MW01056927

This

exeGeses

is the

Possession

of

____

Presented

this ______________________________ *day*

of the ______________________________ *month*

in the ______________________________ *year*

of our

Adonay Yah Shua Messiah;

On the occasion of

____

by

____

True to the work of
Yah Veh Elohim —
Adonay — Eternal I AM —
Creator — Judge.

True to the mission of
Yah Shua Messiah
— Adonay — Eternal I AM
— Creator — Saviour.

exeGeses

ready research BIBLE

a literal translation and transliteration of Scripture

True to the ministry
of the Holy Spirit —
Indwelling Paraclete —
Endower of Spirituals —
Birther of Eternal Life.

True to the enduements
of the Holy Spirit
— Ministries of Service
— Energies of Dynamis
— Attributes of Charismata.

exeGeses
ready research BIBLE

a literal translation and transliteration of Scripture
based on the Authorized King James Version
and keyed to Strong's Concordance.

exeGeses may be freely used and reproduced in part
in the furtherance of the Evangelism of Elohim,
provided that acknowledgement be given
to *exeGeses*.

Less than one year ago, the First Edition titled, "The Authorized King James Version of 1611 in *exeGeses*" was completed. It was offered to the world with the awes of fear and reverence. We now shame for the fear but glory for the reverence, in that the *exeGeses* has been blessed by Elohim and approved by scholars of the Scripture.

Messianic Congregations are using the *exeGeses* in their worship, and Bible Colleges are offering the *exeGeses* to their students as a text.

This Second Edition, titled "*exeGeses ready research BIBLE*" has been thoroughly reedited and reformatted.

The First Edition,
The AUTHORIZED KING JAMES VERSION of 1611 in *exeGeses*, © 1992.

This Second Edition,
exeGeses ready research BIBLE, © 1993.

Library of Congress Catalog Number 93—91350.
Printed in South Korea.

World Bible Publishers
Iowa Falls IA 50126

Acknowledgement

Thank you, Dawn,
for your
encouragement, endurance,
and
editorial excellence.

World Bible Publishers
Iowa Falls IA 50126

In order to straight–cut (rightly divide) what Scripture teaches,
it is necessary to know what Scripture says.

Welcome, Dear Friend,

To *exegeses* – a blessed new experience in Scripture understanding.

In the year 1975, when I entrusted my whole being to Adonay, He instructed me to give up my profession and to hearken to His leading.

Adonay then led me directly to His Word, the Scripture. Even though I had thought of myself as a theologian, I was soon aware of how much I did not know.

Adonay brought this to my attention when I began to diligently search the Scripture to understand what **spirit** and **soul** were, and the difference between them. I soon discovered that most versions translated **nephesh**, the Hebrew word for **soul**, into more than forty different words. Then I discovered that **pneuma**, the Hellenic word for **spirit** was consistently translated **spirit** or **ghost** with one glaring exception; and that one exception, *John* **Yahn** 3:8, is a serious mistranslation.

Now those are just two words. What would I discover if I researched every Hebrew, Aramaic, and Hellenic word of Scripture — more than 14,000 words? And how would I be able to share this knowledge with the world?

Why not take the most revered Version, and insert these exegeses right within the Scripture passage?

That was it! — the Authorized King James Version with its inspiration, and the exegeses with their expositions.

This then, is our purpose — that you hold in your hand, and read the Authorized King James Version exactly as first published — and at the very same moment, and without any further research, have the *exegeses* at your fingertips.

Let's take a step by step journey so that you may better see for yourself all that the *exegeses* affords you – how the *exegeses* will enrich your spiritual life, enlighten your spiritual understanding, and deepen your knowledge of Scripture.

SCRIPTURE is God's inscribed word to humanity. Scripture (singular) consists of 66 volumes of Scriptures (plural).

The Old Covenant was originally inscribed on scrolls in Hebraic, and Aramaic (also known as Chaldean). The New Covenant was inscribed on scrolls in Hebraic, Aramaic, and Hellenic (also known as Bible Greek).

MANUSCRIPT DISTINCTIONS:

All the oldest manuscript copies of both covenants consisted exclusively of **CAPITAL LETTERS** with no **lower case letters.** The Old Covenant manuscripts consisted of consonants only. Vowels were added by a points system in the Masoretic text between the second and fifteenth centuries Anno Domini.

The Authorized King James Version is named after King James who authorized the translation of Scripture into the English language. The Authorized King James Version still stands as the standard of the English speaking world because of its awe and reverence, its beauty of language, and its overall accuracy.

And although the Authorized King James Version is one of the three most accurate Versions ever published, some expressions need a more accurate clarification and correction – hence these exegeses.

DEFINITIONS:

exegeses *plural noun* — the expository critiques of Scripture.

You will quickly appreciate the format of the *exegeses*. As you read the Authorized Version, you will discover the *exegeses* inserted at the point of occurrence.

The portion of the Authorized King James Version *under exegeses is in oblique*, while the **exegeses are inserted at the point of occurence in bold.** Now you can follow along as someone else reads the Authorized King James Version, or read the exegeses by themselves. You may also read the two together and thus enhance your flow of thought.

ready *adjective* — expert; fitted for immediate use; prepared.

research *adjective* — pertaining to exhaustive investigation; studious inquiry.

Bible *proper noun* — Book; the assemblege of Scripture scrolls into a bound format.

literal *adjective* — according to the letter, precise, exact.

Each and every *exegeses* has been thoroughly researched and then translated and/or transliterated as literally as possible.

translation *noun* — the rendering of a **word** from one language to another.

Through the years some words have taken on different meanings. In 1611, **charity** meant **love**; whereas today it means **alms**. *exegeses* presents the distinctions thus: *charity* **love**. Read I Corinthians 13:1. Also, many different manuscriptal words have been translated to the same English word. For example: Where the Authorized Version does not distinguish between the Hellenic verbs **agapao** (love) and **phileo** (befriend), the *exegeses* does. Read *John* **Yahn** 21:15–17.

transliteration *noun* — the rendering of an **alphabet** from one language to another.

Hundreds of words, which in most Versions have been **translated**, are now **transliterated** in the *exegeses*. To mention just a few – **amen**, **apostolize**, **charism**, **charisma**, **Diabolos**, **eucharist**, **Gay Hinnom**, **goyim**, **hades**, **Halalu Yah**, **hanukkah**, **hubris**, **menorah**, **metamorphose**, **parousia**, **shabbath**, **shalom**, **sheol**, **tartarus**, **torah** – all these and more are clearly exposited in the LEXICON.

TRANSLITERATION of NAMES:

TRANSLITERATION is of even more importance when dealing with **names** because of the richness of their meanings.

God the Father first revealed his **name** to Mosheh as **HYH** – the eternal I AM. God the Son also revealed himself as the eternal I AM. Read Exodus 3:13,14, *John* **Yahn** 4:26, 8:58.

The inscribers revealed his **name** as **YHVH** – sequentually as early as Genesis 2:4, and chronologically as early as *Job* **Iyob** 1:6.

The *exegeses* presents his **name** vowel pointed as **Yah Veh**.

Most Versions often render the **name Yah Veh** incorrectly with the **title** ***LORD*** – all capital letters. This is a caving in to the traditions of certain Hebrews who said his **name** was too holy to pronounce. It is more likely that the ancient Hebrews feared the extreme consequences of dishonoring the **name Yah Veh**. For the Hebrews used the **name Yah Veh** to covenant, and whenever the covenant was broken, serious consequences followed. Read Leviticus 19:12.

However, they do transliterate his **name** in very few verses. See Exodus 6:3, Psalm 83:18, *Isaiah* **Yesha Yah** 12:2, 28:4; also see Genesis 22:14, Exodus 17:15, Judges 6:24, Psalm 23:1 for compound **names**.

In most Versions, the **name Yah Veh** is also mistranslated with the **title** *Lord* throughout the New Covenant. One reason is because the Hellene has no equivalent word for **Yah Veh** – and uses *Kurios* throughout.

However there is a clue in the Hellene to distinguish the **name** *LORD* **Yah Veh** from the **title** *Lord* **Adonay**. In almost° every instance where the **title** *Lord* **Adonay** is meant, *Lord* **Adonay** is preceded by the article **the**, or the possessive pronouns **me** or **my**. In almost° every instance where the **name** *LORD* **Yah Veh** is meant, the article or pronouns are absent. Also, the context may indicate whether *Lord* **Adonay** or *LORD* **Yah Veh** is meant. You may confirm this by reading the margins of the Scofield Reference Edition of 1917.

°We say **almost** because of variant manuscripts.

The Hebrew transliteration of the **name** of our *Lord* **Adonay** is **Yah Shua**.

The LEXICON defines **Yah Shua** as **Yah Saves**. With this research, we can now understand the full import of the following verse, which the *exeGeses* presents thus:

And she shall *bring forth* **birth** a son,
and thou shalt call his name *JESUS* **YAH SHUA**:
for he shall save his people from their sins.

Matthew **Matthaios** 1:21

Transliteration is also of utmost importance in the name, *Jew* **Yah Hudah,** his people who are called by His name. Read Genesis 29:35, together with 2 Chronicles 7:14. Also see SUMMARY: YAH HUDAH, YAH HUDIY, YAH HUDIM in the LEXICON.

TRANSLATION and TRANSLITERATION of TITLES:

The *exeGeses* distinguishes between the different Hebrew, and Aramaic words translated *God* – **El, Eli, Elah, Elohim**; as well as the different words translated *Lord* — **adon, adoni, Adonay**.

The *exeGeses* transliterates accurately from the Hebrew the **title** of **Yah Shua Adonay Messiah**. All Messianists will find confirmation of their hope in this *exeGeses*.

LEXICON:

You will particularly appreciate the LEXICON. All the *exeGeses* are verifiable by the expository critiques in the LEXICON, and by Strong's Exhaustive Concordance.

The LEXICON thoroughly explains the importance of the word **word** – and why it is used in both verbal and nounal forms.

Now you can easily satisfy your desire for deeper research – for every word in the LEXICON is number keyed to Strong's Exhaustive Concordance. This is especially helpful because more and more of the old reliable research materials are being republished, also number keyed to Strong's Exhaustive Concordance.

My petition is that Adonay Yah Shua Messiah be pleased to place His seal on my life's work by spiritually enriching your life's work.

In the name of Adonay Yah Shua Messiah,

Herb Jahn, Exegete

I invite all exegetes to critique this Second Edition of *exeGeses* in the hope that future editions may be less imperfect.

Recommended Materials
for
In–Depth Research of Scripture

1. This ***exeGeses ready research BIBLE*** is based on **The Authorized King James Version**: with this ***exeGeses*** one can accurately research every word of Scripture. Published by World Bible Publishers.

2. Strong's Exhaustive Concordance, Complete and Unabridged: this masterpiece is the layperson's key to unlocking the meaning of every word of Scripture. Published by World Bible Publishers.

In order to understand the format of Strong's Exhaustive Concordance, it is of utmost importance to read the General Preface in the front, plus the PLAN OF THE BOOK preceding the Dictionary of the Words in the Hebrew Bible, and preceding the Dictionary of the Words in the Greek Testament in the back of Strong's Exhaustive Concordance. Only then will one be able to distinguish between definitions and renderings.

Beware of some editions which omit important sections of the Concordance.

The following books render in–depth research beyond the scope of Strong's Exhaustive Concordance:

3. Gesenius' Hebrew–Chaldee Lexicon to the Old Testament: a dictionary numerically coded to Strong's Exhaustive Concordance with an exhaustive English index.

4. Thayer's Greek–English Lexicon of the New Testament: a dictionary numerically coded to Strong's Exhaustive Concordance.

5. Theological Wordbook of the Old Testament: compiled by Harris, Archer, and Waltke: a two volume work which presents the Hebrew and Aramaic words by their root families, and distinguishes parts of speech. In the recommended edition, the Index lists the Strong's Exhaustive Concordance number followed by the Theological Wordbook number which directs one to the root word.

6. Vine's Expository Dictionary of Biblical Words: keyed to Strong's Exhaustive Concordance; while the Old Testament section is incomplete, the New Testament section lists the words by their roots, in their most common King James usage, and also lists the parts of speech. The Strong's Exhaustive Concordance key number follows the Greek (Hellenic) spelling. Published by World Bible Publishers.

7. The Englishman's Hebrew and Chaldee Concordance of the Old Testament: by George V. Wigram; numerically coded to Strong's Exhaustive Concordance. The words are listed approximately in the numbering sequence of Strong's Exhaustive Concordance. Following this, every King James rendering of the word is italicized and presented in Scripture sequence.

8. The Englishman's Greek Concordance of the New Testament: by George V. Wigram; numerically coded to Strong's Exhaustive Concordance. The words are listed approximately in the numbering sequence of Strong's Exhaustive Concordance. Following this, every King James rendering of the word is italicized and presented in Scripture sequence.

The preceding books are old standards, painstakingly prepared by patient men. Only the most recent editions have been republished keyed to Strong's Exhaustive Concordance.

9. The Treasury of Scripture Knowledge: a precious book of 500,000 Scripture References and Parallel Passages. With this book, simply select any verse or phrase of Scripture you wish to research, and it lists definitions, explanations, and related verses. This book is ancient and virtually unknown. This book is a light that illuminates in the darkest of darkness. Published by World Bible Publishers.

There they are — nine books – the wealth of thousands of years of research, which one may purchase with minimal sacrifice — the combined knowledge of which will add hundreds of years of research to your life.

What you do with this knowledge is your responsibility — your opportunity .

exeGeses ready research BIBLE

INDEX

****exeGeses*** allots Scripture into Six Subject Headings.

Therefore the **POEMS** of **RUTH** and **LAMENTATIONS** are transplaced to **POETRY**.

And as *JOHN* **YAHN** is the Genesis of the New Covenant, it precedes the synoptic evangelisms. This also allows *LUKE* **LOUKAS and ACTS** to follow in their natural sequence**.** The New Covenant then concludes with the **EPISTLES** and **APOCALYPSE** of *JOHN* **YAHN**.

KEY TO INTERPRETING THE EXEGESES:
King James text is in regular type;
Text under exegeses is in oblique type;
Text of exegeses is in bold type.

CREATION

1 In the beginning
God **Elohim** created the *heaven* **heavens** and the earth.
2 And the earth *was without form* **became waste**, and void;
and darkness was upon the face of the *deep* **abyss.**
And the Spirit of *God* **Elohim**
moved upon the face of the waters.

DAY ONE

3 And *God* **Elohim** said,
Let there be light:
and there *was* **became** light.
4 And *God* **Elohim** saw the light, that it was good:
and *God divided* **Elohim separated**
between the light *from* **and between** the darkness.
5 And *God* **Elohim** called the light Day,
and the darkness he called Night.
And the evening and the morning
were **became** the first day.

DAY TWO

6 And *God* **Elohim** said,
Let there be *a firmament* **an expanse**
in the midst of the waters,
and let it *divide* **separate** the waters from the waters.
7 And *God made* **Elohim worked** the *firmament* **expanse,**
and *divided* **separated** the waters
which were under the *firmament* **expanse**
from the waters
which were above the *firmament* **expanse:**
and *it was so* **thus it became.**
8 And *God* **Elohim** called the *firmament* **expanse**
Heaven **Heavens.**
And the evening and the morning
were **became** the second day.

DAY THREE

9 And *God* **Elohim** said,
Let the waters under the *heaven* **heavens**
be gathered together **congregate** unto one place,
and let the dry *land appear* **be seen:**
and *it was so* **thus it became.**
10 And *God* **Elohim** called the dry *land* Earth;
and the *gathering together* **congregating** of the waters
called he Seas:
and *God* **Elohim** saw that it was good.
11 And *God* **Elohim** said,
Let the earth *bring forth grass* **sprout sprouts,**
the herb *yielding* **seeding** seed,
and the fruit tree *yielding* **working** fruit
after his kind **in species,**
whose seed is in itself, upon the earth:
and *it was so* **thus it became.**
12 And the earth *brought forth grass* **sprouted herbs,**
and herb *yielding* **seeding** seed *after his kind* **in species,**
and the tree *yielding* **working** fruit,
whose seed was in itself, *after his kind* **in species:**
and *God* **Elohim** saw that it was good.
13 And the evening and the morning
were **became** the third day.

DAY FOUR

14 And *God* **Elohim** said,
Let there be lights
in the *firmament* **expanse** of the *heaven* **heavens**
to *divide* **separate between** the day
from **and between** the night;
and let them be for signs, and for seasons,
and for days, and years:
15 And let them be for lights
in the *firmament* **expanse** of the *heaven* **heavens**
to *give light upon* **light up** the earth:
and *it was so* **thus it became.**
16 And *God made* **Elohim worked** two great lights;
the greater light *to rule* **for the reign of** the day,
and the lesser light *to rule* **for the reign of** the night:
he made the stars also.
17 And *God set* **Elohim gave** them
in the *firmament* **expanse** of the *heaven* **heavens**
to *give light upon* **light up** the earth,
18 And to *rule* **reign** over the day and over the night,
and to *divide* **separate between** the light
from **and between** the darkness:
and *God* **Elohim** saw that it was good.
19 And the evening and the morning
were **became** the fourth day.

DAY FIVE

20 And *God* **Elohim** said,
Let the waters *bring forth abundantly* **teem**
the moving creature **with teemers**
that *hath life* **have a living soul,**
and *fowl* **fliers** that may fly above the earth
in the open firmament **upon the face of the expanse**
of *heaven* **the heavens.**
21 And *God* **Elohim** created great *whales* **monsters,**
and every living *creature* **soul** that *moveth* **creepeth,**
which the waters *brought forth abundantly* **teemed,**
after their kind **in species,**
and every winged *fowl after his kind* **flier in species:**
and *God* **Elohim** saw that it was good.
22 And *God* **Elohim** blessed them, saying,
Be fruitful **Bear fruit,** and *multiply* **abound,**
and fill the waters in the seas,
and let *fowl multiply* **fliers abound** in the earth.
23 And the evening and the morning
were **became** the fifth day.

DAY SIX

24 And *God* **Elohim** said,
Let the earth bring forth the living *creature* **soul**
after his kind **in species,**
cattle **animals,** and *creeping thing* **creepers,**
and *beast of* **live beings on** the earth
after his kind **in species:**
and *it was so* **thus it became.**
25 And *God made* **Elohim worked**
the *beast of* **live beings on** the earth *after his kind* **in species,**
and *cattle after their kind* **animals in species,**
and every *thing that creepeth* **creeper** upon the *earth* **soil**
after his kind **in species:**
and *God* **Elohim** saw that it was good.
26 And *God* **Elohim** said,
Let us *make man* **work Adam** in our image,
after our likeness:
and let them *have dominion* **subjugate**
over the fish of the sea,
and over the *fowl* **fliers** of the *air* **heavens,**
and over the *cattle* **animals,** and over all the earth,
and over every *creeping thing* **creeper**
that creepeth upon the earth.
27 So *God* **Elohim** created *man* **Adam** in his *own* image,
in the image of *God* **Elohim** created he him;
male and female created he them.
28 And *God* **Elohim** blessed them,
and *God* **Elohim** said unto them,
Be fruitful **Bear fruit,** and *multiply* **abound,**
and *replenish* **fill** the earth, and subdue it:
and *have dominion* **subjugate** over the fish of the sea,
and over the *fowl* **fliers** of the *air* **heavens,**
and over every *living thing* **live being**
that *moveth* **creepeth** upon the earth.
29 And *God* **Elohim** said, Behold,
I have given you every herb *bearing* **seeding** seed,
which is upon the face of all the earth, and every tree,
in the which is the fruit of a tree *yielding* **seeding** seed;
to you it shall be for *meat* **food.**
30 And to every *beast* **live being** of the earth,
and to every *fowl* **flier** of the *air* **heavens,**
and to every *thing that creepeth* **creeper** upon the earth,
wherein there is *life* **a living soul,**
I have given — every green herb for *meat* **food:**
and *it was so* **thus it became.**
31 And *God* **Elohim**
saw *every thing* **all** that he had *made* **worked,**
and, behold, it was *very* **mighty** good.
And the evening and the morning
were **became** the sixth day.

2 *Thus* the heavens and the earth were finished,
and all the host of them.

DAY SEVEN

2 And on the seventh day
God ended **Elohim finished** his work
which he had *made* **worked**;
and he *rested* **shabbathized** on the seventh day
from all his work which he had *made* **worked**.
3 And *God* **Elohim** blessed the seventh day,
and *sanctified* **hallowed** it:
because that in it
he had *rested* **shabbathized** from all his work
which *God* **Elohim** created and *made* **worked**.

RESUME' OF CREATION

4 These are the generations
of the heavens and of the earth
when they were created,
in the day that *the LORD God* **Yah Veh Elohim**
made **worked** the earth and the heavens,
5 And every *plant* **shrub** of the field
before it was in the earth,
and every herb of the field before it *grew* **sprouted**:
for *the LORD God* **Yah Veh Elohim**
had not caused it to rain upon the earth,
and there was *not a man* **no Adam**
to *till* **serve** the *ground* **soil**.
6 But there *went up* **ascended** a mist from the earth,
and *watered* **moistened** the whole face of the *ground* **soil**.
7 And *the LORD God* **Yah Veh Elohim**
formed *man* **Adam** of the dust of the *ground* **soil**,
and *breathed* **puffed** into his nostrils the breath of life;
and *man* **Adam** became a living soul.

THE GARDEN OF EDEN

8 And *the LORD God* **Yah Veh Elohim**
planted a garden eastward in Eden;
and there he put *the man* **Adam** whom he had formed.
9 And out of the *ground* **soil**
made the LORD God to grow **Yah Veh Elohim sprouted**
every tree that is *pleasant to the sight* **desirable in visage**,
and good for food;
the tree of life also in the midst of the garden,
and the tree of knowledge of good and evil.

FOUR TRIBUTARIES

10 And a river went out of Eden
to *water* **moisten** the garden;
and from thence it *was parted* **separated**,
and became into four heads.
11 The name of the first is *Pison* **Pishon**:
that is it which *compasseth* **surroundeth**
the *whole* land of Havilah,
where there is gold;
12 And the gold of that land is good:
there is bdellium and the onyx stone.
13 And the name of the second river is *Gihon* **Gichon**:
the same is it that *compasseth* **surroundeth**
the *whole* land of *Ethiopia* **Kush**.
14 And the name of the third river is *Hiddekel* **Hiddeqel**:
that is it which goeth toward the east of *Assyria* **Ashshur**.
And the fourth river is Euphrates.
15 And *the LORD God* **Yah Veh Elohim**
took *the man* **Adam**,
and put him into the garden of Eden
to *dress* **serve** it and to *keep* **guard** it.
16 And *the LORD God* **Yah Veh Elohim**
commanded the man **misvahed Adam**, saying,
Of every tree of the garden
in eating, thou mayest *freely* eat:
17 But of the tree of the knowledge of good and evil,
thou shalt not eat of it:
for in the day that thou eatest thereof
in dying, thou shalt *surely* die.
18 And *the LORD God* **Yah Veh Elohim** said,
It is not good that *the man* **Adam** should be alone;
I *will make* **shall work** him an help meet for him.
19 And out of the *ground* **soil**
the LORD God **Yah Veh Elohim**
formed every *beast* **live being** of the field,
and every *fowl* **flier** of the *air* **heavens**;
and brought *them* unto Adam
to see what he *would* **should** call them:
and whatsoever Adam called every living *creature* **soul**,
that was the name thereof.
20 And Adam *gave* **called** names to all *cattle* **animals**,
and to the *fowl* **fliers** of the *air* **heavens**,
and to every *beast* **live being** of the field;
but for Adam there was not found an help meet for him.

WOMAN

21 And *the LORD God* **Yah Veh Elohim**
caused a *deep* **sound** sleep to fall upon Adam,
and he slept:
and he took one of his ribs,
and *closed up* **shut** the flesh *instead* **underneath** thereof;
22 And the rib,
which *the LORD God* **Yah Veh Elohim** had taken
from *man* **Adam**,
made **builded** he a woman,
and brought her unto *the man* **Adam**.
23 And Adam said,
This is *now* **at this time** bone of my bones,
and flesh of my flesh:
she **this** shall be called Woman,
because she was taken out of Man.
24 *Therefore* **Thus** shall a man
leave his father and his mother,
and shall *cleave* **adhere** unto his *wife* **woman**:
and they shall be one flesh.
25 And *they* **the two** were *both* naked,
the man **Adam** and his *wife* **woman**,
and were not ashamed.

FALL OF HUMANITY

3 Now the serpent *was* **became** more subtil
than any *beast* **live being** of the field
which *the LORD God* **Yah Veh Elohim** had *made* **worked**.
And he said unto the woman, Yea, hath *God* **Elohim** said,
Ye shall not eat of every tree of the garden?
2 And the woman said unto the serpent,
We may eat of the fruit of the trees of the garden:
3 But of the fruit of the tree
which is in the midst of the garden,
God **Elohim** hath said, Ye shall not eat of it,
neither shall ye touch it, lest ye die.
4 And the serpent said unto the woman,
In dying, Ye shall not *surely* die:
5 For *God doth know* **Elohim knoweth**
that in the day ye eat thereof,
then your eyes shall be opened,
and ye shall be as *gods* **Elohim**, knowing good and evil.
6 And when the woman saw
that the tree was good for food,
and that it was *pleasant* **desirable** to the eyes,
and a tree to be desired to *make one wise* **comprehend**,
she took of the fruit thereof, and did eat,
and gave also unto her *husband* **man** with her;
and he did eat.
7 And the eyes of *them both* **the two** were opened,
and they knew that they were naked;
and they sewed fig leaves together,
and *made* **worked** themselves *aprons* **girdles**.
8 And they heard the voice
of *the LORD God* **Yah Veh Elohim**
walking in the garden in the *cool* **wind** of the day:
and Adam and his *wife* **woman** hid themselves
from the *presence* **face** of *the LORD God* **Yah Veh Elohim**
amongst the trees of the garden.
9 And *the LORD God* **Yah Veh Elohim** called unto Adam,
and said unto him, Where art thou?
10 And he said, I heard thy voice in the garden,
and I *was afraid* **awed**, because I was naked;
and I hid myself.
11 And he said, Who told thee that thou wast naked?
Hast thou eaten of the tree,
whereof I *commanded* **misvahed** thee
that thou shouldest not eat?
12 And *the man* **Adam** said,
The woman whom thou gavest to be with me,
she gave me of the tree, and I did eat.
13 And *the LORD God* **Yah Veh Elohim**
said unto the woman,
What is this that thou hast *done* **worked**?
And the woman said,
The serpent *beguiled* **deceived** me, and I did eat.
14 And *the LORD God* **Yah Veh Elohim**

said unto the serpent,
Because thou hast *done* **worked** this,
thou art cursed above all *cattle* **animals**,
and above every *beast* **live being** of the field;
upon thy belly shalt thou go,
and dust shalt thou eat all the days of thy life:
15 And I *will* **shall** put enmity
between thee and **between** the woman,
and between thy seed and **between** her seed;
it **he** shall *bruise* **crush** thy head,
and thou shalt *bruise* **crush** his heel.
16 Unto the woman he said,
I will greatly multiply **In abounding, I shall abound**
thy *sorrow* **contortion** and thy conception;
in *sorrow* **contortion**
thou shalt *bring forth children* **bear sons**;
and thy desire shall be to thy *husband* **man**,
and he shall *rule* **reign** over thee.
17 And unto Adam he said,
Because thou hast hearkened
unto the voice of thy *wife* **woman**,
and hast eaten of the tree,
of which I *commanded* **misvahed** thee,
saying, Thou shalt not eat of it:
cursed is the *ground* **soil** for thy sake;
in *sorrow* **contortion** shalt thou eat of it
all the days of thy life;
18 Thorns also and thistles
shall it *bring forth* **sprout** to thee;
and thou shalt eat the herb of the field;
19 In the sweat of thy *face* **nostrils**
shalt thou eat bread,
till thou return unto the *ground* **soil**;
for out of it wast thou taken:
for dust thou art, and unto dust shalt thou return.
20 And Adam called his *wife's* **woman's** name
Eve **Havvah**;
because she was the mother of all living.
21 Unto Adam also and to his *wife* **woman**
did the LORD God **Yah Veh Elohim**
make **worked** coats of skins,
and *clothed* **enrobed** them.
22 And *the LORD God* **Yah Veh Elohim** said,
Behold, *the man* **Adam** is become as one of us,
to know good and evil:
and now, lest he *put forth* **extend** his hand,
and take also of the tree of life, and eat,
and live *for ever:* **eternally** —
23 *Therefore the LORD God* **Yah Veh Elohim**
sent him forth from the garden of Eden,
to *till* **serve** the *ground* **soil** from whence he was taken.
24 So he *drove out the man* **expelled Adam**;
and he *placed* **tabernacled**
at the east of the garden of Eden *Cherubims* **Cherubim**,
and a flaming sword which turned *every way*,
to *keep* **guard** the way of the tree of life.

THE FIRST TWINS

4 And Adam knew *Eve* **Havvah** his *wife* **woman**;
and she conceived, and bare *Cain* **Qayin**, and said,
I have *gotten* **chatteled** a man from *the LORD* **Yah Veh**.
2 And she again bare his brother Abel.
And Abel *was a keeper of sheep* **tended flocks**,
but *Cain was a tiller of* **Qayin served** the *ground* **soil**.
3 And *in process of time* **at day's end** it *came to pass* **became**,
that *Cain* **Qayin** brought of the fruit of the *ground* **soil**
an offering unto *the LORD* **Yah Veh**.
4 And Abel, he also brought of the firstlings of his flock
and of the fat thereof.
And *the LORD* **Yah Veh**
had respect **looked** unto Abel and to his offering:
5 But unto *Cain* **Qayin** and to his offering
he *had not respect* **looked not**.
And *Cain* **Qayin** was *very wroth* **mightily inflamed**,
and his *countenance* **face** fell.
6 And *the LORD* **Yah Veh** said unto *Cain* **Qayin**,
Why art thou *wroth* **inflamed**?
and why is thy *countenance* **face** fallen?
7 If thou *doest* well—**pleasest**,
shalt thou not be *accepted* **exalted**?
and if thou *doest not* well—**pleasest not**,
sin *lieth* **croucheth** at the *door* **portal**.
And unto thee shall be his desire,
and thou shalt *rule* **reign** over him.

FIRST SLAUGHTER

8 And *Cain* **Qayin** talked with Abel his brother:
and it *came to pass* **became**, when they were in the field,
that *Cain* **Qayin** rose up against Abel his brother,
and *slew* **slaughtered** him.
9 And *the LORD* **Yah Veh** said unto *Cain* **Qayin**,
Where is Abel thy brother?
And he said, I know not:
Am I my brother's *keeper* **guardian**?
10 And he said, What hast thou *done* **worked**?
the voice of thy brother's blood
crieth unto me from the *ground* **soil**.
11 And now art thou cursed from the *earth* **soil**,
which hath *opened* **gaped** her mouth
to *receive* **take** thy brother's blood from thy hand;
12 When thou *tillest* **servest** the *ground* **soil**,
it shall not *henceforth* **again**
yield **give** unto thee her *strength* **force**;
a fugitive and a vagabond **to waver and to wander**
shalt thou be in the earth.
13 And *Cain* **Qayin** said unto *the LORD* **Yah Veh**,
My *punishment* **perversity** is greater than I can bear.
14 Behold, thou hast *driven* **expelled** me *out* this day
from the face of the *earth* **soil**;
and from thy face shall I be hid;
and I shall be
a fugitive and a vagabond **to waver and to wander**
in the earth;
and it shall *come to pass* **become**,
that every one that findeth me shall *slay* **slaughter** me.
15 And *the LORD* **Yah Veh** said unto him,
Therefore **Thus**
whosoever *slayeth Cain* **slaughtereth Qayin**,
vengeance shall be taken on him
he shall be avenged sevenfold.
And *the LORD* **Yah Veh** set a *mark* **sign** upon *Cain* **Qayin**,
lest any finding him should *kill* **smite** him.
16 And *Cain* **Qayin** went out
from the *presence* **face** of *the LORD* **Yah Veh**,
and *dwelt* **settled** in the land of Nod, on the east of Eden.
17 And *Cain* **Qayin** knew his *wife* **woman**;
and she conceived, and bare *Enoch* **Hanoch**:
and he builded a city, and called the name of the city,
after the name of his son, *Enoch* **Hanoch**.

GENEALOGY OF HANOCH

18 And unto *Enoch* **Hanoch** was born Irad:
and Irad begat *Mehujael* **Mechuya El**:
and *Mehujael* **Mechuya El** begat *Methusael* **Methusha El**:
and *Methusael* **Methusha El** begat *Lamech* **Lemech**.
19 And *Lamech* **Lemech** took unto him two *wives* **women**:
the name of the one was Adah,
and the name of the *other Zillah* **second Sillah**.
20 And Adah bare *Jabal* **Yabal**:
he was the father of such as *dwell* **settle** in tents,
and of such as *have cattle* **chattel**.
21 And his brother's name was *Jubal* **Yubal**:
he was the father of all such
as *handle* **manipulate** the harp and *organ* **woodwinds**.
22 And *Zillah* **Sillah**, she also bare *Tubalcain* **Tubal Qayin**,
an instructer **a sharpener**
of every artificer in *brass* **copper** and iron:
and the sister of *Tubalcain* **Tubal Qayin** was Naamah.

SECOND SLAUGHTER

23 And *Lamech* **Lemech** said unto his *wives* **women**,
Adah and *Zillah* **Sillah**,
Hear my voice; ye *wives* **women** of *Lamech* **Lemech**,
hearken unto my *speech* **sayings**:
for I have *slain* **slaughtered** a man
to **for** my *wounding* **wound**,
and a *young man to* **child for** my *hurt* **lash**.
24 If *Cain* **Qayin** shall be avenged sevenfold,
truly *Lamech* **Lemech** seventy and sevenfold.

BIRTH OF SHETH

25 And Adam knew his *wife* **woman** again;
and she bare a son, and called his name *Seth* **Sheth**:
For *God* **Elohim**, *said she*,
hath *appointed* **set** me another seed instead of Abel,

whom *Cain slew* **Qayin slaughtered**.
26 And to *Seth* **Sheth**, to him also there was born a son;
and he called his name Enos:
then began *men to call* **the calling**
upon the name of *the LORD* **Yah Veh**.

GENEALOGY OF ADAM

5 This is the *book* **scroll** of the generations of Adam.
In the day that *God* **Elohim** created *man* **Adam**,
in the likeness of *God made* **Elohim worked** he him;
2 Male and female created he them;
and blessed them, and called their name Adam,
in the day when they were created.
3 And Adam lived an hundred and thirty years,
and begat *a son* in his own likeness, and after his image;
and called his name *Seth* **Sheth**:
4 And the days of Adam after he had begotten *Seth* **Sheth**
were eight hundred years:
and he begat sons and daughters:
5 And all the days that Adam lived
were nine hundred **years** and thirty years: and he died.
6 And *Seth* **Sheth** lived an hundred **years** and five years,
and begat Enos:
7 And *Seth* **Sheth** lived after he begat Enos
eight hundred **years** and seven years,
and begat sons and daughters:
8 And all the days of *Seth* **Sheth**
were nine hundred **years** and twelve years: and he died.
9 And Enos lived ninety years, and begat *Cainan* **Qeyan**:
10 And Enos lived after he begat *Cainan* **Qeyan**
eight hundred **years** and fifteen years,
and begat sons and daughters:
11 And all the days of Enos
were nine hundred **years** and five years: and he died.
12 And *Cainan* **Qeyan** lived seventy years,
and begat *Mahalaleel* **Ma Halal El**:
13 And *Cainan* **Qeyan** lived
after he begat *Mahalaleel* **Ma Halal El**
eight hundred **years** and forty years,
and begat sons and daughters:
14 And all the days of *Cainan* **Qeyan**
were nine hundred **years** and ten years: and he died.
15 And *Mahalaleel* **Ma Halal El**
lived sixty **years** and five years, and begat *Jared* **Yered**:
16 And *Mahalaleel* **Ma Halal El** lived
after he begat *Jared* **Yered**
eight hundred **years** and thirty years,
and begat sons and daughters:
17 And all the days of *Mahalaleel* **Ma Halal El**
were eight hundred **years** ninety and five years:
and he died.
18 And *Jared* **Yered** lived
an hundred sixty **years** and two years,
and he begat *Enoch* **Hanoch**:
19 And *Jared* **Yered** lived after he begat *Enoch* **Hanoch**
eight hundred years,
and begat sons and daughters:
20 And all the days of *Jared* **Yered**
were nine hundred **years** sixty and two years:
and he died.
21 And *Enoch* **Hanoch** lived sixty and five years,
and begat *Methuselah* **Methusha Lach**:
22 And *Enoch* **Hanoch** walked with *God* **Elohim**
after he begat *Methuselah* **Methusha Lach**
three hundred years,
and begat sons and daughters:
23 And all the days of *Enoch* **Hanoch**
were three hundred **years** sixty and five years:
24 And *Enoch* **Hanoch** walked with *God* **Elohim**:
and he was not; for *God* **Elohim** took him.
25 And *Methuselah* **Methusha Lach**
lived an hundred **years** eighty and seven years,
and begat *Lamech* **Lemech**.
26 And *Methuselah* **Methusha Lach** lived
after he begat *Lamech* **Lemech**
seven hundred **years** eighty and two years,
and begat sons and daughters:
27 And all the days of *Methuselah* **Methusha Lach**
were nine hundred **years** sixty and nine years:
and he died.
28 And *Lamech* **Lemech** lived
an hundred **years** eighty and two years, and begat a son:
29 And he called his name *Noah* **Noach**, saying,
This *same* **one** shall *comfort* **sigh over** us
concerning our work and *toil* **scars** of our hands,
because of the *ground* **soil**
which *the LORD* **Yah Veh** hath cursed.
30 And *Lamech* **Lemech** lived after he begat *Noah* **Noach**
five hundred **years** ninety and five years,
and begat sons and daughters:
31 And all the days of *Lamech* **Lemech**
were seven hundred **years** seventy and seven years:
and he died.
32 And *Noah* **Noach** was **a son of** five hundred years *old*:
and *Noah* **Noach** begat
Shem, Ham, and *Japheth* **Yepheth**.

SONS OF ELOHIM TAKE DAUGHTERS OF HUMANITY

6 And it *came to pass* **became**,
when *men* **humanity**
began to *multiply* **abound by myriads**
on the face of the *earth* **soil**,
and daughters were born unto them,
2 That the sons of *God* **Elohim**
saw the daughters of *men* **humanity**
that they were *fair* **goodly**;
and they took them *wives* **women**
of all which they chose.

THE SHORTENED LIFE SPAN

3 And *the LORD* **Yah Veh** said,
My spirit shall not *always strive* **eternally plead**
with *man* **humanity**,
for **in their erring inadvertently**, that he *also is* **be** flesh:
yet his days shall be an hundred and twenty years.

THE NEPHILIM

4 There were *giants* **Nephilim** in the earth in those days;
and also *after that* **thus**,
when the sons of *God* **Elohim**
came in unto the daughters of *men* **humanity**,
and they bare *children* to them,
the same became **mighty** *men*
which were of old **originally**, men of *renown* **name**.
5 And *GOD* **Yah Veh** saw
that the *wickedness* **evil** of *man* **humanity**
was great in the earth,
and that every imagination
of the *thoughts* **fabrications** of his heart
was only evil *continually* **every day**.
6 And *it repented the LORD* **Yah Veh sighed**
that he had *made man* **worked humanity** on the earth,
and it *grieved him* **contorted** at his heart.
7 And *the LORD* **Yah Veh** said,
I *will destroy man* **shall wipe out humanity**
whom I have created
from the face of the *earth* **soil**;
both man, and beast **from human to animal**,
and the *creeping thing* **creeper**,
and the *fowls* **fliers** of the *air* **heavens**;
for *it repenteth me* **I sigh** that I have *made* **worked** them.
8 But *Noah* **Noach** found *grace* **charism**
in the eyes of *the LORD* **Yah Veh**.

GENEALOGY OF NOACH

9 These are the generations of *Noah* **Noach**:
Noah **Noach** was a just man
and *perfect* **integrious** in his generations,
and *Noah* **Noach** walked with *God* **Elohim**.
10 And *Noah* **Noach** begat three sons,
Shem, Ham, and *Japheth* **Yepheth**.
11 The earth also was *corrupt* **ruined**
before God **at the face of Elohim**,
and the earth was filled with violence.
12 And *God looked upon* **Elohim saw** the earth,
and, behold, it was *corrupt* **ruined**;
for all flesh had *corrupted* **ruined** his way upon the earth.

THE FLOOD

13 And *God* **Elohim** said unto *Noah* **Noach**,
The end of all flesh is come *before me* **at my face**;
for the earth is filled with violence
through them **at their face**;
and, behold, I *will destroy* **shall ruin** them with the earth.
14 *Make* **Work** thee an ark of gopher *wood* **timber**;
rooms **nests** shalt thou *make* **work** in the ark,

and shalt pitch *it* **the housing**
within and without with pitch.
15 And *this is the fashion which* **thus**
thou shalt *make it of* **work it**:
The length of the ark shall be three hundred cubits,
the breadth of it fifty cubits,
and the height of it thirty cubits.
16 A window shalt thou *make* **work** to the ark,
and in a cubit shalt thou finish it above;
and the *door* **portal** of the ark
shalt thou set in the side thereof;
with *lower* **nether**, second, and third *stories*
shalt thou *make* **work** it.
17 And, behold, I, even I,
do bring a flood of waters upon the earth,
to *destroy* **ruin** all flesh, wherein is the *breath* **spirit** of life,
from under *heaven* **the heavens**;
and every thing **all** that is in the earth shall *die* **expire**.
18 But with thee *will I establish* **shall I raise** my covenant;
and thou shalt come into the ark,
thou, and thy sons, and thy *wife* **woman**,
and thy sons' *wives* **women** with thee.
19 And of every *living thing* **live being** of all flesh,
two of *every sort* **each** shalt thou bring into the ark,
to *keep* **preserve** them alive with thee;
they shall be male and female.
20 Of *fowls after their kind* **fliers in species**,
and of *cattle after their kind* **animals in species**,
of every *creeping thing* **creeper** of the *earth* **soil**
after his kind **in species**,
two of *every sort* **each** shall come unto thee,
to *keep them alive* **live**.
21 And take thou unto thee of all food that is eaten,
and thou shalt gather it to thee;
and it shall be for food for thee, and for them.
22 Thus *did Noah* **Noach worked**;
according to all
that *God commanded* **Elohim misvahed** him,
so *did* **worked** he.

7 And *the LORD* **Yah Veh** said unto *Noah* **Noach**,
Come thou and all thy house into the ark;
for thee have I seen *righteous before me* **just at my face**
in this generation.
2 Of every *clean beast* **pure animal**
thou shalt take to thee *by sevens* **seven by seven**,
the *male* **man** and his *female* **woman**:
and of *beasts* **animals** that are not *clean* **pure** by two,
the *male* **man** and his *female* **woman**.
3 Of *fowls* **fliers** also of the *air* **heavens**
by sevens **seven by seven**, the male and the female;
to keep **that** seed *alive* **might live**
upon the face of all the earth.
4 For *yet* **again** seven days,
and I *will* **shall** cause it to rain upon the earth
forty days and forty nights;
and every *living substance* **risen being**
that I have *made* **worked**
will I destroy **shall I wipe out**
from off the face of the earth.
5 And *Noah did* **Noach worked** according unto all
that *the LORD commanded* **Yah Veh misvahed** him.
6 And *Noah* **Noach** was **a son of** six hundred years *old*
when the flood of waters was upon the earth.
7 And *Noah* **Noach** went in, and his sons,
and his *wife* **woman**, and his sons' *wives* **women**
with him, into the ark,
because **at the face** of the waters of the flood.
8 Of *clean beasts* **pure animals**,
and of *beasts* **animals** that are not *clean* **pure**,
and of *fowls* **fliers**,
and of *every thing* **all** that creepeth upon the *earth* **soil**,
9 There went in two and two
unto *Noah* **Noach** into the ark,
the male and the female,
as *God* **Elohim** had *commanded Noah* **misvahed Noach**.
10 And it *came to pass* **became** after seven days,
that the waters of the flood were upon the earth.
11 In **the year**
— the six hundredth year of *Noah's* **Noach's** life,
in the second month, the seventeenth day of the month,
the same **this** day were all the fountains
of the great *deep broken up* **abyss split**,
and the windows of *heaven were* **the heavens** opened.
12 And the *rain* **downpour** was upon the earth
forty days and forty nights.
13 In the selfsame day entered *Noah* **Noach**,
and Shem, and Ham, and *Japheth* **Yepheth**,
the sons of *Noah* **Noach**,
and *Noah's wife* **Noach's woman**,
and the three *wives* **women** of his sons with them,
into the ark;
14 They, and every *beast* **live being**
after his kind **in species**,
and all the *cattle after their kind* **animals in species**,
and every *creeping thing* **creeper**
that creepeth upon the earth *after his kind* **in species**,
and every *fowl after his kind* **flier in species**,
every bird of every *sort* **wing**.
15 And they went in unto *Noah* **Noach** into the ark,
two and two of all flesh,
wherein is the *breath* **spirit** of life.
16 And they that went in,
went in male and female of all flesh,
as *God* **Elohim** had *commanded* **misvahed** him:
and *the LORD* **Yah Veh** shut him in.
17 And the flood was forty days upon the earth;
and the waters *increased* **abounded**, and bare up the ark,
and it was lift up above the earth.
18 And the waters prevailed **mightily**,
and *were increased greatly* **abounded mightily**
upon the earth;
and the ark went upon the face of the waters.
19 And the waters prevailed **mightily,**
exceedingly **mightily mighty** upon the earth;
and all the high *hills* **mountains**,
that were under the whole *heaven* **heavens**, were covered.
20 Fifteen cubits upward
did the waters prevail **mightily**;
and the mountains were covered.
21 And all flesh *died* **expired**
that *moved* **creeped** upon the earth,
both of *fowl* **fliers**, and of *cattle* **animals**,
and of *beast* **live beings**,
and of every *creeping thing* **teemer**
that *creepeth* **teemeth** upon the earth,
and every *man* **human**:
22 All in whose nostrils was the breath **of the spirit** of life,
of all that was in the *dry land* **parched area**, died.
23 And every *living substance* **risen being**
was *destroyed* **wiped out**
which was upon the face of the *ground* **soil**,
both man **from human**, and *cattle* **animals**,
and the *creeping things* **creepers**,
and the *fowl* **fliers** of the *heaven* **heavens**;
and they were *destroyed* **wiped out** from the earth:
and *Noah* **Noach** only *remained alive* **survived**,
and they that were with him in the ark.
24 And the waters prevailed **mightily** upon the earth
an hundred and fifty days.

8 And *God* **Elohim** remembered *Noah* **Noach**,
and every *living thing* **live being**, and all the *cattle* **animals**
that *was* **were** with him in the ark:
and *God made* **Elohim had** a wind to pass over the earth,
and the waters asswaged;
2 The fountains also of the *deep* **abyss**
and the windows of *heaven* **the heavens**
were *stopped* **shut**,
and the *rain* **downpour** from *heaven* **the heavens**
was restrained;
3 And the waters returned from off the earth
continually **going and returning**:
and after the end of the hundred and fifty days
the waters were abated.
4 And the ark rested in the seventh month,
on the seventeenth day of the month,
upon the mountains of Ararat.
5 And the waters *decreased* **abated**
continually **going and returning** until the tenth month:
in the tenth *month,* on the first *day* of the month,
were the tops of the mountains seen.

6 And it *came to pass* **became** at the end of forty days,
that *Noah* **Noach** opened the window of the ark
which he had *made* **worked**:
7 And he sent forth a raven,
which went forth *to* **going** and *fro* **returning**,
until the waters were dried up from off the earth.
8 Also he sent forth a dove from him,
to see if the waters were abated
from off the face of the *ground* **soil**;
9 But the dove found no rest for the sole of her foot,
and she returned unto him into the ark,
for the waters were on the face of the whole earth:
then he *put forth* **extended** his hand, and took her,
and pulled her in unto him into the ark.
10 And he *stayed* **waited** yet other seven days;
and again he sent forth the dove out of the ark;
11 And the dove came in to him in the evening **time**;
and, *lo* **behold**, in her mouth was an olive leaf pluckt off:
so *Noah* **Noach** knew
that the waters were abated from off the earth.
12 And he *stayed* **waited** yet other seven days;
and sent forth the dove;
which returned not again unto him any more.
13 And it *came to pass* **became**
in the six hundredth and first year,
in the first *month,* the first *day* of the month,
the waters were *dried up* **parched** from off the earth:
and *Noah* **Noach**
removed **turned aside** the covering of the ark,
and *looked* **saw**, and, behold,
the face of the *ground* **soil** was *dry* **parched**.
14 And in the second month,
on the seven and twentieth day of the month,
was the earth dried.
15 And *God spake* **Elohim worded** unto *Noah* **Noach**,
saying,
16 Go forth of the ark, thou, and thy *wife* **woman**,
and thy sons, and thy sons' *wives* **women** with thee.
17 Bring forth with thee
every *living thing* **live being** that is with thee,
of all flesh, *both* of *fowl* **fliers**, and of *cattle* **animals**,
and of every *creeping thing* **creeper**
that creepeth upon the earth;
that they may *breed abundantly* **teem** in the earth,
and *be fruitful* **bear fruit**,
and *multiply* **abound** upon the earth.
18 And *Noah* **Noach** went forth, and his sons,
and his *wife* **woman**,
and his sons' *wives* **women** with him:
19 Every *beast* **live being**, every *creeping thing* **creeper**,
and every *fowl* **flier**,
and *whatsoever* **all that** creepeth upon the earth,
after their kinds **by families**, went forth out of the ark.

NOACH'S SACRIFICE ALTAR

20 And *Noah* **Noach**
builded *an* **a sacrifice** altar unto *the LORD* **Yah Veh**;
and took of every *clean beast* **pure animal**,
and of every *clean fowl* **pure flier**,
and *offered burnt offerings* **holocausted holocausts**
on the **sacrifice** altar.
21 And *the LORD* **Yah Veh**
smelled **scented** a sweet *savour* **scent**;
and *the LORD* **Yah Veh** said in his heart,
I *will* **shall** not again *curse* **abase** the *ground* **soil** *any more*
for *man's* **humanity's** sake;
for the imagination of *man's* **humanity's** heart
is evil from his youth;
neither *will* **shall** I again smite *any more*
every *thing living* **live being**, as I have *done* **worked**.
22 *While* **As yet all the days of** the earth *remaineth*,
seedtime **seed** and harvest, and cold and heat,
and summer and winter, and day and night
shall not *cease* **shabbathize**.

ELOHIM'S BOW COVENANT

9 And *God* **Elohim** blessed *Noah* **Noach** and his sons,
and said unto them, *Be fruitful* **Bear fruit**,
and *multiply* **abound**, and *replenish* **fill** the earth.
2 And the *fear* **awesomeness** of you
and the *dread* **terror** of you
shall be upon every *beast* **live being** of the earth,
and upon every *fowl* **flier** of the *air* **heavens**,
upon all that *moveth* **creepeth** upon the *earth* **soil**,
and upon all the fishes of the sea;
into your hand are they *delivered* **given**.
3 Every *moving thing that liveth* **living creeper**
shall be *meat* for you;
even as the green herb have I given you all *things.*
4 *But* **Only** flesh with the *life* **soul** thereof,
which is the blood thereof, shall ye not eat.
5 And surely your blood of your *lives* **souls**
will **shall** I require;
at the hand of every *beast* **live being**
will **shall** I require it,
and at the hand of *man* **humanity**;
at the hand of every man's brother
will **shall** I require the *life* **soul** of *man* **humanity**.
6 Whoso *sheddeth man's* **poureth human** blood,
by *man* **humanity** shall his blood be *shed* **poured**:
for in the image of *God* **Elohim**
made **worked** he *man* **humanity**.
7 And you, *be ye fruitful* **bear fruit**, and *multiply* **abound**;
bring forth abundantly **teem** in the earth,
and *multiply* **abound** therein.
8 And *God spake* **Elohim said** unto *Noah* **Noach**,
and to his sons with him, saying,
9 And I, behold, I *establish* **raise** my covenant with you,
and with your seed after you;
10 And with every living *creature* **soul** that is with you,
of the *fowl* **fliers**, of the *cattle* **animals**,
and of every *beast* **live being** of the earth with you;
from all that go out of the ark,
to every *beast* **live being** of the earth.
11 And I *will establish* **shall raise** my covenant with you;
neither shall all flesh be cut off any more
by the waters of a flood;
neither shall there any more be a flood
to *destroy* **ruin** the earth.
12 And *God* **Elohim** said,
This is the *token* **sign** of the covenant
which I *make* **set** between me and **between** you
and every living *creature* **soul** that is with you,
for *perpetual* **eternal** generations:
13 I *do set* **give** my bow in the cloud,
and it shall be for a *token* **sign** of a covenant
between me and the earth.
14 And it shall *come to pass* **become**,
when I *bring* **overcloud** a cloud over the earth,
that the bow shall be seen in the cloud:
15 And I *will* **shall** remember my covenant,
which is between me and **between** you
and every living *creature* **soul** of all flesh;
and the waters shall *no more* **never again**
become a flood to *destroy* **ruin** all flesh.
16 And the bow shall be in the cloud;
and I *will look upon* **shall see** it,
that I may remember the *everlasting* **eternal** covenant
between *God* **Elohim**
and **between** every living *creature* **soul** of all flesh
that is upon the earth.
17 And *God* **Elohim** said unto *Noah* **Noach**,
This is the *token* **sign** of the covenant,
which I have *established* **raised** between me
and all flesh that is upon the earth.
18 And the sons of *Noah* **Noach**,
that went forth of the ark,
were Shem, and Ham, and *Japheth* **Yepheth**:
and Ham is the father of *Canaan* **Kenaan**.
19 These are the three sons of *Noah* **Noach**:
and of them was the whole earth *overspread* **scattered**.

NOACH'S INTOXICATION

20 And *Noah* **Noach**
began to be *an husbandman* **a man of the soil**,
and he planted a vineyard:
21 And he drank of the wine,
and *was drunken* **intoxicated**;
and he was *uncovered within* **exposed midst** his tent.
22 And Ham, the father of *Canaan* **Kenaan**,
saw the nakedness of his father,
and told his two brethren without.
23 And Shem and *Japheth* **Yepheth** took a *garment* **cloth**,

and *laid* **set** it
upon *both their* **the** shoulders **of the two of them**,
and went backward,
and covered the nakedness of their father;
and their faces were backward,
and they saw not their father's nakedness.
24 And *Noah* **Noach** awoke from his wine,
and knew what his younger son
had *done* **worked** unto him.
25 And he said, Cursed be *Canaan* **Kenaan**;
a servant of servants shall he be unto his brethren.
26 And he said,
Blessed be *the LORD God* **Yah Veh Elohim** of Shem;
and *Canaan* **Kenaan** shall be his servant.
27 *God* **Elohim** shall enlarge *Japheth* **Yepheth**,
and he shall *dwell* **tabernacle** in the tents of Shem;
and *Canaan* **Kenaan** shall be his servant.
28 And *Noah* **Noach** lived after the flood
three hundred **years** and fifty years.
29 And all the days of *Noah* **Noach**
were nine hundred **years** and fifty years: and he died.

GENEALOGY OF NOACH'S SONS

10 Now these are the generations
of the sons of *Noah* **Noach**,
Shem, Ham, and *Japheth* **Yepheth**:
and unto them were sons born after the flood.
2 The sons of *Japheth* **Yepheth**;
Gomer, and Magog, and *Madai* **Maday**,
and *Javan* **Yavan**, and Tubal,
and Meshech, and Tiras.
3 And the sons of Gomer;
Ashkenaz, and Riphath, and Togarmah.
4 And the sons of *Javan* **Yavan**;
Elishah **Eli Shah**, and Tarshish,
Kittim **Kittiym**, and Dodanim.
5 By these were the isles of the *Gentiles* **goyim**
divided **separated** in their lands;
every one **each man** after his tongue,
after their families, in their *nations* **goyim**.
6 And the sons of Ham;
Cush **Kush**, and *Mizraim* **Misraim**,
and *Phut* **Put**, and *Canaan* **Kenaan**.
7 And the sons of *Cush* **Kush**;
Seba, and Havilah, and Sabtah,
and Raamah, and Sabtechah:
and the sons of Raamah;
Sheba, and Dedan.
8 And *Cush* **Kush** begat Nimrod:
he began to be a mighty *one* in the earth.
9 He was a mighty hunter
before the LORD **at the face of Yah Veh**:
wherefore **thus** it is said,
Even as Nimrod the mighty hunter
before the LORD **at the face of Yah Veh**.
10 And the beginning of his *kingdom* **sovereigndom**
was Babel, and Erech,
and *Accad* **Akkad**, and *Calneh* **Kalneh**,
in the land of Shinar.
11 Out of that land went forth *Asshur* **Ashshur**,
and builded Nineveh,
and the city *Rehoboth* **Rechovoth**, and *Calah* **Kelach**,
12 And Resen between Nineveh and *Calah* **Kelach**:
the same is a great city.
13 And *Mizraim* **Misraim** begat *Ludim* **Ludiym**,
and Anamim, and Lehabim, and *Naphtuhim* **Naphtuchim**,
14 And *Pathrusim* **Pathrsimm**, and *Casluhim* **Kasluhim**,
(out of whom came *Philistim* **Peleshethiym**,)
and *Caphtorim* **Kaphtorim**.
15 And *Canaan* **Kenaan** begat Sidon his firstborn,
and Heth,
16 And the *Jebusite* **Yebusiy**,
and the *Amorite* **Emoriy**, and the *Girgasite* **Girgashiy**,
17 And the *Hivite* **Hivviy**,
and the *Arkite* **Arqiy**, and the *Sinite* **Siniy**,
18 And the *Arvadite* **Arvadiy**,
and the *Zemarite* **Semariy**, and the *Hamathite* **Hamathiy**:
and afterward were the families
of the *Canaanites spread abroad* **Kenaaniy scattered**.
19 And the border of the *Canaanites* **Kenaaniy**
was from Sidon,
as thou comest to Gerar, unto *Gaza* **Azzah**;
as thou goest, unto *Sodom* **Sedom**, and *Gomorrah* **Amorah**,
and Admah, and *Zeboim* **Seboim**,
even unto *Lasha* **Lesha**.
20 These are the sons of Ham,
after their families, after their tongues,
in their *countries* **lands**, *and* in their *nations* **goyim**.
21 Unto Shem also,
the father of all the *children* **sons** of *Eber* **Heber**,
the brother of *Japheth* **Yepheth** the *elder* **greater**,
even to him were *children* born.
22 The *children* **sons** of Shem;
Elam, and *Asshur* **Ashshur**,
and *Arphaxad* **Arpachshad**, and Lud, and Aram.
23 And the *children* **sons** of Aram;
Uz **Us**, and Hul, and Gether, and Mash.
24 And *Arphaxad* **Arpachshad** begat *Salah* **Shelach**;
and *Salah* **Shelach** begat *Eber* **Heber**.
25 And unto *Eber* **Heber** were born two sons:
the name of one was Peleg;
for in his days was the earth divided;
and his brother's name was *Joktan* **Yoqtan**.
26 And *Joktan* **Yoqtan** begat Almodad, and Sheleph,
and *Hazarmaveth* **Hasar Maveth**, and *Jerah* **Yerach**,
27 And *Hadoram* **Hado Ram**,
and Uzal, and *Diklah* **Diqlah**,
28 And Obal, and *Abimael* **Abi Mael**, and Sheba,
29 And Ophir, and Havilah, and *Jobab* **Yobab**:
all these were the sons of *Joktan* **Yoqtan**.
30 And their *dwelling* **settlement** was from Mesha,
as thou goest unto Sephar a mount of the east.
31 These are the sons of Shem,
after their families, after their tongues,
in their lands, after their *nations* **goyim**.
32 These are the families of the sons of *Noah* **Noach**,
after their generations, in their *nations* **goyim**:
and by these were the *nations divided* **goyim separated**
in the earth after the flood.

THE TOWER OF BABEL

11 And the whole earth was of one *language* **lip**,
and of one *speech* **word**.
2 And it *came to pass* **became**,
as they *journeyed* **pulled stakes** from the east,
that they found a *plain* **valley** in the land of Shinar;
and they *dwelt* **settled** there.
3 And they said *one* **man** to *another* **friend**,
Go to **Give**, let us make brick,
and **in burning**, burn them *thoroughly*.
And *they had* **there became** brick for stone,
and *slime had they* **there became bitumin** for morter.
4 And they said, *Go to* **Give**,
let us build us a city and a tower,
whose top may *reach* **be** unto *heaven* **the heavens**;
and let us *make* **work** us a name,
lest we be scattered abroad
upon the face of the whole earth.
5 And *the LORD came down* **Yah Veh descended**
to see the city and the tower,
which the *children* **sons** of *men* **humanity** builded.
6 And *the LORD* **Yah Veh** said, Behold, the people is one,
and they have all one *language* **lip**;
and this they begin to *do* **work**:
and now *nothing* **naught**
will **shall** be *restrained* **clipped** from them,
which they have *imagined* **intrigued** to *do* **work**.
7 *Go to* **Give**, let us *go down* **descend**,
and there *confound* **mix up** their *language* **lip**,
that *they* **man** may not *understand* **hear**
one another's speech **his friend's lip**.
8 So *the LORD* **Yah Veh**
scattered them abroad from thence
upon the face of all the earth:
and they *left off* **ceased** to build the city.
9 Therefore is the name of it called Babel;
because *the LORD* **Yah Veh** did there
confound **mix up** the *language* **lip** of all the earth:
and from thence did *the LORD* **Yah Veh**
scatter them abroad upon the face of all the earth.

GENEALOGY OF SHEM

10 These are the generations of Shem:
Shem was **a son of** an hundred years *old*,
and begat *Arphaxad* **Arpachshad** two years after the flood:
11 And Shem lived after he begat *Arphaxad* **Arpachshad**
five hundred years,
and begat sons and daughters.
12 And *Arphaxad* **Arpachshad** lived five and thirty years,
and begat *Salah* **Shelach**:
13 And *Arphaxad* **Arpachshad** lived
after he begat *Salah* **Shelach**
four hundred **years** and three years,
and begat sons and daughters.
14 And *Salah* **Shelach** lived thirty years,
and begat *Eber* **Heber**:
15 And *Salah* **Shelach** lived after he begat *Eber* **Heber**
four hundred **years** and three years,
and begat sons and daughters.
16 And *Eber* **Heber** lived four and thirty years,
and begat Peleg:
17 And *Eber* **Heber** lived after he begat Peleg
four hundred **years** and thirty years,
and begat sons and daughters.
18 And Peleg lived thirty years, and begat Reu:
19 And Peleg lived after he begat Reu
two hundred **years** and nine years,
and begat sons and daughters.
20 And Reu lived two and thirty years, and begat Serug:
21 And Reu lived after he begat Serug
two hundred **years** and seven years,
and begat sons and daughters.
22 And Serug lived thirty years, and begat *Nahor* **Nachor**:
23 And Serug lived after he begat *Nahor* **Nachor**
two hundred years,
and begat sons and daughters.
24 And *Nahor* **Nachor** lived nine and twenty years,
and begat *Terah* **Terach**:
25 And *Nahor* **Nachor** lived after he begat *Terah* **Terach**
an hundred **years** and nineteen years,
and begat sons and daughters.
26 And *Terah* **Terach** lived seventy years,
and begat Abram, *Nahor* **Nachor**, and Haran.
27 Now these are the generations of *Terah* **Terach**:
Terah **Terach** begat Abram, *Nahor* **Nachor**, and Haran;
and Haran begat Lot.
28 And Haran died
before **at the face of** his father *Terah* **Terach**
in the land of his *nativity* **kindred**,
in Ur of the *Chaldees* **Kesediym**.
29 And Abram and *Nahor* **Nachor**
took them *wives* **women**:
the name of Abram's *wife* **woman** was *Sarai* **Saray**;
and the name of *Nahor's wife* **Nachor's woman**,
Milcah **Milchah**, the daughter of Haran,
the father of *Milcah* **Milchah**,
and the father of *Iscah* **Yiskah**.
30 But *Sarai* **Saray** was *barren* **sterile**; she had no child.
31 And *Terah* **Terach** took Abram his son,
and Lot the son of Haran his son's son,
and *Sarai* **Saray** his daughter in law,
his son Abram's *wife* **woman**;
and they went forth with them
from Ur of the *Chaldees* **Kesediym**,
to go into the land of *Canaan* **Kenaan**;
and they came unto Haran, and *dwelt* **settled** there.
32 And the days of *Terah* **Terach**
were two hundred **years** and five years:
and *Terah* **Terach** died in Haran.

YAH VEH CALLS ABRAM

12 *Now the LORD* **Yah Veh** had said unto Abram,
Get thee out of **Go from** thy *country* **land**,
and from thy kindred, and from thy father's house,
unto a land that I *will shew thee* **shall have thee see**:
2 And I *will make* **shall work** of thee a great *nation* **goyim**,
and I *will* **shall** bless thee,
and *make* **greaten** thy name *great*;
and thou shalt be a blessing:
3 And I *will* **shall** bless them that bless thee,
and curse him that *curseth* **abaseth** thee:
and in thee shall all families of the *earth* **soil** be blessed.
4 So Abram *departed* **went**,
as *the LORD* **Yah Veh** had *spoken* **worded** unto him;
and Lot went with him:
and Abram was **a son of** seventy and five years *old*
when he departed out of Haran.
5 And Abram took *Sarai* **Saray** his *wife* **woman**,
and Lot his brother's son,
and all their *substance* **acquisitions**
that they had *gathered* **acquired**,
and the souls that they had *gotten* **worked** in Haran;
and they went forth
to go into the land of *Canaan* **Kenaan**;
and into the land of *Canaan* **Kenaan** they came.
6 And Abram passed through the land
unto the place of Sichem,
unto the *plain* **mighty oak** of Moreh.
And the *Canaanite* **Kenaaniy** was then in the land.
7 And *the LORD* **Yah Veh**
appeared unto **was seen by** Abram,
and said, Unto thy seed *will* **shall** I give this land:
and there builded he *an* **a sacrifice** altar
unto *the LORD* **Yah Veh**,
who appeared unto him **whom he had seen**.
8 And he removed from thence
unto a mountain on the east of *Bethel* **Beth El**,
and *pitched* **spread** his tent,
having *Bethel on the west* **Beth El seaward**,
and *Hai on the east* **Ay eastward**:
and there he builded *an* **a sacrifice** altar
unto *the LORD* **Yah Veh**,
and called upon the name of *the LORD* **Yah Veh**.
9 And **in pulling stakes,**
Abram *journeyed, going on still* **pulled stakes**,
toward the south.
10 And there was a famine in the land:
and Abram *went down* **descended** into *Egypt* **Misrayim**
to sojourn there;
for the famine was *grievous* **heavy** in the land.
11 And it *came to pass* **became**,
when he *was come near* **approached**
to enter into *Egypt* **Misrayim**,
that he said unto *Sarai* **Saray** his *wife* **woman**,
Behold *now* **I beseech**,
I know that thou art a fair woman *to look upon* **in visage**:
12 Therefore it shall *come to pass* **become**,
when the *Egyptians* **Misrayim** shall see thee,
that they shall say, This is his *wife* **woman**:
and they *will kill* **shall slaughter** me,
but they *will save* **shall preserve** thee alive.
13 Say, I *pray* **beseech** thee, thou art my sister:
that it may *be well with* **well—please** me for thy sake;
and my soul shall live because of thee.
14 And it *came to pass* **became**, that,
when Abram was come into *Egypt* **Misrayim**,
the *Egyptians beheld* **Misrayim saw** the woman
that she was *very* **mighty** fair.
15 The *princes also* **governors** of *Pharaoh* **Paroh** saw her,
and *commended* **halaled** her *before Pharaoh* **unto Paroh**:
and the woman was taken into *Pharaoh's* **Paroh's** house.
16 And he *entreated* **well—pleased** Abram *well* for her sake:
and he had *sheep* **flocks**, and oxen, and he *asses* **burros**,
and *menservants* **servants**, and *maidservants* **maids**,
and she *asses* **burros**, and camels.
17 And *the LORD* **Yah Veh** plagued *Pharaoh* **Paroh**
and his house with great plagues
because of *Sarai* **Saray** Abram's *wife's* **woman's word**.
18 And *Pharaoh* **Paroh** called Abram, and said,
What is this that thou hast *done* **worked** unto me?
why didst thou not tell me that she was thy *wife* **woman**?
19 Why saidst thou, She is my sister?
so I might have taken her to me to *wife* **woman**:
now therefore behold thy *wife* **woman**,
take *her*, and go thy way.
20 And *Pharaoh commanded* **Paroh misvahed** his men
concerning him:
and they sent him away, and his *wife* **woman**,
and all that he had.

ABRAM AND LOT SEPARATE

13 And Abram
went up **ascended** out of *Egypt* **Misrayim**,

he, and his *wife* **woman**, and all that he had,
and Lot with him, *into* **toward** the south.
2 And Abram was *very rich* **mighty heavy**
in *cattle* **chattel**, in silver, and in gold.
3 And he went on his journeys
from the south even to *Bethel* **Beth El**,
unto the place where his tent had been at the beginning,
between *Bethel* **Beth El** and *Hai* **Ai**;
4 Unto the place of the **sacrifice** altar,
which he had *made* **worked** there at the first:
and there Abram
called on the name of *the LORD* **Yah Veh**.
5 And Lot also, which went with Abram,
had flocks, and *herds* **oxen**, and tents.
6 And the land was not able to bear them,
that they might *dwell* **settle** together:
for their *substance* **acquisition** was great,
so that they could not *dwell* **settle** together.
7 And there was a strife
between the *herdmen* **tenders** of Abram's *cattle* **chattel**
and the *herdmen* **tenders** of Lot's *cattle* **chattel**:
and the *Canaanite* **Kenaaniy** and the *Perizzite* **Perizziy**
dwelled **settled** then in the land.
8 And Abram said unto Lot, Let there be no strife,
I *pray* **beseech** thee, between me and **between** thee,
and between my *herdmen* **tenders**
and **between** thy *herdmen* **tenders**;
for we be **men** — brethren.
9 Is not the whole land *before thee* **at thy face**?
separate thyself, I *pray* **beseech** thee, from me:
if *thou wilt take* the left *hand*,
then I *will* **shall** go to the right;
or if *thou depart* to the right *hand*,
then I *will* **shall** go to the left.
10 And Lot lifted up his eyes,
and *beheld* **saw** all the *plain* **environs** of *Jordan* **Yarden**,
that it was *well watered* **moistened** every where,
before the LORD **at the face of Yah Veh**
destroyed Sodom **ruining Sedom** and *Gomorrah* **Amorah**,
even as the garden of *the LORD* **Yah Veh**,
like the land of *Egypt* **Misrayim**,
as thou comest unto *Zoar* **Soar**.
11 Then Lot chose him
all the *plain* **environs** of *Jordan* **Yarden**;
and Lot *journeyed* **pulled stakes** east:
and they separated *themselves*
the one **man** from *the other* **brother**.
12 Abram *dwelled* **settled** in the land of *Canaan* **Kenaan**,
and Lot *dwelled* **settled** in the cities of the *plain* **environs**,
and pitched his tent toward *Sodom* **Sedom**.
13 But the men of *Sodom* **Sedom** were *wicked* **evil**
and *sinners before the LORD exceedingly*
sinned at the face of Yah Veh mightily.
14 And *the LORD* **Yah Veh** said unto Abram,
after that Lot was separated from him,
Lift up *now* thine eyes,
and *look* **see** from the place where thou art
northward, and southward,
and eastward, and *westward* **seaward**:
15 For all the land which thou seest,
to thee *will* **shall** I give it,
and to thy seed *for ever* **unto eternity**.
16 And I *will make* **shall set** thy seed
as the dust of the earth:
so that if a man can number the dust of the earth,
then shall thy seed also be numbered.
17 Arise, walk through the land in the length of it
and in the breadth of it;
for I *will* **shall** give it unto thee.
18 Then Abram removed his tent,
and came and *dwelt* **settled**
in the *plain* **mighty oak** of Mamre, which is in Hebron,
and built there *an* **a sacrifice** altar
unto *the LORD* **Yah Veh**.

ABRAM RESCUES LOT

14 And it *came to pass* **became,**
in the days of Amraphel *king* **sovereign** of Shinar,
Arioch king **Aryoch sovereign** of Ellasar,
Chedorlaomer king **Kedorlaomer sovereign** of Elam,
and Tidal *king* **sovereign** of *nations* **goyim**;
2 That these *made* **worked** war
with Bera *king* **sovereign** of *Sodom* **Sedom**,
and with Birsha *king* **sovereign** of *Gomorrah* **Amorah**,
Shinab *king* **sovereign** of Admah,
and *Shemeber* **Shem Eber**
king **sovereign** of *Zeboiim* **Seboim**,
and the *king* **sovereign** of Bela, which is *Zoar* **Soar**.
3 All these were joined together
in the *vale* **valley** of Siddim, which is the salt sea.
4 Twelve years they served *Chedorlaomer* **Kedorlaomer**,
and in the thirteenth year they rebelled.
5 And in the fourteenth year
came *Chedorlaomer* **Kedorlaomer**,
and the *kings* **sovereigns** that were with him,
and smote the *Rephaims* **Rephaim**
in Ashteroth *Karnaim* **Qarnaim**,
and the *Zuzims* **Zuziym** in Ham,
and the *Emims* **Emim** in Shaveh *Kiriathaim* **Qiryathayim**,
6 And the *Horites* **Horiy** in their mount Seir,
unto *Elparan* **El Paran**, which is by the wilderness.
7 And they returned, and came to *Enmishpat* **En Mishpat**,
which is *Kadesh* **Qadesh**,
and smote all the *country* **field**
of the *Amalekites* **Amaleqiy**,
and also the *Amorites* **Emoriy**,
that *dwelt* **settled** in *Hazezontamar* **Haseson Tamar**.
8 And there went out the *king* **sovereign** of *Sodom* **Sedom**,
and the *king* **sovereign** of *Gomorrah* **Amorah**,
and the *king* **sovereign** of Admah,
and the *king* **sovereign** of *Zeboiim* **Seboim**,
and the *king* **sovereign** of Bela (the same is *Zoar* **Soar**;)
and they *joined battle* **arrayed in war** with them
in the *vale* **valley** of Siddim;
9 With *Chedorlaomer* **Kedorlaomer**
the *king* **sovereign** of Elam,
and with Tidal *king* **sovereign** of *nations* **goyim**,
and Amraphel *king* **sovereign** of Shinar,
and *Arioch king* **Aryoch sovereign** of Ellasar;
four *kings* **sovereigns** with five.
10 And the *vale* **valley** of Siddim
was *full of slimepits* **wells — wells of bitumin**;
and the *kings* **sovereigns**
of *Sodom* **Sedom** and *Gomorrah* **Amorah** fled,
and fell there;
and they that *remained* **survived** fled to the mountain.
11 And they took all the *goods* **acquisitions**
of *Sodom* **Sedom** and *Gomorrah* **Amorah**,
and all their *victuals* **food**, and went their way.
12 And they took Lot, Abram's brother's son,
who *dwelt* **settled** in *Sodom* **Sedom**,
and his *goods* **acquisitions**, and *departed* **went**.
13 And there came *one that had escaped* **an escapee**,
and told Abram the Hebrew;
for he *dwelt* **tabernacled**
in the *plain* **mighty oak** of Mamre the *Amorite* **Emoriy**,
brother of Eshcol, and brother of Aner:
and these were *confederate* **masters of a covenant**
with Abram.
14 And when Abram heard
that his brother was *taken captive* **captured**,
he *armed* **drew** his *trained servants* **hanukked**,
born in his own house,
three hundred and eighteen,
and pursued them unto Dan.
15 And he *divided* **allotted** *himself* against them,
he and his servants, by night,
and smote them, and pursued them unto Hobah,
which is on the left *hand* of *Damascus* **Dammeseq**.
16 And he *brought back* **returned**
all *the goods* **his acquisitions**,
and also *brought again* **returned** his brother Lot,
and his *goods* **acquisitions**,
and the women also, and the people.
17 And the *king* **sovereign** of *Sodom* **Sedom**
went out to meet him
after his return from the *slaughter* **smiting**
of *Chedorlaomer* **Kedorlaomer**,
and of the *kings* **sovereigns** that were with him,
at the valley of Shaveh,
which is *the king's dale* **Ham Melech**.

MALKI SEDEQ

18 And *Melchizedek* **Malki Sedeq**
king **sovereign** of *Salem* **Shalem**
brought forth bread and wine:
and he was the priest of *the most high God* **El Elyon**.
19 And he blessed him, and said,
Blessed be Abram of *the most high God* **El Elyon**,
possessor of heaven **who chatteled the heavens** and earth:
20 And blessed be *the most high God* **El Elyon**,
which hath
delivered thine enemies **bucklered thy tribulators**
into thy hand.
And he gave him tithes of all.
21 And the *king* **sovereign** of *Sodom* **Sedom**
said unto Abram, Give me the *persons* **souls**,
and take the *goods* **acquisitions** to thyself.
22 And Abram said to the *king* **sovereign** of *Sodom* **Sedom**,
I have lift up mine hand unto *the LORD* **Yah Veh**,
the most high God **El Elyon**,
the possessor of heaven **who chatteled the heavens**
and earth,
23 That I *will* **shall** not take from a thread
even to a shoelatchet,
and that I *will* **shall** not take *any thing* **aught** that is thine,
lest thou shouldest say,
I have *made Abram rich* **enriched Abram**:
24 *Save* **Except** only that
which the *young men* **lads** have eaten,
and the *portion* **allotment** of the men
which went with me,
Aner, Eshcol, and Mamre;
let them take their *portion* **allotment**.

YAH VEH'S COVENANT TO ABRAM

15 After these *things* the word of *the LORD* **Yah Veh**
came **became** unto Abram in a vision, saying,
Fear **Awe** not, Abram: I am thy *shield* **buckler**,
and thy *exceeding great reward* **mighty abounding hire**.
2 And Abram said, *Lord GOD* **Adonay Yah Veh**,
what *wilt* **shalt** thou give me, seeing I go *childless* **barren**,
and the *steward* **son of the holdings** of my house
is this *Eliezer* **Eli Ezer** of *Damascus* **Dammeseq**?
3 And Abram said, Behold,
to me thou hast given no seed:
and, *lo* **behold**, *one born in* **a son of** my house
is mine heir **supersedeth me.**
4 And, behold,
the word of *the LORD* **Yah Veh** *came* unto him, saying,
This shall not *be thine heir* **supersede thee**;
but he that shall come forth
out of thine own *bowels* **inwards**
shall *be thine heir* **supersede thee**.
5 And he brought him *forth abroad* **outside**, and said,
Look *now* **I beseech**, toward *heaven* **the heavens**,
and *tell* **scribe** the stars,
if thou be able to *number* **scribe** them:
and he said unto him,
So **Thus** shall thy seed be.
6 And he *believed* **trusted** in *the LORD* **Yah Veh**;
and he *counted* **fabricated** it to him
for *righteousness* **justness**.
7 And he said unto him, *I am the LORD* **I — Yah Veh**
that brought thee out of Ur of the *Chaldees* **Kesediym**,
to give thee this land to *inherit* **possess** it.
8 And he said, *Lord GOD* **Adonay Yah Veh**,
whereby shall I know that I shall *inherit* **possess** it?
9 And he said unto him,
Take me an heifer of three *years old*,
and a she goat of three *years old*,
and a ram of three *years old*,
and a turtledove, and a *young pigeon* **youngling**.
10 And he took unto him all these,
and *divided* **sectioned** them in the midst,
and *laid each piece* **gave the sections**
one against another **man meeting friend**:
but the birds *divided* **sectioned** he not.
11 And when the *fowls* **swoopers**
came down **descended** upon the carcases,
Abram drove them away.
12 And when the sun was going down,
a *deep* **sound** sleep fell upon Abram; and, *lo* **behold**,
an horror **a terror** of great darkness fell upon him.
13 And he said unto Abram,
Know of a surety **In knowing, know**
that thy seed shall be a *stranger* **sojourner**
in a land that is not their's,
and shall serve them;
and they shall *afflict* **humble** them four hundred years;
14 And also that *nation* **goyim**, whom they shall serve,
will I judge **shall I plead their cause**:
and *afterward* **thus** shall they come out
with great *substance* **acquisitions.**
15 And thou shalt go to thy fathers in *peace* **shalom**;
thou shalt be *buried* **entombed**
in a good *old age* **grayness.**
16 But in the fourth generation
they shall *come* **return** hither *again*:
for the *iniquity* **perversity** of the *Amorites* **Emoriy**
is not yet *full* **at shalom.**
17 And it *came to pass* **became,**
that, when the sun went down, and it was *dark* **dusk**,
behold a smoking furnace,
and a *burning lamp* **flambeau of fire**
that passed between those pieces.
18 In *the same* **that** day
the LORD made **Yah Veh cut** a covenant with Abram,
saying, Unto thy seed have I given this land,
from the river of *Egypt* **Misrayim** unto the great river,
the river Euphrates:
19 The *Kenites* **Qeyniy**, and the *Kenizzites* **Qenaziy**,
and the *Kadmonites* **Qadmoniy**,
20 And the *Hittites* **Hethiy**,
and the *Perizzites* **Perizziy**, and the *Rephaims* **Rephaim**,
21 And the *Amorites* **Emoriy**, and the *Canaanites* **Kenaaniy**,
and the *Girgashites* **Girgashiy**, and the *Jebusites* **Yebusiy**.

SARAY AND HAGAR

16 Now *Sarai* **Saray** Abram's *wife* **woman**
bare him no children:
and she had *an handmaid* **a maid**,
an Egyptian **a Misrayim**, whose name was Hagar.
2 And *Sarai* **Saray** said unto Abram,
Behold *now* **I beseech**,
the LORD **Yah Veh** hath restrained me from bearing:
I *pray* **beseech** thee, go in unto my maid;
it may be that **perhaps**
I may *obtain children* **be builded** by her.
And Abram hearkened to the voice of *Sarai* **Saray**.
3 And *Sarai* **Saray** Abram's *wife* **woman**
took Hagar her maid the *Egyptian* **Misrayim**,
after Abram had dwelt ten years
at the end of ten years that Abram had settled
in the land of *Canaan* **Kenaan**,
and gave her to her *husband* **man** Abram
to be his *wife* **woman**.
4 And he went in unto Hagar, and she conceived:
and when she saw that she had conceived,
her *mistress* **lady** was *despised* **abased** in her eyes.
5 And *Sarai* **Saray** said unto Abram,
My *wrong* **violence** be upon thee:
I have given my maid into thy bosom;
and when she saw that she had conceived,
I was *despised* **abased** in her eyes:
the LORD **Yah Veh** judge between me and thee.
6 But Abram said unto *Sarai* **Saray**,
Behold, thy maid is in thy hand;
do **work** to her as *it pleaseth thee* **is good in thine eyes**.
And when *Sarai dealt hardly with* **Saray humbled** her,
she fled from her face.
7 And the angel of *the LORD* **Yah Veh**
found her by a fountain of water in the wilderness,
by the fountain in the way to Shur.
8 And he said, Hagar, *Sarai's* **Saray**'s maid,
whence camest thou?
and whither *wilt* **shalt** thou go?
And she said,
I flee from the face of my *mistress Sarai* **lady Saray**.
9 And the angel of *the LORD* **Yah Veh** said unto her,
Return to thy *mistress* **lady**,
and *submit* **humble** thyself under her hands.
10 And the angel of *the LORD* **Yah Veh** said unto her,
In abounding,

I will multiply **I shall abound** thy seed *exceedingly*,
that it shall not be *numbered* **scribed**
for *multitude* **abundance**.
11 And the angel of *the LORD* **Yah Veh** said unto her,
Behold, thou *art with child* **hast conceived**,
and shalt bear a son,
and shalt call his name *Ishmael* **Yishma El**;
because *the LORD* **Yah Veh**
hath heard thy *affliction* **humiliation**.
12 And he *will* **shall** be a *wild man* **human runner**;
his hand *will* **shall** be against every man,
and every man's hand against him;
and he shall *dwell* **tabernacle**
in the presence **at the face** of all his brethren.
13 And she called the name of *the LORD* **Yah Veh**
that *spake* **worded** unto her, *Thou God seest me* **El Roi**:
for she said,
Have I also here *looked* **seen** after him that seeth me?
14 Wherefore the well was called
Beerlahairoi **Beer Lachay Roi**;
behold, it is between *Kadesh* **Qadesh** and Bered.
15 And Hagar bare Abram a son:
and Abram called his son's name,
which Hagar bare, *Ishmael* **Yishma El**.
16 And Abram
was *fourscore* **a son of eighty** and six years *old*,
when Hagar bare *Ishmael* **Yishma El** to Abram.
17 And when Abram
was **a son of** ninety years and nine **years** *old*,
the LORD appeared to **Yah Veh was seen by** Abram,
and said unto him, *I am the Almighty God* **I — El Shadday**;
walk *before me* **at my face**,
and be thou *perfect* **integrious**.
2 And I *will make* **shall give** my covenant between me
and **between** thee,
and *will multiply* **shall abound** thee
exceedingly **mightily mighty**.

ABRAM IS RENAMED ABRAHAM

3 And Abram fell on his face:
and *God talked* **Elohim worded** with him, saying,
4 *As for me* **Surely — I**, behold, my covenant is with thee,
and thou shalt be a father
of *many nations* **a multitude of goyim**.
5 Neither shall thy name any more be called Abram,
but thy name shall be Abraham;
for a father of *many nations* **a multitude of goyim**
have I *made* **given** thee.
6 And I *will make* **shall give** thee
exceeding fruitful **to mighty mightily bear fruit**,
and I *will make nations of thee* **shall give thee**
to be a goyim,
and *kings* **sovereigns** shall come out of thee.
7 And I *will establish* **shall raise** my covenant
between me and **between** thee
and thy seed after thee in their generations
for an *everlasting* **eternal** covenant,
to be *a God* **Elohim** unto thee, and to thy seed after thee.
8 And I *will* **shall** give unto thee,
and to thy seed after thee,
the land *wherein thou art a stranger* **of thy sojournings**,
all the land of *Canaan* **Kenaan**,
for an *everlasting* **eternal** possession;
and I *will* **shall** be their *God* **Elohim**.

COVENANT OF CIRCUMCISION

9 And *God* **Elohim** said unto Abraham,
Thou shalt *keep* **guard** my covenant therefore,
thou, and thy seed after thee in their generations.
10 This is my covenant, which ye shall *keep* **guard**,
between me and **between** you
and **between** thy seed after thee;
Every *man child* **male** among you shall be circumcised.
11 And ye shall *circumcise* **clip** the flesh of your foreskin;
and it shall be a *token* **sign** of the covenant
betwixt **between** me and **between** you.
12 And he that is **a son of** eight days *old*
shall be circumcised among you,
every *man child* **male** in your generations,
he that is born in the house,
or *bought with money* **a chattel of silver**
of *any* **a son of a** stranger, which is not of thy seed.
13 He that is born in thy house,
and he that is *bought with thy money* **a chattel of silver**,
in circumcising,
must needs **shall certainly** be circumcised:
and my covenant shall be in your flesh
for an *everlasting* **eternal** covenant.
14 And the uncircumcised *man child* **male**
whose flesh of his foreskin is not circumcised,
that soul shall be cut off from his people;
he hath broken my covenant.

SARAY IS RENAMED SARAH

15 And *God* **Elohim** said unto Abraham,
As for *Sarai* **Saray** thy *wife* **woman**,
thou shalt not call her name *Sarai* **Saray**,
but Sarah shall her name be.
16 And I *will* **shall** bless her,
and give thee a son also of her:
yea, I *will* **shall** bless her,
and she shall be a *mother of nations* **goyim**;
kings **sovereigns** of people shall be of her.
17 Then Abraham fell upon his face, and laughed,
and said in his heart,
shall *a child be born unto him* **he bear,**
that is **a son of** an hundred years *old*?
and shall Sarah,
that is **a daughter of** ninety years *old*, bear?
18 And Abraham said unto *God* **Elohim**,
O that *Ishmael* **Yishma El**
might live *before thee* **at thy face**!
19 And *God* **Elohim** said, Sarah thy *wife* **woman**
shall bear thee a son *indeed* **nevertheless**;
and thou shalt call his name *Isaac* **Yischaq**:
and I *will establish* **shall raise** my covenant with him
for an *everlasting* **eternal** covenant,
and with his seed after him.
20 And as for *Ishmael* **Yishma El**, I have heard thee:
Behold, I have blessed him,
and *will make* **shall have** him *fruitful* **bear fruit**,
and *will multiply* **shall abound** him
exceedingly **mightily mighty**;
twelve *princes* **hierarchs** shall he beget,
and I *will make* **shall give** him **for** a great *nation* **goyim**.
21 But my covenant
will I establish **shall I raise** with *Isaac* **Yischaq**,
which Sarah shall bear unto thee
at this *set time* **season** in the next year.
22 And he *left off talking* **finished wording** with him,
and *God went up* **Elohim ascended** from Abraham.
23 And Abraham took *Ishmael* **Yishma El** his son,
and all that were born in his house,
and all that were
bought with his money **a chattel of silver**,
every male among the men of Abraham's house;
and circumcised the flesh of their foreskin
in the selfsame day,
as *God* **Elohim** had *said* **worded** unto him.
24 And Abraham
was **a son of** ninety years *old* and nine **years**,
when he was circumcised in the flesh of his foreskin.
25 And *Ishmael* **Yishma El** his son *was* thirteen *years old*,
when he was circumcised in the flesh of his foreskin.
26 In *the selfsame* **that** day was Abraham circumcised,
and *Ishmael* **Yishma El** his son.
27 And all the men of his house, born in the house,
and *bought with money* **a chattel of silver**
of the **son of a** stranger,
were circumcised with him.

THREE VISITORS

18 And *the LORD* **Yah Veh**
appeared unto **was seen by** him
in the *plains* **mighty oak** of Mamre:
and he sat in the tent *door* **opening** in the heat of the day;
2 And he lift up his eyes and *looked* **saw**, and, *lo* **behold**,
three men *stood* **stationed themselves** by him:
and when he saw them,
he ran to meet them from the tent *door* **opening**,
and *bowed himself* **prostrated** toward the *ground* **earth**,
3 And said, My *Lord* **Adonay**, *if now* **If, I beseech thee,**
I have found *favour* **charism** in thy *sight* **eyes**,
pass not away, I *pray* **beseech** thee, from my servant:

4 Let a little water, I *pray* **beseech** you, be *fetched* **taken**,
and *wash* **bathe** your feet,
and *rest yourselves* **lean** under the tree:
5 And I *will fetch* **shall take** a morsel of bread,
and *comfort* **support** ye your hearts;
after that ye shall pass on:
for therefore are ye *come* **passed** to your servant.
And they said, So *do* **work**, as thou hast *said* **worded**.
6 And Abraham hastened into the tent unto Sarah,
and said, *Make ready quickly* **Hasten**
three *measures* **seahs** of fine *meal* **flour**,
knead *it*, and *make cakes upon the hearth* **work ashcakes**.
7 And Abraham ran unto the *herd* **oxen**,
and *fetcht a calf* **took a son of the oxen** tender and good,
and gave it unto a *young man* **lad**;
and he hasted to *dress* **work** it.
8 And he took butter, and milk,
and the *calf* **son of the oxen**
which he had *dressed* **worked**,
and *set it before them* **gave it at their face**;
and he stood by them under the tree, and they did eat.
9 And they said unto him,
Where is Sarah thy *wife* **woman**?
And he said, Behold, in the tent.
10 And he said,
In returning, I *will certainly* **shall** return unto thee
according to the time of life,
and, *lo* **behold**, Sarah thy *wife* **woman** shall have a son.
And Sarah heard it in the tent *door* **opening**,
which was behind him.
11 Now Abraham and Sarah were *old* **aged**
and well stricken in *age* **days**;
and it ceased to be with Sarah
after the *manner* **way** of women.
12 Therefore Sarah laughed within herself, saying,
After I am *waxed old* **worn out**
shall I have pleasure,
my *lord* **adoni** being *old* **aged** also?
13 And *the LORD* **Yah Veh** said unto Abraham,
Wherefore **Why** did Sarah laugh, saying,
Shall I *of a surety* **truly** bear?
a child, which am old **I — aged**?
14 Is any *thing* **word** too *hard* **marvelous**
for *the LORD* **Yah Veh**?
At the *time appointed* **season** I *will* **shall** return unto thee,
according to the time of life,
and Sarah shall have a son.
15 Then Sarah denied, saying, I laughed not;
for she was *afraid* **awed**.
And he said, Nay; but thou didst laugh.
16 And the men rose up from thence,
and looked toward Sodom **at the face of Sedom**:
and Abraham went with them
to *bring* **send** them on the way.
17 And *the LORD* **Yah Veh** said,
Shall I hide from Abraham that *thing* which I *do* **work**;
18 Seeing that
in becoming, Abraham shall *surely* become
a great and mighty *nation* **goyim**,
and all the *nations* **goyim** of the earth
shall be blessed in him?
19 For I know him,
that he *will command* **shall misvah** his *children* **sons**
and his household after him,
and they shall *keep* **guard** the way of *the LORD* **Yah Veh**,
to *do justice* **work justness** and judgment;
that *the LORD* **Yah Veh** may bring upon Abraham
that which he hath *spoken* **worded** of him.
20 And *the LORD* **Yah Veh** said,
Because the cry of *Sodom* **Sedom** and *Gomorrah* **Amorah**
is great,
and because their sin is *very grievous* **mighty heavy**;
21 I *will go down* **shall descend** now,
and see whether they have *done altogether* **fully worked**
according to the cry of it, which is come unto me;
and if not, I *will* **shall** know.
22 And the men turned their faces from thence,
and went toward *Sodom* **Sedom**:
but Abraham stood *yet* **still**
before the LORD **at the face of Yah Veh**.

ABRAHAM'S INTERCESSION WITH YAH VEH

23 And Abraham drew near, and said,
Wilt **Shalt** thou *also destroy* **scrape away**
the *righteous* **just** with the wicked?
24 Peradventure there be fifty *righteous* **just**
within **midst** the city:
wilt **shalt** thou *also destroy* **scrape away**
and not spare the place
for the fifty *righteous* **just** that are *therein* **within**?
25 *That be far* **Far be it** from thee
to *do after* **work** this *manner* **word**,
to *slay* **deathify** the *righteous* **just** with the wicked:
and that *the righteous* **it** should be,
the just as the wicked,
that be far **far be it** from thee:
Shall not the Judge of all the earth
do right **work judgment**?
26 And *the LORD* **Yah Veh** said,
If I find in *Sodom* **Sedom** fifty *righteous* **just**
within **midst** the city,
then I *will* **shall** spare all the place for their sakes.
27 And Abraham answered and said,
Behold *now* **I beseech**,
I have *taken upon me* **willed** to *speak* **word**
unto *the Lord* **Adonay**,
which am but **I** — dust and ashes:
28 Peradventure there shall lack five
of the fifty *righteous* **just**:
wilt **shalt** thou *destroy* **ruin** all the city for *lack of* five?
And he said, If I find there forty and five,
I *will* **shall** not *destroy* **ruin** it.
29 And he *spake* **worded** unto him yet again, and said,
Peradventure there shall be forty found there.
And he said, I *will* **shall** not *do* **work** it for forty's sake.
30 And he said *unto him, Oh* **I beseech,**
let not *the Lord be angry* **Adonay inflame**,
and I *will speak* **shall word**:
Peradventure there shall thirty be found there.
And he said,
I *will* **shall** not *do* **work** it, if I find thirty there.
31 And he said, Behold *now* **I beseech**,
I have *taken upon me* **willed** to *speak* **word**
unto *the Lord* **Adonay**:
Peradventure there shall be twenty found there.
And he said,
I *will* **shall** not *destroy* **ruin** it for twenty's sake.
32 And he said,
Oh let not *the Lord be angry* **Adonay inflame**,
and I *will speak* **shall word**
yet but this once **only this time**:
Peradventure ten shall be found there.
And he said, I *will* **shall** not *destroy* **ruin** *it* for ten's sake.
33 And *the LORD* **Yah Veh** went his way,
as soon as he had *left communing* **finished wording**
with Abraham:
and Abraham returned unto his place.

SEDOM SCRAPED AWAY

19 And there came two angels
to *Sodom* **Sedom** at even;
and Lot sat in the *gate* **portal** of *Sodom* **Sedom**:
and Lot seeing them rose up to meet them;
and he *bowed himself* **prostrated**
with his *face* **nostrils** toward the *ground* **earth**;
2 And he said, Behold *now* **I beseech**, my *lords* **adonim**,
turn in, I *pray* **beseech** you, into your servant's house,
and *tarry all night* **stay overnight**,
and *wash* **bathe** your feet,
and ye shall *rise up* **start** early, and go on your ways.
And they said, Nay;
but we *will abide* **shall stay**
in the *street all night* **broadway overnight**.
3 And he *pressed upon* **urged** them *greatly* **mightily**;
and they turned in unto him, and entered into his house;
and he *made* **worked** them a *feast* **banquet**,
and did bake *unleavened bread* **matsah**, and they did eat.
4 But before they lay down,
the men of the city, *even* the men of *Sodom* **Sedom**,
compassed **surrounded** the house *round*,
both old and young **from aged to lad**,
all the people from every *quarter* **extremity**:

5 And they called unto Lot, and said unto him,
Where are the men which came in to thee this night?
bring them out unto us, that we may know them.
6 And Lot went out at the *door* **portal** unto them,
and shut the door after him,
7 And said, I *pray* **beseech** you, brethren,
do not so wickedly **vilify not**.
8 Behold *now* **I beseech**,
I have two daughters which have not known man;
let me, I *pray* **beseech** you, bring them out unto you,
and *do* **work** ye to them as is good in your eyes:
only unto these men *do nothing* **work no word**;
for therefore came they
under the shadow of my *roof* **beams**.
9 And they said, *Stand* **Draw** back.
And they said *again,* This one *fellow* came in to sojourn,
and **in judging,** he *will needs be a* **shall** judge:
now *will we deal worse with* **shall we vilify** thee,
(rather) than *with* them.
And they *pressed sore* **urged mightily** upon the man,
even Lot, and came near to break the door.
10 But the men *put forth* **extended** their hand,
and pulled Lot into the house to them,
and shut to the door.
11 And they smote the men
that were at the *door* **portal** of the house with blindness,
both small and great:
so that they wearied themselves to find the *door* **portal**.
12 And the men said unto Lot,
Hast thou here any besides?
son in law, and thy sons, and thy daughters,
and whatsoever thou hast in the city,
bring them out of this place:
13 For we *will destroy* **shall ruin** this place,
because the cry of them *is waxen great* **greateneth**
before **at** the face of *the LORD* **Yah Veh**;
and *the LORD* **Yah Veh** hath sent us to *destroy* **ruin** it.
14 And Lot went out,
and *spake* **worded** unto his *sons in law* **in laws**,
which *married* **had taken** his daughters,
and said, *Up* **Arise**, get you out of this place:
for *the LORD will destroy* **Yah Veh shall ruin** this city.
But he seemed as one that *mocked* **ridiculed**
unto his sons in law **in the eyes of his in laws**.
15 And *when* **as** the *morning arose* **dawn ascended**,
then the angels hastened Lot, saying,
Arise, take thy *wife* **woman**, and thy two daughters,
which are *here* **found**;
lest thou be *consumed* **scraped away**
in the *iniquity* **perversity** of the city.
16 And while he lingered,
the men laid hold upon his hand,
and upon the hand of his *wife* **woman**,
and upon the hand of his two daughters;
the LORD **Yah Veh**
being *merciful* **compassionate** unto him:
and they brought him forth, and set him without the city.
17 And it *came to pass* **became**,
when they had brought them *forth abroad* **out**,
that he said, Escape for thy *life* **soul**;
look not behind thee,
neither stay thou in all the *plain* **environs**;
escape to the mountain,
lest thou be *consumed* **scraped away**.
18 And Lot said unto them,
Oh **I beseech**, not so, my *Lord* **adoni**:
19 Behold *now* **I beseech**,
thy servant hath found *grace* **charism** in thy *sight* **eyes**,
and thou hast *magnified* **greatened** thy mercy,
which thou hast *shewed* **worked** unto me
in *saving* **preserving** my *life* **soul alive**;
and I cannot escape to the mountain,
lest some evil *take me* **adhere**, and I die:
20 Behold *now* **I beseech**,
this city is near to flee unto, and it is a little one:
Oh **I beseech**, let me escape thither,
(is it not a little one?) and my soul shall live.
21 And he said unto him, *See* **Behold**,
I have *accepted thee* **spared thy face**
concerning this *thing* **word** also,
that I *will* **shall** not *overthrow* **overturn** this city,
for the which thou hast *spoken* **worded**.
22 Haste thee, escape thither;
for I *cannot do any thing* **can work no word**
till thou be come thither.
Therefore the name of the city was called *Zoar* **Soar**.
23 The sun was risen upon the earth
when Lot entered into *Zoar* **Soar**.
24 Then *the LORD* **Yah Veh**
rained upon *Sodom* **Sedom** and upon *Gomorrah* **Amorah**
brimstone **sulphur** and fire
from *the LORD* **Yah Veh** out of *heaven* **the heavens**;
25 And he *overthrew* **overturned** those cities,
and all the *plain* **environs**,
and all *the inhabitants of* **that settled** the cities,
and that which *grew* **sprouted** upon the *ground* **soil**.
26 But his *wife* **woman** looked back from behind him,
and she became a *pillar* **statue** of salt.
27 And Abraham *gat up* **started** early in the morning
to the place where he stood
before the LORD **at the face of Yah Veh**:
28 And he looked *toward* **at the face of**
Sodom **Sedom** and *Gomorrah* **Amorah**,
and *toward* **at the face of**
all the land of the *plain* **environs**,
and *beheld* **saw**, and, *lo* **behold**,
the smoke of the *country went up* **land ascended**
as the smoke of a furnace.
29 And it *came to pass* **became**,
when *God* **Elohim**
destroyed **ruined** the cities of the *plain* **environs**,
that *God* **Elohim** remembered Abraham,
and sent Lot out of the midst of the *overthrow* **overturning**,
when he *overthrew* **overturned** the cities
in the which Lot *dwelt* **settled**.
30 And Lot *went up* **ascended** out of *Zoar* **Soar**,
and *dwelt* **settled** in the mountain,
and his two daughters with him;
for he *feared* **awed** to *dwell* **settle** in *Zoar* **Soar**:
and he *dwelt* **settled** in a cave, he and his two daughters.

LOT'S DAUGHTERS' CHILDREN

31 And the firstborn said unto the *younger* **lesser**,
Our father *is old* **hath aged**,
and there is not a man in the earth to come in unto us
after the *manner* **way** of all the earth:
32 *Come* **Go**, let us make our father drink wine,
and we *will* **shall** lie with him,
that we may *preserve* **enliven** seed of our father.
33 And they made their father drink wine that night:
and the firstborn went in, and lay with her father;
and he perceived not when she lay down,
nor when she arose.
34 And it *came to pass* **became** on the morrow,
that the firstborn said unto the *younger* **lesser**,
Behold, I lay yesternight with my father:
let us make him drink wine this night also;
and go thou in, and lie with him,
that we may *preserve* **enliven** seed of our father.
35 And they made their father drink wine that night also:
and the *younger* **lesser** arose, and lay with him;
and he perceived not when she lay down,
nor when she arose.
36 Thus *were both the* **the two** daughters of Lot
with child **conceived** by their father.
37 And the firstborn bare a son,
and called his name Moab:
the same **who** is the father
of the *Moabites* **Moabiym** unto this day.
38 And the *younger* **lesser**, she also bare a son,
and called his name *Benammi* **Ben Ammi**:
the same **who** is the father
of the *children* **sons** of Ammon unto this day.

ABRAHAM PULLS STAKES

20 And Abraham
journeyed **pulled stakes** from thence
toward the south *country* **land**,
and *dwelled* **settled** between *Kadesh* **Qadesh** and Shur,
and sojourned in Gerar.
2 And Abraham said of Sarah his *wife* **woman**,
She is my sister:

and *Abimelech king* **Abi Melech sovereign** of Gerar sent,
and took Sarah.
3 But *God* **Elohim** came to *Abimelech* **Abi Melech**
in a dream by night,
and said to him, Behold, thou *art but a dead man* **diest**,
for the woman which thou hast taken;
for she is *a man's wife* **married to a master**.
4 But *Abimelech* **Abi Melech**
had not *come near* **approached** her:
and he said, *Lord* **Adonay**,
wilt **shalt** thou *slay* **slaughter** also
a *righteous nation* **just goyim**?
5 Said he not unto me, She is my sister?
and she, even she herself said, He is my brother:
in the integrity of my heart
and innocency of my *hands* **palms**
have I *done* **worked** this.
6 And *God* **Elohim** said unto him in a dream,
Yea, I know that thou *didst* **workedst** this
in the integrity of thy heart;
for I also withheld thee from sinning against me:
therefore *suffered* **gave** I thee not to touch her.
7 Now therefore restore the man his *wife* **woman**;
for he is a prophet, and he shall pray for thee,
and thou shalt live:
and if thou restore her not,
know thou that **in dying,** thou shalt *surely* die,
thou, and all that are thine.
8 Therefore *Abimelech* **Abi Melech**
rose **started** early in the morning,
and called all his servants,
and *told* **worded** all these *things* **words** in their ears:
and the men were *sore afraid* **mightily awed**.
9 Then *Abimelech* **Abi Melech** called Abraham,
and said unto him,
What hast thou *done* **worked** unto us?
and what have I *offended* **sinned against** thee,
that thou hast brought on me
and on my *kingdom* **sovereigndom** a great sin?
thou hast *done deeds* **worked works** unto me
that ought not to be *done* **worked**.
10 And *Abimelech* **Abi Melech** said unto Abraham,
What sawest thou,
that thou hast *done* **worked** this *thing* **word**?
11 And Abraham said, Because I *thought* **said**,
Surely **Only** the *fear* **awe** of *God* **Elohim**
is not in this place;
and they *will slay* **shall slaughter** me
for my *wife's sake* **woman's word**.
12 And yet *indeed* **truly** she is my sister;
she is the daughter of my father,
but not the daughter of my mother;
and she became my *wife* **woman**.
13 And it *came to pass* **became**,
when *God* **Elohim** caused me to *wander* **stray**
from my father's house,
that I said unto her,
This is thy *kindness* **mercy**
which thou shalt *shew* **work** unto me;
at every place whither we shall come,
say of me, He is my brother.
14 And *Abimelech* **Abi Melech** took *sheep* **flocks**, and oxen,
and *menservants* **servants**, and *womenservants* **maids**,
and gave them unto Abraham,
and restored him Sarah his *wife* **woman**.
15 And *Abimelech* **Abi Melech** said,
Behold, my land *is before thee* **be at thy face**:
dwell **settle** where it *pleaseth thee* **be good in thine eyes**.
16 And unto Sarah he said, Behold,
I have given thy brother a thousand *pieces of* silver:
behold, he is to thee a covering of the eyes,
unto all that are with thee, and with all *other*:
thus she was reproved.
17 So Abraham prayed unto *God* **Elohim**:
and *God* **Elohim** healed *Abimelech* **Abi Melech**,
and his *wife* **woman**, and his *maidservants* **maids**;
and they bare *children*.
18 For **in restraining,**
the LORD **Yah Veh** had *fast closed up* **restrained**
all the wombs of the house of *Abimelech* **Abi Melech**,
because **for sake of the word** of Sarah
Abraham's *wife* **woman.**

SARAH BIRTHS YISCHAQ

21 And *the LORD* **Yah Veh**
visited Sarah as he had said,
and *the LORD did* **Yah Veh worked** unto Sarah
as he had *spoken* **worded**.
2 For Sarah conceived,
and bare Abraham a son in his old age,
at the *set time* **season**
of which *God* **Elohim** had *spoken* **worded** to him.
3 And Abraham called the name of his son
that was born unto him,
whom Sarah bare to him, *Isaac* **Yischaq**.
4 And Abraham circumcised his son *Isaac* **Yischaq**
being **a son of** eight days *old*,
as *God* **Elohim** had *commanded* **misvahed** him.
5 And Abraham was **a son of** an hundred years *old*,
when his son *Isaac* **Yischaq** was born unto him.
6 And Sarah said,
God **Elohim** hath *made* **worked** me to laugh,
so that all that hear *will* **shall** laugh with me.
7 And she said,
Who *would* **should** have *said* **uttered** unto Abraham,
that Sarah should have *given children suck* **suckled sons**?
for I have born him a son in his old age.
8 And the child grew, and was weaned:
and Abraham *made* **worked** a great *feast* **banquet**
the *same* day that *Isaac* **Yischaq** was weaned.
9 And Sarah saw the son of Hagar the *Egyptian* **Misrayim**,
which she had born unto Abraham, *mocking* **ridiculing**.
10 Wherefore she said unto Abraham,
Cast out **Expel** this *bondwoman* **maid** and her son:
for the son of this *bondwoman* **maid**
shall not *be heir with* **supersede** my son,
even with *Isaac* **Yischaq**.
11 And the *thing* **word** was *very grievous* **mighty evil**
in Abraham's *sight* **eyes**
because of his son.
12 And *God* **Elohim** said unto Abraham,
Let it not be *grievous* **evil** in thy *sight* **eyes**
because of the lad,
and because of thy *bondwoman* **maid**;
in all that Sarah hath said unto thee,
hearken unto her voice;
for in *Isaac* **Yischaq** shall thy seed be called.
13 And also of the son of the *bondwoman* **maid**
will I make a nation **shall I set a goyim**,
because he is thy seed.
14 And Abraham *rose up* **started** early in the morning,
and took bread, and a *bottle* **skin** of water,
and gave it unto Hagar,
putting it on her shoulder, and the child,
and sent her away:
and she *departed* **went**,
and *wandered* **strayed** in the wilderness
of *Beersheba* **Beer Sheba**.
15 And the water
was *spent in* **finished off from** the *bottle* **skin**,
and she cast the child under one of the shrubs.
16 And she went,
and sat her down *over against him* **opposite,**
a good way off **away,** as it were a bowshot:
for she said, Let me not see the death of the child.
And she sat *over against him* **far removed**,
and lift up her voice, and wept.
17 And *God* **Elohim** heard the voice of the lad;
and the angel of *God* **Elohim**
called to Hagar out of *heaven* **the heavens**,
and said unto her, What aileth thee, Hagar? *fear* **awe** not;
for *God* **Elohim** hath heard the voice of the lad
where he is.
18 Arise, lift up the lad,
and *hold* **strengthen** him in thine hand;
for I *will make* **shall set** him a great *nation* **goyim**.
19 And *God* **Elohim** opened her eyes,
and she saw a well of water;
and she went, and filled the *bottle* **skin** with water,
and gave the lad drink.
20 And *God* **Elohim** was with the lad;

and he grew, and *dwelt* **settled** in the wilderness,
and *became an archer* **abounded with the bow.**
21 And he *dwelt* **settled** in the wilderness of Paran:
and his mother took him a *wife* **woman**
out of the land of *Egypt* **Misrayim.**
22 And it *came to pass* **became** at that time,
that *Abimelech* **Abi Melech**
and *Phichol* **Pichol** the *chief captain* **governor** of his host
spake **said** unto Abraham, saying,
God **Elohim** is with thee in all that thou *doest* **workest:**
23 Now therefore *swear* **oath** unto me here by *God* **Elohim**
that thou *wilt* **shalt** not *deal falsely* **falsify** with me,
nor with my *son* **offspring,**
nor with my *son's son* **posterity:**
but according to the *kindness* **mercy**
that I have *done* **worked** unto thee,
thou shalt *do* **work** unto me,
and to the land wherein thou hast sojourned.
24 And Abraham said, I *will swear* **shall oath.**
25 And Abraham reproved *Abimelech* **Abi Melech**
because of a well of water,
which *Abimelech's* **Abi Melech's** servants
had *violently taken away* **stripped.**
26 And *Abimelech* **Abi Melech** said,
I *wot* **perceived** not
who hath *done* **worked** this *thing* **word:**
neither didst thou tell me, neither yet heard I of it,
but **until** to day.
27 And Abraham took *sheep* **flocks** and oxen,
and gave them unto *Abimelech* **Abi Melech;**
and *both* **the two** of them *made* **cut** a covenant.
28 And Abraham
set **stationed** seven ewe lambs of the flock by themselves.
29 And *Abimelech* **Abi Melech** said unto Abraham,
What *mean* — these seven ewe lambs
which thou hast *set* **stationed** by themselves?
30 And he said,
For these seven ewe lambs shalt thou take of my hand,
so that they may be a witness unto me,
that I have digged this well.
31 Wherefore he called that place *Beersheba* **Beer Sheba;**
because there they *sware* **oathed** — *both* **the two** of them.
32 Thus they *made* **cut** a covenant
at *Beersheba* **Beer Sheba:**
then *Abimelech* **Abi Melech** rose up,
and *Phichol* **Pichol** the *chief captain* **governor** of his host,
and they returned
into the land of the *Philistines* **Peleshethiy.**
33 And *Abraham* **he** planted a grove
in *Beersheba* **Beer Sheba,**
and called there on the name of *the LORD* **Yah Veh,**
the *everlasting God* **eternal El.**
34 And Abraham sojourned
in the *Philistines'* land **of the Peleshethiym** many days.

ELOHIM TESTS ABRAHAM

22 And it *came to pass* **became,** after these *things* **words,**
that *God did tempt* **Elohim tested** Abraham,
and said unto him, Abraham:
and he said, Behold, *here I am* — **I.**
2 And he said, Take now thy son,
thine only *son Isaac* **Yischaq,** whom thou lovest,
and *get thee* **go thou** into the land of *Moriah* **Mori Yah;**
and *offer* **holocaust** him there
for a *burnt offering* **holocaust**
upon one of the mountains
which I *will tell thee of* **shall say.**
3 And Abraham *rose up* **started** early in the morning,
and *saddled* **harnessed** his *ass* **he burro,**
and took two of his *young men* **lads** with him,
and *Isaac* **Yischaq** his son,
and *clave* **split** the *wood* **timber**
for the *burnt offering* **holocaust,**
and rose up, and went unto the place
of which *God* **Elohim** had told him.
4 Then on the third day Abraham lifted up his eyes,
and saw the place afar off.
5 And Abraham said unto his *young men* **lads,**
Abide **Sit** ye here with the *ass* **he burro;**
and I and the lad *will* **shall** go *yonder* **thus**
and *worship* **prostrate,**
and *come again* **return** to you.
6 And Abraham took the *wood* **timber**
of the *burnt offering* **holocaust,**
and *laid* **set** it upon *Isaac* **Yischaq** his son;
and he took the fire in his hand, and a knife;
and they went *both* **the two** of them together.
7 And *Isaac spake* **Yischaq said** unto Abraham his father,
and said, My father:
and he said, Here *am* — I, my son.
And he said, Behold the fire and the *wood* **timber:**
but where is the lamb for a *burnt offering* **holocaust?**
8 And Abraham said, My son,
God will provide himself **Elohim shall see** a lamb
for a *burnt offering* **holocaust:**
so they went *both* **the two** of them together.
9 And they came to the place
which *God* **Elohim** had told him of;
and Abraham built *an* **a sacrifice** altar there,
and *laid* **arranged** the *wood* **timber** *in order,*
and bound *Isaac* **Yischaq** his son,
and *laid* **set** him on the **sacrifice** altar
upon **above** the *wood* **timber.**
10 And Abraham *stretched forth* **extended** his hand,
and took the knife to *slay* **slaughter** his son.
11 And the angel of *the LORD* **Yah Veh**
called unto him out of *heaven* **the heavens,**
and said, Abraham, Abraham:
and he said, Here *am* — I.
12 And he said, *Lay* **Extend** not thine hand upon the lad,
neither *do* **work** thou *any thing* **aught** unto him:
for *now* **at this time**
I know that thou *fearest God* **awest Elohim,**
seeing thou hast not withheld thy son,
thine only *son* from me.
13 And Abraham lifted up his eyes,
and *looked* **saw,** and behold,
behind *him* a ram *caught* **held** in a thicket by his horns:
and Abraham went and took the ram,
and *offered* **holocausted** him *up*
for a *burnt offering* **holocaust**
in the stead of his son.
14 And Abraham called the name of that place
Jehovahjireh **Yah Veh Yireh:**
as it is said to this day,
In the mount of *the LORD* **Yah Veh** it shall be seen.
15 And the angel of *the LORD* **Yah Veh**
called unto Abraham out of *heaven* **the heavens**
the second time,
16 And said, By myself have I *sworn* **oathed,**
saith the LORD **an oracle of Yah Veh,**
for because thou hast *done* **worked** this *thing* **word,**
and hast not withheld thy son, thine only *son:*
17 That in blessing, I *will* **shall** bless thee,
and in *multiplying* **abounding,**
I *will multiply* **shall abound** thy seed
as the stars of the *heaven* **heavens,**
and as the sand which is upon the sea *shore* **edge;**
and thy seed shall possess the *gate* **portal** of his enemies;
18 And in thy seed
shall all the *nations* **goyim** of the earth be blessed;
because thou hast *obeyed* **heard** my voice.
19 So Abraham returned unto his *young men* **lads,**
and they rose up
and went together to *Beersheba* **Beer Sheba;**
and Abraham *dwelt* **settled** at *Beersheba* **Beer Sheba.**
20 And it *came to pass* **became,** after these *things* **words,**
that it was told Abraham, saying,
Behold, *Milcah* **Milchah,**
she hath also born *children* **sons**
unto thy brother *Nahor* **Nachor;**
21 Huz his firstborn, and Buz his brother,
and *Kemuel* **Qemu El** the father of Aram,
22 And *Chesed* **Kesed,** and Hazo, and Pildash,
and *Jidlaph* **Yidlaph,** and *Bethuel* **Bethu El.**
23 And *Bethuel* **Bethu El** begat *Rebekah* **Ribqah:**
these eight *Milcah* **Milchah**
did bear to *Nahor* **Nachor,** Abraham's brother.
24 And his concubine, whose name was Reumah,
she bare also *Tebah* **Tebach,** and *Gaham* **Gacham,**
and *Thahash* **Thachash,** and Maachah.

SARAH'S DEATH

23 And **the life of** Sarah was an hundred **years**
and seven **years** and twenty years *old*:
these were — the years of the life of Sarah.
2 And Sarah died in *Kirjatharba* **Qiryath Arba**;
the same is Hebron in the land of *Canaan* **Kenaan**:
and Abraham came to *mourn* **chop** for Sarah,
and to weep for her.
3 And Abraham *stood up* **arose**
from *before* **the face of** his *dead* **who died**,
and *spake* **worded** unto the sons of Heth, saying,
4 I am a *stranger* **sojourner** and a *sojourner* **settler**
with you:
give me a possession of a *buryingplace* **tomb** with you,
that I may *bury my dead* **entomb mine who died**
out of my sight **from my face**.
5 And the *children* **sons** of Heth answered Abraham,
saying unto him,
6 Hear us, my *lord* **adoni**:
thou art a *mighty prince* **hierarch of Elohim** among us:
in the choice of our *sepulchres* **tombs**
bury thy dead **entomb thine who died**;
none **no man** of us
shall *withhold* **restrain** from thee his *sepulchre* **tomb**,
but that thou mayest
bury thy dead **entomb thine who died**.
7 And Abraham *stood up* **arose**,
and *bowed himself* **prostrated** to the people of the land,
even to the *children* **sons** of Heth.
8 And he *communed* **worded** with them, saying,
If it be your *mind* **soul**
that I should *bury my dead* **entomb mine who died**
out of my sight **from my face**;
hear me, and *intreat* **intercede** for me
to Ephron the son of *Zohar* **Sochar**,
9 That he may give me the cave of Machpelah,
which he hath, which is in the end of his field;
for *as much money as it is worth* **its full silver**
he shall give it me
for a possession of a *buryingplace* **tomb** amongst you.
10 And Ephron *dwelt* **settled**
among the *children* **sons** of Heth:
and Ephron the *Hittite* **Hethiy** answered Abraham
in the *audience* **ears** of the *children* **sons** of Heth,
even of all that went in at the *gate* **portal** of his city,
saying,
11 Nay, my *lord* **adoni**, hear me: the field give I thee,
and the cave that is therein, I give it thee;
in the *presence* **eyes** of the sons of my people
give I it thee:
bury thy dead **entomb thine who died**.
12 And Abraham *bowed down himself* **prostrated**
before **at the face of** the people of the land.
13 And he *spake* **worded** unto Ephron
in the *audience* **ears** of the people of the land, saying,
But if **only** thou *wilt give it, I pray thee* **shalt** hear me:
I *will* **shall** give thee *money* **silver** for the field;
take it of me,
and I *will bury* **shall entomb**
my dead **mine who died** there.
14 And Ephron answered Abraham, saying unto him,
15 My *lord* **adoni**, hearken unto me:
the land *is worth* four hundred shekels of silver;
what is that *betwixt* **between** me and thee?
bury therefore thy dead **entomb thine who died**.
16 And Abraham hearkened unto Ephron;
and Abraham weighed to Ephron the silver,
which he had *named* **worded**
in the *audience* **ears** of the sons of Heth,
four hundred shekels of silver,
current money **as passeth** with the merchant.
17 And the field of Ephron
which was in Machpelah,
which was *before* **at the face of** Mamre,
the field, and the cave which was therein,
and all the trees that were in the field,
that were in all the borders round about,
were *made sure* **raised**
18 Unto Abraham for a *possession* **chattel**
in the *presence* **eyes** of the *children* **sons** of Heth,
before all that went in at the *gate* **portal** of his city.
19 And *after this* **thus**,
Abraham *buried* **entombed** Sarah his *wife* **woman**
in the cave of the field of Machpelah
before **at the face of** Mamre:
the same is Hebron in the land of *Canaan* **Kenaan**.
20 And the field, and the cave that is therein,
were *made sure* **raised** unto Abraham
for a possession of a *buryingplace* **tomb**
by the sons of Heth.

YISCHAQ AND RIBQAH

24 And Abraham *was old* **had aged**,
and well stricken in *age* **days**:
and *the LORD* **Yah Veh**
had blessed Abraham in all *things*.
2 And Abraham said
unto his *eldest* **elder** servant of his house,
that *ruled* **reigned** over all that he had,
Put, I pray thee, thy hand under my *thigh* **flank**:
3 And I *will make thee swear* **shall oath thee**
by *the LORD* **Yah Veh**,
the God **Elohim** of *heaven* **the heavens**,
and *the God* **Elohim** of the earth,
that thou shalt not take a *wife* **woman** unto my son
of the daughters of the *Canaanites* **Kenaaniy**,
among whom I *dwell* **settle**:
4 But thou shalt go unto my *country* **land**,
and to my kindred,
and take a *wife* **woman** unto my son *Isaac* **Yischaq**.
5 And the servant said unto him,
Peradventure the woman *will* **willeth** not *be willing*
to *follow* **go after** me unto this land:
in returning, must I *needs bring* **return** thy son *again*
unto the land from whence thou camest?
6 And Abraham said unto him,
Beware **Guard** thou
that thou *bring* **return** not my son thither *again*.
7 *The LORD God* **Yah Veh Elohim** of *heaven* **the heavens**,
which took me from my father's house,
and from the land of my kindred,
and which *spake* **worded** unto me,
and that *sware* **oathed** unto me, saying,
Unto thy seed *will* **shall** I give this land;
he shall send his angel *before thee* **at thy face**,
and thou shalt take a *wife* **woman** unto my son
from thence.
8 And if the woman *will* **willeth** not *be willing*
to *follow* **go after** thee,
then thou shalt be *clear* **exonerated** from this my oath:
only *bring* **return** not my son thither *again*.
9 And the servant put his hand
under the *thigh* **flank** of Abraham his *master* **adoni**,
and *sware* **oathed** to him concerning that *matter* **word**.
10 And the servant took ten camels
of the camels of his *master* **adoni**, and *departed* **went**;
for all the goods of his *master* **adoni** were in his hand:
and he arose, and went to *Mesopotamia* **Aram Naharaim**,
unto the city of *Nahor* **Nachor**.
11 And he made his camels to kneel *down* without the city
by a well of water at the time of the evening,
even the time *that women go out to draw water* **to bail**.
12 And he said, O *LORD God* **Yah Veh Elohim**
of my *master* **adoni** Abraham, I pray thee,
send me good speed **happen upon my face** this day,
and *shew kindness* **work mercy**
unto my *master* **adoni** Abraham.
13 Behold, I *stand here* **station myself**
by the *well* **fountain** of water;
and the daughters of the men of the city
come out to *draw* **bail** water:
14 And let it *come to pass* **become**,
that the *damsel* **lass** to whom I shall say,
Let down **Extend** thy pitcher, I pray thee, that I may drink;
and she shall say,
Drink, and I *will* **shall** give thy camels drink also:
let *the same* be she that thou hast *appointed* **approved**
for thy servant *Isaac* **Yischaq**;
and thereby shall I know
that thou hast *shewed kindness* **worked mercy**
unto my *master* **adoni**.

15 And it *came to pass* **became**,
before he had *done speaking* **finished wording**,
that, behold, *Rebekah* **Ribqah** came out,
who was born to *Bethuel* **Bethu El**, son of *Milcah* **Milchah**,
the *wife* **woman** of *Nahor* **Nachor**, Abraham's brother,
with her pitcher upon her shoulder.
16 And the *damsel* **lass**
was *very fair to look upon* **mighty good looking**,
a virgin, neither had any man known her:
and she *went down* **descended** to the *well* **fountain**,
and filled her pitcher, and *came up* **ascended**.
17 And the servant ran to meet her, and said,
Let me, I *pray* **beseech** thee,
drink a little water of thy pitcher.
18 And she said, Drink, my *lord* **adoni**:
and she hasted,
and *let down* **lowered** her pitcher upon her hand,
and gave him drink.
19 And when she had *done* **finished** giving him drink,
she said, I *will draw water* **shall bail** for thy camels also,
until they have *done* **finished** drinking.
20 And she hasted,
and emptied her pitcher into the trough,
and ran again unto the well to *draw water* **bail**,
and *drew* **bailed** for all his camels.
21 And the man wondering at her *held his peace* **hushed**,
to *wit* **perceive** whether *the LORD* **Yah Veh**
had *made* **prospered** his journey *prosperous* or not.
22 And it *came to pass* **became**,
as the camels had *done* **finished** drinking,
that the man took a golden *earring* **nosering**
of *half a shekel* **a bekah** weight,
and two bracelets for her hands
of ten *shekels* weight of gold;
23 And said, Whose daughter art thou?
tell me, I pray thee:
is there *room* **a place** in thy father's house
for us to *lodge in* **stay overnight**?
24 And she said unto him,
I am the daughter of *Bethuel* **Bethu El**
the son of *Milcah* **Milchah**,
which she bare unto *Nahor* **Nachor**.
25 She said moreover unto him,
We have both **much** straw and provender *enough*,
and *room to lodge in* **place to stay overnight**.
26 And the man bowed *down his head*,
and *worshipped the LORD* **prostrated to Yah Veh**.
27 And he said,
Blessed be *the LORD God* **Yah Veh Elohim**
of my *master* **adoni** Abraham,
who hath not *left destitute* **forsaken** my *master* **adoni**
of his mercy and his truth:
I being in the way, *the LORD* **Yah Veh** led me
to the house of my *master's* **adoni's** brethren.
28 And the *damsel* **lass** ran,
and told them of her mother's house these *things* **words**.
29 And *Rebekah* **Ribqah** had a brother,
and his name was Laban:
and Laban ran out unto the man, unto the *well* **fountain**.
30 And it *came to pass* **became**,
when he saw the *earring* **nosering**
and bracelets upon his sister's hands,
and when he heard the words
of *Rebekah* **Ribqah** his sister, saying,
Thus *spake* **worded** the man unto me;
that he came unto the man; and, behold,
he stood by the camels at the *well* **fountain**.
31 And he said, Come in,
thou blessed of *the LORD* **Yah Veh**;
wherefore standest thou without?
for I have prepared the house,
and *room* **place** for the camels.
32 And the man came into the house:
and he *ungirded* **opened** his camels,
and gave straw and provender for the camels,
and water to *wash* **bathe** his feet,
and the men's feet that were with him.
33 And there was set *meat before him* **at his face** to eat:
but he said, I *will* **shall** not eat,
until I have *told mine errand* **worded my word**.
And he said, *Speak on* **Word**.
34 And he said, I am Abraham's servant.
35 And *the LORD* **Yah Veh**
hath blessed my *master greatly* **adoni mightily**;
and he *is become great* **greatened**:
and he hath given him
flocks, and *herds* **oxen**, and silver, and gold,
and *menservants* **servants**, and *maidservants* **maids**,
and camels, and *asses* **he burros**.
36 And Sarah my *master's wife* **adoni's woman**
bare a son to my *master* **adoni** when she was *old* **aged**:
and unto him hath he given all that he hath.
37 And my *master made me swear* **adoni oathed me**,
saying, Thou shalt not take a *wife* **woman** to my son
of the daughters of the *Canaanites* **Kenaaniy**,
in whose land I *dwell* **settle**:
38 But thou shalt go unto my father's house,
and to my *kindred* **family**,
and take a *wife* **woman** unto my son.
39 And I said unto my *master* **adoni**,
Peradventure
the woman *will* **willeth** not *follow* **to go after** me.
40 And he said unto me,
The LORD **Yah Veh**, *before whom* **at whose face** I walk,
will **shall** send his angel with thee,
and prosper thy way;
and thou shalt take a *wife* **woman** for my son
of my *kindred* **family**, and of my father's house:
41 Then shalt thou be *clear* **exonerated** from *this* my oath,
when thou comest to my *kindred* **family**;
and if they give not thee *one*,
thou shalt be *clear* **exonerated** from my oath.
42 And I came this day unto the *well* **fountain**, and said,
O *LORD God* **Yah Veh Elohim**
of my *master* **adoni** Abraham,
if now thou *do* prosper my way which I go:
43 Behold, I *stand* **station myself**
by the *well* **fountain** of water;
and it shall *come to pass* **become**,
that when the virgin cometh forth to *draw water* **bail**,
and I say to her, Give me, I pray thee,
a little water of thy pitcher to drink;
44 And she say to me, Both drink thou,
and I *will* **shall** also *draw* **bail** for thy camels:
let *the same* **that** be the woman
whom *the LORD* **Yah Veh** hath *appointed out* **approved**
for my *master's* **adoni's** son.
45 And before I had *done speaking* **finished wording**
in mine heart, behold,
Rebekah **Ribqah** came forth
with her pitcher on her shoulder;
and she *went down* **descended** unto the *well* **fountain**,
and *drew water* **bailed**:
and I said unto her, Let me drink, I pray thee.
46 And she *made haste* **hastened**,
and *let down* **lowered** her pitcher *from her shoulder*,
and said, Drink,
and I *will give* **shall water** thy camels *drink* also:
so I drank, and she *made* **watered** the camels *drink* also.
47 And I asked her, and said, Whose daughter art thou?
And she said, the daughter of *Bethuel* **Bethu El**,
Nahor's **Nachor's** son,
whom *Milcah* **Milchah** bare unto him:
and I put the *earring* **nosering** upon her *face* **nostrils**,
and the bracelets upon her hands.
48 And I bowed *down my head*,
and *worshipped the LORD* **prostrated to Yah Veh**,
and blessed *the LORD God* **Yah Veh Elohim**
of my *master* **adoni** Abraham,
which had led me in the *right* way **of truth**
to take my *master's* **adoni's** brother's daughter
unto his son.
49 And now
if ye *will deal kindly* **shall work in mercy** and *truly* **truth**
with my *master* **adoni**, tell me:
and if not, tell me;
that I may *turn* **face** to the right *hand*, or to the left.
50 Then Laban and *Bethuel* **Bethu El** answered and said,
The *thing* **word** proceedeth from *the LORD* **Yah Veh**:
we cannot *speak* **word** unto thee *bad* **evil** or good.

51 Behold, *Rebekah is before* **Ribqah faceth** thee,
take *her,* and go,
and let her be thy *master's* **adoni's** son's *wife* **woman**,
as *the LORD* **Yah Veh** hath *spoken* **worded**.
52 And it *came to pass* **became**,
that, when Abraham's servant heard their words,
he *worshipped the LORD* **prostrated to Yah Veh**,
bowing himself **prostrating** to the earth.
53 And the servant brought forth
jewels **instruments** of silver,
and *jewels* **instruments** of gold,
and *raiment* **clothing**, and gave *them* to *Rebekah* **Ribqah**:
he gave also to her brother and to her mother
precious *things*.
54 And they did eat and drink,
he and the men that were with him,
and *tarried all night* **stayed overnight**;
and they rose up in the morning, and he said,
Send me away unto my *master* **adoni**.
55 And her brother and her mother said,
Let the *damsel abide* **lass sit** with us *a few* days,
at the least **or** ten; after that she shall go.
56 And he said unto them, *Hinder* **Delay** me not,
seeing *the LORD* **Yah Veh** hath prospered my way;
send me away that I may go to my *master* **adoni**.
57 And they said, We *will* **shall** call the *damsel* **lass**,
and *inquire* **ask** at her mouth.
58 And they called *Rebekah* **Ribqah**, and said unto her,
Wilt **Shalt** thou go with this man?
And she said, I *will* **shall** go.
59 And they sent away *Rebekah* **Ribqah** their sister,
and her *nurse* **suckler**,
and Abraham's servant, and his men.
60 And they blessed *Rebekah* **Ribqah**, and said unto her,
Thou art our sister,
be thou *the mother of thousands* **myriads** of millions,
and let thy seed
possess the *gate* **portal** of those which hate them.
61 And *Rebekah* **Ribqah** arose, and her *damsels* **lasses**,
and they rode upon the camels,
and *followed* **went after** the man:
and the servant took *Rebekah* **Ribqah**, and went *his way*.
62 And *Isaac* **Yischaq** came from the way
of *the well Lahairoi* **Beer Lachay Roi**;
for he *dwelt* **settled** in the south *country* **land**.
63 And *Isaac* **Yischaq** went out to meditate in the field
at the *eventide* **face of the evening**:
and he lifted up his eyes, and saw,
and, behold, the camels were coming.
64 And *Rebekah* **Ribqah** lifted up her eyes,
and when she saw *Isaac* **Yischaq**,
she *lighted* **fell** off the camel.
65 For she had said unto the servant,
What **very** man is this
that walketh in the field to meet us?
And the servant had said, It is my *master* **adoni**:
therefore she took a vail, and covered herself.
66 And the servant *told Isaac* **described to Yischaq**
all *things* **words** that he had *done* **worked**.
67 And *Isaac* **Yischaq** brought her
into his mother Sarah's tent,
and took *Rebekah* **Ribqah**,
and she became his *wife* **woman**; and he loved her:
and *Isaac was comforted* **Yischaq sighed**
after his mother's *death*.

ABRAHAM TAKES QETURAH

25 Then again Abraham took a *wife* **woman**,
and her name was *Keturah* **Qeturah**.
2 And she bare him Zimran, and *Jokshan* **Yoqshan**,
and Medan, and *Midian* **Midyan**,
and *Ishbak* **Yishbaq**, and *Shuah* **Shuach**.
3 And *Jokshan* **Yoqshan** begat Sheba, and Dedan.
And the sons of Dedan were *Asshurim* **Ashshuriym**,
and *Letushim* **Letushiym**, and *Leummim* **Leummiym**.
4 And the sons of *Midian* **Midyan**;
Ephah, and Epher, and Hanoch,
and *Abidah* **Abi Dah**, and *Eldaah* **El Daah**.
All these were the *children* **sons** of *Keturah* **Qeturah**.
5 And Abraham gave all that he had unto *Isaac* **Yischaq**.
6 But unto the sons of the concubines,
which Abraham had, Abraham gave gifts,
and sent them away from *Isaac* **Yischaq** his son,
while he yet lived, eastward, unto the east country.

DEATH OF ABRAHAM

7 And these are the days of the years
of Abraham's life which he lived,
an hundred **years**
threescore and fifteen **and seventy years and five** years.
8 Then Abraham *gave up the ghost* **expired**,
and died in a good *old age* **grayness**,
an old man **aged**, and *full of years* **satisfied**;
and was gathered to his people.
9 And his sons *Isaac* **Yischaq** and *Ishmael* **Yishma El**
buried **entombed** him
in the cave of Machpelah,
in the field of Ephron
the son of *Zohar* **Sochar** the *Hittite* **Hethiy**,
which is *before* **at the face of** Mamre;
10 The field which Abraham *purchased* **chatteled**
of the sons of Heth:
there was Abraham *buried* **entombed**,
and Sarah his *wife* **woman**.
11 And it *came to pass* **became,**
after the death of Abraham,
that *God* **Elohim** blessed his son *Isaac* **Yischaq**;
and *Isaac dwelt* **Yischaq settled**
by *the well Lahairoi* **Beer Lachay Roi**.

GENEALOGY OF YISHMA EL

12 Now these are the generations of *Ishmael* **Yishma El**,
Abraham's son, whom Hagar the *Egyptian* **Misrayim**,
Sarah's *handmaid* **maid**, bare unto Abraham:
13 And these are the names
of the sons of *Ishmael* **Yishma El**,
by their names, according to their generations:
the firstborn of *Ishmael* **Yishma El**, *Nebajoth* **Nebayoth**;
and *Kedar* **Qedar**, and *Adbeel* **Adbe El**, and Mibsam,
14 And Mishma, and Dumah, and Massa,
15 Hadar, and Tema,
Jetur **Yetur**, Naphish, and *Kedemah* **Qedemah**:
16 These are the sons of *Ishmael* **Yishma El**,
and these are their names,
by their *towns* **courts**, and by their *castles* **walls**;
twelve *princes* **hierarchs**
according to their *nations* **peoples**.
17 And these are the years of the life of *Ishmael* **Yishma El**,
an hundred **years** and thirty **years** and seven years:
and he *gave up the ghost* **expired** and died;
and was gathered unto his people.
18 And they *dwelt* **tabernacled** from Havilah unto Shur,
that is before Egypt **at the face of Misrayim**,
as thou goest toward *Assyria* **Ashshur**:
and he *died in the presence of* **fell facing** all his brethren.

GENEALOGY OF YISCHAQ

19 And these are the generations of *Isaac* **Yischaq**,
Abraham's son:
Abraham begat *Isaac* **Yischaq**:
20 And *Isaac* **Yischaq** was **a son of** forty years *old*
when he took *Rebekah* **Ribqah** to *wife* **woman**,
the daughter of *Bethuel* **Bethu El**
the *Syrian* **Aramiy** of *Padanaram* **Paddan Aram**,
the sister to Laban the *Syrian* **Aramiy**.
21 And *Isaac* **Yischaq**
intreated *the LORD* **Yah Veh** for his *wife* **woman**,
because she was *barren* **sterile**:
and *the LORD* **Yah Veh** was intreated of him,
and *Rebekah* **Ribqah** his *wife* **woman** conceived.
22 And the *children* **sons**
struggled together **crushed** within her;
and she said, If it be so, why am I thus?
And she went to enquire of *the LORD* **Yah Veh**.
23 And *the LORD* **Yah Veh** said unto her,
Two *nations* **goyim** are in thy *womb* **belly**,
and two *manner of people* **nations**
shall be separated from thy *bowels* **inwards**;
and *the one people* **nation**
shall be stronger than *the other people* **nation**;
and the *elder* **greater** shall serve the *younger* **lesser**.
24 And when her days to be delivered were fulfilled,
behold, *there were* twins in her *womb* **belly**.
25 And the first came out *red* **ruddy**,

all over like an hairy *garment* **mighty mantle**;
and they called his name *Esau* **Esav**.
26 And after that came his brother out,
and his hand took hold on *Esau's* **Esav's** heel;
and his name was called *Jacob* **Yaaqov**:
and *Isaac* **Yischaq** was *threescore* **a son of sixty** years *old*
when she bare them.
27 And the *boys* **lads** grew:
and *Esau* **Esav**
was a *cunning hunter* **man knowing hunting**,
a man of the field;
and *Jacob* **Yaaqov** was *a plain* **an integrious** man,
dwelling **settling** in tents.
28 And *Isaac* **Yischaq** loved *Esau* **Esav**,
because
he did eat of his venison **of the hunt in his mouth**:
but *Rebekah* **Ribqah** loved *Jacob* **Yaaqov**.

ESAV SELLS HIS FIRSTRIGHTS

29 And *Jacob sod* **Yaaqov seethed** pottage:
and *Esau* **Esav** came from the field,
and he was *faint* **languid**:
30 And *Esau* **Esav** said to *Jacob* **Yaaqov**,
Feed me, I *pray* **beseech** thee,
with that same red pottage **of that red, red**;
for am *faint* **languid**:
therefore was his name called Edom.
31 And *Jacob* **Yaaqov** said,
Sell me this day thy *birthright* **firstrights**.
32 And *Esau* **Esav** said, Behold,
I am *at the point* **going** to die:
and what profit shall this *birthright do* **firstrights be** to me?
33 And *Jacob* **Yaaqov** said, *Swear* **Oath** to me this day;
and he *sware* **oathed** unto him:
and he sold his *birthright* **firstrights** unto *Jacob* **Yaaqov**.
34 Then *Jacob* **Yaaqov** gave *Esau* **Esav**
bread and pottage of lentiles;
and he did eat and drink, and rose up, and went his way:
thus *Esau* **Esav** despised his *birthright* **firstrights**.

YISCHAQ AND ABI MELECH

26 And there was a famine in the land,
beside **apart from** the first famine
that was in the days of Abraham.
And *Isaac* **Yischaq** went unto *Abimelech* **Abi Melech**
king **sovereign** of the *Philistines* **Peleshethiym** unto Gerar.
2 And *the LORD appeared unto* **Yah Veh was seen by** him,
and said, *Go* **Descend** not *down* into *Egypt* **Misrayim**;
dwell **tabernacle** in the land which I shall *tell thee of* **say**:
3 Sojourn in this land,
and *I will be* **I AM** with thee, and *will* **shall** bless thee;
for unto thee, and unto thy seed,
I *will* **shall** give all these *countries* **lands**,
and I *will perform* **shall raise** the oath
which I *sware* **oathed** unto Abraham thy father;
4 And I *will make* **shall abound** thy seed *to multiply*
as the stars of *heaven* **the heavens**,
and *will* **shall** give unto thy seed all these countries;
and in thy seed
shall all the *nations* **goyim** of the earth be blessed;
5 Because that Abraham *obeyed* **heard** my voice,
and *kept* **guarded** my *charge* **guard**,
my *commandments* **misvoth**,
my statutes, and my *laws* **torahs**.
6 And *Isaac dwelt* **Yischaq settled** in Gerar:
7 And the men of the place asked him of his *wife* **woman**;
and he said, She is my sister:
for he *feared* **awed** to say, *She is* my *wife* **woman**;
lest, *said he*,
the men of the place should *kill* **slaughter** me
for *Rebekah* **Ribqah**;
because she was *fair to look upon* **good in visage**.
8 And it *came to pass* **became**,
when he had *been there a long time* **prolonged his days**,
that *Abimelech* **Abi Melech**
king **sovereign** of the *Philistines* **Peleshethiym**
looked *out at* **through** a window, and saw, and, behold,
Isaac **Yischaq** was *sporting* **entertaining**
with *Rebekah* **Ribqah** his *wife* **woman**.
9 And *Abimelech* **Abi Melech** called *Isaac* **Yischaq**,
and said, Behold, of a surety she is thy *wife* **woman**:
and how saidst thou, She is my sister?
And *Isaac* **Yischaq** said unto him,
Because I said, Lest I die for her.
10 And *Abimelech* **Abi Melech** said,
What is this thou hast *done* **worked** unto us?
one of the people
might *lightly* have *lien* **lain** with thy *wife* **woman**,
and thou shouldest have brought guiltiness upon us.
11 And *Abimelech* **Abi Melech**
charged **misvahed** all his people, saying,
He that toucheth this man or his *wife* **woman**
in deathifying, shall *surely be put to death* **be deathified**.
12 Then *Isaac sowed* **Yischaq seeded** in that land,
and *received* **found** in the same year an hundredfold:
and *the LORD* **Yah Veh** blessed him.
13 And the man *waxed great* **greatened**,
and went *forward* **walking**,
and *grew until he became very great*
in greatening, he greatened:
14 For he had *possession* **chattel** of flocks,
and *possession* **chattel** of *herds* **oxen**,
and great *store of servants* **servantry**:
and the *Philistines* **Peleshethiym** envied him.
15 For all the wells which his father's servants had digged
in the days of Abraham his father,
the *Philistines* **Peleshethiym** had stopped them,
and filled them with *earth* **dust**.
16 And *Abimelech* **Abi Melech** said unto *Isaac* **Yischaq**,
Go from us; for thou art *much* **mightily** mightier than we.
17 And *Isaac departed* **Yischaq went** thence,
and *pitched his tent* **encamped**
in the *valley* **wadi** of Gerar, and *dwelt* **settled** there.
18 And *Isaac* **Yischaq returned**
and digged *again* the wells of water,
which they had digged in the days of Abraham his father;
for the *Philistines* **Peleshethiym** had stopped them
after the death of Abraham:
and he called their names after the names
by which his father had called them.
19 And *Isaac's* **Yischaq's** servants
digged in the *valley* **wadi**,
and found there a well of *springing* **living** water.
20 And the *herdmen* **tenders** of Gerar
did strive with *Isaac's herdmen* **the tenders of Yischaq**,
saying, The water is ours:
and he called the name of the well *Esek* **Eseq**;
because they *strove* **contended** with him.
21 And they digged another well, and strove for that also:
and he called the name of it Sitnah.
22 And he removed from thence,
and digged another well;
and for that they strove not:
and he called the name of it *Rehoboth* **Rechovoth**;
and he said, *For now* **At this time**
the LORD **Yah Veh** hath *made room* **broadened** for us,
and we shall *be fruitful* **bear fruit** in the land.
23 And he *went up* **ascended** from thence
to *Beersheba* **Beer Sheba**.
24 And *the LORD* **Yah Veh**
appeared unto **was seen by** him the same night,
and said, *I am the God* **I — Elohim** of Abraham thy father:
fear **awe** not, for I am with thee, and *will* **shall** bless thee,
and *multiply* **abound** thy seed
for my servant Abraham's sake.
25 And he builded *an* **a sacrifice** altar there,
and called upon the name of *the LORD* **Yah Veh**,
and *pitched* **spread** his tent there:
and there *Isaac's* **Yischaq's** servants digged a well.

YISCHAQ'S COVENANT WITH ABI MELECH

26 Then *Abimelech* **Abi Melech** went to him from Gerar,
and *Ahuzzath* **Achuz Zath** one of his *friends* **companions**,
and *Phichol* **Pichol**
the *chief captain* **governor** of his *army* **host**.
27 And *Isaac* **Yischaq** said unto them,
Wherefore **Why** come ye to me,
seeing ye hate me, and have sent me away from you?
28 And they said, *We saw certainly* **In seeing, we see**
that *the LORD* **Yah Veh** was with thee: and we said,
Let there be *now* **I beseech,** an oath *betwixt* **between** us,
even betwixt **between** us and thee,
and let us *make* **cut** a covenant with thee;

29 That thou *wilt do* **shalt work** us no *hurt* **evil**,
as we have not touched thee,
and as we have *done* **worked** unto thee
nothing but **only** good,
and have sent thee away in *peace* **shalom**:
thou art *now* **at this time**
the blessed of *the LORD* **Yah Veh**.
30 And he *made* **worked** them a *feast* **banquet**,
and they did eat and drink.
31 And they rose up *betimes* in the morning,
and *sware one* **oathed man** to *another* **brother**:
and *Isaac* **Yischaq** sent them away,
and they *departed* **went** from him in *peace* **shalom**.
32 And it *came to pass* **became** the same day,
that *Isaac's* **Yischaq's** servants came,
and told him concerning the well which they had digged,
and said unto him, We have found water.
33 And he called it *Shebah* **Shibah**:
therefore the name of the city
is *Beersheba* **Beer Sheba** unto this day.
34 And *Esau* **Esav** was **a son of** forty years *old*
when he took to *wife* **woman**
Judith **Yah Hudith**
the daughter of Beeri the *Hittite* **Hethiy**,
and *Bashemath* **Bosmath**
the daughter of Elon the *Hittite* **Hethiy**:
35 Which were a *grief of mind* **bitter spirit**
unto *Isaac* **Yischaq** and to *Rebekah* **Ribqah**.

YISCHAQ'S INADVERTENT BLESSING

27 And it *came to pass* **became**,
that when *Isaac was old* **Yischaq had aged**,
and his eyes were *dim* **weak**, so that he could not see,
he called *Esau* **Esav** his *eldest* **greater** son,
and said unto him, My son:
and he said unto him, Behold, *here am* — I.
2 And he said, Behold now, I *am old* **have aged**,
I know not the day of my death:
3 Now therefore *take* **bear**, I pray thee,
thy *weapons* **instruments**, thy quiver and thy bow,
and go out to the field,
and *take me some venison* **hunt me a hunt**;
4 And *make* **work** me *savoury meat* **delicacies**,
such as I love,
and bring it to me, that I may eat;
that my soul may bless thee before I die.
5 And *Rebekah* **Ribqah** heard
when *Isaac spake* **Yischaq worded** to *Esau* **Esav** his son.
And *Esau* **Esav** went to the field to hunt *for venison* **a hunt**,
and to bring it.
6 And *Rebekah spake* **Ribqah said** unto *Jacob* **Yaaqov**
her son, saying, Behold,
I heard thy father *speak* **word** unto *Esau* **Esav** thy brother,
saying,
7 Bring me *venison* **hunt**,
and *make* **work** me *savoury meat* **delicacies**,
that I may eat,
and bless thee *before the LORD* **at the face of Yah Veh**
before **at the face of** my death.
8 Now therefore, my son, *obey* **hear** my voice
according to that which I *command* **misvah** thee.
9 Go now to the flock,
and *fetch* **take** me from thence two good kids of the goats;
and I *will make* **shall work** them
savoury meat **delicacies** for thy father,
such as he loveth:
10 And thou shalt bring it to thy father, that he may eat,
and that he may bless thee *before* **at the face of** his death.
11 And *Jacob* **Yaaqov** said to *Rebekah* **Ribqah** his mother,
Behold, *Esau* **Esav** my brother is a hairy man,
and I am a smooth man:
12 My father peradventure *will* **shall** feel me,
and I shall seem *to him* **in his eyes** as a deceiver;
and I shall bring *a curse* **an abasement** upon me,
and not a blessing.
13 And his mother said unto him,
Upon me be thy *curse* **abasement**, my son:
only *obey* **hear** my voice, and go *fetch* **take** me them.
14 And he went,
and *fetched* **took**, and brought them to his mother:
and his mother *made savoury meat* **worked delicacies**,
such as his father loved.
15 And *Rebekah* **Ribqah**
took *goodly raiment* **desirable clothing**
of her *eldest son Esau* **greater son Esav**,
which were with her in the house,
and *put them upon Jacob* **enrobed Yaaqov**
her younger son:
16 And she put the skins of the kids of the goats
upon his hands, and upon the smooth of his neck:
17 And she gave
the *savoury meat* **delicacies** and the bread,
which she had *prepared* **worked**,
into the hand of her son *Jacob* **Yaaqov**.
18 And he came unto his father, and said, My father:
and he said, Here *am* — I; who art thou, my son?
19 And *Jacob* **Yaaqov** said unto his father,
I am Esau **I — Esav** thy firstborn;
I have *done* **worked**
according as thou *badest* **wordest** me:
arise, I *pray* **beseech** thee, sit and eat of my *venison* **hunt**,
that thy soul may bless me.
20 And *Isaac* **Yischaq** said unto his son,
How is it that thou hast *found it so quickly* **hasted to find**,
my son?
And he said, Because *the LORD* **Yah Veh** thy *God* **Elohim**
brought it to me **happened at my face**.
21 And *Isaac* **Yischaq** said unto *Jacob* **Yaaqov**,
Come near, I *pray* **beseech** thee,
that I may *feel* **touch** thee, my son,
whether thou be my very son *Esau* **Esav** or not.
22 And *Jacob* **Yaaqov**
went near unto *Isaac* **Yischaq** his father;
and he felt him, and said,
The voice is *Jacob's* **Yaaqov's** voice,
but the hands are the hands of *Esau* **Esav**.
23 And he *discerned* **recognized** him not,
because his hands were hairy,
as his brother *Esau's* **Esav's** hands:
so he blessed him.
24 And he said, Art thou my very son *Esau* **Esav**?
And he said, I *am*.
25 And he said, Bring it near to me,
and I *will* **shall** eat of my son's *venison* **hunt**,
that my soul may bless thee.
And he brought it near to him, and he did eat:
and he brought him wine, and he drank.
26 And his father *Isaac* **Yischaq** said unto him,
Come near *now* **I beseech**, and kiss me, my son.
27 And he came near, and kissed him:
and he *smelled* **scented**
the *smell* **scent** of his *raiment* **clothing**,
and blessed him, and said,
See, the *smell* **scent** of my son
is as the *smell* **scent** of a field
which *the LORD* **Yah Veh** hath blessed:
28 Therefore *God* **Elohim** give thee
of the dew of *heaven* **the heavens**,
and the fatness of the earth,
and *plenty of corn* **an abundance of crop** and *wine* **juice**:
29 Let people serve thee,
and nations *bow down* **prostrate** to thee:
be lord over thy brethren,
and let thy mother's sons *bow down* **prostrate** to thee:
cursed be every one that curseth thee,
and blessed be he that blesseth thee.
30 And it *came to pass* **became**,
as soon as *Isaac* **Yischaq**
had *made an end of* **finished** blessing *Jacob* **Yaaqov**,
and *Jacob* **Yaaqov** was *yet scarce* **hardly** gone out
from the *presence* **face** of *Isaac* **Yischaq** his father,
that *Esau* **Esav** his brother came in from his hunting.
31 And he also had *made savoury meat* **worked delicacies**,
and brought it unto his father, and said unto his father,
Let my father arise, and eat of his son's *venison* **hunt**,
that thy soul may bless me.
32 And *Isaac* **Yischaq** his father said unto him,
Who art thou?
And he said, I am thy son, thy firstborn *Esau* **Esav**.
33 And *Isaac* **Yischaq** trembled
very exceedingly **a mighty great trembling**,

and said, Who?
where is he that hath *taken venison* **hunted the hunt**,
and brought *it* me,
and I have eaten of all before thou camest,
and have blessed him? yea, and he shall be blessed.
34 And when *Esau* **Esav** heard the words of his father,
he cried with a great and *exceeding* **mighty** bitter cry,
and said unto his father,
Bless me, *even* me also, O my father.
35 And he said, Thy brother came with *subtilty* **fraud**,
and hath taken *away* thy blessing.
36 And he said,
Is not he rightly named Jacob?
So that his name be called Yaaqov;
for he hath *supplanted me* **tripped my heel**
these two times:
he took away my *birthright* **firstrights**;
and, behold, now he hath taken away my blessing.
And he said,
Hast thou not *reserved* **set aside** a blessing for me?
37 And *Isaac* **Yischaq** answered and said unto *Esau* **Esav**,
Behold, I have *made* **set** him thy lord,
and all his brethren have I given to him for servants;
and with *corn* **crop** and *wine* **juice** have I sustained him:
and what shall I *do* **work** now unto thee, my son?
38 And *Esau* **Esav** said unto his father,
Hast thou but one blessing, my father?
bless me, *even* — me also, O my father.
And *Esau* **Esav** lifted up his voice, and wept.
39 And *Isaac* **Yischaq** his father answered
and said unto him, Behold,
thy *dwelling* **settlement** shall be the fatness of the earth,
and of the dew of *heaven* **the heavens** from *above* **Elyon**;
40 And by thy sword shalt thou live,
and shalt serve thy brother;
and it shall *come to pass* **become,**
when thou shalt have *the dominion* **rambled on**,
that thou shalt break his yoke from off thy neck.
41 And *Esau hated Jacob* **Esav opposed Yaaqov**
because of the blessing wherewith his father blessed him:
and *Esau* **Esav** said in his heart,
The days of mourning for my father *are at hand* **approach**;
then *will* **shall** I *slay* **slaughter** my brother *Jacob* **Yaaqov**.
42 And these words of *Esau* **Esav** her *elder* **greater** son
were told to *Rebekah* **Ribqah**:
and she sent and called *Jacob* **Yaaqov** her younger son,
and said unto him, Behold, thy brother *Esau* **Esav**,
as touching thee, doth *comfort* **sigh over** himself,
purposing to *kill* **slaughter** thee.
43 Now therefore, my son, *obey* **hear** my voice;
and arise, flee thou to Laban my brother to Haran;
44 And *tarry* **settle** with him a few days,
until thy brother's fury turn away;
45 Until thy brother's *anger* **wrath** turn away from thee,
and he forget that which thou hast *done* **worked** to him:
then I *will* **shall** send, and *fetch* **take** thee from thence:
why should I be *deprived* **bereaved** also
of you *both* **two** in one day?
46 And *Rebekah* **Ribqah** said to *Isaac* **Yischaq**,
I am weary of **abhor** my life
because **at the face** of the daughters of Heth:
if *Jacob* **Yaaqov** take a *wife* **woman**
of the daughters of Heth,
such as these *which are* of the daughters of the land,
what good shall my life do me **why live**?

YAAQOV AT BETH EL

28 And *Isaac* **Yischaq** called *Jacob* **Yaaqov**,
and blessed him, and *charged* **misvahed** him,
and said unto him,
Thou shalt not take a *wife* **woman**
of the daughters of *Canaan* **Kenaan**.
2 Arise, go to *Padanaram* **Paddan Aram**,
to the house of *Bethuel* **Bethu El** thy mother's father;
and take thee a *wife* **woman** from thence
of the daughters of Laban thy mother's brother.
3 And *God Almighty* **El Shadday** bless thee,
and *make* **have** thee *fruitful* **bear fruit**,
and *multiply* **abound** thee,
that thou mayest be a *multitude* **congregation** of people;
4 And give thee the blessing of Abraham,
to thee, and to thy seed with thee;
that thou mayest *inherit* **possess** the land
wherein thou art a stranger **of thy sojournings**,
which *God* **Elohim** gave unto Abraham.
5 And *Isaac* **Yischaq** sent away *Jacob* **Yaaqov**:
and he went to *Padanaram* **Paddan Aram** unto Laban,
son of *Bethuel* **Bethu El** the *Syrian* **Aramiy**,
the brother of *Rebekah* **Ribqah**,
Jacob's **Yaaqov's** and *Esau's* **Esav's** mother.
6 When *Esau* **Esav** saw
that *Isaac* **Yischaq** had blessed *Jacob* **Yaaqov**,
and sent him away to *Padanaram* **Paddan Aram**,
to take him a *wife* **woman** from thence;
and that as he blessed him
he *gave* **misvahed** him *a charge*, saying,
Thou shalt not take a *wife* **woman**
of the daughters of *Canaan* **Kenaan**;
7 And that *Jacob* **Yaaqov**
obeyed **hearkened unto** his father and his mother,
and was gone to *Padanaram* **Paddan Aram**;
8 And *Esau* **Esav**
seeing that the daughters of *Canaan* **Kenaan**
pleased not Isaac **were evil in the eyes of Yischaq**
his father;
9 Then went *Esau* **Esav** unto *Ishmael* **Yishma El**,
and took unto the *wives* **women** which he had
Mahalath **Machalath**
the daughter of *Ishmael* **Yishma El** Abraham's son,
the sister of *Nebajoth* **Nebayoth**, to be his *wife* **woman**.

YAAQOV'S DREAM

10 And *Jacob* **Yaaqov**
went out from *Beersheba* **Beer Sheba**,
and went toward Haran.
11 And he *lighted upon* **encountered** a certain place,
and *tarried* **stayed** there *all night* **overnight**,
because the sun was set;
and he took of the stones of that place,
and *put* **set** them for his *pillows* **headpieces**,
and lay down in that place *to sleep*.
12 And he dreamed,
and behold a ladder *set up* **stationed** on the earth,
and the top of it *reached to heaven* **touched the heavens**:
and behold the angels of *God* **Elohim**
ascending and descending on it.
13 And, behold,
the LORD stood **Yah Veh stationed himself** above it,
and said,
I am the LORD God **I — Yah Veh Elohim**
of Abraham thy father,
and *the God of Isaac* **Elohim of Yischaq**:
the land whereon thou liest,
to thee *will* **shall** I give it, and to thy seed;
14 And thy seed shall be as the dust of the earth,
and thou shalt *spread abroad* **break forth**
to the *west* **sea**, and to the east,
and to the north, and to the south:
and in thee and in thy seed
shall all the families of the *earth* **soil** be blessed.
15 And, behold, I *am* with thee,
and *will keep* **shall guard** thee
in all *places* whither thou goest,
and *will bring* **shall return** thee *again* into this *land* **soil**;
for I *will* **shall** not leave thee,
until I have *done* **worked**
that which I have *spoken* **worded** to thee of.
16 And *Jacob* **Yaaqov** awaked out of his sleep,
and he said, Surely *the LORD* **Yah Veh** is in this place;
and I knew it not.
17 And he *was afraid* **awed**, and said,
How *dreadful* **awesome** is this place!
this is none other but *the house of God* **Beth Elohim**,
and this is the *gate* **portal** of *heaven* **the heavens**.
18 And *Jacob rose up* **Yaaqov started** early in the morning,
and took the stone
that he had *put* **set** for his *pillows* **headpieces**,
and set it up for a *pillar* **monolith**,
and poured oil upon the top of it.
19 And he called the name of that place *Bethel* **Beth El**:
but the name of that city was *called* Luz at the first.
20 And *Jacob* **Yaaqov** vowed a vow, saying,

If *God will* **Elohim shall** be with me,
and *will keep* **shall guard** me in this way that I go,
and *will* **shall** give me bread to eat,
and *raiment* **clothing** to *put on* **enrobe**,
21 So that I *come again* **return** to my father's house
in peace **shalom**;
then shall *the LORD* **Yah Veh** be my *God* **Elohim**:
22 And this stone, which I have set for a *pillar* **monolith**,
shall be *God's house* **Beth Elohim**:
and of all that thou shalt give me
I will surely give the tenth
In tithing, I shall tithe unto thee.

YAAQOV AND RACHEL

29 Then *Jacob* **Yaaqov**
went on his journey **lifted his feet**,
and *came* **went** into the land
of the *people* **sons** of the east.
2 And he *looked* **saw**, and behold, a well in the field,
and, *lo* **behold**,
there were three *flocks* **droves** of *sheep* **flocks**
lying **crouched** by it;
for out of that well
they *watered* **moistened** the *flocks* **droves**:
and a great stone was upon the well's mouth.
3 And thither were all the *flocks* **droves** gathered:
and they rolled the stone from the well's mouth,
and *watered* **moistened** the *sheep* **flock**,
and *put* **returned** the stone *again*
upon the well's mouth in his place.
4 And *Jacob* **Yaaqov** said unto them,
My brethren, whence be ye?
And they said, Of Haran are we.
5 And he said unto them,
Know ye Laban the son of *Nahor* **Nachor**?
And they said, We know him.
6 And he said unto them, Is he *well* **at shalom**?
And they said, He is *well* **at shalom**: and, behold,
Rachel his daughter cometh with the *sheep* **flock**.
7 And he said, *Lo* **Behold**,
it is yet high day **the day is great**,
neither is it time
that the *cattle* **chattel** should be gathered *together*:
water **moisten** ye the *sheep* **flock**,
and go and *feed* **tend** them.
8 And they said, We cannot,
until all the *flocks* **droves** be gathered *together*,
and *till* they roll the stone from the well's mouth;
then we *water* **moisten** the *sheep* **flock**.
9 And while he *yet spake* **still worded** with them,
Rachel came with her father's *sheep* **flock**:
for she *kept* **tended** them.
10 And it *came to pass* **became**,
when *Jacob* **Yaaqov** saw Rachel
the daughter of Laban his mother's brother,
and the *sheep* **flocks** of Laban his mother's brother,
that *Jacob* **Yaaqov** went near,
and rolled the stone from the well's mouth,
and *watered* **moistened** the flock of Laban
his mother's brother.
11 And *Jacob* **Yaaqov** kissed Rachel,
and lifted *up* his voice, and wept.
12 And *Jacob* **Yaaqov** told Rachel
that he was her father's brother,
and that he was *Rebekah's* **Ribqah's** son:
and she ran and told her father.
13 And it *came to pass* **became**,
when Laban heard the *tidings* **report**
of *Jacob* **Yaaqov** his sister's son,
that he ran to meet him, and embraced him,
and kissed him, and brought him to his house.
And he *told* **described to** Laban all these *things* **words**.
14 And Laban said to him,
Surely thou art my bone and my flesh.
And he *abode* **settled** with him
the space of a month **of days**.
15 And Laban said unto *Jacob* **Yaaqov**,
Because thou art my brother,
shouldest thou *therefore* serve me *for nought* **gratuitously**?
tell me, what shall thy *wages* **hire** be?
16 And Laban had two daughters:
the name of the *elder* **greater** was Leah,
and the name of the younger was Rachel.
17 Leah was tender eyed;
but Rachel was beautiful **in form**
and *well favoured* **beautiful in visage**.
18 And *Jacob* **Yaaqov** loved Rachel; and said,
I *will* **shall** serve thee seven years
for Rachel thy younger daughter.
19 And Laban said, It is better that I give her to thee,
than that I should give her to another man:
abide **settle** with me.
20 And *Jacob* **Yaaqov** served seven years for Rachel;
and they *seemed unto him* **were in his eyes**
but a *few days* **day**,
for the **in his** love *he had* to her.
21 And *Jacob* **Yaaqov** said unto Laban,
Give me my *wife* **woman**, for my days are fulfilled,
that I may go in unto her.
22 And Laban gathered *together* all the men of the place,
and *made* **worked** a *feast* **banquet**.
23 And it *came to pass* **became** in the evening,
that he took Leah his daughter, and brought her to him;
and he went in unto her.
24 And Laban gave unto his daughter Leah
Zilpah his maid for *an handmaid* **a maid**.
25 And it *came to pass* **became**,
that in the morning, behold, it was Leah:
and he said to Laban,
What is this thou hast *done* **worked** unto me?
did not I serve with thee for Rachel?
wherefore then hast thou *beguiled* **deceived** me?
26 And Laban said,
It must not be so *done* **worked** in our *country* **place**,
to give the younger *before* **at the face of** the firstborn.
27 Fulfil her week,
and we *will* **shall** give thee this also for the service
which thou shalt serve with me
yet seven other years.
28 And *Jacob did* **Yaaqov worked** so,
and fulfilled her week:
and he gave him Rachel his daughter to *wife* **woman** also.
29 And Laban gave to Rachel his daughter
Bilhah his *handmaid* **maid** to be her maid.
30 And he went in also unto Rachel,
and he loved also Rachel more than Leah,
and served with him yet seven other years.
31 And when *the LORD* **Yah Veh** saw
that Leah was hated,
he opened her womb: but Rachel was *barren* **sterile**.
32 And Leah conceived, and bare a son,
and she called his name *Reuben* **Reu Ben**: for she said,
Surely the LORD **For this cause Yah Veh**
hath *looked upon* **seen** my *affliction* **humiliation**;
now *therefore* **for this cause**
my *husband will* **man shall** love me.
33 And she conceived again, and bare a son; and said,
Because *the LORD* **Yah Veh** hath heard I was hated,
he hath *therefore* given me this *son* also:
and she called his name *Simeon* **Shimon**.
34 And she conceived again, and bare a son; and said,
Now this time
will **shall** my *husband* **man** be joined unto me,
because I have born him three sons:
therefore was his name called Levi.
35 And she conceived again, and bare a son:
and she said,
Now **At this time**
will I praise the LORD **shall I extend hands to Yah Veh**:
therefore she called his name *Judah* **Yah Hudah**°;
and *left* **was stayed from** bearing.

°see Yah Hudah in Lexicon

30 And when Rachel saw
that she bare *Jacob* **Yaaqov** no *children* **sons**,
Rachel envied her sister; and said unto *Jacob* **Yaaqov**,
Give me *children* **sons**, *or else* **and if not** I die.
2 And *Jacob's anger* **Yaaqov's wrath**
was kindled against Rachel:
and he said, Am I in *God's* **Elohim's** stead,
who hath withheld from thee the fruit of the *womb* **belly**?
3 And she said, Behold my maid Bilhah, go in unto her;

and she shall bear upon my knees,
that I may also have children by her.
4 And she gave him Bilhah her *handmaid* **maid**
to *wife* **woman**:
and *Jacob* **Yaaqov** went in unto her.
5 And Bilhah conceived, and bare *Jacob* **Yaaqov** a son.
6 And Rachel said,
God **Elohim** hath *judged me* **pleaded my cause**,
and hath also heard my voice, and hath given me a son:
therefore called she his name Dan.
7 And Bilhah Rachel's maid conceived again,
and bare *Jacob* **Yaaqov** a second son.
8 And Rachel said, With *great* wrestlings **of Elohim**
have I wrestled with my sister, and I have prevailed:
and she called his name Naphtali.
9 When Leah saw that she had *left* **stayed from** bearing,
she took Zilpah her maid,
and gave her *Jacob* **Yaaqov** to *wife* **woman**.
10 And Zilpah Leah's maid bare *Jacob* **Yaaqov** a son.
11 And Leah said, *A troop* **Fortune** cometh:
and she called his name Gad.
12 And Zilpah Leah's maid
bare *Jacob* **Yaaqov** a second son.
13 And Leah said, *Happy* **Blithesome** am I,
for the daughters *will* **shall** call me *blessed* **blithed**:
and she called his name Asher.
14 And *Reuben* **Reu Ben**
went in the days of wheat harvest,
and found mandrakes in the field,
and brought them unto his mother Leah.
Then Rachel said to Leah,
Give me, I *pray* **beseech** thee, of thy son's mandrakes.
15 And she said unto her,
Is it *a small matter* **petty**
that thou hast taken my *husband* **man**?
and *wouldest* **shouldest** thou take *away*
my son's mandrakes also?
And Rachel said,
Therefore he shall lie with thee to night
for thy son's mandrakes.
16 And *Jacob* **Yaaqov** came out of the field in the evening,
and Leah went out to meet him, and said,
Thou must come in unto me;
for surely **in hiring,** I have hired thee
with my son's mandrakes.
And he lay with her that night.
17 And *God* **Elohim** hearkened unto Leah,
and she conceived, and bare *Jacob* **Yaaqov** the fifth son.
18 And Leah said, *God* **Elohim** hath given me my hire,
because I have given my *maiden* **maid**
to my *husband* **man**:
and she called his name *Issachar* **Yissachar**.
19 And Leah conceived again,
and bare *Jacob* **Yaaqov** the sixth son.
20 And Leah said,
God **Elohim** hath *endued* **endowed** me
with a good *dowry* **endowment**;
now will **this time shall** my *husband* **man** dwell with me,
because I have born him six sons:
and she called his name Zebulun.
21 And afterwards she bare a daughter,
and called her name Dinah.
22 And *God* **Elohim** remembered Rachel,
and *God* **Elohim** hearkened to her, and opened her womb.
23 And she conceived, and bare a son; and said,
God **Elohim** hath taken away my *reproach* **disgrace**:
24 And she called his name *Joseph* **Yoseph**; and said,
The LORD **Yah Veh** shall add to me another son.
25 And it *came to pass* **became**,
when Rachel had born *Joseph* **Yoseph**,
that *Jacob* **Yaaqov** said unto Laban, Send me away,
that I may go unto mine own place,
and to my *country* **land**.
26 Give me my *wives* **women** and my children,
for whom I have served thee, and let me go:
for thou knowest my service
which I have *done* **served** thee.
27 And Laban said unto him, I *pray* **beseech** thee,
if I have found *favour* **charism** in thine eyes, *tarry*:
for I have *learned by experience* **prognosticated**
that *the LORD* **Yah Veh** hath blessed me for thy sake.
28 And he said, Appoint me thy *wages* **hire**,
and I *will* **shall** give it.
29 And he said unto him,
Thou knowest how I have served thee,
and how thy *cattle* **chattel** was with me.
30 For it was little which thou hadst
before I came **at my face**,
and it is *now increased* **broken forth**
unto *a multitude* **an abundance**;
and *the LORD* **Yah Veh** hath blessed thee
since my coming **at my foot**:
and now when shall I *provide* **work**
for mine own house also?
31 And he said, What shall I give thee?
And *Jacob* **Yaaqov** said,
Thou shalt not give me *any thing* **aught**:
if thou *wilt do* **shalt work** this *thing* **word** for me,
I *will again feed* **shall return and tend**
and *keep* **guard** thy flock.
32 I *will* **shall** pass through all thy flock to day,
removing **turning aside** from thence
all the *speckled* **branded** and spotted *cattle* **lambs**,
and all the brown *cattle* **lambs** among the *sheep* **lambs**,
and the spotted and *speckled* **branded** among the goats:
and *of such* **they** shall be my hire.
33 *So* **Thus** shall my *righteousness* **justness** answer for me
in *time to come* **the day of the morrow**,
when it shall come for my hire before thy face:
every one **all** that is not *speckled* **branded** and spotted
among the goats,
and brown among the *sheep* **lambs**,
that shall be counted stolen with me.
34 And Laban said, Behold,
I would it might **O that it** be according to thy word.
35 And he *removed* **turned aside** that day
the he goats
that were ringstraked and spotted,
and all the she goats
that were *speckled* **branded** and spotted,
and every one that had *some* white in it,
and all the brown among the *sheep* **lambs**,
and gave them into the hand of his sons.
36 And he set three days' journey
betwixt **between** himself and *Jacob* **between Yaaqov**:
and *Jacob fed* **Yaaqov tended**
the rest of Laban's flocks **that remained**.
37 And *Jacob* **Yaaqov** took him *rods* **sprouts**
of *green* **fresh** poplar, and of the hazel and chestnut tree;
and *pilled* **peeled** white *strakes* **peels** in them,
and *made* **peeled** the white *appear*
which was in the *rods* **sprouts**.
38 And he set the *rods* **sprouts** which he had *pilled* **peeled**
before the flocks in the *gutters* **troughs**
in the watering troughs when the flocks came to drink,
that they should conceive when they came to drink.
39 And the flocks conceived before the *rods* **sprouts**,
and *brought forth cattle* **bare flocks**
ringstraked, *speckled* **branded**, and spotted.
40 And *Jacob* **Yaaqov** did separate the lambs,
and *set* **gave** the faces of the flocks
toward the ringstraked,
and all the brown in the flock of Laban;
and he put his own *flocks* **droves** by themselves,
and put them not unto Laban's *cattle* **flocks**.
41 And it *came to pass* **became**,
whensoever
the *stronger cattle* **conspired flocks** did conceive,
that *Jacob laid* **Yaaqov set** the *rods* **sprouts**
before the eyes of the *cattle* **flocks** in the *gutters* **troughs**,
that they might conceive among the *rods* **sprouts**.
42 But when the *cattle were feeble* **flocks languished**,
he put them not in:
so the *feebler* **languishing** were Laban's,
and the stronger *Jacob's* **Yaaqov's**.
43 And the man *increased* **broke forth**
exceedingly **mightily mighty**,
and had much *cattle* **flocks**,
and *maidservants* **maids**, and *menservants* **servants**,
and camels, and *asses* **he burros**.

YAAQOV FLEES

31 And he heard the words of Laban's sons, saying,
Jacob **Yaaqov** hath taken away all that was our father's;
and of that which was our father's
hath he *gotten* **worked** all this *glory* **honour**.
2 And *Jacob* **Yaaqov**
beheld **saw** the *countenance* **face** of Laban,
and, behold,
it was not toward him as *before* **three yesters ago**.
3 And *the LORD* **Yah Veh** said unto *Jacob* **Yaaqov**,
Return unto the land of thy fathers, and to thy kindred;
and *I will be* **I AM** with thee.
4 And *Jacob* **Yaaqov** sent
and called Rachel and Leah to the field unto his flock,
5 And said unto them,
I see your father's *countenance* **face**,
that it is not toward me as *before* **three yesters ago**;
but *the God* **Elohim** of my father hath been with me.
6 And ye know that with all my *power* **force**
I have served your father.
7 And your father hath *deceived* **mocked** me,
and changed my *wages* **hire** ten times;
but *God suffered* **Elohim gave** him not to *hurt* **vilify** me.
8 If he said thus,
The *speckled* **branded** shall be thy *wages* **hire**;
then all the *cattle* **flocks** bare *speckled* **branded**:
and if he said thus,
The ringstraked shall be thy hire;
then bare all the *cattle* **flocks** ringstraked.
9 Thus *God* **Elohim** hath *taken away* **stripped**
the *cattle* **chattel** of your father, and given them to me.
10 And it *came to pass* **became,**
at the time that the *cattle* **flocks** conceived,
that I lifted up mine eyes, and saw in a dream,
and, behold, the *rams* **he goats**
which *leaped* **ascended** upon the *cattle* **flocks**
were ringstraked, *speckled* **branded**, and grisled.
11 And the angel of *God* **Elohim**
spake **said** unto me in a dream, *saying*, *Jacob* **Yaaqov**:
And I said, Here *am* — I.
12 And he said, Lift up *now* **I beseech,** thine eyes, and see,
all the *rams* **he goats**
which *leap* **ascend** upon the *cattle* **flocks**
are ringstraked, *speckled* **branded**, and grisled:
for I have seen all that Laban *doeth* **worketh** unto thee.
13 *I am the God of Bethel* **I — El of Beth El,**
where thou anointedst the *pillar* **monolith**,
and where thou vowedst a vow unto me:
now arise, get thee out from this land,
and return unto the land of thy kindred.
14 And Rachel and Leah answered and said unto him,
Is there yet any *portion* **allotment** or inheritance for us
in our father's house?
15 Are we not *counted* **fabricated** of him strangers?
for he hath sold us,
and **in consuming,** hath *quite devoured* **consumed**
also our *money* **silver**.
16 For all the riches
which *God* **Elohim** hath *taken* **stripped** from our father,
that is ours, and our *children's* **sons'**:
now then,
whatsoever *God* **Elohim** hath said unto thee, *do* **work**.
17 Then *Jacob* **Yaaqov** rose up,
and *set* **lifted** his sons and his *wives* **women** upon camels;
18 And he *carried away* **drove** all his *cattle* **chattel**,
and all his *goods* **acquisitions**
which he had *gotten* **acquired**,
the *cattle of his getting* **chattel he chatteled**,
which he had *gotten* **acquired**
in *Padanaram* **Paddan Aram**,
for to go to *Isaac* **Yischaq** his father
in the land of *Canaan* **Kenaan**.
19 And Laban went to shear his *sheep* **flock**:
and Rachel had stolen the *images* **teraphim**
that were her father's.
20 And *Jacob* **Yaaqov** stole away
unawares to **the heart of** Laban the *Syrian* **Aramiy**,
in that he told him not that he fled.
21 So he fled with all that he had;
and he rose up, and passed over the river,
and set his face toward the mount *Gilead* **Gilad**.
22 And it was told Laban on the third day
that *Jacob* **Yaaqov** was fled.
23 And he took his brethren with him,
and pursued after him seven days' journey;
and they *overtook* **adhered to** him
in the mount *Gilead* **Gilad**.
24 And *God* **Elohim** came to Laban the *Syrian* **Aramiy**
in a dream by night, and said unto him,
Take heed **Guard** that thou *speak* **word** not
to *Jacob either* **Yaaqov from** good *or bad* **to evil**.
25 Then Laban overtook *Jacob* **Yaaqov**.
Now *Jacob* **Yaaqov**
had *pitched* **staked** his tent in the mount:
and Laban with his brethren
pitched **staked** in the mount of *Gilead* **Gilad**.
26 And Laban said to *Jacob* **Yaaqov**,
What hast thou *done* **worked**,
that thou hast stolen away *unawares to me* **from my heart**,
and *carried away* **driven** my daughters,
as *captives taken* **captured** with the sword?
27 Wherefore didst thou flee away *secretly* **to hide**,
and steal away from me; and didst not tell me,
that I might have sent thee away
with *mirth* **cheerfulness**, and with songs,
with *tabret* **tambourine**, and with harp?
28 And hast not *suffered* **allowed** me
to kiss my sons and my daughters?
thou hast now *done foolishly* **follied** in so *doing* **working**.
29 It is in the *power* **el** of my hand
to *do you hurt* **work you evil**:
but *the God* **Elohim** of your father
spake **worded** unto me yesternight, saying,
Take **Guard** thou *heed* that thou *speak* **word** not
to *Jacob either* **Yaaqov from** good *or bad* **to evil**.
30 And now, *though*
in going, thou *wouldest needs be gone* **goest**,
because **in yearning,** thou *sore longedst* **yearnedst**
after thy father's house,
yet wherefore hast thou stolen my *gods* **elohim**?
31 And *Jacob* **Yaaqov** answered and said to Laban,
Because I *was afraid* **awed**: for I said,
Peradventure **Lest**
thou *wouldest take by force* **shouldest strip**
thy daughters from me.
32 With whomsoever thou findest thy *gods* **elohim**,
let him not live:
before our brethren
discern **recognize** thou what is thine with me,
and take it to thee.
For *Jacob knew* **Yaaqov discerned** not
that Rachel had stolen them.
33 And Laban went into *Jacob's* **Yaaqov's** tent,
and into Leah's tent,
and into the two *maidservants'* **maids'** tents;
but he found them not.
Then went he out of Leah's tent,
and entered into Rachel's tent.
34 Now Rachel had taken the *images* **teraphim**,
and put them in the camel's *furniture* **saddle**,
and sat upon them.
And Laban *searched* **groped** all the tent,
but found them not.
35 And she said to her father,
Let it not *displease* **inflame the eyes of** my *lord* **adoni**
that I cannot rise *up before thee* **at thy face**;
for the *custom* **way** of women is upon me.
And he searched, but found not the *images* **teraphim**.
36 And *Jacob* **Yaaqov** was *wroth* **inflamed**,
and *chode* **chided** with Laban:
and *Jacob* **Yaaqov** answered and said to Laban,
What is my *trespass* **rebellion**?
what is my sin, that thou hast so hotly pursued after me?
37 *Whereas thou hast searched all my stuff,*
For what cause hast thou groped all my instruments?
what hast thou found
of all thy household *stuff* **instruments**?
set it *here* **thus** before my brethren and thy brethren,
that they may *judge* **reprove**
betwixt us both **between the two of us**.

38 This twenty years have I been with thee;
thy ewes and thy she goats
have not *cast their young* **aborted**,
and the rams of thy flock have I not eaten.
39 That which was torn *of beasts*
I brought not unto thee; I bare the loss of it
I brought not unto thee for the sin (offering);
of my hand didst thou *require* **seek** it,
whether stolen by day, or stolen by night.
40 *Thus* I was;
in the day the *drought* **parch** consumed me,
and the frost by night;
and my sleep *departed* **fled** from mine eyes.
41 Thus have I been twenty years in thy house;
I served thee fourteen years for thy two daughters,
and six years for thy *cattle* **flocks**:
and thou hast changed my *wages* **hire** ten times.
42 *Except the God* **Unless Elohim** of my father,
the God **Elohim** of Abraham,
and the fear of *Isaac* **Yischaq**, had been with me,
surely thou hadst sent me away now empty.
God **Elohim** hath seen mine *affliction* **humiliation**
and the labour of my *hands* **palms**,
and *rebuked* **reproved** thee yesternight.
43 And Laban answered and said unto *Jacob* **Yaaqov**,
These daughters are my daughters,
and these *children* **sons** are my *children* **sons**,
and these *cattle* **flocks** are my *cattle* **flocks**,
and all that thou seest is mine:
and what *can I do* **shall I work** this day
unto these my daughters,
or unto their *children* **sons** which they have born?
44 Now therefore *come* **go** thou,
let us *make* **cut** a covenant, I and thou;
and let it be for a witness between me and thee.
45 And *Jacob* **Yaaqov** took a stone,
and *set* **lifted** it *up* for a *pillar* **monolith**.
46 And *Jacob* **Yaaqov** said unto his brethren,
Gather **Glean** stones;
and they took stones, and *made* **worked** an heap:
and they did eat there upon the heap.
47 And Laban called it
Jegarsahadutha **Yegar Sahadutha/Heap of Witness**:
but *Jacob* **Yaaqov** called it
Galeed **Gal Ed/Heap of Witness**.
48 And Laban said,
This heap is a witness
between me and **between** thee this day.
Therefore was the name of it called
Galeed **Gal Ed/Heap of Witness**;

THE MISPEH BENEDICTION

49 And *Mizpah* **Mispeh**; for he said,
The LORD **Yah Veh** watch
between me and **between** thee,
when we are *absent one* **hidden man** from *another* **friend**.
50 If thou shalt *afflict* **humble** my daughters,
or if thou shalt take *other wives* **women**
beside my daughters, no man is with us;
see, *God* **Elohim** is witness
betwixt **between** me and **between** thee.
51 And Laban said to *Jacob* **Yaaqov**,
Behold this heap, and behold this *pillar* **monolith**,
which I have *cast* **poured**
betwixt **between** me and **between** thee:
52 This heap *be* witness,
and this *pillar be* **monolith** witness,
that I *will* **shall** not pass over this heap to thee,
and that thou shalt not pass over this heap
and this *pillar* **monolith** unto me, for *harm* **evil**.
53 *The God* **Elohim** of Abraham,
and *the God* **Elohim** of *Nahor* **Nachor**,
the God **Elohim** of their father, judge *betwixt* **between** us.
And *Jacob sware* **Yaaqov oathed**
by the fear of his father *Isaac* **Yischaq**.
54 Then *Jacob offered* **Yaaqov sacrificed a** sacrifice
upon the mount,
and called his brethren to eat bread:
and they did eat bread,
and *tarried all night* **stayed overnight** in the mount.
55 And early in the morning Laban *rose up* **started**,
and kissed his sons and his daughters, and blessed them:
and Laban *departed* **went**, and returned unto his place.

ANGELS OF ELOHIM ENCOUNTER YAAQOV

32 And *Jacob* **Yaaqov** went on his way,
and the angels of *God met* **Elohim encountered** him.
2 And when *Jacob* **Yaaqov** saw them, he said,
This is *God's host* **Camp Elohim**:
and he called the name of that place
Mahanaim **Machanayim/Double Camp**.
3 And *Jacob* **Yaaqov** sent *messengers* **angels**
before him to Esau **at the face of Esav** his brother
unto the land of Seir, the *country* **field** of Edom.
4 And he *commanded* **misvahed** them, saying,
Thus shall ye *speak* **say** unto my *lord Esau* **adoni Esav**;
Thy servant *Jacob* **Yaaqov** saith thus,
I have sojourned with Laban,
and *stayed* **delayed** there until now:
5 And I have oxen, and *asses* **he burros**, flocks,
and *menservants* **servants**, and *womenservants* **maids**:
and I have sent to tell my *lord* **adoni**,
that I may find *grace* **charism** in thy *sight* **eyes**.
6 And the *messengers* **angels** returned to *Jacob* **Yaaqov**,
saying, We came to thy brother *Esau* **Esav**,
and also he cometh to meet thee,
and four hundred men with him.
7 Then *Jacob* **Yaaqov** was *greatly afraid* **mightily awed**
and *distressed* **depressed**:
and he *divided* **halved** the people that was with him,
and the flocks, and *herds* **oxen**, and the camels,
into two *bands* **camps**;
8 And said,
If *Esau* **Esav** come to the one *company* **camp**,
and smite it,
then the other *company* **camp** which *is left* **surviveth**
shall escape.
9 And *Jacob* **Yaaqov** said,
O *God* **Elohim** of my father Abraham,
and *God* **Elohim** of my father *Isaac* **Yischaq**,
the LORD **Yah Veh** which saidst unto me,
Return unto thy *country* **land**, and to thy kindred,
and I *will deal well with* **shall well—please** thee:
10 I am *not worthy of* **less than** the least
of all the mercies, and of all the truth,
which thou hast *shewed* **worked** unto thy servant;
for with my staff I passed over this *Jordan* **Yarden**;
and now I am become two *bands* **camps**.
11 *Deliver* **Rescue** me, I *pray* **beseech** thee,
from the hand of my brother, from the hand of *Esau* **Esav**:
for I *fear* **awe** him, lest he *will* **shall** come and smite me,
and the mother with the *children* **sons**.
12 And thou saidst,
I will surely do
In well—pleasing, I shall well—please thee *good*,
and *make* **set** thy seed as the sand of the sea,
which cannot be *numbered* **scribed**
for *multitude* **abundance**.
13 And he *lodged* **stayed overnight** there that same night;
and took of that which came to his hand
a present **an offering** for *Esau* **Esav** his brother;
14 Two hundred she goats, and twenty he goats,
two hundred ewes, and twenty rams,
15 Thirty *milch* **suckling** camels with their *colts* **sons**,
forty *kine* **heifer**, and ten *bulls* **bullocks**,
twenty she *asses* **burros**, and ten foals.
16 And he *delivered* **gave** them
into the hand of his servants,
every drove by **drove** *themselves*;
and said unto his servants,
Pass over *before me* **from my face**,
and put *a space* **respiration**
betwixt **between** drove and **between** drove.
17 And he *commanded* **misvahed** the *foremost* **first**,
saying, When *Esau* **Esav** my brother meeteth thee,
and asketh thee, saying,
Whose art thou? and whither goest thou?
and whose are these *before thee* **at thy face**?
18 Then thou shalt say,
They be thy servant *Jacob's* **Yaaqov's**;
it is *a present* **an offering**
sent unto my *lord Esau* **adoni Esav**:

and, behold, also he is behind us.
19 And so *commanded* **misvahed** he the second,
and the third,
and all that *followed* **came after** the droves, saying,
On this manner shall ye speak **Ye shall word this word**
unto *Esau* **Esav**, when ye find him.
20 And say ye moreover,
Behold, thy servant *Jacob* **Yaaqov** is behind us.
For he said,
I *will appease him* **shall kapar/atone at his face**
with the *present* **offering** that goeth *before me* **at my face**,
and afterward I *will* **shall** see his face;
peradventure he *will accept of me* **shall lift at my face**.
21 So *went the present over* **the offering passed**
before him **at his face**:
and himself *lodged* **stayed overnight** that night
in the *company* **camp**.
22 And he rose up that night,
and took his two *wives* **women**,
and his two *womenservants* **maids**,
and his eleven *sons* **children**,
and passed over the ford *Jabbok* **Yabboq**.
23 And he took them,
and *sent* **passed** them over the *brook* **wadi**,
and *sent* **passed** over that he had.

YAAQOV'S WRESTLE

24 And *Jacob was left* **Yaaqov remained** alone;
and there wrestled a man with him
until the *breaking* **ascending** of the *day* **dawn**.
25 And when he saw that he prevailed not against him,
he touched the hollow of his *thigh* **flank**;
and the hollow of *Jacob's thigh* **Yaaqov's flank**
was *out of joint* **dislocated**, as he wrestled with him.
26 And he said, *Let me go* **Send me away**,
for the *day breaketh* **dawn ascendeth**.
And he said, I *will* **shall** not *let thee go* **send thee away**,
except **unless** thou bless me.

YAAQOV IS NAMED YISRA EL

27 And he said unto him, What is thy name?
And he said, *Jacob* **Yaaqov**.
28 And he said, Thy name
shall be *called* **said** no more *Jacob* **Yaaqov**,
but *Israel* **Yisra El**:
for *as a prince hast thou power* **thou hast prevailed**
with *God* **Elohim** and with men,
and hast prevailed.
29 And *Jacob* **Yaaqov** asked him, and said,
Tell me, I *pray* **beseech** thee, thy name.
And he said,
Wherefore is it that thou dost ask after my name?
And he blessed him there.
30 And *Jacob* **Yaaqov** called the name of the place
Peniel **Peni El**:
for I have seen *God* **Elohim** face to face,
and my *life* **soul** is *preserved* **rescued**.
31 And as he passed over *Penuel* **Peni El**
the sun rose upon him,
and he *halted* **limped** upon his *thigh* **flank**.
32 Therefore the *children* **sons** of *Israel* **Yisra El**
eat not of the sinew which *shrank* **shriveled**,
which is upon the hollow of the *thigh* **flank**, unto this day:
because
he touched the hollow of *Jacob's thigh* **Yaaqov's flank**
in the sinew that *shrank* **shriveled**.

YAAQOV MEETS ESAV

33 And *Jacob* **Yaaqov** lifted up his eyes,
and *looked* **saw**, and, behold,
Esau **Esav** came, and with him four hundred men.
And he *divided* **halved** the children unto Leah,
and unto Rachel, and unto the two *handmaids* **maids**.
2 And he put the *handmaids* **maids** and their children
foremost **first**,
and Leah and her children after,
and Rachel and *Joseph hindermost* **Yoseph behind**.
3 And he passed over *before them* **at their face**,
and *bowed himself* **prostrated** to the *ground* **earth**
seven times,
until he came near to his brother.
4 And *Esau* **Esav** ran to meet him, and embraced him,
and fell on his neck, and kissed him: and they wept.
5 And he lifted up his eyes,
and saw the women and the children;
and said, Who are those with thee?
And he said, The children which *God* **Elohim**
hath *graciously given* **granted charism to** thy servant.
6 Then the *handmaidens* **maids** came near,
they and their children,
and they *bowed themselves* **prostrated**.
7 And Leah also with her children came near,
and *bowed themselves* **prostrated**:
and after came *Joseph* **Yoseph** near and Rachel,
and they *bowed themselves* **prostrated**.
8 And he said,
What *meanest thou by* **be to thee**
all this *drove* **camp** which I met?
And he said,
These are to find *grace* **charism**
in the *sight* **eyes** of my *lord* **adoni**.
9 And *Esau* **Esav** said, I have *enough* **much**, my brother;
keep that thou hast unto thyself.
10 And *Jacob* **Yaaqov** said, Nay, I *pray* **beseech** thee,
if, *now* **I beseech**,
I have found *grace* **charism** in *thy sight* **thine eyes**,
then *receive* **take** my *present* **offering** at my hand:
for therefore I have seen thy face,
as *though I had* **having** seen the face of *God* **Elohim**,
and thou wast pleased *with me*.
11 Take, I *pray* **beseech** thee,
my blessing that is brought to thee;
because *God* **Elohim**
hath *dealt graciously with* **granted** me **charism**,
and because I have *enough* **all**.
And he urged him, and he took it.
12 And he said, Let us *take our journey* **pull stakes**,
and let us go, and I *will* **shall** go before thee.
13 And he said unto him,
My *lord* **adoni** knoweth that the children are tender,
and the flocks and *herds* **oxen** with *young* **sucklings**
are with me:
and if men should *overdrive* **beat** them one day,
all the flock *will* **shall** die.
14 Let my *lord* **adoni**, I *pray* **beseech** thee,
pass over *before* **at the face of** his servant:
and I *will lead on softly* **shall guide gently**,
according *as the cattle that goeth* **to the foot of the work**
before me **at my face,**
and **according to the foot of** the children
be able to endure,
until I come unto my *lord* **adoni** unto Seir.
15 And *Esau* **Esav** said, Let me, *now* **I beseech**,
leave with thee *some* of the *folk* **people** that are with me.
And he said, What needeth it?
let me find *grace* **charism**
in the *sight* **eyes** of my *lord* **adoni**.
16 So *Esau* **Esav** returned that day on his way unto Seir.
17 And *Jacob journeyed* **Yaaqov pulled stakes**
to *Succoth* **Sukkoth/Brush Arbors**,
and built him an house,
and *made booths* **worked sukkoth/brush arbors**
for his *cattle* **chattel**:
therefore the name of the place is called
Succoth **Sukkoth/Brush Arbors**.
18 And *Jacob* **Yaaqov** came to Shalem,
a city of Shechem,
which is in the land of *Canaan* **Kenaan**,
when he came from *Padanaram* **Paddan Aram**;
and *pitched his tent* **encamped**
before **at the face of** the city.
19 And he *bought* **chatteled**
a parcel **an allotment** of a field,
where he had spread his tent,
at the hand of the *children* **sons** of Hamor,
Shechem's father,
for an hundred *pieces of money* **ingots**.
20 And he *erected* **stationed** there *an* **a sacrifice** altar,
and called it *EleloheIsrael* **El Elohe Yisra El**.

DINAH IS FOULED

34 And Dinah the daughter of Leah,
which she bare unto *Jacob* **Yaaqov**,
went out to see the daughters of the land.

2 And when Shechem
the son of Hamor the *Hivite* **Hivviy**,
prince **hierarch** of the *country* **land**, saw her,
he took her, and lay with her, and *defiled* **humbled** her.
3 And his soul *clave* **adhered** unto Dinah
the daughter of *Jacob* **Yaaqov**,
and he loved the *damsel* **lass**,
and *spake kindly* **worded**
unto the *damsel* **heart of the lass**.
4 And Shechem *spake* **said** unto his father Hamor,
saying, *Get* **Take** me this *damsel* **child** to *wife* **woman**.
5 And *Jacob* **Yaaqov** heard
that he had *defiled* **fouled** Dinah his daughter:
now his sons were with his *cattle* **chattel** in the field:
and *Jacob held his peace* **Yaaqov hushed**
until they were come.
6 And Hamor the father of Shechem
went out unto *Jacob* **Yaaqov** to *commune* **word** with him.
7 And the sons of *Jacob* **Yaaqov**
came out of the field when they heard it:
and the men *were grieved* **contorted**,
and they were *very wroth* **mighty inflamed**,
because he had *wrought* **worked** folly in *Israel* **Yisra El**
in lying with *Jacob's* **Yaaqov's** daughter;
which *thing* ought not to be *done* **worked**.
8 And Hamor *communed* **worded** with them, saying,
The soul of my son Shechem
longeth for **is attached to** your daughter:
I *pray* **beseech** you give her him to *wife* **woman**.
9 And *make ye marriages* **intermarry** with us,
and give your daughters unto us,
and take our daughters unto you.
10 And ye shall *dwell* **settle** with us:
and the land shall be *before you* **at your face**;
dwell **settle** and *trade* **merchandise** ye therein,
and *get you possessions* **possess** therein.
11 And Shechem
said unto her father and unto her brethren,
Let me find *grace* **charism** in your eyes,
and what ye shall say unto me I *will* **shall** give.
12 *Ask* **Abound upon** me
never so much **a mighty** dowry and gift,
and I *will* **shall** give according as ye shall say unto me:
but give me the *damsel* **lass** to *wife* **woman**.
13 And the sons of *Jacob* **Yaaqov** answered
Shechem and Hamor his father deceitfully,
and *said* **worded**,
because he had *defiled* **fouled** Dinah their sister:
14 And they said unto them,
We cannot *do* **work** this *thing* **word**,
to give our sister to *one* **a man**
that is *uncircumcised* **foreskined**;
for that were a reproach unto us:
15 But in this *will* **shall** we consent unto you:
If ye *will* **shall** be as we be,
that every male of you be circumcised;
16 Then *will* **shall** we give our daughters unto you,
and we *will* **shall** take your daughters to us,
and we *will dwell* **shall settle** with you,
and we *will* **shall** become one people.
17 But if ye *will* **shall** not hearken unto us,
to be circumcised;
then *will* **shall** we take our daughter,
and we *will* **shall** be gone.
18 And their words
pleased **well—pleased the eyes of** Hamor,
and Shechem Hamor's son.
19 And the young *man* **lad**
deferred **delayed** not to *do* **work** the *thing* **word**,
because he had delight in *Jacob's* **Yaaqov's** daughter:
and he was more honourable
than all the house of his father.
20 And Hamor and Shechem his son
came unto the *gate* **portal** of their city,
and *communed* **worded** with the men of their city, saying,
21 These men are *peaceable* **at shalom** with us;
therefore let them *dwell* **settle** in the land,
and *trade* **merchandise** therein;
for the land, behold,
it is *large enough for them* **broadhanded at their face**;
let us take their daughters to us for *wives* **women**,
and let us give them our daughters.
22 Only herein *will* **shall** the men consent unto us
for to *dwell* **settle** with us, to be one people,
if every male among us be circumcised,
as they are circumcised.
23 Shall not their *cattle* **chattel**
and *their substance* **all they chatteled**
and every *beast* **animal** of theirs be ours?
only let us consent unto them,
and they *will dwell* **shall settle** with us.
24 And unto Hamor and unto Shechem his son
hearkened all that went out of the *gate* **portal** of his city;
and every male was circumcised,
all that went out of the *gate* **portal** of his city.
25 And it *came to pass* **became,**
on the third day, when they were *sore* **pained**,
that two of the sons of *Jacob* **Yaaqov**,
Simeon **Shimon** and Levi, Dinah's brethren,
took each man his sword,
and came upon the city *boldly* **confidently**,
and *slew* **slaughtered** all the males.
26 And they *slew* **slaughtered**
Hamor and Shechem his son
with the *edge* **mouth** of the sword,
and took Dinah out of Shechem's house,
and went out.
27 The sons of *Jacob* **Yaaqov** came upon the *slain* **pierced**,
and *spoiled* **plundered** the city,
because they had *defiled* **fouled** their sister.
28 They took their *sheep* **flocks**,
and their oxen, and their *asses* **he burros**,
and that which was in the city,
and that which was in the field,
29 And all their *wealth* **valuables**,
and all their *little ones* **toddlers**,
and **captured** their *wives took captive* **women**,
and *spoiled* **plundered** even all that was in the house.
30 And *Jacob* **Yaaqov** said to *Simeon* **Shimon** and Levi,
Ye have troubled me to make me to stink
among *the inhabitants of* **them that settle** the land,
among the *Canaanites* **Kenaaniy**
and the *Perizzites* **Perizziy**:
and I *being* few **men** in number,
they shall gather *themselves together* against me,
and *slay* **smite** me;
and I shall be *destroyed* **desolated**, I and my house.
31 And they said,
Should he *deal* **work** with our sister
as with *an harlot* **one that whoreth**?

YAAQOV MOVES TO BETH EL

35 And *God* **Elohim** said unto *Jacob* **Yaaqov**, Arise,
go up **ascend** to *Bethel* **Beth El**, and *dwell* **settle** there:
and *make* **work** there *an* **a sacrifice** altar unto *God* **El**,
that *appeared unto* **was seen by** thee
when thou fleddest
from the face of *Esau* **Esav** thy brother.
2 Then *Jacob* **Yaaqov** said unto his household,
and to all that were with him,
Put away **Turn aside** the strange *gods* **elohim**
that are among you,
and be *clean* **purified**, and change your *garments* **clothes**:
3 And let us arise, and *go up* **ascend** to *Bethel* **Beth El**;
and I *will make* **shall work** there
an **a sacrifice** altar unto *God* **El**,
who answered me in the day of my *distress* **tribulation**,
and was with me in the way which I went.
4 And they gave unto *Jacob* **Yaaqov**
all the strange *gods* **elohim** which were in their hand,
and all their *earrings* **noserings** which were in their ears;
and *Jacob hid* **Yaaqov buried** them under the oak
which was by Shechem.
5 And they *journeyed* **pulled stakes**:
and the terror of *God* **Elohim**
was upon the cities that were round about them,
and they did not pursue after the sons of *Jacob* **Yaaqov**.
6 So *Jacob* **Yaaqov** came to Luz,
which is in the land of *Canaan* **Kenaan**,
that is, *Bethel* **Beth El**,
he and all the people that were with him.

7 And he built there *an* **a sacrifice** altar,
and called the place *Elbethel* **El Beth El**:
because there *God* **Elohim**
appeared **exposed himself** unto him,
when he fled from the face of his brother.
8 But Deborah *Rebekah's nurse* **Ribqah's suckler** died,
and she was *buried* **entombed** beneath *Bethel* **Beth El**
under an oak:
and the name of it was called *Allonbachuth* **Allon Bachuth**.
9 And *God* **Elohim**
appeared unto Jacob **was seen by Yaaqov** again,
when he came out of *Padanaram* **Paddan Aram**,
and blessed him.

ELOHIM CONFIRMS THE NAME YISRA EL

10 And *God* **Elohim** said unto him,
Thy name is *Jacob* **Yaaqov**:
thy name shall not be called any more *Jacob* **Yaaqov**,
but *Israel* **Yisra El** shall be thy name:
and he called his name *Israel* **Yisra El**.
11 And *God* **Elohim** said unto him,
I am God Almighty **I — El Shadday**:
be fruitful **bear fruit** and *multiply* **abound**;
a *nation* **goyim**
and a *company* **congregation** of *nations* **goyim**
shall be of thee,
and *kings* **sovereigns** shall come out of thy loins;
12 And the land
which I gave Abraham and *Isaac* **Yischaq**,
to thee I *will* **shall** give it,
and to thy seed after thee *will* **shall** I give the land.
13 And *God went up* **Elohim ascended** from him
in the place where he *talked* **worded** with him.
14 And *Jacob set up* **Yaaqov stationed** a *pillar* **monolith**
in the place where he *talked* **worded** with him,
even a *pillar* **monolith** of stone:
and he *poured* **libated** a *drink offering* **libation** thereon,
and he *poured* **libated** oil thereon.
15 And *Jacob* **Yaaqov** called the name of the place
where *God spake* **Elohim worded** with him,
Bethel **Beth El**.
16 And they *journeyed* **pulled stakes** from *Bethel* **Beth El**;
and there was *but a little way* **still a bit of land**
to come to Ephrath:
and Rachel *travailed* **bore**, and she had hard labour.
17 And it *came to pass* **became**,
when she was in hard labour,
that the *midwife* **accoucheuse** said unto her,
Fear **Awe** not; thou shalt have this son also.
18 And it *came to pass* **became**,
as her soul was in departing, (for she died)
that she called his name *Benoni* **Ben Oni**:
but his father called him *Benjamin* **Ben Yamin**.
19 And Rachel died,
and was *buried* **entombed** in the way to Ephrath,
which is *Bethlehem* **Beth Lechem**.
20 And *Jacob* **Yaaqov**
set a pillar **stationed a monolith** upon her *grave* **tomb**:
that is the *pillar* **monolith** of Rachel's *grave* **tomb**
unto this day.
21 And *Israel journeyed* **Yisra El pulled stakes**,
and spread his tent beyond *the tower of Edar* **Migdal Eder**.
22 And it *came to pass* **became**,
when *Israel dwelt* **Yisra El tabernacled** in that land,
that *Reuben* **Reu Ben** went and lay with Bilhah
his father's concubine:
and *Israel* **Yisra El** heard it.

THE GENEALOGY OF YAAQOV

Now the sons of *Jacob* **Yaaqov** were twelve:
23 The sons of Leah;
Reuben **Reu Ben**, *Jacob's* **Yaaqov's** firstborn,
and *Simeon* **Shimon**, and Levi, and *Judah* **Yah Hudah**,
and *Issachar* **Yissachar**, and Zebulun:
24 The sons of Rachel;
Joseph **Yoseph**, and *Benjamin* **Ben Yamin**:
25 And the sons of Bilhah, Rachel's *handmaid* **maid**;
Dan, and Naphtali:
26 And the sons of Zilpah, Leah's *handmaid* **maid**:
Gad, and Asher:
these are the sons of *Jacob* **Yaaqov**,
which were born to him in *Padanaram* **Paddan Aram**.
27 And *Jacob* **Yaaqov** came unto *Isaac* **Yischaq** his father
unto Mamre,
unto *the city of Arbah* **Qiryath Arba**, which is Hebron,
where Abraham and *Isaac* **Yischaq** sojourned.
28 And the days of *Isaac* **Yischaq**
were an hundred **years** and *fourscore* **eighty** years.
29 And *Isaac gave up the ghost* **Yischaq expired**, and died,
and was gathered unto his people,
being old **aged** and *full* **satisfied** of days:
and his sons *Esau* **Esav** and *Jacob* **Yaaqov**
buried **entombed** him.

THE GENEALOGY OF ESAV

36 Now these are the generations of *Esau* **Esav**,
who is Edom.
2 *Esau* **Esav** took his *wives* **women**
of the daughters of *Canaan* **Kenaan**;
Adah the daughter of Elon the *Hittite* **Hethiy**,
and *Aholibamah* **Oholi Bamah** the daughter of Anah
the daughter of *Zibeon* **Sibon** the *Hivite* **Hivviy**;
3 And *Bashemath* **Bosmath** *Ishmael's* **Yishma El's** daughter,
sister of *Nebajoth* **Nebayoth**.
4 And Adah bare to *Esau* **Esav** *Eliphaz* **Eli Phaz**;
and *Bashemath* **Bosmath** bare *Reuel* **Reu El**;
5 And *Aholibamah* **Oholi Bamah** bare *Jeush* **Yeush**,
and *Jaalam* **Yalam**, and *Korah* **Qorach**:
these are the sons of *Esau* **Esav**,
which were born unto him
in the land of *Canaan* **Kenaan**.
6 And *Esau* **Esav** took his *wives* **women**,
and his sons, and his daughters,
and all the *persons* **souls** of his house,
and his *cattle* **chattel**, and all his *beasts* **animals**,
and all *his substance* **he chatteled**,
which he had *got* **acquired** in the land of *Canaan* **Kenaan**;
and went into the *country* **land**
from the face of his brother *Jacob* **Yaaqov**.
7 For their *riches* **acquisitions** were more
than that they might *dwell* **settle** together;
and the land
wherein they were strangers **of their sojournings**
could not bear them
because **at the face** of their *cattle* **chattel**.
8 Thus *dwelt Esau* **Esav settled** in mount Seir:
Esau **Esav** is Edom.
9 And these are the generations of *Esau* **Esav**
the father of the *Edomites* **Edomiy** in mount Seir:
10 These are the names of *Esau's* **Esav's** sons;
Eliphaz **Eli Phaz** the son of Adah
the *wife* **woman** of *Esau* **Esav**,
Reuel **Reu El** the son of *Bashemath* **Bosmath**
the *wife* **woman** of *Esau* **Esav**.
11 And the sons of *Eliphaz* **Eli Phaz** were
Teman, Omar, *Zepho* **Sepho**, and Gatam,
and *Kenaz* **Qenaz**.
12 And Timna was concubine to *Eliphaz* **Eli Phaz**
Esau's **Esav's** son;
and she bare to *Eliphaz* **Eli Phaz** *Amalek* **Amaleq**:
these were the sons of Adah *Esau's wife* **Esav's woman**.
13 And these are the sons of *Reuel* **Reu El**;
Nahath **Nachath**, and *Zerah* **Zerach**,
Shammah, and Mizzah:
these were the sons of *Bashemath* **Bosmath**
Esau's wife **Esav's woman**.
14 And these were the sons of *Aholibamah* **Oholi Bamah**,
the daughter of Anah the daughter of *Zibeon* **Sibon**,
Esau's wife **Esav's woman**:
and she bare to *Esau* **Esav** *Jeush* **Yeush**,
and *Jaalam* **Yalam**, and *Korah* **Qorach**.
15 These were *dukes* **chiliarchs** of the sons of *Esau* **Esav**:
the sons of *Eliphaz* **Eli Phaz** the firstborn *son* of *Esau* **Esav**;
duke **chiliarch** Teman, *duke* **chiliarch** Omar,
duke Zepho **chiliarch Sepho**,
duke Kenaz **chiliarch Qenaz**,
16 *Duke Korah* **chiliarch Qorach**, *duke* **chiliarch** Gatam,
and duke Amalek **chiliarch Amaleq**:
these are the *dukes* **chiliarchs**
that came of Eliphaz **Eli Phaz** in the land of Edom;
these were the sons of Adah.
17 And these are the sons of *Reuel* **Reu El**
Esau's **Esav's** son;

duke Nahath **chiliarch Nachath**,
duke Zerah **chiliarch Zerach**,
duke **chiliarch** Shammah, *duke* **chiliarch** Mizzah:
these are the *dukes* **chiliarchs** *that came* of *Reuel* **Reu El**
in the land of Edom;
these are the sons of *Bashemath* **Bosmath**
Esau's wife **Esav's woman**.
18 And these are the sons of *Aholibamah* **Oholi Bamah**
Esau's wife **Esav's woman**;
duke Jeush **chiliarch Yeush**, *duke Jaalam* **chiliarch Yalam**,
duke Korah **chiliarch Qorach**:
these were the *dukes* **chiliarchs**
that came Aholibamah of **Oholi Bamah**
the daughter of Anah, *Esau's wife* **Esav's woman**.
19 These are the sons of *Esau* **Esav**, who is Edom,
and these are their *dukes* **chiliarchs**.
20 These are the sons of Seir the *Horite* **Horiy**,
who *inhabited* **settled** the land;
Lotan, and Shobal, and *Zibeon* **Sibon**, and Anah,
21 And Dishon, and *Ezer* **Eser**, and Dishan:
these are the *dukes* **chiliarchs** of the *Horites* **Horiy**,
the *children* **sons** of Seir in the land of Edom.
22 And the *children* **sons** of Lotan were Hori and Hemam;
and Lotan's sister was Timna.
23 And the *children* **sons** of Shobal were these;
Alvan, and *Manahath* **Manachath**, and Ebal,
Shepho, and Onam.
24 And these are the *children* **sons** of *Zibeon* **Sibon**;
both *Ajah* **Ayah**, and Anah:
this was that Anah
that found the *mules* **hot springs** in the wilderness,
as he *fed* **tended** the *asses* **he burros** of *Zibeon* **Sibon**
his father.
25 And the *children* **sons** of Anah were these;
Dishon,
and *Aholibamah* **Oholi Bamah** the daughter of Anah.
26 And these are the *children* **sons** of Dishon;
Hemdan, and Eshban,
and *Ithran* **Yithran**, and *Cheran* **Keran**.
27 The *children* **sons** of *Ezer* **Eser** are these;
Bilhan, and Zaavan, and *Akan* **Aqan**.
28 The *children* **sons** of Dishan are these;
Uz **Us**, and Aran.
29 These are the *dukes* **chiliarchs**
that came of the *Horites* **Horiy**;
duke **chiliarch** Lotan, *duke* **chiliarch** Shobal,
duke Zibeon **chiliarch Sibon**, *duke* **chiliarch** Anah,
30 *Duke* **chiliarch** Dishon, *duke Ezer* **chiliarch Eser**,
duke **chiliarch** Dishan:
these are the *dukes* **chiliarchs** *that came* of Hori,
among their *dukes* **chiliarchs** in the land of Seir.
31 And these are the *kings* **sovereigns**
that reigned in the land of Edom,
before there reigned **at the face of the reign**
of any *king* **sovereign**
over the *children* **sons** of *Israel* **Yisra El**.
32 And Bela the son of Beor reigned in Edom:
and the name of his city was Dinhabah.
33 And Bela died,
and *Jobab* **Yobab**
the son of *Zerah* **Zerach** of *Bozrah* **Bosrah**
reigned in his stead.
34 And *Jobab* **Yobab** died,
and Husham of the land of *Temani* **Temaniy**
reigned in his stead.
35 And Husham died,
and Hadad the son of Bedad,
who smote *Midian* **Midyan** in the field of Moab,
reigned in his stead:
and the name of his city was Avith.
36 And Hadad died,
and Samlah of *Masrekah* **Masreqah**
reigned in his stead.
37 And Samlah died,
and *Saul* **Shaul** of *Rehoboth* **Rechovoth** by the river
reigned in his stead.
38 And *Saul* **Shaul** died,
and *Baalhanan* **Baal Chanan** the son of Achbor
reigned in his stead.
39 And *Baalhanan* **Baal Chanan**
the son of Achbor died,
and Hadar reigned in his stead:
and the name of his city was Pau;
and his *wife's* **woman's** name was *Mehetabel* **Mehetab El**,
the daughter of Matred,
the daughter of *Mezahab* **Me Zahab**.
40 And these are the names
of the *dukes* **chiliarchs** *that came* of *Esau* **Esav**,
according to their families, after their places,
by their names;
duke Timnah **chiliarch Timna**, *duke* **chiliarch** Alvah,
duke Jetheth **chiliarch Yetheth**,
41 *Duke Aholibamah* **chiliarch Oholi Bamah**,
duke **chiliarch** Elah, *duke* **chiliarch** Pinon,
42 *Duke Kenaz* **chiliarch Qenaz**,
duke **chiliarch** Teman, *duke Mibzar* **chiliarch Mibsar**,
43 *Duke Magdiel* **chiliarch Magdi El**, *duke* **chiliarch** Iram:
these be the *dukes* **chiliarchs** of Edom,
according to their *habitations* **settlements**
in the land of their possession:
he is *Esau* **Esav** the father of the *Edomites* **Edomiy**.
37 And *Jacob dwelt* **Yaaqov settled** in the land
wherein his father *was a stranger* **sojourned**,
in the land of *Canaan* **Kenaan**.
2 These are the generations of *Jacob* **Yaaqov**.

THE DREAMS OF YOSEPH

Joseph **Yoseph**, *being* **a son of** seventeen years *old*,
was *feeding* **tending** the flock with his brethren;
and the lad was with the sons of Bilhah,
and with the sons of Zilpah, his father's *wives* **women**:
and *Joseph* **Yoseph** brought unto his father
their *evil report* **slander**.
3 *Now Israel* **Yisra El** loved *Joseph* **Yoseph**
more than all his *children* **sons**,
because he was the son of his old age:
and he *made* **worked** him a **coverall** coat *of many colours*.
4 And when his brethren saw
that their father loved him more than all his brethren,
they hated him,
and could not *speak peaceably* **word shalom** unto him.
5 And *Joseph* **Yoseph** dreamed a dream,
and he told it his brethren:
and they hated him yet *the more* **again**.
6 And he said unto them, Hear, I *pray* **beseech** you,
this dream which I have dreamed:
7 For, behold,
we were *binding* **tying** sheaves *in* **midst** the field,
and, *lo* **behold**, my sheaf arose,
and also *stood upright* **stationed itself**;
and, behold, your sheaves *stood* **turned** round about,
and *made obeisance* **prostrated** to my sheaf.
8 And his brethren said to him,
In reigning,
Shalt thou *indeed* reign over us?
or **in having reign,**
shalt thou *indeed* have *dominion* **reign** over us?
And they hated him yet *the more* **again**
for his dreams, and for his words.
9 And he dreamed yet another dream,
and *told* **described** it **to** his brethren, and said,
Behold, I have dreamed a dream *more* **again**;
and, behold, the sun and the moon and the eleven stars
made obeisance **prostrated** to me.
10 And he *told* **described** it to his father,
and to his brethren:
and his father rebuked him, and said unto him,
What is this dream that thou hast dreamed?
Shall I and thy mother and thy brethren indeed come
to *bow down ourselves* **prostrate** to thee to the earth?
11 And his brethren envied him;
but his father *observed* **guarded** the *saying* **word**.
12 And his brethren went to *feed* **tend** their father's flock
in Shechem.
13 And *Israel* **Yisra El** said unto *Joseph* **Yoseph**,
Do not thy brethren *feed the flock* **tend** in Shechem?
come **go**, and I *will* **shall** send thee unto them.
And he said to him, Here *am* — I.
14 And he said to him, Go, I *pray* **beseech** thee,
see whether it be *well* **shalom** with thy brethren,
and *well* **shalom** with the flocks;

and *bring* **return** me word *again.*
So he sent him out of the *vale* **valley** of Hebron,
and he came to Shechem.
15 And a *certain* man found him,
and, behold, he was wandering in the field:
and the man asked him, saying, What seekest thou?
16 And he said, I seek my brethren:
tell me, I *pray* **beseech** thee,
where they *feed their flocks* **tend**.
17 And the man said,
They *are departed* **have pulled stakes** hence;
for I heard them say, Let us go to Dothan.
And *Joseph* **Yoseph** went after his brethren,
and found them in Dothan.

CONSPIRACY AGAINST YOSEPH

18 And when they saw him afar off,
even before he *came near unto* **approached** them,
they conspired against him to *slay* **deathify** him.
19 And they said *one* **man** to *another* **brother**,
Behold, this *dreamer* **very master of dreams** cometh.
20 *Come* **Go** now therefore, and let us *slay* **slaughter** him,
and cast him into *some pit* **a well**, and we *will* **shall** say,
Some evil *beast* **live being** hath devoured him:
and we shall see what *will* **shall** become of his dreams.
21 And *Reuben* **Reu Ben** heard it,
and he *delivered* **rescued** him out of their hands;
and said, Let us not *kill him* **smite his soul**.
22 And *Reuben* **Reu Ben** said unto them,
Shed **Pour** no blood,
but cast him into this *pit* **well** that is in the wilderness,
and *lay* **extend** no hand upon him;
that he might *rid* **rescue** him out of their hands,
to *deliver* **return** him to his father *again.*
23 And it *came to pass* **became**,
when *Joseph* **Yoseph** was come unto his brethren,
that they stript *Joseph* **Yoseph** out of his coat,
his **the coverall** coat *of many colours* that was on him;
24 And they took him, and cast him into a *pit* **well**:
and the *pit* **well** was empty, there *was* no water in it.
25 And they sat down to eat bread:
and they lifted up their eyes and *looked* **saw**, and, behold,
a *company* **caravan** of *Ishmeelites* **Yishma Eliy**
came from *Gilead* **Gilad** with their camels
bearing spicery and balm and myrrh,
going to *carry it down to Egypt* **descend it to Misrayim**.
26 And *Judah* **Yah Hudah** said unto his brethren,
What *profit* **gain** is it *if we slay* **to slaughter** our brother,
and *conceal* **cover** his blood?
27 *Come* **Go**,
and let us sell him to the *Ishmeelites* **Yishma Eliy**,
and let not our hand be upon him;
for he is our brother and our flesh.
And his brethren *were content* **hearkened**.
28 Then there passed by
Midianites merchantmen **men — Midyaniy merchants**;
and they drew
and *lifted up Joseph* **ascended Yoseph** out of the *pit* **well**,
and sold *Joseph* **Yoseph** to the *Ishmeelites* **Yishma Eliy**
for twenty *pieces of* silver:
and they brought *Joseph* **Yoseph** into *Egypt* **Misrayim**.
29 And *Reuben* **Reu Ben** returned unto the *pit* **well**;
and, behold, *Joseph* **Yoseph** was not in the *pit* **well**;
and he *rent* **ripped** his clothes.
30 And he returned unto his brethren, and said,
The child is not; and I, whither shall I go?
31 And they took *Joseph's* **Yoseph's** coat,
and *killed* **slaughtered** a kid of the goats,
and dipped the coat in the blood;
32 And they sent the **coverall** coat *of many colours,*
and they brought it to their father; and said,
This have we found:
know now **Recognize, I beseech**,
whether it be thy son's coat or no.
33 And he *knew* **recognized** it, and said,
It is my son's coat;
an evil *beast* **live being** hath devoured him;
Joseph is without doubt rent in pieces
in tearing, Yoseph is torn.
34 And *Jacob rent* **Yaaqov ripped** his clothes,
and put *sackcloth* **saq** upon his loins,
and mourned for his son many days.
35 And all his sons and all his daughters
rose *up* to *comfort* **sigh over** him;
but he refused to be *comforted* **sighed over**; and he said,
For I *will go down* **shall descend** into *the grave* **sheol**
unto my son mourning.
Thus his father wept for him.
36 And the *Midianites* **Midyaniym**
sold him into *Egypt* **Misrayim**
unto Potiphar, *an officer* **a eunuch** of *Pharaoh's* **Paroh's**,
and *captain* **governor** of the *guard* **slaughterers**.

YAH HUDAH AND TAMAR

38 And it *came to pass* **became** at that time,
that *Judah* **Yah Hudah**
went down **descended** from his brethren,
and turned in to a *certain Adullamite* **man — an Adullamiy**,
whose name was Hirah.
2 And *Judah* **Yah Hudah** saw there a daughter
of a *certain Canaanite* **man — a Kenaaniy**,
whose name was Shuah;
and he took her, and went in unto her.
3 And she conceived, and bare a son;
and he called his name Er.
4 And she conceived again, and bare a son;
and she called his name Onan.
5 And she yet again *conceived,* and bare a son;
and called his name Shelah:
and he was at *Chezib* **Kezib**, when she bare him.
6 And *Judah* **Yah Hudah**
took a *wife* **woman** for Er his firstborn,
whose name was Tamar.
7 And Er, *Judah's* **Yah Hudah's** firstborn,
was *wicked* **evil** in the *sight* **eyes** of *the LORD* **Yah Veh**;
and *the LORD slew* **Yah Veh deathified** him.
8 And *Judah* **Yah Hudah** said unto Onan,
Go in unto thy brother's *wife* **woman**,
and *marry her* **be her levirate**,
and raise up seed to thy brother.
9 And Onan knew that the seed should not be his;
and it *came to pass* **became**,
when he went in unto his brother's *wife* **woman**,
that he *spilled* **ruined** it on the *ground* **earth**,
lest that he should give seed to his brother.
10 And *the thing* **that** which he *did* **worked**
displeased the LORD **was evil in the eyes of Yah Veh**:
wherefore he *slew* **deathified** him also.
11 Then said *Judah* **Yah Hudah** to Tamar
his daughter in law,
Remain **Settle**, a widow at thy father's house,
till Shelah my son be grown: for he said,
Lest peradventure he die also, as his brethren *did.*
And Tamar went and *dwelt* **settled** in her father's house.
12 And *in process of time* **as the days abounded**
the daughter of Shuah,
Judah's wife **Yah Hudah's woman** died;
and *Judah was comforted* **Yah Hudah sighed**,
and *went up* **ascended**
unto his *sheepshearers* **flockshearers** to *Timnath* **Timnah**,
he and his friend Hirah the *Adullamite* **Adullamiy**.

YAH HUDAH'S WHOREDOM

13 And it was told Tamar, saying, Behold,
thy father in law *goeth up* **ascendeth** to *Timnath* **Timnah**
to shear his *sheep* **flock**.
14 And she
put her widow's garments off from her
turned aside the clothing of her widowhood,
and covered her with a vail, and wrapped herself,
and sat in *an open place* **the portal of the fountain**,
which is by the way to *Timnath* **Timnah**;
for she saw that Shelah was grown,
and she was not given unto him to *wife* **woman**.
15 When *Judah* **Yah Hudah** saw her,
he *thought* **fabricated** her
to be *an harlot* **one that whoreth**;
because she had covered her face.
16 And he turned unto her by the way, and said,
Go to **Give**, I *pray* **beseech** thee,
let me come in unto thee;
(for he knew not that she was his daughter in law.)
And she said, What *wilt* **shalt** thou give me,

that thou mayest come in unto me?
17 And he said, I *will* **shall** send thee
a kid **of the goats** from the flock.
And she said,
Wilt **Shalt** thou give me a pledge, till thou send it?
18 And he said, What pledge shall I give thee?
And she said, Thy *signet* **seal**, and thy *bracelets* **braids**,
and thy *staff* **rod** that is in thine hand.
And he gave it her, and came in unto her,
and she conceived by him.
19 And she arose, and went *away*,
and *laid by* **turned aside** her vail from her,
and *put on* **enrobed**
the *garments* **clothes** of her widowhood.
20 And *Judah* **Yah Hudah** sent the kid **of the goats**
by the hand of his friend the *Adullamite* **Adullamiy**,
to *receive* **take** his pledge from the woman's hand:
but he found her not.
21 Then he asked the men of that place, saying,
Where is the *harlot* **hallowed whore**,
that was *openly* **at the opening of the fountain**
by the way side?
And they said,
There was no *harlot in this place* **hallowed whore here**.
22 And he returned to *Judah* **Yah Hudah**, and said,
I cannot find her;
and also the men of the place said,
that there was no
harlot in this place **hallowed whore here**.
23 And *Judah* **Yah Hudah** said, Let her take it to her,
lest we be *shamed* **a disrespect**:
behold, I sent this kid, and thou hast not found her.
24 And it *came to pass* **became,** about three months after,
that it was told *Judah* **Yah Hudah**, saying,
Tamar thy daughter in law hath *played the harlot* **whored**;
and also, behold,
she *is with child* **hath conceived**
by *whoredom* **whoredoms**.
And *Judah* **Yah Hudah** said,
Bring her forth, and let her be burnt.
25 When she was brought forth,
she sent to her father in law, saying,
By the man, whose these are,
am I with child **have I conceived**:
and she said, *Discern* **Recognize**, I *pray* **beseech** thee,
whose are these,
the *signet* **seal**, and *bracelets* **braids**, and *staff* **rod**.
26 And *Judah acknowledged* **Yah Hudah recognized** them,
and said,
She hath been *more righteous* **justified more** than I;
because that I gave her not to Shelah my son.
And he knew her again no more.
27 And it *came to pass* **became,** in the time of her travail,
that, behold, twins were in her *womb* **belly**.
28 And it *came to pass* **became**, when she travailed,
that the one *put* **gave** out *his* **a** hand:
and the *midwife* **accoucheuse** took
and bound upon his hand *a* scarlet *thread*,
saying, This came out first.
29 And it *came to pass* **became**,
as he *drew* **turned** back his hand,
that, behold, his brother came out:
and she said, How hast thou *broken forth* **breached**?
this breach be upon thee:
therefore his name was called *Pharez* **Peres**.
30 And afterward came out his brother,
that had the scarlet *thread* upon his hand:
and his name was called *Zarah* **Zerach**.

YOSEPH IN MISRAYIM

39 And *Joseph* **Yoseph**
was *brought down* **descended** to *Egypt* **Misrayim**;
and Potiphar, *an officer* **a eunuch** of *Pharaoh* **Paroh**,
captain **governor** of the *guard* **slaughterers**,
an Egyptian **a man — a Misrayim**,
bought **chatteled** him
of the hands of the *Ishmeelites* **Yishma Eliy**,
which had *brought* **descended** him *down* thither.
2 And *the LORD* **Yah Veh** was with *Joseph* **Yoseph**,
and he was a *prosperous* **prospering** man;
and he was in the house of his *master* **adoni**
the *Egyptian* **Misrayim**.
3 And his *master* **adoni**
saw that *the LORD* **Yah Veh** was with him,
and that *the LORD made* **Yah Veh prospered** all
that he *did to prosper* **worked** in his hand.
4 And *Joseph* **Yoseph** found *grace* **charism**
in his *sight* **eyes**,
and he *served* **ministered to** him:
and he *made* **had** him *overseer* **oversee** over his house,
and all that he had he *put* **gave** into his hand.
5 And it *came to pass* **became,**
from the time that he had made him overseer
since he had him oversee
in his house, and *over* all that he had,
that *the LORD* **Yah Veh**
blessed the *Egyptian's* **Misrayim's** house
for *Joseph's* **Yoseph's** sake;
and the blessing of *the LORD* **Yah Veh**
was upon all that he had in the house, and in the field.
6 And he left all that he had in *Joseph's* **Yoseph's** hand;
and he knew not ought he had,
save the bread which he did eat.
And *Joseph* **Yoseph**
was *a goodly person* **beautiful in form**,
and *well favoured* **beautiful in visage**.
7 And it *came to pass* **became,** after these *things* **words**,
that his *master's wife* **adoni's woman**
cast **lifted** her eyes upon *Joseph* **Yoseph**;
and she said, Lie with me.
8 But he refused,
and said unto his *master's wife* **adoni's woman**,
Behold, my master *wotteth* **perceiveth** not
what is with me in the house,
and he hath *committed* **given** all that he hath to my hand;
9 There is none greater in this house than I;
neither hath he *kept back* **withheld**
any thing **aught** from me but thee,
because thou art his *wife* **woman**:
how then can I *do* **work** this great *wickedness* **evil**,
and sin against *God* **Elohim**?
10 And it *came to pass* **became**,
as she *spake* **worded** to *Joseph* **Yoseph** day by day,
that he hearkened not unto her,
to lie *by* **beside** her, or to be with her.
11 And it *came to pass* **became,** *about* this *time* **day**,
that *Joseph* **he** went into the house
to *do* **work** his *business* **work**;
and there was *none* **no man** of the men of the house
there within **the house**.
12 And she *caught* **captured** him by his *garment* **clothes**,
saying, Lie with me:
and he left his *garment* **clothes** in her hand,
and fled, and got him out.
13 And it *came to pass* **became**,
when she saw
that he had left his *garment* **clothes** in her hand,
and *was* fled *forth* **out**,
14 That she called unto the men of her house,
and *spake* **said** unto them, saying,
See, he hath brought in **a man** — an Hebrew unto us
to *mock* **ridicule** us;
he came in unto me to lie with me,
and I *cried* **called** with a *loud* **great** voice:
15 And it *came to pass* **became**,
when he heard that I lifted up my voice and *cried* **called**,
that he left his *garment with* **clothes beside** me,
and fled, and got him out.
16 And she *laid up* **set** his *garment by* **clothes beside** her,
until his *lord* **adoni** came home.
17 And she *spake* **worded** unto him
according to these words, saying,
The Hebrew servant, which thou hast brought unto us,
came in unto me to *mock* **ridicule** me:
18 And it *came to pass* **became**,
as I lifted up my voice and *cried* **called**,
that he left his *garment with* **clothes beside** me,
and fled out.
19 And it *came to pass* **became**,
when his *master* **adoni**
heard the words of his *wife* **woman**,

which she *spake* **worded** unto him, saying,
After this *manner did* **word worked** thy servant to me;
that his wrath was kindled.
20 And *Joseph's master* **Yoseph's adoni** took him,
and *put* **gave** him into the *prison* **tower house**,
a place where the *king's prisoners* **soverign's bound**
were bound:
and he was there in the *prison* **tower house**.
21 But *the LORD* **Yah Veh** was with *Joseph* **Yoseph**,
and *shewed* **extended** him mercy,
and gave him *favour* **charism** in the *sight* **eyes**
of the *keeper* **governor** of the *prison* **tower house**.
22 And the *keeper* **governor** of the *prison* **tower house**
committed to Joseph's **gave into Yoseph's** hand
all *the prisoners* that were **bound**
in the *prison* **tower house**;
and whatsoever they *did* **worked** there,
he was *the doer* **worker** of it.
23 The *keeper* **governor** of the *prison* **tower house**
looked not to any thing **saw after naught**
that was under his hand;
because *the LORD* **Yah Veh** was with him,
and that which he *did* **worked**,
the LORD **Yah Veh** made it to prosper.

YOSEPH INTERPRETS DREAMS

40 And it *came to pass* **became,**
after these *things* **words**,
that the butler of the *king* **sovereign** of *Egypt* **Misrayim**
and his baker had *offended* **sinned against** their *lord* **adoni**
the *king* **sovereign** of *Egypt* **Misrayim.**
2 And *Pharaoh* **Paroh** was *wroth* **enraged**
against two of his *officers* **eunuchs**,
against the *chief* **governor** of the butlers,
and against the *chief* **governor** of the bakers.
3 And he *put* **gave** them *in ward* **under guard**
in the house
of the *captain* **governor** of the *guard* **slaughterers**,
into the *prison* **tower house**,
the place where *Joseph* **Yoseph** was bound.
4 And the *captain* **governor** of the *guard* **slaughterers**
charged Joseph **mustered Yoseph** with them,
and he *served* **ministered to** them:
and they continued a *season in ward* **day under guard**.
5 And they dreamed a dream *both* **the two** of them,
each man his dream in one night,
each man according to the interpretation of his dream,
the butler and the baker
of the *king* **sovereign** of *Egypt* **Misrayim**,
which were bound in the *prison* **tower house**.
6 And *Joseph* **Yoseph** came in unto them in the morning,
and *looked upon* **saw** them,
and, behold, they were *sad* **wroth**.
7 And he asked *Pharaoh's officers* **Paroh's eunuchs**
that were with him
in **under** the *ward* **guard** of his *lord's* **adoni's** house,
saying,
Wherefore *look ye so sadly* **are your faces evil** to day?
8 And they said unto him,
We have dreamed a dream,
and there is no interpreter of it.
And *Joseph* **Yoseph** said unto them,
Do **Be** not interpretations *belong to God* **of Elohim**?
tell **describe** me them, I *pray* **beseech** you.
9 And the *chief butler* **governor of the butlers**
told **described** his dream to *Joseph* **Yoseph**,
and said to him,
In my dream, behold, a vine was *before me* **at my face**;
10 And in the vine were three *branches* **tendrils**:
and it was as *though it budded* **blossoming**,
and her blossoms *shot forth* **ascended**;
and the clusters thereof *brought forth ripe* **ripened** grapes:
11 And *Pharaoh's* **Paroh's** cup was in my hand:
and I took the grapes,
and pressed them into *Pharaoh's* **Paroh's** cup,
and I gave the cup into *Pharaoh's hand* **Paroh's palm**.
12 And *Joseph* **Yoseph** said unto him,
This is the interpretation of it:
The three *branches* **tendrils** are three days:
13 *Yet* **Again** within three days
shall *Pharaoh* **Paroh** lift *up* thine head,
and restore thee unto thy *place* **station**:
and thou shalt *deliver Pharaoh's* **give Paroh's** cup
into his hand,
after the *former manner* **first judgment**
when thou wast his butler.
14 But *think on* **remember** me
when *it shall be well with thee* **thou be well—pleased**,
and *shew kindness* **work mercy**, I *pray* **beseech** thee,
unto me,
and *make mention of* **remember** me unto *Pharaoh* **Paroh**,
and bring me out of this house:
15 For *indeed* **in stealing,** I was stolen *away*
out of the land of the Hebrews:
and here also have I *done nothing* **worked naught**
that they should put me into the *dungeon* **well**.
16 When the *chief baker* **governor of the bakers**
saw that the interpretation was good,
he said unto *Joseph* **Yoseph**,
I also was in my dream, and, behold,
I had three white — **three perforated** baskets on my head:
17 And in the uppermost basket
there was *of all manner of bakemeats* **the work of a baker**
for *Pharaoh* **Paroh**;
and the *birds* **fliers** did eat them
out of the basket upon my head.
18 And *Joseph* **Yoseph** answered and said,
This is the interpretation thereof:
The three baskets are three days:
19 *Yet* **Again** within three days
shall *Pharaoh* **Paroh** lift *up* thy head from off thee,
and shall hang thee on a tree;
and the *birds* **fliers** shall eat thy flesh from off thee.
20 And it *came to pass* **became** the third day,
which was Pharaoh's **Paroh's** birthday,
that he *made* **worked** a *feast* **banquet** unto all his servants:
and he lifted up the head
of the *chief butler* **governor of the butlers**
and **the head**
of the *chief baker* **governor of the bakers**
among his servants.
21 And he restored the *chief butler* **governor of the butlers**
unto his butlership again;
and he gave the cup into *Pharaoh's hand* **Paroh's palm**:
22 But he hanged the *chief baker* **governor of the bakers**:
as *Joseph* **Yoseph** had interpreted to them.
23 Yet did not the *chief butler* **governor of the butlers**
remember *Joseph* **Yoseph**, but forgat him.

PAROH DREAMS

41 And it *came to pass* **became,**
at the end of two *full years* **years of days**,
that *Pharaoh* **Paroh** dreamed:
and, behold, he stood by the river.
2 And, behold, there *came up* **ascended** out of the river
seven *well favoured kine* **heifers beautiful visaged**
and fatfleshed;
and they *fed* **grazed** in *a meadow* **the bulrushes**.
3 And, behold,
seven other *kine came up* **heifers ascended** after them
out of the river,
ill favoured **evil visaged** and *leanfleshed* **thinfleshed**;
and stood by the *other kine* **heifers**
upon the *brink* **edge** of the river.
4 And the *ill favoured* **evil visaged**
and *leanfleshed kine* **thinfleshed heifers**
did eat up the seven
well favoured **beautiful visaged** and fat *kine* **heifers**.
So *Pharaoh* **Paroh** awoke.
5 And he slept and dreamed the second *time*:
and, behold,
seven ears *of corn came up* **ascended** upon one *stalk* **stem**,
rank **fat** and good.
6 And, behold,
seven thin ears and blasted with the *east wind* **easterly**
sprung up after them.
7 And the *seven* thin ears
devoured **swallowed** the seven *rank* **fat** and full ears.
And *Pharaoh* **Paroh** awoke, and, behold, it was a dream.
8 And it *came to pass* **became** in the morning
that his spirit was *troubled* **agitated**;
and he sent and called for

all the magicians of *Egypt* **Misrayim**,
and all the wise *men* thereof:
and *Pharaoh told* **Paroh described** them his dream;
but there was none that could interpret them
unto *Pharaoh* **Paroh**.
9 Then *spake* **worded**
the *chief butler* **governor of the butlers**
unto *Pharaoh* **Paroh**, saying,
I do remember my *faults* **sins** this day:
10 *Pharaoh* **Paroh** was *wroth* **enraged** with his servants,
and *put* **gave** me *in ward* **under guard**
in the *captain* **governor** of the *guard's* **slaughterer's** house,
both me and the *chief baker* **governor of the bakers**:
11 And we dreamed a dream in one night, I and he;
we dreamed each man
according to the interpretation of his dream.
12 And there was there with us a *young man* **lad**,
an Hebrew,
servant to the *captain* **governor** of the *guard* **slaughterers**;
and we *told* **described to** him,
and he interpreted to us our dreams;
to each man according to his dream he did interpret.
13 And it *came to pass* **became**,
as he interpreted to us, so it was;
me he restored unto *mine office* **my station**,
and him he hanged.
14 Then *Pharaoh* **Paroh** sent and called *Joseph* **Yoseph**,
and they *brought* **ran** him *hastily* out of the *dungeon* **well**:
and he shaved *himself*, and changed his *raiment* **clothes**,
and came in unto *Pharaoh* **Paroh**.
15 And *Pharaoh* **Paroh** said unto *Joseph* **Yoseph**,
I have dreamed a dream,
and there is none that can interpret it:
and I have heard say of thee,
that thou *canst understand* **hearest** a dream to interpret it.
16 And *Joseph* **Yoseph** answered *Pharaoh* **Paroh**,
saying, *It is not in me* **Except for I**:
God **Elohim** shall give *Pharaoh* **Paroh**
an answer of *peace* **shalom**.
17 And *Pharaoh said* **Paroh worded** unto *Joseph* **Yoseph**,
In my dream, behold,
I stood upon the *bank* **edge** of the river:
18 And, behold,
there *came up* **ascended** out of the river seven *kine* **heifers**,
fatfleshed and *well favoured* **of beautiful form**;
and they *fed in a meadow* **grazed in the bulrushes**:
19 And, behold,
seven other *kine came up* **heifers ascended** after them,
poor and *very ill favoured* **mighty evil formed**
and *leanfleshed* **emaciated flesh**, such as I never saw
in all the land of *Egypt* **Misrayim** for *badness* **evil**:
20 And the *lean* **emaciated**
and the *ill favoured kine* **evil heifers**
did eat up the first seven fat *kine* **heifers**:
21 And when they had
eaten them up **entered their inwards**,
it could not be known **they were not seen**
that they had eaten them **entering their inwards**;
but they were still *ill favoured* **evil visaged**,
as at the beginning.
So I awoke.
22 And I saw in my dream, and, behold,
seven ears *came up* **ascended** in one *stalk* **stem**,
full and good:
23 And, behold, seven ears, withered, thin,
and blasted with the *east wind* **easterly**,
sprung up after them:
24 And the thin ears
devoured **swallowed** the seven good ears:
and I *told* **said** this unto the magicians;
but there was none *that could declare it* to **tell** me.
25 And *Joseph* **Yoseph** said unto *Pharaoh* **Paroh**,
The dream of *Pharaoh* **Paroh** is one:
God **Elohim** hath *shewed Pharaoh* **told Paroh**
what he is about to *do* **work**.
26 The seven good *kine* **heifer** are seven years;
and the seven good ears are seven years:
the dream is one.
27 And the seven *thin* **emaciated**
and *ill favoured kine* **evil heifers**
that *came up* **ascended** after them are seven years;
and the seven empty ears
blasted with the *east wind* **easterly**
shall be seven years of famine.
28 This is the *thing* **word**
which I have *spoken* **worded** unto *Pharaoh* **Paroh**:
What *God* **Elohim** is about to *do* **work**
he *sheweth unto Pharaoh* **hath Paroh to see**.
29 Behold,
there come seven years of great *plenty* **sufficiency**
throughout all the land of *Egypt* **Misrayim**:
30 And there shall arise after them
seven years of famine;
and all the *plenty* **sufficiency** shall be forgotten
in the land of *Egypt* **Misrayim**;
and the famine shall *consume* **finish off** the land;
31 And the *plenty* **sufficiency**
shall not be known in the land
by reason **at the face** of that famine *following* **thus**;
for it shall be *very grievous* **mighty heavy**.
32 And for that the dream was *doubled* **duplicated**
unto *Pharaoh twice* **Paroh two times**;
it is because the *thing* **word** is established by *God* **Elohim**,
and *God* **Elohim**
will shortly bring it **shall hasten** to *pass* **work**.
33 Now therefore let *Pharaoh look out* **Paroh seek** a man
discreet **discerning** and wise,
and set him over the land of *Egypt* **Misrayim**.
34 Let *Pharaoh do* **Paroh work** this,
and let him *appoint officers* **muster overseers**
over the land,
and take up the fifth part **over a fifth** of the land
of *Egypt* **Misrayim**
in the seven *plenteous* years **of sufficiency**.
35 And let them gather all the food of those good years
that come,
and *lay up corn* **heap grain**
under the hand of *Pharaoh* **Paroh**,
and let them *keep* **guard** food in the cities.
36 And that food shall be for *store* **overseeing** to the land
against the seven years of famine,
which shall be in the land of *Egypt* **Misrayim**;
that the land *perish not* **not be cut** through the famine.
37 And the *thing* **word**
was good in **well—pleased** the eyes of *Pharaoh* **Paroh**,
and *in* the eyes of all his servants.
38 And *Pharaoh* **Paroh** said unto his servants,
Can we find *such a one as this is* **thus**,
a man in whom the Spirit of *God* **Elohim** is?
39 And *Pharaoh* **Paroh** said unto *Joseph* **Yoseph**,
Forasmuch as God **Since Elohim**
hath *shewed thee all this* **made all this known to thee**,
there is none so *discreet* **discerning** and wise as thou *art*:
40 Thou shalt be over my house,
and according unto thy word shall
all my people *be ruled* **shall kiss thy mouth**:
only in the throne *will* **shall** I be greater than thou.
41 And *Pharaoh* **Paroh** said unto *Joseph* **Yoseph**,
See **Behold**,
I have *set* **given** thee over all the land of *Egypt* **Misrayim**.
42 And *Pharaoh* **Paroh**
took off **turned aside** his *ring* **signet** from his hand,
and *put* **gave** it upon *Joseph's* **Yoseph's** hand,
and *arrayed* **enrobed** him
in *vestures* **clothes** of *fine* **white** linen,
and put a gold chain about his neck;
43 And he *made* **caused** him to ride
in the second chariot which he had;
and they *cried before him* **called at his face**,
Bow the knee **Kneel**:
and he *made* **gave** him *ruler*
over all the land of *Egypt* **Misrayim**.
44 And *Pharaoh* **Paroh** said unto *Joseph* **Yoseph**,
I am Pharaoh **I — Paroh**,
and without thee shall no man lift *up* his hand or foot
in all the land of *Egypt* **Misrayim**.
45 And *Pharaoh* **Paroh** called *Joseph's* **Yoseph's** name
Zaphnathpaaneah **Sophnath Paneach**;
and he gave him to *wife* **woman** Asenath
the daughter of *Potipherah* **Poti Phera** priest of On.

And *Joseph* **Yoseph**
went out over *all* the land of *Egypt* **Misrayim**.
46 And *Joseph* **Yoseph** was **a son of** thirty years *old*
when he stood *before Pharaoh* **at the face of Paroh**
king **sovereign** of *Egypt* **Misrayim**.
And *Joseph* **Yoseph** went out
from the *presence* **face** of *Pharaoh* **Paroh**,
and *went throughout* **passed through**
all the land of *Egypt* **Misrayim**.
47 And in the seven *plenteous* years **of sufficiency**
the earth *brought forth* **worked** by handfuls.
48 And he gathered up all the food of the seven years,
which were in the land of *Egypt* **Misrayim**,
and *laid up* **gave** the food in the cities:
the food of the field, which was round about every city,
laid he up in the same **gave he among them**.
49 And *Joseph gathered corn* **Yoseph heaped grain**
as the sand of the sea,
very much **mightily abounding**,
until he *left numbering* **ceased scribing**;
for it was without number — **innumerable**.

YOSEPH BEGETS MENASH SHEH AND EPHRAYIM

50 And unto *Joseph* **Yoseph** were born two sons
before the years of famine came,
which Asenath
the daughter of *Potipherah* **Poti Phera** priest of On
bare unto him.
51 And *Joseph* **Yoseph** called the name of the firstborn
Manasseh **Menash Sheh**:
For *God* **Elohim**, *said he*,
hath made me forget all my *toil* **drudgery**,
and all my father's house.
52 And the name of the second
called he *Ephraim* **Ephrayim**:
For *God* **Elohim** hath caused me to *be fruitful* **bear fruit**
in the land of my *affliction* **humiliation**.
53 And the seven years of *plenteousness* **sufficiency**,
that was in the land of *Egypt* **Misrayim**,
were *ended* **finished**.
54 And the seven years of *dearth* **famine**
began to come **entered**,
according as *Joseph* **Yoseph** had said:
and the *dearth* **famine** was in all lands;
but in all the land of *Egypt* **Misrayim** there was bread.
55 And when all the land of *Egypt* **Misrayim**
was famished,
the people cried to *Pharaoh* **Paroh** for bread:
and *Pharaoh* **Paroh** said unto all the *Egyptians* **Misrayim**,
Go unto *Joseph* **Yoseph**; what he saith to you, *do* **work**.
56 And the famine was over all the face of the earth:
and *Joseph* **Yoseph** opened all the storehouses,
and *sold* **marketed kernels** unto the *Egyptians* **Misrayim**;
and the famine *waxed sore* **prevailed**
in the land of *Egypt* **Misrayim**.
57 And all *countries* **lands** came into *Egypt* **Misrayim**
to *Joseph* **Yoseph** for to *buy corn* **market for kernels**;
because that the famine *was so sore* **prevailed** in all lands.

YOSEPH'S BROTHERS GO TO MISRAYIM

42 Now when *Jacob* **Yaaqov** saw
that there *was corn* **were kernels** in *Egypt* **Misrayim,**
Jacob **Yaaqov** said unto his sons,
Why do ye look one upon another **What see ye**?
2 And he said, Behold,
I have heard that there *is corn* **are kernels**
in *Egypt* **Misrayim**:
get you down **descend** thither,
and *buy* **market for kernels** for us from thence;
that we may live, and not die.
3 And *Joseph's* **Yoseph's** ten brethren
went down **descended**
to *buy corn* **market for kernels of grain** in *Egypt* **Misrayim**.
4 But *Benjamin* **Ben Yamin**, *Joseph's* **Yoseph's** brother,
Jacob **Yaaqov** sent not with his brethren; for he said,
Lest *peradventure* mischief *befall* **confront** him.
5 And the sons of *Israel* **Yisra El** came
to *buy corn* **market for kernels** among those that came:
for the famine was in the land of *Canaan* **Kenaan**.
6 And *Joseph* **Yoseph** was the governor over the land,
and he it was that *sold* **marketed kernels**
to all the people of the land:
and *Joseph's* **Yoseph's** brethren came,
and *bowed down themselves* **prostrated** before him,
with their *faces* **nostrils** to the earth.
7 And *Joseph* **Yoseph** saw his brethren,
and he *knew* **recognized** them,
but *made himself strange unto them*
they recognized him not,
and *spake roughly* **he worded sternly** unto them;
and he said unto them, Whence come ye?
And they said, From the land of *Canaan* **Kenaan**
to *buy* **market for kernels for** food.
8 And *Joseph knew* **Yoseph recognized** his brethren,
but they *knew* **recognized** not him.
9 And *Joseph* **Yoseph** remembered the dreams
which he dreamed of them,
and said unto them, Ye are spies;
to see the nakedness of the land ye are come.
10 And they said unto him, Nay, my *lord* **adoni**,
but to *buy* **market for kernels for** food
are thy servants come.
11 We are all one man's sons;
we are *true men* **upright**, thy servants are no spies.
12 And he said unto them, Nay,
but to see the nakedness of the land ye are come.
13 And they said, Thy servants are twelve brethren,
the sons of one man in the land of *Canaan* **Kenaan**;
and, behold, the youngest is this day with our father,
and one is not.
14 And *Joseph* **Yoseph** said unto them,
That is it that I *spake* **have worded** unto you, saying,
Ye are spies:
15 Hereby ye shall be *proved* **proofed**:
By the *life of Pharaoh* **living Paroh**
ye shall not go *forth* hence,
except your youngest brother come hither.
16 Send one of you, and let him *fetch* **take** your brother,
and ye shall be *kept* **bound** in prison,
that your words may be *proved* **proofed**,
whether there be *any* truth in you:
or else **and if not** by the *life of Pharaoh* **living Paroh**
surely ye are spies.
17 And he *put* **took** them *all together* **away**
into ward **under guard** three days.
18 And *Joseph* **Yoseph** said unto them the third day,
This *do* **work**, and live; for I *fear God* **awe Elohim**:
19 If ye be *true men* **upright**, let one of your brethren
be bound in the house *of your prison* **under guard**:
go ye, carry *corn* **kernels** for the famine of your houses:
20 But bring your youngest brother unto me;
so **thus** shall your words be *verified* **amened**,
and ye shall not die.
And they *did* **worked** so.
21 And they said *one* **man** to *another* **brother**,
We are *verily* **nevertheless** guilty concerning our brother,
in that we saw the *anguish* **tribulation** of his soul,
when he besought us,
and we *would not hear* **hearkened not**;
therefore is this *distress* **tribulation** come upon us.
22 And *Reuben* **Reu Ben** answered them, saying,
Spake **Said** I not unto you, saying,
Do not sin **Sin not** against the child;
and ye *would not hear* **hearkened not**?
therefore, behold, also his blood is required.
23 And they knew not
that *Joseph understood* **Yoseph heard** them;
for *he spake unto them by an interpreter*
a translator was between them.
24 And he turned *himself about* **around** from them,
and wept;
and returned to them *again*,
and *communed* **worded** with them,
and took from them *Simeon* **Shimon**,
and bound him before their eyes.
25 Then *Joseph commanded* **Yoseph misvahed**
to fill their *sacks* **instruments** with *corn* **grain**,
and to restore every man's *money* **silver** into his *sack* **saq**,
and to give them *provision* **hunt** for the way:
and thus *did* **worked** he unto them.
26 And they laded their *asses* **he burros**
with the *corn* **kernels**,

and *departed* **went** thence.
27 And as one of them opened his *sack* **saq**
to give his *ass* **he burro** provender in the *inn* **lodge**,
he *espied* **saw** his *money* **silver**;
for, behold, it was in his sack's mouth.
28 And he said unto his brethren,
My *money* **silver** is restored;
and, *lo* **behold**, it is even in my sack:
and their heart failed them,
and they *were afraid* **trembled**,
saying *one* **man** to *another* **brother**,
What is this that *God* **Elohim** hath *done* **worked** unto us?
29 And they came unto *Jacob* **Yaaqov** their father
unto the land of *Canaan* **Kenaan**,
and told him all that befell unto them; saying,
30 The man, who is the *lord* **adoni** of the land,
spake roughly **worded sternly** to us,
and *took* **gave** us for spies of the *country* **land**.
31 And we said unto him,
We are *true men* **upright**; we are no spies:
32 We be twelve brethren, sons of our father;
one is not, and the youngest is this day with our father
in the land of *Canaan* **Kenaan**.
33 And the man, the *lord* **adoni** of the *country* **land**,
said unto us,
Hereby shall I know that ye are *true men* **upright**;
leave one of your brethren *here* with me,
and take *food* for the famine of your households,
and be gone:
34 And bring your youngest brother unto me:
then shall I know that ye are no spies,
but that ye are *true men* **upright**:
so *will* **shall** I *deliver* **give** you your brother,
and ye shall *traffick* **merchandise** in the land.
35 And it *came to pass* **became**,
as they *emptied* **poured** out their *sacks* **saqs**, that, behold,
every man's bundle of *money* **silver** was in his *sack* **saq**:
and when *both* they and their father
saw the bundles of *money* **silver**, they *were afraid* **awed**.
36 And *Jacob* **Yaaqov** their father said unto them,
Me have ye bereaved *of my children*:
Joseph **Yoseph** is not, and *Simeon* **Shimon** is not,
and ye *will* **shall** take *Benjamin* **Ben Yamin** *away*:
all these *things* are against me.
37 And *Reuben spake* **Reu Ben said** unto his father,
saying, *Slay* **Deathify** my two sons,
if I *bring* **return** him not to thee:
deliver **give** him into my hand,
and I *will bring* **shall return** him to thee *again*.
38 And he said,
My son shall not *go down* **descend** with you;
for his brother is dead, and he *is left* **surviveth** alone:
if mischief *befall* **confront** him
by the way in the which ye go,
then shall ye *bring down* **descend** my *gray hairs* **grayness**
with *sorrow* **grief** to *the grave* **sheol**.

YOSEPH'S BROTHERS RETURN TO MISRAYIM

43 And the famine was *sore* **heavy** in the land.
2 And it *came to pass* **became**,
when they had *eaten up* **finished eating** the *corn* **kernels**
which they had brought out of *Egypt* **Misrayim**,
their father said unto them, *Go again* **Return**,
buy us **market for us kernels for** a little food.
3 And *Judah spake* **Yah Hudah said** unto him, saying,
In witnessing, The man *did solemnly protest* **witnessed**
unto us, saying, Ye shall not see my face,
except **unless** your brother be with you.
4 If thou *wilt* **shalt** send our brother with us,
we *will go down* **shall descend**
and *buy* **market for** thee **kernels for** food:
5 But if thou *wilt* **shalt** not send him,
we *will* **shall** not *go down* **descend**:
for the man said unto us, Ye shall not see my face,
except **unless** your brother be with you.
6 And *Israel* **Yisra El** said,
Wherefore *dealt ye so ill with* **have ye vilified** me,
as to tell the man whether ye had yet a brother?
7 And they said,
In asking, The man asked us *straitly* of our state,
and of our kindred, saying,
Is your father yet alive? have ye *another* **a** brother?
and we told him
according to the *tenor* **mouth** of these words:
In knowing, how could we *certainly* know
that he *would* **should** say,
Bring **Descend** your brother *down*?
8 And *Judah* **Yah Hudah**
said unto *Israel* **Yisra El** his father,
Send the lad with me, and we *will* **shall** arise and go;
that we may live, and not die,
both we, and thou, and also our *little ones* **toddlers**.
9 I *will be surety* **shall pledge** for him;
of my hand shalt thou require him:
if I bring him not unto thee,
and set him *before* **facing** thee,
then *let me bear the blame* **have I sinned against thee**
for ever **all days**:
10 For *except* **if** we had **not** lingered,
surely now **by this time** we had returned this second time.
11 And their father *Israel* **Yisra El** said unto them,
If *it must be* so now, *do* **work** this;
take of the best *fruits* **pluckings** in the land
in your *vessels* **instruments**,
and *carry down* **descend** the man *a present* **an offering**,
a little balm, and a little honey, spices, and myrrh,
nuts **pistachios**, and almonds:
12 And take double *money* **silver** in your hand;
and the *money* **silver** that was *brought again* **returned**
in the mouth of your sacks,
carry it again **return** in your hand;
peradventure it was an *oversight* **error**:
13 Take also your brother,
and arise, *go again* **return** unto the man:
14 And *God Almighty* **El Shadday** give you *mercy* **mercies**
before **at the face of** the man,
that he may send away your other brother,
and *Benjamin* **Ben Yamin**.
If I be bereaved of my children **In bereaving,**
I am bereaved.
15 And the men took that *present* **offering**,
and they took double *money* **silver** in their hand
and *Benjamin* **Ben Yamin**; and rose up,
and *went down* **descended** to *Egypt* **Misrayim**,
and stood *before Joseph* **at the face of Yoseph**.
16 And when *Joseph* **Yoseph**
saw *Benjamin* **Ben Yamin** with them,
he said to the *ruler of* **one over** his house,
Bring these men home,
and *slay* **slaughter a slaughter**, and *make ready* **prepare**;
for these men shall *dine* **eat** with me at noon.
17 And the man *did* **worked** as *Joseph bade* **Yoseph said**;
and the man brought the men
into *Joseph's* **Yoseph's** house.
18 And the men *were afraid* **awed**,
because they were brought into *Joseph's* **Yoseph's** house;
and they said, Because of the *money* **word of the silver**
that was returned in our sacks at the *first time* **beginning**
are we brought in;
that he may *seek occasion* **roll** against us,
and fall upon us,
and take us for *bondmen* **servants**,
and our *asses* **he burros**.
19 And they came near
to the *steward* **man** of *Joseph's* **Yoseph's** house,
and they *communed* **worded** with him
at the *door* **portal** of the house,
20 And said, O *sir* **adoni**,
In descending, we *came indeed down* **descended**
at the *first time* **beginning**
to *buy* **market for kernels for** food:
21 And it *came to pass* **became**,
when we came to the *inn* **lodge**,
that we opened our sacks, and, behold,
every man's *money* **silver** was in the mouth of his sack,
our *money* **silver** in full weight:
and we have *brought* **returned** it *again* in our hand.
22 And other *money* **silver**
have we *brought down* **descended** in our hands
to *buy* **market for kernels for** food:
we *cannot tell* **perceive not**

who put our *money* **silver** in our sacks.
23 And he said, *Peace* **Shalom** be to you, *fear* **awe** not:
your *God* **Elohim**, and the *God* **Elohim** of your father,
hath given you **hidden** treasure in your sacks:
I had your *money* **silver**.
And he brought *Simeon* **Shimon** out unto them.
24 And the man
brought the men into *Joseph's* **Yoseph's** house,
and gave them water, and they *washed* **bathed** their feet;
and he gave their *asses* **he burros** provender.
25 And they *made ready* **prepared** the *present* **offering**
against Joseph **until Yoseph** came at noon:
for they heard that they should eat bread there.
26 And when *Joseph* **Yoseph** came home,
they brought him the *present* **offering**
which was in their hand into the house,
and *bowed themselves* **prostrated** to him to the earth.
27 And he asked them of their *welfare* **shalom**,
and said, Is your father *well* **at shalom**,
the *old man* **elder** of whom ye *spake* **said**?
Is he yet alive?
28 And they *answered* **said**,
Thy servant our father is *in good health* **at shalom**,
he is yet alive.
And they bowed *down their heads*,
and *made obeisance* **prostrated**.
29 And he lifted up his eyes,
and saw his brother *Benjamin* **Ben Yamin**,
his mother's son, and said,
Is this your younger brother,
of whom ye *spake* **said** unto me?
And he said,
God be gracious unto thee **Elohim grant thee charism**,
my son.
30 And *Joseph made haste* **Yoseph hastened**;
for his *bowels* **mercies** did yearn upon his brother:
and he sought where to weep;
and he entered into his chamber, and wept there.
31 And he *washed* **bathed** his face, and went out,
and refrained himself, and said, Set on bread.
32 And they set on for him by himself,
and for them by themselves,
and for the *Egyptians* **Misrayim**,
which did eat with him, by themselves:
because the *Egyptians* **Misrayim**
might **can** not eat bread with the Hebrews;
for that is an *abomination* **abhorrence**
unto the *Egyptians* **Misrayim**.
33 And they sat *before him* **at his face**,
the firstborn according to his *birthright* **firstrights**,
and the *youngest* **lesser** according to his *youth* **youngness**:
and the men marvelled *one at another* **man to friend**.
34 And he *took and sent messes* **loaded loads** unto them
from *before him* **his face**:
but *Benjamin's mess* **Ben Yamin's load**
was **abounded** five *times so much* **hands**
as any of their's **than the loads of all**.
And they drank, and *were merry* **intoxicated** with him.

YOSEPH'S BROTHERS DEPART

44 And he *commanded* **misvahed**
the steward of his house, saying,
Fill the men's sacks with food,
as much as they can *carry* **bear**,
and put every man's *money* **silver** in his sack's mouth.
2 And put my *cup* **bowl**, the silver *cup* **bowl**,
in the sack's mouth of the youngest,
and his *corn money* **kernel silver**.
And he *did* **worked** according to the word
that *Joseph* **Yoseph** had *spoken* **worded**.
3 As soon as the morning was light,
the men were sent away, they and their *asses* **he burros**.
4 And when they were gone out of the city,
and not yet far *off* **removed**,
Joseph **Yoseph** said unto his **house** steward,
Up **Arise**, *follow* **pursue** after the men;
and when thou dost overtake them, say unto them,
Wherefore *have ye rewarded* **shalam ye** evil for good?
5 Is not this it in which my *lord* **adoni** drinketh,
and *whereby indeed he divineth*
in prognosticating, he prognosticateth?
ye have *done evil* **vilified** in so *doing* **working**.
6 And he overtook them,
and he *spake* **worded** unto them these same words.
7 And they said unto him,
Wherefore *saith* **wordeth** my *lord* **adoni** these words?
God forbid **Far be it** that thy servants should *do* **work**
according to this *thing* **word**:
8 Behold, the *money* **silver**,
which we found in our sacks' mouths,
we *brought again* **returned** unto thee
out of the land of *Canaan* **Kenaan**:
how then should we steal
out of thy *lord's* **adoni's** house silver or gold?
9 With whomsoever of thy servants it be found,
both let him die,
and we also
will **shall** be my *lord's bondmen* **adoni's servants**.
10 And he said,
Now also let it be according unto your words:
thus he with whom it is found shall be my servant;
and ye shall be *blameless* **innocent**.
11 Then they *speedily took down* **hastily lowered**
every man his sack to the *ground* **earth**,
and opened every man his sack.
12 And he searched, and began at the *eldest* **greater**,
and *left* **finished** at the youngest:
and the *cup* **bowl** was found
in *Benjamin's* **Ben Yamin's** sack.
13 Then they *rent* **ripped** their clothes,
and laded every man his *ass* **he burro**,
and returned to the city.
14 And *Judah* **Yah Hudah** and his brethren
came to *Joseph's* **Yoseph's** house; for he was yet there:
and they fell *before him* **at his face** on the *ground* **earth**.
15 And *Joseph* **Yoseph** said unto them,
What *deed* **work** is this that ye have *done* **worked**?
wot **know** ye not that such a man as I
can certainly divine **in prognosticating, prognosticateth**?
16 And *Judah* **Yah Hudah** said,
What shall we say unto my *lord* **adoni**?
what shall we *speak* **word**?
or how shall we *clear* **justify** ourselves?
God **Elohim** hath found out
the *iniquity* **perversity** of thy servants:
behold, we are my *lord's* **adoni's** servants,
both we, and he also
with whom **in whose hand** the *cup* **bowl** is found.
17 And he said,
God forbid **Far be it** that I should *do* **work** so:
but the man in whose hand the *cup* **bowl** is found,
he shall be my servant;
and as for you,
get you up **ascend ye** in *peace* **shalom** unto your father.
18 Then *Judah* **Yah Hudah** came near unto him,
and said, Oh my *lord* **adoni**, let thy servant,
I pray thee, speak **word** a word in my *lord's* **adoni's** ears,
and let not *thine anger* **thy wrath**
burn **kindle** against thy servant:
for thou art even as *Pharaoh* **Paroh**.
19 My *lord* **adoni** asked his servants, saying,
Have ye a father, or a brother?
20 And we said unto my *lord* **adoni**,
We have a father, *an old man* **aged**,
and a child of his old age, a *little one* **youngster**;
and his brother is dead,
and he alone *is left* **remaineth** of his mother,
and his father loveth him.
21 And thou saidst unto thy servants,
Bring **Descend** him *down* unto me,
that I may set mine eyes upon him.
22 And we said unto my *lord* **adoni**,
The lad cannot leave his father:
for if he should leave his father,
his father would die **he should die**.
23 And thou saidst unto thy servants,
Except **If** your youngest brother
come down **descend not** with you,
ye shall see my face *no more* **not again**.
24 And it *came to pass* **became**,
when we *came up* **ascended** unto thy servant my father,

we told him the words of my *lord* **adoni**.
25 And our father said, *Go again* **Return**,
and buy us **market us kernels for** a little food.
26 And we said, We cannot *go down* **descend**:
if our youngest brother be with us,
then *will* **shall** we *go down* **descend**:
for we may not see the man's face,
except **unless** our youngest brother be with us.
27 And thy servant my father said unto us,
Ye know that my *wife* **woman** bare me two *sons*:
28 And the one went out from me, and I said,
Surely **In tearing,** he is torn *in pieces*;
and I saw him not since:
29 And if ye take this also from *me* **my face**,
and mischief befall him,
ye shall *bring down* **descend** my *gray hairs* **grayness**
with *sorrow* **evil** to *the grave* **sheol**.
30 Now therefore when I come to thy servant my father,
and the lad be not with us;
seeing that his *life* **soul** is bound up in the lad's *life* **soul**;
31 It shall *come to pass* **become**,
when he seeth that the lad is not *with us*,
that he *will* **shall** die:
and thy servants shall *bring down* **descend**
the *gray hairs* **grayness** of thy servant our father
with *sorrow* **grief** to *the grave* **sheol**.
32 For thy servant *became surety* **pledged**
for the lad unto my father, saying,
If I bring him not unto thee,
then I shall *bear the blame to* **have sinned**
against my father *for ever* **all days**.
33 Now therefore, I *pray* **beseech** thee,
let thy servant *abide* **sit** instead of the lad
a *bondman* **servant** to my *lord* **adoni**;
and let the lad *go up* **ascend** with his brethren.
34 For how shall I *go up* **ascend** to my father,
and the lad be not with me?
lest peradventure I see the evil
that shall *come on* **find** my father.

YOSEPH REVEALS HIS IDENTITY

45 Then *Joseph* **Yoseph** could not refrain himself
before all them that *stood* **stationed themselves** by him;
and he *cried* **called**, Cause every man to go out from me.
And there stood no man with him,
while *Joseph* **Yoseph**
made himself known unto his brethren.
2 And he *wept aloud* **gave his voice in weeping**:
and the *Egyptians* **Misrayim**
and the house of *Pharaoh* **Paroh** heard.
3 And *Joseph* **Yoseph** said unto his brethren,
I am *Joseph* **Yoseph**; doth my father yet live?
And his brethren could not answer him;
for they were *troubled* **terrified** at his *presence* **face**.
4 And *Joseph* **Yoseph** said unto his brethren,
Come near to me, I *pray* **beseech** you.
And they came near.
And he said, I am *Joseph* **Yoseph** your brother,
whom ye sold into *Egypt* **Misrayim**.
5 Now therefore *be not grieved* **neither contort**,
nor *angry with yourselves* **inflame in your eyes**,
that ye sold me hither:
for *God* **Elohim** did send me *before you* **from your face**
to *preserve life* **enliven**.
6 For these two years hath the famine been in the land:
and yet there are five years,
in the which there shall neither be
earing **ploughing** nor harvest.
7 And *God* **Elohim** sent me *before you* **from your face**
to *preserve* **set** you a *posterity* **survivor** in the earth,
and to *save* **preserve** your lives
by a great *deliverance* **escape**.
8 So now it was not you that sent me hither,
but *God* **Elohim**:
and he hath *made* **set** me a father to *Pharaoh* **Paroh**,
and *lord* **adoni** of all his house,
and a *ruler* **sovereign**
throughout all the land of *Egypt* **Misrayim**.
9 Haste ye, and *go up* **ascend** to my father,
and say unto him,
Thus saith thy son *Joseph* **Yoseph**,
God **Elohim** hath *made* **set** me
lord **adoni** of all *Egypt* **Misrayim**:
come down **descend** unto me, *tarry* **stay** not:
10 And thou shalt *dwell* **settle** in the land of Goshen,
and thou shalt be near unto me,
thou, and thy *children* **sons**,
and thy *children's children* **sons' sons**,
and thy flocks, and thy *herds* **oxen**, and all that thou hast:
11 And there *will* **shall** I nourish thee;
for yet there are five years of famine;
lest thou, and thy household, and all that thou hast,
come to poverty **be dispossessed**.
12 And, behold, your eyes see,
and the eyes of my brother *Benjamin* **Ben Yamin**,
that it is my mouth that *speaketh* **wordeth** unto you.
13 And ye shall tell my father
of all my *glory* **honour** in *Egypt* **Misrayim**,
and of all that ye have seen;
and ye shall haste
and *bring down* **descend** my father hither.
14 And he fell
upon his brother *Benjamin's* **Ben Yamin's** neck,
and wept;
and *Benjamin* **Ben Yamin** wept upon his neck.
15 Moreover he kissed all his brethren,
and wept upon them:
and after that his brethren *talked* **worded** with him.
16 And the *fame* **voice** thereof
was heard in *Pharaoh's* **Paroh's** house, saying,
Joseph's **Yoseph's** brethren are come:
and it **well**—pleased **the eyes of** *Pharaoh* **Paroh** *well*,
and **the eyes of** his servants.
17 And *Pharaoh* **Paroh** said unto *Joseph* **Yoseph**,
Say unto thy brethren, This *do* **work** ye;
lade your beasts, and go,
get you unto the land of *Canaan* **Kenaan**;
18 And take your father and your households,
and come unto me:
and I *will* **shall** give you
the good of the land of *Egypt* **Misrayim**,
and ye shall eat the fat of the land.
19 Now thou art *commanded* **misvahed**, this *do* **work** ye;
take you wagons out of the land of *Egypt* **Misrayim**
for your *little ones* **toddlers**, and for your *wives* **women**,
and *bring* **bear** your father, and come.
20 Also *regard* **let** not **your eye spare**
your *stuff* **instruments**;
for the good of all the land of *Egypt* **Misrayim** is your's.
21 And the *children* **sons** of *Israel did* **Yisra El worked** so:
and *Joseph* **Yoseph** gave them wagons,
according to the *commandment* **mouth** of *Pharaoh* **Paroh**,
and gave them *provision* **hunt** for the way.
22 To all of them he gave each man
changes of *raiment* **clothes**;
but to *Benjamin* **Ben Yamin**
he gave three hundred *pieces of* silver,
and five changes of *raiment* **clothes**.
23 And to his father he sent *after this manner* **thus**;
ten *asses* **he burros**
laden with the *good things* **goods** of *Egypt* **Misrayim**,
and ten she *asses* **burros**
laden with *corn* **grain** and bread and *meat* **food**
for his father by the way.
24 So he sent his brethren away, and they *departed* **went**:
and he said unto them,
See that ye *fall not out* **not quiver** by the way.
25 And they *went up* **ascended** out of *Egypt* **Misrayim**,
and came into the land of *Canaan* **Kenaan**
unto *Jacob* **Yaaqov** their father,
26 And told him, saying, *Joseph* **Yoseph** is yet alive,
and he is *governor* **sovereign**
over all the land of *Egypt* **Misrayim**.
And *Jacob's* **Yaaqov's** heart *fainted* **exhausted**,
for he *believed* **trusted** them not.
27 And they *told him* **worded**
all the words of *Joseph* **Yoseph**,
which he had *said* **worded** unto them:
and when he saw the wagons
which *Joseph* **Yoseph** had sent to *carry* **bear** him,
the spirit of *Jacob* **Yaaqov** their father *revived* **enlivened**:

28 And *Israel* **Yisra El** said, *It is enough* **Great**;
Joseph **Yoseph** my son is yet alive:
I *will* **shall** go and see him before I die.

YAAQOV MOVES TO MISRAYIM

46 And *Israel took his journey* **Yisra El pulled stakes**
with all that he had,
and came to *Beersheba* **Beer Sheba**,
and *offered* **sacrificed** sacrifices
unto the *God* **Elohim** of his father *Isaac* **Yischaq**.
2 And *God spake* **Elohim said** unto *Israel* **Yisra El**
in the visions of the night,
and said, *Jacob* **Yaaqov**, *Jacob* **Yaaqov**.
And he said, Here *am* — **I**.
3 And he said, I *am God* — **El**, the *God* **Elohim** of thy father:
fear **awe** not to *go down* **descend** into *Egypt* **Misrayim**;
for I *will* **shall** there *make* **set** of thee a great *nation* **goyim**:
4 I *will go down* **shall descend** with thee
into *Egypt* **Misrayim**;
and **in ascending,**
I *will* **shall** also *surely bring* **ascend** thee *up again*:
and *Joseph* **Yoseph** shall put his hand upon thine eyes.
5 And *Jacob* **Yaaqov** rose up from *Beersheba* **Beer Sheba**:
and the sons of *Israel* **Yisra El**
carried Jacob **bore Yaaqov** their father,
and their *little ones* **toddlers**, and their *wives* **women**,
in the wagons which *Pharaoh* **Paroh** had sent
to *carry* **bear** him.
6 And they took their *cattle* **chattel**,
and their *goods* **acquisitions**,
which they had *gotten* **acquired**
in the land of *Canaan* **Kenaan**,
and came into *Egypt* **Misrayim**,
Jacob **Yaaqov**, and all his seed with him:
7 His sons, and his sons' sons with him,
his daughters, and his sons' daughters,
and all his seed
brought he with him into *Egypt* **Misrayim**.

GENEALOGY OF ALL WHO CAME TO MISRAYIM

8 And these are the names
of the *children* **sons** of *Israel* **Yisra El**,
which came into *Egypt* **Misrayim**,
Jacob **Yaaqov** and his sons:
Reuben **Reu Ben**, *Jacob's* **Yaaqov's** firstborn.
9 And the sons of *Reuben* **Reu Ben**;
Hanoch, and Phallu,
and *Hezron* **Hesron**, and *Carmi* **Karmi**.
10 And the sons of *Simeon* **Shimon**;
Jemuel **Yemu El**, and *Yamin* **Yamiyn**,
and Ohad, and *Jachin* **Yachin**, and *Zohar* **Sochar**,
and Shaul the son of a *Canaanitish* **Kenaaniy** woman.
11 And the sons of Levi;
Gershon, *Kohath* **Qehath**, and Merari.
12 And the sons of *Judah* **Yah Hudah**;
Er, and Onan, and Shelah,
and *Pharez* **Peres**, and *Zarah* **Zerach**:
but Er and Onan died in the land of *Canaan* **Kenaan**.
And the sons of *Pharez* **Peres**
were *Hezron* **Hesron** and Hamul.
13 And the sons of *Issachar* **Yissachar**;
Tola, and *Phuvah* **Puvvah**, and Job, and Shimron.
14 And the sons of Zebulun;
Sered, and Elon, and *Jahleel* **Yachle El**.
15 These be the sons of Leah,
which she bare unto *Jacob* **Yaaqov**
in *Padanaram* **Paddan Aram**,
with his daughter Dinah:
all the souls of his sons and his daughters
were thirty and three.
16 And the sons of Gad;
Ziphion **Siphyon**, and Haggi, Shuni, and *Ezbon* **Esbon**,
Eri **Eriy**, and *Arodi* **Arodiy**, and *Areli* **Ar Eli**.
17 And the sons of Asher;
Jimnah **Yimnah**, and *Ishuah* **Yishvah**,
and *Isui* **Yishviy**, and Beriah,
and *Serah* **Serach** their sister:
and the sons of Beriah;
Heber, and *Malchiel* **Malki El**.
18 These are the sons of Zilpah,
whom Laban gave to Leah his daughter,
and these she bare unto *Jacob* **Yaaqov**, *even* sixteen souls.
19 The sons of Rachel *Jacob's wife* **Yaaqov's woman**;
Joseph **Yoseph**, and *Benjamin* **Ben Yamin**.
20 And unto *Joseph* **Yoseph** in the land of *Egypt* **Misrayim**
were born *Manasseh* **Menash Sheh**
and *Ephraim* **Ephrayim**,
which Asenath
the daughter of *Potipherah* **Poti Phera** priest of On
bare unto him.
21 And the sons of *Benjamin* **Ben Yamin**
were Belah, and Becher, and Ashbel,
Gera, and Naaman, *Ehi* **Achi**, and Rosh,
Muppim, and Huppim, and Ard.
22 These are the sons of Rachel,
which were born to *Jacob* **Yaaqov**:
all the souls were fourteen.
23 And the sons of Dan;
Hushim.
24 And the sons of Naphtali;
Jahzeel **Yachse El**, and Guni, and *Jezer* **Yeser**, and Shillem.
25 These are the sons of Bilhah,
which Laban gave unto Rachel his daughter,
and she bare these unto *Jacob* **Yaaqov**:
all the souls were seven.
26 All the souls
that came with *Jacob* **Yaaqov** into *Egypt* **Misrayim**,
which came out of his *loins* **flank**,
besides *Jacob's* **Yaaqov's** sons' *wives* **women**,
all the souls were *threescore* **sixty** and six;
27 And the sons of *Joseph* **Yoseph**,
which were born him in *Egypt* **Misrayim**, were two souls:
all the souls of the house of *Jacob* **Yaaqov**,
which came into *Egypt* **Misrayim**,
were *threescore and ten* **seventy**.
28 And he sent *Judah* **Yah Hudah**
before him **from his face** unto *Joseph* **Yoseph**,
to direct his face unto Goshen;
and they came into the land of Goshen.
29 And *Joseph made ready* **Yoseph bound** his chariot,
and *went up* **ascended** to meet *Israel* **Yisra El** his father,
to Goshen, and *presented himself unto* **was seen by** him;
and he fell on his neck,
and wept on his neck *a good while* **again**.
30 And *Israel* **Yisra El** said unto *Joseph* **Yoseph**,
Now **This time** let me die, since I have seen thy face,
because thou art *yet* **still** alive.
31 And *Joseph* **Yoseph** said unto his brethren,
and unto his father's house,
I *will go up* **shall ascend**, and *shew Pharaoh* **tell Paroh**,
and say unto him, My brethren, and my father's house,
which were in the land of *Canaan* **Kenaan**,
are come unto me;
32 And the men *are shepherds* **tend flocks**,
for their trade hath been to feed cattle — **men of chattel**;
and they have brought their flocks, and their *herds* **oxen**,
and all that they have.
33 And it shall *come to pass* **become**,
when *Pharaoh* **Paroh** shall call you,
and shall say, What is your *occupation* **work**?
34 That ye shall say,
Thy *servants' trade* **servants**
hath **have** been *about cattle* **men of chattel**
from our youth even until now,
both we, *and* also our fathers:
that ye may *dwell* **settle** in the land of Goshen;
for *every shepherd* **all who tend flocks**
is **are** an *abomination* **abhorrence**
unto the *Egyptians* **Misrayim**.

YAAQOV IN MISRAYIM

47 Then *Joseph* **Yoseph** came and told *Pharaoh* **Paroh**,
and said, My father and my brethren,
and their flocks, and their *herds* **oxen**,
and all that they have,
are come out of the land of *Canaan* **Kenaan**;
and, behold, they are in the land of Goshen.
2 And he took *some* **of the end** of his brethren,
even five men,
and presented them *unto Pharaoh* **at the face of Paroh**.
3 And *Pharaoh* **Paroh** said unto his brethren,
What is your *occupation* **work**?
And they said unto *Pharaoh* **Paroh**,

Thy servants *are shepherds* **tend flocks**,
both we, and also our fathers.
4 They said moreover unto *Pharaoh* **Paroh**,
For to sojourn in the land are we come;
for thy servants have no pasture for their flocks;
for the famine *is sore* **heavy**
in the land of *Canaan* **Kenaan**:
now therefore, we *pray* **beseech** thee,
let thy servants *dwell* **settle** in the land of Goshen.
5 And *Pharaoh spake* **Paroh said** unto *Joseph* **Yoseph**,
saying, Thy father and thy brethren are come unto thee:
6 The land of *Egypt* **Misrayim** is *before thee* **at thy face**;
in the best of the land
make **have** thy father and brethren to *dwell* **settle**;
in the land of Goshen let them *dwell* **settle**:
and if thou knowest *any* men of *activity* **valour**
among them,
then *make* **set** them *rulers* **governors**
over my *cattle* **chattel**.
7 And *Joseph* **Yoseph** brought in *Jacob* **Yaaqov** his father,
and *set* **stood** him *before Pharaoh* **at the face of Paroh**:
and *Jacob* **Yaaqov** blessed *Pharaoh* **Paroh**.
8 And *Pharaoh* **Paroh** said unto *Jacob* **Yaaqov**,
How old art thou
How many are the days of the years of thy life?
9 And *Jacob* **Yaaqov** said unto *Pharaoh* **Paroh**,
The days of the years of my *pilgrimage* **sojournings**
are an hundred **years** and thirty years:
few and evil have the days of the years of my life been,
and have not *attained* **reached**
unto the days of the years of the life of my fathers
in the days of their *pilgrimage* **sojournings**.
10 And *Jacob* **Yaaqov** blessed *Pharaoh* **Paroh**,
and went out from *before Pharaoh* **the face of Paroh**.
11 And *Joseph* **Yoseph**
placed **settled** his father and his brethren,
and gave them a possession
in the land of *Egypt* **Misrayim**,
in the best of the land, in the land of Rameses,
as *Pharaoh* **Paroh** had *commanded* **misvahed**.
12 And *Joseph* **Yoseph** nourished his father,
and his brethren, and all his father's household,
with bread,
according to **the mouths of** their *families* **toddlers**.
13 And there was no bread in all the land;
for the famine was *very sore* **mighty heavy**,
so that the land of *Egypt* **Misrayim**
and *all* the land of *Canaan* **Kenaan**
fainted by reason **were rabid at the face** of the famine.
14 And *Joseph* **Yoseph**
gathered up **gleaned** all the *money* **silver**
that was found in the land of *Egypt* **Misrayim**,
and in the land of *Canaan* **Kenaan**,
for the *corn* **kernels** which they *bought* **marketed**:
and *Joseph* **Yoseph** brought the *money* **silver**
into *Pharaoh's* **Paroh's** house.
15 And when *money* **silver** failed
in the land of *Egypt* **Misrayim**,
and in the land of *Canaan* **Kenaan**,
all the *Egyptians* **Misrayim** came unto *Joseph* **Yoseph**,
and said, Give us bread:
for why should we die in thy presence?
for the *money faileth* **silver is consumed**.
16 And *Joseph* **Yoseph** said, Give your *cattle* **chattel**;
and I *will* **shall** give you for your *cattle* **chattel**,
if *money fail* **silver be consumed**.
17 And they brought their *cattle* **chattel**
unto *Joseph* **Yoseph**:
and *Joseph* **Yoseph** gave them bread
in exchange for horses,
and for the **chattel of the** flocks,
and for the *cattle* **chattel** of the *herds* **oxen**,
and for the *asses* **he burros**:
and he *fed* **sustained** them with bread
for all their *cattle* **chattel** for that year.
18 When that year *was ended* **consumated**,
they came unto him the second year, and said unto him,
We *will* **shall** not *hide* **conceal** it from my *lord* **adoni**,
how that our *money* **silver** is *spent* **consumed**;
my *lord* **adoni** also
hath our *herds* **chattel** of *cattle* **animals**;
there is not ought left **naught surviveth**
in the sight **at the face** of my *lord* **adoni**,
but our bodies, and our *lands* **soil**:
19 Wherefore shall we die before thine eyes,
both we and our *land* **soil**?
buy **chattelize** us and our *land* **soil** for bread,
and we and our *land* **soil**
will **shall** be servants unto *Pharaoh* **Paroh**:
and give us seed, that we may live, and not die,
that the *land* **soil** be not desolate.
20 And *Joseph bought* **Yoseph chatteled**
all the *land* **soil** of *Egypt* **Misrayim** for *Pharaoh* **Paroh**;
for the *Egyptians* **Misrayim** sold every man his field,
because the famine prevailed over them:
so the land became *Pharaoh's* **Paroh's**.
21 And as for the people,
he *removed* **passed** them to cities
from *one* **the** end of the borders of *Egypt* **Misrayim**
even to the *other* end thereof.
22 Only the *land* **soil** of the priests
bought **chatteled** he not;
for the priests had a *portion* **statute**
assigned them of Pharaoh **from Paroh**,
and *did eat* **consumed** their *portion* **statute**
which *Pharaoh* **Paroh** gave them:
wherefore they sold not their *lands* **soil**.
23 Then *Joseph* **Yoseph** said unto the people,
Behold, I have *bought* **chatteled** you this day
and your *land* **soil** for *Pharaoh* **Paroh**:
lo **behold**, *here is* — seed for you,
and ye shall *sow* **seed** the *land* **soil**.
24 And it shall *come to pass* **become**,
in the *increase* **produce**,
that ye shall give the fifth *part* unto *Pharaoh* **Paroh**,
and four *parts* shall be your own, for seed of the field,
and for your food, and for them of your households,
and for food for your *little ones* **toddlers**.
25 And they said, Thou hast *saved* **preserved** our lives:
let us find *grace* **charism**
in the *sight* **eyes** of my *lord* **adoni**,
and we *will* **shall** be *Pharaoh's* **Paroh's** servants.
26 And *Joseph made it* **Yoseph set** a *law* **statute**
over the land of *Egypt* **Misrayim** unto this day,
that *Pharaoh* **Paroh** should have the fifth *part*,
except the *land* **soil** of the priests only,
which became not *Pharaoh's* **Paroh's**.
27 And *Israel* **Yisra El**
dwelt **settled** in the land of *Egypt* **Misrayim**,
in the *country* **land** of Goshen;
and they *had possessions* **possessed** therein,
and *grew* **bore fruit**,
and *multiplied exceedingly* **abounded mightily**.
28 And *Jacob* **Yaaqov**
lived in the land of *Egypt* **Misrayim** seventeen years:
so the *whole age* **days of the years** of *Jacob's* **Yaaqov's life**
was an hundred forty **years** and seven years.
29 And the *time drew nigh* **day approached**
that *Israel must* **Yisra El** die:
and he called his son *Joseph* **Yoseph**, and said unto him,
If now I have found *grace* **charism** in thy *sight* **eyes**,
put, I *pray* **beseech** thee, thy hand under my *thigh* **flank**,
and *deal kindly* **work in mercy** and *truly* **truth** with me;
bury **entomb** me not, I *pray* **beseech** thee,
in *Egypt* **Misrayim**:
30 But I *will* **shall** lie with my fathers,
and thou shalt *carry* **bear** me out of *Egypt* **Misrayim**,
and *bury* **entomb** me in their *buryingplace* **tomb**.
And he said,
I will do as thou hast said **I shall work thy word**.
31 And he said, *Swear* **Oath** unto me.
And he *sware* **oathed** unto him.
And *Israel bowed himself* **Yisra El prostrated**
upon the bed's head.

YISRA EL'S FINAL DAYS

48 And it *came to pass* **became**,
after these *things* **words**,
that one told *Joseph* **Yoseph**, Behold, thy father is sick:
and he took with him his two sons,
Manasseh **Menash Sheh** and *Ephraim* **Ephrayim**.

2 And one told *Jacob* **Yaaqov**, and said,
Behold, thy son *Joseph* **Yoseph** cometh unto thee:
and *Israel* **Yisra El** strengthened himself,
and sat upon the bed.
3 And *Jacob* **Yaaqov** said unto *Joseph* **Yoseph**,
God Almighty appeared unto **El Shadday was seen by** me
at Luz in the land of *Canaan* **Kenaan**, and blessed me,
4 And said unto me, Behold,
I *will make* **shall have** thee *fruitful* **bear fruit**,
and *multiply* **abound** thee,
and I *will make of* **shall give** thee
a *multitude* **congregation** of people;
and *will* **shall** give this land to thy seed after thee
for an *everlasting* **eternal** possession.
5 And now thy two sons,
Ephraim **Ephrayim** and *Manasseh* **Menash Sheh**,
which were born unto thee in the land of *Egypt* **Misrayim**
before **until** I came unto thee into *Egypt* **Misrayim**,
are mine;
as *Reuben* **Reu Ben** and *Simeon* **Shimon**,
they shall be mine.
6 And thy *issue* **kindred**, which thou begettest after them,
shall be thine,
and shall be called after the name of their brethren
in their inheritance.
7 And as for me, when I came from Padan,
Rachel died by me
in the land of *Canaan* **Kenaan** in the way,
when *yet* there was *but a little way* **still a bit of land**
to come unto Ephrath:
and I *buried* **entombed** her there in the way of Ephrath;
the same is *Bethlehem* **Beth Lechem**.
8 And *Israel beheld Joseph's* **Yisra El saw Yoseph's** sons,
and said, Who are these?
9 And *Joseph* **Yoseph** said unto his father,
They are my sons,
whom *God* **Elohim** hath given me *in this place*.
And he said, *Bring* **Take** them, I pray thee, unto me,
and I *will* **shall** bless them.
10 Now the eyes of *Israel* **Yisra El** were *dim* **heavy** for age,
so that he could not see.
And he brought them near unto him;
and he kissed them, and embraced them.
11 And *Israel* **Yisra El** said unto *Joseph* **Yoseph**,
I had not *thought* **prayed** to see thy face: and, *lo* **behold**,
God **Elohim** hath *shewed* me **see** also thy seed.
12 And *Joseph* **Yoseph** brought them out
from between his knees,
and he *bowed* **prostrated** *himself*
with his *face* **nostrils** to the earth.
13 And *Joseph* **Yoseph** took **the two of** them *both*,
Ephraim **Ephrayim** in his right *hand*
toward *Israel's* **Yisra El's** left *hand*,
and *Manasseh* **Menash Sheh** in his left *hand*
toward *Israel's* **Yisra El's** right *hand*,
and brought them near unto him.
14 And *Israel* **Yisra El**
stretched out **extended** his right *hand*,
and *laid* **put** it upon *Ephraim's* **Ephrayim's** head,
who was the *younger* **lesser**,
and his left *hand* upon *Manasseh's* **Menash Sheh's** head,
guiding his hands wittingly **crossing his hands**;
for *Manasseh* **Menash Sheh** was the firstborn.
15 And he blessed *Joseph* **Yoseph**, and said,
God **Elohim**, *before whom* **at whose face**
my fathers Abraham and *Isaac* **Yischaq** did walk,
the God **Elohim** which *fed* **tended** me
all my life long unto this day,
16 The Angel which redeemed me from all evil,
bless the lads;
and let my name be *named* **called** on them,
and the name of my fathers Abraham and *Isaac* **Yischaq**;
and let them *grow* **spawn as fish** into a multitude
in the midst of the earth.
17 And when *Joseph* **Yoseph** saw that his father
laid **put** his right *hand*
upon the head of *Ephraim* **Ephrayim**,
it *displeased him* **was evil in his eyes**:
and he *held up* **upheld** his father's hand,
to *remove it* **turn it aside** from *Ephraim's* **Ephrayim's** head
unto *Manasseh's* **Menash Sheh's** head.
18 And *Joseph* **Yoseph** said unto his father,
Not so, my father: for this is the firstborn;
put thy right *hand* upon his head.
19 And his father refused, and said,
I know *it*, my son, I know *it*:
he also shall become a people,
and he also shall *be great* **greaten**:
but *truly* his younger brother shall be greater than he,
and his seed shall become
a *multitude* **fulness** of *nations* **goyim**.
20 And he blessed them that day, saying,
In thee shall *Israel* **Yisra El** bless, saying,
God make **Elohim set** thee
as *Ephraim* **Ephrayim** and as *Manasseh* **Menash Sheh**:
and he set *Ephraim* **Ephrayim**
before Manasseh **at the face of Menash Sheh**.
21 And *Israel* **Yisra El** said unto *Joseph* **Yoseph**,
Behold, I die: but *God* **Elohim** shall be with you,
and *bring* **return** you *again* unto the land of your fathers.
22 Moreover I have given to thee
one *portion* **shoulder** above thy brethren,
which I took out of the hand of the *Amorite* **Emoriy**
with my sword and with my bow.

YAAQOV BLESSES HIS SONS

49 And *Jacob* **Yaaqov** called unto his sons,
and said, Gather *yourselves together*,
that I may tell you that which shall *befall* **confront** you
in the *last* **final** days.
2 Gather *yourselves together*, and hear,
ye sons of *Jacob* **Yaaqov**;
and hearken unto *Israel* **Yisra El** your father.
3 *Reuben* **Reu Ben**, thou art my firstborn,
my *might* **force**, and the beginning of my strength,
the *excellency* **remainder** of *dignity* **exalting**,
and the *excellency* **remainder** of *power* **strength**:
4 *Unstable* **Frothy** as water,
thou shalt not *excel* **remain**
because thou *wentest up* **ascendest** to thy father's bed;
then *defiledst* **profanest** thou it:
he *went up* **ascended** to my couch.
5 *Simeon* **Shimon** and Levi are brethren;
instruments of *cruelty* **violence**
are *in* their *habitations* **swords**.
6 O my soul, come not thou into their secret;
unto their *assembly* **congregation**,
mine honour, be not thou united:
for in their *anger* **wrath** they *slew* **slaughtered** a man,
and in their *selfwill* **pleasure**
they *digged down a wall* **hamstrung oxen**.
7 Cursed be their *anger* **wrath**, for it was *fierce* **strong**;
and their *wrath* **fury**, for it was *cruel* **hardened**:
I *will divide* **shall allot** them in *Jacob* **Yaaqov**,
and scatter them in *Israel* **Yisra El**.
8 *Judah* **Yah Hudah**,
thou *art he* whom thy brethren shall *praise* **extend hands**:
thy hand shall be in the neck of thine enemies;
thy father's *children* **sons**
shall *bow down* **prostrate** before thee.
9 *Judah* **Yah Hudah** is a lion's whelp:
from the prey, my son, thou art *gone up* **ascended**:
he *stooped down* **kneeled**, he *couched* **crouched** as a lion,
and as *an old* **a roaring** lion;
who shall rouse him *up*?
10 The *sceptre* **scion**
shall not *depart* **turn aside** from *Judah* **Yah Hudah**,
nor a *lawgiver* **statute setter** from between his feet,
until Shiloh come;
and unto him
shall the *gathering* **obedience** of the people be.
11 Binding his foal unto the vine,
and his *ass's colt* **she burro's son** unto the choice *vine*;
he *washed* **laundered** his *garments* **robes** in wine,
and his *clothes* **veil** in the blood of grapes:
12 His eyes shall be *red* **flush** with wine,
and his teeth white with milk.
13 Zebulun shall *dwell* **tabernacle** at the haven of the sea;
and he shall be for an haven of ships;
and his *border* **flank** shall be unto *Zidon* **Sidon**.
14 *Issachar* **Yissachar** is a *strong ass* **bony he burro**

couching down **crouching**
between *two burdens* **the stalls**:
15 And he saw that rest was good,
and the land that it *was pleasant* **pleased**;
and bowed his shoulder to bear,
and became *a servant unto tribute* **to serve as a vassal**.
16 Dan shall *judge* **plead the cause of** his people,
as one of the *tribes* **scions** of *Israel* **Yisra El**.
17 Dan shall be a serpent by the way,
an adder in the path, that biteth the horse heels,
so that his rider shall fall backward.
18 I have *waited for* **awaited** thy salvation,
O *LORD* **Yah Veh**.
19 Gad, a troop shall *overcome* **troop against** him:
but he shall *overcome at the last* **troop against the heel**.
cp Genesis 3:15
20 Out of Asher his bread shall *be fat* **fatten**,
and he shall *yield royal dainties* **give sovereign delicacies**.
21 Naphtali is a hind *let loose* **sent away**:
he giveth *goodly words* **glorious sayings**.
22 *Joseph* **Yoseph** is a fruitful *bough* **son**,
even a fruitful *bough* **son** by a *well* **fountain**;
whose *branches run* **daughters pace** over the wall:
23 The *archers* **masters of arrows**
have *sorely grieved* **embittered** him,
and shot *at him*, and *hated* **opposed** him:
24 But his bow *abode in strength* **settled perrenial**,
and the arms of his hands were *made strong* **solidified**
by the hands
of the *mighty God* **Almighty** of *Jacob* **Yaaqov**;
(from thence is *the shepherd* **he who tendeth**,
the stone of *Israel* **Yisra El**:)
25 *Even* by *the God* **El** of thy father, who shall help thee;
and by *the Almighty* **Shadday**, who shall bless thee
with blessings of *heaven above* **the heavens most high**,
blessings of the *deep* **abyss** that *lieth* **croucheth** under,
blessings of the breasts, and of the womb:
26 The blessings of thy father have prevailed **mightily**
above the blessings of *my progenitors* **whom I conceived**
unto the *utmost bound* **limits**
of the *everlasting* **eternal** hills:
they shall be on the head of *Joseph* **Yoseph**,
and on the *crown of the head* **scalp** of him
that was *separate from* **a Separatist of** his brethren.
27 *Benjamin* **Ben Yamin** shall *ravin* **tear** as a wolf:
in the morning he shall devour the prey,
and at *night* **evening** he shall *divide* **allot** the *spoil* **loot**.
28 All these are the twelve *tribes* **scions** of *Israel* **Yisra El**:
and this is it that their father *spake* **worded** unto them,
and blessed them;
every *one* **man** according to his blessing he blessed them.
29 And he *charged* **misvahed** them, and said unto them,
I am to be gathered unto my people:
bury **entomb** me with my fathers in the cave
that is in the field of Ephron the *Hittite* **Hethiy**,
30 In the cave that is in the field of Machpelah,
which is *before* **at the face of** Mamre,
in the land of *Canaan* **Kenaan**,
which Abraham *bought* **chatteled**
with the field of Ephron the *Hittite* **Hethiy**
for a possession of a *buryingplace* **tomb**.
31 There they *buried* **entombed** Abraham
and Sarah his *wife* **woman**;
there they *buried Isaac* **entombed Yischaq**
and *Rebekah* **Ribqah** his *wife* **woman**;
and there I *buried* **entombed** Leah.
32 The *purchase* **chattel** of the field and of the cave
that is therein was from the *children* **sons** of Heth.
33 And when *Jacob* **Yaaqov**
had *made an end of commanding* **finished misvahing**
his sons,
he gathered up his feet into the bed,
and *yielded up the ghost* **expired**,
and was gathered unto his people.
50 And *Joseph* **Yoseph** fell upon his father's face,
and wept upon him, and kissed him.
2 And *Joseph commanded* **Yoseph misvahed** his servants
the *physicians* **healers** to embalm his father:
and the *physicians* **healers** embalmed *Israel* **Yisra El**.
3 And forty days were fulfilled for him;
for so are fulfilled the days of those which are embalmed:
and the *Egyptians mourned* **Misrayim wept** for him
threescore and ten **seventy** days.
4 And when the days of his *mourning* **weeping** were past,
Joseph spake **Yoseph worded**
unto the house of *Pharaoh* **Paroh**, saying,
If *now* **I beseech,** I have found *grace* **charism** in your eyes,
speak **word**, I *pray* **beseech** you,
in the ears of *Pharaoh* **Paroh**, saying,
5 My father *made me swear* **oathed me**, saying,
Lo **Behold**, I die:
in my *grave* **tomb** which I have digged for me
in the land of *Canaan* **Kenaan**,
there shalt thou *bury* **entomb** me.
Now therefore let me *go up* **ascend**, I *pray* **beseech** thee,
and *bury* **entomb** my father,
and I *will come again* **shall return**.
6 And *Pharaoh* **Paroh** said,
Go up **Ascend**, and *bury* **entomb** thy father,
according as he *made* **oathed** thee *swear*.
7 And *Joseph went up* **Yoseph ascended**
to *bury* **entomb** his father:
and with him *went up* **ascended**
all the servants of *Pharaoh* **Paroh**,
the elders of his house,
and all the elders of the land of *Egypt* **Misrayim**,
8 And all the house of *Joseph* **Yoseph**,
and his brethren, and his father's house:
only their *little ones* **toddlers**, and their flocks,
and their *herds* **oxen**, they left in the land of Goshen.
9 And there *went up* **ascended** with him
both chariots and *horsemen* **cavalry**:
and it was a *very great company* **mighty heavy camp**.
10 And they came to the threshingfloor of *Atad* **Thorns**,
which is beyond *Jordan* **Yarden**,
and there they *mourned* **chopped**
with a great and *very sore* **mighty heavy**
lamentation **chopping**:
and he *made* **worked** a mourning
for his father seven days.
11 And when *the inhabitants of* **they who settled** the land,
the *Canaanites* **Kenaaniy**,
saw the mourning
in the *floor* **threshingfloor** of *Atad* **Thorns**, they said,
This is a *grievous* **heavy** mourning
to the *Egyptians* **Misrayim**:
wherefore
the name of it was called *Abelmizraim* **Abel Misrayim**,
which is beyond *Jordan* **Yarden**.
12 And his sons *did* **worked** unto him
according as he *commanded* **misvahed** them:
13 For his sons *carried* **bore** him
into the land of *Canaan* **Kenaan**,
and *buried* **entombed** him
in the cave of the field of Machpelah,
which Abraham *bought* **chatteled** with the field
for a possession of a *buryingplace* **tomb**
of Ephron the *Hittite* **Hethiy**,
before **at the face of** Mamre.
14 And *Joseph* **Yoseph** returned into *Egypt* **Misrayim**,
he, and his brethren,
and all that *went up* **ascended** with him
to *bury* **entomb** his father,
after he had *buried* **entombed** his father.
15 And when *Joseph's* **Yoseph's** brethren
saw that their father was dead, they said,
Joseph will peradventure hate
What if Yoseph shall oppose us,
and *will certainly requite us* **in returning, shall return**
all the evil which we *did* **dealt** unto him.
16 And they *sent a messenger* **misvahed**
unto *Joseph* **Yoseph**, saying,
Thy father *did command* **misvahed**
before he died **at the face of his death**, saying,
17 *So* **Thus** shall ye say unto *Joseph* **Yoseph**,
Forgive **Bear**, *I pray thee now* **O I beseech, I beseech**,
the *trespass* **rebellion** of thy brethren, and their sin;
for they *did unto* **dealt** thee evil:
and *now* **I beseech**, we *pray* **beseech** thee,
forgive **bear** the *trespass* **rebellion**

of the servants of the *God* **Elohim** of thy father.
And *Joseph* **Yoseph** wept
when they *spake* **worded** unto him.
18 And his brethren also
went and fell down *before* **at** his face;
and they said, Behold, we be thy servants.
19 And *Joseph* **Yoseph** said unto them, *Fear* **Awe** not:
for am I in the place of *God* **Elohim**?
20 But as for you, ye *thought* **fabricated** evil against me;
but *God meant* **Elohim fabricated** it unto good,
to bring to pass **in order to work**, as it is this day,
to *save* **preserve** much people alive.
Romans 8:28
21 Now therefore *fear* **awe** ye not:
I *will* **shall** nourish you, and your *little ones* **toddlers**.
And he *comforted* **sighed over** them,
and *spake kindly* **worded** unto *them* **their heart**.
22 And *Joseph dwelt* **Yoseph settled** in *Egypt* **Misrayim**,
he, and his father's house:
and *Joseph* **Yoseph** lived an hundred and ten years.
23 And *Joseph* **Yoseph**
saw *Ephraim's children* **Ephrayim's sons**
of the third *generation*:
the *children* **sons** also of Machir
the son of *Manasseh* **Menash Sheh**
were *brought up* **borne** upon *Joseph's* **Yoseph's** knees.

DEATH OF YOSEPH

24 And *Joseph* **Yoseph** said unto his brethren, I die:
and *God will surely* **in visiting, Elohim shall** visit you,
and *bring* **ascend** you out of this land
unto the land which he *sware* **oathed** to Abraham,
to *Isaac* **Yischaq**, and to *Jacob* **Yaaqov**.
25 And *Joseph took an oath of* **Yoseph oathed**
the *children* **sons** of *Israel* **Yisra El**, saying,
God will surely
In visiting, Elohim shall visit you,
and ye shall *carry up* **ascend** my bones from hence.
26 So *Joseph* **Yoseph** died,
being **a son of** an hundred and ten years *old*:
and they embalmed him,
and he was put in *a coffin* **an ark** in *Egypt* **Misrayim**.

EXODUS 1

KEY TO INTERPRETING THE EXEGESES:
King James text is in regular type;
Text under exegeses is in oblique type;
Text of exegeses is in bold type.

SONS OF YISRA EL IN MISRAYIM

1 Now these are the names
of the *children* **sons** of *Israel* **Yisra El**,
which came into *Egypt* **Misrayim**;
every man and his household came with *Jacob* **Yaaqov**.
2 *Reuben* **Reu Ben**, *Simeon* **Shimon**,
Levi, and *Judah* **Yah Hudah**,
3 *Issachar* **Yissachar**, Zebulun, and *Benjamin* **Ben Yamin**,
4 Dan, and Naphtali, Gad, and Asher.
5 And all the souls
that came out of the *loins* **flank** of *Jacob* **Yaaqov**
were seventy souls:
for *Joseph* **Yoseph** was in *Egypt* **Misrayim** *already*.
6 And *Joseph* **Yoseph** died,
and all his brethren, and all that generation.
7 And the *children* **sons** of *Israel* **Yisra El**
were fruitful **bore fruit**,
and *increased abundantly* **teemed**,
and *multiplied* **abounded**,
and waxed exceeding mighty **mighty mightily mightier**;
and the land was filled with them.
8 Now there arose up a new *king* **sovereign**
over *Egypt* **Misrayim**,
which knew not *Joseph* **Yoseph**.
9 And he said unto his people,
Behold, the people of the *children* **sons** of *Israel* **Yisra El**
are *more* **greater** and mightier than we:
10 *Come on* **Give**, let us deal wisely with them;
lest they *multiply* **abound**,
and it *come to pass* **become**, that,
when *there falleth out* **we are confronted in** any war,
they *join* **be added** also
unto *our enemies* **them who hate us**,
and fight against us,
and *so get* **ascend** them *up* out of the land.
11 Therefore they did set over them
taskmasters **vassal governors**
to *afflict* **humble** them with their burdens.
And they built for *Pharaoh treasure* **Paroh storage** cities,
Pithom and *Raamses* **Rameses**.
12 But the more they *afflicted* **humbled** them,
the more **thus** they *multiplied* **abounded**
and *grew* **thus they broke forth**.
And they were *grieved* **abhorred**
because **at the face** of the *children* **sons** of *Israel* **Yisra El**.
13 And the *Egyptians* **Misrayim**
made the *children* **sons** of *Israel* **Yisra El**
to serve with *rigour* **tyranny**:
14 And they *made* **embittered** their lives *bitter*
with hard *bondage* **service**, in morter, and in brick,
and in all *manner of* service in the field:
all their service, wherein they made them serve,
was with *rigour* **tyranny**.
15 And the *king* **sovereign** of *Egypt* **Misrayim**
spake **said** to the Hebrew *midwives* **accoucheuses**,
of which the name of the one was Shiphrah,
and the name of the *other* **second** Puah:
16 And he said,
When ye *do the office of a midwife* **accoucheuse**
to the Hebrew *women*,
and see them upon the *stools* **stones**;
if it be a son, then ye shall *kill* **deathify** him:
but if it be a daughter, then she shall live.
17 But the *midwives* **accoucheuses**
feared God **awed Elohim**,
and *did* **worked** not
as the *king* **sovereign** of *Egypt* **Misrayim**
commanded them **had worded**,
but *saved* **preserved** the *men* children alive.
18 And the *king* **sovereign** of *Egypt* **Misrayim**
called for the *midwives* **accoucheuses**,
and said unto them,
Why have ye *done* **worked** this *thing* **word**,
and have *saved* **preserved** the *men* children alive?
19 And the *midwives* **accoucheuses**
said unto *Pharaoh* **Paroh**,

Because the Hebrew *women*
are not as the *Egyptian* **Misrayim** women;
for they are lively, and *are delivered* **birth**
ere the *midwives* **accoucheuses** come in unto them.
20 Therefore *God dealt well* **Elohim was well—pleased**
with the *midwives* **accoucheuses**:
and the people *multiplied* **abounded**,
and waxed very mighty **mighty mightily mightier**.
21 And it *came to pass* **became**,
because the *midwives* **accoucheuses**
feared God **awed Elohim**,
that he *made* **worked** them houses.
22 And *Pharaoh charged* **Paroh misvahed** all his people,
saying, Every son that is born ye shall cast into the river,
and every daughter ye shall *save* **preserve** alive.

BIRTH OF MOSHEH

2 And there went a man of the house of Levi,
and took *to wife* a daughter of Levi.
2 And the woman conceived, and bare a son:
and when she saw him that he was *a* goodly *child*,
she hid him three *months* **moons**.
3 And when she could not *longer* **still** hide him,
she took for him an ark of bulrushes,
and daubed it with *slime* **bitumin** and with *pitch* **asphalt**,
and put the child therein;
and she *laid* **put** it in the *flags* **reeds**
by the river's *brink* **edge**.
4 And his sister stood afar off,
to *wit* **perceive**
what *would* **should** be *done* **worked** to him.
5 And the daughter of *Pharaoh* **Paroh**
came down **descended** to *wash* **bathe** herself at the river;
and her maidens walked along by the river's *side* **hand**;
and when she saw the ark among the *flags* **reeds**,
she sent her maid to *fetch* **take** it.
6 And when she had opened it, she saw the child:
and, behold, the *babe* **lad** wept.
And she had compassion on him, and said,
This is *one* of the Hebrews' children.
7 Then said his sister to *Pharaoh's* **Paroh's** daughter,
shall I go and call to thee a *nurse* **woman suckler**
of the Hebrew *women*,
that she may *nurse* **suckle** the child for thee?
8 And *Pharaoh's* **Paroh's** daughter said to her, Go.
And the *maid* **virgin** went and called the child's mother.
9 And *Pharaoh's* **Paroh's** daughter said unto her,
Take **Carry** this child *away*, and *nurse* **suckle** it for me,
and I *will* **shall** give *thee* thy *wages* **hire**.
And the woman took the child, and *nursed* **suckled** it.
10 And the child grew,
and she brought him unto *Pharaoh's* **Paroh's** daughter,
and he became her son.
And she called his name *Moses* **Mosheh**:
and she said, Because I drew him out of the water.

MOSHEH SMITES A MISRAYIM

11 And it *came to pass* **became** in those days,
when *Moses* **Mosheh** was grown,
that he went out unto his brethren,
and *looked on* **saw** their burdens:
and he *spied an Egyptian* **saw a man — a Misrayim**
smiting **a man** — an Hebrew, one of his brethren.
12 And he *looked this way* **faced thus** and *that way* **thus**,
and when he saw *that there was* no man,
he *slew* **smote** the *Egyptian* **Misrayim**,
and *hid* **buried** him in the sand.
13 And when he went out the second day,
behold, two men of the Hebrews strove together:
and he said to *him that did the wrong* **the wicked**,
Wherefore smitest thou thy *fellow* **friend**?
14 And he said, Who *made* **set** thee
a *prince* **man — a governor** and a judge over us?
intendest **sayest** thou to *kill* **slaughter** me,
as thou *killedst* **slaughteredst** the *Egyptian* **Misrayim**?
And *Moses feared* **Mosheh awed**, and said,
Surely this *thing* **word** is known.
15 Now when *Pharaoh* **Paroh** heard this *thing*,
he sought to *slay Moses* **slaughter Mosheh**.
But *Moses* **Mosheh** fled from the face of *Pharaoh* **Paroh**,
and *dwelt* **settled** in the land of *Midian* **Midyan**:
and he sat down by a well.
16 Now the priest of *Midian* **Midyan** had seven daughters:
and they came and *drew water* **bailed**,
and filled the troughs to *water* **moisten** their father's flock.
17 And the *shepherds* **tenders** came
and *drove* **expelled** them *away*:
but *Moses stood up* **Mosheh rose** and *helped* **saved** them,
and *watered* **moistened** their flock.
18 And when they came to *Reuel* **Reu El** their father,
he said, How is it
that ye *are come so soon* **have hasted to come** to day?
19 And they said, *An Egyptian* **A man — a Misrayim**
delivered **rescued** us
out of the hand of the *shepherds* **tenders**,
and *also drew water enough*
in bailing, he also bailed for us,
and *watered* **moistened** the flock.
20 And he said unto his daughters,
And where is he? why is it that ye have left the man?
call him, that he may eat bread.
21 And *Moses was content* **Mosheh willed**
to *dwell* **settle** with the man:
and he gave *Moses* **Mosheh**
Zipporah **Sipporah** his daughter.
22 And she bare *him* a son,
and he called his name Gershom:
for he said,
I have been a *stranger* **sojourner** in a strange land.
23 And it *came to pass* **became**,
in *process of time* **those many days**,
that the *king* **sovereign** of *Egypt* **Misrayim** died:
and the *children* **sons** of *Israel* **Yisra El** sighed
by reason **because** of the *bondage* **service**, and they cried,
and their cry *came up* **ascended** unto *God* **Elohim**
by reason **because** of the *bondage* **service**.
24 And *God* **Elohim** heard their groaning,
and *God* **Elohim** remembered his covenant
with Abraham, with *Isaac* **Yischaq**,
and with *Jacob* **Yaaqov**.
25 And *God* **Elohim**
looked upon **saw** the *children* **sons** of *Israel* **Yisra El**,
and *God had respect unto them* **Elohim perceived**.

THE BURNING BUSH

3 *Now Moses kept* **Mosheh tended** the flock
of *Jethro* **Yithro** his *father* in law,
the priest of *Midian* **Midyan**:
and he *led* **drove** the flock
to the backside of the *desert* **wilderness**,
and came to the mountain of *God* **Elohim**, *even* to Horeb.
2 And the angel of *the LORD* **Yah Veh**
appeared unto **was seen by** him
in a flame of fire out of the midst of a bush:
and he *looked* **saw**, and, behold,
the bush *burned* **kindled** with fire,
and the bush was not consumed.
3 And *Moses* **Mosheh** said,
I will now **Let me, I beseech thee,** turn aside,
and see this great *sight* **visage**,
why the bush is not *burnt* **consumed**.
4 And when *the LORD* **Yah Veh**
saw that he turned aside to see,
God **Elohim** called unto him out of the midst of the bush,
and said, *Moses* **Mosheh**, *Moses* **Mosheh**.
And he said, Here *am* — I.
5 And he said, *Draw* **Approach** not *nigh* hither:
put off thy shoes from off thy feet,
for the place whereon thou standest is holy *ground* **soil**.
6 Moreover he said, *I am the God* **I — Elohim** of thy father,
the God **Elohim** of Abraham,
the God **Elohim** of *Isaac* **Yischaq**,
and *the God* **Elohim** of *Jacob* **Yaaqov**.
And *Moses* **Mosheh** hid his face;
for he *was afraid* **awed** to look upon *God* **Elohim**.
7 And *the LORD* **Yah Veh** said,
In seeing, I have *surely* seen
the *affliction* **humiliation** of my people
which are in *Egypt* **Misrayim**,
and have heard their cry
by reason **at the face** of their *taskmasters* **exactors**;
for I know their sorrows;
8 And I *am come down* **descend** to deliver them

out of the hand of the *Egyptians* **Misrayim,**
and to *bring* **ascend** them *up* out of that land
unto a good land and *a large* **broad,**
unto a land flowing with milk and honey;
unto the place of the *Canaanites* **Kenaaniy,**
and the *Hittites* **Hethiy,** and the *Amorites* **Emoriy,**
and the *Perizzites* **Perizziy,** and the *Hivites* **Hivviy,**
and the *Jebusites* **Yebusiy.**
9 Now therefore, behold,
the cry of the *children* **sons** of *Israel* **Yisra El**
is come unto me:
and I have also seen the oppression
wherewith the *Egyptians* **Misrayim** oppress them.
10 *Come* **Go** now therefore,
and I *will* **shall** send thee unto *Pharaoh* **Paroh,**
that thou mayest bring forth my people
the *children* **sons** of *Israel* **Yisra El** out of *Egypt* **Misrayim.**
11 And *Moses* **Mosheh** said unto *God* **Elohim,**
Who am I, that I should go unto *Pharaoh* **Paroh,**
and that I should bring forth
the *children* **sons** of *Israel* **Yisra El** out of *Egypt* **Misrayim?**

ELOHIM REVEALS HIMSELF AS I AM WHO I AM

12 And he said,
Certainly I will be **For this cause I AM** with thee;
and this shall be *a token* **the sign** unto thee,
that I have sent thee:
When thou hast brought forth the people
out of *Egypt* **Misrayim,**
ye shall serve *God* **Elohim** upon this mountain.
13 And *Moses* **Mosheh** said unto *God* **Elohim**, Behold,
when I come unto the *children* **sons** of *Israel* **Yisra El,**
and shall say unto them,
The *God* **Elohim** of your fathers hath sent me unto you;
and they shall say to me, What is his name?
what shall I say unto them?
14 And *God* **Elohim** said unto *Moses* **Mosheh,**
I AM *THAT* **WHO** I AM:
and he said,
Thus shalt thou say
unto the *children* **sons** of *Israel* **Yisra El,**
I AM hath sent me unto you.
Read Yahn 8:58
15 And *God* **Elohim**
said *moreover* **again** unto *Moses* **Mosheh,**
Thus shalt thou say
unto the *children* **sons** of *Israel* **Yisra El,**
The LORD God **Yah Veh Elohim** of your fathers,
the God **Elohim** of Abraham,
the God **Elohim** of *Isaac* **Yischaq,**
and *the God* **Elohim** of *Jacob* **Yaaqov,**
hath sent me unto you:
this is my name *for ever* **eternally,**
and this is my memorial
unto all generations **generation to generation.**
16 Go, and gather the elders of *Israel* **Yisra El** *together,*
and say unto them,
The LORD God **Yah Veh Elohim** of your fathers,
the God **Elohim** of Abraham,
of *Isaac* **Yischaq,** and of *Jacob* **Yaaqov,**
appeared unto **was seen by** me, saying,
In visiting, I have *surely* visited you,
and *seen* that which is *done* **worked** to you
in *Egypt* **Misrayim:**
17 And I have said, I *will bring* **shall ascend** you *up*
out of the *affliction* **humiliation** of *Egypt* **Misrayim**
unto the land of the *Canaanites* **Kenaaniy,**
and the *Hittites* **Hethiy,** and the *Amorites* **Emoriy,**
and the *Perizzites* **Perizziy,** and the *Hivites* **Hivviy,**
and the *Jebusites* **Yebusiy,**
unto a land flowing with milk and honey.
18 And they shall hearken to thy voice:
and thou shalt come,
thou and the elders of *Israel* **Yisra El,**
unto the *king* **sovereign** of *Egypt* **Misrayim,**
and ye shall say unto him,
The LORD God **Yah Veh Elohim** of the Hebrews
hath *met with* **happened upon** us:
and now let us go, we beseech thee,
three days' journey into the wilderness,
that we may sacrifice
to *the LORD* **Yah Veh** our *God* **Elohim.**
19 And I am sure
that the *king* **sovereign** of *Egypt* **Misrayim**
will **shall** not *let* **give** you **to** go,
no, not by a *mighty* **strong** hand.
20 And I *will stretch out* **shall extend** my hand,
and smite *Egypt* **Misrayim** with all my *wonders* **marvels**
which I *will do* **shall work** in the midst thereof:
and after that he *will let* **shall send** you *go* **away.**
21 And I *will* **shall** give this people *favour* **charism**
in the *sight* **eyes** of the *Egyptians* **Misrayim:**
and it shall *come to pass* **become,**
that, when ye go, ye shall not go empty:
22 But every woman shall *borrow* **ask**
of her *neighbour* **fellow tabernacler,**
and of her that sojourneth in her house,
jewels **instruments** of silver,
and *jewels* **instruments** of gold,
and *raiment* **clothes:**
and ye shall put them upon your sons,
and upon your daughters;
and *ye* shall *spoil* **strip** the *Egyptians* **Misrayim.**

YAH VEH'S SIGNS TO MOSHEH

4 And *Moses* **Mosheh** answered and said,
But, behold, they *will* **shall** not *believe* **trust** me,
nor hearken unto my voice: for they *will* **shall** say,
The LORD **Yah Veh**
hath not *appeared unto* **been seen by** thee.
2 And *the LORD* **Yah Veh** said unto him,
What is that in thine hand?
And he said, A rod.
3 And he said, Cast it on the *ground* **earth.**
And he cast it on the *ground* **earth,**
and it became a serpent;
and *Moses* **Mosheh** fled from *before* **the face of** it.
4 And *the LORD* **Yah Veh** said unto *Moses* **Mosheh,**
Put forth **Extend** thine hand, and *take* **hold** it by the tail.
And he *put forth* **extended** his hand, and *caught* **held** it,
and it became a rod in his *hand* **palm:**
5 That they may *believe* **trust**
that *the LORD God* **Yah Veh Elohim** of their fathers,
the God **Elohim** of Abraham,
the God **Elohim** of *Isaac* **Yischaq,**
and *the God* **Elohim** of *Jacob* **Yaaqov,**
hath *appeared unto* **been seen by** thee.
6 And *the LORD* **Yah Veh** said *furthermore* **again** unto him,
Put *now* **I beseech thee,** thine hand into thy bosom.
And he put his hand into his bosom:
and when he took it out, behold,
his hand was leprous as snow.
7 And he said,
Put **Return** thine hand into thy bosom *again.*
And he *put* **returned** his hand into his bosom *again;*
and plucked it out of his bosom, and, behold,
it *was turned again* **returned** as his *other* flesh.
8 And it shall *come to pass* **become,**
if they *will* **shall** not *believe* **trust** thee,
neither hearken to the voice of the first sign,
that they *will believe* **shall trust** the voice of the latter sign.
9 And it shall *come to pass* **become,**
if they *will* **shall** not *believe* **trust** also these two signs,
neither hearken unto thy voice,
that thou shalt take of the water of the river,
and pour it upon the dry *land:*
and the water which thou takest out of the river
shall become blood upon the dry *land:*
10 And *Moses* **Mosheh** said unto *the LORD* **Yah Veh,**
O my *Lord* **Adonay,** I am not *eloquent* **a man of words,**
neither *heretofore* **for three yesters ago,**
nor since thou hast *spoken* **worded** unto thy servant:
but I am *slow* **heavy** of *speech* **mouth,**
and of a *slow* **heavy** tongue.
11 And *the LORD* **Yah Veh** said unto him,
Who hath *made man's* **set the human** mouth?
or who *maketh* **setteth** the *dumb* **mute,** or deaf,
or the *seeing* **open—eyed,** or the blind?
have not I *the LORD* **Yah Veh?**
12 Now therefore go, and I *will* **shall** be with thy mouth,
and *teach* **direct** thee what thou shalt *say* **word.**
13 And he said, O my *Lord* **Adonay,**

send, I *pray* **beseech** thee,
by the hand of him whom thou *wilt* **shalt** send.
14 And the *anger* **wrath** of *the LORD* **Yah Veh**
was kindled against *Moses* **Mosheh**, and he said,
Is not *Aaron* **Aharon** the *Levite* **Leviy** thy brother?
I know that **in wording,** he can *speak well* **word**.
And also, behold, he cometh forth to meet thee:
and when he seeth thee,
he *will be glad* **shall cheer** in his heart.
15 And thou shalt *speak* **word** unto him,
and put words in his mouth:
and I *will* **shall** be with thy mouth, and with his mouth,
and *will teach* **shall direct** you what ye shall *do* **work**.
16 And he shall *be thy spokesman* **word for thee**
unto the people:
and he shall be,
even he shall be to thee
instead **in the stead** of a mouth,
and thou shalt be to him
instead **in the stead** of *God* **Elohim**.
17 And thou shalt take this rod in thine hand,
wherewith thou shalt *do* **work** signs.
18 And *Moses* **Mosheh** went
and returned to *Jethro* **Yithro** his *father* in law,
and said unto him, Let me go, I *pray* **beseech** thee,
and return unto my brethren
which are in *Egypt* **Misrayim**,
and see whether they be *yet* **still** alive.
And *Jethro* **Yithro** said to *Moses* **Mosheh**,
Go in *peace* **shalom**.
19 And *the LORD* **Yah Veh** said unto *Moses* **Mosheh**
in *Midian* **Midyan**,
Go, return into *Egypt* **Misrayim**:
for all the men are dead which sought thy *life* **soul**.
20 And *Moses* **Mosheh** took his *wife* **woman** and his sons,
and *set* **rode** them upon *an ass* **a he burro**,
and he returned to the land of *Egypt* **Misrayim**:
and *Moses* **Mosheh** took the rod of *God* **Elohim**
in his hand.
21 And *the LORD* **Yah Veh** said unto *Moses* **Mosheh**,
When thou goest to return into *Egypt* **Misrayim**,
see that thou *do* **work** all those *wonders* **omens**
before Pharaoh **at the face of Paroh**,
which I have put in thine hand:
but I *will harden* **shall callous** his heart,
that he shall not *let* **send** the people *go* **away**.
22 And thou shalt say unto *Pharaoh* **Paroh**,
Thus saith *the LORD* **Yah Veh**,
Israel **Yisra El** is my son, *even* my firstborn:
23 And I say unto thee, *Let* **Send** my son *go* **away**,
that he may serve me:
and if thou refuse to *let* **send** him *go* **away**,
behold, I *will slay* **shall slaughter** thy son,
even thy firstborn.
24 And it *came to pass* **became**,
by the way in the *inn* **lodge**,
that *the LORD* **Yah Veh** met him,
and sought to *kill* **deathify** him.
25 Then *Zipporah* **Sipporah** took a sharp stone,
and cut off the foreskin of her son,
and cast it at **that it touched** his feet, and said,
Surely a bloody *husband* **groom** art thou to me.
26 So he *let* **sent** him *go* **away**:
then she said, A bloody *husband* **groom** *thou art*,
because of the circumcision.
27 And *the LORD* **Yah Veh** said to *Aaron* **Aharon**,
Go into the wilderness to meet *Moses* **Mosheh**.
And he went, and met him in the mount of *God* **Elohim**,
and kissed him.
28 And *Moses* **Mosheh** told *Aaron* **Aharon**
all the words of *the LORD* **Yah Veh** who had sent him,
and all the signs
which he had *commanded* **misvahed** him.
29 And *Moses* **Mosheh** and *Aaron* **Aharon** went
and gathered *together*
all the elders of the *children* **sons** of *Israel* **Yisra El**:
30 And *Aaron spake* **Aharon worded** all the words
which *the LORD* **Yah Veh** had *spoken* **worded**
unto *Moses* **Mosheh**,
and *did* **worked** the signs in the *sight* **eyes** of the people.
31 And the people *believed* **trusted**:
and when they heard that *the LORD* **Yah Veh**
had visited the *children* **sons** of *Israel* **Yisra El**,
and that he had
looked upon **seen** their *affliction* **humiliation,**
then they bowed *their heads* and *worshipped* **prostrated.**

MOSHEH AND AHARON AT THE FACE OF PAROH

5 And afterward
Moses **Mosheh** and *Aaron* **Aharon** went in,
and told *Pharaoh* **Paroh**,
Thus saith *the LORD God* **Yah Veh Elohim**
of *Israel* **Yisra El**,
Let **Send** my people *go* **away**,
that they may *hold a feast* **celebrate** unto me
in the wilderness.
2 And *Pharaoh* **Paroh** said, Who is *the LORD* **Yah Veh**,
that I should *obey* **hear** his voice
to *let Israel go* **send Yisra El away**?
I know not *the LORD* **Yah Veh**,
neither *will I let Israel go* **shall I send Yisra El away**.
3 And they said,
The God **Elohim** of the Hebrews hath met with us:
let us go, we *pray* **beseech** thee,
three days' journey into the *desert* **wilderness**,
and sacrifice unto *the LORD* **Yah Veh** our *God* **Elohim**;
lest he *fall upon* **encounter** us with pestilence,
or with the sword.
4 And the *king* **sovereign** of *Egypt* **Misrayim**
said unto them,
Wherefore do ye, *Moses* **Mosheh** and *Aaron* **Aharon**,
let **expel** the people from their works?
get you **go ye** unto your burdens.
5 And *Pharaoh* **Paroh** said, Behold,
the people of the land now are many,
and ye make them *rest* **shabbathize** from their burdens.
6 And *Pharaoh commanded* **Paroh misvahed** the same day
the *taskmasters* **exactors** of the people, and their officers,
saying,
7 Ye shall *no more* **not again**
give the people straw to make brick,
as *heretofore* **three yesters ago**:
let them go and gather straw for themselves.
8 And the *tale* **quantity** of the bricks,
which they *did make heretofore* **worked three yesters ago**,
ye shall *lay* **set** upon them;
ye shall not diminish *ought* thereof for they be *idle* **lazy**;
therefore they cry, saying,
Let us go and sacrifice to our *God* **Elohim**.
9 Let *there more work* **the service**
be *laid* **heavy** upon the men,
that they may *labour* **work** therein;
and let them not *regard vain* **look unto false** words.
10 And the *taskmasters* **exactors** of the people went out,
and their officers,
and they *spake* **said** to the people, saying,
Thus saith *Pharaoh* **Paroh**, I *will* **shall** not give you straw.
11 Go ye, *get* **take** you straw where ye can find it:
yet not ought **that no word** of your *work* **service**
shall be diminished.
12 So the people were scattered abroad
throughout all the land of *Egypt* **Misrayim**
to gather stubble instead of straw.
13 And the *taskmasters* **exactors** hasted them, saying,
Fulfil **Finish** your works,
your *daily tasks* **day by day words**,
as when there *was* **became** straw.
14 And the officers of the *children* **sons** of *Israel* **Yisra El**,
which *Pharaoh's taskmasters* **Paroh's exactors**
had set over them,
were *beaten* **smitten**, *and demanded* **saying**,
Wherefore have ye not *fulfilled* **finished** your *task* **statute**
in making brick both yesterday and to day,
as *heretofore* **three yesters ago**?
15 Then the officers of the *children* **sons** of *Israel* **Yisra El**
came and cried unto *Pharaoh* **Paroh**, saying,
Wherefore *dealest* **workest** thou thus with thy servants?
16 There is no straw given unto thy servants,
and they say to us, *Make* **Work** brick:
and, behold, thy servants are *beaten* **smitten**;
but the *fault* **sin** is in thine own people.

17 But he said, *Ye are idle* **Lazy**, *ye are idle* **Lazy**:
therefore ye say,
Let us go and *do* sacrifice to *the LORD* **Yah Veh**.
18 Go therefore now, *and work* **serve**;
for there shall no straw be given you,
yet shall ye *deliver* **give** the *tale* **gauge** of bricks.
19 And the officers of the *children* **sons** of *Israel* **Yisra El**
did see that they were in evil *case*, after it was said,
Ye shall not *minish ought* **diminish**
from your bricks of your *daily task* **day by day word**.
20 And they *met* **encountered**
Moses **Mosheh** and *Aaron* **Aharon**,
who *stood* **stationed themselves**
in the way **to confront them**,
as they came forth from *Pharaoh* **Paroh**:
21 And they said unto them,
The LORD look upon you **Yah Veh see thee**, and judge;
because ye have
made our savour to be abhorred **stunk our scent**
in the eyes of *Pharaoh* **Paroh**,
and in the eyes of his servants,
to *put* **give** a sword in their hand to *slay* **slaughter** us.
22 And *Moses* **Mosheh** returned unto *the LORD* **Yah Veh**,
and said, *Lord* **Adonay**,
wherefore hast thou *so evil entreated* **vilified** this people?
why is it that thou hast sent me?
23 For since I came to *Pharaoh* **Paroh**
to *speak* **word** in thy name,
he hath *done evil to* **vilified** this people;
neither hast thou delivered thy people at all
in rescuing, thou hast not rescued thy people.
6 Then *the LORD* **Yah Veh** said unto *Moses* **Mosheh**,
Now shalt thou see
what I *will do* **shall work** to *Pharaoh* **Paroh**:
for with a strong hand
shall he *let* **send** them *go* **away**,
and with a strong hand
shall he *drive* **expel** them out of his land.
2 And *God spake* **Elohim worded** unto *Moses* **Mosheh**,
and said unto him, *I am the LORD* **I — Yah Veh**:
3 And I *appeared unto* **was seen by** Abraham,
unto Isaac **by Yischaq**, and *unto Jacob* **by Yaaqov**,
by the name of God Almighty **as El Shadday**,
but by my name *JEHOVAH* **Yah Veh**
was I not known to them.
4 And I have also *established* **raised** my covenant
with them,
to give them the land of *Canaan* **Kenaan**,
the land of their *pilgrimage* **sojournings**,
wherein they *were strangers* **sojourned**.
5 And I have also heard the groaning
of the *children* **sons** of *Israel* **Yisra El**,
whom the *Egyptians* **Misrayim**
keep in bondage **cause to serve**;
and I have remembered my covenant.
6 *Wherefore say* **Say thus**
unto the *children* **sons** of *Israel* **Yisra El**,
I am the LORD **I — Yah Veh**,
and I *will* **shall** bring you out
from under the burdens of the *Egyptians* **Misrayim**,
and I *will rid* **shall rescue** you
out of their *bondage* **service**,
and I *will* **shall** redeem you
with *a stretched out* **extended** arm,
and with great judgments:
7 And I *will* **shall** take you to me *for* — a people,
and I *will* **shall** be to you *a God* — **Elohim**:
and ye shall know
that I am the LORD **I — Yah Veh** your *God* **Elohim**,
which bringeth you out
from under the burdens of the *Egyptians* **Misrayim**.
8 And I *will* **shall** bring you in unto the land,
concerning the which I *did swear* **lifted my hand**
to give it to Abraham,
to *Isaac* **Yischaq**, and to *Jacob* **Yaaqov**;
and I *will* **shall** give it you for *an heritage* **a possession**:
I am the LORD **I — Yah Veh**.
9 And *Moses spake so* **Mosheh worded thus**
unto the *children* **sons** of *Israel* **Yisra El**:
but they hearkened not unto *Moses* **Mosheh**
for *anguish* **shortness** of spirit,
and for *cruel bondage* **hard service**.
10 And *the LORD spake* **Yah Veh worded**
unto *Moses* **Mosheh**, saying,
11 Go in, *speak* **word** unto *Pharaoh* **Paroh**
king **sovereign** of *Egypt* **Misrayim**,
that he *let* **send**
the *children* **sons** of *Israel go* **Yisra El away** out of his land.
12 And *Moses spake* **Mosheh worded**
before the LORD **at the face of Yah Veh**, saying,
Behold, the *children* **sons** of *Israel* **Yisra El**
have not hearkened unto me;
how then shall *Pharaoh* **Paroh** hear me,
who am — **I** of uncircumcised lips?
13 And *the LORD spake* **Yah Veh worded**
unto *Moses* **Mosheh** and unto *Aaron* **Aharon**,
and *gave* **misvahed** them *a charge*
unto the *children* **sons** of *Israel* **Yisra El**,
and unto *Pharaoh* **Paroh**
king **sovereign** of *Egypt* **Misrayim**,
to bring the *children* **sons** of *Israel* **Yisra El**
out of the land of *Egypt* **Misrayim**.

GENEALOGY OF THE SONS OF YISRA EL

14 These be the heads of their fathers' houses:
The sons of *Reuben* **Reu Ben** the firstborn of *Israel* **Yisra El**;
Hanoch, and Pallu,
Hezron **Hesron**, and *Carmi* **Karmi**:
these be the families of *Reuben* **Reu Ben**.
15 And the sons of *Simeon* **Shimon**;
Jemuel **Yemu El**, and *Jamin* **Yamiyn**,
and Ohad and *Jachin* **Yachin**, and *Zohar* **Sochar**,
and Shaul the son of a *Canaanitish* **Kenaaniy** woman:
these are the families of *Simeon* **Shimon**.
16 And these are the names of the sons of Levi
according to their generations;
Gershon, and *Kohath* **Qehath**, and Merari:
and the years of the life of Levi
were an hundred thirty and seven years.
17 The sons of Gershon;
Libni, and *Shimi* **Shimiy**, according to their families.
18 And the sons of *Kohath* **Qehath**;
Amram **Am Ram**, and *Izhar* **Yishar**,
and Hebron, and *Uzziel* **Uzzi El**:
and the years of the life of *Kohath* **Qehath**
were an hundred thirty and three years.
19 And the sons of Merari;
Mahali **Machli** and Mushi:
these are the families of Levi
according to their generations.
20 And *Amram* **Am Ram** took him *Jochebed* **Yah Chebed**
his *father's sister* **aunt** to *wife* **woman**;
and she bare him *Aaron* **Aharon** and *Moses* **Mosheh**:
and the years of the life of *Amram* **Am Ram**
were an hundred and thirty and seven years.
21 And the sons of *Izhar* **Yishar**;
Korah **Qorach**, and Nepheg, and Zichri.
22 And the sons of *Uzziel* **Uzzi El**;
Mishael **Misha El**,
and *Elzaphan* **El Saphan**, and *Zithri* **Sithri**.
23 And *Aaron* **Aharon** took him *Elisheba* **Eli Sheba**,
daughter of *Amminadab* **Ammi Nadab**,
sister of *Naashon* **Nahshon**, to *wife* **woman**;
and she bare him Nadab, and *Abihu* **Abi Hu**,
Eleazar **El Azar**, and *Ithamar* **Iy Thamar**.
24 And the sons of *Korah* **Qorachiy**;
Assir, and *Elkanah* **El Qanah**, and *Abiasaph* **Abi Asaph**:
these are the families of the *Korhites* **Qorachiy**.
25 And *Eleazar* **El Azar** *Aaron's* **Aharon's** son took him
one of the daughters of *Putiel* **Puti El** to *wife* **woman**;
and she bare him *Phinehas* **Phinechas**:
these are the heads of the fathers of the *Levites* **Leviym**
according to their families.
26 These are that *Aaron* **Aharon** and *Moses* **Mosheh**,
to whom *the LORD* **Yah Veh** said,
Bring out the *children* **sons** of *Israel* **Yisra El**
from the land of *Egypt* **Misrayim**
according to their *armies* **hosts**.
27 These are they which *spake* **worded** to *Pharaoh* **Paroh**
king **sovereign** of *Egypt* **Misrayim**,
to bring out the *children* **sons** of *Israel* **Yisra El**

from *Egypt* **Misrayim**:
these are that *Moses* **Mosheh** and *Aaron* **Aharon**.
28 And it *came to pass* **became** on the day
when *the LORD spake* **Yah Veh worded**
unto *Moses* **Mosheh**
in the land of *Egypt* **Misrayim**,
29 That *the LORD spake* **Yah Veh worded**
unto *Moses* **Mosheh**, saying,
I am the LORD **I — Yah Veh**:
speak **word** thou unto *Pharaoh* **Paroh**
king **sovereign** of *Egypt* **Misrayim**
all that I *say* **speak** unto thee.
30 And *Moses* **Mosheh** said
before the LORD **at the face of Yah Veh**, Behold,
I *am* — of uncircumcised lips,
and how shall *Pharaoh* **Paroh** hearken unto me?

PAROH'S CALLOUSED HEART

7 And *the LORD* **Yah Veh** said unto *Moses* **Mosheh**,
See, I have *made* **given** thee
a god **as Elohim** to *Pharaoh* **Paroh**:
and *Aaron* **Aharon** thy brother shall be thy prophet.
2 Thou shalt *speak* **word** all that I *command* **misvah** thee:
and *Aaron* **Aharon** thy brother
shall *speak* **word** unto *Pharaoh* **Paroh**,
that he send the *children* **sons** of *Israel* **Yisra El**
out of his land.
3 And I *will* **shall** harden *Pharaoh's* **Paroh's** heart,
and *multiply* **abound** my signs and my *wonders* **omens**
in the land of *Egypt* **Misrayim**.
4 But *Pharaoh* **Paroh** shall not hearken unto you,
that I may *lay* **give** my hand upon *Egypt* **Misrayim**,
and bring forth mine *armies* **hosts**,
and my people the *children* **sons** of *Israel* **Yisra El**,
out of the land of *Egypt* **Misrayim** by great judgments.
5 And the *Egyptians* **Misrayim** shall know
that *I am the LORD* **I — Yah Veh**,
when I *stretch forth* **extend** mine hand
upon *Egypt* **Misrayim**,
and bring out the *children* **sons** of *Israel* **Yisra El**
from among them.
6 And *Moses* **Mosheh** and *Aaron did* **Aharon worked**
as *the LORD commanded* **Yah Veh misvahed** them,
so *did* **worked** they.
7 And *Moses* **Mosheh**
was *fourscore* **a son of eighty** years *old*,
and *Aaron* **Aharon**
fourscore **a son of eighty years** and three years *old*,
when they *spake* **worded** unto *Pharaoh* **Paroh**.
8 And *the LORD spake* **Yah Veh said** unto *Moses* **Mosheh**
and unto *Aaron* **Aharon**, saying,
9 When *Pharaoh* **Paroh** shall *speak* **word** unto you,
saying, *Shew a miracle* **Give an omen** for you:
then thou shalt say unto *Aaron* **Aharon**, Take thy rod,
and cast it *before Pharaoh* **at the face of Paroh**,
and it shall become a *serpent* **monster**.
10 And *Moses* **Mosheh** and *Aaron* **Aharon**
went in unto *Pharaoh* **Paroh**, and they *did so* **worked**
as *the LORD* **Yah Veh** had *commanded* **misvahed**:
and *Aaron* **Aharon** cast down his rod
before Pharaoh **at the face of Paroh**,
and *before* **at the face of** his servants,
and it became a *serpent* **monster**.
11 Then *Pharaoh* **Paroh** also
called the wise *men* and the sorcerers:
now the magicians of *Egypt* **Misrayim**,
they also *did in like manner* **worked thus**
with their *enchantments* **flamings**.
12 For they cast down every man his rod,
and they became *serpents* **monsters**:
but *Aaron's* **Aharon's** rod swallowed up their rods.
13 And he *hardened Pharaoh's* **calloused Paroh's** heart,
that he hearkened not unto them;
as *the LORD* **Yah Veh** had *said* **worded**.
14 And *the LORD* **Yah Veh** said unto *Moses* **Mosheh**,
Pharaoh's **Paroh's** heart is *hardened* **calloused**,
he refuseth to *let* **send** the people *go* **away**.
15 *Get* **Go** thee unto *Pharaoh* **Paroh** in the morning;
lo **behold**, he goeth out unto the water;
and thou shalt *stand* **station thyself**
by the river's *brink* **edge** *against he come* **to confront him**;
and the rod which was turned to a serpent
shalt thou take in thine hand.
16 And thou shalt say unto him,
The LORD God **Yah Veh Elohim** of the Hebrews
hath sent me unto thee, saying,
Let **Send** my people *go* **away**,
that they may serve me in the wilderness:
and, behold,
hitherto thus thou *wouldest* **heardest** not *hear*.
17 Thus saith *the LORD* **Yah Veh**,
In this thou shalt know that *I am the LORD* **I — Yah Veh**:
behold, I *will* **shall** smite with the rod that is in mine hand
upon the waters which are in the river,
and they shall be turned to blood.
18 And the fish that is in the river shall die,
and the river shall stink;
and the *Egyptians* **Misrayim**
shall lothe to drink of the water of the river.
19 And *the LORD* **Yah Veh**
spake **said** unto *Moses* **Mosheh**,
Say unto *Aaron* **Aharon**,
Take thy rod, and *stretch out* **extend** thine hand
upon the waters of *Egypt* **Misrayim**,
upon their streams, upon their rivers,
and upon their *ponds* **marshes**,
and upon all their *pools* **congregations** of water,
that they may become blood;
and that there may be blood
throughout all the land of *Egypt* **Misrayim**,
both in *vessels of wood* **timber**, and in *vessels of* stone.
20 And *Moses* **Mosheh** and *Aaron did* **Aharon worked** so,
as *the LORD commanded* **Yah Veh misvahed**;
and he lifted up the rod,
and smote the waters that were in the river,
in the *sight* **eyes** of *Pharaoh* **Paroh**,
and in the *sight* **eyes** of his servants;
and all the waters that were in the river
were turned to blood.
21 And the fish that was in the river died;
and the river stank,
and the *Egyptians* **Misrayim**
could not drink of the water of the river;
and there was blood
throughout all the land of *Egypt* **Misrayim**.
22 And the magicians of *Egypt* **Misrayim**
did **worked** so with their enchantments:
and *Pharaoh's* **Paroh's** heart *was hardened* **calloused**,
neither did he hearken unto them;
as *the LORD* **Yah Veh** had *said* **worded**.
23 And *Pharaoh* **Paroh** turned **his face**
and went into his house,
neither did he set his heart to this also.
24 And all the *Egyptians* **Misrayim**
digged round about the river for water to drink;
for they could not drink of the water of the river.
25 And seven days were fulfilled,
after that *the LORD* **Yah Veh** had smitten the river.
8 And *the LORD spake* **Yah Veh said** unto *Moses* **Mosheh**,
Go unto *Pharaoh* **Paroh**, and say unto him,
Thus saith *the LORD* **Yah Veh**,
Let **Send** my people *go* **away**, that they may serve me.
2 And if thou refuse to *let* **send** them *go* **away**,
behold, I *will* **shall** smite all thy borders with frogs:
3 And the river
shall *bring forth* **teem with** frogs *abundantly*,
which shall *go up* **ascend** and come into thine house,
and into thy bedchamber, and upon thy bed,
and into the house of thy servants, and upon thy people,
and into thine ovens,
and into thy *kneadingtroughs* **doughboards**:
4 And the frogs shall *come up* **ascend** both on thee,
and upon thy people, and upon all thy servants.
5 And *the LORD spake* **Yah Veh said** unto *Moses* **Mosheh**,
Say unto *Aaron* **Aharon**,
Stretch forth **Extend** thine hand with thy rod
over the streams, over the rivers,
and over the *ponds* **marshes**,
and cause frogs to *come up* **ascend**
upon the land of *Egypt* **Misrayim**.
6 And *Aaron stretched out* **Aharon extended** his hand

over the waters of *Egypt* **Misrayim**;
and the frogs *came up* **ascended**,
and covered the land of *Egypt* **Misrayim**.
7 And the magicians *did* **worked** so
with their enchantments,
and *brought up* **ascended** frogs
upon the land of *Egypt* **Misrayim**.
8 Then *Pharaoh* **Paroh**
called for *Moses* **Mosheh** and *Aaron* **Aharon**,
and said, Intreat *the LORD* **Yah Veh**,
that he may *take away* **turn aside** the frogs from me,
and from my people;
and I *will let* **shall send** the people *go* **away**,
that they may *do* sacrifice unto *the LORD* **Yah Veh**.
9 And *Moses* **Mosheh** said unto *Pharaoh* **Paroh**,
Glory **Embellish** over me:
when shall I intreat for thee,
and for thy servants, and for thy people,
to *destroy* **cut** the frogs from thee and thy houses,
that they may *remain* **survive** in the river only?
10 And he said, *To* **By the** morrow.
And he said, Be it according to thy word:
that thou mayest know that there is none
like unto *the LORD* **Yah Veh** our *God* **Elohim**.
11 And the frogs shall *depart* **turn aside** from thee,
and from thy houses,
and from thy servants, and from thy people;
they shall *remain* **survive** in the river only.
12 And *Moses* **Mosheh** and *Aaron* **Aharon**
went out from *Pharaoh* **Paroh**:
and *Moses* **Mosheh** cried unto *the LORD* **Yah Veh**
because **for word** of the frogs
which he had *brought* **set** against *Pharaoh* **Paroh**.
13 And *the LORD did* **Yah Veh worked**
according to the word of *Moses* **Mosheh**;
and the frogs died out of the houses,
out of the *villages* **courts**, and out of the fields.
14 And they *gathered* **heaped** them together upon heaps:
and the land stank.
15 But when *Pharaoh* **Paroh** saw that there was respite,
he *hardened* **calloused** his heart,
and hearkened not unto them;
as *the LORD* **Yah Veh** had *said* **worded**.
16 And *the LORD* **Yah Veh** said unto *Moses* **Mosheh**,
Say unto *Aaron* **Aharon**,
Stretch out **Extend** thy rod, and smite the dust of the land,
that it may become *lice* **stingers**
throughout all the land of *Egypt* **Misrayim**.
17 And they *did* **worked** so;
for *Aaron* **Aharon**
stretched out **extended** his hand with his rod,
and smote the dust of the earth,
and it became *lice* **stingers**
in *man* **humanity**, and in *beast* **animal**;
all the dust of the land became *lice* **stingers**
throughout all the land of *Egypt* **Misrayim**.
18 And the magicians
did **worked** so with their enchantments
to bring forth *lice* **stingers**, but they could not:
so there were *lice* **stingers** upon *man* **humanity**,
and upon *beast* **animal**.
19 Then the magicians said unto *Pharaoh* **Paroh**,
This is the finger of *God* **Elohim**:
and *Pharaoh's* **Paroh's** heart *was hardened* **calloused**,
and he hearkened not unto them;
as *the LORD* **Yah Veh** had *said* **worded**.
20 And *the LORD* **Yah Veh** said unto *Moses* **Mosheh**,
Rise up **Start** early in the morning,
and stand *before Pharaoh* **at the face of Paroh**;
lo **behold**, he cometh forth to the water;
and say unto him, Thus saith *the LORD* **Yah Veh**,
Let **Send** my people *go* **away**, that they may serve me.
21 Else, if thou *wilt* **shalt** not *let* **send** my people *go* **away**,
behold,
I *will* **shall** send *swarms of flies* **swarmers** upon thee,
and upon thy servants, and upon thy people,
and into thy houses:
and the houses of the *Egyptians* **Misrayim**
shall be full of *swarms of flies* **swarmers**,
and also the *ground* **soil** whereon they are.
22 And I *will sever* **shall distinguish** in that day
the land of Goshen,
in which my people *dwell* **stay**,
that no *swarms of flies* **swarmers** shall be there;
to the end **so that** thou mayest know
that *I am the LORD* **I — Yah Veh** in the midst of the earth.
23 And I *will* **shall** put a *division* **redemption**
between my people and **between** thy people:
to **by the** morrow shall this sign be.
24 And *the LORD did* **Yah Veh worked** so;
and there came *a grievous swarm of flies* **heavy swarmers**
into the house of *Pharaoh* **Paroh**,
and into his servants' houses,
and into all the land of *Egypt* **Misrayim**:
the land was *corrupted* **ruined**
by reason **at the face** of the *swarm of flies* **swarmers**.
25 And *Pharaoh* **Paroh**
called for *Moses* **Mosheh** and for *Aaron* **Aharon**, and said,
Go ye, sacrifice to your *God* **Elohim** in the land.
26 And *Moses* **Mosheh** said,
It is not *meet* **established** so to *do* **work**;
for we shall sacrifice
the *abomination* **abhorrence** of the *Egyptians* **Misrayim**
to *the LORD* **Yah Veh** our *God* **Elohim**:
lo **behold**, shall we sacrifice
the *abomination* **abhorrence** of the *Egyptians* **Misrayim**
before their eyes, and *will* **shall** they not stone us?
27 We *will* **shall** go
three days' journey into the wilderness,
and sacrifice to *the LORD* **Yah Veh** our *God* **Elohim**,
as he shall *command* **say to** us.
28 And *Pharaoh* **Paroh** said,
I *will let* **shall send** you *go* **away**,
that ye may sacrifice
to *the LORD* **Yah Veh** your *God* **Elohim**
in the wilderness;
only **in being far removed**,
ye shall not *go very far away* **be far removed**:
intreat for me.
29 And *Moses* **Mosheh** said, Behold, I go out from thee,
and I *will* **shall** intreat *the LORD* **Yah Veh**
that the *swarms of flies* **swarmers**
may *depart* **turn aside** from *Pharaoh* **Paroh**,
from his servants, and from his people, to morrow:
but **only** let not *Pharaoh* **Paroh**
deal deceitfully any more **add to mock again**
in not *letting* **sending** the people *go* **away**
to sacrifice to *the LORD* **Yah Veh**.
30 And *Moses* **Mosheh** went out from *Pharaoh* **Paroh**,
and intreated *the LORD* **Yah Veh**.
31 And *the LORD did* **Yah Veh worked**
according to the word of *Moses* **Mosheh**;
and he *removed* **turned aside**
the *swarms of flies* **swarmers** from *Pharaoh* **Paroh**,
from his servants, and from his people;
there *remained* **survived** not one.
32 And *Pharaoh* **Paroh**
hardened **calloused** his heart at this time also,
neither *would he let* **sent he** the people *go* **away**.

9 Then *the LORD* **Yah Veh** said unto *Moses* **Mosheh**,
Go in unto *Pharaoh* **Paroh**, and *tell* **word** him,
Thus saith *the LORD God* **Yah Veh Elohim**
of the Hebrews,
Let **Send** my people *go* **away**, that they may serve me.
2 For if thou refuse to *let* **send** them *go* **away**,
and *wilt* **shalt** hold them still,
3 Behold, the hand of *the LORD* **Yah Veh**
is **shall be** upon thy *cattle* **chattel** which is in the field,
upon the horses, upon the *asses* **he burros**,
upon the camels, upon the oxen,
and upon the *sheep* **flocks**:
there shall be
a *very grievous murrain* **mighty heavy pestilence**.
4 And *the LORD* **Yah Veh** shall *sever* **distinguish**
between the *cattle* **chattel** of *Israel* **Yisra El**
and the *cattle* **chattel** of *Egypt* **Misrayim**:
and there shall *nothing* **no word** die
of all that is *the children's* **to the sons** of *Israel* **Yisra El**.
5 And *the LORD* **Yah Veh**
appointed a set time **set a season**, saying,

To **By the** morrow
the LORD **Yah Veh** shall *do* **work** this *thing* **word**
in the land.
6 And *the LORD did* **Yah Veh worked** that *thing* **word**
on the morrow,
and all the *cattle* **chattel** of *Egypt* **Misrayim** died:
but of the *cattle* **chattel**
of the *children* **sons** of *Israel* **Yisra El**
died not one.
7 And *Pharaoh* **Paroh** sent, and, behold,
there was not one
of the *cattle* **chattel** of the *Israelites* **Yisra Eliy** dead.
And the heart of *Pharaoh was hardened* **Paroh calloused**,
and he *did* **sent** not *let* the people *go* **away**.
8 And *the LORD* **Yah Veh**
said unto *Moses* **Mosheh** and unto *Aaron* **Aharon**,
Take to you *handfuls* **fists full** of ashes of the furnace,
and let *Moses* **Mosheh** sprinkle it
toward the *heaven* **heavens**
in the *sight* **eyes** of *Pharaoh* **Paroh**.
9 And it shall become small dust
in all the land of *Egypt* **Misrayim**,
and shall be *a boil* **an ulcer**
breaking forth with blains **blossoming pus**
upon *man* **humanity**, and upon *beast* **animal**,
throughout all the land of *Egypt* **Misrayim**.
10 And they took ashes of the furnace,
and stood *before Pharaoh* **at the face of Paroh**;
and *Moses* **Mosheh** sprinkled it *up*
toward *heaven* **the heavens**;
and it became *a boil* **an ulcer**
breaking forth with blains **blossoming pus**
upon *man* **humanity**, and upon *beast* **animal**.
11 And the magicians could not stand
before Moses **at the face of Mosheh**
because of the boils **at the face of the ulcers**;
for the *boil* **ulcer** was upon the magicians,
and upon all the *Egyptians* **Misrayim**.
12 And *the LORD* **Yah Veh**
hardened **calloused** the heart of *Pharaoh* **Paroh**,
and he hearkened not unto them;
as *the LORD* **Yah Veh** had *spoken* **worded**
unto *Moses* **Mosheh**.
13 And *the LORD* **Yah Veh** said unto *Moses* **Mosheh**,
Rise up **Start** early in the morning,
and stand *before Pharaoh* **at the face of Paroh**,
and say unto him,
Thus saith *the LORD God* **Yah Veh Elohim**
of the Hebrews,
Let **Send** my people *go* **away**, that they may serve me.
14 For *I will* **shall** at this time
send all my plagues upon thine heart,
and upon thy servants, and upon thy people;
that thou mayest know that there is none like me
in all the earth.
15 For now I *will stretch out* **shall extend** my hand,
that I may smite thee and thy people with pestilence;
and thou shalt be cut off from the earth.
16 *And in very deed* **But** for this *cause*
have I *raised* **stood** thee *up*,
for to shew in thee **so as to have thee see** my *power* **force**;
and that my name may be *declared* **scribed**
throughout all the earth.
17 As yet exaltest thou thyself against my people,
that thou *wilt* **shalt** not *let* **send** them *go* **away**?
18 Behold, to morrow about this time
I *will* **shall** cause it to rain
a *very grievous* **mighty heavy** hail,
such as hath not been in *Egypt* **Misrayim**
since the foundation **from the day of founding** thereof
even until now.
19 Send therefore now,
and gather **withdraw** thy *cattle* **chattel**,
and all that thou hast in the field;
for upon every *man* **human** and *beast* **animal**
which shall be found in the field,
and shall not be *brought* **gathered** home,
the hail shall *come down* **descend** upon them,
and they shall die.
20 He that *feared* **awed** the word of *the LORD* **Yah Veh**
among the servants of *Pharaoh* **Paroh**
made his servants and his *cattle* **chattel**
flee into the houses:
21 And he that *regarded* **set** not **his heart**
unto the word of *the LORD* **Yah Veh**
left his servants and his *cattle* **chattel** in the field.
22 And *the LORD* **Yah Veh** said unto *Moses* **Mosheh**,
Stretch forth **Extend** thine hand
toward *heaven* **the heavens**,
that there may be hail in all the land of *Egypt* **Misrayim**,
upon *man* **humanity**, and upon *beast* **animal**,
and upon every herb of the field,
throughout **in** the land of *Egypt* **Misrayim**.
23 And *Moses stretched forth* **Mosheh extended** his rod
toward *heaven* **the heavens**:
and *the LORD sent thunder* **Yah Veh gave voice** and hail,
and the fire
ran along upon the ground **came down to earth**;
and *the LORD* **Yah Veh** rained hail
upon the land of *Egypt* **Misrayim**.
24 So there was hail,
and fire *mingled with* **taken midst** the hail,
very grievous **mighty heavy**,
such as there was none like it
in all the land of *Egypt* **Misrayim**
since it became a *nation* **goyim**.
25 And the hail smote
throughout all the land of *Egypt* **Misrayim**
all that was in the field,
both man and beast **from human unto animal**;
and the hail smote every herb of the field,
and brake every tree of the field.
26 Only in the land of Goshen,
where the *children* **sons** of *Israel* **Yisra El** were,
was there no hail.
27 And *Pharaoh* **Paroh** sent,
and called for *Moses* **Mosheh** and *Aaron* **Aharon**,
and said unto them, I have sinned this time:
the LORD **Yah Veh** is *righteous* **just**,
and I and my people are wicked.
28 Intreat *the LORD* **Yah Veh** (for it is *enough* **great**)
that there be no *more*
mighty thunderings **voices of Elohim** and hail;
and I *will let* **shall send** you *go* **away**,
and ye shall *stay no longer* **not add to stay**.
29 And *Moses* **Mosheh** said unto him,
As soon as I am gone out of the city,
I *will* **shall** spread abroad my *hands* **palms**
unto *the LORD* **Yah Veh**;
and the *thunder* **voice** shall cease,
neither shall there be any more hail;
that thou mayest know
how that the earth is *the LORD'S* **Yah Veh's**.
30 But as for thee and thy servants,
I know that ye *will* **shall** not *yet fear* **still awe**
the LORD God **at the face of Yah Veh Elohim**.
31 And the flax and the barley was smitten:
for the barley was *in the ear* **unripened**,
and the flax was *bolled* **budded**.
32 But the wheat and the *rie* **spelt** were not smitten:
for they were not *grown up* **dark**.
33 And *Moses* **Mosheh** went out of the city
from *Pharaoh* **Paroh**,
and spread abroad his *hands* **palms**
unto *the LORD* **Yah Veh**:
and the *thunders* **voices** and hail ceased,
and the rain was not poured upon the earth.
34 And when *Pharaoh* **Paroh** saw that the rain
and the hail and the *thunders* **voices** were ceased,
he *sinned yet more* **added to sin**,
and *hardened* **calloused** his heart, he and his servants.
35 And the heart of *Pharaoh* **Paroh**
was hardened **calloused**,
neither *would* **sent** he *let*
the *children* **sons** of *Israel go* **Yisra El away**;
as *the LORD* **Yah Veh** had *spoken* **worded**
by *Moses* **the hand of Mosheh**.

10 And *the LORD* **Yah Veh** said unto *Moses* **Mosheh**,
Go in unto *Pharaoh* **Paroh**:
for I have *hardened* **calloused** his heart,

and the heart of his servants,
that I might *shew* **set** these my signs
before him **in his midst**:
2 And that thou mayest *tell* **describe**
in the ears of thy son, and of thy son's son,
what *things* I have *wrought* **exploited** in *Egypt* **Misrayim**,
and my signs which I have *done* **set** among them;
that ye may know how that *I am the LORD* **I — Yah Veh**.
3 And *Moses* **Mosheh** and *Aaron* **Aharon**
came in unto *Pharaoh* **Paroh**, and said unto him,
Thus saith *the LORD God* **Yah Veh Elohim**
of the Hebrews,
How long wilt **Until when shalt** thou refuse
to humble thyself *before me* **at my face**?
let **send** my people *go* **away**, that they may serve me.
4 *Else* **Because**,
if thou refuse to *let* **send** my people *go* **away**, behold,
to morrow *will* **shall** I bring the locusts
into thy *coast* **borders**:
5 And they shall cover the *face* **eye** of the earth,
that one cannot be able to see the earth:
and they shall eat
the *residue* **remainder** of that which is escaped,
which *remaineth* **surviveth** unto you from the hail,
and shall eat every tree
which *groweth* **sprouteth** for you out of the field:
6 And they shall fill thy houses,
and the houses of all thy servants,
and the houses of all the *Egyptians* **Misrayim**;
which neither thy fathers, nor thy fathers' fathers
have seen,
since the day that they were upon the *earth* **soil**
unto this day.
And he turned *himself* **his face**,
and went out from *Pharaoh* **Paroh**.
7 And *Pharaoh's* **Paroh's** servants said unto him,
How long shall this man be a snare unto us?
let **send** the men *go* **away**,
that they may serve *the LORD* **Yah Veh** their *God* **Elohim**:
knowest thou not yet that *Egypt* **Misrayim** is destroyed?
8 And *Moses* **Mosheh** and *Aaron* **Aharon**
were *brought again* **returned** unto *Pharaoh* **Paroh**:
and he said unto them,
Go, serve *the LORD* **Yah Veh** your *God* **Elohim**:
but who are they that shall go?
9 And *Moses* **Mosheh** said,
We *will* **shall** go with our *young* **lads**
and with our *old* **aged**,
with our sons and with our daughters,
with our flocks and with our *herds will* **oxen shall** we go;
for *we must hold a feast* **a celebration**
unto *the LORD* **Yah Veh**.
10 And he said unto them,
Let *the LORD* **Yah Veh** be so with you,
as I *will let* **shall send** you *go* **away**,
and your *little ones* **toddlers**:
look to it **see**; for evil is *before* you **at thy face**.
11 Not so: go now ye *that are men* **mighty**,
and serve *the LORD* **Yah Veh**; for that ye did *desire* **seek**.
And they were *driven out* **expelled**
from *Pharaoh's presence* **Paroh's face**.
12 And *the LORD* **Yah Veh** said unto *Moses* **Mosheh**,
Stretch out **Extend** thine hand
over the land of *Egypt* **Misrayim** for the locusts,
that they may *come up* **ascend**
upon the land of *Egypt* **Misrayim**,
and eat every herb of the land,
even all that *the hail hath left* **survived the hail**.
13 And *Moses stretched forth* **Mosheh extended** his rod
over the land of *Egypt* **Misrayim**,
and *the LORD* **Yah Veh**
brought **drove** an east wind upon the land
all that day, and all *that* night;
and when it was morning,
the east wind *brought* **bore** the locusts.
14 And the locusts
went up **ascended** over all the land of *Egypt* **Misrayim**,
and rested in all the *coasts* **borders** of *Egypt* **Misrayim**:
very grievous **mighty heavy** *were they;*
before **facing** them there were no such locusts as they,
neither after them shall be such.
15 For they covered the *face* **eye** of the whole *earth* **land**,
so that the land was darkened;
and they did eat every herb of the land,
and all the fruit of the trees
which *the hail had left* **remained of the hail**:
and there remained not any green *thing* in the trees,
or in the herbs of the field,
through all the land of *Egypt* **Misrayim**.
16 Then *Pharaoh* **Paroh**
called for *Moses* **Mosheh** and *Aaron* **Aharon** in haste;
and he said, I have sinned
against *the LORD* **Yah Veh** your *God* **Elohim**,
and against you.
17 Now therefore *forgive* **bear**, I *pray* **beseech** thee,
my sin only this *once* **one time**,
and intreat *the LORD* **Yah Veh** your *God* **Elohim**,
that he may *take away* **turn aside** from me
this death only.
18 And he went out from *Pharaoh* **Paroh**,
and intreated *the LORD* **Yah Veh**.
19 And *the LORD* **Yah Veh**
turned a mighty strong *west* **seaward** wind,
which *took away* **bore** the locusts,
and *cast* **blast** them into the *Red* **Reed** sea;
there *remained* **survived** not one locust
in all the *coasts* **borders** of *Egypt* **Misrayim**.
20 But *the LORD* **Yah Veh**
hardened Pharaoh's **calloused Paroh's** heart,
so that he *would* **sent** not *let*
the *children* **sons** of *Israel go* **Yisra El away**.
21 And *the LORD* **Yah Veh** said unto *Moses* **Mosheh**,
Stretch out **Extend** thine hand toward *heaven* **the heavens**,
that there may be darkness
over the land of *Egypt* **Misrayim**,
even darkness which may be felt.
22 And *Moses stretched forth* **Mosheh extended** his hand
toward *heaven* **the heavens**;
and there was a *thick* **darkened** darkness
in all the land of *Egypt* **Misrayim** three days:
23 They saw not *one another* **man to brother**,
neither rose any from his place for three days:
but all the *children* **sons** of *Israel* **Yisra El**
had light in their *dwellings* **settlements**.
24 And *Pharaoh* **Paroh** called unto *Moses* **Mosheh**,
and said, Go ye, serve *the LORD* **Yah Veh**;
only let your flocks and your *herds* **oxen** be stayed:
let your *little ones* **toddlers** also go with you.
25 And *Moses* **Mosheh** said,
Thou must give *us* **into our hands**
also sacrifices and *burnt offerings* **holocausts**,
that we may *sacrifice* **work**
unto *the LORD* **Yah Veh** our *God* **Elohim**.
26 Our *cattle* **chattel** also shall go with us;
there shall not an hoof *be left* **survive** behind;
for thereof must we take
to serve *the LORD* **Yah Veh** our *God* **Elohim**;
and we know not
with what we must serve *the LORD* **Yah Veh**,
until we come thither.
27 But *the LORD* **Yah Veh**
hardened Pharaoh's **calloused Paroh's** heart
and he *would* **willed** not *let* **to send** them *go* **away**.
28 And *Pharaoh* **Paroh** said unto him,
Get thee **Go thou** from me,
take heed to **guard** thyself, see my face *no more* **not again**;
for in that day thou seest my face thou shalt die.
29 And *Moses* **Mosheh** said,
Thou hast *spoken well* **worded thus**,
I will **shall** see thy face again no more.
11 And *the LORD* **Yah Veh** said unto *Moses* **Mosheh**,
Yet *will* **shall** I bring one plague *more*
upon *Pharaoh* **Paroh**,
and upon *Egypt* **Misrayim**;
afterwards he *will let* **shall send** you *go* **away** hence:
when he shall *let* **send** you *go* **away**,
in expelling,
he shall *surely thrust* **expel** you *out hence altogether* **fully**.
2 *Speak* **Word** now in the ears of the people,
and let every man *borrow* **ask** of his *neighbour* **friend**,

and every woman of her *neighbour* **friend**,
jewels **instruments** of silver
and *jewels* **instruments** of gold.
3 And *the LORD* **Yah Veh**
gave **granted** the people *favour* **charism**
in the *sight* **eyes** of the *Egyptians* **Misrayim**.
Moreover the man *Moses* **Mosheh**
was *very* **mighty** great in the land of *Egypt* **Misrayim**,
in the *sight* **eyes** of *Pharaoh's* **Paroh's** servants,
and in the *sight* **eyes** of the people.
4 And *Moses* **Mosheh** said, Thus saith *the LORD* **Yah Veh**,
About midnight
will **shall** I go out into the midst of *Egypt* **Misrayim**:
5 And all the firstborn in the land of *Egypt* **Misrayim**
shall die,
from the firstborn of *Pharaoh* **Paroh**
that sitteth upon his throne,
even unto the firstborn of the *maidservant* **maid**
that is behind the *mill* **millstones**;
and all the firstborn of *beasts* **animals**.
6 And there shall be a great cry
throughout all the land of *Egypt* **Misrayim**,
such as there *was* **became** none like it,
nor shall be like it *any more* **again**.
7 But against any of the *children* **sons** of *Israel* **Yisra El**
shall not a dog *move* **point** his tongue,
against man or *beast* **animal**:
that ye may know how that *the LORD* **Yah Veh**
doth put a difference **distinguisheth**
between *the Egyptians* **Misrayim**
and **between** *Israel* **Yisra El**.
8 And all these thy servants
shall *come down* **descend** unto me,
and *bow down themselves* **prostrate** unto me, saying,
Get thee out,
and all the people *that follow thee* **at thy feet**:
and after that I *will* **shall** go out.
And he went out from *Pharaoh* **Paroh**
in a *great anger* **fuming wrath**.
9 And *the LORD* **Yah Veh** said unto *Moses* **Mosheh**,
Pharaoh **Paroh** shall not hearken unto you;
that my *wonders* **omens** may *be multiplied* **abound**
in the land of *Egypt* **Misrayim**.
10 And *Moses* **Mosheh** and *Aaron* **Aharon**
did **worked** all these *wonders* **omens**
before Pharaoh **at the face of Paroh**:
and *the LORD* **Yah Veh**
hardened Pharaoh's **calloused Paroh's** heart,
so that he *would* **should** not *let* **send**
the *children* **sons** of *Israel go* **Yisra El away** out of his land.

PASACH

12 And *the LORD spake* **Yah Veh said**
unto *Moses* **Mosheh** and *Aaron* **Aharon**
in the land of *Egypt* **Misrayim**, saying,
2 This month shall be unto you
the *beginning* **head** of months:
it shall be the first month of the year to you.
3 *Speak* **Word** ye
unto all the *congregation* **witness** of *Israel* **Yisra El**,
saying, In the tenth *day* of this month
they shall take to them every man a lamb,
according to the house of their fathers,
a lamb for an house:
4 And if the household be *too little* **diminished**
for the lamb,
let him and his *neighbour* **fellow tabernacler**
next unto his house
take it according to the *number* **evaluation** of the souls;
every man according to **the food of** his *eating* **mouth**
shall *make your count* **ye estimate** for the lamb.
5 Your lamb shall be *without blemish* **integrious**,
a *male of the first year* **yearling son**:
ye shall take *it* out from the *sheep* **lambs**,
or from the goats:
6 And ye shall *keep* **guard** it *up*
until the fourteenth day of the same month:
and the whole *assembly* **congregation**
of the *congregation* **witness** of *Israel* **Yisra El**
shall *kill* **slaughter** it *in the evening* **between evenings**.
7 And *they* shall take of the blood,
and *strike* **give** it on the two side posts
and on the *upper door post* **lintel** of the houses,
wherein they shall eat it.
8 And they shall eat the flesh in that night,
roast with fire, and *unleavened bread* **matsah**;
and with *bitter herbs* **bitters** they shall eat it.
9 Eat not of it raw,
nor *sodden at all* **in stewing, stewed** with water,
but roast with fire;
his head with his legs,
and with the *purtenance* **inwards** thereof.
10 And ye shall let *nothing* **naught** of it
remain until the morning;
and that which remaineth of it until the morning
ye shall burn with fire.
11 And thus shall ye eat it;
with your loins girded, your shoes on your feet,
and your staff in your hand; and ye shall eat it in haste:
it is *the LORD'S passover* **Yah Veh's pasach**.
12 For I *will* **shall** pass through
the land of *Egypt* **Misrayim** this night,
and *will* **shall** smite all the firstborn
in the land of *Egypt* **Misrayim**,
both *man* **human** and *beast* **animal**;
and against all the *gods* **elohim** of *Egypt* **Misrayim**
I *will execute* **shall work** judgment:
I am the LORD **I — Yah Veh**.
13 And the blood shall be to you
for a *token* **sign** upon the houses where ye are:
and when I see the blood, I *will pass* **shall leap** over you,
and the plague shall not be upon you
to *destroy* **ruin** you,
when I smite the land of *Egypt* **Misrayim**.

MEMORIAL DAY

14 And this day shall be unto you for a memorial;
and ye shall *keep it* **celebrate** a *feast* **celebration**
unto *the LORD* **Yah Veh** throughout your generations;
ye shall *keep it a feast* **celebrate**
by an *ordinance for ever* **eternal statute**.
15 Seven days shall ye eat *unleavened bread* **matsah**;
even **surely** the first day
ye shall *put away leaven* **shabbathize yeast**
out of your houses:
for whosoever eateth *leavened bread* **fermentation**
from the first day until the seventh day,
that soul shall be cut off from *Israel* **Yisra El**.
16 And in the first day there shall be an holy convocation,
and in the seventh day
there shall be an holy convocation to you;
no *manner of* work shall be *done* in them,
save **only** that which every *man* **soul** must eat,
that only may be *done* **worked** of you.
17 And ye shall *observe* **guard**
the *feast of unleavened bread* **matsah**;
for in this selfsame day have I brought your *armies* **hosts**
out of the land of *Egypt* **Misrayim**:
therefore shall ye *observe* **guard** this day
in your generations
by an *ordinance for ever* **eternal statute**.
18 In the first *month*,
on the fourteenth day of the month at even,
ye shall eat *unleavened bread* **matsah**,
until the one and twentieth day of the month at even.
19 Seven days
shall there be no *leaven* **yeast** found in your houses:
for whosoever eateth that which is *leavened* **fermented**,
even that soul shall be cut off
from the *congregation* **witness** of *Israel* **Yisra El**,
whether he be a *stranger* **sojourner**,
or *born* **native** in the land.
20 Ye shall eat *nothing leavened* **naught fermented**;
in all your *habitations* **settlements**
shall ye eat *unleavened bread* **matsah**.
21 Then *Moses* **Mosheh**
called for all the elders of *Israel* **Yisra El**,
and said unto them,
Draw out and take you *a lamb* **of the flock**
according to your families,
and *kill* **slaughter** the *passover* **pasach**.
22 And ye shall take a *bunch* **bundle** of hyssop,

and dip it in the blood that is in the bason,
and *strike* **touch** the lintel and the two side posts
with the blood that is in the bason;
and *none* **no man** of you shall go out
at the *door* **portal** of his house until the morning.
23 For *the LORD will* **Yah Veh shall** pass through
to smite the *Egyptians* **Misrayim**;
and when he seeth the blood upon the lintel,
and on the two side posts,
the LORD **Yah Veh**
will pass **shall leap** over the *door* **portal**,
and *will* **shall** not *suffer* **give** the *destroyer* **ruiner**
to come in unto your houses to smite you.
24 And ye shall *observe* **guard** this *thing* **word**
for an *ordinance* **eternal statute**
to thee and to thy sons *for ever.*
25 And it shall *come to pass* **become**,
when ye be come to the land
which *the LORD will* **Yah Veh shall** give you,
according as he hath *promised* **worded**,
that ye shall *keep* **guard** this service.
26 And it shall *come to pass* **become**,
when your *children* **sons** shall say unto you,
What mean ye by this service?
27 That ye shall say,
It is the sacrifice
of *the LORD'S passover* **Yah Veh's pasach**,
who *passed* **leaped** over the houses
of the *children* **sons** of *Israel* **Yisra El** in *Egypt* **Misrayim**,
when he smote the *Egyptians* **Misrayim**,
and *delivered* **rescued** our houses.
And the people bowed *the head*
and *worshipped* **prostrated**.
28 And the *children* **sons** of *Israel* **Yisra El** went away,
and *did* **worked**
as *the LORD* **Yah Veh** had *commanded* **misvahed**
Moses **Mosheh** and *Aaron* **Aharon**,
so *did* **worked** they.
29 And it *came to pass* **became**, that at midnight
the LORD **Yah Veh** smote all the firstborn
in the land of *Egypt* **Misrayim**,
from the firstborn of *Pharaoh* **Paroh**
that sat on his throne
unto the firstborn of the captive
that was in the *dungeon* **well**;
and all the firstborn of *cattle* **animals**.
30 And *Pharaoh* **Paroh** rose up in the night,
he, and all his servants, and all the *Egyptians* **Misrayim**;
and there was a great cry in *Egypt* **Misrayim**;
for there was not a house
where there was not one *dead* **who died**.
31 And he called for *Moses* **Mosheh** and *Aaron* **Aharon**
by night, and said,
Rise up, and get you forth from among my people,
both ye and the *children* **sons** of *Israel* **Yisra El**;
and go, serve *the LORD* **Yah Veh**,
as ye have *said* **worded**.
32 Also take your flocks and your *herds* **oxen**,
as ye have *said* **worded**, and be gone; and bless me also.
33 And the *Egyptians* **Misrayim**
were urgent **prevailed** upon the people,
that they might send them out of the land in haste;
for they said, We be *all dead men* **about to die**.
34 And the people *took* **bore** their dough
before it was *leavened* **fermented**,
their *kneadingtroughs* **doughboards**
being bound up in their clothes upon their shoulders.
35 And the *children* **sons** of *Israel* **Yisra El**
did **worked** according to the word of *Moses* **Mosheh**;
and they *borrowed* **asked** of the *Egyptians* **Misrayim**
jewels **instruments** of silver,
and *jewels* **instruments** of gold,
and *raiment* **clothes**:
36 And *the LORD* **Yah Veh**
gave **granted** the people *favour* **charism**
in the *sight* **eyes** of the *Egyptians* **Misrayim**,
so that they lent unto them such things as they required.
And they spoiled the Egyptians
— asking and stripping the Misrayim.
37 And the *children* **sons** of *Israel* **Yisra El**
journeyed **pulled stakes** from Rameses
to *Succoth* **Sukkoth/Brush Arbors**,
about six hundred thousand on foot
that were *men* **mighty**,
beside children **apart from toddlers**.
38 And a *mixed multitude* **great rabble**
went up **ascended** also with them;
and flocks, and *herds* **oxen**,
even very much cattle **mighty heavy chattel**.
39 And they baked
unleavened cakes **matsah ashcakes** of the dough
which they brought forth out of *Egypt* **Misrayim**,
for it was not *leavened* **fermented**;
because they were *thrust* **expelled** out of *Egypt* **Misrayim**,
and could not *tarry* **linger**,
neither had they *prepared* **worked** for themselves
any *victual* **hunt**.
40 *Now* the *sojourning* **settlements**
of the *children* **sons** of *Israel* **Yisra El**,
who *dwelt* **settled** in *Egypt* **Misrayim**,
was four hundred **years** and thirty years.
41 And it *came to pass* **became**,
at the end of the four hundred **years** and thirty years,
even the selfsame day it *came to pass* **became**,
that all the hosts of *the LORD* **Yah Veh**
went out from the land of *Egypt* **Misrayim**.
42 It is a night to be *much observed* **guarded**
unto *the LORD* **Yah Veh**
for bringing them out from the land of *Egypt* **Misrayim**:
this is that night of *the LORD* **Yah Veh**
to be *observed* **guarded**
of all the *children* **sons** of *Israel* **Yisra El**
in their generations.
43 And *the LORD* **Yah Veh**
said unto *Moses* **Mosheh** and *Aaron* **Aharon**,
This is the *ordinance* **statute** of the *passover* **pasach**:
There shall no **son of a** stranger eat thereof:
44 But every man's servant
that is *bought for money* **a chattel of silver**,
when thou hast circumcised him,
then shall he eat thereof.
45 A *foreigner* **settler** and an *hired servant* **hireling**
shall not eat thereof.
46 In one house shall it be eaten;
thou shalt not carry forth ought of the flesh
abroad out of the house;
neither shall ye break a bone thereof.
47 All the *congregation* **witness** of *Israel* **Yisra El**
shall *keep* **work** it.
48 And when a *stranger* **sojourner** shall sojourn with thee,
and *will keep* **shall work** the *passover* **pasach**
to *the LORD* **Yah Veh**,
let all his males be circumcised,
and then let him *come near* **approach** and *keep* **work** it;
and he shall be as *one that is born* **a native** in the land:
for no uncircumcised *person* shall eat thereof.
49 One *law* **torah** shall be
to *him that is homeborn* **the native**,
and unto the *stranger* **sojourner**
that sojourneth among you.
50 Thus *did* **worked** all the *children* **sons** of *Israel* **Yisra El**;
as *the LORD commanded* **Yah Veh misvahed**
Moses **Mosheh** and *Aaron* **Aharon**, so *did* **worked** they.
51 And it *came to pass* **became** the selfsame day,
that *the LORD* **Yah Veh**
did bring the *children* **sons** of *Israel* **Yisra El**
out of the land of *Egypt* **Misrayim** by their *armies* **hosts**.

HALLOWING THE FIRSTBORN

13 And *the LORD spake* **Yah Veh worded**
unto *Moses* **Mosheh**, saying,
2 *Sanctify* **Hallow** unto me all the firstborn,
whatsoever openeth **every burster of** the womb
among the *children* **sons** of *Israel* **Yisra El**,
both of man **among human** and *of beast* **among animal**:
it is mine.
3 And *Moses* **Mosheh** said unto the people,
Remember this day,
in which ye came out from *Egypt* **Misrayim**,
out of the house of *bondage* **servants**;
for by strength of hand

the LORD **Yah Veh** brought you out *from this place* **thus**:
there shall no *leavened bread* **fermentation** be eaten.
4 This day came ye out in the month Abib.
5 And it shall be
when *the LORD* **Yah Veh** shall bring thee
into the land of the *Canaanites* **Kenaaniy**,
and the *Hittites* **Hethiy**, and the *Amorites* **Emoriy**,
and the *Hivites* **Hivviy**, and the *Jebusites* **Yebusiy**,
which he *sware* **oathed** unto thy fathers to give thee,
a land flowing with milk and honey,
that thou shalt *keep* **serve** this service in this month.
6 Seven days thou shalt eat *unleavened bread* **matsah**,
and in the seventh day
shall be a *feast* **celebration** to *the LORD* **Yah Veh**.
7 *Unleavened bread* **Matsah** shall be eaten seven days;
and there shall no *leavened bread* **fermentation**
be seen with thee,
neither shall there be *leaven* **yeast** seen with thee
in all thy *quarters* **borders**.
8 And thou shalt *shew* **tell** thy son in that day, saying,
This is done because of that
which the *LORD did* **Yah Veh worked** unto me
when I came forth out of *Egypt* **Misrayim**.
9 And it shall be for a sign unto thee upon thine hand,
and for a memorial between thine eyes,
that *the LORD'S law* **Yah Veh's torah**
may be in thy mouth:
for with a strong hand hath *the LORD* **Yah Veh**
brought thee out of *Egypt* **Misrayim**.
10 Thou shalt therefore *keep* **guard** this *ordinance* **statute**
in his season from *year* **day** to *year* **day**.
11 And it shall be
when *the LORD* **Yah Veh** shall bring thee
into the land of the *Canaanites* **Kenaaniy**,
as he *sware* **oathed** unto thee and to thy fathers,
and shall give it thee,
12 That thou shalt *set apart* **pass** unto *the LORD* **Yah Veh**
all that openeth **every burster of** the matrix,
and every *firstling* **fetus**
that *cometh* **bursteth** of *a beast* **an animal**
which *thou hast* **became thee**;
the males shall be *the LORD'S* **Yah Veh's**.
13 And every *firstling* **burster** of *an ass* **a he burro**
thou shalt redeem with a lamb;
and if thou *wilt* **shalt** not redeem it,
then thou shalt break his neck:
and all the firstborn of *man* **humanity**
among thy *children* **sons** shalt thou redeem.
14 And it shall be
when thy son asketh thee *in time to come* **to morrow**,
saying, What is this?
that thou shalt say unto him, By strength of hand
the LORD **Yah Veh** brought us out from *Egypt* **Misrayim**,
from the house of *bondage* **servants**:
15 And it *came to pass* **became**,
when *Pharaoh* **Paroh**
would hardly let **calloused from sending** us *go* **away**,
that *the LORD slew* **Yah Veh slaughtered** all the firstborn
in the land of *Egypt* **Misrayim**,
both the firstborn of *man* **human**,
and the firstborn of *beast* **animal**:
therefore I sacrifice to *the LORD* **Yah Veh**
all that openeth **every burster of** the matrix, being males;
but all the firstborn of my *children* **sons** I redeem.
16 And it shall be for a *token* **sign** upon thine hand,
and for *frontlets* **phylacteries** between thine eyes:
for by strength of hand
the LORD **Yah Veh** brought us forth
out of *Egypt* **Misrayim**.
17 And it *came to pass* **became**,
when *Pharaoh* **Paroh** had *let* **sent** the people *go* **away**,
that *God* **Elohim** led them not *through* the way
of the land of the *Philistines* **Peleshethiym**,
although **because** that was near;
for God **but because Elohim** said,
Lest peradventure the people *repent* **sigh**
when they see war,
and they return to *Egypt* **Misrayim**:
18 But *God led* **Elohim turned** the people *about* **around**,
through the way of the wilderness of the *Red* **Reed** sea:
and the *children* **sons** of *Israel* **Yisra El**
went up harnessed **ascended in ranks of five**
out of the land of *Egypt* **Misrayim**.
19 And *Moses* **Mosheh**
took the bones of *Joseph* **Yoseph** with him:
for **in oathing,** he had *straitly sworn* **oathed**
the *children* **sons** of *Israel* **Yisra El**, saying,
God will surely **In visiting, Elohim shall** visit you;
and ye shall *carry up* **ascend** my bones
away hence with you.
20 And they *took their journey* **pulled stakes**
from *Succoth* **Sukkoth/Brush Arbors**,
and encamped in Etham,
in the *edge* **end** of the wilderness.
21 And *the LORD* **Yah Veh** went *before them* **at their face**
by day in a pillar of a cloud, to lead them the way;
and by night in a pillar of fire, to give them light;
to go by day and night:
22 He *took* **departed** not *away*
the pillar of the cloud by day,
nor the pillar of fire by night,
from *before* **the face of** the people.

PAROH PURSUES THE SONS OF YISRA EL

14 And *the LORD spake* **Yah Veh worded**
unto *Moses* **Mosheh**, saying,
2 *Speak* **Word** unto the *children* **sons** of *Israel* **Yisra El**,
that they turn and encamp
before Pihahiroth **at the face of Pi Ha Hiroth**,
between Migdol and the sea,
over against Baalzephon **at the face of Baal Sephon**:
before it shall ye encamp by the sea.
3 For *Pharaoh will* **Paroh shall** say
of the *children* **sons** of *Israel* **Yisra El**,
They are entangled in the land,
the wilderness hath shut them in.
4 And I *will harden Pharaoh's* **shall callous Paroh's** heart,
that he shall *follow* **pursue** after them;
and I *will* **shall** be honoured *upon Pharaoh* **through Paroh**,
and *upon* **through** all his *host* **valiant**;
that the *Egyptians* **Misrayim** may know
that *I am the LORD* **I — Yah Veh**.
And they *did* **worked** so.
5 And it was told the *king* **sovereign** of *Egypt* **Misrayim**
that the people fled:
and the heart of *Pharaoh* **Paroh** and of his servants
was turned against the people,
and they said, Why have we *done* **worked** this,
that we have *let Israel go* **sent Yisra El away**
from serving us?
6 And he *made ready* **bound** his chariot,
and took his people with him:
7 And he took six hundred chosen chariots,
and all the chariots of *Egypt* **Misrayim**,
and *captains* **tertiaries** over every one of them.
8 And *the LORD* **Yah Veh**
hardened **calloused** the heart of *Pharaoh* **Paroh**
king **sovereign** of *Egypt* **Misrayim**,
and he pursued after the *children* **sons** of *Israel* **Yisra El**:
and the *children* **sons** of *Israel* **Yisra El**
went out with *an high* **lifted** hand.
9 But the *Egyptians* **Misrayim** pursued after them,
all the horses and chariots of *Pharaoh* **Paroh**,
and his *horsemen* **cavalry**, and his *army* **valiant**,
and overtook them encamping by the sea,
beside *Pihahiroth* **Pi Ha Hiroth**,
before Baalzephon **at the face of Baal Sephon**.
10 And when *Pharaoh drew nigh* **Paroh approached**,
the *children* **sons** of *Israel* **Yisra El** lifted up their eyes,
and, behold,
the *Egyptians marched* **Misrayim pulled stakes** after them;
and they *were sore afraid* **mightily awed**:
and the *children* **sons** of *Israel* **Yisra El**
cried out unto *the LORD* **Yah Veh**.
11 And they said unto *Moses* **Mosheh**,
Because there were no *graves* **tombs** in *Egypt* **Misrayim**,
hast thou taken us away to die in the wilderness?
wherefore hast thou *dealt* **worked** thus with us,
to carry us forth out of *Egypt* **Misrayim**?
12 Is not this the word
that we *did tell* **worded** thee in *Egypt* **Misrayim**,

saying, *Let us alone* **Cease**!,
that we may serve the *Egyptians* **Misrayim**?
For it had been better for us
to serve the *Egyptians* **Misrayim**,
than that we should die in the wilderness.
13 And *Moses* **Mosheh** said unto the people,
Fear **Awe** ye not, stand still,
and see the salvation of *the LORD* **Yah Veh**,
which he *will shew* **shall work** to you to day:
for the *Egyptians* **Misrayim** whom ye have seen to day,
ye shall see them again no more *for ever* **eternally**.
14 *The LORD* **Yah Veh** shall fight for you,
and ye shall *hold your peace* **hush**.
15 And *the LORD* **Yah Veh** said unto *Moses* **Mosheh**,
Wherefore criest thou unto me?
speak **word** unto the *children* **sons** of *Israel* **Yisra El**,
that they *go forward* **pull stakes**:
16 But lift thou up thy rod,
and *stretch out* **extend** thine hand over the sea,
and *divide* **split** it:
and the *children* **sons** of *Israel* **Yisra El**
shall go on dry *ground* through the midst of the sea.
17 And I, behold,
I *will harden* **shall callous** the hearts
of the *Egyptians* **Misrayim**,
and they shall follow them:
and I *will get me honour* **shall be honoured**
upon Pharaoh **through Paroh**,
and *upon* **through** all his *host* **valiant**,
upon **through** his chariots,
and *upon* **through** his *horsemen* **cavalry**.
18 And the *Egyptians* **Misrayim** shall know
that *I am the LORD* **I — Yah Veh**,
when I *have gotten me honour* **shall be honoured**
upon Pharaoh **through Paroh**, *upon* **through** his chariots,
and *upon* **through** his *horsemen* **cavalry**.
19 And the angel of *God* **Elohim**,
which went
before **from the face of** the camp of *Israel* **Yisra El**,
removed **pulled stakes** and went behind them;
and the pillar of the cloud *went* **pulled stakes**
from *before* their face, and stood behind them:
20 And it came
between the camp of the *Egyptians* **Misrayim**
and **between** the camp of *Israel* **Yisra El**;
and it was a cloud and darkness to them,
but it *gave light* **illuminated** by night to these:
so that the one
came **approached** not *near* the other all the night.
21 And *Moses* **Mosheh**
stretched out **extended** his hand over the sea;
and *the LORD* **Yah Veh** caused the sea to go back
by a strong east wind all that night,
and *made* **set** the sea *dry land* **parched**,
and the waters were *divided* **split**.
22 And the *children* **sons** of *Israel* **Yisra El**
went into the midst of the sea upon the dry *ground*:
and the waters were a wall unto them
on their right *hand*, and on their left.
23 And the *Egyptians* **Misrayim** pursued,
and went in after them to the midst of the sea,
even all *Pharaoh's* **Paroh's** horses,
his chariots, and his *horsemen* **cavalry**.
24 And it *came to pass* **became**, that in the morning watch
the LORD **Yah Veh** looked
unto the *host* **camp** of the *Egyptians* **Misrayim**
through the pillar of fire and of the cloud,
and *troubled* **agitated**
the *host* **camp** of the *Egyptians* **Misrayim**,
25 And *took off* **turned aside** their chariot wheels,
that they drave them *heavily* **with heaviness**:
so that the *Egyptians* **Misrayim** said,
Let us flee from the face of *Israel* **Yisra El**;
for *the LORD* **Yah Veh** fighteth for them
against the *Egyptians* **Misrayim**.
26 And *the LORD* **Yah Veh** said unto *Moses* **Mosheh**,
Stretch out **Extend** thine hand over the sea,
that the waters may *come again* **return**
upon the *Egyptians* **Misrayim**,
upon their chariots, and upon their *horsemen* **cavalry**.
27 And *Moses* **Mosheh**
stretched forth **extended** his hand over the sea,
and the sea returned *to his strength* **perrenial**
when **at the face of** the morning *appeared*;
and the *Egyptians* **Misrayim** fled
against **from confronting** it;
and *the LORD* **Yah Veh**
overthrew **shook off** the *Egyptians* **Misrayim**
in the midst of the sea.
28 And the waters returned,
and covered the chariots, and the *horsemen* **cavalry**,
and all the *host* **valiant** of *Pharaoh* **Paroh**
that came into the sea after them;
there *remained* **survived** not *so much as* **even** one of them.
29 But the *children* **sons** of *Israel* **Yisra El**
walked upon dry *land* in the midst of the sea;
and the waters were a wall unto them
on their right *hand*, and on their left.
30 Thus *the LORD* **Yah Veh** saved Israel that day
out of the hand of the *Egyptians* **Misrayim**;
and *Israel* **Yisra El** saw the *Egyptians* **Misrayim**
dead **who died** upon the sea *shore* **edge**.
31 And *Israel* **Yisra El** saw that great *work* **hand**
which *the LORD did* **Yah Veh worked**
upon the *Egyptians* **Misrayim**:
and the people *feared the LORD* **awed Yah Veh**,
and *believed the LORD* **trusted Yah Veh**,
and his servant *Moses* **Mosheh**.

THE SONG OF MOSHEH AND THE SONS OF YISRA EL

15 Then sang *Moses* **Mosheh**
and the *children* **sons** of *Israel* **Yisra El**
this song unto *the LORD* **Yah Veh**, and *spake* **said**, saying,
I *will* **shall** sing unto *the LORD* **Yah Veh**,
for he hath triumphed gloriously:
the horse and his rider
hath he *thrown* **hurled** into the sea.
2 *The LORD* **Yah** is my strength and song,
and he is become my salvation:
he is my *God* **El**,
and I *will prepare* **shall rest** him *an* **in his** habitation;
my father's *God* **Elohim**, and I *will* **shall** exalt him.
3 *The LORD* **Yah Veh** is a man of war:
the LORD **Yah Veh** is his name.
4 *Pharaoh's* **Paroh's** chariots and his *host* **valiant**
hath he *cast* **poured** into the sea:
his chosen *captains* **tertiaries** also
are drowned in the *Red* **Reed** sea.
5 The *depths* **abysses** have covered them:
they *sank* **descended** into the *bottom* **deep** as a stone.
6 Thy right *hand*, O *LORD* **Yah Veh**,
is become *glorious* **mighty** in *power* **force**:
thy right *hand*, O *LORD* **Yah Veh**,
hath *dashed in pieces* **disintegrated** the enemy.
7 And in the *greatness* **abundance**
of *thine excellency* **thy pomp**
thou hast *overthrown* **demolished** them
that rose *up against thee*:
thou sentest forth thy *wrath* **fuming**,
which consumed them as stubble.
8 And with the *blast* **spirit/wind** of thy nostrils
the waters were *gathered together* **heaped**,
the *floods* **flows** stood upright as an heap,
and the *depths* **abysses** were *congealed* **curdled**
in the heart of the sea.
9 The enemy said, I *will* **shall** pursue, I *will* **shall** overtake,
I *will divide* **shall allot** the *spoil* **loot**;
my *lust* **soul** shall be *satisfied upon* **filled of** them;
I *will* **shall** draw my sword,
my hand shall *destroy* **dispossess** them.
10 Thou didst *blow* **puff** with thy *wind* **spirit/wind**,
the sea covered them:
they sank as lead in the mighty waters.
11 Who is like unto thee, O *LORD* **Yah Veh**,
among the *gods* **el**?
who is like thee, *glorious* **mighty** in holiness,
fearful **awesome** in *praises* **halals**,
doing wonders **working marvels**?
12 Thou *stretchedst out* **extendedst** thy right *hand*,
the earth swallowed them.
13 Thou in thy mercy

hast led forth the people which thou hast redeemed:
thou hast guided them in thy strength
unto thy holy habitation **of rest**.
14 The people shall hear, and *be afraid* **quiver**:
sorrow **pangs** shall take hold on
the inhabitants of Palestina **them who settled Peleshesh**.
15 Then the *dukes* **chiliarchs** of Edom
shall be *amazed* **terrified**;
the mighty *men* of Moab,
trembling shall take hold upon them;
all *the inhabitants of Canaan* **they who settled Kenaan**
shall melt away.
16 *Fear* **Terror** and *dread* **fear** shall fall upon them;
by the greatness of thine arm
they shall be as still as a stone;
till thy people pass over, O *LORD* **Yah Veh**,
till the people pass over,
which thou hast *purchased* **chatteled**.
17 Thou shalt bring them in,
and plant them in the mountain of thine inheritance,
in the *place* **establishment**, O *LORD* **Yah Veh**,
which thou hast made for thee to *dwell* **settle** in,
in the *Sanctuary* **Holies**, O *LORD* **Adonay**,
which thy hands have established.
18 *The LORD* **Yah Veh** shall reign
for ever **eternally** and *ever* **eternally**.
19 For the horse of *Pharaoh* **Paroh**
went in with his chariots
and with his *horsemen* **cavalry** into the sea,
and *the LORD* **Yah Veh**
brought again **returned** the waters of the sea upon them;
but the *children* **sons** of *Israel* **Yisra El**
went on dry *land* in the midst of the sea.

THE SONG OF MIRYAM

20 And *Miriam* **Miryam** the prophetess,
the sister of *Aaron* **Aharon**,
took a *timbrel* **tambourine** in her hand;
and all the women went out after her
with *timbrels* **tambourines** and with **round** dances.
21 And *Miriam* **Miryam** answered them,
Sing ye to *the LORD* **Yah Veh**,
for he hath triumphed gloriously;
the horse and his rider
hath he *thrown* **hurled** into the sea.

WATERS OF MARAH

22 So *Moses brought Israel* **Mosheh had Yisra El pull stakes**
from the *Red* **Reed** sea,
and they went out into the wilderness of Shur;
and they went three days in the wilderness,
and found no water.
23 And when they came to Marah,
they could not drink of the waters of Marah,
for they were bitter:
therefore the name of it was called Marah.
24 And the people murmured against *Moses* **Mosheh**,
saying, What shall we drink?
25 And he cried unto *the LORD* **Yah Veh**;
and *the LORD shewed him* **Yah Veh pointed out** a tree,
which when he had cast into the waters,
the waters were *made sweet* **sweetened**:
there he *made* **set** for them
a statute and *an ordinance* **a judgment**,
and there he *proved* **tested** them,
26 And said,
If **in hearkening,** thou *wilt diligently* **shalt** hearken
to the voice of *the LORD* **Yah Veh** thy *God* **Elohim**,
and *wilt do* **shalt work**
that which is *right* **straight** in his *sight* **eyes**,
and *wilt give ear* **shalt hearken**
to his *commandments* **misvoth**,
and *keep* **guard** all his statutes,
I *will* **shall** put none of these *diseases* **sicknesses**
upon thee,
which I have *brought* **put** upon the *Egyptians* **Misrayim**:
for *I am the LORD that healeth thee* **I — Yah Veh Raphah**.
27 And they came to Elim,
where were twelve *wells* **fountains** of water,
and *threescore and ten* **seventy** palm trees:
and they encamped there by the waters.
16 And they *took their journey* **pulled stakes** from Elim,
and all the *congregation* **witness**
of the *children* **sons** of *Israel* **Yisra El**
came unto the wilderness of Sin,
which is between Elim and *Sinai* **Sinay**,
on the fifteenth day of the second month
after their departing out of the land of *Egypt* **Misrayim**.
2 And the whole *congregation* **witness**
of the *children* **sons** of *Israel* **Yisra El**
murmured against *Moses* **Mosheh** and *Aaron* **Aharon**
in the wilderness:
3 And the *children* **sons** of *Israel* **Yisra El** said unto them,
Would to God **O that** we had *died* **given to die**
by the hand of *the LORD* **Yah Veh**
in the land of *Egypt* **Misrayim**,
when we *sat* **settled** by the flesh *pots* **cauldrons**,
and when we did eat bread to *the full* **satiety**;
for ye have brought us forth into this wilderness,
to *kill* **deathify** this whole *assembly* **congregation**
with *hunger* **famine**.

MANNA AND QUAIL

4 Then said *the LORD* **Yah Veh** unto *Moses* **Mosheh**,
Behold,
I *will* **shall** rain bread from *heaven* **the heavens** for you;
and the people shall go out
and *gather a certain rate* **glean their word**
every day **day by day**, that I may *prove* **test** them,
whether they *will* **shall** walk in my *law* **torah**, or no.
5 And it shall *come to pass* **become**, that on the sixth day
they shall prepare that which they bring in;
and it shall be *twice as much* **double**
as they *gather daily* **glean day by day**.
6 And *Moses* **Mosheh** and *Aaron* **Aharon**
said unto all the *children* **sons** of *Israel* **Yisra El**,
At even, then ye shall know that *the LORD* **Yah Veh**
hath brought you out from the land of *Egypt* **Misrayim**:
7 And in the morning,
then ye shall see the *glory* **honour** of *the LORD* **Yah Veh**;
for that he heareth your murmurings
against *the LORD* **Yah Veh**:
and what are we, that ye murmur against us?
8 And *Moses* **Mosheh** said, *This shall be,*
when *the LORD* **Yah Veh** shall give you
in the evening flesh to eat,
and in the morning bread to *the full* **satiety**;
for that *the LORD* **Yah Veh** heareth your murmurings
which ye murmur against him:
and what are we?
your murmurings are not against us,
but against *the LORD* **Yah Veh**.
9 And *Moses spake* **Mosheh said** unto *Aaron* **Aharon**,
Say unto all the *congregation* **witness**
of the *children* **sons** of *Israel* **Yisra El**,
Come near *before the LORD* **at the face of Yah Veh**:
for he hath heard your murmurings.
10 And it *came to pass* **became**,
as *Aaron spake* **Aharon worded**
unto the whole *congregation* **witness**
of the *children* **sons** of *Israel* **Yisra El**,
that they *looked* **set their face** toward the wilderness,
and, behold, the *glory* **honour** of *the LORD* **Yah Veh**
appeared **was seen** in the cloud.
11 And *the LORD spake* **Yah Veh worded**
unto *Moses* **Mosheh**, saying,
12 I have heard the murmurings
of the *children* **sons** of *Israel* **Yisra El**:
speak **word** unto them, saying,
At even **Between evenings** ye shall eat flesh,
and in the morning ye shall *be filled* **satiate** with bread;
and ye shall know
that *I am the LORD* **I — Yah Veh** your *God* **Elohim**.
13 And it *came to pass* **became**,
that at even
the quails *came up* **ascended**, and covered the camp:
and in the morning
the dew lay round about the *host* **camp**.
14 And when the dew that lay *was gone up* **ascended**,
behold, upon the face of the wilderness
there lay a small round thing **a thin shred**,
as *small* **thin** as the hoar frost on the *ground* **earth**.
15 And when the *children* **sons** of *Israel* **Yisra El** saw it,

they said *one* **man** to *another* **brother**, *It is* manna:
for they wist not what it was.
And *Moses* **Mosheh** said unto them, This is the bread
which *the LORD* **Yah Veh** hath given you *to eat* **for food**.
16 This is the *thing* **word**
which *the LORD* **Yah Veh** hath *commanded* **misvahed**,
Gather **Glean** of it every man
according to *his eating* **the food of his mouth**,
an omer *for every man* **per cranium**,
according to the number of your *persons* **souls**;
take ye every man for them which are in his tents.
17 And the *children* **sons** of *Israel did* **Yisra El worked** so,
and *gathered* **gleaned**,
some *more* **greatened**, some *less* **lessened**.
18 And when they *did mete* **measured** it with an omer,
he that *gathered much* **greatened**
had *nothing over* **no leftovers**,
and he that *gathered little* **lessened**
had no lack;
they *gathered* **gleaned** every man
according to *his eating* **the food of his mouth**.
19 And *Moses* **Mosheh** said,
Let no man *leave of it* **let it remain** till the morning.
20 Notwithstanding
they hearkened not unto *Moses* **Mosheh**;
but *some of them left of it* **men let it remain**
until the morning,
and it *bred worms* **raised maggots**, and stank:
and *Moses* **Mosheh** was *wroth* **enraged** with them.
21 And they *gathered* **gleaned** it
every morning **by morning**
every man according to *his eating* **the food of his mouth**:
and when the sun *waxed hot* **heated**, it melted.
22 And it *came to pass* **became**, that on the sixth day
they *gathered twice as much* **gleaned double** bread,
two omers for one *man*:
and all the *rulers* **hierarchs** of the *congregation* **witness**
came and told *Moses* **Mosheh**.
23 And he said unto them,
This is that which *the LORD* **Yah Veh** hath *said* **worded**,
To morrow is the *rest* **shabbathism**
of the holy *sabbath* **shabbath** unto *the LORD* **Yah Veh**:
bake that which ye *will* **shall** bake *to day*,
and *seethe* **stew** that ye *will seethe* **shall stew**;
and *that which remaineth over* **all the leftovers**
lay up **leave** for you to be *kept* **guarded** until the morning.
24 And they *laid it up* **left it** till the morning,
as *Moses bade* **Mosheh misvahed**:
and it did not stink,
neither was there any *worm* **maggot** therein.
25 And *Moses* **Mosheh** said, Eat that to day;
for to day is a *sabbath* **shabbath** unto *the LORD* **Yah Veh**:
to day ye shall not find it in the field.
26 Six days ye shall *gather* **glean** it;
but on the seventh day, *which is* the *sabbath* **shabbath**,
in it there shall be none.
27 And it *came to pass* **became**,
that there went out *some* of the people
on the seventh day for to *gather* **glean**,
and they found none.
28 And *the LORD* **Yah Veh** said unto *Moses* **Mosheh**,
How long refuse ye to *keep* **guard**
my *commandments* **misvoth** and my *laws* **torahs**?
29 See, for that *the LORD* **Yah Veh** hath given you
the *sabbath* **shabbath**,
therefore he giveth you on the sixth day
the bread of two days;
abide ye **sit** — every man in his place,
let no man go out of his place on the seventh day.
30 So the people *rested* **shabbathized** on the seventh day.
31 And the house of *Israel* **Yisra El**
called the name thereof Manna:
and it was like coriander seed, white;
and the taste of it was like wafers *made* with honey.
32 And *Moses* **Mosheh** said, This is *the thing* **that**
which *the LORD commandeth* **Yah Veh misvaheth**,
Fill an omer of it **A full omer**
to be *kept* **guarded** for your generations;
that they may see the bread
wherewith I have fed you in the wilderness,
when I brought you forth
from the land of *Egypt* **Misrayim**.
33 And *Moses* **Mosheh** said unto *Aaron* **Aharon**,
Take a pot, and *put* **give** an omer full of manna therein,
and *lay* **set** it *up before the LORD* **at the face of Yah Veh**,
to be *kept* **guarded** for your generations.
34 As *the LORD* **Yah Veh**
commanded Moses **misvahed Mosheh**,
so *Aaron laid* **Aharon set** it *up*
before the Testimony **at the face of the Witness**,
to be *kept* **guarded**.
35 And the *children* **sons** of *Israel* **Yisra El**
did eat manna forty years,
until they came to a land *inhabited* **settled**;
they did eat manna,
until they came
unto the *borders* **ends** of the land of *Canaan* **Kenaan**.
36 Now an omer is the tenth *part* of an ephah.

WATER FROM THE ROCK

17 And all the *congregation* **witness**
of the *children* **sons** of *Israel* **Yisra El**
journeyed **pulled stakes** from the wilderness of Sin,
after their journeys,
according to
the *commandment* **mouth** of *the LORD* **Yah Veh**,
and *pitched* **encamped** in Rephidim:
and there was no water for the people to drink.
2 Wherefore the people
did chide **chided** with *Moses* **Mosheh**, and said,
Give us water that we may drink.
And *Moses* **Mosheh** said unto them,
Why chide ye with me?
wherefore do ye *tempt the LORD* **test Yah Veh**?
3 And the people thirsted there for water;
and the people murmured against *Moses* **Mosheh**,
and said, Wherefore is this
that thou hast *brought us up* **ascended us**
out of *Egypt* **Misrayim**,
to *kill* **deathify** us and our *children* **sons**
and our *cattle* **chattel** with thirst?
4 And *Moses* **Mosheh** cried unto *the LORD* **Yah Veh**,
saying, What shall I *do* **work** unto this people?
they be almost ready to **in a little they** stone me.
5 And *the LORD* **Yah Veh** said unto *Moses* **Mosheh**,
Go **Pass** on *before* **at the face of** the people,
and take with thee of the elders of *Israel* **Yisra El**;
and thy rod, wherewith thou smotest the river,
take in thine hand, and go.
6 Behold, I *will* **shall** stand *before thee* **at thy face**
there upon the rock in Horeb;
and thou shalt smite the rock,
and there shall come water out of it,
that the people may drink.
And *Moses did* **Mosheh worked** so
in the *sight* **eyes** of the elders of *Israel* **Yisra El**.
7 And he called the name of the place *Massah* **Testing**,
and *Meribah* **Strife**,
because of the *chiding* **striving**
of the *children* **sons** of *Israel* **Yisra El**,
and because they *tempted the LORD* **tested Yah Veh**,
saying, Is *the LORD* **Yah Veh** among us, or not?
8 Then came *Amalek* **Amaleq**,
and fought with *Israel* **Yisra El** in Rephidim.
9 And *Moses* **Mosheh** said unto *Joshua* **Yah Shua**,
Choose us out men, and go out,
fight with *Amalek* **Amaleq**:
to morrow I *will stand* **shall station myself**
on the top of the hill
with the rod of *God* **Elohim** in mine hand.
10 So *Joshua did* **Yah Shua worked**
as *Moses* **Mosheh** had said to him,
and fought with *Amalek* **Amaleq**:
and *Moses* **Mosheh**, *Aaron* **Aharon**, and Hur
went up **ascended** to the top of the hill.
11 And it *came to pass* **became**,
when *Moses held up* **Mosheh lifted** his hand,
that *Israel* **Yisra El** prevailed **mightily**:
and when he *let down* **rested** his hand,
Amalek **Amaleq** prevailed **mightily**.
12 But *Moses* **Mosheh** hands were heavy;

and they took a stone, and put it under him,
and he sat thereon;
and *Aaron* **Aharon** and Hur *stayed up* **upheld** his hands,
the one on *the one* **this** side,
and the *other* **one** on *the other* **that** side;
and his hands were *steady* **trustworthy**
until the going down of the sun.
13 And *Joshua* **Yah Shua**
discomfited Amalek **vanquished Amaleq** and his people
with the *edge* **mouth** of the sword.
14 And *the LORD* **Yah Veh** said unto *Moses* **Mosheh**,
Write **Inscribe** this for a memorial in a *book* **scroll**,
and *rehearse* **set** it in the ears of *Joshua* **Yah Shua**:
for *I will utterly put* **in wiping out, I shall wipe** out
the *remembrance* **memorial** of *Amalek* **Amaleq**
from under *heaven* **the heavens**.
15 And *Moses* **Mosheh** built *an* **a sacrifice** altar,
and called the name of it *Jehovahnissi* **Yah Veh Nissi**:
16 For he said,
Because the LORD hath sworn that
The hand of Yah is my ensign:
the LORD will have **Yah Veh shall** war
with *Amalek* **Amaleq** from generation to generation.

PRIEST YITHRO ADVISES MOSHEH

18 When *Jethro* **Yithro**, the priest of *Midian* **Midyan**,
Moses' **Mosheh's** *father* in law,
heard of all that *God* **Elohim** had *done* **worked**
for *Moses* **Mosheh**, and for *Israel* **Yisra El** his people,
and that *the LORD* **Yah Veh**
had brought *Israel* **Yisra El** out of *Egypt* **Misrayim**;
2 Then *Jethro* **Yithro**, *Moses'* **Mosheh's** *father* in law,
took *Zipporah* **Sipporah**, *Moses' wife* **Mosheh's woman**,
after *he had sent her back* **her dowries**,
3 And her two sons;
of which the name of the one was Gershom;
for he said,
I have been *an alien* **a sojourner** in a strange land:
4 And the name of the *other* **one** was *Eliezer* **Eli Ezer**;
for the *God* **Elohim** of my father, *said he,* was mine help,
and *delivered* **rescued** me
from the sword of *Pharaoh* **Paroh**:
5 And *Jethro* **Yithro**, *Moses'* **Mosheh's** *father* in law,
came with his sons and his *wife* **woman**
unto *Moses* **Mosheh** into the wilderness,
where he encamped at the mount of *God* **Elohim**:
6 And he said unto *Moses* **Mosheh**,
I thy *father* in law *Jethro* **Yithro** am come unto thee,
and thy *wife* **woman**, and her two sons with her.
7 And *Moses* **Mosheh** went out to meet his *father* in law,
and *did obeisance* **prostrated**, and kissed him;
and they asked *each other* **man to friend**
of their *welfare* **shalom**;
and they came into the tent.
8 And *Moses told* **Mosheh described to** his *father* in law
all that *the LORD* **Yah Veh**
had *done* **worked** unto *Pharaoh* **Paroh**
and to the *Egyptians* **Misrayim** for *Israel's* **Yisra El's** sake,
and all the travail
that had *come upon* **found** them by the way,
and how *the LORD delivered* **Yah Veh rescued** them.
9 And *Jethro* **Yithro** rejoiced for all the goodness
which *the LORD* **Yah Veh** had *done* **worked**
to *Israel* **Yisra El**,
whom he had *delivered* **rescued**
out of the hand of the *Egyptians* **Misrayim**.
10 And *Jethro* **Yithro** said, Blessed be *the LORD* **Yah Veh**,
who hath *delivered* **rescued** you
out of the hand of the *Egyptians* **Misrayim**,
and out of the hand of *Pharaoh* **Paroh**,
who hath *delivered* **rescued** the people
from under the hand of the *Egyptians* **Misrayim**.
11 Now I know
that *the LORD* **Yah Veh** is greater than all *gods* **elohim**:
for in the *thing* **word** wherein they *dealt proudly* **seethed**
he was above them.
12 And *Jethro* **Yithro**, *Moses'* **Mosheh's** *father* in law,
took a *burnt offering* **holocaust** and sacrifices
for *God* **Elohim**:
and *Aaron* **Aharon** came,
and all the elders of *Israel* **Yisra El**,
to eat bread with *Moses'* **Mosheh's** *father* in law
before God **at the face of Elohim**.
13 And it *came to pass* **became** on the morrow,
that *Moses* **Mosheh** sat to judge the people:
and the people stood by *Moses* **Mosheh**
from the morning unto the evening.
14 And when *Moses'* **Mosheh's** *father* in law
saw all that he *did* **worked** to the people, he said,
What is this *thing* **word**
that thou *doest* **workest** to the people?
why sittest thou thyself alone,
and all the people *stand* **station themselves** by thee
from morning unto even?
15 And *Moses* **Mosheh** said unto his *father* in law,
Because the people come unto me
to enquire of *God* **Elohim**:
16 When they have a *matter* **word**, they come unto me;
and I judge between *one* **man** and *another* **friend**,
and I do make them know
the statutes of *God* **Elohim**, and his *laws* **torahs**.
17 And *Moses'* **Mosheh's** *father* in law said unto him,
The *thing* **word** that thou *doest* **workest** is not good.
18 *Thou wilt surely wear away*
In wilting, thou shalt wilt
both thou, and this people that is with thee:
for this *thing* **word** is too heavy for thee;
thou art not able to *perform* **work** it thyself alone.
19 Hearken now unto my voice,
I *will* **shall** *give thee* counsel **thee**,
and *God* **Elohim** shall be with thee:
Be thou for the people
to God—ward **in front of Elohim**,
that thou mayest bring the *causes* **words** unto *God* **Elohim**:
20 And thou shalt *teach* **enlighten** them
ordinances **statutes** and *laws* **torahs**,
and shalt *shew them* **make known** the way
wherein they *must* walk,
and the work that they *must do* **work**.
21 Moreover thou shalt *provide* **seek** out of all the people
able **valiant** men,
such as *fear God* **awe Elohim**,
men of truth, hating *covetousness* **greed**;
and *place such* **set** over them,
to be rulers **governors** of thousands,
and *rulers* **governors** of hundreds,
rulers **governors** of fifties,
and *rulers* **governors** of tens:
22 And let them judge the people at all *seasons* **times**:
and it shall be,
that every great *matter* **word** they shall bring unto thee,
but every small *matter* **word** they shall judge:
so shall it be *easier* **lightened** for thyself,
and they shall bear *the burden* with thee.
23 If thou shalt *do* **work** this *thing* **word**,
and *God command* **Elohim misvah** thee so,
then thou shalt be able to *endure* **stand**,
and all this people shall also go to their place
in *peace* **shalom**.
24 So *Moses* **Mosheh** hearkened
to the voice of his *father* in law,
and *did* **worked** all that he had said.
25 And *Moses* **Mosheh** chose *able* **valiant** men
out of all *Israel* **Yisra El**,
and *made* **gave** them heads over the people,
rulers **governors** of thousands,
rulers **governors** of hundreds,
rulers **governors** of fifties,
and *rulers* **governors** of tens.
26 And they judged the people at all *seasons* **times**:
the hard *causes* **words** they brought unto *Moses* **Mosheh**,
but every small *matter* **word** they judged themselves.
27 And *Moses* **Mosheh**
let **sent** his *father* in law *depart* **away**;
and he went his way into his own land.

MOSHEH ON MOUNT SINAY

19 In the third month,
when the *children* **sons** of *Israel* **Yisra El**
were gone forth out of the land of *Egypt* **Misrayim**,
the same day
came they into the wilderness of *Sinai* **Sinay**.

2 For they *were departed* **pulled stakes** from Rephidim,
and were come to the *desert* **wilderness** of *Sinai* **Sinay**,
and had *pitched* **encamped** in the wilderness;
and there *Israel* **Yisra El** camped before the mount.
3 And *Moses went up* **Mosheh ascended** unto *God* **Elohim**,
and *the LORD* **Yah Veh** called unto him
out of the mountain, saying,
Thus shalt thou say to the house of *Jacob* **Yaaqov**,
and tell the *children* **sons** of *Israel* **Yisra El**;
4 Ye have seen
what I *did* **worked** unto the *Egyptians* **Misrayim**,
and how I bare you on eagles' wings,
and brought you unto myself.
5 Now therefore,
if **in hearing,** ye *will obey* **shall hear** my voice *indeed*,
and *keep* **guard** my covenant,
then ye shall be a peculiar *treasure* **possession** unto me
above all people:
for all the earth is mine:
6 And ye shall be unto me
a *kingdom* **sovereigndom** of priests,
and an holy *nation* **goyim**.
These are the words which thou shalt *speak* **word**
unto the *children* **sons** of *Israel* **Yisra El**.
2 Petros 2:9, Apocalypse 1:6
7 And *Moses* **Mosheh** came
and called for the elders of the people,
and *laid* **set** before their faces all these words
which *the LORD commanded* **Yah Veh misvahed** him.
8 And all the people answered together, and said,
All that *the LORD* **Yah Veh** hath *spoken* **worded**
we *will do* **shall work**.
And *Moses* **Mosheh** returned the words of the people
unto *the LORD* **Yah Veh**.
9 And *the LORD* **Yah Veh** said unto *Moses* **Mosheh**,
Lo **Behold**,
I come unto thee in *a thick* **an overclouding** cloud,
that the people may hear when I *speak* **word** with thee,
and *believe* **trust** thee *for ever* **eternally**.
And *Moses* **Mosheh** told the words of the people
unto *the LORD* **Yah Veh**.
10 And *the LORD* **Yah Veh** said unto *Moses* **Mosheh**,
Go unto the people,
and *sanctify* **hallow** them to day and to morrow,
and let them *wash* **launder** their clothes,
11 And be *ready against* **prepared** the third day:
for the third day
the LORD will come down **Yah Veh shall descend**
in the *sight* **eyes** of all the people
upon mount *Sinai* **Sinay**.
12 And thou shalt set *bounds* **borders**
unto the people round about, saying,
Take heed to **Guard** yourselves,
that ye *go* **ascend** not *up* into the mount,
or touch the *border* **end** of it:
whosoever toucheth the mount
in deathifying, shall be *surely put to death* **deathified**:
13 There shall not an hand touch it,
but **in stoning,** he shall *surely* be stoned,
or **in shooting,** shall **be** shot *through*;
whether it be *beast* **animal** or man, it shall not live:
when the *trumpet soundeth long* **jubilee draweth**,
they shall *come up* **ascend** to the mount.
14 And *Moses* **Mosheh**
went down **descended** from the mount unto the people,
and *sanctified* **hallowed** the people;
and they *washed* **laundered** their clothes.
15 And he said unto the people,
Be *ready* **prepared** against the third day:
come not at your *wives* **women**.
16 And it *came to pass* **became,**
on the third day in the morning,
that there were *thunders* **voices** and lightnings,
and a *thick* **heavy** cloud upon the mount,
and the voice of the trumpet
exceeding loud **mighty strong**;
so that all the people that was in the camp trembled.
17 And *Moses* **Mosheh**
brought forth the people out of the camp
to meet with *God* **Elohim**;
and they stood at the nether *part* of the mount.
18 And mount *Sinai* **Sinay**
was altogether *on a smoke* **fuming,**
because the LORD **the face of Yah Veh**
descended upon it in fire:
and the smoke thereof
ascended as the smoke of a furnace,
and the whole mount *quaked greatly* **trembled mightily**.
19 And when the voice of the trumpet
in sounding, sounded long,
and *waxed louder and louder* **mightily mighty**,
Moses spake **Mosheh worded**,
and *God* **Elohim** answered him by a voice.
20 And *the LORD* **Yah Veh**
came down **descended** upon mount *Sinai* **Sinay**,
on the top of the mount:
and *the LORD* **Yah Veh** called *Moses* **Mosheh**
up to the top of the mount;
and *Moses went up* **Mosheh ascended**.
21 And *the LORD* **Yah Veh** said unto *Moses* **Mosheh**,
Go down **Descend**, *charge* **witness to** the people,
lest they break through unto *the LORD* **Yah Veh**
to *gaze* **see,**
and many of them *perish* **fall**.
22 And let the priests also,
which come near to *the LORD* **Yah Veh**,
sanctify **hallow** themselves,
lest *the LORD* **Yah Veh** break forth upon them.
23 And *Moses* **Mosheh** said unto *the LORD* **Yah Veh**,
The people cannot *come up* **ascend** to mount *Sinai* **Sinay**:
for thou *chargedst* **witnessedst to** us, saying,
Set *bounds* **borders** about the mount,
and *sanctify* **hallow** it.
24 And *the LORD* **Yah Veh** said unto him,
Away **Go**, *get thee down* **descend**,
and thou shalt *come up* **ascend**,
thou, and *Aaron* **Aharon** with thee:
but let not the priests and the people break through
to *come up* **ascend** unto *the LORD* **Yah Veh**,
lest he break forth upon them.
25 So *Moses* **Mosheh**
went down **descended** unto the people,
and *spake* **said** unto them.

ELOHIM'S TEN WORDS

20 And *God spake* **Elohim worded** all these words,
saying,
2 *I am the LORD* **I — Yah Veh** thy *God* **Elohim**,
which have brought thee
out of the land of *Egypt* **Misrayim**,
out of the house of *bondage* **servants**.
3 Thou shalt have no other *gods* **elohim**
before me **above my face**.
4 Thou shalt not *make* **work** unto thee
any *graven image* **sculptile**,
or any *likeness of any thing* **similitude**
that is in *heaven* **the heavens** above,
or that is in the earth beneath,
or that is in the water under the earth.
5 Thou shalt not *bow down* **prostrate** thyself to them,
nor serve them:
for I *the LORD* **Yah Veh** thy *God* **Elohim**
am a jealous *God* **El**,
visiting the *iniquity* **perversity** of the fathers
upon the *children* **sons**
unto the third and fourth *generation* of them that hate me;
6 And *shewing* **working** mercy
unto thousands of them that love me,
and *keep* **guard** my *commandments* **misvoth**.
7 Thou shalt not *take* **bear** the name
of *the LORD* **Yah Veh** thy *God* **Elohim**
in *vain* **defamation**;
for *the LORD* **Yah Veh**
will **shall** not *hold* **exonerate** him *guiltless*
that *taketh* **beareth** his name in *vain* **defamation**.
8 Remember the *sabbath* **shabbath** day,
to *keep it holy* **hallow it**.
9 Six days shalt thou *labour* **serve**,
and *do* **work** all thy work:
10 But the seventh day is the *sabbath* **shabbath**
of *the LORD* **Yah Veh** thy *God* **Elohim**:

in it thou shalt not *do* **work** any work,
thou, nor thy son, nor thy daughter,
thy *manservant* **servant**, nor thy *maidservant* **maid**,
nor thy *cattle* **animals**,
nor thy *stranger* **sojourner** that is within thy *gates* **portals**:
11 For in six days *the LORD made* **Yah Veh worked**
heaven **the heavens** and earth,
the sea, and all that in them is,
and rested the seventh day:
wherefore *the LORD* **Yah Veh**
blessed the *sabbath* **shabbath** day, and hallowed it.
12 Honour thy father and thy mother:
that thy days may be *long* **prolonged** upon the *land* **soil**
which *the LORD* **Yah Veh** thy *God* **Elohim** giveth thee.
13 Thou shalt not *kill* **murder**.
14 Thou shalt not *commit adultery* **adulterize**.
15 Thou shalt not steal.
16 Thou shalt not *bear* **answer a** false witness
against thy *neighbour* **friend**.
17 Thou shalt not *covet* **desire**
thy *neighbour's* **friend's** house,
thou shalt not *covet* **desire**
thy *neighbour's wife* **friend's woman**,
nor his *manservant* **servant**, nor his *maidservant* **maid**,
nor his ox, nor his *ass* **he burro**,
nor *any thing* **aught** that is thy *neighbour's* **friend's**.
18 And all the people saw the *thunderings* **voices**,
and the *lightnings* **flambeaus**,
and the *noise* **voice** of the trumpet,
and the mountain smoking:
and when the people saw it,
they *removed* **shook**, and stood afar off.
19 And they said unto *Moses* **Mosheh**,
Speak **Word** thou with us, and we *will* **shall** hear:
but let not *God speak* **Elohim word** with us, lest we die.
20 And *Moses* **Mosheh** said unto the people,
Fear **Awe** not:
for *God* **Elohim** is come **so as** to *prove* **test** you,
and that his *fear* **awe** may be before your faces,
that ye sin not.
21 And the people stood afar off,
and *Moses* **Mosheh** drew near
unto the *thick* **dripping** darkness where *God* **Elohim** was.
22 And *the LORD* **Yah Veh** said unto *Moses* **Mosheh**,
Thus thou shalt say
unto the *children* **sons** of *Israel* **Yisra El**,
Ye have seen that I have *talked* **worded** with you
from *heaven* **the heavens**.
23 Ye shall not *make* **work** with me *gods* **elohim** of silver,
neither shall *make* **work** unto you *gods* **elohim** of gold.
24 *An* **A sacrifice** altar of *earth* **soil**
thou shalt *make* **work** unto me,
and shalt sacrifice thereon thy *burnt offerings* **holocausts**,
and thy *peace offerings* **shelamim**,
thy *sheep* **flocks**, and thine oxen:
in all places where I *record* **memorialize** my name
I *will* **shall** come unto thee, and I *will* **shall** bless thee.
25 And if thou *wilt make* **shalt work** me
an **a sacrifice** altar of stone,
thou shalt not build it of hewn stone:
for if thou *lift up* **shake** thy *tool* **sword** upon it,
thou hast *polluted* **profaned** it.
26 Neither shalt thou *go up by steps* **ascend by degrees**
unto *mine* **my sacrifice** altar,
that thy nakedness be not *discovered* **exposed** thereon.

JUDGMENTS FOR SERVANTS

21 Now these are the judgments
which thou shalt set *before them* **at their face**.
2 If thou *buy* **chattelize** an Hebrew servant,
six years he shall serve:
and in the seventh he shall go out
free for nothing **gratuitously liberated**.
3 If he came in *by himself* **with his body**,
he shall go out *by himself* **with his body**:
if he were *married* **master of a woman**,
then his *wife* **woman** shall go out with him.
4 If his *master* **adoni** have given him a *wife* **woman**,
and she have born him sons or daughters;
the *wife* **woman** and her children
shall be her *master's* **adoni's**,
and he shall go out *by himself* **with his body**.
5 And if the servant **in saying**, shall *plainly* say,
I love my *master* **adoni**,
my *wife* **woman**, and my *children* **sons**;
I *will* **shall** not go out *free* **liberated**:
6 Then his *master* **adoni**
shall bring him unto *the judges* **Elohim**;
he shall also bring him to the door, or unto the door post;
and his *master* **adoni**
shall bore his ear through with an aul;
and he shall serve him *for ever* **eternally**.

JUDGMENTS FOR MAIDS

7 And if a man sell his daughter to be a *maidservant* **maid**,
she shall not go out as the *menservants* **servants** *do*.
8 If she *please not* **be evil in the eyes of** her *master* **adoni**,
who hath betrothed her to himself,
then shall he let her be redeemed:
to sell her unto a strange *nation* **people**
he shall have no *power* **reign**,
seeing he hath dealt *deceitfully* **covertly** with her.
9 And if he have betrothed her unto his son,
he shall deal with her
after the *manner* **judgment** of daughters.
10 If he take him another *wife*;
her *food* **flesh**, her *raiment* **covering**,
and her *duty of marriage* **cohabitation**,
shall he not diminish.
11 And if he *do* **work** not these three unto her,
then shall she go out *free* **gratuitously**
without *money* **silver**.

JUDGMENTS FOR INJURIES

12 He that smiteth a man, so that he die,
in deathifying, he shall be *surely put to death* **deathified**.
13 And if a man *lie not in wait* **lurketh not**,
but *God* **Elohim**
deliver **letteth** him **happen** into his hand;
then I *will appoint* **shall set** thee a place
whither he shall flee.
14 But if a man *come presumptuously* **seethe**
upon his *neighbour* **friend**,
to *slay* **slaughter** him with *guile* **strategy**;
thou shalt take him from *mine* **my sacrifice** altar,
that he may die.
15 And he that smiteth his father, or his mother,
in deathifying, shall be *surely put to death* **deathified**.
16 And he that stealeth a man, and selleth him,
or if he be found in his hand,
in deathifying, he shall *surely be put to death* **be deathified**.
17 And he that *curseth* **abaseth** his father, or his mother,
in deathifying, shall *surely be put to death* **be deathified**.
18 And if men strive together,
and *one* **man** smite *another* **friend** with a stone,
or with his fist,
and he die not, but *keepeth* **falleth on** his bed:
19 If he rise again,
and walk *abroad* **out** upon his *staff* **crutch**,
then shall he that smote him be *quit* **exonerated**:
only he shall *pay* **give**
for *the loss of his time* **his shabbathism**,
and shall cause him to be thoroughly healed.
20 And if a man smite his servant, or his maid,
with a *rod* **scion**, and he die under his hand;
in avenging, he shall be *surely punished* **avenged**.
21 *Notwithstanding* **Only**,
if he *continue a day or two* **stay two days**,
he shall not be *punished* **avenged**:
for he is his *money* **silver**.
22 If men strive,
and *hurt* **smite** a woman *with child* **that she conceive**,
so that her fruit depart from her,
and yet no mischief follow:
in penalizing, he shall be *surely punished* **penalized**,
according as the woman's *husband* **master**
will lay **shall set** upon him;
and he shall *pay* **give** as the judges *determine*.
23 And if any mischief follow,
then thou shalt give *life* **soul** for *life* **soul**,
24 Eye for eye, tooth for tooth,
hand for hand, foot for foot,
25 *Burning* **Blister** for *burning* **blister**,

wound for wound, *stripe* **lash** for *stripe* **lash**.
26 And if a man smite the eye of his servant,
or the eye of his maid, that it *perish* **ruin**;
he shall *let* **send** him *go free* **away liberated**
for his eye's sake.
27 And if he *smite out* **fell** his *manservant's* **servant's** tooth,
or his *maidservant's* **maid's** tooth;
he shall *let* **send** him *go free* **away liberated**
for his tooth's sake.
28 If an ox *gore* **butt** a man or a woman, that they die:
then **in stoning,** the ox shall *surely* be stoned,
and his flesh shall not be eaten;
but the *owner* **master** of the ox shall be *quit* **innocent**.
29 But if the ox
were wont to push **hath butted** with his horn
in time past **three yesters ago**,
and it hath been *testified* **witnessed** to his *owner* **master**,
and he hath not *kept* **guarded** him in,
but that he hath *killed* **deathified** a man or a woman;
the ox shall be stoned,
and his *owner* **master** also
shall be *put to death* **deathified**.
30 If there be *laid* **set** on him
a sum of money **a koper/an atonement**,
then he shall give
for the *ransom* **redemption** of his *life* **soul**
whatsoever is *laid* **set** upon him.
31 *Whether* **If** he have *gored* **butted** a son,
or have *gored* **butted** a daughter,
according to this judgment
shall it be *done* **worked** unto him.
32 If the ox shall *push* **butt** a *manservant* **servant**
or a *maidservant* **maid**;
he shall give unto their *master* **adoni**
thirty shekels of silver,
and the ox shall be stoned.
33 And if a man shall open a *pit* **well**,
or if a man shall dig a *pit* **well**, and not cover it,
and an ox or an *ass* **he burro** fall therein;
34 The *owner* **master** of the *pit* **well**
shall *make it good* **shalam**,
and *give money* **return silver**
unto the *owner* **master** of them;
and *the dead beast* **that which died** shall be his.
35 And if one man's ox *hurt another's* **butt friend's ox**,
that he die;
then they shall sell the live ox,
and *divide* **halve** the *money* **silver** of it;
and *the dead ox* **that which died** also
they shall *divide* **halve**.
36 Or if it be known that the ox
hath *used to push in time past* **butted three yesters ago**,
and his *owner* **master** hath not *kept* **guarded** him in;
in shalam, he shall *surely pay* **shalam**
ox for ox;
and *the dead* **that which died** shall be his own.

JUDGMENTS FOR PROPERTIES

22 If a man shall steal an ox, or a *sheep* **lamb**,
and *kill* **slaughter** it, or sell it;
he shall *restore* **shalam** five oxen for an ox,
and four *sheep* **flocks** for a *sheep* **lamb**.
2 If a thief be found *breaking up* **digging**,
and be smitten that he die,
there shall no blood be *shed* for him.
3 If the sun be risen upon him,
there shall be blood *shed* for him;
for he should make full restitution
in shalam, he shall shalam;
if he have *nothing* **naught**,
then he shall be sold for his theft.
4 If **in finding,**
the theft be *certainly* found in his hand alive,
whether it be **from** ox, or *ass* **he burro**, or *sheep* **lamb**;
he shall *restore double* **shalam twofold**.
5 If a man shall cause a field or vineyard
to be *eaten* **consumed**,
and shall *put* **send** in his beast,
and shall *feed in another man's* **consume another's** field;
of the best of his own field,
and of the best of his own vineyard,
shall he *make restitution* **shalam**.
6 If fire break out, and *catch* **be found** in thorns,
so that the *stacks* **heaps** of corn,
or the *standing corn* **stalks**, or the field,
be consumed *therewith*;
he that kindled the *fire* **kindling**
in shalam, shall *surely make restitution* **shalam**.
7 If a man shall *deliver* **give** unto his *neighbour* **friend**
money **silver** or *stuff* **instruments** to *keep* **guard**,
and it be stolen out of the man's house;
if the thief be found,
let him *pay double* **shalam twofold**.
8 If the thief be not found,
then the master of the house
shall *be brought unto the judges* **approach Elohim**,
to see *whether* **if** he have **not** put his hand
unto his *neighbour's goods* **friend's work**.
9 For *all manner* **every word** of *trespass* **rebellion**,
whether it be for ox, for *ass* **he burro**, for *sheep* **lamb**,
for *raiment* **clothes**, or for any *manner of* lost *thing*,
which another *challengeth* **saith** to be his,
the *cause* **word** of *both* **the two** parties
shall come before *the judges* **Elohim**;
and whom *the judges* **Elohim**
shall *condemn* **declare wicked**,
he shall *pay double* **shalam twofold**
unto his *neighbour* **friend**.
10 If a man *deliver* **give** unto his *neighbour* **friend**
an ass **a he burro**, or an ox, or a *sheep* **lamb**,
or any *beast* **animal**, to *keep* **guard**;
and it die, or be *hurt* **broken**, or *driven away* **captured**,
no man seeing it:
11 Then shall an oath of *the LORD* **Yah Veh**
be between **the two of** them *both*,
that he hath not put his hand
unto his *neighbour's* **friend's** goods;
and the *owner* **master** of it shall *accept* **take** thereof,
and he shall not *make it good* **shalam**.
12 And if **in stealing,** it be stolen from him,
he shall *make restitution* **shalam**
unto the *owner* **master** thereof.
13 If **in tearing,** it be torn *in pieces*,
then let him bring it for witness,
and he shall not *make good* **shalam** that which was torn.
14 And if a man *borrow ought* **ask** of his *neighbour* **friend**,
and it be *hurt* **broken**, or die,
the *owner* **master** thereof being not with it,
in shalam, he shall *surely make it good* **shalam**.
15 But if the *owner* **master** thereof be with it,
he shall not *make it good* **shalam**:
if it be an *hired thing* **hireling**, it came for his hire.

GENERAL JUDGMENTS

16 And if a man *entice* **dupe** a *maid* **virgin**
that is not betrothed, and lie with her,
in endowing,
he shall *surely* endow her to be his *wife* **woman**.
17 If **in refusing,**
her father *utterly* refuse to give her unto him,
he shall *pay money* **weigh silver**
according to the dowry of virgins.
18 Thou shalt not *suffer* **preserve** a *witch* **sorcerer** to live.
19 Whosoever lieth with *a beast* **an animal**,
in deathifying, shall *surely be put to death* **be deathified**.
20 He that sacrificeth unto any *god* **elohim**,
save **except** unto *the LORD* **Yah Veh** only,
in being devoted, he shall be *utterly destroyed* **devoted**.
21 Thou shalt neither *vex* **oppress** a *stranger* **sojourner**,
nor *oppress* **press** him:
for ye were *strangers* **sojourners**
in the land of *Egypt* **Misrayim**.
22 Ye shall not *afflict* **humble** any widow,
or *fatherless child* **orphan**.
23 If **in humbling,** thou *afflict* **humble** them *in any wise*,
and **in crying,** they cry *at all* unto me,
in hearing, I *will* **shall** *surely* hear their cry;
24 And my wrath shall *wax hot* **kindle**,
and I *will kill* **shall slaughter** you with the sword;
and your *wives* **women** shall be widows,
and your *children fatherless* **sons orphans**.
25 If thou lend *money* **silver** to any of my people

that is *poor by* **humbled with** thee,
thou shalt not be to him as *an usurer* **a lender**,
neither shalt *thou lay* **set** upon him usury.
26 If **in pledging,** thou *at all take* **pledgest**
thy *neighbour's raiment* **friend's clothes** *to pledge*,
thou shalt *deliver* **return** it unto him
by that **until** the sun goeth down:
27 For that is his covering only,
it is his *raiment* **clothes** for his skin:
wherein shall he *sleep* **lie down**?
and it shall *come to pass* **become**,
when he crieth unto me, that I *will* **shall** hear;
for I am *gracious* **charismatic**.
28 Thou shalt not *revile the gods* **abase Elohim**,
nor curse the *ruler* **hierarch** of thy people.
29 Thou shalt not delay
to offer the first of thy ripe fruits, and of thy liquors
the fulness of thy juices:
the firstborn of thy sons shalt thou give unto me.
30 *Likewise* **Thus** shalt thou *do* **work**
with thine oxen, and with thy *sheep* **flocks**:
seven days it shall be with his *dam* **mother**;
on the eighth day thou shalt give it me.
31 And ye shall be holy men unto me:
neither shall ye eat any flesh
that is torn *of beasts* in the field;
ye shall cast it to the dogs.

JUDGMENT AND MERCY

23 Thou shalt not *raise a false* **bear a vain** report:
put not thine hand with the wicked
to be *an unrighteous witness* **a witness of violence**.
2 Thou shalt not follow *a multitude* **many** to *do* evil;
neither shalt thou *speak* **witness** in a *cause* **dispute**
to *decline after* **deviate** many to *wrest judgment* **pervert**:
3 Neither shalt thou *countenance a* **esteem the** poor *man*
in his *cause* **dispute**.
4 If thou *meet* **encounter** thine enemy's ox
or his *ass going astray* **he burro straying**,
in returning,
thou shalt *surely bring it back* **return it** to him *again*.
5 If thou see the *ass* **he burro** of him that hateth thee
lying **crouched** under his burden,
and *wouldest forbear* **shouldest cease** to *help* **release** him,
in releasing, thou shalt *surely help with* **release** him.
6 Thou shalt not *wrest* **deviate** the judgment of thy poor
in his *cause* **dispute**.
7 *Keep thee far* **Be thou far removed**
from a false *matter* **word**;
and the innocent and *righteous* **just**
slay **slaughter** thou not:
for I *will* **shall** not justify the wicked.
8 And thou shalt take no *gift* **bribe**:
for the *gift* **bribe** blindeth the *wise* **open—eyed**,
and perverteth the words of the *righteous* **just**.
9 Also thou shalt not oppress a *stranger* **sojourner**:
for ye know the *heart* **soul** of a *stranger* **sojourner**,
seeing **because** ye were *strangers* **sojourners**
in the land of *Egypt* **Misrayim.**
10 And six years thou shalt *sow* **seed** thy land,
and shalt gather in the *fruits* **produce** thereof:
11 But the seventh *year* thou shalt *let it rest* **release it**
and *lie still* **leave it alone**;
that the *poor* **needy** of thy people may eat:
and *what they leave* **the remainder,**
the *beasts* **live beings** of the field shall eat.
In like manner thou shalt *deal* **work** with thy vineyard,
and with thy *oliveyard* **olives**.
12 Six days thou shalt *do* **work** thy work,
and on the seventh day thou shalt *rest* **shabbathize**:
that thine ox and thine *ass* **he burro** may rest,
and the son of thy *handmaid* **maid**,
and the *stranger* **sojourner**, may be refreshed.
13 And in all *things* that I have said unto you
be *circumspect* **on guard**:
and *make no mention of* **memorialize not**
the name of other *gods* **elohim**,
neither let it be heard out of thy mouth.

THREE CELEBRATIONS

14 Three *times* **paces**
thou shalt *keep a feast* **celebrate** unto me in the year.
15 Thou shalt *keep* **guard**
the *feast* **celebration** of *unleavened bread* **matsah**:
(thou shalt eat *unleavened bread* **matsah** seven days,
as I *commanded* **misvahed** thee,
in the *time appointed* **season** of the month Abib;
for in it thou camest out from *Egypt* **Misrayim**:
and none shall *appear* **be seen**
before me **at my face** empty:)
16 And the *feast* **celebration** of harvest,
the firstfruits of thy *labours* **works**,
which thou hast *sown* **seeded** in the field:
and the *feast* **celebration** of ingathering,
which is in the end of the year,
when thou hast gathered in thy *labours* **works**
out of the field.
17 Three times in the year
all thy males shall *appear* **be seen**
before the Lord GOD **at the face of Adonay Yah Veh**.
18 Thou shalt not *offer* **sacrifice** the blood of my sacrifice
with *leavened bread* **fermentation**;
neither shall the *fat of my sacrifice* **celebration**
remain **stay overnight** until the morning.
19 The first of the firstfruits of thy *land* **soil**
thou shalt bring into the house
of *the LORD* **Yah Veh** thy *God* **Elohim**.
Thou shalt not *seethe* **stew** a kid in his mother's milk.

YAH VEH'S ANGEL

20 Behold, I send an Angel *before thee* **at thy face**,
to *keep* **guard** thee in the way,
and to bring thee into the place which I have prepared.
21 *Beware of him* **On guard at his face**,
and *obey* **hear** his voice, *provoke* **embitter** him not;
for he *will* **shall** not *pardon* **bear**
your *transgressions* **rebellions**:
for my name is in *him* **his midst**.
22 But if **in hearing,** thou shalt *indeed obey* **hear** his voice,
and *do* **work** all that I *speak* **word**;
then I *will* **shall** be an enemy unto thine enemies,
and an adversary unto thine adversaries
besiege them who tribulate thee.
23 For mine Angel shall go *before thee* **at thy face**,
and bring thee in unto the *Amorites* **Emoriy**,
and the *Hittites* **Hethiy**, and the *Perizzites* **Perizziy**,
and the *Canaanites* **Kenaaniy**, the *Hivites* **Hivviy**,
and the *Jebusites* **Yebusiy**:
and I *will* **shall** cut them off.
24 Thou shalt not *bow down* **prostrate**
to their *gods* **elohim**,
nor serve them, nor *do* **work** after their works:
but **in demolishing,**
thou shalt *utterly overthrow* **demolish** them,
and **in breaking,**
quite break *down* their *images* **monoliths**.
25 And ye shall serve
the LORD **Yah Veh** your *God* **Elohim**,
and he shall bless thy bread, and thy water;
and I *will take* **shall turn** sickness away
from the midst of thee.
26 There shall *nothing cast their young* **naught abort**,
nor be *barren* **sterile**, in thy land:
the number of thy days I *will* **shall** fulfil.
27 I *will* **shall** send my fear *before thee* **at thy face**,
and *will destroy* **shall agitate** all the people
to whom thou shalt come,
and I *will make* **shall give that** all thine enemies
turn their *backs* **neck** unto thee.
28 And I *will* **shall** send hornets *before thee* **at thy face**,
which shall *drive out* **expel** the *Hivite* **Hivviy**,
the *Canaanite* **Kenaaniy**, and the *Hittite* **Hethiy**,
from *before thee* **thy face**.
29 I *will* **shall** not *drive* **expel** them *out*
from *before thee* **thy face** in one year;
lest the land become desolate,
and the *beast* **live being** of the field
multiply **be many** against thee.
30 By little and little
I *will drive* **shall expel** them *out* from *before thee* **thy face**,
until thou *be increased* **bear fruit**, and inherit the land.
31 And I *will* **shall** set thy *bounds* **borders**
from the *Red* **Reed** sea

even unto the sea of the *Philistines* **Peleshethiym**,
and from the *desert* **wilderness** unto the river:
for I *will deliver the inhabitants of*
shall give them who settled the land
into your hand;
and thou shalt *drive* **expel** them *out*
before thee **from thy face**.
32 Thou shalt *make* **cut** no covenant with them,
nor with their *gods* **elohim**.
33 They shall not *dwell* **settle** in thy land,
lest they *make* **cause** thee **to** sin against me:
for if thou serve their *gods* **elohim**,
it *will surely* **shall** be a snare unto thee.

YAH VEH CUTS A COVENANT

24 And he said unto *Moses* **Mosheh**,
Come up **Ascend** unto *the LORD* **Yah Veh**,
thou, and *Aaron* **Aharon**, Nadab, and *Abihu* **Abi Hu**,
and seventy of the elders of *Israel* **Yisra El**;
and *worship* **prostrate** ye afar off.
2 And *Moses* **Mosheh** alone
shall come near *the LORD* **Yah Veh**:
but they shall not come nigh;
neither shall the people *go up* **ascend** with him.
3 And *Moses* **Mosheh** came
and *told* **described to** the people
all the words of *the LORD* **Yah Veh**,
and all the judgments:
and all the people answered with one voice, and said,
All the words which *the LORD* **Yah Veh** hath *said* **worded**
will **shall** we *do* **work**.
4 And *Moses wrote* **Mosheh inscribed**
all the words of *the LORD* **Yah Veh**,
and *rose up* **started** early in the morning,
and builded *an* **a sacrifice** altar under the *hill* **mountain**,
and twelve *pillars* **monoliths**,
according to the twelve *tribes* **scions** of *Israel* **Yisra El**.
5 And he sent *young men* **lads**
of the *children* **sons** of *Israel* **Yisra El**,
which *offered burnt offerings* **holocausted holocausts**,
and sacrificed **sacrifices**
peace offerings — **shelamim** of *oxen* **bullocks**
unto *the LORD* **Yah Veh**.
6 And *Moses* **Mosheh** took half of the blood,
and put it in *basons* **bowls**;
and half of the blood he sprinkled on the **sacrifice** altar.
7 And he took the *book* **scroll** of the covenant,
and *read* **recalled** in the *audience* **ears** of the people:
and they said,
All that *the LORD* **Yah Veh** hath *said* **worded**
will **shall** we *do* **work**, and *be obedient* **hearken**.
8 And *Moses* **Mosheh** took the blood,
and sprinkled it on the people, and said,
Behold the blood of the covenant,
which *the LORD* **Yah Veh** hath *made* **cut** with you
concerning all these words.
9 Then *went up Moses* **ascended Mosheh**,
and *Aaron* **Aharon**, Nadab, and *Abihu* **Abi Hu**,
and seventy of the elders of *Israel* **Yisra El**:
10 And they saw *the God* **Elohim** of *Israel* **Yisra El**:
and there was under his feet as it were
a *paved* **transparent** work of a sapphire stone,
and as it were the *body* **skeleton** of *heaven* **the heavens**
in his *clearness* **purity**.
11 And upon the nobles
of the *children* **sons** of *Israel* **Yisra El**
he *laid* **extended** not his hand:
also they saw *God* **Elohim**, and did eat and drink.
12 And *the LORD* **Yah Veh** said unto *Moses* **Mosheh**,
Come up **Ascend** to me into the mount, and be there:
and I *will* **shall** give thee *tables* **slabs** of stone,
and a *law* **torah** and *commandments* **misvoth**
which I have *written* **inscribed**;
that thou mayest *teach* **direct** them.
13 And *Moses* **Mosheh** rose up,
and his minister *Joshua* **Yah Shua**:
and *Moses went up* **Mosheh ascended**
into the mount of *God* **Elohim**.
14 And he said unto the elders,
Tarry **Settle** ye here for us,
until we *come again* **return** unto you:
and, behold, *Aaron* **Aharon** and Hur are with you:
if any man *have any matters to do* **be a master of words**,
let him come unto them.
15 And *Moses went up* **Mosheh ascended** into the mount,
and a cloud covered the mount.
16 And the *glory* **honour** of *the LORD* **Yah Veh**
abode **tabernacled** upon mount *Sinai* **Sinay**,
and the cloud covered it six days:
and the seventh day he called unto *Moses* **Mosheh**
out of the midst of the cloud.
17 And the *sight* **visage**
of the *glory* **honour** of *the LORD* **Yah Veh**
was like *devouring* **consuming** fire on the top of the mount
in the eyes of the *children* **sons** of *Israel* **Yisra El**.
18 And *Moses* **Mosheh** went into the midst of the cloud,
and *gat him up* **ascended** into the mount:
and *Moses* **Mosheh** was in the mount
forty days and forty nights.

THE VOLUNTARY EXALTMENT FOR THE HALLOWED REFUGE

25 And *the LORD spake* **Yah Veh worded**
unto *Moses* **Mosheh**, saying,
2 *Speak* **Word** unto the *children* **sons** of *Israel* **Yisra El**,
that they *bring* **take** me an *offering* **exaltment**:
of every man that giveth it willingly with his heart
of all whose heart volunteereth
ye shall take my *offering* **exaltment**.
3 And this is the *offering* **exaltment**
which ye shall take of them;
gold, and silver, and *brass* **copper**,
4 And blue, and purple, and scarlet,
and *fine* **white** linen, and goats' *hair*,
5 And rams' skins *dyed red* **reddened**, and badgers' skins,
and shittim *wood* **timber**,
6 Oil for the light, spices for anointing oil,
and for *sweet* incense **of aromatics**,
7 Onyx stones,
and stones *to be set* — **fillings** in the ephod,
and in the breastplate.
8 And let them *make* **work** me a *sanctuary* **holies**;
that I may *dwell* **tabernacle** among them.
9 According to all that I *shew* **have thee see**,
after the pattern of the tabernacle,
and the pattern of all the instruments thereof,
even so shall ye *make* **work** it.

PATTERN FOR THE ARK

10 And they shall *make* **work**
an ark of shittim *wood* **timber**:
two cubits and a half shall be the length thereof,
and a cubit and a half the breadth thereof,
and a cubit and a half the height thereof.
11 And thou shalt overlay it with pure gold,
within and without shalt thou overlay it,
and shalt *make* **work** upon it
a *crown* **moulding** of gold round about.
12 And thou shalt *cast* **pour**
four *rings* **signets** of gold for it,
and *put* **give** them in the four *corners* **supports** thereof;
and two *rings* **signets** shall be in the one side of it,
and two *rings* **signets** in the *other* **second** side of it.
13 And thou shalt *make* **work** staves
of shittim *wood* **timber**,
and overlay them with gold.
14 And thou shalt put the staves into the *rings* **signets**
by the sides of the ark,
that the ark may be borne with them.
15 The staves shall be in the *rings* **signets** of the ark:
they shall not be *taken* **turned aside** from it.
16 And thou shalt *put* **give** into the ark
the *testimony* **witness** which I shall give thee.
17 And thou shalt *make* **work**
a *mercy seat* **kapporeth** of pure gold:
two cubits and a half shall be the length thereof,
and a cubit and a half the breadth thereof.
18 And thou shalt *make* **work**
two *cherubims* **cherubim** of gold,
of *beaten work* **spinnings** shalt thou *make* **work** them,
in the two ends of the *mercy seat* **kapporeth**.
19 And *make* **work** one cherub on *the one* **this** end,
and *the other* **one** cherub on *the other* **that** end:

even of the *mercy seat* **kapporeth**
shall ye *make* **work** the *cherubims* **cherubim**
on the two ends thereof.
20 And the *cherubims* **cherubim**
shall *stretch forth* **spread** their wings *on high* **upward**,
covering the *mercy seat* **kapporeth** with their wings,
and their faces *shall look one* **man** to *another* **brother**;
toward the *mercy seat* **kapporeth**
shall the faces of the *cherubims* **cherubim** be.
21 And thou shalt *put* **give** the *mercy seat* **kapporeth**
above upon the ark;
and in the ark
thou shalt *put* **give** the *testimony* **witness**
that I shall give thee.
22 And there I *will meet* **shall congregate** with thee,
and I *will commune* **shall word** with thee
from above the *mercy seat* **kapporeth**,
from between the two *cherubims* **cherubim**
which are upon the ark of the *testimony* **witness**,
of all *things* which I *will give* **shall misvah** thee
in commandment
unto the *children* **sons** of *Israel* **Yisra El**.

PATTERN FOR THE TABLE

23 Thou shalt also *make* **work**
a table of shittim *wood* **timber**:
two cubits shall be the length thereof,
and a cubit the breadth thereof,
and a cubit and a half the height thereof.
24 And thou shalt overlay it with pure gold,
and *make* **work** thereto
a *crown* **moulding** of gold round about.
25 And thou shalt *make* **work** unto it a border
of *an hand breadth* **a palm span** round about,
and thou shalt *make* **work** a golden *crown* **moulding**
to the border thereof round about.
26 And thou shalt *make* **work** for it
four *rings* **signets** of gold,
and *put* **give** the *rings* **signets** in the four *corners* **edges**
that are on the four feet thereof.
27 *Over against* **Along side** the border
shall the *rings* **signets** be
for places of the staves to bear the table.
28 And thou shalt *make* **work** the staves
of shittim *wood* **timber**,
and overlay them with gold,
that the table may be borne with them.

PATTERN FOR THE INSTRUMENTS

29 And thou shalt *make* **work** the dishes thereof,
and *spoons* **bowls** thereof, and covers thereof,
and *bowls* **exoneration basins** thereof,
to *cover withal* **libate with**:
of pure gold shalt thou *make* **work** them.
30 And thou shalt *set* **give** upon the table
shewbread **face bread**
before me alway **at my face continually**.
31 And thou shalt *make* **work** a *candlestick* **menorah**
of pure gold:
of *beaten work* **spinning**
shall the *candlestick* **menorah** be *made* **worked**:
his *shaft* **flank**, and his *branches* **stems**, his bowls,
his *knops* **finials**, and his *flowers* **blossoms**,
shall be of the same.
32 And six *branches* **stems** shall come out of the sides of it;
three *branches* **stems** of the *candlestick* **menorah**
out of the one side,
and three *branches* **stems** of the *candlestick* **menorah**
out of the *other* **second** side:
33 Three bowls *made like unto almonds* **almond shaped**,
with a *knop* **finial** and a *flower* **blossom**
in one *branch* **stem**;
and three bowls *made like almonds* **almond shaped**
in *the other branch* **one stem**,
with a *knop* **finial** and a *flower* **blossom**:
so in the six *branches* **stems**
that come out of the *candlestick* **menorah**.
34 And in the *candlestick* **menorah** shall be four bowls
made like unto almonds **almond shaped**,
with their *knops* **finials** and their *flowers* **blossoms**.
35 And there shall be a *knop* **finial**
under two *branches* **stems** of the same,
and a *knop* **finial** under two *branches* **stems** of the same,
and a *knop* **finial** under two *branches* **stems** of the same,
according to the six *branches* **stems**
that proceed out of the *candlestick* **menorah**.
36 Their *knops* **finials** and their *branches* **stems**
shall be of the same:
all it shall be one *beaten work* **spinning** of pure gold.

PATTERN FOR THE LAMPS

37 And thou shalt *make* **work** the seven lamps thereof:
and they shall *light* **holocaust** the lamps thereof,
that they may *give light* **illuminate**
over against **the face of** it.
38 And the tongs thereof, and the *snuffdishes* **trays** thereof,
shall be of pure gold.
39 *Of a talent* **A round** of pure gold shall he *make* **work** it,
with all these *vessels* **instruments**.
40 And *look* **see** that thou *make* **work** them
after their pattern,
which *was shewed thee* **thou sawest** in the mount.

PATTERN FOR THE TABERNACLE

26 Moreover thou shalt *make* **work** the tabernacle
with ten curtains of *fine* **white** twined linen,
and blue, and purple, and scarlet:
with *cherubims* **cherubim,**
of cunning work **the work of a fabricator**
shalt thou *make* **work** them.
2 The length of one curtain
shall be eight and twenty cubits,
and the breadth of one curtain four cubits:
and every one of the curtains shall have one measure.
3 The five curtains shall be *coupled together* **joined**
one **woman** to *another* **sister**;
and *other* five curtains shall be *coupled* **joined**
one **woman** to *another* **sister**.
4 And thou shalt *make* **work** loops of blue
upon the edge of the one curtain
from the *selvedge* **end** in the *coupling* **joint**;
and likewise shalt thou *make* **work**
in the uttermost edge of *another* curtain,
in the *coupling* **joint** of the second.
5 Fifty loops shalt thou *make* **work** in the one curtain,
and fifty loops shalt thou *make* **work**
in the *edge* **end** of the curtain
that is in the *coupling* **joint** of the second;
that the loops may take hold
one **woman** to *another* **sister**.
6 And thou shalt *make* **work** fifty *taches* **hooks** of gold,
and *couple* **join** the curtains
together **woman to sister** with the *taches* **hooks**:
and it shall be one tabernacle.
7 And thou shalt *make* **work** curtains of goats' *hair*
to be a *covering* **tent** upon the tabernacle:
eleven curtains shalt thou *make* **work**.
8 The length of one curtain shall be thirty cubits,
and the breadth of one curtain four cubits:
and the eleven curtains shall be all of one measure.
9 And *thou* shalt *couple* **join** five curtains by themselves,
and six curtains by themselves,
and shalt double the sixth curtain
in the *forefront* **front at the face** of the *tabernacle* **tent**.
10 And thou shalt *make* **work** fifty loops
on the edge of the one curtain
that is outmost in the *coupling* **joint**,
and fifty loops in the edge of the curtain
which coupleth **in the joint of** the second.
11 And thou shalt *make* **work**
fifty *taches* **hooks** of *brass* **copper**,
and put the *taches* **hooks** into the loops,
and *couple* **join** the tent together, that it may be one.
12 And the *remnant that remaineth* **leftover extention**
of the curtains of the tent,
the half curtain *that remaineth* **leftover**,
shall *hang* **extend**
over the *backside* **back** of the tabernacle.
13 And a cubit *on the one side* **from this**,
and a cubit *on the other side of that* **from that**
which *remaineth* **is leftover**
in the length of the curtains of the tent,
it shall *hang* **extend** over the sides of the tabernacle
on **from** this *side* and *on* **from** that *side*, to cover it.

14 And thou shalt *make* **work** a covering for the tent
of rams' skins *dyed red* **reddened**,
and a covering above of badgers' skins.
15 And thou shalt *make* **work** boards for the tabernacle
of shittim *wood* **timber** standing up.
16 Ten cubits shall be the length of a board,
and a cubit and a half *cubit*
shall be the breadth of one board.
17 Two *tenons* **hands** shall there be in one board,
set in order one against another
equidistant woman to sister:
thus shalt thou *make* **work**
for all the boards of the tabernacle.
18 And thou shalt *make* **work** the boards
for the tabernacle,
twenty boards on the south *side* **edge** southward.
19 And thou shalt *make* **work** forty sockets of silver
under the twenty boards;
two sockets under one board
for his two *tenons* **hands**,
and two sockets under *another* **one** board
for his two *tenons* **hands**.
20 And for the second side of the tabernacle
on the north *side* **edge** there shall be twenty boards:
21 And their forty sockets of silver;
two sockets under one board,
and two sockets under *another* **one** board.
22 And for the *sides* **flanks** of the tabernacle
westward **seaward**
thou shalt *make* **work** six boards.
23 And two boards shalt thou *make* **work**
for the corners of the tabernacle in the *two sides* **flanks**.
24 And they shall be
coupled together beneath **twinned downward**,
and they shall be *coupled together* **twinned**
above the head of it unto one *ring* **signet**:
thus shall it be for **the two of** them *both*;
they shall be for the two corners.
25 And they shall be eight boards,
and their sockets of silver, sixteen sockets;
two sockets under one board,
and two sockets under *another* **one** board.
26 And thou shalt *make* **work** bars of shittim *wood* **timber**;
five for the boards of the one side of the tabernacle,
27 And five bars
for the boards of the *other* **second** side of the tabernacle,
and five bars for the boards of the side of the tabernacle,
for the *two sides westward* **flanks seaward**.
28 And the middle bar in the midst of the boards
shall *reach* **extend** from end to end.
29 And thou shalt overlay the boards with gold,
and *make* **work** their *rings* **signets** of gold
for places for the bars:
and thou shalt overlay the bars with gold.
30 And thou shalt *rear up* **raise** the tabernacle
according to the *fashion* **judgment** thereof
which *was shewed thee* **thou sawest** in the mount.
31 And thou shalt *make* **work** a vail of blue,
and purple, and scarlet, and *fine* **white** twined linen
of cunning work **the work of a fabricator**:
with *cherubims* **cherubim** shall it be made:
32 And thou shalt *hang* **give** it
upon four pillars of shittim *wood* overlaid with gold:
their hooks shall be of gold,
upon the four sockets of silver.
33 And thou shalt *hang up* **give** the vail
under the *taches* **hooks**,
that thou mayest bring in thither within the vail
the ark of the *testimony* **witness**:
and the vail shall *divide* **separate** unto you
between the *holy place* **holies**
and **between** the *most holy* **holy of holies**.
34 And thou shalt *put* **give** the *mercy seat* **kapporeth**
upon the ark of the *testimony* **witness**
in the *most holy place* **holy of holies**.
35 And thou shalt set the table without the vail,
and the *candlestick* **menorah** over against the table
on the side of the tabernacle *toward the south* **southward**:
and thou shalt *put* **give** the table on the north side.
36 And thou shalt *make an hanging* **work a covering**
for the *door* **opening** of the tent,
of blue, and purple, and scarlet,
and *fine* **white** twined linen,
wrought with *needlework* **embroidery work**.
37 And thou shalt *make* **work** for the *hanging* **covering**
five pillars of shittim *wood* and overlay them with gold,
and their hooks shall be of gold:
and thou shalt *cast* **pour** five sockets of *brass* **copper**
for them.

PATTERN FOR THE ALTAR

27 And thou shalt *make an* **work a sacrifice** altar
of shittim *wood* **timber**,
five cubits long, and five cubits broad;
the **sacrifice** altar shall be foursquare:
and the height thereof shall be three cubits.
2 And thou shalt *make* **work** the horns of it
upon the four corners thereof:
his horns shall be of the same:
and thou shalt overlay it with *brass* **copper**.
3 And thou shalt *make* **work** his *pans* **cauldrons**
to *receive his ashes* **de—ash,**
and his shovels, and his *basons* **sprinklers**,
and his *fleshhooks* **forks**, and his *firepans* **trays**:
all the *vessels* **instruments** thereof
thou shalt *make* **work** of *brass* **copper**.
4 And thou shalt *make* **work** for it a *grate* **screen**
of network of *brass* **copper**;
and upon the net
shalt thou *make* **work** four *brasen rings* **copper signets**
in the four *corners* **ends** thereof.
5 And thou shalt *put* **give** it under the *compass* **rim**
of the **sacrifice** altar *beneath* **downward**,
that the net may be even to the midst of the **sacrifice** altar.
6 And thou shalt *make* **work** staves
for the **sacrifice** altar,
staves of shittim *wood* **timber**,
and overlay them with *brass* **copper**.
7 And the staves shall be *put*
into the *rings* **signets**,
and the staves shall be
upon the two sides of the **sacrifice** altar, to bear it.
8 Hollow with *boards* **slabs** shalt thou *make* **work** it:
as *it was shewed thee* **thou sawest** in the mount,
so shall they *make* **work** it.

PATTERN FOR THE COURT

9 And thou shalt *make* **work** the court of the tabernacle:
for the south *side* **edge** southward
there shall be hangings for the court
of *fine* **white** twined linen
of an hundred cubits long for one *side* **edge**:
10 And the twenty pillars thereof
and their twenty sockets shall be of *brass* **copper**;
the hooks of the pillars and their *fillets* **attachments**
shall be of silver.
11 And likewise for the north *side* **edge** in length
there shall be hangings of an hundred *cubits* long,
and his twenty pillars and their twenty sockets
of *brass* **copper**;
the hooks of the pillars and their *fillets* **attachments**
of silver.
12 And for the breadth of the court
on the *west side* **seaward edge**
shall be hangings of fifty cubits:
their pillars ten, and their sockets ten.
13 And the breadth of the court
on the east *side eastward* **edge toward the rising**
shall be fifty cubits.
14 The hangings of one *side of the gate* **shoulder**
shall be fifteen cubits:
their pillars three, and their sockets three.
15 And on the *other side* **second shoulder**
shall be hangings fifteen *cubits*:
their pillars three, and their sockets three.
16 And for the *gate* **portal** of the court
shall be *an hanging* **a covering** of twenty cubits,
of blue, and purple, and scarlet,
and *fine* **white** twined linen,
wrought with *needlework* **embroidery work**:
and their pillars shall be four, and their sockets four.
17 All the pillars round about the court

shall be *filleted* **attached** with silver;
their hooks shall be of silver,
and their sockets of *brass* **copper**.
18 The length of the court shall be an hundred cubits,
and the breadth fifty every where,
and the height five cubits of *fine* **white** twined linen,
and their sockets of *brass* **copper**.
19 All the *vessels* **instruments** of the tabernacle
in all the service thereof,
and all the *pins* **stakes** thereof,
and all the *pins* **stakes** of the court,
shall be of *brass* **copper**.
20 And thou shalt *command* **misvah**
the *children* **sons** of *Israel* **Yisra El**,
that they *bring* **take** thee pure oil olive
beaten **pestled** for the light,
to *cause* **holocaust** the lamp *to burn always* **continually**.
21 In the *tabernacle* **tent** of the congregation
without the vail,
which is before the *testimony* **witness**,
Aaron **Aharon** and his sons shall *order* **arrange** it
from evening to morning
before the LORD **at the face of Yah Veh**:
it shall be *a* **an eternal** statute *for ever*
unto their generations
on the behalf of the *children* **sons** of *Israel* **Yisra El**.

PATTERN FOR THE PRIESTAL CLOTHES

28 And *take* **oblate** thou unto thee
Aaron **Aharon** thy brother, and his sons with him,
from among the *children* **sons** of *Israel* **Yisra El**,
that he may *minister unto me in the priest's office*
priest the priesthood unto me,
even *Aaron* **Aharon**, Nadab and *Abihu* **Abi Hu**,
Eleazar **El Azar** and *Ithamar* **Iy Thamar**,
Aaron's **Aharon's** sons.
2 And thou shalt *make* **work** holy *garments* **clothes**
for *Aaron* **Aharon** thy brother
for *glory* **honour** and for *beauty* **adornment**.
3 And thou shalt *speak* **word**
unto all that are wise hearted,
whom I have filled with the spirit of wisdom,
that they may
make Aaron's garments **work Aharon's clothes**
to *consecrate* **hallow** him,
that he may *minister unto me in the priest's office*
priest the priesthood unto me.
4 And these are the *garments* **clothes**
which they shall *make* **work**;
a breastplate, and an ephod, and a *robe* **mantle**,
and a broidered coat, a *mitre* **tiara**, and a girdle:
and they shall *make* **work** holy *garments* **clothes**
for *Aaron* **Aharon** thy brother, and his sons,
that he may *minister unto me in the priest's office*
priest the priesthood unto me.

PATTERN FOR THE EPHOD

5 And they shall take gold, and blue, and purple,
and scarlet, and *fine* **white** linen.
6 And they shall *make* **work** the ephod
of gold, of blue, and of purple, of scarlet,
and *fine* **white** twined linen,
with *cunning* **fabricated** work.
7 It shall have the two shoulderpieces thereof
joined at the two *edges* **ends** thereof;
and *so* it shall be joined *together*.
8 And the *curious* **fabricated** girdle of the ephod,
which is upon it, shall be of the same,
according to the work thereof;
even of gold, of blue, and purple, and scarlet,
and *fine* **white** twined linen.
9 And thou shalt take two onyx stones,
and *grave* **engrave** on them
the names of the *children* **sons** of *Israel* **Yisra El**:
10 Six of their names on one stone,
and *the other* six names *of the rest* **which remain**
on the *other* **second** stone,
according to their *birth* **generations**.
11 With the work of an engraver in stone,
like the engravings of a *signet* **seal**,
shalt thou engrave the two stones
with the names of the *children* **sons** of *Israel* **Yisra El**:
thou shalt *make* **work** them
to be *set in ouches* **surrounded by brocades** of gold.
12 And thou shalt put the two stones
upon the shoulders of the ephod
for stones of memorial
unto the *children* **sons** of *Israel* **Yisra El**:
and *Aaron* **Aharon** shall bear their names
before the LORD **at the face of Yah Veh**
upon his two shoulders for a memorial.
13 And thou shalt *make ouches* **work brocades** of gold;
14 And two chains of pure gold at the ends;
of wreathen work shalt thou *make* **work** them,
and *fasten* **give** the wreathen chains
to the *ouches* **brocades**.

PATTERN FOR THE BREASTPLATE OF JUDGMENT

15 And thou shalt *make* **work** the breastplate of judgment
with *cunning* **fabricated** work;
after the work of the ephod thou shalt *make* **work** it;
of gold, of blue, and of purple, and of scarlet,
and of *fine* **white** twined linen, shalt thou *make* **work** it.
16 Foursquare it shall be being doubled;
a span shall be the length thereof,
and a span shall be the breadth thereof.
17 And thou shalt *set* **fill** in *it*
settings **fillings** of stones,
even four rows of stones:
the *first* row shall be
a sardius, a topaz, and a carbuncle:
this shall be the first row.
18 And the second row shall be
an emerald, a sapphire, and a diamond.
19 And the third row
a ligure **an opal**, an agate, and an amethyst.
20 And the fourth row
a beryl, and an onyx, and a jasper:
they shall be *set* **embroidered** in gold
in their *inclosings* **fillings**.
21 And the stones shall be with the names
of the *children* **sons** of *Israel* **Yisra El**,
twelve, according to their names,
like the engravings of a *signet* **seal**;
every *one* **man** with his name shall they be
according to the twelve *tribes* **scions**.
22 And thou shalt *make* **work** upon the breastplate
chains *at the ends* **twisted** of wreathen work of pure gold.
23 And thou shalt *make* **work** upon the breastplate
two *rings* **signets** of gold,
and shalt *put* **give** the two *rings* **signets**
on the two ends of the breastplate.
24 And thou shalt *put* **give**
the two *wreathen chains* **wreaths** of gold
in the two *rings* **signets**
which are on the ends of the breastplate.
25 And the *other* two ends
of the two *wreathen chains* **wreaths**
thou shalt *fasten* **give** in the two *ouches* **brocades**,
and *put* **give** them on the shoulder pieces of the ephod
before it **at the face of the front**.
26 And thou shalt *make* **work** two *rings* **signets** of gold,
and thou shalt put them
upon the two ends of the breastplate
in the *border* **edge** thereof,
which is *in the side of* **over against**
the ephod *inward* **housing**.
27 And two *other rings* **signets** of gold
thou shalt *make* **work**,
and shalt *put* **give** them on the two *sides* **shoulders**
of the ephod *underneath* **downward**,
toward the forepart **at the face of the front** thereof,
over against **along side** the *other coupling* **joint** thereof,
above the *curious* **fabricated** girdle of the ephod.
28 And they shall bind the breastplate
by the *rings* **signets** thereof
unto the *rings* **signets** of the ephod
with a *lace* **braid** of blue,
that it may be above the *curious* **fabricated** girdle
of the ephod,
and that the breastplate be not *loosed* **removed**
from the ephod.
29 And *Aaron* **Aharon** shall bear

the names of the *children* **sons** of *Israel* **Yisra El**
in the breastplate of judgment upon his heart,
when he goeth in unto the *holy place* **holies,**
for a memorial
before the LORD **at the face of Yah Veh** continually.
30 And thou shalt *put* **give** in the breastplate of judgment
the Urim and the Thummim;
and they shall be upon *Aaron's* **Aharon's** heart,
when he goeth in
before the LORD **at the face of Yah Veh**:
and *Aaron* **Aharon** shall bear the judgment
of the *children* **sons** of *Israel* **Yisra El** upon his heart
before the LORD **at the face of Yah Veh** continually.

PATTERN FOR THE EPHOD MANTLE

31 And thou shalt *make* **work** the *robe* **mantle**
of the ephod *all of* **totally** blue.
32 And there shall be *an hole* **a mouth** in the top of it,
in the midst thereof:
it shall have *a binding* **an edging** of woven work
round about the *hole* **mouth** of it,
as it were the *hole* **mouth** of an habergeon,
that it be not *rent* **ripped.**
33 And *beneath* upon the *hem* **drape** of it
thou shalt *make* **work** pomegranates of blue,
and of purple, and of scarlet,
round about the *hem* **drape** thereof;
and bells of gold *between* **among** them round about:
34 A golden bell and a pomegranate,
a golden bell and a pomegranate,
upon the *hem* **drape** of the *robe* **mantle** round about.
35 And it shall be upon *Aaron* **Aharon** to minister:
and his *sound* **voice** shall be heard when he goeth in
unto the *holy place* **holies**
before the LORD **at the face of Yah Veh,**
and when he cometh out, that he die not.

PATTERN FOR THE TIARA

36 And thou shalt *make* **work**
a *plate* **blossom** of pure gold,
and *grave* **engrave** upon it,
like the engravings of a *signet* **seal,**
HOLINESS TO THE LORD **HOLY TO YAH VEH.**
37 And thou shalt put it on a blue *lace* **braid,**
that it may be upon the *mitre* **tiara;**
upon the forefront **at the face of the front**
of the *mitre* **tiara** it shall be.
38 And it shall be upon *Aaron's* **Aharon's** forehead,
that *Aaron* **Aharon** may bear
the *iniquity* **perversity** of the *holy things* **holies,**
which the *children* **sons** of *Israel* **Yisra El**
shall hallow in all their holy gifts;
and it shall be *always* **continually** upon his forehead,
that they may be *accepted* **pleasing**
before the LORD **at the face of Yah Veh.**
39 And thou shalt embroider the coat of *fine* **white** linen,
and thou shalt *make* **work** the *mitre* **tiara**
of *fine* **white** linen,
and thou shalt *make* **work** the girdle
of *needlework* **embroidery work.**
40 And for *Aaron's* **Aharon's** sons
thou shalt *make* **work** coats,
and thou shalt *make* **work** for them girdles,
and *bonnets* **turbans** shalt thou *make* **work** for them,
for *glory* **honour** and for *beauty* **adornment.**
41 And thou shalt put them
upon *Aaron* **Aharon** thy brother, and his sons with him;
and shalt anoint them,
and *consecrate them* **fill their hand,**
and *sanctify* **hallow** them,
that they may *minister unto me in the priest's office*
priest the priesthood unto me.
42 And thou shalt *make* **work** them linen breeches
to cover **the flesh of** their nakedness;
from the loins even unto the *thighs* **flank** they shall reach:
43 And they shall be upon *Aaron* **Aharon,**
and upon his sons,
when they come in
unto the *tabernacle* **tent** of the congregation,
or when they come near unto the **sacrifice** altar
to minister in the *holy place* **holies;**
that they bear not *iniquity* **perversity,** and die:
it shall be a **an eternal** statute *for ever* unto him
and his seed after him.

HALLOWING THE PRIESTS

29 And this is the *thing* **word**
that thou shalt *do* **work** unto them to hallow them,
to *minister unto me in the priest's office*
priest the priesthood unto me:
Take one *young* bullock **son of the oxen,**
and two **integrious** rams *without blemish,*
2 And *unleavened bread* **matsah,**
and **matsah** cakes *unleavened tempered* **mingled** with oil,
and **matsah** wafers *unleavened* anointed with oil:
of wheaten flour shalt thou *make* **work** them.
3 And thou shalt *put* **give** them into one basket,
and *bring* **oblate** them in the basket,
with the bullock and the two rams.
4 And *Aaron* **Aharon** and his sons thou shalt *bring* **oblate**
unto the *door* **opening**
of the *tabernacle* **tent** of the congregation,
and shalt *wash* **baptize** them with water.
5 And thou shalt take the *garments* **clothes,**
and put upon *Aaron* **Aharon** the coat,
and the *robe* **mantle** of the ephod,
and the ephod, and the breastplate,
and gird him with the *curious* **fabricated** girdle
of the ephod:
6 And thou shalt *put* **give** the *mitre* **tiara** upon his head,
and *put* **give** the holy *crown* **separatism**
upon the *mitre* **tiara.**
7 Then shalt thou take the anointing oil,
and pour it upon his head, and anoint him.
8 And thou shalt *bring* **oblate** his sons,
and put coats upon them.
9 And thou shalt gird them with girdles,
Aaron **Aharon** and his sons,
and *put* **bind** the *bonnets* **turbans** on them:
and the *priest's office* **priesthood** shall be their's
for *a perpetual* **an eternal** statute:
and thou shalt *consecrate Aaron* **fill the hand of Aharon**
and **the hand of** his sons.
10 And thou shalt cause a bullock
to be *brought before* **oblated at the face of**
the *tabernacle* **tent** of the congregation:
and *Aaron* **Aharon** and his sons shall *put* **prop** their hands
upon the head of the bullock.
11 And thou shalt *kill* **slaughter** the bullock
before the LORD **at the face of Yah Veh,**
by the *door* **opening**
of the *tabernacle* **tent** of the congregation.
12 And thou shalt take of the blood of the bullock,
and *put* **give** it upon the horns of the **sacrifice** altar
with thy finger,
and pour all the blood
beside **at the** *bottom* **foundation** of the **sacrifice** altar.
13 And thou shalt take
all the fat that covereth the inwards,
and the caul that is above the liver,
and the two *kidneys* **reins,** and the fat that is upon them,
and *burn* **incense** them upon the **sacrifice** altar.
14 But the flesh of the bullock, and his skin, and his dung,
shalt thou burn with fire without the camp:
it is *a sin offering* **for the sin.**
15 Thou shalt also take one ram;
and *Aaron* **Aharon** and his sons shall *put* **prop** their hands
upon the head of the ram.
16 And thou shalt *slay* **slaughter** the ram,
and thou shalt take his blood,
and sprinkle it round about upon the **sacrifice** altar.
17 And thou shalt
cut the ram in pieces **dismember the members of the ram,**
and *wash* **baptize** the inwards of him, and his legs,
and *put* **give** them unto his *pieces* **members,**
and unto his head.
18 And thou shalt *burn* **incense** the whole ram
upon the **sacrifice** altar:
it is a *burnt offering* **holocaust** unto *the LORD* **Yah Veh:**
it is a *sweet savour* **scent of rest,**
an offering made by fire **a firing** unto *the LORD* **Yah Veh.**
19 And thou shalt take the *other* **second** ram;
and *Aaron* **Aharon** and his sons

shall *put* **prop** their hands upon the head of the ram.
20 Then shalt thou *kill* **slaughter** the ram,
and take of his blood,
and *put* **give** it
upon the tip of the right ear of *Aaron* **Aharon**,
and upon the tip of the right ear of his sons,
and upon the *thumb* **great digit** of their right hand,
and upon the great *toe* **digit** of their right foot,
and sprinkle the blood upon the **sacrifice** altar
round about.
21 And thou shalt take of the blood
that is upon the **sacrifice** altar, and of the anointing oil,
and sprinkle it upon *Aaron* **Aharon**,
and upon his *garments* **clothes**,
and upon his sons,
and upon the *garments* **clothes** of his sons with him:
and he shall be hallowed,
and his *garments* **clothes**,
and his sons, and his sons' *garments* **clothes** with him.
22 Also thou shalt take of the ram the fat and the rump,
and the fat that covereth the inwards,
and the caul above the liver, and the two *kidneys* **reins**,
and the fat that is upon them,
and the right *shoulder* **hindleg**;
for it is a ram of *consecration* **fulfillments**:
23 And one *loaf* **round** of bread,
and one *cake of oiled* bread **of oil**,
and one wafer
out of the basket of the *unleavened bread* **matsah**
that is *before the LORD* **at the face of Yah Veh**:
24 And thou shalt put all
in the *hands* **palms** of *Aaron* **Aharon**,
and in the *hands* **palms** of his sons;
and shalt wave them for a wave *offering*
before the LORD **at the face of Yah Veh.**
25 And thou shalt *receive* **take** them of their hands,
and *burn* **incense** them upon the **sacrifice** altar
for a *burnt offering* **holocaust**,
for a *sweet savour* **scent of rest**
before the LORD **at the face of Yah Veh**:
it is an offering made by fire **a firing**
unto *the LORD* **Yah Veh.**
26 And thou shalt take the breast of the ram
of *Aaron's consecration* **Aharon's fulfillments**,
and wave it for a wave *offering*
before the LORD **at the face of Yah Veh**:
and it shall be thy part.
27 And thou shalt *sanctify* **hallow** the breast
of the wave *offering*,
and the *shoulder* **hindleg** of the *heave offering* **exaltment**,
which is waved, and which is *heaved up* **lifted**,
of the ram of the *consecration* **fulfillments**,
even of that which is for *Aaron* **Aharon**,
and of that which is for his sons:
28 And it shall be *Aaron's* **Aharon's** and his sons'
by a **for an eternal** statute *for ever*
from the *children* **sons** of *Israel* **Yisra El**:
for it is an *heave offering* **exaltment**:
and it shall be an *heave offering* **exaltment**
from the *children* **sons** of *Israel* **Yisra El**
of the sacrifice of their *peace offerings* **shelamim**,
even their *heave offering* **exaltment**
unto *the LORD* **Yah Veh**.
29 And the holy *garments* **clothes** of *Aaron* **Aharon**
shall be his sons' after him,
to be anointed therein,
and to *be consecrated* **fill their hands** in them.
30 And that son that is priest in his stead
shall *put* **enrobe** them *on* seven days,
when he cometh
into the *tabernacle* **tent** of the congregation
to minister in the *holy place* **holies**.
31 And thou shalt take the ram
of the *consecration* **fulfillments**,
and *seethe* **stew** his flesh in the *holy place* **holies**.
32 And *Aaron* **Aharon** and his sons
shall eat the flesh of the ram,
and the bread that is in the basket
by the *door* **opening**
of the *tabernacle* **tent** of the congregation.
33 And they shall eat those *things*
wherewith the atonement was made
which were to kapar/atone,
to *consecrate* **fill their hands** and to *sanctify* **hallow** them:
but a stranger shall not eat thereof,
because they are holy.
34 And if ought of the flesh
of the *consecrations* **fulfillments**,
or of the bread, remain unto the morning,
then thou shalt burn *the remainder* **that which remaineth**
with fire:
it shall not be eaten, because it is holy.
35 And thus shalt thou *do* **work** unto *Aaron* **Aharon**,
and to his sons,
according to all *things*
which I have *commanded* **misvahed** thee:
seven days shalt thou *consecrate them* **fill their hands**.
36 And thou shalt *offer* **work** every day a bullock
for a sin offering for atonement **kippurim for sin**:
and thou shalt *cleanse* **sacrifice for sin**
on the **sacrifice** altar,
when thou *hast made atonement* **shalt kapar/atone** for it,
and thou shalt anoint it, to *sanctify* **hallow** it.
37 Seven days thou shalt *make an atonement* **kapar/atone**
for the **sacrifice** altar, and *sanctify* **hallow** it;
and it shall be *an* **a sacrifice** altar
most holy — **a holy of holies**:
whatsoever toucheth the **sacrifice** altar
shall be *holy* **hallowed.**
38 Now this is that
which thou shalt *offer* **work** upon the **sacrifice** altar;
two lambs *of the first year* **yearling sons**
day by day continually.
39 The one lamb
thou shalt *offer* **work** in the morning;
and the *other* **second** lamb
thou shalt *offer at even* **work between evenings**:
40 And with the one lamb a tenth *deal* of flour
mingled with the fourth *part* of an hin
of *beaten* **pestled** oil;
and the fourth *part* of an hin of wine
for a *drink offering* **libation.**
41 And the *other* **second** lamb
thou shalt *offer at even* **work between evenings**,
and shalt *do* **work** thereto
according to the *meat* **offering** of the morning,
and according to the *drink offering* **libation** thereof,
for a *sweet savour* **scent of rest**,
an offering made by fire **a firing** unto *the LORD* **Yah Veh**.
42 This shall be a continual *burnt offering* **holocaust**
throughout your generations
at the *door* **opening**
of the *tabernacle* **tent** of the congregation
before the LORD **at the face of Yah Veh**:
where **in congregating**,
I *will meet* **shall congregate with** you,
to *speak* **word** there unto thee.
43 And there I *will meet* **shall congregate**
with the *children* **sons** of *Israel* **Yisra El**,
and the tabernacle shall be sanctified **to be hallowed**
by my *glory* **honour**.
44 And I *will sanctify* **shall hallow**
the *tabernacle* **tent** of the congregation,
and the **sacrifice** altar:
I *will sanctify* **shall hallow** also
both *Aaron* **Aharon** and his sons,
to *minister to me in the priest's office*
priest the priesthood unto me.
45 And I *will dwell* **shall tabernacle**
among the *children* **sons** of *Israel* **Yisra El**,
and *will* **shall** be their *God* **Elohim**.
46 And they shall know
that *I am the LORD* **I — Yah Veh** their *God* **Elohim**,
that brought them forth
out of the land of *Egypt* **Misrayim**,
that I may *dwell* **tabernacle** among them:
I am the LORD **I — Yah Veh** their *God* **Elohim**.

PATTERN FOR THE SACRIFICE ALTAR

30 And thou shalt *make an* **work a sacrifice** altar
to *burn* **incence** incense *upon*:

of shittim *wood* **timber** shalt thou *make* **work** it.
2 A cubit shall be the length thereof,
and a cubit the breadth thereof;
foursquare shall it be:
and two cubits shall be the height thereof:
the horns thereof shall be of the same.
3 And thou shalt overlay it with pure gold,
the *top* **roof** thereof,
and the *sides* **walls** thereof round about,
and the horns thereof;
and thou shalt *make* **work** unto it
a *crown* **moulding** of gold round about.
4 And two golden *rings* **signets** shalt thou *make* **work** to it
under the *crown* **moulding** of it,
by the two *corners* **sides** thereof,
upon the two sides of it shalt thou *make* **work** it;
and they shall be for *places* **housings**
for the staves to bear it withal.
5 And thou shalt *make* **work** the staves
of shittim *wood* **timber**,
and overlay them with gold.
6 And thou shalt *put* **give** it *before* **at the face of** the vail
that is by the ark of the *testimony* **witness**,
before **at the face of** the *mercy seat* **kapporeth**
that is over the *testimony* **witness**,
where I *will* **shall** meet with thee.
7 And *Aaron* **Aharon** shall *burn* **incense** thereon
sweet incense **of aromatics**
every morning **by morning**:
when he *dresseth* **well—prepareth** the lamps,
he shall *burn* incense upon it.
8 And when *Aaron lighteth* **Aharon holocausteth** the lamps
at even **between evenings**,
he shall *burn* incense upon it,
a *perpetual* **continual** incense
before the LORD **at the face of Yah Veh**
throughout your generations.
9 Ye shall *offer* **holocaust** no strange incense thereon,
nor *burnt sacrifice* **holocaust**, nor *meat* offering;
neither shall ye
pour drink offering **libate a libation** thereon.
10 And *Aaron* **Aharon**
shall *make an atonement* **kapar/atone**
upon the horns of it once in a year
with the blood
of the *sin offering of atonements* **kippurim for sin**:
once in the year
shall he *make atonement* **kapar/atone** upon it
throughout your generations:
it is *most holy* **a holy of holies** unto *the LORD* **Yah Veh**.

KIPPURIM GIFT

11 And *the LORD spake* **Yah Veh worded**
unto *Moses* **Mosheh**, saying,
12 When thou *takest* **bearest** the *sum* **heads**
of the *children* **sons** of *Israel* **Yisra El**
after their number **who were mustered**,
then shall they give every man
a ransom **a koper/an atonement** for his soul
unto *the LORD* **Yah Veh**,
when thou *numberest* **musterest** them;
that there be no plague among them,
when thou *numberest* **musterest** them.
13 This they shall give,
every one that passeth among them
that are *numbered* **mustered**,
half a shekel after the shekel of the *sanctuary* **holies**:
(a shekel is twenty gerahs:)
an half shekel
shall be the *offering* **exaltment**
of the LORD **unto Yah Veh**.
14 Every one that passeth among them
that are *numbered* **mustered**,
from **sons of** twenty years *old* and above,
shall give an *offering* **exaltment** unto *the LORD* **Yah Veh**.
15 The rich shall not *give more* **abound**,
and the poor
shall not *give less* **diminish** than half a shekel,
when they give an *offering* **exaltment**
unto *the LORD* **Yah Veh**,
to *make an atonement* **kapar/atone** for your souls.
16 And thou shalt take
the *atonement money* **kippurim silver**
of the *children* **sons** of *Israel* **Yisra El**,
and shalt *appoint* **give** it for the service
of the *tabernacle* **tent** of the congregation;
that it may be a memorial
unto the *children* **sons** of *Israel* **Yisra El**
before the LORD **at the face of Yah Veh**,
to *make an atonement* **kapar/atone** for your souls.

PATTERN FOR THE LAVER

17 And *the LORD spake* **Yah Veh worded**
unto *Moses* **Mosheh**, saying,
18 Thou shalt also *make* **work** a laver of *brass* **copper**,
and his *foot also* **base** of *brass* **copper**,
to *wash withal* **baptize**:
and thou shalt *put* **give** it
between the *tabernacle* **tent** of the congregation
and **between** the **sacrifice** altar,
and thou shalt *put* **give** water therein.
19 For *Aaron* **Aharon** and his sons
shall *wash* **baptize** their hands and their feet thereat:
20 When they go
into the *tabernacle* **tent** of the congregation,
they shall *wash* **baptize** with water, that they die not;
or when they come near to the **sacrifice** altar to minister,
to *burn offering made by fire* **incense a firing**
unto *the LORD* **Yah Veh**:
21 So they shall *wash* **baptize** their hands and their feet,
that they die not:
and it shall be *a* **an eternal** statute *for ever* to them,
even to him and to his seed throughout their generations.

FORMULA FOR THE ANOINTING OIL

22 Moreover *the LORD spake* **Yah Veh worded**
unto *Moses* **Mosheh**, saying,
23 Take thou also unto thee *principal* **head** spices,
of *pure* **clear** myrrh five hundred *shekels*,
and of *sweet* **spice** cinnamon half so much,
even two hundred and fifty *shekels*,
and of *sweet calamus* **spice stems**
two hundred and fifty *shekels*,
24 And of cassia five hundred *shekels*,
after the shekel of the *sanctuary* **hallowed refuge**,
and of oil olive an hin:
25 And thou shalt *make* **work** it an oil of holy ointment,
an ointment compound **a perfume of ointments**
after the *art* **work** of the *apothecary* **perfumer**:
it shall be an holy anointing oil.
26 And thou shalt anoint
the *tabernacle* **tent** of the congregation therewith,
and the ark of the *testimony* **witness**,
27 And the table and all his *vessels* **instruments**,
and the *candlestick* **menorah** and his *vessels* **instruments**,
and the **sacrifice** altar of incense,
28 And the **sacrifice** altar of *burnt offering* **holocaust**
with all his *vessels* **instruments**,
and the laver and his *foot* **base**.
29 And thou shalt *sanctify* **hallow** them,
that they may be *most holy* **a holy of holies**:
whatsoever toucheth them shall be *holy* **hallowed**.
30 And thou shalt anoint *Aaron* **Aharon** and his sons,
and *consecrate* **hallow** them, that they may
minister unto me in the priest's office
priest the priesthood unto me.
31 And thou shalt *speak* **word**
unto the *children* **sons** of *Israel* **Yisra El**, saying,
This shall be an holy anointing oil unto me
throughout your generations.
32 Upon *man's* **human** flesh shall it not be poured,
neither shall ye *make* **work** any other like it,
after the composition of it **as this formula**:
it is — holy, and it shall be holy unto you.
33 *Whosoever* **Any man**
compoundeth **who perfumeth** any like it,
or whosoever *putteth any* **giveth** of it upon a stranger,
shall even be cut off from his people.
34 And *the LORD* **Yah Veh** said unto *Moses* **Mosheh**,
Take unto thee *sweet spices* **aromatics**,
stacte, and onycha, and galbanum;
these *sweet spices* **aromatics** with pure frankincense:
of each shall there be a like weight **being equal**:

35 And thou shalt *make* **work** it *a perfume* **an incense**,
a *confection* **perfume**
after the art of the *apothecary* **perfumer**,
tempered together **salted**, pure and holy:
36 And **in pulverizing,**
thou shalt *beat some of it very small* **pulverize it**,
and *put* **give** of it
before the testimony **at the face of the witness**
in the *tabernacle* **tent** of the congregation,
where I *will* **shall** meet with thee:
it shall be unto you *most holy* **a holy of holies**.
37 And as for the *perfume* **incense**
which thou shalt *make* **work**,
ye shall not *make* **work** to yourselves
according to *the composition thereof* **this formula**:
it shall be unto thee holy for *the LORD* **Yah Veh**.
38 *Whosoever* **Any man who**
shall *make* **work** like unto that,
to *smell* **scent** thereto,
shall even be cut off from his people.

BESAL EL IS SPIRIT FILLED

31 And *the LORD spake* **Yah Veh worded**
unto *Moses* **Mosheh**, saying,
2 See, I have called by name *Bezaleel* **Besal El**
the son of Uri, the son of Hur,
of the *tribe* **rod** of *Judah* **Yah Hudah**:
3 And I have filled him with the spirit of *God* **Elohim**,
in wisdom, and in *understanding* **discernment**,
and in knowledge,
and in all *manner of workmanship* **his work**,
4 To *devise cunning works* **fabricate fabrications**,
to work in gold, and in silver, and in *brass* **copper**,
5 And in *cutting* **engraving** of stones, to *set* **fill** them,
and in *carving* **engraving** of timber,
to work in all *manner of workmanship* **work**.
6 And I, behold, I have given with him *Aholiab* **Oholi Ab**,
the son of *Ahisamach* **Achi Samach**, of the *tribe* **rod** of Dan:
and in the hearts of all that are wise hearted
I have *put* **given** wisdom,
that they may *make* **work**
all that I have *commanded* **misvahed** thee;
7 The *tabernacle* **tent** of the congregation,
and the ark of the *testimony* **witness**,
and the *mercy seat* **kapporeth** that is thereupon,
and all the *furniture* **instruments** of the *tabernacle* **tent**,
8 And the table and his *furniture* **instruments**,
and the pure *candlestick* **menorah**
with all his *furniture* **instruments**,
and the **sacrifice** altar of incense,
9 And the **sacrifice** altar of *burnt offering* **holocaust**
with all his *furniture* **instruments**,
and the laver and his *foot* **base**,
10 And the *cloths* **clothes** of *service* **stitching**,
and the holy *garments* **clothes** for *Aaron* **Aharon** the priest,
and the *garments* **clothes** of his sons,
to *minister in the priest's office*
priest the priesthood,
11 And the anointing oil,
and *sweet* incense **of aromatics**
for the *holy place* **holies**:
according to all that I have *commanded* **misvahed** thee
shall they *do* **work**.
12 And *the LORD spake* **Yah Veh worded**
unto *Moses* **Mosheh**, saying,
13 *Speak* **Word** thou also
unto the *children* **sons** of *Israel* **Yisra El**, saying,
Verily **Surely** my *sabbaths* **shabbaths** ye shall *keep* **guard**:
for it is a sign between me and **between** you
throughout your generations;
that ye may know that *I am the LORD* **I — Yah Veh**
that *doth sanctify* **halloweth** you.
14 Ye shall *keep* **guard** the *sabbath* **shabbath** therefore;
for it is holy unto you:
every one that *defileth* **profaneth** it,
in being deathified,
shall *surely be put to death* **be deathified**:
for whosoever *doeth* **worketh** *any* work therein,
that soul shall be cut off from among his people.
15 Six days may work be *done* **worked**;
but in the seventh **day**
is the *sabbath* **shabbath** of *rest* **shabbathism**,
holy to *the LORD* **Yah Veh**:
whosoever *doeth* **worketh** *any* work
in the *sabbath* **shabbath** day,
in being deathified,
he shall *surely be put to death* **be deathified**.
16 *Wherefore* the *children* **sons** of *Israel* **Yisra El**
shall *keep* **guard** the *sabbath* **shabbath**,
to *observe* **work** the *sabbath* **shabbath**
throughout their generations,
for *a perpetual* **an eternal** covenant.
17 It is a sign between me
and **between** the *children* **sons** of *Israel* **Yisra El**
for ever **eternally**:
for in six days *the LORD* **Yah Veh**
made heaven **worked the heavens** and earth,
and on the seventh day he *rested* **shabbathized**,
and *was* refreshed.

THE SLABS OF WITNESS

18 And he gave unto *Moses* **Mosheh**,
when he had
made an end of communing **finished wording**
with him upon mount *Sinai* **Sinay**,
two *tables* **slabs** of *testimony* **witness**, *tables* **slabs** of stone,
written **inscribed** with the finger of *God* **Elohim**.

MOLTEN CALF

32 And when the people saw
that *Moses* **Mosheh** delayed
to *come down* **descend** out of the mount,
the people *gathered themselves together* **congregated**
unto *Aaron* **Aharon**, and said unto him,
Up **Arise**, *make* **work** us *gods* **elohim**,
which shall go *before us* **at our face**;
for as for this *Moses* **Mosheh**,
the man that *brought* **ascended** us *up*
out of the land of *Egypt* **Misrayim**,
we *wot* **know** not what is become of him.
2 And *Aaron* **Aharon** said unto them,
Break off the golden *earrings* **noserings**,
which are in the ears of your *wives* **women**,
of your sons, and of your daughters,
and bring them unto me.
3 And all the people
brake off the golden *earrings* **noserings**
which were in their ears,
and brought them unto *Aaron* **Aharon**.
4 And he *received* **took** them at their hand,
and *fashioned* **formed** it with a *graving tool* **stylus**,
after he had *made* **worked** it a molten calf:
and they said, These be thy *god* **elohim**, O *Israel* **Yisra El**,
which *brought* **ascended** thee *up*
out of the land of *Egypt* **Misrayim**.
5 And when *Aaron* **Aharon** saw it,
he built *an* **a sacrifice** altar *before* **at the face of** it;
and *Aaron made proclamation* **Aharon called**, and said,
To morrow is a *feast* **celebration** to *the LORD* **Yah Veh**.
6 And they *rose up* **started** early on the morrow,
and *offered burnt offerings* **holocausted holocausts**,
and brought *peace offerings* **shelamim**;
and the people sat down to eat and to drink,
and rose up to *play* **entertain**.
7 And the *LORD said* **Yah Veh worded**
unto *Moses* **Mosheh**,
Go, *get thee down* **descend**;
for thy people, which thou *broughtest* **ascendest**
out of the land of *Egypt* **Misrayim**,
have *corrupted* **ruined** themselves:
8 They have turned aside *quickly* **suddenly**
out of the way which I *commanded* **misvahed** them:
they have *made* **worked** them a molten calf,
and have *worshipped* **prostrated** to it,
and have sacrificed thereunto, and said,
These be thy *gods* **elohim**, O *Israel* **Yisra El**,
which have *brought* **ascended** thee *up*
out of the land of *Egypt* **Misrayim**.
9 And *the LORD* **Yah Veh** said unto *Moses* **Mosheh**,
I have seen this people, and, behold,
it is a *stiffnecked* **hard necked** people:
10 Now therefore *let* **leave** me *alone*,
that my wrath may *wax hot* **kindle** against them,

and that I may *consume* **finish** them **off**:
and I *will make* **shall work** of thee a great *nation* **goyim**.

YAH VEH REVEALS HIS GLORY

11 *And Moses besought* **Mosheh stroked the face of**
the LORD **Yah Veh** his *God* **Elohim,** and said,
LORD **O Yah Veh**,
why doth thy wrath *wax hot* **kindle** against thy people,
which thou hast brought forth
out of the land of *Egypt* **Misrayim** with great *power* **force**,
and with a *mighty* **strong** hand?
12 *Wherefore* **Why**
should the *Egyptians speak* **Misrayim say**, and say,
For *mischief* **evil** did he bring them out,
to *slay* **slaughter** them in the mountains,
and to *consume* **finish** them **off**
from the face of the *earth* **soil**?
Turn from thy *fierce* **fuming** wrath,
and *repent* **sigh** of this evil against thy people.
13 Remember Abraham, *Isaac* **Yischaq**, and *Israel* **Yisra El**,
thy servants,
to whom thou *swarest* **oathest** by thine own self,
and *saidst* **wordest** unto them,
I *will multiply* **shall abound** your seed
as the stars of *heaven* **the heavens**,
and all this land that I have *spoken of* **said**
will **shall** I give unto your seed,
and they shall inherit it *for ever* **eternally**.
14 And *the LORD repented* **Yah Veh sighed** of the evil
which he *thought to do* **had worded to work**
unto his people.
15 And *Moses* **Mosheh** turned **his face**,
and *went down* **descended** from the mount,
and the two *tables* **slabs** of the *testimony* **witness**
were in his hand:
the *tables* **slabs** were *written* **inscribed** on both their sides;
on the one side and on the other
were they *written* **inscribed**.
16 And the *tables* **slabs** were the work of *God* **Elohim**,
and the *writing* **inscribing**
was the *writing* **inscibing** of *God* **Elohim**,
graven **engraved** upon the *tables* **slabs**.
17 And when *Joshua* **Yah Shua**
heard the *noise* **voice** of the people as they shouted,
he said unto *Moses* **Mosheh**,
There is a *noise* **voice** of war in the camp.
18 And he said, It is not the voice of them
that *shout* **answer** for *mastery* **might**,
neither is it the voice of them
that *cry* **answer** for being *overcome* **vanquished**:
but the *noise of them that sing* **voice of the humble**
do I hear.
19 And it *came to pass* **became**,
as soon as he *came nigh unto* **approached** the camp,
that he saw the calf, and the **round** dancing:
and *Moses' anger waxed hot* **Mosheh's wrath kindled**,
and he cast the *tables* **slabs** out of his hands,
and brake them beneath the mount.
20 And he took the calf which they had *made* **worked**,
and burnt it in the fire,
and *ground* **pulverized** it *to powder*,
and *strawed* **winnowed** it
upon **the face of** the water,
and made the *children* **sons** of *Israel* **Yisra El** drink of it.
21 And *Moses* **Mosheh** said unto *Aaron* **Aharon**,
What *did* **worked** this people unto thee,
that thou hast brought so great a sin upon them?
22 And *Aaron* **Aharon** said,
Let not the *anger* **wrath** of my *lord wax hot* **adoni kindle**:
thou knowest the people,
that they are set on *mischief* **evil**.
23 For they said unto me, *Make* **Work** us *gods* **elohim**,
which shall go *before us* **at our face**:
for as for this *Moses* **Mosheh**,
the man that *brought us up* **ascended us**
out of the land of *Egypt* **Misrayim**,
we *wot* **know** not what is become of him.
24 And I said unto them,
Whosoever hath any gold, let them break it off.
So they gave it me:
then I cast it into the fire, and there came out this calf.
25 And when *Moses* **Mosheh** saw
that the people were *naked* **exposed**;
(for *Aaron* **Aharon** had *made* **exposed** them *naked*
unto *their shame* **whisperings**
among their *enemies* **uprisers**:)
26 Then *Moses* **Mosheh**
stood in the *gate* **portal** of the camp, and said,
Who is on *the LORD'S* **Yah Veh's** side?
let him come unto me.
And all the sons of Levi
gathered *themselves together* unto him.
27 And he said unto them,
Thus saith *the LORD God* **Yah Veh Elohim**
of *Israel* **Yisra El**,
Put every man his sword by his *side* **flank**,
and *go* **pass** in and *out* **turn** from *gate* **portal** to *gate* **portal**
throughout the camp,
and *slay* **slaughter** every man his brother,
and every man his companion,
and every man his *neighbour* **near friend**.
28 And the *children* **sons** of Levi
did **worked** according to the word of *Moses* **Mosheh**:
and there fell of the people that day
about three thousand men.
29 For *Moses* **Mosheh** had said,
Consecrate yourselves **Fill your hands** to day
to *the LORD* **Yah Veh**,
even every **because** man *upon* **is against** his son,
and *upon* **against** his brother;
that he may *bestow upon* **give** you a blessing this day.
30 And it *came to pass* **became** on the morrow,
that *Moses* **Mosheh** said unto the people,
Ye have sinned a great sin:
and now I *will go up* **shall ascend**
unto *the LORD* **Yah Veh**;
peradventure **perhaps**
I shall *make an atonement* **kapar/atone** for your sin.
31 And *Moses* **Mosheh** returned unto *the LORD* **Yah Veh**,
and said, *Oh* **I beseech**,
this people have sinned a great sin,
and have *made* **worked** them *gods* **elohim** of gold.
32 Yet now, if thou *wilt forgive* **shalt bear** their sin —;
and if not, *blot* **wipe** me, I *pray* **beseech** thee,
out of thy *book* **scroll** which thou hast *written* **inscribed**.
33 And *the LORD* **Yah Veh** said unto *Moses* **Mosheh**,
Whosoever hath sinned against me,
him *will I blot* **shall I wipe** out of my *book* **scroll**.
34 Therefore now go, lead the people unto the place
of which I have *spoken* **worded** unto thee:
behold, mine Angel shall go *before thee* **at thy face**:
nevertheless in the day *when* I visit
I *will* **shall** visit their sin upon them.
35 And *the LORD plagued* **Yah Veh smote** the people,
because they *made* **worked** the calf,
which *Aaron made* **Aharon worked**.

33 And *the LORD* **Yah Veh**
said **worded** unto *Moses* **Mosheh**,
Depart **Go**, and *go up* **ascend** hence,
thou and the people which thou hast *brought up* **ascended**
out of the land of *Egypt* **Misrayim**,
unto the land which I *sware* **oathed** unto Abraham,
to *Isaac* **Yischaq**, and to *Jacob* **Yaaqov**, saying,
Unto thy seed *will* **shall** I give it:
2 And I *will* **shall** send an angel *before thee* **at thy face**;
and I *will drive out* **shall expel**
the *Canaanite* **Kenaaniy**, the *Amorite* **Emoriy**,
and the *Hittite* **Hethiy**, and the *Perizzites* **Perizziy**,
the *Hivite* **Hivviy**, and the *Jebusite* **Yebusiy**:
3 Unto a land flowing with milk and honey:
for I *will* **shall** not *go up* **ascend** in the midst of thee;
for thou art a *stiffnecked* **hard necked** people:
lest I *consume thee* **finish thee off** in the way.
4 And when the people heard these evil *tidings* **words**,
they mourned:
and no man did put on him his ornaments.
5 For *the LORD* **Yah Veh**
had said unto unto *Moses* **Mosheh**,
Say unto the *children* **sons** of *Israel* **Yisra El**,
Ye are a *stiffnecked* **hard necked** people:
I *will come up* **shall ascend** into the midst of thee

in a *moment* **blink**,
and *consume* **finish** thee **off**:
therefore now *put off* **lower** thy ornaments from thee,
that I may know what to *do* **work** unto thee.
6 And the *children* **sons** of *Israel* **Yisra El**
stripped themselves of their ornaments
by the mount Horeb.
7 And *Moses* **Mosheh** took the *tabernacle* **tent**,
and *pitched* **spread** it without the camp,
afar off **far removed** from the camp,
and called it the *Tabernacle* **Tent** of the congregation.
And it *came to pass* **became**,
that every one which sought *the LORD* **Yah Veh**
went out unto the *tabernacle* **tent** of the congregation,
which was without the camp.
8 And it *came to pass* **became**,
when *Moses* **Mosheh** went out unto the *tabernacle* **tent**,
that all the people rose up,
and *stood* **stationed** every man at his tent *door* **opening**,
and looked after *Moses* **Mosheh**,
until he was gone into the *tabernacle* **tent**.
9 And it *came to pass* **became**,
as *Moses* **Mosheh** entered into the *tabernacle* **tent**,
the cloudy pillar descended,
and stood at the *door* **opening** of the *tabernacle* **tent**,
and *the LORD talked* **he worded** with *Moses* **Mosheh**.
10 And all the people saw the cloudy pillar
stand at the *tabernacle door* **tent opening**:
and all the people rose up and *worshipped* **prostrated**,
every man in his tent *door* **opening**.
11 And *the LORD spake* **Yah Veh worded**
unto *Moses* **Mosheh** face to face,
as a man *speaketh* **wordeth** unto his friend.
And he turned again into the camp:
but his *servant Joshua* **minister Yah Shua**,
the son of Nun, a *young man* **lad**,
departed not out of the *tabernacle* **midst of the tent**.
12 And *Moses* **Mosheh** said unto *the LORD* **Yah Veh**,
See, thou sayest unto me, *Bring up* **Ascend** this people:
and thou hast not *let me know* **made known**
whom thou *wilt* **shalt** send with me.
Yet thou hast said, I know thee by name,
and thou hast also found *grace* **charism** in my *sight* **eyes**.
13 Now therefore, I *pray* **beseech** thee,
if I have found *grace* **charism** in thy *sight* **eyes**,
shew me now **make known, I beseech** thy way,
that I may know thee,
that I may find *grace* **charism** in thy *sight* **eyes**:
and *consider* **see** that this *nation* **goyim** is thy people.
14 And he said, My *presence* **face** shall go *with thee,*
and I *will give thee* **shall** rest **thee**.
15 And he said unto him,
If thy *presence* **face** go not *with me,*
carry **ascend** us not *up* hence.
16 For *wherein* **by what** shall it be known here
that I and thy people
have found *grace* **charism** in thy *sight* **eyes**?
is it not in that thou goest with us?
so shall we be separated, I and thy people,
from all the people that are upon the face of the earth.
17 And *the LORD* **Yah Veh** said unto *Moses* **Mosheh**,
I *will do* **shall work** this *thing* **word** also
that thou hast *spoken* **worded**:
for thou hast found *grace* **charism** in my *sight* **eyes**,
and I know thee by name.
18 And he said, I beseech thee,
shew me **have me see** thy *glory* **honour**.
19 And he said,
I *will make* **shall cause** all my goodness pass before thee,
and I *will proclaim* **shall call**
the name of *the LORD before thee* **Yah Veh at thy face**;
and *will be gracious* **shall grant charism**
to whom I *will be gracious* **shall grant charism**,
and *will shew* **shall** mercy
on whom I *will shew* **shall** mercy.
20 And he said, Thou canst not see my face:
for there shall no *man* **human** see me, and live.
21 And *the LORD* **Yah Veh** said, Behold,
there is a place by me,
and thou shalt *stand* **station thyself** upon a rock:
22 And it shall *come to pass* **become**,
while **until** my *glory* **honour** passeth by,
that I *will* **shall** put thee in a clift of the rock,
and *will* **shall** cover thee with my *hand* **palm**
while I pass by:
23 And I *will take* **shall turn** away *mine hand* **my palm**,
and thou shalt see my back *parts*:
but my face shall not be seen.
34 And *the LORD* **Yah Veh** said unto *Moses* **Mosheh**,
Hew **Sculpt** thee two *tables* **slabs** of stone
like unto the first:
and I *will write* **shall inscribe** upon these *tables* **slabs**
the words that were in the first *tables* **slabs**,
which thou brakest.
2 And be *ready* **prepared** in the morning,
and *come up* **ascend** in the morning
unto mount *Sinai* **Sinay**,
and *present* **station** thyself there to me
in the top of the mount.
3 And no man shall *come up* **ascend** with thee,
neither let *any* man be seen throughout all the mount;
neither let the flocks nor *herds feed* **oxen graze**
before **in front of** that mount.
4 And he *hewed* **sculpt** two *tables* **slabs** of stone
like unto the first;
and *Moses rose up* **Mosheh started** early in the morning,
and *went up* **ascended** unto mount *Sinai* **Sinay**,
as *the LORD* **Yah Veh** had *commanded* **misvahed** him,
and took in his hand the two *tables* **slabs** of stone.
5 And *the LORD* **Yah Veh** descended in the cloud,
and stood with him there,
and proclaimed the name of *the LORD* **Yah Veh**.
6 And *the LORD* **Yah Veh** passed by before *him* **his face**,
and *proclaimed* **called**,
The LORD **Yah Veh**, *The LORD God* **Yah Veh El**,
merciful and *gracious* **charismatic**,
longsuffering **slow to wrath**,
and *abundant* **great** in *goodness* **mercy** and truth,
7 *Keeping* **Guarding** mercy for thousands,
forgiving iniquity **bearing perversity**
and *transgression* **rebellion** and sin,
and that *will by no means clear the guilty*
in exonerating, shall not exonerate;
visiting the *iniquity* **perversity** of the fathers
upon the *children* **sons**,
and upon the *children's children* **sons' sons**,
unto the third and to the fourth *generation*.
8 And *Moses made haste* **Mosheh hastened**,
and bowed *his head* toward the earth,
and *worshipped* **prostrated**.
9 And he said, If *now* **I beseech**,
I have found *grace* **charism** in thy *sight* **eyes**,
O *Lord* **Adonay**,
let my *Lord* **Adonay**, I *pray* **beseech** thee, go among us;
for it is a *stiffnecked* **hard necked** people;
and *pardon* **forgive** our *iniquity* **perversity** and our sin,
and *take us for thine inheritance* **inherit us**.

YAH VEH CUTS A COVENANT WITH MOSHEH

10 And he said, Behold, I *make* **cut** a covenant:
before all thy people
I *will do marvels* **shall work wonders**,
such as have not been *done* **created** in all the earth,
nor in any *nation* **goyim**:
and all the people among which thou art
shall see the work of *the LORD* **Yah Veh**:
for it is *a terrible thing* **awesome**
that I *will do* **shall work** with thee.
11 *Observe* **Guard** thou that
which I *command* **misvah** thee this day:
behold, I *drive out before thee* **expel at thy face**
the *Amorite* **Emoriy**, and the *Canaanite* **Kenaaniy**,
and the *Hittite* **Hethiy**, and the *Perizzite* **Perizziy**,
and the *Hivite* **Hivviy**, and the *Jebusite* **Yebusiy**.
12 *Take heed to* **Guard** thyself,
lest thou *make* **cut** a covenant
with *the inhabitants of* **them who settled** the land
whither thou goest,
lest it be for a snare in the midst of thee:
13 But ye shall *destroy* **pull down** their **sacrifice** altars,
break their *images* **monoliths**,

and cut down their *groves* **asherim**:
14 For thou shalt *worship* **prostrate to** no other *god* **el**:
for *the LORD* **Yah Veh**, whose name is Jealous,
is a jealous *God* **El**:
15 Lest thou *make* **cut** a covenant
with *the inhabitants of* **them who settled** the land,
and they *go a whoring* **whore** after their *gods* **elohim**,
and *do* sacrifice unto their *gods* **elohim**,
and *one* call thee, and thou eat of his sacrifice;
16 And thou take of their daughters unto thy sons,
and their daughters
go a whoring **whore** after their *gods* **elohim**,
and make thy sons
go a whoring **whore** after their *gods* **elohim**.
17 Thou shalt *make* **work** thee no molten *gods* **elohim**.
18 The *feast* **celebration** of *unleavened bread* **matsah**
shalt thou *keep* **guard**.
Seven days thou shalt eat *unleavened bread* **matsah**,
as I *commanded* **misvahed** thee,
in the *time* **season** of the month Abib:
for in the month Abib
thou camest out from *Egypt* **Misrayim**.
19 *All that openeth* **Every burster of** the matrix is mine;
and every *firstling* **burster** among thy *cattle* **chattel**,
whether ox or *sheep, that is male* **lamb**.
20 But the *firstling of an ass* **he burro that bursteth**
thou shalt redeem with a lamb:
and if thou redeem him not,
then shalt thou break his neck.
All the firstborn of thy sons thou shalt redeem.
And none shall *appear* **be seen**
before me **at my face** empty.
21 Six days thou shalt *work* **serve**,
but on the seventh day thou shalt *rest* **shabbathize**:
in *earing time* **ploughing** and in harvest,
thou shalt *rest* **shabbathize**.
22 And thou shalt *observe* **work**
the *feast* **celebration** of weeks,
of the firstfruits of wheat harvest,
and the *feast* **celebration** of ingathering
at the *year's end* **revolution of the year**.
23 *Thrice* **Three times** in the year
shall all your *menchildren appear* **male sons be seen**
before the Lord GOD **at the face of Adonay Yah Veh**,
the *God* **Elohim** of *Israel* **Yisra El**.
24 For I *will cast out* **shall dispossess** the *nations* **goyim**
before thee **from thy face**,
and *enlarge* **broaden** thy borders:
neither shall any man desire thy land,
when thou shalt *go up* **ascend** to *appear* **be seen**
before the LORD **at the face of Yah Veh** thy *God* **Elohim**
thrice **three times** in the year.
25 Thou shalt not *offer* **slaughter**
the blood of my sacrifice with *leaven* **fermentation**;
neither shall the sacrifice
of the *feast* **celebration** of the *passover* **pasach**
be left **stay overnight** unto the morning.
26 The first of the firstfruits of thy *land* **soil**
thou shalt bring unto the house
of *the LORD* **Yah Veh** thy *God* **Elohim**.
Thou shalt not *seethe* **stew** a kid in his mother's milk.
27 And *the LORD* **Yah Veh** said unto *Moses* **Mosheh**,
Write **Inscribe** thou these words:
for after the *tenor* **mouth** of these words
I have *made* **cut** a covenant
with thee and with *Israel* **Yisra El**.
28 And he was there with *the LORD* **Yah Veh**
forty days and forty nights;
he did neither eat bread, nor drink water.
And he *wrote* **inscribed** upon the *tables* **slabs**
the words of the covenant, the ten *commandments* **words**.

MOSHEH'S EFFULGENCE

29 And it *came to pass* **became**,
when *Moses came down* **Mosheh descended**
from mount *Sinai* **Sinay**
with the two *tables* **slabs** of *testimony* **witness**
in *Moses'* **Mosheh's** hand,
when he *came down* **descended** from the mount,
that *Moses wist* **Mosheh knew** not
that the skin of his face shone
while he *talked* **worded** with him.
30 And when *Aaron* **Aharon**
and all the *children* **sons** of *Israel* **Yisra El**
saw *Moses* **Mosheh**, behold,
the skin of his face shone;
and they *were afraid* **awed** to come nigh him.
31 And *Moses* **Mosheh** called unto them;
and *Aaron* **Aharon**
and all the *rulers* **hierarchs** of the *congregation* **witness**
returned unto him:
and *Moses talked* **Mosheh worded** with them.
32 And afterward
all the *children* **sons** of *Israel* **Yisra El** came nigh:
and he *gave* **misvahed** them *in commandment*
all that *the LORD* **Yah Veh** had *spoken* **worded** with him
in mount *Sinai* **Sinay**.
33 And till *Moses* **Mosheh**
had *done speaking* **finished wording** with them,
he *put* **gave** a vail on his face.
34 But when *Moses* **Mosheh** went in
before the LORD **at the face of Yah Veh**
to *speak* **word** with him,
he *took the* **turned aside his** vail *off*, until he came out.
And he came out,
and *spake* **worded** unto the *children* **sons** of *Israel* **Yisra El**
that which he was *commanded* **misvahed**.
35 And the *children* **sons** of *Israel* **Yisra El**
saw the face of *Moses* **Mosheh**,
that the skin of *Moses'* **Mosheh's** face shone:
and *Moses put* **Mosheh returned** the vail
upon his face *again*,
until he went in to *speak* **word** with him.

THE SHABBATH OF SHABBATHISM

35 And *Moses* **Mosheh**
gathered **congregated** all the *congregation* **witness**
of the *children* **sons** of *Israel* **Yisra El** *together*,
and said unto them, These are the words
which *the LORD* **Yah Veh** hath *commanded* **misvahed**,
that ye should *do* **work** them.
2 Six days shall **the** work be *done* **worked**,
but on the seventh day
there shall be to you an holy day,
a *sabbath* **shabbath** of *rest* **shabbathism**
to *the LORD* **Yah Veh**:
whosoever *doeth* **worketh the** work therein
shall be *put to death* **deathified**.
3 *Ye* shall kindle no fire
throughout your *habitations* **settlements**
upon the *sabbath* **shabbath** day.

TABERNACLE MATERIALS

4 And *Moses spake* **Mosheh said**
unto all the *congregation* **witness**
of the *children* **sons** of *Israel* **Yisra El**, saying,
This is the *thing* **word**
which *the LORD commanded* **Yah Veh misvahed**, saying,
5 Take ye from among you
an *offering* **exaltment** unto *the LORD* **Yah Veh**:
whosoever is of a willing heart
everyone whose heart volunteereth,
let him bring it,
an *offering of the LORD* **exaltment unto Yah Veh**;
gold, and silver, and *brass* **copper**,
6 And blue, and purple, and scarlet,
and *fine* **white** linen, and goats' *hair*,
7 And rams' skins *dyed red* **reddened**, and badgers' skins,
and shittim *wood* **timber**,
8 And oil for the light, and spices for anointing oil,
and for the *sweet* incense **of aromatics**,
9 And onyx stones,
and stones *to be set* — **fillings** for the ephod,
and for the breastplate.
10 And every wise hearted among you shall come,
and *make* **work** all
that *the LORD* **Yah Veh** hath *commanded* **misvahed**;
11 The tabernacle, his tent, and his covering,
his *taches* **hooks**, and his boards, his bars,
his pillars, and his sockets,
12 The ark, and the staves thereof,
with the mercy seat **kapporeth**,
and the vail of the covering,

13 The table, and his staves,
and all his *vessels* **instruments**,
and the *shewbread* **face bread**,
14 The *candlestick* **menorah** also for the light,
and his *furniture* **instruments**,
and his lamps, with the oil for the light,
15 And the incense **sacrifice** altar, and his staves,
and the anointing oil,
and the *sweet* incense **of aromatics**,
and the *hanging* **covering** for the *door* **opening**,
at the *entering in* **opening** of the tabernacle,
16 The **sacrifice** altar of *burnt offering* **holocaust**,
with his *brasen grate* **copper screen**,
his staves, and all his *vessels* **instruments**,
the laver and his *foot* **base**,
17 The hangings of the court, his pillars, and their sockets,
and the *hanging* **covering** for the *door* **portal** of the court,
18 The *pins* **stakes** of the tabernacle,
and the *pins* **stakes** of the court, and their cords,
19 The *cloths* **clothes** of *service* **stitching**,
to *do service* **minister** in the *holy place* **holies**,
the holy *garments* **clothes** for *Aaron* **Aharon** the priest,
and the *garments* **clothes** of his sons,
to *minister in the priest's office*
priest the priesthood.
20 And all the *congregation* **witness**
of the *children* **sons** of *Israel* **Yisra El**
departed from the *presence* **face** of *Moses* **Mosheh**.
21 And they came,
every one whose heart *stirred him up* **was lifted**,
and every *one* **man**
whom his **whose** spirit *made willing* **volunteered**,
and they brought
the LORD'S offering **Yah Veh's exaltment**
to the work of the *tabernacle* **tent** of the congregation,
and for all his service, and for the holy *garments* **clothes**.
22 And they came, both men and women,
as many as were willing hearted
all whose heart volunteered,
and brought *bracelets* **hooks**, and *earrings* **noserings**,
and rings, and *tablets* **beads**,
all *jewels* **instruments** of gold:
and every man that *offered* **waved**
offered an offering **a wave** of gold
unto *the LORD* **Yah Veh**.
23 And every man, with whom was found blue,
and purple, and scarlet, and *fine* **white** linen,
and goats' *hair*, and *red* **reddened** skins of rams,
and badgers' skins, brought them.
24 Every one that *did offer* **exalted** an *offering* **exaltment**
of silver and *brass* **copper**
brought *the LORD'S offering* **Yah Veh's exaltment**:
and every man,
with whom was found shittim *wood* **timber**
for any work of the service, brought it.
25 And all the women that were wise hearted
did spin with their hands,
and brought *that which they had spun* **their spinning**,
both of blue, and of purple, and of scarlet,
and of *fine* **white** linen.
26 And all the women
whose heart *stirred them up* **was lifted** in wisdom
spun goats' *hair*.
27 And the *rulers* **hierarchs** brought onyx stones,
and stones *to be set*, — **fillings** for the ephod,
and for the breastplate;
28 And spice, and oil for the light,
and for the anointing oil,
and for the *sweet* incense **of aromatics**.
29 The *children* **sons** of *Israel* **Yisra El**
brought a *willing offering* **voluntary**
unto *the LORD* **Yah Veh**,
every man and woman,
whose heart *made them willing* **volunteered**
to bring for all *manner of* work,
which *the LORD* **Yah Veh** had *commanded* **misvahed**
to be *made* **worked** by the hand of *Moses* **Mosheh**.
30 And *Moses* **Mosheh** said
unto the *children* **sons** of *Israel* **Yisra El**,
See,
the LORD **Yah Veh** hath called by name *Bezaleel* **Besal El**
the son of Uri, the son of Hur,
of the *tribe* **rod** of *Judah* **Yah Hudah**;
31 And he hath filled him with the spirit of *God* **Elohim**,
in wisdom, in *understanding* **discernment**,
and in knowledge,
and in all *manner of workmanship* **his work**;
32 And to *devise curious works* **fabricate fabrications**,
to work in gold, and in silver, and in *brass* **copper**,
33 And in the *cutting* **engraving** of stones, to *set* **fill** them,
and in *carving* **engraving** of *wood* **timber**,
to *make* **work** any *manner* **work**
of *cunning work* **fabrications**.
34 And he hath *put* **given** in his heart
that he may *teach* **direct**,
both he, and *Aholiab* **Oholi Ab**,
the son of *Ahisamach* **Achi Samach**, of the *tribe* **rod** of Dan.
35 Them hath he filled with wisdom of heart,
to work all *manner of* work,
of the engraver,
and of the *cunning workman* **work of a fabricator**,
and of the embroiderer,
in blue, and in purple, in scarlet, and in *fine* **white** linen,
and of the weaver,
even of them that do any **workers of every** work,
and of those that
devise cunning work **fabricate fabrications**.

CONSTRUCTION OF THE TABERNACLE

36 Then *wrought* **worked**
Bezaleel **Besal El** and *Aholiab* **Oholi Ab**,
and every wise hearted man,
in whom *the LORD* **Yah Veh**
put **gave** wisdom and *understanding* **discernment**
to know how to work all *manner of* work
for the service of the *sanctuary* **holies**,
according to all
that *the LORD* **Yah Veh** had *commanded* **misvahed**.
2 And *Moses* **Mosheh**
called *Bezaleel* **Besal El** and *Aholiab* **Oholi Ab**,
and every wise hearted man,
in whose heart *the LORD* **Yah Veh** had *put* **given** wisdom,
even every one whose heart *stirred him up* **was lifted**
to *come unto* **approach** the work to *do* **work** it:
3 And they *received* **took at the face** of *Moses* **Mosheh**
all the *offering* **exaltment**,
which the *children* **sons** of *Israel* **Yisra El** had brought
for the work of the service of the *sanctuary* **holies**,
to *make* **work** it *withal*.
And they brought yet unto him *free offerings* **voluntaries**
every morning **morning by morning**.
4 And all the wise *men*,
that *wrought* **worked** all the work of the *sanctuary* **holies**,
came *every man* **man by man** from his work
which they *made* **worked**;
5 And they *spake* **said** unto *Moses* **Mosheh**, saying,
The people
bring much more than **abound in bringing** enough
for the service of the work,
which *the LORD commanded* **Yah Veh misvahed**
to *make* **work**.
6 And *Moses gave commandment* **Mosheh misvahed**,
and they *caused it to be proclaimed* **passed a voice**
throughout the camp, saying,
Let neither man nor woman *make* **work** any more work
for the *offering* **exaltment** of the *sanctuary* **holies**.
So the people were restrained from bringing.
7 For the *stuff* **work** they had
was sufficient for all the work to *make* **work** it,
and *too much* **overflowing**.
8 And *every* **all the** wise hearted *man among them*
that *wrought* **worked** the work of the tabernacle
made **worked** ten curtains of *fine* **white** twined linen,
and blue, and purple, and scarlet:
with *cherubims* **cherubim** of *cunning* **fabricated** work
made **worked** he them.
9 The length of one curtain *was* twenty and eight cubits,
and the breadth of one curtain four cubits:
the curtains were all of one *size* **measure**.
10 And he *coupled* **joined** the five curtains
one *unto another* **to one**:

and the *other* five curtains he *coupled* **joined**
one *unto another* **to one**.
11 And he *made* **worked** loops of blue
on the edge of one curtain
from the *selvedge* **end** in the *coupling* **joint**:
likewise he *made* **worked**
in the uttermost *side* **edge** of *another* **one** curtain,
in the *coupling* **joint** of the second.
12 Fifty loops *made* **worked** he in one curtain,
and fifty loops *made* **worked** he
in the *edge* **end** of the curtain
which was in the *coupling* **joint** of the second:
the loops *held* **took hold** one *curtain* to *another* **one**.
13 And he *made* **worked** fifty *taches* **hooks** of gold,
and *coupled* **joined** the curtains one *unto another* **to one**
with the *taches* **hooks**:
so it became one tabernacle.
14 And he *made* **worked** curtains of goats' *hair*
for the tent over the tabernacle:
eleven curtains he *made* **worked** them.
15 The length of one curtain was thirty cubits,
and four cubits was the breadth of one curtain:
the eleven curtains were of one *size* **measure**.
16 And he *coupled* **joined** five curtains by themselves,
and six curtains by themselves.
17 And he *made* **worked** fifty loops
upon the *uttermost* edge of the curtain
in the *coupling* **joint**,
and fifty loops *made* **worked** he
upon the edge of the curtain
which coupleth **with the joint of** the second.
18 And he *made* **worked** fifty *taches* **hooks** of *brass* **copper**
to *couple* **join** the tent together, that it might be one.
19 And he *made* **worked** a covering for the tent
of rams' skins *dyed red* **reddened**,
and a covering of badgers' skins above that.
20 And he *made* **worked** boards for the tabernacle
of shittim *wood* **timber**, standing up.
21 The length of a board *was* ten cubits,
and the breadth of a board one cubit and a half.
22 One board had two *tenons* **hands**,
equally distant **equidistant** one *from another* **to one**:
thus did he *make* **work** for all the boards of the tabernacle.
23 And he *made* **worked** boards for the tabernacle;
twenty boards for the south *side* **edge** southward:
24 And forty sockets of silver
he *made* **worked** under the twenty boards;
two sockets under one board for
his two *tenons* **hands**,
and two sockets under *another* **one** board
for his two *tenons* **hands**.
25 And for the *other* **second** side of the tabernacle,
which is toward the north *corner* **edge**,
he *made* **worked** twenty boards,
26 And their forty sockets of silver;
two sockets under one board,
and two sockets under *another* **one** board.
27 And for the *sides* **flanks** of the tabernacle
westward **seaward**
he *made* **worked** six boards.
28 And two boards *made* **worked** he
for the corners of the tabernacle in the *two sides* **flanks**.
29 And they were *coupled beneath* **twinned downward**,
and *coupled together* **twinned** at the *head* **top** thereof,
to one *ring* **signet**:
thus he *did* **worked** to *both* **the two** of them
in *both* the **two** corners.
30 And there were eight boards;
and their sockets were sixteen sockets of silver,
under every **one** board two sockets **and two sockets**.
31 And he *made* **worked** bars of shittim *wood* **timber**;
five for the boards
of the one side of the tabernacle,
32 And five bars for the boards
of the *other* **second** side of the tabernacle,
and five bars for the boards
of the tabernacle for the *sides westward* **flanks seaward**.
33 And he *made* **worked** the middle bar
to *shoot through* **extend among** the boards
from *the one* end to *the other* **end**.
34 And he overlaid the boards with gold,
and *made* **worked** their *rings* **signets** of gold
to be *places* **housings** for the bars,
and overlaid the bars with gold.
35 And he *made* **worked** a vail
of blue, and purple, and scarlet,
and *fine* **white** twined linen:
with *cherubims* **cherubim**
made **worked** he it of *cunning* **fabricated** work.
36 And he *made* **worked** thereunto
four pillars of shittim *wood*,
and overlaid them with gold: their hooks were of gold;
and he *cast* **poured** for them four sockets of silver.
37 And he *made an hanging* **worked a covering**
for the *tabernacle door* **tent opening**
of blue, and purple, and scarlet,
and *fine* **white** twined linen,
of *needlework* **embroidery work**;
38 And the five pillars of it with their hooks:
and he overlaid
their *chapiters* **tops** and their *fillets* **attachments** with gold:
but their five sockets were of *brass* **copper**.

CONSTRUCTION OF THE ARK

37 And *Bezaleel* **Besal El**
made **worked** the ark of shittim *wood* **timber**:
two cubits and a half was the length of it,
and a cubit and a half the breadth of it,
and a cubit and a half the height of it:
2 And he overlaid it with pure gold within and without,
and *made* **worked** a *crown* **moulding** of gold to it
round about.
3 And he *cast* **poured** for it four *rings* **signets** of gold,
to be set by the four *corners* **supports** of it;
even two *rings* **signets** upon the one side of it,
and two *rings* **signets** upon the *other* **second** side of it.
4 And he *made* **worked** staves of shittim *wood* **timber**,
and overlaid them with gold.
5 And he put the staves into the *rings* **signets**
by the sides of the ark, to bear the ark.
6 And he *made* **worked** the *mercy seat* **kapporeth**
of pure gold:
two cubits and a half was the length thereof,
and one cubit and a half the breadth thereof.
7 And he *made* **worked** two *cherubims* **cherubim** of gold,
beaten out of one piece **of spinnings**
made **worked** he them,
on the two ends of the *mercy seat* **kapporeth**;
8 One cherub on the end on this side,
and *another* **one** cherub on the *other* end **on that side**:
out of the *mercy seat* **kapporeth**
made **worked** he the *cherubims* **cherubim**
on the two ends thereof.
9 And the *cherubims* **cherubim**
spread out their wings *on high* **upward**,
and covered with their wings
over the *mercy seat* **kapporeth**,
with their faces *one to another* **man toward brother**;
even to **toward** the *mercy seatward* **kapporeth**
were the faces of the *cherubims* **cherubim**.

CONSTRUCTION OF THE TABLE

10 And he *made* **worked** the table of shittim *wood* **timber**:
two cubits *was* the length thereof,
and a cubit the breadth thereof,
and a cubit and a half the height thereof:
11 And he overlaid it with pure gold,
and *made* **worked** thereunto
a *crown* **moulding** of gold round about.
12 Also he *made* **worked** thereunto a border
of *an handbreadth* **a palm span** round about;
and *made a crown* **worked a moulding** of gold
for the border thereof round about.
13 And he *cast* **poured** for it four *rings* **signets** of gold,
and *put* **gave** the *rings* **signets** upon the four *corners* **edges**
that were in the four feet thereof.
14 *Over against* **Along side** the border
were the *rings* **signets**,
the *places* **housings** for the staves to bear the table.
15 And he *made* **worked** the staves
of shittim *wood* **timber**,
and overlaid them with gold, to bear the table.

16 And he *made* **worked** the *vessels* **instruments**
which were upon the table,
his dishes, and his *spoons* **bowls**,
and his *bowls* **exoneration basins**,
and his covers to *cover withal* **libate with**, of pure gold.

CONSTRUCTION OF THE MENORAH

17 And he *made* **worked** the *candlestick* **menorah**
of pure gold:
of *beaten work* **spinnings**
made **worked** he the *candlestick* **menorah**;
his *shaft* **flank**, and his *branch* **stem**, his bowls,
his *knops* **finials**, and his *flowers* **blossoms**,
were of the same:
18 And six *branches* **stems** going out of the sides thereof;
three *branches* **stems** of the *candlestick* **menorah**
out of the one side thereof,
and three *branches* **stems** of the *candlestick* **menorah**
out of the *other* **second** side thereof:
19 Three bowls
made after the fashion of almonds **almond shaped**
in one *branch* **stem**, a *knop* **finial** and a *flower* **blossom**;
and three bowls *made like almonds* **almond shaped**
in *another branch* **one stem**,
a *knop* **finial** and a *flower* **blossom**:
so throughout the six *branches* **stems**
going out of the *candlestick* **menorah**.
20 And in the *candlestick* **menorah** were four bowls
made like almonds **almond shaped**,
his *knops* **finials**, and his *flowers* **blossoms**:
21 And a *knop* **finial**
under two *branches* **stems** of the same,
and a *knop* **finial** under two *branches* **stems** of the same,
and a *knop* **finial** under two *branches* **stems** of the same,
according to the six *branches* **stems** going out of it.
22 Their *knops* **finials** and their *branches* **stems**
were of the same:
all of it was one *beaten work* **spinning** of pure gold.
23 And he *made* **worked** his seven lamps,
and his *snuffers* **tongs**, and his *snuffdishes* **trays**,
of pure gold.
24 Of a *talent* **round** of pure gold *made* **worked** he it,
and all the *vessels* **instruments** thereof.

CONSTRUCTION OF THE INCENSE SACRIFICE ALTAR

25 And he *made* **worked** the incense **sacrifice** altar
of shittim *wood* **timber**:
the length of it *was* a cubit, and the breadth of it a cubit;
it was foursquare; and two cubits was the height of it;
the horns thereof were of the same.
26 And he overlaid it with pure gold,
both the *top* **roof** of it,
and the *sides* **walls** thereof round about,
and the horns of it:
also he *made* **worked** unto it
a *crown* **moulding** of gold round about.
27 And he *made* **worked** two *rings* **signets** of gold for it
under the *crown* **moulding** thereof
by the two *corners* **sides** of it,
upon the two sides thereof,
to be *places* **housings** for the staves to bear it withal.
28 And he *made* **worked** the staves
of shittim *wood* **timber**,
and overlaid them with gold.
29 And he *made* **worked** the holy anointing oil,
and the pure incense of *sweet spices* **aromatics**,
according to the work of the apothecary.

CONSTRUCTION OF THE HOLOCAUST SACRIFICE ALTAR

38 And he *made* **worked** the **sacrifice** altar
of *burnt offering* **holocaust** of shittim *wood* **timber**:
five cubits was the length thereof,
and five cubits the breadth thereof;
it was foursquare; and three cubits the height thereof.
2 And he *made* **worked** the horns thereof
on the four corners of it;
the horns thereof were of the same:
and he overlaid it with *brass* **copper**.
3 And he *made* **worked** all the *vessels* **instruments**
of the **sacrifice** altar,
the *pots* **cauldrons**, and the shovels,
and the *basons* **sprinklers**,
and the *fleshhooks* **forks**, and the *firepans* **trays**:
all the *vessels* **instruments** thereof
made **worked** he of *brass* **copper**.
4 And he *made* **worked** for the **sacrifice** altar
a *brasen grate* **copper screen** of network
under the *compass* **rim** thereof
beneath **downward** unto the midst of it.
5 And he *cast* **poured** four *rings* **signets**
for the four ends of the *grate* **screen** of *brass* **copper**,
to be *places* **housings** for the staves.
6 And he *made* **worked** the staves of shittim *wood* **timber**,
and overlaid them with *brass* **copper**.
7 And he put the staves
into the *rings* **signets** on the sides of the **sacrifice** altar,
to bear it withal;
he *made the altar* **worked it** hollow with *boards* **slabs**.

CONSTRUCTION OF THE LAVER

8 And he *made* **worked** the laver of *brass* **copper**,
and the *foot* **base** of it of *brass* **copper**,
of the *lookingglasses* **mirrors**
of *the women assembling* **those that hosted**,
which *assembled* **hosted** at the *door* **opening**
of the *tabernacle* **tent** of the congregation.

CONSTRUCTION OF THE COURT

9 And he *made* **worked** the court:
on the south *side* **edge** southward
the hangings of the court were of *fine* **white** twined linen,
an hundred cubits:
10 Their pillars were twenty,
and their *brasen* **copper** sockets twenty;
the hooks of the pillars and their *fillets* **attachments**
were of silver.
11 And for the north *side the hangings were* **edge**
an hundred cubits,
their pillars *were* twenty,
and their sockets of *brass* **copper** twenty;
the hooks of the pillars and their *fillets* **attachments**
of silver.
12 And for the *west side were* **seaward edge**
hangings of fifty cubits,
their pillars ten, and their sockets ten;
the hooks of the pillars and their *fillets* **attachments**
of silver.
13 And for the east *side eastward* **edge toward the rising**
fifty cubits.
14 The hangings of the one *side of the gate* **shoulder**
were fifteen cubits;
their pillars three, and their sockets three.
15 And for the *other side* **second shoulder**
of the court *gate* **portal**,
on this *hand* and that,
were hangings of fifteen cubits;
their pillars three, and their sockets three.
16 All the hangings of the court round about
were of *fine* **white** twined linen.
17 And the sockets for the pillars were of *brass* **copper**;
the hooks of the pillars and their *fillets* **attachments**
of silver;
and the overlaying of their *chapiters* **tops** of silver;
and all the pillars of the court
were *filleted* **attached** with silver.
18 And the *hanging* **covering**
for the *gate* **portal** of the court
was *needlework* **embroidery work**,
of blue, and purple, and scarlet,
and *fine* **white** twined linen:
and twenty cubits *was* the length,
and the height in the breadth was five cubits,
answerable to **along side** the hangings of the court.
19 And their pillars were four,
and their sockets of *brass* **copper** four;
their hooks of silver,
and the overlaying of their *chapiters* **tops**
and their *fillets* **attachments** of silver.
20 And all the *pins* **stakes** of the tabernacle,
and of the court round about, *were* of *brass* **copper**.
21 This is the *sum* **muster** of the tabernacle,
even of the tabernacle of *testimony* **witness**,
as it was counted,
according to the *commandment* **mouth** of *Moses* **Mosheh**,

for the service of the *Levites* **Leviym**,
by the hand of *Ithamar* **Iy Thamar**,
son to *Aaron* **Aharon** the priest.
22 And *Bezaleel* **Besal El** the son of Uri, the son of Hur,
of the *tribe* **rod** of *Judah* **Yah Hudah**,
made **worked** all that *the LORD* **Yah Veh**
commanded Moses **misvahed Mosheh**.
23 And with him was *Aholiab* **Oholi Ab**,
son of *Ahisamach* **Achi Samach**, of the *tribe* **rod** of Dan,
an engraver, and a *cunning workman* **fabricator**,
and an embroiderer in blue, and in purple, and in scarlet,
and *fine* **white** linen.
24 All the gold that was *occupied* **worked** for the work
in all the work of the *holy place* **holies**,
even the gold *of* **for** the *offering* **wave**,
was twenty and nine *talents* **rounds**,
and seven hundred and thirty shekels,
after the shekel of the *sanctuary* **holies**.
25 And the silver of them
that were *numbered* **mustered** of the *congregation* **witness**
was an hundred *talents* **rounds**,
and a thousand seven hundred
and *threescore and fifteen* **seventy and five** shekels,
after the shekel of the *sanctuary* **holies**:
26 A bekah *for every man* **per cranium**,
that is, half a shekel,
after the shekel of the *sanctuary* **holies**,
for every one that *went* **passed** to be *numbered* **mustered**,
from **a son of** twenty years *old* and upward,
for six hundred thousand and three thousand
and five hundred and fifty *men*.
27 And of the hundred *talents* **rounds** of silver
were *cast* **poured** the sockets of the *sanctuary* **holies**,
and the sockets of the vail;
an hundred sockets of the hundred *talents* **rounds**,
a *talent* **round** for a socket.
28 And of the thousand seven hundred
seventy and five *shekels*
he *made* **worked** hooks for the pillars,
and overlaid their *chapiters* **tops**,
and *filleted* **attached** them.
29 And the *brass* **copper** of the *offering* **wave**
was seventy *talents* **rounds**,
and two thousand and four hundred shekels.
30 And therewith he *made* **worked** the sockets
to the *door* **opening**
of the *tabernacle* **tent** of the congregation,
and the *brasen* **copper sacrifice** altar,
and the *brasen grate* **copper screen** for it,
and all the *vessels* **instruments** of the **sacrifice** altar,
31 And the sockets of the court round about,
and the sockets of the court *gate* **portal**,
and all the *pins* **stakes** of the tabernacle,
and all the *pins* **stakes** of the court round about.

CONSTRUCTION OF THE CLOTHES

39 And of the blue, and purple, and scarlet,
they *made cloths* **worked clothes** of *service* **stitching**,
to *do service* **minister** in the *holy place* **holies**,
and *made* **worked** the holy *garments* **clothes**
for *Aaron* **Aharon**;
as *the LORD* **Yah Veh**
commanded Moses **misvahed Mosheh**.

CONSTRUCTION OF THE EPHOD

2 And he *made* **worked** the ephod
of gold, blue, and purple, and scarlet,
and *fine* **white** twined linen.
3 And they *did beat* **expanded** the gold
into *thin plates* **sheets**,
and cut it into *wires* **braids**,
to work it in **among** the blue, and *in* **among** the purple,
and *in* **among** the scarlet,
and *in* **among** the *fine* **white** linen,
with *cunning* **fabricated** work.
4 They *made* **worked** shoulderpieces for it,
to *couple* **join** it *together*:
by the two *edges* **ends** was it *coupled* **joined** *together*.
5 And the *curious* **fabricated** girdle of his ephod,
that was upon it,
was of the same, according to the work thereof;
of gold, blue, and purple, and scarlet,
and *fine* **white** twined linen;
as *the LORD* **Yah Veh**
commanded Moses **misvahed Mosheh**.
6 And they *wrought* **worked** onyx stones
inclosed in ouches **surrounded by brocades** of gold,
graven **engraved**, as *signets are graven* **engravings of seals**,
with the names of the *children* **sons** of *Israel* **Yisra El**.
7 And he put them on the shoulders of the ephod,
that they should be stones for a memorial
to the *children* **sons** of *Israel* **Yisra El**;
as *the LORD* **Yah Veh**
commanded Moses **misvahed Mosheh**.

CONSTRUCTION OF THE BREASTPLATE

8 And he *made* **worked** the breastplate
of *cunning* **fabricated** work like the work of the ephod;
of gold, blue, and purple, and scarlet,
and *fine* **white** twined linen.
9 It was foursquare;
they *made* **worked** the breastplate double:
a span *was* the length thereof,
and a span the breadth thereof, *being* doubled.
10 And they *set* **filled** in it four rows of stones:
the first row was a sardius, a topaz, and a carbuncle:
this was the first row.
11 And the second row,
an emerald, a sapphire, and a diamond.
12 And the third row,
a ligure **an opal**, an agate, and an amethyst.
13 And the fourth row,
a beryl, an onyx, and a jasper:
they were *inclosed* **surrounded**
in ouches **by brocades** of gold in their *inclosings* **fillings**.
14 And the stones were according to the names
of the *children* **sons** of *Israel* **Yisra El**,
twelve, according to their names,
like the engravings of a *signet* **seal**,
every *one* **man** with his name,
according to the twelve *tribes* **scions**.
15 And they *made* **worked** upon the breastplate
chains *at the ends* **twisted**, of wreathen work of pure gold.
16 And they *made* **worked** two *ouches* **brocades** of gold,
and two gold *rings* **signets**;
and *put* **gave** the two *rings* **signets**
in the two ends of the breastplate.
17 And they *put* **gave** the two
wreathen chains **wreaths** of gold
in the two *rings* **signets** on the ends of the breastplate.
18 And the two ends of the two *wreathen chains* **wreaths**
they *fastened* **gave** in the two *ouches* **brocades**,
and *put* **gave** them on the shoulderpieces of the ephod,
before it **in front of its face**.
19 And they *made* **worked** two *rings* **signets** of gold,
and put them on the two ends of the breastplate,
upon the *border* **edge** of it,
which was on the side of the ephod *inward* **housing**.
20 And they *made* **worked** two *other* golden *rings* **signets**,
and *put* **gave** them on the two *sides* **shoulders**
of the ephod *underneath* **downward**,
toward the forepart **in front of the face** of it,
over against **along side** the *other coupling* **joint** thereof,
above the *curious* **fabricated** girdle of the ephod.
21 And they did bind the breastplate by his *rings* **signets**
unto the *rings* **signets** of the ephod
with a *lace* **braid** of blue,
that it might be above
the *curious* **fabricated** girdle of the ephod,
and that the breastplate
might not be *loosed* **removed** from the ephod;
as *the LORD* **Yah Veh**
commanded Moses **misvahed Mosheh**.

CONSTRUCTION OF THE MANTLE

22 And he *made* **worked** the *robe* **mantle** of the ephod
of woven work, *all* **totally** of blue.
23 And there was *an hole* **a mouth**
in the midst of the *robe* **mantle**,
as the *hole* **mouth** of an habergeon,
with *a band* **an edging** round about the *hole* **mouth**,
that it should not *rend* **rip**.
24 And they *made* **worked** upon the *hems* **drapes**
of the *robe* **mantle**

pomegranates of blue, and purple, and scarlet,
and twined *linen.*
25 And they *made* **worked** bells of pure gold,
and *put* **gave** the bells *between* **midst** the pomegranates
upon the *hem* **drape** of the *robe* **mantle**,
round about *between* **midst** the pomegranates;
26 A bell and a pomegranate, a bell and a pomegranate,
round about the *hem* **drape** of the *robe* **mantle**
to minister in;
as *the LORD* **Yah Veh**
commanded Moses **misvahed Mosheh**.

CONSTRUCTION OF THE TUNIC, TIARA, AND BREECHES

27 And they *made* **worked** coats
of *fine* **white** linen of woven work
for *Aaron* **Aharon**, and for his sons,
28 And a *mitre* **tiara** of *fine* **white** linen,
and *goodly bonnets* **ornaments of turbans**
of *fine* **white** linen,
and linen breeches of *fine* **white** twined linen,
29 And a girdle of *fine* **white** twined linen,
and blue, and purple, and scarlet,
of *needlework* **embroidery work**;
as *the LORD* **Yah Veh**
commanded Moses **misvahed Mosheh**.

CONSTRUCTION OF THE BLOSSOM OF THE HOLY SEPARATISM

30 And they *made* **worked** the *plate* **blossom**
of the holy *crown* **separatism** of pure gold,
and *wrote* **inscribed** upon it *a writing* **an inscribing**,
like to the engravings of a *signet* **seal**,
HOLINESS TO THE LORD **HOLY TO YAH VEH**.
31 And they *tied* **gave** unto it a *lace* **braid** of blue,
to *fasten* **give** it *on high* **upward** upon the *mitre* **tiara**;
as *the LORD* **Yah Veh**
commanded Moses **misvahed Mosheh**.

INSPECTION OF THE TABERNACLE

32 Thus was all the *work* **service** of the tabernacle
of the tent of the congregation finished:
and the *children* **sons** of *Israel* **Yisra El**
did **worked** according to all
that *the LORD* **Yah Veh**
commanded Moses **misvahed Mosheh**,
so *did* **worked** they.
33 And they brought the tabernacle unto *Moses* **Mosheh**,
the tent, and all his *furniture* **instruments**,
his *taches* **hooks**, his boards, his bars,
and his pillars, and his sockets,
34 And the covering of rams' skins *dyed red* **reddened**,
and the covering of badgers' skins,
and the vail of the covering,
35 The ark of the *testimony* **witness**, and the staves thereof,
and the *mercy seat* **kapporeth**,
36 The table, and all the *vessels* **instruments** thereof,
and the *shewbread* **face bread**,
37 The pure *candlestick* **menorah**, with the lamps thereof,
even with the lamps to be *set in order* **in rows**,
and all the *vessels* **instruments** thereof,
and the oil for light,
38 And the golden **sacrifice** altar, and the anointing oil,
and the *sweet* incense **of aromatics**,
and the *hanging* **covering**
for the *tabernacle door* **tent opening**,
39 The *brasen* **copper sacrifice** altar,
and his *grate* **screen** of *brass* **copper**,
his staves, and all his *vessels* **instruments**,
the laver and his *foot* **base**,
40 The hangings of the court, his pillars, and his sockets,
and the *hanging* **covering** for the court *gate* **portal**,
his cords, and his *pins* **stakes**,
and all *the vessels of* the service of the tabernacle,
for the tent of the congregation,
41 The *cloths* **clothes** of *service* **stitching**
to *do service* **minister** in the *holy place* **holies**,
and the holy *garments* **clothes** for *Aaron* **Aharon** the priest,
and his sons' *garments* **clothes**,
to *minister in the priest's office*
priest the priesthood.
42 According to all that *the LORD* **Yah Veh**
commanded Moses **misvahed Mosheh**,
so the *children* **sons** of *Israel* **Yisra El**
made **worked** all the *work* **service**.
43 And *Moses* **Mosheh** did look upon all the work,
and, behold, they had *done* **worked** it
as *the LORD* **Yah Veh** had *commanded* **misvahed**,
even so **thus** had they *done* **worked** it:
and *Moses* **Mosheh** blessed them.

ERECTION OF THE TABERNACLE

40 And *the LORD spake* **Yah Veh worded**
unto *Moses* **Mosheh**, saying,
2 *On the first day of the first month*
On the first day of the month, on the first of the month
shalt thou *set up* **raise** the tabernacle
of the tent of the congregation.
3 And thou shalt put therein
the ark of the *testimony* **witness**,
and cover the ark with the vail.
4 And thou shalt bring in the table,
and *set in order* **arrange**
the things that are to be set in order upon it
its arrangement;
and thou shalt bring in the *candlestick* **menorah**,
and *light* **holocaust** the lamps thereof.
5 And thou shalt *set* **give** the **sacrifice** altar of gold
for the incense
before **at the face of** the ark of the *testimony* **witness**,
and put the *hanging* **covering**
of the *door* **opening** to the tabernacle.
6 And thou shalt *set* **give** the **sacrifice** altar
of **for** the *burnt offering* **holocaust**
before **at the face of** the *door* **opening**
of the tabernacle of the tent of the congregation.
7 And thou shalt *set* **give** the laver
between the tent of the congregation
and **between** the **sacrifice** altar,
and shalt *put* **give** water therein.
8 And thou shalt set up the court round about,
and *hang up the hanging* **give the covering**
at the court *gate* **portal**.
9 And thou shalt take the anointing oil,
and anoint the tabernacle, and all that is therein,
and shalt hallow it,
and all the *vessels* **instruments** thereof:
and it shall be holy.
10 And thou shalt anoint the **sacrifice** altar
of the burnt offering **for the holocaust**,
and all his *vessels* **instruments**,
and *sanctify* **hallow** the **sacrifice** altar:
and it shall be *an* **a sacrifice** altar
most holy — **a holy of holies**.
11 And thou shalt anoint the laver and his *foot* **base**,
and *sanctify* **hallow** it.
12 And thou shalt *bring Aaron* **oblate Aharon** and his sons
unto the *door* **opening**
of the *tabernacle* **tent** of the congregation,
and *wash* **baptize** them with water.
13 And thou shalt put upon *Aaron* **Aharon**
the holy *garments* **clothes**,
and anoint him, and *sanctify* **hallow** him;
that he may *minister unto me in the priest's office*
priest the priesthood unto me.
14 And thou shalt *bring* **oblate** his sons,
and clothe them with coats:
15 And thou shalt anoint them,
as thou didst anoint their father,
that they may *minister unto me in the priest's office*
priest the priesthood unto me:
for their anointing
shall *surely* be an *everlasting* **eternal** priesthood
throughout their generations.
16 Thus *did Moses* **worked Mosheh**:
according to all
that *the LORD commanded* **Yah Veh misvahed** him,
so *did* **worked** he.
17 And it *came to pass* **became**,
in the first month in the second year,
on the first *day* of the month,
that the tabernacle was *reared up* **raised**.
18 And *Moses reared up* **Mosheh raised** the tabernacle,
and *fastened* **gave** his sockets,

and set up the boards thereof,
and *put* **gave** in the bars thereof,
and *reared up* **raised** his pillars.
19 And he spread abroad the tent over the tabernacle,
and put the covering of the tent above upon it;
as *the LORD commanded Moses* **Yah Veh misvahed Mosheh.**
20 And he took and *put* **gave** the *testimony* **witness**
into the ark,
and set the staves on the ark,
and *put* **gave** the *mercy seat* **kapporeth** above upon the ark:
21 And he brought the ark into the tabernacle,
and set up the vail of the covering,
and covered the ark of the *testimony* **witness**;
as *the LORD commanded Moses* **Yah Veh misvahed Mosheh.**
22 And he *put* **gave** the table
in the tent of the congregation,
upon the *side* **flank** of the tabernacle northward,
without the vail.
23 And he *set* **arranged the arrangement**
of the bread *in order* upon it
before the LORD **at the face of Yah Veh**;
as *the LORD* **Yah Veh**
had commanded Moses **misvahed Mosheh.**
24 And he put the *candlestick* **menorah**
in the tent of the congregation, over against the table,
on the *side* **flank** of the tabernacle southward.
25 And he *lighted* **holocausted** the lamps
before the LORD **at the face of Yah Veh**;
as *the LORD commanded Moses* **Yah Veh misvahed Mosheh.**
26 And he put the golden **sacrifice** altar
in the tent of the congregation
before **at the face of** the vail:
27 And he *burnt* **incensed**
sweet incense **of aromatics** thereon;
as *the LORD commanded Moses* **Yah Veh misvahed Mosheh.**
28 And he set up the *hanging* **covering**
at the *door* **opening** of the tabernacle.
29 And he put the **sacrifice** altar
of *burnt offering* **holocaust** by the *door* **opening**
of the tabernacle of the tent of the congregation,
and *offered* **holocausted** upon it
the *burnt offering* **holocaust** and the *meat* offering;
as *the LORD commanded Moses* **Yah Veh misvahed Mosheh.**
30 And he set the laver
between the tent of the congregation
and **between** the **sacrifice** altar,
and *put* **gave** water there, to *wash* **baptize** *withal.*
31 And *Moses* **Mosheh** and *Aaron* **Aharon** and his sons
washed **baptized** their hands and their feet thereat:
32 When they went into the tent of the congregation,
and when they *came near* **approached**
unto the **sacrifice** altar, they *washed* **baptized**;
as *the LORD commanded Moses* **Yah Veh misvahed Mosheh.**
33 And he *reared up* **raised** the court
round about the tabernacle and the **sacrifice** altar,
and set up the *hanging* **covering** of the court *gate* **portal**.
So *Moses* **Mosheh** finished the work.

YAH VEH'S HONOUR FILLS THE TABERNACLE

34 Then a cloud covered the tent of the congregation,
and the *glory* **honour** of *the LORD* **Yah Veh**
filled the tabernacle.
35 And *Moses* **Mosheh**
was not able to enter into the tent of the congregation,
because the cloud *abode* **tabernacled** thereon,
and the *glory* **honour** of *the LORD* **Yah Veh**
filled the tabernacle.
36 And when the cloud *was taken up* **ascended**
from over the tabernacle,
the *children* **sons** of *Israel* **Yisra El**
went onward **pulled stakes** in all their journeys:
37 But if the cloud *were not taken up* **ascended not**,
then they *journeyed* **pulled stakes** not
till the day that it *was taken up* **ascended.**
38 For the cloud of *the LORD* **Yah Veh**
was upon the tabernacle by day,
and fire was on it by night,
in the *sight* **eyes** of all the house of *Israel* **Yisra El**,
throughout all their journeys.

KEY TO INTERPRETING THE EXEGESES:
King James text is in regular type;
Text under exegeses is in oblique type;
Text of exegeses is in bold type.

OBLATIONS

1 And *the LORD* **Yah Veh** called unto *Moses* **Mosheh**,
and *spake* **worded** unto him
out of the *tabernacle* **tent** of the congregation, saying,
2 *Speak* **Word** unto the *children* **sons** of *Israel* **Yisra El**,
and say unto them,
If any *man* **human** of you
bring an offering **oblate a qorban** unto *the LORD* **Yah Veh**,
ye shall *bring* **oblate** your *offering* **qorban**
of the *cattle* **animals**,
even of the *herd* **oxen**, and of the flock.

HOLOCAUST QORBANS

3 If his *offering* **qorban**
be a *burnt sacrifice* **holocaust** of the *herd* **oxen**,
let him *offer a* **oblate an integrious** male *without blemish*:
he shall *offer* **oblate** it
of his own voluntary will **at his pleasure**
at the *door* **opening**
of the *tabernacle* **tent** of the congregation
before the LORD **at the face of Yah Veh.**
4 And he shall *put* **prop** his hand
upon the head of the *burnt offering* **holocaust**;
and it shall be *accepted* **pleasing** for him
to *make atonement* **kapar/atone** for him.
5 And he shall *kill* **slaughter** the *bullock* **son of the oxen**
before the LORD **at the face of Yah Veh**:
and the priests, *Aaron's* **Aharon's** sons,
shall *bring* **oblate** the blood,
and sprinkle the blood round about
upon the **sacrifice** altar that is by the *door* **opening**
of the *tabernacle* **tent** of the congregation.
6 And he shall *flay* **strip** the *burnt offering* **holocaust**,
and *cut it into* **dismember** his *pieces* **members.**
7 And the sons of *Aaron* **Aharon** the priest
shall *put* **give** fire upon the **sacrifice** altar,
and *lay* **arrange** the *wood in order* **timber** upon the fire:
8 And the priests, *Aaron's* **Aharon's** sons,
shall *lay* **arrange** the *parts* **members**,
the head, and the fat,
in order upon the *wood* **timber** that is on the fire
which is upon the **sacrifice** altar:
9 But his inwards and his legs
shall he *wash* **baptize** in water:
and the priest shall *burn* **incense** all on the **sacrifice** altar,
to be a *burnt sacrifice* **holocaust**,
an offering made by fire **a firing**,
of a *sweet savour* **scent of rest**
unto *the LORD* **Yah Veh.**
10 And if his *offering* **qorban** be of the flocks,
namely, of the *sheep* **lambs**, or of the goats,
for a *burnt sacrifice* **holocaust**;
he shall *bring* **oblate** it
a **an integrious** male *without blemish.*
11 And he shall *kill* **slaughter** it
on the *side* **flank** of the **sacrifice** altar northward
before the LORD **at the face of Yah Veh**:
and the priests, *Aaron's* **Aharon's** sons,
shall sprinkle his blood round about
upon the **sacrifice** altar.
12 And he shall *cut it into* **dismember** his *pieces* **members**,
with his head and his fat:
and the priest shall *lay* **arrange** them *in order*
on the *wood* **timber** that is on the fire
which is upon the **sacrifice** altar:
13 But he shall *wash* **baptize** the inwards and the legs
with water:
and the priest shall *bring* **oblate** it all,
and *burn* **incense** it upon the **sacrifice** altar:
it is a *burnt sacrifice* **holocaust**,
an offering made by fire **a firing**,
of a *sweet savour* **scent of rest**
unto *the LORD* **Yah Veh.**
14 And if the *burnt sacrifice* **holocaust**
for his *offering* **qorban** to *the LORD* **Yah Veh**
be of *fowls* **fliers**,
then he shall *bring* **oblate** his *offering* **qorban**

of turtledoves, or of *young pigeons* **sons of doves**.
15 And the priest shall *bring* **oblate** it
unto the **sacrifice** altar,
and wring off his head,
and *burn* **incense** it on the **sacrifice** altar;
and the blood thereof shall be wrung out
at the *side* **wall** of the **sacrifice** altar:
16 And he shall *pluck* **turn** away his *crop* **craw**
with his *feathers* **plumage**,
and cast it beside the **sacrifice** altar
on the east part **eastward**, by the place of the **fat** ashes:
17 And he shall cleave it with the wings thereof,
but shall not *divide* **separate** it *asunder*:
and the priest shall *burn* **incense** it
upon the **sacrifice** altar,
upon the *wood* **timber** that is upon the fire:
it is a *burnt sacrifice* **holocaust**,
an offering made by fire **a firing**,
of a *sweet savour* **scent of rest**
unto *the LORD* **Yah Veh**.

FLOUR QORBANS

2 And when *any* **a soul**
will offer **shall oblate** a *meat offering* **qorban**
unto *the LORD* **Yah Veh**,
his *offering* **qorban** shall be of *fine* flour;
and he shall pour oil upon it,
and *put* **give** frankincense thereon:
2 And he shall bring it
to *Aaron's* **Aharon's** sons the priests:
and he shall *take* **handle** thereout
his handful of the flour thereof,
and of the oil thereof, with all the frankincense thereof;
and the priest shall *burn* **incense** the memorial of it
upon the **sacrifice** altar,
to be an offering made by fire **a firing**,
of a *sweet savour* **scent of rest**
unto *the LORD* **Yah Veh**:
3 And *the remnant* **that which remaineth**
of the *meat* offering
shall be *Aaron's* **Aharon's** and his sons':
it is a *thing most holy* **holy of holies**
of the *offerings of the LORD made by fire*
firings unto Yah Veh.
4 And if thou *bring an oblation* **oblate a qorban**
of *a meat* **an** offering baken in the oven,
it shall be *unleavened* **matsah** cakes
of *fine* flour mingled with oil,
or *unleavened* **matsah** wafers anointed with oil.
5 And if thy *oblation* **qorban** be *a meat* **an** offering
baken in a pan **on a griddle**,
it shall be of *fine* **matsah** flour *unleavened*,
mingled with oil.
6 Thou shalt part it in *pieces* **morsels**,
and pour oil thereon:
it is *a meat* **an** offering.
7 And if thy *oblation* **qorban** be *a meat* **an** offering
baken in the fryingpan **on a cauldron**,
it shall be *made* **worked** of *fine* flour with oil.
8 And thou shalt bring the *meat* offering
that is *made* **worked** of these *things*
unto *the LORD* **Yah Veh**:
and when it is *presented* **oblated** unto the priest,
he shall bring it unto the **sacrifice** altar.
9 And the priest shall *take* **lift** from the *meat* offering
a memorial thereof,
and shall *burn* **incense** it upon the **sacrifice** altar:
it is *an offering made by fire* **a firing**,
of a *sweet savour* **scent of rest**
unto *the LORD* **Yah Veh**.
10 And that which *is left* **remaineth** of the *meat* offering
shall be *Aaron's* **Aharon's** and his sons':
it is a *thing most holy* **holy of holies**
of the *offerings of the LORD made by fire*
firings unto Yah Veh.
11 No *meat* offering,
which ye shall *bring* **oblate** unto *the LORD* **Yah Veh**,
shall be *made* **worked** with *leaven* **fermentation**:
for ye shall *burn* **incense** no *leaven* **yeast**, nor any honey,
in any *offering of the LORD made by fire*
firing unto Yah Veh.

THE FIRSTS QORBANS

12 As for the *oblation* **qorban** of the *firstfruits* **firsts**,
ye shall *offer* **oblate** them unto *the LORD* **Yah Veh**:
but they shall not be *burnt* **holocausted**
on the **sacrifice** altar for a *sweet savour* **scent of rest**.
13 And every *oblation* **qorban** of thy *meat* offering
shalt thou *season* **salt** with salt;
neither shalt thou *suffer* **shabbathize** the salt
of the covenant of thy *God* **Elohim**
to be lacking from thy *meat* offering:
with all thine *offerings* **qorbans** thou shalt *offer* **oblate** salt.
14 And if thou *offer a meat* **oblate an** offering
of thy firstfruits unto *the LORD* **Yah Veh**,
thou shalt *offer* **oblate** for the *meat* offering of thy firstfruits
green ears of corn **unripened** dried by the fire,
even corn beaten **husks** out of *full ears* **the orchard**.
15 And thou shalt *put* **give** oil upon it,
and *lay* **set** frankincense thereon:
it is *a meat* **an** offering.
16 And the priest shall *burn* **incense** the memorial of it,
part of the *beaten corn* **husks** thereof,
and *part* of the oil thereof,
with all the frankincense thereof:
it is *an offering made by fire* **a firing**
unto *the LORD* **Yah Veh**.

SHELAMIM QORBANS

3 And if his *oblation* **qorban**
be a sacrifice of *peace offering* **shelamim**,
if he *offer* **oblate** it of the *herd* **oxen**;
whether it be a male or female,
he shall *offer* **oblate** it *without blemish* **integrious**
before the LORD **at the face of Yah Veh**.
2 And he shall *lay* **prop** his hand
upon the head of his *offering* **qorban**,
and *kill* **slaughter** it at the *door* **opening**
of the *tabernacle* **tent** of the congregation:
and *Aaron's* **Aharon's** sons the priests
shall sprinkle the blood
upon the **sacrifice** altar round about.
3 And he shall *offer* **oblate**
of the sacrifice of the *peace offering* **shelamim**
an offering made by fire **a firing**
unto *the LORD* **Yah Veh**;
the fat that covereth the inwards,
and all the fat that is upon the inwards,
4 And the two *kidneys* **reins**,
and the fat that is on them, which is by the flanks,
and the caul above the liver, with the *kidneys* **reins**,
it shall he *take away* **twist off**.
5 And *Aaron's* **Aharon's** sons
shall *burn* **incense** it on the **sacrifice** altar
upon the *burnt sacrifice* **holocaust**,
which is upon the *wood* **timber** that is on the fire:
it is *an offering made by fire* **a firing**,
of a *sweet savour* **scent of rest**
unto *the LORD* **Yah Veh**.
6 And if his *offering* **qorban**
for a sacrifice of *peace offering* **shelamim**
unto *the LORD* **Yah Veh** be of the flock; male or female,
he shall *offer* **oblate** it *without blemish* **integrious**.
7 If he *offer* **oblate** a lamb for his *offering* **qorban**,
then shall he *offer* **oblate** it
before the LORD **at the face of Yah Veh**.
8 And he shall *lay* **prop** his hand
upon the head of his *offering* **qorban**,
and *kill* **slaughter** it *before* **at the face of**
the *tabernacle* **tent** of the congregation:
and *Aaron's* **Aharon's** sons
shall sprinkle the blood thereof
round about upon the **sacrifice** altar.
9 And he shall *offer* **oblate**
of the sacrifice of the *peace offering* **shelamim**
an offering made by fire **a firing**
unto *the LORD* **Yah Veh**;
the fat thereof, and the *whole* **integrious** rump,
it shall he *take* **twist** off
hard by **along side** the *backbone* **spine**
and the fat that covereth the inwards,
and all the fat that is upon the inwards,
10 And the two *kidneys* **reins**,

and the fat that is upon them, which is by the flanks,
and the caul above the liver, with the *kidneys* **reins**,
it shall he *take away* **twist off**.
11 And the priest shall *burn* **incense** it
upon the **sacrifice** altar:
it is the *food* **bread** of the *offering made by fire* **firing**
unto *the LORD* **Yah Veh**.
12 And if his *offering* **qorban** be a goat,
then he shall *offer* **oblate** it
before the LORD **at the face of Yah Veh**.
13 And he shall *lay* **prop** his hand upon the head of it,
and *kill* **slaughter** it *before* **at the face of**
the *tabernacle* **tent** of the congregation:
and the sons of *Aaron* **Aharon**
shall sprinkle the blood thereof
upon the **sacrifice** altar round about.
14 And he shall *offer* **oblate** thereof his *offering* **qorban**,
even an offering made by fire **a firing**
unto *the LORD* **Yah Veh**;
the fat that covereth the inwards,
and all the fat that is upon the inwards,
15 And the two *kidneys* **reins**,
and the fat that is upon them, which is by the flanks,
and the caul above the liver, with the *kidneys* **reins**,
it shall he *take away* **twist off**.
16 And the priest shall *burn* **incense** them
upon the **sacrifice** altar:
it is the *food* **bread** of the *offering made by fire* **firing**
for a *sweet savour* **scent of rest**:
all the fat is *the LORD'S* **Yah Veh's**.
17 It shall be *a perpetual* **an eternal** statute
for your generations
throughout all your *dwellings* **settlements**,
that ye eat neither fat nor blood.

PRIESTAL INADVERTENT ERRING QORBANS

4 And *the LORD spake* **Yah Veh worded**
unto *Moses* **Mosheh**, saying,
2 *Speak* **Word** unto the *children* **sons** of *Israel* **Yisra El**,
saying,
If a soul shall sin through *ignorance* **inadvertent error**
against any of the *commandments* **misvoth**
of *the LORD* **Yah Veh**
concerning things which ought not to be *done* **worked**,
and shall *do against any* **work one** of them:
3 If the priest that is anointed do sin
according to the *sin* **guilt** of the people;
then let him *bring* **oblate** for his sin,
which he hath sinned,
a young bullock **son of the oxen**
without blemish **integrious**
unto *the LORD* **Yah Veh** for *a* **his** sin *offering*.
4 And he shall bring the bullock unto the *door* **opening**
of the *tabernacle* **tent** of the congregation
before the LORD **at the face of Yah Veh**;
and shall *lay* **prop** his hand upon the bullock's head,
and *kill* **slaughter** the bullock
before the LORD **at the face of Yah Veh**.
5 And the priest that is anointed
shall take of the bullock's blood,
and bring it to the *tabernacle* **tent** of the congregation:
6 And the priest shall dip his finger in the blood,
and sprinkle of the blood seven times
before the LORD **at the face of Yah Veh**,
before **at the face of** the vail of the *sanctuary* **holies**.
7 And the priest shall *put* **give** some of the blood
upon the horns of the **sacrifice** altar
of *sweet* incense **of aromatics**
before the LORD **at the face of Yah Veh**,
which is in the *tabernacle* **tent** of the congregation;
and shall pour all the blood of the bullock
at the *bottom* **foundation**
of the **sacrifice** altar of the *burnt offering* **holocaust**,
which is at the *door* **opening**
of the *tabernacle* **tent** of the congregation.
8 And he shall *take off* **lift** from it
all the fat of the bullock for the sin *offering*;
the fat that covereth the inwards,
and all the fat that is upon the inwards,
9 And the two *kidneys* **reins**,
and the fat that is upon them, which is by the flanks,
and the caul above the liver, with the *kidneys* **reins**,
it shall he *take away* **twist off**,
10 As it was *taken off* **lifted** from the *bullock* **ox**
of the sacrifice of *peace offerings* **shelamim**:
and the priest shall *burn* **incense** them
upon the **sacrifice** altar of the *burnt offering* **holocaust**.
11 And the skin of the bullock, and all his flesh,
with his head, and with his legs,
and his inwards, and his dung,
12 Even the whole bullock
shall he carry forth without the camp
unto a *clean* **pure** place,
where the **fat** ashes are poured out,
and burn him on the *wood* **timber** with fire:
where the **fat** ashes are poured out shall he be burnt.

CONGREGATIONAL INADVERTENT ERRING QORBANS

13 And if the whole *congregation* **witness** of *Israel* **Yisra El**
sin through ignorance **err inadvertently**,
and the *thing* **word** be *hid* **concealed**
from the eyes of the *assembly* **congregation**,
and they have
done somewhat against any **worked unto one**
of the *commandments* **misvoth** of *the LORD* **Yah Veh**
concerning things which should not be *done* **worked**,
and *are guilty* **have guilted**;
14 When the sin, which they have sinned against it,
is known,
then the congregation shall *offer* **oblate**
a *young* bullock **son of the oxen** for the sin,
and bring him *before* **at the face of**
the *tabernacle* **tent** of the congregation.
15 And the elders of the *congregation* **witness**
shall *lay* **prop** their hands upon the head of the bullock
before the LORD **at the face of Yah Veh**:
and the bullock shall be *killed* **slaughtered**
before the LORD **at the face of Yah Veh**.
16 And the priest that is anointed
shall bring of the bullock's blood
to the *tabernacle* **tent** of the congregation:
17 And the priest shall dip his finger in *some of* the blood,
and sprinkle it seven times
before the LORD **at the face of Yah Veh**,
even before **at the face of** the vail.
18 And he shall *put* **give** *some* of the blood
upon the horns of the **sacrifice** altar
which is *before the LORD* **at the face of Yah Veh**,
that is in the *tabernacle* **tent** of the congregation,
and shall pour out all the blood
at the *bottom* **foundation** of the **sacrifice** altar
of the *burnt offering* **holocaust**,
which is at the *door* **opening**
of the *tabernacle* **tent** of the congregation.
19 And he shall *take* **lift** all his fat from him,
and *burn* **incense** it upon the **sacrifice** altar.
20 And he shall *do with* **work** the bullock
as he *did with* **worked** the bullock
for *a sin offering* **the sin**,
so shall he *do* **work** with this:
and the priest
shall *make an atonement* **kapar/atone** for them,
and it shall be forgiven them.
21 And he shall carry forth the bullock without the camp,
and burn him as he burned the first bullock:
it is *a sin offering* for **the sin of** the congregation.

HIERARCHAL INADVERTENT ERRING QORBANS

22 When a *ruler* **hierarch** hath sinned,
and *done somewhat through ignorance*
hath worked an inadvertent error
against any **in one** of the *commandments* **misvoth**
of *the LORD* **Yah Veh** his *God* **Elohim**
concerning things which should not be *done* **worked**,
and *is guilty* **hath guilted**;
23 Or if his sin, wherein he hath sinned,
come to his knowledge **hath been made known to him**;
he shall bring his *offering* **qorban**, a *kid* **buck** of the goats,
a male *without blemish* **integrious**:
24 And he shall *lay* **prop** his hand
upon the head of the *goat* **buck**,
and *kill* **slaughter** it in the place
where they *kill* **slaughter** the *burnt offering* **holocaust**

before the LORD **at the face of Yah Veh:**
it is *a sin offering* **for the sin.**
25 And the priest shall take of the blood
of the sin offering **for the sin** with his finger,
and *put* **giveth** it upon the horns
of the **sacrifice** altar of *burnt offering* **holocaust**,
and shall pour out his blood
at the *bottom* **foundation**
of the **sacrifice** altar of *burnt offering* **holocaust**.
26 And he shall *burn* **incense** all his fat upon the altar,
as the fat of the sacrifice of *peace offerings* **shelamim**:
and the priest
shall *make an atonement* **kapar/atone** for him
as concerning **for** his sin, and it shall be forgiven him.

SOULICAL INADVERTENT ERRING QORBANS

27 And if *any one* **a soul**
of the *common* people **of the land**
sin *through ignorance* **an inadvertent error**,
while he doeth somewhat against any
and worketh unto one
of the *commandments* **misvoth** of *the LORD* **Yah Veh**
concerning things which ought not to be *done* **worked**,
and *be guilty* **hath guilted**;
28 Or if his sin, which he hath sinned,
come to his knowledge **hath been made known to him**:
then he shall bring his *offering* **qorban**,
a *kid* **doe** of the goats,
a female *without blemish* **integrious**,
for his sin which he hath sinned.
29 And he shall *lay* **prop** his hand
upon the head of *the sin offering* **that for the sin**,
and *slay the sin offering* **slaughter that for the sin**
in the place of the *burnt offering* **holocaust**.
30 And the priest shall take of the blood thereof
with his finger,
and *put* **give** it upon the horns of the **sacrifice** altar
of *burnt offering* **holocaust**,
and shall pour out all the blood thereof
at the *bottom* **foundation** of the **sacrifice** altar.
31 And he shall *take away* **twist off** all the fat thereof,
as the fat is taken away from off the sacrifice
of *peace offerings* **shelamim**;
and the priest shall *burn* **incense** it
upon the **sacrifice** altar
for a *sweet savour* **scent of rest** unto *the LORD* **Yah Veh**;
and the priest
shall *make an atonement* **kapar/atone** for him,
and it shall be forgiven him.
32 And if he bring a lamb for *a sin offering* **the sin**,
he shall bring a female *without blemish* **integrious**.
33 And he shall *lay* **prop** his hand
upon the head of *the sin offering* **that for the sin**,
and *slay it for a sin offering* **slaughter that for the sin**
in the place
where they *kill* **slaughter** the *burnt offering* **holocaust**.
34 And the priest shall take of the blood
of *the sin offering* **that for the sin** with his finger,
and *put* **give** it upon the horns
of the **sacrifice** altar of *burnt offering* **holocaust**,
and shall pour out all the blood thereof
at the *bottom* **foundation** of the altar:
35 And he shall *take away* **twist off** all the fat thereof,
as the fat of the lamb is *taken away* **twisted off**
from the sacrifice of the *peace offerings* **shelamim**;
and the priest shall *burn* **incense** them
upon the **sacrifice** altar,
according to the *offerings made by fire* **firings**
unto *the LORD* **Yah Veh**:
and the priest
shall *make an atonement* **kapar/atone** for his sin
that he hath *committed* **sinned**,
and it shall be forgiven him.

5 And if a soul sin,
and hear the voice of *swearing* **oathing**, and is a witness,
whether **if** he hath seen or known of it;
if he do not *utter* **tell** it,
then he shall bear his *iniquity* **perversity**.
2 Or if a soul touch any *unclean thing* **word of foulness**,
whether it be a carcase
of *an unclean beast* **a live being of foulness**,
or a carcase of *unclean cattle* **animals of foulness**,
or the carcase of *unclean creeping things* **teemers of foulness**,
and if it be *hidden* **concealed** from him;
he also shall be *unclean* **fouled**, and *guilty* **have guilted**.
3 Or if he touch *the uncleanness of man* **human foulness**,
whatsoever *uncleanness* **foulness** it be
that *a man* shall be *defiled withal* **fouled thereby**,
and it be *hid* **concealed** from him;
when he knoweth of it,
then he shall *be guilty* **have guilted**.
4 Or if a soul *swear* **oath**,
pronouncing with his lips
to *do evil* **vilify**, or to *do good* **well—please**,
whatsoever it be
that a *man* **human** shall pronounce with an oath,
and it be *hid* **concealed** from him;
when he knoweth of it,
then he shall *be guilty* **have guilted** in one of these.
5 And it shall be,
when he shall *be guilty* **have guilted** in one of these *things*,
that he shall *confess* **wring hands**
that he hath sinned in that thing
for that wherein he sinned:
6 And he shall bring *his trespass offering* **for his guilt**
unto *the LORD* **Yah Veh** for his sin which he hath sinned,
a female from the flock,
a **ewe** lamb or a *kid* **doe** of the goats,
for *a sin offering* **the sin**;
and the priest
shall *make an atonement* **kapar/atone** for him
concerning **for** his sin.
7 And if *he be not able* **his hand be not sufficient**
to *bring* **touch** a lamb,
then he shall bring for his *trespass* **guilt**,
which he hath *committed* **sinned**,
two turtledoves, or two *young pigeons* **sons of doves**,
unto *the LORD* **Yah Veh**;
one for *a sin offering* **the sin**,
and *the other for a burnt offering* **one for the holocaust**.
8 And he shall bring them unto the priest,
who shall *offer* **oblate** that
which is for the sin *offering* first,
and wring off his head *from* **in front of** his neck,
but shall not divide it asunder:
9 And he shall sprinkle of the blood
of *the sin offering* **that for the sin**
upon the *side* **wall** of the **sacrifice** altar;
and the *rest of the* **surviving** blood shall be wrung out
at the *bottom* **foundation** of the **sacrifice** altar:
it is *a sin offering* **for the sin**.
10 And he shall *offer* **work** the second
for a *burnt offering* **holocaust**,
according to the *manner* **judgment**:
and the priest
shall *make an atonement* **kapar/atone** for him
for his sin which he hath sinned,
and it shall be forgiven him.
11 But if *he be not able* **his hand be not sufficient**
to *bring* **attain** two turtledoves,
or two *young pigeons* **sons of doves**,
then he that sinned shall bring for his *offering* **qorban**
the tenth *part* of an ephah of *fine* flour
for *a sin offering* **the sin**;
he shall put no oil upon it,
neither shall he *put* **give** any frankincense thereon:
for it is *a sin offering* **for the sin**.
12 Then shall he bring it to the priest,
and the priest shall *take* **handle** his handful of it,
even a memorial thereof,
and *burn* **incense** it on the **sacrifice** altar,
according to the *offerings made by fire* **firings**
unto *the LORD* **Yah Veh**:
it is *a sin offering* **for the sin**.
13 And the priest
shall *make an atonement* **kapar/atone** for him
as touching his sin that he hath sinned in one of these,
and it shall be forgiven him:
and *the remnant* shall be the priest's,
as *a meat* **an** offering.
14 And *the LORD spake* **Yah Veh worded**

unto *Moses* **Mosheh**, saying,
15 If a soul *commit* **treason** a *trespass* **treason**,
and sin *through ignorance* **an inadvertent error**,
in the *holy things* **holies** of *the LORD* **Yah Veh**;
then he shall bring for his *trespass* **guilt**
unto *the LORD* **Yah Veh**
a ram *without blemish* **integrious** out of the flocks,
with thy *estimation* **appraisal** by shekels of silver,
after the shekel of the *sanctuary* **holies**,
for *a trespass offering* **the guilt**.
16 And he shall *make amends* **shalam**
for *the harm that he hath done* **that which he sinned**
in the holy thing **against the holies**,
and shall add the fifth *part* thereto,
and give it unto the priest:
and the priest
shall *make an atonement* **kapar/atone** for him
with the ram *of the trespass offering* **for the guilt**,
and it shall be forgiven him.
17 And if a soul sin,
and *commit any* **work one** of these *things*
which are *forbidden* **not** to be *done* **worked**
by the *commandments* **misvoth** of *the LORD* **Yah Veh**;
though he *wist* **knew** it not,
yet *is he guilty* **hath he guilted**,
and shall bear his *iniquity* **perversity**.
18 And he shall bring
a ram *without blemish* **integrious** out of the flock,
with thy *estimation* **appraisal**,
for *a trespass offering* **his guilt**, unto the priest:
and the priest
shall *make an atonement* **kapar/atone** for him
concerning his *ignorance* **inadvertent error**
wherein he erred **inadvertently** and *wist* **knew** it not,
and it shall be forgiven him.
19 It is *a trespass offering* **for his guilt**:
in having guilted,
he hath *certainly trespassed* **guilted**
against *the LORD* **Yah Veh**.
6 And *the LORD spake* **Yah Veh**
worded unto *Moses* **Mosheh**, saying,
If a soul sin, and *commit* **treason** a *trespass* **treason**
against *the LORD* **Yah Veh**,
and *lie unto* **deceive** his *neighbour* **friend**
in that which
was delivered him to keep **he was to oversee**,
or in *fellowship* **placing the hand**,
or *in a thing taken away by violence* **by stripping**,
or hath *deceived* **extorted** his *neighbour* **friend**;
3 Or have found that which was lost,
and *lieth* **deceiveth** concerning it,
and *sweareth* **oatheth** falsely;
in *any* **one** of all these that a *man doeth* **human worketh**,
sinning therein:
4 Then it shall be,
because he hath sinned, and *is guilty* **hath guilted**,
that he shall restore
that which he took violently away
the stripping he stripped,
or the *thing which he hath deceitfully gotten*
extortion he extorted,
or that which
was delivered him to keep **he was overseeing**,
or the lost *thing* which he found,
5 Or all that about which he hath *sworn* **oathed** falsely;
he shall *even restore* **shalam** it *in* **to** the *principal* **top**,
and shall add the fifth *part* more thereto,
and give it unto him to whom it appertaineth,
in the day of his *trespass offering* **guilt**.
6 And he shall bring *his trespass offering* **for his guilt**
unto *the LORD* **Yah Veh**,
a ram *without blemish* **integrious** out of the flock,
with thy *estimation* **appraisal**,
for *a trespass offering* **his guilt**, unto the priest:
7 And the priest shall
make an atonement **kapar/atone** for him
before the LORD **at the face of Yah Veh**:
and it shall be forgiven him
for *any thing* **one** of all that he hath *done* **worked**
in trespassing therein **wherein he hath guilted**.

TORAH OF THE HOLOCAUST

8 And *the LORD spake* **Yah Veh worded**
unto *Moses* **Mosheh**, saying,
9 *Command Aaron* **Misvah Aharon** and his sons, saying,
This is the *law* **torah** of the *burnt offering* **holocaust**:
It is the *burnt offering* **holocaust**,
because of the burning upon the **sacrifice** altar
all night unto the morning,
and the fire of the **sacrifice** altar
shall be burning *in it* **thereon**.
10 And the priest shall *put on* **enrobe**
his linen *garment* **tailoring**,
and his linen breeches shall he *put* **enrobe** upon his flesh,
and *take up* **lift** the **fat** ashes
which the fire hath consumed
with the *burnt offering* **holocaust** on the **sacrifice** altar,
and he shall put them beside the **sacrifice** altar.
11 And he shall *put off* **strip** his *garments* **clothes**,
and *put on* **enrobe** other *garments* **clothes**,
and carry forth the **fat** ashes without the camp
unto a *clean* **pure** place.
12 And the fire upon the **sacrifice** altar
shall be burning in it;
it shall not be put out:
and the priest shall *burn wood* **kindle timber** on it
every morning **by morning**,
and *lay* **arrange** the *burnt offering in order* **holocaust** upon it;
and he shall *burn* **incense** thereon
the fat of the *peace offerings* **shelamim**.
13 The fire shall *ever* **continually** be burning
upon the **sacrifice** altar;
it shall never go out.

TORAH OF THE OFFERING

14 And this is the *law* **torah** of the *meat* offering:
the sons of *Aaron* **Aharon** shall *offer* **oblate** it
before the LORD **at the face of Yah Veh**,
before the **at the face of the sacrifice** altar.
15 And he shall *take* **lift** of it his handful,
of the flour of the *meat* offering, and of the oil thereof,
and all the frankincense which is upon the *meat* offering,
and shall *burn* **incense** it upon the **sacrifice** altar
for a *sweet savour* **scent of rest**,
even the memorial of it, unto *the LORD* **Yah Veh**.
16 And *the remainder* **that which remaineth** thereof
shall *Aaron* **Aharon** and his sons eat:
with *unleavened bread* **matsah** shall it be eaten
in the *holy place* **holies**;
in the court of the *tabernacle* **tent** of the congregation
they shall eat it.
17 It shall not be baken with *leaven* **fermentation**.
I have given it unto them for their *portion* **allotment**
of my *offerings made by fire* **firings**;
it is *most holy* **a holy of holies**
as *is the sin offering* **that for the sin**,
and as *the trespass offering* **that for the guilt**.
18 All the males
among the *children* **sons** of *Aaron* **Aharon** shall eat of it.
It shall be *a* **an eternal** statute *for ever* in your generations
concerning the
offerings of the LORD made by fire **firings unto Yah Veh**
every one that toucheth them shall be *holy* **hallowed**.

TORAH OF THE PRIESTAL QORBAN

19 And *the LORD spake* **Yah Veh worded**
unto *Moses* **Mosheh**, saying,
20 This is the *offering* **qorban**
of *Aaron* **Aharon** and of his sons,
which they shall *offer* **oblate** unto *the LORD* **Yah Veh**
in the day when he is anointed;
the tenth *part* of an ephah of *fine* flour
for a *meat* **continual** offering *perpetual*,
half of it in the morning,
and half thereof *at night* **in the evening**.
21 *In a pan* **On a griddle** it shall be *made* **worked** with oil;
and when it is baken **deep fried**, thou shalt bring it in:
and the *baken pieces* **cakes morsels** of the *meat* offering
shalt thou *offer* **oblate** for a *sweet savour* **scent of rest**
unto *the LORD* **Yah Veh**.
22 And the priest of his sons that is anointed in his stead
shall *offer* **work** it:
it is *a* **an eternal** statute *for ever* unto *the LORD* **Yah Veh**;

it shall be *wholly burnt* **totally incensed.**
23 For every *meat* offering for the priest
shall be *wholly* **totally** burnt:
it shall not be eaten.

TORAH FOR THE SIN

24 And *the LORD spake* **Yah Veh worded**
unto *Moses* **Mosheh**, saying,
25 *Speak* **Word** unto *Aaron* **Aharon** and to his sons,
saying, This is the *law of the sin offering* **torah for the sin**:
In the place
where the *burnt offering* **holocaust** is *killed* **slaughtered**
shall *the sin offering* **that for the sin** be *killed* **slaughtered**
before the LORD **at the face of Yah Veh**:
it is *most holy* **a holy of holies.**
26 The priest *that offereth it for sin* **of that for the sin**
shall eat it:
in the *holy place* **holies** shall it be eaten,
in the court of the *tabernacle* **tent** of the congregation.
27 Whatsoever shall touch the flesh thereof
shall be *holy* **hallowed**:
and when there is sprinkled of the blood thereof
upon any *garment* **clothes**,
thou shalt *wash* **launder** that whereon it was sprinkled
in the *holy place* **holies.**
28 But the *earthen vessel* **pottery instrument**
wherein it is *sodden* **stewed** shall be broken:
and if it be *sodden* **stewed**
in a *brasen pot* **copper instrument**,
it shall be both scoured, and *rinsed* **overflowed** in water.
29 All the males among the priests shall eat thereof:
it is *most holy* **a holy of holies.**
30 And *no sin offering* **naught for the sin**,
whereof *any of* the blood
is brought into the *tabernacle* **tent** of the congregation
to *reconcile withal* **atone** in the *holy place* **holies**,
shall be eaten: it shall be burnt in the fire.

TORAH OF THE GUILT

7 Likewise this is the *law* **torah**
of the trespass offering **for the guilt**:
it is *most holy* **a holy of holies.**
2 In the place where they *kill* **slaughter**
the *burnt offering* **holocaust**
shall they *kill the trespass offering*
slaughter for the guilt:
and the blood thereof
shall he sprinkle round about upon the **sacrifice** altar.
3 And he shall *offer* **oblate** of it all the fat thereof;
the rump, and the fat that covereth the inwards,
4 And the two *kidneys* **reins**,
and the fat that is on them, which is by the flanks,
and the caul that is above the liver,
with the *kidneys* **reins**,
it shall he *take away* **twist off**:
5 And the priest shall *burn* **incense** them
upon the **sacrifice** altar
for *an offering made by fire* **a firing**
unto *the LORD* **Yah Veh**:
it is *a trespass offering* **for the guilt**.
6 Every male among the priests shall eat thereof:
it shall be eaten in the *holy place* **holies**:
it is *most holy* **a holy of holies.**
7 As *the sin offering is* **that for the sin**,
so is *the trespass offering* **that for the guilt**:
there is one *law* **torah** for them:
the priest
that *maketh atonement* **shall kapar/atone** therewith
shall have it.
8 And the priest that *offereth* **oblateth**
any man's *burnt offering* **holocaust,**
even the priest shall have to himself
the skin of the *burnt offering* **holocaust**
which he hath *offered* **oblated**.
9 And all the *meat* offering that is baken in the oven,
and all that is *dressed* **worked** in the *frying pan* **cauldron**,
and *in the pan* **on the griddle**,
shall be the priest's that *offereth* **oblateth** it.
10 And every *meat* offering,
mingled with oil, and *dry* **parched**,
shall all the sons of *Aaron* **Aharon** have,
one as much as another **as man, as brother.**

TORAH OF THE SHELAMIM

11 And this is the *law* **torah**
of the sacrifice of *peace offerings* **shelamim**,
which he shall *offer* **oblate** unto *the LORD* **Yah Veh**.
12 If he *offer* **oblate** it
for *a thanksgiving* **an extended hands praise**,
then he shall *offer* **oblate**
with the sacrifice of *thanksgiving* **extended hands praise**
unleavened **matsah** cakes *mingled* **mixed** with oil,
and *unleavened* **matsah** wafers anointed with oil,
and cakes *mingled* **mixed** with oil, of *fine* flour, **deep** fried.
13 Besides the cakes,
he shall *offer* **oblate** for his *offering* **qorban**
leavened **fermentation** bread
with the sacrifice of *thanksgiving* **extended hands praise**
of his *peace offerings* **shelamim**.
14 And of it he shall *offer* **oblate**
one out of the whole *oblation* **qorban**
for an *heave offering* **exaltment** unto *the LORD* **Yah Veh**,
and it shall be the priest's that sprinkleth the blood
of the *peace offerings* **shelamim**.
15 And the flesh of the sacrifice
of his *peace offerings* **shelamim**
for *thanksgiving* **an extended hands praise**
shall be eaten the same day *that it is offered* **of qorban**;
he shall not leave any of it until the morning.
16 But if the sacrifice of his *offering* **qorban** be a vow,
or a voluntary *offering*,
it shall be eaten the same day
that he *offereth* **oblateth** his sacrifice:
and on the morrow
also *the remainder of it* **that which remaineth**
shall be eaten:
17 But *the remainder* **that which remaineth**
of the flesh of the sacrifice
on the third day shall be burnt with fire.
18 And if *any of* the flesh
of the sacrifice of his *peace offerings* **shelamim,**
in eating, be eaten *at all* on the third day,
it shall not *be accepted* **please**,
neither shall it be *imputed* **fabricated** unto him
that *offereth* **oblateth** it:
it shall be *an abomination* **a stench**,
and the soul that eateth of it
shall bear his *iniquity* **perversity**.
19 And the flesh that toucheth any *unclean thing* **foulness**
shall not be eaten; it shall be burnt with fire:
and as for the flesh,
all that be *clean* **pure** shall eat thereof.
20 But the soul that eateth of the flesh
of the sacrifice of *peace offerings* **shelamim**,
that pertain unto *the LORD* **Yah Veh**,
having his *uncleanness* **foulness** upon him,
even that soul shall be cut off from his people.
21 Moreover the soul
that shall touch any *unclean thing* **foulness**,
as *the uncleanness of man* **human foulness**,
or *any unclean beast* **animal foulness**,
or any abominable *unclean thing* **foulness**,
and eat of the flesh
of the sacrifice of *peace offerings* **shelamim**,
which pertain unto *the LORD* **Yah Veh**,
even that soul shall be cut off from his people.

FORBIDDEN FOODS

22 And *the LORD spake* **Yah Veh worded**
unto *Moses* **Mosheh**, saying,
23 *Speak* **Word** unto the *children* **sons** of *Israel* **Yisra El**,
saying, Ye shall eat no *manner of* fat,
of ox, or of *sheep* **lambs**, or of goat.
24 And the fat of the *beast that dieth of itself* **carcase**,
and the fat of that which is torn *with beasts*,
may be *used* **worked** in any other *use* **work**:
but **in eating,** ye shall *in no wise* **not** eat of it.
25 For whosoever eateth the fat of the *beast* **animal**,
of which men offer an offering made by fire
oblated as a firing unto *the LORD* **Yah Veh**,
even the soul that eateth it
shall be cut off from his people.
26 Moreover ye shall eat no *manner of* blood,
whether it be of *fowl* **flyer** or of *beast* **animal**,

in any of your *dwellings* **settlements**.
27 Whatsoever soul it be
that eateth *any manner of* **whole** blood,
even that soul, shall be cut off from his people.

PRIESTAL PORTIONS

28 And *the LORD spake* **Yah Veh worded**
unto *Moses* **Mosheh**, saying,
29 *Speak* **Word** unto the *children* **sons** of *Israel* **Yisra El**,
saying, He that *offereth* **oblateth**
the sacrifice of his *peace offerings* **shelamim**
unto *the LORD* **Yah Veh**
shall bring his *oblation* **qorban** unto *the LORD* **Yah Veh**
of the sacrifice of his *peace offerings* **shelamim**.
30 His own hands shall bring
the *offerings of the LORD made by fire*
firings unto Yah Veh,
the fat with the breast, it shall he bring,
that the breast may be waved for a wave *offering*
before the LORD **at the face of Yah Veh**.
31 And the priest
shall *burn* **incense** the fat upon the **sacrifice** altar:
but the breast shall be *Aaron's* **Aharon's** and his sons'.
32 And the right *shoulder* **hindleg**
shall ye give unto the priest
for an *heave offering* **exaltment**
of the sacrifices of your *peace offerings* **shelamim**.
33 He among the sons of *Aaron* **Aharon**,
that *offereth* **oblateth** the blood
of the *peace offerings* **shelamim**,
and the fat,
shall have the right *shoulder* **hindleg** for his part.
34 For the wave breast
and the *heave shoulder* **hindleg of the exaltment**
have I taken of the *children* **sons** of *Israel* **Yisra El**
from off the sacrifices of their *peace offerings* **shelamim**,
and have given them
unto *Aaron* **Aharon** the priest and unto his sons
by *a* **an eternal** statute *for ever*
from among the *children* **sons** of *Israel* **Yisra El**.
35 This is *the portion* of the anointing of *Aaron* **Aharon**,
and of the anointing of his sons,
out of the *offerings of the LORD made by fire*
firings unto Yah Veh,
in the day when he *presented* **oblated** them
to *minister unto the LORD in the priest's office*
priest the priesthood unto Yah Veh;
36 Which *the LORD commanded* **Yah Veh misvahed**
to be given them of the *children* **sons** of *Israel* **Yisra El**,
in the day that he anointed them,
by *a* **an eternal** statute *for ever*
throughout their generations.
37 This is the *law* **torah** of the *burnt offering* **holocaust**,
of the *meat* offering,
and *of the sin offering* **that for the sin**,
and *of the trespass offering* **that for the guilt**,
and of the *consecrations* **fulfillments**,
and of the sacrifice of the *peace offerings* **shelamim**;
38 Which *the LORD* **Yah Veh**
commanded Moses **misvahed Mosheh**
in mount *Sinai* **Sinay**,
in the day that he *commanded* **misvahed**
the *children* **sons** of *Israel* **Yisra El**
to *offer* **oblate** their *oblations* **qorbans**
unto *the LORD* **Yah Veh**,
in the wilderness of *Sinai* **Sinay**.

PRIESTS ARE HALLOWED

8 And *the LORD spake* **Yah Veh worded**
unto *Moses* **Mosheh**, saying,
2 Take *Aaron* **Aharon** and his sons with him,
and the *garments* **clothes**, and the anointing oil,
and a bullock for the sin *offering*, and two rams,
and a basket of *unleavened bread* **matsah**;
3 And *gather* **congregate** thou
all the *congregation* **witness** *together*
unto the *door* **opening**
of the *tabernacle* **tent** of the congregation.
4 And *Moses did* **Mosheh worked**
as *the LORD commanded* **Yah Veh misvahed** him;
and the *assembly* **witness**
was gathered together **congregated** unto the *door* **opening**
of the *tabernacle* **tent** of the congregation.
5 And *Moses* **Mosheh** said unto the *congregation* **witness**,
This is the *thing* **word**
which *the LORD commanded* **Yah Veh misvahed**
to be *done* **worked**.

MOSHEH BAPTIZES THE PRIESTS

6 And *Moses* **Mosheh**
brought Aaron **oblated Aharon** and his sons,
and *washed* **baptized** them with water.
7 And he *put* **gave** upon him the coat,
and girded him with the girdle,
and *clothed* **enrobed** him with the *robe* **mantle**,
and *put* **gave** the ephod upon him,
and he girded him
with the *curious* **fabricated** girdle of the ephod,
and bound it unto him therewith.
8 And he put the breastplate upon him:
also he *put* **gave** in the breastplate
the Urim and the Thummim.
9 And he put the *mitre* **tiara** upon his head;
also upon the *mitre* **tiara**, *even* upon his forefront,
did he put the golden *plate* **blossom**,
the holy *crown* **separatism**;
as *the LORD* **Yah Veh**
commanded Moses **misvahed Mosheh**.
10 And *Moses* **Mosheh** took the anointing oil,
and anointed the tabernacle and all that was therein,
and *sanctified* **hallowed** them.
11 And he sprinkled thereof
upon the **sacrifice** altar seven times,
and anointed the **sacrifice** altar
and all his *vessels* **instruments**,
both the laver and his *foot* **base**, to *sanctify* **hallow** them.
12 And he poured of the anointing oil
upon *Aaron's* **Aharon's** head,
and anointed him, to *sanctify* **hallow** him.
13 And *Moses* **Mosheh**
brought Aaron's **oblated Aharon's** sons,
and *put* **enrobed** coats upon them,
and girded them with girdles,
and *put bonnets* **bound turbans** upon them;
as *the LORD* **Yah Veh**
commanded Moses **misvahed Mosheh**.
14 And he brought the bullock for the sin *offering*:
and *Aaron* **Aharon** and his sons *laid* **propped** their hands
upon the head of the bullock for the sin *offering*.
15 And he *slew* **slaughtered** it;
and *Moses* **Mosheh** took the blood,
and *put* **gave** it upon the horns of the **sacrifice** altar
round about with his finger,
and *purified* **for the sin on** the **sacrifice** altar,
and poured the blood
at the *bottom* **foundation** of the **sacrifice** altar,
and *sanctified* **hallowed** it,
to *make reconciliation* **atone** upon it.
16 And he took all the fat that was upon the inwards,
and the caul above the liver,
and the two *kidneys* **reins**, and their fat,
and *Moses burned* **Mosheh incensed** it
upon the **sacrifice** altar.
17 But the bullock,
and his *hide* **skin**, his flesh, and his dung,
he burnt with fire without the camp;
as *the LORD* **Yah Veh**
commanded Moses **misvahed Mosheh**.
18 And he *brought* **oblated** the ram
for the *burnt offering* **holocaust**:
and *Aaron* **Aharon** and his sons
laid **propped** their hands upon the head of the ram.
19 And he *killed* **slaughtered** it;
and *Moses* **Mosheh** sprinkled the blood
upon the **sacrifice** altar round about.
20 And he
cut the ram into pieces **dismembered the ram's members**;
and *Moses burnt* **Mosheh incensed** the head,
and the *pieces* **members**, and the fat.
21 And he *washed* **baptized** the inwards and the legs
in water;
and *Moses burnt* **Mosheh incensed** the whole ram
upon the **sacrifice** altar:

it was a *burnt sacrifice* **holocaust**
for a *sweet savour* **scent of rest**,
and *an offering made by fire* **a firing**
unto *the LORD* **Yah Veh**;
as *the LORD* **Yah Veh**
commanded Moses **misvahed Mosheh**.
22 And he *brought* **oblated** the *other* **second** ram,
the ram of *consecration* **fulfillments**:
and *Aaron* **Aharon** and his sons
laid **propped** their hands upon the head of the ram.
23 And he *slew* **slaughtered** it;
and *Moses* **Mosheh** took of the blood of it,
and *put* **gave** it upon the tip of *Aaron's* **Aharon's** right ear,
and upon the *thumb* **great digit** of his right hand,
and upon the great *toe* **digit** of his right foot.
24 And he *brought Aaron's* **oblated Aharon's** sons,
and *Moses put* **Mosheh gave** of the blood
upon the tip of their right ear,
and upon the *thumbs* **great digits** of their right hands,
and upon the great *toes* **digits** of their right feet:
and *Moses* **Mosheh** sprinkled the blood
upon the **sacrifice** altar round about.
25 And he took the fat, and the rump,
and all the fat that was upon the inwards,
and the caul above the liver,
and the two *kidneys* **reins**, and their fat,
and the right *shoulder* **hindleg**:
26 And out of the basket of *unleavened bread* **matsah**,
that was before the LORD **at the face of Yah Veh**,
he took one *unleavened* **matsah** cake,
and *a* **one** cake of oiled bread, and one wafer,
and put them on the fat,
and upon the right *shoulder* **hindleg**:
27 And he *put* **gave** all
upon *Aaron's hands* **Aharon's palms**,
and upon his sons' *hands* **palms**,
and waved them for a wave *offering*
before the LORD **at the face of Yah Veh**.
28 And *Moses* **Mosheh**
took them from off their *hands* **palms**,
and burnt them on the **sacrifice** altar
upon the *burnt offering* **holocaust**:
they were *consecrations* **fulfillments**
for a *sweet savour* **scent of rest**:
it is *an offering made by fire* **a firing**
unto *the LORD* **Yah Veh**.
29 And *Moses* **Mosheh** took the breast,
and waved it for a wave *offering*
before the LORD **at the face of Yah Veh**:
for of the ram of *consecration* **fulfillments**
it was *Moses'* **Mosheh's** part;
as *the LORD* **Yah Veh**
commanded Moses **misvahed Mosheh**.
30 And *Moses* **Mosheh** took of the anointing oil,
and of the blood which was upon the **sacrifice** altar,
and sprinkled it upon *Aaron* **Aharon**,
and upon his *garments* **clothes**,
and upon his sons,
and upon his sons' *garments* **clothes** with him;
and *sanctified Aaron* **hallowed Aharon**,
and his *garments* **clothes**,
and his sons, and his sons' *garments* **clothes** with him.
31 And *Moses* **Mosheh**
said unto *Aaron* **Aharon** and to his sons,
Boil **Stew** the flesh at the *door* **opening**
of the *tabernacle* **tent** of the congregation:
and there eat it with the bread
that is in the basket of *consecrations* **fulfillments**,
as I *commanded* **misvahed**, saying,
Aaron **Aharon** and his sons shall eat it.
32 And that which remaineth of the flesh and of the bread
shall ye burn with fire.
33 And ye shall not go out of the *door* **opening**
of the *tabernacle* **tent** of the congregation in seven days,
until the days of your *consecration* **fulfillments**
be *at an end* **fulfilled**:
for seven days shall he *consecrate you* **fill your hand**.
34 As he hath *done* **worked** this day,
so *the LORD* **Yah Veh** hath *commanded* **misvahed**
to *do* **work**,
to *make an atonement* **kapar/atone** for you.
35 Therefore shall ye *abide* **sit** at the *door* **opening**
of the *tabernacle* **tent** of the congregation
day and night seven days,
and *keep* **guard** the *charge* **guard** of *the LORD* **Yah Veh**,
that ye die not: for so I am *commanded* **misvahed**.
36 So *Aaron* **Aharon** and his sons
did **worked** all *things* **the words**
which *the LORD commanded* **Yah Veh misvahed**
by the hand of *Moses* **Mosheh.**

ON PRIESTING THE PRIESTHOOD:
SIN AND HOLOCAUST QORBANS

9 And it *came to pass* **became,** on the eighth day,
that *Moses* **Mosheh** called *Aaron* **Aharon** and his sons,
and the elders of *Israel* **Yisra El**;
2 And he said unto *Aaron* **Aharon**,
Take thee a *young calf* **son of the oxen**
for *a sin offering* **the sin**,
and a ram for a *burnt offering* **holocaust**,
without blemish **integrious**,
and *offer* **oblate** them
before the LORD **at the face of Yah Veh**.
3 And unto the *children* **sons** of *Israel* **Yisra El**
thou shalt *speak* **word**, saying,
Take ye a *kid* **buck** of the goats for *a sin offering* **the sin**;
and a calf and a lamb, *both of the first year* **yearling sons**,
without blemish **integrious**, for a *burnt offering* **holocaust**;
4 Also *a bullock* **an ox** and a ram
for *peace offerings* **shelamim**,
to sacrifice *before the LORD* **at the face of Yah Veh**;
and *a meat* **an** offering mingled with oil:
for to day
the LORD will appear unto **Yah Veh shall be seen by** you.
5 And they *brought* **took** that
which *Moses commanded* **Mosheh misvahed**
before **at the face of**
the *tabernacle* **tent** of the congregation:
and all the *congregation drew near* **witness approached**
and stood *before the LORD* **at the face of Yah Veh**.
6 And *Moses* **Mosheh** said,
This is the *thing* **word**
which *the LORD commanded* **Yah Veh misvahed**
that ye should *do* **work**:
and the g*lory* **honour** of *the LORD* **Yah Veh**
shall *appear unto* **be seen by** you.
7 And *Moses* **Mosheh** said unto *Aaron* **Aharon**,
Go unto the **sacrifice** altar,
and *offer thy sin offering* **work for thy sin**,
and thy *burnt offering* **holocaust**,
and *make an atonement* **kapar/atone** for thyself,
and for the people:
and *offer* **work** the *offering* **qorban** of the people,
and *make an atonement* **kapar/atone** for them;
as *the LORD commanded* **Yah Veh misvahed**.
8 *Aaron* **Aharon** *therefore*
went unto **oblated at** the **sacrifice** altar,
and *slew* **slaughtered**
the calf of the sin offering **that for the sin**,
which was for himself.
9 And the sons of *Aaron* **Aharon**
brought **oblated** the blood unto him:
and he dipped his finger in the blood,
and *put* **gave** it upon the horns of the **sacrifice** altar,
and poured out the blood
at the *bottom* **foundation** of the **sacrifice** altar:
10 But the fat, and the *kidneys* **reins**,
and the caul *above* **from** the liver
of the sin offering **for the sin**,
he *burnt* **incensed** upon the **sacrifice** altar;
as *the LORD* **Yah Veh**
commanded Moses **misvahed Mosheh**.
11 And the flesh and the *hide* **skin**
he burnt with fire without the camp.
12 And he *slew* **slaughtered** the *burnt offering* **holocaust**;
and *Aaron's* **Aharon's** sons presented unto him the blood,
which he sprinkled round about upon the **sacrifice** altar.
13 And they presented the *burnt offering* **holocaust**
unto him,
with the *pieces* **members** thereof and the head:
and he *burnt* **incensed** them upon the **sacrifice** altar.

14 And he *did wash* **baptized** the inwards and the legs,
and *burnt* **incensed** them
upon the *burnt offering* **holocaust** on the **sacrifice** altar.
15 And he *brought* **oblated** the people's *offering* **qorban**,
and took the *goat* **buck**,
which was *the sin offering for* **for the sin of** the people,
and *slew it, and offered it for sin*
slaughtered that for the sin,
as the first.
16 And he *brought* **oblated** the *burnt offering* **holocaust**,
and *offered* **worked** it according to the *manner* **decree**.
17 And he *brought* **oblated** the *meat* offering,
and *took an handful thereof* **filled his palm**,
and *burnt* **incensed** it upon the **sacrifice** altar,
beside **apart from**
the *burnt sacrifice* **holocaust** of the morning.
18 He *slew* **slaughtered** also the *bullock* **ox** and the ram
for a sacrifice of *peace offerings* **shelamim**,
which was for the people:
and *Aaron's* **Aharon's** sons presented unto him the blood,
which he sprinkled upon the **sacrifice** altar round about,
19 And the fat of the *bullock* **ox** and of the ram,
the rump, and that which covereth *the inwards*,
and the *kidneys* **reins**, and the caul above the liver:
20 And they put the fat upon the breasts,
and he *burnt* **incensed** the fat upon the **sacrifice** altar:
21 And the breasts and the right *shoulder* **hindleg**
Aaron **Aharon** waved for a wave *offering*
before the LORD **at the face of Yah Veh**;
as *Moses commanded* **Mosheh misvahed.**
22 And *Aaron* **Aharon**
lifted up his hand toward the people, and blessed them,
and *came down* **descended**
from *offering of the sin offering* **working that for the sin**,
and the *burnt offering* **holocaust**,
and *peace offerings* **shelamim**.
23 And *Moses* **Mosheh** and *Aaron* **Aharon**
went into the *tabernacle* **tent** of the congregation,
and came out, and blessed the people:
and the *glory* **honour** of *the LORD* **Yah Veh**
appeared unto **was seen by** all the people.
24 And there came a fire out
from *before the LORD* **the face of Yah Veh**,
and consumed upon the **sacrifice** altar
the *burnt offering* **holocaust** and the fat:
which when all the people saw,
they shouted, and fell on their faces.

SIN AND DEATH OF AHARON'S SONS

10 And Nadab and *Abihu* **Abi Hu**,
the sons of *Aaron* **Aharon**,
took *either of them* **each man** his *censer* **tray**,
and *put* **gave** fire therein, and put incense thereon,
and *offered* **oblated** strange fire
before the LORD **at the face of Yah Veh**,
which he *commanded* **misvahed** them not.
2 And there went out fire
from *the LORD* **the face of Yah Veh**,
and devoured them,
and they died *before the LORD* **at the face of Yah Veh**.
3 Then *Moses* **Mosheh** said unto *Aaron* **Aharon**,
This is it that *the LORD spake* **Yah Veh worded**, saying,
I *will* **shall** be *sanctified* **hallowed** in them
that come nigh me,
and *before* **at the face of** all the people
I *will* **shall** be *glorified* **honoured**.
And *Aaron held his peace* **Aharon hushed**.
4 And *Moses* **Mosheh**
called *Mishael* **Misha El** and *Elzapha* **El Saphan**,
the sons of *Uzziel* **Uzzi El** the uncle of *Aaron* **Aharon**,
and said unto them, Come near,
carry **bear** your brethren
from *before* **the face of** the *sanctuary* **holies**
out of **without** the camp.
5 So they *went near* **approached**,
and *carried* **bore** them in their coats
out of **without** the camp;
as *Moses* **Mosheh** had *said* **worded**.
6 And *Moses* **Mosheh** said unto *Aaron* **Aharon**,
and unto *Eleazar* **El Azar** and unto *Ithamar* **Iy Thamar**,
his sons,
Uncover **Expose** not your heads,
neither *rend* **tear** your clothes;
lest ye die, and lest *wrath* **he be enraged**
come upon all the people **with the witness**:
but let your brethren,
the whole *house of Israel* **Beth Yisra El**,
bewail **weep over** the burning
which *the LORD* **Yah Veh** hath *kindled* **burned**.
7 And *ye* shall not go out from the *door* **opening**
of the *tabernacle* **tent** of the congregation, lest ye die:
for the anointing oil of *the LORD* **Yah Veh** is upon you.
And they *did* **worked**
according to the word of *Moses* **Mosheh**.
8 And *the LORD spake* **Yah Veh worded**
unto *Aaron* **Aharon**, saying,
9 Do not drink wine nor *strong drink* **intoxicants**,
thou, nor thy sons with thee,
when ye go into the *tabernacle* **tent** of the congregation,
lest ye die:
it shall be *a* **an eternal** statute *for ever*
throughout your generations:
10 And that ye may *put difference* **separate**
between holy and *unholy* **profane**,
and between *unclean* **foul** and *clean* **pure**;
11 And that ye may *teach* **point out**
to the *children* **sons** of *Israel* **Yisra El**
all the statutes
which *the LORD* **Yah Veh** hath *spoken* **worded** unto them
by the hand of *Moses* **Mosheh**.
12 And *Moses spake* **Mosheh worded** unto *Aaron* **Aharon**,
and unto *Eleazar* **El Azar** and unto *Ithamar* **Iy Thamar**,
his sons that *were left* **remained**,
Take the *meat* offering that remaineth
of the *offerings of the LORD made by fire*
firings unto Yah Veh,
and eat *it without leaven* **with matsah**
beside the **sacrifice** altar:
for it is *most holy* **a holy of holies**:
13 And ye shall eat it in the *holy place* **holies**,
because it is thy *due* **statute**, and thy sons' *due* **statute**,
of the *sacrifices of the LORD made by fire*
firings unto Yah Veh:
for so I am *commanded* **misvahed**.
14 And the wave breast
and *heave shoulder* **exaltment hindleg**
shall ye eat in a *clean* **pure** place;
thou, and thy sons, and thy daughters with thee:
for they be thy *due* **statute**, and thy sons' *due* **statute**,
which are given out of the sacrifices
of *peace offerings* **shelamim**
of the *children* **sons** of *Israel* **Yisra El**.
15 The *heave shoulder* **exaltment hindleg**
and the wave breast
shall they bring
with the *offerings made by fire* **firings** of the fat,
to wave it for a wave *offering*
before the LORD **at the face of Yah Veh**;
and it shall be thine, and thy sons' with thee,
by *a* **an eternal** statute *for ever*;
as *the LORD* **Yah Veh** hath *commanded* **misvahed**.
16 **And in seeking,**
Moses diligently **Mosheh** sought the goat
of *the sin offering* **that for the sin**,
and, behold, it was burnt:
and he was *angry* **enraged**
with *Eleazar* **El Azar** and *Ithamar* **Iy Thamar**,
the sons of *Aaron* **Aharon** which *were left alive* **remained**,
saying,
17 Wherefore have ye not eaten
the sin offering **that for the sin** in the *holy place* **holies**,
seeing it is *most holy* **a holy of holies**,
and *God* **he** hath given it you to bear
the *iniquity* **perversity** of the *congregation* **witness**,
to *make atonement* **kapar/atone** for them
before the LORD **at the face of Yah Veh**?
18 Behold, the blood of it was not brought in
within the *holy place* **holies**:
in eating, ye should *indeed* have eaten it
in the *holy place* **holies**, as I *commanded* **misvahed**.
19 And *Aaron said* **Aharon worded** unto *Moses* **Mosheh**,

Behold,
this day have they *offered* **oblated for** their sin *offering*
and their *burnt offering* **holocaust**
before the LORD **at the face of Yah Veh;**
and such *things* have *befallen* **confronted** me:
and if I had eaten *the sin offering* **that for the sin** to day,
should it have *been accepted* **well—pleased**
in the *sight* **eyes** of *the LORD* **Yah Veh**?
20 And when *Moses* **Mosheh** heard that,
he was *content* **well—pleased in his eyes.**

FOODS: BIDDEN AND FORBIDDEN

11 And *the LORD spake* **Yah Veh worded**
unto *Moses* **Mosheh** and to *Aaron* **Aharon**,
saying unto them,
2 *Speak* **Word** unto the *children* **sons** of *Israel* **Yisra El**,
saying, These are the *beasts* **live beings** which ye shall eat
among all the *beasts* **animals** that are on the earth.
3 Whatsoever *parteth* **splitteth** the hoof,
and *is clovenfooted* **cleaveth the cleft of the hoof**,
and *cheweth* **regurgitateth** the cud,
among the *beasts* **animals**, that shall ye eat.
4 *Nevertheless* **Only** these shall ye not eat:
of them that *chew* **regurgitate** the cud,
or of them that *divide* **split** the hoof:
as the camel,
because he *cheweth* **regurgitateth** the cud,
but *divideth* **splitteth** not the hoof;
he is *unclean* **fouled** unto you.
5 And the coney,
because he *cheweth* **regurgitateth** the cud,
but *divideth* **splitteth** not the hoof;
he is *unclean* **fouled** unto you.
6 And the hare,
because he *cheweth* **regurgitateth** the cud,
but *divideth* **splitteth** not the hoof;
he is *unclean* **fouled** unto you.
7 And the *swine* **hog**,
though he *divide* **split** the hoof,
and *be clovenfooted* **cleaveth the cleft of the hoof**,
yet he *cheweth* **regurgitateth** not the cud;
he is *unclean* **fouled** to you.
8 Of their flesh shall ye not eat,
and their carcase shall ye not touch;
they are *unclean* **fouled** to you.
9 These shall ye eat of all that are in the waters:
whatsoever hath fins and scales in the waters,
in the seas, and in the *rivers* **wadies**, them shall ye eat.
10 And all that have not fins and scales in the seas,
and in the *rivers* **wadies**,
of all that *move* **teem** in the waters,
and of any living *thing* **soul** which is in the waters,
they shall be an abomination unto you:
11 They shall be even an abomination unto you;
ye shall not eat of their flesh,
but ye shall
have **abominate** their carcases *in abomination*.
12 Whatsoever hath no fins nor scales in the waters,
that shall be an abomination unto you.
13 And these are they
which ye shall *have in abomination* **abominate**
among **of** the *fowls* **fliers**;
they shall not be eaten, they are an abomination:
the eagle, and the ossifrage, and the ospray,
14 And the *vulture* **kite**,
and the *kite after his kind* **hawk in species**;
15 Every raven *after his kind* **in species**;
16 And the **daughter of the** owl, and the night hawk,
and the cuckow, and the hawk *after his kind* **in species**,
17 And the little owl,
and the cormorant, and the great owl,
18 And the swan, and the pelican, and the gier eagle,
19 And the stork, the heron *after her kind* **in species**,
and the *lapwing* **hoopoe**, and the bat.
20 All *fowls* **teemers** that *creep* **fly**, going upon all four,
shall be an abomination unto you.
21 Yet these may ye eat
of every flying *creeping thing* **teemer**
that goeth upon all four,
which have legs above their feet,
to leap withal upon the earth;
22 Even these of them ye may eat;
the locust *after his kind* **in species**,
and the bald locust *after his kind* **in species**,
and the beetle *after his kind* **in species**,
and the grasshopper *after his kind* **in species**.
23 But all *other flying creeping things* **teemers that fly**,
which have four feet, shall be an abomination unto you.
24 And for these ye shall be *unclean* **fouled**:
whosoever toucheth the carcase of them
shall be *unclean* **fouled** until the even.
25 And whosoever beareth *ought* of the carcase of them
shall wash his clothes,
and be *unclean* **fouled** until the even.
26 *The carcases of every beast* **Every animal**
which *divideth* **splitteth** the hoof,
and *is not clovenfooted* **cleaveth not the cleft of the hoof**,
nor *cheweth* **regurgitateth** the cud,
are *unclean* **fouled** unto you:
every one that toucheth them shall be *unclean* **fouled**.
27 And whatsoever goeth upon his paws,
among all *manner of beasts* **live beings** that go on all four,
those are *unclean* **fouled** unto you:
whoso toucheth their carcase
shall be *unclean* **fouled** until the even.
28 And he that beareth the carcase of them
shall wash his clothes,
and be *unclean* **fouled** until the even:
they are *unclean* **fouled** unto you.
29 These also shall be *unclean* **fouled** unto you
among the *creeping things* **teemers**
that *creep* **teem** upon the earth;
the weasel, and the mouse,
and the tortoise *after his kind* **in species**,
30 And the *ferret* **shrieker**, and the chameleon,
and the lizard, and the snail, and the mole.
31 These are *unclean* **fouled** to you
among all *that creep* **the teemers**:
whosoever doth touch them, when they be dead,
shall be *unclean* **fouled** until the even.
32 And upon whatsoever any of them,
when they are dead, doth fall,
it shall be *unclean* **fouled**;
whether it be any *vessel* **instrument** of *wood* **timber**,
or *raiment* **clothes**, or skin, or *sack* **saq**,
whatsoever *vessel* **instrument** it be,
wherein *any* work is *done* **worked**,
it must be put **put it** into water,
and it shall be *unclean* **fouled** until the even;
so **thus** it shall be *cleansed* **purified**.
33 And every *earthen vessel* **pottery instrument**,
whereinto **into the midst** any of them falleth,
whatsoever is in *it* **its midst** shall be *unclean* **fouled**;
and ye shall break it.
34 Of all *meat* **food** which may be eaten,
that on which *such* water cometh shall be *unclean* **fouled**:
and all drink that may be drunk
in every *such vessel* **instrument** shall be *unclean* **fouled**.
35 And *every thing* **all** whereupon
any part of their carcase falleth shall be *unclean* **fouled**;
whether it be oven, or ranges for pots,
they shall be *broken* **pulled** down:
for they are *unclean* **fouled**
and shall be *unclean* **fouled** unto you.
36 Nevertheless a fountain or *pit* **well**,
wherein there is plenty **a congregating** of water,
shall be *clean* **pure**:
but that which toucheth their carcase
shall be *unclean* **fouled**.
37 And if *any part of* their carcase
fall upon any *sowing* **seeding** seed
which is to be *sown* **seeded**,
it shall be *clean* **pure**.
38 But if any water be *put* **given** upon the seed,
and *any part of* their carcase fall thereon,
it shall be *unclean* **fouled** unto you.
39 And if any *beast* **animal**,
of which ye may eat **which is for food**, die;
he that toucheth the carcase thereof
shall be *unclean* **fouled** until the even.
40 And he that eateth of the carcase of it

shall wash his clothes,
and be *unclean* **fouled** until the even:
he also that beareth the carcase of it
shall wash his clothes,
and be *unclean* **fouled** until the even.
41 And every *creeping thing* **teemer**
that *creepeth* **teemeth** upon the earth
shall be an abomination;
it shall not be eaten.
42 Whatsoever goeth upon the belly,
and whatsoever goeth upon all four,
or whatsoever *hath more* **aboundeth** feet
among all *creeping things* **teemers**
that *creep* **teem** upon the earth,
them ye shall not eat; for they are an abomination.
43 Ye shall not
make yourselves abominable **abominate your souls**
with any *creeping thing* **teemer** that *creepeth* **teemeth**,
neither shall ye make yourselves *unclean* **fouled**
with them,
that ye should be *defiled* **fouled** thereby.
44 For *I am the LORD* **I — Yah Veh** your *God* **Elohim**:
ye shall *therefore sanctify* **hallow** yourselves,
and ye shall be holy; for *I am* **I** — holy:
neither shall ye *defile yourselves* **foul your souls**
with any *manner of creeping thing* **teemer**
that creepeth upon the earth.
45 For *I am the LORD* **I — Yah Veh**
that *bringeth* **ascendeth** you *up*
out of the land of *Egypt* **Misrayim**,
to be your *God* **Elohim**:
ye shall therefore be holy, for *I am* **I** — holy:
46 This is the *law* **torah** of the *beasts* **animals**,
and of the *fowl* **fliers**,
and of every living *creature* **soul**
that *moveth* **creepeth** in the waters,
and of every *creature* **soul**
that *creepeth* **teemeth** upon the earth:
47 To *make a difference* **separate** between
the *unclean* **fouled** and **between** the *clean* **pure**,
and between the *beast* **live being** that may be eaten
and **between** the *beast* **live being** that may not be eaten.

TORAH ON BIRTHING

12 And *the LORD spake* **Yah Veh worded**
unto *Moses* **Mosheh**, saying,
2 *Speak* **Word** unto the *children* **sons** of *Israel* **Yisra El**,
saying, If a woman have *conceived seed* **seeded**,
and born a *man child* **male**:
then she shall be *unclean* **fouled** seven days;
according to the days of the *separation* **exclusion**
for her *infirmity* **menstruation** shall she be *unclean* **fouled**.
3 And in the eighth day
the flesh of his foreskin shall be circumcised.
4 And she shall then *continue* **sit**
in the blood of her purifying three **days** and thirty days;
she shall **neither** touch *no hallowed thing* **the holies**,
nor *come into* **enter** the *sanctuary* **holies**,
until the days of her purifying be fulfilled.
5 But if she bear a *maid child* **female**,
then she shall be *unclean* **fouled** two weeks,
as in her *separation* **exclusion**:
and she shall *continue* **sit** in the blood of her purifying
threescore **sixty days** and six days.
6 And when the days of her purifying are fulfilled,
for a son, or for a daughter,
she shall bring a lamb *of the first year* **a yearling son**
for a *burnt offering* **holocaust**,
and a *young pigeon* **son of a dove**, or a turtledove,
for *a sin offering* **the sin**, unto the *door* **opening**
of the *tabernacle* **tent** of the congregation,
unto the priest:
7 Who shall *offer* **oblate** it
before the LORD **at the face of Yah Veh**,
and *make an atonement* **kapar/atone** for her;
and she shall be *cleansed* **purified**
from the *issue* **fountain** of her blood.
This is the *law* **torah** for her
that hath born a male or a female.
8 And if *she be not able* **her hand be not sufficient**
to *bring* **find** a lamb,
then she shall *bring* **take** two *turtles* **turtledoves**,
or two *young pigeons* **sons of doves**;
the one for the *burnt offering* **holocaust**,
and the *other for a sin offering* **one for the sin**:
and the priest shall *make an atonement* **kapar/atone** for her,
and she shall be *clean* **purified**.

TORAH ON LEPROSY

13 And *the LORD spake* **Yah Veh worded**
unto *Moses* **Mosheh** and *Aaron* **Aharon**, saying,
2 When a *man* **human** shall have in the skin of his flesh
a rising **swelling**, a scab, or bright spot,
and it be in the skin of his flesh like the plague of leprosy;
then he shall be brought unto *Aaron* **Aharon** the priest,
or unto one of his sons the priests:
3 And the priest shall *look on* **see** the plague
in the skin of the flesh:
and when the hair in the plague is turned white,
and the plague in *sight* **visage**
be deeper than the skin of his flesh,
it is a plague of leprosy:
and the priest shall *look on* **see** him,
and pronounce him *unclean* **fouled**.
4 If the bright spot be white in the skin of his flesh,
and in *sight* **visage** be not deeper than the skin,
and the hair thereof be not turned white;
then the priest shall shut up him that hath the plague
seven days:
5 And the priest shall *look on* **see** him the seventh day:
and, behold, if the plague in his sight be at a stay,
and the plague spread not in the skin;
then the priest shall shut him up
a second seven days *more*:
6 And the priest shall *look on* **see** him *again*
the **second** seventh day:
and, behold, if the plague be *somewhat dark* **faded**,
and the plague spread not in the skin,
the priest shall pronounce him *clean* **purified**:
it is but a scab:
and he shall *wash* **launder** his clothes,
and be *clean* **purified**.
7 But if **in spreading,**
the scab spread *much abroad* in the skin,
after that he hath been seen of the priest
for his *cleansing* **purifying**,
he shall be seen of the priest *again* **a second time**.
8 And if the priest see that, behold,
the scab spreadeth in the skin,
then the priest shall pronounce him *unclean* **fouled**:
it is a leprosy.
9 When the plague of leprosy is in a *man* **human**,
then he shall be brought unto the priest;
10 And the priest shall see him: and, behold,
if the *rising* **swelling** be white in the skin,
and it have turned the hair white,
and there be *quick raw* **the invigoration of living** flesh
in the *rising* **swelling**;
11 It is an old leprosy in the skin of his flesh,
and the priest shall pronounce him *unclean* **fouled**,
and shall not shut him up: for he is *unclean* **fouled**.
12 And if a leprosy *break out abroad* **in blossoming,**
blossometh in the skin,
and the leprosy cover all the skin
of *him that hath* the plague
from his head even to his foot,
wheresoever the priest looketh
in the visage of the eyes of the priest;
13 Then the priest shall *consider* **see**: and, behold,
if the leprosy have covered all his flesh,
he shall pronounce him *clean* **purified**
that hath the plague:
it is all turned white: he is *clean* **pure**.
14 But *when raw* **in the day living** flesh
appeareth **be seen** in him,
he shall be *unclean* **fouled**.
15 And the priest shall see the *raw* **living** flesh,
and pronounce him to be *unclean* **fouled**:
for the *raw* **living** flesh is *unclean* **fouled**: it is a leprosy.
16 Or if the raw flesh turn again,
and be *changed* **turned** unto white,
he shall come unto the priest;

17 And the priest shall see him: and, behold,
if the plague be turned into white;
then the priest shall pronounce him *clean* **purified**
that hath the plague: he is *clean* **pure**.
18 The flesh also, in which, even in the skin thereof,
was *a boil* **an ulcer**, and is healed,
19 And in the place of the *boil* **ulcer**
there be a white *rising* **swelling**,
or a bright spot, white, and *somewhat* reddish,
and it be *shewed to* **seen by** the priest;
20 And if, when the priest seeth it, behold,
it be in *sight* **visage** lower than the skin,
and the hair thereof be turned white;
the priest shall pronounce him *unclean* **fouled**:
it is a plague of leprosy
broken **blossoming** out of the *boil* **ulcer**.
21 But if the priest *look on it* **see**, and, behold,
there be no white hairs therein,
and if it be not lower than the skin,
but be *somewhat dark* **faded**;
then the priest shall shut him *up* seven days:
22 And if **in spreading,** it spread *much abroad* in the skin,
then the priest shall pronounce him *unclean* **fouled**:
it is a plague.
23 But if the bright spot stay in his place, and spread not,
it is *a burning boil* **an inflamed ulcer**;
and the priest shall pronounce him *clean* **purified**.
24 Or if there be any flesh, in the skin
whereof there is a hot burning — **a burning of fire**,
and the *quick flesh that burneth* **invigoration burning**
have a white bright spot, *somewhat* reddish, or white;
25 Then the priest shall *look upon* **see** it: and, behold,
if the hair in the bright spot be turned white,
and it be in *sight* **visage** deeper than the skin;
it is a leprosy *broken* **blossoming** out of the burning:
wherefore the priest
shall pronounce him *unclean* **fouled**:
it is the plague of leprosy.
26 But if the priest *look on it* **see**, and, behold,
there be no white hair in the bright spot,
and it be no lower than the *other* skin,
but be *somewhat dark* **faded**;
then the priest shall shut him *up* seven days:
27 And the priest shall *look upon* **see** him the seventh day:
and if **in spreading,**
it be spread *much abroad* in the skin,
then the priest shall pronounce him *unclean* **fouled**:
it is the plague of leprosy.
28 And if the bright spot stay in his place,
and spread not in the skin, but it be *somewhat dark* **faded**;
it is a *rising* **swelling** of the burning,
and the priest shall pronounce him *clean* **purified**:
for it is *an inflammation* **inflamed** of the burning.
29 If a man or woman have a plague
upon the head or the beard;
30 Then the priest shall see the plague: and, behold,
if it be in *sight* **visage** deeper than the skin;
and there be in it a yellow thin hair;
then the priest shall pronounce him *unclean* **fouled**:
it is a *dry* scall, even a leprosy upon the head or beard.
31 And if the priest *look on* **see** the plague of the scall,
and, behold, it be not in *sight* **visage** deeper than the skin,
and that there is no *black* **dark** hair in it;
then the priest shall shut *up him that hath*
the plague of the scall seven days:
32 And in the seventh day
the priest shall *look on* **see** the plague: and, behold,
if the scall spread not, and there be in it no yellow hair,
and the scall be not in *sight* **visage** deeper than the skin;
33 He shall be shaven, but the scall shall he not shave;
and the priest shall shut *up him that hath* the scall
a second seven days *more*:
34 And in the seventh day
the priest shall *look on* **see** the scall:
and, behold, if the scall be not spread in the skin,
nor be in *sight* **visage** deeper than the skin;
then the priest shall pronounce him *clean* **purified**:
and he shall *wash* **launder** his clothes,
and be *clean* **purified**.
35 But if **in spreading,**
the scall spread *much* in the skin
after his *cleansing* **purifying**;
36 Then the priest shall *look on* **see** him: and, behold,
if the scall be spread in the skin,
the priest shall not seek for yellow hair;
he is *unclean* **fouled**.
37 But if the scall be in his *sight* **eyes** at a stay,
and that there is *black* **dark** hair
grown up **sprouting** therein;
the scall is healed, he is *clean* **pure**:
and the priest shall pronounce him *clean* **purified**.
38 If a man also or a woman
have in the skin of their flesh bright spots,
even white bright spots;
39 Then the priest shall *look* **see**: and, behold,
if the bright spots in the skin of their flesh
be *darkish* **faded** white;
it is a freckled spot that *groweth* **blossometh** in the skin;
he is *clean* **pure**.
40 And the man
whose *hair is fallen off his* head **baldened**,
he is bald; yet is he *clean* **pure**.
41 And he that hath *his hair fallen off* **baldened**
from the *part* **edge** of his head toward his face,
he is forehead *bald* **high**: yet is he *clean* **pure**.
42 And if there be in the *bald head* **baldness**,
or *bald* **high** forehead,
a white reddish *sore* **plague**;
it is a leprosy *sprung up* **blossoming**
in his *bald head* **baldness**, or his *bald* **high** forehead.
43 Then the priest shall *look upon it* **see**:
and, behold, if the *rising* **swelling** of the *sore* **plague**
be white reddish in his *bald head* **baldness**,
or in his *bald* **high** forehead,
as the **in visage like** leprosy
appeareth in the skin of the flesh;
44 He is a leprous man, he is *unclean* **fouled**:
in fouling,
the priest shall pronounce him *utterly unclean* **fouled**;
his plague is in his head.
45 And the leper in whom the plague is,
his clothes shall be *rent* **torn**,
and his head *bare* **exposed**,
and he shall put a covering upon his upper lip,
and shall *cry* **call**, *Unclean, unclean.* **Fouled! Fouled!**
46 All the days wherein the plague shall be in him
he shall be *defiled* **fouled**; he is *unclean* **fouled**:
he shall *dwell* **settle** alone;
without the camp shall his *habitation* **settlement** be.

TORAH ON LEPROUS CLOTHES

47 The *garment* **clothes** also
that the plague of leprosy is in,
whether it be *a* woollen *garment* **clothes**,
or *a linen garment* **flax clothes**;
48 Whether it be in the warp, or woof;
of *linen* **flax**, or of woollen;
whether in a skin, or in any *thing made* **work** of skin;
49 And if the plague be greenish or reddish
in the *garment* **clothes**, or in the skin,
either **or** in the warp, or in the woof,
or in any *thing* **instrument** of skin;
it is a plague of leprosy,
and *be shewed unto* **shall have** the priest **see**:
50 And the priest shall *look upon* **see** the plague,
and shut *up it that hath* the plague seven days:
51 And he shall *look* **see** on the plague
on the seventh day:
if the plague be spread in the *garment* **clothes**,
either in the warp, or in the woof,
or in a skin, or in any work that is *made* **worked** of skin;
the plague is a *fretting* **bitter** leprosy; it is *unclean* **fouled**.
52 He shall *therefore* burn *that garment* **those clothes**,
whether warp or woof, in woollen or in *linen* **flax**,
or any *thing* **instrument** of skin, wherein the plague is:
for it is a *fretting* **bitter** leprosy;
it shall be burnt in the fire.
53 And if the priest shall *look* **see**, and, behold,
the plague be not spread in the *garment* **clothes**,
either **or** in the warp, or in the woof,
or in any *thing* **instrument** of skin;

54 Then the priest shall *command* **misvah**
that they *wash the thing* **launder that**
wherein the plague is,
and he shall shut it up **a second** seven days *more*:
55 And the priest shall *look on* **see** the plague,
after that it is washed: and, behold,
if the plague have not *changed* **turned** his *colour* **eyes**,
and the plague be not spread; it is *unclean* **fouled**;
thou shalt burn it in the fire; it is *fret inward* **pitted**,
whether it be *bare within* **baldness**
or *without* **high forehead**.
56 And if the priest *look* **see**, and, behold,
the plague be *somewhat dark* **faded**
after *the washing of* it **is laundered**;
then he shall *rend* **rip** it out of the *garment* **clothes**,
or out of the skin, or out of the warp, or out of the woof:
57 And if it *appear* **be seen** still in the *garment* **clothes**,
either in the warp, or in the woof,
or in any *thing* **instrument** of skin;
it is a *spreading plague* **blossoming**:
thou shalt burn that wherein the plague is with fire.
58 And the *garment* **clothes**, either warp, or woof,
or whatsoever *thing* **instrument** of skin it be,
which thou shalt *wash* **launder**,
if the plague be *departed* **turned aside** from them,
then it shall be *washed* **laundered** the second time,
and shall be *clean* **purified**.
59 This is the *law* **torah** of the plague of leprosy
in *a garment* **clothes** of woollen or *linen* **flax**,
either in the warp, or woof,
or any *thing* **instrument** of skins,
to pronounce it *clean* **purified**,
or to pronounce it *unclean* **fouled**.

TORAH ON PURIFYING THE LEPER

14 And *the LORD spake* **Yah Veh worded**
unto *Moses* **Mosheh**, saying,
2 This shall be the *law* **torah** of the leper
in the day of his *cleansing* **purifying**:
He shall be brought unto the priest:
3 And the priest shall go *forth out of* **outside** the camp;
and the priest shall *look* **see**, and, behold,
if the plague of leprosy be healed in the leper;
4 Then shall the priest *command* **misvah**
to take for him that is to be *cleansed* **purified**
two birds *alive* **living** and *clean* **pure**,
and cedar *wood* **timber**, and scarlet, and hyssop:
5 And the priest shall *command* **misvah**
that one of the birds be *killed* **slaughtered**
in *an earthen vessel* **a pottery instrument**
over *running* **living water**:
6 As for the living bird,
he shall take it, and the cedar *wood* **timber**,
and the scarlet, and the hyssop,
and shall dip them and the living bird
in the blood of the bird that was *killed* **slaughtered**
over the *running* **living** water:
7 And he shall sprinkle upon him
that is to be *cleansed* **purified** from the leprosy
seven times,
and shall pronounce him *clean* **purified**,
and shall *let* **send away** the living bird *loose*
into the *open* **face of the** field.
8 And he that is to be *cleansed* **purified**
shall *wash* **launder** his clothes, and shave off all his hair,
and *wash* **baptize** himself in water,
that he may be *clean* **purified**:
and after that he shall come into the camp,
and shall *tarry* **settle**
abroad out of **without** his tent seven days.
9 But it shall be on the seventh day,
that he shall shave all his hair off his head
and his beard and his eyebrows,
even all his hair he shall shave off:
and he shall *wash* **launder** his clothes,
also he shall *wash* **baptize** his flesh in water,
and he shall be *clean* **purified**.
10 And on the eighth day
he shall take two he lambs *without blemish* **integrious**,
and one ewe lamb *of the first year* **a yearling daughter**
without blemish **integrious**,
and three *tenth deals* **tenths** of *fine* flour
for *a meat* **an** offering,
mingled **mixed** with oil, and one log of oil.
11 And the priest that *maketh* **purifieth** him *clean*
shall *present* **stand** the man
that is to be *made clean* **purified**, and those *things*,
before the LORD **at the face of Yah Veh**,
at the *door* **opening**
of the *tabernacle* **tent** of the congregation:
12 And the priest shall take one he lamb,
and *offer* **oblate** him for *a trespass offering* **the guilt**,
and the log of oil,
and wave them for a wave *offering*
before the LORD **at the face of Yah Veh**:
13 And he shall *slay* **slaughter** the lamb
in the place where he shall *kill* **slaughter**
the sin offering **that for the sin**
and the *burnt offering* **holocaust**, in the *holy place* **holies**:
for as *the sin offering* **that for the sin** is the priest's,
so is *the trespass offering* **that for the guilt**:
it is *most holy* **a holy of holies**:
14 And the priest shall take some of the blood
of *the trespass offering* **that for the guilt**,
and the priest shall *put* **give** it
upon the tip of the right ear
of him that is to be *cleansed* **purified**,
and upon the *thumb* **great digit** of his right hand,
and upon the great *toe* **digit** of his right foot:
15 And the priest shall take *some* of the log of oil,
and pour it into the palm of his own left hand:
16 And the priest shall dip his right finger
in the oil that is in his left *hand* **palm**,
and shall sprinkle of the oil with his finger seven times
before the LORD **at the face of Yah Veh**:
17 And of the *rest* **remainder** of the oil
that is in his *hand* **palm**
shall the priest *put* **give** upon the tip of the right ear
of him that is to be *cleansed* **purified**,
and upon the *thumb* **great digit** of his right hand,
and upon the great *toe* **digit** of his right foot,
upon the blood of *the trespass offering* **that for the guilt**:
18 And *the remnant* **that which remaineth**
of the oil that is in the priest's *hand* **palm**
he shall *pour* **give** upon the head of him
that is to be *cleansed* **purified**:
and the priest
shall *make an atonement* **kapar/atone** for him
before the LORD **at the face of Yah Veh**.
19 And the priest shall
offer the sin offering **work that for the sin**,
and *make an atonement* **kapar/atone**
for him that is to be *cleansed* **purified**
from his *uncleanness* **foulness**;
and afterward he shall *kill* **slaughter**
the *burnt offering* **holocaust**:
20 And the priest shall *offer* **holocaust**
the *burnt offering* **holocaust**
and the *meat* offering upon the **sacrifice** altar:
and the priest
shall *make an atonement* **kapar/atone** for him,
and he shall be *clean* **purified**.
21 And if he be poor,
and *cannot get* **his hand hath not attained** so much;
then he shall take one lamb
for *a trespass offering* **the guilt** to be waved,
to *make an atonement* **kapar/atone** for him,
and one tenth *deal of fine* flour *mingled* **mixed** with oil
for *a meat* **an** offering, and a log of oil;
22 And two turtledoves,
or two *young pigeons* **sons of doves**,
such as *he is able to get* **his hand attaineth**;
and the one shall be *a sin offering* **for the sin**,
and the *other a burnt offering* **one for the holocaust**.
23 And he shall bring them on the eighth day
for his *cleansing* **purifying** unto the priest,
unto the *door* **opening**
of the *tabernacle* **tent** of the congregation,
before the LORD **at the face of Yah Veh**.
24 And the priest shall take the lamb
of *the trespass offering* **that for the guilt**, and the log of oil,

and the priest shall wave them for a wave *offering*
before the LORD **at the face of Yah Veh**:
25 And he shall *kill* **slaughter** the lamb
of *the trespass offering* **that for the guilt**,
and the priest shall take *some* of the blood
of *the trespass offering* **that for the guilt**,
and *put* **give** it upon the tip of the right ear
of him that is to be *cleansed* **purified**,
and upon the *thumb* **great digit** of his right hand,
and upon the great *toe* **digit** of his right foot:
26 And the priest shall pour of the oil
into the palm of his own left hand:
27 And the priest shall sprinkle with his right finger
some of the oil that is in his left hand seven times
before the LORD **at the face of Yah Veh**:
28 And the priest shall *put* **give** of the oil
that is in his *hand* **palm**
upon the tip of the right ear
of him that is to be *cleansed* **purified**,
and upon the *thumb* **great digit** of his right hand,
and upon the great *toe* **digit** of his right foot,
upon the place of the blood
of *the trespass offering* **that for the guilt**:
29 And *the rest* **that which remaineth** of the oil
that is in the priest's *hand* **palm**
he shall *put* **give** upon the head of him
that is to be *cleansed* **purified**,
to *make an atonement* **kapar/atone** for him
before the LORD **at the face of Yah Veh**.
30 And he shall *offer* **work** the one of the turtledoves,
or of the *young pigeons* **sons of doves**,
such as *he can get* **his hand attaineth**;
31 Even such as *he is able to get* **his hand attaineth**,
the one for *a sin offering* **the sin**,
and the *other* **one** for *a burnt offering* **the holocaust**,
with the *meat* offering:
and the priest
shall *make an atonement* **kapar/atone** for him
that is to be *cleansed* **purified**
before the LORD **at the face of Yah Veh**.
32 This is the *law of him* **torah**
in whom is the plague of leprosy,
whose hand *is not able to get* **attaineth not**
that which pertaineth to his *cleansing* **purifying**.

TORAH ON PURIFYING THE LEPROUS HOUSE

33 And *the LORD spake* **Yah Veh worded**
unto *Moses* **Mosheh** and unto *Aaron* **Aharon**, saying,
34 When ye be come into the land of *Canaan* **Kenaan**,
which I give to you for a possession,
and I *put* **give** the plague of leprosy
in a house of the land of your possession;
35 And he that owneth the house
shall come and tell the priest, saying,
It seemeth to me there is as it were **I have seen**
a plague in the house:
36 Then the priest shall *command* **misvah**
that they *empty* **prepare** the house,
before the priest go into it to see the plague,
that all that is in the house be not *made unclean* **fouled**:
and afterward the priest shall go in to see the house:
37 And he shall *look on* **see** the plague, and, behold,
if the plague be in the *sides* **walls** of the house
with hollow *strakes* **depressions**, greenish or reddish,
which in *sight* **visage** are lower *than* **from** the wall;
38 Then the priest shall go out of the house
to the *door* **opening** of the house,
and shut up the house seven days:
39 And the priest shall *come again* **return** the seventh day,
and shall *look* **see**: and, behold,
if the plague be spread in the walls of the house;
40 Then the priest shall *command* **misvah**
that they *take away* **strip** the stones
in which the plague is,
and they shall cast them into *an unclean* **a fouled** place
without the city:
41 And he shall cause the house to be scraped
within round about,
and they shall pour out the dust that they scrape off
without the city into *an unclean* **a fouled** place:
42 And they shall take other stones,
and put them in the *place* **stead** of those stones;
and he shall take other *morter* **dust**,
and shall plaister the house.
43 And if the plague *come again* **return**,
and *break out* **blossom** in the house,
after that he hath *taken away* **stripped** the stones,
and after he hath scraped the house,
and after it is plaistered;
44 Then the priest shall come and *look* **see**, and, behold,
if the plague be spread in the house,
it is a *fretting* **bitter** leprosy in the house;
it is *unclean* **fouled**.
45 And he shall *break* **pull** down the house,
the stones of it, and the timber thereof,
and all the *morter* **dust** of the house;
and he shall carry them *forth out of* **without** the city
into *an unclean* **a fouled** place.
46 Moreover he that goeth into the house
all the *while* **days** that it is shut up
shall be *unclean* **fouled** until the even.
47 And he that lieth in the house
shall *wash* **launder** his clothes;
and he that eateth in the house
shall *wash* **launder** his clothes.
48 And if the priest shall come in, and *look upon it* **see**,
and, behold, the plague hath not spread in the house,
after the house was plaistered:
then the priest shall pronounce the house *clean* **purified**,
because the plague is healed.
49 And he shall take *to cleanse* **for the sin of** the house
two birds, and cedar *wood* **timber**,
and scarlet, and hyssop:
50 And he shall *kill* **slaughter** the one of the birds
in *an earthen vessel* **a pottery instrument**
over *running* **living** water
51 And he shall take the cedar *wood* **timber**,
and the hyssop, and the scarlet, and the living bird,
and dip them in the blood of the *slain* **slaughtered** bird,
and in the *running* **living** water,
and sprinkle the house seven times:
52 And he shall *cleanse* **sacrifice for sin for** the house
with the blood of the bird,
and with the *running* **living** water,
and with the living bird, and with the cedar *wood* **timber**,
and with the hyssop, and with the scarlet:
53 But he shall *let go* **send away** the living bird
out of **without** the city into the *open* **face of the** fields,
and *make an atonement* **kapar/atone** for the house:
and it shall be clean.
54 This is the *law* **torah**
for all *manner of* plague of leprosy, and scall,
55 And for the leprosy
of *a garment* **clothes**, and of a house,
56 And for a *rising* **swelling**,
and for a scab, and for a bright spot:
57 To *teach* **point out** when it is *unclean* **fouled**,
and when it is *clean* **pure**:
this is the *law* **torah** of leprosy.

TORAH ON FOULING

15 And *the LORD spake* **Yah Veh worded**
unto *Moses* **Mosheh** and to *Aaron* **Aharon**, saying,
2 *Speak* **Word** unto the *children* **sons** of *Israel* **Yisra El**,
and say unto them, When **a man** — any man
hath a running issue **fluxeth** out of his flesh,
because of his issue he is unclean **his flux is fouled**.
3 And this shall be his *uncleanness* **foulness**
in his *issue* **flux**:
whether his flesh run with his *issue* **flux**,
or his flesh be stopped from his *issue* **flux**,
it is his *uncleanness* **foulness**.
4 Every bed, whereon he lieth that *hath the issue* **fluxeth**,
is *unclean* **fouled**:
and every *thing* **instrument**, whereon he sitteth,
shall be *unclean* **fouled**.
5 And *whosoever* **the man who** toucheth his bed
shall *wash* **launder** his clothes,
and *bathe* **baptize** *himself* in water,
and be *unclean* **fouled** until the even.
6 And he that sitteth on *any thing* **aught**
whereon he sat that *hath the issue* **fluxeth**

shall *wash* **launder** his clothes,
and *bathe* **baptize** *himself* in water,
and be *unclean* **fouled** until the even.
7 And he that toucheth the flesh
of him that *hath the issue* **fluxeth**
shall *wash* **launder** his clothes,
and *bathe* **baptize** *himself* in water,
and be *unclean* **fouled** until the even.
8 And if he that *hath the issue* **fluxeth**
spit upon him that is *clean* **pure**;
then he shall *wash* **launder** his clothes,
and *bathe* **baptize** *himself* in water,
and be *unclean* **fouled** until the even.
9 And *what saddle soever* **whatever chariot**
he rideth upon that *hath the issue* **fluxeth**
shall be *unclean* **fouled.**
10 And whosoever toucheth *any thing* **aught**
that was under him
shall be *unclean* **fouled** until the even:
and he that beareth *any of* those *things*
shall *wash* **launder** his clothes,
and *bathe* **baptize** *himself* in water,
and be *unclean* **fouled** until the even.
11 And whomsoever he toucheth
that *hath the issue* **fluxeth,**
and hath not *rinsed* **overflowed** his hands in water,
he shall *wash* **launder** his clothes,
and *bathe* **baptize** *himself* in water,
and be *unclean* **fouled** until the even.
12 And the *vessel of earth* **pottery instrument,**
that he toucheth which *hath the issue* **fluxeth,**
shall be broken:
and every *vessel* **instrument** of *wood* **timber**
shall be *rinsed* **overflowed** in water.
13 And when he that *hath an issue* **fluxeth**
is *cleansed* **purified** of his *issue* **flux;**
then he shall *number* **scribe** to himself seven days
for his *cleansing* **purifying,**
and *wash* **launder** his clothes,
and *bathe* **baptize** his flesh in *running* **living** water,
and shall be *clean* **purified.**
14 And on the eighth day he shall take to him
two turtledoves, or two *young pigeons* **sons of doves,**
and come *before the LORD* **at the face of Yah Veh**
unto the *door* **opening**
of the *tabernacle* **tent** of the congregation,
and give them unto the priest:
15 And the priest shall *offer* **work** them,
the one for *a sin offering* **the sin,**
and the *other* **one** for a *burnt offering* **holocaust;**
and the priest shall *make an atonement* **kapar/atone**
before the LORD **at the face of Yah Veh** for his *issue* **flux.**
16 And if any man's seed of copulation go out from him,
then he shall *wash* **baptize** all his flesh in water,
and be *unclean* **fouled** until the even.
17 And every *garment* **cloth,** and every skin,
whereon is the seed of copulation,
shall be *washed* **laundered** with water,
and be *unclean* **fouled** until the even.
18 The woman also
with whom man shall lie with seed of copulation,
they shall *both bathe* **baptize** *themselves* in water,
and be *unclean* **fouled** until the even.
19 And if a woman *have an issue* **fluxeth,**
and her *issue* **flux** in her flesh be blood,
she shall be *put apart* **in her exclusion** seven days:
and whosoever toucheth her
shall be *unclean* **fouled** until the even.
20 And *every thing* **all** that she lieth upon
in her *separation* **exclusion** shall be *unclean* **fouled:**
every thing **all** also that she sitteth upon
shall be *unclean* **fouled.**
21 And whosoever toucheth her bed
shall *wash* **launder** his clothes,
and *bathe* **baptize** *himself* in water,
and be *unclean* **fouled** until the even.
22 And whosoever toucheth any *thing* **instrument**
that she sat upon
shall *wash* **launder** his clothes,
and *bathe* **baptize** *himself* in water,
and be *unclean* **fouled** until the even.
23 And if it be on her bed,
or on any *thing* **instrument** whereon she sitteth,
when he toucheth it,
he shall be *unclean* **fouled** until the even.
24 And if **in lying,** any *man lie* **one lie** with her *at all,*
and her *flowers* **exclusion** be upon him,
he shall be *unclean* **fouled** seven days;
and all the bed whereon he lieth shall be *unclean* **fouled.**
25 And if a woman *have an issue* **flux a flux**
of her blood many days
out of **not in** the time of her *separation* **exclusion,**
or if it *run* **flux**
beyond the time of her *separation* **exclusion;**
all the days of the *issue* **flux** of her *uncleanness* **foulness**
shall be as the days of her *separation* **exclusion:**
she shall be *unclean* **fouled.**
26 Every bed whereon she lieth
all the days of her *issue* **flux**
shall be unto her as the bed of her *separation* **exclusion:**
and whatsoever **instrument** she sitteth upon
shall be *unclean* **fouled,**
as the *uncleanness* **foulness** of her *separation* **exclusion.**
27 And whosoever toucheth those *things*
shall be *unclean* **fouled,**
and shall *wash* **launder** his clothes,
and *bathe* **baptize** *himself* in water,
and be *unclean* **fouled** until the even.
28 But if she be *cleansed* **purified** of her *issue* **flux,**
then she shall *number* **scribe** to herself seven days,
and after that she shall be *clean* **purified.**
29 And on the eighth day
she shall take unto her two turtledoves,
or two *young pigeons* **sons of doves,**
and bring them unto the priest,
to the *door* **opening**
of the *tabernacle* **tent** of the congregation.
30 And the priest shall *offer* **work** the one
for *a sin offering* **the sin,**
and the *other* **one** for a *burnt offering* **holocaust;**
and the priest shall *make an atonement* **kapar/atone** for her
before the LORD **at the face of Yah Veh**
for the *issue* **flux** of her *uncleanness* **foulness.**
31 Thus shall ye separate
the *children* **sons** of *Israel* **Yisra El**
from their *uncleanness* **foulness;**
that they die not in their *uncleanness* **foulness,**
when they *defile* **foul** my tabernacle that is among them.
32 This is the *law* **torah** of him that *hath the issue* **fluxeth,**
and of him whose seed **of copulation** goeth from him,
and is *defiled* **fouled** therewith;
33 And of her
that is *sick* **menstrous** of her *flowers* **exclusion,**
and of him that *hath the issue* **fluxeth the flux,**
of the man, and of the *woman* **female,**
and of him that lieth with her that is *unclean* **fouled.**

TORAH ON KIPPURIM/ATONEMENTS: THE SCAPEGOAT

16 And *the LORD* **Yah Veh**
spake **worded** unto *Moses* **Mosheh**
after the death of the two sons of *Aaron* **Aharon,**
when they *offered* **oblated**
before the LORD **at the face of Yah Veh,** and died;
2 And *the LORD* **Yah Veh** said unto *Moses* **Mosheh,**
Speak **Word** unto *Aaron* **Aharon** thy brother,
that he come not at all times
into the *holy place within* **holies that houseth** the vail
before **at the face of** the *mercy seat* **kapporeth,**
which is upon the ark; that he die not:
for I *will appear* **shall be seen** in the cloud
upon the *mercy seat* **kapporeth.**
3 Thus shall *Aaron* **Aharon**
come into the *holy place* **holies:**
with a *young* bullock **son of the oxen**
for *a sin offering* **the sin,**
and a ram for a *burnt offering* **holocaust.**
4 He shall *put on* **enrobe** the holy linen coat,
and he shall have the linen breeches upon his flesh,
and shall be girded with a linen girdle,
and with the linen *mitre* **tiara** shall he be attired:
these are holy *garments* **clothes;**

therefore shall he *wash* **baptize** his flesh in water,
and *so put* **thus enrobe** them *on*.
5 And he shall take of the *congregation* **witness**
of the *children* **sons** of *Israel* **Yisra El**
two *kids* **bucks** of the goats for *a sin offering* **the sin**,
and one ram for a *burnt offering* **holocaust**.
6 And *Aaron* **Aharon** shall *offer* **oblate** his bullock
of the sin offering **for the sin**, which is for himself,
and *make an atonement* **kapar/atone** for himself,
and for his house.
7 And he shall take the two *goats* **bucks**,
and *present* **stand** them
before the LORD **at the face of Yah Veh**
at the *door* **opening**
of the *tabernacle* **tent** of the congregation.
8 And *Aaron* **Aharon** shall *cast lots* **give pebbles**
upon the two *goats* **bucks**;
one *lot* **pebble** for *the LORD* **Yah Veh**,
and *the other lot* **one pebble** for the scapegoat.
9 And *Aaron* **Aharon** shall *bring* **oblate** the *goat* **buck**
upon which
the LORD'S lot fell **Yah Veh's pebble ascended**,
and *offer* **work** him for *a sin offering* **the sin**.
10 But the *goat* **buck**,
on which the *lot fell* **pebble ascended**
to be the scapegoat,
shall be *presented* **stood** alive
before the LORD **at the face of Yah Veh**,
to *make an atonement* **kapar/atone** with him,
and to *let him go* **send him away** for a scapegoat
into the wilderness.
11 And *Aaron* **Aharon** shall *bring* **oblate** the bullock
of the sin offering **for the sin**,
which is for himself,
and shall *make an atonement* **kapar/atone** for himself,
and for his house,
and shall *kill* **slaughter** the bullock
of the sin offering **for the sin**
which is for himself:
12 And he shall take a *censer* **tray**
full of burning coals of fire from off the **sacrifice** altar
before the LORD **at the face of Yah Veh**,
and his *hands* **fists** full
of *sweet* incense **of aromatics** beaten *small* **thin**,
and bring it *within* **to the housing of** the vail:
13 And he shall *put* **give** the incense upon the fire
before the LORD **at the face of Yah Veh**,
that the cloud of the incense
may cover the *mercy seat* **kapporeth**
that is upon the *testimony* **witness**, that he die not:
14 And he shall take of the blood of the bullock,
and sprinkle it with his finger
upon the *mercy seat* **face of the kapporeth** eastward;
and *before* **upon the face**
of the *mercy seat* **kapporeth**
shall he sprinkle of the blood with his finger seven times.
15 Then shall he *kill* **slaughter** the *goat* **buck**
of the sin offering **for the sin**,
that is for the people,
and bring his blood within **the housing of** the vail,
and *do with* **work** that blood
as he *did with* **worked** the blood of the bullock,
and sprinkle it upon the *mercy seat* **kapporeth**,
and *before* **at the face of** the *mercy seat* **kapporeth**:
16 And he shall *make an atonement* **kapar/atone**
for the *holy place* **holies**,
because of the *uncleanness* **foulness**
of the *children* **sons** of *Israel* **Yisra El**,
and because of their *transgressions* **rebellions**
in all their sins:
and so shall he *do* **work**
for the *tabernacle* **tent** of the congregation,
that *remaineth* **tabernacleth** among them
in the midst of their *uncleanness* **foulness**.
17 And there shall be no *man* **human**
in the *tabernacle* **tent** of the congregation
when he goeth in
to *make an atonement* **kapar/atone** in the *holy place* **holies**,
until he come out,
and *have made an atonement* **kapar/atone** for himself,
and for his household,
and for all the congregation of *Israel* **Yisra El**.
18 And he shall go out unto the **sacrifice** altar
that is before the LORD **at the face of Yah Veh**,
and *make an atonement* **kapar/atone** for it;
and shall take of the blood of the bullock,
and of the blood of the *goat* **buck**,
and *put* **give** it
upon the horns of the **sacrifice** altar round about.
19 And he shall sprinkle of the blood upon it
with his finger seven times, and *cleanse* **purify** it,
and hallow it from the *uncleanness* **foulness**
of the *children* **sons** of *Israel* **Yisra El**.
20 And when he hath
made an end of reconciling **finished to kapar/atone**
in the *holy place* **holies**,
and the *tabernacle* **tent** of the congregation,
and the **sacrifice** altar,
he shall *bring* **oblate** the live *goat* **buck**:
21 And *Aaron* **Aharon** shall *lay both* **prop** his **two** hands
upon the head of the live *goat* **buck**,
and *confess* **wring hands** over him
all the *iniquities* **perversities**
of the *children* **sons** of *Israel* **Yisra El**,
and all their *transgressions* **rebellions** in all their sins,
putting **and give** them upon the head of the *goat* **buck**,
and shall send him away
by the hand of a *fit* **timely** man into the wilderness:
22 And the *goat* **buck** shall bear upon him
all their *iniquities* **perversities**
unto a land *not inhabited* **of separation**:
and he shall *let go* **send away** the *goat* **buck**
in the wilderness.
23 And *Aaron* **Aharon** shall come
into the *tabernacle* **tent** of the congregation,
and shall *put off* **strip** the linen *garments* **clothes**,
which he *put on* **enrobed**
when he went into the *holy place* **holies**,
and shall *leave* **set** them there:
24 And he shall *wash* **baptize** his flesh with water
in the *holy place* **holies**,
and *put on* **enrobe** his *garments* **clothes**, and come forth,
and *offer* **work** his *burnt offering* **holocaust**,
and the *burnt offering* **holocaust** of the people,
and *make an atonement* **kapar/atone** for himself,
and for the people.
25 And the fat of *the sin offering* **that for the sin**
shall he *burn* **incense** upon the **sacrifice** altar.
26 And he that *let go* **sent forth** the *goat* **buck**
for the scapegoat
shall *wash* **launder** his clothes,
and *wash* **baptize** his flesh in water,
and afterward come into the camp.
27 And the bullock for the sin *offering*,
and the *goat* **buck** for the sin *offering*,
whose blood was brought in
to *make atonement* **kapar/atone** in the *holy place* **holies**,
shall one carry *forth* without the camp;
and they shall burn in the fire their skins,
and their flesh, and their dung.
28 And he that burneth them
shall *wash* **launder** his clothes,
and *wash* **baptize** his flesh in water,
and afterward he shall come into the camp.

ANNUAL KOPER/ATONEMENT

29 And this shall be *a* **an eternal** statute *for ever* unto you:
that in the seventh month, on the tenth *day* of the month,
ye shall *afflict* **humble** your souls,
and *do* **work** no work *at all*,
whether it be one of your own country — **native**,
or *a stranger* **sojourner** that sojourneth among you:
30 For on that day
shall *the priest make an atonement* **he kapar/atone** for you,
to *cleanse* **purify** you,
that ye may be *clean* **purified** from all your sins
before the LORD **at the face of Yah Veh**.
31 It shall be a *sabbath* **shabbath**
of rest — **a shabbathism** unto you,
and ye shall *afflict* **humble** your souls,
by *a* **an eternal** statute *for ever*.

32 And the priest, whom he shall anoint,
and whom he shall *consecrate* **fill his hand**
to *minister in the priest's office* **priest the priesthood**
in his father's stead,
shall *make the atonement* **kapar/atone**,
and shall *put on* **enrobe** the linen clothes,
even the holy *garments* **clothes**:
33 And he shall *make an atonement* **kapar/atone**
for the *holy sanctuary* **holy of holies**,
and he shall *make an atonement* **kapar/atone**
for the *tabernacle* **tent** of the congregation,
and for the **sacrifice** altar,
and he shall
make an atonement **kapar/atone** for the priests,
and for all the people of the congregation.
34 And this shall be
an *everlasting* **eternal** statute unto you,
to *make an atonement* **kapar/atone**
for the *children* **sons** of *Israel* **Yisra El**
for all their sins once a year.
And he *did* **worked** as *the LORD* **Yah Veh**
commanded Moses **misvahed Mosheh**.

TORAH ON SLAUGHTER

17 And *the LORD spake* **Yah Veh worded**
unto *Moses* **Mosheh**, saying,
2 *Speak* **Word** unto *Aaron* **Aharon**, and unto his sons,
and unto all the *children* **sons** of *Israel* **Yisra El**,
and say unto them; This is the *thing* **word**
which *the LORD* **Yah Veh** hath *commanded* **misvahed**,
saying,
3 *What man soever* **A man — any man**
there be of the house of *Israel* **Yisra El**,
that *killeth* **slaughtereth** an ox, or lamb, or goat,
in the camp,
or that *killeth* **slaughtereth** it *out of* **without** the camp,
4 And bringeth it not unto the *door* **opening**
of the *tabernacle* **tent** of the congregation,
to *offer an offering* **oblate a qorban**
unto *the LORD* **Yah Veh**
before **at the face of** the tabernacle of *the LORD* **Yah Veh**;
blood shall be *imputed* **fabricated** unto that man;
he hath *shed* **poured** blood;
and that man shall be cut off from among his people:
5 To the end that the *children* **sons** of *Israel* **Yisra El**
may bring their sacrifices, which they *offer* **sacrifice**
in the open **at the face of the** field,
even that they may bring them unto *the LORD* **Yah Veh**,
unto the *door* **opening**
of the *tabernacle* **tent** of the congregation, unto the priest,
and *offer* **sacrifice** them for *peace offerings* **shelamim**
unto *the LORD* **Yah Veh**.
6 And the priest shall sprinkle the blood
upon the **sacrifice** altar of *the LORD* **Yah Veh**
at the *door* **opening**
of the *tabernacle* **tent** of the congregation,
and *burn* **incense** the fat
for a *sweet savour* **scent of rest** unto *the LORD* **Yah Veh**.
7 And they shall no more
offer **sacrifice** their sacrifices unto *devils* **bucks**,
after whom they have *gone a whoring* **whored**.
This shall be *a* **an eternal** statute *for ever*
unto them throughout their generations.

THE SOUL OF THE FLESH

8 And thou shalt say unto them,
Whatsoever man **A man — any man**
there be of the house of *Israel* **Yisra El**,
or of the *strangers* **sojourners** which sojourn among you,
that *offereth* **holocausteth**
a *burnt offering* **holocaust** or sacrifice,
9 And bringeth it not unto the *door* **opening**
of the *tabernacle* **tent** of the congregation,
to *offer* **work** it unto *the LORD* **Yah Veh**;
even that man shall be cut off from among his people.
10 And *whatsoever man* **a man — any man**
there be of the house of *Israel* **Yisra El**,
or of the *strangers* **sojourners** that sojourn among you,
that eateth any manner of blood;
I *will* **shall** even *set* **give** my face
against that soul that eateth blood,
and *will* **shall** cut him off from among his people.
11 For the *life* **soul** of the flesh is in the blood:
and I have given it to you upon the **sacrifice** altar
to *make an atonement* **kapar/atone** for your souls:
for it is the blood
that *maketh an atonement* **shall kapar/atone** for the soul.
12 Therefore
I said unto the *children* **sons** of *Israel* **Yisra El**,
No soul of you shall eat blood,
neither shall any *stranger* **sojourner**
that sojourneth among you eat blood.
13 And *whatsoever man* **a man — any man**
there be of the *children* **sons** of *Israel* **Yisra El**,
or of the *strangers* **sojourners** that sojourn among you,
which hunteth *and catcheth* **to hunt**
any *beast* **live being** or *fowl* **flyer** that may be eaten;
he shall *even* pour out the blood thereof,
and cover it with dust.
14 For it is the *life* **soul** of all flesh;
the blood of it is for the *life* **soul** thereof:
therefore I said unto the *children* **sons** of *Israel* **Yisra El**,
Ye shall eat the blood of no *manner of* flesh:
for the *life* **soul** of all flesh is the blood thereof:
whosoever eateth it shall be cut off.
15 And every soul
that eateth *that which died of itself* **of a carcase**,
or that which was torn *with beasts*,
whether it be one of your own country **native**,
or a *stranger* **sojourner**,
he shall *both wash* **launder** his clothes,
and *bathe* **baptize** *himself* in water,
and be *unclean* **fouled** until the even:
then shall he be *clean* **purified**.
16 But if he *wash* **launder** them not,
nor *bathe* **baptize** his flesh;
then he shall bear his *iniquity* **perversity**.

18 And *the LORD spake* **Yah Veh worded**
unto *Moses* **Mosheh**, saying,
2 *Speak* **Word** unto the *children* **sons** of *Israel* **Yisra El**,
and say unto them,
I am the LORD **I — Yah Veh** your *God* **Elohim**.
3 After the *doings* **works** of the land of *Egypt* **Misrayim**,
wherein ye *dwelt* **settled**, shall ye not *do* **work**:
and after the *doings* **works** of the land of *Canaan* **Kenaan**,
whither I bring you, shall ye not *do* **work**:
neither shall ye walk in their *ordinances* **statutes**.
4 Ye shall *do* **work** my judgments,
and *keep* **guard** mine ordinances, to walk therein:
I am the LORD **I — Yah Veh** your *God* **Elohim**.
5 Ye shall *therefore keep* **guard** my statutes,
and my judgments:
which if a *man do* **human work**, he shall live in them:
I am the LORD **I — Yah Veh**.

TORAH ON EXPOSING NAKEDNESS

6 *None of you* **Man — no man** shall approach
to any that is *near of kin* **kinflesh** to him,
to *uncover* **expose** their nakedness:
I am the LORD **I — Yah Veh**.
7 The nakedness of thy father,
or the nakedness of thy mother,
shalt thou not *uncover* **expose**:
she is thy mother;
thou shalt not *uncover* **expose** her nakedness.
8 The nakedness of thy father's *wife* **woman**
shalt thou not *uncover* **expose**:
it is thy father's nakedness.
9 The nakedness of thy sister,
the daughter of thy father, or daughter of thy mother,
whether she be born at **kindred of** home,
or *born abroad* **kindred without**,
even their nakedness thou shalt not *uncover* **expose**.
10 The nakedness of thy son's daughter,
or of thy daughter's daughter,
even their nakedness thou shalt not *uncover* **expose**:
for theirs is thine own nakedness.
11 The nakedness of thy father's *wife's* **woman's** daughter,
begotten **kindred** of thy father, she is thy sister,
thou shalt not *uncover* **expose** her nakedness.
12 Thou shalt not *uncover* **expose**
the nakedness of thy father's sister:
she is thy father's *near kinswoman* **kinflesh**.

13 Thou shalt not *uncover* **expose**
the nakedness of thy mother's sister:
for she is thy mother's *near kinswoman* **kinflesh**.
14 Thou shalt not *uncover* **expose**
the nakedness of thy father's brother,
thou shalt not approach to his *wife* **woman**:
she is thine aunt.
15 Thou shalt not *uncover* **expose**
the nakedness of thy daughter in law:
she is thy son's *wife* **woman**;
thou shalt not *uncover* **expose** her nakedness.
16 Thou shalt not *uncover* **expose**
the nakedness of thy brother's *wife* **woman**:
it is thy brother's nakedness.
17 Thou shalt not *uncover* **expose**
the nakedness of a woman and her daughter,
neither shalt thou take her son's daughter,
or her daughter's daughter,
to *uncover* **expose** her nakedness;
for they are her *near kinswomen* **kin**:
it is *wickedness* **intrigue.**
18 Neither shalt thou take a *wife* **woman** to her sister,
to *vex* **tribulate** her,
to *uncover* **expose** her nakedness,
beside the other in her life *time*.
19 Also thou shalt not approach unto a woman
to *uncover* **expose** her nakedness,
as long as she is *put apart* **in exclusion**
for her *uncleanness* **foulness**.
20 Moreover
thou shalt not *lie carnally with* **copulate to give seed**
to thy *neighbour's wife* **friend's woman**,
to *defile* **foul** thyself with her.
21 And thou shalt not *let* **give** any of thy seed
to pass through *the fire* to Molech,
neither shalt thou profane the name of thy *God* **Elohim**:
I am the LORD **I — Yah Veh**.

ON HOMOSEXUALITY AND BESTIALITY

22 Thou shalt not lie with *mankind* **male**,
as **bedding** with *womankind* **a woman**:
it is *abomination* **abhorrent**.
23 Neither shalt thou *lie* **give to copulate**
with any *beast* **animal** to *defile* **foul** thyself therewith:
neither shall any woman stand
before a beast **to face an animal**
to *lie down thereto* **copulate**:
it is *confusion* **comingling.**
24 *Defile* **Foul** not ye yourselves in any of these *things*:
for in all these the *nations* **goyim** are *defiled* **fouled**
which I *cast out before you* **sent away from your face**:
25 And the land is *defiled* **fouled**:
therefore
I do visit the *iniquity* **perversity** thereof upon it,
and the land itself vomiteth *out*
her inhabitants **them who settle her**.
26 Ye shall *therefore keep* **guard** my statutes
and my judgments,
and shall not *commit* **work**
any of these *abominations* **abhorrences**;
neither any of your own nation **native**,
nor *any stranger* **sojourner** that sojourneth among you:
27 (For all these *abominations* **abhorrences**
have the men of the land *done* **worked**,
which were *before* you **at your face**,
and the land is *defiled* **fouled**;)
28 *That* **Lest** the land *spue not you out also* **vomit you**,
when ye *defile* **foul** it,
as it *spued* **vomited** *out* the *nations* **goyim**
that were before you **at your face**.
29 For whosoever shall *commit* **work**
any of these *abominations* **abhorrences**,
even the souls that *commit* **work** them
shall be cut off from among their people.
30 Therefore shall ye
keep mine ordinance **guard my guard**,
that ye *commit not any one* **work none** of these
abominable customs **abhorrent statutes**,
which were *committed before you* **worked at your face**,
and that ye *defile* **foul** not yourselves therein:
I am the LORD **I — Yah Veh** your *God* **Elohim**.

CALL TO HOLINESS

19 And *the LORD spake* **Yah Veh worded**
unto *Moses* **Mosheh**, saying,
2 *Speak* **Word** unto all the *congregation* **witness**
of the *children* **sons** of *Israel* **Yisra El**,
and say unto them, Ye shall be holy:
for **I** *the LORD* **Yah Veh** your *God* **Elohim** am holy.
3 Ye shall *fear* **awe** every man his mother, and his father,
and *keep* **guard** my *sabbaths* **shabbaths**:
I am the LORD **I — Yah Veh** your *God* **Elohim**.
4 Turn ye not **your face** unto idols,
nor *make* **work** to yourselves molten *gods* **elohim**:
I am the LORD **I — Yah Veh** your *God* **Elohim**.
5 And if ye *offer* **sacrifice** a sacrifice
of *peace offerings* **shelamim** unto *the LORD* **Yah Veh**,
ye shall *offer* **sacrifice** it at your *own will* **pleasure**.
6 It shall be eaten the same day ye *offer* **sacrifice** it,
and on the morrow:
and if ought remain until the third day,
it shall be burnt in the fire.
7 And if **in eating,** it be eaten *at all* on the third day,
it is *abominable* **a stench**;
it shall not *be accepted* **please**.
8 *Therefore every one* **He** that eateth it
shall bear his *iniquity* **perversity**,
because he hath profaned
the *hallowed thing* **holies** of *the LORD* **Yah Veh**:
and that soul shall be cut off from among his people.
9 And when ye *reap* **harvest** the harvest of your land,
thou shalt not *wholly* **finish off**
reap **harvesting** the *corners* **edges** of thy field,
neither shalt thou *gather* **glean**
the gleanings of thy harvest.
10 And thou shalt not *glean* **exploit** thy vineyard,
neither shalt thou *gather every grape* **glean the stray fruit**
of thy vineyard;
thou shalt leave them
for the *poor* **humbled** and *stranger* **sojourner**:
I am the LORD **I — Yah Veh** your *God* **Elohim**.
11 Ye shall not steal, neither *deal falsely* **deceive**,
neither *lie one* **falsify man** to *another* **friend**.

ON OATHING BY YAH VEH'S NAME

12 And ye shall not *swear* **oath** by my name falsely,
neither shalt thou profane the name of thy *God* **Elohim**:
I am the LORD **I — Yah Veh**.
13 Thou shalt not *defraud* **extort** thy *neighbour* **friend**,
neither *rob* **strip** him:
the *wages of him that is hired* **deeds of an hireling**
shall not *abide* **stay** with thee
all night **overnight** until the morning.
14 Thou shalt not *curse* **abase** the deaf,
nor *put* **give** a stumblingblock before the blind,
but shalt *fear* **awe** thy *God* **Elohim**:
I am the LORD **I — Yah Veh**.
15 Ye shall *do* **work** no *unrighteousness* **wickedness**
in judgment:
thou shalt not *respect* **exalt** the *person* **face** of the poor,
nor *honor* **esteem** the *person* **face** of the *mighty* **greater**:
but in *righteousness* **justness**
shalt thou judge thy *neighbour* **friend.**
16 Thou shalt not *go up and down as* **be** a talebearer
among thy people:
neither shalt thou stand
against the blood of thy *neighbour* **friend**;
I am the LORD **I — Yah Veh**.
17 Thou shalt not hate thy brother in thine heart:
thou shalt in *any wise* **reproving,**
rebuke **reprove** thy *neighbour* **friend**,
and not *suffer* **exalt his** sin *upon him*.
18 Thou shalt not avenge,
nor *bear any grudge* **guard**
against the *children* **sons** of thy people,
but thou shalt love thy *neighbour* **friend** as thyself:
I am the LORD **I — Yah Veh**.
19 Ye shall *keep* **guard** my statutes.
Thou shalt not let thy *cattle gender* **animals copulate**
with *a diverse kind* **heterogenetic inductions**:
thou shalt not *sow* **seed** thy *field* **seed**
with *mingled seed* **heterogenetic inductions**:
neither shall *a garment* **clothes**

mingled **with heterogenetic inductions**
of *linen and woollen* **linsey—woolsey**
come upon **ascend** thee.
20 And *whosoever* **any man who**
lieth carnally **giveth seed of copulation**
with **to** a woman, that is a *bondmaid* **maid**,
betrothed to an husband **exposed by a man**,
and **in redeeming**, not *at all* redeemed,
nor *freedom* **liberty** given her;
she shall be scourged **let there be an inquisition**;
they shall not be *put to death* **deathified**,
because she was not *free* **liberated**.
21 And he shall bring
his trespass offering **that for his guilt**
unto *the LORD* **Yah Veh**,
unto the *door* **opening**
of the *tabernacle* **tent** of the congregation,
even a ram for *a trespass offering* **the guilt**.
22 And the priest
shall *make an atonement* **kapar/atone** for him
with the ram *of the trespass offering* **for his guilt**
before the LORD **at the face of Yah Veh**
for his sin which he hath *done* **sinned**:
and the sin which he hath *done* **sinned**
shall be forgiven him.
23 And when ye shall come into the land,
and shall have planted all *manner of* trees for food,
then ye shall count
the fruit thereof as uncircumcised
as uncircumcised, the uncircumcision of the fruit:
three years shall it be as uncircumcised unto you:
it shall not be eaten of.
24 But in the fourth year all the fruit thereof shall be holy
to praise the LORD withal — **halals to Yah Veh**.
25 And in the fifth year shall ye eat of the fruit thereof,
that it may *yield* **add** unto you
the *increase* **produce** thereof:
I am the LORD **I — Yah Veh** your *God* **Elohim**.
26 Ye shall not eat *any thing* **aught** with the blood:
neither shall ye *use enchantment* **prognosticate**,
nor observe times.
27 Ye shall not *round* **ruin** the *corners* **edges** of your heads,
neither shalt thou *mar* **ruin** the *corners* **edges** of thy beard.
28 Ye shall not *make any cuttings* **give incisions**
in your flesh for the *dead* **soul**,
nor *print any marks* **give an inscription of a tattoo**
upon you:
I am the LORD **I — Yah Veh**.
29 Do not *prostitute* **profane** thy daughter,
to cause her to *be a* whore;
lest the land *fall to whoredom* **whore**,
and the land become full of *wickedness* **intrigue**.
30 Ye shall *keep* **guard** my *sabbaths* **shabbaths**,
and *reverence* **awe** my *sanctuary* **holies**:
I am the LORD **I — Yah Veh**.
31 *Regard not them that have familiar spirits*
Neither face necromancers,
neither seek after *wizards* **knowers**,
to be *defiled* **fouled** by them:
I am the LORD **I — Yah Veh** your *God* **Elohim**.
32 Thou shalt rise up
before the hoary head **at the face of the grayed**,
and *honour* **esteem** the face of the *old man* **aged**,
and *fear* **awe** thy *God* **Elohim**:
I am the LORD **I — Yah Veh**.
33 And if a *stranger* **sojourner**
sojourn with thee in your land,
ye shall not *vex* **oppress** him.
34 But the *stranger* **sojourner**
that *dwelleth* **sojourneth** with you
shall be unto you as *one born* **a native** among you,
and thou shalt love him as thyself;
for ye were *strangers* **sojourners**
in the land of *Egypt* **Misrayim**:
I am the LORD **I — Yah Veh** your *God* **Elohim**.
35 Ye shall *do* **work** no *unrighteousness* **wickedness**
in judgment, in *meteyard* **measurement**,
in weight, or in *measure* **quantity**.
36 *Just balances* **Balances of justness**,
just weights **stones of justness**,
a just ephah **an ephah of justness**,
and a *just hin* **hin of justness**, shall ye have:
I am the LORD **I — Yah Veh** your *God* **Elohim**,
which brought you out of the land of *Egypt* **Misrayim**.
37 *Therefore* shall ye *observe* **guard** all my statutes,
and all my judgments, and *do* **work** them:
I am the LORD **I — Yah Veh**.

ON IDOLATRY

20 And *the LORD spake* **Yah Veh worded**
unto *Moses* **Mosheh**, saying,
2 Again, thou shalt say
to the *children* **sons** of *Israel* **Yisra El**,
Whosoever he be of the *children* **sons** of *Israel* **Yisra El**,
or of the *strangers* **sojourners**
that sojourn in *Israel* **Yisra El**,
that giveth any of his seed unto Molech;
in deathifying, he shall *surely* be *put to death* **deathified**:
the people of the land shall stone him with stones.
3 And I *will set* **shall give** my face against that man,
and *will* **shall** cut him off from among his people;
because he hath given of his seed unto Molech,
to *defile* **foul** my *sanctuary* **holies**,
and to profane my holy name.
4 And if the people of the land
do any ways hide **in vailing, vail** their eyes from the man,
when he giveth of his seed unto Molech,
and *kill* **deathify** him not:
5 Then I *will* **shall** set my face against that man,
and against his family,
and *will* **shall** cut him off,
and all that *go a whoring* **whore** after him,
to *commit whoredom* **whore** with Molech,
from among their people.
6 And the soul that turneth **the face**
after such as have familiar spirits **from necromancers**,
and *after wizards* **from knowers**,
to *go a whoring* **whore** after them,
I *will* **shall** even set my face against that soul,
and *will* **shall** cut him off from among his people.
7 *Sanctify* **Hallow** yourselves therefore, and be ye holy:
for *I am the LORD* **I — Yah Veh** your *God* **Elohim**.
8 And ye shall *keep* **guard** my statutes, and *do* **work** them:
I am the LORD which sanctify **I — Yah Veh hallow** you.
9 For *every one* **man — every man**
that *curseth* **abaseth** his father or his mother
in deathifying, shall be *surely put to death* **deathified**:
he hath *cursed* **abased** his father or his mother;
his blood shall be upon him.
10 And the man that *committeth adultery* **adulterizeth**
with *another* **a** man's *wife* **woman**,
even he that *committeth adultery* **adulterizeth**
with his *neighbour's wife* **friend's woman**,
the adulterer and the adulteress
in deathifying, shall *surely* be *put to death* **deathified**.
11 And the man that lieth with his father's *wife* **woman**
hath *uncovered* **exposed** his father's nakedness:
both **the two** of them
in deathifying, shall *surely* be *put to death* **deathified**;
their blood shall be upon them.
12 And if a man lie with his daughter in law,
both **the two** of them
in deathifying, shall *surely* be *put to death* **deathified**:
they have *wrought confusion* **worked comingling**;
their blood shall be upon them.
13 If a man also lie with *mankind* **male**,
as *he lieth with* **bedding with** a woman,
both **the two** of them
have *committed an abomination* **done an abhorrence**:
in deathifying, they shall *surely* be *put to death* **deathified**;
their blood shall be upon them.
14 And if a man take a *wife* **woman** and her mother,
it is *wickedness* **intrigue**:
they shall be burnt with fire, both he and they;
that there be no *wickedness* **intrigue** among you.
15 And if a man **giveth to** lie with *a beast* **an animal**,
in deathifying, he shall *surely* be *put to death* **deathified**:
and ye shall *slay* **slaughter** the *beast* **animal**.
16 And if a woman approach unto any *beast* **animal**,
and *lie down thereto* **copulate**,
thou shalt *kill* **slaughter** the woman,

and the *beast* **animal**:
in deathifying, they shall *surely* be *put to death* **deathified**;
their blood shall be upon them.
17 And if a man shall take his sister,
his father's daughter, or his mother's daughter,
and see her nakedness, and she see his nakedness;
it is a *wicked thing* **shame**;
and they shall be cut off in the *sight* **eyes** of their people:
he hath *uncovered* **exposed** his sister's nakedness;
he shall bear his *iniquity* **perversion**.
18 And if a man shall lie with a woman
having her sickness — **menstrous**,
and shall *uncover* **expose** her nakedness;
he hath *discovered* **stripped naked** her fountain,
and she hath *uncovered* **exposed**
the fountain of her blood:
and *both* **the two** of them shall be cut off
from among **the sons of** their people.
19 And thou shalt not *uncover* **expose** the nakedness
of thy mother's sister, nor of thy father's sister:
for he *uncovereth* **hath stripped naked**
his *near kin* **kinflesh**:
they shall bear their *iniquity* **perversion**.
20 And if a man shall lie with his uncle's *wife* **woman**,
he hath *uncovered* **exposed** his uncle's nakedness:
they shall bear their sin; they shall die *childless* **barren**.
21 And if a man shall take his brother's *wife* **woman**,
it is an *unclean thing* **exclusion**:
he hath *uncovered* **exposed** his brother's nakedness;
they shall be *childless* **barren**.
22 Ye shall *therefore keep* **guard** all my statutes,
and all my judgments, and *do* **work** them:
that the land, whither I bring you to *dwell* **settle** therein,
spue **vomit** you not *out*.
23 And ye shall not walk
in the *manners* **statutes** of the *nation* **goyim**,
which I cast out *before* you **from your face**:
for they *committed* **have worked** all these *things*,
and therefore I abhorred them.
24 But I have said unto you,
Ye shall *inherit* **possess** their *land* **soil**,
and I *will* **shall** give it unto you to possess it,
a land that floweth with milk and honey:
I am the LORD **I — Yah Veh** your *God* **Elohim**,
which have separated you from *other* people.
25 Ye shall therefore *put difference* **separate**
between *clean beasts* **pure animals**
and *unclean* **between fouled**,
and between *unclean fowls* **fouled fliers**
and *clean* **between pure**:
and ye shall not *make* **abominate** your souls *abominable*
by *beast* **animal**, or by *fowl* **flier**,
or by any *manner of living thing* **live being**
that creepeth on the *ground* **soil**,
which I have separated from you as *unclean* **fouled**.
26 And ye shall be holy unto me:
for I *the LORD* **Yah Veh** am holy,
and have *severed* **separated** you from *other* people,
that ye should be mine.
27 A man *also* or woman
that hath a familiar spirit — **a necromancer**,
or that is a *wizard* **knower**,
in deathifying, shall *surely* be *put to death* **deathified**:
they shall stone them with stones:
their blood shall be upon them.

ON THE PRIESTHOOD

21 And *the LORD* **Yah Veh** said unto *Moses* **Mosheh**,
Speak **Say** unto the priests the sons of *Aaron* **Aharon**,
and say unto them,
There shall none be *defiled* **fouled**
for *the dead* **a soul** among his people:
2 *But* **Except** for his *kin* **kinflesh**, that is near unto him,
that is, for his mother, and for his father,
and for his son, and for his daughter, and for his brother.
3 And for his sister a virgin, that is nigh unto him,
which hath had no *husband* **man**;
for her may he be *defiled* **fouled**.
4 But *he* **a master** shall not *defile* **foul** himself,
being a chief man among his people, to profane himself.
5 They shall not *make baldness upon* **balden** their head,
neither shall they shave off the *corner* **edge** of their beard,
nor *make* **incise** any *cuttings* **incisions** in their flesh.
6 They shall be holy unto their *God* **Elohim**,
and not profane the name of their *God* **Elohim**:
for the *offerings of the LORD made by fire*
firings unto Yah Veh,
and the bread of their *God* **Elohim**, they do *offer* **oblate**:
therefore they shall be holy.
7 They shall not take a *wife* **woman** that is a whore,
or profane;
neither shall they take a woman
put away **expelled** from her *husband* **man**:
for he is holy unto his *God* **Elohim**.
8 Thou shalt *sanctify* **hallow** him *therefore*;
for he *offereth* **oblateth** the bread of thy *God* **Elohim**:
he shall be holy unto thee:
for *I the LORD* **I — Yah Veh**,
which *sanctify* **halloweth** you, am holy.
9 And the daughter of *any* **a man** — **a** priest,
if she profane herself by *playing the whore* **whoring**,
she profaneth her father: she shall be burnt with fire.
10 And he that is the *high* **great** priest among his brethren,
upon whose head the anointing oil was poured,
and *that is consecrated* **hath filled his hand**
to *put on the garments* **enrobe the clothes**,
shall not *uncover* **expose** his head,
nor *rend* **tear** his clothes;
11 Neither shall he go in to any *dead body* **soul that died**,
nor *defile* **foul** himself for his father, or for his mother;
12 Neither shall he go out of the *sanctuary* **holies**,
nor profane the *sanctuary* **holies** of his *God* **Elohim**;
for the *crown* **separatism** of the anointing oil
of his *God* **Elohim** is upon him:
I am the LORD **I — Yah Veh**.
13 And he shall take a *wife* **woman** in her virginity.
14 A widow, or *a divorced woman* **expelled**,
or profane, or *an harlot* **that whoreth**,
these shall he not take:
but he shall take a virgin of his own people
to *wife* **woman**.
15 Neither shall he profane his seed among his people:
for I *the LORD do sanctify* **Yah Veh hallow** him.
16 And *the LORD spake* **Yah Veh worded**
unto *Moses* **Mosheh**, saying,
17 *Speak* **Word** unto *Aaron* **Aharon**, saying,
Whosoever he be **Any man** of thy seed
in their generations that hath any blemish,
let him not approach
to *offer* **oblate** the bread of his *God* **Elohim**.
18 For whatsoever man he be that hath a blemish,
he shall not approach:
a blind man, or a lame,
or *he that hath a flat nose* **disfigured**,
or *any thing superfluous* **extended**,
19 Or a man that is brokenfooted, or brokenhanded,
20 Or *crookbackt* **archbacked**, or *a dwarf* **thin**,
or that hath a *blemish* **cataract** in his eye,
or be scurvy, or scabbed,
or hath his *stones broken* **testicles castrated**;
21 No man that hath a blemish
of the seed of *Aaron* **Aharon** the priest
shall come nigh to *offer* **oblate**
the *offerings of the LORD made by fire*
firings unto Yah Veh:
he hath a blemish;
he shall not come nigh
to *offer* **oblate** the bread of his *God* **Elohim**.
22 He shall eat the bread of his *God* **Elohim**,
both of the *most holy* **holy of holies**,
and of the *holy* **holies**.
23 Only he shall not go in unto the vail,
nor come nigh unto the **sacrifice** altar,
because he hath a blemish;
that he profane not my *sanctuaries* **holies**:
for I *the LORD do sanctify* **Yah Veh hallow** them.
24 And *Moses told it* **Mosheh worded** unto *Aaron* **Aharon**,
and to his sons,
and unto all the *children* **sons** of *Israel* **Yisra El**.
22 And *the LORD spake* **Yah Veh worded**
unto *Moses* **Mosheh**, saying,

2 *Speak* **Word** unto *Aaron* **Aharon** and to his sons,
that they separate themselves from the *holy things* **holies**
of the *children* **sons** of *Israel* **Yisra El**,
and that they profane not my holy name *in those things*
which they hallow unto me:
I am the LORD **I — Yah Veh**.
3 Say unto them,
Whosoever he be **The man** of all your seed
among your generations,
that *goeth unto* **approacheth** the *holy things* **holies**,
which the *children* **sons** of *Israel* **Yisra El**
hallow unto *the LORD* **Yah Veh**,
having his *uncleanness* **foulness** upon him,
that soul shall be cut off from my *presence* **face**:
I am the LORD **I — Yah Veh**.
4 *What man soever* **Man — whatever man**
of the seed of *Aaron* **Aharon** is a leper,
or *hath a running issue* **fluxeth**;
he shall not eat of the *holy things* **holies**,
until he be *clean* **purified**.
And whoso toucheth *any thing* **aught**
that is *unclean* **fouled** by the *dead* **soul**,
or a man whose seed **of copulation** goeth from him;
5 Or *whosoever* **whatever man**
toucheth any *creeping thing* **teemer**,
whereby he may be *made unclean* **fouled**,
or a *man* **human**
of *whom he may take uncleanness* **his foulness**,
whatsoever *uncleanness* **foulness** he hath;
6 The soul which hath touched any such
shall be *unclean* **fouled** until even,
and shall not eat of the *holy things* **holies**,
unless he *wash* **baptize** his flesh with water.
7 And when the sun is down, he shall be *clean* **purified**,
and shall afterward eat of the *holy things* **holies**;
because it is his *food* **bread**.
8 That *which dieth of itself* **carcase**, or *is* torn *with beasts*,
he shall not eat to *defile* **foul** himself therewith;
I am the LORD **I — Yah Veh**.
9 They shall *therefore*
keep mine ordinance **guard my guard**,
lest they bear sin for it, and die therefore, if they profane it:
I *the LORD do sanctify* **Yah Veh hallow** them.
10 There shall no stranger eat of the *holy thing* **holies**:
a *sojourner* **settler** of the priest,
or an *hired servant* **hireling**,
shall not eat of the *holy thing* **holies**.
11 But if the priest *buy* **chattelize** any soul
with his money **— a chattel of silver**, he shall eat of it,
and he that is born in his house:
they shall eat of his *meat* **bread**.
12 If the priest's daughter also
be married **becometh a man's**
unto a stranger **— a stranger's**,
she may not eat
of an *heave offering* **exaltment** of the *holy things* **holies**.
13 But if the priest's daughter be a widow,
or *divorced* **expelled**, and have no *child* **seed**,
and is returned unto her father's house, as in her youth,
she shall eat of her father's *meat* **bread**:
but there shall be no stranger eat thereof.
14 And if a man eat of the *holy thing* **holies**
unwittingly **erring inadvertently**,
then he shall *put* **add** the fifth *part* thereof *unto it* **thereto**,
and shall give *it* unto the priest with the *holy thing* **holies**.
15 And they shall not profane the *holy things* **holies**
of the *children* **sons** of *Israel* **Yisra El**,
which they *offer* **lift** unto *the LORD* **Yah Veh**;
16 Or *suffer* **cause** them to bear
the *iniquity* **perversity** of *trespass* **guilt**,
when they eat their *holy things* **holies**:
for I *the LORD do sanctify* **Yah Veh hallow** them.
17 And *the LORD spake* **Yah Veh worded**
unto *Moses* **Mosheh**, saying,
18 *Speak* **Word** unto *Aaron* **Aharon**, and to his sons,
and unto all the *children* **sons** of *Israel* **Yisra El**,
and say unto them,
Whatsoever he be **Man — whatever man**
of the house of *Israel* **Yisra El**,
or of the *strangers* **sons of sojourners** in *Israel* **Yisra El**,
that *will offer* **shall oblate** his *oblation* **qorban**
for all his vows,
and for all his *freewill offerings* **voluntaries**,
which they *will offer* **shall oblate** unto *the LORD* **Yah Veh**
for a *burnt offering* **holocaust**;
19 *Ye shall offer* at your *own will* **pleasure**
a male *without blemish* **integrious**,
of the *beeves* **oxen**, of the *sheep* **lambs**, or of the goats.
20 But whatsoever hath a blemish,
that shall ye not *offer* **oblate**:
for it shall not be *acceptable* **pleasing** for you.
21 And *whosoever offereth* **the man that oblateth**
a sacrifice of *peace offerings* **shelamim**
unto *the LORD* **Yah Veh**
to accomplish his **— a marvelous** vow,
or a *freewill offering* **voluntary**
in *beeves* **oxen** or *sheep* **flocks**,
it shall be *perfect* **integrious** to be *accepted* **pleasing**;
there shall be no blemish therein.
22 Blind, or broken, or *maimed* **cut**,
or *having a wen* **pussed**, or scurvy, or scabbed,
ye shall not *offer* **oblate** these unto *the LORD* **Yah Veh**,
nor *make an offering by fire* **give firings** of them
upon the **sacrifice** altar unto *the LORD* **Yah Veh**.
23 Either *a bullock* **an ox** or a lamb
that hath *any thing superfluous* **extended**
or *lacking in his parts* **maimed**,
that mayest thou *offer* **work**
for a *freewill offering* **voluntary**;
but for a vow it shall not be *accepted* **pleasing**.
24 Ye shall not *offer* **oblate** unto *the LORD* **Yah Veh**
that which is *bruised* **pinched**, or crushed,
or *broken* **torn**, or cut;
neither shall ye *make any offering thereof* **work**
in your land.
25 Neither from a stranger's hand
shall ye *offer* **oblate** the bread of your *God* **Elohim**
of any of these;
because their *corruption* **ruin** is in them,
and blemishes be in them:
they shall not be *accepted* **pleasing** for you.
26 And *the LORD spake* **Yah Veh worded**
unto *Moses* **Mosheh**, saying,
27 When *a bullock* **an ox**, or a *sheep* **lamb**,
or a goat, is *brought forth* **born**,
then it shall be seven days under the *dam* **mother**;
and from the eighth day and *thenceforth* **beyond**
it shall be *accepted* **pleasing** for *an offering* **a qorban**
made by fire **a firing** unto *the LORD* **Yah Veh**.
28 And *whether it be cow* **ox**, or *ewe* **lamb**,
ye shall not *kill* **slaughter** it and her *young* **sons**
both in one day.
29 And when ye *will offer* **shall sacrifice** a sacrifice
of thanksgiving **— an extended hands praise**
unto *the LORD* **Yah Veh**,
offer **sacrifice** it at your *own will* **pleasure**.
30 On the same day it shall be eaten up;
ye shall *leave* **let** none of it **remain** until the morrow:
I am the LORD **I — Yah Veh**.
31 Therefore shall ye *keep* **guard**
my *commandments* **misvoth**, and *do* **work** them:
I am the LORD **I — Yah Veh**.
32 Neither shall ye profane my holy name;
but I *will* **shall** be hallowed
among the *children* **sons** of *Israel* **Yisra El**:
I am the LORD **I — Yah Veh** which hallow you,
33 That brought you out of the land of *Egypt* **Misrayim**,
to be your *God* **Elohim**:
I am the LORD **I — Yah Veh**.

TORAH ON SEASONS

23 And *the LORD spake* **Yah Veh worded**
unto *Moses* **Mosheh**, saying,
2 *Speak* **Word** unto the *children* **sons** of *Israel* **Yisra El**,
and say unto them,
Concerning the *feasts* **seasons** of *the LORD* **Yah Veh**,
which ye shall *proclaim* **recall** to be holy convocations,
even these are my *feasts* **seasons**.

SEASON OF SHABBATH

3 Six days shall work be *done* **worked**:
but the seventh day

is the *sabbath* **shabbath** of *rest* **shabbathism**,
an holy convocation;
ye shall *do* **work** no work *therein*:
it is the *sabbath* **shabbath** of *the LORD* **Yah Veh**
in all your *dwellings* **settlements**.
4 These are the *feasts* **seasons** of *the LORD* **Yah Veh**,
even holy convocations,
which ye shall *proclaim* **recall** in their seasons.

SEASON OF PASACH

5 *In the fourteenth day of the first month*
In the first month, on the fourteenth of the month,
at even **between evenings**
is *the LORD'S passover* **Yah Veh's pasach**.

SEASON OF MATSAH

6 And on the fifteenth day of the same month
is the *feast* **celebration** of *unleavened bread* **matsah**
unto *the LORD* **Yah Veh**:
seven days ye *must* **shall** eat *unleavened bread* **matsah**.
7 In the first day ye shall have an holy convocation:
ye shall *do* **work** no *servile* **service** work therein.
8 But ye shall *offer an offering made by fire* **oblate a firing**
unto *the LORD* **Yah Veh** seven days:
in the seventh day is an holy convocation:
ye shall *do* **work** no *servile* **service** work *therein*.

SEASON OF HARVEST FIRSTS

9 And *the LORD spake* **Yah Veh**
worded unto *Moses* **Mosheh**, saying,
10 *Speak* **Word** unto the *children* **sons** of *Israel* **Yisra El**,
and say unto them,
When ye be come into the land which I give unto you,
and shall *reap* **harvest** the harvest thereof,
then ye shall bring *a sheaf* **an omer**
of the *firstfruits* **firsts** of your harvest unto the priest:
11 And he shall wave the *sheaf* **omer**
before the LORD **at the face of Yah Veh**,
to be accepted for you **at your pleasure**:
on the morrow after the *sabbath* **shabbath**
the priest shall wave it.
12 And ye shall *offer* **work** that day
when ye wave the *sheaf* **omer**
an he lamb *without blemish* **integrious**
of the first year — **a yearling son**
for a *burnt offering* **holocaust** unto *the LORD* **Yah Veh**.
13 And the *meat* offering thereof
shall be two *tenth deals of fine* **tenths** flour
mingled **mixed** with oil,
an offering made by fire **a firing** unto *the LORD* **Yah Veh**
for a *sweet savour* **scent of rest**:
and the *drink offering* **libation** thereof shall be of wine,
the fourth *part* of an hin.
14 And ye shall eat neither bread, nor parched *corn*,
nor *green ears* **of the orchard**,
until *the selfsame* **that** day that ye have brought
an *offering* **qorban** unto your *God* **Elohim**:
it shall be *a* **an eternal** statute *for ever*
throughout your generations
in all your *dwellings* **settlements**.

SEASON OF PENTECOST

15 And ye shall *count* **scribe** unto you
from the morrow after the *sabbath* **shabbath**,
from the day
that ye brought the *sheaf* **omer** of the wave *offering*;
seven *sabbaths* **shabbaths** shall be *complete* **integrious**:
16 Even unto the morrow
after the seventh *sabbath* **shabbath**
shall ye *number* **scribe** fifty days;
and ye shall *offer* **oblate** a new *meat* offering
unto *the LORD* **Yah Veh**.
17 Ye shall bring out of your *habitations* **settlements**
two wave *loaves* **breads** of two *tenth deals* **tenths**;
they shall be of *fine* flour;
they shall be baken with *leaven* **fermentation**;
they are the firstfruits unto *the LORD* **Yah Veh**.
18 And ye shall *offer* **oblate** with the bread
seven lambs *without blemish* **integrious**
of the first year — **yearling sons**,
and one *young* bullock **son of the oxen**, and two rams:
they shall be for a *burnt offering* **holocaust**
unto *the LORD* **Yah Veh**,
with their *meat* offering, and their *drink offerings* **libations**,
even an offering made by fire **a firing**,
of sweet savour **a scent of rest** unto *the LORD* **Yah Veh**.
19 Then ye shall *sacrifice* **work** one *kid* **buck** of the goats
for *a sin offering* **the sin**,
and two lambs *of the first year* **yearling sons**
for a sacrifice of *peace offerings* **shelamim**.
20 And the priest shall wave them
with the bread of the firstfruits for a wave *offering*
before the LORD **at the face of Yah Veh**,
with the two lambs:
they shall be holy to *the LORD* **Yah Veh** for the priest.
21 And ye shall proclaim on the selfsame day,
that it may be an holy convocation unto you:
ye shall *do* **work** no *servile* **service** work *therein*:
it shall be *a* **an eternal** statute *for ever*
in all your *dwellings* **settlements**
throughout your generations.
22 And when ye *reap* **harvest** the harvest of your land,
thou shalt not *make clean riddance of* **finish off**
the *corners* **edges** of thy field
when thou *reapest* **harvestest**,
neither shalt thou *gather* **glean**
any gleaning of thy harvest:
thou shalt leave them unto the *poor* **humbled**,
and to the *stranger* **sojourner**:
I am the LORD **I — Yah Veh** your *God* **Elohim**.

SEASON OF BLASTING

23 And *the LORD spake* **Yah Veh worded**
unto *Moses* **Mosheh**, saying,
24 *Speak* **Word** unto the *children* **sons** of *Israel* **Yisra El**,
saying,
In the seventh month, in the first *day* of the month,
shall ye have a *sabbath* **shabbathism**,
a memorial of *blowing of trumpets* **blasting**,
an holy convocation.
25 Ye shall *do* **work** no *servile* **service** work *therein*:
but ye shall *offer an offering made by fire* **oblate a firing**
unto *the LORD* **Yah Veh**.

SEASON OF YOM KIPPURIM

26 And *the LORD spake* **Yah Veh worded**
unto *Moses* **Mosheh**, saying,
27 *Also* **Only** on the tenth *day* of this seventh month
there shall be *a day of atonement* **Yom Kippurim**:
it shall be an holy convocation unto you;
and ye shall *afflict* **humble** your souls,
and *offer an offering made by fire* **oblate a firing**
unto *the LORD* **Yah Veh**.
28 And ye shall *do* **work** no work in that same day:
for it is *a day of atonement* **Yom Kippurim**,
to *make an atonement* **kapar/atone for you**
before the LORD **at the face of Yah Veh** your *God* **Elohim**.
29 For whatsoever soul it be
that shall not be *afflicted* **humbled** in that same day,
he shall be cut off from among his people.
30 And whatsoever soul it be
that *doeth* **worketh** any work in that same day,
the same soul *will* **shall** I destroy from among his people.
31 Ye shall *do* **work** no *manner of* work:
it shall be *a* **an eternal** statute *for ever*
throughout your generations
in all your *dwellings* **settlements**.
32 It shall be unto you
a *sabbath* **shabbath** of *rest* **shabbathism**,
and ye shall *afflict* **humble** your souls:
in the ninth *day* of the month at even,
from even unto even,
shall ye *celebrate* **shabbathize** your *sabbath* **shabbath**.

SEASON OF SUKKOTH/BRUSH ARBORS

33 And *the LORD spake* **Yah Veh worded**
unto *Moses* **Mosheh**, saying,
34 *Speak* **Word** unto the *children* **sons** of *Israel* **Yisra El**,
saying,
The fifteenth day of this seventh month
shall be the *feast* **celebration**
of *tabernacles* **sukkoth/brush arbors**
for seven days unto *the LORD* **Yah Veh**.
35 On the first day shall be an holy convocation:
ye shall *do* **work** no *servile* **service** work *therein*.
36 Seven days ye shall
offer an offering made by fire **oblate a firing**

unto *the LORD* **Yah Veh**:
on the eighth day shall be an holy convocation unto you;
and ye shall *offer an offering made by fire* **oblate a firing**
unto *the LORD* **Yah Veh**:
it is *a solemn assembly* **an abstinence**;
and ye shall *do* **work** no *servile* **service** work *therein*.
37 These are the *feasts* **seasons** of *the LORD* **Yah Veh**,
which ye shall *proclaim* **recall** to be holy convocations,
to *offer an offering made by fire* **oblate a firing**
unto *the LORD* **Yah Veh**,
a *burnt offering* **holocaust**, and *a meat* **an** offering,
a sacrifice, and *drink offerings* **libations**,
every *thing upon his day* **word day by day**:
38 Beside the *sabbaths* **shabbaths** of *the LORD* **Yah Veh**,
and beside your gifts, and beside all your vows,
and beside all your *freewill offerings* **voluntaries**,
which ye give unto *the LORD* **Yah Veh**.

SEASON OF SHABBATHISM

39 Also in the fifteenth day of the seventh month,
when ye have gathered in the *fruit* **produce** of the land,
ye shall *keep* **celebrate** a *feast* **celebration**
unto *the LORD* **Yah Veh** seven days:
on the first day shall be a *sabbath* **shabbathism**,
and on the eighth day shall be a *sabbath* **shabbathism**.
40 And ye shall take you on the first day
the boughs of *goodly* **majestic** trees,
branches **palms** of palm trees,
and the *boughs* **fruit** of thick trees,
and willows of the *brook* **wadi**;
and ye shall *rejoice* **cheer**
before the LORD **at the face of Yah Veh** your *God* **Elohim**
seven days.
41 And ye shall *keep it* **celebrate** a *feast* **celebration**
unto *the LORD* **Yah Veh** seven days in the year.
It shall be *a* **an eternal** statute *for ever* in your generations:
ye shall celebrate it in the seventh month.
42 Ye shall *dwell* **sit** in *booths* **sukkoth/brush arbors**
seven days;
all that are *Israelites* **Yisra Eliy** born
shall *dwell* **sit** in *booths* **sukkoth/brush arbors**:
43 That your generations may know
that I *made* **caused** the *children* **sons** of *Israel* **Yisra El**
to *dwell* **sit** in *booths* **sukkoth/brush arbors**,
when I brought them out of the land of *Egypt* **Misrayim**:
I am the LORD **I — Yah Veh** your *God* **Elohim**.
44 And *Moses declared* **Mosheh worded**
unto the *children* **sons** of *Israel* **Yisra El**
the *feasts* **seasons** of *the LORD* **Yah Veh**.

CONGREGATIONAL TENT MENORAH

24 And *the LORD spake* **Yah Veh worded**
unto *Moses* **Mosheh**, saying,
2 *Command* **Misvah** the *children* **sons** of *Israel* **Yisra El**,
that they *bring* **take** unto thee
pure oil olive *beaten* **pestled** for the light,
to cause the lamps to *burn* **holocaust** continually.
3 Without the vail of the *testimony* **witness**,
in the *tabernacle* **tent** of the congregation,
shall *Aaron order* **Aharon arrange** it
from the evening unto the morning
before the LORD **at the face of Yah Veh** continually:
it shall be *a* **an eternal** statute *for ever* in your generations.
4 He shall *order* **arrange** the lamps
upon the pure *candlestick* **menorah**
before the LORD **at the face of Yah Veh** continually.

CONGREGATIONAL TENT CAKES

5 And thou shalt take *fine* flour,
and bake twelve cakes thereof:
two *tenth deals* **tenths** shall be in one cake.
6 And thou shalt set them in two rows, six on a row,
upon the pure table
before the LORD **at the face of Yah Veh**.
7 And thou shalt *put* **give** pure frankincense
upon each row,
that it may be on the bread for a memorial,
even *an offering made by fire* **a firing**
unto *the LORD* **Yah Veh**.
8 *Every sabbath* **On the shabbath — every shabbath day**
he shall *set it in order* **arrange it**
before the LORD **at the face of Yah Veh** continually,
being taken from the *children* **sons** of *Israel* **Yisra El**
by an *everlasting* **eternal** covenant.
9 And it shall be *Aaron's* **Aharon's** and his sons';
and they shall eat it in the *holy place* **holies**:
for it is *most holy* **a holy of holies** unto him
of the *offering of the LORD made by fire*
firing unto Yah Veh
by a perpetual **— an eternal** statute.

AN ABASER IS STONED

10 And the son of an *Israelitish* **Yisra Eliy** woman,
whose father was an Egyptian
a son of a man — a Misrayim,
went out among the *children* **sons** of *Israel* **Yisra El**:
and this son of the *Israelitish woman* **Yisra Eliy**
and *a man of Israel* **an Yisra Eliy man**
strove together in the camp;
11 And the *Israelitish* **Yisra Eliy** woman's son
blasphemed **pierced** the name *of the Lord*,
and *cursed* **abased**.
And they brought him unto *Moses* **Mosheh**:
(and his mother's name was Shelomith,
the daughter of Dibri, of the *tribe* **rod** of Dan:)
12 And they *put* **set** him *in ward* **under guard**,
that the *mind* **mouth** of *the LORD* **Yah Veh**
might be *shewed them* **expressed**.
13 And *the LORD spake* **Yah Veh worded**
unto *Moses* **Mosheh**, saying,
14 Bring forth
him that hath *cursed* **abased** without the camp;
and let all that heard him
lay **prop** their hands upon his head,
and let all the *congregation* **witness** stone him.
15 And thou shalt *speak* **word**
unto the *children* **sons** of *Israel* **Yisra El**, saying,
Whosoever **A man — any man**
curseth **that abaseth** his *God* **Elohim** shall bear his sin.
16 And he that *blasphemeth* **pierceth**
the name of *the LORD* **Yah Veh**,
in deathifying, he shall *surely* be *put to death* **deathified**,
and all the *congregation* **witness**
in stoning, shall *certainly* stone him:
as well the *stranger* **sojourner**,
as he that is born in the land,
when he *blasphemeth* **pierceth** the name *of the LORD*,
shall be *put to death* **deathified**.
17 And *he* **a man**
that *killeth any man* **smiteth a human soul,**
in deathifying, shall *surely* be *put to death* **deathified**.
18 And he that
killeth a beast **smiteth the soul of an animal**
shall *make it good* **shalam for it**; *beast* **soul** for *beast* **soul**.
19 And if a man
cause **give** a blemish in his *neighbour* **friend**;
as he hath *done* **worked**,
so shall it be *done* **worked** to him;
20 Breach for breach, eye for eye, tooth for tooth:
as he hath *caused* **given** a blemish in a *man* **human**,
so shall it be *done* **given** to him again.
21 And he that *killeth a beast* **smiteth an animal**,
he shall *restore* **shalam** it:
and he that *killeth a man* **smiteth a human**,
he shall be *put to death* **deathified**.
22 Ye shall have one *manner of law* **judgment**,
as well for the *stranger* **sojourner**,
as for one of your own country:
for *I am the LORD* **I — Yah Veh** your *God* **Elohim**.
23 And *Moses spake* **Mosheh worded**
to the *children* **sons** of *Israel* **Yisra El**,
that they should bring forth him that had *cursed* **abased**
out of **without** the camp, and stone him with stones.
And the *children* **sons** of *Israel did* **Yisra El worked**
as *the LORD* **Yah Veh**
commanded Moses **misvahed Mosheh**.

SHABBATH YEAR

25 And *the LORD spake* **Yah Veh worded**
unto *Moses* **Mosheh** in mount *Sinai* **Sinay**, saying,
2 *Speak* **Word** unto the *children* **sons** of *Israel* **Yisra El**,
and say unto them,
When ye come into the land which I give you,
then shall the land *keep* **shabbathize** a *sabbath* **shabbath**
unto *the LORD* **Yah Veh**.

3 Six years thou shalt *sow* **seed** thy field,
and six years thou shalt *prune* **pluck** thy vineyard,
and gather in the *fruit* **produce** thereof;
4 But in the seventh year
shall be a *sabbath* **shabbath**
of rest — **a shabbathism** unto the land,
a *sabbath* **shabbath** for *the LORD* **Yah Veh**:
thou shalt neither *sow* **seed** thy field,
nor *prune* **pluck** thy vineyard.
5 That *which groweth of its own accord*
spontaneous growth of thy harvest,
thou shalt not *reap* **harvest**,
neither *gather* **clip** the grapes
of thy *vine undressed* **separatism**:
for it is a year of *rest* **shabbathism** unto the land.
6 And the *sabbath* **shabbath** of the land
shall be *meat* **food** for you;
for thee, and for thy servant, and for thy maid,
and for thy *hired servant* **hireling**,
and for thy *stranger* **settler** that sojourneth with thee.
7 And for thy *cattle* **animals**,
and for the *beast* **live beings** that are in thy land,
shall all the *increase* **produce** thereof be *meat* **to eat.**

BLASTING

8 And thou shalt *number* **scribe**
seven *sabbaths* **shabbaths** of years unto thee,
seven times seven years;
and the *space* **days**
of the seven *sabbaths* **shabbaths** of years
shall be unto thee forty and nine years.
9 Then shalt thou cause the trumpet of the *jubile* **blasting**
to *sound* **pass**
on the tenth day of the seventh month
in the seventh month, on the tenth of the month,
in *the day of atonement* **Yom Kippurim**
shall ye *make* **pass** the trumpet *sound*
throughout all your land.
10 And ye shall hallow **that year** — the fiftieth year,
and *proclaim* **call** liberty throughout all the land
unto all *the inhabitants* **who settle** thereof:
it shall be a jubile unto you;
and ye shall return every man unto his possession,
and ye shall return every man unto his family.
11 A jubile shall that **year** — **the** fiftieth year be unto you:
ye shall not *sow* **seed**, neither *reap* **harvest**
that which groweth of itself in it **the spontaneous growth**,
nor *gather the grapes* **clip** in it
of thy *vine undressed* **separatism**.
12 For it is the jubile; it shall be holy unto you:
ye shall eat the *increase* **produce** thereof out of the field.
13 In the year of this jubile
ye shall return every man unto his possession.
14 And if **in selling**,
thou *sell ought* **sellest** unto thy *neighbour* **friend**,
or *buyest ought* **chattelizest**
of thy *neighbour's* **friend's** hand,
ye shall not oppress *one another* **man to brother**:
15 According to the number of years after the jubile
thou shalt *buy* **chattelize** of thy *neighbour* **friend**,
and according
unto the number of years of the *fruits* **produce**
he shall sell unto thee:
16 According to the *multitude* **abundance** of years
thou shalt *increase* **greaten** the *price* **equity** thereof,
and according to the *fewness* **diminishing** of years
thou shalt diminish the *price* **equity** of it:
for according
to the number *of the years* of the *fruits* **produce**
doth he sell unto thee.
17 Ye shall not therefore
oppress *one another* **man to friend**;
but thou shalt *fear* **awe** thy *God* **Elohim**
for *I am the LORD* **I — Yah Veh** your *God* **Elohim**.
18 *Wherefore* ye shall *do* **work** my statutes,
and *keep* **guard** my judgments, and *do* **work** them;
and ye shall *dwell* **settle** in the land *in safety* **confidently**.
19 And the land shall *yield* **give** her fruit,
and ye shall eat *your fill* **to satiety**,
and *dwell therein in safety* **settle confidently**.
20 And if ye shall say,
What shall we eat the seventh year?
behold, we shall not *sow* **seed**,
nor gather in our *increase* **produce**:
21 Then I *will command* **shall misvah** my blessing
upon you in the sixth year,
and it shall *bring forth fruit* **work** fruit for three years.
22 And ye shall *sow* **seed** the eighth year,
and eat yet of old *fruit* **produce** until the ninth year;
until her *fruits* **produce** come in,
ye shall eat of the old *store*.
23 The land shall not be sold *for ever* **ad infinitum**:
for the land is mine,
for ye are *strangers* **sojourners**
and *sojourners* **settlers** with me.
24 And in all the land of your possession
ye shall *grant* **give** a redemption for the land.
25 If thy brother be *waxen poor* **impoverished**,
and hath sold *away some* of his possession,
and if any of his **near of** kin come to redeem it,
then shall he redeem that which his brother sold.
26 And if *the man* **his hand**
have none **findeth not sufficient** to redeem it,
and *himself* **his own hand**
be able **hath attaineth** to redeem it;
27 Then let him *count* **fabricate**
the years of the sale thereof,
and restore the *overplus* **leftovers**
unto the man to whom he sold it;
that he may return unto his possession.
28 But if *he be not able* **his hand findeth not sufficient**
to restore it to him,
then that which is sold shall remain
in the hand of him that hath *bought* **chatteled** it
until the year of jubile:
and in the jubile it shall go out,
and he shall return unto his possession.
29 And if a man
sell a *dwelling* **settlement** house in a walled city,
then he may redeem it
within a whole year **until the consumation of the year**
after it is sold;
within a full year may he — **days to** redeem it.
30 And if it be not redeemed
within the *space of a full* **fulfilling of an integrious** year,
then the house that is in the walled city
shall be *established for ever* **raised ad infinitum**
to him that *bought* **chatteled** it throughout his generations:
it shall not go out in the jubile.
31 But the houses of the *villages* **courts**
which have no wall round about them
shall be *counted* **fabricated**
as the fields of the *country* **land**:
they may be redeemed,
and they shall go out in the jubile.
32 Notwithstanding the cities of the *Levites* **Leviym**,
and the houses of the cities of their possession,
may the *Levites* **Leviym** redeem *at any time* **eternally**.
33 And *if a man* **as for him**
purchase **that redeemeth** of the *Levites* **Leviym**,
then the house that was sold,
and the city of his possession,
shall go out in the *year of* jubile:
for the houses of the cities of the *Levites* **Leviym**
are their possession
among the *children* **sons** of *Israel* **Yisra El**.
34 But the field of the suburbs of their cities
may not be sold;
for it is their *perpetual* **eternal** possession.
35 And if thy brother be *waxen poor* **impoverished**,
and *fallen in decay* **his hand shaketh** with thee;
then thou shalt *relieve* **strengthen** him:
yea, *though he be a stranger* **as a sojourner**,
or *a sojourner* **as a settler**;
that he may live with thee.
36 Take thou no usury of him, or *increase* **bounty**:
but *fear* **awe** thy *God* **Elohim**;
that thy brother may live with thee.
37 Thou shalt not give him thy *money* **silver** upon usury,
nor *lend* **give** him thy *victuals* **food** for increase.
38 *I am the LORD* **I — Yah Veh** your *God* **Elohim**,

which brought you forth
out of the land of *Egypt* **Misrayim**,
to give you the land of *Canaan* **Kenaan**,
and to be your *God* **Elohim**.
39 And if thy brother *that dwelleth* by thee
be *waxen poor* **impoverished**, and be sold unto thee;
thou shalt not compel him to serve as a bondservant
he shall not serve the service of a servant:
40 But as an *hired servant* **hireling**,
and as a *sojourner* **settler**,
he shall be with thee,
and shall serve thee unto the year of jubile.
41 And then shall he depart from thee,
both he and his *children* **sons** with him,
and shall return unto his own family,
and unto the possession of his fathers shall he return.
42 For they are my servants,
which I brought forth out of the land of *Egypt* **Misrayim**:
they shall not be *sold as bondmen* **the sale of servants**.
43 Thou shalt not *rule over* **subjugate** him
with *rigour* **tyranny**;
but shalt *fear* **awe** thy *God* **Elohim**.
44 Both thy *bondmen* **servants**, and thy *bondmaids* **maids**,
which thou shalt have,
shall be of the *heathen* **goyim** that are round about you;
of them shall ye *buy bondmen* **chattelize servants**
and *bondmaids* **maids**.
45 Moreover of the *children* **sons** of the *strangers* **settlers**
that do sojourn among you,
of them shall ye *buy* **chattelize**,
and of their families that are with you,
which they begat in your land:
and they shall be your possession.
46 And ye shall *take* **inherit** them *as an inheritance*
for your *children* **sons** after you,
to *inherit* **possess** them for a possession;
they shall *be your bondmen for ever* **serve you eternally**:
but over your brethren the *children* **sons** of *Israel* **Yisra El**,
ye shall not *rule* **subjugate**
one over another **man to brother** with *rigour* **tyranny**.
47 And if **the hand of** a sojourner or *stranger* **settler**
wax rich **hath attained** by thee,
and thy brother *that dwelleth* by him
wax poor **be impoverished**,
and sell himself
unto the *stranger* **sojourner** or *sojourner* **settler** by thee,
or *to the stock of the stranger's family*
the sojourner's family be uprooted:
48 After that he is sold he may be redeemed again;
one of his brethren may redeem him:
49 Either his uncle, or his uncle's son, may redeem him,
or *any that is nigh of kin unto him* **kinflesh** of his family
may redeem him;
or if *he be able* **his hand hath attained**,
he may redeem *himself*.
50 And he shall *reckon* **fabricate** with him
that *bought* **chatteled** him
from the year that he was sold to him
unto the year of jubile:
and the *price* **silver** of his sale
shall be according unto the number of years,
according to the *time* **days** of an *hired servant* **hireling**
shall it be with him.
51 If there be yet many years *behind*,
according unto **the mouth of** them
he shall *give again the price of* **return** his redemption
out of the *money* **silver**
that he was bought for **for which he became a chattel**.
52 And if there *remain* **survive** but few years
unto the year of jubile,
then he shall *count* **fabricate** with him,
and according unto **the mouth of** his years
shall *he give* **return to** him *again*
the price of **for** his redemption.
53 And as a *yearly hired servant* **year by year hireling**
shall he be with him:
and the other shall not
rule with rigour over **subjugate** him **with tyranny**
in thy *sight* **eyes**.
54 And if he be not redeemed in these *years*,
then he shall go out in the year of jubile,
both he, and his *children* **sons** with him.
55 For unto me the *children* **sons** of *Israel* **Yisra El**
are servants;
they are my servants whom I brought forth
out of the land of *Egypt* **Misrayim**:
I am the LORD **I — Yah Veh** your *God* **Elohim**.

BLESSING OF OBEDIENCE

26 Ye shall *make* **work** you no idols
nor *graven image* **sculptile**,
neither *rear you up* **raise** a *standing image* **monolith**,
neither shall ye *set up* **give** any *image* **imagery** of stone
in your land,
to *bow down* **prostrate** unto it:
for *I am the LORD* **I — Yah Veh** your *God* **Elohim**.
2 Ye shall *keep* **guard** my *sabbaths* **shabbaths**,
and *reverence* **awe** my *sanctuary* **holies**:
I am the LORD **I — Yah Veh**.
3 If ye walk in my statutes,
and *keep* **guard** my *commandments* **misvoth**,
and *do* **work** them;
4 Then I *will* **shall** give you *rain* **downpour**
in *due season* **time**,
and the land shall *yield* **give** her *increase* **produce**,
and the trees of the field shall *yield* **give** their fruit.
5 And your threshing shall reach
unto the *vintage* **crop**,
and the *vintage* **crop** shall reach
unto the *sowing time* **seeding**:
and ye shall eat your bread to *the full* **satiety**,
and *dwell* **settle** in your land *safely* **confidently**.
6 And I *will* **shall** give *peace* **shalom** in the land,
and ye shall lie down,
and none shall *make* **tremble** you *afraid*:
and I *will rid evil beasts* **shall cause the evil live being**
to shabbathize out of the land,
neither shall the sword *go* **pass** through your land.
7 And ye shall *chase* **pursue** your enemies,
and they shall fall *before you* **at your face** by the sword.
8 And five of you shall *chase* **pursue** an hundred,
and an hundred of you
shall *put ten thousand to flight* **pursue a myriad**:
and your enemies shall fall *before you* **at your face**
by the sword.
9 For I *will have respect* **shall turn my face**
unto **toward** you,
and make you fruitful **that you bear fruit**,
and *multiply* **abound** you,
and *establish* **raise** my covenant with you.
10 And ye shall eat old store,
and bring forth the old *because of* **at the face of** the new.
11 And I *will set* **shall give** my tabernacle among you:
and my soul shall not *abhor* **loathe** you.
12 And I *will* **shall** walk among you,
and *will be your God* **shall be to you, Elohim**,
and ye shall *be my people* **be to me, people**.
13 *I am the LORD* **I — Yah Veh** your *God* **Elohim**,
which brought you forth
out of the land of *Egypt* **Misrayim**,
that ye should not be their *bondmen* **servants**;
and I have broken the *bands* **yoke poles** of your yoke,
and *made you go upright* **carried you erect**.

DISCIPLINE OF DISOBEDIENCE

14 But if ye *will* **shall** not hearken unto me,
and *will* **shall** not *do* **work**
all these *commandments* **misvoth**;
15 And if ye shall *despise* **spurn** my statutes,
or if your soul *abhor* **loathe** my judgments,
so that ye *will* **shall** not
do **work** all my *commandments* **misvoth**,
but that ye break my covenant:
16 I also *will do* **shall work** this unto you;
I *will even appoint* **shall visit** over you terror,
consumption **emaciation**, and the burning ague,
that shall *consume* **finish off** the eyes,
and cause *sorrow* **moping** of *heart* **soul**:
and ye shall *sow* **seed** your seed in vain,
for your enemies shall eat it.
17 And I *will set* **shall give** my face against you,
and ye shall be *slain* **smitten**

before **at the face of** your enemies:
they that hate you shall *reign over* **subjugate** you;
and ye shall flee when none pursueth you.
18 And if ye *will* **shall** not yet for all this hearken unto me,
then I *will punish* **shall add to discipline** you
seven times *more* for your sins.
19 And I *will* **shall** break
the *pride* **pomp** of your *power* **strength**;
and I *will make* **shall give** your *heaven* **heavens** as iron,
and your earth as *brass* **copper**:
20 And your *strength* **force**
shall be *spent* **consumed** in vain:
for **that** your land
shall not *yield* **give** her *increase* **produce**,
neither shall the trees of the land *yield* **give** their fruits.
21 And if ye walk contrary unto me,
and *will* **shall** not hearken unto me;
I *will bring* **shall add** seven *times more plagues* **strokes**
upon you according to your sins.
22 I *will* **shall** also send
wild beasts **live beings of the field** among you,
which shall *rob* **bereave** you *of your children*,
and *destroy* **cut** your *cattle* **animals**,
and *make* **diminish** you *few in number*;
and
your high ways shall be desolate **shall desolate your ways**.
23 And if ye *will* **shall** not be *reformed* **disciplined** by me
by these *things*,
but *will* **shall** walk contrary unto me;
24 Then *will* **shall** I also walk contrary unto you,
and *will punish* **shall smite** you
yet seven *times* for your sins.
25 And I *will* **shall** bring a sword upon you,
that shall avenge the *quarrel* **avenging** of my covenant:
and when ye are gathered *together within* **unto** your cities,
I *will* **shall** send the pestilence among you;
and ye shall be *delivered* **given**
into the hand of the enemy.
26 And when I have broken the *staff* **rod** of your bread,
ten women shall bake your bread in one oven,
and they shall *deliver you* **restore** your bread *again*
by weight:
and ye shall eat, and not *be satisfied* **satiate**.
27 And if ye *will* **shall** not for all this hearken unto me,
but walk contrary unto me;
28 Then I *will* **shall** walk contrary unto you also in fury;
and I, *even* **yea** I,
will chastise **shall discipline** you seven *times* for your sins.
29 And ye shall eat the flesh of your sons,
and the flesh of your daughters shall ye eat.
30 And I *will* **shall** destroy your *high places* **bamahs**,
and cut down your *images* **sun icons**,
and *cast* **give** your carcases
upon the carcases of your idols,
and my soul shall *abhor* **loathe** you.
31 And I *will make* **shall give** your cities
waste **parched areas**,
and *bring your sanctuaries unto desolation*
desolate your holies,
and I *will* **shall** not *smell* **scent**
the savour of your sweet odours **your scent of rest**.
32 And I *will* **shall**
bring the land into desolation **desolate the land**:
and your enemies which *dwell* **settle** therein
shall be *astonished at it* **desolated**.
33 And I *will* **shall** scatter you among the *heathen* **goyim**,
and *will* **shall** draw out a sword after you:
and your land shall be desolate,
and your cities *waste* **parched areas**.
34 Then shall the land
enjoy **be pleased in** her *sabbaths* **shabbaths**,
as long as it *lieth desolate* **desolateth**,
and ye be in your enemies' land;
even then shall the land *rest* **shabbathize**,
and *enjoy* **be pleased in** her *sabbaths* **shabbaths**.
35 As long as it *lieth desolate* **desolateth**
it shall *rest* **shabbathize**;
because it did not *rest* **shabbathize**
in your *sabbaths* **shabbaths**,
when ye *dwelt* **settled** upon it.
36 And upon them that *are left alive* **survive** of you
I *will* **shall** send a *faintness* **timidity** into their hearts
in the lands of their enemies;
and the *sound* **voice** of a *shaken* **driven** leaf
shall *chase* **pursue** them;
and they shall flee, as *fleeing* **retreating** from a sword;
and they shall fall when none pursueth.
37 And they shall *fall* **falter**
one upon another — **man to brother**,
as it were *before* **at the face of** a sword,
when none pursueth:
and ye shall have no *power to stand* **resistance**
before **at the face of** your enemies.
38 And ye shall *perish* **destruct** among the *heathen* **goyim**,
and the land of your enemies shall eat you up.
39 And they that *are left* **survive** of you
shall pine away in their *iniquity* **perversity**
in your enemies' lands;
and also in the *iniquities* **perversities** of their fathers
shall they pine away with them.

THE REWARD FOR WRINGING HANDS

40 If they shall *confess* **wring hands**
for their *iniquity* **perversity**,
and the *iniquity* **perversity** of their fathers,
with their *trespass* **treason**
which they *trespassed* **treasoned** against me,
and that also they have walked contrary unto me;
41 And that I also have walked contrary unto them,
and have brought them into the land of their enemies;
if then their uncircumcised hearts be humbled,
and they then *accept of* **be pleased**
in the punishment of their *iniquity* **perversity**:
42 Then *will* **shall** I remember
my covenant with *Jacob* **Yaaqov**,
and also my covenant with *Isaac* **Yischaq**,
and also my covenant with Abraham
will **shall** I remember;
and I *will* **shall** remember the land.
43 The land also shall be left of them,
and shall *enjoy* **be pleased in** her *sabbaths* **shabbaths**,
while she lieth desolate without them:
and they shall *accept* **be pleased**
of the punishment of their iniquity **in their perversity**:
because,
even because they *despised* **spurned** my judgments,
and because their soul *abhorred* **loathed** my statutes.
44 And *yet* **yea** for all that,
when they be in the land of their enemies,
I *will* **shall** not *cast* **spurn** them *away*,
neither *will* **shall** I *abhor* **loathe** them,
to *destroy* **finish** them *utterly* **off**,
and to break my covenant with them:
for *I am the LORD* **I — Yah Veh** their *God* **Elohim**.
45 But I *will* **shall** for their sakes
remember the covenant of their *ancestors* **first**,
whom I brought forth out of the land of *Egypt* **Misrayim**
in the *sight* **eyes** of the *heathen* **goyim**,
that I might be their *God* **Elohim**:
I am the LORD **I — Yah Veh**.
46 These are the statutes and judgments and *laws* **torahs**,
which *the LORD made* **Yah Veh gave** between him
and **between** the *children* **sons** of *Israel* **Yisra El**
in mount *Sinai* **Sinay** by the hand of *Moses* **Mosheh**.

TORAH ON VOWS

27 And *the LORD spake* **Yah Veh worded**
unto *Moses* **Mosheh**, saying,
2 *Speak* **Word** unto the *children* **sons** of *Israel* **Yisra El**,
and say unto them,
When a man shall *make a singular* **marvel** a vow,
the *persons* **souls** shall be for *the LORD* **Yah Veh**
by thy *estimation* **appraisal**.
3 And thy *estimation* **appraisal** shall be
of the male *from* **a son of** twenty years *old*
even unto **a son of** sixty years *old*,
even thy *estimation* **appraisal** shall be
fifty shekels of silver,
after the shekel of the *sanctuary* **holies**.
4 And if it be a female,
then thy *estimation* **appraisal** shall be
thirty shekels.

5 And if it be *from* **a son of** five years *old*
even unto **a son of** twenty years *old,*
then thy *estimation* **appraisal** shall be
of the male twenty shekels,
and for the female ten shekels.
6 And if *it be from* **a son of** a month *old*
even unto **a son of** five years *old,*
then thy *estimation* **appraisal** shall be
of the male five shekels of silver,
and for the female thy *estimation* **appraisal** shall be
three shekels of silver.
7 And if it be *from* **a son of** sixty years *old* and above;
if it be a male,
then thy *estimation* **appraisal** shall be
fifteen shekels,
and for the female ten shekels.
8 But if he be *poorer* **impoverished**
than thy estimation **beyond thy appraisal,**
then he shall *present* **stand** *himself*
before **at the face of** the priest,
and the priest shall *value* **appraise** him;
according to his *ability* **mouth as his hand hath attained**
that vowed shall the priest *value* **appraise** him.
9 And if it be *a beast* **an animal,**
whereof *men bring an offering* **he oblate a qorban**
unto *the LORD* **Yah Veh,**
all that *any man* **he** giveth of such
unto *the LORD* **Yah Veh** shall be holy.
10 He shall not *alter* **change** it,
nor *change* **exchange** it,
a good for *a bad* **an evil**, or *a bad* **an evil** for a good:
and if **in exchanging,** he shall *at all change* **exchange**
beast **animal** for *beast* **animal**,
then it and the exchange thereof shall be holy.
11 And if it be any *unclean beast* **fouled animal**,
of which they do not *offer* **oblate** a *sacrifice* **qorban**
unto *the LORD* **Yah Veh,**
then he shall *present* **stand** the *beast* **animal**
before **at the face of** the priest:
12 And the priest shall *value* **appraise** it,
whether it be good or *bad* **evil**:
as *thou valuest it* **thy appraisal**, who art the priest,
so shall it be.
13 But if **in redeeming,** he *will at all* **shall** redeem it,
then he shall add a fifth *part* thereof
unto thy *estimation* **appraisal**.
14 And when a man shall *sanctify* **hallow** his house
to be holy unto *the LORD* **Yah Veh,**
then the priest shall *estimate* **appraise** it,
whether it be good or *bad* **evil**:
as the priest shall *estimate* **appraise** it,
so shall it *stand* **be raised**.
15 And if he that *sanctified* **hallowed** it
will **shall** redeem his house,
then he shall add the fifth *part* of the *money* **silver**
of thy *estimation* **appraisal** unto it,
and it shall be his.
16 And if a man
shall *sanctify* **hallow** unto *the LORD* **Yah Veh**
some part of a field of his possession,
then thy *estimation* **appraisal** shall be
according to the **mouth of the** seed thereof:
an homer **a chomer** of barley seed
shall be valued at fifty shekels of silver.
17 If he *sanctify* **hallow** his field from the year of jubile,
according to thy *estimation* **appraisal**
it shall *stand* **be raised**.
18 But if he *sanctify* **hallow** his field after the jubile,
then the priest
shall *reckon* **fabricate** unto him the *money* **silver**
according to the **mouth of the** years that remain,
even unto the year of the jubile,
and it shall be abated from thy *estimation* **appraisal**.
19 And if he that *sanctified* **hallowed** the field
will in any wise **in redeeming, shall** redeem it,
then he shall add the fifth *part* of the *money* **silver**
of thy *estimation* **appraisal** unto it,
and it shall be *assured* **raised** to him.
20 And if he *will* **shall** not redeem the field,
or if he have sold the field to another man,
it shall not be redeemed any more.
21 But the field, when it goeth out in the jubile,
shall be holy unto *the LORD* **Yah Veh**, as a field devoted;
the possession thereof shall be the priest's.
22 And if *a man sanctify* **one hallow** unto *the LORD* **Yah Veh**
a field *which he hath bought* **of his chattel,**
which is not of the fields of his possession;
23 Then the priest shall *reckon* **fabricate** unto him
the worth of thy *estimation* **appraisal,**
even unto the year of the jubile:
and he shall give thine *estimation* **appraisal** in that day,
as a *holy thing* **holies** unto *the LORD* **Yah Veh.**
24 In the year of the jubile the field shall return unto him
of whom it was *bought* **chatteled,**
even to him
to whom the possession of the land *did belong* **be.**
25 And all thy *estimations* **appraisals**
shall be according to the shekel of the *sanctuary* **holies**:
twenty gerahs shall be the shekel.
26 Only the firstling of the *beasts* **animals,**
which should be *the LORD'S* **Yah Veh's** firstling,
no man shall *sanctify* **hallow** it;
whether it be ox, or *sheep* **lamb**:
it is *the LORD'S* **Yah Veh's.**
27 And if it be of *an unclean beast* **a fouled animal,**
then he shall redeem it
according to thine *estimation* **appraisal,**
and shall add a fifth *part of it* thereto:
or if it be not redeemed,
then it shall be sold according to thy *estimation* **appraisal.**
28 Notwithstanding *no* **naught** devoted *thing,*
that a man shall devote unto *the LORD* **Yah Veh**
of all that he hath,
both of man and beast **from human to animal,**
and of the field of his possession,
shall be sold or redeemed:
every **all** devoted *thing*
is *most holy* **a holy of holies** unto *the LORD* **Yah Veh.**
29 *None* **Naught** devoted,
which shall be devoted of *men* **humanity,**
shall be redeemed;
but **in deathifying,** shall *surely* be *put to death* **deathified.**
30 And all the tithe of the land,
whether of the seed of the land, or of the fruit of the tree,
is *the LORD'S* **Yah Veh's:**
it is — holy unto *the LORD* **Yah Veh.**
31 And if **in redeeming,**
a man will at all **he shall** redeem *ought* of his tithes,
he shall add thereto the fifth *part* thereof.
32 And concerning the tithe of the *herd* **oxen,**
or of the flock,
even of whatsoever passeth under the *rod* **scion,**
the tenth shall be holy unto *the LORD* **Yah Veh.**
33 He shall not search whether it be good or *bad* **evil,**
neither shall he change it:
and if **in changing,** he change it *at all,*
then both it and the change thereof shall be holy;
it shall not be redeemed.
34 These are the *commandments* **misvoth,**
which *the LORD* **Yah Veh**
commanded Moses **misvahed Mosheh**
for the *children* **sons** of *Israel* **Yisra El**
in mount *Sinai* **Sinay.**

KEY TO INTERPRETING THE EXEGESES:
King James text is in regular type;
Text under exegeses is in oblique type;
Text of exegeses is in bold type.

CENSUS OF THE SONS OF YISRA EL

1 And *the LORD spake* **Yah Veh worded**
unto *Moses* **Mosheh** in the wilderness of *Sinai* **Sinay**,
in the *tabernacle* **tent** of the congregation,
on the first *day* of the second month, in the second year
after they were come out
of the land of *Egypt* **Misrayim**, saying,
2 *Take* **Bear** ye the sum of all the *congregation* **witness**
of the *children* **sons** of *Israel* **Yisra El**,
after **by** their families, by the house of their fathers,
with the number of their names,
every male by their *polls* **craniums**;
3 *From* **Sons of** twenty years *old* and upward,
all that are able to go forth to *war* **hostility**
in *Israel* **Yisra El**:
thou and *Aaron* **Aharon**
shall *number* **muster** them by their *armies* **hosts**.
4 And with you there shall be a man *of every tribe* **per rod**;
every one head of the house of his fathers.
5 And these are the names of the men
that shall stand with you:
of the tribe of Reuben **Of Reu Ben**;
Elizur **Eli Sur** the son of *Shedeur* **Shedey Ur**.
6 Of *Simeon* **Shimon**;
Shelumiel **Shelumi El** the son of *Zurishaddai* **Suri Shadday**.
7 Of *Judah* **Yah Hudah**;
Nahshon the son of *Amminadab* **Ammi Nadab**.
8 Of *Issachar* **Yissachar**;
Nethaneel **Nethan El** the son of *Zuar* **Suar**.
9 Of Zebulun;
Eliab **Eli Ab** the son of Helon.
10 Of the *children* **sons** of *Joseph* **Yoseph**:
of *Ephraim* **Ephrayim**;
Elishama **Eli Shama** the son of *Ammihud* **Ammi Hud**:
of *Manasseh* **Menash Sheh**;
Gamaliel **Gamli El** the son of *Pedahzur* **Pedah Sur**.
11 Of *Benjamin* **Ben Yamin**;
Abidan **Abi Dan** the son of *Gideoni* **Gidoni**.
12 Of Dan;
Ahiezer **Achi Ezer** the son of *Ammishaddai* **Ammi Shaday**.
13 Of Asher;
Pagiel **Pagi El** the son of *Ocran* **Ochran**.
14 Of Gad;
Eliasaph **Eli Yasaph** the son of *Deuel* **Deu El**.
15 Of Naphtali;
Ahira **Achi Ra** the son of Enan.
16 These were the *renowned* **called**
of the *congregation* **witness**,
princes **hierarchs** of the *tribes* **rods** of their fathers,
heads of thousands in *Israel* **Yisra El**.
17 And *Moses* **Mosheh** and *Aaron* **Aharon** took these men
which are *expressed* **appointed** by their names:
18 And they *assembled* **congregated**
all the *congregation* **witness** *together*
on the first *day* of the second month,
and they declared their *pedigrees after* **births**
by their families, by the house of their fathers,
according to the number of the names,
from **sons of** twenty years *old* and upward,
by their *polls* **craniums**.
19 As *the LORD* **Yah Veh**
commanded Moses **misvahed Mosheh**,
so he *numbered* **mustered** them
in the wilderness of *Sinai* **Sinay**.
20 And the *children* **sons** of *Reuben* **Reu Ben**,
Israel's eldest son **Yisra El's firstborn**,
by their generations, *after* **by** their families,
by the house of their fathers,
according to the number of the names,
by their *polls* **craniums**,
every male **son** from twenty years *old* and upward,
all that were able to go forth to *war* **hostility**;
21 Those that were *numbered* **mustered** of them,
even of the *tribe* **rod** of *Reuben* **Reu Ben**,
were forty and six thousand and five hundred.
22 Of the *children* **sons** of *Simeon* **Shimon**,
by their generations, *after* **by** their families,
by the house of their fathers,
those that were *numbered* **mustered** of them,
according to the number of the names,
by their *polls* **craniums**,
every male **son** from twenty years *old* and upward,
all that were able to go forth to *war* **hostility**;
23 Those that were *numbered* **mustered** of them,
even of the *tribe* **rod** of *Simeon* **Shimon**,
were fifty and nine thousand and three hundred.
24 Of the *children* **sons** of Gad,
by their generations, *after* **by** their families,
by the house of their fathers,
according to the number of the names,
from **sons of** twenty years *old* and upward,
all that were able to go forth to *war* **hostility**;
25 Those that were *numbered* **mustered** of them,
even of the *tribe* **rod** of Gad,
were forty and five thousand six hundred and fifty.
26 Of the *children* **sons** of *Judah* **Yah Hudah**,
by their generations, *after* **by** their families,
by the house of their fathers,
according to the number of the names,
from **sons of** twenty years *old* and upward,
all that were able to go forth to *war* **hostility**;
27 Those that were *numbered* **mustered** of them,
even of the *tribe* **rod** of *Judah* **Yah Hudah**,
were *threescore and fourteen* **seventy and four** thousand
and six hundred.
28 Of the *children* **sons** of *Issachar* **Yissachar**,
by their generations, *after* **by** their families,
by the house of their fathers,
according to the number of the names,
from **sons of** twenty years *old* and upward,
all that were able to go forth to *war* **hostility**;
29 Those that were *numbered* **mustered** of them,
even of the *tribe* **rod** of *Issachar* **Yissachar**,
were fifty and four thousand and four hundred.
30 Of the *children* **sons** of Zebulun, by their generations,
after **by** their families, by the house of their fathers,
according to the number of the names,
from **sons of** twenty years *old* and upward,
all that were able to go forth to *war* **hostility**;
31 Those that were *numbered* **mustered** of them,
even of the *tribe* **rod** of Zebulun,
were fifty and seven thousand and four hundred.
32 Of the *children* **sons** of *Joseph* **Yoseph**, *namely*,
of the *children* **sons** of *Ephraim* **Ephrayim**,
by their generations, *after* **by** their families,
by the house of their fathers,
according to the number of the names,
from **sons of** twenty years *old* and upward,
all that were able to go forth to *war* **hostility**;
33 Those that were *numbered* **mustered** of them,
even of the *tribe* **rod** of *Ephraim* **Ephrayim**,
were forty thousand and five hundred.
34 Of the *children* **sons** of *Manasseh* **Menash Sheh**,
by their generations, *after* **by** their families,
by the house of their fathers,
according to the number of the names,
from **sons of** twenty years *old* and upward,
all that were able to go forth to *war* **hostility**;
35 Those that were *numbered* **mustered** of them,
even of the *tribe* **rod** of *Manasseh* **Menash Sheh**,
were thirty and two thousand and two hundred.
36 Of the *children* **sons** of *Benjamin* **Ben Yamin**,
by their generations, *after* **by** their families,
by the house of their fathers,
according to the number of the names,
from sons of twenty years *old* and upward,
all that were able to go forth to *war* **hostility**;
37 Those that were *numbered* **mustered** of them,
even of the *tribe* **rod** of *Benjamin* **Ben Yamin**,
were thirty and five thousand and four hundred.
38 Of the *children* **sons** of Dan, by their generations,
after **by** their families, by the house of their fathers,
according to the number of the names,
from **sons of** twenty years *old* and upward,
all that were able to go forth to *war* **hostility**;
39 Those that were *numbered* **mustered** of them,

even of the *tribe* **rod** of Dan,
were *threescore* **sixty** and two thousand
and seven hundred.
40 Of the *children* **sons** of Asher,
by their generations, *after* **by** their families,
by the house of their fathers,
according to the number of the names,
from **sons of** twenty years *old* and upward,
all that were able to go forth to *war* **hostility**;
41 Those that were *numbered* **mustered** of them,
even of the *tribe* **rod** of Asher,
were forty and one thousand and five hundred.
42 Of the *children* **sons** of Naphtali,
throughout their generations, *after* **by** their families,
by the house of their fathers,
according to the number of the names,
from **sons of** twenty years *old* and upward,
all that were able to go forth to *war* **hostility**;
43 Those that were *numbered* **mustered** of them,
even of the *tribe* **rod** of Naphtali,
were fifty and three thousand and four hundred.
44 These are those that were *numbered* **mustered**,
which *Moses* **Mosheh** and *Aaron* **Aharon**
numbered **mustered**,
and the *princes* **hierarchs** of *Israel* **Yisra El**,
being twelve men:
each *one* **man** was for the house of his fathers.
45 So were all those that were *numbered* **mustered**
of the *children* **sons** of *Israel* **Yisra El**,
by the house of their fathers,
from **sons of** twenty years *old* and upward,
all that were able to go forth to *war* **hostility**
in *Israel* **Yisra El**;
46 Even all they that were *numbered* **mustered**
were six hundred thousand and three thousand
and five hundred and fifty.
47 But the *Levites* **Leviym**
after **by** the *tribe* **rod** of their fathers
were not *numbered* **mustered** among them.
48 For *the LORD* **Yah Veh** had *spoken* **worded**
unto *Moses* **Mosheh**, saying,
49 Only thou shalt not *number* **muster**
the *tribe* **rod** of Levi,
neither *take* **lift** the *sum* **heads** of them
among the *children* **sons** of *Israel* **Yisra El**:
50 But thou shalt *appoint* **have** the *Levites* **Leviym**
oversee over the tabernacle of *testimony* **witness**,
and over all the *vessels* **instruments** thereof,
and over all *things* that belong to it:
they shall bear the tabernacle,
and all the *vessels* **instruments** thereof;
and they shall minister unto it,
and shall encamp round about the tabernacle.
51 And when the tabernacle *setteth forward* **pulleth stakes**,
the *Levites* **Leviym** shall *take it down* **lower it**:
and when the tabernacle is *to be pitched* **encamped**,
the *Levites* **Leviym** shall *set* **raise** it *up*:
and the stranger that *cometh nigh* **approacheth**
shall be *put to death* **deathified**.
52 And the *children* **sons** of *Israel* **Yisra El**
shall *pitch their tents* **encamp**,
every man by his own camp,
and every man by his own *standard* **banner**,
throughout their hosts.
53 But the *Levites* **Leviym** shall *pitch* **encamp**
round about the tabernacle of *testimony* **witness**,
that there be no *wrath* **rage**
upon the *congregation* **witness**
of the *children* **sons** of *Israel* **Yisra El**:
and the *Levites* **Leviym** shall *keep* **guard** the *charge* **guard**
of the tabernacle of *testimony* **witness**.
54 And the *children* **sons** of *Israel* **Yisra El**
did **worked** according to all that *the LORD* **Yah Veh**
commanded Moses **misvahed Mosheh**,
so *did* **worked** they.

CAMPS OF THE SONS OF YISRA EL

2 And *the LORD spake* **Yah Veh worded**
unto *Moses* **Mosheh** and unto *Aaron* **Aharon**, saying,
2 Every man of the *children* **sons** of *Israel* **Yisra El**
shall *pitch* **encamp** by his own *standard* **banner**,
with the ensign of their father's house:
far off about **in front and round about**
the *tabernacle* **tent** of the congregation
shall they *pitch* **encamp**.
3 And on the east side toward the rising *of the sun*
shall they of the *standard* **banner**
of the camp of *Judah* **Yah Hudah**
pitch throughout their *armies* **hosts**:
and Nahshon the son of *Amminadab* **Ammi Nadab**,
shall be *captain* **hierarch**
of the *children* **sons** of *Judah* **Yah Hudah**.
4 And his host,
and those that were *numbered* **mustered** of them,
were threescore and fourteen **seventy and four** thousand
and six hundred.
5 And those that do pitch next unto him
shall be the *tribe* **rod** of *Issachar* **Yissachar**:
and *Nethaneel* **Nethan El** the son of *Zuar* **Suar,**
shall be *captain* **hierarch**
of the *children* **sons** of *Issachar* **Yissachar**.
6 And his host,
and those that were *numbered* **mustered** thereof,
were fifty and four thousand and four hundred.
7 Then the *tribe* **rod** of Zebulun:
and *Eliab* **Eli Ab** the son of Helon,
shall be *captain* **hierarch** of the *children* **sons** of Zebulun.
8 And his host,
and those that were *numbered* **mustered** thereof,
were fifty and seven thousand and four hundred.
9 All that were *numbered* **mustered**
in the camp of *Judah* **Yah Hudah**
were an hundred thousand and *fourscore* **eighty** thousand
and six thousand and four hundred,
throughout their *armies* **hosts**.
These shall first *set forth* **pull stakes**.
10 *On the south side* **Southward,**
shall be the *standard* **banner**
of the camp of *Reuben* **Reu Ben**
according to their *armies* **hosts**:
and the *captain* **hierarch**
of the *children* **sons** of *Reuben* **Reu Ben,**
shall be *Elizur* **Eli Sur** the son of *Shedeur* **Shedey Ur**.
11 And his host,
and those that were *numbered* **mustered** thereof,
were forty and six thousand and five hundred.
12 And those which pitch by him
shall be the *tribe* **rod** of *Simeon* **Shimon**:
and the *captain* **hierarch**
of the *children* **sons** of *Simeon* **Shimon,**
shall be *Shelumiel* **Shelumi El**
the son of *Zurishaddai* **Suri Shadday**.
13 And his host,
and those that were *numbered* **mustered** of them,
were fifty and nine thousand and three hundred.
14 Then the *tribe* **rod** of Gad:
and the *captain* **hierarch** of the sons of Gad,
shall be *Eliasaph* **Eli Yasaph** the son of *Reuel* **Reu El**.
15 And his host,
and those that were *numbered* **mustered** of them,
were forty and five thousand and six hundred and fifty.
16 All that were *numbered* **mustered**
in the camp of *Reuben* **Reu Ben**
were an hundred thousand and fifty and one thousand
and four hundred and fifty,
throughout their *armies* **hosts**.
And they shall *set forth* **pull stakes** in the second *rank*.
17 Then the *tabernacle* **tent** of the congregation
shall *set forward* **pull stakes**
with the camp of the *Levites* **Leviym**
in the midst of the camp:
as they encamp, so shall they *set forward* **pull stakes**,
man — every man *in his place* **at hand**
by their *standards* **banners**.
18 *On the west side* **Seaward,**
shall be the *standard* **banner**
of the camp of *Ephraim* **Ephrayim**
according to their *armies* **hosts**:
and the *captain* **hierarch** of the sons of *Ephraim* **Ephrayim,**
shall be *Elishama* **Eli Shama**
the son of *Ammihud* **Ammi Hud**.

19 And his host,
and those that were *numbered* **mustered** of them,
were forty thousand and five hundred.
20 And by him
shall be the *tribe* **rod** of *Manasseh* **Menash Sheh**:
and the *captain* **hierarch**
of the *children* **sons** of *Manasseh* **Menash Sheh**
shall be *Gamaliel* **Gamli El**
the son of *Pedahzur* **Pedah Sur**.
21 And his host,
and those that were *numbered* **mustered** of them,
were thirty and two thousand and two hundred.
22 Then the *tribe* **rod** of *Benjamin* **Ben Yamin**:
and the *captain* **hierarch** of the sons of *Benjamin* **Ben Yamin,**
shall be *Abidan* **Abi Dan** the son of *Gideoni* **Gidoni**.
23 And his host,
and those that were *numbered* **mustered** of them,
were thirty and five thousand and four hundred.
24 All that were *numbered* **mustered**
of the camp of *Ephraim* **Ephrayim**
were an hundred thousand
and eight thousand and an hundred,
throughout their *armies* **hosts**.
And they shall *go forward* **pull stakes** in the third *rank*.
25 The *standard* **banner** of the camp of Dan,
shall be on the north side by their *armies* **hosts**:
and the *captain* **hierarch** of the *children* **sons** of Dan,
shall be *Ahiezer* **Achi Ezer**
the son of *Ammishaddai* **Ammi Shaday**.
26 And his host,
and those that were *numbered* **mustered** of them,
were threescore **sixty** and two thousand
and seven hundred.
27 And those that encamp by him,
shall be the *tribe* **rod** of Asher:
and the *captain* **hierarch** of the *children* **sons** of Asher,
shall be *Pagiel* **Pagi El** the son of *Ocran* **Ochran**.
28 And his host,
and those that were *numbered* **mustered** of them,
were forty and one thousand and five hundred.
29 Then the *tribe* **rod** of Naphtali:
and the *captain* **hierarch** of the *children* **sons** of Naphtali,
shall be *Ahira* **Achi Ra** the son of Enan.
30 And his host,
and those that were *numbered* **mustered** of them,
were fifty and three thousand and four hundred.
31 All they that were *numbered* **mustered**
in the camp of Dan,
were an hundred thousand and fifty and seven thousand
and six hundred.
They shall *go hindmost* **pull stakes behind**
with their *standards* **banners**.
32 These are those which were *numbered* **mustered**
of the *children* **sons** of *Israel* **Yisra El**
by the house of their fathers:
all those that were *numbered* **mustered**
of the camps throughout their hosts,
were six hundred thousand and three thousand
and five hundred and fifty.
33 But the *Levites* **Leviym** were not *numbered* **mustered**
among the *children* **sons** of *Israel* **Yisra El**;
as *the LORD* **Yah Veh**
commanded Moses **misvahed Mosheh**.
34 And the *children* **sons** of *Israel* **Yisra El**
did **worked** according to all
that *the LORD* **Yah Veh**
commanded Moses **misvahed Mosheh**:
so they *pitched* **encamped** by their *standards* **banners**,
and so they *set forward* **pulled stakes**,
every one after **man — every man by** their families,
according to the house of their fathers.

PRIESTS OF THE SONS OF YISRA EL

3 These also are the generations
of *Aaron* **Aharon** and *Moses* **Mosheh**
in the day that *the LORD spake* **Yah Veh worded**
with *Moses* **Mosheh** in mount *Sinai* **Sinay**.
2 And these are the names of the sons of *Aaron* **Aharon**;
Nadab the firstborn, and *Abihu* **Abi Hu**,
Eleazar **El Azar**, and *Ithamar* **Iy Thamar**.
3 These are the names of the sons of *Aaron* **Aharon**,
the priests which were anointed,
whom he consecrated **whose hand he filled**
to *minister in the priest's office* **priest the priesthood**.
4 And Nadab and *Abihu* **Abi Hu**
died *before the LORD* **at the face of Yah Veh**,
when they *offered* **oblated** strange fire
before the LORD **at the face of Yah Veh**,
in the wilderness of *Sinai* **Sinay**,
and they had no *children* **sons**:
and *Eleazar* **El Azar** and *Ithamar* **Iy Thamar**
ministered in the priest's office **priested the priesthood**
in the sight of Aaron **at the face of Aharon** their father.
5 And *the LORD spake* **Yah Veh worded**
unto *Moses* **Mosheh,** saying,
6 *Bring* **Oblate** the *tribe* **rod** of Levi *near*,
and *present* **stand** them
before Aaron **at the face of Aharon** the priest,
that they may minister unto him.
7 And they shall *keep* **guard** his *charge* **guard**,
and the *charge* **guard** of the whole *congregation* **witness**
before **at the face**
of the *tabernacle* **tent** of the congregation,
to *do* **serve** the service of the tabernacle.
8 And they shall *keep* **guard** all the instruments
of the *tabernacle* **tent** of the congregation,
and the *charge* **guard**
of the *children* **sons** of *Israel* **Yisra El**,
to *do* **serve** the service of the tabernacle.
9 And thou shalt give the *Levites* **Leviym**
unto *Aaron* **Aharon** and to his sons:
in giving, they are *wholly* given unto him
out of the *children* **sons** of *Israel* **Yisra El**.
10 And thou shalt
appoint Aaron **muster Aharon** and his sons,
and they shall
wait on **guard** their *priest's office* **priesthood**:
and the stranger that *cometh nigh* **approacheth,**
shall be *put to death* **deathified**.
11 And *the LORD spake* **Yah Veh worded**
unto *Moses* **Mosheh,** saying,
12 And I, behold, I have taken the *Levites* **Leviym**
from among the *children* **sons** of *Israel* **Yisra El**
instead of all the firstborn that *openeth* **bursteth** the matrix
among the *children* **sons** of *Israel* **Yisra El**:
therefore the *Levites* **Leviym** shall be mine;
13 Because all the firstborn are mine;
for on the day that I smote all the firstborn
in the land of *Egypt* **Misrayim**
I hallowed unto me all the firstborn in *Israel* **Yisra El**,
both man and beast **from human to animal**:
mine shall they be:
I am the LORD **I — Yah Veh**.
14 And *the LORD spake* **Yah Veh worded**
unto *Moses* **Mosheh** in the wilderness of *Sinai* **Sinay**,
saying,
15 *Number* **Muster** the *children* **sons** of Levi
after **by** the house of their fathers, by their families:
every male, *from* **a son of** a month *old* and upward,
shalt thou *number* **muster** them.
16 And *Moses numbered* **Mosheh mustered** them
according to the *word* **mouth** of *the LORD* **Yah Veh**,
as he was *commanded* **misvahed**.
17 And these were the sons of Levi by their names;
Gershon, and *Kohath* **Qehath**, and Merari.
18 And these are the names of the sons of Gershon
by their families;
Libni, and *Shimei* **Shimiy**.
19 And the sons of *Kohath* **Qehath** by their families;
Amram **Am Ram**, and *Izehar* **Yishar**,
Hebron, and *Uzziel* **Uzzi El**.
20 And the sons of Merari by their families;
Mahli **Machli**, and Mushi.
These are the families of the *Levites* **Leviym**
according to the house of their fathers.
21 Of Gershon was the family of the *Libnites* **Libniy**,
and the family of the *Shimites* **Shimiy**:
these are the families of the *Gershonites* **Gershoniy**.
22 Those that were *numbered* **mustered** of them,
according to the number of all the males,
from **sons of** a month *old* and upward,

even those that were *numbered* **mustered** of them
were seven thousand and five hundred.
23 The families of the *Gershonites* **Gershoniy**
shall *pitch* **encamp**
behind the tabernacle *westward* **seaward**.
24 And the *chief* **hierarch**
of the house of the father of the *Gershonites* **Gershoniy,**
shall be *Eliasaph* **Eli Yasaph** the son of *Lael* **La El**.

SERVICE OF THE SONS OF GERSHON

25 And the *charge* **guard** of the sons of Gershon
in the *tabernacle* **tent** of the congregation,
shall be the tabernacle, and the tent,
the covering thereof,
and the *hanging* **covering** for the *door* **opening**
of the *tabernacle* **tent** of the congregation,
26 And the hangings of the court,
and the *curtain* **covering** for the *door* **opening** of the court,
which is by the tabernacle,
and by the **sacrifice** altar round about,
and the cords of it for all the service thereof.
27 And of *Kohath* **Qehath**
was the family of the *Amramites* **Am Ramiy**,
and the family of the *Izeharites* **Yishariy**,
and the family of the *Hebronites* **Hebroniy**,
and the family of the *Uzzielites* **Uzzi Eliy**:
these are the families of the *Kohathites* **Qehathiy**.
28 In the number of all the males,
from **sons of** a month *old* and upward,
were eight thousand and six hundred,
keeping **guarding** the *charge* **guard** of the *sanctuary* **holies**.
29 The families of the sons of *Kohath* **Qehath**
shall *pitch* **encamp** on the *side* **flank** of the tabernacle
southward.
30 And the *chief* **hierarch** of the house
of the father of the families of the *Kohathites* **Qehathiy,**
shall be *Elizaphan* **El Saphan** the son of *Uzziel* **Uzzi El**.
31 And their *charge* **guard** shall be the ark, and the table,
and the *candlestick* **menorah**, and the **sacrifice** altars,
and the *vessels* **instruments** of the *sanctuary* **holies**
wherewith they minister,
and the *hanging* **covering**, and all the service thereof.
32 And *Eleazar* **El Azar** the son of *Aaron* **Aharon** the priest,
shall be *chief* **hierarch**
over the *chief* **hierarchy** of the *Levites* **Leviym**,
and have the oversight of them
that *keep* **guard** the *charge* **guard** of the *sanctuary* **holies.**
33 Of Merari was the family of the *Mahlites* **Machliy**,
and the family of the *Mushites* **Mushiy**:
these are the families of Merari.
34 And those that were *numbered* **mustered** of them,
according to the number of all the males,
from **sons of** a month *old* and upward,
were six thousand and two hundred.
35 And the *chief* **hierarch** of the house
of the father of the families of Merari,
was Zuriel **Suri El** the son of *Abihail* **Abi Hail**:
these shall *pitch* **encamp**
on the *side* **flank** of the tabernacle northward.
36 And under the *custody* **oversight** and *charge* **guard**
of the sons of Merari,
shall be the boards of the tabernacle,
and the bars thereof,
and the pillars thereof, and the sockets thereof,
and all the *vessels* **instruments** thereof,
and all *that serveth* **the service** thereto,
37 And the pillars of the court round about,
and their sockets, and their *pins* **stakes**, and their cords.
38 But those that encamp
before **at the face of** the tabernacle toward the *east* **rising**,
even before **at the face of**
the *tabernacle* **tent** of the congregation
eastward **dawnward**,
shall be *Moses* **Mosheh**, and *Aaron* **Aharon** and his sons,
keeping **guarding** the *charge* **guard** of the *sanctuary* **holies**
for the *charge* **guard** of the *children* **sons** of *Israel* **Yisra El**;
and the stranger that cometh nigh
shall be *put to death* **deathified**.
39 All that were *numbered* **mustered** of the *Levites* **Leviym**,
which *Moses* **Mosheh** and *Aaron* **Aharon**
numbered **mustered**
at the *commandment* **mouth** of *the LORD* **Yah Veh**,
throughout their families,
all the males *from* **sons of** a month *old* and upward,
were twenty and two thousand.
40 And *the LORD* **Yah Veh** said unto *Moses* **Mosheh**,
Number **Muster** all the firstborn of the males
of the *children* **sons** of *Israel* **Yisra El**
from **sons of** a month *old* and upward,
and *take* **bear** the number of their names.
41 And thou shalt take the *Levites* **Leviym** for me
(*I am the LORD* **I — Yah Veh**)
instead of all the firstborn
among the *children* **sons** of *Israel* **Yisra El**;
and the *cattle* **animals** of the *Levites* **Leviym**
instead of all the firstlings among the *cattle* **animals**
of the *children* **sons** of *Israel* **Yisra El**.
42 And *Moses numbered* **Mosheh mustered,**
as *the LORD commanded* **Yah Veh misvahed** him,
all the firstborn among the *children* **sons** of *Israel* **Yisra El**.
43 And all the firstborn males by the number of names,
from **sons of** a month *old* and upward,
of those that were *numbered* **mustered** of them,
were twenty and two thousand two hundred
and *threescore and thirteen* **seventy and three**.
44 And *the LORD spake* **Yah Veh worded**
unto *Moses* **Mosheh,** saying,
45 Take the *Levites* **Leviym** instead of all the firstborn
among the *children* **sons** of *Israel* **Yisra El**,
and the *cattle* **animals** of the *Levites* **Leviym**
instead of their *cattle* **animals**;
and the *Levites* **Leviym** shall be mine:
I am the LORD **I — Yah Veh**.
46 And for those that are to be redeemed
of the two hundred
and *threescore and thirteen* **seventy and three**
of the firstborn of the *children* **sons** of *Israel* **Yisra El**,
which are *more than* **left over of** the *Levites* **Leviym**;
47 Thou shalt even take
five — five shekels *apiece by the poll* **per cranium**,
after the shekel of the *sanctuary* **holies**
shalt thou take them:
(the shekel is twenty gerahs:)
48 And thou shalt give the *money* **silver**,
wherewith *the odd number of them* **they who are left over**
is **are** to be redeemed,
unto *Aaron* **Aharon** and to his sons.
49 And *Moses* **Mosheh** took the redemption *money* **silver**
of them that were *over and above* **left over of** them
that were redeemed by the *Levites* **Leviym**:
50 Of the firstborn of the *children* **sons** of *Israel* **Yisra El**
took he the *money* **silver**;
a thousand three hundred
and *threescore* **sixty** and five *shekels*,
after the shekel of the *sanctuary* **holies**:
51 And *Moses* **Mosheh** gave the *money* **silver**
of *them that were redeemed* **redemption**
unto *Aaron* **Aharon** and to his sons,
according to the *word* **mouth** of *the LORD* **Yah Veh**,
as *the LORD* **Yah Veh**
commanded Moses **misvahed Mosheh**.

SERVICE OF THE SONS OF QEHATH

4 And *the LORD spake* **Yah Veh worded**
unto *Moses* **Mosheh** and unto *Aaron* **Aharon**, saying,
2 *Take* **Bear** the *sum* **heads** of the sons of *Kohath* **Qehath**
from among the sons of Levi,
after **by** their families, by the house of their fathers,
3 *From* **Sons of** thirty years *old* and upward
even until **sons of** fifty years *old*,
all that enter into the host,
to *do* **work** the work
in the *tabernacle* **tent** of the congregation.
4 This shall be the service of the sons of *Kohath* **Qehath**
in the *tabernacle* **tent** of the congregation,
about the *most holy things* **holy of holies**:
5 And when the camp *setteth forward* **pulleth stakes**,
Aaron **Aharon** shall come, and his sons,
and they shall *take down* **lower** the covering vail,
and cover the ark of *testimony* **witness** with it:
6 And shall *put* **give** thereon
the covering of badgers' skins,

and shall spread over it a cloth *wholly of* **totally** blue,
and shall put in the staves thereof.
7 And upon the table of *shewbread* **face bread**
they shall spread a cloth of blue,
and *put* **give** thereon the dishes, and the spoons,
and the *bowls* **exoneration basins**,
and covers *to cover withal* **of libation**:
and the continual bread shall be thereon:
8 And they shall spread upon them a cloth of scarlet,
and cover the same with a covering of badgers' skins,
and shall put in the staves thereof.
9 And they shall take a cloth of blue,
and cover the *candlestick* **menorah** of the light,
and his lamps, and his tongs, and his *snuffdishes* **trays**,
and all the oil *vessels* **instruments** thereof,
wherewith they minister unto it:
10 And they shall *put* **give** it
and all the *vessels* **instruments** thereof
within a covering of badgers' skins,
and shall *put* **give** it upon a *bar* **pole**.
11 And upon the golden **sacrifice** altar
they shall spread a cloth of blue,
and cover it with a covering of badgers' skins,
and shall put to the staves thereof:
12 And they shall take all the instruments of ministry,
wherewith they minister in the *sanctuary* **holies**,
and *put* **give** them in a cloth of blue,
and cover them with a covering of badgers' skins,
and shall *put* **give** them on a *bar* **pole**:
13 And they shall
take away the ashes from **de—fat** the **sacrifice** altar,
and spread a purple cloth thereon:
14 And they shall *put* **give** upon it
all the *vessels* **instruments** thereof,
wherewith they minister about it,
even the *censers* **trays**, the *fleshhooks* **forks**,
and the shovels, and the *basons* **sprinklers**,
all the *vessels* **instruments** of the **sacrifice** altar;
and they shall spread upon it
a covering of badgers' skins,
and put to the staves of it.
15 And when *Aaron* **Aharon** and his sons
have *made an end of* **finished**
covering the *sanctuary* **holies**,
and all the *vessels* **instruments** of the *sanctuary* **holies**,
as the camp is to *set forward* **pull stakes**;
after that,
the sons of *Kohath* **Qehath** shall come to bear it:
but they shall not touch *any holy thing* **the holies**,
lest they die.
These *things* are the burden of the sons of *Kohath* **Qehath**
in the *tabernacle* **tent** of the congregation.
16 And to the *office* **oversight** of *Eleazar* **El Azar**
the son of *Aaron* **Aharon** the priest
pertaineth the oil for the light,
and the *sweet* incense **of aromatics**,
and the *daily meat* **continual** offering,
and the anointing oil,
and the oversight of all the tabernacle,
and of all that therein is, in the *sanctuary* **holies**,
and in the *vessels* **instruments** thereof.
17 And *the LORD spake* **Yah Veh worded**
unto *Moses* **Mosheh** and unto *Aaron* **Aharon**, saying,
18 Cut ye not off
the *tribe* **scion** of the families of the *Kohathites* **Qehathiy**
from among the *Levites* **Leviym**:
19 But thus *do* **work** unto them,
that they may live, and not die,
when they approach
unto the *most holy things* **holy of holies**:
Aaron **Aharon** and his sons shall go in,
and *appoint* **set** them *every one* **man by man**
to his service and to his burden:
20 But they shall not go in to see
when the *holy things* **holies** are *covered* **swallowed**,
lest they die.

SERVICE OF THE SONS OF GERSHON

21 And *the LORD spake* **Yah Veh worded**
unto *Moses* **Mosheh,** saying,
22 *Take* **Bear** also the *sum* **heads** of the sons of Gershon,
throughout the houses of their fathers, by their families;
23 *From* **Sons of** thirty years *old* and upward
until **sons of** fifty years *old*
shalt thou *number* **muster** them;
all that enter in to *perform* **host** the *service* **hosting**,
to *do* **serve** the work
in the *tabernacle* **tent** of the congregation.
24 This is the service
of the families of the *Gershonites* **Gershoniy**,
to serve, and for burdens:
25 And they shall bear the curtains of the tabernacle,
and the *tabernacle* **tent** of the congregation, his covering,
and the covering of the badgers' skins
that is above upon it,
and the *hanging* **covering** for the *door* **opening**
of the *tabernacle* **tent** of the congregation,
26 And the hangings of the court,
and the *hanging* **covering** for the *door* **opening**
of the *gate* **portal** of the court,
which is by the tabernacle
and by the **sacrifice** altar round about,
and their cords, and all the instruments of their service,
and all that is *made* **worked** for them: so shall they serve.
27 At the *appointment* **mouth**
of *Aaron* **Aharon** and his sons shall be all the service
of the sons of the *Gershonites* **Gershoniy**,
in all their burdens, and in all their service:
and ye shall *appoint* **muster** unto them
in charge **guard of** all their burdens.
28 This is the service
of the families of the sons of Gershon
in the *tabernacle* **tent** of the congregation:
and their *charge* **guard** shall be
under the hand of *Ithamar* **Iy Thamar**
the son of *Aaron* **Aharon** the priest.

SERVICE OF THE SONS OF MERARI

29 As for the sons of Merari,
thou shalt *number* **muster** them *after* **by** their families,
by the house of their fathers;
30 *From* **Sons of** thirty years *old* and upward
even unto **sons of** fifty years *old*
shalt thou *number* **muster** them,
every one that entereth into the *service* **hosting**,
to *do the work* **serve the service**
of the *tabernacle* **tent** of the congregation.
31 And this is the *charge* **guard** of their burden,
according to all their service
in the *tabernacle* **tent** of the congregation;
the boards of the tabernacle, and the bars thereof,
and the pillars thereof, and sockets thereof,
32 And the pillars of the court round about,
and their sockets, and their *pins* **stakes**, and their cords,
with all their instruments, and with all their service:
and by name,
ye shall *reckon* **muster** the instruments
of the *charge* **guard** of their burden.
33 This is the service of the families of the sons of Merari,
according to all their service,
in the *tabernacle* **tent** of the congregation,
under the hand of *Ithamar* **Iy Thamar**
the son of *Aaron* **Aharon** the priest.

MUSTERING OF THE PRIESTS

34 And *Moses* **Mosheh** and *Aaron* **Aharon**
and the *chief* **hierarch** of the *congregation* **witness**
numbered **mustered** the sons of the *Kohathites* **Qehathiy**
after **by** their families,
and *after* **by** the house of their fathers,
35 *From* **Sons of** thirty years *old* and upward
even unto **sons of** fifty years *old*,
every one that entereth into the *service* **hosting**,
for the *work* **service**
in the *tabernacle* **tent** of the congregation:
36 And those that were *numbered* **mustered** of them
by their families,
were two thousand seven hundred and fifty.
37 These were they that were *numbered* **mustered**
of the families of the *Kohathites* **Qehathiy**,
all that might *do service* **serve**
in the *tabernacle* **tent** of the congregation,
which *Moses* **Mosheh** and *Aaron* **Aharon**

did number **mustered** according to
the *commandment* **mouth** of *the LORD* **Yah Veh**
by the hand of *Moses* **Mosheh**.
38 And those that were *numbered* **mustered**
of the sons of Gershon,
throughout their families, and by the house of their fathers,
39 *From* **Sons of** thirty years *old* and upward
even unto **sons of** fifty years *old*,
every one that entereth into the *service* **hosting**,
for the *work* **service**
in the *tabernacle* **tent** of the congregation,
40 Even those that were *numbered* **mustered** of them,
throughout their families, by the house of their fathers,
were two thousand and six hundred and thirty.
41 These are they that were *numbered* **mustered**
of the families of the sons of Gershon,
of all that might *do service* **serve**
in the *tabernacle* **tent** of the congregation,
whom *Moses* **Mosheh** and *Aaron* **Aharon**
did number **mustered** according to
the *commandment* **mouth** of *the LORD* **Yah Veh**.
42 And those that were *numbered* **mustered**
of the families of the sons of Merari,
throughout their families, by the house of their fathers,
43 *From* **Sons of** thirty years *old* and upward
even unto **sons of** fifty years *old*,
every one that entereth into the *service* **hosting**,
for the *work* **service**
in the *tabernacle* **tent** of the congregation,
44 Even those that were *numbered* **mustered** of them
after **by** their families,
were three thousand and two hundred.
45 These be those that were *numbered* **mustered**
of the families of the sons of Merari,
whom *Moses* **Mosheh** and *Aaron* **Aharon**
numbered **mustered**
according to the *word* **mouth** of *the LORD* **Yah Veh**
by the hand of *Moses* **Mosheh**.
46 All those that were *numbered* **mustered**
of the *Levites* **Leviym**,
whom *Moses* **Mosheh** and *Aaron* **Aharon**
and the *chief* **hierarch** of *Israel* **Yisra El**
numbered **mustered**,
after **by** their families,
and *after* **by** the house of their fathers,
47 *From* **Sons of** thirty years *old* and upward
even unto **sons of** fifty years *old*,
every one that came
to *do* **serve** the service *of the ministry*,
and the service of the burden
in the *tabernacle* **tent** of the congregation.
48 Even those that were *numbered* **mustered** of them,
were eight thousand
and five hundred and *fourscore* **eighty**,
49 According to
the *commandment* **mouth** of *the LORD* **Yah Veh**
they were *numbered* **mustered**
by the hand of *Moses* **Mosheh**,
every one **man by man** according to his service,
and according to his burden:
thus were they *numbered* **mustered** of him,
as *the LORD* **Yah Veh**
commanded Moses **misvahed Mosheh**.

PURIFYING THE CAMP

5 And *the LORD spake* **Yah Veh worded**
unto *Moses* **Mosheh,** saying,
2 *Command* **Misvah** the *children* **sons** of *Israel* **Yisra El**,
that they *put* **send forth** out of the camp every leper,
and every one that *hath the issue* **fluxeth**,
and whosoever is defiled by the *dead* **soul**:
3 *Both* **From** male *and* **to** female
shall ye *put out* **send forth**,
without the camp shall ye *put* **send** them **forth**;
that they *defile* **foul** not their camps,
in the midst whereof I *dwell* **tabernacle**.
4 And the *children* **sons** of *Israel did* **Yisra El worked** so,
and *put* **sent** them *out* **forth** without the camp:
as *the LORD spake* **Yah Veh worded** unto *Moses* **Mosheh**,
so *did* **worked** the *children* **sons** of *Israel* **Yisra El**.
5 And *the LORD spake* **Yah Veh worded**
unto *Moses* **Mosheh,** saying,
6 *Speak* **Word** unto the *children* **sons** of *Israel* **Yisra El**,
When a man or woman shall *commit* **work** any sin
that men commit **of humanity**,
to *do* **treason** a *trespass* **treason**
against *the LORD* **Yah Veh**,
and that *person be guilty* **soul hath guilted**;
7 Then they shall *confess* **wring hands for** their sin
which they have *done* **worked**:
and he shall *recompense his trespass* **restore for his guilt**
with the principal thereof **to the top**,
and add unto it the fifth *part* thereof,
and give it unto him
against whom he hath *trespassed* **guilted**.
8 But if the man have no *kinsman* **redeemer**
to recompense *the trespass unto* **for his guilt**,
let *the trespass* **that for the guilt**
be *recompensed* **returned** unto *the LORD* **Yah Veh**,
even to the priest;
beside the ram of the *atonement* **kippurim**,
whereby
an atonement shall be made for him **he shall be atoned**.
9 And every *offering* **exaltment** of all the *holy thing* **holies**
of the *children* **sons** of *Israel* **Yisra El**,
which they *bring* **oblate** unto the priest, shall be his.
10 And every man's *hallowed thing* **holies** shall be his:
whatsoever *any* man giveth the priest, it shall be his.

THE TORAH OF SUSPICIONS

11 And *the LORD spake* **Yah Veh worded**
unto *Moses* **Mosheh,** saying,
12 *Speak* **Word** unto the *children* **sons** of *Israel* **Yisra El**,
and say unto them,
If **a man** — any man's *wife go aside* **woman deviate**,
and *commit* **treason** a *trespass* **treason** against him,
13 And a man lie
with her carnally **to give her seed of copulation**,
and it be *hid* **concealed**
from the eyes of her *husband* **man**,
and be *kept close* **hidden**, and she be *defiled* **fouled**,
and there be no witness against her,
neither she be *taken with the manner* **manipulated**;
14 And the spirit of *jealousy* **suspicion**
come **pass** upon him,
and he *be jealous of* **suspect** his *wife* **woman**,
and she be *defiled* **fouled**:
or if the spirit of *jealousy come* **suspicion pass** upon him,
and he *be jealous of* **suspect** his *wife* **woman**,
and she be not *defiled* **fouled**:
15 Then shall the man
bring his *wife* **woman** unto the priest,
and he shall bring her *offering* **qorban** for her,
the tenth *part* of an ephah of barley *meal* **flour**;
he shall pour no oil upon it,
nor put frankincense thereon;
for it is an offering of *jealousy* **suspicion**,
an offering of memorial,
bringing *iniquity* **perversity** to remembrance.
16 And the priest shall *bring* **oblate** her *near*,
and *set* **stand** her *before the LORD* **at the face of Yah Veh**:
17 And the priest shall take holy water
in *an earthen vessel* **a pottery instrument**;
and of the dust that is in the floor of the tabernacle
the priest shall take, and *put* **give** it into the water:
18 And the priest shall *set* **stand** the woman
before the LORD **at the face of Yah Veh**,
and *uncover* **expose** the woman's head,
and *put* **give** the offering of memorial in her *hands* **palms**,
which is the *jealousy* **suspicion** offering:
and the priest shall have in his hand
the bitter water that *causeth the curse* **curseth**:
19 And the priest shall *charge* **oath** her *by an oath*,
and say unto the woman, If no man have lain with thee,
and if thou hast not
gone aside **deviated** to *uncleanness* **foulness**
with another instead of thy *husband* **man**,
be thou *free* **exonerated** from this bitter water
that *causeth the curse* **curseth**:
20 But if thou hast *gone aside* **deviated**
to another instead of thy husband **from thy man**,
and if thou be *defiled* **fouled**,

and some man have *lain* **given to copulate** with thee
beside thine husband **except thy man**:
21 Then the priest shall *charge* **oath** the woman
with an oath *of cursing,*
and the priest shall say unto the woman,
The LORD make **Yah Veh give** thee *a curse* **an oath**
and an oath among thy people,
when *the LORD doth make* **Yah Veh giveth**
thy *thigh to rot* **flank to fall off**, and thy belly to swell;
22 And this water that *causeth the curse* **curseth**
shall go into thy *bowels* **inwards**,
to make thy belly to swell,
and thy *thigh to rot* **flank to fall off**:
And the woman shall say, Amen, amen.
23 And the priest
shall *write* **inscribe** these *curses* **oaths** in a *book* **scroll**,
and he shall *blot* **wipe** them out with the bitter water:
24 And he shall cause the woman
to drink the bitter water that *causeth the curse* **curseth**:
and the water that *causeth the curse* **curseth**
shall enter into her, and *become bitter* **embitter**.
25 Then the priest
shall take the *jealousy* **suspicion** offering
out of the woman's hand,
and shall wave the offering
before the LORD **at the face of Yah Veh**,
and *offer* **oblate** it upon the **sacrifice** altar:
26 And the priest
shall *take an handful of* **handle** the offering,
even the memorial thereof,
and *burn* **incense** it upon the **sacrifice** altar,
and afterward shall cause the woman to drink the water.
27 And when he hath made her to drink the water,
then it shall *come to pass* **become**, that,
if she be *defiled* **fouled**,
and have *done trespass* **treasoned a treason**
against her *husband* **man**,
that the water that *causeth the curse* **curseth**
shall enter into her, and b*become bitter* **embitter**,
and her belly shall swell,
and her *thigh* **flank** shall *rot* **fall off**:
and the woman shall be *a curse* **an oath**
among her people.
28 And if the woman be not *defiled* **fouled**,
but be *clean* **pure**;
then she shall be *free* **exonerated**,
and shall *conceive* **seed** seed.
29 This is the *law* **torah** of *jealousies* **suspicions**,
when a *wife goeth aside* **woman** *to another* **deviateth**
instead of her *husband* **man**, and is *defiled* **fouled**;
30 Or when the spirit of *jealousy* **suspicion**
cometh **passeth** upon *him* **a man**,
and he be *jealous* **suspicious** over his *wife* **woman**,
and shall *set* **stand** the woman
before the LORD **at the face of Yah Veh**,
and the priest shall *execute* **work** upon her
all this *law* **torah**.
31 Then shall the man
be *guiltless* **exonerated** from *iniquity* **perversity**,
and this woman shall bear her *iniquity* **perversity**.

THE SEPARATIST VOW OF SEPARATISM

6 And *the LORD spake* **Yah Veh worded**
unto *Moses* **Mosheh,** saying,
2 *Speak* **Word** unto the *children* **sons** of *Israel* **Yisra El**,
and say unto them,
When either man or woman shall separate *themselves*
to vow a vow — **the vow** of a *Nazarite* **Separatist**,
to *separate themselves* **marvel** unto *the LORD* **Yah Veh**:
3 He shall separate *himself*
from wine and *strong drink* **intoxicants**,
and shall drink no *vinegar of* **fermented** wine,
or *vinegar of strong drink* **fermented intoxicants**,
neither shall he drink any *liquor* **steepings** of grapes,
nor *eat moist* grapes, *or* dried **or fresh**.
4 All the days of his *separation* **separatism**
shall he eat *nothing* **naught**
that is *made* **worked** of the **wine of the** vine *tree*,
from the kernels even to the husk.
5 All the days of the vow of his *separation* **separatism**
there shall no razor *come* **pass** upon his head:
until the days be fulfilled,
in the which he separateth *himself*
unto *the LORD* **Yah Veh**,
he shall be holy,
and shall let the locks of the hair of his head grow.
6 All the days
that he separateth himself **of his vow of separatism**
unto *the LORD* **Yah Veh**
he shall come at no *dead body* **soul that died**.
7 He shall not *make* **foul** himself *unclean*
for his father, or for his mother,
for his brother, or for his sister, when they *die* **are dead**:
because the *consecration* **separatism** of his *God* **Elohim**
is upon his head.
8 All the days of his *separation* **separatism**
he is holy unto *the LORD* **Yah Veh**.
9 And if **in dying,**
any *man* **one** die *very suddenly* **in a blink** by him,
and he hath *defiled* **fouled**
the head of his *consecration* **separatism**;
then he shall shave his head
in the day of his *cleansing* **purifying**,
on the seventh day shall he shave it.
10 And on the eighth day
he shall bring two *turtles* **turtledoves**,
or two *young pigeons* **sons of doves**, to the priest,
to the *door* **opening**
of the *tabernacle* **tent** of the congregation:
11 And the priest shall *offer* **work** the one
for *a sin offering* **the sin**,
and the *other* **one** for *a burnt offering* **the holocaust**,
and *make an atonement* **kapar/atone** for him,
for that he sinned by the *dead* **soul**,
and shall hallow his head that same day.
12 And he shall
consecrate **separate** unto *the LORD* **Yah Veh**
the days of his *separation* **separatism**,
and shall bring a lamb *of the first year* **a yearling son**
for *a trespass offering* **his guilt**:
but the **first** days *that were before* shall be *lost* **fallen**,
because his *separation* **separatism** was defiled.
13 And this is the *law* **torah** of the *Nazarite* **Separatist**,
when **in** the days of his *separation* **separatism**
the days are fulfilled:
he shall be brought unto the *door* **opening**
of the *tabernacle* **tent** of the congregation:
14 And he shall *offer* **oblate** his *offering* **qorban**
unto *the LORD* **Yah Veh**,
one he lamb
of the first year without blemish
an integrious yearling son
for *a burnt offering* **the holocaust**,
and one ewe lamb
of the first year without blemish
an integrious yearling daughter
for *a sin offering* **the sin**,
and one ram *without blemish* **integrious**
for *peace offerings* **shelamim**,
15 And a basket of *unleavened bread* **matsah**,
cakes of *fine* flour *mingled* **mixed** with oil,
and wafers of *unleavened bread* **matsah** anointed with oil,
and their *meat* offering, and their *drink offerings* **libations**.
16 And the priest shall *bring* **oblate** them
before the LORD **at the face of Yah Veh**,
and shall *offer his sin offering* **work for his sin**,
and his *burnt offering* **holocaust**:
17 And he shall *offer* **work** the ram
for a sacrifice of *peace offerings* **shelamim**
unto *the LORD* **Yah Veh**,
with the basket of *unleavened bread* **matsah**:
the priest shall *offer* **work** also his *meat* offering,
and his *drink offering* **libation**.
18 And the *Nazarite* **Separatist**
shall shave the head of his *separation* **separatism**
at the *door* **opening**
of the *tabernacle* **tent** of the congregation,
and shall take the hair
of the head of his *separation* **separatism**,
and *put* **give** it in the fire which is under the sacrifice
of the *peace offerings* **shelamim**.

19 And the priest shall take
the *sodden shoulder* **stewed foreleg** of the ram,
and one *unleavened* **matsah** cake out of the basket,
and one *unleavened* **matsah** wafer,
and shall *put* **give** them
upon the *hands* **palms** of the *Nazarite* **Separatist**,
after *the hair of his separation* **his separatism** is shaven:
20 And the priest shall wave them for a wave *offering*
before the LORD **at the face of Yah Veh**:
this is holy for the priest,
with the wave breast and *heave shoulder* **hindleg**
of the exaltment:
and after that the *Nazarite* **Separatist** may drink wine.
21 This is the *law* **torah**
of the *Nazarite* **Separatist** who hath vowed,
and of his *offering* **qorban** unto *the LORD* **Yah Veh**
for his *separation* **separatism**,
beside that that his hand shall *get* **attain**:
according to the **mouth of the** vow which he vowed,
so he *must do* **shall work**
after the *law* **torah** of his *separation* **separatism**.

A BENEDICTION

22 And *the LORD spake* **Yah Veh worded**
unto *Moses* **Mosheh**, saying,
23 *Speak* **Word** unto *Aaron* **Aharon** and unto his sons,
saying,
On this wise **Thus** ye shall bless
the *children* **sons** of *Israel* **Yisra El**,
saying unto them,
24 *The LORD* **Yah Veh** bless thee,
and *keep* **guard** thee:
25 *The LORD make* **Yah Veh illuminate** his face *shine*
upon thee,
and *be gracious unto thee* **grant thee charism**:
26 *The LORD* **Yah Veh** lift up his *countenance* **face**
upon thee,
and *give* **set** thee *peace* **shalom**.
27 And they shall put my name
upon the *children* **sons** of *Israel* **Yisra El**,
and I *will* **shall** bless them.

HANUKKAH OF THE TABERNACLE

7 And it *came to pass* **became** on the day
that *Moses* **Mosheh** had *fully* **finished**
set up **raising** the tabernacle,
and had anointed it, and *sanctified* **hallowed** it,
and all the instruments thereof,
both the **sacrifice** altar
and all the *vessels* **instruments** thereof ,
and had anointed them, and *sanctified* **hallowed** them;
2 That the *princes* **hierarchs** of *Israel* **Yisra El**,
heads of the house of their fathers,
who were the *princes* **hierarchs** of the *tribes* **rods**,
and *were* **stood** over them that were *numbered* **mustered**,
offered **oblated**:
3 And they *brought* **oblated** their *offering* **qorban**
before the LORD **at the face of Yah Veh**,
six covered wagons, and twelve oxen;
a wagon for two of the *princes* **hierarchs**,
and for each one an ox:
and they brought them
before **at the face of** the tabernacle.
4 And the *LORD spake* **Yah Veh said**
unto *Moses* **Mosheh**, saying,
5 Take it of them,
that they may be to *do* **serve** the service
of the *tabernacle* **tent** of the congregation;
and thou shalt give them unto the *Levites* **Leviym**,
to every man according to **the mouth of** his service.
6 And *Moses* **Mosheh** took the wagons and the oxen,
and gave them unto the *Levites* **Leviym**.
7 Two wagons and four oxen
he gave unto the sons of Gershon,
according to **the mouth of** their service:
8 And four wagons and eight oxen
he gave unto the sons of Merari,
according unto **the mouth of** their service,
under the hand of *Ithamar* **Iy Thamar**
the son of *Aaron* **Aharon** the priest.
9 But unto the sons of *Kohath* **Qehath** he gave none:
because the service of the *sanctuary* **holies**
belonging unto them
was that they should bear upon their shoulders.

THE HANUKKAH OF THE SACRIFICE ALTAR

10 And the *princes offered* **hierarchs oblated**
for *dedicating* **the hanukkah** of the **sacrifice** altar
in the day that it was anointed,
even the *princes* **hierarchs**
offered **oblated** their *offering* **qorban**
before the **at the face of the sacrifice** altar.
11 And *the LORD* **Yah Veh** said unto *Moses* **Mosheh**,
They shall *offer* **oblate** their *offering* **qorban**,
each prince on his day
one hierarch a day — one hierarch a day,
for the *dedicating* **hanukkah** of the **sacrifice** altar.
12 And he that *offered* **oblated** his *offering* **qorban**
the first day
was Nahshon the son of *Amminadab* **Ammi Nadab**,
of the *tribe* **rod** of *Judah* **Yah Hudah**:
13 And his *offering* **qorban** was one silver *charger* **dish**,
the weight thereof *was* an hundred and thirty *shekels*,
one silver *bowl* **sprinkler** of seventy shekels,
after the shekel of the *sanctuary* **holies**;
both **the two** of them were full of *fine* flour
mingled **mixed** with oil for *a meat* **an** offering:
14 One *spoon* **bowl** of ten *shekels* gold, full of incense:
15 One *young* bullock **son of the oxen**, one ram,
one lamb *of the first year* **a yearling son**
for a *burnt offering* **holocaust**:
16 One *kid* **buck** of the goats for *a sin offering* **the sin**:
17 And for a sacrifice of *peace offerings* **shelamim**,
two oxen, five rams, five he goats,
five lambs *of the first year* **yearling sons**:
this was the *offering* **qorban** of Nahshon
the son of *Amminadab* **Ammi Nadab**.
18 On the second day
Nethaneel **Nethan El** the son of *Zuar* **Suar**,
prince **hierarch** of *Issachar* **Yissachar**, *did offer* **oblated**:
19 He *offered* **oblated** for his *offering* **qorban**
one silver *charger* **dish**,
the weight whereof was an hundred and thirty *shekels*,
one silver *bowl* **sprinkler** of seventy shekels,
after the shekel of the *sanctuary* **holies**;
both **the two** of them were full of *fine* flour
mingled **mixed** with oil for *a meat* **an offering**:
20 One *spoon* **bowl** of gold of ten *shekels*, full of incense:
21 One *young* bullock **son of the oxen**, one ram,
one lamb *of the first year* **a yearling son**
for a *burnt offering* **holocaust**:
22 One *kid* **buck** of the goats for *a sin offering* **the sin**:
23 And for a sacrifice of *peace offerings* **shelamim**,
two oxen, five rams, five he goats,
five lambs *of the first year* **yearling sons**:
this was the *offering* **qorban** of *Nethaneel* **Nethan El**
the son of *Zuar* **Suar**.
24 On the third day
Eliab **Eli Ab** the son of Helon,
prince **hierarch** of the *children* **sons** of Zebulun, *did offer*:
25 And his *offering* **qorban** was one silver *charger* **dish**,
the weight whereof was an hundred and thirty *shekels*,
one silver *bowl* **sprinkler** of seventy shekels,
after the shekel of the *sanctuary* **holies**;
both **the two** of them were full of *fine* flour
mingled with oil for *a meat* **an offering**:
26 One golden *spoon* **bowl** of ten *shekels*, full of incense:
27 One *young* bullock **son of the oxen**, one ram,
one lamb *of the first year* **a yearling son**
for a *burnt offering* **holocaust**:
28 One *kid* **buck** of the goats for *a sin offering* **the sin**:
29 And for a sacrifice of *peace offerings* **shelamim**,
two oxen, five rams, five he goats,
five lambs *of the first year* **yearling sons**:
this was the *offering* **qorban** of *Eliab* **Eli Ab**
the son of Helon.
30 On the fourth day
Elizur **Eli Sur** the son of *Shedeur* **Shedey Ur**,
prince **hierarch** of the *children* **sons** of *Reuben* **Reu Ben**
did offer:
31 And his *offering* **qorban** was one silver *charger* **dish**
of the weight of an hundred and thirty *shekels*,
one silver *bowl* **sprinkler** of seventy shekels,

after the shekel of the *sanctuary* **holies**;
both **the two** of them were full of *fine* flour
mingled with oil for *a meat* **an offering**:
32 One golden *spoon* **bowl** of ten *shekels*, full of incense:
33 One *young* bullock **son of the oxen**, one ram,
one lamb *of the first year* **a yearling son**
for a *burnt offering* **holocaust**:
34 One *kid* **buck** of the goats for *a sin offering* **the sin**:
35 And for a sacrifice of *peace offerings* **shelamim**,
two oxen, five rams, five he goats,
five lambs *of the first year* **yearling sons**:
this was the *offering* **qorban** of *Elizur* **Eli Sur**
the son of *Shedeur* **Shedey Ur**.
36 On the fifth day
Shelumiel **Shelumi El** the son of *Zurishaddai* **Suri Shadday**,
prince **hierarch** of the *children* **sons** of *Simeon* **Shimon**
did offer:
37 And his *offering* **qorban** was one silver *charger* **dish**,
the weight whereof was an hundred and thirty *shekels*,
one silver *bowl* **sprinkler** of seventy shekels,
after the shekel of the *sanctuary* **holies**;
both **the two** of them were full of *fine* flour
mingled with oil for *a meat* **an** offering:
38 One golden *spoon* **bowl** of ten *shekels*, full of incense:
39 One *young* bullock **son of the oxen**, one ram,
one lamb *of the first year* **a yearling son**
for a *burnt offering* **holocaust**:
40 One *kid* **buck** of the goats for *a sin offering* **the sin**:
41 And for a sacrifice of *peace offerings* **shelamim**,
two oxen, five rams, five he goats,
five lambs *of the first year* **yearling sons**:
this was the *offering* **qorban** of *Shelumiel* **Shelumi El**
the son of *Zurishaddai* **Suri Shadday**.
42 On the sixth day
Eliasaph **Eli Yasaph** the son of *Deuel* **Deu El**,
prince **hierarch** of the *children* **sons** of Gad, *offered*:
43 His *offering* **qorban** was one silver *charger* **dish**,
of the weight of an hundred and thirty *shekels*,
a silver *bowl* **sprinkler** of seventy shekels,
after the shekel of the *sanctuary* **holies**;
both **the two** of them were full of *fine* flour
mingled **mixed** with oil for *a meat* **an offering**:
44 One golden *spoon* **bowl** of ten *shekels*, full of incense:
45 One *young* bullock **son of the oxen**, one ram,
one lamb *of the first year* **a yearling son**
for a *burnt offering* **holocaust**:
46 One *kid* **buck** of the goats for *a sin offering* **the sin**:
47 And for a sacrifice of *peace offerings* **shelamim**,
two oxen, five rams, five he goats,
five lambs *of the first year* **yearling sons**:
this was the *offering* **qorban** of *Eliasaph* **Eli Yasaph**
the son of *Deuel* **Deu El**.
48 On the seventh day
Elishama **Eli Shama** the son of *Ammihud* **Ammi Hud**,
prince **hierarch** of the *children* **sons** of *Ephraim* **Ephrayim**,
offered:
49 His *offering* **qorban** was one silver *charger* **dish**,
the weight whereof was an hundred and thirty *shekels*,
one silver *bowl* **sprinkler** of seventy shekels,
after the shekel of the *sanctuary* **holies**;
both **the two** of them were full of *fine* flour
mingled **mixed** with oil for *a meat* **an offering:**
50 One golden *spoon* **bowl** of ten *shekels*, full of incense:
51 One *young* bullock **son of the oxen**, one ram,
one lamb *of the first year* **a yearling son**
for a *burnt offering* **holocaust**:
52 One *kid* **buck** of the goats for *a sin offering* **the sin**:
53 And for a sacrifice of *peace offerings* **shelamim**,
two oxen, five rams, five he goats,
five lambs *of the first year* **yearling sons**:
this was the *offering* **qorban** of *Elishama* **Eli Shama**
the son of *Ammihud* **Ammi Hud**.
54 On the eighth day
offered Gamaliel **Gamli El** the son of *Pedahzur* **Pedah Sur**,
prince **hierarch**
of the *children* **sons** of *Manasseh* **Menash Sheh**:
55 His *offering* **qorban** was one silver *charger* **dish**
of the weight of an hundred and thirty *shekels*,
one silver *bowl* **sprinkler** of seventy shekels,
after the shekel of the *sanctuary* **holies**;
both **the two** of them were full of *fine* flour
mingled **mixed** with oil for *a meat* **an offering**:
56 One golden *spoon* **bowl** of ten *shekels*, full of incense:
57 One *young* bullock **son of the oxen**, one ram,
one lamb *of the first year* **a yearling son**,
for a *burnt offering* **holocaust**:
58 One *kid* **buck** of the goats for *a sin offering* **the sin**:
59 And for a sacrifice of *peace offerings* **shelamim**,
two oxen, five rams, five he goats,
five lambs *of the first year* **yearling sons**:
this was the *offering* **qorban** of *Gamaliel* **Gamli El**
the son of *Pedahzur* **Pedah Sur**.
60 On the ninth day
Abidan **Abi Dan** the son of *Gideoni* **Gidoni**,
prince **hierarch**
of the *children* **sons** of *Benjamin* **Ben Yamin**, *offered*:
61 His *offering* **qorban** was one silver *charger* **dish**,
the weight whereof was an hundred and thirty *shekels*,
one silver *bowl* **sprinkler** of seventy shekels,
after the shekel of the *sanctuary* **holies**;
both **the two** of them were full of *fine* flour
mingled **mixed** with oil for *a meat* **an offering**:
62 One golden *spoon* **bowl** of ten *shekels*, full of incense:
63 One *young* bullock **son of the oxen**, one ram,
one lamb *of the first year* **a yearling son**
for a *burnt offering* **holocaust**:
64 One *kid* **buck** of the goats for *a sin offering* **the sin**:
65 And for a sacrifice of *peace offerings* **shelamim**,
two oxen, five rams, five he goats,
five lambs *of the first year* **yearling sons**:
this was the *offering* **qorban** of *Abidan* **Abi Dan**
the son of *Gideoni* **Gidoni**.
66 On the tenth day
Ahiezer **Achi Ezer** the son of *Ammishaddai* **Ammi Shaday**,
prince **hierarch** of the *children* **sons** of Dan, *offered*:
67 His *offering* **qorban** was one silver *charger* **dish**,
the weight whereof was an hundred and thirty *shekels*,
one silver *bowl* **sprinkler** of seventy shekels,
after the shekel of the *sanctuary* **holies**;
both **the two** of them were full of *fine* flour
mingled **mixed** with oil for *a meat* **an** offering:
68 One golden *spoon* **bowl** of ten *shekels*, full of incense:
69 One *young* bullock **son of the oxen**, one ram,
one lamb *of the first year* **a yearling son**
for a *burnt offering* **holocaust**:
70 One *kid* **buck** of the goats for *a sin offering* **the sin**:
71 And for a sacrifice of *peace offerings* **shelamim**,
two oxen, five rams, five he goats,
five lambs *of the first year* **yearling sons**:
this was the *offering* **qorban** of *Ahiezer* **Achi Ezer**
the son of *Ammishaddai* **Ammi Shaday**.
72 On the **day — the** eleventh day
Pagiel **Pagi El** the son of *Ocran* **Ochran**,
prince **hierarch** of the *children* **sons** of Asher, *offered*:
73 His *offering* **qorban** was one silver *charger* **dish**,
the weight whereof was an hundred and thirty *shekels*,
one silver *bowl* **sprinkler** of seventy shekels,
after the shekel of the *sanctuary* **holies**;
both **the two** of them were full of *fine* flour
mingled **mixed** with oil for *a meat* **an** offering:
74 One golden *spoon* **bowl** of ten *shekels*, full of incense:
75 One *young* bullock **son of the oxen**, one ram,
one lamb *of the first year* **a yearling son**
for a *burnt offering* **holocaust**:
76 One *kid* **buck** of the goats for *a sin offering* **the sin**:
77 And for a sacrifice of *peace offerings* **shelamim**,
two oxen, five rams, five he goats,
five lambs *of the first year* **yearling sons**:
this was the *offering* **qorban** of *Pagiel* **Pagi El**
the son of *Ocran* **Ochran**.
78 On the **day — the** twelfth day
Ahira **Achi Ra** the son of Enan,
prince **hierarch** of the *children* **sons** of Naphtali, *offered*:
79 His *offering* **qorban** was one silver *charger* **dish**,
the weight whereof was an hundred and thirty *shekels*,
one silver *bowl* **sprinkler** of seventy shekels,
after the shekel of the sanctuary holies;
both **the two** of them were full of *fine* flour
mingled **mixed** with oil for *a meat* **an** offering:
80 One golden *spoon* **bowl** of ten *shekels*, full of incense:

81 One *young* bullock **son of the oxen,** one ram,
one lamb *of the first year* **a yearling son**
for a *burnt offering* **holocaust**:
82 One *kid* **buck** of the goats for *a sin offering* **the sin**:
83 And for a sacrifice of *peace offerings* **shelamim,**
two oxen, five rams, five he goats,
five lambs *of the first year* **yearling sons**:
this was the *offering* **qorban** of *Ahira* **Achi Ra**
the son of Enan.
84 This was the *dedicating* **hanukkah** of the **sacrifice** altar,
in the day when it was anointed,
by the *princes* **hierarchs** of *Israel* **Yisra El**:
twelve *chargers* **dishes** of silver,
twelve silver *bowls* **sprinklers**, twelve spoons of gold:
85 Each *charger* **dish** of silver
weighing an hundred and thirty *shekels*,
each *bowl* **sprinkler** seventy:
all the silver *vessels* **instruments** *weighed*
two thousand and four hundred *shekels*,
after the shekel of the *sanctuary* **holies**:
86 The golden *spoons* **bowls** were twelve, full of incense,
weighing ten shekels apiece **each bowl, ten, ten,**
after the shekel of the *sanctuary* **holies**:
all the gold of the *spoons* **bowls**
was an hundred and twenty *shekels*.
87 All the oxen for the *burnt offering* **holocaust**
were twelve bullocks, the rams twelve,
the lambs *of the first year* **yearling sons** twelve,
with their *meat* offering:
and the *kids* **bucks** of the goats *for sin offering* **for the sin**
twelve.
88 And all the oxen
for the sacrifice of the *peace offerings* **shelamim**
were twenty and four bullocks,
the rams sixty, the he goats sixty,
the lambs *of the first year* **yearling sons** sixty.
This was the *dedicating* **hanukkah** of the **sacrifice** altar,
after that it was anointed.
89 And when *Moses* **Mosheh**
was gone into the *tabernacle* **tent** of the congregation
to *speak* **word** with him,
then he heard the voice of one *speaking* **wording** unto him
from off the *mercy seat* **kapporeth**
that was upon the ark of *testimony* **witness**,
from between the two *cherubims* **cherubim**:
and he *spake* **worded** unto him.

HOLOCAUST OF THE LAMPS OF THE MENORAH

8 And *the LORD spake* **Yah Veh worded**
unto *Moses* **Mosheh,** saying,
2 *Speak* **Word** unto *Aaron* **Aharon** and say unto him,
When thou *lightest* **holocaustest** the lamps,
the seven lamps shall *give light* **illuminate**
over against **in front of the face of**
the *candlestick* **menorah**.
3 And *Aaron did* **Aharon worked** so;
he *lighted* **holocausted** the lamps thereof
over against **in front of the face of**
the *candlestick* **menorah**,
as *the LORD* **Yah Veh**
commanded Moses **misvahed Mosheh**.
4 And this work of the *candlestick* **menorah**
was of *beaten* **spun** gold,
unto the shaft **flank** thereof,
unto the *flowers* **blossoms** thereof, was *beaten work* **spun**:
according unto the *pattern* **vision**
which *the LORD* **Yah Veh**
had *shewed Moses* **Mosheh see**,
so he *made* **worked** the *candlestick* **menorah**.

PURIFYING THE LEVIYM

5 And *the LORD spake* **Yah Veh worded**
unto *Moses* **Mosheh,** saying,
6 Take the *Levites* **Leviym**
from among the *children* **sons** of *Israel* **Yisra El,**
and *cleanse* **purify** them.
7 And thus shalt thou *do* **work** unto them,
to *cleanse* **purify** them:
Sprinkle water *of purifying* **for the sin** upon them,
and let them *shave* **pass a razor over** all their flesh,
and let them *wash* **launder** their clothes,
and so *make* **purify** themselves *clean*.
8 Then let them take a *young* bullock **son of the oxen**
with his *meat* offering,
even *fine* flour *mingled* **mixed** with oil,
and *another young* **a second** bullock **son of the oxen**
shalt thou take for *a sin offering* **the sin.**
9 And thou shalt *bring* **oblate** the *Levites* **Leviym**
before **at the face of**
the *tabernacle* **tent** of the congregation:
and thou shalt *gather* **congregate**
the *whole assembly* **witness**
of the *children* **sons** of *Israel* **Yisra El** *together*:
10 And thou shalt *bring* **oblate** the *Levites* **Leviym**
before the LORD **at the face of Yah Veh**:
and the *children* **sons** of *Israel* **Yisra El**
shall *put* **prop** their hands upon the *Levites* **Leviym**:
11 And *Aaron* **Aharon** shall *offer* **wave** the *Levites* **Leviym**
before the LORD **at the face of Yah Veh**
for *an offering* **a wave**
of the *children* **sons** of *Israel* **Yisra El,**
that they may *execute* **serve**
the service of *the LORD* **Yah Veh**.
12 And the *Levites* **Leviym** shall *lay* **prop** their hands
upon the heads of the bullocks:
and thou shalt *offer* **work** the one for *a sin offering* **the sin,**
and the *other* **one** for *a burnt offering* **holocaust,**
unto *the LORD* **Yah Veh,**
to *make an atonement* **kapar/atone** for the *Levites* **Leviym.**
13 And thou shalt *set* **stand** the *Levites* **Leviym**
before Aaron **at the face of Aharon,**
and *before* **at the face of** his sons,
and *offer* **wave** them
for *an offering* **a wave** unto *the LORD* **Yah Veh.**
14 Thus shalt thou separate the *Levites* **Leviym**
from among the *children* **sons** of *Israel* **Yisra El**:
and the *Levites* **Leviym** shall be mine.
15 And after that shall the *Levites* **Leviym** go in
to *do* **serve** the service
of the *tabernacle* **tent** of the congregation:
and thou shalt *cleanse* **purify** them,
and *offer* **wave** them for *an offering* **a wave.**
16 For **in giving,** they are *wholly* given unto me
from among the *children* **sons** of *Israel* **Yisra El**;
instead of *such as open every* **every burster of the** womb,
even instead of the firstborn
of all the *children* **sons** of *Israel* **Yisra El,**
have I taken them unto me.
17 For all the firstborn of the *children* **sons** of *Israel* **Yisra El**
are mine,
both man **human** and *beast* **animal**:
on the day that I smote every firstborn
in the land of *Egypt* **Misrayim**
I *sanctified* **hallowed** them for myself.
18 And I have taken the *Levites* **Leviym**
for all the firstborn of the *children* **sons** of *Israel* **Yisra El.**
19 And I have given the *Levites* **Leviym**
as a gift to Aaron — **given to Aharon** and to his sons
from among the *children* **sons** of *Israel* **Yisra El,**
to *do* **serve** the service
of the *children* **sons** of *Israel* **Yisra El**
in the *tabernacle* **tent** of the congregation,
and to *make an atonement* **kapar/atone**
for the *children* **sons** of *Israel* **Yisra El**:
that there be no plague
among the *children* **sons** of *Israel* **Yisra El,**
when the *children* **sons** of *Israel* **Yisra El**
come nigh **approach** unto the *sanctuary* **holies**.
20 And *Moses* **Mosheh**, and *Aaron* **Aharon,**
and all the *congregation* **witness**
of the *children* **sons** of *Israel* **Yisra El,**
did **worked** to the *Levites* **Leviym**
according unto all that *the LORD* **Yah Veh**
commanded Moses **misvahed Mosheh**
concerning the *Levites* **Leviym,**
so *did* **worked** the *children* **sons** of *Israel* **Yisra El**
unto them.
21 And the *Levites* **Leviym,** *were purified,* **for the sin,**
and they washed **laundered** their clothes;
and *Aaron offered* **Aharon waved** them
as *an offering* **a wave**
before the LORD **at the face of Yah Veh**;

and *Aaron* **Aharon**
made an atonement **did kapar/atone** for them
to *cleanse* **purify** them.
22 And after that went the *Levites* **Leviym** in
to *do* **serve** their service
in the *tabernacle* **tent** of the congregation
before Aaron **at the face of Aharon**,
and *before* **at the face of** his sons:
as *the LORD* **Yah Veh**
had *commanded Moses* **misvahed Mosheh**
concerning the *Levites* **Leviym**,
so *did* **worked** they unto them.
23 And *the LORD spake* **Yah Veh worded**
unto *Moses* **Mosheh**, saying,
24 This is it that belongeth unto the *Levites* **Leviym**:
from **a son of** twenty and five years *old* and upward
they shall go in to *wait upon* **host** the *service* **hosting**
of the *tabernacle* **tent** of the congregation:
25 And *from the age* **a son** of fifty years
they shall *cease* **turn away**
waiting upon **from hosting** the service *thereof*,
and shall serve no more:
26 But shall minister with their brethren
in the *tabernacle* **tent** of the congregation,
to *keep* **guard** the *charge* **guard**,
and shall *do* **serve** no service.
Thus shalt thou *do* **work** unto the *Levites* **Leviym**
touching **regarding** their *charge* **guard**.

THE PASACH

9 And *the LORD spake* **Yah Veh worded**
unto *Moses* **Mosheh** in the wilderness of *Sinai* **Sinay**,
in the first month of the second year
after they were come out of the land of *Egypt* **Misrayim**,
saying,
2 Let the *children* **sons** of *Israel* **Yisra El**
also *keep* **work** the *passover* **pasach**
at his *appointed* season.
3 In the fourteenth day of this month,
at even **between evenings**,
ye shall *keep* **work** it in his *appointed* season:
according to all the *rites* **statutes** of it,
and according to all the *ceremonies* **judgments** thereof,
shall ye *keep* **work** it.
4 And *Moses spake* **Mosheh worded**
unto the *children* **sons** of *Israel* **Yisra El**,
that they should *keep* **work** the *passover* **pasach**.
5 And they *kept* **worked** the *passover* **pasach**
on the fourteenth day of the first month
at even **between evenings**
in the wilderness of *Sinai* **Sinay**:
according to all that *the LORD* **Yah Veh**
commanded Moses **misvahed Mosheh**,
so *did* **worked** the *children* **sons** of *Israel* **Yisra El**.
6 And there were *certain* **men**,
who were defiled by the *dead body* **soul** of a *man* **human**,
that they could not *keep* **work** the *passover* **pasach**
on that day
came before Moses **approached at the face of Mosheh**
and *before Aaron* **at the face of Aharon** on that day:
7 And those men said unto him,
We are defiled by the *dead body* **soul** of a *man* **human**:
wherefore are we kept back,
that we may not *offer an offering* **oblate a qorban**
of *the LORD* **Yah Veh** in his *appointed* season
among the *children* **sons** of *Israel* **Yisra El**?
8 And *Moses* **Mosheh** said unto them, Stand still,
and I *will* **shall** hear
what *the LORD will command* **Yah Veh shall misvah**
concerning you.
9 And *the LORD spake* **Yah Veh worded**
unto *Moses* **Mosheh**, saying,
10 *Speak* **Word** unto the *children* **sons** of *Israel* **Yisra El**,
saying,
If **a man** — any man of you or of your *posterity* **generation**
shall be *unclean* **fouled** by *reason of a dead body* **a soul**,
or be in a journey afar off,
yet he shall *keep* **work** the *passover* **pasach**
unto *the LORD* **Yah Veh**.
11 The fourteenth day of the second month
at even **between evenings** they shall *keep* **work** it,
and eat it
with *unleavened bread* **matsah** and *bitter herbs* **bitters**.
12 They shall *leave* **let** none of it **survive**
unto the morning,
nor break any bone of it:
according to all the *ordinances* **statutes**
of the *passover* **pasach**
they shall *keep* **work** it.
13 But the man that is *clean* **pure**, and is not in a journey,
and *forbeareth* **ceaseth** to *keep* **work** the *passover* **pasach**,
even the same soul
shall be cut off from among his people:
because he *brought* **oblated** not
the *offering* **qorban** of *the LORD* **Yah Veh**
in his *appointed* season,
that man shall bear his sin.
14 And if a *stranger* **sojourner** shall sojourn among you,
and *will keep* **shall work** the *passover* **pasach**
unto *the LORD* **Yah Veh**;
according to the *ordinance* **statute** of the *passover* **pasach**,
and according to the *manner* **judgment** thereof,
so **thus** shall he *do* **work**:
ye shall have one *ordinance* **statute**,
both for the *stranger* **sojourner**,
and for *him that was born in the land* **the native**.

TABERNACLE CLOUD COVER

15 And on the day that the tabernacle was *reared up* **raised**
the cloud covered the tabernacle,
namely, the tent of the *testimony* **witness**:
and at even there was upon the tabernacle
as *it were the appearance* **the visage** of fire,
until the morning.
16 So it was *alway* **continually**:
the cloud covered it *by day*,
and the *appearance* **visage** of fire by night.
17 And when the **mouth of the** cloud
was taken up **ascended** from the *tabernacle* **tent**,
then after that
the *children* **sons** of *Israel journeyed* **Yisra El pulled stakes**:
and in the place where the cloud *abode* **tabernacled**,
there the *children* **sons** of *Israel* **Yisra El**
pitched their tents **encamped**.
18 At the *commandment* **mouth** of *the LORD* **Yah Veh**
the *children* **sons** of *Israel journeyed* **Yisra El pulled stakes**,
and at the *commandment of the LORD* **mouth of Yah Veh**
they *pitched* **encamped**:
as long as **all the days**
the cloud *abode* **tabernacled** upon the tabernacle
they *rested in their tents* **encamped**.
19 And when the cloud
tarried long **prolonged** upon the tabernacle many days,
then the *children* **sons** of *Israel* **Yisra El**
kept **guarded** the *charge* **guard** of *the LORD* **Yah Veh**,
and *journeyed* **pulled stakes** not.
20 And so it was, when the cloud
was a *few* **number of** days upon the tabernacle;
according to
the *commandment* **mouth** of *the LORD* **Yah Veh**
they *abode in their tents* **encamped**,
and according to
the *commandment* **mouth** of *the LORD* **Yah Veh**
they *journeyed* **pulled stakes**.
21 And so *it was*, when the cloud
abode **became** from even unto the morning,
and that the cloud *was taken up* **ascended** in the morning,
then they *journeyed* **pulled stakes**:
whether it was by day or by night
that the cloud *was taken up* **ascended**,
they *journeyed* **pulled stakes**.
22 *Or whether it were* — two days, or a month, or a year,
that the cloud *tarried* **prolonged** upon the tabernacle,
remaining **tabernacling** thereon,
the *children* **sons** of *Israel* **Yisra El**
abode in their tents **encamped**,
and *journeyed* **pulled stakes** not:
but when it *was taken up* **ascended**,
they *journeyed* **pulled stakes**.
23 At the *commandment* **mouth** of *the LORD* **Yah Veh**
they *rested in the tents* **encamped**,
and at the *commandment* **mouth** of *the LORD* **Yah Veh**

they *journeyed* **pulled stakes**:
they *kept* **guarded** the *charge* **guard** of *the LORD* **Yah Veh**,
at the *commandment* **mouth** of *the LORD* **Yah Veh**
by the hand of *Moses* **Mosheh**.

BLASTING OF TRUMPETS

10 And *the LORD spake* **Yah Veh worded**
unto *Moses* **Mosheh,** saying,
2 *Make* **Work** thee two trumpets of silver;
of *a whole piece* **spinning** shalt thou *make* **work** them:
that thou mayest use them
for the *calling* **convocation** of the *assembly* **witness**,
and for the journeying of the camps.
3 And when they shall *blow* **blast** with them,
all the *assembly* **witness**
shall *assemble* **congregate** *themselves* to thee
at the *door* **opening**
of the *tabernacle* **tent** of the congregation.
4 And if they *blow* **blast** but *with* one *trumpet*,
then the *princes* **hierarchs**,
which are heads of the thousands of *Israel* **Yisra El**,
shall *gather* **congregate** *themselves* unto thee.
5 When ye *blow an alarm* **blast blast**,
then the camps that lie *on the east parts* **eastward**
shall *go forward* **pull stakes**.
6 When ye *blow an alarm* **blast blast** the second time,
then the camps that lie *on the south side* **southward**
shall *take their journey* **pull stakes**:
they shall *blow an alarm* **blast blast** for their journeys.
7 But when the congregation
is to be *gathered* **congregated** *together*,
ye shall *blow* **blast**,
but ye shall not *sound an alarm* **blast blast**.
8 And the sons of *Aaron* **Aharon**, the priests,
shall *blow* **blast** with the trumpets;
and they shall be to you
for an *ordinance for ever* **eternal statute**
throughout your generations.
9 And if ye go to war in your land
against the *enemy* **tribulator**
that *oppresseth* **tribulateth** you,
then ye shall *blow an alarm* **blast blast** with the trumpets;
and ye shall be remembered
before the LORD **at the face of Yah Veh** your *God* **Elohim**,
and ye shall be saved from your enemies.
10 Also in the day of your *gladness* **cheerfulness**,
and in your *solemn days* **seasons**,
and in the *beginnings* **heads** of your months,
ye shall *blow* **blast** with the trumpets
over your *burnt offerings* **holocausts**,
and over the sacrifices of your *peace offerings* **shelamim**;
that they may be to you for a memorial
before **at the face of** your *God* **Elohim**:
I am the LORD **I — Yah Veh** your *God* **Elohim**.

SONS OF YISRA EL PULL STAKES FROM SINAY

11 And it *came to pass* **became,**
on the twentieth day of the second month
in the second month, on the twentieth of the month,
in the second year,
that the cloud *was taken up* **ascended**
from off the tabernacle of the *testimony* **witness**.
12 And the *children* **sons** of *Israel* **Yisra El**
took **pulled stakes in** their journeys
out of the wilderness of *Sinai* **Sinay**;
and the cloud *rested* **tabernacled**
in the wilderness of Paran.
13 And they first *took their journey* **pulled stakes**
according to
the *commandment* **mouth** of *the LORD* **Yah Veh**
by the hand of *Moses* **Mosheh**.
14 *In the first place* **The first to pull stakes**
went **was** the standard of the camp
of the *children* **sons** of *Judah* **Yah Hudah**
according to their *armies* **hosts**:
and over his host was Nahshon
the son of *Amminadab* **Ammi Nadab**.
15 And over the host of the *tribe* **rod**
of the *children* **sons** of *Issachar* **Yissachar**
was *Nethaneel* **Nethan El** the son of *Zuar* **Suar**.
16 And over the host of the *tribe* **rod**
of the *children* **sons** of Zebulun
was *Eliab* **Eli Ab** the son of Helon.
17 And the tabernacle was *taken down* **lowered**;
and the sons of Gershon and the sons of Merari
set forward **pulled stakes**, bearing the tabernacle.
18 And the standard of the camp of *Reuben* **Reu Ben**
set forward **pulled stakes** according to their *armies* **hosts**:
and over his host was *Elizur* **Eli Sur**
the son of *Shedeur* **Shedey Ur**.
19 And over the host of the *tribe* **rod**
of the *children* **sons** of *Simeon* **Shimon**
was *Shelumiel* **Shelumi El**
the son of *Zurishaddai* **Suri Shadday**.
20 And over the host of the *tribe* **rod**
of the *children* **sons** of Gad
was *Eliasaph* **Eli Yasaph** the son of *Deuel* **Deu El**.
21 And the *Kohathites set forward* **Qehathiy pulled stakes**,
bearing the *sanctuary* **holies**:
and *the other did set up* **raised** the tabernacle
against they came **as they arrived**.
22 And the standard of the camp
of the *children* **sons** of *Ephraim* **Ephrayim**
set forward **pulled stakes** according to their *armies* **hosts**:
and over his host was *Elishama* **Eli Shama**
the son of *Ammihud* **Ammi Hud**.
23 And over the host of the *tribe* **rod**
of the *children* **sons** of *Manasseh* **Menash Sheh**
was *Gamaliel* **Gamli El** the son of *Pedahzur* **Pedah Sur**.
24 And over the host of the *tribe* **rod**
of the *children* **sons** of *Benjamin* **Ben Yamin**
was *Abidan* **Abi Dan** the son of *Gideoni* **Gidoni**.
25 And the standard of the camp
of the *children* **sons** of Dan *set forward* **pulled stakes**,
which *was the rereward* **gathered rearward**
of all the camps throughout their hosts:
and over his host was *Ahiezer* **Achi Ezer**
the son of *Ammishaddai* **Ammi Shaday**.
26 And over the host of the *tribe* **rod**
of the *children* **sons** of Asher
was *Pagiel* **Pagi El** the son of *Ocran* **Ochran**.
27 And over the host of the *tribe* **rod**
of the *children* **sons** of Naphtali
was *Ahira* **Achi Ra** the son of Enan.
28 Thus were the journeyings
of the *children* **sons** of *Israel* **Yisra El**
according to their *armies* **hosts**,
when they *set forward* **pulled stakes**.
29 And *Moses* **Mosheh** said unto Hobab,
the son of *Raguel* **Reu El** the *Midianite* **Midyaniy**,
Moses' **Mosheh's** *father* in law,
We are *journeying* **pulling stakes**
unto the place of which *the LORD* **Yah Veh** said,
I *will* **shall** give it you:
come **go** thou with us, and we *will* **shall** do thee good:
for *the LORD* **Yah Veh** hath *spoken* **worded** good
concerning *Israel* **Yisra El**.
30 And he said unto him, I *will* **shall** not go;
but I *will depart* **shall go** to mine own land,
and to my kindred.
31 And he said, Leave us not, I *pray* **beseech** thee;
forasmuch **for thus** as thou knowest
how we are to encamp in the wilderness,
and thou mayest be to us instead of eyes.
32 And it shall be, if thou go with us, yea,
it shall be, that what goodness
the LORD **Yah Veh** shall *do unto* **well—please** us,
the same will **that good shall** we do unto thee.
33 And they *departed* **pulled stakes**
from the mount of *the LORD* **Yah Veh** three days' journey:
and the ark of the covenant of *the LORD* **Yah Veh**
went before them **pulled stakes at their face**
in the three days' journey,
to *search* **explore** a *resting place* **rest** for them.
34 And the cloud of *the LORD* **Yah Veh**
was upon them by day,
when they *went* **pulled stakes** out of the camp.
35 And it *came to pass* **became**,
when the ark *set forward* **pulled stakes**,
that *Moses* **Mosheh** said, Rise up, *LORD* **O Yah Veh**,
and let thine enemies be scattered;
and let them that hate thee flee *before thee* **thy face**.

36 And when it rested, he said, Return, O *LORD* **Yah Veh**,
unto the *many thousands* **myriads** of *Israel* **Yisra El**.

YAH VEH'S CONSUMING FIRE

11 And when the people complained,
it *displeased the LORD* **was evil in Yah Veh's ears**:
and *the LORD* **Yah Veh** heard it;
and his *anger* **wrath** was kindled;
and the fire of *the LORD* **Yah Veh**
burnt **kindled** among them,
and consumed *them*
that were in the uttermost parts **the ends** of the camp.
2 And the people cried unto *Moses* **Mosheh**;
and when *Moses* **Mosheh** prayed unto *the LORD* **Yah Veh**,
the fire was quenched.
3 And he called the name of the place Taberah:
because the fire of *the LORD* **Yah Veh**
burnt **kindled** among them.

SONS OF YISRA EL COMPLAIN ABOUT THE MANNA

4 And the *mixt multitude* **gathering**
that was *among them* **in their midst**
fell a lusting **desired a desire**:
and the *children* **sons** of *Israel* **Yisra El**
wept again **turned to weep also**, and said,
Who shall *give* **feed** us flesh *to eat*?
5 We remember the fish,
which we did eat in *Egypt freely* **Misrayim gratuitously**;
the cucumbers, and the melons,
and the leeks, and the onions, and the garlick:
6 But now our soul is dried away:
there is *nothing* **naught** at all, *beside* **except** this manna,
before our eyes.
7 And the manna was as coriander seed,
and the *colour* **eye** thereof as the *colour* **eye** of bdellium.
8 And the people *went about* **flitted**,
and *gathered* **gleaned** it,
and ground it in *mills* **millstones**, or beat it in a mortar,
and *baked* **stewed** it in *pans* **skillets**,
and *made cakes* **worked ashcakes** of it:
and the taste of it was as the taste of *fresh* **juicy** oil.
9 And when the dew
fell **descended** upon the camp in the night,
the manna *fell* **descended** upon it.
10 Then *Moses* **Mosheh** heard the people weep
throughout their families,
every man in the *door* **opening** of his tent:
and the *anger* **wrath** of *the LORD* **Yah Veh**
was kindled *greatly* **mightily**;
Moses also was displeased
And it was vilifying in Mosheh's eyes.
11 And *Moses* **Mosheh** said unto *the LORD* **Yah Veh**,
Wherefore hast thou *afflicted* **vilified** thy servant?
and wherefore
have I not found *favour* **charism** in thy *sight* **eyes**,
that thou *layest* **settest** the burden of all this people
upon me?
12 Have I conceived all this people?
have I *begotten* **borne** them,
that thou shouldest say unto me,
Carry **Bear** them in thy bosom,
as a *nursing father* **fosterer**
beareth the sucking child **the suckling**,
unto the *land* **soil**
which thou *swarest* **oathest** unto their fathers?
13 Whence should I have flesh to give unto all this people?
for they weep unto me, saying,
Give us flesh, that we may eat.
14 I am not able to bear all this people alone,
because it is too heavy for me.
15 And if thou *deal* **work** thus with me, *kill* **slaughter** me,
I *pray* **beseech** thee, *out of hand* **slaughter me**,
if I have found *favour* **charism** in thy *sight* **eyes**;
and let me not see my *wretchedness* **evil**.

YAH VEH PROMISES FLESH TO EAT

16 And *the LORD* **Yah Veh** said unto *Moses* **Mosheh**,
Gather unto me seventy men
of the elders of *Israel* **Yisra El**,
whom thou knowest to be the elders of the people,
and officers over them;
and *bring* **take** them
unto the *tabernacle* **tent** of the congregation,
that they may stand there with thee.
17 And I *will come down* **shall descend**
and *talk* **word** with thee there:
and I *will take* **shall set aside** of the spirit
which is upon thee,
and *will* **shall** put it upon them;
and they shall bear the burden of the people with thee,
that thou bear it not thyself alone.
18 And say thou unto the people,
sanctify yourselves against to **hallow by the** morrow,
and ye shall eat flesh:
for ye have wept in the ears of *the LORD* **Yah Veh**,
saying, Who shall *give* **feed** us flesh *to eat*?
for it was *well* **good** with us in *Egypt* **Misrayim**:
therefore *the LORD will* **Yah Veh shall** give you flesh,
and ye shall eat.
19 Ye shall not eat one day, nor two days,
nor five days, neither ten days, nor twenty days;
20 But even a *whole* month **of days**,
until it come out at your nostrils,
and it be *loathsome* **strange** unto you:
because that ye have
despised the LORD **spurned Yah Veh**
which is among you,
and have wept *before him* **at his face**, saying,
Why came we forth out of *Egypt* **Misrayim**?
21 And *Moses* **Mosheh** said,
The people, among whom I am,
are six hundred thousand *footmen* **on foot**;
and thou hast said, I *will* **shall** give them flesh,
that they may eat a *whole* month **of days**.
22 Shall the flocks and the *herds* **oxen** be slain for them,
to *suffice* **be found for** them?
or shall all the fish of the sea
be gathered *together* for them,
to *suffice* **be found for** them?
23 And *the LORD* **Yah Veh** said unto *Moses* **Mosheh**,
Is *the LORD'S* **Yah Veh's** hand *waxed short* **curtailed**?
thou shalt see now whether my word
shall *come to pass unto* **befall** thee or not.
24 And *Moses* **Mosheh** went out,
and *told* **worded** the people
the words of *the LORD* **Yah Veh**,
and gathered the seventy men of the elders of the people,
and *set* **stood** them round about the *tabernacle* **tent**.
25 And *the LORD* **Yah Veh**
came down **descended** in a cloud,
and *spake* **worded** unto him,
and *took* **set aside** of the spirit that was upon him,
and gave it unto the seventy **men** — elders:
and it *came to pass* **became**, that,
when the spirit rested upon them, they prophesied,
and did not cease **but not again**.
26 But there *remained* **survived**
two of the men in the camp,
the name of the one was *Eldad* **El Dad**,
and the name of the *other* **second** Medad:
and the spirit rested upon them;
and they were of them that were *written* **inscribed**,
but went not out unto the *tabernacle* **tent**:
and they prophesied in the camp.
27 And there ran a *young man* **lad**,
and told *Moses* **Mosheh**, and said,
Eldad **El Dad** and Medad *do* prophesy in the camp.
28 And *Joshua* **Yah Shua** the son of Nun,
the *servant* **minister** of *Moses* **Mosheh**,
one of his *young men* **youths**, answered and said,
My *lord Moses* **adoni Mosheh**, *forbid* **restrain** them.
29 And *Moses* **Mosheh** said unto him,
Enviest thou for my sake?
would God **O to give**
that all *the LORD's* **Yah Veh's** people were prophets,
and that *the LORD would put* **Yah Veh should give**
his spirit upon them!
30 And *Moses gat* **Mosheh gathered** him into the camp,
he and the elders of *Israel* **Yisra El**.

YAH VEH PROVIDES QUAILS

31 And *there went forth a wind from the LORD*
Yah Veh pulled a wind,
and brought quails from the sea,

and *let them fall* **left them** by the camp,
as it were a day's journey *on this side* **thus,**
and as it were a day's journey *on the other side* **thus,**
round about the camp,
and as it were two cubits high upon the face of the earth.
32 And the people *stood up* **rose** all that day,
and all that night,
and all the *next* **morrow** day, and they gathered the quails:
he that *gathered least* **lessened**
gathered ten *homers* **chomers**:
and **in spreading,** they spread them *all abroad*
for themselves round about the camp.
33 And while the flesh was yet between their teeth,
ere it was *chewed* **cut,**
the wrath of *the LORD* **Yah Veh**
was kindled against the people,
and *the LORD* **Yah Veh** smote the people
with a *very* **mighty** great *plague* **stroke.**
34 And he called the name of that place
Kibrothhattaavah **Qibroth Hat Taavah**:
because there
they *buried* **entombed** the people that *lusted* **desired.**
35 And the people *journeyed* **pulled stakes**
from *Kibrothhattaavah* **Qibroth Hat Taavah**
unto *Hazeroth* **Haseroth**;
and abode at *Hazeroth* **Haseroth.**

MIRYAM AND AHARON WORD AGAINST MOSHEH

12 And *Miriam* **Miryam** and *Aaron* **Aharon**
spake **worded** against *Moses* **Mosheh**
because of **concerning** the *Ethiopian* **Kushiy** woman
whom he had *married* **taken**:
for he had *married an Ethiopian* **taken a Kushiy** woman.
2 And they said, Hath *the LORD* **Yah Veh** *indeed*
spoken **worded** only by *Moses* **Mosheh**?
hath he not *spoken* **worded** also by us?
And *the LORD* **Yah Veh** heard it.
3 (*Now the man Moses* **Mosheh the man**
was *very meek* **mighty humble,**
above all *the men* **humanity**
which were upon the face of the *earth* **soil.**)
4 And *the LORD spake* **Yah Veh said** suddenly
unto *Moses* **Mosheh,**
and unto *Aaron* **Aharon,** and unto *Miriam* **Miryam,**
Come out ye three
unto the *tabernacle* **tent** of the congregation.
And they three came out.
5 And *the LORD came down* **Yah Veh descended**
in the pillar of the cloud,
and stood in the *door* **opening** of the *tabernacle* **tent,**
and called *Aaron* **Aharon** and *Miriam* **Miryam**:
and *they both* **the two** came forth.
6 And he said, Hear *now* **I beseech,** my words:
If there be a prophet *among you,*
I the LORD **I — Yah Veh**
will **shall** make myself known unto him in a vision,
and *will speak* **shall word** unto him in a dream.
7 My servant *Moses* **Mosheh** is not so,
who is *faithful* **trustworthy** in all mine house.
8 With him *will I speak* **shall I word** mouth to mouth,
even apparently **by vision,**
and not in *dark speeches* **riddles**;
and the similitude of *the LORD* **Yah Veh**
shall he *behold* **look at**:
wherefore then were ye not *afraid* **awed**
to *speak* **word** against my servant *Moses* **Mosheh**?
9 And the *anger* **wrath** of *the LORD* **Yah Veh**
was kindled against them; and he *departed* **went.**
10 And the cloud *departed* **turned aside**
from off the *tabernacle* **tent**; and, behold,
Miriam **Miryam** became leprous, *white* as snow:
and *Aaron looked upon Miriam* **Aharon faced Miryam,**
and, behold, she was leprous.
11 And *Aaron* **Aharon** said unto *Moses* **Mosheh,**
Alas, my *lord* **adoni,** I beseech thee,
lay **set** not the sin upon us,
wherein we have *done foolishly* **follied,**
and wherein we have sinned.
12 Let **I pray,** her not be as one *dead* **that died,**
of whom the flesh is half consumed
when he cometh out of his mother's womb.
13 And *Moses* **Mosheh** cried unto the *LORD* **Yah Veh,**
saying,
Heal her *now* **I beseech,** O *God* **El,** I beseech thee.
14 And *the LORD* **Yah Veh** said unto *Moses* **Mosheh,**
If **in spitting,** her father had but spit in her face,
should she not be ashamed seven days?
let her be shut *out from* **without** the camp seven days,
and after that let her be *received in again* **gathered.**
15 And *Miriam* **Miryam**
was shut *out from* **without** the camp seven days:
and the people *journeyed* **pulled stakes** not
till *Miriam* **Miryam** was brought in *again.*
16 And afterward the people
removed **pulled stakes** from *Hazeroth* **Haseroth,**
and *pitched* **encamped** in the wilderness of Paran.

EXPLORATION OF KENAAN

13 And *the LORD spake* **Yah Veh worded**
unto *Moses* **Mosheh,** saying,
2 Send thou men,
that they may *search* **explore** the land of *Canaan* **Kenaan,**
which I give unto the *children* **sons** of *Israel* **Yisra El**:
of every *tribe* **rod** of their fathers
shall ye send *a man, every one* **one man — one man,**
a ruler among them.
3 And *Moses* **Mosheh**
by the *commandment* **mouth** of *the LORD* **Yah Veh**
sent them from the wilderness of Paran:
all those men were heads
of the *children* **sons** of *Israel* **Yisra El.**
4 And these were their names:
of the *tribe* **rod** of *Reuben* **Reu Ben,**
Shammua the son of *Zaccur* **Zakkur.**
5 Of the *tribe* **rod** of *Simeon* **Shimon,**
Shaphat the son of Hori.
6 Of the *tribe* **rod** of *Judah* **Yah Hudah,**
Caleb **Kaleb** the son of *Jephunneh* **Yephunneh.**
7 Of the *tribe* **rod** of *Issachar* **Yissachar,**
Igal **Yigal** the son of *Joseph* **Yoseph.**
8 Of the *tribe* **rod** of *Ephraim* **Ephrayim,**
Oshea **Hoshea** the son of Nun.
9 Of the *tribe* **rod** of *Benjamin* **Ben Yamin,**
Palti the son of Raphu.
10 Of the *tribe* **rod** of Zebulun,
Gaddiel **Gadi El** the son of Sodi.
11 Of the *tribe* **rod** of *Joseph* **Yoseph,**
namely, of the *tribe* **rod** of *Manasseh* **Menash Sheh,**
Gaddi the son of Susi.
12 Of the *tribe* **rod** of Dan,
Ammiel **Ammi El** the son of Gemalli.
13 Of the *tribe* **rod** of Asher,
Sethur the son of *Michael* **Michah El.**
14 Of the *tribe* **rod** of Naphtali,
Nahbi **Nachbi** the son of Vophsi.
15 Of the *tribe* **rod** of Gad,
Geuel **Geu El** the son of Machi.
16 These are the names of the men
which *Moses* **Mosheh** sent to *spy out* **explore** the land.
And *Moses* **Mosheh** called *Oshea* **Hoshea** the son of Nun
Jehoshua **Yah Shua.**
17 And *Moses* **Mosheh** sent them
to *spy out* **explore** the land of *Canaan* **Kenaan,**
and said unto them,
Get you up **Ascend** this way southward,
and *go up* **ascend** into the mountain:
18 And see the land, what it is,
and the people that *dwelleth* **settleth** therein,
whether they be strong or weak, few or many;
19 And what the land is that they *dwell* **settle** in,
whether it be good or *bad* **evil**;
and what cities they be that they *dwell* **settle** in,
whether in *tents* **camps,** or in *strong holds* **fortresses;**
20 And what the land is,
whether it be fat or *lean* **emaciated,**
whether there be *wood* **timber** therein, or not.
And *be ye of good courage* **prevail ye,**
and *bring* **take** of the fruit of the land.
Now the time was the *time* **days**
of the *firstripe* **firstfruits** grapes.
21 So they *went up* **ascended,**
and *searched* **explored** the land

from the wilderness of *Zin* **Sin** unto *Rehob* **Rechob**,
as men come to Hamath.
22 And they ascended by the south,
and came unto Hebron;
where *Ahiman* **Achi Man**, *Sheshai* **Sheshay**,
and *Talmai* **Talmay**,
the *children* **born** of Anak, were.
(*Now* Hebron was built seven years
before Zoan **at the face of Soan** in *Egypt* **Misrayim**.)
23 And they came unto the *brook* **wadi** of Eshcol,
and cut down from thence
a *branch* **twig** with one cluster of grapes,
and they bare it between two upon a *staff* **pole**;
and they brought **also** of the pomegranates, and of the figs.
24 The place was called the *brook* **wadi** Eshcol,
because of the *cluster of grapes* **clusters**
which the *children* **sons** of *Israel* **Yisra El**
cut down from thence.
25 And they returned from *searching of* **exploring** the land
after **at the end of** forty days.

EXPLORERS RETURN WORD

26 And they went
and came to *Moses* **Mosheh**, and to *Aaron* **Aharon**,
and to all the *congregation* **witness**
of the *children* **sons** of *Israel* **Yisra El**,
unto the wilderness of Paran, to *Kadesh* **Qadesh**;
and *brought back* **returned** word unto them,
and unto all the *congregation* **witness**,
and *shewed them* **had them see** the fruit of the land.
27 And they *told* **described to** him, and said,
We came unto the land whither thou sentest us,
and surely it floweth with milk and honey;
and this is the fruit of it.
28 *Nevertheless* **Finally**
the people be strong that *dwell* **settle** in the land,
and the cities are *walled* **fortified**, and *very* **mighty** great:
and moreover we saw the *children* **born** of Anak there.
29 *The Amalekites* **Amaleq**
dwell **settleth** in the land of the south:
and the *Hittites* **Hethiy**, and the *Jebusites* **Yebusiy**,
and the *Amorites* **Emoriy**, *dwell* **settle** in the mountains:
and the *Canaanites dwell* **Kenaaniy settle** by the sea,
and by the *coast* **hand** of *Jordan* **Yarden**.
30 And *Caleb* **Kaleb** stilled the people
before *Moses* **Mosheh**, and said,
In ascending, Let us *go up at once* **ascend**, and possess it;
for we are well able to *overcome it* **prevail**.
31 But the men that *went up* **ascended** with him said,
We be not able to *go up* **ascend** against the people;
for they are stronger than we.
32 And they brought up *an evil report* **a slander** of the land
which they had *searched* **explored**
unto the *children* **sons** of *Israel* **Yisra El**,
saying, The land,
through which we have *gone* **passed** to *search* **explore** it,
is a land that eateth *up*
the inhabitants thereof **them who settled**;
and all the people that we saw in *it* **their midst**
are men of *a great stature* **measure**.
33 And there we saw the *giants* **Nephilim**,
the sons of Anak, which come of the *giants* **Nephilim**:
and we were in our own *sight* **eyes** as grasshoppers,
and so we were in their *sight* **eyes**.

THE SONS OF YISRA EL MURMUR

14 And all the *congregation* **witness**
lifted up **and gave** their voice, and cried;
and the people wept that night.
2 And all the *children* **sons** of *Israel* **Yisra El** murmured
against *Moses* **Mosheh** and against *Aaron* **Aharon**:
and the whole *congregation* **witness** said unto them,
Would God **O** that we had died
in the land of *Egypt* **Misrayim**!
or *would God* **O that** we had died in this wilderness!
3 And wherefore hath *the LORD* **Yah Veh**
brought us unto this land, to fall by the sword,
that our *wives* **women** and our children
should be a *prey* **plunder**?
were it not better for us to return into *Egypt* **Misrayim**?
4 And they said *one* **man** to *another* **brother**,
Let us *make a captain* **give a head**,
and let us return into *Egypt* **Misrayim**.
5 Then *Moses* **Mosheh** and *Aaron* **Aharon**
fell *on their faces before* **at the face of** all the
assembly **congregation** of the *congregation* **witness**
of the *children* **sons** of *Israel* **Yisra El**.
6 And *Joshua* **Yah Shua** the son of Nun,
and *Caleb* **Kaleb** the son of *Jephunneh* **Yephunneh**,
which were of them that *searched* **explored** the land,
rent **ripped** their clothes:
7 And they *spake* **said** unto all the *company* **witness**
of the *children* **sons** of *Israel* **Yisra El**, saying,
The land, which we passed through to *search it* **explore**,
is *an exceeding* **a mighty mighty** good land.
8 If *the LORD* **Yah Veh** delight in us,
then he *will* **shall** bring us into this land, and give it us;
a land which floweth with milk and honey.
9 Only rebel not ye against *the LORD* **Yah Veh**,
neither *fear* **awe** ye the people of the land;
for they are bread for us:
their defence is *departed* **turned aside** from them,
and *the LORD* **Yah Veh** is with us: *fear* **awe** them not.
10 But all the *congregation* **witness**
bade **said to** stone them with stones.
And the *glory* **honour** of *the LORD* **Yah Veh**
appeared **was seen**
in the *tabernacle* **tent** of the congregation
before **at the face of** all the *children* **sons** of *Israel* **Yisra El**.
11 And *the LORD* **Yah Veh** said unto *Moses* **Mosheh**,
How long *will* **shall** this people *provoke* **scorn** me?
and how long *will* **shall** it be ere they *believe* **trust** me,
for all the signs
which I have *shewed* **worked** among them?
12 I *will* **shall** smite them with the pestilence,
and *disinherit* **dispossess** them,
and *will make* **shall work** of thee a greater *nation* **goyim**
and mightier than they.

MOSHEH PLEADS FOR THE SONS OF YISRA EL

13 And *Moses* **Mosheh** said unto *the LORD* **Yah Veh**,
Then the *Egyptians* **Misrayim** shall hear it,
(for thou *broughtest up* **ascendest** this people
in thy *might* **force** from among them;)
14 And they *will* **shall** tell it
to *the inhabitants of* **them that settled** this land:
for they have heard that thou *LORD* **Yah Veh**
art among this people,
that thou *LORD* **Yah Veh** art seen *face* **eye** to *face* **eye**,
and that thy cloud standeth over them,
and that thou goest *before them* **at their face**,
by day *time* in a pillar of a cloud,
and in a pillar of fire by night.
15 Now if thou shalt *kill* **deathify** all this people
as one man,
then the *nations* **goyim**
which have heard the *fame* **report** of thee
will speak **shall say**, saying,
16 *Because the LORD* **Yah Veh** was not able
to bring this people
into the land which he *sware* **oathed** unto them,
therefore he hath *slain* **slaughtered** them in the wilderness.
17 And now, I beseech thee,
let the *power* **force** of my *Lord be great* **Adonay greaten**,
according as thou hast *spoken* **worded**, saying,
18 *The LORD* **Yah Veh** is *longsuffering* **slow to wrath**,
and of great mercy,
forgiving iniquity **bearing perversity**
and *transgression* **rebellion**,
and *by no means clearing the guilty*
in exonerating, exonerateth not,
visiting the *iniquity* **perversity** of the fathers
upon the *children* **sons**
unto the third and fourth *generation*.
19 *Pardon* **Forgive**, I beseech thee,
the *iniquity* **perversity** of this people
according unto the greatness of thy mercy,
and as thou hast *forgiven* **borne** this people,
from *Egypt* **Misrayim** even until now.

YAH VEH FORGIVES THE SONS OF YISRA EL

20 And *the LORD* **Yah Veh** said,
I have *pardoned* **forgiven** according to thy word:
21 But as truly as I live,

all the earth shall be filled
with the *glory* **honour** of *the LORD* **Yah Veh**.
22 Because all those men
which have seen my *glory* **honour**, and my *miracles* **signs**,
which I *did* **worked**
in *Egypt* **Misrayim** and in the wilderness,
and have *tempted* **tested** me now these ten times,
and have not hearkened to my voice;
23 Surely they shall not see the land
which I *sware* **oathed** unto their fathers,
neither shall any of them that *provoked* **scorned** me see it:
24 But my servant *Caleb* **Kaleb**,
because he had another spirit with him,
and hath followed me fully,
him *will* **shall** I bring into the land whereinto he went;
and his seed shall possess it.
25 (Now the *Amalekites* **Amaleqiy**
and the *Canaanites dwelt* **Kenaaniy settled** in the valley.)
To morrow *turn* you **shall pull stakes**,
and get you into **unto the face of** the wilderness
by the way of the *Red* **Reed** sea.
26 And *the LORD spake* **Yah Veh worded**
unto *Moses* **Mosheh** and unto *Aaron* **Aharon**, saying,
27 How long *shall I bear with*
— this evil *congregation* **witness**,
which murmur against me?
I have heard the murmerings
of the *children* **sons** of *Israel* **Yisra El**,
which they murmur against me.
28 Say unto them, *As truly as I live* **I live**,
saith the LORD **an oracle of Yah Veh**,
as ye have *spoken* **worded** in mine ears,
so *will* **shall** I *do* **work** to you:
29 Your carcases shall fall in this wilderness;
and all that were *numbered* **mustered** of you,
according to your whole number,
from **sons of** twenty years *old* and upward
which have *murmured* **complained** against me.
30 Doubtless ye shall not come into the land,
concerning which I *sware* **lifted my hand**
to make **that** you *dwell* **tabernacle** therein,
save Caleb **except Kaleb**
the son of *Jephunneh* **Yephunneh**,
and *Joshua* **Yah Shua** the son of Nun.
31 But your *little ones* **toddlers**,
which ye said should be a *prey* **plunder**,
them *will* **shall** I bring in,
and they shall know the land
which ye have *despised* **spurned**.
32 But as for you, your carcases,
they shall fall in this wilderness.
33 And your *children* **sons**
shall *wander* **tend** in the wilderness forty years,
and bear your whoredoms,
until your carcases be *wasted* **consumed** in the wilderness.
34 After the number of the days
in which ye *searched* **explored** the land, even forty days,
each day for a year **a day for a year, a day for a year**,
shall ye bear your *iniquities* **perversities**,
even — forty years,
and ye shall know my *breach of promise* **alienation**.
35 I *the LORD* **Yah Veh** have *said* **worded**,
I will surely do it **If I work not**
unto all this evil *congregation* **witness**,
that are *gathered together* **congregated** against me:
in this wilderness they shall be consumed,
and there they shall die.
36 And the men,
which *Moses* **Mosheh** sent to *search* **explore** the land,
who returned,
and made all the *congregation* **witness**
to murmur against him,
by bringing up a slander upon the land,
37 Even those men
that did bring up the *evil report* **slander** upon the land,
died by the plague
before the LORD **at the face of Yah Veh**.
38 But *Joshua* **Yah Shua** the son of Nun,
and *Caleb* **Kaleb** the son of *Jephunneh* **Yephunneh**,
which were of the men
that went to *search* **explore** the land,
lived *still*.
39 And *Moses told* **Mosheh worded** these *sayings* **words**
unto all the *children* **sons** of *Israel* **Yisra El**:
and the people mourned *greatly* **mightily**.
40 And they *rose up* **started** early in the morning,
and *gat them up* **ascended** into the top of the mountain,
saying, *Lo* **Behold**, we be here,
and *will go up* **shall ascend** unto the place
which *the LORD* **Yah Veh** hath *promised* **said**:
for we have sinned.
41 And *Moses* **Mosheh** said,
Wherefore now do ye *transgress* **trespass**
the *commandment* **mouth** of *the LORD* **Yah Veh**?
but it shall not prosper.
42 *Go not up* **Ascend not**,
for *the LORD* **Yah Veh** is not among you;
that ye be not smitten *before* **at the face of** your enemies.
43 For the *Amalekites* **Amaleqiy**
and the *Canaanites* **Kenaaniy**
are there *before you* **at your face**,
and ye shall fall by the sword:
because ye are turned *away*
from *the LORD* **following Yah Veh**,
therefore *the LORD will* **Yah Veh shall** not be with you.
44 But **in ascending,** they *presumed to go up* **ascended**
unto the *hill* **mountain** top:
nevertheless the ark of the covenant
of *the LORD* **Yah Veh**, and *Moses* **Mosheh**,
departed not out of the camp.
45 Then the *Amalekites came down* **Amaleqiy descended**,
and the *Canaanites* **Kenaaniy**
which *dwelt* **settled** in that *hill* **mountain**,
and smote them, and *discomfited* **crushed** them,
even unto Hormah.

CELEBRATION SEASONS

15 And *the LORD spake* **Yah Veh worded**
unto *Moses* **Mosheh,** saying,
2 *Speak* **Word** unto the *children* **sons** of *Israel* **Yisra El**,
and say unto them,
When ye *be come* **have entered**
into the land of your *habitations* **settlements**,
which I give unto you,
3 And *will make an offering by fire* **shall work a firing**
unto *the LORD* **Yah Veh**,
a *burnt offering* **holocaust**, or a sacrifice,
in performing **or marvel** a vow,
or in a *freewill offering* **voluntary**,
or in your *solemn feasts* **seasons**,
to *make* **work** a *sweet savour* **scent of rest**
unto *the LORD* **Yah Veh**,
of the *herd* **oxen**, or of the flock:
4 Then shall he that *offereth* **oblateth** his *offering* **qorban**
unto *the LORD* **Yah Veh**
bring a meat **oblateth an** offering of a tenth *deal* of flour
mingled **mixed** with the fourth *part* of an hin of oil.
5 And the fourth *part* of an hin of wine
for a *drink offering* **libation** shalt thou *prepare* **work**
with the *burnt offering* **holocaust** or sacrifice,
for one lamb.
6 Or for a ram,
thou shalt *prepare* **work** for *a meat* **an** offering
two *tenth deals* **tenths** of flour
mingled **mixed** with the third *part* of an hin of oil.
7 And for a *drink offering* **libation**
thou shalt *offer* **oblate** the third *part* of an hin of wine,
for a *sweet savour* **scent of rest** unto *the LORD* **Yah Veh**.
8 And when thou *preparest* **workest**
a *bullock* **son of the oxen**
for a *burnt offering* **holocaust**,
or for a sacrifice *in performing* **or marvel** a vow,
or *peace offerings* **shelamim** unto *the LORD* **Yah Veh**:
9 Then shall he *bring* **oblate** with a *bullock* **son of the oxen**
a meat **an** offering of three *tenth deals* **tenths** of flour
mingled **mixed** with half an hin of oil.
10 And thou shalt *bring* **oblate** for a *drink offering* **libation**
half an hin of wine,
for *an offering made by fire* **a firing**,
of a *sweet savour* **scent of rest** unto *the LORD* **Yah Veh**.
11 Thus shall it be *done* **worked** for one *bullock* **ox**,

or for one ram, or for a lamb **of the sheep**,
or *a kid* **of the goats**.
12 According to the number that ye shall *prepare* **work**,
so **thus** shall ye *do* **work** to every one
according to their number.
13 *All that are born of the country* **Each native**
shall *do* **work** these *things* after this manner,
in *offering an offering made by fire* **oblating a firing**,
of a *sweet savour* **scent of rest** unto *the LORD* **Yah Veh**.
14 And if a *stranger* **sojourner** sojourn with you,
or whosoever be among you in your generations,
and *will offer an offering made by fire* **shall work a firing**,
of a *sweet savour* **scent of rest** unto *the LORD* **Yah Veh**;
as ye *do* **work**, so he shall *do* **work**.
15 One *ordinance* **statute**
shall be *both* for you of the congregation,
and also for the *stranger* **sojourner**
that sojourneth with you,
an *ordinance for ever* **eternal statute** in your generations:
as ye are, so shall the *stranger* **sojourner** be
before the LORD **at the face of Yah Veh**.
16 One *law* **torah** and one *manner* **judgment**
shall be for you,
and for the *stranger* **sojourner** that sojourneth with you.
17 And *the LORD spake* **Yah Veh worded**
unto *Moses* **Mosheh**, saying,
18 *Speak* **Word** unto the *children* **sons** of *Israel* **Yisra El**,
and say unto them,
When ye come into the land whither I bring you,
19 Then it shall be, that,
when ye eat of the bread of the land,
ye shall *offer up* **exalt** an *heave offering* **exaltment**
unto *the LORD* **Yah Veh**.
20 Ye shall *offer up* **exalt** a cake of the first of your dough
for an *heave offering* **exaltment**:
as *ye do*
the *heave offering* **exaltment** of the threshingfloor,
so shall ye *heave* **exalt** it.
21 Of the first of your dough
ye shall give unto *the LORD* **Yah Veh**
an *heave offering* **exaltment** in your generations.
22 And if ye have erred **inadvertently**,
and not *observed* **worked**
all these *commandments* **misvoth**,
which *the LORD* **Yah Veh**
hath *spoken* **worded** unto *Moses* **Mosheh**,
23 Even all that *the LORD* **Yah Veh**
hath *commanded* **misvahed** you
by the hand of *Moses* **Mosheh**,
from the day that *the LORD* **Yah Veh**
commanded Moses **misvahed**,
and *henceforward* **beyond** among your generations;
24 Then it shall be,
if ought be *committed* **worked**
by *ignorance* **inadvertent error**
without the knowledge **from the eyes**
of the *congregation* **witness**,
that all the *congregation* **witness**
shall *offer* **work** one *young* bullock **son of the oxen**
for a *burnt offering* **holocaust**,
for a *sweet savour* **scent of rest** unto *the LORD* **Yah Veh**,
with his *meat* offering, and his *drink offering* **libation**,
according to the *manner* **judgment**,
and one *kid* **buck** of the goats for *a sin offering* **the sin**.
25 And the priest shall *make an atonement* **kapar/atone**
for all the *congregation* **witness**
of the *children* **sons** of *Israel* **Yisra El**,
and it shall be forgiven them;
for it is *ignorance* **inadvertent error**:
and they shall bring their *offering* **qorban**,
a *sacrifice made by fire* **firing** unto *the LORD* **Yah Veh**,
and *their sin offering* **that for their sin**
before the LORD **at the face of Yah Veh**,
for their *ignorance* **inadvertent error**:
26 And it shall be forgiven all the *congregation* **witness**
of the *children* **sons** of *Israel* **Yisra El**,
and the *stranger* **sojourner** that sojourneth among them;
seeing all the people were in *ignorance* **inadvertent error**.
27 And if *any* **one** soul sin
through ignorance **by inadvertent error**,
then he shall *bring* **oblate of the goats**,
a *she goat of the first year* **yearling daughter**
for *a sin offering* **the sin**.
28 And the priest
shall *make an atonement* **kapar/atone** for the soul
that *sinneth ignorantly* **erreth inadvertently**,
when he sinneth by *ignorance* **inadvertent error**
before the LORD **at the face of Yah Veh**,
to *make an atonement* **kapar/atone** for him;
and it shall be forgiven him.
29 Ye shall have one *law* **torah** for him
that *sinneth through ignorance* **worketh inadvertent error**,
both for *him that is born* **the native**
among the *children* **sons** of *Israel* **Yisra El**,
and for the *stranger* **sojourner**
that sojourneth among them.
30 But the soul that *doeth ought* **worketh**
presumptuously **with lifted hand**,
whether he be born in the land **of native**,
or *a stranger* **of sojourner**,
the same reproacheth *the LORD* **Yah Veh**;
and that soul shall be cut off from among his people.
31 Because he hath despised
the word of *the LORD* **Yah Veh**,
and hath broken his *commandment* **misvah**,
in cutting, that soul shall *utterly* be cut off;
his *iniquity* **perversity** shall be upon him.
32 And while the *children* **sons** of *Israel* **Yisra El**
were in the wilderness,
they found a man that gathered *sticks* **timber**
upon the *sabbath* **shabbath** day.
33 And they that found him gathering *sticks* **timber**
brought him **had him approach**
unto *Moses* **Mosheh** and *Aaron* **Aharon**,
and unto all the *congregation* **witness**.
34 And they *put* **set** him *in ward* **under guard**,
because it was not *declared* **expressed**
what should be *done* **worked** to him.
35 And *the LORD* **Yah Veh** said unto *Moses* **Mosheh**,
In deathifying,
The man shall be *surely put to death* **deathified**:
all the *congregation* **witness** shall stone him with stones
without the camp.
36 And all the *congregation* **witness**
brought him without the camp,
and stoned him with stones, and he died;
as *the LORD* **Yah Veh**
commanded Moses **misvahed Mosheh**.
37 And *the LORD spake* **Yah Veh worded**
unto *Moses* **Mosheh**, saying,
38 *Speak* **Word** unto the *children* **sons** of *Israel* **Yisra El**,
and *bid them* **say** that they *make* **work** them *fringes* **tassels**
in the borders of their *garments* **clothes**
throughout their generations,
and that they *put* **give** upon the *fringe* **tassel** of the borders
a *ribband* **braid** of blue:
39 And it shall be unto you for a *fringe* **tassel**,
that ye may *look upon it* **see**, and remember
all the *commandments* **misvoth** of *the LORD* **Yah Veh**,
and *do* **work** them;
and that ye *seek* **explore** not
after your own heart and **after** your own eyes,
after which ye *use to go a whoring* **whored**:
40 That ye may remember,
and *do* **work** all my *commandments* **misvoth**,
and be holy unto your *God* **Elohim**.
41 *I am the LORD* **I — Yah Veh** your *God* **Elohim**,
which brought you out of the land of *Egypt* **Misrayim**,
to be your *God* **Elohim**:
I am the LORD **I — Yah Veh** your *God* **Elohim**.

REBELLION OF QORACH

16 Now *Korah* **Qorach**, the son of *Izhar* **Yishar**,
the son of *Kohath* **Qehath**, the son of Levi,
and Dathan and *Abiram* **Abi Ram**, the sons of *Eliab* **Eli Ab**,
and On, the son of Peleth, sons of *Reuben* **Reu Ben**,
took *men*:
2 And they rose up *before Moses* **at the face of Mosheh**,
with certain of the *children* **sons** of *Israel* **Yisra El**,
two hundred and fifty *princes* **hierarchs**
of the *assembly* **witness**,

famous in **the called of** the congregation,
men of *renown* **name**:
3 And they *gathered themselves together* **congregated**
against *Moses* **Mosheh** and against *Aaron* **Aharon**,
and said unto them, *Ye take* too much upon you,
seeing all the *congregation* **witness** are holy,
every one of them,
and *the LORD* **Yah Veh** is among them:
wherefore then *lift* **exalt** ye *up* yourselves
above the congregation of *the LORD* **Yah Veh**?
4 And when *Moses* **Mosheh** heard it, he fell upon his face:
5 And he *spake* **worded** unto *Korah* **Qorach**
and unto all his *company* **witness**, saying,
Even to morrow
the LORD will shew **Yah Veh shall make known**
who are his, and who is holy;
and *will* **shall** cause him to *come near unto* **approach** him:
even him whom he hath chosen
will **shall** he cause to *come near unto* **approach** him.
6 This *do* **work**; Take you *censers* **trays**,
Korah **Qorach**, and all his *company* **witness**;
7 And *put* **give** fire therein, and put incense in them
before the LORD **at the face of Yah Veh** to morrow:
and it shall be
that the man whom *the LORD* **Yah Veh** doth choose,
he shall be holy:
ye take too much upon you, ye sons of Levi.
8 And *Moses* **Mosheh** said unto *Korah* **Qorach**,
Hear, I *pray* **beseech** you, ye sons of Levi:
9 Seemeth it but *a small thing* **petty** unto you,
that *the God* **Elohim** of *Israel* **Yisra El** hath separated you
from the *congregation* **witness** of *Israel* **Yisra El**,
to *bring* **oblate** you *near* to himself
to *do* **serve** the service of the tabernacle
of *the LORD* **Yah Veh**,
and to stand *before* **at the face of** the *congregation* **witness**
to minister unto them?
10 And he hath
brought thee near to **thee to approach** him,
and all thy brethren the sons of Levi with thee:
and seek ye the priesthood also?
11 *For which cause both* **Thus** thou
and all thy *company* **witness**
are *gathered* **congregated** *together*
against *the LORD* **Yah Veh**:
and what is *Aaron* **Aharon**, that ye murmur against him?
12 And *Moses* **Mosheh**
sent to call Dathan and *Abiram* **Abi Ram**,
the sons of *Eliab* **Eli Ab**: which said,
We *will* **shall** not *come up* **ascend**:
13 Is it *a small thing* **petty**
that thou hast *brought us up* **ascended us**
out of a land that floweth with milk and honey,
to *kill* **deathify** us in the wilderness,
except **for which cause**
thou make thyself altogether a prince
in marshalling, thou marshallest over us?
14 *Moreover* **Also** thou hast not brought us
into a land that floweth with milk and honey,
or given us inheritance of fields and vineyards:
wilt **shalt** thou *put* **bore** out the eyes of these men?
we *will* **shall** not *come up* **ascend**.
15 And *Moses* **Mosheh** was *very wroth* **mighty inflamed**,
and said unto *the LORD* **Yah Veh**,
Respect not thou **Turn not thy face to** their offering:
I have not *taken* **lifted** one *ass* **he burro** from them,
neither have I *hurt* **vilified** one of them.
16 And *Moses* **Mosheh** said unto *Korah* **Qorach**,
Be thou and all thy *company* **witness**
before the LORD **at the face of Yah Veh**,
thou, and they, and *Aaron* **Aharon**, to morrow:
17 And take every man his *censer* **tray**,
and *put* **give** incense in them,
and *bring* **oblate** ye
before the LORD **at the face of Yah Veh**
every man his *censer* **tray**,
two hundred and fifty *censers* **trays**;
thou also, and *Aaron* **Aharon**,
each of you **every man** his *censer* **tray**.
18 And they took every man his *censer* **tray**,
and *put* **gave** fire in them, and *laid* **set** incense thereon,
and stood in the *door* **opening**
of the *tabernacle* **tent** of the congregation
with *Moses* **Mosheh** and *Aaron* **Aharon**.
19 And *Korah gathered* **Qorach congregated**
all the *congregation* **witness** against them
unto the *door* **opening**
of the *tabernacle* **tent** of the congregation:
and the *glory* **honour** of *the LORD* **Yah Veh**
appeared unto **was seen by** all the *congregation* **witness**.
20 And *the LORD spake* **Yah Veh worded**
unto *Moses* **Mosheh** and unto *Aaron* **Aharon**, saying,
21 Separate yourselves
from among this *congregation* **witness**,
that I may *consume* **finish** them **off** in a *moment* **blink**.
22 And they fell upon their faces, and said,
O *God* **El**, the *God* **Elohim** of the spirits of all flesh,
shall one man sin,
and *wilt* thou be *wroth* **enraged**
with all the *congregation* **witness**?
23 And *the LORD spake* **Yah Veh worded**
unto *Moses* **Mosheh,** saying,
24 *Speak* **Word** unto the *congregation* **witness**, saying,
Get you up **Ascend ye**
from **round** about the tabernacle of *Korah* **Qorach**,
Dathan, and *Abiram* **Abi Ram**.
25 And *Moses* **Mosheh** rose up
and went unto Dathan and *Abiram* **Abi Ram**;
and the elders of *Israel followed* **Yisra El went after** him.
26 And he *spake* **worded** unto the *congregation* **witness**,
saying, *Depart* **Turn aside**, I *pray* **beseech** you,
from the tents of these wicked men,
and touch *nothing* **naught** of theirs,
lest ye be *consumed* **scraped away** in all their sins.
27 So they *gat up* **ascended** from the tabernacle
of *Korah* **Qorach**, Dathan, and *Abiram* **Abi Ram**,
on every side **round about**:
and Dathan and *Abiram* **Abi Ram** came out,
and *stood* **stationed themselves**
in the *door* **opening** of their tents,
and their *wives* **women**,
and their sons, and their *little children* **toddlers**.
28 And *Moses* **Mosheh** said,
Hereby ye shall know
that *the LORD* **Yah Veh** hath sent me
to *do* **work** all these works;
for I have not done them **and not** of mine own *mind* **heart**.
29 If these men die
the common death of all *men* **humanity**,
or if they be visited
after the visitation of all *men* **humanity**;
then *the LORD* **Yah Veh** hath not sent me.
30 But if *the LORD* **Yah Veh**
make a new thing **create a creature**,
and the *earth open* **soil gape** her mouth,
and swallow them up,
with all that *appertain unto them* **they have**,
and they *go down quick* **descend alive** into *the pit* **sheol**;
then ye shall understand that these men
have *provoked the LORD* **scorned Yah Veh**.
31 And it *came to pass* **became**,
as he had *made an end* **finished**
of speaking **wording** all these words,
that the *ground clave asunder* **soil split**
that was under them:
32 And the earth opened her mouth,
and swallowed them up, and their houses,
and all *the men* **humanity**
that *appertained unto Korah* **were for Qorach**,
and all their *goods* **acquisitions**.
33 They, and all *that appertained to them* **they had**,
went down **descended** alive into the pit,
and the earth closed upon them:
and they *perished* **destructed**
from among the congregation.
34 And all *Israel* **Yisra El** that were round about them
fled at the *cry* **voice** of them:
for they said, Lest the earth swallow us up *also*.
35 And there came out a fire from *the LORD* **Yah Veh**,
and consumed the two hundred and fifty men

that *offered* **oblated** incense.
36 And *the LORD spake* **Yah Veh worded**
unto *Moses* **Mosheh,** saying,
37 *Speak* **Say** unto *Eleazar* **El Azar**
the son of *Aaron* **Aharon** the priest,
that he *take up* **lift** the *censers* **trays**
out of **between** the burning,
and *scatter* **winnow** thou the fire yonder;
for they are hallowed.
38 The *censers* **trays** of these sinners
against their own souls,
let them *make* **work** them *broad plates* **expanded sheets**
for *a covering* **an overlay** of the **sacrifice** altar:
for they *offered* **oblated** them
before the LORD **at the face of Yah Veh,**
therefore they are hallowed:
and they shall be a sign
unto the *children* **sons** of *Israel* **Yisra El.**
39 And *Eleazar* **El Azar** the priest
took the *brasen censers* **copper trays,**
wherewith they that were burnt had *offered* **oblated;**
and they *were made broad plates* **expanded them**
for a covering of the **to overlay the sacrifice** altar:
40 To be a memorial
unto the *children* **sons** of *Israel* **Yisra El,**
so that no **man** — stranger,
which is not of the seed of *Aaron* **Aharon,**
come near **approach** to offer incense
before the LORD **at the face of Yah Veh;**
that he be not as *Korah* **Qorach,**
and as his *company* **witness:**
as *the LORD said* **Yah Veh worded** to him
by the hand of *Moses* **Mosheh.**

SONS OF YISRA EL MURMUR

41 But on the morrow
all the *congregation* **witness**
of the *children* **sons** of *Israel* **Yisra El** murmured
against *Moses* **Mosheh** and against *Aaron* **Aharon,** saying,
Ye have *killed* **deathified**
the people of *the LORD* **Yah Veh.**
42 And it *came to pass* **became,**
when the *congregation was gathered* **witness congregated**
against *Moses* **Mosheh** and against *Aaron* **Aharon,**
that they *looked* **turned their face**
toward the *tabernacle* **tent** of the congregation:
and, behold, the cloud covered it,
and the *glory* **honour** of *the LORD* **Yah Veh**
appeared **was seen.**
43 And *Moses* **Mosheh** and *Aaron* **Aharon** came
before **at the face**
of the *tabernacle* **tent** of the congregation.
44 And *the LORD spake* **Yah Veh worded**
unto *Moses* **Mosheh,** saying,
45 Get you up from among this *congregation* **witness,**
that I may *consume* **finish** them **off** as in a *moment* **blink.**
And they fell upon their faces.
46 And *Moses* **Mosheh** said unto *Aaron* **Aharon,**
Take a *censer* **tray,**
and *put* **give** fire therein from off the **sacrifice** altar,
and put on incense,
and *go* **carry it** quickly unto the *congregation* **witness,**
and *make an atonement* **kapar/atone** for them:
for there is *wrath* **rage** gone out
from the *LORD* **face of Yah Veh;**
the plague is begun.
47 And *Aaron* **Aharon** took
as *Moses commanded* **Mosheh worded,**
and ran into the midst of the congregation;
and, behold, the plague was begun among the people:
and he *put on* **gave** incense,
and *made an atonement* **did kapar/atone** for the people.
48 And he stood
between *the dead* **those that died** and the living;
and the plague was *stayed* **restrained.**
49 Now they that died in the plague
were fourteen thousand and seven hundred,
beside them that died
about the *matter* **word** of *Korah* **Qorach.**
50 And *Aaron* **Aharon** returned unto *Moses* **Mosheh**
unto the *door* **opening**
of the *tabernacle* **tent** of the congregation:
and the plague was *stayed* **restrained.**

AHARON'S ROD BLOSSOMS

17 And *the LORD spake* **Yah Veh worded**
unto *Moses* **Mosheh,** saying,
2 *Speak* **Word** unto the *children* **sons** of *Israel* **Yisra El,**
and take of every one of them a rod — **a rod**
according to the house of their fathers,
of all their *princes* **hierarchs**
according to the house of their fathers twelve rods:
write **inscribe** thou every man's name upon his rod.
3 And thou shalt *write Aaron's* **inscribe Aharon's** name
upon the rod of Levi:
for one rod shall be for the head
of the house of their fathers.
4 And thou shalt *lay* **set** them *up*
in the *tabernacle* **tent** of the congregation
before **at the face of** the *testimony* **witness,**
where I *will* **shall** meet with you.
5 And it shall *come to pass* **become,**
that the man's rod, whom I shall choose, shall blossom:
and I *will make* **shall cause** to cease from me
the murmerings of the *children* **sons** of *Israel* **Yisra El,**
whereby they murmur against you.
6 And *Moses spake* **Mosheh worded**
unto the *children* **sons** of *Israel* **Yisra El,**
and every one of their *princes* **hierarchs**
gave him a rod apiece,
for each prince one
one rod per hierarch — one rod per hierarch,
according to their fathers' houses, even twelve rods:
and the rod of *Aaron* **Aharon** was among their rods.
7 And *Moses laid up* **Mosheh set** the rods
before the LORD **at the face of Yah Veh**
in the *tabernacle* **tent** of witness.
8 And it *came to pass* **became,** that on the morrow
Moses **Mosheh** went into the *tabernacle* **tent** of witness;
and, behold,
the rod of *Aaron* **Aharon** for the house of Levi
was budded **blossomed,**
and brought forth *buds* **blossoms,**
and *bloomed* **blossomed** blossoms, and yielded almonds.
9 And *Moses* **Mosheh** brought out all the rods
from *before the LORD* **the face of Yah Veh**
unto all the *children* **sons** of *Israel* **Yisra El:**
and they *looked* **saw,** and took every man his rod.
10 And *the LORD* **Yah Veh** said unto *Moses* **Mosheh,**
Bring Aaron's **Return Aharon's** rod *again*
before the testimony **at the face of the witness,**
to be *kept* **guarded** for a *token* **sign**
against the *rebels* **sons of rebellion;**
and thou shalt *quite take away* **finish off**
their murmurings from me, that they die not.
11 And *Moses did so* **Mosheh worked:**
as *the LORD commanded* **Yah Veh misvahed** him,
so *did* **worked** he.
12 And the *children* **sons** of *Israel* **Yisra El**
spake **said** unto *Moses* **Mosheh,** saying,
Behold, we *die* **expire,**
we *perish* **destruct,** we all *perish* **destruct.**
13 Whosoever
cometh any thing near unto **in approaching, approacheth**
the tabernacle of *the LORD* **Yah Veh** shall die:
shall we be consumed *with dying* — **to expire?**

MINISTRY OF THE TENT OF WITNESS

18 And *the LORD* **Yah Veh** said unto *Aaron* **Aharon,**
Thou and thy sons and thy father's house with thee
shall bear the *iniquity* **perversity** of the *sanctuary* **holies:**
and thou and thy sons with thee
shall bear the *iniquity* **perversity** of your priesthood.
2 And thy brethren also of the *tribe* **rod** of Levi,
the *tribe* **scion** of thy father, *bring* **oblate** thou with thee,
that they may be joined unto thee, and minister unto thee:
but thou and thy sons with thee *shall minister*
before **at the face of** the *tabernacle* **tent** of witness.
3 And they shall *keep* **guard** thy *charge* **guard,**
and the *charge* **guard** of all the *tabernacle* **tent:**
only they shall not *come nigh* **approach**
the *vessels* **instruments**
of the *sanctuary* **holies** and the **sacrifice** altar,

that neither they, nor ye also, die.
4 And they shall be joined unto thee,
and *keep* **guard** the *charge* **guard**
of the *tabernacle* **tent** of the congregation,
for all the service of the *tabernacle* **tent**:
and a stranger shall not *come nigh* **approach** unto you.
5 And *ye* shall *keep* **guard**
the *charge* **guard** of the *sanctuary* **holies**,
and the *charge* **guard** of the **sacrifice** altar:
that there be no *wrath* **rage** any more
upon the *children* **sons** of *Israel* **Yisra El**.
6 And I, behold,
I have taken your brethren the *Levites* **Leviym**
from among the *children* **sons** of *Israel* **Yisra El**:
to you they are given as a gift for *the LORD* **Yah Veh**,
to *do* **serve** the service
of the *tabernacle* **tent** of the congregation.
7 Therefore thou and thy sons with thee
shall *keep* **guard** your *priest's office* **priesthood**
for every *thing* **word** of the **sacrifice** altar,
and *within* **housing** the vail; and ye shall serve:
I have given your *priest's office* **priesthood** unto you
as a service of gift:
and the stranger that *cometh nigh* **approacheth**
shall be *put to death* **deathified**.
8 And *the LORD spake* **Yah Veh worded**
unto *Aaron* **Aharon**, Behold,
I also have given thee
the *charge* **guard** of mine *heave offering* **exaltment**
of all the *hallowed things* **holies**
of the *children* **sons** of *Israel* **Yisra El**;
unto thee have I given them
by reason of **for** the anointing,
and to thy sons, by an *ordinance for ever* **eternal statute**.
9 This shall be thine of the *most holy things* **holy of holies**,
reserved from the fire:
every *oblation* **qorban** of theirs,
every *meat* offering of theirs,
and *every sin offering of theirs* **all that for their sin**,
and *every trespass offering of theirs* **all that for their guilt**
which they shall *render* **return** unto me,
shall be *most holy* **a holy of holies**
for thee and for thy sons.
10 In the *most holy place* **holy of holies** shalt thou eat it;
every male shall eat it:
it shall be holy unto thee.
11 And this is thine;
the *heave offering* **exaltment** of their gift,
with all the *wave offerings* **waves**
of the *children* **sons** of *Israel* **Yisra El**:
I have given them unto thee,
and to thy sons and to thy daughters with thee,
by *a* **an eternal** statute *for ever*:
every one that is *clean* **pure** in thy house shall eat of it.
12 All the *best* **fat** of the oil,
and all the *best* **fat** of the *wine* **juice**,
and of the *wheat* **crop**,
the *firstfruits* **firstlings** of them
which they shall *offer* **give** unto *the LORD* **Yah Veh**,
them have I given thee.
13 And whatsoever is *first ripe* **firstfruits** in *the* **their** land,
which they shall bring unto *the LORD* **Yah Veh**,
shall be thine;
every one that is clean in thine house shall eat of it.
14 *Every thing* **All that is** devoted in *Israel* **Yisra El**
shall be thine.
15 *Every thing* **All** that *openeth* **bursteth** the matrix
in all flesh,
which they *bring* **oblate** unto *the LORD* **Yah Veh**,
whether it be of men or beasts **human or animal**,
shall be thine:
nevertheless **in redeeming,**
the firstborn of *man* **humanity** shalt thou *surely* redeem,
and the firstling of *unclean beasts* **fouled animals**
shalt thou redeem.
16 And those that are to be redeemed
from **sons of** a month *old* shalt thou redeem,
according to thine *estimation* **appraisal**,
for the *money* **silver** of five shekels,
after the shekel of the *sanctuary* **holies**,
which is twenty gerahs.
17 But the firstling of *a cow* **an ox**,
or the firstling of a *sheep* **lamb**, or the firstling of a goat,
thou shalt not redeem; they are holy:
thou shalt sprinkle their blood upon the **sacrifice** altar,
and shalt *burn* **incense** their fat
for *an offering made by fire* **a firing**,
for a *sweet savour* **scent of rest** unto *the LORD* **Yah Veh**.
18 And the flesh of them shall be thine,
as the wave breast and as the right *shoulder* **hindleg**
are thine.
19 All the *heave offerings* **exaltments**
of the *holy things* **holies**,
which the *children* **sons** of *Israel* **Yisra El**
offer **exalt** unto *the LORD* **Yah Veh**,
have I given thee,
and thy sons and thy daughters with thee,
by *a* **an eternal** statute *for ever*:
it is a covenant of salt *for ever* **eternal**
before the LORD **at the face of Yah Veh**
unto thee and to thy seed with thee.
20 And *the LORD spake* **Yah Veh said** unto *Aaron* **Aharon**,
Thou shalt *have no inheritance in* **not inherit** their land,
neither shalt thou have any *part* **allotment** among them:
I am *thy part* **thine allotment** and thine inheritance
among the *children* **sons** of *Israel* **Yisra El**.
21 And, behold, I have given the *children* **sons** of Levi
all the tenth in *Israel* **Yisra El** for an inheritance,
in exchange for their service which they serve,
even the service
of the *tabernacle* **tent** of the congregation.
22 Neither *must* **shall** the *children* **sons** of *Israel* **Yisra El**
henceforth come nigh **ever again approach**
the *tabernacle* **tent** of the congregation,
lest they bear sin, and die.
23 But the *Levites* **Leviym** shall *do* **serve** the service
of the *tabernacle* **tent** of the congregation,
and they shall bear their *iniquity* **perversity**:
it shall be *a* **an eternal** statute *for ever*
throughout your generations,
that among the *children* **sons** of *Israel* **Yisra El**
they *have* **shall inherit** no inheritance.
24 But the tithes of the *children* **sons** of *Israel* **Yisra El**,
which they *offer* **exalt**
as an *heave offering* **exaltment** unto *the LORD* **Yah Veh**,
I have given to the *Levites* **Leviym** to inherit:
therefore I have said unto them,
Among the *children* **sons** of *Israel* **Yisra El**
they shall *have* **inherit** no inheritance.
25 And *the LORD spake* **Yah Veh worded**
unto *Moses* **Mosheh,** saying,
26 Thus *speak* **word** unto the *Levites* **Leviym**,
and say unto them,
When ye take of the *children* **sons** of *Israel* **Yisra El**
the tithes which I have given you from them
for your inheritance,
then ye shall *offer up* **exalt**
an *heave offering* **exaltment** of it
for the LORD **unto Yah Veh**,
even a *tenth part* **tithe** of the tithe.
27 And this your *heave offering* **exaltment**
shall be *reckoned* **fabricated** unto you,
as *though it were* the *corn* **crop** of the threshingfloor,
and as the fulness of the *winepress* **trough**.
28 Thus ye also shall
offer **exalt** an *heave offering* **exaltment**
unto *the LORD* **Yah Veh** of all your tithes,
which ye *receive* **take**
of the *children* **sons** of *Israel* **Yisra El**;
and ye shall give thereof
the LORD'S heave offering **Yah Veh's exaltment**
to *Aaron* **Aharon** the priest.
29 Out of all your gifts ye shall *offer* **exalt**
every heave offering **the whole exaltment**
of *the LORD* **Yah Veh**,
of all the *best* **fat** thereof,
even the *hallowed part* **holies** thereof out of it.
30 *Therefore* thou shalt say unto them,
When ye have *heaved* **lifted** the *best* **fat** thereof from it,
then it shall be *counted* **fabricated** unto the *Levites* **Leviym**

as the *increase* **produce** of the threshingfloor,
and as the *increase* **produce** of the *winepress* **trough**.
31 And ye shall eat it in every place,
ye and your households:
for it is your *reward* **hire in exchange** for your service
in the *tabernacle* **tent** of the congregation.
32 And ye shall bear no sin by reason of it,
when ye have *heaved* **lifted** from it the *best* **fat** of it:
neither shall ye *pollute* **profane** the *holy things* **holies**
of the *children* **sons** of *Israel* **Yisra El**, lest ye die.

THE WATER OF EXCLUSION

19 And *the LORD spake* **Yah Veh worded**
unto *Moses* **Mosheh** and unto *Aaron* **Aharon**, saying,
2 This is the *ordinance* **statute** of the *law* **torah**
which *the LORD* **Yah Veh** hath *commanded* **misvahed**,
saying,
Speak **Word** unto the *children* **sons** of *Israel* **Yisra El**,
that they *bring* **take** thee a red heifer
without spot **integrious**, wherein is no blemish,
and upon which never *came* **ascended a** yoke:
3 And ye shall give her unto *Eleazar* **El Azar** the priest,
that he may bring her forth without the camp,
and *one* shall *slay* **slaughter** her *before* **at** his face:
4 And *Eleazar* **El Azar** the priest
shall take of her blood with his finger,
and sprinkle of her blood *directly before* **toward the face of** the *tabernacle* **tent** of the congregation seven times:
5 And *one* shall burn the heifer in his *sight* **eyes**;
her skin, and her flesh, and her blood, with her dung,
shall he burn:
6 And the priest shall take cedar *wood* **timber**,
and hyssop, and scarlet,
and cast it into the midst of the burning of the heifers.
7 Then the priest shall *wash* **launder** his clothes,
and he shall *bathe* **baptize** his flesh in water,
and afterward he shall come into the camp,
and the priest shall be *unclean* **fouled** until the even.
8 And he that burneth her
shall *wash* **launder** his clothes in water,
and *bathe* **baptize** his flesh in water,
and shall be *unclean* **fouled** until the even.
9 And a man that is *clean* **pure**
shall gather *up* the ashes of the heifers,
and *lay* **set** them *up*
without the camp in a *clean* **pure** place,
and it shall be *kept* **guarded**
for the *congregation* **witness**
of the *children* **sons** of *Israel* **Yisra El**
for a water of *separation* **exclusion**:
it is *a purification for sin* **for the sin**.
10 And he that gathereth the ashes of the heifer
shall *wash* **launder** his clothes,
and be *unclean* **fouled** until the even:
and it shall be unto the *children* **sons** of *Israel* **Yisra El**,
and unto the *stranger* **sojourner**
that sojourneth among them,
for *a* **an eternal** statute *for ever*.
11 He that toucheth
the *dead body of any man* **human soul that died**
shall be *unclean* **fouled** seven days.
12 He shall purify *himself* **for his sin** with it
on the third day,
and on the seventh day he shall be *clean* **purified**:
but if he purify not *himself* **for his sin** the third day,
then the seventh day he shall not be *clean* **purified**.
13 Whosoever toucheth
the *dead body of any man* **human soul that died**
— that is dead,
and purifieth not *himself* **for his sin**,
defileth **fouleth** the tabernacle of *the LORD* **Yah Veh**;
and that soul shall be cut off from *Israel* **Yisra El**:
because the water of *separation* **exclusion**
was not sprinkled upon him,
he shall be *unclean* **fouled**;
his *uncleanness* **foulness** is yet upon him.
14 This is the *law* **torah**,
when a *man* **human** dieth in a tent:
all that come into the tent, and all that is in the tent,
shall be *unclean* **fouled** seven days.
15 And every open *vessel* **instrument**,
which hath no *covering bound* **clasp braided** upon it,
is *unclean* **fouled**.
16 And whosoever toucheth one
that is *slain* **pierced** with a sword
in the *open* **face of the** fields,
or *a dead body* **that which died**,
or a bone of a *man* **human**, or a *grave* **tomb**,
shall be *unclean* **fouled** seven days.
17 And for *an unclean person* **the fouled**
they shall take of the *ashes* **dust**
of the *burnt* **burning** heifer of purification for sin,
and *running* **living** water shall be *put* **given** thereto
in *a vessel* **an instrument**:
18 And a *clean person* **pure man** shall take hyssop,
and dip it in the water,
and sprinkle it upon the tent,
and upon all the *vessels* **instruments**,
and upon the *persons* **souls** that were there,
and upon him that touched a bone, or one *slain* **pierced**,
or *one dead* **that which died**, or a *grave* **tomb**:
19 And the *clean person* **pure**
shall sprinkle upon the *unclean* **fouled**
on the third day, and on the seventh day:
and on the seventh day
he shall *purify himself* **sacrifice for his sin**,
and *wash* **launder** his clothes,
and *bathe* **baptize** *himself* in water,
and shall be *clean* **purified** at even.
20 But the man that shall be *unclean* **fouled**,
and shall not purify *himself* **for his sin**,
that soul shall be cut off from among the congregation,
because he hath *defiled* **fouled**
the *sanctuary* **holies** of *the LORD* **Yah Veh**:
the water of *separation* **exclusion**
hath not been sprinkled upon him;
he is *unclean* **fouled**.
21 And it shall be *a perpetual* **an eternal** statute unto them,
that he that sprinkleth the water of *separation* **exclusion**
shall *wash* **launder** his clothes;
and he that toucheth the water of *separation* **exclusion**
shall be *unclean* **fouled** until even.
22 And whatsoever the *unclean person* **fouled** toucheth
shall be *unclean* **fouled**;
and the soul that toucheth it
shall be *unclean* **fouled** until even.

DEATH OF MIRYAM

20 Then came the *children* **sons** of *Israel* **Yisra El**,
even the whole *congregation* **witness**,
into the desert of *Zin* **Sin** in the first month:
and the people *abode* **settled** in *Kadesh* **Qadesh**;
and *Miriam* **Miryam** died there,
and was *buried* **entombed** there.
2 And there was no water for the *congregation* **witness**:
and they gathered *themselves together*
against *Moses* **Mosheh** and against *Aaron* **Aharon**.
3 And the people *chode* **chided** with *Moses* **Mosheh**,
and spake, saying,
Would God **O** that we had *died* **expired**
when our brethren *died* **expired**
before the LORD **at the face of Yah Veh**!
4 And why have ye brought up
the congregation of *the LORD* **Yah Veh**
into this wilderness,
that we and our *cattle* **beasts** should die there?
5 And wherefore have ye *made* **ascended** us *to come up*
out of *Egypt* **Misrayim**,
to bring us in unto this evil place?
it is no place of seed,
or of figs, or of vines, or of pomegranates;
neither is there any water to drink.
6 And *Moses* **Mosheh** and *Aaron* **Aharon**
went from the *presence* **face** of the *assembly* **congregation**
unto the *door* **opening**
of the *tabernacle* **tent** of the congregation,
and they fell upon their faces:
and the *glory* **honour** of *the LORD* **Yah Veh**
appeared unto **was seen by** them.

WATER OF MERIBAH/STRIFE

7 And *the LORD spake* **Yah Veh worded**
unto *Moses* **Mosheh,** saying,

8 Take the rod,
and *gather* **congregate** thou the *assembly* **witness** *together,*
thou, and *Aaron* **Aharon** thy brother,
and *speak* **word** ye unto the rock before their eyes;
and it shall give forth his water,
and thou shalt bring forth to them water out of the rock:
so **thus** thou shalt give
the *congregation* **witness** and their beasts drink.
9 And *Moses* **Mosheh** took the rod
from *before the LORD* **the face of Yah Veh,**
as he *commanded* **misvahed** him.
10 And *Moses* **Mosheh** and *Aaron* **Aharon**
gathered **congregated** the congregation *together*
before **at the face of** the rock,
and he said unto them, Hear *now* **I beseech**, ye rebels;
must we fetch you water out of this rock?
11 And *Moses* **Mosheh** lifted up his hand,
and with his rod he smote the rock *twice* **two times**:
and *the* **much** water came out *abundantly,*
and the *congregation* **witness** drank, and their beasts also.
12 And *the LORD spake* **Yah Veh said**
unto *Moses* **Mosheh** and *Aaron* **Aharon,**
Because ye *believed* **trusted** me not,
to *sanctify* **hallow** me
in the eyes of the *children* **sons** of *Israel* **Yisra El,**
therefore ye shall not bring this congregation
into the land which I have given them.
13 This is the water of *Meribah* **Meribah/Strife**;
because the *children* **sons** of *Israel* **Yisra El**
strove with *the LORD* **Yah Veh,**
and he was *sanctified* **hallowed** in them.
14 And *Moses* **Mosheh** sent *messengers* **angels**
from *Kadesh* **Qadesh** unto the *king* **sovereign** of Edom,
Thus saith thy brother *Israel* **Yisra El,**
Thou knowest all the travail that hath *befallen* **found** us:
15 How our fathers
went down **descended** into *Egypt* **Misrayim,**
and we have *dwelt* **settled** in *Egypt* **Misrayim**
a long time **many days**;
and the *Egyptians vexed* **Misrayim vilified** us,
and our fathers:
16 And when we cried unto *the LORD* **Yah Veh,**
he heard our voice, and sent an angel,
and hath brought us forth out of *Egypt* **Misrayim**:
and, behold, we are in *Kadesh* **Qadesh,**
a city in the *uttermost* **end** of thy border:
17 Let us pass, I *pray* **beseech** thee,
through thy *country* **land**:
we *will* **shall** not pass through the fields,
or through the vineyards,
neither *will* **shall** we drink of the water of the wells:
we *will* **shall** go by the *king's high* **sovereign's** way,
we *will* **shall** not *turn* **deviate**
to the right *hand* nor to the left,
until we have passed thy borders.
18 And Edom said unto him, Thou shalt not pass by me,
lest I come out *against* **confronting** thee with the sword.
19 And the *children* **sons** of *Israel* **Yisra El** said unto him,
We *will go* **shall ascend** by the high way:
and if I and my *cattle* **chattel** drink of thy water,
then I *will pay for it* **shall give their price**:
I *will* **shall** only, without *doing any thing else* **a word,**
go **pass** through on my feet.
20 And he said, Thou shalt not *go* **pass** through.
And Edom came out *against* **confronting** him
with much **heavy with** people, and with a strong hand.
21 Thus Edom refused
to *give Israel passage* **let Yisra El pass** through his border:
wherefore *Israel turned away* **Yisra El deviated** from him.

DEATH OF AHARON

22 And the *children* **sons** of *Israel* **Yisra El,**
even the whole *congregation* **witness,**
journeyed **pulled stakes** from *Kadesh* **Qadesh,**
and came unto mount Hor.
23 And *the LORD spake* **Yah Veh said**
unto *Moses* **Mosheh** and *Aaron* **Aharon** in mount Hor,
by the *coast* **border** of the land of Edom, saying,
24 *Aaron* **Aharon** shall be gathered unto his people:
for he shall not enter
into the land which I have given
unto the *children* **sons** of *Israel* **Yisra El,**
because ye rebelled against my *word* **mouth**
at the water of *Meribah* **Strife.**
25 Take *Aaron* **Aharon** and *Eleazar* **El Azar** his son,
and *bring* **ascend** them *up* unto mount Hor:
26 And strip *Aaron* **Aharon** of his *garments* **clothes,**
and put them upon *Eleazar* **El Azar** his son:
and *Aaron* **Aharon** shall be gathered *unto his people,*
and shall die there.
27 And *Moses did* **Mosheh worked**
as *the LORD commanded* **Yah Veh misvahed**:
and they *went up* **ascended** into mount Hor
in the *sight* **eyes** of all the *congregation* **witness.**
28 And *Moses* **Mosheh** stripped *Aaron* **Aharon**
of his *garments* **clothes,**
and *put* **enrobed** them upon *Eleazar* **El Azar** his son;
and *Aaron* **Aharon** died there in the top of the mount:
and *Moses* **Mosheh** and *Eleazar* **El Azar**
came down **descended** from the mount.
29 And when all the *congregation* **witness** saw
that *Aaron was dead* **Aharon had expired,**
they *mourned* **wept** for *Aaron* **Aharon** thirty days,
even all the house of *Israel* **Yisra El.**

21

And when *king* **sovereign** Arad
the *Canaanite* **Kenaaniy,**
which *dwelt* **settled** in the south,
heard tell that *Israel* **Yisra El** came
by the way of *the spies* **Atharim**;
then he fought against *Israel* **Yisra El,**
and *took some* **captured** of them *prisoners* **captives.**
2 And *Israel* **Yisra El** vowed a vow
unto *the LORD* **Yah Veh,** and said,
If **in giving,** thou *wilt indeed deliver* **shalt give** this people
into my hand,
then I *will utterly destroy* **shall devote** their cities.
3 And *the LORD* **Yah Veh**
hearkened to the voice of *Israel* **Yisra El,**
and *delivered up* **gave** the *Canaanites* **Kenaaniy**;
and they *utterly destroyed* **devoted** them and their cities:
and he called the name of the place Hormah.

YAH VEH SENDS SERAPH SERPENTS

4 And they *journeyed* **pulled stakes** from mount Hor
by the way of the *Red* **Reed** sea,
to *compass* **surround** the land of Edom:
and the soul of the people
was *much discouraged* **curtailed** because of the way.
5 And the people *spake* **worded**
against *God* **Elohim,** and against *Moses* **Mosheh,**
Wherefore have ye *brought* **ascended** us *up*
out of *Egypt* **Misrayim** to die in the wilderness?
for there is no bread, neither *is there any* water;
and our soul *loatheth* **abhorreth** this light bread.
6 And *the LORD* **Yah Veh** sent *fiery* **seraph** serpents
among the people, and they bit the people;
and much people of *Israel* **Yisra El** died.
7 Therefore the people came to *Moses* **Mosheh,** and said,
We have sinned,
for we have *spoken* **worded**
against *the LORD* **Yah Veh,** and against thee;
pray unto *the LORD* **Yah Veh,**
that he *take away* **turn aside** the serpents from us.
And *Moses* **Mosheh** prayed for the people.
8 And *the LORD* **Yah Veh** said unto *Moses* **Mosheh,**
Make **Work** thee a *fiery serpent* **seraph,**
and set it upon a pole:
and it shall *come to pass* **become,**
that every one that is bitten,
when he *looketh upon it* **seeth,** shall live.
9 And *Moses made* **Mosheh worked**
a serpent of *brass* **copper,** and put it upon a pole,
and it *came to pass* **became,**
that if a serpent had bitten any man,
when he *beheld* **looked at** the serpent of *brass* **copper,**
he lived.

SONS OF YISRA EL PULL STAKES

10 And the *children* **sons** of *Israel* **Yisra El**
set forward **pulled stakes,**
and *pitched* **encamped** in Oboth.
11 And they *journeyed* **pulled stakes** from Oboth,
and *pitched* **encamped** at *Ijeabarim* **Iye Ha Abiram,**

in the wilderness which is *before* **at the face of** Moab,
toward the *sunrising* **sun dawnward**.
2 From thence they *removed* **pulled stakes**,
and *pitched* **encamped** in the *valley* **wadi** of Zared.
3 From thence they *removed* **pulled stakes**,
and *pitched* **encamped** on the other side of Arnon,
which is in the wilderness that cometh out
of the *coasts* **borders** of the *Amorites* **Emoriy**:
for Arnon is the border of Moab,
between Moab and the *Amorites* **Emoriy**.
4 Wherefore it is said
in the *book* **scroll** of the wars of *the LORD* **Yah Veh**,
What he did **Vaheb** in the *Red* **Reed** sea,
and in the *brooks* **wadies** of Arnon,
5 And at the stream of the *brooks* **storm channels**
that *goeth down* **extendeth**
to the *dwelling of* **settlement at** Ar,
and lieth upon the border of Moab.
6 And from thence *they went to Beer* **to the well**:
that is the well whereof
the LORD spake **Yah Veh said** unto *Moses* **Mosheh**,
Gather the people together,
and I *will* **shall** give them water.
7 Then *Israel* **Yisra El** sang this song,
Spring up **Ascend**, O well; *sing ye* **answer** unto it:
8 The *princes* **governors** digged the well,
the *nobles* **volunteers** of the people digged it,
by the *direction of the lawgiver* **statute setter**,
with their *staves* **crutches**.
And from the wilderness they went to Mattanah:
19 And from Mattanah to *Nahaliel* **Nachali El**:
and from *Nahaliel* **Nachali El** to Bamoth:
20 And from Bamoth in the valley,
that is in the *country* **field** of Moab, to the top of Pisgah,
which looketh toward Jeshimon
at the face of the desolation.
21 And *Israel* **Yisra El** sent *messengers* **angels**
unto *Sihon* **Sichon** *king* **sovereign** of the *Amorites* **Emoriy**,
saying,
22 Let me pass through thy land:
we *will* **shall** not *turn* **deviate** into the fields,
or into the vineyards;
we *will* **shall** not drink of the waters of the well:
but we *will* **shall** go along by the *king's high* **sovereign's** way,
until we *be past* **pass** thy borders.
23 And *Sihon* **Sichon**
would not suffer Israel **gave not Yisra El**
to pass through his border:
but *Sihon* **Sichon** gathered all his people together,
and went out *against Israel* **confronting Yisra El**
into the wilderness:
and he came to *Jahaz* **Yahsah**,
and fought against *Israel* **Yisra El**.
24 And *Israel* **Yisra El** smote him
with the *edge* **mouth** of the sword,
and possessed his land from Arnon unto *Jabbok* **Yabboq**,
even unto the *children* **sons** of Ammon:
for the border of the *children* **sons** of Ammon was strong.
25 And *Israel* **Yisra El** took all these cities:
and *Israel dwelt* **Yisra El settled** in all the cities
of the *Amorites* **Emoriy**,
in Heshbon, and in all the *villages* **daughters** thereof.
26 For Heshbon was the city of *Sihon* **Sichon**
the *king* **sovereign** of the *Amorites* **Emoriy**,
who had fought against
the *former king* **head sovereign** of Moab,
and taken all his land out of his hand, even unto Arnon.
27 Wherefore
they that *speak in proverbs* **proverbialize** say,
Come into Heshbon,
let the city of *Sihon* **Sichon** be built and prepared:
28 For there is a fire gone out of Heshbon,
a flame from the city of *Sihon* **Sichon**:
it hath consumed Ar of Moab,
and the *lords* **masters** of the *high places* **bamahs** of Arnon.
29 Woe to thee, Moab! thou art *undone* **destroyed**,
O people of *Chemosh* **Kemosh**:
he hath given his sons that escaped, and his daughters,
into captivity unto *Sihon* **Sichon**
king **sovereign** of the *Amorites* **Emoriy**.
30 We have shot at them;
Heshbon is *perished* **destroyed** even unto Dibon,
and we have *laid* **desolated** them *waste*
even unto *Nophah* **Nophach**,
which reacheth unto Medeba.
31 Thus *Israel dwelt* **Yisra El settled**
in the land of the *Amorites* **Emoriy**.
32 And *Moses* **Mosheh** sent to spy out *Jaazer* **Yazer**,
and they *took* **captured** the *villages* **daughters** thereof,
and *drove out* **dispossessed** the *Amorites* **Emoriy**
that were there.
33 And *they turned and went up*
from their face they ascended by the way of Bashan:
and Og the *king* **sovereign** of Bashan
went out *against* **confronting** them,
he, and all his people, to the *battle* **war** at Edrei.
34 And *the LORD* **Yah Veh** said unto *Moses* **Mosheh**,
Fear **Awe** him not:
for I have *delivered* **given** him into thy hand,
and all his people, and his land;
and thou shalt *do* **work** to him
as thou *didst* **workedst** unto *Sihon* **Sichon**
king **sovereign** of the *Amorites* **Emoriy**,
which *dwelt* **settled** at Heshbon.
35 So they smote him, and his sons, and all his people,
until *there was none left him alive* **no survivor survived**:
and they possessed his land.

BALAQ AND BILAM

22 And the *children* **sons** of *Israel* **Yisra El**
set forward **pulled stakes**,
and *pitched* **encamped** in the plains of Moab
on this side *Jordan* **Yarden** by *Jericho* **Yericho**.
2 And *Balak* **Balaq** the son of *Zippor* **Sippor**
saw all that *Israel* **Yisra El** had *done* **worked**
to the *Amorites* **Emoriy**.
3 And Moab was *sore* **mighty** afraid
at the face of the people,
because they were many:
and Moab was *distressed* **abhorred**
because **at the face** of the *children* **sons** of *Israel* **Yisra El**.
4 And Moab said unto the elders of *Midian* **Midyan**,
Now shall this *company* **congregation**
lick up all that are round about us,
as the ox licketh up the *grass* **green** of the field.
And *Balak* **Balaq** the son of *Zippor* **Sippor**
was *king* **sovereign** of *the Moabites* **Moab** at that time.
5 He sent *messengers* **angels** *therefore*
unto *Balaam* **Bilam** the son of Beor to Pethor,
which is by the river
of the land of the *children* **sons** of his people,
to call him, saying, Behold,
there is a people come out from *Egypt* **Misrayim**:
behold, they cover the *face* **eye** of the earth,
and they *abide over against* **settle in front of** me:
6 *Come* **Go** now therefore, I *pray* **beseech** thee,
curse me this people; for they are too mighty for me:
peradventure I shall prevail, that we may smite them,
and that I may drive them out of the land:
for I *wot* **know** that he whom thou blessest is blessed,
and he whom thou cursest is cursed.
7 And the elders of Moab
and the elders of *Midian* **Midyan**
departed **went** with the *rewards of* divination
in their hand;
and they came unto *Balaam* **Bilam**,
and *spake* **worded** unto him the words of *Balak* **Balaq**.
8 And he said unto them,
Lodge **Stay** here *this night* **overnight**,
and I *will bring* **shall return** you word *again*,
as *the LORD* **Yah Veh** shall *speak* **word** unto me:
and the *princes* **governors** of Moab
abode **settled** with *Balaam* **Bilam**.
9 And *God* **Elohim** came unto *Balaam* **Bilam**, and said,
What men are these with thee?
10 And *Balaam* **Bilam** said unto *God* **Elohim**,
Balak **Balaq** the son of *Zippor* **Sippor**,
king **sovereign** of Moab, hath sent unto me, *saying*,
11 Behold, there is a people come out of *Egypt* **Misrayim**,
which covereth the *face* **eye** of the earth:
come **go** now, curse me them;

peradventure
I shall *be able* **prevail** to *overcome* **fight** them,
and *drive* **expel** them *out*.
12 And *God* **Elohim** said unto *Balaam* **Bilam**,
Thou shalt not go with them;
thou shalt not curse the people: for they are blessed.
13 And *Balaam* **Bilam** rose up in the morning,
and said unto the *princes* **governors** of *Balak* **Balaq**,
Get you **Go** into your land:
for *the LORD* **Yah Veh** refuseth
to *give me leave* **allow me** to go with you.
14 And the *princes* **governors** of Moab rose up,
and they went unto *Balak* **Balaq**, and said,
Balaam **Bilam** refuseth to come with us.
15 And *Balak* **Balaq** sent yet again *princes* **governors**,
more **greater**, and more honourable than they.
16 And they came to *Balaam* **Bilam**, and said to him,
Thus saith *Balak* **Balaq** the son of *Zippor* **Sippor**,
Let *nothing* **naught**, I *pray* **beseech** thee,
hinder thee from coming unto me:
17 For **in honouring,**
I will promote thee unto very great honour
I shall honour thee mightily,
and I *will do* **shall work** whatsoever thou sayest unto me:
come therefore **go**, I *pray* **beseech** thee,
curse me this people.
18 And *Balaam* **Bilam** answered
and said unto the servants of *Balak* **Balaq**,
If *Balak would* **Balaq should** give me
his house full of silver and gold,
I cannot *go beyond* **trespass** the *word* **mouth**
of *the LORD* **Yah Veh** my *God* **Elohim**,
to *do* **work** less or *more* **greater**.
19 Now therefore, I *pray* **beseech** you,
tarry **settle** ye also here this night,
that I may know what *the LORD* **Yah Veh**
will say **shall word** unto me *more* **again**.

BILAM AND THE ANGEL OF YAH VEH

20 And *God* **Elohim** came unto *Balaam* **Bilam** at night,
and said unto him,
If the men come to call thee, rise up, and go with them;
but yet **surely** the word which I shall *say* **word** unto thee,
that shalt thou *do* **work**.
21 And *Balaam* **Bilam** rose up in the morning,
and *saddled* **harnessed** his *ass* **she burro**,
and went with the *princes* **governors** of Moab.
22 And *God's anger* **Elohim's wrath** was kindled
because he went:
and the angel of *the LORD* **Yah Veh** stood in the way
for *an adversary* **a satan** against him.
Now he was riding upon his *ass* **she burro**,
and his two *servants were* **lads** with him.
23 And the *ass* **she burro**
saw the angel of *the LORD* **Yah Veh**
standing **stationed** in the way,
and his sword drawn in his hand:
and the *ass* **she burro**
turned aside **deviated** out of the way,
and went into the field:
and *Balaam* **Bilam** smote the *ass* **she burro**,
to *turn* **deviate** her into the way.
24 But the angel of *the LORD* **Yah Veh**
stood in a path of the vineyards,
a wall being on this side, and a wall on that side.
25 And when the *ass* **she burro**
saw the angel of *the LORD* **Yah Veh,**
she *thrust* **pressed** *herself* unto the wall,
and *crushed Balaam's* **pressed Bilam's** foot
against the wall:
and he smote her again.
26 And the angel of *the LORD* **Yah Veh**
went further **passed again**,
and stood in a *narrow* **constricted** place,
where was no way to turn
either to the right *hand* or to the left.
27 And when the *ass* **she burro**
saw the angel of *the LORD* **Yah Veh**,
she *fell down* **crouched** under *Balaam* **Bilam**:
and *Balaam's anger was* **Bilam's wrath** kindled,
and he smote the *ass* **she burro** with a staff.
28 And *the LORD* **Yah Veh**
opened the mouth of the *ass* **she burro**,
and she said unto *Balaam* **Bilam**,
What have I *done* **worked** unto thee,
that thou hast smitten me these three *times* **paces**?
29 And *Balaam* **Bilam** said unto the *ass* **she burro**,
Because thou hast *mocked* **exploited** me:
I would **O that** there were a sword in mine hand,
for now *would I kill* **should I have slaughtered** thee.
30 And the *ass* **she burro** said unto *Balaam* **Bilam**,
Am not I *thine ass* **thy she burro**,
upon which thou hast ridden
ever since I was thine unto this day?
was I ever wont to do so unto thee
In using, have I ever been used to work so unto thee?
And he said, Nay.
31 Then *the LORD* **Yah Veh**
opened **exposed** the eyes of *Balaam* **Bilam**,
and he saw the angel of *the LORD* **Yah Veh**
standing **stationed** in the way,
and his sword drawn in his hand:
and he bowed *down his head*,
and *fell flat* **prostrated** on his *face* **nostrils**.
32 And the angel of *the LORD* **Yah Veh** said unto him,
Wherefore hast thou smitten thine *ass* **she burro**
these three *times* **paces**?
behold, I went out to *withstand* **be a satan to** thee,
because thy way is *perverse* **precipitous** before me:
33 And the *ass* **she burro** saw me,
and *turned* **deviated her face** from me
these three *times* **paces**:
unless she had **if she had not**
turned **deviated her face** from me,
surely now also I had *slain* **slaughtered** thee,
and *saved* **preserved** her alive.
34 And *Balaam* **Bilam**
said unto the angel of *the LORD* **Yah Veh**,
I have sinned;
for I knew not
that thou *stoodest* **stationest thyself** in the way
against **to confront** me:
now therefore,
if it *displease thee* **be vilifying in thine eyes**,
I *will get me back again* **shall return**.
35 And the angel of *the LORD* **Yah Veh**
said unto *Balaam* **Bilam**,
Go with the men:
but only **finally** the word that I shall *speak* **word** unto thee,
that thou shalt *speak* **word**.
So *Balaam* **Bilam** went
with the *princes* **governors** of *Balak* **Balaq**.
36 And when *Balak* **Balaq** heard
that *Balaam* **Bilam** was come,
he went out to meet him unto a city of Moab,
which is in the border of Arnon,
which is in the *utmost coast* **end border**.
37 And *Balak* **Balaq** said unto *Balaam* **Bilam**,
In sending,
Did I not *earnestly* send unto thee to call thee?
wherefore camest thou not unto me?
am I not able *indeed* **truly**
to promote thee to honour **thee**?
38 And *Balaam* **Bilam** said unto *Balak* **Balaq**,
lo **behold**, I am come unto thee:
have I now any power at all to say any thing
in being able, am I able to word aught?
the word that *God* **Elohim** putteth in my mouth,
that shall I *speak* **word**.
39 And *Balaam* **Bilam** went with *Balak* **Balaq**,
and they came unto *Kirjathhuzoth* **Qiryath Husoth**.
40 And *Balak* **Balaq**
offered **sacrificed** oxen and *sheep* **flocks**,
and sent to *Balaam* **Bilam**,
and to the *princes* **governors** that were with him.
41 And it *came to pass* **became** on the morrow,
that *Balak* **Balaq** took *Balaam* **Bilam**,
and *brought* **ascended** him *up*
into the high places of Baal **unto Bamah Baal**,
that thence he might see
the *utmost part* **ends** of the people.

BILAM'S ORACLES

23 And *Balaam* **Bilam** said unto *Balak* **Balaq**,
Build me here seven **sacrifice** altars,
and prepare me here seven *oxen* **bullocks** and seven rams.
2 And *Balak did* **Balaq worked**
as *Balaam* **Bilam** had *spoken* **worded**;
and *Balak* **Balaq** and *Balaam* **Bilam**
offered **holocausted** on every **sacrifice** altar
a bullock and a ram.
3 And *Balaam* **Bilam** said unto *Balak* **Balaq**,
Stand by thy *burnt offering* **holocaust**, and I *will* **shall** go:
peradventure
the LORD will come **Yah Veh shall happen** to meet me:
and whatsoever **word** he *sheweth me* **he hath me see**
I *will* **shall** tell thee.
And he went to *an high place* **the barrens**.
4 And *God met Balaam* **Elohim happened upon Bilam**:
and he said unto him,
I have *prepared* **arranged** seven **sacrifice** altars,
and I have *offered* **holocausted** upon every **sacrifice** altar
a bullock and a ram.
5 And *the LORD* **Yah Veh**
put a word in *Balaam's* **Bilam's** mouth, and said,
Return unto *Balak* **Balaq**, and thus thou shalt *speak* **word**.
6 And he returned unto him, and, *lo* **behold**,
he *stood* **stationed himself**
by his *burnt sacrifice* **holocaust**,
he, and all the *princes* **governors** of Moab.
7 And he *took up* **lifted** his *parable* **proverb**, and said,
Balak **Balaq** the *king* **sovereign** of Moab
hath *brought* **led** me from Aram,
out of the mountains of the east, *saying*,
Come **Go**, curse me *Jacob* **Yaaqov**,
and *come* **go**, *defy Israel* **enrage Yisra El**.
8 How shall I *curse* **pierce**, whom *God* **El** hath not cursed?
or how shall I *defy* **enrage**,
whom *the LORD* **Yah Veh** hath not *defied* **enraged**?
9 For from the top of the rocks I see him,
and from the hills I *behold* **observe** him:
lo **behold**, the people shall *dwell* **tabernacle** alone,
and shall not be *reckoned* **fabricated**
among the *nations* **goyim**.
10 Who can *count* **number** the dust of *Jacob* **Yaaqov**,
and the number of the fourth *part* of *Israel* **Yisra El**?
Let *me* **my soul** die the death of the *righteous* **straight**,
and let my *last end* **finality** be like his!
11 And *Balak* **Balaq** said unto *Balaam* **Bilam**,
What hast thou *done* **worked** unto me?
I took thee to curse mine enemies, and, behold,
in blessing, thou hast blessed them *altogether*.
12 And he answered and said,
Must **Shall** I not *take heed* **guard** to *speak* **word**
that which *the LORD* **Yah Veh** hath put in my mouth?
13 And *Balak* **Balaq** said unto him,
Come **Go**, I *pray* **beseech** thee,
with me unto another place,
from whence thou mayest see them:
thou shalt see but the *utmost part* **final end** of them,
and shalt not see them all:
and curse me them from thence.
14 And he *brought* **took** him
into the field of *Zophim* **Watchers**, to the top of Pisgah,
and built seven **sacrifice** altars,
and *offered* **holocausted** a bullock and a ram
on every **sacrifice** altar.
15 And he said unto *Balak* **Balaq**,
Stand *here* **thus** by thy *burnt offering* **holocaust**,
while I *meet the LORD yonder* **happen over there**.
16 And *the LORD* **Yah Veh**
met Balaam **happened upon Bilam**,
and put a word in his mouth, and said,
Go again **Return** unto *Balak* **Balaq**, and *say* **word** thus.
17 And when he came to him, behold,
he *stood* **stationed himself** by his *burnt offering* **holocaust**,
and the *princes* **governors** of Moab with him.
And *Balak* **Balaq** said unto him,
What hath *the LORD spoken* **Yah Veh worded**?
18 And he took up his *parable* **proverb**, and said,
Rise up, *Balak* **Balaq**, and hear;
hearken unto me, thou son of *Zippor* **Sippor**:
19 *God* **El** is not a man, that he should lie;
neither the son of *man* **humanity**,
that he should *repent* **sigh**:
hath he said, and shall he not *do* **work** it?
or hath he *spoken* **worded**,
and shall he not *make it good* **raise**?
20 Behold, I have *received commandment* **taken** to bless:
and he hath blessed; and I cannot *reverse* **turn** it.
21 He hath not *beheld iniquity* **looked at the mischief**
in *Jacob* **Yaaqov**,
neither hath he seen *perverseness* **drudgery**
in *Israel* **Yisra El**:
the LORD **Yah Veh** his *God* **Elohim** is with him,
and the shout of a *king* **sovereign** is among them.
22 *God* **El** brought them out of *Egypt* **Misrayim**;
he hath as *it were* the strength of *an unicorn* **a reem**.
23 Surely there is no *enchantment* **prognostication**
against *Jacob* **Yaaqov**,
neither is there any divination against *Israel* **Yisra El**:
according to this time
it shall be said of *Jacob* **Yaaqov** and of *Israel* **Yisra El**,
What hath *God wrought* **El done**!
24 Behold, the people shall rise up as a *great* **roaring** lion,
and lift up himself as a *young* lion:
he shall not lie down until he eat of the prey,
and drink the blood of the *slain* **pierced**.
25 And *Balak* **Balaq** said unto *Balaam* **Bilam**,
Neither *curse* **pierce** them at all, nor bless them at all.
26 But *Balaam* **Bilam** answered and said unto *Balak* **Balaq**,
Told **Worded** not I **to** thee, saying,
All that *the LORD speaketh* **Yah Veh wordeth**,
that I *must do* **work**?
27 And *Balak* **Balaq** said unto *Balaam* **Bilam**,
Come **Go**, I *pray* **beseech** thee,
I *will bring* **shall take** thee unto another place;
peradventure it will **perhaps it shall be straight**
please God **in the eyes of Elohim**
that thou mayest curse me them from thence.
28 And *Balak brought Balaam* **Balaq took Bilam**
unto the top of Peor,
that looketh toward Jeshimon
at the face of the desolation.
29 And *Balaam* **Bilam** said unto *Balak* **Balaq**,
Build me here seven **sacrifice** altars,
and prepare me here seven bullocks and seven rams.
30 And *Balak did* **Balaq worked** as *Balaam* **Bilam** had said,
and offered a bullock and a ram
on every **sacrifice** altar.
24 And when *Balaam* **Bilam** saw
that it *pleased the LORD* **was good in the eyes of Yah Veh**
to bless *Israel* **Yisra El**,
he went not, as *at other times* **time by time**,
to *seek for enchantments* **confront prognostications**,
but he set his face toward the wilderness.
2 And *Balaam* **Bilam** lifted up his eyes,
and he saw *Israel abiding in his tents* **Yisra El tabernacling**
according to their *tribes* **scions**;
and the spirit of *God* **Elohim** came upon him.
3 And he *took up* **lifted** his *parable* **proverb**, and said,
Balaam **An oracle of Bilam** the son of Beor *hath said*,
and the man **An oracle of the master**
whose eyes **were shut**
are open hath said **but now unveiled**:
4 *He hath said*, **An oracle of him**
which heard the *words* **sayings** of *God* **El**,
which saw the vision of *the Almighty* **Shadday**,
falling *into a trance*, but having his eyes *open* **exposed**:
5 How goodly are thy tents, O *Jacob* **Yaaqov**,
and thy tabernacles, O *Israel* **Yisra El**!
6 As the *valleys* **wadies** are they spread forth,
as gardens by the river's side,
as the *trees of lign* aloes
which *the LORD* **Yah Veh** hath planted,
and as cedar trees beside the waters.
7 He shall *pour* **flow** the water out of his *buckets* **pails**,
and his seed shall be in many waters,
and his *king* **sovereign**
shall be *higher* **more exalted** than Agag,
and his *kingdom* **sovereigndom** shall be exalted.
8 *God* **El** brought him forth out of *Egypt* **Misrayim**;

he hath as *it were* the strength of *an unicorn* **a reem**:
he shall eat *up* the *nations* **goyim** his *enemies* **tribulators**,
and shall *break* **craunch** their bones,
and *pierce* **strike** *them through* with his arrows.
9 He *couched* **kneeled**, he lay down as a lion,
and as a *great* **roaring** lion:
who shall *stir* **rouse** him *up*?
Blessed is he that blesseth thee,
and cursed is he that curseth thee.
10 And *Balak's anger* **Balaq's wrath**
was kindled against *Balaam* **Bilam**,
and he *smote* **clapped** his *hands* **palms** together:
and *Balak* **Balaq** said unto *Balaam* **Bilam**,
I called thee to curse mine enemies, and, behold,
in blessing,
thou hast *altogether* blessed them these three times.
11 Therefore now flee thou to thy place:
I thought to promote thee unto great honour
I had said, In honouring, I honour thee;
but, *lo* **behold**,
the LORD **Yah Veh** hath *kept* **withheld** thee *back*
from honour.
12 And *Balaam* **Bilam** said unto *Balak* **Balaq**,
Spake **Worded** I not also to thy *messengers* **angels**
which thou sentest unto me, saying,
13 If *Balak would* **Balaq should** give me
his house full of silver and gold,
I cannot *go beyond* **trespass**
the *commandment* **mouth** of *the LORD* **Yah Veh**,
to *do either* **work** good or *bad* **evil**
of mine own *mind* **heart**;
but what *the LORD saith* **Yah Veh wordeth**,
that *will* **shall** I *speak* **word**?
14 And now, behold, I go unto my people:
come **go** *therefore*, and I *will advertise* **shall counsel** thee
what this people shall *do* **work** to thy people
in the *latter* **final** days.

ORACLE OF BILAM TO THE SON OF BEOR

15 And he *took up* **lifted** his *parable* **proverb**, and said,
Balaam **An oracle of Bilam** the son of Beor *hath said*,
and the man **An oracle of the master**
whose eyes **were shut**
are open hath said **but now unveiled**:
16 *He hath said,* **An oracle of him**
which heard the *words* **sayings** of *God* **El**,
and knew the knowledge of *the most High* **Elyon**,
which saw the vision of *the Almighty* **Shadday**,
falling *into a trance*, but having his eyes *open* **uncovered**:
17 I shall see him, but not now:
I shall *behold* **observe** him, but not nigh:
there shall *come* **tread** a Star out of *Jacob* **Yaaqov**,
and a *Sceptre* **Scion** shall rise out of *Israel* **Yisra El**,
and shall *smite* **strike** the *corners* **edges** of Moab,
and *destroy* **undermine** all the *children* **sons** of Sheth.

ORACLE OF BILAM TO YISRA EL

18 And Edom shall be a possession,
Seir also shall be a possession for his enemies;
and *Israel* **Yisra El** shall *do* **work** valiantly.
19 Out of *Jacob* **Yaaqov**
shall come he that shall have dominion,
and shall destroy him that *remaineth* **surviveth** of the city.

ORACLE OF BILAM TO AMALEQ

20 And when he *looked on Amalek* **saw Amaleq**,
he *took up* **lifted** his *parable* **proverb**, and said,
Amalek **Amaleq** was the first of the *nations* **goyim**;
but his *latter end* **finality**
shall be *that he perish for ever* **eternal destruction**.

ORACLE OF BILAM TO THE QAYINIY

21 And he *looked on the Kenites* **saw the Qayiniy**,
and *took up* **lifted** his *parable* **proverb**, and said,
Strong is **Perrenial be** thy *dwellingplace* **settlement**,
and thou puttest thy nest in a rock.
22 Nevertheless
the *Kenite* **Qayiniy** shall be *wasted* **consumed**,
until Asshur **when Ashshur**
shall *carry thee away captive* **capture thee**.
23 And he *took up* **lifted** his *parable* **proverb**,
and said, *Alas* **Woe**,
who shall live when *God doeth* **El setteth** this!
24 And ships *shall come*
from the *coast* **hand** of *Chittim* **Kittim**,
and shall *afflict Asshur* **humble Ashshur**,
and shall *afflict Eber* **humble Heber**,
and he also shall *perish for ever* **be to eternal destruction**.
25 And *Balaam* **Bilam** rose up,
and went and returned to his place:
and *Balak* **Balaq** also went his way.

YISRA EL JOINS BAAL PEOR

25 And *Israel abode* **Yisra El settled** in Shittim,
and the people began to *commit whoredom* **whore**
with the daughters of Moab.
2 And they called the people
unto the sacrifices of their *gods* **elohim**:
and the people did eat,
and *bowed down* **prostrated** to their *gods* **elohim**.
3 And *Israel* **Yisra El**
joined himself unto *Baalpeor* **Baal Peor**:
and the *anger* **wrath** of *the LORD* **Yah Veh**
was kindled against *Israel* **Yisra El**.
4 And *the LORD* **Yah Veh** said unto *Moses* **Mosheh**,
Take all the heads of the people,
and *hang* **impale** them *up*
before the LORD **at the face of Yah Veh** against the sun,
that the *fierce anger* **fuming wrath** of *the LORD* **Yah Veh**
may be turned away from *Israel* **Yisra El**.
5 And *Moses* **Mosheh**
said unto the judges of *Israel* **Yisra El**,
Slay ye every one his **Men, slaughter your** men
that were joined unto *Baalpeor* **Baal Peor**.
6 And, behold,
one **a man** of the *children* **sons** of *Israel* **Yisra El** came
and *brought unto* **approached** his brethren
with a *Midianitish* **Midyaniy** woman
in the *sight* **eyes** of *Moses* **Mosheh**,
and in the *sight* **eyes** of all the *congregation* **witness**
of the *children* **sons** of *Israel* **Yisra El**,
who were weeping before the *door* **opening**
of the *tabernacle* **tent** of the congregation.
7 And when *Phinehas* **Phinechas**,
the son of *Eleazar* **El Azar**,
the son of *Aaron* **Aharon** the priest, saw it,
he rose up from among the *congregation* **witness**,
and took a javelin in his hand;
8 And he went after the man of *Israel* **Yisra El**
into the *tent* **belly**,
and *thrust both* **stabbed the two** of them through,
the man of *Israel* **Yisra El**,
and the woman *through* **into** her belly.
So the plague was *stayed* **restrained**
from the *children* **sons** of *Israel* **Yisra El**.
9 And those that died in the plague
were twenty and four thousand.
10 And *the LORD spake* **Yah Veh worded**
unto *Moses* **Mosheh**, saying,
11 *Phinehas* **Phinechas**, the son of *Eleazar* **El Azar**,
the son of *Aaron* **Aharon** the priest,
hath turned my *wrath* **fury** away
from the *children* **sons** of *Israel* **Yisra El**,
while he *was zealous for my sake* **envied over my envy**
among them,
that I *consumed not* **finished not off**
the *children* **sons** of *Israel* **Yisra El** in my *jealousy* **envy**.
12 Wherefore say, Behold,
I give unto him my covenant of *peace* **shalom**:
13 And he shall have it, and his seed after him,
even the covenant of an *everlasting* **eternal** priesthood;
because he *was zealous* **envied** for his *God* **Elohim**,
and *made an atonement* **did kapar/atone**
for the *children* **sons** of *Israel* **Yisra El**.
14 Now the name of the **man**
Israelite — **the Yisra Eliy** that was *slain* **smitten**,
even that was slain with the *Midianitish* **Midyaniy** woman,
was Zimri, the son of *Salu* **Sallu**,
a *prince* **hierarch** of a *chief* **father's** house
among the *Simeonites* **Shimoniy**.
15 And the name of the *Midianitish* **Midyaniy** woman
that was *slain* **smitten** was *Cozbi* **Kozbi**,
the daughter of *Zur* **Sur**;
he was head over a *people* **peoples**,
and *of a chief* **hierarch of a father's** house in *Midian* **Midyan**.

16 And *the LORD spake* **Yah Veh worded**
unto *Moses* **Mosheh,** saying,
17 *Vex* **Tribulate** the *Midianites* **Midyaniy**, and smite them:
18 For they *vex* **tribulate** you with their *wiles* **deceit**,
wherewith they have *beguiled* **deceived** you
in the *matter* **word** of Peor,
and in the *matter* **word** of *Cozbi* **Kozbi**,
the daughter of a *prince* **hierarch** of *Midian* **Midyan**,
their sister,
which was slain in the day of the plague
for Peor's *sake* **word**.

SECOND MUSTER OF THE SONS OF YISRA EL

26 And it *came to pass* **became**, after the plague,
that *the LORD spake* **Yah Veh worded**
unto *Moses* **Mosheh** and unto *Eleazar* **El Azar**
the son of *Aaron* **Aharon** the priest, saying,
2 *Take* **Bear** the *sum* **heads** of all the *congregation* **witness**
of the *children* **sons** of *Israel* **Yisra El**,
from **sons of** twenty years *old* and upward,
throughout **by** their fathers' house,
all that are able to go to *war* **the hostility** in *Israel* **Yisra El**.
3 And *Moses* **Mosheh** and *Eleazar* **El Azar** the priest
spake **worded** with them in the plains of Moab
by *Jordan* **Yarden** near *Jericho* **Yericho**, saying,
4 *Take the sum of the people,*
from **Sons of** twenty years *old* and upward;
as *the LORD* **Yah Veh**
commanded Moses **misvahed Mosheh**
and the *children* **sons** of *Israel* **Yisra El**,
which went forth out of the land of *Egypt* **Misrayim**.

MUSTER OF THE SONS OF REU BEN

5 *Reuben* **Reu Ben**,
the *eldest son* **firstborn** of *Israel* **Yisra El**:
the *children* **sons** of *Reuben* **Reu Ben**;
Hanoch,
of *whom cometh* the family of the *Hanochites* **Hanochiy**:
of Pallu, the family of the *Palluites* **Palluiy**:
6 Of *Hezron* **Hesron**,
the family of the *Hezronites* **Hesroniy**:
of *Carmi* **Karmi**, the family of the *Carmites* **Karmiy**.
7 These are the families of the *Reubenites* **Reu Beniy**:
and they that were *numbered* **mustered** of them
were forty and three thousand
and seven hundred and thirty.

MUSTER OF THE SONS OF PALLU

8 And the sons of Pallu;
Eliab **Eli Ab**.

MUSTER OF THE SONS OF ELI AB

9 And the sons of *Eliab* **Eli Ab**;
Nemuel **Nemu El**, and Dathan, and *Abiram* **Abi Ram**.
This is that Dathan and *Abiram* **Abi Ram**,
which were *famous* **called** in the *congregation* **witness**,
who strove
against *Moses* **Mosheh** and against *Aaron* **Aharon**
in the *company* **witness** of *Korah* **Qorach**,
when they strove against *the LORD* **Yah Veh**:
10 And the earth opened her mouth,
and swallowed them up together with *Korah* **Qorach**,
when that company died **at that witness's death**,
what time **and** the fire *devoured* **consumed**
two hundred and fifty men:
and they became a sign.
11 *Notwithstanding*
the *children* **sons** of *Korah* **Qorach** died not.

MUSTER OF THE SONS OF SHIMON

12 The sons of *Simeon after their* **Shimon by** families:
of *Nemuel* **Nemu El**,
the family of the *Nemuelites* **Nemu Eliy**:
of *Yamin* **Yamiyn**, the family of the *Jaminites* **Yamiyniy**:
of *Jachin* **Yachin**, the family of the *Jachinites* **Yachiniy**:
13 Of *Zerah* **Zerach**, the family of the *Zarhites* **Zerachiy**:
of Shaul, the family of the *Shaulites* **Shauliy**.
14 These are the families of the *Simeonites* **Shimoniy**,
twenty and two thousand and two hundred.

MUSTER OF THE SONS OF GAD

15 The *children* **sons** of Gad *after their* **by** families:
of *Zephon* **Sephoniy**,
the family of the *Zephonites* **Sephoniy**:
of Haggi, the family of the *Haggites* **Haggiy**:
of Shuni, the family of the *Shunites* **Shuniy**:
16 Of Ozni, the family of the *Oznites* **Ozniy**:
of *Eri* **Eriy**, the family of the *Erites* **Eriy**:
17 Of *Arod* **Arodi**, the family of the *Arodites* **Arodiy**:
of Areli, the family of the *Arelites* **Areliy**.
18 These are the families of the *children* **sons** of Gad
according to those that were *numbered* **mustered** of them,
forty thousand and five hundred.
19 The sons of *Judah* **Yah Hudah** were Er and Onan:
and Er and Onan died in the land of *Canaan* **Kenaan**.

MUSTER OF THE SONS OF YAH HUDAH

20 And the sons of *Judah* **Yah Hudah**
after their **by** families were;
of Shelah, the family of the *Shelanites* **Shelaniy**:
of *Pharez* **Peres**, the family of the *Pharzites* **Peresiy**:
of *Zerah* **Zerach**, the family of the *Zarhites* **Zerachiy**.
21 And the sons of *Pharez* **Peres** were;
of *Hezron* **Hesron**, the family of the *Hezronites* **Hezroniy**:
of Hamul, the family of the *Hamulites* **Hamuliy**.
22 These are the families of *Judah* **Yah Hudah**
according to those *that were numbered* **mustered** of them,
threescore and sixteen **seventy and six** thousand
and five hundred.

MUSTER OF THE SONS OF YISSACHAR

23 Of the sons of *Issachar after their* **Yissachar by** families:
of Tola, the family of the *Tolaites* **Tolaiy**:
of *Pua* **Puah**, the family of the *Punites* **Puniy**:
24 Of *Jashub* **Yashub**,
the family of the *Jashubites* **Yashubiy**:
of Shimron, the family of the *Shimronites* **Shimroniy**.
25 These are the families of *Issachar* **Yissachar**
according to those that were *numbered* **mustered** of them,
threescore **sixty** and four thousand and three hundred.

MUSTER OF THE SONS OF ZEBULUN

26 Of the sons of Zebulun *after their* **by** families:
of Sered, the family of the *Sardites* **Sardiy**:
of Elon, the family of the *Elonites* **Eloniy**:
of *Jahleel* **Yachle El**,
the family of the *Jahleelites* **Yachle Eliy**.
27 These are the families of the *Zebulunites* **Zebuluniy**
according to those that were *numbered* **mustered** of them,
threescore **sixty** thousand and five hundred.

MUSTER OF THE SONS OF MENASH SHEH
THE SON OF YOSEPH

28 The sons of *Joseph after their* **Yoseph by** families
were *Manasseh* **Menash Sheh** and *Ephraim* **Ephrayim**.
29 Of the sons of *Manasseh* **Menash Sheh**:
of Machir, the family of the *Machirites* **Machiriy**:
and Machir begat *Gilead* **Gilad**:
of *Gilead* **Gilad** *come* the family of the *Gileadites* **Giladiy**.
30 These are the sons of *Gilead* **Gilad**:
of *Jeezer* **Iy Ezer**, the family of the *Jeezerites* **Iy Ezeriy**:
of *Helek* **Heleq**, the family of the *Helekites* **Heleqiy**:
31 And of *Asriel* **Asri El**,
the family of the *Asrielites* **Asri Eliy**
and of Shechem,
the family of the *Shechemites* **Shechemiy**
32 And of *Shemida* **Shemiyda**,
the family of the *Shemidaites* **Shemidaiy**:
and of Hepher, the family of the *Hepherites* **Hepheriy**.
33 And *Zelophehad* **Seloph Had** the son of Hepher
had no sons, but daughters:
and the names of the daughters
of *Zelophehad* **Seloph Had**
were *Mahlah* **Machlah**, and Noah,
Hoglah, *Milcah* **Milchah**, and *Tirzah* **Tirsah**.
34 These are the families of *Manasseh* **Menash Sheh**,
and those that were *numbered* **mustered** of them,
fifty and two thousand and seven hundred.

MUSTER OF THE SONS OF EPHRAYIM
THE SON OF YOSEPH

35 These are the sons of *Ephraim* **Ephrayim**
after their **by** families:
of *Shuthelah* **Shu Telach**,
the family of the *Shuthalhites* **Shu Telachiy**:
of Becher, the family of the *Bachrites* **Becheriy**:
of *Tahan* **Tachan**, the family of the *Tahanites* **Tachaniy**.
36 And these are the sons of *Shuthelah* **Shu Thelach**:
of Eran, the family of the *Eranites* **Eraniy**.
37 These are the families of the sons of *Ephraim* **Ephrayim**
according to those that were *numbered* **mustered** of them,

thirty and two thousand and five hundred.
These are the sons of *Joseph after their* **Yoseph by** families.

MUSTER OF THE SONS OF BEN YAMIN

38 The sons of *Benjamin after their* **Ben Yamin by** families:
of Bela, the family of the *Belaites* **Belaiy**:
of Ashbel, the family of the *Ashbelites* **Ashbeliy**:
of *Ahiram* **Achi Ramiy**,
the family of the *Ahiramites* **Ach Ramiy**:
39 Of *Shupham* **Shuphupham**,
the family of the *Shuphamites* **Shuphuphamiy**:
of Hupham, the family of the *Huphamites* **Huphamiy**.
40 And the sons of Bela were Ard and Naaman:
of Ard, the family of the *Ardites* **Ardiy**:
and of Naaman, the family of the *Naamites* **Naamiy**.
41 These are the sons of *Benjamin* **Ben Yamin**
after their **by** families:
and they that were *numbered* **mustered** of them
were forty and five thousand and six hundred.

MUSTER OF THE SONS OF DAN

42 These are the sons of Dan *after their* **by** families:
of *Shuham* **Shucham**,
the family of the *Shuhamites* **Shuchamiy**.
These are the families of Dan *after their* **by** families.
43 All the families of the *Shuhamites* **Shuchamiy**,
according to those that were *numbered* **mustered** of them,
were threescore **sixty** and four thousand and four hundred.

MUSTER OF THE SONS OF ASHER

44 Of the *children* **sons** of Asher *after their* **by** families:
of *Jimna* **Yimnah**, the family of the *Jimnites* **Yimnahy**:
of *Jesui* **Yishvi**, the family of the *Jesuites* **Yishviy**:
of Beriah, the family of the *Beriites* **Beriiy**.
45 Of the sons of Beriah:
of Heber, the family of the *Heberites* **Heberiy**:
of *Malchiel* **Malki El**,
the family of the *Malchielites* **Malki Eliy**.
46 And the name of the daughter of Asher
was *Sarah* **Serach**.
47 These are the families of the sons of Asher
according to those that were *numbered* **mustered** of them;
who were fifty and three thousand and four hundred.

MUSTER OF THE SONS OF NAPHTALI

48 Of the sons of Naphtali *after their* **by** families:
of *Jahzeel* **Yachse El**,
the family of the *Jahzeelites* **Yachse Eliy**:
of Guni, the family of the *Gunites* **Guniy**:
49 Of *Jezer* **Yeser**, the family of the *Jezerites* **Yeseriy**:
of Shillem, the family of the *Shillemites* **Shillemiy**.
50 These are the families of Naphtali
according to their **by** families:
and they that were *numbered* **mustered** of them
were forty and five thousand and four hundred.
51 These were the *numbered* **mustered**
of the *children* **sons** of *Israel* **Yisra El**,
six hundred thousand
and a thousand seven hundred and thirty.
52 And *the LORD spake* **Yah Veh worded**
unto *Moses* **Mosheh,** saying,
53 Unto these the land shall be *divided* **apportioned**
for an inheritance according to the number of names.
54 To many
thou shalt *give the more* **greaten the** inheritance,
and to few
thou shalt *give the less* **diminish the** inheritance:
to every *one* **man** shall his inheritance be given
according to **the mouth of** those
that were *numbered* **mustered** of him.
55 Notwithstanding
the land shall be *divided* **apportioned** by *lot* **pebble**:
according to the names of the *tribes* **rods** of their fathers
they shall inherit.
56 According to the *lot* **mouth of the pebble**
shall the *possession* **inheritance** thereof
be *divided* **apportioned** between many and few.

MUSTER OF THE LEVIYM

57 And these are they that were *numbered* **mustered**
of the *Levites after their* **Leviym by** families:
of Gershon, the family of the *Gershonites* **Gershoniy**:
of *Kohath* **Qehath**, the family of the *Kohathites* **Qehathiy**:
of Merari, the family of the *Merarites* **Merariy**.
58 These are the families of the *Levites* **Leviym**:
the family of the *Libnites* **Libniy**,
the family of the *Hebronites* **Hebroniy**,
the family of the *Mahlites* **Machliy**,
the family of the *Mushites* **Mushiy**,
the family of the *Korathites* **Qorachiy**.
And *Kohath* **Qehath** begat *Amram* **Am Ram**.
59 And the name of *Amram's wife* **Am Ram's woman**
was *Jochebed* **Yah Chebed**, the daughter of Levi,
whom her mother who bare to Levi in *Egypt* **Misrayim**:
and she bare unto *Amram* **Am Ram**
Aaron **Aharon** and *Moses* **Mosheh**,
and *Miriam* **Miryam** their sister.
60 And unto *Aaron* **Aharon** was born
Nadab, and *Abihu* **Abi Hu**,
Eleazar **El Azar**, and *Ithamar* **Iy Thamar**.
61 And Nadab and *Abihu* **Abi Hu** died,
when they *offered* **oblated** strange fire
before the LORD **at the face of Yah Veh**.
62 And those that were *numbered* **mustered** of them
were twenty and three thousand,
all males *from* **sons of** a month *old* and upward:
for they were not *numbered* **mustered**
among the *children* **sons** of *Israel* **Yisra El**,
because there was no inheritance given them
among the *children* **sons** of *Israel* **Yisra El**.
63 These are they that were *numbered* **mustered**
by *Moses* **Mosheh** and *Eleazar* **El Azar** the priest,
who *numbered* **mustered**
the *children* **sons** of *Israel* **Yisra El**
in the plains of Moab
by *Jordan* **Yarden** near *Jericho* **Yericho**.
64 But among these there was not a man of them
whom *Moses* **Mosheh** and *Aaron* **Aharon** the priest
numbered **mustered**,
when they *numbered* **mustered**
the *children* **sons** of *Israel* **Yisra El**
in the wilderness of *Sinai* **Sinay**.
65 For *the LORD* **Yah Veh** had said of them,
In deathifying, They shall *surely die* **be deathified**
in the wilderness.
And there *was* **remained** not *left* a man of them,
save Caleb **except Kaleb**
the son of *Jephunneh* **Yephunneh**,
and *Joshua* **Yah Shua** the son of Nun.

INHERITANCE OF THE DAUGHTERS OF YISRA EL

27 Then *came* **approached**
the daughters of *Zelophehad* **Seloph Had**,
the son of Hepher, the son of *Gilead* **Gilad**,
the son of Machir,
the son of *Manasseh* **Menash Sheh**,
of the families of *Manasseh* **Menash Sheh**
the son of *Joseph* **Yoseph**:
and these are the names of his daughters;
Mahlah **Machlah**, Noah, and Hoglah,
and *Milcah* **Milchah**, and *Tirzah* **Tirsah**.
2 And they stood *before Moses* **at the face of Mosheh**,
and *before Eleazar* **at the face of El Azar** the priest,
and *before the princes* **at the face of the hierarchs**
and all the *congregation* **witness**,
by the *door* **opening**
of the *tabernacle* **tent** of the congregation, saying,
3 Our father died in the wilderness,
and he was not *in* **in midst** the *company* **witness**
of them that *gathered* **congregated** *themselves together*
against *the LORD* **Yah Veh**
in the *company* **witness** of *Korah* **Qorach**;
but died in his own sin, and had no sons.
4 Why should the name of our father
be done away from among his family,
because he hath no son?
Give unto us *therefore* a possession
among the brethren of our father.
5 And *Moses* **Mosheh**
brought **oblated** their *cause* **judgment**
before the LORD **at the face of Yah Veh**.
6 And *the LORD spake* **Yah Veh said** unto *Moses* **Mosheh**,
saying,
7 The daughters of *Zelophehad* **Seloph Had**
speak right **have worded thus**:
in giving, thou shalt *surely* give them a possession

of an inheritance among their father's brethren;
and thou shalt cause the inheritance of their father
to pass unto them.
8 And thou shalt *speak* **word**
unto the *children* **sons** of *Israel* **Yisra El**, saying,
If a man die, and have no son,
then ye shall cause his inheritance
to pass unto his daughter.
9 And if he have no daughter,
then ye shall give his inheritance unto his brethren.
10 And if he have no brethren,
then ye shall give his inheritance
unto his father's brethren.
11 And if his father have no brethren,
then ye shall give his inheritance
unto *his kinsman that is next to him* **the kinflesh**
of his family,
and he shall possess it:
and it shall be unto the *children* **sons** of *Israel* **Yisra El**
a statute of judgment,
as *the LORD* **Yah Veh**
commanded Moses **misvahed Mosheh**.
12 And *the LORD* **Yah Veh** said unto *Moses* **Mosheh**,
Get thee up **Ascend** into this mount Abarim,
and see the land which I have given
unto the *children* **sons** of *Israel* **Yisra El**.
13 And when thou hast seen it,
thou also shalt be gathered unto thy people,
as *Aaron* **Aharon** thy brother was gathered.
14 For ye rebelled against my *commandment* **mouth**
in the *desert* **wilderness** of *Zin* **Sin**,
in the strife of the *congregation* **witness**,
to *sanctify* **hallow** me at the water before their eyes:
that is the water of *Meribah* **Strife**
in *Kadesh* **Qadesh** in the wilderness of *Zin* **Sin**.

MOSHEH MISVAHS YAH SHUA

15 And *Moses spake* **Mosheh worded**
unto *the LORD* **Yah Veh**, saying,
16 Let *the LORD* **Yah Veh**,
the *God* **Elohim** of the spirits of all flesh,
set **muster** a man over the *congregation* **witness**,
17 Which may go out *before them* **at their face**,
and which may go in *before them* **at their face**,
and which may lead them out,
and which may bring them in;
that the *congregation* **witness** of *the LORD* **Yah Veh**
be not as *sheep* **flocks** which have no *shepherd* **tender**.
18 And *the LORD* **Yah Veh** said unto *Moses* **Mosheh**,
Take thee *Joshua* **Yah Shua** the son of Nun,
a man in whom is the spirit,
and *lay* **prop** thine hand upon him;
19 And *set* **stand** him
before Eleazar **at the face of El Azar** the priest,
and *before* **at the face of** all the *congregation* **witness**;
and *give* **misvah** him *a charge* in their *sight* **eyes**.
20 And thou shalt *put* **give**
some of thine *honour* **majesty** upon him,
that all the *congregation* **witness**
of the *children* **sons** of *Israel* **Yisra El**
may *be obedient* **hearken**.
21 And he shall stand
before Eleazar **at the face of El Azar** the priest,
who shall ask *counsel* for him
after the judgment of Urim
before the LORD **at the face of Yah Veh**:
at his *word* **mouth** shall they go out,
and at his *word* **mouth** they shall come in,
both he,
and all the *children* **sons** of *Israel* **Yisra El** with him,
even all the *congregation* **witness**.
22 And *Moses did* **Mosheh worked**
as *the LORD commanded* **Yah Veh misvahed** him:
and he took *Joshua* **Yah Shua**,
and *set* **stood** him
before Eleazar **at the face of El Azar** the priest,
and *before* **at the face of** all the *congregation* **witness**:
23 And he *laid* **propped** his hands upon him,
and *gave* **misvahed** him *a charge*,
as *the LORD commanded* **Yah Veh worded**
by the hand of *Moses* **Mosheh**.

DAILY OBLATIONS UNTO YAH VEH

28 And *the LORD spake* **Yah Veh worded**
unto *Moses* **Mosheh**, saying,
2 *Command* **Misvah** the *children* **sons** of *Israel* **Yisra El**,
and say unto them,
My *offering* **qorban**,
and my bread for my *sacrifices made by fire* **firings**,
for a *sweet savour unto me* **scent of my rest**,
shall ye *observe* **guard**
to *offer* **oblate** unto me in their *due* season.
3 And thou shalt say unto them,
This is the *offering made by fire* **firing**
which ye shall *offer* **oblate** unto *the LORD* **Yah Veh**;
two lambs
of the first year without spot **yearling sons integrious**
day by day **daily**, for a continual *burnt offering* **holocaust**.
4 The one lamb shalt thou *offer* **work** in the morning,
and the *other* **second** lamb
shalt thou *offer at even* **work between evenings**;
5 And a tenth *part* of an ephah of flour
for *a meat* **an** offering,
mingled **mixed** with
the fourth *part* of an hin of *beaten* **pestled** oil.
6 It is a continual *burnt offering* **holocaust**,
which was *ordained* **worked** in mount *Sinai* **Sinay**
for a *sweet savour* **scent of rest**,
a *sacrifice made by fire* **firing** unto *the LORD* **Yah Veh**.
7 And the *drink offering* **libation** thereof
shall be the fourth *part* of an hin for the one lamb:
in the *holy place* **holies**
shalt thou cause the *strong wine* **intoxicants**
to be *poured* **libated** unto *the LORD* **Yah Veh**
for a *drink offering* **libation**.
8 And the *other* **second** lamb
shalt thou *offer at even* **work between evenings**:
as the *meat* offering of the morning,
and as the *drink offering* **libation** thereof,
thou shalt *offer* **work** it, a *sacrifice made by fire* **firing**,
of a *sweet savour* **scent of rest** unto *the LORD* **Yah Veh**.

SHABBATH OBLATIONS UNTO YAH VEH

9 And on the *sabbath* **shabbath** day
two lambs
of the first year without spot **yearling sons integrious**,
and two *tenth deals* **tenths** of flour for *a meat* **an** offering,
mingled **mixed** with oil,
and the *drink offering* **libation** thereof:
10 This is the *burnt offering* **holocaust**
of *every sabbath* **the shabbath on the shabbath**,
beside the continual *burnt offering* **holocaust**,
and his *drink offering* **libation**.

MONTHLY OBLATIONS UNTO YAH VEH

11 And in the *beginnings* **heads** of your months
ye shall *offer* **oblate** a *burnt offering* **holocaust**
unto *the LORD* **Yah Veh**;
two *young bullocks* **son bullocks of the oxen**,
and one ram,
seven lambs
of the first year without spot **yearling sons integrious**;
12 And three *tenth deals* **tenths** of flour
for *a meat* **an** offering,
mingled **mixed** with oil, for one bullock;
and two *tenth deals* **tenths** of flour for *a meat* **an** offering,
mingled **mixed** with oil, for one ram;
13 And a *several tenth deal* **tenth and a tenth** of flour
mingled **mixed** with oil
for *a meat* **an** offering unto one lamb;
for a *burnt offering* **holocaust**
of a *sweet savour* **scent of rest**,
a *sacrifice made by fire* **firing** unto *the LORD* **Yah Veh**.
14 And their *drink offerings* **libations**
shall be half an hin of wine unto a bullock,
and the third *part* of an hin unto a ram,
and a fourth *part* of an hin unto a lamb:
this is the *burnt offering* **holocaust**
of *every* month **by month**
throughout the months of the year.
15 And one *kid* **buck** of the goats for *a sin offering* **the sin**
unto *the LORD* **Yah Veh** shall be *offered* **worked**,
beside the continual *burnt offering* **holocaust**,
and his *drink offering* **libation**.

Pasach unto Yah Veh

16 *And in the fourteenth day of the first month*
And in the first month,
on the fourteenth day of the month
is the *passover* **pasach** of *the LORD* **Yah Veh.**
17 And in the fifteenth day of this month
is the *feast* **celebration**:
seven days shall *unleavened bread* **matsah** be eaten.
18 In the first day shall be an holy convocation;
ye shall *do* work
no *manner* **work** of *servile therein* **service**:
19 But ye shall *offer* **oblate** a *sacrifice made by fire* **firing**
for a *burnt offering* **holocaust** unto *the LORD* **Yah Veh**;
two *young bullocks* **sons of the oxen**, and one ram,
and seven lambs *of the first year* **yearling sons**:
they shall be unto you *without blemish* **integrious**:
20 And their *meat* offering shall be of flour
mingled **mixed** with oil:
three *tenth deals* **tenths** shall ye *offer* **work** for a bullock,
and two *tenth deals* **tenths** for a ram;
21 A *several tenth deal* **tenth and a tenth**
shalt thou *offer* **work** for *every* **one** lamb,
throughout the seven lambs:
22 And one *goat for a sin offering* **buck for the sin**,
to *make an atonement* **kapar/atone** for you.
23 Ye shall *offer* **work** these
beside the *burnt offering* **holocaust** in the morning,
which is for a continual *burnt offering* **holocaust**.
24 *After* **As** this *manner* ye shall *offer* **work** daily,
throughout the seven days,
the *meat* **bread** of the *sacrifice made by fire* **firing**,
of a *sweet savour* **scent of rest** unto *the LORD* **Yah Veh**:
it shall be *offered* **worked**
beside the continual *burnt offering* **holocaust**,
and his *drink offering* **libation**.
25 And on the seventh day
ye shall have an holy convocation;
ye shall *do no servile* work **no work of service**.

Weeks Offering unto Yah Veh

26 Also in the day of the firstfruits,
when ye *bring* **oblate** a new *meat* offering
unto *the LORD* **Yah Veh**,
after your weeks *be out*,
ye shall have an holy convocation;
ye shall *do no servile* work **no work of service**:
27 But ye shall *offer* **oblate** the *burnt offering* **holocaust**
for a *sweet savour* **scent of rest** unto *the LORD* **Yah Veh**;
two *young* **son** bullocks **of the oxen**,
one ram, seven lambs *of the first year* **yearling sons**;
28 And their *meat* offering of flour *mingled* **mixed** with oil,
three *tenth deals* **tenths** unto one bullock,
two *tenth deals* **tenths** unto one ram,
29 A *several tenth deal* **tenth and a tenth** unto one lamb,
throughout **for** the seven lambs;
30 And one *kid* **buck** of the goats,
to *make an atonement* **kapar/atone** for you.
31 Ye shall *offer* **work** them
beside the continual *burnt offering* **holocaust**,
and his *meat* offering,
(they shall be unto you *without blemish* **integrious**)
and their *drink offerings* **libations**.

Blastings unto Yah Veh

29 And in the seventh month,
on the first *day* of the month,
ye shall have an holy convocation;
ye shall *do no servile* work **no work of service**:
it is a day of *blowing the trumpets* **blastings** unto you.
2 And ye shall *offer* **work** a *burnt offering* **holocaust**
for a *sweet savour* **scent of rest** unto *the LORD* **Yah Veh**;
one *young* bullock **son of the oxen**, one ram,
and seven lambs
of the first year without blemish **yearling sons integrious**:
3 And their *meat* offering
shall be of flour *mingled* **mixed** with oil,
three *tenth deals* **tenths** for a bullock,
and two *tenth deals* **tenths** for a ram,
4 And one tenth *deal* for one lamb,
throughout the seven lambs:
5 And one *kid* **buck** of the goats for *a sin offering* **the sin**,
to *make an atonement* **kapar/atone** for you:
6 Beside the *burnt offering* **holocaust** of the month,
and his *meat* offering,
and the *daily burnt offering* **continual holocaust**,
and his *meat* offering,
and their *drink offerings* **libations**,
according unto their *manner* **judgment**,
for a *sweet savour* **scent of rest**,
a *sacrifice made by fire* **firing** unto *the LORD* **Yah Veh**.

Holy Convocations unto Yah Veh

7 And ye shall have
on the tenth *day* of this seventh month
an holy convocation;
and ye shall *afflict* **humble** your souls:
ye shall *not do any* **work no** work *therein*:
8 But ye shall *offer* **oblate** a *burnt offering* **holocaust**
unto *the LORD* **Yah Veh** for a *sweet savour* **scent of rest**;
one *young* bullock **son of the oxen**, one ram,
and seven lambs *of the first year* **yearling sons**;
they shall be unto you *without blemish* **integrious**:
9 And their *meat* offering
shall be of flour *mingled* **mixed** with oil,
three *tenth deals* **tenths** to a bullock,
and two *tenth deals* **tenths** to one ram,
10 A *several tenth deal* **tenth and a tenth** for one lamb,
throughout the seven lambs:
11 One *kid* **buck** of the goats for *a sin offering* **the sin**;
beside *the sin offering* **that for the sin**
of *atonement* **kippurim**,
and the continual *burnt offering* **holocaust**,
and the *meat* offering of it,
and their *drink offerings* **libations**.
12 And on the fifteenth day of the seventh month
ye shall have an holy convocation;
ye shall *do no servile* work **no work of service**,
and ye shall *keep* **celebrate** a *feast* **celebration**
unto *the LORD* **Yah Veh** seven days:
13 And ye shall *offer* **oblate** a *burnt offering* **holocaust**,
a *sacrifice made by fire* **firing**,
of a *sweet savour* **scent of rest** unto *the LORD* **Yah Veh**;
thirteen *young* bullocks **sons of the oxen**, two rams,
and fourteen lambs *of the first year* **yearling sons**;
they shall be *without blemish* **integrious**:
14 And their *meat* offering
shall be of flour *mingled* **mixed** with oil,
three *tenth deals* **tenths** unto *every* **each** bullock
of the thirteen bullocks,
two *tenth deals* **tenths** to each ram of the two rams,
15 And a *several tenth deal* **tenth and a tenth** to each lamb
of the fourteen lambs:
16 And one *kid* **buck** of the goats for *a sin offering* **the sin**;
beside the continual *burnt offering* **holocaust**,
his *meat* offering, and his *drink offering* **libation**.
17 And on the second day
ye shall offer twelve *young* bullocks **sons of the oxen**,
two rams, fourteen lambs
of the first year without spot **yearling sons integrious**:
18 And their *meat* offering
and their *drink offerings* **libations**
for the bullocks, for the rams, and for the lambs,
shall be according to their number,
after the *manner* **judgment**:
19 And one *kid* **buck** of the goats for *a sin offering* **the sin**;
beside the continual *burnt offering* **holocaust**,
and the *meat* offering thereof,
and their *drink offerings* **libations**.
20 And on the third day eleven bullocks, two rams,
fourteen lambs
of the first year without blemish **yearling sons integrious**;
21 And their *meat* offering
and their *drink offerings* **libations**
for the bullocks, for the rams, and for the lambs,
shall be according to their number,
after the *manner* **judgment**:
22 And one *goat for a sin offering* **buck for the sin**;
beside the continual *burnt offering* **holocaust**,
and his *meat* offering, and his *drink offering* **libation**.
23 And on the fourth day ten bullocks, two rams,
and fourteen lambs
of the first year without blemish **yearling sons integrious**:
24 Their *meat* offering and their *drink offerings* **libations**

for the bullocks, for the rams, and for the lambs,
shall be according to their number,
after the *manner* **judgment**:
25 And one *kid* **buck** of the goats for *a sin offering* **the sin**;
beside the continual *burnt offering* **holocaust**,
his *meat* offering, and his *drink offering* **libation**.
26 And on the fifth day nine bullocks, two rams,
and fourteen lambs
of the first year without blemish **yearling sons integrious**:
27 And their *meat* offering
and their *drink offerings* **libations**
for the bullocks, for the rams, and for the lambs,
shall be according to their number,
after the *manner* **judgment**:
28 And one *goat for a sin offering* **buck for the sin**;
beside the continual *burnt offering* **holocaust**,
and his *meat* offering, and his *drink offering* **libation**.
29 And on the sixth day eight bullocks, two rams,
and fourteen lambs
of the first year without blemish **yearling sons integrious**:
30 And their *meat* offering
and their *drink offerings* **libations**
for the bullocks, for the rams, and for the lambs,
shall be according to their number,
after the *manner* **judgment**:
31 And one *goat for a sin offering* **buck for the sin**;
beside the continual *burnt offering* **holocaust**,
his *meat* offering, and his *drink offering* **libation**.
32 And on the seventh day seven bullocks, two rams,
and fourteen lambs
of the first year without blemish **yearling sons integrious**:
33 And their *meat* offering
and their drink *offerings* **libations**
for the bullocks, for the rams, and for the lambs,
shall be according to their number,
after the *manner* **judgment**:
34 And one *goat for a sin offering* **buck for the sin**;
beside the continual *burnt offering* **holocaust**,
his *meat* offering, and his *drink offering* **libation**.
35 On the eighth day
ye shall have *a solemn assembly* **an abstinence**:
ye shall *do no servile* work **no work of service** *therein*:
36 But ye shall *offer a burnt offering* **oblate a holocaust**,
a sacrifice made by fire **firing**,
of a *sweet savour* **scent of rest** unto *the LORD* **Yah Veh**:
one bullock, one ram,
seven lambs
of the first year without blemish **yearling sons integrious**:
37 Their *meat* offering and their *drink offerings* **libations**
for the bullock, for the ram, and for the lambs,
shall be according to their number,
after the *manner* **judgment**:
38 And one *goat for a sin offering* **buck for the sin**;
beside the continual *burnt offering* **holocaust**,
and his *meat* offering, and his *drink offering* **libation**.
39 These *things* ye shall *do* **work**
unto *the LORD* **Yah Veh** in your *set feasts* **seasons**,
beside your vows, and your *freewill offerings* **voluntaries**,
for your *burnt offerings* **holocausts**,
and for your *meat* offerings,
and for your *drink offerings* **libations**,
and for your *peace offerings* **shelamim**.
40 And *Moses* **Mosheh**
told the *children* **sons** of *Israel* **Yisra El**
according to all that *the LORD* **Yah Veh**
commanded Moses **misvahed Mosheh**.

VOWS UNTO YAH VEH

30 And *Moses spake* **Mosheh worded**
unto the heads of the *tribes* **rods**
concerning the *children* **sons** of *Israel* **Yisra El**, saying,
This is the *thing* **word**
which *the LORD* **Yah Veh** hath *commanded* **misvahed**.
2 If a man vow a vow unto *the LORD* **Yah Veh**,
or *swear* **oath** an oath to bind his soul with a bond;
he shall not *break* **profane** his word,
he shall *do* **work** according to all
that proceedeth out of his mouth.
3 If a woman also vow a vow unto *the LORD* **Yah Veh**,
and bind *herself* by a bond,
being in her father's house in her youth;
4 And her father hear her vow,
and her bond wherewith she hath bound her soul,
and her father shall *hold his peace at her* **hush**;
then all her vows shall *stand* **be raised**,
and every bond wherewith she hath bound her soul
shall *stand* **be raised**.
5 But if her father disallow her in the day that he heareth;
not any of her vows,
or of her bonds wherewith she hath bound her soul,
shall *stand* **be raised**:
and *the LORD* **Yah Veh** shall forgive her,
because her father disallowed her.
6 And if she *had at all an husband* **became a man's**,
when *she vowed* **her vows were upon her**,
or *uttered ought out* **the utterance** of her lips,
wherewith she bound her soul;
7 And her *husband* **man** heard it,
and *held his peace* **hushed** at her
in the day that he heard it:
then her vows shall *stand* **be raised**,
and her bonds wherewith she bound her soul
shall *stand* **be raised**.
8 But if her *husband* **man** disallowed her
on the day that he heard it;
then he shall *make* **break** her vow which she vowed,
and *that which she uttered with* **the utterance of** her lips,
wherewith she bound her soul, *of none effect*:
and *the LORD* **Yah Veh** shall forgive her.
9 But every vow of a widow,
and of her that is divorced **or expelled**,
wherewith they have bound their souls,
shall *stand* **be raised** against her.
10 And if she vowed in her *husband's* **man's** house,
or bound her soul by a bond with an oath;
11 And her *husband* **man** heard it,
and *held his peace* **hushed** at her, and disallowed her not:
then all her vows shall *stand* **be raised**,
and every bond wherewith she bound her soul
shall *stand* **be raised**.
12 But if **in breaking,**
her *husband* **man** hath *utterly made* **broken** them *void*
on the day he heard them;
then whatsoever proceeded out of her lips
concerning her vows,
or concerning the bond of her soul,
shall not *stand* **be raised**:
her *husband* **man** hath *made* **broken** them *void*;
and *the LORD* **Yah Veh** shall forgive her.
13 Every vow, and every *binding* **bonded** oath
to *afflict* **humble** the soul,
her *husband* **man** may *establish* **raise** it,
or her *husband* **man** may *make it void* **break**.
14 But **if in hushing,**
her *husband altogether hold his peace* **man husheth**
at her from day by day;
then he *establisheth* **raiseth** all her vows, or all her bonds,
which *are* **be** upon her:
he *confirmeth* **raiseth** them,
because he *held his peace* **hushed** at her
in the day that he heard them.
15 But if **in breaking**
he shall *any ways make them void* **break them**
after that he hath heard them;
then he shall bear her *iniquity* **perversity**.
16 These are the statutes,
which *the LORD* **Yah Veh**
commanded Moses **misvahed Mosheh**,
between a man and his *wife* **woman**,
between the father and his daughter,
being yet in her youth in her father's house.

SONS OF YISRA EL AVENGE THE MIDYANIY

31 And *the LORD spake* **Yah Veh worded**
unto *Moses* **Mosheh, saying,**
2 Avenge the **avengement**
of the *children* **sons** of *Israel* **Yisra El**
of the *Midianites* **Midyaniy**:
afterward shalt thou be gathered unto thy people.
3 And *Moses spake* **Mosheh worded** unto the people,
saying,
Arm some **Equip men** of yourselves unto the *war* **hostility**,

and let them go against *the Midianites* **Midyaniy**,
and *avenge the LORD* **give the avengement of Yah**
of Midian **on Midyan**.
4 *Of every tribe a thousand*
A thousand per rod — a thousand per rod,
throughout all the *tribes* **rods** of *Israel* **Yisra El**,
shall ye send to the *war* **hostility**.
5 So there were *delivered* **set apart**
out of the thousands of *Israel* **Yisra El**,
a thousand *slain of every tribe* **pierced per rod**,
twelve thousand *armed* **equipped** for *war* **hostility**.
6 And *Moses* **Mosheh** sent them to the *war* **hostility**,
a thousand *of every tribe* **per rod**,
them and *Phinehas* **Phinechas**
the son of *Eleazar* **El Azar** the priest,
to the *war* **hostility**,
with the holy instruments,
and the trumpets to *blow* **blast** in his hand.
7 And they *warred* **hosted** against the *Midianites* **Midyaniy**,
as *the LORD* **Yah Veh**
commanded Moses **misvahed Mosheh**;
and they *slew* **slaughtered** all the males.
8 And they *slew* **slaughtered**
the *kings* **sovereigns** of *Midian* **Midyan**,
beside the rest of them that were *slain* **pierced**; *namely,*
Evi, and *Rekem* **Reqem**, and *Zur* **Sur**, and Hur, and Reba,
five *kings* **sovereigns** of *Midian* **Midyan**:
Balaam **Bilam** also the son of Beor
they *slew* **slaughtered** with the sword.
9 And the *children* **sons** of *Israel* **Yisra El**
took **captured** all the women of *Midian* **Midyan** *captives*,
and their *little ones* **toddlers**,
and took the *spoil* **plunder** of all their *cattle* **animals**,
and all their *flocks* **chattel**, and all their *goods* **valuables**.
10 And they burnt all their cities
wherein they dwelt **of their settlements**,
and all their *goodly castles* **walls**, with fire.
11 And they took all the *spoil* **loot**, and all the prey,
both of men **human** and *of beasts* **animal**.
12 And they brought the captives,
and the prey, and the *spoil* **loot**,
unto *Moses* **Mosheh** and *Eleazar* **El Azar** the priest,
and unto the *congregation* **witness**
of the *children* **sons** of *Israel* **Yisra El**,
unto the camp at the plains of Moab,
which are by *Jordan* **Yarden** near *Jericho* **Yericho**.
13 And *Moses* **Mosheh**, and *Eleazar* **El Azar** the priest,
and all the *princes* **hierarchs** of the *congregation* **witness**,
went forth to meet them without the camp.
14 And *Moses* **Mosheh** was *wroth* **enraged**
with *the officers of the host* **them who oversee the valiant**,
with the *captains* **governors** over thousands,
and *captains* **governors** over hundreds,
which came from the *battle* **hostility of war**.
15 And *Moses* **Mosheh** said unto them,
Have ye *saved* **preserved** all the *women* **females** alive?
16 Behold, these *caused* **became**
to the *children* **sons** of *Israel* **Yisra El**,
through the *counsel* **word** of *Balaam* **Bilam**,
to *commit trespass* **set treason** against *the LORD* **Yah Veh**
in the *matter* **word** of Peor,
and there was a plague
among the *congregation* **witness** of *the LORD* **Yah Veh**.
17 Now therefore
kill **slaughter** every male among the *little ones* **toddlers**,
and *kill* **slaughter** every woman that hath known man
by *lying* **bedding** with *him* **a male**.
18 But all the
women children **toddlers among the women**,
that have not known
a man by lying with him **bedding with a male**,
keep **preserve** alive for yourselves.
19 And *do* ye *abide* **encamp** without the camp seven days:
whosoever hath *killed* **slaughtered** any *person* **soul**,
and whosoever hath touched any *slain* **pierced**,
purify *both yourselves* **for your sins** and your captives
on the third day, and on the seventh day.
20 And purify **for your sins** your *raiment* **clothes**,
and all *that is made* **instruments** of skins,
and all work of goats' *hair*,
and all *things* **instruments** made of *wood* **timber**.
21 And *Eleazar* **El Azar** the priest
said unto the men of *war* **hostility**
which went to the *battle* **war**,
This is the *ordinance* **statute** of the *law* **torah**
which *the LORD* **Yah Veh**
commanded Moses **misvahed Mosheh**;
22 Only the gold, and the silver, the *brass* **copper**,
the iron, the tin, and the lead,
23 Every *thing* **word** that may abide the fire,
ye shall *make* **pass** it *go* through the fire,
and it shall be *clean* **purified**:
nevertheless it shall be purified **for your sins**
with the water of *separation* **exclusion**:
and all that abideth not the fire
ye shall *make go* **pass** through the water.
24 And ye shall *wash* **launder** your clothes
on the seventh day,
and ye shall be *clean* **purified**,
and afterward ye shall come into the camp.

HALVING THE PREY

25 And *the LORD spake* **Yah Veh said**
unto *Moses* **Mosheh**, saying,
26 *Take* **Bear** the *sum* **top** of the prey
that was taken **of the captives**,
both *of man* **human** and *of beast* **animal**,
thou, and *Eleazar* **El Azar** the priest,
and the *chief* **head** fathers of the *congregation* **witness**:
27 And *divide* **halve** the prey into two parts;
between them that *took* **manipulated** the war upon them,
who went out to *battle* **the hostility**,
and between all the *congregation* **witness**:
28 And *levy a tribute* **lift an assessment**
unto *the LORD* **Yah Veh**
of the men of war which went out to battle:
one soul of five hundred,
both of the *persons* **humans**, and of the *beeves* **oxen**,
and of the *asses* **he burros**, and of the *sheep* **flocks**:
29 Take it of their half,
and give it unto *Eleazar* **El Azar** the priest,
for an *heave offering* **exaltment**
of the LORD **unto Yah Veh**.
30 And of the *children* **sons** of *Israel's* **Yisra El's** half,
thou shalt take one *portion* **possession** of fifty,
of the *persons* **humans**,
of the *beeves* **oxen**, of the *asses* **he burros**,
and of the flocks, of all *manner of beasts* **animals**,
and give them unto the *Levites* **Leviym**,
which *keep* **guard** the *charge* **guard**
of the tabernacle of *the LORD* **Yah Veh**.
31 And *Moses* **Mosheh** and *Eleazar* **El Azar** the priest
did **worked** as *the LORD* **Yah Veh**
commanded Moses **misvahed Mosheh**.
32 And the *booty* **prey**,
being the *rest* **remainder** of the *prey* **plunder**
which the men of *war* **hostility** had *caught* **plundered**,
was six hundred thousand and seventy thousand
and five thousand *sheep* **flocks**,
33 And *threescore and twelve* **seventy and two** thousand
beeves **oxen**,
34 And *threescore* **sixty** and one thousand *asses* **he burros**,
35 And *thirty and two thousand in all,*
of women that had not known man
by *lying* **bedding** with him **and of human souls,**
— all the souls are thirty and two thousand.
36 And the half,
which was the *portion* **allotment** of them
that went out to *war* **the hostility**,
was in number three hundred thousand
and seven and thirty thousand
and five hundred *sheep* **flocks**:
37 And *the LORD'S tribute* **Yah Veh's assessment**
of the *sheep* **flocks** was six hundred
and *threescore and fifteen* **seventy and five**.
38 And the *beeves* **oxen** were thirty and six thousand;
of which *the LORD'S tribute* **Yah Veh's assessment**
was *threescore and twelve* **seventy and two**.
39 And the *asses* **he burros**
were thirty thousand and five hundred;
of which *the LORD'S tribute* **Yah Veh's assessment**

was *threescore* **sixty** and one.
40 And the *persons* **souls of humanity**
were sixteen thousand;
of which *the LORD'S tribute* **Yah Veh's assessment**
was thirty and two *persons* **souls**.
41 And *Moses* **Mosheh** gave the *tribute* **assessment**,
which was
the LORD'S heave offering **Yah Veh's exaltment**,
unto *Eleazar* **El Azar** the priest,
as *the LORD* **Yah Veh**
commanded Moses **misvahed Mosheh**.
42 And of the *children* **sons** of *Israel's* **Yisra El's** half,
which *Moses divided* **Mosheh halved**
from the men that *warred* **hosted**,
43 (*Now* the half
that pertained unto the congregation **for the witness**
was three hundred thousand and thirty thousand
and seven thousand and five hundred
sheep **of the flocks**,
44 And thirty and six thousand *beeves* **oxen**,
45 And thirty thousand *asses* **he burros** and five hundred,
46 And sixteen thousand *persons* **souls of humanity**;)
47 Even of the *children* **sons** of *Israel's* **Yisra El's** half,
Moses **Mosheh** took one *portion* **possession** of fifty,
both of man **human** and *of beast* **animal**,
and gave them unto the *Levites* **Leviym**,
which *kept* **guarded** the *charge* **guard**
of the tabernacle of *the LORD* **Yah Veh**;
as *the LORD* **Yah Veh**
commanded Moses **misvahed Mosheh**.
48 And *the officers which were over* **they who oversaw**
thousands of the host,
the *captains* **governors** of thousands,
and *captains* **governors** of hundreds,
came near unto *Moses* **Mosheh**:
49 And they said unto *Moses* **Mosheh**,
Thy servants have *taken* **lifted** the *sum* **heads**
of the men of war which are under our *charge* **hand**,
and *there lacketh not one* **no** man of us **was oversighted**.
50 We have *therefore*
brought an oblation **oblated a qorban**
for *the LORD* **Yah Veh**,
what every man hath *gotten* **found**,
of *jewels* **instruments** of gold, *chains* **anklets**,
and bracelets, *rings* **signets**, earrings, and *tablets* **beads**,
to *make an atonement* **kapar/atone** for our souls
before the LORD **at the face of Yah Veh**.
51 And *Moses* **Mosheh** and *Eleazar* **El Azar** the priest
took the gold of them,
even all *wrought jewels* **works of instruments**.
52 And all the gold of the *offering* **exaltment**
that they *offered up to the LORD* **exalted unto Yah Veh**,
of the *captains* **governors** of thousands,
and of the *captains* **governors** of hundreds,
was sixteen thousand seven hundred and fifty shekels.
53 (For the men of *war* **hostility**
had *taken spoil* **plundered**, every man for himself.)
54 And *Moses* **Mosheh** and *Eleazar* **El Azar** the priest
took the gold
of the *captains* **governors** of thousands and of hundreds,
and brought it into the *tabernacle* **tent** of the congregation,
for a memorial for the *children* **sons** of *Israel* **Yisra El**
before the LORD **at the face of Yah Veh**.

SONS OF YISRA EL DISPUTE OVER LAND

32 Now the *children* **sons** of *Reuben* **Reu Ben**
and the *children* **sons** of Gad
had *a very great multitude of cattle*
mighty mighty many chattel:
and when they saw the land of *Jazer* **Yazer**,
and the land of *Gilead* **Gilad**,
that, behold, the place was a place for *cattle* **chattel**;
2 The *children* **sons** of Gad
and the *children* **sons** of *Reuben* **Reu Ben** came
and *spake* **said** unto *Moses* **Mosheh**,
and to *Eleazar* **El Azar** the priest,
and unto the *princes* **hierarchs**
of the *congregation* **witness**, saying,
3 Ataroth, and Dibon, and *Jazer* **Yazer**,
and Nimrah, and Heshbon, and *Elealeh* **El Aleh**,
and *Shebam* **Sebam**, and Nebo, and Beon,
4 Even the country which *the LORD* **Yah Veh** smote
before **at the face**
of the *congregation* **witness** of *Israel* **Yisra El**,
is a land for *cattle* **chattel**,
and thy servants have *cattle* **chattel**:
5 Wherefore, said they,
if we have found *grace* **charism** in thy *sight* **eyes**,
let this land be given unto thy servants for a possession,
and *bring* **pass** us not over *Jordan* **Yarden**.
6 And *Moses* **Mosheh** said unto the *children* **sons** of Gad
and to the *children* **sons** of *Reuben* **Reu Ben**,
Shall your brethren go to war, and shall ye sit here?
7 And wherefore discourage ye the heart
of the *children* **sons** of *Israel* **Yisra El**
from *going over* **passing** into the land
which *the LORD* **Yah Veh** hath given them?
8 Thus *did* **worked** your fathers,
when I sent them from *Kadeshbarnea* **Qadesh Barnea**
to see the land.
9 For when they *went up* **ascended**
unto the *valley* **wadi** of Eshcol,
and saw the land,
they discouraged the heart
of the *children* **sons** of *Israel* **Yisra El**,
that they should not go into the land
which *the LORD* **Yah Veh** had given them.
10 And *the LORD'S anger* **Yah Veh's wrath**
was kindled *the same time* **that day**,
and he *sware* **oathed**, saying,
11 Surely none of the men
that *came up* **ascended** out of *Egypt* **Misrayim**,
from **sons of** twenty years *old* and upward,
shall see the *earth* **soil**
which I *sware* **oathed** unto Abraham,
unto *Isaac* **Yischaq**, and unto *Jacob* **Yaaqov**;
because they have not
wholly followed **fulfilled to follow** me:
12 Save *Caleb* **Kaleb**
the son of *Jephunneh* **Yephunneh** the *Kenezite* **Qenaziy**,
and *Joshua* **Yah Shua** the son of Nun:
for they have
wholly followed the LORD **fulfilled to follow Yah Veh**.
13 And *the LORD'S anger* **Yah Veh's wrath**
was kindled against *Israel* **Yisra El**,
and he made them wander in the wilderness forty years,
until all the generation,
that had *done* **worked** evil
in the *sight* **eyes** of *the LORD* **Yah Veh**, was consumed.
14 And, behold, ye are risen up in your fathers' stead,
an *increase* **abundance** of sinful men,
to *augment* **scrape together** yet
the *anger* **fuming wrath** of *the LORD* **Yah Veh**
toward *Israel* **Yisra El**.
15 For if ye turn away from after him,
he *will yet again* **shall add**
to leave them in the wilderness;
and ye shall *destroy* **ruin** all this people.
16 And they came near unto him, and said,
We *will* **shall** build
sheepfolds **flock walls** here for our *cattle* **chattel**,
and cities for our *little ones* **toddlers**:
17 But we ourselves *will* **shall** go ready *armed* **equipped**
before **at the face of** the *children* **sons** of *Israel* **Yisra El**,
until we have brought them unto their place:
and our *little ones* **toddlers** shall *dwell* **settle**
in the *fenced* **fortified** cities
because of the **at the face of them**
inhabitants of **who settled** the land.
18 We *will* **shall** not return unto our houses,
until the *children* **sons** of *Israel* **Yisra El**
have inherited every man his inheritance.
19 For we *will* **shall** not inherit with them
on yonder side *Jordan* **Yarden**, or *forward* **beyond**;
because our inheritance is fallen to us
on this side *Jordan eastward* **Yarden toward the rising**.
20 And *Moses* **Mosheh** said unto them,
If ye *will do* **shall work** this *thing* **word**,
if ye *will* **shall** go *armed* **equipped**
before the LORD **at the face of Yah Veh** to war,
21 And *will go* **shall pass** all of you

armed **equipped** over *Jordan* **Yarden**
before the LORD **at the face of Yah Veh,**
until he hath *driven out* **dispossessed** his enemies
from *before him* **his face,**
22 And the land be subdued
before the LORD **at the face of Yah Veh:**
then afterward ye shall return,
and be *guiltless* **innocent**
before the LORD **at the face of Yah Veh,**
and *before Israel* **at the face of Yisra El;**
and this land shall be your possession
before the LORD **at the face of Yah Veh.**
23 But if ye *will* **shall** not *do* **work** so, behold,
ye have sinned against *the LORD* **Yah Veh:**
and *be sure* **perceive that** your sin *will* **shall** find you out.
24 Build you cities for your *little ones* **toddlers,**
and *folds* **walls** for your *sheep* **flocks;**
and *do* **work** that
which hath proceeded out of your mouth.
25 And the *children* **sons** of Gad
and the *children* **sons** of *Reuben* **Reu Ben**
spake **said** unto *Moses* **Mosheh,** saying,
Thy servants *will do* **shall work**
as my *lord commandeth* **adoni misvaheth.**
26 Our *little ones* **toddlers,** our *wives* **women,**
our *flocks* **chattel,** and all our *cattle* **animals,**
shall be there in the cities of *Gilead* **Gilad:**
27 But thy servants *will* **shall** pass over,
every man *armed* **equipped** for *war* **hostility,**
before the LORD **at the face of Yah Veh** to *battle* **war,**
as my *lord saith* **adoni wordeth.**
28 So concerning them
Moses commanded **Mosheh misvahed**
Eleazar **El Azar** the priest,
and *Joshua* **Yah Shua** the son of Nun,
and the *chief* **head** fathers of the *tribes* **rods**
of the *children* **sons** of *Israel* **Yisra El:**
29 And *Moses* **Mosheh** said unto them,
If the *children* **sons** of Gad
and the *children* **sons** of *Reuben* **Reu Ben**
will **shall** pass with you over *Jordan* **Yarden,**
every man *armed* **equipped** to *battle* **war,**
before the LORD **at the face of Yah Veh,**
and the land shall be subdued *before you* **at your face;**
then ye shall give them the land of *Gilead* **Gilad**
for a possession:
30 But if they *will* **shall** not pass over with you
armed **equipped,**
they shall *have possessions* **possess** among you
in the land of *Canaan* **Kenaan.**
31 And the *children* **sons** of Gad
and the *children* **sons** of *Reuben* **Reu Ben** answered,
saying,
As *the LORD* **Yah Veh** hath *said* **worded** unto thy servants,
so *will* **shall** we *do* **work.**
32 We *will* **shall** pass over *armed* **equipped**
before the LORD **at the face of Yah Veh**
into the land of *Canaan* **Kenaan,**
that the possession of our inheritance
on this side *Jordan* **Yarden** may be ours.
33 And *Moses* **Mosheh** gave unto them,
even to the *children* **sons** of Gad,
and to the *children* **sons** of *Reuben* **Reu Ben,**
and unto half the *tribe* **scion** of *Manasseh* **Menash Sheh**
the son of *Joseph* **Yoseph,**
the *kingdom* **sovereigndom** of Siho
king **sovereign** of the *Amorites* **Emoriy,**
and the *kingdom* **sovereigndom** of Og
king **sovereign** of Bashan,
the land, with the cities thereof in the *coasts* **borders,**
even the cities of the *country* **land** round about.
34 And the *children* **sons** of Gad
built Dibon, and Ataroth, and Aroer,
35 And Atroth, Shophan, and *Jaazer* **Yazer,** and Jogbehah,
36 And *Bethnimrah* **Beth Nimrah,**
and *Bethharan* **Beth Ha Ran,**
fenced **fortified** cities: and *folds* **walls** for *sheep* **flocks.**
37 And the *children* **sons** of *Reuben* **Reu Ben**
built Heshbon, and *Elealeh* **El Aleh,**
and *Kirjathaim* **Qiryathaim,**
38 And Nebo, and *Baalmeon* **Baal Meon,**
(their names being *changed* **turned around,**)
and *Shibmah* **Sibmah:**
and *gave other names* **called by name,**
the names unto the cities which they builded.
39 And the *children* **sons** of Machir
the son of *Manasseh* **Menash Sheh**
went to *Gilead* **Gilad,** and *took* **captured** it,
and dispossessed the *Amorite* **Emoriy** which was in it.
40 And *Moses* **Mosheh** gave *Gilead* **Gilad**
unto Machir the son of *Manasseh* **Menash Sheh;**
and he *dwelt* **settled** therein.
41 And *Jair* **Yair** the son of *Manasseh* **Menash Sheh**
went and *took* **captured**
the *small towns* **living areas** thereof,
and called them *Havothjair* **Havoth Yair.**
42 And *Nobah* **Nobach** went
and *took Kenath* **captured Qenath,**
and the *villages* **daughters** thereof,
and called it *Nobah* **Nobach,** after his own name.

RESUME' OF THE JOURNEYS OF THE SONS OF YISRA EL

33 These are the journeys
of the *children* **sons** of *Israel* **Yisra El,**
which went forth out of the land of *Egypt* **Misrayim**
with their *armies* **hosts**
under the hand of *Moses* **Mosheh** and *Aaron* **Aharon.**
2 And *Moses wrote* **Mosheh inscribed**
their *goings out* **proceedings** according to their journeys
by the *commandment* **mouth** of *the LORD* **Yah Veh:**
and these are their journeys
according to their *goings out* **proceedings.**
3 And they *departed* **pulled stakes** from Rameses
in the first month, on the fifteenth day of the first month;
on the morrow after the *passover* **pasach**
the *children* **sons** of *Israel* **Yisra El**
went out with *an high* **lifted** hand
in the *sight* **eyes** of all the *Egyptians* **Misrayim.**
4 For the *Egyptians* **Misrayim**
buried **entombed** all their firstborn,
which *the LORD* **Yah Veh** had smitten among them:
upon their *gods* **elohim** also
the LORD executed **Yah Veh worked** judgments.
5 And the *children* **sons** of *Israel* **Yisra El**
removed **pulled stakes** from Rameses,
and *pitched* **encamped** in *Succoth* **Sukkoth/Brush Arbors.**
6 And they *departed* **pulled stakes**
from *Succoth* **Sukkoth/Brush Arbors,**
and *pitched* **encamped** in Etham,
which is in the *edge* **end** of the wilderness.
7 And they *removed* **pulled stakes** from Etham,
and turned again unto *Pihahiroth* **Pi Ha Hiroth,**
which is *before Baalzephon* **at the face of Baal Sephon:**
and they *pitched before* **encamped at the face of** Migdol.
8 And they *departed* **pulled stakes**
from *before Pihahiroth* **the face of Piha Hiroth,**
and passed through the midst of the sea
into the wilderness,
and went three days' journey in the wilderness of Etham,
and *pitched* **encamped** in Marah.
9 And they *removed* **pulled stakes** from Marah,
and came unto Elim:
and in Elim were twelve fountains of water,
and *threescore and ten* **seventy** palm trees;
and they *pitched* **encamped** there.
10 And they *removed* **pulled stakes** from Elim,
and encamped by the *Red* **Reed** sea.
11 And they *removed* **pulled stakes** from the *Red* **Reed** sea,
and encamped in the wilderness of Sin.
12 And they *took their journey* **pulled stakes**
out of the wilderness of Sin,
and encamped in *Dophkah* **Dophqah.**
13 And they *departed* **pulled stakes**
from *Dophkah* **Dophqah,**
and encamped in Alush.
14 And they *removed* **pulled stakes** from Alush,
and encamped at Rephidim,
where was no water for the people to drink.
15 And they *departed* **pulled stakes** from Rephidim,
and *pitched* **encamped** in the wilderness of *Sinai* **Sinay.**
16 And they *removed* **pulled stakes**

from the *desert* **wilderness** of *Sinai* **Sinay**,
and *pitched* **encamped**
at *Kibrothhattaavah* **Qibroth Hat Taavah**.
17 And they *departed* **pulled stakes**
from *Kibrothhattaavah* **Qibroth Hat Taavah**,
and encamped at *Hazeroth* **Haseroth**.
18 And they *departed* **pulled stakes**
from *Hazeroth* **Haseroth**,
and *pitched* **encamped** in Rithmah.
19 And they *departed* **pulled stakes** from Rithmah,
and *pitched* **encamped** at *Rimmonparez* **Rimmon Phares**.
20 And they *departed* **pulled stakes**
from *Rimmonparez* **Rimmon Phares**,
and *pitched* **encamped** in Libnah.
21 And they *removed* **pulled stakes** from Libnah,
and *pitched* **encamped** at Rissah.
22 And they *journeyed* **pulled stakes** from Rissah,
and *pitched* **encamped** in *Kehelathah* **Qehelathah**.
23 And they *went* **pulled stakes**
from *Kehelathah* **Qehelathah**,
and *pitched* **encamped** in mount *Shapher* **Shepher**.
24 And they *removed* **pulled stakes**
from mount *Shapher* **Shepher**,
and encamped in Haradah.
25 And they *removed* **pulled stakes** from Haradah,
and *pitched* **encamped** in *Makheloth* **Maqheloth**.
26 And they *removed* **pulled stakes**
from *Makheloth* **Maqheloth**,
and encamped at *Tahath* **Tachath**.
27 And they *departed* **pulled stakes** from *Tahath* **Tachath**,
and *pitched* **encamped** at *Tarah* **Terach**.
28 And they *removed* **pulled stakes** from *Tarah* **Terach**,
and *pitched* **encamped** in *Mithcah* **Mithqah**.
29 And they *went* **pulled stakes** from *Mithcah* **Mithqah**,
and *pitched* **encamped** in Hashmonah.
30 And they *departed* **pulled stakes** from Hashmonah,
and encamped at Moseroth.
31 And they *departed* **pulled stakes** from Moseroth,
and *pitched* **encamped** in *Benejaakan* **Bene Yaaqan**.
32 And they *removed* **pulled stakes**
from *Benejaakan* **Bene Yaaqan**,
and encamped at *Horhagidgad* **Hor Hag Gidgad**.
33 And they *went* **pulled stakes**
from *Horhagidgad* **Hor Hag Gidgad**,
and *pitched* **encamped** in *Jotbathah* **Yotbathah**.
34 And they *removed* **pulled stakes**
from *Jotbathah* **Yotbathah**,
and encamped at *Ebronah* **Hebronah**.
35 And they *departed* **pulled stakes**
from *Ebronah* **Hebronah**,
and encamped at *Eziongaber* **Esyon Geber**.
36 And they *removed* **pulled stakes**
from *Eziongaber* **Esyon Geber**,
and *pitched* **encamped** in the wilderness of *Zin* **Sin**,
which is *Kadesh* **Qadesh**.
37 And they *removed* **pulled stakes** from *Kadesh* **Qadesh**,
and *pitched* **encamped** in mount Hor,
in the *edge* **end** of the land of Edom.
38 And *Aaron* **Aharon** the priest
went up **ascended** into mount Hor
at the *commandment* **mouth** of *the LORD* **Yah Veh**,
and died there,
in the fortieth year after the *children* **sons** of *Israel* **Yisra El**
were come out of the land of *Egypt* **Misrayim**,
in the first *day* of the fifth month.
39 And *Aaron* **Aharon**
was **a son** an hundred and twenty and three years *old*
when he died **at his death** in mount Hor.
40 And *king* **sovereign** Arad the *Canaanite* **Kenaaniy**,
which *dwelt* **settled** in the south
in the land of *Canaan* **Kenaan**,
heard of the coming of the *children* **sons** of *Israel* **Yisra El**.
41 And they *departed* **pulled stakes** from mount Hor,
and *pitched* **encamped** in *Zalmonah* **Sal Monah**.
42 And they *departed* **pulled stakes**
from *Zalmonah* **Sal Monah**,
and *pitched* **encamped** in Punon.
43 And they *departed* **pulled stakes** from Punon,
and *pitched* **encamped** in Oboth.
44 And they *departed* **pulled stakes** from Oboth,
and *pitched* **encamped** in *Ijeabarim* **Iye Ha Abiram**,
in the border of Moab.
45 And they *departed* **pulled stakes** from *Iim* **Iyiy**,
and *pitched* **encamped** in Dibongad.
46 And they *removed* **pulled stakes** from Dibongad,
and encamped in *Almondiblathaim* **Almon Diblathaim**.
47 And they *removed* **pulled stakes**
from *Almondiblathaim* **Almon Diblathaim**,
and *pitched* **encamped** in the mountains of Abarim,
before **at the face of** Nebo.
48 And they *departed* **pulled stakes**
from the mountains of Abarim,
and *pitched* **encamped** in the plains of Moab
by *Jordan* **Yarden** near *Jericho* **Yericho**.
49 And they *pitched* **encamped** by *Jordan* **Yarden**,
from *Bethjesimoth* **Beth Ha Yeshimoth**
even unto *Abelshittim* **Abel Hash Shittim**
in the plains of Moab.
50 And *the LORD spake* **Yah Veh worded**
unto *Moses* **Mosheh** in the plains of Moab
by *Jordan* **Yarden** near *Jericho* **Yericho**, saying,
51 *Speak* **Word** unto the *children* **sons** of *Israel* **Yisra El**,
and say unto them,
When ye are passed over *Jordan* **Yarden**
into the land of *Canaan* **Kenaan**;
52 Then ye shall *drive out* **dispossess**
the inhabitants of **who settled** the land
from *before you* **your face**,
and destroy all their *pictures* **imageries**,
and *destroy* **desolate** all their molten images,
and *quite pluck down* **desolate**
all their *high places* **bamahs**:
53 And ye shall dispossess the *inhabitants of the* land,
and *dwell* **settle** therein:
for I have given you the land to possess it.
54 And ye shall *divide* **inherit** the land by *lot* **pebble**
for an inheritance among your families:
and to the more
ye shall *give the more* **greaten the** inheritance,
and to the fewer
ye shall *give the less* **diminish the** inheritance:
every man's *inheritance*
shall be in the place where his *lot* **pebble** falleth;
according to the *tribes* **rods** of your fathers
ye shall inherit.
55 But if ye *will* **shall** not *drive out* **dispossess**
the inhabitants of **them who settled** the land
from *before you* **your face**;
then it shall *come to pass* **become**,
that those which ye let remain of them
shall be *pricks* **barbs** in your eyes,
and thorns in your sides,
and shall *vex* **tribulate** you
in the land wherein ye *dwell* **settle**.
cp 2 Corinthians 12:7
56 Moreover it shall *come to pass* **become**,
that I shall *do* **work** unto you,
as I thought to *do* **work** unto them.

ALLOTTING THE BORDERS OF KENAAN TO THE SONS OF YISRA EL

34 And *the LORD spake* **Yah Veh worded**
unto *Moses* **Mosheh**, saying,
2 *Command* **Misvah** the *children* **sons** of *Israel* **Yisra El**,
and say unto them,
When ye come into the land of *Canaan* **Kenaan**;
(this is the land that shall fall unto you for an inheritance,
even the land of *Canaan* **Kenaan**
with the *coasts* **borders** thereof:)
3 Then your south *quarter* **edge**
shall be from the wilderness of *Zin* **Sin**
along by the *coast* **hand** of Edom,
and your south border
shall be the *outmost coast* **ends** of the salt sea eastward:
4 And your border shall *turn* **surround** from the south
to the ascent of Akrabbim, and pass on to *Zin* **Sin**:
and the *going forth* **exits** thereof shall be
from the south to *Kadeshbarnea* **Qadesh Barnea**,
and shall go on to *Hazaraddar* **Hasar Addar**,
and pass on to *Azmon* **Asmon**:
5 And the border

shall *fetch a compass* **surround** from *Azmon* **Asmon**
unto the *river* **wadi** of *Egypt* **Misrayim**,
and the *goings out of it* **exits** shall be at the sea.
6 And as for the *western* **seaward** border,
ye shall even have the great sea for a border:
this shall be your *west* **seaward** border.
7 And this shall be your north border:
from the great sea
shall *point out* **survey** for you mount Hor:
8 From mount Hor ye shall *point out your border* **survey**
unto the entrance of Hamath;
and the *goings forth* **exits** of the border
shall be to *Zedad* **Sedad**:
9 And the border shall go on to Ziphron,
and the *goings out of it* **exits**
shall be at *Hazarenan* **Hasar Enan**:
this shall be your north border.
10 And ye shall *point* **mark** out your east border
from *Hazarenan* **Hasar Enan** to Shepham:
11 And the *coast* **border** shall *go down* **descend**
from Shepham to Riblah, on the east side of *Ain* **Ayin**;
and the border shall descend,
and shall *reach* **extend** unto the *side* **shoulder**
of the sea of *Chinnereth* **Kinneroth** eastward:
12 And the border shall *go down* **descend**
to *Jordan* **Yarden**,
and the *goings out of it* **exits** shall be at the salt sea:
this shall be your land
with the *coasts* **borders** thereof round about.
13 And *Moses commanded* **Mosheh misvahed**
the *children* **sons** of *Israel* **Yisra El**, saying,
This is the land which ye shall inherit by *lot* **pebble**,
which *the LORD commanded* **Yah Veh misvahed**
to give unto the nine *tribes* **rods**, and to the half *tribe* **rod**:
14 For the *tribe* **rod**
of the *children* **sons** of *Reuben* **Reu Ben**
according to the house of their fathers,
and the *tribe* **rod** of the *children* **sons** of Gad
according to the house of their fathers,
have *received their inheritance* **taken**;
and half the *tribe* **rod** of *Manasseh* **Menash Sheh**
have *received* **taken** their inheritance:
15 The two *tribes* **rods** and the half *tribe* **rod**
have *received* **taken** their inheritance
on this side *Jordan* **Yarden** near *Jericho* **Yericho** eastward,
toward the *sunrising* **rising**.
16 And *the LORD spake* **Yah Veh worded**
unto *Moses* **Mosheh**, saying,
17 These are the names of the men
which shall *divide* **inherit** the land unto you:
Eleazar **El Azar** the priest,
and *Joshua* **Yah Shua** the son of Nun.
18 And ye shall take
one prince **one hierarch — one hierarch**
of every *tribe* **rod**,
to *divide the land by inheritance* **inherit the land**.
19 And the names of the men are these:
Of the *tribe* **rod** of *Judah* **Yah Hudah**,
Caleb **Kaleb** the son of *Jephunneh* **Yephunneh**.
20 And of the *tribe* **rod**
of the *children* **sons** of *Simeon* **Shimon**,
Shemuel **Shemu El** the son of *Ammihud* **Ammi Hud**.
21 Of the *tribe* **rod** of *Benjamin* **Ben Yamin**,
Elidad **Eli Dad** the son of *Chislon* **Kislon**.
22 And the *prince* **hierarch** of the *tribe* **rod**
of the *children* **sons** of Dan,
Bukki **Buqqi** the son of *Jogli* **Yogli**.
23 The *prince* **hierarch**
of the *children* **sons** of *Joseph* **Yoseph**,
for the *tribe* **rod**
of the *children* **sons** of *Manasseh* **Menash Sheh**,
Hanniel **Hanni El** the son of Ephod.
24 And the *prince* **hierarch** of the *tribe* **rod**
of the *children* **sons** of *Ephraim* **Ephrayim**,
Kemuel **Qemu El** the son of Shiphtan.
25 And the *prince* **hierarch** of the *tribe* **rod**
of the *children* **sons** of Zebulun,
Elizaphan **El Saphan** the son of Parnach.
26 And the *prince* **hierarch** of the *tribe* **rod**
of the *children* **sons** of *Issacha* **Yissachar**,
Paltiel **Palti El** the son of Azzan.
27 And the *prince* **hierarch** of the *tribe* **rod**
of the *children* **sons** of Asher,
Ahihud **Achi Hud** the son of Shelomi.
28 And the *prince* **hierarch** of the *tribe* **rod**
of the *children* **sons** of Naphtali,
Pedahel **Pedah El** the son of *Ammihud* **Ammi Hud**.
29 These are they
whom *the LORD commanded* **Yah Veh misvahed**
to divide the inheritance unto the children of Israel
the sons of Yisra El to inherit
in the land of *Canaan* **Kenaan**.

ALLOTTING CITIES OF THE LEVIYM

35 And *the LORD spake* **Yah Veh worded**
unto *Moses* **Mosheh** in the plains of Moab
by *Jordan* **Yarden** near *Jericho* **Yericho**, saying,
2 *Command* **Misvah** the *children* **sons** of *Israel* **Yisra El**,
that they give unto the *Levites* **Leviym**
of the inheritance of their possession
cities to *dwell* **settle** in;
and ye shall give also unto the *Levites* **Leviym**
suburbs for the cities round about them.
3 And the cities shall they have to *dwell* **settle** in;
and the suburbs of them shall be for their *cattle* **animals**,
and for their *goods* **acquisitions**,
and for all their *beasts* **live beings**.
4 And the suburbs of the cities,
which ye shall give unto the *Levites* **Leviym**,
shall *reach* **be** from the wall of the city and outward
a thousand cubits round about.
5 And ye shall measure from without the city
on the east *side* **edge** two thousand cubits,
and on the south *side* **edge** two thousand cubits,
and on the *west side* **seaward edge** two thousand cubits,
and on the north *side* **edge** two thousand cubits;
and the city shall be in the midst:
this shall be to them the suburbs of the cities.

ALLOTTING CITIES OF REFUGE TO THE LEVIYM

6 And among the cities
which ye shall give unto the *Levites* **Leviym,**
there shall be six cities for refuge,
which ye shall *appoint* **give** for the *manslayer* **murderer**,
that he may flee thither:
and to them ye shall *add* **give** forty and two cities.
7 So all the cities which ye shall give to the *Levites* **Leviym**
shall be forty and eight cities:
them *shall ye give* with their suburbs.
8 And the cities which ye shall give
shall be of the possession
of the *children* **sons** of *Israel* **Yisra El**:
from them that have many ye shall *give many* **greaten**;
but from *them that have* few ye shall *give few* **lessen**:
every *one* **man** shall give of his cities
unto the *Levites* **Leviym**
according to **the mouth of** his inheritance
which he inheriteth.
9 And *the LORD spake* **Yah Veh worded**
unto *Moses* **Mosheh,** saying,
10 *Speak* **Word** unto the *children* **sons** of *Israel* **Yisra El**,
and say unto them,
When ye *be come* **pass** over *Jordan* **Yarden**
into the land of *Canaan* **Kenaan**;
11 *Then ye shall appoint you* **And happen upon** cities
to be cities of refuge for you;
that the *slayer* **murderer** may flee thither,
which *killeth any person* **smiteth a soul**
at unawares **by inadvertent error**.
12 And they shall be unto you
cities for refuge from the *avenger* **redeemer**;
that the *manslayer* **murderer** die not,
until he stand
before **at the face of** the *congregation* **witness**
in judgment.
13 And of these cities which ye shall give
six cities shall *ye have* **be** for refuge.
14 Ye shall give three cities on this side *Jordan* **Yarden**,
and three cities shall ye give
in the land of *Canaan* **Kenaan**,
which shall be cities of refuge.
15 These six cities shall be a refuge,

both for the *children* **sons** of *Israel* **Yisra El,**
and for the *stranger* **sojourner,**
and for the *sojourner* **settler** among them:
that every one that *killeth any person* **smiteth a soul**
unawares may **by inadvertent error** flee thither.
16 And if he smite him with an instrument of iron,
so that he die, he is a murderer:
in deathifying,
the murderer shall *surely be put to death* **be deathified.**
17 And if he smite him *with throwing* **by handling** a stone,
wherewith he may die, and he die, he is a murderer:
in deathifying,
the murderer shall *surely be put to death* **be deathified.**
18 Or if he smite him
with an hand *weapon* **instrument** of *wood* **timber,**
wherewith he may die, and he die, he is a murderer:
in deathifying,
the murderer shall *surely be put to death* **be deathified.**
19 The *revenger* **redeemer** of blood himself
shall *slay* **deathify** the murderer:
when he *meeteth* **encountereth** him,
he shall *slay* **deathify** him.
20 But if he *thrust* **shove** him of hatred,
or hurl at him by *laying of wait* **lurking,** that he die;
21 Or in enmity smite him with his hand, that he die:
in deathifying,
he that smote him
shall *surely be put to death* **be deathified;**
for he is a murderer:
the *revenge* **redeemer** of blood
shall *slay* **deathify** the murderer,
when he *meeteth* **encountereth** him.
22 But if he *thrust* **shove** him *suddenly* **in a blink**
without enmity,
or have cast upon him any *thing* **instrument**
without *laying of wait* **lurking,**
23 Or with any stone, wherewith a man may die,
seeing him not, and *cast it upon* **it felleth** him, that he die,
and was not his enemy, neither sought his *harm* **evil:**
24 Then the *congregation* **witness** shall judge
between *the slayer* **him who smote**
and the *revenger* **redeemer** of blood
according to these judgments:
25 And the *congregation* **witness**
shall *deliver* **rescue** the *slayer* **murderer**
out of the hand of the *revenger* **redeemer** of blood,
and the *congregation* **witness** shall restore him
to the city of his refuge, whither he was fled:
and he shall *abide* **settle** in it
unto the death of the *high* **great** priest,
which was anointed with the holy oil.
26 But if the *slayer* **murderer** shall at any time
come without the border of the city of his refuge,
whither he was fled;
27 And the *revenger* **redeemer** of blood
find him without the borders of the city of his refuge,
and the *revenger* **redeemer** of blood
kill **murder** the *slayer* **murderer;**
he shall not be guilty of blood:
28 Because he should have *remained* **settled**
in the city of his refuge
until the death of the *high* **great** priest:
but after the death of the *high* **great** priest
the *slayer* **murderer** shall return
into the land of his possession.
29 So these *things* shall be for a statute of judgment
unto you
throughout your generations
in all your *dwellings* **settlements.**
30 Whoso *killeth any person* **smiteth a soul,**
the murderer shall be *put to death* **murdered**
by the mouth of witnesses:
but one witness shall not *testify* **answer**
against *any person* **a soul**
to cause him to die **unto his death.**
31 Moreover
ye shall take no *satisfaction* **koper/atonement**
for the *life* **soul** of a murderer,
which is *guilty of* **wicked unto** death:
but **in being deathified,**
he shall be *surely put to death* **deathified.**
32 And ye shall take no *satisfaction* **koper/atonement**
for him that is fled to the city of his refuge,
that he should *come again* **return**
to *dwell* **settle** in the land,
until the death of the priest.
33 So ye shall not *pollute* **profane** the land wherein ye are:
for blood it *defileth* **profaneth** the land:
and the land cannot be *cleansed* **kapar/atoned**
of **for** the blood that is *shed* **poured** therein,
but **except** by the blood of him that *shed* **poured** it.
34 *Defile* **Foul** not *therefore*
the land which ye shall *inhabit* **settle,**
wherein I dwell **midst I tabernacle:**
for *I the LORD* **I — Yah Veh**
dwell **tabernacle** among the *children* **sons** of *Israel* **Yisra El.**

ALLOTMENT OF THE DAUGHTERS OF YISRA EL

36 And the *chief* **heads of the** fathers
of the families of the *children* **sons** of *Gilead* **Gilad,**
the son of Machir,
the son of *Manasseh* **Menash Sheh,**
of the families of the sons of *Joseph* **Yoseph,**
came near **approached,**
and *spake before Moses* **worded at the face of Mosheh,**
and *before the princes* **at the face of the hierarchs,**
the *chief* **heads of the** fathers
of the *children* **sons** of *Israel* **Yisra El:**
2 And they said,
The LORD commanded **Yah Veh misvahed** my *lord* **adoni**
to give the land for an inheritance by *lot* **pebble**
to the *children* **sons** of *Israel* **Yisra El:**
and my *lord* **adoni**
was *commanded* **misvahed** by *the LORD* **Yah Veh**
to give the inheritance
of *Zelophehad* **Seloph Had** our brother
unto his daughters.
3 And if they be *married* **women** to any of the sons
of the *other tribes* **scions**
of the *children* **sons** of *Israel* **Yisra El,**
then shall their inheritance
be taken from the inheritance of our fathers,
and shall be *put* **added** to the inheritance
of the *tribe* **rod** whereunto they are received:
so **thus** shall it be taken
from the *lot* **pebble** of our inheritance.
4 And when the jubile
of the *children* **sons** of *Israel* **Yisra El** shall be,
then shall their inheritance
be *put* **added** unto the inheritance
of the *tribe* **rod** whereunto they are received:
so shall their inheritance be taken away
from the inheritance of the *tribe* **rod** of our fathers.
5 And *Moses commanded* **Mosheh misvahed**
the *children* **sons** of *Israel* **Yisra El**
according to the *word* **mouth** of *the LORD* **Yah Veh,**
saying,
The *tribe* **rod** of the sons of *Joseph* **Yoseph**
hath *said* **worded** *well.*
6 This is the *thing* **word**
which *the LORD doth command* **Yah Veh misvaheth**
concerning the daughters of *Zelophehad* **Seloph Had,**
saying, Let them *marry* **be women**
to whom they think best **of whom is good in their eyes;**
only to the family of the *tribe* **rod** of their father
shall they *marry* **be women.**
7 *So* **Thus** shall not the inheritance
of the *children* **sons** of *Israel* **Yisra El**
remove **turn around** from *tribe* **rod** to *tribe* **rod:**
for every *one* **man** of the *children* **sons** of *Israel* **Yisra El**
shall *keep himself* **adhere** to the inheritance
of the *tribe* **rod** of his fathers.
8 And every daughter, that possesseth an inheritance
in any *tribe* **rod** of the *children* **sons** of *Israel* **Yisra El,**
shall be *wife* **woman** unto one of the family
of the *tribe* **rod** of her father,
that the *children* **sons** of *Israel* **Yisra El**
may *enjoy* **possess** every man
the inheritance of his fathers.
9 Neither shall the inheritance *remove* **turn around**
from *one tribe to another tribe* **rod to rod;**

but every *one* **man** of the *tribes* **rods**
of the *children* **sons** of *Israel* **Yisra El**
shall *keep himself* **adhere** to his own inheritance.
10 Even as *the LORD* **Yah Veh**
commanded Moses **misvahed Mosheh**,
so *did* **worked** the daughters of *Zelophehad* **Seloph Had**:
11 For *Mahlah* **Machlah**, *Tirzah* **Tirsah**, and Hoglah,
and *Milcah* **Milchah**, and Noah,
the daughters of *Zelophehad* **Seloph Had**,
were *married* **women**
unto their *father's brothers'* **uncle's** sons:
12 And they *were married into* **became women**
of the families of the sons of *Manasseh* **Menash Sheh**
the son of *Joseph* **Yoseph**,
and their inheritance remained
in the *tribe* **rod** of the family of their father.
13 These are the *commandments* **misvoth**
and the judgments,
which *the LORD commanded* **Yah Veh misvahed**
by the hand of *Moses* **Mosheh**
unto the *children* **sons** of *Israel* **Yisra El**
in the plains of Moab
by *Jordan* **Yarden** near *Jericho* **Yericho**.

KEY TO INTERPRETING THE EXEGESES:
King James text is in regular type;
Text under exegeses is in oblique type;
Text of exegeses is in bold type.

RESUME' OF THE SONS OF YISRA EL

1 These be the words
which *Moses spake* **Mosheh worded**
unto all *Israel* **Yisra El**
on this side *Jordan* **Yarden** in the wilderness,
in the plain *over against* **opposite** the *Red sea* **reeds**,
between Paran, and Tophel, and Laban,
and Hazeroth, and *Dizahab* **Di Zahab**.
2 (There are eleven days' *journey* from Horeb
by the way of mount Seir
unto *Kadeshbarnea* **Qadesh Barnea**.)
3 And it *came to pass* **became**, in the fortieth year,
in the eleventh month, on the first *day* of the month,
that *Moses spake* **Mosheh worded**
unto the *children* **sons** of *Israel* **Yisra El**,
according unto all that the *LORD* **Yah Veh**
had *given in commandment* **misvahed**
unto **concerning** them;
4 After he had *slain Sihon* **smitten Sichon**
the *king* **sovereign** of the *Amorites* **Emoriy**,
which *dwelt* **settled** in Heshbon,
and Og the *king* **sovereign** of Bashan,
which *dwelt* **settled** at Astaroth in Edrei:
5 On this side *Jordan* **Yarden**, in the land of Moab,
began Moses **Mosheh willed**
to *declare* **explain** this *law* **torah**, saying,
6 *The LORD* **Yah Veh** our *God* **Elohim**
spake **worded** unto us in Horeb, saying,
ye have *dwelt long enough* **settled too much**
in this mount:
7 Turn *you* **your face**, and *take your journey* **pull stakes**,
and go to the mount of the *Amorites* **Emoriy**,
and unto all the *places* **tabernacles** nigh thereunto,
in the plain, in the *hills* **mountains**,
and in the *vale* **lowlands**, and in the south,
and by the sea *side* **haven**,
to the land of the *Canaanites* **Kenaaniy**, and unto Lebanon,
unto the great river, the river Euphrates.
8 *Behold* **See**,
I have *set* **given** the land *before you* **at your face**:
go in and possess the land
which *the LORD sware* **Yah Veh oathed** unto your fathers,
Abraham, *Isaac* **Yischaq**, and *Jacob* **Yaaqov**,
to give unto them and to their seed after them.
9 And I *spake* **said** unto you at that time, saying,
I am not able to bear you myself alone:

RESUME' ON DELEGATING JUDGMENT

10 *The LORD* **Yah Veh** your *God* **Elohim**
hath *multiplied* **abounded** you, and, behold,
ye are this day as the stars of *heaven* **the heavens**
for *multitude* **abundance**.
11 (*The LORD God* **Yah Veh Elohim** of your fathers
make **add to** you a thousand times
so many *more* as ye are,
and bless you, as he hath *promised* **worded** you!)
12 How can I myself alone bear your cumbrance,
and your burden, and your *strife* **dispute**?
13 *Take* **Give** you wise men,
and *understanding* **discerning**,
and known among your *tribes* **scions**,
and I *will make* **shall set** them *rulers* **heads** over you.
14 And ye answered me, and said,
The *thing* **word** which thou hast spoken
is good *for us* to *do* **work**.
15 So I took the *chief* **head** of your *tribes* **scions**,
wise men, and known,
and *made* **gave** them heads over you,
captains **governors** over thousands,
and *captains* **governors** over hundreds,
and *captains* **governors** over fifties,
and *captains* **governors** over tens,
and officers among your *tribes* **scions**.
16 And I *charged* **misvahed** your judges at that time,
saying, *Hear the causes* **Hearken**
between your brethren,
and judge *righteously* **justness**

between every man and his brother,
and the *stranger* **sojourner** that is with him.
17 Ye shall not
respect persons **recognize faces** in judgment;
but ye shall hear the small as well as the great;
ye shall not *be afraid of* **fear** the face of man;
for the judgment is *God's* **Elohim's**:
and the *cause* **word** that is too hard for you,
bring **approach** it unto me, and I *will* **shall** hear it.
18 And I *commanded* **misvahed** you at that time
all the *things* **words** which ye should *do* **work**.

RESUME' ON SENDING EXPLORERS TO ESHCOL

19 And when we *departed* **pulled stakes** from Horeb,
we went through
all that great and *terrible* **awesome** wilderness,
which ye saw by the way
of the mountain of the *Amorites* **Emoriy**,
as *the LORD* **Yah Veh** our *God* **Elohim**
commanded **misvahed** us;
and we came to *Kadeshbarnea* **Qadesh Barnea**.
20 And I said unto you,
ye are come unto the mountain of the *Amorites* **Emoriy**,
which *the LORD* **Yah Veh** our *God* **Elohim**
doth **shall** give unto us.
21 *Behold* **See**, *the LORD* **Yah Veh** thy *God* **Elohim**
hath *set* **given** the land *before thee* **at thy face**:
go up **ascend** and possess it,
as *the LORD God* **Yah Veh Elohim** of thy fathers
hath *said* **worded** unto thee;
fear **awe** not, neither be *discouraged* **dismayed**.
22 And ye *came near* **approached** unto me
every one of you, and said,
We *will* **shall** send men *before us* **from our face**,
and they shall *search us out* **explore** the land,
and *bring us* **return** word *again* **to us**
by what way we *must go up* **shall ascend**,
and into what cities we shall come.
23 And the *saying* **word**
pleased me well **well—pleased my eyes**:
and I took twelve men of you,
one *of a tribe* **man per scion**:
24 And they turned **their face**,
and *went up* **ascended** into the mountain,
and came unto the *valley* **wadi** of Eshcol,
and *searched* **spied** it out.
25 And they took of the fruit of the land in their hands,
and *brought* **descended** it *down* unto us,
and *brought us* **returned** word *again* **unto us**,
and said, It is a good land
which *the LORD* **Yah Veh** our *God* **Elohim**
doth **shall** give us.

RESUME' OF THE REBELLION OF THE SONS OF YISRA EL

26 Notwithstanding
ye *would not go up* **willed to not ascend**,
but rebelled against the *commandment* **mouth**
of *the LORD* **Yah Veh** your *God* **Elohim**:
27 And ye murmured in your tents, and said,
Because *the LORD hated us* **of Yah Veh's hatred**,
he hath brought us forth out of the land of *Egypt* **Misrayim**,
to *deliver* **give** us into the hand of the *Amorites* **Emoriy**,
to *destroy* **desolate** us.
28 Whither shall we *go up* **ascend**?
our brethren have *discouraged* **melted** our heart, saying,
The people is greater and *taller* **more exalted** than we;
the cities are great and *walled* **fortified**
up to *heaven* **the heavens**;
and moreover
we have seen the sons of the *Anakims* **Anakiy** there.
29 Then I said unto you, Dread not,
neither *be afraid of* **awe** them.
30 *The LORD* **Yah Veh** your *God* **Elohim**
which goeth *before you* **at your face**,
he shall fight for you,
according to all
that he *did* **worked** for you in *Egypt* **Misrayim**
before your eyes;
31 And in the wilderness, where thou hast seen
how that *the LORD* **Yah Veh** thy *God* **Elohim** bare thee,
as a man doth bear his son,
in all the way that ye went, until ye came into this place.
32 Yet in this *thing* **word** ye did not *believe* **trust**
the LORD **Yah Veh** your *God* **Elohim**,
33 Who went in the way *before you* **at your face**,
to *search* **explore** you out a place
to *pitch your tents in* **encamp**,
in fire by night,
to *shew* **have** you **see** by what way ye should go,
and in a cloud by day.
34 And *the LORD* **Yah Veh** heard the voice of your words,
and *was wroth* **enraged**, and *sware* **oathed**, saying,
35 Surely *there* shall not one of these men
of this evil generation see that good land,
which I *sware* **oathed** to give unto your fathers.
36 *Save Caleb* **Except Kaleb**
the son of *Jephunneh* **Yephunneh**;
he shall see it,
and to him *will* **shall** I give the land
that he hath trodden upon,
and to his *children* **sons**,
because he hath
wholly followed the LORD **fulfilled to follow Yah Veh**.
37 Also *the LORD* **Yah Veh** was angry with me
for your sakes, saying,
Thou also shalt not go in thither.
38 But *Joshua* **Yah Shua** the son of Nun,
which standeth *before thee* **at your face**,
he shall go in thither:
encourage **strengthen** him:
for he shall cause *Israel* **Yisra El** to inherit it.
39 Moreover your *little ones* **toddlers**,
which ye said, should be a *prey* **plunder**,
and your *children* **sons**,
which in that day
had no knowledge between good and evil,
they shall go in thither,
and unto them *will* **shall** I give it,
and they shall possess it.
40 But as for you, turn *you* **your face**,
and *take your journey* **pull stakes** into the wilderness
by the way of the *Red* **Reed** sea.
41 Then ye answered and said unto me,
We have sinned against *the LORD* **Yah Veh**,
we *will go up* **shall ascend** and fight,
according to all that *the LORD* **Yah Veh** our *God* **Elohim**
commanded **misvahed** us.
And when ye had girded on every man
his *weapons* **instruments** of war,
ye were ready to *go up* **ascend** into the *hill* **mountain**.
42 And *the LORD* **Yah Veh** said unto me, Say unto them,
Go not up **Ascend not**, neither fight;
for I am not among you;
lest ye be smitten *before* **at the face of** your enemies.
43 So I *spake* **worded** unto you;
and ye *would not hear* **hearkened not**,
but rebelled
against the *commandment* **mouth** of *the LORD* **Yah Veh**,
and *went presumptuously up* **ascended seething**
into the *hill* **mountain**.
44 And the *Amorites* **Emoriy**,
which *dwelt* **settled** in that mountain,
came out *against* **confronting** you,
and *chased* **pursued** you, as bees *do* **work**,
and *destroyed* **crushed** you in Seir, even unto Hormah.
45 And ye returned and wept
before the LORD **at the face of Yah Veh**;
but *the LORD* **Yah Veh**
would not hearken **hearkened not** to your voice,
nor *give ear* **hearkened** unto you.
46 So ye *abode* **settled** in *Kadesh* **Qadesh** many days,
according unto the days that ye *abode* **settled** there.

RESUME' OF THE WANDERINGS OF THE SONS OF YISRA EL

2 Then we turned **our face**,
and *took our journey* **pulled stakes** into the wilderness
by the way of the *Red* **Reed** sea,
as *the LORD spake* **Yah Veh worded** unto me:
and we *compassed* **surrounded** mount Seir many days.
2 And *the LORD spake* **Yah Veh said** unto me, saying,
3 Ye have *compassed* **surrounded** this mountain
long enough **too much**:

turn *you* **your face** northward.
4 And *command* **misvah** thou the people, saying,
ye are to pass through the *coast* **border** of your brethren
the *children* **sons** of *Esau* **Esav**, which *dwell* **settle** in Seir;
and they shall *be afraid of* **awe** you:
take ye good heed unto yourselves **guard mightily**
therefore:
5 *Meddle not with* **Throttle** them **not**;
for I *will* **shall** not give you of their land, no,
not so much as a *foot breadth* **step of the sole of a foot**;
because I have given mount Seir unto *Esau* **Esav**
for a possession.
6 Ye shall *buy meat* **market for kernels for food** of them
for *money* **silver**, that ye may eat;
and ye shall also *buy* **dig** water of them
for *money* **silver**, that ye may drink.
7 For *the LORD* **Yah Veh** thy *God* **Elohim**
hath blessed thee in all the works of thy hand:
he knoweth thy walking through this great wilderness:
these forty years
the LORD **Yah Veh** thy *God* **Elohim** hath been with thee;
thou hast lacked *nothing* **no word**.
8 And when we passed by from our brethren
the *children* **sons** of *Esau* **Esav**, which *dwelt* **settled** in Seir,
through the way of the plain from Elath,
and from *Eziongaber* **Esyon Geber**,
we turned **our face**
and passed by the way of the wilderness of Moab.
9 And *the LORD* **Yah Veh** said unto me,
Distress **Besiege** not *the Moabites* **Moabiy**,
neither *contend with* **throttle** them in *battle* **war**:
for I *will* **shall** not give thee of their land for a possession;
because I have given Ar
unto the *children* **sons** of Lot for a possession.
10 The *Emims dwelt* **Emim settled** therein
in times past **at their face**,
a people great, and many, and *tall* **exalted**,
as the *Anakims* **Anakiy**;
11 Which also were *accounted giants* **fabricated Rephaim**,
as the *Anakims* **Anakiy**;
but the *Moabites* **Moabiy** call them *Emims* **Emim**.
12 The *Horims* **Horim** also *dwelt* **settled** in Seir
beforetime **at their face**;
but the *children* **sons** of *Esau* **Esav** succeeded them,
when they had *destroyed* **desolated** them
from *before them* **their face**,
and *dwelt* **settled** in their stead;
as *Israel did* **Yisra El worked**
unto the land of his possession,
which *the LORD* **Yah Veh** gave unto them.
13 Now rise up, *said I*,
and *get* **pass** you over the *brook* **wadi** Zered.
And we *went* **passed** over the *brook* **wadi** Zered.
14 And the *space* **day**
in which we came from *Kadeshbarnea* **Qadesh Barnea**,
until we were *come* **passed** over the *brook* **wadi** Zered,
was thirty and eight years;
until all the generation of the men of war
were *wasted* **consumed** out from among the *host* **camp**,
as *the LORD sware* **Yah Veh oathed** unto them.
15 For indeed the hand of *the LORD* **Yah Veh**
was against them,
to *destroy* **agitate** them from among the *host* **camp**,
until they were consumed.
16 So it *came to pass* **became**,
when all the men of war were consumed
and *dead* **died** from among the people,
17 That *the LORD spake* **Yah Veh worded** unto me, saying,
18 *Thou art to* pass over through Ar,
the *coast* **border** of Moab, this day:
19 And when thou *comest nigh* **approachest**
over against **opposite** the *children* **sons** of Ammon,
distress **besiege** them not, nor *meddle with* **throttle** them:
for I *will* **shall** not give thee of the land
of the *children* **sons** of Ammon any possession;
because I have given it unto the *children* **sons** of Lot
for a possession.
20 (That also was *accounted* **fabricated**
a land of *giants* **Rephaim**:
giants dwelt **Rephaim settled** therein
in old time **at their face**;
and the *Ammonites* **Ammoniy** call them
Zamzummims **Zamzomiym**;
21 A people great, and many, and *tall* **exalted**,
as the *Anakims* **Anakiy**;
but *the LORD destroyed* **Yah Veh desolated** them
before them **at their face**;
and they succeeded them, and *dwelt* **settled** in their stead:
22 As he *did* **worked** to the *children* **sons** of *Esau* **Esav**,
which *dwelt* **settled** in Seir,
when he destroyed the *Horims* **Horim**
from *before them* **their face**;
and they succeeded them,
and *dwelt* **settled** in their stead even unto this day:
23 And the *Avims* **Avvim**
which *dwelt* **settled** in *Hazerim* **Haserim**,
even unto Azzah,
the *Caphtorims* **Kaphtorim**,
which came forth out of *Caphtor* **Kaphtor**,
destroyed them, and *dwelt* **settled** in their stead.)

RESUME' OF THE DEFEAT OF SICHON

24 Rise ye up, *take your journey* **pull stakes**,
and pass over the *river* **wadi** Arnon: *behold* **see**,
I have given into thine hand
Sihon **Sichon** the *Amorite* **Emoriy**,
king **sovereign** of Heshbon, and his land:
begin to possess it,
and *contend with* **throttle** him in *battle* **war**.
25 This day *will* **shall** I begin
to *put* **give** the *dread* **fear** of thee and the *fear* **awe** of thee
upon the *nations* **face of the people**
that are under the whole *heaven* **of the heavens**,
who shall hear report of thee, and shall *tremble* **quiver**,
and *be in anguish because of thee* **writhe at thy face**.
26 And I sent *messengers* **angels**
out of the wilderness of *Kedemoth* **Qedemoth**
unto *Sihon king* **Sichon sovereign** of Heshbon
with words of *peace* **shalom**, saying,
27 Let me pass through thy land:
I *will* **shall** go along **the way** by the *high* way,
I *will* **shall** neither turn **aside**
unto the right *hand* nor to the left.
28 Thou shalt *sell* **market** me *meat* **kernels for my food**
for *money* **silver**, that I may eat;
and give me water for *money* **silver**, that I may drink:
only I *will* **shall** pass through on my feet;
29 (As the *children* **sons** of *Esau* **Esav**
which *dwell* **settle** in Seir,
and the *Moabites* **Moabiy** which *dwell* **settle** in Ar,
did **worked** unto me;)
until I shall pass over *Jordan* **Yarden** into the land
which *the LORD* **Yah Veh** our *God* **Elohim** giveth us.
30 But *Sihon king* **Sichon sovereign** of Heshbon
would **willed to** not let us pass by him:
for *the LORD* **Yah Veh** thy *God* **Elohim** hardened his spirit,
and *made* **strengthened** his heart *obstinate*,
that he might *deliver* **give** him into thy hand,
as *appeareth* this day.
31 And *the LORD* **Yah Veh** said unto me, *Behold* **See**,
I have begun to give *Sihon* **Sichon** and his land
before thee **at thy face**:
begin to possess, that thou mayest *inherit* **possess** his land.
32 Then *Sihon* **Sichon** came out *against* **confronting** us,
he and all his people, to *fight* **war** at *Jahaz* **Yahsah**.
33 And *the LORD* **Yah Veh** our *God* **Elohim**
delivered **gave** him *before us* **at our face**;
and we smote him, and his sons, and all his people.
34 And we *took* **captured** all his cities at that time,
and *utterly destroyed* **devoted** the **few** men,
and the women, and the *little ones* **toddlers**, of every city,
we left *none* **no survivors** to *remain* **survive**:
35 Only the *cattle* **animals**
we *took for a prey* **plundered** unto ourselves,
and the *spoil* **loot** of the cities which we *took* **captured**.
36 From Aroer,
which is by the *brink* **edge** of the *river* **wadi** of Arnon,
and from the city that is by the *river* **wadi**,
even unto *Gilead* **Gilad**,
there was not one city too *strong* **lofted** for us:
the LORD **Yah Veh** our *God* **Elohim**

delivered **gave** all *unto us* **at our face**:
37 Only unto the land of the *children* **sons** of Ammon
thou *camest* **approachest** not,
nor unto any *place* **hand** of the *river Jabbok* **wadi Yabboq**,
nor unto the cities in the mountains,
nor unto whatsoever
the LORD **Yah Veh** our *God forbad* **Elohim misvahed** us.

RESUME' OF THE DEFEAT OF OG

3 Then we turned **our face**,
and *went up* **ascended** the way to Bashan:
and Og the *king* **sovereign** of Bashan
came out *against* **confronting** us,
he and all his people, to *battle* **war** at Edrei.
2 And *the LORD* **Yah Veh** said unto me, *Fear* **Awe** him not:
for I *will deliver* **shall give** him,
and all his people, and his land, into thy hand;
and thou shalt *do* **work** unto him
as thou *didst* **workedst** unto *Sihon* **Sichon**
king **sovereign** of the *Amorites* **Emoriy**,
which *dwelt* **settled** at Heshbon.
3 So *the LORD* **Yah Veh** our *God* **Elohim**
delivered **gave** into our hands Og also,
the *king* **sovereign** of Bashan, and all his people:
and we smote him until
none was left to him remaining **no survivors survived**.
4 And we *took* **captured** all his cities at that time,
there was not a city which we took not from them,
threescore **sixty** cities, all the *region* **boundaries** of Argob,
the *kingdom* **sovereigndom** of Og in Bashan.
5 All these cities were *fenced* **fortified**
with high walls, gates, and bars;
beside *unwalled towns* **suburban cities**
a great many **mightily abounding**.
6 And we *utterly destroyed* **devoted** them,
as we *did* **worked** unto *Sihon* **Sichon**
king **sovereign** of Heshbon,
utterly destroying **devoting** the **few** men,
women, and *children* **toddlers**, of every city.
7 But all the *cattle* **animals**, and the *spoil* **loot** of the cities,
we *took for a prey* **plundered** to ourselves.
8 And we took at that time out of the hand
of the two *kings* **sovereigns** of the *Amorites* **Emoriy**
the land that was on this side *Jordan* **Yarden**,
from the *river* **wadi** of Arnon unto mount Hermon;
9 (Which Hermon the *Sidonians* **Sidoniy** call Sirion;
and the *Amorites* **Emoriy** call it Shenir;)
10 All the cities of the plain,
and all *Gilead* **Gilad**, and all Bashan,
unto Salchah and Edrei,
cities of the *kingdom* **sovereigndom** of Og in Bashan.
11 For only Og *king* **sovereign** of Bashan
remained **survived**
of the remnant of *giants* **Rephaim**;
behold his bedstead was a bedstead of iron;
is it not in *Rabbath* **Rabbah**
of the *children* **sons** of Ammon?
nine cubits was the length thereof,
and four cubits the breadth of it, after the cubit of a man.

RESUME' OF THE ALLOTMENT OF LAND

12 And this land, which we possessed at that time,
from Aroer, which is by the *river* **wadi** Arnon,
and half mount *Gilead* **Gilad**, and the cities thereof,
gave I unto the *Reubenites* **Reu Beniy**
and to the *Gadites* **Gadiy**.
13 And the *rest* **remainder** of *Gilead* **Gilad**, and all Bashan,
being the *kingdom* **sovereigndom** of Og,
gave I unto the half *tribe* **scion** of *Manasseh* **Menash Sheh**;
all the *region* **boundaries** of Argob, with all Bashan,
which was called the land of *giants* **Rephaim**.
14 *Jair* **Yair** the son of *Manasseh* **Menash Sheh**
took all the *country* **boundaries** of Argob
unto the *coasts* **borders** of *Geshuri* **the Geshuriy**
and *Maachathi Maachahiy*;
and called them after his own name,
Bashanhavothjair **Bashan Havoth Yair**, unto this day.
15 And I gave *Gilead* **Gilad** unto Machir.
16 And unto the *Reubenites* **Reu Beniy**
and unto the *Gadites* **Gadiy**
I gave from *Gilead* **Gilad** even unto the *river* **wadi** Arnon
half **midst** the *valley* **wadi**,
and the border even unto the *river Jabbok* **wadi Yabboq**,
which is the border of the *children* **sons** of Ammon;
17 The plain also, and *Jordan* **Yarden**,
and the *coast* **border** *thereof*,
from *Chinnereth* **Kinneroth** even unto the sea of the plain,
even the salt sea,
under *Ashdothpisgah* **Ashdoth Pisgah**
eastward **toward the rising**.
18 And I *commanded* **misvahed** you at that time, saying,
the LORD **Yah Veh** your *God* **Elohim**
hath given you this land to possess it:
ye shall pass over *armed* **equipped**
before **at the face of** your brethren
the *children* **sons** of *Israel* **Yisra El**,
all that are *meet for the war* **sons of valour**.
19 But your *wives* **women**, and your *little ones* **toddlers**,
and your *cattle* **chattel**,
(for I know that ye have much *cattle* **chattel**,)
shall *abide* **settle** in your cities which I have given you;
20 Until *the LORD* **Yah Veh**
have given rest unto your brethren, as well as unto you,
and until they also possess the land
which *the LORD* **Yah Veh** your *God* **Elohim**
hath given them beyond *Jordan* **Yarden**:
and then shall ye return every man unto his possession,
which I have given you.

RESUME' OF YAH VEH'S FORBIDDING MOSHEH

21 And I *commanded Joshua* **misvahed Yah Shua**
at that time, saying,
Thine eyes have seen
all that *the LORD* **Yah Veh** your *God* **Elohim**
hath *done* **worked** unto these two *kings* **sovereigns**:
so shall *the LORD do* **Yah Veh work**
unto all the *kingdoms* **sovereigndoms**
whither thou passest.
22 Ye shall not *fear* **awe** them:
for *the LORD* **Yah Veh** your *God* **Elohim**
he shall fight for you.
23 And I besought *the LORD* **Yah Veh** at that time, saying,
24 O *Lord GOD* **Adonay Yah Veh**,
thou hast begun to
shew **have** thy servant **see** thy greatness,
and thy *mighty* **strong** hand:
for what *God* **El** is there in *heaven* **the heavens** or in earth,
that can *do* **work** according to thy works,
and according to thy might?
25 I *pray* **beseech** thee, let me *go* **pass** over,
and see the good land that is beyond *Jordan* **Yarden**,
that goodly mountain, and Lebanon.
26 But *the LORD was wroth with* **Yah Veh passed over** me
for your sakes **because of you**,
and *would not hear me* **heard me not**:
and *the LORD* **Yah Veh** said unto me,
Let it suffice thee **Too much**;
speak no more **word not again**
unto me of this *matter* **word**.
27 *Get* **Ascend** thee *up* into the top of Pisgah,
and lift up thine eyes *westward* **seaward**,
and northward and southward,
and *eastward* **toward the rising**,
and *behold* **see** it with thine eyes:
for thou shalt not *go* **pass** over this *Jordan* **Yarden**.
28 But *charge Joshua* **misvah Yah Shua**,
and *encourage* **strengthen** him,
and *strengthen* **toughen** him:
for he shall *go* **pass** over *before* **at the face of** this people,
and he shall cause them to inherit the land
which thou shalt see.
29 So we *abode* **settled** in the valley
over against Bethpeor **opposite Beth Peor**.

MOSHEH LAYS OUT THE TORAH

4 Now therefore hearken, O *Israel* **Yisra El**,
unto the statutes and unto the judgments,
which I teach you, for to *do* **work** them, that ye may live,
and go in and possess the land
which *the LORD God* **Yah Veh Elohim** of your fathers
giveth you.
2 Ye shall not add unto the word
which I *command* **misvah** you,
neither shall ye diminish *ought* from it,

that ye may *keep* **guard** the *commandments* **misvoth**
of *the LORD* **Yah Veh** your *God* **Elohim**
which I *command* **misvah** you.
3 Your eyes have seen
what *the LORD did* **Yah Veh worked**
because of *Baalpeor* **Baal Peor**:
for all the men
that *followed Baalpeor* **went after Baal Peor**,
the LORD **Yah Veh** thy *God* **Elohim**
hath destroyed them from among you.
4 But ye that did *cleave* **adhere**
unto *the LORD* **Yah Veh** your *God* **Elohim**
are alive every one of you this day.
5 *Behold* **See**, I have taught you statutes and judgments,
even as *the LORD* **Yah Veh** my *God* **Elohim**
commanded **misvahed** me,
that ye should *do so in* **so work midst** the land
whither ye go to possess it.
6 *Keep* **Guard** *therefore* and *do* **work** them;
for this is your wisdom
and your *understanding* **discernment**
in the *sight* **eyes** of the *nations* **people**,
which shall hear all these statutes, and say,
Surely this great *nation* **goyim**
is a wise and *understanding* **discerning** people.
7 For what *nation* **goyim** is there so great,
who hath *God* **Elohim** so nigh unto them,
as *the LORD* **Yah Veh** our *God* **Elohim** is in all *things*
that we call upon him for?
8 And what *nation* **goyim** is there so great,
that hath statutes and judgments so *righteous* **just**
as all this *law* **torah**,
which I set *before you* **at your face** this day?
9 Only *take heed to* **guard** thyself,
and *keep* **guard** thy soul *diligently* **mightily**,
lest thou forget the *things* **words**
which thine eyes have seen,
and lest they *depart* **turn aside** from thy heart
all the days of thy life:
but teach them thy sons, and thy sons' sons;
10 *Specially* the day
that thou stoodest *before* **at the face of**
the LORD **Yah Veh** thy *God* **Elohim** in Horeb,
when *the LORD* **Yah Veh** said unto me,
Gather me **Congregate** the people *together*,
and I *will* **shall** make them hear my words,
that they may learn to *fear* **awe** me
all the days that they shall live upon the *earth* **soil**,
and that they may teach their *children* **sons**.
11 And ye *came near* **approached**
and stood under the mountain;
and the mountain *burned* **kindled** with fire
unto the *midst* **heart** of *heaven* **the heavens**,
with darkness, clouds, and *thick* **dripping** darkness.
12 And *the LORD spake* **Yah Veh worded** unto you
out of the midst of the fire:
ye heard the voice of the words,
but saw no *similitude* **manifestation**;
only ye heard **except** a voice.
13 And he *declared* **told** unto you his covenant,
which he *commanded* **misvahed** you to *perform* **work**,
even ten *commandments* **words**;
and he *wrote* **inscribed** them
upon two *tables* **slabs** of stone.
14 And *the LORD commanded* **Yah Veh misvahed** me
at that time
to teach you statutes and judgments,
that ye might *do* **work** them
in the land whither ye *go* **pass** over to possess it.

MOSHEH WARNS AGAINST IDOLATRY

15 *Take ye therefore good heed unto yourselves*
Guard your souls mightily;
for ye saw no *manner of similitude* **manifestation**
on the day
that *the LORD spake* **Yah Veh worded** unto you in Horeb
out of the midst of the fire:
16 Lest ye *corrupt* **ruin** *yourselves*,
and *make* **work** you a *graven image* **sculptile**,
the *similitude* **manifestation** of any *figure* **figurine**,
the *likeness* **pattern** of male or female,
17 The *likeness* **pattern** of any *beast* **animal**
that is on the earth,
the *likeness* **pattern** of any winged fowl
that flieth in the *air* **heavens**,
18 The *likeness* **pattern** of *any thing* **aught**
that creepeth on the *ground* **soil**,
the *likeness* **pattern** of any fish
that is in the waters beneath the earth:
19 And lest thou lift up thine eyes
unto *heaven* **the heavens**,
and when thou seest the sun, and the moon, and the stars,
even all the host of *heaven* **the heavens**,
shouldest be driven to *worship* **prostrate to** them,
and serve them,
which *the LORD* **Yah Veh** thy *God* **Elohim**
hath *divided* **allotted** unto all *nations* **people**
under the whole *heaven* **of the heavens**.
20 But *the LORD* **Yah Veh** hath taken you,
and brought you forth out of the iron furnace,
even out of *Egypt* **Misrayim**,
to be unto him a people of inheritance, as ye are this day.
21 Furthermore *the LORD* **Yah Veh** was angry with me
for **because of** your *sakes* **words**,
and *sware* **oathed**
that I should not *go* **pass** over *Jordan* **Yarden**,
and that I should not go in unto that good land,
which *the LORD* **Yah Veh** thy *God* **Elohim**
giveth thee for an inheritance:
22 But I *must* die in this land,
I *must* **shall** not *go* **pass** over *Jordan* **Yarden**:
but ye shall *go* **pass** over, and possess that good land.
23 *Take heed* **Guard** unto yourselves,
lest ye forget the covenant
of *the LORD* **Yah Veh** your *God* **Elohim**,
which he *made* **cut** with you,
and *make* **work** you a *graven image* **sculptile**,
or *the likeness of any thing* **manifestation**,
which *the LORD* **Yah Veh** thy *God* **Elohim**
hath *forbidden* **misvahed** thee.
24 For *the LORD* **Yah Veh** thy *God* **Elohim**
is a consuming fire, *even* a jealous *God* **El**.
25 When thou shalt beget *children* **sons**,
and *children's children* **sons' sons**,
and ye shall have *remained long* **lingered** in the land,
and shall *corrupt* **ruin** *yourselves*,
and make a *graven image* **sculptile**,
or the *likeness of any thing* **manifestation**,
and shall *do* **work** evil
in the *sight* **eyes** of *the LORD* **Yah Veh** thy *God* **Elohim**,
to *provoke* **vex** him to *anger* **wrath**:
26 I call *heaven* **the heavens** and earth
to witness against you this day,
that **in destructing**,
ye shall *soon utterly perish* **suddenly destruct**
from off the land
whereunto ye *go* **pass** over *Jordan* **Yarden** to possess it;
ye shall not prolong your days upon it,
but **in desolating**, shall *utterly be destroyed* **be desolated**.
27 And *the LORD* **Yah Veh** shall scatter you
among the nations,
and ye shall be *left few* **few men** in number
that survive among the *heathen* **people**,
whither *the LORD* **Yah Veh** shall *lead* **drive** you.
28 And there ye shall serve *gods* **elohim**,
the work of *men's* **human** hands, *wood* **timber** and stone,
which neither see, nor hear, nor eat, nor *smell* **scent**.
29 But if from thence
thou shalt seek *the LORD* **Yah Veh** thy *God* **Elohim**,
thou shalt find *him*,
if thou seek him with all thy heart and with all thy soul.
30 When thou art in tribulation,
and all these *things* **words**
are come upon **have found** thee,
even in the *latter* **final** days,
if thou turn to *the LORD* **Yah Veh** thy *God* **Elohim**,
and shalt *be obedient* **hearken** unto his voice;

YAH VEH, A MERCIFUL EL

31 (For *the LORD* **Yah Veh** thy *God* **Elohim**
is a merciful *God* **El**;)
he *will* **shall** not *forsake thee* **let thee loose**,

neither *destroy* **ruin** thee,
nor forget the covenant of thy fathers
which he *sware* **oathed** unto them.
32 For ask *now* **I beseech**,
of the *days that are past* **first days**,
which were *before thee* **at thy face**,
since the day that
God **Elohim** created *man* **humanity** upon the earth,
and *ask* from the *one side* **end** of *heaven* **the heavens**
unto the *other* **end of the heavens**,
whether there hath *been* **become** *any such thing*
as this great *thing* **word** is, or hath been heard like it?
33 Did ever people hear the voice of *God* **Elohim**
speaking **wording** out of the midst of the fire,
as thou hast heard, and live?
34 Or hath *God assayed* **Elohim tested**
to go and take him a *nation* **goyim**
from the midst of *another nation* **goyim**,
by *temptations* **testings**, by signs, and by *wonders* **omens**,
and by war, and by a *mighty* **strong** hand,
and by a *stretched out* **extended** arm,
and by great *terrors* **awesomenesses**,
according to all that *the LORD* **Yah Veh** your *God* **Elohim**
did **worked** for you in *Egypt before* **Misrayim in** your eyes?
35 *Unto thee it was shewed* **You have seen**,
that thou mightest know
that *the LORD* **Yah Veh** he is *God* **Elohim**;
there is none else beside him.
36 Out of *heaven* **the heavens**
he *made* **had** thee to hear his voice,
that he might *instruct* **discipline** thee:
and upon earth he *shewed* **had** thee **to see** his great fire;
and thou heardest his words out of the midst of the fire.
37 And because he loved thy fathers,
therefore he chose their seed after them,
and brought thee out *in his sight* **at his face**
with his mighty *power* **force** out of *Egypt* **Misrayim**;
38 To *drive out nations* **dispossess goyim**
from *before thee* **thy face**
greater and mightier than thou art,
to bring thee in, to give thee their land for an inheritance,
as it is this day.
39 Know therefore this day,
and *consider it* **let it return** in thine heart,
that *the LORD* **Yah Veh**
he is *God* **Elohim** in *heaven* **the heavens** above,
and upon the earth beneath: there is none else.
40 Thou shalt *keep* **guard** therefore his statutes,
and his *commandments* **misvoth**,
which I *command* **misvah** thee this day,
that it may *go well with* **well—please** thee,
and with thy *children* **sons** after thee,
and that thou mayest prolong thy days upon the *earth* **soil**,
which *the LORD* **Yah Veh** thy *God* **Elohim** giveth thee,
for ever **all days**.

MOSHEH SEPARATES CITIES OF REFUGE

41 Then *Moses severed* **Mosheh separated** three cities
on this side *Jordan* **Yarden** toward the sunrising;
42 That the *slayer* **murderer** might flee thither,
which should *kill* **murder** his *neighbour* **friend**
unawares **unknowingly**,
and hated him not *in times past* **three yesters ago**;
and that fleeing unto one of these cities he might live:
43 *Namely*, *Bezer* **Beser** in the wilderness,
in the plain *country* **land**, of the *Reubenites* **Reu Beniy**;
and Ramoth in *Gilead* **Gilad**, of the *Gadites* **Gadiy**;
and Golan in Bashan, of the *Manassites* **Menash Shehiy**.

RESUME' OF THE TORAH

44 And this is the *law* **torah** which *Moses* **Mosheh** set
before **at the face of** the *children* **sons** of *Israel* **Yisra El**:
45 These are the *testimonies* **witnesses**,
and the statutes, and the judgments,
which *Moses spake* **Mosheh worded**
unto the *children* **sons** of *Israel* **Yisra El**,
after they came forth out of *Egypt* **Misrayim**.
46 On this side *Jordan* **Yarden**,
in the valley *over against Bethpeor* **opposite Beth Peor**,
in the land of *Sihon* **Sichon**
king **sovereign** of the *Amorites* **Emoriy**,
who *dwelt* **settled** at Heshbon,
whom *Moses* **Mosheh**
and the *children* **sons** of *Israel* **Yisra El** smote,
after they were come forth out of *Egypt* **Misrayim**:
47 And they possessed his land,
and the land of Og *king* **sovereign** of Bashan,
two *kings* **sovereigns** of the *Amorites* **Emoriy**,
which were on this side *Jordan* **Yarden**
toward the sunrising;
48 From Aroer,
which is by the *bank* **edge** of the *river* **wadi** Arnon,
even unto mount Sion, which is Hermon,
49 And all the plain on this side *Jordan* **Yarden**
eastward **toward the rising**,
even unto the sea of the plain, under the springs of Pisgah.

RESUME' OF STATUTES AND JUDGMENTS

5 And *Moses* **Mosheh** called all *Israel* **Yisra El**,
and said unto them, Hear, O *Israel* **Yisra El**,
the statutes and judgments
which I *speak* **word** in your ears this day,
that ye may learn them,
and *keep* **guard**, *and do* **work** them.
2 *The LORD* **Yah Veh** our *God* **Elohim**
made **cut** a covenant with us in Horeb.
3 *The LORD made* **Yah Veh cut** not this covenant
with our fathers, but with us,
even us, who are all of us here alive this day.
4 *The LORD talked* **Yah Veh worded** with you
face to face in the mount out of the midst of the fire,
5 (I stood between *the LORD* **Yah Veh** and you
at that time,
to *shew* **tell** you the word of *the LORD* **Yah Veh**:
for ye *were afraid by reason* **awed at the face** of the fire,
and *went* **ascended** not *up* into the mount;) saying,
6 *I am the LORD thy God* **I — Yah Veh thy Elohim**,
which brought thee out of the land of *Egypt* **Misrayim**,
from the house of *bondage* **servants**.
7 Thou shalt have none other *gods* **elohim** before me.
8 Thou shalt not
make **work** thee any *graven image* **sculptile**,
or any *likeness of any thing* **manifestation**
that is in *heaven* **the heavens** above,
or that is in the earth beneath,
or that is in the waters beneath the earth:
9 Thou shalt not
bow down **prostrate** *thyself* unto them, nor serve them:
for *I the LORD thy God* **I — Yah Veh thy Elohim**
am a jealous *God* **El**,
visiting the *iniquity* **perversity** of the fathers
upon the *children* **sons**
unto the third and fourth *generation* of them that hate me,
10 And *shewing* **working** mercy
unto thousands of them that love me
and *keep* **guard** my *commandments* **misvoth**.
11 Thou shalt not
take **bear** the name of *the LORD* **Yah Veh** thy *God* **Elohim**
in *vain* **defamation**:
for *the LORD* **Yah Veh**
will **shall** not *hold him guiltless* **exonerate him**
that *taketh* **beareth** his name in *vain* **defamation**.
12 *Keep* **Guard** the *sabbath* **shabbath** day
to *sanctify* **hallow** it,
as *the LORD* **Yah Veh** thy *God* **Elohim**
hath *commanded* **misvahed** thee.
13 Six days thou shalt *labour* **serve**,
and *do* **work** all thy work:
14 But the seventh day is the *sabbath* **shabbath**
of *the LORD* **Yah Veh** thy *God* **Elohim**:
in it thou shalt not *do* **work** any work,
thou, nor thy son, nor thy daughter,
nor thy *manservant* **servant**, nor thy *maidservant* **maid**,
nor thine ox, nor thine *ass* **he burro**,
nor any of thy *cattle* **animals**,
nor thy *stranger* **sojourner** that is within thy *gates* **portals**;
that thy *manservant* **servant** and thy *maidservant* **maid**
may rest as well as thou.
15 And remember that thou wast a servant
in the land of *Egypt* **Misrayim**,
and that *the LORD* **Yah Veh** thy *God* **Elohim**
brought thee out thence
through a *mighty* **strong** hand

and by *a stretched out* **an extended** arm:
therefore *the LORD* **Yah Veh** thy *God* **Elohim**
commanded **misvahed** thee
to *keep* **guard** the *sabbath* **shabbath** day.
16 Honour thy father and thy mother,
as *the LORD* **Yah Veh** thy *God* **Elohim**
hath *commanded* **misvahed** thee;
that thy days may be prolonged,
and that it may *go well with* **well—please** thee,
in the *land* **soil**
which *the LORD* **Yah Veh** thy *God* **Elohim** giveth thee.
17 Thou shalt not *kill* **murder**.
18 Neither shalt thou *commit adultery* **adulterize**.
19 Neither shalt thou steal.
20 Neither shalt thou *bear false* **answer a vain** witness
against thy *neighbour* **friend**.
21 Neither shalt thou desire
thy *neighbour's wife* **friend's woman**,
neither shalt thou *covet* **desire**
thy *neighbour's* **friend's** house,
his field, or his *manservant* **servant**,
or his *maidservant* **maid**, his ox, or his *ass* **he burro**,
or *any thing* **aught** that is thy *neighbour's* **friend's**.
22 These words *the LORD spake* **Yah Veh worded**
unto all your *assembly* **congregation**
in the mount out of the midst of the fire,
of the cloud, and of the *thick* **dripping** darkness,
with a great voice: and he added *no more* **not**.
And he *wrote* **inscribed** them in two *tables* **slabs** of stone,
and *delivered* **gave** them unto me.
23 And it *came to pass* **became**,
when ye heard the voice out of the midst of the darkness,
(for the mountain *did burn* **kindled** with fire,)
that ye *came near unto* **approached** me,
even all the heads of your *tribes* **scions**, and your elders;
24 And ye said, Behold,
the LORD **Yah Veh** our *God* **Elohim**
hath *shewed* us **see** his *glory* **honour** and his greatness,
and we have heard his voice out of the midst of the fire:
we have seen this day
that *God doth talk* **Elohim wordeth** with *man* **humanity**,
and he liveth.
25 Now therefore why should we die?
for this great fire *will* **shall** consume us:
if we hear the voice
of *the LORD* **Yah Veh** our *God any more* **Elohim again**,
then we shall die.
26 For who is there of all flesh,
that hath heard the voice of the living *God* **Elohim**
speaking **wording** out of the midst of the fire,
as we have, and lived?
27 Go thou near, and hear all
that *the LORD* **Yah Veh** our *God* **Elohim** shall say:
and *speak* **word** thou unto us
all that *the LORD* **Yah Veh** our *God* **Elohim**
shall *speak* **word** unto thee;
and we *will* **shall** hear it, and *do* **work** it.
28 And *the LORD* **Yah Veh** heard the voice of your words,
when ye *spake* **worded** unto me;
and *the LORD* **Yah Veh** said unto me,
I have heard the voice of the words of this people,
which they have *spoken* **worded** unto thee:
they have well—**pleasingly** said
all that they have *spoken* **worded**.
29 O **give** that there were such an heart in them,
that they *would fear* **should awe** me,
and *keep* **guard** all my *commandments* **misvoth**
always **all days**,
that it might *be well with* **well—please** them,
and with their *children for ever* **sons eternally**!
30 Go say to them, *Get* **Return** you into your tents *again*.
31 But as for thee, stand thou here by me,
and I *will speak* **shall word** unto thee
all the *commandments* **misvoth**,
and the statutes, and the judgments,
which thou shalt teach them,
that they may *do* **work** them
in the land which I give them to possess it.
32 Ye shall *observe* **guard** to *do* **work** *therefore*
as *the LORD* **Yah Veh** your *God* **Elohim**
hath *commanded* **misvahed** you:
Ye shall not turn aside to the right *hand* or to the left.
33 ye shall walk in all the ways
which *the LORD* **Yah Veh** your *God* **Elohim**
hath *commanded* **misvahed** you,
that ye may live, and that it may be *well* **good** with you,
and that ye may prolong your days
in the land which ye shall possess.
6 Now these are the *commandments* **misvoth**,
the statutes, and the judgments,
which *the LORD* **Yah Veh** your *God* **Elohim**
commanded **misvahed** to teach you,
that ye might *do* **work** them
in the land whither ye *go* **pass over** to possess it:
2 That thou mightest *fear* **awe**
the LORD **Yah Veh** thy *God* **Elohim**,
to *keep* **guard** all his statutes
and his *commandments* **misvoth**,
which I *command* **misvah** thee,
thou, and thy son, and thy son's son,
all the days of thy life;
and that thy days may be prolonged.
3 Hear *therefore*, O *Israel* **Yisra El**,
and *observe* **guard** to *do* **work** it;
that it may *be well with* **well—please** thee,
and that ye may *increase* **abound** mightily,
as *the LORD God* **Yah Veh Elohim** of thy fathers
hath *promised* **worded unto** thee,
in the land that floweth with milk and honey.
4 Hear, O *Israel* **Yisra El**:
The LORD **Yah Veh** our *God* **Elohim**
is one *LORD* **Yah Veh**:
5 And thou shalt love *the LORD* **Yah Veh** thy *God* **Elohim**
with all thine heart, and with all thy soul,
and with all thy might.
6 And these words,
which I *command* **misvah** thee this day,
shall be in thine heart:
7 And thou shalt *teach* **point** them *diligently*
unto thy *children* **sons**,
and shalt *talk* **word** of them
when thou sittest in thine house,
and when thou walkest by the way,
and when thou liest down,
and when thou risest up.
8 And thou shalt bind them for a sign upon thine hand,
and they shall be
as frontlets **phylacteries** between thine eyes.
9 And thou shalt *write* **inscribe** them
upon the posts of thy house, and on thy *gates* **portals**.
10 And it shall be,
when *the LORD* **Yah Veh** thy *God* **Elohim**
shall have brought thee into the land
which he *sware* **oathed** unto thy fathers,
to Abraham, to *Isaac* **Yischaq**, and to *Jacob* **Yaaqov**,
to give thee great and goodly cities,
which thou buildedst not,
11 And houses full of all good *things*,
which thou filledst not,
and wells *digged* **hewn**,
which thou *diggedst* **hewest** not,
vineyards and olive trees,
which thou plantedst not;
when thou shalt have eaten and be *full* **satiated**;
12 Then *beware* **guard** lest thou forget *the LORD* **Yah Veh**,
which brought thee forth
out of the land of *Egypt* **Misrayim**,
from the house of *bondage* **servants**.
13 Thou shalt *fear* **awe**
the LORD **Yah Veh** thy *God* **Elohim**,
and serve him, and shalt *swear* **oath** by his name.
14 Ye shall not go after other *gods* **elohim**,
of the *gods* **elohim** of the people
which are round about you;
15 (For *the LORD* **Yah Veh** thy *God* **Elohim**
is a jealous *God* **El** among you)
lest the *anger* **wrath** of *the LORD* **Yah Veh** thy *God* **Elohim**
be kindled against thee,
and destroy thee from off the face of the *earth* **soil**.
16 Ye shall not *tempt* **test**

the *LORD* **Yah Veh** your *God* **Elohim**,
as **,in testing** ye *tempted* **tested** him *in Massah*.
17 **In guarding,** ye shall *diligently keep* **guard**
the *commandments* **misvoth**
of *the LORD* **Yah Veh** your *God* **Elohim,**
and his *testimonies* **witnesses**, and his statutes,
which he hath *commanded* **misvahed** thee.
18 *And* thou shalt *do* **work**
that which is *right* **straight** and good
in the *sight* **eyes** of *the LORD* **Yah Veh**:
that it may *be well with* **well—please** thee,
and that thou mayest go in and possess the good land
which *the LORD sware* **Yah Veh oathed** unto thy fathers.
19 To *cast out* **expel** all thine enemies
from *before thee* **thy face,**
as *the LORD* **Yah Veh** hath *spoken* **worded.**
20 And when thy son asketh thee
in time to come **on the morrow**, saying,
What mean the *testimonies* **witnesses**,
and the statutes, and the judgments,
which *the LORD* **Yah Veh** our *God* **Elohim**
hath *commanded* **misvahed** you?
21 Then thou shalt say unto thy son,
We were *Pharaoh's bondmen* **Paroh's servants**
in *Egypt* **Misrayim;**
and *the LORD* **Yah Veh** brought us out of *Egypt* **Misrayim**
with a *mighty* **strong** hand:
22 And *the LORD* **Yah Veh**
shewed **gave** signs and *wonders* **omens**,
great and *sore* **evil**,
upon *Egypt* **Misrayim**, upon *Pharaoh* **Paroh**,
and upon all his household, before our eyes:
23 And he brought us out from thence,
that he might bring us in, to give us the land
which he *sware* **oathed** unto our fathers.
24 And *the LORD commanded* **Yah Veh misvahed** us
to *do* **work** all these statutes,
to *fear the LORD* **awe Yah Veh** our *God* **Elohim**,
for our good *always* **all days**,
that he might preserve us alive, as it is at this day.
25 And it shall be our *righteousness* **justness**,
if we *observe* **guard** to *do* **work**
all these *commandments* **misvoth**
before the LORD **at the face of Yah Veh** our *God* **Elohim**,
as he hath *commanded* **misvahed** us.

THE TORAH ON MINGLING

7 When *the LORD* **Yah Veh** thy *God* **Elohim**
shall bring thee into the land whither thou goest
to possess it,
and hath *cast* **plucked** *out* many *nations* **goyim**
before thee **at thy face**,
the *Hittites* **Hethiy**, and the *Girgashites* **Girgashiy**
and the *Amorites* **Emoriy**, and the *Canaanites* **Kenaaniy**,
and the *Perizzites* **Perizziy**, and the *Hivites* **Hivviy**,
and the *Jebusites* **Yebusiy**,
seven *nations* **goyim** greater and mightier than thou;
2 And when *the LORD* **Yah Veh** thy *God* **Elohim**
shall *deliver* **give** them *before thee* **at thy face**;
thou shalt smite them,
and *utterly destroy* **in devoting, devote** them;
thou shalt *make* **cut** no covenant with them,
nor *shew mercy* **grant charism** unto them:
3 Neither shalt *thou make marriages* **intermarry** with them;
thy daughter thou shalt not give unto his son,
nor his daughter shalt thou take unto thy son.
4 For they *will* **shall** turn *away* **aside** thy son
from following me,
that they may serve other *gods* **elohim**:
so *will* **shall** the *anger* **wrath** of *the LORD* **Yah Veh**
be kindled against you, and destroy thee suddenly.
5 But thus shall ye *deal* **work** with them;
ye shall *destroy* **pull down** their **sacrifice** altars,
and break down their *images* **monoliths**,
and cut down their *groves* **asherim**,
and burn their *graven images* **sculptiles** with fire.
6 For thou art an holy people
unto *the LORD* **Yah Veh** thy *God* **Elohim**:
the LORD **Yah Veh** thy *God* **Elohim** hath chosen thee
to be a *special* **peculiar** people unto himself,
above all people that are upon the face of the *earth* **soil**.
7 *The LORD* **Yah Veh**
did not *set his love upon* **attach himself to** you,
nor *choose* **chose** you,
because ye were more *in number* **abundant**
than any people;
for ye were the fewest of all people:
8 But because *the LORD loved* **of Yah Veh's love to** you,
and because he *would keep* **should guard** the oath
which he had *sworn* **oathed** unto your fathers,
hath *the LORD* **Yah Veh** brought you out
with a *mighty* **strong** hand,
and redeemed you out of the house of *bondmen* **servants**,
from the hand of *Pharaoh* **Paroh**
king **sovereign** of *Egypt* **Misrayim.**
9 Know therefore that *the LORD* **Yah Veh** thy *God* **Elohim**,
he is *God* **Elohim**, the *faithful God* **trustworthy El**,
which *keepeth* **guardeth** covenant and mercy
with them that love him
and *keep* **guard** his *commandments* **misvoth**
to a thousand generations;
10 And *repayeth* **doth shalam** them
that hate him to their face, to destroy them:
he *will* **shall** not *be slack* **delay** to him that hateth him,
he *will repay* **shall shalam** him to his face.
11 Thou shalt *therefore*
keep **guard** the *commandments* **misvoth**,
and the statutes, and the judgments,
which I *command* **misvah** thee this day, to *do* **work** them.
12 Wherefore it shall *come to pass* **become**,
if **because** ye hearken to these judgments,
and *keep* **guard**, and *do* **work** them,
that *the LORD* **Yah Veh** thy *God* **Elohim**
shall *keep* **guard** unto thee the covenant and the mercy
which he *sware* **oathed** unto thy fathers:
13 And he *will* **shall** love thee, and bless thee,
and *multiply* **abound** thee:
he *will* **shall** also bless the fruit of thy *womb* **belly**,
and the fruit of thy *land* **soil**,
thy *corn* **crop**, and thy *wine* **juice**, and thine oil,
the *increase* **fetus** of thy *kine* **yoke**,
and the *flocks* **riches** of thy *sheep* **flocks**,
in the *land* **soil** which he *sware* **oathed** unto thy fathers
to give thee.
14 Thou shalt be blessed above all people:
there shall not be male **sterile** or female *barren* **sterile**
among you, or among your *cattle* **animals**.
15 And *the LORD* **Yah Veh**
will take **shall turn** away from thee all sickness,
and *will* **shall** put none
of the evil diseases of *Egypt* **Misrayim**,
which thou knowest, upon thee;
but *will lay* **shall give** them upon all them that hate thee.
16 And thou shalt consume all the people
which *the LORD* **Yah Veh** thy *God* **Elohim**
shall *deliver* **give** thee;
thine eye shall *have no pity upon* **not spare** them:
neither shalt thou serve their *gods* **elohim**;
for that *will* **shall** be a snare unto thee.
17 If thou shalt say in thine heart,
These *nations* **goyim** are *more* **greater** than I;
how can I dispossess them?
18 Thou shalt not *be afraid of* **awe** them:
but shalt well remember
what *the LORD* **Yah Veh** thy *God* **Elohim**
did **worked** unto *Pharaoh* **Paroh**,
and unto all *Egypt* **Misrayim;**
19 The great *temptations* **testings** which thine eyes saw,
and the signs, and the *wonders* **omens**,
and the *mighty* **strong** hand,
and the *stretched out* **extended** arm,
whereby *the LORD* **Yah Veh** thy *God* **Elohim**
brought thee out:
so shall *the LORD* **Yah Veh** thy *God* **Elohim**
do **work** unto all the people
of whom thou art afraid **whose face thou awest**.
20 *Moreover the LORD* **Yah Veh** thy *God* **Elohim**
will **shall** send the hornet among them,
until they that *are left* **survive**,
and hide themselves from *thee* **thy face**,
be destroyed.

21 Thou shalt not be *affrighted* **terrified** at *them* **their face**:
for *the LORD* **Yah Veh** thy *God* **Elohim** is among you,
a *mighty God* **great El** and *terrible* **awesome**.
22 And *the LORD* **Yah Veh** thy *God* **Elohim**
will put out **shall pluck** those *nations* **goyim**
before thee **from thy face**
by little and little **bit by bit**:
thou mayest not **be able**
consume them at once **to finish them off suddenly**,
lest the *beasts* **live beings** of the field
increase **abound** upon thee.
23 But *the LORD* **Yah Veh** thy *God* **Elohim**
shall *deliver* **give** them unto *thee* **thy face**,
and shall *destroy* **quake** them
with a *mighty destruction* **great confusion**,
until they be *destroyed* **desolated**.
24 And he shall *deliver* **give** their *kings* **sovereigns**
into thine hand,
and thou shalt destroy their name
from under *heaven* **the heavens**:
there shall no man be able to stand
before thee **at thy face**,
until thou have *destroyed* **desolated** them.
25 The *graven images* **sculptiles** of their *gods* **elohim**
shall ye burn with fire:
thou shalt not desire the silver or gold that is on them,
nor take it unto thee, lest thou be snared therein:
for it is an *abomination* **abhorrence**
to *the LORD* **Yah Veh** thy *God* **Elohim**.
26 Neither shalt thou bring an *abomination* **abhorrence**
into thine house,
lest thou be *a cursed thing* **devoted** like it:
but **in abominating,** thou shalt *utterly detest* **abominate** it,
and **in abhorring,** thou shalt *utterly* abhor it;
for it is *a cursed thing* **devoted**.

ON GUARDING THE MISVOTH

8 All the *commandments* **misvoth**
which I *command* **misvah** thee this day
shall ye *observe* **guard** to *do* **work**,
that ye may live, and *multiply* **abound**,
and go in and possess the land
which *the LORD sware* **Yah Veh oathed** unto your fathers.
2 And thou shalt remember all the way
which *the LORD* **Yah Veh** thy *God* **Elohim**
led **carried** thee these forty years in the wilderness,
to humble thee, and to *prove* **test** thee,
to know what was in thine heart,
whether thou *wouldest*
keep **guard** his *commandments* **misvoth**, or no.
3 And he humbled thee,
and *suffered* **famished** thee *to hunger*,
and fed thee with manna, which thou knewest not,
neither did thy fathers know;
that he might make **known to** thee *know*
that *man* **humanity** doth not live by bread only,
but by *every word* **all**
that proceedeth out of the mouth of *the LORD* **Yah Veh**
doth *man* **humanity** live.
4 Thy *raiment* **clothes**
waxed not old **neither wore out** upon thee,
neither did thy foot swell, these forty years.
5 Thou shalt also consider in thine heart,
that, as a man *chasteneth* **disciplineth** his son,
so *the LORD* **Yah Veh** thy *God* **Elohim**
chasteneth **disciplineth** thee.
6 *Therefore*
thou shalt *keep* **guard** the *commandments* **misvoth**
of *the LORD* **Yah Veh** thy *God* **Elohim**,
to walk in his ways, and to *fear* **awe** him.
7 For *the LORD* **Yah Veh** thy *God* **Elohim**
bringeth thee into a good land,
a land of *brooks* **wadies** of water,
of fountains and *depths* **abysses**
that spring out of valleys and *hills* **mountains**;
8 A land of wheat, and barley,
and vines, and *fig trees* **figs**, and pomegranates;
a land of oil olive, and honey;
9 A land wherein thou shalt eat bread
without *scarceness* **poverty**,
thou shalt not lack *any thing* **aught** in it;
a land whose stones are iron,
and out of whose *hills* **mountains**
thou mayest *dig brass* **hew copper**.
10 When thou hast eaten and art *full* **satiated**,
then thou shalt bless *the LORD* **Yah Veh** thy *God* **Elohim**
for the good land which he hath given thee.
11 *Beware* **Guard** that thou forget not
the LORD **Yah Veh** thy *God* **Elohim**,
in not *keeping* **guarding** his *commandments* **misvoth**,
and his judgments, and his statutes,
which I *command* **misvah** thee this day:
12 Lest when thou hast eaten and art *full* **satiated**,
and hast built goodly houses, and *dwelt* **settled** *therein*;
13 And when thy *herds* **oxen** and thy flocks
multiply **abound**,
and thy silver and thy gold *is multiplied* **aboundeth**,
and all that thou hast *is multiplied* **aboundeth**;
14 Then thine heart be lifted up,
and thou forget *the LORD* **Yah Veh** thy *God* **Elohim**,
which brought thee forth
out of the land of *Egypt* **Misrayim**,
from the house of *bondage* **servants**;
15 Who *led* **carried** thee through
that great and *terrible* **awesome** wilderness,
wherein were *fiery* **seraph** serpents, and scorpions,
and *drought* **thirst**, where there was no water;
who brought thee forth water out of the rock of flint;
16 Who fed thee in the wilderness with manna,
which thy fathers knew not,
that he might humble thee,
and that he might *prove* **test** thee,
to *do* **well—please** thee *good* at thy latter end;
17 And thou say in thine heart,
My *power* **force** and the might of mine hand
hath *gotten* **worked** me this *wealth* **valour**.
18 But thou shalt remember
the LORD **Yah Veh** thy *God* **Elohim**:
for it is he that giveth thee *power* **force**
to *get wealth* **work valour**,
that he may *establish* **raise** his covenant
which he *sware* **oathed** unto thy fathers, as it is this day.
19 And it shall be,
if **in forgetting,** thou *do at all* forget
the LORD **Yah Veh** thy *God* **Elohim**,
and walk after other *gods* **elohim**, and serve them,
and *worship* **prostrate to** them,
I *testify* **witness** against you this day
that **in destructing,** ye shall *surely perish* **destruct**.
20 As the *nations* **goyim**
which *the LORD* **Yah Veh** destroyeth
before your face **at thy face**, so shall ye *perish* **destruct**;
because ye *would not be obedient* **hearkened not**
unto the voice of *the LORD* **Yah Veh** your *God* **Elohim**.

RESUME' OF YAH VEH'S INTERVENTIONS

9 Hear, O *Israel* **Yisra El**:
Thou art to pass over *Jordan* **Yarden** this day,
to go in to possess *nations* **goyim**
greater and mightier than thyself,
cities great and *fenced* **fortified** up to *heaven* **the heavens**,
2 A people great and *tall* **exalted**,
the *children* **sons** of the *Anakims* **Anakiy**,
whom thou knowest,
and of whom thou hast heard *say*,
Who can stand
before **at the face of** the *children* **sons** of Anak!
3 Understand therefore this day,
that *the LORD* **Yah Veh** thy *God* **Elohim**
is he which *goeth* **passeth** over *before* thee **at thy face**;
as a consuming fire he shall *destroy* **desolate** them,
and he shall *bring* **subdue** them *down before* **at** thy face:
so **thus** shalt thou *drive* **dispossess** them *out*,
and destroy them *quickly* **suddenly**,
as *the LORD* **Yah Veh** hath *said* **worded** unto thee.
4 *Speak* **Say** not thou in thine heart,
after that *the LORD* **Yah Veh** thy *God* **Elohim**
hath *cast* **expelled** them *out* from *before thee* **thy face**,
saying, For my *righteousness* **justness**
the *LORD* **Yah Veh** hath brought me in
to possess this land:
but for the wickedness of these *nations* **goyim**

the LORD doth drive **Yah Veh dispossesseth** them *out*
from *before thee* **thy face.**
5 Not for thy *righteousness* **justness,**
or for the *uprightness* **straightness** of thine heart,
dost thou go to possess their land:
but for the wickedness of these *nations* **goyim**
the LORD **Yah Veh** thy *God* **Elohim**
doth drive **dispossesseth** them *out*
from *before thee* **thy face,**
and that he may *perform* **raise** the word
which *the LORD sware* **Yah Veh oathed** unto thy fathers,
Abraham, *Isaac* **Yischaq,** and *Jacob* **Yaaqov.**
6 Understand therefore,
that *the LORD* **Yah Veh** thy *God* **Elohim**
giveth thee not this good land to possess it
for thy *righteousness* **justness;**
for thou art a *stiffnecked* **hard necked** people.

RESUME' OF IDOLATRIES

7 Remember, and forget not,
how thou *provokedst* **enragedst**
the LORD thy God to wrath **Yah Veh thy Elohim**
in the wilderness:
from the day that thou
didst depart out of the land of *Egypt* **Misrayim,**
until ye came unto this place,
ye have been rebellious against *the LORD* **Yah Veh.**
8 Also in Horeb
ye *provoked the LORD* **enraged Yah Veh** *to wrath,*
so that *the LORD* **Yah Veh** was angry with you
to have *destroyed* **desolated** you.
9 When I *was gone up* **ascended** into the mount
to *receive* **take** the *tables* **slabs** of stone,
even the *tables* **slabs** of the covenant
which *the LORD made* **Yah Veh cut** with you,
then I *abode* **settled** in the mount
forty days and forty nights,
I neither did eat bread nor drink water:
10 And *the LORD delivered* **Yah Veh gave** unto me
two *tables* **slabs** of stone
written **inscribed** with the finger of *God* **Elohim;**
and on them *was written* according to all the words,
which *the LORD spake* **Yah Veh worded** with you
in the mount out of the midst of the fire
in the day of the *assembly* **congregation.**
11 And it *came to pass* **became,**
at the end of forty days and forty nights,
that *the LORD* **Yah Veh**
gave me the two *tables* **slabs** of stone,
even the *tables* **slabs** of the covenant.
12 And *the LORD* **Yah Veh** said unto me, Arise,
get thee down quickly **descend suddenly** from hence;
for thy people
which thou hast brought forth out of *Egypt* **Misrayim**
have *corrupted* **ruined** *themselves;*
they are *quickly* **suddenly** turned aside
out of the way which I *commanded* **misvahed** them;
they have *made* **worked** them a molten *image.*
13 *Furthermore the LORD spake* **Yah Veh said** unto me,
saying, I have seen this people, and, behold,
it is a *stiffnecked* **hard necked** people:
14 Let me alone, that I may *destroy* **desolate** them,
and *blot* **wipe** out their name from under *heaven* **the heavens:**
and I *will make* **shall work** of thee a *nation* **goyim**
mightier and greater than they.
15 So I turned **my face**
and *came down* **descended** from the mount,
and the mount *burned* **kindled** with fire:
and the two *tables* **slabs** of the covenant
were in my two hands.
16 And I *looked* **saw,** and, behold,
ye had sinned
against *the LORD* **Yah Veh** your *God* **Elohim,**
and had *made* **worked** you a molten calf:
ye had turned aside *quickly* **suddenly** out of the way
which *the LORD* **Yah Veh**
had *commanded* **misvahed** you.
17 And I *took* **manipulated** the two *tables* **slabs,**
and cast them out of my two hands,
and brake them before your eyes.
18 And I fell down
before the LORD **at the face of Yah Veh,**
as at the first, forty days and forty nights:
I did neither eat bread, nor drink water,
because of all your sins which ye sinned,
in *doing wickedly* **working evil**
in the *sight* **eyes** of *the LORD* **Yah Veh,**
to *provoke him to anger* **vex him.**
19 For I was afraid *of* **to face**
the *anger* **wrath** and *hot displeasure* **fury,**
wherewith *the LORD* **Yah Veh**
was *wroth* **enraged** against you to *destroy* **desolate** you.
But *the LORD* **Yah Veh**
hearkened unto me at that time also.
20 And *the LORD* **Yah Veh**
was *very* **mighty** angry with *Aaron* **Aharon**
to have *destroyed* **desolated** him:
and I prayed for *Aaron* **Aharon** also the same time.
21 And I took your sin,
the calf which ye had *made* **worked,**
and burnt it with fire, and *stamped* **crushed** it,
and ground it *very small* **well,**
even until it was *as small* **pulverized** as dust:
and I cast the dust thereof into the *brook* **wadi**
that descended out of the mount.
22 And at Taberah, and at *Massah* **Testing,**
and at *Kibrothhattaavah* **Qibroth Hat Taavah,**
ye *provoked the LORD to wrath* **enraged Yah Veh.**
23 Likewise when *the LORD* **Yah Veh** sent you
from *Kadeshbarnea* **Qadesh Barnea,**
saying, *Go up* **Ascend**
and possess the land which I have given you;
then ye rebelled against the *commandment* **mouth**
of *the LORD* **Yah Veh** your *God* **Elohim,**
and ye *believed* **trusted** him not,
nor hearkened to his voice.
24 Ye have been rebellious against *the LORD* **Yah Veh**
from the day that I knew you.
25 Thus I fell down
before the LORD **at the face of Yah Veh**
forty days and forty nights, as I fell down *at the first;*
because *the LORD* **Yah Veh** had said
he would destroy **to desolate** you.
26 I prayed therefore unto *the LORD* **Yah Veh,**
and said, O *Lord GOD* **Adonay Yah Veh,**
destroy **ruin** not thy people and thine inheritance,
which thou hast redeemed through thy greatness,
which thou hast brought forth out of *Egypt* **Misrayim**
with a *mighty* **strong** hand.
27 Remember thy servants,
Abraham, *Isaac* **Yischaq,** and *Jacob* **Yaaqov;**
look **turn** not **your face**
unto the stubbornness of this people,
nor to their wickedness, nor to their sin:
28 Lest the land whence thou broughtest us out say,
Because *the LORD* **Yah Veh** was not able to bring them
into the land which he *promised* **worded** them,
and because *he hated them* **of his hatred,**
he hath brought them out
to *slay* **deathify** them in the wilderness.
29 Yet they are thy people and thine inheritance,
which thou broughtest out
by thy *mighty power* **great force**
and by thy *stretched out* **extended** arm.

RESUME' OF THE SECOND TWO SLABS

10 At that time *the LORD* **Yah Veh** said unto me,
Hew **Sculpt** thee two *tables* **slabs** of stone
like unto the first,
and *come up* **ascend** unto me into the mount,
and *make* **work** thee an ark of *wood* **timber.**
2 And I *will write* **shall inscribe** on the *tables* **slabs**
the words that were in the first *tables* **slabs**
which thou brakest,
and thou shalt put them in the ark.
3 And I *made* **worked** an ark of shittim *wood* **timber,**
and *hewed* **sculpt** two *tables* **slabs** of stone
like unto the first,
and *went up* **ascended** into the mount,
having the two *tables* **slabs** in mine hand.
4 And he *wrote* **inscribed** on the *tables* **slabs,**
according to the first *writing* **inscribing,**

the ten *commandments* **words**,
which *the LORD spake* **Yah Veh worded** unto you
in the mount out of the midst of the fire
in the day of the *assembly* **congregation**:
and *the LORD* **Yah Veh** gave them unto me.
5 And I turned *myself* **my face**
and *came down* **descended** from the mount,
and put the *tables* **slabs** in the ark
which I had *made* **worked**;
and there they be,
as *the LORD commanded* **Yah Veh misvahed** me.
6 And the *children* **sons** of *Israel* **Yisra El**
took their journey **pulled stakes** from
Beeroth of the children of Jaakan **Beeroth Bene Yaaqan**
to *Mosera* **Moserah**:
there *Aaron* **Aharon** died,
and there he was *buried* **entombed**;
and *Eleazar* **El Azar** his son
ministered in the priest's office **priested the priesthood**
in his stead.
7 From thence they *journeyed* **pulled stakes**
unto Gudgodah;
and from Gudgodah to *Jotbathah* **Yotbathah**,
a land of *rivers* **wadies** of waters.
8 At that time
the LORD **Yah Veh** separated the *tribe* **scion** of Levi,
to bear the ark of the covenant of *the LORD* **Yah Veh**,
to stand *before the LORD* **at the face of Yah Veh**
to minister unto him, and to bless in his name,
unto this day.
9 Wherefore Levi hath no *part* **allotment** nor inheritance
with his brethren;
the LORD **Yah Veh** is his inheritance,
according as *the LORD* **Yah Veh** thy *God* **Elohim**
promised **had worded to** him.
10 And I stayed in the mount,
according to the first *time* **days**,
forty days and forty nights;
and *the LORD* **Yah Veh** hearkened unto me
at that time also,
and *the LORD would* **Yah Veh willed**
to not *destroy* **ruin** thee.
11 And *the LORD* **Yah Veh** said unto me,
Arise, take thy journey *before* **at the face of** the people,
that they may go in and possess the land,
which I *sware* **oathed** unto their fathers to give unto them.

AWE YAH VEH

12 And now, *Israel* **Yisra El**,
what doth *the LORD* **Yah Veh** thy *God* **Elohim**
require **ask** of thee,
but to *fear the LORD* **awe Yah Veh** thy *God* **Elohim**,
to walk in all his ways, and to love him,
and to serve *the LORD* **Yah Veh** thy *God* **Elohim**
with all thy heart and with all thy soul,
13 To *keep* **guard** the *commandments* **misvoth**
of *the LORD* **Yah Veh**, and his statutes,
which I *command* **misvah** thee this day for thy good?
14 Behold, the *heaven* **heavens**
and the *heaven* **heavens of the** heavens
is the LORD'S **are to Yah Veh** thy *God* **Elohim**,
the earth also, with all that therein is.
15 Only *the LORD* **Yah Veh**
had a delight in **attached himself to** thy fathers
to love them,
and he chose their seed after them,
even you above all people, as it is this day.
16 Circumcise therefore the foreskin of your heart,
and be no more *stiffnecked* **hard necked**.
17 For *the LORD* **Yah Veh** your *God* **Elohim**
is *God of gods* **Elohim of elohim**,
and *Lord of lords* **Adonay of adonim**,
a great *God* **El**, a mighty, and *a terrible* **awesome**,
which *regardeth* **lifteth** not *persons* **faces**,
nor taketh *reward* **bribe**:
18 He *doth execute* **worketh** the judgment
of the *fatherless* **orphan** and widow,
and loveth the *stranger* **sojourner**,
in giving him *food* **bread** and *raiment* **clothes**.
19 Love ye *therefore* the *stranger* **sojourner**:
for ye were strangers **sojourners**
in the land of *Egypt* **Misrayim**.
20 Thou shalt *fear* **awe**
the LORD **Yah Veh** thy *God* **Elohim**;
him shalt thou serve, and to him shalt thou *cleave* **adhere**,
and *swear* **oath** by his name.
21 He is thy *praise* **halal**, and he is thy *God* **Elohim**,
that hath *done* **worked** for thee
these great and *terrible* **awesome** *things*,
which thine eyes have seen.
22 Thy fathers *went down* **descended** into *Egypt* **Misrayim**
with *threescore and ten persons* **seventy souls**;
and now *the LORD* **Yah Veh** thy *God* **Elohim**
hath *made* **set** thee as the stars of *heaven* **the heavens**
for *multitude* **abundance**.

LOVE YAH VEH

11 *Therefore*
thou shalt love *the LORD* **Yah Veh** thy *God* **Elohim**,
and *keep* **guard** his *charge* **guard**,
and his statutes, and his judgments,
and his *commandments* **misvoth**, *alway* **all days**.
2 And know ye this day:
for I speak — not with your *children* **sons**
which have not known,
and which have not seen the *chastisement* **discipline**
of *the LORD* **Yah Veh** your *God* **Elohim**,
his greatness, his *mighty* **strong** hand,
and his *stretched out* **extended** arm,
3 And his *miracles* **signs**, and his *acts* **works**,
which he *did* **worked** in the midst of *Egypt* **Misrayim**
unto *Pharaoh* **Paroh** the *king* **sovereign** of *Egypt* **Misrayim**,
and unto all his land;
4 And what he *did* **worked**
unto the *army* **valiant** of *Egypt* **Misrayim**,
unto their horses, and to their chariots;
how he *made* **overflowed** the water of the *Red* **Reed** sea
to overflow **at the face of** them as they pursued after you,
and how *the LORD* **Yah Veh** hath destroyed them
unto this day;
5 And what he *did* **worked** unto you in the wilderness,
until ye came into this place;
6 And what he *did* **worked**
unto Dathan and *Abiram* **Abi Ram**,
the sons of *Eliab* **Eli Ab**, the son of *Reuben* **Reu Ben**:
how the earth *opened* **gaped** her mouth,
and swallowed them up,
and their households, and their tents,
and *all the substance* **every risen being**
that was *in* **at** their *possession* **feet**,
in the midst of all *Israel* **Yisra El**:
7 But your eyes have seen
all the great *acts* **works** of *the LORD* **Yah Veh**
which he *did* **worked**.
8 *Therefore*
shall ye *keep* **guard** all the *commandments* **misvoth**
which I *command* **misvah** you this day,
that ye may *be strong* **prevail**,
and go in and possess the land,
whither ye go pass over to possess it;
9 And that ye may prolong your days in the *land* **soil**,
which *the LORD sware* **Yah Veh oathed** unto your fathers
to give unto them and to their seed,
a land that floweth with milk and honey.
10 For the land, whither thou goest in to possess it,
is not as the land of *Egypt* **Misrayim**,
from whence ye came out,
where thou *sowedst* **seededst** thy seed,
and *wateredst* **moistenedst** it with thy foot,
as a garden of herbs:
11 But the land, whither ye *go* **pass over** to possess it,
is a land of *hills* **mountains** and valleys,
and drinketh water of the rain of *heaven* **the heavens**:
12 A land which *the LORD* **Yah Veh** thy *God* **Elohim**
careth for **seeketh**:
the eyes of *the LORD* **Yah Veh** thy *God* **Elohim**
are *always* **continually** upon it,
from the beginning of the year
even unto the end of the year.
13 And it shall *come to pass* **become**,
if **in hearing,**
ye shall *hearken diligently unto* **hear**

my *commandments* **misvoth**
which I *command* **misvah** you this day,
to love *the LORD* **Yah Veh** your *God* **Elohim**,
and to serve him with all your heart and with all your soul,
14 That I *will* **shall** give you
the rain of your land in his *due season* **time**,
the *first* **early** rain and the *latter* **after** rain,
that thou mayest gather in thy *corn* **crop**,
and thy *wine* **juice**, and thine oil.
15 And I *will send grass* **shall give herbage** in thy fields
for thy *cattle* **animals**,
that thou mayest eat and *be full* **satiate**.
16 *Take heed* **Guard** to yourselves,
that your heart be not *deceived* **deluded**,
and ye turn aside,
and serve other *gods* **elohim**,
and *worship* **prostrate to** them;
17 And then *the LORD'S* **Yah Weh's** wrath
be kindled against you,
and he *shut up* **restrain** the *heaven* **heavens**,
that there be no rain,
and that the *land yield* **soil give** not her *fruit* **produce**;
and lest ye *perish* **destruct** quickly from off the good land
which *the LORD* **Yah Veh** giveth you.
18 *Therefore* shall ye *lay up* **set** these my words
in your heart and in your soul,
and bind them for a sign upon your hand,
that they may be as *frontlets* **phylacteries**
between your eyes.
19 And ye shall teach them your *children* **sons**,
speaking **wording** of them
when thou sittest in thine house,
and when thou walkest by the way,
when thou liest down, and when thou risest up.
20 And thou shalt *write* **inscribe** them
upon the door posts of thine house,
and upon thy *gates* **portals**:
21 That your days may *be multiplied* **abound**,
and the days of your *children* **sons**,
in the *land* **soil** which *the LORD sware* **Yah Veh oathed**
unto your fathers to give them,
as the days of *heaven* **the heavens** upon the earth.
22 For if **in guarding,**
ye shall *diligently keep* **guard**
all these *commandments* **misvoth**
which I *command* **misvah** you, to *do* **work** them,
to love *the LORD* **Yah Veh** your *God* **Elohim**,
to walk in all his ways, and to *cleave* **adhere** unto him;
23 Then *will the LORD* **shall Yah Veh**
drive out **dispossess** all these *nations* **goyim**
from *before you* **your face**,
and ye shall possess greater *nations* **goyim**
and mightier than yourselves.
24 Every place whereon the soles of your feet shall tread
shall be yours:
from the wilderness and Lebanon,
from the river, the river Euphrates,
even unto the *uttermost* **latter** sea
shall your *coast* **border** be.
25 There shall no man be able to stand
before you **at thy face**:
for *the LORD* **Yah Veh** your *God* **Elohim**
shall *lay* **give** the fear of you
and the *dread* **awesomeness** of you
upon **the face of** all the land that ye shall tread upon,
as he hath *said* **worded** unto you.
26 *Behold* **See**, I set *before you* **at thy face** this day
a blessing and *a curse* **an abasement**;
27 A blessing,
if ye *obey* **hear** the *commandments* **misvoth**
of *the LORD* **Yah Veh** your *God* **Elohim**,
which I *command* **misvah** you this day:
28 And *a curse* **an abasement**,
if ye *will* **shall** not *obey* **hear** the *commandments* **misvoth**
of *the LORD* **Yah Veh** your *God* **Elohim**,
but turn aside out of the way
which I *command* **misvah** you this day,
to go after other *gods* **elohim**, which ye have not known.
29 And it shall *come to pass* **become**,
when *the LORD* **Yah Veh** thy *God* **Elohim**
hath brought thee in unto the land
whither thou goest to possess it,
that thou shalt *put* **give** the blessing upon mount Gerizim,
and the *curse* **abasement** upon mount Ebal.
30 Are they not on the other side *Jordan* **Yarden**,
by **after** the way
where the sun goeth down **of the entrance of the sun**,
in the land of the *Canaanites* **Kenaaniy**,
which *dwell* **settle** in the *champaign* **plains**
over against **opposite** Gilgal,
beside the *plains* **mighty oaks** of Moreh?
31 For ye shall pass over *Jordan* **Yarden**
to go in to possess the land
which *the LORD* **Yah Veh** your *God* **Elohim** giveth you,
and ye shall possess it, and *dwell* **settle** therein.
32 And ye shall *observe* **guard** to *do* **work**
all the statutes and judgments
which I set *before you* **at thy face** this day.

THE TORAH ON POSSESSING THE LAND

12 These are the statutes and judgments,
which ye shall *observe* **guard** to *do* **work** in the land,
which *the LORD God* **Yah Veh Elohim** of thy fathers
giveth thee to possess it,
all the days that ye live upon the *earth* **soil**.
2 **In destroying,** Ye shall *utterly* destroy all the places,
wherein the *nations* **goyim** which ye shall possess
served their *gods* **elohim**,
upon the *high* **exalted** mountains, and upon the hills,
and under every green tree:
3 And ye shall *overthrow* **pull down** their **sacrifice** altars,
and break their *pillars* **monoliths**,
and burn their *groves* **asherim** with fire;
and ye shall *hew* **cut** down the *graven images* **sculptiles**
of their *gods* **elohim**,
and destroy the names of them out of that place.
4 Ye shall not *do* **work** so
unto *the LORD* **Yah Veh** your *God* **Elohim**.
5 But unto the place
which *the LORD* **Yah Veh** your *God* **Elohim** shall choose
out of all your *tribes* **scions** to put his name there,
even unto his *habitation* **tabernacle** shall ye seek,
and thither thou shalt come:
6 And thither
ye shall bring your *burnt offerings* **holocausts**,
and your sacrifices, and your tithes,
and *heave offerings* **exaltments** of your hand,
and your vows, and your *freewill offerings* **voluntaries**,
and the firstlings of your *herds* **oxen** and of your flocks:
7 And there ye shall eat
before the LORD **at the face of Yah Veh** your *God* **Elohim**,
and ye shall *rejoice* **cheer**
in all that ye put **unto every extending of** your hand *unto*,
ye and your households,
wherein *the LORD* **Yah Veh** thy *God* **Elohim**
hath blessed thee.
8 Ye shall not *do* **work** after all *the things* **those**
that we *do* **work** here this day,
every man whatsoever is *right* **straight** in his own eyes.
9 For ye are not as yet come
to the rest and to the inheritance,
which *the LORD* **Yah Veh** your *God* **Elohim** giveth you.
10 But when ye *go* **pass** over *Jordan* **Yarden**,
and *dwell* **settle** in the land
which *the LORD* **Yah Veh** your *God* **Elohim**
giveth **hath** you to inherit,
and when he giveth you rest
from all your enemies round about,
so that ye *dwell in safety* **settle confidently**;
11 Then there shall be a place
which *the LORD* **Yah Veh** your *God* **Elohim** shall choose
to cause his name to *dwell* **tabernacle** there;
thither shall ye bring all that I *command* **misvah** you;
your *burnt offerings* **holocausts**, and your sacrifices,
your tithes,
and the *heave offering* **exaltment** of your hand,
and all your choice vows
which ye vow unto *the LORD* **Yah Veh**:
12 And ye shall *rejoice* **cheer**
before the LORD **at the face of Yah Veh** your *God* **Elohim**,
ye, and your sons, and your daughters,

and your *menservants* **servants**,
and your *maidservants* **maids**,
and the *Levite* **Leviy** that is within your *gates* **portals**;
forasmuch as **for which cause**
he hath no *part* **allotment** nor inheritance with you.
13 *Take heed to* **Guard** thyself that thou
offer **holocaust** not thy *burnt offerings* **holocausts**
in every place that thou seest:
14 But in the place
which *the LORD* **Yah Veh** shall choose
in one of thy *tribes* **scions**,
there thou shalt
offer **holocaust** thy *burnt offerings* **holocausts,**
and there thou shalt
do **work** all that I *command* **misvah** thee.
15 Notwithstanding
thou mayest *kill* **sacrifice** and eat flesh
in all thy *gates* **portals**,
whatsoever thy soul *lusteth after* **desireth**,
according to the blessing
of *the LORD* **Yah Veh** thy *God* **Elohim**
which he hath given thee:
the *unclean* **fouled** and the *clean* **pure** may eat thereof,
as of the *roebuck* **gazelle**, and as of the hart.
16 Only ye shall not eat the blood;
ye shall pour it upon the earth as water.
17 Thou mayest not eat within thy *gates* **portals**
the tithe of thy *corn* **crop**,
or of thy *wine* **juice**, or of thy oil,
or the firstlings of thy *herds* **oxen,** or of thy flock,
nor any of thy vows which thou vowest,
nor thy *freewill offerings* **voluntaries**,
or *heave offering* **exaltment** of thine hand:
18 But thou *must* eat them
before the LORD **at the face of Yah Veh** thy *God* **Elohim**
in the place which *the LORD* **Yah Veh** thy *God* **Elohim**
shall choose,
thou, and thy son, and thy daughter,
and thy *manservant* **servant**, and thy *maidservant* **maid**,
and the *Levite* **Leviy** that is within thy *gates* **portals**:
and thou shalt *rejoice* **cheer**
before the LORD **at the face of Yah Veh** thy *God* **Elohim**
in all that thou *puttest* **extendest** thine hands *unto*.
19 *Take heed to* **Guard** thyself
that thou forsake not the *Levite* **Leviy**
as long as thou livest **all thy days** upon the *earth* **soil**.
20 When *the LORD* **Yah Veh** thy *God* **Elohim**
shall *enlarge* **broaden** thy border,
as he hath *promised* **worded unto** thee,
and thou shalt say, I *will* **shall** eat flesh,
because thy soul *longeth* **desireth** to eat flesh;
thou mayest eat flesh,
whatsoever thy soul *lusteth after* **desireth**.
21 If the place which *the LORD* **Yah Veh** thy *God* **Elohim**
hath chosen to put his name there
be too far **removed** from thee,
then thou shalt *kill* **sacrifice**
of thy *herd* **oxen** and of thy flock,
which *the LORD* **Yah Veh** hath given thee,
as I have *commanded* **misvahed** thee,
and thou shalt eat in thy *gates* **portals**
whatsoever thy soul *lusteth after* **desireth**.
22 Even as the *roebuck* **gazelle** and the hart is eaten,
so thou shalt eat them:
the *unclean* **fouled** and the *clean* **pure**
shall eat of them *alike* **together**.
23 Only *be sure* **prevail** that thou eat not the blood:
for the blood is the *life* **soul**;
and thou mayest not eat the *life* **soul** with the flesh.
24 Thou shalt not eat it;
thou shalt pour it upon the earth as water.
25 Thou shalt not eat it;
that it may *go well with* **well—please** thee,
and *with* thy *children* **sons** after thee,
when thou shalt *do that which is right* **work straight**
in the *sight* **eyes** of *the LORD* **Yah Veh**.
26 Only thy *holy things* **holies** which thou hast,
and thy vows,
thou shalt *take* **bear**,
and go unto the place
which *the LORD* **Yah Veh** shall choose:
27 And thou shalt
offer **work** thy *burnt offerings* **holocausts**,
the flesh and the blood,
upon the **sacrifice** altar
of *the LORD* **Yah Veh** thy *God* **Elohim**:
and the blood of thy sacrifices shall be poured *out*
upon the **sacrifice** altar
of *the LORD* **Yah Veh** thy *God* **Elohim**,
and thou shalt eat the flesh.
28 *Observe* **Guard** and hear all these words
which I *command* **misvah** thee,
that it may *go well with* **well—please** thee,
and with thy *children* **sons** after thee *for ever* **eternally**,
when thou *doest* **workest**
that which is good and *right* **straight**
in the *sight* **eyes** of *the LORD* **Yah Veh** thy *God* **Elohim**.
29 When *the LORD* **Yah Veh** thy *God* **Elohim**
shall cut off the *nations* **goyim** from *before thee* **thy face**,
whither thou goest to possess them,
and thou *succeedest* **possessest** them,
and *dwellest* **settlest** in their land;
30 *Take heed to* **Guard** thyself
that thou be not snared by following them,
after that they be *destroyed* **desolated**
from *before thee* **thy face**;
and that thou enquire not after their *gods* **elohim**, saying,
How did these *nations* **goyim** serve their *god* **elohim**?
even so *will* **shall** I *do* **work** likewise.
31 Thou shalt not *do* **work** so
unto *the LORD* **Yah Veh** thy *God* **Elohim**:
for every *abomination* **abhorrence** to *the LORD* **Yah Veh**,
which he hateth,
have they *done* **worked** unto their *gods* **elohim**;
for even their sons and their daughters
they have burnt in the fire to their *gods* **elohim.**
32 What *thing* **word** soever I *command* **misvah** you,
observe **guard** to *do* **work** it:
thou shalt not add thereto, nor diminish from it.

THE TORAH ON IDOLATRY

13 If there arise among you a prophet,
or a dreamer of dreams,
and giveth thee a sign or *a wonder* **an omen**,
2 And the sign or the *wonder* **omen**
come to pass **becometh**,
whereof he *spake* **worded** unto thee, saying,
Let us go after other *gods* **elohim**,
which thou hast not known, and let us serve them;
3 Thou shalt not hearken unto the words of that prophet,
or that dreamer of dreams:
for *the LORD* **Yah Veh** your *God* **Elohim**
proveth **testeth** you,
to know
whether ye love *the LORD* **Yah Veh** your *God* **Elohim**
with all your heart and with all your soul.
4 Ye shall walk after *the LORD* **Yah Veh** your *God* **Elohim**,
and *fear* **awe** him,
and *keep* **guard** his *commandments* **misvoth**,
and *obey* **hear** his voice,
and ye shall serve him, and *cleave* **adhere** unto him.
5 And that prophet, or that dreamer of dreams,
shall be *put to death* **deathified**;
because he hath *spoken* **worded**
to turn you away **that you revolt**
from *the LORD* **Yah Veh** your *God* **Elohim**,
which brought you out of the land of *Egypt* **Misrayim**,
and redeemed you out of the house of *bondage* **servants**,
to *thrust* **drive** thee out of the way
which *the LORD* **Yah Veh** thy *God* **Elohim**
commanded **misvahed** thee to walk in.
So **Thus** shalt thou *put the* **burn** evil away
from the midst of thee.
6 If thy brother, the son of thy mother, or thy son,
or thy daughter, or the *wife* **woman** of thy bosom,
or thy friend, which is as thine own soul,
entice **goad** thee *secretly* **covertly**, saying,
Let us go and serve other *gods* **elohim**,
which thou hast not known, thou, nor thy fathers;
7 *Namely*, of the *gods* **elohim** of the people
which are round about you,

nigh unto thee, or far off from thee,
from the *one* end of the earth
even unto the *other* end of the earth;
8 Thou shalt not *consent* **will** unto him,
nor hearken unto him;
neither shall thine eye pity him, neither shalt thou spare,
neither shalt thou *conceal* **cover** him:
9 But **in slaughtering,** thou shalt *surely kill* **slaughter** him;
thine hand shall be first upon him
to *put him to death* **deathify him,**
and afterwards the hand of all the people.
10 And thou shalt stone him with stones, that he die;
because he hath sought to *thrust* **drive** thee away
from *the LORD* **Yah Veh** thy *God* **Elohim,**
which brought thee out of the land of *Egypt* **Misrayim,**
from the house of *bondage* **servants.**
11 And all *Israel* **Yisra El** shall hear, and *fear* **awe,**
and shall *do no more* **add not to work**
any such wickedness **according to this evil word**
as this is among you.
12 If thou shalt hear *say* in one of thy cities,
which *the LORD* **Yah Veh** thy *God* **Elohim**
hath given thee to *dwell* **settle** there, saying,
13 *Certain* men, *the children* **sons** of *Belial* **Beli Yaal,**
are gone out from among you,
and have *withdrawn* **driven**
the inhabitants of **them that settled** their city, saying,
Let us go and serve other *gods* **elohim,**
which ye have not known;
14 Then shalt thou enquire,
and *make search* **probe,** and ask *diligently* **well;**
and, behold, if it be truth,
and the *thing certain* **word established,**
that such *abomination* **abhorrence**
is *wrought* **worked** among you;
15 **In smiting,** Thou shalt *surely* smite
the inhabitants of **them that settled that** city
with the *edge* **mouth** of the sword,
destroying it utterly **devoting it,** and all that is therein,
and the *cattle* **animals** thereof,
with the *edge* **mouth** of the sword.
16 And thou shalt gather all the *spoil* **loot** of it
into the midst of the *street* **broadway** thereof,
and shalt burn with fire the city,
and all the *spoil* **loot** thereof *every whit* **totally,**
for *the LORD* **Yah Veh** thy *God* **Elohim:**
and it shall be an heap for *ever* **eternity;**
it shall not be built again.
17 And there shall *cleave* **adhere**
nought of the *cursed* **devoted** *thing* to thine hand:
that *the LORD* **Yah Veh** may turn
from *the fierceness of his anger* **his fuming wrath,**
and *shew* **give** thee *mercy* **mercies,**
and *have compassion upon* **mercy** thee,
and *multiply* **abound** thee,
as he hath *sworn* **oathed** unto thy fathers;
18 When thou shalt hearken
to the voice of *the LORD* **Yah Veh** thy *God* **Elohim,**
to *keep* **guard** all his *commandments* **misvoth**
which I *command* **misvah** thee this day,
to *do* **work** that which is *right* **straight**
in the eyes of *the LORD* **Yah Veh** thy *God* **Elohim.**

THE TORAH ON MUTILATION

14 Ye are the *children* **sons**
of *the LORD* **Yah Veh** your *God* **Elohim:**
ye shall not cut yourselves,
nor *make* **set** any baldness between your eyes
for *the dead* **that which died.**
2 For thou art an holy people
unto *the LORD* **Yah Veh** thy *God* **Elohim,**
and *the LORD* **Yah Veh** hath chosen thee
to be a peculiar people unto himself,
above all the *nations* **goyim**
that are upon the *earth* **face of the soil.**

THE TORAH ON EATING

3 Thou shalt not eat any *abominable thing* **abhorrence.**
4 These are the *beasts* **animals** which ye shall eat:
the ox, the *sheep* **lamb of the lambs,**
and the *goat* **lamb of the goats,**
5 The hart, and the *roebuck* **gazelle,**
and the fallow deer, and the wild goat,
and the pygarg, and the wild ox, and the chamois.
6 And every *beast* **animal** that *parteth* **splitteth** the hoof,
and cleaveth the cleft into two *claws* **hoofs,**
and *cheweth* **regurgitateth** the cud
among the *beasts* **animals,**
that ye shall eat.
7 Nevertheless these ye shall not eat:
of them that *chew* **regurgitate** the cud,
or of them that *divide* **split** the cloven hoof;
as the camel, and the hare, and the coney:
for they *chew* **regurgitate** the cud, but divide not the hoof;
therefore they are *unclean* **fouled** unto you.
8 And the *swine* **hog,**
because it *divideth* **splitteth** the hoof,
yet cheweth not the cud,
it is unclean unto you:
ye shall *not* **neither** eat of their flesh,
nor touch their *dead* carcase.
9 These ye shall eat of all that are in the waters:
all that have fins and scales, shall ye eat:
10 And whatsoever hath not fins and scales,
ye may not eat; it is *unclean* **fouled** unto you.
11 Of all *clean* **pure** birds ye shall eat.
12 But these are they of which ye shall not eat:
the eagle, and the ossifrage, and the ospray,
13 And the glede, and the kite,
and the vulture *after his kind* **in species,**
14 And every raven *after his kind* **in species,**
15 And the **daughter of the** owl, and the night hawk,
and the cuckow, and the hawk *after his kind* **in species,**
16 The little owl, and the great owl, and the swan,
17 And the pelican, and the gier eagle, and the cormorant,
18 And the stork, and the heron *after her kind* **in species,**
and the lapwing, and the bat.
19 And every creeping *thing that flieth* **flier**
is *unclean* **fouled** unto you:
they shall not be eaten.
20 But of all *clean fowls* **pure fliers,** ye may eat.
21 Ye shall not eat of any *thing that dieth of itself* **carcase:**
thou shalt give it unto the *stranger* **sojourner**
that is in thy *gates* **portals,** that he may eat it;
or thou mayest sell it unto *an alien* **a stranger:**
for thou art an holy people
unto *the LORD* **Yah Veh** thy *God* **Elohim.**
Thou shalt not *seethe* **stew** a kid in his mother's milk.

THE TORAH ON TITHING

22 **In tithing,**
Thou shalt *truly* tithe all the *increase* **produce** of thy seed,
that the field bringeth forth year by year.
23 And thou shalt eat *before* **at the face of**
the LORD **Yah Veh** thy *God* **Elohim,**
in the place which he shall choose
to *place* **tabernacle** his name there,
the tithe of thy *corn* **crop,**
of thy *wine* **juice,** and of thine oil,
and the firstlings of thy *herds* **oxen** and of thy flocks;
that thou mayest learn to *fear* **awe**
the LORD **Yah Veh** thy *God always* **Elohim all days.**
24 And if the way *be too long* **abound** for thee,
so that thou art not able to *carry* **bear** it;
or if the place be too far **removed** from thee,
which *the LORD* **Yah Veh** thy *God* **Elohim**
shall choose to set his name there,
when *the LORD* **Yah Veh** thy *God* **Elohim**
hath blessed thee:
25 Then shalt thou *turn* **give** it into *money* **silver,**
and bind up the *money* **silver** in thine hand,
and shalt go unto the place
which *the LORD* **Yah Veh** thy *God* **Elohim** shall choose:
26 And thou shalt *bestow* **give** that *money* **silver**
for whatsoever thy soul *lusteth after* **desireth,**
for oxen, or for *sheep* **flocks,**
or for wine, or for *strong drink* **intoxicants,**
or for whatsoever thy soul *desireth* **asketh:**
and thou shalt eat there
before the LORD **at the face of Yah Veh** thy *God* **Elohim,**
and thou shalt *rejoice* **cheer,** thou, and thine household,
27 And the *Levite* **Leviy** that is within thy *gates* **portals;**
thou shalt not forsake him;

for he hath no *part* **allotment** nor inheritance with thee.
28 At the end of three years
thou shalt bring forth
all the tithe of thine *increase* **produce** the same year,
and shalt *lay* **set** it *up* within thy *gates* **portals**:
29 And the *Levite* **Leviy**,
(because he hath no *part* **allotment** nor inheritance
with thee,)
and the *stranger* **sojourner**, and the *fatherless* **orphan**,
and the widow, which are within thy *gates* **portals**,
shall come, and shall eat and *be satisfied* **satiate**;
that *the LORD* **Yah Veh** thy *God* **Elohim** may bless thee
in all the work of thine hand which thou *doest* **workest**.

THE TORAH ON DEBT RELEASE

15 At the end of *every* seven years **work**
thou shalt *make* **work** a release.
2 And this is the *manner* **word** of the release:
Every *creditor that* **master whose hand** lendeth ought
unto his *neighbour* **friend** shall release it;
he shall not exact it of his *neighbour* **friend**,
or of his brother;
because it is called *the LORD'S* **Yah Veh's** release.
3 Of a *foreigner* **stranger** thou mayest exact it *again*:
but that which is thine with thy brother
thine hand shall release;
4 *Save when* **Finally,**
that there shall be no *poor* **needy** among you;
for *the LORD* **Yah Veh** shall greatly bless thee
in the land which *the LORD* **Yah Veh** thy *God* **Elohim**
giveth thee for an inheritance to possess it:
5 Only if **in hearing,**
thou *carefully hearken unto* **hearest**
the voice of *the LORD* **Yah Veh** thy *God* **Elohim,**
to *observe* **guard** to *do* **work**
all these *commandments* **misvoth**
which I *command* **misvah** thee this day.
6 For *the LORD* **Yah Veh** thy *God* **Elohim** blesseth thee,
as he *promised* **worded** thee:
and thou shalt *lend* **pledge** unto many *nations* **goyim**,
but thou shalt not *borrow* **pawn**;
and thou shalt reign over many *nations* **goyim**
but they shall not reign over thee.
7 If there be among you
a poor man **needy** of one of thy brethren
within *any* **one** of thy *gates* **portals** in thy land
which *the LORD* **Yah Veh** thy *God* **Elohim** giveth thee,
thou shalt not *harden* **strengthen** thine heart,
nor shut thine hand from thy *poor* **needy** brother:
8 But thou shalt open thine hand wide unto him,
and **in pledging,** shalt *surely lend* **pledge** him
sufficient for his *need* **lack**,
in that which he *wanteth* **lacketh**.
9 *Beware* **Guard** that there be not a *thought* **word**
in thy *wicked* heart **of Beli Yaal**, saying,
The seventh year, the year of release,
is at hand **approacheth**;
and thine eye *be evil* **vilify** against thy *poor* **needy** brother,
and thou givest him nought;
and he *cry* **call** unto *the LORD* **Yah Veh** against thee,
and it be sin unto thee.
10 **In giving,** Thou shalt *surely* give him,
and thine heart shall not be *grieved* **vilified**
when thou givest unto him:
because that for this *thing* **word**
the LORD **Yah Veh** thy *God* **Elohim**
shall bless thee in all thy works,
and in all that thou *puttest* **extendest** thine hand *unto*.
11 For the *poor* **needy** shall never cease out of the land:
therefore I *command* **misvah** thee, saying,
Thou shalt open thine hand wide unto thy brother,
to thy *poor* **humbled**, and to thy needy, in thy land.
12 And if thy brother, an Hebrew *man*,
or an *Hebrew woman* **Hebrewess**,
be sold unto thee, and serve thee six years;
then in the seventh year
thou shalt *let him go* **send him forth**
free **liberated** from thee.
13 And when thou sendest him *out* **forth**
free **liberated** from thee,
thou shalt not *let him go away* **send him forth** empty:
14 **In adorning,** Thou shalt *furnish* **adorn** him *liberally*
out of thy flock, and out of thy **threshing** floor,
and out of thy *winepress* **trough**:
of that wherewith
the LORD **Yah Veh** thy *God* **Elohim** hath blessed thee
thou shalt give unto him.
15 And thou shalt remember
that thou wast a *bondman* **servant**
in the land of *Egypt* **Misrayim**,
and *the LORD* **Yah Veh** thy *God* **Elohim** redeemed thee:
therefore I *command* **misvah** thee this *thing* **word** to day.
16 And it shall be, if he say unto thee,
I *will* **shall** not go away from thee;
because he loveth thee and thine house,
because he is *well* **good** with thee;
17 Then thou shalt take an aul,
and *thrust* **give** it through his ear unto the door,
and he shall be thy servant *for ever* **eternally**.
And also unto thy *maidservant* **maid**
thou shalt *do* **work** likewise.
18 It shall not *seem* **be** hard *unto thee* **in thine eyes**,
when thou sendest him away *free* **liberated** from thee;
for he hath been *worth*
a double *hired servant* **hire of an hireling** *to thee*,
in serving thee six years:
and *the LORD* **Yah Veh** thy *God* **Elohim**
shall bless thee in all that thou *doest* **workest**.
19 All the firstling males
that come **born** of thy *herd* **oxen** and of thy flock,
thou shalt *sanctify* **hallow**
unto *the LORD* **Yah Veh** thy *God* **Elohim**:
thou shalt *do no work* **not serve**
with the firstling of thy *bullock* **ox**,
nor shear the firstling of thy *sheep* **flocks**.
20 Thou shalt eat it
before the LORD **at the face of Yah Veh** thy *God* **Elohim**
year by year
in the place which *the LORD* **Yah Veh** shall choose,
thou and thy household.
21 And if there be any blemish therein,
as if it be lame, or blind, or have any *ill* **evil** blemish,
thou shalt not sacrifice it
unto *the LORD* **Yah Veh** thy *God* **Elohim**.
22 Thou shalt eat it within thy *gates* **portals**:
the *unclean* **fouled** and the *clean person* **pure**
shall eat it alike **together**,
as the *roebuck* **gazelle**, and as the hart.
23 Only thou shalt not eat the blood thereof;
thou shalt pour it upon the *ground* **earth** as water.

THE TORAH ON PREPARING THE PASACH

16 *Observe* **Guard** the month of Abib,
and *keep* **work** the *passover* **pasach**
unto *the LORD* **Yah Veh** thy *God* **Elohim**:
for in the month of Abib
the LORD **Yah Veh** thy *God* **Elohim**
brought thee forth out of *Egypt* **Misrayim** by night.
2 Thou shalt therefore sacrifice the *passover* **pasach**
unto *the LORD* **Yah Veh** thy *God* **Elohim**,
of the flock and the *herd* **oxen**,
in the place which *the LORD* **Yah Veh** shall choose
to *place* **tabernacle** his name there.
3 Thou shalt eat no *leavened bread* **fermentation** with it;
seven days
shalt thou eat *unleavened bread* **matsah** *therewith*,
even the bread of *affliction* **humiliation**;
for thou camest forth
out of the land of *Egypt* **Misrayim** in haste:
that thou mayest remember the day
when thou camest forth out of the land of *Egypt* **Misrayim**
all the days of thy life.
4 And there shall be no *leavened bread* **yeast**
seen with thee in all thy *coast* **border** seven days;
neither shall *there any thing* **aught** of the flesh,
which thou sacrificedst the first day at even,
remain **stay** overnight all night until the morning.
5 Thou *mayest* **canst** not sacrifice the *passover* **pasach**
within *any* **one** of thy *gates* **portals**,
which *the LORD* **Yah Veh** thy *God* **Elohim** giveth thee:
6 But at the place
which *the LORD* **Yah Veh** thy *God* **Elohim** shall choose

to *place* **tabernacle** his name in,
there thou shalt sacrifice the *passover* **pasach** at even,
at the going down of the sun,
at the season
that thou camest forth out of *Egypt* **Misrayim**.
7 And thou shalt *roast* **stew** and eat it in the place
which *the LORD* **Yah Veh** thy *God* **Elohim** shall choose:
and thou shalt turn **thy face** in the morning,
and go unto thy tents.
8 Six days thou shalt eat *unleavened bread* **matsah**:
and on the seventh day
shall be *a solemn assembly* **an abstinence**
to *the LORD* **Yah Veh** thy *God* **Elohim**:
thou shalt *do* **work** no work *therein*.

THE TORAH ON THE CELEBRATION OF WEEKS

9 Seven weeks shalt thou *number* **scribe** unto thee:
begin to *number* **scribe** the seven weeks
from *such time as* **when**
thou beginnest *to put* the sickle to the *corn* **stalks**.
10 And thou shalt *keep* **work**
the *feast* **celebration** of weeks
unto *the LORD* **Yah Veh** thy *God* **Elohim voluntarily**
with a *tribute of a freewill offering* **voluntary**
of thine hand,
which thou shalt give *unto the Lord thy God*,
according as *the LORD* **Yah Veh** thy *God* **Elohim**
hath blessed thee:
11 And thou shalt *rejoice* **cheer**
before the LORD **at the face of Yah Veh** thy *God* **Elohim**,
thou, and thy son, and thy daughter,
and thy *manservant* **servant**, and thy *maidservant* **maid**,
and the *Levite* **Leviy** that is within thy *gates* **portals**,
and the *stranger* **sojourner**, and the *fatherless* **orphan**,
and the widow, that are among you,
in the place which *the LORD* **Yah Veh** thy *God* **Elohim**
hath chosen to *place* **tabernacle** his name there.
12 And thou shalt remember
that thou wast a *bondman* **servant** in *Egypt* **Misrayim**:
and thou shalt *observe* **guard** and *do* **work** these statutes.

THE TORAH ON THE CELEBRATION OF SUKKOTH/BRUSH ARBORS

13 Thou shalt *observe* **work** the *feast* **celebration**
of *tabernacles* **Sukkoth/Brush Arbors** seven days,
after that thou hast gathered in
thy *corn* **threshingfloor** and thy *wine* **trough**:
14 And thou shalt *rejoice* **cheer** in thy *feast* **celebration**,
thou, and thy son, and thy daughter,
and thy *manservant* **servant**, and thy *maidservant* **maid**,
and the *Levite* **Leviy**, the *stranger* **sojourner**,
and the *fatherless* **orphan**, and the widow,
that are within thy *gates* **portals**.
15 Seven days shalt thou *keep a solemn feast* **celebrate**
unto *the LORD* **Yah Veh** thy *God* **Elohim**
in the place which *the LORD* **Yah Veh** shall choose:
because *the LORD* **Yah Veh** thy *God* **Elohim**
shall bless thee in all thine *increase* **produce**,
and in all the works of thine hands,
therefore thou shalt *surely rejoice* **be cheerful**.
16 Three times in a year shall all thy males *appear* **be seen**
before the LORD **at the face of Yah Veh** thy *God* **Elohim**
in the place which he shall choose;
in the *feast* **celebration** of *unleavened bread* **matsah**,
and in the *feast* **celebration** of weeks,
and in the *feast* **celebration**
of *tabernacles* **Sukkoth/Brush Arbors**:
and they shall not *appear* **be seen**
before the LORD **at the face of Yah Veh** empty:
17 Every man
shall give as he **as the gift of his hand** is able,
according to the blessing
of *the LORD* **Yah Veh** thy *God* **Elohim**
which he hath given thee.

THE TORAH ON SETTING JUDGES AND OFFICERS

18 Judges and officers shalt thou *make* **give** thee
in all thy *gates* **portals**,
which *the LORD* **Yah Veh** thy *God* **Elohim** giveth thee,
throughout thy *tribes* **scions**:
and they shall judge the people
with *just* judgment **of justness**.
19 Thou shalt not *wrest* **deviate** judgment;
thou shalt not *respect persons* **recognize faces**,
neither take a *gift* **bribe**:
for a *gift* **bribe** doth blind the eyes of the wise,
and pervert the words of the *righteous* **just**.
20 *That which is altogether just shalt thou follow*
Justness — pursue justness,
that thou mayest live, and *inherit* **possess** the land
which *the LORD* **Yah Veh** thy *God* **Elohim** giveth thee.

THE TORAH ON IDOLATRY

21 Thou shalt not plant thee *a grove* **an asherah**
of any trees *near unto* **beside** the **sacrifice** altar
of *the LORD* **Yah Veh** thy *God* **Elohim**,
which thou shalt *make thee* **work**.
22 Neither shalt thou
set thee up any image **raise a monolith**;
which *the LORD* **Yah Veh** thy *God* **Elohim** hateth.

THE TORAH ON SACRIFICES

17 Thou shalt not sacrifice
unto *the LORD* **Yah Veh** thy *God* **Elohim**
any *bullock* **ox**, or *sheep* **lamb**,
wherein is blemish, or any *evilfavouredness* **evil word**:
for that is an *abomination* **abhorrence**
unto *the LORD* **Yah Veh** thy *God* **Elohim**.

THE TORAH ON APOSTATES

2 If there be found among you,
within *any* **one** of thy *gates* **portals**
which *the LORD* **Yah Veh** thy *God* **Elohim** giveth thee,
man or woman,
that hath *wrought wickedness* **worked evil**
in the *sight* **eyes** of *the LORD* **Yah Veh** thy *God* **Elohim**,
in *transgressing* **trespassing** his covenant,
3 And hath gone and served other *gods* **elohim**,
and *worshipped* **prostrated to** them,
either the sun, or moon,
or any of the host of *heaven* **the heavens**,
which I have not *commanded* **misvahed**;
4 And it be told thee, and thou hast heard of it,
and enquired *diligently* **well**, and, behold,
it be *true* **truth**, and the *thing certain* **word established**,
that such *abomination* **abhorrence**
is *wrought* **worked** in *Israel* **Yisra El**:
5 Then shalt thou bring forth that man or that woman,
which have *committed* **worked**
that *wicked thing* **evil word**,
unto thy *gates* **portals**,
even that man or that woman,
and shalt stone them with stones, till they die.
6 At the mouth of two witnesses, or three witnesses,
shall he that is *worthy of death* **to be deathified**
be *put to death* **deathified**;
but at the mouth of one witness
he shall not be *put to death* **deathified**.
7 The hands of the witnesses shall be first upon him
to *put him to death* **deathify him**,
and afterward the hands of all the people.
So thou shalt *put* **burn** the evil away from among you.

THE TORAH ON JUDGMENT

8 If there arise a *matter* **word**
too hard for **that marveleth** thee in judgment,
between blood and blood, between plea and plea,
and between *stroke* **plague** and *stroke* **plague**,
being *matters* **words** of *controversy* **dispute**
within thy *gates* **portals**:
then shalt thou arise,
and *get thee up* **ascend** into the place
which *the LORD* **Yah Veh** thy *God* **Elohim** shall choose;
9 And thou shalt come unto the priests the *Levites* **Leviym**,
and unto the judge that shall be in those days,
and enquire;
and they shall *shew* **tell** thee
the *sentence* **word** of *the mouth* **judgment**:
10 And thou shalt *do* **work**
according to the *sentence* **word** of *judgment* **his mouth**,
which they of that place
which *the LORD* **Yah Veh** shall choose
shall *shew* **tell** thee;
and thou shalt *observe* **guard** to *do* **work**
according to all that they *inform* **point out to** thee:
11 According to the *sentence* **mouth** of the *law* **torah**
which they shall *teach* **point out to** thee,

and according to the judgment which they shall tell thee,
thou shalt *do* **work**:
thou shalt not *decline* **turn aside**
from the *sentence* **word** which they shall *shew* **tell** thee,
to the right *hand,* nor to the left.
12 And the man
that *will do presumptuously* **shall work arrogance**,
and *will* **shall** not hearken unto the priest
that standeth to minister there
before the LORD **at the face of Yah Veh** thy *God* **Elohim**,
or unto the judge, even that man shall die:
and thou shalt *put* **burn** away the evil from *Israel* **Yisra El**.
13 And all the people shall hear, and *fear* **awe**,
and *do no more presumptuously* **not seethe**.

THE TORAH ON SOVEREIGNS

14 When thou art come unto the land
which *the LORD* **Yah Veh** thy *God* **Elohim** giveth thee,
and shalt possess it, and shalt *dwell* **settle** therein,
and shalt say, I *will* **shall** set a *king* **sovereign** over me,
like as all the *nations* **goyim** that are *about* **all around** me;
15 **In setting,**
Thou shalt *in any wise* set him *king* **sovereign** over thee,
whom *the LORD* **Yah Veh** thy *God* **Elohim** shall choose:
one from among thy brethren
shalt thou set *king* **sovereign** over thee:
thou *mayest* **canst** not *set* **give a man**
—a stranger over thee, which is not thy brother.
16 But he shall not *multiply* **abound** horses to himself,
nor cause the people to return to *Egypt* **Misrayim**,
to the end that he should *multiply* **abound** horses:
forasmuch as *the LORD* **Yah Veh** hath said unto you,
Ye shall henceforth return *no more* **not again** that way.
17 Neither shall he
multiply wives **abound women** to himself,
that his heart turn not away:
neither shall he *greatly multiply* **mightily abound**
to himself silver and gold.
18 And it shall be,
when he sitteth upon the throne
of his *kingdom* **sovereigndom**,
that he shall *write* **inscribe** him
a *copy* **duplicate** of this *law* **torah** in a *book* **scroll**
out of that
which is *before* **at the face of** the priests the *Levites* **Leviym**:
19 And it shall be with him,
and he shall *read* **recall** therein all the days of his life:
that he may learn
to *fear the LORD* **awe Yah Veh** his *God* **Elohim**,
to *keep* **guard** all the words
of this *law* **torah** and these statutes,
to *do* **work** them:
20 That his heart be not lifted up above his brethren,
and that he turn not aside from the *commandment* **misvah**,
to the right *hand,* or to the left:
to the end that he may prolong his days
in his *kingdom* **sovereigndom**,
he, and his *children* **sons**, in the midst of *Israel* **Yisra El**.

THE TORAH ON THE PRIESTAL ALLOTMENTS

18 The priests the *Levites* **Leviym**,
and all the *tribe* **scion** of Levi,
shall have no *part* **allotment** nor inheritance
with *Israel* **Yisra El**:
they shall eat
the *offerings of the LORD made by fire*
firings unto Yah Veh,
and his inheritance.
2 Therefore
shall they have no inheritance among their brethren:
the LORD **Yah Veh** is their inheritance,
as he hath *said* **worded** unto them.
3 And this shall be the priest's *due* **judgment**
from the people,
from them that *offer* **sacrifice** a sacrifice,
whether it be ox or *sheep* **lamb**;
and they shall give unto the priest the *shoulder* **foreleg**,
and the two cheeks, and the *maw* **belly**.
4 The *firstfruit* **firstling** also of thy *corn* **crop**,
of thy *wine* **juice**, and of thine oil,
and the first of the *fleece* **shearing** of thy sheep,
shalt thou give him.
5 For *the LORD* **Yah Veh** thy *God* **Elohim**
hath chosen him out of all thy *tribes* **scions**,
to stand to minister in the name of *the LORD* **Yah Veh**,
him and his sons *for ever* **all days**.
6 And if a *Levite* **Leviy**
come from *any* **one** of thy *gates* **portals**
out of all *Israel* **Yisra El**, where he sojourned,
and come with all the desire of his *mind* **soul**
unto the place which *the LORD* **Yah Veh** shall choose;
7 Then he shall minister
in the name of *the LORD* **Yah Veh** his *God* **Elohim**,
as all his brethren the *Levites* **Leviym** do,
which stand there
before the LORD **at the face of Yah Veh**.
8 They shall have
like portions **allotment by allotment** to eat,
beside that which cometh of *the sale* **his sales**
of *his patrimony* **the fathers'**.

THE TORAH ON APOSTATIZING

9 When thou art come into the land
which *the LORD* **Yah Veh** thy *God* **Elohim** giveth thee,
thou shalt not learn to *do* **work**
after the *abominations* **abhorrences**
of those *nations* **goyim**.
10 There shall not be found among you any one
that *maketh* **passeth** his son or his daughter *to pass*
through the fire,
or that *useth* **divineth** divination,
or *an observer of times* **a cloudgazer**,
or *an enchanter* **a prognosticater**, or a *witch* **sorcerer**.
11 Or a charmer **that charms**,
or *a consulter with familiar spirits*
an inquirer of a necromancer,
or a *wizard* **knower**,
or *a necromancer* **an inquirer of the deathified**.
12 For all that *do* **work** these *things*
are an *abomination* **abhorrence** unto *the LORD* **Yah Veh**:
and because of these *abominations* **abhorrences**
the LORD **Yah Veh** thy *God* **Elohim**
doth *drive* **dispossess** them *out* from *before thee* **thy face**.
13 Thou shalt be *perfect* **integrious**
with *the LORD* **Yah Veh** thy *God* **Elohim**.
14 For these *nations* **goyim**, which thou shalt possess,
hearkened unto *observers of times* **cloudgazers**,
and unto diviners:
but as for thee,
the LORD **Yah Veh** thy *God* **Elohim**
hath not *suffered* **given** thee so to do.

THE TORAH ON PROPHETS

15 *The LORD* **Yah Veh** thy *God* **Elohim**
will **shall** raise *up* unto thee a Prophet
from the midst of thee,
of thy brethren, like unto me; unto him ye shall hearken;
16 According to all that thou *desiredst* **askedst**
of *the LORD* **Yah Veh** thy *God* **Elohim** in Horeb
in the day of the *assembly* **congregation**, saying,
Let me not hear again
the voice of *the LORD* **Yah Veh** my *God* **Elohim**,
neither let me see this great fire any more, that I die not.
17 And *the LORD* **Yah Veh** said unto me,
They have *well spoken* **well—pleased**
that which they have *spoken* **worded**.
18 I *will* **shall** raise them up a Prophet
from among their brethren, like unto thee,
and *will put* **shall give** my words in his mouth;
and he shall *speak* **word** unto them all
that I shall *command* **misvah** him.
19 And it shall *come to pass* **become**,
that *whosoever* **what man**
will **shall** not hearken unto my words
which he shall *speak* **word** in my name,
I *will* **shall** require it of him.
20 But the prophet,
which shall *presume* **seethe**
to *speak* **word** a word in my name,
which I have not *commanded* **misvahed** him
to *speak* **word**,
or that shall *speak* **word**
in the name of other *gods* **elohim**,
even that prophet shall die.

THE TEST OF THE PROPHET
21 And if thou say in thine heart,
How shall we know the word
which *the LORD* **Yah Veh** hath not spoken?
22 When a prophet *speaketh* **wordeth**
in the name of *the LORD* **Yah Veh**,
if the *thing follow* **word become** not,
nor *come to pass* **arrive**,
that is the *thing* **word**
which *the LORD* **Yah Veh** hath not spoken,
but the prophet hath
spoken it presumptuously **worded arrogance**:
thou shalt not *be afraid of* **fear** him.
THE TORAH ON CITIES OF REFUGE
19 When *the LORD* **Yah Veh** thy *God* **Elohim**
hath cut off the *nations* **goyim**,
whose land
the LORD **Yah Veh** thy *God* **Elohim** giveth thee,
and thou *succeedest* **possessest** them,
and *dwellest* **settlest** in their cities, and in their houses;
2 Thou shalt separate three cities for thee
in the midst of thy land,
which *the LORD* **Yah Veh** thy *God* **Elohim**
giveth thee to possess it.
3 Thou shalt prepare thee a way,
and divide the *coasts* **borders** of thy land,
which *the LORD* **Yah Veh** thy *God* **Elohim**
giveth thee to inherit, into *three parts* **thirds**,
that every *slayer* **murderer** may flee thither.
4 And this is the *case* **word** of the *slayer* **murderer**,
which shall flee thither, that he may live:
Whoso *killeth* **smiteth** his *neighbour* **friend**
ignorantly **unknowingly**,
whom he hated not *in time past* **three yesters ago**;
5 As when a man goeth into the *wood* **forest**
with his *neighbour* **friend** to *hew wood* **chop timber**,
and his hand *fetcheth a stroke with* **driveth** the axe
to cut down the tree,
and the *head* **iron** slippeth from the *helve* **timber**,
and *lighteth upon* **findeth** his *neighbour* **friend**,
that he die;
he shall flee unto one of those cities, and live:
6 Lest the *avenger* **redeemer** of the blood
pursue the *slayer* **murderer**,
while his heart is hot, and overtake him,
because the way *is long* **aboundeth**,
and *slay him* **smite his soul**
whereas he was not worthy **when he had no judgment**
of death,
inasmuch as **because** he hated him not
in time past **three yesters ago**.
7 Wherefore I *command* **misvah** thee, saying,
Thou shalt separate three cities for thee.
8 And if *the LORD* **Yah Veh** thy *God* **Elohim**
enlarge **broaden** thy *coast* **border**,
as he hath *sworn* **oathed** unto thy fathers,
and give thee all the land
which he *promised* **worded** to give unto thy fathers;
9 If thou shalt *keep* **guard**
all these *commandments* **misvoth** to *do* **work** them,
which I *command* **misvah** thee this day,
to love *the LORD* **Yah Veh** thy *God* **Elohim**,
and to walk *ever* **all days** in his ways;
then shalt thou add three cities more for thee,
beside these three:
10 That innocent blood be not *shed* **poured** in thy land,
which *the LORD* **Yah Veh** thy *God* **Elohim**
giveth thee for an inheritance,
and so blood be upon thee.
11 But if any man hate his *neighbour* **friend**,
and *lie in wait* **lurk** for him, and rise up against him,
and smite *him mortally* **his soul** that he die,
and fleeth into one of these cities:
12 Then the elders of his city
shall send and *fetch* **take** him thence,
and *deliver* **give** him
into the hand of the *avenger* **redeemer** of blood,
that he may die.
13 Thine eye shall not *pity* **spare** him,
but thou shalt *put* **burn** away
the guilt of **for the** innocent blood from *Israel* **Yisra El**,
that it may *go well* **be good** with thee.
THE TORAH ON LAND BORDERS
14 Thou shalt not remove
thy *neighbour's landmark* **friend's border**,
which they *of old time* **at the first** have set
in thine inheritance,
which thou shalt inherit in the land
that *the LORD* **Yah Veh** thy *God* **Elohim**
giveth thee to possess it.
THE TORAH ON WITNESSES
15 One witness shall not rise *up* against a man
for any *iniquity* **perversity**, or for any sin,
in any sin that he sinneth:
at the mouth of two witnesses,
or at the mouth of three witnesses,
shall the *matter* **word** be *established* **raised**.
16 If a *false witness* **witness of violence** rise *up*
against any man
to *testify* **answer** against him
that which is *wrong* **revolting**;
17 Then *both* the **two** men,
between whom the *controversy* **dispute** is,
shall stand *before the LORD* **at the face of Yah Veh**,
before **at the face of** the priests and the judges,
which shall be in those days;
18 And the judges shall
make diligent inquisition **inquire well**:
and, behold, if the witness be a false witness,
and hath *testified* **witnessed** falsely against his brother;
19 Then shall ye *do* **work** unto him,
as he had *thought* **intrigued**
to have *done* **worked** unto his brother:
so shalt thou put the evil away from among you.
20 And those which *remain* **survive** shall hear,
and *fear* **awe**,
and shall henceforth *commit* **add to work**
no *more any* such **word of** evil among you.
21 Thine eye shall not *pity* **spare**;
but life shall go for life **soul for soul**, eye for eye,
tooth for tooth, hand for hand, foot for foot.
THE TORAH ON WARRING
20 When thou goest out to *battle* **war**
against thine enemies,
and seest horses, and chariots,
and a people more than thou,
be not afraid of **awe** them **not**:
for *the LORD* **Yah Veh** thy *God* **Elohim** is with thee,
which *brought* **ascended** thee *up*
out of the land of *Egypt* **Misrayim**.
2 And it shall be,
when ye *are come nigh* **approach** unto the *battle* **war**,
that the priest shall approach
and *speak* **word** unto the people,
3 And shall say unto them, Hear, O *Israel* **Yisra El**,
ye approach this day unto battle against your enemies:
let not your hearts *faint* **tenderize**,
fear **awe** not, and do not *tremble* **hasten**,
neither be ye terrified *because of them* **at their face**;
4 For *the LORD* **Yah Veh** your *God* **Elohim**
is he that goeth with you,
to fight for you against your enemies, to save you.
5 And the officers shall *speak* **word** unto the people,
saying, What man is there that hath built a new house,
and hath not *dedicated* **hanukkahed** it?
let him go and return to his house,
lest he die in the *battle* **war**,
and another man *dedicate* **hanukkah** it.
6 And what man is he that hath planted a vineyard,
and hath not yet *eaten* **plucked** of it?
let him *also* go and return unto his house,
lest he die in the *battle* **war**,
and another man *eat* **pluck** of it.
7 And what man is there
that hath betrothed a *wife* **woman**,
and hath not taken her?
let him go and return unto his house,
lest he die in the *battle* **war**, and another man take her.
8 And the officers
shall *speak further* **word again** unto the people,

and they shall say,
What man is there that *is fearful* **aweth**
and *fainthearted* **tender of heart?**
let him go and return unto his house,
lest his brethren's heart *faint* **melt** as well as his heart.
9 And it shall be,
when the officers
have *made an end of speaking* **finished wording**
unto the people
that they shall *make captains* **muster governors**
of the *armies* **hosts** to *lead* **head** the people.
10 When thou *comest nigh* **approachest** unto a city
to fight against it,
then *proclaim peace* **call shalom** unto it.
11 And it shall be,
if it make thee answer of *peace* **shalom,**
and open unto thee,
then it shall be,
that all the people that is found therein
shall be *tributaries* **vassals** unto thee,
and they shall serve thee.
12 And if it *will make no peace* **shall not shalam** with thee,
but *will make* **shall work** war against thee,
then thou shalt besiege it:
13 And when *the LORD* **Yah Veh** thy *God* **Elohim**
hath *delivered* **given** it into thine hands,
thou shalt smite every male thereof
with the *edge* **mouth** of the sword:
14 But the women, and the *little ones* **toddlers,**
and the *cattle* **animals**, and all that is in the city,
even all the *spoil* **loot** thereof,
shalt thou *take* **plunder** unto thyself;
and thou shalt eat the *spoil* **loot** of thine enemies,
which *the LORD* **Yah Veh** thy *God* **Elohim**
hath given thee.
15 Thus shalt thou *do* **work** unto all the cities
which are *very* **mighty** far off from thee,
which are not of the cities of these *nations* **goyim**.
16 But of the cities of these people,
which *the LORD* **Yah Veh** thy *God* **Elohim**
doth give thee for an inheritance,
thou shalt *save* **preserve** alive
nothing **naught** that breatheth:
17 But **in devoting,** thou shalt *utterly destroy* **devote** them;
namely, the *Hittites* **Hethiy**, and the *Amorites* **Emoriy**,
the *Canaanites* **Kenaaniy**, and the *Perizzites* **Perizziy**,
the *Hivites* **Hivviy**, and the *Jebusites* **Yebusiy**;
as *the LORD* **Yah Veh** thy *God* **Elohim**
hath *commanded* **misvahed** thee:
18 That they teach you not to *do* **work**
after all their *abominations* **abhorrences,**
which they have *done* **worked** unto their *gods* **elohim**;
so should **and thus** sin
against *the LORD* **Yah Veh** your *God* **Elohim**.
19 When thou shalt besiege a city *a long time* **many days,**
in *making war* **fighting** against it to *take* **capture** it,
thou shalt not *destroy* **ruin** the trees thereof
by *forcing* **driving** an axe against them:
for thou mayest eat of them,
and shalt not cut them down
(for the tree of the field is man's life)
to employ them in the siege
O humanity,
face ye the tree of the field to besiege you?:
20 Only the trees which thou knowest
that they be not trees for *meat* **food,**
thou shalt *destroy* **ruin** and cut them down;
and thou shalt build *bulwarks* **sieges**
against the city that *maketh* **worketh** war with thee,
until it *be subdued* **topple.**

THE TORAH ON UNKNOWN ASSASSINS

21 If one be found *slain* **pierced** in the *land* **soil**
which *the LORD* **Yah Veh** thy *God* **Elohim**
giveth thee to possess it, *lying* **fallen** in the field,
and it be not known who hath slain him:
2 Then thy elders and thy judges shall come forth,
and they shall measure unto the cities
which are round about him that is *slain* **pierced:**
3 And it shall be,
that the city
which is *next* **near** unto the *slain man* **pierced,**
even the elders of that city
shall take an heifer **of the oxen,**
which hath not *been wrought with* **served,**
and which hath not drawn in the yoke;
4 And the elders of that city
shall *bring down* **descend** the heifer
unto a *rough valley* **perrenial wadi,**
which is neither *eared* **served** nor *sown* **seeded,**
and shall *strike off* **break** the heifer's neck
there in the *valley* **wadi:**
5 And the priests the sons of Levi shall come near;
for them *the LORD* **Yah Veh** thy *God* **Elohim**
hath chosen to minister unto him,
and to bless in the name of *the LORD* **Yah Veh;**
and by their *word* **mouth**
shall every *controversy* **dispute**
and every *stroke* **plague** be *tried:*
6 And all the elders of that city,
that are *next* **near** unto the *slain man* **pierced,**
shall *wash* **baptize** their hands over the heifer
that is beheaded **whose neck is broken** in the *valley* **wadi:**
7 And they shall answer and say,
Our hands have not *shed* **poured** this blood,
neither have our eyes seen it.
8 *Be merciful* **Kapar/Atone,** O *LORD* **Yah Veh,**
unto thy people *Israel* **Yisra El,**
whom thou hast redeemed,
and *lay* **give** not innocent blood
unto thy people *of Israel's charge* **midst Yisra El.**
And the blood shall *be forgiven them* **kapar/atone.**
9 So shalt thou *put* **burn** away
the *guilt of* innocent blood from among you,
when thou shalt *do that which is right* **work straight**
in the *sight* **eyes** of *the LORD* **Yah Veh.**

THE TORAH ON THE CAPTURED WOMAN

10 When thou goest forth to war against thine enemies,
and *the LORD* **Yah Veh** thy *God* **Elohim**
hath *delivered* **given** them into thine hands,
and thou hast *taken* **captured** them *captive,*
11 And seest among the captives
a *beautiful* woman **fair in form,**
and hast *a desire* **attached** unto her,
that thou *wouldest have* **shouldest take** her
to **as** thy *wife* **woman;**
12 Then thou shalt bring her home *to* **midst** thine house,
and she shall shave her head, and *pare* **work** her nails;
13 And she shall *put* **turn aside**
the *raiment* **clothes** of her captivity *from off her,*
and shall *remain* **settle** in thine house,
and *bewail* **weep over** her father and her mother
a *full month* **moon of days:**
and after that thou shalt go in unto her,
and *be* **marry** her *husband,*
and she shall be thy *wife* **woman.**
14 And it shall be, if thou have no delight in her,
then thou shalt *let* **send** her *go* **away**
whither she will **as her soul desireth;**
but **in selling,** thou shalt not sell her *at all*
for *money* **silver,**
thou shalt not *make merchandise of* **tyrranize** her,
because thou hast humbled her.

THE TORAH ON FIRSTBORN

15 If a man have two *wives* **women,**
one beloved, and *another* **one** hated,
and they have born him *children* **sons,**
both the beloved and the hated;
and if the firstborn son be hers that was hated:
16 Then it shall be,
when he maketh **the day** his sons *to* inherit
that which he hath,
that he *may* **can** not make the son of the beloved firstborn
before **face** the son of the hated,
which is indeed — the firstborn:
17 But he shall *acknowledge* **recognize**
the son of the hated for the firstborn,
by giving him a *double portion* **twofold mouth**
of all that *he hath* **be found with him:**
for he is the beginning of his strength;
the *right of the firstborn* **judgment of firstrights** is his.

THE TORAH ON REVOLTING AND REBELLIOUS SONS

18 If a man have a *stubborn* **revolting** and rebellious son,
which *will* **shall** not *obey* **hearken**
to the voice of his father, or the voice of his mother,
and that, when they have *chastened* **disciplined** him,
will **shall** not hearken unto them:
19 Then shall his father and his mother
lay hold on **capture** him,
and bring him out unto the elders of his city,
and unto the *gate* **portal** of his place;
20 And they shall say unto the elders of his city,
This our son is *stubborn* **revolting** and rebellious,
he *will* **doth** not *obey* **hearken to** our voice;
he is a glutton, and a *drunkard* **carouser**.
21 And all the men of his city shall stone him with stones,
that he die:
so shalt thou *put* **burn** evil away from among you;
and all *Israel* **Yisra El** shall hear, and *fear* **awe**.

THE TORAH ON EXECUTION

22 And if a man *have committed* **becometh** a sin
worthy — **a judgment** of death,
and he be to be *put to death* **deathified**,
and thou hang him on a tree:
23 His *body* **carcase**
shall not *remain all night* **stay overnight** upon the tree,
but **in entombing,**
thou shalt *in any wise bury* **entomb** him that day;
(for he that is hanged
is accursed **hath an abasement** of *God* **Elohim**;)
that thy *land* **soil** be not defiled,
which *the LORD* **Yah Veh** thy *God* **Elohim**
giveth thee for an inheritance.

THE TORAH ON SUNDRY MATTERS

22 Thou shalt not see
thy brother's ox or his *sheep go astray* **lamb driven**,
and *hide* **conceal** thyself from them:
in returning,
thou shalt *in any case bring* **return** them *again*
unto thy brother.
2 And if thy brother be not nigh unto thee,
or if thou know him not,
then thou shalt *bring* **gather** it
unto **the midst of** thine own house,
and it shall be with thee until thy brother seek after it,
and thou shalt restore it to him again.
3 *In like manner* **Thus** shalt thou *do* **work**
with his *ass* **he burro**;
and *so* **thus** shalt thou *do* **work** with his *raiment* **clothes**;
and with all lost *thing* of thy brother's,
which he hath lost, and thou hast found,
shalt thou *do* **work** likewise:
thou *mayest not hide* **art not able to conceal** thyself.
4 Thou shalt not see thy brother's *ass* **he burro**
or his ox fall down by the way,
and *hide* **conceal** thyself from them:
in raising,
thou shalt *surely help him to lift* **raise** them *up again*.
5 The woman shall not *wear* **bear**
that which pertaineth unto a man **a mighty's instruments**,
neither shall a *man* **mighty**
put on **enrobe** a woman's *garment*:
for all that *do* **work** so are *abomination* **abhorrence**
unto *the LORD* **Yah Veh** thy *God* **Elohim**.
6 If a bird's nest *chance to be before thee* **confront thy face**
in the way in any tree, or on the *ground* **earth**,
whether they be young ones **chicks**, or eggs,
and the *dam sitting* **mother crouching**
upon the *young* **chicks**, or upon the eggs,
thou shalt not take the *dam* **mother** with the *young* **son**:
7 But **in sending away,**
thou shalt
in any wise let the dam go **send away the mother**,
and take the *young* **son** to thee;
that it may *be well with* **well—please** thee,
and that thou mayest prolong thy days.
8 When thou buildest a new house,
then thou shalt
make a battlement **work a parapet** for thy roof,
that thou *bring* **set** not blood upon thine house,
if **in falling,** any man fall from thence.
9 Thou shalt not *sow* **seed** thy vineyard
with *divers seeds* **heterogenetic inductions**:
lest the *fruit* **fulness** of thy seed
which thou hast *sown* **seeded**,
and the *fruit* **produce** of thy vineyard, be defiled.
10 Thou shalt not plow
with an ox and *an ass* **a he burro** together.
11 Thou shalt not
wear a garment of divers sorts **enrobe linsey woolsey**,
as of woollen and *linen* **flax** together.
12 Thou shalt *make* **work** thee *fringes* **threads**
upon the four *quarters* **borders** of thy *vesture* **covering**,
wherewith thou coverest *thyself*.

THE TORAH ON VIRGINITY

13 If any man take a *wife* **woman**,
and go in unto her, and hate her,
14 And *give occasions* **set exploitations** of *speech* **words**
against her,
and bring up an evil name upon her, and say,
I took this woman, and when I *came to* **approached** her,
I found *her not a maid* **no virginity in her**:
15 Then shall the father of the *damsel* **lass**,
and her mother,
take and bring forth
the tokens of the *damsel's* **lass'** virginity
unto the elders of the city in the *gate* **portal**:
16 And the damsel's father shall say unto the elders,
I gave my daughter unto this man to *wife* **woman**,
and he hateth her;
17 And, *lo* **behold**,
he hath *given occasions* **set exploitations** of *speech* **words**
against her, saying,
I found
not thy daughter a maid **no virginity in thy daughter**;
and yet these are *the tokens* of my daughter's virginity.
And they shall spread the cloth
before **at the face of** the elders of the city.
18 And the elders of that city shall take that man
and *chastise* **discipline** him;
19 And they shall *amerce* **penalize** him
in an hundred *shekels of* silver,
and give them unto the father of the *damsel* **lass**,
because he hath brought up an evil name
upon a virgin of *Israel* **Yisra El**:
and she shall be his *wife* **woman**;
he *may* **can** not *put* **send** her away all his days.
20 But if this *thing* **word** be *true* **truth**,
and *the tokens of* virginity
be not found for the *damsel* **lass**:
21 Then they shall bring out the *damsel* **lass**
to the *door* **opening** of her father's house,
and the men of her city
shall stone her with stones that she die:
because she hath *wrought* **worked** folly in *Israel* **Yisra El**,
to *play the* whore in her father's house:
so shalt thou *put* **burn** evil away from among you.
22 If a man be found lying with a woman
married to *an husband* **a master**,
then they shall *both* **the two** of them die,
both the man that lay with the woman, and the woman:
so shalt thou *put* **burn** away evil from *Israel* **Yisra El**.
23 If a *damsel* **lass** that is a virgin
be betrothed unto an *husband* **man**,
and a man find her in the city, and lie with her;
24 Then ye shall bring **the two of** them *both*
out unto the *gate* **portal** of that city,
and ye shall stone them with stones that they die;
the *damsel* **lass**,
because **for the word that** she cried not, being in the city;
and the man,
because **for the word that**
he hath humbled his *neighbour's wife* **friend's woman**:
so shalt thou *put* **burn** away evil from among you.
25 But if a man find a betrothed *damsel* **lass** in the field,
and the man *force* **take strong hold of** her,
and lie with her:
then the man only that lay with her shall die.
26 But unto the *damsel* **lass**
thou shalt *do nothing* **work no word**;

there is in the *damsel* **lass** no sin *worthy* of death:
for as when a man riseth against his *neighbour* **friend**,
and *slayeth him* **murdureth his soul**,
even so is this *matter* **word**:
27 For he found her in the field,
and the betrothed *damsel* **lass** cried,
and there was none to save her.
28 If a man find a *damsel* **lass** that is a virgin,
which is not betrothed,
and *lay hold on* **capture** her, and lie with her,
and they be found;
29 Then the man that lay with her
shall give unto the *damsel's* **lass's** father
fifty *shekels of* silver,
and she shall be his *wife* **woman**;
because he hath humbled her,
he *may* **can** not *put* **send** her away all his days.
30 A man shall not take his father's *wife* **woman**,
nor *discover* **expose** his father's *skirt* **border**.

THE TORAH ON CONGREGATIONAL EXCLUSIONS

23 He that is wounded *in the stones* **or castrated,**
or hath his *privy member* **penis** cut off,
shall not enter
into the congregation of *the LORD* **Yah Veh**.
2 A bastard shall not enter
into the congregation of *the LORD* **Yah Veh**;
even to his tenth generation shall he not enter
into the congregation of *the LORD* **Yah Veh**.
3 An *Ammonite* **Ammoniy** or *Moabite* **Moabiy**
shall not enter
into the congregation of *the LORD* **Yah Veh**;
even to their tenth generation shall they not enter
into the congregation of *the LORD* **Yah Veh**
for ever **eternally**:
4 *Because* **For word that** they *met* **anticipated** you not
with bread and with water in the way,
when ye came forth out of *Egypt* **Misrayim**;
and because they hired against thee
Balaam **Bilam** the son of Beor of Pethor
of *Mesopotamia* **Aram Naharaim**, to *curse* **abase** thee.
5 Nevertheless *the LORD* **Yah Veh** thy *God* **Elohim**
would **willed to** not hearken unto *Balaam* **Bilam**;
but *the LORD* **Yah Veh** thy *God* **Elohim**
turned the *curse* **abasement** into a blessing unto thee,
because *the LORD* **Yah Veh** thy *God* **Elohim** loved thee.
6 Thou shalt not seek their *peace* **shalom**
nor their *prosperity* **good** all thy days *for ever* **eternally**.
7 Thou shalt not abhor an *Edomite* **Edomiy**;
for he is thy brother:
thou shalt not abhor *an Egyptian* **a Misrayim**;
because thou wast a *stranger* **sojourner** in his land.
8 The *children* **sons** that are *begotten* **born** of them
shall enter into the congregation of *the LORD* **Yah Veh**
in their third generation.

THE TORAH ON SANITATION

9 When the *host* **camp** goeth forth against thine enemies,
then *keep* **guard** thee from every *wicked thing* **evil word**.
10 If there be among you any man,
that is not *clean* **pure**
by reason of uncleanness that chanceth him by night
from happenings of the night,
then shall he go *abroad out of* **outside** the camp,
he shall not come *within* **midst** the camp:
11 But it shall be,
when **at the face of** evening *cometh on*,
he shall *wash* **baptize** *himself* with water:
and when the sun is down,
he shall come *into* **midst** the camp again.

ON SANITATION ECOLOGY

12 Thou shalt have a *place* **hand** also without the camp,
whither thou shalt go *forth abroad* **without**:
13 And thou shalt
have a paddle **take** upon thy *weapon* **ear**;
and it shall be,
when thou *wilt ease thyself abroad* **shalt sit without**,
thou shalt dig therewith,
and shalt turn back
and cover *that which cometh from thee* **thy excrement**:
14 For *the LORD* **Yah Veh** thy *God* **Elohim**
walketh in the midst of thy camp, to *deliver* **rescue** thee,
and to give up thine enemies *before thee* **at thy face**;
therefore shall thy camp be holy:
that he see no *unclean thing* **word of nakedness** in thee,
and turn away *from* **after** thee.

THE TORAH ON SERVANTS

15 Thou shalt not deliver unto his *master* **adoni**
the servant which is escaped from his *master* **adoni**
unto thee:
16 He shall *dwell* **settle** with thee, even among you,
in that place which he shall choose
in one of thy *gates* **portals**,
where it *liketh him best* **is good for him**:
thou shalt not oppress him.

THE TORAH ON HALLOWED WHORES

17 There shall be no **hallowed** whore
of the daughters of *Israel* **Yisra El**,
nor a *sodomite* **hallowed whoremaster**
of the sons of *Israel* **Yisra El**.
18 Thou shalt not bring the *hire* **payoff**
of *a whore* **one that whoreth**, or the price of a dog,
into the house of *the LORD* **Yah Veh** thy *God* **Elohim**
for any vow:
for even *both* these **two** are *abomination* **an abhorrence**
unto *the LORD* **Yah Veh** thy *God* **Elohim**.

THE TORAH ON USUARY

19 Thou shalt not *lend upon usury to* **usure** thy brother;
usury of *money* **silver**, usury of *victuals* **food**,
usury of any
thing that is lent upon usury **word of a usurer**:
20 Unto a stranger, thou mayest *lend upon usury* **usure**;
but unto thy brother, thou shalt not *lend upon usury* **usure**:
that *the LORD* **Yah Veh** thy *God* **Elohim** may bless thee
in *all that thou settest* **every extending of** thine hand
in the land whither thou goest to possess it.

THE TORAH ON VOWS

21 When thou shalt vow a vow
unto *the LORD* **Yah Veh** thy *God* **Elohim**,
thou shalt not *slack* **delay** to *pay* **shalam** it:
for **in requiring**,
the LORD **Yah Veh** thy *God* **Elohim**
will **shall** *surely* require it of thee;
and it *would* be sin in thee.
22 But if thou shalt *forbear* **cease** to vow,
it shall be no sin in thee.
23 That which *is gone* **proceeded** out of thy lips
thou shalt *keep* **guard** and *perform* **work**;
even a *freewill offering* **voluntary**,
according as thou hast vowed
unto *the LORD* **Yah Veh** thy *God* **Elohim**,
which thou hast *promised* **worded** with thy mouth.

THE TORAH ON GLEANING

24 When thou comest
into thy *neighbour's* **friend's** vineyard,
then thou mayest eat grapes
thy fill at thine own pleasure **to fill thy soul**;
but thou shalt not *put* **give** any in thy *vessel* **instrument**.
25 When thou comest
into the *standing corn* **stalks** of thy *neighbour* **friend**,
then thou mayest pluck the ears with thine hand;
but thou shalt not move a sickle
unto thy *neighbour's standing corn* **friend's stalks**.

THE TORAH ON THE SCROLL OF DIVORCEMENT

24 When a man hath taken a *wife* **woman**
and married her,
and it *come to pass* **becometh,**
that she find no *favour* **charism** in his eyes,
because he hath found some
uncleanness **word of nakedness** in her:
then let him *write* **inscribe** her a *bill* **scroll** of divorcement,
and give it in her hand, and send her out of his house.
2 And when she is departed out of his house,
she may go and be another man's *wife*.
3 And if the latter *husband* **man** hate her,
and *write* **inscribe** her a *bill* **scroll** of divorcement,
and giveth it in her hand,
and sendeth her out of his house;
or if the latter *husband* **man** die,
which took her to be his *wife* **woman**;
4 Her *former husband* **first master**, which sent her away,
may **can** not **return to** take her *again*

to be **as** his *wife* **woman**,
after that she is *defiled* **fouled**;
for that is *abomination* **abhorrence**
before the LORD **at the face of Yah Veh**:
and thou shalt not cause the land to sin,
which *the LORD* **Yah Veh** thy *God* **Elohim**
giveth thee for an inheritance.

THE TORAH ON SUNDRY MATTERS

5 When a man hath taken a new *wife* **woman**,
he shall not go out to *war* **the hostility**,
neither shall he
be charged with **pass** any *business* **word over him**:
but he shall be *free* **exonerated** at home one year,
and shall cheer *up* his *wife* **woman** which he hath taken.
6 No man shall take the *nether* **millstone**
or the upper millstone to pledge:
for he taketh a *man's life* **soul** to pledge.
7 If a man be found stealing *any* **a soul** of his brethren
of the *children* **sons** of *Israel* **Yisra El**,
and *maketh merchandise of* **tyrranizeth** him,
or selleth him;
then that thief shall die;
and thou shalt *put* **burn** evil away from among you.
8 *Take heed* **On guard** in the plague of leprosy,
that thou *observe diligently* **guard mightily**,
and *do* **work** according to all
that the priests the *Levites* **Leviym**
shall *teach* **point out to** you:
as I *commanded* **misvahed** them,
so ye shall *observe* **guard** to *do* **work**.
9 Remember what *the LORD* **Yah Veh** thy *God* **Elohim**
did **worked** unto *Miriam* **Miryam** by the way,
after that ye were come forth out of *Egypt* **Misrayim**.
10 When thou dost lend
thy *brother any thing* **friend a loan**,
thou shalt not go into his house
to *fetch* **pledge** his pledge.
11 Thou shalt stand *abroad* **without**,
and the man to whom thou dost lend
shall bring out the pledge *abroad* **without** unto thee.
12 And if the man be *poor* **humbled**,
thou shalt not *sleep* **lie down** with his pledge:
13 In *any case* **returning**,
thou shalt *deliver* **return** him the pledge *again*
when the sun goeth down,
that he may *sleep* **lie down** in his own *raiment* **clothes**,
and bless thee:
and it shall be *righteousness* **justness** unto thee
before the LORD **at the face of Yah Veh** thy *God* **Elohim**.
14 Thou shalt not oppress an *hired servant* **hireling**
that is *poor* **humbled** and needy,
whether he be of thy brethren,
or of thy *strangers* **sojourners**
that are in thy land within thy *gates* **portals**:
15 At his day thou shalt give him his hire,
neither shall the sun go down upon it;
for he is *poor* **humbled**,
and *setteth* **lifteth** his *heart* **soul** upon it:
lest he *cry* **call** against thee unto *the LORD* **Yah Veh**,
and it be sin unto thee.
16 The fathers
shall not be *put to death* **deathified** for the *children* **sons**,
neither shall the *children* **sons**
be *put to death* **deathified** for the fathers:
every man
shall be *put to death* **deathified** for his own sin.
17 Thou shalt not *pervert* **deviate** the judgment
of the *stranger* **sojourner**, nor of the *fatherless* **orphan**;
nor take a widow's *raiment* **clothes** to pledge:
18 But thou shalt remember
that thou wast a *bondman* **servant** in *Egypt* **Misrayim**,
and *the LORD* **Yah Veh** thy *God* **Elohim**
redeemed thee thence:
therefore I *command* **misvah** thee
to *do* **work** this *thing* **word**.
19 When thou *cuttest down* **harvestest** thine harvest
in thy field,
and hast forgot *a sheaf* **an omer** in the field,
thou shalt not *go again* **return** to *fetch* **take** it:
it shall be for the *stranger* **sojourner**,
for the *fatherless* **orphan**, and for the widow:
that *the LORD* **Yah Veh** thy *God* **Elohim** may bless thee
in all the work of thine hands.
20 When thou beatest thine olive tree,
thou shalt not *go over the boughs again* **shake after thee**:
it shall be for the *stranger* **sojourner**,
for the *fatherless* **orphan**, and for the widow.
21 When thou *gatherest* **clippest** the grapes
of thy vineyard,
thou shalt not *glean it afterward* **exploit after thee**:
it shall be for the *stranger* **sojourner**,
for the *fatherless* **orphan**, and for the widow.
22 And thou shalt remember
that thou wast a *bondman* **servant**
in the land of *Egypt* **Misrayim**:
therefore I *command* **misvah** thee
to *do* **work** this *thing* **word**.

25 If there be a *controversy* **dispute** between men,
and they come unto judgment,
that *the judges may judge them* **they be judged**;
then they shall justify the *righteous* **just**,
and *condemn* **declare wicked** the wicked.
2 And it shall be,
if the wicked *man be worthy to be beaten* **son be smitten**,
that the judge shall cause him to *lie down* **fall**,
and to be *beaten before* **smitten at** his face,
sufficient according to his *fault* **wickedness**,
by a certain number.
3 Forty *stripes he may give him* **smites**,
and not *exceed* **add**:
lest, if he should *exceed* **add**,
and *beat* **smite** him above these with many *stripes* **strokes**,
then thy brother
should *seem vile unto thee* **be abased in thine eyes**.
4 Thou shalt not muzzle the ox
when he *treadeth* **thresheth** out the corn.

THE TORAH ON THE LEVIRATE

5 If brethren *dwell* **settle** together,
and one of them die, and have no *child* **son**,
the *wife of the dead* **woman of him who died**
shall not marry *without unto* **an outsider man**
—a stranger:
her *husband's brother* **levirate** shall go in unto her,
and take her to him to *wife* **woman**,
and *perform the duty of an husband's brother unto her*
be her levirate.
6 And it shall be,
that the firstborn which she beareth
shall *succeed* **be raised** in the name of his brother
which is dead **who died**,
that his name be not *put* **wiped** out of *Israel* **Yisra El**.
7 And if the man *like not* **be not delighted**
to *take his brother's wife* **become a levirate**,
then let *his brother's wife* **her of the levirate**
go up **ascend** to the *gate* **portal** unto the elders,
and say, My *husband's brother* **levirate**
refuseth to raise up unto his brother
a name in *Israel* **Yisra El**,
he will not perform the duty of my husband's brother
he willeth to not be my levirate.
8 Then the elders of his city shall call him,
and *speak* **word** unto him:
and if he stand to it, and say,
I *like* **delight** not to take her;
9 Then shall *his brother's wife* **the woman of the levirate**
come unto him in the *presence* **eyes** of the elders,
and *loose* **strippeth** his shoe from off his foot,
and spit in his face, and shall answer and say,
So **Thus** shall it be *done* **worked** unto that man
that *will* **shall** not build *up* his brother's house.
10 And his name shall be called in *Israel* **Yisra El**,
The house of him that hath his shoe loosed.

THE TORAH ON SUNDRY MATTERS

11 When men strive together one with another,
and the *wife* **woman** of the one *draweth near* **approacheth**
for to *deliver* **rescue** her *husband* **man**
out of the hand of him that smiteth him,
and *putteth forth* **extendeth** her hand,
and *taketh him by the secrets* **layeth hold on his pudenda**:
12 Then thou shalt cut off her *hand* **palm**,

thine eye shall not *pity* **spare** her.
13 Thou shalt not have in thy *bag* **pouch**
divers weights **a stone and a stone**,
a great and a small.
14 Thou shalt not have in thine house
divers measures **an ephah and an ephah**,
a great and a small.
15 But thou shalt have
a perfect and just weight
a stone of shalom and justness,
a perfect and just measure
an ephah of shalom and justness
shalt thou have:
that thy days may be *lengthened* **prolonged**
in the *land* **soil**
which *the LORD* **Yah Veh** thy *God* **Elohim** giveth thee.
16 For all that *do* **work** such *things*,
and all that *do unrighteously* **work wickedness**,
are an *abomination* **abhorrence**
unto *the LORD* **Yah Veh** thy *God* **Elohim**.
17 Remember what *Amalek did* **Amaleq worked** unto thee
by the way,
when ye were come forth out of *Egypt* **Misrayim**;
18 How he *met* **happened upon** thee by the way,
and *smote the hindmost of* **curtailed** thee,
even all that were *feeble* **weak** behind thee,
when thou wast *faint* **languid** and *weary* **belaboured**;
and he *feared* **awed** not *God* **Elohim**.
19 Therefore it shall be,
when *the LORD* **Yah Veh** thy *God* **Elohim**
hath *given thee rest* **rested thee**
from all thine enemies round about,
in the land which *the LORD* **Yah Veh** thy *God* **Elohim**
giveth thee for an inheritance to possess it,
that thou shalt *blot* **wipe** out
the *remembrance* **memorial** of *Amalek* **Amaleq**
from under *heaven* **the heavens**;
thou shalt not forget it.

THE TORAH ON FIRSTS AND TITHES

26 And it shall be,
when thou art come in unto the land
which *the LORD* **Yah Veh** thy *God* **Elohim**
giveth thee for an inheritance,
and possessest it, and *dwellest* **settlest** therein;
2 That thou shalt take
of the first of all the fruit of the *earth* **soil**,
which thou shalt bring of thy land
that *the LORD* **Yah Veh** thy *God* **Elohim** giveth thee,
and shalt put it in a basket,
and shalt go unto the place
which *the LORD* **Yah Veh** thy *God* **Elohim**
shall choose to place his name there.
3 And thou shalt go unto the priest
that shall be in those days,
and say unto him,
I *profess* **tell** this day
unto *the LORD* **Yah Veh** thy *God* **Elohim**,
that I am come unto the *country* **land**
which *the LORD sware* **Yah Veh oathed** unto our fathers
for to give us.
4 And the priest shall take the basket out of thine hand,
and set it *down before the* **at the face of the sacrifice** altar
of *the LORD* **Yah Veh** thy *God* **Elohim**.
5 And thou shalt *speak* **answer** and say
before the LORD **at the face of Yah Veh** thy *God* **Elohim**,
A Syrian ready to perish **A destroyed Aramiy**
was my father,
and he *went down* **descended** into *Egypt* **Misrayim**,
and sojourned there with a few **men**,
and became there a *nation* **goyim**,
great, mighty, and *populous* **many**:
6 And the *Egyptians* **Misrayim** evil entreated us,
and *afflicted* **humbled** us,
and *laid* **gave** upon us hard *bondage* **service**:
7 And when we cried
unto *the LORD God* **Yah Veh Elohim** of our fathers,
the LORD **Yah Veh** heard our voice,
and *looked on* **saw** our *affliction* **humiliation**,
and our *labour* **drudgery**, and our oppression:
8 And *the LORD* **Yah Veh**
brought us forth out of *Egypt* **Misrayim**
with a *mighty* **strong** hand,
and with an *outstretched* **extended** arm,
and with great *terribleness* **awesomeness**,
and with signs, and with *wonders* **omens**:
9 And he hath brought us into this place,
and hath given us this land,
even a land that floweth with milk and honey.
10 And now, behold,
I have brought the *firstfruits* **firsts of the fruit**
of the *land* **soil**,
which thou, O *LORD* **Yah Veh**, hast given me.
And thou shalt *set* **leave** it
before the LORD **at the face of Yah Veh** thy *God* **Elohim**,
and *worship* **prostrate**
before the LORD **at the face of Yah Veh** thy *God* **Elohim**:
11 And thou shalt *rejoice* **cheer** in every good *thing*
which *the LORD* **Yah Veh** thy *God* **Elohim**
hath given unto thee, and unto thine house,
thou, and the *Levite* **Leviy**,
and the *stranger* **sojourner** that is among you.
12 When thou hast *made an end of* **finished off**
tithing all the tithes of thine *increase* **produce**
the third year, which is the year of tithing,
and hast given it unto the *Levite* **Leviy**,
the *stranger* **sojourner**,
the *fatherless* **orphan**, and the widow,
that they may eat within thy *gates* **portals**,
and *be filled* **satiate**;
13 Then thou shalt say
before the LORD **at the face of Yah Veh** thy *God* **Elohim**,
I have *brought* **burnt** away the *hallowed things* **holies**
out of mine house,
and also have given them unto the *Levite* **Leviy**,
and unto the *stranger* **sojourner**,
to the *fatherless* **orphan**, and to the widow,
according to all thy *commandments* **misvoth**
which thou hast *commanded* **misvahed** me:
I have not *transgressed* **trespassed**
thy *commandments* **misvoth**,
neither have I forgotten them.
14 I have not eaten thereof in my *mourning* **mischief**,
neither have I *taken* **burnt** away *ought* thereof
for any *unclean* **fouled** use,
nor given *ought thereof for the dead* **for them that died**:
but I have hearkened
to the voice of *the LORD* **Yah Veh** my *God* **Elohim**,
and have *done* **worked** according to all
that thou hast *commanded* **misvahed** me.
15 Look down from thy holy habitation,
from *heaven* **the heavens**,
and bless thy people *Israel* **Yisra El**,
and the *land* **soil** which thou hast given us,
as thou *swarest* **oathest** unto our fathers,
a land that floweth with milk and honey.
16 This day *the LORD* **Yah Veh** thy *God* **Elohim**
hath *commanded* **misvahed** thee
to *do* **work** these statutes and judgments:
thou shalt therefore *keep* **guard** and *do* **work** them
with all thine heart, and with all thy soul.
17 Thou hast *avouched the LORD* **said** this day
to be **that Yah Veh become** thy *God* **Elohim**,
and to walk in his ways, and to *keep* **guard** his statutes,
and his *commandments* **misvoth**, and his judgments,
and to hearken unto his voice:
18 And *the LORD* **Yah Veh** hath *avouched* **said** this day
to be **that thou become** his peculiar people,
as he hath *promised* **worded unto** thee,
and that thou shouldest
keep **guard** all his *commandments* **misvoth**;
19 And to *make* **give** thee **most** high
above all *nations* **goyim** which he hath *made* **worked**,
in *praise* **halal**, and in name, and in *honour* **adornment**;
and that thou mayest be an holy people
unto *the LORD* **Yah Veh** thy *God* **Elohim**,
as he hath *spoken* **worded**.

THE STONES OF THE WORDS OF THE TORAH

27 And *Moses* **Mosheh** with the elders of *Israel* **Yisra El**
commanded **misvahed** the people, saying,
Keep **Guard** all the *commandments* **misvoth**

which I *command* **misvah** you this day.
2 And it shall be
on the day when ye shall pass over *Jordan* **Yarden**
unto the land
which *the LORD* **Yah Veh** thy *God* **Elohim** giveth thee,
that thou shalt *set* **raise** thee *up* great stones,
and plaister them with plaister:
3 And thou shalt *write* **inscribe** upon them
all the words of this *law* **torah**,
when thou art passed over,
that thou mayest go in unto the land
which *the LORD* **Yah Veh** thy *God* **Elohim** giveth thee,
a land that floweth with milk and honey;
as *the LORD God* **Yah Veh Elohim** of thy fathers
hath *promised* **worded** unto thee.
4 Therefore it shall be
when ye be *gone* **passed** over *Jordan* **Yarden**,
that ye shall *set up* **raise** these stones,
which I *command* **misvah** you this day, in mount Ebal,
and thou shalt plaister them with plaister.

THE SACRIFICE ALTAR OF STONES

5 And there shalt thou build *an* **a sacrifice** altar
unto *the LORD* **Yah Veh** thy *God* **Elohim**,
an **a sacrifice** altar of stones:
thou shalt not lift *up* any iron *tool* upon them.
6 Thou shalt build the **sacrifice** altar
of *the LORD* **Yah Veh** thy *God* **Elohim**
of *whole* stones **of shalom**:
and thou shalt *offer burnt offerings* **holocaust holocausts**
thereon
unto *the LORD* **Yah Veh** thy *God* **Elohim**:
7 And thou shalt *offer peace offerings* **sacrifice shelamim**,
and shalt eat there, and *rejoice* **cheer**
before the LORD **at the face of Yah Veh** thy *God* **Elohim**.
8 And thou shalt *write* **inscribe** upon the stones
all the words of this *law very plainly* **torah well explained**.
9 And *Moses* **Mosheh** and the priests the *Levites* **Leviym**
spake **worded** unto all *Israel* **Yisra El**, saying,
Take heed, and hearken, O *Israel* **Yisra El**;
this day thou art become
the people of *the LORD* **Yah Veh** thy *God* **Elohim**.
10 Thou shalt therefore *obey* **hear** the voice
of *the LORD* **Yah Veh** thy *God* **Elohim**,
and *do* **work** his *commandments* **misvoth**
and his statutes,
which I *command* **misvah** thee this day.

THE TWELVE CURSES FROM MOUNT EBAL

11 And *Moses* **Mosheh**
charged **misvahed** the people the same day, saying,
12 These shall stand upon mount Gerizim
to bless the people,
when ye are *come* **passed** over *Jordan* **Yarden**;
Simeon **Shimon**, and Levi, and *Judah* **Yah Hudah**,
and *Issachar* **Yissachar**, and *Joseph* **Yoseph**,
and *Benjamin* **Ben Yamin**:
13 And these shall stand upon mount Ebal
to curse **for the abasement**;
Reuben **Reu Ben**, Gad, and Asher,
and Zebulun, Dan, and Naphtali.
14 And the *Levites* **Leviym** shall *speak* **answer**,
and say unto all the men of *Israel* **Yisra El**
with *a loud* **lifted** voice,
15 Cursed be the man
that *maketh* **worketh** any *graven* **sculptile** or molten *image*,
an *abomination* **abhorrence** unto *the LORD* **Yah Veh**,
the work of the hands of the *craftsman* **engraver**,
and putteth it in a *secret place* **hideout**.
And all the people shall answer and say, Amen.
16 Cursed be he
that *setteth light* **be abased** by his father or his mother.
And all the people shall say, Amen.
17 Cursed be he
that removeth his *neighbour's landmark* **friend's border**.
And all the people shall say, Amen.
18 Cursed be he
that *maketh* **causeth** the blind to *wander* **err inadvertently**
out of the way.
And all the people shall say, Amen.
19 Cursed be he
that *perverteth* **deviateth** the judgment
of the *stranger* **sojourner**,
fatherless **orphan**, and widow.
And all the people shall say, Amen.
20 Cursed be he
that lieth with his father's *wife* **woman**;
because he *uncovereth* **exposeth** his father's *skirt* **border**.
And all the people shall say, Amen.
21 Cursed be he
that lieth with any *manner of beast* **animal**.
And all the people shall say, Amen.
22 Cursed be he
that lieth with his sister,
the daughter of his father, or the daughter of his mother.
And all the people shall say, Amen.
23 Cursed be he
that lieth with his *mother* in law.
And all the people shall say, Amen.
24 Cursed be he
that smiteth his *neighbour secretly* **friend covertly**.
And all the people shall say, Amen.
25 Cursed be he
that taketh *reward* **a bribe**
to *slay* **smite** an innocent *person* **soul**.
And all the people shall say, Amen.
26 Cursed be he
that *confirmeth* **raiseth** not
all the words of this *law* **torah** to *do* **work** them.
And all the people shall say, Amen.

THE BLESSINGS OF OBEDIENCE

28 And it shall *come to pass* **become**,
if **in hearkening,** thou shalt hearken *diligently*
unto the voice of *the LORD* **Yah Veh** thy *God* **Elohim**,
to *observe* **guard** and to *do* **work**
all his *commandments* **misvoth**
which I *command* **misvah** thee this day,
that *the LORD* **Yah Veh** thy *God* **Elohim**
will set **shall give** thee *on* **most** high
above all *nations* **goyim** of the earth:
2 And all these blessings shall come on thee,
and overtake thee,
if thou shalt hearken
unto the voice of *the LORD* **Yah Veh** thy *God* **Elohim**.
3 Blessed shalt thou be in the city,
and blessed shalt thou be in the field.
4 Blessed shall be the fruit of thy *body* **belly**,
and the fruit of thy *ground* **soil**,
and the fruit of thy *cattle* **animals**,
the *increase* **fetus** of thy *kine* **yoke**,
and the *flocks* **riches** of thy *sheep* **flocks**.
5 Blessed shall be thy basket and thy *store* **doughboard**.
6 Blessed shalt thou be when thou comest in,
and blessed shalt thou be when thou goest out.
7 *The LORD* **Yah Veh** shall *cause* **give** thine enemies
that rise up against thee
to be smitten *before* **at** thy face:
they shall come out against thee one way,
and flee *before thee* **thy face** seven ways.
8 *The LORD* **Yah Veh**
shall *command* **misvah** the blessing upon thee
in thy *storehouses* **ingatherings**,
and in all that thou *settest* **extendest** thine hand *unto*;
and he shall bless thee in the land
which *the LORD* **Yah Veh** thy *God* **Elohim** giveth thee.
9 *The LORD* **Yah Veh** shall *establish* **raise** thee
an holy people unto himself,
as he hath *sworn* **oathed** unto thee,
if thou shalt *keep* **guard** the *commandments* **misvoth**
of *the LORD* **Yah Veh** thy *God* **Elohim**,
and walk in his ways.
10 And all people of the earth shall see
that thou art called by the name of the LORD
that the name of Yah Veh be called upon thee;
and they shall *be afraid of* **awe** thee.
11 And *the LORD* **Yah Veh**
shall *make* **overflow** thee *plenteous* in goods,
in the fruit of thy *body* **belly**,
and in the fruit of thy *cattle* **animals**,
and in the fruit of thy *ground* **soil**,
in the *land* **soil**
which *the LORD sware* **Yah Veh oathed** unto thy fathers

to give thee.
12 *The LORD* **Yah Veh** shall open unto thee
his good treasure,
the *heaven* **heavens**
to give the rain unto thy land in his *season* **time**,
and to bless all the work of thine hand:
and thou shalt lend unto many *nations* **goyim**,
and thou shalt not borrow.
13 And *the LORD* **Yah Veh** shall *make* **give** thee the head,
and not the tail;
and thou shalt be above only,
and thou shalt not be *beneath* **downward**;
if that thou hearken unto the *commandments* **misvoth**
of *the LORD* **Yah Veh** thy *God* **Elohim**,
which I *command* **misvah** thee this day,
to *observe* **guard** and to *do* **work** them:
14 And thou shalt not *go* **turn** aside from any of the words
which I *command* **misvah** thee this day,
to the right *hand*, or to the left,
to go after other *gods* **elohim** to serve them.

THE CURSINGS OF DISOBEDIENCE

15 But it shall *come to pass* **become,**
if thou *wilt* **shalt** not hearken
unto the voice of *the LORD* **Yah Veh** thy *God* **Elohim**,
to *observe* **guard** to *do* **work**
all his *commandments* **misvoth** and his statutes
which I *command* **misvah** thee this day;
that all these *curses* **abasements** shall come upon thee,
and overtake thee:
16 Cursed shalt thou be in the city,
and cursed shalt thou be in the field.
17 Cursed shall be thy basket and thy *store* **doughboard**.
18 Cursed shall be the fruit of thy *body* **belly**,
and the fruit of thy *land* **soil**,
the *increase* **fetus** of thy *kine* **yoke**,
and the *flocks* **riches** of thy *sheep* **flocks**.
19 Cursed shalt thou be when thou comest in,
and cursed shalt thou be when thou goest out.
20 *The LORD* **Yah Veh** shall send upon thee cursing,
vexation **confusion**, and rebuke,
in all that thou *settest* **extendest** thine hand unto
for to *do* **work**,
until thou be *destroyed* **desolated**,
and until thou *perish quickly* **destruct suddenly**;
because **at the face**
of the *wickedness* **evil** of thy *doings* **exploits**,
whereby thou hast forsaken me.
21 *The LORD* **Yah Veh**
shall make the pestilence cleave unto thee,
until he have *consumed* **finished** thee **off**
from *off* the *land* **soil**,
whither thou goest to possess it.
22 *The LORD* **Yah Veh** shall smite thee
with *a consumption* **an emaciation**,
and with a fever, and with an inflammation,
and with *an extreme burning* **a fevered fever**,
and with the sword,
and with blasting, and with *mildew* **palegreen**;
and they shall pursue thee until thou *perish* **destruct**.
23 And thy *heaven that is* **heavens** over thy head
shall be *brass* **copper**,
and the earth that is under thee shall be iron.
24 *The LORD* **Yah Veh** shall *make* **give** the rain of thy land
powder and dust:
from *heaven* **the heavens**
shall it *come down* **descend** upon thee,
until thou be *destroyed* **desolated**.
25 *The LORD* **Yah Veh** shall *cause* **give** thee to be smitten
before **at the face of** thine enemies:
thou shalt go out one way against them,
and flee seven ways *before them* **from their face**:
and shalt be removed
into all the *kingdoms* **sovereigndoms** of the earth.
26 And thy carcase shall be *meat* **for food**
unto all *fowls* **fliers** of the *air* **heavens**,
and unto the *beasts* **animals** of the earth,
and no man shall *fray* **cause** them *away* **to tremble**.
27 *The LORD will* **Yah Veh shall** smite thee
with the *botch* **ulcer** of *Egypt* **Misrayim**,
and with the *emerods* **hemorrhoids**,
and with the *scab* **scurvy**, and with the itch,
whereof thou canst not be healed.
28 *The LORD* **Yah Veh** shall smite thee
with *madness* **insanity**, and blindness,
and *astonishment* **consternation** of heart:
29 And thou shalt grope at *noonday* **noon**,
as the blind gropeth in darkness,
and thou shalt not prosper in thy ways:
and thou shalt be only
oppressed and *spoiled evermore* **stripped all days**,
and no man shall save thee.
30 Thou shalt betroth a *wife* **woman**,
and another man shall *lie with* **rape** her:
thou shalt build an house,
and thou shalt not *dwell* **settle** therein:
thou shalt plant a vineyard,
and shalt not *gather the grapes* **pluck** thereof.
31 Thine ox shall be *slain* **slaughtered**
before **at the face of** thine eyes,
and thou shalt not eat hereof:
thine *ass* **he burro** shall be *violently taken away* **stripped**
from *before* thy face,
and shall not be *restored* **returned** to thee:
thy *sheep* **flocks** shall be given unto thine enemies,
and thou shalt have none to *rescue* **save** them.
32 Thy sons and thy daughters
shall be given unto another people,
and thine eyes shall *look* **see**,
and fail *with longing* for them all the day long;
and there shall be no *might* **El** in thine hand.
33 The fruit of thy *land* **soil**, and all thy labours,
shall a *nation* **people** which thou knowest not eat up;
and thou shalt be only oppressed and crushed
always **all days**:
34 So that thou shalt be *mad* **insane**
for the *sight* **visage** of thine eyes which thou shalt *see*.
35 *The LORD* **Yah Veh** shall smite thee
in the knees, and in the legs,
with *a sore botch* **an evil ulcer** that cannot be healed,
from the sole of thy foot
unto *the top of thy head* **thy scalp**.
36 *The LORD* **Yah Veh**
shall *bring* **carry** thee, and thy *king* **sovereign**
which thou shalt *set* **raise** over thee,
unto a *nation* **goyim**
which neither thou nor thy fathers have known;
and there shalt thou serve other *gods* **elohim**,
wood **timber** and stone.
37 And thou shalt become *an astonishment* **a desolation**,
a proverb, and a *byword* **gibe**, among all *nations* **people**
whither *the LORD* **Yah Veh** shall *lead* **drive** thee.
38 Thou shalt carry much seed out into the field,
and shalt gather but little in;
for the locust shall consume it.
39 Thou shalt plant vineyards, and *dress* **servest** them,
but shalt neither drink of the wine, nor gather the grapes;
for the *worms* **maggots** shall eat them.
40 Thou shalt have *olive trees* **olives**
throughout all thy *coasts* **borders**,
but thou shalt not anoint *thyself* with the oil;
for thine olive shall *cast his fruit* **slip**.
41 Thou shalt beget sons and daughters,
but thou shalt not enjoy them;
for they shall go into captivity.
42 All thy trees and fruit of thy *land* **soil**
shall the locust *consume* **possess**.
43 The *stranger that is within thee* **sojourner in thy midst**
shall *get up above thee* **ascend**
very high **upward and upward**;
and thou shalt *come down* **descend**
very low **downward and downward**.
44 He shall lend to thee, and thou shalt not lend to him:
he shall be the head, and thou shalt be the tail.
45 Moreover all these *curses* **abasements**
shall come upon thee,
and shall pursue thee, and overtake thee,
till thou be *destroyed* **desolated**;
because thou hearkenedst not
unto the voice of *the LORD* **Yah Veh** thy *God* **Elohim**,
to *keep* **guard** his *commandments* **misvoth**

and his statutes which he *commanded* **misvahed** thee:
46 And they shall be upon thee
for a sign and for *a wonder* **an omen**,
and upon thy seed *for ever* **eternally**.
47 Because thou servedst not
the LORD **Yah Veh** thy *God* **Elohim**
with *joyfulness* **cheerfulness**,
and with *gladness* **goodness** of heart,
for the abundance of all *things*;
48 Therefore shalt thou serve thine enemies
which *the LORD* **Yah Veh** shall send against thee,
in *hunger* **famine**, and in thirst, and in nakedness,
and in want of all *things*:
and he shall *put* **give** a yoke of iron upon thy neck,
until he have *destroyed* **desolated** thee.
49 *The LORD* **Yah Veh**
shall *bring* **lift** a *nation* **goyim** against thee from far,
from the end of the earth, *as swift as* the eagle flieth;
a *nation* **goyim**
whose tongue thou shalt not *understand* **hear**;
50 A *nation* **goyim** *of fierce countenance* **strong of face**,
which shall not *regard* **exalt**
the *person* **face** of the *old* **aged**,
nor *shew favour* **grant charism** to the *young* **lads**:
51 And he shall eat the fruit of thy *cattle* **animals**,
and the fruit of thy *land* **soil**,
until thou be *destroyed* **desolated**:
which also **and there** shall not *leave thee* **survive**
either corn **crop**, *wine* **juice**, or oil,
or the *increase* **fetus** of thy *kine* **yoke**,
or *flocks* **riches** of thy *sheep* **flocks**,
until he have destroyed thee.
52 And he shall *besiege* **tribulate** thee
in all thy *gates* **portals**,
until thy high and *fenced* **fortified** walls
come down **topple**,
wherein thou *trustedst* **confidest**, throughout all thy land:
and he shall *besiege* **tribulate** thee in all thy *gates* **portals**
throughout all thy land,
which *the LORD* **Yah Veh** thy *God* **Elohim**
hath given thee.
53 And thou shalt eat the fruit of thine own *body* **belly**,
the flesh of thy sons and of thy daughters,
which *the LORD* **Yah Veh** thy *God* **Elohim**
hath given thee,
in the siege, and in the *straitness* **distress**,
wherewith thine enemies shall distress thee:
54 So that the man that is tender among you,
and *very* **mighty** delicate,
his eye shall be evil toward his brother,
and toward the *wife* **woman** of his bosom,
and toward the remnant of his *children* **sons**
which *he* shall *leave* **remain:**
55 So that he *will* **shall** not give *to any* **one** of them
of the flesh of his *children* **sons** whom he shall eat:
because he hath *nothing left* **naught to survive** him
in the siege, and in the *straitness* **distress**,
wherewith thine enemies shall distress thee
in all thy *gates* **portals.**
56 The tender and delicate *woman* among you,
which *would* **should** not *adventure* **test**
to set the sole of her foot upon the *ground* **earth**
for delicateness and tenderness,
her eye shall be evil
toward the *husband* **man** of her bosom,
and toward her son, and toward her daughter,
57 And toward her *young one* **fetus**
that cometh out from between her feet,
and toward her *children* **sons** which she shall bear:
for she shall eat them for *want* **lack** of all *things*
secretly **covertly** in the siege and *straitness* **distress**,
wherewith thine enemy shall distress thee
in thy *gates* **portals.**
58 If thou *wilt* **shalt** not *observe* **guard**
to *do* **work** all the words of this *law* **torah**
that are *written* **inscribed** in this *book* **scroll**,
that thou mayest *fear* **awe**
this *glorious* **honoured** and *terrible* **awesome** name,
THE LORD THY GOD **YAH VEH THY ELOHIM**;
59 Then *the LORD* **Yah Veh**
will **shall** make thy *plagues wonderful* **strokes marvelous**,
and the *plagues* **strokes** of thy seed,
even great *plagues* **strokes**,
and of long continuance — **trustworthy**,
and *sore* **evil** sicknesses,
and of long continuance — **trustworthy**.
60 *Moreover* he *will bring* **shall restore** upon thee
all the diseases of *Egypt* **Misrayim**,
which thou wast afraid of **at their face**;
and they shall *cleave* **adhere** unto thee.
61 Also every sickness, and every *plague* **stroke**,
which is not *written* **inscribed**
in the *book* **scroll** of this *law* **torah**,
them *will the LORD* **shall Yah Veh**
bring **ascend** upon thee,
until thou be *destroyed* **desolated**.
62 And ye shall *be left* **survive** few **men** in number,
whereas ye were as the stars of *heaven* **the heavens**
for *multitude* **abundance**;
because thou *wouldest* **heardest** not *obey* the voice
of *the LORD* **Yah Veh** thy *God* **Elohim**.
63 And it shall *come to pass* **become**,
that as *the LORD* **Yah Veh** rejoiced over you
to *do you good* **well—please you**,
and to *multiply* **abound** you;
so *the LORD will* **Yah Veh shall** rejoice over you
to destroy you,
and to *bring* **desolate** you *to nought*;
and ye shall be *plucked* **uprooted** from off the *land* **soil**
whither thou goest to possess it.
64 And *the LORD* **Yah Veh** shall scatter thee
among all people,
from the *one* end of the earth
even unto the *other* **end of the earth**;
and there thou shalt serve other *gods* **elohim**,
which neither thou nor thy fathers have known,
even wood **timber** and stone.
65 And among these *nations* **goyim**
shalt thou *find no ease* **not blink**,
neither shall the sole of thy foot *have* rest:
but *the LORD* **Yah Veh** shall give thee there
a *trembling* **quivering** heart,
and failing of eyes, and sorrow of *mind* **soul**:
66 And thy life shall *hang in doubt* **be in suspense**
before thee;
and thou shalt fear day and night,
and shalt *none assurance* **have no trust** of thy life:
67 In the morning thou shalt say,
Would God **O that it be given that** it were even!
and at even thou shalt say,
would God **O that it be given that** it were morning!
for the fear of thine heart wherewith thou shalt fear,
and for the *sight* **vision** of thine eyes which thou shalt see.
68 And *the LORD* **Yah Veh** shall *bring* **return** thee
into *Egypt* **Misrayim** again with ships,
by the way whereof I *spake* **said** unto thee,
Thou shalt see it *no more* **not** again:
and there ye shall be ye sold unto your enemies
for *bondmen* **servants** and *bondwomen* **maids**,
and no man shall *buy* **chattel** you.

YAH VEH CUTS ANOTHER COVENANT

29 These are the words of the covenant,
which *the LORD* **Yah Veh**
commanded Moses **misvahed Mosheh**
to *make* **cut** with the *children* **sons** of *Israel* **Yisra El**
in the land of Moab,
beside the covenant which he *made* **cut**
with them in Horeb.
2 And *Moses* **Mosheh** called unto all *Israel* **Yisra El**,
and said unto them, Ye have seen all
that *the LORD did* **Yah Veh worked** before your eyes
in the land of *Egypt* **Misrayim** unto *Pharaoh* **Paroh**,
and unto all his servants, and unto all his land;
3 The great *temptations* **testings**
which thine eyes have seen,
the signs, and those great *miracles* **omens**:
4 Yet *the LORD* **Yah Veh** hath not given you
an heart to perceive, and eyes to see, and ears to hear,
unto this day.
5 And I have *led* **carried** you forty years in the wilderness:

your clothes are not *waxen old* **worn out** upon you,
and thy shoe is not *waxen old* **worn out** upon thy foot.
6 Ye have not eaten bread,
neither have ye drunk wine or *strong drink* **intoxicants**:
that ye might know
that *I am the LORD* **I — Yah Veh** your *God* **Elohim**.
7 And when ye came unto this place,
Sihon **Sichon** the *king* **sovereign** of Heshbon,
and Og the *king* **sovereign** of Bashan,
came out *against* **confronting** us unto *battle* **war**,
and we smote them:
8 And we took their land, and gave it for an inheritance
unto the *Reubenites* **Reu Beniy** and to the *Gadites* **Gadiy**,
and to the half *tribe* **scion** of *Manasseh* **Menash Shiy**.
9 *Keep* **Guard** *therefore* the words of this covenant,
and *do* **work** them,
that ye may *prosper* **comprehend** in all that ye *do* **work**.
10 Ye stand this day all of you
before the LORD **at the face of Yah Veh** your *God* **Elohim**;
your *captains* **heads** of your *tribes* **scions**,
your elders, and your officers,
with all the men of *Israel* **Yisra El**,
11 Your *little ones* **toddlers**, your *wives* **women**,
and thy *stranger* **sojourner** that is *in* **within** thy camp,
from the hewer of thy *wood* **timber**
unto the drawer of thy water:
12 That thou shouldest *enter* **pass** into covenant
with *the LORD* **Yah Veh** thy *God* **Elohim**,
and into his oath,
which *the LORD* **Yah Veh** thy *God* **Elohim**
maketh **cutteth** with thee this day:
13 That he may *establish* **raise** thee to day
for a people unto himself,
and that he may be unto thee *a God* **— Elohim**,
as he hath *said* **worded** unto thee,
and as he hath *sworn* **oathed** unto thy fathers,
to Abraham, to *Isaac* **Yischaq**, and to *Jacob* **Yaaqov**.
14 Neither with you only
do I *make* **cut** this covenant and this oath;
15 But with him that standeth here with us this day
before the LORD **at the face of Yah Veh** our *God* **Elohim**,
and also with him that is not here with us this day:
16 (For ye know how we have *dwelt* **settled**
in the land of *Egypt* **Misrayim**;
and how we came *through* **midst** the *nations* **goyim**
which ye passed by;
17 And ye have seen their *abominations* **abhorrences**,
and their idols,
wood **timber** and stone, silver and gold,
which were among them:)
18 Lest there should be among you
man, or woman, or family, or *tribe* **scion**,
whose heart turneth *away* this day
from *the LORD* **the face of Yah Veh** our *God* **Elohim**,
to go and serve the *gods* **elohim** of these *nations* **goyim**;
lest there should be among you
a root that beareth *gall* **the fruit of rosh** and wormwood;
19 And it *come to pass* **becometh**,
when he heareth the words of this *curse* **oath**,
that he bless himself in his heart, saying,
I shall have *peace* **shalom**,
though I walk in the *imagination* **warp** of mine heart,
to *add drunkenness* **scrape together satiation** to thirst:
20 *The LORD will* **Yah Veh shall** not *spare* **forgive** him,
but then the *anger* **wrath** of *the LORD* **Yah Veh**
and his jealousy shall *smoke* **fume** against that man,
and all the *curses* **oaths**
that are *written* **inscribed** in this *book* **scroll**
shall *lie* **crouch** upon him,
and *the LORD* **Yah Veh** shall *blot* **wipe** out his name
from under *heaven* **the heavens**.
21 And *the LORD* **Yah Veh** shall separate him unto evil
out of all the *tribes* **scions** of *Israel* **Yisra El**,
according to all the *curses* **oaths** of the covenant
that are *written* **inscribed**
in this *book* **scroll** of the *law* **torah**:
22 So that the **latter** generation *to come*
of your *children* **sons** that shall rise *up* after you,
and the stranger that shall come from a far land,
shall say, when they see the *plagues* **strokes** of that land,
and the sicknesses
which *the LORD* **Yah Veh** hath *laid* **stroked** upon it;
23 And that the whole land thereof
is *brimstone* **sulphur**, and salt, and burning,
that it is not *sown* **seeded**, nor *beareth* **sprouteth**,
nor any *grass groweth* **herbage ascendeth** therein,
like the overthrow of
Sodom **Sedom**, and *Gomorrah* **Amorah**,
Admah, and *Zeboim* **Seboim**,
which *the LORD overthrew* **Yah Veh overturned**
in his *anger* **wrath**, and in his *wrath* **fury**:
24 Even all *nations* **goyim** shall say,
Wherefore hath *the LORD* **Yah Veh**
done **worked** thus unto this land?
what meaneth the heat of — this great *anger* **fuming wrath**?
25 Then men shall say,
Because they have forsaken the covenant
of *the LORD God* **Yah Veh Elohim** of their fathers,
which he *made* **cut** with them
when he brought them forth
out of the land of *Egypt* **Misrayim**:
26 For they went and served other *gods* **elohim**,
and *worshipped* **prostrated to** them,
gods **elohim** whom they knew not,
and whom he had not *given* **allotted** unto them:
27 And the *anger* **wrath** of *the LORD* **Yah Veh**
was kindled against this land,
to bring upon it all the *curses* **abasements**
that are *written* **inscribed** in this *book* **scroll**:
28 And *the LORD rooted* **Yah Veh uprooted** them
out of their *land* **soil** in *anger* **wrath**,
and in wrath, and in great *indignation* **rage**,
and cast them into another land, as it is this day.
29 The *secret things* **hidden** belong unto
the LORD **Yah Veh** our *God* **Elohim**:
but those *things* which are *revealed* **exposed**
belong unto us and to our *children for ever* **sons eternally**,
that we may *do* **work** all the words of this *law* **torah**.

YAH VEH'S OPEN INVITATION

30 And it shall *come to pass* **become**,
when all these *things* **words** are come upon thee,
the blessing and the *curse* **abasement**,
which I have *set before thee* **given at thy face**,
and thou shalt *call* **restore** them to *mind* **heart**
among all the *nations* **goyim**,
whither *the LORD* **Yah Veh** thy *God* **Elohim**
hath driven thee,
2 And shalt return
unto *the LORD* **Yah Veh** thy *God* **Elohim**,
and shalt *obey* **hear** his voice
according to all that I *command* **misvah** thee this day,
thou and thy *children* **sons**,
with all thine heart, and with all thy soul;
3 That then *the LORD* **Yah Veh** thy *God* **Elohim**
will **shall** turn thy captivity,
and *have compassion upon* **shall mercy** thee,
and *will* **shall** return and gather thee
from all the *nations* **goyim**,
whither *the LORD* **Yah Veh** thy *God* **Elohim**
hath scattered thee.
4 If any of thine be driven out
unto the *outmost parts* **ends** of *heaven* **the heavens**,
from thence *will the LORD* **shall Yah Veh** thy *God* **Elohim**
gather thee,
and from thence *will* **shall** he *fetch* **take** thee:
5 And *the LORD* **Yah Veh** thy *God* **Elohim**
will **shall** bring thee
into the land which thy fathers possessed,
and thou shalt possess it;
and he *will do thee good* **shall well—please thee**,
and *multiply* **abound** thee above thy fathers.
6 And *the LORD* **Yah Veh** thy *God* **Elohim**
will **shall** circumcise thine heart,
and the heart of thy seed,
to love *the LORD* **Yah Veh** thy *God* **Elohim**
with all thine heart, and with all thy soul,
that thou mayest live **for thy life**.
7 And *the LORD* **Yah Veh** thy *God* **Elohim**
will put **shall give** all these *curses* **oaths**
upon thine enemies, and on them that hate thee,

which *persecuted* **pursued** thee.
8 And thou shalt return
and *obey* **hear** the voice of *the LORD* **Yah Veh**,
and *do* **work** all his *commandments* **misvoth**
which I *command* **misvah** thee this day.
9 And *the LORD* **Yah Veh** thy *God* **Elohim**
will make thee plenteous **shall overflow thee**
in every work of thine hand,
in the fruit of thy *body* **belly**,
and in the fruit of thy *cattle* **animals**,
and in the fruit of thy *land* **soil**, for good:
for *the LORD* **Yah Veh**
will again **shall return to** rejoice over thee for good,
as he rejoiced over thy fathers:
10 If thou shalt hearken unto the voice
of *the LORD* **Yah Veh** thy *God* **Elohim**,
to *keep* **guard**
his *commandments* **misvoth** and his statutes
which are *written* **inscribed**
in this *book* **scroll** of the *law* **torah**,
and if thou turn unto *the LORD* **Yah Veh** thy *God* **Elohim**
with all thine heart, and with all thy soul.
11 For this *commandment* **misvah**
which I *command* **misvah** thee this day,
it is not *hidden from* **too marvelous for** thee,
neither is it far off.
12 It is not in *heaven* **the heavens**,
that thou shouldest say **saying**,
Who shall *go up* **ascend** for us to *heaven* **the heavens**,
and *bring* **take** it unto us,
that we may hear it, and *do* **work** it?
13 Neither is it beyond the sea,
that thou shouldest say **saying**,
Who shall *go* **pass** over the sea for us,
and *bring* **take** it unto us,
that we may hear it, and *do* **work** it?
14 But the word is *very* **mighty** nigh unto thee,
in thy mouth, and in thy heart,
that thou mayest *do* **work** it.
cp Romans 10:6—9

YAH VEH'S OFFER OF LIFE AND GOOD

15 See, I have *set before thee* **given at thy face** this day
life and good, and death and evil;
16 In that I *command* **misvah** thee this day
to love *the LORD* **Yah Veh** thy *God* **Elohim**,
to walk in his ways,
and to *keep* **guard** his *commandments* **misvoth**
and his statutes and his judgments,
that thou mayest live and *multiply* **increase**:
and *the LORD* **Yah Veh** thy *God* **Elohim** shall bless thee
in the land whither thou goest to possess it.
17 But if thine heart turn *away*,
so that thou *wilt* **shalt** not hear,
but shalt be *drawn away* **driven**,
and *worship* **prostrate to** other *gods* **elohim**,
and serve them;
18 I *denounce* **tell** unto you this day,
that **in destructing**, ye shall *surely perish* **destruct**,
and that ye shall not
prolong your days upon the *land* **soil**,
whither thou passest over *Jordan* **Yarden**
to go to possess it.
19 I call *heaven* **the heavens** and earth
to *record* **witness** this day against you,
that I have *set before you* **given at your face**
life and death, blessing and *cursing* **abasement**:
therefore choose life,
that both thou and thy seed may live:
20 That thou mayest love
the LORD **Yah Veh** thy *God* **Elohim**,
and that thou mayest *obey* **hear** his voice,
and that thou mayest *cleave* **adhere** unto him:
for he is thy life, and the length of thy days:
that thou mayest *dwell* **settle** in the *land* **soil**
which *the LORD sware* **Yah Veh oathed** unto thy fathers,
to Abraham, to *Isaac* **Yischaq**, and to *Jacob* **Yaaqov**,
to give them.

MOSHEH CALLS YAH SHUA

31 And *Moses* **Mosheh** went
and *spake* **worded** these words unto all *Israel* **Yisra El**.
2 And he said unto them,
I am **a son of** an hundred and twenty years *old* this day;
I can no more go out and come in:
also *the LORD* **Yah Veh** hath said unto me,
Thou shalt not *go* **pass** over this *Jordan* **Yarden**.
3 *The LORD* **Yah Veh** thy *God* **Elohim**,
he *will go* **shall pass** over *before thee* **at thy face**,
and he *will destroy* **shall desolate** these *nations* **goyim**
from *before thee* **thy face**,
and thou shalt possess them:
and *Joshua* **Yah Shua**,
he shall go over *before thee* **at thy face**,
as *the LORD* **Yah Veh** hath *said* **worded**.
4 And *the LORD* **Yah Veh** shall *do* **work** unto them
as he *did* **worked** to *Sihon* **Sichon** and to Og,
kings **sovereigns** of the *Amorites* **Emoriy**,
and unto the land of them, whom he destroyed.
5 And *the LORD* **Yah Veh** shall give them up
before **at** your face,
that ye may *do* **work** unto them
according unto all the *commandments* **misvoth**
which I have *commanded* **misvahed** you.
6 *Be strong and of a good courage*
In strenthening, be strengthened,
fear not **neither awe**, nor *be afraid of them* **awe their face**:
for *the LORD* **Yah Veh** thy *God* **Elohim**,
he it is that doth go with thee;
he *will* **shall** not *fail* **let loose of** thee,
nor forsake thee.
7 And Moses **Mosheh** called unto *Joshua* **Yah Shua**,
and said unto him in the *sight* **eyes** of all *Israel* **Yisra El**,
Be strong and of a good courage
In strenthening, be strengthened:
for thou *must* **shalt** go with this people unto the land
which *the LORD* **Yah Veh**
hath *sworn* **oathed** unto their fathers to give them;
and thou shalt cause them to inherit it.
8 And *the LORD* **Yah Veh**,
he it is that doth go *before thee* **at thy face**;
he *will* **shall** be with thee,
he *will* **shall** not *fail thee* **let thee loose**,
neither forsake thee:
fear **awe** not, neither be *dismayed* **terrified**.

MOSHEH INSCRIBES THE TORAH

9 And *Moses wrote* **Mosheh inscribed** this *law* **torah**,
and *delivered* **gave** it unto the priests the sons of Levi,
which bare the ark of the covenant of *the LORD* **Yah Veh**,
and unto all the elders of *Israel* **Yisra El**.
10 And *Moses commanded* **Mosheh misvahed** them,
saying, At the end of *every* seven years,
in the *solemnity* **season** of the year of release,
in the *feast* **celebration**
of *tabernacles* **Sukkoth/Brush Arbors**,
11 When all *Israel* **Yisra El** is come to *appear* **be seen**
before the LORD **at the face of Yah Veh** thy *God* **Elohim**
in the place which he shall choose,
thou shalt *read* **recall** this *law* **torah**
before all *Israel* **Yisra El** in their *hearing* **ears**.
12 *Gather* **Congregate** the people *together*,
men and women, and *children* **toddlers**,
and thy *stranger* **sojourner** that is within thy *gates* **portals**,
that they may hear, and that they may learn,
and *fear the LORD* **awe Yah Veh** your *God* **Elohim**,
and *observe* **guard** to *do* **work**
all the words of this *law* **torah**:
13 And that their *children* **sons**,
which have not known *any thing*,
may hear, and learn
to *fear* **awe** *the LORD* **Yah Veh** your *God* **Elohim**,
as long as **all days** ye live in the *land* **soil**
whither ye *go* **pass** over *Jordan* **Yarden** to possess it.

YAH VEH SPEAKS TO MOSHEH AND YAH SHUA

14 And *the LORD* **Yah Veh** said unto *Moses* **Mosheh**,
Behold, thy days approach that thou *must* die:
call *Joshua* **Yah Shua**, and *present* **station** yourselves
in the *tabernacle* **tent** of the congregation,
that I may *give* **misvah** him *a charge*.
And *Moses* **Mosheh** and *Joshua* **Yah Shua** went,
and *presented* **stationed** themselves
in the *tabernacle* **tent** of the congregation.

15 And *the LORD appeared* **Yah Veh was seen**
in the *tabernacle* **tent** in a pillar of a cloud:
and the pillar of the cloud
stood over the *door* **opening** of the *tabernacle* **tent**.
16 And *the LORD* **Yah Veh** said unto *Moses* **Mosheh**,
Behold, thou shalt *sleep* **lie** with thy fathers;
and this people *will* **shall** rise up,
and *go a whoring* **whore** after the *gods* **elohim**
of the strangers of the land,
whither they go to be among them,
and *will* **shall** forsake me,
and break my covenant
which I have *made* **cut** with them.
17 Then my *anger* **wrath**
shall be kindled against them in that day,
and I *will* **shall** forsake them,
and I *will* **shall** hide my face from them,
and they shall be devoured,
and many evils and *troubles* **tribulations**
shall *befall* **find** them;
so that they *will* **shall** say in that day,
Are not these evils come upon us,
because our *God* **Elohim** is not among us?
18 And **in hiding,**
I *will surely* **shall** hide my face in that day
for all the evils which they shall have *wrought* **worked**,
in that they are turned unto **the face of** other *gods* **elohim**.

THE NEW SONG

19 Now therefore *write* **inscribe** ye this song for you,
and teach it the *children* **sons** of *Israel* **Yisra El**:
put it in their mouths,
that this song may be a witness for me
against the *children* **sons** of *Israel* **Yisra El**.
20 For when I shall have brought them into the *land* **soil**
which I *sware* **oathed** unto their fathers,
that floweth with milk and honey;
and they shall have eaten and *filled themselves* **satiated**,
and *waxen fat* **fattened**;
then *will* **shall** they turn
unto **the face of** other *gods* **elohim**,
and serve them,
and *provoke* **scorn** me, and break my covenant.
21 And it shall *come to pass* **become**,
when many evils and *troubles* **tribulations**
are befallen **have found** them,
that this song shall *testify* **answer**
against them **at their face** as a witness;
for it shall not be forgotten
out of the mouths of their seed:
for I know their imagination which they *go about* **work**,
even now **this day**,
before I have brought them
into the land which I *sware* **oathed**.
22 *Moses therefore wrote* **Mosheh inscribed** this song
the same day,
and taught it the *children* **sons** of *Israel* **Yisra El**.
23 And he *gave Joshua* **misvahed Yah Shua** the son of Nun
a charge, and said,
Be strong and of a good courage
In strengthening, be strengthened:
for thou shalt bring the *children* **sons** of *Israel* **Yisra El**
into the land which I *sware* **oathed** unto them:
and I *will* **shall** be with thee.
24 And it *came to pass* **became**,
when *Moses* **Mosheh** had *made an end* **finished**
of writing **inscribing** the words of this *law* **torah**
in a *book* **scroll**,
until they were *finished* **consumated**,
25 That *Moses* **Mosheh**
commanded **misvahed** the *Levites* **Leviym**,
which bare the ark of the covenant of *the LORD* **Yah Veh**,
saying,
26 Take this *book* **scroll** of the *law* **torah**,
and put it in the side of the ark of the covenant
of *the LORD* **Yah Veh** your *God* **Elohim**,
that it may be there for a witness against thee.
27 For I know thy rebellion, and thy *stiff* **hard** neck:
behold, while I am yet alive with you this day,
ye have been rebellious against *the LORD* **Yah Veh**;
and how much more after my death?
28 *Gather* **Congregate** unto me
all the elders of your *tribes* **scions**, and your officers,
that I may speak these words in their ears,
and call *heaven* **the heavens** and earth
to record against them.
29 For I know that after my death
ye will utterly corrupt yourselves
in ruining, ye shall ruin,
and turn aside from the way
which I have *commanded* **misvahed** you;
and evil *will befall* **shall confront** you
in the *latter* **final** days;
because ye *will do* **shall work** evil
in the *sight* **eyes** of *the LORD* **Yah Veh**,
to *provoke* **vex** him *to anger*
through the work of your hands.
30 And *Moses spake* **Mosheh worded**
in the ears of all the congregation of *Israel* **Yisra El**
the words of this song, until they were *ended* **consumated**.

cp Apocalypse 15:3,4

MOSHEH SINGS THE NEW SONG

32 *Give ear* **Hearken**, O ye heavens,
and I *will speak* **shall word**;
and hear, O earth,
the *words* **sayings** of my mouth.
2 My doctrine shall *drop* **drip** as the rain,
my *speech* **sayings** shall *distil* **flow** as the dew,
as the *small rain* **shower** upon the tender *herb* **sprout**,
and as the showers upon the *grass* **herbage**:
3 Because I *will publish* **shall recall**
the name of *the LORD* **Yah Veh**:
ascribe **give** ye greatness unto our *God* **Elohim**.
4 *He is* the Rock, his *work is perfect* **deed is integrious**:
for all his ways are judgment:
a God **an El** of *truth* **trust** and without *iniquity* **wickedness**,
just and *right* **straight** is he.
5 They have *corrupted* **ruined to** themselves,
their spot is not the spot of his children
they are not his sons:
they are a *perverse* **pervert**
and *crooked* **twisted** generation.
6 *Do* **Deal** ye thus *requite the LORD* **unto Yah Veh**,
O foolish people and unwise?
is not he thy father that hath *bought* **chatteled** thee?
hath he not *made* **worked** thee, and established thee?
7 Remember the days *of old* **eternal**,
consider **discern** the years
of many generations — **the years generation to generation**:
ask thy father, and he *will shew* **shall tell** thee;
thy elders, and they *will tell thee* **shall say**.
8 When *the Most High* **Elyon**
divided to the nations their inheritance
had the goyim to inherit,
when he separated the sons of *Adam* **humanity**,
he *set* **stationed** the *bounds* **borders** of the people
according to the number
of the *children* **sons** of *Israel* **Yisra El**.
9 For *the LORD'S portion* **Yah Veh's allotment**
is his people;
Jacob **Yaaqov** is the *lot* **boundary** of his inheritance.
10 He found him in a *desert* **wilderness** land,
and in the waste howling *wilderness* **desolation**;
he *led* **turned** him *about* **around**,
he *instructed him* **had him discern**,
he *kept* **guarded** him as the *apple* **pupil** of his eye.
11 As an eagle *stirreth up* **waketh** her nest,
fluttereth over her *young* **younglings**,
spreadeth abroad her wings,
taketh them, beareth them on her *wings* **pinions**:
12 So *the LORD* **Yah Veh** alone did lead him,
and there was no strange *god* **el** with him.
13 He *made* **had** him ride
on the *high places* **bamahs** of the earth,
that he might eat the *increase* **produce** of the fields;
and he *made* **had** him to suck honey out of the rock,
and oil out of the flinty rock;
14 Butter of *kine* **oxen**, and milk of *sheep* **flocks**,
with fat of *lambs* **rams**,
and rams of the *breed* **sons** of Bashan,
and **he** goats, with the fat of *kidneys* **reins** of wheat;

and thou didst drink the *pure* **fermented** blood
of the grape.
15 But *Jeshurun waxed fat* **Yeshurun fattened**, and kicked:
thou art *waxen fat* **fattened**,
thou art *grown thick* **thickened**,
thou art *covered with fatness* **fattened**;
then he forsook *God* **Elohah** which *made* **worked** him,
and *lightly esteemed* **disgraced** the Rock of his salvation.
16 They *provoked him to* **aroused his** jealousy
with *strange gods* **strangers**,
with abominations *provoked* **vexed** they him *to anger*.
17 They sacrificed unto *devils* **demons**, not to *God* **Elohah**;
to *gods* **elohim** whom they knew not,
to new gods that came newly up **new — from nearby**,
whom your fathers feared not
who whirled not away your fathers.
18 *Of* **Remember** the Rock that begat thee
thou art unmindful,
and **thou** hast forgotten *God* **El** that formed thee.
19 And when *the LORD* **Yah Veh** saw it,
he *abhorred* **scorned** them,
because of the *provoking* **vexation** of his sons,
and of his daughters.
20 And he said, I *will* **shall** hide my face from them,
I *will* **shall** see *what their end shall be* **their finality**:
for they are a very froward generation,
children in whom is no faith **sons — not trustworthy**.
21 They have moved me to jealousy
with *that which is not God* **their non—el**;
they have *provoked* **vexed** me *to anger* with their vanities:
and I *will* **shall** move them to jealousy
with those which are not a people;
I *will provoke* **shall vex** them *to anger*
with a foolish *nation* **goyim**.
22 For a fire is kindled in *mine anger* **my wrath**,
and shall burn unto the *lowest hell* **nethermost sheol**,
and shall consume the earth with her *increase* **produce**,
and *set on fire* **inflame** the foundations of the mountains.
23 I *will heap mischiefs* **shall scrape together evils**
upon them;
I *will spend* **shall finish off** mine arrows upon them.
24 They shall be *burnt* **exhausted** with *hunger* **famine**,
and devoured with burning heat,
and with bitter *destruction* **ruin**:
I *will* **shall** also send the teeth of *beasts* **animals**
upon them,
with the poison of *serpents* **creepers** of the dust.
25 The sword without,
and terror *within* **from the chambers**,
shall *destroy both* **bereave**
the *young man* **youth** and the virgin,
the suckling also with the man of *gray hairs* **grayness**.
26 I said,
I *would scatter* **should blow** them *into corners* **away**,
I would make the remembrance of them to cease
I should shabbathize their memorial from among men:
27 *Were it not that I* **If I had not** feared
the *wrath* **vexation** of the enemy,
lest their *adversaries* **tribulators**
should *behave themselves strangely* **discern**
and lest they should say, Our hand is *high* **lifted**,
and *the LORD* **Yah Veh** hath not done all this.
28 For they are a *nation void* **goyim destroyed** of counsel,
neither is there *any understanding* **discernment** in them.
29 O that they were wise,
that they *understood* **comprehended** this,
that they *would consider* **should discern**
their *latter end* **finality**!
30 How should one *chase* **pursue** a thousand,
and two *put ten thousand to flight* **pursue a myriad**,
except **unless** their Rock had sold them,
and *the LORD* **Yah Veh** had shut them up?
31 For their rock is not as our Rock,
even our enemies themselves being judges.
32 For their vine is of the vine of *Sodom* **Sedom**,
and of the fields of *Gomorrah* **Amorah**:
their grapes are grapes of *gall* **rosh**,
their clusters are bitter:
33 Their wine is the poison of *dragons* **monsters**,
and the cruel *venom* **rosh** of asps.
34 Is not this *laid up in store* **stored** with me,
and sealed up among my treasures?
35 *To me belongeth vengeance* **Mine be the avenging**
and *recompence* **retribution**;
their foot shall *slide in due* **slip in** time:
for the day of their calamity is *at hand* **near**,
and *the things* **those** that shall *come* **impend** upon them
make haste **hasten**.
36 For *the LORD* **Yah Veh** shall judge his people,
and *repent himself* **sigh** for his servants,
when he seeth that their *power* **hand** is *gone* **disappeared**,
and there is none *shut up* **that is restrained**, or left.
37 And he shall say, Where are their *gods* **elohim**,
their rock in whom they *trusted* **sought refuge**,
38 Which did eat the fat of their sacrifices,
and drank the wine of their *drink offerings* **libation**?
let them rise up and help you,
and be your *protection* **covert**.
39 See now that I, even I, am he,
and there is no *god* **elohim** with me:
I *kill* **deathify**, and I *make alive* **enliven**;
I *wound* **strike**, and I heal:
neither is there any
that can *deliver* **escape** out of my hand.
40 For I lift up my hand to *heaven* **the heavens**,
and say, I live *for ever* **eternally**.
41 If I *whet* **pointen**
my glittering **the lightning of my** sword,
and mine hand take hold on judgment;
I *will render vengeance* **shall return avengement**
to *mine enemies* **my tribulators**,
and *will reward* **shall shalam** them that hate me.
42 I *will* **shall** make mine arrows
drunk **intoxicate** with blood,
and my sword shall devour flesh;
and that with the blood of the *slain* **pierced**
and of the captives,
from the *beginning of revenges* **heads of the leaders**
upon the enemy.
43 *Rejoice* **Shout**, O ye *nations* **goyim**, with his people:
for he *will* **shall** avenge the blood of his servants,
and *will render vengeance* **shall return avengement**
to his *adversaries* **tribulators**,
and *will be merciful* **shall kapar/atone** unto his *land* **soil**,
and to his people.
44 And *Moses* **Mosheh** came and *spake* **worded**
all the words of this song in the ears of the people,
he, and *Hoshea* **Yah Shua** the son of Nun.
45 And *Moses* **Mosheh**
made an end of speaking **finished wording** all these words
to all *Israel* **Yisra El**:
46 And he said unto them,
Set your hearts unto all the words
which I *testify* **witness** among you this day,
which ye shall *command* **misvah** your *children* **sons**
to *observe* **guard** to *do* **work**,
all the words of this *law* **torah**.
47 For it is not a vain *thing* **word** for you;
because it is your life:
and through this *thing* **word**
ye shall prolong your days in the *land* **soil**,
whither ye *go* **pass** over *Jordan* **Yarden** to possess it.

MOSHEH TO ASCEND MOUNT NEBO

48 And *the LORD spake* **Yah Veh worded**
unto *Moses* **Mosheh** that selfsame day, saying,
49 *Get thee up* **Ascend** into this mountain Abarim,
unto mount Nebo, which is in the land of Moab,
that is over against Jericho **at the face of Yericho**;
and *behold* **see** the land of *Canaan* **Kenaan**,
which I give unto the *children* **sons** of *Israel* **Yisra El**
for a possession:
50 And die in the mount whither thou *goest up* **ascendest**,
and be gathered unto thy people;
as *Aaron* **Aharon** thy brother died in mount Hor,
and was gathered unto his people:
51 Because ye *trespassed* **treasoned** against me
among the *children* **sons** of *Israel* **Yisra El**
at the waters of *Meribah—Kadesh* **Strife at Qadesh**,
in the wilderness of *Zin* **Sin**;
because ye *sanctified* **hallowed** me not

in the midst of the *children* **sons** of *Israel* **Yisra El**.
52 Yet thou shalt see the land before thee;
but thou shalt not go thither unto the land
which I give the *children* **sons** of *Israel* **Yisra El**.

MOSHEH'S BLESSINGS ON THE SONS OF YISRA EL

33 And this is the blessing,
wherewith *Moses* **Mosheh** the man of *God* **Elohim**
blessed the *children* **sons** of *Israel* **Yisra El**
before **at the face of** his death.
2 And he said, *the LORD* **Yah Veh** came from *Sinai* **Sinay**,
and rose up from Seir unto them;
he shined forth from mount Paran,
and he came with *ten thousands* **myriads** of *saints* **holy**:
from his right *hand*
went a *fiery law* **decree of fire** for them.
3 Yea, he *loved* **cherished** the people;
all his *saints* **holy** are in thy hand:
and they *sat down* **camped** at thy feet;
every one shall *receive* **bear** of thy words.
4 *Moses commanded* **Mosheh misvahed** us a *law* **torah**,
even the *inheritance* **possession**
of the congregation of *Jacob* **Yaaqov**.
5 And he was *king* **sovereign** in *Jeshurun* **Yeshurun**,
when the heads of the people
and the *tribes* **scions** of *Israel* **Yisra El**
were gathered *together*.
6 Let *Reuben* **Reu Ben** *live*, and not die;
and let *not* his men be *few* **a number**.
7 And this is *the blessing of Judah* **Yah Hudah**:
and he said, Hear, *LORD* **O Yah Veh**,
the voice of *Judah* **Yah Hudah**,
and bring him unto his people:
let his hands be *sufficient* **great** for him;
and be thou an help to him from his *enemies* **tribulators**.
8 And of Levi he said,
Let thy Thummim and thy Urim
be with thy *holy one* **men of mercy**,
whom thou didst *prove* **test**
at *Massah* **Testing**,
and with whom thou didst strive
at the waters of *Meribah* **Strife**;
9 Who said unto his father and to his mother,
I have not seen him;
neither *did he acknowledge* **recognized he** his brethren,
nor knew his own *children* **sons**:
for they have *observed* **guarded** thy *word* **sayings**,
and *kept* **guarded** thy covenant.
10 They shall *teach* **point out**
Jacob **to Yaaqov** thy judgments,
and *Israel* **Yisra El** thy *law* **torah**:
they shall put incense *before thee* **at thy nostrils**,
and whole burnt sacrifice **totally**
upon *thine* **thy sacrifice** altar.
11 Bless, *LORD* **Yah Veh**, his *substance* **valour**,
and *accept the work* **be pleased in the deeds** of his hands;
smite **strike** *through* the loins of them that rise against him,
and of them that hate him,
that they rise not **from rising** again.
12 And of *Benjamin* **Ben Yamin** he said,
The beloved of *the LORD* **Yah Veh**
shall *dwell in safety* **tabernacle confidently** by him;
and *the Lord* shall cover him all the day long,
and he shall *dwell* **tabernacle** between his shoulders.
13 And of *Joseph* **Yoseph** he said,
Blessed of *the LORD* **Yah Veh** be his land,
for the precious *things* of *heaven* **the heavens**,
for the dew,
and for the *deep* **abyss** that *coucheth* **croucheth** beneath,
14 And for the precious *fruits* **produce**
brought forth by the sun,
and for the precious *things*
put **thrust** forth by the moon,
15 And for the *chief things* **tops**
of the ancient mountains,
and for the precious *things*
of the *lasting* **eternal** hills,
16 And for the precious *things*
of the earth and fulness thereof,
and for the *good will* **pleasure** of him
that *dwelt* **tabernacleth** in the bush:
let *the blessing* it come upon the head of *Joseph* **Yoseph**,
and upon the *top of the head* **scalp** of him
that was *separated* **a Separatist** from his brethren.
17 His *glory* **majesty** is like the firstling of his *bullock* **ox**,
and his horns are like the horns of *unicorns* **a reem**:
with them he shall *push* **butt** the people together
to the *ends* **finality** of the earth:
and they are
the *ten thousands* **myriads** of *Ephraim* **Ephrayim**,
and they are
the thousands of *Manasseh* **Menash Sheh**.
18 And of Zebulun he said,
Rejoice **Cheer**, Zebulun, in thy going out;
and, *Issachar* **Yissachar**, in thy tents.
19 They shall call the people unto the mountain;
there they shall
offer **sacrifice** sacrifices of *righteousness* **justness**:
for they shall suck of the *abundance* **bounty** of the seas,
and of *treasures hid* **that covered and buried** in the sand.
20 And of Gad he said,
Blessed be he that *enlargeth* **broadeneth** Gad:
he *dwelleth* **tabernacleth** as a *roaring* lion,
and teareth the arm
with the crown of the head — **yea the scalp**.
21 And he *provided* **seeth to** the first *part* for himself,
because there,
in *a portion* **an allotment** of the *lawgiver* **statute setter**,
was he *seated* **covered**;
and he came with the heads of the people,
he *executed* **worked**
the *justice* **justness** of *the LORD* **Yah Veh**,
and his judgments with *Israel* **Yisra El**.
22 And of Dan he said,
Dan is a lion's whelp: he shall leap from Bashan.
23 And of Naphtali he said,
O Naphtali, satisfied with *favour* **pleasure**,
and full with the blessing of *the LORD* **Yah Veh**:
possess thou the *west* **seaward** and the south.
24 And of Asher he said,
Let Asher be blessed with *children* **sons**;
let him be *acceptable* **pleasing** to his brethren,
and let him dip his foot in oil.
25 Thy shoes shall be iron and *brass* **copper**;
and as thy days, *so* shall thy strength be.
26 There is none like
unto the *God* **El** of *Jeshurun* **Yeshurun**,
who rideth upon the *heaven* **heavens** in thy help,
and in his *excellency* **pomp** on the *sky* **vapour**.
27 The *eternal God* **ancient Elohim**
is thy *refuge* **habitation**,
and underneath are the *everlasting* **eternal** arms:
and he shall *thrust out* **expel** the enemy
from *before thee* **thy face**;
and shall say, *Destroy them* **Desolate**.
28 *Israel* **Yisra El** then
shall *dwell in safety* **tabernacle confidently** alone:
the fountain of *Jacob* **Yaaqov**
shall be upon a land of *corn* **crop** and *wine* **juice**;
also his heavens shall *drop down* **drip** dew.
29 *Happy* **Blithe** art thou, O *Israel* **Yisra El**:
who is like unto thee,
O people saved by *the LORD* **Yah Veh**,
the *shield* **buckler** of thy help,
and who is the sword of thy *excellency* **pomp**!
and thine enemies
shall be *found liars unto* **disowned before** thee;
and thou shalt tread upon their *high places* **bamahs**.

MOSHEH ASCENDS MOUNT NEBO

34 And *Moses* **Mosheh**
went up **ascended** from the plains of Moab
unto the mountain of Nebo, to the top of Pisgah,
that is over against Jericho **at the face of Yericho**.
And *the LORD* **Yah Veh**
shewed him **had him see** all the land of *Gilead* **Gilad**,
unto Dan,
2 And all Naphtali, and the land of *Ephraim* **Ephrayim**,
and *Manasseh* **Menash Sheh**,
and all the land of *Judah* **Yah Hudah**,
unto the *utmost* **latter** sea,
3 And the south,

and the *plain* **environs** of the valley of *Jericho* **Yericho**,
the city of palm trees **Ir Hat Temarim**, unto *Zoar* **Soar**.
4 And *the LORD* **Yah Veh** said unto him,
This is the land which I *sware* **oathed** unto Abraham,
unto *Isaac* **Yischaq**, and unto *Jacob* **Yaaqov**,
saying, I *will* **shall** give it unto thy seed:
I have caused thee to see it with thine eyes,
but thou shalt not *go* **pass** over thither.

THE DEATH OF MOSHEH

5 So *Moses* **Mosheh** the servant of *the LORD* **Yah Veh**
died there in the land of Moab,
according to the *word* **mouth** of *the LORD* **Yah Veh**.
6 And he *buried* **entombed** him
in a valley in the land of Moab,
over against Bethpeor **in front of Beth Peor**:
but no man knoweth of his *sepulchre* **tomb** unto this day.
7 And *Moses* **Mosheh**
was **a son of** an hundred and twenty years *old*
when he died **at his death**:
his eye was not *dim* **weak**,
nor his *natural force abated* **freshness fled**.
8 And the *children* **sons** of *Israel* **Yisra El**
wept for *Moses* **Mosheh** in the plains of Moab thirty days:
so the days of weeping and mourning for *Moses* **Mosheh**
were *ended* **consumated**.
9 And *Joshua* **Yah Shua** the son of Nun
was full of the spirit of wisdom;
for *Moses* **Mosheh** had *laid* **propped** his hands upon him:
and the *children* **sons** of *Israel* **Yisra El**
hearkened unto him,
and *did* **worked** as *the LORD* **Yah Veh**
commanded Moses **misvahed Mosheh**.
10 And there arose not a prophet *since* **again**
in *Israel* **Yisra El** like unto *Moses* **Mosheh**,
whom *the LORD* **Yah Veh** knew face to face,
11 In all the signs and the *wonders* **omens**,
which *the LORD* **Yah Veh** sent him to *do* **work**
in the land of *Egypt* **Misrayim** to *Pharaoh* **Paroh**,
and to all his servants, and to all his land,
12 And in all that *mighty* **strong** hand,
and in all the great *terror* **awesomeness**
which *Moses shewed* **Mosheh worked**
in the *sight* **eyes** of all *Israel* **Yisra El**.

KEY TO INTERPRETING THE EXEGESES:
King James text is in regular type;
Text under exegeses is in oblique type;
Text of exegeses is in bold type.

YAH VEH MISVAHS YAH SHUA

1 Now after the death of *Moses* **Mosheh**
the servant of *the LORD* **Yah Veh**
it *came to pass* **became**,
that *the LORD spake* **Yah Veh said** unto *Joshua* **Yah Shua**
the son of Nun, Moses' minister, saying,
2 *Moses* **Mosheh** my servant *is dead* **died**;
now therefore arise, *go* **pass** over this *Jordan* **Yarden**,
thou, and all this people,
unto the land which I do give to them,
even to the *children* **sons** of *Israel* **Yisra El**.
3 Every place that the sole of your foot shall tread *upon*,
that have I given unto you,
as I *said* **worded** unto *Moses* **Mosheh**.
4 From the wilderness and this Lebanon
even unto the great river,
the river Euphrates, all the land of the *Hittites* **Hethiy**,
and unto the great sea
toward the *going down* **entry** of the sun,
shall be your *coast* **border**.
5 There shall not any man be able to stand
before thee **at thy face** all the days of thy life:
as I was with *Moses* **Mosheh**, so I *will* **shall** be with thee:
I will **shall** not *fail* **let** thee **down**, nor forsake thee.
6 Be *strong* **strengthened**
and *of a good courage* **encouraged**:
for unto this people
shalt thou divide for an inheritance the land,
which I *sware* **oathed** unto their fathers to give them.
7 Only be thou *strong* **strengthened**
and *very courageous* **mightily encouraged**,
that thou mayest *observe* **guard** to *do* **work**
according to all the *law* **torah**,
which *Moses* **Mosheh** my servant
commanded **misvahed** thee:
turn not **aside** from it to the right *hand* or to the left,
that thou mayest *prosper* **comprehend**
whithersoever thou goest.
8 *This book* **The scroll** of *the law* **this torah**
shall not depart out of thy mouth;
but thou shalt meditate therein **by** day and **by** night,
that thou mayest *observe* **guard** to *do* **work**
according to all that is *written* **inscribed** therein:
for then thou shalt *make thy way prosperous* **prosper**,
and then thou shalt *have good success* **comprehend**.
9 Have not I *commanded* **misvahed** thee?
Be *strong* **strengthened**
and *of a good courage* **encouraged**;
be not *afraid* **awed**, neither be thou *dismayed* **terrified**:
for *the LORD* **Yah Veh** thy *God* **Elohim** is with thee
whithersoever thou goest.

YAH SHUA MISVAHS

10 Then *Joshua* **Yah Shua**
commanded **misvahed** the officers of the people, saying,
11 Pass *through* **over midst** the *host* **camp**,
and *command* **misvah** the people, saying,
Prepare you *victuals* **hunt**;
for within three days
ye shall pass over this *Jordan* **Yarden**,
to go in to possess the land,
which *the LORD* **Yah Veh** your *God* **Elohim**
giveth you to possess it.
12 And to the *Reubenites* **Reu Beniy**,
and to the *Gadites* **Gadiy**,
and to half the *tribe* **scion** of *Manasseh* **Menash Sheh**,
spake Joshua **said Yah Shua**, saying,
13 Remember the word which *Moses* **Mosheh**
the servant of *the LORD* **Yah Veh**
commanded **misvahed** you, saying,
The LORD **Yah Veh** your *God* **Elohim**
hath *given you rest* **rested thee**,
and hath given you this land.
14 Your *wives* **women**, your *little ones* **toddlers**,
and your *cattle* **chattel**, shall *remain* **settle** in the land
which *Moses* **Mosheh** gave you
on this side *Jordan* **Yarden**;
but ye shall pass *before* **at the face of** your brethren
armed **in ranks of five**,
all the mighty *men* of valour, and help them;
15 Until *the LORD* **Yah Veh**
have given **hath rested** your brethren *rest*,
as *he hath given* you,
and they also have possessed the land
which *the LORD* **Yah Veh** your *God* **Elohim** giveth them:
then ye shall return unto the land of your possession,
and *enjoy* **possess** it,
which *Moses* **Mosheh**, *the LORD'S* **Yah Veh's** servant
gave you on this side *Jordan* **Yarden**
toward the sunrising **from the rising sun**.
16 And they answered *Joshua* **Yah Shua**, saying,
All that thou *commandest* **misvahest** us
we *will do* **shall work**,
and whithersoever thou sendest us, we *will* **shall** go.
17 According as we hearkened unto *Moses* **Mosheh**
in all *things*,
so *will* **shall** we hearken unto thee:
only *the LORD* **Yah Veh** thy *God* **Elohim** be with thee,
as he was with *Moses* **Mosheh**.
18 *Whosoever he be* **Every man** that doth rebel
against thy *commandment* **mouth**,
and *will* **shall** not hearken unto thy words
in all that thou *commandest* **misvahest** him,
he shall be *put to death* **deathified**:
only be *strong* **strengthend**
and *of a good courage* **encouraged**.

RACHAB PROTECTS THE SPIES

2 And *Joshua* **Yah Shua** the son of Nun
sent out of Shittim
two men to spy *secretly* **quietly**, saying,
Go *view* **see** the land, even *Jericho* **Yericho**.
And they went,
and came into *an harlot's* **a woman whore's** house,
named *Rahab* **Rachab**, and *lodged* **lay down** there.
2 And it was *told* **said**
to the *king* **sovereign** of *Jericho* **Yericho**, saying,
Behold, there came men in hither to night
of the *children* **sons** of *Israel* **Yisra El**
to *search out* **explore** the *country* **land**.
3 And the *king* **sovereign** of *Jericho* **Yericho**
sent unto *Rahab* **Rachab**, saying,
Bring forth the men that are come to thee,
which are entered into thine house:
for they be come
to *search out* **explore** all the *country* **land**.
4 And the woman took the two men, and hid them,
and said thus,
There came men unto me,
but I *wist* **knew** not whence they were:
5 And it *came to pass* **became**,
about the time of **at the** shutting of the *gate* **portal**,
when it was dark, that the men went out:
whither the men went I *wot* **know** not:
pursue after them *quickly* **hastily**;
for ye shall overtake them.
6 But she had *brought* **ascended** them *up*
to the roof of the house,
and hid them with the *stalks* **timbers** of flax,
which she had *laid in order* **aligned** upon the roof.
7 And the men pursued after them
the way to *Jordan* **Yarden** unto the *fords* **passages**:
and as soon as they which pursued after them
were gone out,
they shut the *gate* **portal**.
8 And before they were laid down,
she *came up* **ascended** unto them upon the roof;
9 And she said unto the men,
I know that *the LORD* **Yah Veh** hath given you the land,
and that your terror is fallen upon us,
and that all the *inhabitants* **settlers** of the land
faint because of you **melt at thy face**.
10 For we have heard how *the LORD* **Yah Veh**
dried up **withered** the water of the *Red* **Reed** sea
for you **at thy face**,
when ye *came* **went** out of *Egypt* **Misrayim**;
and what ye *did* **worked**
unto the two *kings* **sovereigns** of the *Amorites* **Emoriy**,

that were on the other side *Jordan* **Yarden**,
Sihon **Sichon** and Og, whom ye *utterly destroyed* **devoted**.
1 And as soon as we had heard *these things*,
our hearts did melt,
neither did there *remain* **rise up** any more
courage **spirit/wind** in any man,
because of you **at thy face**:
for *the LORD* **Yah Veh** your *God* **Elohim**,
he is *God* **Elohim** in *heaven* **the heavens** above,
and in earth beneath.
12 Now therefore, I *pray* **beseech** you,
swear **oath** unto me by *the LORD* **Yah Veh**,
since **surely** I have *shewed* **worked** you *kindness* **mercy**,
that ye *will* **shall** also *shew kindness* **work mercy**
unto my father's house,
and give me a true *token* **sign**:
13 And that ye *will* **shall** save alive
my father, and my mother,
and my brethren, and my sisters, and all that they have,
and *deliver* **rescue** our *lives* **souls** from death.
14 And the men *answered* **said to** her,
Our *life for your's* **soul instead of your's to die**,
if ye *utter* **tell** not this our *business* **word**.
And it shall *be* **give**,
when *the LORD* **Yah Veh** hath given us the land,
that we *will deal kindly* **shall work mercifully**
and truly with thee.
15 Then she *let* **descended** them *down* by a cord
through the window:
for her house was upon the *town* wall,
and she *dwelt* **settled** upon the wall.
16 And she said unto them, *Get you* **Go** to the mountain,
lest the pursuers meet you;
and hide yourselves there three days,
until the pursuers be returned:
and afterward may ye go your way.
17 And the men said unto her,
We *will* **shall** be *blameless* **innocent** of this thine oath
which thou hast made us *swear* **oath**.
18 Behold, when we come into the land,
thou shalt bind this *line* **cord** of scarlet thread
in the window
by which thou *didst let* **descended** us *down by*:
and thou shalt *bring* **gather** thy father, and thy mother,
and thy brethren, and all thy father's household,
home unto thee **unto thy house**.
19 And it shall *be* **become**,
that whosoever
shall go out of the doors of thy house
into the street **outside**,
his blood shall be upon his head,
and we *will* **shall** be *guiltless* **innocent**:
and whosoever shall be with thee in the house,
his blood shall be on our head, if any hand be upon him.
20 And if thou *utter* **tell** this our *business* **word**,
then we *will* **shall** be *quit* **innocent** of thine oath
which thou hast made us to *swear* **oath**.
21 And she said, According unto your words, so be it.
And she sent them away, and they *departed* **went**:
and she bound the scarlet *line* **cord** in the window.
22 And they went, and came unto the mountain,
and *abode* **settled** there three days,
until the pursuers *were* returned:
and the pursuers sought them throughout all the way,
but found them not.
23 So the two men returned,
and descended from the mountain,
and passed over,
and came to *Joshua* **Yah Shua** the son of Nun,
and *told* **scribed** him all *things* that *befell* **found** them:
24 And they said unto *Joshua* **Yah Shua**,
Truly the LORD **Surely Yah Veh**
hath *delivered* **given** into our hands all the land;
for even all the *inhabitants* **settlers** of the *country* **land**
do faint because of us **melt at our face**.

SONS OF YISRA EL PASS OVER YARDEN

3 And *Joshua rose* **Yah Shua started** early in the morning;
and they *removed* **pulled stakes** from Shittim,
and came to *Jordan* **Yarden**,
he and all the *children* **sons** of *Israel* **Yisra El**,
and *lodged* **stayed overnight** there
before they passed over.
2 And it *came to pass* **became**,
after **at the end of** three days,
that the officers *went* **passed over**
through **midst** the *host* **camp**;
3 And they *commanded* **misvahed** the people, saying,
When ye see the ark of the covenant
of *the LORD* **Yah Veh** your *God* **Elohim**,
and the priests the *Levites* **Leviym** bearing it,
then ye shall *remove* **pull stakes** from your place,
and go after it.
4 Yet there shall be a *space* **distance** between you and it,
about two thousand cubits by measure:
come **approach** not *near* unto it,
that ye may know the way by which ye must go:
for ye have not passed this way
heretofore **three yesters ago**.
5 And *Joshua* **Yah Shua** said unto the people,
Sanctify **Hallow** yourselves:
for to morrow
the LORD will do wonders **Yah Veh shall work marvels**
among you.
6 And *Joshua spake* **Yah Shua said** unto the priests, saying,
Take up **Lift** the ark of the covenant,
and pass over *before* **at the face of** the people.
And they *took up* **lifted** the ark of the covenant,
and went *before* **at the face of** the people.
7 And *the LORD* **Yah Veh** said unto *Joshua* **Yah Shua**,
This day *will* **shall** I begin to *magnify* **greaten** thee
in the *sight* **eyes** of all *Israel* **Yisra El**,
that they may know that,
as I was with *Moses* **Mosheh**, so I *will* **shall** be with thee.
8 And thou shalt *command* **misvah** the priests
that bear the ark of the covenant, saying,
When ye are come
to the *brink* **edge** of the water of *Jordan* **Yarden**,
ye shall stand still in *Jordan* **Yarden**.
9 And *Joshua* **Yah Shua**
said unto the *children* **sons** of *Israel* **Yisra El**,
Come *hither* **near**, and hear the words
of *the LORD* **Yah Veh** your *God* **Elohim**.
10 And *Joshua* **Yah Shua** said,
Hereby ye shall know
that the living *God* **El** is among you,
and that **in dispossessing**,
he *will without fail drive out* **shall dispossess**
from *before you* **your face**
the *Canaanites* **Kenaaniy**, and the *Hittites* **Hethiy**,
and the *Hivites* **Hivviy**, and the *Perizzites* **Perizziy**,
and the *Girgashites* **Girgashiy**, and the *Amorites* **Emoriy**,
and the *Jebusites* **Yebusiy**.
11 Behold,
the ark of the covenant of *the Lord* **Adonay** of all the earth
passeth over *before you* **at thy face** into *Jordan* **Yarden**.
12 Now therefore take you twelve men
out of the *tribes* **scions** of *Israel* **Yisra El**,
out of every *tribe* **a scion one** man.
13 And it shall *come to pass* **become**,
as soon as the soles of the feet
of the priests that bear the ark of *the LORD* **Yah Veh**,
the Lord **Adonay** of all the earth,
shall rest in the waters of *Jordan* **Yarden**,
that the waters of *Jordan* **Yarden** shall be cut off
from – the waters that *come down* **descend** from above;
and they shall stand *upon an heap* – **one heap**.
14 And it *came to pass* **became**,
when the people *removed* **pulled stakes** from their tents,
to pass over *Jordan* **Yarden**,
and the priests bearing the ark of the covenant
before **at the face of** the people;
15 And as they that bare the ark
were come unto *Jordan* **Yarden**,
and the feet of the priests that bare the ark
were dipped in the *brim* **edge** of the water,
(for *Jordan overfloweth* **Yarden filleth over** all his banks
all the *time* **day** of harvest,)
16 That the waters which came down from above
stood and rose *up upon an heap* – **one heap**
very far **mighty far removed** from the city Adam,

that is beside *Zaretan* **Sarethan**:
and those that *came down* **descended**
toward the sea of the plain, *even* the salt sea,
failed **consumated**, and were cut off:
and the people passed over right against *Jericho* **Yericho**.
17 And the priests
that bare the ark of the covenant of *the LORD* **Yah Veh**
stood *firm* **established** on *dry ground* **a parched area**
in the midst of *Jordan* **Yarden**,
and all the *Israelites* **Yisra Eliy** passed over
on *dry ground* **a parched area**,
until all the *people* **goyim**
were *passed clean* **finished passing**
over *Jordan* **Yarden**.

MEMORIAL STONES

4 And it *came to pass* **became**,
when all the *people* **goyim**
were *clean passed* **finished passing**
over *Jordan* **Yarden**,
that *the LORD* **Yah Veh**
spake **said** unto *Joshua* **Yah Shua**, saying,
2 Take you twelve men out of the people,
out of every *tribe a* **scion one** man,
3 And *command* **misvah** ye them, saying,
Take **Lift** you hence out of the midst of *Jordan* **Yarden**,
out of the place
where the priests' feet stood *firm* **established**,
twelve stones,
and ye shall *carry* **pass** them over with you,
and leave them in the *lodging place* **lodge**,
where ye shall *lodge* **stay overnight** this night.
4 Then *Joshua* **Yah Shua** called the twelve men,
whom he had prepared
of the *children* **sons** of *Israel* **Yisra El**,
out of every *tribe a* **scion one** man:
5 And *Joshua* **Yah Shua** said unto them,
Pass over *before* **at the face of** the ark
of *the LORD* **Yah Veh** your *God* **Elohim**
into the midst of *Jordan* **Yarden**,
and *take you up* **lift** every man of you
a **one** stone upon his shoulder,
according unto the number of the *tribes* **scions**
of the *children* **sons** of *Israel* **Yisra El**:
6 That this may be a sign among you,
that when your *children* **sons** ask *their fathers*
in time to come **to morrow**, saying,
What mean ye by these stones?
7 Then ye shall *answer* **say to** them,
That the waters of *Jordan* **Yarden** were cut off
before **at the face of** the ark of the covenant
of *the LORD* **Yah Veh**;
when it passed over *Jordan* **Yarden**,
the waters of *Jordan* **Yarden** were cut off:
and these stones shall be for a memorial
unto the *children* **sons** of *Israel for ever* **Yisra El eternally**.
8 And the *children* **sons** of *Israel did so* **Yisra El worked**
as *Joshua commanded* **Yah Shua misvahed**,
and *took up* **lifted** twelve stones
out of the midst of *Jordan* **Yarden**,
as *the LORD spake* **Yah Veh worded**
unto *Joshua* **Yah Shua**,
according to the number of the *tribes* **scions**
of the *children* **sons** of *Israel* **Yisra El**,
and *carried* **passed** them over with them
unto the place where they lodged,
and *laid them down* **set them** there.
9 And *Joshua set up* **Yah Shua raised** twelve stones
in the midst of *Jordan* **Yarden**,
in the place where the feet of the priests
which bare the ark of the covenant stood:
and they are there unto this day.
10 For the priests which bare the ark
stood in the midst of *Jordan* **Yarden**,
until every *thing* **word** was finished
that *the LORD* **Yah Veh**
commanded Joshua **misvahed Yah Shua**
to *speak* **word** unto the people,
according to all that
Moses commanded Joshua **Mosheh misvahed Yah Shua**:
and the people hasted and passed over.
11 And it *came to pass* **became**,
when all the people
were *clean passed* **finished passing** over,
that the ark of *the LORD* **Yah Veh** passed over,
and the priests, *in the presence* **at the face** of the people.
12 And the *children* **sons** of *Reuben* **Reu Ben**,
and the *children* **sons** of Gad,
and half the *tribe* **scion** of *Manasseh* **Menash Sheh**,
passed over *armed* **in ranks of five**
before **at the face of** the *children* **sons** of *Israel* **Yisra El**,
as *Moses spake* **Mosheh worded** unto them:
13 About forty thousand
prepared **equipped** for *war* **hostility**
passed over *before the LORD* **at the face of Yah Veh**
unto *battle* **war**, to the plains of *Jericho* **Yericho**.
14 On that day
the LORD magnified Joshua **Yah Veh greatened Yah Shua**
in the *sight* **eyes** of all *Israel* **Yisra El**;
and they *feared* **awed** him,
as they *feared Moses* **awed Mosheh**,
all the days of his life.
15 And *the LORD* **Yah Veh**
spake **said** unto *Joshua* **Yah Shua**, saying,
16 *Command* **Misvah** the priests
that bear the ark of the *testimony* **witness**,
that they *come up* **ascend** out of *Jordan* **Yarden**.
17 *Joshua* **Yah Shua** therefore
commanded **misvahed** the priests, saying,
Come **Ascend** ye *up* out of *Jordan* **Yarden**.
18 And it *came to pass* **became**,
when the priests
that bare the ark of the covenant of *the LORD* **Yah Veh**
were *come up* **ascended**
out of the midst of *Jordan* **Yarden**,
and the soles of the priests' feet
were *lifted up* **torn** unto the *dry land* **parched area**,
that the waters of *Jordan* **Yarden**
returned unto their place,
and *flowed* **went** over all his banks,
as *they did before* **three yesters ago**.
19 And the people *came up* **ascended** out of *Jordan* **Yarden**
on the tenth *day* of the first month,
and encamped in Gilgal,
in the east border **from the rising** of *Jericho* **Yericho**.
20 And those twelve stones,
which they took out of *Jordan* **Yarden**,
did Joshua pitch **Yah Shua raised** in Gilgal.
21 And he *spake* **said** unto
the *children* **sons** of *Israel* **Yisra El**, saying,
When your *children* **sons** shall ask their fathers
in time to come **to morrow**, saying,
What mean these stones?
22 Then ye shall let your *children* **sons** know, saying,
Israel came **Yisra El passed** over this *Jordan* **Yarden**
on dry *land*.
23 For *the LORD* **Yah Veh** your *God* **Elohim**
dried up **withered** the waters of *Jordan* **Yarden**
from *before you* **your face**, until ye were passed over,
as *the LORD* **Yah Veh** your *God* **Elohim**
did **worked** to the *Red* **Reed** sea,
which he *dried up* **withered** from *before us* **our face**,
until we *were gone* **passed** over:
24 That all the people of the earth might know
the hand of *the LORD* **Yah Veh**, that it is *mighty* **strong**:
that ye might *fear* **awe**
the LORD **Yah Veh** your *God for ever* **Elohim all days**.
5 And it *came to pass* **became**,
when all the *kings* **sovereigns** of the *Amorites* **Emoriy**,
which were
on the side of *Jordan westward* **Yarden seaward**,
and all the *kings* **sovereigns** of the *Canaanites* **Kenaaniy**,
which were by the sea,
heard that *the LORD* **Yah Veh**
had *dried up* **withered** the waters of *Jordan* **Yarden**
from *before* **the face of** the *children* **sons** of *Israel* **Yisra El**,
until we were passed over,
that their heart melted,
neither was there *spirit* **spirit/wind** in them any more,
because **at the face** of the *children* **sons** of *Israel* **Yisra El**.

SONS OF YISRA EL CIRCUMCISED

2 At that time
the LORD **Yah Veh** said unto *Joshua* **Yah Shua**,
Make **Work** thee *sharp knives* **swords of rocks**,
and *circumcise again* **return and circumcise**
the *children* **sons** of *Israel* **Yisra El** the second time.
3 And *Joshua* **Yah Shua**
made **worked** him *sharp knives* **swords of rocks**,
and circumcised the *children* **sons** of *Israel* **Yisra El**
at the hill of the foreskins
at Gibeah Haaraloth/Hill of the Foreskins.
4 And this is the *cause* **word**
why *Joshua* **Yah Shua** did circumcise:
All the people that *came* **went** out of *Egypt* **Misrayim**,
that were males, *even* all the men of war,
died in the wilderness by the way,
after they *came* **went** out of *Egypt* **Misrayim**.
5 *Now* **Surely** all the people that *came out* **went**
were circumcised:
but all the people that were born in the wilderness
by the way
as they *came forth* **went** out of *Egypt* **Misrayim**,
them they had not circumcised.
6 For the *children* **sons** of *Israel* **Yisra El**
walked forty years in the wilderness,
till all the *people* **goyim** that were men of war,
which *came* **went** out of *Egypt* **Misrayim**, were consumed,
because they *obeyed* **hearkened** not
unto the voice of *the LORD* **Yah Veh**:
unto whom *the LORD sware* **Yah Veh oathed**
that he *would* **shall** not *shew* **have** them **see** the land,
which *the LORD sware* **Yah Veh oathed** unto their fathers
that he *would* **shall** give us,
a land that floweth with milk and honey.
7 And their *children* **sons**,
whom he raised up in their stead,
them *Joshua* **Yah Shua** circumcised:
for they were uncircumcised,
because they had not circumcised them by the way.
8 And it *came to pass* **became**,
when they had *done* **consumated**
circumcising all the *people* **goyim**,
that they *abode* **settled** in their places in the camp,
till they *were whole* **revived**.
9 And *the LORD* **Yah Veh** said unto *Joshua* **Yah Shua**,
This day have I rolled away
the reproach of *Egypt* **Misrayim** from off you.
Wherefore the name of the place is called Gilgal
unto this day.

THE MANNA CEASES

10 And the *children* **sons** of *Israel* **Yisra El**
encamped in Gilgal,
and *kept* **worked** the *passover* **pasach**
on the fourteenth day of the month at *even* **evening**
in the plains of *Jericho* **Yericho**.
11 And they did eat of the *old corn* **leftovers** of the land
on the morrow after the *passover* **pasach**,
unleavened cakes **matsahs**,
and *parched corn* **scorched** in the selfsame day.
12 And the manna ceased on the morrow
after they had eaten of the *old corn* **leftovers** of the land;
neither had the *children* **sons** of *Israel* **Yisra El** manna
any more;
but they did eat of the *fruit* **produce**
of the land of *Canaan* **Kenaan** that year.

YERICHO FALLS

13 And it *came to pass* **became**,
when *Joshua* **Yah Shua** was by *Jericho* **Yericho**,
that he lifted up his eyes and *looked* **saw**, and, behold,
there stood a man over against him
with his sword drawn in his hand:
and *Joshua* **Yah Shua** went unto him, and said unto him,
Art thou for us, or for our *adversaries* **tribulators**?
14 And he said, Nay; but as *captain* **governor**
of *the host of the LORD* **Yah Veh Sabaoth** am I now come.
And *Joshua* **Yah Shua** fell on his face to the earth,
and *did worship* **prostrated**, and said unto him,
What *saith* **wordeth** my *lord* **adoni** unto his servant?
15 And the *captain* **governor**
of *the LORD'S host* **Yah Veh Sabaoth**
said unto *Joshua* **Yah Shua**,
Loose **Pluck** thy shoe from off thy foot;
for the place whereon thou standest is holy.
And *Joshua did so* **Yah Shua worked thus**.
6 *Now Jericho* **In shutting, Yericho** was *straitly* shut up
because **from the face**
of the *children* **sons** of *Israel* **Yisra El**:
none went out, and none came in.
2 And *the LORD* **Yah Veh** said unto *Joshua* **Yah Shua**,
See, I have given into thine hand *Jericho* **Yericho**,
and the *king* **sovereign** thereof,
and the mighty *men* of valour.
3 And ye shall *compass* **surround** the city,
all ye men of war,
and go round about the city *once* **one time**.
Thus shalt thou *do* **work** six days.
4 And seven priests shall bear *before* **at the face of** the ark
seven trumpets of *rams' horns* **jubile**:
and the seventh day
ye shall *compass* **surround** the city seven times,
and the priests shall *blow* **blast** with the trumpets.
5 And it shall *come to pass* **become**,
that when they
make a long blast with the ram's **draw on the jubile** horn,
and when ye hear the *sound* **voice** of the trumpet,
all the people shall shout with a great *shout* **shouting**;
and the wall of the city shall fall *down flat* **under it**,
and the people shall ascend *up*
every man straight before him.
6 And *Joshua* **Yah Shua** the son of Nun called the priests,
and said unto them, *Take up* **Lift** the ark of the covenant,
and let seven priests
bear seven trumpets of *rams' horns* **jubile**
before **at the face of** the ark of *the LORD* **Yah Veh**.
7 And he said unto the people,
Pass on, and *compass* **surround** the city,
and let him that is *armed* **equipped** pass on
before **at the face of** the ark of *the LORD* **Yah Veh**.
8 And it *came to pass* **became**,
when *Joshua had spoken* **Yah Shua said** unto the people,
that the seven priests
bearing the seven trumpets of *rams' horns* **jubile**
passed on *before the LORD* **at the face of Yah Veh**,
and *blew* **blast** with the trumpets:
and the ark of the covenant of *the LORD* **Yah Veh**
followed **walked after** them.
9 And the *armed men went* **equipped walked**
before **at the face of** the priests
that *blew* **blast** with the trumpets,
and the *rereward came* **gathering walked** after the ark,
the priests going on,
and *blowing* **blasting** with the trumpets.
10 And *Joshua* **Yah Shua**
had *commanded* **misvahed** the people, saying,
Ye shall not shout,
nor *make any noise with* **let** your voice **be heard**,
neither shall any word *proceed* **go** out of your mouth,
until the day I *bid you* **say** shout; then shall ye shout.
11 So the ark of *the LORD* **Yah Veh**
compassed **surrounded** the city,
going about it *once* **one time**:
and they came into the camp,
and *lodged* **stayed overnight** in the camp.
12 And *Joshua rose* **Yah Shua started** early in the morning,
and the priests
took up **lifted** the ark of *the LORD* **Yah Veh**.
13 And seven priests
bearing seven trumpets of *rams' horns* **jubile**
before **at the face of** the ark of *the LORD* **Yah Veh**
went on continually **in walking, walked**,
and *blew* **blast** with the trumpets:
and the *armed men* **equipped** went *before* **from their face**;
but the *rereward* **gathering**
came after the ark of *the LORD* **Yah Veh**,
the priests going on,
and *blowing* **blasting** with the trumpets.
14 And the second day
they *compassed* **surrounded** the city *once* **one time**,
and returned into the camp:
so they *did* **worked** six days.

15 And it *came to pass* **became,** on the seventh day,
that they *rose* **started** early
about the *dawning* **ascending** of *the day* **dawn,**
and *compassed* **surrounded** the city
after the same *manner* **judgment** seven times:
only on that day
they *compassed* **surrounded** the city seven times.
16 And it *came to pass* **became,** at the seventh time,
when the priests *blew* **blast** with the trumpets,
Joshua **Yah Shua** said unto the people, Shout;
for *the LORD* **Yah Veh** hath given you the city.
17 And the city shall *be accursed* **become devoted,**
even it, and all that are therein, to *the LORD* **Yah Veh**:
only *Rahab* **Rachab** the *harlot* **whore** shall live,
she and all that are with her in the house,
because she hid the *messengers* **angels** that we sent.
18 And ye, *in any wise keep* **only guard** *yourselves*
from the *accursed thing* **devoted,**
lest ye *make yourselves accursed* **become devoted,**
when ye take of the *accursed thing* **devotement,**
and *make* **set** the camp of *Israel* **Yisra El**
a *curse* **devotement**, and trouble it.
19 But all the silver, and gold,
and *vessels* **instruments** of *brass* **copper** and iron,
are *consecrated* **holy** unto *the LORD* **Yah Veh**:
they shall come into the treasury of *the LORD* **Yah Veh.**
20 So the people shouted
when the priests blew **and blast** with the trumpets:
and it *came to pass* **became,**
when the people heard the *sound* **voice** of the trumpet,
and the people shouted with a great *shout* **shouting,**
that the wall fell *down* flat,
so that the people *went up* **ascended** into the city,
every man straight before him,
and they took **captured** the city.
21 And they *utterly destroyed* **devoted**
all that was in the city,
both man and woman,
young and old **from lad and to old man,**
and ox, and *sheep* **lamb**, and *ass* **he burro,**
with the *edge* **mouth** of the sword.
22 But *Joshua* **Yah Shua** had said
unto the two men that had spied out the *country* **land,**
Go into the *harlot's* **woman's** house,
and bring out thence the woman, and all that she hath,
as ye *sware* **oathed** unto her.
23 And the *young men* **lads** that were spies went in,
and brought out *Rahab* **Rachab,**
and her father, and her mother,
and her brethren, and all that she had;
and they brought out all her *kindred* **family,**
and left them without the camp of *Israel* **Yisra El.**
24 And they burnt the city with fire,
and all that was therein:
only the silver, and the gold,
and the *vessels* **instruments** of *brass* **copper** and of iron,
they *put* **gave** into the treasury
of the house of *the LORD* **Yah Veh.**
25 And *Joshua* **Yah Shua**
saved *Rahab* **Rachab** the *harlot* **whore** alive,
and her father's household, and all that she had;
and she *dwelleth in Israel* **settleth within Yisra El**
even unto this day;
because she hid the *messengers* **angels,**
which *Joshua* **Yah Shua** sent to spy out *Jericho* **Yericho.**
26 And *Joshua adjured* **Yah Shua oathed** them at that time,
saying,
Cursed be the man
before the LORD **from the face of Yah Veh,**
that riseth up and buildeth this city *Jericho* **Yericho**:
he shall lay the foundation thereof in his firstborn,
and in his *youngest son* **lesser**
shall he *set up* **station** the *gates* **doors.**
27 So *the LORD* **Yah Veh** was with *Joshua* **Yah Shua**;
and his fame *was noised* **became**
throughout all the *country* **land.**

ACHAN'S TREASON

7 But the *children* **sons** of *Israel* **Yisra El**
committed **treasoned** a *trespass* **treason**
in the *accursed thing* **devotement:**
for Achan, the son of *Carmi* **Karmi,**
the son of Zabdi, the son of *Zerah* **Zerach,**
of the *tribe* **rod** of *Judah* **Yah Hudah,**
took of the *accursed thing* **devotement:**
and the *anger* **wrath** of *the LORD* **Yah Veh**
was kindled against the *children* **sons** of *Israel* **Yisra El.**
2 And *Joshua* **Yah Shua** sent men from *Jericho* **Yericho**
to *Ai* **Ay**, which is beside *Bethaven* **Beth Aven,**
on the east *side* of *Bethel* **Beth El,**
and *spake* **said** unto them, saying,
Go up **Ascend** and *view* **spy** the *country* **land.**
And the men *went up* **ascended** and *viewed Ai* **spied Ay.**
3 And they returned to *Joshua* **Yah Shua,**
and said unto him, Let not all the people *go up* **ascend;**
but let about two or three thousand men
go up **ascend** and smite *Ai* **Ay;**
and make not all the people to labour thither;
for they are *but* few.
4 So there *went up* **ascended** thither of the people
about three thousand men:
and they fled *before* **from the face of** the men of *Ai* **Ay.**
5 And the men of *Ai* **Ay**
smote of them about thirty and six men:
for they *chased* **pursued** them
from *before* **the face of** the *gate* **portal**
even unto Shebarim,
and smote them in the *going down* **descent:**
wherefore the hearts of the people melted,
and became as water.
6 And *Joshua rent* **Yah Shua ripped** his clothes,
and fell to the earth upon his face
before **at the face of** the ark of *the LORD* **Yah Veh**
until the *eventide* **evening,**
he and the elders of *Israel* **Yisra El,**
and *put* **ascended** dust upon their heads.
7 And *Joshua* **Yah Shua** said,
Alas **Aha,** O *Lord GOD* **Adonay Yah Veh,**
wherefore **in passing, why** hast thou *at all brought* **passed**
this people over *Jordan* **Yarden,**
to *deliver* **give** us into the hand of the *Amorites* **Emoriy,**
to destroy us?
would to GOD **if only** we had *been content* **willed,**
and *dwelt* **settled** on the other side *Jordan* **Yarden!**
8 O *Lord* **Adonay**, what shall I say,
when *Israel* **Yisra El** turneth **back** their *backs* **necks**
before **at the face of** their enemies!
9 For the *Canaanites* **Kenaaniy**
and all the *inhabitants* **settlers** of the land shall hear of it,
and shall *environ* **surround** us *round,*
and cut off our name from the earth:
and what *wilt* **shalt** thou *do* **work** unto thy great name?
10 And *the LORD* **Yah Veh** said unto *Joshua* **Yah Shua,**
Get thee up **Arise;**
wherefore *liest* **fallest** thou thus upon thy face?
11 *Israel* **Yisra El** hath sinned,
and they have also *transgressed* **trespassed** my covenant
which I *commanded* **misvahed** them:
for they have even taken
of the *accursed thing* **devotement,**
and have also stolen, and *dissembled* **deceived** also,
and they have *put* **set** it
even among their own *stuff* **instruments.**
12 Therefore the *children* **sons** of *Israel* **Yisra El**
could not *stand* **rise**
before **at the face of** their enemies,
but turned their *backs* **necks**
before **at the face of** their enemies,
because they were *accursed* **devoted:**
neither *will* **shall** I be with you *any more* **again,**
except **unless** ye *destroy* **desolate**
the *accursed* **devotement** from among you.
13 *Up* **Arise**, *sanctify* **hallow** the people, and say,
Sanctify **Hallow** yourselves against to morrow:
for thus saith
the LORD God **Yah Veh Elohim** of *Israel* **Yisra El,**
There is *an accursed thing* **a devotement**
in the midst of thee, O *Israel* **Yisra El:**
thou canst not *stand* **rise**
before **at the face of** thine enemies,
until ye *take away* **turn aside**

the *accursed thing* **devotement** from among you.
14 In the morning therefore
ye shall *be brought* **approach**
according to your *tribes* **scions**:
and it shall *be* **become**,
that the *tribe* **scion**
which *the LORD taketh* **Yah Veh captureth**
shall *come* **approach** according to the families thereof;
and the family
which *the LORD* **Yah Veh** shall *take* **capture**
shall *come* **approach** by households;
and the household
which *the LORD* **Yah Veh** shall *take* **capture**
shall *come man* **approach mighty** by *man* **mighty**.
15 And it shall be,
that he that is *taken* **captured**
with the *accursed thing* **devotement**
shall be burnt with fire, he and all that he hath:
because he hath *transgressed* **trespassed**
the covenant of *the LORD* **Yah Veh**,
and because he hath *wrought* **worked** folly
in *Israel* **Yisra El**.
16 So *Joshua* **Yah Shua**
rose up **started** early in the morning,
and *brought Israel* **approached Yisra El**
by their *tribes* **scions**;
and the *tribe* **scion** of *Judah* **Yah Hudah**
was *taken* **captured**:
17 And he *brought* **approached**
the family of *Judah* **Yah Hudah**;
and he *took* **captured** the family of the *Zarhites* **Zerachiy**:
and he *brought* **approached**
the family of the *Zarhites* **Zerachiy**
man **mighty** by *man* **mighty**;
and Zabdi was *taken* **captured**:
18 And he *brought* **approached** his household
man **mighty** by *man* **mighty**;
and Achan, the son of *Carmi* **Karmi**,
the son of Zabdi, the son of *Zerah* **Zerach**,
of the *tribe* **rod** of *Judah* **Yah Hudah**, was *taken* **captured**.
19 And *Joshua* **Yah Shua** said unto Achan,
My son, *give* **set**, I *pray* **beseech** thee,
glory **honour** to *the LORD God* **Yah Veh Elohim**
of *Israel* **Yisra El**,
and *make confession* **place extended hands** unto him;
and tell me now what thou hast *done* **worked**;
hide **conceal** it not from me.
20 And Achan answered *Joshua* **Yah Shua**, and said,
Indeed **Truly** I have sinned against
the LORD God **Yah Veh Elohim** of *Israel* **Yisra El**,
and thus and thus have I *done* **worked**:
21 When I saw among the spoils
a goodly *Babylonish garment* **Babel mighty mantle**,
and two hundred shekels of silver,
and *a wedge* **one tongue** of gold of fifty shekels weight,
then I *coveted* **desired** them, and took them;
and, behold,
they are hid in the earth in the midst of my tent,
and the silver under it.
22 So *Joshua* **Yah Shua** sent *messengers* **angels**,
and they ran unto the tent;
and, behold, it was hid in his tent, and the silver under it.
23 And they took them out of the midst of the tent,
and brought them unto *Joshua* **Yah Shua**,
and unto all the *children* **sons** of *Israel* **Yisra El**,
and *laid* **poured** them out
before the LORD **at the face of Yah Veh**.
24 And *Joshua* **Yah Shua**, and all *Israel* **Yisra El** with him,
took Achan the son of *Zerah* **Zerach**,
and the silver, and the *garment* **mighty mantle**,
and the *wedge* **tongue** of gold,
and his sons, and his daughters,
and his oxen, and his *asses* **he burros**,
and his *sheep* **flock**, and his tent, and all that he had:
and they *brought* **ascended** them
unto the valley of Achor.
25 And *Joshua* **Yah Shua** said, Why hast thou troubled us?
the LORD **Yah Veh** shall trouble thee this day.
And all *Israel* **Yisra El** stoned him with stones,
and burned them with fire,
after they had stoned them with stones.
26 And they raised over him
a great heap of stones unto this day.
So *the LORD* **Yah Veh** turned
from the *fierceness* **fuming** of his *anger* **wrath**.
Wherefore the name of that place was called,
The valley of Achor, unto this day.

SONS OF YISRA EL CONQUER AY

8 And *the LORD* **Yah Veh** said unto *Joshua* **Yah Shua**,
Fear **Awe** not, neither be thou *dismayed* **terrified**:
take all the people of war with thee,
and arise, *go up* **ascend** to *Ai* **Ay**: see,
I have given into thy hand the *king* **sovereign** of *Ai* **Ay**,
and his people, and his city, and his land:
2 And thou shalt *do* **work** to *Ai* **Ay** and her *king* **sovereign**
as thou *didst* **workedst** unto *Jericho* **Yericho**
and her *king* **sovereign**:
only the spoil thereof, and the *cattle* **animals** thereof,
shall *ye take for a prey* **plunder ye** unto yourselves:
lay thee an ambush **lurk** for the city behind it.
3 So *Joshua* **Yah Shua** arose, and all the people of war,
to *go up* **ascend** against *Ai* **Ay**:
and *Joshua* **Yah Shua**
chose out thirty thousand mighty men of valour,
and sent them away by night.
4 And he *commanded* **misvahed** them, saying, *Behold* **See**,
ye shall *lie in wait* **lurk** against the city,
even behind the city:
go not *very* **mighty** far **removed** from the city,
but be ye all *ready* **prepared**:
5 And I, and all the people that are with me,
will **shall** approach unto the city:
and it shall *come to pass* **become**,
when they *come out against* **go to confront** us,
as at the first,
that we *will* **shall** flee *before them* **from their face**,
6 (For they *will come out* **shall go** after us)
till we have *drawn* **torn** them from the city;
for they *will* **shall** say,
They flee *before us* **from our face**, as at the first:
therefore we *will* **shall** flee *before them* **from their face**.
7 Then ye shall rise up from the *ambush* **lurk**,
and *seize upon* **possess** the city:
for *the LORD* **Yah Veh** your *God* **Elohim**
will deliver **shall give** it into your hand.
8 And it shall be,
when ye have *taken* **apprehended** the city,
that ye shall *set* **burn** the city on fire:
according to the *commandment* **word**
of *the LORD* **Yah Veh**
shall ye *do* **work**.
See, I have *commanded* **misvahed** you.
9 *Joshua* **Yah Shua** therefore sent them forth:
and they went to *lie in ambush* **lurk**,
and *abode* **settled** between *Bethel* **Beth El** and *Ai* **Ay**,
on the west side **seaward** of *Ai* **Ay**:
but *Joshua lodged* **Yah Shua stayed overnight** that night
among the people.
10 And *Joshua* **Yah Shua**
rose up **started** early in the morning,
and *numbered* **mustered** the people,
and *went up* **ascended**, he and the elders of *Israel* **Yisra El**,
before **at the face of** the people to *Ai* **Ay**.
11 And all the people, *even the people* of war
that were with him,
went up **ascended**, and drew *nigh* **near**,
and came before the city,
and *pitched* **encamped** on the north *side* of *Ai* **Ay**:
now there was a valley between them and *Ai* **Ay**.
12 And he took about five thousand men,
and set them to *lie in ambush* **lurk**
between *Bethel* **Beth El** and *Ai* **Ay**,
on the west side **seaward** of the city.
13 And when they had set the people,
even all the *host* **camp** that was on the north of the city,
and their *liers in wait* **heel trippers**
on the west **seaward** of the city,
Joshua **Yah Shua** went that night
into the midst of the valley.
14 And it *came to pass* **became**,

when the *king* **sovereign** of *Ai* **Ay** saw it,
that they hasted and *rose up* **started** early,
and the men of the city went out
against Israel **to meet Yisra El** to *battle* **war**,
he and all his people,
at a *time appointed* **season**, *before* **at the face of** the plain;
but he *wist* **knew** not
that there were *liers in ambush* **lurkers** against him
behind the city.
15 And *Joshua* **Yah Shua** and all *Israel* **Yisra El**
made **appeared** as *if they were beaten* **to be touched**
before them **at their face**,
and fled by the way of the wilderness.
16 And all the people that were in *Ai* **Ay**
were called together **cried** to pursue after them:
and they pursued after *Joshua* **Yah Shua**,
and were *drawn* **torn** away from the city.
17 And there *was* **survived** not a man *left*
in *Ai* **Ay** or *Bethel* **Beth El**,
that went not out after *Israel* **Yisra El**:
and they left the city open,
and pursued after *Israel* **Yisra El**.
18 And *the LORD* **Yah Veh** said unto *Joshua* **Yah Shua**,
Stretch out the *spear* **dart** that is in thy hand
toward *Ai* **Ay**;
for I *will* **shall** give it into thine hand.
And *Joshua* **Yah Shua**
stretched out the *spear* **dart** that he had in his hand
toward *the city* **Ay**.
19 And the *ambush* **lurkers**
arose quickly out of their place,
and they ran as soon as he had stretched out his hand:
and they entered into the city, and *took* **captured** it,
and hasted and *set* **burned** the city on fire.
20 And when the men of *Ai looked* **Ay faced** behind them,
they saw, and, behold,
the smoke of the city ascended *up* to *heaven* **the heavens**,
and they had no *power* **hand** to flee
this way **here** or *that way* **there**:
and the people that fled to the wilderness
turned back upon the pursuers.
21 And when *Joshua* **Yah Shua** and all *Israel* **Yisra El**
saw that the *ambush* **lurkers** had *taken* **captured** the city,
and that the smoke of the city ascended,
then they turned *again* **back**,
and *slew* **smote** the men of *Ai* **Ay**.
22 And the other *issued* **went** out of the city
against **to meet** them;
so they were in the midst of *Israel* **Yisra El**,
some **these** on this side, and *some* **those** on that side:
and they smote them,
so that they let none of them remain or escape
so that no escapee survived.
23 And the *king* **sovereign** of *Ai* **Ay**
they *took* **apprehended** alive,
and *brought* **approached** him to *Joshua* **Yah Shua**.
24 And it *came to pass* **became**,
when *Israel* **Yisra El**
had *made an end of slaying* **finished slaughtering**
all the *inhabitants* **settlers** of *Ai* **Ay** in the field,
in the wilderness wherein they *chased* **pursued** them,
and when they were all fallen
on the *edge* **mouth** of the sword,
until they were consumed,
that all the *Israelites* **Yisra Eliy** returned unto *Ai* **Ay**,
and smote it with the *edge* **mouth** of the sword.
25 And *so* it *was* **became**,
that all that fell that day, both of men and women,
were twelve thousand, *even* all the men of *Ai* **Ay**.
26 For *Joshua drew* **Yah Shua turned** not his hand back,
wherewith he stretched out the spear,
until he had *utterly destroyed* **devoted**
all the *inhabitants* **settlers** of *Ai* **Ay**.
27 Only the *cattle* **animals** and the spoil of that city
Israel took for a prey **Yisra El plundered** unto themselves,
according unto the word of *the LORD* **Yah Veh**
which he *commanded Joshua* **misvahed Yah Shua**.
28 And *Joshua* **Yah Shua** burnt *Ai* **Ay**,
and *made* **set** it an heap for *ever* **eternity**,
even a desolation unto this day.
29 And the *king* **sovereign** of *Ai* **Ay**
he hanged on a tree until *eventide* **evening time**:
and as soon as the sun was down,
Joshua commanded **Yah Shua misvahed**
that they should *take* **bring** his carcase
down from the tree,
and cast it
at the *entering* **opening** of the *gate* **portal** of the city,
and raise thereon a great heap of stones,
that remaineth unto this day.

YAH SHUA'S ALTAR TO YAH VEH

30 Then *Joshua* **Yah Shua** built *an* **a sacrifice** altar
unto *the LORD God* **Yah Veh Elohim** of *Israel* **Yisra El**
in mount Ebal,
31 As *Moses* **Mosheh** the servant of *the LORD* **Yah Veh**
commanded **misvahed** the *children* **sons** of *Israel* **Yisra El**,
as it is *written* **inscribed**
in the *book* **scroll** of the *law* **torah** of *Moses* **Mosheh**,
an **a sacrifice** altar of *whole* **complete** stones,
over which no man hath *lift up any* **waved** iron:
and they *offered* **holocausted** thereon
burnt offerings **holocausts** unto *the LORD* **Yah Veh**,
and sacrificed *peace offerings* **shelamim**.
32 And he *wrote* **inscribed** there upon the stones
a *copy* **duplicate** of the *law* **torah** of *Moses* **Mosheh**,
which he *wrote* **inscribed**
in the *presence* **face** of the *children* **sons** of *Israel* **Yisra El**.
33 And all *Israel* **Yisra El**,
and their elders, and officers, and their judges,
stood on this side the ark and on that side
before the priests the *Levites* **Leviym**,
which bare the ark of the covenant of *the LORD* **Yah Veh**,
as well the *stranger* **sojourner**,
as *he that was born among them* **the native**;
half of them *over against* **toward** mount Gerizim,
and half of them *over against* **toward** mount Ebal;
as *Moses* **Mosheh** the servant of *the LORD* **Yah Veh**
had *commanded before* **first misvahed**,
that they should bless the people of *Israel* **Yisra El**.
34 And afterward
he *read* **called out** all the words of the *law* **torah**,
the blessings and *cursings* **abasements**,
according to all that is *written* **inscribed**
in the *book* **scroll** of the *law* **torah**.
35 There was not a word
of all that *Moses commanded* **Mosheh misvahed**,
which *Joshua read* **Yah Shua called** not **out**
before all the congregation of *Israel* **Yisra El**,
with the women, and the *little ones* **toddlers**,
and the *strangers* **sojourners**
that *were conversant* **walked** among them.

PEOPLES UNITE AGAINST YAH SHUA AND YISRA EL

9 And it *came to pass* **became**,
when all the *kings* **sovereigns**
which were on this side *Jordan* **Yarden**,
in the *hills* **mountains**, and in the *valleys* **lowlands**,
and in all the *coasts* **havens** of the great sea
over *against* **toward** Lebanon,
the *Hittite* **Hethiy**, and the *Amorite* **Emoriy**,
the *Canaanite* **Kenaaniy**, the *Perizzite* **Perizziy**,
the *Hivite* **Hivviy**, and the *Jebusite* **Yebusiy**, heard thereof;
2 That they gathered themselves together,
to fight with *Joshua* **Yah Shua** and with *Israel* **Yisra El**,
with one *accord* **mouth**.

THE STRATEGY OF THE SETTLERS OF GIBON

3 And when the *inhabitants* **settlers** of *Gibeon* **Gibon**
heard what *Joshua* **Yah Shua** had *done* **worked**
unto *Jericho* **Yericho** and to *Ai* **Ay**,
4 They did work *wilily* **strategy**,
and went and made as if they had been ambassadors,
and took *old sacks* **worn out saqs**
upon their *asses* **he burros**,
and wine *bottles* **skins**,
old **worn out**, and *rent* **split**, and bound up;
5 And *old* **worn out** shoes
and *clouted* **patched** upon their feet,
and *old garments* **worn out clothes** upon them;
and all the bread of their *provision* **hunt**
was *dry* **withered** and *mouldy* **crumbly**.
6 And they went to *Joshua* **Yah Shua**

unto the camp at Gilgal,
and said unto him, and to the men of *Israel* **Yisra El**,
We be come from a far *country* **land**:
now therefore *make* **cut** ye a *league* **covenant** with us.
7 And the men of *Israel* **Yisra El**
said unto the *Hivites* **Hivviy**,
Peradventure **Perhaps** ye *dwell* **settle** among us;
and how shall we *make* **cut** a *league* **covenant** with you?
8 And they said unto *Joshua* **Yah Shua**,
We *are* **be** thy servants.
And *Joshua* **Yah Shua** said unto them,
Who are ye? and from whence come ye?
9 And they said unto him,
From a *very far country* **mighty far land**
thy servants are come
because of the name
of *the LORD* **Yah Veh** thy *God* **Elohim**:
for we have heard the fame of him,
and all that he *did* **worked** in *Egypt* **Misrayim**,
10 And all that he *did* **worked**
to the two *kings* **sovereigns** of the *Amorites* **Emoriy**,
that were beyond *Jordan* **Yarden**,
to *Sihon king* **Sichon sovereign** of Heshbon,
and to Og *king* **sovereign** of Bashan,
which was at Ashtaroth.
11 Wherefore our elders
and all the *inhabitants* **settlers** of our *country* **land**
spake **said** to us, saying,
Take *victuals with you* **hunt in your hand** for the journey,
and go to meet them, and say unto them,
We *are your* **be thy** servants:
therefore now *make* **cut** ye *a league* **covenant** with us.
12 This our bread we took *hot* **warm** for our provision
out of our houses
on the day we *came forth* **went** to go unto you;
but now, behold,
it is *dry* **withered**, and it is *mouldy* **crumbly**:
13 And these *bottles* **skins** of wine,
which we filled, were new;
and, behold, they be *rent* **split**:
and these our *garments* **clothes** and our shoes
are become *old* **worn out**
by *reason of the very long* **the mighty great** journey.
14 And the men took of their *victuals* **hunt**,
and asked not *counsel* at the mouth of *the LORD* **Yah Veh**.
15 And *Joshua* **Yah Shua**
made peace **worked shalom** with them,
and *made* **cut** a *league* **covenant** with them,
to let them live:
and the *princes* **hierarchs** of the *congregation* **witness**
sware **oathed** unto them.

SONS OF YISRA EL HONOUR THEIR OATH

16 And it *came to pass* **became,** at the end of three days
after they had *made* **cut** a *league* **covenant** with them,
that they heard that they were their neighbours,
and that they *dwelt* **settled** among them.
17 And the *children* **sons** of *Israel* **Yisra El**
journeyed **pulled stakes**,
and came unto their cities on the third day.
Now their cities were *Gibeon* **Gibon**,
and *Chephirah* **Kephirah**, and Beeroth,
and *Kirjathjearim* **Kirjath Arim**.
18 And the *children* **sons** of *Israel* **Yisra El** smote them not,
because the *princes* **hierarchs** of the *congregation* **witness**
had *sworn* **oathed** unto them
by *the LORD God* **Yah Veh Elohim** of *Israel* **Yisra El**.
And all the *congregation* **witness**
murmured against the *princes* **hierarchs**.
19 But all the *princes* **hierarchs**
said unto all the *congregation* **witness**,
We have *sworn* **oathed** unto them
by *the LORD God* **Yah Veh Elohim** of *Israel* **Yisra El**:
now therefore we *may* **are** not **able to** touch them.
20 This we *will do* **shall work** to them;
we *will* **shall** even let them live,
lest *wrath* **rage** be upon us,
because of the oath which we *sware* **oathed** unto them.
21 And the *princes* **hierarchs** said unto them,
Let them live;
but let them be *hewers* **choppers** of *wood* **timber**
and *drawers* **bailers** of water
unto all the *congregation* **witness**;
as the *princes* **hierarchs** had *promised* **worded** them.
22 And *Joshua* **Yah Shua** called for them,
and he *spake* **worded** unto them, saying,
Wherefore have ye *beguiled* **deceived** us, saying,
We are *very* **mighty** far from you;
when ye *dwell* **settle** among us?
23 Now therefore ye are cursed,
and there shall none of you be *freed* **cut off**
from being *bondmen* **servants**,
and *hewers* **choppers** of *wood* **timber**
and *drawers* **bailers** of water
for the house of my *God* **Elohim**.
24 And they answered *Joshua* **Yah Shua**, and said,
In telling, *Because* it was *certainly* told thy servants,
how that *the LORD* **Yah Veh** thy *God* **Elohim**
commanded **misvahed** his servant *Moses* **Mosheh**
to give you all the land,
and to *destroy* **desolate**
all the *inhabitants* **settlers** of the land
from *before you* **thy face**,
therefore we were *sore afraid* **mighty awed**
of our *lives because of you* **souls at thy face**,
and have *done* **worked** this *thing* **word**.
25 And now, behold, we are in thine hand:
as it seemeth good and *right* **straight**
unto thee **in thine eyes** to *do* **work** unto us, *do* **work**.
26 And so *did* **worked** he unto them,
and delivered them out of the hand
of the *children* **sons** of *Israel* **Yisra El**,
that they *slew* **slaughtered** them not.
27 And *Joshua made* **Yah Shua gave** them that day
hewers **choppers** of *wood* **timber**
and *drawers* **bailers** of water
for the *congregation* **witness**,
and for the **sacrifice** altar of *the LORD* **Yah Veh**,
even unto this day, in the place which he should choose.

THE DAY THE SUN STOOD STILL

10 Now it *came to pass* **became**,
when *Adonizedec* **Adoni Sedeq**
king **sovereign** of *Jerusalem* **Yeru Shalem**
had heard how **surely**
Joshua **Yah Shua** had *taken Ai* **captured Ay**,
and had *utterly destroyed* **devoted** it;
as he had *done* **worked**
to *Jericho* **Yericho** and her *king* **sovereign**,
so he had *done* **worked** to *Ai* **Ay** and her *king* **sovereign**;
and how the *inhabitants* **settlers** of *Gibeon* **Gibon**
had made peace **did shalam** with *Israel* **Yisra El**,
and were among them;
2 That they *feared greatly* **awed mightily**,
because *Gibeon* **Gibon** was a great city,
as one of the royal cities,
and because it was greater than *Ai* **Ay**,
and all the men thereof were mighty.
3 Wherefore *Adonizedec* **Adoni Sedeq,**
king **sovereign** of *Jerusalem* **Yeru Shalem**,
sent unto Hoham *king* **sovereign** of Hebron,
and unto Piram *king* **sovereign** of *Jarmuth* **Yarmuth**,
and unto *Japhia* **Yaphia**, *king* **sovereign** of Lachish,
and unto Debir *king* **sovereign** of Eglon, saying,
4 *Come up* **Ascend** unto me, and help me,
that we may smite *Gibeon* **Gibon**:
for it *hath made peace* **did shalam** with *Joshua* **Yah Shua**
and with the *children* **sons** of *Israel* **Yisra El**.
5 Therefore
the five *kings* **sovereigns** of the *Amorites* **Emoriy**,
the *king* **sovereign** of *Jerusalem* **Yeru Shalem**,
the *king* **sovereign** of Hebron,
the *king* **sovereign** of *Jarmuth* **Yarmuth**,
the *king* **sovereign** of Lachish,
the *king* **sovereign** of Eglon,
gathered themselves together, and *went up* **ascended**,
they and all their *hosts* **camps**,
and encamped *before Gibeon* **against Gibon**,
and *made war* **fought** against it.
6 And the men of *Gibeon* **Gibon**
sent unto *Joshua* **Yah Shua** to the camp to Gilgal,
saying, Slack not thy hand from thy servants;

come up **ascend** to us quickly, and save us, and help us:
for all the *kings* **sovereigns** of the *Amorites* **Emoriy**
that *dwell* **settle** in the mountains
are gathered together against us.
7 So *Joshua* **Yah Shua** ascended from Gilgal,
he, and all the people of war with him,
and all the mighty *men* of valour.
8 And *the LORD* **Yah Veh** said unto *Joshua* **Yah Shua**,
Fear **Awe** them not:
for I have *delivered* **given** them into thine hand;
there shall not a man of them
stand *before thee* **at thy face.**
9 *Joshua* **Yah Shua** therefore came unto them suddenly,
and *went up* **ascended** from Gilgal all night.
10 And *the LORD discomfited* **Yah Veh agitated** them
before Israel **at the face of Yisra El**,
and *slew* **smote** them with a great *slaughter* **stroke**
at *Gibeon* **Gibon**,
and *chased* **pursued** them along the way
that goeth up to Bethhoron **of the ascent of Beth Horon**,
and smote them to *Azekah* **Azeqah**,
and unto *Makkedah* **Maqqedah**.
11 And it *came to pass* **became**,
as they fled from *before Israel* **the face of Yisra El**,
and were in
the *going down to Bethhoron* **descent of Beth Horon**,
that *the LORD* **Yah Veh** cast down great stones
from *heaven* **the heavens**
upon them unto *Azekah* **Azeqah**, and they died:
they were *more* **greater** which died with hailstones
than they whom the *children* **sons** of *Israel* **Yisra El**
slew **slaughtered** with the sword.
12 Then *spake Joshua* **worded Yah Shua**
to *the LORD* **Yah Veh** in the day
when *the LORD* **Yah Veh**
delivered up **gave** the *Amorites* **Emoriy**
before **at the face of** the *children* **sons** of *Israel* **Yisra El**,
and he said in the *sight* **eyes** of *Israel* **Yisra El**,
Sun, stand thou still upon *Gibeon* **Gibon**;
and thou, Moon, in the valley of *Ajalon* **Ayalon**.
13 And the sun stood still, and the moon stayed,
until the *people* **goyim** had avenged themselves
upon their enemies.
Is not this *written* **inscribed**
in the *book* **scroll** of *Jasher* **the straight**?
So the sun stood still in the midst of *heaven* **the heavens**,
and hasted not to go down
about *a whole* **an integrious** day.
14 And there was no day like that
before **at the face of** it or after it,
that *the LORD* **Yah Veh**
hearkened unto the voice of a man:
for *the LORD* **Yah Veh** fought for *Israel* **Yisra El**.
15 And *Joshua* **Yah Shua** returned,
and all *Israel* **Yisra El** with him, unto the camp to Gilgal.

FIVE SOVEREIGNS HIDE

16 But these five *kings* **sovereigns** fled,
and hid themselves in a cave at *Makkedah* **Maqqedah**.
17 And it was told *Joshua* **Yah Shua**, saying,
The five *kings* **sovereigns** are found
hid in a cave at *Makkedah* **Maqqedah**.
18 And *Joshua* **Yah Shua** said,
Roll great stones upon the mouth of the cave,
and *set* **oversee** men by it for to *keep* **guard** them:
19 And stay ye not, but pursue after your enemies,
and *smite the hindmost of* **curtail** them;
suffer **give** them not to enter into their cities:
for *the LORD* **Yah Veh** your *God* **Elohim**
hath *delivered* **given** them into your hand.
20 And it *came to pass* **became**,
when *Joshua* **Yah Shua**
and the *children* **sons** of *Israel* **Yisra El**
had *made an end of slaying* **finished smiting** them
with a *very* **mighty** great *slaughter* **stroke**,
till they were consumed,
that the *rest* **survivors** which *remained* **survived** of them
entered into *fenced* **fortified** cities.
21 And all the people returned to the camp
to *Joshua* **Yah Shua** at *Makkedah* **Maqqedah**
in *peace* **shalom**:
none *moved* **pointened** his tongue
against any **man** of the *children* **sons** of *Israel* **Yisra El**.

FIVE SOVEREIGNS SLAUGHTERED

22 Then said *Joshua* **Yah Shua**,
Open the mouth of the cave,
and bring out those five *kings* **sovereigns** unto me
out of the cave.
23 And they *did* **worked** so,
and brought forth those five *kings* **sovereigns** unto him
out of the cave,
the *king* **sovereign** of *Jerusalem* **Yeru Shalem**,
the *king* **sovereign** of Hebron,
the *king* **sovereign** of *Jarmuth* **Yarmuth**,
the *king* **sovereign** of Lachish,
and the *king* **sovereign** of Eglon.
24 And it *came to pass* **became**,
when they brought out those *kings* **sovereigns**
unto *Joshua* **Yah Shua**,
that *Joshua* **Yah Shua**
called for all the men of *Israel* **Yisra El**,
and said unto the *captains* **commanders**
of the men of war
which went with him, *Come near* **Approach**,
put **set** your feet
upon the necks of these *kings* **sovereigns**.
And they *came near* **approached**,
and *put* **set** their feet upon the necks of them.
25 And *Joshua* **Yah Shua** said unto them,
Fear **Awe** not, nor be *dismayed* **terrified**,
be *strong* **strengthened** and *of good courage* **encouraged**:
for thus shall *the LORD* **Yah Veh**
do **work** to all your enemies against whom ye fight.
26 And afterward *Joshua* **Yah Shua** smote them,
and *slew* **deathified** them, and hanged them on five trees:
and they were hanging upon the trees until the evening.
27 And it *came to pass* **became,**
at the time of the going down of the sun,
that *Joshua commanded* **Yah Shua misvahed**,
and they *took* **brought** them down off the trees,
and cast them into the cave wherein they had been hid,
and *laid* **set** great stones in the cave's mouth,
which remain until this *very* **selfsame** day.
28 And that day
Joshua took Makkedah **Yah Shua captured Maqqedah**,
and smote it with the *edge* **mouth** of the sword,
and the *king* **sovereign** thereof
he *utterly destroyed* **devoted**,
them, and all the souls that were therein;
he let none remain **no survivors survived**:
and he *did* **worked**
to the *king* **sovereign** of *Makkedah* **Maqqedah**
as he *did* **worked**
unto the *king* **sovereign** of *Jericho* **Yericho**.

YAH SHUA CONQUERS SOUTHERN PELESHETH

29 Then *Joshua* **Yah Shua**
passed from *Makkedah* **Maqqedah**,
and all *Israel* **Yisra El** with him, unto Libnah,
and fought against Libnah:
30 And *the LORD delivered* **Yah Veh gave** it also,
and the *king* **sovereign** thereof,
into the hand of *Israel* **Yisra El**;
and he smote it with the *edge* **mouth** of the sword,
and all the souls that were therein;
he let none remain in it **no survivors survived**;
but *did* **worked** unto the *king* **sovereign** thereof
as he *did* **worked**
unto the *king* **sovereign** of *Jericho* **Yericho**.
31 And *Joshua* **Yah Shua** passed from Libnah,
and all *Israel* **Yisra El** with him, unto Lachish,
and encamped against it, and fought against it:
32 And *the LORD delivered* **Yah Veh gave** Lachish
into the hand of *Israel* **Yisra El**,
which *took* **captured** it on the second day,
and smote it with the *edge* **mouth** of the sword,
and all the souls that were therein,
according to all that he had *done* **worked** to Libnah.
33 Then Horam *king* **sovereign** of Gezer
came up **ascended** to help Lachish;
and *Joshua* **Yah Shua** smote him and his people,
until *he had left him none remaining* **no survivors survived**.

34 And from Lachish *Joshua* **Yah Shua** passed unto Eglon,
and all *Israel* **Yisra El** with him;
and they encamped against it, and fought against it:
35 And they *took* **captured** it on that day,
and smote it with the *edge* **mouth** of the sword,
and all the souls that were therein
he *utterly destroyed* **devoted** that day,
according to all that he had *done* **worked** to Lachish.
36 And *Joshua went up* **Yah Shua ascended** from Eglon,
and all *Israel* **Yisra El** with him, unto Hebron;
and they fought against it:
37 And they *took* **captured** it,
and smote it with the *edge* **mouth** of the sword,
and the *king* **sovereign** thereof, and all the cities thereof,
and all the souls that were therein;
he left none remaining **no survivors survived**,
according to all that he had *done* **worked** to Eglon;
but *destroyed it utterly* **devoted it**,
and all the souls that were therein.
38 And *Joshua* **Yah Shua** returned,
and all *Israel* **Yisra El** with him, to Debir;
and fought against it:
39 And he *took* **captured** it,
and the *king* **sovereign** thereof, and all the cities thereof;
and they smote them with the *edge* **mouth** of the sword,
and *utterly destroyed* **devoted** all the souls
that were therein;
he left none remaining **no survivors survived**:
as he had *done* **worked** to Hebron,
so he *did* **worked** to Debir,
and to the *king* **sovereign** thereof;
as he had *done* **worked** also to Libnah,
and to her *king* **sovereign**.
40 So *Joshua* **Yah Shua** smote all the *country* **land**
of the *hills* **mountains**, and of the south,
and of the *vale* **lowland**, and of the springs,
and all their *kings* **sovereigns**:
he left none remaining **no survivors survived**,
but *utterly destroyed all that breathed* **devoted all breath**,
as *the LORD God* **Yah Veh Elohim** of *Israel* **Yisra El**
commanded **misvahed**.
41 And *Joshua* **Yah Shua** smote them
from *Kadeshbarnea* **Qadesh Barnea**
even unto *Gaza* **Azzah**,
and all the *country* **land** of Goshen,
even unto *Gibeon* **Gibon**.
42 And all these *kings* **sovereigns** and their land
did *Joshua take* **Yah Shua capture** at one time,
because *the LORD God* **Yah Veh Elohim** of *Israel* **Yisra El**
fought for *Israel* **Yisra El**.
43 And *Joshua* **Yah Shua** returned,
and all *Israel* **Yisra El** with him, unto the camp to Gilgal.

YAH SHUA CONQUERS NORTHERN PELESHETH

11 And it *came to pass* **became**,
when *Jabin king* **Yabyn sovereign** of *Hazor* **Hasor**
had heard those *things*,
that he sent to *Jobab* **Yobab**, *king* **sovereign** of Madon,
and to the *king* **sovereign** of Shimron,
and to the *king* **sovereign** of Achshaph,
2 And to the *kings* **sovereigns**
that were on the north of the mountains,
and of the plains south of *Chinneroth* **Kinneroth**,
and in the *valley* **lowland**,
and in the *borders* **heights** of Dor *on the west* **seaward**,
3 And to the *Canaanite* **Kenaaniy**
on **from** the *east* **rising** and *on the west* **seaward**,
and to the *Amorite* **Emoriy**, and the *Hittite* **Hethiy**,
and the *Perizzite* **Perizziy**, and the *Jebusite* **Yebusiy**
in the mountains,
and to the *Hivite* **Hivviy** under Hermon
in the land of *Mizpeh* **Mispeh**.
4 And they went out,
they and all their *hosts* **camps** with them, much people,
even as the sand that is upon the sea *shore* **lip**
in *multitude* **abundance**,
with horses and chariots *very* **mighty** many.
5 And when all these *kings* **sovereigns**
were *met together* **congregated**,
they came and *pitched* **encamped** together
at the waters of Merom, to fight against *Israel* **Yisra El**.
6 And *the LORD* **Yah Veh** said unto *Joshua* **Yah Shua**,
Be **Awe** not *afraid because of them* **their face**:
for to morrow about this time
will **shall** I *deliver* **give** them *up*
all *slain before Israel* **pierced at the face of Yisra El**:
thou shalt *hough* **hamstring** their horses,
and burn their chariots with fire.
7 So *Joshua* **Yah Shua** came,
and all the people of war with him,
against them by the waters of Merom suddenly;
and they fell upon them.
8 And *the LORD delivered* **Yah Veh gave** them
into the hand of *Israel* **Yisra El**,
who smote them,
and *chased* **pursued** them unto great *Zidon* **Sidon**,
and unto *Misrephothmaim* **Misrephoth Mayim**,
and unto the valley of *Mizpeh* **Mispeh**
eastward **from the rising**;
and they smote them,
until *they left them none remaining* **no survivors survived**.
9 And *Joshua did* **Yah Shua worked** unto them
as *the LORD bade* **Yah Veh said to** him:
he *houghed* **hamstrung** their horses,
and burnt their chariots with fire.
10 And *Joshua* **Yah Shua** at that time turned back,
and *took Hazor* **captured Hasor**,
and smote the *king* **sovereign** thereof with the sword:
for *Hazor beforetime* **Hasor formerly**
was the head of all those *kingdoms* **sovereigndoms**.
11 And they smote all the souls that were therein
with the *edge* **mouth** of the sword,
utterly destroying **devoting** them:
there was *not any left to breathe* **no survivor with breath**:
and he burnt *Hazor* **Hasor** with fire.
12 And all the cities of those *kings* **sovereigns**,
and all the *kings* **sovereigns** of them,
did *Joshua take* **Yah Shua capture**
and smote them with the *edge* **mouth** of the sword,
and he *utterly destroyed* **devoted** them,
as *Moses* **Mosheh** the servant of *the LORD* **Yah Veh**
commanded **misvahed**.
13 But *as for* the cities
that stood still *in their strength* **on their heap**,
Israel **Yisra El** burned none of them,
save Hazor **except Hasor** only;
that did *Joshua* **Yah Shua** burn.
14 And all the spoil of these cities, and the *cattle* **animals**,
the *children* **sons** of *Israel* **Yisra El**
took for a prey **plundered** unto themselves;
but every *man* **human**
they smote with the *edge* **mouth** of the sword,
until they had *destroyed* **desolated** them,
neither left they any *to breathe* **survivor with breath**.
15 As *the LORD* **Yah Veh**
commanded Moses **misvahed Mosheh** his servant,
so *did Moses command Joshua* **Mosheh misvahed Yah Shua**,
and so *did Joshua* **Yah Shua worked**;
he left *nothing undone* **no word turned aside**
of all that *the LORD* **Yah Veh**
commanded Moses **misvahed Mosheh**.
16 So *Joshua* **Yah Shua** took all that land,
the *hills* **mountains**, and all the south *country* **land**,
and all the land of Goshen, and the *valley* **lowland**,
and the plain, and the mountain of *Israel* **Yisra El**,
and the *valley of the same* **lowland**;
17 *Even* from the mount Halak,
that *goeth up* **ascendeth** to Seir,
even unto *Baalgad* **Baal Gad**
in the valley of Lebanon under mount Hermon:
and all their *kings* **sovereigns** he *took* **captured**,
and smote them, and *slew* **deathified** them.
18 *Joshua made* **Yah Shua worked** war
a long time **many days**
with all those *kings* **sovereigns**.
19 There was not a city that *made peace* **did shalam**
with the *children* **sons** of *Israel* **Yisra El**,
save the *Hivites* **Hivviy**
the *inhabitants* **settlers** of *Gibeon* **Gibon**:
all *other* they took in *battle* **war**.
20 For it was of *the LORD* **Yah Veh**

to *harden* **callous** their hearts,
that they should *come against Israel* **meet Yisra El**
in *battle* **war**,
that he might *destroy* **devote** them *utterly*,
and that they might have no *favour* **supplication**,
but that he might destroy them,
as *the LORD* **Yah Veh**
commanded Moses **misvahed Mosheh**.
21 And at that time came *Joshua* **Yah Shua**,
and cut off the *Anakims* **Anaqiy** from the mountains,
from Hebron, from Debir, from Anab,
and from all the mountains of *Judah* **Yah Hudah**,
and from all the mountains of *Israel* **Yisra El**:
Joshua destroyed **Yah Shua devoted** them *utterly*
with their cities.
22 There was none of the *Anakims left* **Anaqiy survived**
in the land of the *children* **sons** of *Israel* **Yisra El**:
only in *Gaza* **Azzah**, in Gath, and in Ashdod,
there *remained* **survived**.
23 So *Joshua* **Yah Shua** took the whole land,
according to all that *the LORD said* **Yah Veh worded**
unto *Moses* **Mosheh**;
and *Joshua* **Yah Shua** gave it for an inheritance
unto *Israel* **Yisra El**
according to their *divisions* **allotment**
by their *tribes* **scions**.
And the land rested from war.

WORDS OF THE DAYS OF THE DEFEATED SOVEREIGNS

12 Now these are the *kings* **sovereigns** of the land,
which the *children* **sons** of *Israel* **Yisra El** smote,
and possessed their land on the other side *Jordan* **Yarden**
toward **from** the rising of the sun,
from the *river* **wadi** Arnon unto mount Hermon,
and all the plain *on the east* **from the rising**:
2 *Sihon* **Sichon**, *king* **sovereign** of the *Amorites* **Emoriy**,
who dwelt **settled** in Heshbon,
and ruled **reigning** from Aroer,
which is upon the *bank* **lip** of the *river* **wadi** Arnon,
and from the middle of the *river* **wadi**,
and from half *Gilead* **Gilad**,
even unto the *river Jabbok* **wadi Yabboq**,
which is the border of the *children* **sons** of Ammon;
3 And from the plain to the sea of *Chinneroth* **Kinneroth**
on the east **from the rising**, and unto the sea of the plain,
even the salt sea *on the east* **from the rising**,
the way to *Bethjeshimoth* **Beth Ha Yeshimoth**;
and *from the south* **southward**,
under *Ashdothpisgah* **Ashdoth Pisgah**:
4 And the *coast* **border** of Og, *king* **sovereign** of Bashan,
which was of the remnant of the *giants* **Rephaim**,
that *dwelt* **settled** at Ashtaroth and at Edrei,
5 And reigned in mount Hermon,
and in *Salcah* **Salchah**, and in all Bashan,
unto the border of the *Geshurites* **Geshuriy**
and the *Maachathites* **Maachahiy**, and half *Gilead* **Gilad**,
the border of *Sihon king* **Sichon sovereign** of Heshbon.
6 Them did
Moses **Mosheh** the servant of *the LORD* **Yah Veh**
and the *children* **sons** of *Israel* **Yisra El** smite:
and *Moses* **Mosheh** the servant of *the LORD* **Yah Veh**
gave it for a possession unto the *Reubenites* **Reu Beniy**,
and the *Gadites* **Gadiy**,
and the half *tribe* **scion** of *Manasseh* **Menash Sheh**.
7 And these are the *kings* **sovereigns** of the *country* **land**
which *Joshua* **Yah Shua**
and the *children* **sons** of *Israel* **Yisra El**
smote on this side *Jordan on the west* **Yarden seaward**,
from *Baalgad* **Baal Gad** in the valley of Lebanon
even unto the mount Halak,
that *goeth up* **ascendeth** to Seir;
which *Joshua* **Yah Shua** gave
unto the *tribes* **scions** of *Israel* **Yisra El**
for a possession according to their *divisions* **allotment**;
8 In the mountains, and in the *valleys* **lowlands**,
and in the plains, and in the springs,
and in the wilderness, and in the south *country* **land**;
the *Hittites* **Hethiy**, the *Amorites* **Emoriy**,
and the *Canaanites* **Kenaaniy**, the *Perizzites* **Perizziy**,
the *Hivites* **Hivviy**, and the *Jebusites* **Yebusiy**:
9 The *king* **sovereign** of *Jericho* **Yericho**, one;
the *king* **sovereign** of *Ai* **Ay**,
which is beside *Bethel* **Beth El**, one;
10 The *king* **sovereign** of *Jerusalem* **Yeru Shalem**, one;
the *king* **sovereign** of Hebron, one;
11 The *king* **sovereign** of *Jarmuth* **Yarmuth**, one;
the *king* **sovereign** of Lachish, one;
12 The *king* **sovereign** of Eglon, one;
the *king* **sovereign** of Gezer, one;
13 The *king* **sovereign** of Debir, one;
the *king* **sovereign** of Geder, one;
14 The *king* **sovereign** of Hormah, one;
the *king* **sovereign** of Arad, one;
15 The *king* **sovereign** of Libnah, one;
the *king* **sovereign** of Adullam, one;
16 The *king* **sovereign** of *Makkedah* **Maqqedah**, one;
the *king* **sovereign** of *Bethel* **Beth El**, one;
17 The *king* **sovereign** of *Tappuah* **Tappuach**, one;
the *king* **sovereign** of Hepher, one;
18 The *king* **sovereign** of *Aphek* **Apheq**, one;
the *king* **sovereign** of Lasharon, one;
19 The *king* **sovereign** of Madon, one;
the *king* **sovereign** of *Hazor* **Hasor**, one;
20 The *king* **sovereign** of *Shimronmeron* **Shimron Meron**,
one;
the *king* **sovereign** of Achshaph, one;
21 The *king* **sovereign** of Taanach, one;
the *king* **sovereign** of Megiddo, one;
22 The *king* **sovereign** of *Kedesh* **Qedesh**, one;
the *king* **sovereign** of *Jokneam* **Yoqne Am**
of *Carmel* **Karmel**, one;
23 The *king* **sovereign** of Dor in the *coast* **heights** of Dor,
one;
the *king* **sovereign** of the *nations* **goyim** of Gilgal, one;
24 The *king* **sovereign** of *Tirzah* **Tirsah**, one:
all the *kings* **sovereigns** thirty and one.

PELESHETH REMAINS TO BE CONQUERED

13 Now *Joshua* **Yah Shua**
was old and stricken in *years* **days**;
and *the LORD* **Yah Veh** said unto him,
Thou art old and stricken in *years* **days**,
and there *remaineth* **surviveth** yet
very much **a mighty abounding** of land to be possessed.
2 This is the land that yet *remaineth* **surviveth**:
all the *borders* **region** of the *Philistines* **Peleshethiy**,
and all Geshuri,
3 From *Sihor* **Shichor**,
which is *before Egypt* **at the face of Misrayim**,
even unto the borders of *Ekron* **Eqron** northward,
which is *counted* **fabricated** to the *Canaanite* **Kenaaniy**:
five *lords* **ringleaders** of the *Philistines* **Peleshethiy**;
the *Gazathites* **Azzahiy**, and the *Ashdothites* **Ashdodiy**,
the *Eshkalonites* **Ashqeloniy**, the *Gittites* **Gittiy**,
and the *Ekronites* **Eqroniy**; also the *Avites* **Avviy**:
4 *From the south* **Southward**,
all the land of the *Canaanites* **Kenaaniy**,
and *Mearah* **the cave** that is beside the *Sidonians* **Sidoniy**
unto *Aphek* **Apheq**, to the borders of the *Amorites* **Emoriy**:
5 And the land of the *Giblites* **Gibliy**, and all Lebanon,
toward **from** the *sunrising* **rising sun**,
from *Baalgad* **Baal Gad** under mount Hermon
unto the entering into Hamath.
6 All the *inhabitants* **settlers** of the *hill country* **mountains**
from Lebanon unto *Misrephothmaim* **Misrephoth Mayim**,
and all the *Sidonians* **Sidoniy**,
them *will* **shall** I *drive out* **dispossess**
from *before* **the face of** the *children* **sons** of *Israel* **Yisra El**:
only *divide thou it by lot* **let it fall**
unto the *Israelites* **Yisra Eliy** for an inheritance,
as I have *commanded* **misvahed** thee.
7 Now therefore *divide* **allot** this land
for an inheritance unto the nine *tribes* **scions**,
and the half *tribe* **scion** of *Manasseh* **Menash Sheh**,
8 With whom
the *Reubenites* **Reu Beniy** and the *Gadites* **Gadiy**
have *received* **taken** their inheritance,
which *Moses* **Mosheh** gave them,
beyond *Jordan eastward* **Yarden from the rising**,
even as *Moses* **Mosheh** the servant of *the LORD* **Yah Veh**
gave them;
9 From Aroer,

that is upon the *bank* **lip** of the *river* **wadi** Arnon,
and the city that is in the midst of the *river* **wadi**,
and all the plain of Medeba unto Dibon;
10 And all the cities of *Sihon* **Sichon**
king **sovereign** of the *Amorites* **Emoriy**,
which reigned in Heshbon,
unto the border of the *children* **sons** of Ammon;
11 And *Gilead* **Gilad**,
and the border of the *Geshurites* **Geshuriy**
and *Maachathites* **Maachahiy**, and all mount Hermon,
and all Bashan unto *Salcah* **Salchah**;
12 All the *kingdom* **sovereigndom** of Og in Bashan,
which reigned in Ashtaroth and in Edrei,
who *remained* **survived**
of the remnant of the *giants* **Rephaim**:
for these did *Moses* **Mosheh** smite,
and *cast them out* **dispossess**.
13 Nevertheless the *children* **sons** of *Israel* **Yisra El**
expelled not the *Geshurites* **Geshuriy**,
nor the *Maachathites* **Maachahiy**:
but the *Geshurites* **Geshuriy**
and *the Maachathites* **Maakaiy**
dwell **settle** among the *Israelites* **Yisra Eliy** until this day.
14 Only unto the *tribe* **scion** of Levi
he gave none inheritance;
the sacrifices of the LORD God of Israel made by fire
the firings of Yah Veh Elohim of Yisra El
are their inheritance, as he *said* **worded** unto them.
15 And *Moses* **Mosheh** gave
unto the *tribe* **rod** of the *children* **sons** of *Reuben* **Reu Ben**
inheritance according to their families.
16 And their *coast* **border** was from Aroer,
that is on the *bank* **lip** of the *river* **wadi** Arnon,
and the city that is in the midst of the *river* **wadi**,
and all the plain by Medeba;
17 Heshbon, and all her cities that are in the plain;
Dibon, and *Bamoth—baal* **Bahmah Baal**,
and *Beth—baal—meon* **Beth Baal Meon**,
18 And *Jahaza* **Yahsah**,
and *Kedemoth* **Qedemoth**, and Mephaath,
19 And *Kirjathaim* **Kirjathaim**, and Sibmah,
and *Zarethshahar* **Sereth Hash Shachar**
in the mount of the valley,
20 And *Bethpeor* **Beth Peor**,
and *Ashdothpisgah* **Ashdoth Pisgah**,
and *Bethjeshimoth* **Beth Ha Yeshimoth**,
21 And all the cities of the plain,
and all the *kingdom* **sovereigndom** of *Sihon* **Sichon**
king **sovereign** of the *Amorites* **Emoriy**,
which reigned in Heshbon,
whom *Moses* **Mosheh** smote
with the *princes* **hierarchs** of *Midian* **Midyan**,
Evi, and *Rekem* **Reqem**, and *Zur* **Sur**, and Hur, and Reba,
which were *dukes* **libates** of *Sihon* **Sichon**,
dwelling **settling** in the *country* **land**.
22 *Balaam* **Bilam** also the son of Beor,
the *soothsayer* **diviner**,
did the *children* **sons** of *Israel* **Yisra El**
slay **slaughter** with the sword
among them that were *slain* **pierced** by them.
23 And the border of the *children* **sons** of *Reuben* **Reu Ben**
was *Jordan* **Yarden**, and the border thereof.
This was the inheritance
of the *children* **sons** of *Reuben* **Reu Ben** after their families,
the cities and the *villages* **courts** thereof.
24 And *Moses* **Mosheh** gave *inheritance*
unto the *tribe* **rod** of Gad,
even unto the *children* **sons** of Gad
according to their families.
25 And their *coast* **border** was *Jazer* **Yazer**,
and all the cities of *Gilead* **Gilad**,
and half the land of the *children* **sons** of Ammon,
unto Aroer that is *before* **at the face of** Rabbah;
26 And from Heshbon
unto *Ramathmizpeh* **Ramah Ham Mispeh**, and Betonim;
and from *Mahanaim* **Machanayim**
unto the border of Debir;
27 And in the valley, *Betharam* **Beth Ha Ram**,
and *Bethnimrah* **Beth Nimrah**,
and *Succoth* **Sukkoth/Brush Arbors**, and *Zaphon* **Saphon**,
the rest of the *kingdom* **sovereigndom** of *Sihon* **Sichon**
king **sovereign** of Heshbon,
Jordan **Yarden** and his border,
even unto the edge of the sea of *Chinnereth* **Kinneroth**
on the other side *Jordan eastward* **Yarden from the rising**.
28 This is the inheritance
of the *children* **sons** of Gad after their families,
the cities, and their *villages* **courts**.
29 And *Moses* **Mosheh** gave *inheritance*
unto the half *tribe* **rod** of *Manasseh* **Menash Sheh**:
and this was the possession of the half *tribe* **scion**
of the *children* **sons** of *Manasseh* **Menash Sheh**
by their families.
30 And their *coast* **border**
was from *Mahanaim* **Machanayim**, all Bashan,
all the *kingdom* **sovereigndom**
of Og *king* **sovereign** of Bashan,
and all the *towns* **living areas** of *Jair* **Yair**,
which are in Bashan, *threescore* **sixty** cities:
31 And half *Gilead* **Gilad**, and Ashtaroth, and Edrei,
cities of the *kingdom* **sovereigndom** of Og in Bashan,
were pertaining unto the children **sons** of Machir
the son of *Manasseh* **Menash Sheh**,
even to the one half of the *children* **sons** of Machir
by their families.
32 These *are the countries which Moses* **Mosheh**
did distribute for inheritance in the plains of Moab,
on the other side *Jordan* **Yarden**,
by *Jericho* **Yericho**, *eastward* **from the rising**.
33 But unto the *tribe* **scion** of Levi
Moses **Mosheh** gave *not any* **no** inheritance:
the LORD God **Yah Veh Elohim** of *Israel* **Yisra El**
was their inheritance, as he *said* **worded** unto them.

ALLOTMENT OF THE LAND OF KENAAN

14 And these *are the countries which*
the *children* **sons** of *Israel* **Yisra El** inherited
in the land of *Canaan* **Kenaan**,
which *Eleazar* **El Azar** the priest,
and *Joshua* **Yah Shua** the son of Nun,
and the heads of the fathers
of the *tribes* **rods** of the *children* **sons** of *Israel* **Yisra El**,
distributed for inheritance to them.
2 By *lot* **pebble** was their inheritance,
as *the LORD commanded* **Yah Veh misvahed**
by the hand of *Moses* **Mosheh**,
for the nine *tribes* **rods**, and for the half *tribe* **rod**.
3 For *Moses* **Mosheh** had given the inheritance
of two *tribes* **rods** and an half *tribe* **rod**
on the other side *Jordan* **Yarden**:
but unto the *Levites* **Leviym**
he gave none inheritance among them.
4 For the *children* **sons** of *Joseph* **Yoseph**
were two *tribes* **rods**,
Manasseh **Menash Sheh** and *Ephraim* **Ephrayim**:
therefore they gave no *part* **allotment**
unto the *Levites* **Leviym** in the land,
save cities to *dwell in* **settle**, with their suburbs
for their *cattle* **chattel**
and for their substance **which they chatteled**.
5 As *the LORD* **Yah Veh**
commanded Moses **misvahed Mosheh**,
so the *children* **sons** of *Israel did* **Yisra El worked**,
and they *divided* **allotted** the land.

KALEB'S CLAIM

6 Then the *children* **sons** of *Judah* **Yah Hudah**
came **near** unto *Joshua* **Yah Shua** in Gilgal:
and *Caleb* **Kaleb**
the son of *Jephunneh* **Yephunneh** the *Kenezite* **Qenaziy**
said unto him,
Thou knowest the *thing* **word**
that *the LORD said* **Yah Veh worded**
unto *Moses* **Mosheh** the man of *God* **Elohim**
concerning me and thee in *Kadeshbarnea* **Qadesh Barnea**.
7 **I was a son of** Forty years *old was I*
when *Moses* **Mosheh** the servant of *the LORD* **Yah Veh**
sent me from *Kadeshbarnea* **Qadesh Barnea**
to espy out the land;
and I *brought* **returned** him word *again*
as it was in mine heart.
8 Nevertheless my brethren

that *went up* **ascended** with me
made the heart of the people melt:
but I *wholly* **fully** followed **after**
the LORD **Yah Veh** my *God* **Elohim**.
9 And *Moses sware* **Mosheh oathed** on that day, saying,
Surely the land whereon thy feet have trodden
shall be thine inheritance,
and thy *children's for ever* **son's eternally**,
because thou hast *wholly* **fully** followed **after**
the LORD **Yah Veh** my *God* **Elohim**.
10 And now, behold,
the LORD **Yah Veh** hath kept me alive,
as he *said* **worded**, these forty and five years,
even since the LORD **when Yah Veh**
spake **worded** this word unto *Moses* **Mosheh**,
while *the children of Israel* **Yisra El**
wandered **walked** in the wilderness:
and now, *lo* **behold**, I am this day
fourscore **a son of eighty** and five years *old*.
11 As yet I am as strong this day
as I was in the day that *Moses* **Mosheh** sent me:
as my *strength* **force** was then,
even so is my *strength* **force** now,
for war, *both* to go out, and to come in.
12 Now therefore give me this mountain,
whereof *the LORD spake* **Yah Veh worded** in that day;
for thou heardest in that day
how the *Anakims* **Anaqiy** were there,
and that the cities were great and *fenced* **cut off**:
if so be the LORD will **perhaps Yah Veh shall** be with me,
then I shall *be able to drive them out* **dispossess them**,
as *the LORD said* **Yah Veh worded**.
13 And *Joshua* **Yah Shua** blessed him,
and gave unto *Caleb* **Kaleb**
the son of *Jephunneh* **Yephunneh**
Hebron for an inheritance.
14 Hebron therefore
became the inheritance of *Caleb* **Kaleb**
the son of *Jephunneh* **Yephunneh** the *Kenezite* **Qenaziy**
unto this day,
because that he *wholly* **fully** followed **after**
the LORD God **Yah Veh Elohim** of *Israel* **Yisra El**.
15 And the name of Hebron before
was *Kirjatharba* **Qiryath Arba**;
which Arba was a great man – **a great human**
among the *Anakims* **Anaqiy**.
And the land *had rest* **rested** from war.

YAH HUDAH'S ALLOTMENT

15 This then was the *lot* **pebble**
of the *tribe* **rod** of the *children* **sons** of *Judah* **Yah Hudah**
by their families;
even to the border of Edom
the wilderness of *Zin* **Sin** southward
was the *uttermost part* **extremity**
of the *south coast* **southward border**.
2 And their south border
was from the *shore* **end** of the salt sea,
from the *bay that looketh* **tongue at the face** southward:
3 And it went out to the south side
to *Maalehacrabbim* **Maaleh Acrabbim**,
and passed along to *Zin* **Sin**,
and ascended *up* on the south side
unto *Kadeshbarnea* **Qadesh Barnea**,
and passed along to *Hezron* **Hesron**,
and *went up* **ascended** to *Adar* **Addar**,
and *fetched a compass* **turned about** to *Karkaa* **Qarqa**:
4 *From thence* it passed toward *Azmon* **Asmon**,
and went out unto the *river* **wadi** of *Egypt* **Misrayim**;
and the *goings out* **exits** of that *coast* **border**
were at the sea:
this shall be your *south coast* **southward** border.
5 And the east border was the salt sea,
even unto the end of *Jordan* **Yarden**.
And their border in the north *quarter* **edge**
was from the *bay* **tongue** of the sea
at the *uttermost part* **extremity** of *Jordan* **Yarden**:
6 And the border
went up **ascended** to *Bethhogla* **Beth Chogla**,
and passed along
by the north of *Betharabah* **Beth Arabah**;
and the border *went up* **ascended**
to the stone of Bohan the son of *Reuben* **Reu Ben**:
7 And the border *went up* **ascended** toward Debir
from the valley of Achor,
and so northward, *looking toward* **at the face of** Gilgal,
that is before
the *going up to Adummim* **Ascent of Adummim**,
which is on the south side of the *river* **wadi**:
and the border
passed toward the waters of *Enshemesh* **En Shemesh**,
and the *goings out* **exits** thereof were at *Enrogel* **En Rogel**:
8 And the border *went up* **ascended**
by the valley of the son of *Hinnom* **Hinnom/Burning**
unto the south *side* **shoulder** of the *Jebusite* **Yebusiy**;
the same is *Jerusalem* **Yeru Shalem**:
and the border *went up* **ascended**
to the top of the mountain
that lieth before **at the face of**
the valley of *Hinnom* **Hinnom/Burning**
westward **seaward**,
which is at the end of
the valley of the giants **Gaymek Rephaim** northward:
9 And the border was *drawn* **surveyed**
from the top of the *hill* **mountain**
unto the fountain
of *the water of Nephtoah* **Mayim Nephtoach**,
and went out to the cities of mount Ephron;
and the border was *drawn* **surveyed** to *Baalah* **Baal Ah**,
which is *Kirjathjearim* **Qiryath Arim**:
10 And the border *compassed* **went about**
from *Baalah westward* **Baal Ah seaward** unto mount Seir,
and passed along
unto the *side* **shoulder** of mount *Jearim* **Yearim**,
which is *Chesalon* **Kesalon**, on the north *side*,
and *went down* **descended**
to *Bethshemesh* **Beth Shemesh**,
and passed on to Timnah:
11 And the border went out
unto the *side* **shoulder** of *Ekron* **Eqron** northward:
and the border was *drawn* **surveyed** to *Shicron* **Shikkeron**,
and passed along to mount *Baalah* **Baal Ah**,
and went out unto *Jabneel* **Yabne El**;
and the *goings out* **exits** of the border were at the sea.
12 And the *west* **seaward** border was to the great sea,
and the *coast* **border** thereof.
This is the *coast* **border**
of the *children* **sons** of *Judah* **Yah Hudah**
round about according to their families.
13 And unto *Caleb* **Kaleb** the son of *Jephunneh* **Yephunneh**
he gave *a part* **an allotment**
among the *children* **sons** of *Judah* **Yah Hudah**,
according to
the *commandment* **mouth** of the *LORD* **Yah Veh**
to *Joshua* **Yah Shua**,
even the city of Arba **Qiryath Arba**
the father of *Anak* **Anaq**, which *city* is Hebron.
14 And *Caleb* **Kaleb**
drove **dispossessed** thence the three sons of *Anak* **Anaq**,
Sheshai **Sheshay**, and *Ahiman* **Achiy Man**,
and *Talmai* **Talmay**,
the *children* **born** of *Anak* **Anaq**.
15 And he *went up* **ascended** thence
to the *inhabitants* **settlers** of Debir:
and the name of Debir before
was *Kirjathsepher* **Qiryath Sepher**.
16 And *Caleb* **Kaleb** said,
He that smiteth *Kirjathsepher* **Qiryath Sepher**,
and *taketh* **captureth** it,
to him *will* **shall** I give Achsah my daughter
to *wife* **woman**.
17 And *Othniel* **Othni El** the son of *Kenaz* **Qenaz**,
the brother of *Caleb* **Kaleb**, *took* **captured** it:
and he gave him Achsah his daughter
to *wife* **woman**.
18 And it *came to pass* **became**, as she came *unto him*,
that she *moved* **goaded** him to ask of her father a field:
and she *lighted* **alighted** off her *ass* **he burro**;
and *Caleb* **Kaleb** said unto her,
What *wouldest thou* – **to thee?**
19 Who *answered* **said**, Give me a blessing;

for thou hast given me a south land;
give me also *springs* **fountains** of water.
And he gave her the upper *springs* **fountains**,
and the *nether springs* **nethermost fountains**.
20 This is the inheritance
of the *tribe* **rod** of the *children* **sons** of *Judah* **Yah Hudah**
according to their families.
21 And the *uttermost* **extremity** cities
of the *tribe* **rod** of the *children* **sons** of *Judah* **Yah Hudah**
toward the *coast* **border** of Edom southward
were *Kabzeel* **Qabse El**, and Eder, and *Jagur* **Yagur**,
22 And *Kinah* **Qinah**, and Dimonah, and Adadah,
23 And *Kedesh* **Qedesh**,
and *Hazor* **Hasor**, and *Ithnan* **Yithnan**,
24 Ziph, and Telem, and Bealoth,
25 And *Hazor* **Hasor**, Hadattah, and *Kerioth* **Qerioth**,
and *Hezron* **Hesron**, which is *Hazor* **Hasor**,
26 Amam, and Shema, and Moladah,
27 And *Hasargaddah* **Hasar Gaddah**,
and Heshmon, and *Bethpalet* **Beth Palet**,
28 And *Hasarshual* **Hasar Shual**,
and *Beersheba* **Beer Sheba**, and *Bizjothjah* **Bizyoth Yah**,
29 *Baalah* **Baal Ah**, and *Iim* **Iyim**, and *Azem* **Esem**,
30 And *Eltolad* **El Tolad**, and *Chesil* **Kesil**, and Hormah,
31 And *Ziklag* **Siqlag**, and Madmannah, and Sansannah,
32 And Lebaoth, and *Shilhim* **Shilchim**,
and *Ain* **Ayin**, and Rimmon:
all the cities are twenty and nine,
with their *villages* **courts**:
33 And in the *valley* **lowland**,
Eshtaol, and *Zoreah* **Sorah**, and Ashnah,
34 And *Zanoah* **Zanoach**, and *Engannim* **En Gannim**,
Tappuah **Tappuach**, and *Enam* **En Am**,
35 *Jarmuth* **Yarmuth**, and Adullam,
Socoh **Sochoh**, and *Azekah* **Azeqah**,
36 And *Sharaim* **Shaarayim**, and *Adithaim* **Adithayim**,
and Gederah, and *Gederothaim* **Gederothayim**;
fourteen cities with their *villages* **courts**:
37 *Zenan* **Senan**, and Hadashah,
and *Migdalgad* **Migdal Gad**,
38 And *Dilean* **Dilan**,
and *Mizpeh* **Mispeh**, and *Joktheel* **Yoqthe El**,
39 Lachish, and *Bozkath* **Bosqath**, and Eglon,
40 And *Cabbon* **Kabbon**,
and *Lahmam* **Lachmam**, and Kithlish,
41 And Gederoth, *Bethdagon* **Beth Dagon**,
and Naamah, and *Makkedah* **Maqqedah**;
sixteen cities with their *villages* **courts**:
42 Libnah, and Ether, and Ashan,
43 And *Jiphtah* **Yiphtach**, and Ashnah, and *Nezib* **Nesib**,
44 And *Keilah* **Qeilah**, and Achzib, and Mareshah;
nine cities with their *villages* **courts**:
45 *Ekron* **Eqron**,
with her *towns* **daughters** and her *villages* **courts**:
46 From *Ekron* **Eqron** even unto the sea,
all *that lay near* **at the hand of** Ashdod,
with their *villages* **courts**:
47 Ashdod
with her *towns* **daughters** and her *villages* **courts**,
Gaza **Azzah**
with her *towns* **daughters** and her *villages* **courts**,
unto the *river* **wadi** of *Egypt* **Misrayim**,
and the *great sea*, **sea of the** border thereof:
48 And in the mountains,
Shamir, and *Jattir* **Yattir**, and *Socoh* **Sochoh**,
49 And Dannah,
and *Kirjathsannah* **Qiryath Sannah**, which is Debir,
50 And Anab, and Eshtemoh, and Anim,
51 And Goshen, and Holon, and Giloh;
eleven cities with their *villages* **courts**:
52 Arab, and Dumah, and *Eshean* **Eshan**,
53 And *Janum* **Yanim**,
and *Bethtappuah* **Beth Tappuach**, and *Aphekah* **Apheqah**,
54 And Humtah,
and *Kirjatharba* **Qiryath Arba**, which is Hebron,
and *Zior* **Sior**;
nine cities with their *villages* **courts**:
55 Maon, *Carmel* **Karmel**, and Ziph, and *Juttah* **Yuttah**,
56 And *Jezreel* **Yizre El**,
and *Jokdeam* **Yoqde Am**, and *Zanoah* **Zanoach**,
57 *Cain* **Qayin**, *Gibeah* **Gibah**, and Timnah;
ten cities with their *villages* **courts**:
58 *Halhul* **Halchul**, *Bethzur* **Beth Sur**, and Gedor,
59 And Maarath,
and *Bethanoth* **Beth Anoth**, and *Eltekon* **El Teqon**;
six cities with their *villages* **courts**:
60 *Kirjathbaal* **Qiryath Baal**,
which is *Kirjathjearim* **Qiryath Arim**,
and Rabbah;
two cities with their *villages* **courts**:
61 In the wilderness,
Betharabah **Beth Arabah**, Middin, and *Secacah* **Sechachah**,
62 And Nibshan,
and *the city of Salt* **Ir Ham Melach**, and *Engedi* **En Gedi**;
six cities with their *villages* **courts**.
63 As for the *Jebusites* **Yebusiy**
the *inhabitants* **settlers** of *Jerusalem* **Yeru Shalem**,
the *children* **sons** of *Judah* **Yah Hudah**
could not *drive* **dispossess** them *out*;
but the *Jebusites* **Yebusiy**
dwell **settle** with the *children* **sons** of *Judah* **Yah Hudah**
at *Jerusalem* **Yeru Shalem** unto this day.

YOSEPH'S BOUNDARIES

16 And the *lot* **pebble**
of the *children* **sons** of *Joseph* **Yoseph**
fell **goeth** from *Jordan* **Yarden** by *Jericho* **Yericho**,
unto the water of *Jericho* **Yericho** *on* **from** the *east* **rising**,
to the wilderness
that *goeth up* **ascendeth** from *Jericho* **Yericho**
throughout mount *Bethel* **Beth El**,
2 And goeth *out* from *Bethel* **Beth El** to Luz,
and passeth along
unto the borders of *Archi* **Arki** to Ataroth,
3 And *goeth down westward* **descendeth seaward**
to the *coast* **border** of *Japhleti* **Yaphletiy**,
unto the *coast* **border**
of *Bethhoron* **Beth Horon** the nether,
and to Gezer;
and the *goings out* **exits** thereof are at the sea.
4 So the *children* **sons** of *Joseph* **Yoseph**,
Manasseh **Menash Sheh** and *Ephraim* **Ephrayim**,
took their inheritance.

EPHRAYIM'S BOUNDARIES

5 And the border of the *children* **sons** of *Ephraim* **Ephrayim**
according to their families *was thus*:
even the border of their inheritance
on the east side **from the rising**
was *Atarothaddar* **Atroth Addar**,
unto *Bethhoron the upper* **Beth Horon Elyon**;
6 And the border went out toward the sea
to Michmethah on the north *side*;
and the border went about *eastward* **from the rising**
unto *Taanathshiloh* **Taanath Shiloh**,
and passed by it *on the east* **from the rising**
to *Janohah* **Yanochah**;
7 And it *went down* **descended**
from *Janohah* **Yanochah** to Ataroth,
and to *Naarath* **Naarah**,
and *came* **reached** to *Jericho* **Yericho**,
and went out at *Jordan* **Yarden**.
8 The border went out
from *Tappuah westward* **Tappuach seaward**
unto the *river Kanah* **wadi Qanah**;
and the *goings out* **exits** thereof were at the sea.
This is the inheritance
of the *tribe* **rod** of the *children* **sons** of *Ephraim* **Ephrayim**
by their families.
9 And the separate cities
for the *children* **sons** of *Ephraim* **Ephrayim**
were among the inheritance
of the *children* **sons** of *Manasseh* **Menash Sheh**,
all the cities with their *villages* **courts**.
10 And they *drave* **dispossessed** not *out*
the *Canaanites* **Kenaaniy** that *dwelt* **settled** in Gezer:
but the *Canaanites* **Kenaaniy**
dwell **settle** among the *Ephraimites* **Ephrayimiy**
unto this day,
and serve *under tribute* **a vassal**.

MENASH SHEH'S BOUNDARIES

17 There was also a *lot* **pebble**
for the *tribe* **rod** of *Manasseh* **Menash Sheh**;
for he was the firstborn of *Joseph* **Yoseph**; *to wit,*
for Machir the firstborn of *Manasseh* **Menash Sheh**,
the father of *Gilead* **Gilad**:
because he was a man of war,
therefore he had *Gilead* **Gilad** and Bashan.
2 There was also
a lot for the rest of **remaining for**
the *children* **sons** of *Manasseh* **Menash Sheh**
by their families;
for the *children* **sons** of *Abiezer* **Abi Ezer**,
and for the *children* **sons** of *Helek* **Heleq**,
and for the *children* **sons** of *Asriel* **Asri El**,
and for the *children* **sons** of Shechem,
and for the *children* **sons** of Hepher,
and for the *children* **sons** of *Shemida* **Shemi Da**:
these were the male *children* **sons**
of *Manasseh* **Menash Sheh**
the son of *Joseph* **Yoseph** by their families.
3 But *Zelophehad* **Seloph Had**, the son of Hepher,
the son of *Gilead* **Gilad**, the son of Machir,
the son of *Manasseh* **Menash Sheh**,
had no sons, but daughters:
and these are the names of his daughters,
Mahlah **Machlah**, and Noah,
Hoglah, *Milcah* **Milchah**, and *Tirzah* **Tirsah**.
4 And they *came near* **approached**
before Eleazar **at the face of El Azar** the priest,
and *before Joshua* **at the face of Yah Shua** the son of Nun,
and *before the princes* **at the face of the hierarchs**, saying,
the LORD commanded Moses **Yah Veh misvahed Mosheh**
to give us an inheritance among our brethren.
Therefore according
to the *commandment* **mouth** of *the LORD* **Yah Veh**
he gave them an inheritance
among the brethren of their father.
5 And there fell ten *portions* **boundaries**
to *Manasseh* **Menash Sheh**,
beside the land of *Gilead* **Gilad** and Bashan,
which were on the other side *Jordan* **Yarden**;
6 Because the daughters of *Manasseh* **Menash Sheh**
had **inherited** an inheritance among his sons:
and the *rest* **remaining** of *Manasseh's* **Menash Sheh's** sons
had the land of *Gilead* **Gilad**.
7 And the *coast* **border** of *Manasseh* **Menash Sheh**
was from Asher to Michmethah,
that lieth before **at the face of** Shechem;
and the border went along on the right *hand*
unto the *inhabitants* **settlers** of *Entappuah* **En Tappuach**.
8 *Now Manasseh* **Menash Sheh**
had the land of *Tappuah* **Tappuach**:
but *Tappuah* **Tappuach**
on the border of *Manasseh* **Menash Sheh**
belonged **was** to the *children* **sons** of *Ephraim* **Ephrayim**;
9 And the *coast* **border** descended
unto the *river Kanah* **wadi Qanah**,
southward of the *river* **wadi**:
these cities of *Ephraim* **Ephrayim**
are among the cities of *Manasseh* **Menash Sheh**:
the *coast* **border** of *Manasseh* **Menash Sheh** also
was on the north *side* of the *river* **wadi**,
and the *outgoings* **exits** of it were at the sea:
10 Southward it was *Ephraim's* **Ephrayim's**,
and northward it was *Manasseh's* **Menash Sheh's**,
and the sea is his border;
and they met together in Asher on the north,
and in *Issachar on* **Yissachar from** the *east* **rising**.
11 And *Manasseh* **Menash Sheh**
had in *Issachar* **Yissachar** and in Asher
Bethshean **Beth Shaan** and her *towns* **daughters**,
and *Ibleam* **Yible Am** and her *towns* **daughters**,
and the *inhabitants* **settlers** of Dor
and her *towns* **daughters**,
and the *inhabitants* **settlers** of *Endor* **En Dor**
and her *towns* **daughters**,
and the *inhabitants* **settlers** of Taanach
and her *towns* **daughters**,
and the *inhabitants* **settlers** of Megiddo
and her *towns* **daughters**,
even three *countries* **hills**.
12 Yet the *children* **sons** of *Manasseh* **Menash Sheh**
could not
drive out the inhabitants of **dispossess** those cities;
but the *Canaanites* **Kenaaniy**
would dwell **willed to settle** in that land.
13 Yet it *came to pass* **became**,
when the *children* **sons** of *Israel* **Yisra El**
were *waxen strong* **strengthened**,
that they *put* **gave** the *Canaanites* **Kenaaniy**
to *tribute* **vassal**,
but **in dispossessing**,
did not *utterly drive* **dispossess** them *out*.
14 And the *children* **sons** of *Joseph* **Yoseph**
spake **worded** unto *Joshua* **Yah Shua**, saying,
Why hast thou given me but one *lot* **pebble**
and one *portion to inherit* **boundary of inheritance**,
seeing I am a great people,
forasmuch as the LORD **even as Yah Veh**
hath blessed me hitherto?
15 And *Joshua answered* **Yah Shua said to** them,
If thou be a great people,
then *get thee up* **ascend** to the *wood country* **forest**,
and cut down for thyself there
in the land of the *Perizzites* **Perizziy**
and of the *giants* **Rephaim**,
if mount *Ephraim* **Ephrayim**
be too *narrow* **pressed** for thee.
16 And the *children* **sons** of *Joseph* **Yoseph** said,
The *hill* **mountain** is not *enough* **found** for us:
and all the *Canaanites* **Kenaaniy**
that *dwell* **settle** in the land of the valley
have chariots of iron,
both they who are of *Bethshean* **Beth Shaan**
and her *towns* **daughters**,
and they who are of the valley of *Jezreel* **Yizre El**.
17 And *Joshua spake* **Yah Shua said**
unto the house of *Joseph* **Yoseph**,
even to *Ephraim* **Ephrayim** and to *Manasseh* **Menash Sheh**,
saying,
Thou art a great people, and hast great *power* **force**:
thou shalt not have one *lot only* **pebble**:
18 But the mountain shall be thine;
for it is a *wood* **forest**, and thou shalt cut it down:
and the *outgoings* **exits** of it shall be thine:
for thou shalt
drive out **dispossess** the *Canaanites* **Kenaaniy**,
though they have iron chariots,
and though they be strong.

THE ALLOTMENT OF THE REST OF THE LAND

18 And the whole *congregation* **witness**
of the *children* **sons** of *Israel* **Yisra El**
assembled **congregated** *together* at Shiloh,
and *set up* **tabernacled**
the *tabernacle* **tent** of the congregation there.
And the land was subdued *before them* **at their face**.
2 And there remained
among the *children* **sons** of *Israel* **Yisra El**
seven *tribes* **scions**,
which had not yet *received* **allotted** their inheritance.
3 And *Joshua* **Yah Shua** said
unto the *children* **sons** of *Israel* **Yisra El**,
How long are ye slack to go to possess the land,
which *the LORD God* **Yah Veh Elohim** of your fathers
hath given you?
4 Give out from among you
three men for *each tribe* **a scion**:
and I *will* **shall** send them,
and they shall rise, and *go* **walk** through the land,
and *describe* **chart** it **by mouth**
according to the inheritance of them;
and they shall come *again* to me.
5 And they shall *divide* **allot** it into seven *parts* **allotments**:
Judah **Yah Hudah**
shall *abide* **stand** in their *coast* **border** on the south,
and the house of *Joseph* **Yoseph**
shall *abide* **stand** in their *coast* **border** on the north.
6 Ye shall therefore *describe* **chart** the land
into seven *parts* **allotments**,

and bring *the description* hither to me,
that I may cast *lots* **pebbles** for you here
before the LORD **at the face of Yah Veh** our *God* **Elohim**.
7 But the *Levites* **Leviym**
have no *part* **allotment** among you;
for the priesthood of *the LORD* **Yah Veh**
is their inheritance:
and Gad, and *Reuben* **Reu Ben**,
and half the *tribe* **scion** of *Manasseh* **Menash Sheh**,
have *received* **taken** their inheritance
beyond *Jordan* **Yarden** on the east,
which *Moses* **Mosheh** the servant of *the LORD* **Yah Veh**
gave them.

THE LAND IS CHARTED

8 And the men arose, and went away:
and *Joshua charged* **Yah Shua misvahed** them
that went to *describe* **chart** the land, saying,
Go and walk through the land, and *describe* **chart** it,
and *come again* **return** to me,
that I may here cast *lots* **pebbles** for you
before the LORD **at the face of Yah Veh** in Shiloh.
9 And the men went and passed through the land,
and *described* **charted** it by cities
into seven *parts* **allotments** in a *book* **scroll**,
and came again to *Joshua* **Yah Shua**
to the *host* **camp** at Shiloh.
10 And *Joshua* **Yah Shua**
cast *lots* **pebbles** for them in Shiloh
before the LORD **at the face of Yah Veh**:
and there *Joshua divided* **Yah Shua allotted** the land
unto the *children* **sons** of *Israel* **Yisra El**
according to their *divisions* **allotment**.

BEN YAMIN'S PEBBLE

11 And the *lot* **pebble** of the *tribe* **rod**
of the *children* **sons** of *Benjamin* **Ben Yamin**
came up **ascended** according to their families:
and the *coast* **border** of their *lot came forth* **pebble went**
between the *children* **sons** of *Judah* **Yah Hudah**
and the *children* **sons** of *Joseph* **Yoseph**.
12 And their border on the north *side* **edge**
was from *Jordan* **Yarden**;
and the border *went up* **ascended**
to the *side* **shoulder** of *Jericho* **Yericho** on the north *side*,
and *went up* **ascended** through the mountains
westward **seaward**;
and the *goings out* **exits** thereof
were at the wilderness of *Bethaven* **Beth Aven**.
13 And the border *went* **passed** over
from thence toward Luz,
to the *side* **shoulder** of Luz, which is *Bethel* **Beth El**,
southward;
and the border descended to *Atarothadar* **Ataroth Addar**,
near the *hill* **mountain**
that lieth on the south side
of the nether *Bethhoron* **Beth Horon**.
14 And the border was *drawn thence* **surveyed**,
and *compassed* **went about** the *corner* **edge** of the sea
southward,
from the *hill* **mountain**
that lieth before Bethhoron **at the face of Beth Horon**
southward;
and the *goings out* **exits** thereof
were at *Kirjathbaal* **Qiryath Baal**,
which is *Kirjathjearim* **Qiryath Arim**,
a city of the *children* **sons** of *Judah* **Yah Hudah**:
this was the *west quarter* **sea edge**.
15 And the south *quarter* **edge**
was from the end of *Kirjathjearim* **Qiryath Arim**,
and the border went out on the *west* **sea**,
and went out to the *well* **fountain**
of *waters of Nephtoah* **Mayim Nephtoach**:
16 And the border *came down* **descended**
to the end of the mountain
that lieth before **at the face**
of the valley of the son of *Hinnom* **Hinnom/Burning**,
and which is in the valley of *the giants* **Rephaim**
on the north,
and descended to the valley of *Hinnom* **Hinnom/Burning**,
to the *side* **shoulder** of *Jebusi* **Yebusi** on the south,
and descended to *Enrogel* **En Rogel**,
17 And was *drawn* **surveyed** from the north,
and went forth to *Enshemesh* **En Shemesh**,
and went forth toward Geliloth,
which is over against the *going up* **ascent** of Adummim,
and descended to the stone of Bohan
the son of *Reuben* **Reu Ben**,
18 And passed along toward the *side* **shoulder**
over against Arabah **toward the plain** northward,
and *went down* **descended** unto *Arabah* **the plain**:
19 And the border passed along
to the *side* **shoulder** of *Bethhogla* **Beth Chogla** northward:
and the *outgoings* **exits** of the border
were at the north *bay* **tongue** of the salt sea
at the south end of *Jordan* **Yarden**:
this was the south *coast* **border**.
20 And *Jordan* **Yarden** was the border of it
on the east *side* **edge**.
This was the inheritance
of the *children* **sons** of *Benjamin* **Ben Yamin**,
by the *coasts* **borders** thereof round about,
according to their families.

BEN YAMIN'S CITIES

21 Now the cities of the *tribe* **rod**
of the *children* **sons** of *Benjamin* **Ben Yamin**
according to their families were *Jericho* **Yericho**,
and *Bethhogla* **Beth Chogla**, and the valley of *Keziz* **Qesis**,
22 And *Betharabah* **Beth Arabah**,
and *Zemaraim* **Semarayim**, and *Bethel* **Beth El**,
23 And *Avim* **Avviy**, and Parah, and Ophrah,
24 And *Chepharhaammonai* **Kephar Ammonai**,
and *Ophni* **Opheniy**, and *Gaba* **Geba**;
twelve cities with their *villages* **courts**:
25 *Gibeon* **Gibon**, and Ramah, and Beeroth,
26 And *Mizpeh* **Mispeh**, and *Chephirah* **Kephirah**,
and *Mozah* **Mosah**,
27 And *Rekem* **Reqem**, and *Irpeel* **Yirpe El**, and Taralah,
28 And *Zelah* **Sela**, *Eleph* **Chiliarch**,
and *Jebusi* **Yebusi**, which is *Jerusalem* **Yeru Shalem**,
Gibeath **Gibath**, and *Kirjath* **Qiryath**;
fourteen cities with their *villages* **courts**.
This is the inheritance
of the *children* **sons** of *Benjamin* **Ben Yamin**
according to their families.

SHIMON'S PEBBLE

19 And the second *lot* **pebble**
came forth **went** to *Simeon* **Shimon**,
even for the *tribe* **rod**
of the *children* **sons** of *Simeon* **Shimon**
according to their families:
and their inheritance was within the inheritance
of the *children* **sons** of *Judah* **Yah Hudah**.
2 And they had in their inheritance *Beersheba* **Beer Sheba**,
and Sheba, and Moladah,
3 And *Hasarshual* **Hasar Shual**,
and Balah, and *Azem* **Esem**,
4 And *Eltolad* **El Tolad**, and *Bethul* **Bethu El**, and Hormah,
5 And *Ziklag* **Siqlag**, and *Bethmarcaboth* **Beth Markaboth**,
and *Hasarsusah* **Hasar Susah**,
6 And *Bethlebaoth* **Beth Lebaoth**,
and *Sharuhen* **Sharuchen**;
thirteen cities and their *villages* **courts**:
7 *Ain* **Ayin**, *Remmon* **Rimmon**, and Ether, and Ashan;
four cities and their *villages* **courts**:
8 And all the *villages* **courts**
that were round about these cities
to *Baalathbeer* **Baalath Beer**,
Ramath **Ramah** of the south.
This is the inheritance
of the *tribe* **rod** of the *children* **sons** of *Simeon* **Shimon**
according to their families.
9 Out of the *portion* **boundaries**
of the *children* **sons** of *Judah* **Yah Hudah**
was the inheritance
of the *children* **sons** of *Simeon* **Shimon**:
for the *part* **allotment**
of the *children* **sons** of *Judah* **Yah Hudah**
was too much for them:
therefore the *children* **sons** of *Simeon* **Shimon**
had their inheritance within the inheritance of them.

ZEBULUN'S PEBBLE

10 And the third *lot* **pebble**
came up **ascended** for the *children* **sons** of Zebulun
according to their families:
and the border of their inheritance was unto Sarid:
11 And their border *went up* **ascended** toward the sea,
and Maralah, and reached to *Dabbasheth* **Dabbesheth**,
and reached to the *river* **wadi**
that is before Jokneam **at the face of Yoqne Am**;
12 And turned from Sarid eastward
toward the *sunrising* **rising sun**
unto the border of *Chislothtabor* **Kisloth Tabor**,
and then goeth *out* to Daberath,
and *goeth up* **ascendeth** to *Japhia* **Yaphia**,
13 And from thence passeth on along
on the east **from the rising**
to Gittahhepher, to *Ittahkazin* **Eth Qasin**,
and goeth *out* to *Remmonmethoar* **Rimmon**
which is surveyed to Neah;
14 And the border *compasseth* **surroundeth** it
on the north *side* to Hannathon:
and the *outgoings* **exits** thereof
are in the valley of *Jiphthahel* **Yiphtach El**:
15 And *Kattath* **Qattath**, and Nahallal, and Shimron,
and *Idalah* **Yidalah**, and *Bethlehem* **Beth Lechem**:
twelve cities with their *villages* **courts**.
16 This is the inheritance of the *children* **sons** of Zebulun
according to their families,
these cities with their *villages* **courts**.

YISSACHAR'S PEBBLE

17 *And* the fourth *lot* **pebble**
came out **went** to *Issachar* **Yissachar**,
for the *children* **sons** of *Issachar* **Yissachar**
according to their families.
18 And their border was toward *Jezreel* **Yizre El**,
and *Chesulloth* **Kesulloth**, and Shunem,
19 And *Haphraim* **Haphrayim**,
and *Shihon* **Shiyon**, and *Anaharath* **Anacharath**,
20 And Rabbith, and *Kishion* **Qishyon**, and *Abez* **Abes**,
21 And Remeth, and *Engannim* **En Gannim**,
and *Enhaddah* **En Haddah**, and *Bethpazzez* **Beth Patses**;
22 And the *coast* **border** reacheth to Tabor,
and *Shahazimah* **Shachasom**,
and *Bethshemesh* **Beth Shemesh**;
and the *outgoings* **exits** of their border
were at *Jordan* **Yarden**:
sixteen cities with their *villages* **courts**.
23 This is the inheritance
of the *tribe* **rod** of the *children* **sons** of *Issachar* **Yissachar**
according to their families,
the cities and their *villages* **courts**.

ASHER'S PEBBLE

24 And the fifth *lot* **pebble**
came out **went** for the *tribe* **rod** of the *children* **sons** of Asher
according to their families.
25 And their border was *Helkath* **Helqath**,
and Hali, and Beten, and Achshaph,
26 And *Alammelech* **Alam Melech**, and Amad, and Misheal;
and reacheth to *Carmel westward* **Karmel seaward**,
and to *Shihorlibnath* **Shichor Libnath**;
27 And turneth toward the *sunrising* **rising sun**
to *Bethdagon* **Beth Dagon**, and reacheth to Zebulun,
and to the valley of *Jiphthahel* **Yiphtach El**
toward the north *side* of *Bethemek* **Beth Ha Emeq**,
and *Neiel* **Nei El**,
and goeth *out* to *Cabul* **Kabul** on the left *hand*,
28 And *Hebron* **Ebron**, and *Rehob* **Rechob**,
and Hammon, and *Kanah* **Qanah**,
even unto great *Zidon* **Sidon**;
29 And *then* the *coast* **border** turneth to Ramah,
and to the *strong* **fortified** city *Tyre* **Sor**;
and the *coast* **border** turneth to Hosah;
and the *outgoings* **exits** thereof are at the sea
from the *coast region* **border boundaries** to Achzib:
30 Ummah also, and *Aphek* **Apheq**, and *Rehob* **Rechob**:
twenty and two cities with their *villages* **courts**.
31 This is the inheritance of the *tribe* **rod**
of the *children* **sons** of Asher
according to their families,
these cities with their *villages* **courts**.

NAPHTALI'S PEBBLE

32 The sixth *lot* **pebble**
came out **went** to the *children* **sons** of Naphtali,
even for the *children* **sons** of Naphtali
according to their families.
33 And their *coast* **border** was from Heleph,
from Allon to *Zaanannim* **Saanannim**, and Adami,
Nekeb **Neqeb**, and *Jabneel* **Yabne El**,
unto *Lakum* **Laqqum**;
and the *outgoings* **exits** thereof were at *Jordan* **Yarden**:
34 And *then* the *coast* **border** turneth *westward* **seaward**
to *Aznothtabor* **Aznoth Tabor**,
and goeth *out* from thence to *Hukkok* **Huqqoq**,
and reacheth to Zebulun on the south *side*,
and reacheth to Asher on the *west* **sea** *side*,
and to *Judah* **Yah Hudah** upon *Jordan* **Yarden**
toward the *sunrising* **rising sun**.
35 And the *fenced* **fortified** cities are *Ziddim* **Siddim**,
Zer **Ser**, and Hammath,
Rakkath **Raqqath**, and *Chinnereth* **Kinneroth**,
36 And Adamah, and Ramah, and *Hazor* **Hasor**,
37 And *Kedesh* **Qedesh**, and Edrei, and *Enhazor* **En Hasor**,
38 And *Iron* **Yiron**, and *Migdalel* **Migdal El**,
Horem, and *Bethanath* **Beth Anath**,
and *Bethshemesh* **Beth Shemesh**;
nineteen cities with their *villages* **courts**.
39 This is the inheritance of the *tribe* **rod**
of the *children* **sons** of Naphtali
according to their families,

DAN'S PEBBLE

40 *And* the seventh *lot* **pebble**
came out **went** for the *tribe* **rod**
of the *children* **sons** of Dan
according to their families.
41 And the *coast* **border** of their inheritance
was *Zorah* **Sorah**, and Eshtaol,
and *Irshemesh* **Ir Shemesh**,
42 And *Shaalabbin* **Shaalbim**,
and *Ajalon* **Ayalon**, and *Jethlah* **Yithlah**,
43 And Elon, and *Thimnathah* **Timnah**, and *Ekron* **Eqron**,
44 And *Eltekeh* **El Teqeh**, and Gibbethon, and Baalath,
45 And *Jehud* **Yah Hudah**, and *Beneberak* **Bene Beraq**,
and *Gathrimmon* **Gath Rimmon**,
46 And *Mejarkon* **Me Hay Yarqon**, and *Rakkon* **Raqqon**,
with the border *before Japho* **toward Yapho**.
47 And the *coast* **border** of the *children* **sons** of Dan
went out *too little* for them:
therefore the *children* **sons** of Dan
went up **ascended** to fight against Leshem,
and *took* **captured** it,
and smote it with the *edge* **mouth** of the sword,
and possessed it, and *dwelt* **settled** therein,
and called Leshem, Dan,
after the name of Dan their father.
48 This is the inheritance of the *tribe* **rod**
of the *children* **sons** of Dan
according to their families,
these cities with their *villages* **courts**.

YAH SHUA'S PEBBLE

49 When they had *made an end of* **finished**
dividing the land for inheritance
by their *coasts* **borders**,
the *children* **sons** of *Israel* **Yisra El** gave an inheritance
to *Joshua* **Yah Shua** the son of Nun among them:
50 According to the *word* **mouth** of *the LORD* **Yah Veh**
they gave him the city which he asked,
even *Timnathserah* **Timnah Heres**
in mount *Ephraim* **Ephrayim**:
and he built the city, *and dwelt* **settled** therein.
51 These are the inheritances,
which *Eleazar* **El Azar** the priest,
and *Joshua* **Yah Shua** the son of Nun,
and the heads of the fathers of the *tribes* **rods**
of the *children* **sons** of *Israel* **Yisra El**,
divided for an inheritance by *lot* **pebble** in Shiloh
before the LORD **at the face of Yah Veh**,
at the *door* **opening**
of the *tabernacle* **tent** of the congregation.
So they *made an end of* **finished**
dividing **allotting** the *country* **land**.

CITIES OF REFUGE

20 *The LORD* **Yah Veh**
also *spake* **worded** unto *Joshua* **Yah Shua**, saying,
2 *Speak* **Word** to the *children* **sons** of *Israel* **Yisra El**,
saying, *Appoint* **Give** out for you cities of refuge,
whereof I *spake* **worded** unto you
by the hand of *Moses* **Mosheh**:
3 That the *slayer* **murderer**
that *killeth any person* **smiteth a soul**
unawares and unwittingly
by inadvertent error unknowingly
may flee thither:
and they shall be your refuge
from the *avenger* **redeemer** of blood.
4 And when he that doth flee unto one of those cities
shall stand at the *entering* **portal**
of the *gate* **portal** of the city,
and shall *declare* **word** his *cause* **word**
in the ears of the elders of that city,
they shall *take* **gather** him into the city unto them,
and give him a place,
that he may *dwell* **settle** among them.
5 And if the *avenger* **redeemer** of blood pursue after him,
then they shall not *deliver* **shut** the *slayer* **murderer** *up*
into his hand;
because he smote his *neighbour* **friend**
unwittingly **unknowingly**,
and hated him not *beforetime* **three yesters ago**.
6 And he shall *dwell* **settle** in that city,
until he stand
before **at the face of** the *congregation* **witness**
for judgment,
and until the death of the *high* **great** priest
that shall be in those days:
then shall the *slayer* **murderer** return,
and come unto his own city, and unto his own house,
unto the city from whence he fled.
7 And they *appointed* **hallowed**
Kedesh **Qedesh** in *Galilee* **Galiyl** in mount Naphtali,
and Shechem in mount *Ephraim* **Ephrayim**,
and *Kirjatharba* **Qiryath Arba**, which is Hebron,
in the mountain of *Judah* **Yah Hudah**.
8 And on the other side *Jordan* **Yarden**
by *Jericho eastward* **Yericho toward the rising**,
they *assigned Bezer* **gave Beser**
in the wilderness upon the plain
out of the *tribe* **rod** of *Reuben* **Reu Ben**,
and Ramoth in *Gilead* **Gilad** out of the *tribe* **rod** of Gad,
and Golan in Bashan
out of the *tribe* **rod** of *Manasseh* **Manesh Sheh**.
9 These were the cities appointed
for all the *children* **sons** of *Israel* **Yisra El**,
and for the *stranger* **sojourner**
that sojourneth among them,
that whosoever *killeth any person* **smiteth a soul**
at unawares **by inadvertent error** might flee thither,
and not die
by the hand of the *avenger* **redeemer** of blood,
until he stood
before **at the face of** the *congregation* **witness**.

LEVIYM'S PEBBLE

21 Then came near
the heads of the fathers of the *Levites* **Leviym**
unto *Eleazar* **El Azar** the priest,
and unto *Joshua* **Yah Shua** the son of Nun,
and unto the heads of the fathers
of the *tribes* **rods** of the *children* **sons** of *Israel* **Yisra El**;
2 And they *spake* **worded** unto them at Shiloh
in the land of *Canaan* **Kenaan**, saying,
the LORD commanded **Yah Veh misvahed**
by the hand of *Moses* **Mosheh**
to give us cities to *dwell* **settle** in,
with the suburbs thereof for our *cattle* **animals**.
3 And the *children* **sons** of *Israel* **Yisra El**
gave unto the *Levites* **Leviym** out of their inheritance,
at the *commandment* **mouth** of *the LORD* **Yah Veh**,
these cities and their suburbs.

QOHATHIY'S PEBBLE

4 And the *lot came out* **pebble went**
for the families of the *Kohathites* **Qohathiy**:
and the *children* **sons** of *Aaron* **Aharon** the priest,
which were of the *Levites* **Leviym**,
had by *lot* **pebble**
out of the *tribe* **rod** of *Judah* **Yah Hudah**,
and out of the *tribe* **rod** of *Simeon* **Shimoniy**,
and out of the *tribe* **rod** of *Benjamin* **Ben Yamin**,
thirteen cities.
5 And the *rest* **remaining**
of the children **sons** of *Kohath* **Qohath**
had by *lot* **pebble** out of the families
of the *tribe* **rod** of *Ephraim* **Ephrayim**,
and out of the *tribe* **rod** of Dan,
and out of the half *tribe* **rod** of *Manasseh* **Menash Sheh**,
ten cities.

GERSHON'S PEBBLE

6 And the *children* **sons** of Gershon
had by *lot* **pebble** out of the families
of the *tribe* **rod** of *Issachar* **Yissachar**,
and out of the *tribe* **rod** of Asher,
and out of the *tribe* **rod** of Naphtali,
and out of the half *tribe* **rod** of *Manasseh* **Menash Sheh**
in Bashan, thirteen cities.

MERARI'S PEBBLE

7 The *children* **sons** of Merari by their families
had out of the *tribe* **rod** of *Reuben* **Reu Ben**,
and out of the *tribe* **rod** of Gad,
and out of the *tribe* **rod** of Zebulun,
twelve cities.
8 And the *children* **sons** of *Israel* **Yisra El**
gave by *lot* **pebble** unto the *Levites* **Leviym**
these cities with their suburbs,
as *the LORD commanded* **Yah Veh misvahed**
by the hand of *Moses* **Mosheh**.

AHARON'S PEBBLE

9 And they gave out of the *tribe* **rod**
of the *children* **sons** of *Judah* **Yah Hudah**,
and out of the *tribe* **rod**
of the *children* **sons** of *Simeon* **Shimon**,
these cities which are *here mentioned* **called** by name.
10 Which the *children* **sons** of *Aaron* **Aharon**,
being of the families of the *Kohathites* **Qehathiy**,
who were of the *children* **sons** of Levi, had:
for theirs was the first *lot* **pebble**.
11 And they gave them *the city of Arba* **Qiryath Arba**
the father of *Anak* **Anaq**, which *city* is Hebron,
in the *hill country* **mountains** of *Judah* **Yah Hudah**,
with the suburbs thereof round about it.
12 But the fields of the city,
and the *villages* **courts** thereof,
gave they to *Caleb* **Kaleb**
the son of *Jephunneh* **Yephunneh** for his possession.
13 Thus they gave
to the *children* **sons** of *Aaron* **Aharon** the priest
Hebron with her suburbs,
to be a city of refuge for the *slayer* **murderer**;
and Libnah with her suburbs,
14 And *Jattir* **Yattir** with her suburbs,
and Eshtemoa with her suburbs,
15 And Holon with her suburbs,
and Debir with her suburbs,
16 And *Ain* **Ayin** with her suburbs,
and *Juttah* **Yuttah** with her suburbs,
and Bethshemesh **Beth Shemesh** with her suburbs;
nine cities out of those two *tribes* **scions**.
17 And out of the *tribe* **rod** of *Benjamin* **Ben Yamin**,
Gibeon **Gibon** with her suburbs,
Geba with her suburbs,
18 Anathoth with her suburbs,
and Almon with her suburbs;
four cities.
19 All the cities
of the *children* **sons** of *Aaron* **Aharon**, the priests,
were thirteen cities with their suburbs.

QEHATH'S PEBBLE

20 And the families of the *children* **sons** of *Kohath* **Qehath**,
the *Levites* **Leviym** which remained
of the *children* **sons** of *Kohath* **Qehath**,
even they had the cities of their *lot* **pebble**
out of the *tribe* **rod** of *Ephraim* **Ephrayim**.
21 For they gave them Shechem

with her suburbs in mount *Ephraim* **Ephrayim**,
to be a city of refuge for the *slayer* **murderer**;
and Gezer with her suburbs,
22 And *Kibzaim* **Qibsayim** with her suburbs,
and *Bethhoron* **Beth Horon** with her suburbs;
four cities.
23 And out of the *tribe* **rod** of Dan,
Eltekeh **El Teqeh** with her suburbs,
Gibbethon with her suburbs,
24 *Aijalon* **Ayalon** with her suburbs,
Gat—rimmon **Gath Rimmon** πwith her suburbs;
four cities.
25 And out of the half *tribe* **rod**
of *Manasseh* **Menash Sheh**,
Tanach **Taanach** with her suburbs,
and *Gathrimmon* **Gath Rimmon** with her suburbs;
two cities.
26 All the cities were ten with their suburbs
for the families of the *children* **sons** of *Kohath* **Qehath**
that remained.

GERSHON'S PEBBLE

27 And unto the *children* **sons** of Gershon,
of the families of the *Levites* **Leviym**,
out of the *other* half *tribe* **rod** of *Manasseh* **Menash Sheh**
they gave Golan in Bashan with her suburbs,
to be a city of refuge for the *slayer* **murderer**;
and *Beeshterah* **Beesh Terah** with her suburbs;
two cities.
28 And out of the *tribe* **rod** of *Issachar* **Yissachar**,
Kishon **Qishyon** with her suburbs,
Dabareh **Dabarath** with her suburbs,
29 *Jarmuth* **Yarmuth** with her suburbs,
Engannim **En Gannim** with her suburbs;
four cities.
30 And out of the *tribe* **rod** of Asher,
Mishal with her suburbs,
Abdon with her suburbs,
31 *Helkath* **Helqath** with her suburbs,
and *Rehob* **Rechob** with her suburbs;
four cities.
32 And out of the *tribe* **rod** of Naphtali,
Kedesh in Galilee **Qedesh Galiyl** with her suburbs,
to be a city of refuge for the *slayer* **murderer**;
and *Hammothdor* **Hammoth Dor** with her suburbs,
and *Kartan* **Qartan** with her suburbs;
three cities.
33 All the cities of the *Gershonites* **Gershoniy**
according to their families
were thirteen cities with their suburbs.

MERARI'S PEBBLE

34 And unto the families of the *children* **sons** of Merari,
the rest **remaining** of the *Levites* **Leviym**,
out of the *tribe* **rod** of Zebulun,
Jokneam **Yoqne Am** with her suburbs,
and *Kartah* **Qartah** with her suburbs,
35 Dimnah with her suburbs,
Nahalal with her suburbs;
four cities.
36 And out of the *tribe* **rod** of *Reuben* **Reu Ben**,
Bezer with her suburbs,
and Jahazah with her suburbs,
37 Kedemoth with her suburbs,
and Mephaath with her suburbs;
four cities.
38 And out of the *tribe* **rod** of Gad,
Ramoth in *Gilead* **Gilad** with her suburbs,
to be a city of refuge for the *slayer* **murderer**;
and *Mahanaim* **Machanayim** with her suburbs,
39 Heshbon with her suburbs,
Jazer **Yazer** with her suburbs;
four cities in all.
40 So all the cities
for the *children* **sons** of Merari by their families,
which were remaining
of the families of the *Levites* **Leviym**,
were by their *lot* **pebble** twelve cities.
41 All the cities of the *Levites* **Leviym**
within the possession of the *children* **sons** of *Israel* **Yisra El**
were forty and eight cities with their suburbs.
42 These cities were *every one* **city by city**
with their suburbs round about them:
thus were all these cities.
43 And *the LORD* **Yah Veh** gave unto *Israel* **Yisra El**
all the land which he *sware* **oathed**
to give unto their fathers;
and they possessed it, and *dwelt* **settled** therein.
44 And *the LORD* **Yah Veh** gave them rest round about,
according to all that he *sware* **oathed** unto their fathers:
and there stood not a man of all their enemies
before them **at their face**;
the LORD delivered **Yah Veh gave** all their enemies
into their hand.
45 There *failed* **fell** not ought of any good *thing* **word**
which *the LORD* **Yah Veh** had *spoken* **worded**
unto the house of *Israel* **Yisra El**; all *came to pass* **became**.

SOME RODS RETURN HOME

22 Then *Joshua* **Yah Shua** called
the *Reubenites* **Reu Beniy**, and the *Gadites* **Gadiy**,
and the half *tribe* **rod** of *Manasseh* **Menash Sheh**,
2 And said unto them, ye have *kept* **guarded** all
that *Moses* **Mosheh** the servant of *the LORD* **Yah Veh**
commanded **misvahed** you,
and have *obeyed* **heard** my voice
in all that I *commanded* **misvahed** you:
3 Ye have not left your brethren these many days
unto this day,
but have *kept* **guarded** the *charge* **guard**
of the *commandment* **misvah**
of *the LORD* **Yah Veh** your *God* **Elohim**.
4 And now *the LORD* **Yah Veh** your *God* **Elohim**
hath *given rest unto* **rested** your brethren,
as he *promised* **worded** them:
therefore now *return* **face** ye,
and *get you* **go** unto your tents,
and unto the land of your possession,
which *Moses* **Mosheh** the servant of *the LORD* **Yah Veh**
gave you on the other side *Jordan* **Yarden**.
5 But *take diligent heed* **guard mightily**
to *do* **work** the *commandment* **misvah** and the *law* **torah**,
which *Moses* **Mosheh** the servant of *the LORD* **Yah Veh**
charged **misvahed** you,
to love *the LORD* **Yah Veh** your *God* **Elohim**,
and to walk in all his ways,
and to *keep* **guard** his *commandments* **mitsvoth**,
and to *cleave* **adhere** unto him,
and to serve him
with all your heart and with all your soul.
6 So *Joshua* **Yah Shua** blessed them, and sent them away:
and they went unto their tents.
7 Now to the *one* half
of the *tribe* **scion** of *Manasseh* **Menash Sheh**
Moses **Mosheh** had given *possession* in Bashan:
but unto the *other* half thereof
gave *Joshua* **Yah Shua** among their brethren
on this side *Jordan westward* **Yarden seaward**.
And when *Joshua* **Yah Shua**
sent them away also unto their tents,
then he blessed them,
8 And he *spake* **said** unto them, saying,
Return with much *riches* **holdings** unto your tents,
and with *very* **mighty** much *cattle* **chattel**,
with silver, and with gold,
and with *brass* **copper**, and with iron,
and with
very much raiment **a mighty abounding of clothes**:
divide **allot** the spoil of your enemies with your brethren.
9 And the *children* **sons** of *Reuben* **Reu Ben**
and the *children* **sons** of Gad
and the half *tribe* **scion** of *Manasseh* **Menash Sheh**
returned,
and *departed* **went** from the *children* **sons** of *Israel* **Yisra El**
out of Shiloh, which is in the land of *Canaan* **Kenaan**,
to go unto the *country* **land** of *Gilead* **Gilad**,
to the land of their possession,
whereof they were possessed,
according to the *word* **mouth** of *the LORD* **Yah Veh**
by the hand of *Moses* **Mosheh**.

THE REBEL ALTAR

10 And when they came
unto the *borders* **region** of *Jordan* **Yarden**,

that are in the land of *Canaan* **Kenaan**,
the *children* **sons** of *Reuben* **Reu Ben**
and the *children* **sons** of Gad
and the half *tribe* **scion** of *Manasseh* **Menash Sheh**
built there *an* **a sacrifice** altar by *Jordan* **Yarden**,
a great **sacrifice** altar to *see to* **the sight**.
11 And the *children* **sons** of *Israel* **Yisra El** heard say,
Behold, the *children* **sons** of *Reuben* **Reu Ben**
and the *children* **sons** of Gad
and the half *tribe* **scion** of *Manasseh* **Menash Sheh**
have built *an* **a sacrifice** altar
over *against* **toward** the land of *Canaan* **Kenaan**,
in the *borders* **region** of *Jordan* **Yarden**,
at the passage **on this side**
of the *children* **sons** of *Israel* **Yisra El**.
12 And when the *children* **sons** of *Israel* **Yisra El** heard of it,
the whole *congregation* **witness**
of the *children* **sons** of *Israel* **Yisra El**
gathered **congregated** themselves together at Shiloh,
to *go up* **ascend** to *war* **host** against them.
13 And the *children* **sons** of *Israel* **Yisra El**
sent unto the *children* **sons** of *Reuben* **Reu Ben**,
and to the *children* **sons** of Gad,
and to the half *tribe* **scion** of *Manasseh* **Menash Sheh**,
into the land of *Gilead* **Gilad**,
Phinehas **Pinechas** the son of *Eleazar* **El Azar** the priest,
14 And with him ten *princes* **hierarchs**,
of each *chief house* **house of the fathers,**
a prince **one hierarch**
throughout all the *tribes* **rods** of *Israel* **Yisra El**;
and each *one* **man** was an head
of the house of their fathers
among the thousands of *Israel* **Yisra El**.
15 And they came
unto the *children* **sons** of *Reuben* **Reu Ben**,
and to the *children* **sons** of Gad,
and to the half *tribe* **scion** of *Manasseh* **Menash Sheh**,
unto the land of *Gilead* **Gilad**,
and they *spake* **worded** with them, saying,
16 Thus saith the whole *congregation* **witness**
of *the LORD* **Yah Veh**,
What *trespass* **treason** is this
that ye have *committed* **treasoned**
against *the God* **Elohim** of *Israel* **Yisra El**,
to turn away this day
from *following the LORD* **after Yah Veh**,
in that ye have builded you *an* **a sacrifice** altar,
that ye might rebel this day against *the LORD* **Yah Veh**?
17 Is the *iniquity* **perversity** of Peor too little for us,
from which we are not *cleansed* **purified** until this day,
although there was a plague
in the *congregation* **witness** of *the LORD* **Yah Veh**,
18 But that ye must turn away this day
from *following the LORD* **after Yah Veh**?
and it *will* **shall** be,
seeing ye rebel to day against *the LORD* **Yah Veh**,
that to morrow he *will* **shall** be *wroth* **enraged**
with the whole *congregation* **witness** of *Israel* **Yisra El**.
19 *Notwithstanding* **Surely**,
if the land of your possession be *unclean* **foul**,
then pass ye over unto the land
of the possession of *the LORD* **Yah Veh**,
wherein *the LORD'S* **Yah Veh's** tabernacle
dwelleth **tabernacleth**,
and take possession among us:
but rebel not against *the LORD* **Yah Veh**,
nor rebel against us,
in building you *an* **a sacrifice** altar
beside the **sacrifice** altar
of *the LORD* **Yah Veh** our *God* **Elohim**.
20 Did not Achan the son of *Zerah* **Zerach**
commit **treason** a *trespass* **treason**
in the *accursed thing* **devotement**,
and *wrath* **rage** fell
on all the *congregation* **witness** of *Israel* **Yisra El**?
and that man *perished* **expired** not alone
in his *iniquity* **perversity**.
21 Then the *children* **sons** of *Reuben* **Reu Ben**
and the *children* **sons** of Gad
and the half *tribe* **scion** of *Manasseh* **Menash Sheh**
answered, and *said* **worded**
unto the heads of the thousands of *Israel* **Yisra El**,
22 *The LORD God of gods* **Yah Veh El of elohim**,
the LORD God of gods **Yah Veh El of elohim**,
he knoweth,
and *Israel* **Yisra El** he shall know; if it be in rebellion,
or if in *transgression* **treason** against *the LORD* **Yah Veh**,
(save us not this day,)
23 That we have built us *an* **a sacrifice** altar
to turn from *following the LORD* **after Yah Veh**,
or if to *offer thereon burnt offering* **holocaust a holocaust**
or *meat* offering,
or if to *offer peace offerings* **work shelamim** thereon,
let *the LORD* **Yah Veh** himself *require* **beseech** it;
24 And if we have not *rather done* **worked** it
for *fear* **concern** of this *thing* **word**, saying,
In time to come **To morrow**
your *children* **sons** might *speak* **say** unto our *children* **sons**,
saying, What have ye to do
with *the LORD God* **Yah Veh Elohim** of *Israel* **Yisra El**?
25 For *the LORD* **Yah Veh** hath *made Jordan* **given Yarden**
a border between us and you,
ye *children* **sons** of *Reuben* **Reu Ben**
and *children* **sons** of Gad;
ye have no *part* **allotment** in *the LORD* **Yah Veh**:
so **thus** shall your *children* **sons**
make our *children* **sons** cease
from fearing the LORD **in not awing Yah Veh**.
26 Therefore we said,
Let us now *prepare* **work** to build us *an* **a sacrifice** altar,
not for *burnt offering* **holocaust**, nor for sacrifice:
27 But that it may be a witness between us, and you,
and our generations after us,
that we might *do* **serve** the service of *the LORD* **Yah Veh**
before him **at his face** with our *burnt offerings* **holocausts**,
and with our sacrifices,
and with our *peace offerings* **shelamim**;
that your *children* **sons** may not say to our *children* **sons**
in time to come **to morrow**,
ye have no *part* **allotment** in *the LORD* **Yah Veh**.
28 Therefore said we, that it shall be,
when they should *so* say to us
or to our generations *in time to come* **to morrow**,
that we may say *again*,
Behold **See** the pattern
of the **sacrifice** altar of *the LORD* **Yah Veh**,
which our fathers *made* **worked**,
not for *burnt offerings* **holocausts**, nor for sacrifices;
but it is a witness between us and you.
29 *God forbid* **Far be it**
that we should rebel against *the LORD* **Yah Veh**,
and turn this day from *following the LORD* **after Yah Veh**,
to build *an* **a sacrifice** altar for *burnt offerings* **holocausts**,
for *meat* offerings, or for sacrifices,
beside **apart from** the **sacrifice** altar
of *the LORD* **Yah Veh** our *God* **Elohim**
that is before **at the face of** his tabernacle.
30 And when *Phinehas* **Pinechas** the priest,
and the *princes* **hierarchs** of the *congregation* **witness**
and heads of the thousands of *Israel* **Yisra El**
which were with him,
heard the words that the *children* **sons** of *Reuben* **Reu Ben**
and the *children* **sons** of Gad
and the *children* **sons** of *Manasseh* **Menash Sheh**
spake **worded**,
it *pleased them* **well—pleased their eyes**.
31 And *Phinehas* **Pinechas**
the son of *Eleazar* **El Azar** the priest
said unto the *children* **sons** of *Reuben* **Reu Ben**,
and to the *children* **sons** of Gad,
and to the *children* **sons** of *Manasseh* **Menash Sheh**,
This day
we perceive that *the LORD* **Yah Veh** is among us,
because ye have not
committed **treasoned** this *trespass* **treason**
against *the LORD* **Yah Veh**:
now **then** ye have *delivered* **rescued**
the *children* **sons** of *Israel* **Yisra El**
out of the hand of *the LORD* **Yah Veh**.
32 And *Phinehas* **Pinechas**

the son of *Eleazar* **El Azar** the priest,
and the *princes* **hierarchs,**
returned from the *children* **sons** of *Reuben* **Reu Ben,**
and from the *children* **sons** of Gad,
out of the land of *Gilead* **Gilad,**
unto the land of *Canaan* **Kenaan,**
to the *children* **sons** of *Israel* **Yisra El,**
and *brought* **returned** them word *again.*
33 And the *thing pleased* **word well—pleased**
the eyes of the *children* **sons** of *Israel* **Yisra El;**
and the *children* **sons** of *Israel* **Yisra El**
blessed *God* **Elohim,**
and did not *intend* **say** to *go up* **ascend** against them
in *battle* **hosting,**
to *destroy* **ruin** the land
wherein the *children* **sons** of *Reuben* **Reu Ben** and Gad
dwelt **settled.**
34 And the *children* **sons** of *Reuben* **Reu Ben**
and the *children* **sons** of Gad called the **sacrifice** altar
Ed **Witness:**
for it shall *be a* witness between us
that *the LORD* **Yah Veh** is *God* **Elohim.**

23 And it *came to pass* **became,**
a long time after **after many days**
that *the LORD* **Yah Veh**
had *given rest unto Israel* **rested Yisra El**
from all their enemies round about,
that *Joshua* **Yah Shua** waxed old
and stricken *in age* **and come into days.**
2 And *Joshua* **Yah Shua** called for all *Israel* **Yisra El,**
and for their elders, and for their heads,
and for their judges, and for their officers,
and said unto them,
I am old and stricken *in age* **and come into days:**
3 And ye have seen all
that *the LORD* **Yah Veh** your *God* **Elohim**
hath *done* **worked** unto all these *nations* **goyim**
because of you **at thy face;**
for *the LORD* **Yah Veh** your *God* **Elohim**
is he that hath fought for you.
4 *Behold* **See,** I have *divided* **felled** unto you *by lot*
these *nations* **goyim** that *remain* **survive,**
to be an inheritance for your *tribes* **scions,**
from *Jordan* **Yarden,**
with all the *nations* **goyim** that I have cut off,
even unto the great sea *westward* **at the entry of the sun.**
5 And *the LORD* **Yah Veh** your *God* **Elohim,**
he shall expel them from *before you* **thy face,**
and *drive* **dispossess** them from *out of your sight* **thy face;**
and ye shall possess their land,
as *the LORD* **Yah Veh** your *God* **Elohim**
hath *promised* **worded** unto you.
6 Be ye therefore *very courageous* **mighty strong**
to *keep* **guard** and to *do* **work** all that is *written* **inscribed**
in the *book* **scroll** of the *law* **torah** of *Moses* **Mosheh,**
that ye turn not aside therefrom
to the right *hand* or to the left;
7 That ye come not among these *nations* **goyim,**
these that *remain* **survive** among you;
neither *make mention of* **memorialize**
the name of their *gods* **elohim,**
nor *cause to swear* **oath** by them, neither serve them,
nor *bow* **prostrate** yourselves unto them:
8 But *cleave* **adhere**
unto *the LORD* **Yah Veh** your *God* **Elohim,**
as ye have *done* **worked** unto this day.
9 For *the LORD* **Yah Veh**
hath *driven out* **dispossessed** from *before you* **thy face**
great *nations* **goyim** and *strong* **mighty:**
but *as for* you,
no man hath been able to stand *before you* **at thy face**
unto this day.
10 One man of you shall *chase* **pursue** a thousand:
for *the LORD* **Yah Veh** your *God* **Elohim,**
he *it is that* fighteth for you,
as he hath *promised* **worded** you.
11 *Take good heed* **Guard mightily** therefore
unto *yourselves* **your souls,**
that ye love *the LORD* **Yah Veh** your *God* **Elohim.**
12 Else if **in turning back,** ye *do in any wise go* **turn** back,
and *cleave* **adhere**
unto the remnant of these *nations* **goyim,**
even these that *remain* **survive** among you,
and shall *make marriages* **intermarry** with them,
and go in unto them, and they to you:
13 **In knowing,** Know *for a certainty*
that *the LORD* **Yah Veh** your *God* **Elohim**
will no more drive out **shall not add to dispossess**
any of these *nations* **goyim** from *before you* **thy face;**
but they shall be snares, *and traps* **snares** unto you,
and scourges in your sides, and thorns in your eyes,
until ye *perish* **destruct** from off this good *land* **soil**
which *the LORD* **Yah Veh** your *God* **Elohim**
hath given you.
14 And, behold,
this day I am going the way of all the earth:
and ye know in all your hearts and in all your souls,
that not one *thing* **word** hath *failed* **fallen**
of all the good *things* **words**
which *the LORD* **Yah Veh** your *God spake* **Elohim worded**
concerning you;
all are come *to pass* unto you,
and not one *thing* **word** hath *failed* **fallen** thereof.
15 Therefore it shall *come to pass* **become,**
that as all good *things* **words** are come upon you,
which *the LORD* **Yah Veh** your *God* **Elohim**
promised **worded** you;
so **thus** shall *the LORD* **Yah Veh**
bring upon you all evil *things* **words,**
until he have *destroyed* **desolated** you
from off this good *land* **soil**
which *the LORD* **Yah Veh** your *God* **Elohim**
hath given you.
16 When ye have *transgressed* **trespassed** the covenant
of *the LORD* **Yah Veh** your *God* **Elohim,**
which he *commanded* **misvahed** you,
and have gone and served other *gods* **elohim,**
and bowed yourselves to them;
then shall the *anger* **wrath** of *the LORD* **Yah Veh**
be kindled against you,
and ye shall *perish* **destruct** quickly
from off the good land
which he hath given unto you.

YAH SHUA'S REVIEW

24 And *Joshua* **Yah Shua**
gathered all the *tribes* **scions** of *Israel* **Yisra El**
to Shechem,
and called for the elders of *Israel* **Yisra El,**
and for their heads,
and for their judges, and for their officers;
and they *presented* **set** *themselves*
before God **at the face of Elohim.**
2 And *Joshua* **Yah Shua** said unto all the people,
Thus saith
the LORD God **Yah Veh Elohim** of *Israel* **Yisra El,**
Your fathers *dwelt* **settled**
on the other side of the *flood in old time* **river originally,**
even Terah **Terach,**
the father of Abraham, and the father of Nachor:
and they served other *gods* **elohim.**
3 And I took your father Abraham
from the other side of the *flood* **river,**
and *led* **walked** him
throughout all the land of *Canaan* **Kenaan,**
and *multiplied* **abounded** his seed,
and gave him *Isaac* **Yischaq.**
4 And I gave unto *Isaac* **Yischaq**
Jacob **Yaaqov** and *Esau* **Esav:**
and I gave unto *Esau* **Esav** mount Seir, to possess it;
but *Jacob* **Yaaqov** and his *children* **sons**
went down **descended** into *Egypt* **Misrayim.**
5 I sent *Moses* **Mosheh** also and *Aaron* **Aharon,**
and I *plagued Egypt* **smote Misrayim,**
according to that which I *did* **worked** among them:
and afterward I brought you out.
6 And I brought your fathers out of *Egypt* **Misrayim:**
and ye came unto the sea;
and the *Egyptians* **Misrayim** pursued after your fathers
with chariots and *horsemen* **cavalry**
unto the *Red* **Reed** sea.

7 And when they cried unto *the LORD* **Yah Veh**,
he *put* **set** darkness between you
and **between** the *Egyptians* **Misrayim**,
and brought the sea upon them, and covered them;
and your eyes have seen
what I have *done* **worked** in *Egypt* **Misrayim**:
and ye *dwelt* **settled** in the wilderness
a long season **many days**.
8 And I brought you into the land of the *Amorites* **Emoriy**,
which *dwelt* **settled** on the other side *Jordan* **Yarden**;
and they fought with you:
and I gave them into your hand,
that ye might possess their land;
and I *destroyed* **desolated** them from *before you* **thy face**.
9 Then *Balak* **Balaq** the son of *Zippor* **Sippor**,
king **sovereign** of Moab,
arose and *warred* **fought** against *Israel* **Yisra El**,
and sent and called *Balaam* **Bilam** the son of Beor
to *curse* **abase** you:
10 But I *would* **willed to** not hearken unto *Balaam* **Bilam**;
therefore **in blessing,** he blessed you *still*:
so I delivered you out of his hand.
11 And you *went* **passed** over *Jordan* **Yarden**,
and came unto *Jericho* **Yericho**:
and the *men* **masters** of *Jericho* **Yericho**
fought against you,
the *Amorites* **Emoriy**, and the *Perizzites* **Perizziy**
and the *Canaanites* **Kenaaniy**, and the *Hittites* **Hethiy**,
and the *Girgashites* **Girgashiy**, the *Hivites* **Hivviy**,
and the *Jebusites* **Yebusiy**;
and I *delivered* **gave** them into your hand.
12 And I sent the hornet *before you* **from thy face**,
which drave them out from *before you* **thy face**,
even the two *kings* **sovereigns** of the *Amorites* **Emoriy**;
but not with thy sword, nor with thy bow.
13 And I have given you a land for which ye did not labour,
and cities which ye built not, and ye *dwell* **settle** in them;
of the vineyards and oliveyards which ye planted not
do ye eat.

YAH SHUA'S CHALLENGE

14 Now therefore *fear the LORD* **awe Yah Veh**,
and serve him in *sincerity* **integrity** and in truth:
and *put away* **turn aside**
the *gods* **elohim** which your fathers served
on the other side of the *flood* **river**,
and in *Egypt* **Misrayim;**
and serve ye *the LORD* **Yah Veh**.
15 And if it *seem evil unto you* **vilify your eyes**
to serve *the LORD* **Yah Veh**,
choose you this day *whom* **ever** ye *will* **shall** serve;
whether the *gods* **elohim** which your fathers served
that were on the other side of the *flood* **river**,
or the *gods* **elohim** of the *Amorites* **Emoriy**,
in whose land ye *dwell* **settle**:
but as for me and my house,
we *will* **shall** serve *the LORD* **Yah Veh**.
16 And the people answered and said,
God forbid **Far be it**
that we should forsake *the LORD* **Yah Veh**,
to serve other *gods* **elohim**;
17 For *the LORD* **Yah Veh** our *God* **Elohim**,
he *it is that brought* **ascended** us *up* and our fathers
out of the land of *Egypt* **Misrayim**,
from the house of *bondage* **servants**,
and which *did* **worked** those great signs in our *sight* **eyes**,
and *preserved* **guarded** us in all the way wherein we went,
and among all the people
through **among** whom we passed:
18 And *the LORD* **Yah Veh**
drave out from *before us* **our face** all the people,
even the *Amorites* **Emoriy** which *dwelt* **settled** in the land:
therefore will we also **shall** serve *the LORD* **Yah Veh**;
for he is our *God* **Elohim**.
19 And *Joshua* **Yah Shua** said unto the people,
Ye cannot serve *the LORD* **Yah Veh**:
for he is an holy *God* **Elohim**; he is a jealous *God* **El**;
he *will* **shall** not *forgive* **lift** your *transgressions* **rebellions**
nor your sins.
20 If ye forsake *the LORD* **Yah Veh**,
and serve strange *gods* **elohim**,
then he *will* **shall** turn and *do you hurt* **vilify you**,
and *consume you* **finish you off**,
after that he hath *done you good* **well—pleased you**.
21 And the people said unto *Joshua* **Yah Shua**,
Nay; but we *will* **shall** serve *the LORD* **Yah Veh**.
22 And *Joshua* **Yah Shua** said unto the people,
ye are witnesses against yourselves
that ye have chosen you *the LORD* **Yah Veh**,
to serve him.
And they said, We are witnesses.
23 Now therefore *put away* **turn aside**, *said he*,
the strange *gods* **elohim** which are among you,
and *incline* **extend** your heart
unto *the LORD God* **Yah Veh Elohim** of *Israel* **Yisra El**.
24 And the people said unto *Joshua* **Yah Shua**,
The LORD **Yah Veh** our *God will* **Elohim shall** we serve,
and his voice *will* **shall** we *obey* **hear**.
25 So *Joshua made* **Yah Shua cut** a covenant
with the people that day,
and set them a statute and *an ordinance* **a judgment**
in Shechem.
26 And *Joshua wrote* **Yah Shua inscribed** these words
in the *book* **scroll** of the *law* **torah** of *God* **Elohim**,
and took a great stone,
and *set* **raised** it up there under an oak,
that was by the *sanctuary* **holies** of *the LORD* **Yah Veh**.
27 And *Joshua* **Yah Shua** said unto all the people,
Behold, this stone shall be a witness unto us;
for it hath heard
all the *words* **sayings** of *the LORD* **Yah Veh**
which he *spake* **worded** unto us:
it shall be therefore a witness unto you,
lest ye deny your *God* **Elohim**.
28 So *Joshua let* **Yah Shua sent** the people *depart* **away**,
every man unto his inheritance.

YAH SHUA'S ENTOMBMENT

29 And it *came to pass* **became**, after these *things* **words**,
that *Joshua* **Yah Shua** the son of Nun,
the servant of *the LORD* **Yah Veh**, died,
being **a son of** an hundred and ten years *old*.
30 And they *buried* **entombed** him
in the border of his inheritance
in *Timnathserah* **Timnah Heres**,
which is in mount *Ephraim* **Ephrayim**,
on the north *side* of the *hill* **mountain** of Gaash.

YISRA EL'S FIDELITY

31 And *Israel* **Yisra El** served *the LORD* **Yah Veh**
all the days of *Joshua* **Yah Shua**,
and all the days of the elders
that *overlived Joshua* **prolonged Yah Shua**,
and which had known
all the works of *the LORD* **Yah Veh**,
that he had *done* **worked** for *Israel* **Yisra El**.
32 And the bones of *Joseph* **Yoseph**,
which the *children* **sons** of *Israel* **Yisra El**
brought up **ascended** out of *Egypt* **Misrayim**,
buried **entombed** they in Shechem,
in a *parcel* **field** of *ground* **allotment**
which *Jacob bought* **Yaaqov chatteled**
of the sons of Hamor the father of Shechem
for an hundred *pieces of silver* **ingots**:
and it became the inheritance
of the *children* **sons** of *Joseph* **Yoseph**.
33 And *Eleazar* **El Azar** the son of *Aaron* **Aharon** died;
and they *buried* **entombed** him in a hill
that pertained to Phinehas **of Pinechas** his son,
which was given him in mount *Ephraim* **Ephrayim**.

KEY TO INTERPRETING THE EXEGESES:
King James text is in regular type;
Text under exegeses is in oblique type;
Text of exegeses is in bold type.

YISRA EL CAPTURES KENAAN

1 Now after the death of *Joshua* **Yah Shua**
it *came to pass* **became,**
that the *children* **sons** of *Israel* **Yisra El**
asked *the LORD* **Yah Veh**, saying,
Who shall *go up* **ascend** for us
against the *Canaanites* **Kenaaniy**
first, **to begin** to fight against them?
2 And *the LORD* **Yah Veh** said,
Judah **Yah Hudah** shall *go up* **ascend**:
behold, I have *delivered* **given** the land into his hand.
3 And *Judah* **Yah Hudah**
said unto *Simeon* **Shimon** his brother,
Come up **Ascend** with me into my *lot* **pebble**,
that we may fight against the *Canaanites* **Kenaaniy**;
and I likewise *will* **shall** go with thee into thy *lot* **pebble**.
So *Simeon* **Shimon** went with him.
4 And *Judah went up* **Yah Hudah ascended**;
and *the LORD delivered* **Yah Veh gave**
the *Canaanites* **Kenaaniy** and the *Perizzites* **Perizziy**
into their hand:
and they *slew* **smote** of them in *Bezek* **Bezeq**
ten thousand men.
5 And they found *Adonibezek* **Adoni Bezeq**
in *Bezek* **Bezeq**:
and they fought against him,
and they *slew* **smote** the *Canaanites* **Kenaaniy**
and the *Perizzites* **Perizziy**.
6 But *Adonibezek* **Adoni Bezeq** fled;
and they pursued after him, and *caught* **possessed** him,
and *cut* **chopped** off
his thumbs and his great toes
the great digits of his hands and of his feet.
7 And *Adonibezek* **Adoni Bezeq** said,
Threescore and ten kings **Seventy sovereigns,**
having *their thumbs and their great toes*
the great digits of their hands and of their feet
cut **chopped** off,
gathered their meat **gleaned** under my table:
as I have *done* **worked**,
so *God hath requited* **Elohim did shalam** me.
And they brought him to *Jerusalem* **Yeru Shalem**,
and there he died.

YAH HUDAH CAPTURES YERU SHALEM

8 Now the *children* **sons** of *Judah* **Yah Hudah**
had fought against *Jerusalem* **Yeru Shalem**,
and had *taken* **captured** it,
and smitten it with the *edge* **mouth** of the sword,
and *set* **sent** the city on fire.
9 And afterward the *children* **sons** of *Judah* **Yah Hudah**
went down **descended** to fight
against the *Canaanites* **Kenaaniy**,
that *dwelt* **settled** in the mountain,
and in the south, and in the *valley* **lowland**.
10 And *Judah* **Yah Hudah**
went against the *Canaanites* **Kenaaniy**
that *dwelt* **settled** in Hebron:
(now the name of Hebron before
was *Kirjatharba* **Qiryath Arba**:)
and they *slew Sheshai* **smote Sheshay**,
and *Ahiman* **Achiy Man**, and *Talmai* **Talmay**.

KALEB CAPTURES DEBIR

11 And from thence
he went against the *inhabitants* **settlers** of Debir:
and the name of Debir before
was *Kirjathsepher* **Qiryath Sepher**:
12 And *Caleb* **Kaleb** said,
He that smiteth *Kirjathsepher* **Qiryath Sepher**
and *taketh* **captureth** it,
to him *will* **shall** I give Achsah my daughter
to *wife* **woman**.
13 And *Othniel* **Othni El** the son of *Kenaz* **Qenaz**,
Caleb's **Kaleb's** younger brother, *took* **captured** it:
and he gave him Achsah his daughter
to *wife* **woman**.

ACHSAH'S SEDUCTION

14 And it *came to pass* **became**, when she came *to him*,
that she *moved* **goaded** him to ask of her father a field:
and she *lighted* **alighted** from off her *ass* **he burro**;
and *Caleb* **Kaleb** said unto her,
What *wilt thou* **is to thee**?
15 And she said unto him, Give me a blessing:
for thou hast given me a south land;
give me also *springs* **fountains** of water.
And *Caleb* **Kaleb** gave her the upper *springs* **fountains**
and the nether *springs* **fountains**.
16 And the *children* **sons** of the *Kenite* **Qayiniy**,
Moses' **Mosheh's** father in law,
went up **ascended**
out of *the city of palm trees* **Ir Hat Temarim**
with the *children* **sons** of *Judah* **Yah Hudah**
into the wilderness of *Judah* **Yah Hudah**,
which *lieth* **be** in the south of Arad;
and they went and *dwelt* **settled** among the people.

YAH HUDAH DEVOTES SEPHATH

17 And *Judah* **Yah Hudah**
went with *Simeon* **Shimon** his brother,
and they *slew* **smote** the *Canaanites* **Kenaaniy**
that *inhabited Zephath* **settled Sephath**,
and *utterly destroyed* **devoted** it.
And the name of the city was called Hormah.

THE CAPTURED CITIES

18 Also *Judah took* **Yah Hudah captured**
Gaza **Azzah** with the *coast* **border** thereof,
and *Askelon* **Ashqelon** with the *coast* **border** thereof,
and *Ekron* **Eqron** with the *coast* **border** thereof.
19 And *the LORD* **Yah Veh** was with *Judah* **Yah Hudah**;
and he *drave out* **dispossessed**
the *inhabitants of* mountain;
but could not *drive out* **dispossess**
the *inhabitants* **settlers** of the valley,
because they had chariots of iron.
20 And they gave Hebron unto *Caleb* **Kaleb**,
as *Moses said* **Mosheh worded**:
and he *expelled* **dispossessed** thence
the three sons of *Anak* **Anaq**.
21 And the *children* **sons** of *Benjamin* **Ben Yamin**
did not *drive out* **dispossess** the *Jebusites* **Yebusiy**
that *inhabited Jerusalem* **settled Yeru Shalem**;
but the *Jebusites* **Yebusiy**
dwell **settle** with the *children* **sons** of *Benjamin* **Ben Yamin**
in *Jerusalem* **Yeru Shalem** unto this day.
22 And the house of *Joseph* **Yoseph**,
they also *went up* **ascended** against *Bethel* **Beth El**:
and *the LORD* **Yah Veh** was with them.
23 And the house of *Joseph* **Yoseph**
sent to *descry Bethel* **explore Beth El**.
(Now the name of the city before was Luz.)
24 And the *spies* **guards** saw a man
come forth out of **leave** the city,
and they said unto him,
Shew us **Let us see**, we *pray* **beseech** thee,
the entrance into the city,
and we *will shew* **shall work** thee mercy.
25 And when he *shewed them* **let them see**
the entrance into the city,
they smote the city with the *edge* **mouth** of the sword;
but they *let go* **sent away** the man and all his family.
26 And the man went into the land of the *Hittites* **Hethiy**,
and built a city, and called the name thereof Luz:
which is the name thereof unto this day.

THE UNCONQUERED CITIES

27 Neither did *Manasseh* **Menash Sheh**
drive out **dispossess**
the inhabitants of Bethshean **Beth Shean**
and her *towns* **daughters**,
nor Taanach and her *towns* **daughters**,
nor the *inhabitants* **settlers** of Dor
and her *towns* **daughters**,
nor the *inhabitants* **settlers** of *Ibleam* **Yible Am**
and her *towns* **daughters**,
nor the *inhabitants* **settlers** of Megiddo
and her *towns* **daughters**:
but the *Canaanites* **Kenaaniy**

would dwell **willed to settle** in that land.
28 And it *came to pass* **became,**
when *Israel was strong* **Yisra El strengthened,**
that they *put* **set** the *Canaanites* **Kenaaniy** to *tribute* **vassal,**
and **in dispossessing,**
did not *utterly drive* **dispossess** them *out.*
29 Neither did *Ephraim drive out* **Ephrayim dispossess**
the *Canaanites* **Kenaaniy** that *dwelt* **settled** in Gezer;
but the *Canaanites* **Kenaaniy**
dwelt **settled** in Gezer among them.
30 Neither did Zebulun *drive out* **dispossess**
the *inhabitants* **settlers** of *Kitron* **Qitron,**
nor the *inhabitants* **settlers** of Nahalol;
but the *Canaanites dwelt* **Kenaaniy settled** among them,
and became *tributaries* **vassals.**
31 Neither did Asher *drive out* **dispossess**
the *inhabitants* **settlers** of *Accho* **Akko,**
nor the *inhabitants* **settlers** of *Zidon* **Sidon,**
nor of *Ahlab* **Ach Lab,** nor of Achzib,
nor of Helbah, nor of *Aphik* **Aphek,** nor of *Rehob* **Rechob:**
32 But the *Asherites* **Asheriy**
dwelt **settled** among the *Canaanites* **Kenaaniy,**
the *inhabitants* **settlers** of the land:
for they did not *drive* **dispossess** them *out.*
33 Neither did Naphtali *drive out* **dispossess**
the *inhabitants* **settlers** of *Bethshemesh* **Beth Shemesh,**
nor the *inhabitants* **settlers** of *Bethanath* **Beth Anath;**
but he *dwelt* **settled** among the *Canaanites* **Kenaaniy,**
the *inhabitants* **settlers** of the land:
nevertheless the *inhabitants* **settlers**
of *Bethshemesh* **Beth Shemesh**
and of *Bethanath* **Beth Anath**
became *tributaries* **vassals** unto them.
34 And the *Amorites* **Emoriy**
forced **pressed** the *children* **sons** of Dan
into the mountain:
for they *would not suffer* **did not allow** them
to *come down* **descend** to the valley:
35 But the *Amorites would dwell* **Emoriy willed to settle**
in mount Heres in *Aijalon* **Ayalon,** and in Shaalbim:
yet the hand of the house of *Joseph* **Yoseph**
prevailed **was heavy,**
so that they became *tributaries* **vassals.**
36 And the *coast* **border** of the *Amorites* **Emoriy**
was from the *going up to Akrabbim* **ascent of Acrabbim,**
from the rock, and upward.

YAH VEH'S ANGEL AT BOCHIM

2 And an angel of *the LORD* **Yah Veh**
came up **ascended** from Gilgal to Bochim,
and said,
I made you to *go up* **ascend** out of *Egypt* **Misrayim,**
and have brought you unto the land
which I *sware* **oathed** unto your fathers; and I said,
I *will never* **shall not** break my covenant with you
eternally.
2 And ye shall *make* **cut** no *league* **covenant**
with the *inhabitants* **settlers** of this land;
ye shall *throw* **pull** down their **sacrifice** altars:
but ye have not *obeyed* **hearkened unto** my voice:
why have ye *done* **worked** this?
3 Wherefore I also said,
I *will* **shall** not *drive* **dispossess** them *out*
from *before you* **thy face;**
but they shall be *as thorns* in your sides,
and their *gods* **elohim** shall be a snare unto you.
4 And it *came to pass* **became,**
when the angel of *the LORD* **Yah Veh**
spake **worded** these words
unto all the *children* **sons** of *Israel* **Yisra El,**
that the people lifted up their voice, and wept.
5 And they called the name of that place Bochim:
and they sacrificed there unto *the LORD* **Yah Veh.**

YAH SHUA'S DEATH

6 And when *Joshua* **Yah Shua**
had *let* **sent** the people *go* **away,**
the *children* **sons** of *Israel* **Yisra El** went
every man unto his inheritance to possess the land.
7 And the people served *the LORD* **Yah Veh**
all the days of *Joshua* **Yah Shua,**
and all the days of the elders
that *outlived Joshua* **prolonged days after Yah Shua,**
who had seen all the great works of *the LORD* **Yah Veh,**
that he *did* **worked** for *Israel* **Yisra El.**
8 And *Joshua* **Yah Shua** the son of Nun,
the servant of *the LORD* **Yah Veh,** died,
being **a son of** an hundred and ten years *old.*
9 And they *buried* **entombed** him
in the border of his inheritance
in *Timnathheres* **Timnah Heres,**
in the mount of *Ephraim* **Ephrayim,**
on the north *side* of *the hill* **Mount** Gaash.

THE NEW GENERATIONS SERVE BAALIM

10 And also all that generation
were gathered unto their fathers:
and there arose another generation after them,
which knew not *the LORD* **Yah Veh,**
nor yet the works
which he had *done* **worked** for *Israel* **Yisra El.**
11 And the *children* **sons** of *Israel did* **Yisra El worked** evil
in the *sight* **eyes** of *the LORD* **Yah Veh,**
and served Baalim:
12 And they forsook
the LORD God **Yah Veh Elohim** of their fathers,
which brought them out of the land of *Egypt* **Misrayim,**
and *followed* **went after** other *gods* **elohim,**
of the *gods* **elohim** of the people
that were round about them,
and *bowed* **prostrated** themselves unto them,
and *provoked the LORD to anger* **vexed Yah Veh.**
13 And they forsook *the LORD* **Yah Veh,**
and served Baal and Ashtaroth.
14 And the *anger* **wrath** of *the LORD* **Yah Veh**
was hot **kindled** against *Israel* **Yisra El,**
and he *delivered* **gave** them
into the hands of *spoilers* **plunderers**
that *spoiled* **plundered** them,
and he sold them
into the hands of their enemies round about,
so that they could not *any longer* **still** stand
before **at the face of** their enemies.
15 Whithersoever they went out,
the hand of *the LORD* **Yah Veh** was against them for evil,
as *the LORD* **Yah Veh** had *said* **worded,**
and as *the LORD* **Yah Veh** had *sworn* **oathed** unto them:
and they were *greatly distressed* **mightily depressed.**

YAH VEH RAISES JUDGES

16 Nevertheless *the LORD* **Yah Veh** raised up judges,
which *delivered* **saved** them
out of the hand of those that *spoiled* **plundered** them.
17 And yet they *would* **did** not hearken unto their judges,
but they *went a whoring* **whored** after other *gods* **elohim,**
and *bowed* **prostrated** themselves unto them:
they turned *quickly* **hastily aside**
out of the way which their fathers walked in,
obeying **hearing** the *commandments* **mitsvoth**
of *the LORD* **Yah Veh;**
but they *did* **worked** not so.
18 And when *the LORD* **Yah Veh** raised them up judges,
then *the LORD* **Yah Veh** was with the judge,
and *delivered* **saved** them out of the hand of their enemies
all the days of the judge:
for *it repented the LORD* **Yah Veh sighed**
because of their groanings
by reason of them that oppressed them
at the face of their oppressors
and *vexed* **oppressed** them.
19 And it *came to pass* **became,** when the judge was dead,
that they returned,
and *corrupted* **ruined** *themselves* more than their fathers,
in *following* **going after** other *gods* **elohim** to serve them,
and to *bow down* **prostrate** unto them;
they *ceased* **fell** not from their *own doings* **exploits,**
nor from their *stubborn* **hard** way.
20 And the *anger* **wrath** of *the LORD* **Yah Veh**
was hot **kindled** against *Israel* **Yisra El;** and he said,
Because that this *people* **goyim**
hath *transgressed* **trespassed** my covenant
which I *commanded* **misvahed** their fathers,
and have not hearkened unto my voice;
21 I also *will* **shall** not **add to**

henceforth drive out any **dispossess man**
from *before them* **their face** of the *nations* **goyim**
which *Joshua* **Yah Shua** left when he died:
22 That through them I may *prove Israel* **test Yisra El**,
whether they *will keep* **shall guard**
the way of *the LORD* **Yah Veh** to walk therein,
as their fathers *did keep it* **guarded**, or not.
23 Therefore *the LORD* **Yah Veh**
left **set** those *nations* **goyim**,
without driving **by not dispossessing** them *out* hastily;
neither *delivered* **gave** he them
into the hand of *Joshua* **Yah Shua**.

YAH VEH TESTS YISRA EL

3 *Now* these are the *nations* **goyim**
which *the LORD left* **Yah Veh set**,
to *prove Israel* **test Yisra El** by them,
even as many *of Israel* as had not known
all the wars of *Canaan* **Kenaan**;
2 Only that the generations
of the *children* **sons** of *Israel* **Yisra El** might know,
to teach them war,
at the least **only** such
as *before* **formerly** knew *nothing* **naught** thereof;
3 *Namely*,
five *lords* **ringleaders** of the *Philistines* **Peleshethiy**,
and all the *Canaanites* **Kenaaniy**,
and the *Sidonians* **Sidoniy**,
and the *Hivites* **Hivviy**
that *dwelt* **settled** in mount Lebanon,
from mount *Baalhermon* **Baal Hermon**
unto the entering in of Hamath.
4 And they were to *prove Israel* **test Yisra El** by them,
to know whether they *would* **should** hearken
unto the *commandments* **mitsvoth** of *the LORD* **Yah Veh**,
which he *commanded* **misvahed** their fathers
by the hand of *Moses* **Mosheh**.
5 And the *children* **sons** of *Israel* **Yisra El**
dwelt **settled** among
the *Canaanites* **Kenaaniy**, *Hittites* **Hethiy**,
and *Amorites* **Emoriy**, and *Perizzites* **Perizziy**,
and *Hivites* **Hivviy**, and *Jebusites* **Yebusiy**:
6 And they took their daughters to be their *wives* **women**,
and gave their daughters to their sons,
and served their *gods* **elohim**.

JUDGE OTHNI EL

7 And the *children* **sons** of *Israel* **Yisra El**
did **worked** evil in the *sight* **eyes** of *the LORD* **Yah Veh**,
and forgat *the LORD* **Yah Veh** their *God* **Elohim**,
and served Baalim and the *groves* **asherim**.
8 Therefore the *anger* **wrath** of *the LORD* **Yah Veh**
was hot **kindled** against *Israel* **Yisra El**,
and he sold them into the hand of
Chushanrishathaim **Kushan Rishathaim**
king **sovereign** of *Mesopotamia* **Aram Naharaim**:
and the *children* **sons** of *Israel* **Yisra El**
served *Chushanrishathaim* **Kushan Rishathaim** eight years.
9 And when the *children* **sons** of *Israel* **Yisra El**
cried unto *the LORD* **Yah Veh**,
the LORD **Yah Veh** raised up a *deliverer* **saviour**
to the *children* **sons** of *Israel* **Yisra El**,
who *delivered* **saved** them,
even *Othniel* **Othni El** the son of *Kenaz* **Qenaz**,
Caleb's **Kaleb's** younger brother.
10 And the Spirit of *the LORD* **Yah Veh** came upon him,
and he judged *Israel* **Yisra El**, and went out to war:
and *the LORD delivered* **Yah Veh gave**
Chushanrishathaim **Kushan Rishathaim,**
king **sovereign** of *Mesopotamia* **Aram** into his hand;
and his hand prevailed
against *Chushanrishathaim* **Kushan Rishathaim**.
11 And the land *had rest* **rested** forty years.
And *Othniel* **Othni El** the son of *Kenaz* **Qenaz** died.

YISRA EL IN SERVITUDE

12 And the *children* **sons** of *Israel* **Yisra El**
did **added to work** evil *again*
in the *sight* **eyes** of *the LORD* **Yah Veh**:
and *the LORD* **Yah Veh** strengthened Eglon
the *king* **sovereign** of Moab against *Israel* **Yisra El**,
because they had *done* **worked** evil
in the *sight* **eyes** of *the LORD* **Yah Veh**.
13 And he gathered unto him
the *children* **sons** of Ammon and *Amalek* **Amaleq**,
and went and smote *Israel* **Yisra El**,
and possessed *the city of palm trees* **Ir Hat Temarim**.
14 So the *children* **sons** of *Israel* **Yisra El**
served Eglon the *king* **sovereign** of Moab eighteen years.

EHUD THE SAVIOUR

15 But when the *children* **sons** of *Israel* **Yisra El**
cried unto *the LORD* **Yah Veh**,
the LORD **Yah Veh** raised them up a *deliverer* **saviour**,
Ehud the son of Gera, a *Benjamite* **Ben Yaminiy**,
a man *lefthanded* **shut of his right hand**:
and *by him* **in his hand** the *children* **sons** of *Israel* **Yisra El**
sent *a present* **an offering** unto Eglon
the *king* **sovereign** of Moab.
16 But Ehud *made* **worked** him a *dagger* **sword**
which had two edges, of a *cubit* **span** length;
and he did gird it under his *raiment* **tailoring**
upon his right *thigh* **flank**.
17 And he *brought* **oblated** the *present* **offering**
unto Eglon *king* **sovereign** of Moab:
and Eglon was a *very* **mighty** fat man.
18 And when he had *made an end* **finished**
to offer **oblating** the *present* **offering**,
he sent away the people that bare the *present* **offering**.
19 But he himself turned *again* from the *quarries* **sculptiles**
that were by Gilgal, and said,
I have a *secret errand* **covert word** unto thee,
O *king* **sovereign**:
who said, *Keep silence* **Hush**.
And all that stood by him went out from him.
20 And Ehud came unto him;
and he *was sitting* **settled**
in *a summer parlour* **an upper room of cooling**,
which he had for himself alone.
And Ehud said,
I have a *message* **word** from *God* **Elohim** unto thee.
And he arose out of his *seat* **throne**.
21 And Ehud *put* **sent** forth his left *hand*,
and took the *dagger* **sword** from his right *thigh* **flank**,
and *thrust* **staked** it into his belly:
22 And the *haft* **handle** also went in after the blade;
and the fat *closed upon* **shut through** the blade,
so that he could not draw the *dagger* **sword**
out of his belly;
and *the dirt* **it** came out **at the anus**.
23 Then Ehud went forth through the *porch* **portico**,
and shut the doors of the *parlour* **upper room** upon him,
and *locked* **enclosed** them.
24 When he *was gone out* **went**, his servants came;
and when they saw that, behold,
the doors of the *parlour* **upper room**
were *locked* **enclosed**, they said,
Surely he covereth his feet
in his *summer* **cooling** chamber.
25 And they *tarried* **waited** till they were *ashamed* **shamed**:
and, behold,
he opened not the doors of the *parlour* **upper room**;
therefore they took a key, and opened *them*: and, behold,
their *lord* **adoni** was fallen down
dead **having died** on the earth.
26 And Ehud escaped while they *tarried* **lingered**,
and passed beyond the *quarries* **sculptiles**,
and escaped unto *Seirath* **Seirah**.
27 And it *came to pass* **became**, when he was come,
that he *blew* **blast** a trumpet
in the mountain of *Ephraim* **Ephrayim**,
and the *children* **sons** of *Israel* **Yisra El**
went down **descended** with him from the mount,
and he *before them* **at their face**.
28 And he said unto them, *Follow* **Pursue** after me:
for *the LORD* **Yah Veh** hath *delivered* **given**
your enemies the *Moabites* **Moabiy**
into your hand.
And they *went down* **descended** after him,
and *took* **captured** the *fords* **passages** of *Jordan* **Yarden**
toward Moab,
and *suffered* **allowed** not a man to pass over.
29 And they *slew* **smote** of Moab at that time
about ten thousand men,

all *lusty* **fat**, and all men of valour;
and there escaped not a man.
30 So Moab was subdued that day
under the hand of *Israel* **Yisra El**.
And the land *had rest fourscore* **rested eighty** years.

SHAMGAR

31 And after him was Shamgar the son of Anath,
which *slew* **smote** of the *Philistines* **Peleshethiy**
six hundred men with an ox goad:
and he also *delivered Israel* **saved Yisra El**.

SONS OF YISRA EL ARE SOLD

4 And the *children* **sons** of *Israel* **Yisra El**
again did **added to work** evil
in the *sight* **eyes** of *the LORD* **Yah Veh**,
when Ehud *was dead* **died**.
2 And *the LORD* **Yah Veh** sold them
into the hand of *Jabin* **Yabyn**
king **sovereign** of *Canaan* **Kenaan**,
that reigned in *Hazor* **Hasor**;
the *captain* **governor** of whose host was Sisera,
which *dwelt* **settled**
in Harosheth **by Harosheth/Engravers**
of the *Gentiles* **Goyim**.
3 And the *children* **sons** of *Israel* **Yisra El**
cried unto *the LORD* **Yah Veh**:
for he had nine hundred chariots of iron;
and twenty years he *mightily* **strongly** oppressed
the *children* **sons** of *Israel* **Yisra El**.

DEBORAH

4 And Deborah, a **woman** prophetess,
the *wife* **woman** of *Lapidoth* **Lappidoth**,
she judged *Israel* **Yisra El** at that time.
5 And she *dwelt* **settled** under the palm tree of Deborah
between Ramah and *Bethel* **Beth El**
in mount *Ephraim* **Ephrayim**:
and the *children* **sons** of *Israel* **Yisra El**
came up **ascended** to her for judgment.
6 And she sent and called *Barak* **Baraq**
the son of *Abinoam* **Abi Noam**
out of *Kedeshnaphtali* **Kedesh Naphtali**,
and said unto him,
Hath not *the LORD God* **Yah Veh Elohim** of *Israel* **Yisra El**
commanded **misvahed**, *saying,*
Go and draw toward mount Tabor,
and take with thee ten thousand men
of the *children* **sons** of Naphtali
and of the *children* **sons** of Zebulun?
7 And I *will* **shall** draw unto thee
to the *river Kishon* **wadi Qishon** Sisera,
the *captain* **governor** of *Jabin's army* **Yabyn's host**,
with his chariots and his multitude;
and I *will deliver* **shall give** him into thine hand.
8 And *Barak* **Baraq** said unto her,
If thou *wilt* **shalt** go with me, then I *will* **shall** go:
but if thou *wilt* **shalt** not go with me,
then I will **I shall** not go.
9 And she said, **In walking,**
I *will surely go* **shall walk** with thee:
notwithstanding **finally**
the journey that thou *takest* **walkest**
shall not be for thine *honour* **adornment**;
for *the LORD* **Yah Veh** shall sell Sisera
into the hand of a woman.
And Deborah arose,
and went with *Barak* **Baraq** to *Kedesh* **Qedesh**.
10 And *Barak* **Baraq**
called **cried unto** Zebulun and Naphtali
to *Kedesh* **Qedesh**;
and he *went up* **ascended**
with ten thousand men at his feet:
and Deborah *went up* **ascended** with him.
11 Now Heber the *Kenite* **Qayiniy**,
which was of the *children* **sons** of Hobab
the father in law of *Moses* **Mosheh**,
had *severed* **separated** himself from the *Kenites* **Qayiniy**,
and *pitched* **stretched** his tent
unto the *plain* **mighty oaks** of *Zaanaim* **Saanayim**,
which is by *Kedesh* **Qedesh**.
12 And they *shewed* **told** Sisera
that *Barak* **Baraq** the son of *Abinoam* **Abi Noam**
was gone up **ascended** to mount Tabor.
13 And Sisera *gathered together* **cried for** all his chariots,
even nine hundred chariots of iron,
and all the people that were with him,
from *Harosheth* **the engravers** of the *Gentiles* **goyim**
unto the river of *Kishon* **Qishon**.
14 And Deborah said unto *Barak* **Baraq**, *Up* **Arise**;
for this is the day in which *the LORD* **Yah Veh**
hath *delivered* **given** Sisera into thine hand:
is not *the LORD* **Yah Veh**
gone out *before thee* **at thy face**?
So *Barak went down* **Baraq descended** from mount Tabor,
and ten thousand men after him.
15 And *the LORD discomfited* **Yah Veh agitated** Sisera,
and all his chariots, and all his *host* **camp**,
with the *edge* **mouth** of the sword
before Barak **at the face of Baraq**;
so that Sisera *lighted down* **descended** off his chariot,
and fled away on his feet.
16 But *Barak* **Baraq** pursued after the chariots,
and after the *host* **camp**,
unto *Harosheth* **the engravers** of the *Gentiles* **goyim**:
and all the *host* **camp** of Sisera
fell upon the *edge* **mouth** of the sword;
and *there was not a man left* **not one survived**.
17 Howbeit Sisera fled away on his feet
to the tent of *Jael* **Yael**
the *wife* **woman** of Heber the *Kenite* **Qayiniy**:
for there was *peace* **shalom**
between *Jabin* **Yabyn** the *king* **sovereign** of *Hazor* **Hasor**
and the house of Heber the *Kenite* **Qayiniy**.
18 And *Jael* **Yael** went out to meet Sisera,
and said unto him,
Turn in, my *lord* **adoni**, turn in to me; *fear* **awe** not.
And when he had turned in unto her into the tent,
she covered him with a *mantle* **blanket**.
19 And he said unto her, Give me, I *pray* **beseech** thee,
a little water to drink; for I *am thirsty* **thirst**.
And she opened a *bottle* **skin** of milk,
and gave him drink, and covered him.
20 Again he said unto her,
Stand in the *door* **opening** of the tent, and it shall be,
when any man doth come and *enquire* **ask** of thee,
and say, Is there any man here? that thou shalt say, No.
21 Then *Jael* **Yael** Heber's *wife* **woman**
took a *nail* **stake** of the tent,
and *took* **set** an hammer in her hand,
and went *softly* **quietly** unto him,
and *smote* **staked** the *nail* **stake** into his temples,
and *fastened* **drove** it into the *ground* **earth**:
for he was *fast* **sound** asleep and *weary* **fluttered**.
So he died.
22 And, behold, as *Barak* **Baraq** pursued Sisera,
Jael came out **Yael went** to meet him,
and said unto him, Come,
and I *will shew thee* **shall have thee see**
the man whom thou seekest.
And when he came into her *tent*,
behold, Sisera *lay dead* **had fallen and died**,
and the *nail* **stake** was in his temples.
23 So *God* **Elohim** subdued on that day
Jabin **Yabyn** the *king* **sovereign** of *Canaan* **Kenaan**
before **at the face of** the *children* **sons** of *Israel* **Yisra El**.
24 And the hand of the *children* **sons** of *Israel* **Yisra El**
prospered **in going, did go**,
and *prevailed* **did go hard** against *Jabin* **Yabyn**
the *king* **sovereign** of *Canaan* **Kenaan**,
until they had *destroyed Jabin* **cut off Yabyn**
king **sovereign** of *Canaan* **Kenaan**.

THE SONG OF DEBORAH AND BARAQ

5 Then sang Deborah and *Barak* **Baraq**
the son of *Abinoam* **Abi Noam** on that day, saying,
2 *Praise* **Bless** *ye the LORD* **Yah Veh**
for *the avenging* **leading the leaders** of *Israel* **Yisra El**,
when the people *willingly offered* **volunteered** themselves.
3 Hear, O ye *kings* **sovereigns**;
give ear **hearken**, O ye *princes* **potentates**;
I, *even I, will* — **I shall** sing unto *the LORD* **Yah Veh**;
I *will sing praise* **shall pluck**
to *the LORD God* **Yah Veh Elohim** of *Israel* **Yisra El**.

4 *LORD* **O Yah Veh**, when thou wentest out of Seir,
when thou *marchedst* **pacedst** out of the field of Edom,
the earth *trembled* **quaked**, and the heavens dropped,
the **thick** clouds also dropped water.
5 The mountains *melted* **flowed**
from *before the LORD* **the face of Yah Veh**,
even that *Sinai* **Sinay** from *before* **the face of**
the LORD God **Yah Veh Elohim** of *Israel* **Yisra El**.
6 In the days of Shamgar the son of Anath,
in the days of *Jael* **Yael**,
the highways were *unoccupied* **abandoned**,
and the *travellers* **walkers of paths**
walked through *byways* **crooked ways**.
7 The *inhabitants of the villages* **suburbanites** ceased,
they ceased in *Israel* **Yisra El**, until that I Deborah arose,
that I arose a mother in *Israel* **Yisra El**.
8 They chose new *gods* **elohim**;
then was *war* **fighting** in the *gates* **portals**:
was there a *shield* **buckler** or *spear* **javelin** seen
among forty thousand in *Israel* **Yisra El**?
9 My heart is toward
the *governors* **statute setters** of *Israel* **Yisra El**,
that *offered themselves willingly* **volunteered**
among the people.
Bless ye *the LORD* **Yah Veh**.
10 *Speak* **Meditate**, ye that ride on white *asses* **she burros**,
ye that *sit in judgment* **settle in tailoring**,
and walk by the way.
11 *They that are delivered from the noise of archers*
By the voice in rank
in the *places of drawing water* **troughs**,
there shall they *rehearse* **celebrate**
the *righteous acts* **justnesses** of *the LORD* **Yah Veh**,
even the *righteous acts* **justnesses**
toward the *inhabitants of his villages* **suburbanites**
in *Israel* **Yisra El**:
then shall the people of *the LORD* **Yah Veh**
go down **descend** to the *gates* **portals**.
12 Awake, awake, Deborah:
awake, awake, *utter* **word** a song:
arise, *Barak* **Baraq**, and lead thy captivity captive,
thou son of *Abinoam* **Abi Noam**.
13 Then he made him that *remaineth* **surviveth**
have dominion **subjugate** over the nobles
among the people:
the LORD **Yah Veh**
made me *have dominion* **subjugate** over the mighty.
14 Out of *Ephraim* **Ephrayim**
was there a root of them against *Amalek* **Amaleq**;
after thee, *Benjamin* **Ben Yamin**, among thy people;
out of Machir
came down governors **descended the statute setters**,
and out of Zebulun
they that *handle* **draw with** the *pen* **scion**
of the *writer* **scribe**.
15 And the *princes* **governors** of *Issachar* **Yissachar**
were with Deborah;
even *Issachar* **Yissachar**, and also *Barak* **Baraq**:
he was sent on foot into the valley.
For the divisions of *Reuben* **Reu Ben**
there were great *thoughts* **statutes** of heart.
16 Why *abodest* **seatest** thou
among **between** the *sheepfolds* **stalls**,
to hear the *bleatings* **hisses** of the *flocks* **droves**?
For the divisions of *Reuben* **Reu Ben**
there were great *searchings* **probings** of heart.
17 *Gilead abode* **Gilad tabernacled** beyond *Jordan* **Yarden**:
and why did Dan *remain* **sojourn** in ships?
Asher *continued* **settled** on the sea *shore* **haven**,
and *abode* **tabernacled** in his *breaches* **breakwater**.
18 Zebulun and Naphtali were a people
that jeoparded **exposed to reproach** their *lives* **souls**
unto *the death* **dying** in the high places of the field.
19 The *kings* **sovereigns** came and fought,
then fought the *kings* **sovereigns** of *Canaan* **Kenaan**
in Taanach by the waters of Megiddo;
they took no gain of *money* **silver**.
20 They fought from *heaven* **the heavens**;
the stars in their *courses* **highways** fought against Sisera.
21 The *river* **wadi** of *Kishon* **Qishon**
swept **bore** them away,
that ancient *river* **wadi**, the *river Kishon* **wadi Qishon**.
O my soul, thou hast trodden down strength.
22 Then were the *horsehoofs* **horse heelprints**
broken **hammered** by the means of the pransings,
the pransings of their mighty ones.
23 Curse ye Meroz, said the angel of *the LORD* **Yah Veh**,
in cursing, curse ye *bitterly* the *inhabitants* **settlers** thereof;
because they came not to the help of *the LORD* **Yah Veh**,
to the help of *the LORD* **Yah Veh** against the mighty.
24 Blessed above women shall *Jael* **Yael**
the *wife* **woman** of Heber the *Kenite* **Qayiniy** be,
blessed shall she be above women in the tent.
25 He asked water, and she gave *him* milk;
she *brought forth* **approached with** butter
in a *lordly dish* **mighty bason**.
26 She *put* **extended** her hand to the *nail* **stake**,
and her right *hand* to the *workmen's* **toiler's** hammer;
and *with the hammer she smote* **she hammered** Sisera,
she *smote off* **crushed** his head,
when she had *pierced* **struck**
and *stricken* **passed** through his temples.
27 At her feet he bowed, he fell, he lay down:
at her feet he bowed, he fell:
where he bowed, there he fell down *dead* **ravaged**.
28 The mother of Sisera looked out at a window,
and cried through the lattice,
Why is his chariot *so long* **delayed** in coming?
why *tarry* **delay** the *wheels* **steps** of his chariots?
29 Her wise *ladies* **governesses** answered her,
yea, she returned *answer* **sayings** to herself,
30 Have they not *sped* **found**?
have they *not divided* **allotted** the *prey* **spoil**;
to *every man* **the head mighty**
a *damsel* **maiden** or two **maidens**;
to Sisera a *prey* **spoil** of *divers colours* **dyes**,
a *prey* **spoil** of *divers colours* **dyes**
of *needlework* **embroidery**
of *divers colours* **dyes** of *needlework* **embroidery**
on both sides,
meet for the necks of *them that take the spoil* **the spoilers**?
31 So let all thine enemies *perish* **destruct**,
O *LORD* **Yah Veh**:
but let them that love him be as the sun
when he goeth *forth* in his might.
And the land *had rest* **rested** forty years.

A PERSECUTION OF THE MIDYANIY, THE AMALEKIY, AND THE SONS OF THE EAST

6 And the *children* **sons** of *Israel did* **Yisra El worked** evil
in the *sight* **eyes** of *the LORD* **Yah Veh**:
and *the LORD delivered* **Yah Veh gave** them
into the hand of *Midian* **Midyan** seven years.
2 And the hand of *Midian* **Midyan**
prevailed against *Israel* **Yisra El**:
and *because* **at the face** of the *Midianites* **Midyaniy**
the *children* **sons** of *Israel made* **Yisra El worked** them
the *dens* **caverns** which are in the mountains,
and caves, and *strong holds* **huntholds**.
3 And so it was, when *Israel* **Yisra El** had *sown* **seeded**,
that the *Midianites came up* **Midyan ascended**,
and the *Amalekites* **Amalekiy**,
and the *children* **sons** of the east,
even they *came up* **ascended** against them;
4 And they encamped against them,
and *destroyed* **ruined** the *increase* **produce** of the earth,
till thou come unto *Gaza* **Azzah**,
and *left no sustenance* **no invigoration survived**
for *Israel* **Yisra El**,
neither *sheep* **lamb**, nor ox, nor *ass* **he burro**.
5 For they *came up* **ascended**
with their *cattle* **chattel** and their tents,
and they came as *grasshoppers* **locusts**
enough for *multitude* **abundance**;
for both they and their camels were without number:
and they entered into the land to *destroy* **ruin** it.
6 And *Israel* **Yisra El**
was *greatly impoverished* **mighty lanquished**
because **at the face** of the *Midianites* **Midyaniy**;
and the *children* **sons** of *Israel* **Yisra El**
cried unto *the LORD* **Yah Veh**.

GIDON

7 And it *came to pass* **became,**
when the *children* **sons** of *Israel* **Yisra El**
cried unto *the LORD* **Yah Veh**
because of *the Midianites* **Midyan,**
8 That *the LORD* **Yah Veh** sent **a man** — a prophet
unto the *children* **sons** of *Israel* **Yisra El,**
which said unto them, Thus saith
the LORD God **Yah Veh Elohim** of *Israel* **Yisra El,**
I *brought* **ascended** you *up* from *Egypt* **Misrayim,**
and brought you forth
out of the house of *bondage* **servants;**
9 And I *delivered* **rescued** you
out of the hand of the *Egyptians* **Misrayim,**
and out of the hand of all that oppressed you,
and drave them out from *before you* **thy face,**
and gave you their land;
10 And I said unto you,
I am the LORD **I — Yah Veh** your *God* **Elohim;**
fear **awe** not the *gods* **elohim** of the *Amorites* **Emoriy,**
in whose land ye *dwell* **settle:**
but ye have not *obeyed* **hearkened unto** my voice.

YAH VEH'S ANGEL VISITS GIDON

11 And there came an angel of *the LORD* **Yah Veh,**
and sat **settled** under an oak which was in Ophrah,
that pertained unto Joash **of Yah Ash**
the *Abiezrite* **Abi Ezeriy:**
and his son *Gideon* **Gidon**
threshed wheat by the winepress,
to *hide it* **cause it to flee**
from **the face of** the *Midianites* **Midyaniy.**
12 And the angel of *the LORD* **Yah Veh**
appeared unto **was seen by** him, and said unto him,
The LORD **Yah Veh** is with thee,
thou mighty *man* of valour.
13 And *Gideon* **Gidon** said unto him, Oh my *Lord* **Adonay,**
if *the LORD* **Yah Veh** be with us,
why then is all this *befallen us* **present?**
and where be all his *miracles* **marvels**
which our fathers *told us of* **scribed us,** saying,
Did not *the LORD* **Yah Veh**
bring **ascend** us *up* from *Egypt* **Misrayim?**
but now *the LORD* **Yah Veh** hath forsaken us,
and *delivered* **given** us
into the *hands* **palms** of the *Midianites* **Midyaniy.**
14 And *the LORD looked upon* **Yah Veh faced** him,
and said, Go in this thy *might* **force,**
and thou shalt save *Israel* **Yisra El**
from the *hand* **palm** of the *Midianites* **Midyaniy:**
have not I sent thee?
15 And he said unto him, Oh my *Lord* **Adonay,**
wherewith shall I save *Israel* **Yisra El?** behold,
my *family* **thousand** is poor in *Manasseh* **Menash Sheh,**
and I am the *least* **lesser** in my father's house.
16 And *the LORD* **Yah Veh** said unto him,
Surely I *will* **shall** be with thee,
and thou shalt smite the *Midianites* **Midyaniy** as one man.
17 And he said unto him,
If now I have found *grace* **charism** in thy *sight* **eyes,**
then *shew* **work** me a sign
that thou *talkest* **wordest** with me.
18 Depart not hence, I *pray* **beseech** thee,
until I come unto thee,
and bring forth my *present* **offering,**
and set it *before thee* **at thy face.**
And he said,
I *will tarry* **shall settle** until thou *come again* **return.**
19 And *Gideon* **Gidon** went in,
and *made ready* **worked** a *kid* **doe goat,**
and *unleavened cakes* **matsahs** of an ephah of flour:
the flesh he *put* **set** in a basket,
and he *put* **set** the broth in a *pot* **skillet,**
and brought it out unto him under the oak,
and *presented it* **approached.**
20 And the angel of *God* **Elohim** said unto him,
Take the flesh and the *unleavened cakes* **matsahs,**
and *lay them* **set** upon this rock, and pour out the broth.
And he *did* **worked** so.
21 Then the angel of *the LORD* **Yah Veh**
put **sent** forth the end of the staff that was in his hand,
and touched the flesh and the *unleavened cakes* **matsahs;**
and there *rose up* **ascended** fire out of the rock,
and consumed the flesh
and the *unleavened cakes* **matsahs.**
Then the angel of *the LORD* **Yah Veh**
departed out of his sight **went from his eyes.**
22 And when *Gideon* **Gidon**
perceived **saw** that he was an angel of *the LORD* **Yah Veh,**
Gideon **Gidon** said, *Alas* **Aha,**
O *Lord GOD* **Adonay Yah Veh!**
for *because* **thus**
I have seen an angel of *the LORD* **Yah Veh** face to face.
23 And *the LORD* **Yah Veh** said unto him,
Peace **Shalom** be unto thee; *fear* **awe** not:
thou shalt not die.
24 Then *Gideon* **Gidon** built *an* **a sacrifice** altar there
unto *the LORD* **Yah Veh,**
and called it *Jehovahshalom* **Yah Veh Shalom:**
unto this day
it is yet in Ophrah of the *Abiezrites* **Abi Ezeriy.**
25 And it *came to pass* **became,** the same night,
that *the LORD* **Yah Veh** said unto him,
Take thy father's young *bullock* **steer ox,**
even the second bullock of seven years *old,*
and *throw down* **demolish** the **sacrifice** altar of Baal
that thy father hath,
and cut down the *grove* **asherah** that is by it:
26 And build *an* **a sacrifice** altar
unto *the LORD* **Yah Veh** thy *God* **Elohim**
upon the top of this *rock* **stronghold,**
in the ordered place **by the arrangement,**
and take the second bullock,
and *offer* **holocaust** a *burnt sacrifice* **holocaust**
with the *wood* **timber** of the *grove* **asherah**
which thou shalt cut down.
27 Then *Gideon* **Gidon** took ten men of his servants,
and *did* **worked**
as *the LORD* **Yah Veh** had *said* **worded** unto him:
and so *it was* **became,**
because he *feared* **awed** his father's household,
and the men of the city,
that he could not *do* **work** it by day,
that he *did* **worked** it by night.
28 And when the men of the city
arose **started** early in the morning, behold,
the **sacrifice** altar of Baal was *cast* **pulled** down,
and the *grove* **asherah** was cut down that was by it,
and the second bullock
was *offered* **holocausted**
upon the **sacrifice** altar *that was* built.
29 And they said *one* **man** to *another* **friend,**
Who hath *done* **worked** this *thing* **word?**
And when they enquired and *asked* **sought,** they said,
Gideon **Gidon** the son of *Joash* **Yah Ash**
hath *done* **worked** this *thing* **word.**
30 Then the men of the city said unto *Joash* **Yah Ash,**
Bring out thy son, that he may die:
because he hath *cast* **pulled** down
the **sacrifice** altar of Baal,
and because he hath cut down
the *grove* **asherah** that was by it.
31 And *Joash* **Yah Ash** said unto all that stood against him,
Will **Shall** ye plead for Baal? *will* **shall** ye save him?
he that *will* **shall** plead for him,
let him be *put to death* **deathified** whilst it is *yet* morning:
if he be *a god* **an elohim,** let him plead for himself,
because *one* **he** hath *cast* **pulled** down his **sacrifice** altar.
32 Therefore on that day
he called him *Jerubbaal* **Yerub Baal,** saying,
Let Baal plead against him,
because he hath *thrown* **pulled** down his **sacrifice** altar.
33 Then all *the Midianites* **Midyaniy**
and *the Amalekites* **Amaleqiy**
and the *children* **sons** of the east were gathered together,
and *went* **passed** over,
and *pitched* **encamped** in the valley of *Jezreel* **Yizre El.**
34 But the Spirit of *the LORD* **Yah Veh**
came upon Gideon **enrobed Gidon,**
and he *blew* **blast** a trumpet;
and *Abiezer was gathered* **Abi Ezer cried** after him.

35 And he sent *messengers* **angels**
throughout all *Manasseh* **Menash Sheh**;
who also *was gathered* **cried** after him:
and he sent *messengers* **angels** unto Asher,
and unto Zebulun, and unto Naphtali;
and they *came up* **ascended** to meet them.

GIDON AND THE SHEARING

36 And *Gideon* **Gidon** said unto *God* **Elohim**,
If thou *wilt* **shalt** save *Israel* **Yisra El** by mine hand,
as thou hast *said* **worded**,
37 Behold, I *will put* **shall place** a *fleece* **shearing** of wool
in the *floor* **threshingfloor**;
and if the dew be on the *fleece* **shearing** only,
and *it be dry* **parched** upon all the earth *beside*,
then shall I know that
thou *wilt* **shalt** save *Israel* **Yisra El** by mine hand,
as thou hast *said* **worded**.
38 And it *was* **became** so:
for he *rose up* **started** early on the morrow,
and *thrust* **squeezed** the *fleece* **shearing** together,
and wringed the dew out of the *fleece* **shearing**,
a *bowl* **bason** full of water.
39 And *Gideon* **Gidon** said unto *God* **Elohim**,
Let not *thine anger be hot* **thy wrath kindle** against me,
and I *will speak* **shall word** but this *once* **one time**:
let me *prove* **test**, I *pray* **beseech** thee,
but this *once* **one time** with the *fleece* **shearing**;
let it now be *dry* **parched** only upon the *fleece* **shearing**,
and upon all the *ground* **earth** let there be dew.
40 And *God did* **Elohim worked** so that night:
for it was *dry* **parched** upon the *fleece* **shearing** only,
and there was dew on all the *ground* **earth**.

GIDON DEFEATS THE MIDYANIY

7 Then *Jerubbaal* **Yerub Baal**, who is *Gideon* **Gidon**,
and all the people that were with him,
rose up **started** early,
and *pitched* **encamped**
beside *the well of Harod* **En Harod**:
so that the *host* **camp** of the *Midianites* **Midyaniy**
were on the north *side* of them,
by the hill of Moreh, in the valley.
2 And *the LORD* **Yah Veh** said unto *Gideon* **Gidon**,
The people that are with thee are too many for me
to give the *Midianites* **Midyaniy** into their hands,
lest *Israel vaunt* **Yisra El boast** themselves against me,
saying, Mine own hand hath saved me.
3 Now therefore *go to* **I beseech**,
proclaim **call out** in the ears of the people, saying,
Whosoever *is fearful* **aweth** and *afraid* **trembleth**,
let him return
and *depart early* **skip about** from mount *Gilead* **Gilad**.
And there returned of the people
twenty and two thousand;
and there *remained* **survived** ten thousand.
4 And *the LORD* **Yah Veh** said unto *Gideon* **Gidon**,
The people are yet *too* many;
bring them down unto the water,
and I *will try* **shall refine** them for thee there:
and it shall be, *that* of whom I say unto thee,
This shall go with thee, the same shall go with thee;
and of whomsoever I say unto thee,
This shall not go with thee, the same shall not go.
5 So he brought down the people unto the water:
and *the LORD* **Yah Veh** said unto *Gideon* **Gidon**,
Every one that lappeth of the water with his tongue,
as a dog lappeth, him shalt thou set by himself;
likewise
every one that boweth down upon his knees to drink.
6 And the number of them that lapped,
putting their hand to their mouth,
were three hundred men:
but all the rest of the people
bowed down upon their knees to drink water.
7 And *the LORD* **Yah Veh** said unto *Gideon* **Gidon**,
By the three hundred men that lapped
will **shall** I save you,
and *deliver* **give** the *Midianites* **Midyaniy** into thine hand:
and let all the other people go every man unto his place.
8 So the people took *victuals* **hunt** in their hand,
and their trumpets:
and he sent *all the rest of Israel*
every man **of Yisra El** unto his tent,
and *retained* **upheld** those three hundred men:
and the *host* **camp** of *Midian* **Midyaniy**
was beneath him in the valley.
9 And it *came to pass* **became**, the same night,
that *the LORD* **Yah Veh** said unto him,
Arise, *get* **descend** thee *down* unto the *host* **camp**;
for I have *delivered* **given** it into thine hand.
10 But if thou *fear* **awe** to *go down* **descend**,
go **descend** thou with *Phurah* **Purah** thy *servant* **lad**
down to the *host* **camp**:
11 And thou shalt hear what they *say* **word**;
and afterward shall thine hands be strengthened
to *go down* **descend** unto the *host* **camp**.
Then *went* **descended** he *down*
with *Phurah* **Purah** his *servant* **lad**
unto the *outside* **edge** of the armed men
that were in the *host* **camp**.
12 And the *Midianites* **Midyaniy** and the *Amalekites* **Amaleqiy**
and all the *children* **sons** of the east
lay along **are fallen** in the valley
like *grasshoppers* **locusts** for *multitude* **abundance**;
and their camels were without number,
as the sand by the sea *side* **lip** for *multitude* **abundance**.
13 And when *Gideon* **Gidon** was come, behold,
there *was* a man
that *told* **scribed** a dream unto his *fellow* **friend**,
and said, Behold, I dreamed a dream, and, *lo* **behold**,
a cake of barley bread *tumbled* **overturned**
into the *host* **camp** of *Midian* **Midyaniy**,
and came unto a tent, and smote it that it fell,
and overturned it **upward**, that the tent *lay along* **fell**.
14 And his *fellow* **friend** answered and said,
This is *nothing* **naught** else
save the sword of *Gideon* **Gidon**
the son of *Joash* **Yah Ash**, a man of *Israel* **Yisra El**:
for into his hand
hath *God delivered Midian* **Elohim given Midyaniy**,
and all the *host* **camp**.
15 And it was *so*,
when *Gideon* **Gidon**
heard the *telling* **renumerating** of the dream,
and the *interpretation* **breaking forth** thereof,
that he *worshipped* **prostrated**,
and returned into the *host* **camp** of *Israel* **Yisra El**,
and said, Arise;
for *the LORD* **Yah Veh**
hath *delivered* **given** into your hand
the *host* **camp** of *Midian* **Midyaniy**.
16 And he divided the three hundred men
into three *companies* **heads**,
and he *put* **gave** a trumpet in every man's hand,
with empty pitchers,
and *lamps* **flambeaus** within the pitchers.
17 And he said unto them, *Look on* **See unto** me,
and *do* **work** likewise: and, behold,
when I come to the *outside* **edge** of the camp,
it shall be that, as I *do* **work**, so shall ye *do* **work**.
18 When I *blow* **blast** with a trumpet,
I and all that are with me,
then *blow* **blast** ye the trumpets also
on every side of **round about** all the camp, and say,
The sword of the LORD **Of Yah Veh**,
and of *Gideon* **Gidon**.
19 So *Gideon* **Gidon**,
and the hundred men that were with him,
came unto the *outside* **edge** of the camp
in the beginning of the middle watch;
and **in raising,**
they had *but newly set* **raised** the *watch* **guard**:
and they *blew* **blast** the trumpets,
and *brake* **shattered** the pitchers that were in their hands.
20 And the three *companies* **heads**
blew **blast** the trumpets, and brake the pitchers,
and held the *lamps* **flambeaus** in their left hands,
and the trumpets in their right hands to *blow* **blast** *withal*:
and they *cried* **called out**,
The sword of *the LORD* **Yah Veh**, and of *Gideon* **Gidon**.
21 And they stood every man in his place

round about the camp;
and all the *host* **camp** ran, and *cried* **shouted**, and fled.
22 And the three hundred *blew* **blast** the trumpets,
and *the LORD* **Yah Veh**
set every man's sword against his *fellow* **friend**,
even throughout all the *host* **camp**:
and the *host* **camp** fled to *Bethshittah* **Beth Hath Shittah**
in *Zererath* **Seredah**,
and to the *border* **lip** of *Abelmeholah* **Abel Mecholah**,
unto Tabbath.
23 And the men of *Israel* **Yisra El**
gathered themselves together **cried** out of Naphtali,
and out of Asher, and out of all *Manasseh* **Menash Sheh**,
and pursued after the *Midianites* **Midyaniy**.
24 And *Gideon* **Gidon** sent *messengers* **angels**
throughout all mount *Ephraim* **Ephrayim**, saying,
Come down **Descend**
against **to meet** the *Midianites* **Midyaniy**,
and *take* **capture** before them
the waters unto *Bethbarah* **Beth Barah** and *Jordan* **Yarden**.
Then all the men of *Ephraim* **Ephrayim**
gathered themselves together **cried out**,
and *took* **captured** the waters
unto *Bethbarah* **Beth Barah** and *Jordan* **Yarden**.
25 And they *took* **captured** two *princes* **governors**
of the *Midianites* **Midyaniy**, Oreb and Zeeb;
and they *slew* **slaughtered** Oreb
upon the rock Oreb,
and Zeeb they *slew* **slaughtered**
at the *winepress* **trough** of Zeeb,
and pursued *Midian* **Midyaniy**,
and brought the heads of Oreb and Zeeb
to *Gideon* **Gidon** on the other side *Jordan* **Yarden**.

MEN OF EPHRAYIM FEEL SLIGHTED

8 And the men of *Ephraim* **Ephrayim** said unto him,
In working,
Why hast thou *served us thus* **worked this word**,
that thou calledst us not,
when thou wentest to fight with the *Midianites* **Midyaniy**?
And they *did chide* **contended** with him *sharply* **strongly**.
2 And he said unto them,
What have I *done* **worked** now in comparison of you?
Is not the gleaning of *the grapes of Ephraim* **Ephrayim**
better than the *vintage* **crop** of *Abiezer* **Abi Ezer**?
3 *God* **Elohim** hath *delivered* **given** into your hands
the *princes* **governors** of *Midian* **Midyaniy**, Oreb and Zeeb:
and what was I able to *do* **work** in comparison of you?
Then their *anger was abated* **spirit slackened** toward him,
when he had *said* **worded** that **word**.
4 And *Gideon* **Gidon** came to *Jordan* **Yarden**,
and passed over,
he, and the three hundred men that were with him,
faint **languid**, yet pursuing them.
5 And he said
unto the men of *Succoth* **Sukkoth/Brush Arbors**,
Give, I *pray* **beseech** you, *loaves* **rounds** of bread
unto the people *that follow me* **at my feet**;
for they be *faint* **languid**,
and I am pursuing
after *Zebah* **Zebach** and *Zalmunna* **Sal Munna**,
kings **sovereigns** of *Midian* **Midyaniy**.
6 And the *princes* **governors**
of *Succoth* **Sukkoth/Brush Arbors** said,
Are the *hands* **palms**
of *Zebah* **Zebach** and *Zalmunna* **Sal Munna**
now in thine hand,
that we should give bread unto thine *army* **host**?
7 And *Gideon* **Gidon** said,
Therefore when *the LORD* **Yah Veh** hath *delivered* **given**
Zebah **Zebach** and *Zalmunna* **Sal Munna**
into mine hand,
then I *will tear* **shall thresh** your flesh
with the thorns of the wilderness and with *briers* **flints**.
8 And he *went up* **ascended** thence to *Penuel* **Penu El**,
and *spake* **worded** unto them *likewise* **thus**:
and the men of *Penuel* **Penu El** answered him
as the men of *Succoth* **Sukkoth/Brush Arbors**
had answered *him*.
9 And he *spake* **said** also unto the men of *Penuel* **Penu El**,
saying, When I *come again* **return** in *peace* **shalom**,
I *will break* **shall pull** down this tower.
10 Now *Zebah* **Zebach** and *Zalmunna* **Sal Munna**
were in *Karkor* **Qarqor**,
and their *hosts* **camps** with them,
about fifteen thousand *men*,
all that *were left* **remained** of all the *hosts* **camps**
of the *children* **sons** of the east:
for there fell an hundred and twenty thousand men
that drew sword.
11 And *Gideon went up* **Gidon ascended**
by the way of them that *dwelt* **tabernacled** in tents
on the east of *Nobah* **Nobach** and *Jogbehah* **Yogbehah**,
and smote the *host* **camp**; for the *host* **camp** was secure.
12 And when
Zebah **Zebach** and *Zalmunna* **Sal Munna** fled,
he pursued after them, and *took* **captured**
the two *kings* **sovereigns** of *Midian* **Midyaniy**,
Zebah **Zebach** and *Zalmunna* **Sal Munna**,
and *discomfited* **trembled** all the *host* **camp**.
13 And *Gideon* **Gidon** the son of *Joash* **Yah Ash**
returned from *battle* **war**
before the **ascent of the** sun *was up*,
14 And *caught* **captured** a *young man* **lad**
of the men of *Succoth* **Sukkoth/Brush Arbors**,
and *enquired* **asked** of him:
and he *described* **inscribed** unto him
the *princes* **governors** of *Succoth* **Sukkoth/Brush Arbors**,
and the elders thereof,
even threescore and seventeen **seventy seven** men.
15 And he came unto the men
of *Succoth* **Sukkoth/Brush Arbors**, and said,
Behold *Zebah* **Zebach** and *Zalmunna* **Sal Munna**,
with whom ye *did upbraid* **reproached** me, saying,
Are the *hands* **palms**
of *Zebah* **Zebach** and *Zalmunna* **Sal Munna**
now in thine hand,
that we should give bread unto thy men that are weary?
16 And he took the elders of the city,
and thorns of the wilderness and *briers* **flints**,
and with them he *taught* **caused** the men
of *Succoth* **Sukkoth/Brush Arbors to know**.
17 And he *beat* **pulled** down the tower of *Penuel* **Penu El**,
and *slew* **slaughtered** the men of the city.
18 Then said he
unto *Zebah* **Zebach** and *Zalmunna* **Sal Munna**,
What manner of men **Who** were they
whom ye *slew* **slaughtered** at Tabor?
And they *answered* **said**, As thou *art*, so were they **thus**;
each one *resembled* **according to the form**
of the *children* **sons** of *a king* **one sovereign**.
19 And he said, They were my brethren,
even the sons of my mother:
as *the LORD* **Yah Veh** liveth, if ye had saved them alive,
I *would* **should** not *slay* **slaughter** you.
20 And he said unto *Jether* **Yether** his firstborn,
Up **Arise**, *and slay* **slaughter** them.
But the *youth* **lad** drew not his sword:
for he *feared* **awed**, because he was yet a *youth* **lad**.
21 Then *Zebah* **Zebach** and *Zalmunna* **Sal Munna** said,
Rise thou, and *fall* **encounter** upon us:
for as the man *is, so is* **thus** his *strength* **might**.
And *Gideon* **Gidon** arose, and *slew* **slaughtered**
Zebah **Zebach** and *Zalmunna* **Sal Munna**,
and took away the *ornaments* **pendants**
that were on their camels' necks.

GIDON'S EPHOD

22 Then the men of *Israel* **Yisra El**
said unto *Gideon* **Gidon**,
Rule **Reign** thou over us,
both thou, and thy son, and thy son's son also:
for thou hast *delivered* **saved** us
from the hand of *Midian* **Midyaniy**.
23 And *Gideon* **Gidon** said unto them,
I *will* **shall** not *rule* **reign** over you,
neither shall my son *rule* **reign** over you:
the LORD **Yah Veh** shall *rule* **reign** over you.
24 And *Gideon* **Gidon** said unto them,
I *would desire a request* **ask a petition** of you,
that ye *would* **should** give me every man
the *earrings* **noserings** of his *prey* **spoil**.

(For they had golden *earrings* **noserings**,
because they were *Ishmaelites* **Yishma Eliy**.)
25 And they *answered* **said**,
In giving, We *will willingly* **shall** give them.
And they spread a *garment* **cloth**,
and did cast therein every man
the *earrings* **noserings** of his *prey* **spoil**.
26 And the weight of the golden *earrings* **noserings**
that he *requested* **asked**
was a thousand and seven hundred *shekels* of gold;
beside *ornaments* **crescents**, and *collars* **pendants**,
and purple *raiment* **covering**
that was on the *kings* **sovereigns** of *Midian* **Midyaniy**,
and beside the *chains* **chokers**
that were about their camels' necks.
27 And *Gideon made* **Gidon worked** an ephod thereof,
and *put* **placed** it in his city, even in Ophrah:
and all *Israel* **Yisra El**
went thither a whoring **whored** after it:
which *thing* became a snare unto *Gideon* **Gidon**,
and to his house.

SUMMARY

28 Thus was *Midian* **Midyaniy** subdued
before **at the face of** the *children* **sons** of *Israel* **Yisra El**,
so that they *lifted up* **added to not lift** their heads *no more*.
And the *country was in quietness* **land rested** forty years
in the days of *Gideon* **Gidon**.
29 And *Jerubbaal* **Yerub Baal** the son of *Joash* **Yah Ash**
went and *dwelt* **settled** in his own house.
30 And *Gideon* **Gidon** had *threescore and ten* **seventy** sons
of his body begotten **going out of his flank**:
for he had many *wives* **women**.
31 And his concubine that was in Shechem,
she also bare him a son,
whose name he *called Abimelech* **set Abi Melech**.

GIDON'S DEATH

32 And *Gideon* **Gidon** the son of *Joash* **Yah Ash**
died in a good *old age* **grayness**,
and was *buried* **entombed**
in the *sepulchre* **tomb** of *Joash* **Yah Ash** his father,
in Ophrah of the *Abiezrites* **Abi Ezeriy**.

YISRA EL WHORES

33 And it *came to pass* **became**,
as soon as *Gideon was dead* **Gidon had died**,
that the *children* **sons** of *Israel* **Yisra El** turned *again* **back**,
and *went a whoring* **whored** after Baalim,
and *made Baalberith* **set Baal Berith** their *god* **elohim**.
34 And the *children* **sons** of *Israel* **Yisra El**
remembered not *the LORD* **Yah Veh** their *God* **Elohim**,
who had *delivered* **rescued** them out of the hands
of all their enemies *on every side* **round about**:
35 Neither *shewed* **worked** they *kindness* **mercy**
to the house of *Jerubbaal* **Yerub Baal**,
namely, Gideon **Gidon**,
according to all the goodness
which he had *shewed* **worked** unto *Israel* **Yisra El**.

ABI MELECH'S CONSPIRACY

9 And *Abimelech* **Abi Melech**
the son of *Jerubbaal* **Yerub Baal**
went to Shechem unto his mother's brethren,
and *communed* **worded** with them,
and with all the family
of the house of his mother's father, saying,
2 *Speak* **Word**, I *pray* **beseech** you,
in the ears of all the *men* **masters** of Shechem,
Whether is better for you,
either that all the sons of *Jerubbaal* **Yerub Baal**,
which are *threescore and ten persons* **seventy men**,
reign over you,
or that one reign over you?
remember also that I am your bone and your flesh.
3 And his mother's brethren *spake* **worded** of him
in the ears of all the *men* **masters** of Shechem
all these words:
and their hearts *inclined* **stretched**
to follow *Abimelech* **after Abi Melech**;
for they said, He is our brother.
4 And they gave him
threescore and ten **seventy** *pieces* of silver
out of the house of *Baalberith* **Baal Berith**,
wherewith *Abimelech* **Abi Melech**
hired vain and *light persons* **frothy men**,
which *followed* **went after** him.
5 And he went unto his father's house at Ophrah,
and *slew* **slaughtered** his brethren
the sons of *Jerubbaal* **Yerub Baal**,
being threescore and ten persons **seventy men**,
upon one stone:
notwithstanding
yet *Jotham* **Yah Tham**
the youngest son of *Jerubbaal* **Yerub Baal**
was left **remained**; for he hid himself.
6 And all the *men* **masters** of Shechem
gathered together,
and all the house of Millo, and went,
and *made Abimelech king* **reigned Abi Melech sovereign**,
by the *plain* **mighty oak** of the *pillar* **station**
that was in Shechem.
7 And when they told it to *Jotham* **Yah Tham**,
he went and stood in the top of mount Gerizim,
and lifted up his voice, and *cried* **called out**,
and said unto them, Hearken unto me,
ye *men* **masters** of Shechem,
that *God* **Elohim** may hearken unto you.
8 **In going**, The trees *went forth on a time* **have gone**
to anoint a *king* **sovereign** over them;
and they said unto the olive tree, Reign thou over us.
9 But the olive tree said unto them,
should I *leave* **forsake** my fatness,
wherewith by me they honour *God* **Elohim** and man,
and go to *be promoted* **wave** over the trees?
10 And the trees said to the fig tree,
Come thou, and reign over us.
11 But the fig tree said unto them,
should I forsake my sweetness,
and my good *fruit* **produce**,
and go to *be promoted* **wave** over the trees?
12 Then said the trees unto the vine,
Come thou, and reign over us.
13 And the vine said unto them,
should I *leave* **forsake** my *wine* **juice**,
which cheereth *God* **Elohim** and man,
and go to *be promoted* **wave** over the trees?
14 Then said all the trees unto the *bramble* **thorn**,
Come thou, and reign over us.
15 And the *bramble* **thorn** said unto the trees,
If in truth ye anoint me *king* **sovereign** over you,
then *come and put your trust* **seek refuge** in my shadow:
and if not, let fire *come* **go** out of the *bramble* **thorn**,
and devour the cedars of Lebanon.
16 Now therefore,
if ye have *done* **worked** truly and *sincerely* **integriously**,
in that ye have *made Abimelech king* **Abi Melech to reign**,
and if ye have *dealt well* **worked good**
with *Jerubbaal* **Yerub Baal** and his house,
and have *done* **worked** unto him
according to the *deserving* **dealing** of his hands;
17 (For my father fought for you,
and *adventured his life far* **cast his soul from him**,
and *delivered* **rescued** you
out of the hand of *Midian* **Midyaniy**:
18 And ye are risen up against my father's house this day,
and have *slain* **slaughtered** his sons,
threescore and ten persons **seventy men**, upon one stone,
and have made *Abimelech* **Abi Melech**,
the son of his *maidservant* **maid**,
king **to reign** over the *men* **masters** of Shechem,
because he is your brother;)
19 If ye then
have *dealt* **worked** truly and *sincerely* **integriously**
with *Jerubbaal* **Yerub Baal** and with his house this day,
then *rejoice* **cheer** ye in *Abimelech* **Abi Melech**,
and let him also *rejoice* **cheer** in you:
20 But if not,
let fire *come out* **go** from *Abimelech* **Abi Melech**,
and devour the *men* **masters** of Shechem,
and the house of Millo;
and let fire *come out* **go**
from the *men* **masters** of Shechem,
and from the house of Millo,

and devour *Abimelech* **Abi Melech**.
1 And *Jotham ran away* **Yah Tham fled**,
and fled, and went to Beer, and *dwelt* **settled** there,
for fear **from the face** of *Abimelech* **Abi Melech** his brother.

THE FALL OF ABI MELECH AND SHECHEM

2 When *Abimelech* **Abi Melech**
had *reigned* **dominated** three years over *Israel* **Yisra El**,
3 Then *God* **Elohim** sent an evil spirit
between *Abimelech* **Abi Melech**
and the *men* **masters** of Shechem;
and the *men* **masters** of Shechem
dealt *treacherously* **covertly** with *Abimelech* **Abi Melech**:
4 That the *cruelty* **violence** done
to the *threescore and ten* **seventy** sons
of *Jerubbaal* **Yerub Baal** might come,
and their blood
be *laid* **set** upon *Abimelech* **Abi Melech** their brother,
which *slew* **slaughtered** them;
and upon the *men* **masters** of Shechem,
which *aided him* **strengthened his hands**
in the *killing* **slaughter** of his brethren.
5 And the *men* **masters** of Shechem
set *liers in wait* **lurkers** for him
in the top of the mountains,
and they *robbed* **stripped** all
that *came* **passed** along that way by them:
and it was told *Abimelech* **Abi Melech**.
6 And Gaal the son of Ebed came with his brethren,
and *went* **passed** over to Shechem:
and the *men* **masters** of Shechem
put their confidence **confided** in him.
7 And they went out into the fields,
and *gathered* **clipped** their vineyards,
and *trode the grapes* **treaded**,
and *made merry* **worked halals**,
and went into the house of their *god* **elohim**,
and did eat and drink,
and *cursed Abimelech* **belittled Abi Melech**.
8 And Gaal the son of Ebed said,
Who is *Abimelech* **Abi Melech**,
and who is Shechem, that we should serve him?
is not he the son of *Jerubbaal* **Yerub Baal**?
and Zebul his *officer* **overseer**?
serve the men of Hamor the father of Shechem:
for why should we serve him?
9 *And would to God* **O that Elohim give**
that this people were under my hand!
then *would* **should** I
remove Abimelech **turn aside Abi Melech**.
And he said to *Abimelech* **Abi Melech**,
Increase thine army **Greaten thy host**, and *come out* **go**.
30 And when Zebul the *ruler* **governor** of the city
heard the words of Gaal the son of Ebed,
his *anger* **wrath** was kindled.
31 And he sent *messengers* **angels**
unto *Abimelech* **Abi Melech**
privily **deceitfully/to Tormah**, saying, Behold,
Gaal the son of Ebed and his brethren
be come to Shechem; and, behold,
they *fortify* **besiege** the city against thee.
32 Now therefore *up* **arise** by night,
thou and the people that is with thee,
and *lie in wait* **lurk** in the field:
33 And it shall be, that in the morning,
as soon as the sun *is up* **riseth**, thou shalt *rise* **start** early,
and *set upon* **spread over** the city: and, behold,
when he and the people that is with him
come out **go** against thee,
then mayest thou *do* **work** to them
as thou shalt find occasion.
34 And *Abimelech* **Abi Melech** rose up,
and all the people that were with him, by night,
and they *laid wait* **lurked** against Shechem
in four *companies* **heads**.
35 And Gaal the son of Ebed went out,
and stood in the *entering* **opening**
of the *gate* **portal** of the city:
and *Abimelech* **Abi Melech** rose up,
and the people that were with him,
from *lying in wait* **lurking**.
36 And when Gaal saw the people, he said to Zebul,
Behold, *there come* people **descend** *down*
from the top of the mountains.
And Zebul said unto him,
Thou seest the shadow of the mountains
as *if they were* men.
37 And Gaal *spake* **worded** again, and said,
See *there come* people **descend** *down*
by the *middle* **summit** of the land,
and *another company* **one head** come *along* **journeying**
by the *plain* **mighty oak** of Meonenim.
38 Then said Zebul unto him,
Where is now thy mouth, wherewith thou saidst,
Who is *Abimelech* **Abi Melech**, that we should serve him?
is not this the people that thou hast *despised* **spurned**?
go out, I *pray* **beseech** now, and fight with them.
39 And Gaal went out *before* **at the face**
of the *men* **masters** of Shechem,
and fought with *Abimelech* **Abi Melech**.
40 And *Abimelech chased* **Abi Melech pursued** him,
and he fled *before him* **from his face**,
and many were *overthrown* **fallen** and *wounded* **pierced**,
even unto the *entering* **opening** of the *gate* **portal**.
41 And *Abimelech dwelt* **Abi Melech settled** at Arumah:
and Zebul *thrust* **drove** *out* Gaal and his brethren,
that they should not *dwell* **settle** in Shechem.
42 And it *came to pass* **became,** on the morrow,
that the people went out into the field;
and they told *Abimelech* **Abi Melech**.
43 And he took the people,
and divided them into three *companies* **heads**,
and *laid wait* **lurked** in the field, and *looked* **saw**,
and, behold,
the people were *come* **gone** *forth* out of the city;
and he rose up against them, and smote them.
44 And *Abimelech* **Abi Melech**,
and the *company* **head** that was with him,
rushed **spread** forward,
and stood in the *entering* **opening**
of the *gate* **portal** of the city:
and the two *other companies* **heads**
ran upon **stripped** all *the people* that were in the fields,
and *slew* **smote** them.
45 And *Abimelech* **Abi Melech**
fought against the city all that day;
and he *took* **captured** the city,
and *slew* **slaughtered** the people that was therein,
and *beat* **pulled** down the city,
and *sowed* **seeded** it with salt.
46 And when all the *men* **masters**
of the tower of Shechem heard that,
they entered into *an hold* **a tower**
of *the house of the god* **Beth El** Berith.
47 And it was told *Abimelech* **Abi Melech**,
that all the *men* **masters** of the tower of Shechem
were gathered together.
48 And *Abimelech* **Abi Melech**
gat **ascended** him *up* to mount *Zalmon* **Salmon**,
he and all the people that were with him;
and *Abimelech* **Abi Melech** took an ax in his hand,
and cut down a *bough* **branch** from the trees,
and *took* **lifted** it, and *laid* **set** it on his shoulder,
and said unto the people that were with him,
What ye have seen me *do* **work**,
make haste **hasten**, and *do* **work** as I have *done*.
49 And all the people likewise
cut down every man his *bough* **branch**,
and *followed Abimelech* **went after Abi Melech**,
and *put* **set** them to the *hold* **tower**,
and *set* **burnt** the *hold* **tower** on fire upon them;
so that all the men
of the tower of Shechem died also,
about a thousand men and women.
50 Then went *Abimelech* **Abi Melech** to *Thebez* **Tebes**,
and encamped against *Thebez* **Tebes**,
and *took* **captured** it.
51 But there was a *strong tower* **tower of strength**
within the city,
and thither fled all the men and women,
and all *they* **the masters** of the city, and shut it to them,

and *gat* **ascended** them *up* to the *top* **roof** of the tower.
52 And *Abimelech* **Abi Melech** came unto the tower,
and fought against it,
and *went hard* **came near**
unto the *door* **portal** of the tower to burn it with fire.
53 And *a certain* **one** woman
cast a *piece* **slice** of *a* **an upper** millstone
upon *Abimelech's* **Abi Melech's** head,
and all to *brake* **crush** his *skull* **cranium**.
54 Then he called *hastily* **quickly** unto the *young man* **lad**
his *armourbearer* **instrument bearer**, and said unto him,
Draw thy sword, and *slay* **deathify** me,
that men say not of me, A women *slew* **slaughtered** him.
And his *young man thrust* **lad stabbed** him through,
and he died.
55 And when the men of *Israel* **Yisra El**
saw that *Abimelech was dead* **Abi Melech had died**,
they *departed* **went** every man unto his place.
56 Thus *God rendered* **Elohim turned back**
the *wickedness* **evil** of *Abimelech* **Abi Melech**,
which he *did* **worked** unto his father,
in *slaying* **slaughtering** his seventy brethren:
57 And all the evil of the men of Shechem
did God render **Elohim turned back** upon their heads:
and upon them came the *curse* **abasement**
of *Jotham* **Yah Tham** the son of *Jerubbaal* **Yerub Baal**.

JUDGE TOLA

10 And after *Abimelech* **Abi Melech**
there arose to *defend Israel* **save Yisra El**
Tola the son of Puah, the son of Dodo,
a man of *Issachar* **Yissachar**;
and he *dwelt* **settled** in Shamir
in mount *Ephraim* **Ephrayim**.
2 And he judged *Israel* **Yisra El** twenty and three years,
and died, and was *buried* **entombed** in Shamir.

JUDGE YAIR

3 And after him arose *Jair* **Yair**, a *Gileadite* **Giladiy**,
and judged *Israel* **Yisra El** twenty and two years.
4 And he had thirty sons that rode on thirty *ass* colts,
and they had thirty cities,
which are called *Havothjair* **Havoth Yair** unto this day,
which are in the land of *Gilead* **Gilad**.
5 And *Jair* **Yair** died,
and was *buried* **entombed** in *Camon* **Qamon**.

YISRA EL ABANDONS YAH VEH

6 And the *children* **sons** of *Israel* **Yisra El**
did **added to work** evil *again*
in the *sight* **eyes** of *the LORD* **Yah Veh**,
and served Baalim, and Ashtaroth,
and the *gods* **elohim** of *Syria* **Aram**,
and the *gods* **elohim** of *Zidon* **Sidon**,
and the *gods* **elohim** of Moab,
and the *gods* **elohim** of the *children* **sons** of Ammon,
and the *gods* **elohim** of the *Philistines* **Peleshethiy**,
and forsook *the LORD* **Yah Veh**, and served not him.
7 And the *anger* **wrath** of *the LORD* **Yah Veh**
was hot **kindled** against *Israel* **Yisra El**,
and he sold them
into the hands of the *Philistines* **Peleshethiy**,
and into the hands of the *children* **sons** of Ammon.
8 And that year
they *vexed* **harassed** and *oppressed* **crushed**
the *children* **sons** of *Israel* **Yisra El**:
eighteen years, all the *children* **sons** of *Israel* **Yisra El**
that were on the other side *Jordan* **Yarden**
in the land of the *Amorites* **Emoriy**,
which is in *Gilead* **Gilad**.
9 Moreover the *children* **sons** of Ammon
passed over *Jordan* **Yarden**
to fight also against *Judah* **Yah Hudah**,
and against *Benjamin* **Ben Yamin**,
and against the house of *Ephraim* **Ephrayim**;
so that *Israel* **Yisra El**
was *sore distressed* **mightily depressed**.
10 And the *children* **sons** of *Israel* **Yisra El**
cried unto *the LORD* **Yah Veh**, saying,
We have sinned against thee,
both because we have forsaken our *God* **Elohim**,
and also served Baalim.
11 And *the LORD* **Yah Veh**
said unto the *children* **sons** of *Israel* **Yisra El**,
Did not I *deliver you* from the *Egyptians* **Misrayim**,
and from the *Amorites* **Emoriy**,
from the *children* **sons** of Ammon,
and from the *Philistines* **Peleshethiy**?
12 The *Zidonians* **Sidoniy** also,
and *the Amalekites* **Amaleq**,
and *the Maonites* **Maon**, did oppress you;
and ye cried to me,
and I *delivered* **saved** you out of their hand.
13 Yet ye have forsaken me,
and served other *gods* **elohim**:
wherefore I *will deliver you no more* **add not to save you**.
14 Go and cry unto the *gods* **elohim**
which ye have chosen;
let them *deliver* **save** you in the time of your tribulation.
15 And the *children* **sons** of *Israel* **Yisra El**
said unto *the LORD* **Yah Veh**, We have sinned:
do **work** thou unto us
whatsoever seemeth good *unto thee* **in thine eyes**;
deliver **rescue** us only, we *pray* **beseech** thee, this day.
16 And they *put away* **turned aside**
the *strange gods* **elohim of strangers** from among them,
and served *the LORD* **Yah Veh**:
and his soul was *grieved* **shortened**
for the *misery* **toil** of *Israel* **Yisra El**.

JUDGE YIPHTACH

17 Then the *children* **sons** of Ammon
were gathered together **cried out**,
and encamped in *Gilead* **Gilad**.
And the *children* **sons** of *Israel* **Yisra El**
assembled **gathered** *themselves together*,
and encamped in *Mizpeh* **Mispeh**.
18 And the people and *princes* **governors** of *Gilead* **Gilad**
said *one* **man** to *another* **friend**,
What man *is he that will* **shall** begin to fight
against the *children* **sons** of Ammon?
he shall be head
over all the *inhabitants* **settlers** of *Gilead* **Gilad**.
11 Now *Jephthah* **Yiphtach** the *Gileadite* **Giladiy**
was a mighty *man* of valour,
and he was the son of *an harlot* **a whore**:
and *Gilead* **Gilad** begat *Jephthah* **Yiphtach**.
2 And *Gilead's wife* **Gilad's woman** bare him sons;
and his *wife's* **woman's** sons grew up,
and they *thrust out Jephthah* **expelled Yiphtach**,
and said unto him,
Thou shalt not inherit in our father's house;
for thou art the son of *a strange* **another** woman.
3 Then *Jephthah* **Yiphtach**
fled from **the face of** his brethren,
and *dwelt* **settled** in the land of Tob:
and there were gathered vain men to *Jephthah* **Yiphtach**,
and went out with him.
4 And it *came to pass* **became**,
in process of time **after days**,
that the *children* **sons** of Ammon
made war **fought** against *Israel* **Yisra El**.
5 And it *was so* **became**,
that when the *children* **sons** of Ammon
made war **fought** against *Israel* **Yisra El**,
the elders of *Gilead* **Gilad**
went to *fetch Jephthah* **take Yiphtach**
out of the land of Tob:
6 And they said unto *Jephthah* **Yiphtach**,
Come, and be our *captain* **commander**,
that we may fight with the *children* **sons** of Ammon.
7 And *Jephthah* **Yiphtach**
said unto the elders of *Gilead* **Gilad**,
Did not ye hate me,
and expel me out of my father's house?
and why are ye come unto me now
when ye *are in distress* **tribulate**?
8 And the elders of *Gilead* **Gilad**
said unto *Jephthah* **Yiphtach**,
Therefore we turn *again* **back** to thee now,
that thou mayest go with us,
and fight *against* the *children* **sons** of Ammon,
and be our head
over all the *inhabitants* **settlers** of *Gilead* **Gilad**.

9 And *Jephthah* **Yiphtach**
said unto the elders of *Gilead* **Gilad**,
If ye *bring me home again* **turn me back**
to fight *against* the *children* **sons** of Ammon,
and *the LORD deliver* **Yah Veh give** them
before me **at my face**,
shall I be your head?
10 And the elders of *Gilead* **Gilad**
said unto *Jephthah* **Yiphtach**,
The LORD be witness **Yah Veh hearken** between us,
if we *do* **work** not so according to thy words.
11 Then *Jephthah* **Yiphtach**
went with the elders of *Gilead* **Gilad**,
and the people *made* **set** him
head and *captain* **commander** over them:
and *Jephthah uttered* **Yiphtach worded** all his words
before the LORD **at the face of Yah Veh**
in *Mizpeh* **Mispeh**.
12 And *Jephthah* **Yiphtach** sent *messengers* **angels**
unto the *king* **sovereign** of the *children* **sons** of Ammon,
saying, What hast thou to do with me,
that thou art come against me to fight in my land?
13 And the *king* **sovereign** of the *children* **sons** of Ammon
answered **said**
unto the *messengers* **angels** of *Jephthah* **Yiphtach**,
Because *Israel* **Yisra El** took away my land,
when they *came up* **ascended** out of *Egypt* **Misrayim**,
from Arnon even unto *Jabbok* **Yabboq**,
and unto *Jordan* **Yarden**:
now therefore restore those *lands* again
peaceably **in shalom**.

JUDGE YIPHTACH DEFENDS YISRA EL'S HONOUR

14 And *Jephthah* **Yiphtach** sent *messengers* **angels** again
unto the *king* **sovereign** of the *children* **sons** of Ammon:
15 And said unto him, Thus saith *Jephthah* **Yiphtach**,
Israel **Yisra El** took not away the land of Moab,
nor the land of the *children* **sons** of Ammon:
16 But when *Israel* **Yisra El**
came up **ascended** from *Egypt* **Misrayim**,
and walked through the wilderness
unto the *Red* **Reed** sea, and came to *Kadesh* **Qadesh**;
17 Then *Israel* **Yisra El** sent *messengers* **angels**
unto the *king* **sovereign** of Edom, saying,
Let me, I *pray* **beseech** thee, pass through thy land:
but the *king* **sovereign** of Edom
would not hearken **hearkened not** thereto.
And in like manner
they sent unto the *king* **sovereign** of Moab:
but he *would not consent* **willed not**:
and *Israel abode* **Yisra El settled** in *Kadesh* **Qadesh**.
18 Then they went along through the wilderness,
and *compassed* **surrounded** the land of Edom,
and the land of Moab,
and came by the *east side* **rising of the sun**
of the land of Moab,
and *pitched* **encamped** on the other side of Arnon,
but came not within the border of Moab:
for Arnon was the border of Moab.
19 And *Israel* **Yisra El** sent *messengers* **angels**
unto *Sihon king* **Sichon sovereign** of the *Amorites* **Emoriy**,
the *king* **sovereign** of Heshbon;
and *Israel* **Yisra El** said unto him,
Let us pass, we *pray* **beseech** thee,
through thy land *into* **unto** my place.
20 But *Sihon* **Sichon** trusted not *Israel* **Yisra El**
to pass through his *coast* **border**:
but *Sihon* **Sichon** gathered all his people together,
and *pitched* **encamped** in *Jahaz* **Yahsah**,
and fought against *Israel* **Yisra El**.
21 And *the LORD God* **Yah Veh Elohim** of *Israel* **Yisra El**
delivered Sihon **gave Sichon** and all his people
into the hand of *Israel* **Yisra El**, and they smote them:
so *Israel* **Yisra El** possessed
all the land of the *Amorites* **Emoriy**,
the *inhabitants* **settlers** of that *country* **land**.
22 And they possessed
all the *coasts* **borders** of the *Amorites* **Emoriy**,
from Arnon even unto *Jabbok* **Yabboq**,
and from the wilderness even unto *Jordan* **Yarden**.
23 So now
the LORD God **Yah Veh Elohim** of *Israel* **Yisra El**
hath dispossessed the *Amorites* **Emoriy**
from *before* **the face of** his people *Israel* **Yisra El**,
and shouldest thou possess it?
24 *Wilt* **Shalt** not thou possess that
which *Chemosh* **Kemosh** thy *god* **elohim**
giveth thee to possess?
So whomsoever *the LORD* **Yah Veh** our *God* **Elohim**
shall *drive out* **dispossess** from *before us* **our face**,
them *will* **shall** we possess.
25 And now art thou any *thing* better than *Balak* **Balaq**
the son of *Zippor* **Sippor**, *king* **sovereign** of Moab?
in striving, did he *ever* strive against *Israel* **Yisra El**,
or **in fighting,** did he *ever* fight against them,
26 While *Israel dwelt* **Yisra El settled**
in Heshbon and her *towns* **daughters**,
and in Aroer and her *towns* **daughters**,
and in all the cities
that be along by the *coasts* **hand** of Arnon,
three hundred years?
why therefore
did ye not *recover* **rescue** them within that time?
27 Wherefore I have not sinned against thee,
but thou *doest* **workest** me *wrong* **evil**
to *war* **fight** against me:
the LORD **Yah Veh** the Judge be judge this day
between
the *children* **sons** of *Israel* **Yisra El**
and the *children* **sons** of Ammon.
28 Howbeit the *king* **sovereign**
of the *children* **sons** of Ammon
hearkened not unto the words of *Jephthah* **Yiphtach**
which he sent him.
29 Then the Spirit of *the LORD* **Yah Veh**
came upon *Jephthah* **Yiphtach**,
and he passed over *Gilead* **Gilad**,
and *Manasseh* **Menash Sheh**,
and passed over *Mizpeh* **Mispeh** of *Gilead* **Gilad**,
and from *Mizpeh* **Mispeh** of *Gilead* **Gilad**
he passed over *unto* the *children* **sons** of Ammon.

JUDGE YIPHTACH'S VOW

30 And *Jephthah* **Yiphtach**
vowed a vow unto *the LORD* **Yah Veh**, and said,
If **in giving,** thou shalt *without fail deliver* **give**
the *children* **sons** of Ammon into mine hands,
31 Then it shall be,
that *whatsoever cometh forth* **which goeth**
of the doors of my house to meet me,
when I return in *peace* **shalom**
from the *children* **sons** of Ammon,
shall surely be *the LORD'S* **Yah Veh's**,
and I *will offer* **shall holocaust** it *up*
for a *burnt offering* **holocaust**.
32 So *Jephthah* **Yiphtach** passed over
unto the *children* **sons** of Ammon to fight against them;
and *the LORD* **Yah Veh**
delivered **gave** them into his hands.
33 And he smote them from Aroer,
even till thou come to Minnith, *even* twenty cities,
and unto *the plain of the vineyards* **Abel Keramin**,
with a *very* **mighty** great *slaughter* **stroke**.
Thus the *children* **sons** of Ammon were subdued
before **at the face of** the *children* **sons** of *Israel* **Yisra El**.

JUDGE YIPHTACH'S DAUGHTER

34 And *Jephthah* **Yiphtach** came to *Mizpeh* **Mispeh**
unto his house, and, behold,
his daughter *came out* **went** to meet him
with *timbrels* **tambourines** and with **round** dances:
and she was his only child;
beside her he had neither son nor daughter.
35 And it *came to pass* **became**, when he saw her,
that he *rent* **ripped** his clothes, and said,
Alas **Aha**, my daughter!
in kneeling,
thou hast *brought me very low* **caused me to kneel**,
and thou art one of them that trouble me:
for I have *opened* **gaped** my mouth
unto *the LORD* **Yah Veh**,
and I cannot *go* **turn** back.
36 And she said unto him, My father,

if thou hast *opened* **gaped** thy mouth
unto *the LORD* **Yah Veh**,
do **work** to me according to that
which *hath proceeded* **went** out of thy mouth;
forasmuch as the LORD **since Yah Veh**
hath *taken* **worked** vengeance for thee of thine enemies,
even of the *children* **sons** of Ammon.
37 And she said unto her father,
Let this *thing* **word** be *done* **worked** for me:
let me *alone* **loose** two months,
that I may *go up* **ascend** and *down* **descend**
upon the mountains,
and *bewail* **weep over** my virginity,
I and my *fellows* **friends**.
38 And he said, Go.
And he sent her away for two months:
and she went with her *companions* **friends**,
and *bewailed* **wept over** her virginity upon the mountains.
39 And it *came to pass* **became**, at the end of two months,
that she returned unto her father,
who *did* **worked** with her
according to his vow which he had vowed:
and she knew no man.
And it was a *custom* **statute** in *Israel* **Yisra El**,
40 That the daughters of *Israel* **Yisra El**
went *yearly* **from days by days**
to *lament* **celebrate** the daughter of *Jephthah* **Yiphtach**
the *Gileadite* **Giladiy** four days in a year.

THE EPHRAYIM FEEL SLIGHTED

12 And the men of *Ephraim* **Ephrayim**
gathered themselves together **were summoned**,
and *went* **passed over** northward,
and said unto *Jephthah* **Yiphtach**,
Wherefore passedst thou over
to fight against the *children* **sons** of Ammon,
and didst not call us to go with thee?
we *will* **shall** burn thine house upon thee with fire.
2 And *Jephthah* **Yiphtach** said unto them,
I and my people were *at great* **men of mighty** strife
with the *children* **sons** of Ammon;
and when I *called* **cried to** you,
ye *delivered* **saved** me not out of their hands.
3 And when I saw that ye *delivered* **saved** me not,
I *put* **set** my *life* **soul** in my *hands* **palms**,
and passed over against the *children* **sons** of Ammon,
and *the LORD* **Yah Veh**
delivered **gave** them into my hand:
wherefore then are ye *come up* **ascended** unto me
this day, to fight against me?

JUDGE YIPHTACH FIGHTS WITH EPHRAYIM

4 Then *Jephthah* **Yiphtach** gathered together
all the men of *Gilead* **Gilad**,
and fought with *Ephraim* **Ephrayim**:
and the men of *Gilead* **Gilad** smote *Ephraim* **Ephrayim**,
because they said, ye *Gileadites* **Giladiy**
are *fugitives* **escapees** of *Ephraim* **Ephrayim**
among the *Ephraimites* **Ephrayimiy**,
and among the *Manassites* **Menash Shiy**.
5 And the *Gileadites* **Giladiy**
took **captured** the passages of *Jordan* **Yarden**
before the *Ephraimites* **Ephrayimiy**:
and it *was so* **became**,
that when those *Ephraimites* **Ephrayimiy**
which were escaped **escapees** said,
Let me *go* **pass** over;
that the men of *Gilead* **Gilad** said unto him,
Art thou an *Ephraimite* **Ephrayim**?
If he said, Nay;
6 Then said they unto him, Say now Shibboleth:
and he said Sibboleth:
for he could not *frame* **prepare** to *pronounce it* **word** right.
Then they *took* **held** him, and *slew* **slaughtered** him
at the passages of *Jordan* **Yarden**:
and there fell at that time of the *Ephraimites* **Ephrayimiy**
forty and two thousand.

JUDGE YIPHTACH'S DEATH

7 And *Jephthah* **Yiphtach** judged *Israel* **Yisra El** six years.
Then died *Jephthah* **Yiphtach** the *Gileadite* **Giladiy**,
and was *buried* **entombed**
in *one of* the cities of *Gilead* **Gilad**.

JUDGE IBSAN

8 And after him *Ibzan* **Ibsan** of *Bethlehem* **Beth Lechem**
judged *Israel* **Yisra El**.
9 And he had thirty sons,
and thirty daughters, *whom* he sent abroad,
and took in thirty daughters from abroad for his sons.
And he judged *Israel* **Yisra El** seven years.
10 Then died *Ibzan* **Ibsan**,
and was *buried* **entombed** at *Bethlehem* **Beth Lechem**.

JUDGE ELON

11 And after him Elon, a *Zebulonite* **Zebuluniy**,
judged *Israel* **Yisra El**;
and he judged *Israel* **Yisra El** ten years.
12 And Elon the *Zebulonite* **Zebuluniy** died,
and was *buried* **entombed** in *Aijalon* **Ayalon**
in the *country* **land** of Zebulun.

JUDGE ABDON

13 And after him Abdon the son of Hillel,
a *Pirathonite* **Pirathoniy**, judged *Israel* **Yisra El**.
14 And he had forty sons and thirty *nephews* **sons' sons**,
that rode on *threescore and ten ass* **seventy** colts:
and he judged *Israel* **Yisra El** eight years.
15 And Abdon the son of Hillel the *Pirathonite* **Pirathoniy**
died, and was *buried* **entombed** in Pirathon
in the land of *Ephraim* **Ephrayim**,
in the mount of the *Amalekites* **Amaleqiy**.

SONS OF YISRA EL GIVEN OVER TO THE PELESHETHIY

13 And the *children* **sons** of *Israel* **Yisra El**
did **added to work** evil *again*
in the *sight* **eyes** of *the LORD* **Yah Veh**;
and *the LORD delivered* **Yah Veh gave** them
into the hand of the *Philistines* **Peleshethiy** forty years.

SHIMSHON'S BIRTH FORETOLD

2 And there was *a certain* **one** man of *Zorah* **Sorah**,
of the family of *the Danites* **Daniy**,
whose name was *Manoah* **Manoach**;
and his *wife* **woman** was *barren* **sterile**, and bare not.
3 And the angel of *the LORD* **Yah Veh**
appeared unto **was seen by** the woman, and said unto her,
Behold now, thou art *barren* **sterile**, and bearest not:
but thou shalt conceive, and bear a son.
4 Now therefore *beware* **guard**, I *pray* **beseech** thee,
and drink not wine nor *strong drink* **intoxicants**,
and eat not any *unclean thing* **foulness**:
5 For, *lo* **behold**,
thou shalt conceive, and bear a son;
and no razor shall *come* **ascend** on his head:
for the *child* **lad** shall be a *Nazarite* **Separatist**
unto *God* **Elohim** from the *womb* **belly**:
and he shall begin to *deliver Israel* **save Yisra El**
out of the hand of the *Philistines* **Peleshethiy**.
6 Then the woman came
and *told* **said to** her *husband* **man**, saying,
A man of *God* **Elohim** came unto me,
and his *countenance* **visage**
was like the *countenance* **visage**
of an angel of *God* **Elohim**,
very terrible **mighty awesome**:
but I asked him not whence he was,
neither told he me his name:
7 But he said unto me,
Behold, thou shalt conceive, and bear a son;
and now drink no wine nor *strong drink* **intoxicants**,
neither eat any *unclean thing* **foulness**:
for the *child* **lad** shall be a *Nazarite* **Separatist**
to *God* **Elohim** from the *womb* **belly**
to the day of his death.
8 Then *Manoah* **Manoach** intreated *the LORD* **Yah Veh**,
and said, O my *Lord* **Adonay**, let **I beseech**,
the man of *God* **Elohim** which thou didst send
come again unto us,
and *teach* **direct** us what we shall *do* **work**
unto the *child* **lad** that shall be born.
9 And *God* **Elohim**
hearkened to the voice of *Manoah* **Manoach**;
and the angel of *God* **Elohim** came again unto the woman
as she *sat* **settled** in the field:
but *Manoah* **Manoach** her *husband* **man** was not with her.
10 And the woman made haste, and ran,
and *shewed* **told** her *husband* **man**, and said unto him,

Behold, the man *hath appeared unto* **was seen by** me,
that came unto me *the other* **that** day.
11 And *Manoah* **Manoach** arose,
and went after his *wife* **woman,**
and came to the man, and said unto him,
Art thou the man that *spakest* **wordest** unto the woman?
And he said, I am.
12 And *Manoah* **Manoach** said,
Now let thy words *come to pass* **become**.
How shall we order the child,
and how shall we do unto him
What is the judgment of the lad, and his work?
13 And the angel of *the LORD* **Yah Veh**
said unto *Manoah* **Manoach,**
Of all that I said unto the woman let her *beware* **guard.**
14 She may not eat of *any thing* **aught**
that *cometh* **goeth** of the vine,
neither let her drink wine or *strong drink* **intoxicants,**
nor eat any *unclean thing* **foulness**:
all that I *commanded* **misvahed** her let her *observe* **guard.**
15 And *Manoah* **Manoach**
said unto the angel of *the LORD* **Yah Veh,**
I *pray* **beseech** thee, let us detain **restrain** thee,
until we shall have *made ready* **worked** a *kid* **doe goat**
for thee **at thy face.**
16 And the angel of *the LORD* **Yah Veh**
said unto *Manoah* **Manoach,**
Though thou *detain* **restrain** me,
I *will* **shall** not eat of thy bread:
and if thou *wilt offer* **shalt work** a *burnt offering* **holocaust,**
thou must *offer it* **shalt holocaust** unto *the LORD* **Yah Veh.**
For *Manoah* **Manoach** knew not
that he was an angel of *the LORD* **Yah Veh.**
17 And *Manoah* **Manoach**
said unto the angel of *the LORD* **Yah Veh,**
What is thy name,
that when thy *sayings* **words** come to *pass* **be,**
we may do thee honour?
18 And the angel of *the LORD* **Yah Veh** said unto him,
Why askest thou thus after my name,
seeing it is *secret* **marvellous**?
19 So *Manoah* **Manoach**
took a *kid* **doe goat** with *a meat* **an** offering,
and *offered it* **holocausted** upon a rock
unto *the LORD* **Yah Veh**:
and the angel did wonderously
and in working, he worked marvellously;
and *Manoah* **Manoach** and his *wife* **woman**
looked on **saw.**
20 For it *came to pass* **became,**
when the flame *went up* **ascended**
toward *heaven* **the heavens** from off the **sacrifice** altar,
that the angel of *the LORD* **Yah Veh**
ascended in the flame of the **sacrifice** altar.
And *Manoah* **Manoach** and his *wife* **woman**
looked on it **saw,**
and fell on their faces to the *ground* **earth.**
21 But the angel of *the LORD* **Yah Veh**
did no more appear **added not to be seen**
to *Manoah* **Manoach** and to his *wife* **woman.**
Then *Manoah* **Manoach** knew
that he was an angel of *the LORD* **Yah Veh.**
22 And *Manoah* **Manoach** said unto his *wife* **woman,**
In dying, We shall *surely* die,
because we have seen *God* **Elohim.**
23 But his *wife* **woman** said unto him,
If *the LORD* **Yah Veh** were *pleased* **delighted**
to *kill* **deathify** us,
he *would* **should** not have *received* **taken**
a *burnt offering* **holocaust** and *a meat* **an** offering
at our hands,
neither *would* **should** he have *shewed us* **us see**
all these *things,*
nor *would* **should** as at this time
have *told us such things as these* **us hear thus.**

SHIMSHON'S BIRTH

24 And the woman bare a son,
and called his name *Samson* **Shimshon**:
and the *child* **lad** grew,
and *the LORD* **Yah Veh** blessed him.
25 And the Spirit of *the LORD* **Yah Veh**
began to *move* **agitate** him at times in the camp of Dan
between *Zorah* **Sorah** and Eshtaol.

SHIMSHON'S MARRIAGE

14 And *Samson* **Shimshon**
went down **descended** to *Timnath* **Timnah,**
and saw a woman in *Timnath* **Timnah**
of the daughters of the *Philistines* **Peleshethiy.**
2 And he *came up* **ascended,**
and told his father and his mother, and said,
I have seen a woman in *Timnath* **Timnah**
of the daughters of the *Philistines* **Peleshethiy**:
now therefore *get* **take** her for me to *wife* **woman.**
3 Then his father and his mother said unto him,
Is there *never* **not** a woman
among the daughters of thy brethren,
or among all my people,
that thou goest to take a *wife* **woman**
of the uncircumcised *Philistines* **Peleshethiy**?
And *Samson* **Shimshon** said unto his father,
Get **Take** her for me;
for she *pleaseth me well* **be straight in mine eyes.**
4 But his father and his mother
knew not that it was of *the LORD* **Yah Veh,**
that he sought an occasion
against the *Philistines* **Peleshethiy**:
for at that time the *Philistines* **Peleshethiy**
had dominion **reigned** over *Israel* **Yisra El.**
5 Then *went Samson down* **Shimshon descended,**
and his father and his mother, to *Timnath* **Timnah,**
and came to the vineyards of *Timnath* **Timnah**:
and, behold,
a *young lion* **whelp of the lionesses**
roared *against* **in meeting** him.
6 And the Spirit of *the LORD* **Yah Veh**
came mightily upon **prospered over** him,
and he *rent* **clove** him
as he *would have rent* **had cloven** a kid,
and he had *nothing* **naught** in his hand:
but he told not his father or his mother
what he had *done* **worked.**
7 And he *went down* **descended,**
and *talked* **worded** with the woman;
and she *pleased* **was straight**
Samson well **in the eyes of Shimshon.**
8 And after *a time* **many days** he returned to take her,
and he turned aside to see the *carcase* **ruin** of the lion:
and, behold,
there was a *swarm* **witness** of bees and honey
in the *carcase* **body** of the lion.
9 And he *took* **crumbled** thereof in his *hands* **palms,**
and **in walking,** *went* **walked** on eating,
and *came* **went** to his father and mother,
and he gave them, and they did eat:
but he told not them
that he had *taken* **crumbled** the honey
out of the *carcase* **body** of the lion.
10 So his father *went down* **descended** unto the woman:
and *Samson made* **Shimshon worked** there
a *feast* **banquet;**
for so used the *young men* **youths** to *do* **work.**
11 And it *came to pass* **became,** when they saw him,
that they *brought* **took** thirty companions to be with him.
12 And *Samson* **Shimshon** said unto them,
I *will* **shall** now *put forth* **propound** a riddle unto you:
if **in telling,** ye can *certainly declare* **tell** me it
within the seven days of the *feast* **banquet,**
and find it out,
then I *will* **shall** give you thirty *sheets* **wraps**
and thirty change of *garments* **clothes**:
13 But if ye cannot *declare* **tell** it me,
then shall ye give me thirty *sheets* **wraps**
and thirty change of *garments* **clothes.**
And they said unto him,
Put forth **Propound** thy riddle, that we may hear it.
14 And he said unto them,
Out of the eater *came forth meat* **went food,**
and out of the strong *came forth* **went** sweetness.
And they could not in three days *expound* **tell** the riddle.
15 And it *came to pass* **became,** on the seventh day,

that they said unto *Samson's wife* **Shimshon's woman**,
Entice thy *husband* **man**,
that he may *declare* **tell** unto us the riddle,
lest we burn thee and thy father's house with fire:
have ye called us to take that we *have* **possess**?
is it not so?
16 And *Samson's wife* **Shimshon's woman**
wept before him, and said,
Thou dost but hate me, and lovest me not:
thou hast *put forth* **propounded** a riddle
unto the *children* **sons** of my people,
and hast not told it me.
And he said unto her, Behold,
I have not told it my father nor my mother,
and shall I tell it thee?
17 And she wept before him the seven days,
while their *feast lasted* **banquet became**:
and it *came to pass* **became,** on the seventh day,
that he told her,
because she *lay sore upon* **oppressed** him:
and she told the riddle to the *children* **sons** of her people.
18 And the men of the city said unto him
on the seventh day before the sun went down,
What is sweeter than honey?
And what is stronger than a lion?
and he said unto them,
If ye had not plowed with my heifer,
ye had not found out my riddle.
19 And the Spirit of *the LORD* **Yah Veh**
came upon **prospered over** him,
and he *went down* **descended** to *Ashkelon* **Ashqelon**,
and *slew* **smote** thirty men of them,
and took their *spoil* **clothes**,
and gave *change of garments* **changes** unto them
which *expounded* **told** the riddle.
And his *anger was* **wrath** kindled,
and he *went up* **ascended** to his father's house.
20 But *Samson's wife* **Shimshon's woman**
was given to his companion,
whom he had *used as his friend* **befriended**.

SHIMSHON AVENGES THE PELESHETHIY

15 But it *came to pass* **became,**
within a while after **days later,**
in the *time of* wheat harvest,
that *Samson* **Shimshon** visited his *wife* **woman**
with a *kid* **doe goat**; and he said,
I *will* **shall** go in to my *wife* **woman** into the chamber.
But her father *would not suffer* **allowed** him **not** to go in.
2 And her father said,
In saying, I *verily thought* **had said**
that **in hating,** thou hadst *utterly* hated her;
therefore I gave her to thy companion:
is not her younger sister *fairer* **better** than she?
take her, I *pray* **beseech** thee, instead of her.
3 And *Samson* **Shimshon** said concerning them,
Now **This time** shall I be more *blameless* **exonerated**
than the *Philistines* **Peleshethiy**,
though I *do* **work** them *a displeasure* **evil**.
4 And *Samson* **Shimshon** went
and *caught* **captured** three hundred foxes,
and took *firebrands* **flambeaus**,
and *turned* **faced them** tail to tail,
and *put a firebrand* **set one flambeau** in the midst
between two tails.
5 And when he had
set **burnt** the *brands* **flambeaus** on fire,
he *let* **sent** them *go* **away**
into the *standing corn* **stalks** of the *Philistines* **Peleshethiy**,
and burnt up *both* the *shocks* **heaps**,
and also the *standing corn* **stalks**,
with the vineyards and olives.
6 Then the *Philistines* **Peleshethiy** said,
Who hath *done* **worked** this?
And they *answered* **said**, *Samson* **Shimshon**,
the son in law of the *Timnite* **Timnahiy**,
because he had taken his *wife* **woman**,
and given her to his companion.
And the *Philistines came up* **Peleshethiy ascended**,
and burnt her and her father with fire.
7 And *Samson* **Shimshon** said unto them,
Though ye have *done* **worked** this,
yet *will* **shall** I be avenged of you,
and after that I *will* **shall** cease.
8 And he smote them *hip and thigh* **leg unto flank**
with a great *slaughter* **stroke**:
and he *went down* **descended**
and *dwelt* **settled** in the *top* **cleft** of the rock Etam.
9 Then the *Philistines went up* **Peleshethiy ascended**,
and *pitched* **encamped** in *Judah* **Yah Hudah**,
and spread themselves in *Lehi* **Lechi**.
10 And the men of *Judah* **Yah Hudah** said,
Why are ye *come up* **ascended** against us?
And they *answered* **said**,
To bind *Samson* **Shimshon** are we *come up* **ascended**,
to *do* **work** to him as he hath *done* **worked** to us.
11 Then three thousand men of *Judah* **Yah Hudah**
went **descended** to the *top* **cleft** of the rock Etam,
and said to *Samson* **Shimshon**,
Knowest thou not that the *Philistines* **Peleshethiy**
are *rulers* **sovereigns** over us?
what is this that thou hast *done* **worked** unto us?
And he said unto them,
As they *did* **worked** unto me,
so have I *done* **worked** unto them.
12 And they said unto him,
We *are come down* **descended** to bind thee,
that we may *deliver* **give** thee
into the hand of the *Philistines* **Peleshethiy**.
And *Samson* **Shimshon** said unto them,
Swear **Oath** unto me,
that ye *will* **shall** not *fall* **encounter** upon me yourselves.
13 And they *spake* **said** unto him, saying, No;
but **in binding,** we *will* **shall** bind thee *fast*,
and *deliver* **give** thee into their hand:
but **in killing,** *surely* we *will* **shall** not kill thee.
And they bound him with two new *cords* **ropes**,
and *brought* **ascended** him *up* from the rock.
14 And when he came unto *Lehi* **Lechi**,
the *Philistines* **Peleshethiy** shouted *against* **meeting** him:
and the Spirit of *the LORD* **Yah Veh**
came mightily upon **prospered over** him,
and the *cords* **ropes** that were upon his arms
became as flax that was burnt with fire,
and his bands *loosed* **melted** from off his hands.
15 And he found a *new jawbone* **fresh jaw**
of *an ass* **a he burro**,
and *put* **sent** forth his hand, and took it,
and *slew* **smote** a thousand men therewith.
16 And *Samson* **Shimshon** said,
With the *jawbone* **jaw** of *an ass* **a he burro**,
heaps upon heaps,
with the jaw of *an ass* **a he burro**
have I *slain* **smitten** a thousand men.
17 And it *came to pass* **became**,
when he had *made an end of speaking* **finished wording**,
that he cast away the *jawbone* **jaw** out of his hand,
and called that place *Ramathlehi* **Ramah Lechi**.
18 And he was *sore athirst* **mighty thirsty**,
and called on *the LORD* **Yah Veh**, and said,
Thou hast given this great *deliverance* **salvation**
into the hand of thy servant:
and now shall I die for thirst,
and fall into the hand of the uncircumcised?
19 But *God clave an hollow place* **Elohim split a socket**
that was in the jaw,
and there *came* **went** water *thereout*;
and when he had drunk, his spirit *came again* **returned**,
and he *revived* **enlivened**:
wherefore he called the name thereof
Enhakkore **En Hak Qore**,
which is in *Lehi* **Lechi** unto this day.
20 And he judged *Israel* **Yisra El**
in the days of the *Philistines* **Peleshethiy** twenty years.

SHIMSHON AND THE LURKERS

16 Then went *Samson* **Shimshon** to *Gaza* **Azzah**,
and saw there *an harlot* **a woman whore**,
and went in unto her.
2 *And it was told the Gazites,* saying, **The Azzahiy say,**
Samson **Shimshon** is come hither.
And they *compassed him in,* **surrounded**

and *laid wait* **lurked** for him all night
in the *gate* **portal** of the city,
and *were quiet* **hushed** all the night, saying,
In the morning, when it is *day* **light**,
we shall *kill* **slaughter** him.
3 And *Samson* **Shimshon** lay till midnight,
and arose at midnight,
and *took* **possessed** the doors of the *gate* **portal** of the city,
and the two posts,
and *went away with them* **pulled**, bar and all,
and *put* **set** them upon his shoulders,
and *carried* **ascended** them *up*
to the top of *an hill* **a mountain**
that is before **at the face of** Hebron.

SHIMSHON AND DELILAH

4 And it *came to pass* **became,** afterward,
that he loved a woman in the *valley* **wadi** of *Sorek* **Soreq**,
whose name was Delilah.
5 And the *lords* **ringleaders** of the *Philistines* **Peleshethiy**
came up **ascended** unto her, and said unto her,
Entice him, and see wherein his great *strength* **force** *lieth*,
and by what *means* we may prevail against him,
that we may bind him to *afflict* **humble** him;
and we *will* **shall** give thee every *one* **man** of us
eleven hundred *pieces of* silver.
6 And Delilah said to *Samson* **Shimshon**,
Tell me, I *pray* **beseech** thee,
wherein thy great *strength* **force** *lieth*,
and wherewith thou mightest be bound
to *afflict* **humble** thee.
7 And *Samson* **Shimshon** said unto her,
If they bind me with seven *green withs* **fresh cords**
that were never *dried* **parched**,
then shall I be *weak* **worn**,
and be as *another man* **one human**.
8 Then the *lords* **ringleaders** of the *Philistines* **Peleshethiy**
brought up **ascended** to her seven *green withs* **fresh cords**
which had not been *dried* **parched**,
and she bound him with them.
9 Now there were men *lying in wait* **lurking**,
abiding **settling** with her in the chamber.
And she said unto him,
The *Philistines* **Peleshethiy** be upon thee,
Samson **Shimshon**.
And he *brake* **tore** the *withs* **cords**,
as a *thread* **braid** of *tow* **tuft** is *broken* **torn**
when it *toucheth* **scenteth** the fire.
So his *strength* **force** was not known.
10 And Delilah said unto *Samson* **Shimshon**,
Behold, thou hast mocked me, and *told me* **worded** lies:
now tell me, I *pray* **beseech** thee,
wherewith thou mightest be bound.
11 And he said unto her,
If **in binding,** they bind me *fast* with new ropes
that never were occupied
wherewith work hath never been done,
then shall I be *weak* **worn**, and be as *another* **one** man.
12 Delilah therefore took new ropes
and bound him therewith,
and said unto him,
The *Philistines* **Peleshethiy** be upon thee,
Samson **Shimshon**.
And there were *liers in wait* **lurkers**
abiding **settling** in the chamber.
And he *brake* **tore** them from off his arms like a thread.
13 And Delilah said unto *Samson* **Shimshon**,
Hitherto **Thither** thou hast mocked me,
and *told* **worded** me lies:
tell me wherewith thou mightest be bound.
And he said unto her,
If thou weavest the seven *locks* **braids** of my head
with the web.
14 And she *fastened* **staked** it with the *pin* **stake**,
and said unto him,
The *Philistines* **Peleshethiy** be upon thee,
Samson **Shimshon**.
And he awaked out of his sleep,
and *went away* **pulled**
with the *pin* **stake** of the *beam* **weaver**, and with the web.
15 And she said unto him,
How canst thou say, I love thee,
when thine heart is not with me?
thou hast mocked me these three times,
and hast not told me
wherein thy great *strength* **force** *lieth*.
16 And it *came to pass* **became**,
when she *pressed* **oppressed** him *daily* **all days**
with her words, and urged him,
so that his soul was *vexed unto death* **shortened to die**;
17 That he told her all his heart, and said unto her,
There hath not *come* **ascended** a razor upon mine head;
for I have been a *Nazarite* **Separatist** unto *God* **Elohim**
from my mother's *womb* **belly**:
if I be shaven,
then my *strength will go* **force shall turn aside** from me,
and I shall become *weak* **worn**,
and be like any *other man* **one human**.
18 And when Delilah saw
that he had told her all his heart,
she sent and called for the *lords* **ringleaders**
of the *Philistines* **Peleshethiy**, saying,
Come up **Ascend** this *once* **one time**,
for he hath *shewed* **told** me all his heart.
Then the *lords* **ringleaders** of the *Philistines* **Peleshethiy**
came up **ascended** unto her,
and *brought money* **ascended silver** in their hand.
19 And she made him sleep upon her knees;
and she called for a man,
and she caused him
to shave off the seven *locks* **braids** of his head;
and she began to *afflict* **abase** him,
and his *strength went* **force turned aside** from him.
20 And she said, The *Philistines* **Peleshethiy** be upon thee,
Samson **Shimshon**.
And he awoke out of his sleep, and said,
I *will* **shall** go out as *at other times before* **time by time**,
and shake myself.
And he *wist* **knew** not that *the LORD* **Yah Veh**
was departed **had turned aside** from him.
21 But the *Philistines took* **Peleshethiy possessed** him,
and *put* **bore** out his eyes,
and brought him down to *Gaza* **Azzah**,
and bound him with fetters of *brass* **copper**;
and he did grind in the *prison house* **house of binding**.
22 Howbeit the hair of his head
began to *grow again* **sprout** after he was shaven.

SHIMSHON'S DEATH

23 Then the *lords* **ringleaders** of the *Philistines* **Peleshethiy**
gathered them together
for to *offer* **sacrifice** a great sacrifice
unto Dagon their *god* **elohim**,
and to *rejoice* **cheer**:
for they said, Our *god* **elohim**
hath *delivered Samson* **given Shimshon** our enemy
into our hand.
24 And when the people saw him,
they *praised* **halaled** their *god* **elohim**: for they said,
Our *god* **elohim** hath delivered into our hands our enemy,
and the *destroyer* **parcher** of our *country* **land**,
which *slew many of us* **abounded our pierced**.
25 And it *came to pass* **became**,
when their hearts were *merry* **goodly**, that they said,
Call for *Samson* **Shimshon**,
that he may *make* **entertain** us *sport*.
And they called for *Samson* **Shimshon**
out of the *prison house* **house of binding**;
and he *made* **entertained** them *sport*:
and they *set* **stood** him between the pillars.
26 And *Samson* **Shimshon**
said unto the lad that held him by the hand,
Suffer **Allow** me that I may *feel* **touch** the pillars
whereupon the house *standeth* **be established**,
that I may lean upon them.
27 Now the house was *full* **filled** of men and women;
and all the *lords* **ringleaders** of the *Philistines* **Peleshethiy**
were there;
and there were upon the roof
about three thousand men and women,
that *beheld* **saw**
while *Samson made sport* **Shimshon entertained**.

28 And *Samson* **Shimshon** called unto *the LORD* **Yah Veh**,
and said, O *Lord GOD* **Adonay Yah Veh**,
remember me, I *pray* **beseech** thee,
and strengthen me, I *pray* **beseech** thee,
only this *once* **one time**, O *God* **Elohim**,
that I may *be at once avenged* **avenge the avengement**
of the *Philistines* **Peleshethiy** for my two eyes.
29 And *Samson* **Shimshon**
took hold of **clasped** the two middle pillars
upon which the house *stood* **was established**,
and on which it was *borne up* **propped**,
of the one with his right *hand*,
and of the *other* **one** with his left.
30 And *Samson* **Shimshon** said,
Let *me* **my soul** die with the *Philistines* **Peleshethiy**.
And he *bowed* **extended** himself with *all his* might **force**;
and the house fell upon the *lords* **ringleaders**,
and upon all the people that were therein.
So the dead which he *slew* **deathified** at his death
were *more* **greater** than they
which he *slew* **deathified** in his life.
31 Then his brethren and all the house of his father
came down **descended**,
and *took* **lifted** him, and *brought* **ascended** him *up*,
and *buried* **entombed** him
between *Zorah* **Sorah** and Eshtaol
in the *buryingplace* **tomb** of *Manoah* **Manoach** his father.
And he judged *Israel* **Yisra El** twenty years.

MICHAH YAH'S IDOLS

17 And there was a man of mount *Ephraim* **Ephrayim**,
whose name was *Micah* **Michah Yah**.
2 And he said unto his mother,
The eleven hundred shekels of silver
that were taken from thee, about which thou cursedst,
and *spakest* **said** of also in mine ears, behold,
the silver is with me; I took it.
And his mother said,
Blessed be thou of *the LORD* **Yah Veh**, my son.
3 And when he had restored
the eleven hundred *shekels of* silver to his mother,
his mother said,
In hallowing, I had *wholly dedicated* **hallowed** the silver
unto *the LORD* **Yah Veh** from my hand for my son,
to *make a graven image* **work a sculptile**
and a *molten image* **molting**:
now therefore I *will* **shall** restore it unto thee.
4 Yet he restored the *money* **silver** unto his mother;
and his mother took two hundred *shekels of* silver,
and gave them to the *founder* **refiner**,
who *made* **worked** thereof a *graven image* **sculptile**
and a *molten image* **molting**:
and they were in the house of *Micah* **Michah Yah**.
5 And the man *Micah* **Michah Yah**
had an house of *gods* **elohim**,
and *made* **worked** an ephod, and teraphim,
and *consecrated* **filled the hand of** one of his sons,
who became his priest.
6 In those days
there was no *king* **sovereign** in *Israel* **Yisra El**,
but every man *did* **worked**
that which was *right* **straight** in his own eyes.
7 And there was a *young man* **lad**
out of *Bethlehemjudah* **Beth Lechem Yah Hudah**
of the family of *Judah* **Yah Hudah**,
who was a *Levite* **Leviy**, and he sojourned there.
8 And the man *departed* **went** out of the city
from *Bethlehemjudah* **Beth Lechem Yah Hudah**
to sojourn where he could find *a place*:
and he came to mount *Ephraim* **Ephrayim**
to the house of *Micah* **Michah Yah**,
as he *journeyed* **worked his way**.
9 And *Micah* **Michah Yah** said unto him,
Whence comest thou?
And he said unto him, I am a *Levite* **Leviy**
of *Bethlehemjudah* **Beth Lechem Yah Hudah**,
and I go to sojourn where I may find *a place*.
10 And *Micah* **Michah Yah** said unto him,
Dwell **Settle** with me,
and be unto me a father and a priest,
and I *will* **shall** give thee ten *shekels of* silver
by the year **daily**,
and *a suit* **an appraisal** of *apparel* **clothes**,
and thy *victuals* **invigoration**. So the *Levite* **Leviy** went in.
11 And the *Levite* **Leviy**
was content **willed** to *dwell* **settle** with the man;
and the *young man* **lad** was unto him as one of his sons.
12 And *Micah* **Michah Yah**
consecrated **filled the hand of** the *Levite* **Leviy**;
and the *young man* **lad** became his priest,
and was in the house of *Micah* **Michah Yah**.
13 Then said *Micah* **Michah Yah**, Now know I
that *the LORD will do me good* **Yah Veh is well—pleased**,
seeing I have a *Levite* **Leviy** to my priest.

THE SCION OF THE DANIY SEEK AN INHERITANCE

18 In those days
there was no *king* **sovereign** in *Israel* **Yisra El**:
and in those days the *tribe* **scion** of the *Danites* **Daniy**
sought them an inheritance to *dwell* **settle** in;
for unto that day
all their inheritance had not fallen unto them
among the *tribes* **scions** of *Israel* **Yisra El**.
2 And the *children* **sons** of Dan
sent of their family five men from their *coasts* **ends**,
men **sons** of valour, from *Zorah* **Sorah**, and from Eshtaol,
to spy out the land, and to *search* **probe** it;
and they said unto them, Go, *search* **probe** the land:
who when they came to mount *Ephraim* **Ephrayim**,
to the house of *Micah* **Michah Yah**,
they *lodged* **stayed overnight** there.
3 When they were by the house of *Micah* **Michah Yah**,
they *knew* **recognized** the voice
of the *young man* **lad** the *Levite* **Leviy**:
and they turned in thither, and said unto him,
Who brought thee hither?
and what *makest* **workest** thou in this *place*?
and what hast thou here?
4 And he said unto them,
Thus and thus *dealeth* **worketh**
Micah with **Michah Yah unto** me,
and hath hired me, and I am his priest.
5 And they said unto him,
Ask counsel, we *pray* **beseech** thee, of *God* **Elohim**,
that we may know whether our way which we go
shall *be prosperous* **prosper**.
6 And the priest said unto them, Go in *peace* **shalom**:
before *the LORD is* **Yah Veh be** your way wherein ye go.

THE SCION OF THE DANIY COME TO LAISH

7 Then the five men *departed* **went**, and came to Laish,
and saw the people that were *therein* **within**,
how they *dwelt careless* **settled confidently**,
after the *manner* **judgment** of the *Zidonians* **Sidoniy**,
quiet **rested** and *secure* **confident**;
and there was no *magistrate* **restrainer** in the land,
that might *put them to* shame **them** in *any thing* **word**;
and they were far from the *Zidonians* **Sidoniy**,
and had no *business* **word** with *any man* **human**.
8 And they came unto their brethren
to *Zorah* **Sorah** and Eshtaol:
and their brethren said unto them, What say ye?
9 And they said,
Arise, that we may *go up* **ascend** against them:
for we have seen the land, and, behold,
it is *very* **mighty** good:
and *are ye still* **hush ye**?
be not slothful to go, *and* to enter to possess the land.
10 When ye go,
ye shall come unto a people *secure* **confident**,
and to a *large* land **broad of hands**:
for *God* **Elohim** hath given it into your hands;
a place where there is no *want* **lack** of any *thing* **word**
that is in the earth.
11 And there *went* **pulled** from thence
of the family of the *Danites* **Daniy**,
out of *Zorah* **Sorah** and out of Eshtaol,
six hundred men
appointed **girded** with *weapons* **instruments** of war.
12 And they *went up* **ascended**,
and *pitched* **encamped** in *Kirjathjearim* **Qiryath Arim**,
in *Judah* **Yah Hudah**:
wherefore they called that place

Mahanehdan **Machaneh Dan** unto this day: behold,
it is behind *Kirjathjearim* **Qiryath Arim**.
13 And they passed thence
unto mount *Ephraim* **Ephrayim**,
and came unto the house of *Micah* **Michah Yah**.
14 Then answered the five men
that went to spy out the *country* **land** of Laish,
and said unto their brethren,
Do ye know that there is in these houses an ephod,
and teraphim, and a *graven image* **sculptile**,
and a molten *image*?
now therefore *consider* **perceive** what ye have to *do* **work**.
15 And they turned *thitherward* **aside**,
and came to the house
of the *young man* **lad** the *Levite* **Leviy**,
even unto the house of *Micah* **Michah Yah**,
and *saluted him* **asked of him shalom**.
16 And the six hundred men
appointed **girded** with their *weapons* **instruments** of war,
which were of the *children* **sons** of Dan,
stood **stationed themselves**
by the *entering* **opening** of the *gate* **portal**.
17 And the five men that went to spy out the land
went up **ascended**, and came in thither,
and took the *graven image* **sculptile**, and the ephod,
and the teraphim, and the molten *image*:
and the priest *stood* **stationed himself**
in the *entering* **opening** of the *gate* **portal**
with the six hundred men that *were appointed* **girded**
with *weapons* **instruments** of war.
18 And these went
into *Micah's house* **the house of Michah Yah**,
and *fetched* **took** the *carved image* **sculptile**, the ephod,
and the teraphim, and the molten *image*.
Then said the priest unto them, What *do* **work** ye?
19 And they said unto him, *Hold thy peace* **Hush**,
lay **set** thine hand upon thy mouth, and go with us,
and be to us a father and a priest:
is it better for thee to be a priest
unto the house of one man,
or that thou be a priest
unto a *tribe* **scion** and a family in *Israel* **Yisra El**?
20 And the priest's heart was *glad* **well—pleased**,
and he took the ephod, and the teraphim,
and the *graven image* **sculptile**,
and went in the midst of the people.
21 So they turned **face** and *departed* **went**,
and *put* **set** the *little ones* **toddlers** and the *cattle* **chattel**
and the *carriage before* **honourable at the face of** them.
22 And when they were *a good way* **far removed**
from the house of *Micah* **Michah Yah**,
the men that were in the houses
near *to Micah's house* **the house of Michah Yah**
were gathered together **cried out**,
and *overtook* **adhered to** the *children* **sons** of Dan.
23 And they cried **out** unto the *children* **sons** of Dan.
And they turned their faces,
and said unto *Micah* **Michah Yah**, What aileth thee,
that thou *comest with such a company* **criest out**?
24 And he said,
ye have taken away my *gods* **elohim**
which I *made* **worked**,
and the priest, and ye *are gone away* **have gone**:
and what have I more?
and what is this that ye say unto me, What aileth thee?
25 And the *children* **sons** of Dan said unto him,
Let not thy voice be heard among us,
lest *angry fellows* **men bitter of soul**
run upon **encounter** thee,
and *thou lose thy life* **thy soul be gathered**,
with the *lives* **souls** of thy household.
26 And the *children* **sons** of Dan went their way:
and when *Micah* **Michah Yah** saw
that they were too strong for him,
he turned **face** and *went* **turned** back unto his house.
27 And they took *the things* **those**
which *Micah* **Michah Yah** had *made* **worked**,
and the priest which he had, and came unto Laish,
unto a people
that *were at quiet and secure* **rested confidently**:
and they smote them with the *edge* **mouth** of the sword,
and burnt the city with fire.
28 And there was no *deliverer* **rescuer**,
because it was far from *Zidon* **Sidon**,
and they had no *business* **word** with *any man* **human**;
and it was in the valley *that lieth*
by *Bethrehob* **Beth Rechob**.
And they built a city, and *dwelt* **settled** therein.
29 And they called the name of the city Dan,
after the name of Dan their father,
who was born unto *Israel* **Yisra El**:
howbeit **but** the name of the city was Laish at the first.
30 And the *children* **sons** of Dan
set up **raised** the *graven image* **sculptile**:
and *Jonathan* **Yah Nathan**,
the son of Gershom, the son of *Manasseh* **Menash Sheh**,
he and his sons were priests to the *tribe* **scion** of Dan
until the day of the *captivity* **exile** of the land.
31 And they set them up
Micah's graven image **Michah's sculptile**,
which he *made* **worked**,
all the *time* **days**
that the house of *God* **Elohim** was in Shiloh.

A LEVIY'S WHORING CONCUBINE

19 And it *came to pass* **became**, in those days,
when there was no *king* **sovereign** in *Israel* **Yisra El**,
that there was a *certain Levite*, **man — a Leviy**
sojourning on the *side* **flank** of mount *Ephraim* **Ephrayim**,
who took to him **a woman** — a concubine
out of *Bethlehemjudah* **Beth Lechem Yah Hudah**.
2 And his concubine played the whore against him,
and went away from him unto her father's house
to *Bethlehemjudah* **Beth Lechem Yah Hudah**,
and was there four *whole* months **of days**.
3 And her *husband* **man** arose, and went after her,
to *speak friendly* **word** unto her **heart**,
and to *bring* **return** her *again*,
having his *servant* **lad** with him,
and a *couple* **pair** of *asses* **he burros**:
and she brought him into her father's house:
and when the father of the *damsel* **lass** saw him,
he *rejoiced* **cheered** to meet him.
4 And his father in law, the *damsel's* **lass'** father,
retained **held** him;
and he *abode* **settled** with him three days:
so they did eat and drink,
and *lodged* **stayed overnight** there.
5 And it *came to pass* **became**, on the fourth day,
when they *arose* **started** early in the morning,
that he rose up to *depart* **go**:
and the *damsel's* **lass'** father said unto his son in law,
Comfort **Support** thine heart with a morsel of bread,
and afterward go your way.
6 And they *sat down* **settled**,
and did eat and drink both of them together:
for the *damsel's* **lass'** father had said unto the man,
Be content, I *pray* **beseech** thee,
and tarry all night **that thou willest to stay overnight**,
and let thine heart be *merry* **well—pleased**.
7 And when the man rose up to *depart* **go**,
his father in law urged him:
therefore
he *lodged there again* **returned and stayed overnight**.
8 And he *arose* **started** early in the morning
on the fifth day to *depart* **go**;
and the *damsel's* **lass'** father said,
Comfort **Support** thine heart, I *pray* **beseech** thee.
And they *tarried* **lingered** until *afternoon* **the day declined**,
and they did eat both of them.
9 And when the man rose up to *depart* **go**,
he, and his concubine, and his servant,
his father in law, the *damsel's* **lass'** father, said unto him,
Behold, now the day *draweth* **slacketh** toward evening,
I *pray* **beseech** you *tarry all night* **stay overnight**:
behold, the day *groweth to an end* **encampeth**,
lodge **stay overnight** here,
that thine heart may be *merry* **well—pleased**;
and to morrow *get you* **start** early on your way,
that thou mayest go *home* **to thy tent**.
10 But the man *would* **willed to** not

tarry that night **stay overnight**,
but he rose up and *departed* **went**,
and came over against *Jebus* **Yebus**,
which is *Jerusalem* **Yeru Shalem**;
and there were with him
two asses saddled **a pair of he burros harnessed**,
his concubine also was with him.
11 And when they were by *Jebus* **Yebus**,
the day was *far spent* **mightily subdued**;
and the *servant* **lad** said unto his *master* **adoni**,
Come, I *pray* **beseech** thee,
and let us turn in into this city of the *Jebusites* **Yebusiy**,
and *lodge* **stay overnight** in it.
12 And his *master* **adoni** said unto him,
We *will* **shall** not turn aside hither
into the city of a stranger,
that is not of the *children* **sons** of *Israel* **Yisra El**;
we *will* **shall** pass over to *Gibeah* **Gibah**.
13 And he said unto his *servant* **lad**, Come,
and let us *draw near* **approach** to one of these places
to *lodge all night* **stay overnight**,
in *Gibeah* **Gibah**, or in Ramah.
14 And they passed on and went their way;
and the sun went down upon them
when they were by Gibeah **beside Gibah**,
which *belongeth* **be** to *Benjamin* **Ben Yamin**.
15 And they turned aside thither,
to go in and to *lodge* **stay overnight** in *Gibeah* **Gibah**:
and when he went in,
he *sat him down* **seated** in a *street* **broadway** of the city:
for there was no man
that *took* **gathered** them into his house
to *lodging* **stay overnight**.
16 And, behold,
there came an old man from his work
out of the field at even,
which was *also* **a man** of mount *Ephraim* **Ephrayim**;
and he sojourned in *Gibeah* **Gibah**:
but the men of the place were *Benjamites* **Ben Yaminiy**.
17 And when he had lifted up his eyes,
he saw a *wayfaring* **caravan,**
a man in the *street* **broadway** of the city:
and the old man said,
Whither goest thou? and whence comest thou?
18 And he said unto him,
We are passing
from *Bethlehemjudah* **Beth Lechem Yah Hudah**
toward the *side* **flank** of mount *Ephraim* **Ephrayim**;
from thence am I:
and I went to *Bethlehemjudah* **Beth Lechem Yah Hudah**,
but I am *now* going to the house of *the LORD* **Yah Veh**;
and there is no man that *receiveth* **gathereth** me to house.
19 Yet there is both straw and provender
for our *asses* **he burros**;
and there is bread and wine also for me,
and for thy *handmaid* **maid**,
and for the young man which is with thy *servants* **lads**:
there is no *want* **lack** of any *thing* **word**.
20 And the old man said, *Peace* **Shalom** be with thee;
howsoever let **only** all thy *wants lie* **lacks be** upon me;
only *lodge* **stay overnight** not in the *street* **broadway**.
21 So he brought him into his house,
and *gave provender unto* **foddered**
the *asses* **he burros**:
and they *washed* **baptised** their feet,
and did eat and drink.

THE SONS OF BELI YAAL EXPLOIT THE CONCUBINE

22 Now as they were
making **well—preparing** their hearts *merry*,
behold, the men of the city,
certain **men,** sons of *Belial* **Beli Yaal**,
beset the house round about, and beat at the door,
and *spake* **said** to the *master* **man** of the house,
the old man, saying,
Bring forth the man that came into thine house,
that we may know him.
23 And the man, the master of the house,
went out unto them, and said unto them,
Nay **No**, my brethren, *nay*,
I *pray* **beseech** you, *do* **vilify** not *so wickedly*;
seeing **after** that this man is come into mine house,
do **work** not this folly.
24 Behold, *here is* my daughter a *maiden* **virgin**,
and his concubine;
them I *will* **shall** bring out now,
and *humble* ye **abase** them,
and *do* **work** with them
what seemeth good *unto you* **in your eyes**:
but unto this man *do* **work** not
so vile a thing **this word of folly**.
25 But the men *would* **willed to** not hearken to him:
so the man *took* **held** his concubine,
and brought her *forth* **out** unto them;
and they knew her,
and *abused* **exploited** her all the night until the morning:
and when the *day began to spring* **dawn ascended**,
they *let* **sent** her *go* **away**.
26 Then came the woman
in the dawning **at the turning of the face**
of the *day* **morning**,
and fell down at the *door* **portal** of the man's house
where her *lord* **adoni** was, till it was light.
27 And her *lord* **adoni** rose up in the morning,
and opened the doors of the house,
and went out to go his way: and, behold,
the woman his concubine
was fallen down at the *door* **portal** of the house,
and her hands were upon the threshold.
28 And he said unto her, *Up* **Arise**, and let us be going.
But none answered.
Then the man took her up upon *an ass* **a he burro**,
and the man rose up, and *gat* **went** him unto his place.
29 And when he was come into his house,
he took a knife,
and laid hold on his concubine,
and *divided* **dismembered** her, *together* with her bones,
into twelve *pieces* **members**,
and sent her into all the *coasts* **borders** of *Israel* **Yisra El**.
30 And it *was so* **became**, that all that saw it said,
There was no such deed done **Thus hath not been** nor seen
from the day that the *children* **sons** of *Israel* **Yisra El**
came up **ascended** out of the land of *Egypt* **Misrayim**
unto this day:
consider of **set to yourselves upon it**,
take advice **consult**, and *speak your minds* **word**.

THE SONS OF YISRA EL ATTACK THE SONS OF BEN YAMIN

20 Then all the *children* **sons** of *Israel* **Yisra El** went out,
and the *congregation* **witnesses**
was gathered **congregated** *together* as one man,
from Dan even to *Beersheba* **Beer Sheba**,
with the land of *Gilead* **Gilad**,
unto *the LORD* **Yah Veh** in *Mizpeh* **Mispeh**.
2 And the chief of all the people,
even of all the *tribes* **scions** of *Israel* **Yisra El**,
presented **set** *themselves* in the *assembly* **congregation**
of the people of *God* **Elohim**,
four hundred thousand footmen that drew sword.
3 (Now the *children* **sons** of *Benjamin* **Ben Yamin**
heard that the *children* **sons** of *Israel* **Yisra El**
were gone up **ascended** to *Mizpeh* **Mispeh**.)
Then said the *children* **sons** of *Israel* **Yisra El**,
Tell **Word** *us*, how was this *wickedness* **evil**?
4 And the *Levite* **Leviy**,
the *husband* **man** of the woman that was *slain* **murdered**,
answered and said,
I came into *Gibeah* **Gibah**
that belongeth to *Benjamin* **Ben Yamin**,
I and my concubine, to *lodge* **stay overnight**.
5 And the *men* **masters** of *Gibeah* **Gibah** rose against me,
and *beset* **surrounded** the house *round about*
upon me by night,
and *thought to have slain* **considered slaughtering** me:
and my concubine have they *forced* **abased**,
that she *is dead* **died**.
6 And I *took* **possessed** my concubine,
and *cut her in pieces* **dismembered her**,
and sent her throughout all the *country* **fields**
of the inheritance of *Israel* **Yisra El**:
for they have *committed lewdness* **worked intrigue**

and folly in *Israel* **Yisra El.**
7 Behold, ye are all *children* **sons** of *Israel* **Yisra El;**
give here your *advice* **word** and counsel.
8 And all the people arose as one man, saying,
We will not any **No man shall** go to his tent,
neither *will* **shall** *we* any **man** *of us*
turn **aside** into his house.
9 But now this shall be the *thing* **word**
which we *will do* **shall work** to *Gibeah* **Gibah;**
we will go up by lot — **by pebble** against it;
10 And we *will* **shall** take ten men of an hundred
throughout all the *tribes* **scions** of *Israel* **Yisra El,**
and an hundred of a thousand,
and a thousand out of *ten thousand* **a myriad,**
to *fetch victual* **take hunt** for the people,
that they may *do* **work,**
when they come to *Gibeah* **Gibah** of *Benjamin* **Ben Yamin,**
according to all the folly
that they have *wrought* **worked** in *Israel* **Yisra El.**
11 So all the men of *Israel* **Yisra El**
were gathered against the city,
knit together **companions** as one man.
12 And the *tribes* **scions** of *Israel* **Yisra El** sent men
through all the *tribe* **scion** of *Benjamin* **Ben Yamin,** saying,
What *wickedness* **evil** is this that is *done* among you?
13 Now therefore *deliver us* **give** the men,
the *children* **sons** of *Belial* **Beli Yaal,**
which are in *Gibeah* **Gibah,**
that we may *put* **deathify** them *to death,*
and *put* **burn** away evil from *Israel* **Yisra El.**
But the *children* **sons** of *Benjamin* **Ben Yamin**
would **willed to** not hearken to the voice of their brethren
the *children* **sons** of *Israel* **Yisra El.**
14 But the *children* **sons** of *Benjamin* **Ben Yamin**
gathered themselves *together* out of the cities
unto *Gibeah* **Gibah,**
to go out to *battle* **war** against
the *children* **sons** of *Israel* **Yisra El.**
15 And the *children* **sons** of *Benjamin* **Ben Yamin**
were *numbered at that time* **mustered daily**
out of the cities
twenty and six thousand men that drew sword,
beside the *inhabitants* **settlers** of *Gibeah* **Gibah,**
which were *numbered* **mustered**
seven hundred chosen men.
16 Among all this people
there were seven hundred chosen men
lefthanded **bound of their right hand;**
every one could sling stones at an hair *breadth,*
and not *miss* **sin.**
17 And the men of *Israel* **Yisra El,**
beside *Benjamin* **Ben Yamin,**
were *numbered* **mustered** four hundred thousand men
that drew sword: all these were men of war.
18 And the *children* **sons** of *Israel* **Yisra El** arose,
and *went up* **ascended** to the house of *God* **Elohim,**
and asked counsel of *God* **Elohim,** and said,
Which **Whoever** of us shall go *up first* **at the beginning**
to *the battle* **war**
against the *children* **sons** of *Benjamin* **Ben Yamin?**
And *the LORD* **Yah Veh** said,
Judah shall go up first **Yah Hudah, at the beginning.**
19 And the *children* **sons** of *Israel* **Yisra El**
rose up in the morning,
and encamped against *Gibeah* **Gibah.**
20 And the men of *Israel* **Yisra El**
went out to *battle* **war** against *Benjamin* **Ben Yamin;**
and the men of *Israel* **Yisra El**
put themselves in array **lined up**
to *fight* **war** against them at *Gibeah* **Gibah.**
21 And the *children* **sons** of *Benjamin* **Ben Yamin**
came forth **went** out of *Gibeah* **Gibah,**
and *destroyed* **ruined** down to the *ground* **earth**
of the *Israelites* **Yisra Eliy** that day
twenty and two thousand men.
22 And the people the men of *Israel* **Yisra El**
encouraged **strengthened** themselves,
and *set their battle in array* **lined up to war** again
in the place
where they *put themselves in array* **lined up** the first day.
23 (And the *children* **sons** of *Israel* **Yisra El**
went up **ascended**
and wept *before the LORD* **at the face of Yah Veh**
until even,
and asked counsel of *the LORD* **Yah Veh,** saying,
Shall I *go up* **approach** again to *battle* **war**
against the *children* **sons** of *Benjamin* **Ben Yamin**
my brother?
And *the LORD* **Yah Veh** said, *Go up* **Ascend** against him.)
24 And the *children* **sons** of *Israel* **Yisra El**
came near **approached**
against the *children* **sons** of *Benjamin* **Ben Yamin**
the second day.
25 And *Benjamin* **Ben Yamin** went forth
against **meeting** them out of *Gibeah* **Gibah**
the second day,
and *destroyed* **ruined** down to the *ground* **earth**
of the *children* **sons** of *Israel* **Yisra El** again
eighteen thousand men; all these drew the sword.
26 Then all the *children* **sons** of *Israel* **Yisra El,**
and all the people, *went up* **ascended,**
and came unto the house of *God* **Elohim,** and wept,
and *sat* **settled** there
before the LORD **at the face of Yah Veh,**
and fasted that day until even,
and *offered burnt offerings* **holocausted holocausts**
and *peace offerings* **shelamim**
before the LORD **at the face of Yah Veh.**
27 And the *children* **sons** of *Israel* **Yisra El**
enquired **asked** of *the LORD* **Yah Veh,**
(for the ark of the covenant of *God* **Elohim**
was there in those days,
28 And *Phinehas* **Pinechas,**
the son of *Eleazar* **El Azar,** the son of *Aaron* **Aharon,**
stood *before* **at the face of** it in those days,) saying,
Shall I yet again go out to *battle* **war**
against the *children* **sons** of *Benjamin* **Ben Yamin**
my brother,
or shall I cease?
And *the LORD* **Yah Veh** said, *Go up* **Ascend;**
for to morrow
I *will deliver* **shall give** them into thine hand.
29 And *Israel* **Yisra El** set *liers in wait* **lurkers**
round about *Gibeah* **Gibah.**
30 And the *children* **sons** of *Israel* **Yisra El**
went up **ascended**
against the *children* **sons** of *Benjamin* **Ben Yamin**
on the third day,
and *put themselves in array* **lined up**
against *Gibeah* **Gibah,** as *at other times* **time by time.**
31 And the *children* **sons** of *Benjamin* **Ben Yamin**
went out *against* **to meet** the people,
and were *drawn* **torn** away from the city;
and they began to smite of the people, and *kill* **pierce,**
as *at other times* **time by time,** in the highways,
of which one *goeth up* **ascendeth**
to the house of *God* **Elohim,**
and *the other* **one** to *Gibeah* **Gibah** in the field,
about thirty men of *Israel* **Yisra El.**
32 And the *children* **sons** of *Benjamin* **Ben Yamin** said,
They are smitten down *before us* **at our face,** as at the first.
But the *children* **sons** of *Israel* **Yisra El** said, Let us flee,
and *draw* **tear** them **away** from the city
unto the highways.
33 And all the men of *Israel* **Yisra El**
rose up out of their place,
and *put themselves in array* **lined up**
at *Baaltamar* **Baal Tamar:**
and the *liers in wait* **lurkers** of *Israel* **Yisra El**
came forth out of their places,
even out of the *meadows* **barrens** of *Gibeah* **Gibah.**
34 And there came against *Gibeah* **Gibah**
ten thousand chosen men out of all *Israel* **Yisra El,**
and the *battle* **war** was *sore* **heavy:**
but they knew not that evil *was near* **touched** them.
35 And *the LORD* **Yah Veh** smote *Benjamin* **Ben Yamin**
before Israel **at the face of Yisra El:**
and the *children* **sons** of *Israel* **Yisra El**
destroyed **ruined** of the *Benjamites* **Ben Yaminiy** that day
twenty and five thousand and an hundred men:

all these drew the sword.
36 So the *children* **sons** of *Benjamin* **Ben Yamin**
saw that they were smitten:
for the men of *Israel* **Yisra El**
gave place to the *Benjamites* **Ben Yaminiy**,
because they *trusted* **confided**
unto the *liers in wait* **lurkers**
which they had set beside *Gibeah* **Gibah**.
37 And the *liers in wait* **lurkers** hasted,
and *rushed* **spread** upon *Gibeah* **Gibah**;
and the *liers in wait* **lurkers** drew *themselves* along,
and smote all the city with the *edge* **mouth** of the sword.
38 Now there was *an appointed sign* **a season**
between the men of *Israel* **Yisra El**
and the *liers in wait* **lurkers**,
that they should make
a great flame **an abounding heaviness**
with smoke *rise up* **ascending** out of the city.
39 And when the men of *Israel* **Yisra El**
retired **returned** in the *battle* **war**,
Benjamin **Ben Yamin** began to smite and *kill* **pierce**
of the men of *Israel* **Yisra El** about thirty persons:
for they said,
Surely **In being smitten,** they are smitten down
before us **at our face**, as in the first *battle* **war**.
40 But when the *flame* **signal** began to *arise up* **ascend**
out of the city with a pillar of smoke,
the *Benjamites looked* **Ben Yaminiy turned face**
behind them, and, behold,
the *flame of the* city **totally** ascended *up*
to *heaven* **the heavens**.
41 And when the men of *Israel* **Yisra El** turned again,
the men of *Benjamin were amazed* **Ben Yamin hastened**:
for they saw that evil *was come* **touched** upon them.
42 Therefore they turned *their backs*
before **at the face of** the men of *Israel* **Yisra El**
unto the way of the wilderness;
but the *battle* **war** overtook them;
and them which came out of the cities
they *destroyed* **ruined** in the midst of them.
43 Thus they *inclosed* **surrounded**
the *Benjamites* **Ben Yaminiy** *round about,*
and *chased* **pursued** them,
and trode them down with ease
over against *Gibeah* **Gibah**
toward **from** the *sunrising* **rising sun**.
44 And there fell of *Benjamin* **Ben Yamin**
eighteen thousand men;
all these were men of valour.
45 And they turned **face** and fled toward the wilderness
unto the rock of Rimmon:
and they gleaned of them in the highways
five thousand men;
and *pursued hard* **adhered** after them unto Gidom,
and *slew* **smote** two thousand men of them.
46 So that all which fell that day of *Benjamin* **Ben Yamin**
were twenty and five thousand men that drew the sword;
all these were men of valour.
47 But six hundred men turned **face**
and fled to the wilderness unto the rock Rimmon,
and *abode* **settled** in the rock Rimmon four months.
48 And the men of *Israel turned again* **Yisra El returned**
upon the *children* **sons** of *Benjamin* **Ben Yamin**,
and smote them with the *edge* **mouth** of the sword,
as well the *men* **integrious** of *every* city,
as the beast **even animals**,
and all that *came to hand* **were found**:
also they set on fire all the cities that they *came to* **found**.

THE OVERSIGHTED SCION OF YISRA EL

21 Now the men of *Israel* **Yisra El**
had *sworn* **oathed** in *Mizpeh* **Mispeh**, saying,
There shall not *any* **a man** of us give his daughter
unto *Benjamin* **Ben Yamin** to *wife* **woman**.
2 And the people came to the house of *God* **Elohim**,
and *abode* **settled** there till even
before God **at the face of Elohim**,
and lifted up their voices, and wept *sore* **a great weeping**;
3 And said,
O *LORD God* **Yah Veh Elohim** of *Israel* **Yisra El**,
why is this *come to pass* **become** in *Israel* **Yisra El**,
that there should be to day one *tribe* **scion**
lacking **oversighted** in *Israel* **Yisra El**?
4 And it *came to pass* **became,** on the morrow,
that the people *rose* **started** early,
and built there *an* **a sacrifice** altar,
and *offered burnt offerings* **holocausted holocausts**
and *peace offerings* **shelamim**.
5 And the *children* **sons** of *Israel* **Yisra El** said,
Who is there among all the *tribes* **scions** of *Israel* **Yisra El**
that *came* **ascended** not *up* with the congregation
unto *the LORD* **Yah Veh**?
For they had made a great oath concerning him
that *came* **ascended** not *up*
to *the LORD* **Yah Veh** to *Mizpeh* **Mispeh**, saying,
In deathifying, He shall *surely* be *put to death* **deathified**.
6 And the *children* **sons** of *Israel* **Yisra El**
repented them **sighed**
for *Benjamin* **Ben Yamin** their brother, and said,
There is one *tribe* **scion** cut off from *Israel* **Yisra El** this day.
7 How shall we *do* **work** for *wives* **women**
for them that remain,
seeing we have *sworn* **oathed** by *the LORD* **Yah Veh**
that we *will* **shall** not give them of our daughters
to *wives* **women**?
8 And they said,
What one is there of the *tribes* **scions** of *Israel* **Yisra El**
that *came* **ascended** not *up* to *Mizpeh* **Mispeh**
to *the LORD* **Yah Veh**?
And, behold, there came *none* **no man** to the camp
from *Jabeshgilead* **Yabesh Gilad**
to the *assembly* **congregation**.
9 For the people were *numbered* **mustered,**
and, behold, there were *none* **no man**
of the *inhabitants* **settlers** of *Jabeshgilead* **Yabesh Gilad**
there.
10 And the *congregation* **witnesses** sent thither
twelve thousand men of the *valiantest* **sons of valour**,
and *commanded* **misvahed** them, saying,
Go and smite
the *inhabitants* **settlers** of *Jabeshgilead* **Yabesh Gilad**
with the *edge* **mouth** of the sword,
with the women and the *children* **toddlers**.
11 And this is the *thing* **word** that ye shall *do* **work**,
ye shall *utterly destroy* **devote** every male,
and every woman
that hath *lain by man* **known bedding with male**.
12 And they found among
the *inhabitants* **settlers** of *Jabeshgilead* **Yabesh Gilad**
four hundred *young* **lass** virgins,
that had known no man by *lying* **bedding** with any male:
and they brought them unto the camp to Shiloh,
which is in the land of *Canaan* **Kenaan**.
13 And the whole *congregation* **witness**
sent *some* to *speak* **word**
to the *children* **sons** of *Benjamin* **Ben Yamin**
that were in the rock Rimmon,
and to call *peaceably* **shalom** unto them.
14 And *Benjamin* **Ben Yamin**
came again **returned** at that time;
and they gave them *wives* **women**
which they had saved alive
of the women of *Jabeshgilead* **Yabesh Gilad**:
and yet so they *sufficed them not* **found not so for them.**
15 And the people
repented them **sighed** for *Benjamin* **Ben Yamin**,
because that *the LORD* **Yah Veh**
had *made* **worked** a breach
in the *tribes* **scions** of *Israel* **Yisra El**.
16 Then the elders of the *congregation* **witness** said,
How shall we *do* **work**
for *wives* **women** for them that remain,
seeing the women are *destroyed* **desolated**
out of *Benjamin* **Ben Yamin**?
17 And they said,
There must be an inheritance **A possession** for them
that be escaped **of the escapees** of *Benjamin* **Ben Yamin**,
that *a tribe* **no scion**
be *not destroyed* **wiped** out of *Israel* **Yisra El**.
18 Howbeit
we *may* **can** not give them *wives* **women** of our daughters:

for the *children* **sons** of *Israel* **Yisra El** have *sworn* **oathed**,
saying, Cursed be he
that giveth a *wife* **woman** to *Benjamin* **Ben Yamin**.
19 Then they said, Behold,
there is a *feast* **celebration** of *the LORD* **Yah Veh**
in Shiloh *yearly* **from days by days**
in a place which is on the north *side* of Beth El,
on the east side **toward the sun rising** of the highway
that *goeth up* **ascendeth**
from *Bethel* **Beth El** to Shechem,
and on the south of Lebonah.
20 Therefore they *commanded* **misvahed**
the *children* **sons** of *Benjamin* **Ben Yamin**, saying,
Go and *lie in wait* **lurk** in the vineyards;
21 And see, and, behold, if the daughters of Shiloh
come out to dance **go and whirl** in **round** dances,
then *come* **go** ye *out of* **from** the vineyards,
and catch you every man his *wife* **woman**
of the daughters of Shiloh,
and go to the land of *Benjamin* **Ben Yamin**.
22 And it shall be, when their fathers or their brethren
come unto us to *complain* **contend**,
that we *will* **shall** say unto them,
Be favourable **Grant charism** unto them for our sakes:
because we *reserved* **took** not
to each man his *wife* **woman** in the war:
for ye did not give unto them at this time,
that ye should be guilty.
23 And the *children* **sons** of *Benjamin* **Ben Yamin**
did **worked** so,
and *took* **lifted** them *wives* **women**,
according to their number,
of them that *danced* **whirled**, whom they *caught* **stripped**:
and they went and returned unto their inheritance,
and *repaired* **strengthened** the cities,
and *dwelt* **settled** in them.
24 And the *children* **sons** of *Israel* **Yisra El**
departed **walked** thence at that time,
every man to his *tribe* **scion** and to his family,
and they went out from thence
every man to his inheritance.
25 In those days
there was no *king* **sovereign** in *Israel* **Yisra El**:
every man *did* **worked**
that which was *right* **straight** in his own eyes.

KEY TO INTERPRETING THE EXEGESES:
King James text is in regular type;
Text under exegeses is in oblique type;
Text of exegeses is in bold type.

EL QANAH'S WOMEN

1 Now there was *a certain* **one** man
of *Ramathaimzophim* **Ramahayim Sophim**,
of mount *Ephraim* **Ephrayim**,
and his name was *Elkanah* **El Qanah**,
the son of *Jeroham* **Yerocham**,
the son of *Elihu* **Eli Hu**, the son of *Tohu* **Tochu**,
the son of *Zuph* **Suph**, an *Ephrathite* **Ephrathiy**:
2 And he had two *wives* **women**;
the name of the one was Hannah,
and the name of the *other* **second** Peninnah:
and Peninnah had children, but Hannah had no children.
3 And this man
went up **ascended** out of his city *yearly* **days by days**
to *worship* **prostrate** and to sacrifice
unto *the LORD of hosts* **Yah Veh Sabaoth** in Shiloh.
And the two sons of Eli, Hophni and *Phinehas* **Pinechas**,
the priests of *the LORD* **Yah Veh**, were there.
4 And when the *time was* **day became**
that *Elkanah offered* **El Qanah sacrificed**,
he gave to Peninnah his *wife* **woman**,
and to all her sons and her daughters, portions:
5 But unto Hannah
he gave *a worthy* **one double faced** portion;
for he loved Hannah:
but *the LORD* **Yah Veh** had shut up her womb.
6 And her *adversary* **tribulator**
also *provoked* **vexed** her *sore* **to vexation**,
for to *make* **irritate** her *fret*,
because *the LORD* **Yah Veh**
had shut *up* **through** her womb.
7 And *as he did so* **so he worked** year by year,
when she *went up* **ascended often enough**
to the house of *the LORD* **Yah Veh**,
so she *provoked* **vexed** her;
therefore she wept, and did not eat.
8 Then said *Elkanah* **El Qanah** her *husband* **man** to her,
Hannah, why weepest thou? and why eatest thou not?
and why is thy heart *grieved* **evil**?
am not I better to thee than ten sons?
9 So Hannah rose up after they had eaten in Shiloh,
and after they had drunk.
Now Eli the priest *sat* **settled** upon a *seat* **throne**
by a post of the *temple* **manse** of *the LORD* **Yah Veh**.
10 And she was *in bitterness* **bitter** of soul,
and prayed unto *the LORD* **Yah Veh**,
and **in weeping,** wept *sore*.
11 And she vowed a vow, and said,
O *LORD of hosts* **Yah Veh Sabaoth**,
if **in seeing,** thou *wilt indeed look* **seest**
on the *affliction* **humiliation** of *thine handmaid* **thy maid**,
and remember me,
and not forget *thine handmaid* **thy maid**,
but *wilt* **shalt** give unto *thine handmaid* **thy maid**
a man *child* **seed**,
then I *will* **shall** give him unto *the LORD* **Yah Veh**
all the days of his life,
and there shall no razor *come* **ascend** upon his head.
12 And it *came to pass* **became**,
as she *continued praying* **abounded to pray**
before the LORD **at the face of Yah Veh**,
that Eli *marked* **guarded** her mouth.

HANNAH'S VEXATION

13 Now Hannah, she *spake* **worded** in her heart;
only her lips *moved* **wavered**,
but her voice was not heard:
therefore Eli *thought* **fabricated**
she had been *drunken* **intoxicated**.
14 And Eli said unto her,
How long *wilt* **shalt** thou be *drunken* **intoxicated**?
put away **turn aside** thy wine from thee.
15 And Hannah answered and said, No, my *lord* **adoni**,
I am a woman of a *sorrowful* **hard** spirit:
I have drunk neither wine nor *strong drink* **intoxicants**,
but have poured out my soul
before the LORD **at the face of Yah Veh**.

16 *Count* **Give** not *thine handmaid* **thy maid**
for **as at the face of** a daughter of *Belial* **Beli Yaal**:
for out of the abundance of my *complaint* **meditation**
and *grief* **vexation** have I *spoken* **worded** hitherto.
17 Then Eli answered and said, Go in *peace* **shalom**:
and the *God* **Elohim** of *Israel* **Yisra El**
grant **give** thee thy petition that thou hast asked of him.
18 And she said, Let *thine handmaid* **thy maid**
find *grace* **charism** in thy *sight* **eyes**.
So the woman went her way, and did eat,
and her *countenance* **face** was no more *sad*.

SHEMU EL'S BIRTH

19 And they rose up in the morning early,
and *worshipped* **prostrated**
before the LORD **at the face of Yah Veh**,
and returned, and came to their house to Ramah:
and *Elkanah* **El Qanah** knew Hannah his *wife* **woman**;
and *the LORD* **Yah Veh** remembered her.
20 Wherefore it *came to pass* **became**,
when the time was come about **in revolution of days**
after Hannah had conceived, that she bare a son,
and called his name *Samuel* **Shemu El**, *saying*,
Because I have asked him of *the LORD* **Yah Veh**.
21 And the man *Elkanah* **El Qanah**, and all his house,
went up **ascended**
to *offer* **sacrifice** unto *the LORD* **Yah Veh**
the *yearly sacrifice* **sacrifice of days**, and his vow.
22 But Hannah *went* **ascended** not *up*;
for she said unto her *husband* **man**,
I will not go up until the child **When the lad** be weaned,
and then I *will* **shall** bring him,
that he may *appear* **be seen**
before the LORD **at the face of Yah Veh**,
and there *abide for ever* **settle eternally**.
23 And *Elkanah* **El Qanah** her *husband* **man** said unto her,
Do **Work** what seemeth *thee* good **in thine eyes**;
tarry **settle** until thou have weaned him;
only *the LORD establish* **Yah Veh raise** his word.
So the woman *abode* **settled**,
and *gave* **suckled** her son *suck* until she weaned him.
24 And when she had *weaned him* **dealt**,
she *took him* **ascended** him *up* with her,
with three bullocks,
and one ephah of flour, and a *bottle* **bag** of wine,
and brought him
unto the house of *the LORD* **Yah Veh** in Shiloh:
and the *child* **lad** was *young* **but a lad**.
25 And they *slew* **slaughtered** a bullock,
and brought the *child* **lad** to Eli.
26 And she said, Oh my *lord* **adoni**,
as thy soul liveth, my *lord* **adoni**,
I am the woman that *stood* **stationed** by thee here,
praying unto *the LORD* **Yah Veh**.
27 For this *child* **lad** I prayed;
and *the LORD* **Yah Veh** hath given me my petition
which I asked of him:
28 Therefore also I have lent him to *the LORD* **Yah Veh**;
as long as **all the days** he liveth
he shall be lent to *the LORD* **Yah Veh**.
And he *worshipped* **prostrated**
the LORD **to Yah Veh** there.

HANNAH'S PRAYER OF PRAISE

2 And Hannah prayed, and said,
My heart *rejoiceth* **jumpeth for joy** in *the LORD* **Yah Veh**,
mine horn is exalted in *the LORD* **Yah Veh**:
my mouth is enlarged over mine enemies;
because I *rejoice* **cheer** in thy salvation.
2 There is none holy as *the LORD* **Yah Veh**:
for there is none *beside* **except** thee:
neither is there any rock like our *God* **Elohim**.
3 *Talk no more* **Abound not thy word**
so *exceeding proudly* **high and lofty**;
let not *arrogancy come out* **impudence go** of your mouth:
for *the LORD* **Yah Veh** is *a God* **an El** of knowledge,
and by him *actions* **exploits** are *weighed* **gauged**.
4 The bows of the mighty *men* are *broken* **crushed**,
and they that stumbled are girded with *strength* **valour**.
5 They that were *full* **satisfied**
have hired out themselves for bread;
and they that were *hungry* **famished** ceased:
so that the *barren* **sterile** hath born seven;
and she that hath many *children* **sons**
is waxed feeble **languisheth**.
6 *The LORD killeth* **Yah Veh deathifieth**,
and *maketh alive* **enliveneth**:
he *bringeth down* **descendeth** to *the grave* **sheol**,
and *bringeth up* **ascendeth**.
7 *The LORD maketh poor* **Yah Veh dispossesseth**,
and *maketh rich* **enricheth**:
he *bringeth low* **abaseth**, and lifteth *up*.
8 He raiseth *up* the poor out of the dust,
and lifteth *up* the *beggar* **needy** from the dunghill,
to set them among *princes* **volunteers**,
and to make them inherit the throne of *glory* **honour**:
for the pillars of the earth are *the LORD'S* **Yah Veh's**,
and he hath set the world upon them.
9 He *will keep* **shall guard** the feet of his *saints* **mercied**,
and the wicked shall be *silent* **hushed** in darkness;
for by *strength* **force** shall no man prevail **mightily**.
10 The *adversaries* **contenders** of *the LORD* **Yah Veh**
shall be *broken to pieces* **terrified**;
out of *heaven* **the heavens** shall he thunder upon them:
the LORD **Yah Veh** shall *judge* **rule**
the *ends* **finality** of the earth;
and he shall give strength unto his *king* **sovereign**,
and exalt the horn of his anointed.
11 And *Elkanah* **El Qanah** went to Ramah to his house.
And the *child* **lad** did minister unto *the LORD* **Yah Veh**
before **at the face of** Eli the priest.

ELI'S SONS

12 Now the sons of Eli were sons of *Belial* **Beli Yaal**;
they knew not *the LORD* **Yah Veh**.
13 And the priest's *custom* **judgment** with the people was,
that, when any man *offered* **sacrificed** sacrifice,
the priest's *servant* **lad** came,
while the flesh was *in seething* **stewing**,
with a *fleshhook* **fork** of three teeth in his hand;
14 And he *struck* **smote** it into the *pan* **laver**,
or *kettle* **boiler**, or caldron, or *pot* **skillet**;
all that the *fleshhook brought up* **fork ascended**
the priest took for himself.
So they *did* **worked** in Shiloh
unto all the *Israelites* **Yisra Eliy** that came thither.
15 Also before they *burnt* **incensed** the fat,
the priest's *servant* **lad** came,
and said to the man that sacrificed,
Give flesh to roast for the priest;
for he *will not have sodden* **shall take no stewed** flesh
of thee,
but *raw* **live**.
16 And if any man said unto him,
In incensing, Let them *not fail to burn* **incense** the fat
presently **as on this day**,
and *then* take as *much as* thy soul desireth;
then he *would answer* **should say** to him, *Nay*;
but thou shalt give it me now:
and if not, I *will* **shall** take it by *force* **strength**.
17 Wherefore the sin of the *young men* **lads**
was *very* **mighty** great
before the LORD **at the face of Yah Veh**:
for men *abhorred* **scorned**
the offering of *the LORD* **Yah Veh**.

SHEMU EL'S LADHOOD MINISTRY

18 But *Samuel* **Shemu El** ministered
before the LORD **at the face of Yah Veh**,
being a child — **a lad**, girded with a linen ephod.
19 Moreover his mother
made **worked** him a little *coat* **mantle**,
and *brought* **ascended** it to him
from year to year **days by days**,
when she *came up* **ascended** with her *husband* **man**
to *offer* **sacrifice** the *yearly* sacrifice **of days**.
20 And Eli blessed *Elkanah* **El Qanah** and his *wife* **woman**,
and said,
The LORD give **Yah Veh set** thee seed of this woman
for the *loan* **petition** which is lent to *the LORD* **Yah Veh**.
And they went unto their *own home* **place**.
21 *And the LORD* **Surely Yah Veh** visited Hannah,
so that she conceived,
and bare three sons and two daughters.

And the *child Samuel* **lad Shemu El** grew
before the LORD **at the face of Yah Veh**.
22 Now Eli was *very* **mighty** old,
and heard
all that his sons *did* **worked** unto all *Israel* **Yisra El**;
and how they lay with the women that *assembled* **hosted**
at the *door* **opening**
of the *tabernacle* **tent** of the congregation.
23 And he said unto them,
Why *do* **work** ye *such things* **according to these words**?
for I hear of your evil *dealings* **words** by all this people.
24 Nay, my sons; for it is no good report that I hear:
ye make *the LORD'S* **Yah Veh's** people
to *transgress* **trespass**.
25 If one man sin against *another* **man**,
the judge **Elohim** shall *judge* **pray for** him:
but if a man sin against *the LORD* **Yah Veh**,
who shall *intreat* **pray** for him?
Notwithstanding
they hearkened not unto the voice of their father,
because *the LORD* **Yah Veh**
would slay **desired to deathify** them.
26 And the *child Samuel grew* **lad Shemu El walked** on
and greatened,
and was *in favour* **goodly** both with *the LORD* **Yah Veh**,
and also with men.

PROPHECY AGAINST ELI'S HOUSEHOLD

27 And there came a man of *God* **Elohim** unto Eli,
and said unto him, Thus saith *the LORD* **Yah Veh**,
Did I plainly appear **In exposing, exposed I**
unto the house of thy father,
when they were in *Egypt* **Misrayim**
in *Pharaoh's* **Paroh's** house?
28 And did I choose him
out of all the *tribes* **scions** of *Israel* **Yisra El** to be my priest,
to *offer* **holocaust** upon *mine* **my sacrifice** altar,
to *burn* **incense** incense,
to *wear* **bear** an ephod *before me* **at my face**?
and did I give unto the house of thy father
all the *offerings made by fire* **firings**
of the *children* **sons** of *Israel* **Yisra El**?
29 Wherefore *kick* **trample** ye
at my sacrifice and at mine offering,
which I have *commanded* **misvahed** in my habitation;
and honourest thy sons above me,
to *make yourselves fat with the chiefest* **cut the firstlings**
of all the offerings of *Israel* **Yisra El** my people?
30 *Wherefore* **Therefore**,
the LORD God of Israel saith
an oracle of Yah Veh Elohim of Yisra El,
In saying, I said *indeed* that thy house,
and the house of thy father,
should walk *before me for ever* **at my face eternally**:
but now *the LORD saith* **an oracle of Yah Veh**,
Be it far from me;
for them that honour me I *will* **shall** honour,
and they that despise me shall *be lightly esteemed* **I abase**.
31 Behold, the days come,
that I *will* **shall** cut off thine arm,
and the arm of thy father's house,
that there shall not be an old man in thine house.
32 And thou shalt *see an enemy* **look at the tribulation**
in **of** my habitation,
in all *the wealth* which *God* **Elohim**
shall *give Israel* **well—prepare for Yisra El**:
and there shall not be an old man in thine house
for ever **all days**.
33 And the man of thine,
whom I shall not cut off from *mine* **my sacrifice** altar,
shall *be to consume* **finish off** thine eyes,
and *to grieve thine heart* **lanquish thy soul**:
and all the increase of thine house
shall **these men** die *in the flower of their age*.
34 And this shall be a sign unto thee,
that shall come upon thy two sons,
on Hophni and *Phinehas* **Pinechas**;
in one day they shall die both of them.
35 And I *will* **shall** raise me up a *faithful* **trustworthy** priest,
that shall *do* **work** according to that which is in mine heart
and in my *mind* **soul**:
and I *will* **shall** build him a *sure* **permanent** house;
and he shall walk *before* **at the face of** mine anointed
for ever **all days**.
36 And it shall *come to pass* **become**,
that every one that *is left* **remaineth** in thine house
shall come and *crouch* **prostrate** to him
for a *piece* **coin** of silver and a *morsel* **round** of bread,
and shall say, *Put* **Scrape** me, I *pray* **beseech** thee,
into one of the *priests' offices* **priesthood's**,
that I may eat a *piece* **morsel** of bread.

SHEMU EL'S CALLING

3 And the *child Samuel* **lad Shemu El**
ministered unto *the LORD* **Yah Veh**
before **at the face of** Eli.
And the word of *the LORD* **Yah Veh**
was *precious* **esteemed** in those days;
there was no *open* vision **broken forth**.
2 And it *came to pass* **became**, at that *time* **day**,
when Eli was laid down in his place,
and his eyes began to *wax dim* **fade**, that he could not see;
3 And ere the lamp of *God went out* **Elohim quenched**
in the *temple* **manse** of *the LORD* **Yah Veh**,
where the ark of *God* **Elohim** was,
and *Samuel* **Shemu El** was laid down *to sleep*;
4 That *the LORD* **Yah Veh** called *Samuel* **Shemu El**:
and he *answered* **said**, *Here am I* **Behold, I**.
5 And he ran unto Eli, and said,
Here am I **Behold, I**; for thou calledst me.
And he said, I called not; **turn back**, lie down *again*.
And he went and lay down.
6 And *the LORD* **Yah Veh** called yet again,
Samuel **Shemu El**.
And *Samuel* **Shemu El** arose and went to Eli, and said,
Here am I **Behold, I**; for thou didst call me.
And he *answered* **said**, I called not, my son;
turn back, lie down *again*.
7 Now *Samuel* **Shemu El**
did not yet know *the LORD* **Yah Veh**,
neither was the word of *the LORD* **Yah Veh**
yet *revealed* **exposed** unto him.
8 And *the LORD* **Yah Veh**
called *Samuel* **Shemu El** again the third time.
And he arose and went to Eli, and said,
Here am I **Behold, I**; for thou didst call me.
And Eli *perceived* **discerned**
that *the LORD* **Yah Veh** had called the *child* **lad**.
9 Therefore Eli said unto *Samuel* **Shemu El**, Go, lie down:
and it shall be, if he call thee,
that thou shalt say, *Speak* **Word**, *LORD* **O Yah Veh**;
for thy servant heareth.
So *Samuel* **Shemu El** went and lay down in his place.
10 And *the LORD* **Yah Veh** came, and stood,
and called as *at other times* **time by time**,
Samuel **Shemu El**, *Samuel* **Shemu El**.
Then *Samuel answered* **Shemu El said**, *Speak* **Word**;
for thy servant heareth.
11 And *the LORD* **Yah Veh** said to *Samuel* **Shemu El**,
Behold, I *will do* **shall work** a *thing* **word** in *Israel* **Yisra El**,
at which both the ears of every one that heareth it
shall tingle.
12 In that day I *will perform* **shall raise** against Eli
all *things* **those** which I have *spoken* **worded**
concerning his house:
when I begin, I *will* **shall** also *make an end* **finish**.
13 *For I have told* **And I tell** him
that I *will* **shall** judge his house *for ever* **eternally**
for the *iniquity* **perversity** which he knoweth;
because his sons *made* **abased** themselves *vile*,
and he *restrained* **dimmed** them not.
14 And therefore
I have *sworn* **oathed** unto the house of Eli,
that the *iniquity* **perversity** of Eli's house
shall not *be purged* **kapar/atone** with sacrifice nor offering
for ever **eternally**.
15 And *Samuel* **Shemu El** lay until the morning,
and opened the doors of the house of *the LORD* **Yah Veh**.
And *Samuel feared* **Shemu El awed**
to *shew* **tell** Eli the vision.
16 Then Eli called *Samuel* **Shemu El**, and said,
Samuel **Shemu El**, my son.

And he *answered* **said**, *Here am I* **Behold, I.**
17 And he said, What is the *thing* **word**
that *the LORD hath said* **he hath worded** unto thee?
I *pray* **beseech** thee *hide* **conceal** it not from me:
God do **Elohim work** so to thee, and *more* **so add** also,
if thou *hide any thing* **conceal a word** from me
of all the *things* **words** that he *said* **hath worded** unto thee.
18 And *Samuel* **Shemu El** told him every *whit* **word**,
and *hid nothing* **concealed naught** from him.
And he said, It is *the LORD* **Yah Veh**:
let him *do* **work** what seemeth *him* good **in his eyes**.
19 And *Samuel* **Shemu El** grew,
and *the LORD* **Yah Veh** was with him,
and did let none of his words fall to the *ground* **earth**.
20 And all *Israel* **Yisra El**
from Dan even to *Beersheba* **Beer Sheba**
knew that *Samuel* **Shemu El** was *established* **trustworthy**
to be a prophet of *the LORD* **Yah Veh**.
21 And *the LORD* **Yah Veh**
appeared again **added to be seen** in Shiloh:
for *the LORD* **Yah Veh**
revealed himself **exposed** to *Samuel* **Shemu El**
in Shiloh by the word of *the LORD* **Yah Veh**.
4 And the word of *Samuel* **Shemu El**
came to all *Israel* **Yisra El**.

THE ARK CAPTURED

Now *Israel* **Yisra El** went out
against **to meet** the *Philistines* **Peleshethiy** to *battle* **war**,
and *pitched* **encamped** beside *Ebenezer* **Eben Ezer**:
and the *Philistines* **Peleshethiy**
pitched **encamped** in *Aphek* **Apheq**.
2 And the *Philistines* **Peleshethiy**
put themselves in array **lined up**
against Israel **to meet Yisra El**:
and when they *joined battle* **allowed war**,
Israel **Yisra El** was smitten
before **at the face of** the *Philistines* **Peleshethiy**:
and they *slew* **smote** of the *army* **ranks** in the field
about four thousand men.
3 And when the people were come into the camp,
the elders of *Israel* **Yisra El** said,
Wherefore hath *the LORD* **Yah Veh** smitten us to day
before **at the face of** the *Philistines* **Peleshethiy**?
Let us *fetch* **take**
the ark of the covenant of *the LORD* **Yah Veh**
out of Shiloh unto us,
that, when it cometh among us,
it may save us out of the *hand* **palm** of our enemies.
4 So the people sent to Shiloh,
that they might *bring* **bear** from thence
the ark of the covenant
of *the LORD of hosts* **Yah Veh Sabaoth**,
which *dwelleth* **settleth** between the *cherubims* **cherubim**:
and the two sons of Eli, Hophni and *Phinehas* **Pinechas**,
were there with the ark of the covenant of *God* **Elohim**.
5 And when the ark of the covenant of *the LORD* **Yah Veh**
came into the camp,
all *Israel* **Yisra El** shouted with a great *shout* **shouting**,
so that the earth *rang again* **quaked**.
6 And when the *Philistines* **Peleshethiy**
heard the *noise* **voice** of the *shout* **shouting**, they said,
What *meaneth* **be** the *noise* **voice**
of this great *shout* **shouting** in the camp of the Hebrews?
And they *understood* **knew**
that the ark of *the LORD* **Yah Veh**
was come into the camp.
7 And the *Philistines were afraid* **Peleshethiy awed**,
for they said, *God* **Elohim** is come into the camp.
And they said, Woe unto us!
for there hath not been such *a thing*
heretofore **since three yesters ago**.
8 Woe unto us! who shall *deliver* **rescue** us
out of the hand of these mighty *Gods* **Elohim**?
these are the *Gods* **Elohim**
that smote the *Egyptians* **Misrayim**
with all the *plagues* **strokes** in the wilderness.
9 Be strong and *quit yourselves like* **be** men,
O ye *Philistines* **Peleshethiy**,
that ye be not servants unto the Hebrews,
as they have *been to* **served** you:
quit yourselves like **be** men, and fight.
10 And the *Philistines* **Peleshethiy** fought,
and *Israel* **Yisra El** was smitten,
and they fled every man into his tent:
and there was a *very* **mighty** great *slaughter* **stroke**;
for there fell of *Israel* **Yisra El**
thirty thousand *footmen* **on foot**.
11 And the ark of *God* **Elohim** was taken;
and the two sons of Eli, Hophni and *Phinehas* **Pinechas**,
were *slain* **deathified**.

ELI'S DEATH

12 And there ran a man of *Benjamin* **Ben Yamin**
out of the *army* **ranks**,
and came to Shiloh the same day
with his *clothes rent* **tailoring ripped**,
and with *earth* **soil** upon his head.
13 And when he came, *lo* **behold**,
Eli *sat* **settled** upon a *seat* **throne**
by the *wayside* **hand of the way** watching:
for his heart trembled for the ark of *God* **Elohim**.
And when the man came into the city, and told it,
all the city cried out.
14 And when Eli heard the *noise* **voice** of the *crying* **cry**,
he said, What *meaneth the noise* **is the voice**
of this *tumult* **multitude**?
And the man came in hastily, and told Eli.
15 Now Eli was **a son of** ninety and eight years *old*;
and his eyes *were dim* **arose**, that he could not see.
16 And the man said unto Eli,
I am he that came out of the *army* **ranks**,
and I fled to day out of the *army* **ranks**.
And he said, What is *there done* **the word**, my son?
17 And *the messenger* **he who evangelized**
answered and said, *Israel* **Yisra El** is fled
before the Philistines **at the face of the Peleshethiy**,
and there hath been also a great *slaughter* **plague**
among the people,
and thy two sons also, Hophni and *Phinehas* **Pinechas**,
are *dead* **deathified**,
and the ark of *God* **Elohim** is taken.
18 And it *came to pass* **became**,
when he *made mention of* **remembered**
the ark of *God* **Elohim**,
that he fell from off the *seat* **throne** backward
by **through** the *side* **handle** of the *gate* **portal**,
and his neck brake, and he died:
for he was an old man, and heavy.
And he had judged *Israel* **Yisra El** forty years.

IY CHABOD'S BIRTH

19 And his daughter in law,
Phinehas' wife **Pinechas' woman**,
was with child **conceived**, near to *be delivered* **birth**:
and when she heard the *tidings* **report**
that the ark of *God* **Elohim** was taken,
and that her father in law and her *husband* **man**
were *dead* **deathified**,
she bowed herself and *travailed* **birthed**;
for her pains *came* **turned** upon her.
20 And about the time *of her death* **she died**
the women *that stood* **stationed** by her
said **worded** unto her,
Fear **Awe** not; for thou hast born a son.
But she answered not,
neither did she *regard it* **set her heart**.
21 And she *named* **called** the *child Ichabod* **lad Iy Chabod**,
saying,
The *glory* **honour** is *departed* **exiled** from *Israel* **Yisra El**:
because the ark of *God* **Elohim** was taken,
and because of her father in law and her *husband* **man**.
22 And she said,
The *glory* **honour** is *departed* **exiled** from *Israel* **Yisra El**:
for the ark of *God* **Elohim** is taken.

THE ARK REMOVED

5 And the *Philistines* **Peleshethiy**
took the ark of *God* **Elohim**,
and brought it from *Ebenezer* **Eben Ezer** unto Ashdod.
2 When the *Philistines* **Peleshethiy**
took the ark of *God* **Elohim**,
they brought it into the house of Dagon,
and set it *by* **beside** Dagon.

3 And when *they of Ashdod* **the Ashdodiy**
arose **started** early on the morrow, behold,
Dagon was fallen upon his face to the earth
before **at the face of** the ark of *the LORD* **Yah Veh**.
And they took Dagon,
and *set* **turned** him **back** in his place *again*.
4 And when they
arose **started** early on the morrow morning, behold,
Dagon was fallen upon his face to the *ground* **earth**
before **at the face of** the ark of *the LORD* **Yah Veh**;
and the head of Dagon and both the palms of his hands
were cut off upon the threshold;
only *the stump of* Dagon *was left* **survived** to him.
5 Therefore neither the priests of Dagon,
nor any that come into Dagon's house,
tread on the threshold of Dagon in Ashdod unto this day.
6 But the hand of *the LORD* **Yah Veh**
was heavy upon them of Ashdod,
and he *destroyed* **desolated** them,
and smote them with *emerods* **hemorrhoids**,
even Ashdod and the *coasts* **borders** thereof.
7 And when the men of Ashdod saw that it was so,
they said, The ark of the *God* **Elohim** of *Israel* **Yisra El**
shall not *abide* **settle** with us:
for his hand is *sore* **hard** upon us,
and upon Dagon our *god* **elohim**.
8 They sent therefore and gathered all the *lords* **ringleaders**
of the *Philistines* **Peleshethiy** unto them, and said,
What shall we *do* **work**
with the ark of *the God* **Elohim** of *Israel* **Yisra El**?
And they *answered* **said**,
Let the ark of *the God* **Elohim** of *Israel* **Yisra El**
be carried about **go** unto Gath.
And they *carried* **turned** the ark
of *the God* **Elohim** of *Israel* **Yisra El** about *thither*.
9 And it *was so* **became**, that,
after they had *carried* **turned** it about,
the hand of *the LORD* **Yah Veh** was against the city
with a *very* **mighty** great *destruction* **confusion**:
and he smote the men of the city, both small and great,
and *they had emerods in their secret parts*
hemorrhoids erupted.
10 Therefore they sent the ark of *God* **Elohim**
to *Ekron* **Eqron**.
And it *came to pass* **became**,
as the ark of *God* **Elohim** came to *Ekron* **Eqron**,
that the *Ekronites* **Eqroniy** cried out, saying,
They have *brought* **turned** about the ark
of *the God* **Elohim** of *Israel* **Yisra El** to us,
to *slay* **deathify** us and our people.
11 So they sent and gathered together
all the *lords* **ringleaders** of the *Philistines* **Peleshethiy**,
and said,
Send away the ark of *the God* **Elohim** of *Israel* **Yisra El**,
and let it *go again* **return** to his own place,
that it *slay* **deathify** us not, and our people:
for there was a *deadly destruction* **confusion of death**
throughout all the city;
the hand of *God* **Elohim** was *very* **mighty** heavy there.
12 And the men that died not
were smitten with the *emerods* **hemorrhoids**:
and the cry of the city
went up **ascended** to *heaven* **the heavens**.

THE ARK RETURNED

6 And the ark of *the LORD* **Yah Veh**
was in the *country* **field** of the *Philistines* **Peleshethiy**
seven months.
2 And the *Philistines* **Peleshethiy**
called for the priests and the diviners, saying,
What shall we *do* **work** to the ark of *the LORD* **Yah Veh**?
tell us **have us know**
wherewith we shall send it to his place.
3 And they said,
If ye send away
the ark of *the God* **Elohim** of *Israel* **Yisra El**,
send it not empty;
but in **returning**, *any wise* return him
a trespass offering **for the guilt**:
then ye shall be healed,
and it shall be known to you
why his hand is not *removed* **turned aside** from you.
4 Then said they,
What shall be *the trespass offering* **for the guilt**
which we shall return to him?
They *answered* **said**,
Five golden *emerods* **hemorrhoids**, and five golden mice,
according to the number
of the *lords* **ringleaders** of the *Philistines* **Peleshethiy**:
for one plague was on you all,
and on your *lords* **ringleaders**.
5 Wherefore ye shall *make* **work**
images of your *emerods* **hemorrhoids**,
and images of your mice that *mar* **ruin** the land;
and ye shall give *glory* **honour**
unto *the God* **Elohim** of *Israel* **Yisra El**:
peradventure
he *will lighten* **shall slighten** his hand from off you,
and from off your *gods* **elohim**, and from off your land.
6 Wherefore then do ye *harden* **callous** your hearts,
as the *Egyptians* **Misrayim** and *Pharaoh* **Paroh**
hardened **calloused** their hearts?
when he had *wrought wonderfully* **exploited** among them,
did they not *let* **send** the people *go* **away**,
and they *departed* **went**?
7 Now therefore *make a* **work one** new *cart* **wagon**,
and take two *milch kine* **suckling heifers**,
on which there hath *come* **ascended** no yoke,
and *tie* **hitch** the *kine* **heifers** to the *cart* **wagon**,
and *bring* **turn** their *calves* **sons**
home from them **afterward to their house**:
8 And take the ark of *the LORD* **Yah Veh**,
and *lay* **give** it upon the *cart* **wagon**;
and *put* **set** the *jewels* **instruments** of gold,
which ye return him for *a trespass offering* **the guilt**,
in a coffer by the side thereof;
and send it away, that it may go.
9 And see,
if it *goeth up* **ascendeth**
by the way of his own *coast* **border**
to *Bethshemesh* **Beth Shemesh**,
then he hath *done* **worked** us this great evil:
but if not,
then we shall know
that it is not his hand that *smote* **touched** us:
it was a *chance* **happening** that happened to us.
10 And the men *did* **worked** so;
and took two *milch kine* **suckling heifers**,
and *tied* **hitched** them to the *cart* **wagon**,
and *shut up* **restrained** their *calves* **sons**
at *home* **the house**:
11 And they *laid* **set** the ark of *the LORD* **Yah Veh**
upon the *cart* **wagon**,
and the coffer with the mice of gold
and the images of their *emerods* **hemorrhoids**.
12 And the *kine* **heifers** took the straight way
to the way of *Bethshemesh* **Beth Shemesh**,
and *went along the highway* **in going, did go on one path**,
lowing **bellowing** as they went,
and turned not aside to the right *hand* or to the left;
and the *lords* **ringleaders** of the *Philistines* **Peleshethiy**
went after them
unto the border of *Bethshemesh* **Beth Shemesh**.
13 And they of *Bethshemesh* **Beth Shemesh**
were *reaping* **harvesting** their wheat harvest in the valley:
and they lifted up their eyes,
and saw the ark, and *rejoiced* **cheered** to see it.
14 And the *cart* **wagon** came into the field
of *Joshua* **Yah Shua**, a *Bethshemite* **Beth Shemeshiy**,
and stood there, where there was a great stone:
and they *clave* **split** the *wood* **timber** of the *cart* **wagon**,
and *offered* **holocausted** the *kine* **heifers**
a *burnt offering* **holocaust** unto *the LORD* **Yah Veh**.
15 And the *Levites* **Leviym**
took down **descended** the ark of *the LORD* **Yah Veh**,
and the coffer that was with it,
wherein the *jewels* **instruments** of gold were,
and *put* **set** them on the great stone:
and the men of *Bethshemesh* **Beth Shemesh**
offered burnt offerings **holocausted holocausts**
and sacrificed sacrifices

the same day unto *the LORD* **Yah Veh**.
16 And when the five *lords* **ringleaders**
of the *Philistines* **Peleshethiy** had seen it,
they returned to *Ekron* **Eqron** the same day.
17 And these are the golden *emerods* **hemorrhoids**
which the *Philistines* **Peleshethiy** returned
for *a trespass offering* **the guilt** unto *the LORD* **Yah Veh**;
for Ashdod one, for *Gaza* **Azzah** one,
for *Askelon* **Ashqelon** one, for Gath one,
for *Ekron* **Eqron** one;
18 And the golden mice,
according to the number
of all the cities of the *Philistines* **Peleshethiy**
belonging to the five *lords* **ringleaders**,
both of *fenced* **fortified** cities,
and of *country* villages **of the suburbs**,
even unto the great *stone of* Abel,
whereon
they *set down* **descended** the ark of *the LORD* **Yah Veh**:
which stone remaineth unto this day
in the field of *Joshua* **Yah Shua**,
the *Bethshemite* **Beth Shemeshiy**.
19 And he smote the men of *Bethshemesh* **Beth Shemesh**,
because they had *looked* **seen**
into the ark of *the LORD* **Yah Veh**,
even he smote of the people fifty thousand
and *threescore and ten* **seventy** men:
and the people *lamented* **mourned**,
because *the LORD* **Yah Veh** had smitten
many of the people with a great *slaughter* **stroke**.
20 And the men of *Bethshemesh* **Beth Shemesh** said,
Who is able to stand *before* **at the face**
of this holy *LORD God* **Yah Veh Elohim**?
and to whom shall he *go up* **ascend** from us?
21 And they sent *messengers* **angels**
to the *inhabitants* **settlers** of *Kirjathjearim* **Qiryath Arim**,
saying, The *Philistines* **Peleshethiy**
have brought again the ark of *the LORD* **Yah Veh**;
come **descend** ye *down*, and *fetch* **ascend** it *up* to you.
7 And the men of *Kirjathjearim* **Qiryath Arim** came,
and *fetched up* **ascended** the ark of *the LORD* **Yah Veh**,
and brought it into the house of *Abinadab* **Abi Nadab**
in *the hill* **Gibah**,
and *sanctified Eleazar* **hallowed El Azar** his son
to *keep* **guard** the ark of *the LORD* **Yah Veh**.
2 And it *came to pass* **became**,
while **from the day**
the ark *abode* **settled** in *Kirjathjearim* **Qiryath Arim**,
that the *time was long* **days abounded**;
for it was twenty years:
and all the house of *Israel* **Yisra El**
lamented after *the LORD* **Yah Veh**.
3 And *Samuel spake* **Shemu El said**
unto all the house of *Israel* **Yisra El**, saying,
If ye do return unto *the LORD* **Yah Veh**
with all your hearts,
then *put away* **turn aside**
the strange *gods* **elohim** and Ashtaroth from among you,
and prepare your hearts unto *the LORD* **Yah Veh**,
and serve him only:
and he *will deliver* **shall rescue** you
out of the hand of the *Philistines* **Peleshethiy**.
4 Then the *children* **sons** of *Israel* **Yisra El**
did put away **turned aside** Baalim and Ashtaroth,
and served *the LORD* **Yah Veh** only.
5 And *Samuel* **Shemu El** said,
Gather all *Israel* **Yisra El** to *Mizpeh* **Mispeh**,
and I *will* **shall** pray for you unto *the LORD* **Yah Veh**.
6 And they gathered together to *Mizpeh* **Mispeh**,
and *drew* **bailed** water, and poured it out
before the LORD **at the face of Yah Veh**,
and fasted on that day, and said there,
We have sinned against *the LORD* **Yah Veh**.
And *Samuel* **Shemu El**
judged the *children* **sons** of *Israel* **Yisra El**
in *Mizpeh* **Mispeh**.

PELESHETHIY SUBDUED

7 And when the *Philistines* **Peleshethiy** heard
that the *children* **sons** of *Israel* **Yisra El**
were gathered *together* to *Mizpeh* **Mispeh**,
the *lords* **ringleaders** of the *Philistines* **Peleshethiy**
went up **ascended** against *Israel* **Yisra El**.
And when the *children* **sons** of *Israel* **Yisra El** heard it,
they *were afraid* **awed**
at the face of the *Philistines* **Peleshethiy**.
8 And the *children* **sons** of *Israel* **Yisra El**
said to *Samuel* **Shemu El**,
Cease **Hush** not to cry
unto *the LORD* **Yah Veh** our *God* **Elohim** for us,
that he *will* **shall** save us
out of the hand of the *Philistines* **Peleshethiy**.
9 And *Samuel* **Shemu El** took *a sucking* **one milking** lamb,
and *offered it for a burnt offering* **holocausted a holocaust**
wholly **totally** unto *the LORD* **Yah Veh**:
and *Samuel* **Shemu El**
cried unto *the LORD* **Yah Veh** for *Israel* **Yisra El**;
and *the LORD heard* **Yah Veh answered** him.
10 And as *Samuel* **Shemu El**
was offering up **holocausted** the *burnt offering* **holocaust**,
the *Philistines* **Peleshethiy** drew near
to *battle* **war** against *Israel* **Yisra El**:
but *the LORD* **Yah Veh** thundered
with a great *thunder* **voice** on that day
upon the *Philistines* **Peleshethiy**,
and *discomfited* **agitated** them;
and they were smitten *before Israel* **at the face of Yisra El**.
11 And the men of *Israel* **Yisra El**
went out of *Mizpeh* **Mispeh**,
and pursued the *Philistines* **Peleshethiy**, and smote them,
until they came under *Bethcar* **Beth Kar**.
12 Then *Samuel* **Shemu El** took *a* **one** stone,
and set it between *Mizpeh* **Mispeh** and Shen,
and called the name of it *Ebenezer* **Eben Ezer**, saying,
Hitherto hath *the LORD* **Yah Veh** helped us.
13 So the *Philistines* **Peleshethiy** were subdued,
and they *came no more* **added not to come**
into the *coast* **border** of *Israel* **Yisra El**:
and the hand of *the LORD* **Yah Veh**
was against the *Philistines* **Peleshethiy**
all the days of *Samuel* **Shemu El**.
14 And the cities which the *Philistines* **Peleshethiy**
had taken from *Israel* **Yisra El**
were restored to *Israel* **Yisra El**,
from *Ekron* **Eqron** even unto Gath;
and the *coasts* **borders** thereof
did *Israel deliver* **Yisra El rescue**
out of the hands of the *Philistines* **Peleshethiy**.
And there *was peace* **became shalom**
between *Israel* **Yisra El** and the *Amorites* **Emoriy**.
15 And *Samuel* **Shemu El** judged *Israel* **Yisra El**
all the days of his life.
16 And he went **enough** from year to year
in circuit **and turned around** to *Bethel* **Beth El**,
and Gilgal, and *Mizpeh* **Mispeh**,
and judged *Israel* **Yisra El** in all those places.
17 And his return was to Ramah; for there was his house;
and there he judged *Israel* **Yisra El**;
and there he built *an* **a sacrifice** altar
unto *the LORD* **Yah Veh**.

SHEMU EL'S DISHONEST SONS

8 And it *came to pass* **became**,
when *Samuel* **Shemu El** was old,
that he *made* **set** his sons judges over *Israel* **Yisra El**.
2 Now the name of his firstborn **son** was *Joel* **Yah El**;
and the name of his second, *Abiah* **Abi Yah**:
they were judges in *Beersheba* **Beer Sheba**.
3 And his sons walked not in his ways,
but *turned aside* **extended** after *lucre* **greed**,
and took bribes, and perverted judgment.

ELDERS OF YISRA EL REQUEST A SOVEREIGN

4 Then all the elders of *Israel* **Yisra El**
gathered themselves together,
and came to *Samuel* **Shemu El** unto Ramah,
5 And said unto him, Behold, thou art old,
and thy sons walk not in thy ways:
now *make* **set** us a *king* **sovereign** to judge us
like all the *nations* **goyim**.
6 But the *thing* **word**
displeased Samuel **was evil in the eyes of Shemu El**,
when they said, Give us a *king* **sovereign** to judge us.

And *Samuel* **Shemu El** prayed unto *the LORD* **Yah Veh**.
7 And *the LORD* **Yah Veh** said unto *Samuel* **Shemu El**,
Hearken unto the voice of the people
in all that they say unto thee:
for they have not *rejected* **refused** thee,
but they have *rejected* **refused** me,
that I should not reign over them.
8 According to all the works which they have *done* **worked**
since the day
that I *brought* **ascended** them *up* out of *Egypt* **Misrayim**
even unto this day,
wherewith they have forsaken me,
and served other *gods* **elohim**,
so *do* **work** they also unto thee.
9 Now therefore hearken unto their voice:
howbeit yet protest solemnly
only in witnessing, witness unto them,
and *shew* **tell** them the *manner* **judgment**
of the *king* **sovereign** that shall reign over them.
10 And *Samuel* **Shemu El**
told **said** all the words of *the LORD* **Yah Veh**
unto the people that asked of him a *king* **sovereign**.
11 And he said, This *will* **shall** be the *manner* **judgment**
of the *king* **sovereign** that shall reign over you:
He *will* **shall** take your sons,
and *appoint* **set** them for himself,
for his chariots, and to be his *horsemen* **cavalry**;
and some shall run before **at the face of** his chariots.
12 And he *will appoint* **shall set** him
captains **governors** over thousands,
and *captains* **governors** over fifties;
and *will* **shall** set them
to *ear* **plough** his *ground* **ploughing**,
and to *reap* **harvest** his harvest,
and to *make* **work** his instruments of war,
and instruments of his chariots.
13 And he *will* **shall** take your daughters
to be *confectionaries* **perfumers**,
and to be *cooks* **slaughterers**, and to be bakers.
14 And he *will* **shall** take your fields, and your vineyards,
and your oliveyards, *even* the best of them,
and give them to his servants.
15 And he *will* **shall** take the *tenth* **tithe** of your seed,
and of your vineyards,
and give to his *officers* **eunuchs**, and to his servants.
16 And he *will* **shall** take your *menservants* **servants**,
and your *maidservants* **maids**,
and your goodliest *young men* **youths**,
and your *asses* **he burros**, and *put* **work** them to his work.
17 He *will* **shall** take the *tenth* **tithe** of your *sheep* **flock**:
and ye shall be his servants.
18 And ye shall cry out in that day
because **at the face** of your *king* **sovereign**
which ye shall have chosen you;
and *the LORD* **Yah Veh**
will **shall** not *hear you* **answer you** in that day.
19 Nevertheless the people refused to *obey* **hear**
the voice of *Samuel* **Shemu El**;
and they said, Nay;
but we *will* **shall** have a *king* **sovereign** over us;
20 That we also may be like all the *nations* **goyim**;
and that our *king* **sovereign** may judge us,
and go out *before us* **from our face**,
and fight our *battles* **wars**.
21 And *Samuel* **Shemu El**
heard all the words of the people,
and he *rehearsed* **worded** them
in the ears of *the LORD* **Yah Veh**.
22 And *the LORD* **Yah Veh** said to *Samuel* **Shemu El**,
Hearken unto their voice,
and make them a king **that they have a sovereign reign**.
And *Samuel* **Shemu El** said unto the men of *Israel* **Yisra El**,
Go ye every man unto his city.

SHEMU EL ANOINTS SHAUL

9 Now there was a man of *Benjamin* **Ben Yamin**,
whose name was *Kish* **Qish**,
the son of *Abiel* **Abi El**, the son of *Zeror* **Seror**,
the son of Bechorath,
the son of *Aphiah* **Aphiach**,
a *Benjamite* **Ben Yaminiy**, a mighty *man* of *power* **valour**.
2 And he had a son, whose name was *Saul* **Shaul**,
a *choice young man* **youth**, and *a* goodly:
and there was not
among the *children* **sons** of *Israel* **Yisra El**
a goodlier *person* **man** than he:
from his shoulders and upward
he was higher than any of the people.
3 And the *asses* **she burros** of *Kish* **Qish**
Saul's **Shaul's** father were lost.
And *Kish* **Qish** said to *Saul* **Shaul** his son,
Take now one of the *servants* **lads** with thee, and arise,
go seek the *asses* **she burros**.
4 And he passed through mount *Ephraim* **Ephrayim**,
and passed through the land of *Shalisha* **Shalishah**,
but they found them not:
then they passed through the land of *Shalim* **Shaalim**,
and there they were not:
and he passed through the land
of the *Benjamites* **Ben Yaminiy**,
but they found them not.
5 And when they were come to the land of *Zuph* **Suph**,
Saul **Shaul** said to his *servant* **lad** that was with him,
Come, and let us return;
lest my father *leave caring* **cease** for the *asses* **she burros**,
and *take thought* **be concerned** for us.
6 And he said unto him, Behold now,
there is in this city a man of *God* **Elohim**,
and he is an honourable man;
all that he *saith cometh* **wordeth** surely *to pass* **becometh**:
now let us go thither;
peradventure he can *shew* **tell** us
our way that we should go.
7 Then said *Saul* **Shaul** to his *servant* **lad**, But, behold,
if we go, what shall we bring the man?
for the bread
is spent **hath disappeared** in our *vessels* **instruments**,
and there is not a *present* **gift** to bring
to the man of *God* **Elohim**:
what have we?
8 And the *servant* **lad added**
and answered *Saul* **Shaul** *again*, and said, Behold,
I have here at **There is found in my** hand
the fourth *part* of a shekel of silver:
that *will* **shall** I give to the man of *God* **Elohim**,
to tell us our way.
9 (*Beforetime in Israel* **At the face of Yisra El**,
when a man went to enquire of *God* **Elohim**,
thus he *spake* **saith**,
Come, and let us go to the seer:
for *he that is now called a* **the** Prophet **of today**
was *beforetime* **formerly** called *a* **the** Seer.)
10 Then said *Saul* **Shaul** to his *servant* **lad**,
Well said **Good word**; come, let us go.
So they went unto the city
where the man of *God* **Elohim** was.
11 *And* as they *went up* **ascended**
the *hill to* **ascent of** the city,
they found *young maidens* **lasses**
going out to *draw* **bail** water,
and said unto them, Is the seer here?
12 And they answered them, and said, He is;
behold, he is *before you* **at thy face**:
make haste now, for he came to day to the city;
for there is a sacrifice of the people
to day in the *high place* **bamah**:
13 As soon as ye be come into the city,
thus ye shall *straightway* find him,
before he *go up* **ascendeth** to the *high place* **bamah** to eat:
for the people *will* **shall** not eat until he come,
because he doth bless the sacrifice;
and *afterwards* **thus** they eat that be *bidden* **called**.
Now therefore *get you up* **ascend ye**;
for *about this time* **to day** ye shall find him.
14 And they *went up* **ascended** into the city:
and when they were come into **the midst of** the city,
behold,
Samuel came out against **Shemu El went to meet** them,
for to *go up* **ascend** to the *high place* **bamah**.
15 Now *the LORD* **Yah Veh**
had *told Samuel* **exposed to Shemu El** in his ear

a **one** day *before Saul came* **at the face of Shaul's coming,**
saying,
16 To morrow about this time
I *will* **shall** send thee a man
out of the land of *Benjamin* **Ben Yamin,**
and thou shalt anoint him
to be *captain* **eminent** over my people *Israel* **Yisra El,**
that he may save my people
out of the hand of the *Philistines* **Peleshethiy:**
for I have *looked upon* **seen** my people,
because their cry is come unto me.
17 And when *Samuel* **Shemu El** saw *Saul* **Shaul,**
the LORD said unto **Yah Veh answered** him,
Behold the man whom I *spake* **said** to thee of!
this same shall *reign over* **restrain** my people.
18 Then *Saul* **Shaul** drew near to *Samuel* **Shemu El**
in **the midst of** the *gate* **portal,** and said,
Tell me, I *pray* **beseech** thee, where the seer's house is.
19 And *Samuel* **Shemu El** answered *Saul* **Shaul,**
and said, I am the seer:
go up before me **ascend at my face**
unto the *high place* **bamah;**
for ye shall eat with me to day,
and *to morrow* **in the morning**
I *will let* **shall send** thee *go* **away,**
and *will* **shall** tell thee all that is in thine heart.
20 And as for *thine asses* **thy she burros**
that were lost three days ago,
set not thy *mind* **heart** on them; for they are found.
And on whom is all the desire of *Israel* **Yisra El?**
Is it not on thee, and on all thy father's house?
21 And *Saul* **Shaul** answered and said,
Am not I a *Benjamite* **Ben Yaminiy,**
of the smallest of the *tribes* **scions** of *Israel* **Yisra El?**
and my family the *least* **lesser** of all the families
of the *tribe* **scion** of *Benjamin* **Ben Yamin?**
wherefore then *speakest* **wordest** thou so to me?
22 And *Samuel* **Shemu El**
took *Saul* **Shaul** and his *servant* **lad,**
and brought them into the *parlour* **chamber,**
and *made* **gave** them *sit in the chiefest* **head** place
among them that were *bidden* **called,**
which were about thirty *persons* **men.**
23 And *Samuel* **Shemu El** said unto the *cook* **slaughterer,**
Bring **Give** the portion which I gave thee,
of which I said unto thee, Set it by thee.
24 And the *cook* **slaughterer**
took up **lifted** the *shoulder* **leg,**
and that which was upon it,
and set it *before Saul* **at the face of Shaul.**
And *Samuel* **he** said, Behold that which *is left* **surviveth!**
set it *before thee* **at thy face,** and eat:
for unto this *time* **season**
hath it been *kept* **guarded** for thee since I said,
I have *invited* **called** the people.
So *Saul* **Shaul** did eat with *Samuel* **Shemu El** that day.
25 And when they *were come down* **descended**
from the *high place* **bamah** into the city,
Samuel communed **he worded** with *Saul* **Shaul**
upon the *top of the house* **roof.**
26 And they *arose* **started** early:
and it *came to pass* **became,**
about the *spring* **ascent** of the *day* **dawn,**
that *Samuel* **Shemu El** called *Saul* **Shaul**
to the *top of the house* **roof,** saying,
Up **Arise,** that I may send thee away.
And *Saul* **Shaul** arose, and they went out both of them,
he and *Samuel* **Shemu El,** *abroad* **out.**
27 And as they were *going down* **descending**
to the end of the city,
Samuel **Shemu El** said to *Saul* **Shaul,**
Bid the servant **Say that the lad** pass on
before us **from our face,**
(and he passed on), but stand thou still *a while* **today,**
that I may *shew* **have** thee **hear** the word of *God* **Elohim.**

SHAUL'S ANOINTING

10 Then *Samuel* **Shemu El** took a *vial* **flask** of oil,
and poured it upon his head, and kissed him, and said,
Is it not because *the LORD* **Yah Veh** hath anointed thee
to be *captain* **eminent** over his inheritance?
2 When thou art *departed* **gone** from me to day,
then thou shalt find two men by Rachel's *sepulchre* **tomb**
in the border of *Benjamin* **Ben Yamin** at *Zelzah* **Selsach;**
and they *will* **shall** say unto thee,
The *asses* **she burros** which thou wentest to seek
are found: and, *lo* **behold,**
thy father hath left the *care* **word** of the *asses* **she burros,**
and *sorroweth* **is concerned** for you, saying,
What shall I *do* **work** for my son?
3 Then shalt thou *go on forward* **pass beyond** from thence,
and thou shalt come to the *plain* **mighty oak** of Tabor,
and there *shall meet thee* **shalt thou find** three men
going up **ascending** to *God* **Elohim** to *Bethel* **Beth El,**
one *carrying* **bearing** three kids,
and *another carrying* **one bearing**
three *loaves* **rounds** of bread,
and *another carrying* **one bearing** a *bottle* **bag** of wine:
4 And they *will salute* **shall ask shalom of** thee,
and give thee two *loaves of* bread;
which thou shalt *receive* **take** of their hands.
5 After that thou shalt come to the hill of *God* **Elohim,**
where is the *garrison* **station** of the *Philistines* **Peleshethiy:**
and it shall *come to pass* **become,**
when thou art come thither to the city,
that thou shalt meet a *company* **line** of prophets
coming down **descending** from the *high place* **bamah**
with a *psaltery* **bagpipe,** and a *tabret* **tambourine,**
and a *pipe* **flute,** and a harp, *before them* **at their face;**
and they shall prophesy:
6 And the Spirit of *the LORD* **Yah Veh**
will come **shall prosper** upon thee,
and thou shalt prophesy with them,
and shalt be turned into another man.
7 And let it be, when these signs are come unto thee,
that thou *do* **work**
as *occasion serve thee* **thy hand findeth;**
for *God* **Elohim** is with thee.
8 And thou shalt *go down* **descend**
before me **at my face** to Gilgal; and, behold,
I *will come down* **shall descend** unto thee,
to *offer burnt offerings* **holocaust holocausts,**
and to sacrifice sacrifices of *peace offerings* **shelamim:**
seven days shalt thou *tarry* **wait,** till I come to thee,
and *shew* **have** thee **know** what thou shalt *do* **work.**
9 And it *was so* **became,**
that when he had turned **to face** his *back* **shoulder**
to go from *Samuel* **Shemu El,**
God gave **Elohim turned to** him another heart:
and all those signs *came to pass* **became** that day.
10 And when they came thither to *the hill* **Gibah,**
behold, a *company* **line** of prophets met him;
and the Spirit of *God came* **Elohim prospered** upon him,
and he prophesied among them.
11 And it *came to pass* **became,**
when all that knew him *beforetime* **three yesters ago**
saw that, behold,
he prophesied among the prophets,
then the people said *one* **man** to *another* **friend,**
What is this that is come unto the son of *Kish* **Qish?**
Is *Saul* **Shaul** also among the prophets?
12 And *one* **a man** of the same place answered and said,
But who is their father?
Therefore it became a proverb,
Is *Saul* **Shaul** also among the prophets?
13 And when he had
made an end of **finished** prophesying,
he came to the *high place* **bamah.**
14 And *Saul's* **Shaul's** uncle
said unto him and to his *servant* **lad,**
Whither went ye?
And he said, To seek the *asses* **she burros:**
and when we saw that they were no where,
we came to *Samuel* **Shemu El.**
15 And *Saul's* **Shaul's** uncle said, Tell me, I pray thee,
what *Samuel* **Shemu El** said unto you.
16 And *Saul* **Shaul** said unto his uncle,
In telling, He told us *plainly*
that the *asses* **she burros** were found.
But of the *matter* **word** of the *kingdom* **sovereigndom,**
whereof *Samuel spake* **Shemu El saith,** he told him not.

SHAUL SET AS SOVEREIGN
17 And *Samuel* **Shemu El**
called **summoned** the people together
unto *the LORD* **Yah Veh** to *Mizpeh* **Mispeh**;
18 And said unto the *children* **sons** of *Israel* **Yisra El**,
Thus saith
the LORD God **Yah Veh Elohim** of *Israel* **Yisra El**,
I *brought up Israel* **ascended Yisra El**
out of *Egypt* **Misrayim**,
and *delivered* **rescued** you
out of the hand of *the Egyptians* **Misrayim**,
and out of the hand of all *kingdoms* **sovereigndoms**,
and of them that oppressed you:
19 And ye have this day *rejected* **refused** your *God* **Elohim**,
who himself saved you
out of all your *adversities* **evils** and your tribulations;
and ye have said unto him, *Nay*,
but set a *king* **sovereign** over us.
Now therefore *present* **set** yourselves
before the LORD **at the face of Yah Veh**
by your *tribes* **scions**, and by your thousands.
20 And when *Samuel* **Shemu El** had *caused*
all the *tribes* **scions** of *Israel* **Yisra El**
to *come near* **approach**,
the *tribe* **scion** of *Benjamin* **Ben Yamin**
was *taken* **captured.**
21 When he had *caused*
the *tribe* **scion** of *Benjamin* **Ben Yamin**
to *come near* **approach** by their families,
the family of Matri was *taken* **captured**,
and *Saul* **Shaul** the son of *Kish* **Qish** was *taken* **captured**:
and when they sought him, he could not be found.
22 Therefore
they *enquired* **asked** of *the LORD* **Yah Veh** further,
if the man should yet come *thither* **hither**.
And *the LORD answered* **Yah Veh said**,
Behold he hath hid himself among the *stuff* **instruments**.
23 And they ran and *fetched* **took** him thence:
and when he stood among the people,
he was higher than any of the people
from his shoulders and upward.
24 And *Samuel* **Shemu El** said to all the people,
See ye him whom *the LORD* **Yah Veh** hath chosen,
that there is none like him among all the people?
And all the people shouted, and said,
God save the king **Elohim, let the sovereign live**.
25 Then *Samuel told* **Shemu El worded to** the people
the *manner* **judgment** of the *kingdom* **sovereigndom**,
and *wrote it* **inscribed** in a *book* **scroll**,
and *laid* **set** it *up before the LORD* **at the face of Yah Veh**.
And *Samuel* **Shemu El** sent all the people away,
every man to his house.
26 And *Saul* **Shaul** also
went *home* **to his house** to *Gibeah* **Gibah**;
and there went with him *a band of* **valiant** men,
whose hearts *God* **Elohim** had touched.
27 But the *children* **sons** of *Belial* **Beli Yaal** said,
How shall this man save us?
And they despised him, and brought no *presents* **offerings**.
But he *held his peace* **hushed**.

SHAUL DEFEATS THE AMMONIY
11 Then *Nahash* **Nachash** the *Ammonite* **Ammoniy**
came up **ascended**,
and encamped against *Jabeshgilead* **Yabesh Gilad**:
and all the men of *Jabesh* **Yabesh**
said unto *Nahash* **Nachash**,
Make **Cut** a covenant with us,
and we *will* **shall** serve thee.
2 And *Nahash* **Nachash** the *Ammonite* **Ammoniy**
answered **said to** them,
On **By** this *condition*
will **shall** I *make a covenant* **cut** with you,
that I may *thrust* **bore** out all your right eyes,
and lay it for a reproach upon all *Israel* **Yisra El**.
3 And the elders of *Jabesh* **Yabesh** said unto him,
Give us seven days' respite **Let us go seven days**,
that we may send *messengers* **angels**
unto all the *coasts* **borders** of *Israel* **Yisra El**:
and then, if there be no man to save us,
we *will come out* **shall go** to thee.
4 Then came the *messengers* **angels**
to *Gibeah* **Gibah** of *Saul* **Shaul**,
and *told the tidings* **worded the words**
in the ears of the people:
and all the people lifted up their voices, and wept.
5 And, behold,
Saul **Shaul** came after the *herd* **oxen** out of the field;
and *Saul* **Shaul** said,
What *aileth* **be to** the people that they weep?
And they *told* **scribed** him
the *tidings* **words** of the men of *Jabesh* **Yabesh**.
6 And the Spirit of *God* **Elohim**
came **prospered** upon *Saul* **Shaul**
when he heard those *tidings* **words**,
and his *anger* **wrath** was kindled *greatly* **mightily**.
7 And he took a yoke of oxen,
and *hewed* **dismembered** them *in pieces*,
and sent them
throughout all the *coasts* **borders** of *Israel* **Yisra El**
by the hands of *messengers* **angels**, saying,
Whosoever *cometh* **goeth** not *forth*
after *Saul* **Shaul** and after *Samuel* **Shemu El**,
so shall it be *done* **worked** unto his oxen.
And the fear of *the LORD* **Yah Veh** fell on the people,
and they *came out with* **went as** one *consent* **man**.
8 And when he *numbered* **mustered** them in *Bezek* **Bezeq**,
the *children* **sons** of *Israel* **Yisra El**
were three hundred thousand,
and the men of *Judah* **Yah Hudah** thirty thousand.
9 And they said unto the *messengers* **angels** that came,
Thus shall ye say
unto the men of *Jabeshgilead* **Yabesh Gilad**,
To morrow, by that *time* the sun be hot,
ye shall have *help* **salvation**.
And the *messengers* **angels** came
and *shewed* **told** it to the men of *Jabesh* **Yabesh**;
and they *were glad* **cheered**.
10 Therefore the men of *Jabesh* **Yabesh** said,
To morrow we *will come out* **shall go** unto you,
and ye shall *do* **work** with us
all that seemeth good *unto you* **in your eyes**.
11 And it was so on the morrow,
that *Saul put* **Shaul set** the people
in three *companies* **heads**;
and they came into the midst of the *host* **camp**
in the morning watch,
and *slew* **smote** the *Ammonites* **Ammoniy**
until the heat of the day:
and it *came to pass* **became**,
that they which *remained* **survived** were scattered,
so that two of them *were not left* **survived not** together.
12 And the people said unto *Samuel* **Shemu El**,
Who is he that said, shall *Saul* **Shaul** reign over us?
bring **give** the men,
that we may *put* **deathify** them *to death*.
13 And *Saul* **Shaul** said,
There shall not a man be *put to death* **deathified** this day:
for to day *the LORD* **Yah Veh**
hath *wrought* **worked** salvation in *Israel* **Yisra El**.
14 Then said *Samuel* **Shemu El** to the people,
Come, and let us go to Gilgal,
and renew the *kingdom* **sovereigndom** there.
15 And all the people went to Gilgal;
and there they *made Saul king* **had Shaul reign**
before the LORD **at the face of Yah Veh** in Gilgal;
and there they sacrificed
sacrifices of *peace offerings* **shelamim**
before the LORD **at the face of Yah Veh**;
and there *Saul* **Shaul** and all the men of *Israel* **Yisra El**
rejoiced greatly **cheered mightily**.

SHEMU EL'S FAREWELL
12 And *Samuel* **Shemu El** said unto all *Israel* **Yisra El**,
Behold, I have hearkened unto your voice
in all that ye said unto me,
and have *made a king* **a sovereign to reign** over you.
2 And now, behold,
the *king* **sovereign** walketh *before you* **at thy face**:
and I am old and *grayheaded* **grayed**;
and, behold, my sons are with you:
and I have walked *before you* **at thy face**

from my *childhood* **youth** unto this day.
3 Behold, here I am:
witness **answer** against me before *the LORD* **Yah Veh**,
and before his anointed:
whose ox have I taken?
or whose *ass* **he burro** have I taken?
or whom have I *defrauded* **extorted**?
whom have I *oppressed* **crushed**?
or of whose hand
have I *received any bribe* **taken a koper/an atonement**
to *blind* **veil** mine eyes therewith?
and I *will* **shall** restore it you.
4 And they said, Thou hast not *defrauded* **extorted** us,
nor *oppressed* **crushed** us,
neither hast thou taken ought of any man's hand.
5 And he said unto them,
The LORD **Yah Veh** is witness against you,
and his anointed is witness this day,
that ye have not found ought in my hand.
And they *answered* **said**, He is witness.
6 And *Samuel* **Shemu El** said unto the people,
It is *the LORD* **Yah Veh**
that *advanced Moses* **worked Mosheh** and *Aaron* **Aharon**,
and that *brought* **ascended** your fathers *up*
out of the land of *Egypt* **Misrayim**.
7 Now therefore stand still,
that I may *reason* **judge** with you
before the LORD **at the face of Yah Veh**
of all the *righteous acts* **justnesses** of *the LORD* **Yah Veh**,
which he *did* **worked** to you and to your fathers.
8 When *Jacob* **Yaaqov** was come into *Egypt* **Misrayim**,
and your fathers cried unto *the LORD* **Yah Veh**,
then *the LORD* **Yah Veh**
sent *Moses* **Mosheh** and *Aaron* **Aharon**,
which brought forth your fathers out of *Egypt* **Misrayim**,
and *made* **settled** them *dwell* in this place.
9 And when they forgat
the LORD **Yah Veh** their *God* **Elohim**,
he sold them into the hand of Sisera,
captain **governor** of the host of *Hazor* **Hasor**,
and into the hand of the *Philistines* **Peleshethiy**,
and into the hand of the *king* **sovereign** of Moab,
and they fought against them.
10 And they cried unto *the LORD* **Yah Veh**,
and said, We have sinned,
because we have forsaken *the LORD* **Yah Veh**,
and have served Baalim and Ashtaroth:
but now *deliver* **rescue** us out of the hand of our enemies,
and we *will* **shall** serve thee.
11 And *the LORD* **Yah Veh** sent *Jerubbaal* **Yerub Baal**,
and Bedan, and *Jephthah* **Yiphtach**, and *Samuel* **Shemu El**,
and *delivered* **rescued** you
out of the hand of your enemies
on every side **round about**,
and ye *dwelled safe* **settled securely**.
12 And when ye saw that *Nahash* **Nachash**
the *king* **sovereign** of the *children* **sons** of Ammon
came against you,
ye said unto me, Nay;
but a *king* **sovereign** shall reign over us:
when *the LORD* **Yah Veh** your *God* **Elohim**
was your *king* **sovereign**.
13 Now therefore
behold the *king* **sovereign** whom ye have chosen,
and whom ye have *desired* **asked**! and, behold,
the LORD **Yah Veh**
hath *set* **given** a *king* **sovereign** over you.
14 If ye *will fear the LORD* **shall awe Yah Veh**,
and serve him, and *obey* **hear** his voice,
and not rebel
against the *commandment* **mouth** of *the LORD* **Yah Veh**,
then shall both ye
and also the *king* **sovereign** that reigneth over you
continue *following* **after**
the LORD **Yah Veh** your *God* **Elohim**:
15 But if ye *will* **shall** not
obey **hear** the voice of *the LORD* **Yah Veh**,
but rebel against
the *commandment* **mouth** of *the LORD* **Yah Veh**,
then shall the hand of *the LORD* **Yah Veh**
be against you, as it was against your fathers.
16 Now *therefore* **however**
stand and see this great *thing* **word**,
which *the LORD* **Yah Veh**
will do **shall work** before your eyes.
17 Is it not wheat harvest to day?
I *will* **shall** call unto *the LORD* **Yah Veh**,
and he shall *send thunder* **give voice** and rain;
that ye may perceive and see
that your *wickedness* **evil** is great,
which ye have *done* **worked**
in the *sight* **eyes** of *the LORD* **Yah Veh**,
in asking you a *king* **sovereign**.
18 So *Samuel* **Shemu El** called unto *the LORD* **Yah Veh**;
and *the LORD* **Yah Veh**
sent thunder **gave voice** and rain that day:
and all the people *greatly feared* **mightily awed**
the LORD **Yah Veh** and *Samuel* **Shemu El**.
19 And all the people said unto *Samuel* **Shemu El**,
Pray for thy servants
unto *the LORD* **Yah Veh** thy *God* **Elohim**, that we die not:
for we have added unto all our sins this evil,
to ask us a *king* **sovereign**.
20 And *Samuel* **Shemu El** said unto the people,
Fear **Awe** not:
ye have *done* **worked** all this *wickedness* **evil**:
yet turn not aside from *following the LORD* **after Yah Veh**,
but serve *the LORD* **Yah Veh** with all your heart;
21 And turn ye not aside:
for then should ye go after *vain things* **wasteness**,
which cannot *profit* **benefit** nor *deliver* **rescue**;
for they are *vain* **waste**.
22 For *the LORD* **Yah Veh**
will **shall** not *forsake* **abandon** his people
for his great name's sake:
because *it hath pleased the LORD* **Yah Veh hath willed**
to *make* **work** you his people.
23 Moreover as for me,
God forbid **Far be it**
that I should sin against *the LORD* **Yah Veh**
in ceasing to pray for you:
but I *will teach* **shall direct** you
the good and the *right* **straight** way:
24 Only *fear the LORD* **awe Yah Veh**,
and serve him in truth with all your heart:
for *consider* **see** how great *things* he hath done for you.
25 But if **in vilifying**, ye shall *still do wickedly* **vilify**,
ye shall be *consumed* **scraped away**,
both ye and your *king* **sovereign**.

WAR WITH THE PELESHETHIY

13 *Saul reigned one year*
Shaul was a son of a year in his reigning;
and when he had reigned two years over *Israel* **Yisra El**,
2 *Saul* **Shaul** chose him
three thousand *men* of *Israel* **Yisra El**;
whereof two thousand were with *Saul* **Shaul** in Michmash
and in mount *Bethel* **Beth El**,
and a thousand were with *Jonathan* **Yah Nathan**
in *Gibeah* **Gibah** of *Benjamin* **Ben Yamin**:
and the rest of the people he sent every man to his tent.
3 And *Jonathan* **Yah Nathan** smote the *garrison* **station**
of the *Philistines* **Peleshethiy** that was in Geba,
and the *Philistines* **Peleshethiy** heard of it.
And *Saul blew* **Shaul blast** the trumpet
throughout all the land, saying,
Let the Hebrews hear.
4 And all *Israel* **Yisra El** heard say
that *Saul* **Shaul** had smitten
a *garrison* **station** of the *Philistines* **Peleshethiy**,
and that *Israel* **Yisra El** also *was had in abomination* **stank**
with the *Philistines* **Peleshethiy**.
And the people were *called together* **summoned**
after *Saul* **Shaul** to Gilgal.
5 And the *Philistines* **Peleshethiy**
gathered *themselves together* to fight with *Israel* **Yisra El**,
thirty thousand chariots,
and six thousand *horsemen* **cavalry**,
and people as the sand which is on the sea *shore* **lip**
in *multitude* **abundance**:
and they *came up* **ascended**,

and *pitched* **encamped** in Michmash,
eastward from *Bethaven* **Beth Aven**.
6 When the men of *Israel* **Yisra El**
saw that they were *in a strait* **tribulated**,
(for the people were *distressed* **exacted**,)
then the people did hide themselves in caves,
and in *thickets* **crevices**, and in rocks,
and in *high places* **towers**, and in *pits* **wells**.
7 And *some of* the Hebrews
went **passed** over *Jordan* **Yarden**
to the land of Gad and *Gilead* **Gilad**.
As for *Saul* **Shaul**, he was yet in Gilgal,
and all the people *followed* **trembled after** him *trembling*.
8 And he *tarried* **waited** seven days
according to the *set time* **season**
that Samuel had appointed **with Shemu El**:
but *Samuel* **Shemu El** came not to Gilgal;
and the people were scattered from him.
9 And *Saul* **Shaul** said,
Bring *hither* **near** a *burnt offering* **holocaust** to me,
and *peace offerings* **shelamim**.
And he *offered* **holocausted** the *burnt offering* **holocaust**.
10 And it *came to pass* **became**,
that as soon as he had *made an end of* **finished**
offering **holocausting** the *burnt offering* **holocaust**,
behold, *Samuel* **Shemu El** came;
and *Saul* **Shaul** went out to meet him,
that he might *salute* **bless** him.
11 And *Samuel* **Shemu El** said,
What hast thou *done* **worked**?
And *Saul* **Shaul** said,
Because I saw that the people were scattered from me,
and that thou camest not
within the *days appointed* **season of days**,
and that the *Philistines* **Peleshethiy**
gathered themselves *together* at Michmash;
12 Therefore said I, The *Philistines* **Peleshethiy**
will come down **shall descend** now upon me to Gilgal,
and I have not
made supplication **stroked the face**
unto the LORD **of Yah Veh**:
I *forced* **restrained** myself *therefore*,
and *offered* **holocausted** a *burnt offering* **holocaust**.
13 And *Samuel* **Shemu El** said to *Saul* **Shaul**,
Thou hast *done foolishly* **follied**:
thou hast not *kept* **guarded** the *commandment* **misvah**
of *the LORD* **Yah Veh** thy *God* **Elohim**,
which he *commanded* **misvahed** thee:
for now *would the LORD* **should Yah Veh**
have established thy *kingdom* **sovereigndom**
upon *Israel for ever* **Yisra El eternally**.
14 But now thy *kingdom* **sovereigndom**
shall not *continue* **rise**:
the LORD **Yah Veh**
hath sought him a man after his own heart,
and *the LORD* **Yah Veh** hath *commanded* **misvahed** him
to be captain **eminence** over his people,
because thou hast not *kept* **guarded** that
which *the LORD commanded* **Yah Veh misvahed** thee.
15 And *Samuel* **Shemu El** arose,
and *gat* **ascended** him *up* from Gilgal
unto *Gibeah* **Gibah** of *Benjamin* **Ben Yamin**.
And *Saul numbered* **Shaul mustered** the people
that were *present* **found** with him, about six hundred men.
16 And *Saul* **Shaul**, and *Jonathan* **Yah Nathan** his son,
and the people that were *present* **found** with them,
abode **settled** in *Gibeah* **Gibah** of *Benjamin* **Ben Yamin**:
but the *Philistines* **Peleshethiy** encamped in Michmash.
17 And *the spoilers came* **ruiners went** out of the camp
of the *Philistines* **Peleshethiy** in three *companies* **heads**:
one *company* **head** turned to **face**
unto the way *that leadeth* to Ophrah,
unto the land of Shual:
18 And *another company* **one head** turned to **face**
the way to *Bethhoron* **Beth Horon**:
and *another company* **one head** turned to **face**
the way of the border
that looketh to the valley of *Zeboim* **Seboim**
toward the wilderness.
19 Now there was no *smith* **artificer** found
throughout all the land of *Israel* **Yisra El**:
for the *Philistines* **Peleshethiy** said,
Lest the Hebrews *make* **work** *them* swords or spears:
20 But all the *Israelites* **Yisra Eliy**
went down **descended** to the *Philistines* **Peleshethiy**,
to sharpen every man his share,
and his *coulter* **plowshare**,
and his ax, and his *mattock* **pick**.
21 Yet they had a file **with mouths** for the mattocks,
and for the *coulters* **plowshares**, and for the **triple** forks,
and for the axes, and to *sharpen* **station** the goads.
22 So it *came to pass* **became,** in the day of *battle* **war**,
that there was neither sword nor spear
found in the hand of any of the people
that were with *Saul* **Shaul** and *Jonathan* **Yah Nathan**:
but with *Saul* **Shaul** and with *Jonathan* **Yah Nathan** his son
was there found.
23 And the *garrison* **standing camp**
of the *Philistines* **Peleshethiy**
went out to the passage of Michmash.

YAH NATHAN'S VICTORY

14 Now it *came to pass* **became,** upon a day,
that *Jonathan* **Yah Nathan** the son of *Saul* **Shaul** said
unto the *young man* **lad** that bare his *armour* **instruments**,
Come, and let us *go* **pass** over
to the *Philistines' garrison* **Peleshethiy's standing camp**,
that is *on the other side* **beyond this**.
But he told not his father.
2 And *Saul tarried* **Shaul settled**
in the *uttermost part* **extremity** of *Gibeah* **Gibah**
under a pomegranate tree which is in Migron:
and the people that were with him
were about six hundred men;
3 And *Ahiah* **Achiy Yah**, the son of *Ahitub* **Achiy Tub**,
Ichabod's **Iy Chabod's** brother,
the son of *Phinehas* **Pinechas**, the son of Eli,
the LORD'S **Yah Veh's** priest in Shiloh,
wearing **bearing** an ephod.
And the people knew not
that *Jonathan* **Yah Nathan** was gone.
4 And between the passages,
by which *Jonathan* **Yah Nathan** sought to *go* **pass** over
unto the *Philistines' garrison* **Peleshethiy's standing camp**,
there was a *sharp* **tooth of the** rock on the one side,
and a *sharp* **tooth of the** rock on the *other* **one** side:
and the name of the one was *Bozez* **Boses**
and the name of the *other* **one** Seneh.
5 The *forefront* **tooth** of the one
was *situate* **pillared** northward
over against **opposite** Michmash,
and the *other* **one** southward
over against Gibeah **opposite Gibah**.
6 And *Jonathan* **Yah Nathan** said
to the *young man* **lad** that bare his *armour* **instruments**,
Come, and let us *go* **pass** over
unto the *garrison* **standing camp** of these uncircumcised:
it may be **perhaps**
that the LORD will **Yah Veh shall** work for us:
for there is no *restraint* **hindrance** to *the LORD* **Yah Veh**
to save by many or by few.
7 And his *armourbearer* **instrument bearer** said unto him,
Do **Work** all that is in thine heart:
turn thee **stretch**; behold,
I am with thee according to thy heart.
8 Then said *Jonathan* **Yah Nathan**,
Behold, we *will* **shall** pass over unto these men,
and *we will discover* **shall expose** *ourselves* unto them.
9 If they say thus unto us,
Tarry **Be still** until we *come to* **touch** you;
then we *will* **shall** stand still in our place,
and *will* **shall** not *go up* **ascend** unto them.
10 But if they say thus, *Come up* **Ascend** unto us;
then we *will go up* **shall ascend**:
for *the LORD* **Yah Veh**
hath *delivered* **given** them into our hand:
and this shall be a sign unto us.
11 And both of them *discovered* **exposed** *themselves*
unto the *garrison* **standing camp**
of the *Philistines* **Peleshethiy**:
and the *Philistines* **Peleshethiy** said, Behold,

the Hebrews *come forth* **go** out of the holes
where they had hid themselves.
12 And the men of the *garrison* **station**
answered *Jonathan* **Yah Nathan**
and his *armourbearer* **instrument bearer**, and said,
Come up **Ascend** to us, and we
will shew you a thing **shall have you know a word**.
And *Jonathan* **Yah Nathan** said
unto his *armourbearer* **instrument bearer**,
Come up **Ascend** after me:
for *the LORD* **Yah Veh** hath *delivered* **given** them
into the hand of *Israel* **Yisra El**.
13 And *Jonathan* **Yah Nathan**
climbed up **ascended** upon his hands and upon his feet,
and his *armourbearer* **instrument bearer** after him:
and they fell *before Jonathan* **at the face of Yah Nathan**;
and his *armourbearer* **instrument bearer**
slew **deathified** after him.
14 And that first *slaughter* **stroke**,
which *Jonathan* **Yah Nathan**
and his *armourbearer made* **instrument bearer smote**,
was about twenty men,
within as it were an half **furrow of an** acre of *land* **field**,
which **of** a yoke *of oxen might plow*.
15 And there was trembling in the *host* **camp**,
in the field, and among all the people:
the *garrison* **standing camp**, and the *spoilers* **ruiners**,
they also trembled, and the earth quaked:
so it was a *very great* trembling **of Elohim**.
16 And the *watchmen* **watchers** of *Saul* **Shaul**
in *Gibeah* **Gibah** of *Benjamin looked* **Ben Yamin saw**;
and, behold, the multitude melted away, and they went on
beating down one another **descending and hammering**.
17 Then said *Saul* **Shaul**
unto the people that were with him,
Number **Muster** now, and see who is gone from us.
And when they had *numbered* **mustered**, behold,
Jonathan **Yah Nathan**
and his *armourbearer* **instrument bearer** were not *there*.
18 And *Saul* **Shaul** said unto *Ahiah* **Achiy Yah**,
Bring *hither* **near** the ark of *God* **Elohim**.
For the ark of *God* **Elohim** was at that *time* **day**
with the *children* **sons** of *Israel* **Yisra El**.
19 And it *came to pass* **became**,
while *Saul talked* **Shaul worded** unto the priest,
that the *noise* **multitude**
that was in the *host* **camp** of the *Philistines* **Peleshethiy**
went **in walking, walked** on and *increased* **greatened**:
and *Saul* **Shaul** said unto the priest,
Withdraw **Gather away** thine hand.
20 And *Saul* **Shaul** and all the people that were with him
assembled themselves **cried out together**,
and they came to the *battle* **war**: and, behold,
every man's sword was against his *fellow* **friend**,
and there was a *very* **mighty** great *discomfiture* **confusion**.
21 Moreover
the Hebrews that were with the *Philistines* **Peleshethiy**
before that time **three yesters ago**,
which *went up* **ascended** with them into the camp
from the country round about,
even they also *turned to be* **became**
with the *Israelites* **Yisra Eliy**
that were with *Saul* **Shaul** and *Jonathan* **Yah Nathan**.
22 Likewise all the men of *Israel* **Yisra El**
which had hid themselves in mount *Ephraim* **Ephrayim**,
when they heard that the *Philistines* **Peleshethiy** fled,
even they also
followed hard **adhered** after them in the *battle* **war**.
23 So *the LORD* **Yah Veh** saved *Israel* **Yisra El** that day:
and the *battle* **war** passed over unto *Bethaven* **Beth Aven**.
24 And the men of *Israel* **Yisra El**
were distressed **exacted** that day:
for *Saul* **Shaul** had *adjured* **oathed** the people, saying,
Cursed be the man
that eateth *any food* **bread** until evening,
that I may be avenged on mine enemies.
So none of the people tasted *any food* **bread**.
25 And all *they of* the land came to a *wood* **forest**;
and there was honey upon the *ground* **face of the field**.
26 And when the people were come into the *wood* **forest**,
behold, *the honey dropped* **a flowing of honey**;
but no man *put* **reached** his hand to his mouth:
for the people *feared* **awed** the oath.
27 But *Jonathan* **Yah Nathan** heard not
when his father *charged* **oathed** the people with the oath:
wherefore
he *put* **sent** forth the end of the rod that was in his hand,
and dipped it in an *honeycomb* **forest**,
and *put* **returned** his hand to his mouth;
and his eyes were enlightened.
28 Then answered *one* **a man** of the people, and said,
In oathing,
Thy father *straitly charged* **oathed** the people with an oath,
saying, Cursed be the man that eateth *any* food this day.
And the people were *faint* **fluttered**.
29 Then said *Jonathan* **Yah Nathan**,
My father hath troubled the land:
see, I *pray* **beseech** you,
how mine eyes have been enlightened,
because I tasted a little of this honey.
30 *How much more* **Also**, if *haply* **only** the people
in eating, had eaten *freely* to day
of the spoil of their enemies which they found?
for had there not been now a much greater slaughter
for now, hath not the stroke greatened
among the *Philistines* **Peleshethiy**?
31 And they smote the *Philistines* **Peleshethiy** that day
from Michmash to *Aijalon* **Ayalon**:
and the people were *very faint* **mighty fluttered**.
32 And the people *flew* **worked** upon the spoil,
and took *sheep* **flock**, and oxen, and *calves* **sons of oxen**,
and *slew* **slaughtered** them on the *ground* **earth**:
and the people did eat them with the blood.
33 Then they told *Saul* **Shaul**, saying, Behold,
the people sin against *the LORD* **Yah Veh**,
in that they eat with the blood.
And he said, Ye have *transgressed* **concealed**:
roll a great stone unto me this day.
34 And *Saul* **Shaul** said,
Disperse **Scatter** yourselves among the people,
and say unto them,
Bring me *hither* **near** every man his ox,
and every man his *sheep* **lamb**,
and *slay* **slaughter** *them* here, and eat;
and sin not against *the LORD* **Yah Veh**
in eating with the blood.
And all the people brought **near**
every man his ox *with him* **in his hand** that night,
and *slew* **slaughtered** *them* there.
35 And *Saul* **Shaul** built *an* **a sacrifice** altar
unto *the LORD* **Yah Veh**:
the same was the first **he began to build the sacrifice** altar
that he built unto *the LORD* **Yah Veh**.
36 And *Saul* **Shaul** said,
Let us *go down* **descend** after the *Philistines* **Peleshethiy**
by night,
and *spoil* **plunder** them until the morning light,
and let us not *leave* **survive** a man of them.
And they said,
Do **Work** whatsoever seemeth good
unto thee **in thine eyes**.
Then said the priest,
Let us *draw near* **approach** hither unto *God* **Elohim**.
37 And *Saul* **Shaul** asked counsel of *God* **Elohim**,
shall I *go down* **descend** after the *Philistines* **Peleshethiy**?
wilt **shalt** thou *deliver* **give** them
into the hand of *Israel* **Yisra El**?
But he answered him not that day.
38 And *Saul* **Shaul** said,
Draw ye near hither, all the chief of the people:
and know and see wherein this sin hath been this day.
39 For, *as the LORD* **Yah Veh** liveth,
which saveth *Israel* **Yisra El**,
though it be in *Jonathan* **Yah Nathan** my son,
in dying, he shall *surely* die.
But there was not a man among all the people
that answered him.
40 Then said he unto all *Israel* **Yisra El**,
Be ye on one side,
and I and *Jonathan* **Yah Nathan** my son

will **shall** be on *the other* **one** side.
And the people said unto *Saul* **Shaul**,
Do **Work** what seemeth good *unto thee* **in thine eyes**.
41 Therefore *Saul* **Shaul** said
unto *the LORD God* **Yah Veh Elohim** of *Israel* **Yisra El**,
Give a perfect lot **Show integrity**.
And *Saul* **Shaul** and *Jonathan* **Yah Nathan**
were *taken* **captured**:
but the people *escaped* **went**.
42 And *Saul* **Shaul** said,
Cast lots **Fell** between me
and *Jonathan* **Yah Nathan** my son.
And *Jonathan* **Yah Nathan** was *taken* **captured**.
43 Then *Saul* **Shaul** said to *Jonathan* **Yah Nathan**,
Tell me what thou hast *done* **worked**.
And *Jonathan* **Yah Nathan** told him, and said,
I did but taste **In tasting, I tasted** a little honey
with the end of the rod that was in mine hand,
and, lo **behold**, I must die.
44 And *Saul answered* **Shaul said**,
God do so and more **Elohim work thus and add** also:
for **in dying,** thou shalt *surely* die, *Jonathan* **Yah Nathan**.
45 And the people said unto *Saul* **Shaul**,
shall *Jonathan* **Yah Nathan** die,
who hath *wrought* **worked** this great salvation
in *Israel* **Yisra El**?
God forbid **Far be it**: *as the LORD* — **Yah Veh** liveth,
there shall not one hair of his head
fall to the *ground* **earth**;
for he hath *wrought* **worked** with *God* **Elohim** this day.
So the people *rescued Jonathan* **redeemed Yah Nathan**,
that he died not.
46 Then *Saul went up* **Shaul ascended**
from *following* **after** the *Philistines* **Peleshethiy**:
and the *Philistines* **Peleshethiy** went to their own place.
47 So *Saul* **Shaul**
took **captured** the *kingdom* **sovereigndom**
over *Israel* **Yisra El**,
and fought against all his enemies
on every side **round about**,
against Moab,
and against the *children* **sons** of Ammon,
and against Edom,
and against the *kings* **sovereigns** of *Zobah* **Sobah**,
and against the *Philistines* **Peleshethiy**:
and whithersoever he turned *himself* **his face**,
he *vexed them* **dealt wickedly**.
48 And he *gathered an host* **worked valour**,
and smote the *Amalekites* **Amaleq**,
and *delivered Israel* **rescued Yisra El**
out of the hands of them that *spoiled* **plundered** them.
49 Now the sons of *Saul* **Shaul** were *Jonathan* **Yah Nathan**,
and *Ishui* **Yishvi**, and *Melchishua* **Malki Shua**:
and the names of his two daughters were these;
the name of the firstborn Merab,
and the name of the younger Michal:
50 And the name of *Saul's wife* **Shaul's woman**
was *Ahinoam* **Achiy Noam**,
the daughter of *Ahimaaz* **Achiy Maas**:
and the name of the *captain* **governor** of his host
was *Abner* **Abi Ner**, the son of Ner, *Saul's* **Shaul's** uncle.
51 And *Kish* **Qish** was the father of *Saul* **Shaul**;
and Ner the father of *Abner* **Abi Ner**
was the son of *Abiel* **Abi El**.
52 And there was *sore* **tough** war
against the *Philistines* **Peleshethiy**
all the days of *Saul* **Shaul**:
and when *Saul* **Shaul** saw any *strong* **mighty** man,
or any *valiant man* **son of valour**,
he *took* **gathered** him unto him.

YAH VEH REJECTS SHAUL AS SOVEREIGN

15 *Samuel* **Shemu El** also said unto *Saul* **Shaul**,
The LORD **Yah Veh** sent me to anoint thee
to be *king* **sovereign** over his people, over *Israel* **Yisra El**:
now therefore hearken thou unto the voice
of the words of *the LORD* **Yah Veh**.
2 Thus saith *the LORD of hosts* **Yah Veh Sabaoth**,
I remember **visit** that
which *Amalek did* **Amaleq worked** to *Israel* **Yisra El**,
how he *laid wait* **set** for him in the way,
when he *came up* **ascended** from *Egypt* **Misrayim**.
3 Now go and smite *Amalek* **Amaleq**,
and *utterly destroy* **devote** all that they have,
and spare them not;
but slay **deathify** both man and woman,
infant and suckling **from suckling and infant**,
ox and *sheep* **lamb**, camel and *ass* **he burro**.
4 And *Saul gathered* **Shaul heard** the people *together*,
and *numbered* **mustered** them in Telaim,
two hundred thousand *footmen* **on foot**,
and ten thousand men of *Judah* **Yah Hudah**.
5 And *Saul* **Shaul** came to a city of *Amalek* **Amaleq**,
and *laid wait* **lurked** in the *valley* **wadi**.
6 And *Saul* **Shaul** said unto the *Kenites* **Qayiniy**,
Go, *depart* **turn aside**, *get you down* **descend ye**
from among the *Amalekites* **Amaleq**,
lest I *destroy* **gather** you with them:
for ye *shewed kindness* **worked mercy**
to all the *children* **sons** of *Israel* **Yisra El**,
when they *came up* **ascended** out of *Egypt* **Misrayim**.
So the *Kenites departed* **Qayiniy turned aside**
from among the *Amalekites* **Amaleq**.
7 And *Saul* **Shaul** smote the *Amalekites* **Amaleq**
from Havilah until thou comest to Shur,
that is *over against Egypt* **at the face of Misrayim**.
8 And he *took* **apprehended** Agag
the *king* **sovereign** of the *Amalekites* **Amaleq** alive,
and *utterly destroyed* **devoted** all the people
with the *edge* **mouth** of the sword.
9 But *Saul* **Shaul** and the people spared Agag,
and the best of the *sheep* **flock**, and of the oxen,
and of the *fatlings* **second sort**, and the *lambs* **rams**,
and all that was good,
and *would* **willed to** not *utterly destroy* **devote** them:
but *every thing* **all** that was vile and *refuse* **molten**,
that they *destroyed utterly* **devoted**.
10 Then came the word of *the LORD* **Yah Veh**
unto *Samuel* **Shemu El**, saying,
11 *It repenteth me* **I sigh**
that I have *set up Saul to be king* **Shaul to reign sovereign**:
for he is turned back from *following* **after** me,
and hath not *performed* **raised** my *commandments* **words**.
And it *grieved Samuel* **inflamed Shemu El**;
and he cried unto *the LORD* **Yah Veh** all night.
12 And when *Samuel rose* **Shemu El started** early
to meet *Saul* **Shaul** in the morning,
it was told *Samuel* **Shemu El**, saying,
Saul **Shaul** came to *Carmel* **Karmel**, and, behold,
he *set him up a place* **stationed him a hand**,
and is gone about, and passed on,
and *gone down* **descended** to Gilgal.
13 And *Samuel* **Shemu El** came to *Saul* **Shaul**:
and *Saul* **Shaul** said unto him,
Blessed be thou of *the LORD* **Yah Veh**:
I have *performed* **raised**
the *commandment* **word** of *the LORD* **Yah Veh**.
14 And *Samuel* **Shemu El** said, What *meaneth* then
this *bleating* **voice** of the *sheep* **flock** in mine ears,
and the *lowing* **voice** of the oxen which I hear?
15 And *Saul* **Shaul** said,
They have brought them from the *Amalekites* **Amaleqiy**:
for the people spared
the best of the *sheep* **flock** and of the oxen,
to sacrifice unto *the LORD* **Yah Veh** thy *God* **Elohim**;
and the *rest* **remainder** we have *utterly destroyed* **devoted**.
16 Then *Samuel* **Shemu El** said unto *Saul* **Shaul**,
Stay **Loosen up**, and I *will* **shall** tell thee
what *the LORD* **Yah Veh**
hath *said* **worded** to me this night.
And he said unto him, *Say on* **Word**.
17 And *Samuel* **Shemu El** said,
When thou wast little in thine own *sight* **eyes**,
wast thou not *made* the head
of the *tribes* **scions** of *Israel* **Yisra El**,
and *the LORD* **Yah Veh** anointed thee *king* **sovereign**
over *Israel* **Yisra El**?
18 And *the LORD* **Yah Veh** sent thee on a journey,
and said,
Go and *utterly destroy* **devote**
the sinners the *Amalekites* **Amaleq**,

and fight against them
until they be *consumed* **finished off**.
19 Wherefore then didst thou not
obey **hear** the voice of *the LORD* **Yah Veh**,
but didst *fly* **swoop** upon the spoil,
and *didst* **workest** evil
in the *sight* **eyes** of *the LORD* **Yah Veh**?
20 And *Saul* **Shaul** said unto *Samuel* **Shemu El**,
Yea, I have *obeyed* **heard** the voice of *the LORD* **Yah Veh**,
and *have gone* **went** the way
which *the LORD* **Yah Veh** sent me,
and have brought Agag
the *king* **sovereign** of *Amalek* **Amaleq**,
and have *utterly destroyed* **devoted**
the Amalekites **Amaleq**.
21 But the people took of the spoil, *sheep* **flock** and oxen,
the *chief of the things* **firstlings**
which should have been *utterly destroyed* **devoted**,
to sacrifice unto *the LORD* **Yah Veh** thy *God* **Elohim**
in Gilgal.
22 And *Samuel* **Shemu El** said,
Hath *the LORD as great* **Yah Veh** delight
in *burnt offerings* **holocausts** and sacrifices,
as in *obeying* **hearing** the voice of *the LORD* **Yah Veh**?
Behold, to *obey* **hear** is better than sacrifice,
and to hearken than the fat of rams.
23 For rebellion
is *as* the sin of *witchcraft* **divination**,
and stubbornness
is *as iniquity* **mischief** and *idolatry* **teraphim**.
Because thou hast *rejected* **refused**
the word of *the LORD* **Yah Veh**,
he hath also *rejected* **refused** thee
from being *king* **sovereign**.
24 And *Saul* **Shaul** said unto *Samuel* **Shemu El**,
I have sinned: for I have *transgressed* **trespassed**
the *commandment* **mouth** of *the LORD* **Yah Veh**,
and thy words:
because I *feared* **awed** the people,
and *obeyed* **heard** their voice.
25 Now therefore, I *pray* **beseech** thee, *pardon* **lift** my sin,
and turn *again* **back** with me,
that I may *worship the LORD* **prostrate to Yah Veh**.
26 And *Samuel* **Shemu El** said unto *Saul* **Shaul**,
I *will* **shall** not return with thee:
for thou hast *rejected* **refused**
the word of *the LORD* **Yah Veh**,
and *the LORD* **Yah Veh** hath *rejected* **refused** thee
from being *king* **sovereign** over *Israel* **Yisra El**.
27 And as *Samuel* **Shemu El** turned about to go away,
he laid hold upon the *skirt* **borders** of his mantle,
and it *rent* **ripped**.
28 And *Samuel* **Shemu El** said unto him,
The LORD **Yah Veh** hath *rent* **ripped**
the *kingdom* **sovereigndom** of *Israel* **Yisra El**
from thee this day,
and hath given it to a *neighbour* **friend** of thine,
that is better than thou.
29 And also the *Strength* **Perpetuity** of *Israel* **Yisra El**
will **shall** not *lie* **falsify** nor *repent* **sigh**:
for he is not a *man* **human**, that he should *repent* **sigh**.
30 Then he said, I have sinned:
yet honour me now, I *pray* **beseech** thee,
before the elders of my people, and before *Israel* **Yisra El**,
and turn *again* **back** with me,
that I may *worship* **prostrate**
the LORD **to Yah Veh** thy *God* **Elohim**.
31 So *Samuel* **Shemu El** turned *again* **back** after *Saul* **Shaul**;
and *Saul* **Shaul**
worshipped the LORD **prostrated to Yah Veh**.
32 Then said *Samuel* **Shemu El**,
Bring ye *hither* **near** to me Agag
the *king* **sovereign** of the *Amalekites* **Amaleq**.
And Agag came unto him delicately.
And Agag said,
Surely the bitterness of death is *past* **turned aside**.
33 And *Samuel* **Shemu El** said,
As the sword hath *made* **bereaved** women *childless*,
so shall thy mother be *childless* **bereft** among women.
And *Samuel hewed* **Shemu El cleaved** Agag in pieces
before the LORD **at the face of Yah Veh** in Gilgal.
34 Then *Samuel* **Shemu El** went to Ramah;
and *Saul went up* **Shaul ascended** to his house
to *Gibeah* **Gibah** of *Saul* **Shaul**.
35 And *Samuel* **Shemu El**
came no more **added not** to see *Saul* **Shaul**
until the day of his death:
nevertheless Samuel **surely Shemu El**
mourned for *Saul* **Shaul**:
and *the LORD repented* **Yah Veh sighed**
that he had *made Saul king* **Shaul reign**
over *Israel* **Yisra El**.

SHEMU EL IN BETH LECHEM

16 And *the LORD* **Yah Veh** said unto *Samuel* **Shemu El**,
How long *wilt* **shalt** thou mourn for *Saul* **Shaul**,
seeing I have *rejected* **refused** him
from reigning over *Israel* **Yisra El**?
fill thine horn with oil, and go,
I *will* **shall** send thee to *Jesse* **Yishay**
the *Bethlehemite* **Beth Lechemiy**:
for I have *provided* **seen** me
a *king* **sovereign** among his sons.
2 And *Samuel* **Shemu El** said, How *can* **shall** I go?
if *Saul* **Shaul** hear *it*, he *will kill* **shall slaughter** me.
And *the LORD* **Yah Veh** said,
Take an heifer *with thee* **of the ox in thy hand**, and say,
I am come to sacrifice to *the LORD* **Yah Veh**.
3 And call *Jesse* **Yishay** to the sacrifice,
and I *will shew thee* **shall have thee know**
what thou shalt *do* **work**:
and thou shalt anoint unto me
him whom I *name* **say** unto thee.
4 And *Samuel did* **Shemu El worked**
that which *the LORD spake* **Yah Veh worded**,
and came to *Bethlehem* **Beth Lechem**.
And the elders of the *town* **city**
trembled *at his coming* **to meet him**, and said,
Comest thou *peaceably* **in shalom**?
5 And he said, *Peaceably* **In shalom**:
I am come to sacrifice unto *the LORD* **Yah Veh**:
sanctify **hallow** yourselves,
and come with me to the sacrifice.
And he *sanctified Jesse* **hallowed Yishay** and his sons,
and called them to the sacrifice.
6 And it *came to pass* **became**, when they were come,
that he *looked on Eliab* **saw Eli Ab**, and said,
Surely *the LORD'S* **Yah Veh's** anointed is before him.
7 But *the LORD* **Yah Veh** said unto *Samuel* **Shemu El**,
Look not on his *countenance* **visage**,
or on the height of his *stature* **height**;
because I have refused him:
for the LORD seeth — not as *man* **humanity** seeth;
for *man* **humanity**
looketh on **seeth** the *outward appearance* **eyes**,
but *the LORD looketh on* **Yah Veh seeth** the heart.
8 Then *Jesse* **Yishay** called *Abinadab* **Abi Nadab**,
and made him pass
before Samuel **at the face of Shemu El**.
And he said, Neither hath *the LORD* **Yah Veh** chosen this.
9 Then *Jesse* **Yishay** made Shammah to pass by.
And he said, Neither hath *the LORD* **Yah Veh** chosen this.
10 Again, *Jesse* **Yishay** made seven of his sons
to pass *before Samuel* **at the face of Shemu El**.
And *Samuel* **Shemu El** said unto *Jesse* **Yishay**,
The LORD **Yah Veh** hath not chosen these.
11 And *Samuel* **Shemu El** said unto *Jesse* **Yishay**,
Are here all thy *children* **integrious lads**?
And he said, There *remaineth* **surviveth** yet the youngest,
and, behold, he *keepeth* **tendeth** the *sheep* **flock**.
And *Samuel* **Shemu El** said unto *Jesse* **Yishay**,
Send and *fetch* **take** him:
for we *will* **shall** not *sit down* **turn around**
till he come hither.

DAVID ANOINTED

12 And he sent, and brought him in. Now he was ruddy,
and withal of *a* beautiful *countenance* **eyes**,
and goodly to *look to* **see**.
And *the LORD* **Yah Veh** said, Arise, anoint him:
for this is he.
13 Then *Samuel* **Shemu El** took the horn of oil,

and anointed him in the midst of his brethren:
and the Spirit of *the LORD* **Yah Veh**
came **prospered** upon David
from that day *forward* **onward.**
So *Samuel* **Shemu El** rose up, and went to Ramah.

AN EVIL SPIRIT FROM YAH VEH

14 But the Spirit of *the LORD* **Yah Veh**
departed **turned aside** from *Saul* **Shaul**,
and an evil spirit from *the LORD* **Yah Veh**
troubled **frightened** him.
15 And *Saul's* **Shaul's** servants said unto him, Behold now,
an evil spirit from *God troubleth* **Elohim frighteneth** thee.
16 Let our *lord* **adoni** now *command* **say to** thy servants,
which are *before thee* **at thy face**, to seek out a man,
who is a cunning player **a knowing strummer** on an harp:
and it shall *come to pass* **become**,
when the evil spirit from *God* **Elohim** is upon thee,
that he shall *play* **strum** with his hand,
and thou shalt be *well* **good**.
17 And *Saul* **Shaul** said unto his servants,
Provide **See** me now a man
that can play well **well—prepared and a good strummer**,
and bring him to me.
18 Then answered one of the *servants* **lads**,
and said, Behold,
I have seen a son of *Jesse* **Yishay**
the *Bethlehemite* **Beth Lechemiy**,
that is cunning in playing **a knowledgeable strummer**,
and a mighty valiant *man*, and a man of war,
and *prudent* **discerning** in *matters* **words**,
and a *comely person* **man of form**,
and *the LORD* **Yah Veh** is with him.
19 Wherefore *Saul* **Shaul**
sent *messengers* **angels** unto *Jesse* **Yishay**, and said,
Send me David thy son, which is with the *sheep* **flock**.
20 And *Jesse* **Yishay** took *an ass laden* **a he burro**
with bread, and a *bottle* **skin** of wine,
and *a kid* **one doe goat**,
and sent them by **the hand of** David his son
unto *Saul* **Shaul**.
21 And David came to *Saul* **Shaul**,
and stood *before him* **at his face**:
and he loved him *greatly* **mightily**;
and he became his *armourbearer* **instrument bearer**.
22 And *Saul* **Shaul** sent to *Jesse* **Yishay**, saying,
Let David, I *pray* **beseech** thee,
stand *before me* **at my face**;
for he hath found *favour* **charism** in my *sight* **eyes**.
23 And it *came to pass* **became**,
when the *evil* spirit from *God* **Elohim**
was upon *Saul* **Shaul**,
that David took an harp,
and *played* **strummed** with his hand:
so *Saul was refreshed* **Shaul respired**, and was *well* **good**,
and the evil spirit *departed* **turned aside** from him.

DAVID AND GOLYATH

17 Now the *Philistines* **Peleshethiy**
gathered *together* their *armies* **camps** to *battle* **war**,
and were gathered *together* at *Shochoh* **Sochoh**,
which *belongeth* **be** to *Judah* **Yah Hudah**,
and *pitched* **encamped**
between *Shochoh* **Sochoh** and *Azekah* **Azeqah**,
in *Ephesdammim* **Ephes Dammim**.
2 And *Saul* **Shaul** and the men of *Israel* **Yisra El**
were gathered *together*,
and *pitched* **encamped** by the valley of Elah,
and *set the battle in array* **lined up for war**
against **to meet** the *Philistines* **Peleshethiy**.
3 And the *Philistines* **Peleshethiy** stood on a mountain
on *the one* **this** side,
and *Israel* **Yisra El** stood on a mountain
on *the other* **that** side:
and there was a valley between them.
4 And there went out a *champion* **man of double size**
out of the camp of the *Philistines* **Peleshethiy**,
named *Goliath* **Golyath**, of Gath,
whose height was six cubits and a span.
5 And he had an helmet of *brass* **copper** upon his head,
and he was *armed* **enrobed** with a *coat* **habergeon** of mail;
and the weight of the *coat* **habergeon**
was five thousand shekels of *brass* **copper**.
6 And he had *greaves* **shinguards** of *brass* **copper**
upon his *legs* **feet**,
and a *target* **dart** of *brass* **copper**
between his shoulders.
7 And the *staff* **timber** of his spear
was like a weaver's beam;
and his spear's *head weighed* **blade**
be six hundred shekels of iron:
and one bearing a shield
went *before* **at the face of** him.
8 And he stood and *cried* **called out**
unto the *armies* **ranks** of *Israel* **Yisra El**,
and said unto them,
Why are ye *come* **gone** *out*
to *set your battle in array* **line up for war**?
am not I a *Philistine* **Peleshethiy**,
and ye servants to *Saul* **Shaul**?
choose **cut** you a man for you,
and let him *come down* **descend** to me.
9 If he be able to fight with me, and to *kill* **smite** me,
then *will* **shall** we be your servants:
but if I prevail against him, and *kill* **smite** him,
then shall ye be our servants, and serve us.
10 And the *Philistine* **Peleshethiy** said,
I *defy* **reproach** the *armies* **ranks** of *Israel* **Yisra El** this day;
give me a man, that we may fight together.
11 When *Saul* **Shaul** and all *Israel* **Yisra El**
heard those words of the *Philistine* **Peleshethiy**,
they were *dismayed* **terrified**,
and *greatly afraid* **mighty awed**.
12 Now David was the son of **a man,**
that Ephrathite **— an Ephrathiy**
of *Bethlehemjudah* **Beth Lechem Yah Hudah**,
whose name was *Jesse* **Yishay**; and he had eight sons:
and the man went among men for an old man
in the days of *Saul* **Shaul**.
13 And the three *eldest* **greatest** sons of *Jesse* **Yishay** went
and *followed Saul* **went after Shaul** to the *battle* **war**:
and the names of his three sons
that went to the *battle* **war** were
Eliab **Eli Ab** the firstborn,
and *next unto him Abinadab* **second Abi Nadab**,
and the third Shammah.
14 And David was the youngest:
and the three *eldest* **greatest**
followed Saul **went after Shaul**.
15 But David went and returned from *Saul* **Shaul**
to *feed* **tend** his father's *sheep* **flock**
at *Bethlehem* **Beth Lechem**.
16 And the *Philistine* **Peleshethiy** drew near
morning **starting early** and evening,
and *presented* **set** himself forty days.
17 And *Jesse* **Yishay** said unto David his son,
Take now for thy brethren an ephah of this parched *corn*,
and these ten *loaves* **bread**,
and run to the camp of thy brethren;
18 And carry these ten *cheeses* **slices of milk**
unto the *captain* **governor** of their thousand,
and *look how* **visit** thy brethren *fare* **for shalom**,
and take their pledge.
19 Now *Saul* **Shaul**, and they,
and all the men of *Israel* **Yisra El**,
were in the valley of Elah,
fighting with the *Philistines* **Peleshethiy**.
20 And David *rose up* **started** early in the morning,
and left the *sheep* **flock** with a *keeper* **guard**,
and *took* **lifted**, and went,
as *Jesse* **Yishay** had *commanded* **misvahed** him;
and he came to the *trench* **route**,
as the *host* **valiant** was going forth to the *fight* **ranks**,
and shouted for the *battle* **war**.
21 For *Israel* **Yisra El** and the *Philistines* **Peleshethiy**
had *put the battle in array* **lined up**,
army against army **ranks meeting ranks**.
22 And David left his *carriage* **instrument**
in the hand of the *keeper* **guard** of the *carriage* **instrument**,
and ran into the *army* **ranks**,
and came and *saluted* **asked** his brethren **of shalom**.
23 And as he *talked* **worded** with them, behold,

there *came up* **ascended**
the *champion* **man of double size**,
the *Philistine* **Peleshethiy** of Gath,
Goliath **Golyath** by name,
out of the *armies* **ranks** of the *Philistines* **Peleshethiy**,
and *spake according to the same* **worded these words**:
and David heard them.
24 And all the men of *Israel* **Yisra El**,
when they saw the man,
fled from *him* **his face**,
and were *sore afraid* **mightily awed**.
25 And the men *of Israel* **— the Yisra Eliy** said,
Have ye seen this man that *is come up* **ascended**?
surely to *defy Israel* **reproach Yisra El**
is he *come up* **ascended**:
and it shall be, that the man who *killeth* **smiteth** him,
the *king will* **sovereign shall** enrich him with great riches,
and *will* **shall** give him his daughter,
and *make* **work** his father's house *free* **liberated**
in *Israel* **Yisra El**.
26 And David *spake* **said** to the men that stood by him,
saying, What shall be *done* **worked** to the man
that *killeth* **smiteth** this *Philistine* **Peleshethiy**,
and *taketh away* **turneth aside** the reproach
from *Israel* **Yisra El**?
for who is this uncircumcised *Philistine* **Peleshethiy**,
that he should *defy* **reproach** the *armies* **ranks**
of the living *God* **Elohim**?
27 And the people *answered* **said to** him
after this *manner* **word**, saying,
So **Thus** shall it be *done* **worked**
to the man that killeth him.
28 And *Eliab* **Eli Ab** his *eldest* **greatest** brother
heard when he *spake* **worded** unto the men;
and *Eliab's anger* **Eli Ab's wrath**
was kindled against David, and he said,
Why *camest* **descendest** thou *down* hither?
and with whom
hast thou left those few *sheep* **flock** in the wilderness?
I know thy *pride* **arrogance**,
and the *naughtiness* **evil** of thine heart;
for thou art *come down* **descended**
that thou mightest see the *battle* **war**.
29 And David said, What have I now *done* **worked**?
Is there not a *cause* **word**?
30 And he turned from **beside** him toward another,
and *spake* **said** after the same *manner* **word**:
and the people *answered him again* **returned word**
after the former *manner* **word**.
31 And when the words were heard
which David *spake* **worded**,
they *rehearsed* **told** them *before Saul* **at the face of Shaul**:
and he *sent for* **took** him.
32 And David said to *Saul* **Shaul**,
Let no *man's* **human's** heart *fail* **fall** because of him;
thy servant *will* **shall** go
and fight with this *Philistine* **Peleshethiy**.
33 And *Saul* **Shaul** said to David,
Thou art not able to go against this *Philistine* **Peleshethiy**
to fight with him:
for thou art *but* a *youth* **lad**,
and he a man of war from his youth.
34 And David said unto *Saul* **Shaul**,
Thy servant *kept* **was tending** his father's *sheep* **flock**,
and there came a lion, and a bear,
and *took* **lifted** a lamb out of the *flock* **drove**:
35 And I went out after him, and smote him,
and *delivered* **rescued** it out of his mouth:
and when he arose against me,
I *caught* **held** him by his beard,
and smote him, and *slew* **deathified** him.
36 Thy servant *slew* **smote** both the lion and the bear:
and this uncircumcised *Philistine* **Peleshethiy**
shall be as one of them,
seeing he hath *defied* **reproached** the *armies* **ranks**
of the living *God* **Elohim**.
37 David said moreover,
The LORD **Yah Veh** that *delivered* **rescued** me
out of the *paw* **hand** of the lion,
and out of the *paw* **hand** of the bear,
he *will deliver* **shall rescue** me
out of the hand of this *Philistine* **Peleshethiy**.
And *Saul* **Shaul** said unto David,
Go, and *the LORD* **Yah Veh** be with thee.
38 And *Saul armed* **Shaul enrobed** David
with his *armour* **uniform**,
and he *put* **gave** an helmet of *brass* **copper** upon his head;
also he *armed* **enrobed** him
with a *coat* **habergeon** of mail.
39 And David girded his sword upon his *armour* **uniform**,
and he *assayed* **willed** to go;
for he had not *proved* **tested** *it*.
And David said unto *Saul* **Shaul**, I cannot go with these;
for I have not *proved* **tested** them.
And David *put* **turned** them *off him* **aside**.
40 And he took his staff in his hand,
and chose him five smooth stones out of the *brook* **wadi**,
and *put* **set** them in a *shepherd's bag* **tender's instrument**
which he had, even in a *scrip* **pouch**;
and his sling was in his hand:
and he drew near to the *Philistine* **Peleshethiy**.
41 And **in walking,**
the *Philistine came* **Peleshethiy walked** on
and *drew near* **approached** unto David;
and the man that bare the shield
went before him **at his face**.
42 And when the *Philistine* **Peleshethiy** looked about,
and saw David, he *disdained* **despised** him:
for he was *but* a *youth* **lad**, and ruddy,
and of a *fair countenance* **handsome visage**.
43 And the *Philistine* **Peleshethiy** said unto David,
Am I a dog, that thou comest to me with staves?
And the *Philistine cursed* **Peleshethiy belittled** David
by his *gods* **elohim**.
44 And the *Philistine* **Peleshethiy** said to David,
Come to me, and I *will* **shall** give thy flesh
unto the *fowls* **flyers** of the *air* **heavens**,
and to the *beasts* **animals** of the field.
45 Then said David to the *Philistine* **Peleshethiy**,
Thou comest to me with a sword,
and with a spear, and with a *shield* **dart**:
but I come to thee
in the name of *the LORD of hosts* **Yah Veh Sabaoth**,
the *God* **Elohim** of the *armies* **ranks** of *Israel* **Yisra El**,
whom thou hast *defied* **reproached**.
46 This day *will the LORD* **shall Yah Veh**
deliver **shut** thee into mine hand;
and I *will* **shall** smite thee,
and *take* **turn aside** thine head from thee;
and I *will* **shall** give the carcases
of the *host* **camp** of the *Philistines* **Peleshethiy** this day
unto the *fowls* **flyers** of the *air* **heavens**,
and to the *wild beasts* **live beings** of the earth;
that all the earth may know
that there is *a God* **an Elohim** in *Israel* **Yisra El**.
47 And all this *assembly* **congregation** shall know
that *the LORD* **Yah Veh** saveth not with sword and spear:
for the *battle is the LORD'S* **war be Yah Veh's**,
and he *will* **shall** give you into our hands.
48 And it *came to pass* **became**,
when the *Philistine* **Peleshethiy** arose, and came,
and *drew nigh* **approached** to meet David,
that David hasted,
and ran toward the *army* **ranks**
to meet the *Philistine* **Peleshethiy**.
49 And David *put* **extended** his hand
in his *bag* **instrument**,
and took thence a stone, and slang it,
and smote the *Philistine* **Peleshethiy** in his forehead,
that the stone sunk into his forehead;
and he fell upon his face to the earth.
50 So David prevailed over the *Philistine* **Peleshethiy**
with a sling and with a stone,
and smote the *Philistine* **Peleshethiy**,
and *slew* **deathified** him;
but there was no sword in the hand of David.
51 Therefore David ran,
and stood upon the *Philistine* **Peleshethiy**,
and took his sword, and drew it out of the sheath thereof,
and *slew* **deathified** him, and cut off his head therewith.

And when the *Philistines* **Peleshethiy**
saw their *champion was dead* **mighty had died**, they fled.
52 And the men of *Israel* **Yisra El** and of *Judah* **Yah Hudah**
arose, and shouted,
and pursued the *Philistines* **Peleshethiy**,
until thou come to the valley,
and to the *gates* **portals** of *Ekron* **Eqron**.
And the *wounded* **pierced** of the *Philistines* **Peleshethiy**
fell down **descended** by the way to *Shaaraim* **Shaarayim**,
even unto Gath, and unto *Ekron* **Eqron**.
53 And the *children* **sons** of *Israel* **Yisra El** returned
from *chasing* **hotly pursuing**
after the *Philistines* **Peleshethiy**,
and they *spoiled* **plundered** their *tents* **camps**.
54 And David took the head of the *Philistine* **Peleshethiy**,
and brought it to *Jerusalem* **Yeru Shalem**;
but he *put* **set** his *armour* **instruments** in his tent.
55 And when *Saul* **Shaul** saw David go forth
against **to meet** the *Philistine* **Peleshethiy**,
he said unto *Abner* **Abi Ner**,
the *captain* **governor** of the host,
Abner **Abi Ner**, whose son is this *youth* **lad**?
And *Abner* **Abi Ner** said, *As* thy soul liveth,
O *king* **sovereign**, I *cannot tell* **know not**.
56 And the *king* **sovereign** said,
Enquire **Ask** thou whose son the *stripling* **lad** is.
57 And as David returned
from *the slaughter of* **smiting** the *Philistine* **Peleshethiy**,
Abner **Abi Ner** took him,
and brought him *before Saul* **at the face of Shaul**
with the head of the *Philistine* **Peleshethiy** in his hand.
58 And *Saul* **Shaul** said to him,
Whose son art thou, thou *young man* **lad**?
And David *answered* **said**,
I am the son of thy servant *Jesse* **Yishay**
the *Bethlehemite* **Beth Lechemiy**.

DAVID AND YAH NATHAN

18 And it *came to pass* **became**,
when he had *made an end of speaking* **finished wording**
unto *Saul* **Shaul**,
that the soul of *Jonathan* **Yah Nathan**
was *knit* **bound** with the soul of David,
and *Jonathan* **Yah Nathan** loved him as his own soul.
2 And *Saul* **Shaul** took him that day,
and *would let him go no more home*
gave him not to return to his father's house.
3 Then *Jonathan* **Yah Nathan** and David
made **cut** a covenant,
because he loved him as his own soul.
4 And *Jonathan* **Yah Nathan**
stripped himself of the *robe* **mantle** that was upon him,
and gave it to David, and his *garments* **uniform**,
even to his sword, and to his bow, and to his girdle.
5 And David went out whithersoever *Saul* **Shaul** sent him,
and *behaved himself wisely* **comprehended**:
and *Saul* **Shaul** set him over the men of war,
and he was *accepted* **well—pleasing**
in the *sight* **eyes** of all the people,
and also in the *sight* **eyes** of *Saul's* **Shaul's** servants.
6 And it *came to pass* **became**, as they came,
when David was returned
from *the slaughter of* **smiting** the *Philistine* **Peleshethiy**,
that the women
came **went** out of all cities of *Israel* **Yisra El**,
singing and **round** dancing,
to meet *king Saul* **sovereign Shaul**,
with *tabrets* **tambourines**, with *joy* **cheer**,
and with *instruments of musick* **triangles**.
7 And the women answered *one another*
as they *played* **entertained**, and said,
Saul **Shaul** hath *slain* **smitten** his thousands,
and David his *ten thousands* **myriads**.
8 And *Saul* **Shaul** was *very wroth* **mighty inflamed**,
and the *saying displeased him* **word was evil in his eyes**;
and he said,
They have *ascribed* **given** unto David
ten thousands **myriads**,
and to me they have
ascribed but **given** thousands:
and what *can he have* more
but the *kingdom* **sovereigndom**?
9 And *Saul* **Shaul** eyed David from that
day and *forward* **beyond**.

SHAUL FEARS DAVID

10 And it *came to pass* **became**, on the morrow,
that the evil spirit from *God* **Elohim**
came **prospered** upon *Saul* **Shaul**,
and he prophesied in the midst of the house:
and David *played* **strummed** with his hand,
as *at other times* **day by day**:
and there was a *javelin* **spear** in *Saul's* **Shaul's** hand.
11 And *Saul* **Shaul** cast the *javelin* **spear**; for he said,
I *will* **shall** smite David even to the wall *with it*.
And David *avoided* **turned aside**
out of his presence twice **from his face two times**.
12 And *Saul was afraid* **Shaul awed at the face** of David,
because *the LORD* **Yah Veh** was with him,
and was *departed* **turned aside** from *Saul* **Shaul**.
13 Therefore
Saul removed him **Shaul turned aside** from him,
and *made* **set** him his *captain* **governor** over a thousand;
and he went out and came in
before **at the face of** the people.
14 And David *behaved himself wisely* **comprehended**
in all his ways;
and *the LORD* **Yah Veh** was with him.
15 Wherefore when *Saul* **Shaul** saw that he
behaved himself very wisely **comprehended mightily**,
he *was afraid of him* **sojourned from his face**.
16 But all *Israel* **Yisra El** and *Judah* **Yah Hudah**
loved David,
because he went out and came in
before them **at their face**.
17 And *Saul* **Shaul** said to David,
Behold my *elder* **greater** daughter Merab,
her *will* **shall** I give thee to *wife* **woman**:
only be thou *valiant* **a son of valour** for me,
and fight *the LORD'S battles* **Yah Veh's wars**.
For *Saul* **Shaul** said, Let not mine hand
be upon him,
but let the hand of the *Philistines* **Peleshethiy**
be upon him.
18 And David said unto *Saul* **Shaul**, Who am I?
and what is my life, or my father's family in *Israel* **Yisra El**,
that I should be son in law to the *king* **sovereign**?
19 But it *came to pass* **became**,
at the time when Merab *Saul's* **Shaul's** daughter
should have been given to David,
that she was given unto *Adriel* **Adri El**
the *Meholathite* **Mecholathiy** to *wife* **woman**.
20 And Michal *Saul's* **Shaul's** daughter loved David:
and they told *Saul* **Shaul**,
and the *thing pleased him* **word was straight in his eyes**.
21 And *Saul* **Shaul** said, I *will* **shall** give him her,
that she may be a snare to him,
and that the hand of the *Philistines* **Peleshethiy**
may be against him.
Wherefore *Saul* **Shaul** said to David **a second time**,
Thou shalt this day be my son in law
in the one of the twain.
22 And *Saul commanded* **Shaul misvahed** his servants,
saying, Commune **Word** with David *secretly* **undercover**,
and say, Behold, the *king* **sovereign** hath delight in thee,
and all his servants love thee:
now therefore be the *king's* **sovereign's** son in law.
23 And *Saul's* **Shaul's** servants
spake **worded** those words in the ears of David.
And David said, Seemeth it *to you* **in your eyes**
a light thing **trifling** to be a *king's* **sovereign's** son in law,
seeing that I am *a poor man* **impoverished**,
and *lightly esteemed* **abased**?
24 And the servants of *Saul* **Shaul** told him, saying,
On this manner **According to these words**
spake **worded** David.
25 And *Saul* **Shaul** said, Thus shall ye say say to David,
The *king desireth* **sovereign delighteth** not any dowry,
but an hundred foreskins of the *Philistines* **Peleshethiy**,
to be avenged of the *king's* **sovereign's** enemies.
But *Saul thought* **Shaul fabricated** to make David fall
by the hand of the *Philistines* **Peleshethiy**.

26 And when his servants told David these words,
it pleased David well
the word was straight in David's eyes
to be the *king's* **sovereign's** son in law:
and the days were not *expired* **fulfilled**.
27 Wherefore David arose and went, he and his men,
and *slew* **smote** of the *Philistines* **Peleshethiy**
two hundred men;
and David brought their foreskins,
and they gave them *in full tale* **fully** to the *king* **sovereign**,
that he might be the *king's* **sovereign's** son in law.
And *Saul* **Shaul** gave him Michal
his daughter to *wife* **woman**.
28 And *Saul* **Shaul** saw and knew
that *the LORD* **Yah Veh** was with David,
and that Michal *Saul's* **Shaul's** daughter loved him.
29 And *Saul was yet the more afraid of*
Shaul added to awe to face David;
and *Saul* **Shaul** became David's enemy
continually **all days**.
30 Then the *princes* **governors**
of the *Philistines* **Peleshethiy** went forth:
and it *came to pass* **became**, after they went forth,
that David
behaved himself more wisely **comprehended more**
than all the servants of *Saul* **Shaul**;
so that his name was *much set by* **mightily esteemed**.

SHAUL ATTEMPTS TO DEATHIFY DAVID

19 And *Saul* **Shaul**
spake **worded** to *Jonathan* **Yah Nathan** his son,
and to all his servants,
that they should *kill* **deathify** David.
2 But *Jonathan* **Yah Nathan**, *Saul's* **Shaul's** son
delighted *much* **mightily** in David:
and *Jonathan* **Yah Nathan** told David, saying,
Saul **Shaul** my father seeketh to *kill* **deathify** thee:
now therefore, I *pray* **beseech** thee,
take *heed* **guard** to thyself until the morning,
and *abide in a secret place* **settle covertly**,
and hide thyself:
3 And I *will* **shall** go out
and stand *beside* **at the hand of** my father
in the field where thou art,
and I *will commune* **shall word** with my father of thee;
and what I see, that I *will* **shall** tell thee.
4 And *Jonathan spake* **Yah Nathan worded** good of David
unto *Saul* **Shaul** his father, and said unto him,
Let not the *king* **sovereign** sin against his servant,
against David;
because he hath not sinned against thee,
and because his works
have been *to thee—ward* very *good* **mighty toward thee**:
5 For he *did put his life* **set his soul** in his *hand* **palm**,
and *slew* **smote** the *Philistine* **Peleshethiy**,
and *the LORD wrought* **Yah Veh worked** a great salvation
for all *Israel* **Yisra El**:
thou sawest it, and didst *rejoice* **cheer**:
wherefore then *wilt* **shalt** thou sin against innocent blood,
to *slay* **deathify** David *without a cause* **gratuitously**?
6 And *Saul* **Shaul**
hearkened unto the voice of *Jonathan* **Yah Nathan**:
and *Saul sware* **Shaul oathed**,
As the LORD **Yah Veh** liveth,
he shall not be *slain* **deathified**.
7 And *Jonathan* **Yah Nathan** called David,
and *Jonathan shewed* **Yah Nathan told** him
all those *things* **words**.
And *Jonathan* **Yah Nathan** brought David to *Saul* **Shaul**,
and he was *in his presence* **at his face**,
as *in times past* **three yesters ago**.
8 And there *was war again* **added to be war**:
and David went out,
and fought with the *Philistines* **Peleshethiy**,
and *slew* **smote** them with a great *slaughter* **stroke**;
and they fled from *him* **his face**.
9 And the evil spirit from *the LORD* **Yah Veh**
was upon *Saul* **Shaul**,
as he *sat* **settled** in his house
with his *javelin* **spear** in his hand:
and David *played* **strummed** with his hand.
10 And *Saul* **Shaul** sought to smite David
even to the wall with the *javelin* **spear**:
but he *slipped away* **burst forth**
out of Saul's presence **from Shaul's face**,
and he smote the *javelin* **spear** into the wall:
and David fled, and escaped that night.
11 *Saul* **Shaul** also sent *messengers* **angels**
unto David's house, to *watch* **guard** him,
and to *slay* **deathify** him in the morning:
and Michal David's *wife* **woman** told him, saying,
If thou *save* **rescue** not thy *life* **soul** to night,
to morrow thou shalt be *slain* **deathified**.
12 So Michal *let* **descended** David *down*
through a window:
and he went, and fled, and escaped.
13 And Michal took *an image* **a teraphim**,
and *laid it* **set** in the bed,
and *put a pillow* **set a mattress** of *goats' hair* **doe goats**
for his *bolster* **headpieces**,
and covered *it* **them** with a cloth.
14 And when *Saul* **Shaul**
sent *messengers* **angels** to take David,
she said, He is sick.
15 And *Saul* **Shaul** sent the *messengers* **angels** *again*
to see David, saying,
Bring **Ascend** him *up* to me in the bed,
that I may *slay* **deathify** him.
16 And when the *messengers* **angels** were come in,
behold, there was *an image* **a teraphim** in the bed,
with a *pillow* **mattress** of *goats' hair* **doe goats'**
for his *bolster* **headpieces**.
17 And *Saul* **Shaul** said unto Michal,
Why hast thou deceived me so,
and sent away mine enemy, that he is escaped?
And Michal *answered Saul* **said to Shaul**,
He said unto me, *Let me go* **Send me away**;
why should I *kill* **deathify** thee?
18 So David fled, and escaped,
and came to *Samuel* **Shemu El** to Ramah,
and told him all that *Saul* **Shaul** had *done* **worked** to him.
And he and *Samuel* **Shemu El** went
and *dwelt* **settled** in *Naioth* **Navith**.
19 And it was told *Saul* **Shaul**, saying,
Behold, David is at *Naioth* **Navith** in Ramah.
20 And *Saul* **Shaul** sent *messengers* **angels** to take David:
and when they saw the *company* **assembly** of the prophets
prophesying,
and *Samuel* **Shemu El**
standing *as appointed* **stationed** over them,
the Spirit of *God* **Elohim**
was upon the *messengers* **angels** of *Saul* **Shaul**,
and they also prophesied.
21 And when it was told *Saul* **Shaul**,
he sent other *messengers* **angels**,
and they prophesied likewise.
And *Saul* **Shaul** sent *messengers* **angels** *again*
the third time,
and they prophesied also.
22 Then went he also to Ramah,
and came to a great well that is in Sechu:
and he asked and said,
Where are *Samuel* **Shemu El** and David?
And one said, Behold, they be at *Naioth* **Navith** in Ramah.
23 And he went thither to *Naioth* **Navith** in Ramah:
and the Spirit of *God* **Elohim** was upon him also,
and *he went* **in walking, he walked** on, and prophesied,
until he came to *Naioth* **Navith** in Ramah.
24 And he stripped off his clothes also,
and prophesied *before Samuel* **at the face of Shemu El**
in like manner **also**,
and *lay down* **fell** naked all that day and all that night.
Wherefore they say,
Is *Saul* **Shaul** also among the prophets?

DAVID AND YAH NATHAN CUT A COVENANT

20 And David fled from *Naioth* **Navith** in Ramah,
and came and said
before Jonathan **at the face of Yah Nathan**,
What have I *done* **worked**?
what is *mine iniquity* **my perversion**?
and what is my sin *before* **at the face of** thy father,

that he seeketh my *life* **soul**?
2 And he said unto him, *God forbid* **Far be it**;
thou shalt not die:
behold, my father *will do nothing* **shall work naught**
either — great **word** or small **word**,
but that he *will shew it me* **shall expose in mine ear**:
and why should my father hide this *thing* **word** from me?
it is not so.
3 And David *sware* **oathed** moreover, and said,
In knowing, Thy father *certainly* knoweth
that I have found *grace* **charism** in thine eyes;
and he saith, Let not *Jonathan* **Yah Nathan** know this,
lest he be *grieved* **contorted**:
but truly as *the LORD* **Yah Veh** liveth,
and as thy soul liveth,
there is but a *step* **stride** between me and death.
4 Then said *Jonathan* **Yah Nathan** unto David,
Whatsoever thy soul *desireth* **saith**,
I *will even do* **shall work** it for thee.
5 And David said unto *Jonathan* **Yah Nathan**,
Behold, to morrow is the new moon,
and I should *not fail to sit* **settle**
with the *king at meat* **sovereign to eat**:
but let me go **send me away**,
that I may hide myself in the field
unto the third *day* at even.
6 If **in visiting,** thy father *at all miss me* **visit me**,
then say,
In asking, David *earnestly* asked *leave* of me
that he might run to *Bethlehem* **Beth Lechem** his city:
for there is a *yearly sacrifice* **sacrifice of days** there
for all the family.
7 If he say thus, *It is well* **Good**;
thy servant shall have *peace* **shalom**:
but if **in inflaming,** he be *very wroth* **inflamed**,
then *be sure* **know** that evil is *determined* **finished** by him.
8 Therefore
thou shalt *deal kindly* **work mercy** with thy servant;
for thou hast brought thy servant
into a covenant of *the LORD* **Yah Veh** with thee:
notwithstanding, if there be in me *iniquity* **perversity**,
slay **deathify** me thyself;
for why shouldest thou bring me to thy father?
9 And *Jonathan* **Yah Nathan** said, Far be it from thee:
for if **in knowing,** I knew *certainly*
that evil were *determined* **finished** by my father
to come upon thee,
then *would* **should** not I tell it thee?
10 Then said David to *Jonathan* **Yah Nathan**,
Who shall tell me?
or what if thy father answer thee *roughly* **hardly**?
11 And *Jonathan* **Yah Nathan** said unto David,
Come, and let us go out into the field.
And they went out both of them into the field.
12 And *Jonathan* **Yah Nathan** said unto David,
O *LORD God* **Elohim** of *Israel* **Yisra El**,
when I have *sounded* **probed** my father about to morrow
any time, or the third *day*,
and, behold, if there be good toward David,
and I then send not unto thee,
and *shew it thee* **expose it in thine ear**;
13 *The LORD* **Yah Veh**
do so and much more **work thus and add**
to *Jonathan* **Yah Nathan**:
but if it *please* **well—please** my father
to *do thee evil* **vilify thee**,
then I *will shew it thee* **shall expose it in thine ear**,
and send thee away,
that thou mayest go in *peace* **shalom**:
and *the LORD* **Yah Veh** be with thee,
as he hath been with my father.
14 And thou shalt not only while yet I live
shew **work** me the *kindness* **mercy** of *the LORD* **Yah Veh**,
that I die not:
15 But also thou shalt not cut off thy *kindness* **mercy**
from my house *for ever* **eternally**:
no, not when *the LORD* **Yah Veh**
hath cut off the enemies of David
every *one* **man** from the face of the *earth* **soil**.
16 *So Jonathan made a covenant* **And Yah Nathan cut**
with the house of David, *saying*,
Let *the LORD even require* **Yah Veh seek** it
at the hand of David's enemies.
17 And *Jonathan* **Yah Nathan**
caused David to *swear again* **add an oath**,
because he loved him:
for he loved him as he loved his own soul.
18 Then *Jonathan* **Yah Nathan** said to David,
To morrow is the new moon:
and thou shalt be *missed* **inspected**,
because thy seat *will* **shall** be *empty* **inspected**.
19 And when thou hast stayed three days,
then thou shalt *go down quickly* **descend mightily**,
and come to the place where thou didst hide thyself
when the business was in hand **in the day of work**,
and shalt *remain by* **settle beside** the stone Ezel.
20 And I *will* **shall** shoot three arrows on the side thereof,
as *though I shot* **sent** at a *mark* **target**.
21 And, behold, I *will* **shall** send a lad,
saying, Go, find out the arrows.
If **in saying,** I *expressly* say unto the lad,
Behold, the arrows are on this side of thee, take them;
then come thou:
for there is *peace* **shalom** to thee, and no *hurt* **word**;
as the LORD **Yah Veh** liveth.
22 But if I say thus unto the *young man* **lad**,
Behold, the arrows are beyond thee; go thy way:
for *the LORD* **Yah Veh** hath sent thee away.
23 And *as touching the matter* **the word**
which thou and I have *spoken of* **worded**, behold,
the LORD **Yah Veh** be between thee and me
for ever **eternally**.
24 So David hid himself in the field:
and when the new moon was come,
the *king sat him* **sovereign settled** down to eat *meat* **bread**.
25 And the *king sat* **sovereign settled** upon his seat
as *at other times* **time by time**,
even upon a seat by the wall:
and *Jonathan* **Yah Nathan** arose,
and *Abner sat* **Abi Ner settled** by *Saul's* **Shaul's** side,
and David's place was *empty* **inspected**.
26 Nevertheless
Saul spake not any thing **Shaul worded naught** that day:
for he *thought* **said**,
Something **A happening** hath *befallen* **happened** him,
he is not *clean* **pure**; surely he is not *clean* **pure**.
27 And it *came to pass* **became,** on the morrow,
which was the second *day* of the month,
that David's place was *empty* **inspected**:
and *Saul* **Shaul** said unto *Jonathan* **Yah Nathan** his son,
Wherefore
cometh not the son of *Jesse* **Yishay** to *meat* **bread**,
neither yesterday, nor to day?
28 And *Jonathan* **Yah Nathan** answered *Saul* **Shaul**,
In asking, David *earnestly* asked *leave* of me
to go to *Bethlehem* **Beth Lechem**:
29 And he said, *Let me go* **Send me away**,
I *pray* **beseech** thee;
for our family hath a sacrifice in the city;
and my brother,
he hath *commanded* **misvahed** me *to be there*:
and now, if I have found *favour* **charism** in thine eyes,
let me *get away* **escape**, I *pray* **beseech** thee,
and see my brethren.
Therefore he cometh not unto the *king's* **sovereign's** table.
30 Then *Saul's anger* **Shaul's wrath**
was kindled against *Jonathan* **Yah Nathan**,
and he said unto him,
Thou son of the *perverse* **perverted** rebellious *woman*,
do not I know
that thou hast chosen the son of *Jesse* **Yishay**
to thine own *confusion* **shame**,
and unto the *confusion* **shame** of thy mother's nakedness?
31 For *as long as* **all the days**
the son of *Jesse* **Yishay** liveth upon the *ground* **soil**,
thou shalt not be established,
nor thy *kingdom* **sovereigndom**.
Wherefore now send and *fetch* **take** him unto me,
for he *shall surely die* **is a son of death**.
32 And *Jonathan* **Yah Nathan**

answered *Saul* **Shaul** his father,
and said unto him,
Wherefore shall he be *slain* **deathified**?
what hath he *done* **worked**?
33 And *Saul* **Shaul** cast a *javelin* **spear** at him to smite him:
whereby *Jonathan* **Yah Nathan** knew that it was
determined **fully finished** of his father
to *slay* **deathify** David.
34 So *Jonathan* **Yah Nathan**
arose from the table in *fierce anger* **fuming wrath**,
and did eat no *meat* **bread** the second day of the month:
for he was *grieved* **contorted** for David,
because his father had *done* **shamed** him *shame*.
35 And it *came to pass* **became,** in the morning,
that *Jonathan* **Yah Nathan** went out into the field
at the *time appointed* **season** with David,
and a little lad with him.
36 And he said unto his lad,
Run, find out now the arrows which I shoot.
And as the lad ran,
he shot an arrow *beyond* **to pass over** him.
37 And when the lad was come to the place of the arrow
which *Jonathan* **Yah Nathan** had shot,
Jonathan cried **Yah Nathan called out** after the lad,
and said, Is not the arrow beyond thee?
38 And *Jonathan cried* **Yah Nathan called out** after the lad,
Make speed **Quickly**, *haste* **hasten**, stay not.
And *Jonathan's* **Yah Nathan's** lad gathered up the arrows,
and came to his *master* **adoni**.
39 But the lad knew *not any thing* **naught**:
only *Jonathan* **Yah Nathan** and David
knew the *matter* **word**.
40 And *Jonathan* **Yah Nathan**
gave his *artillery* **instrument** unto his lad,
and said unto him, Go, carry them to the city.
41 And as soon as the lad was gone,
David arose *out of a place toward* **beside** the south,
and fell on his *face* **nostrils** to the *ground* **earth**,
and *bowed* **prostrated** himself three times:
and they kissed *one another* **man to friend**,
and wept *one with another* **man to friend**,
until David *exceeded* **greatened**.
42 And *Jonathan* **Yah Nathan** said to David,
Go in *peace* **shalom**,
forasmuch as we have *sworn* **oathed** both of us
in the name of *the LORD* **Yah Veh**, saying,
The LORD **Yah Veh** be between me and thee,
and between my seed and thy seed *for ever* **eternally**.
And he arose and *departed* **went**:
and *Jonathan* **Yah Nathan** went into the city.

HOLY BREAD

21 Then came David to Nob
to *Ahimelech* **Achiy Melech** the priest:
and *Ahimelech* **Achiy Melech**
was afraid **trembled** at the meeting of David,
and said unto him,
Why art thou alone, and no man with thee?
2 And David said unto *Ahimelech* **Achiy Melech** the priest,
The *king* **sovereign**
hath *commanded* **misvahed** me a *business* **word**,
and hath said unto me, Let no man know *any thing* **aught**
of the *business* **word** whereabout I send thee,
and what I have *commanded* **misvahed** thee:
and I have *appointed* my *servants* **lads to know**
to **at** such and such a place.
3 Now therefore what is under thine hand?
give me five *loaves of* bread in mine hand,
or what there is *present* **found**.
4 And the priest answered David, and said,
There is no *common* **profane** bread under mine hand,
but there is *hallowed* **holy** bread;
if the *young men* **lads** have *kept* **guarded** themselves
at least **only** from women.
5 And David answered the priest, and said unto him,
Of a truth women have been *kept* **restrained** from us
about these three days **as three yesters ago**,
since I *came out* **went**,
and the *vessels* **instruments** of the *young men* **lads**
are holy,
and *the bread is* in a *manner common* **profane way**,
yea, though it were *sanctified* **hallowed** this day
in the *vessel* **instrument**.
6 So the priest gave him *hallowed bread* **the holy**:
for there was no bread there
but the *shewbread* **face bread**,
that was *taken* **twisted off**
from before the LORD **at the face of Yah Veh**,
to *put* **set** hot bread in the day when it was taken away.
7 Now a *certain* man of the servants of *Saul* **Shaul**
was there that day,
detained **restrained**
before the LORD **at the face of Yah Veh**;
and his name was Doeg, an *Edomite* **Edomiy**,
the *chiefest* **mighty** of the *herdmen* **tenders**
that belonged to Saul **of Shaul**.
8 And David said unto *Ahimelech* **Achiy Melech**,
And is there not here under thine hand spear or sword?
for I have neither *brought* **taken** my sword
nor my *weapons with me* **instruments in my hand**,
because the *king's business* **sovereign's word**
required haste **be urgent**.
9 And the priest said,
The sword of *Goliath* **Golyath** the *Philistine* **Peleshethiy**,
whom thou *slewest* **smotest** in the valley of Elah, behold,
it is here *wrapped* **veiled** in a cloth behind the ephod:
if thou *wilt* **shalt** take that, take it:
for there is no other *save that here* **except thus**.
And David said, There is none like that; give it me.
10 And David arose and fled that day
for fear **from the face** of *Saul* **Shaul**,
and went to Achish the *king* **sovereign** of Gath.
11 And the servants of Achish said unto him,
Is not this David the *king* **sovereign** of the land?
did they not *sing* **answer** one to another *of him*
thus in **round** dances, saying,
Saul **Shaul** hath *slain* **smitten** his thousands,
and David his *ten thousands* **myriads**?
12 And David *laid* **set** up these words in his heart,
and was *sore afraid* **mightily awed**
at the face of Achish the *king* **sovereign** of Gath.
13 And he changed his *behaviour* **perception**
before them **at their eyes**,
and *feigned himself mad* **halaled** in their hands,
and *scrabbled* **marked** on the doors of the *gate* **portal**,
and let his *spittle fall down* **saliva descend** upon his beard.
14 Then said Achish unto his servants,
Lo **Behold**, ye see the man is *mad* **insane**:
wherefore *then* have ye brought him to me?
15 *Have I need of mad men* **Lack I insanity**,
that ye have brought this *fellow*
to play *the mad man* **insane** in my presence?
shall this *fellow* come into my house?

DAVID AT CAVE ADULLAM AND MISPEH

22 David *therefore departed* **went** thence,
and escaped to the cave Adullam:
and when his brethren and all his father's house heard it,
they *went down* **descended** thither to him.
2 And every *one* **man** that was in distress,
and every *one* **man** that *was in debt* **had an exactor**,
and every *one* **man** that was *discontented* **bitter of soul**,
gathered themselves unto him;
and he became a *captain* **governor** over them:
and there were with him about four hundred men.
3 And David went thence to *Mizpeh* **Mispeh** of Moab:
and he said unto the *king* **sovereign** of Moab,
Let my father and my mother, I *pray* **beseech** thee,
come forth, and be **go** with you,
till I know what *God will do* **Elohim shall work** for me.
4 And he *brought* **led** them
before the king **at the face of the sovereign** of Moab:
and they *dwelt* **settled** with him all the *while* **day**
that David was in the hold.
5 And the prophet Gad said unto David,
Abide **Settle** not in the hold; *depart* **go**,
and get thee into the land of *Judah* **Yah Hudah**.
Then David *departed* **went**,
and came into the forest of Hareth.

SHAUL DEATHIFIES THE PRIESTS OF NOB

6 When *Saul* **Shaul** heard
that David was *discovered* **known**,

and the men that were with him,
(now *Saul abode* **Shaul settled** in *Gibeah* **Gibah**
under a *tree* **grove** in Ramah, having his spear in his hand,
and all his servants were *standing* **stationed** about him;)
7 Then *Saul* **Shaul** said unto his servants
that stood **stationed** about him,
Hear now, ye *Benjamites* **Ben Yaminiy**;
will **shall** the son of *Jesse* **Yishay**
give every one of you fields and vineyards,
and *make* **set** you all *captains* **governors** of thousands,
and *captains* **governors** of hundreds;
8 That all of you have conspired against me,
and there is none that *sheweth me* **exposeth in mine ear**
that my son hath *made a league* **cut**
with the son of *Jesse* **Yishay**,
and there is none of you that is *sorry* **sick** for me,
or *sheweth unto me* **exposeth in mine ear**
that my son hath *stirred* **raised** up my servant against me,
to *lie in wait* **lurk**, as at this day?
9 Then answered Doeg the *Edomite* **Edomiy**,
which was *set* **stationed** over the servants of *Saul* **Shaul**,
and said, I saw the son of *Jesse* **Yishay** coming to Nob,
to *Ahimelech* **Achiy Melech** the son of *Ahitub* **Achiy Tub**.
10 And he *enquired* **asked** of *the LORD* **Yah Veh** for him,
and gave him *victuals* **hunt**, and gave him the sword
of *Goliath* **Golyath** the *Philistine* **Peleshethiy**.
11 Then the *king* **sovereign** sent to call
Ahimelech **Achiy Melech** the priest,
the son of *Ahitub* **Achiy Tub**,
and all his father's house, the priests that were in Nob:
and they came all of them to the *king* **sovereign**.
12 And *Saul* **Shaul** said,
Hear now, thou son of *Ahitub* **Achiy Tub**.
And he *answered* **said**, Here I am, my *lord* **adoni**.
13 And *Saul* **Shaul** said unto him,
Why have ye conspired against me,
thou and the son of *Jesse* **Yishay**,
in that thou hast given him bread, and a sword,
and hast *enquired* **asked** of *God* **Elohim** for him,
that he should rise against me,
to *lie in wait* **lurk**, as at this day?
14 Then *Ahimelech* **Achiy Melech**
answered the *king* **sovereign**, and said,
And who is *so faithful* **amenable** among all thy servants
as David,
which is the *king's* **sovereign's** son in law,
and *goeth at thy bidding* **turneth aside at hearing thee**,
and is honourable in thine house?
15 Did I *then* **daily** begin to *enquire* **ask** of *God* **Elohim**
for him?
be it far from me:
let not the *king impute* **sovereign set** any *thing* **word**
unto his servant,
nor to all the house of my father:
for thy servant knew *nothing* **no word** of all this,
less or *more* **great**.
16 And the *king* **sovereign** said,
In dying, Thou shalt *surely* die,
Ahimelech **Achiy Melech**, thou, and all thy father's house.
17 And the *king* **sovereign** said unto the *footmen* **runners**
that *stood* **stationed** about him,
Turn, and *slay* **deathify** the priests of *the LORD* **Yah Veh**:
because their hand also is with David,
and because they knew when he fled,
and *did not shew it to me* **exposed it not in mine ear**.
But the servants of the *king* **sovereign**
would not put **willed to not send** forth their hand
to *fall* **encounter** upon the priests of *the LORD* **Yah Veh**.
18 And the *king* **sovereign** said to Doeg,
Turn thou, and *fall* **encounter** upon the priests.
And Doeg the *Edomite* **Edomiy** turned,
and he *fell* **encountered** upon the priests,
and *slew* **deathified** on that day
fourscore **eighty** and five *persons* **men**
that *did wear* **bore** a linen ephod.
19 And Nob, the city of the priests,
smote he with the *edge* **mouth** of the sword,
both men and women, *children* **infants** and sucklings,
and oxen, and *asses* **he burros**, and *sheep* **lambs**,
with the *edge* **mouth** of the sword.
20 And one of the sons of *Ahimelech* **Achiy Melech**
the son of *Ahitub* **Achiy Tub**, named *Abiathar* **Abi Athar**,
escaped, and fled after David.
21 And *Abiathar shewed* **Abi Athar told** David
that *Saul* **Shaul**
had *slain the LORD'S* **slaughtered Yah Veh's** priests.
22 And David said unto *Abiathar* **Abi Athar**,
I knew it that day,
when Doeg the *Edomite* **Edomiy** was there,
that **in telling,** he *would surely* **should** tell *Saul* **Shaul**:
I have *occasioned the death* **gone about**
of all the *persons* **souls** of thy father's house.
23 *Abide* **Settle** thou with me, *fear* **awe** not:
for he that seeketh my *life* **soul** seeketh thy *life* **soul**:
but with me thou shalt be in *safeguard* **guard**.

DAVID SAVES QEILAH

23 Then they told David, saying, Behold,
the *Philistines* **Peleshethiy** fight against *Keilah* **Qeilah**,
and they *rob* **plunder** the threshingfloors.
2 Therefore David *enquired* **asked** of *the LORD* **Yah Veh**,
saying, shall I go and smite these *Philistines* **Peleshethiy**?
And *the LORD* **Yah Veh** said unto David,
Go, and smite the *Philistines* **Peleshethiy**,
and save *Keilah* **Qeilah**.
3 And David's men said unto him,
Behold, we be *afraid* **awed** here in *Judah* **Yah Hudah**:
how much more then if we come to *Keilah* **Qeilah**
against the *armies* **ranks** of the *Philistines* **Peleshethiy**?
4 Then David
enquired of the LORD yet again
added yet to ask of Yah Veh.
And *the LORD* **Yah Veh** answered him and said,
Arise, *go down* **descend** to *Keilah* **Qeilah**;
for I *will deliver* **shall give** the *Philistines* **Peleshethiy**
into thine hand.
5 So David and his men went to *Keilah* **Qeilah**,
and fought with the *Philistines* **Peleshethiy**,
and *brought away* **drove** their *cattle* **chattel**,
and smote them with a great *slaughter* **stroke**.
So David saved the *inhabitants* **settlers** of *Keilah* **Qeilah**.

SHAUL PURSUES DAVID

6 And it *came to pass* **became**, when *Abiathar* **Abi Athar**
the son of *Ahimelech* **Achiy Melech**
fled to David to *Keilah* **Qeilah**,
that he *came down* **descended** with an ephod in his hand.
7 And it was told *Saul* **Shaul**
that David was come to *Keilah* **Qeilah**.
And *Saul* **Shaul** said,
God **Elohim** hath *delivered* **recognized** him
into mine hand; for he is shut in,
by entering into a *town* **city**
that hath *gates* **doors** and bars.
8 And *Saul* **Shaul**
called **hearkened** all the people together to war,
to *go down* **descend** to *Keilah* **Qeilah**,
to besiege David and his men.
9 And David knew that *Saul* **Shaul**
secretly practised mischief **plotted evil** against him;
and he said to *Abiathar* **Abi Athar** the priest,
Bring *hither* **near** the ephod.
10 Then said David,
O *LORD God* **Yah Veh Elohim** of *Israel* **Yisra El**,
In hearing, thy servant hath *certainly* heard
that *Saul* **Shaul** seeketh to come to *Keilah* **Qeilah**,
to *destroy* **ruin** the city for my sake.
11 *Will* **Shall** the *men* **masters** of *Keilah* **Qeilah**
deliver **shut** me up into his hand?
will Saul come down **shall Shaul descend**,
as thy servant hath heard?
O *LORD God* **Yah Veh Elohim** of *Israel* **Yisra El**,
I beseech thee, tell thy servant.
And *the LORD* **Yah Veh** said,
He *will come down* **shall descend**.
12 Then said David,
Will **Shall** the *men* **masters** of *Keilah* **Qeilah**
deliver **shut** me and my men into the hand of *Saul* **Shaul**?
And *the LORD* **Yah Veh** said,
They *will deliver* **shall shut** thee up.
13 Then David and his men,
which were about six hundred **men**,

arose and *departed* **went** out of *Keilah* **Qeilah**,
and *went whithersoever they could go*
in walking, they walked.
And it was told *Saul* **Shaul**
that David was escaped from *Keilah* **Qeilah**;
and he *forbare* **ceased** to go forth.
14 And David *abode* **settled** in the wilderness
in *strong holds* **huntholds**,
and *remained* **settled** in a mountain
in the wilderness of Ziph.
And *Saul* **Shaul** sought him every day,
but *God delivered* **Elohim gave** him not into his hand.
15 And David saw that *Saul* **Shaul**
was come out **went** to seek his *life* **soul**:
and David was in the wilderness of Ziph in a *wood* **forest**.
16 And *Jonathan* **Yah Nathan,** *Saul's* **Shaul's** son arose,
and went to David into the *wood* **forest**,
and strengthened his hand in *God* **Elohim**.
17 And he said unto him, *Fear* **Awe** not:
for the hand of *Saul* **Shaul** my father shall not find thee;
and thou shalt *be king* **reign** over *Israel* **Yisra El**,
and I shall be *next* **second** unto thee;
and that also *Saul* **Shaul** my father knoweth.
18 And they two *made* **cut** a covenant
before the LORD **at the face of Yah Veh**:
and David *abode* **settled** in the *wood* **forest**,
and *Jonathan* **Yah Nathan** went to his house.
19 Then *came up* **ascended** the *Ziphites* **Ziphiy**
to *Saul* **Shaul** to *Gibeah* **Gibah**, saying,
Doth not David hide himself with us
in *strong holds* **huntholds** in the *wood* **forest**,
in the hill of Hachilah,
which is on the *south* **right** of *Jeshimon* **Yeshimon**?
20 Now therefore, O *king* **sovereign**,
come down **descend**
according to all the *desire* **yearning** of thy soul
to *come down* **descend**;
and our part shall be
to *deliver* **shut** him into the *king's* **sovereign's** hand.
21 And *Saul* **Shaul** said,
Blessed be ye of *the LORD* **Yah Veh**;
for ye have compassion on me.
22 Go, I *pray* **beseech** you, prepare yet,
and know and see his place where his *haunt* **foot** is,
and who hath seen him there:
for it is *told* **said to** me
that *he dealeth very subtilly*
in strategizing, he strategizeth.
23 See therefore, and *take knowledge* **know**
of all the *lurking places* **refuges** where he hideth himself,
and *come* **return** ye *again* to me
with the certainty **prepared**,
and I *will* **shall** go with you:
and it shall *come to pass* **become**, if he be in the land,
that I *will* **shall** search him out
throughout all the thousands of *Judah* **Yah Hudah**.
24 And they arose, and went to Ziph
before Saul **from the face of Shaul**:
but David and his men were in the wilderness of Maon,
in the plain on the *south* **right** of *Jeshimon* **Yeshimon**.
25 *Saul* **Shaul** also and his men went to seek him.
And they told David:
wherefore he *came down* **descended** into a rock,
and *abode* **settled** in the wilderness of Maon.
And when *Saul* **Shaul** heard that,
he pursued after David in the wilderness of Maon.
26 And *Saul* **Shaul** went on this side of the mountain,
and David and his men on that side of the mountain:
and David *made haste* **hastened**
to *get away for fear of Saul* **go from the face of Shaul**;
for *Saul* **Shaul** and his men
compassed **surrounded** David and his men *round about*
to take **apprehend** them.
27 But there came *a messenger* **an angel** unto *Saul* **Shaul**,
saying, Haste thee, and come;
for the *Philistines* **Peleshethiy**
have *invaded* **stripped** the land.
28 Wherefore *Saul* **Shaul** returned
from pursuing after David,
and went *against* **to meet** the *Philistines* **Peleshethiy**:
therefore they called that place
Selahammahlekoth
Sela Ham Machleqoth/The Rock of Allotments.
29 And David *went up* **ascended** from thence,
and *dwelt* **settled** in *strong holds* **huntholds**
at *Engedi* **En Gedi**.

DAVID SPARES SHAUL'S LIFE

24 And it *came to pass* **became**,
when *Saul* **Shaul** was returned
from *following* **after** the *Philistines* **Peleshethiy**,
that it was told him, saying, Behold,
David is in the wilderness of *Engedi* **En Gedi**.
2 Then *Saul* **Shaul** took three thousand chosen men
out of all *Israel* **Yisra El**,
and went to seek David and his men
upon **the face of** the rocks of the *wild goats* **ibexes**.
3 And he came to the *sheepcotes* **flock walls** by the way,
where was a cave;
and *Saul* **Shaul** went in to cover his feet:
and David and his men
remained **settled** in the *sides* **flanks** of the cave.
4 And the men of David said unto him,
Behold the day
of which *the LORD* **Yah Veh** said unto thee,
Behold,
I *will deliver* **shall give** thine enemy into thine hand,
that thou mayest *do* **work** to him
as it shall *seem good unto thee* **well—please thine eyes**.
Then David arose, and cut off the *skirt* **border**
of *Saul's robe privily* **Shaul's mantle undercover**.
5 And it *came to pass* **became,** afterward,
that David's heart smote him,
because he had cut off *Saul's skirt* **Shaul's border**.
6 And he said unto his men,
The LORD forbid **Far be it**
that I should *do* **work** this *thing* **word**
unto my *master* **adoni**,
the LORD'S **Yah Veh's** anointed,
to *stretch* **send** forth mine hand against him,
seeing he is the anointed of *the LORD* **Yah Veh**.
7 So David *stayed* **cleaved** his *servants* **men**
with these words,
and *suffered* **allowed** them not to rise against *Saul* **Shaul**.
But *Saul* **Shaul** rose up out of the cave,
and went on his way.
8 David also arose afterward, and went out of the cave,
and *cried* **called out** after *Saul* **Shaul**, saying,
My *lord* **adoni** the *king* **sovereign**.
And when *Saul* **Shaul** looked behind him,
David *stooped* **bowed** with his *face* **nostrils** to the earth,
and *bowed himself* **prostrated**.
9 And David said to *Saul* **Shaul**,
Wherefore hearest thou *men's* **human** words, saying,
Behold, David seeketh thy *hurt* **evil**?
10 Behold, this day thine eyes have seen
how that *the LORD* **Yah Veh**
had *delivered* **given** thee to day
into mine hand in the cave:
and *some bade me kill* **said to slaughter** thee:
but *mine eye* spared thee;
and I said,
I *will* **shall** not *put* **send** forth mine hand
against my *lord* **adoni**;
for he is *the LORD'S* **Yah Veh's** anointed.
11 Moreover, my father, see, yea,
see the *skirt* **borders** of thy *robe* **mantle** in my hand:
for in that I cut off the *skirt* **border** of thy *robe* **mantle**,
and *killed* **slaughtered** thee not,
know thou and see that there is neither evil
nor *transgression* **rebellion** in mine hand,
and I have not sinned against thee;
yet thou *huntest* **lurkest** my soul to take it.
12 *The LORD* **Yah Veh** judge between me and thee,
and *the LORD* **Yah Veh** avenge me of thee:
but mine hand shall not be upon thee.
13 As saith the proverb of the ancients,
Wickedness *proceedeth* **goeth** from the wicked:
but mine hand shall not be upon thee.
14 After whom
is the *king* **sovereign** of *Israel come out* **Yisra El gone**?

after whom dost thou pursue?
after a dead dog, after *a* **one** flea.
15 *The LORD* **Yah Veh** therefore be *judge* **advocate**,
and judge between me and thee, and see,
and plead my *cause* **plea**,
and *deliver* **judge** me out of thine hand.
16 And it *came to pass* **became**,
when David
had *made an end of speaking* **finished wording**
these words unto *Saul* **Shaul**, that *Saul* **Shaul** said,
Is this thy voice, my son David?
And *Saul* **Shaul** lifted up his voice, and wept.
17 And he said to David,
Thou art more *righteous* **just** than I:
for thou hast *rewarded* **dealt** me good,
whereas I have *rewarded* **dealt** thee evil.
18 And thou hast *shewed* **told** this day
how that thou hast *dealt well* **worked good** with me:
forasmuch as when *the LORD* **Yah Veh**
had *delivered* **shut** me into thine hand,
thou *killedst* **slaughteredst** me not.
19 For if a man find his enemy,
will he let him go **shall he send him away**
well away **in a good way**?
wherefore *the LORD reward* **Yah Veh shalam** thee *good*
for that thou hast *done* **worked** unto me this day.
20 And now, behold, I know well
that **in reigning**, thou shalt *surely be king* **reign**,
and that the *kingdom* **sovereigndom** of *Israel* **Yisra El**
shall *be established* **rise** in thine hand.
21 *Swear* **Oath** now therefore unto me
by *the LORD* **Yah Veh**,
that thou *wilt* **shalt** not cut off my seed after me,
and that thou *wilt* **shalt** not *destroy* **desolate** my name
out of my father's house.
22 And David *sware* **oathed** unto *Saul* **Shaul**.
And *Saul* **Shaul** went *home* **to his house**;
but David and his men
gat **ascended** them *up* unto the hold.

SHEMU EL'S DEATH

25 And *Samuel* **Shemu El** died;
and all the *Israelites* **Yisra Eliy** were gathered *together*,
and *lamented* **chopped over** him,
and *buried* **entombed** him in his house at Ramah.
And David arose,
and *went down* **descended** to the wilderness of Paran.
2 And there was a man in Maon,
whose *possessions* **works** were in *Carmel* **Karmel**;
and the man was *very* **mighty** great,
and he had three thousand *sheep* **flock**,
and a thousand **doe** goats:
and he was shearing his *sheep* **flock** in *Carmel* **Karmel**.
3 Now the name of the man was Nabal;
and the name of his *wife Abigail* **woman Abi Gail**:
and she was a woman
of good *understanding* **comprehension**,
and of a beautiful *countenance* **form**:
but the man was *churlish* **hard** and evil
in his *doings* **exploits**;
and he was *of the house of Caleb* **a Kalebiy**.
4 And David heard in the wilderness
that Nabal did shear his *sheep* **flock**.
5 And David sent out ten *young men* **lads**,
and David said unto the *young men* **lads**,
Get you up **Ascend** to *Carmel* **Karmel**, and go to Nabal,
and *greet him* **ask him of shalom** in my name:
6 And thus shall ye say to him that liveth *in prosperity*,
Peace be **Shalom** both to thee,
and *peace be* **shalom** to thine house,
and *peace be* **shalom** unto all that thou hast.
7 And now I have heard that thou hast shearers:
now thy *shepherds* **tenders** which were with us,
we *hurt* **shamed** them not,
neither was there ought *missing* **overseen** unto them,
all the *while* **days** they were in *Carmel* **Karmel**.
8 Ask thy *young men* **lads**,
and they *will shew* **shall tell** thee.
Wherefore
let the *young men* **lads** find *favour* **charism** in thine eyes:
for we come in a good day:
give, I *pray* **beseech** thee,
whatsoever *cometh to* thine hand **findeth**
unto thy servants, and to thy son David.
9 And when David's *young men* **lads** came,
they *spake* **worded** to Nabal according to all those words
in the name of David, and *ceased* **rested**.
10 And Nabal answered David's servants, and said,
Who is David? and who is the son of *Jesse* **Yishay**?
there *be many* **abound by the myriads**
servants now a days that break away every man
from **the face of** his *master* **adoni**.
11 Shall I *then* take my bread, and my water,
and my *flesh* **slaughter** that I have *killed* **slaughtered**
for my shearers,
and give it unto men, whom I know not whence they be?
12 So David's *young men* **lads** turned their way,
and *went again* **turned back**,
and came and told him all those *sayings* **words**.
13 And David said unto his men,
Gird ye on every man his sword.
And they girded on every man his sword;
and David also girded on his sword:
and there *went up* **ascended** after David
about four hundred men;
and two hundred *abode* **settled** by the *stuff* **instruments**.
14 But one **lad** of the *young men* **lads**
told *Abigail* **Abi Gail**, Nabal's *wife* **woman**, saying,
Behold,
David sent *messengers* **angels** out of the wilderness
to *salute* **bless** our *master* **adoni**;
and he *railed on* **swooped upon** them.
15 But the men were *very* **mighty** good unto us,
and we were not *hurt* **shamed**,
neither *missed we any thing* **was aught overseen**,
as long as **all the days**
we *were conversant* **walked** with them,
when we were in the fields:
16 They were a wall unto us both by night and **by** day,
all the *while* **days** we were with them
keeping **tending** the *sheep* **flock**.
17 Now therefore know and *consider* **see**
what thou *wilt do* **shalt work**;
for evil is *determined* **finished** against our *master* **adoni**,
and against all his household:
for he is *such* **too much of** a son of *Belial* **Beli Yaal**,
that a man cannot speak to him **to word to**.
18 Then *Abigail made haste* **Abi Gail hastened**,
and took two hundred *loaves* **breads**,
and two *bottles* **bags** of wine,
and five *sheep ready dressed* **flock worked**,
and five *measures* **seahs** of parched *corn*,
and an hundred *clusters of raisins* **raisincakes**,
and two hundred *cakes* **lumps** of figs,
and *laid* **set** them on *asses* **he burros**.
19 And she said unto her *servants* **lads**,
Go on before me **Pass over at my face**;
behold, I come after you.
But she told not her *husband* **man** Nabal.
20 And it *was so* **became**, *as* she rode on the *ass* **he burro**,
that she *came down* **descended**
by the covert of the *hill* **mountain**, and, behold,
David and his men
came down against **descended to meet** her;
and she met them.
21 Now David had said, Surely in *vain* **falsehood**
have I *kept* **guarded**
all that this *fellow* hath in the wilderness,
so that *nothing* **naught** was *missed* **overseen**
of all that *pertained unto him* **he hath**:
and he hath *requited* **turned back to** me evil for good.
22 *So and more also do God* **Thus add Elohim to work**
unto the enemies of David,
if I *leave* **let survive** of all that *pertain to him* **he hath**
by **toward** the morning light
any that *pisseth* **urinateth** against the wall.
23 And when *Abigail* **Abi Gail** saw David, she hasted,
and *lighted* **descended** off the *ass* **he burro**,
and fell *before* **at the nostrils of** David on her face,
and *bowed* **prostrated** herself to the *ground* **earth**,
24 And fell at his feet, and said, Upon me, my *lord* **adoni**,

upon me let this *iniquity* **perversity** be:
and let *thine handmaid* **thy maid**, I *pray* **beseech** thee,
speak **word** in thine *audience* **ears**,
and hear the words of *thine handmaid* **thy maid**.
25 Let not my *lord* **adoni**, I *pray* **beseech** thee,
regard **set to his heart** this man of *Belial* **Beli Yaal**,
even Nabal: for as his name is, so is he;
Nabal is his name, and folly is with him:
but I *thine handmaid* **thy maid**
saw not the *young men* **lads** of my *lord* **adoni**,
whom thou didst send.
26 Now therefore, my *lord* **adoni**,
as *the LORD* **Yah Veh** liveth, and as thy soul liveth,
seeing *the LORD* **Yah Veh** hath withholden thee
from coming to *shed* blood,
and from *avenging* **saving** thyself with thine own hand,
now let thine enemies,
and they that seek evil to my *lord* **adoni**, be as Nabal.
27 And now this blessing which *thine handmaid* **thy maid**
hath brought unto my *lord* **adoni**,
let it even be given unto the *young men* **lads**
that *follow* **walk at the feet of** my *lord* **adoni**.
28 I *pray* **beseech** thee, *forgive* **lift** the *trespass* **rebellion**
of *thine handmaid* **thy maid**:
for *the LORD will certainly make*
in working, Yah Veh shall work
my *lord a sure* **adoni an amenable** house;
because my *lord* **adoni**
fighteth the *battles* **wars** of *the Lord* **Yah Veh**,
and evil hath not been found in thee all thy days.
29 Yet a *man* **human** is risen to pursue thee,
and to seek thy soul:
but the soul of my *lord* **adoni**
shall be bound in the bundle of life
with *the LORD* **Yah Veh** thy *God* **Elohim**;
and the souls of thine enemies,
them shall he sling *out*,
as *out* **in the midst** of the *middle* **hollow** of a sling.
30 And it shall *come to pass* **become**,
when *the LORD* **Yah Veh**
shall have *done* **worked** to my *lord* **adoni**
according to all the good that he hath *spoken* **worded**
concerning thee,
and shall have *appointed* **misvahed** thee
ruler **eminent** over *Israel* **Yisra El**;
31 That this shall *be no grief unto* **not stagger** thee,
nor *offence* **a stumblingblock** of heart unto my *lord* **adoni**,
either that thou hast *shed* **poured** blood
causeless **gratuitously**,
or that my *lord* **adoni** hath *avenged* **saved** himself:
but when *the LORD* **Yah Veh**
shall have dealt *well* **well—pleasingly** with my *lord* **adoni**,
then remember *thine handmaid* **thy maid**.
32 And David said to *Abigail* **Abi Gail**,
Blessed
be *the LORD God* **Yah Veh Elohim** of *Israel* **Yisra El**,
which sent thee this day to meet me:
33 And blessed be thy *advice* **perception**,
and blessed be thou,
which *hast kept* **restrained** me this day
from coming to *shed* blood,
and from *avenging* **saving** myself with mine own hand.
34 *For in very deed* **But**,
as *the LORD God* **Yah Veh Elohim** of *Israel* **Yisra El** liveth,
which hath *kept* **withheld** me *back*
from *hurting* **vilifying** thee,
except **unless** thou hadst hasted and come to meet me,
surely there had not *been left* **remained** unto Nabal
by the morning light
any that *pisseth* **urinateth** against the wall.
35 So David *received* **took** of her hand
that which she had brought him, and said unto her,
Go up **Ascend** in *peace* **shalom** to thine house;
see, I have hearkened to thy voice,
and have *accepted* **spared** thy *person* **face**.
36 And *Abigail* **Abi Gail** came to Nabal;
and, behold, he held a *feast* **banquet** in his house,
like the *feast* **banquet** of a *king* **sovereign**;
and Nabal's heart was *merry* **good** within him,
for he was *very drunken* **mighty intoxicated**:
wherefore she told him *nothing* **no word**,
less or *more* **great**, until the morning light.
37 But it *came to pass* **became,** in the morning,
when the wine was gone out of Nabal,
and his *wife* **woman** had told him these *things* **words**,
that his heart died within him, and he became as a stone.
38 And it *came to pass* **became,** about ten days *after*,
that *the LORD* **Yah Veh** smote Nabal, and he died.
39 And when David heard that Nabal *was dead* **had died**,
he said, Blessed be *the LORD* **Yah Veh**,
that hath pleaded the *cause* **plea** of my reproach
from the hand of Nabal,
and hath *kept* **restrained** his servant from evil:
for *the LORD* **Yah Veh**
hath returned the *wickedness* **evil** of Nabal
upon his own head.
And David sent
and *communed* **worded** with *Abigail* **Abi Gail**,
to take her to him to *wife* **woman**.
40 And when the servants of David
were come to *Abigail* **Abi Gail** to *Carmel* **Karmel**,
they *spake* **worded** unto her, saying,
David sent us unto thee,
to take thee to him to *wife* **woman**.
41 And she arose, and *bowed* **prostrated** herself
on her *face* **nostrils** to the earth, and said, Behold,
let *thine handmaid* **thy maid** be a *servant* **maid**
to *wash* **bathe** the feet of the servants of my *lord* **adoni**.
42 And *Abigail* **Abi Gail** hasted,
and arose and rode upon *an ass* **a he burro**,
with five *damsels* **lasses** of hers
that went *after her* **at her feet**;
and she went after the *messengers* **angels** of David,
and became his *wife* **woman**.
43 David also took
Ahinoam **Achiy Noam** of *Jezreel* **Yizre El**;
and they were also both of them his *wives* **women**.
44 But *Saul* **Shaul** had given Michal his daughter,
David's *wife* **woman**,
to Phalti the son of Laish, which was of Gallim.

DAVID SPARES SHAUL AGAIN

26 And the *Ziphites* **Ziphiy** came unto *Saul* **Shaul**
to *Gibeah* **Gibah**, saying,
Doth not David hide himself
in the hill of Hachilah,
which is before Jeshimon **at the face of Yeshimon**?
2 Then *Saul* **Shaul** arose,
and *went down* **descended** to the wilderness of Ziph,
having three thousand chosen men of *Israel* **Yisra El**
with him,
to seek David in the wilderness of Ziph.
3 And *Saul pitched* **Shaul encamped**
in the hill of Hachilah,
which is before Jeshimon **at the face of Yeshimon,**
by the way.
But David *abode* **settled** in the wilderness,
and he saw that *Saul* **Shaul** came after him
into the wilderness.
4 David therefore sent out spies,
and *understood* **knew** that *Saul* **Shaul**
was come *in very deed* **prepared**.
5 And David arose, and came to the place
where *Saul* **Shaul** had *pitched* **encamped**:
and David *beheld* **saw** the place where *Saul* **Shaul** lay,
and *Abner* **Abi Ner** the son of Ner,
the *captain* **governor** of his host:
and *Saul* **Shaul** lay in the *trench* **route**,
and the people *pitched* **encamped** round about him.
6 Then answered David
and said to *Ahimelech* **Achiy Melech** the *Hittite* **Hethiy**,
and to *Abishai* **Abi Shai** the son of *Zeruiah* **Seruyah**,
brother to *Joab* **Yah Ab**, saying,
Who *will go down* **shall descend** with me
to *Saul* **Shaul** to the camp?
And *Abishai* **Abi Shai** said,
I *will go down* **shall descend** with thee.
7 So David and *Abishai* **Abi Shai**
came to the people by night: and, behold,
Saul **Shaul** lay sleeping within the *trench* **route**,
and his spear *stuck* **pierced** in the *ground* **earth**

at his *bolster* **headpieces**:
but *Abner* **Abi Ner** and the people lay round about him.
8 Then said *Abishai* **Abi Shai** to David,
God **Elohim** hath *delivered* **shut up** thine enemy
into thine hand this day:
now therefore let me smite him, I *pray* **beseech** thee,
with the spear even to the earth *at once* **one time**,
and *I will* not *smite him* the second time.
9 And David said to *Abishai* **Abi Shai**,
Destroy **Ruin** him not:
for who can *stretch* **send** forth his hand
against *the LORD'S* **Yah Veh's** anointed,
and be *guiltless* **exonorated**?
10 David said furthermore, *As the LORD* **Yah Veh** liveth,
the LORD **Yah Veh** shall smite him;
or his day shall come to die;
or he shall descend into *battle* **war**,
and *perish* **be scraped away**.
11 *The LORD forbid* **Far be it**
that I should *stretch* **send** forth mine hand
against *the LORD'S* **Yah Veh's** anointed:
but, I *pray* **beseech** thee,
take thou now the spear that is at his *bolster* **headpieces**,
and the cruse of water, and let us go.
12 So David took the spear and the cruse of water
from *Saul's bolster* **Shaul's headpieces**;
and they *gat them away* **went**,
and no man saw it, nor knew it, neither awaked:
for they were all asleep;
because a *deep* **sound** sleep from *the LORD* **Yah Veh**
was fallen upon them.
13 Then David *went* **passed** over to the other side,
and stood on the top of *an hill* **a mountain** afar off;
a great *space* **place** *being* between them:
14 And David *cried* **called out** to the people,
and to *Abner* **Abi Ner** the son of Ner, saying,
Answerest thou not, *Abner* **Abi Ner**?
Then *Abner* **Abi Ner** answered and said,
Who art thou that *criest* **callest out** to the *king* **sovereign**?
15 And David said to *Abner* **Abi Ner**,
Art not thou a *valiant* man?
and who is like to thee in *Israel* **Yisra El**?
wherefore then hast thou not *kept* **guarded**
thy *lord* **adoni** the *king* **sovereign**?
for there came one of the people in
to *destroy* **ruin** the *king* **sovereign** thy *lord* **adoni**.
16 This *thing* **word** is not good
that thou hast *done* **worked**.
As the LORD **Yah Veh** liveth,
ye are *worthy to die* **sons of death**,
because ye have not *kept* **guarded** your *master* **adoni**,
the LORD'S **Yah Veh's** anointed.
And now see where the *king's* **sovereign's** spear is,
and the cruse of water that was at his *bolster* **headpieces**.
17 And *Saul knew* **Shaul recognized** David's voice,
and said, Is this thy voice, my son David?
And David said, It is my voice,
my *lord* **adoni**, O *king* **sovereign**.
18 And he said, Wherefore doth my *lord* **adoni**
thus pursue after his servant?
for what have I *done* **worked**?
or what evil is in mine hand?
19 Now therefore, I *pray* **beseech** thee,
let my *lord* **adoni** the *king* **sovereign**
hear the words of his servant.
If *the LORD* **Yah Veh**
have *stirred* **goaded** thee *up* against me,
let him *accept* **scent** an offering:
but if they be the *children* **sons** of *men* **humanity**,
cursed be they *before the LORD* **at the face of Yah Veh**;
for they have driven me out this day
from *abiding* **being scraped**
in the inheritance of *the LORD* **Yah Veh**, saying,
Go, serve other *gods* **elohim**.
20 Now therefore, let not my blood fall to the earth
before **at** the face of *the LORD* **Yah Veh**:
for the *king* **sovereign** of *Israel* **Yisra El**
is *come out* **gone** to seek *a* **one** flea,
as when one *doth hunt* **pursueth** a partridge
in the mountains.
21 Then said *Saul* **Shaul**, I have sinned:
return, my son David:
for I *will* **shall vilify thee** no more *do thee harm*,
because my soul was *precious* **valued** in thine eyes
this day: behold,
I have *played the fool* **follied**,
and have **inadvertently** erred
exceedingly **mightily abounding**.
22 And David answered and said,
Behold the *king's* **sovereign's** spear!
and let one of the *young men* **lads**
come **pass** over and *fetch* **take** it.
23 *The LORD render* **Yah Veh turn back** to every man
his *righteousness* **justness**
and his *faithfulness* **trustworthiness**;
for *the LORD* **Yah Veh**
delivered **gave** thee into my hand to day,
but I *would not stretch* **willed to not send** forth mine hand
against *the LORD'S* **Yah Veh's** anointed.
24 And, behold, as thy *life* **soul** was *much set by* **greatened**
this day in mine eyes,
so let my *life* **soul** be *much set by* **greatened**
in the eyes of *the LORD* **Yah Veh**,
and let him *deliver* **rescue** me out of all tribulation.
25 Then *Saul* **Shaul** said to David,
Blessed be thou, my son David:
in working, thou shalt *both do great things* **work**,
and **in prevailing,** *also* shalt *still* prevail.
So David went on his way,
and *Saul* **Shaul** returned to his place.

DAVID AND THE PELESHETHIY

27 And David said in his heart,
I shall now *perish* **be scraped away** one day
by the hand of *Saul* **Shaul**:
there is *nothing* **naught** better for me
than that I should speedily escape
into the land of the *Philistines* **Peleshethiy**;
and *Saul* **Shaul** shall *despair of me* **quit me**,
to seek me any more in any *coast* **border** of *Israel* **Yisra El**:
so **in escaping,** shall I escape out of his hand.
2 And David arose, and he passed over
with the six hundred men that were with him
unto Achish, the son of Maoch,
king **sovereign** of Gath.
3 And David *dwelt* **settled** with Achish at Gath,
he and his men, every man with his household,
even David with his two *wives* **women**,
Ahinoam **Achiy Noam** the *Jezreelitess* **Yizre Eliyth**,
and *Abigail* **Abi Gail** the *Carmelitess* **Karmeliyth**,
Nabal's *wife* **woman**.
4 And it was told *Saul* **Shaul** that David was fled to Gath:
and he *sought no more again* **added not to seek** for him.
5 And David said unto Achish,
If I have now found *grace* **charism** in thine eyes,
let them give me a place
in *some town in the country* **one of the cities of the field**,
that I may *dwell* **settle** there:
for why should thy servant *dwell* **settle**
in the *royal* **sovereigndom** city with thee?
6 Then Achish gave him *Ziklag* **Siqlag** that day:
wherefore *Ziklag pertaineth* **Siqlag becometh**
unto the *kings* **sovereigns** of *Judah* **Yah Hudah**
unto this day.
7 And the *time* **number of days** that David *dwelt* **settled**
in the *country* **field** of the *Philistines* **Peleshethiy**
was a full year **of days** and four months.
8 And David and his men *went up* **ascended**,
and *invaded* **stripped** the *Geshurites* **Geshuriy**,
and the *Gezrites* **Gezeriy**, and the *Amalekites* **Amaleqiy**:
for *those nations were of old* **they were originally**
the *inhabitants* **settlers** of the land,
as thou goest to Shur,
even unto the land of *Egypt* **Misrayim**.
9 And David smote the land,
and left neither man nor woman alive,
and took away the *sheep* **flock**, and the oxen,
and the *asses* **he burros**, and the camels,
and the *apparel* **covering**,
and returned, and came to Achish.
10 And Achish said,

Whither have ye *made a road* **stripped** to day?
And David said, Against the south of *Judah* **Yah Hudah**,
and against the south of the *Jerahmeelites* **Yerachme Eliy**,
and against the south of the *Kenites* **Qayiniy**.
11 And David *saved* **let** neither man nor woman *alive* **live**,
to bring *tidings* to Gath, saying, Lest they should tell on us,
saying, So *did* **worked** David,
and *so will* **thus shall** be his *manner* **judgment**
all the *while* **days** he *dwelleth* **settleth**
in the *country* **field** of the *Philistines* **Peleshethiy**.
12 And Achish *believed* **trusted** David, saying,
He hath made his people Israel utterly to abhor him;
In stinking, he stinketh among his people Yisra El;
therefore he shall be my servant *for ever* **eternally**.

THE NECROMANCER OF EN DOR

28 And it *came to pass* **became,** in those days,
that the *Philistines* **Peleshethiy**
gathered their *armies* **camps** *together* for *warfare* **hostility**,
to fight with *Israel* **Yisra El**.
And Achish said unto David,
In knowing, Know thou *assuredly* **this**
that thou shalt go out with me *to battle* **into the camp**,
thou and thy men.
2 And David said to Achish,
Surely **Thus** thou shalt know
what thy servant can *do* **work**.
And Achish said to David,
Therefore *will I make* **I shall set** thee
keeper **guard** of mine head *for ever* **all days**.
3 Now *Samuel was dead* **Shemu El died**,
and all *Israel had lamented* **Yisra El chopped over** him,
and *buried* **entombed** him in Ramah, even in his own city.
And *Saul* **Shaul** had *put away* **turned aside**
those that had familiar spirits **the necromancers**,
and the *wizards* **knowers**, out of the land.
4 And the *Philistines* **Peleshethiy**
gathered *themselves together*,
and came and *pitched* **encamped** in Shunem:
and *Saul* **Shaul** gathered all *Israel* **Yisra El** *together*,
and they *pitched* **encamped** in Gilboa.
5 And when *Saul* **Shaul** saw
the *host* **camp** of the *Philistines* **Peleshethiy**,
he *was afraid* **awed**,
and his heart *greatly* **mightily** trembled.
6 And when *Saul* **Shaul**
enquired **asked** of *the LORD* **Yah Veh**,
the LORD **Yah Veh** answered him not,
neither by dreams, nor by Urim, nor by prophets.
7 Then said *Saul* **Shaul** unto his servants,
Seek me a woman
that hath a familiar spirit — **a baalah**,
that I may go to her, and enquire of her.
And his servants said to him, Behold, there is a woman
that hath a familiar spirit — **a baalah**
at *Endor* **En Dor**.
8 And *Saul disguised himself* **Shaul searched**,
and *put on* **enrobed** other *raiment* **clothes**,
and he went, and two men with him,
and they came to the woman by night:
and he said, I *pray* **beseech** thee,
divine unto me by the *familiar spirit* **necromancer**,
and *bring me him up* **ascend him to me**,
whom I shall *name* **say** unto thee.
9 And the woman said unto him, Behold,
thou knowest what *Saul* **Shaul** hath *done* **worked**,
how he hath cut off
those that have familiar spirits **the necromancers**,
and the *wizards* **knowers**, out of the land:
wherefore then layest thou a snare for my *life* **soul**,
to *cause me to die* **deathify me**?
10 And *Saul sware* **Shaul oathed** to her
by *the LORD* **Yah Veh**, saying,
As the LORD **Yah Veh** liveth,
there shall no punishment **perversion** happen to thee
for this *thing* **word**.
11 Then said the woman,
Whom shall I *bring up* **ascend** unto thee?
And he said, *Bring me up Samuel* **Ascend Shemu El**.
12 And when the woman saw *Samuel* **Shemu El**,
she cried with a *loud* **great** voice:
and the woman *spake* **said** to *Saul* **Shaul**, saying,
Why hast thou deceived me? for thou art *Saul* **Shaul**.
13 And the *king* **sovereign** said unto her,
Be not *afraid* **awed**: for what sawest thou?
And the woman said unto *Saul* **Shaul**,
I saw *gods* **elohim** ascending out of the earth.
14 And he said unto her, What **be his** form *is he of*?
And she said, An old man *cometh up* **ascendeth**;
and he is covered with a mantle.
And *Saul* **Shaul** perceived that it was *Samuel* **Shemu El**,
and he *stooped* **bowed**
with his *face* **nostrils** to the *ground* **earth**,
and *bowed* **prostrated** himself.
15 And *Samuel* **Shemu El** said to *Saul* **Shaul**,
Why hast thou *disquieted* **quivered** me,
to *bring* **ascend** me *up*?
And *Saul answered* **Shaul said**,
I am *sore* **mighty** distressed;
for the *Philistines make war* **Peleshethiy fight** against me,
and *God* **Elohim** is *departed* **turned aside** from me,
and answereth me no more,
neither by **the hand of** prophets, nor by dreams:
therefore I have called thee,
that thou mayest make known unto me
what I shall *do* **work**.
16 Then said *Samuel* **Shemu El**,
Wherefore then dost thou ask of me,
seeing *the LORD* **Yah Veh** is *departed* **turned aside** from thee,
and is become thine enemy?
17 And *the LORD* **Yah Veh** hath *done* **worked** to him,
as he *spake* **worded** by *me* **my hand**:
for *the LORD* **Yah Veh** hath *rent* **ripped**
the *kingdom* **sovereigndom** out of thine hand,
and given it to thy *neighbour* **friend**, *even* to David:
18 Because thou *obeyedst* **heardest** not
the voice of *the LORD* **Yah Veh**,
nor *executedst* **workedst** his *fierce* **fuming** wrath
upon *Amalek* **Amaleq**,
therefore hath *the LORD* **Yah Veh**
done **worked** this *thing* **word** unto thee this day.
19 Moreover *the LORD* **Yah Veh**
will **shall** also *deliver Israel* **give Yisra El** with thee
into the hand of the *Philistines* **Peleshethiy**:
and to morrow shalt thou and thy sons be with me:
the LORD **Yah Veh** also
shall *deliver* **give** the *host* **camp** of *Israel* **Yisra El**
into the hand of the *Philistines* **Peleshethiy**.
20 Then *Saul* **Shaul** fell *straightway* **hastily**
all **the fulness of his stature** along on the earth,
and was *sore afraid* **mighty awed**,
because of the words of *Samuel* **Shemu El**:
and there was no *strength* **force** in him;
for he had eaten no bread all the day, nor all the night.
21 And the woman came unto *Saul* **Shaul**,
and saw that he was *sore troubled* **mighty terrified**,
and said unto him, Behold,
thine handmaid **thy maid** hath *obeyed* **heard** thy voice,
and I have *put* **set** my *life* **soul** in my *hand* **palm**,
and have hearkened unto thy words
which thou *spakest* **wordest** unto me.
22 Now therefore, I *pray* **beseech** thee,
hearken thou also
unto the voice of *thine handmaid* **thy maid**,
and let me set a morsel of bread *before thee* **at thy face**;
and eat, that thou mayest have *strength* **force**,
when thou goest on thy way.
23 But he refused, and said, I *will* **shall** not eat.
But his servants, together with the woman,
compelled **urged** him;
and he hearkened unto their voice.
So he arose from the earth, and *sat* **settled** upon the bed.
24 And the woman had a *fat calf* **calf of the stall**
in the house;
and she hasted, and *killed* **sacrificed** it,
and took flour, and kneaded,
and did bake *unleavened bread* **matsah** thereof:
25 And she brought it **near**
before Saul **at the face of Shaul**,
and *before* **at the face of** his servants; and they did eat.
Then they rose up, and went away that night.

PELESHETHIY DISTRUST DAVID

29 Now the *Philistines* **Peleshethiy** gathered *together*
all their *armies* **camps** to *Aphek* **Apheq**:
and the *Israelites* **Yisra Eliy**
pitched **encamped** by a fountain
which is in *Jezreel* **Yizre El**.
2 And the *lords* **ringleaders** of the *Philistines* **Peleshethiy**
passed on by hundreds, and by thousands:
but David and his men passed on
in the rereward **afterward** with Achish.
3 Then said
the *princes* **governors** of the *Philistines* **Peleshethiy**,
What *do* **be** these Hebrews *here*?
And Achish said
unto the *princes* **governors** of the *Philistines* **Peleshethiy**,
Is not this David, the servant of *Saul* **Shaul**
the *king* **sovereign** of *Israel* **Yisra El**,
which hath been with me these days, or these years,
and I have found *no fault* **naught** in him
since **from the day** he fell *unto me* **away** unto this day?
4 And the *princes* **governors** of the *Philistines* **Peleshethiy**
were *wroth* **enraged** with him;
and the *princes* **governors** of the *Philistines* **Peleshethiy**
said unto him, Make this *fellow* **man** return,
that he may *go again* **turn back** to his place
which thou hast *appointed* **overseen for** him,
and let him not *go down* **descend** with us to *battle* **war**,
lest in the *battle* **war** he be *an adversary* **a satan** to us:
for wherewith should he *reconcile* **satisfy** himself
unto his *master* **adoni**?
should it not be with the heads of these men?
5 Is not this David,
of whom they *sang* **answered** one to another
in **round** dances, saying,
Saul slew **Shaul smote** his thousands,
and David his *ten thousands* **myriads**?
6 Then Achish called David, and said unto him,
Surely, as *the LORD* **Yah Veh** liveth,
thou hast been *upright* **straight**,
and thy going out and thy coming in with me
in the *host* **camp** is good in my *sight* **eyes**:
for I have not found evil in thee
since the day of thy coming unto me unto this day:
nevertheless *the lords favour thee not*
in the eyes of the ringleaders thou art not good.
7 Wherefore now return, and go in *peace* **shalom**,
that thou *displease not the lords*
work not evil in the eyes of the ringleaders
of the *Philistines* **Peleshethiy**.
8 And David said unto Achish,
But what have I *done* **worked**?
and what hast thou found in thy servant
so long **from the day** as I have been *with thee* **at thy face**
unto this day,
that I may not go fight against the enemies
of my *lord* **adoni** the *king* **sovereign**?
9 And Achish answered and said to David,
I know that thou art good in my *sight* **eyes**,
as an angel of *God* **Elohim**:
notwithstanding
the *princes* **governors** of the *Philistines* **Peleshethiy**
have said,
He shall not *go up* **ascend** with us to the *battle* **war**.
10 Wherefore now *rise up* **start** early in the morning
with thy *master's* **adoni's** servants that are come with thee:
and as soon as ye *be up* **start** early in the morning,
and have light, *depart* **go**.
11 So David and his men *rose up* **started** early
to *depart* **go** in the morning,
to return into the land of the *Philistines* **Peleshethiy**.
And the *Philistines* **Peleshethiy**
went up **ascended** to *Jezreel* **Yizre El**.

DAVID DESTROYS THE AMALEQIY

30 And it *came to pass* **became**,
when David and his men
were come to *Ziklag* **Siqlag** on the third day,
that the *Amalekites* **Amaleqiy**
had *invaded* **stripped** the south, and *Ziklag* **Siqlag**,
and smitten *Ziklag* **Siqlag**, and burned it with fire;
2 And had taken the women captives, that were therein:
they *slew not any* **deathified no man**, either great or small,
but *carried* **drove** them away, and went on their way.
3 So David and his men came to the city,
and, behold, it was burned with fire;
and their *wives* **women**,
and their sons, and their daughters
were *taken captives* **captured**.
4 Then David and the people that were with him
lifted up their voice and wept,
until they had no more *power* **force** to weep.
5 And David's two *wives* **women**
were *taken captives* **captured**,
Ahinoam **Achiy Noam** the *Jezreelitess* **Yizre Eliyth**,
and *Abigail* **Abi Gail**
the *wife* **woman** of Nabal the *Carmelite* **Karmeliy**.
6 And David was *greatly distressed* **mighty depressed**;
for the people *spake* **said** of stoning him,
because the soul of all the people was *grieved* **embittered**,
every man for his sons and for his daughters:
but David *encouraged* **strengthened** *himself*
in *the LORD* **Yah Veh** his *God* **Elohim**.
7 And David said to *Abiathar* **Abi Athar** the priest,
Ahimelech's **Achiy Melech's** son,
I *pray* **beseech** thee, bring me *hither* **near** the ephod.
And *Abiathar* **Abi Athar** brought *thither* **near** the ephod
to David.
8 And David *enquired* **asked** at *the LORD* **Yah Veh**, saying,
Shall I pursue after this troop? shall I overtake them?
And he *answered* **said to** him, Pursue:
for **in overtaking,** thou shalt *surely* overtake them,
and **in rescuing,** *without fail recover all* **rescue**.
9 So David went,
he and the six hundred men that were with him,
and came to the *brook* **wadi** Besor,
where those that *were left behind* **remained** stayed.
10 But David pursued, he and four hundred men:
for two hundred *abode* **stayed** behind,
which were so *faint* **exhausted**
that they could not *go* **pass** over the *brook* **wadi** Besor.
11 And they found *an Egyptian* **a man — a Misrayim**
in the field,
and *brought* **took** him to David, and gave him bread,
and he did eat; and they made him drink water;
12 And they gave him a *piece* **slice** of a *cake* **lump** of figs,
and two *clusters of raisins* **raisincakes**:
and when he had eaten,
his spirit *came again* **returned** to him:
for he had eaten no bread, nor drunk *any* water,
three days and three nights.
13 And David said unto him,
To whom *belongest* **be** thou? and whence *art* **be** thou?
And he said, I am a *young man of Egypt* **lad — a Misrayim**,
servant to **a man,** an *Amalekite* **Amaleqiy**;
and my *master* **adoni** left me,
because three days agone I fell sick.
14 We *made an invasion upon* **stripped**
the south of the *Cherethites* **Kerethiy**,
and upon *the coast*
which *belongeth* **be** to *Judah* **Yah Hudah**,
and upon the south of *Caleb* **Kaleb**;
and we burned *Ziklag* **Siqlag** with fire.
15 And David said to him,
Canst thou bring me down to this *company* **troop**?
And he said, *Swear* **Oath** unto me by *God* **Elohim**,
that thou *wilt* **shalt** neither *kill* **deathify** me,
nor *deliver* **shut** me into the hands of my *master* **adoni**,
and I *will bring* **shall descend** thee *down*
to this *company* **troop**.
16 And when he had *brought* **descended** him *down*,
behold, they were *spread abroad* **left**
upon **the face of** all the earth,
eating and drinking, and *dancing* **celebrating**,
because of all the great spoil that they had taken
out of the land of the *Philistines* **Peleshethiy**,
and out of the land of *Judah* **Yah Hudah**.
17 And David smote them
from the *twilight* **evening breeze**
even unto the evening of the *next day* **morrow**:
and there escaped not a man of them,
save four hundred *young men* **lads**,

which rode upon camels, and fled.
18 And David *recovered* **rescued** all
that the *Amalekites* **Amaleqiy** had *carried away* **taken**:
and David rescued his two *wives* **women**.
19 And there was *nothing* **naught** lacking to them,
neither **from** small *nor* **to** great,
neither sons nor daughters, neither spoil,
nor *any thing* **aught** that they had taken to them:
David *recovered* **returned** all.
20 And David took all the flocks and the *herds* **oxen**,
which they drave
before **at the face of** those *other cattle* **chattel**,
and said, This is David's spoil.
21 And David came to the two hundred men,
which were so *faint* **exhausted**
that they could not *follow* **go after** David,
whom they had *made also to abide* **settled**
at the *brook* **wadi** Besor:
and they went forth to meet David,
and to meet the people that were with him:
and when David came near to the people,
he *saluted* **asked** them **of shalom**.
22 Then answered all the *wicked* **evil** men
and men of Belial **of Beli Yaal**,
of those **men** that went with David, and said,
Because they went not with us,
we *will* **shall** not give them ought of the spoil
that we have *recovered* **rescued**,
save to every man his *wife* **woman** and his *children* **sons**,
that they may *lead* **drive** them away, and *depart* **go**.
23 Then said David,
Ye shall not *do so* **work thus**, my brethren,
with that which *the LORD* **Yah Veh** hath given us,
who hath *preserved* **guarded** us,
and *delivered* **given** the *company* **troop**
that came against us into our hand.
24 For who *will* **shall** hearken unto you
in this *matter* **word**?
but as his *part* **allotment** is
that *goeth down* **descendeth** to the *battle* **war**,
so **thus** shall his *part* **allotment** be
that *tarrieth* **settleth** by *the stuff* **his instruments**:
they shall *part alike* **allot unitedly**.
25 And *it was so* **thus it became**
from that day *forward* **and onward**,
that he *made* **set** it a statute and *an ordinance* **a judgment**
for *Israel* **Yisra El** unto this day.
26 And when David came to *Ziklag* **Siqlag**,
he sent of the spoil unto the elders of *Judah* **Yah Hudah**,
even to his friends, saying,
Behold a *present* **blessing** for you
of the spoil of the enemies of *the LORD* **Yah Veh**;
27 To them *which were* in *Bethel* **Beth El**,
and to them *which were* in south Ramoth,
and to them *which were* in *Jattir* **Yattir**,
28 And to them *which were* in Aroer,
and to them *which were* in Siphmoth,
and to them *which were* in Eshtemoa,
29 And to them *which were* in Rachal,
and to them *which were* in the cities
of the *Jerahmeelites* **Yerachme Eliy**,
and to them *which were*
in the cities of the *Kenites* **Qayiniy**,
30 And to them *which were* in Hormah,
and to them *which were* in *Chorashan* **Kor Ashan**,
and to them *which were* in Athach,
31 And to them *which were* in Hebron,
and to all the places where David himself
and his men *were wont to haunt* **had walked**.

THE DEATH OF SHAUL

31 Now the *Philistines* **Peleshethiy**
fought against *Israel* **Yisra El**:
and the men of *Israel* **Yisra El** fled
from *before* **the face of** the *Philistines* **Peleshethiy**,
and fell *down slain* **pierced** in mount Gilboa.
2 And the *Philistines* **Peleshethiy**
followed hard **adhered** upon *Saul* **Shaul**
and upon his sons;
and the *Philistines* **Peleshethiy**
slew Jonathan **smote Yah Nathan**,
and *Abinadab* **Abi Nadab**, and *Melchishua* **Malki Shua**,
Saul's **Shaul's** sons.
3 And the *battle went sore* **war was heavy**
against *Saul* **Shaul**,
and the *archers hit* **men bow shooters found** him;
and he was *sore wounded* **mighty writhed**
of the *archers* **shooters**.
4 Then said *Saul* **Shaul**
unto his *armourbearer* **instrument bearer**,
Draw thy sword, and *thrust* **stab** me *through* therewith;
lest these uncircumcised
come and *thrust* **stab** me *through*,
and *abuse* **exploit** me.
But his *armourbearer would* **instrument bearer willed** not;
for he was *sore afraid* **mighty awed**.
Therefore *Saul* **Shaul** took a sword, and fell upon it.
5 And when his *armourbearer* **instrument bearer**
saw that *Saul was dead* **Shaul had died**,
he fell likewise upon his sword, and died with him.
6 So *Saul* **Shaul** died, and his three sons,
and his *armourbearer* **instrument bearer**, and all his men,
that same day together.
7 And when the men of *Israel* **Yisra El**
that were on the other side of the valley,
and *they that were* on the other side *Jordan* **Yarden**,
saw that the men of *Israel* **Yisra El** fled,
and that *Saul* **Shaul** and his sons *were dead* **had died**,
they forsook the cities, and fled;
and the *Philistines* **Peleshethiy**
came and *dwelt* **settled** in them.
8 And it *came to pass* **became,** on the morrow,
when the *Philistines* **Peleshethiy**
came to strip the *slain* **pierced**,
that they found *Saul* **Shaul** and his three sons
fallen in mount Gilboa.
9 And they cut off his head,
and stripped off his *armour* **instruments**,
and sent into the land of the *Philistines* **Peleshethiy**
round about,
to *publish* **evangelize** it in the house of their idols,
and among the people.
10 And they *put* **set** his *armour* **instruments**
in the house of Ashtaroth:
and they *fastened* **staked** his body
to the wall of *Bethshan* **Beth Shaan**.
11 And when the *inhabitants* **settlers**
of *Jabeshgilead* **Yabesh Gilad**
heard of that which the *Philistines* **Peleshethiy**
had *done* **worked** to *Saul* **Shaul**;
12 All the *valiant* men **of valour** arose,
and went all night,
and took the body of *Saul* **Shaul** and the bodies of his sons
from the wall of *Bethshan* **Beth Shaan**,
and came to *Jabesh* **Yabesh**, and burnt them there.
13 And they took their bones,
and *buried* **entombed** them under a *tree* **grove**
at *Jabesh* **Yabesh**, and fasted seven days.

KEY TO INTERPRETING THE EXEGESES:
King James text is in regular type;
Text under exegeses is in oblique type;
Text of exegeses is in bold type.

DAVID HEARS OF SHAUL'S DEATH

1 Now it *came to pass* **became,**
after the death of *Saul* **Shaul,**
when David was returned
from the *slaughter* **smiting** of the *Amalekites* **Amaleqiy,**
and David had *abode* **settled** two days in *Ziklag* **Siqlag;**
2 It *came even to pass* **became,** on the third day,
that, behold, a man came out of the camp from *Saul* **Shaul**
with his clothes *rent* **ripped,** and *earth* **soil** upon his head:
and *so it was* **became,** when he came to David,
that he fell to the earth, and *did obeisance* **prostrated.**
3 And David said unto him, From whence comest thou?
And he said unto him,
Out of the camp of *Israel* **Yisra El** am I escaped.
4 And David said unto him,
How went the *matter* **word**? I *pray* **beseech** thee, tell me.
And he *answered* **said,**
That the people are fled from the *battle* **war,**
and *many* **an abounding** of the people also are fallen
and *dead* **die;**
and *Saul* **Shaul** and *Jonathan* **Yah Nathan** his son
are dead **have died** also.
5 And David said unto the *young man* **lad** that told him,
How knowest thou
that *Saul* **Shaul** and *Jonathan* **Yah Nathan** his son
be dead **have died?**
6 And the young man that told him said,
As I happened by chance **In meeting,**
as I met upon mount Gilboa, behold,
Saul **Shaul** leaned upon his spear; and, *lo* **behold,**
the chariots and *horsemen* **masters of the cavalry**
followed hard **adhered** after him.
7 And when he *looked* **faced** behind him, he saw me,
and called unto me. And I *answered* **said,** Here am I.
8 And he said unto me, Who art thou?
And I *answered* **said to** him, I am an *Amalekite* **Amaleqiy.**
9 He said unto me again,
Stand, I *pray* **beseech** thee, upon me, and slay me:
for *anguish is come upon*
my embroidered mail possesseth me,
because my *life* **soul** is yet whole in me.
10 So I stood upon him, and *slew* **deathified** him,
because I *was sure* **knew** that he could not live
after that he was fallen:
and I took the *crown* **separatism** that was upon his head,
and the *bracelet* **anklet** that was on his arm,
and have brought them hither unto my *lord* **adoni.**
11 Then David took hold on his clothes,
and *rent* **ripped** them;
and likewise all the men that were with him:
12 And they *mourned* **chopped,** and wept,
and fasted until even,
for *Saul* **Shaul,** and for *Jonathan* **Yah Nathan** his son,
and for the people of *the LORD* **Yah Veh,**
and for the house of *Israel* **Yisra El;**
because they were fallen by the sword.
13 And David said unto the young man that told him,
Whence art thou?
And he *answered* **said,**
I am the son of a *stranger* **man, a sojourner,**
an *Amalekite* **Amaleqiy.**
14 And David said unto him,
How wast thou not *afraid* **awed**
to *stretch* **send** forth thine hand
to *destroy the LORD'S* **ruin Yah Veh's** anointed?
15 And David called one of the *young men* **lads,**
and said, Go near, *and fall* **encounter** upon him.
And he smote him that he died.
16 And David said unto him,
Thy blood be upon thy head;
for thy mouth hath *testified* **answered** against thee, saying,
I have *slain the LORD'S* **deathified Yah Veh's** anointed.

DAVID'S LAMENTATION

17 And David lamented with this lamentation
over *Saul* **Shaul** and over *Jonathan* **Yah Nathan** his son:
18 (Also he *bade them* **said**
to teach the *children* **sons** of *Judah* **Yah Hudah**
the use of the bow:
behold, it is *written* **inscribed**
in the *book* **scroll** of *Jasher* **the straight.**)
Apocalypse 20:12
19 The *beauty* **splendour** of *Israel* **Yisra El** is *slain* **pierced**
upon thy *high places* **bamahs:**
how are the mighty fallen!
20 Tell it not in Gath,
publish **evangelize** it not
in the *streets* **outskirts** of *Askelon* **Ashqelon;**
lest the daughters of the *Philistines* **Peleshethiy**
rejoice **cheer,**
lest the daughters of the uncircumcised
triumph **jump for joy.**
21 Ye mountains of Gilboa,
let there be no — **neither** dew,
neither *let there be* rain, upon you,
nor fields of *offerings* **exaltments:**
for there the *shield* **buckler** of the mighty
is vilely cast away **loatheth,**
the *shield* **buckler** of *Saul* **Shaul,**
as *though he had* not been anointed with oil.
22 From the blood of the *slain* **pierced,**
from the fat of the mighty,
the bow of *Jonathan* **Yah Nathan**
turned **retreated** not *back,*
and the sword of *Saul* **Shaul**
returned not empty.
23 *Saul* **Shaul** and *Jonathan* **Yah Nathan**
were lovely and pleasant in their lives,
and in their death they were not *divided* **separated:**
they were swifter than eagles,
they *were stronger than* **prevailed mightily over** lions.
24 Ye daughters of *Israel* **Yisra El,** weep over *Saul* **Shaul,**
who *clothed* **enrobed** you in scarlet,
with *other delights* **pleasures,**
who *put on* **ascended** ornaments of gold
upon your *apparel* **robe.**
25 How are the mighty fallen
in the midst of the *battle* **war!**
O *Jonathan* **Yah Nathan,**
thou wast *slain* **pierced** in *thine high places* **thy bamahs.**
26 I am distressed for thee,
my brother *Jonathan* **Yah Nathan:**
very pleasant **mighty pleasing** hast thou been unto me:
thy love to me was *wonderful* **marvellous,**
passing the love of women.
27 How are the mighty fallen,
and the *weapons* **instruments** of war *perished* **destroyed!**

DAVID ANOINTED SOVEREIGN

2 And it *came to pass* **became,** after this,
that David *enquired* **asked** of *the LORD* **Yah Veh,** saying,
shall I *go up* **ascend**
into *any* **one** of the cities of *Judah* **Yah Hudah?**
And *the LORD* **Yah Veh** said unto him, *Go up* **Ascend.**
And David said, Whither shall I *go up* **ascend?**
And he said, Unto Hebron.
2 So David *went up* **ascended** thither,
and his two *wives* **women** also,
Ahinoam **Achiy Noam** the *Jezreelitess* **Yizre Eliyth,**
and *Abigail* **Abi Gail**
Nabal's *wife* **woman** the *Carmelite* **Karmeliy.**
3 And his men that were with him
did David *bring up* **ascend,**
every man with his household:
and they *dwelt* **settled** in the cities of Hebron.
4 And the men of *Judah* **Yah Hudah** came,
and there they anointed David
king **sovereign** over the house of *Judah* **Yah Hudah.**
And they told David, saying,
That the men of *Jabeshgilead* **Yabesh Gilad**
were they that *buried Saul* **entombed Shaul.**
5 And David sent *messengers* **angels**
unto the men of *Jabeshgilead* **Yabesh Gilad,**
and said unto them, Blessed be ye of *the LORD* **Yah Veh,**
that ye have *shewed* **worked** this *kindness* **mercy**
unto your *lord* **adoni,** even unto *Saul* **Shaul,**
and have *buried* **entombed** him.
6 And now *the LORD* **Yah Veh**

shew kindness **work mercy** and truth unto you:
and I also
will requite **shall work** you this *kindness* **goodness**,
because ye have *done* **worked** this *thing* **word**.
7 Therefore now let your hands be strengthened,
and be ye *valiant* **sons of valour**:
for your *master Saul is dead* **adoni Shaul hath died**,
and also the house of *Judah* **Yah Hudah**
have anointed me *king* **sovereign** over them.

SHAUL'S SON REIGNS OVER YISRA EL

8 But *Abner* **Abi Ner** the son of Ner,
captain **governor** of *Saul's* **Shaul**'s host,
took *Ishbosheth* **Ish Bosheth** the son of *Saul* **Shaul**,
and *brought* **passed** him over to *Mahanaim* **Machanayim**;
9 And *made* **caused** him *king* **to reign** over *Gilead* **Gilad**,
and over the *Ashurites* **Ashshuriy**,
and over *Jezreel* **Yizre El**,
and over *Ephraim* **Ephrayim**,
and over *Benjamin* **Ben Yamin**,
and over all *Israel* **Yisra El**.
10 *Ishbosheth Saul's* **Ish Bosheth Shaul's** son
was **a son of** forty years *old*
when he began to reign over *Israel* **Yisra El**,
and reigned two years.
But the house of *Judah* **Yah Hudah**
followed **went after** David.
11 And the *time* **number of days**
that David was *king* **sovereign** in Hebron
over the house of *Judah* **Yah Hudah**
was seven years and six months.

CIVIL WAR

12 And *Abner* **Abi Ner** the son of Ner,
and the servants of *Ishbosheth* **Ish Bosheth**
the son of *Saul* **Shaul**,
went out from *Mahanaim* **Machanayim** to *Gibeon* **Gibon**.
13 And *Joab* **Yah Ab** the son of *Zeruiah* **Seruyah**,
and the servants of David,
went out, and met together by the pool of *Gibeon* **Gibon**:
and they *sat down* **settled**,
the one
on the one side of the pool **by the pool here**,
and the *other* **one**
on the other side of the pool **by the pool there**.
14 And *Abner* **Abi Ner** said to *Joab* **Yah Ab**,
Let the *young men* **lads** now arise,
and *play before us* **entertain at our face**.
And *Joab* **Yah Ab** said, Let them arise.
15 Then there arose and *went* **passed** over by number
twelve of *Benjamin* **Ben Yamin**,
which pertained to Ishbosheth **of Ish Bosheth**
the son of *Saul* **Shaul**,
and twelve of the servants of David.
16 And *they caught every one* **each man held**
his *fellow* **friend** by the head,
and *thrust* his sword in his *fellow's* **friend's** side;
so they fell *down* together:
wherefore that place was called
Helkathhazzurim **Helgath Hats Surim**,
which is in *Gibeon* **Gibon**.
17 And there was a *very sore battle* **mighty hard war**
that day;
and *Abner* **Abi Ner** was *beaten* **smitten**,
and the men of *Israel* **Yisra El**,
before **at the face of** the servants of David.
18 And there were three sons of *Zeruiah* **Seruyah** there,
Joab **Yah Ab**, and *Abishai* **Abi Shai**, and *Asahel* **Asa El**:
and *Asahel* **Asa El** was as *light* **swift** of foot
as *a wild roe* **one of the gazelles in the field**.
19 And *Asahel* **Asa El** pursued after *Abner* **Abi Ner**;
and in going
he *turned* **extended** not to the right *hand* nor to the left
from following Abner **after Abi Ner**.
20 Then *Abner looked* **Abi Ner faced** behind him,
and said, Art thou *Asahel* **Asa El**?
And he *answered* **said**, *I am*.
21 And *Abner* **Abi Ner** said to him,
Turn thee aside **Extend** to thy right *hand* or to thy left,
and lay thee hold on one of the *young men* **lads**,
and take thee his *armour* **clothes**.
But *Asahel would* **Asa El willed to** not turn aside
from *following of* **after** him.
22 And *Abner* **Abi Ner**
said again **added to say** to *Asahel* **Asa El**,
Turn thee aside from *following* **after** me:
wherefore should I smite thee to the *ground* **earth**?
how then should I *hold up* **lift** my face
to *Joab* **Yah Ab** thy brother?
23 Howbeit he refused to turn aside:
wherefore *Abner* **Abi Ner**
with the *hinder end* **back** of the spear
smote him under the fifth *rib*,
that the spear *came out* **went** behind him;
and he fell *down* there,
and died *in the same place* **under it**:
and it *came to pass* **became**,
that as many as came to the place
where *Asahel* **Asa El** fell *down* and died stood still.
24 *Joab* **Yah Ab** also and *Abishai* **Abi Shai**
pursued after *Abner* **Abi Ner**:
and the sun *went down* **descended**
when they were come to the hill of Ammah,
that lieth before Giah **at the face of Giach**
by the way of the wilderness of *Gibeon* **Gibon**.
25 And the *children* **sons** of *Benjamin* **Ben Yamin**
gathered themselves together after *Abner* **Abi Ner**,
and became one *troop* **band**,
and stood on the top of *an* **one** hill.
26 Then *Abner* **Abi Ner** called to *Joab* **Yah Ab**, and said,
Shall the sword devour *for ever* **in perpetuity**?
knowest thou not
that it *will* **shall** be *bitterness* **bitter** in the latter end?
how long shall it be then, ere thou *bid* **say to** the people
return from *following* **after** their brethren?
27 And *Joab* **Yah Ab** said, *As God* **Elohim** liveth,
unless thou hadst *spoken* **worded**,
surely then in the morning
the people had *gone up* **ascended**
every one **each man** from *following* **after** his brother.
28 So *Joab blew* **Yah Ab blast** a trumpet,
and all the people stood still,
and pursued after *Israel* **Yisra El** no more,
neither *fought they any more* **added they yet to fight**.
29 And *Abner* **Abi Ner** and his men
walked all that night through the plain,
and passed over *Jordan* **Yarden**,
and went through all Bithron,
and they came to *Mahanaim* **Machanayim**.
30 And *Joab* **Yah Ab** returned
from *following Abner* **after Abi Ner**:
and when he had gathered all the people *together*,
there *lacked* **mustered** of David's servants
nineteen men and *Asahel* **Asa El**.
31 But the servants of David had smitten
of *Benjamin* **Ben Yamin**, and of *Abner's* **Abi Ner's** men,
so that three hundred and *threescore* **sixty** men died.
32 And they *took up Asahel* **lifted Asa El**,
and *buried* **entombed** him
in the *sepulchre* **tomb** of his father,
which was in *Bethlehem* **Beth Lechem**.
And *Joab* **Yah Ab** and his men went all night,
and they came to Hebron at *break of day* **light**.

DAVID'S HOUSEHOLD STRENGTHENED

3 Now there was long war
between the house of *Saul* **Shaul** and the house of David:
but David
waxed stronger and stronger **walked on strengthened**,
and the house of Saul
waxed weaker and weaker **walked on poor**.

DAVID GENDERS SONS

2 And unto David were sons born in Hebron:
and his firstborn was Amnon,
of *Ahinoam* **Achiy Noam** the *Jezreelitess* **Yizre Eliyth**;
3 And his second, *Chileab* **Kil Ab**, of *Abigail* **Abi Gail**
the *wife* **woman** of Nabal the *Carmelite* **Karmeliy**;
and the third,
Absalom **Abi Shalom** the son of Maachah
the daughter of *Talmai king* **Talmay sovereign** of Geshur;
4 And the fourth,
Adonijah **Adoni Yah** the son of Haggith;
and the fifth,

Shephatiah **Shaphat Yah** the son of *Abital* **Abi Tal**;
5 And the sixth,
Ithream **Yithre Am**, by Eglah David's *wife* **woman**.
These were born to David in Hebron.

ABI NER UNITES WITH DAVID

6 And it *came to pass* **became**, while there was war
between the house of *Saul* **Shaul** and the house of David,
that *Abner made* **Abi Ner strengthened** himself *strong*
for the house of *Saul* **Shaul**.
7 And *Saul* **Shaul** had a concubine,
whose name was *Rizpah* **Rispah**,
the daughter of *Aiah* **Ajah**:
and *Ishbosheth* **he** said to *Abner* **Abi Ner**,
Wherefore hast thou gone in unto my father's concubine?
8 Then was *Abner very wroth* **Abi Ner mighty inflamed**
for the words of *Ishbosheth* **Ish Bosheth**,
and said, *Am* I a dog's head,
which against *Judah* **Yah Hudah**
do shew kindness **worketh mercy** this day
unto the house of *Saul* **Shaul** thy father,
to his brethren, and to his *friends* **companions**,
and have not *delivered* **presented** thee
into the hand of David,
that thou *chargest* **visitest** me to day
with a *fault* **perversion** concerning this woman?
9 So *do God* **work Elohim** to *Abner* **Abi Ner**,
and *more* **add** also, except,
as *the LORD* **Yah Veh** hath *sworn* **oathed** to David,
even so I *do* **work** to him;
10 To *translate* **pass over** the *kingdom* **sovereigndom**
from the house of *Saul* **Shaul**,
and to *set up* **raise** the throne of David
over *Israel* **Yisra El** and over *Judah* **Yah Hudah**,
from Dan even to *Beersheba* **Beer Sheba**.
11 And he could not
answer Abner **return Abi Ner** a word *again*,
because he *feared* **awed** him.
12 And *Abner* **Abi Ner**
sent *messengers* **angels** to David on his behalf,
saying, Whose is the land?
saying *also*, *Make* **Cut** thy *league* **covenant** with me,
and, behold, my hand shall be with thee,
to *bring* **turn** about all *Israel* **Yisra El** unto thee.
13 And he said, *Well* **Good**;
I *will make* **shall cut** a *league* **covenant** with thee:
but one *thing* **word** I *require* **ask** of thee, *that is* **saying**,
Thou shalt not see my face,
except thou first bring
Michal *Saul's* **Shaul's** daughter,
when thou comest to see my face.
14 And David sent *messengers* **angels**
to *Ishbosheth* **Ish Bosheth,** *Saul's* **Shaul's** son, saying,
Deliver **Give** me my *wife* **woman** Michal,
which I *espoused* **betrothed** to me
for an hundred foreskins of the *Philistines* **Peleshethiy**.
15 And *Ishbosheth* **Ish Bosheth** sent,
and took her from her *husband* **man**,
even from *Phaltiel* **Phalti El** the son of *Laish* **Lush**.
16 And her *husband* **man** went with her
along **walking and** weeping behind her
to *Bahurim* **Bachurim.**
Then said *Abner* **Abi Ner** unto him, Go, return.
And he returned.
17 And *Abner* **Abi Ner** had *communication* **word**
with the elders of *Israel* **Yisra El**, saying,
ye sought for David *in times past* **three yesters ago**
to be *king* **sovereign** over you:
18 Now then *do* **work** it:
for *the LORD* **Yah Veh** hath *spoken* **said** of David,
saying, By the hand of my servant David
I *will* **shall** save my people *Israel* **Yisra El**
out of the hand of the *Philistines* **Peleshethiy**,
and out of the hand of all their enemies.
19 And *Abner* **Abi Ner**
also *spake* **worded** in the ears of *Benjamin* **Ben Yamin**:
and *Abner* **Abi Ner** went also
to *speak* **word** in the ears of David in Hebron
all that seemed good *to Israel* **in the eyes of Yisra El**,
and that seemed good
to **in the eyes of** the whole house of *Benjamin* **Ben Yamin**.
20 So *Abner* **Abi Ner** came to David to Hebron,
and twenty men with him.
And David *made Abner* **worked Abi Ner**
and the men that were with him a *feast* **banquet**.
21 And *Abner* **Abi Ner** said unto David,
I *will* **shall** arise and go,
and *will* **shall** gather all *Israel* **Yisra El**
unto my *lord* **adoni** the *king* **sovereign**,
that they may *make* **cut** a *league* **covenant** with thee,
and that thou mayest reign
over all that *thine heart* **thy soul** desireth.
And David sent *Abner* **Abi Ner** away;
and he went in *peace* **shalom**.

YAH AB DEATHIFIES ABI NER

22 And, behold, the servants of David and *Joab* **Yah Ab**
came from *pursuing* a troop,
and brought in a great spoil with them:
but *Abner* **Abi Ner** was not with David in Hebron;
for he had sent him away,
and he was gone in *peace* **shalom**.
23 When *Joab* **Yah Ab** and all the host that was with him
were come,
they told *Joab* **Yah Ab**, saying,
Abner **Abi Ner** the son of Ner came to the *king* **sovereign**,
and he hath sent him away,
and he is gone in *peace* **shalom**.
24 Then *Joab* **Yah Ab** came to the *king* **sovereign**,
and said, What hast thou *done* **worked**?
behold, *Abner* **Abi Ner** came unto thee;
why is it that thou hast sent him away,
and *he is quite gone* **in walking, he hath walked away**?
25 Thou knowest *Abner* **Abi Ner** the son of Ner,
that he came to *deceive* **entice** thee,
and to know
thy *going out* **rising** and thy *coming in* **entering**,
and to know all that thou *dost* **workest**.
26 And when *Joab* **Yah Ab**
was come out **went** from David,
he sent *messengers* **angels** after *Abner* **Abi Ner**,
which *brought* **turned** him *again* from the well of Sirah:
but David knew it not.
27 And when *Abner* **Abi Ner** was returned to Hebron,
Joab took **Yah Ab turned** him aside
in the *gate* **midst of the portal**
to *speak* **word** with him *quietly* **serenely**,
and smote him there under the fifth *rib*, that he died,
for the blood of *Asahel* **Asa El** his brother.
28 And afterward when David heard it, he said,
I and my *kingdom* **sovereigndom** are *guiltless* **innocent**
before the LORD for ever **at the face of Yah Veh eternally**
from the blood of *Abner* **Abi Ner** the son of Ner:
29 *Let it rest* **It waiteth** on the head of *Joab* **Yah Ab**,
and on all his father's house;
and let there not *fail* **be cut off**
from the house of *Joab* **Yah Ab**
one that *hath an issue* **floweth**, or that is a leper,
or that *leaneth on* **holdeth** a *staff* **crutch**,
or that falleth on the sword, or that lacketh bread.
30 So *Joab* **Yah Ab**, and *Abishai* **Abi Shai** his brother
slew Abner **slaughtered Abi Ner**,
because he had *slain* **deathified**
their brother *Asahel* **Asa El**
at *Gibeon* **Gibon** in the *battle* **war**.
31 And David said to *Joab* **Yah Ab**,
and to all the people that were with him,
Rend **Rip** your clothes, and gird you with *sackcloth* **saq**,
and *mourn before Abner* **chop at the face of Abi Ner**.
And *king* **sovereign** David *himself*
followed the bier **walked after the bed**.
32 And they *buried Abner* **entombed Abi Ner** in Hebron:
and the *king* **sovereign** lifted *up* his voice,
and wept at the *grave* **tomb** of *Abner* **Abi Ner**;
and all the people wept.
33 And the *king* **sovereign** lamented over *Abner* **Abi Ner**,
and said, *Died as a fool dieth Abner*
Dieth Abi Ner the death of a fool?
34 Thy hands were not bound,
nor thy feet *put into fetters* **approached copper**:
as a man falleth *before* **at the face of** wicked *men* **sons**,
so fellest thou.

And all the people *wept again* **added to weep** over him.
35 And when all the people came
to cause David to *eat meat* **chew bread**
while it was *yet* **still** day,
David *sware* **oathed**, saying,
So do God **Thus work Elohim** to me,
and *more* may **add** also,
if I taste bread, or ought *else* **at all**,
till **the face of** the sun be down.
36 And all the people *took notice of* **recognized** it,
and it *pleased them* **was good in their eyes**:
as whatsoever the *king did* **sovereign worked**
pleased **was good in the eyes of** all the people.
37 For all the people and all *Israel* **Yisra El**
understood **knew** that day
that it was not of the *king* **sovereign**
to *slay Abner* **deathify Abi Ner** the son of Ner.
38 And the *king* **sovereign** said unto his servants,
Know ye not
that there is a *prince* **governor** and a great man
fallen this day in *Israel* **Yisra El**?
39 And I am this day *weak* **tender**,
though anointed *king* **sovereign**;
and these men the sons of *Zeruiah* **Seruyah**
be too hard for me:
the LORD **Yah Veh** shall *reward* **shalam**
the *doer* **worker** of evil according to his *wickedness* **evil**.

ISH BOSHETH IS DEATHIFIED

4 And when *Saul's* **Shaul's** son heard
that *Abner was dead* **Abi Ner died** in Hebron,
his hands *were feeble* **slackened**,
and all the *Israelites* **Yisra Eliy** were *troubled* **terrified**.
2 And *Saul's* **Shaul's** son had two men
that were *captains* **governors** of *bands* **troops**:
the name of the one was Baanah,
and the name of the *other* **second** Rechab,
the sons of Rimmon a *Beerothite* **Beerothiy**,
of the *children* **sons** of *Benjamin* **Ben Yamin**:
(for Beeroth also was *reckoned* **fabricated**
to *Benjamin* **Ben Yamin**.
3 And the *Beerothites* **Beerothiy** fled to *Gittaim* **Gittayim**,
and were sojourners there until this day.)
4 And *Jonathan* **Yah Nathan**, *Saul's* **Shaul's** son,
had a son that was *lame* **smitten** of his feet.
He was **a son of** five years *old*
when the *tidings* **reports** came
of *Saul* **Shaul** and *Jonathan* **Yah Nathan**
out of *Jezreel* **Yizre El**,
and his *nurse took* **foster lifted** him *up*, and fled:
and it *came to pass* **became**, as she made haste to flee,
that he fell, and *became lame* **limped**.
And his name was *Mephibosheth* **Mephi Bosheth**.
5 And the sons of Rimmon the *Beerothite* **Beerothiy**,
Rechab and Baanah, went,
and came about the heat of the day
to the house of *Ishbosheth* **Ish Bosheth**,
who lay on a bed at noon.
6 And they came thither into the midst of the house,
as though they *would have fetched* **should take** wheat;
and they smote him under the fifth *rib*:
and Rechab and Baanah his brother escaped.
7 For when they came into the house,
he lay on his bed in his bedchamber,
and they smote him, and *slew* **deathified** him,
and *beheaded him* **twisted off his head**,
and took his head,
and *gat them away* **journeyed** through the plain all night.
8 And they brought the head of *Ishbosheth* **Ish Bosheth**
unto David to Hebron, and said to the *king* **sovereign**,
Behold the head of *Ishbosheth* **Ish Bosheth**
the son of *Saul* **Shaul** thine enemy,
which sought thy *life* **soul**;
and *the LORD hath avenged* **Yah Veh giveth avengements**
to my *lord* **adoni** the *king* **sovereign** this day
of *Saul* **Shaul**, and of his seed.
9 And David answered Rechab
and Baanah his brother,
the sons of Rimmon the *Beerothite* **Beerothiy**,
and said unto them, *As the LORD* **Yah Veh** liveth,
who hath redeemed my soul
out of all *adversity* **tribulation**,
10 When one told me, saying,
Behold, *Saul is dead* **Shaul died**,
thinking to have brought good tidings
who in his own eyes became a bringer of evangelism,
I took hold of him,
and *slew* **slaughtered** him in *Ziklag* **Siqlag**,
who thought that I would have given him a reward
instead of giving him for his *tidings* **evangelism**:
11 *How much more* **Also**, when wicked men
have *slain* **slaughtered** a *righteous person* **just man**
in his own house upon his bed?
shall I not *therefore now require* **seek** his blood
of your hand,
and *take* **burn** you away from the earth?
12 And David *commanded* **misvahed** his *young men* **lads**,
and they *slew* **slaughtered** them,
and *cut* **chopped** off their hands and their feet,
and hanged them up over the pool in Hebron.
But they took the head of *Ishbosheth* **Ish Bosheth**,
and *buried* **entombed** it
in the *sepulchre* **tomb** of *Abner* **Abi Ner** in Hebron.

DAVID ANOINTED SOVEREIGN

5 Then came all the *tribes* **scions** of *Israel* **Yisra El**
to David unto Hebron, and *spake* **said**, saying,
Behold, we are thy bone and thy flesh.
2 Also *in time past* **three yesters ago**,
when *Saul* **Shaul** was *king* **sovereign** over us,
thou wast he that *leddest* **broughtest** out
and broughtest in *Israel* **Yisra El**:
and *the LORD* **Yah Veh** said to thee,
Thou shalt *feed* **tend** my people *Israel* **Yisra El**,
and thou shalt be *a captain* **eminent** over *Israel* **Yisra El**.
3 So all the elders of *Israel* **Yisra El**
came to the *king* **sovereign** to Hebron;
and *king* **sovereign** David
made **cut** a *league* **covenant** with them in Hebron
before the LORD **at the face of Yah Veh**:
and they anointed David
king **sovereign** over *Israel* **Yisra El**.
4 David was **a son of** thirty years *old*
when he began to reign,
and he reigned forty years.
5 In Hebron he reigned over *Judah* **Yah Hudah**
seven years and six months:
and in *Jerusalem* **Yeru Shalem**
he reigned thirty and three years
over all *Israel* **Yisra El** and *Judah* **Yah Hudah**.
6 And the *king* **sovereign** and his men
went to *Jerusalem* **Yeru Shalem** unto the *Jebusites* **Yebusiy**,
the *inhabitants* **settlers** of the land:
which *spake* **said** unto David, saying,
Except thou *take away* **turn aside** the blind and the lame,
thou shalt not come in hither:
thinking **saying**, David cannot come in hither.
7 *Nevertheless*
David *took* **captured** the strong hold of *Zion* **Siyon**:
the same is **being** the city of David.
8 And David said on that day,
Whosoever *getteth up* **toucheth** to the *gutter* **culvert**,
and smiteth the *Jebusites* **Yebusiy**,
and the lame and the blind,
that are hated of David's soul,
he shall be chief and captain.
Wherefore they said,
The blind and the lame shall not come into the house.
9 So David *dwelt* **settled** in the *fort* **stronghold**,
and called it the city of David.
And David built round about from Millo
and inward **the house**.
10 And **in walking,** David *went* **walked** on,
and *grew great* **walked and greatened**,
and *the LORD God of hosts* **Yah Veh Elohim Sabaoth**
was with him.
11 And Hiram *king* **sovereign** of *Tyre* **Sor**
sent *messengers* **angels** to David,
and cedar trees, and *carpenters* **artificers of timber**,
and *masons* **artificers of the stone for the wall**:
and they built David an house.
12 And David perceived that *the LORD* **Yah Veh**

had established him *king* **sovereign** over *Israel* **Yisra El**,
and that he had *exalted* **lifted** his *kingdom* **sovereigndom**
for his people *Israel's* **Yisra El's** sake.
13 And David took him
more concubines and *wives* **women**
out of *Jerusalem* **Yeru Shalem**,
after he was come from Hebron:
and there were yet sons and daughters born to David.
14 And these be the names of those
that were born unto him in *Jerusalem* **Yeru Shalem**;
Shammuah, and Shobab,
and Nathan, and *Solomon* **Shelomoh**,
15 *Ibhar* **Yibchar** also, and *Elishua* **Eli Shua**,
and Nepheg, and *Japhia* **Yaphia**,
16 And *Elishama* **Eli Shama**, and *Eliada* **El Ad**,
and *Eliphalet* **Eli Phelet**.
17 But when the *Philistines* **Peleshethiy** heard
that they had anointed David
king **sovereign** over *Israel* **Yisra El**,
all the *Philistines* **Peleshethiy**
came up **ascended** to seek David;
and David heard of it,
and *went down* **descended** to the hold.
18 The *Philistines* **Peleshethiy** also came
and *spread* **dispersed** *themselves* in the valley of Rephaim.
19 And David *enquired* **asked** of *the LORD* **Yah Veh**,
saying,
Shall I *go up* **ascend** to the *Philistines* **Peleshethiy**?
wilt **shalt** thou *deliver* **give** them into mine hand?
And *the LORD* **Yah Veh** said unto David, *Go up* **Ascend**:
for **in giving,** I *will doubtless deliver* **shall give**
the *Philistines* **Peleshethiy** into thine hand.
20 And David came to *Baalperazim* **Baal Perasim**,
and David smote them there, and said,
The LORD **Yah Veh**
hath *broken forth* **breached** upon mine enemies
before me **at my face**, as the breach of waters.
Therefore he called the name of that place
Baalperazim **Baal Perasim**.
21 And there they left their *images* **idols**,
and David and his men *burned* **lifted** them **away**.
22 And the *Philistines* **Peleshethiy**
came up yet again **added to ascend**,
and *spread* **dispersed** *themselves* in the valley of Rephaim.
23 And when David *enquired* **asked** of *the LORD* **Yah Veh**,
he said, Thou shalt not *go up* **ascend**;
but *fetch a compass* **go about** behind them,
and come upon them
over against **opposite** the *mulberry trees* **weepers**.
24 And *let it be* **it becometh**,
when thou hearest the *sound* **voice** of *a going* **marching**
in the tops of the *mulberry trees* **weepers**,
that then thou shalt *bestir thyself* **point**:
for then shall *the LORD* **Yah Veh**
go *out before thee* **at thy face**,
to smite the *host* **camp** of the *Philistines* **Peleshethiy**.
25 And David *did* **worked** so,
as *the LORD* **Yah Veh** had *commanded* **misvahed** him;
and smote the *Philistines* **Peleshethiy**
from Geba until thou come to *Gazer* **Gezer**.

ARK BROUGHT TO YERU SHALEM

6 *Again*, David *gathered together* **added to gather**
all the chosen *men* of *Israel* **Yisra El**, thirty thousand.
2 And David arose, and went with all the people
that were with him from Baale *of Judah* **Yah Hudah**,
to *bring up* **ascend** from thence the ark of *God* **Elohim**,
whose name is called by the name of
the LORD of hosts **Yah Veh Sabaoth**
that *dwelleth* **settleth**
between **upon** the *cherubims* **cherubim**.
3 And they *set* **rode** the ark of *God* **Elohim**
upon a new *cart* **wagon**,
and *brought* **lifted** it out
of the house of *Abinadab* **Abi Nadab**
that was in *Gibeah* **Gibah**:
and Uzzah and *Ahio* **Achyo**,
the sons of *Abinadab* **Abi Nadab**,
drave the new *cart* **wagon**.
4 And they *brought* **lifted** it out
of the house of *Abinadab* **Abi Nadab**
which was at *Gibeah* **Gibah**,
accompanying the ark of *God* **Elohim**:
and *Ahio went before* **Achyo walked at the face of** the ark.
5 And David and all the house of *Israel* **Yisra El**
played **entertained**
before the LORD **at the face of Yah Veh**
on all manner of
instruments made of fir wood **cypress timber**,
even on harps, and on *psalteries* **bagpipes**,
and on *timbrels* **tambourines**, and on *cornets* **sistrums**,
and on cymbals.
6 And when they came
to Nachon's threshingfloor,
Uzzah *put* **sent** forth *his hand* to the ark of *God* **Elohim**,
and took hold of it; for the oxen *shook* **released** it.
7 And the *anger* **wrath** of *the LORD* **Yah Veh**
was kindled against Uzzah;
and *God* **Elohim** smote him there for his *error* **deception**;
and there he died by the ark of *God* **Elohim**.
8 And David was *displeased* **inflamed**,
because *the LORD* **Yah Veh**
had *made* **breached** a breach upon Uzzah:
and he called the name of the place
Perezuzzah **Peres Uzzah** to this day.
9 And David
was *afraid of the LORD* **awed of Yah Veh** that day,
and said,
How shall the ark of *the LORD* **Yah Veh** come to me?
10 So David *would* **willed to** not *remove* **turn aside**
the ark of *the LORD* **Yah Veh** unto him
into the city of David:
but David *carried aside* **extended** it into
the house of *Obededom* **Obed Edom** the *Gittite* **Gittiy**.
11 And the ark of *the LORD continued* **Yah Veh settled**
in the house of *Obededom* **Obed Edom** the *Gittite* **Gittiy**
three months:
and *the LORD* **Yah Veh** blessed *Obededom* **Obed Edom**,
and all his household.
12 And it was told *king* **sovereign** David, saying,
The LORD **Yah Veh** hath blessed
the house of *Obededom* **Obed Edom**,
and all that *pertaineth* **be** unto him,
because of the ark of *God* **Elohim**.
So David went
and *brought up* **ascended** the ark of *God* **Elohim**
from the house of *Obededom* **Obed Edom**
into the city of David with *gladness* **cheerfulness**.
13 And it *was so* **became**,
that when they that bare the ark of *the LORD* **Yah Veh**
had *gone* **paced** six paces, he sacrificed oxen and fatlings.
14 And David *danced* **twirled**
before the LORD **at the face of Yah Veh**
with all *his might* **strength**;
and David was girded with a linen ephod.
15 So David and all the house of *Israel* **Yisra El**
brought up **ascended** the ark of *the LORD* **Yah Veh**
with shouting,
and with the *sound* **voice** of the trumpet.
16 And as the ark of *the LORD* **Yah Veh**
came into the city of David,
Michal *Saul's* **Shaul's** daughter
looked through a window,
and saw *king* **sovereign** David
leaping and *dancing* **twirling**
before the LORD **at the face of Yah Veh**;
and she despised him in her heart.
17 And they brought in the ark of *the LORD* **Yah Veh**,
and set it in his place, in the midst of the *tabernacle* **tent**
that David had *pitched* **stretched** for it:
and David *offered burnt offerings* **holocausted holocausts**
and *peace offerings* **shelamim**
before the LORD **at the face of Yah Veh**.
18 And as soon as David *had made an end of* **finished**
offering burnt offerings **holocausting holocausts**
and *peace offerings* **shelamim**,
he blessed the people
in the name of *the LORD of hosts* **Yah Veh Sabaoth**.
19 And he *dealt* **allotted** among all the people,
even among the whole multitude of *Israel* **Yisra El**,
as well to the women as men,

to every *one a* **man one** cake of bread,
and *a good piece* **one portion** *of flesh*,
and *a flagon* **one cake** of *wine* **bread**.
So all the people *departed* **went**
every one **each man** to his house.
20 Then David returned to bless his household.
And Michal the daughter of *Saul* **Shaul**
came out **went** to meet David, and said,
How *glorious* **honourable**
was the *king* **sovereign** of *Israel* **Yisra El** to day,
who *uncovered* **exposed** himself to day
in the eyes of the *handmaids* **maids** of his servants,
as one of the vain *fellows* shamelessly uncovereth himself!
21 And David said unto Michal,
It was *before the LORD* **at the face of Yah Veh**,
which chose me before thy father,
and before all his house,
to *appoint* **misvah** me *ruler* **eminent**
over the people of *the LORD* **Yah Veh**,
over *Israel* **Yisra El**:
therefore *will* **shall** I *play* **entertain**
before the LORD **at the face of Yah Veh**.
22 And I *will* **shall** *yet* be more *vile* **abased** than thus,
and *will* **shall** be *base* **lowly** in mine own *sight* **eyes**:
and of the *maidservants* **maids**
which thou hast *spoken of* **said**,
of them shall I be *had in honour* **honoured**.
23 Therefore Michal the daughter of *Saul* **Shaul**
had no child unto the day of her death.

YAH VEH'S HOUSE

7 And it *came to pass* **became**,
when the *king sat* **sovereign settled** in his house,
and *the LORD* **Yah Veh** had given him rest round about
from all his enemies;
2 That the *king* **sovereign** said unto Nathan the prophet,
See now, I *dwell* **settle** in an house of cedar,
but the ark of *God* **Elohim**
dwelleth **settleth** within curtains.
3 And Nathan said to the *king* **sovereign**, Go,
do **work** all that is in thine heart;
for *the LORD* **Yah Veh** is with thee.
4 And it *came to pass* **became,** that night,
that the word of *the LORD* **Yah Veh**
came unto Nathan, saying,
5 Go and *tell* **say to** my servant David,
Thus saith *the LORD* **Yah Veh**,
Shalt thou build me an house for me to *dwell* **settle** in?
6 Whereas I have not *dwelt* **settled** in *any* **a** house
since **from** the *time* **day** that I *brought up* **ascended**
the *children* **sons** of *Israel* **Yisra El** out of *Egypt* **Misrayim**,
even to this day,
but have walked in a tent and in a tabernacle.
7 In all *the places* wherein I have walked
with all the *children* **sons** of *Israel* **Yisra El**
spake **worded** I a word
with *any* **one** of the *tribes* **scions** of *Israel* **Yisra El**,
whom I *commanded* **misvahed**
to *feed* **tend** my people *Israel* **Yisra El**, saying,
Why build ye not me an house of cedar?

YAH VEH SABAOTH CUTS A COVENANT WITH DAVID

8 Now therefore
so **thus** shalt thou say unto my servant David,
Thus saith *the LORD of hosts* **Yah Veh Sabaoth**,
I took thee from the *sheepcote* **habitation of rest**,
from *following* **after** the *sheep* **flock**,
to be *ruler* **eminent** over my people, over *Israel* **Yisra El**:
9 And I was with thee whithersoever thou wentest,
and have cut off all thine enemies
out of **from** thy *sight* **face**,
and have *made* **worked** thee a great name,
like unto the name of the great *men* that are in the earth.
10 Moreover I *will appoint* **shall set** a place
for my people *Israel* **Yisra El**,
and *will* **shall** plant them,
that they may *dwell* **tabernacle** in a place of their own,
and *move* **quiver** no more;
neither shall the *children* **sons** of wickedness
afflict **add to abase** them *any more*,
as *beforetime* **formerly**,
11 And as *since* **from** the *time* **day**
that I *commanded* **misvahed** judges
to be over my people *Israel* **Yisra El**,
and have caused thee to rest from all thine enemies.
Also *the LORD* **Yah Veh** telleth thee
that he *will make* **shall work** thee an house.
12 And when thy days be fulfilled,
and thou shalt *sleep* **lie down** with thy fathers,
I *will set up* **shall raise** thy seed after thee,
which shall *proceed* **go** out of thy *bowels* **inwards**,
and I *will* **shall** establish his *kingdom* **sovereigndom**.
13 He shall build an house for my name,
and I *will stablish* **shall establish** the throne
of his *kingdom for ever* **sovereigndom eternally**.
14 I *will* **shall** be *his* **for him,** father,
and he shall be *my* **for me,** son.
If he *commit iniquity* **pervert**,
I *will chasten* **shall reprove** him
with the *rod* **scion** of men,
and with the *stripes* **plagues**
of the *children* **sons** of *men* **humanity**:
15 But my mercy
shall not *depart away* **turn aside** from him,
as I *took* **turned** it **aside** from *Saul* **Shaul**,
whom I *put away before thee* **turned aside from thy face**.
16 And thine house and thy *kingdom* **sovereigndom**
shall be *established for ever* **permanent eternally**
before thee **at thy face**:
thy throne shall be established *for ever* **eternally**.
17 According to all these words,
and according to all this vision,
so did Nathan *speak* **word** unto David.

DAVID'S PRAYER

18 Then went *king* **sovereign** David in,
and *sat before the LORD* **settled at the face of Yah Veh**,
and he said, Who am I, O *Lord GOD* **Adonay Yah Veh**?
and what is my house, that thou hast brought me hitherto?
19 And this was yet *a small thing* **little** in thy *sight* **eyes**,
O *Lord GOD* **Adonay Yah Veh**;
but thou hast *spoken* **worded** also of thy servant's house
for a great while to come **afar off.**
And is this the *manner* **torah** of *man* **humanity**,
O *Lord GOD* **Adonay Yah Veh**?
20 And what *can* **addeth** David
say more **to word** unto thee?
for thou, *Lord GOD* **Adonay Yah Veh**,
knowest thy servant.
21 For thy word's sake, and according to thine own heart,
hast thou *done* **worked** all these *great things* **greatnesses**,
to make thy servant know them.
22 Wherefore thou art great,
O *LORD God* **Yah Veh Elohim**:
for there is none like thee,
neither *is* **be** there *any God* **elohim** beside thee,
according to all that we have heard with our ears.
23 And what one *nation* **goyim** in the earth
is *like* **as** thy people, *even like Israel* **as Yisra El**,
whom *God* **Elohim** went to redeem
for a people to himself,
and to *make* **set** him a name,
and to *do* **work** for you great *things* and *terrible* **awesome**,
for thy land, *before* **at the face of** thy people,
which thou redeemedst to thee from *Egypt* **Misrayim**,
from the *nations* **goyim** and their *gods* **elohim**?
24 For thou hast *confirmed* **established** to thyself
thy people *Israel* **Yisra El**
to be a people unto thee *for ever* **eternally**:
and thou, *LORD* **Yah Veh**, art become their *God* **Elohim**.
25 And now, O *LORD God* **Yah Veh Elohim**,
the word that thou hast *spoken* **worded**
concerning thy servant,
and concerning his house,
establish **raise** it *for ever* **eternally**,
and *do* **work** as thou hast *said* **worded**.
26 And let thy name
be *magnified for ever* **greatened eternally**, saying,
The LORD of hosts **Yah Veh Sabaoth**
is *the God* **Elohim** over *Israel* **Yisra El**:
and let the house of thy servant David
be established *before thee* **at thy face**.
27 For thou, O *LORD of hosts* **Yah Veh Sabaoth**,

God **Elohim** of *Israel* **Yisra El**,
hast *revealed to* **exposed in the ear of** thy servant, saying,
I *will* **shall** build thee an house:
therefore hath thy servant found in his heart
to pray this prayer unto thee.
28 And now, O *Lord GOD* **Adonay Yah Veh**,
thou art that *God* **Elohim**, and thy words be true,
and thou hast *promised* **worded** this goodness
unto thy servant:
29 Therefore now *let it please thee* **mayest thou will**
to bless the house of thy servant,
that it may continue *for ever* **eternally**
before thee **at thy face**:
for thou, O *Lord GOD* **Adonay Yah Veh**,
hast *spoken* **worded** it:
and with thy blessing let the house of thy servant
be blessed *for ever* **eternally**.

DAVID'S TRIUMPHS

8 And after this it *came to pass* **became**,
that David smote the *Philistines* **Peleshethiy**,
and subdued them:
and David took *Methegammah* **Metheg Ha Ammah**
out of the hand of the *Philistines* **Peleshethiy**.
2 And he smote Moab, and measured them with a line,
casting **making** them **lie** down to the *ground* **earth**;
even with two lines measured he to *put to death* **deathify**,
and with one full line to keep alive.
And *so* the *Moabites* **Moabiy** became David's servants,
and *brought gifts* **lifted offerings**.
3 David smote also *Hadadezer* **Hadad Ezer**,
the son of *Rehob* **Rechob**, *king* **sovereign** of *Zobah* **Sobah**,
as he went to *recover* **turn back** his *border* **hand**
at the river Euphrates.
4 And David *took* **captured** from him a thousand *chariots*,
and seven hundred *horsemen* **cavalry**,
and twenty thousand *footmen*: **men on foot**
and David *houghed* **uprooted/hamstrung**
all the chariot *horses*,
but *reserved* **retained** of them *for* an hundred chariots.
5 And when the *Syrians* **Aramiy** of *Damascus* **Dammeseq**
came to *succour Hadadezer* **help Hadad Ezer**,
king **sovereign** of *Zobah* **Sobah**,
David *slew* **smote** of the *Syrians* **Aramiy**
two and twenty thousand men.
6 Then David *put garrisons* **set stations**
in *Syria* **Aram** of *Damascus* **Dammeseq**:
and the *Syrians* **Aramiy** became servants to David,
and *brought gifts* **lifted offerings**.
And *the LORD preserved* **Yah Veh saved** David
whithersoever he went.
7 And David took the shields of gold
that were on the servants of *Hadadezer* **Hadad Ezer**,
and brought them to *Jerusalem* **Yeru Shalem**.
8 And from *Betah* **Betach**, and from Berothai,
cities of *Hadadezer* **Hadad Ezer**,
king **sovereign** David took
exceeding much brass **mighty abounding copper**.
9 When Toi *king* **sovereign** of Hamath
heard that David had smitten all the *host* **valiant**
of *Hadadezer* **Hadad Ezer**,
10 Then Toi sent *Joram* **Yah Ram** his son
unto *king* **sovereign** David,
to *salute* **ask of** him **shalom**, and to bless him,
because he had fought against *Hadadezer* **Hadad Ezer**,
and smitten him:
for *Hadadezer* **Hadad Ezer**
had **been a man of** wars with Toi.
And *Joram brought with him* **in his hand were**
vessels **instruments** of silver,
and *vessels* **instruments** of gold,
and *vessels* **instruments** of *brass* **copper**:
11 Which also *king* **sovereign** David
did dedicate **hallowed** unto *the LORD* **Yah Veh**,
with the silver and gold that he had *dedicated* **hallowed**
of all *nations* **goyim** which he subdued;
12 Of *Syria* **Aram**, and of Moab,
and of the *children* **sons** of Ammon,
and of the *Philistines* **Peleshethiy**, and of *Amalek* **Amaleq**,
and of the spoil of *Hadadezer* **Hadad Ezer**,
son of *Rehob* **Rechob**, *king* **sovereign** of *Zobah* **Sobah**.
13 And David *gat* **worked** him a name
when he returned from smiting of the *Syrians* **Aramiy**
in the *valley of salt* **Valley of Salt/Gay Melach**,
being eighteen thousand *men*.
14 And he *put garrisons* **set stations** in Edom;
throughout all Edom *put* **set** he *garrisons* **stations**,
and all they of Edom became David's servants.
And *the LORD preserved* **Yah Veh saved** David
whithersoever he went.
15 And David reigned over all *Israel* **Yisra El**;
and David *executed* **worked** judgment and *justice* **justness**
unto all his people.
16 And *Joab* **Yah Ab** the son of *Zeruiah* **Seruyah**
was over the host;
and *Jehoshaphat* **Yah Shaphat** the son of *Ahilud* **Achiy Lud**
was *recorder* **remembrancer**;
17 And *Zadok* **Sadoq** the son of *Ahitub* **Achiy Tub**,
and *Ahimelech* **Achiy Melech**
the son of *Abiathar* **Abi Athar**, were the priests;
and *Seraiah* **Sera Yah** was the scribe;
18 And *Benaiah* **Bena Yah** the son of *Jehoiada* **Yah Yada**
was over both the *Cherethites* **executioners**
and the *Pelethites* **couriers**;
and David's sons were *chief rulers* **priests**.

DAVID'S MERCY

9 And David said, Is there yet any that *is left* **remain**
of the house of *Saul* **Shaul**,
that I may *shew* **work** him *kindness* **mercy**
for *Jonathan's* **Yah Nathan's** sake?
2 And there was of the house of *Saul* **Shaul** a servant
whose name was *Ziba* **Siba**.
And when they had called him unto David,
the *king* **sovereign** said unto him, Art thou *Ziba* **Siba**?
And he said, Thy servant *is he*.
3 And the *king* **sovereign** said,
Is there *not yet any* **finally**
a man of the house of *Saul* **Shaul**,
that I may *shew* **work** the *kindness* **mercy** of *God* **Elohim**
unto him?
And *Ziba* **Siba** said unto the *king* **sovereign**,
Jonathan **Yah Nathan** hath yet a son,
which is lame on his **with smitten** feet.
4 And the *king* **sovereign** said unto him, Where is he?
And *Ziba* **Siba** said unto the *king* **sovereign**, Behold,
he is in the house of Machir,
the son of *Ammiel* **Ammi El**, in *Lodebar* **Lo Debar**.
5 Then *king* **sovereign** David sent,
and *fetched* **took** him out of the house of Machir,
the son of *Ammiel* **Ammi El**, from *Lodebar* **Lo Debar**.
6 Now when *Mephibosheth* **Mephi Bosheth**,
the son of *Jonathan* **Yah Nathan**, the son of *Saul* **Shaul**,
was come unto David,
he fell on his face, and *did reverence* **prostrated**.
And David said, *Mephibosheth* **Mephi Bosheth**.
And he *answered* **said**, Behold thy servant!
7 And David said unto him, *Fear* **Awe** not:
for **in working**,
I *will surely shew* **shall work** thee *kindness* **mercy**
for *Jonathan* **Yah Nathan** thy father's sake,
and *will* **shall** restore thee
all the *land* **field** of *Saul* **Shaul** thy father;
and thou shalt eat bread at my table continually.
8 And he *bowed* **prostrated** himself, and said,
What is thy servant,
that thou shouldest *look upon* **face**
such a dead dog as I *am*?
9 Then the *king* **sovereign** called to *Ziba* **Siba**,
Saul's servant **Shaul's lad**, and said unto him,
I have given unto thy *master's* **adoni's** son
all that *pertained* **became** to *Saul* **Shaul**
and to all his house.
10 Thou therefore, and thy sons, and thy servants,
shall *till* **serve** the *land* **soil** for him,
and thou shalt bring in *the fruits*,
that thy *master's* **adoni's** son may have *food* **bread** to eat:
but *Mephibosheth* **Mephi Bosheth** thy *master's* **adoni's** son
shall eat bread *alway* **continually** at my table.
Now *Ziba* **Siba** had fifteen sons and twenty servants.
11 Then said *Ziba* **Siba** unto the *king* **sovereign**,
According to all that my *lord* **adoni** the *king* **sovereign**

hath *commanded* **misvahed** his servant,
so **thus** shall thy servant *do* **work**.
As for *Mephibosheth* **Mephi Bosheth**, *said the king*,
he shall eat at my table,
as one of the *king's* **sovereign's** sons.
12 And *Mephibosheth* **Mephi Bosheth** had a young son,
whose name was *Micha* **Michah Yah**.
And all that *dwelt* **were seated** in the house of *Ziba* **Siba**
were servants unto *Mephibosheth* **Mephi Bosheth**.
13 So *Mephibosheth* **Mephi Bosheth**
dwelt **settled** in *Jerusalem* **Yeru Shalem**:
for he did eat continually at the *king's* **sovereign's** table;
and was lame on both his feet.

DAVID DEFEATS THE SONS OF AMMON AND THE ARAMIY

10 And it *came to pass* **became,** after this,
that the *king* **sovereign**
of the *children* **sons** of Ammon died,
and Hanun his son reigned in his stead.
2 Then said David, I *will shew kindness* **shall work mercy**
unto Hanun the son of *Nahash* **Nachash**,
as his father *shewed kindness* **worked mercy** unto me.
And David sent to *comfort* **sigh over** him
by the hand of his servants for his father.
And David's servants
came into the land of the *children* **sons** of Ammon.
3 And the *princes* **governors**
of the *children* **sons** of Ammon
said unto Hanun their *lord* **adoni**,
Thinkest thou that **In thine eyes**
honoureth David *doth honour* thy father,
that he hath sent *comforters unto* **to sigh over** thee?
hath not David *rather* sent his servants unto thee,
so as to *search* **probe** the city, and to spy it out,
and to *overthrow* **overturn** it?
4 Wherefore Hanun took David's servants,
and shaved off the one half of their beards,
and cut off their garments in the middle,
even to their buttocks, and sent them away.
5 When they told it unto David, he sent to meet them,
because the men were *greatly* **mighty** ashamed:
and the *king* **sovereign** said, *Tarry* **Settle** at *Jericho* **Yericho**
until your beards *be grown* **sprout**, and *then* return.
6 And when the *children* **sons** of Ammon
saw that they stank before David,
the *children* **sons** of Ammon sent
and hired the *Syrians* **Aramiy** of *Bethrehob* **Beth Rechob**
and the *Syrians* **Aramiy** of *Zoba* **Sobah**,
twenty thousand *footmen* **on foot**,
and of *king* **sovereign** Maachah a thousand men,
and of *Ishtob* **Ish Tob** twelve thousand men.
7 And when David heard of it,
he sent *Joab* **Yah Ab**, and all the host of the mighty *men*.
8 And the *children* **sons** of Ammon *came out* **went**,
and *put the battle in array* **lined up for war**
at the *entering in* **opening** of the *gate* **portal**:
and the *Syrians* **Aramiy** of *Zoba* **Sobah**,
and of *Rehob* **Rechob**,
and *Ishtob* **Ish Tob**, and Maachah,
were *by themselves* **alone** in the field.
9 When *Joab* **Yah Ab** saw
that the *front* **face** of the *battle* **war** was against him
before **at their face** and behind,
he chose of all the *choice men* **chosen** of *Israel* **Yisra El**,
and *put* **lined** them *in array* **up**
against **to meet** the *Syrians* **Aramiy**:
10 And the rest of the people he *delivered* **gave**
into the hand of *Abishai* **Abi Shai** his brother,
that he might *put* **line** them *in array* **up**
against **to meet** the *children* **sons** of Ammon.
11 And he said,
If the *Syrians be too strong for* **Aramiy prevail over** me,
then thou shalt *help* **save** me:
but if the *children* **sons** of Ammon
be too strong for **prevail over** thee,
then I *will* **shall** come and *help* **save** thee.
12 *Be of good courage* **Strengthen**,
and let us play the men — **strengthen** for our people,
and for the cities of our *God* **Elohim**:
and *the LORD* **Yah Veh** do that
which *seemeth him* **be** good **in his eyes**.
13 And *Joab* **Yah Ab** drew nigh,
and the people that were with him,
unto the *battle* **war** against the *Syrians* **Aramiy**:
and they fled *before him* **from his face**.
14 And when the *children* **sons** of Ammon
saw that the *Syrians* **Aramiy** *were* fled,
then fled they also
before Abishai **from the face of Abi Shai**,
and entered into the city.
So *Joab* **Yah Ab**
returned from the *children* **sons** of Ammon,
and came to *Jerusalem* **Yeru Shalem**.
15 And when the *Syrians* **Aramiy**
saw that they were smitten
before Israel **at the face of Yisra El**,
they gathered *themselves* together.
16 And *Hadarezer* **Hadar Ezer** sent,
and brought out the *Syrians* **Aramiy**
that were beyond the river:
and they came to Helam;
and Shobach
the *captain* **governor** of the host of *Hadarezer* **Hadar Ezer**
went *before them* **from their face**.
17 And when it was told David,
he gathered all *Israel* **Yisra El** *together*,
and passed over *Jordan* **Yarden**, and came to Helam.
And the *Syrians* **Aramiy**
set themselves in array against **lined up to meet** David,
and fought with him.
18 And the *Syrians* **Aramiy**
fled *before Israel* **from the face of Yisra El**;
and David *slew* **slaughtered**
the men of seven hundred chariots of the *Syrians* **Arami**,
and forty thousand *horsemen* **cavalry**,
and smote Shobach
the *captain* **governor** of their host, who died there.
19 And when all the *kings* **sovereigns**
that were servants to *Hadarezer* **Hadar Ezer**
saw that they were smitten
before Israel **at the face of Yisra El**,
they *made peace* **did shalam** with *Israel* **Yisra El**,
and served them.
So the *Syrians feared* **Aramiy awed**
to *help* **save** the *children* **sons** of Ammon any more.

DAVID AND BATH SHEBA

11 And it *came to pass* **became**,
after **at the turn of** the year *was expired*,
at the time when *kings* **angels** go forth *to battle*,
that David sent *Joab* **Yah Ab**, and his servants with him,
and all *Israel* **Yisra El**;
and they *destroyed* **ruined** the *children* **sons** of Ammon,
and besieged Rabbah.
But David *tarried* **settled** still at *Jerusalem* **Yeru Shalem**.
2 And it *came to pass* **became,**
in an eveningtide **at evening time**,
that David arose from off his bed,
and walked upon the roof of the *king's* **sovereign's** house:
and from the roof he saw a woman
washing **baptizing** herself;
and the woman
was *very beautiful to look upon* **of mighty good visage**.
3 And David sent and enquired after the woman.
And *one* said, Is not this *Bathsheba* **Bath Sheba**,
the daughter of *Eliam* **Eli Am**,
the *wife* **woman** of *Uriah* **Uri Yah** the *Hittite* **Hethiy**?
4 And David sent *messengers* **angels**, and took her;
and she came in unto him, and he lay with her;
for she was *purified* **hallowed**
from her *uncleanness* **foulness**:
and she returned unto her house.
5 And the woman conceived, and sent and told David,
and said, I *am with child* **have conceived**.
6 And David sent to *Joab* **Yah Ab**, *saying*,
Send me *Uriah* **Uri Yah** the *Hittite* **Hethiy**.
And *Joab* **Yah Ab** sent *Uriah* **Uri Yah** to David.
7 And when *Uriah* **Uri Yah** was come unto him,
David *demanded* **asked** *of him*
how Joab did **of the shalom of Yah Ab**,
and *how* **of the shalom of** the people *did*,

and *how* **of the shalom of** the war *prospered.*
8 And David said to *Uriah* **Uri Yah**,
Go down **Descend** to thy house,
and *wash* **baptize** thy feet.
And *Uriah* **Uri Yah**
departed **went** out of the *king's* **sovereign's** house,
and there *followed* **went out after** him
a *mess of meat* **signal** from the *king* **sovereign**.
9 But *Uriah slept* **Uri Yah laid**
at the *door* **portal** of the *king's* **sovereign's** house
with all the servants of his *lord* **adoni**,
and *went* **descended** not *down* to his house.
10 And when they had told David, saying,
Uriah went **Uri Yah descended** not *down* unto his house,
David said unto *Uriah* **Uri Yah**,
Camest thou not from *thy* **a** journey?
why *then* didst thou not
go down **descend** unto thine house?
11 And *Uriah* **Uri Yah** said unto David,
The ark, and *Israel* **Yisra El**, and *Judah* **Yah Hudah**,
abide **settle** in *tents* **brush arbors**;
and my *lord Joab* **adoni Yah Ab**,
and the servants of my *lord* **adoni**,
are encamped *in* **upon** the *open* **face of the** fields;
shall I then go into mine house, to eat and to drink,
and to lie with my *wife* **woman**?
as thou livest, and *as* thy soul liveth,
I will **shall** not *do this thing* **work such word**.
12 And David said to *Uriah* **Uri Yah**,
Tarry **Settle** here to day also,
and to morrow I *will let* **shall send** thee *depart* **away**.
So *Uriah abode* **Uri Yah settled** in *Jerusalem* **Yeru Shalem**
that day, and the morrow.
13 And when David had called him,
he did eat and drink *before him* **at his face**;
and he *made* **intoxicated** him *drunk*:
and at even he went out to lie on his bed
with the servants of his *lord* **adoni**,
but *went* **descended** not *down* to his house.
14 And it *came to pass* **became,** in the morning,
that David *wrote* **inscribed** a *letter* **scroll** to *Joab* **Yah Ab**,
and sent it by the hand of *Uriah* **Uri Yah**.
15 And he *wrote* **inscribed** in the *letter* **scroll**, saying,
Set **Give** ye *Uriah* **Uri Yah**
in the forefront **at the face**
of the *hottest battle* **strongest war**,
and *retire* **turn** ye **back** from **after** him,
that he may be smitten, and die.
16 And it *came to pass* **became,**
when *Joab observed* **Yah Ab guarded** the city,
that he *assigned Uriah* **gave Uri Yah** unto a place
where he knew that valiant men were.
17 And the men of the city went out,
and fought with *Joab* **Yah Ab**:
and there fell *some* of the people of the servants of David;
and *Uriah* **Uri Yah** the *Hittite* **Hethiy** died also.
18 Then *Joab* **Yah Ab** sent and told David
all the *things* **words** concerning the war;
19 And *charged* **misvahed** the *messenger* **angel**, saying,
When thou hast *made an end of* **finished**
telling **wording** the *matters* **words** of the war
unto the *king* **sovereign**,
20 And if *so be* **it becometh**
that the *king's wrath arise* **sovereign's fury ascend**,
and he say unto thee,
Wherefore approached ye so nigh unto the city
when ye did fight?
knew ye not that they *would* **should** shoot from the wall?
21 Who smote *Abimelech* **Abi Melech**
the son of *Jerubbesheth* **Yerub Besheth**?
did not a woman cast a *piece* **slice** of *a* **an upper** millstone
upon him from the wall, that he died in *Thebez* **Tebes**?
why *went* **approached** ye *nigh* the wall?
then say thou,
Thy servant *Uriah* **Uri Yah** the *Hittite* **Hethiy**
is dead **hath died** also.
22 So the *messenger* **angel** went,
and came and *shewed* **told** David all
that *Joab* **Yah Ab** had sent him for.
23 And the *messenger* **angel** said unto David,
Surely the men prevailed **mightily** against us,
and *came out* **went** unto us into the field,
and we were upon them
even unto the *entering* **opening** of the *gate* **portal**.
24 And the shooters shot from off the wall
upon thy servants;
and some of the *king's* **sovereign's** servants *be dead* **died**,
and thy servant *Uriah* **Uri Yah** the *Hittite* **Hethiy**
is dead **died** also.
25 Then David said unto the *messenger* **angel**,
Thus shalt thou say unto *Joab* **Yah Ab**,
Let not this *thing displease thee* **word be evil in thine eyes**,
for the sword devoureth one *as well as another* **thus**:
make **strengthen** thy *battle more strong* **warfare**
against the city, and *overthrow* **demolish** it:
and *encourage* **strengthen** thou him.
26 And when the *wife* **woman** of *Uriah* **Uri Yah** heard
that *Uriah* **Uri Yah** her *husband was dead* **man died**,
she *mourned* **chopped** for her *husband* **master**.
27 And when the mourning was past,
David sent and *fetched* **gathered** her to his house,
and she became his *wife* **woman**, and bare him a son.
But the *thing* **word** that David had *done* **worked**
displeased the LORD **was evil in the eyes of Yah Veh**.

NATHAN REBUKES DAVID

12 And *the LORD* **Yah Veh** sent Nathan unto David.
And he came unto him, and said unto him,
There were two men in one city;
the one rich, and the *other poor* **one impoverished**.
2 The rich *man* had *exceeding many* **mighty abounding**
flocks and *herds* **oxen**:
3 But the *poor* **impoverished** *man* had *nothing* **naught**,
save one little ewe lamb,
which he had *bought* **chatteled** and *nourished up* **livened**:
and it grew up together with him,
and with his *children* **sons**;
it did eat of his own *meat* **morsel**,
and drank of his own cup,
and lay in his bosom, and was unto him as a daughter.
4 And there came a *traveller* **wayfarer** unto the rich man,
and he spared
to take of his own flock and of his own *herd* **oxen**,
to *dress* **work** for the *wayfaring man* **caravan**
that was come unto him;
but took the *poor* **impoverished** man's **ewe** lamb,
and *dressed* **worked** it for the man that was come to him.
5 And David's *anger was greatly* **wrath** kindled **mightily**
against the man;
and he said to Nathan, *As the LORD* **Yah Veh** liveth,
the man that hath *done* **worked** this *thing*
shall surely die **is a son of death**:
6 And he shall *restore* **shalam**
for the **ewe** lamb fourfold,
because he *did* **worked** this *thing* **word**,
and *because* **finally,** he had no *pity* **compassion**.
7 And Nathan said to David, Thou art the man.
Thus saith
the LORD God **Yah Veh Elohim** of *Israel* **Yisra El**,
I anointed thee *king* **sovereign** over *Israel* **Yisra El**,
and I *delivered* **rescued** thee out of the hand of *Saul* **Shaul**;
8 And I gave thee thy *master's* **adoni's** house,
and thy *master's wives* **adoni's women** into thy bosom,
and gave thee
the house of *Israel* **Yisra El** and of *Judah* **Yah Hudah**;
and if that had been too little,
I *would moreover have given* **had added** unto thee
such **these** and *such* **those** *things.*
9 Wherefore hast thou despised
the *commandment* **word** of *the LORD* **Yah Veh**,
to *do* **work** evil in his *sight* **eyes**?
thou hast *killed* **smitten**
Uriah **Uri Yah** the *Hittite* **Hethiy** with the sword,
and hast taken his *wife* **woman** to be thy *wife* **woman**,
and hast *slain* **slaughtered** him
with the sword of the *children* **sons** of Ammon.
10 Now therefore the sword
shall *never depart* **not turn aside eternally**
from thine house;
because **finally,** thou hast despised me,
and hast taken the *wife* **woman**

of *Uriah* **Uri Yah** the *Hittite* **Hethiy**
to be thy *wife* **woman**.
11 Thus saith *the LORD* **Yah Veh**, Behold,
I *will* **shall** raise up evil against thee
out of thine own house,
and I *will* **shall** take thy *wives* **women** before thine eyes,
and give them unto thy *neighbour* **friend**,
and he shall lie with thy *wives* **women**
in the *sight* **eyes** of this sun.
12 For thou *didst* **workedst** it *secretly* **covertly**:
but I *will do* **shall work** this *thing* **word**
before all *Israel* **Yisra El**, and before the sun.
13 And David said unto Nathan,
I have sinned against *the LORD* **Yah Veh**.
And Nathan said unto David,
The LORD **Yah Veh**
also hath *put away* **passed over** thy sin;
thou shalt not die.
14 *Howbeit* **Finally**,
because by this *deed* **word** thou hast given great occasion
to the enemies of *the LORD* **Yah Veh** to *blaspheme* **scorn**,
the *child* **son** also that is born unto thee
in dying, shall *surely* die.
15 And Nathan *departed* **went** unto his house.
And *the LORD struck* **Yah Veh smote** the child
that *Uriah's wife* **Uri Yah's woman** bare unto David,
and it was very sick.
16 David therefore besought *God* **Elohim** for the *child* **lad**;
and David fasted **a fast**, and went in,
and *lay all night* **stayed overnight** upon the earth.
17 And the elders of his house arose, *and went* to him,
to raise him up from the earth: but he *would* **willed** not,
neither did he *eat* **chew** bread with them.
18 And it *came to pass* **became,** on the seventh day,
that the child died.
And the servants of David
feared **awed** to tell him that the child *was dead* **died**:
for they said, Behold,
while the child was yet alive, we *spake* **worded** unto him,
and he *would* **hearkened** not *hearken* unto our voice:
how *will* **shall** he then *vex himself* **work himself evil**,
if we *tell* **say to** him that the child *is dead* **died**?
19 But when David saw
that his servants *whispered* **enchanted**,
David *perceived* **discerned** that the child *was dead* **died**:
therefore David said unto his servants,
Is **Hath** the child *dead* **died**?
And they said, He *is dead* **died**.
20 Then David arose from the earth,
and *washed* **baptized**, and anointed *himself*,
and *changed* **passed** his *apparel* **clothes**,
and came into the house of *the LORD* **Yah Veh**,
and *worshipped* **prostrated**:
then he came to his own house;
and when he *required* **asked**, they set bread before him,
and he did eat.
21 Then said his servants unto him,
What *thing* word is this that thou hast *done* **worked**?
thou didst fast and weep for the child,
while it was **being** alive;
but when the child *was dead* **died,**
thou didst rise and eat bread.
22 And he said, While the child was yet alive,
I fasted and wept:
for I said, Who *can tell* **knoweth**
whether *GOD* **Yah Veh**
will be gracious to me **shall grant me charism**,
that the child may live?
23 But now he *is dead* **died**, wherefore should I fast?
can I *bring* **return** him *back again*?
I shall go to him, but he shall not return to me.

SHELOMOH'S BIRTH

24 And David *comforted* **sighed over**
Bathsheba **Bath Sheba** his *wife* **woman**,
and went in unto her, and lay with her:
and she bare a son,
and he called his name *Solomon* **Shelomoh**:
and *the LORD* **Yah Veh** loved him.
25 And he sent by the hand of Nathan the prophet;
and he called his name *Jedidiah* **Yedid Yah**,
because of *the LORD* **Yah Veh**.
26 And *Joab* **Yah Ab**
fought against Rabbah of the *children* **sons** of Ammon,
and *took* **captured** the *royal* **sovereigndom** city.
27 And *Joab* **Yah Ab** sent *messengers* **angels** to David,
and said, I have fought against Rabbah,
and *have taken* **captured** the city of waters.
28 Now therefore gather the rest of the people *together*,
and encamp against the city, and *take* **capture** it:
lest I *take* **capture** the city, and it be called after my name.
29 And David gathered all the people *together*,
and went to Rabbah, and fought against it,
and *took* **captured** it.
30 And he took their *king's* **sovereign's** crown
from off his head,
the weight *whereof was a talent* **— a round** of gold
with the *precious* **esteemed** stones:
and it was *set* on David's head.
And he brought forth the spoil of the city
in great abundance **mightily abounding**.
31 And he brought forth the people that were therein,
and *put* **set** them under saws,
and under *harrows* **slicers** of iron, and under axes of iron,
and made them pass through the brickkiln:
and thus *did* **worked** he unto all the cities
of the *children* **sons** of Ammon.
So David and all the people
returned unto *Jerusalem* **Yeru Shalem**.

AMNON AND TAMAR

13 And it *came to pass* **became** after this,
that *Absalom* **Abi Shalom** the son of David
had a *fair* **beautiful** sister, whose name was Tamar;
and Amnon the son of David loved her.
2 And Amnon was so *vexed* **depressed**,
that he fell sick for his sister Tamar; for she was a virgin;
and Amnon thought it hard
and it was marvellous in the eyes of Amnon
for him to *do any thing* **work aught** to her.
3 But Amnon had a friend,
whose name was *Jonadab* **Yah Nadab**,
the son of *Shimeah* **Shimah** David's brother:
and *Jonadab* **Yah Nadab**
was a *very subtil* **mighty wise** man.
4 And he said unto him,
Why art thou, *being* the *king's* **sovereign's** son,
lean from day to day **poor morning by morning**?
wilt **shalt** thou not tell me?
And Amnon said unto him,
I love Tamar, my brother *Absalom's* **Abi Shalom's** sister.
5 And *Jonadab* **Yah Nadab** said unto him,
Lay thee down on thy bed, and make thyself sick:
and when thy father cometh to see thee, say unto him,
I pray thee, let my sister Tamar come,
and *give* **cut** me *meat* **bread to chew**,
and *dress the meat* **work cuttings** in my *sight* **eyes**,
that I may see it, and eat it at her hand.
6 So Amnon lay down, and made himself sick:
and when the *king* **sovereign** was come to see him,
Amnon said unto the *king* **sovereign**, I pray thee,
let Tamar my sister come,
and *make* **bake** me a couple of cakes in my *sight* **eyes**,
that I may *eat* **chew** at her hand.
7 Then David sent home to Tamar, saying,
Go now to thy brother Amnon's house,
and *dress* **work** him *meat* **cuttings**.
8 So Tamar went to her brother Amnon's house;
and he was laid down.
And she took *flour* **dough**, and kneaded it,
and *made cakes* **baked** in his *sight* **eyes**,
and *did bake* **ripened** the cakes.
9 And she took a pan,
and poured them out *before him* **at his face**;
but he refused to eat.
And Amnon said, *Have out* **Bring** all men from me.
And they went out every man from him.
10 And Amnon said unto Tamar,
Bring the *meat* **cuttings** into the chamber,
that I may *eat* **chew** of thine hand.
And Tamar took the cakes which she had *made* **worked**,
and brought them into the chamber to Amnon her brother.

11 And when she had brought them **near** unto him to eat,
he took hold of her, and said unto her,
Come lie with me, my sister.
12 And she *answered* **said to** him,
Nay, my brother, do not *force* **humble** me;
for *no such thing ought* **such ought not**
to be *done* **worked** in *Israel* **Yisra El**:
do **work** not thou this folly.
13 And I, whither shall I cause my *shame* **reproach** to go?
and as for thee,
thou shalt be as one of the fools in *Israel* **Yisra El**.
Now therefore, I pray thee,
speak **word** unto the *king* **sovereign**;
for he *will* **shall** not withhold me from thee.
14 Howbeit he *would* **willed**
to not hearken unto her voice:
but, being *stronger* **tougher** than she,
forced **humbled** her, and lay with her.
15 Then Amnon hated her *exceedingly* **mightily**;
so that the hatred wherewith he hated her
was greater than the love wherewith he had loved her.
And Amnon said unto her, Arise, *be gone* **go**.
16 And she said unto him, There is no *cause* **concern**:
this evil in sending me away
is greater than the other that thou *didst* **workedst** unto me.
But he *would* **willed to** not hearken unto her.
17 Then he called his *servant* **lad** that ministered unto him,
and said, *Put* **Send away** now this *woman* out from me,
and *bolt* **enclose** the door after her.
18 And she had a *garment of divers colours* **coverall coat**
upon her:
for with such *robes* **mantles**
were the *king's* **sovereign's** daughters
that *were* virgins *apparelled* **enrobed**.
Then his *servant* **minister** brought her out,
and *bolted* **enclosed** the door after her.
19 And Tamar *put* **took** ashes on her head,
and *rent* **ripped**
her *garment of divers colours* **coverall coat**
that was on her,
and *laid* **set** her hand on her head,
and *went* **in walking, walked** on crying.
20 And *Absalom* **Abi Shalom** her brother said unto her,
Hath Amnon thy brother been with thee?
but *hold now thy peace* **hush now**, my sister:
he is thy brother;
regard not this thing **set not thy heart to this word**.
So Tamar *remained* **settled** desolate
in her brother *Absalom's* **Abi Shalom's** house.
21 But when *king* **sovereign** David
heard of all these *things* **words**,
he was *very wroth* **mightily inflamed**.
22 And *Absalom* **Abi Shalom**
spake **worded** unto his brother Amnon
neither good nor *bad* **evil**:
for *Absalom* **Abi Shalom** hated Amnon,
because **for word that**
he had *forced* **abased** his sister Tamar.

ABI SHALOM DEATHIFIES AMNON

23 And it *came to pass* **became,**
after two *full years* **years of days,**
that *Absalom* **Abi Shalom** had sheepshearers
in *Baalhazor* **Baal Hasor,**
which is beside *Ephraim* **Ephrayim**:
and *Absalom* **Abi Shalom**
invited **called** all the *king's* **sovereign's** sons.
24 And *Absalom* **Abi Shalom** came to the *king* **sovereign,**
and said, Behold now, thy servant hath sheepshearers;
let the *king* **sovereign,** I beseech thee,
and his servants go with thy servant.
25 And the *king* **sovereign** said to *Absalom* **Abi Shalom,**
Nay, my son, let us not all now go,
lest we be *chargeable* **too heavy** unto thee.
And he *pressed* **breached** him:
howbeit he *would* **willed to** not go, but blessed him.
26 Then said *Absalom* **Abi Shalom,**
If not, I pray thee, let my brother Amnon go with us.
And the *king* **sovereign** said unto him,
Why should he go with thee?
27 But *Absalom pressed* **Abi Shalom breached** him,
that he *let* **sent away** Amnon
and all the *king's* **sovereign's** sons *go* with him.
28 Now *Absalom* **Abi Shalom**
had *commanded* **misvahed** his *servants* **lads,** saying,
Mark **See** ye now
when Amnon's heart is *merry* **good** with wine,
and when I say unto you, Smite Amnon;
then kill **deathify** him, *fear* **awe** not:
have not I *commanded* **misvahed** you?
be courageous **strengthen,** and be *valiant* **sons of valour.**
29 And the *servants* **lads** of *Absalom* **Abi Shalom**
did **worked** unto Amnon
as *Absalom* **Abi Shalom** had *commanded* **misvahed.**
Then all the *king's* **sovereign's** sons arose,
and every man *gat him up* **rode** upon his mule, and fled.
30 And it *came to pass* **became,**
while they were in the way,
that *tidings* **reports** came to David, saying,
Absalom **Abi Shalom**
hath *slain* **smitten** all the *king's* **sovereign's** sons,
and there is not one of them *left* **remaining.**
31 Then the *king* **sovereign** arose,
and *tare* **ripped** his *garments* **clothes,** and lay on the earth;
and all his servants *stood* **stationed** by
with their clothes *rent* **ripped.**
32 And *Jonadab* **Yah Nadab,**
the son of *Shimeah* **Shimah** David's brother,
answered and said, Let not my *lord suppose* **adoni say**
that they have *slain* **deathified** all the *young men* **lads**
the *king's* **sovereign's** sons;
for Amnon only *is dead* **died:**
for by the *appointment* **mouth** of *Absalom* **Abi Shalom**
this hath been *determined* **set**
from the day that he *forced* **abased** his sister Tamar.
33 Now therefore let not my *lord* **adoni** the *king* **sovereign**
take **set** the *thing* **word** to his heart, *to think* **saying**
that all the *king's* **sovereign's** sons *are dead* **died:**
for Amnon only *is dead* **died.**
34 But *Absalom* **Abi Shalom** fled.
And the *young man* **lad** that *kept the watch* **watched**
lifted up his eyes, and *looked* **saw,** and, behold,
there came much people
by the way of the *hill* **mountain** side behind him.
35 And *Jonadab* **Yah Nadab** said unto the *king* **sovereign,**
Behold, the *king's* **sovereign's** sons come:
as **according to the word of** thy servant *said,*
so it *is* **becometh.**
36 And it *came to pass* **became,**
as soon as he had
made an end of speaking **finished wording,**
that, behold, the *king's* **sovereign's** sons came,
and lifted up their voice and wept:
and the *king* **sovereign** also and all his servants
wept *very sore* **a mighty great weeping.**
37 But *Absalom* **Abi Shalom** fled,
and went to *Talmai* **Talmay,**
the son of *Ammihud* **Ammi Hud,**
king **sovereign** of Geshur.
And *David* mourned for his son every day.
38 So *Absalom* **Abi Shalom** fled, and went to Geshur,
and was there three years.
39 And *the soul of king* **sovereign** David
longed **concluded** to go forth unto *Absalom* **Abi Shalom:**
for he *was comforted* **sighed** concerning Amnon,
seeing he *was dead* **died.**

WISE WOMAN OF TEQOHA

14 Now *Joab* **Yah Ab** the son of *Zeruiah* **Seruyah**
perceived that the *king's* **sovereign's** heart
was toward *Absalom* **Abi Shalom.**
2 And *Joab* **Yah Ab** sent to *Tekoah* **Teqoha,**
and *fetched* **took** thence a wise woman, and said unto her,
I pray thee, feign thyself to be a mourner,
and *put on* **enrobe** now mourning *apparel* **clothes,**
and anoint not thyself with oil,
but be as a woman
that had *a long time* **many days** mourned for the dead:
3 And come to the *king* **sovereign,**
and *speak on* **word** this *manner* **word** unto him.
So *Joab put* **Yah Ab set** the words in her mouth.
4 And when the woman *of Tekoah* **Teqohiy**

spake **said** to the *king* **sovereign**,
she fell on her *face* **nostrils** to the *ground* **earth**,
and *did obeisance* **prostrated**, and said,
Help **Save**, O *king* **sovereign**.
5 And the *king* **sovereign** said unto her, What aileth thee?
And she *answered* **said**,
I am *indeed* **nevertheless** a widow woman,
and *mine husband is dead* **my man has died**.
6 And thy *handmaid* **maid** had two sons,
and they two strove together in the field,
and there was *none to part* **no rescuer between** them,
but the one smote the *other* **first**, and *slew* **deathified** him.
7 And, behold,
the whole family is risen against *thine handmaid* **thy maid**,
and they said, *Deliver* **Give** him that smote his brother,
that we may *kill* **deathify** him,
for the *life* **soul** of his brother whom he *slew* **slaughtered**;
and we *will destroy* **shall desolate** the *heir* **successor** also:
and so they shall quench my coal which *is left* **surviveth**,
and shall *not leave to my husband* **set to my man**
neither name nor *remainder* **survivors**
upon the *earth* **face of the soil**.
8 And the *king* **sovereign** said unto the woman,
Go to thine house,
and I *will give charge* **shall misvah** concerning thee.
9 And the woman *of Tekoah* **Teqohiy**
said unto the *king* **sovereign**,
My *lord* **adoni**, O *king* **sovereign**,
the *iniquity* **perversion** be on me,
and on my father's house:
and the *king* **sovereign** and his throne
be *guiltless* **innocent**.
10 And the *king* **sovereign** said,
Whosoever *saith* **wordeth** *ought* unto thee,
bring him to me,
and he shall **be added to** not touch thee *any more*.
11 Then said she, I pray thee,
let the *king* **sovereign**
remember *the LORD* **Yah Veh** thy *God* **Elohim**,
that *thou wouldest not suffer*
the *revengers* **redeemers** of blood
to destroy any more **not abound to ruin**,
lest they destroy my son.
And he said, *As the LORD* **Yah Veh** liveth,
there shall not one hair of thy son fall to the earth.
12 Then the woman said, Let *thine handmaid* **thy maid**,
I pray thee, *speak one* **word a** word
unto my *lord* **adoni** the *king* **sovereign**.
And he said, *Say* **Word** on.
13 And the woman said,
Wherefore then hast thou *thought* **fabricated**
such a *thing* **word** against the people of *God* **Elohim**?
for the *king* **sovereign** doth *speak* **word** this *thing* **word**
as one which is *faulty* **guilty**,
in that the *king* **sovereign**
doth not fetch home again **hath not returned**
his *banished* **expelled**.
14 For **in dying,** we *must needs* die,
and are as water *spilt* **poured** on the *ground* **earth**,
which cannot be gathered up again;
neither doth God respect **because Elohim taketh not away**
any person **a soul**:
yet doth he *devise means* **fabricate fabrications**,
that his *banished* **expelled** be not expelled from him.
15 Now therefore that I am come
to *speak of* **word** this *thing* **word**
unto my *lord* **adoni** the *king* **sovereign**,
it is because the people
have *made* **caused** me *afraid* **to awe**:
and thy *handmaid* **maid** said,
I *will* **shall** now *speak* **word** unto the *king* **sovereign**;
that it may be that the *king* **sovereign**
will perform **shall work** the *request* **word**
of his *handmaid* **maid**.
16 For the *king will* **sovereign shall** hear,
to *deliver* **rescue** his *handmaid* **maid**
out of the *hand* **palm** of the man
that *would destroy* **should desolate** me and my son
together out of the inheritance of *God* **Elohim**.
17 Then *thine handmaid* **thy maid** said,
The word of my *lord* **adoni** the *king* **sovereign**
shall now *be comfortable* **rest**:
for as an angel of *God* **Elohim**,
so is my *lord* **adoni** the *king* **sovereign**
to *discern* **hear** good and *bad* **evil**:
therefore *the LORD* **Yah Veh** thy *God* **Elohim**
will **shall** be with thee.
18 Then the *king* **sovereign** answered
and said unto the woman,
Hide **Conceal** not from me, I pray thee,
the *thing* **word** that I shall ask thee.
And the woman said,
Let my *lord* **adoni** the *king* **sovereign** now *speak* **word**.
19 And the *king* **sovereign** said,
Is *not* the hand of *Joab* **Yah Ab** with thee in all this?
And the woman answered and said,
As thy soul liveth, my *lord* **adoni** the *king* **sovereign**,
none **no man** can turn to the right *hand* or to the left
from ought that my *lord* **adoni** the *king* **sovereign**
hath *spoken* **worded**:
for thy servant *Joab* **Yah Ab**, he *bade* **misvahed** me,
and he *put* **set** all these words
in the mouth of *thine handmaid* **thy maid**:
20 *To fetch* **So as to go** about
this form **the face** of *speech* **this word**
hath thy servant *Joab* **Yah Ab**
done **worked** this *thing* **word**:
and my *lord* **adoni** is wise,
according to the wisdom of an angel of *God* **Elohim**,
to know all *things* that are in the earth.
21 And the *king* **sovereign** said unto *Joab* **Yah Ab**,
Behold now, I have *done* **worked** this *thing* **word**:
go therefore,
bring **return** the *young man Absalom* **lad Abi Shalom**
again.
22 And *Joab* **Yah Ab** fell to the *ground* **earth** on his face,
and *bowed* **prostrated** *himself*,
and *thanked* **blessed** the *king* **sovereign**:
and *Joab* **Yah Ab** said,
To day thy servant knoweth
that I have found *grace* **charism** in thy *sight* **eyes**,
my *lord* **adoni**, O *king* **sovereign**,
in that the *king* **sovereign**
hath *fulfilled* **worked** the *request* **word** of his servant.
23 So *Joab* **Yah Ab** arose and went to Geshur,
and brought *Absalom* **Abi Shalom**
to *Jerusalem* **Yeru Shalem**.
24 And the *king* **sovereign** said,
Let him turn to his own house,
and let him not see my face.
So *Absalom* **Abi Shalom** returned to his own house,
and saw not the *king's* **sovereign's** face.
25 But in all *Israel* **Yisra El** there was *none* **no man**
to be *much praised* **mightily halaled**
as *Absalom* **Abi Shalom**
for his beauty **there was not as handsome a man**:
from the sole of his foot
even to *the crown of his head* **his scalp**
there was no blemish in him.
26 And when he *polled* **shaved** his head,
(for it was at *every year's end* **the end of days by days**
that he *polled* **shaved** it:
because *the hair* **it** was heavy on him,
therefore he *polled* **shaved** it:)
he weighed the hair of his head at two hundred shekels
after the *king's weight* **sovereign's stone**.
27 And unto *Absalom* **Abi Shalom**
there were born three sons,
and one daughter, whose name was Tamar:
she was a woman of *a fair countenance* **beautiful visage**.
28 So *Absalom dwelt* **Abi Shalom settled**
two *full* years **of days** in *Jerusalem* **Yeru Shalem**,
and saw not the *king's* **sovereign's** face.
29 Therefore *Absalom* **Abi Shalom** sent for *Joab* **Yah Ab**,
to have sent him to the *king* **sovereign**;
but he *would* **willed to** not come to him:
and when he sent again the second time,
he *would* **willed to** not come.
30 Therefore he said unto his servants,
See, *Joab's field* **Yah Ab's allotment** is near mine **hand**,

and he hath barley there; go and *set* **burn** it on fire.
And *Absalom's* **Abi Shalom's** servants
set the *field* **allotment** on fire.
31 Then *Joab* **Yah Ab** arose,
and came to *Absalom* **Abi Shalom** unto his house,
and said unto him, Wherefore have thy servants
set my field **burnt mine allotment** on fire?
32 And *Absalom* **Abi Shalom**
answered Joab **said to Yah Ab**, Behold,
I sent unto thee, saying, Come hither,
that I may send thee to the *king* **sovereign**, to say,
Wherefore am I come from Geshur?
it had been good for me to have been there still:
now therefore let me see the *king's* **sovereign's** face;
and if there be *any iniquity* **perversity** in me,
let him *kill* **deathify** me.
33 So *Joab* **Yah Ab** came to the *king* **sovereign**,
and told him:
and when he had called for *Absalom* **Abi Shalom**,
he came to the *king* **sovereign**,
and *bowed* **prostrated** himself on his *face* **nostrils**
to the *ground* **earth**
before the king **at the face of the sovereign**:
and the *king* **sovereign** kissed *Absalom* **Abi Shalom**.

ABI SHALOM'S CONSPIRACY

15 And it *came to pass* **became** after this,
that *Absalom prepared* **Abi Shalom worked** him
chariots and horses,
and fifty men to run *before him* **at his face**.
2 And *Absalom rose up* **Abi Shalom started** early,
and stood *beside* **at hand by** the way of the *gate* **portal**:
and it *was so* **became**,
that when any man that had a controversy
came to the *king* **sovereign** for judgment,
then *Absalom* **Abi Shalom** called unto him, and said,
Of what city art thou?
And he said,
Thy servant is of one of the *tribes* **scions** of *Israel* **Yisra El**.
3 And *Absalom* **Abi Shalom** said unto him,
See, thy *matters* **words** are good and *right* **straightforward**;
but there is no man *deputed* of the *king* **sovereign**
to hear thee.
4 *Absalom* **Abi Shalom** said moreover,
Oh that I were made **Who setteth me** judge in the land,
that every man
which hath any *suit* **plea** or *cause* **judgment**
might come unto me,
and I *would do him justice* **should justify him**!
5 And it *was so* **became**,
that when any man *came nigh to* **approached** him
to *do* **prostrate to** him *obeisance*,
he *put* **sent** forth his hand,
and *took* **held** him, and kissed him.
6 And on this *manner* **word**
did Absalom **worked Abi Shalom** to all *Israel* **Yisra El**
that came to the *king* **sovereign** for judgment:
so *Absalom* **Abi Shalom**
stole the hearts of the men of *Israel* **Yisra El**.
7 And it *came to pass* **became**,
after **at the end of** forty years,
that *Absalom* **Abi Shalom** said unto the *king* **sovereign**,
I pray thee, let me go and *pay* **shalam** my vow,
which I have vowed unto *the LORD* **Yah Veh**, in Hebron.
8 For thy servant vowed a vow
while I *abode* **settled** at Geshur in *Syria* **Aram**, saying,
If the LORD shall bring me again indeed
If in returning, Yah Veh shall return me
to *Jerusalem* **Yeru Shalem**,
then I *will* **shall** serve *the LORD* **Yah Veh**.
9 And the *king* **sovereign** said unto him,
Go in *peace* **shalom**.
So he arose, and went to Hebron.
10 But *Absalom* **Abi Shalom** sent spies
throughout all the *tribes* **scions** of *Israel* **Yisra El**, saying,
As soon as ye hear the *sound* **voice** of the trumpet,
then ye shall say,
Absalom **Abi Shalom** reigneth in Hebron.
11 And with *Absalom* **Abi Shalom**
went two hundred men out of *Jerusalem* **Yeru Shalem**,
that were called;
and they went in their *simplicity* **integrity**,
and they knew not *any thing* **a word**.
12 And *Absalom* **Abi Shalom**
sent for *Ahithophel* **Achiy Thophel** the *Gilonite* **Gilohiy**,
David's counsellor, from his city, *even* from Giloh,
while he *offered* **sacrificed** sacrifices.
And the conspiracy was strong;
for the **many** people *increased continually* **walked**
with *Absalom* **Abi Shalom**.

DAVID FLEES YERU SHALEM

13 And there came a *messenger* **teller** to David, saying,
The hearts of the men of *Israel* **Yisra El**
are after *Absalom* **Abi Shalom**.
14 And David said unto all his servants
that were with him at *Jerusalem* **Yeru Shalem**,
Arise, and let us flee;
for **in escaping,** we shall not *else* escape
from *Absalom* **the face of Abi Shalom**:
make speed **hasten** to *depart* **go**,
lest he **hasten and** overtake us *suddenly*,
and *bring* **drive** evil upon us,
and smite the city with the *edge* **mouth** of the sword.
15 And the *king's* **sovereign's** servants
said unto the *king* **sovereign**, Behold,
thy servants *are ready to* **shall** do whatsoever
my *lord* **adoni** the *king* **sovereign** shall *appoint* **choose**.
16 And the *king* **sovereign** went forth,
and all his household *after him* **at his feet**.
And the *king* **sovereign** left ten women,
which were — concubines, to *keep* **guard** the house.
17 And the *king* **sovereign** went forth,
and all the people *after him* **at his feet**,
and *tarried* **stayed** in a *place* **house** that was far off.
18 And all his servants passed on *beside him* **at his hand**;
and all the *Cherethites* **executioners**,
and all the *Pelethites* **couriers**, and all the *Gittites* **Gittiy**,
six hundred men
which came *after him* **at his feet** from Gath,
passed on *before* **at the face of** the *king* **sovereign**.
19 Then said the *king* **sovereign**
to *Ittai* **Ittay** the *Gittite* **Gittiy**,
Wherefore goest thou also with us?
return to thy place,
and *abide* **settle** with the *king* **sovereign**:
for thou art a stranger, and also an exile.
20 Whereas thou camest *but* yesterday,
should I this day
make **have** thee *go up and down* **wander in going** with us?
seeing I go whither I may **go**,
return thou, and *take* **turn** back thy brethren:
mercy and truth be with thee.
21 And *Ittai* **Ittay** answered the *king* **sovereign**, and said,
As the LORD **Yah Veh** liveth,
and *as my lord* **adoni** the *king* **sovereign** liveth,
surely in what place
my *lord* **adoni** the *king* **sovereign** shall be,
whether in death or life,
even there also *will* **shall** thy servant be.
22 And David said to *Ittai* **Ittay**, Go and pass over.
And *Ittai* **Ittay** the *Gittite* **Gittiy** passed over,
and all his men,
and all the *little ones* **toddlers** that were with him.
23 And all the *country* **land** wept with a *loud* **great** voice,
and all the people passed over:
the *king* **sovereign** also *himself*
passed over the *brook Kidron* **wadi Qidron**,
and all the people passed over,
toward **upon the face of** the way of the wilderness.
24 And *lo Zadok* **behold Sadoq** also,
and all the *Levites* **Leviym** were with him,
bearing the ark of the covenant of *God* **Elohim**:
and they *set down* **firmed** the ark of *God* **Elohim**;
and *Abiathar went up* **Abi Athar ascended**,
until all the people had *done* **consumated**
passing out of the city.
25 And the *king* **sovereign** said unto *Zadok* **Sadoq**,
Carry **Turn** back the ark of *God* **Elohim** into the city:
if I shall find *favour* **charism**
in the eyes of *the LORD* **Yah Veh**,
he *will bring* **shall turn** me *again* **back**,

and *shew* **have** me *both* **see** it, and his habitation **of rest**:
26 But if he thus say, I have no delight in thee;
behold, *here am* I,
let him *do* **work** to me
as seemeth good *unto him* **in his eyes**.
27 The *king* **sovereign**
said also unto *Zadok* **Sadoq** the priest,
Art *not* thou a seer?
return into the city in *peace* **shalom**,
and your two sons with you,
Ahimaaz **Achiy Maas** thy son,
and *Jonathan* **Yah Nathan** the son of *Abiathar* **Abi Athar**.
28 See, I *will tarry* **shall linger**
in the plain of the wilderness,
until there come word from you to *certify* **tell** me.
29 *Zadok* **Sadoq** therefore and *Abiathar* **Abi Athar**
carried **turned back** the ark of *God* **Elohim**
to *Jerusalem* **Yeru Shalem**: and they *tarried* **settled** there.
30 And David *went up* **ascended**
by the ascent of *mount Olivet* **the Olives**,
and wept as he *went up* **ascended**,
and had his head covered,
and he *went barefoot* **walked unshod**:
and all the people that was with him
covered every man his head,
and they *went up* **ascended**,
weeping as they *went up* **ascended**.
31 And one told David, saying,
Ahithophel **Achiy Thophel** is among the conspirators
with *Absalom* **Abi Shalom**.
And David said, O *LORD* **Yah Veh**, I pray thee,
turn the counsel of Ahithophel into follishness
in follying, folly the counsel of Achiy Thophel.
32 And it *came to pass* **became**,
that when David was come to the top *of the mount*,
where he *worshipped God* **prostrated to Elohim**, behold,
Hushai **Hushay** the *Archite* **Arkiy** came to meet him
with his coat *rent* **ripped**, and *earth* **soil** upon his head:
33 Unto whom David said, If thou passest on with me,
then thou shalt be a burden unto me:
34 But if thou return to the city,
and say unto *Absalom* **Abi Shalom**,
I *will* **shall** be thy servant, O *king* **sovereign**;
as I have been thy father's servant *hitherto* **since then**,
so *will* **shall** I now also be thy servant:
then mayest thou for me
defeat **break down** the counsel
of *Ahithophel* **Achiy Thophel**.
35 And hast thou not there with thee
Zadok **Sadoq** and *Abiathar* **Abi Athar** the priests?
therefore it shall be,
that what *thing* **word** soever thou shalt hear
out of the *king's* **sovereign's** house,
thou shalt tell it
to *Zadok* **Sadoq** and *Abiathar* **Abi Athar** the priests.
36 Behold, they have there with them their two sons,
Ahimaaz **Achiy Maas,** *Zadok's* **Sadoq's** *son*,
and *Jonathan* **Yah Nathan,** *Abiathar's* **Abi Athar's** *son*;
and by *them* **their hand**
ye shall send unto me every *thing* **word** that ye can hear.
37 So *Hushai* **Hushay** David's friend
came into the city,
and *Absalom* **Abi Shalom**
came into *Jerusalem* **Yeru Shalem**.

DAVID AND SIBA

16 And when David was a little past the top *of the hill*,
behold,
Ziba **Siba** the *servant* **lad** of *Mephibosheth* **Mephi Bosheth**
met him,
with a *couple* **pair** of *asses saddled* **he burros harnessed**,
and upon them two hundred *loaves of* bread,
and an hundred *bunches of raisins* **raisincakes**,
and an hundred of summer fruits,
and a *bottle* **bag** of wine.
2 And the *king* **sovereign** said unto *Ziba* **Siba**,
What meanest thou by these?
And *Ziba* **Siba** said, The *asses* **he burros**
be for the *king's* **sovereign's** household to ride on;
and the bread and summer fruit
for the *young men* **lads** to eat;
and the wine,
that such as be *faint* **weary** in the wilderness may drink.
3 And the *king* **sovereign** said,
And where is thy *master's* **adoni's** son?
And *Ziba* **Siba** said unto the *king* **sovereign**, Behold,
he *abideth* **settleth** at *Jerusalem* **Yeru Shalem**:
for he said, To day shall the house of *Israel* **Yisra El**
restore me the *kingdom* **sovereigndom** of my father.
4 Then said the *king* **sovereign** to *Ziba* **Siba**, Behold,
thine are all *that pertained*
unto *Mephibosheth* **Mephi Bosheth**.
And *Ziba* **Siba** said, I *humbly beseech* **prostrate to** thee
that I may find *grace* **charism** in thy *sight* **eyes**,
my *lord* **adoni**, O *king* **sovereign**.

SHIMI ABASES DAVID

5 And when *king* **sovereign** David
came to *Bahurim* **Bachurim**, behold,
thence *came out* **went** a man
of the family of the house of *Saul* **Shaul**,
whose name was *Shimei* **Shimi**, the son of Gera:
he *came forth* **went**,
and *cursed still* **abased** as he *came* **went**.
6 And he *cast* **stoned** stones at David,
and at all the servants of *king* **sovereign** David:
and all the people and all the mighty *men*
were on his right *hand* and on his left.
7 And thus said *Shimei* **Shimi** when he *cursed* **abased**,
Come out **Go**, *come out* **go**, thou bloody man,
and thou man of *Belial* **Beli Yaal**:
8 *The LORD* **Yah Veh** hath returned upon thee
all the blood of the house of *Saul* **Shaul**,
in whose stead thou hast reigned;
and *the LORD* **Yah Veh**
hath *delivered* **given** the *kingdom* **sovereigndom**
into the hand of *Absalom* **Abi Shalom** thy son:
and, behold, thou art *taken* in thy *mischief* **evil**,
because thou art a bloody man.
9 Then said *Abishai* **Abi Shai** the son of *Zeruiah* **Seruyah**
unto the *king* **sovereign**,
Why should this dead dog
curse **abase** my *lord* **adoni** the *king* **sovereign**?
let me *go* **pass** over, I pray thee,
and *take* **twist** off his head.
10 And the *king* **sovereign** said,
What have I to do with you, ye sons of *Zeruiah* **Seruyah**?
so let him *curse* **abase**,
because *the LORD* **Yah Veh** hath said unto him,
Curse **Abase** David.
Who shall then say, Wherefore hast thou *done* **worked** so?
11 And David said to *Abishai* **Abi Shai**,
and to all his servants, Behold,
my son, which *came forth* **went** of my *bowels* **inwards**,
seeketh my *life* **soul**:
how much more now
may this *Benjamite* **Ben Yaminiy** do it?
let him alone, and let him curse **allow him to abase**;
for the *LORD* **Yah Veh** hath *bidden* **said to** him.
12 *It may be that the LORD* **Perhaps Yah Veh**
will look on mine affliction **shall see my humiliation**,
and that *the LORD* **Yah Veh**
will requite **shall return** me good
for his *cursing* **abasing** this day.
13 And as David and his men went by the way,
Shimei **Shimi** went along on the *hill's* **mountain** side
over against **beside** him,
and *cursed* **abased** as he went,
and *threw* **stoned** stones *at* **beside** him,
and *cast* **dusted** dust.
14 And the *king* **sovereign**,
and all the people that were with him,
came *weary* **languid**, and refreshed themselves there.

ABI SHALOM APPROACHES YERU SHALEM

15 And *Absalom* **Abi Shalom**,
and all the people of the men of *Israel* **Yisra El**,
came to *Jerusalem* **Yeru Shalem**,
and *Ahithophel* **Achiy Thophel** with him.
16 And it *came to pass* **became**,
when *Hushai* **Hushay** the *Archite* **Arkiy**, David's friend,
was come unto *Absalom* **Abi Shalom**,
that *Hushai* **Hushay** said unto *Absalom* **Abi Shalom**,

God save the king **Let the sovereign live,**
God save the king **Let the sovereign live.**
17 And *Absalom* **Abi Shalom** said to *Hushai* **Hushay**,
Is this thy *kindness* **mercy** to thy friend?
why wentest thou not with thy friend?
18 And *Hushai* **Hushay** said unto *Absalom* **Abi Shalom**,
Nay; but whom *the LORD* **Yah Veh**, and this people,
and all the men of *Israel* **Yisra El**, choose,
his *will* **shall** I be, and with him *will* **shall** I *abide* **settle**.
19 And *again* **secondly**, whom should I serve?
should I not *serve in* **at** the *presence* **face** of his son?
as I have served *in* **at** thy father's *presence* **face**,
so *will* **shall** I be *in* **at** thy *presence* **face**.
20 Then said *Absalom* **Abi Shalom**
to *Ahithophel* **Achiy Thophel**,
Give counsel among you what we shall *do* **work**.
21 And *Ahithophel* **Achiy Thophel**
said unto *Absalom* **Abi Shalom,**
Go in unto thy father's concubines,
which he hath *left* **allowed** to *keep* **guard** the house;
and all *Israel* **Yisra El** shall hear
that thou *art abhorred* **stinkest** of thy father:
then shall the hands of all that are with thee
be *strong* **strengthened**.
22 So they spread *Absalom* **Abi Shalom** a tent
upon the *top of the house* **roof**;
and *Absalom* **Abi Shalom**
went in unto his father's concubines
in the *sight* **eyes** of all *Israel* **Yisra El**.
23 And the counsel of *Ahithophel* **Achiy Thophel**,
which he counselled in those days,
was as if a man had *enquired* **asked**
at the *oracle* **word** of *God* **Elohim**:
so was all the counsel of *Ahithophel* **Achiy Thophel**
both with David and with *Absalom* **Abi Shalom**.

HUSHAY'S COUNSEL

17 Moreover
Ahithophel **Achiy Thophel** said unto *Absalom* **Abi Shalom**,
Let me now choose out twelve thousand men,
and I *will* **shall** arise and pursue after David this night:
2 And I *will* **shall** come upon him
while he is *weary* **belaboured** and weak handed,
and *will make* **shall cause** him *afraid* **to tremble**:
and all the people that are with him shall flee;
and I *will* **shall** smite the *king* **sovereign** only:
3 And I *will bring back* **shall return** all the people
unto thee:
the man whom thou seekest is as if all returned:
so all the people shall be in *peace* **shalom**.
4 And the *saying pleased* **word was right**
Absalom well **in the eyes of Abi Shalom**,
and **in the eyes of** all the elders of *Israel* **Yisra El**.
5 Then said *Absalom* **Abi Shalom**,
Call now *Hushai* **Hushay** the *Archite* **Arkiy** also,
and let us hear likewise what *he saith* **is in his mouth**.
6 And when *Hushai* **Hushay**
was come to *Absalom* **Abi Shalom**,
Absalom spake **Abi Shalom said** unto him, saying,
Ahithophel **Achiy Thophel**
hath *spoken* **worded** after this *manner* **word**:
shall we *do* **work** after his *saying* **word**?
if not; *speak* **word** thou.
7 And *Hushai* **Hushay** said unto *Absalom* **Abi Shalom**,
The counsel
that *Ahithophel* **Achiy Thophel** hath *given* **counselled**
is not good at this time.
8 For, said *Hushai* **Hushay**,
thou knowest thy father and his men,
that they be mighty *men*,
and they be *chafed in their minds* **bitter of soul**,
as a bear *robbed of her whelps* **bereft** in the field:
and thy father is a man of war,
and *will* **shall** not *lodge* **stay overnight** with the people.
9 Behold, he is hid now in *some pit* **one of the pits**,
or in *some other place* **one of the places**:
and it *will come to pass* **shall become**,
when some of them be *overthrown* **fallen**
at the *first* **beginning**,
that **in hearing,**
whosoever heareth it will **a hearer shall** say,
There is a *slaughter* **plague** among the people
that *follow Absalom* **go after Abi Shalom**.
10 And he also that is *valiant* **a son of valour**,
whose heart is as the heart of a lion,
in melting, shall *utterly* melt:
for all *Israel* **Yisra El** knoweth
that thy father is *a* mighty *man*,
and they which be with him
are *valiant men* **sons of valour**.
11 Therefore I counsel that all *Israel* **Yisra El**
in gathering, be *generally* gathered unto thee,
from Dan even to *Beersheba* **Beer Sheba**,
as the sand that is by the sea for *multitude* **abundance**;
and that thou go to *battle* **war**
in thine own person **by yourself**.
12 So shall we come upon him
in *some place* **one of the places** where he shall be found,
and we *will* **shall** light upon him
as the dew falleth on the *ground* **soil**:
and of him and of all the men that are with him
there shall not *be left so much as* **remain even** one.
13 Moreover, if he be *gotten* **gathered** into a city,
then shall all *Israel* **Yisra El**
bring ropes **bear lines** to that city,
and we *will draw* **shall drag** it into the *river* **wadi**,
until there be not *one small stone* **even a bundle**
found there.
14 And *Absalom* **Abi Shalom**
and all the men of *Israel* **Yisra El** said,
The counsel of *Hushai* **Hushay** the *Archite* **Arkiy**
is better than the counsel of *Ahithophel* **Achiy Thophel**.
For *the LORD* **Yah Veh**
had *appointed* **misvahed** to *defeat* **break down**
the good counsel of *Ahithophel* **Achiy Thophel,**
to the intent **so** that *the LORD* **Yah Veh**
might bring evil upon *Absalom* **Abi Shalom**.
15 Then said *Hushai* **Hushay** unto *Zadok* **Sadoq**
and to *Abiathar* **Abi Athar** the priests,
Thus and thus did *Ahithophel* **Achiy Thophel** counsel
Absalom **Abi Shalom** and the elders of *Israel* **Yisra El**;
and thus and thus have I counselled.
16 Now therefore send quickly, and tell David, saying,
Lodge **Stay** not **overnight**
this night in the plains of the wilderness,
but **in passing,** *speedily* pass over;
lest the *king* **sovereign** be swallowed up,
and all the people that are with him.
17 Now *Jonathan* **Yah Nathan** and *Ahimaaz* **Achiy Maas**
stayed by *Enrogel* **En Rogel**;
for they *might* **could** not be seen to come into the city:
and a *wench* **maid** went and told them;
and they went and told *king* **sovereign** David.
18 Nevertheless a lad saw them,
and told *Absalom* **Abi Shalom**:
but they went both of them away quickly,
and came to a man's house in *Bahurim* **Bachurim**,
which had a well in his court;
whither they *went down* **descended**.
19 And the woman took
and spread a covering over the well's *mouth* **face**,
and spread *ground corn* **grits** thereon;
and the *thing* **word** was not known.
20 And when *Absalom's* **Abi Shalom's** servants
came to the woman to the house, they said,
Where is *Ahimaaz* **Achiy Maas** and *Jonathan* **Yah Nathan**?
And the woman said unto them,
They be *gone* **passed** over the *brook* **streamlet** of water.
And when they had sought and could not find them,
they returned to *Jerusalem* **Yeru Shalem**.
21 And it *came to pass* **became**,
after they *were departed* **went**,
that they *came up* **ascended** out of the well,
and went and told *king* **sovereign** David,
and said unto David,
Arise, and pass quickly over the water:
for thus hath *Ahithophel* **Achiy Thophel**
counselled against you.
22 Then David arose,
and all the people that were with him,
and they passed over *Jordan* **Yarden**:

by the morning light there lacked not one of them
that was not *gone* **passed** over *Jordan* **Yarden**.
23 And when *Ahithophel* **Achiy Thophel**
saw that his counsel was not *followed* **worked**,
he *saddled* **harnessed** his *ass* **he burro**, and arose,
and *gat him home* **went** to his house, to his city,
and *put his household in order*
misvahed concerning his house,
and *hanged* **strangled** himself, and died,
and was *buried* **entombed**
in the *sepulchre* **tomb** of his father.
24 Then David came to *Mahanaim* **Machanayim**.
And *Absalom* **Abi Shalom** passed over *Jordan* **Yarden**,
he and all the men of *Israel* **Yisra El** with him.
25 And *Absalom* **Abi Shalom**
made **set** Amasa captain of the host
instead of *Joab* **Yah Ab**:
which Amasa was a man's son,
whose name was *Ithra* **Yithra** an *Israelite* **Yisra Eliy**,
that went in to *Abigail* **Abi Gail**
the daughter of *Nahash* **Nachash**,
sister to *Zeruiah* **Seruyah**, *Joab's* **Yah Ab's** mother.
26 So *Israel* **Yisra El** and *Absalom* **Abi Shalom**
pitched **encamped** in the land of *Gilead* **Gilad**.
27 And it *came to pass* **became**,
when David was come to *Mahanaim* **Machanayim**,
that Shobi the son of *Nahash* **Nachash** of Rabbah
of the *children* **sons** of Ammon,
and Machir the son of *Ammiel* **Ammi El**
of *Lodebar* **Lo Debar**,
and *Barzillai* **Barzillay** the *Gileadite* **Giladiy** of Rogelim,
28 Brought **near** beds, and basons,
and *earthen vessels* **formed instruments**,
and wheat, and barley, and flour, and parched *corn*,
and beans, and lentiles, and parched *pulse*,
29 And honey, and butter, and *sheep* **flock**,
and cheese of *kine* **oxen**,
for David, and for the people that were with him, to eat:
for they said, The people is *hungry* **famished**,
and *weary* **languid**, and thirsty, in the wilderness.

DAVID LINES UP FOR WAR

18 And David *numbered* **mustered** the people
that were with him,
and set *captains* **governors** of thousands,
and *captains* **governors** of hundreds over them.
2 And David sent forth a third *part* of the people
under the hand of *Joab* **Yah Ab**,
and a third *part* under the hand of *Abishai* **Abi Shai**
the son of *Zeruiah* **Seruyah**, *Joab's* **Yah Ab's** brother,
and a third *part*
under the hand of *Ittai* **Ittay** the *Gittite* **Gittiy**.
And the *king* **sovereign** said unto the people,
In going, I *will* **shall** *surely* go *forth* with you
myself — **I** also.
3 But the people *answered* **said**, Thou shalt not go forth:
for if **in fleeing,** we flee *away*,
they *will* **shall** not *care for* **set their heart on** us;
neither if half of us die,
will **shall** they *care for* **set their heart on** us:
but now thou art *worth* **as** ten thousand of us:
therefore now
it is better that thou *succour* **help** us out of the city.
4 And the *king* **sovereign** said unto them,
What *seemeth you best* **well—pleaseth your eyes**
I *will do* **shall work**.
And the *king* **sovereign**
stood by the *gate side* **portal handle**,
and all the people *came out* **went**
by hundreds and by thousands.
5 And the *king commanded* **sovereign misvahed**
Joab **Yah Ab** and *Abishai* **Abi Shai** and *Ittai* **Ittay**, saying,
Deal gently for my sake with the *young man* **lad**,
even with *Absalom* **Abi Shalom**.
And all the people heard when the *king* **sovereign**
gave **misvahed** all the *captains charge* **governors**
the word concerning *Absalom* **Abi Shalom**.
6 So the people went out into the field
against Israel **to meet Yisra El**:
and the *battle* **war**
was in the *wood* **forest** of *Ephraim* **Ephrayim**;
7 Where the people of *Israel* **Yisra El** were *slain* **smitten**
before **at the face of** the servants of David,
and there was there a great *slaughter* **plague** that day
of twenty thousand *men*.
8 For the *battle* **war** was there scattered
over the face of all the *country* **land**:
and the *wood* **forest abounded**
and devoured more people that day
than the sword devoured.

ABI SHALOM'S DEATH

9 And *Absalom* **Abi Shalom**
met **faced** the servants of David.
And *Absalom* **Abi Shalom** rode upon a mule,
and the mule
went under the *thick boughs* **thicket** of a great oak,
and his head caught hold of the oak,
and he was *taken* **given** up
between the *heaven* **heavens** and the earth;
and the mule that was under him *went away* **passed on**.
10 And *a certain* **one** man saw it, and told *Joab* **Yah Ab**,
and said, Behold,
I saw *Absalom* **Abi Shalom** hanged in an oak.
11 And *Joab* **Yah Ab** said unto the man that told him,
And, behold, thou sawest him,
and why didst thou not smite him there
to the *ground* **earth**?
and I *would* **should** have given thee
ten *shekels* of silver, and *a* **one** girdle.
12 And the man said unto *Joab* **Yah Ab**,
Though **If** I should *receive* **weigh**
a thousand *shekels of* silver *in mine hand* **upon my palm**,
yet would **should** I not *put* **send** forth mine hand
against the *king's* **sovereign's** son:
for in our *hearing* **ears**
the *king charged* **sovereign misvahed** thee
and *Abishai* **Abi Shai** and *Ittai* **Ittay**, saying,
Beware that none touch the young man Absalom
Guard against the lad — against Abi Shalom.
13 Otherwise I should have *wrought* **worked** falsehood
against mine own *life* **soul**:
for there is no *matter* **word**
hid **concealed** from the *king* **sovereign**,
and thou thyself
wouldest **shouldest** have set thyself against me.
14 Then said *Joab* **Yah Ab**,
I may not *tarry* **wait** thus *with thee* **at thy face**.
And he took three *darts* **scions** in his *hand* **palm**,
and *thrust* **staked** them
through the heart of *Absalom* **Abi Shalom**,
while he was yet alive in the *midst* **heart** of the oak.
15 And ten *young men* **lads**
that bare *Joab's armour* **Yah Ab's instruments**
compassed **surrounded** about
and smote *Absalom* **Abi Shalom**, and *slew* **deathified** him.
16 And *Joab blew* **Yah Ab blast** the trumpet,
and the people returned from pursuing after *Israel* **Yisra El**:
for *Joab held back* **Yah Ab restrained** the people.
17 And they took *Absalom* **Abi Shalom**,
and cast him into a great pit in the *wood* **forest**,
and *laid* **stationed**
a *very* **mighty** great heap of stones upon him:
and all *Israel* **Yisra El** fled every *one* **man** to his tent.
18 Now *Absalom* **Abi Shalom** in his lifetime
had taken and *reared up* **stationed** for himself
a *pillar* **monolith**,
which is in *the king's dale* **Sovereign's Valley**:
for he said, I have no son
to *keep* **memorialize** my name *in remembrance*:
and he called the *pillar* **monolith** after his own name:
and it is called unto this day,
Absalom's place **The Hand of Abi Shalom**.
19 Then said *Ahimaaz* **Achiy Maas**
the son of *Zadok* **Sadoq**,
Let me now run,
and bear the *king tidings* **sovereign the evangelism**,
how that *the LORD* **Yah Veh** hath *avenged* **judged** him
from the hand of his enemies.
20 And *Joab* **Yah Ab** said unto him,
Thou shalt not
bear tidings **be a man evangelizing** this day,

but thou shalt *bear tidings* **evangelize** another day:
but this day thou shalt *bear no tidings* **not evangelize**,
because the *king's* **sovereign's** son *is dead* **died**.
21 Then said *Joab* **Yah Ab** to *Cushi* **Kushiy**,
Go tell the *king* **sovereign** what thou hast seen.
And *Cushi* **Kushiy**
bowed **prostrated** himself unto *Joab* **Yah Ab**, and ran.
22 Then *said Ahimaaz* **Achiy Maas** the son of *Zadok* **Sadoq**
yet again to Joab **added to say to Yah Ab**,
But howsoever,
let me, I pray thee, also run after *Cushi* **Kushiy**.
And *Joab* **Yah Ab** said,
Wherefore *wilt* **shalt** thou run, my son,
seeing that thou
hast no *tidings ready* **evangelism to present**?
23 But howsoever, *said he*, let me run.
And he said unto him, Run.
Then *Ahimaaz* **Achiy Maas**
ran by the way of the *plain* **environ**,
and *overran Cushi* **passed Kushiy**.
24 And David *sat* **settled** between the two *gates* **portals**:
and the *watchman* **watcher** went up to the roof
over the *gate* **portal** unto the wall, and lifted up his eyes,
and *looked* **saw**, and behold a man running alone.
25 And the *watchman cried* **watcher called out**,
and told the *king* **sovereign**.
And the *king* **sovereign** said,
If he be alone, there is *tidings* **evangelism** in his mouth.
And *he came apace* **in walking, he walked**,
and *drew near* **approached**.
26 And the *watchman* **watcher** saw another man running:
and the *watchman* **watcher** called unto the porter,
and said, Behold *another* **a** man running alone.
And the *king* **sovereign** said,
He also *bringeth tidings* **evangelizeth**.
27 And the *watchman* **watcher** said,
Me thinketh the running **I see the racing**
of the *foremost* **first**
is like the *running* **racing** of *Ahimaaz* **Achiy Maas**
the son of *Zadok* **Sadoq**.
And the *king* **sovereign** said, He is a good man,
and cometh with good *tidings* **evangelism**.
28 And *Ahimaaz* **Achiy Maas** called,
and said unto the *king* **sovereign**, *All is well* **Shalom**.
And he *fell down* **prostrated** to the earth
upon his *face* **nostrils**
before **at the face of** the *king* **sovereign**, and said,
Blessed be *the LORD* **Yah Veh** thy *God* **Elohim**,
which hath *delivered* **shut** up the men
that lifted up their hand
against my *lord* **adoni** the *king* **sovereign**.
29 And the *king* **sovereign** said,
Is the *young man Absalom safe* **lad Abi Shalom at shalom**?
And *Ahimaaz answered* **Achiy Maas said**,
When *Joab* **Yah Ab** sent the *king's* **sovereign's** servant,
and *me* thy servant,
I saw a great *tumult* **multitude**, but I knew not what it was.
30 And the *king* **sovereign** said *unto him*,
Turn *aside* **around**, and stand *here* **thus**.
And he turned *aside* **around**, and stood still.
31 And, behold, *Cushi* **Kushiy** came;
and *Cushi* **Kushiy** said, *Tidings* **Evangelism** is brought,
my *lord* **adoni** the *king* **sovereign**:
for *the LORD* **Yah Veh** hath *avenged* **judged** thee this day
from the hand of all them that rose up against thee.
32 And the *king* **sovereign** said unto *Cushi* **Kushiy**,
Is the *young man Absalom safe* **lad Abi Shalom at shalom**?
And *Cushi answered* **Kushiy said**,
The enemies of my *lord* **adoni** the *king* **sovereign**,
and all that rise against thee to *do* **vilify** thee *hurt*,
be as that *young man* **lad** is.
33 And the *king was much moved* **sovereign quivered**,
and *went up* **ascended**
to the *chamber* **upper room** over the *gate* **portal**,
and wept:
and as he went, thus he said,
O my son *Absalom* **Abi Shalom**, my son,
my son *Absalom* **Abi Shalom**!
would God **O that** I had died for thee,
O *Absalom* **Abi Shalom**, my son, my son!

DAVID REBUKED FOR MOURNING

19 And it was told *Joab* **Yah Ab**, Behold,
the *king* **sovereign** weepeth and mourneth
for *Absalom* **Abi Shalom**.
2 And the *victory* **salvation** that day
was *turned* into mourning unto all the people:
for the people heard say that day
how the *king was grieved* **sovereign writhed** for his son.
3 And the people gat them by stealth that day into the city,
as people being ashamed steal away
when they flee in *battle* **war**.
4 But the *king covered* **sovereign muffled** his face,
and the *king* **sovereign** cried with a *loud* **great** voice,
O my son *Absalom* **Abi Shalom**,
O *Absalom* **Abi Shalom**, my son, my son!
5 And *Joab* **Yah Ab** came into the house
to the *king* **sovereign**, and said,
Thou hast shamed this day the faces of all thy servants,
which this day have *saved* **rescued** thy *life* **soul**,
and the *lives* **souls** of thy sons and of thy daughters,
and the *lives* **souls** of thy *wives* **women**,
and the *lives* **souls** of thy concubines;
6 In that thou lovest thine *enemies* **haters**,
and hatest thy *friends* **beloved**.
For thou hast *declared* **told** this day,
that thou regardest neither *princes* **governors** nor servants:
for this day I perceive,
that if *Absalom* **Abi Shalom** had lived,
and all we had died this day,
then it had *pleased thee well* **been straight in thine eyes**.
7 Now therefore arise, go forth,
and *speak comfortably* **word**
unto **the heart of** thy servants:
for **I** *swear* **oath** by *the LORD* **Yah Veh**,
if thou go not forth,
there will not tarry one **no man shall stay overnight**
with thee this night:
and that *will* **shall** be *worse* **more vilified** unto thee
than all the evil that befell thee from thy youth until now.
8 Then the *king* **sovereign** arose,
and *sat* **settled** in the *gate* **portal**.
And they told unto all the people, saying, Behold,
the *king* **sovereign** doth *sit* **settle** in the *gate* **portal**.
And all the people came
before **at the face of** the *king* **sovereign**:
for *Israel* **Yisra El** had fled every man to his tent.

DAVID'S SOVEREIGNDOM RESTORED

9 And all the people *were at strife* **pleaded**
throughout all the *tribes* **scions** of *Israel* **Yisra El**, saying,
The *king saved* **sovereign rescued** us
out of the *hand* **palm** of our enemies,
and he *delivered* **rescued** us
out of the *hand* **palm** of the *Philistines* **Peleshethiy**;
and now he is fled
out of the land for *Absalom* **Abi Shalom**.
10 And *Absalom* **Abi Shalom**, whom we anointed over us,
is dead **hath died** in *battle* **war**.
Now therefore why *speak ye not a word* **hush ye**
of *bringing* **returning** the *king back* **sovereign**?
11 And *king* **sovereign** David
sent to *Zadok* **Sadoq** and to *Abiathar* **Abi Athar** the priests,
saying, *Speak* **Word** unto the elders of *Judah* **Yah Hudah**,
saying, Why are ye the last
to *bring* **return** the *king* **sovereign** *back* to his house?
(*seeing the speech* **and the word** of all *Israel* **Yisra El**
is come to the *king* **sovereign**, *even* to his house.)
12 Ye are my brethren, ye are my bones and my flesh:
wherefore then are ye the last
to *bring back* **return** the *king* **sovereign**?
13 And say ye to Amasa,
Art thou not of my bone, and of my flesh?
God do **Elohim work** so to me, and *more* **add** also,
if thou be not *captain* **governor** of the host
before me continually **at my face all days**
in the room of Joab **under Yah Ab**.
14 And he *bowed* **extended** the heart
of all the men of *Judah* **Yah Hudah**,
even as *the heart of* one man;
so that they sent *this word* unto the *king* **sovereign**,
Return thou, and all thy servants.

15 So the *king* **sovereign** returned,
and came to *Jordan* **Yarden.**
And *Judah* **Yah Hudah** came to Gilgal,
to go to meet the *king* **sovereign**,
to *conduct* **pass** the *king* **sovereign** over *Jordan* **Yarden**.
16 And *Shimei* **Shimi** the son of Gera,
a *Benjamite* **Ben Yaminiy**, which was of *Bahurim* **Bachurim**,
hasted and *came down* **descended**
with the men of *Judah* **Yah Hudah**
to meet *king* **sovereign** David.
17 And there were
a thousand men of *Benjamin* **Ben Yamin** with him,
and *Ziba* **Siba** the *servant* **lad** of the house of *Saul* **Shaul**,
and his fifteen sons and his twenty servants with him;
and they *went* **prospered** over *Jordan* **Yarden**
before **at the face of** the *king* **sovereign**.
18 And there *went* **passed** over a *ferry boat* **raft**
to *carry* **pass** over the *king's* **sovereign's** household,
and to *do what he thought* **work** good **in his eyes**.
And *Shimei* **Shimi** the son of Gera fell down
before **at the face of** the *king* **sovereign**,
as he was *come* **passed** over *Jordan* **Yarden**;
19 And said unto the *king* **sovereign**,
Let not my *lord* **adoni**
impute iniquity **fabricate perversity** unto me,
neither do thou remember
that which thy servant did *perversely* **pervert**
the day that my *lord* **adoni** the *king* **sovereign**
went out of *Jerusalem* **Yeru Shalem**,
that the *king* **sovereign** should *take* **set** it to his heart.
20 For thy servant doth know that I have sinned:
therefore, behold,
I am come the first this day
of all the house of *Joseph* **Yoseph**
to *go down* **descend**
to meet my *lord* **adoni** the *king* **sovereign**.
21 But *Abishai* **Abi Shai** the son of *Zeruiah* **Seruyah**
answered and said,
Shall not *Shimei* **Shimi** be *put to death* **deathified** for this,
because he *cursed* **abased**
the LORD'S **Yah Veh's** anointed?
22 And David said,
What have I to do with you, ye sons of *Zeruiah* **Seruyah**,
that ye should this day be *adversaries* **satans** unto me?
shall there any man be *put to death* **deathified**
this day in *Israel* **Yisra El**?
for do not I know that I am this day
king **sovereign** over *Israel* **Yisra El**?
23 Therefore the *king* **sovereign** said unto *Shimei* **Shimi**,
Thou shalt not die.
And the *king sware* **sovereign oathed** unto him.
24 And *Mephibosheth* **Mephi Bosheth**
the son of *Saul* **Shaul**
came down **descended** to meet the *king* **sovereign**,
and had neither *dressed* **worked** his feet,
nor *trimmed* **worked** his *beard* **upper lip**,
nor *washed* **laundered** his clothes,
from the day the *king departed* **sovereign went**
until the day he came *again* in *peace* **shalom**.
25 And it *came to pass* **became**,
when he was come to *Jerusalem* **Yeru Shalem**
to meet the *king* **sovereign**,
that the *king* **sovereign** said unto him,
Wherefore wentest not thou with me,
Mephibosheth **Mephi Bosheth**?
26 And he *answered* **said**, My *lord* **adoni**,
O *king* **sovereign**, my servant deceived me:
for thy servant said,
I *will saddle* **shall harness** me *an ass* **a he burro**,
that I may ride thereon, and go to the *king* **sovereign**;
because thy servant is lame.
27 And he hath *slandered* **treaded upon** thy servant
unto my *lord* **adoni** the *king* **sovereign**;
but my *lord* **adoni** the *king* **sovereign**
is as an angel of *God* **Elohim**:
do **work** therefore what is good in thine eyes.
28 For all of my father's house
were **naught** but *dead men* **men of death**
before my lord **to my adoni** the *king* **sovereign**:
yet didst thou set thy servant
among them that did eat at thine own table.
What *right* **justness** therefore have I yet
to cry any more unto the *king* **sovereign**?
29 And the *king* **sovereign** said unto him,
Why *speakest* **wordest** thou any more
of thy *matters* **words**?
I have said, Thou and *Ziba divide* **Siba allot** the *land* **field**.
30 And *Mephibosheth* **Mephi Bosheth**
said unto the *king* **sovereign**, Yea, let him take all,
forasmuch as **since** my *lord* **adoni** the *king* **sovereign**
is come again in *peace* **shalom** unto his own house.
31 And *Barzillai* **Barzillay** the *Gileadite* **Giladiy**
came down **descended** from Rogelim,
and *went* **passed** over *Jordan* **Yarden**
with the *king* **sovereign**,
to *conduct* **send** him over *Jordan* **Yarden**.
32 Now *Barzillai* **Barzillay**
was *a very aged man* **mighty old**,
even fourscore — **a son of eighty** years *old*:
and he had *provided* **sustained** the *king* **sovereign**
of sustenance
while he *lay* **resided** at *Mahanaim* **Machanayim**;
for he was a *very* **mighty** great man.
33 And the *king* **sovereign** said unto *Barzillai* **Barzillay**,
Come **Pass** thou over with me,
and I *will feed* **shall sustain** thee with me
in *Jerusalem* **Yeru Shalem**.
34 And *Barzillai* **Barzillay** said unto the *king* **sovereign**,
How long have I to live
How many days are the years of my life,
that I should *go up* **ascend** with the *king* **sovereign**
unto *Jerusalem* **Yeru Shalem**?
35 I am this day *fourscore* **a son of eighty** years *old*:
and can I *discern* **know** between good and evil?
can thy servant taste what I eat or what I drink?
can I hear any more the voice of *singing men* **songsters**
and *singing women* **songstresses**?
wherefore then should thy servant
be yet a burden unto my *lord* **adoni** the *king* **sovereign**?
36 Thy servant
will go **shall pass** a little way over *Jordan* **Yarden**
with the *king* **sovereign**:
and why, **in dealing,**
should the *king* **sovereign**
recompense it me with such a reward **deal with me thus**?
37 Let thy servant, I pray thee, turn back again,
that I may die in mine own city,
and be buried by the *grave* **tomb**
of my father and of my mother.
But behold thy servant *Chimham* **Kimham**;
let him *go* **pass** over
with my *lord* **adoni** the *king* **sovereign**;
and *do* **work** to him
what shall seem good *unto thee* **in thine eyes**.
38 And the *king answered* **sovereign said**,
Chimham **Kimham** shall *go* **pass** over with me,
and I *will do* **shall work** to him
that which shall seem good
unto thee **in thine eyes**:
and whatsoever thou shalt *require* **choose** of me,
that *will* **shall** I *do* **work** for thee.
39 And all the people *went* **passed** over *Jordan* **Yarden**.
And when the *king was come* **sovereign passed** over,
the *king* **sovereign** kissed *Barzillai* **Barzillay**,
and blessed him;
and he returned unto his own place.
40 Then the *king went on* **sovereign passed over** to Gilgal,
and *Chimham went on* **Kimham passed over** with him:
and all the people of *Judah* **Yah Hudah**
conducted **passed** the *king* **sovereign over,**
and also half the people of *Israel* **Yisra El**.
41 And, behold,
all the men of *Israel* **Yisra El** came to the *king* **sovereign**,
and said unto the *king* **sovereign**,
Why have our brethren the men of *Judah* **Yah Hudah**
stolen thee away,
and have *brought* **passed** the *king* **sovereign**,
and his household, and all David's men with him,
over *Jordan* **Yarden**?
42 And all the men of *Judah* **Yah Hudah**

answered the men of *Israel* **Yisra El**,
Because the *king* **sovereign** is near *of kin* to us:
wherefore then be ye *angry* **inflamed** for this *matter* **word**?
in eating, have we eaten *at all*
of the *king's* **sovereign's** *cost*?
or hath he *given* **borne** us any *gift* **offering**?
43 And the men of *Israel* **Yisra El**
answered the men of *Judah* **Yah Hudah**, and said,
We have ten *parts* **hands** in the *king* **sovereign**,
and we have also more *right* in David than ye:
why then did ye *despise* **belittle** us,
that our *advice* **word** should not be first had
in *bringing back* **returning** our *king* **sovereign**?
And the words of the men of *Judah* **Yah Hudah**
were *fiercer* **harder**
than the words of the men of *Israel* **Yisra El**.

SHEBA REBELS

20 And there *happened to be* **was called** there
a man of *Belial* **Beli Yaal**, whose name was Sheba,
the son of Bichri, a *Benjamite* **Ben Yaminiy**:
and he *blew* **blast** a trumpet, and said,
We have no *part* **allotment** in David,
neither have we inheritance in the son of *Jesse* **Yishay**:
every man to his tents, O *Israel* **Yisra El**.
2 So every man of *Israel* **Yisra El**
went up **ascended** from after David,
and *followed* **went after** Sheba the son of Bichri:
but the men of *Judah* **Yah Hudah**
clave **adhered** unto their *king* **sovereign**,
from *Jordan* **Yarden** even to *Jerusalem* **Yeru Shalem**.
3 And David came to his house at *Jerusalem* **Yeru Shalem**;
and the *king* **sovereign**
took the ten women *his* concubines,
whom he had *left* **allowed** to *keep* **guard** the house,
and *put* **gave** them in *ward* **a house of guard**,
and *fed* **sustained** them, but went not in unto them.
So they were *shut up* **bound**
unto the day *of their death* **they died**,
living in widowhood.
4 Then said the *king* **sovereign** to Amasa,
Assemble **Cry out unto** me the men of *Judah* **Yah Hudah**
within three days,
and *be* **stand** thou here *present*.
5 So Amasa *went to assemble*
the men of Judah **cried out unto Yah Hudah**:
but he *tarried* **lingered**
longer than **beyond** the *set time* **season**
which he had appointed him **to congregate**.
6 And David said to *Abishai* **Abi Shai**,
Now shall Sheba the son of Bichri do
us more *harm* **evil** than did *Absalom* **Abi Shalom**:
take thou thy *lord's* **adoni's** servants, and pursue after him,
lest he *get* **find** him *fenced* **protected** cities,
and *escape us* **deliver himself from our eyes**.
7 And there went out after him *Joab's* **Yah Ab's** men,
and the *Cherethites* **executioners**,
and the *Pelethites* **couriers**, and all the mighty *men*:
and they went out of *Jerusalem* **Yeru Shalem**,
to pursue after Sheba the son of Bichri.
8 When they were at the great stone
which is in *Gibeon* **Gibon**,
Amasa went *before them* **at their face**.
And *Joab's garment* **Yah Ab's tailoring**
that he had *put on* **enrobed**
was girded unto him, and upon it a girdle with a sword
fastened **joined** upon his loins in the sheath thereof;
and as he went forth it fell out.
9 And *Joab* **Yah Ab** said to Amasa,
Art thou in *health* **shalom**, my brother?
And *Joab took* **Yah Ab held** Amasa by the beard
with the right *hand* to kiss him.
10 But Amasa *took no heed to* **regarded not** the sword
that was in *Joab's* **Yah Ab's** hand:
so he smote him therewith in the fifth *rib*,
and *shed* **poured** out his *bowels* **inwards**
to the *ground* **earth**,
and *struck him not again* **repeated not**; and he died.
So *Joab* **Yah Ab** and *Abishai* **Abi Shai** his brother
pursued after Sheba the son of Bichri.
11 And *one* **a man** of *Joab's men* **Yah Ab's lads**
stood by him, and said,
He that favoureth Joab **Whoever delighteth in Yah Ab**,
and *he that is* **whoever be** for David,
let him go after *Joab* **Yah Ab**.
12 And Amasa *wallowed* **rolled** in blood
in the midst of the highway.
And when the man saw that all the people stood still,
he *removed* **turned** Amasa out of the highway
into the field, and cast a cloth upon him,
when he saw that every one that came by him stood still.
13 When he was removed out of the highway,
all the *people went on* **men passed over** after *Joab* **Yah Ab**,
to pursue after Sheba the son of Bichri.
14 And he *went* **passed** through
all the *tribes* **scions** of *Israel* **Yisra El** unto Abel,
and to *Bethmaachah* **Beth Maachah**,
and all the *Berites* **Beriy**:
and they *were gathered together* **congregated**,
and went also after him.
15 And they came and besieged him
in Abel of *Bethmaachah* **Beth Maachah**,
and they *cast up* **poured** a *bank* **mound** against the city,
and it stood in the trench:
and all the people that were with *Joab* **Yah Ab**
battered **ruined** the wall, *to throw it down* **and felled it**.
16 Then *cried* **called out** a wise woman out of the city,
Hear, hear; say, I pray you, unto *Joab* **Yah Ab**,
Come near **Approach** hither,
that I may *speak* **word** with thee.
17 And when he *was come near* **approached** unto her,
the woman said, Art thou *Joab* **Yah Ab**?
And he *answered* **said**, I *am he*.
Then she said unto him,
Hear the words of *thine handmaid* **thy maid**.
And he *answered* **said**, I *do* hear.
18 Then she *spake* **said**, saying,
In wording, They *were wont to speak* **worded**
in *old time* **the beginning**, saying,
In asking, They shall *surely* ask *counsel* at Abel:
and so they *ended* **consumated** *the matter*.
19 I *am one of them that are peaceable* **do shalam**
and *faithful in Israel* **am amenable in Yisra El**:
thou seekest to *destroy* **deathify** a city
and a mother in *Israel* **Yisra El**:
why *wilt* **shalt** thou swallow *up*
the inheritance of *the LORD* **Yah Veh**?
20 And *Joab* **Yah Ab** answered and said,
Far be it, far be it from me,
that I should swallow up or *destroy* **ruin**.
21 The *matter* **word** is not so:
but a man of mount *Ephraim* **Ephrayim**,
Sheba the son of Bichri by name,
hath lifted up his hand against the *king* **sovereign**,
even against David: *deliver* **give** him only,
and I *will depart* **shall go** from the city.
And the woman said unto *Joab* **Yah Ab**, Behold,
his head shall be thrown to thee *over* **through** the wall.
22 Then the woman
went unto all the people in her wisdom.
And they cut off the head of Sheba the son of Bichri,
and cast it out to *Joab* **Yah Ab**.
And he *blew* **blast** a trumpet,
and they *retired* **scattered** from the city,
every man to his tent.
And *Joab* **Yah Ab** returned to *Jerusalem* **Yeru Shalem**
unto the *king* **sovereign**.
23 Now *Joab* **Yah Ab**
was over all the host of *Israel* **Yisra El**:
and *Benaiah* **Bena Yah** the son of *Jehoiada* **Yah Yada**
was over the *Cherethites* **executioners**
and over the *Pelethites* **couriers**:
24 And *Adoram* **Adoni Ram** was over the *tribute* **vassal**:
and *Jehoshaphat* **Yah Shaphat** the son of *Ahilud* **Achiy Lud**
was *recorder* **remembrancer**:
25 And *Sheva* **Sheya** was scribe:
and *Zadok* **Sadoq** and *Abiathar* **Abi Athar** were the priests:
26 And Ira also the *Jairite* **Yairiy**
was a *chief ruler* **priest** about David.

GIBONIY REVENGE

21 Then there was a famine in the days of David
three years, year after year;
and David
enquired of the LORD **sought the face of Yah Veh**.
And *the LORD answered* **Yah Veh said**,
It is for *Saul* **Shaul**, and for *his* **the** bloody house,
because he *slew* **deathified** the *Gibeonites* **Giboniy**.
2 And the *king* **sovereign** called the *Gibeonites* **Giboniy**,
and said unto them;
(now the *Gibeonites* **Giboniy**
were not of the *children* **sons** of *Israel* **Yisra El**,
but of the remnant of the *Amorites* **Emoriy**;
and the *children* **sons** of *Israel* **Yisra El**
had *sworn* **oathed** unto them:
and *Saul* **Shaul** sought to *slay* **smite** them
in his *zeal* **jealousy**
to the *children* **sons** of *Israel* **Yisra El**
and *Judah* **Yah Hudah**.)
3 Wherefore David said unto the *Gibeonites* **Giboniy**,
What shall I *do* **work** for you?
and wherewith
shall I *make the atonement* **kapar/atone for you**,
that ye may bless the inheritance of *the LORD* **Yah Veh**?
4 And the *Gibeonites* **Giboniy** said unto him,
We *will* **shall** have no silver nor gold of *Saul* **Shaul**,
nor of his house;
neither for us
shalt thou *kill* **deathify** any man in *Israel* **Yisra El**.
And he said, What ye shall say,
that *will* **shall** I *do* **work** for you.
5 And they *answered* **said to** the *king* **sovereign**,
The man that *consumed* **finished** us **off**,
and that *devised* **considered** against us
that we should be *destroyed* **desolated**
from *remaining* **standing by**
in any of the *coasts* **borders** of *Israel* **Yisra El**,
6 Let seven men of his sons be *delivered* **given** unto us,
and we *will hang* **shall impale** them *up*
unto *the LORD* **Yah Veh** in *Gibeah* **Gibah** of *Saul* **Shaul**,
whom *the LORD* **Yah Veh** did choose.
And the *king* **sovereign** said, I *will* **shall** give them.
7 But the *king* **sovereign**
spared *Mephibosheth* **Mephi Bosheth**,
the son of *Jonathan* **Yah Nathan** the son of *Saul* **Shaul**,
because of *the LORD'S* **Yah Veh's** oath
that was between them,
between David and *Jonathan* **Yah Nathan**
the son of *Saul* **Shaul**.
8 But the *king* **sovereign**
took the two sons of *Rizpah* **Rispah**
the daughter of *Aiah* **Ajah**,
whom she bare unto *Saul* **Shaul**,
Armoni and *Mephibosheth* **Mephi Bosheth;**
and the five sons of Michal
the daughter of *Saul* **Shaul**,
whom she *brought up* **bore** for *Adriel* **Adri El**
the son of *Barzillai* **Barzillay** the *Meholathite* **Mecholathiy**:
9 And he *delivered* **gave** them
into the hands of the *Gibeonites* **Giboniy**,
and they *hanged* **impaled** them in the *hill* **mountain**
before the LORD **at the face of Yah Veh**:
and they fell *all seven* **sevenfold** together,
and were *put to death* **deathified** in the days of harvest,
in the first *days*, in the beginning of barley harvest.
10 And *Rizpah* **Rispah** the daughter of *Aiah* **Ajah**
took *sackcloth* **saq**, and spread it for her upon the rock,
from the beginning of harvest
until water *dropped* **poured** upon them
out of *heaven* **the heavens**,
and *suffered* **gave**
neither the *birds* **flyers** of the *air* **heavens**
to rest on them by day,
nor the *beasts* **live beings** of the field by night.
11 And it was told David
what *Rizpah* **Rispah** the daughter of *Aiah* **Ajah**,
the concubine of *Saul* **Shaul**, had *done* **worked**.
12 And David went and took the bones of *Saul* **Shaul**
and the bones of *Jonathan* **Yah Nathan** his son
from the *men* **masters** of *Jabeshgilead* **Yabesh Gilad**,
which had stolen them
from the *street* **broadway** of *Bethshan* **Beth Shaan**,
where the *Philistines* **Peleshethiy** had hanged them,
in the day when the *Philistines* **Peleshethiy**
had *slain Saul* **smitten Shaul** in Gilboa:
13 And he *brought up* **ascended** from thence
the bones of *Saul* **Shaul**
and the bones of *Jonathan* **Yah Nathan** his son;
and they gathered the bones
of them that were *hanged* **impailed**.
14 And the bones of *Saul* **Shaul**
and *Jonathan* **Yah Nathan** his son
buried **entombed** they
in the *country* **land** of *Benjamin* **Ben Yamin** in *Zelah* **Sela**,
in the *sepulchre* **tomb** of *Kish* **Qish** his father:
and they performed
all that the *king commanded* **sovereign misvahed**.
And after that *God* **Elohim** was intreated for the land.
15 Moreover the *Philistines* **Peleshethiy**
had yet war again with *Israel* **Yisra El;**
and David *went down* **descended**,
and his servants with him,
and fought against the *Philistines* **Peleshethiy**:
and David *waxed faint* **fluttered**.
16 And *Ishbibenob* **Yishbo Be Nob**,
which was *of the sons of the giant* **born to Rapha**,
the weight of whose spear
weighed three hundred *shekels of brass* **copper** in weight,
he being girded with a new *sword*,
thought **said** to have *slain* **smitten** David.
17 But *Abishai* **Abi Shai** the son of *Zeruiah* **Seruyah**
succoured **helped** him,
and smote the *Philistine* **Peleshethiy**,
and *killed* **deathified** him.
Then the men of David *sware* **oathed** unto him, saying,
Thou shalt go no more out with us to *battle* **war**,
that thou quench not the *light* **lamp** of *Israel* **Yisra El**.
18 And it *came to pass* **became** after this,
that there was again
a *battle* **war** with the *Philistines* **Peleshethiy** at Gob:
then *Sibbechai* **Sibbechay** the *Hushathite* **Hushathiy**
slew **smote** Saph,
which was *of the sons of the giant* **born to Rapha**.
19 And there was again a *battle* **war** in Gob
with the *Philistines* **Peleshethiy**,
where *Elhanan* **El Hanan**
the son of *Jaareoregim* **Yaare Oregim**,
a *Bethlehemite* **Beth Lechemiy**,
slew the brother of Goliath **smote Golyath**
the *Gittite* **Gittiy**,
the *staff* **timber** of whose spear was like a weaver's beam.
20 And there was yet a *battle* **war** in Gath,
where was a man of *great stature* **measure**,
that had on every hand six fingers
and the digits of his hands were six,
and on every foot six toes
and the digits of his feet were six,
four and twenty in number;
and he also was born to *the giant* **Rapha**.
21 And when he *defied Israel* **reproached Yisra El**,
Jonathan **Yah Nathan**
the son of *Shimeah* **Shimah** the brother of David
slew **smote** him.
22 These four were born to *the giant* **Rapha** in Gath,
and fell by the hand of David,
and by the hand of his servants.

DAVID'S SONG OF HALAL

22 And David *spake* **worded** unto *the LORD* **Yah Veh**
the words of this song in the day
that *the LORD* **Yah Veh** had delivered **rescued** him
out of the *hand* **palm** of all his enemies,
and out of the *hand* **palm** of *Saul* **Shaul**:
2 And he said, *The LORD* **Yah Veh** is my rock,
and my *fortress* **stronghold**, and my *deliverer* **escape**;
3 The *God* **Elohim** of my rock;
in him *will* **shall** I *trust* **seek refuge**:
he is my *shield* **buckler**, and the horn of my salvation,
my *high tower* **secure loft**, and my *refuge* **retreat**,
my saviour; thou savest me from violence.
4 I *will* **shall** call on *the LORD* **Yah Veh**,

who is worthy to be praised **the halaled**:
so shall I be saved from mine enemies.
5 When the waves of death *compassed* **surrounded** me,
the *floods* **wadies** of *ungodly men* **Beli Yaal**
made me afraid **frightened me**;
6 The *sorrows* **cords** of *hell* **sheol**
compassed me about **surrounded me**;
the snares of death
prevented **confronted** me;
7 In my *distress* **tribulation**
I called upon *the LORD* **Yah Veh**,
and cried to my *God* **Elohim**:
and he did hear my voice out of his *temple* **manse**,
and my cry *did enter into* **be in** his ears.
8 Then the earth shook and *trembled* **quaked**;
the foundations of *heaven* **the heavens**
moved **quaked** and shook,
because he was *wroth* **inflamed**.
9 There *went up* **ascended** a smoke out of his nostrils,
and fire out of his mouth devoured:
coals were *kindled* **burnt away** by it.
10 He *bowed* **extended** the heavens also,
and *came down* **descended**;
and **dripping** darkness was under his feet.
11 And he rode upon a cherub, and did fly:
and he was seen
upon the wings of the *wind* **spirit/wind**.
12 And he *made* **placed** darkness
pavilions **brush arbors** round about him,
dark waters, and thick clouds of *the skies* **vapour**.
13 Through the *brightness* **brilliancy** before him
were coals of fire *kindled* **burnt away**.
14 *The LORD* **Yah Veh**
thundered from *heaven* **the heavens**,
and *the most High uttered* **Elyon gave** his voice.
15 And he sent out arrows, and scattered them;
lightning, and *discomfited* **agitated** them.
16 And the *channels* **reservoirs** of the sea
appeared **were seen**,
the foundations of the world
were *discovered* **exposed**,
at the rebuking of *the LORD* **Yah Veh**,
at the *blast* **breath** of the *breath* **spirit/wind** of his nostrils.
17 He sent from *above* **high**, he took me;
he drew me out of *many* **great** waters;
18 He *delivered* **rescued** me from my strong enemy,
and from them that hated me:
for they were too strong for me.
19 They *prevented* **confronted** me
in the day of my calamity:
but *the LORD* **Yah Veh** was my *stay* **support**.
20 He brought me forth also into *a large place* **an expanse**:
he *delivered* **rescued** me, because he delighted in me.
21 *The LORD rewarded* **Yah Veh dealt** me
according to my *righteousness* **justness**:
according to the *cleanness* **purity** of my hands
hath he *recompensed* **returned to** me.
22 For I have *kept* **guarded**
the ways of *the LORD* **Yah Veh**,
and have not *wickedly departed* **done wickedly**
from **against** my *God* **Elohim**.
23 For all his judgments were before me:
and *as for* his statutes,
I *did not depart* **turned not aside** from them.
24 I was also *upright* **integrious** before him,
and have *kept* **guarded** myself
from *mine iniquity* **my perversity**.
25 Therefore
the LORD **Yah Veh** hath *recompensed* **returned to** me
according to my *righteousness* **justness**;
according to my *cleanness* **purity**
in *his eye sight* **front of his eyes**.
26 With the merciful
thou *wilt* **shalt** shew thyself merciful,
and with the *upright man* **mighty integrious**
thou *wilt* **shalt** shew thyself *upright* **integrious**.
27 With the pure
thou *wilt* **shalt** shew thyself pure;
and with the *froward* **perverted**
thou *wilt* **shalt** shew thyself *unsavoury* **wrestlest**.
28 And the *afflicted* **humble** people
thou *wilt* **shalt** save:
but thine eyes are upon the *haughty* **lofty**,
that thou mayest *bring* **descend** them *down* **low**.
29 For thou art my lamp, O *LORD* **Yah Veh**:
and *the LORD* **Yah Veh**
will lighten **shall illuminate** my darkness.
30 For by thee I have run through a troop:
by my *God* **Elohim** have I leaped over a wall.
31 *As for God* **El**, his way is *perfect* **integrious**;
the *word* **sayings** of *the LORD is tried* **Yah Veh be refined**:
he is a buckler to all them that *trust* **seek refuge** in him.
32 For who is *God* **El**, *save the LORD* **except Yah Veh**?
and who is a rock, *save* **except** our *God* **Elohim**?
33 *God* **El** is my *strength* **stronghold** and *power* **valour**:
and he *maketh* **looseth** my way *perfect* **integrious**.
34 He *maketh* **equalizeth** my feet like hinds' *feet*:
and *setteth* **standeth** me upon my *high places* **bamahs**.
35 He teacheth my hands to war;
so that a bow of *steel* **copper** is *broken* **bent** by mine arms.
36 Thou hast also given me
the *shield* **buckler** of thy salvation:
and thy *gentleness* **humbling**
hath *made* **abounded** me *great*.
37 Thou hast enlarged my *steps* **paces** under me;
so that my *feet did not slip* **ankles wavered not**.
38 I have pursued mine enemies,
and *destroyed* **desolated** them;
and turned not *again* **back**
until I had *consumed* **finished** them **off**.
39 And I have *consumed* **finished** them **off**,
and *wounded* **stricken** them, that they could not arise:
yea, they are fallen under my feet.
40 For thou hast girded me
with *strength* **valour** to *battle* **war**:
them that rose up against me
hast thou *subdued* **caused to bow** under me.
41 Thou hast also given me the necks of mine enemies,
that I might *destroy* **exterminate** them that hate me.
42 They looked, but there was none to save;
even unto *the LORD* **Yah Veh**,
but he answered them not.
43 Then *did I beat* **I pulverized** them
as small as the dust of the earth,
I *did stamp* **pulverized** them
as the mire of the *street* **outway**,
and *did spread* **expanded** them *abroad*.
44 Thou also hast *delivered* **slipped** me **out**
from the strivings of my people,
thou hast *kept* **guarded** me
to be head of the *heathen* **goyim**:
a people *which* I knew not shall serve me.
45 *Strangers* **Sons of the stranger**
shall *submit* **deny** themselves unto me:
as soon as they hear **at the hearing of the ear**,
they shall *be obedient* **hearken** unto me.
46 *Strangers* **Sons of the stranger** shall *fade away* **wither**,
and they shall
be afraid out of their close places **gird their borders**.
47 *The LORD* **Yah Veh** liveth; and blessed be my rock;
and exalted be the *God* **Elohim**
of the rock of my salvation.
48 *It is God that avengeth* **El giveth avengement for** me,
and that bringeth down the people under me.
49 And that bringeth me forth from mine enemies:
thou also hast lifted me up on high
above them that rose up against me:
thou hast *delivered* **rescued** me
from the *violent man* **man of violence**.
50 Therefore
I *will give thanks* **shall extend hands** unto thee,
O *LORD* **Yah Veh**, among the *heathen* **goyim**,
and I *will sing praises* **shall pluck** unto thy name.
51 He *is the tower of* **greateneth** salvation
for his *king* **sovereign**:
and *sheweth* **worketh** mercy
to his anointed, unto David,
and to his seed *for evermore* **eternally**.

DAVID'S FINAL WORDS

23 Now these be the last words of David.
An oracle of David the son of *Jesse said* **Yishay**,
and **an oracle of** the *man* **mighty**
who was raised up on high,
the anointed of the *God* **Elohim** of *Jacob* **Yaaqov**,
and the *sweet psalmist* **pleasantness of the psalms**
of *Israel* **Yisra El**, *said*,
2 The Spirit of *the LORD spake* **Yah Veh worded** by me,
and his *word* **utterance** was in my tongue.
3 The *God* **Elohim** of *Israel* **Yisra El** said,
the Rock of *Israel spake* **Yisra El worded** to me,
He that ruleth over men **The sovereign over humanity**
must be just,
ruling **reigning** in the *fear* **awe** of *God* **Elohim**.
4 And he shall be as the light of the morning,
when the sun riseth,
even a morning without **thick** clouds;
as the tender grass springing **the sprouts** out of the earth
by *clear shining* **brilliancy** after rain.
5 Although my house be not so with *God* **El**;
yet he hath *made* **set** with me
an *everlasting* **eternal** covenant,
ordered **aligned** in all *things*, and *sure* **guarded**:
for this is all my salvation, and all my *desire* **delight**,
although he make it not to *grow* **sprout**.
6 But *the sons* of *Belial* **Beli Yaal**
shall be all of them as thorns *thrust* **fled** *away*,
because they cannot be taken with hands:
7 But the man that shall touch them
must be *fenced* **filled** with iron
and the *staff* **timber** of a spear;
and **in burning,** they shall be *utterly burned* **burnt** with fire
in the *same place* **seat**.

DAVID'S MIGHTY

8 These be the names of the mighty *men* whom David had:
The Tachmonite that sat in the seat
Tachkemoniy Yosheb Bash Shabbath,
chief **head** among the *captains* **tertiaries**;
the same was Adino
the *Eznite; he lift up his spear* **spearer**
against eight hundred,
whom he *slew* **pierced** at one time.
9 And after him was *Eleazar* **El Azar**
the son of Dodo the *Ahohite* **Ach Oachiy**,
one of the three mighty *men* with David,
when they *defied* **reproached** the *Philistines* **Peleshethiy**
that were there gathered together to *battle* **war**,
and the men of *Israel* **Yisra El**
were gone away **had ascended**:
10 He arose, and smote the *Philistines* **Peleshethiy**
until his hand was *weary* **belaboured**,
and his hand *clave* **adhered** unto the sword:
and *the LORD* **Yah Veh**
wrought **worked** a great *victory* **salvation** that day;
and the people returned after him only to *spoil* **strip**.
11 And after him was Shammah
the son of *Agee* **Age** the *Hararite* **Harariy**.
And the *Philistines* **Peleshethiy**
were gathered *together into a troop* **alive**,
where was *a piece of ground* **an allotment of field**
full of lentiles:
and the people fled
from **the face of** the *Philistines* **Peleshethiy**.
12 But he stood in the midst of the *ground* **allotment**,
and *defended* **rescued** it,
and *slew* **smote** the *Philistines* **Peleshethiy**:
and *the LORD* **Yah Veh**
wrought **worked** a great *victory* **salvation**.
13 And three of the thirty *chief* **heads**
went down **descended**, and came to David
in the harvest time unto the cave of Adullam:
and the *troop* **living** of the *Philistines* **Peleshethiy**
pitched **encamped** in the valley of Rephaim.
14 And David was then in an hold,
and the *garrison* **standing camp** of the *Philistines* **Peleshethiy**
was then *in Bethlehem* **Beth Lechem**.
15 And David *longed* **desired**, and said,
Oh that one *would* **should** give me drink
of the water of the well of *Bethlehem* **Beth Lechem**,
which is by the *gate* **portal**!
16 And the three mighty *men brake through* **split**
the *host* **camp** of the *Philistines* **Peleshethiy**,
and *drew* **bailed** water
out of the well of *Bethlehem* **Beth Lechem**,
that was by the *gate* **portal**,
and *took* **lifted** it, and brought it to David:
nevertheless he *would* **willed to** not drink thereof,
but poured it out unto *the LORD* **Yah Veh**.
17 And he said, Be it far from me, O *LORD* **Yah Veh**,
that I should *do* **work** this:
is *not* this the blood of the men
that went *in jeopardy of their lives* **with their souls**?
therefore he *would* **willed to** not drink it.
These *things did* **worked** these three mighty *men*.
18 And *Abishai* **Abi Shai**, the brother of *Joab* **Yah Ab**,
the son of *Zeruiah* **Seruyah**, was *chief* **head** among three.
And he *lifted up* **wakened** his spear against three hundred,
and *slew* **pierced** them, and had the name among three.
19 Was he not most honourable of three?
therefore he was their *captain* **governor**:
howbeit he attained not unto the *first* three.
20 And *Benaiah* **Bena Yah** the son of *Jehoiada* **Yah Yada**,
the son of a valiant man, of *Kabzeel* **Qabse El**,
who had done many *acts* **deeds**,
he *slew* **smote** two *lionlike men* **Ari Eliy** of Moab:
he *went down* **descended** also and *slew* **smote** a lion
in the midst of a *pit* **well** in *time* **a day** of snow:
21 And he *slew an Egyptian* **smote a man, a Misrayim**,
a *goodly man* **man of visage**:
and the *Egyptian* **Misrayim** had a spear in his hand;
but he *went down* **descended** to him with a *staff* **scion**,
and *plucked* **stripped** the spear
out of the *Egyptian's* **Misrayim's** hand,
and *slew* **slaughtered** him with his own spear.
22 These *things did Benaiah* **worked Bena Yah**
the son of *Jehoiada* **Yah Yada**,
and had the name among three mighty *men*.
23 He was more honourable than the thirty,
but he attained not to the *first* three.
And David set him over his guard.
24 *Asahel* **Asa El** the brother of *Joab* **Yah Ab**
was one of the thirty;
Elhanan **El Hanan**
the son of Dodo of *Bethlehem* **Beth Lechem**,
25 Shammah the *Harodite* **Harodiy**,
Elika **Eli Qa** the *Harodite* **Harodiy**,
26 *Helez* **Heles** the *Paltite* **Paltiy**,
Ira the son of *Ikkesh* **Iqqesh** the *Tekoite* **Teqohiy**,
27 *Abiezer* **Abi Ezer** the *Anethothite* **Anathothiy**,
Mebunnai **Mebunnay** the *Hushathite* **Hushathiy**,
28 *Zalmon* **Salmon** the *Ahohite* **Ach Oachiy**,
Maharai **Maharay** the *Netophathite* **Netophathiy**,
29 Heleb the son of Baanah, a *Netophathite* **Netophathiy**,
Ittai **Ittay** the son of *Ribai* **Ribay** out of *Gibeah* **Gibah**
of the *children* **sons** of *Benjamin* **Ben Yamin**,
30 *Benaiah* **Bena Yah** the *Pirathonite* **Pirathoniy**,
Hiddai of the *brooks* **wadies** of Gaash,
31 *Abialbon* **Abi Albon** the *Arbathite* **Arabahiy**,
Azmaveth the *Barhumite* **Barhumiy**,
32 *Eliahba* **El Yachba** the *Shaalbonite* **Shaalbimiy**,
of the sons of *Jashen* **Yashen**,
Jonathan **Yah Nathan**,
33 Shammah the *Hararite* **Harariy**,
Ahiam **Achiy Am** the son of Sharar the *Hararite* **Harariy**,
34 *Eliphelet* **Eli Phelet** the son of *Ahasbai* **Achasbay**,
the son of the *Maachathite* **Maachahiy**,
Eliam **Eli Am**
the son of *Ahithophel* **Achiy Thophel** the *Gilonite* **Gilohiy**,
35 *Hezrai* **Hesro** the *Carmelite* **Karmeliy**,
Paarai **Paaray** the *Arbite* **Arbiy**,
36 *Igal* **Yigal** the son of Nathan of *Zobah* **Sobah**,
Bani the *Gadite* **Gadiy**,
37 *Zelek* **Seleq** the *Ammonite* **Ammoniy**,
Nahari **Nachray** the *Beerothite* **Beerothiy**,
armourbearer **instrument bearer** to *Joab* **Yah Ab**
the son of *Zeruiah* **Seruyah**,
38 Ira an *Ithrite* **Yetheriy**, Gareb an *Ithrite* **Yetheriy**,
39 *Uriah* **Uri Yah** the *Hittite* **Hethiy**:
thirty and seven in all.

DAVID MUSTERS YISRA EL

24 And *again* the *anger* **wrath** of *the LORD* **Yah Veh**
was **added to be** kindled against *Israel* **Yisra El**,
and he *moved* **goaded** David against them to say,
Go, number *Israel* **Yisra El** and *Judah* **Yah Hudah**.
2 For the *king* **sovereign** said to *Joab* **Yah Ab**
the *captain* **governor** of the *host* **valiant**,
which was with him,
Go **Flit** now
through all the *tribes* **scions** of *Israel* **Yisra El**,
from Dan even to *Beersheba* **Beer Sheba**,
and number ye the people,
that I may know the number of the people.
3 And *Joab* **Yah Ab** said unto the *king* **sovereign**,
Now *the LORD* **Yah Veh** thy *God* **Elohim**
add unto the people,
how many soever they be,
an hundredfold **a hundred times**,
and that the eyes of my *lord* **adoni** the *king* **sovereign**
may see it:
but why doth my *lord* **adoni** the *king* **sovereign**
delight in this *thing* **word**?
4 Notwithstanding
the *king's* **sovereign's** word prevailed against *Joab* **Yah Ab**,
and against the *captains* **governors** of the *host* **valiant**.
And *Joab* **Yah Ab**
and the *captains* **governors** of the *host* **valiant**
went out from the *presence* **face** of the *king* **sovereign**,
to *number* **muster** the people of *Israel* **Yisra El**.
5 And they passed over *Jordan* **Yarden**,
and *pitched* **encamped** in Aroer,
on the right side of the city
that lieth in the midst of the *river* **wadi** of Gad,
and toward *Jazer* **Yazer**:
6 Then they came to *Gilead* **Gilad**,
and to the land of *Tahtimhodshi* **Tahtim Hodshi**;
and they came to *Danjaan* **Dan Yaan**,
and about to *Zidon* **Sidon**,
7 And came to the *strong hold* **fortress** of *Tyre* **Sor**,
and to all the cities of the *Hivites* **Hivviy**,
and of the *Canaanites* **Kenaaniy**:
and they went out to the south of *Judah* **Yah Hudah**,
even to *Beersheba* **Beer Sheba**.
8 So when they had *gone* **flitted** through all the land,
they came to *Jerusalem* **Yeru Shalem**
at the end of nine months and twenty days.
9 And *Joab* **Yah Ab** gave up the *sum* **number**
of the *number* **census** of the people
unto the *king* **sovereign**:
and there were in *Israel* **Yisra El**
eight hundred thousand valiant *men* that drew the sword;
and the men of *Judah* **Yah Hudah**
were five hundred thousand men.
10 And David's heart smote him
after that he had *numbered* **scribed** the people.
And David said unto *the LORD* **Yah Veh**,
I have sinned *greatly* **mightily** in that I have *done* **worked**:
and now, I beseech thee, O *LORD* **Yah Veh**,
take away **pass over** the *iniquity* **perversity** of thy servant;
for I *have done very foolishly* **follied mightily**.
11 For when David *was up* **arose** in the morning,
the word of *the LORD* **Yah Veh**
came unto the prophet Gad, David's seer, saying,
12 Go and *say* **word** unto David,
Thus saith *the LORD* **Yah Veh**,
I *offer* **lift** thee **these** three *things*;
choose thee one of them, that I may *do* **work** *it* unto thee.
13 So Gad came to David, and told him,
and said unto him,
Shall seven years of famine come unto thee in thy land?
or *wilt* **shalt** thou flee three months
before thine enemies **at the face of thy tribulators**,
while they pursue thee?
or that there be three days' pestilence in thy land?
now *advise* **perceive**, and see
what *answer* **word** I shall return to him that sent me.
14 And David said unto Gad,
I *am in a great strait* **tribulate mightily**:
let us fall now into the hand of *the LORD* **Yah Veh**;
for his mercies are *great* **many**:
and let me not fall into the hand of *man* **humanity**.
15 So *the LORD* **Yah Veh**
sent **gave** a pestilence upon *Israel* **Yisra El**
from the morning even to the time *appointed* **of season**:
and there died of the people
from Dan even to *Beersheba* **Beer Sheba**
seventy thousand men.
16 And when the angel *stretched out* **extended** his hand
upon *Jerusalem* **Yeru Shalem** to *destroy* **ruin** it,
the LORD repented **Yah Veh sighed** him of the evil,
and said to the angel that *destroyed* **ruined** the people,
It is enough: *stay* **slacken** now thine hand.
And the angel of *the LORD* **Yah Veh**
was by the threshingplace
of *Araunah* **Aravnah** the *Jebusite* **Yebusiy**.
17 And David *spake* **said** unto *the LORD* **Yah Veh**
when he saw the angel that smote the people,
and said, *Lo* **Behold**,
I have sinned, and I have *done wickedly* **perverted**:
but these *sheep* **flock**, what have they *done* **worked**?
let thine hand, I pray thee,
be against me, and against my father's house.
18 And Gad came that day to David, and said unto him,
Go up **Ascend**,
rear an **raise a sacrifice** altar unto *the LORD* **Yah Veh**
in the threshingfloor
of *Araunah* **Aravnah** the *Jebusite* **Yebusiy**.
19 And David, according to the *saying* **word** of Gad,
went up **ascended**
as *the LORD commanded* **Yah Veh misvahed**
20 And *Araunah* **Aravnah** looked,
and saw the *king* **sovereign** and his servants
coming on **passing over** toward him:
and *Araunah* **Aravnah** went out,
and *bowed* **prostrated** himself before the *king* **sovereign**
on his *face* **nostrils** upon the *ground* **earth**.
21 And *Araunah* **Aravnah** said,
Wherefore is my *lord* **adoni** the *king* **sovereign**
come to his servant?
And David said, To *buy* **chattel** the threshingfloor of thee,
to build *an* **a sacrifice** altar unto *the LORD* **Yah Veh**,
that the plague may be *stayed* **restrained** from the people.
22 And *Araunah* **Aravnah** said unto David,
Let my *lord* **adoni** the *king* **sovereign**
take and *offer up* **holocaust**
what *seemeth* **be** good *unto him* **in his eyes**:
behold, here be **see** — oxen for *burnt sacrifice* **holocaust**,
and threshing *instruments* **sledges**
and *other* instruments of the oxen for *wood* **timber**.
23 All these *things* did *Araunah* **Aravnah**,
as a *king* **sovereign**, give unto the *king* **sovereign**.
And *Araunah* **Aravnah** said unto the *king* **sovereign**,
The LORD **Yah Veh** thy *God accept* **Elohim please** thee.
24 And the *king* **sovereign** said unto *Araunah* **Aravnah**,
Nay; but **in chatteling**,
I *will surely buy* **shall chattel** it of thee at a price:
neither *will* **shall** I
offer burnt offerings **holocaust holocausts**
unto *the LORD* **Yah Veh** my *God* **Elohim**
of that which *doth cost me nothing* **be gratuitous**.
So David *bought* **chatteled** the threshingfloor and the oxen
for fifty shekels of silver.
25 And David built there *an* **a sacrifice** altar
unto *the LORD* **Yah Veh**,
and *offered burnt offerings* **holocausted holocausts**
and *peace offerings* **shelamim**.
So *the LORD* **Yah Veh** was intreated for the land,
and the plague was *stayed* **restrained** from *Israel* **Yisra El**.

KEY TO INTERPRETING THE EXEGESES:
King James text is in regular type;
Text under exegeses is in oblique type;
Text of exegeses is in bold type.

DAVID AGES

1 Now *king* **sovereign** David was old
and stricken in *years* **days**;
and they covered him with clothes,
but he *gat* **had** no heat.
2 Wherefore his servants said unto him,
Let there be sought for my *lord* **adoni** the *king* **sovereign**
a *young* **lass** virgin:
and let her stand *before* **at the face of** the *king* **sovereign**,
and let her *cherish* **be accustomed to** him,
and let her lie in thy bosom,
that my *lord* **adoni** the *king* **sovereign** may *get* **have** heat.
3 So they sought for a *fair damsel* **beautiful lass**
throughout all the *coasts* **borders** of *Israel* **Yisra El**,
and found *Abishag* **Abi Shag** a *Shunammite* **Shunemiyth**,
and brought her to the *king* **sovereign**.
4 And the *damsel* **lass** was *very fair* **mighty beautiful**,
and *cherished* **was accustomed to** the *king* **sovereign**,
and ministered to him:
but the *king* **sovereign** knew her not.

ADONI YAH USURPS LEADERSHIP

5 Then *Adonijah* **Adoni Yah** the son of Haggith
exalted **lifted** himself, saying, I *will be king* **shall reign**:
and he *prepared* **worked** him
chariots and *horsemen* **cavalry**,
and fifty men to run *before him* **at his face**.
6 And his father had not *displeased* **contorted** him
at any time in **all his days** saying,
Why hast thou *done* **worked** so?
and he also was *a very goodly man* **mighty good of form**;
and *his mother bare him* **he bore**
after *Absalom* **Abi Shalom**.
7 And *he conferred* **his words were** with *Joab* **Yah Ab**
the son of *Zeruiah* **Seruyah**,
and with *Abiathar* **Abi Athar** the priest:
and they *following Adonijah* **after Adoni Yah** helped him.
8 But *Zadok* **Sadoq** the priest,
and *Benaiah* **Bena Yah** the son of *Jehoiada* **Yah Yada**,
and Nathan the prophet, and *Shimei* **Shimi**, and Rei,
and the mighty *men which belonged to* **of** David,
were not with *Adonijah* **Adoni Yah**.
9 And *Adonijah* **Adoni Yah**
slew sheep **sacrificed flock** and oxen and *fat cattle* **fatlings**
by the stone of *Zoheleth* **Zocheleth**,
which is by *Enrogel* **En Rogel**,
and called all his brethren
the *king's* **sovereign's** sons,
and all the men of *Judah* **Yah Hudah**
the *king's* **sovereign's** servants:
10 But Nathan the prophet, and *Benaiah* **Bena Yah**,
and the mighty *men*, and *Solomon* **Shelomoh** his brother,
he called not.

NATHAN AND BATH SHEBA

11 Wherefore
Nathan *spake* **said** unto *Bathsheba* **Bath Sheba**
the mother of *Solomon* **Shelomoh**, saying,
Hast thou not heard
that *Adonijah* **Adoni Yah** the son of Haggith doth reign,
and David our *lord* **adoni** knoweth it not?
12 Now therefore come,
let me, I pray thee, give thee counsel,
that thou mayest *save* **rescue** thine own *life* **soul**,
and the *life* **soul** of thy son *Solomon* **Shelomoh**.
13 Go and get thee in unto *king* **sovereign** David,
and say unto him,
Didst not thou, my *lord* **adoni**, O *king* **sovereign**,
swear **oath** unto *thine handmaid* **thy maid**, saying,
Assuredly *Solomon* **Shelomoh** thy son shall reign after me,
and he shall *sit* **settle** upon my throne?
why then doth *Adonijah* **Adoni Yah** reign?
14 Behold, while thou yet *talkest* **wordest** there
with the *king* **sovereign**,
I also *will* **shall** come in after thee,
and *confirm* **fill up** thy words.
15 And *Bathsheba* **Bath Sheba**
went in unto the *king* **sovereign** into the chamber:
and the *king* **sovereign** was *very* **mighty** old;
and *Abishag* **Abi Shag** the *Shunammite* **Shunemiyth**
ministered unto the *king* **sovereign**.
16 And *Bathsheba* **Bath Sheba** bowed,
and *did obeisance* **prostrated** unto the *king* **sovereign**.
And the *king* **sovereign** said,
What *wouldest thou* **be it to thee**?
17 And she said unto him, My *lord* **adoni**,
thou *swarest* **oathest**
by *the LORD* **Yah Veh** thy *God* **Elohim**
unto *thine handmaid* **thy maid**, *saying,*
Assuredly
Solomon **Shelomoh** thy son shall reign after me,
and he shall *sit* **settle** upon my throne.
18 And now, behold, *Adonijah* **Adoni Yah** reigneth;
and now, my *lord* **adoni** the *king* **sovereign**,
thou knowest it not:
19 And he hath *slain* **sacrificed** oxen and *fat cattle* **fatlings**
and *sheep* **flocks** in abundance,
and hath called all the sons of the *king* **sovereign**,
and *Abiathar* **Abi Athar** the priest,
and *Joab* **Yah Ab** the *captain* **governor** of the host:
but *Solomon* **Shelomoh** thy servant hath he not called.
20 And thou, my *lord* **adoni**, O *king* **sovereign**,
the eyes of all *Israel* **Yisra El** are upon thee,
that thou shouldest tell them who shall *sit* **settle**
on the throne of my *lord* **adoni** the *king* **sovereign**
after him.
21 Otherwise it shall *come to pass* **become**,
when my *lord* **adoni** the *king* **sovereign**
shall *sleep* **lie** with his fathers,
that I and my son *Solomon* **Shelomoh**
shall be *counted offenders* **as sinners**.
22 And, *lo* **behold**,
while she yet *talked* **worded** with the *king* **sovereign**,
Nathan the prophet also came in.
23 And they told the *king* **sovereign**, saying,
Behold Nathan the prophet.
And when he was come in
before **at the face of** the *king* **sovereign**,
he *bowed* **prostrated** himself
before **at the face of** the *king* **sovereign**
with his *face* **nostrils** to the *ground* **earth**.
24 And Nathan said, My *lord* **adoni**, O *king* **sovereign**,
hast thou said, *Adonijah* **Adoni Yah** shall reign after me,
and he shall *sit* **settle** upon my throne?
25 For he *is gone down* **descended** this day,
and hath *slain* **sacrificed** oxen and *fat cattle* **fatlings**
and *sheep* **flocks** in abundance,
and hath called all the *king's* **sovereign's** sons,
and the *captains* **governors** of the host,
and *Abiathar* **Abi Athar** the priest;
and, behold, they eat and drink *before him* **at his face**,
and say,
God save king Adonijah **Sovereign Adoni Yah liveth**.
26 But me, *even* me thy servant,
and *Zadok* **Sadoq** the priest,
and *Benaiah* **Bena Yah** the son of *Jehoiada* **Yah Yada**,
and thy servant *Solomon* **Shelomoh**, hath he not called.
27 Is this *thing* **word**
done by my lord **of my adoni** the *king* **sovereign**,
and thou hast not *shewed* **revealed** it unto thy servant,
who should *sit* **settle** on the throne
of my *lord* **adoni** the *king* **sovereign** after him?
28 Then *king* **sovereign** David answered and said,
Call me *Bathsheba* **Bath Sheba**.
And she came
into **at the face of** the *king's presence* **sovereign**,
and stood *before* **at the face of** the *king* **sovereign**.
29 And the *king sware* **sovereign oathed**, and said,
As the LORD **Yah Veh** liveth,
that hath redeemed my soul out of all *distress* **tribulation**,
30 Even as I *sware* **oathed** unto thee
by *the LORD God* **Yah Veh Elohim** of *Israel* **Yisra El**,
saying, Assuredly
Solomon **Shelomoh** thy son shall reign after me,
and he shall *sit* **settle** upon my throne in my stead;
even so **in working**,
will I certainly do **shall I work** this day.
31 Then *Bathsheba* **Bath Sheba** bowed

with *her face* **nostrils** to the earth,
and *did reverence* **prostrated** to the *king* **sovereign**,
and said, Let my *lord king* **adoni sovereign** David
live *for ever* **eternally**.
32 And *king* **sovereign** David said,
Call me *Zadok* **Sadoq** the priest, and Nathan the prophet,
and *Benaiah* **Bena Yah** the son of *Jehoiada* **Yah Yada**.
And they came *before* **at the face of** the *king* **sovereign**.
33 The *king* **sovereign** also said unto them,
Take with you the servants of your *lord* **adoni**,
and cause *Solomon* **Shelomoh** my son
to ride upon mine own mule,
and *bring* **descend** him *down* to *Gihon* **Gichon**:
34 And let *Zadok* **Sadoq** the priest and Nathan the prophet
anoint him there *king* **sovereign** over *Israel* **Yisra El**:
and *blow* **blast** ye with the trumpet, and say,
God save king Solomon **Sovereign Shelomoh liveth**.
35 Then ye shall *come up* **ascend** after him,
that he may come and *sit* **settle** upon my throne;
for he shall *be king* **reign** in my stead:
and I have *appointed* **misvahed** him
to *be ruler* **have eminence**
over *Israel* **Yisra El** and over *Judah* **Yah Hudah**.
36 And *Benaiah* **Bena Yah** the son of *Jehoiada* **Yah Yada**
answered the *king* **sovereign**, and said, Amen:
the LORD God **Yah Veh Elohim**
of my *lord* **adoni** the *king* **sovereign**
say so too **sayeth thus**.
37 As *the LORD* **Yah Veh**
hath been with my *lord* **adoni** the *king* **sovereign**,
even so be he with *Solomon* **Shelomoh**,
and make his throne greater
than the throne of my *lord king* **adoni sovereign** David.
38 So *Zadok* **Sadoq** the priest, and Nathan the prophet,
and *Benaiah* **Bena Yah** the son of *Jehoiada* **Yah Yada**,
and the *Cherethites* **executioners**,
and the *Pelethites* **couriers**,
went down **descended**,
and caused *Solomon* **Shelomoh**
to ride upon *king* **sovereign** David's mule,
and *brought* **walked** him to *Gihon* **Gichon**.
39 And *Zadok* **Sadoq** the priest
took an horn of oil out of the *tabernacle* **tent**,
and anointed *Solomon* **Shelomoh**.
And they *blew* **blast** the trumpet; and all the people said,
God save king Solomon **Sovereign Shelomoh liveth**.
40 And all the people *came up* **ascended** after him,
and the people *piped* **fluted** with *pipes* **flutes**,
and *rejoiced* **cheered** with great *joy* **cheer**,
so that the earth *rent* **split** with the *sound* **voice** of them.
41 And *Adonijah* **Adoni Yah**
and all the *guests* **called** that were with him
heard it as they had *made an end of* **finished** eating.
And when *Joab* **Yah Ab**
heard the *sound* **voice** of the trumpet, he said,
Wherefore is this *noise* **voice** of the city
being in an uproar **roaring**?
42 And while he yet *spake* **worded**, behold,
Jonathan **Yah Nathan**
the son of *Abiathar* **Abi Athar** the priest came;
and *Adonijah* **Adoni Yah** said unto him, Come in;
for thou art a valiant man,
and bringest good *tidings* **evangelism**.
43 And *Jonathan* **Yah Nathan** answered
and said to *Adonijah* **Adoni Yah**,
Verily **Nevertheless,** our *lord king* **adoni sovereign** David
hath *made Solomon king* **Shelomoh to reign**.
44 And the *king* **sovereign** hath sent with him
Zadok **Sadoq** the priest, and Nathan the prophet,
and *Benaiah* **Bena Yah** the son of *Jehoiada* **Yah Yada**,
and the *Cherethites* **executioners**,
and the *Pelethites* **couriers**,
and they have caused him
to ride upon the *king's* **sovereign's** mule:
45 And *Zadok* **Sadoq** the priest and Nathan the prophet
have anointed him *king* **sovereign** in *Gihon* **Gichon**:
and they are *come up* **ascended** from thence
rejoicing **cheering**,
so that the city *rang again* **quaked**.
This is the *noise* **voice** that ye have heard.
46 And also *Solomon sitteth* **Shelomoh settleth**
on the throne of the *kingdom* **sovereigndom**.
47 And moreover the *king's* **sovereign's** servants
came to bless our *lord king* **adoni sovereign** David, saying,
God make **Elohim well—prepare**
the name of *Solomon* **Shelomoh**
better than thy name,
and make his throne greater than thy throne.
And the *king* **sovereign**
bowed **prostrated** himself upon the bed.
48 And also thus said the *king* **sovereign**,
Blessed be
the LORD God **Yah Veh Elohim** of *Israel* **Yisra El**,
which hath given one to *sit* **settle** on my throne this day,
mine eyes even seeing it.
49 And all the *guests* **called**
that were with *Adonijah* **Adoni Yah**
were afraid **trembled**, and rose up,
and went every man his way.
50 And *Adonijah* **Adoni Yah**
feared because **awed at the face** of *Solomon* **Shelomoh**,
and arose, and went,
and caught hold on the horns of the **sacrifice** altar.
51 And it was told *Solomon* **Shelomoh**, saying, Behold,
Adonijah **Adoni Yah**
feareth king Solomon **aweth sovereign Shelomoh**:
for, *lo* **behold**,
he hath caught hold on the horns of the **sacrifice** altar,
saying,
Let *king Solomon* **sovereign Shelomoh**
swear **oath** unto me to day
that he *will* **shall** not *slay* **deathify** his servant
with the sword.
52 And *Solomon* **Shelomoh** said,
If he *will* **shall** shew himself a *worthy man* **son of valour**,
there shall not an hair of him fall to the earth:
but if *wickedness* **evil** shall be found in him, he shall die.
53 So *king Solomon* **sovereign Shelomoh** sent,
and they *brought* **descended** him *down*
from the **sacrifice** altar.
And he came and *bowed* **prostrated** *himself*
to *king Solomon* **sovereign Shelomoh**:
and *Solomon* **Shelomoh** said unto him, Go to thine house.

DAVID COMMANDS SHELOMOH

2 Now the days of David *drew nigh* **approached**
that he should die;
and he *charged Solomon* **misvahed Shelomoh** his son,
saying,
2 I go the way of all the earth:
be thou strong **strengthen** *therefore*,
and *shew thyself* **be** a man;
3 And *keep* **guard** the *charge* **guard**
of *the LORD* **Yah Veh** thy *God* **Elohim**,
to walk in his ways, to *keep* **guard** his statutes,
and his *commandments* **mitsvoth**,
and his judgments, and his *testimonies* **witnesses**,
as it is *written* **inscribed**
in the *law* **torah** of *Moses* **Mosheh**,
that thou mayest *prosper* **comprehend**
in all that thou *doest* **workest**,
and whithersoever thou *turnest* **facest** *thyself*:
4 That *the LORD* **Yah Veh** may *continue* **raise** his word
which he *spake* **worded** concerning me, saying,
If thy *children take heed to* **sons guard** their way,
to walk *before me* **at my face** in truth
with all their heart and with all their soul,
there shall not *fail* **be cut off from** thee
(said he) a man on the throne of *Israel* **Yisra El**.
5 Moreover thou knowest also
what *Joab* **Yah Ab** the son of *Zeruiah* **Seruyah**
did **worked** to me,
and — what he *did* **worked** to the two *captains* **governors**
of the hosts of *Israel* **Yisra El**,
unto *Abner* **Abi Ner** the son of Ner,
and unto Amasa the son of *Jether* **Yether**,
whom he *slew* **slaughtered**,
and *shed* **set** the blood of war in *peace* **shalom**,
and *put* **gave** the blood of war
upon his girdle that was about his loins,
and in his shoes that were on his feet.

6 *Do* **Work** therefore according to thy wisdom,
and let not his *hoar head* **grayness**
go down **descend** to *the grave* **sheol** in *peace* **shalom**.
7 But *shew kindness* **work mercy**
unto the sons of *Barzillai* **Barzillay** the *Gileadite* **Giladiy**,
and let them be of those that eat at thy table:
for so they *came* **approached** to me
when I fled *because* **from the face** of *Absalom* **Abi Shalom**
thy brother.
8 And, behold,
thou hast with thee *Shimei* **Shimi** the son of Gera,
a *Benjamite* **Ben Yaminiy** of *Bahurim* **Bachurim**,
which *cursed* **abased** me
with a *grievous curse* **reinforced abasement**
in the day when I went to *Mahanaim* **Machanayim**:
but he *came down* **descended**
to meet me at *Jordan* **Yarden**,
and I *sware* **oathed** to him by *the LORD* **Yah Veh**, saying,
I will **shall** not *put* **deathify** thee *to death* with the sword.
9 Now therefore *hold* **exonerate** him not *guiltless*:
for thou art a wise man,
and knowest what thou oughtest to *do* **work** unto him;
but his *hoar head* **grayness**
bring thou down **descend** to *the grave* **sheol** with blood.
10 So David *slept* **laid** with his fathers,
and was *buried* **entombed** in the city of David.
11 And the days that David reigned over *Israel* **Yisra El**
were forty years:
seven years reigned he in Hebron,
and thirty and three years reigned he
in *Jerusalem* **Yeru Shalem**.
12 Then *sat Solomon* **settled Shelomoh**
upon the throne of David his father;
and his *kingdom* **sovereigndom**
was established *greatly* **mightily**.

ADONI YAH APPROACHES BATH SHEBA

13 And *Adonijah* **Adoni Yah** the son of Haggith
came to *Bathsheba* **Bath Sheba**
the mother of *Solomon* **Shelomoh**.
And she said, Comest thou *peaceably* **in shalom**?
And he said, *Peaceably* **In shalom**.
14 He said moreover,
I have *somewhat to say* **a word** unto thee.
And she said, *Say* **Word** on.
15 And he said,
Thou knowest that the *kingdom* **sovereigndom** was mine,
and that all *Israel* **Yisra El** set their faces on me,
that I should reign:
howbeit the *kingdom* **sovereigndom** is turned about,
and is become my brother's:
for it was his from *the LORD* **Yah Veh**.
16 And now I ask one petition of thee,
deny me **turn** not **away my face**.
And she said unto him, *Say* **Word** on.
17 And he said, *Speak* **Say**, I pray thee,
unto *Solomon* **Shelomoh** the *king* **sovereign**,
(for he *will* **shall** not *say thee nay* **turn away thy face**,)
that he give me *Abishag* **Abi Shag**
the *Shunammite* **Shunemiyth** to *wife* **woman**.
18 And *Bathsheba* **Bath Sheba** said, *Well* **Good**;
I *will speak* **shall word** for thee unto the *king* **sovereign**.
19 *Bathsheba* **Bath Sheba** *therefore*
went unto *king Solomon* **sovereign Shelomoh**,
to *speak* **word** unto him for *Adonijah* **Adoni Yah**.
And the *king* **sovereign** rose up to meet her,
and *bowed* **prostrated** himself unto her,
and *sat down* **settled** on his throne,
and caused a seat to be set
for the *king's* **sovereign's** mother;
and she *sat* **settled** on his right *hand*.
20 Then she said, I *desire* **ask** one small petition of thee;
I pray thee, say me not nay **Turn not away my face**.
And the *king* **sovereign** said unto her, Ask on, my mother:
for I *will* **shall** not *say thee nay* **turn away thy face**.
21 And she said,
Let *Abishag* **Abi Shag** the *Shunammite* **Shunemiyth**
be given to *Adonijah* **Adoni Yah** thy brother
to *wife* **woman**.
22 And *king Solomon* **sovereign Shelomoh** answered
and said unto his mother,
And why dost thou ask
Abishag **Abi Shag** the *Shunammite* **Shunemiyth**
for *Adonijah* **Adoni Yah**?
ask for him the *kingdom* **sovereigndom** also;
for he is *mine elder* **my greater** brother;
even for him, and for *Abiathar* **Abi Athar** the priest,
and for *Joab* **Yah Ab** the son of *Zeruiah* **Seruyah**.
23 Then *king Solomon* **sovereign Shelomoh**
sware **oathed** by *the LORD* **Yah Veh**, saying,
God do **Elohim work** so to me, and *more* **add** also,
if *Adonijah* **Adoni Yah** have not *spoken* **worded** this word
against his own *life* **soul**.
24 Now therefore, *as the LORD* **Yah Veh** liveth,
which hath established me,
and set me on the throne of David my father,
and who hath *made* **worked** me an house,
as he *promised* **worded**,
Adonijah **Adoni Yah** shall be *put to death* **deathified**
this day.
25 And *king Solomon* **sovereign Shelomoh** sent
by the hand of *Benaiah* **Bena Yah**
the son of *Jehoiada* **Yah Yada**;
and he *fell* **encountered** upon him that he died.
26 And unto *Abiathar* **Abi Athar** the priest
said the *king* **sovereign**,
Get thee **Go** to Anathoth, unto thine own fields;
for thou art *worthy* **a man** of death:
but I *will* **shall** not
at this time put thee to death **deathify thee today**,
because thou barest the ark
of *the Lord GOD* **Adonay Yah Veh**
before **at the face of** David my father,
and because thou hast been *afflicted* **humbled**
in all wherein my father was *afflicted* **humbled**.
27 So *Solomon* **Shelomoh**
thrust out Abiathar **expelled Abi Athar**
from being priest unto *the LORD* **Yah Veh**;
that he might fulfil the word of *the LORD* **Yah Veh**,
which he *spake* **worded**
concerning the house of Eli in Shiloh.

YAH AB IS DEATHIFIED

28 Then *tidings* **reports** came to *Joab* **Yah Ab**:
for *Joab* **Yah Ab**
had *turned* **extended** after *Adonijah* **Adoni Yah**,
though he *turned* **extended** not after *Absalom* **Abi Shalom**.
And *Joab* **Yah Ab** fled
unto the *tabernacle* **tent** of *the LORD* **Yah Veh**,
and caught hold on the horns of the **sacrifice** altar.
29 And it was told *king Solomon* **sovereign Shelomoh**
that *Joab* **Yah Ab** was fled
unto the *tabernacle* **tent** of *the LORD* **Yah Veh**;
and, behold, *he is by* **beside** the **sacrifice** altar.
Then *Solomon* **Shelomoh**
sent *Benaiah* **Bena Yah** the son of *Jehoiada* **Yah Yada**,
saying, Go, *fall* **encounter** upon him.
30 And *Benaiah* **Bena Yah**
came to the *tabernacle* **tent** of *the LORD* **Yah Veh**,
and said unto him,
Thus saith the *king* **sovereign**, *Come forth* **Go**.
And he said, Nay; but I *will* **shall** die here.
And *Benaiah* **Bena Yah**
brought the king **returned** word *again* **to the sovereign**,
saying, Thus *said Joab* **worded Yah Ab**,
and thus he answered me.
31 And the *king* **sovereign** said unto him,
Do **Work** as he hath *said* **worded**,
and *fall* **encounter** upon him, and *bury* **entomb** him;
that thou mayest *take away* **turn aside**
the *innocent* **gratuitous** blood,
which *Joab shed* **Yah Ab poured**,
from me, and from the house of my father.
32 And *the LORD* **Yah Veh**
shall return his blood upon his own head,
who *fell upon* **encountered** two men
more *righteous* **just** and better than he,
and *slew* **slaughtered** them with the sword,
my father David not knowing thereof, *to wit*,
Abner **Abi Ner** the son of Ner,
captain **governor** of the host of *Israel* **Yisra El**,
and Amasa the son of *Jether* **Yether**,

captain **governor** of the host of *Judah* **Yah Hudah.**
33 Their blood shall *therefore* return
upon the head of *Joab* **Yah Ab,**
and upon the head of his seed *for ever* **eternally**:
but upon David, and upon his seed,
and upon his house, and upon his throne,
shall there be *peace for ever* **shalom eternally**
from *the LORD* **Yah Veh.**
34 So *Benaiah* **Bena Yah** the son of *Jehoiada* **Yah Yada**
went up **ascended,**
and *fell upon* **encountered** him, and *slew* **deathified** him:
and he was *buried* **entombed** in his own house
in the wilderness.
35 And the *king* **sovereign**
put Benaiah **gave Bena Yah** the son of *Jehoiada* **Yah Yada**
in his room over the host:
and *Zadok* **Sadoq** the priest
did the *king put* **sovereign give**
in the room of *Abiathar* **Abi Athar.**

SHIMI IS DEATHIFIED

36 And the *king* **sovereign** sent
and called for *Shimei* **Shimi**, and said unto him,
Build thee an house in *Jerusalem* **Yeru Shalem,**
and *dwell* **settle** there,
and go not forth thence any *whither* **where.**
37 For it shall be, that on the day thou goest out,
and passest over the *brook Kidron* **wadi Qidron,**
in knowing, thou shalt know *for certain*
that **in dying,** thou shalt *surely* die:
thy blood shall be upon thine own head.
38 And *Shimei* **Shimi** said unto the *king* **sovereign,**
The *saying* **word** is good:
as my *lord* **adoni** the *king* **sovereign** hath *said* **worded,**
so *will* **shall** thy servant *do* **work.**
And *Shimei dwelt* **Shimi settled** in *Jerusalem* **Yeru Shalem**
many days.
39 And it *came to pass* **became,** at the end of three years,
that two of the servants of *Shimei* **Shimi**
ran away **fled** unto Achish
son of Maachah *king* **sovereign** of Gath.
And they told *Shimei* **Shimi**, saying,
Behold, thy servants be in Gath.
40 And *Shimei* **Shimi** arose,
and *saddled* **harnessed** his *ass* **he burro,**
and went to Gath to Achish to seek his servants:
and *Shimei* **Shimi** went,
and brought his servants from Gath.
41 And it was told *Solomon* **Shelomoh**
that *Shimei* **Shimi**
had gone from *Jerusalem* **Yeru Shalem** to Gath,
and *was come again* **returned.**
42 And the *king* **sovereign** sent
and called for *Shimei* **Shimi**, and said unto him,
Did I not make thee to *swear* **oath** by *the LORD* **Yah Veh,**
and *protested* **witnessed** unto thee, saying,
In knowing, Know *for a certain,* on the day thou goest out,
and walkest abroad any *whither* **where,**
that **in dying,** thou shalt *surely* die?
and thou saidst unto me,
The word that I have heard is good.
43 Why then hast thou not *kept* **guarded**
the oath of *the LORD* **Yah Veh,**
and the *commandment* **misvah**
that I have *charged* **misvahed** thee with?
44 The *king* **sovereign** said *moreover* to *Shimei* **Shimi,**
Thou knowest all the *wickedness* **evil**
which thine heart *is privy to* **perceiveth,**
that thou *didst* **workedst** to David my father:
therefore
the LORD **Yah Veh** shall return thy *wickedness* **evil**
upon thine own head;
45 And *king Solomon shall be blessed*
blessed be sovereign Shelomoh,
and *the throne of David shall be established*
established be the throne of David
before the LORD for ever **at the face of Yah Veh eternally.**
46 So the *king commanded* **sovereign misvahed**
Benaiah **Bena Yah** the son of *Jehoiada* **Yah Yada;**
which went out,
and *fell* **encountered** upon him, that he died.
And the *kingdom* **sovereigndom**
was established in the hand of *Solomon* **Shelomoh.**

SHELOMOH REQUESTS WISDOM

3 And *Solomon made affinity* **Shelomoh intermarried**
with *Pharaoh* **Paroh,** *king* **sovereign** of *Egypt* **Misrayim,**
and took *Pharaoh's* **Paroh's** daughter,
and brought her into the city of David,
until he had *made an end of* **finished**
building his own house,
and the house of *the LORD* **Yah Veh,**
and the wall of *Jerusalem* **Yeru Shalem** round about.
2 Only the people sacrificed in *high places* **bamahs,**
because there was no house built
unto the name of *the LORD* **Yah Veh**, until those days.
3 And *Solomon* **Shelomoh** loved *the LORD* **Yah Veh,**
walking in the statutes of David his father:
only he sacrificed and *burnt incense* **incensed**
in *high places* **bamahs.**
4 And the *king* **sovereign** went to *Gibeon* **Gibon**
to sacrifice there;
for that was the great *high place* **bamah**:
a thousand *burnt offerings* **holocausts**
did Solomon offer **Shelomoh holocausted**
upon that **sacrifice** altar.
5 In *Gibeon* **Gibon,**
the LORD **Yah Veh**
appeared to Solomon **was seen by Shelomoh**
in a dream by night:
and *God* **Elohim** said, Ask what I shall give thee.
6 And *Solomon* **Shelomoh** said,
Thou hast *shewed* **worked**
unto thy servant David my father great mercy,
according as he walked *before thee* **at thy face** in truth,
and in *righteousness* **justness,**
and in *uprightness* **straightness** of heart with thee;
and thou hast *kept* **guarded** for him
this great *kindness* **mercy,**
that thou hast given him a son to *sit* **settle** on his throne,
as *it is* this day.
7 And now, O *LORD* **Yah Veh** my *God* **Elohim,**
thou hast *made* thy servant *king* **reign**
instead of David my father:
and I am *but* a little *child* **lad**:
I know not *how* to go out or come in.
8 And thy servant is in the midst of thy people
which thou hast chosen,
a great people, that cannot be numbered
nor *counted* **scribed** for *multitude* **abundance.**
9 Give therefore thy servant
an understanding **a hearing** heart to judge thy people,
that I may discern between good and *bad* **evil**:
for who is able to judge this
thy *so great a* **grievous** people?
10 And the *speech* **word**
pleased the Lord **well—pleased the eyes of Adonay,**
that *Solomon* **Shelomoh** had asked this *thing* **word.**
11 And *God* **Elohim** said unto him,
Because thou hast asked this *thing* **word,**
and hast not asked for thyself *long life* **many days;**
neither hast asked riches for thyself,
nor hast asked the *life* **soul** of thine enemies;
but hast asked for thyself *understanding* **discernment**
to *discern* **hear** judgment;
12 Behold, I have *done* **worked** according to thy words:
lo **behold,** I have given thee
a wise and *an understanding* **discerning** heart;
so that there was none like thee *before thee* **at thy face,**
neither after thee shall any arise like unto thee.
13 And I have also given thee
that which thou hast not asked,
both riches, and honour:
so that there shall *not be any* **be no man**
among the *kings* **sovereigns**
like unto thee all thy days.
14 And if thou *wilt* **shalt** walk in my ways,
to *keep* **guard** my statutes
and my *commandments* **mitsvoth,**
as thy father David did walk,
then I *will lengthen* **shall prolong** thy days.
15 And *Solomon* **Shelomoh** awoke;

and, behold, *it was* a dream.
And he came to *Jerusalem* **Yeru Shalem**,
and stood
before **at the face of** the ark of the covenant
of *the LORD* **Yah Veh**,
and *offered up burnt offerings* **holocausted holocausts**,
and *offered peace offerings* **worked shelamim**,
and *made* **worked** a feast to all his servants.

SHELOMOH'S FIRST CASE

16 Then came there two women,
that were harlots — **whores**,
unto the *king* **sovereign**, and stood *before him* **at his face**.
17 And the one woman said, O my *lord* **adoni**,
I and this woman *dwell* **settle** in one house;
and I *was delivered of a child* **birthed**
with her in the house.
18 And it *came to pass* **became,**
the third day after that I *was delivered* **birthed**,
that this woman *was delivered* **birthed** also:
and we were together;
there was no stranger with us in the house,
save **except** we two in the house.
19 And this woman's *child* **son** died in the night;
because she *overlaid* **layed down upon** it.
20 And she arose *at midnight* **in the middle of the night**,
and took my son from beside me,
while *thine handmaid* **thy maid** slept,
and laid it in her bosom,
and laid her dead *child* **son** in my bosom.
21 And when I rose in the morning
to *give my child suck* **suckle my son**,
behold, it *was dead* **had died**:
but when I had *considered* **discerned** it in the morning,
behold, it was not my son, which I did bear.
22 And the other woman said, Nay;
but the living is my son, and the dead is thy son.
And this said, No;
but the dead is thy son, and the living is my son.
Thus they *spake* **worded**
before **at the face of** the *king* **sovereign**.

SHELOMOH'S FIRST JUDGMENT

23 Then said the *king* **sovereign**,
The one **This** saith,
This is my son that liveth, and thy son is the dead:
and *the other* **that** saith,
Nay; but thy son is the dead, and my son is the living.
24 And the *king* **sovereign** said, *Bring* **Take** me a sword.
And they brought a sword
before **at the face of** the *king* **sovereign**.
25 And the *king* **sovereign** said,
Divide **Cut** the living child in two,
and give half to the one, and half to the *other* **one**.
26 Then *spake* **said** the woman
whose the living *child* **son** was unto the *king* **sovereign**,
for her *bowels* **mercies** yearned upon her son,
and she said,
O my *lord* **adoni**, give her the living *child* **begotten**,
and in *no wise slay it* **deathifying, deathify it not**.
But the other said,
Let it be neither mine nor thine, *but divide* **cut** it.
27 Then the *king* **sovereign** answered and said,
Give her the living *child* **begotten**,
and *in no wise slay it* **in deathifying, deathify it not**:
she is the mother thereof.
28 And all *Israel* **Yisra El** heard of the judgment
which the *king* **sovereign** had judged;
and they *feared* **awed at the face of** the *king* **sovereign**:
for they saw that the wisdom of *God* **Elohim**
was in *him* **his midst**, to *do* **work** judgment.

SHELOMOH'S GOVERNORS

4 So *king Solomon* **sovereign Shelomoh**
was *king* **sovereign** over all *Israel* **Yisra El**.
2 And these were the *princes* **governors** which he had;
Azariah **Azar Yah** the son of *Zadok* **Sadoq** the priest,
3 *Elihoreph* **Eli Horeph** and *Ahiah* **Achiy Yah**,
the sons of Shisha, scribes;
Jehoshaphat **Yah Shaphat** the son of *Ahilud* **Achiy Lud**,
the *recorder* **remembrancer**.
4 And *Benaiah* **Bena Yah** the son of *Jehoiada* **Yah Yada**
was over the host:
and *Zadok* **Sadoq** and *Abiathar* **Abi Athar** *were* the priests:
5 And *Azariah* **Azar Yah** the son of Nathan
was over the *officers* **stationed**:
and Zabud the son of Nathan was *principal officer* **priest**,
and the *king's* **sovereign's** friend:
6 And *Ahishar* **Achiy Shar** *was* over the household:
and *Adoniram* **Adoni Ram** the son of Abda
was over the *tribute* **vassal**.

SHELOMOH'S STATIONED

7 And *Solomon* **Shelomoh**
had twelve *officers* **stationed** over all *Israel* **Yisra El**,
which *provided victuals for* **sustained** the *king* **sovereign**
and his household:
each man his month in a year made provision
each one sustained one month per year.
8 And these are their names:
The son of Hur **Ben Hur**, in mount *Ephraim* **Ephrayim**:
9 *The son of Dekar* **Ben Deqer**, in *Makaz* **Maqas**,
and in Shaalbim and *Bethshemesh* **Beth Shemesh**,
and *Elonbethhanan* **Elon Beth Hanan**:
10 *The son of Hesed* **Ben Hesed**, in *Aruboth* **Arubboth**;
to him *pertained* Sochoh,
and all the land of Hepher:
11 *The son of Abinadab* **Ben Abi Nadab**,
in all the *region* **heights** of Dor;
which had Taphath the daughter of *Solomon* **Shelomoh**
to *wife* **woman**:
12 Baana the son of *Ahilud* **Achiy Lud**;
to him *pertained* Taanach and Megiddo,
and all *Bethshean* **Beth Shaan**,
which is *by Zartanah* **beside Sarethan**
beneath *Jezreel* **Yizre El**,
from *Bethshean* **Beth Shaan**
to *Abelmeholah* **Abel Mecholah**,
even unto the place that is beyond *Jokneam* **Yoqme Am**:
13 *The son of Geber* **Ben Geber**,
in *Ramothgilead* **Ramoth Gilad**;
to him *pertained* the *towns* **living areas** of *Jair* **Yair**
the son of *Manasseh* **Menash Sheh**,
which are in *Gilead* **Gilad**;
to him *also pertained* the *region* **boundaries** of Argob,
which is in Bashan,
threescore **sixty** great cities
with walls and *brasen* **copper** bars:
14 *Ahinadab* **Achiy Nadab** the son of Iddo
had *Mahanaim* **Machanayim**:
15 *Ahimaaz* **Achiy Maas** was in Naphtali;
he also took *Basmath* **Bosmath**
the daughter of *Solomon* **Shelomoh** to *wife* **woman**:
16 Baanah the son of *Hushai* **Hushay**
was in Asher and in *Aloth* **Bealoth**:
17 *Jehoshaphat* **Yah Shaphat** the son of *Paruah* **Paruach**,
in *Issachar* **Yissachar**:
18 *Shimei* **Shimi** the son of *Elah* **Ela**,
in *Benjamin* **Ben Yamin**:
19 Geber the son of Uri
was in the *country* **land** of *Gilead* **Gilad**,
in the *country* **land** of *Sihon* **Sichon**
king **sovereign** of the *Amorites* **Emoriy**,
and of Og *king* **sovereign** of Bashan;
and he was the *only officer* **one prefect**
which was in the land.

SHELOMOH'S REIGN

20 *Judah* **Yah Hudah** and *Israel* **Yisra El** were many,
as the sand which is by the sea in *multitude* **abundance**,
eating and drinking, and *making merry* **cheering**.
21 And *Solomon* **Shelomoh**
reigned **was sovereign** over all *kingdoms* **sovereigndoms**
from the river unto the land of the *Philistines* **Peleshethiy**,
and unto the border of *Egypt* **Misrayim**:
they brought *presents* **near offerings**,
and served *Solomon* **Shelomoh** all the days of his life.

SHELOMOH'S BREAD

22 And *Solomon's provision* **Shelomoh's bread** for one day
was thirty *measures* **kors** of *fine* flour,
and *threescore measures* **sixty kors** of *meal* **flour**,
23 Ten fat oxen, and twenty oxen out of the pastures,
and an hundred *sheep* **flocks**,
beside harts, and *roebucks* **gazelles**,
and fallowdeer, and *fatted* **foddered** fowl.

24 For he *had dominion* **subjugated** over all *the region*
on this side the river,
from *Tiphsah* **Tiphsach** even to Azzah,
over all the *kings* **sovereigns** on this side the river:
and he had *peace* **shalom**
on all sides **from all his servants** round about him.
25 And *Judah* **Yah Hudah** and *Israel* **Yisra El**
dwelt safely **settled confidently**,
every man under his vine and under his fig tree,
from Dan even to *Beersheba* **Beer Sheba**,
all the days of *Solomon* **Shelomoh**.
26 And *Solomon* **Shelomoh**
had forty thousand stalls of horses for his chariots,
and twelve thousand *horsemen* **cavalry**.
27 And those *officers* **stationed**
provided victual for king Solomon
sustained sovereign Shelomoh,
and for all that *came* **approached**
unto *king Solomon's* **sovereign Shelomoh's** table,
every man in his month:
they lacked *nothing* **no word**.
28 Barley also and straw
for the horses and *dromedaries* **stallions**
brought they unto the place where *the officers* **they** were,
every man according to his *charge* **judgment**.

SHELOMOH'S WISDOM

29 And *God* **Elohim** gave *Solomon* **Shelomoh**
wisdom and *understanding* **discernment**
exceeding much **mightily abounding**,
and *largeness* **breadth** of heart,
even as the sand that is on the sea *shore* **lip**.
30 And *Solomon's* **Shelomoh's** wisdom *excelled* **abounded**
above the wisdom of all
the *children* **sons** of the east *country* **land**,
and all the wisdom of *Egypt* **Misrayim**.
31 For he was *wiser* **enwisened**
than **above** all *men* **humanity**;
than Ethan the *Ezrahite* **Zerachiy**, and Heman,
and *Chalcol* **Kalkol**, and Darda,
the sons of *Mahol* **Machol**:
and his fame was in all *nations* **goyim** round about.
32 And he *spake* **worded** three thousand proverbs:
and his songs were a thousand and five.
33 And he *spake* **worded** of trees,
from the cedar tree that is in Lebanon
even unto the hyssop
that *springeth* **emergeth** out of the wall:
he *spake also* **worded** of *beasts* **animals**,
and of *fowl* **flyers**,
and of *creeping things* **creepers**, and of fishes.
34 And there came of all people
to hear the wisdom of *Solomon* **Shelomoh**,
from all *kings* **sovereigns** of the earth,
which had heard of his wisdom.

SHELOMOH'S ALLIANCE WITH SOVEREIGN HIRAM

5 And Hiram *king* **sovereign** of *Tyre* **Sor**
sent his servants unto *Solomon* **Shelomoh**;
for he had heard
that they had anointed him *king* **sovereign**
in the *room* **stead** of his father:
for Hiram was *ever* **all days** a lover of David.
2 And *Solomon* **Shelomoh** sent to Hiram, saying,
3 Thou knowest how that David my father
could not build an house
unto the name of *the LORD* **Yah Veh** his *God* **Elohim**
for **at the face of** the wars
which *were about* **surrounded** him on every side,
until *the LORD* **Yah Veh**
put **gave** them under the soles of his feet.
4 But now *the LORD* **Yah Veh** my *God* **Elohim**
hath given me rest *on every side* **round about**,
so that there is neither *adversary* **a satan**
nor evil *occurrent* **incident**.
5 And, behold, I *purpose* **said** to build an house
unto the name of *the LORD* **Yah Veh** my *God* **Elohim**,
as *the LORD spake* **Yah Veh worded**
unto David my father, saying, Thy son,
whom I *will set* **shall give** upon thy throne in thy room,
he shall build an house unto my name.
6 Now *therefore command* **misvah** thou
that they *hew* **cut** me cedar trees out of Lebanon;
and my servants shall be with thy servants:
and unto thee *will* **shall** I give hire for thy servants
according to all that thou shalt *appoint* **say**:
for thou knowest that there is not among us
any **a man** that *can skill* **knoweth** to *hew* **cut** timber
like unto the *Sidonians* **Sidoniy**.
7 And it *came to pass* **became**,
when Hiram heard the words of *Solomon* **Shelomoh**,
that he *rejoiced greatly* **cheered mightily**, and said,
Blessed be *the LORD* **Yah Veh** this day,
which hath given unto David
a wise son over this great people.
8 And Hiram sent to *Solomon* **Shelomoh**, saying,
I have *considered the things* **heard those**
which thou sentest to me for:
and I *will do* **shall work** all thy *desire* **delight**
concerning timber of cedar,
and concerning timber of *fir* **cypress**.
9 My servants shall *bring* **descend** them *down*
from Lebanon unto the sea:
and I *will convey* **shall set** them by sea in *floats* **rafts**
unto the place that thou shalt *appoint* **send** me,
and *will* **shall** cause them
to be *discharged* **scattered** there,
and thou shalt *receive* **lift** them:
and thou shalt *accomplish* **work** my *desire* **delight**,
in giving *food* **bread** for my household.
10 So Hiram gave *Solomon* **Shelomoh** cedar trees
and *fir* **cypress** trees according to all his *desire* **delight**.
11 And *Solomon* **Shelomoh** gave Hiram
twenty thousand *measures* **kors** of wheat
for food **nourishment** to his household,
and twenty *measures* **kors** of *pure* **pestled** oil:
thus gave *Solomon* **Shelomoh** to Hiram year by year.
12 And *the LORD* **Yah Veh**
gave *Solomon* **Shelomoh** wisdom,
as he *promised* **worded** him:
and there was *peace* **shalom**
between Hiram and *Solomon* **Shelomoh**;
and they two *made* **cut** a *league* **covenant** *together*.

DRAFTING THE VASSAL

13 And *king Solomon* **sovereign Shelomoh**
raised **ascended** a *levy* **vassal** out of all *Israel* **Yisra El**;
and the *levy* **vassal** was thirty thousand men.
14 And he sent them to Lebanon,
ten thousand a month by *courses* **changes**:
a month they were in Lebanon,
and two months at *home* **their house**:
and *Adoniram* **Adoni Ram** was over the *levy* **vassal**.
15 And *Solomon* **Shelomoh**
had *threescore and ten* **seventy** thousand
that bare burdens **burdenbearers**,
and *fourscore* **eighty** thousand hewers in the mountains;
16 Beside the *chief* **governor**
of *Solomon's officers* **Shelomoh's stationed**
which were over the work,
three thousand and three hundred,
which *ruled* **subjugated** over the people
that *wrought* **worked** in the work.
17 And the *king commanded* **sovereign misvahed**,
and they *brought* **pulled** great stones,
costly **precious** stones, and hewed stones,
to lay the foundation of the house.
18 And *Solomon's* **Shelomoh's** builders
and Hiram's builders *did hew them*,
and the *stonesquarers* **Gibliy sculpted**:
so they prepared timber and stones to build the house.

THE BUILDING OF THE HOUSE OF YAH VEH

6 And it *came to pass* **became**,
in the four hundred and eightieth year
after the *children* **sons** of *Israel* **Yisra El**
were *come* **gone** out of the land of *Egypt* **Misrayim**,
in the fourth year
of *Solomon's* **Shelomoh's** reign over *Israel* **Yisra El**,
in the month Zif, which is the second month,
that he began to build the house of *the LORD* **Yah Veh**.
2 And the house which *king Solomon* **sovereign Shelomoh**
built for *the LORD* **Yah Veh**,
the length thereof *was threescore* **sixty** cubits,

and the breadth thereof twenty *cubits,*
and the height thereof thirty cubits.
3 And the porch
before **at the face of** the *temple* **manse** of the house,
twenty cubits was the length thereof,
according to **at the face of** the breadth of the house;
and ten cubits was the breadth thereof
before **at the face of** the house.
4 And for the house he *made windows* **worked lookouts**
of *narrow* **shuttered** lights.
5 And against the wall of the house
he built chambers round about,
against the walls of the house round about,
both of the *temple* **manse** and of the *oracle* **pulpit**:
and he *made chambers* **worked ribs** round about:
6 The nethermost chamber was five cubits broad,
and the middle was six cubits broad,
and the third was seven cubits broad:
for without *in the wall of* the house
he *made narrowed rests* **gave ledges** round about,
that the beams should not be fastened
not held in the walls of the house.
7 And the house,
when it was in building, was built of stone
made ready before it was brought thither
which they did shalam at the quarry:
so that there was neither hammer nor ax
nor *any tool* **instrument** of iron heard in the house,
while it was in building.
8 The *door* **portal** for the middle *chamber* **rib**
was in the right *side* **shoulder** of the house:
and they *went up* **ascended** with *winding* **spiral** stairs
into the middle *chamber,*
and out of the middle into the third.
9 So he built the house, and finished it;
and *covered* **cieled** the house
with *beams* **carvings** and *boards* **shingles** of cedar.
10 And then he built chambers against all the house,
five cubits high:
and they *rested* **took hold** on the house
with timber of cedar.
11 And the word of *the LORD* **Yah Veh**
came to *Solomon* **Shelomoh**, saying,
12 *Concerning* this house which thou art in building,
if thou *wilt* **shalt** walk in my statutes,
and *execute* **work** my judgments,
and *keep* **guard** all my *commandments* **misvoth**
to walk in them;
then *will* **shall** I *perform* **raise** my word with thee,
which I *spake* **worded** unto David thy father:
13 And I *will dwell* **shall tabernacle**
among the *children* **sons** of *Israel* **Yisra El**,
and *will* **shall** not forsake my people *Israel* **Yisra El**.
14 So *Solomon* **Shelomoh** built the house, and finished it.
15 And he built the walls of the house within
with *boards* **ribs** of cedar,
both the floor of the house, and the walls of the ceiling:
and he *covered* **overlaid** them on the *inside* **house**
with *wood* **timber**,
and *covered* **overlaid** the floor of the house
with *planks* **ribs** of *fir* **cypress**.
16 And he built twenty cubits
on the *sides* **flanks** of the house,
both **from** the floor *and* **to** the walls
with *boards* **ribs** of cedar:
he even built them for it *within* **a house,**
even for the *oracle* **pulpit**,
even for the *most holy place* **Holy of Holies**.
17 And the house, that is,
the *temple before it* **manse at the face in front**,
was forty cubits *long.*
18 And the cedar of the house within
was carved **were carvings**
with *knops* **knobs** and open *flowers* **blossoms**:
all was cedar; there was no stone seen.
19 And the *oracle* **pulpit**
he prepared in **the midst of** the house within,
to *set* **give** there
the ark of the covenant of *the LORD* **Yah Veh**.
20 And the *oracle in the forepart* **face of the pulpit**
was twenty cubits in length, and twenty cubits in breadth,
and twenty cubits in the height thereof:
and he overlaid it with *pure* **concentrated** gold;
and *so covered* **overlaid** the **sacrifice** altar
which was of **with** cedar.
21 So *Solomon* **Shelomoh** overlaid the house within
with *pure* **concentrated** gold:
and he made *a partition* **an overpass** by the chains of gold
before **at the face of** the *oracle* **pulpit**;
and he overlaid it with gold.
22 And the whole house he overlaid with gold,
until he had *finished* **consumated** all the house:
also the whole **sacrifice** altar that was by the *oracle* **pulpit**
he overlaid with gold.
23 And within the *oracle* **pulpit**
he *made* **worked** two *cherubims* **cherubim**
of *olive* **oil** tree, *each* ten cubits high.
24 And five cubits was the one wing of the cherub,
and five cubits the *other* **second** wing of the cherub:
from the *uttermost part* **end** of the one wing
unto the *uttermost part* **end** of the *other* **wing**
were ten cubits.
25 And the *other* **second** cherub was ten cubits:
both the *cherubims* **cherubim**
were of one measure and one *size* **shape**.
26 The height of the one cherub was ten cubits,
and *so was it of the other* **thus the second** cherub.
27 And he *set* **gave** the *cherubims* **cherubim**
within the inner house:
and they *stretched* **spread** forth the wings
of the *cherubims* **cherubim**,
so that the wing of the one touched the one wall,
and the wing of the *other* **second** cherub
touched the *other* **second** wall;
and their wings touched *one another* **wing to wing**
in the midst of the house.
28 And he overlaid the *cherubims* **cherubim** with gold.
29 And he carved all the walls of the house round about
with *carved figures* **carvings** of *cherubims* **cherubim**
and palm trees and open *flowers* **blossoms**,
within and without.
30 And the floor of the house he overlaid with gold,
within and without.
31 And for the *entering* **portal** of the *oracle* **pulpit**
he *made* **worked** doors of *olive* **oil** tree:
the *lintel* **pilaster** and side posts
were a fifth *part of the wall.*
32 The two doors also were of *olive* **oil** tree;
and he carved upon them carvings of *cherubims* **cherubim**
and palm trees and open *flowers* **blossoms**,
and overlaid them with gold,
and *spread* **overlaid** gold upon the *cherubims* **cherubim**,
and upon the palm trees.
33 So also *made* **worked** he
for the *door* **opening** of the *temple* **manse**
posts of *olive* **oil** tree, a fourth *part of the wall.*
34 And the two doors were of *fir* **cypress** tree:
the two *leaves* **ribs** of the one door were folding,
and the two *leaves* **hangings** of the *other* **second** door
were folding.
35 And he carved *thereon cherubims* **cherubim**
and palm trees and open *flowers* **blossoms**:
and *covered* **overlaid** them with gold
fitted **straight** upon the *carved* **engraved** work.
36 And he built the inner court
with three rows of hewed stone,
and a row of cedar beams.
37 In the fourth year
was the foundation of the house
of *the LORD* **Yah Veh** laid,
in the month Zif:
38 And in the eleventh year, in the month *Bul* **Buwl**,
which is the eighth month,
was the house finished
throughout all the *parts* **word** thereof,
and according to all *the fashion* **judgment** of it.
So was he seven years in building it.

THE BUILDING OF THE HOUSE OF SHELOMOH

7 But *Solomon* **Shelomoh**
was building his own house thirteen years,

and he finished all his house.
2 He built also the house of the forest of Lebanon;
the length thereof *was* an hundred cubits,
and the breadth thereof fifty cubits,
and the height thereof thirty cubits,
upon four rows of cedar pillars,
with cedar beams upon the pillars.
3 And it was *covered* **cieled** with cedar
above upon the *beams* **ribs**,
that *lay* on forty five pillars, fifteen in a row.
4 And there were *windows* **lookouts** in three rows,
and *light* **window** was against *light* **window**
in three *ranks* **steps**.
5 And all the *doors* **portals** and posts were square,
with the *windows* **lookouts**:
and *light* **window** was against *light* **window**
in three *ranks* **steps**.
6 And he *made* **worked** a porch of pillars;
the length thereof *was* fifty cubits,
and the breadth thereof thirty cubits:
and the porch was *before them* **at their face**:
and the *other* pillars and the thick beam
were *before them* **at their face**.
7 Then he *made* **worked** a porch for the throne
where he might judge, *even* the porch of judgment:
and it was *covered* **cieled** with cedar
from *one side of the floor to the other* **floor to floor**.
8 And his house where he *dwelt* **settled**
had another court *within* **to house** the porch,
which was of the like work.
Solomon made **Shelomoh worked** also an house
for *Pharaoh's* **Paroh's** daughter,
whom he had taken *to wife*, like unto this porch.
9 All these were of *costly* **precious** stones,
according to the measures of hewed stones,
sawed with saws,
within and without **the house**,
even from the foundation unto the *coping* **support**,
and so on the outside toward the great court.
10 And the foundation was of *costly* **precious** stones,
even great stones,
stones of ten cubits, and stones of eight cubits.
11 And above were *costly* **precious** stones,
after the measures of hewed stones, and cedars.
12 And the great court round about
was with three rows of hewed stones,
and a row of cedar beams,
both for the inner court
of the house of *the LORD* **Yah Veh**,
and for the porch of the house.

THE FURNISHINGS OF THE HOUSE OF SHELOMOH

13 And *king Solomon* **sovereign Shelomoh**
sent and *fetched* **took** Hiram out of *Tyre* **Sor**.
14 He was a *widow's* **woman's** son
of the *tribe* **rod** of Naphtali,
and his father was a *man of Tyre* **Soriy**,
a worker in brass **an engraver in copper**:
and he was filled with wisdom,
and *understanding* **discernment**, and *cunning* **knowledge**
to work all works in *brass* **copper**.
And he came to *king Solomon* **sovereign Shelomoh**,
and *wrought* **worked** all his work.
15 For he *cast* **formed** two pillars of *brass* **copper**,
of eighteen cubits high *apiece*
was the height of one pillar:
and a *line* **thread** of twelve cubits
did compass either of them about
surrounded the second pillar.
16 And he *made* **worked**
two *chapiters* **caps** of *molten brass* **poured copper**,
to *set* **give** upon the tops of the pillars:
the height of the one *chapiter* **cap**
was five cubits,
and the height of the *other chapiter* **second cap**
was five cubits:
17 And nets of *checker* **net** work,
and *wreaths* **threads** of chain work,
for the *chapiters* **caps**
which were upon the top of the pillars;
seven for the one *chapiter* **cap**,
and seven for the *other chapiter* **second cap**.
18 And he *made* **worked** the pillars,
and two rows round about upon the one *network* **net**,
to cover the *chapiters* **caps** that were upon the top,
with pomegranates:
and so *did* **worked** he for the *other chapiter* **second cap**.
19 And the *chapiters* **caps**
that were upon the top of the pillars
were of lily work in the porch, four cubits.
20 And the *chapiters* **caps** upon the two pillars
had pomegranates also above,
over against **beside** the belly
which was *by* **beside** the *network* **net**:
and the pomegranates
were two hundred in rows round about
upon the *other chapiter* **second cap**.
21 And he *set up* **raised** the pillars
in the porch of the *temple* **manse**:
and he *set up* **raised** the right pillar,
and called the name thereof *Jachin* **Yachin**:
and he *set up* **raised** the left pillar,
and called the name thereof Boaz.
22 And upon the top of the pillars was lily work:
so was the work of the pillars *finished* **consumated**.
23 And he *made* **worked** a *molten* **poured** sea,
ten cubits from *the one brim to the other* **lip to lip**:
it was round *all* **round** about,
and his height was five cubits:
and a line of thirty cubits
did *compass* **surround** it round about.
24 And under the *brim* **lip** of it round about
there were *knops compassing* **knobs surrounding** it,
ten in a cubit,
compassing **surrounding** the sea round about:
the *knops* **knobs** were *cast* **poured** in two rows,
when it was *cast* **founded**.
25 It stood upon twelve oxen,
three *looking* **at the face** toward the north,
and three *looking* **at the face** toward the *west* **sea**,
and three *looking* **at the face** toward the south,
and three *looking* **at the face** toward the *east* **rising**:
and the sea was *set* above upon them,
and all their *hinder parts* **backs**
were *inward* **toward the house**.
26 And it was *an hand breadth* **a palm span** thick,
and the *brim* **lip** thereof
was wrought like the *brim* **work of the lip** of a cup,
with *flowers* **blossoms** of lilies:
it contained two thousand baths.
27 And he *made* **worked** ten bases of *brass* **copper**;
four cubits was the length of one base,
and four cubits the breadth thereof,
and three cubits the height of it.
28 And the work of the bases was *on this manner* **thus**:
they had borders,
and the borders were between the ledges:
29 And on the borders that were between the ledges
were lions, oxen, and *cherubims* **cherubim**:
and upon the ledges there was a base above:
and beneath the lions and oxen
were *certain additions made* **wreaths** of *thin* **festoon** work.
30 And *every* **one** base had four *brasen* **copper** wheels,
and *plates* **axles** of *brass* **copper**:
and the four *corners* **supports** thereof
had *undersetters* **shoulder pieces**:
under the laver
were *undersetters molten* **shoulder pieces poured**,
at the side of *every addition* **each man a wreath**.
31 And the mouth of it *within* **housing** the *chapiter* **cap**
and above was a cubit:
but the mouth thereof was round
after the work of the base, a cubit and *a half* **a cubit**:
and also upon the mouth of it were *gravings* **carvings**
with their borders, foursquare, not round.
32 And under the borders were four wheels;
and the *axletrees* **hands** of the wheels
were *joined* to the base:
and the height of *a* **one** wheel was a cubit and half a cubit.
33 And the work of the wheels
was like the work of a chariot wheel:

their *axletrees* **hands**, and their *naves* **rims**,
and their *felloes* **spokes**, and their *spokes* **hubs**,
were all *molten* **poured**.
34 And there were four *undersetters* **shoulder pieces**
to the four corners of one base:
and the *undersetters* **shoulder pieces**
were of the very base itself.
35 And in the top of the base
was *there a round compass* **round about**
of half a cubit high:
and on the top of the base the *ledges* **hands** thereof
and the borders thereof were of the same.
36 For on the *plates* **slabs** of the *ledges* **hands** thereof,
and on the borders thereof,
he *graved* **engraved**
cherubims **cherubim**, lions, and palm trees,
according to the *proportion* **nakedness** of *every one* **man**,
and *additions* **wreaths** round about.
37 *After this manner* **Thus** he *made* **worked** the ten bases:
all of them had one casting,
one measure, *and* one *size* **shape**.
38 Then *made* **worked** he ten lavers of *brass* **copper**:
one laver contained forty baths:
and every **one** laver was four cubits:
and upon every one of the ten bases one laver.
39 And he *put* **gave** five bases
on the right *side* **shoulder** of the house,
and five on the left *side* **shoulder** of the house:
and he *set* **gave** the sea
on the right *side* **shoulder** of the house
eastward *over against* **toward** the south.
40 And Hiram *made* **worked** the lavers,
and the shovels, and the *basons* **sprinklers**.
So Hiram *made an end* **finished**
of doing **working** all the work that he *made* **worked**
king Solomon **for sovereign Shelomoh**
for the house of *the LORD* **Yah Veh**:
41 The two pillars, and the *two* bowls of the *chapiters* **caps**
that were on the top of the two pillars;
and the two *networks* **nets**,
to cover the two bowls of the *chapiters* **caps**
which were upon the top of the pillars;
42 And four hundred pomegranates
for the two *networks* **nets**,
even two rows of pomegranates for one *network* **net**,
to cover the two bowls of the *chapiters* **caps**
that were upon **the face of** the pillars;
43 And the ten bases, and ten lavers on the bases;
44 And one sea, and twelve oxen under the sea;
45 And the *pots* **caldrons**, and the shovels,
and the *basons* **sprinklers**:
and all these *vessels* **instruments**,
which Hiram *made* **worked**
to *king Solomon* **sovereign Shelomoh**
for the house of *the LORD* **Yah Veh**,
were of *bright brass* **polished copper**.
46 In the *plain* **environs** of *Jordan* **Yarden**
did the *king cast* **sovereign pour** them,
in the *clay ground* **compacted soil**
between *Succoth* **Sukkoth/Brush Arbors**
and *Zarthan* **Sarethan**.
47 And *Solomon* **Shelomoh**
left **set** all the *vessels* **instruments** *unweighed,*
because they were exceeding many
for the mighty mighty abundance:
neither was the weight of the *brass* **copper**
found out **probed**.
48 And *Solomon* **Shelomoh**
made **worked** all the *vessels* **instruments**
that *pertained unto* **be in** the house of *the LORD* **Yah Veh**:
the **sacrifice** altar of gold, and the table of gold,
whereupon the *shewbread* **face bread** was,
49 And the *candlesticks* **menorahs**
of *pure* **concentrated** gold,
five on the right *side,* and five on the left,
before **at the face of** the *oracle* **pulpit**,
with the *flowers* **blossoms**,
and the lamps, and the tongs of gold,
50 And the *bowls* **basons**, and the *snuffers* **tweezers**,
and the *basons* **sprinklers**, and the *spoons* **bowls**,
and the *censers* **trays** of *pure* **concentrated** gold;
and the hinges of gold,
both for the doors of the inner house,
the *most holy place* **Holy of Holies**,
and for the doors of the house,
to wit, of the *temple* **manse**.
51 So *was ended* **doth shalam** all the work
that *king Solomon made* **sovereign Shelomoh worked**
for the house of *the LORD* **Yah Veh**.
And *Solomon* **Shelomoh** brought in
the *things which* **holies of** David his father
had dedicated;
even the silver, and the gold, and the *vessels* **instruments**,
did he *put* **give** among the treasures
of the house of *the LORD* **Yah Veh**.

THE ARK IN THE HOUSE OF YAH VEH

8 Then *Solomon* **Shelomoh**
assembled **congregated** the elders of *Israel* **Yisra El**,
and all the heads of the *tribes* **rods**,
the *chief* **hierarchs** of the fathers
of the *children* **sons** of *Israel* **Yisra El**,
unto *king Solomon* **sovereign Shelomoh**
in *Jerusalem* **Yeru Shalem**,
that they might *bring up* **ascend**
the ark of the covenant of *the LORD* **Yah Veh**
out of the city of David, which is *Zion* **Siyon**.
2 And all the men of *Israel* **Yisra El**
assembled themselves **congregated**
unto *king Solomon* **sovereign Shelomoh**
at the *feast* **celebration**
in the month Ethanim, which is the seventh month.
3 And all the elders of *Israel* **Yisra El** came,
and the priests *took up* **lifted** the ark.
4 And they *brought up* **ascended**
the ark of *the LORD* **Yah Veh**,
and the *tabernacle* **tent** of the congregation,
and all the holy *vessels* **instruments**
that were in the *tabernacle* **tent**,
even those did the priests and the *Levites* **Leviym**
bring up **ascend**.
5 And *king Solomon* **sovereign Shelomoh**,
and all the *congregation* **witness** of *Israel* **Yisra El**,
that *were assembled* **congregated** unto him,
were with him *before* **at the face of** the ark,
sacrificing *sheep* **flock** and oxen,
that could not be *told* **scribed** nor numbered
for *multitude* **abundance**.
6 And the priests brought in
the ark of the covenant of *the LORD* **Yah Veh**
unto his place,
into the *oracle* **pulpit** of the house,
to the *most holy place* **Holy of Holies**,
even under the wings of the *cherubims* **cherubim**.
7 For the *cherubims* **cherubim** spread forth their two wings
over the place of the ark,
and the *cherubims* **cherubim**
covered the ark and the staves thereof above.
8 And they *drew out* **lengthened** the staves,
that the *ends* **heads** of the staves were seen
out in the *holy place* **holies**
before **at the face of** the *oracle* **pulpit**,
and they were not seen without:
and there they are unto this day.
9 There was *nothing* **naught** in the ark
save **only** the two *tables* **slabs** of stone,
which *Moses put* **Mosheh set** there at Horeb,
when *the LORD made a covenant* **Yah Veh cut**
with the *children* **sons** of *Israel* **Yisra El**,
when they *came* **went** out of the land of *Egypt* **Misrayim**.
10 And it *came to pass* **became**,
when the priests
were *come* **gone** out of the *holy place* **holies**,
that the cloud filled the house of *the LORD* **Yah Veh**,
11 So that the priests could not stand to minister
because **at the face** of the cloud:
for the *glory* **honour** of *the LORD* **Yah Veh**
had filled the house of *the LORD* **Yah Veh**.
12 Then *spake Solomon* **said Shelomoh**,
The LORD **Yah Veh** said
that he *would dwell* **should tabernacle**

in the *thick* **dripping** darkness.
13 **In building,** I have *surely* built thee an house
to *dwell* **reside** in,
a settled place **an establishment** for thee
to *abide* **settle** in *for ever* **eternally**.
14 And the *king* **sovereign** turned his face about,
and blessed all the congregation of *Israel* **Yisra El**:
(and all the congregation of *Israel* **Yisra El** stood;)
15 And he said, Blessed be
the LORD God **Yah Veh Elohim** of *Israel* **Yisra El**,
which *spake* **worded** with his mouth
unto David my father,
and hath with his hand fulfilled it, saying,
16 Since the day
that I brought forth my people *Israel* **Yisra El**
out of *Egypt* **Misrayim**,
I chose no city out of all the *tribes* **scions** of *Israel* **Yisra El**
to build an house, that my name might be therein;
but I chose David to be over my people *Israel* **Yisra El**.
17 And it was in the heart of David my father
to build an house for the name of
the LORD God **Yah Veh Elohim** of *Israel* **Yisra El**.
18 And *the LORD* **Yah Veh** said unto David my father,
Whereas **Because** it was in thine heart
to build an house unto my name,
thou didst *well* **good** that it was in thine heart.
19 *Nevertheless* **Only** thou shalt not build the house;
but thy son that shall *come* **go** forth out of thy loins,
he shall build the house unto my name.
20 And *the LORD* **Yah Veh**
hath *performed* **raised** his word that he *spake* **worded**,
and I am risen *up* in the *room* **stead** of David my father,
and *sit* **settle** on the throne of *Israel* **Yisra El**,
as *the LORD promised* **Yah Veh worded**,
and have built an house for the name
of *the LORD God* **Yah Veh Elohim** of *Israel* **Yisra El**.
21 And I have set there a place for the ark,
wherein is the covenant of *the LORD* **Yah Veh**,
which he *made* **cut** with our fathers,
when he brought them out of the land of *Egypt* **Misrayim**.

SHELOMOH'S PRAYER OF HANUKKAH FOR THE HOUSE

22 And *Solomon* **Shelomoh** stood
before **at the face of the sacrifice** altar
of *the LORD* **Yah Veh**
in *the presence* **front**
of all the congregation of *Israel* **Yisra El**,
and spread forth his *hands* **palms**
toward *heaven* **the heavens**:
23 And he said,
LORD God **Yah Veh Elohim** of *Israel* **Yisra El**,
there is no *God* **Elohim** like thee,
in *heaven* **the heavens** above, or on earth beneath,
who *keepest* **guardest** covenant and mercy
with thy servants
that walk *before thee* **at thy face** with all their heart:
24 Who hast *kept* **guarded**
with thy servant David my father
that thou *promisedst* **wordest** him:
thou *spakest* **wordest** also with thy mouth,
and hast fulfilled it with thine hand, as *it is* this day.
25 Therefore now,
LORD God **Yah Veh Elohim** of *Israel* **Yisra El**,
keep **guard** with thy servant David my father
that thou *promisedst* **wordedst** him, saying,
There shall not *fail* **be cut off from** thee
a man in my *sight* **face**
to *sit* **settle** on the throne of *Israel* **Yisra El**;
so that **only if** thy
children take heed to **sons guard** their way,
that they walk *before me* **at my face**
as thou hast walked *before me* **at my face**.
26 And now, O *God* **Elohim** of *Israel* **Yisra El**,
let thy word, I *pray* **beseech** thee, be *verified* **amenable**,
which thou *spakest* **wordest**
unto thy servant David my father.
27 But *will God* **shall Elohim**
indeed dwell **truly settle** on the earth?
behold, the *heaven* **heavens**
and *heaven* **the heavens of the** heavens
cannot contain thee;
how much less **also** this house that I have builded?
28 Yet *have thou respect* **face thou**
unto the prayer of thy servant,
and to his supplication,
O *LORD* **Yah Veh** my *God* **Elohim**,
to hearken unto the *cry* **shout** and to the prayer,
which thy servant prayeth *before thee* **at thy face** to day:
29 That thine eyes may be open
toward this house night and day,
even toward the place of which thou hast said,
My name shall be there:
that thou mayest hearken unto the prayer
which thy servant shall *make* **pray** toward this place.
30 And hearken thou to the supplication of thy servant,
and of thy people *Israel* **Yisra El**,
when they shall pray toward this place:
and hear thou in *heaven* **the heavens**
the place of thy *dwelling place* **settlement**:
and when thou hearest, forgive.
31 If any man *trespass* **sin** against his *neighbour* **friend**,
and an oath be laid upon him to cause him to *swear* **oath**,
and the oath come
before thine **at the face of thy sacrifice** altar in this house:
32 Then hear thou in *heaven* **the heavens**, and *do* **work**,
and judge thy servants
condemning **declaring wicked** the wicked,
to *bring* **give** his way upon his head;
and justifying the *righteous* **just**,
to give him according to his *righteousness* **justness**.
33 When thy people *Israel* **Yisra El** be smitten down
before **at the face of** the enemy,
because they have sinned against thee,
and shall turn again to thee,
and *confess* **extend hands to** thy name, and pray,
and *make supplication* **beseech** unto thee in this house:
34 Then hear thou in *heaven* **the heavens**,
and forgive the sin of thy people *Israel* **Yisra El**,
and *bring* **return** them *again* unto the *land* **soil**
which thou gavest unto their fathers.
35 When *heaven is shut up* **the heavens be restrained**,
and there is no rain,
because they have sinned against thee;
if they pray toward this place,
and *confess* **extend hands to** thy name,
and turn from their sin,
when thou *afflictest* **humblest** them:
36 Then hear thou in *heaven* **the heavens**,
and forgive the sin of thy servants,
and of thy people *Israel* **Yisra El**,
that thou *teach* **direct** them the good way
wherein they should walk,
and give rain upon thy land,
which thou hast given to thy people for an inheritance.
37 If there be in the land famine, if there be pestilence,
blasting, *mildew* **pale green**, locust,
or if there be caterpiller;
if their enemy *besiege* **tribulate** them
in the land of their *cities* **portals**;
whatsoever plague, whatsoever *sickness* **disease** *there be*;
38 What prayer and supplication soever
be *made* by any man,
or by all thy people *Israel* **Yisra El**,
which shall know every *man* **human**
the plague of his own heart,
and spread forth his *hands* **palms** toward this house:
39 Then hear thou in *heaven* **the heavens**
the place of thy *dwelling place* **settlement**,
and forgive, and *do* **work**,
and give to every man according to his ways,
whose heart thou knowest;
(for thou, even thou only, knowest the hearts
of all the *children* **sons** of *men* **humanity**;)
40 That they may *fear* **awe** thee
all the days that they live
in the land **upon the face of the soil**
which thou gavest unto our fathers.
41 Moreover concerning a stranger,
that is not of thy people *Israel* **Yisra El**,
but cometh out of a far *country* **land** for thy name's sake;
42 (For they shall hear of thy great name,

and of thy strong hand, and of thy stretched out arm;)
when he shall come and pray toward this house;
43 Hear thou in *heaven* **the heavens**
the place of thy *dwelling place* **settlement**,
and *do* **work** according to all
that the stranger calleth to thee for:
that all people of the earth may know thy name,
to *fear* **awe** thee, as *do* thy people *Israel* **Yisra El**;
and that they may know that this house,
which I have builded, is called by thy name.
44 If thy people go out to *battle* **war** against their enemy,
whithersoever **in the way which** thou shalt send them,
and shall pray unto *the LORD* **Yah Veh**
toward the city which thou hast chosen,
and toward the house that I have built for thy name:
45 Then hear thou in *heaven* **the heavens**
their prayer and their supplication,
and *maintain* **work** their *cause* **judgment**.
46 If they sin against thee,
(for there is no *man* **human** that sinneth not,)
and thou be angry with them,
and *deliver* **give** them to **face** the enemy,
so that
they carry them away captives **their captors capture them**
unto the land of the enemy, far or near;
47 *Yet* if they shall
bethink themselves in **return their hearts to** the land
whither they were *carried captives* **captured**,
and *repent* **turn**, and *make supplication* **beseech** unto thee
in the land of them that *carried* **captured** them *captives*,
saying, We have sinned,
and have *done perversely* **perverted**,
we have *committed wickedness* **done wickedly**;
48 And *so* return unto thee with all their heart,
and with all their soul, in the land of their enemies,
which *led* **captured** them *away captive*,
and pray unto thee toward their land,
which thou gavest unto their fathers,
the city which thou hast chosen,
and the house which I have built for thy name:
49 Then hear thou their prayer and their supplication
in *heaven* **the heavens**
the place of thy *dwelling place* **settlement**,
and *maintain* **work** their *cause* **judgment**,
50 And forgive thy people that have sinned against thee,
and all their *transgressions* **rebellions**
wherein they have *transgressed* **rebelled** against thee,
and give them *compassion* **mercies**
before **at the face of** them
who *carried* **captured** them *captive*,
that they may *have compassion on* **mercy** them:
51 For they be thy people, and thine inheritance,
which thou broughtest forth out of *Egypt* **Misrayim**,
from the midst of the furnace of iron:
52 That thine eyes may be open
unto the supplication of thy servant,
and unto the supplication of thy people *Israel* **Yisra El**,
to hearken unto them in all that they call for unto thee.
53 For thou didst separate them
from among all the people of the earth,
to be thine inheritance,
as thou *spakest* **wordest**
by the hand of *Moses* **Mosheh** thy servant,
when thou broughtest our fathers out of *Egypt* **Misrayim**,
O *Lord GOD* **Adonay Yah Veh**.
54 And it *was so* **became**, that *when Solomon* **Shelomoh**
had *made an end of* **finished** praying all this prayer
and supplication unto *the LORD* **Yah Veh**,
he arose from
before **the face of** the **sacrifice** altar of *the LORD* **Yah Veh**,
from *kneeling* **bowing** on his knees
with his *hands* **palms** spread up to *heaven* **the heavens**.
55 And he stood,
and blessed all the congregation of *Israel* **Yisra El**
with a *loud* **great** voice, saying,
56 Blessed be *the LORD* **Yah Veh**,
that hath given rest unto his people *Israel* **Yisra El**,
according to all that he *promised* **worded**:
there hath not *failed* **fallen**
one word of all his good *promise* **word**,
which he *promised* **worded**
by the hand of *Moses* **Mosheh** his servant.
57 *The LORD* **Yah Veh** our *God* **Elohim** be with us,
as he was with our fathers:
let him not leave us, nor forsake us:
58 That he may *incline* **extend** our hearts unto him,
to walk in all his ways,
and to *keep* **guard** his *commandments* **misvoth**,
and his statutes, and his judgments,
which he *commanded* **misvahed** our fathers.
59 And let these my words,
wherewith I have *made supplication* **besought**
before the LORD **at the face of Yah Veh**,
be nigh unto *the LORD* **Yah Veh** our *God* **Elohim**
day and night,
that he *maintain* **work** the *cause* **judgment** of his servant,
and the *cause* **judgment** of his people *Israel* **Yisra El**
at all times **the day by day word**,
as the *matter* **word** shall require:
60 That all the people of the earth may know
that *the LORD* **Yah Veh** is *God* **Elohim**,
and that there is — none else.
61 Let your heart therefore be *perfect* **at shalom**
with *the LORD* **Yah Veh** our *God* **Elohim**,
to walk in his statutes,
and to *keep* **guard** his *commandments* **misvoth**,
as at this day.

THE HANUKKAH

62 And the *king* **sovereign**, and all *Israel* **Yisra El** with him,
offered **sacrificed** sacrifice
before the LORD **at the face of Yah Veh**.
63 And *Solomon offered* **Shelomoh sacrificed**
a sacrifice of *peace offerings* **shelamim**,
which he *offered* **sacrificed** unto *the LORD* **Yah Veh**,
two and twenty thousand oxen,
and an hundred and twenty thousand *sheep* **flocks**.
So the *king* **sovereign**
and all the *children* **sons** of *Israel* **Yisra El**
dedicated **hanukkahed** the house of *the LORD* **Yah Veh**.
64 The same day did the *king* **sovereign**
hallow the middle of the court that was
before **at the face** the house of *the LORD* **Yah Veh**:
for there he *offered burnt offerings* **worked holocausts**,
and *meat* offerings,
and the fat of the *peace offerings* **shelamim**:
because the *brasen* **copper sacrifice** altar
that was before the LORD **at the face of Yah Veh**
was too little
to *receive* **contain** the *burnt offerings* **holocausts**,
and *meat* offerings,
and the fat of the *peace offerings* **shelamim**.
65 And at that time
Solomon held **Shelomoh worked** a *feast* **celebration**,
and all *Israel* **Yisra El** with him, a great congregation,
from the entering in of Hamath
unto the *river* **wadi** of *Egypt* **Misrayim**,
before the LORD **at the face of Yah Veh** our *God* **Elohim**,
seven days and seven days, *even* fourteen days.
66 On the eighth day he sent the people away:
and they blessed the *king* **sovereign**,
and went unto their tents *joyful* **cheerful**
and *glad* **good** of heart
for all the goodness
that *the LORD* **Yah Veh** had *done* **worked**
for David his servant, and for *Israel* **Yisra El** his people.

YAH VEH IS SEEN BY SHELOMOH

9 And it *came to pass* **became**,
when *Solomon* **Shelomoh** had finished
the building of the house of *the LORD* **Yah Veh**,
and the *king's* **sovereign's** house,
and all *Solomon's* **Shelomoh's** desire
which he *was pleased* **delighted** to *do* **work**,
2 That *the LORD* **Yah Veh**
appeared to Solomon **was seen by Shelomoh**
the second time,
as he *had appeared unto* **was seen by** him
at *Gibeon* **Gibon**.
3 And *the LORD* **Yah Veh** said unto him,
I have heard thy prayer and thy supplication,
that thou hast *made before me* **besought at my face**:

I have hallowed this house, which thou hast built,
to *put* **set** my name there *for ever* **eternally**;
and mine eyes and mine heart
shall be there *perpetually* **all days**.
4 And if thou *wilt* **shalt** walk *before me* **at my face**,
as David thy father walked,
in integrity of heart, and in *uprightness* **straightness**,
to *do* **work**
according to all that I have *commanded* **misvahed** thee,
and *wilt keep* **shalt guard** my statutes and my judgments:
5 Then I *will establish* **shall raise** the throne
of thy *kingdom* **sovereigndom**
upon *Israel for ever* **Yisra El eternally**,
as I *promised* **worded** to David thy father, saying,
There shall not *fail* **be cut off from** thee
a man upon the throne of *Israel* **Yisra El**.
6 But if **in turning,**
ye shall *at all* turn from *following* **after** me,
ye or your *children* **sons**,
and *will* **shall** not
keep **guard** my *commandments* **misvoth** and my statutes
which I have *set before you* **given at thy face**,
but go and serve other *gods* **elohim**,
and *worship* **prostrate to** them:
7 Then *will* **shall** I cut off *Israel* **Yisra El**
out **from the face** of the *land* **soil**
which I have given them;
and this house, which I have hallowed for my name,
will I cast out of my sight **shall I send away from my face**;
and *Israel* **Yisra El** shall be a proverb and *a byword* **gibe**
among all people:
8 And at this house, *which is high* **Elyon,**
every one that passeth by it
shall be *astonished* **desolated**, and shall hiss;
and they shall say,
Why hath *the LORD done* **Yah Veh worked** thus
unto this land, and to this house?
9 And they shall *answer* **say**,
Because they forsook
the LORD **Yah Veh** their *God* **Elohim**,
who brought forth their fathers
out of the land of *Egypt* **Misrayim**,
and have taken hold upon other *gods* **elohim**,
and have *worshipped* **prostrated to** them,
and served them:
therefore
hath *the LORD* **Yah Veh** brought upon them all this evil.
10 And it *came to pass* **became,** at the end of twenty years,
when *Solomon* **Shelomoh** had built the two houses,
the house of *the LORD* **Yah Veh**,
and the *king's* **sovereign's** house,
11 (*Now* Hiram the *king* **sovereign** of *Tyre* **Sor**
had *furnished Solomon* **loaded Shelomoh**
with cedar trees and *fir* **cypress** trees, and with gold,
according to all his desire,)
that then *king Solomon* **sovereign Shelomoh** gave Hiram
twenty cities in the land of *Galilee* **Galiyl**.
12 And Hiram *came out* **went** from *Tyre* **Sor**
to see the cities which *Solomon* **Shelomoh** had given him;
and they *pleased him not* **were not straight in his eyes**.
13 And he said,
What cities are these which thou hast given me,
my brother?
And he called them the land of *Cabul* **Kabul** unto this day.
14 And Hiram sent to the *king* **sovereign**
sixscore talents **an hundred and twenty rounds** of gold.
15 And this is the *reason* **word** of the *levy* **vassal**
which *king Solomon raised* **sovereign Shelomoh lifted**;
for to build the house of *the LORD* **Yah Veh**,
and his own house, and Millo,
and the wall of *Jerusalem* **Yeru Shalem**,
and *Hazor* **Hasor**, and Megiddo, and Gezer.
16 *For Pharaoh* **Paroh,** *king* **sovereign** of *Egypt* **Misrayim**
had *gone up* **ascended**, and *taken* **captured** Gezer,
and burnt it with fire,
and *slain* **slaughtered** the *Canaanites* **Kenaaniy**
that *dwelt* **settled** in the city,
and given it for *a present* **dowries** unto his daughter,
Solomon's wife **Shelomoh's woman**.
17 And *Solomon* **Shelomoh** built Gezer,
and *Bethhoron* **Beth Horon** the nether,
18 And Baalath, and Tadmor in the wilderness, in the land,
19 And all the cities of *store* **storage**
that *Solomon* **Shelomoh** had,
and cities for his chariots,
and cities for his *horsemen* **cavalry**,
and *that which Solomon* **the desire of Shelomoh**
that he desired to build in *Jerusalem* **Yeru Shalem**,
and in Lebanon, and in all the land of his *dominion* **reign**.
20 *And* all the people that *were left* **remained**
of the *Amorites* **Emoriy**,
Hittites **Hethiy**, *Perizzites* **Perizziy**,
Hivites **Hivviy**, and *Jebusites* **Yebusiy**,
which were not of the *children* **sons** of *Israel* **Yisra El**,
21 Their *children* **sons** that *were left* **remained** after them
in the land,
whom the *children* **sons** of *Israel* **Yisra El** also
were not able *utterly to destroy* **to devote**,
upon those did *Solomon* **Shelomoh**
levy a tribute **ascend a vassal** of *bondservice* **service**
unto this day.
22 But of the *children* **sons** of *Israel* **Yisra El**
did Solomon make **Shelomoh gave** no *bondmen* **servants**:
but they were men of war,
and his servants, and his *princes* **governors**,
and his *captains* **tertiaries**,
and *rulers* **governors** of his chariots,
and his *horsemen* **cavalry**.
23 These were the *chief of the officers* **governors**
that were **stationed** over *Solomon's* **Shelomoh's** work,
five hundred and fifty,
which *bare rule over* **subjugated** the people
that *wrought* **worked** in the work.
24 But *Pharaoh's* **Paroh's** daughter
came up **ascended** out of the city of David unto her house
which *Solomon* **he** had built for her:
then did he build Millo.
25 And three times in a year *did Solomon* **Shelomoh**
offer burnt offerings **holocausted holocausts**
and *peace offerings* **shelamim**
upon the **sacrifice** altar
which he built unto *the LORD* **Yah Veh**,
and he *burnt incense upon the altar* **incensed thereon**
that was before the LORD **at the face of Yah Veh**.
So **did** he *finished* **shalam** the house.
26 And *king Solomon* **sovereign Shelomoh**
made **worked** a navy of ships in *Eziongeber* **Esyon Geber**,
which is beside Eloth,
on the *shore* **lip** of the *Red* **Reed** sea, in the land of Edom.
27 And Hiram sent in the *navy* **ships** his servants,
shipmen **men of ships**
that *had knowledge of* **knew** the sea,
with the servants of *Solomon* **Shelomoh**.
28 And they came to Ophir,
and *fetched* **took** from thence gold,
four hundred and twenty *talents* **rounds**,
and brought it to *king Solomon* **sovereign Shelomoh**.

THE SOVEREIGNESS OF SHEBA

10 And when the *queen* **sovereigness** of Sheba
heard of the fame of *Solomon* **Shelomoh**
concerning the name of *the LORD* **Yah Veh**,
she came to *prove* **test** him with *hard questions* **riddles**.
2 And she came to *Jerusalem* **Yeru Shalem**
with *a very great train* **mighty heavy valuables**,
with camels that bare spices,
and *very* **mighty** much gold, and precious stones:
and when she was come to *Solomon* **Shelomoh**,
she *communed* **worded** with him
of all that was in her heart.
3 And *Solomon* **Shelomoh** told her all her *questions* **words**:
there was *not any thing hid* **no word concealed**
from the *king* **sovereign**, which he told her not.
4 And when the *queen* **sovereigness** of Sheba
had seen all *Solomon's* **Shelomoh's** wisdom,
and the house that he had built,
5 And the *meat* **food** of his table,
and the *sitting* **settlement** of his servants,
and the *attendance* **function** of his ministers,
and their *apparel* **robes**, and his *cupbearers* **butlers**,
and his ascent by which he *went up* **ascended**

unto the house of *the LORD* **Yah Veh**;
there was no more spirit in her.
6 And she said to the *king* **sovereign**,
It was a true *report* **word** that I heard in mine own land
of thy *acts* **words** and of thy wisdom.
7 Howbeit I *believed* **trusted** not the words,
until I came, and mine eyes had seen it:
and, behold, the half was not told me:
thy **thou hast added** wisdom
and *prosperity exceedeth* **goodness**
to the *fame* **report** which I heard.
8 *Happy* **Blithe** are thy men,
happy **blithe** are these thy servants,
which stand continually *before thee* **at thy face**,
and that hear thy wisdom.
9 Blessed be *the LORD* **Yah Veh** thy *God* **Elohim**,
which delighted in thee,
to *set* **give** thee on the throne of *Israel* **Yisra El**:
because *the LORD* **Yah Veh**
loved *Israel for ever* **Yisra El eternally**,
therefore *made* **set** he thee *king* **sovereign**,
to *do* **work** judgment and *justice* **justness**.
10 And she gave the *king* **sovereign**
an hundred and twenty *talents* **rounds** of gold,
and of spices *very* **a mighty** great *store* **abundance**,
and precious stones:
there came no more such abundance of spices as these
which the *queen* **sovereigness** of Sheba gave
to *king Solomon* **sovereign Shelomoh**.
11 And the *navy* **ships** also of Hiram,
that *brought* **lifted** gold from Ophir,
brought in from Ophir
great plenty of almug trees
a mighty abundance of algumim,
and precious stones.
12 And the *king* **sovereign**
made **worked** of the *almug trees* **algumim**
pillars **banisters** for the house of *the LORD* **Yah Veh**,
and for the *king's* **sovereign's** house,
harps also and *psalteries* **bagpipes** for singers:
there came no such *almug trees* **algumim**,
nor were seen unto this day.
13 And *king Solomon* **sovereign Shelomoh**
gave unto the *queen* **sovereigness** of Sheba
all her *desire* **delight**, whatsoever she asked,
beside that which *Solomon* **Shelomoh** gave her
of the hand of his *royal* **sovereign** bounty.
So she *turned* **faced** and went to her own *country* **land**,
she and her servants.

THE WEALTH AND WISDOM OF SHELOMOH

14 Now the weight of gold
that came to *Solomon* **Shelomoh** in one year
was six hundred *threescore* **sixty** and six
talents **rounds** of gold,
15 Beside that *he had* **of** the *merchantmen* **men explorers**,
and of the *traffick* **merchandising** of the *spice* merchants,
and of all the *kings* **sovereigns** of *Arabia* **the mongrels**,
and of the governors of the *country* **land**.
16 And *king Solomon* **sovereign Shelomoh**
made **worked** two hundred *targets* **shields** of beaten gold:
six hundred *shekels of* gold
went **ascended** to one *target* **shield**.
17 And *he made* three hundred *shields* **bucklers**
of beaten gold;
three *pound* **maneh** of gold
went **ascended** to one *shield* **buckler**:
and the *king put* **sovereign gave** them
in the house of the forest of Lebanon.
18 Moreover
the *king made* **sovereign worked** a great throne of ivory,
and overlaid it with *the best* **purified** gold.
19 The throne had six steps,
and the top of the throne was round behind:
and there were *stays* **hands**
on either side **here and there** on the place of the seat,
and two lions stood beside the *stays* **hands**.
20 And twelve lions stood there
on the one side and on the other **here and there**
upon the six steps:
there was not *the like made* **such worked**
in any *kingdom* **sovereigndom**.
21 And all *king Solomon's* **sovereign Sholomoh's**
drinking *vessels* **instruments** were of gold,
and all the *vessels* **instruments**
of the house of the forest of Lebanon
were of *pure* **concentrated** gold; none were of silver:
it was *nothing accounted of* **not fabricated**
in the days of *Solomon* **Shelomoh**.
22 For the *king* **sovereign** had at sea
a navy **the ships** of Tarshish with the *navy* **ships** of Hiram:
once in three years came the *navy* **ships** of Tarshish,
bringing **bearing** gold, and silver,
ivory **tusks**, and apes, and peacocks.
23 So *king Solomon* **sovereign Shelomoh**
exceeded **greatened**
above all the *kings* **sovereigns** of the earth
for riches and for wisdom.
24 And all the earth
sought *to Solomon* **the face of Shelomoh**,
to hear his wisdom,
which *God* **Elohim** had *put* **given** in his heart.
25 And they brought every man his *present* **offering**,
vessels **instruments** of silver,
and *vessels* **instruments** of gold,
and *garments* **clothes**, and armour,
and spices, horses, and mules,
a *rate* year by year **word**.
26 And *Solomon* **Shelomoh** gathered *together*
chariots and *horsemen* **cavalry**:
and he had a thousand and four hundred chariots,
and twelve thousand *horsemen* **cavalry**,
whom he *bestowed* **guided** in the cities for chariots,
and with the *king* **sovereign** at *Jerusalem* **Yeru Shalem**.
27 And the *king made* **sovereign gave** silver
to be in *Jerusalem* **Yeru Shalem** as stones,
and cedars *made* **gave** he *to be* as the sycomore trees
that are in the *vale* **lowland**, for abundance.
28 And *Solomon* **Shelomoh** had horses
brought **proceed** out of *Egypt* **Misrayim**,
and *linen yarn* **troops**:
the *king's* **sovereign's** merchants
received the linen yarn **took the troops** at a price.
29 And a chariot *came up* **ascended**
and went out of *Egypt* **Misrayim**
for six hundred *shekels* of silver,
and an horse for an hundred and fifty:
and so for all the *kings* **sovereigns** of the *Hittites* **Hethiy**,
and for the *kings* **sovereigns** of *Syria* **Aram**,
did they bring them out by *their means* **hand**.

THE WOMEN OF SHELOMOH

11 But *king Solomon* **sovereign Shelomoh**
loved many strange women,
together with the daughter of *Pharaoh* **Paroh**,
women of the *Moabites* **Moabiy**,
Ammonites **Ammoniy**, *Edomites* **Edomiy**,
Zidonians **Sidoniy**, and *Hittites* **Hethiy**:
2 Of the *nations* **goyim**
concerning which *the LORD* **Yah Veh** said
unto the *children* **sons** of *Israel* **Yisra El**,
Ye shall not go in to them,
neither shall they come in unto you:
for surely they *will turn away* **shall pervert** your heart
after their *gods* **elohim**:
Solomon clave **Shelomoh adhered** unto these in love.
3 And he had seven hundred *wives* **women**,
princesses **governesses**, and three hundred concubines:
and his *wives turned away* **women perverted** his heart.
4 For it *came to pass* **became**,
when Solomon **the time Shelomoh** was **of** old **age**,
that his *wives turned away* **women perverted** his heart
after other *gods* **elohim**:
and his heart was not *perfect* **at shalom**
with *the LORD* **Yah Veh** his *God* **Elohim**,
as was the heart of David his father.
5 For *Solomon* **Shelomoh** went after Ashtoreth
the *goddess* **elohim** of the *Zidonians* **Sidoniy**,
and after *Milcom* **Milchom**
the abomination of the *Ammonites* **Ammoniy**.
6 And *Solomon did* **Shelomoh worked** evil
in the *sight* **eyes** of *the LORD* **Yah Veh**,

and *went* **fulfilled** not *fully* after *the LORD* **Yah Veh**,
as did David his father.
7 Then did *Solomon* **Shelomoh**
build *an high place* **a bamah** for *Chemosh* **Kemosh**,
the abomination of Moab,
in the *hill* **mountain**
that is before Jerusalem **at the face of Yeru Shalem**,
and for Molech,
the abomination of the *children* **sons** of Ammon.
8 And likewise
did **worked** he for all his strange *wives* **women**,
which *burnt incense* **incensed** and sacrificed
unto their *gods* **elohim**.
9 And *the LORD* **Yah Veh**
was angry with *Solomon* **Shelomoh**,
because his heart was *turned* **extended**
from *the LORD God* **Yah Veh Elohim** of *Israel* **Yisra El**,
which *had appeared unto* **was seen by** him
twice **two times**,
10 And had *commanded* **misvahed** him
concerning this *thing* **word**,
that he should not go after other *gods* **elohim**:
but he *kept* **guarded** not
that which *the LORD commanded* **Yah Veh misvahed**.
11 Wherefore
the LORD **Yah Veh** said unto *Solomon* **Shelomoh**,
Forasmuch as this is done of thee,
and thou hast not *kept* **guarded**
my covenant and my statutes,
which I have *commanded* **misvahed** thee,
in ripping, I *will surely rend* **shall rip**
the *kingdom* **sovereigndom** from thee,
and *will* **shall** give it to thy servant.
12 Notwithstanding
in thy days I *will* **shall** not *do* **work** it
for David thy father's sake:
but I *will rend* **shall rip** it out of the hand of thy son.
13 *Howbeit* **Only**
I *will* **shall** not *rend* **rip** away
all the *kingdom* **sovereigndom**;
but *will* **shall** give one *tribe* **scion** to thy son
for David my servant's sake,
and for *Jerusalem's* **Yeru Shalem's** sake
which I have chosen.

A SATAN RAISED UNTO SHELOMOH

14 And *the LORD* **Yah Veh**
stirred up an adversary **raised a satan**
unto *Solomon* **Shelomoh**,
Hadad the *Edomite* **Edomiy**:
he was of the *king's* **sovereign's** seed in Edom.
15 For it *came to pass* **became**, when David was in Edom,
and *Joab* **Yah Ab** the *captain* **governor** of the host
was gone up **ascended** to *bury* **entomb** the *slain* **pierced**,
after he had smitten every male in Edom;
16 (For six months did *Joab remain* **Yah Ab settle** there
with all *Israel* **Yisra El**,
until he had cut off every male in Edom:)
17 That Hadad fled,
he and *certain Edomites* **men — Edomiy**
of his father's servants with him,
to go into *Egypt* **Misrayim**;
Hadad *being* yet a little *child* **lad**.
18 And they arose out of *Midian* **Midyaniy**,
and came to Paran:
and they took men with them out of Paran,
and they came to *Egypt* **Misrayim**,
unto Pharaoh *king* **sovereign** of *Egypt* **Misrayim**;
which gave him an house,
and *appointed* **said for** him *victuals* **bread**,
and gave him land.
19 And Hadad found *great favour* **mighty charism**
in the *sight* **eyes** of *Pharaoh* **Paroh**,
so that he gave him to *wife* **woman**
the sister of his own *wife* **woman**,
the sister of *Tahpenes* **Tachpenes** the *queen* **lady**.
20 And the sister of *Tahpenes* **Tachpenes**
bare him Genubath his son,
whom *Tahpenes* **Tachpenes** weaned
in Pharaoh's **midst Paroh's** house:
and Genubath was in *Pharaoh's* **Paroh's** household
among the sons of *Pharaoh* **Paroh**.
21 And when Hadad heard in *Egypt* **Misrayim**
that David *slept* **laid** with his fathers,
and that *Joab* **Yah Ab** the captain of the host
was dead **died**,
Hadad said to *Pharaoh* **Paroh**,
Let me depart **Send me away**,
that I may go to mine own *country* **land**.
22 Then *Pharaoh* **Paroh** said unto him,
But what hast thou lacked with me, that, behold,
thou seekest to go to thine own *country* **land**?
And he *answered* **said**, *Nothing* **Naught**:
howbeit
let me go in any wise **in sending away, send me away**.
23 And *God* **Elohim**
stirred **raised** him up *another adversary* **a satan**,
Rezon the son of *Eliadah* **Eli Ada**,
which fled from his *lord Hadadezer* **adoni Hadad Ezer**
king **sovereign** of *Zobah* **Sobah**:
24 And he gathered men unto him,
and became *captain* **governor** over a *band* **troop**,
when David *slew* **slaughtered** them *of Zobah*:
and they went to *Damascus* **Dammeseq**,
and *dwelt* **settled** *therein*,
and reigned in *Damascus* **Dammeseq**.
25 And he was *an adversary* **a satan** to *Israel* **Yisra El**
all the days of *Solomon* **Shelomoh**,
beside the *mischief* **evil** that Hadad did:
and he abhorred *Israel* **Yisra El**,
and reigned over *Syria* **Aram**.

YAROB AM REBELS AGAINST SHELOMOH

26 And *Jeroboam* **Yarob Am** the son of Nebat,
an *Ephrathite* **Ephrathiy** of *Zereda* **Seredah**,
Solomon's **Shelomoh's** servant,
whose mother's name was *Zeruah* **Seruah**,
a widow woman,
even he lifted up *his* **a** hand against the *king* **sovereign**.
27 And this was the *cause* **word**
that he lifted up *his* **a** hand against the *king* **sovereign**:
Solomon **Shelomoh** built Millo,
and *repaired* **shut** the breaches
of the city of David his father.
28 And the man *Jeroboam* **Yarob Am**
was *a* mighty *man* of valour:
and *Solomon* **Shelomoh**
seeing the *young man* **lad** that he *was industrious* **worked**,
he made him *ruler* **overseer**
over all the *charge* **burden** of the house of *Joseph* **Yoseph**.
29 And it *came to pass* **became** at that time
when *Jeroboam* **Yarob Am**
went out of *Jerusalem* **Yeru Shalem**,
that the prophet *Ahijah* **Achiy Yah** the *Shilonite* **Shilohiy**
found him in the way;
and he *had clad* **covered** himself
with *a* new *garment* **clothes**;
and they two were alone in the field:
30 And *Ahijah* **Achiy Yah**
caught **manipulated** the new *garment* **clothes**
that was on him,
and *rent* **shreaded** it in twelve *pieces* **shreads**:
31 And he said to *Jeroboam* **Yarob Am**,
Take thee ten *pieces* **shreads**:
for thus saith *the LORD* **Yah Veh**,
the *God* **Elohim** of *Israel* **Yisra El**, Behold,
I *will rend* **shall shread** the *kingdom* **sovereigndom**
out of the hand of *Solomon* **Shelomoh**,
and *will* **shall** give ten *tribes* **scions** to thee:
32 (But he shall have one *tribe* **scion**
for my servant David's sake,
and for *Jerusalem's* **Yeru Shalem's** sake,
the city which I have chosen
out of all the *tribes* **scions** of *Israel* **Yisra El**:)
33 Because that they have forsaken me,
and have *worshipped* **prostrated to** Ashtoreth
the *goddess* **elohim** of the *Zidonians* **Sidoniy**,
Chemosh **Kemosh**
the *god* **elohim** of the *Moabites* **Moabiy**,
and *Milcom* **Milchom**
the *god* **elohim** of the *children* **sons** of Ammon,
and have not walked in my ways,

to *do* **work** that which is *right* **straight** in mine eyes,
and *to keep* **in** my statutes and **in** my judgments,
as did David his father.
34 Howbeit
I *will* **shall** not take the whole *kingdom* **sovereigndom**
out of his hand:
but I *will make* **shall set** him
prince **hierarch** all the days of his life
for David my servant's sake, whom I chose,
because he *kept* **guarded**
my *commandments* **misvoth** and my statutes:
35 But I *will* **shall** take the *kingdom* **sovereigndom**
out of his son's hand,
and *will* **shall** give it unto thee, *even* ten *tribes* **scions**.
36 And unto his son *will* **shall** I give one *tribe* **scion**,
that David my servant
may have a *light alway* **lamp all days**
before me **at my face** in *Jerusalem* **Yeru Shalem**,
the city which I have chosen me to *put* **set** my name there.
37 And I *will* **shall** take thee,
and thou shalt reign according to all that thy soul desireth,
and shalt be *king* **sovereign** over *Israel* **Yisra El**.
38 And it shall be,
if thou *wilt* **shalt** hearken unto all
that I *command* **misvah** thee,
and *wilt* **shalt** walk in my ways,
and *do* **work** that is *right* **straight** in my *sight* **eyes**,
to *keep* **guard**
my statutes and my *commandments* **misvoth**,
as David my servant *did* **worked**;
that I *will* **shall** be with thee,
and build thee a *sure* **trustworthy** house,
as I built for David,
and *will* **shall** give *Israel* **Yisra El** unto thee.
39 And I *will* **shall** for this *afflict* **humble** the seed of David,
but not *for ever* **all days**.
40 *Solomon* **Shelomoh** sought therefore
to *kill Jeroboam* **deathify Yarob Am**.
And *Jeroboam* **Yarob Am** arose,
and fled into *Egypt* **Misrayim**,
unto Shishak *king* **sovereign** of *Egypt* **Misrayim**,
and was in *Egypt* **Misrayim**
until the death of *Solomon* **Shelomoh**.
41 And the rest of the *acts* **words** of *Solomon* **Shelomoh**,
and all that he *did* **worked**, and his wisdom,
are they not *written* **inscribed** in the *book* **scroll**
of the *acts* **words** of *Solomon* **Shelomoh**?
42 And the *time* **days** that *Solomon* **Shelomoh** reigned
in *Jerusalem* **Yeru Shalem** over all *Israel* **Yisra El**
was forty years.
43 And *Solomon slept* **Shelomoh laid** with his fathers,
and was *buried* **entombed** in the city of David his father:
and *Rehoboam* **Rechab Am** his son reigned in his stead.

YISRA EL REBELS AGAINST RECHAB AM

12 And *Rehoboam* **Rechab Am**
went to Shechem:
for all *Israel* **Yisra El** were come to Shechem
to *make* **have** him *king* **reign**.
2 And it *came to pass* **became**,
when *Jeroboam* **Yarob Am** the son of Nebat,
who was yet in *Egypt* **Misrayim**, heard of it,
(for he was fled from the *presence* **face**
of *king Solomon* **sovereign Shelomoh**,
and *Jeroboam dwelt* **Yarob Am settled** in *Egypt* **Misrayim**;)
3 That they sent and called him.
And *Jeroboam* **Yarob Am**
and all the congregation of *Israel* **Yisra El** came,
and *spake* **worded** unto *Rehoboam* **Rechab Am**, saying,
4 Thy father *made* **hardened** our yoke *grievous*:
now therefore *make* **hardenen** thou
the *grievous* service of thy father,
and his heavy yoke which he *put* **gave** upon us, *lighter*,
and we *will* **shall** serve thee.
5 And he said unto them, *Depart* **Go** yet for three days,
then *come again* **return** to me.
And the people *departed* **went**.
6 And *king Rehoboam* **sovereign Rechab Am**
consulted **counselled** with the old men,
that stood *before Solomon* **at the face of Shelomoh**
his father while he yet lived, *and said* **saying**,
How do ye *advise* **counsel**
that I may *answer* **return word to** this people?
7 And they *spake* **worded** unto him, saying,
If thou *wilt* **shalt** be a servant unto this people this day,
and *wilt* **shalt** serve them, and answer them,
and *speak* **word** good words to them,
then they *will* **shall** be thy servants *for ever* **all days**.
8 But he forsook the counsel of the old men,
which they had *given* **counselled** him,
and *consulted* **counselled** with the *young men* **children**
that were grown up with him,
and which stood *before him* **at his face**:
9 And he said unto them, What counsel give ye
that we may *answer* **return word** to this people,
who have *spoken* **worded** to me, saying,
Make **Swiften** the yoke
which thy father *did put* **gave** upon us *lighter*?
10 And the *young men* **children**
that were grown up with him *spake* **worded** unto him,
saying, Thus shalt thou *speak* **say** unto this people
that *spake* **worded** unto thee, saying,
Thy father made our yoke heavy,
but *make* **swiften** thou it *lighter* unto us;
thus shalt thou *say* **word** unto them,
My *little finger* **pinky** shall be thicker
than my father's loins.
11 And now whereas my father
did lade you with a heavy yoke,
I *will* **shall** add to your yoke:
my father hath *chastised* **disciplined** you with whips,
but I *will chastise* **shall discipline** you with scorpions.
12 So *Jeroboam* **Yarob Am** and all the people
came to *Rehoboam* **Rechab Am** the third day,
as the *king* **sovereign** had *appointed* **worded**, saying,
Come **Return** to me *again* the third day.
13 And the *king* **sovereign**
answered the people *roughly* **hard**,
and forsook the old men's counsel
that they *gave* **counselled** him;
14 And *spake* **worded** to them
after the counsel of the *young men* **children**, saying,
My father made your yoke heavy,
and I *will* **shall** add to your yoke:
my father *also chastised* **disciplined** you with whips,
but I *will chastise* **shall discipline** you with scorpions.
15 Wherefore
the *king* **sovereign** hearkened not unto the people;
for the *cause* **turn** was from *the LORD* **Yah Veh**,
that he might *perform* **raise** his *saying* **word**,
which *the LORD spake* **Yah Veh worded**
by *Ahijah* **the hand of Achiy Yah** the *Shilonite* **Shilohiy**
unto *Jeroboam* **Yarob Am** the son of Nebat.

THE SOVEREIGNDOM DIVIDED

16 So when all *Israel* **Yisra El** saw
that the *king* **sovereign** hearkened not unto them,
the people *answered* **returned word to** the *king* **sovereign**,
saying, What *portion* **allotment** have we in David?
neither have we inheritance in the son of *Jesse* **Yishay**:
to your tents, O *Israel* **Yisra El**:
now see to thine own house, David.
So *Israel departed* **Yisra El went** unto their tents.
17 But as for the *children* **sons** of *Israel* **Yisra El**
which *dwelt* **settled** in the cities of *Judah* **Yah Hudah**,
Rehoboam **Rechab Am** reigned over them.
18 Then *king Rehoboam* **sovereign Rechab Am**
sent *Adoram* **Adoni Ram**,
who was over the *tribute* **vassal**;
and all *Israel* **Yisra El** stoned him with stones, that he died.
Therefore *king Rehoboam* **sovereign Rechab Am**
made speed **strengthened himself**
to *get him up* **ascend** to his chariot,
to flee to *Jerusalem* **Yeru Shalem**.
19 So *Israel* **Yisra El**
rebelled against the house of David unto this day.
20 And it *came to pass* **became**, when all *Israel* **Yisra El** heard
that *Jeroboam was come again* **Yarob Am had returned**,
that they sent and called him
unto the *congregation* **witness**,
and *made* **had** him *king* **reign** over all *Israel* **Yisra El**:
there was none *that followed* **after** the house of David,

but **except** the *tribe* **scion** of *Judah* **Yah Hudah** only.
21 And when *Rehoboam* **Rechab Am**
was come to *Jerusalem* **Yeru Shalem**,
he *assembled* **congregated**
all the house of *Judah* **Yah Hudah**,
with the *tribe* **scion** of *Benjamin* **Ben Yamin**,
an hundred and *fourscore* **eighty** thousand chosen men,
which *were warriors* **worked war**,
to fight against the house of *Israel* **Yisra El**,
to *bring* **return** the *kingdom* **sovereigndom** *again*
to *Rehoboam* **Rechab Am** the son of *Solomon* **Shelomoh**.
22 But the word of *God* **Elohim**
came unto *Shemaiah* **Shema Yah** the man of *God* **Elohim**,
saying,
23 *Speak* **Say** unto *Rehoboam* **Rechab Am**,
the son of *Solomon* **Shelomoh**,
king **sovereign** of *Judah* **Yah Hudah**,
and unto all the house
of *Judah* **Yah Hudah** and *Benjamin* **Ben Yamin**,
and to the remnant of the people, saying,
24 Thus saith *the LORD* **Yah Veh**,
Ye shall not *go up* **ascend**, nor fight
against your brethren the *children* **sons** of *Israel* **Yisra El**:
return every man to his house;
for this *thing* **word** is from me.
They hearkened therefore to the word of *the LORD* **Yah Veh**,
and returned to *depart* **go**,
according to the word of *the LORD* **Yah Veh**.

YAROB AM'S ALTAR OF SACRIFICE

25 Then *Jeroboam* **Yarob Am**
built Shechem in mount *Ephraim* **Ephrayim**,
and *dwelt* **settled** therein;
and went out from thence, and built *Penuel* **Penu El**.
26 And *Jeroboam* **Yarob Am** said in his heart,
Now shall the *kingdom* **sovereigndom** return
to the house of David:
27 If this people *go up* **ascend** to *do* **work** sacrifice
in the house of *the LORD* **Yah Veh**
at *Jerusalem* **Yeru Shalem**,
then shall the heart of this people
turn again **return** unto their *lord* **adoni**,
even unto *Rehoboam* **Rechab Am**,
king **sovereign** of *Judah* **Yah Hudah**,
and they shall *kill* **slaughter** me,
and *go again* **return** to *Rehoboam* **Rechab Am**,
king **sovereign** of *Judah* **Yah Hudah**.
28 Whereupon the *king* **sovereign** took counsel,
and *made* **worked** two calves of gold, and said unto them,
It is too much for you
to *go up* **ascend** to *Jerusalem* **Yeru Shalem**:
behold thy *gods* **Elohim**, O *Israel* **Yisra El**,
which *brought* **ascended** thee *up*
out of the land of *Egypt* **Misrayim**.
29 And he set the one in *Bethel* **Beth El**,
and the *other put* **one gave** he in Dan.
30 And this *thing* **word** became a sin:
for the people went
to worship before **at the face of** the one, *even* unto Dan.
31 And he *made* **worked** an house of *high places* **bamahs**,
and *made* **worked** priests of the *lowest* **end** of the people,
which were not of the sons of Levi.
32 And *Jeroboam* **Yarob Am**
ordained **worked** a *feast* **celebration**
in the eighth month, on the fifteenth day of the month,
like unto the *feast* **celebration** that is in *Judah* **Yah Hudah**,
and he *offered* **holocausted** upon the **sacrifice** altar.
So *did* **worked** he in *Bethel* **Beth El**,
sacrificing unto the calves that he had *made* **worked**:
and he *placed* **stood** in *Bethel* **Beth El**
the priests of the *high places* **bamahs**
which he had *made* **worked**.
33 So he *offered* **holocausted** upon the **sacrifice** altar
which he had *made* **worked** in *Bethel* **Beth El**
the fifteenth day of the eighth month,
even in the month
which he had *devised* **contrived** of his own heart;
and *ordained* **worked** a *feast* **celebration**
unto the *children* **sons** of *Israel* **Yisra El**:
and he *offered* **holocausted** upon the **sacrifice** altar,
and *burnt incense* **incensed**.

THE MAN OF ELOHIM WITH THE WORD OF YAH VEH

13 And, behold,
there came a man of *God* **Elohim** out of *Judah* **Yah Hudah**
by the word of *the LORD* **Yah Veh** unto *Bethel* **Beth El**:
and *Jeroboam* **Yarob Am** stood by the **sacrifice** altar
to *burn* incense.
2 And he *cried* **called out** against the **sacrifice** altar
in the word of *the LORD* **Yah Veh**, and said,
O **sacrifice** altar, **sacrifice** altar,
thus saith *the LORD* **Yah Veh**; Behold,
a *child* **son** shall be born unto the house of David,
Josiah **Yoshi Yah** by name;
and upon thee shall he *offer* **sacrifice**
the priests of the *high places* **bamahs**
that *burn* incense upon thee,
and *men's* **human** bones shall be burnt upon thee.
3 And he gave *a sign* **an omen** the same day, saying,
This is the *sign* **omen**
which *the LORD* **Yah Veh** hath *spoken* **worded**;
Behold, the **sacrifice** altar shall be *rent* **ripped**,
and the *ashes that are* **fat** upon it shall be poured out.
4 And it *came to pass* **became**,
when *king Jeroboam* **sovereign Yarob Am**
heard the *saying* **word** of the man of *God* **Elohim**,
which *had cried* **called out**
against the **sacrifice** altar in *Bethel* **Beth El**,
that he *put* **sent** forth his hand from the **sacrifice** altar,
saying, *Lay hold on* **Apprehend** him.
And his hand, which he *put* **sent** forth against him,
dried up **withered**,
so that he could not *pull it in again* **turn it back** to him.
5 The **sacrifice** altar also was *rent* **ripped**,
and the *ashes* **fat** poured out from the **sacrifice** altar,
according to the *sign* **omen**
which the man of *God* **Elohim** had given
by the word of *the LORD* **Yah Veh**.
6 And the *king* **sovereign** answered
and said unto the man of *God* **Elohim**,
Intreat **Stroke** now
the face of *the LORD* **Yah Veh** thy *God* **Elohim**,
and pray for me, that my hand may be restored me *again*.
And the man of *God* **Elohim**
besought the LORD **stroked the face of Yah Veh**,
and the *king's* **sovereign's** hand was restored him *again*,
and became as *it was before* **formerly**.
7 And the *king* **sovereign**
said **worded** unto the man of *God* **Elohim**,
Come home with me, and *refresh* **support** thyself,
and I *will* **shall** give thee a *reward* **gift**.
8 And the man of *God* **Elohim**
said unto the *king* **sovereign**,
If thou *wilt* **shalt** give me half thine house,
I *will* **shall** not go in with thee,
neither *will* **shall** I eat bread nor drink water in this place:
9 For so was it *charged* **misvahed** me
by the word of *the LORD* **Yah Veh**, saying,
Eat no bread, nor drink water,
nor *turn again* **return** by the same way that thou camest.
10 So he went another way, and returned not
by the way that he came to *Bethel* **Beth El**.

THE DISOBEDIENT PROPHET

11 Now there *dwelt an* **settled one** old prophet
in *Bethel* **Beth El**;
and his *sons* **son** came and *told* **scribed** him all the works
that the man of *God* **Elohim**
had *done* **worked** that day in *Bethel* **Beth El**:
the words which he had *spoken* **worded**
unto the *king* **sovereign**,
them they *told* **scribed** also to their father.
12 And their father *said* **worded** unto them,
What way went he?
For his sons had seen
what way the man of *God* **Elohim** went,
which came from *Judah* **Yah Hudah**.
13 And he said unto his sons,
Saddle me the ass **Harness my he burro**.
So they *saddled him the ass* **harnessed his he burro**:
and he rode thereon,
14 And went after the man of *God* **Elohim**,
and found him *sitting* **settled** under an oak:

and he said unto him,
Art thou the man of *God* **Elohim**
that camest from *Judah* **Yah Hudah**?
And he said, I *am*.
15 Then he said unto him,
Come home with me, and eat bread.
16 And he said, I may not return with thee,
nor go in with thee:
neither *will* **shall** I eat bread nor drink water with thee
in this place:
17 For it was *said* **worded** to me
by the word of *the LORD* **Yah Veh**,
Thou shalt eat no bread nor drink water there,
nor *turn again* **return** to go by the way that thou camest.
18 He said unto him, I am a prophet also as thou *art*;
and an angel *spake* **worded** unto me
by the word of *the LORD* **Yah Veh**, saying,
Bring **Return** him *back* with thee into thine house,
that he may eat bread and drink water.
But he *lied unto* **had deceived** him.
19 So he *went back* **returned** with him,
and did eat bread in his house, and drank water.
20 And it *came to pass* **became**,
as they *sat* **settled** at the table,
that the word of *the LORD* **Yah Veh**
came unto the prophet
that *brought him back* **returned him**:
21 And he *cried* **called out** unto the man of *God* **Elohim**
that came from *Judah* **Yah Hudah**, saying,
Thus saith *the LORD* **Yah Veh**,
Forasmuch **Because** as thou hast *disobeyed* **rebelled**
the mouth of *the LORD* **Yah Veh**,
and hast not *kept* **guarded** the *commandment* **misvah**
which *the LORD* **Yah Veh** thy *God* **Elohim**
commanded **misvahed** thee,
22 But *camest back* **returnest**,
and hast eaten bread and drunk water in the place,
of the which *the LORD did say* **he worded** to thee,
Eat no bread, and drink no water;
thy carcase shall not come
unto the *sepulchre* **tomb** of thy fathers.
23 And it *came to pass* **became**,
after he had eaten bread, and after he had drunk,
that he *saddled for him the ass* **harnessed his he burro**,
to wit,
for the prophet whom he had *brought back* **returned**.
24 And when he was gone,
a lion *met* **found** him by the way,
and *slew* **deathified** him:
and his carcase was cast in the way,
and the *ass* **he burro** stood *by* **beside** it,
the lion also stood *by* **beside** the carcase.
25 And, behold, men passed by,
and saw the carcase cast in the way,
and the lion standing *by* **beside** the carcase:
and they came and *told* **worded** it
in the city where the old prophet *dwelt* **settled**.
26 And when the prophet
that *brought* **returned** him *back* from the way
heard thereof,
he said, It is the man of *God* **Elohim**,
who *was disobedient* **rebelled**
unto the *word* **mouth** of *the LORD* **Yah Veh**:
therefore *the LORD* **Yah Veh**
hath *delivered* **given** him unto the lion,
which hath *torn* **broken** him, and *slain* **deathifed** him,
according to the word of *the LORD* **Yah Veh**,
which he *spake* **worded** unto him.
27 And he *spake* **worded** to his sons, saying,
Saddle me the ass **Harness my he burro**.
And they *saddled* **harnessed** *him*.
28 And he went and found his carcase cast in the way,
and the *ass* **he burro** and the lion
standing *by* **beside** the carcase:
the lion had not eaten the carcase,
nor *torn* **broken** the *ass* **he burro**.
29 And the prophet *took up* **lifted** the carcase
of the man of *God* **Elohim**,
and *laid* **set** it upon the *ass* **he burro**,
and *brought* **returned** it *back*:
and the old prophet came to the city,
to *mourn* **chop** and to *bury* **entomb** him.
30 And he *laid* **set** his carcase in his own *grave* **tomb**;
and they *mourned* **chopped** over him,
saying, *Alas* **Ho**, my brother!
31 And it *came to pass* **became**,
after he had *buried* **entombed** him,
that he *spake* **said** to his sons, saying,
When I *am dead* **die**,
then *bury* **entomb** me in the *sepulchre* **tomb**
wherein the man of *God* **Elohim** is *buried* **entombed**;
lay **set** my bones beside his bones:
32 For the *saying* **word** which he *cried* **called out**
by the word of *the LORD* **Yah Veh**
against the **sacrifice** altar in *Bethel* **Beth El**,
and against all the houses of the *high places* **bamahs**
which are in the cities of *Samaria* **Shomeron**,
shall surely *come to pass* **become**.
33 After this *thing* **word**
Jeroboam **Yarob Am** returned not from his evil way,
but *made again* **returned and worked**
of the *lowest* **end** of the people
priests of the *high places* **bamahs**:
whosoever *would* **delighted**,
he *consecrated him* **filled his hand**,
and he became *one* of the priests
of the *high places* **bamahs**.
34 And this *thing* **word** became sin
unto the house of *Jeroboam* **Yarob Am**, even to cut it off,
and to *destroy* **desolate** it
from off the face of the *earth* **soil**.

ACHIY YAH'S PROPHECY AGAINST YAROB AM

14 At that time
Abijah **Abi Yah** the son of *Jeroboam* **Yarob Am** fell sick.
2 And *Jeroboam* **Yarob Am** said to his *wife* **woman**,
Arise, I *pray* **beseech** thee, and *disguise* **alter** thyself,
that *thou be not known* **they not know thee**
to be the *wife* **woman** of *Jeroboam* **Yarob Am**;
and *get thee* **go** to Shiloh:
behold, there is *Ahijah* **Achiy Yah** the prophet,
which *told* **worded** me
that I should be *king* **sovereign** over this people.
3 And take *with thee* **in thine hand** ten *loaves* **bread**,
and *cracknels* **crumbs**, and a cruse bottle of honey,
and go to him:
he shall tell thee what shall become of the *child* **lad**.
4 And *Jeroboam's wife* **Yarob Am's woman**
did **worked** so and arose, and went to Shiloh,
and came to the house of *Ahijah* **Achiy Yah**.
But *Ahijah* **Achiy Yah** could not see;
for his eyes *were set* **arose** by reason of his *age* **grayness**.
5 And *the LORD* **Yah Veh** said unto *Ahijah* **Achiy Yah**,
Behold, the *wife* **woman** of *Jeroboam* **Yarob Am** cometh
to *ask* **enquire** a *thing* **word** of thee for her son;
for he is sick:
thus and thus shalt thou *say* **word** unto her:
for it shall be, when she cometh in,
that she shall *feign* **estrange** herself to be another *woman*.
6 And it *was so* **became**,
when *Ahijah* **Achiy Yah** heard the *sound* **voice** of her feet,
as she came in at the *door* **portal**, that he said,
Come in, thou *wife* **woman** of *Jeroboam* **Yarob Am**;
why *feignest* **estrangest** thou thyself to be another?
for I am sent to thee with *heavy tidings* **hardness**.
7 Go, *tell Jeroboam* **say to Yarob Am**,
Thus saith
the LORD God **Yah Veh Elohim** of *Israel* **Yisra El**,
Forasmuch as **Because** I exalted thee
from among the people,
and *made* **gave** thee *prince* **eminence**
over my people *Israel* **Yisra El**,
8 And *rent* **ripped** the *kingdom* **sovereigndom**
away from the house of David, and gave it thee:
and *yet* thou hast not been as my servant David,
who *kept* **guarded** my *commandments* **misvoth**,
and who *followed* **went after** me with all his heart,
to *do* **work** that only
which was *right* **straight** in mine eyes;
9 But hast *done evil* **vilified to work**
above all that were *before thee* **at thy face**:

for thou hast gone and *made* **worked** thee
other *gods* **elohim**, and molten *images*,
to *provoke* **vex** me *to anger*,
and hast cast me behind thy back:
10 Therefore, behold,
I *will* **shall** bring evil
upon the house of *Jeroboam* **Yarob Am**,
and *will* **shall** cut off from *Jeroboam* **Yarob Am**
him that *pisseth* **urinateth** against the wall,
and him that is *shut up* **restrained**
and left in *Israel* **Yisra El**,
and *will take* **shall burn** away the *remnant* **posterity**
of the house of *Jeroboam* **Yarob Am**,
as a man *taketh* **burneth** away dung **balls**,
till it be *all gone* **consumed**.
11 Him that dieth of *Jeroboam* **Yarob Am** in the city
shall the dogs *eat* **devour**;
and him that dieth in the field
shall the *fowls* **flyers** of the *air eat* **heavens devour**:
for *the LORD* **Yah Veh** hath *spoken* **worded** it.
12 Arise thou therefore, *get thee* **go** to thine own house:
and when thy feet enter into the city, the child shall die.
13 And all *Israel* **Yisra El** shall *mourn for* **chop over** him,
and *bury* **entomb** him:
for he only of *Jeroboam* **Yarob Am**
shall come to the *grave* **tomb**,
because in him there is found *some* **a** good *thing* **word**
toward *the LORD God* **Yah Veh Elohim** of *Israel* **Yisra El**
in the house of *Jeroboam* **Yarob Am**.
14 Moreover *the LORD* **Yah Veh**
shall raise him *up* a *king* **sovereign** over *Israel* **Yisra El**,
who shall cut off the house of *Jeroboam* **Yarob Am**
that day:
but what? even now.
15 For *the LORD* **Yah Veh** shall smite *Israel* **Yisra El**,
as a *reed is shaken* **stalk wags** in the water,
and he shall *root up Israel* **uproot Yisra El**
out of this good *land* **soil**,
which he gave to their fathers,
and shall scatter them beyond the river,
because they have *made* **worked** their *groves* **asherim**,
provoking the LORD to anger **vexing Yah Veh**.
16 And he shall give *Israel* **Yisra El** up
because of the sins of *Jeroboam* **Yarob Am**,
who did sin, and who made *Israel* **Yisra El** to sin.
17 And *Jeroboam's wife* **Yarob Am's woman** arose,
and *departed* **went**, and came to *Tirzah* **Tirsah**:
and when she came to the threshold of the *door* **house**,
the *child* **lad** died;
18 And they *buried* **entombed** him;
and all *Israel mourned for* **Yisra El chopped over** him,
according to the word of *the LORD* **Yah Veh**,
which he *spake* **worded** by the hand of his servant
Ahijah **Achiy Yah** the prophet.
19 And the rest of the *acts* **words** of *Jeroboam* **Yarob Am**,
how he *warred* **fought**, and how he reigned, behold,
they are *written* **inscribed** in the *book* **scroll**
of the *chronicles* **words of the days**
of the *kings* **sovereigns** of *Israel* **Yisra El**.
20 And the days which *Jeroboam* **Yarob Am** reigned
were two and twenty years:
and he *slept* **laid** with his fathers,
and Nadab his son reigned in his stead.

THE REIGN OF RECHAB AM OVER YAH HUDAH

21 And *Rehoboam* **Rechab Am**
the son of *Solomon* **Shelomoh**
reigned in *Judah* **Yah Hudah**.
Rehoboam **Rechab Am**
was **a son of** forty and one years *old*
when he began to reign,
and he reigned seventeen years in *Jerusalem* **Yeru Shalem**,
the city which *the LORD* **Yah Veh** did choose
out of all the *tribes* **scions** of *Israel* **Yisra El**,
to *put* **set** his name there.
And his mother's name was Naamah
an *Ammonitess* **Ammoniyth**.
22 And *Judah did* **Yah Hudah worked** evil
in the *sight* **eyes** of *the LORD* **Yah Veh**,
and they *provoked* **caused** him to *jealousy* **be jealous**
with their sins which they had *committed* **sinned**,
above all that their fathers had *done* **worked**.
23 For they also built them *high places* **bamahs**,
and *images* **monoliths**, and *groves* **asherim**,
on every high hill, and under every green tree.
24 And there were also
sodomites **hallowed whoremongers** in the land:
and they *did* **worked** according
to all the *abominations* **abhorrences** of the *nations* **goyim**
which *the LORD cast out* **Yah Veh dispossessed**
before **at the face of** the *children* **sons** of *Israel* **Yisra El**.
25 And it *came to pass* **became**,
in the fifth year of *king Rehoboam* **sovereign Rechab Am**,
that Shishak *king* **sovereign** of *Egypt* **Misrayim**
came up **ascended** against *Jerusalem* **Yeru Shalem**:
26 And he took away the treasures
of the house of *the LORD* **Yah Veh**,
and the treasures of the *king's* **sovereign's** house;
he even took away all:
and he took away all the *shields* **bucklers** of gold
which *Solomon* **Shelomoh** had *made* **worked**.
27 And *king Rehoboam* **sovereign Rechab Am**
made **worked** in their stead
brasen shields **copper bucklers**,
and *committed* **oversaw** *them*
unto the hands of the *chief* **governor** of the *guard* **runners**,
which *kept* **guarded** the *door* **portal**
of the *king's* **sovereign's** house.
28 And it *was so* **became**, when the *king* **sovereign**
went into the house of *the LORD* **Yah Veh**,
that the *guard* **runners** bare them,
and *brought* **turned** them back
into the *guard* **runners** chamber.
29 Now the rest of the *acts* **words**
of *Rehoboam* **Rechab Am**,
and all that he *did* **worked**,
are they not *written* **inscribed** in the *book* **scroll**
of the *chronicles* **words of the days**
of the *kings* **sovereigns** of *Judah* **Yah Hudah**?
30 And there was war
between *Rehoboam* **Rechab Am** and *Jeroboam* **Yarob Am**
all *their* days.
31 And *Rehoboam* **Rechab Am**
slept **laid** with his fathers,
and was *buried* **entombed** with his fathers
in the city of David.
And his mother's name was Naamah
an *Ammonitess* **Ammoniyth**.
And *Abijam* **Abi Yam** his son reigned in his stead.

THE REIGN OF ABI YAM OVER YAH HUDAH

15 Now in the eighteenth year
of *king Jeroboam* **sovereign Yarob Am** the son of Nebat
reigned *Abijam* **Abi Yam** over *Judah* **Yah Hudah**.
2 Three years reigned he in *Jerusalem* **Yeru Shalem**.
and his mother's name was Maachah,
the daughter of *Abishalom* **Abi Shalom**.
3 And he walked in all the sins of his father,
which he had *done before him* **worked at his face**:
and his heart was not *perfect* **at shalom**
with *the LORD* **Yah Veh** his *God* **Elohim**,
as the heart of David his father.
4 Nevertheless for David's sake
did the LORD **Yah Veh** his *God* **Elohim**
give **gave** him a lamp in *Jerusalem* **Yeru Shalem**,
to *set up* **raise** his son after him,
and to *establish Jerusalem* **station Yeru Shalem**:
5 Because David *did* **worked** that which was *right* **straight**
in the eyes of *the LORD* **Yah Veh**,
and turned not aside from *any thing* **all**
that he *commanded* **misvahed** him all the days of his life,
save only
in the *matter* **word** of *Uriah* **Uri Yah** the *Hittite* **Hethiy**.
6 And there was war
between *Rehoboam* **Rechab Am** and *Jeroboam* **Yarob Am**
all the days of his life.
7 Now the rest of the *acts* **words** of *Abijam* **Abi Yam**,
and all that he *did* **worked**,
are they not *written* **inscribed** in the *book* **scroll**
of the *chronicles* **words of the days**
of the *kings* **sovereigns** of *Judah* **Yah Hudah**?
And there was war

between *Abijam* **Abi Yam** and *Jeroboam* **Yarob Am**.
8 And *Abijam slept* **Abi Yam laid** with his fathers;
and they *buried* **entombed** him in the city of David:
and Asa his son reigned in his stead.

THE REIGN OF ASA OVER YAH HUDAH

9 And in the twentieth year of *Jeroboam* **Yarob Am**,
king **sovereign** of *Israel* **Yisra El**
reigned Asa over *Judah* **Yah Hudah**.
10 And forty and one years reigned he
in *Jerusalem* **Yeru Shalem**.
And his mother's name was Maachah,
the daughter of *Abishalom* **Abi Shalom**.
11 And Asa *did* **worked** that which was *right* **straight**
in the eyes of *the LORD* **Yah Veh**, as *did* David his father.
12 And he *took* **passed** *away*
the *sodomites* **hallowed whoremongers** out of the land,
and *removed* **turned aside** all the idols
that his fathers had *made* **worked**.
13 And also Maachah his mother,
even her he *removed* **turned aside** from being *queen* **lady**,
because she had *made* **worked** an idol **of awe**
in *a grove* **an asherah**;
and Asa *destroyed* **cut off** her idol **of awe**,
and burnt it by the *brook Kidron* **wadi Qidron**.
14 But the *high places* **bamahs**
were not *removed* **turned aside**:
nevertheless Asa's heart was *perfect* **at shalom**
with *the LORD* **Yah Veh** all his days.
15 And he brought in
the *things which* **holies** of his father *had dedicated*,
and
the things which himself had dedicated **his own holies**,
into the house of *the LORD* **Yah Veh**,
silver, and gold, and *vessels* **instruments**.
16 And there was war between Asa
and *Baasha king* **Basha sovereign** of *Israel* **Yisra El**
all their days.
17 And *Baasha king* **Basha sovereign** of *Israel* **Yisra El**
went up **ascended** against *Judah* **Yah Hudah**,
and built Ramah,
that he might not *suffer* **give** any to go out or come in
to Asa *king* **sovereign** of *Judah* **Yah Hudah**.
18 Then Asa took all the silver and the gold
that *were left* **remained** in the treasures
of the house of *the LORD* **Yah Veh**,
and the treasures of the *king's* **sovereign's** house,
and *delivered* **gave** them into the hand of his servants:
and *king* **sovereign** Asa
sent them to *Benhadad* **Ben Hadad**,
the son of *Tabrimon* **Tab Rimon**,
the son of *Hezion* **Hezyon**,
king **sovereign** of *Syria* **Aram**,
that *dwelt* **settled** at *Damascus* **Dammeseq**, saying,
19 There is a *league* **covenant** between me and thee,
and between my father and thy father: behold,
I have sent unto thee a *present* **bribe** of silver and gold;
come and break thy *league* **covenant**
with *Baasha king* **Basha sovereign** of *Israel* **Yisra El**,
that he may *depart* **ascend** from me.
20 So *Benhadad* **Ben Hadad**
hearkened unto *king* **sovereign** Asa,
and sent the *captains* **governors** of the *hosts* **valiant**
which he had against the cities of *Israel* **Yisra El**,
and smote *Ijon* **Iyon**, and Dan,
and *Abelbethmaachah* **Abel Beth Maachah**,
and all *Cinneroth* **Kinneroth**, with all the land of Naphtali.
21 And it *came to pass* **became**,
when *Baasha* **Basha** heard thereof,
that he *left off* **ceased** building of Ramah,
and *dwelt* **settled** in *Tirzah* **Tirsah**.
22 Then *king* **sovereign** Asa
made a proclamation throughout all Judah
had all Yah Hudah hear;
none was *exempted* **exonerated**:
and they *took away* **lifted** the stones of Ramah,
and the timber thereof,
wherewith *Baasha* **Basha** had builded;
and *king* **sovereign** Asa built with them
Geba of *Benjamin* **Ben Yamin**, and *Mizpah* **Mispeh**.
23 The rest of all the *acts* **words** of Asa, and all his might,
and all that he *did* **worked**, and the cities which he built,
are they not *written* **inscribed** in the *book* **scroll**
of the *chronicles* **words of the days**
of the *kings* **sovereigns** of *Judah* **Yah Hudah**?
Nevertheless in the time of his old age
he was *diseased* **sick** in his feet.
24 And Asa *slept* **laid** with his fathers,
and was *buried* **entombed** with his fathers
in the city of David his father:
and *Jehoshaphat* **Yah Shaphat** his son reigned in his stead.

THE REIGN OF NADAB OVER YAH HUDAH

25 And Nadab the son of *Jeroboam* **Yarob Am**
began to reign **reigned** over *Israel* **Yisra El**
in the second year of Asa
king **sovereign** of *Judah* **Yah Hudah**,
and reigned over *Israel* **Yisra El** two years.
26 And he *did* **worked** evil
in the *sight* **eyes** of *the LORD* **Yah Veh**,
and walked in the way of his father,
and in his sin wherewith he made *Israel* **Yisra El** to sin.
27 And *Baasha* **Basha** the son of *Ahijah* **Achiy Yah**,
of the house of *Issachar* **Yissachar**, conspired against him;
and *Baasha* **Basha** smote him at Gibbethon,
which *belonged* **was** to the *Philistines* **Peleshethiy**;
for Nadab and all *Israel* **Yisra El**
laid siege to **besieged** Gibbethon.
28 Even in the third year of Asa
king **sovereign** of *Judah* **Yah Hudah**
did Baasha slay **Basha deathified** him,
and reigned in his stead.
29 And it *came to pass* **became**, when he reigned,
that he smote all the house of *Jeroboam* **Yarob Am**;
he left not to *Jeroboam* **Yarob Am** any **survivors**
that *breathed* **hath breath**,
until he had *destroyed* **desolated** him,
according unto the *saying* **word** of *the LORD* **Yah Veh**,
which he *spake* **worded** by **the hand of** his servant
Ahijah **Achiy Yah** the *Shilonite* **Shilohiy**:
30 Because of the sins of *Jeroboam* **Yarob Am**
which he sinned,
and which he made *Israel* **Yisra El** sin,
by his *provocation* **vexation**
wherewith he *provoked* **vexed**
the LORD God **Yah Veh Elohim** of *Israel* **Yisra El** *to anger*.
31 Now the rest of the *acts* **words** of Nadab,
and all that he *did* **worked**,
are they not *written* **inscribed** in the *book* **scroll**
of the *chronicles* **words of the days**
of the *kings* **sovereigns** of *Israel* **Yisra El**?
32 And there was war between Asa
and *Baasha king* **Basha sovereign** of *Israel* **Yisra El**
all their days.

THE REIGN OF BASHA OVER YISRA EL

33 In the third year of Asa
king **sovereign** of *Judah* **Yah Hudah**
began *Baasha* **Basha** the son of *Ahijah* **Achiy Yah**
to reign over all *Israel* **Yisra El** in *Tirzah* **Tirsah**,
twenty and four years.
34 And he *did* **worked** evil
in the *sight* **eyes** of *the LORD* **Yah Veh**,
and walked in the way of *Jeroboam* **Yarob Am**,
and in his sin
wherewith he made *Israel* **Yisra El** to sin.

16 Then the word of *the LORD* **Yah Veh**
came to *Jehu* **Yah Hu**
the son of Hanani against *Baasha* **Basha**, saying,
2 Forasmuch as I exalted thee out of the dust,
and *made* **gave** thee *prince* **eminence**
over my people *Israel* **Yisra El**;
and thou hast walked in the way of *Jeroboam* **Yarob Am**,
and hast made my people *Israel* **Yisra El** to sin,
to *provoke* **vex** me *to anger* with their sins;
3 Behold, I *will take* **shall burn** away
the posterity of *Baasha* **Basha**,
and the posterity of his house;
and *will make* **shall give** thy house
like the house of *Jeroboam* **Yarob Am** the son of Nebat.
4 Him that dieth of *Baasha* **Basha** in the city
shall the dogs *eat* **devour**;
and him that dieth of his in the fields

shall the *fowls* **flyers** of the *air eat* **heavens devour**.
5 Now the rest of the *acts* **words** of *Baasha* **Basha**,
and what he *did* **worked**, and his might,
are they not *written* **inscribed** in the *book* **scroll**
of the *chronicles* **words of the days**
of the *kings* **sovereigns** of *Israel* **Yisra El**?
6 So *Baasha slept* **Basha laid** with his fathers,
and was *buried* **entombed** in *Tirzah* **Tirsah**:
and Elah his son reigned in his stead.
7 And also by the hand of the prophet
Jehu **Yah Hu** the son of Hanani
came the word of *the LORD* **Yah Veh**
against *Baasha* **Basha**, and against his house,
even for all the evil that he *did* **worked**
in the *sight* **eyes** of *the LORD* **Yah Veh**
in *provoking* **vexing** him *to anger*
with the work of his hands,
in being like the house of *Jeroboam* **Yarob Am**;
and because he *killed* **smote** him.

THE REIGN OF ELAH OVER YISRA EL

8 In the twenty and sixth year
of Asa *king* **sovereign** of *Judah* **Yah Hudah**
began Elah the son of *Baasha* **Basha**
to reign over *Israel* **Yisra El** in *Tirzah* **Tirsah**, two years.
9 And his servant Zimri,
captain **governor** of half his chariots,
conspired against him, as he was in *Tirzah* **Tirsah**,
drinking himself *drunk* **intoxicated**
in the house of *Arza* **Arsa**
steward of *his* **the** house in *Tirzah* **Tirsah**.
10 And Zimri went in and smote him,
and *killed* **deathified** him,
in the twenty and seventh year of Asa
king **sovereign** of *Judah* **Yah Hudah**,
and reigned in his stead.
11 And it *came to pass* **became**, when he began to reign,
as soon as he *sat* **settled** on his throne,
that he *slew* **smote** all the house of *Baasha* **Basha**:
he *left him* **let survive**
not one that *pisseth* **urinateth** against a wall,
neither of his *kinsfolks* **redeemers**, nor of his friends.
12 Thus did Zimri
destroy **desolate** all the house of *Baasha* **Basha**,
according to the word of *the LORD* **Yah Veh**,
which he *spake* **worded** against *Baasha* **Basha**
by *Jehu* **the hand of Yah Hu** the prophet.
13 For all the sins of *Baasha* **Basha**,
and the sins of Elah his son,
by which they sinned,
and by which they made *Israel* **Yisra El** to sin,
in *provoking* **vexing**
the LORD God **Yah Veh Elohim** of *Israel* **Yisra El** *to anger*
with their vanities.
14 Now the rest of the *acts* **words** of Elah,
and all that he *did* **worked**,
are they not *written* **inscribed** in the *book* **scroll**
of the *chronicles* **words of the days**
of the *kings* **sovereigns** of *Israel* **Yisra El**?

THE REIGN OF ZIMRI OVER YISRA EL

15 In the twenty and seventh year of Asa
king **sovereign** of *Judah* **Yah Hudah**
did Zimri reign seven days in *Tirzah* **Tirsah**.
And the people were encamped against Gibbethon,
which *belonged* **be** to the *Philistines* **Peleshethiy**.
16 And the people that were encamped heard say,
Zimri hath conspired,
and hath also *slain* **smitten** the *king* **sovereign**:
wherefore all *Israel* **Yisra El** made Omri,
the *captain* **governor** of the host,
king **reign** over *Israel* **Yisra El** that day in the camp.
17 And Omri *went up* **ascended** from Gibbethon,
and all *Israel* **Yisra El** with him,
and they besieged *Tirzah* **Tirsah**.
18 And it *came to pass* **became**,
when Zimri saw that the city was *taken* **captured**,
that he went
into the *palace* **citadel** of the *king's* **sovereign's** house,
and burnt the *king's* **sovereign's** house over him with fire,
and died.
19 For his sins which he sinned in *doing* **working** evil
in the *sight* **eyes** of *the LORD* **Yah Veh**,
in walking in the way of *Jeroboam* **Yarob Am**,
and in his sin which he *did* **worked**,
to make *Israel* **Yisra El** to sin.
20 Now the rest of the *acts* **words** of Zimri,
and his *treason* **conspiracy** that he *wrought* **conspired**,
are they not *written* **inscribed** in the *book* **scroll**
of the *chronicles* **words of the days**
of the *kings* **sovereigns** of *Israel* **Yisra El**?

THE REIGN OF OMRI OVER YISRA EL

21 Then were the people of *Israel* **Yisra El**
divided **allotted** into two parts:
half of the people *followed* **were after** Tibni
the son of Ginath, to make him *king* **reign**;
and half *followed* **were after** Omri.
22 But the people that *followed* **were after** Omri
prevailed against the people
that *followed* **were after** Tibni the son of Ginath:
so Tibni died, and Omri reigned.
23 In the thirty and first year of Asa
king **sovereign** of *Judah* **Yah Hudah**
began Omri to reign over *Israel* **Yisra El**, twelve years:
six years reigned he in *Tirzah* **Tirsah**.
24 And he *bought* **chatteled**
the hill Samaria **mount Shomeron**
of Shemer for two *talents* **rounds** of silver,
and built on the *hill* **mount**,
and called the name of the city which he built,
after the name of Shemer,
owner **adoni** of the *hill* **mount**, *Samaria* **Shomeron**.
25 But Omri *wrought* **worked** evil
in the eyes of *the LORD* **Yah Veh**,
and *did worse* **vilified**
than that were before him **above all at their face**.
26 For he walked in all the way of *Jeroboam* **Yarob Am**
the son of Nebat,
and in his sin wherewith he made *Israel* **Yisra El** to sin,
to *provoke* **vex**
the LORD God **Yah Veh Elohim** of *Israel* **Yisra El** *to anger*
with their vanities.
27 Now the rest of the *acts* **words** of Omri
which he *did* **worked**,
and his might that he *shewed* **worked**,
are they not *written* **inscribed** in the *book* **scroll**
of the *chronicles* **words of the days**
of the *kings* **sovereigns** of *Israel* **Yisra El**?
28 So Omri *slept* **laid** with his fathers,
and was *buried* **entombed** in *Samaria* **Shomeron**:
and *Ahab* **Ach Ab** his son reigned in his stead.

THE REIGN OF ACH AB OVER YISRA EL

29 And in the thirty and eighth year of Asa
king **sovereign** of *Judah* **Yah Hudah**
began *Ahab* **Ach Ab** the son of Omri
to reign over *Israel* **Yisra El**:
and *Ahab* **Ach Ab** the son of Omri
reigned over *Israel* **Yisra El** in *Samaria* **Shomeron**
twenty and two years.
30 And *Ahab* **Ach Ab** the son of Omri *did* **worked** evil
in the *sight* **eyes** of *the LORD* **Yah Veh**
above all that were *before him* **at his face**.
31 And it *came to pass* **became**,
as if it had been *a light thing* **trifle**
for him to walk in the sins of *Jeroboam* **Yarob Am**
the son of Nebat,
that he took to *wife* **woman**
Jezebel **Iy Zebel** the daughter of *Ethbaal* **Eth Baal**
king **sovereign** of the *Zidonians* **Sidoniy**,
and went and served Baal,
and *worshipped* **prostrated** to him.
32 And he *reared up an* **raised a sacrifice** altar for Baal
in the house of Baal,
which he had built in *Samaria* **Shomeron**.
33 And *Ahab made a grove* **Ach Ab worked an asherah**;
and *Ahab did more* **Ach Ab added to work**
to *provoke* **vex**
the LORD God **Yah Veh Elohim** of *Israel* **Yisra El** *to anger*
than all the *kings* **sovereigns** of *Israel* **Yisra El**
that were before him **at their face**.
34 In his days did *Hiel* **Hi El** the *Bethelite* **Beth Eliy**
build *Jericho* **Yericho**:

he laid the foundation thereof
in *Abiram* **Abi Ram** his firstborn,
and *set up* **stationed** the *gates* **doors** thereof
in his *youngest* **lesser** *son* Segub,
according to the word of *the LORD* **Yah Veh**,
which he *spake* **worded**
by *Joshua* **the hand of Yah Shua** the son of Nun.

RAVENS SUSTAIN ELI YAH

17 And *Elijah* **Eli Yah** the *Tishbite* **Tisbehiy**,
who was of the *inhabitants* **settlers** of *Gilead* **Gilad**,
said unto *Ahab* **Ach Ab**,
As the LORD God **Yah Veh Elohim** of *Israel* **Yisra El** liveth,
before whom **at whose face** I stand,
there shall not be dew nor rain these years,
but according to my *word* **mouth**.
2 And the word of *the LORD* **Yah Veh** came unto him,
saying,
3 *Get thee* **Go** hence, and *turn* **face** thee eastward,
and hide thyself by the *brook Cherith* **wadi Kerith**,
that is before Jordan **at the face of Yarden**.
4 And it shall be, that thou shalt drink of the *brook* **wadi**;
and I have *commanded* **misvahed** the ravens
to *feed* **sustain** thee there.
5 So he went and *did* **worked**
according unto the word of *the LORD* **Yah Veh**:
for he went and *dwelt* **settled**
by the *brook Cherith* **wadi Kerith**,
that is before Jordan **at the face of Yarden**.
6 And the ravens brought him
bread and flesh in the morning,
and bread and flesh in the evening;
and he drank of the *brook* **wadi**.
7 And it *came to pass* **became,**
after a while **at the end of days**,
that the *brook dried up* **wadi withered**,
because there had been no rain in the land.
8 And the word of *the LORD* **Yah Veh** came unto him,
saying,
9 Arise, *get thee* **go** to *Zarephath* **Sarephath**,
which *belongeth* **be** to *Zidon* **Sidon**,
and *dwell* **settle** there: behold,
I have *commanded* **misvahed** a widow woman there
to sustain thee.
10 So he arose and went to *Zarephath* **Sarephath**.
And when he came to the *gate* **portal** of the city, behold,
the widow woman was there gathering *of sticks* **timber**:
and he called to her, and said,
Fetch **Take** me, I *pray* **beseech** thee,
a little water in *a vessel* **an instrument**, that I may drink.
11 And as she was going to *fetch* **take** it,
he called to her, and said,
Bring **Take** me, I *pray* **beseech** thee,
a morsel of bread in thine hand.
12 And she said,
As the LORD **Yah Veh** thy *God* **Elohim** liveth,
I have *not a cake* **no bakings**,
but *an handful* **a palmful** of *meal* **flour** in a *barrel* **pitcher**,
and a little oil in a cruse: and, behold,
I am gathering two *sticks* **timbers**,
that I may go in and *dress* **work** it for me and my son,
that we may eat it, and die.
13 And *Elijah* **Eli Yah** said unto her, *Fear* **Awe** not;
go and *do* **work** as thou hast *said* **worded**:
but *make* **work** me thereof a little *cake* **ashcake** first,
and bring it unto me,
and after *make* **work** for thee and for thy son.
14 For thus saith
the LORD God **Yah Veh Elohim** of *Israel* **Yisra El**,
The *barrel* **pitcher** of *meal* **flour** shall not *waste* **finish**,
neither shall the cruse of oil *fail* **lack**,
until the day that *the LORD sendeth* **Yah Veh giveth** rain
upon the *earth* **face of the soil**.
15 And she went and *did* **worked**
according to the *saying* **word** of *Elijah* **Eli Yah**:
and she, and he, and her house, did eat *many* days.
16 And the *barrel* **pitcher** of *meal* **flour**
wasted **finished** not,
neither did the cruse of oil *fail* **lack**,
according to the word of *the LORD* **Yah Veh**,
which he *spake* **worded** by *Elijah* **the hand of Eli Yah**.

ELI YAH ENLIVENS THE WIDOW'S SON

17 And it *came to pass* **became,** after these *things* **words**,
that the son of the woman,
the *mistress* **baalah** of the house, fell sick;
and his sickness was *so sore* **mighty strong**,
that *there was* **remained** no breath *left* in him.
18 And she said unto *Elijah* **Eli Yah**,
What have I to do with thee, O thou man of *God* **Elohim**?
art thou come unto me
to call my *sin* **perversity** to remembrance,
and to *slay* **deathify** my son?
19 And he said unto her, Give me thy son.
And he took him out of her bosom,
and *carried* **ascended** him *up* into *a loft* **an upper room**,
where he *abode* **settled**, and laid him upon his own bed.
20 And he *cried* **called out** unto *the LORD* **Yah Veh**,
and said, O *LORD* **Yah Veh** my *God* **Elohim**,
hast thou also *brought evil upon* **vilified** the widow
with whom I sojourn, by *slaying* **deathifying** her son?
21 And he *stretched* **measured** himself upon the child
three times,
and *cried* **called out** unto *the LORD* **Yah Veh**, and said,
O *LORD* **Yah Veh** my *God* **Elohim**, I *pray* **beseech** thee,
let this child's soul *come* **return**
into *him again* **his inwards**.
22 And *the LORD* **Yah Veh**
heard the voice of *Elijah* **Eli Yah**;
and the soul of the child *came* **returned**
into *him again* **his inwards**,
and he *revived* **lived**.
23 And *Elijah* **Eli Yah** took the child,
and *brought* **descended** him *down*
out of the *chamber* **upper room** into the house,
and *delivered* **gave** him unto his mother:
and *Elijah* **Eli Yah** said, See, thy son liveth.
24 And the woman said to *Elijah* **Eli Yah**,
Now by this I know that thou art a man of *God* **Elohim**,
and that the word of *the LORD* **Yah Veh** in thy mouth
is truth.

ELI YAH AND OBAD YAH

18 And it *came to pass* **became,** after many days,
that the word of *the LORD* **Yah Veh** came to *Elijah* **Eli Yah**
in the third year, saying,
Go, *shew thyself unto Ahab* **be seen by Ach Ab**;
and I *will send* **shall give** rain
upon the *earth* **face of the soil**.
2 And *Elijah* **Eli Yah** went
to *shew himself unto Ahab* **be seen of Ach Ab**.
And there was a *sore* **strong** famine in *Samaria* **Shomeron**.
3 And *Ahab* **Ach Ab** called *Obadiah* **Obad Yah**,
which was the governor of *his* **the** house.
(Now *Obadiah* **Obad Yah**
feared the LORD greatly **awed Yah Veh mightily**:
4 For it *was so* **became**,
when *Jezebel* **Iy Zebel**
cut off the prophets of *the LORD* **Yah Veh**,
that *Obadiah* **Obad Yah** took an hundred prophets,
and hid them by fifty **men** in a cave,
and *fed* **sustained** them with bread and water.)
5 And *Ahab* **Ach Ab** said unto *Obadiah* **Obad Yah**,
Go into the land,
unto all fountains of water, and unto all *brooks* **wadies**:
peradventure **perhaps** we may find *grass* **leeks**
to save the horses and mules alive,
that we *lose* not **cut off** all the *beasts* **animals**.
6 So they *divided* **allotted** the land between them
to pass throughout it:
Ahab **Ach Ab** went one way by himself,
and *Obadiah* **Obad Yah** went *another* **one** way by himself.
7 And as *Obadiah* **Obad Yah** was in the way, behold,
Elijah **Eli Yah** met him: and he *knew* **recognized** him,
and fell on his face, and said,
Art thou that my *lord Elijah* **adoni Eli Yah**?
8 And he *answered* **said to** him, I *am*:
go, *tell* **say to** thy *lord* **adoni**, Behold,
Elijah **Eli Yah** is here.
9 And he said, What have I sinned,
that thou *wouldest* **shouldest** deliver thy servant
into the hand of *Ahab* **Ach Ab**, to *slay* **deathify** me?
10 *As the LORD* **Yah Veh** thy *God* **Elohim** liveth,

there is no *nation* **goyim** or *kingdom* **sovereigndom**,
whither my *lord* **adoni** hath not sent to seek thee:
and when they said, *He is not there* **No**;
he *took an oath* **oathed**
of the *kingdom* **sovereigndom** and *nation* **goyim**,
that they found thee not.
11 And now thou sayest, Go, *tell* **say to** thy *lord* **adoni**,
Behold, *Elijah* **Eli Yah** *is here*.
12 And it shall *come to pass* **become**,
as soon as I am gone from thee,
that the Spirit of *the LORD* **Yah Veh** shall *carry* **lift** thee
whither I know not;
and *so* when I come and tell *Ahab* **Ach Ab**,
and he cannot find thee, he shall *slay* **slaughter** me:
but I thy servant
fear the LORD **awe Yah Veh** from my youth.
13 Was it not told my *lord* **adoni** what I *did* **worked**
when *Jezebel* **Iy Zebel**
slew **slaughtered** the prophets of *the LORD* **Yah Veh**,
how I hid an hundred men
of *the LORD'S* **Yah Veh's** prophets
by fifty **men** in a cave,
and *fed* **sustained** them with bread and water?
14 And now thou sayest, Go, *tell* **say to** thy *lord* **adoni**,
Behold, *Elijah* **Eli Yah** *is here*:
and he shall *slay* **slaughter** me.
15 And *Elijah* **Eli Yah** said,
As the LORD of hosts **Yah Veh Sabaoth** liveth,
before whom **at whose face** I stand,
I will **shall** surely *shew myself unto* **be seen by** him to day.
16 So *Obadiah* **Obad Yah** went to meet *Ahab* **Ach Ab**,
and told him:
and *Ahab* **Ach Ab** went to meet *Elijah* **Eli Yah**.
17 And it *came to pass* **became**,
when *Ahab* **Ach Ab** saw *Elijah* **Eli Yah**,
that *Ahab* **Ach Ab** said unto him,
Art thou he that troubleth *Israel* **Yisra El**?
18 And he *answered* **said**,
I have not troubled *Israel* **Yisra El**;
but thou, and thy father's house,
in that ye have forsaken
the *commandments* **misvoth** of *the LORD* **Yah Veh**,
and thou hast *followed* **walked after** Baalim.
19 Now therefore send,
and gather to me all *Israel* **Yisra El**
unto mount *Carmel* **Karmel**,
and the prophets of Baal four hundred and fifty,
and the prophets of the *groves* **asherim** four hundred,
which eat at *Jezebel's* **Iy Zebel's** table.
20 So *Ahab* **Ach Ab**
sent unto all the *children* **sons** of *Israel* **Yisra El**,
and gathered the prophets
together unto mount *Carmel* **Karmel**.
21 And *Elijah* **Eli Yah** came **near** unto all the people,
and said,
How long *halt* **limp** ye *between* **divided in** two *opinions*?
if *the LORD* **Yah Veh** be *God* **Elohim**, *follow* **go after** him:
but if Baal, *then follow* **go after** him.
And the people answered him not a word.
22 Then said *Elijah* **Eli Yah** unto the people,
I, *even* I only, remain a prophet of *the LORD* **Yah Veh**;
but Baal's prophets are four hundred and fifty men.
23 Let them therefore give us two bullocks;
and let them choose one bullock for themselves,
and *cut* **dismember** it *in pieces*,
and *lay* **set** it on *wood* **timber**, and *put* **set** no fire *under*:
and I *will dress the other* **shall work one** bullock,
and *lay* **give** it on *wood* **timber**, and *put* **set** no fire *under*:
24 And call ye on the name of your *gods* **elohim**,
and I *will* **shall** call on the name of *the LORD* **Yah Veh**:
and the *God* **elohim** that answereth by fire,
let him be *God* **Elohim**.
And all the people answered and said,
It is well spoken **Good word**.
25 And *Elijah* **Eli Yah** said unto the prophets of Baal,
Choose you one bullock for yourselves,
and *dress* **work** it first;
for ye are many;
and call on the name of your *gods* **elohim**,
but *put* **set** no fire *under*.
26 And they took the bullock
which *was given* **he gave** them,
and they *dressed* **worked** it,
and called on the name of Baal
from morning even until noon, saying,
O Baal, *hear* **answer** us.
But there was no voice, nor any that answered.
And they leaped upon the **sacrifice** altar
which was *made* **worked**.
27 And it *came to pass* **became** at noon,
that *Elijah* **Eli Yah** mocked them, and said,
Cry aloud **Call out with a great voice**:
for he is *a god* **elohim**;
either he *is talking* **meditateth**,
or he *is pursuing* **withdraweth**, or he is in a journey,
or *peradventure* **perhaps** he sleepeth,
and must be awaked.
28 And they *cried aloud* **called out with a great voice**,
and *cut* **incised** themselves after their *manner* **judgment**
with *knives* **swords** and *lancets* **javelins**,
till the blood *gushed* **poured** out upon them.
29 And it *came to pass* **became**,
when *midday* **noon** was past,
and they prophesied until *the time of*
the *offering* **holocaust** of the *evening sacrifice* **offering**,
that there was neither voice, nor any to answer,
nor any that *regarded* **hearkened**.
30 And *Elijah* **Eli Yah** said unto all the people,
Come near unto me.
And all the people came near unto him.
And he *repaired* **healed**
the **sacrifice** altar of *the LORD* **Yah Veh**
that was *broken down* **demolished**.
31 And *Elijah* **Eli Yah** took twelve stones,
according to the number
of the *tribes* **scions** of the sons of *Jacob* **Yaaqov**,
unto whom the word of *the LORD* **Yah Veh** came, saying,
Israel **Yisra El** shall be thy name:
32 And with the stones he built *an* **a sacrifice** altar
in the name of *the LORD* **Yah Veh**:
and he *made* **worked** a *trench* **channel**
round about the **sacrifice** altar,
as great as would contain **to house**
two *measures* **seahs** of seed.
33 And he *put* **lined up** the *wood* **timber** *in order*,
and *cut* **dismembered** the bullock *in pieces*,
and *laid* **set** him on the *wood* **timber**, and said,
Fill four *barrels* **pitchers** with water,
and pour it on the *burnt sacrifice* **holocaust**,
and on the *wood* **timber**.
34 And he said, *Do it the second time* **Double**.
And they *did it the second time* **doubled**.
And he said, *Do it the third time* **Triple**.
And they *did it the third time* **tripled**.
35 And the water *ran* **went** round about the **sacrifice** altar;
and he filled the *trench* **channel** also with water.
36 And it *came to pass* **became**,
at the *time of the offering* **holocaust**
of the *evening sacrifice* **offering**,
that *Elijah* **Eli Yah** the prophet came near, and said,
LORD God **Yah Veh Elohim** of Abraham,
Isaac **Yischaq**, and of *Israel* **Yisra El**,
let it be known this day
that thou art *God* **Elohim** in *Israel* **Yisra El**,
and that I am thy servant,
and that I have *done* **worked** all these *things* at thy word.
37 *Hear* **Answer** me, O *LORD* **Yah Veh**, *hear* **answer** me,
that this people may know
that thou art *the LORD God* **Yah Veh Elohim**,
and that thou hast turned their heart *back again* **backward**.
38 Then the fire of *the LORD* **Yah Veh** fell,
and consumed the *burnt sacrifice* **holocaust**,
and the *wood* **timber**, and the stones, and the dust,
and licked up the water that was in the *trench* **channel**.
39 And when all the people saw it, they fell on their faces:
and they said,
The LORD **Yah Veh**, he is *the God* **Elohim**;
the LORD **Yah Veh**, he is *the God* **Elohim**.
40 And *Elijah* **Eli Yah** said unto them,
Take **Apprehend** the prophets of Baal;

let not *one* **a man** of them escape.
And they *took* **apprehended** them:
and *Elijah brought* **Eli Yah descended** them *down*
to the *brook Kishon* **wadi Qishon,**
and *slew* **slaughtered** them there.
41 And *Elijah* **Eli Yah** said unto *Ahab* **Ach Ab,**
Get thee up **Ascend**, eat and drink;
for there is a *sound* **voice** of *abundance* **multitude** of rain.
42 So *Ahab went up* **Ach Ab ascended** to eat and to drink.
And *Elijah went up* **Eli Yah ascended**
to the top of *Carmel* **Karmel**;
and he *cast* **prostrated** himself *down* upon the earth,
and *put* **set** his face between his knees,
43 And said to his *servant* **lad**, *Go up* **Ascend** now,
look *toward* **the way of** the sea.
And he *went up* **ascended**, and looked, and said,
There is *nothing* **naught**.
And he said, *Go again* **Turn back** seven times.
44 And it *came to pass* **became,**
at the seventh *time,* that he said, Behold,
there *ariseth* **ascendeth** a little **thick** cloud out of the sea,
like **as** a man's *hand* **palm**.
And he said, *Go up* **Ascend**, say unto *Ahab* **Ach Ab**,
Prepare **Bind** *thy chariot,*
and *get thee down* **descend**
that the rain *stop* **restrain** thee not.
45 And it *came to pass in the mean while* **became thus,**
that the *heaven was black* **heavens were darkened**
with **thick** clouds and wind, and there was a great rain.
And *Ahab* **Ach Ab** rode, and went to *Jezreel* **Yizre El.**
46 And the hand of *the LORD* **Yah Veh**
was on *Elijah* **Eli Yah**;
and he girded up his loins,
and ran *before Ahab* **at the face of Ach Ab**
to the entrance of *Jezreel* **Yizre El.**

ELI YAH FLEES FROM IY ZEBEL

19 And *Ahab* **Ach Ab** told *Jezebel* **Iy Zebel**
all that *Elijah* **Eli Yah** had *done* **worked**,
and withal how he had *slain* **slaughtered** all the prophets
with the sword.
2 Then *Jezebel* **Iy Zebel**
sent *a messenger* **an angel** unto *Elijah* **Eli Yah**, saying,
So let the *gods do* **elohim work** *to me,*
and *more* **add** also,
if I *make* **set** not thy *life* **soul** as the *life* **soul** of one of them
by to morrow about this time.
3 And when he saw that, he arose,
and went for his *life* **soul**,
and came to *Beersheba* **Beer Sheba**,
which *belongeth* **be** to *Judah* **Yah Hudah**,
and *left* **set** his *servant* **lad** there.
4 But he himself went a day's journey into the wilderness,
and came and *sat down* **settled** under *a* **one** juniper *tree*:
and he *requested* **asked** for *himself* **his soul**
that he might die; and said, *It is* enough;
now, O *LORD* **Yah Veh**, take away my *life* **soul**;
for I am not better than my fathers.
5 And as he lay and slept under *a* **one** juniper *tree*, behold,
then an angel touched him,
and said unto him, Arise and eat.
6 And he looked, and, behold,
there was *a cake* **an ashcake**
baken on the *coals* **red hot stones**,
and a cruse of water at his head **pieces**.
And he did eat and drink,
and **returned and** laid him down *again.*
7 And the angel of *the LORD* **Yah Veh**
came again **returned** the second time,
and touched him, and said,
Arise and eat; because the journey is too great for thee.

ELI YAH IN MOUNT HOREB

8 And he arose, and did eat and drink,
and went in the *strength* **substance** of that *meat* **food**
forty days and forty nights
unto Horeb the mount of *God* **Elohim.**
9 And he came thither unto a cave,
and *lodged* **stayed overnight** there; and, behold,
the word of *the LORD* **Yah Veh** *came* to him,
and he said unto him,
What dost thou here, *Elijah* **Eli Yah**?
10 And he said,
In being jealous, I have been *very* jealous
for *the LORD God of hosts* **Yah Veh Elohim Sabaoth**:
for the *children* **sons** of *Israel* **Yisra El**
have forsaken thy covenant,
thrown down thine **demolished thy sacrifice** altars,
and *slain* **slaughtered** thy prophets with the sword;
and I, *even* I only, *am left* **remain**;
and they seek my *life* **soul**, to take it away.
11 And he said, Go forth,
and stand upon the mount
before the LORD **at the face of Yah Veh.**
And, behold, *the LORD* **Yah Veh** passed by,
and a great and strong wind *rent* **split** the mountains,
and brake *in pieces* the rocks
before the LORD **at the face of Yah Veh**;
but the LORD **Yah Veh** was not in the wind:
and after the wind *an earthquake* **a quake**;
but the LORD **Yah Veh** was not in the *earthquake* **quake**:
12 And after the *earthquake* **quake** a fire;
but the LORD **Yah Veh** was not in the fire:
and after the fire a still *small* **thin** voice.
13 And it *was so* **became**, when *Elijah* **Eli Yah** heard it,
that he *wrapped* **veiled** his face in his **mighty** mantle,
and went out,
and stood in the *entering in* **opening** of the cave.
And, behold, *there came* a voice unto him, and said,
What dost thou here, *Elijah* **Eli Yah**?
14 And he said,
In being jealous, I have been *very* jealous
for *the LORD God of hosts* **Yah Veh Elohim Sabaoth**:
because the *children* **sons** of *Israel* **Yisra El**
have forsaken thy covenant,
thrown down thine **demolished thy sacrifice** altars,
and *slain* **slaughtered** thy prophets with the sword;
and I, *even* I only, *am left* **remain**;
and they seek my *life* **soul**, to take it away.
15 And *the LORD* **Yah Veh** said unto him, Go,
return on thy way
to the wilderness of *Damascus* **Dammeseq**:
and when thou comest, anoint *Hazael* **Haza El**
to be *king* **sovereign** over *Syria* **Aram**:
16 And *Jehu* **Yah Hu** the son of Nimshi
shalt thou anoint to be *king* **sovereign** over *Israel* **Yisra El**:
and *Elisha* **Eli Shua**
the son of Shaphat of *Abelmeholah* **Abel Mecholah**
shalt thou anoint to be prophet in thy *room* **stead**.
17 And it shall *come to pass* **become**,
that him that escapeth the sword of *Hazael* **Haza El**
shall *Jehu slay* **Yah Hu deathify**
and him that escapeth from the sword of *Jehu* **Yah Hu**
shall *Elisha slay* **Eli Shua deathify**.
18 Yet I have *left* **survived** me
seven thousand in *Israel* **Yisra El**,
all the knees which have not bowed unto Baal,
and every mouth which hath not kissed him.
19 So he *departed* **went** thence,
and found *Elisha* **Eli Shua** the son of Shaphat,
who was plowing with twelve yoke *of oxen*
before him **at his face**, and he with the twelfth:
and *Elijah* **Eli Yah** passed by him,
and cast his **mighty** mantle upon him.
20 And he left the oxen, and ran after *Elijah* **Eli Yah**,
and said, Let me, I *pray* **beseech** thee,
kiss my father and my mother,
and *then I will follow* **I shall go after** thee.
And he said unto him, Go *back again* **return**:
for what have I *done* **worked** to thee?
21 And he returned *back* **afterward** from him,
and took a yoke of oxen, and *slew* **sacrificed** them,
and *boiled* **stewed** their flesh
with the instruments of the oxen,
and gave unto the people, and they did eat.
Then he arose, and went after *Elijah* **Eli Yah**,
and ministered unto him.

ARAM ATTACKS SHOMERON

20 And *Benhadad* **Ben Hadad**
the *king* **sovereign** of *Syria* **Aram**
gathered all his *host* **valiant** together:
and there were thirty and two *kings* **sovereigns** with him,

and horses, and chariots;
and he *went up* **ascended**
and besieged *Samaria* **Shomeron**,
and *warred* **fought** against it.
2 And he sent *messengers* **angels** to *Ahab* **Ach Ab**,
king **sovereign** of *Israel* **Yisra El** into the city,
and said unto him, Thus saith *Benhadad* **Ben Hadad**,
3 Thy silver and thy gold is mine;
thy *wives* **women** also and thy *children* **sons**,
even the goodliest, are mine.
4 And the *king* **sovereign** of *Israel* **Yisra El**
answered and said,
My *lord* **adoni**, O *king* **sovereign**,
according to thy *saying* **word**, I am thine,
and all that I have.
5 And the *messengers came again* **angels returned**,
and said,
Thus *speaketh Benhadad* **saith Ben Hadad**, saying,
Although I have sent unto thee, saying,
Thou shalt *deliver* **give** me thy silver, and thy gold,
and thy *wives* **women**, and thy *children* **sons**;
6 Yet I *will* **shall** send my servants unto thee
to morrow about this time,
and they shall search thine house,
and the houses of thy servants;
and it shall be,
that whatsoever is *pleasant in* **the desire of** thine eyes,
they shall *put* **set** it in their hand, and take it away.
7 Then the *king* **sovereign** of *Israel* **Yisra El**
called all the elders of the land,
and said, *Mark* **Perceive**, I *pray* **beseech** you,
and see how this *man* seeketh *mischief* **evil**:
for he sent unto me for my *wives* **women**,
and for my *children* **sons**,
and for my silver, and for my gold;
and I *denied* **withheld** him not.
8 And all the elders and all the people said unto him,
Hearken not *unto him*, nor *consent* **will**.
9 Wherefore he said
unto the *messengers* **angels** of *Benhadad* **Ben Hadad**,
Tell **Say to** my *lord* **adoni** the *king* **sovereign**,
All that thou didst send for to thy servant at the first
I *will do* **shall work**:
but this *thing* **word** I *may* **shall** not *do* **work**.
And the *messengers departed* **angels went**,
and *brought* **returned** him word *again*.
10 And *Benhadad* **Ben Hadad** sent unto him, and said,
The *gods do* **elohim work** so unto me, and *more* **add** also,
if the dust of *Samaria* **Shomeron**
shall suffice for *handfuls* **palmfuls**
for all the people *that follow me* **at my feet**.
11 And the *king* **sovereign** of *Israel* **Yisra El**
answered and said,
Tell **Word** him, Let not him that girdeth *on his harness*
boast **halal** himself as he that *putteth it off* **openeth**.
12 And it *came to pass* **became**,
when *Benhadad* **he** heard this *message* **word**,
as he was drinking,
he and the *kings* **sovereigns** in the *pavilions* **brush arbors**,
that he said unto his servants,
Set yourselves in array **Line up**.
And they *set themselves in array* **lined up** against the city.

ARAM DEFEATED

13 And, behold, there *came a* **approached one** prophet
unto *Ahab king* **Ach Ab sovereign** of *Israel* **Yisra El**, saying,
Thus saith *the LORD* **Yah Veh**,
Hast thou seen all this great multitude? behold,
I *will* **shall** deliver it into thine hand this day;
and thou shalt know that I am *the LORD* **Yah Veh**.
14 And *Ahab* **Ach Ab** said, By whom?
And he said, Thus saith *the LORD* **Yah Veh**,
Even by the *young men* **lads**
of the *princes* **governors** of the *provinces* **jurisdictions**.
Then he said, Who shall *order* **bind** the *battle* **war**?
And he *answered* **said**, Thou.
15 Then he *numbered* **mustered** the *young men* **lads**
of the *princes* **governors** of the *provinces* **jurisdictions**,
and they were two hundred and thirty two:
and after them he *numbered* **mustered** all the people,
even all the *children* **sons** of *Israel* **Yisra El**,
being seven thousand.
16 And they went out at noon.
But *Benhadad* **Ben Hadad**
was drinking himself *drunk* **intoxicated**
in the *pavilions* **brush arbors**,
he and the *kings* **sovereigns**,
the thirty and two *kings* **sovereigns** that helped him.
17 And the *young men* **lads**
of the *princes* **governors** of the *provinces* **jurisdictions**
went out first;
and *Benhadad* **Ben Hadad** sent out,
and they told him, saying,
There are men *come* **gone** out of *Samaria* **Shomeron**.
18 And he said,
Whether they be *come* **gone** out for *peace* **shalom**,
take **apprehend** them alive;
or whether they be *come* **gone** out for war,
take **apprehend** them alive.
19 So these *young men* **lads**
of the *princes* **governors** of the *provinces* **jurisdictions**
came **went** out of the city,
and the *army which followed* **valiant after** them.
20 And they *slew* **smote** every one his man:
and the *Syrians* **Aramiy** fled;
and *Israel* **Yisra El** pursued them:
and *Benhadad* **Ben Hadad**,
the *king* **sovereign** of *Syria* **Aram**,
escaped on an horse with the *horsemen* **cavalry**.
21 And the *king* **sovereign** of *Israel* **Yisra El** went out,
and smote the horses and chariots,
and *slew* **smote** the *Syrians* **Aramiy**
with a great *slaughter* **stroke**.
22 And the prophet came **near**
to the *king* **sovereign** of *Israel* **Yisra El**, and said unto him,
Go, strengthen *thyself*, and *mark* **perceive**,
and see what thou *doest* **workest**:
for at the *return* **turn** of the year
the *king* **sovereign** of *Syria* **Aram**
will come up **shall ascend** against thee.
23 And the servants of the *king* **sovereign** of *Syria* **Aram**
said unto him,
Their *gods* **elohim** are *gods* **elohim** of the *hills* **mountains**;
therefore they *were stronger than we* **prevailed over us**;
but let us fight against them in the plain,
and surely **unless**
we shall *be stronger than they* **prevail over them**.
24 And *do* **work** this *thing* **word**,
Take **Turn aside** the *kings* **sovereigns** *away*,
every man out of his place,
and *put captains* **set governors** in their rooms:
25 And number thee *an army* **the valiant**,
like the *army* **valiant** that *thou hast lost* **hath fallen**,
horse for horse, and chariot for chariot:
and we *will* **shall** fight against them in the plain,
and surely we shall
be stronger than they **prevail over them**.
And he hearkened unto their voice, and *did* **worked** so.
26 And it *came to pass* **became**,
at the *return* **turn** of the year,
that *Benhadad* **Ben Hadad**
numbered **mustered** the *Syrians* **Aramiy**,
and *went up* **ascended** to *Aphek* **Apheq**,
to *fight* **war** against *Israel* **Yisra El**.
27 And the *children* **sons** of *Israel* **Yisra El**
were *numbered* **mustered**,
and *were all present* **maintained**,
and went *against* **to meet** them:
and the *children* **sons** of *Israel* **Yisra El**
pitched **encamped** before them
like two *little flocks of kids* **bare doe goats**;
but the *Syrians* **Aramiy** filled the *country* **land**.
28 And there came **near** a man of *God* **Elohim**,
and *spake* **said** unto the *king* **sovereign** of *Israel* **Yisra El**,
and said, Thus saith *the LORD* **Yah Veh**,
Because the *Syrians* **Aramiy** have said,
The LORD **Yah Veh** is *God* **Elohim** of the *hills* **mountains**,
but he is not *God* **Elohim** of the valleys,
therefore *will* **shall** I
deliver **give** all this great multitude into thine hand,
and ye shall know *that I am the LORD* **I — Yah Veh**.

29 And they *pitched* **encamped** one over against the other
seven days.
And *so it was* **became**,
that in the seventh day
the *battle was joined* **war approached**:
and the *children* **sons** of *Israel* **Yisra El**
slew **smote** of the *Syrians* **Aramiy**
an hundred thousand *footmen* **on foot** in one day.
30 But the *rest* **remaining** fled to *Aphek* **Apheq**,
into the city;
and there a wall fell upon twenty and seven thousand
of the men that *were left* **remained**.
And *Benhadad* **Ben Hadad** fled,
and came into the city, into an inner chamber.
31 And his servants said unto him, Behold now,
we have heard
that the *kings* **sovereigns** of the house of *Israel* **Yisra El**
are merciful *kings* **sovereigns**:
let us, I *pray* **beseech** thee,
put sackcloth **set saq** on our loins,
and *ropes* **lines** upon our heads,
and go out to the *king* **sovereign** of *Israel* **Yisra El**:
peradventure he *will save thy life* **shall let thy soul live**.
32 So they girded *sackcloth* **saq** on their loins,
and put *ropes* **lines** on their heads,
and came to the *king* **sovereign** of *Israel* **Yisra El**, and said,
Thy servant *Benhadad* **Ben Hadad** saith,
I *pray* **beseech** thee, let *me* **my soul** live.
And he said, Is he yet alive? he is my brother.
33 Now the men
did diligently observe
whether any thing would come from him
prognosticated of him,
and *did hastily catch* **they hasted and snatched** it:
and they said, Thy brother *Benhadad* **Ben Hadad**.
Then he said, Go ye, *bring* **take** him.
Then *Benhadad came forth* **Ben Hadad went** to him;
and he caused him to *come up* **ascend** into the chariot.
34 And *Benhadad* said unto him,
The cities, which my father took from thy father,
I *will* **shall** restore;
and thou shalt *make streets* **set outways** for thee
in *Damascus* **Dammeseq**,
as my father *made* **set** in *Samaria* **Shomeron**.
Then said *Ahab* **he**,
I *will* **shall** send thee away with this covenant.
So he *made* **cut** a covenant with him, and sent him away.

A SON OF THE PROPHETS ORDERS A SMITING

35 And *a certain* **one** man of the sons of the prophets
said unto his *neighbour* **friend**
in the word of *the LORD* **Yah Veh**,
Smite me, I *pray* **beseech** thee.
And the man refused to smite him.
36 Then said he unto him,
Because thou hast not *obeyed* **hearkened**
to the voice of *the LORD* **Yah Veh**, behold,
as soon as thou art *departed* **gone** from me,
a lion shall *slay* **smite** thee.
And as soon as he was *departed* **gone** from *him* **his side**,
a lion found him, and *slew* **smote** him.
37 Then he found another man,
and said, Smite me, I *pray* **beseech** thee.
And the man smote him,
so that in smiting he wounded him.
38 So the prophet *departed* **went**,
and *waited* **stood by** for the *king* **sovereign** by the way,
and disguised himself with ashes upon his *face* **eyes**.
39 And as the *king* **sovereign** passed by,
he cried unto the *king* **sovereign**: and he said,
Thy servant went out into the midst of the *battle* **war**;
and, behold, a man turned aside,
and brought a man unto me, and said,
Keep **Guard** this man:
if **in missing**, *by any means* he be missing,
then shall thy *life* **soul** be for his *life* **soul**,
or else thou shalt *pay a talent* **weigh out a round** of silver.
40 And as thy servant was *busy* **working** here and there,
he was *gone* **not**.
And the *king* **sovereign** of *Israel* **Yisra El** said unto him,
So **Thus** shall thy judgment be;
thyself hast *decided* **appointed** *it*.
41 And he hasted,
and *took* **turned aside** the ashes *away* from his *face* **eyes**;
and the *king* **sovereign** of *Israel* **Yisra El**
discerned **recognized** him that he was of the prophets.
42 And he said unto him, Thus saith *the LORD* **Yah Veh**,
Because thou hast *let go* **sent away** out of thy hand
a man whom I *appointed to utter* **devoted to** destruction,
therefore thy *life* **soul** shall go for his *life* **soul**,
and thy people for his people.
43 And the *king* **sovereign** of *Israel* **Yisra El**
went to his house *heavy* **peeved** and *displeased* **enraged**,
and came to *Samaria* **Shomeron**.

ACH AB COVETS NABOTH'S VINEYARD

21 And it *came to pass* **became**, after these *things* **words**,
that Naboth the *Jezreelite* **Yizre Eliy** had a vineyard,
which was in *Jezreel* **Yizre El**,
hard by **beside** the *palace* **temple** of *Ahab* **Ach Ab**
king **sovereign** of *Samaria* **Shomeron**.
2 And *Ahab spake* **Ach Ab worded** unto Naboth, saying,
Give me thy vineyard,
that I may have it for a garden of *herbs* **greens**,
because it is near *unto* **beside** my house:
and I *will* **shall** give thee for it a better vineyard than it;
or, if it seem good *to thee* **in thine eyes**,
I *will* **shall** give thee the *worth* **price** of it in *money* **silver**.
3 And Naboth said to *Ahab* **Ach Ab**,
The LORD forbid it me **Far be it**,
that I should give the inheritance of my fathers unto thee.
4 And *Ahab* **Ach Ab** came into his house
heavy **peeved** and *displeased* **enraged**
because of the word
which Naboth the *Jezreelite* **Yizre Eliy**
had *spoken* **worded** to him:
for he had said,
I *will* **shall** not give thee the inheritance of my fathers.
And he laid him down upon his bed,
and turned away his face, and *would eat* **ate** no bread.
5 But *Jezebel* **Iy Zebel** his *wife* **woman** came to him,
and *said* **worded** unto him,
Why is thy spirit so *sad* **peeved**, that thou eatest no bread?
6 And he said unto her,
Because I *spake* **worded**
unto Naboth the *Jezreelite* **Yizre Eliy**,
and said unto him, Give me thy vineyard for *money* **silver**;
or else, if it *please* **delight** thee,
I *will* **shall** give thee *another* **a** vineyard for it:
and he *answered* **said**,
I *will* **shall** not give thee my vineyard.
7 And *Jezebel* **Iy Zebel** his *wife* **woman** said unto him,
Dost thou now *govern* **work**
the *kingdom* **sovereigndom** of *Israel* **Yisra El**?
arise, *and* eat bread,
and let thine heart be *merry* **well—pleased**:
I *will* **shall** give thee the vineyard
of Naboth the *Jezreelite* **Yizre Eliy**.
8 So she *wrote letters* **inscribed scrolls**
in *Ahab's* **Ach Ab's** name,
and sealed them with his seal,
and sent the *letters* **scrolls**
unto the elders and to the nobles that were in his city,
dwelling **settling** with Naboth.
9 And she *wrote* **inscribed** in the *letters* **scrolls**, saying,
Proclaim **Call** a fast, and *set* **seat** Naboth
on high among **the head of** the people:
10 And set two men, sons of *Belial* **Beli Yaal**, before him,
to bear witness against him, saying,
Thou didst *blaspheme* **bless**
God **Elohim** and the *king* **sovereign**.
And then *carry* **bring** him out,
and stone him, that he may die.
11 And the men of his city, *even* the elders and the nobles
who *were the inhabitants* **settled** in his city,
did **worked** as *Jezebel* **Iy Zebel** had sent unto them,
and as it was *written* **inscribed** in the *letters* **scrolls**
which she had sent unto them.
12 They *proclaimed* **called** a fast,
and *set* **seated** Naboth
on high among **the head of** the people.
13 And there came in two men,

children **sons** of *Belial* **Beli Yaal**,
and *sat* **settled** before him:
and the men of *Belial* **Beli Yaal** witnessed against him,
even against Naboth, in the presence of the people,
saying, Naboth *did blaspheme God* **blessed Elohim**
and the *king* **sovereign**.
Then they *carried* **brought** him forth out of the city,
and stoned him with stones, that he died.
14 Then they sent to *Jezebel* **Iy Zebel**, saying,
Naboth is stoned, and *is dead* **hath died**.
15 And it *came to pass* **became**,
when *Jezebel* **Iy Zebel** heard that Naboth was stoned,
and *was dead* **had died**,
that *Jezebel* **Iy Zebel** said to *Ahab* **Ach Ab**, Arise,
take possession of the vineyard
of Naboth the *Jezreelite* **Yizre Eliy**,
which he refused to give thee for *money* **silver**:
for Naboth is not alive, but *dead* **hath died**.
16 And it *came to pass* **became**,
when *Ahab* **Ach Ab** heard that Naboth *was dead* **died**,
that *Ahab* **Ach Ab** rose *up* to *go down* **descend**
to the vineyard of Naboth the *Jezreelite* **Yizre Eliy**,
to take possession of it.
17 And the word of *the LORD* **Yah Veh**
came to *Elijah* **Eli Yah** the *Tishbite* **Tisbehiy**, saying,
18 Arise, *go down* **descend** to meet *Ahab* **Ach Ab**
king **sovereign** of *Israel* **Yisra El**,
which is in *Samaria* **Shomeron**:
behold, he is in the vineyard of Naboth,
whither he *is gone down* **hath descended** to possess it.
19 And thou shalt *speak* **word** unto him, saying,
Thus saith *the LORD* **Yah Veh**,
Hast thou *killed* **murdered**, and also taken possession?
And *thou* shalt *speak* **word thou** unto him, saying,
Thus saith *the LORD* **Yah Veh**,
In the place
where dogs *licked* **lapped** the blood of Naboth
shall dogs *lick* **lap** thy blood, even thine.
20 And *Ahab* **Ach Ab** said to *Elijah* **Eli Yah**,
Hast thou found me, O mine enemy?
And he *answered* **said**, I have found thee:
because thou hast sold thyself to work evil
in the *sight* **eyes** of *the LORD* **Yah Veh**.
21 Behold, I *will* **shall** bring evil upon thee,
and *will take* **shall burn** away thy posterity,
and *will* **shall** cut off from *Ahab* **Ach Ab**
him that *pisseth* **urinateth** against the wall,
and him that is *shut up* **restrained**
and left in *Israel* **Yisra El**,
22 And *will make* **shall give** thine house
like the house of *Jeroboam* **Yarob Am** the son of Nebat,
and like the house of *Baasha* **Basha**
the son of *Ahijah* **Achiy Yah**,
for the *provocation* **vexation**
wherewith thou hast *provoked* **vexed** me *to anger*,
and made *Israel* **Yisra El** to sin.
23 And of *Jezebel* **Iy Zebel** also
spake the LORD **worded Yah Veh**, saying,
The dogs shall *eat Jezebel* **devour Iy Zebel**
by the *wall* **trench** of *Jezreel* **Yizre El**.
24 Him that dieth of *Ahab* **Ach Ab** in the city
the dogs shall *eat* **devour**;
and him that dieth in the field
shall the *fowls* **flyers** of the *air eat* **heavens devour**.
25 But there was none like unto *Ahab* **Ach Ab**,
which did sell himself to work *wickedness* **evil**
in the *sight* **eyes** of *the LORD* **Yah Veh**,
whom *Jezebel* **Iy Zebel** his *wife stirred up* **woman goaded**.
26 And he did *very abominably* **mighty abhorrently**
in *following* **going after** idols,
according to all *things*
as *did* **worked** the *Amorites* **Emoriy**,
whom *the LORD cast out* **Yah Veh dispossessed**
before **at the face of** the *children* **sons** of *Israel* **Yisra El**.
27 And it *came to pass* **became**,
when *Ahab* **Ach Ab** heard those words,
that he *rent* **ripped** his clothes,
and *put sackcloth* **set saq** upon his flesh, and fasted,
and lay in *sackcloth* **saq**, and *went softly* **walked gently**.
28 And the word of *the LORD* **Yah Veh**
came to *Elijah* **Eli Yah** the *Tishbite* **Tisbehiy**, saying,
29 Seest thou how *Ahab* **Ach Ab** humbleth himself
before me **at my face**?
because he humbleth himself *before me* **at my face**,
I *will* **shall** not bring the evil in his days:
but in his son's days
will **shall** I bring the evil upon his house.

ACH AB'S THIRD WAR WITH ARAM

22 And they *continued* **settled** three years without war
between *Syria* **Aram** and *Israel* **Yisra El**.
2 And it *came to pass* **became**, in the third year,
that *Jehoshaphat* **Yah Shaphat**,
the *king* **sovereign** of *Judah* **Yah Hudah**
came down **descended**
to the *king* **sovereign** of *Israel* **Yisra El**.
3 And the *king* **sovereign** of *Israel* **Yisra El**
said unto his servants,
Know ye that Ramoth in *Gilead* **Gilad** is ours,
and we be *still* **hushed**, and take it not
out of the hand of the *king* **sovereign** of *Syria* **Aram**?
4 And he said unto *Jehoshaphat* **Yah Shaphat**,
Wilt **Shalt** thou go with me to *battle* **war**
to *Ramothgilead* **Ramoth Gilad**?
And *Jehoshaphat* **Yah Shaphat**
said to the *king* **sovereign** of *Israel* **Yisra El**,
I *am* as thou *art*,
my people as thy people, my horses as thy horses.
5 And *Jehoshaphat* **Yah Shaphat**
said unto the *king* **sovereign** of *Israel* **Yisra El**,
Enquire, I *pray* **beseech** thee,
at the word of *the LORD* **Yah Veh** to day.
6 Then the *king* **sovereign** of *Israel* **Yisra El**
gathered the prophets *together*,
about four hundred men, and said unto them,
Shall I go against *Ramothgilead* **Ramoth Gilad**
to *battle* **war**,
or shall I *forbear* **cease**?
And they said, *Go up* **Ascend**;
for *the Lord* **Adonay** shall *deliver* **give** it
into the hand of the *king* **sovereign**.
7 And *Jehoshaphat* **Yah Shaphat** said,
Is there not here a prophet of *the LORD* **Yah Veh** *besides*,
that we might enquire of him?
8 And the *king* **sovereign** of *Israel* **Yisra El**
said unto *Jehoshaphat* **Yah Shaphat**,
There is yet one man,
Micaiah **Michah Yah** the son of *Imlah* **Yimlah**,
by whom we may enquire of *the LORD* **Yah Veh**:
but I hate him;
for he doth not prophesy good concerning me, but evil.
And *Jehoshaphat* **Yah Shaphat** said,
Let not the *king* **sovereign** say so.
9 Then the *king* **sovereign** of *Israel* **Yisra El**
called *an officer* **one eunuch**, and said,
Hasten *hither Micaiah* **Michah Yah** the son of *Imlah* **Yimlah**.
10 And the *king* **sovereign** of *Israel* **Yisra El**
and *Jehoshaphat* **Yah Shaphat**
the *king* **sovereign** of *Judah* **Yah Hudah**
sat **settled** each **man** on his throne,
having *put on* **enrobed** their *robes* **clothes**,
in a *void place* **threshingfloor**
in the *entrance* **opening**
of the *gate* **portal** of *Samaria* **Shomeron**;
and all the prophets prophesied *before them* **at their face**.
11 And *Zedekiah* **Sidqi Yah**
the son of *Chenaanah* **Kenaanah**
made **worked** him horns of iron:
and he said, Thus saith *the LORD* **Yah Veh**,
With these shalt thou *push* **butt** the *Syrians* **Aramiy**,
until thou have *consumed* **finished** them **off**.
12 And all the prophets prophesied so, saying,
Go up **Ascend** to *Ramothgilead* **Ramoth Gilad**,
and prosper:
for *the LORD* **Yah Veh** shall *deliver* **give** it
into the *king's* **sovereign's** hand.

MICHAH YAH PROPHESIES DEFEAT

13 And the *messenger* **angel**
that was gone to call *Micaiah* **Michah Yah**
spake **worded** unto him, saying,
Behold now, the words of the prophets

declare **are** good unto the *king* **sovereign** with one mouth:
let thy word, I *pray* **beseech** thee,
be like the word of one of them,
and *speak* **word** that which is good.
14 And *Micaiah* **Michah Yah** said,
As the LORD **Yah Veh** liveth,
what *the LORD* **Yah Veh** saith unto me,
that *will* **shall** I *speak* **word**.
15 So he came to the *king* **sovereign**.
And the *king* **sovereign** said unto him, *Micaiah* **Michah Yah**,
shall we go against *Ramothgilead* **Ramoth Gilad**
to *battle* **war**, or shall we *forbear* **cease**?
And he *answered* **said to** him, *Go* **Ascend**, and prosper:
for *the LORD* **Yah Veh**
shall *deliver* **give** it into the hand of the *king* **sovereign**.
16 And the *king* **sovereign** said unto him,
How many times shall I *adjure* **oath** thee
that thou *tell* **word** me *nothing* **naught**
but that which is *true* **truth**
in the name of *the LORD* **Yah Veh**?
17 And he said,
I saw all *Israel* **Yisra El** scattered upon the *hills* **mountains**,
as *sheep* **flocks** that have *not a shepherd* **no tender**:
and *the LORD* **Yah Veh** said, These have no *master* **adoni**:
let them return every man to his house in *peace* **shalom**.
18 And the *king* **sovereign** of *Israel* **Yisra El**
said unto *Jehoshaphat* **Yah Shaphat**,
Did I not *tell* **say to** thee
that he *would* **should** prophesy no good concerning me,
but evil?
19 And he said,
Hear thou therefore the word of *the LORD* **Yah Veh**:
I saw *the LORD sitting* **Yah Veh settled** on his throne,
and all the host of *heaven* **the heavens** standing by him
on his right *hand* and on his left.
20 And *the LORD* **Yah Veh** said,
Who shall *persuade Ahab* **entice Ach Ab**,
that he may *go up* **ascend**
and fall at *Ramothgilead* **Ramoth Gilad**?
And **this** one said *on this manner* **thus**,
and *another* **that one** said *on that manner* **thus**.
21 And there *came forth* **went** a spirit,
and stood *before the LORD* **at the face of Yah Veh**,
and said, I *will persuade* **shall entice** him.
22 And *the LORD* **Yah Veh** said unto him, Wherewith?
And he said, I *will* **shall** go forth,
and I *will be* **shall become** a *lying* **false** spirit
in the mouth of all his prophets.
And he said,
Thou shalt *persuade* **entice** him, and prevail also:
go forth, and *do* **work** so.
23 Now therefore, behold,
the LORD **Yah Veh** hath *put* **given** a *lying* **false** spirit
in the mouth of all these thy prophets,
and *the LORD* **Yah Veh** hath *spoken* **worded** evil
concerning thee.
24 But *Zedekiah* **Sidqi Yah**
the son of *Chenaanah went* **Kenaanah came** near,
and smote *Micaiah* **Michah Yah** on the cheek, and said,
Which way went **Where passed**
the Spirit of *the LORD* **Yah Veh** from me
to *speak* **word** unto thee?
25 And *Micaiah* **Michah Yah** said, Behold,
thou shalt see in that day,
when thou shalt go into an inner chamber to hide thyself.
26 And the *king* **sovereign** of *Israel* **Yisra El** said,
Take *Micaiah* **Michah Yah**,
and *carry* **return** him *back*
unto Amon the governor of the city,
and to *Joash* **Yah Ash** the *king's* **sovereign's** son;
27 And say, Thus saith the *king* **sovereign**,
Put **Set** this *fellow* **one** in the prison **house**,
and *feed him with* **have him eat**
bread of *affliction* **oppression**
and *with* water of *affliction* **oppression**,
until I come in *peace* **shalom**.
28 And *Micaiah* **Michah Yah** said,
If **in returning,** thou return *at all* in *peace* **shalom**,
the LORD **Yah Veh** hath not *spoken* **worded** by me.
And he said, Hearken, O people, every one of you.

ACH AB DEATHIFIED

29 So the *king* **sovereign** of *Israel* **Yisra El**
and *Jehoshaphat* **Yah Shaphat,**
the *king* **sovereign** of *Judah* **Yah Hudah**
went up **ascended** to *Ramothgilead* **Ramoth Gilad**.
30 And the *king* **sovereign** of *Israel* **Yisra El**
said unto *Jehoshaphat* **Yah Shaphat**,
I *will* **shall** disguise myself, and enter into the *battle* **war**;
but *put* **enrobe** thou *on* thy *robes* **clothes**.
And the *king* **sovereign** of *Israel* **Yisra El** disguised himself,
and went into the *battle* **war**.
31 But the *king* **sovereign** of *Syria* **Aram**
commanded **misvahed**
his thirty and two *captains* **governors**
that had rule over his chariots, saying,
Fight neither with small nor great,
save only with the *king* **sovereign** of *Israel* **Yisra El**.
32 And it *came to pass* **became**,
when the *captains* **governors** of the chariots
saw *Jehoshaphat* **Yah Shaphat**, that they said,
Surely it is the *king* **sovereign** of *Israel* **Yisra El**.
And they turned aside to fight against him:
and *Jehoshaphat* **Yah Shaphat** cried out.
33 And it *came to pass* **became**,
when the *captains* **governors** of the chariots *perceived* **saw**
that it was not the *king* **sovereign** of *Israel* **Yisra El**,
that they turned back from *pursuing* **after** him.
34 And a *certain* man
drew a bow *at a venture* **in his integrity**,
and smote the *king* **sovereign** of *Israel* **Yisra El**
between the joints of the *harness* **habergeon**:
wherefore he said unto *the driver of* his *chariot* **charioteer**,
Turn thine hand, and *carry* **bring** me out of the *host* **camp**;
for I am *wounded* **sick**.
35 And the *battle increased* **war ascended** that day:
and the *king* **sovereign**
was stayed up in his chariot against the *Syrians* **Aramiy**,
and died at even:
and the blood *ran* **poured** out of the *wound* **stroke**
into the *midst* **bosom** of the chariot.
36 And there *went* **passed** a *proclamation* **shout**
throughout the *host* **camp**
about the *going down* **descent** of the sun, saying,
Every man to his city,
and every man to his own *country* **land**.
37 So the *king* **sovereign** died,
and was brought to *Samaria* **Shomeron**;
and they *buried* **entombed** the *king* **sovereign**
in *Samaria* **Shomeron**.
38 And *one washed* **overflowed** the chariot
in the pool of *Samaria* **Shomeron**;
and the dogs *licked* **lapped** up his blood;
and they *washed* **bathed** his armour;
according unto the word of *the LORD* **Yah Veh**
which he *spake* **worded**.
39 Now the rest of the *acts* **words** of *Ahab* **Ach Ab**,
and all that he *did* **worked**,
and the ivory house which he *made* **built**,
and all the cities that he built,
are they not *written* **inscribed** in the *book* **scroll**
of the *chronicles* **words of the days**
of the *kings* **sovereigns** of *Israel* **Yisra El**?
40 So *Ahab slept* **Ach Ab laid** with his fathers;
and *Ahaziah* **Achaz Yah** his son reigned in his stead.

YAH SHAPHAT REIGNS OVER YISRA EL

41 And *Jehoshaphat* **Yah Shaphat** the son of Asa
began to reign over *Judah* **Yah Hudah**
in the fourth year
of *Ahab* **Ach Ab** *king* **sovereign** of *Israel* **Yisra El**.
42 *Jehoshaphat* **Yah Shaphat**
was **a son of** thirty and five years *old*
when he began to reign;
and he reigned twenty and five years
in *Jerusalem* **Yeru Shalem**.
And his mother's name was Azubah
the daughter of *Shilhi* **Shilchi**.
43 And he walked in all the ways of Asa his father;
he turned not aside from it,
doing **working** that which was *right* **straight**
in the eyes of *the LORD* **Yah Veh**:

nevertheless the *high places* **bamahs**
were not *taken away* **turned aside;**
for the people
offered **sacrificed** and *burnt incense* **incensed**
yet in the *high places* **bamahs.**
44 And *Jehoshaphat made peace* **Yah Shaphat did shalam**
with the *king* **sovereign** of *Israel* **Yisra El.**
45 Now the rest of the *acts* **words**
of *Jehoshaphat* **Yah Shaphat,**
and his might that he *shewed* **worked,**
and how he *warred* **fought,**
are they not *written* **inscribed** in the *book* **scroll**
of the *chronicles* **words of the days**
of the *kings* **sovereigns** of *Judah* **Yah Hudah?**
46 And the remnant
of the *sodomites* **hallowed whoremongers,**
which *remained* **survived** in the days of his father Asa,
he *took* **burnt** out of the land.
47 There was then no *king* **sovereign** in Edom:
a deputy was king **one was stationed as sovereign.**
48 *Jehoshaphat* **Yah Shaphat**
made **worked ten** ships of *Tharshish* **Tarshish**
to go to Ophir for gold: but they went not;
for the ships were broken at *Eziongeber* **Esyon Geber.**
49 Then said *Ahaziah* **Achaz Yah** the son of *Ahab* **Ach Ab**
unto *Jehoshaphat* **Yah Shaphat,**
Let my servants go with thy servants in the ships.
But *Jehoshaphat would* **Yah Shaphat willed** not.
50 And *Jehoshaphat* **Yah Shaphat**
slept **laid** with his fathers,
and was *buried* **entombed** with his fathers
in the city of David his father:
and *Jehoram* **Yah Ram** his son reigned in his stead.

ACHAZ YAH REIGNS OVER YISRA EL

51 *Ahaziah* **Achaz Yah** the son of *Ahab* **Ach Ab**
began to reign over *Israel* **Yisra El** in *Samaria* **Shomeron**
the seventeenth year of *Jehoshaphat* **Yah Shaphat,**
king **sovereign** of *Judah* **Yah Hudah,**
and reigned two years over *Israel* **Yisra El.**
52 And he *did* **worked** evil
in the *sight* **eyes** of *the LORD* **Yah Veh,**
and walked in the way of his father,
and in the way of his mother,
and in the way of *Jeroboam* **Yarob Am** the son of Nebat,
who made *Israel* **Yisra El** to sin:
53 For he served Baal, and *worshipped* **prostrated to** him,
and *provoked to anger* **vexed**
the LORD God **Yah Veh Elohim** of *Israel* **Yisra El,**
according to all that his father had *done* **worked.**

KEY TO INTERPRETING THE EXEGESES:
King James text is in regular type;
Text under exegeses is in oblique type;
Text of exegeses is in bold type.

YAH VEH JUDGES ACHAZ YAH

1 Then Moab rebelled against *Israel* **Yisra El**
after the death of *Ahab* **Ach Ab.**
2 And *Ahaziah* **Achaz Yah**
fell down **descended** through a lattice
in his upper *chamber* **room**
that was in *Samaria* **Shomeron,** and was sick:
and he sent *messengers* **angels,** and said unto them,
Go, enquire of *Baalzebub* **Baal Zebub**
the *god* **elohim** of *Ekron* **Eqron**
whether I shall *recover* **live** of this *disease* **sickness.**
3 But the angel of *the LORD* **Yah Veh**
said **worded** to *Elijah* **Eli Yah** the *Tishbite* **Tisbehiy,**
Arise, *go up* **ascend** to meet the *messengers* **angels**
of the *king* **sovereign** of *Samaria* **Shomeron,**
and *say* **word** unto them,
Is it not because
there is not *a God* **Elohim** in *Israel* **Yisra El,**
that ye go to enquire
of *Baalzebub* **Baal Zebub** the *god* **elohim** of *Ekron* **Eqron?**
4 Now therefore thus saith *the LORD* **Yah Veh,**
Thou shalt not *come down* **descend**
from that bed on which thou art *gone up* **ascended,**
but **in dying,** shalt *surely* die.
And *Elijah departed* **Eli Yah went.**
5 And when the *messengers* **angels** turned back unto him,
he said unto them, Why are ye *now* **thus** turned back?
6 And they said unto him,
There *came* **ascended** a man *up* to meet us,
and said unto us, Go,
turn again **return** unto the *king* **sovereign** that sent you,
and *say* **word** unto him, Thus saith *the LORD* **Yah Veh,**
Is it not because
there is not a *God* **Elohim** in *Israel* **Yisra El,**
that thou sendest to enquire
of *Baalzebub* **Baal Zebub** the *god* **elohim** of *Ekron* **Eqron?**
therefore thou shalt not *come down* **descend**
from that bed on which thou art *gone up* **ascended,**
but **in dying,** shalt *surely* die.
7 And he *said* **worded** unto them,
What *manner* **judgment** of man *was he*
which *came up* **ascended** to meet you,
and *told* **worded** you these words?
8 And they *answered* **said to** him,
He was *an hairy man* **a man, a master of hair,**
and girt with a girdle of *leather* **skin** about his loins.
And he said, It is *Elijah* **Eli Yah** the *Tishbite* **Tisbehiy.**
9 Then the *king* **sovereign** sent unto him
a *captain* **governor** of fifty with his fifty.
And he *went up* **ascended** to him: and, behold,
he *sat* **settled** on the top of *an hill* **a mountain.**
And he *spake* **worded** unto him,
Thou man of *God* **Elohim,**
the *king* **sovereign** hath *said* **worded,**
Come down **Descend.**
10 And *Elijah* **Eli Yah** answered and *said* **worded**
to the *captain* **governor** of fifty,
If I be a man of *God* **Elohim,**
then let fire
come down **descend** from *heaven* **the heavens,**
and consume thee and thy fifty.
And there *came down* **descended** fire
from *heaven* **the heavens,**
and consumed him and his fifty.
11 *Again also* **And** he **returned and** sent unto him
another *captain* **governor** of fifty with his fifty.
And he answered and *said* **worded** unto him,
O man of *God* **Elohim,** thus hath the *king* **sovereign** said,
Come down **Descend** quickly.
12 And *Elijah* **Eli Yah**
answered and *said* **worded** unto them,
If I be a man of *God* **Elohim,**
let fire *come down* **descend** from *heaven* **the heavens,**
and consume thee and thy fifty.
And the fire of *God* **Elohim**
came down **descended** from *heaven* **the heavens,**

and consumed him and his fifty.
13 And he **returned and** sent *again*
a *captain* **governor** of the third fifty with his fifty.
And the third *captain* **governor** of fifty *went up* **ascended**,
and came and *fell* **bowed** on his knees
before Elijah **in front of Eli Yah**,
and besought him, and *said* **worded** unto him,
O man of *God* **Elohim**, I *pray* **beseech** thee,
let my *life* **soul**, and the *life* **soul** of these fifty thy servants,
be precious in thy *sight* **eyes**.
14 Behold, there *came* **descended** fire *down*
from *heaven* **the heavens**,
and *burnt up* **consumed** the two *captains* **governors**
of the former fifties with their fifties:
therefore let my *life* **soul**
now be precious in thy *sight* **eyes**.
15 And the angel of *the LORD* **Yah Veh**
said **worded** unto *Elijah* **Eli Yah**,
Go down **Descend** with him:
be not *afraid of* **awed to face** him.
And he arose, and *went down* **descended** with him
unto the *king* **sovereign**.
16 And he *said* **worded** unto him,
Thus saith *the LORD* **Yah Veh**,
Forasmuch as thou hast sent *messengers* **angels** to enquire
of *Baalzebub* **Baal Zebub** the *god* **elohim** of *Ekron* **Eqron**,
is it not because there is no *God* **Elohim** in *Israel* **Yisra El**
to enquire of his word?
therefore thou shalt not *come down* **descend** off that bed
on which thou art *gone up* **ascended**,
but **in dying,** shalt *surely* die.
17 So he died according to the word of *the LORD* **Yah Veh**
which *Elijah* **Eli Yah** had *spoken* **worded**.
And *Jehoram* **Yah Ram** reigned in his stead
in the second year of *Jehoram* **Yah Ram**
the son of *Jehoshaphat* **Yah Shaphat,**
king **sovereign** of *Judah* **Yah Hudah**;
because he had no son.
18 Now the rest of the *acts* **words** of *Ahaziah* **Achaz Yah**
which he *did* **worked**,
are they not *written* **inscribed** in the *book* **scroll**
of the *chronicles* **words of the days**
of the *kings* **sovereigns** of *Israel* **Yisra El**?

ELI YAH ASCENDS TO THE HEAVENS

2 And it *came to pass* **became**,
when *the LORD would take up Elijah*
Yah Veh should ascend Eli Yah
into *heaven* **the heavens** by a *whirlwind* **storm**,
that *Elijah* **Eli Yah** went with *Elisha* **Eli Shua** from Gilgal.
2 And *Elijah* **Eli Yah** said unto *Elisha* **Eli Shua**,
Tarry **Settle** here, I *pray* **beseech** thee;
for *the LORD* **Yah Veh** hath sent me to *Bethel* **Beth El**.
And *Elisha* **Eli Shua** said *unto him*,
As the LORD **Yah Veh** liveth, and *as* thy soul liveth,
I *will* **shall** not leave thee.
So they *went down* **descended** to *Bethel* **Beth El**.
3 And the sons of the prophets that were at *Bethel* **Beth El**
came forth **went** to *Elisha* **Eli Shua**, and said unto him,
Knowest thou that *the LORD* **Yah Veh**
will **shall** take *away* thy *master* **adoni**
from thy head to day?
And he said, Yea, I know it; *hold ye your peace* **hush**.
4 And *Elijah* **Eli Yah** said unto him,
Elisha **Eli Shua**, *tarry* **settle** here, I *pray* **beseech** thee;
for *the LORD* **Yah Veh** hath sent me to *Jericho* **Yericho**.
And he said,
As the LORD **Yah Veh** liveth, and *as* thy soul liveth,
I *will* **shall** not leave thee.
So they came to *Jericho* **Yericho**.
5 And the sons of the prophets that were at *Jericho* **Yericho**
came **near** to *Elisha* **Eli Shua**, and said unto him,
Knowest thou that *the LORD* **Yah Veh**
will **shall** take *away* thy *master* **adoni**
from thy head to day?
And he *answered* **said**,
Yea, I know it; *hold* ye *your peace* **hush**.
6 And *Elijah* **Eli Yah** said unto him,
Tarry **Settle**, I *pray* **beseech** thee, here;
for *the LORD* **Yah Veh** hath sent me to *Jordan* **Yarden**.
And he said,
As the LORD **Yah Veh** liveth, and *as* thy soul liveth,
I *will* **shall** not leave thee. And they two went on.
7 And fifty men of the sons of the prophets went,
and stood *to view* **over against** afar off:
and they two stood by *Jordan* **Yarden**.
8 And *Elijah* **Eli Yah** took his **mighty** mantle,
and *wrapped it together* **rolled it up**,
and smote the waters,
and they were *divided* **halved** hither and thither,
so that they two *went* **passed** over
on *dry ground* **parched area**.
9 And it *came to pass* **became**,
when they were *gone* **passed** over,
that *Elijah* **Eli Yah** said unto *Elisha* **Eli Shua**,
Ask what I shall *do* **work** for thee,
before I be taken away from thee.
And *Elisha* **Eli Shua** said, I *pray* **beseech** thee,
let a *double portion* **twofold mouth** of thy spirit
be upon me.
10 And he said, Thou hast asked a hard *thing*:
nevertheless, if thou see me *when I am* taken from thee,
it shall be so unto thee **so be it**;
but if not, *it shall not be* **so be it not**.
11 And it *came to pass* **became**,
as they still went **in walking, as they walked** on,
and *talked* **worded**, that, behold,
there appeared a chariot of fire, and horses of fire,
and *parted* **separated between** them both *asunder*;
and *Elijah went up* **Eli Yah ascended** by a *whirlwind* **storm**
into *heaven* **the heavens**.
12 And *Elisha* **Eli Shua** saw it, and he cried,
My father, my father, the chariot of *Israel* **Yisra El**,
and the *horsemen* **cavalry** thereof.
And he saw him no more:
and he took hold of his own clothes,
and *rent* **shreaded** them in two *pieces* **shreads**.
13 He *took up* **lifted** also
the **mighty** mantle of *Elijah* **Eli Yah** that fell from him,
and *went back* **returned**,
and stood by the *bank* **lip** of *Jordan* **Yarden**;
14 And he took the **mighty** mantle of *Elijah* **Eli Yah**
that fell from him,
and smote the waters, and said,
Where is *the LORD God* **Yah Veh Elohim** of *Elijah* **Eli Yah**?
and when he also had smitten the waters,
they *parted* **halved** hither and thither:
and *Elisha went* **Eli Shua passed** over.
15 And when the sons of the prophets
which were *to view* **opposite** at *Jericho* **Yericho** saw him,
they said,
The spirit of *Elijah* **Eli Yah** doth rest on *Elisha* **Eli Shua**.
And they came to meet him,
and *bowed* **prostrated** themselves to the *ground* **earth**
before him.
16 And they said unto him, Behold now,
there be with thy servants fifty *strong men* **sons of valour**;
let them go, we *pray* **beseech** thee,
and seek thy *master* **adoni**:
lest *peradventure* the Spirit of *the LORD* **Yah Veh**
hath *taken* **lifted** him *up*,
and cast him upon *some* **one** mountain,
or into *some* **one** valley.
And he said, ye shall not send.
17 And when they urged him till he was *ashamed* **shamed**,
he said, Send. They sent therefore fifty men;
and they sought three days, but found him not.
18 And when they *came* **returned** *again* to him,
(for he *tarried* **settled** at *Jericho* **Yericho**,)
he said unto them, Did I not say unto you, Go not?

WATERS HEALED

19 And the men of the city said unto *Elisha* **Eli Shua**,
Behold, I *pray* **beseech** thee,
the *situation* **site** of this city is *pleasant* **good**,
as my *lord* **adoni** seeth:
but the water is *naught* **evil**,
and the *ground barren* **earth aborteth**.
20 And he said, *Bring* **Take** me a new cruse,
and *put* **set** salt therein.
And they *brought* **took** it to him.
21 And he went forth unto the spring of the waters,

and cast the salt in there, and said,
Thus saith *the LORD* **Yah Veh**, I have healed these waters;
there shall not be *from thence any* **no** more death
or barren *land*.
22 So the waters were healed unto this day,
according to the *saying* **word** of *Elisha* **Eli Shua**
which he *spake* **worded**.

ELI SHUA RIDICULED

23 And he *went up* **ascended** from thence
unto *Bethel* **Beth El**:
and as he was *going up* **ascending** by the way,
there *came forth* **went** little *children* **lads** out of the city,
and *mocked* **ridiculed** him, and said unto him,
Go up **Ascend**, *thou bald head* **baldy**;
go up **ascend**, *thou bald head* **baldy**.
24 And he *turned* **faced** back, and *looked on* **saw** them,
and *cursed* **abased** them
in the name of *the LORD* **Yah Veh**.
And there *came forth* **went**
two she bears out of the *wood* **forest**,
and *tare* **split** forty and two children of them.
25 And he went from thence to mount *Carmel* **Karmel**,
and from thence he returned to *Samaria* **Shomeron**.

THE REIGN OF YAH RAM OVER YISRA EL

3 Now *Jehoram* **Yah Ram** the son of *Ahab* **Ach Ab**
began to reign over *Israel* **Yisra El** in *Samaria* **Shomeron**
the eighteenth year of *Jehoshaphat* **Yah Shaphat**
king **sovereign** of *Judah* **Yah Hudah**,
and reigned twelve years.
2 And he *wrought* **worked** evil
in the *sight* **eyes** of *the LORD* **Yah Veh**;
but not like his father, and like his mother:
for he *put away* **turned aside** the *image* **monolith** of Baal
that his father had *made* **worked**.
3 Nevertheless he *cleaved* **adhered** unto the sins
of *Jeroboam* **Yarob Am** the son of Nebat,
which made *Israel* **Yisra El** to sin;
he *departed* **turned** not **aside** therefrom.

MOAB'S REBELLION

4 And Mesha *king* **sovereign** of Moab
was a *sheepmaster* **brander**,
and *rendered* **returned**
unto the *king* **sovereign** of *Israel* **Yisra El**
an hundred thousand *lambs* **rams**,
and an hundred thousand rams, with the wool.
5 But it *came to pass* **became**,
when *Ahab* **Ach Ab** was dead,
that the *king* **sovereign** of Moab
rebelled against the *king* **sovereign** of *Israel* **Yisra El**.
6 And *king Jehoram* **sovereign Yah Ram**
went out of *Samaria* **Shomeron** the same *time* **day**,
and *numbered* **mustered** all *Israel* **Yisra El**.
7 And he went and sent to *Jehoshaphat* **Yah Shaphat**
the *king* **sovereign** of *Judah* **Yah Hudah**, saying,
The *king* **sovereign** of Moab hath rebelled against me:
wilt **shalt** thou go with me against Moab to *battle* **war**?
And he said, I *will go up* **shall ascend**: I *am* as thou *art*,
my people as thy people, *and* my horses as thy horses.
8 And he said, Which way shall we *go up* **ascend**?
And he *answered* **said**,
The way through the wilderness of Edom.
9 So the *king* **sovereign** of *Israel* **Yisra El** went,
and the *king* **sovereign** of *Judah* **Yah Hudah**,
and the *king* **sovereign** of Edom:
and they *fetched a compass* **went**
of **about** seven days' journey:
and there was no water for the *host* **camp**,
and for the *cattle* **animals** that followed *them* **at their feet**.
10 And the *king* **sovereign** of *Israel* **Yisra El** said, *Alas* **Aha**!
that *the LORD* **Yah Veh** hath called
these three *kings* **sovereigns** together,
to *deliver* **give** them into the hand of Moab!
11 But *Jehoshaphat* **Yah Shaphat** said,
Is there not here a prophet of *the LORD* **Yah Veh**,
that we may enquire of *the LORD* **Yah Veh** by him?
And one of the *king* **sovereign** of *Israel's* **Yisra El's** servants
answered and said,
Here is *Elisha* **Eli Shua** the son of Shaphat,
which poured water on the hands of *Elijah* **Eli Yah**.
12 And *Jehoshaphat* **Yah Shaphat** said,
The word of *the LORD is* **Yah Veh be** with him.
So the *king* **sovereign** of *Israel* **Yisra El**
and *Jehoshaphat* **Yah Shaphat**
and the *king* **sovereign** of Edom
went down **descended** to him.
13 And *Elisha* **Eli Shua**
said unto the *king* **sovereign** of *Israel* **Yisra El**,
What have I to do with thee?
get thee **go** to the prophets of thy father,
and to the prophets of thy mother.
And the *king* **sovereign** of *Israel* **Yisra El** said unto him,
Nay: for *the LORD* **Yah Veh**
hath called these three *kings* **sovereigns** together,
to deliver them into the hand of Moab.
14 And *Elisha* **Eli Shua** said,
As the LORD of hosts **Yah Veh Sabaoth** liveth,
before **at the face of** whom I stand, *surely*,
were it not that **for unless** I
regard the presence **lift the face**
of *Jehoshaphat* **Yah Shaphat**,
the *king* **sovereign** of *Judah* **Yah Hudah**,
I *would* **should** not look toward thee, nor see thee.
15 But now *bring* **take** me a *minstrel* **strummer**.
And it *came to pass* **became**,
when the *minstrel played* **strummer strummed**,
that the hand of *the LORD* **Yah Veh** came upon him.
16 And he said, Thus saith *the LORD* **Yah Veh**,
Make **Work** this *valley* **wadi** full of *ditches* **dugouts**.
17 For thus saith *the LORD* **Yah Veh**,
ye shall not see wind, neither shall ye see rain;
yet that *valley* **wadi** shall be filled with water,
that ye may drink, both ye,
and your *cattle* **chattel**, and your *beasts* **animals**.
18 And this is *but a light thing* **a trifle**
in the *sight* **eyes** of *the LORD* **Yah Veh**:
he *will deliver* **shall give**
the *Moabites* **Moabiy** also into your hand.
19 And ye shall smite every *fenced* **fortified** city,
and every choice city, and shall fell every good tree,
and stop all *wells* **fountains** of water,
and *mar* **pain** every good *piece of land* **allotment**
with stones.
20 And it *came to pass* **became**, in the morning,
when the *meat* offering was *offered* **holocausted**,
that, behold, there came water by the way of Edom,
and the *country* **land** was filled with water.
21 And when all the *Moabites* **Moabiy** heard
that the *kings* **sovereigns**
were come up **ascended** to fight against them,
they *gathered* **called together**
all that were able to *put on armour* **gird a girdle**,
and upward,
and stood in the border.
22 And they *rose up* **started** early in the morning,
and the sun *shone* **rose** upon the water,
and the *Moabites* **Moabiy** saw the water
on the other side **in front** as red as blood:
23 And they said, This is blood:
in being desolated,
the *kings* **sovereigns** are *surely slain* **desolated,**
and they have smitten *one another* **man his friend**:
now therefore, Moab, to the spoil.
24 And when they came to the camp of *Israel* **Yisra El**,
the *Israelites* **Yisra Eliy** rose up
and smote the *Moabites* **Moabiy**,
so that they fled *before them* **from their face**:
but they went forward smiting **and they smote**
the *Moabites* **Moabiy** *even in their country*.
25 And they *beat down* **demolished** the cities,
and on every good *piece of land* **allotment**
cast every man his stone, and filled it;
and they stopped all the *wells* **fountains** of water,
and felled all the good trees:
only in *Kirharaseth* **Qir Hareseth**
left they the stones thereof;
howbeit the slingers went about it, and smote it.
26 And when the *king* **sovereign** of Moab saw
that the *battle* **war** was too *sore* **strong** for him,
he took with him seven hundred men that drew swords,
to *break* **split** *through*

even unto the *king* **sovereign** of Edom:
but they could not.
27 Then he took his *eldest* **firstborn** son
that should have reigned in his stead,
and *offered* **holocausted** him for a *burnt offering* **holocaust**
upon the wall.
And there was great *indignation* **rage**
against *Israel* **Yisra El**:
and they *departed* **pulled stakes** from him,
and returned to their *own* land.

THE WIDOW'S OIL

4 Now there cried
a certain **one** woman of the *wives* **women**
of the sons of the prophets unto *Elisha* **Eli Shua**, saying,
Thy servant my *husband is dead* **man has died**;
and thou knowest that thy servant
did *fear the LORD* **awe Yah Veh**:
and the *creditor* **exactor** is come to take unto him
my two *sons* **children** to be *bondmen* **servants**.
2 And *Elisha* **Eli Shua** said unto her,
What shall I *do* **work** for thee?
tell me, what hast thou in the house?
And she said,
Thine handmaid **Thy maid** hath *not any thing* **naught**
in the house,
save *a pot* **except an anointing flask** of oil.
3 Then he said, Go, *borrow* **ask** thee *vessels* **instruments**
abroad **out** of all thy *neighbours* **fellow tabernaclers**,
even empty *vessels* **instruments**;
borrow not a few **diminish not**.
4 And when thou art come in,
thou shalt shut the door upon thee and upon thy sons,
and shalt pour out into all those *vessels* **instruments**,
and thou shalt *set aside* **pluck** that which is full.
5 So she went from him,
and shut the door upon her and upon her sons,
who brought **near** *the vessels* to her; and she poured out.
6 And it *came to pass* **became**,
when the *vessels* **instruments** were *full* **filled**,
that she said unto her son,
Bring **near** me yet *a vessel* **an instrument**.
And he said unto her,
There is not *a vessel* **an instrument** more.
And the oil stayed.
7 Then she came and told the man of *God* **Elohim**.
And he said, Go, sell the oil,
and *pay* **shalam** thy *debt* **lender**,
and live thou and thy *children* **sons** of the rest.

ELI SHUA'S UPPER ROOM

8 And it fell on a day,
that *Elisha* **Eli Shua** passed to Shunem,
where was a great woman;
and she *constrained* **laid hold on** him to eat bread.
And so it *was* **became**,
that as oft as he passed by,
he turned in thither to eat bread.
9 And she said unto her *husband* **man**, Behold now,
I perceive that this is an holy man of *God* **Elohim**,
which passeth by us continually.
10 Let us *make* **work** a little *chamber* **upper room**,
I *pray* **beseech** thee, on the wall;
and let us set for him there a bed, and a table,
and a *stool* **throne**, and a *candlestick* **menorah**:
and it shall be, when he cometh to us,
that he shall turn in thither.

A SON IS PROPHESIED, AND BORN

11 And it fell on a day, that he came thither,
and he turned **aside** into the *chamber* **upper room**,
and lay there.
12 And he said to *Gehazi* **Gay Chazi** his *servant* **lad**,
Call this *Shunammite* **Shunemiyth**.
And when he had called her,
she stood *before him* **at his face**.
13 And he said unto him, Say now unto her, Behold,
thou hast *been careful* **trembled** for us
with all this *care* **trembling**;
what is to be *done* **worked** for thee?
wouldest **shouldest** thou
be spoken for **that we word** to the *king* **sovereign**,
or to the *captain* **governor** of the host?
And she *answered* **said**,
I *dwell* **settle** among mine own people.
14 And he said, What then is to be *done* **worked** for her?
And *Gehazi answered* **Gay Chazi said**,
Verily **Nevertheless**
she hath no *child* **son**, and her *husband* **man** is old.
15 And he said, Call her.
And when he had called her, she stood in the *door* **portal**.
16 And he said, About this season,
according to the time of life, thou shalt embrace a son.
And she said, Nay, my *lord* **adoni**,
thou man of *God* **Elohim**,
do not lie unto *thine handmaid* **thy maid**.
17 And the woman conceived,
and bare a son at that season
that *Elisha* **Eli Shua** had *said* **worded** unto her,
according to the time of life.

THE SON DIES

18 And when the child was grown, it fell on a day,
that he went out to his father to the *reapers* **harvesters**.
19 And he said unto his father, My head, my head.
And he said to a lad, *Carry* **Lift** him to his mother.
20 And when he had *taken* **lifted** him,
and brought him to his mother,
he *sat* **settled** on her knees till noon, and *then* died.
21 And she *went up* **ascended**,
and laid him on the bed of the man of *God* **Elohim**,
and shut *the door* upon him, and went out.
22 And she called unto her *husband* **man**, and said,
Send me, I *pray* **beseech** *thee*,
one of the *young men* **lads**,
and one of the *asses* **she burros**,
that I may run to the man of *God* **Elohim**,
and *come again* **return**.
23 And he said,
Wherefore *wilt* **shalt** thou go to him to day?
it is neither new moon, nor *sabbath* **shabbath**.
And she said, *It shall be well* **Shalom**.
24 Then she *saddled an ass* **harnessed a she burro**,
and said to her *servant* **lad**, Drive, and go forward;
slack **restrain** not thy riding for me, except I *bid* **say to** thee.
25 So she went and came unto the man of *God* **Elohim**
to mount *Carmel* **Karmel**.
And it *came to pass* **became**,
when the man of *God* **Elohim** saw her afar off,
that he said to *Gehazi* **Gay Chazi** his *servant* **lad**,
Behold, *yonder is* that *Shunammite* **Shunemiyth**:
26 Run now, I *pray* **beseech** thee, to meet her,
and say unto her,
Is it well **Shalom** with thee?
is it well **Shalom** with thy *husband* **man**?
is it *well* **Shalom** with the child?
And she *answered* **said**, *It is well* **Shalom**:
27 And when she came to the man of *God* **Elohim**
to the *hill* **mountain**, she *caught* **held** him by the feet:
but *Gehazi* **Gay Chazi** came near to *thrust* **expel** her *away*.
And the man of *God* **Elohim** said, *Let* **Loose** her *alone*;
for her soul is *vexed* **embittered** within her:
and *the LORD* **Yah Veh** hath *hid* **concealed** it from me,
and hath not told me.
28 Then she said, Did I *desire* **ask** a son of my *lord* **adoni**?
did I not say, Do not *deceive* **mislead** me?
29 Then he said to *Gehazi* **Gay Chazi**, Gird up thy loins,
and take my staff in thine hand, and go thy way:
if thou *meet any* **find a** man, *salute* **bless** him not;
and if *any salute* **a man bless** thee, answer him not *again*:
and *lay* **set** my staff upon the face of the *child* **lad**.
30 And the mother of the *child* **lad** said,
As the LORD **Yah Veh** liveth, and *as* thy soul liveth,
I *will* **shall** not leave thee.
And he arose, and *followed* **went after** her.
31 And *Gehazi* **Gay Chazi** passed on
before them **from their face**,
and *laid* **set** the staff upon the face of the *child* **lad**;
but there was neither voice, nor *hearing* **hearkening**.
Wherefore he *went again* **turned back** to meet him,
and told him, saying, The *child* **lad** is not awaked.
32 And when *Elisha* **Eli Shua** was come into the house,
behold, the *child was dead* **lad had died**,
and laid upon his bed.

THE SON ENLIVENED

33 He went in therefore,
and shut the door upon them *twain* **both**,
and prayed unto *the LORD* **Yah Veh**.
34 And he *went up* **ascended**, and lay upon the child,
and *put* **set** his mouth upon his mouth,
and his eyes upon his eyes,
and his *hands* **palms** upon his *hands* **palms**:
and *stretched* **prostrated** himself upon the child;
and the flesh of the child *waxed warm* **heated**.
35 Then he returned, and walked in the house
to and fro **once hither and once thither**;
and *went up* **ascended**,
and *stretched* **prostrated** himself upon him:
and the *child* **lad** sneezed seven times,
and the *child* **lad** opened his eyes.
36 And he called *Gehazi* **Gay Chazi**, and said,
Call this *Shunammite* **Shunemiyth**.
So he called her.
And when she was come in unto him, he said,
Take up **Lift** thy son.
37 Then she went in, and fell at his feet,
and *bowed* **prostrated** herself to the *ground* **earth**,
and *took up* **lifted** her son, and went out.

ELI SHUA PURGES THE POTTAGE

38 And *Elisha came again* **Eli Shua returned** to Gilgal:
and there was a *dearth* **famine** in the land;
and the sons of the prophets
were sitting before him **settled at his face**:
and he said unto his *servant* **lad**,
Set on the great *pot* **caldron**,
and *seethe* **stew** pottage for the sons of the prophets.
39 And one went out into the field to gather herbs,
and found a *wild vine* **vine of the field**,
and gathered thereof *wild gourds* **cucumbers of the field**
his *lap* **coverall** full, and came and *shred* **cleaved** them
into the *pot* **caldron** of pottage:
for they knew them not.
40 So they poured out for the men to eat.
And it *came to pass* **became**,
as they were eating of the pottage,
that they cried out, and said,
O *thou* man of *God* **Elohim**,
there is death in the *pot* **caldron**.
And they could not eat thereof.
41 But he said, *Then bring meal* **Take flour**.
And he cast it into the *pot* **caldron**;
and he said, Pour out for the people, that they may eat.
And there was no *harm* **evil word** in the *pot* **caldron**.
42 And there came a man
from *Baalshalisha* **Baal Shalishah**,
and brought the man of *God* **Elohim** bread of the firstfruits,
twenty *loaves* **bread** of barley,
and *full ears of corn* **of the orchard**
in the *husk* **sack** thereof. And he said,
Give unto the people, that they may eat.
43 And his *servitor* **minister** said,
What, should I *set* **give** this
before **at the face of** an hundred men?
He said again, Give the people, that they may eat:
for thus saith *the LORD* **Yah Veh**, They shall eat,
and **there** shall *leave* **remain** thereof.
44 So he *set it before them* **gave it at their face**,
and they did eat,
and *left* **there remained** thereof,
according to the word of *the LORD* **Yah Veh**.

ELI SHUA HEALS NAAMAN

5 Now Naaman, *captain* **governor** of the host
of the *king* **sovereign** of *Syria* **Aram**,
was a great man *with* **at the face of** his *master* **adoni**,
and honourable **accepted of face**,
because by him
the LORD **Yah Veh** had given *deliverance* **salvation**
unto *Syria* **Aram**:
he was also a mighty man in valour, *but he was* — a leper.
2 And the *Syrians* **Aramiy**
had gone out by *companies* **troops**,
and had *brought away captive* **captured**
out of the land of *Israel* **Yisra El** a little *maid* **lass**;
and she waited *on* **at the face of** Naaman's *wife* **woman**.
3 And she said unto her *mistress* **lady**,
Would God my lord **O that my adoni**
were with **faced** the prophet that is in *Samaria* **Shomeron**!
for he would recover **that he gather** him of his leprosy.
4 And one went in, and told his *lord* **adoni**, saying,
Thus and thus *said* **worded** the *maid* **lass**
that is of the land of *Israel* **Yisra El**.
5 And the *king* **sovereign** of *Syria* **Aram** said, Go to,
go, and I *will* **shall** send a *letter* **scroll**
unto the *king* **sovereign** of *Israel* **Yisra El**.
And he *departed* **went**,
and took *with him* **in his hand** ten *talents* **rounds** of silver,
and six thousand *pieces* of gold,
and ten changes of *raiment* **clothes**.
6 And he brought the *letter* **scroll**
to the *king* **sovereign** of *Israel* **Yisra El**, saying,
Now when this *letter* **scroll** is come unto thee, behold,
I have *therewith* sent Naaman my servant to thee,
that thou mayest *recover* **gather** him of his leprosy.
7 And it *came to pass* **became**,
when the *king* **sovereign** of *Israel* **Yisra El**
had *read* **called out** the *letter* **scroll**,
that he *rent* **ripped** his clothes, and said,
Am I *God* **Elohim**, to *kill* **deathify** and to make alive,
that this man doth send unto me
to *recover* **gather** a man of his leprosy?
wherefore consider **only perceive**, I *pray* **beseech** *you*,
and see how he *seeketh a quarrel* **happeneth** against me.
8 And it *was so* **became**,
when *Elisha* **Eli Shua** the man of *God* **Elohim** had heard
that the *king* **sovereign** of *Israel* **Yisra El**
had *rent* **ripped** his clothes,
that he sent to the *king* **sovereign**, saying,
Wherefore hast thou *rent* **ripped** thy clothes?
let him come now to me,
and he shall know that there is a prophet in *Israel* **Yisra El**.
9 So Naaman came with his horses and with his chariot,
and stood at the *door* **portal**
of the house of *Elisha* **Eli Shua**.
10 And *Elisha* **Eli Shua**
sent *a messenger* **an angel** unto him, saying,
Go and *wash* **baptise** in *Jordan* **Yarden** seven times,
and thy flesh shall *come again* **return** to thee,
and thou shalt be *clean* **purified**.
11 But Naaman was *wroth* **enraged**, and went away,
and said, Behold, I *thought* **said**,
That in coming, He *will* **shall** *surely* come out to me,
and stand and call on the name
of *the LORD* **Yah Veh** his *God* **Elohim**,
and *strike* **wave** his hand over the place,
and *recover* **gather** the leper.
12 Are not *Abana* **Amanah** and *Pharpar* **Parpar**,
rivers of *Damascus* **Dammeseq**,
better than all the waters of *Israel* **Yisra El**?
may I not *wash* **baptise** in them, and be *clean* **purified**?
So he turned **from his face** and went away in a *rage* **fury**.
13 And his servants came near,
and *spake* **worded** unto him, and said, My father,
if the prophet had *bid* **worded** thee
do some **a** great *thing* **word**,
wouldest **shouldest** thou not have *done* **worked** it?
how much rather then **also**, when he saith to thee,
Wash **Baptise**, and be *clean* **purified**?
14 Then *went* **descended** he *down*,
and dipped himself seven times in *Jordan* **Yarden**,
according to the *saying* **word** of the man of *God* **Elohim**:
and his flesh *came again* **returned**
like unto the flesh of a little *child* **lad**,
and he was *clean* **purified**.
15 And he returned to the man of *God* **Elohim**,
he and all his *company* **camp**, and came,
and stood *before him* **at his face**: and he said, Behold,
now I know that there is no *God* **Elohim** in all the earth,
but **except** in *Israel* **Yisra El**:
now therefore, I *pray* **beseech** thee,
take a blessing of thy servant.
16 But he said, *As the LORD* **Yah Veh** liveth,
before whom **at whose face** I stand,
I *will receive* **shall take** none.
And he urged him to take it; but he refused.

17 And Naaman said,
Shall there not then **If not**, I *pray* **beseech** thee,
let there be given to thy servant
two **a pair of** mules' burden of *earth* **soil**?
for thy servant *will* **shall** henceforth *offer* **work**
neither *burnt offering* **holocaust** nor sacrifice
unto other *gods* **elohim**, but unto *the LORD* **Yah Veh**.
18 In this *thing* **word**
the LORD pardon **Yah Veh forgive** thy servant,
that when my *master* **adoni**
goeth into the house of Rimmon
to *worship* **prostrate** there,
and he leaneth on my hand,
and I *bow* **prostrate** myself in the house of Rimmon:
when I *bow down* **prostrate** myself
in the house of Rimmon,
the LORD pardon **Yah Veh forgive** thy servant
in this *thing* **word**.
19 And he said unto him, Go in *peace* **shalom**.
So he *departed* **went** from him a *little way* **bit of earth**.
20 But *Gehazi* **Gay Chazi**, the *servant* **lad** of *Elisha* **Eli Shua**
the man of *God* **Elohim**, said,
Behold, my *master* **adoni** hath *spared* **restrained**
Naaman this *Syrian* **Aramiy**,
in not receiving **from taking** at his hands
that which he brought:
but, *as the LORD* **Yah Veh** liveth, I *will* **shall** run after him,
and take *somewhat* of him.
21 So *Gehazi followed* **Gay Chazi pursued** after Naaman.
And when Naaman saw him running after *him*,
he *lighted down* **fell away** from the chariot to meet him,
and said, *Is all well* **Shalom**?
22 And he said, *All is well* **Shalom**.
My *master* **adoni** hath sent me, saying, Behold,
even now there be come to me
from mount *Ephraim* **Ephrayim**
two *young men* **lads** of the sons of the prophets:
give them, I *pray* **beseech** thee, a *talent* **round** of silver,
and two changes of *garments* **clothes**.
23 And Naaman said,
Be content **If you will**, take two *talents* **rounds**.
And he *urged* **breached** him,
and bound *two talents* **rounds** of silver
in two *bags* **pouches**,
with two changes of *garments* **clothes**,
and *laid* **gave** them upon two of his *servants* **lads**;
and they bare them *before him* **at his face**.
24 And when he came to the *tower* **mound**,
he took them from their hand,
and *bestowed* **visited** them in the house:
and he *let* **sent** the men *go* **away**,
and they *departed* **went**.
25 But he went in, and stood before his *master* **adoni**.
And *Elisha* **Eli Shua** said unto him,
Whence *comest thou, Gehazi* **Gay Chazi**?
And he said, Thy servant went no *whither* **where**.
26 And he said unto him, Went not mine heart *with thee*,
when the man turned again from his chariot to meet thee?
Is it a time to *receive money* **take silver**,
and to *receive garments* **take clothes**,
and oliveyards, and vineyards, and *sheep* **flock**, and oxen,
and *menservants* **servants**, and *maidservants* **maids**?
27 The leprosy *therefore* of Naaman
shall *cleave* **adhere** unto thee,
and unto thy seed *for ever* **eternally**.
And he went out from his *presence* **face**
a leper *as white* as snow.

THE FLOATING IRON

6 And the sons of the prophets said unto *Elisha* **Eli Shua**,
Behold now,
the place where we *dwell with thee* **settle at thy face**
is *too strait* **tribulated** for us.
2 Let us go, we *pray* **beseech** *thee*, unto *Jordan* **Yarden**,
and take thence every man *a* **one** beam,
and let us *make* **work** us a place there,
where we may *dwell* **settle**.
And he *answered* **said**, Go ye.
3 And one said,
Be content **If you will**, I *pray* **beseech** *thee*,
and go with thy servants.
And he *answered* **said**, I *will* **shall** go.
4 So he went with them.
And when they came to *Jordan* **Yarden**,
they cut down *wood* **trees**.
5 But as one was felling a beam,
the *ax head* **iron** fell into the water: and he cried, and said,
Alas **Aha**, *master* **adoni**! for it was *borrowed* **lent**.
6 And the man of *God* **Elohim** said, Where fell it?
And he *shewed him* **had him see** the place.
And he *cut down* **clipped** a *stick* **tree**,
and cast it in thither;
and the iron did *swim* **float**.
7 Therefore said he, Take it up to thee.
And he *put out* **extended** his hand, and took it.
8 Then the *king* **sovereign** of *Syria* **Aram**
warred **fought** against *Israel* **Yisra El**,
and *took counsel* **counselled** with his servants, saying,
In such and such a place shall be my *camp* **encampment**.
9 And the man of *God* **Elohim**
sent unto the *king* **sovereign** of *Israel* **Yisra El**, saying,
Beware **Guard** that thou pass not *such a* **this** place;
for thither the *Syrians are come down* **Aramiy descend**.
10 And the *king* **sovereign** of *Israel* **Yisra El**
sent to the place
which the man of *God told* **Elohim said**
and *warned* **enlightened** him of,
and *saved* **guarded** himself there,
not once nor twice.
11 Therefore the heart of the *king* **sovereign** of *Syria* **Aram**
was sore troubled **stormed** for this *thing* **word**;
and he called his servants, and said unto them,
will **shall** ye not *shew* **tell** me
which of us is for the *king* **sovereign** of *Israel* **Yisra El**?
12 And one of his servants said,
None, my *lord* **adoni**, O *king* **sovereign**:
but *Elisha* **Eli Shua**, the prophet that is in *Israel* **Yisra El**,
telleth the *king* **sovereign** of *Israel* **Yisra El**
the words that thou *speakest* **wordest** in thy bedchamber.
13 And he said, Go and *spy* **see** where he is,
that I may send and *fetch* **take** him.
And it was told him, saying, Behold, *he is* in Dothan.
14 Therefore sent he thither horses, and chariots,
and *a great host* **heavy valiant**: and they came by night,
and *compassed* **surrounded** the city about.
15 And when the *servant* **lad** of the man of *God* **Elohim**
was risen **had started** early, and gone forth, behold,
an host compassed **the valiant surrounded** the city
both with horses and chariots.
And his *servant* **minister** said unto him,
Alas **Aha**, my *master* **adoni**! how shall we *do* **work**?
16 And he *answered* **said**, *Fear* **Awe** not:
for they that be with us
are *more* **greater** than they that be with them.
17 And *Elisha* **Eli Shua** prayed, and said,
LORD **Yah Veh**, I *pray* **beseech** *thee*,
open his eyes, that he may see.
And *the LORD* **Yah Veh**
opened the eyes of the *young man* **lad**;
and he saw: and, behold,
the mountain was *full of* **filled**
with horses and chariots of fire
round about *Elisha* **Eli Shua**.
18 And when they *came down* **descended** to him,
Elisha **Eli Shua** prayed unto *the LORD* **Yah Veh**, and said,
Smite this *people* **goyim**, I *pray* **beseech** *thee*,
with blindness.
And he smote them with blindness
according to the word of *Elisha* **Eli Shua**.
19 And *Elisha* **Eli Shua** said unto them,
This is not the way, neither is this the city:
follow **come** ye **after** me,
and I *will bring* **shall walk** you to the man whom ye seek.
But he *led* **walked** them to *Samaria* **Shomeron**.
20 And it *came to pass* **became**,
when they were come into *Samaria* **Shomeron**,
that *Elisha* **Eli Shua** said, *LORD* **Yah Veh**,
open the eyes of these *men*, that they may see.
And *the LORD* **Yah Veh** opened their eyes, and they saw;
and, behold, they were in the midst of *Samaria* **Shomeron**.
21 And the *king* **sovereign** of *Israel* **Yisra El**

said unto *Elisha* **Eli Shua**, when he saw them,
My father, shall I smite them? shall I smite them?
22 And he *answered* **said**, Thou shalt not smite them:
wouldest **shouldest** thou smite those
whom thou hast *taken captive* **captured**
with thy sword and with thy bow?
set bread and water *before them* **at their face**,
that they may eat and drink, and go to their *master* **adoni**.
23 And he *prepared* **digged** great provision for them:
and when they had eaten and drunk, he sent them away,
and they went to their *master* **adoni**.
So the *bands* **troops** of *Syria* **Aram**
came no more **added not to come**
into the land of *Israel* **Yisra El**.

FAMINE IN SHOMERON

24 And it *came to pass* **became** after this,
that *Benhadad* **Ben Hadad,** *king* **sovereign** of *Syria* **Aram**
gathered all his *host* **camp**,
and *went up* **ascended**, and besieged *Samaria* **Shomeron**.
25 And there was a great famine in *Samaria* **Shomeron**:
and, behold, they besieged it,
until *an ass's* **a he burro's** head
was *sold for fourscore* **eighty** *pieces of* silver,
and the fourth *part of a cab* **qab** of dove's *dung* **dungs**
for five *pieces of* silver.
26 And as the *king* **sovereign** of *Israel* **Yisra El**
was passing by upon the wall,
there cried a woman unto him, saying,
Help **Save**, my *lord* **adoni**, O *king* **sovereign**.
27 And he said,
If *the LORD* **Yah Veh** do not *help* **save** thee ,
whence shall I *help* **save** thee?
out of the *barnfloor* **threshingfloor**,
or out of the *winepress* **trough**?
28 And the *king* **sovereign** said unto her, What aileth thee?
And she *answered* **said**, This woman said unto me,
Give thy son, that we may eat him to day,
and *we will* **shall** eat my son to morrow.
29 So we *boiled* **stewed** my son, and did eat him:
and I said unto her on the next day,
Give thy son, that we may eat him:
and she hath hid her son.
30 And it *came to pass* **became**,
when the *king* **sovereign** heard the words of the woman,
that he *rent* **ripped** his clothes;
and he passed by upon the wall,
and the people *looked* **saw**, and, behold,
he had *sackcloth within* **saq housed** upon his flesh.
31 Then he said, *God do* **Elohim work** so
and *more* **add** also to me,
if the head of *Elisha* **Eli Shua** the son of Shaphat
shall stand on him this day.
32 But *Elisha sat* **Eli Shua settled** in his house,
and the elders *sat* **settled** with him;
and *the king* sent a man from *before him* **his face**:
but ere the *messenger* **angel** came to him,
he said to the elders,
See ye how this son of a murderer
hath sent to *take away* **turn aside** mine head?
look **see**, when the *messenger* **angel** cometh,
shut the door, and *hold him fast* **press him** at the door:
is not the *sound* **voice** of his *master's* **adoni's** feet
behind **after** him?
33 And while he yet *talked* **worded** with them, behold,
the *messenger came down* **angel descended** unto him:
and he said, Behold, this evil is of *the LORD* **Yah Veh**;
what should I *wait for the LORD* **await Yah Veh**
any longer?

ELI SHUA PROPHESIES FOOD

7 Then *Elisha* **Eli Shua** said,
Hear ye the word of *the LORD* **Yah Veh**;
Thus saith *the LORD* **Yah Veh**,
To morrow about this time
shall a *measure* **seah** of *fine* flour be *sold* for a shekel,
and two *measures* **seahs** of barley for a shekel,
in the *gate* **portal** of *Samaria* **Shomeron**.
2 Then a *lord* **tertiary**
on whose hand the *king* **sovereign** leaned
answered the man of *God* **Elohim**, and said, Behold,
if the LORD **though Yah Veh**
would make **should work** windows
in *heaven* **the heavens**,
might this *thing* **word** be?
And he said, Behold, thou shalt see *it* with thine eyes,
but shalt not eat hereof.
3 And there were four leprous men
at the *entering in* **opening** of the *gate* **portal**:
and they said *one* **man** to *another* **friend**,
Why *sit* **settle** we here until we die?
4 If we say, We *will* **shall** enter into the city,
then the famine is in the city, and we shall die there:
and if we *sit still* **settle** here, we die also.
Now therefore come,
and let us fall unto the *host* **camp** of the *Syrians* **Aramiy**:
if they save us alive, we shall live;
and if they *kill* **deathify** us, we shall *but* die.
5 And they rose up in the *twilight* **evening breeze**,
to go unto the camp of the *Syrians* **Aramiy**:
and when they were come
to the *uttermost part* **extremity** of the camp of *Syria* **Aram**,
behold, there was no man there.
6 For *the Lord* **Adonay**
had *made* the *host* **camp** of the *Syrians* **Aramiy**
to hear a *noise* **voice** of chariots,
and a *noise* **voice** of horses,
even the *noise* **voice** of a great *host* **valiant**:
and they said *one* **man** to *another* **brother**,
Lo **Behold**, the *king* **sovereign** of *Israel* **Yisra El**
hath hired against us
the *kings* **sovereigns** of the *Hittites* **Hethiy**,
and the *kings* **sovereigns** of the *Egyptians* **Misrayim**,
to come upon us.
7 Wherefore they arose
and fled in the *twilight* **evening breeze**,
and left their tents,
and their horses, and their *asses* **he burros**,
even the camp as it was, and fled for their *life* **soul**.
8 And when these lepers
came to the *uttermost part* **extremity** of the camp,
they went into one tent, and did eat and drink,
and *carried* **lifted** thence silver, and gold,
and *raiment* **clothes**, and went and hid it;
and *came again* **returned**, and entered into another tent,
and *carried* **lifted** thence *also*, and went and hid it.
9 Then they said *one* **man** to *another* **friend**,
We *do* **work** not well:
this day is a day of *good tidings* **evangelism**,
and we *hold our peace* **hush**:
if we *tarry* **wait** till the morning light,
some mischief will come upon **perversion shall find** us:
now therefore come,
that we may go and tell the *king's* **sovereign's** household.
10 So they came and called unto the porter of the city:
and they told them, saying,
We came to the camp of the *Syrians* **Aramiy**, and, behold,
there was no man there, neither voice of *man* **human**,
but horses *tied* **bound**, and *asses tied* **he burros bound**,
and the tents as they were.
11 And he called the porters;
and they told it to the *king's* **sovereign's** house within.
12 And the *king* **sovereign** arose in the night,
and said unto his servants,
I *will* **shall** now *shew* **tell** you
what the *Syrians* **Aramiy** have *done* **worked** to us.
They know that we be *hungry* **famished**;
therefore are they gone out of the camp
to hide themselves in the field, saying,
When they *come* **go** out of the city,
we shall *catch* **apprehend** them alive, and get into the city.
13 And one of his servants answered and said,
Let some take, I *pray* **beseech** thee,
five of the horses that *remain* **survive**,
which *are left* **survive** in the city,
(behold, they are as all the multitude of *Israel* **Yisra El**
that *are left* **survive** in it: behold, *I say*,
they are even as all the multitude of the *Israelites* **Yisra Eliy**
that are consumed:)
and let us send and see.
14 They took therefore two chariot horses;
and the *king* **sovereign**

sent after the *host* **camp** of the *Syrians* **Aramiy**, saying,
Go and see.
15 And they went after them unto *Jordan* **Yarden**:
and, *lo* **behold**, all the way
was full of *garments* **clothes** and *vessels* **instruments**,
which the *Syrians* **Aramiy** had cast away in their haste.
And the *messengers* **angels** returned,
and told the *king* **sovereign**.
16 And the people went out,
and *spoiled* **plundered**
the *tents* **camps** of the *Syrians* **Aramiy**.
So a *measure* **seah** of *fine* flour was *sold* for a shekel,
and two *measures* **seahs** of barley for a shekel,
according to the word of *the LORD* **Yah Veh**.
17 And the *king appointed* **sovereign mustered**
the *lord* **tertiary** on whose hand he leaned
to *have the charge of* **oversee** the *gate* **portal**:
and the people *trode upon* **trampled** him
in the *gate* **portal**, and he died,
as the man of *God* **Elohim** had *said* **worded**,
who *spake* **worded**
when the *king came down* **sovereign descended** to him.
18 And it *came to pass* **became,**
as the man of *God* **Elohim**
had *spoken* **worded** to the *king* **sovereign**, saying,
Two *measures* **seahs** of barley for a shekel,
and a *measure* **seah** of *fine* flour for a shekel,
shall be to morrow about this time
in the *gate* **portal** of *Samaria* **Shomeron**:
19 And that *lord* **tertiary** answered the man of *God* **Elohim**,
and said, Now, behold,
if the LORD **though Yah Veh**
should *make* **work** windows in *heaven* **the heavens**,
might such a *thing* **word** be?
And he said, Behold,
thou shalt see it with thine eyes, but shalt not eat thereof.
20 And so it fell out unto him:
for the people *trode* **trampled** *upon* him in the *gate* **portal**,
and he died.

ELI SHUA PROPHESIES FAMINE

8 Then *spake Elisha* **worded Eli Shua** unto the woman,
whose son he had *restored to life* **enlivened,** saying,
Arise, and go thou and thine household,
and sojourn wheresoever thou canst sojourn:
for *the LORD* **Yah Veh** hath called for a famine;
and it shall also come upon the land seven years.
2 And the woman arose, and *did* **worked**
after the *saying* **word** of the man of *God* **Elohim**:
and she went with her household,
and sojourned in the land of the *Philistines* **Peleshethiy**
seven years.

WOMAN'S LAND RESTORED

3 And it *came to pass* **became,** at the seven years' end,
that the woman returned
out of the land of the *Philistines* **Peleshethiy**:
and she went forth to cry unto the *king* **sovereign**
for her house and for her *land* **field**.
4 And the *king* **sovereign**
talked **worded** with *Gehazi* **Gay Chazi**
the *servant* **lad** of the man of *God* **Elohim**, saying,
Tell **Scribe** me, I *pray* **beseech** *thee*,
all the great *things* that *Elisha* **Eli Shua** hath *done* **worked**.
5 And it *came to pass* **became,**
as he was *telling* **scribing to** the *king* **sovereign**
how he had *restored a dead body to life* **enlivened the dead**,
that, behold, the woman,
whose son he had *restored to life* **enlivened**,
cried to the *king* **sovereign**
for her house and for her *land* **field**.
And *Gehazi* **Gay Chazi** said,
My *lord* **adoni**, O *king* **sovereign**,
this is the woman, and this is her son,
whom *Elisha restored to life* **Eli Shua enlivened**.
6 And when the *king* **sovereign** asked the woman,
she *told* **scribed to** him.
So the *king* **sovereign**
appointed **gave** unto her *a certain officer* **one eunuch**,
saying, Restore all that was hers,
and all the *fruits* **produce** of the field
since the day that she left the land, even until now.

ELI SHUA PROPHESIES EVIL

7 And *Elisha* **Eli Shua** came to *Damascus* **Dammeseq**;
and *Benhadad* **Ben Hadad**
the *king* **sovereign** of *Syria* **Aram** was sick;
and it was told him, saying,
The man of *God* **Elohim** is come hither.
8 And the *king* **sovereign** said unto *Hazael* **Haza El**,
Take *a present* **an offering** in thine hand, and go,
meet the man of *God* **Elohim**,
and enquire of *the LORD* **Yah Veh** by him, saying,
shall I *recover* **live** of this *disease* **sickness**?
9 So *Hazael* **Haza El** went to meet him,
and took *a present with him* **an offering in his hand**,
even of every good *thing* of *Damascus* **Dammeseq**,
forty camels' burden,
and came and stood *before him* **at his face**, and said,
Thy son *Benhadad* **Ben Hadad**
king **sovereign** of *Syria* **Aram** hath sent me to thee, saying,
shall I *recover* **live** of this *disease* **sickness**?
10 And *Elisha* **Eli Shua** said unto him, Go, say unto him,
In living, Thou *mayest certainly recover* **shalt live**:
howbeit *the LORD* **Yah Veh** hath *shewed* me **see**
that **in dying,** he shall *surely* die.
11 And he
settled his countenance stedfastly **stood setting his face,**
until he was *ashamed* **shamed**:
and the man of *God* **Elohim** wept.
12 And *Hazael* **Haza El** said, Why weepeth my *lord* **adoni**?
And he *answered* **said**, Because I know the evil
that thou *wilt do* **shalt work**
unto the *children* **sons** of *Israel* **Yisra El**:
their *strong holds* **fortresses**
wilt **shalt** thou *set* **send** on fire,
and their *young men* **youths**
wilt **shalt** thou *slay* **slaughter** with the sword,
and *wilt dash* **shalt splatter** their *children* **sucklings**,
and *rip up* **splittest open**
their *women with child* **conceivers**.
13 And *Hazael* **Haza El** said,
But what, is thy servant a dog,
that he should *do* **work** this great *thing* **word**?
And *Elisha answered* **Eli Shua** said,
The LORD **Yah Veh** hath *shewed* me **see**
that thou shalt be *king* **sovereign** over *Syria* **Aram**.
14 So he *departed* **went** from *Elisha* **Eli Shua**,
and came to his *master* **adoni**; who said to him,
What said *Elisha* **Eli Shua** to thee?
And he *answered* **said**, He *told* **said to** me
that **in living,** thou shouldest *surely recover* **live.**
15 And it *came to pass* **became,** on the morrow,
that he took a *thick cloth* **net**, and dipped it in water,
and spread it on his face, so that he died:
and *Hazael* **Haza El** reigned in his stead.

YAH RAM REIGNS OVER YAH HUDAH

16 And in the fifth year of *Joram* **Yah Ram**
the son of *Ahab king* **Ach Ab sovereign** of *Israel* **Yisra El**,
Jehoshaphat **Yah Shaphat**
being *then king* **sovereign** of *Judah* **Yah Hudah**,
Jehoram **Yah Ram** the son of *Jehoshaphat* **Yah Shaphat,**
king **sovereign** of *Judah* **Yah Hudah** began to reign.
17 **A son of** Thirty and two years *old*
was he when he began to reign;
and he reigned eight years in *Jerusalem* **Yeru Shalem**.
18 And he walked in the way
of the *kings* **sovereigns** of *Israel* **Yisra El**,
as *did* **worked** the house of *Ahab* **Ach Ab**:
for the daughter of *Ahab* **Ach Ab** was his *wife* **woman**:
and he *did* **worked** evil
in the *sight* **eyes** of *the LORD* **Yah Veh.**
19 Yet *the LORD would* **Yah Veh willed to**
not *destroy Judah* **ruin Yah Hudah**
for David his servant's sake,
as he *promised* **said to** him
to give him *alway a light* **all days a lamp**,
and to his *children* **sons**.
20 In his days Edom *revolted* **rebelled**
from under the hand of *Judah* **Yah Hudah**,
and *made* **had** a *king* **sovereign reign** over themselves.
21 So *Joram went* **Yah Ram passed** over to *Zair* **Sair**,
and all the chariots with him:

and he rose by night,
and smote the *Edomites* **Edomiy**
which *compassed* **surrounded** him *about,*
and the *captains* **governors** of the chariots:
and the people fled into their tents.
22 Yet Edom *revolted* **rebelled**
from under the hand of *Judah* **Yah Hudah** unto this day.
Then Libnah *revolted* **rebelled** at the same time.
23 And the rest of the *acts* **words** of *Joram* **Yah Ram,**
and all that he *did* **worked,**
are they not *written* **inscribed** in the *book* **scroll**
of the *chronicles* **words of the days**
of the *kings* **sovereigns** of *Judah* **Yah Hudah**?
24 And *Joram slept* **Yah Ram laid** with his fathers,
and was *buried* **entombed** with his fathers
in the city of David:
and *Ahaziah* **Achaz Yah** his son reigned in his stead.

ACHAZ YAH REIGNS OVER YAH HUDAH

25 In the twelfth year of *Joram* **Yah Ram**
the son of *Ahab king* **Ach Ab sovereign** of *Israel* **Yisra El**
did *Ahaziah* **Achaz Yah** the son of *Jehoram* **Yah Ram,**
king **sovereign** of *Judah* **Yah Hudah** begin to reign.
26 **A son of** Two and twenty years *old*
was *Ahaziah* **Achaz Yah** when he began to reign;
and he reigned one year in *Jerusalem* **Yeru Shalem**.
And his mother's name was *Athaliah* **Athal Yah,**
the daughter of Omri *king* **sovereign** of *Israel* **Yisra El**.
27 And he walked in the way
of the house of *Ahab* **Ach Ab,**
and *did* **worked** evil
in the *sight* **eyes** of *the LORD* **Yah Veh,**
as did the house of *Ahab* **Ach Ab**:
for he was the son in law of the house of *Ahab* **Ach Ab.**
28 And he went with *Joram* **Yah Ram**
the son of *Ahab* **Ach Ab**
to the war against *Hazael* **Haza El**
king **sovereign** of *Syria* **Aram**
in *Ramothgilead* **Ramoth Gilad**;
and the *Syrians wounded Joram* **Aramiy smote Yah Ram**.
29 And *king Joram went back* **sovereign Yah Ram returned**
to be healed in *Jezreel* **Yizre El** of the *wounds* **strokes**
which the *Syrians* **Aramiy** had *given him* **smitten**
at Ramah,
when he fought against *Hazael* **Haza El**
king **sovereign** of *Syria* **Aram**.
And *Ahaziah* **Achaz Yah** the son of *Jehoram* **Yah Ram**
king **sovereign** of *Judah* **Yah Hudah**
went down **descended** to see *Joram* **Yah Ram**
the son of *Ahab* **Ach Ab** in *Jezreel* **Yizre El,**
because he was sick.

YAH HU REIGNS OVER YAH HUDAH

9 And *Elisha* **Eli Shua** the prophet
called one of the *children* **sons** of the prophets,
and said unto him, Gird up thy loins,
and take this *box* **flask** of oil in thine hand,
and go to *Ramothgilead* **Ramoth Gilad**:
2 And when thou comest thither,
look out **see** there *Jehu* **Yah Hu**
the son of *Jehoshaphat* **Yah Shaphat** the son of Nimshi,
and go in,
and make him arise up from among his brethren,
and carry him to an inner chamber;
3 Then take the *box* **flask** of oil, and pour *it* on his head,
and say, Thus saith *the LORD* **Yah Veh,**
I have anointed thee *king* **sovereign** over *Israel* **Yisra El**.
Then open the door, and flee, and *tarry* **wait** not.
4 So the *young man* **lad,**
even the *young man* **lad** the prophet,
went to *Ramothgilead* **Ramoth Gilad**.
5 And when he came, behold,
the *captains* **governors** of the *host* **valiant**
were *sitting* **settled**; and he said,
I have *an errand* **a word** to thee, O captain.
And *Jehu* **Yah Hu** said, Unto which of all us?
And he said, To thee, O *captain* **governor**.
6 And he arose, and went into the house;
and he poured the oil on his head, and said unto him,
Thus saith
the LORD God **Yah Veh Elohim** of *Israel* **Yisra El,**
I have anointed thee *king* **sovereign**
over the people of *the LORD* **Yah Veh,**
even over *Israel* **Yisra El**.
7 And thou shalt smite
the house of *Ahab* **Ach Ab** thy *master* **adoni,**
that I may avenge the blood of my servants the prophets,
and the blood of all the servants of *the LORD* **Yah Veh,**
at the hand of *Jezebel* **Iy Zebel**.
8 For the whole house of *Ahab* **Ach Ab**
shall *perish* **destruct**:
and I *will* **shall** cut off from *Ahab* **Ach Ab**
him that *pisseth* **urinateth** against the wall,
and him that is *shut up* **restrained**
and left in *Israel* **Yisra El**:
9 And I *will make* **shall give** the house of *Ahab* **Ach Ab**
like the house of *Jeroboam* **Yarob Am** the son of Nebat,
and like the house of *Baasha* **Basha**
the son of *Ahijah* **Achiy Yah**:
10 And the dogs shall *eat Jezebel* **devour Iy Zebel**
in the *portion* **allotment** of *Jezreel* **Yizre El,**
and there shall be none to *bury* **entomb** her.
And he opened the door, and fled.
11 Then *Jehu came forth* **Yah Hu went**
to the servants of his *lord* **adoni**:
and *one* said unto him, *Is all well* **Shalom**?
wherefore came this *mad fellow* **insane** to thee?
And he said unto them,
ye know the man, and his communication.
12 And they said, It is false; tell us now.
And he said, Thus and thus *spake* **said** he to me, saying,
Thus saith *the LORD* **Yah Veh,**
I have anointed thee *king* **sovereign** over *Israel* **Yisra El**.
13 Then they hasted,
and took every man his *garment* **clothes,**
and *put* **set** it under him
on the *top* **bone** of the *stairs* **steps,**
and *blew* **blast** with trumpets, saying,
Jehu is king **Yah Hu reigneth.**

YAH HU DEATHIFIES YAH RAM AND ACHAZ YAH

14 So *Jehu* **Yah Hu** the son of *Jehoshaphat* **Yah Shaphat**
the son of Nimshi conspired against *Joram* **Yah Ram**.
(Now *Joram* **Yah Ram**
had *kept Ramothgilead* **guarded Ramoth Gilad,**
he and all *Israel* **Yisra El,**
because **at the face** of *Hazael* **Haza El,**
king **sovereign** of *Syria* **Aram**.
15 But *king Joram* **sovereign Yah Ram**
was returned to be healed in *Jezreel* **Yizre El**
of the *wounds* **strokes**
which the *Syrians* **Aramiy** had *given him* **smitten,**
when he fought with *Hazael* **Haza El**
king **sovereign** of *Syria* **Aram.)**
And *Jehu* **Yah Hu** said, If it be your *minds* **souls,**
then let *none* **no escapee** go forth *nor escape*
out of the city to go to tell it in *Jezreel* **Yizre El**.
16 So *Jehu* **Yah Hu** rode in a chariot,
and went to *Jezreel* **Yizre El**;
for *Joram* **Yah Ram** lay there.
And *Ahaziah* **Achaz Yah**
king **sovereign** of *Judah* **Yah Hudah**
was come down **descended** to see *Joram* **Yah Ram**.
17 And there stood a *watchman* **watcher**
on the tower in *Jezreel* **Yizre El,**
and he *spied* **saw** the *company* **throng** of *Jehu* **Yah Hu**
as he came,
and said, I see a *company* **throng**.
And *Joram* **Yah Ram** said, Take *an horseman* **a charioteer,**
and send to meet them,
and let him say, *Is it peace* **Shalom**?
18 So there went one
on horseback **riding on a horse** to meet him, and said,
Thus saith the *king* **sovereign,** *Is it peace* **Shalom**?
And *Jehu* **Yah Hu** said,
What hast thou to do with *peace* **shalom**?
turn thee behind me.
And the *watchman* **watcher** told, saying,
The *messenger* **angel** came to them,
but he *cometh not again* **returneth not**.
19 Then he sent out a second
on horseback **riding on a horse,**
which came to them, and said,

Thus saith the *king* **sovereign**, *Is it peace* **Shalom**?
And *Jehu answered* **Yah Hu said**,
What hast thou to do with *peace* **shalom**?
turn thee behind me.
20 And the *watchman* **watcher** told, saying,
He came even unto them,
and *cometh not again* **returneth not**:
and the driving
is like the driving of *Jehu* **Yah Hu** the son of Nimshi;
for he driveth *furiously* **insanely**.
21 And *Joram* **Yah Ram** said, *Make ready* **Bind**.
And his chariot was *made ready* **bound**.
And *Joram* **Yah Ram** *king* **sovereign** of *Israel* **Yisra El**
and *Ahaziah* **Achaz Yah**
king **sovereign** of *Judah* **Yah Hudah**
went out, each **man** in his chariot,
and they went out *against Jehu* **to meet Yah Hu**,
and *met* **found** him in the *portion* **allotment** of Naboth
the *Jezreelite* **Yizre Eliy**.
22 And it *came to pass* **became**,
when *Joram* **Yah Ram** saw *Jehu* **Yah Hu**,
that he said, *Is it peace* **Shalom**, *Jehu* **Yah Hu**?
And he *answered* **said**, What *peace* **shalom**,
so *long as* **that** the whoredoms
of thy mother *Jezebel* **Iy Zebel**
and her *witchcrafts* **sorceries** are *so* many?
23 And *Joram* **Yah Ram** turned his hands, and fled,
and said to *Ahaziah* **Achaz Yah**,
There is *treachery* **fraud**, O *Ahaziah* **Achaz Yah**.
24 And *Jehu* **Yah Hu**
drew a bow with his full strength
filled his hand with a bow,
and smote *Jehoram* **Yah Ram** between his arms,
and the arrow went out at his heart,
and he *sunk* **bowed** down in his chariot.
25 Then said *Jehu* **he** to *Bidkar* **Bidqar** his *captain* **tertiary**,
Take up **Lift**,
and cast him in the *portion* **allotment** of the field
of Naboth the *Jezreelite* **Yizre Eliy**:
for remember how that,
when I and thou rode *together* **paired**
after *Ahab* **Ach Ab** his father,
the LORD **Yah Veh** laid this burden upon him;
26 Surely I have seen *yesterday* **yesternight**
the blood of Naboth, and the blood of his sons,
saith the LORD **an oracle of Yah Veh**;
and I *will requite* **shall shalam** thee in this *plat* **allotment**,
saith the LORD **an oracle of Yah Veh**.
Now therefore *take* **lift**
and cast him into the *plat of ground* **allotment**,
according to the word of *the LORD* **Yah Veh**.
27 But when *Ahaziah* **Achaz Yah**,
the *king* **sovereign** of *Judah* **Yah Hudah** saw this,
he fled by the way of the garden house.
And *Jehu followed* **Yah Hu pursued** after him, and said,
Smite him also in the chariot.
And they did so at the *going up* **ascent** to Gur,
which is by *Ibleam* **Yible Am**.
And he fled to Megiddo, and died there.
28 And his servants *carried* **rode** him in a chariot
to *Jerusalem* **Yeru Shalem**,
and *buried* **entombed** him in his *sepulchre* **tomb**
with his fathers in the city of David.

ACHAZ YAH REIGNS OVER YAH HUDAH

29 And in the eleventh year of *Joram* **Yah Ram**
the son of *Ahab* **Ach Ab**
began *Ahaziah* **Achaz Yah** to reign over *Judah* **Yah Hudah**.

IY ZEBEL DEATHIFIED

30 And when *Jehu* **Yah Hu** was come to *Jezreel* **Yizre El**,
Jezebel **Iy Zebel** heard of it;
and she *painted* **set** her *face* **eyes in stibium**,
and *tired* **well—prepared** her head,
and looked out at a window.
31 And as *Jehu* **Yah Hu** entered in at the *gate* **portal**,
she said, Had Zimri *peace* **shalom**,
who *slew* **slaughtered** his *master* **adoni**?
32 And he lifted up his face to the window, and said,
Who is on my side? who?
And there looked out to him two or three eunuchs.
33 And he said, *Throw her down* **Release her**.
So they *threw her down* **released her**:
and *some of* her blood was sprinkled on the wall,
and on the horses:
and he *trode* **trampled** her under foot.
34 And when he was come in, he did eat and drink,
and said, *Go, see* **Visit** now this cursed *woman*,
and *bury* **entomb** her:
for she is a *king's* **sovereign's** daughter.
35 And they went to *bury* **entomb** her:
but they found no more of her than the *skull* **cranium**,
and the feet, and the palms of her hands.
36 Wherefore they *came again* **returned**, and told him.
And he said, This is the word of *the LORD* **Yah Veh**,
which he *spake* **worded** by **the hand of** his servant
Elijah **Eli Yah** the *Tishbite* **Tisbehiy**, saying,
In the *portion* **allotment** of *Jezreel* **Yizre El**
shall dogs *eat* **devour** the flesh of *Jezebel* **Iy Zebel**:
37 And the carcase of *Jezebel* **Iy Zebel** shall be as dung
upon the face of the field
in the *portion* **allotment** of *Jezreel* **Yizre El**;
so that they shall not say, This is *Jezebel* **Iy Zebel**.

ACH AB'S HOUSEHOLD DEATHIFIED

10 And *Ahab* **Ach Ab**
had seventy sons in *Samaria* **Shomeron**.
And *Jehu wrote letters* **Yah Hu inscribed scrolls**,
and sent to *Samaria* **Shomeron**,
unto the *rulers* **governors** of *Jezreel* **Yizre El**, to the elders,
and to them
that *brought up Ahab's children* **be amenable to Ach Ab**,
saying,
2 Now as soon as this *letter* **scroll** cometh to you,
seeing your *master's* **adoni's** sons are with you,
and there are with you chariots and horses,
a *fenced* **fortified** city also, and armour;
3 Look even out the best and *meetest* **straightest**
of your *master's* **adoni's** sons,
and set him on his father's throne,
and fight for your *master's* **adoni's** house.
4 But they were *exceedingly afraid* **mighty awed**,
and said, Behold,
two *kings* **sovereigns** stood not *before him* **at his face**:
how then shall *we* stand?
5 And he that was over the house,
and he that was over the city, the elders also,
and the *bringers up of the children* **amenable**,
sent to *Jehu* **Yah Hu**, saying, We are thy servants,
and *will do* **shall work** all that thou shalt *bid* **say to** us;
we *will not make any king* **shall have no man to reign**:
do **work** thou that which is good in thine eyes.
6 Then he *wrote* **inscribed** a *letter* **scroll**
the second time to them, saying,
If ye be mine, and if ye *will* **shall** hearken unto my voice,
take ye the heads of the men your *master's* **adoni's** sons,
and come to me to *Jezreel* **Yizre El** by to morrow this time.
Now the *king's* **sovereign's** sons,
being seventy *persons* **men**,
were with the great men of the city,
which *brought* **greatened** them *up*.
7 And it *came to pass* **became**,
when the *letter* **scroll** came to them,
that they took the *king's* **sovereign's** sons,
and *slew* **slaughtered** seventy *persons* **men**,
and *put* **set** their heads in *baskets* **boilers**,
and sent him them to *Jezreel* **Yizre El**.
8 And there came *a messenger* **an angel**,
and told him, saying,
They have brought the heads
of the *king's* **sovereign's** sons.
And he said, *Lay* **Set** ye them in two heaps
at the *entering in* **opening** of the *gate* **portal**
until the morning.
9 And it *came to pass* **became**, in the morning,
that he went out, and stood, and said to all the people,
ye be *righteous* **just**: behold,
I conspired against my *master* **adoni**,
and *slew* **slaughtered** him: but who *slew* **smote** all these?
10 Know now that there shall fall unto the earth
nothing **naught** of the word of *the LORD* **Yah Veh**,
which *the LORD spake* **Yah Veh worded**
concerning the house of *Ahab* **Ach Ab**:

for *the LORD* **Yah Veh** hath *done* **worked**
that which he *spake* **worded**
by **the hand of** his servant *Elijah* **Eli Yah**.
11 So *Jehu slew* **Yah Hu smote** all that *remained* **survived**
of the house of *Ahab* **Ach Ab** in *Jezreel* **Yizre El**,
and all his great men, and *his kinsfolks* **those he knew**,
and his priests,
until **in surviving**, he left him none *remaining* **surviving**.
12 And he arose and departed,
and came to *Samaria* **Shomeron**.
And as he was at
the *shearing* **tenders'** house **of binding/Beth Eqed**
in the way,
13 *Jehu* **Yah Hu**
met with **found** the brethren of *Ahaziah* **Achaz Yah**,
king **sovereign** of *Judah* **Yah Hudah**, and said,
Who are ye?
And they *answered* **said**,
We are the brethren of *Ahaziah* **Achaz Yah**;
and we *go down* **descend** to *salute* **bid shalom**
to the *children* **sons** of the *king* **sovereign**
and the *children* **sons** of the *queen* **lady**.
14 And he said, *Take* **Apprehend** them alive.
And they *took* **apprehended** them alive,
and *slew* **slaughtered** them
at the *pit* **well** of the *shearing* house **of binding/Beth Eqed**,
even two and forty men;
neither *left he* **survived** any of them.
15 And when he was *departed* **gone** thence,
he *lighted on Jehonadab* **found Yah Nadab**
the son of Rechab coming to meet him:
and he *saluted* **blessed** him, and said to him,
Is thine heart *right* **straight**, as my heart is with thy heart?
And *Jehonadab answered* **Yah Nadab said**, It is.
If it be, give *me* thine hand.
And he gave *him* his hand;
and he *took* **ascended** him *up* to him into the chariot.
16 And he said, Come with me,
and see my zeal for *the LORD* **Yah Veh**.
So they made him ride in his chariot.
17 And when he came to *Samaria* **Shomeron**,
he *slew* **smote** all that *remained* **survived**
unto *Ahab* **Ach Ab** in *Samaria* **Shomeron**,
till he had *destroyed* **desolated** him,
according to the *saying* **word** of *the LORD* **Yah Veh**,
which he *spake* **worded** to *Elijah* **Eli Yah**.
18 And *Jehu* **Yah Hu** gathered all the people *together*,
and said unto them, *Ahab* **Ach Ab** served Baal a little;
but Jehu **Yah Hu** shall serve him *much* **aboundingly**.
19 Now therefore call unto me all the prophets of Baal,
all his servants, and all his priests;
let *none* **no man** be *wanting* **missing**:
for I have a great sacrifice *to do* to Baal;
whosoever shall be *wanting* **missing**, he shall not live.
But *Jehu did* **Yah Hu worked** it in *subtilty* **trickery**,
to the intent
that he might destroy the *worshippers* **servants** of Baal.
20 And *Jehu* **Yah Hu** said,
Proclaim **Hallow** a *solemn* **private** assembly for Baal.
And they *proclaimed* **called** it.
21 And *Jehu* **Yah Hu** sent through all *Israel* **Yisra El**:
and all the *worshippers* **servants** of Baal came,
so that there was not a man *left* **surviving** that came not.
And they came into the house of Baal;
and the house of Baal was *full* **filled**
from *one end* **mouth** to *another* **mouth**.
22 And he said unto him
that was over the *vestry* **wardrobe**,
Bring forth *vestments* **robes**
for all the *worshippers* **servants** of Baal.
And he brought them forth *vestments* **robes**.
23 And *Jehu* **Yah Hu** went,
and *Jehonadab* **Yah Nadab** the son of Rechab,
into the house of Baal,
and said unto the *worshippers* **servants** of Baal,
Search, and *look* **see** that there be here with you
none of the servants of *the LORD* **Yah Veh**,
but the *worshippers* **servants** of Baal only.
24 And when they went in
to *offer* **work** sacrifices and *burnt offerings* **holocausts**,
Jehu appointed fourscore **Yah Hu set eighty** men without,
and said,
If *any* **a man**
of the men whom I have brought into your hands escape,
he that letteth him go,
his *life* **soul** shall be for *the life of him* **his soul**.
25 And it *came to pass* **became**,
as soon as he had *made an end of* **finished**
offering **working** the *burnt offering* **holocaust**,
that *Jehu* **Yah Hu** said to the *guard* **runners**
and to the *captains* **tertiaries**,
Go in, and *slay* **smite** them;
let *none come forth* **no man go**.
And they smote them with the *edge* **mouth** of the sword;
and the *guard* **runners** and the *captains* **tertiaries**
cast them out,
and went to the city of the house of Baal.
26 And they brought forth the *images* **monoliths**
out of the house of Baal, and burned them.
27 And they
brake **pulled** down the *image* **monolith** of Baal,
and *brake* **pulled** down the house of Baal,
and *made* **set** it a *draught house* **sewer** unto this day.
28 Thus *Jehu destroyed* **Yah Hu desolated** Baal
out of *Israel* **Yisra El**.
29 Howbeit *from* the sins of *Jeroboam* **Yarob Am**
the son of Nebat,
who made *Israel* **Yisra El** to sin,
Jehu departed not **Yah Hu turned not aside**
from after them, *to wit*,
the golden calves that were in *Bethel* **Beth El**,
and that were in Dan.
30 And *the LORD* **Yah Veh** said unto *Jehu* **Yah Hu**,
Because thou hast done *well* **good**
in *executing that which is right* **working straight**
in mine eyes,
and hast *done* **worked** unto the house of *Ahab* **Ach Ab**
according to all that was in mine heart,
thy *children* **sons** of the fourth *generation*
shall *sit* **settle** on the throne of *Israel* **Yisra El**.
31 But *Jehu took no heed* **Yah Hu guarded not**
to walk in the *law* **torah**
of *the LORD God* **Yah Veh Elohim** of *Israel* **Yisra El**
with all his heart:
for he *departed* **turned** not **aside**
from the sins of *Jeroboam* **Yarob Am**,
which made *Israel* **Yisra El** to sin.
32 In those days *the LORD* **Yah Veh**
began to cut *Israel short* **Yisra El off**:
and *Hazael* **Haza El** smote them
in all the *coasts* **borders** of *Israel* **Yisra El**;
33 From *Jordan* **Yarden**
eastward **toward the rising of the sun**,
all the land of *Gilead* **Gilad**, the *Gadites* **Gadiy**,
and the *Reubenites* **Reu Beniy**,
and the *Manassites* **Menash Shiy**,
from Aroer, which is by the *river* **wadi** Arnon,
even *Gilead* **Gilad** and Bashan.
34 Now the rest of the *acts* **words** of *Jehu* **Yah Hu**,
and all that he *did* **worked**, and all his might,
are they not *written* **inscribed** in the *book* **scroll**
of the *chronicles* **words of the days**
of the *kings* **sovereigns** of *Israel* **Yisra El**?
35 And *Jehu slept* **Yah Hu laid** with his fathers:
and they *buried* **entombed** him in *Samaria* **Shomeron**.
And *Jehoahaz* **Yah Achaz** his son reigned in his stead.
36 And the *time* **day**
that *Jehu* **Yah Hu** reigned over *Israel* **Yisra El**
in *Samaria* **Shomeron** was twenty and eight years.

ATHAL YAH REIGNS OVER YAH HUDAH

11 And when *Athaliah* **Athal Yah**
the mother of *Ahaziah* **Achaz Yah**
saw that her son *was dead* **died**,
she arose
and destroyed all the seed *royal* **of the sovereigndom**.
2 But *Jehosheba* **Yah Sheba**,
the daughter of *king Joram* **sovereign Yah Ram**,
sister of *Ahaziah* **Achaz Yah**,
took *Joash* **Yah Ash** the son of *Ahaziah* **Achaz Yah**,
and stole him from among the *king's* **sovereign's** sons

which were *slain* **deathified**;
and they hid him, *even* him and his *nurse* **suckler**,
in the bedchamber from *Athaliah* **the face of Athal Yah**,
so that he was not *slain* **deathified**.
3 And he was with her
hid in the house of *the LORD* **Yah Veh** six years.
And *Athaliah* **Athal Yah** did reign over the land.
4 And the seventh year *Jehoiada* **Yah Yada** sent
and *fetched* **took** the *rulers* **governors** over hundreds,
with the *captains* **executioners** and the *guard* **runners**,
and brought them to him
into the house of *the LORD* **Yah Veh**,
and *made* **cut** a covenant with them,
and *took an oath* **oathed** of them
in the house of *the LORD* **Yah Veh**,
and *shewed them* **had them see** the *king's* **sovereign's** son.
5 And he *commanded* **misvahed** them, saying,
This is the *thing* **word** that ye shall *do* **work**;
A third *part* of you that enter in on the *sabbath* **shabbath**
shall even *be keepers of the watch* **guard the guard**
of the *king's* **sovereign's** house;
6 And a third *part* shall be at the *gate* **portal** of Sur;
and a third *part* at the *gate* **portal** behind the *guard* **runners**:
so shall ye *keep* **guard** the *watch* **guard** of the house,
that it be not *broken down* **uprooted**.
7 And two *parts* **hands** of all you
that go forth on the *sabbath* **shabbath**,
even they shall *keep* **guard** the *watch* **guard**
of the house of *the LORD* **Yah Veh**
about the *king* **sovereign**.
8 And ye shall *compass* **surround** the *king* **sovereign**
round about,
every man with his *weapons* **instruments** in his hand:
and he that cometh within the *ranges* **ranks**,
let him be *slain* **deathified**:
and be ye with the *king* **sovereign**
as he goeth out and as he cometh in.
9 And the *captains* **governors** over the hundreds
did **worked** according to all *things*
that *Jehoiada* **Yah Yada** the priest *commanded* **misvahed**:
and they took every man his men
that were to come in on the *sabbath* **shabbath**,
with them that should go out on the *sabbath* **shabbath**,
and came to *Jehoiada* **Yah Yada** the priest.
10 And to the *captains* **governors** over hundreds
did the priest
give *king* **sovereign** David's spears and shields,
that were in the *temple* **house** of *the LORD* **Yah Veh**.
11 And the *guard* **runners** stood,
every man with his *weapons* **instruments** in his hand,
round about the *king* **sovereign**,
from the right *corner* **shoulder** of the *temple* **house**
to the left *corner* **shoulder** of the *temple* **house**,
along by the **sacrifice** altar and the *temple* **house**.
12 And he brought forth the *king's* **sovereign's** son,
and *put* **gave** the *crown* **separatism** upon him,
and *gave him the testimony* **the witness**;
and they made him *king* **reign**, and anointed him;
and they *clapped* **smote** their *hands* **palms**, and said,
God save the king **The sovereign liveth**.
13 And when *Athaliah* **Athal Yah**
heard the noise of the *guard* **runners** and of the people,
she came to the people
into the *temple* **house** of *the LORD* **Yah Veh**.
14 And when she *looked* **saw**, behold,
the *king* **sovereign** stood by a pillar,
as the *manner* **judgment** was,
and the *princes* **governors** and the trumpeters
by the *king* **sovereign**,
and all the people of the land *rejoiced* **cheered**
and *blew* **blast** with trumpets:
and *Athaliah* rent **Athal Yah ripped** her clothes,
and *cried* **called out**,
Treason, Treason. **Conspiracy! Conspiracy!**
15 But *Jehoiada* **Yah Yada** the priest *commanded* **misvahed**
the *captains* **governors** of the hundreds,
the *officers* **overseers** of the *host* **valiant**,
and said unto them,
Have her forth without the ranges
Bring out her house by ranks:
and him that *followeth her* **goeth after**,
kill **deathify** with the sword.
For the priest had said,
Let her not be slain **Deathify her not**
in the house of *the LORD* **Yah Veh**.
16 And they *laid* **set** hands on her;
and she went by the way
by the *which* **entrance of** the horses *came*
into the *king's* **sovereign's** house:
and there was she *slain* **deathified**.
17 And *Jehoiada made* **Yah Yada cut** a covenant
between *the LORD* **Yah Veh** and the *king* **sovereign**
and the people,
that they should be *the LORD'S* **Yah Veh's** people;
between the *king* **sovereign** also and the people.
18 And all the people of the land
went into the house of Baal, and *brake* **pulled** it down;
his **sacrifice** altars and his images
brake they *in pieces* thoroughly,
and *slew* **slaughtered** Mattan the priest of Baal
before **at the face of** the **sacrifice** altars.
And the priest *appointed officers* **set overseers**
over the house of *the LORD* **Yah Veh**.
19 And he took the *rulers* **governors** over hundreds,
and the *captains* **executioners**, and the *guard* **runners**,
and all the people of the land;
and they *brought down* **descended** the *king* **sovereign**
from the house of *the LORD* **Yah Veh**,
and came by the way
of the *gate* **portal** of the *guard* **runners**
to the *king's* **sovereign's** house.
And he *sat* **settled** on the throne of the *kings* **sovereigns**.
20 And all the people of the land *rejoiced* **cheered**,
and the city *was in quiet* **rested**:
and they *slew Athaliah* **deathified Athal Yah**
with the sword beside the *king's* **sovereign's** house.

YAH ASH REIGNS OVER YAH HUDAH

21 **A son of** Seven years *old* was *Jehoash* **Yah Ash**
when he began to reign.
12 In the seventh year of *Jehu* **Yah Hu**
Jehoash **Yah Ash** began to reign;
and forty years reigned he in *Jerusalem* **Yeru Shalem**.
And his mother's name was *Zibiah* **Zib Yah**
of *Beersheba* **Beer Sheba**.
2 And *Jehoash did* **Yah Ash worked**
that which was *right* **straight**
in the *sight* **eyes** of *the LORD* **Yah Veh** all his days
wherein *Jehoiada* **Yah Yada** the priest
instructed **taught** him.
3 But the *high places* **bamahs**
were not *taken away* **turned aside**:
the people still sacrificed and *burnt incense* **incensed**
in the *high places* **bamahs**.
4 And *Jehoash* **Yah Ash** said to the priests,
All the *money* **silver** of the *dedicated things* **holies**
that is brought into the house of *the LORD* **Yah Veh**,
even the *money* **silver** of every *one* **man** that passeth
the account,
the *money* **silver**
that every man is set at **of the appraisal of his soul**,
and all the *money* **silver**
that *cometh* **ascendeth** into any man's heart
to bring into the house of *the LORD* **Yah Veh**,
5 Let the priests take it to them,
every man of his acquaintance:
and let them *repair* **strengthen** the breaches of the house,
wheresoever any breach shall be found.
6 But it *was so* **became**,
that in the three and twentieth year
of *king Jehoash* **sovereign Yah Ash**,
the priests had not *repaired* **strengthened**
the breaches of the house.
7 Then *king Jehoash* **sovereign Yah Ash**
called for *Jehoiada* **Yah Yada** the priest,
and the *other* priests, and said unto them,
Why *repair* **strengthen** ye not the breaches of the house?
now therefore
receive **take** no *more money* **silver** of your acquaintance,
but *deliver* **give** it for the breaches of the house.
8 And the priests consented

to receive **take** no *more money* **silver** of the people,
neither *to repair* **strengthen** the breaches of the house.
9 But *Jehoiada* **Yah Yada** the priest took *a chest* **one ark**,
and bored a hole in the *lid* **door** of it,
and *set* **gave** it beside the **sacrifice** altar, on the right side
as *one* **man** cometh into the house of *the LORD* **Yah Veh**:
and the priests that *kept* **guarded** the *door* **threshold**
put **gave** therein all the *money* **silver**
that was brought into the house of *the LORD* **Yah Veh**.
10 And it *was so* **became**,
when they saw
that there was much *money* **silver** in the *chest* **ark**,
that the *king's* **sovereign's** scribe and the *high* **great** priest
came up **ascended**,
and they *put up in bags* **bound it up**,
and *told* **numbered** the *money* **silver**
that was found in the house of *the LORD* **Yah Veh**.
11 And they gave the *money* **silver**, being *told* **gauged**,
into the hands of them that *did* **worked** the work,
that had the oversight **the overseers**
of the house of *the LORD* **Yah Veh**:
and they *laid it out* **brought it**
to the *carpenters* **carvers of timber** and builders,
that *wrought* **worked**
upon the house of *the LORD* **Yah Veh**,
12 And to *masons* **wallers**, and hewers of stone,
and to *buy* **chattel** timber and hewed stone
to *repair* **strengthen** the breaches
of the house of *the LORD* **Yah Veh**,
and for all that *was laid out* **went** for the house
to *repair* **strengthen** it.
13 Howbeit there were not *made* **worked**
for the house of *the LORD* **Yah Veh**
bowls **basons** of silver, *snuffers* **tweezers**,
basons **sprinklers**, trumpets,
any *vessels* **instruments** of gold,
or *vessels* **instruments** of silver,
of the *money* **silver**
that was brought into the house of *the LORD* **Yah Veh**:
14 But they gave that
to *the workmen* **those doing the work**,
and *repaired* **strengthened** therewith
the house of *the LORD* **Yah Veh**.
15 Moreover they *reckoned* **fabricated** not with the men,
into whose hand they *delivered* **gave** the *money* **silver**
to be *bestowed* **given**
on workmen **to those doing the work**:
for they *dealt faithfully* **worked trustworthily**.
16 The *trespass money* **silver for the guilt**
and *sin money* **the silver for the sin**
was not brought into the house of *the LORD* **Yah Veh**:
it was the priests'.
17 Then *Hazael* **Haza El**
king **sovereign** of *Syria went up* **Aram ascended**,
and fought against Gath, and *took* **captured** it:
and *Hazael* **Haza El** set his face
to *go up* **ascend** to *Jerusalem* **Yeru Shalem**.
18 And *Jehoash* **Yah Ash**
king **sovereign** of *Judah* **Yah Hudah**
took all the *hallowed things* **holies**
that *Jehoshaphat* **Yah Shaphat**, and *Jehoram* **Yah Ram**,
and *Ahaziah* **Achaz Yah**, his fathers,
kings **sovereigns** of *Judah* **Yah Hudah**,
had *dedicated* **hallowed**,
and his own *hallowed things* **holies**,
and all the gold that was found in the treasures
of the house of *the LORD* **Yah Veh**,
and in the *king's* **sovereign's** house,
and sent it to *Hazael* **Haza El**
king **sovereign** of *Syria* **Aram**:
and he *went away* **ascended** from *Jerusalem* **Yeru Shalem**.
19 And the rest of the *acts* **words** of *Joash* **Yah Ash**,
and all that he *did* **worked**,
are they not *written* **inscribed** in the *book* **scroll**
of the *chronicles* **words of the days**
of the *kings* **sovereigns** of *Judah* **Yah Hudah**?
20 And his servants arose,
and *made* **conspired** a conspiracy,
and *slew Joash* **smote Yah Ash** in the house of Millo,
which *goeth down* **descendeth** to Silla.
21 For *Jozachar* **Yah Zachar** the son of Shimeath,
and *Jehozabad* **Yah Zabad** the son of Shomer, his servants,
smote him, and he died;
and they *buried* **entombed** him with his fathers
in the city of David:
and *Amaziah* **Amaz Yah** his son reigned in his stead.

YAH ACHAZ REIGNS OVER YISRA EL

13 In the three and twentieth year of *Joash* **Yah Ash**
the son of *Ahaziah* **Achaz Yah**
king **sovereign** of *Judah* **Yah Hudah**,
Jehoahaz **Yah Achaz** the son of *Jehu* **Yah Hu**
began to reign over *Israel* **Yisra El** in *Samaria* **Shomeron**,
and reigned seventeen years.
2 And he *did* **worked** that which was evil
in the *sight* **eyes** of *the LORD* **Yah Veh**,
and *followed* **walked after** the sins of *Jeroboam* **Yarob Am**
the son of Nebat, which made *Israel* **Yisra El** to sin;
he *departed* **turned** not **aside** therefrom.
3 And the *anger* **wrath** of *the LORD* **Yah Veh**
was kindled against *Israel* **Yisra El**,
and he *delivered* **gave** them into the hand
of *Hazael* **Haza El** *king* **sovereign** of *Syria* **Aram**,
and into the hand
of *Benhadad* **Ben Hadad** the son of *Hazael* **Haza El**,
all their days.
4 And *Jehoahaz* **Yah Achaz**
besought the LORD **stroked the face of Yah Veh**,
and *the LORD* **Yah Veh** hearkened unto him:
for he saw the oppression of *Israel* **Yisra El**,
because the *king* **sovereign** of *Syria* **Aram** oppressed them.
5 (And *the LORD* **Yah Veh** gave *Israel* **Yisra El** a saviour,
so that they went out
from under the hand of the *Syrians* **Aramiy**:
and the *children* **sons** of *Israel* **Yisra El**
dwelt **settled** in their tents,
as *beforetime* **three yesters ago**.
6 Nevertheless they *departed* **turned** not **aside**
from the sins of the house of *Jeroboam* **Yarob Am**,
who made *Israel* **Yisra El** sin, but walked therein:
and there *remained* **stood** the *grove* **asherah** also
in *Samaria* **Shomeron**.)
7 Neither *did* **let** he *leave* **survive** of the people
to *Jehoahaz* **Yah Achaz** but fifty *horsemen* **cavalry**,
and ten chariots, and ten thousand *footmen* **on foot**;
for the *king* **sovereign** of *Syria* **Aram** had destroyed them,
and had *made* **set** them like the dust by threshing.
8 Now the rest of the *acts* **words** of *Jehoahaz* **Yah Achaz**,
and all that he *did* **worked**, and his might,
are they not *written* **inscribed** in the *book* **scroll**
of the *chronicles* **words of the days**
of the *kings* **sovereigns** of *Israel* **Yisra El**?
9 And *Jehoahaz slept* **Yah Achaz laid** with his fathers;
and they *buried* **entombed** him in *Samaria* **Shomeron**:
and *Joash* **Yah Ash** his son reigned in his stead.

YAH ASH REIGNS OVER YISRA EL

10 In the thirty and seventh year of *Joash* **Yah Ash**,
king **sovereign** of *Judah* **Yah Hudah**
began *Jehoash* **Yah Ash** the son of *Jehoahaz* **Yah Achaz**
to reign over *Israel* **Yisra El** in *Samaria* **Shomeron**,
and reigned sixteen years.
11 And he *did* **worked** that which was evil
in the *sight* **eyes** of *the LORD* **Yah Veh**;
he *departed* **turned** not **aside**
from all the sins of *Jeroboam* **Yarob Am** the son of Nebat,
who made *Israel* **Yisra El** sin: but he walked therein.
12 And the rest of the *acts* **words** of *Joash* **Yah Ash**,
and all that he *did* **worked**, and his might
wherewith he fought against *Amaziah* **Amaz Yah**,
king **sovereign** of *Judah* **Yah Hudah**,
are they not *written* **inscribed** in the *book* **scroll**
of the *chronicles* **words of the days**
of the *kings* **sovereigns** of *Israel* **Yisra El**?
13 And *Joash slept* **Yah Ash laid** with his fathers;
and *Jeroboam sat* **Yarob Am seated** upon his throne:
and *Joash* **Yah Ash**
was *buried* **entombed** in *Samaria* **Shomeron**
with the *kings* **sovereigns** of *Israel* **Yisra El**.

ELI SHUA'S FINAL COUNSEL

14 Now *Elisha* **Eli Shua** was fallen sick
of his sickness whereof he died.

And *Joash* **Yah Ash,** the *king* **sovereign** of *Israel* **Yisra El**
came down **descended** unto him, and wept over his face,
and said, O my father, my father,
the chariot of *Israel* **Yisra El**,
and the *horsemen* **cavalry** thereof.
15 And *Elisha* **Eli Shua** said unto him,
Take bow and arrows.
And he took unto him bow and arrows.
16 And he said to the *king* **sovereign** of *Israel* **Yisra El**,
Put **Drive** thine hand upon the bow.
And he *put* **drove** his hand upon it:
and *Elisha* **Eli Shua** put his hands
upon the *king's* **sovereign's** hands.
17 And he said, Open the window eastward.
And he opened it.
Then *Elisha* **Eli Shua** said, Shoot.
And he shot. And he said,
The arrow of *the LORD'S deliverance* **Yah Veh's salvation**,
and the arrow of *deliverance* **salvation** from *Syria* **Aram**:
for thou shalt smite the *Syrians* **Aramiy** in *Aphek* **Apheq**,
till thou have *consumed* **finished** them **off**.
18 And he said, Take the arrows. And he took them.
And he said unto the *king* **sovereign** of *Israel* **Yisra El**,
Smite upon the *ground* **earth**.
And he smote *thrice* **three times**, and stayed.
19 And the man of *God* **Elohim**
was *wroth* **enraged** with him, and said,
Thou shouldest have smitten **By smiting** five or six times;
then hadst thou smitten *Syria* **Aram**
till thou hadst *consumed* **finished** it **off**:
whereas now
thou shalt smite *Syria but thrice* **Aram three times**.

ELI SHUA'S DEATH

20 And *Elisha* **Eli Shua** died,
and they *buried* **entombed** him.
And the *bands* **troops** of the *Moabites* **Moabiy**
invaded the land at the coming in of the year.
21 And it *came to pass* **became**,
as they were *burying* **entombing** a man, that, behold,
they *spied a band of men* **saw a troop**;
and they cast the man
into the *sepulchre* **tomb** of *Elisha* **Eli Shua**:
and when the man was *let down* **descended**,
and touched the bones of *Elisha* **Eli Shua**,
he *revived* **enlivened**, and *stood up* **arose** on his feet.
22 But *Hazael* **Haza El** *king* **sovereign** of *Syria* **Aram**
oppressed *Israel* **Yisra El**
all the days of *Jehoahaz* **Yah Achaz**.
23 And *the LORD* **Yah Veh**
was gracious **granted charism** unto them,
and *had compassion on* **mercied** them,
and *had respect* **turned his face** unto them,
because of his covenant
with Abraham, *Isaac* **Yischaq**, and *Jacob* **Yaaqov**,
and *would* **willed to** not *destroy* **ruin** them,
neither cast he them from his *presence* **face** as yet.

BEN HADAD REIGNS OVER ARAM

24 So *Hazael* **Haza El** *king* **sovereign** of *Syria* **Aram** died;
and *Benhadad* **Ben Hadad** his son reigned in his stead.
25 And *Jehoash* **Yah Ash** the son of *Jehoahaz* **Yah Achaz**
took again **returned and took** out of the hand
of *Benhadad* **Ben Hadad** the son of *Hazael* **Haza El**
the cities,
which he had taken out of the hand
of *Jehoahaz* **Yah Achaz** his father by war.
Three times did *Joash beat* **Yah Ash smite** him,
and *recovered* **returned** the cities of *Israel* **Yisra El**.

AMAZ YAH REIGNS OVER YAH HUDAH

14 In the second year of *Joash* **Yah Ash**
son of *Jehoahaz* **Yah Achaz**
king **sovereign** of *Israel* **Yisra El**
reigned *Amaziah* **Amaz Yah**
the son of *Joash* **Yah Ash**
king **sovereign** of *Judah* **Yah Hudah**.
2 He was **a son of** twenty and five years *old*
when he began to reign,
and reigned twenty and nine years
in *Jerusalem* **Yeru Shalem**.
And his mother's name was *Jehoaddan* **Yah Addan**
of *Jerusalem* **Yeru Shalem**.
3 And he *did* **worked** that which was right **straight**
in the *sight* **eyes** of *the LORD* **Yah Veh**,
yet **only** not like David his father:
he *did* **worked** according to all *things*
as *Joash* **Yah Ash** his father *did* **worked.**
4 Howbeit
the *high places* **bamahs** were not *taken away* **turned aside**:
as yet **still** the people did sacrifice
and *burnt incense* **incensed** on the *high places* **bamahs**.
5 And it *came to pass* **became**,
as soon as the *kingdom* **sovereigndom**
was *confirmed* **strong** in his hand,
that he *slew* **smote** his servants
which had *slain* **smitten** the *king* **sovereign** his father.
6 But the *children* **sons** of the *murderers* **smiters**
he *slew* **deathified** not:
according unto that which is *written* **inscribed**
in the *book* **scroll** of the *law* **torah** of *Moses* **Mosheh**,
wherein *the LORD commanded* **Yah Veh misvahed**, saying,
The fathers shall not be *put to death* **deathified**
for the *children* **sons,**
nor the *children be put to death* **sons deathified**
for the fathers;
but every man shall be *put to death* **deathified**
for his own sin.
7 He *slew* **smote** of Edom
in *the valley of salt* **Gay Melach/Valley of Salt**
ten thousand,
and *took Selah* **apprehended the rock** by war,
and called the name of it *Joktheel* **Yoqthe El** unto this day.
8 Then *Amaziah* **Amaz Yah** sent *messengers* **angels**
to *Jehoash* **Yah Ash**, the son of *Jehoahaz* **Yah Achaz**
son of *Jehu* **Yah Hu**, *king* **sovereign** of *Israel* **Yisra El**,
saying, Come, let us *look* **see** one another in the face.
9 And *Jehoash* **Yah Ash** the *king* **sovereign** of *Israel* **Yisra El**
sent to *Amaziah* **Amaz Yah**
king **sovereign** of *Judah* **Yah Hudah**, saying,
The *thistle* **thorn** that was in Lebanon
sent to the cedar that was in Lebanon, saying,
Give thy daughter to my son to *wife* **woman**:
and there passed by a *wild beast* **live being of the field**
that was in Lebanon,
and *trode down* **trampled** the *thistle* **thorn.**
10 **In smiting,** Thou hast *indeed* smitten Edom,
and thine heart hath lifted thee up:
glory of this **be honoured**,
and *tarry* **settle** at *home* **thy house**:
for why shouldest thou *meddle to thy hurt* **coax to evil**,
that thou shouldest fall,
even thou, and *Judah* **Yah Hudah** with thee?
11 But *Amaziah would not hear* **Amaz Yah hearkened not**.
Therefore *Jehoash* **Yah Ash**
king **sovereign** of *Israel went up* **Yisra El ascended**;
and he and *Amaziah* **Amaz Yah**,
king **sovereign** of *Judah* **Yah Hudah**
looked **saw** one another in the face
at *Bethshemesh* **Beth Shemesh**,
which *belongeth* **be** to *Judah* **Yah Hudah**.
12 And *Judah* **Yah Hudah**
was *put to the worse* **smitten**
before Israel **at the face of Yisra El**;
and they fled every man to their tents.
13 And *Jehoash* **Yah Ash** *king* **sovereign** of *Israel* **Yisra El**
took Amaziah **apprehended Amaz Yah,**
king **sovereign** of *Judah* **Yah Hudah**,
the son of *Jehoash* **Yah Ash** the son of *Ahaziah* **Achaz Yah**,
at *Bethshemesh* **Beth Shemesh**,
and came to *Jerusalem* **Yeru Shalem**,
and brake down the wall of *Jerusalem* **Yeru Shalem**
from the *gate* **portal** of *Ephraim* **Ephrayim**
unto the corner *gate* **portal**, four hundred cubits.
14 And he took all the gold and silver,
and all the *vessels* **instruments**
that were found in the house of *the LORD* **Yah Veh**,
and in the treasures of the *king's* **sovereign's** house,
and *hostages* **sons as pledges**,
and returned to *Samaria* **Shomeron**.
15 Now the rest of the *acts* **words** of *Jehoash* **Yah Ash**
which he *did* **worked**, and his might,
and how he fought with *Amaziah* **Amaz Yah,**

king **sovereign** of *Judah* **Yah Hudah**,
are they not *written* **inscribed** in the *book* **scroll**
of the *chronicles* **words of the days**
of the *kings* **sovereigns** of *Israel* **Yisra El**?
16 And *Jehoash slept* **Yah Ash laid** with his fathers,
and was *buried* **entombed** in *Samaria* **Shomeron**
with the *kings* **sovereigns** of *Israel* **Yisra El**;
and *Jeroboam* **Yarob Am** his son reigned in his stead.
17 And *Amaziah* **Amaz Yah** the son of *Joash* **Yah Ash**,
king **sovereign** of *Judah* **Yah Hudah**
lived after the death of *Jehoash* **Yah Ash**
son of *Jehoahaz* **Yah Achaz**
king **sovereign** of *Israel* **Yisra El** fifteen years.
18 And the rest of the *acts* **words** of *Amaziah* **Amaz Yah**,
are they not *written* **inscribed** in the *book* **scroll**
of the *chronicles* **words of the days**
of the *kings* **sovereigns** of *Judah* **Yah Hudah**?
19 Now they *made* **conspired** a conspiracy against him
in *Jerusalem* **Yeru Shalem**: and he fled to Lachish;
but they sent after him to Lachish,
and *slew* **deathified** him there.
20 And they *brought* **lifted** him on horses:
and he was *buried* **entombed** at *Jerusalem* **Yeru Shalem**
with his fathers in the city of David.

AZAR YAH REIGNS OVER YAH HUDAH

21 And all the people of *Judah* **Yah Hudah**
took *Azariah* **Azar Yah**,
which was **a son of** sixteen years *old*,
and made him *king* **reign**
instead of his father *Amaziah* **Amaz Yah**.
22 He built *Elath* **Eloth**,
and restored it to *Judah* **Yah Hudah**,
after that the *king* **sovereign**
slept **laid** with his fathers.

YAROB AM REIGNS OVER YAH HUDAH

23 In the fifteenth year of *Amaziah* **Amaz Yah**
the son of *Joash* **Yah Ash**
king **sovereign** of *Judah* **Yah Hudah**
Jeroboam **Yarob Am** the son of *Joash* **Yah Ash**
king **sovereign** of *Israel* **Yisra El**
began to reign in *Samaria* **Shomeron**,
and reigned forty and one years.
24 And he *did* **worked** that which was evil
in the *sight* **eyes** of *the LORD* **Yah Veh**:
he *departed* **turned** not **aside** from all the sins
of *Jeroboam* **Yarob Am** the son of Nebat,
who made *Israel* **Yisra El** to sin.
25 He restored the *coast* **border** of *Israel* **Yisra El**
from the entering of Hamath unto the sea of the plain,
according to the word
of *the LORD God* **Yah Veh Elohim** of *Israel* **Yisra El**,
which he *spake* **worded**
by the hand of his servant *Jonah* **Yonah**,
the son of *Amittai* **Amittay**, the prophet,
which was of Gathhepher.
26 For *the LORD* **Yah Veh**
saw the *affliction* **humiliation** of *Israel* **Yisra El**,
that it was *very bitter* **mighty rebelling**:
for there was not any *shut up* **finally restrained**,
nor any **finally** left
nor any helper for *Israel* **Yisra El**.
27 And *the LORD said* **Yah Veh worded** not
that he *would* **should**
blot **wipe** out the name of *Israel* **Yisra El**
from under *heaven* **the heavens**:
but he saved them by the hand of *Jeroboam* **Yarob Am**
the son of *Joash* **Yah Ash**.
28 Now the rest of the *acts* **words** of *Jeroboam* **Yarob Am**,
and all that he *did* **worked**,
and his might, how he *warred* **fought**,
and how he *recovered Damascus* **returned Dammeseq**,
and Hamath, *which belonged to Judah* **Yah Hudah**,
for *Israel* **Yisra El**,
are they not *written* **inscribed** in the *book* **scroll**
of the *chronicles* **words of the days**
of the *kings* **sovereigns** of *Israel* **Yisra El**?
29 And *Jeroboam* **Yarob Am**
slept **laid** with his fathers,
even with the *kings* **sovereigns** of *Israel* **Yisra El**;
and *Zachariah* **Zechar Yah** his son reigned in his stead.

AZAR YAH REIGNS OVER YAH HUDAH

15 In the twenty and seventh year of *Jeroboam* **Yarob Am**
king **sovereign** of *Israel* **Yisra El**
began *Azariah* **Azar Yah** son of *Amaziah* **Amaz Yah**
king **sovereign** of *Judah* **Yah Hudah** to reign.
2 **A son of** Sixteen years *old* was he
when he began to reign,
and he reigned two and fifty years
in *Jerusalem* **Yeru Shalem**.
And his mother's name was *Jecholiah* **Yechol Yah**
of *Jerusalem* **Yeru Shalem**.
3 And he *did* **worked** that which was *right* **straight**
in the *sight* **eyes** of *the LORD* **Yah Veh**,
according to all that his father *Amaziah* **Amaz Yah**
had *done* **worked**;
4 *Save* **Except** that the *high places* **bamahs**
were not *removed* **turned aside**:
the people sacrificed and *burnt incense* **incensed** still
on the *high places* **bamahs**.
5 And *the LORD smote* **Yah Veh touched** the *king* **sovereign**,
so that he was a leper unto the day of his death,
and *dwelt* **settled** in a *several* **liberty** house.
And *Jotham* **Yah Tham** the *king's* **sovereign's** son
was over the house, judging the people of the land.
6 And the rest of the *acts* **words** of *Azariah* **Azar Yah**,
and all that he *did* **worked**,
are they not *written* **inscribed** in the *book* **scroll**
of the *chronicles* **words of the days**
of the *kings* **sovereigns** of *Judah* **Yah Hudah**?
7 So *Azariah slept* **Azar Yah laid** with his fathers;
and they *buried* **entombed** him with his fathers
in the city of David:
and *Jotham* **Yah Tham** his son reigned in his stead.

ZECHAR YAH REIGNS OVER YAH HUDAH

8 In the thirty and eighth year of *Azariah* **Azar Yah**,
king **sovereign** of *Judah* **Yah Hudah**
did *Zachariah* **Zechar Yah** the son of *Jeroboam* **Yarob Am**
reign over *Israel* **Yisra El** in *Samaria* **Shomeron** six months.
9 And he *did* **worked** that which was evil
in the *sight* **eyes** of *the LORD* **Yah Veh**,
as his fathers had *done* **worked**:
he *departed* **turned** not **aside**
from the sins of *Jeroboam* **Yarob Am** the son of Nebat,
who made *Israel* **Yisra El** to sin.
10 And Shallum the son of *Jabesh* **Yabesh**
conspired against him, and smote him
before **in front of** the people,
and *slew* **deathified** him, and reigned in his stead.
11 And the rest of the *acts* **words** of *Zachariah* **Zechar Yah**,
behold, they are *written* **inscribed** in the *book* **scroll**
of the *chronicles* **words of the days**
of the *kings* **sovereigns** of *Israel* **Yisra El**.
12 This was the word of *the LORD* **Yah Veh**
which he *spake* **worded** unto *Jehu* **Yah Hu**, saying,
Thy sons shall *sit* **settle** on the throne of *Israel* **Yisra El**
unto the fourth *generation*.
And so it *came to pass* **became**.

SHALLUM REIGNS OVER YAH HUDAH

13 Shallum the son of *Jabesh* **Yabesh** began to reign
in the nine and thirtieth year of *Uzziah* **Uzzi Yah**,
king **sovereign** of *Judah* **Yah Hudah**;
and he reigned a *full month* **month of days**
in *Samaria* **Shomeron**.
14 For *Menahem* **Menachem** the son of Gadi
went up **ascended** from *Tirzah* **Tirsah**,
and came to *Samaria* **Shomeron**,
and smote Shallum the son of *Jabesh* **Yabesh**
in *Samaria* **Shomeron**,
and *slew* **slaughtered** him, and reigned in his stead.
15 And the rest of the *acts* **words** of Shallum,
and his conspiracy which he *made* **conspired**, behold,
they are *written* **inscribed** in the *book* **scroll**
of the *chronicles* **words of the days**
of the *kings* **sovereigns** of *Israel* **Yisra El**.
16 Then *Menahem* **Menachem** smote *Tiphsah* **Tiphsach**,
and all that were therein,
and the *coasts* **borders** thereof from *Tirzah* **Tirsah**:
because they opened not to him, therefore he smote it;
and all the *women therein that were with child* **conceivers**
he *ripped up* **split**.

MENACHEM REIGNS OVER YAH HUDAH

17 In the nine and thirtieth year of *Azariah* **Azar Yah**,
king **sovereign** of *Judah* **Yah Hudah**
began *Menahem* **Menachem** the son of Gadi
to reign over *Israel* **Yisra El**,
and reigned ten years in *Samaria* **Shomeron**.
18 And he *did* **worked** that which was evil
in the *sight* **eyes** of *the LORD* **Yah Veh**:
he *departed* **turned** not **aside** all his days
from the sins of *Jeroboam* **Yarob Am** the son of Nebat,
who made *Israel* **Yisra El** to sin.
19 *And* Pul the *king* **sovereign** of *Assyria* **Ashshur**
came against the land:
and *Menahem* **Menachem** gave Pul
a thousand *talents* **rounds** of silver,
that his hand might be with him
to *confirm* **uphold** the *kingdom* **sovereigndom** in his hand.
20 And *Menahem* **Menachem**
exacted **brought** the *money* **silver** of *Israel* **Yisra El**,
even of all the mighty *men* of *wealth* **valuables**,
of *each* **one** man fifty shekels of silver,
to give to the *king* **sovereign** of *Assyria* **Ashshur**.
So the *king* **sovereign** of *Assyria* **Ashshur** turned back,
and stayed not there in the land.
21 And the rest of the *acts* **words** of *Menahem* **Menachem**,
and all that he *did* **worked**,
are they not *written* **inscribed** in the *book* **scroll**
of the *chronicles* **words of the days**
of the *kings* **sovereigns** of *Israel* **Yisra El**?
22 And *Menahem* **Menachem**
slept **laid** with his fathers;
and *Pekahiah* **Peqach Yah** his son reigned in his stead.

PEQACH YAH REIGNS OVER YAH HUDAH

23 In the fiftieth year of *Azariah* **Azar Yah**
king **sovereign** of *Judah* **Yah Hudah**
Pekahiah **Peqach Yah** the son of *Menahem* **Menachem**
began to reign over *Israel* **Yisra El** in *Samaria* **Shomeron**,
and reigned two years.
24 And he *did* **worked** that which was evil
in the *sight* **eyes** of *the LORD* **Yah Veh**:
he *departed* **turned** not **aside**
from the sins of *Jeroboam* **Yarob Am** the son of Nebat,
who made *Israel* **Yisra El** to sin.
25 But *Pekah* **Peqach** the son of *Remaliah* **Remal Yah**,
a *captain* **tertiary** of his, conspired against him,
and smote him in *Samaria* **Shomeron**,
in the *palace* **citadel** of the *king's* **sovereign's** house,
with Argob and *Arieh* **Aryah**,
and with him fifty men
of the *Gileadites* **sons of the Giladiy**:
and he *killed* **deathified** him,
and reigned in his *room* **stead**.
26 And the rest of the *acts* **words** of *Pekahiah* **Peqach Yah**,
and all that he *did* **worked**, behold,
they are *written* **inscribed** in the *book* **scroll**
of the *chronicles* **words of the days**
of the *kings* **sovereigns** of *Israel* **Yisra El**.

PEQACH REIGNS OVER YISRA EL

27 In the two and fiftieth year of *Azariah* **Azar Yah**,
king **sovereign** of *Judah* **Yah Hudah**,
Pekah **Peqach** the son of *Remaliah* **Remal Yah**
began to reign over *Israel* **Yisra El** in *Samaria* **Shomeron**,
and reigned twenty years.
28 And he *did* **worked** that which was evil
in the *sight* **eyes** of *the LORD* **Yah Veh**:
he *departed* **turned** not **aside**
from the sins of *Jeroboam* **Yarob Am** the son of Nebat,
who made *Israel* **Yisra El** to sin.
29 In the days of *Pekah* **Peqach**
king **sovereign** of *Israel* **Yisra El**
came *Tiglathpileser* **Tilgath Pileser**,
king **sovereign** of *Assyria* **Ashshur**, and took *Ijon* **Iyon**,
and *Abelbethmaachah* **Abel Beth Maachah**,
and *Janoah* **Yanochah**, and *Kedesh* **Qedesh**,
and *Hazor* **Hasor**, and *Gilead* **Gilad**, and *Galilee* **Galiyl**,
all the land of Naphtali,
and *carried* **exiled** them *captive* to *Assyria* **Ashshur**.
30 And Hoshea the son of Elah
made **conspired** a conspiracy
against *Pekah* **Peqach** the son of *Remaliah* **Remal Yah**,
and smote him, and *slew* **deathified** him,
and reigned in his stead,
in the twentieth year of *Jotham* **Yah Tham**
the son of *Uzziah* **Uzzi Yah**.
31 And the rest of the *acts* **words** of *Pekah* **Peqach**,
and all that he *did* **worked**, behold,
they are *written* **inscribed** in the *book* **scroll**
of the *chronicles* **words of the days**
of the *kings* **sovereigns** of *Israel* **Yisra El**.

YAH THAM REIGNS OVER YAH HUDAH

32 In the second year of *Pekah* **Peqach**
the son of *Remaliah* **Remal Yah**
king **sovereign** of *Israel* **Yisra El**
began *Jotham* **Yah Tham** the son of *Uzziah* **Uzzi Yah**
king **sovereign** of *Judah* **Yah Hudah** to reign.
33 **A son of** Five and twenty years *old*
was he when he began to reign,
and he reigned sixteen years in *Jerusalem* **Yeru Shalem**.
And his mother's name was *Jerusha* **Yerushah**,
the daughter of *Zadok* **Sadoq**.
34 And he *did* **worked** that which was *right* **straight**
in the *sight* **eyes** of *the LORD* **Yah Veh**:
he *did* **worked** according to all
that his father *Uzziah* **Uzzi Yah** had *done* **worked**.
35 Howbeit
the *high places* **bamahs** were not *removed* **turned aside**:
the people sacrificed and *burned incense* **incensed** still
in the *high places* **bamahs**.
He built *the higher gate* **Elyon Portal**
of the house of the *LORD* **Yah Veh**.
36 Now the rest of the *acts* **words** of *Jotham* **Yah Tham**,
and all that he *did* **worked**,
are they not *written* **inscribed** in the *book* **scroll**
of the *chronicles* **words of the days**
of the *kings* **sovereigns** of *Judah* **Yah Hudah**?
37 In those days *the LORD* **Yah Veh** began to send
against *Judah* **Yah Hudah**
Rezin **Resin** the *king* **sovereign** of *Syria* **Aram**,
and *Pekah* **Peqach** the son of *Remaliah* **Remal Yah**.
38 And *Jotham slept* **Yah Tham laid** with his fathers,
and was *buried* **entombed** with his fathers
in the city of David his father:
and *Ahaz* **Achaz** his son reigned in his stead.

ACHAZ REIGNS OVER YAH HUDAH

16 In the seventeenth year of *Pekah* **Peqach**
the son of *Remaliah* **Remal Yah**,
Ahaz **Achaz** the son of *Jotham* **Yah Tham**,
king **sovereign** of *Judah* **Yah Hudah** began to reign.
2 **A son of** Twenty years *old* was *Ahaz* **Achaz**
when he began to reign,
and reigned sixteen years in *Jerusalem* **Yeru Shalem**,
and *did* **worked** not that which was *right* **straight**
in the *sight* **eyes** of *the LORD* **Yah Veh** his *God* **Elohim**,
like David his father.
3 But he walked in the way
of the *kings* **sovereigns** of *Israel* **Yisra El**, yea,
and made his son to pass through the fire,
according to the *abominations* **abhorrences**
of the *heathen* **goyim**,
whom *the LORD cast out* **Yah Veh dispossessed**
from *before* **the face of** the *children* **sons** of *Israel* **Yisra El**.
4 And he sacrificed and *burnt incense* **incensed**
in the *high places* **bamahs**,
and on the hills, and under every green tree.
5 Then *Rezin* **Resin** *king* **sovereign** of *Syria* **Aram**,
and *Pekah* **Peqach** son of *Remaliah* **Remal Yah**,
king **sovereign** of *Israel* **Yisra El**
came up **ascended** to *Jerusalem* **Yeru Shalem** to war:
and they besieged *Ahaz* **Achaz**,
but could not *overcome* **fight** him.
6 At that time *Rezin* **Resin** *king* **sovereign** of *Syria* **Aram**
recovered Elath **restored Eloth** to *Syria* **Aram**,
and *drave* **plucked** the *Jews* **Yah Hudiym** from *Elath* **Eloth**:
and the *Syrians* **Edomiy** came to *Elath* **Eloth**,
and *dwelt* **settled** there unto this day.
7 So *Ahaz* **Achaz** sent *messengers* **angels**
to *Tiglathpileser* **Tilgath Pileser**
king **sovereign** of *Assyria* **Ashshur**, saying,
I am thy servant and thy son: *come up* **ascend**,
and save me out of the *hand* **palm**

of the *king* **sovereign** of *Syria* **Aram**,
and out of the *hand* **palm**
of the *king* **sovereign** of *Israel* **Yisra El**,
which rise up against me.
8 And *Ahaz* **Achaz** took the silver and gold
that was found in the house of *the LORD* **Yah Veh**,
and in the treasures of the *king's* **sovereign's** house,
and sent it for a *present* **bribe**
to the *king* **sovereign** of *Assyria* **Ashshur**.
9 And the *king* **sovereign** of *Assyria* **Ashshur**
hearkened unto him:
for the *king* **sovereign** of *Assyria* **Ashshur**
went up **ascended** against *Damascus* **Dammeseq**,
and *took* **apprehended** it,
and *carried the people of it captive* **captured it** to *Kir* **Qir**,
and *slew Rezin* **deathified Resin**.
10 And *king Ahaz* **sovereign Achaz**
went to *Damascus* **Dammeseq**
to meet *Tiglathpileser* **Tilgath Pileser**,
king **sovereign** of *Assyria* **Ashshur**,
and saw *an* **a sacrifice** altar
that was at *Damascus* **Dammeseq**:
and *king Ahaz* **sovereign Achaz**
sent to *Urijah* **Uri Yah** the priest
the *fashion* **likeness** of the **sacrifice** altar,
and the pattern of it,
according to all the *workmanship* **works** thereof.
11 And *Urijah* **Uri Yah** the priest built *an* **a sacrifice** altar
according to all that *king Ahaz* **sovereign Achaz**
had sent from *Damascus* **Dammeseq**:
so *Urijah* **Uri Yah** the priest *made* **worked** it
against king Ahaz came
unto the coming of sovereign Achaz
from *Damascus* **Dammeseq**.
12 And when the *king* **sovereign**
was come from *Damascus* **Dammeseq**,
the *king* **sovereign** saw the **sacrifice** altar:
and the *king* **sovereign** approached to the **sacrifice** altar,
and *offered* **holocausted** thereon.
13 And he *burnt* **incensed** his *burnt offering* **holocaust**
and his *meat* offering,
and poured his *drink offering* **libation**,
and sprinkled the blood of his *peace offerings* **shelamim**,
upon the **sacrifice** altar.
14 And he *brought* **approached** also
the *brasen* **copper sacrifice** altar,
which was before the LORD **at the face of Yah Veh**,
from the *forefront* **face** of the house,
from between the **sacrifice** altar
and the house of *the LORD* **Yah Veh**,
and *put* **gave** it
on the north *side* **flank** of the **sacrifice** altar.
15 And *king Ahaz* **sovereign Achaz**
commanded Urijah **misvahed Uri Yah** the priest, saying,
Upon the great **sacrifice** altar
burn **incense** the morning *burnt offering* **holocaust**,
and the evening *meat* offering,
and the *king's burnt sacrifice* **sovereign's holocaust**,
and his *meat* offering,
with the *burnt offering* **holocaust**
of all the people of the land,
and their *meat* offering,
and their *drink offerings* **libations**;
and sprinkle upon it
all the blood of the *burnt offering* **holocaust**,
and all the blood of the sacrifice:
and the *brasen* **copper sacrifice** altar
shall be for me to *enquire* **search** by.
16 Thus *did Urijah* **worked Uri Yah** the priest,
according to all
that *king Ahaz commanded* **sovereign Achaz misvahed**.
17 And *king Ahaz* **sovereign Achaz**
cut **chopped** off the borders of the bases,
and *removed* **twisted off** the laver from off them;
and *took down* **descended** the sea
from off the *brasen* **copper** oxen that were under it,
and *put* **gave** it upon the pavement of stones.
18 And the *covert* **portico** for the *sabbath* **shabbath**
that they had built in the house,
and the *king's* **sovereign's** entry without,
turned he
from **the face of** the house of *the LORD* **Yah Veh**
for the king of Assyria
at the face of the sovereign of Ashshur.
19 Now the rest of the *acts* **words** of *Ahaz* **Achaz**
which he *did* **worked**,
are they not *written* **inscribed** in the *book* **scroll**
of the *chronicles* **words of the days**
of the *kings* **sovereigns** of *Judah* **Yah Hudah**?
20 And *Ahaz slept* **Achaz laid** with his fathers,
and was *buried* **entombed** with his fathers
in the city of David:
and *Hezekiah* **Yechizqi Yah** his son reigned in his stead.

HOSHEA REIGNS OVER YISRA EL

17 In the twelfth year of *Ahaz* **Achaz**,
king **sovereign** of *Judah* **Yah Hudah**
began Hoshea the son of Elah
to reign in *Samaria* **Shomeron**
over *Israel* **Yisra El** nine years.
2 And he *did* **worked** that which was evil
in the *sight* **eyes** of *the LORD* **Yah Veh**,
but not as the *kings* **sovereigns** of *Israel* **Yisra El**
that were *before him* **at his face**.
3 Against him *came up* **ascended** Shalmaneser
king **sovereign** of *Assyria* **Ashshur**;
and Hoshea became his servant,
and *gave* **returned** him *presents* **offerings**.
4 And the *king* **sovereign** of *Assyria* **Ashshur**
found conspiracy in Hoshea:
for he had sent *messengers* **angels** to So,
king **sovereign** of *Egypt* **Misrayim**,
and *brought* **holocausted** no *present* **offering**
to the *king* **sovereign** of *Assyria* **Ashshur**,
as *he had done* year by year:
therefore the *king* **sovereign** of *Assyria* **Ashshur**
shut **restrained** him *up*,
and bound him in **the house of** prison.
5 Then the *king* **sovereign** of *Assyria* **Ashshur**
came up **ascended** throughout all the land,
and *went up* **ascended** to *Samaria* **Shomeron**,
and besieged it three years.

YISRA EL EXILED

6 In the ninth year of Hoshea
the *king* **sovereign** of *Assyria* **Ashshur**
took Samaria **captured Shomeron**,
and *carried Israel away* **exiled Yisra El**
into *Assyria* **Ashshur**,
and *placed* **set** them in *Halah* **Halach**
and in Habor by the river of Gozan,
and in the cities of the *Medes* **Madaim**.
7 For *so it was* **it became**,
that the *children* **sons** of *Israel* **Yisra El**
had sinned against *the LORD* **Yah Veh** their *God* **Elohim**,
which had *brought* **ascended** them *up*
out of the land of *Egypt* **Misrayim**,
from under the hand of *Pharaoh* **Paroh**,
king **sovereign** of *Egypt* **Misrayim**,
and had *feared* **awed** other *gods* **elohim**,
8 And walked in the statutes of the *heathen* **goyim**,
whom *the LORD cast out* **Yah Veh dispossessed**
from *before* **the face of** the *children* **sons** of *Israel* **Yisra El**,
and of the *kings* **sovereigns** of *Israel* **Yisra El**,
which they had *made* **worked**.
9 And the *children* **sons** of *Israel* **Yisra El**
did *secretly* **covertly** those *things* **words** that were not right
against *the LORD* **Yah Veh** their *God* **Elohim**
and they built them *high places* **bamahs** in all their cities,
from the tower of the *watchmen* **guards**
to the *fenced* **fortified** city.
10 And they *set* **stationed** them *up images* **monoliths**
and *groves* **asherim** in every high hill,
and under every green tree:
11 And there they *burnt incense* **incensed**
in all the *high places* **bamahs**,
as did the *heathen* **goyim**
whom *the LORD carried away* **Yah Veh exiled**
before them **from their face**;
and *wrought wicked things* **worked evil words**
to *provoke the LORD to anger* **vex Yah Veh**:
12 For they served idols,

whereof *the LORD* **Yah Veh** had said unto them,
ye shall not *do* **work** this *thing* **word**.
13 Yet *the LORD testified* **Yah Veh witnessed**
against *Israel* **Yisra El**, and against *Judah* **Yah Hudah**,
by **the hand of** all the prophets, and by all the seers,
saying, Turn ye from your evil ways,
and *keep* **guard**
my *commandments* **misvoth** and my statutes,
according to all the *law* **torah**
which I *commanded* **misvahed** your fathers,
and which I sent to you by **the hand of** my servants
the prophets.
14 Notwithstanding they *would not hear* **hearkened not**,
but hardened their necks, like to the neck of their fathers,
that did not *believe* **trust**
in *the LORD* **Yah Veh** their *God* **Elohim**.
15 And they *rejected* **refused** his statutes,
and his covenant that he *made* **cut** with their fathers,
and his *testimonies* **witnesses**
which he *testified* **witnessed** against them;
and they *followed* **went after** vanity, and became vain,
and went after the *heathen* **goyim**
that were round about them,
concerning whom
the LORD **Yah Veh** had *charged* **misvahed** them,
that they should not *do* **work** like them.
16 And they left all the *commandments* **misvoth**
of *the LORD* **Yah Veh** their *God* **Elohim**
and *made* **worked** them molten *images, even* two calves,
and *made a grove* **worked an asherah**,
and *worshipped* **prostrated**
to all the host of *heaven* **the heavens**,
and served Baal.
17 And they caused their sons and their daughters
to pass through the fire,
and *used* **divined** divination
and *enchantments* **prognostications**,
and sold themselves
to *do* **work** evil in the *sight* **eyes** of *the LORD* **Yah Veh**,
to *provoke* **vex** him *to anger*.
18 Therefore *the LORD* **Yah Veh**
was *very* **mighty** angry with *Israel* **Yisra El**,
and *removed* **turned** them **aside** out of his *sight* **face**:
there was none left **none survived**
but the *tribe* **scion** of *Judah* **Yah Hudah** only.
19 Also *Judah* **Yah Hudah**
kept **guarded** not the *commandments* **misvoth**
of *the LORD* **Yah Veh** their *God* **Elohim**
but walked in the statutes of *Israel* **Yisra El**
which they *made* **worked**.
20 And *the LORD* **Yah Veh**
rejected **refused** all the seed of *Israel* **Yisra El**,
and *afflicted* **humbled** them,
and *delivered* **gave** them
into the hand of *spoilers* **plunderers**,
until he had cast them out of his *sight* **face**.
21 For he *rent Israel* **ripped Yisra El**
from the house of David;
and they made *Jeroboam* **Yarob Am** the son of Nebat
king **to reign**:
and *Jeroboam drave Israel* **Yarob Am banished Yisra El**
from *following the LORD* **going after Yah Veh**,
and made them sin a great sin.
22 For the *children* **sons** of *Israel* **Yisra El**
walked in all the sins of *Jeroboam* **Yarob Am**
which he *did* **worked**;
they *departed* **turned** not **aside** from them;
23 Until *the LORD removed* **Yah Veh turned aside**
Israel **Yisra El** out of his *sight* **face**,
as he had *said* **worded**
by **the hand of** all his servants the prophets.
So was *Israel carried away* **Yisra El exiled**
out of their own *land* **soil**
to *Assyria* **Ashshur** unto this day.

GOYIM SETTLE IN SHOMERON

24 And the *king* **sovereign** of *Assyria* **Ashshur**
brought *men* from *Babylon* **Babel**, and from *Cuthah* **Kuth**,
and from *Ava* **Avva**, and from Hamath,
and from *Sepharvaim* **Sepharvayim**,
and *placed* **set** them in the cities of *Samaria* **Shomeron**
instead of the *children* **sons** of *Israel* **Yisra El**:
and they possessed *Samaria* **Shomeron**,
and *dwelt* **settled** in the cities thereof.
25 And *so* it *was* **became**
at the beginning of their *dwelling* **settling** there,
that they *feared* **awed** not *the LORD* **Yah Veh**:
therefore *the LORD* **Yah Veh** sent lions among them,
which *slew some of* **slaughtered among** them.
26 Wherefore they *spake* **said**
to the *king* **sovereign** of *Assyria* **Ashshur**, saying,
The *nations* **goyim** which thou hast *removed* **exiled**,
and *placed* **set** in the cities of *Samaria* **Shomeron**,
know not the *manner* **judgment**
of the *God* **Elohim** of the land:
therefore he hath sent lions among them, and, behold,
they *slay* **deathify** them,
because they know not the *manner* **judgment**
of the *God* **Elohim** of the land.
27 Then the *king* **sovereign** of *Assyria* **Ashshur**
commanded **misvahed**, saying,
Carry **Walk** thither one of the priests
whom ye *brought* **exiled** from thence;
and let them go and *dwell* **settle** there,
and let him *teach* **direct** them
the *manner* **judgment** of the *God* **Elohim** of the land.
28 Then one of the priests
whom they had *carried away* **exiled**
from *Samaria* **Shomeron**
came and *dwelt* **settled** in *Bethel* **Beth El**,
and *taught* **directed** them
how they should *fear the LORD* **awe Yah Veh**.
29 Howbeit *every nation* **goyim by goyim**
made gods **worked elohim** of their own,
and *put* **set** them in the houses of the *high places* **bamahs**
which the *Samaritans* **Shomeroniy** had *made* **worked**,
every nation **goyim by goyim**
in their cities wherein they *dwelt* **settled**.
30 And the men of *Babylon* **Babel**
made Succothbenoth **worked Sukkoth Benoth**,
and the men of *Cuth made* **Kuth worked** Nergal,
and the men of Hamath *made* **worked** Ashima,
31 And the *Avites* **Avviy**
made Nibhaz **worked Nibchaz** and *Tartak* **Tartaq**,
and the *Sepharvites* **Sepharviy**
burnt their *children* **sons** in fire
to *Adrammelech* **Adram Melech**
and *Anammelech* **Anam Melech**,
the *gods* **elohim** of *Sepharvaim* **Sepharvayim**.
32 So they *feared the LORD* **awed Yah Veh**,
and *made* **worked** unto themselves
of the *lowest* **end** of them
priests of the *high places* **bamahs**,
which *sacrificed* **worked** for them
in the houses of the *high places* **bamahs**.
33 They *feared the LORD* **awed Yah Veh**,
and served their own *gods* **elohim**,
after the *manner* **judgment** of the *nations* **goyim**
whom they *carried away* **exiled** from thence.
34 Unto this day
they *do* **work** after the former *manners* **judgments**:
they *fear* **awe** not *the LORD* **Yah Veh**,
neither *do* **work** they after their statutes,
or after their *ordinances* **judgments**,
or after the *law* **torah** and *commandment* **misvah**
which *the LORD* **Yah Veh**
commanded **misvahed** the *children* **sons** of *Jacob* **Yaaqov**,
whom he named Israel **on whose name he set, Yisra El**;
35 With whom
the LORD **Yah Veh** had *made* **cut** a covenant,
and *charged* **misvahed** them, saying,
Ye shall not *fear* **awe** other *gods* **elohim**,
nor *bow* **prostrate** yourselves to them,
nor serve them, nor sacrifice to them:
36 But *the LORD* **Yah Veh**,
who *brought* **ascended** you *up*
out of the land of *Egypt* **Misrayim**
with great *power* **force** and a stretched out arm,
him shall ye *fear* **awe**,
and **to** him shall ye *worship* **prostrate**,
and to him shall ye *do* sacrifice.

37 And the statutes, and the *ordinances* **judgments**,
and the *law* **torah**, and the *commandment* **misvah**,
which he *wrote* **inscribed** for you,
ye shall *observe* **guard** to *do for evermore* **work all days**;
and ye shall not *fear* **awe** other *gods* **elohim**.
38 And the covenant that I have *made* **cut** with you
ye shall not forget;
neither shall ye *fear* **awe** other *gods* **elohim**.
39 But *the LORD* **Yah Veh** your *God* **Elohim**
ye shall *fear* **awe**;
and he shall *deliver* **rescue** you
out of the hand of all your enemies.
40 Howbeit they did not hearken,
but they *did* **worked** after their former *manner* **judgment**.
41 So these *nations* **goyim**
feared the LORD **awed Yah Veh**,
and served their *graven images* **sculptiles**,
both their *children* **sons**,
and their *children's children* **son's sons**:
as *did* **worked** their fathers, so *do* **work** they unto this day.

YECHIZQI YAH REIGNS IN YERU SHALEM

18 Now it *came to pass* **became**,
in the third year of Hoshea son of Elah
king **sovereign** of *Israel* **Yisra El**,
that *Hezekiah* **Yechizqi Yah** the son of *Ahaz* **Achaz**,
king **sovereign** of *Judah* **Yah Hudah** began to reign.
2 **A son of** Twenty and five years *old*
was he when he began to reign;
and he reigned twenty and nine years
in *Jerusalem* **Yeru Shalem**.
His mother's name also was Abi,
the daughter of *Zachariah* **Zechar Yah**.
3 And he *did* **worked** that which was right **straight**
in the *sight* **eyes** of *the LORD* **Yah Veh**,
according to all that David his father *did* **worked**.
4 He *removed* **turned aside** the *high places* **bamahs**,
and brake the *images* **monoliths**,
and cut down the *groves* **asherim**,
and *brake in pieces* **crushed** the *brasen* **copper** serpent
that *Moses* **Mosheh** had *made* **worked**:
for unto those days the *children* **sons** of *Israel* **Yisra El**
did burn incense **incensed** to it:
and he called it *Nehushtan* **Coppery/Nechustan**.
5 He *trusted* **confided**
in *the LORD God* **Yah Veh Elohim** of *Israel* **Yisra El**;
so that after him was none like him
among all the *kings* **sovereigns** of *Judah* **Yah Hudah**,
nor *any* that were *before him* **at his face**.
6 For he *clave* **adhered** to *the LORD* **Yah Veh**,
and *departed* **turned** not **aside** from *following* **after** him,
but *kept* **guarded** his *commandments* **misvoth**,
which *the LORD* **Yah Veh**
commanded Moses **misvahed Mosheh**.
7 And *the LORD* **Yah Veh** was with him;
and he *prospered* **comprehended**
whithersoever he went forth:
and he rebelled
against the *king* **sovereign** of *Assyria* **Ashshur**,
and served him not.
8 He smote the *Philistines* **Peleshethiy**,
even unto *Gaza* **Azzah**, and the borders thereof,
from the tower of the *watchmen* **guards**
to the *fenced* **fortified** city.
9 And it *came to pass* **became**,
in the fourth year
of *king Hezekiah* **sovereign Yechizqi Yah**,
which was the seventh year of Hoshea
son of Elah *king* **sovereign** of *Israel* **Yisra El**,
that Shalmaneser *king* **sovereign** of *Assyria* **Ashshur**
came up **ascended** against *Samaria* **Shomeron**,
and besieged it.
10 And at the end of three years they *took* **captured** it:
even in the sixth year of *Hezekiah* **Yechizqi Yah**,
that is in the ninth year of Hoshea
king **sovereign** of *Israel* **Yisra El**,
Samaria **Shomeron** was *taken* **captured**.
11 And the *king* **sovereign** of *Assyria* **Ashshur**
did carry away Israel **exiled Yisra El** unto *Assyria* **Ashshur**,
and *put* **guided** them in *Halah* **Halach**
and in Habor by the river of Gozan,
and in the cities of the *Medes* **Madaim**:
12 Because they *obeyed* **heard** not
the voice of *the LORD* **Yah Veh** their *God* **Elohim**
but *transgressed* **trespassed** his covenant,
and all that *Moses* **Mosheh**
the servant of *the LORD commanded* **Yah Veh misvahed**,
and *would not hear them* **hearkened not**,
nor *do* **worked** them.
13 Now in the fourteenth year
of *king Hezekiah* **sovereign Yechizqi Yah**
did *Sennacherib* **Sancherib**
king **sovereign** of *Assyria* **Ashshur**
come up **ascend** against all the *fenced* **cut off** cities
of *Judah* **Yah Hudah**, and *took* **apprehended** them.
14 And *Hezekiah* **Yechizqi Yah**
king **sovereign** of *Judah* **Yah Hudah**
sent to the *king* **sovereign** of *Assyria* **Ashshur** to Lachish,
saying, I have *offended* **sinned**; return from me:
that which thou *puttest* **givest** on me *will* **shall** I bear.
And the *king* **sovereign** of *Assyria* **Ashshur**
appointed **set** unto *Hezekiah* **Yechizqi Yah,**
king **sovereign** of *Judah* **Yah Hudah**
three hundred *talents* **rounds** of silver
and thirty *talents* **rounds** of gold.
15 And *Hezekiah* **Yechizqi Yah** gave him all the silver
that was found in the house of *the LORD* **Yah Veh**,
and in the treasures of the *king's* **sovereign's** house.
16 At that time did *Hezekiah* **Yechizqi Yah**
cut **chop** off *the gold from* the doors
of the *temple* **manse** of *the LORD* **Yah Veh**,
and *from* the pillars
which *Hezekiah* **Yechizqi Yah**
king **sovereign** of *Judah* **Yah Hudah** had *overlaid* **watched**,
and gave it to the *king* **sovereign** of *Assyria* **Ashshur**.
17 And the *king* **sovereign** of *Assyria* **Ashshur**
sent Tartan *and Rabsaris* **the chief eunuch**
and *Rabshakeh* **Rab Shaqeh/the chief butler**
from Lachish to *king Hezekiah* **sovereign Yechizqi Yah**
with *a great host* **heavy valiant**
against *Jerusalem* **Yeru Shalem**.
And they *went up* **ascended**
and came to *Jerusalem* **Yeru Shalem**.
And when they *were come up* **ascended**,
they came and stood by the *conduit* **channel**
of *the upper pool* **Pool Elyon**,
which is in the highway of the fuller's field.
18 And when they had called to the *king* **sovereign**,
there *came* **went** out to them *Eliakim* **El Yaqim**
the son of *Hilkiah* **Hilqi Yah**,
which was over the household,
and Shebna the scribe,
and *Joah* **Yah Ach** the son of Asaph
the *recorder* **remembrancer**.
19 And *Rabshakeh* **Rab Shaqeh/the chief butler**
said unto them,
Speak **Say** ye now to *Hezekiah* **Yechizqi Yah**,
Thus saith the great *king* **sovereign**,
the *king* **sovereign** of *Assyria* **Ashshur**,
What confidence is this wherein thou *trustest* **confidest**?
20 Thou sayest,
(but they are but *vain* words **of lips**,)
I have counsel and *strength* **might** for the war.
Now on whom dost thou *trust* **confide**,
that thou rebellest against me?
21 Now, behold,
thou *trustest* **confidest** upon the staff
of this *bruised reed* **crushed stalk**,
even upon *Egypt* **Misrayim**,
on which if a man *lean* **prop**,
it *will* **shall** go into his *hand* **palm**, and pierce it:
so is *Pharaoh* **Paroh**, *king* **sovereign** of *Egypt* **Misrayim**
unto all that *trust* **confide** on him.
22 But if ye say unto me,
We *trust* **confide** in *the LORD* **Yah Veh** our *God* **Elohim**:
is not that he,
whose *high places* **bamahs** and whose **sacrifice** altars
Hezekiah **Yechizqi Yah** hath *taken away* **turned aside**,
and hath said to *Judah* **Yah Hudah**
and *Jerusalem* **Yeru Shalem**,
Ye shall *worship before* **prostrate at the face**

of this **sacrifice** altar in *Jerusalem* **Yeru Shalem**?
23 Now therefore, I *pray* **beseech** thee,
give pledges **pledge** to my *lord* **adoni**
the *king* **sovereign** of *Assyria* **Ashshur**,
and I *will deliver* **shall give** thee two thousand horses,
if thou be able on thy part to *set* **give** riders upon them.
24 How then *wilt* **shalt** thou turn away
the face of one *captain* **governor**
of the least of my *master's* **adoni's** servants,
and *put thy trust* **confide** on *Egypt* **Misrayim**
for chariots and for *horsemen* **cavalry**?
25 *Am I now come up* **Ascend I now**
without *the LORD* **Yah Veh**
against this place to *destroy* **ruin** it?
The LORD **Yah Veh** said to me,
Go up **Ascend** against this land, and *destroy* **ruin** it.
26 Then said *Eliakim* **El Yaqim**
the son of *Hilkiah* **Hilqi Yah**,
and Shebna, and *Joah* **Yah Ach**,
unto *Rabshakeh* **Rab Shaqeh/the chief butler**,
Speak **Word**, I *pray* **beseech** thee,
to thy servants in *the Syrian language* **Aramaic**;
for we *understand* **hear** it:
and *talk* **word** not with us
in *the Jews' language* **Yah Hudaic**
in the ears of the people that are on the wall.
27 But *Rabshakeh* **Rab Shaqeh/the chief butler**
said unto them,
Hath my *master* **adoni** sent me to thy master, and to thee,
to *speak* **word** these words?
hath he not *sent me* to the men
which *sit* **settle** on the wall,
that they may eat their own *dung* **dungs**,
and drink *their own piss* **the urine at their feet** with you?
28 Then *Rabshakeh* **Rab Shaqeh/the chief butler**
stood and *cried* **called out**
with a *loud* **great** voice in *the Jews' language* **Yah Hudaic**,
and *spake* **worded**, saying,
Hear the word of the great *king* **sovereign**,
the *king* **sovereign** of *Assyria* **Ashshur**:
29 Thus saith the *king* **sovereign**,
Let not *Hezekiah* **Yechizqi Yah** deceive you:
for he shall not be able to *deliver* **rescue** you
out of his hand:
30 Neither let *Hezekiah* **Yechizqi Yah**
make you *trust* **confide** in *the LORD* **Yah Veh**, saying,
In rescuing,
The LORD will surely deliver **Yah Veh shall rescue** us,
and this city shall not be *delivered* **given**
into the hand of the *king* **sovereign** of *Assyria* **Ashshur**.
31 Hearken not to *Hezekiah* **Yechizqi Yah**:
for thus saith the *king* **sovereign** of *Assyria* **Ashshur**,
Make an agreement **Work** with me by a *present* **blessing**,
and *come* **go** out to me,
and then eat ye every man of his own vine,
and every *one* **man** of his fig tree,
and drink ye every *one* **man** the waters of his *cistern* **well**:
32 Until I come and take you away
to a land like your own land,
a land of *corn* **crop** and *wine* **juice**,
a land of bread and vineyards,
a land of oil olive and of honey,
that ye may live, and not die:
and hearken not unto *Hezekiah* **Yechizqi Yah**,
when he *persuadeth* **goadeth** you, saying,
The LORD will deliver **Yah Veh shall rescue** us.
33 **In rescuing,**
Hath any of the *gods* **elohim** *of the nations* **goyim**
delivered at all **rescued a man** his land
out of the hand of the *king* **sovereign** of *Assyria* **Ashshur**?
34 Where are the *gods* **elohim** of Hamath, and of Arpad?
where are the *gods* **elohim** of *Sepharvaim* **Sepharvayim**,
Hena, and *Ivah* **Avva**?
have they *delivered Samaria* **rescued Shomeron**
out of mine hand?
35 Who are they
among all the *gods* **elohim** of the *countries* **lands**,
that have *delivered* **rescued** their *country* **land**
out of mine hand,
that *the LORD* **Yah Veh**
should *deliver Jerusalem* **rescue Yeru Shalem**
out of mine hand?
36 But the people *held their peace* **hushed**,
and answered him not a word:
for the *king's commandment* **sovereign's misvah** was,
saying, Answer him not.
37 Then came *Eliakim* **El Yaqim**
the son of *Hilkiah* **Hilqi Yah**,
which was over the household, and Shebna the scribe,
and *Joah* **Yah Ach** the son of Asaph
the *recorder* **remembrancer**,
to *Hezekiah* **Yechizqi Yah** with their clothes *rent* **ripped**,
and told him the words
of *Rabshakeh* **Rab Shaqeh/the chief butler**.

19

And it *came to pass* **became**,
when *king Hezekiah* **sovereign Yechizqi Yah** heard it,
that he *rent* **ripped** his clothes,
and covered himself with *sackcloth* **saq**,
and went into the house of *the LORD* **Yah Veh**.
2 And he sent *Eliakim* **El Yaqim**,
which was over the household,
and Shebna the scribe, and the elders of the priests,
covered with *sackcloth* **saq**,
to *Isaiah* **Yesha Yah** the prophet the son of *Amoz* **Amos**.
3 And they said unto him,
Thus saith *Hezekiah* **Yechizqi Yah**,
This day is a day of *trouble* **tribulation**,
and of *rebuke* **reproof**, and *blasphemy* **scorning**;
for the *children* **sons** are come to the *birth* **matrix**,
and there is not *strength* **force** to *bring forth* **birth**.
4 *It may be the LORD* **Perhaps Yah Veh** thy *God* **Elohim**
will **shall** hear all the words
of *Rabshakeh* **Rab Shaqeh/the chief butler**,
whom the *king* **sovereign** of *Assyria* **Ashshur**
his *master* **adoni**
hath sent to reproach the living *God* **Elohim**;
and *will* **shall** reprove the words
which *the LORD* **Yah Veh** thy *God* **Elohim** hath heard:
wherefore lift up *thy* prayer
for the *remnant* **survivors** that are *left* **found**.
5 So the servants of *king Hezekiah* **sovereign Yechizqi Yah**
came to *Isaiah* **Yesha Yah**.
6 And *Isaiah* **Yesha Yah** said unto them,
Thus shall ye say to your *master* **adoni**,
Thus saith *the LORD* **Yah Veh**,
Be **Awe** not *afraid* **at the face** of the words
which thou hast heard,
with which the *servants* **lads**
of the *king* **sovereign** of *Assyria* **Ashshur**
have blasphemed me.
7 Behold, I *will send* **shall give**
a *blast* **spirit/wind** upon him,
and he shall hear a *rumour* **report**,
and shall return to his own land;
and I *will* **shall** cause him to fall by the sword
in his own land.
8 So *Rabshakeh* **Rab Shaqeh/the chief butler** returned,
and found the *king* **sovereign** of *Assyria* **Ashshur**
warring **fighting** against Libnah:
for he had heard
that he *was departed* **had pulled stakes** from Lachish.
9 And when he heard say of *Tirhakah* **Tirhaqah**
king **sovereign** of *Ethiopia* **Kush**, Behold,
he is *come out* **gone** to fight against thee:
he **returned and** sent *messengers* **angels** *again*
unto *Hezekiah* **Yechizqi Yah**, saying,
10 Thus shall ye *speak* **say** to *Hezekiah* **Yechizqi Yah**,
king **sovereign** of *Judah* **Yah Hudah**, saying,
Let not thy *God* **Elohim** in whom thou *trustest* **confidest**
deceive thee, saying,
Jerusalem **Yeru Shalem** shall not be *delivered* **given**
into the hand of the *king* **sovereign** of *Assyria* **Ashshur**.
11 Behold, thou hast heard
what the *kings* **sovereigns** of *Assyria* **Ashshur**
have *done* **worked** to all lands,
by *destroying* **devoting** them *utterly*:
and shalt thou be *delivered* **rescued**?
12 Have the *gods* **elohim** of the *nations* **goyim**
delivered **rescued** them
which my fathers have *destroyed* **ruined**;

as Gozan, and Haran, and *Rezeph* **Reseph**,
and the *children* **sons** of Eden which were in Thelasar?
13 Where is the *king* **sovereign** of Hamath,
and the *king* **sovereign** of Arpad,
and the *king* **sovereign**
of the city of *Sepharvaim* **Sepharvayim**,
of Hena, and *Ivah* **Avva**?
14 And *Hezekiah* **Yechizqi Yah**
received **took** the *letter* **scroll**
of the hand of the *messengers* **angels**,
and *read* **called** it **out**:
and *Hezekiah* **Yechizqi Yah**
went up **ascended** into the house of *the LORD* **Yah Veh**,
and spread it *before the LORD* **at the face of Yah Veh**.
15 And *Hezekiah* **Yechizqi Yah**
prayed *before the LORD* **at the face of Yah Veh**, and said,
O *LORD God* **Yah Veh Elohim** of *Israel* **Yisra El**,
which *dwellest* **settlest** between the *cherubims* **cherubim**,
thou art the *God* **Elohim**, *even* thou alone,
of all the *kingdoms* **sovereigndoms** of the earth;
thou hast *made heaven* **worked the heavens** and earth.
16 *LORD* **Yah Veh**, *bow down* **extend** thine ear, and hear:
open, *LORD* **Yah Veh**, thine eyes, and see:
and hear the words of *Sennacherib* **Sancherib**,
which hath sent him to reproach the living *God* **Elohim**.
17 *Of a truth* **Truly**, *LORD* **Yah Veh**,
the *kings* **sovereigns** of *Assyria* **Ashshur**
have *destroyed* **desolated** the *nations* **goyim**
and their lands,
18 And have *cast* **given** their *gods* **elohim** into the fire:
for they were no *gods* **elohim**,
but the work of *men's* **human** hands,
wood **timber** and stone:
therefore they **and** have destroyed them.
19 Now *therefore*, O *LORD* **Yah Veh** our *God* **Elohim**,
I beseech thee, save thou us out of his hand,
that all the *kingdoms* **sovereigndoms** of the earth
may know that thou art *the LORD God* **Yah Veh Elohim**,
even thou only.
20 Then *Isaiah* **Yesha Yah** the son of *Amoz* **Amos**
sent to *Hezekiah* **Yechizqi Yah**, saying,
Thus saith
the LORD God **Yah Veh Elohim** of *Israel* **Yisra El**,
That which thou hast prayed to me
against *Sennacherib* **Sancherib**,
king **sovereign** of *Assyria* **Ashshur**
I have heard.
21 This is the word
that *the LORD* **Yah Veh** hath *spoken* **worded**
concerning him;
The virgin the daughter of *Zion* **Siyon** hath despised thee,
and *laughed* **derided** thee *to scorn*;
the daughter of *Jerusalem* **Yeru Shalem**
hath shaken her head *at* **after** thee.
22 Whom hast thou reproached and blasphemed?
and against whom hast thou exalted thy voice,
and lifted up thine eyes on high?
even against the Holy *One* of *Israel* **Yisra El**.
23 By **the hand of** thy *messengers* **angels**
thou hast reproached *the Lord* **Adonay**, and hast said,
With the *multitude* **abundance** of my chariots
I *am come up* **ascend** to the height of the mountains,
to the *sides* **flanks** of Lebanon,
and *will* **shall** cut down
the *tall* **height of** cedar trees thereof,
and the choice *fir* **cypress** trees thereof:
and I *will* **shall** enter
into the lodgings of his *borders* **edges**,
and into the forest of his *Carmel* **Karmel/orchard**.
24 I have digged and drunk strange waters,
and with the sole of my *feet* **steps**
have I *dried up* **parched** all the rivers
of *besieged places* **seige/Masor**.
25 Hast thou not heard *long ago* **from afar**
how I have *done* **worked** it,
and of ancient *times* **days** that I have formed it?
now have I brought it to *pass* **be**,
that thou shouldest be to lay waste
fenced **cut off** cities into *ruinous* **desolate** heaps.
26 *Therefore* **And** their *inhabitants* **settlers**
were *of small power* **short of hand**,
they were *dismayed* **terrified** and *confounded* **shamed**;
they were as the *grass* **herb** of the field,
and as the green *herb* **sprouts**,
as the *grass* **leeks** on the *house tops* **roofs**,
and as corn blasted *before it be grown up*
at the face of her stalks.
27 But I know thy *abode* **settlement**, and thy going out,
and thy coming in, and thy *rage* **quaking** against me.
28 Because thy *rage* **quaking** against me
and thy *tumult* **uproar**
is come up **ascendeth** into mine ears,
therefore I *will put* **shall set** my hook in thy *nose* **nostrils**,
and my *bridle* **bit** in thy lips,
and I *will* **shall** turn thee back
by the way by which thou camest.
29 And this shall be a sign unto thee,
Ye shall eat this year
such things as grow of themselves
of the spontaneous growth,
and in the second year
that which springeth of the same
of the spontaneous sprout;
and in the third year *sow* **seed** ye, and *reap* **harvest**,
and plant vineyards, and eat the fruits thereof.
30 And the *remnant* **escapees** that *is escaped* **survived**
of the house of *Judah* **Yah Hudah**
shall yet again take root downward,
and *bear* **work** fruit upward.
31 For out of *Jerusalem* **Yeru Shalem**
shall go forth a *remnant* **survivor**,
and *they that escape* **the escapees**
out of mount *Zion* **Siyon**:
the zeal of *the LORD of hosts* **Yah Veh Sabaoth**
shall *do* **work** this.
32 Therefore thus saith *the LORD* **Yah Veh**
concerning the *king* **sovereign** of *Assyria* **Ashshur**,
He shall not come into this city,
nor shoot an arrow there,
nor *come before* **precede** it with *shield* **buckler**,
nor *cast* **pour** a *bank* **mound** against it.
33 By the way that he came, by the same shall he return,
and shall not come into this city,
saith the LORD **an oracle of Yah Veh**.
34 For I *will defend* **shall garrison** this city, to save it,
for mine own sake, and for my servant David's sake.
35 And it *came to pass* **became** that night,
that the angel of *the LORD* **Yah Veh** went out,
and smote in the camp of the *Assyrians* **Ashshuri**
an hundred *fourscore* **eighty** and five thousand:
and when they *arose* **started** early in the morning, behold,
they were all dead *corpses* **carcases**.
36 So *Sennacherib* **Sancherib**,
king **sovereign** of *Assyria departed* **Ashshur pulled stakes**,
and went and returned, and *dwelt* **settled** at Nineveh.
37 And it *came to pass* **became**,
as he was *worshipping* **prostrating**
in the house of Nisroch his *god* **elohim**,
that *Adrammelech* **Adram Melech** and *Sharezer* **Shareser**
his sons smote him with the sword:
and they escaped into the land of *Armenia* **Ararat**.
And *Esarhaddon* **Esar Chaddon** his son
reigned in his stead.

YECHIZQI YAH'S SICKNESS

20 In those days
was *Hezekiah* **Yechizqi Yah** sick unto death.
And the prophet *Isaiah* **Yesha Yah** the son of *Amoz* **Amos**
came to him, and said unto him,
Thus saith *the LORD* **Yah Veh**,
Set **Misvah concerning** thine house *in order*
for thou shalt die, and not live.
2 Then he turned his face to the wall,
and prayed unto *the LORD* **Yah Veh**, saying,
3 I beseech thee, O *LORD* **Yah Veh**,
remember now
how I have walked *before thee* **at thy face** in truth
and with a *perfect heart* **heart at shalom**,
and have *done* **worked**
that which is good in thy *sight* **eyes**.
And *Hezekiah* **Yechizqi Yah** wept *sore* **a great weeping**.

4 And it *came to pass* **became,**
afore *Isaiah* **Yesha Yah** was gone out
into the middle *court* **city,**
that the word of *the LORD* **Yah Veh** came to him, saying,
5 Turn *again* **back,**
and *tell Hezekiah* **say to Yechizqi Yah**
the *captain* **eminent** of my people,
Thus saith *the LORD* **Yah Veh,**
the *God* **Elohim** of David thy father,
I have heard thy prayer, I have seen thy tears:
behold, I *will* **shall** heal thee:
on the third day thou shalt *go up* **ascend**
unto the house of *the LORD* **Yah Veh.**
6 And I *will* **shall** add unto thy days fifteen years;
and I *will deliver* **shall rescue** thee and this city
out of the *hand* **palm**
of the *king* **sovereign** of *Assyria* **Ashshur;**
and I *will defend* **shall garrison** this city
for mine own sake,
and for my servant David's sake.
7 And *Isaiah* **Yesha Yah** said, Take a *lump* **cake** of figs.
And they took and *laid* **set** it on the *boil* **ulcer,**
and he *recovered* **enlivened.**
8 And *Hezekiah* **Yechizqi Yah** said unto *Isaiah* **Yesha Yah,**
What shall be the sign
that *the LORD will* **Yah Veh shall** heal me,
and that I shall *go up* **ascend**
into the house of *the LORD* **Yah Veh** the third day?
9 And *Isaiah* **Yesha Yah** said,
This sign shalt thou have of *the LORD* **Yah Veh,**
that *the LORD* **Yah Veh**
will do the thing **shall work the word**
that he hath *spoken* **worded:**
shall the shadow go forward ten degrees,
or *go* **turn** back ten degrees?
10 And *Hezekiah answered* **Yechizqi Yah said,**
It is a *light thing* **trifle**
for the shadow to *go down* **extend** ten degrees:
nay, but let the shadow return backward ten degrees.
11 And *Isaiah* **Yesha Yah** the prophet
cried **called out** unto *the LORD* **Yah Veh:**
and he *brought* **turned** the shadow ten degrees backward,
by **the degrees** which it had *gone down* **descended**
in the *dial* **degrees** of *Ahaz* **Achaz.**

THE BABEL ENVOYS

12 At that time *Berodachbaladan* **Berodach Bel Adoni,**
the son of *Baladan* **Bel Adan,**
king **sovereign** of *Babylon* **Babel,**
sent *letters* **scrolls** and *a present* **an offering**
unto *Hezekiah* **Yechizqi Yah:**
for he had heard
that *Hezekiah* **Yechizqi Yah** had been sick.
13 And *Hezekiah* **Yechizqi Yah** hearkened unto them,
and *shewed them* **had them see**
all the house of his *precious things* **spicery,**
the silver, and the gold,
and the spices, and the *precious* **best** ointment,
and all the house of his *armour* **instruments,**
and all that was found in his treasures:
there was *nothing* **no word** in his house,
nor in all his *dominion* **reign,**
that *Hezekiah* **Yechizqi Yah**
shewed them not **had them not see.**
14 Then came *Isaiah* **Yesha Yah** the prophet
unto *king Hezekiah* **sovereign Yechizqi Yah,**
and said unto him,
What said these men?
and from whence came they unto thee?
And *Hezekiah* **Yechizqi Yah** said,
They are come from a far *country* **land,**
even from *Babylon* **Babel.**
15 And he said, What have they seen in thine house?
And *Hezekiah answered* **Yechizqi Yah said,**
All *the things* that are in mine house have they seen:
there is *nothing* **no word** among my treasures
that I have not *shewed them* **had them see.**
16 And *Isaiah* **Yesha Yah**
said unto *Hezekiah* **Yechizqi Yah,**
Hear the word of *the LORD* **Yah Veh.**
17 Behold, the days come, that all that is in thine house,
and that which thy fathers
have *laid up in store* **treasured** unto this day,
shall be *carried* **lifted** into *Babylon* **Babel:**
nothing **no word** shall *be left* **remain,**
saith *the LORD* **Yah Veh.**
18 And of thy sons that shall *issue* **emerge** from thee,
which thou shalt beget, shall they take away;
and they shall be eunuchs in the *palace* **temple**
of the *king* **sovereign** of *Babylon* **Babel.**
19 Then said *Hezekiah* **Yechizqi Yah**
unto *Isaiah* **Yesha Yah,**
Good is the word of *the LORD* **Yah Veh**
which thou hast *spoken* **worded.**
And he said, Is it not *good,*
if *peace* **shalom** and truth be in my days?

THE DEATH OF YECHIZQI YAH

20 And the rest of the *acts* **words**
of *Hezekiah* **Yechizqi Yah,**
and all his might, and how he *made* **worked** a pool,
and a *conduit* **channel,** and brought water into the city,
are they not *written* **inscribed** in the *book* **scroll**
of the *chronicles* **words of the days**
of the *kings* **sovereigns** of *Judah* **Yah Hudah?**
21 And *Hezekiah* **Yechizqi Yah**
slept **laid** with his fathers:
and *Manasseh* **Menash Sheh** his son reigned in his stead.

MENASH SHEH REIGNS IN YERU SHALEM

21 *Manasseh* **Menash Sheh**
was **a son of** twelve years *old*
when he began to reign,
and reigned fifty and five years in *Jerusalem* **Yeru Shalem.**
And his mother's name was *Hephzibah* **Hephsi Bah.**
2 And he *did* **worked** that which was evil
in the *sight* **eyes** of *the LORD* **Yah Veh,**
after the *abominations* **abhorrences** of the *heathen* **goyim,**
whom *the LORD cast out* **Yah Veh dispossessed**
before **at the face of** the *children* **sons** of *Israel* **Yisra El.**
3 For he *built up again* **returned and built**
the *high places* **bamahs**
which *Hezekiah* **Yechizqi Yah** his father had destroyed;
and he *reared up* **raised sacrifice** altars for Baal,
and *made a grove* **worked an asherah,**
as *did Ahab* **worked Ach Ab**
king **sovereign** of *Israel* **Yisra El;**
and *worshipped* **prostrated**
to all the host of *heaven* **the heavens,**
and served them.
4 And he built **sacrifice** altars
in the house of *the LORD* **Yah Veh,**
of which *the LORD* **Yah Veh** said,
In *Jerusalem will I put* **Yeru Shalem shall I set** my name.
5 And he built **sacrifice** altars
for all the host of *heaven* **the heavens**
in the two courts of the house of *the LORD* **Yah Veh.**
6 And he made his son pass through the fire,
and *observed times* **cloudgazed,**
and *used enchantments* **prognosticated,**
and *dealt* **worked** with *familiar spirits* **necromancers**
and *wizards* **knowers:**
he *wrought much wickedness* **abounded to work evil**
in the *sight* **eyes** of *the LORD* **Yah Veh,**
to *provoke* **vex** him *to anger.*
7 And he set a *graven image* **sculptile** of the *grove* **asherah**
that he had *made* **worked** in the house,
of which *the LORD* **Yah Veh** said to David,
and to *Solomon* **Shelomoh** his son,
In this house, and in *Jerusalem* **Yeru Shalem,**
which I have chosen
out of all *tribes* **scions** of *Israel* **Yisra El,**
will I put **shall I set** my name *for ever* **eternally:**
8 Neither *will* **shall** I make the feet of *Israel* **Yisra El**
move any more **waver again**
out of the *land* **soil** which I gave their fathers;
only if they *will observe* **shall guard** to *do* **work**
according to all that I have *commanded* **misvahed** them,
and according to all the *law* **torah**
that my servant *Moses* **Mosheh**
commanded **misvahed** them.
9 But they hearkened not:
and *Manasseh seduced* **Menash Sheh strayed** them

to *do* **work** more evil than did the *nations* **goyim**
whom *the LORD destroyed* **Yah Veh desolated**
before **at the face of** the *children* **sons** of *Israel* **Yisra El**.
10 And *the LORD spake* **Yah Veh worded**
by **the hand of** his servants the prophets, saying,
11 Because *Manasseh* **Menash Sheh,**
king **sovereign** of *Judah* **Yah Hudah**
hath *done* **worked** these *abominations* **abhorrences**,
and hath *done wickedly* **vilified** above all
that the *Amorites did* **Emoriy worked**,
which were *before him* **at his face**,
and hath made *Judah* **Yah Hudah** also to sin with his idols:
12 Therefore thus saith
the LORD God **Yah Veh Elohim** of *Israel* **Yisra El**,
Behold, I am bringing *such* evil
upon *Jerusalem* **Yeru Shalem** and *Judah* **Yah Hudah**,
that whosoever heareth of it, both his ears shall tingle.
13 And I *will* **shall** stretch over *Jerusalem* **Yeru Shalem**
the line of *Samaria* **Shomeron**,
and the *plummet* **plumb line** of the house of *Ahab* **Ach Ab**:
and I *will* **shall** wipe *Jerusalem* **Yeru Shalem**
as *a man wipeth a dish* **wiping a bowl**, wiping it,
and turning it *upside down* **to descend upon its face**.
14 And I *will forsake* **shall abandon**
the *remnant* **survivors** of mine inheritance,
and *deliver* **give** them into the hand of their enemies;
and they shall become a *prey* **plunder**
and a *spoil* **plunder** to all their enemies;
15 Because they have *done* **worked** that which was evil
in my *sight* **eyes**,
and have *provoked* **vexed** me *to anger since* **from** the day
their fathers *came forth* **went** out of *Egypt* **Misrayim**,
even unto this day.
16 Moreover *Manasseh* **Menash Sheh**
shed **poured** innocent blood
very much **mighty aboundingly**,
till he had filled *Jerusalem* **Yeru Shalem**
from one end **mouth** to *another* **mouth**;
beside his sin wherewith he made *Judah* **Yah Hudah** to sin,
in *doing* **working** that which was evil
in the *sight* **eyes** of *the LORD* **Yah Veh**.
17 Now the rest of the *acts* **words**
of *Manasseh* **Menash Sheh**,
and all that he *did* **worked**, and his sin that he sinned,
are they not *written* **inscribed** in the *book* **scroll**
of the *chronicles* **words of the days**
of the *kings* **sovereigns** of *Judah* **Yah Hudah**?
18 And *Manasseh* **Menash Sheh** *slept* **laid** with his fathers,
and was *buried* **entombed** in the garden of his own house,
in the garden of Uzza:
and Amon his son reigned in his stead.

AMON REIGNS IN YERU SHALEM

19 Amon was **a son of** twenty and two years *old*
when he began to reign,
and he reigned two years in *Jerusalem* **Yeru Shalem**.
And his mother's name was Meshullemeth,
the daughter of *Haruz* **Harus** of *Jotbah* **Yotbah**.
20 And he *did* **worked** that which was evil
in the *sight* **eyes** of *the LORD* **Yah Veh**,
as his father *Manasseh did* **Menash Sheh worked**.
21 And he walked in all the way that his father walked in,
and served the idols that his father served,
and *worshipped* **prostrated to** them:
22 And he forsook
the LORD God **Yah Veh Elohim** of his fathers,
and walked not in the way of *the LORD* **Yah Veh**.
23 And the servants of Amon conspired against him,
and *slew* **deathified** the *king* **sovereign** in his own house.
24 And the people of the land *slew* **smote** all them
that had conspired against *king* **sovereign** Amon;
and the people of the land made *Josiah* **Yoshi Yah** his son
king **to reign** in his stead.
25 Now the rest of the *acts* **words** of Amon
which he *did* **worked**,
are they not *written* **inscribed** in the *book* **scroll**
of the *chronicles* **words of the days**
of the *kings* **sovereigns** of *Judah* **Yah Hudah**?
26 And he was *buried* **entombed** in his *sepulchre* **tomb**
in the garden of Uzza:
and *Josiah* **Yoshi Yah** his son reigned in his stead.

YOSHI YAH REIGNS IN YERU SHALEM

22 *Josiah* **Yoshi Yah** was **a son of** eight years *old*
when he began to reign,
and he reigned thirty and one years
in *Jerusalem* **Yeru Shalem**.
And his mother's name was *Jedidah* **Yedidah**,
the daughter of *Adaiah* **Ada Yah** of *Boscath* **Bosqath**.
2 And he *did* **worked** that which was *right* **straight**
in the *sight* **eyes** of *the LORD* **Yah Veh**,
and walked in all the way of David his father,
and turned not aside to the right *hand* or to the left.
3 And it *came to pass* **became**,
in the eighteenth year of *king Josiah* **sovereign Yoshi Yah**,
that the *king* **sovereign** sent Shaphan
the son of *Azaliah* **Asal Yah**, the son of Meshullam,
the scribe,
to the house of *the LORD* **Yah Veh**, saying,
4 *Go up* **Ascend** to *Hilkiah* **Hilqi Yah** the *high* **great** priest,
that he may *sum* **consumate** the silver
which is brought into the house of *the LORD* **Yah Veh**,
which the *keepers* **guards** of the *door* **threshold**
have gathered of the people:
5 And let them *deliver* **give** it
into the hand of the *doers* **workers** of the work,
that *have the oversight of* **oversee**
the house of *the LORD* **Yah Veh**:
and let them give it to the *doers* **workers** of the work
which is in the house of *the LORD* **Yah Veh**,
to *repair* **strengthen** the breaches of the house,
6 Unto *carpenters* **carvers**,
and builders, and *masons* **wallers**,
and to *buy* **chattel** timber and hewn stone
to *repair* **strengthen** the house.
7 Howbeit
there was no *reckoning made* **fabricating** with them
of the *money* **silver**
that was *delivered* **given** into their hand,
because they *dealt faithfully* **worked trustworthily**.
8 And *Hilkiah* **Hilqi Yah** the *high* **great** priest
said unto Shaphan the scribe,
I have found the *book* **scroll** of the *law* **torah**
in the house of *the LORD* **Yah Veh**.
And *Hilkiah* **Hilqi Yah** gave the *book* **scroll** to Shaphan,
and he *read* **called** it **out**.
9 And Shaphan the scribe came to the *king* **sovereign**,
and *brought the king word again*
returned word to the sovereign, and said,
Thy servants have *gathered* **melted** the *money* **silver**
that was found in the house,
and have *delivered* **given** it
into the hand of them that *do* **work** the work,
that *have the oversight of* **oversee**
the house of *the LORD* **Yah Veh**.
10 And Shaphan the scribe
shewed **told** the *king* **sovereign**, saying,
Hilkiah **Hilqi Yah** the priest
hath *delivered* **given** me a *book* **scroll**.
And Shaphan *read* **called** it **out**
before **at the face of** the *king* **sovereign**.
11 And it *came to pass* **became**,
when the *king* **sovereign** had heard
the words of the *book* **scroll** of the *law* **torah**,
that he *rent* **ripped** his clothes.
12 And the *king commanded* **sovereign misvahed**
Hilkiah **Hilqi Yah** the priest,
and *Ahikam* **Achiy Qam** the son of Shaphan,
and Achbor the son of *Michaiah* **Michah Yah**,
and Shaphan the scribe,
and *Asahiah* **Asah Yah** a servant of the *king's* **sovereign's**,
saying,
13 Go ye, enquire of *the LORD* **Yah Veh** for me,
and for the people, and for all *Judah* **Yah Hudah**,
concerning the words of this *book* **scroll** that is found:
for great is the *wrath* **fury** of *the LORD* **Yah Veh**
that is kindled against us,
because our fathers have not hearkened
unto the words of this *book* **scroll**,
to *do* **work** according unto all
that which is *written* **inscribed** concerning us.
14 So *Hilkiah* **Hilqi Yah** the priest,

and *Ahikam* **Achiy Qam**, and Achbor,
and Shaphan, and *Asahiah* **Asah Yah**,
went unto Huldah the prophetess,
the *wife* **woman** of Shallum the son of *Tikvah* **Tiqvah**,
the son of *Harhas* **Harchas**,
keeper **guard** of the *wardrobe* **clothes**;
(now she *dwelt* **settled** in *Jerusalem* **Yeru Shalem**
in the *college* **second part**;)
and they *communed* **worded** with her.
15 And she said unto them,
Thus saith
the LORD God **Yah Veh Elohim** of *Israel* **Yisra El**,
Tell **Say to** the man that sent you to me,
16 Thus saith *the LORD* **Yah Veh**, Behold,
I *will* **shall** bring evil upon this place,
and upon the *inhabitants* **settlers** thereof,
even all the words of the *book* **scroll**
which the *king* **sovereign** of *Judah* **Yah Hudah**
hath *read* **called out**:
17 Because they have forsaken me,
and have *burned incense* **incensed**
unto other *gods* **elohim**,
that they might *provoke* **vex** me *to anger*
with all the works of their hands;
therefore my *wrath* **fury** shall be kindled against this place,
and shall not be quenched.
18 But to the *king* **sovereign** of *Judah* **Yah Hudah**
which sent you to enquire of *the LORD* **Yah Veh**,
thus shall ye say to him,
Thus saith
the LORD God **Yah Veh Elohim** of *Israel* **Yisra El**,
As touching the words which thou hast heard;
19 Because thine heart was *tender* **tenderized**,
and thou hast humbled thyself
before the LORD **at the face of Yah Veh**,
when thou heardest
what I *spake* **worded** against this place,
and against the *inhabitants* **settlers** thereof,
that they should become
a desolation and *a curse* **an abasement**,
and hast *rent* **ripped** thy clothes,
and wept *before me* **at my face**;
I also have heard *thee*,
saith the LORD **an oracle of Yah Veh**.
20 Behold therefore,
I *will* **shall** gather thee unto thy fathers,
and thou shalt be gathered into thy *grave* **tomb**
in *peace* **shalom**;
and thine eyes shall not see all the evil
which I *will* **shall** bring upon this place.
And they
brought the king word again **returned word to the sovereign**.

YOSHI YAH CUTS A COVENANT

23 And the *king* **sovereign** sent,
and they gathered unto him all the elders
of *Judah* **Yah Hudah** and of *Jerusalem* **Yeru Shalem**.
2 And the *king* **sovereign**
went up **ascended** into the house of *the LORD* **Yah Veh**,
and all the men of *Judah* **Yah Hudah**
and all the *inhabitants* **settlers** of *Jerusalem* **Yeru Shalem**
with him,
and the priests, and the prophets, and all the people,
both small and great:
and he *read* **called out** in their ears
all the words of the *book* **scroll** of the covenant
which was found in the house of *the LORD* **Yah Veh**.
3 And the *king* **sovereign** stood by a pillar,
and *made* **cut** a covenant
before the LORD **at the face of Yah Veh**,
to walk after *the LORD* **Yah Veh**,
and to *keep* **guard** his *commandments* **misvoth**
and his *testimonies* **witnesses** and his statutes
with all their heart and all their soul,
to *perform* **raise** the words of this covenant
that were *written* **inscribed** in this *book* **scroll**.
And all the people stood to the covenant.
4 And the *king commanded* **sovereign misvahed**
Hilkiah **Hilqi Yah** the *high* **great** priest,
and the priests of the second order,
and the *keepers* **guards** of the *door* **threshold**,
to bring forth
out of the *temple* **manse** of *the LORD* **Yah Veh**
all the *vessels* **instruments** that were *made* **worked**
for Baal, and for the *grove* **asherah**,
and for all the host of *heaven* **the heavens**:
and he burned them without *Jerusalem* **Yeru Shalem**
in the fields of *Kidron* **Qidron**,
and *carried* **lifted** the *ashes* **dust** of them
unto *Bethel* **Beth El**.
5 And he *put down* **caused to cease**
the *idolatrous priests* **ascetics**,
whom the *kings* **sovereigns** of *Judah* **Yah Hudah**
had *ordained* **given**
to *burn* incense in the *high places* **bamahs**
in the cities of *Judah* **Yah Hudah**,
and in the places round about *Jerusalem* **Yeru Shalem**;
them also that *burned incense* **incensed** unto Baal,
to the sun, and to the moon,
and to the *planets* **constellations**,
and to all the host of *heaven* **the heavens**.
6 And he brought out the *grove* **asherah**
from the house of *the LORD* **Yah Veh**,
without *Jerusalem* **Yeru Shalem**,
unto the *brook Kidron* **wadi Qidron**,
and burned it at the *brook Kidron* **wadi Qidron**,
and *stamped* **pulverized** it *small to powder* **into dust**,
and cast the *powder* **dust** thereof
upon the *graves* **tombs** of the *children* **sons** of the people.
7 And he *brake* **pulled** down the houses
of the *sodomites* **hallowed whoremongers**,
that were by the house of *the LORD* **Yah Veh**,
where the women
wove *hangings* **housings** for the *grove* **asherah**.
8 And he brought all the priests
out of the cities of *Judah* **Yah Hudah**,
and *defiled* **fouled** the *high places* **bamahs**
where the priests had *burned incense* **incensed**,
from Geba to *Beersheba* **Beer Sheba**,
and *brake* **pulled** down
the *high places* **bamahs** of the *gates* **portals**
that were in the *entering in* **opening** of the *gate* **portal**
of *Joshua* **Yah Shua** the governor of the city,
which were on a man's left *hand*
at the *gate* **portal** of the city.
9 Nevertheless the priests of the *high places* **bamahs**
came **ascended** not *up*
to the **sacrifice** altar of *the LORD* **Yah Veh**
in *Jerusalem* **Yeru Shalem**,
but they did eat of the *unleavened bread* **matsah**
among their brethren.
10 And he *defiled* **fouled** Topheth,
which is in the valley
of the *children* **sons** of *Hinnom* **burning**,
that no man might make his son or his daughter
to pass through the fire to Molech.
11 And he *took away* **caused to cease** the horses
that the *kings* **sovereigns** of *Judah* **Yah Hudah**
had given to the sun,
at the entering in of the house of *the LORD* **Yah Veh**,
by the chamber of
Nathanmelech **Nathan Melech** the *chamberlain* **eunuch**,
which was in the suburbs,
and burned the chariots of the sun with fire.
12 And the **sacrifice** altars that were on the *top* **roof**
of the upper *chamber* **room** of *Ahaz* **Achaz**,
which the *kings* **sovereigns** of *Judah* **Yah Hudah**
had *made* **worked**,
and the **sacrifice** altars
which *Manasseh* **Menash Sheh** had *made* **worked**
in the two courts of the house of *the LORD* **Yah Veh**,
did the *king beat* **sovereign pull** down,
and *brake them down* **ran** from thence,
and cast the dust of them
into the *brook Kidron* **wadi Qidron**.
13 And the *high places* **bamahs**
that were *before Jerusalem* **at the face of Yeru Shalem**,
which were on the right *hand*
of the mount of *corruption* **ruin**,
which *Solomon* **Shelomoh**
the *king* **sovereign** of *Israel* **Yisra El**

had builded for Ashtoreth
the abomination of the *Zidonians* **Sidoniy**,
and for *Chemosh* **Kemosh**
the abomination of the *Moabites* **Moabiy**,
and for *Milcom* **Milchom**
the *abomination* **abhorrence**
of the *children* **sons** of Ammon,
did the *king defile* **sovereign foul**.
14 And he brake *in pieces* the *images* **monoliths**,
and cut down the *groves* **asherim**,
and filled their places with the bones of *men* **humans**.
15 *Moreover* the **sacrifice** altar that was at *Bethel* **Beth El**,
and the *high place* **bamah**
which *Jeroboam* **Yarob Am** the son of Nebat,
who made *Israel* **Yisra El** to sin, had *made* **worked**,
both that **sacrifice** altar and the *high place* **bamah**
he *brake* **pulled** down, and burned the *high place* **bamah**,
and *stamped* **pulverized** it *small to powder* **into dust**,
and burned the *grove* **asherah**.
16 And as *Josiah* **Yoshi Yah** turned *himself* **his face**,
he *spied* **saw** the *sepulchres* **tombs**
that were there in the mount,
and sent, and took the bones out of the *sepulchres* **tombs**,
and burned them upon the **sacrifice** altar,
and *polluted* **fouled** it,
according to the word of *the LORD* **Yah Veh**
which the man of *God proclaimed* **Elohim called out**,
who *proclaimed* **called out** these words.
17 Then he said, What *title* **monument** is that that I see?
And the men of the city *told* **said to** him,
It is the *sepulchre* **tomb** of the man of *God* **Elohim**,
which came from *Judah* **Yah Hudah**,
and *proclaimed* **called out** these *things* **words**
that thou hast *done* **worked**
against the **sacrifice** altar of *Bethel* **Beth El**.
18 And he said, Let him alone;
let no man *move* **shake** his bones.
So they let his bones *alone* **escape**,
with the bones of the prophet
that came out of *Samaria* **Shomeron**.
19 And all the houses also of the *high places* **bamahs**
that were in the cities of *Samaria* **Shomeron**,
which the *kings* **sovereigns** of *Israel* **Yisra El**
had *made* **worked**
to *provoke the LORD to anger* **vex**,
Josiah took away **Yoshi Yah turned aside**,
and *did* **worked** to them according to all the *acts* **works**
that he had done in *Bethel* **Beth El**.
20 And he *slew* **sacrificed**
all the priests of the *high places* **bamahs**
that were there upon the **sacrifice** altars,
and burned *men's* **human** bones upon them,
and returned to *Jerusalem* **Yeru Shalem**.
21 And the *king* **sovereign**
commanded **misvahed** all the people, saying,
Keep **Work** the *passover* **pasach**
unto *the LORD* **Yah Veh** your *God* **Elohim**,
as it is *written* **inscribed**
in the *book* **scroll** of this covenant.
22 Surely
there was not *holden* **worked** such a *passover* **pasach**
from the days of the judges that judged *Israel* **Yisra El**,
nor in all the days of the *kings* **sovereigns** of *Israel* **Yisra El**,
nor of the *kings* **sovereigns** of *Judah* **Yah Hudah**;
23 But in the eighteenth year
of *king Josiah* **sovereign Yoshi Yah**,
wherein this *passover* **pasach** was *holden* **worked**
to *the LORD* **Yah Veh** in *Jerusalem* **Yeru Shalem**.
24 *Moreover*
the *workers with familiar spirits* **necromancers**,
and the *wizards* **knowers**,
and the *images* **teraphim**, and the idols,
and all the abominations that were *spied* **seen**
in the land of *Judah* **Yah Hudah**
and in *Jerusalem* **Yeru Shalem**,
did Josiah put away **Yoshi Yah burnt**,
that he might *perform* **raise** the words of the *law* **torah**
which were *written* **inscribed** in the *book* **scroll**
that *Hilkiah* **Hilqi Yah** the priest
found in the house of *the LORD* **Yah Veh**.
25 And like unto him
was there no *king before him* **sovereign at his face**,
that turned to *the LORD* **Yah Veh** with all his heart,
and with all his soul, and with all his might,
according to all the *law* **torah** of *Moses* **Mosheh**;
neither after him arose there any like him.
26 *Notwithstanding the LORD* **Only Yah Veh**
turned not from the *fierceness* **fuming** of his great wrath,
wherewith his *anger* **wrath** was kindled
against *Judah* **Yah Hudah**,
because of all the *provocations* **vexations**
that *Manasseh* **Menash Sheh** had *provoked* **vexed** him *withal*.
27 And *the LORD* **Yah Veh** said,
I *will remove Judah* **shall turn aside Yah Hudah** also
out of my *sight* **face**,
as I have *removed Israel* **turned aside Yisra El**,
and *will cast off* **shall spurn**
this city *Jerusalem* **Yeru Shalem** which I have chosen,
and the house of which I said, My name shall be there.
28 Now the rest of the *acts* **words** of *Josiah* **Yoshi Yah**,
and all that he *did* **worked**,
are they not *written* **inscribed** in the *book* **scroll**
of the *chronicles* **words of the days**
of the *kings* **sovereigns** of *Judah* **Yah Hudah**?
29 In his days *Pharaoh* **Paroh** Nechoh,
king **sovereign** of *Egypt went up* **Misrayim ascended**
against the *king* **sovereign** of *Assyria* **Ashshur**
to the river Euphrates:
and *king Josiah* **sovereign Yoshi Yah**
went *against* **to meet** him;
and he *slew* **deathified** him at Megiddo,
when he had seen him.
30 And his servants *carried* **rode** him in a chariot
dead from Megiddo,
and brought him to *Jerusalem* **Yeru Shalem**,
and *buried* **entombed** him in his own *sepulchre* **tomb**.
And the people of the land
took *Jehoahaz* **Yah Achaz** the son of *Josiah* **Yoshi Yah**,
and anointed him,
and *made him king* **had him reign** in his father's stead.

YAH ACHAZ REIGNS IN YERU SHALEM

31 *Jehoahaz* **Yah Achaz**
was **a son of** twenty and three years *old*
when he began to reign;
and he reigned three months in *Jerusalem* **Yeru Shalem**.
And his mother's name was Hamutal,
the daughter of *Jeremiah* **Yirme Yah** of Libnah.
32 And he *did* **worked** that which was evil
in the *sight* **eyes** of *the LORD* **Yah Veh**,
according to all that his fathers had *done* **worked**.
33 And *Pharaoh* **Paroh** Nechoh
put him in bands **bound him** at Riblah
in the land of Hamath,
that he might not reign in *Jerusalem* **Yeru Shalem**;
and *put* **gave** the land to a *tribute* **penalty**
of an hundred *talents* **rounds** of silver,
and a *talent* **round** of gold.
34 And *Pharaoh* **Paroh** Nechoh
made Eliakim **had El Yaqim** the son of *Josiah* **Yoshi Yah**
king **reign** in the *room* **stead** of *Josiah* **Yoshi Yah** his father,
and turned his name to *Jehoiakim* **Yah Yaqim**,
and took *Jehoahaz* **Yah Achaz** away:
and he came to *Egypt* **Misrayim**, and died there.
35 And *Jehoiakim* **Yah Yaqim**
gave the silver and the gold to *Pharaoh* **Paroh**;
but he *taxed* **appraised** the land to give the *money* **silver**
according to the *commandment* **mouth** of *Pharaoh* **Paroh**:
he exacted the silver and the gold
of the people of the land,
of *every one* **man** according to his *taxation* **appraisal**,
to give it unto *Pharaoh* **Paroh** Nechoh.
36 *Jehoiakim* **Yah Yaqim**
was **a son of** twenty and five years *old*
when he began to reign;
and he reigned eleven years in *Jerusalem* **Yeru Shalem**.
And his mother's name was *Zebudah* **Zebidah**,
the daughter of *Pedaiah* **Pedah Yah** of Rumah.
37 And he *did* **worked** that which was evil
in the *sight* **eyes** of *the LORD* **Yah Veh**,
according to all that his fathers had *done* **worked**.

24 In his days *Nebuchadnezzar* **Nebukadnets Tsar**
king **sovereign** of *Babylon came up* **Babel ascended**,
and *Jehoiakim* **Yah Yaqim** became his servant three years:
then he turned and rebelled against him.
2 And *the LORD* **Yah Veh** sent against him
bands **troops** of the *Chaldees* **Kasdiy**,
and *bands* **troops** of the *Syrians* **Aramiy**,
and *bands* **troops** of the *Moabites* **Moabiy**,
and *bands* **troops** of the *children* **sons** of Ammon,
and sent them against *Judah* **Yah Hudah** to destroy it,
according to the word of *the LORD* **Yah Veh**,
which he *spake* **worded**
by **the hand of** his servants the prophets.
3 Surely at the *commandment* **mouth** of *the LORD* **Yah Veh**
came this upon *Judah* **Yah Hudah**,
to *remove* **turn** them **aside** out of his *sight* **face**,
for the sins of *Manasseh* **Menash Sheh**,
according to all that he *did* **worked**;
4 And also for the innocent blood that he *shed* **poured**:
for he filled *Jerusalem* **Yeru Shalem** with innocent blood;
which *the LORD would* **Yah Veh willed**
not *pardon* **to forgive**.
5 Now the rest of the *acts* **words** of *Jehoiakim* **Yah Yaqim**,
and all that he *did* **worked**,
are they not *written* **inscribed** in the *book* **scroll**
of the *chronicles* **words of the days**
of the *kings* **sovereigns** of *Judah* **Yah Hudah**?
6 So *Jehoiakim slept* **Yah Yaqim laid** with his fathers:
and *Jehoiachin* **Yah Yachin** his son reigned in his stead.
7 And the *king* **sovereign** of *Egypt* **Misrayim**
came **added** not *again* **to go** any more out of his land:
for the *king* **sovereign** of *Babylon* **Babel** had taken
from the *river* **wadi** of *Egypt* **Misrayim**
unto the river Euphrates
all that pertained to the *king* **sovereign** of *Egypt* **Misrayim**.

YAH YACHIN REIGNS IN YERU SHALEM

8 *Jehoiachin* **Yah Yachin** was **a son of** eighteen years *old*
when he began to reign,
and he reigned in *Jerusalem* **Yeru Shalem** three months.
And his mother's name was *Nehushta* **Nechushta**,
the daughter of *Elnathan* **El Nathan**
of *Jerusalem* **Yeru Shalem**.
9 And he *did* **worked** that which was evil
in the *sight* **eyes** of *the LORD* **Yah Veh**,
according to all that his father had *done* **worked**.
10 At that time the servants of
Nebuchadnezzar **Nebukadnets Tsar**
king **sovereign** of *Babylon* **Babel**
came up **ascended** against *Jerusalem* **Yeru Shalem**
and the city was besieged.
11 And *Nebuchadnezzar* **Nebukadnets Tsar**
king **sovereign** of *Babylon* **Babel**
came against the city, and his servants did besiege it.
12 And *Jehoiachin* **Yah Yachin**
the *king* **sovereign** of *Judah* **Yah Hudah**
went out to the *king* **sovereign** of *Babylon* **Babel**,
he, and his mother, and his servants,
and his *princes* **governors**, and his *officers* **eunuchs**:
and the *king* **sovereign** of *Babylon* **Babel**
took him in the eighth year of his reign.
13 And he *carried out* **brought** thence
all the treasures of the house of *the LORD* **Yah Veh**,
and the treasures of the *king's* **sovereign's** house,
and *cut in pieces* **chopped**
all the *vessels* **instruments** of gold
which *Solomon king* **Shelomoh sovereign** of *Israel* **Yisra El**
had *made* **worked**
in the *temple* **manse** of *the LORD* **Yah Veh**,
as *the LORD* **Yah Veh** had *said* **worded**.
14 And he *carried away* **exiled** all *Jerusalem* **Yeru Shalem**,
and all the *princes* **governors**,
and all the mighty *men* of valour,
even ten thousand *captives* **exiles**,
and all the *craftsmen* **artificers** and *smiths* **locksmiths**:
none *remained* **survived**,
save **except** the poorest sort of the people of the land.
15 And he *carried away Jehoiachin* **exiled Yah Yachin**
to *Babylon* **Babel**,
and the *king's* **sovereign's** mother,
and the *king's wives* **sovereign's women**,
and his *officers* **eunuchs**, and the mighty of the land,
those *carried* **walked** he into *captivity* **exile**
from *Jerusalem* **Yeru Shalem** to *Babylon* **Babel**.
16 And all the men of *might* **valour**, even seven thousand,
and *craftsmen* **atificers** and *smiths* **locksmiths** a thousand,
all that were *strong* **mighty** and *apt for* **worked** war,
even them the *king* **sovereign** of *Babylon* **Babel**
brought captive **exiled** to *Babylon* **Babel**.
17 And the *king* **sovereign** of *Babylon* **Babel**
made *Mattaniah* **Mattan Yah** his *father's brother* **uncle**
king **reign** in his stead,
and *changed* **turned** his name to *Zedekiah* **Sidqi Yah**.

SIDQI YAH REIGNS IN YERU SHALEM

18 *Zedekiah* **Sidqi Yah**
was **a son of** twenty and one years *old*
when he began to reign,
and he reigned eleven years in *Jerusalem* **Yeru Shalem**.
And his mother's name was Hamutal,
the daughter of *Jeremiah* **Yirme Yah** of Libnah.
19 And he *did* **worked** that which was evil
in the *sight* **eyes** of *the LORD* **Yah Veh**,
according to all
that *Jehoiakim* **Yah Yaqim** had *done* **worked**.
20 For through the *anger* **wrath** of *the LORD* **Yah Veh**
it *came to pass* **became**
in *Jerusalem* **Yeru Shalem** and *Judah* **Yah Hudah**,
until he had cast them out from his *presence* **face**,
that *Zedekiah* **Sidqi Yah** rebelled
against the *king* **sovereign** of *Babylon* **Babel**.

THE FALL OF YERU SHALEM

25 And it *came to pass* **became**,
in the ninth year of his reign,
in the tenth month, in the tenth *day* of the month,
that *Nebuchadnezzar* **Nebukadnets Tsar**,
king **sovereign** of *Babylon* **Babel** came,
he, and all his *host* **valiant**,
against *Jerusalem* **Yeru Shalem**,
and *pitched* **encamped** against it;
and they built forts against it round about.
2 And the city was besieged unto the eleventh year
of *king Zedekiah* **sovereign Sidqi Yah**.
3 And on the ninth *day* of the *fourth* month
the famine prevailed in the city,
and there was no bread for the people of the land.
4 And the city was *broken up* **split**,
and all the men of war *fled* by night
by the way of the *gate* **portal** between two walls,
which is by the *king's* **sovereign's** garden:
(now the *Chaldees* **Kasdiy**
were against the city round about:)
and *the king* went the way toward the plain.
5 And the *army* **valiant** of the *Chaldees* **Kasdiy**
pursued after the *king* **sovereign**,
and overtook him in the plains of *Jericho* **Yericho**:
and all his *army* **valiant** were scattered from him.
6 So they *took* **apprehended** the *king* **sovereign**,
and *brought* **ascended** him *up*
to the *king* **sovereign** of *Babylon* **Babel** to Riblah;
and they *gave* **worded** judgment upon him.
7 And they *slew* **slaughtered**
the sons of *Zedekiah* **Sidqi Yah** before his eyes,
and *put out* **blinded** the eyes of *Zedekiah* **Sidqi Yah**,
and bound him with fetters of *brass* **copper**,
and carried him to *Babylon* **Babel**.
8 And in the fifth month, on the seventh *day* of the month,
which is the nineteenth year
of *king Nebuchadnezzar* **sovereign Nebukadnets Tsar**
king **sovereign** of *Babylon* **Babel**,
came *Nebuzaradan* **Nebu Zaradan**,
captain of the guard **the great slaughterer**,
a servant of the *king* **sovereign** of *Babylon* **Babel**,
unto *Jerusalem* **Yeru Shalem**:
9 And he burnt the house of *the LORD* **Yah Veh**,
and the *king's* **sovereign's** house,
and all the houses of *Jerusalem* **Yeru Shalem**,
and every great *man's* house burnt he with fire.
10 And all the *army* **valiant** of the *Chaldees* **Kasdiy**,
that were with the *captain of the guard* **great slaughterer**,
brake **pulled** down the walls of *Jerusalem* **Yeru Shalem**

round about.
11 Now the rest of the people
that *were left* **survived** in the city,
and the fugitives that fell away
to the *king* **sovereign** of *Babylon* **Babel**,
with the remnant of the multitude,
did *Nebuzaradan* **Nebu Zaradan**
the *captain of the guard* **great slaughterer**
carry away **exile**.
12 But the *captain of the guard* **great slaughterer**
left **let survive** of the poor of the land
to be vinedressers and *husbandmen* **plowers**.
13 And the pillars of *brass* **copper**
that were in the house of *the LORD* **Yah Veh**,
and the bases, and the *brasen* **copper** sea
that was in the house of *the LORD* **Yah Veh**,
did the *Chaldees* **Kasdiy** break *in pieces*,
and *carried* **lifted** the *brass* **copper** of them
to *Babylon* **Babel**.
14 And the *pots* **caldrons**, and the shovels,
and the *snuffers* **tweezers**, and the *spoons* **bowls**,
and all the *vessels* **instruments** of *brass* **copper**
wherewith they ministered, took they away.
15 And the *firepans* **trays**, and the *bowls* **sprinklers**,
and such *things* as were of gold, in gold,
and of silver, in silver,
the *captain of the guard* **great slaughterer** took away.
16 The two pillars, one sea, and the bases
which *Solomon* **Shelomoh** had *made* **worked**
for the house of *the LORD* **Yah Veh**;
the *brass* **copper** of all these *vessels* **instruments**
was *without weight* **not weighed**.
17 The height of the one pillar was eighteen cubits,
and the *chapiter* **cap** upon it was *brass* **copper**:
and the height of the *chapiter* **cap** three cubits;
and the *wreathen work* **netting**,
and pomegranates upon the *chapiter* **cap** round about,
all of *brass* **copper**:
and like unto these
had the second pillar with *wreathen work* **netting**.
18 And the *captain of the guard* **great slaughterer**
took *Seraiah* **Sera Yah** the *chief* **head** priest,
and *Zephaniah* **Sephan Yah** the second priest,
and the three *keepers* **guards** of the *door* **threshold**:
19 And out of the city he took *an officer* **one eunuch**
that was *set* **overseer** over the men of war,
and five men of them
that *were in* **saw** the *king's presence* **sovereign's face**,
which were found in the city,
and the *principal* scribe **of the governor** of the host,
which *mustered* **hosted** the people of the land,
and *threescore* **sixty** men of the people of the land
that were found in the city:
20 And *Nebuzaradan* **Nebu Zaradan**
captain of the *guard* **slaughterers** took these,
and *brought* **walked** them
to the *king* **sovereign** of *Babylon* **Babel** to Riblah:
21 And the *king* **sovereign** of *Babylon* **Babel** smote them,
and *slew* **deathified** them at Riblah in the land of Hamath.
So *Judah* **Yah Hudah** was *carried away* **exiled**
out of their *land* **soil**.
22 And as for the people
that *remained* **survived** in the land of *Judah* **Yah Hudah**,
whom *Nebuchadnezzar* **Nebukadnets Tsar**
king **sovereign** of *Babylon had left* **Babel let survive**,
even over them he made *Gedaliah* **Gedal Yah**
the son of *Ahikam* **Achiy Qam**, the son of Shaphan,
ruler **overseer**.
23 And when
all the *captains* **governors** of the *armies* **valiant**,
they and their men,
heard that the *king* **sovereign** of *Babylon* **Babel**
had made *Gedaliah governor* **Gedal Yah overseer**,
there came to *Gedaliah* **Gedal Yah** to *Mizpah* **Mispeh**,
even *Ishmael* **Yishma El** the son of *Nethaniah* **Nethan Yah**,
and *Johanan* **Yah Hanan** the son of *Careah* **Qareach**,
and *Seraiah* **Sera Yah** the son of *Tanhumeth* **Tanchumeth**
the *Netophathite* **Netophathiy**,
and *Jaazaniah* **Yaazan Yah**
the son of a *Maachathite* **Maachahiy**,
they and their men.
24 And *Gedaliah sware* **Gedal Yah oathed** to them,
and to their men, and said unto them,
Fear **Awe** not to be the servants of the *Chaldees* **Kasdiy**:
dwell **settle** in the land,
and serve the *king* **sovereign** of *Babylon* **Babel**;
and it shall be *well* **well—pleasing** with you.
25 But it *came to pass* **became**, in the seventh month,
that *Ishmael* **Yishma El** the son of *Nethaniah* **Nethan Yah**,
the son of *Elishama* **Eli Shama**,
of the seed *royal* **of the sovereigndom**, came,
and ten men with him,
and smote *Gedaliah* **Gedal Yah**, that he died,
and the *Jews* **Yah Hudiym** and the *Chaldees* **Kasdiym**
that were with him at *Mizpah* **Mispeh**.
26 And all the people, both small and great,
and the *captains* **governors** of the *armies* **valiant**,
arose, and came to *Egypt* **Misrayim**:
for they *were afraid of* **awed to face** the *Chaldees* **Kasdiy**.
27 And it *came to pass* **became**,
in the seven and thirtieth year
of the *captivity* **exile** of *Jehoiachin* **Yah Yachin**
king **sovereign** of *Judah* **Yah Hudah**,
in the twelfth month,
on the seven and twentieth *day* of the month,
that Evilmerodach **Evil Merodakch**
king **sovereign** of *Babylon* **Babel**
in the year that he began to reign
did lift up the head of *Jehoiachin* **Yah Yachin**
king **sovereign** of *Judah* **Yah Hudah**
out of **the house of** prison;
28 And he *spake kindly* **worded good** to him,
and *set* **gave** his throne
above the throne of the *kings* **sovereigns**
that were with him in *Babylon* **Babel**;
29 And changed his prison *garments* **clothes**:
and he did eat bread continually *before him* **at his face**
all the days of his life.
30 And his *allowance* **ration**
was a continual *allowance* **ration**
given him of the *king* **sovereign**,
a daily rate for every day **the word day by day**,
all the days of his life.

KEY TO INTERPRETING THE EXEGESES:
King James text is in regular type;
Text under exegeses is in oblique type;
Text of exegeses is in bold type.

GENEALOGIES:

GENEALOGY OF ADAM

1 Adam, Sheth, Enosh,
2 *Kenan* **Qeynan**, *Mahalaleel* **Ma Halal El**, *Jered* **Yered**,
3 Hanoch, *Methuselah* **Methu Shelach**,
Lamech **Lemech**,
4 *Noah* **Noach**, Shem, Ham, and *Japheth* **Yepheth**.

GENEALOGY OF YEPHETH

5 The sons of *Japheth* **Yepheth**;
Gomer, and Magog, and *Madai* **Maday**, and *Javan* **Yavan**,
and Tubal, and Meshech, and Tiras.
6 And the sons of Gomer;
Ashchenaz **Ashkenaz**,
and *Riphath* **Diphath**, and Togarmah.
7 And the sons of *Javan* **Yavan**;
Elishah **Eli Shah**, and Tarshish, *Kittim* **Kittiy**, and Dodanim.

GENEALOGY OF HAM

8 The sons of Ham;
Cush **Kush**, and *Misraim* **Misrayim**,
Put, and *Canaan* **Kenaan**.
9 And the sons of *Cush* **Kush**;
Seba, and Havilah, and Sabta,
and Raamah, and Sabtecha.
And the sons of Raamah;
Sheba, and Dedan.
10 And *Cush* **Kush** begat Nimrod:
he began to be mighty upon the earth.
11 And *Misraim* **Misrayim** begat *Ludim* **Ludiym**,
and Anamim, and Lehabim, and *Naphtuhim* **Naphtuchim**,
12 And *Pathrusim* **Pathrosiym**, and *Casluhim* **Kasluhim**,
(of whom *came* **went** the *Philistines* **Peleshethiym**,)
and *Caphthorim* **Kaphtorim**.
13 And *Canaan* **Kenaan**
begat *Zidon* **Sidon** his firstborn, and Heth,
14 The *Jebusite* **Yebusiy** also,
and the *Amorite* **Emoriy**, and the *Girgashite* **Girgashiy**,
15 And the *Hivite* **Hivviy**, and the *Arkite* **Arqiy**,
and the *Sinite* **Siniy**,
16 And the *Arvadite* **Arvadiy**, and the *Zemarite* **Semariy**,
and the *Hamathite* **Hamath**.

GENEALOGY OF SHEM

17 The sons of Shem;
Elam, and *Asshur* **Ashshur**, and *Arphaxad* **Arpachshad**,
and Lud, and Aram, and *Uz* **Us**, and Hul, and Gether,
and *Meshech* **Meshek**.
18 And *Arphaxad* **Arpachshad** begat *Shelah* **Shelach**,
and *Shelah* **Shelach** begat *Eber* **Heber**.
19 And unto *Eber* **Heber** were born two sons:
the name of the one was Peleg;
because in his days the earth was *divided* **split**:
and his brother's name was *Joktan* **Yoqtan**.
20 And *Joktan* **Yoqtan** begat Almodad, and Sheleph
and *Hazarmaveth* **Hasar Maveth**, and *Jerah* **Yerach**,
21 Hadoram also, and Uzal, and *Diklah* **Diqlah**,
22 And Ebal, and *Abimael* **Abi Mael**, and Sheba,
23 And Ophir, and Havilah, and *Jobab* **Yobab**.
All these were the sons of *Joktan* **Yoqtan**.
24 Shem, *Arphaxad* **Arpachshad**, *Shelah* **Shelach**,
25 *Eber* **Heber**, Peleg, Reu,
26 Serug, Nahor, *Terah* **Terach**,
27 Abram; the same is Abraham.

GENEALOGY OF ABRAHAM

28 The sons of Abraham;
Isaac **Yischaq**, and *Ishmael* **Yishma El**.
29 These are their generations:
The firstborn of *Ishmael* **Yishma El**, *Nebaioth* **Nebayoth**;
then *Kedar* **Qedar**, and *Adbeel* **Adbe El**, and Mibsam,
30 Mishma, and Dumah, Massa, Hadad, and Tema,
31 *Jetur* **Yetur**, Naphish, and *Kedemah* **Qedemah**.
These are the sons of *Ishmael* **Yishma El**.
32 Now the sons of *Keturah* **Qeturah**,
Abraham's concubine:
she bare Zimran, and *Jokshan* **Yoqshan**, and Medan,
and *Midian* **Midyan**, and *Ishbak* **Yishbaq**,
and *Shuah* **Shuach**.
And the sons of *Jokshan* **Yoqshan**;
Sheba, and Dedan.
33 And the sons of *Midian* **Midyan**;
Ephah, and Epher, and Hanoch ,
and *Abida* **Abi Dah**, and Eldaah.
All these are the sons of *Keturah* **Qeturah**.
34 And Abraham begat *Isaac* **Yischaq**.
The sons of *Isaac* **Yischaq**;
Esau **Esav** and *Israel* **Yisra El**.
35 The sons of *Esau* **Esav**;
Eliphaz **Eli Phaz**, *Reuel* **Reu El**, and *Jeush* **Yeush**,
and *Jaalam* **Yalam**, and *Korah* **Qorach**.
36 The sons of *Eliphaz* **Eli Phaz**;
Teman, and Omar, *Zephi* **Sephi**, and Gatam,
Kenaz **Qenaz**, and Timna, and *Amalek* **Amaleq**.
37 The sons of *Reuel* **Reu El**;
Nahath **Nachath**, *Zerah* **Zerach**, Shammah, and Mizzah.
38 And the sons of Seir;
Lotan, and Shobal, and *Zibeon* **Sibon**, and Anah,
and Dishon, and *Ezar* **Esar**, and Dishan.
39 And the sons of Lotan;
Hori, and Homam:
and Timna was Lotan's sister.
40 The sons of Shobal;
Alian **Alyan**, and *Manahath* **Manachath**, and Ebal,
Shephi, and Onam.
and the sons of *Zibeon* **Sibon**;
Aiah **Ayah**, and Anah.
41 The sons of Anah;
Dishon.
And the sons of Dishon;
Amram **Hamram**, and Eshban,
and *Ithran* **Yithran**, and *Cheran* **Keran**.
42 The sons of *Ezar* **Esar**;
Bilhan, and Zavan, and *Jakan* **Yaaqan**.
The sons of Dishan;
Uz **Us**, and Aran.

GENEALOGY OF THE SOVEREIGNS OF EDOM

43 Now these are the *kings* **sovereigns**
that reigned in the land of Edom
before **at the face of** any *king* **sovereign that** reigned
over the *children* **sons** of *Israel* **Yisra El**;
Bela the son of Beor:
and the name of his city was Dinhabah.
44 And when Bela *was dead* **died**,
Jobab **Yobab** the son of *Zerah* **Zerach** of Bozrah
reigned in his stead.
45 And when *Jobab was dead* **Yobab died**,
Husham of the land of the *Temanites* **Temaniy**
reigned in his stead.
46 And when Husham *was dead* **died**,
Hadad the son of Bedad,
which smote *Midian* **Midyan** in the field of Moab,
reigned in his stead:
and the name of his city was Avith.
47 And when Hadad *was dead* **died**,
Samlah of *Masrekah* **Masreqah** reigned in his stead.
48 And when Samlah *was dead* **died**,
Shaul of *Rehoboth* **Rechovoth** by the river
reigned in his stead.
49 And when Shaul *was dead* **died**,
Baalhanan **Baal Hanan** the son of Achbor
reigned in his stead.
50 And when *Baalhanan was dead* **Baal Hanan died**,
Hadad reigned in his stead:
and the name of his city was Pai;
and his *wife's* **woman's** name was *Mehetabel* **Mehetab El**,
the daughter of Matred,
the daughter of *Mezahab* **Me Zahab**.
51 Hadad died also.

GENEALOGY OF THE CHILIARCHS OF EDOM

And the *dukes* **chiliarchs** of Edom *were*;
duke Timnah **chiliarch Timna**,
duke Aliah **chiliarch Alvah**,
duke Jetheth **chiliarch Yetheth**,
52 *Duke Aholibamah* **chiliarch Oholi Bamah**,
duke **chiliarch** Elah, *duke* **chiliarch** Pinon,
53 *Duke Kenaz* **chiliarch Qenaz**,
duke **chiliarch** Teman, *duke Mibzar* **chiliarch Mibsar**,
54 *Duke Magdiel* **chiliarch Magdi El**, *duke* **chiliarch** Iram.
These are the *dukes* **chiliarchs** of Edom.

GENEALOGY OF THE SONS OF YISRA EL
2 These are the sons of *Israel* **Yisra El**;
Reuben **Reu Ben**, *Simeon* **Shimon**, Levi,
and *Judah* **Yah Hudah**, *Issachar* **Yissachar**, and Zebulun,
2 Dan, *Joseph* **Yoseph**, and *Benjamin* **Ben Yamin**,
Naphtali, Gad, and Asher.
3 The sons of *Judah* **Yah Hudah**;
Er, and Onan, and Shelah:
which three were born unto him
of *the daughter of Shua* **Bath Shua**
the *Canaanitess* **Kenaaniyth**.
And Er, the firstborn of *Judah* **Yah Hudah**,
was evil in the *sight* **eyes** of *the LORD* **Yah Veh**;
and he *slew* **deathified** him.
4 And Tamar his daughter in law bare him
Pharez **Peres** and *Zerah* **Zerach**.
All the sons of *Judah* **Yah Hudah** were five.
5 The sons of *Pharez* **Peres**;
Hezron **Hesron**, and Hamul.
6 And the sons of *Zerah* **Zerach**;
Zimri, and Ethan, and Heman,
and *Calcol* **Kalkol**, and Dara:
five of them in all.
7 And the sons of *Carmi* **Karmi**;
Achar, the troubler of *Israel* **Yisra El**,
who *transgressed* **treasoned** in the *thing accursed* **devoted**.
8 And the sons of Ethan;
Azariah **Azar Yah**.
9 The sons also of *Hezron* **Hesron**,
that were born unto him;
Jerahmeel **Yerachme El**, and Ram, and *Chelubai* **Kelubay**.
10 And Ram begat *Amminadab* **Ammi Nadab**;
and *Amminadab* **Ammi Nadab** begat Nahshon,
prince **hierarch** of the *children* **sons** of *Judah* **Yah Hudah**;
11 And Nahshon begat Salma, and Salma begat Boaz,
12 And Boaz begat Obed, and Obed begat *Jesse* **Yishay**,
13 And *Jesse* **Yishay** begat his firstborn *Eliab* **Eli Ab**,
and *Abinadab* **Abi Nadab** the second,
and *Shimma* **Shimah** the third,
14 *Nethaneel* **Nethan El** the fourth,
Raddai **Radday** the fifth,
15 *Ozem* **Osem** the sixth, David the seventh:
16 Whose sisters were *Zeruiah* **Seruyah**,
and *Abigail* **Abi Gail**.
And the sons of *Zeruiah* **Seruyah**;
Abishai **Abi Shai**, and *Joab* **Yah Ab**,
and *Asahel* **Asa El**, three.
17 And *Abigail* **Abi Gail** bare Amasa:
and the father of Amasa
was *Jether* **Yether** the *Ishmaelite* **Yishma Eliy**.
18 And *Caleb* **Kaleb** the son of *Hezron* **Hesron**
begat *children* of Azubah his *wife* **woman**,
and of *Jerioth* **Yerioth**:
her sons are these;
Jesher **Yesher**, and Shobab, and Ardon.
19 And when Azubah *was dead* **died**,
Caleb **Kaleb** took unto him *Ephrath* **Ephratha**,
which bare him Hur.
20 And Hur begat Uri, and Uri begat *Bezaleel* **Besal El**.
21 And afterward *Hezron* **Hesron**
went in to the daughter
of Machir the father of *Gilead* **Gilad**,
whom he married **and he took her**
when he was *threescore* **a son of sixty** years *old*;
and she bare him Segub.
22 And Segub begat *Jair* **Yair**,
who had three and twenty cities
in the land of *Gilead* **Gilad**.
23 And he took Geshur, and Aram,
with the *towns* **living areas** of *Jair* **Yair**, from them,
with *Kenath* **Qenath**, and the *towns* **daughters** thereof,
even threescore **sixty** cities.
All these *belonged to* **of** the sons of Machir
the father of *Gilead* **Gilad**.
24 And after that *Hezron was dead* **Hesron died**
in *Calebephratah* **Kaleb Ephrath**,
then *Abiah Hezron's wife* **Abi Yah Hesron's woman**
bare him *Ashur* **Ashchur** the father of *Tekoa* **Teqoha**.
25 And the sons of *Jerahmeel* **Yerachme El**
the firstborn of *Hezron* **Hesron** *were*,
Ram the firstborn, and Bunah, and Oren,
and *Ozem* **Osem**, and *Ahijah* **Achiy Yah**.
26 *Jerahmeel* **Yerachme El** had also another *wife* **woman**,
whose name was Atarah; she was the mother of Onam.
27 And the sons of Ram
the firstborn of *Jerahmeel* **Yerachme El** *were*,
Maaz **Maas**, and *Jamin* **Yamin**, and *Eker* **Eqer**.
28 And the sons of Onam *were*,
Shammai **Shammay**, and *Jada* **Yada**.
And the sons of *Shammai* **Shammay**;
Nadab and *Abishur* **Abi Shur**.
29 And the name of the *wife* **woman** of *Abishur* **Abi Shur**
was *Abihail* **Abi Hail**,
and she bare him *Ahban* **Ach Ban**, and Molid.
30 And the sons of Nadab;
Seled, and *Appaim* **Appayim**:
but Seled died without *children* **sons**.
31 And the sons of *Appaim* **Appayim**;
Ishi **Yishi**.
And the sons of *Ishi* **Yishi**;
Sheshan.
And the *children* **sons** of Sheshan;
Ahlai **Achiy Lay**.
32 And the sons of *Jada* **Yada**
the brother of *Shammai* **Shammay**;
Jether **Yether**, and *Jonathan* **Yah Nathan**:
and *Jether* **Yether** died without *children* **sons**.
33 And the sons of *Jonathan* **Yah Nathan**;
Peleth, and Zaza.
These were the sons of *Jerahmeel* **Yerachme El**.
34 Now Sheshan had no sons, but daughters.
And Sheshan had a servant, *an Egyptian* **a Misrayim**,
whose name was *Jarha* **Yarcha**.
35 And Sheshan gave his daughter
to *Jarha* **Yarcha** his servant to *wife* **woman**;
and she bare him *Attai* **Attay**.
36 And *Attai* **Attay** begat Nathan,
and Nathan begat Zabad,
37 And Zabad begat Ephlal,
and Ephlal begat Obed,
38 And Obed begat *Jehu* **Yah Hu**,
and *Jehu* **Yah Hu** begat *Azariah* **Azar Yah**,
39 And *Azariah* **Azar Yah** begat *Helez* **Heles**,
and *Helez* **Heles** begat *Eleasah* **El Asah**,
40 And *Eleasah* **El Asah** begat *Sisamai* **Sismay**,
and *Sisamai* **Sismay** begat Shallum,
41 And Shallum begat *Jekamiah* **Yeqam Yah**,
and *Jekamiah* **Yeqam Yah** begat *Elishama* **Eli Shama**.
42 Now the sons of *Caleb* **Kaleb**
the brother of *Jerahmeel* **Yerachme El** *were*,
Mesha his firstborn, which was the father of Ziph;
and the sons of Mareshah the father of Hebron.
43 And the sons of Hebron;
Korah **Qorach**, and *Tappuah* **Tappuach**,
and *Rekem* **Reqem**, and Shema.
44 And Shema begat *Raham* **Racham**,
the father of *Jorkoam* **Yorqe Am**:
and *Rekem* **Reqem** begat *Shammai* **Shammay**.
45 And the son of *Shammai* **Shammay** was Maon:
and Maon was the father of *Bethzur* **Beth Sur**.
46 And Ephah, *Caleb's* **Kaleb's** concubine,
bare Haran, and *Moza* **Mosa**, and Gazez:
and Haran begat Gazez.
47 And the sons of *Jahdai* **Yah Dai**;
Regem, and *Jotham* **Yah Tham**, and *Gesham* **Geshan**,
and Pelet, and Ephah, and Shaaph.
48 Maachah, *Caleb's* **Kaleb's** concubine,
bare Sheber, and *Tirhanah* **Tirchanah**.
49 She bare also Shaaph the father of Madmannah,
Sheva the father of Machbenah,
and the father of *Gibea* **Giba**:
and the daughter of *Caleb* **Kaleb** was Achsah.
50 These were the sons of *Caleb* **Kaleb** the son of Hur,
the firstborn of *Ephratah* **Ephratha**;
Shobal the father of *Kirjathjearim* **Qiryath Arim**.
51 Salma the father of *Bethlehem* **Beth Lechem**,
Hareph the father of *Bethgader* **Beth Gader**.
52 And Shobal the father of *Kirjathjearim* **Qiryath Arim**
had sons;
Haroeh **Roeh**,

and *half of the Manahethites* **Hatzi Ham Menuchoth**.
53 And the families of *Kirjathjearim* **Qiryath Arim**;
the *Ithrites* **Yetheriy**, and the *Puhites* **Puthiy**,
and the *Shumathites* **Shumahiy**,
and the *Mishraites* **Mishraiy**;
of them *came* **went** the *Zareathites* **Sorahiy**,
and the *Eshtaulites* **Eshtaoliy**,
54 The sons of Salma;
Bethlehem **Beth Lechem**,
and the *Netophathites* **Netophathiy**,
Ataroth **Atroth**, the house of *Joab* **Yah Ab**,
and *half of the Manahethites* **Hasi Ham Menuchiy**,
the *Zorites* **Sorahiy**.
55 And the families of the scribes
which *dwelt* **settled** at *Jabez* **Yabes**;
the *Tirathites* **Tirahiy**, the *Shimeathites* **Shimahiy**,
and *Suchathites* **Suchahiy**.
These are the *Kenites* **Qayiniy**
that came of *Hemath* **Hammath**,
the father of the house of Rechab.

GENEALOGY OF THE SONS OF DAVID

3 Now these were the sons of David,
which were born unto him in Hebron;
the firstborn Amnon,
of *Ahinoam* **Achiy Noam** the *Jezreelitess* **Yizre Eliyth**;
the second, *Daniel* **Dani El**,
of *Abigail* **Abi Gail** the *Carmelitess* **Karmeliyth**:
2 The third, *Absalom* **Abi Shalom**
the son of Maachah
the daughter of *Talmai* **Talmay** *king* **sovereign** of Geshur:
the fourth, *Adonijah* **Adoni Yah** the son of Haggith:
3 The fifth, *Shephatiah* **Shaphat Yah** of *Abital* **Abi Tal**:
the sixth, *Ithream* **Yithre Am** by Eglah his *wife* **woman**.
4 These six were born unto him in Hebron;
and there he reigned seven years and six months:
and in *Jerusalem* **Yeru Shalem**
he reigned thirty and three years.
5 And these were born unto him in *Jerusalem* **Yeru Shalem**;
Shimea **Shimah**, and Shobab, and Nathan,
and *Solomon* **Shelomoh**, four,
of *Bathshua* **Bath Shua** the daughter of *Ammiel* **Ammi El**:
6 *Ibhar* **Yibchar** also, and *Elishama* **Eli Shama**,
and *Eliphelet* **Eli Phelet**,
7 And Nogah, and Nepheg, and *Japhia* **Yaphia**,
8 And *Elishama* **Eli Shama**, and *Eliada* **Eli Ada**,
and *Eliphelet* **Eli Phelet**, nine.
9 These were all the sons of David,
beside the sons of the concubines, and Tamar their sister.

GENEALOGY OF THE SOVEREIGNS OF YAH HUDAH

10 And *Solomon's* **Sholomoh's** son
was *Rehoboam* **Rechab Am**,
Abia **Abi Yah** his son, Asa his son,
Jehoshaphat **Yah Shaphat** his son,
11 *Joram* **Yah Ram** his son,
Ahaziah **Achaz Yah** his son, *Joash* **Yah Ash** his son,
12 *Amaziah* **Amaz Yah** his son,
Azariah **Azar Yah** his son, *Jotham* **Yah Tham** his son,
13 *Ahaz* **Achaz** his son,
Hezekiah **Yechizqi Yah** his son,
Manasseh **Menash Sheh** his son,
14 Amon his son,
Josiah **Yoshi Yah** his son.
15 And the sons of *Josiah* **Yoshi Yah** *were*,
the firstborn *Johanan* **Yah Hanan**,
the second *Jehoiakim* **Yah Aqim**,
the third *Zedekiah* **Sidqi Yah**,
the fourth Shallum.
16 And the sons of *Jehoiakim* **Yah Aqim**:
Jeconiah **Yechon Yah** his son,
Zedekiah **Sidqi Yah** his son.
17 And the sons of *Jeconiah* **Yechon Yah**;
Assir, *Salathiel* **Shealti El** his son,
18 *Malchiram* **Malki Ram** also, and *Pedaiah* **Pedah Yah**,
and *Shenazar* **Shenassar**, *Jecamiah* **Yeqam Yah**,
Hoshama **Yah Shama**, and *Nedabiah* **Nedab Yah**.
19 And the sons of *Pedaiah* **Pedah Yah** *were*,
Zerubbabel **Zerub Babel**, and *Shimei* **Shimi**:
and the sons of *Zerubbabel* **Zerub Babel**;
Meshullam, and *Hananiah* **Hanan Yah**,
and Shelomith their sister:
20 And Hashubah, and Ohel, and *Berechiah* **Berech Yah**,
and *Hasadiah* **Hasad Yah**, *Jushabhesed* **Yushab Hesed**,
five.
21 And the sons of *Hananiah* **Hanan Yah**;
Pelatiah **Pelat Yah**, and *Jesaiah* **Yesha Yah**:
the sons of *Rephaiah* **Repha Yah**,
the sons of Arnan,
the sons of *Obadiah* **Obad Yah**,
the sons of *Shechaniah* **Shechan Yah**.
22 And the sons of *Shechaniah* **Shechan Yah**;
Shemaiah **Shema Yah**:
and the sons of *Shemaiah* **Shema Yah**;
Hattush, and *Igeal* **Yigal**, and *Bariah* **Bariach**,
and *Neariah* **Near Yah**, and Shaphat, six.
23 And the sons of *Neariah* **Near Yah**;
Elioenai **El Ya Enay**, and *Hezekiah* **Yechizqi Yah**,
and *Azrikam* **Ezri Qam**, three.
24 And the sons of *Elioenai* **El Ya Enay** *were*,
Hodaiah **Hodav Yah**, and *Eliashib* **El Yashib**,
and *Pelaiah* **Pela Yah**, and *Akkub* **Aqqub**,
and *Johanan* **Yah Hanan**, and *Dalaiah* **Dela Yah**,
and Anani, seven.

GENEALOGY OF THE SONS OF YAH HUDAH

4 The sons of *Judah* **Yah Hudah**;
Pharez **Peres**, *Hezron* **Hesron**,
and *Carmi* **Karmi**, and Hur, and Shobal.
2 And *Reaiah* **Rea Yah** the son of Shobal
begat *Jahath* **Yachath**;
and *Jahath* **Yachath** begat *Ahumai* **Ach Umay**, and Lahad.
These are the families of the *Zorathites* **Sorahiy**.
3 And these were of the father of Etam;
Jezreel **Yizre El**, and *Ishma* **Yishma**, and *Idbash* **Yidbash**:
and the name of their sister was *Hazelelponi* **Selel Poni**:
4 And *Penuel* **Penu El** the father of Gedor,
and Ezer the father of Hushah.
These are the sons of Hur,
the firstborn of *Ephratah* **Ephratha**,
the father of *Bethlehem* **Beth Lechem**.
5 And *Ashur* **Ashchur** the father of *Tekoa* **Teqoha**
had two *wives* **women**, Helah and Naarah.
6 And Naarah bare him *Ahuzam* **Achuz Zam**, and Hepher,
and Temeni, and *Haahashtari* **Achashtariy**.
These were the sons of Naarah.
7 And the sons of Helah *were*,
Zereth **Sereth**, and *Jezoar* **Sochar**, and Ethnan.
8 And *Coz* **Qos** begat Anub, and *Zobebah* **Sobebah**,
and the families of *Aharhel* **Ach Archel** the son of Harum.
9 And *Jabez* **Yabes** was more honourable than his brethren:
and his mother called his name *Jabez* **Yabes**, saying,
Because I bare him with *sorrow* **contortion**.
10 And *Jabez* **Yabes**
called on *the God* **Elohim** of *Israel* **Yisra El**, saying,
Oh that **in blessing,** thou *wouldest* bless me *indeed*,
and *enlarge* **abound** my *coast* **border**,
and that thine hand might be with me,
and that thou *wouldest keep* **work** me from evil,
that it may not *grieve* **contort** me!
And *God* **Elohim** granted him
that which he *requested* **asked**.
11 And *Chelub* **Kelub** the brother of *Shuah* **Shuach**
begat *Mehir* **Mechir**,
which was the father of Eshton.
12 And Eshton begat *Bethrapha* **Beth Rapha**,
and *Paseah* **Paseach**,
and *Tehinnah* **Techinnah**
the father of *Irnahash* **Ir Nachash**.
These are the men of Rechah.
13 And the sons of *Kenaz* **Qenaz**;
Othniel **Othni El**, and *Seraiah* **Sera Yah**:
and the sons of *Othniel* **Othni El**;
Hathath.
14 And *Meonothai* **Meonothay** begat Ophrah:
and *Seraiah* **Sera Yah** begat *Joab* **Yah Ab**,
the father of the
valley of Charashim **Gay Harashim/Valley of Engravers**;
for they were *craftsmen* **engravers**.
15 And the sons of *Caleb* **Kaleb**
the son of *Jephunneh* **Yephunneh**;
Iru, Elah, and Naam:
and the sons of Elah, even *Kenaz* **Qenaz**.

16 And the sons of *Jehaleleel* **Ye Halal El**;
Ziph, and Ziphah, *Tiria* **Tireya**, and *Asareel* **Asar El**.
17 And the sons of *Ezra* **Ezrah** *were*,
Jether **Yether**, and Mered, and Epher, and *Jalon* **Yalon**:
and she *bare Miriam* **conceived Miryam**,
and *Shammai* **Shammay**,
and *Ishbah* **Yishbach** the father of Eshtemoa.
18 And his *wife Jehudijah* **woman Yah Hudahi Yah**
bare *Jered* **Yered** the father of Gedor,
and Heber the father of Sochoh,
and *Jekuthiel* **Yequthi El** the father of *Zanoah* **Zanoach**.
And these are the sons of *Bithiah* **Bith Yah**
the daughter of *Pharaoh* **Paroh**, which Mered took.
19 And the sons of his *wife Hodiah* **woman Hodi Yah**
the sister of *Naham* **Nacham**,
the father of *Keilah* **Qeilah** the *Garmite* **Garmiy**,
and Eshtemoa the *Maachathite* **Maachahiy**.
20 And the sons of Shimon *were*,
Amnon, and Rinnah,
Benhanan **Ben Hanan**, and *Tilon* **Tulon**.
And the sons of *Ishi* **Yishi** *were*,
Zoheth **Zoheth**, and *Benzoheth* **Ben Zoheth**.
21 The sons of Shelah the son of *Judah* **Yah Hudah** *were*,
Er the father of *Lecah* **Lechah**,
and *Laadah* **Ladah** the father of Mareshah,
and the families of the house
of *them that wrought fine* **the service of bleached** linin,
of the house of Ashbea,
22 And *Jokim* **Yah Qim**, and the men of *Chozeba* **Kozeba**,
and *Joash* **Yah Ash**, and Saraph,
who *had the dominion* **mastered** in Moab,
and *Jashubilehem* **Yashubi Lechem**.
And these are *ancient things* **words of antiquity**.
23 These were the *potters* **formers**,
and those that *dwelt* **settled**
among plants and *hedges* **walls**:
there they *dwelt* **settled** with the *king* **sovereign**
for his work.

GENEALOGY OF THE SONS OF SHIMON

24 The sons of *Simeon* **Shimon** *were*,
Nemuel **Nemu El**, and *Jamin* **Yamin**,
Jarib **Yarib**, *Zerah* **Zerach**, and Shaul:
25 Shallum his son, Mibsam his son, Mishma his son.
26 And the sons of Mishma;
Hamuel **Hammu El** his son, *Zacchur* **Zakkur** his son,
Shimei **Shimi** his son.
27 And *Shimei* **Shimi** had sixteen sons and six daughters:
but his brethren had not many *children* **sons**,
neither did all their family *multiply* **abound**,
like to the *children* **sons** of *Judah* **Yah Hudah**.
28 And they *dwelt* **settled** at *Beersheba* **Beer Sheba**,
and Moladah, and *Hazarshual* **Hasar Shual**,
29 And at Bilhah, and at *Ezem* **Esem**, and at Tolad,
30 And at *Bethuel* **Bethu El**,
and at Hormah, and at *Ziklag* **Siqlag**,
31 And at *Bethmarcaboth* **Beth Markaboth**,
and *Hazarsusim* **Hasar Susim**,
and at *Bethbirei* **Beth Biri**, and at *Shaaraim* **Shaarayim**.
These were their cities unto the reign of David.
32 And their *villages* **courts** *were*,
Etam, and *Ain* **Ayin**, Rimmon,
and Tochen, and Ashan, five cities:
33 And all their *villages* **courts**
that were round about the same cities, unto Baal.
These were their *habitations* **sites**, and their genealogy.
34 And Meshobab, and *Jamlech* **Yamlech**,
and *Joshah* **Yah Shah**, the son of *Amaziah* **Amaz Yah**,
35 And *Joel* **Yah El**,
and *Jehu* **Yah Hu** the son of *Josibiah* **Yoshib Yah**,
the son of *Seraiah* **Sera Yah**, the son of *Asiel* **Asi El**,
36 And *Elioenai* **El Ya Enay**, and *Jaakobah* **Yaaqovah**,
and *Jeshohaiah* **Yeshocha Yah**, and *Asaiah* **Asah Yah**,
and *Adiel* **Adi El**, and *Jesimiel* **Yesima El**,
and *Benaiah* **Bena Yah**,
37 And Ziza the son of Shiphi,
the son of Allon, the son of *Jedaiah* **Yeda Yah**,
the son of Shimri, the son of *Shemaiah* **Shema Yah**;
38 These mentioned by their names
were *princes* **hierarchs** in their families:
and the house of their fathers
increased greatly **breached with greatness**.
39 And they went to the entrance of Gedor,
even unto the east side **from the rising** of the valley,
to seek pasture for their flocks.
40 And they found fat pasture and good,
and the land was *wide* **broad of hands**,
and *quiet* **at rest**, and *peaceable* **serene**;
for they of Ham had *dwelt* **settled** there
of old **from the first**.
41 And these *written* **inscribed** by name
came in the days of *Hezekiah* **Yechizqi Yah**,
king **sovereign** of *Judah* **Yah Hudah**,
and smote their tents,
and the habitations that were found there,
and *destroyed them utterly* **they are devoted** unto this day,
and *dwelt* **settled** in their *rooms* **stead**:
because there was pasture there for their flocks.
42 And *some* of them, *even* of the sons of *Simeon* **Shimon**,
five hundred men, went to mount Seir,
having for their *captains* **heads**
Pelatiah **Pelat Yah**, and *Neariah* **Near Yah**,
and *Rephaiah* **Repha Yah**, and *Uzziel* **Uzzi El**,
the sons of *Ishi* **Yishi**.
43 And they smote
the *rest* **survivors** of the *Amalekites* **Amaleqiy**
that were escaped **of the escapees**,
and *dwelt* **settled** there unto this day.

GENEALOGY OF THE SONS OF REU BEN

5 Now the sons of *Reuben* **Reu Ben**
the firstborn of *Israel* **Yisra El**,
(for he was the firstborn;
but forasmuch
as he *defiled* **profaned** his father's *bed* **chamber**,
his *birthright* **firstright** was given
unto the sons of *Joseph* **Yoseph**
the son of *Israel* **Yisra El**:
and the genealogy is not to be *reckoned* **genealogized**
after the *birthright* **firstrights**.
2 For *Judah* **Yah Hudah**
prevailed **mightily** above his brethren,
and of him *came the chief ruler* **eminent**;
but the birthright was *Joseph's* **Yoseph's**:)
3 The sons, *I say*, of *Reuben* **Reu Ben**
the firstborn of *Israel* **Yisra El** *were*,
Hanoch Hanoch and Pallu,
Hezron **Hesron**, and *Carmi* **Karmi**.
4 The sons of *Joel* **Yah El**;
Shemaiah **Shema Yah** his son,
Gog his son, *Shimei* **Shimi** his son,
5 *Micah* **Michah Yah** his son,
Reaia **Rea Yah** his son, Baal his son,
6 Beerah his son,
whom *Tilgathpilneser* **Tilgath Pileser**,
king **sovereign** of *Assyria* **Ashshur**
carried away captive **exiled**:
he was *prince* **hierarch** of the *Reubenites* **Reu Beniy**.
7 And his brethren by their families,
when the genealogy of their generations
was *reckoned* **genealogized**,
were the *chief* **head**,
Jeiel **Yei El**, and *Zechariah* **Zechar Yah**,
8 And Bela the son of Azaz,
the son of Shema, the son of *Joel* **Yah El**,
who *dwelt* **settled** in Aroer,
even unto Nebo and *Baalmeon* **Baal Meon**:
9 And *eastward* **from the rising**
he *inhabited* **settled** unto the entering in of the wilderness
from the river Euphrates:
because their *cattle* **chattel**
were multiplied **abounded** in the land of *Gilead* **Gilad**.
10 And in the days of *Saul* **Shaul**
they *made* **worked** war with the *Hagarites* **Hagariy**,
who fell by their hand:
and they *dwelt* **settled** in their tents
throughout **upon the face of** all the east *land*
of *Gilead* **Gilad**.

GENEALOGY OF THE SONS OF GAD

11 And the *children* **sons** of Gad
dwelt **settled** over against them,
in the land of Bashan unto *Salcah* **Salchah**:

12 *Joel* **Yah El** the *chief* **head,**
and Shapham *the next* **second,**
and *Jaanai* **Yaanay,** and Shaphat in Bashan.
13 And their brethren of the house of their fathers *were,*
Michael **Michah El,** and Meshullam, and Sheba,
and *Jorai* **Yoray,** and *Jachan* **Yakan,** and Zia, and Heber,
seven.
14 These are the *children* **sons** of *Abihail* **Abi Hail**
the son of Huri, the son of *Jaroah* **Yaroach,**
the son of *Gilead* **Gilad,** the son of *Michael* **Michah El,**
the son of *Jeshishai* **Yeshishay,** the son of *Jahdo* **Yachdo,**
the son of Buz;
15 *Ahi* **Achiy** the son of *Abdiel* **Abdi El,** the son of Guni,
chief **head** of the house of their fathers.
16 And they *dwelt* **settled** in *Gilead* **Gilad** in Bashan,
and in her *towns* **daughters,**
and in all the suburbs of Sharon,
upon their *borders* **exits.**
17 All these were *reckoned by genealogies* **genealogized**
in the days of *Jotham* **Yah Tham,**
king **sovereign** of *Judah* **Yah Hudah,**
and in the days of *Jeroboam* **Yarob Am**
king **sovereign** of *Israel* **Yisra El.**
18 The sons of *Reuben* **Reu Ben,** and the *Gadites* **Gadiy,**
and half the *tribe* **scion** of *Manasseh* **Menash Sheh,**
of valiant men **sons of valour,**
men able to bear buckler and sword,
and to *shoot* **arch** with bow, and *skilful* **taught** in war,
were four and forty thousand
seven hundred and *threescore* **sixty,**
that went out to the *war* **host.**
19 And they *made* **worked** war with the *Hagarites* **Hagariy,**
with *Jetur* **Yetur,** and Nephish, and Nodab.
20 And they were helped against them,
and the *Hagarites* **Hagariy**
were *delivered* **given** into their hand,
and all that were with them:
for they cried to *God* **Elohim** in the *battle* **war,**
and he was intreated of them;
because they *put their trust* **confided** in him.
21 And they *took away* **captured** their *cattle* **chattel;**
of their camels fifty thousand,
and of *sheep* **flocks** two hundred and fifty thousand,
and of *asses* **he burros** two thousand,
and of *men* **souls of humanity** an hundred thousand.
22 For there fell down many *slain* **pierced,**
because the war was of *God* **Elohim.**
And they *dwelt* **settled** in their steads
until the *captivity* **exile.**

GENEALOGY OF THE SONS OF THE HALF SCION OF MENASH SHEH

23 And the *children* **sons**
of the half *tribe* **scion** of *Manasseh* **Menash Sheh**
dwelt **settled** in the land:
they *increased* **abounded** from Bashan
unto *Baalhermon* **Baal Hermon** and Senir,
and unto mount Hermon.
24 And these were the heads of the house of their fathers,
even Epher, and *Ishi* **Yishi,** and *Eliel* **Eli El,**
and *Azriel* **Ezri El,** and *Jeremiah* **Yirme Yah,**
and *Hodaviah* **Hodav Yah,** and *Jahdiel* **Yachdi El,**
mighty men of valour, *famous* men **of name,**
and heads of the house of their fathers.
25 And they *transgressed* **treasoned**
against *the God* **Elohim** of their fathers,
and *went a whoring* **whored** after the *gods* **elohim**
of the people of the land,
whom *God destroyed* **Elohim desolated**
before them **at their face.**
26 And *the God* **Elohim** of *Israel* **Yisra El**
stirred up **wakened** the spirit of Pul
king **sovereign** of *Assyria* **Ashshur,**
and the spirit of *Tilgathpilneser* **Tilgath Pileser,**
king **sovereign** of *Assyria* **Ashshur,**
and he *carried* **exiled** them *away,*
even the *Reubenites* **Reu Beniy,** and the *Gadites* **Gadiy,**
and the half *tribe* **scion** of *Manasseh* **Menash Sheh,**
and brought them unto *Halah* **Halach,** and Habor,
and Hara, and to the river Gozan, unto this day.

GENEALOGY OF THE SONS OF LEVI

6 The sons of Levi;
Gershon, *Kohath* **Qehath,** and Merari.
2 And the sons of *Kohath* **Qehath;**
Amram **Am Ram,** *Izhar* **Yishar,**
and Hebron, and *Uzziel* **Uzzi El.**
3 And the *children* **sons** of *Amram* **Am Ram;**
Aaron **Aharon,** and *Moses* **Mosheh,** and *Miriam* **Miryam.**
The sons also of *Aaron* **Aharon;**
Nadab, and *Abihu* **Abi Hu,**
Eleazar **El Azar,** and *Ithamar* **Iy Thamar.**
4 *Eleazar* **El Azar** begat *Phinehas* **Pinechas,**
Phinehas **Pinechas** begat *Abishua* **Abi Shua,**
5 And *Abishua* **Abi Shua** begat *Bukki* **Buqqi,**
and *Bukki* **Buqqi** begat Uzzi,
6 And Uzzi begat *Zerahiah* **Zerach Yah,**
and *Zerahiah* **Zerach Yah** begat *Meraioth* **Merayoth,**
7 *Meraioth* **Merayoth** begat *Amariah* **Amar Yah,**
and *Amariah* **Amar Yah** begat *Ahitub* **Achiy Tub,**
8 And *Ahitub* **Achiy Tub** begat *Zadok* **Sadoq,**
and *Zadok* **Sadoq** begat *Ahimaaz* **Achiy Maas,**
9 And *Ahimaaz* **Achiy Maas** begat *Azariah* **Azar Yah,**
and *Azariah* **Azar Yah** begat *Johanan* **Yah Hanan,**
10 And *Johanan* **Yah Hanan** begat *Azariah* **Azar Yah,**
he it is that *executed the priest's office* **priested**
in the *temple* **house**
that *Solomon* **Shelomoh** built in *Jerusalem* **Yeru Shalem:)**
11 And *Azariah* **Azar Yah** begat *Amariah* **Amar Yah,**
and *Amariah* **Amar Yah** begat *Ahitub* **Achiy Tub,**
12 And *Ahitub* **Achiy Tub** begat *Zadok* **Sadoq,**
and *Zadok* **Sadoq** begat Shallum,
13 And Shallum begat *Hilkiah* **Hilqi Yah,**
and *Hilkiah* **Hilqi Yah** begat *Azariah* **Azar Yah,**
14 And *Azariah* **Azar Yah** begat *Seraiah* **Sera Yah,**
and *Seraiah* **Sera Yah** begat *Jehozadak* **Yah Sadaq,**
15 And *Jehozadak* **Yah Sadaq** went *into captivity,*
when *the LORD carried away* **Yah Veh exiled**
Judah **Yah Hudah** and *Jerusalem* **Yeru Shalem**
by the hand of *Nebuchadnezzar* **Nebukadnets Tsar.**
16 The sons of Levi;
Gershom, *Kohath* **Qehath,** and Merari.
17 And these be the names of the sons of Gershom;
Libni, and *Shimei* **Shimi.**
18 And the sons of *Kohath* **Qehath** *were,*
Amram **Am Ram,** and *Izhar* **Yishar,**
and Hebron, and *Uzziel* **Uzzi El.**
19 The sons of Merari;
Mahli **Machli,** and Mushi.
And these are the families of the *Levites* **Leviym**
according to their fathers.
20 Of Gershom;
Libni his son, *Jahath* **Yachath** his son, Zimmah his son,
21 *Joah* **Yah Ach** his son, Iddo his son,
Zerah **Zerach** his son, *Jeaterai* **Jeatheray** his son.
22 The sons of *Kohath* **Qehath;**
Amminadab **Ammi Nadab** his son,
Korah **Qorach** his son, Assir his son,
23 *Elkanah* **El Qanah** his son,
and *Ebiasaph* **Abi Asaph** his son, and Assir his son,
24 *Tahath* **Tachath** his son, *Uriel* **Uri El** his son,
Uzziah **Uzzi Yah** his son, and Shaul his son.
25 And the sons of *Elkanah* **El Qanah;**
Amasai **Amasay,** and *Ahimoth* **Achiy Moth.**
26 *As for Elkanah* **El Qanah:** the sons of *Elkanah* **El Qanah;**
Zophai **Suph** his son, and *Nahath* **Nachath** his son,
27 *Eliab* **Eli Ab** his son,
Jeroham **Yerocham** his son, *Elkanah* **El Qanah** his son.
28 And the sons of *Samuel* **Shemu El;**
the firstborn Vashni, and *Abiah* **Abi Yah.**
29 The sons of Merari;
Mahli **Machli,** Libni his son,
Shimei **Shimi** his son, Uzza his son,
30 *Shimea* **Shimah** his son, *Haggiah* **Haggi Yah** his son,
Asaiah **Asah Yah** his son.

GENEALOGY OF THE SONG LEADERS

31 And these are they whom David *set* **stood**
over the *service* **hand** of song
in the house of *the LORD* **Yah Veh,**
after that the ark *had rest* **rested.**

32 And they ministered
before the dwelling place **at the face of the tabernacle**
of the *tabernacle* **tent** of the congregation
with *singing* **song**,
until *Solomon* **Shelomoh**
had built the house of *the LORD* **Yah Veh**
in *Jerusalem* **Yeru Shalem**:
and then they *waited* **stood** on their *office* **service**
according to their *order* **judgment**.
33 And these are they
that *waited* **stood** with their *children* **sons**.
Of the sons of the *Kohathites* **Qehathiy**:
Heman a singer,
the son of *Joel* **Yah El**, the son of *Shemuel* **Shemu El**,
34 The son of *Elkanah* **El Qanah**,
the son of *Jeroham* **Yerocham**,
the son of *Eliel* **Eli El**, the son of *Toah* **Toach**,
35 The son of *Zuph* **Suph**, the son of *Elkanah* **El Qanah**,
the son of *Mahath* **Machath**, the son of *Amasai* **Amasay**,
36 The son of *Elkanah* **El Qanah**, the son of *Joel* **Yah El**,
the son of *Azariah* **Azar Yah**,
the son of *Zephaniah* **Sephan Yah**,
37 The son of *Tahath* **Tachath**, the son of Assir,
the son of *Ebiasaph* **Abi Asaph**, the son of *Korah* **Qorach**,
38 The son of *Izhar* **Yishar**, the son of *Kohath* **Qehath**,
the son of Levi, the son of *Israel* **Yisra El**.
39 And his brother Asaph, who stood on his right *hand*,
even Asaph the son of *Berechiah* **Berech Yah**,
the son of *Shimea* **Shimah**,
40 The son of *Michael* **Michah El**,
the son of *Baaseiah* **Baase Yah**,
the son of *Malchiah* **Malki Yah**,
41 The son of Ethni, the son of *Zerah* **Zerach**,
the son of *Adaiah* **Ada Yah**,
42 The son of Ethan,
the son of Zimmah, the son of *Shimei* **Shimi**,
43 The son of *Jahath* **Yachath**,
the son of Gershom, the son of Levi.
44 And their brethren the sons of Merari
stood on the left *hand*:
Ethan the son of *Kishi* **Qishi**,
the son of Abdi, the son of Malluch,
45 The son of *Hashabiah* **Hashab Yah**,
the son of *Amaziah* **Amaz Yah**,
the son of *Hilkiah* **Hilqi Yah**,
46 The son of *Amzi* **Amsi**,
the son of Bani, the son of *Shamer* **Shemer**,
47 The son of *Mahli* **Machli**, the son of Mushi,
the son of Merari, the son of Levi.

GENEALOGY OF THE LEADERS OF TABERNACLE SERVICE

48 Their brethren also the *Levites* **Leviym**
were *appointed* **given** unto all manner of service
of the tabernacle of the house of *God* **Elohim**.
49 But *Aaron* **Aharon** and his sons *offered* **incensed**
upon the **sacrifice** altar of the *burnt offering* **holocaust**,
and on the **sacrifice** altar of incense,
and were appointed for all the work
of the *place most holy* **Holy of Holies**,
and to *make an atonement* **kapar/atone** for *Israel* **Yisra El**,
according to all
that *Moses* **Mosheh** the servant of *God* **Elohim**
had *commanded* **misvahed**.
50 And these are the sons of *Aaron* **Aharon**;
Eleazar **El Azar** his son,
Phinehas **Pinechas** his son, *Abishua* **Abi Shua** his son,
51 *Bukki* **Buqqi** his son, Uzzi his son,
Zerahiah **Zerach Yah** his son,
52 *Meraioth* **Merayoth** his son,
Amariah **Amar Yah** his son, *Ahitub* **Achiy Tub** his son,
53 *Zadok* **Sadoq** his son, *Ahimaaz* **Achiy Maas** his son.
54 Now these are their *dwelling places* **sites**
throughout their *castles* **walls** in their *coasts* **borders**,
of the sons of *Aaron* **Aharon**,
of the families of the *Kohathites* **Qehathiy**:
for their's was the *lot* **pebble**.
55 And they gave them Hebron
in the land of *Judah* **Yah Hudah**,
and the suburbs thereof round about it.
56 But the fields of the city, and the *villages* **courts** thereof,
they gave to *Caleb* **Kaleb**
the son of *Jephunneh* **Yephunneh**.
57 And to the sons of *Aaron* **Aharon**
they gave the cities of *Judah* **Yah Hudah**,
namely, Hebron, *the city* of refuge,
and Libnah with her suburbs,
and *Jattir* **Yattir**, and Eshtemoa, with their suburbs,
58 And Hilen with her suburbs, Debir with her suburbs,
59 And Ashan with her suburbs,
and *Bethshemesh* **Beth Shemesh** with her suburbs:
60 And out of the *tribe* **rod** of *Benjamin* **Ben Yamin**;
Geba with her suburbs, and Alemeth with her suburbs,
and Anathoth with her suburbs.
All their cities throughout their families
were thirteen cities.
61 And unto the sons of *Kohath* **Qehath**,
which *were left* **remained** of the family of that *tribe* **rod**,
were cities given out of the half *tribe* **rod**, *namely*,
out of the half *tribe* of *Manasseh* **Menash Sheh**,
by *lot* **pebble**, ten cities.
62 And to the sons of Gershom throughout their families
out of the *tribe* **rod** of *Issachar* **Yissachar**,
and out of the *tribe* **rod** of Asher,
and out of the *tribe* **rod** of Naphtali,
and out of the *tribe* **rod** of *Manasseh* **Menash Sheh**
in Bashan, thirteen cities.
63 Unto the sons of Merari *were given* by *lot* **pebble**,
throughout their families,
out of the *tribe* **rod** of *Reuben* **Reu Ben**,
and out of the *tribe* **rod** of Gad,
and out of the *tribe* **rod** of Zebulun, twelve cities.
64 And the *children* **sons** of *Israel* **Yisra El**
gave to the *Levites* **Leviym** these cities with their suburbs.
65 And they gave by *lot* **pebble**
out of the *tribe* **rod**
of the *children* **sons** of *Judah* **Yah Hudah**,
and out of the *tribe* **rod**
of the *children* **sons** of *Simeon* **Shimon**,
and out of the *tribe* **rod**
of the *children* **sons** of *Benjamin* **Ben Yamin**,
these cities, which are called by *their* names.
66 And *the residue of* the families
of the sons of *Kohath* **Qehath**
had cities of their *coasts* **borders**
out of the *tribe* **rod** of *Ephraim* **Ephrayim**.
67 And they gave unto them, *of* the cities of refuge,
Shechem in mount *Ephraim* **Ephrayim**
with her suburbs;
they gave also Gezer with her suburbs,
68 And *Jokmeam* **Yoqme Am** with her suburbs,
and *Bethhoron* **Beth Horon** with her suburbs,
69 And *Aijalon* **Ayalon** with her suburbs,
and *Gathrimmon* **Gath Rimmon** with her suburbs:
70 And out of the half *tribe* **rod** of *Manasseh* **Menash Sheh**;
Aner with her suburbs,
and *Bileam* **Balaam** with her suburbs,
for the family *of the remnant* **remaining**
of the sons of *Kohath* **Qehath**.
71 Unto the sons of Gershom *were given*
out of the family
of the half *tribe* **rod** of *Manasseh* **Menash Sheh**,
Golan in Bashan with her suburbs,
and Ashtaroth with her suburbs:
72 And out of the *tribe* **rod** of *Issachar* **Yissachar**;
Kedesh with her suburbs, Daberath with her suburbs,
73 And Ramoth with her suburbs,
and Anem with her suburbs:
74 And out of the *tribe* **rod** of Asher;
Mashal with her suburbs, and Abdon with her suburbs,
75 And *Hukok* **Huqqoq** with her suburbs,
and *Rehob* **Rechob** with her suburbs:
76 And out of the *tribe* **rod** of Naphtali;
Kedesh in *Galilee* **Galiyl** with her suburbs,
and Hammon with her suburbs,
and *Kirjathaim* **Qiryathaim** with her suburbs.
77 Unto the *rest of the children* **remaining sons** of Merari
were given out of the *tribe* **rod** of Zebulun,
Rimmon with her suburbs, Tabor with her suburbs:
78 And on the other side *Jordan* **Yarden**
by *Jericho* **Yericho**,
on the east side **from the rising** of *Jordan* **Yarden**,

were given them out of the tribe **rod** of Reuben **Reu Ben**,
Bezer in the wilderness with her suburbs,
and Jahzah **Yahsah** with her suburbs,
79 Kedemoth **Qedemoth** also with her suburbs,
and Mephaath with her suburbs:
80 And out of the tribe **rod** of Gad;
Ramoth in Gilead **Gilad** with her suburbs,
and Mahanaim **Machanayim** with her suburbs,
81 And Heshbon with her suburbs,
and Jazer **Yazer** with her suburbs.

GENEALOGY OF THE SONS OF YISSACHAR

7 Now the sons of Issachar **Yissachar** were,
Tola, and Puah, Jashub **Yashub**, and Shimrom, four.
2 And the sons of Tola;
Uzzi, and Rephaiah **Repha Yah**, and Jeriel **Yeri El**,
and Jahmai **Yachmay**, and Jibsam **Yibsam**,
and Shemuel **Shemu El**,
heads of their father's house, to wit, of Tola:
they were valiant men of might **and mighty mighty**
in their generations;
whose number was in the days of David
two and twenty thousand and six hundred.
3 And the sons of Uzzi;
Izrahiah **Yizrach Yah**:
and the sons of Izrahiah **Yizrach Yah**;
Michael **Michah El**, and Obadiah **Obad Yah**, and Joel **Yah El**,
Ishiah **Yishshi Yah**, five: all of them chief men **heads**.
4 And with them, by their generations,
after the house of their fathers,
were bands **troops** of soldiers **hosts** for war,
six and thirty thousand men:
for they had many wives **abounded with women** and sons.
5 And their brethren
among all the families of Issachar **Yissachar**
were valiant men of might **mighty mighty**,
reckoned in all by their genealogies **all genealogized**
fourscore **eighty** and seven thousand.

GENEALOGY OF THE SONS OF BEN YAMIN

6 The sons of Benjamin **Ben Yamin**;
Bela, and Becher, and Jediael **Yedia El**, three.
7 And the sons of Bela;
Ezbon **Esbon**, and Uzzi, and Uzziel **Uzzi El**,
and Jerimoth **Yerimoth**, and Iri, five;
heads of the house of their fathers,
mighty men of valour;
and were reckoned by their genealogies **genealogized**
twenty and two thousand and thirty and four.
8 And the sons of Becher;
Zemira **Zemirah**, and Joash **Yah Ash**,
and Eliezer **Eli Ezer**, and Elioenai **El Ya Enay**,
and Omri, and Jerimoth **Yerimoth**,
and Abiah **Abi Yah**, and Anathoth, and Alameth **Alemeth**.
All these are the sons of Becher.
9 And the number of them,
after their genealogy **genealogized** by their generations,
heads of the house of their fathers,
mighty men of valour,
was twenty thousand and two hundred.
10 The sons also of Jediael **Yedia El**;
Bilhan:
and the sons of Bilhan;
Jeush **Yeush**, and Benjamin **Ben Yamin**, and Ehud,
and Chenaanah **Kenaanah**, and Zethan,
and Tharshish **Tarshish**, and Ahishahar **Achiy Shachar**.
11 All these the sons of Jediael **Yedia El**,
by the heads of their fathers, mighty men of valour,
were seventeen thousand and two hundred soldiers,
fit to go out for war **hostility** and battle **war**.
12 Shuppim also, and Huppim, the children **sons** of Ir,
and Hushim, the sons of Aher **Acher**.

GENEALOGY OF THE SONS OF NAPHTALI

13 The sons of Naphtali;
Jahziel **Yachsi El**, and Guni, and Jezer **Yeser**, and Shallum,
the sons of Bilhah.

GENEALOGY OF THE SONS OF MENASH SHEH

14 The sons of Manasseh **Menash Sheh**;
Ashriel **Asri El**, whom she bare:
(but his concubine the Aramitess **Aramiy**
bare Machir the father of Gilead **Gilad**:
15 And Machir took to wife **woman**
the sister of Huppim and Shuppim,
whose sister's name was Maachah;)
and the name of the second was Zelophehad **Seloph Had**:
and Zelophehad **Seloph Had** had daughters.
16 And Maachah
the wife **woman** of Machir bare a son,
and she called his name Peresh;
and the name of his brother was Sheresh;
and his sons were Ulam and Rakem **Reqem**.
17 And the sons of Ulam;
Bedan.
These were the sons of Gilead **Gilad**,
the son of Machir,
the son of Manasseh **Menash Sheh**.
18 And his sister Hammoleketh **Molecheth**
bare Ishod **Ish Hod**,
and Abiezer **Abi Ezer**, and Mahalah **Machlah**.
19 And the sons of Shemidah **Shemi Da** were,
Ahian **Achyan**, and Shechem,
and Likhi **Liqchi**, and Aniam **Ani Am**.

GENEALOGY OF THE SONS OF EPHRAYIM

20 And the sons of Ephraim **Ephrayim**;
Shuthelah **Shuthelach**, and Bered his son,
and Tahath **Tachath** his son,
and Eladah **El Adah** his son, and Tahath **Tachath** his son,
21 And Zabad his son, and Shuthelah **Shuthelach** his son,
and Ezer, and Elead **El Ad**,
whom the men of Gath that were born in that land
slew **slaughtered**,
because they came down **descended**
to take away their cattle **chattel**.
22 And Ephraim **Ephrayim** their father
mourned many days,
and his brethren came to comfort **sigh over** him.
23 And when he went in to his wife **woman**,
she conceived, and bare a son,
and he called his name Beriah,
because it went evil with his house.
24 (And his daughter was Sherah **Sheerah**,
who built Bethhoron **Beth Horon**
the nether, and the upper,
and Uzzensherah **Uzzen Sheerah**.)
25 And Rephah **Rephach** was his son, also Resheph,
and Telah **Telach** his son, and Tahan **Tachan** his son.
26 Laadan **Ladan** his son, Ammihud **Ammi Hud** his son,
Elishama **Eli Shama** his son.
27 Non his son, Jehoshuah **Yah Shua** his son.
28 And their possessions and habitations **sites** were,
Bethel **Beth El** and the towns **daughters** thereof,
and eastward **from the rising** Naaran,
and westward **duskward** Gezer,
with the towns **daughters** thereof;
Shechem also and the towns **daughters** thereof,
unto Gaza **Azzah** and the towns **daughters** thereof:
29 And by the borders **hand**
of the children **sons** of Manasseh **Menash Sheh**,
Bethshean **Beth Shaan** and her towns **daughters**,
Taanach and her towns **daughters**,
Megiddo and her towns **daughters**,
Dor and her towns **daughters**.
In these dwelt **settled** the children **sons** of Joseph **Yoseph**
the son of Israel **Yisra El**.

GENEALOGY OF THE SONS OF ASHER

30 The sons of Asher;
Imnah **Yimnah**, and Isuah **Yishvah**,
and Ishuai **Yishvi**, and Beriah,
and Serah **Serach** their sister.
31 And the sons of Beriah;
Heber, and Malchiel **Malki El**,
who is the father of Birzavith **Birzoth**.
32 And Heber begat Japhlet **Yaphlet**,
and Shomer, and Hotham,
and Shua their sister.
33 And the sons of Japhlet **Yaphlet**;
Pasach, and Bimhal, and Ashvath.
These are the children **sons** of Japhlet **Yaphlet**.
34 And the sons of Shamer **Shemer**;
Ahi **Achiy**, and Rohgah **Rohagah**,
Jehubbah **Jechubbah**, and Aram.
35 And the sons of his brother Helem;

Zophah **Sophach**, and *Imna* **Yimna**,
and Shelesh, and Amal.
36 The sons of *Zophah* **Sophach**;
Suah **Suach**, and Harnepher,
and Shual, and Beri, and *Imrah* **Yimrah**,
37 Bezer, and Hod, and Shamma,
and Shilshah, and *Ithran* **Yithran**, and Beera.
38 And the sons of *Jether* **Yether**;
Jephunneh **Yephunneh**, and Pispah, and Ara.
39 And the sons of Ulla;
Arah **Arach**, and *Haniel* **Hani El**, and *Rezia* **Risya**.
40 All these were the *children* **sons** of Asher,
heads of *their* father's house,
choice **pure** and mighty *men* of valour,
chief **head** of the *princes* **hierarchs**.
And the number
throughout the genealogy of them **genealogized**
that were apt to the *war* **hostility** and to *battle* **war**
was twenty and six thousand men.

GENEALOGY OF THE SONS OF BEN YAMIN

8 Now *Benjamin* **Ben Yamin** begat Bela his firstborn,
Ashbel the second, and *Aharah* **Ach Rach** the third,
2 *Nohah* **Nochah** the fourth, and Rapha the fifth.
3 And the sons of Bela *were*,
Addar, and Gera, and *Abihud* **Abi Hud**,
4 And *Abishua* **Abi Shua**,
and Naaman, and *Ahoah* **Ach Oach**,
5 And Gera, and Shephuphan, and *Huram* **Hiram**.
6 And these are the sons of *Ehud* **Echud**:
these are the heads of the fathers
of the *inhabitants* **settlers** of Geba,
and they *removed* **exiled** them to *Manahath* **Manachath**:
7 And Naaman, and *Ahiah* **Achiy Yah**, and Gera,
he *removed* **exiled** them,
and begat Uzza, and *Ahihud* **Achiy Chud**.
8 And *Shaharaim* **Shacharayim** begat *children*
in the *country* **field** of Moab,
after he had sent them away;
Hushim and Baara were his *wives* **women**.
9 And he begat of Hodesh his *wife* **woman**,
Jobab **Yobab**, and *Zibia* **Sibya**,
and Mesha, and Malcham,
10 And *Jeuz* **Yeus**,
and *Shachia* **Shobyah**, and *Mirma* **Mirmah**.
These were his sons, heads of the fathers.
11 And of Hushim
he begat *Abitub* **Abi Tub**, and *Elpaal* **El Paal**.
12 The sons of *Elpaal* **El Paal**;
Eber **Heber**, and Misham, and *Shamed* **Shemer**,
who built Ono, and Lod,
with the *towns* **daughters** thereof:
13 Beriah also, and Shema,
who were heads of the fathers
of the *inhabitants* **settlers** of *Aijalon* **Ayalon**,
who *drove away* **made flee**
the *inhabitants* **settlers** of Gath:
14 And *Ahio* **Achyo**, *Shashak* **Shashaq**,
and *Jeremoth* **Yeremoth**,
15 And *Zebadiah* **Zebad Yah**, and Arad, and *Ader* **Eder**,
16 And *Michael* **Michah El**,
and *Ispah* **Yishpah**, and *Joha* **Yah Ha**,
the sons of Beriah;
17 And *Zebadiah* **Zebad Yah**, and Meshullam,
and *Hezeki* **Hezqi**, and Heber,
18 *Ishmerai* **Yishmeray** also,
and *Jezliah* **Yizliah**, and *Jobab* **Yobab**,
the sons of *Elpaal* **El Paal**;
19 And *Jakim* **Yaqim**, and Zichri, and Zabdi,
20 And *Elienai* **Eli Enay**,
and *Zilthai* **Sillethay**, and *Eliel* **Eli El**,
21 And *Adaiah* **Ada Yah**,
and *Beraiah* **Bera Yah**, and Shimrath,
the sons of Shimhi;
22 And *Ishpan* **Yishpan**, and Heber, and *Eliel* **Eli El**,
23 And Abdon, and Zichri, and Hanan,
24 And *Hananiah* **Hanan Yah**,
and Elam, and *Antothijah* **Anthothi Yah**,
25 And *Iphedeiah* **Yiphde Yah**, and *Penuel* **Penu El**,
the sons of *Shashak* **Shashaq**;
26 And *Shamsherai* **Shamsheray**,
and *Shehariah* **Shechar Yah**, and *Athaliah* **Athal Yah**,
27 And *Jaresiah* **Yaaresh Yah**,
and *Eliah* **Eli Yah**, and Zichri,
the sons of *Jeroham* **Yerocham**.
28 These were heads of the fathers, by their generations,
chief **heads** *men*.
These *dwelt* **settled** in *Jerusalem* **Yeru Shalem**.
29 And at *Gibeon* **Gibon**
dwelt **settled** the father of *Gibeon* **Gibon**;
whose *wife's* **woman's** name was Maachah:
30 And his firstborn son Abdon,
and *Zur* **Sur**, and *Kish* **Qish**, and Baal, and Nadab,
31 And Gedor, and *Ahio* **Achyo**, and *Zacher* **Zecher**.
32 And *Mikloth* **Miqloth** begat *Shimeah* **Shimah**.
And these also *dwelt* **settled** with their brethren
in *Jerusalem* **Yeru Shalem**, over against them.
33 And Ner begat *Kish* **Qish**,
and *Kish* **Qish** begat *Saul* **Shaul**,
and *Saul* **Shaul** begat *Jonathan* **Yah Nathan**,
and *Malchishua* **Malki Shua**, and *Abinadab* **Abi Nadab**,
and *Eshbaal* **Esh Baal**.
34 And the son of *Jonathan* **Yah Nathan,**
was Meribbaal **Merib Baal**;
and *Meribbaal* **Merib Baal** begat *Micah* **Michah Yah**.
35 And the sons of *Micah* **Michah Yah** *were*,
Pithon, and Melech,
and *Tarea* **Taarea**, and *Ahaz* **Achaz**.
36 And *Ahaz* **Achaz** begat *Jehoadah* **Yah Addah**;
and *Jehoadah* **Yah Addah** begat Alemeth,
and Azmaveth, and Zimri;
and Zimri begat *Moza* **Mosa**,
37 And *Moza* **Mosa** begat *Binea* **Binah**:
Rapha was his son,
Eleasah **El Asah** his son, *Azel* **Asel** his son:
38 And Azel had six sons, whose names are these,
Azrikam **Ezri Qam**, Bocheru,
and *Ishmael* **Yishma El**, and *Sheariah* **Shear Yah**,
and *Obadiah* **Obad Yah**, and Hanan.
All these were the sons of Azel.
39 And the sons of *Eshek* **Esheq** his brother *were*,
Ulam his firstborn, *Jehush* **Yeush** the second,
and *Eliphelet* **Eli Phelet** the third.
40 And the sons of Ulam
were mighty *men* of valour, *archers* **bowmen**,
and *had many* **abounded with** sons, and sons' sons,
an hundred and fifty.
All these are of the sons of *Benjamin* **Ben Yamin**.

GENEALOGIES INSCRIBED IN THE SCROLLS OF THE SOVEREIGNS OF YISRA EL AND YAH HUDAH

9 So all *Israel* **Yisra El**
were *reckoned by genealogies* **genealogized**;
and, behold,
they were *written* **inscribed** in the *book* **scroll**
of the *kings* **sovereigns**
of *Israel* **Yisra El** and *Judah* **Yah Hudah**,
who were *carried away* **exiled** to *Babylon* **Babel**
for their *transgression* **treason**.

GENEALOGY OF THE YISRA ELIY

2 Now the first *inhabitants that dwelt* **settlers**
in their possessions in their cities *were*,
the *Israelites* **Yisra Eliy**, the priests, *Levites* **Leviym**,
and the *Nethinims* **Nethinim**.
3 And in *Jerusalem dwelt* **Yeru Shalem settled**
of the *children* **sons** of *Judah* **Yah Hudah**,
and of the *children* **sons** of *Benjamin* **Ben Yamin**,
and of the *children* **sons** of *Ephraim* **Ephrayim**,
and *Manasseh* **Menash Sheh**;
4 *Uthai* **Uthay** the son of *Ammihud* **Ammi Hud**,
the son of Omri, the son of Imri, the son of Bani,
of the *children* **sons** of *Pharez* **Peres**
the son of *Judah* **Yah Hudah**.
5 And of the *Shilonites* **Shilohiy**;
Asaiah **Asah Yah** the firstborn, and his sons.
6 And of the sons of *Zerah* **Zerach**;
Jeuel **Yeu El**, and their brethren,
six hundred and ninety.
7 And of the sons of *Benjamin* **Ben Yamin**;
Sallu the son of Meshullam,
the son of *Hodaviah* **Hodav Yah**,
the son of *Hasenuah* **Senuah**,

8 And *Ibneiah* **Yibne Yah** the son of *Jeroham* **Yerocham**,
and Elah the son of Uzzi, the son of Michri,
and Meshullam the son of *Shephathiah* **Shaphat Yah**,
the son of *Reuel* **Reu El**, the son of *Ibnijah* **Yibni Yah**;
9 And their brethren, according to their generations,
nine hundred and fifty and six.
All these men were *chief* **head** of the fathers
in the house of their fathers.

GENEALOGY OF THE PRIESTS

10 And of the priests;
Jedaiah **Yeda Yah**,
and *Jehoiarib* **Yah Arib**, and *Jachin* **Yachin**,
11 And *Azariah* **Azar Yah** the son of *Hilkiah* **Hilqi Yah**,
the son of Meshullam, the son of *Zadok* **Sadoq**,
the son of *Meraioth* **Merayoth**,
the son of *Ahitub* **Achiy Tub**,
the ruler **eminent** of the house of *God* **Elohim**;
12 And *Adaiah* **Ada Yah** the son of *Jeroham* **Yerocham**,
the son of *Pashur* **Pashchur**,
the son of *Malchijah* **Malki Yah**,
and *Maasiai* **Masay** the son of *Adiel* **Adi El**,
the son of *Jahzerah* **Yachzerah**, the son of Meshullam,
the son of Meshillemith, the son of Immer;
13 And their brethren, heads of the house of their fathers,
a thousand and seven hundred and *threescore* **sixty**;
very able men **mighty of valour**
for the work of the service of the house of *God* **Elohim**.

GENEALOGY OF THE LEVIYM

14 And of the *Levites* **Leviym**;
Shemaiah **Shema Yah** the son of *Hasshub* **Hashshub**,
the son of *Azrikam* **Ezri Qam**,
the son of *Hashabiah* **Hashab Yah**, of the sons of Merari;
15 And *Bakbakkar* **Baqbaqqar**, Heresh, and Galal,
and *Mattaniah* **Mattan Yah** the son of *Micah* **Michah Yah**,
the son of Zichri, the son of Asaph;
16 And *Obadiah* **Obad Yah**
the son of *Shemaiah* **Shema Yah**,
the son of Galal, the son of *Jeduthun* **Yeduthun**,
and *Berechiah* **Berech Yah** the son of Asa,
the son of *Elkanah* **El Qanah**,
that *dwelt* **settled** in the *villages* **courts**
of the *Netophathites* **Netophathiy**.
17 And the porters *were*,
Shallum, and *Akkub* **Aqqub**,
and Talmon, and *Ahiman* **Achiy Man**,
and their brethren: Shallum was the *chief* **head**;
18 *Who hitherto waited in the king's gate eastward*
At the sovereign's portal from the rising:
they were porters in the *companies* **camps**
of the *children* **sons** of Levi.
19 And Shallum the son of *Kore* **Qore**,
the son of *Ebiasaph* **Abi Asaph**,
the son of *Korah* **Qorach** and his brethren,
of the house of his father, the *Korahites* **Qorachiy**,
were over the work of the service,
keepers **guards**
of the *gates* **thresholds** of the *tabernacle* **tent**:
and their fathers,
being over the *host* **camp** of *the LORD* **Yah Veh**,
were *keepers* **guards** of the entry.
20 And *Phinehas* **Pinechas** the son of *Eleazar* **El Azar**
was *the ruler* **eminent** over them *in time past* **formerly**,
and the LORD **Yah Veh** was with him.
21 *And Zechariah* **Zechar Yah**
the son of *Meshelemiah* **Meshelem Yah**
was porter of the *door* **opening**
of the *tabernacle* **tent** of the congregation.
22 All these which were *chosen* **purified**
to be porters in the *gates* **thresholds**
were two hundred and twelve.
These were *reckoned by their genealogy* **genealogized**
in their *villages* **courts**,
whom David and *Samuel* **Shemu El** the seer
did ordain **founded** in their *set office* **trustworthiness**.
23 So they and their *children* **sons**
had the oversight of **were over** the *gates* **portals**
of the house of *the LORD* **Yah Veh**, *namely*,
the house of the *tabernacle* **tent**, by *wards* **guards**.
24 In four *quarters* **winds** were the porters,
toward the east **from the rising**, *west* **seaward**,
north, and south.
25 And their brethren, *which were* in their *villages* **courts**,
were to come
after seven days from time to time with them.
26 For these *Levites* **Leviym**, the four *chief* **mighty** porters,
were *in their set office* **trustworthy**,
and were over the chambers and treasuries
of the house of *God* **Elohim**.
27 And they *lodged* **stayed overnight**
round about the house of *God* **Elohim**,
because the *charge* **guard** was upon them,
and the *opening* **key** thereof
every morning **by morning** pertained to them.
28 And *certain* of them
had the charge of **were over**
the *ministering vessels* **instruments of service**,
that they should bring them *in and out by tale* **by number**.
29 *Some* of them also were *appointed* **numbered**
to oversee **over** the *vessels* **instruments**,
and all the instruments of the *sanctuary* **holies**,
and the *fine* flour, and the wine, and the oil,
and the frankincense, and the spices.
30 And *some* of the sons of the priests
made **perfumed** the ointment of the spices.
31 And *Mattithiah* **Mattith Yah**, *one* of the *Levites* **Leviym**,
who was the firstborn of Shallum the *Korahite* **Qorachiy**,
had the *set office* **trustworthiness**
over the *things that were made in the pans* **griddle work**.
32 And *other* of their brethren,
of the sons of the *Kohathites* **Qehathiy**,
were over the *shewbread* **bread of arrangement**,
to prepare it every *sabbath* **shabbath**.
33 And these are the singers,
chief **head** of the fathers of the *Levites* **Leviym**,
who remaining in the chambers were *free* **liberated**:
for they were employed in that work **by** day and night.
34 These *chief* **head** fathers of the *Levites* **Leviym**
were *chief* **head** throughout their generations;
these *dwelt* **settled** at *Jerusalem* **Yeru Shalem**.

GENEALOGY OF YEI EL

35 And in *Gibeon* **Gibon**
dwelt **settled** the father of *Gibeon* **Gibon**, *Jehiel* **Yei El**,
whose *wife's* **woman's** name was Maachah:
36 And his firstborn son Abdon,
then *Zur* **Sur**, and *Kish* **Qish**,
and Baal, and Ner, and Nadab.
37 And Gedor, and *Ahio* **Achyo**,
and *Zechariah* **Zechar Yah**, and *Mikloth* **Miqloth**.
38 And *Mikloth* **Miqloth** begat *Shimeam* **Shimam**.
And they also *dwelt* **settled** with their brethren
at *Jerusalem* **Yeru Shalem**, over against their brethren.
39 And Ner begat *Kish* **Qish**;
and *Kish* **Qish** begat *Saul* **Shaul**;
and *Saul* **Shaul** begat *Jonathan* **Yah Nathan**,
and *Malchishua* **Malki Shua**,
and *Abinadab* **Abi Nadab**, and *Eshbaal* **Esh Baal**.
40 And the son of *Jonathan* **Yah Nathan**,
was Meribbaal **Meri Baal**:
and *Meribbaal* **Meri Baal** begat *Micah* **Michah Yah**.
41 And the sons of *Micah* **Michah Yah** *were*,
Pithon, and Melech,
and *Tahrea* **Tachrea**, *and Ahaz*.
42 And *Ahaz***Achaz** begat *Jarah* **Yarah**;
and *Jarah* **Yarah** begat Alemeth, and Azmaveth, and Zimri;
and Zimri begat *Moza* **Mosa**;
43 And *Moza* **Mosa** begat *Binea* **Bina**;
and *Rephaiah* **Repha Yah** his son,
Eleasah **El Asah** his son, Azel his son.
44 And Azel had six sons, whose names are these,
Azrikam **Ezri Qam**, Bocheru,
and *Ishmael* **Yishma El**, and *Sheariah* **Shear Yah**,
and *Obadiah* **Obad Yah**, and Hanan:
these were the sons of Azel.

THE DEATH OF SHAUL

10 Now the *Philistines* **Peleshethiy**
fought against *Israel* **Yisra El**;
and the men of *Israel* **Yisra El**
fled from *before* **the face of** the *Philistines* **Peleshethiy**,
and fell down *slain* **pierced** in mount Gilboa.
2 And the *Philistines* **Peleshethiy**

followed hard **adhered** after *Saul* **Shaul**, and after his sons;
and the *Philistines* **Peleshethiy**
slew Jonathan **smote Yah Nathan**,
and *Abinadab* **Abi Nadab**, and *Malchishua* **Malki Shua**,
the sons of *Saul* **Shaul**.
And the *battle went sore* **war was heavy**
against *Saul* **Shaul**,
and the *archers hit* **bowmen found** him,
and he was *wounded* **writhed** of the archers.
4 Then said *Saul* **Shaul**
to his *armourbearer* **instrument bearer**,
Draw thy sword, and *thrust me through* **stab me** therewith;
lest these uncircumcised come and *abuse* **exploit** me.
But his *armourbearer would* **instrument bearer willed** not;
for he was *sore afraid* **mighty awed**.
So *Saul* **Shaul** took a sword, and fell upon it.
5 And when his *armourbearer* **instrument bearer**
saw that *Saul was dead* **Shaul died**,
he fell likewise on the sword, and died.
6 So *Saul* **Shaul** died, and his three sons,
and all his house died together.
7 And when all the men of *Israel* **Yisra El**
that were in the valley saw that they fled,
and that *Saul* **Shaul** and his sons *were dead* **had died**,
then they forsook their cities, and fled:
and the *Philistines* **Peleshethiy** came
and *dwelt* **settled** in them.
8 And it *came to pass* **became**, on the morrow,
when the *Philistines* **Peleshethiy**
came to strip the *slain* **pierced**,
that they found *Saul* **Shaul** and his sons
fallen in mount Gilboa.
9 And when they had stripped him,
they *took* **lifted** his head, and his *armour* **instruments**,
and sent into the land of the *Philistines* **Peleshethiy**
round about,
to *carry tidings* **evangelize** unto their idols,
and to the people.
10 And they *put* **set** his *armour* **instruments**
in the house of their *gods* **elohim**,
and *fastened* **staked** his *head* **cranium**
in the *temple* **house** of Dagon.
11 And when all *Jabeshgilead* **Yabesh Gilad**
heard all that the *Philistines* **Peleshethiy**
had *done* **worked** to *Saul* **Shaul**,
12 They arose, all the valiant men,
and *took away* **lifted** the *body* **carcase** of *Saul* **Shaul**,
and the *bodies* **carcases** of his sons,
and brought them to *Jabesh* **Yabesh**,
and *buried* **entombed** their bones
under the oak in *Jabesh* **Yabesh**,
and fasted seven days.
13 So *Saul* **Shaul** died for his *transgression* **treason**
which he *committed* **treasoned**
against *the LORD* **Yah Veh**,
even against the word of *the LORD* **Yah Veh**,
which he *kept* **guarded** not, and also for asking *counsel*
of *one that had a familiar spirit* **a necromancer**,
to enquire of it;
14 And enquired not of *the LORD* **Yah Veh**:
therefore he *slew* **deathified** him,
and turned the *kingdom* **sovereigndom** unto David
the son of *Jesse* **Yishay**.

DAVID REIGNS OVER YISRA EL

11 Then all *Israel* **Yisra El**
gathered *themselves* to David unto Hebron, saying,
Behold, *we are* thy bone and thy flesh.
2 *And moreover in time past* **Also three yesters ago**,
even when *Saul* **Shaul** was *king* **sovereign**,
thou wast he
that leddest out and broughtest in *Israel* **Yisra El**:
and *the LORD* **Yah Veh** thy *God* **Elohim** said unto thee,
Thou shalt *feed* **tend** my people *Israel* **Yisra El**,
and thou shalt be *ruler* **eminent**
over my people *Israel* **Yisra El**.
3 Therefore came all the elders of *Israel* **Yisra El**
to the *king* **sovereign** to Hebron;
and David *made* **cut** a covenant with them in Hebron
before the LORD **at the face of Yah Veh**;
and they anointed David
king **sovereign** over *Israel* **Yisra El**,
according to the word of *the LORD* **Yah Veh**
by *Samuel* **the hand of Shemu El**.
4 And David and all *Israel* **Yisra El**
went to *Jerusalem* **Yeru Shalem**, which is *Jebus* **Yebus**;
where the *Jebusites* **Yebusiy** were,
the *inhabitants* **settlers** of the land.
5 And the *inhabitants* **settlers** of *Jebus* **Yebus** said to David,
Thou shalt not come hither.
Nevertheless
David *took* **captured** the *castle* **net** of *Zion* **Siyon**,
which is the city of David.
6 And David said,
Whosoever smiteth the *Jebusites* **Yebusiy** first
shall be *chief* **head** and *captain* **governor**.
So *Joab* **Yah Ab** the son of *Zeruiah* **Seruyah**
went **ascended** first *up*, and was *chief* **head**.
7 And David *dwelt* **settled** in the *castle* **hunthold**;
therefore they called it the city of David.
8 And he built the city round about,
even from Millo round about:
and *Joab repaired* **Yah Ab enlivened**
the *rest* **survivors** of the city.
9 *So* **In walking,** David *waxed* **walked** greater and greater:
for *the LORD of hosts* **Yah Veh Sabaoth** was with him.

THE HEADS OF THE MIGHTY OF DAVID

10 These also are the *chief* **head**
of the mighty *men* whom David had,
who strengthened themselves with him
in his *kingdom* **sovereigndom**, and with all *Israel* **Yisra El**,
to *make* **have** him *king* **reign**,
according to the word of *the LORD* **Yah Veh**
concerning *Israel* **Yisra El**.
11 And this is the number of the mighty *men*
whom David had;
Jashobeam **Yashob Am**,
an Hachmonite **a son of the Hachmoniy**,
the *chief* **head** of the *captains* **tertiaries**:
he *lifted up* **wakened** his spear against three hundred
slain **pierced** *by him* at one time.
12 And after him was *Eleazar* **El Azar** the son of Dodo,
the *Ahohite* **Ach Oachiy**,
who was one of the three *mighties* **mighty**.
13 He was with David at *Pasdammim* **Pas Dammin**,
and there the *Philistines* **Peleshethiy**
were gathered *together* to *battle* **war**,
where was
a parcel **an allotment** of *ground* **field** full of barley;
and the people fled
from *before* **the face of** the *Philistines* **Peleshethiy**.
14 And they set themselves
in the midst of that *parcel* **allotment**,
and *delivered* **rescued** it,
and slew the *Philistines* **Peleshethiy**;
and *the LORD* **Yah Veh** saved them
by a great *deliverance* **salvation**.
15 Now three of the thirty *captains* **heads**
went down **descended** to the rock to David,
into the cave of Adullam;
and the *host* **camp** of the *Philistines* **Peleshethiy**
encamped in the valley of Rephaim.
16 And David was then in the hold,
and the *Philistines' garrison* **Peleshethiy station**
was then at *Bethlehem* **Beth Lechem**.
17 And David *longed* **desired**, and said,
Oh that one *would* give me drink of the water
of the well of *Bethlehem* **Beth Lechem**,
that is at the *gate* **portal**!
18 And the three *brake* **split** through the *host* **camp**
of the *Philistines* **Peleshethiy**,
and *drew* **bailed** water
out of the well of *Bethlehem* **Beth Lechem**,
that was by the *gate* **portal**,
and *took* **lifted** *it*, and brought *it* to David:
but David *would* **willed to** not drink of it,
but poured it out to *the LORD* **Yah Veh**.
19 And said, My *God* **Elohim**, *forbid it* **far be it from** me,
that I should *do* **work** this *thing*:
shall I drink the blood of these men
that have put their lives in jeopardy **with their souls**?

for with *the jeopardy of their lives* **their souls**
they brought it.
Therefore he *would* **willed to** not drink it.
These *things did* **worked** these three *mightiest* **mighty**.
20 And *Abishai* **Abi Shai** the brother of *Joab* **Yah Ab**,
he was *chief* **head** of the three:
for *lifting up* **wakening** his spear against three hundred,
he *slew* **pierced** them, and had a name among the three.
21 Of the three, he was more honourable than the two;
for he was their *captain* **governor**:
howbeit he attained not to the *first* three.
22 *Benaiah* **Bena Yah** the son of *Jehoiada* **Yah Yada**,
the son of a valiant man of *Kabzeel* **Qabse El**,
who had done many acts — **great of deeds**;
he *slew* **smote** two *lionlike men* **Ariel** of Moab:
also he *went down* **descended** and *slew* **smote** a lion
in a *pit* **well** in a *snowy* day **of snow**.
23 And he *slew an Egyptian* **smote a man — a Misrayim**,
a man of *great stature* **measure**, five cubits high;
and in the *Egyptian's* **Misrayim's** hand
was a spear like a weaver's beam;
and he *went down* **descended** to him with a *staff* **scion**,
and *plucked* **stripped** the spear
out of the *Egyptian's* **Misrayim's** hand,
and *slew* **slaughtered** him with his own spear.
24 These *things did Benaiah* **worked Bena Yah**
the son of *Jehoiada* **Yah Yada**,
and had the name among the three *mighties* **mighty**.
25 Behold, he was honourable among the thirty,
but attained not to the *first* three:
and David set him over his guard.
26 Also the *valiant men of the armies* **mighty of valour** *were*,
Asahel **Asa El** the brother of *Joab* **Yah Ab**,
Elhanan **El Hanan** the son of Dodo
of *Bethlehem* **Beth Lechem**,
27 Shammoth the *Harorite* **Haroriy**,
Helez **Heles** the *Pelonite* **Paloniy**,
28 Ira the son of *Ikkesh* **Iqqesh** the *Tekoite* **Teqohiy**,
Abiezer **Abi Ezer** the *Antothite* **Anathothiy**,
29 *Sibbecai* **Sibbechay** the *Hushathite* **Hushathiy**,
Ilai **Ilay** the *Ahohite* **Ach Oachiy**,
30 *Maharai* **Maharay** the *Netophathite* **Netophathiy**,
Heled the son of Baanah the *Netophathite* **Netophathiy**,
31 *Ithai* **Ittay** the son of *Ribai* **Ribay** of *Gibeah* **Gibah**,
that pertained to the children **of the sons**
of *Benjamin* **Ben Yamin**,
Benaiah **Bena Yah** the *Pirathonite* **Pirathoniy**,
32 Hurai of the *brooks* **wadies** of Gaash,
Abiel **Abi El** the *Arbathite* **Arabahiy**,
33 Azmaveth the *Baharumite* **Bachurimiy**,
Eliahba **El Yachba** the *Shaalbonite* **Shaalbimiy**,
34 The sons of Hashem the *Gizonite* **Gizohiy**,
Jonathan **Yah Nathan**
the son of Shage the *Hararite* **Harariy**,
35 *Ahiam* **Achiy Am**
the son of *Sacar* **Sachar** the *Hararite* **Harariy**,
Eliphal **Eli Phal** the son of Ur,
36 Hepher the *Mecherathite* **Mecherahiy**,
Ahijah **Achiy Yah** the *Pelonite* **Paloniy**,
37 *Hezro* **Hesro** the *Carmelite* **Karmeliy**,
Naarai **Naaray** the son of Ezbai,
38 *Joel* **Yah El** the brother of Nathan,
Mibhar **Mibchar** the son of *Haggeri* **Hagariy**,
39 *Zelek* **Seleq** the *Ammonite* **Ammoniy**,
Naharai **Nachray** the *Berothite* **Berothiy**,
the *armourbearer* **instrument bearer** of *Joab* **Yah Ab**
the son of *Zeruiah* **Seruyah**,
40 Ira the *Ithrite* **Yetheriy**,
Gareb the *Ithrite* **Yetheriy**,
41 *Uriah* **Uri Yah** the *Hittite* **Hethiy**,
Zabad the son of *Ahlai* **Achiy Lay**,
42 Adina the son of Shiza the *Reubenite* **Reu Beniy**,
a *captain* **head** of the *Reubenites* **Reu Beniy**,
and thirty with him,
43 Hanan the son of Maachah,
and *Joshaphat* **Yah Shaphat** the *Mithnite* **Mithniy**,
44 *Uzzia* **Uzzi Yah** the *Ashterathite* **Ashtarothiy**,
Shama and *Jehiel* **Yei El**
the sons of Hothan the *Aroerite* **Aroeriy**,
45 *Jediael* **Yedia El** the son of Shimri,
and *Joha* **Yah Ha** his brother, the *Tizite* **Tisiy**,
46 *Eliel* **Eli El** the *Mahavite* **Machaviy**,
and *Jeribai* **Yeribay**, and *Joshaviah* **Yah Shavah**,
the sons of *Elnaam* **El Naam**,
and *Ithmah* **Yithmah** the *Moabite* **Moabiy**,
47 *Eliel* **Eli El**, and Obed,
and *Jasiel* **Yaasi El** the *Mesobaite* **Mesoba Yah**.

DAVID'S WARRIORS OF SIQLAG

12 Now these are they
that came to David to *Ziklag* **Siqlag**,
while he yet *kept himself close* **refrained**
because **from the face** of *Saul* **Shaul** the son of *Kish* **Qish**:
and they were among the mighty *men*, helpers of the war.
2 They were *armed* **kissed** with bows,
and could use both the right *hand* and the left
in *hurling* stones and *shooting* arrows out of a bow,
even of *Saul's* **Shaul's** brethren of *Benjamin* **Ben Yamin**.
3 The *chief* **head**
was *Ahiezer* **Achiy Ezer**, then *Joash* **Yah Ash**,
the sons of Shemaah the *Gibeathite* **Gibathiy**;
and *Jeziel* **Yezav El**, and Pelet, the sons of Azmaveth;
and Berachah,
and *Jehu* **Yah Hu** the *Antothite* **Anathothiy**.
4 And *Ismaiah* **Yishma Yah** the *Gibeonites* **Giboniy**,
a mighty *man* among the thirty, and over the thirty;
and *Jeremiah* **Yirme Yah**, and *Jahaziel* **Yachazi El**,
and *Johanan* **Yah Hanan**,
and *Josabad* **Yah Zabad** the *Gederathite* **Gederahiy**,
5 *Eluzai* **El Uzay**, and *Jerimoth* **Yerimoth**,
and *Bealiah* **Beal Yah**, and *Shemariah* **Shemar Yah**,
and *Shephatiah* **Shaphat Yah** the *Haruphite* **Haruphiy**,
6 *Elkanah* **El Qanah**, and *Jesiah* **Yishshi Yah**,
and *Azareel* **Azar El**, and *Joezer* **Yah Ezer**,
and *Jashobeam* **Yashob Am**, the *Korhites* **Qorachiy**,
7 And *Joelah* **Yoelah**, and *Zebadiah* **Zebad Yah**,
the sons of *Jeroham* **Yerocham** of Gedor.
8 And of the *Gadites* **Gadiy**
there separated themselves unto David
into the *hold* **hunthold** to the wilderness
men of might **mighty of valour**, and men of *war* **hostility**
fit for the *battle* **war**,
that could *handle* **line up** shield and *buckler* **javelin**,
whose faces were *like* the faces of lions,
and *were* as swift
as the *roes* **gazelles** upon the mountains;
9 Ezer the *first* **head**, *Obadiah* **Obad Yah** the second,
Eliab **Eli Ab** the third,
10 Mishmannah the fourth, *Jeremiah* **Yirme Yah** the fifth,
11 *Attai* **Attay** the sixth, *Eliel* **Eli El** the seventh,
12 *Johanan* **Yah Hanan** the eighth,
Elzabad **El Zabad** the ninth,
13 *Jeremiah* **Yirme Yah** the tenth,
Machbanai **Machbenaiy** the eleventh.
14 These were of the sons of Gad,
captains **heads** of the host:
one of the least was over an hundred,
and the greatest over a thousand.
15 These are they
that *went* **passed** over *Jordan* **Yarden** in the first month,
when it had *overflown* **overflowed** all his banks;
and they *put* **caused** to *flight* **flee** all them of the valleys,
both toward the east **from the rising**,
and *toward the west* **from the dusk**.
16 And there came of the *children* **sons**
of *Benjamin* **Ben Yamin** and *Judah* **Yah Hudah**
to the *hold* **hunthold** unto David.
17 And David went out *to meet them* **at their face**,
and answered and said unto them,
If ye be come *peaceably* **in shalom** unto me to help me,
mine heart shall be *knit* **altogether** unto you:
but if *ye be come* to *betray* **hurl** me
to *mine enemies* **my tribulators**,
seeing there is no *wrong* **violence**
in *mine hands* **my palms**,
the *God* **Elohim** of our fathers *look* **see** *thereon*,
and *rebuke* **reprove** it.
18 Then the spirit *came upon Amasai* **enrobed Amasay**,
who was chief **head** of the *captains* **tertiaries**, *and he said*,
Thine *are we*, David, and on thy side,
thou son of *Jesse* **Yishay**:

peace **shalom**, *peace* **shalom** be unto thee,
and *peace* **shalom** be to thine helpers;
for thy *God* **Elohim** helpeth thee.
Then David *received* **took** them,
and *made* **gave** them *captains* **heads** of the *band* **troop**.
19 And there fell
some of *Manasseh* **Menash Sheh** to David,
when he came with the *Philistines* **Peleshethiy**
against *Saul* **Shaul** to *battle* **war**:
but they helped them not:
for the *lords* **ringleaders** of the *Philistines* **Peleshethiy**
upon *advisement* **counsel** sent him away, saying,
He *will* **shall** fall to his *master Saul* **adoni Shaul**
to *the jeopardy of* our heads.
20 As he went to *Ziklag* **Siqlag**,
there fell to him of *Manasseh* **Menash Sheh**,
Adnah, and *Jozabad* **Yah Zabad**, and *Jediael* **Yedia El**,
and *Michael* **Michah El**, and *Jozabad* **Yah Zabad**,
and *Elihu* **Eli Hu**, and *Zilthai* **Sillethay**,
captains **heads** of the thousands
that were of *Manasseh* **Menash Sheh**.
21 And they helped David
against the *band* **troop** *of the rovers*:
for they were all mighty *men* of valour,
and were *captains* **governors** in the host.
22 For at that time day by day
there came to David to help him,
until it was a great *host* **camp**,
like the *host* **camp** of *God* **Elohim**.

DAVID'S WARRIORS OF THE SONS OF YISRA EL

23 And these are the numbers of the *bands* **heads**
that were ready armed **equipped** to the *war* **hostility**,
and came to David to Hebron,
to turn the *kingdom* **sovereigndom** of *Saul* **Shaul** to him,
according to the *word* **mouth** of *the LORD* **Yah Veh**.
24 The *children* **sons** of *Judah* **Yah Hudah**
that bare shield and *spear* **javelin**
were six thousand and eight hundred,
ready armed **equipped** to the *war* **hostility**.
25 Of the *children* **sons** of *Simeon* **Shimon**,
mighty *men* of valour for the *war* **hostility**,
seven thousand and one hundred.
26 Of the *children* **sons** of Levi,
four thousand and six hundred.
27 And *Jehoiada* **Yah Yada**
was *the leader* **eminent** of the *Aaronites* **Aharoniy**,
and with him were three thousand and seven hundred;
28 And *Zadok* **Sadoq**, a *young man* **lad** mighty of valour,
and of his father's house
twenty and two *captains* **governors**.
29 And of the *children* **sons** of *Benjamin* **Ben Yamin**
the *kindred* **brothers** of *Saul* **Shaul**,
three thousand:
for hitherto the *greatest part* **increase** *of them*
had *kept* **guarded** the *ward* **guard**
of the house of *Saul* **Shaul**.
30 And of the *children* **sons** of *Ephraim* **Ephrayim**
twenty thousand and eight hundred,
mighty *men* of valour,
famous **men of name** throughout the house of their fathers.
31 And of the half *tribe* **rod** of *Manasseh* **Menash Sheh**
eighteen thousand,
which were *expressed* **appointed** by name,
to come and make David *king* **reign**.
32 And of the *children* **sons** of *Issachar* **Yissachar**,
which were men
that *had understanding* **knew discernment** of the times,
to know what *Israel* **Yisra El** ought to *do* **work**;
the heads of them were two hundred;
and all their brethren were at their *commandment* **mouth**.
33 Of Zebulun, such as went forth to *battle* **hostility**,
expert in war **lined up for battle**,
with all instruments of war,
fifty thousand,
which could *keep rank* **line up for battle**:
they were not of double heart.
34 And of Naphtali a thousand *captains* **governors**,
and with them with shield and spear
thirty and seven thousand.
35 And of the *Danites* **Daniy**
expert in war **lined up in battle**
twenty and eight thousand and six hundred.
36 And of Asher, such as went forth to *battle* **hostility**,
expert in war **to line up for battle**,
forty thousand.
37 And on the other side of *Jordan* **Yarden**,
of the *Reubenites* **Reu Beniy**, and the *Gadites* **Gadiy**,
and of the half *tribe* **scion** of *Manasseh* **Menash Sheh**,
with all manner of instruments of *war* **hostility**
for the *battle* **war**,
an hundred and twenty thousand.
38 All these men of war,
that could *keep rank* **line up for battle**,
came with a *perfect heart* **heart at shalom** to Hebron,
to make David *king* **reign** over all *Israel* **Yisra El**:
and all the rest also of *Israel* **Yisra El** were of one heart
to make David *king* **reign**.
39 And there they were with David three days,
eating and drinking:
for their brethren had prepared for them.
40 Moreover they that were nigh them,
even unto *Issachar* **Yissachar** and Zebulun and Naphtali,
brought bread on *asses* **he burros**,
and on camels, and on mules, and on oxen,
and *meat* **food**, *meal* **flour**, *cakes* **lumps** of figs,
and *bunches of raisins* **raisincakes**, and wine, and oil,
and oxen, and *sheep abundantly* **flocks in abundance**:
for there was *joy* **cheer** in *Israel* **Yisra El**.

THE RETURN OF THE ARK

13 And David *consulted* **counselled**
with the *captains* **governors** of thousands and hundreds,
and with every *leader* **eminence**.
2 And David said
unto all the congregation of *Israel* **Yisra El**,
If it *seem* **be** good unto you,
and that it be of *the LORD* **Yah Veh** our *God* **Elohim**,
let us send *abroad* **and break forth**
unto our brethren every where,
that *are left* **survive** in all the land of *Israel* **Yisra El**,
and with them *also* to the priests and *Levites* **Leviym**
which are in their cities and suburbs,
that they may gather themselves unto us:
3 And let us *bring again* **return**
the ark of our *God* **Elohim** to us:
for we enquired not at it in the days of *Saul* **Shaul**.
4 And all the congregation
said that they *would* **should** *do* **work** so:
for the *thing* **word** was *right* **straight**
in the eyes of all the people.
5 So David *gathered* **congregated**
all *Israel* **Yisra El** *together*,
from *Shihor* **Shichor** of *Egypt* **Misrayim**
even unto the entering of *Hemath* **Hamath**,
to bring the ark of *God* **Elohim**
from *Kirjathjearim* **Qiryath Arim**.
6 And David *went up* **ascended**, and all *Israel* **Yisra El**,
to *Baalah* **Baal Ah**, *that is*, to *Kirjathjearim* **Qiryath Arim**,
which *belonged* **be** to *Judah* **Yah Hudah**,
to *bring up* **ascend** thence
the ark of *God the LORD* **Elohim Yah Veh**,
that *dwelleth* **settleth** between the *cherubims* **cherubim**,
whose name is called on it.
7 And they *carried* **rode** the ark of *God* **Elohim**
in a new *cart* **wagon**
out of the house of *Abinadab* **Abi Nadab**:
and Uzza and *Ahio* **Achyo** drave the *cart* **wagon**.
8 And David and all *Israel* **Yisra El**
played before God **entertained at the face of Elohim**
with all their *might* **strength**, and with *singing* **songs**,
and with harps, and with *psalteries* **bagpipes**,
and with *timbrels* **tambourines**, and with cymbals,
and with trumpets.
9 And when they came
unto the threshingfloor of *Chidon* **Kidon**,
Uzza *put* **sent** *forth* his hand to hold the ark;
for the oxen *stumbled* **released it**.
10 And the *anger* **wrath** of *the LORD* **Yah Veh**
was kindled against Uzza, and he smote him,
because he *put* **extended** his hand to the ark:
and there he died *before God* **at the face of Elohim**.

11 And David was *displeased* **inflamed**,
because *the LORD* **Yah Veh**
had *made* **breached** a breach upon Uzza:
wherefore that place is called *Perezuzza* **Peres Uzza**
to this day.
12 And David *was afraid* **awed** of *God* **Elohim** that day,
saying,
How shall I bring the ark of *God* **Elohim** *home* to me?
13 So David *brought* **returned** not the ark *home* to himself
to the city of David,
but *carried it aside* **extended it** into the house
of *Obededom* **Obed Edom** the *Gittite* **Gittiy**.
14 And the ark of *God remained* **Elohim settled**
with the *family* **house** of *Obededom* **Obed Edom**
in his house three months.
And *the LORD* **Yah Veh**
blessed the house of *Obededom* **Obed Edom**,
and all that he had.

THE GENEALOGY OF DAVID'S EXPANDED FAMILY

14 Now Hiram *king* **sovereign** of *Tyre* **Sor**
sent *messengers* **angels** to David, and timber of cedars,
with *masons* **artificers of walls**
and *carpenters* **artificers of timber**,
to build him an house.
2 And David perceived
that *the LORD* **Yah Veh** had *confirmed* **established** him
king **sovereign** over *Israel* **Yisra El**,
for his *kingdom* **sovereigndom**
was lifted up *on high* **above**,
because of his people *Israel* **Yisra El**.
3 And David took more *wives* **women**
at *Jerusalem* **Yeru Shalem**:
and David begat more sons and daughters.
4 Now these are the names of his *children* **begotten**
which he had in *Jerusalem* **Yeru Shalem**;
Shammua, and Shobab,
Nathan, and *Solomon* **Shelomoh**,
5 And *Ibhar* **Yibchar**, and *Elishua* **Eli Shua**,
and *Elpalet* **Eli Phelet**,
6 And Nogah, and Nepheg, and *Japhia* **Yaphia**,
7 And *Elishama* **Eli Shama**,
and *Beeliada* **Baal Yada**, and *Eliphalet* **Eli Phelet**.

DAVID DEFEATS THE PELESHETHIY

8 And when the *Philistines* **Peleshethiy**
heard that David was anointed
king **sovereign** over all *Israel* **Yisra El**,
all the *Philistines* **Peleshethiy**
went up **ascended** to seek David.
And David heard of it,
and went out *against them* **at their face**.
9 And the *Philistines* **Peleshethiy** came
and spread themselves in the valley of Rephaim.
10 And David *enquired* **asked** of *God* **Elohim**, saying,
shall I *go up* **ascend** against the *Philistines* **Peleshethiy**?
And *wilt* **shalt** thou *deliver* **give** them into mine hand?
And *the LORD* **Yah Veh** said unto him, *Go up* **Ascend**;
for I *will deliver* **shall give** them into thine hand.
11 So they *came up* **ascended**
to *Baalperazim* **Baal Perasim**;
and David smote them there.
Then David said,
God **Elohim** hath *broken in* **breached** upon mine enemies
by mine hand like the breaking forth of waters:
therefore they called the name of that place
Baalperazim **Baal Perasim**.
12 And when they had left their *gods* **elohim** there,
David *gave a commandment* **said**,
and they were burned with fire.
13 And the *Philistines yet again* **Peleshethiy added yet**
to spread themselves *abroad* **out** in the valley.
14 Therefore David *enquired* **asked** again of *God* **Elohim**;
and *God* **Elohim** said unto him,
Go **Ascend** not *up* after them;
turn away from them, and come upon them
over against **opposite** the *mulberry trees* **weepers**.
15 And it shall be,
when thou shalt hear a *sound* **voice** of *going* **marching**
in the tops of the *mulberry trees* **weepers**,
that then thou shalt go out to *battle* **war**:
for *God* **Elohim** is gone forth *before thee* **at thy face**
to smite the *host* **camp** of the *Philistines* **Peleshethiy**.
16 David *therefore did* **worked**
as *God commanded* **Elohim misvahed** him:
and they smote
the *host* **camp** of the *Philistines* **Peleshethiy**
from *Gibeon* **Gibon** even to *Gazer* **Gezer**.
17 And the fame of David went out into all lands;
and *the LORD brought* **Yah Veh gave** the fear of him
upon all *nations* **goyim**.

THE ARK IN YERU SHALEM

15 And *David made* **he worked** him houses
in the city of David,
and prepared a place for the ark of *God* **Elohim**,
and *pitched* **stretched** for it a tent.
2 Then David said,
None ought to *carry* **lift** the ark of *God* **Elohim**
but the *Levites* **Leviym**:
for them hath *the LORD* **Yah Veh** chosen
to *carry* **lift** the ark of *God* **Elohim**,
and to minister unto him *for ever* **eternally**.
3 And David
gathered **congregated** all *Israel* **Yisra El** *together*
to *Jerusalem* **Yeru Shalem**,
to *bring up* **ascend** the ark of *the LORD* **Yah Veh**
unto his place,
which he had prepared for it.
4 And David *assembled* **gathered** the *children* **sons**
of *Aaron* **Aharon**, and the *Levites* **Leviym**:
5 Of the sons of *Kohath* **Qehath**;
Uriel **Uri El** the *chief* **governor**,
and his brethren an hundred and twenty:
6 Of the sons of Merari;
Asaiah **Asah Yah** the *chief* **governor**,
and his brethren two hundred and twenty:
7 Of the sons of Gershom;
Joel **Yah El** the *chief* **governor**,
and his brethren an hundred and thirty:
8 Of the sons of *Elizaphan* **El Saphan**;
Shemaiah **Shema Yah** the *chief* **governor**,
and his brethren two hundred:
9 Of the sons of Hebron;
Eliel **Eli El** the *chief* **governor**,
and his brethren *fourscore* **eighty**:
10 Of the sons of *Uzziel* **Uzzi El**;
Amminadab **Ammi Nadab** the *chief* **governor**,
and his brethren an hundred and twelve.
11 And David called for *Zadok* **Sadoq**
and *Abiathar* **Abi Athar** the priests,
and for the *Levites* **Leviym**,
for *Uriel* **Uri El**, *Asaiah* **Asah Yah**, and *Joel* **Yah El**,
Shemaiah **Shema Yah**, and *Eliel* **Eli El**,
and *Amminadab* **Ammi Nadab**,
12 And said unto them,
ye are the *chief* **head** of the fathers of the *Levites* **Leviym**:
sanctify **hallow** yourselves, *both* ye and your brethren,
that ye may *bring* **ascend** *up* the ark
of *the LORD God* **Yah Veh Elohim** of *Israel* **Yisra El**
unto the place that I have prepared for it.
13 For because ye did it not at the first,
the LORD **Yah Veh** our *God* **Elohim**
made **breached** a breach upon us,
for that we sought him not after the *due order* **judgment**.
14 So the priests and the *Levites* **Leviym**
sanctified **hallowed** themselves
to *bring up* **ascend** the ark
of *the LORD God* **Yah Veh Elohim** of *Israel* **Yisra El**.
15 And the *children* **sons** of the *Levites* **Leviym**
bare the ark of *God* **Elohim**
upon their shoulders with the *staves* **yoke poles** *thereon*,
as *Moses commanded* **Mosheh misvahed**
according to the word of *the LORD* **Yah Veh**.
16 And David
spake **said** to the *chief* **governor** of the *Levites* **Leviym**
to *appoint* **stand** their brethren
to be the singers with instruments of *musick* **song**,
psalteries **bagpipes** and harps and cymbals,
sounding **heard**, by lifting up the voice with *joy* **cheer**.
17 So the *Levites* **Leviym**
appointed **stood** Heman the son of *Joel* **Yah El**;
and of his brethren,

Asaph the son of *Berechiah* **Berech Yah**;
and of the sons of Merari their brethren,
Ethan the son of *Kushaiah* **Qusha Yah**;
18 And with them their brethren of the second *degree*,
Zechariah **Zechar Yah**, Ben, and *Jaaziel* **Yaazi El**,
and *Shemiramoth* **Shemi Ramoth**, and *Jehiel* **Yechi El**,
and Unni, *Eliab* **Eli Ab**, and *Benaiah* **Bena Yah**,
and *Maaseiah* **Maase Yah**, and *Mattithiah* **Mattith Yah**,
and *Elipheleh* **Eli Phelehu**, and *Mikneiah* **Miqne Yah**,
and *Obededom* **Obed Edom**, and *Jehiel* **Yei El**, the porters.
19 So the singers, Heman, Asaph, and Ethan,
were *appointed to sound* **heard**
with cymbals of *brass* **copper**;
20 And *Zechariah* **Zechar Yah**, and *Aziel* **Azi El**,
and *Shemiramoth* **Shemi Ramoth**, and *Jehiel* **Yechi El**,
and Unni, and *Eliab* **Eli Ab**,
and *Maaseiah* **Maase Yah**, and *Benaiah* **Bena Yah**,
with *psalteries on Alamoth* **bagpipes besides virgins**;
21 And *Mattithiah* **Mattith Yah**, and *Elipheleh* **Eli Phelehu**,
and *Mikneiah* **Miqne Yah**, and *Obededom* **Obed Edom**,
and *Jeiel* **Yei El**, and *Azaziah* **Azaz Yah**,
with harps on the *Sheminith* **octave** to *excel* **oversee**.
22 And *Chenaniah* **Kenan Yah**,
chief **governor** of the *Levites* **Leviym**,
was for *song* **burden**:
he *instructed* **disciplined** about the *song* **burden**,
because he was *skilful* **discerning**.
23 And *Berechiah* **Berech Yah** and *Elkanah* **El Qanah**
were *doorkeepers* **porters** for the ark.
24 And *Shebaniah* **Sheban Yah**,
and *Jehoshaphat* **Yah Shaphat**,
and *Nethaneel* **Nethan El**, and *Amasai* **Amasay**,
and *Zechariah* **Zechar Yah**, and *Benaiah* **Bena Yah**,
and *Eliezer* **Eli Ezer**, the priests,
did blow with **trumpeted** the trumpets
before **at the face of** the ark of *God* **Elohim**:
and *Obededom* **Obed Edom** and *Jehiah* **Yechi Yah**
were *doorkeepers* **porters** for the ark.
25 So David, and the elders of *Israel* **Yisra El**,
and the *captains* **governors** over thousands,
went to *bring* **ascend** *up*
the ark of the covenant of *the LORD* **Yah Veh**
out of the house of *Obededom* **Obed Edom**
with *joy* **cheer**.
26 And it *came to pass* **became**,
when *God* **Elohim** helped the *Levites* **Leviym**
that bare the ark of the covenant of *the LORD* **Yah Veh**,
that they *offered* **sacrificed**
seven bullocks and seven rams.
27 And David was *clothed* **cloaked**
with a *robe* **mantle** of *fine* **bleached** linin,
and all the *Levites* **Leviym** that bare the ark,
and the singers,
and *Chenaniah* **Kenan Yah**
the *master* **governor** of the *song* **burden** with the singers:
David also had upon him an ephod of linen.
28 Thus all *Israel brought up* **Yisra El ascended** the ark
of the covenant of *the LORD* **Yah Veh** with shouting,
and with *sound* **voice** of the *cornet* **trumpet**,
and with trumpets, and with cymbals,
making a noise **heard** with *psalteries* **bagpipes** and harps.

DAVID'S CELEBRATION

29 And it *came to pass* **became**,
as the ark of the covenant of *the LORD* **Yah Veh**
came to the city of David,
that Michal, the daughter of *Saul* **Shaul**
looking out at a window saw *king* **sovereign** David
dancing and *playing* **entertaining**:
and she despised him in her heart.
16 So they brought the ark of *God* **Elohim**,
and set it in the midst of the tent
that David had *pitched* **stretched** for it:
and they *offered burnt sacrifices* **oblated holocausts**
and *peace offerings* **shelamim**
before God **at the face of Elohim**.
2 And when David had *made an end* **finished**
of offering **holocausting** the *burnt offerings* **holocausts**
and the *peace offerings* **shelamim**,
he blessed the people in the name of *the LORD* **Yah Veh**.
3 And he *dealt* **allotted** to every *one* **man** of *Israel* **Yisra El**,
both man and woman,
to every *one* **man** a *loaf* **round** of bread,
and a *good piece of flesh* **portion**,
and a *flagon* **cake** *of wine*.
4 And he *appointed* **gave**
certain of the *Levites* **Leviym** to minister
before **at the face of** the ark of *the LORD* **Yah Veh**,
and to *record* **memorialize**, and to *thank* **extend hands**
and *praise* **halal**
the LORD God **Yah Veh Elohim** of *Israel* **Yisra El**:
5 Asaph the *chief* **head**,
and *next to him Zechariah* **second Zechar Yah**,
Jeiel **Yei El**, and *Shemiramoth* **Shemi Ramoth**,
and *Jehiel* **Yechi El**, and *Mattithiah* **Mattith Yah**,
and *Eliab* **Eli Ab**, and *Benaiah* **Bena Yah**,
and *Obededom* **Obed Edom**:
and *Jeiel* **Yei El**
with *psalteries* **instruments of bagpipes** and with harps;
but Asaph *made a sound* **was heard** with cymbals;
6 *Benaiah* **Bena Yah** also
and *Jahaziel* **Yachazi El** the priests
with trumpets continually
before **at the face**
of the ark of the covenant of *God* **Elohim**.

DAVID'S EXTENDING OF HANDS

7 Then on that day
David *delivered first this psalm* **gave at the beginning**
to *thank the LORD* **extend hands to Yah Veh**
into the hand of Asaph and his brethren.
8 *Give thanks* **Extend hands** unto *the LORD* **Yah Veh**,
call upon his name,
make known his *deeds* **exploits** among the people.
9 Sing unto him, sing psalms unto him,
talk **meditate** ye of all his *wondrous* **marvellous** works.
10 *Glory* **Halal** ye in his holy name:
let the heart of them *rejoice* **cheer**
that seek *the LORD* **Yah Veh**.
11 Seek *the LORD* **Yah Veh** and his strength,
seek his face continually.
12 Remember his marvellous works
that he hath *done* **worked**,
his *wonders* **omens**, and the judgments of his mouth;
13 O ye seed of *Israel* **Yisra El** his servant,
ye *children* **sons** of *Jacob* **Yaaqov**, his chosen ones.
14 He is *the LORD* **Yah Veh** our *God* **Elohim**;
his judgments are in all the earth.
15 *Be ye mindful always of* **Remember eternally**
his covenant;
the word which he *commanded* **misvahed**
to a thousand generations;
16 *Even of the covenant*
which he *made* **cut** with Abraham,
and of his oath unto *Isaac* **Yischaq**;
17 And hath *confirmed the same* **stood** to *Jacob* **Yaaqov**
for a *law* **statute**,
and to Israel **Yisra El** for an *everlasting* **eternal** covenant,
18 Saying,
Unto thee *will* **shall** I give the land of *Canaan* **Kenaan**,
the *lot* **cords** of your inheritance;
19 When ye were but *few* **men of number**,
even a few, and *strangers* **sojourners** in it.
20 And *when* they went
from *nation* **goyim** to *nation* **goyim**,
and from *one kingdom* **sovereigndom** to another people;
21 He *suffered* **allowed** no man to *do* **oppress** them *wrong*:
yea, he reproved *kings* **sovereigns** for their sakes,
22 *Saying*, Touch not mine anointed,
and do **nor vilify** my prophets *no harm*.
23 Sing unto *the LORD* **Yah Veh**, all the earth;
shew forth **evangelize** from day to day his salvation.
24 *Declare* **Scribe** his *glory* **honour**
among the *heathen* **goyim**;
his marvellous works among all nations.
25 For great is *the LORD* **Yah Veh**,
and *greatly* **mighty** to be *praised* **halaled**:
he also is to be *feared* **awed** above all *gods* **elohim**.
26 For all the *gods* **elohim** of the people are idols:
but *the LORD made* **Yah Veh worked** the heavens.
27 *Glory* **Grandeur** and *honour* **majesty**
are *in* **at** his *presence* **face**;

strength and *gladness* **rejoicing**
are in his place.
28 Give unto *the LORD* **Yah Veh**,
ye *kindreds* **families** of the people,
give unto *the LORD* **Yah Veh**
glory **honour** and strength.
29 Give unto *the LORD* **Yah Veh**
the *glory* **honour** *due* unto his name:
bring **lift** an offering,
and come *before him* **at his face**:
worship the LORD **prostrate to Yah Veh**
in the *beauty* **majesty** of holiness.
30 *Fear before* **Whirl at the face of** him, all the earth:
the world also shall be *stable* **established**,
that it be not *moved* **toppled**.
31 Let the heavens *be glad* **cheer**,
and let the earth *rejoice* **twirl**:
and let men say among the *nations* **goyim**,
The LORD **Yah Veh** reigneth.
32 Let the sea *roar* **thunder**, and the fulness thereof:
let the fields *rejoice* **jump for joy**, and all that is therein.
33 Then shall the trees of the *wood sing out* **forest shout**
at the *presence* **face** of *the LORD* **Yah Veh**,
because he cometh to judge the earth.
34 *O give thanks* **Extend hands** unto *the LORD* **Yah Veh**;
for he is good;
for his *mercy endureth for ever* **eternal mercy**.
35 And say ye, Save us,
O *God* **Elohim** of our salvation,
and gather us *together*,
and *deliver* **rescue** us from the *heathen* **goyim**,
that we may *give thanks* **extend hands** to thy holy name,
and *glory* **laud** in thy *praise* **halal**.
36 Blessed
be *the LORD God* **Yah Veh Elohim** of *Israel* **Yisra El**
for ever **eternally** and *ever* **eternally**.
And all the people said, Amen,
and *praised the LORD* **halaled Yah Veh**.
37 So he left there *before* **at the face**
of the ark of the covenant of *the LORD* **Yah Veh**
Asaph and his brethren,
to minister *before* **at the face of** the ark continually,
as every day's work required **the day by day word**:
38 And *Obededom* **Obed Edom** with their brethren,
threescore **sixty** and eight;
Obededom **Obed Edom** also
the son of *Jeduthun* **Yeduthun** and Hosah
to be porters:
39 And *Zadok* **Sadoq** the priest,
and his brethren the priests,
before **at the face**
of the tabernacle of *the LORD* **Yah Veh**
in the *high place* **bamah** that was at *Gibeon* **Gibon**,
40 To *offer burnt offerings* **holocaust holocausts**
unto *the LORD* **Yah Veh**
upon the **sacrifice** altar of the *burnt offering* **holocaust**
continually morning and evening,
and to do according to all that is *written* **inscribed**
in the *law* **torah** of *the LORD* **Yah Veh**,
which he *commanded Israel* **misvahed Yisra El**;
41 And with them Heman and *Jeduthun* **Yeduthun**,
and the *rest* **survivors** that were *chosen* **purified**,
who were *expressed* **appointed** by name
to *give thanks* **extend hands** to *the LORD* **Yah Veh**,
because his mercy endureth for ever **for his eternal mercy**;
42 And with them Heman and *Jeduthun* **Yeduthun**
with trumpets and cymbals
for those that should *make a sound* **be heard**,
and with *musical instruments* **instruments of song**
of *God* **Elohim**.
And the sons of *Jeduthun* **Yeduthun**
were *porters* **for the portal**.
43 And all the people *departed* **went** *every man*
to his house:
and David returned to bless his house.

DAVID'S SON TO BUILD THE HOUSE OF YAH VEH

17 Now it *came to pass* **became**,
as David *sat* **settled** in his house,
that David said to Nathan the prophet,
Lo **Behold**, I *dwell* **settle** in an house of cedars,
but the ark of the covenant of *the LORD* **Yah Veh**
remaineth **be** under curtains.
2 Then Nathan said unto David,
Do **Work** all that is in thine heart;
for *God* **Elohim** is with thee.
3 And it *came to pass* **became**, the same night,
that the word of *God* **Elohim** came to Nathan, saying,
4 Go and *tell* **say to** David my servant,
Thus saith *the LORD* **Yah Veh**,
Thou shalt not build me an house to *dwell* **settle** in:
5 For I have not *dwelt* **settled** in an house
since the day that I *brought up Israel* **ascended Yisra El**
unto this day;
but have gone from tent to tent,
and from *one* tabernacle *to another*.
6 Wheresoever I have walked with all *Israel* **Yisra El**,
spake **worded** I a word
to *any* **one** of the judges of *Israel* **Yisra El**,
whom I *commanded* **misvahed** to *feed* **tend** my people,
saying, Why have ye not built me an house of cedars?
7 Now therefore thus shalt thou say
unto my servant David,
Thus saith *the LORD of hosts* **Yah Veh Sabaoth**,
I took thee from the *sheepcote* **habitation of rest**,
even from *following* **after** the *sheep* **flock**,
that thou shouldest be *ruler* **eminent**
over my people *Israel* **Yisra El**:
8 And I have been with thee
whithersoever thou hast walked,
and have cut off all thine enemies
from *before thee* **thy face**,
and have *made* **worked** thee a name
like the name of the great men that are in the earth.
9 Also I *will ordain* **shall set** a place
for my people *Israel* **Yisra El**,
and *will* **shall** plant them,
and they shall *dwell* **tabernacle** in their place,
and shall *be moved* **quiver** no more;
neither shall the *children* **sons** of wickedness
waste them any more **add to wear them out**,
as at the beginning,
10 And since the *time* **days**
that I *commanded* **misvahed** judges
to be over my people *Israel* **Yisra El**.
Moreover I *will* **shall** subdue all thine enemies.
Furthermore I tell thee
that *the LORD will* **Yah Veh shall** build thee an house.
11 And it shall *come to pass* **become**,
when thy days be *expired* **fulfilled**
that thou must go to be with thy fathers,
that I *will* **shall** raise up thy seed after thee,
which shall be of thy sons;
and I *will* **shall** establish his *kingdom* **sovereigndom**.
12 He shall build me an house,
and I *will* **shall** stablish his throne *for ever* **eternally**.
13 I *will be his father* **shall be to him, father**,
and he shall be *my son* **to me, son**:
and I *will* **shall** not *take* **turn aside** my mercy *away*
from him,
as I *took* **turned** it **aside**
from him that was *before thee* **at thy face**:
14 But I *will settle* **shall stand** him in mine house
and in my *kingdom for ever* **sovereigndom eternally**:
and his throne shall be established *for ever* **eternally**.
15 According to all these words,
and according to all this vision,
so did Nathan *speak* **word** unto David.
16 And David the *king* **sovereign** came
and *sat before the LORD* **settled at the face of Yah Veh**,
and said, Who am I, O *LORD God* **Yah Veh Elohim**,
and what is mine house,
that thou hast brought me hitherto?
17 And *yet* this was *a small thing* **little** in thine eyes,
O *God* **Elohim**;
for thou hast *also spoken* **worded** of thy servant's house
for a great while to come **from afar off**,
and hast *regarded* **seen** me according to the *estate* **manner**
of a *man* **human** of high degree,
O *LORD God* **Yah Veh Elohim**.
18 What can David *speak* **add** more to thee

for the honour of thy servant?
for thou knowest thy servant.
19 O *LORD* **Yah Veh**, for thy servant's sake,
and according to thine own heart,
hast thou *done* **worked** all this greatness,
in making known all these *great things* **greatnesses**.
20 O *LORD* **Yah Veh**, there is none like thee,
neither is there any *God* **Elohim** beside thee,
according to all that we have heard with our ears.
21 And what one *nation* **goyim** in the earth
is like thy people *Israel* **Yisra El**,
whom *God* **Elohim** went to redeem to be his own people,
to *make* **set** thee a name
of greatness and *terribleness* **awesomeness**,
by driving out *nations* **goyim**
from *before* **the face of** thy people,
whom thou hast redeemed out of *Egypt* **Misrayim**?
22 For thy people *Israel* **Yisra El**
didst thou *make* **give** thine own people *for ever* **eternally**;
and thou, *LORD* **Yah Veh**, becamest their *God* **Elohim**.
23 Therefore now, *LORD* **Yah Veh**,
let the *thing* **word** that thou hast *spoken* **worded**
concerning thy servant and concerning his house
be *established for ever* **amened eternally**,
and *do* **work** as thou hast *said* **worded**.
24 Let it even be *established* **amened**,
that thy name
may be *magnified for ever* **greatened eternally**, saying,
The LORD of hosts **Yah Veh Sabaoth**
is the God — **Elohim** of *Israel* **Yisra El**,
even a God — **Elohim** to *Israel* **Yisra El**:
and let the house of David thy servant
be established *before thee* **at thy face**.
25 For thou, O my *God* **Elohim**,
hast *told* **exposed in the ear of** thy servant
that thou *wilt* **shalt** build him an house:
therefore thy servant hath found in his heart
to pray *before thee* **at thy face**.
26 And now, *LORD* **Yah Veh**, thou *art God* **Elohim**,
and hast *promised* **worded** this goodness unto thy servant:
27 Now therefore let it *please thee* **be thy will**
to bless the house of thy servant,
that it may be *before thee for ever* **at thy face eternally**:
for thou blessest, O *LORD* **Yah Veh**,
and it shall be blessed *for ever* **eternally**.

DAVID EXPANDS HIS DOMINION

18 Now after this it *came to pass* **became**,
that David smote the *Philistines* **Peleshethiy**,
and subdued them,
and took Gath and her *towns* **daughters**
out of the hand of the *Philistines* **Peleshethiy**.
2 And he smote Moab;
and the *Moabites* **Moabiy** became David's servants,
and *brought gifts* **bore offerings**.
3 And David smote *Hadarezer* **Hadar Ezer**
king **sovereign** of *Zobah* **Sobah** unto Hamath,
as he went to *stablish* **station** his *dominion* **hand**
by the river Euphrates.
4 And David *took* **captured** from him a thousand chariots,
and seven thousand *horsemen* **cavalry**,
and twenty thousand footmen:
David also *houghed* **uprooted/hamstrung**
all the chariot *horses*,
but *reserved* **remained** of them an hundred chariots.
5 And when the *Syrians* **Aramiy** of *Damascus* **Dammeseq**
came to help *Hadarezer* **Hadar Ezer**,
king **sovereign** of *Zobah* **Sobah**,
David *slew* **smote** of the *Syrians* **Aramiy**
two and twenty thousand men.
6 Then David *put garrisons* **set**
in *Syria—damascus* **Aram Dammeseq**;
and the *Syrians* **Aramiy** became David's servants,
and *brought gifts* **bore offerings**.
Thus *the LORD preserved* **Yah Veh saved** David
whithersoever he went.
7 And David took the shields of gold
that were on the servants of *Hadarezer* **Hadar Ezer**,
and brought them to *Jerusalem* **Yeru Shalem**.
8 Likewise from *Tibhath* **Tibchath**, and from *Chun* **Kun**,
cities of *Hadarezer* **Hadar Ezer**,
brought **took** David *very* **mighty** much *brass* **copper**,
wherewith *Solomon* **Shelomoh**
made **worked** the *brasen* **copper** sea, and the pillars,
and the *vessels* **instruments** of *brass* **copper**.
9 Now when Tou *king* **sovereign** of Hamath
heard how David had smitten all the *host* **valiant**
of *Hadarezer* **Hadar Ezer**, *king* **sovereign** of *Zobah* **Sobah**;
10 He sent Hadoram his son to *king* **sovereign** David,
to *enquire* **ask** of his *welfare* **shalom**,
and to *congratulate* **bless** him,
because he had fought against *Hadarezer* **Hadar Ezer**,
and smitten him;
(for *Hadarezer had war* **Hadar Ezer was a man of wars**
with Tou;)
and *with him* all manner of *vessels* **instruments**
of gold and silver and *brass* **copper**.
11 Them also *king* **sovereign** David
dedicated **hallowed** unto the *LORD* **Yah Veh**,
with the silver and the gold
that he *brought* **lifted** from all *these nations* **goyim**;
from Edom, and from Moab,
and from the *children* **sons** of Ammon,
and from the *Philistines* **Peleshethiy**,
and from *Amalek* **Amaleq**.
12 Moreover *Abishai* **Abi Shai** the son of *Zeruiah* **Seruyah**
slew **smote** of the *Edomites* **Edomiy**
in *the valley of salt* **Gay Melach/Valley of Salt**
eighteen thousand.
13 And he *put garrisons* **set stations** in Edom;
and all the *Edomites* **Edomiy** became David's servants.
Thus *the LORD preserved* **Yah Veh saved** David
whithersoever he went.
14 So David reigned over all *Israel* **Yisra El**,
and *executed* **worked** judgment and *justice* **justness**
among all his people.
15 And *Joab* **Yah Ab**
the son of *Zeruiah* **Seruyah** was over the host;
and *Jehoshaphat* **Yah Shaphat**
the son of *Ahilud* **Achiy Lud**, *recorder* **remembrancer**.
16 And *Zadok* **Sadoq** the son of *Ahitub* **Achiy Tub**,
and *Abimelech* **Abi Melech** the son of *Abiathar* **Abi Athar**,
were the priests; and Shavsha was scribe;
17 And *Benaiah* **Bena Yah** the son of *Jehoiada* **Yah Yada**
was over
the *Cherethites* **executioners** and the *Pelethites* **couriers**;
and the sons of David
were *chief about* **heads at the hand of** the *king* **sovereign**.

SONS OF AMMON REJECT DAVID'S MERCY

19 Now it *came to pass* **became** after this,
that *Nahash* **Nachash**
the *king* **sovereign** of the *children* **sons** of Ammon died,
and his son reigned in his stead.
2 And David said, I *will shew kindness* **shall work mercy**
unto Hanun the son of *Nahash* **Nachash**,
because his father *shewed kindness* **worked mercy** to me.
And David sent *messengers* **angels**
to *comfort* **sigh over** him concerning his father.
So the servants of David came into the land
of the *children* **sons** of Ammon to Hanun,
to *comfort* **sigh over** him.
3 But the *princes* **governors** of the *children* **sons** of Ammon
said to Hanun, *Thinkest thou* **In thine eyes**
that David doth **doth David** honour thy father,
that he hath sent *comforters unto* **to sigh over** thee?
are not his servants come unto thee for to *search* **probe**,
and to *overthrow* **overturn**, and to spy out the land?
4 Wherefore Hanun took David's servants,
and shaved them,
and cut off their garments in the midst
hard by their *buttocks* **crotches**,
and sent them away.
5 Then there went *certain*,
and told David how the men were served.
And he sent to meet them:
for the men were *greatly* **mighty** ashamed.
And the *king* **sovereign** said,
Tarry **Settle** at *Jericho* **Yericho**
until your beards *be grown* **sprout**,
and *then* return.
6 And when the *children* **sons** of Ammon

saw that they had made themselves
odious **a stink** to David,
Hanun and the *children* **sons** of Ammon
sent a thousand *talents* **rounds** of silver
to hire them chariots and *horsemen* **cavalry**
out of *Mesopotamia* **Aram Naharaim**,
and out of *Syriamaachah* **Aram Maachah**,
and out of *Zobah* **Sobah**.
7 So they hired thirty and two thousand chariots,
and the *king* **sovereign** of Maachah
and his people;
who came and *pitched* **camped**
before **at the face of** Medeba.
And the *children* **sons** of Ammon
gathered *themselves together* from their cities,
and came to *battle* **war**.

DAVID'S HOST LINES UP AGAINST THE SONS OF AMMON

8 And when David heard of it,
he sent *Joab* **Yah Ab**, and all the host of the mighty *men*.
9 And the *children* **sons** of Ammon *came out* **went**,
and *put the battle in array* **lined up for war**
before the *gate* **portal** of the city:
and the *kings* **sovereigns** that were come
were by themselves in the field.
10 Now when *Joab* **Yah Ab** saw
that the *battle* **face of the war** was set against him
before **at his face** and behind,
he chose out of all the *choice* **chosen** of *Israel* **Yisra El**,
and *put* **lined** them *in array* **up**
against **to meet** the *Syrians* **Aramiy**.
11 And the rest of the people he *delivered* **gave**
unto the hand of *Abishai* **Abi Shai** his brother,
and they *set themselves in array* **lined up**
against **to meet** the *children* **sons** of Ammon.
12 And he said, If the *Syrians* **Aramiy** be too strong for me,
then thou shalt *help* **save** me:
but if the *children* **sons** of Ammon be too strong for thee,
then I *will help* **shall save** thee.
13 *Be of good courage* **Strengthen**,
and let us *behave ourselves valiantly* **toughen**
for our people,
and for the cities of our *God* **Elohim**:
and let *the LORD* **Yah Veh**
do **work** that which is good in his *sight* **eyes**.
14 So *Joab* **Yah Ab** and the people that were with him
drew nigh *before* **at the face of** the *Syrians* **Aramiy**
unto the *battle* **war**;
and they fled *before him* **from his face**.
15 And when the *children* **sons** of Ammon
saw that the *Syrians* **Aramiy** were fled,
they likewise fled
before Abishai **from the face of Abi Shai** his brother,
and entered into the city.
Then *Joab* **Yah Ab** came to *Jerusalem* **Yeru Shalem**.
16 And when the *Syrians* **Aramiy** saw
that they were *put to the worse* **smitten**
before Israel **at the face of Yisra El**,
they sent *messengers* **angels**,
and *drew forth* **brought** the *Syrians* **Aramiy**
that were beyond the river:
and Shophach the *captain* **governor**
of the host of *Hadarezer* **Hadar Ezer**
went *before them* **at their face**.
17 And it was told David;
and he gathered all *Israel* **Yisra El**,
and passed over *Jordan* **Yarden**, and came upon them,
and *set the battle in array* **lined up** against them.
So when David had
put the battle in array **lined up for war**
. *against* **to meet** the *Syrians* **Aramiy**,
they fought with him.
18 But the *Syrians* **Aramiy** fled
before Israel **from the face of Yisra El**;
and David *slew* **slaughtered** of the *Syrians* **Aramiy**
seven thousand *men which fought* in chariots,
and forty thousand footmen,
and *killed* **deathified** Shophach
the *captain* **governor** of the host.
19 And when the servants of *Hadarezer* **Hadar Ezer**
saw that they were *put to the worse* **smitten**
before Israel **at the face of Yisra El**,
they *made peace* **did shalam** with David,
and became his servants:
neither *would* **willed** the *Syrians* **Aramiy**
help **to save** the *children* **sons** of Ammon any more.

DAVID'S HOST RUINS THE SONS OF AMMON

20 And it *came to pass* **became**,
that after the **turn of the** year *was expired*,
at the time that *kings* **sovereigns** go out *to battle*,
Joab led forth **Yah Ab drove**
the *power* **valiant** of the *army* **hosts**,
and *wasted* **ruined** the *country* **land**
of the *children* **sons** of Ammon,
and came and besieged Rabbah.
But David *tarried* **settled** at *Jerusalem* **Yeru Shalem**.
And *Joab* **Yah Ab** smote Rabbah,
and *destroyed* **demolished** it.
2 And David took the crown of their *king* **sovereign**
from off his head,
and found it
to weigh a talent **the weight of a round** of gold,
and there were precious stones in it;
and it was set upon David's head:
and he brought also
exceeding much **a mighty abounding of** spoil
out of the city.
3 And he brought out the people that were in it,
and *cut* **sawed** them with saws,
and with *harrows* **slicers** of iron, and with *axes* **saws**.
Even so *dealt* **worked** David
with all the cities of the *children* **sons** of Ammon.
And David and all the people
returned to *Jerusalem* **Yeru Shalem**.

DAVID WARS WITH THE PELESHETHIY AND THE RAPHAIY

4 And it *came to pass* **became** after this,
that there *arose* **stood** war at Gezer
with the *Philistines* **Peleshethiy**;
at which time Sibbechai **when Sibbechay**
the *Hushathite slew Sippai* **Hushathiy smote Sippay**,
that was **born** of *the children of the giant* **Rapha**:
and they were subdued.
5 And there was war again with the *Philistines* **Peleshethiy**;
and *Elhanan* **El Hanan** the son of *Jair* **Yaur**
slew Lahmi **smote Lachmi**
the brother of *Goliath* **Golyath** the *Gittite* **Gittiy**,
whose spear *staff* **timber** was like a weaver's beam.
6 And yet again there was war at Gath,
where was a man of *great stature* **measure**,
whose *fingers and toes* **digits** were four and twenty,
six *on each hand*, and six *on each foot*:
and he also was *the son* **born** of *the giant* **Rapha**.
7 But when he *defied Israel* **reproached Yisra El**,
Jonathan **Yah Nathan**
the son of *Shimea* **Shimah** David's brother
slew **smote** him.
8 These were born unto *the giant* **Rapha** in Gath;
and they fell by the hand of David,
and by the hand of his servants.

SATAN GOADS DAVID TO NUMBER YISRA EL

21 And Satan stood up against *Israel* **Yisra El**,
and *provoked* **goaded** David to number *Israel* **Yisra El**.
2 And David said to *Joab* **Yah Ab**
and to the *rulers* **governors** of the people,
Go, number **and scribe** *Israel* **Yisra El**
from *Beersheba* **Beer Sheba** even to Dan;
and bring the number of them to me, that I may know it.
3 And *Joab answered* **Yah Ab said**,
The LORD make **Yah Veh add to** his people
an hundred times so many *more* as they be:
but, my *lord* **adoni** the *king* **sovereign**,
are they not all my *lord's* **adoni's** servants?
why then doth my *lord require* **adoni seek** this *thing*?
why *will* **shall** he be a cause of *trespass* **guilt**
to *Israel* **Yisra El**?
4 Nevertheless the *king's* **sovereign's** word
prevailed against *Joab* **Yah Ab**.
Wherefore Joab departed **Yah Ab went**,
and went throughout all *Israel* **Yisra El**,
and came to *Jerusalem* **Yeru Shalem**.

5 And *Joab* **Yah Ab**
gave the *sum* **number** of the *number* **census** of the people
unto David.
And all *they of Israel* **Yisra El** were a thousand thousand
and an hundred thousand men that drew sword:
and *Judah* **Yah Hudah**
was four hundred *threescore and ten* **seventy**
thousand men that drew sword.
6 But Levi and *Benjamin* **Ben Yamin**
counted **mustered** he not among them:
for the *king's* **sovereign's** word
was *abominable* **abhorrent** to *Joab* **Yah Ab**.
7 *And God was displeased with this thing*
And this word was evil in the eyes of Elohim;
therefore he smote *Israel* **Yisra El**.
8 And David said unto *God* **Elohim**,
I have sinned *greatly* **mightily**,
because I have *done* **worked** this *thing* **word**:
but now, I beseech thee,
do away **pass over** the *iniquity* **perversity** of thy servant;
for I *have done very foolishly* **follied mightily**.
9 And *the LORD spake* **Yah Veh worded** unto Gad,
David's seer, saying,
10 Go and *tell* **word to** David, saying,
Thus saith *the LORD* **Yah Veh**,
I *offer* **stretch out to** thee three *things*:
choose thee one of these, that I may *do* **work** it unto thee.
11 So Gad came to David, and said unto him,
Thus saith *the LORD* **Yah Veh**, *Choose* **Take to** thee
12 Either three years' famine;
or three months to be *destroyed* **scraped away**
before **at the face of** thy *foes* **tribulators**,
while that the sword of thine enemies overtaketh thee;
or else three days the sword of *the LORD* **Yah Veh**,
even the pestilence, in the land,
and the angel of *the LORD destroying* **Yah Veh ruining**
throughout all the *coasts* **borders** of *Israel* **Yisra El**.
Now therefore *advise thyself* **see** what word
I shall *bring again* **return** to him that sent me.
13 And David said unto Gad,
I am *in a great strait* **mighty tribulated:**
let me fall now into the hand of *the LORD* **Yah Veh**;
for *very great* **mighty many** are his mercies:
but let me not fall into the hand of *man* **humanity**.
14 So *the LORD* **Yah Veh**
sent **gave** pestilence upon *Israel* **Yisra El**:
and there fell of *Israel* **Yisra El** seventy thousand men.
15 And *God* **Elohim**
sent an angel unto *Jerusalem* **Yeru Shalem**
to *destroy* **ruin** it:
and as he was *destroying* **ruining**,
the LORD beheld **Yah Veh saw**,
and he *repented* **sighed** *him* of the evil,
and said to the angel that *destroyed* **ruined**,
It is enough, **Enough!** *stay* **Slacken** now thine hand.
And the angel of *the LORD* **Yah Veh**
stood by the threshingfloor of Ornan the *Jebusite* **Yebusiy**.
16 And David lifted up his eyes,
and saw the angel of *the LORD* **Yah Veh**
stand between the earth and the *heaven* **heavens**,
having *a drawn sword* **his sword drawn** in his hand
stretched out over *Jerusalem* **Yeru Shalem**.
Then David and the elders *of Israel*,
who were *clothed* **covered** in *sackcloth* **saq**,
fell upon their faces.
17 And David said unto *God* **Elohim**,
Is it not I
that *commanded* **said** the people to be numbered?
even I it is that have sinned
and *done evil indeed* **in vilifying, have vilified**;
but as for *these sheep* **this flock**,
what have they *done* **worked**?
let thine hand, I *pray* **beseech** thee,
O *LORD* **Yah Veh** my *God* **Elohim**,
be on me, and on my father's house;
but not on thy people, that they should be plagued.
18 Then the angel of *the LORD* **Yah Veh**
commanded **said to** Gad to say to David,
that David should *go up* **ascend**,
and *set up an* **raise a sacrifice** altar
unto *the LORD* **Yah Veh**
in the threshingfloor of Ornan the *Jebusite* **Yebusiy**.
19 And David *went up* **ascended**
at the *saying* **word** of Gad,
which he *spake* **worded**
in the name of *the LORD* **Yah Veh**.
20 And Ornan turned back, and saw the angel;
and his four sons with him hid themselves.
Now Ornan was threshing wheat.
21 And as David came to Ornan,
Ornan looked and saw David,
and went out of the threshingfloor,
and bowed himself to David
with *his face* **nostrils** to the *ground* **earth**.
22 Then David said to Ornan,
Grant **Give** me the place of *this* **the** threshingfloor,
that I may build *an* **a sacrifice** altar therein
unto *the LORD* **Yah Veh**:
thou shalt *grant* **give** it me for the full *price* **silver**:
that the plague may be *stayed* **restrained** from the people.
23 And Ornan said unto David, Take it to thee,
and let my *lord* **adoni** the *king* **sovereign**
do **work** that which is good in his eyes: *lo* **see**,
I give thee the oxen also for *burnt offerings* **holocausts**,
and the threshing *instruments* **sledges** for *wood* **timber**,
and the wheat for the *meat* offering; I give it all.
24 And *king* **sovereign** David said to Ornan, Nay;
but **in chatteling,** I *will verily buy* **shall chattel** it
for the full *price* **silver**:
for I *will* **shall** not *take* **lift** that which is thine
for *the LORD* **Yah Veh**,
nor *offer burnt offerings* **holocaust holocausts**
without cost **gratuitously**.
25 So David gave to Ornan for the place
six hundred shekels of gold by weight.
26 And David built there
an **a sacrifice** altar unto *the LORD* **Yah Veh**,
and *offered burnt offerings* **holocausted holocausts**
and *peace offerings* **shelamim**,
and called upon *the LORD* **Yah Veh**;
and he answered him from *heaven* **the heavens** by fire
upon the **sacrifice** altar of *burnt offering* **holocaust**.
27 And *the LORD commanded* **Yah Veh said to** the angel;
and he *put up* **turned back** his sword *again*
into the sheath thereof.
28 At that time when David saw
that *the LORD* **Yah Veh** had answered him
in the threshingfloor of Ornan the *Jebusite* **Yebusiy**,
then he sacrificed there.
29 For the tabernacle of *the LORD* **Yah Veh**,
which *Moses made* **Mosheh worked** in the wilderness,
and the **sacrifice** altar of the *burnt offering* **holocaust**,
were at that *season* **time**
in the *high place* **bamah** at *Gibeon* **Gibon**.
30 But David could not go *before it* **at its face**
to enquire of *God* **Elohim**:
for he was *afraid* **frightened**
because **from the face** of the sword
of the angel of *the LORD* **Yah Veh**.

DAVID PREPARES TO BUILD THE HOUSE OF ELOHIM

22 Then David said,
This is the house of *the LORD God* **Yah Veh Elohim**,
and this is the **sacrifice** altar
of the *burnt offering* **holocaust** for *Israel* **Yisra El**.
2 And David *commanded* **said**
to gather *together* the *strangers* **sojourners**
that were in the land of *Israel* **Yisra El**;
and he *set masons* **stood hewers**
to hew *wrought* **hewed** stones
to build the house of *God* **Elohim**.
3 And David prepared iron in abundance
for the nails for the doors of the *gates* **portals**,
and for the *joinings* **joints**;
and *brass* **copper** in abundance without weight;
4 Also cedar trees *in abundance* **without number**:
for the *Zidonians* **Sidoniy** and *they of Tyre* **the Soriy**
brought *much* **in abundance** cedar *wood* **timber** to David.
5 And David said,
Solomon **Shelomoh** my son is *young* **a lad** and tender,
and the house that is to be builded for *the LORD* **Yah Veh**

must be exceeding magnifical **is to greaten upward**,
of *fame* **name** and of *glory* **adornment**
throughout all *countries* **lands**:
I *will* **shall** *therefore* now *make preparation* **prepare** for it.
So David prepared *abundantly* **in abundance**
before **at the face of** his death.
6 Then he called for *Solomon* **Shelomoh** his son,
and *charged* **misvahed** him to build an house
for *the LORD God* **Yah Veh Elohim** of *Israel* **Yisra El**.
7 And David said to *Solomon* **Shelomoh**,
My son, as for me,
it was in *my mind* **heart** to build an house
unto the name of *the LORD* **Yah Veh** my *God* **Elohim**:
8 But the word of *the LORD* **Yah Veh** came to me, saying,
Thou hast *shed* **poured** blood *abundantly* **in abundance**,
and hast *made* **worked** great wars:
thou shalt not build an house unto my name,
because thou hast *shed* **poured** much blood
upon the earth in my *sight* **face**.
9 Behold, a son shall be born to thee,
who shall be a man of rest;
and I *will* **shall** *give him* rest **him**
from all his enemies round about:
for his name shall be *Solomon* **Shelomoh**,
and I *will* **shall** give *peace* **shalom** and *quietness* **rest**
unto *Israel* **Yisra El** in his days.
10 He shall build an house for my name;
and he shall be *my son* **to me, son**,
and I *will* **shall** be *his father* **to him, father**;
and I *will* **shall** establish
the throne of his *kingdom* **sovereigndom**
over *Israel for ever* **Yisra El eternally**.
11 Now, my son, *the LORD* **Yah Veh** be with thee;
and prosper thou,
and build the house
of *the LORD* **Yah Veh** thy *God* **Elohim**,
as he hath *said* **worded** of thee.
12 Only *the LORD* **Yah Veh** give thee
wisdom **comprehension** and *understanding* **discernment**,
and *give* **misvah** thee *charge* concerning *Israel* **Yisra El**,
that thou mayest *keep* **guard** the *law* **torah**
of *the LORD* **Yah Veh** thy *God* **Elohim**.
13 Then shalt thou prosper,
if thou *takest heed* **guardest**
to *fulfil* **work** the statutes and judgments
which *the LORD* **Yah Veh**
charged Moses with **misvahed Mosheh**
concerning *Israel* **Yisra El**:
be strong **strengthen**, *and of good courage* **encourage**;
dread **awe** not, nor *be dismayed* **terrify**.
14 Now, behold, in my *trouble* **humiliation**
I have prepared for the house of *the LORD* **Yah Veh**
an hundred thousand *talents* **rounds** of gold,
and a thousand thousand *talents* **rounds** of silver;
and of *brass* **copper** and iron without weight;
for it is in abundance:
timber also and stone have I prepared;
and thou mayest add thereto.
15 Moreover there are *workmen* **doers of the work**
with thee in abundance,
hewers and *workers* **artificers** of stone and timber,
and all manner of *cunning men* **wise**
for every manner of work.
16 Of the gold, the silver,
and the *brass* **copper**, and the iron, there is no number.
Arise *therefore*, and *be doing* **work**,
and *the LORD* **Yah Veh** be with thee.
17 David also *commanded* **misvahed**
all the *princes* **governors** of *Israel* **Yisra El**
to help *Solomon* **Shelomoh** his son, *saying*,
18 Is not *the LORD* **Yah Veh** your *God* **Elohim** with you?
and hath he not given you rest *on every side* **round about**?
for he hath given the *inhabitants* **settlers** of the land
into mine hand;
and the land is subdued
before the LORD **at the face of Yah Veh**,
and *before* **at the face of** his people.
19 Now *set* **give** your heart and your soul
to seek *the LORD* **Yah Veh** your *God* **Elohim**;
arise therefore, and build ye the *sanctuary* **holies**
of *the LORD God* **Yah Veh Elohim**,
to bring the ark of the covenant of *the LORD* **Yah Veh**,
and the holy *vessels* **instruments** of *God* **Elohim**,
into the house that is to be built
to the name of *the LORD* **Yah Veh**.

DAVID MAKES SHELOMOH TO REIGN OVER YISRA EL

23 So when David was old and *full* **satisfied** of days,
he made *Solomon* **Shelomoh** his son
king **to reign** over *Israel* **Yisra El**.
2 And he gathered *together*
all the *princes* **governors** of *Israel* **Yisra El**,
with the priests and the *Levites* **Leviym**.

SCRIBING THE LEVIYM

3 Now the *Levites* **Leviym** were *numbered* **scribed**
from *the age* **sons** of thirty years and upward:
and their number *by their polls* **per cranium**,
man **mighty** by *man* **mighty**,
was thirty and eight thousand.
4 Of *which* **these**,
twenty and four thousand were to *set forward* **oversee**
the work of the house of *the LORD* **Yah Veh**;
and six thousand were officers and judges:
5 Moreover four thousand were porters;
and four thousand *praised the LORD* **halaled Yah Veh**
with the instruments which I *made* **worked**, *said David*,
to *praise* **halal** *therewith*.
6 And David *divided* **allotted** them *into courses* **allotments**
among the sons of Levi,
namely, Gershon, *Kohath* **Qehath**, and Merari.

SCRIBING THE GERSHONIY

7 Of the *Gershonites* **Gershoniy** *were*,
Laadan **Ladan**, and *Shimei* **Shimi**.
8 The sons of *Laadan* **Ladan**;
the *chief* **head** was *Jehiel* **Yechi El**,
and Zetham, and *Joel* **Yah El**, three.
9 The sons of *Shimei* **Shimi**;
Shelomith **Shelomoth**,
and *Haziel* **Hazi El**, and Haran, three.
These were the *chief* **head** of the fathers of *Laadan* **Ladan**.
10 And the sons of *Shimei* **Shimi** *were*,
Jahath **Yachath**, Zina, and *Jeush* **Yeush**, and Beriah.
These four were the sons of *Shimei* **Shimi**.
11 And *Jahath* **Yachath** was the *chief* **head**,
and Zizah the second:
but *Jeush* **Yeush** and Beriah
had not many **abounded not** sons;
therefore they were in one *reckoning* **mustering**,
according to *their* father's house.

SCRIBING THE SONS OF QEHATH

12 The sons of *Kohath* **Qehath**;
Amram **Am Ram**, *Izhar* **Yishar**,
Hebron, and *Uzziel* **Uzzi El**, four.
13 The sons of *Amram* **Am Ram**;
Aaron **Aharon** and *Moses* **Mosheh**:
and *Aaron* **Aharon** was separated,
that he should *sanctify* **hallow**
the *most holy things* **Holy of Holies**,
he and his sons *for ever* **eternally**,
to *burn* incense *before the LORD* **at the face of Yah Veh**,
to minister unto him,
and to bless in his name *for ever* **eternally**.
14 Now *concerning*
Moses **Mosheh** the man of *God* **Elohim**,
his sons were *named* **called** of the *tribe* **scion** of Levi.
15 The sons of *Moses* **Mosheh** *were*,
Gershom, and *Eliezer* **Eli Ezer**.
16 Of the sons of Gershom,
Shebuel **Shebu El** was the *chief* **head**.
17 And the sons of *Eliezer* **Eli Ezer** *were*,
Rehabiah **Rechab Yah** the *chief* **head**.
And *Eliezer* **Eli Ezer** had none other sons:
but the sons of *Rehabiah* **Rechab Yah**
were very many **abounded above**.
18 Of the sons of *Izhar* **Yishar**;
Shelomith the *chief* **head**.
19 Of the sons of Hebron;
Jeriah **Yeri Yah** the *first* **head**,
Amariah **Amar Yah** the second,
Jahaziel **Yachazi El** the third,
and *Jekameam* **Yeqam Am** the fourth.

20 Of the sons of *Uzziel* **Uzzi El**;
Micah **Michah Yah** the *first* **head**,
and *Jesiah* **Yishshi Yah** the second.

SCRIBING THE SONS OF MERARI

21 The sons of Merari;
Mahli **Machli**, and Mushi.
The sons of *Mahli* **Machli**;
Eleazar **El Azar**, and *Kish* **Qish**.
22 And *Eleazar* **El Azar** died,
and had no sons, but daughters:
and their brethren the sons of *Kish took* **Qish lifted** them.
23 The sons of Mushi;
Mahli **Machli**, and Eder, and *Jeremoth* **Yeremoth**, three.

THE NEW SERVICE OF THE LEVIYM

24 These were the sons of Levi
after the house of their fathers;
even the *chief* **head** of the fathers,
as they were *counted* **mustered** by number of names
by their polls **per cranium**, that *did* **worked** the work
for the service of the house of *the LORD* **Yah Veh**,
from *the age* **sons** of twenty years and upward.
25 For David said,
The LORD God **Yah Veh Elohim** of *Israel* **Yisra El**
hath *given rest unto* **rested** his people,
that they may *dwell* **tabernacle** in *Jerusalem* **Yeru Shalem**
for ever **eternally**:
26 And also unto the *Levites* **Leviym**;
they shall *no more carry* **neither bear** the tabernacle,
nor any *vessels* **instruments** of it for the service thereof.
27 For by the last words of David
the *Levites* **sons of Levi** were numbered
from **sons** of twenty years *old* and above:
28 Because their *office* **function**
was *to wait on* **at the hand of** the sons of *Aaron* **Aharon**
for the service of the house of *the LORD* **Yah Veh**,
in the courts, and in the chambers,
and in the purifying of all *holy things* **the holies**,
and the work of the service of the house of *God* **Elohim**;
29 Both for the *shewbread* **bread arrangement**,
and for the *fine* flour for *meat* offering,
and for the *unleavened cakes* **matsah wafers**,
and for that which is *baked in the pan* **griddled**,
and for that which is **deep** fried,
and for all manner of measure and *size* **measure**;
30 And to stand *every* morning **by morning**
to *thank* **extend hands**
and *praise the LORD* **halal Yah Veh**,
and likewise at even:
31 And to *offer* **holocaust** all *burnt sacrifices* **holocausts**
unto *the LORD* **Yah Veh** in the *sabbaths* **shabbaths**,
in the new moons, *and on the set feasts* **festivals**,
by number,
according to the *order commanded* **judgment** unto them,
continually *before the LORD* **at the face of Yah Veh**:
32 And that they should *keep* **guard** the *charge* **guard**
of the *tabernacle* **tent** of the congregation,
and the *charge* **guard** of the *holy place* **holies**,
and the *charge* **guard** of the sons of *Aaron* **Aharon**
their brethren,
in the service of the house of *the LORD* **Yah Veh**.

THE ALLOTMENTS OF THE SONS OF AHARON

24 Now these are the *divisions* **allotments**
of the sons of *Aaron* **Aharon**.
The sons of *Aaron* **Aharon**;
Nadab, and *Abihu* **Abi Hu**,
Eleazar **El Azar**, and *Ithamar* **Iy Thamar**.
2 But Nadab and *Abihu* **Abi Hu** died
before **at the face of** their father,
and had no *children* **sons**:
therefore *Eleazar* **El Azar** and *Ithamar* **Iy Thamar**
executed the priest's office **priested**.
3 And David *distributed* **allotted** them,
both *Zadok* **Sadoq** of the sons of *Eleazar* **El Azar**,
and *Ahimelech* **Achiy Melech**
of the sons of *Ithamar* **Iy Thamar**,
according to their *offices* **overseeing** in their service.
4 And there were
more chief men **many head mighty** found
of the sons of *Eleazar* **El Azar**
than of the sons of *Ithamar* **Iy Thamar**;
and thus were they *divided* **allotted**.
Among the sons of *Eleazar* **El Azar**
there were sixteen *chief* **head** men
of the house of their fathers,
and eight among the sons of *Ithamar* **Iy Thamar**
according to the house of their fathers.
5 Thus were they *divided* **allotted** by *lot* **pebble**,
one sort with *another* **these**;
for the governors of the *sanctuary* **holies**,
and governors of *the house God* **Elohim**,
were of the sons of *Eleazar* **El Azar**,
and of the sons of *Ithamar* **Iy Thamar**.
6 And *Shemaiah* **Shema Yah**
the son of *Nethaneel* **Nethan El** the scribe,
one of the *Levites* **Leviym**,
wrote **inscribed** them
before **at the face of** the *king* **sovereign**,
and the *princes* **governors**, and *Zadok* **Sadoq** the priest,
and *Ahimelech* **Achiy Melech**
the son of *Abiathar* **Abi Athar**,
and *before* the *chief* **head** of the fathers
of the priests and *Levites* **Leviym**:
one *principal household* **house of the fathers**
being taken **possessed** for *Eleazar* **El Azar**,
and one *taken* **possessed** for *Ithamar* **Iy Thamar**.
7 Now the first *lot* **pebble**
came forth **went** to *Jehoiarib* **Yah Arib**,
the second to *Jedaiah* **Yeda Yah**,
8 The third to Harim,
the fourth to Seorim,
9 The fifth to *Malchijah* **Malki Yah**,
the sixth to *Mijamin* **Mi Yamin**,
10 The seventh to *Hakkoz* **Qos**,
the eighth to *Abijah* **Abi Yah**,
11 The ninth to *Jeshuah* **Yah Shua**,
the tenth to *Shecaniah* **Shechan Yah**,
12 The eleventh to *Eliashib* **El Yashib**,
the twelfth to *Jakim* **Yaqim**,
13 The thirteenth to Huppah,
the fourteenth to *Jeshebeab* **Yesheb Ab**,
14 The fifteenth to Bilgah,
the sixteenth to Immer,
15 The seventeenth to Hezir,
the eighteenth to *Aphses* **Pisses**,
16 The nineteenth to *Pethahiah* **Pethach Yah**,
the twentieth to *Jehezekel* **Yechezq El**,
17 The one and twentieth to *Jachin* **Yachin**,
the two and twentieth to Gamul,
18 The three and twentieth to *Delaiah* **Dela Yah**,
the four and twentieth to *Maaziah* **Maaz Yah**.
19 These were the *orderings* **overseeings** of them
in their service
to come into the house of *the LORD* **Yah Veh**,
according to their *manner* **judgment**,
under Aaron **by the hand of Aharon** their father,
as *the LORD God* **Yah Veh Elohim** of *Israel* **Yisra El**
had *commanded* **misvahed** him.
20 And *the rest* **remaining** of the sons of Levi *were these*:
Of the sons of *Amram* **Am Ram**;
Shubael **Shuba El**:
of the sons of *Shubael* **Shuba El**;
Jehdeiah **Yachdi Yah**.
21 *Concerning Rehabiah* **Of Rechab Yah**:
of the sons of *Rehabiah* **Rechab Yah**,
the *first* **head** was *Isshiah* **Yishshi Yah**.
22 Of the *Izharites* **Yishariy**;
Shelomoth:
of the sons of Shelomoth;
Jahath **Yachath**.
23 And the sons of *Hebron; Jeriah the first,* **Yeri Yah;**
Amariah **Amar Yah** the second,
Jahaziel **Yachazi El** the third,
Jekameam **Yeqam Am** the fourth.
24 Of the sons of *Uzziel* **Uzzi El**;
Michah:
of the sons of Michah;
Shamir **Shamur**.
25 The brother of Michah was *Isshiah* **Yishshi Yah**:
of the sons of *Isshiah* **Yishshi Yah**;
Zechariah **Zechar Yah**.

26 The sons of Merari *were*;
Mahli **Machli** and Mushi:
the sons of *Jaaziah* **Yaazi Yah**;
Beno.
27 The sons of Merari by *Jaaziah* **Yaazi Yah**;
Beno, and Shoham, and *Zaccur* **Zakkur**, and Ibri.
28 Of *Mahli* **Machli** *came Eleazar* **El Azar**,
who had no sons.
29 Concerning *Kish* **Qish**:
the son of *Kish* **Qish** was *Jerahmeel* **Yerachme El**.
30 The sons also of Mushi;
Mahli **Machli**, and Eder, and *Jerimoth* **Yerimoth**.
These were the sons of the *Levites* **Leviym**
after the house of their fathers.
31 These likewise *cast lots* **felled pebbles**
over against **beside** their brethren
the sons of *Aaron* **Aharon**
in the *presence* **face** of David the *king* **sovereign**,
and *Zadok* **Sadoq**, and *Ahimelech* **Achiy Melech**,
and the *chief* **head** of the fathers
of the priests and *Levites* **Leviym**,
even the *principal* **head** fathers
over against **beside** their younger brethren.

DAVID SEPARATES THE PROPHET MUSICIANS

25 Moreover
David and the *captains* **governors** of the host
separated to the service of the sons of Asaph,
and of Heman, and of *Jeduthun* **Yeduthun**,
who should prophesy — **prophets** with harps,
with *psalteries* **bagpipes**, and with cymbals:
and the number of the workmen
according to their service was:
2 Of the sons of Asaph;
Zaccur **Zakkur**, and *Joseph* **Yoseph**,
and *Nethaniah* **Nethan Yah**, and *Asarelah* **Ashar Elah**,
the sons of Asaph under the hands of Asaph,
which prophesied
according to the *order* **hand** of the *king* **sovereign**.
3 Of *Jeduthun* **Yeduthun**: the sons of *Jeduthun* **Yeduthun**;
Gedaliah **Gedal Yah**, and *Zeri* **Seri**,
and *Jeshaiah* **Yesha Yah**, *Hashabiah* **Hashab Yah**,
and *Mattithiah* **Mattith Yah**, six,
under the hands of their father *Jeduthun* **Yeduthun**,
who prophesied with a harp, to *give thanks* **extend hands**
and to *praise the LORD* **halal Yah Veh**.
4 Of Heman: the sons of Heman:
Bukkiah **Buqqi Yah**, *Mattaniah* **Mattan Yah**,
Uzziel **Uzzi El**, *Shebuel* **Shebu El**, and *Jerimoth* **Yerimoth**,
Hananiah **Hanan Yah**, Hanani, *Eliathah* **Eli Athah**,
Giddalti, and *Romamtiezer* **Romamti Ezer**,
Joshbekashah **Yoshbe Qashah**, Mallothi, Hothir,
and *Mahazioth* **Machazioth**:
5 All these were the sons of Heman
the *king's* **sovereign's** seer in the words of *God* **Elohim**,
to lift up the horn.
And *God* **Elohim** gave to Heman
fourteen sons and three daughters.
6 All these were under the hands of their father
for song in the house of *the LORD* **Yah Veh**,
with cymbals, *psalteries* **bagpipes**, and harps,
for the service of the house of *God* **Elohim**,
according **by the hands**
to the king's order **of the sovereign**
to Asaph, *Jeduthun* **Yeduthun**, and Heman.
7 So the number of them, with their brethren
that were *instructed* **taught**
in the songs of *the LORD* **Yah Veh**,
even all that were *cunning* **discerning**,
was two hundred *fourscore* **eighty** and eight.
8 And they *cast lots* **felled pebbles**,
ward against ward **guard by guard**,
as well the small as the great,
the *teacher* **discerner** as the scholar.
9 Now the first *lot* **pebble**
came forth **went** for Asaph to *Joseph* **Yoseph**:
the second to *Gedaliah* **Gedal Yah**,
who with his brethren and sons were twelve:
10 The third to *Zaccur* **Zakkur**,
he, his sons, and his brethren, *were* twelve:
11 The fourth to *Izri* **Yisri**,
he, his sons, and his brethren, *were* twelve:
12 The fifth to *Nethaniah* **Nethan Yah**,
he, his sons, and his brethren, *were* twelve:
13 The sixth to *Bukkiah* **Buqqi Yah**,
he, his sons, and his brethren, *were* twelve:
14 The seventh to *Jesharelah* **Yesar Elah**,
he, his sons, and his brethren, *were* twelve:
15 The eighth to *Jeshaiah* **Yesha Yah**,
he, his sons, and his brethren, *were* twelve:
16 The ninth to *Mattaniah* **Mattan Yah**,
he, his sons, and his brethren, *were* twelve:
17 The tenth to *Shimei* **Shimi**,
he, his sons, and his brethren, *were* twelve:
18 The eleventh to *Azareel* **Azar El**,
he, his sons, and his brethren, *were* twelve:
19 The twelfth to *Hashabiah* **Hashab Yah**,
he, his sons, and his brethren, *were* twelve:
20 The thirteenth to *Shubael* **Shuba El**,
he, his sons, and his brethren, *were* twelve:
21 The fourteenth to *Mattithiah* **Mattith Yah**,
he, his sons, and his brethren, *were* twelve:
22 The fifteenth to *Jeremoth* **Yeremoth**,
he, his sons, and his brethren, *were* twelve:
23 The sixteenth to *Hananiah* **Hanan Yah**,
he, his sons, and his brethren, *were* twelve:
24 The seventeenth to *Joshbekashah* **Yoshbe Qashah**,
he, his sons, and his brethren, *were* twelve:
25 The eighteenth to Hanani,
he, his sons, and his brethren, *were* twelve:
26 The nineteenth to Mallothi,
he, his sons, and his brethren, *were* twelve:
27 The twentieth to *Eliathah* **Eli Athah**,
he, his sons, and his brethren, *were* twelve:
28 The one and twentieth to Hothir,
he, his sons, and his brethren, *were* twelve:
29 The two and twentieth to Giddalti,
he, his sons, and his brethren, *were* twelve:
30 The three and twentieth to Mahazioth,
he, his sons, and his brethren, *were* twelve:
31 The four and twentieth to *Romamtiezer* **Romamti Ezer**,
he, his sons, and his brethren, *were* twelve.

ALLOTMENTS OF THE PORTERS

26 *Concerning* the *divisions* **allotments** of the porters:
Of the *Korhites* **Qorachiy**,
was Meshelemiah **Meshelem Yah** the son of *Kore* **Qore**,
of the sons of Asaph.
2 And the sons of *Meshelemiah* **Meshelem Yah** *were*,
Zechariah **Zechar Yah** the firstborn,
Jediael **Yedia El** the second,
Zebadiah **Zebad Yah** the third,
Jathniel **Yathni El** the fourth,
3 Elam the fifth,
Jehohanan **Yah Hanan** the sixth,
Elioenai **El Ya Enay** the seventh.
4 Moreover the sons of *Obededom* **Obed Edom** *were*,
Shemaiah **Shema Yah** the firstborn,
Jehozabad **Yah Zabad** the second,
Joah **Yah Ach** the third,
and *Sacar* **Sachar** the fourth,
and *Nethaneel* **Nethan El** the fifth.
5 *Ammiel* **Ammi El** the sixth,
Issachar **Yissachar** the seventh,
Peulthai **Peullthay** the eighth:
for *God* **Elohim** blessed him.
6 Also unto *Shemaiah* **Shema Yah** his son were sons born,
that *ruled* **reigned** throughout the house of their father:
for they were mighty *men* of valour.
7 The sons of *Shemaiah* **Shema Yah**;
Othni, and *Rephael* **Repha El**,
and Obed, *Elzabad* **El Zabad**,
whose brethren were *strong men* **valiant sons**,
Elihu **Eli Hu**, and *Semachiah* **Semach Yah**.
8 All these of the sons of *Obededom* **Obed Edom**:
they and their sons and their brethren,
able **valiant** men *for strength* **of force** for the service,
were *threescore* **sixty** and two of *Obededom* **Obed Edom**.
9 And *Meshelemiah* **Meshelem Yah** had sons and brethren,
strong men **valiant sons**, eighteen.
10 Also Hosah, of the *children* **sons** of Merari, had sons;
Simri **Shimri** the *chief* **head**,

(*for though* he was not the firstborn,
yet his father *made* **set** him the *chief* **head**;)
11 *Hilkiah* **Hilqi Yah** the second,
Tebaliah **Tebal Yah** the third,
Zechariah **Zechar Yah** the fourth:
all the sons and brethren of Hosah were thirteen.
12 Among these
were the *divisions* **allotments** of the porters,
even among the *chief men* **head mighty**,
having wards one against another **guards beside brethren**,
to minister in the house of *the LORD* **Yah Veh**.
13 And they *cast lots* **felled pebbles**,
as well the small as the great,
according to the house of their fathers,
for every gate **portal by portal**.
14 And the *lot eastward* **pebble from the rising**
fell to *Shelemiah* **Shelem Yah**.
Then for *Zechariah* **Zechar Yah** his son,
a *wise* counsellor **of comprehension**,
they *cast lots* **felled pebbles**;
and his *lot came out* **pebble went** northward.
15 To *Obededom* **Obed Edom** southward;
and to his sons the house of *Asuppim* **Gatherings**.
16 To Shuppim and Hosah
the lot came forth westward **duskward**,
with the *gate* **portal** Shallecheth,
by the *causeway* **highway** of the *going up* **ascent**,
ward against ward **guard by guard**.
17 *Eastward were* **From the rising**, six *Levites* **Leviym**,
northward four a day, southward four a day,
and *toward Asuppim* **to the Gatherings,** two and two.
18 At *Parbar westward* **the suburb duskward**,
four at the *causeway* **highway**,
and two at *Parbar* **the suburb**.
19 These are the *divisions* **allotments** of the porters
among the *sons of Kore* **Qorachiy**,
and among the sons of Merari.

THE TREASURERS OF BETH ELOHIM AND THE HOLIES

20 And of the *Levites* **Leviym**,
Ahijah **Achiy Yah**
was over the treasures of the house of *God* **Elohim**,
and over the treasures of the *dedicated things* **holies**.
21 *As concerning* the sons of *Laadan* **Ladan**;
the sons of the *Gershonite Laadan* **Gershoniy Ladan**,
chief **head** fathers,
even of *Laadan* **Ladan** the *Gershonite* **Gershoniy**,
were Jehieli **Yechi Eliy**.
22 The sons of *Jehieli* **Yechi Eliy**;
Zetham, and *Joel* **Yah El** his brother,
which were over the treasures
of the house of *the LORD* **Yah Veh**.
23 Of the *Amramites* **Am Ramiy**, and the *Izharites* **Yishariy**,
the *Hebronites* **Hebroniy**, *and* the *Uzzielites* **Uzzi Eliy**:
24 And *Shebuel* **Shebu El** the son of Gershom,
the son of *Moses* **Mosheh**,
was ruler **eminent** of the treasures.
25 And his brethren by *Eliezer* **Eli Ezer**;
Rehabiah **Rechab Yah** his son,
and *Jeshaiah* **Yesha Yah** his son,
and *Joram* **Yah Ram** his son,
and Zichri his son,
and *Shelomith* **Shelomoth** his son.
26 Which *Shelomith* **Shelomoth** and his brethren
were over all the treasures of the *dedicated things* **holies**,
which David the *king* **sovereign**,
and the *chief* **head** fathers,
the *captains* **governors** over thousands and hundreds,
and the *captains* **governors** of the host,
had *dedicated* **hallowed**.
27 Out of the spoils won in *battles* **wars**
did they *dedicate* **hallow**
to *maintain* **strengthen** the house of *the LORD* **Yah Veh**.
28 And all that *Samuel* **Shemu El** the seer,
and *Saul* **Shaul** the son of *Kish* **Qish**,
and *Abner* **Abi Ner** the son of Ner,
and *Joab* **Yah Ab** the son of *Zeruiah* **Seruyah**,
had *dedicated* **hallowed**;
and whosoever had *dedicated* **hallowed** *any thing*,
it was under the hand of Shelomith, and of his brethren.
29 Of the *Izharites* **Yishariy**,
Chenaniah **Kenan Yah** and his sons
were for the *outward business* **outside work**
over *Israel* **Yisra El**,
for officers and judges.
30 *And* of the *Hebronites* **Hebroniy**,
Hashabiah **Hashab Yah** and his brethren,
men **sons** of valour,
a thousand and seven hundred,
were *officers* **overseers** among them of *Israel* **Yisra El**
on this side *Jordan westward* **Yarden duskward**
in all the *business* **work** of *the LORD* **Yah Veh**,
and in the service of the *king* **sovereign**.
31 Among the *Hebronites* **Hebroniy**
was *Jerijah* **Yeri Yah** the *chief* **head**,
even among the *Hebronites* **Hebroniy**,
according to the generations of his fathers.
In the fortieth year of the *reign* **sovereigndom** of David
they were sought for,
and there were found among them mighty *men* of valour
at *Jazer* **Yazer** of *Gilead* **Gilad**.
32 And his brethren, *men* **sons** of valour,
were two thousand and seven hundred *chief* **head** fathers,
whom *king* **sovereign** David made *rulers* **overseers**
over the *Reubenites* **Reu Beniy**, the *Gadites* **Gadiy**,
and the half *tribe* **scion** of *Manasseh* **Menash Shiy**,
for every *matter pertaining to God* **word of Elohim**,
and affairs of the *king* **sovereign**.

THE DIVISIONS OF THE CHILIARCHS AND CENTURIANS

27 Now the *children* **sons** of *Israel* **Yisra El**
after their number, *to wit*,
the *chief* **head** fathers
and *captains* **governors** of thousands and hundreds,
and their officers
that *served* **ministered to** the *king* **sovereign**
in any *matter* **word** of the *courses* **allotments**,
which came in and went out month by month
throughout all the months of the year,
of *every course* **one allotment**
were twenty and four thousand.
2 Over the first *course* **allotment** for the first month
was *Jashobeam* **Yashob Am** the son of *Zabdiel* **Zabdi El**:
and in his *course* **allotment**
were twenty and four thousand.
3 Of the *children* **sons** of *Perez* **Peres**
was the *chief* **head**
of all the *captains* **governors** of the host
for the first month.
4 And over the *course* **allotment** of the second month
was *Dodai* **Doday** an *Ahohite* **Ach Oachiy**,
and of his *course* **allotment**
was *Mikloth* **Miqloth** also the *ruler* **eminent**:
in his *course* **allotment** likewise
were twenty and four thousand.
5 The third *captain* **governor** of the host for the third month
was *Benaiah* **Bena Yah** the son of *Jehoiada* **Yah Yada**,
a *chief* **head** priest:
and in his *course* **allotment**
were twenty and four thousand.
6 This *is that Benaiah* **Bena Yah**,
who was mighty among the thirty, and above the thirty:
and in his *course* **allotment**
was *Ammizabad* **Ammi Zabad** his son.
7 The fourth *captain* for the fourth month
was *Asahel* **Asa El** the brother of *Joab* **Yah Ab**,
and *Zebadiah* **Zebad Yah** his son after him:
and in his *course* **allotment**
were twenty and four thousand.
8 The fifth *captain* **governor** for the fifth month
was Shamhuth the *Izrahite* **Yizrach**:
and in his *course* **allotment**
were twenty and four thousand.
9 The sixth *captain* for the sixth month
was Ira the son of *Ikkesh* **Iqqesh** the *Tekoite* **Teqohiy**:
and in his *course* **allotment**
were twenty and four thousand.
10 The seventh *captain* for the seventh month
was *Helez* **Heles** the *Pelonite* **Paloniy**,
of the *children* **sons** of *Ephraim* **Ephrayim**:
and in his *course* **allotment**

were twenty and four thousand.
11 The eighth *captain* for the eighth month
was *Sibbecai* **Sibbechay** the *Hushathite* **Hushathiy**,
of the *Zarhites* **Zerachiy**:
and in his *course* **allotment**
were twenty and four thousand.
12 The ninth *captain* for the ninth month
was *Abiezer* **Abi Ezer** the *Anetothite* **Anathothiy**,
of the *Benjamites* **Ben Yaminiy**:
and in his *course* **allotment**
were twenty and four thousand.
13 The tenth *captain* for the tenth month
was *Maharai* **Maharay** the *Netophathite* **Netophathiy**,
of the *Zarhites* **Zerachiy**:
and in his *course* **allotment**
were twenty and four thousand.
14 The eleventh *captain* for the eleventh month
was *Benaiah* **Bena Yah** the *Pirathonite* **Pirathoniy**,
of the *children* **sons** of *Ephraim* **Ephrayim**:
and in his *course* **allotment**
were twenty and four thousand.
15 The twelfth *captain* for the twelfth month
was *Heldai* **Helday** the *Netophathite* **Netophathiy**,
of *Othniel* **Othni El**:
and in his *course* **allotment**
were twenty and four thousand.

OVERSEERS OF THE SCIONS OF YISRA EL

16 Furthermore over the *tribes* **scions** of *Israel* **Yisra El**:
the *ruler* **eminent** of the *Reubenites* **Reu Beniy**
was *Eliezer* **Eli Ezer** the son of Zichri:
of the *Simeonites* **Shimoniy**,
Shephatiah **Shaphat Yah** the son of Maachah:
17 Of the *Levites* **Leviym**,
Hashabiah **Hashab Yah** the son of *Kemuel* **Qemu El**:
of the *Aaronites* **Aharoniy**,
Zadok **Sadoq**:
18 Of *Judah* **Yah Hudah**,
Elihu **Eli Hu**, *one* of the brethren of David:
of *Issachar* **Yissachar**,
Omri the son of *Michael* **Michah El**:
19 Of Zebulun,
Ishmaiah **Yishma Yah** the son of *Obadiah* **Obad Yah**:
of Naphtali,
Jerimoth **Yerimoth** the son of *Azriel* **Ezri El**:
20 Of the *children* **sons** of *Ephraim* **Ephrayim**,
Hoshea the son of *Azaziah* **Azaz Yah**:
of the half *tribe* **scion** of *Manasseh* **Menash Sheh**,
Joel **Yah El** the son of *Pedaiah* **Pedah Yah**:
21 Of the half *tribe* of *Manasseh* **Menash Sheh**
in *Gilead* **Gilad**,
Iddo **Yiddo** the son of *Zechariah* **Zechar Yah**:
of *Benjamin* **Ben Yamin**,
Jaasiel **Yaasi El** the son of *Abner* **Abi Ner**:
22 Of Dan,
Azareel **Azar El** the son of *Jeroham* **Yerocham**.
These were the *princes* **governors**
of the *tribes* **scions** of *Israel* **Yisra El**.
23 But David *took* **spared** not the number of them
sons from twenty years *old* and *under* **downward**:
because *the LORD* **Yah Veh** had said
he *would increase Israel* **should abound Yisra El**
like to the stars of the heavens.
24 *Joab* **Yah Ab** the son of *Zeruiah* **Seruyah**
began to number, but he finished not,
because there fell *wrath* **rage** for it against *Israel* **Yisra El**;
neither was the number *put* **ascended** in the account
of the *chronicles* **words of the days**
of *king* **sovereign** David.

OVERSEERS OF THE SOVEREIGN'S TREASURES

25 And over the *king's* **sovereign's** treasures
was Azmaveth the son of *Adiel* **Adi El**:
and over the *storehouses* **treasures** in the fields,
in the cities, and in the villages, and in the *castles* **towers**,
was Jehonathan the son of *Uzziah* **Uzzi Yah**:
26 And over them that *did* **worked** the work of the field
for *tillage* **service** of the *ground* **soil**
was Ezri the son of *Chelub* **Kelub**:
27 And over the vineyards
was *Shimei* **Shimi** the *Ramathite* **Ramahiy**:
over the increase of the vineyards
for the wine *cellars* **treasures**
was Zabdi the *Shiphmite* **Shephamiy**:
28 And over the olive trees and the sycomore trees
that were in the *low plains* **lowlands**
was *Baalhanan* **Baal Hanan** the *Gederite* **Gederiy**:
and over the *cellars* **treasures** of oil was *Joash* **Yah Ash**:
29 And over the *herds* **oxen** that *fed* **grazed** in Sharon
was *Shitrai* **Shitray** the *Sharonite* **Sharoniy**:
and over the *herds* **oxen** that were in the valleys
was Shaphat the son of *Adlai* **Adlay**:
30 Over the camels also
was Obil the *Ishmaelite* **Yishma Eliy**:
and over the *asses* **she burros**
was *Jehdeiah* **Yachdi Yah** the *Meronothite* **Meronothiy**:
31 And over the flocks
was *Jaziz* **Yaziz** the *Hagerite* **Hagariy**.
All these were the *rulers* **governors**
of the *substance* **acquisition**
which was *king* **sovereign** David's.
32 Also *Jonathan* **Yah Nathan** David's uncle
was a counsellor,
a *wise* **discerning** man, and a scribe:
and *Jehiel* **Yechi El** the son of *Hachmoni* **Hachmoniy**
was with the *king's* **sovereign's** sons:
33 And *Ahithophel* **Achiy Thophel**
was the *king's* **sovereign's** counsellor:
and *Hushai* **Hushay** the *Archite* **Arkiy**
was the *king's companion* **sovereign's friend**:
34 And after *Ahithophel* **Achiy Thophel**
was *Jehoiada* **Yah Yada** the son of *Benaiah* **Bena Yah**,
and *Abiathar* **Abi Athar**:
and the *general* **governor**
of the *king's army* **sovereign's host** was *Joab* **Yah Ab**.

DAVID CHARGES SHELOMOH

28 And David *assembled* **congregated**
all the *princes* **governors** of *Israel* **Yisra El**,
the *princes* **governors** of the *tribes* **scions**,
and the *captains* **governors** of the *companies* **allotments**
that ministered to the *king* **sovereign** *by course*,
and the *captains* **governors** over the thousands,
and *captains* **governors** over the hundreds,
and the *stewards* **governors**
over all the *substance* **acquisition**
and *possession* **chattel** of the *king* **sovereign**,
and of his sons,
with the *officers* **eunuchs**, and with the mighty *men*,
and with all the *valiant men* **mighty of valour**,
unto *Jerusalem* **Yeru Shalem**.
2 Then David the *king* **sovereign**
stood up **arose** upon his feet, and said,
Hear me, my brethren, and my people:
As for me, I had in mine heart to build an house of rest
for the ark of the covenant of *the LORD* **Yah Veh**,
and for the *footstool* **stool of the feet** of our *God* **Elohim**,
and had *made ready* **prepared** for the building:
3 But *God* **Elohim** said unto me,
Thou shalt not build an house for my name,
because thou hast been a man of war,
and hast *shed* **poured** blood.
4 Howbeit
the LORD God **Yah Veh Elohim** of *Israel* **Yisra El**
chose me before all the house of my father
to be *king* **sovereign** over *Israel for ever* **Yisra El eternally**:
for he hath chosen *Judah* **Yah Hudah**
to be the *ruler* **eminent**;
and of the house of *Judah* **Yah Hudah**,
the house of my father;
and among the sons of my father he *liked me* **was pleased**
to *make* **have** me *king* **reign** over all *Israel* **Yisra El**:
5 And of all my sons,
(for *the LORD* **Yah Veh** hath given me many sons,)
he hath chosen *Solomon* **Shelomoh** my son
to *sit* **settle** upon the throne of the *kingdom* **sovereigndom**
of *the LORD* **Yah Veh** over *Israel* **Yisra El**.
6 And he said unto me, *Solomon* **Shelomoh** thy son,
he shall build my house and my courts:
for I have chosen him to be *my son* **to me, son**,
and I *will* **shall** be *his father* **to him, father**.
7 Moreover
I *will* **shall** establish his *kingdom* **sovereigndom**

for ever **eternally**,
if he *be constant* **strenghthen** to *do* **work**
my *commandments* **misvoth** and my judgments,
as at this day.
8 Now therefore in the *sight* **eyes** of all *Israel* **Yisra El**
the congregation of *the LORD* **Yah Veh**,
and in the *audience* **ears** of our *God* **Elohim**,
keep **guard** and seek for all the *commandments* **misvoth**
of *the LORD* **Yah Veh** your *God* **Elohim**:
that ye may possess this good land,
and leave it for an inheritance
for your *children* **sons** after you *for ever* **eternally**.
9 And thou, *Solomon* **Shelomoh** my son,
know thou the *God* **Elohim** of thy father,
and serve him with a *perfect heart* **heart of shalom**
and with a *willing mind* **soul of desire**:
for *the LORD searcheth* **Yah Veh examineth** all hearts,
and *understandeth* **discerneth**
all the imaginations of *the thoughts* **fabrications**:
if thou seek him, he *will* **shall** be found of thee;
but if thou forsake him,
he *will cast* **shall abandon** thee *off for ever* **eternally**.
10 *Take heed* **See** now;
for *the LORD* **Yah Veh** hath chosen thee
to build an house for the *sanctuary* **holies**:
be strong **strengthen**, and *do* **work** it.
11 Then David gave to *Solomon* **Shelomoh** his son
the pattern of the porch, and of the houses thereof,
and of the treasuries thereof,
and of the upper *chambers* **rooms** thereof,
and of the inner *parlours* **chambers** thereof,
and of the *place* **house** of the *mercy seat* **kapporeth**,
12 And the pattern of all that he had by the spirit,
of the courts of the house of *the LORD* **Yah Veh**,
and of all the chambers round about,
of the treasuries of the house of *God* **Elohim**,
and of the treasuries of the *dedicated things* **holies**:
13 Also for the *courses* **allotments**
of the priests and the *Levites* **Leviym**,
and for all the work of the service
of the house of *the LORD* **Yah Veh**,
and for all the *vessels* **instruments** of service
in the house of *the LORD* **Yah Veh**.
14 *He gave* of gold by weight for *things* **that** of gold,
for all instruments of *all manner of* service **and service**;
silver also for all instruments of silver by weight,
for all instruments of *every kind of* service **and service**:
15 Even the weight for the *candlesticks* **menorah** of gold,
and for their lamps of gold,
by weight *for every candlestick* **menorah by menorah**,
and for the lamps thereof:
and for the *candlesticks* **menorah** of silver by weight,
both for the *candlestick* **menorah**,
and *also* for the lamps thereof,
according to the *use* **service**
of every candlestick **menorah by menorah**.
16 And by weight *he gave*
gold for the tables of *shewbread* **arrangement**,
for every table **by table**;
and *likewise* silver for the tables of silver:
17 Also pure gold for the *fleshhooks* **forks**,
and the *bowls* **sprinklers**, and the *cups* **covers**:
and for the golden *basons* **tankards**
he gave gold by weight
for every bason **tankard by tankard**;
and *likewise silver* by weight
for every bason **tankard by tankard** of silver:
18 And for the **sacrifice** altar of incense refined gold
by weight;
and gold for the pattern
of the chariot of the *cherubims* **cherubim**,
that spread out *their wings*,
and covered
the ark of the covenant of *the LORD* **Yah Veh**.
19 All *this, said David*,
the LORD **Yah Veh** made me *understand* **comprehend**
in *writing* **inscribing** by his hand upon me,
even all the works of this pattern.
20 And David said to *Solomon* **Shelomoh** his son,
Be strong and of good courage **Strengthen, encourage**,
and *do* **work** *it*:
fear **awe** not, nor be *dismayed* **terrified**:
for *the LORD God* **Yah Veh Elohim**,
even my *God* **Elohim**, *will* **shall** be with thee;
he *will* **shall** not *fail* **let thee down**, nor forsake thee,
until thou hast finished all the work for the service
of the house of *the LORD* **Yah Veh**.
21 And, behold, the *courses* **allotments**
of the priests and the *Levites* **Leviym**,
even they shall be with thee
for all the service of the house of *God* **Elohim**:
and there shall be with thee
for all *manner of workmanship* **work**
every *willing skilful man* **volunteer in wisdom**,
for any manner of service:
also the *princes* **governors** and all the people
will **shall** be wholly at thy *commandment* **word**.

DAVID CHARGES THE CONGREGATION TO BUILD THE HOUSE OF YAH VEH ELOHIM

29 Furthermore David the *king* **sovereign**
said unto all the congregation,
Solomon **Shelomoh** my son,
whom *alone* **as one,** *God* **Elohim** hath chosen,
is yet young **a lad** and tender,
and the work is great:
for the palace is not for *man* **humanity**,
but for *the LORD God* **Yah Veh Elohim**.
2 Now I have prepared with all my *might* **force**
for the house of my *God* **Elohim**
the gold for things to be made of gold **gold for the gold**,
and the silver for things of silver **silver for the silver**,
and the brass for things of brass **copper for the copper**,
the iron for things of iron **iron for the iron**,
and wood for things of wood **timber for the timber**;
onyx stones, and *stones to be set* **fillings**,
glistering **stibium** stones,
and of *divers colours* **embroidery**,
and all manner of precious stones,
and marble stones in abundance.
3 Moreover, because I *have set my affection* **am pleased**
to **in** the house of my *God* **Elohim**,
I have of mine own *proper good* **peculiar treasure**,
of gold and silver,
which I have given to the house of my *God* **Elohim**,
over and above all that I have prepared for the holy house.
4 *Even* three thousand *talents* **rounds** of gold,
of the gold of Ophir,
and seven thousand *talents* **rounds** of refined silver,
to *overlay* **plaister** the walls of the houses *withal*:
5 *The gold for things of gold* **Gold for the gold**,
and the silver for things of silver **silver for the silver**,
and for all manner of work
to be made by **of** the hands of artificers.
And who *then is willing* **volunteereth**
to *consecrate* **fill** his *service* **hand** this day
unto *the LORD* **Yah Veh**?
6 Then the *chief* **governor** of the fathers
and *princes* **governors**
of the *tribes* **scions** of *Israel* **Yisra El**,
and the *captains* **governors** of thousands and of hundreds,
with the *rulers* **governors** of the *king's* **sovereign's** work,
offered willingly **volunteered**,
7 And gave for the service of the house of *God* **Elohim**
of gold five thousand *talents* **rounds**
and ten thousand *drams* **darics**,
and of silver *ten thousand talents* **a myriad rounds**,
and of *brass* **copper**
eighteen thousand talents
a myriad and eight thousand rounds,
and one hundred thousand *talents* **rounds** of iron.
8 And they with whom *precious* stones were found
gave them to the treasure
of the house of *the LORD* **Yah Veh**,
by the hand of *Jehiel* **Yechi El** the *Gershonite* **Gershoniy**.
9 Then the people *rejoiced* **cheered**,
for that they *offered willingly* **volunteered**,
because with *perfect* **a** heart **at shalom**
they *offered willingly* **volunteered** to *the LORD* **Yah Veh**:
and David the *king* **sovereign**
also *rejoiced* **cheered** with great *joy* **cheer**.

DAVID BLESSES YAH VEH ELOHIM OF YISRA EL

10 Wherefore David blessed *the LORD* **Yah Veh**
before **in the eyes of** all the congregation:
and David said, Blessed be thou,
LORD God **Yah Veh Elohim** of *Israel* **Yisra El** our father,
for ever **eternally** and *ever* **eternally**.
11 Thine, O *LORD* **Yah Veh** is the greatness,
and the *power* **might**, and the *glory* **adornment**,
and the victory **in perpetuity**, and the majesty:
for all that is in the *heaven* **heavens** and in the earth
is thine;
thine is the *kingdom* **sovereigndom**, O *LORD* **Yah Veh**,
and thou art *exalted* **lifted** as head above all.
12 Both riches and honour *come of thee* **be from thy face**,
and thou reignest over all;
and in thine hand is *power* **force** and might;
and in thine hand it is to *make great* **greaten**,
and to *give strength unto* **strengthen** all.
13 Now therefore, our *God* **Elohim**,
we *thank* **extend hands to** thee,
and *praise* **halal** thy glorious name.
14 But who am I, and what is my people,
that *we* should
be able to offer so willingly **restrain from volunteering**
after this sort?
for all *things come* **be** of thee,
and of thine *own* **hand** have we given thee.
15 For we are *strangers before thee* **sojourners at thy face**,
and *sojourners* **settlers**, as *were* all our fathers:
our days on the earth are as a shadow,
and there is *none abiding* **no expectation**.
16 O *LORD* **Yah Veh** our *God* **Elohim**,
all this *store* **multitude** that we have prepared
to build thee an house for thine holy name
cometh **be** of thine hand, and is all thine own.
17 I know also, my *God* **Elohim**,
that thou *triest* **proofest** the heart
and hast pleasure in *uprightness* **straightness**.
As for me, in the *uprightness* **straightness** of mine heart
I have *willingly offered* **volunteered** all these *things*:
and now have I seen with *joy* **cheer** thy people,
which are *present* **found** here,
to *offer willingly* **volunteer** unto thee.
18 O *LORD God* **Yah Veh Elohim** of Abraham,
Isaac **Yischaq**, and of *Israel* **Yisra El**, our fathers,
keep **guard** this *for ever* **eternally**
in the imagination of the *thoughts* **fabrications**
of the heart of thy people,
and prepare their heart unto thee:
19 And give unto *Solomon* **Shelomoh** my son
a *perfect* heart **of shalom**,
to *keep* **guard** thy *commandments* **misvoth**,
thy *testimonies* **witnesses**, and thy statutes,
and to *do* **work** all these *things*, and to build the palace,
for the which I have *made provision* **prepared**.
20 And David said to all the congregation,
Now bless *the LORD* **Yah Veh** your *God* **Elohim**.
And all the congregation
blessed *the LORD God* **Yah Veh Elohim** of their fathers,
and bowed *down their heads*,
and *worshipped the LORD* **prostrated to Yah Veh**,
and the *king* **sovereign**.

SHELOMOH ANOINTED UNTO YAH VEH

21 And they sacrificed sacrifices unto *the LORD* **Yah Veh**,
and *offered burnt offerings* **holocausted holocausts**
unto *the LORD* **Yah Veh**,
on the morrow after that day,
even a thousand bullocks, a thousand rams,
and a thousand lambs, with their *drink offerings* **libations**,
and sacrifices in abundance for all *Israel* **Yisra El**:
22 And did eat and drink
before the LORD **at the face of Yah Veh**
on that day with great *gladness* **cheerfulness**.
And they *made Solomon* **had Shelomoh** the son of David
king **reign** the second time,
and anointed him unto *the LORD* **Yah Veh**
to be the *chief governor* **eminent**,
and *Zadok* **Sadoq** to be priest.
23 Then *Solomon* **Shelomoh**
sat **settled** on the throne of *the LORD* **Yah Veh**
as *king* **sovereign**
instead of David his father, and prospered;
and all *Israel obeyed* **Yisra El hearkened to** him.
24 And all the *princes* **governors**, and the mighty *men*,
and all the sons likewise of *king* **sovereign** David,
submitted themselves **gave their hand**
unto Solomon **under Shelomoh** the *king* **sovereign**.
25 And *the LORD* **Yah Veh**
magnified Solomon **greatened Shelomoh**
exceedingly **over** in the *sight* **eyes** of all *Israel* **Yisra El**,
and *bestowed* **gave** upon him
such royal majesty **the majesty of the sovereigndom**
as had not been on any *king* **sovereign**
before him **at his face** in *Israel* **Yisra El**.

THE DEATH OF DAVID

26 Thus David the son of *Jesse* **Yishay**
reigned over all *Israel* **Yisra El**.
27 And the *time* **days** that he reigned over *Israel* **Yisra El**
was forty years;
seven years reigned he in Hebron,
and thirty and three *years*
reigned he in *Jerusalem* **Yeru Shalem**.
28 And he died in a good *old age* **grayness**,
full **satisfied** of days, riches, and honour:
and *Solomon* **Shelomoh** his son reigned in his stead.
29 Now the *acts* **words** of David the *king* **sovereign**,
first and last, behold,
they are *written* **inscribed**
in the *book* **words** of *Samuel* **Shemu El** the seer,
and in the *book* **words** of Nathan the prophet,
and in the *book* **words** of Gad the seer.
30 With all his *reign* **sovereigndom** and his might,
and the times that *went* **passed** over him,
and over *Israel* **Yisra El**,
and over all the *kingdoms* **sovereigndoms**
of the *countries* **lands**.

EY TO INTERPRETING THE EXEGESES:
ing James text is in regular type;
ext under exegeses is in oblique type;
ext of exegeses is in bold type.

SHELOMOH'S SOVEREIGNDOM STRENGTHENED

1 And *Solomon* **Shelomoh** the son of David
was strengthened in his *kingdom* **sovereigndom**,
and *the LORD* **Yah Veh** his *God* **Elohim** was with him,
and *magnified* **greatened** him exceedingly.

SHELOMOH HOLOCAUSTS UPON THE SACRIFICE ALTAR

Then *Solomon* **Shelomoh**
spake **said** unto all *Israel* **Yisra El**,
to the *captains* **governors** of thousands and of hundreds,
and to the judges,
and to every *governor* **hierarch** in all *Israel* **Yisra El**,
the *chief* **head** of the fathers.
3 So *Solomon* **Shelomoh**,
and all the congregation with him,
went to the *high place* **bamah** that was at *Gibeon* **Gibon**;
for there was the *tabernacle* **tent**
of the congregation of *God* **Elohim**,
which *Moses* **Mosheh** the servant of *the LORD* **Yah Veh**
had *made* **worked** in the wilderness.
4 *But* **Nevertheless**
the ark of *God* **Elohim** had David *brought up* **ascended**
from *Kirjathjearim* **Qiryath Arim**
to the place which **when** David had prepared for it:
for he had *pitched* **stretched** a tent for it
at *Jerusalem* **Yeru Shalem**.
5 Moreover the *brasen* **copper sacrifice** altar,
that *Bezaleel* **Besal El** the son of Uri, the son of Hur,
had *made* **worked**,
he *put before* **set at the face**
of the tabernacle of *the LORD* **Yah Veh**:
and *Solomon* **Shelomoh** and the congregation
sought unto it.
6 And *Solomon went up* **Shelomoh holocausted** thither
to the *brasen* **copper sacrifice** altar
before the LORD **at the face of Yah Veh**,
which was at the *tabernacle* **tent** of the congregation,
and *offered* **holocausted**
a thousand *burnt offerings* **holocausts** upon it.

SHELOMOH ASKS FOR WISDOM

7 In that night *did God appear* **Elohim was seen**
unto Solomon **by Shelomoh**,
and said unto him, Ask what I shall give thee.
8 And *Solomon* **Shelomoh** said unto *God* **Elohim**,
Thou hast *shewed* **worked** great mercy
unto David my father,
and hast made me to reign in his stead.
9 Now, O *LORD God* **Yah Veh Elohim**,
let thy *promise* **word** unto David my father
be *established* **amened**:
for thou hast made me *king* **reign** over *a* **much** people
like the dust of the earth *in multitude*.
10 Give me now wisdom and knowledge,
that I may go out and come in
before **at the face of** this people:
for who can judge this thy people, that is so great?
11 And *God* **Elohim** said to *Solomon* **Shelomoh**,
Because this was in thine heart,
and thou hast not asked riches,
wealth **holdings**, or honour,
nor the *life* **soul** of *thine enemies* **thy haters**,
neither yet hast asked *long life* **many days**;
but hast asked wisdom and knowledge for thyself,
that thou mayest judge my people,
over whom I have made thee *king* **reign**:
12 Wisdom and knowledge is *granted* **given** unto thee;
and I *will* **shall** give thee riches,
and *wealth* **holdings**, and honour,
such as none of the *kings* **sovereigns** have had
that have *been before thee* **at thy face**,
neither shall there any after thee have the like.
13 Then *Solomon* **Shelomoh** came *from his journey*
to the *high place* **bamah** that was at *Gibeon* **Gibon**
to *Jerusalem* **Yeru Shalem**,
from *before* **the face of**
the *tabernacle* **tent** of the congregation,
and reigned over *Israel* **Yisra El**.
14 And *Solomon* **Shelomoh**
gathered chariots and *horsemen* **cavalry**:
and he had a thousand and four hundred chariots,
and twelve thousand *horsemen* **cavalry**,
which he *placed* **set** in the chariot cities,
and with the *king* **sovereign** at *Jerusalem* **Yeru Shalem**.
15 And the *king made* **sovereign gave** silver and gold
at *Jerusalem* **Yeru Shalem** *as plenteous* as stones,
and cedar trees *made* **gave** he as the sycomore trees
that are in the *vale* **lowland** for abundance.
16 And *Solomon* **Shelomoh** had horses
brought **proceed** out of *Egypt* **Misrayim**,
and *linen yarn* **troops**:
the *king's* **sovereign's** merchants
received **took** the *linen yarn* **troops** at a price.
17 And they *fetched up* **ascended**,
and brought forth out of *Egypt* **Misrayim**
a chariot for six hundred *shekels of* silver,
and an horse for an hundred and fifty:
and so brought they out *horses*
for all the *kings* **sovereigns** of the *Hittites* **Hethiy**,
and for the *kings* **sovereigns** of *Syria* **Aram**,
by their *means* **hand**.

SHELOMOH PREPARES TO BUILD THE HOUSE OF YAH VEH

2 And *Solomon determined* **Shelomoh said**
to build an house for the name of *the LORD* **Yah Veh**,
and an house for his *kingdom* **sovereigndom**.
2 And *Solomon* **Shelomoh**
told out threescore and ten **scribed seventy** thousand men
to bear burdens **— burdenbearers**,
and *fourscore* **eighty** thousand **men**
to hew in the mountain,
and three thousand and six hundred to oversee them.
3 And *Solomon* **Shelomoh** sent to *Huram* **Hiram**
the *king* **sovereign** of *Tyre* **Sor**, saying,
As thou didst *deal* **work** with David my father,
and didst send him cedars
to build him an house to *dwell* **settle** therein,
even so deal with me.
4 Behold, I build an house
to the name of *the LORD* **Yah Veh** my *God* **Elohim**,
to *dedicate* **hallow** it to him,
and to *burn before him* **incense at his face**
sweet incense **of aromatics**,
and for the continual *shewbread* **arrangement**,
and for the *burnt offerings* **holocausts**
morning and evening,
on the *sabbaths* **shabbaths**, and on the new moons,
and on the *solemn feasts* **festivals**
of *the LORD* **Yah Veh** our *God* **Elohim**.
This is *an ordinance for ever to Israel* **eternal to Yisra El**.
5 And the house which I build is great:
for great is our *God* **Elohim** above all *gods* **elohim**.
6 But who *is able* **hath obtained force**
to build him an house,
seeing the *heaven* **heavens**
and *heaven* **the heavens** of *heavens* **the heavens**
cannot contain him?
who am I then, that I should build him an house,
save only to burn sacrifice **except to incense**
before him **at his face**?
7 Send me now therefore a man
cunning **wise** to work in gold,
and in silver, and in *brass* **copper**, and in iron,
and in purple, and crimson, and blue,
and that *can skill* **percieveth** to *grave* **engrave engravings**
with the *cunning men* **wise** that are with me
in *Judah* **Yah Hudah** and in *Jerusalem* **Yeru Shalem**,
whom David my father *did provide* **prepared**.
8 Send me also cedar trees, *fir* **cypress** trees,
and *algum* **algumim** trees, out of Lebanon:
for I know that thy servants
can skill **perceive** to cut timber in Lebanon; and, behold,
my servants shall be with thy servants,
9 Even to prepare me timber in abundance:
for the house which I am about to build
shall be *wonderful* **marvellous and** great.
10 And, behold, I *will* **shall** give to thy servants,
the *hewers* **choppers** that cut timber,

twenty thousand *measures* **kors** of *beaten* **struck** wheat,
and twenty thousand *measures* **kors** of barley,
and twenty thousand baths of wine,
and twenty thousand baths of oil.
11 Then *Huram* **Hiram,** the *king* **sovereign** of *Tyre* **Sor**
answered **said** in *writing* **inscribings,**
which he sent to *Solomon* **Shelomoh,**
Because *the LORD* **Yah Veh** hath loved his people,
he hath *made* **given** thee *king* **sovereign** over them.
12 *Huram* **Hiram** said *moreover,*
Blessed be
the LORD God **Yah Veh Elohim** of *Israel* **Yisra El,**
that *made heaven* **worked the heavens** and earth,
who hath given to David the *king* **sovereign** a wise son,
endued with prudence **knowing comprehension**
and *understanding* **discernment,**
that might build an house for *the LORD* **Yah Veh,**
and an house for his *kingdom* **sovereigndom.**
13 And now I have sent a *cunning* **wise** man,
endued with understanding **knowing discernment,**
of *Huram* **Hiram** my father's,
14 The son of a woman of the daughters of Dan,
and his father was a *man of Tyre* **Soriy,**
skilful **perceiving** to work in gold, and in silver,
in *brass* **copper,** in iron, in stone, and in timber,
in purple, in blue, and in *fine* **bleached** linen,
and in crimson;
also to *grave* **engrave** any *manner of graving* **engraving,**
and to *find out every device* **fabricate any fabrication**
which shall *put to* **be given** him,
with thy *cunning men* **wise,**
and with the *cunning men* **wise**
of my *lord* **adoni** David thy father.
15 Now therefore
the wheat, and the barley, the oil, and the wine,
which my *lord* **adoni** hath *spoken of* **said,**
let him send unto his servants:
16 And we *will* **shall** cut *wood* **timber** out of Lebanon,
as much as thou shalt need:
and we *will* **shall** bring it to thee in *flotes* **rafts** by sea
to *Joppa* **Yapho;**
and thou shalt *carry* **ascend** it *up*
to *Jerusalem* **Yeru Shalem.**
17 And *Solomon* **Shelomoh**
numbered **scribed** all the *strangers* **men sojourners**
that were in the land of *Israel* **Yisra El,**
after the *numbering* **scribing**
wherewith David his father had *numbered* **scribed** them;
and they were found an hundred and fifty thousand
and three thousand and six hundred.
18 And he *set* **worked**
threescore and ten **seventy** thousand of them
to be *bearers of burdens* **burdenbearers,**
and *fourscore* **eighty** thousand
to be hewers in the mountain,
and three thousand and six hundred overseers
to *set* **serve** the people *a work* **who serve.**

SHELOMOH BEGINS TO BUILD THE HOUSE OF YAH VEH

3 Then *Solomon* **Shelomoh** began to build
the house of *the LORD* **Yah Veh**
at *Jerusalem* **Yeru Shalem** in mount *Moriah* **Mori Yah,**
where the LORD appeared **which was seen**
unto **by** David his father,
in the place that David had prepared
in the threshingfloor of Ornan the *Jebusite* **Yebusiy.**
2 And he began to build
in the second *day* of the second month,
in the fourth year of his *reign* **sovereigndom.**

THE DIMENSIONS OF THE HOUSE OF YAH VEH

3 Now these are *the things* **those**
wherein *Solomon* **Shelomoh** was *instructed* **founded**
for the building of the house of *God* **Elohim.**
The length by cubits after the first measure
was *threescore* **sixty** cubits,
and the breadth twenty cubits.
4 And the porch
that was *in the front* **at the face** *of the house,*
the length **at the face** of it
was *according to* **as** the breadth of the house,
twenty cubits,
and the height was an hundred and twenty:
and he overlaid it within with pure gold.
5 And the greater house
he *cieled* **covered** with *fir* **cypress** tree,
which he *overlaid* **covered** with *fine* **the best** gold,
and *set* **ascended** thereon palm trees and chains.
6 And he *garnished* **overlaid** the house
with precious stones for *beauty* **adornment:**
and the gold was gold of *Parvaim* **Parvayim.**
7 He *overlaid* **covered** *also* the house,
the beams,the *posts* **thresholds,** and the walls thereof,
and the doors thereof, with gold;
and *graved cherubims* **engraved cherubim** on the walls.
8 And he *made* **worked**
the *most holy house* **Holy of Holies,**
the length *whereof* **at the face**
was *according to* **as** the breadth of the house,
twenty cubits, and the breadth thereof twenty cubits:
and he *overlaid* **covered** it with *fine* **the best** gold,
amounting to six hundred *talents* **rounds.**
9 And the weight of the nails was fifty shekels of gold.
And he *overlaid* **covered** the upper *chambers* **rooms**
with gold.
10 And in the *most holy house* **Holy of Holies**
he *made* **worked**
two *cherubims* **cherubim** of *image* **carved** work,
and overlaid them with gold.
11 And the wings of the *cherubims* **cherubim**
were twenty cubits long:
one wing *of the one cherub* was five cubits,
reaching **touching** to the wall of the house:
and the other wing was *likewise* five cubits,
reaching **touching** to the wing of the *other* **one** cherub.
12 And *one* **the** wing of the *other* **one** cherub
was five cubits,
reaching **touching** to the wall of the house:
and the *other* **one** wing was five cubits *also,*
joining **adhering** to the wing of the *other* **one** cherub.
13 The wings of these *cherubims* **cherubim**
spread themselves forth twenty cubits:
and they stood on their feet,
and their faces were *inward* **toward the house.**
14 And he *made* **worked** the vail of blue, and purple,
and crimson, and *fine* **bleached** linen,
and *wrought cherubims* **ascended cherubim** thereon.
15 Also he *made before* **worked at the face of** the house
two pillars of thirty and five cubits *high* **in length,**
and the *chapiter* **cap** that was on the top of each of them
was five cubits.
16 And he *made* **worked** chains, as in the *oracle* **pulpit,**
and *put* **gave** them on the heads of the pillars;
and *made* **worked** an hundred pomegranates,
and *put* **gave** them on the chains.
17 And he *reared* **raised** up the pillars
before **at the face of** the *temple* **manse,**
one on the right *hand,* and *the other* **one** on the left;
and called the name of that on the right *hand*
Jachin **Yachin,**
and the name of that on the left
Boaz.

THE FURNISHINGS OF THE HOUSE OF YAH VEH

4 Moreover
he *made an* **worked a sacrifice** altar of *brass* **copper,**
twenty cubits the length thereof,
and twenty cubits the breadth thereof,
and ten cubits the height thereof.
2 Also he *made* **worked** a *molten* **poured** sea
of ten cubits from *brim* **lip** to *brim* **lip,**
round **about** in compass,
and five cubits the height thereof;
and a line of thirty cubits
did compass **surrounded** it round about.
3 And under it was the *similitude* **likeness** of oxen,
which *did compass* **surrounded** it round about:
ten in a cubit,
compassing **surrounding** the sea round about.
Two rows of oxen were *cast* **poured,**
when it was cast **in casting.**
4 It stood upon twelve oxen,
three *looking* toward **the face of** the north,

and three *looking* toward **the face of** the *west* **sea**,
and three *looking* toward **the face of** the south,
and three *looking* toward **the face of** the *east* **rising**:
and the sea was *set* above upon them,
and all their *hinder parts* **backs**
were *inward* **toward the house**.
And the thickness of it was *an handbreadth* **a palm span**,
and the *brim* **lip** of it like the work of the *brim* **lip** of a cup,
with *flowers* **blossoms** of lilies;
and it *received* **prevailed**
and *held* **contained** three thousand baths.
He *made* **worked** also ten lavers,
and *put* **gave** five on the right *hand*, and five on the left,
to *wash* **baptise** in them:
such *things* as they *offered* **worked**
for the *burnt offering* **holocaust**
they *washed* **cleansed** in them;
but the sea was for the priests to *wash* **baptize** in.
And he *made* **worked** ten *candlesticks* **menorah** of gold
according to their *form* **judgment**,
and *set* **gave** them in the *temple* **manse**,
five on the right *hand*, and five on the left.
He *made* **worked** also ten tables,
and *placed* **set** them in the *temple* **manse**,
five on the right *side*, and five on the left.
And he *made* **worked**
an hundred *basons* **sprinklers** of gold.
Furthermore he *made* **worked** the court of the priests,
and the great court, and doors for the court,
and overlaid the doors of them with *brass* **copper**.
0 And he *set* **gave** the sea
on the right *side of the east end* **shoulder toward the east**,
over against **toward** the south.
1 And *Huram made* **Hiram worked** the *pots* **caldrons**,
and the shovels, and the *basons* **sprinklers**.
And *Huram* **Hiram** finished the work
that he was to *make* **work**
for *king Solomon* **sovereign Shelomoh**
for the house of *God* **Elohim**;
2 *To wit*, the two pillars, and the *pommels* **bowls**,
and the *chapiters* **caps**
which were on the top of the two pillars,
and the two *wreaths* **nets** to cover the two *pommels* **bowls**
of the *chapiters* **caps** which were on the top of the pillars;
3 And four hundred pomegranates
on the two *wreaths* **nets**;
two rows of pomegranates on *each wreath* **one net**,
to cover the two *pommels* **bowls** of the *chapiters* **caps**
which were upon **the face of** the pillars.
4 He *made* **worked** also bases,
and lavers *made* **worked** he upon the bases;
5 One sea, and twelve oxen under it.
6 The *pots* **caldrons** also, and the shovels,
and the *fleshhooks* **forks**, and all their instruments,
did *Huram* **Hiram** his father *make* **work**
to *king Solomon* **sovereign Shelomoh**
for the house of *the LORD* **Yah Veh**
of *bright brass* **scoured copper**.
7 In the *plain* **environ** of *Jordan* **Yarden**
did the *king cast* **sovereign pour** them,
in the *clay ground* **thicknesses of the soil**
between *Succoth* **Sukkoth/Brush Arbors**
and *Zeredathah* **Seredah**.
18 Thus *Solomon* **Shelomoh**
made **worked** all these *vessels* **instruments**
in *great* **mighty** abundance:
for the weight of the *brass* **copper**
could not be *found out* **probed**.
19 And *Solomon* **Shelomoh**
made **worked** all the *vessels* **instruments**
that were for the house of *God* **Elohim**,
the golden **sacrifice** altar also,
and the tables whereon the *shewbread* **facebread** was *set*;
20 *Moreover* the *candlesticks* **menorah** with their lamps,
that they should burn after the *manner* **judgment**
before **at the face of** the *oracle* **pulpit**,
of *pure* **concentrated** gold;
21 And the *flowers* **blossoms**,
and the lamps, and the tongs,
made he of gold, *and that perfect* — **the perfection of** gold;
22 And the *snuffers* **tweezers**, and the *basons* **sprinklers**,
and the *spoons* **bowls**, and the *censers* **trays**,
of pure **concentrated** gold:
and the *entry* **portal** of the house,
the inner doors thereof
for the *most holy place* **Holy of Holies**,
and the doors of the house of the *temple* **manse**,
were of gold.

THE ARK BROUGHT INTO THE HOUSE OF YAH VEH

5 Thus all the work
that *Solomon made* **Shelomoh worked**
for the house of *the LORD* **Yah Veh**
was finished **they did shalam**:
and *Solomon* **Shelomoh** brought in
all the *things that* **holies of** David his father *had dedicated*;
and the silver, and the gold, and all the instruments,
put **gave** he among the treasures
of the house of *God* **Elohim**.
2 Then *Solomon assembled* **Shelomoh congregated**
the elders of *Israel* **Yisra El**,
and all the heads of the *tribes* **rods**,
the *chief* **hierarch** of the fathers
of the *children* **sons** of *Israel* **Yisra El**,
unto *Jerusalem* **Yeru Shalem**,
to *bring up* **ascend**
the ark of the covenant of *the LORD* **Yah Veh**
out of the city of David, which is *Zion* **Siyon**.
3 Wherefore all the men of *Israel* **Yisra El**
assembled **congregated** *themselves*
unto the *king* **sovereign**
in the *feast* **celebration** which was in the seventh month.
4 And all the elders of *Israel* **Yisra El** came;
and the *Levites took up* **Leviym bore** the ark.
5 And they *brought up* **ascended** the ark,
and the *tabernacle* **tent** of the congregation,
and all the holy *vessels* **instruments**
that were in the *tabernacle* **tent**,
these did the priests and the *Levites* **Leviym**
bring up **ascend**.
6 Also *king Solomon* **sovereign Shelomoh**,
and all the *congregation* **witness** of *Israel* **Yisra El**
that were *assembled* **congregated** unto him
before **at the face of** the ark,
sacrificed *sheep* **flock** and oxen,
which could not be *told* **scribed** nor numbered
for *multitude* **abundance**.
7 And the priests brought in
the ark of the covenant of *the LORD* **Yah Veh**
unto his place,
to the *oracle* **pulpit** of the house,
into the *most holy place* **Holy of Holies**,
even under the wings of the *cherubims* **cherubim**:
8 For the *cherubims* **cherubim**
spread forth their wings over the place of the ark,
and the *cherubims* **cherubim**
covered the ark and the staves thereof above.
9 And they *drew out* **lengthened** the staves *of the ark*,
that the *ends* **heads** of the staves were seen from the ark
before **at the face of** the *oracle* **pulpit**;
but they were not seen without.
And there it is unto this day.
10 There was *nothing* **naught** in the ark
save **except** the two *tables* **slabs**
which *Moses put* **Mosheh gave** therein at Horeb,
when *the LORD made* **Yah Veh cut** *a covenant*
with the *children* **sons** of *Israel* **Yisra El**,
when they *came* **went** out of *Egypt* **Misrayim**.

THE HONOUR OF YAH VEH
FILLS THE HOUSE OF YAH VEH

11 And it *came to pass* **became**,
when the priests
were *come* **gone** out of the *holy place* **holies**:
(for all the priests that were *present* **found**
were *sanctified* **hallowed**,
and did not then *wait* **guard** by *course* **allotment**:
12 Also the *Levites* **Leviym** which were the singers,
all of them of Asaph, of Heman, of *Jeduthun* **Yeduthun**,
with their sons and their brethren,
being arrayed **enrobed** in *white* **bleached** linen,
having cymbals and *psalteries* **bagpipes** and harps,

stood at the *east end* **rising** of the **sacrifice** altar,
and with them an hundred and twenty priests
sounding **trumpeting** with trumpets:)
13 It *came even to pass* **became**,
as the trumpeters and singers were as one,
to make one *sound* **voice** to be heard in *praising* **halaling**
and *thanking the LORD* **extending hands to Yah Veh**;
and when they lifted *up* their voice with the trumpets
and cymbals and instruments of *musick* **song**,
and *praised the LORD* **halaled Yah Veh**, *saying*,
For he is good; for his mercy *endureth for ever* **be eternal**:
that then the house was filled with a cloud,
even the house of *the LORD* **Yah Veh**;
14 So that the priests could not stand to minister
by reason **at the face** of the cloud:
for the *glory* **honour** of *the LORD* **Yah Veh**
had filled the house of *God* **Elohim**.

SHELOMOH RECOUNTS YAH VEH'S PROMISES

6 Then said *Solomon* **Shelomoh**,
The LORD **Yah Veh** hath said
that he *would dwell* **should tabernacle**
in the *thick* **dripping** darkness.
2 But I have built an house of habitation for thee,
and *a place* **an establishment** for thy *dwelling* **settling**
for ever **eternally**.
3 And the *king* **sovereign** turned his face,
and blessed the whole congregation of *Israel* **Yisra El**:
and all the congregation of *Israel* **Yisra El** stood.
4 And he said,
Blessed be
the LORD God **Yah Veh Elohim** of *Israel* **Yisra El**,
who hath with his hands
fulfilled that which he *spake* **worded** with his mouth
to my father David, saying,
5 Since the day that I brought forth my people
out of the land of *Egypt* **Misrayim**
I chose no city among all the *tribes* **scions** of *Israel* **Yisra El**
to build an house in, that my name might be there;
neither chose I any man to be *a ruler* **eminent**
over my people *Israel* **Yisra El**:
6 But I have chosen *Jerusalem* **Yeru Shalem**,
that my name might be there;
and have chosen David
to be over my people *Israel* **Yisra El**.
7 Now it was in the heart of David my father
to build an house for the name
of *the LORD God* **Yah Veh Elohim** of *Israel* **Yisra El**.
8 But *the LORD* **Yah Veh** said to David my father,
Forasmuch as it was in thine heart
to build an house for my name,
thou didst *well* **good** in that it was in thine heart:
9 *Notwithstanding* **Only** thou shalt not build the house;
but thy son which shall *come* **go** forth out of thy loins,
he shall build the house for my name.
10 *The LORD* **Yah Veh** *therefore*
hath *performed* **raised** his word
that he hath *spoken* **worded**:
for I am risen up in the room of David my father,
and am *set* **settled** on the throne of *Israel* **Yisra El**,
as *the LORD promised* **Yah Veh worded**,
and have built the house for the name
of *the LORD God* **Yah Veh Elohim** of *Israel* **Yisra El**.
11 And *in it* **therein** have I *put* **set** the ark,
wherein is the covenant of *the LORD* **Yah Veh**,
that he *made* **cut** with the *children* **sons** of *Israel* **Yisra El**.

SHELOMOH'S PRAYER OF HANUKKAH

12 And he stood *before* **at the face of** the **sacrifice** altar
of *the LORD* **Yah Veh**
in the presence of all the congregation of *Israel* **Yisra El**,
and spread forth his *hands* **palms**:
13 For *Solomon* **Shelomoh**
had *made* **worked** a *brasen scaffold* **copper laver**,
of five cubits long, and five cubits broad,
and three cubits high,
and had *set* **given** it in the midst of the court:
and upon it he stood, and kneeled down upon his knees
before all the congregation of *Israel* **Yisra El**,
and spread forth his *hands* **palms**
toward *heaven* **the heavens**.
14 And said,
O *LORD God* **Yah Veh Elohim** of *Israel* **Yisra El**,
there is no *God* **Elohim** like thee
in the *heaven* **heavens**, nor in the earth;
which *keepest* **guardest** covenant,
and *shewest mercy unto* **merciest** thy servants,
that walk *before thee* **at thy face** with all their hearts:
15 Thou which hast *kept* **guarded**
with thy servant David my father
that which thou hast *promised* **worded** him;
and *spakest* **wordest** with thy mouth,
and hast fulfilled it with thine hand, as *it is* this day.
16 Now *therefore*,
O *LORD God* **Yah Veh Elohim** of *Israel* **Yisra El**,
keep **guard** with thy servant David my father
that which thou hast *promised* **worded** him, saying,
There shall not *fail* **be cut off** to thee
a man in my *sight* **face**
to *sit* **settle** upon the throne of *Israel* **Yisra El**;
yet so that **only if** thy *children* **sons**
take heed to **guard** their way to walk in my *law* **torah**,
as thou hast walked *before me* **at my face**.
17 Now *then*,
O *LORD God* **Yah Veh Elohim** of *Israel* **Yisra El**,
let thy word be *verified* **amened**,
which thou hast *spoken* **worded** unto thy servant David.
18 But *will God* **shall Elohim**
in very deed dwell **truly settle** with *men* **humanity**
on the earth?
behold, *heaven* **the heavens**
and the *heaven* **heavens** of *heavens* **the heavens**
cannot contain thee;
how much less this house which I have built!
19 *Have respect* **Face** *therefore* to the prayer of thy servant,
and to his supplication,
O *LORD* **Yah Veh** my *God* **Elohim**,
to hearken unto the *cry* **shout** and the prayer
which thy servant prayeth *before thee* **at thy face**:
20 That thine eyes may be open upon this house
by day and night,
upon the place whereof thou hast said
that thou *wouldest put* **shouldest set** thy name there;
to hearken unto the prayer
which thy servant prayeth toward this place.
21 Hearken therefore unto the supplications of thy servant,
and of thy people *Israel* **Yisra El**,
which they shall *make* **pray** toward this place:
hear thou
from *thy dwelling place* **the place of thy settlement**,
even from *heaven* **the heavens**;
and when thou hearest, forgive.
22 If a man sin against his *neighbour* **friend**,
and an oath be laid upon him
to *make him swear* **oath him**,
and the oath come
before thine **at the face of thy sacrifice** altar in this house;
23 Then hear thou from *heaven* **the heavens**, and *do* **work**,
and judge thy servants,
by *requiting* **turning back** the wicked,
by *recompensing* **giving** his way upon his own head;
and by justifying the *righteous* **just**,
by giving him according to his *righteousness* **justness**.
24 And if thy people *Israel* **Yisra El**
be *put to the worse* **smitten**
before **at the face of** the enemy,
because they have sinned against thee;
and shall return and *confess* **extend hands to** thy name,
and pray and *make supplication* **ask charism**
before thee **at thy face** in this house;
25 Then hear thou from the heavens,
and forgive the sin of thy people *Israel* **Yisra El**,
and *bring* **return** them *again* unto the *land* **soil**
which thou gavest to them and to their fathers.
26 When the *heaven is shut up* **heavens be restrained**,
and there is no rain,
because they have sinned against thee;
yet if they pray toward this place,
and *confess* **extend hands to** thy name,
and turn from their sin,
when thou *dost afflict* **shalt humble** them;
27 Then hear thou from *heaven* **the heavens**,

and forgive the sin of thy servants,
and of thy people *Israel* **Yisra El**,
when thou hast *taught* **directed** them the good way,
wherein they should walk;
and *send* **give** rain upon thy land,
which thou hast given unto thy people for an inheritance.
28 If there be *dearth* **famine** in the land,
if there be pestilence,
if there be blasting, or *mildew* **pale green**,
locusts, or caterpillers;
if their enemies *besiege* **tribulate** them
in the *cities* **land** of their *land* **portals**;
whatsoever *sore* **plague**
or whatsoever *sickness* **disease** there be:
29 Then what prayer or what supplication soever
shall be made of any *man* **human**,
or of all thy people *Israel* **Yisra El**,
when *every one* **man** shall know
his own *sore* **plague** and his own *grief* **sorrow**,
and shall spread forth his *hands* **palms** in this house:
30 Then hear thou from *heaven* **the heavens**
thy dwelling place **the place of thy settlement**,
and forgive,
and *render* **give** unto every man
according unto all his ways,
whose heart thou knowest;
(for thou only knowest the hearts
of the *children* **sons** of *men* **humanity**:)
31 That they may *fear* **awe** thee, to walk in thy ways,
so long as **all the days** they live
in the land **upon the face of the soil**
which thou gavest unto our fathers.
32 Moreover concerning the stranger,
which is not of thy people *Israel* **Yisra El**,
but is come from a far *country* **land**
for thy great name's sake,
and thy *mighty* **strong** hand, and thy stretched out arm;
if they come and pray in this house;
33 Then hear thou from the heavens,
even from *thy dwelling place* **the place of thy settlement**,
and *do* **work** according to all
that the stranger calleth to thee for;
that all people of the earth may know thy name,
and *fear* **awe** thee,
as doth thy people *Israel* **Yisra El**,
and may know that this house which I have built
is called by thy name.
34 If thy people go out to war against their enemies
by the way that thou shalt send them,
and they pray unto thee *toward* **by the way of** this city
which thou hast chosen,
and the house which I have built for thy name;
35 Then hear thou from the heavens
their prayer and their supplication,
and *maintain* **work** their *cause* **judgment**.
36 If they sin against thee,
(for there is no *man* **human** which sinneth not,)
and thou be angry with them,
and *deliver* **give** them over
before **at the face of** their enemies,
and they *carry* **capture** them *away captives*
unto a land far off or near;
37 Yet if they *bethink themselves* **bring back to their heart**
in the land whither they are *carried captive* **captured**,
and turn and pray *unto thee* in the land of their captivity,
saying, We have sinned,
we have *done amiss* **distorted**, and have dealt wickedly;
38 If they return to thee
with all their heart and with all their soul
in the land of their captivity,
whither they have *carried* **captured** them *captives*,
and pray *toward* **in the way of** their land,
which thou gavest unto their fathers,
and *toward* the city which thou hast chosen,
and *toward* the house which I have built for thy name:
39 Then hear thou from the heavens,
even from *thy dwelling place* **the place of thy settlement**,
their prayer and their supplications,
and *maintain* **work** their *cause* **judgment**,
and forgive thy people which have sinned against thee.
40 Now, my *God* **Elohim**,
let, I beseech thee, thine eyes be open,
and let thine ears *be attent* **hearken**
unto the prayer *that is made* in this place.
41 Now therefore arise, O *LORD God* **Yah Veh Elohim**,
into thy *resting place* **rest**,
thou, and the ark of thy strength:
let thy priests, O *LORD God* **Yah Veh Elohim**,
be *clothed* **enrobed** with salvation,
and let thy *saints rejoice* **mercied cheer** in goodness.
42 O *LORD God* **Yah Veh Elohim**,
turn not away the face of thine anointed:
remember the mercies of David thy servant.

THE HANUKKAH OF THE HOUSE OF YAH VEH

7 Now when *Solomon* **Shelomoh**
had *made an end of* **finished** praying,
the fire *came down* **descended** from *heaven* **the heavens**,
and consumed
the *burnt offering* **holocaust** and the sacrifices;
and the *glory* **honour** of *the LORD* **Yah Veh** filled the house.
2 And the priests could not enter
into the house of *the LORD* **Yah Veh**,
because the *glory* **honour** of *the LORD* **Yah Veh**
had filled the *LORD'S house* **house of Yah Veh**.
3 And when all the *children* **sons** of *Israel* **Yisra El**
saw how the fire *came down* **descended**,
and the *glory* **honour** of *the LORD* **Yah Veh** upon the house,
they bowed themselves
with their *faces* **nostrils** to the *ground* **earth**
upon the pavement, and *worshipped* **prostrated**,
and *praised the LORD* **extended hands to Yah Veh**,
saying, For he is good;
for his mercy *endureth for ever* **is eternal**.
4 Then the *king* **sovereign** and all the people
offered **sacrificed** sacrifices
before the LORD **at the face of Yah Veh**.
5 And *king Solomon* **sovereign Shelomoh**
offered **sacrificed** a sacrifice
of twenty and two thousand oxen,
and an hundred and twenty thousand *sheep* **flocks**:
so the *king* **sovereign** and all the people
dedicated **hanukkahed** the house of *God* **Elohim**.
6 And the priests *waited* **stood** on their *offices* **guards**:
the *Levites* **Leviym** also with instruments of *musick* **song**
of *the LORD* **Yah Veh**,
which David the *king* **sovereign** had *made* **worked**
to *praise the LORD* **extend hands to Yah Veh**,
because **for** his mercy *endureth for ever* **is eternal**,
when David *praised* **halaled** by their *ministry* **hand**;
and the priests *sounded* **trumpeted** trumpets before them,
and all *Israel* **Yisra El** stood.
7 *Moreover Solomon* **Shelomoh**
hallowed the middle of the court
that was before **at the face of** the house of *the LORD* **Yah Veh**:
for there he *offered burnt offerings* **worked holocausts**,
and the fat of the *peace offerings* **shelamim**,
because the *brasen* **copper sacrifice** altar
which *Solomon* **Shelomoh** had *made* **worked**
was not able to *receive* **contain**
the *burnt offerings* **holocausts**,
and the *meat* offerings, and the fat.
8 Also at the same time *Solomon* **Shelomoh**
kept **worked** the *feast* **celebration** seven days,
and all *Israel* **Yisra El** with him,
a *very* **mighty** great congregation,
from the entering in of Hamath
unto the *river* **wadi** of *Egypt* **Misrayim**.
9 And in the eighth day
they *made* **worked** a *solemn* **private** assembly:
for they *kept* **worked** the *dedication* **hanukkah**
of the **sacrifice** altar seven days,
and the *feast* **celebration** seven days.
10 And on the three and twentieth day
of the seventh month
he sent the people away into their tents,
glad **cheerful** and *merry* **goodly** in heart
for the goodness
that *the LORD* **Yah Veh** had *shewed* **worked**
unto David, and to *Solomon* **Shelomoh**,
and to *Israel* **Yisra El** his people.

YAH VEH IS SEEN BY SHELOMOH

11 Thus *Solomon* **Shelomoh** finished
the house of *the LORD* **Yah Veh**,
and the *king's* **sovereign's** house:
and all that came into *Solomon's* **Sholomoh's** heart
to *make* **work** in the house of *the LORD* **Yah Veh**,
and in his own house, he *prosperously effected* **prospered**.
12 And *the LORD* **Yah Veh**
appeared to Solomon **was seen by Shelomoh** by night,
and said unto him, I have heard thy prayer,
and have chosen this place to myself
for an house of sacrifice.
13 If I *shut up heaven* **restrain the heavens**
that there be no rain,
or if I *command* **misvah** the locusts to devour the land,
or if I send pestilence among my people;
14 If my people,
which are called by my name
upon whom my name is called°,
shall humble themselves, and pray, and seek my face,
and turn from their *wicked* **evil** ways;
then *will* **shall** I hear from *heaven* **the heavens**,
and *will* **shall** forgive their sin,
and *will* **shall** heal their land.
°see: Yah Hudah in Lexicon
15 Now mine eyes shall be open,
and mine ears *attent* **hearken** unto the prayer
that is made in this place.
16 For now
have I chosen and *sanctified* **hallowed** this house,
that my name may be there *for ever* **eternally**:
and mine eyes and mine heart
shall be there *perpetually* **all days**.
17 And as for thee,
if thou *wilt* **shalt** walk *before me* **at my face**,
as David thy father walked,
and *do* **work** according to all
that I have *commanded* **misvahed** thee,
and shalt *observe* **guard** my statutes and my judgments;
18 Then *will* **shall** I *stablish* **raise**
the throne of thy *kingdom* **sovereigndom**,
according as I have *covenanted* **cut** with David thy father,
saying, There shall not *fail* **be cut off to** thee a man,
to *be ruler* **reign** in *Israel* **Yisra El**.
19 But if ye turn away,
and forsake my statutes and my *commandments* **misvoth**,
which I have *set before you* **given at thy face**,
and shall go and serve other *gods* **elohim**,
and worship them;
20 Then *will* **shall** I
pluck them up by the roots **uproot them**
out of my *land* **soil** which I have given them;
and this house,
which I have *sanctified* **hallowed** for my name,
will **shall** I cast out of my *sight* **face**,
and *will make* **shall give** it
to be a proverb and a *byword* **gibe**
among all *nations* **the peoples**.
21 And this house, which is *high* **become Elyon**,
shall be *an astonishment* **desolated**
to every one that passeth by it;
so that he shall say,
Why hath *the LORD done* **Yah Veh worked** thus
unto this land, and unto this house?
22 And it shall be *answered* **said**,
Because they forsook *the LORD God* **Yah Veh Elohim**
of their fathers,
which brought them forth
out of the land of *Egypt* **Misrayim**,
and laid hold on other *gods* **elohim**,
and *worshipped* **prostrated to** them, and served them:
therefore hath he brought all this evil upon them.

THE FAME OF SHELOMOH

8 And it *came to pass* **became**,
at the end of twenty years,
wherein *Solomon* **Shelomoh** had built
the house of *the LORD* **Yah Veh**, and his own house,
2 That the cities which *Huram* **Hiram**
had *restored* **given** to *Solomon* **Shelomoh**,
Solomon **Shelomoh** built them,
and caused the *children* **sons** of *Israel* **Yisra El**
to *dwell* **settle** there.
3 And *Solomon* **Shelomoh**
went to *Hamathzobah* **Hamath Sobah**,
and prevailed against it.
4 And he built Tadmor in the wilderness,
and all the *store* **storage** cities, which he built in Hamath.
5 Also he built *Bethhoron* **Beth Horon** the upper
and *Bethhoron* **Beth Horon** the nether,
fenced **rampart** cities, with walls, *gates* **doors**, and bars;
6 And Baalath,
and all the *store* **storage** cities
that *Solomon* **Shelomoh** had,
and all the chariot cities,
and the cities of the *horsemen* **cavalry**,
and all that *Solomon desired* **Shelomoh attached** to build
in *Jerusalem* **Yeru Shalem**, and in Lebanon,
and throughout all the land of his *dominion* **reign**.
7 *As for* all the people *that were left* **remaining**
of the *Hittites* **Hethiy**, and the *Amorites* **Emoriy**,
and the *Perizzites* **Perizziy**, and the *Hivites* **Hivviy**,
and the *Jebusites* **Yebusiy**,
which were not of *Israel* **Yisra El**,
8 *But* of their *children* **sons**,
who *were left* **remained** after them in the land,
whom the *children* **sons** of *Israel* **Yisra El**
consumed **finished** not,
them did *Solomon* **Shelomoh**
make **cause** *to pay tribute* **ascend a vassal** until this day.
9 But of the *children* **sons** of *Israel* **Yisra El**
did Solomon make **Shelomoh gave**
no servants for his work;
but they were men of war,
and *chief* **governor** of his *captains* **tertiaries**,
and *captains* **governors**
of his chariots and *horsemen* **cavalry**.
10 And these were the *chief* **governor**
of *king Solomon's* **sovereign Sholomoh's**
officers **station prefects**,
even two hundred and fifty,
that *bare rule* **subjugated** over the people.
11 And *Solomon brought up* **Shelomoh ascended**
the daughter of *Pharaoh* **Paroh** out of the city of David
unto the house that he had built for her:
for he said, My *wife* **woman** shall not *dwell* **settle**
in the house of David *king* **sovereign** of *Israel* **Yisra El**,
because *the places are holy* **of the holies**,
whereunto the ark of *the LORD* **Yah Veh** hath come.
12 Then *Solomon* **Shelomoh**
offered burnt offerings **holocausted holocausts**
unto *the LORD* **Yah Veh**
on the **sacrifice** altar of *the LORD* **Yah Veh**,
which he had built *before* **at the face of** the porch,
13 Even after a *certain rate every day* **day by day word**,
offering **holocausting**
according to the *commandment* **misvah** of *Moses* **Mosheh**,
on the *sabbaths* **shabbaths**, and on the new moons,
and on the *solemn feasts* **seasons**, three times in the year,
even in the *feast* **celebration** of *unleavened bread* **matsah**,
and in the *feast* **celebration** of weeks,
and in the *feast* **celebration**
of *tabernacles* **sukkoth/brush arbors**.
14 And he *appointed* **stood**,
according to the *order* **judgment** of David his father,
the *courses* **allotments** of the priests to their service,
and the *Levites* **Leviym** to their *charges* **guards**,
to *praise* **halal** and minister before the priests,
as the *duty of every day required* **day by day word**:
the porters also by their *courses* **allotments**
at every gate **portal by portal**:
for so *had David the man of God commanded*
was the misvah of David the man of Elohim.
15 And they *departed* **turned** not **aside**
from the *commandment* **misvah** of the *king* **sovereign**
unto the priests and *Levites* **Leviym**
concerning any *matter* **word**, or concerning the treasures.
16 Now all the work of *Solomon* **Shelomoh**
was prepared unto the day of the foundation
of the house of *the LORD* **Yah Veh**,
and until it was finished.

So the house of *the LORD* **Yah Veh**
was *perfected* **at shalom**.
17 Then went *Solomon* **Shelomoh**
to *Eziongeber* **Esyon Geber**, and to Eloth,
at the sea *side* **lip** in the land of Edom.
18 And *Huram* **Hiram** sent him
by the hands of his servants ships,
and servants that *had knowledge of* **knew** the sea;
and they went with the servants of *Solomon* **Shelomoh**
to Ophir,
and took thence
four hundred and fifty *talents* **rounds** of gold,
and brought them to *king Solomon* **sovereign Shelomoh**.

THE SOVEREIGNESS OF SHEBA

9 And when the *queen* **sovereigness** of Sheba
heard of the fame of *Solomon* **Shelomoh**,
she came to *prove Solomon* **test Shelomoh**
with *hard questions* **riddles** at *Jerusalem* **Yeru Shalem**,
with *a very great company* **mighty heavy valuables**,
and camels that bare spices,
and gold in abundance, and precious stones:
and when she was come to *Solomon* **Shelomoh**,
she *communed* **worded** with him
of all that was in her heart.
2 And *Solomon* **Shelomoh** told her all her *questions* **words**:
and there was *nothing hid* **no word concealed**
from *Solomon* **Shelomoh** which he told her not.
3 And when the *queen* **sovereigness** of Sheba
had seen the wisdom of *Solomon* **Shelomoh**,
and the house that he had built,
4 And the *meat* **food** of his table,
and the *sitting* **seat** of his servants,
and the *attendance* **function** of his ministers
and their *apparel* **robes**;
his *cupbearers* **butlers** also, and their *apparel* **robes**;
and his *ascent* **holocausts**
by which he *went up* **holocausted**
into the house of *the LORD* **Yah Veh**;
there was no more spirit in her.
5 And she said to the *king* **sovereign**,
It was a true *report* **word** which I heard in mine own land
of *thine acts* **thy words**, and of thy wisdom:
6 Howbeit I *believed* **trusted** not their words,
until I came, and mine eyes had seen it: and, behold,
the one half of the *greatness* **increase** of thy wisdom
was not told me:
for thou *exceedest the fame* **addest to the report**
that I heard.
7 *Happy* **Blithe** are thy men,
and *happy* **blithe** are these thy servants,
which stand continually *before thee* **at thy face**,
and hear thy wisdom.
8 Blessed be *the LORD* **Yah Veh** thy *God* **Elohim**,
which delighted in thee to *set* **give** thee on his throne,
to be *king* **sovereign**
for *the LORD* **Yah Veh** thy *God* **Elohim**:
because thy *God* **Elohim** loved *Israel* **Yisra El**,
to *establish* **stand** them *for ever* **eternally**,
therefore *made* **gave** he thee *king* **sovereign** over them,
to *do* **work** judgment and *justice* **justness**.
9 And she gave the *king* **sovereign**
an hundred and twenty *talents* **rounds** of gold,
and of spices *great* **mighty** abundance,
and precious stones:
neither was there any such spice
as the *queen* **sovereigness** of Sheba
gave *king Solomon* **sovereign Shelomoh**.
10 And the servants also of *Huram* **Hiram**,
and the servants of *Solomon* **Shelomoh**,
which brought gold from Ophir,
brought *algum* **algumim** trees and precious stones.
11 And the *king* **sovereign**
made **worked** of the *algum* **algumim** trees
terraces **highways** to the house of *the LORD* **Yah Veh**,
and to the *king's palace* **house of the sovereign**,
and harps and *psalteries* **bagpipes** for singers:
and there were none such *seen* **as these**
before in **at the face of** the land of *Judah* **Yah Hudah**.
12 And *king Solomon* **sovereign Shelomoh**
gave to the *queen* **sovereigness** of Sheba
all her *desire* **delight**, whatsoever she asked,
beside that which she had brought
unto the *king* **sovereign**.
So she turned, and went away to her own land,
she and her servants.
13 Now the weight of gold
that came to *Solomon* **Shelomoh** in one year
was six hundred and *threescore* **sixty** and six
talents **rounds** of gold;
14 Beside that
which *chapmen* **explorer men**
and merchants brought.
And all the *kings* **sovereigns** of Arabia
and governors of the *country* **land**
brought gold and silver to *Solomon* **Shelomoh**.
15 And *king Solomon* **sovereign Shelomoh**
made **worked** two hundred *targets* **shields** of beaten gold:
six hundred *shekels* of beaten gold
went **ascended** to one *target* **shield**.
16 And three hundred *shields* **bucklers**
made he of beaten gold:
three hundred *shekels of* gold
went **ascended** to one *shield* **buckler**.
And the *king put* **sovereign gave** them
in the house of the forest of Lebanon.
17 Moreover
the *king made* **sovereign worked** a great throne of ivory,
and overlaid it with pure gold.
18 And there were six steps to the throne,
with a footstool of gold,
which were fastened to the throne,
and *stays* **handles** on each side of the *sitting* **seated** place,
and two lions standing by the *stays* **handles**:
19 And twelve lions stood *there on the one side* **here**
and *on the other* **there** upon the six steps.
There was not the like
made **worked** in any *kingdom* **sovereigndom**.
20 And all the drinking *vessels* **instruments**
of *king Solomon* **sovereign Shelomoh** were *of* gold,
and all the *vessels* **instruments**
of the house of the forest of Lebanon
were of *pure* **concentrated** gold: none were of silver;
it was *not any thing accounted of* **naught fabricated**
in the days of *Solomon* **Shelomoh**.
21 For the *king's* **sovereign's** ships went to Tarshish
with the servants of *Huram* **Hiram**:
every three years once came the ships of Tarshish
bringing **bearing** gold, and silver,
ivory **tusks**, and apes, and peacocks.
22 And *king Solomon* **sovereign Shelomoh**
passed **greatened**
above all the *kings* **sovereigns** of the earth
in riches and wisdom.
23 And all the *kings* **sovereigns** of the earth
sought the *presence* **face** of *Solomon* **Shelomoh**,
to hear his wisdom,
that *God* **Elohim** had *put* **given** in his heart.
24 And they brought every man his *present* **offering**,
vessels **instruments** of silver,
and *vessels* **instruments** of gold,
and *raiment* **clothes**, *harness* **armour**,
and spices, horses, and mules,
a *rate* **word** year by year.
25 And *Solomon* **Shelomoh**
had four thousand stalls for horses and chariots,
and twelve thousand *horsemen* **cavalry**;
whom he *bestowed* **set** in the chariot cities,
and with the *king* **sovereign** at *Jerusalem* **Yeru Shalem**.
26 And he *reigned* **was sovereign**
over all the *kings* **sovereigns** from the river
even unto the land of the *Philistines* **Peleshethiy**,
and to the border of *Egypt* **Misrayim**.
27 And the *king* **sovereign**
made **gave** silver in *Jerusalem* **Yeru Shalem** as stones,
and cedar trees *made* **gave** he as the sycomore trees
that are in the *low plains* **lowlands** in abundance.
28 And they brought unto *Solomon* **Shelomoh**
horses out of *Egypt* **Misrayim**, and out of all lands.

THE DEATH OF SHELOMOH

29 Now the *rest* **remainder**
of the *acts* **words** of *Solomon* **Shelomoh**,
first and last,
are they not *written* **inscribed**
in the *book* **words** of Nathan the prophet,
and in the prophecy
of *Ahijah* **Achiy Yah** the *Shilonite* **Shilohiy**,
and in the visions of *Iddo* **Yedi** the seer
against *Jeroboam* **Yarob Am** the son of Nebat?
30 And *Solomon* **Shelomoh**
reigned in *Jerusalem* **Yeru Shalem** over all *Israel* **Yisra El**
forty years.
31 And *Solomon slept* **Shelomoh laid** with his fathers,
and he was *buried* **entombed**
in the city of David his father:
and *Rehoboam* **Rechab Am** his son reigned in his stead.

RECHAB AM REIGNS OVER YERU SHALEM

10 And *Rehoboam* **Rechab Am**
went to Shechem:
for to Shechem were all *Israel* **Yisra El** come
to *make* **have** him *king* **reign**.
2 And it *came to pass* **became**,
when *Jeroboam* **Yarob Am** the son of Nebat,
who was in *Egypt* **Misrayim**,
whither he had fled from the *presence* **face**
of *Solomon* **Shelomoh** the *king* **sovereign**, heard it,
that *Jeroboam* **Yarob Am** returned out of *Egypt* **Misrayim**.
3 And they sent and called him.
So *Jeroboam* **Yarob Am** and all *Israel* **Yisra El** came
and *spake* **worded** to *Rehoboam* **Rechab Am**, saying,
4 Thy father made our yoke *grievous* **hard**:
now therefore *ease* **slacken** thou *somewhat*
the *grievous servitude* **hard service** of thy father,
and his heavy yoke that he *put* **gave** upon us,
and we *will* **shall** serve thee.
5 And he said unto them,
Come again **Return** unto me after three days.
And the people *departed* **went**.
6 And *king Rehoboam* **sovereign Rechab Am** took counsel
with the old men that had stood
before Solomon **at the face of Shelomoh** his father
while he yet lived, saying,
What counsel give **How counsel** ye me
to return *answer* **word** to this people?
7 And they *spake* **worded** unto him, saying,
If thou be *kind* **good** to this people, and please them,
and *speak* **word** good words to them,
they *will* **shall** be thy servants *for ever* **all days**.
8 But he forsook the counsel
which the old men *gave him* **counselled**,
and *took counsel* **counselled** with the *young men* **children**
that were *brought* **grown** up with him,
that stood *before him* **at his face**.
9 And he said unto them,
What advice give **How counsel** ye
that we may return *answer* **word** to this people,
which have *spoken* **worded** to me, saying,
Ease somewhat **Slacken** the yoke
that thy father *did put* **gave** upon us?
10 And the *young men* **children**
that were *brought* **grown** up with him
spake **worded** unto him, saying,
Thus shalt thou *answer* **say to** the people
that *spake* **worded** unto thee, saying,
Thy father made our yoke heavy,
but *make* **slacken** thou it *somewhat lighter* for us;
thus shalt thou say unto them,
My *little finger shall be* **pinky is** thicker
than my father's loins.
11 For *whereas* **from the time**
my father *put* **loaded** a heavy yoke upon you,
I *will put more* **shall add** to your yoke:
my father *chastised* **disciplined** you with whips,
but I *will chastise* **shall discipline** you with scorpions.
12 So *Jeroboam* **Yarob Am** and all the people
came to *Rehoboam* **Rechab Am** on the third day,
as the *king bade* **sovereign worded**, saying,
Come again **Return** to me on the third day.
13 And the *king* **sovereign** answered them *roughly* **hardly**;
and *king Rehoboam* **sovereign Rechab Am**
forsook the counsel of the old men,
14 And *answered* **worded** them
after the *advice* **counsel** of the *young men* **children**,
saying, My father made your yoke heavy,
but I *will* **shall** add thereto:
my father *chastised* **disciplined** you with whips,
but I *will chastise* **shall discipline** *you* with scorpions.
15 So the *king* **sovereign** hearkened not unto the people:
for the cause was of *God* **Elohim**,
that *the LORD* **Yah Veh** might *perform* **raise** his word,
which he *spake* **worded**
by the hand of *Ahijah* **Achiy Yah** the *Shilonite* **Shilohiy**
to *Jeroboam* **Yarob Am** the son of Nebat.
16 And when all *Israel* **Yisra El** saw
that the *king* **sovereign**
would not hearken **hearkened not** unto them,
the people
answered the king **turned back to the sovereign**, saying,
What *portion* **allotment** have we in David?
and we have none inheritance in the son of *Jesse* **Yishay**:
every man to your tents, O *Israel* **Yisra El**:
and now, David, see to thine own house.
So all *Israel* **Yisra El** went to their tents.
17 But *as for* the *children* **sons** of *Israel* **Yisra El**
that *dwelt* **settled** in the cities of *Judah* **Yah Hudah**,
Rehoboam **Rechab Am** reigned over them.
18 Then *king Rehoboam* **sovereign Rechab Am**
sent Hadoram that was over the *tribute* **vassal**;
and the *children* **sons** of *Israel* **Yisra El**
stoned him with stones, that he died.
But *king Rehoboam* **sovereign Rechab Am**
made speed **strengthened himself**
to *get* **ascend** him *up* to his chariot,
to flee to *Jerusalem* **Yeru Shalem**.
19 And *Israel* **Yisra El** rebelled against the house of David
unto this day.

RECHAB AM RETURNS TO YERU SHALEM

11 And when *Rehoboam* **Rechab Am**
was come to *Jerusalem* **Yeru Shalem**,
he *gathered* **congregated**
of the house of *Judah* **Yah Hudah** and *Benjamin* **Ben Yamin**
an hundred and *fourscore* **eighty** thousand chosen *men*,
which were warriors **working war**,
to fight against *Israel* **Yisra El**,
that he might *bring* **return** the *kingdom* **sovereigndom**
again to *Rehoboam* **Rechab Am**.
2 But the word of *the LORD* **Yah Veh**
came to *Shemaiah* **Shema Yah** the man of *God* **Elohim**,
saying,
3 *Speak* **Say** unto *Rehoboam* **Rechab Am**
the son of *Solomon* **Shelomoh**,
king **sovereign** of *Judah* **Yah Hudah**,
and to all *Israel* **Yisra El** in *Judah* **Yah Hudah**
and *Benjamin* **Ben Yamin**, saying,
4 Thus saith *the LORD* **Yah Veh**,
Ye shall not *go up* **ascend**, nor fight against your brethren:
return every man to his house:
for this *thing is done* **word be** of me.
And they *obeyed* **heard** the words of *the LORD* **Yah Veh**,
and returned from going against *Jeroboam* **Yarob Am**.
5 And *Rehoboam* **Rechab Am**
dwelt **settled** in *Jerusalem* **Yeru Shalem**,
and built cities for *defence* **rampart** in *Judah* **Yah Hudah**.
6 He built even *Bethlehem* **Beth Lechem**,
and Etam, and *Tekoa* **Teqoha**,
7 And *Bethzur* **Beth Sur**, and *Shoco* **Sochoh**, and Adullam,
8 And Gath, and Mareshah, and Ziph,
9 And *Adoraim* **Adorayim**,
and Lachish, and *Azekah* **Azeqah**,
10 And *Zorah* **Sorah**, and *Aijalon* **Ayalon**, and Hebron,
which are in
Judah **Yah Hudah** and in *Benjamin* **Ben Yamin**
fenced **rampart** cities.
11 And he *fortified* **strengthened**
the *strong holds* **ramparts**,
and *put captains* **gave eminence** in them,
and *store* **treasure** of *victual* **food**, and of oil and wine.
12 And *in every several city* **city by city**
he put shields and *spears* **javelins**,

and *made* **strengthened** them
exceeding strong **aboundingly mighty,**
having *Judah* **Yah Hudah** and *Benjamin* **Ben Yamin**
on his side.
13 And the priests and the *Levites* **Leviym**
that were in all *Israel* **Yisra El** *resorted* **stood** to him
out of all their *coasts* **borders**.
14 For the *Levites* **Leviym**
left their suburbs and their possession,
and came to *Judah* **Yah Hudah**
and *Jerusalem* **Yeru Shalem**:
for *Jeroboam* **Yarob Am** and his sons
had *cast* **adandoned** them *off*
from *executing the priest's office* **priesting**
unto *the LORD* **Yah Veh**:
15 And he *ordained* **stood** him priests
for the *high places* **bamahs**,
and for the *devils* **bucks**, and for the calves
which he had *made* **worked**.
16 And after them
out of all the *tribes* **scions** of *Israel* **Yisra El**
such as *set* **gave** their hearts
to seek *the LORD God* **Yah Veh Elohim** of *Israel* **Yisra El**
came to *Jerusalem* **Yeru Shalem**,
to sacrifice
unto *the LORD God* **Yah Veh Elohim** of their fathers.
17 So they strengthened
the *kingdom* **sovereigndom** of *Judah* **Yah Hudah**,
and *made Rehoboam* **strengthened Rechab Am**
the son of *Solomon* **Shelomoh** *strong, three years*:
for three years
they walked in the way of David and *Solomon* **Shelomoh**.
18 And *Rehoboam* **Rechab Am**
took him *Mahalath* **Machalath**
the daughter of *Jerimoth* **Yerimoth**
the son of David to *wife* **woman**,
and *Abihail* **Abi Hail**
the daughter of *Eliab* **Eli Ab** the son of *Jesse* **Yishay**;
19 Which bare him *children* **sons**;
Jeush **Yeush**, and *Shamariah* **Shemar Yah**, and Zaham.
20 And after her he took Maachah
the daughter of *Absalom* **Abi Shalom**;
which bare him *Abijah* **Abi Yah**, and *Attai* **Attay**,
and Ziza, and Shelomith.
21 And *Rehoboam* **Rechab Am** loved Maachah
the daughter of *Absalom* **Abi Shalom**
above all his *wives* **women** and his concubines:
(for he *took* **bore** eighteen *wives* **women**,
and *threescore* **sixty** concubines;
and begat twenty and eight sons,
and *threescore* **sixty** daughters.)
22 And *Rehoboam* **Rechab Am**
made Abijah **stood Abi Yah**
the son of Maachah the *chief* **head**,
to be *ruler* **eminent** among his brethren:
for he thought to make him king **to have him reign**.
23 And he *dealt wisely* **discerned**,
and *dispersed of* **separated** all his *children* **sons**
throughout all the *countries* **lands**
of *Judah* **Yah Hudah** and *Benjamin* **Ben Yamin**,
unto every *fenced* **rampart** city:
and he gave them *victual* **food** in abundance.
And he *desired many wives* **asked a multitude of women**.

RECHAB AM FORSAKES THE TORAH

12 And it *came to pass* **became**,
when *Rehoboam* **Rechab Am**
had established the *kingdom* **sovereigndom**,
and had strengthened himself,
he forsook the *law* **torah** of *the LORD* **Yah Veh**,
and all *Israel* **Yisra El** with him.

SOVEREIGN OF MISRAYIM ASCENDS AGAINST YERU SHALEM

2 And it *came to pass* **became**, *that* in the fifth year
of *king Rehoboam* **sovereign Rechab Am**
Shishak *king* **sovereign** of *Egypt* **Misrayim**
came up **ascended** against *Jerusalem* **Yeru Shalem**,
because they had
transgressed **treasoned** against *the LORD* **Yah Veh**,
3 With twelve hundred chariots,
and *threescore* **sixty** thousand *horsemen* **cavalry**:
and the people were without number
that came with him out of *Egypt* **Misrayim**;
the *Lubims* **Lubiym**, the *Sukkiims* **Sukkiym**,
and the *Ethiopians* **Kushiym**.
4 And he *took* **captured** the *fenced* **rampart** cities
which *pertained* **be** to *Judah* **Yah Hudah**,
and came to *Jerusalem* **Yeru Shalem**.
5 Then came *Shemaiah* **Shema Yah** the prophet
to *Rehoboam* **Rechab Am**,
and to the *princes* **governors** of *Judah* **Yah Hudah**,
that were gathered *together* to *Jerusalem* **Yeru Shalem**
because **from the face** of Shishak, and said unto them,
Thus saith *the LORD* **Yah Veh**, ye have forsaken me,
and therefore have I also left you in the hand of Shishak.
6 Whereupon the *princes* **governors** of *Israel* **Yisra El**
and the *king* **sovereign** humbled themselves;
and they said, *The LORD is righteous* **Yah Veh is just**.
7 And when *the LORD* **Yah Veh**
saw that they humbled themselves,
the word of *the LORD* **Yah Veh**
came to *Shemaiah* **Shema Yah**, saying,
They have humbled themselves;
therefore I *will* **shall** not *destroy* **ruin** them,
but I *will grant* **shall give** them
some deliverance **a little escape**;
and my *wrath* **fury** shall not be poured out
upon *Jerusalem* **Yeru Shalem** by the hand of Shishak.
8 Nevertheless they shall be his servants;
that they may know my service,
and the service
of the *kingdoms* **sovereigndoms** of the *countries* **lands**.
9 So Shishak *king* **sovereign** of *Egypt* **Misrayim**
came up **ascended** against *Jerusalem* **Yeru Shalem**,
and took away the treasures
of the house of *the LORD* **Yah Veh**,
and the treasures
of the *king's* **sovereign's** house; he took all:
he *carried* **took** *away* also the *shields* **bucklers** of gold
which *Solomon* **Shelomoh** had *made* **worked**.
10 Instead of which *king Rehoboam* **sovereign Rechab Am**
made shields **worked bucklers** of *brass* **copper**,
and *committed* **oversaw** them
to the hands of the *chief* **governor** of the *guard* **runners**,
that *kept* **guarded** the *entrance* **portal**
of the *king's* **sovereign's** house.
11 And when the *king* **sovereign**
entered into the house of *the LORD* **Yah Veh**,
the *guard* **runners** came and *fetched* **lifted** them,
and *brought* **returned** them *again*
into the *guard* **runners** chamber.
12 And when he humbled himself,
the wrath of *the LORD* **Yah Veh** turned from him,
that he *would* **should** not *destroy* **ruin** him *altogether* **fully**:
and also in *Judah things* **Yah Hudah all** went *well* **good**.
13 So *king Rehoboam* **sovereign Rechab Am**
strengthened himself in *Jerusalem* **Yeru Shalem**,
and reigned:
for *Rehoboam* **Rechab Am**
was **a son of** one and forty years *old*
when he began to reign,
and he reigned seventeen years in *Jerusalem* **Yeru Shalem**,
the city which *the LORD* **Yah Veh** had chosen
out of all the *tribes* **scions** of *Israel* **Yisra El**,
to *put* **set** his name there.
And his mother's name was Naamah
an *Ammonitess* **Ammoniyth**.
14 And he *did* **worked** evil,
because he prepared not his heart
to seek *the LORD* **Yah Veh**.
15 Now the *acts* **words** of *Rehoboam* **Rechab Am**,
first and last,
are they not *written* **inscribed**
in the *book* **words** of *Shemaiah* **Shema Yah** the prophet,
and of Iddo the seer
concerning genealogies **genealogized**?
And there were wars between *Rehoboam* **Rechab Am**
and *Jeroboam continually* **Yarob Am all days**.
16 And *Rehoboam slept* **Rechab Am laid** with his fathers,
and was *buried* **entombed** in the city of David:
and *Abijah* **Abi Yah** his son reigned in his stead.

ABI YAH REIGNS OVER YAH HUDAH

13 Now in the eighteenth year
of *king Jeroboam* **sovereign Yarob Am**
began *Abijah* **Abi Yah** to reign over *Judah* **Yah Hudah**.
2 He reigned three years in *Jerusalem* **Yeru Shalem**.
His mother's name also was *Michaiah* **Michah Yah**
the daughter of *Uriel* **Uri El** of *Gibeah* **Gibah**.
And there was war
between *Abijah* **Abi Yah** and *Jeroboam* **Yarob Am**.
3 And *Abijah* **Abi Yah**
set the battle in array **lined up for war**
with an army of *valiant men of war* **mighty of valour**,
even four hundred thousand chosen men:
Jeroboam **Yarob Am** also
set the battle in array **lined up in war**
against him with eight hundred thousand chosen men,
being mighty *men* of valour.
4 And *Abijah stood up* **Abi Yah arose**
upon mount *Zemaraim* **Semarayim**,
which is in mount *Ephraim* **Ephrayim**, and said,
Hear me, thou *Jeroboam* **Yarob Am**, and all *Israel* **Yisra El**;
5 Ought ye not to know
that *the LORD God* **Yah Veh Elohim** of *Israel* **Yisra El**
gave the *kingdom* **sovereigndom** over *Israel* **Yisra El**
to David *for ever* **eternally**,
even to him and to his sons by a covenant of salt?
6 Yet *Jeroboam* **Yarob Am** the son of Nebat,
the servant of *Solomon* **Shelomoh** the son of David,
is risen up, and hath rebelled against his *lord* **adoni**.
7 And there are gathered unto him vain men,
the *children* **sons** of *Belial* **Beli Yaal**,
and have strengthened themselves
against *Rehoboam* **Rechab Am**
the son of *Solomon* **Shelomoh**,
when *Rehoboam* **Rechab Am**
was *young and tenderhearted* **a lad of tender heart**,
and could not
withstand them **strengthen himself at their face**.
8 And now ye *think* **say** to *withstand* **strengthen yourselves**
at the face of
the *kingdom* **sovereigndom** of *the LORD* **Yah Veh**
in the hand of the sons of David;
and ye be a great multitude,
and there are with you golden calves,
which *Jeroboam* **Yarob Am**
made **worked** you for *gods* **elohim**.
9 Have ye not *cast out* **expelled**
the priests of *the LORD* **Yah Veh**,
the sons of *Aaron* **Aharon**, and the *Levites* **Leviym**,
and have *made* **worked** you priests
after the manner of the nations of *other* lands?
so that whosoever cometh
to *consecrate himself* **fill his hand**
with a *young bullock* **steer the son of an ox**
and seven rams,
the same may be a priest
of *them that are no gods* **non—elohim**.
10 But as for us, *the LORD* **Yah Veh** is our *God* **Elohim**,
and we have not forsaken him;
and the priests, which minister unto *the LORD* **Yah Veh**,
are the sons of *Aaron* **Aharon**,
and the *Levites* **Leviym** wait upon *their business* **work**:
11 And they *burn* **incense** unto *the LORD* **Yah Veh**
every morning **by morning** and *every* evening **by evening**
burnt sacrifices **holocausts**
and *sweet* incense **of aromatics**:
the *shewbread* **arrangement bread**
also set they in order upon the pure table;
and the *candlestick* **menorah** of gold
with the lamps thereof,
to burn *every* evening **by evening**:
for we *keep* **guard** the *charge* **guard**
of *the LORD* **Yah Veh** our *God* **Elohim**;
but ye have forsaken him.
12 And, behold,
God **Elohim** himself is with us for *our captain* **head**,
and his priests with *sounding* **blasting** trumpets
to *cry alarm* **blast** against you.
O *children* **sons** of *Israel* **Yisra El**,
fight ye not against
the LORD God **Yah Veh Elohim** of your fathers;
for ye shall not prosper.
13 But *Jeroboam* **Yarob Am**
caused an ambushment to come about **lurked around**
behind them:
so they were *before Judah* **at the face of Yah Hudah**,
and *the ambushment was* **they lurked** behind them.
14 And when *Judah* **Yah Hudah**
looked **turned to face** back, behold,
the *battle* **war** was *before* **at their face** and behind:
and they cried unto *the LORD* **Yah Veh**,
and the priests *sounded with* **trumpeted** the trumpets.
15 Then the *men of Judah* **Yah Hudiy** gave a shout:
and as the *men of Judah* **Yah Hudiy** shouted,
it *came to pass* **became**,
that *God* **Elohim**
smote *Jeroboam* **Yarob Am** and all *Israel* **Yisra El**
before Abijah **at the face of**
Abi Yah and *Judah* **Yah Hudah**.
16 And the *children* **sons** of *Israel* **Yisra El**
fled *before Judah* **from the face of Yah Hudah**:
and *God delivered* **Elohim gave** them into their hand.
17 And *Abijah* **Abi Yah** and his people
slew **smote** them with a great *slaughter* **stroke**:
so there fell down *slain* **pierced** of *Israel* **Yisra El**
five hundred thousand chosen men.
18 Thus the *children* **sons** of *Israel* **Yisra El**
were *brought under* **subdued** at that time,
and the *children* **sons** of *Judah* **Yah Hudah**
prevailed **strengthened**,
because they *relied* **leaned**
upon *the LORD God* **Yah Veh Elohim** of their fathers.
19 And *Abijah* **Abi Yah** pursued after *Jeroboam* **Yarob Am**,
and *took* **captured** cities from him,
Bethel **Beth El** with the *towns* **daughters** thereof,
and *Jeshanah* **Yeshanah** with the *towns* **daughters** thereof,
and Ephrain with the *towns* **daughters** thereof.
20 Neither did *Jeroboam* **Yarob Am**
recover strength again **retain force**
in the days of *Abijah* **Abi Yah**:
and *the LORD struck* **Yah Veh smote** him, and he died.
21 But *Abijah waxed mighty* **Abi Yah strengthened**,
and *married* **bore him** fourteen *wives* **women**,
and begat twenty and two sons, and sixteen daughters.
22 And the rest of the *acts* **words** of *Abijah* **Abi Yah**,
and his ways, and his *sayings* **words**,
are *written* **inscribed**
in the *story* **commentary** of the prophet Iddo.

THE DEATH OF ABI YAH

14 So *Abijah slept* **Abi Yah laid** with his fathers,
and they *buried* **entombed** him in the city of David:
and Asa his son reigned in his stead.
In his days the land *was quiet* **rested** ten years.

ASA REIGNS OVER YAH HUDAH

2 And Asa *did* **worked**
that which was good and *right* **straight**
in the eyes of *the LORD* **Yah Veh** his *God* **Elohim**:
3 For he *took away* **turned aside**
the **sacrifice** altars of the strange *gods*,
and the *high places* **bamahs**,
and brake down the *images* **monoliths**,
and cut down the *groves* **asherim**:
4 And *commanded Judah* **said to Yah Hudah**
to seek *the LORD God* **Yah Veh Elohim** of their fathers,
and to *do* **work**
the *law* **torah** and the *commandment* **misvah**.
5 Also he *took away* **turned aside**
out of all the cities of *Judah* **Yah Hudah**
the *high places* **bamahs** and the *images* **sun icons**:
and the *kingdom* **sovereigndom**
was quiet before him **rested at his face**.
6 And he built *fenced* **rampart** cities in *Judah* **Yah Hudah**:
for the land *had rest* **rested**,
and he had no war in those years;
because *the LORD* **Yah Veh**
had *given him rest* **rested him**.
7 Therefore he said unto *Judah* **Yah Hudah**,
Let us build these cities,
and *make* **turn** about *them*
walls, and towers, *gates* **doors**, and bars,

while the land is yet *before us* **at our face**;
because we have sought
the LORD **Yah Veh** our *God* **Elohim**,
we have sought him,
and he hath
given us rest on every side **rested us round about**.
So they built and prospered.
8 And Asa had *an army of men* **mighty of valour**
that bare *targets* **shields** and *spears* **javelins**,
out of *Judah* **Yah Hudah** three hundred thousand;
and out of *Benjamin* **Ben Yamin**,
that bare *shields* **bucklers** and *drew* **arched** bows,
two hundred and *fourscore* **eighty** thousand:
all these were mighty *men* of valour.
9 And there *came out* **went** against them
Zerah **Zerach** the *Ethiopian* **Kushiy**
with *an host of* a thousand thousand **valiant**,
and three hundred chariots; and came unto Mareshah.
10 Then Asa went out *against him* **at his face**,
and they *set the battle in array* **lined up for war**
in the valley of *Zephathah* **Sephathah** at Mareshah.
11 And Asa
cried **called** unto *the LORD* **Yah Veh** his *God* **Elohim**,
and said, *LORD* **Yah Veh**,
it is *nothing* **naught** with thee to help,
whether with **between** many,
or *with* them that have no *power* **force**:
help us, O *LORD* **Yah Veh** our *God* **Elohim**;
for we *rest* **lean** on thee,
and in thy name we go against this multitude.
O *LORD* **Yah Veh**, thou art our *God* **Elohim**;
let no **mortal** man *prevail* **restrain** against thee.
12 So *the LORD* **Yah Veh** smote the *Ethiopians* **Kushiy**
before **at the face of** Asa,
and *before Judah* **at the face of Yah Hudah**;
and the *Ethiopians* **Kushiy** fled.
13 And Asa and the people that were with him
pursued them unto Gerar:
and the *Ethiopians* **Kushiy** were *overthrown* **felled**,
that they
could not recover themselves **had no invigoration**;
for they were *destroyed* **broken**
before the LORD **at the face of Yah Veh**,
and *before* **at the face of** his *host* **camp**;
and they *carried* **bore** away
very much spoil **a mighty abundance of plunder**.
14 And they smote all the cities round about Gerar;
for the fear of *the LORD* **Yah Veh** came upon them:
and they *spoiled* **plundered** all the cities;
for there was exceeding much spoil in them.
15 They smote also the tents of *cattle* **chattel**,
and *carried away* **captured**
sheep **flocks** and camels in abundance,
and returned to *Jerusalem* **Yeru Shalem**.

AZAR YAH AT THE FACE OF ASA

15 And the Spirit of *God* **Elohim**
came upon *Azariah* **Azar Yah** the son of Oded:
2 And he went out *to meet* **at the face of** Asa,
and said unto him, Hear ye me, Asa,
and all *Judah* **Yah Hudah** and *Benjamin* **Ben Yamin**;
The LORD **Yah Veh** is with you, while ye be with him;
and if ye seek him, he *will* **shall** be found of you;
but if ye forsake him, he *will* **shall** forsake you.
3 Now for *a long season* **many days**
Israel **Yisra El** hath been without the true *God* **Elohim**,
and without a teaching priest, and without *law* **torah**.
4 But when they in their *trouble* **tribulation** did turn
unto *the LORD God* **Yah Veh Elohim** of *Israel* **Yisra El**,
and sought him, he was found of them.
5 And in those times there was no *peace* **shalom**
to him that went out, nor to him that came in,
but great *vexations were* **confusion**
upon all the *inhabitants* **settlers** of the *countries* **lands**.
6 And *nation was destroyed of nation*
goyim crushed goyim, and city of city:
for *God did vex* **Elohim agitated** them
with all *adversity* **tribulation**.
7 *Be ye strong therefore* **Strengthen**,
and let not your hands *be weak* **slacken**:
for your *work* **hire** shall be *rewarded* **to your deed**.

THE REFORM OF ASA

8 And when Asa heard these words,
and the prophecy of Oded the prophet,
he *took courage* **strengthened**,
and *put* **passed** *away* the *abominable idols* **abominations**
out of all the land
of *Judah* **Yah Hudah** and *Benjamin* **Ben Yamin**,
and out of the cities which he *had taken* **captured**
from mount *Ephraim* **Ephrayim**,
and renewed the **sacrifice** altar of *the LORD* **Yah Veh**,
that was *before* **at the face**
of the porch of *the LORD* **Yah Veh**.
9 And he gathered
all *Judah* **Yah Hudah** and *Benjamin* **Ben Yamin**,
and the *strangers* **sojourners** with them
out of *Ephraim* **Ephrayim** and *Manasseh* **Menash Sheh**,
and out of *Simeon* **Shimon**:
for they fell to him out of *Israel* **Yisra El** in abundance,
when they saw
that *the LORD* **Yah Veh** his *God* **Elohim** was with him.
10 So they gathered *themselves together*
at *Jerusalem* **Yeru Shalem** in the third month,
in the fifteenth year of the *reign* **sovereigndom** of Asa.
11 And they *offered* **sacrificed** unto *the LORD* **Yah Veh**
the same *time* **day**,
of the spoil which they had brought,
seven hundred oxen and seven thousand *sheep* **flocks**.
12 And they entered into a covenant
to seek *the LORD God* **Yah Veh Elohim** of their fathers
with all their heart and with all their soul;
13 That whosoever *would* **should** not seek
the LORD God **Yah Veh Elohim** of *Israel* **Yisra El**
should be *put to death* **deathified**,
whether **from** small or great,
whether **from** man or woman.
14 And they *sware* **oathed** unto *the LORD* **Yah Veh**
with a *loud* **great** voice, and with shouting,
and with trumpets, and with *cornets* **trumpets**.
15 And all *Judah rejoiced* **Yah Hudah cheered** at the oath:
for they had *sworn* **oathed** with all their heart,
and sought him with their whole *desire* **pleasure**;
and he was found of them:
and *the LORD gave* **Yah Veh rested** them *rest*
round about.
16 And also *concerning* Maachah
the mother of Asa the *king* **sovereign**,
he *removed* **turned** her **aside** from being *queen* **lady**,
because she had *made* **worked** an idol **of awe**
in *a grove* **an asherah**:
and Asa cut down her idol **of awe**,
and *stamped* **pulverized** it,
and burnt it at the *brook Kidron* **wadi Qidron**.
17 But the *high places* **bamahs**
were not *taken away* **turned aside** out of *Israel* **Yisra El**:
nevertheless the heart of Asa
was *perfect* **at shalom** all his days.
18 And he brought into the house of *God* **Elohim**
the *things that* **holies of** his father *had dedicated*,
and *that he himself had dedicated* **holies of his own**,
silver, and gold, and *vessels* **instruments**.
19 And there was no *more* war
unto the five and thirtieth year
of the *reign* **sovereigndom** of Asa.

THE SOVEREIGN OF YISRA EL COMES AGAINST YAH HUDAH

16 In the six and thirtieth year
of the *reign* **sovereigndom** of Asa,
Baasha king **Basha sovereign** of *Israel* **Yisra El**
came up **ascended** against *Judah* **Yah Hudah**,
and built Ramah,
to the intent **until** that he might *let* **give that**
none go out or come in
to Asa *king* **sovereign** of *Judah* **Yah Hudah**.
2 Then Asa brought out silver and gold
out of the treasures of the house of *the LORD* **Yah Veh**
and of the *king's* **sovereign's** house,
and sent to *Benhadad* **Ben Hadad**,
king **sovereign** of *Syria* **Aram**,
that *dwelt* **settled** at *Damascus* **Dammeseq**, saying,
3 There is a *league* **covenant** between me and thee,

as there was between my father and thy father:
behold, I have sent thee silver and gold;
go, break thy *league* **covenant**
with *Baasha king* **Basha sovereign** of *Israel* **Yisra El**,
that he may *depart* **ascend** from me.
4 And *Benhadad* **Ben Hadad**
hearkened unto *king* **sovereign** Asa,
and sent the *captains* **governors** of his *armies* **valiant**
against the cities of *Israel* **Yisra El**;
and they smote *Ijon* **Iyon**,
and Dan, and *Abelmaim* **Abel Maim**,
and all the *store* **storage** cities of Naphtali.
5 And it *came to pass* **became**,
when *Baasha* **Basha** heard *it*,
that he *left off* **ceased** building of Ramah,
and *let* **ceased** his work *cease*.
6 Then Asa the *king* **sovereign** took all *Judah* **Yah Hudah**;
and they *carried* **lifted** *away*
the stones of Ramah, and the timber thereof,
wherewith *Baasha* **Basha** was building;
and he built therewith Geba and *Mizpah* **Mispeh**.
7 And at that time Hanani the seer came to Asa
king **sovereign** of *Judah* **Yah Hudah**, and said unto him,
Because thou hast *relied* **leaned**
on the *king* **sovereign** of *Syria* **Aram**,
and not *relied* **leaned**
on *the LORD* **Yah Veh** thy *God* **Elohim**,
therefore
is the *host* **valiant** of the *king* **sovereign** of *Syria* **Aram**
escaped out of thine hand.
8 Were not the *Ethiopians* **Kushiy** and the *Lubims* **Lubiy**
a huge host **an abundance of valiant**,
with *very many* **a mighty abundance of** chariots
and *horsemen* **cavalry**?
yet, because thou didst *rely* **lean** on *the LORD* **Yah Veh**,
he *delivered* **gave** them into thine hand.
9 For the eyes of *the LORD* **Yah Veh**
run to and fro **flit** throughout the whole earth,
to shew himself strong **strengthened** in the behalf of them
whose heart is *perfect* **at shalom** toward him.
Herein thou hast *done foolishly* **follied**:
therefore from *henceforth* **this time** thou shalt have wars.
10 Then Asa was *wroth* **vexed** with the seer,
and *put* **gave** him in a *prison* **stock** house;
for he was in a rage with him because of this *thing*.
And Asa *oppressed* **crushed** *some* of the people
the same time.
11 And, behold, the *acts* **words** of Asa, first and last,
lo **behold**, they are *written* **inscribed**
in the *book* **scroll** of the *kings* **sovereigns**
of *Judah* **Yah Hudah** and *Israel* **Yisra El**.

THE DEATH OF ASA

12 And Asa
in the thirty and ninth year of his *reign* **sovereigndom**
was diseased in his feet,
until his *disease* **sickness** was *exceeding great* **severe**:
yet in his *disease* **sickness**
he sought not to *the LORD* **Yah Veh**,
but to the *physicians* **healers**.
13 And Asa *slept* **laid** with his fathers,
and died in the one and fortieth year of his reign.
14 And they *buried* **entombed** him
in his own *sepulchres* **tombs**,
which he had *made* **digged** for himself
in the city of David,
and laid him in the bed
which was filled with *sweet odours* **spices**
and divers kinds of spices **species by species**
prepared by the apothecaries' art **of perfumed ointment**:
and they
made a very **burnt a mighty** great burning for him.

YAH SHAPHAT REIGNS OVER YAH HUDAH

17 And *Jehoshaphat* **Yah Shaphat** his son
reigned in his stead,
and strengthened himself against *Israel* **Yisra El**.
2 And he *placed forces* **gave the valiant**
in all the *fenced* **fortified** cities of *Judah* **Yah Hudah**,
and *set garrisons* **gave stations**
in the land of *Judah* **Yah Hudah**,
and in the cities of *Ephraim* **Ephrayim**,
which Asa his father had *taken* **captured**.
3 And *the LORD* **Yah Veh**
was with *Jehoshaphat* **Yah Shaphat**,
because he walked in the first ways of his father David,
and sought not unto Baalim;
4 But sought to *the LORD God* **Elohim** of his father,
and walked in his *commandments* **misvoth**,
and not after the *doings* **works** of *Israel* **Yisra El**.
5 Therefore *the LORD* **Yah Veh**
stablished the *kingdom* **sovereigndom** in his hand;
and all *Judah* **Yah Hudah**
brought to Jehoshaphat presents
gave Yah Shaphat offerings;
and he had riches and honour in abundance.
6 And his heart was *lifted up* **exalted**
in the ways of *the LORD* **Yah Veh**:
moreover he *took away* **turned aside**
the *high places* **bamahs** and *groves* **asherim**
out of *Judah* **Yah Hudah**.
7 Also in the third year of his reign
he sent to his *princes* **governors**,
even to *Benhail* **Ben Hail**, and to *Obadiah* **Obad Yah**,
and to *Zechariah* **Zechar Yah**, and to *Nethaneel* **Nethan El**,
and to *Michaiah* **Michah Yah**,
to teach in the cities of *Judah* **Yah Hudah**.
8 And with them *he sent Levites* **Leviym**,
even Shemaiah **Shema Yah**, and *Nethaniah* **Nethan Yah**,
and *Zebadiah* **Zebad Yah**, and *Asahel* **Asa El**,
and *Shemiramoth* **Shemi Ramoth**,
and *Jehonathan* **Yah Nathan**, and *Adonijah* **Adoni Yah**,
and *Tobijah* **Tobi Yah**, and *Tobadonijah* **Tob Adoni Yah**,
Levites **Leviym**;
and with them *Elishama* **Eli Shama** and *Jehoram* **Yah Ram**,
priests.
9 And they taught in *Judah* **Yah Hudah**,
and had the *book* **scroll**
of the *law* **torah** of *the LORD* **Yah Veh** with them,
and went about
throughout all the cities of *Judah* **Yah Hudah**,
and taught the people.
10 And the fear of *the LORD* **Yah Veh**
fell upon all the *kingdoms* **sovereigndoms** of the lands
that were round about *Judah* **Yah Hudah**,
so that they *made no war* **fought not**
against *Jehoshaphat* **Yah Shaphat**.
11 Also *some* of the *Philistines* **Peleshethiy**
brought *Jehoshaphat* **Yah Shaphat**
presents **offerings**, and *tribute* **burden** silver;
and the *Arabians* **Arabiy** brought him flocks,
seven thousand and seven hundred rams,
and seven thousand and seven hundred he goats.
12 And *Jehoshaphat* **Yah Shaphat**
waxed great exceedingly **walked and greatened upward**;
and he built in *Judah castles* **Yah Hudah palaces**,
and cities of *store* **storage**.
13 And he had much *business* **work**
in the cities of *Judah* **Yah Hudah**:
and the men of war, mighty *men* of valour,
were in *Jerusalem* **Yeru Shalem**.
14 And these are the *numbers of them* **mustered**
according to the house of their fathers:
Of *Judah* **Yah Hudah**,
the *captains* **governors** of thousands;
Adnah the *chief* **governor**,
and with him mighty *men* of valour
three hundred thousand.
15 And *next to him* **at his hand**
was *Jehohanan* **Yah Hanan** the *captain* **governor**,
and with him two hundred and *fourscore* **eighty** thousand.
16 And *next him* **at his hand**
was *Amasiah* **Amas Yah** the son of Zichri,
who *willingly offered himself* **volunteered**
unto *the LORD* **Yah Veh**;
and with him
two hundred thousand mighty *men* of valour.
17 And of *Benjamin* **Ben Yamin**;
Eliada **Eli Ada** *a* mighty *man* of valour,
and with him
armed men **them kissed** with bow and *shield* **buckler**
two hundred thousand.

18 And *next him* **at his hand** was *Jehozabad* **Yah Zabad**,
and with him an hundred and *fourscore* **eighty** thousand
ready prepared **equipped** for *the war* **hostility**.
19 These *waited on* **ministered to** the *king* **sovereign**,
beside those whom the *king put* **sovereign gave**
in the *fenced* **fortified** cities
throughout all *Judah* **Yah Hudah**.

YAH SHAPHAT INTERMARRIES WITH ACH AB

18 Now *Jehoshaphat* **Yah Shaphat**
had riches and honour in abundance,
and *joined affinity* **intermarried** with *Ahab* **Ach Ab**.
2 And *after certain* **at the end of** years
he *went down* **descended** to *Ahab* **Ach Ab**
to *Samaria* **Shomeron**.
And *Ahab killed sheep* **Ach Ab sacrificed flocks** and oxen
for him in abundance,
and for the people *that he had* with him,
and *persuaded* **goaded** him to *go up* **ascend** *with him*
to *Ramothgilead* **Ramoth Gilad**.
3 And *Ahab* **Ach Ab** *king* **sovereign** of *Israel* **Yisra El**
said unto *Jehoshaphat* **Yah Shaphat**
king **sovereign** of *Judah* **Yah Hudah**,
wilt **shalt** thou go with me
to *Ramothgilead* **Ramoth Gilad**?
And he *answered* **said to** him,
I am as thou art **As I, so thou,**
and my people as thy people **as thy people, so my people**;
and we *will* **shall even** be with thee in the war.
4 And *Jehoshaphat* **Yah Shaphat**
said unto the *king* **sovereign** of *Israel* **Yisra El**,
Enquire, *I pray* **beseech** thee,
at the word of *the LORD* **Yah Veh** to day.
5 *Therefore* the *king* **sovereign** of *Israel* **Yisra El**
gathered *together* of prophets four hundred men,
and said unto them,
shall *we* go to *Ramothgilead* **Ramoth Gilad** to *battle* **war**,
or shall I *forbear* **cease**?
And they said, *Go up* **Ascend**;
for *God will deliver* **Elohim shall give** it
into the *king's* **sovereign's** hand.
6 But *Jehoshaphat* **Yah Shaphat** said,
Is there not here a prophet of *the LORD* **Yah Veh** besides,
that we might enquire of him?
7 And the *king* **sovereign** of *Israel* **Yisra El**
said unto *Jehoshaphat* **Yah Shaphat**,
There is yet one man,
by whom we may enquire of *the LORD* **Yah Veh**:
but I hate him;
for he never prophesied good unto me,
but *always* **all his days** evil:
the same is *Micaiah* **Michah Yah** the son of *Imla* **Yimlah**.
And *Jehoshaphat* **Yah Shaphat** said,
Let not the *king* **sovereign** say so.
8 And the *king* **sovereign** of *Israel* **Yisra El**
called for one *of his officers* **eunuch**, and said,
Fetch quickly Micaiah **Hasten Michah Yah**
the son of *Imla* **Yimlah**.
9 And the *king* **sovereign** of *Israel* **Yisra El**
and *Jehoshaphat* **Yah Shaphat,**
king **sovereign** of *Judah* **Yah Hudah**
sat either of them **settled each man** on his throne,
clothed **enrobed** in their *robes* **clothes**,
and they *sat* **settled** in a *void place* **threshingfloor**
at the *entering in* **opening** of the *gate* **portal**
of *Samaria* **Shomeron**;
and all the prophets prophesied *before them* **at their face**.
10 And *Zedekiah* **Sidqi Yah**
the son of *Chenaanah* **Kenaanah**
had *made* **worked** him horns of iron, and said,
Thus saith *the LORD* **Yah Veh**,
With these thou shalt *push Syria* **butt Aram**
until they be *consumed* **finished off**.
11 And all the prophets prophesied so, saying,
Go up **Ascend** to *Ramothgilead* **Ramoth Gilad**,
and prosper:
for *the LORD* **Yah Veh** shall *deliver* **give** it
into the hand of the *king* **sovereign**.
12 And the *messenger* **angel**
that went to call *Micaiah* **Michah Yah**
spake **worded** to him, saying, Behold,
the words of the prophets
declare **are** good to the *king* **sovereign**
with one *assent* **mouth**;
let thy word *therefore, I pray* **beseech** thee,
be like one of their's, and *speak* **word** thou good.
13 And *Micaiah* **Michah Yah** said,
As the LORD **Yah Veh** liveth,
even what my *God* **Elohim** saith,
that *will* **shall** I *speak* **word**.
14 And when he was come to the *king* **sovereign**,
the *king* **sovereign** said unto him, *Micaiah* **Michah Yah**,
shall we go to *Ramothgilead* **Ramoth Gilad** to *battle* **war**,
or shall I forbear?
And he said, *Go ye up* **Ascend**, and prosper,
and they shall be *delivered* **given** into your hand.
15 And the *king* **sovereign** said to him,
How many times shall I *adjure* **oath** thee
that thou *say nothing* **word naught** but the truth to me
in the name of *the LORD* **Yah Veh**?
16 Then he said, I did see all *Israel* **Yisra El**
scattered upon the mountains,
as *sheep* **flocks** that have no *shepherd* **tender**:
and *the LORD* **Yah Veh** said, These have no *master* **adoni**;
let them return *therefore*
every man to his house in *peace* **shalom**.
17 And the *king* **sovereign** of *Israel* **Yisra El**
said to *Jehoshaphat* **Yah Shaphat**, Did I not *tell* **say to** thee
that he *would* **should** not prophesy good unto me,
but evil?
18 Again he said,
Therefore hear the word of *the LORD* **Yah Veh**;
I saw *the LORD sitting* **Yah Veh seated** upon his throne,
and all the host of *heaven* **the heavens**
standing on his right *hand* and on his left.
19 And *the LORD* **Yah Veh** said,
Who shall entice *Ahab* **Ach Ab,**
king **sovereign** of *Israel* **Yisra El,**
that he may *go up* **ascend**
and fall at *Ramothgilead* **Ramoth Gilad**?
And one *spake* **said,** saying *after this manner* **thus**,
and another saying *after that manner* **thus.**
20 Then there *came out* **went** a spirit,
and stood *before the LORD* **at the face of Yah Veh,**
and said, I *will* **shall** entice him.
And *the LORD* **Yah Veh** said unto him, Wherewith?
21 And he said, I *will* **shall** go out,
and be a *lying* **false** spirit in the mouth of all his prophets.
And *the LORD* **he** said,
Thou shalt entice him, **Entice!**
and thou shalt also prevail: **Prevail!**
go out, **Go!** *and do even so.* **Work!**
22 Now *therefore*, behold,
the LORD **Yah Veh** hath *put* **given** a *lying* **false** spirit
in the mouth of these thy prophets,
and *the LORD* **Yah Veh** hath *spoken* **worded** evil
against thee.
23 Then *Zedekiah* **Sidqi Yah**
the son of *Chenaanah* **Kenaanah** came near,
and smote *Micaiah* **Michah Yah** upon the cheek, and said,
Which way *went* **passed** the Spirit of *the LORD* **Yah Veh**
from me to *speak* **word** unto thee?
24 And *Micaiah* **Michah Yah** said, Behold,
thou shalt see on that day
when thou shalt go into an inner chamber to hide thyself.
25 Then the *king* **sovereign** of *Israel* **Yisra El** said,
Take ye *Micaiah* **Michah Yah,**
and *carry* **turn** him back to Amon
the governor of the city,
and to *Joash* **Yah Ash,** the *king's* **sovereign's** son;
26 And say, Thus saith the *king* **sovereign**,
Put **Set** this *fellow* in the prison **house,**
and *feed him with* **have him eat**
bread of *affliction* **oppression**
and *with* water of *affliction* **oppression**,
until I return in *peace* **shalom**.
27 And *Micaiah* **Michah Yah** said,
If **in returning,**
thou *certainly* **shalt** return in *peace* **shalom**,
then hath not *the LORD spoken* **Yah Veh worded** by me.
And he said, Hearken, all ye people.

THE DEATH OF ACH AB

28 So the *king* **sovereign** of *Israel* **Yisra El**
and *Jehoshaphat* **Yah Shaphat,**
the *king* **sovereign** of *Judah* **Yah Hudah**
went up **ascended** to *Ramothgilead* **Ramoth Gilad.**
29 And the *king* **sovereign** of *Israel* **Yisra El**
said unto *Jehoshaphat* **Yah Shaphat,**
I *will* **shall** disguise myself,
and I *will* **shall** go to the *battle* **war;**
but *put thou on* **enrobe** thy *robes* **clothes.**
So the *king* **sovereign** of *Israel* **Yisra El** disguised himself;
and they went to the *battle* **war.**
30 Now the *king* **sovereign** of *Syria* **Aram**
had *commanded* **misvahed**
the *captains* **governors** of the chariots that were with him,
saying, Fight ye not with small or great,
save only **except** with the *king* **sovereign** of *Israel* **Yisra El.**
31 And it *came to pass* **became,**
when the *captains* **governors** of the chariots
saw *Jehoshaphat* **Yah Shaphat,**
that they said, It is the *king* **sovereign** of *Israel* **Yisra El.**
Therefore they *compassed about* **surrounded** him to fight:
but *Jehoshaphat* **Yah Shaphat** cried out,
and *the LORD* **Yah Veh** helped him;
and *God moved* **Elohim goaded** them *to depart* from him.
32 For it *came to pass* **became,** that,
when the *captains* **governors** of the chariots *perceived* **saw**
that it was not the *king* **sovereign** of *Israel* **Yisra El,**
they turned back again from *pursuing* **after** him.
33 And a *certain* man drew a bow
at a venture **in his integrity,**
and smote the *king* **sovereign** of *Israel* **Yisra El**
between the joints of the *harness* **habergeon:**
therefore he said to his *chariot man* **charioteer,**
Turn thine hand,
that thou mayest *carry* **bring** me out of the *host* **camp;**
for I am *wounded* **sickened.**
34 And the *battle increased* **war ascended** that day:
howbeit the *king* **sovereign** of *Israel* **Yisra El**
stayed *himself* up in his chariot
against the *Syrians* **Aramiy** until the even:
and about the time of the sun *going down* **descending**
he died.

YAH SHAPHAT APPOINTS JUDGES

19 And *Jehoshaphat* **Yah Shaphat,**
the *king* **sovereign** of *Judah* **Yah Hudah**
returned to his house in *peace* **shalom**
to *Jerusalem* **Yeru Shalem.**
2 And *Jehu* **Yah Hu** the son of Hanani the seer
went out to *meet* **face** him,
and said to *king Jehoshaphat* **sovereign Yah Shaphat,**
shouldest thou help the *ungodly* **wicked,**
and love them that hate *the LORD* **Yah Veh?**
therefore is wrath **this rage be** upon thee
from *before the LORD* **the face of Yah Veh.**
3 Nevertheless there are good *things* **words** found in thee,
in that thou hast *taken* **burnt** away
the *groves* **asherim** out of the land,
and hast prepared thine heart to seek *God* **Elohim.**
4 And *Jehoshaphat* **Yah Shaphat**
dwelt **settled** at *Jerusalem* **Yeru Shalem:**
and he *went out again* **returned and went out**
through the people
from *Beersheba* **Beer Sheba** to mount *Ephraim* **Ephrayim,**
and *brought* **returned** them *back*
unto *the LORD God* **Yah Veh Elohim** of their fathers.
5 And he *set* **stood** judges in the land
throughout
all the *fenced* **fortified** cities of *Judah* **Yah Hudah,**
city by city,
6 And said to the judges, *Take heed* **See** what ye *do* **work:**
for ye judge not for *man* **humanity,**
but for *the LORD* **Yah Veh,**
who is with you in the judgment.
7 Wherefore
now let the fear of *the LORD* **Yah Veh** be upon you;
take heed **guard** and *do* **work** it:
for there is no *iniquity* **wickedness**
with *the LORD* **Yah Veh** our *God* **Elohim,**
nor *respect* **partiality** of *persons* **faces,**
nor *taking* **receiving** of *gifts* **bribes.**
8 Moreover in *Jerusalem* **Yeru Shalem**
did Jehoshaphat **Yah Shaphat**
set **stood** of the *Levites* **Leviym,** and of the priests,
and of the *chief* **head** of the fathers of *Israel* **Yisra El,**
for the judgment of *the LORD* **Yah Veh,**
and for controversies,
when they returned to *Jerusalem* **Yeru Shalem.**
9 And he *charged* **misvahed** them, saying,
Thus shall ye *do* **work**
in the *fear* **awe** of *the LORD* **Yah Veh,**
faithfully **trustworthily,**
and with a *perfect heart* **heart at shalom.**
10 And what *cause* **strife** soever shall come to you
of your brethren that *dwell* **settle** in your cities,
between blood and blood,
between *law* **torah** and *commandment* **misvah,**
statutes and judgments,
ye shall *even warn* **enlighten** them
so that they *trespass* **guilt** not against *the LORD* **Yah Veh,**
and so *wrath* **rage**
come upon you, and upon your brethren:
this do **work thus,** and ye shall not *trespass* **guilt.**
11 And, behold,
Amariah **Amar Yah** the *chief* **head** priest is over you
in all *matters* **words** of *the LORD* **Yah Veh;**
and *Zebadiah* **Zebad Yah** the son of *Ishmael* **Yishma El,**
the *ruler* **eminent** of the house of *Judah* **Yah Hudah,**
for all the *king's matters* **sovereign's words:**
also the *Levites* **Leviym** shall be officers
before you **at thy face.**
Deal courageously **Strengthen and work,**
and *the LORD* **Yah Veh** shall be with the good.

SONS OF MOAB AND AMMON COME AGAINST YAH SHAPHAT

20 It *came to pass* **became,** after this also,
that the *children* **sons** of Moab,
and the *children* **sons** of Ammon,
and with them *other* beside the *Ammonites* **Ammoniy,**
came against *Jehoshaphat* **Yah Shaphat** to *battle* **war.**
2 Then there came some
that told *Jehoshaphat* **Yah Shaphat,** saying,
There cometh a great multitude against thee
from beyond the sea on this side *Syria* **Aram;** and, behold,
they be in *Hazazontamar* **Haseson Tamar,**
which is *Engedi* **En Gedi.**
3 And *Jehoshaphat feared* **Yah Shaphat awed,**
and *set himself* **gave his face** to seek *the LORD* **Yah Veh,**
and *proclaimed* **called** a fast
throughout **concerning** all *Judah* **Yah Hudah.**
4 And *Judah* **Yah Hudah** gathered *themselves together,*
to *ask help of the LORD* **seek Yah Veh:**
even out of all the cities of *Judah* **Yah Hudah**
they came to seek *the LORD* **Yah Veh.**
5 And *Jehoshaphat* **Yah Shaphat** stood in the congregation
of *Judah* **Yah Hudah** and *Jerusalem* **Yeru Shalem,**
in the house of *the LORD* **Yah Veh,**
before **at the face of** the new court,
6 And said, O *LORD God* **Yah Veh Elohim** of our fathers,
art not thou *God* **Elohim** in *heaven* **the heavens?**
and *rulest* **reignest** not thou over all
the *kingdoms* **sovereigndoms** of the *heathen* **goyim?**
and in thine hand is there not *power* **force** and might,
so that none is able to withstand thee?
7 Art not thou our *God* **Elohim,**
who *didst drive out* **dispossessed**
the *inhabitants* **settlers** of this land
before **at the face of** thy people *Israel* **Yisra El,**
and gavest it to the seed of Abraham thy *friend* **beloved**
for ever **eternally?**
8 And they *dwelt* **settled** therein,
and have built thee
a *sanctuary* **holies** therein for thy name, saying,
9 If, *when* evil cometh upon us,
as the sword, judgment, or pestilence, or famine,
we stand *before* **at the face of** this house,
and *in* **at** thy *presence* **face,**
(for thy name is in this house,)
and cry unto thee in our *affliction* **tribulation,**
then thou *wilt* **shalt** hear and *help* **save.**

10 And now, behold,
the *children* **sons** of Ammon and Moab and mount Seir,
whom thou *wouldest* **shouldest** not
let Israel **give Yisra El to** invade,
when they came out of the land of *Egypt* **Misrayim**,
but they turned **aside** from them,
and *destroyed* **desolated** them not;
11 Behold, *I say*, how they *reward* **deal** us,
to come to *cast* **expel** us out of thy possession,
which thou hast given us to *inherit* **possess**.
12 O our *God* **Elohim**, *wilt* **shalt** thou not judge them?
for we have no might **force**
against **at the face of** this great *company* **multitude**
that cometh against us;
neither know we what to *do* **work**:
but our eyes are upon thee.
13 And all *Judah* **Yah Hudah**
stood *before the LORD* **at the face of Yah Veh**,
with their *little ones* **toddlers**,
their *wives* **women**, and their *children* **sons**.
14 Then upon *Jahaziel* **Yachazi El**
the son of *Zechariah* **Zechar Yah**,
the son of *Benaiah* **Bena Yah**, the son of *Jeiel* **Yei El**,
the son of *Mattaniah* **Mattan Yah**,
a *Levite* **Leviy** of the sons of Asaph,
came the Spirit of *the LORD* **Yah Veh**
in the midst of the congregation;
15 And he said, Hearken ye, all *Judah* **Yah Hudah**,
and ye *inhabitants* **settlers** of *Jerusalem* **Yeru Shalem**,
and thou *king Jehoshaphat* **sovereign Yah Shaphat**,
Thus saith *the LORD* **Yah Veh** unto you,
Be not afraid **Awe not**, nor *dismayed* **terrify**
by reason **at the face** of this great multitude;
for the *battle* **war** is not yours, but *God's* **Elohim's**.
16 To morrow *go* **descend** ye *down* against them: behold,
they *come up* **ascend** by the *cliff* **ascent** of *Ziz* **Sis**;
and ye shall find them at the end of the *brook* **wadi**,
before **at the face of** the wilderness of *Jeruel* **Yeru El**.
17 Ye shall not *need to* fight in this *battle*:
set yourselves, stand ye *still*,
and see the salvation of *the LORD* **Yah Veh** with you,
O *Judah* **Yah Hudah** and *Jerusalem* **Yeru Shalem**:
fear **awe** not, nor *be dismayed* **terrify**;
to morrow go out *against them* **at their face**:
for *the LORD will* **Yah Veh shall** be with you.
18 And *Jehoshaphat* **Yah Shaphat** bowed *his head*
with *his face* **nostrils** to the *ground* **earth**:
and all *Judah* **Yah Hudah**
and the *inhabitants* **settlers** of *Jerusalem* **Yeru Shalem**
fell *before the LORD* **at the face of Yah Veh**,
worshipping the LORD **prostrating to Yah Veh**.
19 And the *Levites* **Leviym**,
of the *children* **sons** of the *Kohathites* **Qehathiy**,
and of the *children* **sons** of the *Korhites* **Qorachiy**,
stood up **arose** to *praise* **halal**
the LORD God **Yah Veh Elohim** of *Israel* **Yisra El**
with a *loud* **great** voice *on high* **above**.
20 And they *rose* **started** early in the morning,
and went forth into the wilderness of *Tekoa* **Teqoha**:
and as they went forth,
Jehoshaphat **Yah Shaphat** stood and said,
Hear me, O *Judah* **Yah Hudah**,
and ye *inhabitants* **settlers** of *Jerusalem* **Yeru Shalem**;
Believe **Trust** in *the LORD* **Yah Veh** your *God* **Elohim**,
so shall ye be *established* **amenable**;
believe **trust** his prophets, so shall ye prosper.
21 And when he had
consulted **counselled** with the people,
he *appointed* **stood** singers unto *the LORD* **Yah Veh**,
and that should
praise **halal** the *beauty* **majesty** of holiness,
as they went out *before* **at the face of** the *army* **equipped**,
and to say, *Praise the LORD* **Extend hands to Yah Veh**;
for his mercy *endureth for ever* **is eternal**.
22 And *when* **in the time that** they began
to *sing* **shout** and to *praise* **halal**
the LORD set ambushments **Yah Veh lurked**
against the *children* **sons** of Ammon,
Moab, and mount Seir,
which were come against *Judah* **Yah Hudah**;
and they *were smitten* **smote one another**.
23 For the *children* **sons** of Ammon and Moab
stood up against the *inhabitants* **settlers** of mount Seir,
utterly to *slay* **devote** and *destroy* **desolate** them:
and when they had *made an end of* **finished off**
the *inhabitants* **settlers** of Seir,
every one **each man** helped
to destroy another **against his friend for ruin**.
24 And when *Judah* **Yah Hudah**
came toward *the watch tower* **Mispeh** in the wilderness,
they *looked* **faced** unto the multitude, and, behold,
they were *dead bodies* **carcases** fallen to the earth,
and none escaped.
25 And when *Jehoshaphat* **Yah Shaphat** and his people
came to *take away* **plunder** the spoil of them,
they found among them in abundance
both *riches* **acquisitions** with the *dead bodies* **carcases**,
and *precious jewels* **desirable instruments**,
which they stripped off for themselves,
more than they could carry away **without burden**:
and they were three days
in *gathering* **plundering** of the spoil, it was so much.
26 And on the fourth day
they *assembled* **congregated** *themselves*
in the valley of *Berachah* **Berachah /Blessing**;
for there they blessed *the LORD* **Yah Veh**:
therefore the name of the same place was called,
The valley of *Berachah* **Berachah/Blessing**, unto this day.
27 Then they returned, every man
of *Judah* **Yah Hudah** and *Jerusalem* **Yeru Shalem**,
and *Jehoshaphat* **Yah Shaphat**
in the forefront **at the head** of them,
to *go again* **return** to *Jerusalem* **Yeru Shalem**
with *joy* **cheer**;
for *the LORD* **Yah Veh** had *made* **caused** them
to *rejoice* **cheer** over their enemies.
28 And they came to *Jerusalem* **Yeru Shalem**
with *psalteries* **bagpipes** and harps and trumpets
unto the house of *the LORD* **Yah Veh**
29 And the fear of *God* **Elohim**
was on all the *kingdoms* **sovereigndoms**
of those *countries* **lands**,
when they had heard that *the LORD* **Yah Veh**
fought against the enemies of *Israel* **Yisra El**.
30 So the *realm* **sovereigndom** of *Jehoshaphat* **Yah Shaphat**
was quiet **rested**:
for his *God gave him rest* **Elohim rested him** round about.

THE DEATH OF YAH SHAPHAT

31 And *Jehoshaphat* **Yah Shaphat**
reigned over *Judah* **Yah Hudah**:
he was **a son of** thirty and five years *old*
when he began to reign,
and he reigned
twenty and five years in *Jerusalem* **Yeru Shalem**.
And his mother's name was Azubah
the daughter of *Shilhi* **Shilchi**.
32 And he walked in the way of Asa his father,
and *departed not* **turned not aside** from it,
doing **working** that which was *right* **straight**
in the *sight* **eyes** of *the LORD* **Yah Veh**.
33 Howbeit the *high places* **bamahs**
were not *taken away* **turned aside**:
for as yet the people had not prepared their hearts
unto the *God* **Elohim** of their fathers.
34 Now the rest of the *acts* **words**
of *Jehoshaphat* **Yah Shaphat**, first and last, behold,
they are *written* **inscribed**
in the *book* **words** of *Jehu* **Yah Hu** the son of Hanani,
who is *mentioned* **ascended** in the *book* **scroll**
of the *kings* **sovereigns** of *Israel* **Yisra El**.
35 And after this did *Jehoshaphat* **Yah Shaphat**
king **sovereign** of *Judah* **Yah Hudah**
join himself with *Ahaziah* **Achaz Yah**
king **sovereign** of *Israel* **Yisra El**,
who *did very* **worked** wickedly.
36 And he joined himself with him
to *make* **work** ships to go to Tarshish:
and they *made* **worked** the ships
in *Eziongaber* **Esyon Geber**.
37 Then *Eliezer* **Eli Ezer**

the son of *Dodavah* **Doda Yah** of Mareshah
prophesied against *Jehoshaphat* **Yah Shaphat**, saying,
Because thou hast joined thyself with *Ahaziah* **Achaz Yah**,
the LORD **Yah Veh** hath *broken* **breached** thy works.
And the ships were broken,
that they *were not able* **retained not** to go to Tarshish.

YAH RAM REIGNS OVER YAH HUDAH

21 Now *Jehoshaphat* **Yah Shaphat**
slept **laid** with his fathers,
and was *buried* **entombed** with his fathers
in the city of David.
And *Jehoram* **Yah Ram** his son reigned in his stead.
2 And he had brethren
the sons of *Jehoshaphat* **Yah Shaphat**,
Azariah **Azar Yah**, and *Jehiel* **Yechi El**,
and *Zechariah* **Zechar Yah**, and *Azariah* **Azar Yah**,
and *Michael* **Michah El**, and *Shephatiah* **Shaphat Yah**:
all these were the sons of *Jehoshaphat* **Yah Shaphat**,
king **sovereign** of *Israel* **Yisra El**.
3 And their father gave them great gifts
of silver, and of gold, and *of* precious *things*,
with *fenced* **rampart** cities in *Judah* **Yah Hudah**:
but the *kingdom* **sovereigndom**
gave he to *Jehoram* **Yah Ram**;
because he was the firstborn.
4 Now when *Jehoram* **Yah Ram**
was risen up to the *kingdom* **sovereigndom** of his father,
he strengthened himself,
and *slew* **slaughtered** all his brethren with the sword,
and *divers* also of the *princes* **governors** of *Israel* **Yisra El**.
5 *Jehoram* **Yah Ram** was **a son of** thirty and two years *old*
when he began to reign,
and he reigned eight years in *Jerusalem* **Yeru Shalem**.
6 And he walked in the way
of the *kings* **sovereigns** of *Israel* **Yisra El**,
like as *did* **worked** the house of *Ahab* **Ach Ab**:
for he had the daughter of *Ahab* **Ach Ab** to *wife* **woman**:
and he *wrought* **worked** that which was evil
in the eyes of *the LORD* **Yah Veh**.
7 Howbeit *the LORD* **Yah Veh**
would **willed to** not *destroy* **ruin** the house of David,
because of the covenant that he had *made* **cut** with David,
and as he *promised* **said**
to give a *light* **lamp** to him and to his sons
for ever **all days**.
8 In his days the *Edomites revolted* **Edomiy rebelled**
from under the *dominion* **hand** of *Judah* **Yah Hudah**,
and *made themselves a king*
had a sovereign reign over them.
9 Then *Jehoram went forth* **Yah Ram passed over**
with his *princes* **governors**, and all his chariots with him:
and he rose up by night, and smote the *Edomites* **Edomiy**
which *compassed* **surrounded** him *in*,
and the *captains* **governors** of the chariots.
10 So the *Edomites revolted* **Edomiy rebelled**
from under the hand of *Judah* **Yah Hudah** unto this day.
The same time also
did Libnah *revolt* **rebelled** from under his hand;
because he had forsaken
the LORD God **Yah Veh Elohim** of his fathers.
11 Moreover he *made high places* **worked bamahs**
in the mountains of *Judah* **Yah Hudah**
and caused
the *inhabitants* **settlers** of *Jerusalem* **Yeru Shalem**
to *commit fornication* **whore**,
and *compelled Judah* **drove Yah Hudah** *thereto*.
12 And there came *a writing* **inscribed** to him
from *Elijah* **Eli Yah** the prophet, saying,
Thus saith
the LORD God **Yah Veh Elohim** of David thy father,
Because thou hast not walked in the ways
of *Jehoshaphat* **Yah Shaphat** thy father,
nor in the ways
of Asa *king* **sovereign** of *Judah* **Yah Hudah**,
13 But hast walked in the way
of the *kings* **sovereigns** of *Israel* **Yisra El**,
and hast made *Judah* **Yah Hudah**
and the *inhabitants* **settlers** of *Jerusalem* **Yeru Shalem**
to *go a whoring* **whore**,
like to the *whoredoms* **whoring**
of the house of *Ahab* **Ach Ab**,
and also hast *slain* **slaughtered**
thy brethren of thy father's house,
which were better than thyself:
14 Behold, with a great plague
will the LORD **shall Yah Veh** smite thy people,
and thy *children* **sons**, and thy *wives* **women**,
and all thy *goods* **acquisitions**:
15 And thou shalt have great sickness by disease
of thy *bowels* **inwards**, until thy *bowels fall out* **inwards go**
by reason of the sickness day by day.
16 Moreover *the LORD* **Yah Veh**
stirred up **wakened** against *Jehoram* **Yah Ram**
the spirit of the *Philistines* **Peleshethiy**,
and of the *Arabians* **Arabiy**,
that were *near* **alongside**
by the hand of the *Ethiopians* **Kushiy**:
17 And they *came up* **ascended** into *Judah* **Yah Hudah**,
and *brake into* **split** it,
and *carried away* **captured** all the *substance* **acquisition**
that was found in the *king's* **sovereign's** house,
and his sons also, and his *wives* **women**;
so that *there was never a* **no** son *left* **survived** him,
save Jehoahaz **except Yah Achaz**, the youngest of his sons.
18 And after all this
the LORD **Yah Veh** smote him in his *bowels* **inwards**
with *an incurable disease* **a nonhealing sickness**.
19 And it *came to pass* **became**,
that *in process of time* **day by day**,
after the end **in the going out** of two years,
his *bowels fell out* **inwards went** by reason of his sickness:
so he died of *sore diseases* **evil sicknesses**.
And his people *made* **worked** no burning for him,
like the burning of his fathers.
20 **A son of** Thirty and two years *old* was he
when he began to reign,
and he reigned in *Jerusalem* **Yeru Shalem** eight years,
and *departed* **went** without being desired.
Howbeit they *buried* **entombed** him in the city of David,
but not in the *sepulchres* **tombs** of the *kings* **sovereigns**.

ACHAZ YAH REIGNS OVER YAH HUDAH

22 And the *inhabitants* **settlers**
of *Jerusalem* **Yeru Shalem**
made *Ahaziah* **Achaz Yah** his youngest son
king **reign** in his stead:
for the *band of men* **troops**
that came with the *Arabians* **Arabiy** to the camp
had *slain* **slaughtered** all the *eldest* **heads**.
So *Ahaziah* **Achaz Yah** the son of *Jehoram* **Yah Ram**,
king **sovereign** of *Judah* **Yah Hudah** reigned.
2 **A son of** Forty and two years *old*
was *Ahaziah* **Achaz Yah** when he began to reign,
and he reigned one year in *Jerusalem* **Yeru Shalem**.
His mother's name also was *Athaliah* **Athal Yah**
the daughter of Omri.
3 He also walked in the ways
of the house of *Ahab* **Ach Ab**:
for his mother was his counsellor to do wickedly.
4 Wherefore he *did* **worked** evil
in the *sight* **eyes** of *the LORD* **Yah Veh**
like the house of *Ahab* **Ach Ab**:
for they were his counsellors after the death of his father
to his *destruction* **ruin**.
5 He walked also after their counsel,
and went with *Jehoram* **Yah Ram** the son of *Ahab* **Ach Ab**,
king **sovereign** of *Israel* **Yisra El**
to war against *Hazael* **Haza El**,
king **sovereign** of *Syria* **Aram**
at *Ramothgilead* **Ramoth Gilad**:
and the *Syrians* **Aramiy** smote *Joram* **Yah Ram**.
6 And he returned to be healed in *Jezreel* **Yizre El**
because of the *wounds* **strokes**
which *were given* **they smote** him at Ramah,
when he fought with *Hazael* **Haza El**,
king **sovereign** of *Syria* **Aram**.
And *Azariah* **Azar Yah** the son of *Jehoram* **Yah Ram**,
king **sovereign** of *Judah went down* **Yah Hudah descended**
to see *Jehoram* **Yah Ram** the son of *Ahab* **Ach Ab**
at *Jezreel* **Yizre El**, because he was sick.
7 And the *destruction* **trampling** of *Ahaziah* **Achaz Yah**

was of *God* **Elohim** by coming to *Joram* **Yah Ram**:
for when he was come,
he went out with *Jehoram* **Yah Ram**
against *Jehu* **Yah Hu** the son of Nimshi,
whom *the LORD* **Yah Veh** had anointed
to cut off the house of *Ahab* **Ach Ab**.
8 And it *came to pass* **became**, that,
when *Jehu was executing judgment* **Yah Hu judged**
upon the house of *Ahab* **Ach Ab**,
and found the *princes* **governors** of *Judah* **Yah Hudah**,
and the sons of the brethren of *Ahaziah* **Achaz Yah**,
that ministered to *Ahaziah* **Achaz Yah**,
he *slew* **slaughtered** them.
9 And he sought *Ahaziah* **Achaz Yah**:
and they *caught* **captured** him,
(for he was hid in *Samaria* **Shomeron**,)
and brought him to *Jehu* **Yah Hu**:
and when they had *slain* **deathified** him,
they *buried* **entombed** him:
Because, said they,
he is the son of *Jehoshaphat* **Yah Shaphat**,
who sought *the LORD* **Yah Veh** with all his heart.
So the house of *Ahaziah* **Achaz Yah** had no *power* **force**
to *keep still* **retain** the *kingdom* **sovereigndom**.
10 But when *Athaliah* **Athal Yah**
the mother of *Ahaziah* **Achaz Yah**
saw that her son *was dead* **had died**,
she arose and *destroyed* **worded to**
all the *seed royal* **sovereigndom seed**
of the house of *Judah* **Yah Hudah**.
11 But *Jehoshabeath* **Yah Shabath**,
the daughter of the *king* **sovereign**,
took *Joash* **Yah Ash** the son of *Ahaziah* **Achaz Yah**,
and stole him from among the *king's* **sovereign's** sons
that were *slain* **deathified**,
and *put* **gave** him and his *nurse* **suckler** in a bedchamber.
So *Jehoshabeath* **Yah Shabath**,
the daughter of *king Jehoram* **sovereign Yah Ram**,
the *wife* **woman** of *Jehoiada* **Yah Yada** the priest,
(for she was the sister of *Ahaziah* **Achaz Yah**,)
hid him from *Athaliah* **the face of Athal Yah**,
so that she *slew* **deathified** him not.
12 And he was with them
hid in the house of *God* **Elohim** six years:
and *Athaliah* **Athal Yah** reigned over the land.

YAH YADA SETS YAH ASH TO REIGN OVER YAH HUDAH

23 And in the seventh year
Jehoiada **Yah Yada** strengthened himself,
and took the *captains* **governors** of hundreds,
Azariah **Azar Yah** the son of *Jeroham* **Yerocham**,
and *Ishmael* **Yishma El** the son of *Jehohanan* **Yah Hanan**,
and *Azariah* **Azar Yah** the son of Obed,
and *Maaseiah* **Maase Yah** the son of *Adaiah* **Ada Yah**
and *Elishaphat* **Eli Shaphat** the son of Zichri,
into covenant with him.
2 And they went about in *Judah* **Yah Hudah**,
and gathered the *Levites* **Leviym**
out of all the cities of *Judah* **Yah Hudah**,
and the *chief* **head** of the fathers of *Israel* **Yisra El**,
and they came to *Jerusalem* **Yeru Shalem**.
3 And all the congregation *made* **cut** a covenant
with the *king* **sovereign** in the house of *God* **Elohim**.
And he said unto them, Behold,
the *king's* **sovereign's** son shall reign,
as *the LORD* **Yah Veh**
hath *said* **worded** of the sons of David.
4 This is the *thing* **word** that ye shall *do* **work**;
A third *part* of you entering on the *sabbath* **shabbath**,
of the priests and of the *Levites* **Leviym**,
shall be porters of the *doors* **thresholds**;
5 And a third *part* shall be at the *king's* **sovereign's** house;
and a third *part* at the *gate* **portal** of the foundation:
and all the people shall be in the courts
of the house of *the LORD* **Yah Veh**.
6 But let none come into the house of *the LORD* **Yah Veh**,
save **except** the priests,
and they that minister of the *Levites* **Leviym**;
they shall go in, for they are holy:
but all the people
shall *keep* **guard** the *watch* **guard** of *the LORD* **Yah Veh**.
7 And the *Levites* **Leviym**
shall *compass* **surround** the *king* **sovereign** round about,
every man with his *weapons* **instruments** in his hand;
and whosoever *else* cometh into the house,
he shall be *put to death* **deathified**:
but be ye with the *king* **sovereign**
when he cometh in, and when he goeth out.
8 So the *Levites* **Leviym** and all *Judah* **Yah Hudah**
did **worked** according to all *things*
that *Jehoiada* **Yah Yada** the priest
had *commanded* **misvahed**,
and took every man his men
that were to come in on the *sabbath* **shabbath**,
with them that were to go out on the *sabbath* **shabbath**:
for *Jehoiada* **Yah Yada** the priest
dismissed **liberated** not the *courses* **allotments**.
9 Moreover *Jehoiada* **Yah Yada** the priest
delivered **gave** to the *captains* **governors** of hundreds
spears, and bucklers, and shields,
that had been *king* **sovereign** David's,
which were in the house of *God* **Elohim**.
10 And he *set* **stood** all the people,
every man having his *weapon* **spear** in his hand,
from the right *side* **shoulder** of the *temple* **house**
to the left *side* **shoulder** of the *temple* **house**,
along by the **sacrifice** altar and the *temple* **house**,
by the *king* **sovereign** round about.
11 Then they brought out the *king's* **sovereign's** son,
and *put* **gave** upon him the *crown* **separatism**,
and *gave him* the *testimony* **witness**,
and *made* **had** him *king* **reign**.
And *Jehoiada* **Yah Yada** and his sons anointed him,
and said, *God save the king* **The sovereign liveth**.
12 Now when *Athaliah* **Athal Yah**
heard the *noise* **voice** of the people running
and *praising* **halaling** the *king* **sovereign**,
she came to the people
into the house of *the LORD* **Yah Veh**:
13 And she *looked* **saw**, and, behold,
the *king* **sovereign** stood at his pillar
at the *entering in* **entrance**,
and the *princes* **governors** and the trumpets
by the *king* **sovereign**:
and all the people of the land *rejoiced* **cheered**,
and *sounded* **blast** with trumpets,
also the singers with instruments of *musick* **song**,
and such as *taught to sing praise* **made known to halal**.
Then *Athaliah rent* **Athal Yah ripped** her clothes, and said,
Treason, Treason. **Conspiracy! Conspiracy!**
14 Then *Jehoiada* **Yah Yada** the priest
brought out the *captains* **governors** of hundreds
that *were set over* **oversaw** the *host* **valiant**,
and said unto them,
Have **Bring** her *forth* **out of the house** of the *ranges* **ranks**:
and whoso *followeth* **goeth after** her,
let him be *slain* **deathified** with the sword.
For the priest said,
Slay her **Deathify** not in the house of *the LORD* **Yah Veh**.
15 So they *laid* **set** hands on her;
and when she was come to the *entering* **entrance**
of the horse *gate* **portal** by the *king's* **sovereign's** house,
they *slew* **deathified** her there.
16 And *Jehoiada* **Yah Yada**
made **cut** a covenant between him,
and between all the people,
and between the *king* **sovereign**,
that they should be *the LORD'S* **Yah Veh's** people.
17 Then all the people went to the house of Baal,
and *brake* **pulled** it down,
and brake his **sacrifice** altars and his images in pieces,
and *slew* **slaughtered** Mattan the priest of Baal
before **at the face of** the **sacrifice** altars.
18 Also *Jehoiada* **Yah Yada**
appointed **set** the *offices* **overseers**
of the house of *the LORD* **Yah Veh**
by the hand of the priests the *Levites* **Leviym**,
whom David had *distributed* **allotted**
in the house of *the LORD* **Yah Veh**,
to *offer* **holocaust** the *burnt offerings* **holocausts**
of *the LORD* **Yah Veh**,

as *it is written* **inscribed**
in the *law* **torah** of *Moses* **Mosheh**,
with *rejoicing* **cheer** and with singing,
as it was ordained by **the hand of** David.
19 And he *set* **stood** the porters at the *gates* **portals**
of the house of *the LORD* **Yah Veh**,
that none which was *unclean* **foul** in any *thing* **word**
should enter in.
20 And he took the *captains* **governors** of hundreds,
and the *nobles* **mighty**,
and the *governors* **sovereigns** of the people,
and all the people of the land,
and *brought down* **descended** the *king* **sovereign**
from the house of *the LORD* **Yah Veh**:
and they came *through the high gate* **within Elyon Portal**
into the *king's* **sovereign's** house,
and *set* **settled** the *king* **sovereign**
upon the throne of the *kingdom* **sovereigndom**.
21 And all the people of the land *rejoiced* **cheered**:
and the city *was quiet* **rested**,
after that they *had slain Athaliah* **deathified Athal Yah**
with the sword.

YAH ASH REIGNS IN YERU SHALEM

24 *Joash* **Yah Ash** was **a son of** seven years *old*
when he began to reign,
and he reigned forty years in *Jerusalem* **Yeru Shalem**.
His mother's name also was *Zibiah* **Zib Yah**
of *Beersheba* **Beer Sheba**.
2 And *Joash* **Yah Ash**
did **worked** that which was *right* **straight**
in the *sight* **eyes** of *the LORD* **Yah Veh**
all the days of *Jehoiada* **Yah Yada** the priest.
3 And *Jehoiada* **Yah Yada**
took **bore** for him two *wives* **women**;
and he begat sons and daughters.

YAH ASH RENEWS THE HOUSE OF YAH VEH

4 And it *came to pass* **became**, after this,
that *Joash was minded* **it was in the heart of Yah Ash**
to *repair* **renew** the house of *the LORD* **Yah Veh**.
5 And he gathered *together*
the priests and the *Levites* **Leviym**, and said to them,
Go out unto the cities of *Judah* **Yah Hudah**,
and gather of all *Israel* **Yisra El** *money* **silver**
to *repair* **strengthen** the house of your *God* **Elohim**
from **enough** year to year,
and see that ye hasten the *matter* **word**.
Howbeit the *Levites* **Leviym** hastened it not.
6 And the *king* **sovereign**
called for *Jehoiada* **Yah Yada** the *chief* **head**,
and said unto him,
Why hast thou not required
of the *Levites* **Leviym** to bring in
out of *Judah* **Yah Hudah** and out of *Jerusalem* **Yeru Shalem**
the *collection* **burden**,
according to *the commandment of Moses* **Mosheh**
the servant of *the LORD* **Yah Veh**,
and of the congregation of *Israel* **Yisra El**,
for the *tabernacle* **tent** of witness?
7 For the sons of *Athaliah* **Athal Yah**, that wicked *woman*,
had *broken up* **breached** the house of *God* **Elohim**;
and also all the *dedicated things* **holies**
of the house of *the LORD* **Yah Veh**
did they *bestow* **work** upon Baalim.
8 And at the *king's commandment* **sovereign's saying**
they *made a chest* **worked one ark**,
and *set* **gave** it without
at the *gate* **portal** of the house of *the LORD* **Yah Veh**.
9 And they *made a proclamation* **gave voice**
through *Judah* **Yah Hudah** and *Jerusalem* **Yeru Shalem**,
to bring in to *the LORD* **Yah Veh** the *collection* **burden**
that *Moses* **Mosheh** the servant of *God* **Elohim**
laid upon *Israel* **Yisra El** in the wilderness.
10 And all the *princes* **governors** and all the people
rejoiced **cheered**, and brought in,
and cast into the *chest* **ark**,
until they had *made an end* **finished**.
11 Now it *came to pass* **became**,
that at what time the *chest* **ark** was brought
unto the *king's office* **sovereign's oversight**
by the hand of the *Levites* **Leviym**,
and when they saw that there was much *money* **silver**,
the *king's* **sovereign's** scribe
and the *high* **head** priest's *officer* **overseer**
came and emptied the *chest* **ark**, and *took* **lifted** it,
and *carried* **returned** it to his place *again*.
Thus they *did* **worked** day by day,
and gathered *money* **silver** in abundance.
12 And the *king* **sovereign** and *Jehoiada* **Yah Yada**
gave it to such as *did* **worked** the work
of the service of the house of *the LORD* **Yah Veh**,
and hired *masons* **hewers** and *carpenters* **artificers**
to *repair* **renew** the house of *the LORD* **Yah Veh**,
and also
such as wrought **artificers of** iron and *brass* **copper**
to *mend* **strengthen** the house of *the LORD* **Yah Veh**.
13 So the *workmen wrought* **workers worked**,
and the work was perfected by them
and healing ascended upon the work of their hand,
and they *set* **stood** the house of *God* **Elohim**
in *his state* **quantity**, and strengthened it.
14 And when they had finished it,
they brought the *rest* **remainder** of the *money* **silver**
before **at the face**
of the *king* **sovereign** and *Jehoiada* **Yah Yada**,
whereof were *made vessels* **worked instruments**
for the house of *the LORD* **Yah Veh**,
even vessels to minister **instruments of ministry**,
and to *offer* **holocaust** *withal*,
and *spoons* **bowls**,
and *vessels* **instruments** of gold and silver.
And they *offered burnt offerings* **holocausted holocausts**
in the house of *the LORD* **Yah Veh** continually
all the days of *Jehoiada* **Yah Yada**.
15 But *Jehoiada waxed old* **Yah Yada aged**,
and was *full* **satisfied** of days when he died;
a son of an hundred and thirty years *old*
was he when he died.
16 And they *buried* **entombed** him in the city of David
among the *kings* **sovereigns**,
because he had *done* **worked** good in *Israel* **Yisra El**,
both toward *God* **Elohim**, and toward his house.
17 Now after the death of *Jehoiada* **Yah Yada**
came the *princes* **governors** of *Judah* **Yah Hudah**,
and *made obeisance* **prostrated** to the *king* **sovereign**.
Then the *king* **sovereign** hearkened unto them.
18 And they left
the house of *the LORD God* **Yah Veh Elohim**
of their fathers,
and served *groves* **asherim** and idols:
and *wrath* **rage**
came upon *Judah* **Yah Hudah** and *Jerusalem* **Yeru Shalem**
for this their *trespass* **guilt**.
19 Yet he sent prophets to them,
to *bring* **return** them *again* unto *the LORD* **Yah Veh**;
and they *testified* **witnessed** against them:
but they *would not give ear* **hearkened not**.
20 And the Spirit of *God* **Elohim**
came upon Zechariah **enrobed Zechar Yah**
the son of *Jehoiada* **Yah Yada** the priest,
which stood above the people, and said unto them,
Thus saith *God* **Elohim**, Why *transgress* **trespass** ye
the *commandments* **misvoth** of *the LORD* **Yah Veh**,
that ye cannot prosper?
because ye have forsaken *the LORD* **Yah Veh**,
he hath also forsaken you.
21 And they conspired against him,
and stoned him with stones
at the *commandment* **misvah** of the *king* **sovereign**
in the court of the house of *the LORD* **Yah Veh**.
22 Thus *Joash* **Yah Ash** the *king* **sovereign**
remembered not the *kindness* **mercy**
which *Jehoiada* **Yah Yada** his father
had *done* **worked** to him,
but *slew* **slaughtered** his son.
And when he died, he said,
The LORD look **Yah Veh see** upon it, and require it.

ARAM ASCENDS AGAINST YAH HUDAH AND YERU SHALEM

23 And it *came to pass* **became**,
at the *end* **revolution** of the year,

that the *host* **valiant** of *Syria* **Aram**
came up **ascended** against him:
and they came
to *Judah* **Yah Hudah** and *Jerusalem* **Yeru Shalem**,
and *destroyed* **ruined**
all the *princes* **governors** of the people
from among the people,
and sent all the spoil of them
unto the *king* **sovereign** of *Damascus* **Dammeseq**.
24 For the *army* **valiant** of *the Syrians* **Aram**
came with *a small company of* **little** men,
and *the LORD delivered* **Yah Veh gave**
a *very* **mighty** great *host* **valiant** into their hand,
because they had forsaken
the LORD God **Yah Veh Elohim** of their fathers.
So they *executed judgment* **worked judgements**
against *Joash* **Yah Ash**.

THE DEATH OF YAH ASH

25 And when they *were departed* **went** from him,
(for they left him in great diseases,)
his own servants conspired against him
for the blood of the sons of *Jehoiada* **Yah Yada** the priest,
and *slew* **slaughtered** him on his bed, and he died:
and they *buried* **entombed** him in the city of David,
but they *buried* **entombed** him not
in the *sepulchres* **tombs** of the *kings* **sovereigns**.
26 And these are they that conspired against him;
Zabad the son of Shimeath an *Ammonitess* **Ammoniyth**,
and *Jehozabad* **Yah Zabad** the son of Shimrith
a *Moabitess* **Moabiyth**.
27 Now *concerning* his sons,
and the *greatness of the* **greatened** burdens *laid* upon him,
and the *repairing* **foundation** of the house of *God* **Elohim**,
behold,
they are *written* **inscribed** in the *story* **commentary**
of the *book* **scroll** of the *kings* **sovereigns**.
And *Amaziah* **Amaz Yah** his son reigned in his stead.

AMAZ YAH REIGNS IN YERU SHALEM

25 *Amaziah* **Amaz Yah**
was **a son of** twenty and five years *old*
when he began to reign,
and he reigned twenty and nine years
in *Jerusalem* **Yeru Shalem**.
And his mother's name was *Jehoaddan* **Yah Addan**
of *Jerusalem* **Yeru Shalem**.
2 And he *did* **worked** that which was *right* **straight**
in the *sight* **eyes** of *the LORD* **Yah Veh**,
but not with a *perfect heart* **heart at shalom**.
3 Now it *came to pass* **became**,
when the *kingdom* **sovereigndom**
was *established to* **strong upon** him,
that he *slew* **slaughtered** his servants
that had *killed* **smitten** the *king* **sovereign** his father.
4 But he *slew* **deathified** not their *children* **sons**,
but did as *it is written* **inscribed** in the *law* **torah**
in the *book* **scroll** of *Moses* **Mosheh**,
where *the LORD commanded* **Yah Veh misvahed**, saying,
The fathers shall not die for the *children* **sons**,
neither shall the *children* **sons** die for the fathers,
but *every man* **each** shall die for his own sin.
5 *Moreover Amaziah* **Amaz Yah**
gathered *Judah* **Yah Hudah** *together*,
and *made* **stood** them *captains* **governors** over thousands,
and *captains* **governors** over hundreds,
according to the houses of their fathers,
throughout
all *Judah* **Yah Hudah** and *Benjamin* **Ben Yamin**:
and he *numbered* **mustered** them
from **sons of** twenty years *old* and above,
and found them three hundred thousand
choice men **chosen**,
able to go forth to *war* **hostility**,
that could *handle spear* **hold javelin** and shield.
6 He hired also an hundred thousand mighty *men* of valour
out of *Israel* **Yisra El**
for an hundred *talents* **rounds** of silver.
7 But there came a man of *God* **Elohim** to him, saying,
O *king* **sovereign**,
let not the *army* **host** of *Israel* **Yisra El** go with thee;
for *the LORD* **Yah Veh** is not with *Israel* **Yisra El**, *to wit*,
with all the *children* **sons** of *Ephraim* **Ephrayim**.
8 But if thou *wilt* **shalt** go, *do* **work** it;
be strong **strengthen** for the *battle* **war**:
God **Elohim** shall *make* **stumble** *thee fall*
before **at the face of** the enemy:
for *God* **Elohim** hath *power* **force** to help,
and to *cast down* **stumble**.
9 And *Amaziah* **Amaz Yah** said to the man of *God* **Elohim**,
But what shall we *do* **work** for the hundred *talents* **rounds**
which I have given to the *army* **troop** of *Israel* **Yisra El**?
And the man of *God answered* **Elohim said**,
The LORD **Yah Veh** is able to give thee
much **aboundingly** more than this.
10 Then *Amaziah* **Amaz Yah** separated them, *to wit*,
the *army* **troop** that was come to him
out of *Ephraim* **Ephrayim**,
to go *home* **to their place** again:
wherefore their *anger* **wrath** was *greatly* **mightily** kindled
against *Judah* **Yah Hudah**,
and they returned *home* **to their place**
in *great anger* **fuming wrath**.
11 And *Amaziah* **Amaz Yah** strengthened himself,
and *led forth* **drove** his people,
and went to *the valley of salt* **Gay Melach/Valley of Salt**,
and smote of the *children* **sons** of Seir ten thousand.
12 And *other* ten thousand *left* alive
did the *children* **sons** of *Judah* **Yah Hudah**
carry away captive **capture**,
and brought them unto the top of the rock,
and cast them down from the top of the rock,
that they all were *broken in pieces* **split**.
13 But the *soldiers* **sons of the band** of the *army* **troop**
which *Amaziah sent* **Amaz Yah turned** back,
that they should not go with him to *battle* **war**,
fell upon **stripped** the cities of *Judah* **Yah Hudah**,
from *Samaria* **Shomeron**
even unto *Bethhoron* **Beth Horon**,
and smote three thousand of them,
and *took* **plundered** much spoil.
14 Now it *came to pass* **became**,
after that *Amaziah* **Amaz Yah** was come
from the *slaughter* **smiting** of the *Edomites* **Edomiy**,
that he brought the *gods* **elohim**
of the *children* **sons** of Seir,
and *set* **stood** them *up* to be his *gods* **elohim**,
and *bowed down himself before them*
prostrated at their face,
and *burned incense* **incensed** unto them.
15 *Wherefore* the *anger* **wrath** of *the LORD* **Yah Veh**
was kindled against *Amaziah* **Amaz Yah**,
and he sent unto him a prophet, which said unto him,
Why hast thou sought after the *gods* **elohim** of the people,
which could not *deliver* **rescue** their own people
out of thine hand?
16 And it *came to pass* **became**,
as he *talked* **worded** with him,
that *the king* **he** said unto him,
Art thou *made* **given**
of the king's counsel **to be counsellor to the sovereign**?
forbear **cease**; why shouldest thou be smitten?
Then the prophet *forbare* **ceased**, and said,
I know that *God* **Elohim**
hath *determined* **counselled** to *destroy* **ruin** *thee*,
because thou hast *done* **worked** this,
and hast not hearkened unto my counsel.

THE SOVEREIGN OF YAH HUDAH
CHALLENGES THE SOVEREIGN OF YISRA EL

17 Then *Amaziah* **Amaz Yah**,
king **sovereign** of *Judah* **Yah Hudah**
took advice **counselled**,
and sent to *Joash* **Yah Ash**,
the son of *Jehoahaz* **Yah Achaz**, the son of *Jehu* **Yah Hu**,
king **sovereign** of *Israel* **Yisra El**, saying,
Come, let us see one another in the face.
18 And *Joash* **Yah Ash**,
king **sovereign** of *Israel* **Yisra El**
sent to *Amaziah* **Amaz Yah**,
king **sovereign** of *Judah* **Yah Hudah**, saying,
The *thistle* **thorn** that was in Lebanon
sent to the cedar that was in Lebanon, saying,

Give thy daughter to my son to *wife* **woman**:
and there passed by a *wild beast* **live being of the field**
that was in Lebanon,
and *trode down* **trampled** the *thistle* **thorn**.
19 Thou sayest, *Lo* **Behold**,
thou hast smitten the *Edomites* **Edomiy**;
and thine heart lifteth thee *up* to *boast* **honour**:
abide **settle** now *at home* **in thy house**;
why shouldest thou *meddle to thine hurt* **coax evil**,
that thou shouldest fall, *even* thou,
and *Judah* **Yah Hudah** with thee?
20 But *Amaziah would not hear* **Amaz Yah hearkened not**;
for it *came* **be** of *God* **Elohim**,
that he might *deliver* **give** them into the hand
of their enemies,
because they sought after the *gods* **elohim** of Edom.
21 So *Joash* **Yah Ash**, the *king* **sovereign** of *Israel* **Yisra El**
went up **ascended**;
and they saw one another in the face,
both he and *Amaziah* **Amaz Yah**,
king **sovereign** of *Judah* **Yah Hudah**,
at *Bethshemesh* **Beth Shemesh**,
which *belongeth* **be** to *Judah* **Yah Hudah**.
22 And *Judah* **Yah Hudah**
was *put to the worse* **smitten**
before Israel **at the face of Yisra El**,
and they fled every man to his tent.
23 And *Joash* **Yah Ash**, the *king* **sovereign** of *Israel* **Yisra El**
took Amaziah **apprehended Amaz Yah**,
king **sovereign** of *Judah* **Yah Hudah**,
the son of *Joash* **Yah Ash**, the son of *Jehoahaz* **Yah Achaz**,
at *Bethshemesh* **Beth Shemesh**,
and brought him to *Jerusalem* **Yeru Shalem**,
and brake down the wall of *Jerusalem* **Yeru Shalem**
from the *gate* **portal** of *Ephraim* **Ephrayim**
to the *corner gate* **portal at the face**, four hundred cubits.
24 And *he took* all the gold and the silver,
and all *the vessels* **instruments** that were found
in the house of *God* **Elohim** with *Obededom* **Obed Edom**,
and the treasures of the *king's* **sovereign's** house,
the *hostages* **sons as pledges** also,
and returned to *Samaria* **Shomeron**.
25 And *Amaziah* **Amaz Yah** the son of *Joash* **Yah Ash**,
king **sovereign** of *Judah* **Yah Hudah**
lived after the death of *Joash* **Yah Ash**,
son of *Jehoahaz* **Yah Achaz**,
king **sovereign** of *Israel* **Yisra El** fifteen years.
26 Now the rest of the *acts* **words** of *Amaziah* **Amaz Yah**,
first and last, behold,
are they not *written* **inscribed**
in the *book* **scroll** of the *kings* **sovereigns**
of *Judah* **Yah Hudah** and *Israel* **Yisra El**?
27 Now after the time
that *Amaziah* **Amaz Yah** did turn *away* **aside**
from *following the LORD* **after Yah Veh**
they *made* **conspired** a conspiracy against him
in *Jerusalem* **Yeru Shalem**;
and he fled to Lachish: but they sent to Lachish after him,
and *slew* **deathified** him there.
28 And they *brought* **lifted** him upon horses,
and *buried* **entombed** him with his fathers
in the city of *Judah* **Yah Hudah**.

UZZI YAH REIGNS OVER YAH HUDAH

26 Then all the people of *Judah* **Yah Hudah**
took *Uzziah* **Uzzi Yah**,
who was **a son of** sixteen years *old*,
and *made* **had** him *king* **reign**
in the *room* **stead** of his father *Amaziah* **Amaz Yah**.
2 He built Eloth, and restored it to *Judah* **Yah Hudah**,
after that the *king slept* **sovereign laid** with his fathers.
3 **A son of** Sixteen years *old*
was *Uzziah* **Uzzi Yah** when he began to reign,
and he reigned fifty and two years
in *Jerusalem* **Yeru Shalem**.
His mother's name also was *Jecoliah* **Yechol Yah**
of *Jerusalem* **Yeru Shalem**.
4 And he *did* **worked** that which was *right* **straight**
in the *sight* **eyes** of *the LORD* **Yah Veh**,
according to all
that his father *Amaziah did* **Amaz Yah worked**.
5 And he sought *God* **Elohim**
in the days of *Zechariah* **Zechar Yah**,
who had *understanding* **discernment**
in the *visions* **seeings** of *God* **Elohim**:
and *as long as he* **in the days of his**
sought the LORD **seeking Yah Veh**,
God **Elohim** made him to prosper.
6 And he went forth
and *warred* **fought** against the *Philistines* **Peleshethiy**,
and brake down the wall of Gath,
and the wall of *Jabneh* **Yabneh**,
and the wall of Ashdod,
and built cities about Ashdod,
and among the *Philistines* **Peleshethiy**.
7 And *God* **Elohim** helped him
against the *Philistines* **Peleshethiy**,
and against the *Arabians* **Arabiy**
that *dwelt* **settled** in *Gurbaal* **Gur Baal**,
and the *Mehunims* **Maoniy**.
8 And the *Ammonites* **Ammoniy**
gave *gifts* **offerings** to *Uzziah* **Uzzi Yah**:
and his name *spread abroad* **went out**
even to the entering in of *Egypt* **Misrayim**;
for he strengthened *himself exceedingly* **above**.
9 *Moreover Uzziah* **Uzzi Yah**
built towers in *Jerusalem* **Yeru Shalem**
at the corner *gate* **portal**,
and at the valley *gate* **portal**,
and at the *turning of the wall* **corners**,
and *fortified* **strengthened** them.
10 Also he built towers in the *desert* **wilderness**,
and *digged* **hewed** many wells:
for he had much *cattle* **chattel**,
both in the *low country* **lowlands**, and in the plains:
husbandmen **cultivators** *also*,
and vine dressers in the mountains,
and in *Carmel* **orchards/Karmel**:
for he loved *husbandry* **the soil**.
11 Moreover *Uzziah* **Uzzi Yah**
had an host of *fighting men* **valiant warriors working war**,
that went out to *war* **the hostility** by *bands* **troops**,
according to the number *of their account* **mustered**
by the hand of *Jeiel* **Yei El** the scribe
and *Maaseiah* **Maase Yah** the *ruler* **officer**,
under the hand of *Hananiah* **Hanan Yah**,
one of the *king's captains* **sovereign's governors**.
12 The whole number of the *chief* **head** of the fathers
of the mighty *men* of valour
were two thousand and six hundred.
13 And under their hand was *an army* **a host**,
three hundred thousand
and seven thousand and five hundred,
that *made* **worked** war with *mighty power* **valiant force**,
to help the *king* **sovereign** against the enemy.
14 And *Uzziah* **Uzzi Yah**
prepared for them throughout all the host
shields **bucklers**, and *spears* **javelins**,
and helmets, and habergeons,
and bows, and *slings to cast stones* **stones for slings**.
15 And he *made* **worked** in *Jerusalem* **Yeru Shalem**
engines **fabrications**,
invented by cunning men — **the fabrication of fabricators**,
to be on the towers and upon the *bulwarks* **corners**,
to *shoot* **flow** arrows and great stones withal.
And his name *spread far abroad* **went forth afar off**;
for he was marvellously helped,
till he *was strong* **prevailed**.
16 But when he *was strong* **strengthened**,
his heart *was lifted up* **exalted** to *his destruction* **ruin him**:
for he *transgressed* **treasoned**
against *the LORD* **Yah Veh** his *God* **Elohim**,
and went into the *temple* **manse** of *the LORD* **Yah Veh**
to *burn* incense upon the **sacrifice** altar of incense.
17 And *Azariah* **Azar Yah** the priest went in after him,
and with him
fourscore **eighty** priests of *the LORD* **Yah Veh**,
that were valiant *men* **sons**:
18 And they withstood
Uzziah **Uzzi Yah** the *king* **sovereign**, and said unto him,
It *appertaineth* **becometh** not unto thee, *Uzziah* **Uzzi Yah**,

to *burn* incense unto *the LORD* **Yah Veh**,
but to the priests the sons of *Aaron* **Aharon**,
that are *consecrated* **hallowed** to *burn* incense:
go out of the *sanctuary* **holies**;
for thou hast *trespassed* **treasoned**;
neither shall it be for thine honour
from *the LORD God* **Yah Veh Elohim**.
19 Then *Uzziah* **Uzzi Yah** was *wroth* **enraged**,
and had a censer in his hand to *burn* incense:
and while he was *wroth* **enraged** with the priests,
the leprosy even rose up in his forehead
before **at the face of** the priests
in the house of *the LORD* **Yah Veh**,
from beside the incense **sacrifice** altar.
20 And *Azariah* **Azar Yah**, the *chief* **head** priest,
and all the priests, *looked upon* **faced** him, and, behold,
he was leprous in his forehead,
and they *thrust* **hasted** him *out* from thence;
yea, himself hasted also to go out,
because *the LORD* **Yah Veh** had *smitten* **touched** him.
21 And *Uzziah* **Uzzi Yah**, the *king* **sovereign**
was a leper unto the day of his death,
and *dwelt* **settled** in a *several* **liberty** house, *being* a leper;
for he was cut off from the house of *the LORD* **Yah Veh**:
and *Jotham* **Yah Tham** his son
was over the *king's* **sovereign's** house,
judging the people of the land.
22 Now the rest of the *acts* **words** of *Uzziah* **Uzzi Yah**,
first and last, did *Isaiah* **Yesha Yah** the prophet,
the son of *Amoz* **Amos**, *write* **inscribe**.
23 So *Uzziah slept* **Uzzi Yah laid** with his fathers,
and they *buried* **entombed** him with his fathers
in the field of the *burial* **tomb**
which *belonged to the kings* **be the sovereigns**;
for they said, He is a leper:
and *Jotham* **Yah Tham** his son reigned in his stead.

YAH THAM REIGNS IN YERU SHALEM

27 *Jotham* **Yah Tham**
was **a son of** twenty and five years *old*
when he began to reign,
and he reigned sixteen years in *Jerusalem* **Yeru Shalem**.
His mother's name also was *Jerushah* **Yerushah**,
the daughter of *Zadok* **Sadoq**.
2 And he *did* **worked** that which was *right* **straight**
in the *sight* **eyes** of *the LORD* **Yah Veh**,
according to all
that his father *Uzziah did* **Uzzi Yah worked**:
howbeit he entered not
into the *temple* **manse** of *the LORD* **Yah Veh**.
And the people *did yet corruptly* **ruined**.
3 He built *the high gate* **Elyon Portal**
of the house of *the LORD* **Yah Veh**,
and on the wall of Ophel he built *much* **abundantly**.
4 Moreover
he built cities in the mountains of *Judah* **Yah Hudah**,
and in the forests he built *castles* **palaces** and towers.
5 He fought also
with the *king* **sovereign** of the *Ammonites* **sons of Ammon**,
and prevailed against them.
And the *children* **sons** of Ammon gave him the same year
an hundred *talents* **rounds** of silver,
and ten thousand *measures* **kors** of wheat,
and ten thousand of barley.
So much **This** did the *children* **sons** of Ammon
pay **return** unto him,
both the second year, and the third.
6 So *Jotham became mighty* **Yah Tham prevailed**,
because he prepared his ways
before the LORD **at the face of Yah Veh** his *God* **Elohim**.
7 Now the rest of the *acts* **words** of *Jotham* **Yah Tham**,
and all his wars, and his ways, *lo* **behold**,
they are *written* **inscribed**
in the *book* **scroll** of the *kings* **sovereigns**
of *Israel* **Yisra El** and *Judah* **Yah Hudah**.
8 He was **a son of** five and twenty years *old*
when he began to reign,
and reigned sixteen years in *Jerusalem* **Yeru Shalem**.
9 And *Jotham slept* **Yah Tham laid** with his fathers,
and they *buried* **entombed** him in the city of David:
and *Ahaz* **Achaz** his son reigned in his stead.

ACHAZ REIGNS IN YERU SHALEM

28 *Ahaz* **Achaz** was **a son of** twenty years *old*
when he began to reign,
and he reigned sixteen years in *Jerusalem* **Yeru Shalem**:
but he *did* **worked** not that which was *right* **straight**
in the *sight* **eyes** of *the LORD* **Yah Veh**,
like David his father:
2 For he walked in the ways
of the *kings* **sovereigns** of *Israel* **Yisra El**,
and *made* **worked** also *molten images* **moltens** for Baalim.
3 Moreover he *burnt incense* **incensed**
in the valley of the son of *Hinnom* **burning**,
and burnt his *children* **sons** in the fire,
after the *abominations* **abhorrences** of the *heathen* **goyim**
whom *the LORD* **Yah Veh** had *cast out* **dispossessed**
before **at the face of** the *children* **sons** of *Israel* **Yisra El**.
4 He sacrificed also and *burnt incense* **incensed**
in the *high places* **bamahs**, and on the hills,
and under every green tree.
5 Wherefore *the LORD* **Yah Veh** his *God* **Elohim**
delivered **gave** him into the hand
of the *king* **sovereign** of *Syria* **Aram**;
and they smote him,
and *carried away* **captured**
a great multitude of them *captives*,
and brought *them* to *Damascus* **Dammeseq**.
And he was also *delivered* **given**
into the hand of the *king* **sovereign** of *Israel* **Yisra El**,
who smote him with a great *slaughter* **stroke**.
6 For *Pekah* **Peqach** the son of *Remaliah* **Remal Yah**
slew **slaughtered** in *Judah* **Yah Hudah**
an hundred and twenty thousand in one day,
which *were* all valiant *men* **sons**;
because they had forsaken
the LORD God **Yah Veh Elohim** of their fathers.
7 And Zichri, *a* mighty *man* of *Ephraim* **Ephrayim**,
slew Maaseiah **slaughtered Maase Yah**
the *king's* **sovereign's** son,
and *Azrikam* **Ezri Qam** the *governor* **eminent** of the house,
and *Elkanah* **El Qanah**
that was *next* **second** to the *king* **sovereign**.
8 And the *children* **sons** of *Israel* **Yisra El**
carried away captive **captured** of their brethren
two hundred thousand, women, sons, and daughters,
and *took* **plundered** also *away* much spoil from them,
and brought the spoil to *Samaria* **Shomeron**.
9 But a prophet of *the LORD* **Yah Veh** was there,
whose name was Oded:
and he went out *before* **at the face of** the host
that came to *Samaria* **Shomeron**, and said unto them,
Behold,
because *the LORD God* **Yah Veh Elohim** of your fathers
was wroth **in his fury** with *Judah* **Yah Hudah**,
he hath *delivered* **given** them into your hand,
and ye have *slain* **slaughtered** them in a rage
that *reacheth up* **toucheth** unto *heaven* **the heavens**.
10 And now ye *purpose* **say** to *keep under* **subdue**
the *children* **sons** of *Judah* **Yah Hudah**
and *Jerusalem* **Yeru Shalem**
for *bondmen* **servants** and *bondwomen* **maids** unto you:
but are there not with you, *even* **only** with you,
sins **guilt** against *the LORD* **Yah Veh** your *God* **Elohim**?
11 Now hear me therefore,
and *deliver* **return** the captives *again*,
which ye have *taken captive* **captured** of your brethren:
for the *fierce* **fuming** wrath of *the LORD* **Yah Veh**
is upon you.
12 Then *certain* **men**
of the heads of the *children* **sons** of *Ephraim* **Ephrayim**,
Azariah **Azar Yah** the son of *Johanan* **Yah Hanan**,
Berechiah **Berech Yah** the son of Meshillemoth,
and *Jehizkiah* **Yechizqi Yah** the son of Shallum,
and Amasa the son of Hadlai,
stood up **arose** against them
that came from the *war* **hostility**,
13 And said unto them,
ye shall not bring *in* the captives hither:
for whereas we have *offended* **guilted**
against *the LORD* **Yah Veh** *already*,
ye *intend* **say** to add *more*

to our sins and to our *trespass* **guilt**:
for our *trespass* **guilt** is great,
and there is *fierce* **fuming** wrath against *Israel* **Yisra El**.
14 So the *armed men* **equipped**
left the captives and the *spoil* **plunder**
before **at the face of** the *princes* **governors**
and all the congregation.
15 And the men which were *expressed* **appointed** by name
rose up, and *took* **held** the captives,
and with the spoil
clothed **enrobed** all that were naked among them,
and *arrayed* **enrobed** them, and *shod* **enclosed** them,
and gave them to eat and to drink, and anointed them,
and *carried* **guided** all *the feeble of* them **that faltered**
upon *asses* **he burros**,
and brought them to *Jericho* **Yericho**,
the city of palm trees, *to* **beside** their brethren:
then they returned to *Samaria* **Shomeron**.
16 At that time did *king Ahaz* **sovereign Achaz**
send unto the *kings* **sovereigns** of *Assyria* **Ashshur**
to help him.
17 For again the *Edomites* **Edomiy** had come
and smitten *Judah* **Yah Hudah**,
and *carried away* **captured** captives.
18 The *Philistines* **Peleshethiy** also
had *invaded* **stripped** the cities
of the *low country* **lowlands**,
and of the south of *Judah* **Yah Hudah**,
and had *taken Bethshemesh* **captured Beth Shemesh**,
and *Ajalon* **Aijalon**, and Gederoth,
and *Shocho* **Sochoh** with the *villages* **daughters** thereof,
and Timnah with the *villages* **daughters** thereof,
Gimzo also and the *villages* **daughters** thereof:
and they *dwelt* **settled** there.
19 For *the LORD* **Yah Veh**
brought Judah low **humbled Yah Hudah**
because of *Ahaz* **Achaz**, *king* **sovereign** of *Israel* **Yisra El**;
for he *made Judah naked* **exposed Yah Hudah**,
and *transgressed sore* **in treasoning, treasoned**
against *the LORD* **Yah Veh**.
20 And *Tilgathpilneser* **Tilgath Pileser**,
king **sovereign** of *Assyria* **Ashshur** came unto him,
and *distressed* **besieged** him, but strengthened him not.
21 For *Ahaz took away a portion* **Achaz allotted**
out of the house of *the LORD* **Yah Veh**,
and *out* of the house of the *king* **sovereign**,
and of the *princes* **governors**,
and gave it unto the *king* **sovereign** of *Assyria* **Ashshur**:
but he helped him not.
22 And in the time of his distress
did he *trespass yet more* **add to treason**
against *the LORD* **Yah Veh**:
this is that *king Ahaz* **sovereign Achaz**.
23 For he sacrificed
unto the *gods* **elohim** of *Damascus* **Dammeseq**,
which smote him: and he said,
Because the *gods* **elohim**
of the *kings* **sovereigns** of *Syria* **Aram** help them,
therefore *will* **shall** I sacrifice to them,
that they may help me.
But they *were the ruin of* **stumbled** him,
and of all *Israel* **Yisra El**.
24 And *Ahaz* **Achaz** gathered *together*
the *vessels* **instruments** of the house of *God* **Elohim**,
and *cut* **chopped** in pieces the *vessels* **instruments**
of the house of *God* **Elohim**,
and shut up the doors of the house of *the LORD* **Yah Veh**,
and he *made* **worked** him **sacrifice** altars
in every corner of *Jerusalem* **Yeru Shalem**.
25 And in *every several city* **city by city**
of *Judah* **Yah Hudah**
he *made high places* **worked bamahs**
to *burn* incense unto other *gods* **elohim**,
and *provoked to anger* **vexed**
the LORD God **Yah Veh Elohim** of his fathers.

THE DEATH OF ACHAZ

26 Now the rest of his *acts* **words** and of all his ways,
first and last, behold,
they are *written* **inscribed**
in the *book* **scroll** of the *kings* **sovereigns**
of *Judah* **Yah Hudah** and *Israel* **Yisra El**.
27 And *Ahaz slept* **Achaz laid** with his fathers,
and they *buried* **entombed** him in the city,
even in *Jerusalem* **Yeru Shalem**:
but they brought him not into the *sepulchres* **tombs**
of the *kings* **sovereigns** of *Israel* **Yisra El**:
and *Hezekiah* **Yechizqi Yah** his son reigned in his stead.

YECHIZQI YAH REIGNS IN YERU SHALEM

29 *Hezekiah* **Yechizqi Yah** began to reign
when he was **a son of** five and twenty years *old*,
and he reigned nine and twenty years
in *Jerusalem* **Yeru Shalem**.
And his mother's name was *Abijah* **Abi Yah**,
the daughter of *Zechariah* **Zechar Yah**.
2 And he *did* **worked** that which was *right* **straight**
in the *sight* **eyes** of *the LORD* **Yah Veh**,
according to all that David his father had *done* **worked**.

YECHIZQI YAH STRENGTHENS THE HOUSE OF YAH VEH

3 He in the first year of his reign, in the first month,
opened the doors of the house of *the LORD* **Yah Veh**,
and *repaired* **strengthened** them.
4 And he brought in the priests and the *Levites* **Leviym**,
and gathered them *together*
into the *east street* **broadway toward the rising**,
5 And said unto them, Hear me, ye *Levites* **Leviym**,
sanctify **hallow** now yourselves,
and *sanctify* **hallow** the house
of *the LORD God* **Yah Veh Elohim** of your fathers,
and *carry forth* **bring** the *filthiness* **exclusion**
out of the *holy place* **holies**.
6 For our fathers have *trespassed* **treasoned**,
and *done* **worked** that which was evil
in the eyes of *the LORD* **Yah Veh** our *God* **Elohim**,
and have forsaken him,
and have turned away their faces
from the *habitation* **tabernacle** of *the LORD* **Yah Veh**
and *turned* **gave** their *backs* **necks**.
7 Also they have shut up the doors of the porch,
and *put out* **quenched** the lamps,
and have not *burned* **incensed** incense
nor *offered burnt offerings* **holocausted holocausts**
in the *holy place* **holies**
unto *the God* **Elohim** of *Israel* **Yisra El**.
8 Wherefore the *wrath* **rage** of *the LORD* **Yah Veh**
was upon *Judah* **Yah Hudah** and *Jerusalem* **Yeru Shalem**,
and he hath *delivered* **given** them *to trouble* **agitation**,
to *astonishment* **desolation**, and to hissing,
as ye see with your eyes.
9 For, *lo* **behold**, our fathers have fallen by the sword,
and our sons and our daughters and our *wives* **women**
are in captivity for this.
10 Now it is in mine heart to *make* **cut** a covenant
with *the LORD God* **Yah Veh Elohim** of *Israel* **Yisra El**,
that his *fierce* **fuming** wrath may turn away from us.
11 My sons, be not now *negligent* **misled**:
for *the LORD* **Yah Veh** hath chosen you
to stand *before him* **at his face**,
to *serve* **minister unto** him,
and that ye should minister unto him, and *burn* incense.
12 Then the *Levites* **Leviym** arose,
Mahath **Machath** the son of *Amasai* **Amasay**,
and *Joel* **Yah El** the son of *Azariah* **Azar Yah**,
of the sons of the *Kohathites* **Qehathiy**:
and of the sons of Merari, *Kish* **Qish** the son of Abdi,
and *Azariah* **Azar Yah** the son of *Jehaleleel* **ye Halal El**:
and of the *Gershonites* **Gershoniy**;
Joah **Yah Ach** the son of Zimmah,
and Eden the son of *Joah* **Yah Ach**:
13 And of the sons of *Elizaphan* **El Saphan**;
Shimri, and *Jeiel* **Yei El**:
and of the sons of Asaph;
Zechariah **Zechar Yah**, and *Mattaniah* **Mattan Yah**:
14 And of the sons of Heman;
Jehi El **Yechi El**, and *Shimei* **Shimi**:
and of the sons of *Jeduthun* **Yeduthun**;
Shemaiah **Shema Yah**, and *Uzziel* **Uzzi El**.
15 And they gathered their brethren,
and *sanctified* **hallowed** themselves, and came,
according to
the *commandment* **misvah** of the *king* **sovereign**,

by the words of *the LORD* **Yah Veh**,
to *cleanse* **purify** the house of *the LORD* **Yah Veh**.
6 And the priests went *into the inner part of* **within**
the house of *the LORD* **Yah Veh**, to *cleanse* **purify** it,
and brought out all the *uncleanness* **foulness**
that they found in the *temple* **manse** of *the LORD* **Yah Veh**
into the court of the house of *the LORD* **Yah Veh**.
And the *Levites* **Leviym** took it,
to *carry* **bring** it out *abroad*
into the *brook Kidron* **wadi Qidron**.
17 Now they began on the first *day* of the first month
to *sanctify* **hallow**,
and on the eighth day of the month
came they to the porch of *the LORD* **Yah Veh**:
so they *sanctified* **hallowed**
the house of *the LORD* **Yah Veh** in eight days;
and in the sixteenth day of the first month
they *made an end* **finished**.
18 Then they went in
to *Hezekiah* **Yechizqi Yah** the *king* **sovereign**, and said,
We have *cleansed* **purified**
all the house of *the LORD* **Yah Veh**,
and the **sacrifice** altar of *burnt offering* **holocaust**,
with all the *vessels* **instruments** thereof,
and the *shewbread* **arrangement** table,
with all the *vessels* **instruments** thereof.
19 Moreover all the *vessels* **instruments**,
which *king Ahaz* **sovereign Achaz**
in his *reign* **sovereigndom**
did cast away **abandoned** in his *transgression* **treason**,
have we prepared and *sanctified* **hallowed**, and, behold,
they are *before* **at the face of** the **sacrifice** altar
of *the LORD* **Yah Veh**.

YECHIZQ YAH RESTORES WORSHIP IN THE HOUSE OF YAH VEH

20 Then *Hezekiah* **Yechizqi Yah**, the *king* **sovereign**
rose **started** early,
and gathered the *rulers* **governors** of the city,
and *went up* **ascended** to the house of *the LORD* **Yah Veh**.
21 And they brought seven bullocks,
and seven rams, and seven lambs,
and seven *he goats* **buck goats of the doe goats**,
for *a sin offering* **the sin**
for the *kingdom* **sovereigndom**,
and for the *sanctuary* **holies**, and for *Judah* **Yah Hudah**.
And he *commanded* **said to** the priests
the sons of *Aaron* **Aharon**
to *offer* **holocaust** them
on the **sacrifice** altar of *the LORD* **Yah Veh**.
22 So they *killed* **slaughtered** the *bullocks* **oxen**,
and the priests *received* **took** the blood,
and sprinkled it on the **sacrifice** altar:
likewise, when they had *killed* **slaughtered** the rams,
they sprinkled the blood upon the **sacrifice** altar:
they *killed* **slaughtered** also the lambs,
and they sprinkled the blood upon the altar.
23 And they brought *forth* **near** the he *goats* **bucks**
for the sin *offering*
before **at the face of** the *king* **sovereign**
and the congregation;
and they *laid* **propped** their hands upon them:
24 And the priests *killed* **slaughtered** them,
and they *made reconciliation* **cleansed**
with their blood upon the **sacrifice** altar,
to *make an atonement* **kapar/atone** for all *Israel* **Yisra El**:
for the *king commanded* **sovereign said**
that the *burnt offering* **holocaust**
and **that for** the sin *offering*
should be *made* for all *Israel* **Yisra El**.
25 And he *set* **stood** the *Levites* **Leviym**
in the house of *the LORD* **Yah Veh**
with cymbals, with *psalteries* **bagpipes**, and with harps,
according to the *commandment* **misvah** of David,
and of Gad the *king's* **sovereign's** seer,
and Nathan the prophet:
for so was the *commandment* **misvah**
by the hand of *the LORD* **Yah Veh**,
by **the hand of** his prophets.
26 And the *Levites* **Leviym** stood
with the instruments of David,
and the priests with the trumpets.
27 And *Hezekiah commanded* **Yechizqi Yah said**
to *offer* **holocaust** the *burnt offering* **holocaust**
upon the **sacrifice** altar.
And *when* **at the time** the *burnt offering* **holocaust** began,
the song of *the LORD* **Yah Veh** began *also*
with the trumpets,
and with **by the hand of** the instruments *ordained*
by **of** David *king* **sovereign** of *Israel* **Yisra El**.
28 And all the congregation *worshipped* **prostrated**,
and the singers sang,
and the trumpeters *sounded* **trumpeted**:
and all *this continued*
until the *burnt offering* **holocaust** was finished.
29 And when they had
made an end of offering **finished holocausting**,
the *king* **sovereign**
and all that were *present* **found** with him
bowed *themselves*, and *worshipped* **prostrated**.
30 Moreover *Hezekiah* **Yechizqi Yah**, the *king* **sovereign**
and the *princes* **governors**
commanded **said to** the *Levites* **Leviym**
to *sing praise* **halal** unto *the LORD* **Yah Veh**
with the words of David, and of Asaph the seer.
And they *sang praises* **halaled** with *gladness* **cheerfulness**,
and they bowed *their heads* and *worshipped* **prostrated**.
31 Then *Hezekiah* **Yechizqi Yah** answered and said,
Now ye have *consecrated yourselves* **filled your hand**
unto *the LORD* **Yah Veh**,
come near and bring sacrifices
and *thank offerings* **extended hands**
into the house of *the LORD* **Yah Veh**.
And the congregation brought in sacrifices
and *thank offerings* **extended hands**;
and as many as were of a *free* **voluntary** heart
burnt offerings **holocausted**.
32 And the number of the *burnt offerings* **holocausts**,
which the congregation brought,
was *threescore and ten bullocks* **seventy oxen**,
an hundred rams, and two hundred lambs:
all these were for a *burnt offering* **holocaust**
to *the LORD* **Yah Veh**.
33 And the *consecrated things* **holies**
were six hundred oxen and three thousand *sheep* **flocks**.
34 But the priests were too few,
so that they could not *flay* **strip**
all the *burnt offerings* **holocausts**:
wherefore their brethren the *Levites* **Leviym**
did help **strengthened** them,
till the work was *ended* **finished**,
and until the *other* priests
had *sanctified* **hallowed** themselves:
for the *Levites* **Leviym** were more *upright* **straight** in heart
to *sanctify* **hallow** themselves than the priests.
35 And also the *burnt offerings* **holocausts**
were in abundance,
with the fat of the *peace offerings* **shelamim**,
and the *drink offerings* **libations**
for *every burnt offering* **the holocaust**.
So the service of the house of *the LORD* **Yah Veh**
was *set in order* **established**.
36 And *Hezekiah rejoiced* **Yechizqi Yah cheered**,
and all the people,
that *God* **Elohim** had prepared the people:
for the *thing* **word** was *done* suddenly.

YECHIZQI YAH WORKS THE PASACH

30 And *Hezekiah* **Yechizqi Yah**
sent to all *Israel* **Yisra El** and *Judah* **Yah Hudah**,
and *wrote letters* **inscribed epistles** also
to *Ephraim* **Ephrayim** and *Manasseh* **Menash Sheh**,
that they should come to the house of *the LORD* **Yah Veh**
at *Jerusalem* **Yeru Shalem**,
to *keep* **work** the *passover* **pasach**
unto *the LORD God* **Yah Veh Elohim** of *Israel* **Yisra El**.
2 For the *king* **sovereign** had taken counsel,
and his *princes* **governors**,
and all the congregation in *Jerusalem* **Yeru Shalem**,
to *keep* **work** the *passover* **pasach** in the second month.
3 For they could not *keep* **work** it at that time,
because the priests

had not *sanctified* **hallowed** themselves sufficiently,
neither had the people
gathered *themselves together* to *Jerusalem* **Yeru Shalem**.
4 And the *thing pleased* **word was straight**
in the eyes of the *king* **sovereign**
and **in the eyes of** all the congregation.
5 So they *established* **stood** a *decree* **word**
to *make proclamation* **pass the voice**
throughout all *Israel* **Yisra El**,
from *Beersheba* **Beer Sheba** even to Dan,
that they should come to *keep* **work** the *passover* **pasach**
unto *the LORD God* **Yah Veh Elohim** of *Israel* **Yisra El**
at *Jerusalem* **Yeru Shalem**:
for they had not *done* **worked** it
of a long time **in abundance**
in such sort as it was *written* **inscribed**.
6 So the *posts* **runners** went with the *letters* **epistles**
from **the hand of** the *king* **sovereign**
and his *princes* **governors**
throughout all *Israel* **Yisra El** and *Judah* **Yah Hudah**,
and according to
the *commandment* **misvah** of the *king* **sovereign**, saying,
Ye *children* **sons** of *Israel* **Yisra El**,
turn again **return** unto *the LORD God* **Yah Veh Elohim**
of Abraham, *Isaac* **Yischaq**, and *Israel* **Yisra El**,
and he *will* **shall** return to the *remnant* **survivors** of you,
that are *escaped* **escapees** out of the *hand* **palm**
of the *kings* **sovereigns** of *Assyria* **Ashshur**.
7 And be not ye like your fathers, and like your brethren,
which *trespassed* **treasoned**
against *the LORD God* **Yah Veh Elohim** of their fathers,
who therefore gave them up to desolation, as ye see.
8 Now *be* ye *not stiffnecked* **harden not your necks**
as your fathers *were*,
but yield yourselves **give your hand**
unto *the LORD* **Yah Veh**,
and enter into his *sanctuary* **holies**,
which he hath *sanctified for ever* **hallowed eternally**:
and serve *the LORD* **Yah Veh** your *God* **Elohim**,
that the *fierceness* **fuming** of his wrath
may turn *away* from you.
9 For if ye *turn again* **return** unto *the LORD* **Yah Veh**,
your brethren and your *children* **sons**
shall *find compassion* **be mercied**
before them that lead them captive
at the face of their captors,
so that they shall *come again* **return** into this land:
for *the LORD* **Yah Veh** your *God* **Elohim**
is *gracious* **charismatic** and merciful,
and *will* **shall** not turn *away* **aside** his face from you,
if ye return unto him.
10 So the *posts* **runners** passed from city to city
through the *country* **land** of *Ephraim* **Ephrayim**
and *Manasseh* **Menash Sheh** even unto Zebulun:
but they *laughed* **ridiculed** them *to scorn*,
and *mocked* **derided** them.
11 Nevertheless
divers **men** of Asher and *Manasseh* **Menash Sheh**
and of Zebulun humbled themselves,
and came to *Jerusalem* **Yeru Shalem**.
12 Also in *Judah* **Yah Hudah**
the hand of *God* **Elohim** was to give them one heart
to *do* **work** the *commandment* **misvah**
of the *king* **sovereign** and of the *princes* **governors**,
by the word of *the LORD* **Yah Veh**.
13 And there *assembled* **gathered**
at *Jerusalem* **Yeru Shalem** much people to *keep* **work**
the *feast* **celebration** of *unleavened bread* **matsah**
in the second month, a *very* **mighty** great congregation.
14 And they arose
and *took away* **turned aside** the **sacrifice** altars
that were in *Jerusalem* **Yeru Shalem**,
and all the *altars for incense* **censers**
took **turned** they *away* **aside**,
and cast them into the *brook Kidron* **wadi Qidron**.
15 Then they *killed* **slaughtered** the *passover* **pasach**
on the fourteenth *day* of the second month:
and the priests and the *Levites* **Leviym** were ashamed,
and *sanctified* **hallowed** themselves,
and brought in the *burnt offerings* **holocausts**
into the house of *the LORD* **Yah Veh**.
16 And they stood in their *place* **stations**
after their *manner* **judgment**,
according to the *law* **torah** of *Moses* **Mosheh**
the man of *God* **Elohim**:
the priests sprinkled the blood,
which they received of the hand of the *Levites* **Leviym**.
17 For there were many in the congregation
that were not *sanctified* **hallowed**:
therefore the *Levites* **Leviym** had the charge
of the *killing* **slaughter** of the *passovers* **pasachs**
for every one that was not *clean* **pure**,
to *sanctify* **hallow** them unto *the LORD* **Yah Veh**.
18 For *a multitude* **an increase** of the people,
even many of *Ephraim* **Ephrayim**,
and *Manasseh* **Menash Sheh**,
Issachar **Yissachar**, and Zebulun,
had not *cleansed* **purified** *themselves*,
yet did they eat the *passover* **pasach**
otherwise than it was written **not as inscribed**.
But *Hezekiah* **Yechizqi Yah** prayed for them, saying,
The good *LORD pardon* **Yah Veh kapar/atone** every one
19 That prepareth his heart to seek *God* **Elohim**,
the LORD God **Yah Veh Elohim** of his fathers,
though he be not *cleansed*
according to the purification of the *sanctuary* **holies**.
20 And *the LORD* **Yah Veh**
hearkened to *Hezekiah* **Yechizqi Yah**,
and healed the people.
21 And the *children* **sons** of *Israel* **Yisra El**
that were *present* **found** at *Jerusalem* **Yeru Shalem**
kept **worked**
the *feast* **celebration** of *unleavened bread* **matsah**
seven days with great *gladness* **cheerfulness**:
and the *Levites* **Leviym** and the priests
praised the LORD **halaled Yah Veh** day by day,
singing with loud instruments **with instruments of strength**
unto *the LORD* **Yah Veh**.
22 And *Hezekiah spake comfortably* **Yechizqi Yah worded**
unto **the heart of** all the *Levites* **Leviym**
that *taught* **comprehended**
the good *knowledge* **comprehension**
of *the LORD* **Yah Veh**:
and they did eat throughout the *feast* **festival** seven days,
offering **sacrificing the sacrifices**
peace offerings **of shelamim**,
and *making confession* **extended hands**
to *the LORD God* **Yah Veh Elohim** of their fathers.
23 And the whole *assembly* **congregation**
took counsel **counselled**
to *keep* **work** other seven days:
and they *kept* **worked** *other* seven days
with *gladness* **cheerfulness**.
24 For *Hezekiah* **Yechizqi Yah**,
king **sovereign** of *Judah* **Yah Hudah**
did give **lifted up** to the congregation
a thousand bullocks and seven thousand *sheep* **flocks**;
and the *princes* **governors**
gave **lifted up** to the congregation
a thousand bullocks and ten thousand *sheep* **flocks**:
and *a great number* **an abundance** of priests
sanctified **hallowed** themselves.
25 And all the congregation of *Judah* **Yah Hudah**,
with the priests and the *Levites* **Leviym**,
and all the congregation that came out of *Israel* **Yisra El**,
and the *strangers* **sojourners**
that came out of the land of *Israel* **Yisra El**,
and that *dwelt* **settled** in *Judah* **Yah Hudah**,
rejoiced **cheered**.
26 So there was great *joy* **cheer** in *Jerusalem* **Yeru Shalem**:
for since the *time* **day** of *Solomon* **Shelomoh**
the son of David *king* **sovereign** of *Israel* **Yisra El**
there was not the like in *Jerusalem* **Yeru Shalem**.
27 Then the priests the *Levites* **Leviym** arose
and blessed the people:
and their voice was heard, and their prayer came *up*
to *his holy dwelling place* **the habitation of his holiness**,
even unto *heaven* **the heavens**.

YISRA EL DESTROYS THE MONOLITHS,
ASHERIM, AND BAMAHS
31 Now when all this was finished,
all *Israel* **Yisra El** that were *present* **found**
went out to the cities of *Judah* **Yah Hudah**,
and brake the *images* **monoliths** in pieces,
and cut down the *groves* **asherim**,
and *threw* **pulled** down the *high places* **bamahs**
and the **sacrifice** altars
out of all *Judah* **Yah Hudah** and *Benjamin* **Ben Yamin**,
in *Ephraim* **Ephrayim** also and *Manasseh* **Menash Sheh**,
until they had *utterly destroyed* **finished** them *all* **off**.
Then all the *children* **sons** of *Israel* **Yisra El** returned,
every man to his possession, into their own cities.
2 And *Hezekiah* **Yechizqi Yah**
appointed **stationed** the *courses* **allotments**
of the priests and the *Levites* **Leviym**
after their *courses* **allotments**,
every man according to **the mouth of** his service,
the priests and *Levites* **Leviym**
for *burnt offerings* **holocausts**
and for *peace offerings* **shelamim**,
to minister,
and to *give thanks* **extend hands**, and to *praise* **halal**
in the *gates* **portals**
of the *tents* **camps** of *the LORD* **Yah Veh**.
3 *He appointed* also
the *king's portion* **sovereign's allotment**
of his *substance* **acquisition**
for the *burnt offerings* **holocausts**, *to wit,*
for the morning and evening *burnt offerings* **holocausts**,
and the *burnt offerings* **holocausts**
for the *sabbaths* **shabbaths**,
and for the new moons, and for the *set feasts* **festivals**,
as it is *written* **inscribed**
in the *law* **torah** of *the LORD* **Yah Veh**.
4 Moreover he *commanded* **said to** the people
that *dwelt* **settled** in *Jerusalem* **Yeru Shalem**
to give the *portion* **allotment**
of the priests and the *Levites* **Leviym**,
that they might be *encouraged* **strengthened**
in the *law* **torah** of *the LORD* **Yah Veh**.
5 And as soon as the
commandment came abroad **word broke forth**,
the *children* **sons** of *Israel* **Yisra El**
brought in abundance **abounded**
the *firstfruits* **firstlings** of *corn* **crop**
wine **juice**, and oil, and honey,
and of all the *increase* **produce** of the field;
and the tithe of all *things* brought they
in *abundantly* **abundance**.
6 And *concerning*
the *children* **sons** of *Israel* **Yisra El** and *Judah* **Yah Hudah**,
that *dwelt* **settled** in the cities of *Judah* **Yah Hudah**,
they also brought in the tithe of oxen and *sheep* **flock**,
and the tithe of *holy things* **holies**
which were *consecrated* **hallowed**
unto *the LORD* **Yah Veh** their *God* **Elohim**
and *laid* **gave** them by heaps.
7 In the third month
they began to lay the foundation of the heaps,
and finished them in the seventh month.
8 And when *Hezekiah* **Yechizqi Yah**
and the *princes* **governors** came and saw the heaps,
they blessed *the LORD* **Yah Veh**,
and his people *Israel* **Yisra El**.
9 Then *Hezekiah* **Yechizqi Yah** questioned
with the priests and the *Levites* **Leviym**
concerning the heaps.
10 And *Azariah* **Azar Yah**
the *chief* **head** priest of the house of *Zadok* **Sadoq**
answered **said to** him, and said,
Since *the people began to bring* **bringing**
the *offerings* **exaltments**
into the house of *the LORD* **Yah Veh**,
we *have had enough to eat* **be satisfied**,
and have *left plenty* **remaining abundantly**:
for *the LORD* **Yah Veh** hath blessed his people;
and that which *is left* **remaineth**
is this great *store* **multitude**.
11 Then *Hezekiah commanded* **Yechizqi Yah said**
to prepare chambers in the house of *the LORD* **Yah Veh**;
and they prepared them,
12 And brought in the *offerings* **exaltments** and the tithes
and the *dedicated things faithfully* **holies trustworthily**:
over which
Cononiah **Konan Yah** the *Levite* **Leviy** was *ruler* **eminent**,
and *Shimei* **Shimi** his brother was the *next* **second**.
13 And *Jehiel* **Yechi El**, and *Azaziah* **Azaz Yah**,
and *Nahath* **Nachath**, and *Asahel* **Asa El**,
and *Jerimoth* **Yerimoth**, and *Jozabad* **Yah Zabad**,
and *Eliel* **Eli El**, and *Ismachiah* **Yismach Yah**,
and *Mahath* **Machath**, and *Benaiah* **Bena Yah**,
were overseers under the hand
of *Cononiah* **Konan Yah** and *Shimei* **Shimi** his brother,
at the *commandment* **mandate**
of *Hezekiah* **Yechizqi Yah** the *king* **sovereign**,
and *Azariah* **Azar Yah** the *ruler* **eminent**
of the house of *God* **Elohim**.
14 And *Kore* **Qore**
the son of *Imnah* **Yimlah** the *Levite* **Leviy**,
the porter toward the *east* **rising**,
was over the *freewill offerings* **voluntaries** of *God* **Elohim**,
to *distribute* **give**
the *oblations* **exaltments** of *the LORD* **Yah Veh**,
and the *most holy things* **holies**.
15 And *next him* **at his hand**
were Eden, and *Miniamin* **Min Yamin**,
and *Jeshua* **Yah Shua**, and *Shemaiah* **Shema Yah**,
Amariah **Amar Yah**, and *Shecaniah* **Shechan Yah**,
in the cities of the priests, in their *set office* **trust**,
to give to their brethren by *courses* **allotments**,
as well to the great as to the small:
16 Beside their *genealogy of* **genealogized** males,
from **sons of** three years *old* and upward,
even unto every one
that entereth into the house of *the LORD* **Yah Veh**,
his daily *portion* **word** for their **day by day** service
in their *charges* **guards**
according to their *courses* **allotments**;
17 Both to the *genealogy* **genealogized** of the priests
by the house of their fathers, and the *Levites* **Leviym**
from **sons of** twenty years *old* and upward,
in their *charges* **guards** by their *courses* **allotments**;
18 And to the *genealogy* **genealogized**
of all their *little ones* **toddlers**, their *wives* **women**,
and their sons, and their daughters,
through all the congregation:
for in their *set office* **trust**
they *sanctified* **hallowed** themselves in holiness:
19 Also of the sons of *Aaron* **Aharon** the priests,
which were in the fields of the suburbs of their cities,
in every several city **city by city**,
the men that were *expressed* **appointed** by name,
to give portions to all the males among the priests,
and to all that were *reckoned by genealogies* **genealogized**
among the *Levites* **Leviym**.
20 And thus *did Hezekiah* **worked Yechizqi Yah**
throughout all *Judah* **Yah Hudah**,
and *wrought* **worked**
that which was good and *right* **straight** and truth
before the LORD **at the face of Yah Veh** his *God* **Elohim**.
21 And in every work that he began
in the service of the house of *God* **Elohim**,
and in the *law* **torah**, and in the *commandments* **misvoth**,
to seek his *God* **Elohim**,
he *did* **worked** it with all his heart, and prospered.

THE SOVEREIGN OF ASHSHUR
ENCAMPS AGAINST YERU SHALEM
32 After these *things* **words**,
and the *establishment* **truth** thereof,
Sennacherib **Sancherib**, *king* **sovereign** of *Assyria* **Ashshur**
came, and entered into *Judah* **Yah Hudah**,
and encamped against the *fenced* **cut off** cities,
and *thought to win* **said to split** them for himself.
2 And when *Hezekiah* **Yechizqi Yah** saw
that *Sennacherib* **Sancherib** was come,
and that *he was purposed* **his face was**
to *fight* **war** against *Jerusalem* **Yeru Shalem**,
3 He *took counsel* **counselled** with his *princes* **governors**

and his mighty *men* to stop the waters of the fountains
which were without the city: and they did help him.
4 So there was gathered much people together,
who stopped all the fountains,
and the *brook* **wadi** that *ran* **overflowed**
through the midst of the land, saying,
Why should the *kings* **sovereigns** of *Assyria* **Ashshur**
come, and find much water?
5 Also he strengthened himself,
and built up all the wall that was broken,
and *raised* **ascended** it *up* to the towers,
and another wall without,
and *repaired* **strengthened** Millo *in* the city of David,
and *made* **worked**
darts **spears** and *shields* **bucklers** in abundance.
6 And he *set captains* **gave governors** of war
over the people,
and gathered them *together* to him
in the *street* **broadway** of the *gate* **portal** of the city,
and *spake comfortably* **worded** to *them* **their heart**,
saying,
7 *Be strong and courageous* **Strengthen, encourage**,
be not afraid **neither awe** nor *dismayed* **terrify**
for the king of Assyria
at the face of the sovereign of Ashshur,
nor *for* **at the face of** all the multitude that is with him:
for there be *more* **greater** with us than with him:
8 With him is an arm of flesh;
but with us
is *the LORD* **Yah Veh** our *God* **Elohim** to help us,
and to fight our *battles* **wars**.
And the people *rested* **propped** *themselves*
upon the words of *Hezekiah* **Yechizqi Yah**
king **sovereign** of *Judah* **Yah Hudah**.
9 After this did *Sennacherib* **Sancherib**
king **sovereign** of *Assyria* **Ashshur**
send his servants to *Jerusalem* **Yeru Shalem**,
(but he *himself laid siege* against Lachish,
and all his *power* **reign** with him,)
unto *Hezekiah* **Yechizqi Yah**
king **sovereign** of *Judah* **Yah Hudah**,
and unto all *Judah* **Yah Hudah**
that were at *Jerusalem* **Yeru Shalem**, saying,
10 Thus saith *Sennacherib* **Sancherib**
king **sovereign** of *Assyria* **Ashshur**,
Whereon *do ye trust* **confide ye**,
that ye *abide* **settle** in the siege in *Jerusalem* **Yeru Shalem**?
11 Doth not *Hezekiah persuade* **Yechizqi Yah goad** you
to give over yourselves to die by famine and by thirst,
saying, *the LORD* **Yah Veh** our *God* **Elohim**
shall *deliver* **rescue** us out of the *hand* **palm**
of the *king* **sovereign** of *Assyria* **Ashshur**?
12 Hath not the same *Hezekiah* **Yechizqi Yah**
taken away **turned aside**
his *high places* **bamahs** and his **sacrifice** altars,
and *commanded Judah* **said to Yah Hudah**
and *Jerusalem* **Yeru Shalem**, saying,
Ye shall worship *before* **at the face of** one **sacrifice** altar,
and *burn* incense upon it?
13 Know ye not what I and my fathers have *done* **worked**
unto all the people of other lands?
were the *gods* **elohim** of the *nations* **goyim** of those lands
any ways **at all** able to *deliver* **rescue** their lands
out of mine hand?
14 Who was there
among all the *gods* **elohim** of those *nations* **goyim**
that my fathers *utterly destroyed* **devoted**,
that could *deliver* **rescue** his people out of mine hand,
that your *God* **Elohim** should be able to *deliver* **rescue** you
out of mine hand?
15 Now therefore
let not *Hezekiah* **Yechizqi Yah** deceive you,
nor *persuade* **goad** you *on this manner* **thus**,
neither yet *believe* **trust** him:
for no *god* **elohah**
of any *nation* **goyim** or *kingdom* **sovereigndom**
was able to *deliver* **rescue** his people out of mine hand,
and out of the hand of my fathers:
how much less **neither** shall your *God* **Elohim**
deliver **rescue** you out of mine hand?
16 And his servants *spake* **worded** yet *more*
against *the LORD God* **Yah Veh Elohim**,
and against his servant *Hezekiah* **Yechizqi Yah**.
17 He *wrote* **inscribed** also *letters* **scrolls**
to *rail on* **reproach**
the LORD God **Yah Veh Elohim** of *Israel* **Yisra El**,
and to *speak* **say** against him, saying,
As the *gods* **elohim** of the *nations* **goyim** of other lands
have not *delivered* **rescued** their people out of mine hand,
so shall not *the God* **Elohim** of *Hezekiah* **Yechizqi Yah**
deliver **rescue** his people out of mine hand.
18 Then they *cried* **called out**
with a *loud* **great** voice in *the Jews' speech* **Yah Hudahaic**
unto the people of *Jerusalem* **Yeru Shalem**
that were on the wall,
to *affright* **awe** them, and to *trouble* **terrify** them;
that they might *take* **capture** the city.
19 And they *spake* **worded**
against the *God* **Elohim** of *Jerusalem* **Yeru Shalem**,
as against the *gods* **elohim** of the people of the earth,
which were the work of the hands of *man* **humanity**.
20 And for this cause
Hezekiah **Yechizqi Yah** the *king* **sovereign**,
and the prophet *Isaiah* **Yesha Yah** the son of *Amoz* **Amos**,
prayed and cried to *heaven* **the heavens**.
21 And *the LORD* **Yah Veh** sent an angel,
which cut off all the mighty *men* of valour,
and the *leaders* **eminent** and *captains* **governors**
in the camp of the *king* **sovereign** of *Assyria* **Ashshur**.
So he returned with shame of face to his own land.
And when he was come into the house of his *god* **elohim**,
they that came forth **the offspring**
of his *own bowels* **inwards**
slew **felled** him there with the sword.
22 Thus *the LORD* **Yah Veh** saved *Hezekiah* **Yechizqi Yah**
and the *inhabitants* **settlers** of *Jerusalem* **Yeru Shalem**
from the hand of *Sennacherib* **Sancherib**
the *king* **sovereign** of *Assyria* **Ashshur**,
and from the hand of all other,
and guided them *on every side* **round about**.
23 And many brought *gifts* **offerings**
unto *the LORD* **Yah Veh** to *Jerusalem* **Yeru Shalem**,
and *presents* **preciousnesses** to *Hezekiah* **Yechizqi Yah**
king **sovereign** of *Judah* **Yah Hudah**:
so that he was *magnified* **lifted up**
in the *sight* **eyes** of all *nations* **goyim**
from thenceforth **thereafter**.
24 In those days *Hezekiah* **Yechizqi Yah**
was sick to *the death* **die**,
and prayed unto *the LORD* **Yah Veh**:
and he *spake* **said** unto him,
and he gave him *a sign* **an omen**.
25 But *Hezekiah* **Yechizqi Yah**
rendered **returned** not *again*
according to the *benefit done* **dealing** unto him;
for his heart was lifted *up*:
therefore there was *wrath* **rage** upon him,
and upon *Judah* **Yah Hudah** and *Jerusalem* **Yeru Shalem**.
26 Notwithstanding
Hezekiah **Yechizqi Yah** humbled himself
for the *pride* **haughtiness** of his heart,
both he
and the *inhabitants* **settlers** of *Jerusalem* **Yeru Shalem**,
so that the *wrath* **rage** of *the LORD* **Yah Veh**
came not upon them
in the days of *Hezekiah* **Yechizqi Yah**.
27 And *Hezekiah* **Yechizqi Yah**
had exceeding much **abounded mightily**
in riches and honour:
and he *made* **worked** himself treasuries
for silver, and for gold, and for *precious* **esteemed** stones,
and for spices, and for *shields* **bucklers**,
and for all manner
of *pleasant jewels* **instruments of desire**;
28 *Storehouses* **Storage** *also* for the *increase* **produce**
of *corn* **crop**, and *wine* **juice**, and oil;
and stalls for *all manner of beasts* **animal by animal**,
and *cotes* **stalls** for *flocks* **droves**.
29 Moreover he *provided* **worked** him cities,
and *possessions* **chattels** of flocks and *herds* **oxen**

in abundance:
for *God* **Elohim** had given him
substance very **mighty** much **acquisition**.
30 This same *Hezekiah* **Yechizqi Yah** also stopped
the upper *watercourse* **water springs** of *Gihon* **Gichon**,
and brought it *straight down* **downward**
to the west side **duskward** of the city of David.
And *Hezekiah* **Yechizqi Yah** prospered in all his works.
31 *Howbeit* **Thus**
in the business of the ambassadors **by the interpreters**
of the *princes* **governors** of *Babylon* **Babel**,
who sent unto him to enquire
of the *wonder* **omen** that was *done* in the land,
God **Elohim** left him, to *try* **test** him,
that he might know all that was in his heart.

THE DEATH OF YECHIZQI YAH

32 Now the rest of the *acts* **words**
of *Hezekiah* **Yechizqi Yah**,
and his *goodness* **mercy**, behold,
they are *written* **inscribed** in the vision
of *Isaiah* **Yesha Yah** the prophet, the son of *Amoz* **Amos**,
and in the *book* **scroll** of the *kings* **sovereigns**
of *Judah* **Yah Hudah** and *Israel* **Yisra El**.
33 And *Hezekiah* **Yechizqi Yah**
slept **laid** with his fathers,
and they buried him in the *chiefest* **ascent**
of the *sepulchres* **tombs** of the sons of David:
and all *Judah* **Yah Hudah**
and the *inhabitants* **settlers** of *Jerusalem* **Yeru Shalem**
did **worked** him honour at his death.
And *Manasseh* **Menash Sheh** his son reigned in his stead.

MENASH SHEH REIGNS IN YERU SHALEM

33 *Manasseh* **Menash Sheh**
was **a son of** twelve years *old* when he began to reign,
and he reigned fifty and five years
in *Jerusalem* **Yeru Shalem**:
2 But *did* **worked** that which was evil
in the *sight* **eyes** of *the LORD* **Yah Veh**,
like unto the *abominations* **abhorrence**
of the *heathen* **goyim**,
whom *the LORD* **Yah Veh** had *cast out* **dispossessed**
before **at the face of** the *children* **sons** of *Israel* **Yisra El**.
3 For he **returned and** built *again* the *high places* **bamahs**
which *Hezekiah* **Yechizqi Yah** his father
had *broken* **pulled** *down*,
and he *reared up* **raised sacrifice** altars for Baalim,
and *made groves* **worked asherim**,
and *worshipped* **prostrated**
to all the host of *heaven* **the heavens**,
and served them.
4 Also he built **sacrifice** altars
in the house of *the LORD* **Yah Veh**,
whereof *the LORD* **Yah Veh** had said,
In *Jerusalem* **Yeru Shalem**
shall my name be *for ever* **eternally**.
5 And he built **sacrifice** altars
for all the host of *heaven* **the heavens**
in the two courts of the house of *the LORD* **Yah Veh**.
6 And he caused his *children* **sons** to pass through the fire
in the valley of the son of *Hinnom* **burning**:
also he *observed times* **cloudglazed**,
and *used enchantments* **prognosticated**,
and *used witchcraft* **sorcered**,
and *dealt* **worked** with a *familiar spirit* **necromancer**,
and with *wizards* **knowers**:
he *wrought much* **abounded to work** evil
in the *sight* **eyes** of *the LORD* **Yah Veh**,
to *provoke* **vex** him *to anger*.
7 And he set a *carved image* **sculptile**,
the *idol* **figurine** which he had *made* **worked**,
in the house of *God* **Elohim**,
of which *God* **Elohim** had said to David
and to *Solomon* **Shelomoh** his son,
In this house, and in *Jerusalem* **Yeru Shalem**,
which I have chosen
before all the *tribes* **scions** of *Israel* **Yisra El**,
will **shall** I *put* **set** my name *for ever* **eternally**:
8 Neither *will* **shall** I *any more remove* **turn aside**
the foot of *Israel* **Yisra El** from out of the *land* **soil**
which I have *appointed* **stood** for your fathers;
so that they *will take heed* **shall guard**
to *do* **work** all that I have *commanded* **misvahed** them,
according to the whole *law* **torah**
and the statutes and the *ordinances* **judgments**
by the hand of *Moses* **Mosheh**.
9 So *Manasseh* **Menash Sheh** made *Judah* **Yah Hudah**
and the *inhabitants* **settlers** of *Jerusalem* **Yeru Shalem**
to *err* **stray**,
and to *do worse than* **work evil above** the *heathen* **goyim**,
whom *the LORD* **Yah Veh** had *destroyed* **desolated**
before **at the face of** the *children* **sons** of *Israel* **Yisra El**.
10 And *the LORD spake* **Yah Veh worded**
to *Manasseh* **Menash Sheh**, and to his people:
but they *would not hearken* **hearkened not**.
11 Wherefore *the LORD* **Yah Veh** brought upon them
the *captains* **governors** of the host
of the *king* **sovereign** of *Assyria* **Ashshur**,
which *took Manasseh* **captured Menash Sheh**
among the thorns,
and bound him with *fetters* **copper**,
and *carried* **walked** him to *Babylon* **Babel**.
12 And when he was *in affliction* **tribulated**,
he *besought* **stroked the face**
the LORD **of Yah Veh** his *God* **Elohim**,
and humbled himself *greatly* **mightily**
before the God **at the face of Elohim** of his fathers,
13 And prayed unto him:
and he was intreated of him, and heard his supplication,
and *brought* **returned** him *again* to *Jerusalem* **Yeru Shalem**
into his *kingdom* **sovereigndom**.
Then *Manasseh* **Menash Sheh** knew
that *the LORD* **Yah Veh** he was *God* **Elohim**.
14 Now after this he built a wall without the city of David,
on the west side **duskward** of *Gihon* **Gichon**,
in the *valley* **wadi**,
even to the *entering in* **entrance** at the fish *gate* **portal**,
and *compassed* **surrounded** about Ophel,
and *raised* **heightened** it *up a very great height* **mightily**,
and *put captains* **set governors** of *war* **valour**
in all the *fenced* **cut off** cities of *Judah* **Yah Hudah**.
15 And he *took away* **turned aside**
the strange *gods* **elohim**, and the *idol* **figurine**
out of the house of *the LORD* **Yah Veh**,
and all the **sacrifice** altars that he had built
in the mount of the house of *the LORD* **Yah Veh**,
and in *Jerusalem* **Yeru Shalem**,
and cast them *out of* **without** the city.
16 And he *repaired* **built**
the **sacrifice** altar of *the LORD* **Yah Veh**,
and sacrificed thereon
peace offerings **sacrifices of shelamim**
and *thank offerings* **sacrifices of extended hands**,
and *commanded Judah* **said to Yah Hudah**
to serve *the LORD God* **Yah Veh Elohim** of *Israel* **Yisra El**.
17 Nevertheless the people did sacrifice still
in the *high places* **bamahs**,
yet unto *the LORD* **Yah Veh** their *God* **Elohim** only.
18 Now the rest of the *acts* **words**
of *Manasseh* **Menash Sheh**,
and his prayer unto his *God* **Elohim**,
and the words of the seers that *spake* **worded** to him
in the name
of *the LORD God* **Yah Veh Elohim** of *Israel* **Yisra El**,
behold, they are *written* in the *book* **words**
of the *kings* **sovereigns** of *Israel* **Yisra El**.
19 His prayer also,
and *how God was intreated of him* **his entreaty**,
and all his sins, *and his trespass* **treason**,
and the places wherein he built *high places* **bamahs**,
and *set up groves* **stood asherim**
and *graven images* **sculptiles**,
before he was **at the face of his being** humbled:
behold, they are *written* **inscribed**
among the *sayings* **words** of *the seers* **seers/Hozay**.
20 So *Manasseh* **Menash Sheh**
slept **laid** with his fathers,
and they *buried* **entombed** him in his own house:
and Amon his son reigned in his stead.

AMON REIGNS IN YERU SHALEM

21 Amon was **a son of** two and twenty years *old*
when he began to reign,
and reigned two years in *Jerusalem* **Yeru Shalem**.
22 But he *did* **worked** that which was evil
in the *sight* **eyes** of *the LORD* **Yah Veh**,
as *did Manasseh* **worked Menash Sheh** his father:
for Amon sacrificed unto all the *carved images* **sculptiles**
which *Manasseh* **Menash Sheh** his father
had *made* **worked**, and served them;
23 And humbled not himself
before the LORD **at the face of Yah Veh**,
as *Manasseh* **Menash Sheh** his father
had humbled himself;
but Amon *trespassed more and more* **abounded his guilt**.
24 And his servants conspired against him,
and *slew* **deathified** him in his own house.
25 But the people of the land *slew* **smote**
all them that had conspired against *king* **sovereign** Amon;
and the people of the land
made Josiah **had Yoshi Yah** his son *king* **reign** in his stead.

YOSHI YAH REIGNS IN YERU SHALEM

34 *Josiah* **Yoshi Yah** was **a son of** eight years *old*
when he began to reign,
and he reigned in *Jerusalem* **Yeru Shalem**
one and thirty years.
2 And he *did* **worked** that which was *right* **straight**
in the *sight* **eyes** of *the LORD* **Yah Veh**,
and walked in the ways of David his father,
and *declined* **turned aside**
neither to the right *hand*, nor to the left.
3 For in the eighth year of his reign,
while he was yet *young* **a lad**,
he began to seek after the *God* **Elohim** of David his father:
and in the twelfth year he began to *purge* **purify**
Judah **Yah Hudah** and *Jerusalem* **Yeru Shalem**
from the *high places* **bamahs**, and the *groves* **asherim**,
and the *carved images* **sculptiles**, and the molten *images*.
4 And they *brake* **pulled** down
the **sacrifice** altars of Baalim *in his presence* **from his face**;
and the *images* **sun icons**,
that were *on high* **over** above them, he cut down;
and the *groves* **asherim**, and the *carved images* **sculptiles**,
and the molten *images*, he *brake in pieces* **pulled**,
and *made dust* **pulverized** *of them*,
and *strowed* **sprinkled** *it*
upon the *graves* **face of the tombs** of them
that had sacrificed unto them.
5 And he burnt the bones of the priests
upon their **sacrifice** altars,
and *cleansed* **purified**
Judah **Yah Hudah** and *Jerusalem* **Yeru Shalem**.
6 And *so did he* in the cities of *Manasseh* **Menash Sheh**,
and *Ephraim* **Ephrayim**, and *Simeon* **Shimon**,
even unto Naphtali,
with their *mattocks* **swords** round about.
7 And when he had *broken* **pulled** down
the **sacrifice** altars and the *groves* **asherim**,
and had *beaten* **crushed** the *graven images* **sculptiles**
into powder **and pulverized**,
and cut down all the *idols* **sun icons**
throughout all the land of *Israel* **Yisra El**,
he returned to *Jerusalem* **Yeru Shalem**.
8 Now in the eighteenth year of his reign,
when he had *purged* **purified** the land, and the house,
he sent Shaphan the son of *Azaliah* **Asal Yah**,
and *Maaseiah* **Maase Yah** the governor of the city,
and *Joah* **Yah Ach** the son of *Joahaz* **Yah Achaz**
the *recorder* **remembrancer**,
to *repair* **strengthen**
the house of *the LORD* **Yah Veh** his *God* **Elohim**.
9 And when they came
to *Hilkiah* **Hilqi Yah** the *high* **great** priest,
they *delivered* **gave** the *money* **silver**
that was brought into the house of *God* **Elohim**,
which the *Levites* **Leviym**
that *kept* **guarded** the *doors* **thresholds** had gathered
of the hand
of *Manasseh* **Menash Sheh** and *Ephraim* **Ephrayim**,
and of all the *remnant* **survivors** of *Israel* **Yisra El**,
and of all *Judah* **Yah Hudah** and *Benjamin* **Ben Yamin**;
and they *returned to Jerusalem* **settled in Yeru Shalem**.
10 And they *put* **gave** *it*
in the hand of the *workmen* **workers**
that *had the oversight of* **oversaw**
the house of *the LORD* **Yah Veh**,
and they gave it to the *workmen* **workers**
that wrought in the house of *the LORD* **Yah Veh**,
to repair and *amend* **strengthen** the house:
11 Even to the artificers and builders gave they it,
to *buy* **chattel** hewn stone, and timber for *couplings* **joints**,
and to *floor* **beam** the houses
which the *kings* **sovereigns** of *Judah* **Yah Hudah**
had *destroyed* **ruined**.
12 And the men
did **worked** the work *faithfully* **trustworthily**:
and the overseers of them
were *Jahath* **Yachath** and *Obadiah* **Obad Yah**,
the *Levites* **Leviym**, of the sons of Merari;
and *Zechariah* **Zechar Yah** and Meshullam,
of the sons of the *Kohathites* **Qehathiy**,
to *set it forward* **oversee**;
and *other* of the *Levites* **Leviym**,
all that could *skill* **discern** of instruments of *musick* **song**.
13 Also
they were over the *bearers of burdens* **burdenbearers**,
and were overseers of all that *wrought* **worked** the work
in any manner of service **by service**:
and of the *Levites* **Leviym** there were scribes,
and officers, and porters.

THE SCROLL OF THE TORAH IS FOUND

14 And when they brought out the *money* **silver**
that was brought into the house of *the LORD* **Yah Veh**,
Hilkiah **Hilqi Yah** the priest
found a *book* **scroll** of the *law* **torah** of *the LORD* **Yah Veh**
given by Moses **by the hand of Mosheh**.
15 And *Hilkiah* **Hilqi Yah** answered
and said to Shaphan the scribe,
I have found the *book* **scroll** of the *law* **torah**
in the house of *the LORD* **Yah Veh**.
And *Hilkiah* **Hilqi Yah**
delivered **gave** the *book* **scroll** to Shaphan.
16 And Shaphan
carried the *book* **scroll** to the *king* **sovereign**,
and *brought the king word back again*
returned word to the sovereign, saying,
All that was *committed* **given** to **the hand of** thy servants,
they *do* **work** it.
17 And they have
gathered together **poured out** the *money* **silver**
that was found in the house of *the LORD* **Yah Veh**,
and have *delivered* **given** it into the hand of the overseers,
and to the hand of the *workmen* **workers**.
18 Then Shaphan the scribe told the *king* **sovereign**,
saying,
Hilkiah **Hilqi Yah** the priest hath given me a *book* **scroll**.
And Shaphan *read it* **called it out**
before **at the face of** the *king* **sovereign**.
19 And it *came to pass* **became**,
when the *king* **sovereign**
had heard the words of the *law* **torah**,
that he *rent* **ripped** his clothes.
20 And the *king* **sovereign**
commanded Hilkiah **misvahed Hilqi Yah**,
and *Ahikam* **Achiy Qam** the son of Shaphan,
and Abdon the son of *Micah* **Michah Yah**,
and Shaphan the scribe,
and *Asaiah* **Asah Yah** a servant of the *king's* **sovereign's**,
saying,
21 Go, enquire of *the LORD* **Yah Veh** for me,
and for them that *are left* **survive**
in *Israel* **Yisra El** and in *Judah* **Yah Hudah**,
concerning the words of the *book* **scroll** that is found:
for great is the *wrath* **fury** of *the LORD* **Yah Veh**
that is poured out upon us,
because our fathers
have not *kept* **guarded** the word of *the LORD* **Yah Veh**,
to *do* **work**
after all that is *written* **inscribed** in this *book* **scroll**.
22 And *Hilkiah* **Hilqi Yah**,

and they *that the king had appointed* **of the sovereign,**
went to Huldah the prophetess,
the *wife* **woman** of Shallum the son of *Tikvath* **Tiqvah,**
the son of Hasrah, *keeper* **guard** of the *wardrobe* **clothes;**
(now she *dwelt* **settled** in *Jerusalem* **Yeru Shalem**
in the *college* **second part:)**
and they *spake* **worded that** to her *to that effect.*
23 And she *answered* **said to** them,
Thus saith
the LORD God **Yah Veh Elohim** of *Israel* **Yisra El,**
Tell ye **Say to** the man that sent you to me,
24 Thus saith *the LORD* **Yah Veh,**
Behold, I *will* **shall** bring evil upon this place,
and upon the *inhabitants* **settlers** thereof,
even all the *curses* **oaths**
that are *written* **inscribed** in the *book* **scroll**
which they have *read* **called out**
before **at the face of**
the *king* **sovereign** of *Judah* **Yah Hudah:**
25 Because they have forsaken me,
and have *burned incense* **incensed**
unto other *gods* **elohim,**
that they might *provoke* **vex** me *to anger*
with all the works of their hands;
therefore my *wrath* **fury**
shall be poured out upon this place,
and shall not be quenched.
26 And as for the *king* **sovereign** of *Judah* **Yah Hudah,**
who sent you to enquire of *the LORD* **Yah Veh,**
so **thus** shall ye say unto him,
Thus saith
the LORD God **Yah Veh Elohim** of *Israel* **Yisra El**
concerning the words which thou hast heard;
27 Because thine heart was *tender* **tenderized,**
and thou didst humble thyself
before God **at the face of Elohim,**
when thou heardest his words against this place,
and against the *inhabitants* **settlers** thereof,
and humbledst thyself *before me* **at my face,**
and didst *rend* **rip** thy clothes,
and weep *before* **at my face;**
I have even heard thee also,
saith the LORD **an oracle of Yah Veh.**
28 Behold, I *will* **shall** gather thee to thy fathers,
and thou shalt be — gathered to thy *grave* **tomb**
in *peace* **shalom,**
neither shall thine eyes see all the evil
that I *will* **shall** bring upon this place,
and upon the *inhabitants* **settlers** of the same.
So they
brought the king word again
returned word to the sovereign.
29 Then the *king* **sovereign** sent and gathered *together*
all the elders
of *Judah* **Yah Hudah** and *Jerusalem* **Yeru Shalem.**
30 And the *king went up* **sovereign ascended**
into the house of *the LORD* **Yah Veh,**
and all the *men of Judah* **Yah Hudiy,**
and the *inhabitants* **settlers** of *Jerusalem* **Yeru Shalem,**
and the priests, and the *Levites* **Leviym,** and all the people,
from great *and* **to** small:
and he *read* **called out** in their ears
all the words of the *book* **scroll** of the covenant
that was found in the house of *the LORD* **Yah Veh.**
31 And the *king* **sovereign** stood in his *place* **station,**
and *made* **cut** a covenant
before the LORD **at the face of Yah Veh,**
to walk after *the LORD* **Yah Veh,**
and to *keep* **guard** his *commandments* **misvoth,**
and his *testimonies* **witnesses,** and his statutes,
with all his heart, and with all his soul,
to *perform* **work** the words of the covenant
which are written **inscribed** in this *book* **scroll.**
32 And he caused all that were *present* **found**
in *Jerusalem* **Yeru Shalem** and *Benjamin* **Ben Yamin**
to stand to it.
And the *inhabitants* **settlers** of *Jerusalem* **Yeru Shalem**
did **worked** according to the covenant of *God* **Elohim,**
the *God* **Elohim** of their fathers.
33 And *Josiah took away* **Yoshi Yah turned aside**
all the *abominations* **abhorrences**
out of all the *countries that pertained* **lands**
to the children **of the sons** of *Israel* **Yisra El,**
and made all that were *present* **found** in *Israel* **Yisra El**
to serve,
even — to serve *the LORD* **Yah Veh** their *God* **Elohim.**
And all his days they *departed not* **turned not aside**
from *following the LORD* **after Yah Veh,**
the *God* **Elohim** of their fathers.

YOSHI YAH WORKS THE PASACH

35 Moreover
Josiah kept **Yoshi Yah worked** a *passover* **pasach**
unto *the LORD* **Yah Veh** in *Jerusalem* **Yeru Shalem:**
and they *killed* **slaughtered** the *passover* **pasach**
on the fourteenth *day* of the first month.
2 And he *set* **stood** the priests in their *charges* **guards,**
and *encouraged* **strengthened** them to the service
of the house of *the LORD* **Yah Veh,**
3 And said unto the *Levites* **Leviym**
that taught all *Israel* **Yisra El,**
which were holy unto *the LORD* **Yah Veh,**
Put **Give** the holy ark in the house
which *Solomon* **Shelomoh** the son of David
king **sovereign** of *Israel* **Yisra El** did build;
it shall not be a burden upon your shoulders:
serve now *the LORD* **Yah Veh** your *God* **Elohim,**
and his people *Israel* **Yisra El,**
4 And prepare *yourselves* by the houses of your fathers,
after your *courses* **allotments,**
according to the *writing* **inscribing**
of David *king* **sovereign** of *Israel* **Yisra El,**
and according to the *writing* **inscribing**
of *Solomon* **Shelomoh** his son.
5 And stand in the *holy place* **holies**
according to the divisions
of the *families* **house** of the fathers of your brethren
the **sons of the** people,
and *after the division* **the allotment**
of the *families* **house of the fathers** of the *Levites* **Leviym.**
6 So *kill* **slaughter** the *passover* **pasach,**
and *sanctify* **hallow** yourselves, and prepare your brethren,
that they may *do* **work**
according to the word of *the LORD* **Yah Veh**
by the hand of *Moses* **Mosheh.**
7 And *Josiah* **Yoshi Yah**
gave **lifted** to the **sons of the** people,
of the flock, lambs and *kids* **sons of doe goats,**
all for the *passover* **pasach** *offerings,*
for all that were present,
to the number of thirty thousand,
and three thousand *bullocks* **oxen:**
these were of the *king's substance* **sovereign's acquisition.**
8 And his *princes gave willingly* **governors volunteered**
unto the people, to the priests, and to the *Levites* **Leviym:**
Hilkiah **Hilqi Yah**
and *Zechariah* **Zechar Yah** and *Jehiel* **Yechi El,**
rulers **eminent** of the house of *God* **Elohim,**
gave **lifted up** unto the priests
for the *passover* **pasach** *offerings*
two thousand and six hundred *small cattle*
and three hundred oxen.
9 *Cononiah* **Konan Yah** also, and *Shemaiah* **Shema Yah**
and *Nethaneel* **Nethan El,** his brethren,
and *Hashabiah* **Hashab Yah** and *Jeiel* **Yei El**
and *Jozabad* **Yah Zabad,**
chief **governor** of the *Levites* **Leviym,**
gave **lifted up** unto the *Levites* **Leviym**
for *passover* **pasach** *offerings*
five thousand *small cattle,* and five hundred oxen.
10 So the service was prepared,
and the priests stood in their *place* **station,**
and the *Levites* **Leviym** in their *courses* **allotments,**
according to the *king's commandment* **sovereign's misvah.**
11 And they *killed* **slaughtered** the *passover* **pasach,**
and the priests sprinkled *the blood* from their hands,
and the *Levites flayed* **Leviym stripped** them.
12 And they *removed* **turned aside**
the *burnt offerings* **holocausts,**
that they might give according to the divisions
of the *families* **house of the fathers**

of the **sons of the** people,
to *offer* **oblate** unto *the LORD* **Yah Veh**,
as it is *written* **inscribed** in the *book* **scroll** of *Moses* **Mosheh**.
And so did they with the oxen.
13 And they *roasted* **stewed** the *passover* **pasach** with fire
according to the *ordinance* **judgment**:
but the *other holy offerings* **holies**
sod **stewed** they in *pots* **caldrons**,
and in *caldrons* **boilers**, and in *pans* **skillets**,
and *divided* **ran** them *speedily*
among all the **sons of the** people.
14 And afterward they *made ready* **prepared**
for themselves, and for the priests:
because the priests the sons of *Aaron* **Aharon**
were busied in offering of burnt offerings
holocausted holocausts and the fat until night;
therefore the *Levites* **Leviym** prepared for themselves,
and for the priests the sons of *Aaron* **Aharon**.
15 And the singers the sons of Asaph
were in their *place* **function**,
according to the *commandment* **misvah**
of David, and Asaph, and Heman,
and *Jeduthun* **Yeduthun** the *king's* **sovereign's** seer;
and the porters *waited at every gate* **at portal by portal**;
they might not *depart* **turn aside** from their service;
for their brethren the *Levites* **Leviym** prepared for them.
16 So all the service of *the LORD* **Yah Veh**
was prepared the same day,
to *keep* **work** the *passover* **pasach**,
and to *offer burnt offerings* **holocaust holocausts**
upon the **sacrifice** altar of *the LORD* **Yah Veh**,
according to the *commandment* **misvah**
of *king Josiah* **sovereign Yoshi Yah**.
17 And the *children* **sons** of *Israel* **Yisra El**
that were *present* **found**
kept **worked** the *passover* **pasach** at that time,
and the *feast* **celebration** of *unleavened bread* **matsah**
seven days.
18 And there was no *passover like to* **pasach such as** that
kept **worked** in *Israel* **Yisra El**
from the days of *Samuel* **Shemu El** the prophet;
neither did all the *kings* **sovereigns** of *Israel* **Yisra El**
keep **work** such a *passover* **pasach**
as *Josiah kept* **Yoshi Yah worked**,
and the priests, and the *Levites* **Leviym**,
and all *Judah* **Yah Hudah** and *Israel* **Yisra El**
that were present,
and the *inhabitants* **settlers** of *Jerusalem* **Yeru Shalem**.
19 In the eighteenth year
of the *reign* **sovereigndom** of *Josiah* **Yoshi Yah**
was this *passover kept* **pasach worked**.

THE DEATH OF YOSHI YAH

20 After all this,
when *Josiah* **Yoshi Yah** had prepared the *temple* **house**,
Necho *king* **sovereign** of *Egypt* **Misrayim**
came up **ascended** to fight
against *Charchemish* **Karchemish** by Euphrates:
and *Josiah* **Yoshi Yah** went out *against* **to meet** him.
21 But he sent *ambassadors* **angels** to him, saying,
What have I to do with thee,
thou *king* **sovereign** of *Judah* **Yah Hudah**?
I come — not against thee this day,
but against the house wherewith I have war:
for *God commanded* **Elohim said to** me to make haste:
forbear **cease** thee from *meddling with God* **Elohim**,
who is with me,
that he *destroy* **ruin** thee not.
22 Nevertheless
Josiah would not turn **Yoshi Yah turned not**
his face from him,
but disguised *himself*, that he might fight with him,
and hearkened not unto the words of Necho
from the mouth of *God* **Elohim**,
and came to fight in the valley of Megiddo.
23 And the *archers* **shooters**
shot at *king Josiah* **sovereign Yoshi Yah**;
and the *king* **sovereign** said to his servants,
Have me away **Pass me over**;
for I am *sore wounded* **mighty sick**.
24 His servants therefore
took **passed** him out of that chariot,
and *put* **rode** him in the second chariot that he had;
and they *brought* **walked** him to *Jerusalem* **Yeru Shalem**,
and he died,
and was *buried* **entombed**
in *one of the sepulchres* **tombs** of his fathers.
And all *Judah* **Yah Hudah** and *Jerusalem* **Yeru Shalem**
mourned for *Josiah* **Yoshi Yah**.
25 And *Jeremiah* **Yirme Yah** lamented for *Josiah* **Yoshi Yah**:
and all the *singing men* **songsters**
and the *singing women* **songstresses**
spake **say** of *Josiah* **Yoshi Yah** in their lamentations
to this day,
and *made* **gave** them *an ordinance* **a statute**
in *Israel* **Yisra El**: and, behold,
they are *written* **inscribed** in the lamentations.
26 Now the rest of the *acts* **words** of *Josiah* **Yoshi Yah**,
and his *goodness* **mercy**,
according to that which was *written* **inscribed**
in the *law* **torah** of *the LORD* **Yah Veh**,
27 And his *deeds* **words**, first and last, behold,
they are *written* **inscribed**
in the *book* **scroll** of the *kings* **sovereigns**
of *Israel* **Yisra El** and *Judah* **Yah Hudah**.

YAH ACHAZ REIGNS IN YERU SHALEM

36 Then the people of the land
took *Jehoahaz* **Yah Achaz** the son of *Josiah* **Yoshi Yah**,
and *made king* **had him reign**
in his father's stead in *Jerusalem* **Yeru Shalem**.
2 *Jehoahaz* **Yah Achaz**
was **a son of** twenty and three years *old*
when he began to reign,
and he reigned three months in *Jerusalem* **Yeru Shalem**.
3 And the *king* **sovereign** of *Egypt* **Misrayim**
put him down **turned him aside** at *Jerusalem* **Yeru Shalem**,
and *condemned* **penalized** the land
in an hundred *talents* **rounds** of silver
and a *talent* **round** of gold.

YAH YAQIM REIGNS IN YERU SHALEM

4 And the *king* **sovereign** of *Egypt* **Misrayim**
made Eliakim **had El Yaqim** his brother *king* **reign**
over *Judah* **Yah Hudah** and *Jerusalem* **Yeru Shalem**,
and turned his name to *Jehoiakim* **Yah Yaqim**.
And Necho took *Jehoahaz* **Yah Achaz** his brother,
and carried him to *Egypt* **Misrayim**.
5 *Jehoiakim* **Yah Yaqim**
was **a son of** twenty and five years *old*
when he began to reign,
and he reigned eleven years in *Jerusalem* **Yeru Shalem**:
and he *did* **worked** that which was evil
in the *sight* **eyes** of *the LORD* **Yah Veh** his *God* **Elohim**.
6 Against him *came up* **ascended**
Nebuchadnezzar **Nebukadnets Tsar,**
king **sovereign** of *Babylon* **Babel**,
and bound him in *fetters* **copper**,
to *carry him* **go** to *Babylon* **Babel**.
7 *Nebuchadnezzar* **Nebukadnets Tsar**
also carried of the *vessels* **instruments**
of the house of *the LORD* **Yah Veh** to *Babylon* **Babel**,
and *put* **gave** them in his *temple* **manse** at *Babylon* **Babel**.
8 Now the rest of the *acts* **words** of *Jehoiakim* **Yah Yaqim**,
and his *abominations* **abhorrences** which he *did* **worked**,
and that which was found in him, behold,
they are *written* **inscribed**
in the *book* **scroll** of the *kings* **sovereigns**
of *Israel* **Yisra El** and *Judah* **Yah Hudah**:
and *Jehoiachin* **Yah Yachin** his son reigned in his stead.
9 *Jehoiachin* **Yah Yachin** was **a son of** eight years *old*
when he began to reign,
and he reigned three months and ten days
in *Jerusalem* **Yeru Shalem**:
and he *did* **worked** that which was evil
in the *sight* **eyes** of *the LORD* **Yah Veh**.
10 And *when the year was expired* **at the turn of the year**,
king Nebuchadnezzar **sovereign Nebukadnets Tsar** sent,
and brought him to *Babylon* **Babel**,
with the *goodly vessels* **instruments of desire**
of the house of *the LORD* **Yah Veh,**
and *made Zedekiah* **had Sidqi Yah** his brother *king* **reign**
over *Judah* **Yah Hudah** and *Jerusalem* **Yeru Shalem**.

SIDQI YAH REIGNS IN YERU SHALEM
11 *Zedekiah* **Sidqi Yah**
was **a son of** one and twenty years *old*
when he began to reign,
and reigned eleven years in *Jerusalem* **Yeru Shalem**.
12 And he *did* **worked** that which was evil
in the *sight* **eyes** of *the LORD* **Yah Veh** his *God* **Elohim**,
and humbled not himself
before Jeremiah **at the face of Yirme Yah** the prophet
speaking from the mouth of *the LORD* **Yah Veh**.
13 And he also rebelled against
king Nebuchadnezzar **sovereign Nebukadnets Tsar**,
who had made him *swear* **oath** by *God* **Elohim**:
but he *stiffened* **hardened** his neck,
and *hardened* **strengthened** his heart from turning
unto *the LORD God* **Yah Veh Elohim** of *Israel* **Yisra El**.
14 Moreover all the *chief* **governor** of the priests,
and the people,
transgressed very much
in treasoning, abounded to treason
after all the *abominations* **abhorrences**
of the *heathen* **goyim**;
and *polluted* **fouled** the house of *the LORD* **Yah Veh**
which he had hallowed in *Jerusalem* **Yeru Shalem**.
THE FURY OF YAH VEH AGAINST HIS PEOPLE
15 And *the LORD God* **Yah Veh Elohim** of their fathers
sent to them by **the hand of** his *messengers* **angels**,
rising up betimes **starting early**, and sending;
because he had compassion on his people,
and on his *dwelling place* **habitation**:
16 But they *mocked* **derided**
the *messengers* **angels** of *God* **Elohim**,
and despised his words,
and *misused* **deceived** his prophets,
until the *wrath* **fury** of *the LORD* **Yah Veh**
arose **ascended** against his people,
till there was no *remedy* **healing**.
17 Therefore he *brought* **ascended** upon them
the *king* **sovereign** of the *Chaldees* **Kasdiy**,
who *slew* **slaughtered** their *young men* **youths**
with the sword
in the house of their *sanctuary* **holies**,
and had no compassion
upon *young man* **youth** or *maiden* **virgin**,
old man, or *him that stooped for age* **aged**:
he gave them all into his hand.
18 And all the *vessels* **instruments**
of the house of *God* **Elohim**, great and small,
and the treasures of the house of *the LORD* **Yah Veh**,
and the treasures of the *king* **sovereign**,
and of his *princes* **governors**;
all these he brought to *Babylon* **Babel**.
19 And they burnt the house of *God* **Elohim**,
and *brake* **pulled** down
the wall of *Jerusalem* **Yeru Shalem**,
and burnt all the *palaces* **citadels** thereof with fire,
and *destroyed* **ruined**
all the *goodly vessels* **instruments of desire** thereof.
20 And *them that had escaped* **the survivors**
from the sword
carried he away **exiled he** to *Babylon* **Babel**;
where they were servants to him and his sons
until the reign of the *kingdom* **sovereigndom** of Persia:
21 To fulfil the word of *the LORD* **Yah Veh**
by the mouth of *Jeremiah* **Yirme Yah**,
until the land
had *enjoyed* **pleased** her *sabbaths* **shabbaths**:
for as long as **all the days** she *lay desolate* **desolated**
she *kept sabbath* **shabbathized**,
to fulfil *threescore and ten* **seventy** years.
KORESH IS MUSTERED TO BUILD THE HOUSE OF YAH VEH
22 Now in the first year of *Cyrus* **Koresh**,
king **sovereign** of Persia,
that the word of *the LORD* **Yah Veh**
spoken by the mouth of *Jeremiah* **Yirme Yah**
might be *accomplished* **finished**,
the LORD **Yah Veh**
stirred up **wakened** the spirit of *Cyrus* **Koresh**,
king **sovereign** of Persia,
that he *made a proclamation* **passed a voice**
throughout all his *kingdom* **sovereigndom**,
and *put it also in writing* **also inscribed**, saying,
23 Thus saith *Cyrus king* **Koresh sovereign** of Persia,
All the *kingdoms* **sovereigndoms** of the earth hath
the LORD God **Yah Veh Elohim** of *heaven* **the heavens**
given me;
and he hath *charged* **mustered** me
to build him an house in *Jerusalem* **Yeru Shalem**,
which is in *Judah* **Yah Hudah**.
Who is there among you of all his people?
The LORD **Yah Veh** his *God* **Elohim** be with him,
and let him *go up* **ascend**.

KEY TO INTERPRETING THE EXEGESES:
King James text is in regular type;
Text under exegeses is in oblique type;
Text of exegeses is in bold type.

KORESH IS MUSTERED TO BUILD THE HOUSE OF YAH VEH

1 Now in the first year of *Cyrus* **Koresh**
king **sovereign** of Persia,
that the word of *the LORD* **Yah Veh**
by the mouth of *Jeremiah* **Yirme Yah**
might be *fulfilled* **finished,**
the LORD stirred up **Yah Veh wakened** the spirit
of *Cyrus king* **Koresh sovereign** of Persia,
that he *made* **passed** a *proclamation* **voice**
throughout all his *kingdom* **sovereigndom,**
and *put it* also *in writing* **inscribing**, saying,
2 Thus saith *Cyrus king* **Koresh sovereign** of Persia,
The LORD God **Yah Veh Elohim** of *heaven* **the heavens**
hath given me
all the *kingdoms* **sovereigndoms** of the earth;
and he hath *charged* **mustered** me
to build him an house at *Jerusalem* **Yeru Shalem,**
which is in *Judah* **Yah Hudah.**
3 Who is there among you of all his people?
his *God* **Elohim** be with him,
and let him *go up* **ascend** to *Jerusalem* **Yeru Shalem,**
which is in *Judah* **Yah Hudah,**
and build the house of *the LORD God* **Yah Veh Elohim**
of *Israel* **Yisra El,**
(he is *the God* **Elohim**,)
which is in *Jerusalem* **Yeru Shalem.**
4 And whosoever *remaineth* **surviveth** in any place
where he sojourneth,
let the men of his place
help **lift** him with silver, and with gold,
and with *goods* **acquisitions**, and with *beasts* **animals**,
beside the *freewill offering* **voluntary**
for the house of *God* **Elohim**
that is in *Jerusalem* **Yeru Shalem.**

THE RESTORATION OF THE INSTRUMENTS

5 Then rose up
the *chief* **head** of the fathers of *Judah* **Yah Hudah**
and *Benjamin* **Ben Yamin,**
and the priests, and the *Levites* **Leviym,**
with all them
whose spirit *God* **Elohim** had *raised* **wakened,**
to *go up* **ascend** to build the house of *the LORD* **Yah Veh**
which is in *Jerusalem* **Yeru Shalem.**
6 And all they that were **round** about them
strengthened their hands
with *vessels* **instruments** of silver, with gold,
with *goods* **acquisitions**, and with *beasts* **animals**,
and with *precious things* **preciousnesses,**
beside all that was *willingly offered* **volunteered.**
7 Also *Cyrus* **Koresh** the *king* **sovereign**
brought forth the *vessels* **instruments**
of the house of *the LORD* **Yah Veh,**
which *Nebuchadnezzar* **Nebukadnets Tsar**
had brought forth out of *Jerusalem* **Yeru Shalem,**
and had *put* **given** them in the house of his *gods* **elohim;**
8 Even those did *Cyrus king* **Koresh sovereign** of Persia
bring forth by the hand of Mithredath the treasurer,
and *numbered* **scribed** them
unto *Sheshbazzar* **Sheshbats Tsar,**
the *prince* **hierarch** of *Judah* **Yah Hudah.**
9 And this is the number of them:
thirty *chargers* **basins** of gold,
a thousand *chargers* **basins** of silver,
nine and twenty knives,
10 Thirty *basons* **tankards** of gold,
silver *basons* **tankards** of a second *sort*
four hundred and ten,
and other *vessels* **instruments** a thousand.
11 All the *vessels* **instruments** of gold and of silver
were five thousand and four hundred.
All these did *Sheshbazzar* **Sheshbats Tsar**
bring up **ascend** with them of the *captivity* **exile**
that were *brought up* **ascended** from *Babylon* **Babel**
unto *Jerusalem* **Yeru Shalem.**

THE RESTORATION OF THE PEOPLE

2 Now these are
the *children* **sons** of the *province* **jurisdiction**
that *went up* **ascended** out of the captivity,
of those which had been *carried away* **exiled,**
whom *Nebuchadnezzar* **Nebukadnets Tsar,**
the *king* **sovereign** of *Babylon* **Babel**
had *carried away* **exiled** unto *Babylon* **Babel,**
and *came again* **returned**
unto *Jerusalem* **Yeru Shalem** and *Judah* **Yah Hudah,**
every *one* **man** unto his city;
2 Which came with *Zerubbabel* **Zerub Babel**:
Jeshua **Yah Shua**, *Nehemiah* **Nechem Yah,**
Seraiah **Sera Yah**, *Reelaiah* **Reela Yah,**
Mordecai **Mordechay**, Bilshan, Mizpar,
Bigvai **Bigvay**, *Rehum* **Rechum**, Baanah.
The number of the men of the people of *Israel* **Yisra El**:
3 The *children* **sons** of Parosh,
two thousand an hundred seventy and two.
4 The *children* **sons** of *Shephatiah* **Shaphat Yah,**
three hundred seventy and two.
5 The *children* **sons** of *Arah* **Arach,**
seven hundred seventy and five.
6 The *children* **sons** of *Pahathmoab* **Pachath Moab,**
of the *children* **sons** of *Jeshua* **Yah Shua** and *Joab* **Yah Ab,**
two thousand eight hundred and twelve.
7 The *children* **sons** of Elam,
a thousand two hundred fifty and four.
8 The *children* **sons** of Zattu,
nine hundred forty and five.
9 The *children* **sons** of *Zaccai* **Zakkay,**
seven hundred and *threescore* **sixty.**
10 The *children* **sons** of Bani,
six hundred forty and two.
11 The *children* **sons** of *Bebai* **Bebay,**
six hundred twenty and three.
12 The *children* **sons** of Azgad,
a thousand two hundred twenty and two.
13 The *children* **sons** of *Adonikam* **Adoni Qam,**
six hundred sixty and six.
14 The *children* **sons** of *Bigvai* **Bigvay,**
two thousand fifty and six.
15 The *children* **sons** of Adin,
four hundred fifty and four.
16 The *children* **sons** of Ater of *Hezekiah* **Yechizqi Yah,**
ninety and eight.
17 The *children* **sons** of *Bezai* **Besay,**
three hundred twenty and three.
18 The *children* **sons** of *Jorah* **Yorah,**
an hundred and twelve.
19 The *children* **sons** of Hashum,
two hundred twenty and three.
20 The *children* **sons** of Gibbar,
ninety and five.
21 The *children* **sons** of *Bethlehem* **Beth Lechem,**
an hundred twenty and three.
22 The men of Netophah,
fifty and six.
23 The men of Anathoth,
an hundred twenty and eight.
24 The *children* **sons** of Azmaveth,
forty and two.
25 The *children* **sons** of Kirjatharim,
Chephirah **Kephirah**, and Beeroth,
seven hundred and forty and three.
26 The *children* **sons** of Ramah and *Gaba* **Geba,**
six hundred twenty and one.
27 The men of Michmas,
an hundred twenty and two.
28 The men of *Bethel* **Beth El** and *Ai* **Ay,**
two hundred twenty and three.
29 The *children* **sons** of Nebo,
fifty and two.
30 The *children* **sons** of Magbish,
an hundred fifty and six.
31 The *children* **sons** of the other Elam,
a thousand two hundred fifty and four.
32 The *children* **sons** of Harim,
three hundred and twenty.

33 The *children* **sons** of Lod, Hadid, and Ono,
seven hundred twenty and five.
34 The *children* **sons** of *Jericho* **Yericho**,
three hundred forty and five.
35 The *children* **sons** of Senaah,
three thousand and six hundred and thirty.
36 The priests:
the *children* **sons** of *Jedaiah* **Yeda Yah**,
of *the house of Jeshua* **Beth Yah Shua**,
nine hundred seventy and three.
37 The *children* **sons** of Immer,
a thousand fifty and two.
38 The *children* **sons** of *Pashur* **Pashchur**,
a thousand two hundred forty and seven.
39 The *children* **sons** of Harim,
a thousand and seventeen.
40 The *Levites* **Leviym**:
the *children* **sons** of *Jeshua* **Yah Shua**
and *Kadmiel* **Qadmi El**,
of the *children* **sons** of *Hodaviah* **Hodav Yah**,
seventy and four.
41 The singers:
the *children* **sons** of Asaph,
an hundred twenty and eight.
42 The *children* **sons** of the porters:
the *children* **sons** of Shallum, the *children* **sons** of Ater,
the *children* **sons** of Talmon,
the *children* **sons** of *Akkub* **Aqqub**,
the *children* **sons** of Hatita,
the *children* **sons** of *Shobai* **Shobay**,
in all an hundred thirty and nine.
43 The *Nethinims* **Dedicates**:
the *children* **sons** of *Ziha* **Sicha**,
the *children* **sons** of *Hasupha* **Hashupha**,
the *children* **sons** of Tabbaoth,
44 The *children* **sons** of *Keros* **Qeros**,
the *children* **sons** of Siaha, the *children* **sons** of Padon,
45 The *children* **sons** of Lebanah,
the *children* **sons** of Hagabah,
the *children* **sons** of *Akkub* **Aqqub**,
46 The *children* **sons** of Hagab,
the *children* **sons** of *Shalmai* **Shalmay**,
the *children* **sons** of Hanan,
47 The *children* **sons** of Giddel,
the *children* **sons** of *Gahar* **Gachar**,
the *children* **sons** of *Reaiah* **Rea Yah**,
48 The *children* **sons** of *Rezin* **Resin**,
the *children* **sons** of Nekoda,
the *children* **sons** of Gazzam,
49 The *children* **sons** of Uzza,
the *children* **sons** of *Paseah* **Paseach**,
the *children* **sons** of *Besai* **Besay**,
50 The *children* **sons** of Asnah,
the *children* **sons** of *Mehunim* **Maoniym**,
the *children* **sons** of *Nephusim* **Nephisim**,
51 The *children* **sons** of *Bakbuk* **Baqbuq**,
the *children* **sons** of *Hakupha* **Haqupha**,
the *children* **sons** of *Harhur* **Harchur**,
52 The *children* **sons** of *Bazluth* **Basluth**,
the *children* **sons** of *Mehida* **Mechida**,
the *children* **sons** of Harsha,
53 The *children* **sons** of *Barkos* **Barqos**,
the *children* **sons** of Sisera,
the *children* **sons** of *Thamah* **Temach**,
54 The *children* **sons** of *Neziah* **Nesiach**,
the *children* **sons** of Hatipha.
55 The *children* **sons** of *Solomon's* **Sholomoh's** servants:
the *children* **sons** of *Sotai* **Sotay**,
the *children* **sons** of Sophereth,
the *children* **sons** of Peruda,
56 The *children* **sons** of *Jaalah* **Yaalah**,
the *children* **sons** of *Darkon* **Darqon**,
the *children* **sons** of Giddel,
57 The *children* **sons** of *Shephatiah* **Shaphat Yah**,
the *children* **sons** of Hattil,
the *children* **sons** of
Pochereth of *Zebaim* **Sebayim**,
the *children* **sons** of Ami.
58 All the *Nethinims* **Dedicates**,
and the *children* **sons** of *Solomon's* **Sholomoh's** servants,
were three hundred ninety and two.
59 And these were they which *went up* **ascended**
from *Telmelah* **Tel Melach**, *Telharsa* **Tel Harsha**,
Cherub, Addan, and Immer:
but they could not *shew* **tell** their father's house,
and their seed,
whether they were of *Israel* **Yisra El**:
60 The *children* **sons** of *Delaiah* **Dela Yah**,
the *children* **sons** of *Tobiah* **Tobi Yah**,
the *children* **sons** of Nekoda,
six hundred fifty and two.
61 And of the *children* **sons** of the priests:
the *children* **sons** of *Habaiah* **Haba Yah**,
the *children* **sons** of *Koz* **Qos**,
the *children* **sons** of *Barzillai* **Barzillay**;
which took a *wife* **woman** of the daughters
of *Barzillai* **Barzillay** the *Gileadite* **Giladiy**,
and was called after their name:
62 These sought their *register* **inscribings** among those
that were *reckoned by genealogy* **genealogized**,
but they were not found:
therefore were they,
as *polluted, put* **profaned** from the priesthood.
63 And the *Tirshatha* **governor** said unto them,
that they should not eat
of the *most holy things* **Holy of Holies**,
till there stood up a priest with Urim and with Thummim.
64 The whole congregation *together* **as one**
was *forty* **four myriads**
and two thousand three hundred *and threescore* **sixty**,
65 Beside their servants and their maids,
of *whom* **these** there were
seven thousand three hundred thirty and seven:
and there were among them two hundred
singing men **songsters** and *singing women* **songstresses**.
66 Their horses were seven hundred thirty and six;
their mules, two hundred forty and five;
67 Their camels, four hundred thirty and five;
their asses **he burros**,
six thousand seven hundred and twenty.
68 And *some* of the *chief* **head** of the fathers,
when they came to the house of *the LORD* **Yah Veh**
which is at *Jerusalem* **Yeru Shalem**,
offered freely **volunteered** for the house of *God* **Elohim**
to *set it up in his place* **establish it on its base**.
69 They gave *after their ability* **of their substance**
unto the treasure of the work
threescore **six myriads**
and one thousand *drams* **drachmim** of gold,
and five thousand *pound* **maneh** of silver,
and one hundred priests' *garments* **coats**.
70 So the priests, and the *Levites* **Leviym**,
and *some* of the people, and the singers,
and the porters, and the *Nethinims* **Dedicates**,
dwelt **settled** in their cities,
and all *Israel* **Yisra El** in their cities.

THE RESTORATION OF THE ALTAR

3 And when the seventh month *was come* **had touched**,
and the *children* **sons** of *Israel* **Yisra El** were in the cities,
the people gathered themselves together as one man
to *Jerusalem* **Yeru Shalem**.
2 Then *stood up Jeshua* **arose Yah Shua**
the son of *Jozadak* **Yah Sadaq**,
and his brethren the priests,
and *Zerubbabel* **Zerub Babel**
the son of *Shealtiel* **Shealti El**,
and his brethren,
and builded the **sacrifice** altar
of *the God* **Elohim** of *Israel* **Yisra El**,
to *offer burnt offerings* **holocaust holocausts** thereon,
as it is *written* **inscribed**
in the *law* **torah** of *Moses* **Mosheh**
the man of *God* **Elohim**.
3 And they *set* **established** the **sacrifice** altar
upon his bases;
for *fear* **terror** was upon them
because of the people of those *countries* **lands**:
and they *offered burnt offerings* **holocausted holocausts**
thereon unto *the LORD* **Yah Veh**,
even *burnt offerings* **holocausts for** morning and evening.

THE RESTORATION OF THE WORSHIP
4 They *kept* **worked** also
the *feast* **celebration** of *tabernacles* **sukkoth/brush arbors**,
as it is *written* **inscribed**,
and *offered the daily burnt offerings*
the day by day holocausts by number,
according to the *custom* **judgment**,
as the *duty* **word** of every day required;

THE RESTORATION OF THE HALLOWED FESTIVALS OF YAH VEH
5 And afterward
offered the continual *burnt offering* **holocaust**,
both of the new moons,
and of all the *set feasts* **festivals** of *the LORD* **Yah Veh**
that were *consecrated* **hallowed**,
and of every one that *willingly offered* **volunteered**
a *freewill offering* **voluntary** unto *the LORD* **Yah Veh**.
6 From the first day of the seventh month
began they to *offer burnt offerings* **holocaust holocausts**
unto *the LORD* **Yah Veh**.
But the foundation
of the *temple* **manse** of *the LORD* **Yah Veh**
was not yet laid.
7 They gave *money* **silver** also unto the *masons* **hewers**,
and to the *carpenters* **artificers**;
and meat **food**, and drink, and oil,
unto *them of Zidon* **the Sidoniy**,
and to *them of Tyre* **the Soriy**,
to bring cedar trees from Lebanon
to the sea of *Joppa* **Yapho**,
according to the *grant* **permit** that they had
of *Cyrus king* **Koresh sovereign** of Persia.

THE FOUNDATION OF THE HOUSE OF YAH VEH LAID
8 Now in the second year of their coming
unto the house of *God* **Elohim** at *Jerusalem* **Yeru Shalem**,
in the second month,
began *Zerubbabel* **Zerub Babel**
the son of *Shealtiel* **Shealti El**,
and *Jeshua* **Yah Shua** the son of *Jozadak* **Yah Sadaq**,
and the *remnant* **survivors** of their brethren
the priests and the *Levites* **Leviym**,
and all they that were come out of the captivity
unto *Jerusalem* **Yeru Shalem**;
and *appointed* **stood** the *Levites* **Leviym**,
from **sons of** twenty years *old* and upward,
to *set forward* **oversee** the work
of the house of *the LORD* **Yah Veh**.
9 Then stood *Jeshua* **Yah Shua**
with his sons and his brethren,
Kadmiel **Qadmi El** and his sons,
the sons of *Judah* **Yah Hudah**, *together* **as one**,
to *set forward* **oversee** the *workmen* **doers of the work**
in the house of *God* **Elohim**:
the sons of Henadad,
with their sons and their brethren the *Levites* **Leviym**.
10 And when the builders laid the foundation
of the *temple* **manse** of *the LORD* **Yah Veh**,
they *set* **stood** the priests
in their apparel **enrobed** with trumpets,
and the *Levites* **Leviym** the sons of Asaph with cymbals,
to *praise the LORD* **halal Yah Veh**,
after the *ordinance* **hand**
of David *king* **sovereign** of *Israel* **Yisra El**.
11 And they *sang* **answered** together by course
in *praising* **halaling**
and *giving thanks* **extending hands**
unto *the LORD* **Yah Veh**;
because he is good,
for his mercy *endureth for ever* **is eternal**
toward *Israel* **Yisra El**.
And all the people shouted with a great *shout* **shouting**,
when they *praised the LORD* **halaled Yah Veh**,
because the foundation
of the house of *the LORD* **Yah Veh** was laid.
12 But many of the priests and *Levites* **Leviym**
and *chief* **head** of the fathers,
who were ancient men **elders**,
that had seen the first house,
when the foundation of this house
was laid before their eyes,
wept with a *loud* **great** voice;
and many shouted
aloud for joy **and cheered with lifted voice**:
13 So that the people could not *discern* **recognize**
the *noise* **voice** of the shout of *joy* **cheering**
from the *noise* **voice** of the weeping of the people:
for the people shouted with a *loud shout* **great shouting**,
and the *noise* **voice** was heard afar off.

YAH HUDAH AND BEN YAMIN TRIBULATE AGAINST THE MANSE OF YAH VEH
4 Now when the *adversaries* **tribulators**
of *Judah* **Yah Hudah** and *Benjamin* **Ben Yamin**
heard that the *children* **sons** of the *captivity* **exile**
builded the *temple* **manse**
unto *the LORD God* **Yah Veh Elohim** of *Israel* **Yisra El**;
2 Then they came **near** to *Zerubbabel* **Zerub Babel**,
and to the *chief* **head** of the fathers,
and said unto them,
Let us build with you:
for we seek your *God* **Elohim**, as ye *do*;
and we *do* sacrifice unto him
since the days of *Esarhaddon* **Esar Chaddon**
king **sovereign** of *Assur* **Ashshur**,
which *brought* **ascended** us *up* hither.
3 But *Zerubbabel* **Zerub Babel**, and *Jeshua* **Yah Shua**,
and the *rest* **survivors**
of the *chief* **head** of the fathers of *Israel* **Yisra El**,
said unto them, ye have *nothing* **naught** to do with us
to build an house unto our *God* **Elohim**;
but we ourselves together
will **shall** build
unto *the LORD God* **Yah Veh Elohim** of *Israel* **Yisra El**,
as *king Cyrus* **sovereign Koresh**
the *king* **sovereign** of Persia
hath *commanded* **misvahed** us.
4 Then the people of the land
weakened **slackened** the hands
of the people of *Judah* **Yah Hudah**,
and *troubled* **terrified** them in building,
5 And hired counsellors against them,
to *frustrate* **break down** their *purpose* **counsel**,
all the days of *Cyrus* **Koresh** *king* **sovereign** of Persia,
even until the *reign* **sovereigndom** of *Darius* **Daryavesh**,
king **sovereign** of Persia.

ACHASH ROSH TRIBULATES AGAINST THE HOUSE OF YAH VEH
6 And in the *reign* **sovereigndom**
of *Ahasuerus* **Achash Rosh**,
in the beginning of his *reign* **sovereigndom**,
wrote **inscribed** they unto him an *accusation* **opposition**
against the *inhabitants* **settlers**
of *Judah* **Yah Hudah** and *Jerusalem* **Yeru Shalem**.
7 And in the days of *Artaxerxes* **Artach Shashta**
wrote **inscribed** Bishlam, Mithredath, *Tabeel* **Tabe El**,
and the *rest* **survivors** of their *companions* **colleagues**,
unto *Artaxerxes king* **Artach Shashta sovereign** of Persia;
and the *writing* **inscribing** of the *letter* **epistle**
was *written* **inscribed** in *the Syrian tongue* **Aramaic**,
and *interpreted* **translated** in *the Syrian tongue* **Aramaic**.
8 *Rehum* **Rechum** the *chancellor* **master of decrees**
and *Shimshai* **Shimshay** the scribe
wrote a letter **inscribed one epistle**
against *Jerusalem* **Yeru Shalem**
to *Artaxerxes* **Artach Shashta** the *king* **sovereign**
in this sort **thus**:
9 Then *wrote Rehum* **Rechum**
the *chancellor* **master of decrees**,
and *Shimshai* **Shimshay** the scribe,
and the *rest* **survivors** of their *companions* **colleagues**;
the *Dinaites* **Dinaiy**, the *Apharsathchites* **Apharesiym**,
the *Tarpelites* **Tarpeliy**, the *Apharsites* **Apharsiy**,
the *Archevites* **Archeviy**, the *Babylonians* **Babeliy**,
the *Susanchites* **Shushanchiy**, the *Dehavites* **Dehaviy**,
and the *Elamites* **Elamiy**,
10 And the *rest* **survivors** of the nations
whom the great and *noble Asnapper* **esteemed Osnapper**
brought over **revealed**,
and *set* **settled** in the cities of *Samaria* **Shomeron**,
and the *rest* **survivors** that are on this side the river,
and *at such a time* **et cetera**.

ARTACH SHASHTA TRIBULATES AGAINST THE HOUSE OF YAH VEH

11 This is the *copy* **transcript** of the *letter* **epistle**
that they sent unto him,
even unto *Artaxerxes* **Artach Shashta** the *king* **sovereign**;
Thy servants the men on this side the river,
and *at such a time* **et cetera**.
12 Be it known unto the *king* **sovereign**,
that the *Jews* **Yah Hudiym**
which *came up* **ascended** from thee to us
are come unto *Jerusalem* **Yeru Shalem**,
building the rebellious and the *bad* **wicked** city,
and *have set up* **finished** the walls thereof,
and joined the foundations.
13 Be it known now unto the *king* **sovereign**, that,
if this city be builded, and the walls *set up* **finished** *again*,
then *will* **shall** they not *pay toll* **give tribute**,
tribute **excise**, and custom,
and *so* **thus** thou shalt endamage the revenue
of the *kings* **sovereigns**.
14 Now because we
have maintenance from the king's palace
are salted with the salt of the manse,
and it was not *meet* **convenient** for us
to see the *king's dishonour* **sovereign's nakedness**,
therefore have we sent
and *certified the king* **made known to the sovereign**;
15 That search may be made
in the *book* **scroll** of the records of thy fathers:
so shalt thou find in the *book* **scroll** of the records,
and know that this city is a rebellious city,
and *hurtful* **damaging**
unto *kings* **sovereigns** and *provinces* **jurisdictions**,
and that they have *moved sedition* **rebelled**
within the same of old time
in the midst thereof **from eternal days**:
for which cause was this city *destroyed* **desolated**.
16 We *certify the king* **have the sovereign know** that,
if this city be builded *again*,
and the walls thereof *set up* **finished**,
by this means **therefore** thou shalt have no portion
on this side the river.
17 Then sent the *king an answer* **sovereign a decision**
unto *Rehum* **Rechum** the *chancellor* **master of decrees**,
and *to Shimshai* **Shimshay** the scribe,
and to the *rest* **survivors** of their *companions* **colleagues**
that *dwell* **settle** in *Samaria* **Shomeron**,
and unto the *rest* **survivors** beyond the river,
Peace **Shalom**, and *at such a time* **et cetera**.
18 The *letter* **epistle** which ye sent unto us
hath been *plainly read* **distinctly called out**
before **in front of** me.
19 And I *commanded* **have set a decree**,
and search hath been made,
and it is found that this city *of old time* **from eternal days**
hath *made insurrection* **lifted itself**
against *kings* **sovereigns**,
and that rebellion and sedition have been made therein.
20 There have been mighty *kings* **sovereigns**
also over *Jerusalem* **Yeru Shalem**,
which have ruled over all *countries* beyond the river;
and *toll* **tribute**, *tribute* **excise**, and custom,
was *paid* **given** unto them.
21 *Give* **Set** ye now *commandment* **a decree**
to cause these men to *cease* **stop**,
and that this city be not builded,
until another *commandment* **decree**
shall be *given* **set** from me.
22 *Take heed now* **Be enlightened**
that ye *fail not to do* **not err about** this:
why should damage *grow* **increase**
to the *hurt* **damage** of the *kings* **sovereigns**?

THE SERVICE OF THE HOUSE OF YAH VEH STOPPED

23 *Now* **Then** when the *copy* **transcript**
of *king Artaxerxes'* **sovereign Artach Shashta's**
letter **epistle** was *read* **called out**
before Rehum **in front of Rechum**,
and *Shimshai* **Shimshay** the scribe,
and their *companions* **colleagues**,
they went up in haste to *Jerusalem* **Yeru Shalem**
unto the *Jews* **Yah Hudiym**,
and made them to *cease* **stop**
by *force* **arm** and *power* **valour**.
24 Then *ceased* **stopped** the *work* **service**
of the house of *God* **Elah**
which is at *Jerusalem* **Yeru Shalem**.
So it *ceased* **stopped** unto the second year
of the *reign* **sovereigndom** of *Darius* **Daryavesh**
king **sovereign** of Persia.

THE BUILDING OF THE HOUSE OF YAH VEH STARTED

5 Then the prophets, *Haggai* **Haggay** the prophet,
and *Zechariah* **Zechar Yah** the son of Iddo,
prophesied unto the *Jews* **Yah Hudiym**
that were in *Judah* **Yah Hudah** and *Jerusalem* **Yeru Shalem**
in the name of the *God* **Elah** of *Israel* **Yisra El**,
even unto them.
2 Then rose up *Zerubbabel* **Zerub Babel**
the son of *Shealtiel* **Shealti El**,
and *Jeshua* **Yah Shua** the son of *Jozadak* **Yah Sadaq**,
and *began* **released** to build the house of *God* **Elah**
which is at *Jerusalem* **Yeru Shalem**:
and with them were the prophets of *God* **Elah**
helping **upholding** them.
3 At the same *time* **appointment**
came to them *Tatnai* **Tattenay**,
governor on this side the river,
and *Shetharboznai* **Shethar Bozenay**
and their *companions* **colleagues**,
and said thus unto them,
Who hath *commanded you* **set you a decree**
to build this house, and to *make up* **finish** this wall?
4 Then said we unto them *after this manner* **thus**,
What **Who** are the names
of the men that *make* **build** this building?
5 But the eye of their *God* **Elah**
was upon the elders of the *Jews* **Yah Hudiym**,
that they could not cause them to *cease* **stop**,
till the *matter* **decree**
came **was brought** to *Darius* **Daryavesh**:
and then they *returned answer* **responded** by *letter* **epistle**
concerning this *matter*.

THE EPISTLE OF TATTENAY TO DARYAVESH

6 The *copy* **transcript** of the *letter* **epistle**
that *Tatnai* **Tattenay**, governor on this side the river,
and *Shetharboznai* **Shethar Bozenay**
and his *companions* **colleagues**
the *Apharsachites* **Apharsechiy**,
which were on this side the river,
sent unto *Darius* **Daryavesh** the *king* **sovereign**:
7 They sent a *letter* **decision** unto him,
wherein was written **midst which was inscribed** thus;
Unto *Darius* **Daryavesh** the *king* **sovereign**,
all *peace* **shalom**.
8 Be it known unto the *king* **sovereign**,
that we went
into the *province* **jurisdiction** of *Judea* **Yah Hudah**,
to the **great** house of *the great God* **Elah**,
which is builded with *great* **round** stones,
and timber is *laid* **set** in the walls,
and this *work goeth fast on* **service keepeth on diligently**,
and prospereth in their hands.
9 Then asked we those elders, and said unto them thus,
Who *commanded you* **set you a decree**
to build this house, and to *make up* **finish** these walls?
10 We asked their names also,
to *certify thee* **have thee know**,
that we might *write* **inscribe** the names of the men
that were the *chief* **head** of them.
11 And thus they returned us *answer* **a decision**, saying,
We are the servants
of *the God* **Elah** of *heaven* **the heavens** and earth,
and build the house
that was builded these many years *ago* **prior**,
which a great *king* **sovereign** of *Israel* **Yisra El**
builded and *set up* **finished**.
12 *But* **Except** after that our fathers had *provoked* **caused**
the God **Elah** of *heaven unto wrath* **the heavens to quiver**,
he gave them into the hand
of *Nebuchadnezzar* **Nebukadnets Tsar**,
the *king* **sovereign** of *Babylon* **Babel**,

the *Chaldean* **Kasdiy**,
who *destroyed* **demolished** this house,
and *carried* **exiled** the people *away* into *Babylon* **Babel**.
13 *But* **However** in the first year of *Cyrus* **Koresh**
the *king* **sovereign** of *Babylon* **Babel**
the same king Cyrus — **sovereign Koresh**
made **set** a decree to build this house of *God* **Elah**.
14 And the vessels also of gold and silver
of the house of *God* **Elah**,
which *Nebuchadnezzar* **Nebukadnets Tsar**
took **removed** out of the *temple* **manse**
that was in *Jerusalem* **Yeru Shalem**,
and brought them
into the *temple* **manse** of *Babylon* **Babel**,
those did *Cyrus* **Koresh** the *king* **sovereign**
take **remove** out of the *temple* **manse** of *Babylon* **Babel**,
and they were *delivered* **given** unto one,
whose name was *Sheshbazzar* **Sheshbats Tsar**,
whom he had *made* **set** governor;
15 And said unto him, *Take* **Lift** these vessels,
go, *carry* **deposit** them into the *temple* **manse**
that is in *Jerusalem* **Yeru Shalem**,
and let the house of *God* **Elah** be builded in his place.
16 Then came *the same Sheshbazzar* **this Sheshbats Tsar**,
and laid the foundation of the house of *God* **Elah**
which is in *Jerusalem* **Yeru Shalem**:
and *since that time* **from then** even until now
hath it been in building,
and *yet* it is not *finished* **shalamed**.
17 Now therefore, if it *seem* **be** good to the *king* **sovereign**,
let there be search made
in the *king's* **sovereign's** treasure house,
which is there at *Babylon* **Babel**,
whether it **though there** be *so*,
that a decree was *made* **set**
of *Cyrus* **Koresh** the *king* **sovereign**
to build this house of *God* **Elah** at *Jerusalem* **Yeru Shalem**,
and let the *king* **sovereign**
send his *pleasure* **intention** to us concerning this matter.

DARYAVESH SETS A DECREE

6 Then *Darius* **Daryavesh** the *king* **sovereign**
made **set** a decree,
and search was made in the house of the *rolls* **scrolls**,
where the treasures were *laid up* **deposited**
in *Babylon* **Babel**.
2 And there was found at *Achmetha* **Ach Metha**,
in the palace
that is in the *province* **jurisdiction** of the *Medes* **Maday**,
a **one** roll,
and *therein* **in the midst of it** was a record
thus *written* **inscribed**:
3 In the first year of *Cyrus* **Koresh** the *king* **sovereign**
the same Cyrus **Koresh** the *king* **sovereign**
made **set** a decree concerning the house of *God* **Elah**
at *Jerusalem* **Yeru Shalem**,
Let the house be builded,
the place where they *offered* **sacrificed** sacrifices,
and let the foundations thereof be *strongly laid* **erected**;
the height thereof *threescore* **sixty** cubits,
and the *breadth* **width** thereof *threescore* **sixty** cubits;
4 With three *rows* **layers** of *great* **round** stones,
and a row of new timber:
and let the expenses
be given out of the *king's* **sovereign's** house:
5 And also let the golden and silver vessels
of the house of *God* **Elah**,
which *Nebuchadnezzar* **Nebukadnets Tsar**
took forth **removed** out of the *temple* **manse**
which is at *Jerusalem* **Yeru Shalem**,
and brought unto *Babylon* **Babel**, be restored,
and brought again
unto the *temple* **manse** which is at *Jerusalem* **Yeru Shalem**,
every one to his place,
and *place* **deposit** them in the house of *God* **Elah**.
6 Now *therefore*,
Tatnai **Tattenay**, governor beyond the river,
Shetharboznai **Shethar Bozenay**,
and your *companions* **colleagues**
the *Apharsachites* **Apharsechiy**,
which are beyond the river, be ye far from thence:
7 Let the *work* **service** of this house of *God* **Elah** alone;
let the governor of the *Jews* **Yah Hudiym**
and the elders of the *Jews* **Yah Hudiym**
build this house of *God* **Elah** in his place.
8 *Moreover* I *make* **set** a decree
what ye shall do to the elders of these *Jews* **Yah Hudiym**
for the building of this house of *God* **Elah**:
that of the *king's goods* **sovereign's holdings**,
even of the tribute beyond the river,
forthwith **diligently** expenses be given unto these men,
that they *be not hindered* **not cease**.
9 And that which they have need of,
both young bullocks **sons of bulls**, and rams, and lambs,
for the *burnt offerings* **holocausts**
of the *God* **Elah** of *heaven* **the heavens**,
wheat, salt, *wine* **fermentation**, and **anointing** oil,
according to the *appointment* **edict** of the priests
which are at *Jerusalem* **Yeru Shalem**,
let it be given them day by day *without fail* **with no error**:
10 That they may *offer* **oblate**
sacrifices of *sweet* savours **of rest**
unto *the God* **Elah** of *heaven* **the heavens**,
and pray for the life of the *king* **sovereign**,
and of his sons.
11 *Also* I have *made* **set** a decree,
that *whosoever* **any man who** shall alter
this *word* **decision**,
let timber be *pulled down* **uprooted** from his house,
and being *set up* **lifted**, let him be *hanged* **struck** thereon;
and let his house be made *a dunghill* **cesspools** for this.
12 And *the God* **Elah**
that hath caused his name to *dwell* **tabernacle** there
destroy **overthrow** all *kings* **sovereigns** and people,
that shall *put to* **send forth** their hand
to alter and to *destroy* **despoil** this house of *God* **Elah**:
which is at *Jerusalem* **Yeru Shalem**.
I *Darius* **Daryavesh** have *made* **set** a decree;
let it be *done with speed* **serviced diligently**.
13 Then *Tatnai* **Tattenay**, governor on this side the river,
Shetharboznai **Shethar Bozenay**,
and their *companions* **colleagues**,
according to that
which *Darius* **Daryavesh** the *king* **sovereign** had sent,
so **thus** they did *speedily* **diligently**.
14 And the elders of the *Jews* **Yah Hudiym** builded,
and they prospered
through the prophesying of *Haggai* **Haggay** the prophet
and *Zechariah* **Zechar Yah** the son of Iddo.
And they builded, and finished it,
according to the *commandment* **decree**
of *the God* **Elah** of *Israel* **Yisra El**,
and according to the *commandment* **decree**
of *Cyrus* **Koresh**, and *Darius* **Daryavesh**,
and *Artaxerxes* **Artach Shashta** *king* **sovereign** of Persia.

THE HOUSE OF YAH VEH FINISHED

15 And this house was finished
on the third day of the month Adar,
which was in the sixth year of the *reign* **sovereigndom**
of *Darius* **Daryavesh** the *king* **sovereign**.

THE HOUSE OF YAH VEH HANUKKAHED

16 And the *children* **sons** of *Israel* **Yisra El**,
the priests, and the *Levites* **Leviym**,
and the *rest* **survivors**
of the *children* **sons** of the *captivity* **exile**,
kept the *dedication* **hanukkah** of this house of *God* **Elah**:
with *joy* **rejoicing**.
17 And *offered* **oblated** at the *dedication* **hanukkah**
of this house of *God* **Elah**:
an hundred *bullocks* **bulls**,
two hundred rams, four hundred lambs;
and for *a sin offering* **the sin** for all *Israel* **Yisra El**,
twelve *he goats* **buck goats of the doe goats**,
according to the *number* **enumeration**
of the *tribes* **scions** of *Israel* **Yisra El**.
18 And they *set* **raised** the priests in their divisions,
and the *Levites* **Leviym** in their *courses* **allotments**,
for the service of *God* **Elah**,
which is at *Jerusalem* **Yeru Shalem**;
as it is written **according to the inscribing**
in the *book* **scroll** of *Moses* **Mosheh**.

THE PASACH WORKED

19 And the *children* **sons** of the *captivity* **exile**
kept **worked** the *passover* **pasach**
upon the fourteenth *day* of the first month.
20 For the priests and the *Levites* **Leviym**
were purified *together,*
all **each one** of them *were* pure,
and *killed* **slaughtered** the *passover* **pasach**
for all the *children* **sons** of *the captivity* **exile**,
and for their brethren the priests, and for themselves.
21 And the *children* **sons** of *Israel* **Yisra El**,
which *were come again* **returned** out of *captivity* **exile**,
and all such as had separated themselves unto them
from the *filthiness* **foulness**
of the *heathen* **goyim** of the land,
to seek *the LORD God* **Yah Veh Elohim** of *Israel* **Yisra El**,
did eat,
22 And *kept* **worked**
the *feast* **celebration** of *unleavened bread* **matsah**
seven days with *joy* **cheer**:
for *the LORD* **Yah Veh** had *made* **cheered** them *joyful,*
and turned the heart
of the *king* **sovereign** of *Assyria* **Ashshur** unto them,
to strengthen their hands
in the work of the house of *God* **Elohim**,
the *God* **Elohim** of *Israel* **Yisra El**.

EZRA COMES TO YERU SHALEM

7 Now after these *things* **words**,
in the *reign* **sovereigndom** of *Artaxerxes* **Artach Shashta**,
king **sovereign** of Persia,
Ezra the son of *Seraiah* **Sera Yah**,
the son of *Azariah* **Azar Yah**, the son of *Hilkiah* **Hilqi Yah**,
2 The son of Shallum,
the son of *Zadok* **Sadoq**, the son of *Ahitub* **Achiy Tub**,
3 The son of *Amariah* **Amar Yah**,
the son of *Azariah* **Azar Yah**,
the son of *Meraioth* **Merayoth**,
4 The son of *Zerahiah* **Zerach Yah**,
the son of Uzzi, the son of *Bukki* **Buqqi**,
5 The son of *Abishua* **Abi Shua**,
the son of *Phinehas* **Pinechas**, the son of *Eleazar* **El Azar**,
the son of *Aaron* **Aharon** the *chief* **head** priest:
6 This Ezra *went up* **ascended** from *Babylon* **Babel**;
and he was a *ready* **skillful** scribe
in the *law* **torah** of *Moses* **Mosheh**,
which *the LORD God* **Yah Veh Elohim** of *Israel* **Yisra El**
had given:
and the *king granted* **sovereign gave** him all his request,
according to the hand
of *the LORD* **Yah Veh** his *God* **Elohim** upon him.
7 And there *went up* **ascended**
some of the *children* **sons** of *Israel* **Yisra El**,
and of the priests, and the *Levites* **Leviym**,
and the singers, and the porters,
and the *Nethinims* **Dedicates**,
unto *Jerusalem* **Yeru Shalem**,
in the seventh year
of *Artaxerxes* **Artach Shashta** the *king* **sovereign**.
8 And he came to *Jerusalem* **Yeru Shalem**
in the fifth month,
which was in the seventh year of the *king* **sovereign**.
9 For upon the first *day* of the first month
began he to go up from Babylon
he founded the ascent to Babel,
and on the first *day* of the fifth month
came he to *Jerusalem* **Yeru Shalem**,
according to the good hand of his *God* **Elohim** upon him.
10 For Ezra had prepared his heart
to seek the *law* **torah** of *the LORD* **Yah Veh**,
and to *do* **work** it,
and to teach in *Israel* **Yisra El** statutes and judgments.

THE EPISTLE OF ARTACH SHASHTA TO EZRA

11 Now this is the *copy* **transcript** of the *letter* **epistle**
that the *king Artaxerxes* **sovereign Artach Shashta**
gave unto Ezra the priest, the scribe,
even a scribe of the words
of the *commandments* **misvoth** of *the LORD* **Yah Veh**,
and of his statutes to *Israel* **Yisra El**.
12 *Artaxerxes* **Artach Shashta**,
king **sovereign** of *kings* **sovereigns**,
unto Ezra the priest,
a scribe of the *law* **edict**
of *the God* **Elah** of *heaven* **the heavens**,
perfect **consummate** *peace,* and *at such a time* **et cetera**.
13 I *make* **set** a decree,
that all they of the people of *Israel* **Yisra El**,
and *of* his priests and *Levites* **Leviym**,
in my *realm* **sovereigndom**,
which *are minded of their own freewill* **volunteer**
to *go up* **bring** to *Jerusalem* **Yeru Shalem**,
go **bring** with thee.
14 *Forasmuch* **Because** as thou art sent
from *in front* of the *king* **sovereign**,
and of his seven counsellors,
to *enquire* **search**
concerning *Judah* **Yah Hudah** and *Jerusalem* **Yeru Shalem**,
according to the *law* **edict** of thy *God* **Elah**
which is in thine hand;
15 And to *carry* **bring** the silver and gold,
which the *king* **sovereign** and his counsellors
have *freely offered* **volunteered**
unto *the God* **Elah** of *Israel* **Yisra El**,
whose *habitation* **tabernacle** is in *Jerusalem* **Yeru Shalem**,
16 And all the silver and gold that thou canst find
in all the *province* **jurisdiction** of *Babylon* **Babel**,
with the *freewill offering* **voluntary** of the people,
and of the priests,
offering willingly **volunteered** for the house of their *God* **Elah**
which is in *Jerusalem* **Yeru Shalem**:
17 *That* **Therefore**
thou mayest buy *speedily* **diligently** with this *money* **silver**
bullocks **bulls**, rams, lambs,
with their *meat* offerings and their *drink offerings* **libations**,
and *offer* **oblate** them upon the **sacrifice** altar
of the house of your *God* **Elah**
which is in *Jerusalem* **Yeru Shalem**.
18 And whatsoever shall *seem good to* **well—please** thee,
and *to* thy brethren,
to do with the *rest* **surviving** of the silver and the gold,
that do after the *will* **intention** of your *God* **Elah**.
19 The vessels also that are given thee
for the service of the house of thy *God* **Elah**,
those *deliver* **shalam** thou
before the God **in front of the Elah** of *Jerusalem* **Yeru Shalem**.
20 And *whatsoever more shall be needful*
the rest of the needs
for the house of thy *God* **Elah**,
which *thou shalt have occasion* **shall befall thee**
to *bestow* **give**,
bestow **give** it out of the *king's* **sovereign's** treasure house.
21 And *I* **from me**,
even I *Artaxerxes* **Artach Shashta** the *king* **sovereign**,
do make **set** a decree to all the treasurers
which are beyond the river,
that *whatsoever* **all that** Ezra the priest,
the scribe of the *law* **edict**
of *the God* **Elah** of *heaven* **the heavens**,
shall *require* **ask** of you, it be done *speedily* **diligently**,
22 Unto an hundred *talents* **rounds** of silver,
and to an hundred measures of wheat,
and to an hundred baths of *wine* **fermentation**,
and to an hundred baths of **anointing** oil,
and salt *without prescribing how much* **not scribed**.
23 *Whatsoever is commanded* **All that is of the decree**
by *the God* **Elah** of *heaven* **the heavens**,
let it be diligently done
for the house of *the God* **Elah** of *heaven* **the heavens**:
for why should there be *wrath* **rage**
against the *realm* **sovereigndom**
of the *king* **sovereign** and his sons?
24 Also we *certify* **have** you **know**,
that touching any of the priests and *Levites* **Leviym**,
singers **pluckers**, *porters* **portal guards**,
Nethinims **Dedicates**,
or *ministers* **servers** of this house of *God* **Elah**,
it shall not be *lawful* **permissible**
to *impose toll* **assess tribute**, or custom, upon them.
25 And thou, Ezra,
after the wisdom of thy *God* **Elah**, that is in thine hand,
set magistrates **appoint judges** and *judges* **advocates**,

which may *judge* **plead**
for all the people that are beyond the river,
all such as know the *laws* **edicts** of thy *God* **Elah**;
and *teach* ye **have** them **know** that know them not.
26 And whosoever *will* **shall** not do
the *law* **edict** of thy *God* **Elah**,
and the *law* **edict** of the *king* **sovereign**,
let *judgment* **penalty**
be *executed speedily* **served diligently** *upon him*,
whether *it be* unto death,
or to banishment **whether to uproot**,
or **whether** to confiscation *of goods* **holdings**,
or to imprisonment **whether to bonds**.
27 Blessed be
the LORD God **Yah Veh Elohim** of our fathers,
which hath *put* **given** such *a thing* as this
in the *king's* **sovereign's** heart,
to *beautify* **adorn** the house of *the LORD* **Yah Veh**
which is in *Jerusalem* **Yeru Shalem**:
28 And hath extended mercy unto me
before **at the face of** the *king* **sovereign**,
and his counsellors,
and *before* **at the face**
of all the *king's* **sovereign's** mighty *princes* **governors**.
And I was strengthened as the hand
of *the LORD* **Yah Veh** my *God* **Elohim** was upon me,
and I gathered *together* out of *Israel* **Yisra El**
chief men **heads** to *go up* **ascend** with me.

THE GENEALOGIZED THAT ASCENDED FROM BABEL

8 These are now the *chief* **head** of their fathers,
and *this is* **these are** the *genealogy of them* **genealogized**
that *went up* **ascended** with me from *Babylon* **Babel**,
in the *reign* **sovereigndom**
of *Artaxerxes* **Artach Shashta** the *king* **sovereign**.
2 Of the sons of *Phinehas* **Pinechas**;
Gershom:
of the sons of *Ithamar* **Iy Thamar**;
Daniel:
of the sons of David;
Hattush.
3 Of the sons of *Shechaniah* **Shechan Yah**,
of the sons of Pharosh;
Zechariah **Zechar Yah**:
and with him
were *reckoned by genealogy* **genealogized** of the males
an hundred and fifty.
4 Of the sons of *Pahathmoab* **Pachath Moab**;
Elioenai **El Ya Enay** the son of *Zerahiah* **Zerach Yah**,
and with him two hundred males.
5 Of the sons of *Shechaniah* **Shechan Yah**;
the son of *Jahaziel* **Yachazi El**,
and with him three hundred males.
6 Of the sons also of Adin;
Ebed the son of *Jonathan* **Yah Nathan**,
and with him fifty males.
7 And of the sons of Elam;
Jeshaiah **Yesha Yah** the son of *Athaliah* **Athal Yah**,
and with him seventy males.
8 And of the sons of *Shephatiah* **Shaphat Yah**;
Zebadiah **Zebad Yah** the son of *Michael* **Michah El**,
and with him *fourscore* **eighty** males.
9 Of the sons of *Joab* **Yah Ab**;
Obadiah **Obad Yah** the son of *Jehiel* **Yechi El**,
and with him two hundred and eighteen males.
10 And of the sons of Shelomith;
the son of *Josiphiah* **Yosiph Yah**,
and with him an hundred and *threescore* **sixty** males.
11 And of the sons of *Bebai* **Bebay**;
Zechariah **Zechar Yah** the son of *Bebai* **Bebay**,
and with him twenty and eight males.
12 And of the sons of Azgad;
Johanan **Yah An** the son of *Hakkatan* **Qatan**,
and with him an hundred and ten males.
13 And of the last sons of *Adonikam* **Adoni Qam**,
whose names are these,
Eliphelet **Eli Phelet**, *Jeiel* **Yei El** and *Shemaiah* **Shema Yah**,
and with them *threescore* **sixty** males.
14 Of the sons also of *Bigvai* **Bigvay**;
Uthai, and *Zabbud* **Zakkur**,
and with them seventy males.
15 And I gathered them *together*
to the river that runneth to Ahava;
and there *abode* **encamped** we *in tents* three days:
and I *viewed* **discerned** the people, and the priests,
and found there none of the sons of Levi.
16 Then sent I for *Eliezer* **Eli Ezer**,
for *Ariel* **Ari El**, for *Shemaiah* **Shema Yah**,
and for *Elnathan* **El Nathan**, and for *Jarib* **Yarib**,
and for *Elnathan* **El Nathan**, and for Nathan,
and for *Zechariah* **Zechar Yah**, and for Meshullam,
chief men **heads**;
also for *Joiarib* **Yah Jarib**, and for *Elnathan* **El Nathan**,
men of understanding **discerners**.
17 And I *sent* **misvahed** them *with commandment*
unto Iddo
the *chief* **head** at the place *Casiphia* **Kasiphia**,
and I *told them* **set in their mouth**
what **words** they should *say* **word** unto Iddo,
and to his brethren the *Nethinims* **Dedicates**,
at the place *Casiphia* **Kasiphia**,
that they should bring unto us ministers
for the house of our *God* **Elohim**.
18 And by the good hand of our *God* **Elohim** upon us
they brought us a man of *understanding* **comprehension**,
of the sons of *Mahli* **Machli**,
the son of Levi, the son of *Israel* **Yisra El**;
and *Sherebiah* **Shereb Yah**, with his sons and his brethren,
eighteen;
19 And *Hashabiah* **Hashab Yah**,
and with him *Jeshaiah* **Yesha Yah** of the sons of Merari,
his brethren and their sons,
twenty;
20 Also of the *Nethinims* **Dedicates**,
whom David and the *princes* **governors**
had *appointed* **given** for the service of the *Levites* **Leviym**,
two hundred and twenty *Nethinims* **Dedicates**:
all of them were *expressed* **appointed** by name.
21 Then I *proclaimed* **called** a fast there,
at the river of Ahava,
that we might *afflict* **humble** ourselves
before **at the face of** our *God* **Elohim**,
to seek of him a *right* **straight** way for us,
and for our *little ones* **toddlers**,
and for all our *substance* **acquisition**.
22 For I was *ashamed* **shamed**
to *require* **ask** of the *king* **sovereign**
a band of soldiers **valiant men** and *horsemen* **cavalry**
to help us against the enemy in the way:
because we had *spoken* **said** unto the *king* **sovereign**,
saying, The hand of our *God* **Elohim**
is upon all them for good that seek him;
but his *power* **strength** and his wrath
is against all them that forsake him.
23 So we fasted and besought our *God* **Elohim** for this:
and he was intreated of us.
24 Then I separated
twelve of the *chief* **governors** of the priests,
Sherebiah **Shereb Yah**, *Hashabiah* **Hashab Yah**,
and ten of their brethren with them,
25 And weighed unto them the silver, and the gold,
and the *vessels* **instruments**,
even the *offering* **exaltment**
of the house of our *God* **Elohim**,
which the *king* **sovereign**, and his counsellors,
and his *lords* **governors**,
and all *Israel* **Yisra El** *there* present, had *offered* **lifted**:
26 I even weighed unto their hand
six hundred and fifty *talents* **rounds** of silver,
and silver *vessels* **instruments** an hundred *talents* **rounds**,
and of gold an hundred *talents* **rounds**;
27 Also twenty *basons* **tankards** of gold,
of a thousand *drams* **darics**;
and two *vessels* **instruments** of *fine* **best yellow** copper,
precious **desirable** as gold.
28 And I said unto them,
ye are holy unto *the LORD* **Yah Veh**;
the *vessels* **instruments** are holy also;
and the silver and the gold
are a *freewill offering* **voluntary**

unto *the LORD God* **Yah Veh Elohim** of your fathers.
29 Watch ye, and *keep* **guard** them,
until ye weigh them
before **at the face of** the *chief* **governor**
of the priests and the *Levites* **Leviym**,
and *chief* **governor** of the fathers of *Israel* **Yisra El**,
at *Jerusalem* **Yeru Shalem**,
in the chambers of the house of *the LORD* **Yah Veh**.
30 So took the priests and the *Levites* **Leviym**
the weight of the silver, and the gold,
and the *vessels* **instruments**,
to bring them to *Jerusalem* **Yeru Shalem**
unto the house of our *God* **Elohim**.
31 Then we *departed* **pulled stakes** from the river of Ahava
on the twelfth *day* of the first month,
to go unto *Jerusalem* **Yeru Shalem**:
and the hand of our *God* **Elohim** was upon us,
and he *delivered* **rescued** us
from the *hand* **palm** of the enemy,
and of such as *lay in wait* **lurked** by the way.
32 And we came to *Jerusalem* **Yeru Shalem**,
and *abode* **settled** there three days.
33 Now on the fourth day
was the silver and the gold and the *vessels* **instruments**
weighed in the house of our *God* **Elohim**
by the hand of Meremoth
the son of *Uriah* **Uri Yah** the priest;
and with him was *Eleazar* **El Azar**
the son of *Phinehas* **Pinechas**;
and with them was *Jozabad* **Yah Zabad**
the son of *Jeshua* **Yah Shua**,
and *Noadiah* **Noad Yah** the son of *Binnui* **Binnuy**,
Levites **Leviym**;
34 By number and by weight of every one:
and all the weight was *written* **inscribed** at that time.
35 Also the *children* **sons** of those
that had been *carried away* **exiled**,
which were come out of the captivity,
offered burnt offerings **oblated holocausts**
unto *the God* **Elohim** of *Israel* **Yisra El**,
twelve bullocks for all *Israel* **Yisra El**,
ninety and six rams, seventy and seven lambs,
twelve *he* **buck** goats for *a sin offering* **the sin**:
all this
was a *burnt offering* **holocaust** unto *the LORD* **Yah Veh**.
36 And they *delivered* **gave**
the *king's commissions* **sovereign's edicts**
unto the *king's lieutenants* **sovereign's satraps**,
and to the governors on this side the river:
and they *furthered* **lifted** the people,
and the house of *God* **Elohim**.

EZRA'S PRAYER CONCERNING INTERMINGLING

9 Now when these *things* were *done* **finished**,
the *princes* **governors** came **near** to me, saying,
The people of *Israel* **Yisra El**,
and the priests, and the *Levites* **Leviym**,
have not separated themselves
from the people of the lands,
doing according to their *abominations* **abhorrences**,
even of the *Canaanites* **Kenaaniy**, the *Hittites* **Hethiy**,
the *Perizzites* **Perizziy**, the *Jebusites* **Yebusiy**,
the *Ammonites* **Ammoniy**, the *Moabites* **Moabiy**,
the *Egyptians* **Misrayim**, and the *Amorites* **Emoriy**.
2 For they have *taken* **spared** of their daughters
for themselves, and for their sons:
so that the holy seed have mingled themselves
with the people of those lands:
yea, the hand of the *princes* **governors** and *rulers* **prefects**
hath been *chief* **head** in this *trespass* **treason**.
3 And when I heard this *thing* **word**,
I *rent* **ripped** my *garment* **clothes** and my mantle,
and *plucked off* **baldened** the hair
of my head and of my beard,
and sat down astonied.
4 Then were *assembled* **gathered** unto me
every one that trembled at the words
of *the God* **Elohim** of *Israel* **Yisra El**,
because of the *transgression* **treason**
of those that had been *carried away* **exiled**;
and I sat astonied until the evening *sacrifice* **offering**.
5 And at the evening *sacrifice* **offering**
I arose up *from my heaviness* **fasting**;
and having *rent* **ripped**
my *garment* **clothes** and my mantle,
I *fell* **bowed** upon my knees,
and spread out my *hands* **palms**
unto *the LORD* **Yah Veh** my *God* **Elohim**,
6 And said, O my *God* **Elohim**,
I am *ashamed* **shamed** and blush to lift up my face to thee,
my *God* **Elohim**:
for our *iniquities* **perversities**
are increased **abound** over our head,
and our *trespass* **guilt** is grown up unto the heavens.
7 Since the days of our fathers
have we been in a great *trespass* **guilt** unto this day;
and for our *iniquities* **perversities** have we,
our *kings* **sovereigns**, and our priests,
been *delivered* **given** into the hand
of the *kings* **sovereigns** of the lands,
to the sword, to captivity, and to a *spoil* **plunder**,
and to *confusion of* **shamed** face, as it is this day.
8 And now for a little *space* **blink**
grace **supplication** hath been *shewed*
from *the LORD* **Yah Veh** our *God* **Elohim**,
to leave *us a remnant* **escapees** to *escape* **survive**,
and to give us a *nail* **stake** in his *holy place* **holies**,
that our *God* **Elohim** may lighten our eyes,
and give us a little *reviving* **invigoration**
in our *bondage* **servitude**.
9 For we were *bondmen* **servants**;
yet our *God* **Elohim** hath not forsaken us
in our *bondage* **servitude**,
but hath extended mercy unto us
in the *sight* **face** of the *kings* **sovereigns** of Persia,
to give us *a reviving* **an invigoration**,
to *set up* **lift** the house of our *God* **Elohim**,
and to *repair* **stand** the *desolations* **parched areas** thereof,
and to give us a wall
in *Judah* **Yah Hudah** and in *Jerusalem* **Yeru Shalem**.
10 And now, O our *God* **Elohim**,
what shall *we say* after this?
for we have forsaken thy *commandments* **misvoth**,
11 Which thou hast *commanded* **misvahed**
by **the hand of** thy servants the prophets, saying,
The land, unto which ye go to possess it,
is *an unclean land with the filthiness* **a land of exclusion**
of the people of the lands,
with their *abominations* **abhorrences**,
which have filled it from *one end* **mouth** to *another* **mouth**
with their *uncleanness* **foulness**.
12 Now *therefore* give not your daughters unto their sons,
neither *take* **bear** their daughters unto your sons,
nor seek their *peace* **shalom** or their *wealth* **goodness**
for ever **eternally**:
that ye may *be strong* **strengthen**,
and eat the good of the land,
and leave it for an inheritance to your children for ever
for your sons to possess eternally.
13 And after all that is come upon us
for our evil *deeds* **works**, and for our great *trespass* **guilt**,
seeing that thou our *God* **Elohim** hast
punished us less than our iniquities deserve
spared us from our downward perversities,
and hast given us such *deliverance* **an escape** as this;
14 Should we *again* **return**
to break thy *commandments* **misvoth**,
and *join in affinity* **intermarry**
with the people of these *abominations* **abhorrences**?
wouldest **shouldest** not thou be angry with us
till thou hadst *consumed* **finished** us **off**,
so that there should be no *remnant* **survivors**
nor escaping?
15 O *LORD God* **Yah Veh Elohim** of *Israel* **Yisra El**,
thou art *righteous* **just**:
for we *remain* **survive** yet escaped as it is this day: behold,
we are *before thee* **at thy face** in our *trespasses* **guilt**:
for we cannot stand *before thee* **at thy face**
because of this.

10
A MIGHTY CONGREGATION WEEPS
Now when Ezra had prayed,
and when he had *confessed* **extended hands**,
weeping and *casting himself* **falling** down
before **at the face of** the house of *God* **Elohim**,
there *assembled* **gathered** unto him out of *Israel* **Yisra El**
a *very* **mighty** great congregation
of men and women and children:
for **in weeping**, the people wept *very sore* **aboundingly**.
2 And *Shechaniah* **Shechan Yah** the son of *Jehiel* **Yechi El**,
one of the sons of Elam, answered and said unto Ezra,
We have *trespassed* **treasoned** against our *God* **Elohim**,
and have *taken* **settled** strange *wives* **women**
of the people of the land:
yet now there is *hope* **expectation** in *Israel* **Yisra El**
concerning this *thing*.
3 Now therefore
let us *make* **cut** a covenant with our *God* **Elohim**
to *put away* **bring** all the *wives* **women**,
and such as are born of them,
according to the counsel of my *Lord* **Adonay**,
and of those that tremble
at the *commandment* **misvah** of our *God* **Elohim**;
and let it be *done* **worked** according to the *law* **torah**.
4 Arise; for this *matter belongeth* **word be** unto thee:
we also *will* **shall** be with thee:
be of good courage **strengthen**, and *do* **work** *it*.
5 Then arose Ezra, and made the *chief* **governor** priests,
the *Levites* **Leviym**, and all *Israel* **Yisra El**,
to *swear* **oath**
that they should *do* **work** according to this word.
And they *sware* **oathed**.
6 Then Ezra rose *up*
from *before* **the face of** the house of *God* **Elohim**,
and went into the chamber
of *Johanan* **Yah Hanan** the son of *Eliashib* **El Yashib**:
and when he came thither,
he did eat no bread, nor drink water:
for he mourned because of the *transgression* **treason**
of them that had been *carried away* **exiled**.
7 And they *made proclamation* **passed a voice**
throughout *Judah* **Yah Hudah** and *Jerusalem* **Yeru Shalem**
unto all the *children* **sons** of the *captivity* **exile**,
that they should gather *themselves together*
unto *Jerusalem* **Yeru Shalem**;
8 And that whosoever
would **should** not come within three days,
according to the counsel
of the *princes* **governors** and the elders,
all his *substance* should **acquisition** be *forfeited* **devoted**,
and himself separated from the congregation
of those that had been *carried away* **exiled**.
9 Then all the men
of *Judah* **Yah Hudah** and *Benjamin* **Ben Yamin**
gathered *themselves together* unto *Jerusalem* **Yeru Shalem**
within three days.
It was the ninth month, on the twentieth *day* of the month;
and all the people *sat* **settled** in the *street* **broadway**
of the house of *God* **Elohim**,
trembling because of this *matter* **word**,
and for the great rain.
10 And Ezra the priest *stood up* **arose**, and said unto them,
ye have *transgressed* **treasoned**,
and have *taken* **settled** strange *wives* **women**,
to *increase* **add to** the *trespass* **guilt** of *Israel* **Yisra El**.
11 Now therefore *make confession* **give extended hands**
unto *the LORD God* **Yah Veh Elohim** of your fathers,
and *do* **work** his pleasure:
and separate yourselves from the people of the land,
and from the strange *wives* **women**.
12 Then all the congregation answered
and said with a *loud* **great** voice,
As thou hast said **According to thy word**,
so must we do **we work**.
13 *But* **Nevertheless** the people are many,
and it is a time of much rain,
and we *are not able* **have no force** to stand without,
neither is this a work of one day or two:
for we *are many* **abound**
that have *transgressed* **rebelled** in this *thing* **word**.
14 Let now
our *rulers* **governors** of all the congregation stand,
and let all them
which have *taken* **settled** strange *wives* **women**
in our cities come at appointed times,
and with them the elders *of every city* **city by city**,
and the judges thereof,
until the *fierce* **fuming** wrath of our *God* **Elohim**
for this *matter* **word** be turned from us.
15 Only *Jonathan* **Yah Nathan** the son of *Asahel* **Asa El**
and *Jahaziah* **Yachazi Yah** the son of *Tikvah* **Tiqvah**
were employed **stood** about this *matter*:
and Meshullam and *Shabbethai* **Shabbethay**
the *Levite* **Leviy** helped them.
16 And the *children* **sons** of the *captivity* **exile**
did **worked** so.
And Ezra the priest,
with *certain chief* **head men** of the fathers,
after the house of their fathers,
and all of them by *their* names,
were separated and *sat down* **settled**
in the first day of the tenth month
to examine the *matter* **word**.
17 And they *made an end* **finished** with all the men
that had *taken* **settled** strange *wives* **women**
by the first day of the first month.

THE INTERMINGLERS
18 And among the sons of the priests there were found
that had *taken* **settled** strange *wives* **women**: *namely*,
of the sons of *Jeshua* **Yah Shua**
the son of *Jozadak* **Yah Sadaq**,
and his brethren;
Maaseiah **Maase Yah**, and *Eliezer* **Eli Ezer**,
and *Jarib* **Yarib**, and *Gedaliah* **Gedal Yah**.
19 And they gave their hands
that they *would* **should**
put away **bring** their *wives* **women**;
and *being guilty* **for their guilt**,
they offered a ram of the flock for their *trespass* **guilt**.
20 And of the sons of Immer;
Hanani, and *Zebadiah* **Zebad Yah**.
21 And of the sons of Harim;
Maaseiah **Maase Yah**, and *Elijah* **Eli Yah**,
and *Shemaiah* **Shema Yah**, and *Jehiel* **Yechi El**,
and *Uzziah* **Uzzi Yah**.
22 And of the sons of *Pashur* **Paschur**;
Elioenai **El Ya Enay**, *Maaseiah* **Maase Yah**,
Ishmael **Yishma El**, *Nethaneel* **Nethan El**,
Jozabad **Yah Zabad**, and *Elasah* **El Asah**.
23 Also of the *Levites* **Leviym**;
Jozabad **Yah Zabad**, and *Shimei* **Shimi**,
and *Kelaiah* **Qelayah**, (the same is *Kelita* **Qelita**,)
Pethahiah **Pethach Yah**, *Judah* **Yah Hudah**,
and *Eliezer* **Eli Ezer**.
24 Of the singers also;
Eliashib **El Yashib**:
and of the porters;
Shallum, and Telem, and Uri.
25 *Moreover* **Also** of *Israel* **Yisra El**:
of the sons of Parosh;
Ramiah **Ram Yah**, and *Jeziah* **Yezav Yah**,
and *Malchiah* **Malki Yah**, and *Miamin* **Mi Yamin**,
and *Eleazar* **El Azar**, and *Malchijah* **Malki Yah**,
and *Benaiah* **Bena Yah**.
26 And of the sons of Elam;
Mattaniah **Mattan Yah**, *Zechariah* **Zechar Yah**,
and *Jehiel* **Yechi El**, and Abdi,
and *Jeremoth* **Yeremoth**, and *Eliah* **Eli Yah**.
27 And of the sons of Zattu;
Elioenai **El Ya Enay** *Eliashib* **El Yashib**,
Mattaniah **Mattan Yah**, and *Jeremoth* **Yeremoth**,
and Zabad, and Aziza.
28 Of the sons also of *Bebai* **Bebay**;
Jehohanan **Yah Hanan**, *Hananiah* **Hanan Yah**,
Zabbai **Zakkay**, and *Athlai* **Athlay**.
29 And of the sons of Bani;
Meshullam, Malluch, and *Adaiah* **Ada Yah**,
Jashub **Yashub**, and Sheal, and Ramoth.
30 And of the sons of *Pahathmoab* **Pachath Moab**;
Adna, and *Chelal* **Kelal**,

Benaiah **Bena Yah**, *Maaseiah* **Maase Yah**,
Mattaniah **Mattan Yah**, *Bezaleel* **Besal El**,
and *Binnui* **Binnuy**, and *Manasseh* **Menash Sheh**.
31 And *of* the sons of Harim;
Eliezer **Eli Ezer**, *Ishijah* **Yishshi Yah**,
Malchiah **Malki Yah**, *Shemaiah* **Shema Yah**,
Shimeon **Shimon**,
32 *Benjamin* **Ben Yamin**, Malluch,
and *Shemariah* **Shemar Yah**.
33 Of the sons of Hashum;
Mattenai **Mattenay**, *Mattathah* **Mattattah**,
Zabad, *Eliphelet* **Eli Phelet**, *Jeremai* **Yeremay**,
Manasseh **Menash Sheh**, and *Shimei* **Shimi**.
34 Of the sons of Bani;
Maadai **Maaday**, *Amram* **Am Ram**, and Uel,
35 *Benaiah* **Bena Yah**, *Bedeiah* **Bede Yah**,
Chelluh **Keluhay**,
36 *Vaniah* **Van Yah**, Meremoth, *Eliashib* **El Yashib**,
37 *Mattaniah* **Mattan Yah**, *Mattenai* **Mattenay**,
and *Jaasau* **Yaasu**,
38 And Bani, and *Binnui* **Binnuy**, *Shimei* **Shimi**,
39 And *Shelemiah* **Shelem Yah**, and Nathan,
and *Adaiah* **Ada Yah**,
40 *Machnadebai* **Mach Nadbay**,
Shashai **Shashay**, *Sharai* **Sharay**,
41 *Azareel* **Azar El**, and *Shelemiah* **Shelem Yah**,
Shemariah **Shemar Yah**,
42 Shallum, *Amariah* **Amar Yah**, and *Joseph* **Yoseph**.
43 Of the sons of Nebo;
Jeiel **Yei El**, *Mattithiah* **Mattith Yah**,
Zabad, Zebina, *Jadau* **Yiddo**,
and *Joel* **Yah El**, *Benaiah* **Bena Yah**.
44 All these *had taken* **bore** strange *wives* **women**:
and *some* of them had *wives* **women**
by whom they *had children* **set sons**.

KEY TO INTERPRETING THE EXEGESES:
King James text is in regular type;
Text under exegeses is in oblique type;
Text of exegeses is in bold type.

NECHEM YAH WEEPS OVER THE SURVIVORS

1 The words of *Nehemiah* **Nechem Yah**
the son of *Hachaliah* **Hachal Yah**.
And it *came to pass* **became**, in the month *Chisleu* **Kislav**,
in the twentieth year, as I was in Shushan the palace,
2 That Hanani, one of my brethren, came,
he and *certain* men of *Judah* **Yah Hudah**;
and I asked them
concerning the *Jews* **Yah Hudiym** that had escaped,
which *were left* **survived** of the captivity,
and concerning *Jerusalem* **Yeru Shalem**.
3 And they said unto me,
The *remnant* **survivors**
that *are left* **survived** of the captivity
there in the *province* **jurisdiction**
are in great *affliction* **evil** and reproach:
the wall of *Jerusalem* **Yeru Shalem** also is broken down,
and the *gates* **portals** thereof are burned with fire.
4 And it *came to pass* **became**, when I heard these words,
that I *sat down* **settled** and wept,
and mourned *certain* days, and fasted, and prayed
before **at the face of**
the God **Elohim** of *heaven* **the heavens**,
5 And said, I beseech thee,
O *LORD God* **Yah Veh Elohim** of *heaven* **the heavens**,
the great and *terrible God* **awesome El**,
that *keepeth* **guardeth** covenant and mercy
for them that love him
and *observe* **guard** his *commandments* **misvoth**:
6 Let thine ear now *be attentive* **hearken**,
and thine eyes open,
that thou mayest hear the prayer of thy servant,
which I pray *before thee now* **at thy face this day**,
by day and **by** night,
for the *children* **sons** of *Israel* **Yisra El** thy servants,
and *confess* **extend hands for** the sins
of the *children* **sons** of *Israel* **Yisra El**,
which we have sinned against thee:
both I and my father's house have sinned.
7 **In despoiling,**
We have *dealt very corruptly* **despoiled** against thee,
and have not *kept* **guarded** the *commandments* **misvoth**,
nor the statutes, nor the judgments,
which thou
commandedst **misvahedst** thy servant *Moses* **Mosheh**.
8 Remember, I beseech thee,
the word that thou *commandedst* **misvahedst**
thy servant *Moses* **Mosheh**, saying,
If ye *transgress* **treason**,
I *will* **shall** scatter you abroad among the *nations* **people**:
9 But if ye turn unto me,
and *keep* **guard** my *commandments* **misvoth**,
and *do* **work** them;
though there were of you *cast out* **expelled**
unto the *uttermost part* **extremity** of the *heaven* **heavens**,
yet *will* **shall** I gather them from thence,
and *will* **shall** bring them unto the place that I have chosen
to *set* **tabernacle** my name there.
10 Now these are thy servants and thy people,
whom thou hast redeemed
by thy great *power* **force**, and by thy strong hand.
11 O *Lord* **Adonay**, I beseech thee,
let now thine ear *be attentive* **hearken**
to the prayer of thy servant,
and to the prayer of thy servants,
who *desire* **delight** to *fear* **awe** thy name:
and prosper, I *pray* **beseech** thee, thy servant this day,
and *grant* **give** him *mercy* **mercies**
in the *sight* **face** of this man.
For I was the *king's cupbearer* **sovereign's butler**.

ARTACH SHASHTA SENDS NECHEM YAH TO YERU SHALEM

2 And it *came to pass* **became**, in the month Nisan,
in the twentieth year
of *Artaxerxes* **Artach Shashta** the *king* **sovereign**,
that wine was *before him* **at his face**:

and I *took up* **lifted** the wine,
and gave it unto the *king* **sovereign**.
Now I had not been *beforetime*
sad in **evil at** his *presence* **face**.
2 Wherefore the *king* **sovereign** said unto me,
Why is thy *countenance sad* **face evil**,
seeing thou art not sick?
this is *nothing* **naught** *else* but *sorrow of* **an evil** heart.
Then I was *very sore afraid* **mighty aboundingly awed**,
3 And said unto the *king* **sovereign**,
Let the king live for ever **The sovereign liveth eternally**:
why should not my *countenance* **face** be *sad* **evil**,
when the city,
the *place* **house** of my fathers' *sepulchres* **tombs**,
lieth waste **be parched**,
and the *gates* **portals** thereof are consumed with fire?
4 Then the *king* **sovereign** said unto me,
For what *dost thou make request* **seekest thou**?
So I prayed to *the God* **Elohim** of *heaven* **the heavens**.
5 And I said unto the *king* **sovereign**,
If it *please* **be good with** the *king* **sovereign**,
and if thy servant *have found favour* **be well—pleased**
in **at** thy *sight* **face**,
that thou *wouldest* **shouldest** send me
unto *Judah* **Yah Hudah**,
unto the city of my fathers' *sepulchres* **tombs**,
that I may build it.
6 And the *king* **sovereign** said unto me,
(the *queen* **mistress** also *sitting* **settled** by him,)
For how long shall thy *journey* **walk** be?
and when *wilt* **shalt** thou return?
So it *pleased* **was good at the face of** the *king* **sovereign**
to send me;
and I *set* **gave** him *a time* **an appointment**.
7 Moreover I said unto the *king* **sovereign**,
If it *please* **be good with** the *king* **sovereign**,
let *letters* **epistles** be given me
to the governors beyond the river,
that they may *convey* **pass** me over
till I come into *Judah* **Yah Hudah**;
8 And *a letter* **an epistle** unto Asaph
the *keeper* **guard** of the *king's forest* **sovereign's paradise**,
that he may give me timber
to *make* **fell** beams for the *gates* **portals** of the palace
which *appertained* **be** to the house,
and for the wall of the city,
and for the house that I shall enter into.
And the *king granted* **sovereign gave** me,
according to the good hand of my *God* **Elohim** upon me.
9 Then I came to the governors beyond the river,
and gave them the *king's letters* **sovereign's epistles**.
Now the *king* **sovereign** had sent *captains* **governors**
of the *army* **valiant men** and *horsemen* **cavalry** with me.
10 When Sanballat the *Horonite* **Horoniy**,
and *Tobiah* **Tobi Yah** the servant,
the *Ammonite* **Ammoniy**, heard of it,
it grieved them exceedingly
in being evil, it was evil to them
that there was come a *man* **human**
to seek the *welfare* **good**
of the *children* **sons** of *Israel* **Yisra El**.

NECHEM YAH EXAMINES THE RUINED WALLS

11 So I came to *Jerusalem* **Yeru Shalem**,
and was there three days.
12 And I arose in the night, I and some few men with me;
neither told I any *man* **human**
what my *God* **Elohim** had *put* **given** in my heart
to *do* **work** at *Jerusalem* **Yeru Shalem**:
neither was there any *beast* **animal** with me,
save the *beast* **animal** that I rode upon.
13 And I went out by night by the *gate* **portal** of the valley,
even before **at the face of**
the *dragon well* **monster fountain**,
and to the *dung port* **dunghill portal**,
and *viewed* **was examining**
the walls of *Jerusalem* **Yeru Shalem**,
which were broken down,
and the *gates* **portals** thereof were consumed with fire.
14 Then I *went* **passed** on to the *gate* **portal** of the fountain,
and to the *king's* **sovereign's** pool:
but there was no place
for the *beast* **animal** that was under me to pass.
15 Then *went I up* **I ascended** in the night
by the *brook* **wadi**,
and *viewed* **examined** the wall, and turned back,
and entered by the *gate* **portal** of the valley,
and *so* returned.
16 And the *rulers* **prefects** knew not whither I went,
or what I *did* **worked**;
neither had I *as yet* **thus** told it to the *Jews* **Yah Hudiym**,
nor to the priests, nor to the nobles,
nor to the *rulers* **prefects**, nor to the rest
that *did* **worked** the work.
17 Then said I unto them,
ye see the *distress* **evil** that we are in,
how *Jerusalem lieth waste* **Yeru Shalem be parched**,
and the *gates* **portals** thereof *are* burned with fire: come,
and let us build up the wall of *Jerusalem* **Yeru Shalem**,
that we be no more a reproach.
18 Then I told them of the hand of my *God* **Elohim**
which was good upon me;
as also the *king's* **sovereign's** words
that he had *spoken* **said** unto me.
And they said, Let us rise up and build.
So they strengthened their hands for this good *work*.
19 But when Sanballat the *Horonite* **Horoniy**,
and *Tobiah* **Tobi Yah** the servant,
the *Ammonite* **Ammoniy**,
and Geshem the *Arabian* **Arabiy**, heard it,
they *laughed* **derided** us *to scorn*, and despised us,
and said, What is this *thing* **word** that ye *do* **work**?
will **shall** ye rebel against the *king* **sovereign**?
20 Then *answered I them* **returned I word**,
and said unto them,
The *God* **Elohim** of *heaven* **the heavens**,
he *will* **shall** prosper us;
therefore we his servants *will* **shall** arise and build:
but ye have no *portion* **allotment**, nor *right* **justness**,
nor memorial, in *Jerusalem* **Yeru Shalem**.

THE WALL BUILDERS

3 Then *Eliashib* **El Yashib** the *high* **great** priest
rose *up* with his brethren the priests,
and they builded the *sheep gate* **flock portal**;
they *sanctified* **hallowed** it,
and *set up* **stood** the doors of it;
even unto the tower of Meah they *sanctified* **hallowed** it,
unto the tower of *Hananeel* **Hanan El**.
2 And *next unto him* **at his hand**
builded the men of *Jericho* **Yericho**.
And *next to them* **at their hand**
builded *Zaccur* **Zakkur** the son of Imri.
3 But the fish *gate* **portal**
did the sons of *Hassenaah* **Senaah** build,
who *also laid* **felled** the beams thereof,
and *set up* **stood** the doors thereof,
the locks thereof, and the bars thereof.
4 And *next unto them* **at their hand**
repaired **strengthened** Meremoth
the son of *Urijah* **Uri Yah**, the son of *Koz* **Qos**.
And *next unto them* **at their hand**
repaired **strengthened** Meshullam
the son of *Berechiah* **Berech Yah**,
the son of *Meshezabeel* **Meshezab El**.
And *next unto them* **at their hand**
repaired Zadok **strengthened Sadoq** the son of Baana.
5 And *next unto them* **at their hand**
the *Tekoites repaired* **Teqoaiy strengthened**;
but their *nobles* **mighty** put not their necks
to the *work* **service** of their *Lord* **Adonay**.
6 Moreover the old *gate* **portal**
repaired Jehoiada **strengthened Yah Yada**
the son of *Paseah* **Paseach**,
and Meshullam the son of *Besodeiah* **Besod Yah**;
they *laid* **felled** the beams thereof,
and *set up* **stood** the doors thereof,
and the locks thereof, and the bars thereof.
7 And *next unto them* **at their hand**
repaired **strengthened**
Melatiah **Melat Yah** the *Gibeonite* **Giboniy**,
and *Jadon* **Yadon** the *Meronothite* **Meronothiy**,

the men of *Gibeon* **Gibon**, and of *Mizpah* **Mispeh**,
unto the throne of the governor on this side the river.
8 *Next unto him* **At his hand**
repaired Uzziel **strengthened Uzzi El**
the son of *Harhaiah* **Harha Yah**, of the *goldsmiths* **refiners**.
Next unto him **At his hand**
also *repaired Hananiah* **strengthened Hanan Yah**
the son of *one of* the *apothecaries* **perfumers**,
and they *fortified Jerusalem* **left Yeru Shalem**
unto the broad wall.
9 And *next unto them* **at their hand**
repaired Rephaiah **strengthened Repha Yah**
the son of Hur, the *ruler* **governor**
of the half *part* **circuit** of *Jerusalem* **Yeru Shalem**.
10 And *next unto them* **at their hand**
repaired Jedaiah **strengthened Yeda Yah**
the son of *Harumaph* **Harum Aph**,
even over against his house.
And *next unto him* **at his hand**
repaired **strengthened** Hattush
the son of *Hashabniah* **Hashabne Yah**.
11 *Malchijah* **Malki Yah** the son of Harim,
and *Hashub* **Hashshub**
the son of *Pahathmoab* **Pachath Moab**,
repaired **strengthened** the *other piece* **second measure**,
and the tower of the furnaces.
12 And *next unto him* **at his hand**
repaired **strengthened** Shallum
the son of *Halohesh* **Lochesh**, the *ruler* **governor**
of the half *part* **circuit** of *Jerusalem* **Yeru Shalem**,
he and his daughters.
13 The valley *gate repaired* **portal strengthened** Hanun,
and the *inhabitants* **settlers** of *Zanoah* **Zanoach**;
they built it, and *set up* **stood** the doors thereof,
the locks thereof, and the bars thereof,
and a thousand cubits on the wall
unto the *dung gate* **dunghill portal**.
14 But the *dung gate* **dunghill portal**
repaired Malchiah **strengthened Malki Yah**
the son of Rechab,
the *ruler* **governor** of *part* **the circuit**
of *Bethhaccerem* **Beth Hak Kerem**;
he built it, and *set up* **stood** the doors thereof,
the locks thereof, and the bars thereof.
15 But the *gate* **portal** of the fountain
repaired **strengthened** Shallun
the son of *Colhozeh* **Kol Hozeh**,
the *ruler* **governor** of *part* **the circuit** of *Mizpah* **Mispeh**;
he built it, and covered it,
and *set up* **stood** the doors thereof,
the locks thereof, and the bars thereof,
and the wall of the pool of *Siloah* **Shiloach**
by the *king's* **sovereign's** garden,
and unto the *stairs* **steps**
that *go down* **descend** from the city of David.
16 After him
repaired Nehemiah **strengthened Nechem Yah**
the son of *Azbuk* **Az Buq**, the *ruler* **governor**
of the half *part* **circuit** of *Bethzur* **Beth Sur**,
unto *the place* over against the *sepulchres* **tombs** of David,
and to the pool that was *made* **worked**,
and unto the house of the mighty.
17 After him *repaired* **strengthened** the *Levites* **Leviym**,
Rehum **Rechum** the son of Bani.
Next unto him **At his hand**
repaired Hashabiah **strengthened Hashab Yah**,
the *ruler* **governor** of the half *part* **circuit** of *Keilah* **Qeilah**,
in his *part* **circuit**.
18 After him *repaired* **strengthened** their brethren,
Bavai **Bavay** the son of Henadad,
the *ruler* **governor** of the half *part* **circuit** of *Keilah* **Qeilah**.
19 And *next to him* **at his hand**
repaired **strengthened** Ezer the son of *Jeshua* **Yah Shua**,
the *ruler* **governor** of *Mizpah* **Mispeh**,
another piece **a second measure**
over against the *going up* **ascent** to the armoury
at the *turning of the wall* **corner**.
20 After him Baruch the son of *Zabbai* **Zakkay**
earnestly repaired **kindled to strengthen**
the *other piece* **second measure**,
from the *turning of the wall* **corner** unto the *door* **portal**
of the house of *Eliashib* **El Yashib** the *high* **great** priest.
21 After him *repaired* **strengthened** Meremoth
the son of *Urijah* **Uri Yah** the son of *Koz* **Qos**
another piece **a second measure**,
from the *door* **portal** of the house of *Eliashib* **El Yashib**
even to the *end* **conclusion**
of the house of *Eliashib* **El Yashib**.
22 And after him *repaired* **strengthened** the priests,
the men of the *plain* **environs**.
23 After him *repaired* **strengthened**
Benjamin **Ben Yamin** and *Hashub* **Hashshub**
over against their house.
After him *repaired Azariah* **strengthened Azar Yah**
the son of *Maaseiah* **Maase Yah**
the son of *Ananiah* **Anan Yah** by his house.
24 After him *repaired* **strengthened**
Binnui **Binnuy** the son of Henadad
another piece **a second measure**,
from the house of *Azariah* **Azar Yah**
unto the *turning of the wall* **corner**, even unto the corner.
25 Palal the son of Uzai,
over against the *turning of the wall* **corner**,
and the tower which *lieth* **goeth** *out*
from the *king's* **sovereign's** high house,
that was by the court of the *prison* **guard yard**.
After him *Pedaiah* **Pedah Yah** the son of Parosh.
26 *Moreover*
the *Nethinims dwelt* **Dedicates settled** in Ophel,
unto the place over against the water *gate* **portal**
toward the *east* **rising**, and the tower *that lieth* **goeth** out.
27 After them the *Tekoites* **Teqoaiy**
repaired another piece **strengthened a second measure**,
over against the great tower that *lieth* **goeth** out,
even unto the wall of Ophel.
28 From above the horse *gate* **portal**
repaired **strengthened** the priests,
every one **each man** over against his house.
29 After them *repaired* **strengthened**
Zadok **Sadoq** the son of Immer
over against his house.
After him *repaired* **strengthened**
also *Shemaiah* **Shema Yah**
the son of *Shechaniah* **Shechan Yah**,
the *keeper* **guard** of the *east gate* **portal toward the rising**.
30 After him *repaired Hananiah* **strengthened Hanan Yah**
the son of *Shelemiah* **Shelem Yah**,
and Hanun the sixth son of *Zalaph* **Salaph**
another piece **a second measure**.
After him *repaired* **strengthened** Meshullam
the son of *Berechiah* **Berech Yah** over against his chamber.
31 After him *repaired Malchiah* **strengthened Malki Yah**
the *goldsmith's* **refiner's** son
unto the *place* **house** of the *Nethinims* **Dedicates**,
and of the merchants,
over against the *gate* **portal** Miphkad,
and to the *going up* **upper room** of the corner.
32 And between the *going up* **upper room** of the corner
unto the *sheep gate* **flock portal**
repaired **strengthened**
the *goldsmiths* **refiners** and the merchants.

THE YAH HUDIYM DERIDED

4 But it *came to pass* **became**,
that when Sanballat heard that we builded the wall,
he was *wroth* **inflamed**,
and *took great indignation* **his vexation abounded**,
and *mocked* **derided** the *Jews* **Yah Hudiym**.
2 And he *spake before* **said at the face of** his brethren
and the *army* **valiant men** of *Samaria* **Shomeron**,
and said,
What *do* **work** these *feeble Jews* **languid Yah Hudiym**?
will **shall** they *fortify* **be left to** themselves?
will **shall** they sacrifice?
will **shall** they *make an end* **finish** in a day?
will **shall** they *revive* **enliven** the stones
out of the heaps of the *rubbish* **dust** which are burned?
3 Now *Tobiah* **Tobi Yah** the *Ammonite* **Ammoniy**
was by him, and he said,
Even that which they build, if a fox *go up* **ascend**,
he shall even *break down* **split** their stone wall.

4 Hear, O our *God* **Elohim**;
for we are *despised* **disrespected**:
and turn their reproach upon their own head,
and give them for *a prey* **plunder** in the land of captivity:
5 And cover not their *iniquity* **perversity**,
and let not their sin be *blotted out* **wiped away**
from *before thee* **thy face**:
for they have *provoked* **vexed** thee *to anger*
before the builders.
6 So built we the wall;
and all the wall was *joined* **bound** *together*
unto the half thereof:
for the people had a *mind* **heart** to work.
7 But it *came to pass* **became**,
that when Sanballat, and *Tobiah* **Tobi Yah**,
and the *Arabians* **Arabiy**, and the *Ammonites* **Ammoniy**,
and the *Ashdodites* **Ashdodiy**,
heard that the walls of *Jerusalem* **Yeru Shalem**
were *made up* **ascended**,
and that the breaches began to be stopped,
then they were *very wroth* **mightily inflamed**,
8 And conspired all of them together
to come and to fight against *Jerusalem* **Yeru Shalem**,
and to *hinder* **work error to** it.
9 Nevertheless we *made our prayer* **prayed**
unto our *God* **Elohim**,
and *set a watch* **stood an underguard** against them
by day and **by** night, *because of them* **at their face**.

THE YAH HUDIYM DISCOURAGED

10 And *Judah* **Yah Hudah** said,
The *strength* **force**
of the *bearers of burdens* **burdenbearers**
is *decayed* **faltered**,
and *there is much rubbish* **dust aboundeth**;
so that we are not able to build the wall.
11 And our *adversaries* **tribulators** said,
They shall not know, neither see,
till we come in the midst among them,
and *slay* **slaughter** them, and cause the work to cease.
12 And it *came to pass* **became**,
that when the *Jews* **Yah Hudiym**
which *dwelt* **settled** by them came,
they said unto us ten times,
From all places whence ye shall return unto us —
they will be upon you.
13 Therefore *set* **stood** I
in the *lower* **nether parts of the** places behind the wall,
and on the *higher places* **clearing**,
I even *set* **stood** the people after their families
with their swords, their *spears* **javelins**, and their bows.
14 And I *looked* **saw**, and rose *up*,
and said unto the nobles, and to the *rulers* **prefects**,
and to the rest of the people,
Be not ye *afraid of them* **Awe ye not at their face**:
remember *the Lord* **Adonay**,
which is great and *terrible* **awesome**,
and fight for your brethren, your sons, and your daughters,
your *wives* **women**, and your houses.
15 And it *came to pass* **became**,
when our enemies heard that it was known unto us,
and *God* **Elohim** had *brought* **broken** their counsel
to nought,
that we returned all of us to the wall,
every one **each man** unto his work.
16 And it *came to pass* **became**, from that *time* **day** forth,
that the half of my *servants* **lads**
wrought **worked** in the work,
and the other half of them held both the *spears* **javelins**,
the *shields* **bucklers**, and the bows, and the habergeons;
and the *rulers* **governors** were behind
all the house of *Judah* **Yah Hudah**.
17 They which builded on the wall,
and they that bare burdens, with those that laded,
every one with one *of his hands* **hand**
wrought **worked** in the work,
and with *the other* **one** *hand* held a *weapon* **spear**.
18 For the builders, *every one* **each man** had his sword
girded by **bound on** his *side* **loins**, and so builded.
And he that *sounded* **blast** the trumpet was by me.
19 And I said unto the nobles, and to the rulers,
and to the rest of the people,
The work is *great* **abundant** and large,
and we are separated upon the wall,
one **man** far from *another* **brother**.
20 In what place *therefore*
ye hear the *sound* **voice** of the trumpet,
resort **gather** ye thither unto us:
our *God* **Elohim** shall fight for us.
21 So we *laboured* **worked** in the work:
and half of them held the *spears* **javelins**
from the *rising* **ascending** of the *morning* **dawn**
till the stars *appeared* **went**.
22 Likewise at the same time said I unto the people,
Let *every one* **each man** with his *servant* **lad**
lodge **stay overnight** within *Jerusalem* **Yeru Shalem**,
that in the night they may be *a guard* **an underguard** to us,
and *labour* **work** on the day.
23 So neither I, nor my brethren, nor my *servants* **lads**,
nor the men of the *guard* **underguard**
which followed **after** me,
none of us *put off* **stripped** our clothes,
saving that every one put them off for washing
each man went with his spear for water.

THE YAH HUDIYM ARE REGRETFUL

5 And there *was* **became** a great cry
of the people and of their *wives* **women**
against their brethren the *Jews* **Yah Hudiym.**
2 For there were that said,
We, our sons, and our daughters, are many:
therefore we take up *corn* **crop** *for them,*
that we may eat, and live.
3 *Some* also there were that said,
We have *mortgaged* **pledged** our *lands* **fields**,
vineyards, and houses,
that we might *buy corn* **take crop**,
because of the *dearth* **famine**.
4 There were also that said,
We have borrowed *money* **silver**
for the *king's tribute* **sovereign's measure**,
and that upon our *lands* **fields** and vineyards.
5 Yet now our flesh is as the flesh of our brethren,
our *children* **sons** as their *children* **sons**:
and, *lo* **behold**, we *bring into bondage* **subdue**
our sons and our daughters to be servants,
and *some* of our daughters
are *brought unto bondage* **subdued** *already*:
neither is it in *our power* **the El of our hands**
to redeem them;
for other men have our *lands* **fields** and vineyards.
6 And I was *very angry* **mighty inflamed**
when I heard their cry and these words.
7 Then *I consulted* **my heart reigned** with myself,
and I *rebuked* **contended**
with the nobles, and the *rulers* **prefects**,
and said unto them,
Ye *exact usury* **bear interest**,
every one **each man** of his brother.
And I *set* **gave** a great *assembly* **congregation**
against them.
8 And I said unto them,
We after our *ability* **sufficiency**
have *redeemed* **chatteled** our brethren
the *Jews* **Yah Hudiym**
which were sold unto the *heathen* **goyim**;
and *will* **shall** ye *even* sell your brethren?
or shall they be sold unto us?
Then *held they their peace* **they hushed**,
and found *nothing to answer* **no word**.
9 Also I said,
The word that ye work It is not good *that ye do*:
ought ye not to walk in the *fear* **awe** of our *God* **Elohim**
because of the reproach
of the *heathen* **goyim** our enemies?
10 I likewise, and my brethren, and my *servants* **lads**,
might exact of them *money* **silver** and *corn* **crop**:
I *pray* **beseech** you, let us leave off this *usury* **interest**.
11 Restore, I *pray* **beseech** you, to them, even this day,
their *lands* **fields**, their vineyards,
their oliveyards, and their houses,
also the hundredth *part* of the *money* **silver**,

and of the *corn* **crop**, the *wine* **juice**, and the oil,
that ye exact of them.
12 Then said they, We *will* **shall** restore them,
and *will require nothing* **shall seek naught** of them;
so *will* **shall** we *do* **work** as thou sayest.
Then I called the priests, and *took an oath of* **oathed** them,
that they should *do* **work** according to this *promise* **word**.
13 Also I shook my *lap* **bosom**, and said,
So *God* **Elohim** shake out every man from his house,
and from his labour,
that *performeth* **raiseth** not this *promise* **word**,
even thus be he shaken out, and emptied.
And all the congregation said, Amen,
and *praised the LORD* **halaled Yah Veh**.
And the people *did* **worked**
according to this *promise* **word**.
14 Moreover from the *time* **day**
that I was *appointed* **misvahed** to be their governor
in the land of *Judah* **Yah Hudah**,
from the twentieth year
even unto the two and thirtieth year
of *Artaxerxes* **Artach Shashta** the *king* **sovereign**,
that is, twelve years,
I and my brethren
have not eaten the bread of the governor.
15 But the former governors
that had been before me **at my face**
were *chargeable* **heavy** unto the people,
and had taken of them bread and wine,
beside **after** forty shekels of silver; *yea* **however**,
even their *servants* **lads**
bare rule **dominated** over the people:
but so *did* **worked** not I,
because **at the face** of the *fear* **awe** of *God* **Elohim**.
16 Yea, also I *continued* **held fast** in the work of this wall,
neither *bought* **chatteled** we any *land* **field**:
and all my *servants* **lads**
were gathered thither unto the work.
17 *Moreover*
there were at my table an hundred and fifty **men**
of the *Jews* **Yah Hudiym** and *rulers* **prefects**,
beside those that came unto us
from among the *heathen* **goyim** that are **round** about us.
18 Now that which was *prepared* **worked**
for me *daily* **one day**
was one ox and six *choice sheep* **pure flock**;
also *fowls* **birds** were *prepared* **worked** for me,
and once in ten days
store **aboundance** of all sorts of wine:
yet for all this
required **sought** not I the bread of the governor,
because the *bondage* **service** was heavy upon this people.
19 *Think* **Remember** upon me, my *God* **Elohim**, for good,
according to all that I have *done* **worked** for this people.

THE YAH HUDIYM ACCUSED

6 Now it *came to pass* **became**,
when Sanballat, and *Tobiah* **Tobi Yah**,
and Geshem the *Arabian* **Arabiy**,
and the rest of our enemies,
heard that I had builded the wall,
and that there was no breach *left* **remaining** therein;
(*though at* **however until** that time
I had not *set up* **stood** the doors upon the *gates* **portals**;)
2 That Sanballat and Geshem sent unto me, saying, Come,
let us *meet* **congregate** *together*
in some *one* of the villages in the *plain* **valley** of Ono.
But they *thought* **fabricated** to *do* **work** me *mischief* **evil**.
3 And I sent *messengers* **angels** unto them, saying,
I am *doing* **working** a great work,
so that I cannot *come down* **descend**:
why should the work cease,
whilst I *leave* **slacken** it, and *come down* **descend** to you?
4 Yet they sent unto me four times
after this *sort* **word**;
and I *answered* **returned** them
after the same *manner* **word**.
5 Then sent Sanballat his *servant* **lad** unto me
in like *manner* **word** the fifth time
with an open *letter* **epistle** in his hand;
6 Wherein was *written* **inscribed**,
It is *reported* **heard** among the *heathen* **goyim**,
and Gashmu saith it,
that thou and the *Jews* **Yah Hudiym**
think **fabricate** to rebel:
for *which cause* **thus** thou buildest the wall,
that thou mayest be their *king* **sovereign**,
according to these words.
7 And thou hast also *appointed* **stood** prophets
to *preach* **call out** of thee at *Jerusalem* **Yeru Shalem**,
saying, There is a *king* **sovereign** in *Judah* **Yah Hudah**:
and now shall it be *reported* **heard**
to **by** the *king* **sovereign** according to these words.
Come now therefore, and let us *take* counsel together.
8 Then I sent unto him, saying,
There are no such *things done* **words** as thou sayest,
but thou *feignest* **contrivest** them out of thine own heart.
9 For they all *made* **awe** us *afraid*, saying,
Their hands shall *be weakened* **slacken** from the work,
that it be not *done* **worked**.
Now therefore, *O God*,
strengthen my hands.
10 Afterward
I came unto the house of *Shemaiah* **Shema Yah**
the son of *Delaiah* **Dela Yah**
the son of *Mehetabeel* **Mehetab El**,
who was *shut up* **restrained**;
and he said, Let us *meet* **congregate** *together*
in the house of *God* **Elohim**, within the *temple* **manse**,
and let us shut the doors of the *temple* **manse**:
for they *will* **shall** come to *slay* **slaughter** thee; yea,
in the night *will* **shall** they come to *slay* **slaughter** thee.
11 And I said, should such a man as I flee?
and who is there, that, *being* as I *am*,
would **should** go into the *temple* **manse**
to *save his life* **live**?
I *will* **shall** not go in.
12 And, *lo* **behold**,
I *perceived* **recognized**
that *God* **Elohim** had not sent him;
but that he *pronounced* **worded** this prophecy against me:
for *Tobiah* **Tobi Yah** and Sanballat had hired him.
13 Therefore was he hired, that I should be *afraid* **awed**,
and *do* **work** so, and sin,
and that they might *have matter* **become**
for an evil *report* **name**,
that they might reproach me.
14 My *God* **Elohim**,
think **remember** thou upon *Tobiah* **Tobi Yah** and Sanballat
according to these their works,
and on the prophetess *Noadiah* **Noad Yah**,
and the rest of the prophets,
that *would have put me in fear* **should have me awe**.
15 So the wall *was finished* **they did shalam**
in the twenty and fifth *day* of *the month* Elul,
in fifty and two days.
16 And it *came to pass* **became**,
that when all our enemies heard thereof,
and all the *heathen* **goyim** that were **round** about us
saw these *things*,
they were *much cast down* **mightily fallen**
in their own eyes:
for they perceived that this work
was *wrought* **worked** of our *God* **Elohim**.
17 Moreover
in those days the nobles of *Judah* **Yah Hudah**
sent many letters **abounded passing their epistles**
unto *Tobiah* **Tobi Yah**,
and *the letters* **those** of *Tobiah* **Tobi Yah** came unto them.
18 For there were many **masters** in *Judah* **Yah Hudah**
sworn **oathed** unto him,
because he was the son in law of *Shechaniah* **Shechan Yah**
the son of *Arah* **Arach**;
and his son *Johanan* **Yah Hanan**
had taken the daughter of Meshullam
the son of *Berechiah* **Berech Yah**.
19 Also they *reported* **said** his good deeds
before me **at my face**,
and *uttered* **brought** my words to him.
And *Tobiah* **Tobi Yah** sent *letters* **epistles**
to *put me in fear* **have me awe**.

NECHEM YAH COMMANDS HANANI AND HANAN YAH CONCERNING YERU SHALEM

7 Now it *came to pass* **became,**
when the wall was built,
and I had *set up* **stood** the doors,
and the porters and the singers and the *Levites* **Leviym**
were *appointed* **mustered,**
2 That I *gave* **misvahed** my brother Hanani,
and *Hananiah* **Hanan Yah**
the *ruler* **governor** of the palace,
charge over Jerusalem **concerning Yeru Shalem**:
for he was a *faithful man* **man of truth,**
and *feared God* **awed Elohim** above many.
3 And I said unto them,
Let not
the *gates* **portals** of *Jerusalem* **Yeru Shalem** be opened
until the sun be hot;
and while they stand by,
let them shut the doors, and *bar* **hold** them:
and *appoint watches* **stand guards**
of the *inhabitants* **settlers** of *Jerusalem* **Yeru Shalem,**
every one **each man** in his *watch* **underguard,**
and *every one* **each man** to be over against his house.
4 Now the city was *large* **broad in space** and great:
but the people were few therein,
and the houses were not builded.

THE GENEALOGY OF THE EXILED

5 And my *God put* **Elohim gave** into mine heart
to gather *together* the nobles,
and the *rulers* **prefects,** and the people,
that they might be *reckoned by genealogy* **genealogized.**
And I found a *register* **scroll** of the genealogy of them
which *came up* **ascended** at the first,
and found *written* **inscribed** therein,
6 These are the *children* **sons** of the *province* **jurisdiction,**
that *went up* **ascended** out of the captivity,
of those that had been *carried away* **exiled,**
whom *Nebuchadnezzar* **Nebukadnets Tsar,**
the *king* **sovereign** of *Babylon* **Babel**
had *carried away* **exiled,**
and *came again* **returned**
to *Jerusalem* **Yeru Shalem** and to *Judah* **Yah Hudah,**
every one **each man** unto his city;
7 Who came with *Zerubbabel* **Zerub Babel,**
Jeshua **Yah Shua,** *Nehemiah* **Nechem Yah,**
Azariah **Azar Yah,** *Raamiah* **Raam Yah,**
Nahamani **Nachamani,** *Mordecai* **Mordechay,** Bilshan,
Mispereth, *Bigvai* **Bigvay,** *Nehum* **Nechum,** Baanah.
The number, *I say,*
of the men of the people of *Israel* **Yisra El** *was this;*
8 The *children* **sons** of Parosh,
two thousand an hundred seventy and two.
9 The *children* **sons** of *Shephatiah* **Shaphat Yah,**
three hundred seventy and two.
10 The *children* **sons** of *Arah* **Arach,**
six hundred fifty and two.
11 The *children* **sons** of *Pahathmoab* **Pachath Moab**
of the *children* **sons** of *Jeshua* **Yah Shua** and *Joab* **Yah Ab,**
two thousand and eight hundred and eighteen.
12 The *children* **sons** of Elam
a thousand two hundred fifty and four.
13 The *children* **sons** of Zattu,
eight hundred forty and five.
14 The *children* **sons** of *Zaccai* **Zakkay,**
seven hundred and *threescore* **sixty.**
15 The *children* **sons** of *Binnui* **Binnuy,**
six hundred forty and eight.
16 The *children* **sons** of *Bebai* **Bebay,**
six hundred twenty and eight.
17 The *children* **sons** of Azgad,
two thousand three hundred twenty and two.
18 The *children* **sons** of *Adonikam* **Adoni Qam,**
six hundred *threescore* **sixty** and seven.
19 The *children* **sons** of *Bigvai* **Bigvay,**
two thousand *threescore* **sixty** and seven.
20 The *children* **sons** of Adin,
six hundred fifty and five.
21 The *children* **sons** of Ater
of *Hezekiah* **Yechizqi Yah,**
ninety and eight.
22 The *children* **sons** of Hashum,
three hundred twenty and eight.
23 The *children* **sons** of *Bezai* **Besay,**
three hundred twenty and four.
24 The *children* **sons** of Hariph,
an hundred and twelve.
25 The *children* **sons** of *Gibeon* **Gibon,**
ninety and five.
26 The men of *Bethlehem* **Beth Lechem** and Netophah,
an hundred *fourscore* **eighty** and eight.
27 The men of Anathoth,
an hundred twenty and eight.
28 The men of *Bethazmaveth* **Beth Azmaveth,**
forty and two.
29 The men of *Kirjathjearim* **Qiryath Arim,**
Chephirah **Kephirah,** and Beeroth,
seven hundred forty and three.
30 The men of Ramah and *Gaba* **Geba,**
six hundred twenty and one.
31 The men of Michmas,
an hundred and twenty and two.
32 The men of *Bethel* **Beth El** and *Ai* **Ay,**
an hundred twenty and three.
33 The men of the other Nebo,
fifty and two.
34 The *children* **sons** of the other Elam,
a thousand two hundred fifty and four.
35 The *children* **sons** of Harim,
three hundred and twenty.
36 The *children* **sons** of *Jericho* **Yericho,**
three hundred forty and five.
37 The *children* **sons** of Lod, Hadid, and Ono,
seven hundred twenty and one.
38 The *children* **sons** of Senaah,
three thousand nine hundred and thirty.
39 The priests:
the *children* **sons** of *Jedaiah* **Yeda Yah,**
of *the house of Jeshua* **Beth Yah Shua,**
nine hundred seventy and three.
40 The *children* **sons** of Immer,
a thousand fifty and two.
41 The *children* **sons** of *Pashur* **Pashchur,**
a thousand two hundred forty and seven.
42 The *children* **sons** of Harim,
a thousand and seventeen.
43 The *Levites* **Leviym**:
the *children* **sons** of *Jeshua* **Yah Shua,**
of *Kadmiel* **Qadmi El,**
and of the *children* **sons** of *Hodevah* **Hode Yah,**
seventy and four.
44 The singers:
the *children* **sons** of Asaph,
an hundred forty and eight.
45 The porters:
the *children* **sons** of Shallum,
the *children* **sons** of Ater,
the *children* **sons** of Talmon,
the *children* **sons** of *Akkub* **Aqqub,**
the *children* **sons** of Hatita,
the *children* **sons** of *Shobai* **Shobay,**
an hundred thirty and eight.
46 The *Nethinims* **Dedicates**:
the *children* **sons** of *Ziha* **Sicha,**
the *children* **sons** of Hashupha,
the *children* **sons** of Tabbaoth,
47 The *children* **sons** of *Keros* **Qeros,**
the *children* **sons** of Sia,
the *children* **sons** of Padon,
48 The *children* **sons** of Lebana,
the *children* **sons** of *Hagaba* **Hagabah,**
the *children* **sons** of *Shalmai* **Salmay,**
49 The *children* **sons** of Hanan,
the *children* **sons** of Giddel,
the *children* **sons** of *Gahar* **Gachar,**
50 The *children* **sons** of *Reaiah* **Rea Yah,**
the *children* **sons** of *Rezin* **Resin,**
the *children* **sons** of Nekoda,
51 The *children* **sons** of Gazzam,
the *children* **sons** of Uzza,
the *children* **sons** of *Phaseah* **Paseach,**

52 The *children* **sons** of *Besai* **Besay**,
the *children* **sons** of *Meunim* **Maoniym**,
the *children* **sons** of *Nephishesim* **Nephisim**,
53 The *children* **sons** of *Bakbuk* **Baqbuq**,
the *children* **sons** of *Hakupha* **Haqupha**,
the *children* **sons** of *Harhur* **Harchur**,
54 The *children* **sons** of *Bazlith* **Baslith**,
the *children* **sons** of *Mehida* **Mechida**,
the *children* **sons** of Harsha,
55 The *children* **sons** of *Barkos* **Barqos**,
the *children* **sons** of Sisera,
the *children* **sons** of *Tamah* **Temach**,
56 The *children* **sons** of *Neziah* **Nesiach**,
the *children* **sons** of Hatipha.
57 The *children* **sons** of *Solomon's* **Sholomoh's** servants:
the *children* **sons** of *Sotai* **Sotay**,
the *children* **sons** of Sophereth,
the *children* **sons** of Perida,
58 The *children* **sons** of *Jaala* **Yaalah**,
the *children* **sons** of *Darkon* **Darqon**,
the *children* **sons** of Giddel,
59 The *children* **sons** of *Shephatiah* **Shaphat Yah**,
the *children* **sons** of Hattil,
the *children* **sons** of
Pochereth of *Zebaim* **Sebayim**,
the *children* **sons** of Amon.
60 All the *Nethinims* **Dedicates**,
and the *children* **sons** of *Solomon's* **Sholomoh's** servants,
were three hundred ninety and two.
61 And these were they which *went up* **ascended** *also*
from *Telmelah* **Tel Melach**, *Telharesha* **Tel Harsha**,
Cherub, Addon, and Immer:
but they could not *shew* **tell** their father's house,
nor their seed,
whether they were of *Israel* **Yisra El**.
62 The *children* **sons** of *Delaiah* **Dela Yah**,
the *children* **sons** of *Tobiah* **Tobi Yah**,
the *children* **sons** of Nekoda,
six hundred forty and two.
63 And of the priests:
the *children* **sons** of *Habaiah* **Haba Yah**,
the *children* **sons** of *Koz* **Qos**,
the *children* **sons** of *Barzillai* **Barzillay**,
which took *one* of the daughters
of *Barzillai* **Barzillay** the *Gileadite* **Giladiy** to *wife* **woman**,
and was called after their name.
64 These sought their *register* **inscribings** among those
that were *reckoned by genealogy* **genealogized**,
but it was not found:
therefore were they, *as polluted,*
put **profaned** from the priesthood.
65 And the *Tirshatha* **governor** said unto them,
that they should not eat
of the *most holy things* **Holy of Holies**,
till there stood *up* a priest with Urim and Thummim.
66 The whole congregation *together* **as one**
was *forty* **four myriads**
and two thousand three hundred and *threescore* **sixty**,
67 Beside
their *manservants* **servants** and their *maidservants* **maids**,
of whom there were
seven thousand three hundred thirty and seven:
and they had two hundred forty and five
singing men **songsters** and *singing women* **songstresses**.
68 Their horses, seven hundred thirty and six:
their mules, two hundred forty and five:
69 Their camels, four hundred thirty and five:
six thousand seven hundred and twenty *asses* **he burros**.
70 And *some* **part** of the *chief* **head** of the fathers
gave unto the work.
The *Tirshatha* **governor** gave to the treasure
a thousand *drams* **drachmim** of gold,
fifty *basons* **sprinklers**,
five hundred and thirty priests' *garments* **coats**.
71 And *some* of the *chief* **head** of the fathers
gave to the treasure of the work
twenty thousand drams **two myriads drachmim** of gold,
and two thousand and two hundred *pound* **maneh**
of silver.
72 And that which the *rest* **survivors** of the people gave
was *twenty thousand drams* **two myriads drachmim**
of gold,
and two thousand *pound* **maneh** of silver,
and *threescore* **sixty** and seven priests' *garments* **coats**.
73 So the priests, and the *Levites* **Leviym**, and the porters,
and the singers, and *some* of the people,
and the *Nethinims* **Dedicates**, and all *Israel* **Yisra El**,
dwelt **settled** in their cities;
and when the seventh month *came* **touched**,
the *children* **sons** of *Israel* **Yisra El** were in their cities.

EZRA CALLS OUT THE TORAH

8 And all the people
gathered *themselves together* as one man
into the *street* **broadway**
that was *before* **at the face of** the water *gate* **portal**;
and they *spake* **said** unto Ezra the scribe
to bring the *book* **scroll**
of the *law* **torah** of *Moses* **Mosheh**,
which *the LORD* **Yah Veh** had *commanded* **misvahed**
to *Israel* **Yisra El**.
2 And Ezra the priest brought the *law* **torah**
before **at the face of** the congregation
both of men and women,
and all that *could hear* **discerned**
with understanding **hearkened**,
upon the first day of the seventh month.
3 And he *read* **called out** therein
before **at the face of** the *street* **broadway**
that was *before* **at the face of** the water *gate* **portal**
from the *morning* **light** until midday,
before **in front of** the men and the women,
and those that *could understand* **discerned**;
and the ears of all the people
were attentive unto the *book* **scroll** of the *law* **torah**.
4 And Ezra the scribe
stood upon a *pulpit* **tower** of *wood* **timber**,
which they had *made* **worked** for the *purpose* **word**;
and beside him stood *Mattithiah* **Mattith Yah**,
and Shema, and *Anaiah* **Ana Yah**,
and *Urijah* **Uri Yah**, and *Hilkiah* **Hilqi Yah**,
and *Maaseiah* **Maase Yah**, on his right *hand*;
and on his left *hand*, *Pedaiah* **Pedah Yah**,
and *Mishael* **Misha El**, and *Malchiah* **Malki Yah**,
and Hashum, and *Hashbadana* **Hashbad Danah**,
Zechariah **Zechar Yah**, and Meshullam.
5 And Ezra opened the *book* **scroll**
in the *sight* **eyes** of all the people;
(for he was above all the people;)
and when he opened it, all the people stood *up*:
6 And Ezra blessed *the LORD* **Yah Veh**,
the great *God* **Elohim**.
And all the people answered, Amen, Amen,
with lifting up **raising** their hands:
and they bowed their heads,
and *worshipped the LORD* **prostrated to Yah Veh**
with their *faces* **nostrils** to the *ground* **earth**.
7 Also *Jeshua* **Yah Shua**, and Bani,
and *Sherebiah* **Shereb Yah**, *Jamin* **Yamin**, *Akkub* **Aqqub**,
Shabbethai **Shabbethay**, *Hodijah* **Hodi Yah**,
Maaseiah **Maase Yah**, *Kelita* **Qelita**, *Azariah* **Azar Yah**,
Jozabad **Yah Zabad**, Hanan, *Pelaiah* **Pela Yah**,
and the *Levites* **Leviym**,
caused the people to *understand* **discern** the *law* **torah**:
and the people *stood* in their *place* **station**.
8 So they *read* **called out** in the *book* **scroll**
in the *law* **torah** of *God distinctly* **Elohim expressly**,
and *gave* **set** the *sense* **comprehension**,
and caused them
to *understand* **discern** the *reading* **convocation**.
9 And *Nehemiah* **Nechem Yah**,
which is the *Tirshatha* **governor**,
and Ezra the priest the scribe,
and the *Levites* **Leviym** that *taught* **had** the people **discern**,
said unto all the people,
This day is holy
unto *the LORD* **Yah Veh** your *God* **Elohim**;
mourn not, nor weep.
For all the people wept,
when they heard the words of the *law* **torah**.
10 Then he said unto them, Go your way,

eat the fat, and drink the sweet,
and send portions unto them
for whom *nothing* **naught** is prepared:
for this day is holy unto our *Lord* **Adonay**:
neither *be* ye *sorry* **contort**;
for the *joy* **rejoicing** of *the LORD* **Yah Veh**
is your *strength* **stronghold**.
11 So the *Levites stilled* **Leviym hushed** all the people,
saying, *Hold your peace* **Hush**, for the day is holy;
neither *be* ye *grieved* **contort**.
12 And all the people went their way to eat, and to drink,
and to send portions, and to *make* **work** great *mirth* **cheer**,
because they had *understood* **discerned** the words
that were *declared* **made known** unto them.
13 And on the second day were gathered *together*
the *chief* **head** of the fathers of all the people,
the priests, and the *Levites* **Leviym**, unto Ezra the scribe,
even to *understand* **comprehend**
the words of the *law* **torah**.

THE CELEBRATION OF SUKKOTH/BRUSH ARBORS

14 And they found *written* **inscribed** in the *law* **torah**
which *the LORD* **Yah Veh** had *commanded* **misvahed**
by *Moses* **the hand of Mosheh**,
that the *children* **sons** of *Israel* **Yisra El**
should *dwell* **settle** in *booths* **sukkoth/brush arbors**
in the *feast* **celebration** of the seventh month:
15 And that they should *publish* **hear**
and *proclaim* **pass a voice** in all their cities,
and in *Jerusalem* **Yeru Shalem**, saying,
Go forth unto the mount, and fetch olive *branches* **leaves**,
and *pine branches* **leaves of oil trees**,
and myrtle *branches* **leaves**,
and palm *branches* **tree leaves**,
and *branches* **leaves** of thick trees,
to *make booths* **work sukkoth/brush arbors**,
as *it is written* **inscribed**.
16 So the people went forth, and brought *them*,
and *made* **worked** themselves
booths **sukkoth/brush arbors**,
every one **each man** upon the roof of his house,
and in their courts,
and in the courts of the house of *God* **Elohim**,
and in the *street* **broadway**
of the water *gate* **portal**,
and in the *street* **broadway**
of the *gate* **portal** of *Ephraim* **Ephrayim**.
17 And all the congregation of them
that *were come again* **returned** out of the captivity
made booths **worked sukkoth/brush arbors**,
and *sat* **settled** under the *booths* **sukkoth/brush arbors**:
for since the days of *Jeshua* **Yah Shua** the son of Nun
unto that day
had not the *children* **sons** of *Israel* **Yisra El**
done **worked** so.
And there was *very* **mighty** great *gladness* **cheerfulness**.
18 Also day by day, from the first day unto the last day,
he *read* **called out**
in the *book* **scroll** of the *law* **torah** of *God* **Elohim**.
And they *kept* **worked** the *feast* **celebration** seven days;
and on the eighth day was a *solemn* **private** assembly,
according unto the *manner* **judgment**.

THE SONS OF YISRA EL FAST

9 Now in the twenty and fourth day of this month
the *children* **sons** of *Israel* **Yisra El**
were *assembled* **gathered** with fasting,
and with *sackclothes* **saqs**, and *earth* **soil** upon them.
2 And the seed of *Israel* **Yisra El** separated *themselves*
from all **sons of** strangers,
and stood and *confessed* **extended hands for** their sins,
and the *iniquities* **perversities** of their fathers.
3 And they *stood up* **arose** in their *place* **station**,
and *read* **called out** in the *book* **scroll** of the *law* **torah**
of *the LORD* **Yah Veh** their *God* **Elohim**
one **a** fourth *part* of the day;
and *another* **a** fourth *part* they *confessed* **extended hands**,
and *worshipped* **prostrated**
to *the LORD* **Yah Veh** their *God* **Elohim.**
4 Then *stood up* **arose** upon the *stairs* **ascent**,
of the *Levites* **Leviym**,
Jeshua **Yah Shua**, and Bani,
Kadmiel **Qadmi El**, *Shebaniah* **Sheban Yah**, Bunni,
Sherebiah **Shereb Yah**, Bani, and *Chenani* **Kenani**,
and cried with a *loud* **great** voice
unto *the LORD* **Yah Veh** their *God* **Elohim**.
5 Then the *Levites* **Leviym**,
Jeshua **Yah Shua**, and *Kadmiel* **Qadmi El**, Bani,
Hashabniah **Hashabne Yah**, *Sherebiah* **Shereb Yah**,
Hodijah **Hodi Yah**, *Shebaniah* **Sheban Yah**,
and *Pethahiah* **Pethach Yah**, said,
Stand up **Arise**
and bless *the LORD* **Yah Veh** your *God* **Elohim**
for ever **eternally** and *ever* **eternally**:
and blessed be *thy glorious name* **the name of thy honour**,
which is exalted above all blessing and *praise* **halal**.
6 Thou, *even* thou, *art LORD* **Yah Veh** alone;
thou hast *made heaven* **worked the heavens**,
the *heaven* **heavens** of *heavens* **the heavens**,
with all their host,
the earth, and all *things* that are therein,
the seas, and all that is therein,
and thou *preservest* **enlivenest** them all;
and the host of *heaven* **the heavens**
worshippeth **prostrateth to** thee.
7 Thou art *the LORD the God* **Yah Veh Elohim**,
who didst choose Abram,
and broughtest him forth out of Ur of the *Chaldees* **Kasdiy**,
and *gavest* **settest** him the name of Abraham;
8 And foundest his heart
faithful before thee **amenable at thy face**,
and *madest* **cuttest** a covenant with him
to give the land of the *Canaanites* **Kenaaniy**,
the *Hittites* **Hethiy**, the *Amorites* **Emoriy**,
and the *Perizzites* **Perizziy**, and the *Jebusites* **Yebusiy**,
and the *Girgashites* **Girgashiy**,
to give it, *I say*, to his seed,
and hast *performed* **raised** thy words;
for thou art *righteous* **just**:
9 And didst see the *affliction* **humiliation** of our fathers
in *Egypt* **Misrayim**,
and heardest their cry by the *Red* **Reed** sea;
10 And *shewedst* **gavest** signs and *wonders* **omens**
upon *Pharaoh* **Paroh**, and on all his servants,
and on all the people of his land:
for thou knewest
that they *dealt proudly* **seethed** against them.
So didst thou *get* **work** thee a name, as it is this day.
11 And thou didst *divide* **split** the sea
before them **at their face**,
so that they *went* **passed** through the midst of the sea
on the dry *land*;
and their *persecutors* **pursuers**
thou threwest into the deeps,
as a stone into the *mighty* **strong** waters.
12 Moreover thou leddest them
in the **by** day by a *cloudy* pillar **of cloud**;
and *in the* **by** night by a pillar of fire,
to give them light in the way wherein they should go.
13 Thou *camest down* **descendest** also
upon mount *Sinai* **Sinay**,
and *spakest* **wordest** with them from *heaven* **the heavens**,
and gavest them *right* **straight** judgments,
and true *laws* **torahs**,
good statutes and *commandments* **misvoth**:
14 And madest known unto them
thy holy *sabbath* **shabbath**,
and *commandedst* **misvahedst** them
precepts **misvoth**, statutes, and *laws* **torah**,
by the hand of *Moses* **Mosheh** thy servant:
15 And gavest them bread from *heaven* **the heavens**
for their *hunger* **famine**,
and broughtest forth water for them out of the rock
for their thirst,
and *promisedst* **saidst to** them
that they should go in to possess the land
which thou hadst *sworn* **lifted thy hand** to give them.
16 But they and our fathers *dealt proudly* **seethed**,
and hardened their necks,
and hearkened not to thy *commandments* **misvoth**,
17 And refused to *obey* **hear**,
neither *were mindful of* **remembered** thy *wonders* **marvels**

that thou *didst* **workedst** among them;
but hardened their necks,
and in their rebellion
appointed a captain **gave a head**
to return to their *bondage* **servitude**:
but thou art
a God ready to pardon **an Elohah of forgivenesses**,
gracious **charismatic** and merciful, slow to *anger* **wrath**,
and of great *kindness* **mercy**, and forsookest them not.
18 Yea, when they had *made* **worked** them a molten calf,
and said, This is thy *God* **Elohim**
that *brought* **ascended** thee *up* out of *Egypt* **Misrayim**,
and had *wrought* **worked** great *provocations* **scornings**;
19 Yet thou in thy *manifold* **abundant** mercies
forsookest them not in the wilderness:
the pillar of the cloud
departed **turned** not **aside** from them by day,
to lead them in the way;
neither the pillar of fire by night,
to shew them light,
and the way wherein they should go.
20 Thou gavest also thy good spirit
to *instruct* **have** them **comprehend**,
and withheldest not thy manna from their mouth,
and gavest them water for their thirst.
21 Yea, forty years
didst thou sustain them in the wilderness,
so that they lacked *nothing* **naught**;
their clothes *waxed not old* **wore not out**,
and their feet swelled not.
22 Moreover thou gavest them
kingdoms **sovereigndoms** and *nations* **people**,
and *didst divide* **allottedst** them *into corners* **to the edges**:
so they possessed the land of *Sihon* **Sichon**,
and the land of the *king* **sovereign** of Heshbon,
and the land of Og *king* **sovereign** of Bashan.
23 Their *children* **sons** also *multipliedst* **aboundedst** thou
as the stars of *heaven* **the heavens**,
and broughtest them into the land,
concerning which
thou hadst *promised* **said** to their fathers,
that they should go in to possess it.
24 So the *children* **sons** went in and possessed the land,
and thou subduedst *before them* **at their face**
the *inhabitants* **settlers** of the land,
the *Canaanites* **Kenaaniy**,
and gavest them into their hands,
with their *kings* **sovereigns**, and the people of the land,
that they might *do* **work** with them as they *would* **pleased**.
25 And they *took strong* **captured cut off** cities,
and a fat *land* **soil**, and possessed houses full of all goods,
wells *digged* **hewed**, vineyards, and oliveyards,
and *fruit* **food** trees in abundance:
so they did eat, and were *filled* **satisfied**,
and *became fat* **fattened**,
and *delighted* **pleased** themselves in thy great goodness.
26 Nevertheless they were *disobedient* **rebellious**,
and rebelled against thee,
and cast thy *law* **torah** behind their backs,
and *slew* **slaughtered** thy prophets
which *testified* **witnessed** against them
to turn them to thee,
and they *wrought* **worked** great *provocations* **scornings**.
27 Therefore thou *deliveredst* **gavest** them
into the hand of their *enemies* **tribulators**,
who *vexed* **tribulated** them:
and in the time of their *trouble* **tribulation**,
when they cried unto thee,
thou heardest *them* from *heaven* **the heavens**;
and according to thy *manifold* **abundant** mercies
thou gavest them saviours, who saved them
out of the hand of their *enemies* **tribulators**.
28 But after they had *rest* **rested**,
they *did* **returned to work** evil *again*
before thee **at thy face**:
therefore leftest thou them in the hand of their enemies,
so that they had *the dominion over* **subjugated** them:
yet when they returned, and cried unto thee,
thou heardest *them* from *heaven* **the heavens**;
and many times didst thou *deliver* **rescue** them
according to thy mercies;
29 And *testifiedst* **witnessedst** against them,
that thou mightest *bring* **return** them *again*
unto thy *law* **torah**:
yet they *dealt proudly* **seethed**,
and hearkened not unto thy *commandments* **misvoth**,
but sinned against thy judgments,
(which if a *man do* **human work**, he shall live in them;)
and *withdrew the* **they gave a revolting** shoulder,
and hardened their neck,
and *would not hear* **hearkened not**.
30 Yet many years didst thou *forbear* **draw** them,
and *testifiedst* **witnessedst** against them by thy spirit
in **the hand of** thy prophets:
yet *would they not give ear* **they hearkened not**:
therefore gavest thou them
into the hand of the people of the lands.
31 Nevertheless for thy great mercies' sake
thou didst not *utterly consume* **fully work** them **over**,
nor forsake them;
for thou art a *gracious* **charismatic** and merciful *God* **El**.
32 Now therefore, our *God* **Elohim**,
the great, the mighty, and the *terrible God* **awesome El**,
who *keepest* **guardest** covenant and mercy,
let not all the *trouble seem little* **travail diminish**
before thee **at thy face**,
that hath *come* **been found** upon us,
on our *kings* **sovereigns**, on our *princes* **governors**,
and on our priests, and on our prophets,
and on our fathers, and on all thy people,
since the *time* **day**
of the *kings* **sovereigns** of *Assyria* **Ashshur**
unto this day.
33 Howbeit thou art just in all that is brought upon us;
for thou hast *done right* **worked true**,
but we have done wickedly:
34 Neither have our *kings* **sovereigns**,
our *princes* **governors**, our priests,
nor our fathers, *kept* **worked** thy *law* **torah**,
nor hearkened unto thy *commandments* **misvoth**
and thy *testimonies* **witnesses**,
wherewith thou *didst testify* **witnessed** against them.
35 For they have not served thee
in their *kingdom* **sovereigndom**,
and in thy great goodness that thou gavest them,
and in the large and fat land
which thou gavest *before them* **at their face**,
neither turned they from their *wicked works* **evil exploits**.
36 Behold, we are servants this day,
and *for* the land that thou gavest unto our fathers
to eat the fruit thereof and the good thereof,
behold, we are servants in it:
37 And it *yieldeth much increase* **aboundeth produce**
unto the *kings* **sovereigns**
whom thou hast *set* **given** over us because of our sins:
also they *have dominion* **reign** over our bodies,
and over our *cattle* **animals**, at their pleasure,
and we are in great *distress* **tribulation**.

AN AMANAH CUT, INSCRIBED, AND SEALED

38 And because of all this
we *make a sure covenant* **cut an amanah**,
and *write* **inscribe** it;
and our *princes* **governors**,
Levites **Leviym**, and priests, seal unto it.

10 Now those that sealed *were*,
Nehemiah **Nechem Yah**, the *Tirshatha* **governor**,
the son of *Hachaliah* **Hachal Yah**, and *Zidkijah* **Sidqi Yah**,
2 *Seraiah* **Sera Yah**,
Azariah **Azar Yah**, *Jeremiah* **Yirme Yah**,
3 *Pashur* **Pashchur**,
Amariah **Amar Yah**, *Malchijah* **Malki Yah**,
4 Hattush, *Shebaniah* **Sheban Yah**, Malluch,
5 Harim, Meremoth, *Obadiah* **Obad Yah**,
6 *Daniel* **Dani El**, Ginnethon, Baruch,
7 Meshullam, *Abijah* **Abi Yah**, *Mijamin* **Mi Yamin**,
8 *Maaziah* **Maaz Yah**, *Bilgai* **Bilgay**, *Shemaiah* **Shema Yah**:
these were the priests.
9 And the *Levites* **Leviym**:
both *Jeshua* **Yah Shua** the son of *Azaniah* **Azan Yah**,
Binnui **Binnuy** of the sons of Henadad, *Kadmiel* **Qadmi El**;

10 And their brethren,
Shebaniah **Sheban Yah**, *Hodijah* **Hodi Yah**,
Kelita **Qelita**, *Pelaiah* **Pela Yah**, Hanan,
11 *Micha* **Michah Yah**, *Rehob* **Rechob**,
Hashabiah **Hashab Yah**,
12 *Zaccur* **Zakkur**,
Sherebiah **Shereb Yah**, *Shebaniah* **Sheban Yah**,
13 *Hodijah* **Hodi Yah**, Bani, *Beninu* **Ben Inu**.
14 The *chief* **head** of the people;
Parosh, *Pahathmoab* **Pachath Moab**, Elam, Zatthu, Bani,
15 Bunni, Azgad, *Bebai* **Bebay**,
16 *Adonijah* **Adoni Yah**, *Bigvai* **Bigvay**, Adin,
17 Ater, *Hizkijah* **Yechizqi Yah**, Azzur,
18 *Hodijah* **Hodi Yah**, Hashum, *Bezai* **Besay**,
19 Hariph, Anathoth, *Nebai* **Nobay**,
20 *Magpiash* **Magpi Ash**, Meshullam, Hezir,
21 *Meshezabeel* **Meshezab El**,
Zadok **Sadoq**, *Jaddua* **Yaddua**,
22 *Pelatiah* **Pelat Yah**, Hanan, *Anaiah* **Ana Yah**,
23 Hoshea, *Hananiah* **Hanan Yah**, *Hashub* **Hashshub**,
24 *Halohesh* **Lochesh**, *Pileha* **Pilcha**, *Shobek* **Shobeq**,
25 *Rehum* **Rechum**, Hashabnah, *Maaseiah* **Maase Yah**,
26 And *Ahijah* **Achiy Yah**, Hanan, Anan,
27 Malluch, Harim, Baanah.
28 And the *rest* **survivors** of the people,
the priests, the *Levites* **Leviym**,
the porters, the singers, the *Nethinims* **Dedicates**,
and all they that had separated themselves
from the people of the lands
unto the *law* **torah** of *God* **Elohim**,
their *wives* **women**, their sons, and their daughters,
every one *having knowledge* **who knoweth**,
and *having understanding* **discerneth**;
29 They *clave* **held** to their brethren, their *nobles* **mighty**,
and *entered into a curse, and into an oath* **oathed an oath**,
to walk in *God's law* **the torah of Elohim**,
which was given by *Moses* **the hand of Mosheh**
the servant of *God* **Elohim**,
and to *observe* **guard** and *do* **work**
all the *commandments* **misvoth**
of *the LORD* **Yah Veh** our *Lord* **Adonay**,
and his judgments and his statutes;
30 And that we *would* **should** not give our daughters
unto the people of the land,
nor take their daughters for our sons:
31 And if the people of the land bring *ware* **merchandises**
or any *victuals* **kernels** on the *sabbath* **shabbath** day to sell,
that we *would* **should** not *buy* **take** it of them
on the *sabbath* **shabbath**, or on the holy day:
and that we *would* **should** leave the seventh year,
and the *exaction* **burden** of every *debt* **hand**.
32 Also we *made ordinances* **stood misvoth** for us,
to *charge* **give** ourselves yearly
with the third *part* of a shekel
for the service of the house of our *God* **Elohim**;
33 For the *shewbread* **bread of arangement**,
and for the continual *meat* offering,
and for the continual *burnt offering* **holocaust**,
of the *sabbaths* **shabbaths**, of the new moons,
for the *set feasts* **festivals**, and for the *holy things* **holies**,
and for the sin *offerings*
to *make an atonement* **kapar/atone** for *Israel* **Yisra El**,
and *for* all the work of the house of our *God* **Elohim**.
34 And we *cast* **felled** the *lots* **pebbles** among the priests,
the *Levites* **Leviym**, and the people,
for the *wood offering* **qorban of timber**,
to bring it into the house of our *God* **Elohim**,
after the houses of our fathers,
at times appointed year by year,
to burn upon the **sacrifice** altar
of *the LORD* **Yah Veh** our *God* **Elohim**,
as it is *written* **inscribed** in the *law* **torah**:
35 And to bring the firstfruits of our *ground* **soil**,
and the firstfruits of all fruit of all trees, year by year,
unto the house of *the LORD* **Yah Veh**:
36 Also the firstborn of our sons, and of our *cattle* **animals**,
as it is *written* **inscribed** in the *law* **torah**,
and the firstlings of our *herds* **oxen** and of our flocks,
to bring to the house of our *God* **Elohim**,
unto the priests that minister
in the house of our *God* **Beth Elohim**:
37 And that we should bring
the *firstfruits* **firstlings** of our dough,
and our *offerings* **exaltments**,
and the fruit of all manner of trees,
of *wine* **juice** and of oil, unto the priests,
to the chambers of the house of our *God* **Elohim**;
and the tithes of our *ground* **soil** unto the *Levites* **Leviym**,
that the same *Levites* **Leviym** might have the tithes
in all the cities of our *tillage* **service**.
38 And the priest the son of *Aaron* **Aharon**
shall be with the *Levites* **Leviym**,
when the *Levites* **Leviym** take tithes:
and the *Levites* **Leviym**
shall *bring up* **ascend** the tithe of the tithes
unto the house of our *God* **Elohim**,
to the chambers, into the treasure house.
39 For the *children* **sons** of *Israel* **Yisra El**
and the *children* **sons** of Levi
shall bring the *offering* **exaltment** of the *corn* **crop**,
of the *new wine* **juice**, and the oil, unto the chambers,
where are the *vessels* **instruments** of the *sanctuary* **holies**,
and the priests that minister,
and the porters, and the singers:
and we *will* **shall** not forsake
the house of our *God* **Elohim**.

THE SETTLERS OF YERU SHALEM

11 And the *rulers* **governors** of the people
dwelt **settled** at *Jerusalem* **Yeru Shalem**:
the *rest* **survivors** of the people
also *cast lots* **felled pebbles**,
to bring one of ten
to *dwell* **settle** in *Jerusalem* **Yeru Shalem** the holy city,
and nine *parts to dwell in* **hands to** other cities.
2 And the people blessed all the men,
that *willingly offered themselves* **volunteered**
to *dwell* **settle** at *Jerusalem* **Yeru Shalem**.
3 Now these are the *chief* **head** of the *province* **jurisdiction**
that *dwelt* **settled** in *Jerusalem* **Yeru Shalem**:
but in the cities of *Judah* **Yah Hudah**
dwelt every one **settled each man**
in his possession in their cities, *to wit*,
Israel **Yisra El**, the priests, and the *Levites* **Leviym**,
and the *Nethinims* **Dedicates**,
and the *children* **sons** of *Solomon's* **Sholomoh's** servants.
4 And at *Jerusalem dwelt* **Yeru Shalem settled**
certain of the *children* **sons** of *Judah* **Yah Hudah**,
and of the *children* **sons** of *Benjamin* **Ben Yamin**.
Of the *children* **sons** of *Judah* **Yah Hudah**;
Athaiah **Atha Yah** the son of *Uzziah* **Uzzi Yah**,
the son of *Zechariah* **Zechar Yah**,
the son of *Amariah* **Amar Yah**,
the son of *Shephatiah* **Shaphat Yah**,
the son of *Mahalaleel* **Ma Halal El**,
of the *children* **sons** of *Perez* **Peres**;
5 And *Maaseiah* **Maase Yah** the son of Baruch,
the son of *Colhozeh* **Kol Hozeh**,
the son of *Hazaiah* **Haza Yah**,
the son of *Adaiah* **Ada Yah**,
the son of *Joiarib* **Yah Yarib**,
the son of *Zechariah* **Zechar Yah**,
the son of *Shiloni* **Shilohiy**.
6 All the sons of *Perez* **Peres**
that *dwelt* **settled** at *Jerusalem* **Yeru Shalem**
were four hundred *threescore* **sixty** and eight valiant men.
7 And these are the sons of *Benjamin* **Ben Yamin**;
Sallu the son of Meshullam, the son of *Joed* **Yoed**,
the son of *Pedaiah* **Pedah Yah**,
the son of *Kolaiah* **Qola Yah**,
the son of *Maaseiah* **Maase Yah**,
the son of *Ithiel* **Ithi El**,
the son of *Jesaiah* **Yesha Yah**.
8 And after him *Gabbai* **Gabbay**, *Sallai* **Sallay**,
nine hundred twenty and eight.
9 And *Joel* **Yah El** the son of Zichri was their overseer:
and *Judah* **Yah Hudah** the son of Senuah
was second over the city.
10 Of the priests:
Jedaiah **Yeda Yah** the son of *Joiarib* **Yah Yarib**,
Jachin **Yachin**.

11 *Seraiah* **Sera Yah** the son of *Hilkiah* **Hilqi Yah**,
the son of Meshullam,
the son of *Zadok* **Sadoq**,
the son of *Meraioth* **Merayoth**,
the son of *Ahitub* **Achiy Tub**,
was the *ruler* **eminent** of the house of *God* **Elohim**.
12 And their brethren
that *did* **worked** the work of the house
were eight hundred twenty and two:
and *Adaiah* **Ada Yah** the son of *Jeroham* **Yerocham**,
the son of *Pelaliah* **Pelal Yah**,
the son of *Amzi* **Amsi**,
the son of *Zechariah* **Zechar Yah**,
the son of *Pashur* **Pashchur**,
the son of *Malchiah* **Malki Yah**.
13 And his brethren, *chief* **head** of the fathers,
two hundred forty and two:
and *Amashai* **Amashsay** the son of *Azareel* **Azar El**,
the son of *Ahasai* **Ach Zay**,
the son of Meshillemoth,
the son of Immer,
14 And their brethren, mighty *men* of valour,
an hundred twenty and eight:
and their overseer was *Zabdiel* **Zabdi El**,
the son of *one of* the great men.
15 Also of the *Levites* **Leviym**:
Shemaiah **Shema Yah** the son of *Hashub* **Hashshub**,
the son of *Azrikam* **Ezri Qam**,
the son of *Hashabiah* **Hashab Yah**,
the son of Bunni;
16 And *Shabbethai* **Shabbethay** and *Jozabad* **Yah Zabad**,
of the *chief* **head** of the *Levites* **Leviym**,
had the oversight of the *outward business* **outside work**
of the house of *God* **Elohim**.
17 And *Mattaniah* **Mattan Yah** the son of *Micha* **Michah Yah**,
the son of Zabdi,
the son of Asaph,
was the *principal to begin* **head at the beginning**
the thanksgiving **in giving extended hands** in prayer:
and *Bakbukiah* **Baqbuk Yah** the second
among his brethren,
and Abda the son of Shammua,
the son of Galal,
the son of *Jeduthun* **Yeduthun**.
18 All the *Levites* **Leviym** in the holy city
were two hundred *fourscore* **eighty** and four.
19 Moreover the porters, *Akkub* **Aqqub**, Talmon,
and their brethren that *kept* **guarded** the *gates* **portals**,
were an hundred seventy and two.

THE SETTLERS OF THE CITIES OF YAH HUDAH

20 And the *residue* **survivors** of *Israel* **Yisra El**,
of the priests, and the *Levites* **Leviym**,
were in all the cities of *Judah* **Yah Hudah**,
every one **each man** in his inheritance.
21 But the *Nethinims dwelt* **Dedicates settled** in Ophel:
and *Ziha* **Sicha** and *Gispa* **Gishpa**
were over the *Nethinims* **Dedicates**.
22 The overseer also of the *Levites* **Leviym**
at *Jerusalem* **Yeru Shalem**
was Uzzi the son of Bani,
the son of *Hashabiah* **Hashab Yah**,
the son of *Mattaniah* **Mattan Yah**,
the son of *Micha* **Michah Yah**.
Of the sons of Asaph,
the singers were *over* **in front of** the *business* **work**
of the house of *God* **Elohim**.
23 For it was the *king's commandment* **sovereign's misvah**
concerning them,
that *a certain portion* **an amanah** should be for the singers,
due for every day **a day by day word**.
24 And *Pethahiah* **Pethach Yah**
the son of *Meshezabeel* **Meshezab El**,
of the *children* **sons** of *Zerah* **Zerach**
the son of *Judah* **Yah Hudah**,
was at the *king's* **sovereign's** hand
in all *matters* **words** concerning the people.
25 And for the *villages* **courts**, with their fields,
some of the *children* **sons** of *Judah* **Yah Hudah**
dwelt **settled** at *Kirjatharba* **Qiryath Arba**,
and in the *villages* **courts** thereof,
and at Dibon, and in the *villages* **courts** thereof,
and at *Jekabzeel* **Yeqabse El**,
and in the *villages* **courts** thereof,
26 And at *Jeshua* **Yah Shua**,
and at Moladah, and at *Bethphelet* **Beth Palet**,
27 And at *Hazarshual* **Hasar Shual**,
and at *Beersheba* **Beer Sheba**,
and in the *villages* **daughters** thereof,
28 And at *Ziklag* **Siqlag**, and at Mekonah,
and in the *villages* **daughters** thereof,
29 And at *Enrimmon* **En Rimmon**,
and at *Zareah* **Sorah**, and at *Jarmuth* **Yarmuth**,
30 *Zanoah* **Zanoach**, Adullam, and *in* their *villages* **courts**,
at Lachish, and the fields thereof,
at *Azekah* **Azeqah**, and in the *villages* **daughters** thereof.
And they *dwelt* **encamped** from *Beersheba* **Beer Sheba**
unto *the*
valley of Hinnom **Gay Hinnom/Valley of Burning**.
31 The *children* **sons** also of *Benjamin* **Ben Yamin**
from Geba
dwelt at Michmash, and *Aija* **Aya**, and *Bethel* **Beth El**,
and in their *villages* **daughters**.
32 And at Anathoth, Nob, *Ananiah* **Anan Yah**,
33 *Hazor* **Hasor**, Ramah, *Gittaim* **Gittayim**,
34 Hadid, *Zeboim* **Seboim**, Neballat,
35 Lod, and Ono,
the *valley of craftsmen* **Gay Harashim/Valley of Engravers**.
36 And of the *Levites* **Leviym**
were *divisions* **allotments** in *Judah* **Yah Hudah**,
and in *Benjamin* **Ben Yamin**.

THE PRIESTS AND LEVIYM WHO SETTLED YERU SHALEM

12 Now these are the priests and the *Levites* **Leviym**
that *went up* **ascended** with *Zerubbabel* **Zerub Babel**
the son of *Shealtiel* **Shealti El**, and *Jeshua* **Yah Shua**:
Seraiah **Sera Yah**, *Jeremiah* **Yirme Yah**, Ezra,
2 *Amariah* **Amar Yah**, Malluch, Hattush,
3 *Shechaniah* **Shechan Yah**, *Rehum* **Rechum**, Meremoth,
4 Iddo, Ginnetho, *Abijah* **Abi Yah**,
5 *Miamin* **Mi Yamin**, *Maadiah* **Maad Yah**, Bilgah,
6 *Shemaiah* **Shema Yah**,
and *Joiarib* **Yah Yarib**, *Jedaiah* **Yeda Yah**,
7 Sallu, *Amok* **Amoq**, *Hilkiah* **Hilqi Yah**, *Jedaiah* **Yeda Yah**.
These were the *chief* **head** of the priests
and of their brethren in the days of *Jeshua* **Yah Shua**.
8 Moreover the *Levites* **Leviym**:
Jeshua **Yah Shua**, *Binnui* **Binnuy**, *Kadmiel* **Qadmi El**,
Sherebiah **Shereb Yah**, *Judah* **Yah Hudah**,
and *Mattaniah* **Mattan Yah**,
which was over the *thanksgiving* **choir**,
he and his brethren.
9 Also *Bakbukiah* **Baqbuk Yah** and Unni, their brethren,
were over against them in the *watches* **guards**.
10 And *Jeshua* **Yah Shua** begat *Joiakim* **Yah Yaqim**,
Joiakim **Yah Yaqim** also begat *Eliashib* **El Yashib**,
and *Eliashib* **El Yashib** begat *Joiada* **Yah Yada**,
11 And *Joiada* **Yah Yada** begat *Jonathan* **Yah Nathan**,
and *Jonathan* **Yah Nathan** begat *Jaddua* **Yaddua**.
12 And in the days of *Joiakim* **Yah Yaqim** were priests,
the *chief* **head** of the fathers:
of *Seraiah* **Sera Yah**, *Meraiah* **Merayah**;
of *Jeremiah* **Yirme Yah**, *Hananiah* **Hanan Yah**;
13 Of Ezra, Meshullam;
of *Amariah* **Amar Yah**, *Jehohanan* **Yah Hanan**;
14 Of *Melicu* **Meloochi**, *Jonathan* **Yah Nathan**;
of *Shebaniah* **Sheban Yah**, *Joseph* **Yoseph**;
15 Of Harim, Adna;
of *Meraioth* **Merayoth**, *Helkai* **Helqai**;
16 Of Iddo, *Zechariah* **Zechar Yah**;
of Ginnethon, Meshullam;
17 Of *Abijah* **Abi Yah**, Zichri;
of *Miniamin* **Min Yamin**, of *Moadiah* **Moad Yah**,
Piltai **Piltay**:
18 Of Bilgah, Shammua;
of *Shemaiah* **Shema Yah**, *Jehonathan* **Yah Nathan**;
19 And of *Joiarib* **Yah Yarib**, *Mattenai* **Mattenay**;
of *Jedaiah* **Yeda Yah**, Uzzi;
20 Of *Sallai* **Sallay**, *Kallai* **Qallay**;
of *Amok* **Amoq**, *Eber* **Heber**;
21 Of *Hilkiah* **Hilqi Yah**, *Hashabiah* **Hashab Yah**;
of *Jedaiah* **Yeda Yah**, *Nethaneel* **Nethan El**.

22 The *Levites* **Leviym** in the days of *Eliashib* **El Yashib**,
Joiada **Yah Yada**,
and *Johanan* **Yah An**, and *Jaddua* **Yaddua**,
were *recorded chief* **inscribed head** of the fathers:
also the priests,
to the *reign* **sovereigndom** of *Darius* **Daryavesh**
the Persian.
23 The sons of Levi, the *chief* **head** of the fathers,
were *written* **inscribed** in the *book* **scroll**
of the *chronicles* **words of the days**,
even until the days of *Johanan* **Yah Hanan**
the son of *Eliashib* **El Yashib**.
24 And the *chief* **head** of the *Levites* **Leviym**:
Hashabiah **Hashab Yah**, *Sherebiah* **Shereb Yah**,
and *Jeshua* **Yah Shua** the son of *Kadmiel* **Qadmi El**,
with their brethren over against them,
to *praise* **halal** and to *give thanks* **extend hands**,
according to the *commandment* **misvah** of David
the man of *God* **Elohim**,
ward over against ward **underguard by underguard**.
25 *Mattaniah* **Mattan Yah**, and *Bakbukiah* **Baqbuk Yah**,
Obadiah **Obad Yah**, Meshullam, Talmon, *Akkub* **Aqqub**,
were porters *keeping* **guarding** the *ward* **underguard**
at the *thresholds* **gatherings** of the *gates* **portals**.
26 These were in the days of *Joiakim* **Yah Yaqim**
the son of *Jeshua* **Yah Shua**, the son of *Jozadak* **Yah Sadaq**,
and in the days of *Nehemiah* **Nechem Yah** the governor,
and of Ezra the priest, the scribe.

HANUKKAH OF THE WALL OF YERU SHALEM

27 And at the *dedication* **hanukkah**
of the wall of *Jerusalem* **Yeru Shalem**
they sought the *Levites* **Leviym** out of all their places,
to bring them to *Jerusalem* **Yeru Shalem**,
to *keep* **work** the *dedication* **hanukkah**
with *gladness* **cheer**,
both with *thanksgivings* **extended hands**, and with singing,
with cymbals, *psalteries* **bagpipes**, and with harps.
28 And the sons of the singers
gathered *themselves together*,
both out of the *plain country* **environs of the land**
round about *Jerusalem* **Yeru Shalem**,
and from the *villages* **courts** of Netophathi;
29 Also from the house of *Gilgal* **Hag Gilgal**,
and out of the fields of Geba and Azmaveth:
for the singers had builded them *villages* **courts**
round about *Jerusalem* **Yeru Shalem**.
30 And the priests and the *Levites* **Leviym**
purified themselves,
and purified the people,
and the *gates* **portals**, and the wall.
31 Then I *brought up* **ascended**
the *princes* **governors** of *Judah* **Yah Hudah** upon the wall,
and *appointed* **stood** two great
companies of them that gave thanks **extenders of hands**,
whereof one went
— processions on the right *hand* upon the wall
toward the *dung gate* **dunghill portal**:
32 And after them went *Hoshaiah* **Hosha Yah**,
and half of the *princes* **governors** of *Judah* **Yah Hudah**,
33 And *Azariah* **Azar Yah**, Ezra, and Meshullam,
34 *Judah* **Yah Hudah**, and *Benjamin* **Ben Yamin**,
and *Shemaiah* **Shema Yah**, and *Jeremiah* **Yirme Yah**,
35 And *certain* of the priests' sons with trumpets; *namely*,
Zechariah **Zechar Yah** the son of *Jonathan* **Yah Nathan**,
the son of *Shemaiah* **Shema Yah**,
the son of *Mattaniah* **Mattan Yah**,
the son of *Michaiah* **Michah Yah**,
the son of *Zaccur* **Zakkur**,
the son of Asaph:
36 And his brethren,
Shemaiah **Shema Yah**, and *Azarael* **Azar El**,
Milalai **Milalay**, *Gilalai* **Gilalay**,
Maai, *Nethaneel* **Nethan El**,
and *Judah* **Yah Hudah**, Hanani,
with the *musical instruments* **instruments of song**
of David the man of *God* **Elohim**,
and Ezra the scribe *before them* **at their face**.
37 And at the fountain *gate* **portal**,
which was over against them,
they *went up* **ascended**
by the *stairs* **steps** of the city of David,
at the *going up* **ascent** of the wall,
above the house of David,
even unto the water *gate* **portal**
eastward **toward the rising**.
38 And the *other* **second**
company of them that gave thanks **extenders of hands**
went *over against* **opposite** them, and I after them,
and the half of the people upon the wall,
from beyond the tower of the furnaces
even unto the broad wall;
39 And from above the *gate* **portal** of *Ephraim* **Ephrayim**,
and above the old *gate* **portal**,
and above the fish *gate* **portal**,
and the tower of *Hananeel* **Hanan El**,
and the tower of Meah,
even unto the *sheep gate* **flock portal**:
and they stood still in the *prison gate* **guard yard portal**.
40 So stood the two
companies of them that gave thanks **extenders of hands**
in the house of *God* **Elohim**,
and I, and the half of the *rulers* **prefects** with me:
41 And the priests;
Eliakim **El Yaqim**, *Maaseiah* **Maase Yah**,
Miniamin **Min Yamin**, *Michaiah* **Michah Yah**,
Elioenai **El Ya Enay**, *Zechariah* **Zechar Yah**,
and *Hananiah* **Hanan Yah**, with trumpets;
42 And *Maaseiah* **Maase Yah**, and *Shemaiah* **Shema Yah**,
and *Eleazar* **El Azar**, and Uzzi,
and *Jehohanan* **Yah Hanan**, and *Malchijah* **Malki Yah**,
and Elam, and Ezer.
And the singers *sang loud* **voiced to be heard**,
with *Jezrahiah* **Yizrach Yah** their overseer.
43 Also that day they *offered* **sacrificed** great sacrifices,
and *rejoiced* **cheered**:
for *God* **Elohim**
had *made* them *rejoice* **cheer** with great *joy* **cheer**:
the *wives* **women** also and the children *rejoiced* **cheered**:
so that the *joy* **cheer** of *Jerusalem* **Yeru Shalem**
was heard even afar off.
44 And at that *time* **day**
were *some appointed over* **men to oversee** the chambers
for the treasures, for the *offerings* **exaltments**,
for the *firstfruits* **firstlings**, and for the tithes,
to gather into them out of the fields of the cities
the *portions* **allotments** of the *law* **torah**
for the priests and *Levites* **Leviym**:
for *Judah rejoiced* **the cheer of Yah Hudah** for the priests
and for the *Levites* **Leviym** that *waited* **stood**.
45 And both the singers and the porters
kept **guarded** the *ward* **guard** of their *God* **Elohim**,
and the *ward* **guard** of the purification,
according to the commandment of David,
and of *Solomon* **Shelomoh** his son.
46 For in the days of David and Asaph of *old* **antiquity**
there were *chief* **head** of the singers,
and songs of *praise* **halal** and *thanksgiving* **extended hands**
unto *God* **Elohim**.
47 And all *Israel* **Yisra El**
in the days of *Zerubbabel* **Zerub Babel**
and in the days of *Nehemiah* **Nechem Yah**,
gave the *portions* **allotments** of the singers and the porters,
every day **day by day** his *portion* **word**:
and they *sanctified holy things* **hallowed**
unto the *Levites* **Leviym**;
and the *Levites sanctified* **Leviym hallowed** them
unto the *children* **sons** of *Aaron* **Aharon**.

MONGRELS SEPARATED FROM YISRA EL

13 On that day they *read* **called out**
in the *book* **scroll** of *Moses* **Mosheh**
in the *audience* **ears** of the people;
and therein was found *written* **inscribed**
that the *Ammonite* **Ammoniy** and the *Moabite* **Moabiy**
should not come into the congregation of *God* **Elohim**
for ever **eternally**;
2 Because they *met* **anticipated** not
the *children* **sons** of *Israel* **Yisra El**
with bread and with water,
but hired *Balaam* **Bilam** against them,
that he should *curse* **abase** them:

howbeit our *God* **Elohim**
turned the *curse* **abasement** into a blessing.
3 Now it *came to pass* **became,**
when they had heard the *law* **torah**,
that they separated from *Israel* **Yisra El**
all the *mixed multitude* **mongrels**.
4 And *before* **at the face of** this,
Eliashib **El Yashib** the priest,
having **given** the oversight of the chamber
of the house of our *God* **Elohim,**
was *allied* **near** unto *Tobiah* **Tobi Yah**:
5 And he had *prepared* **worked** for him a great chamber,
where *aforetime* **formerly**
they *laid* **gave** the *meat* offerings,
the frankincense, and the *vessels* **instruments**,
and the tithes of the *corn* **crop**,
the *new wine* **juice**, and the oil,
which was commanded to be given **the misvah**
to **of** the *Levites* **Leviym**, and the singers, and the porters;
and the *offerings* **exaltments** of the priests.
6 But in all this *time* was not I at *Jerusalem* **Yeru Shalem**:
for in the two and thirtieth year
of *Artaxerxes* **Artach Shashta**
king **sovereign** of *Babylon* **Babel**
came I unto the *king* **sovereign**,
and *after certain* **at the end of** days
obtained I leave **I asked** of the *king* **sovereign**:
7 And I came to *Jerusalem* **Yeru Shalem**,
and *understood* **discerned** of the evil
that *Eliashib did* **El Yashib worked**
for Tobiah **unto Tobi Yah,**
in *preparing* **working** him a chamber
in the courts of the house of *God* **Elohim**.
8 And it *grieved me sore* **was mighty evil to me**:
therefore I cast forth all the household *stuff* **instruments**
to *Tobiah* **Tobi Yah** out of the chamber.
9 Then I *commanded* **said**,
and they *cleansed* **purified** the chambers:
and thither brought I again
the *vessels* **instruments** of the house of *God* **Elohim**,
with the *meat* offering and the frankincense.
10 And I perceived
that the *portions* **allotments** of the *Levites* **Leviym**
had not been given them:
for the *Levites* **Leviym** and the singers,
that *did* **worked** the work,
were fled *every one* **each man** to his field.
11 Then contended I with the *rulers* **prefects**, and said,
Why is the house of *God* **Elohim** forsaken?
And I gathered them *together*,
and *set* **stood** them in their *place* **station**.
12 Then brought all *Judah* **Yah Hudah**
the tithe of the *corn* **crop**
and the *new wine* **juice** and the oil unto the treasuries.
13 And I made treasurers over the treasuries,
Shelemiah **Shelem Yah** the priest,
and *Zadok* **Sadoq** the scribe,
and of the *Levites* **Leviym**, *Pedaiah* **Pedah Yah**:
and *next to them* **at their hand** was Hanan
the son of *Zaccur* **Zakkur**,
the son of *Mattaniah* **Mattan Yah**:
for they were *counted faithful* **fabricated amenable**,
and their office was to *distribute* **allot** unto their brethren.
14 Remember me, O my *God* **Elohim**, concerning this,
and wipe not out my *good deeds* **mercies**
that I have *done* **worked** for the house of my *God* **Elohim**,
and for the *offices* **underguard** thereof.
15 In those days saw I in *Judah* **Yah Hudah**
some treading wine presses on the *sabbath* **shabbath**,
and bringing in *sheaves* **heaps**, and lading *asses* **he burros**;
as also wine, grapes, and figs, and all *manner of* burdens,
which they brought into *Jerusalem* **Yeru Shalem**
on the *sabbath* **shabbath** day:
and I *testified against them* **witnessed**
in the day wherein they sold *victuals* **hunt**.
16 There *dwelt men of Tyre* **settled the Soriy** also therein,
which brought fish, and all manner of *ware* **price**,
and sold on the *sabbath* **shabbath**
unto the *children* **sons** of *Judah* **Yah Hudah**,
and in *Jerusalem* **Yeru Shalem**.
17 Then I contended with the nobles of *Judah* **Yah Hudah**,
and said unto them,
What evil *thing* **word** is this that ye *do* **work**,
and profane the *sabbath* **shabbath** day?
18 *Did* **Worked** not your fathers thus,
and did not our *God* **Elohim** bring all this evil upon us,
and upon this city?
yet ye *bring more wrath* **add fuming** upon *Israel* **Yisra El**
by profaning the *sabbath* **shabbath**.
19 And it *came to pass* **became,**
that when the *gates* **portals** of *Jerusalem* **Yeru Shalem**
began to *be dark* **overshadow**
before **at the face of** the *sabbath* **shabbath,**
I *commanded* **said** that the gates should be shut,
and *charged* **said** that they should not be opened
till after the *sabbath* **shabbath**:
and *some* of my *servants* **lads**
set **stood** I at the *gates* **portals**,
that there should no burden be brought in
on the *sabbath* **shabbath** day.
20 So the merchants and sellers of all *kind of ware* **sold**
lodged **stayed overnight** without *Jerusalem* **Yeru Shalem**
once **one time** or twice.
21 Then I *testified* **witnessed** against them,
and said unto them,
Why *lodge* **stay** ye **overnight** *about* **over against** the wall?
if ye *do so again* **repeat**,
I *will lay* **shall extend** hands on you.
From that time forth
came they *no more* **not** on the *sabbath* **shabbath**.
22 And I *commanded* **said to** the *Levites* **Leviym**
that they should *cleanse* **purify** *themselves*,
and that they should come
and *keep* **guard** the *gates* **portals**,
to *sanctify* **hallow** the *sabbath* **shabbath** day.
Remember me, O my *God* **Elohim**, *concerning* this also,
and spare me according to the greatness of thy mercy.
23 In those days also saw I *Jews* **Yah Hudiym** that had
married wives **settled with women** of *Ashdod* **Ashdodiy**,
of *Ammon* **Ammoniy**, and of *Moab* **Moabiy**:
24 And their *children* **sons**
spake **worded** half in the speech of Ashdod,
and *could* **recognized** not
speak **to word** in *the Jews' language* **Yah Hudaic**,
but according to the language of *each* people **by people**.
25 And I contended with them, and *cursed* **abased** them,
and smote *certain* **men** of them,
and *plucked off their hair* **baldened them**,
and made them *swear* **oath** by *God* **Elohim**, saying,
ye shall not give your daughters unto their sons,
nor *take* **bear** their daughters unto your sons,
or for yourselves.
26 Did not *Solomon* **Shelomoh,**
king **sovereign** of *Israel* **Yisra El** sin by these *things*?
yet among many *nations* **goyim**
was there no *king* **sovereign** like him,
who was beloved of his *God* **Elohim**,
and *God made* **Elohim gave** him
king **sovereign** over all *Israel* **Yisra El**:
nevertheless even him
did *outlandish* **strange** women cause to sin.
27 Shall we then hearken unto you
to *do* **work** all this great evil,
to *transgress* **treason** against our *God* **Elohim**
in *marrying* **settling with** strange *wives* **women**?
28 And *one* of the sons of *Joiada* **Yah Yada**,
the son of *Eliashib* **El Yashib** the *high* **great** priest,
was son in law to Sanballat the *Horonite* **Horoniy**:
therefore I *chased* **fled** him from me.
29 Remember them, O my *God* **Elohim**,
because they have *defiled* **profaned** the priesthood,
and the covenant of the priesthood,
and of the *Levites* **Leviym**.
30 Thus *cleansed* **purified** I them from all strangers,
and *appointed* **stationed** the *wards* **guards**
of the priests and the *Levites* **Leviym**,
every one **each man** in his *business* **work**;
31 And for the *wood offering* **qorban of timber**,
at times appointed, and for the *firstfruits* **firstlings**.
Remember me, O my *God* **Elohim**, for good.

KEY TO INTERPRETING THE EXEGESES:
King James text is in regular type;
Text under exegeses is in oblique type;
Text of exegeses is in bold type.

RUTH AND NOOMIY

1 Now it *came to pass* **became,**
in the days when the judges *ruled* **judged,**
that there was a famine in the land.
And a *certain* man
of *Bethlehemjudah* **Beth Lechem Yah Hudah**
went to sojourn in the *country* **fields** of Moab,
he, and his *wife* **woman**, and his two sons.
2 And the name of the man was *Elimelech* **Eli Melech**,
and the name of his *wife Naomi* **woman Noomiy**,
and the name of his two sons
Mahlon **Machlon** and *Chilion* **Kilyon**,
Ephrathites **Ephrathiy**
of *Bethlehemjudah* **Beth Lechem Yah Hudah**.
And they came into the *country* **fields** of Moab,
and continued there.
3 And *Elimelech* **Eli Melech**
Naomi's husband **Noomiy's man** died;
and she *was left* **survived**, and her two sons.
4 And they *took them wives of the* **bore** women of Moab:
the name of the one was Orpah,
and the name of the *other* **second** Ruth:
and they *dwelled* **settled** there about ten years.
5 And *Mahlon* **Machlon** and *Chilion* **Kilyon**
died also both of them;
and the woman *was left* **survived**
of her two *sons* **children** and her *husband* **man**.
6 Then she arose with her daughters in law,
that she might return from the *country* **fields** of Moab:
for she had heard in the *country* **fields** of Moab
how that *the LORD* **Yah Veh** had visited his people
in giving them bread.
7 Wherefore she went forth
out of the place where she was,
and her two daughters in law with her;
and they went on the way
to return unto the land of *Judah* **Yah Hudah**.
8 And *Naomi* **Noomiy**
said unto her two daughters in law,
Go, return each **woman** to her mother's house:
the LORD deal kindly **Yah Veh work mercy** with you,
as ye have *dealt* **worked** with the dead, and with me.
9 *The LORD grant* **Yah Veh give** you
that ye may find rest,
each *of you* **woman** in the house of her *husband* **man**.
Then she kissed them;
and they lifted up their voice, and wept.
10 And they said unto her,
Surely we *will* **shall** return with thee unto thy people.
11 And *Naomi* **Noomiy** said,
Turn *again* **back**, my daughters:
why *will* **shall** ye go with me?
are there yet *any more* sons in my *womb* **inwards**,
that they may be your *husbands* **men**?
12 Turn *again* **back**, my daughters, go *your way*;
for I am too old to have *an husband* **a man**.
If I should say, I have hope,
if I should have *an husband* **a man** also to night,
and should also bear sons;
13 *Would* **Should** ye *tarry for* **expect** them
till they were grown?
would **should** ye *stay for* **ban** them
from having *husbands* **men**?
nay, my daughters;
for it *grieveth* **embittereth** me *much* **mightily**
for your sakes
that the hand of *the LORD* **Yah Veh**
is gone *out* against me.
14 And they lifted up their voice, and wept again:
and Orpah kissed her mother in law;
but Ruth *clave* **adhered** unto her.
15 And she said, Behold,
thy sister in law is *gone back* **returned** unto her people,
and unto her *gods* **elohim**:
return thou after thy sister in law.
16 And Ruth said, *Intreat* **Intercede** me not to leave thee,
or to return from following after thee:
for whither thou goest, I *will* **shall** go;
and where thou *lodgest* **stayest overnight**,
I *will lodge* **shall stay overnight**:
thy people shall be my people,
and thy *God* **Elohim** my *God* **Elohim**:
17 Where thou diest, *will* **shall** I die,
and there *will* **shall** I be *buried* **entombed**:
the LORD do so **Yah Veh work** to me, and *more* **add** also,
if ought but death *part* **separate** thee and me.
18 When she saw that she
was stedfastly minded **strengthened herself**
to go with her,
then she *left speaking* **ceased wording** unto her.
19 So they two went
until they came to *Bethlehem* **Beth Lechem**.
And it *came to pass* **became**,
when they were come to *Bethlehem* **Beth Lechem**,
that all the city *was moved* **quaked** about them,
and they said, Is this *Naomi* **Noomiy**?
20 And she said unto them, Call me not *Naomi* **Noomiy**,
call me *Mara* **Bitter**:
for *the Almighty* **Shadday**
hath *dealt very bitterly with* **mightily embittered** me.
21 I went out full
and *the LORD* **Yah Veh**
hath *brought me home again empty* **turned me back**:
why *then* call ye me *Naomi* **Noomiy**,
seeing *the LORD* **Yah Veh**
hath *testified* **answered** against me,
and *the Almighty* **Shadday** hath *afflicted* **vilified** me?
22 So *Naomi* **Noomiy** returned,
and Ruth the *Moabitess* **Moabiyth**, her daughter in law,
with her,
which returned out of the *country* **fields** of Moab:
and they came to *Bethlehem* **Beth Lechem**
in the beginning of barley harvest.

RUTH AND BOAZ

2 And *Naomi* **Noomiy** had a *kinsman* **kin**
of her *husband's* **man**,
a mighty man of *wealth* **valuables**,
of the family of *Elimelech* **Eli Melech**;
and his name was Boaz.
2 And Ruth the *Moabitess* **Moabiyth**
said unto *Naomi* **Noomiy**,
Let me now go to the field,
and glean ears *of corn* after him
in whose *sight* **eyes** I shall find *grace* **charism**.
And she said unto her, Go, my daughter.
3 And she went, and came,
and gleaned in the field after the *reapers* **harvesters**:
and her *hap was* **happening happened** to light
on *a part* **an allotment** of the field *belonging* unto Boaz,
who was of the *kindred* **family** of *Elimelech* **Eli Melech**.
4 And, behold, Boaz came from *Bethlehem* **Beth Lechem**,
and said unto the *reapers* **harvesters**,
The LORD **Yah Veh** be with you.
And they *answered* **said to** him,
The LORD **Yah Veh** bless thee.
5 Then said Boaz unto his *servant* **lad**
that was *set* **stationed** over the *reapers* **harvesters**,
Whose *damsel* **lass** is this?
6 And the *servant* **lad**
that was *set* **stationed** over the *reapers* **harvesters**
answered and said,
It is the Moabitish *damsel* **lass**
that *came back* **returned** with *Naomi* **Noomiy**
out of the *country* **fields** of Moab:
7 And she said, I *pray* **beseech** you,
let me glean and gather after the *reapers* **harvesters**
among the *sheaves* **omers**:
so she came, and hath *continued* **stayed**
even from the morning until now,
that she *tarried* **settled** a little in the house.
8 Then said Boaz unto Ruth,
Hearest thou not, my daughter?
Go not to glean in another field,
neither *go* **pass** from hence,
but *abide* **adhere** here *fast* by my *maidens* **lasses**:
9 Let thine eyes be on the field that they do *reap* **harvest**,

and go thou after them:
have I not *charged* **misvahed** the *young men* **lads**
that they shall not touch thee?
and when thou *art athirst* **thirstest**,
go unto the *vessels* **instruments**, and drink of that
which the *young men* **lads** have *drawn* **bailed**.
10 Then she fell on her face,
and *bowed* **prostrated** herself to the *ground* **earth**,
and said unto him,
Why have I found *grace* **charism** in thine eyes,
that thou shouldest *take knowledge of* **recognize** me,
seeing I am a stranger?
11 And Boaz answered and said unto her,
In being told, It hath *fully* been *shewed* **told** me,
all that thou hast *done* **worked** unto thy mother in law
since the death of *thine husband* **thy man**:
and how thou hast left thy father and thy mother,
and the land of thy nativity,
and art come unto a people which thou knewest not
heretofore **three yesters ago**.
12 *The LORD* **Yah Veh**
recompense **shalam** thy *work* **deed**,
and a *full reward* **complete hire** be given thee
of *the LORD God* **Yah Veh Elohim** of *Israel* **Yisra El**,
under whose wings thou art come to *trust* **seek refuge**.
13 Then she said,
Let me find *favour* **charism** in thy *sight* **eyes**,
my *lord* **adoni**;
for that thou hast *comforted* **sighed over** me,
and for that
thou hast *spoken friendly* **worded to the heart**
unto *thine handmaid* **thy maid**,
though I be not
like unto one of *thine handmaidens* **thy maids**.
14 And Boaz said unto her,
At *mealtime come thou hither* **foodtime approach**,
and eat of the bread,
and dip thy morsel in the *vinegar* **fermentation**.
And she *sat* **settled** beside the *reapers* **harvesters**:
and he *reached* **snatched** her parched *corn*,
and she did eat, and was *sufficed* **satisfied**,
and *left* **remained**.
15 And when she was risen up to glean,
Boaz *commanded* **misvahed** his *young men* **lads**, saying,
Let her glean even among the *sheaves* **omers**,
and *reproach* **shame** her not:
16 And *let fall also some of the handfuls of purpose*
of the spoilings, let fistfuls be spoiled for her,
and leave them, that she may glean them,
and rebuke her not.
17 So she gleaned in the field until even,
and *beat out* **threshed** that she had gleaned:
and it was about an ephah of barley.
18 And she *took* **lifted** it *up*, and went into the city:
and her mother in law saw what she had gleaned:
and she brought forth,
and gave to her that *she had reserved* **which remained**
after she was *sufficed* **satisfied**.
19 And her mother in law said unto her,
Where hast thou gleaned to day?
and where *wroughtest* **workedst** thou?
blessed be he that *did take knowledge of* **recognized** thee.
And she *shewed* **told** her mother in law
with whom she had *wrought* **worked**, and said,
The man's name with whom I *wrought* **worked** to day
is Boaz.
20 And *Naomi* **Noomiy** said unto her daughter in law,
Blessed be he of *the LORD* **Yah Veh**,
who hath not left off his *kindness* **mercy**
to the living and to the dead.
And *Naomi* **Noomiy** said unto her,
The man is near *of kin* unto us,
one of our *next kinsmen* **redeemers**.
21 And Ruth the *Moabitess* **Moabiyth** said,
He said unto me also,
Thou shalt *keep fast* **stick** by my *young men* **lads**,
until they have *ended* **finished** all my harvest.
22 And *Naomi* **Noomiy**
said unto Ruth her daughter in law,
It is good, my daughter,
that thou go *out* with his *maidens* **lasses**,
that they meet thee not in any other field.
23 So she *kept fast* **stuck** by the *maidens* **lasses** of Boaz
to glean unto the *end* **finish**
of barley harvest and of wheat harvest;
and *dwelt* **settled** with her mother in law.

BOAZ REDEEMS RUTH

3 Then *Naomi* **Noomiy** her mother in law
said unto her,
My daughter, shall I not seek rest for thee,
that it may *be well with* **well—please** thee?
2 And now is not Boaz of our *kindred* **kin**,
with whose *maidens* **lasses** thou wast?
Behold,
he winnoweth barley to night in the threshingfloor.
3 *Wash* **Baptise** thyself therefore, and anoint thee,
and *put* **set** thy *raiment* **clothes** upon thee,
and *get* **descend** thee *down* to the *floor* **threshingfloor**:
but make not thyself known unto the man,
until he shall have *done* **finished** eating and drinking.
4 And it shall be, when he lieth down,
that thou shalt *mark* **know** the place where he shall lie,
and thou shalt go in, and *uncover* **expose** his feet,
and lay thee down;
and he *will* **shall** tell thee what thou shalt *do* **work**.
5 And she said unto her,
All that thou sayest unto me I *will do* **shall work**.
6 And she *went down* **descended**
unto the *floor* **threshingfloor**,
and *did* **worked** according to all
that her mother in law *bade* **misvahed** her.
7 And when Boaz had eaten and drunk,
and his heart was *merry* **well—pleased**,
he went to lie down at the end of the *heap of corn* **heaps**:
and she came *softly* **undercover**,
and *uncovered* **exposed** his feet, and laid her down.
8 And it *came to pass* **became,** at midnight,
that the man *was afraid* **trembled**,
and *turned himself* **clasped on**:
and, behold, a woman lay at his feet.
9 And he said, Who art thou?
And she *answered* **said**,
I am Ruth *thine handmaid* **thy maid**:
spread therefore thy *skirt* **wing**
over *thine handmaid* **thy maid**;
for thou art a *near kinsman* **redeemer**.
10 And he said,
Blessed be thou of *the LORD* **Yah Veh**, my daughter:
for thou hast *shewed* **well—pleased** more *kindness* **mercy**
in the latter end than at the beginning,
inasmuch as
thou *followedst* **goest** not *young men* **after youths**,
whether poor or rich.
11 And now, my daughter, *fear* **awe** not;
I *will do* **shall work** to thee all that thou *requirest* **sayest**:
for all the *city* **portal** of my people
doth know that thou art a virtuous woman.
12 And now *it is true that* **truly**
I am thy *near kinsman* **redeemer**:
howbeit there is a *kinsman* **redeemer** nearer than I.
13 *Tarry this night* **Stay overnight**,
and it shall be in the morning,
that if he
will perform unto thee the part of a kinsman, well
shall redeem thee, good;
let him *do the kinsman's part* **redeem thee**:
but if he *will* **shall** not **delight**
do the part of a kinsman to **redeem** thee,
then *will I do the part of a kinsman to* **shall I redeem** thee,
as *the LORD* **Yah Veh** liveth:
lie down until the morning.
14 And she lay at his feet until the morning:
and she rose up
before one could know another **ere man recognized friend**.
And he said, Let it not be known
that a woman came into the *floor* **threshingfloor**.
15 Also he said,
Bring the vail that thou hast **Give the cloak** upon thee,
and hold it.
And when she held it,

he measured six *measures of* barley,
and *laid* **placed** it on her:
and she went into the city.
16 And when she came to her mother in law, she said,
Who art thou, my daughter?
And she told her
all that the man had *done* **worked** to her.
17 And she said,
These six *measures of* barley gave he me;
for he said to me, Go not empty unto thy mother in law.
18 Then said she, *Sit still* **Settle**, my daughter,
until thou know how the *matter will* **word shall** fall:
for the man *will* **shall** not *be in* rest,
until he have finished the *thing* **word** this day.

BOAZ MARRIES RUTH

4 Then *went* Boaz **ascended** *up* to the *gate* **portal**,
and *sat him down* **settled** there: and, behold,
the *kinsman* **redeemer** of whom Boaz *spake* **worded**
came **passed** by;
unto whom he said, Ho, such a one!
turn aside, *sit down* **settle** here.
And he turned aside, and *sat down* **settled**.
2 And he took ten men of the elders of the city,
and said, *Sit* **Settle** ye *down* here.
And they *sat down* **settled**.
3 And he said unto the *kinsman* **redeemer**,
Naomi **Noomiy**,
that *is come again* **returned**
out of the *country* **fields** of Moab,
selleth *a parcel* **an allotment** of *land* **field**,
which was our brother *Elimelech's* **Eli Melech's**:
4 And I *thought* **said** to *advertise thee* **expose in thine ear**,
saying,
Buy it **Chattel** before the *inhabitants* **settlers**,
and before the elders of my people.
If thou *wilt* **shalt** redeem it, redeem it:
but if thou *wilt* **shalt** not redeem it,
then tell me, that I may know:
for there is none to redeem it *beside* **except** thee;
and I am after thee.
And he said, I *will* **shall** redeem it.
5 Then said Boaz,
What day thou *buyest* **chattelest** the field
of the hand of *Naomi* **Noomiy**,
thou *must buy it* **chattelest** also
of Ruth the *Moabitess* **Moabiyth**,
the *wife* **woman** of the dead,
to raise up the name of the dead upon his inheritance.
6 And the *kinsman* **redeemer** said,
I cannot redeem it for myself,
lest I *mar* **ruin** mine own inheritance:
redeem thou my *right* **redemption** to thyself;
for I cannot redeem it.
7 Now this was
the manner in former time in Israel **at the face of Yisra El**
concerning redeeming
and concerning *changing* **exchanging**,
for to confirm all *things* **words**;
a man *plucked* **drew** off his shoe,
and gave it to his *neighbour* **friend**:
and this was a *testimony* **witness** in *Israel* **Yisra El**.
8 Therefore the *kinsman* **redeemer** said unto Boaz,
Buy it **Chattel** for thee. So he drew off his shoe.
9 And Boaz said unto the elders, and *unto* all the people,
ye are witnesses this day,
that I have *bought* **chatteled** all
that was *Elimelech's* **Eli Melech's**,
and all that was *Chilion's* **Kilyon's**
and *Mahlon's* **Machlon's**,
of the hand of *Naomi* **Noomiy**.
10 Moreover Ruth the *Moabitess* **Moabiyth**,
the *wife* **woman** of *Mahlon* **Machlon**,
have I *purchased* **chatteled** to be my *wife* **woman**,
to raise up the name of the dead upon his inheritance,
that the name of the dead be not cut off
from among his brethren,
and from the *gate* **portal** of his place:
ye are witnesses this day.
11 And all the people that were in the *gate* **portal**,
and the elders, said, We are witnesses.
The LORD **Yah Veh**
make **give** the woman that is come into thine house
like Rachel and like Leah,
which two did build the house of *Israel* **Yisra El**:
and *do* **work** thou
worthily **to get valuables** in *Ephratah* **Ephrath**,
and *be famous* **call out thy name**
in *Bethlehem* **Beth Lechem**:
12 And let thy house be like the house of *Pharez* **Peres**,
whom Tamar bare unto *Judah* **Yah Hudah**,
of the seed which *the LORD* **Yah Veh** shall give thee
of this *young woman* **lass**.
13 So Boaz took Ruth, and she was his *wife* **woman**:
and when he went in unto her,
the LORD **Yah Veh** gave her conception,
and she bare a son.
14 And the women said unto *Naomi* **Noomiy**,
Blessed be *the LORD* **Yah Veh**,
which hath not *left* **ceased** thee this day
without a *kinsman* **redeemer**,
that his name may be *famous* **called out** in *Israel* **Yisra El**.
15 And he shall be unto thee a restorer of thy *life* **soul**,
and a *nourisher* **sustainer** of *thine old age* **thy grayness**:
for thy daughter in law, which loveth thee,
which is better to thee than seven sons, hath born him.
16 And *Naomi* **Noomiy** took the child,
and *laid* **placed** it in her bosom,
and *became nurse unto* **nursed** it.
17 And the women her *neighbours* **fellow tabernaclers**
gave it a name **called out**, saying,
There is a son born to *Naomi* **Noomiy**;
and they called his name Obed:
he is the father of *Jesse* **Yishay**, the father of David.

THE GENERATIONS OF PERES

18 Now these are the generations of *Pharez* **Peres**:
Pharez **Peres** begat *Hezron* **Hesron**,
19 And *Hezron* **Hesron** begat Ram,
and Ram begat *Amminadab* **Ammi Nadab**,
20 And *Amminadab* **Ammi Nadab** begat Nahshon,
and Nahshon begat *Salmon* **Salmah**,
21 And *Salmon* **Salmah** begat Boaz,
and Boaz begat Obed,
22 And Obed begat *Jesse* **Yishay**,
and *Jesse* **Yishay** begat David.

KEY TO INTERPRETING THE EXEGESES:
King James text is in regular type;
Text under exegeses is in oblique type;
Text of exegeses is in bold type.

VASHTI THE SOVEREIGNESS

1
Now it *came to pass* **became,**
in the days of *Ahasuerus* **Achash Rosh**,
(this is *Ahasuerus* **Achash Rosh** which reigned,
from *India* **Hodu** even unto *Ethiopia* **Kush**,
over an hundred and seven and twenty
provinces **jurisdictions**:)
2 That in those days,
when the *king Ahasuerus* **sovereign Achash Rosh**
sat **settled** on the throne of his *kingdom* **sovereigndom**,
which was in Shushan the palace,
3 In the third year of his reign,
he *made* **worked** a *feast* **banquet**
unto all his *princes* **governors** and his servants;
the *power* **virtue** of Persia and *Media* **Maday**,
the nobles and *princes* **governors**
of the *provinces* **jurisdictions,**
being before him **at his face**:
4 When he *shewed* **had them see** the riches
of the honour of his *glorious kingdom* **sovereigndom**
and the *honour* **esteem**
of the adornment of his *excellent majesty* **greatness**
many days,
even an hundred and *fourscore* **eighty** days.
5 And when these days were *expired* **fulfilled**,
the *king made* **sovereign worked** a *feast* **banquet**
unto all the people
that were *present* **found** in Shushan the palace,
both unto great and small, seven days,
in the court of the garden
of the *king's* **sovereign's** palace;
6 Where were white, *green* **byssus**, and blue, *hangings*,
fastened **held** with cords
of *fine linen* **bleached cotton** and purple
to silver rings and pillars of **white** marble:
the beds were of gold and silver,
upon a pavement of *red* **bright**,
and *blue* **white marble**, and *white* **pearl**,
and *black, marble* **black tile**.
7 And they gave them drink
in *vessels* **instruments** of gold,
(the *vessels* **instruments**
being diverse one **differing** from *another* **instruments**,)
and *royal* wine **of the sovereigndom** in abundance,
according to the *state* **hand** of the *king* **sovereign**.
8 And the drinking was according to the *law* **edict**;
none *did compel* **insisted**:
for so the *king* **sovereign** had *appointed* **founded**
to all the *officers* **great** of his house,
that they should *do* **work** according to
every man's **the** pleasure **of man to man**.
9 Also Vashti the *queen* **sovereigness**
made **worked** a *feast* **banquet** for the women
in the *royal* house **of the sovereigndom**
which belonged to king Ahasuerus
of sovereign Achash Rosh.
10 On the seventh day,
when the heart of the *king* **sovereign**
was *merry* **good** with wine,
he *commanded* **said to** Mehuman,
Biztha, Harbona, Bigtha, and Abagtha,
Zethar, and *Carcas* **Karcas**,
the seven *chamberlains* **eunuchs** that *served* **ministered**
in the presence **at the face**
of *Ahasuerus* **Achash Rosh** the *king* **sovereign**,
11 To bring Vashti the *queen* **sovereigness**
before **at the face of** the *king* **sovereign**
with the *crown royal* **diadem of the sovereigndom**,
to *shew* **have** the people and the *princes* **governors**
see her beauty:
for she was *fair to look on* **good of visage**.
12 But the *queen* **sovereigness** Vashti refused
to come at the *king's commandment* **sovereign's word**
by **the hand of** his *chamberlains* **eunuchs**:
therefore
was the *king very wroth* **sovereign mighty enraged**,
and his *anger* **fury** burned in him.
13 Then the *king* **sovereign** said to the wise men,
which knew the times,
(for so was the *king's manner* **sovereign's word**
toward **at the face of** all
that knew *law* **edict** and *judgment* **pleading**:
14 And *the next* **near** unto him was *Carshena* **Karshena**,
Shethar, Admatha, Tarshish,
Meres, Marsena, and *Memucan* **Memuchan**,
the seven *princes* **governors** of Persia and *Media* **Maday**,
which saw the *king's* **sovereign's** face,
and *which sat* **settled** the first
in the *kingdom* **sovereigndom**;)
15 What shall we *do* **work**
unto the *queen* **sovereigness** Vashti
according to *law* **edict**,
because
she hath not *performed* **worked** the *commandment* **edict**
of the *king Ahasuerus* **sovereign Achash Rosh**
by **the hand of** the *chamberlains* **eunuchs**?
16 And *Memucan answered* **Memuchan said**
before **at the face**
of the *king* **sovereign** and the *princes* **governors**,
Vashti the *queen* **sovereigness**
hath not *done wrong* **bent** to the *king* **sovereign** only,
but also to all the princes,
and to all the people
that are in all the *provinces* **jurisdictions**
of the *king Ahasuerus* **sovereign Achash Rosh.**
17 For this *deed* **word** of the *queen* **sovereigness**
shall *come abroad* **go** unto all women,
so that they shall despise their *husbands* **masters**
in their eyes,
when it shall be reported **saying,**
The king Ahasuerus **Sovereign Achash Rosh**
commanded **said to** Vashti the *queen* **sovereigness**
to be brought in *before him* **at his face**,
but she came not.
18 Likewise shall the *ladies* **governesses** of Persia
and *Media* **Maday** say this day
unto all the *king's princes* **sovereign's governors**,
which have heard
of the *deed* **word** of the *queen* **sovereigness**.
Thus shall there arise
too much contempt **enough despite** and *wrath* **rage**.
19 If it *please* **be good with** the *king* **sovereign**,
let there go
a *royal commandment* **word of the sovereigndom**
from *him* **his face**,
and let it be *written* **inscribed** among the *laws* **edicts**
of the Persians and the *Medes* **Maday**,
that it *be not altered* **pass not away**,
That Vashti come no more
before **at the face of**
king Ahasuerus **sovereign Achash Rosh**;
and let the *king* **sovereign**
give her *royal estate* **sovereigndom**
unto *another* **her friend** that is better than she.
20 And when the *king's decree* **sovereign's sentence**
which he shall *make* **work**
shall be *published* **heard**
throughout all his *empire* **sovereigndom,**
(for it is great,)
all the *wives* **women**
shall give to their *husbands honour* **masters esteem**,
both to great and small.
21 And the *saying* **word**
well—pleased the eyes of the *king* **sovereign**
and the *princes* **governors**;
and the *king did* **sovereign worked**
according to the word of *Memucan* **Memuchan**:
22 For he sent *letters* **scrolls**
into all the *king's provinces* **sovereign's jurisdictions**,
into every province — **jurisdiction by jurisdiction**
according to the *writing* **inscribing** thereof,
and to *every people* **people by people**
after their *language* **tongue**,
that every man should bear rule in his own house,
and that it should be *published* **worded**
according to the *language* **tongue** of every people.

A SOVEREIGNESS IS SOUGHT

2 After these *things* **words**,
when the *wrath* **fury**
of *king Ahasuerus* **sovereign Achash Rosh**
was *appeased* **assuaged**,
he remembered Vashti, and what she had *done* **worked**,
and what was *decreed* **cut** against her.
2 Then said the *king's servants* **sovereign's lads**
that ministered unto him,
Let there be *fair young* **lasses of good visage**
— virgins sought for the *king* **sovereign**:
3 And let the *king* **sovereign**
appoint officers **oversee overseers**
in all the *provinces* **jurisdictions**
of his *kingdom* **sovereigndom**,
that they may gather together
all the *fair young* **lasses of good visage**
— virgins unto Shushan the palace,
to the house of the women,
unto the *custody* **hand** of Hege
the *king's chamberlain* **sovereign's eunuch**,
keeper **guard** of the women;
and let their *things for* purification be given them:
4 And let the *maiden* **lass**
which **well—**pleaseth **the eyes of** the *king* **sovereign**
be queen **reign** instead of Vashti.
And the *thing* **word**
well—pleased **the eyes of** the *king* **sovereign**;
and he *did* **worked** so.
5 Now in Shushan the palace
there was a *certain Jew* **man — a Yah Hudiy**,
whose name was *Mordecai* **Mordekay**,
the son of *Jair* **Yair**, the son of *Shimei* **Shimi**,
the son of *Kish* **Qish**, a *Benjamite* **man of Ben Yamin**;
6 Who had been *carried away* **exiled**
from *Jerusalem* **Yeru Shalem** with the *captivity* **exile**
which had been *carried away* **exiled**
with *Jeconiah* **Yekon Yah**
king **sovereign** of *Judah* **Yah Hudah**,
whom *Nebuchadnezzar* **Nebukadnets Tsar**
the *king* **sovereign** of *Babylon* **Babel**
had *carried away* **exiled**.
7 And he *brought up* **fostered** Hadassah,
that is, *Esther* **Ester**, his uncle's daughter:
for she had neither father nor mother,
and the *maid* **lass** was *fair* **beautiful of form**
and *beautiful* **good of visage**;
whom *Mordecai* **Mordekay**,
when her father and mother *were dead* **died**,
took for his own daughter.

ESTER WELL—PLEASES THE SOVEREIGN'S EYES

8 So it *came to pass* **became**,
when the *king's commandment* **sovereign's word**
and his *decree* **edict** was heard,
and when many *maidens* **lasses** were gathered *together*
unto Shushan the palace, to the *custody* **hand** of Hegai,
that *Esther* **Ester** was *brought* **taken** *also*
unto the *king's* **sovereign's** house,
to the *custody* **hand** of Hegai,
keeper **guard** of the women.
9 And the *maiden* **lass well—**pleased *him* **his eyes**,
and she *obtained kindness of him* **bore mercy at his face**;
and he *speedily gave her* **hastened**
her *things for purification* **purifications**,
with *such things as belonged to her* **her portions**,
and seven *maidens* **lasses**,
which were *meet* **seen** to be given her,
out of the *king's* **sovereign's** house:
and he *preferred* **changed** her and her *maids* **lasses**
unto the best *place* of the house of the women.
10 *Esther* **Ester** had not *shewed* **told** her people
nor her kindred:
for *Mordecai* **Mordekay** had *charged* **misvahed** her
that she should not *shew* **tell** it.
11 And *Mordecai* **Mordekay** walked *every* day **by day**
before **at the face of** the court of the women's house,
to know *how Esther did* **the shalom of Ester**,
and what should *become* **be worked** of her.
12 Now when every *maid's* **lasses'** turn
was *come* **reached**
to go in to *king Ahasuerus* **sovereign Achash Rosh**,
after that she had been **at the end of** twelve months,
according to the *manner* **edict** of the women,
(for so were the days of their purifications
accomplished **fulfilled**, *to wit*,
six months with oil of myrrh,
and six months with *sweet odours* **spices**,
and with other *things for the purifying* **purifications**
of the women;)
13 Then thus came *every maiden* **the lasses**
unto the *king* **sovereign**;
whatsoever she *desired* **said** was given her
to go with her out of the house of the women
unto the *king's* **sovereign's** house.
14 In the evening she went,
and on the *morrow* **morning** she returned
into the second house of the women,
to the *custody* **hand** of Shaashgaz,
the *king's chamberlain* **sovereign's eunuch**,
which *kept* **guarded** the concubines:
she came in unto the *king* **sovereign** no more,
except the *king* **sovereign** delighted in her,
and that she were called by name.
15 Now when the turn of *Esther* **Ester**,
the daughter of *Abihail* **Abi Hail**
the uncle of *Mordecai* **Mordekay**,
who had taken her for his daughter,
was *come* **reached** to go in unto the *king* **sovereign**,
she *required nothing* **besought no word**
but what Hegai
the *king's chamberlain* **sovereign's eunuch**,
the *keeper* **guard** of the women, *appointed* **said**.
And *Esther obtained favour* **Ester bore charism**
in the *sight* **eyes** of all them that *looked upon* **saw** her.
16 So *Esther* **Ester** was taken
unto *king Ahasuerus* **sovereign Achash Rosh**
into *his house royal* **the house of his sovereigndom**
in the tenth month, which is the month Tebeth,
in the seventh year of his *reign* **sovereigndom**.

SOVEREIGNESS ESTER

17 And the *king* **sovereign**
loved *Esther* **Ester** above all the women,
and she *obtained grace* **bore charism** and *favour* **mercy**
in his sight **at his face** more than all the virgins;
so that he set
the *royal crown* **diadem of the sovereigndom**
upon her head,
and made her *queen* **reign** instead of Vashti.
18 Then the *king* **sovereign**
made **worked** a great *feast* **banquet**
unto all his *princes* **governors** and his servants,
even *Esther's feast* **Ester's banquet**;
and he *made* **worked** a *release* **rest**
to the *provinces* **jurisdictions**,
and gave *gifts* **loads**,
according to the *state* **hand** of the *king* **sovereign**.

MORDEKAY SAVES THE SOVEREIGN

19 And when the virgins
were gathered *together* the second time,
then *Mordecai* **Mordekay**
sat **settled** in the *king's gate* **sovereign's portal**.
20 *Esther* **Ester** had not *yet shewed* **told** her kindred
nor her people;
as *Mordecai* **Mordekay** had *charged* **misvahed** her:
for *Esther did* **Ester worked**
the *commandment* **edict** of *Mordecai* **Mordekay**,
like as when she was *brought up with* **tutored by** him.
21 In those days,
while *Mordecai* **Mordekay**
sat **settled** in the *king's gate* **sovereign's portal**,
two of the *king's chamberlains* **sovereign's eunuchs**,
Bigthan and Teresh,
of those which kept **guards of** the *door* **threshold**,
were *wroth* **enraged**,
and sought to *lay* **send forth their** hand
on *the king Ahasuerus* **sovereign Achash Rosh**.
22 And the *thing* **word** was known to *Mordecai* **Mordekay**,
who told it unto *Esther* **Ester** the *queen* **sovereigness**;
and *Esther certified* **Ester said to** the *king* **sovereign** thereof
in *Mordecai's* **Mordekay's** name.

23 And when *inquisition* **the word**
was *made of the matter* **researched**,
it was found out;
therefore they were both hanged on a tree:
and it was *written* **inscribed** in the *book* **scroll**
of the *chronicles* **words of the days**
before **at the face of** the *king* **sovereign**.

HAMAN PLOTS AGAINST THE YAH HUDIY

3 After these *things* **words**
did king Ahasuerus **sovereign Achash Rosh**
promote **greatened** Haman
the son of *Hammedatha* **Medatha** the *Agagite* **Agagiy**,
and *advanced* **lifted** him,
and set his seat
above all the *princes* **governors** that were with him.
2 And all the *king's* **sovereign's** servants,
that were in the *king's gate* **sovereign's portal**,
bowed, and *reverenced* **prostrated to** Haman:
for the *king* **sovereign** had so *commanded* **misvahed**
concerning him.
But *Mordecai* **Mordekay** bowed not,
nor *did him reverence* **prostrated**.
3 Then the *king's* **sovereign's** servants,
which were in the *king's gate* **sovereign's portal**,
said unto *Mordecai* **Mordekay**,
Why *transgressest* **trespassest** thou
the *king's commandment* **sovereign's misvah**?
4 Now it *came to pass* **became**,
when they *spake daily* **said day by day** unto him,
and he hearkened not unto them, that they told Haman,
to see whether *Mordecai's matters* **Mordekay's words**
would **should** stand:
for he had told them that he was *a Jew* **Yah Hudiy**.
5 And when Haman saw
that *Mordecai* **Mordekay** bowed not,
nor *did him reverence* **prostrated to him**,
then was Haman *full of wrath* **filled with fury**.
6 And *he thought scorn* **despicable in his eyes**
to *lay* **send forth** hands on *Mordecai* **Mordekay** alone;
for they had *shewed* **told** him **of** the people
of *Mordecai* **Mordekay**:
wherefore Haman
sought to *destroy* **desolate** all the *Jews* **Yah Hudiym**
that were throughout the whole *kingdom* **sovereigndom**
of *Ahasuerus* **Achash Rosh**,
even the people of *Mordecai* **Mordekay**.
7 In the first month, that is, the month Nisan,
in the twelfth year
of *king Ahasuerus* **sovereign Achash Rosh**,
they *cast* **felled** Pur, that is, the *lot* **pebble**,
before **at the face of** Haman from day to day,
and from month to month,
to the twelfth *month*, that is, the month Adar.
8 And Haman said
unto *king Ahasuerus* **sovereign Achash Rosh**,
There is *a certain* **one** people scattered *abroad*
and *dispersed* **spread** among the people
in all the *provinces* **jurisdictions**
of thy *kingdom* **sovereigndom**;
and their *laws* **edicts** are diverse from all people;
neither *keep* **work** they the *king's laws* **sovereign's edicts**:
therefore it is not **equated**
for the *king's profit* **sovereign** to *suffer* **allow** them.
9 If it *please* **be good with** the *king* **sovereign**,
let it be *written* **inscribed** that they may be destroyed:
and I *will pay* **shall weigh**
ten thousand *talents* **rounds** of silver
to the hands of *those that have the charge* **the workers**
of the *business* **work**,
to bring it into the *king's* **sovereign's** treasuries.
10 And the *king* **sovereign**
took **twisted off** his *ring* **signet** from his hand,
and gave it unto Haman
the son of *Hammedatha* **Medatha** the *Agagite* **Agagiy**,
the *Jews' enemy* **Yah Hudiym's tribulator**.
11 And the *king* **sovereign** said unto Haman,
The silver is given to thee, the people also,
to *do* **work** with them
as it seemeth good *to thee* **in thine eyes**.
12 Then were the *king's* **sovereign's** scribes called
on the thirteenth *day* of the first month,
and there was *written* **inscribed**
according to all that Haman had *commanded* **misvahed**
unto the *king's lieutenants* **sovereign's satraps**,
and to the governors that were over
every province **jurisdiction by jurisdiction**,
and to the *rulers* **governors**
of *every people* **people by people**
of *every province* **jurisdiction by jurisdiction**
according to the *writing* **inscribings** thereof,
and to *every people* **people by people**
after their *language* **tongue**;
in the name of *king Ahasuerus* **sovereign Achash Rosh**
was it *written* **inscribed**,
and sealed with the *king's ring* **sovereign's signet**.
13 And the *letters* **scrolls** were sent
by *posts* **the hand of runners**
into all the *king's provinces* **sovereign's jurisdictions**,
to *destroy* **desolate**, to *kill* **slaughter**,
and to *cause to perish* **destroy**, all *Jews* **Yah Hudiym**,
both young and old **from lad to old man**,
little children **toddlers** and women, in one day,
even upon the thirteenth *day* of the twelfth month,
which is the month Adar,
and *to take the spoil of them for a prey* **spoil their plunder**.
14 The *copy* **transcript** of the *writing* **inscribings**
for *a commandment* **an edict** to be given
in every province **jurisdiction by jurisdiction**
was *published* **exposed** unto all people,
that they should be ready against that day.
15 The *posts* **runners** went out,
being hastened
by the *king's commandment* **sovereign's word**,
and the *decree* **edict** was given in Shushan the palace.
And the *king* **sovereign** and Haman sat *down* to drink;
but the city Shushan was perplexed.

ESTER TOLD OF HAMAN'S PLOT

4 When *Mordecai* **Mordekay**
perceived all that was *done* **worked**,
Mordecai rent **Mordekay ripped** his clothes,
and *put on sackcloth* **enrobed saq** with ashes,
and went out into the midst of the city,
and cried with a *loud* **great** and a bitter cry;
2 And came even
before **at the face of** the *king's gate* **sovereign's portal**:
for none might enter
into the *king's gate* **sovereign's portal**
clothed **robed** with *sackcloth* **saq**.
3 And in *every province* **jurisdiction by jurisdiction**,
whithersoever **whatever place**
the *king's commandment* **sovereign's word**
and his *decree came* **edict touched**,
there was great mourning among the *Jews* **Yah Hudiym**,
and fasting, and weeping, and *wailing* **chopping**;
and many *lay* **spread** in *sackcloth* **saq** and ashes.
4 So *Esther's maids* **Ester's lasses**
and her *chamberlains* **eunuchs** came and told *it* her.
Then was the *queen* **sovereigness**
exceedingly grieved **mightily writhed**;
and she sent *raiment* **clothes**
to *clothe Mordecai* **enrobe Mordekay**,
and to *take away* **turn aside** his *sackcloth* **saq** from him:
but he *received* **took** it not.
5 Then called *Esther* **Ester** for *Hatach* **Hathach**,
one of the *king's chamberlains* **sovereign's eunuchs**,
whom he had *appointed* **stood** to *attend upon* **face** her,
and *gave him a commandment* **misvahed**
to Mordecai **for Mordekay**,
to know what it was, and why it was.
6 So *Hatach* **Hathach** went forth to *Mordecai* **Mordekay**
unto the *street* **broadway** of the city,
which was before **at the face**
of the *king's gate* **sovereign's portal**.
7 And *Mordecai* **Mordekay** told him
of all that had happened unto him,
and of the sum of the *money* **silver**
that Haman had *promised* **said**
to *pay* **weigh** to the *king's* **sovereign's** treasuries
for the *Jews* **Yah Hudiym**, to destroy them.
8 Also he gave him

the *copy* **transcript** of the *writing* **inscribing**
of the *decree* **edict** that was given at Shushan
to *destroy* **desolate** them,
to *shew it unto Esther* **have Ester see**,
and to declare it unto her,
and to *charge* **misvah** her
that she should go in unto the *king* **sovereign**,
to *make supplication unto* **beseech charism of** him,
and to *make request before him* **beseech at his face**
for her people.
9 And *Hatach* **Hathach** came and told *Esther* **Ester**
the words of *Mordecai* **Mordekay**.
10 Again *Esther spake* **Ester said** unto *Hatach* **Hathach**,
and *gave him commandment* **misvahed**
unto Mordecai **for Mordekay**;
11 All the *king's* **sovereign's** servants, and the people
of the *king's provinces* **sovereign's jurisdictions**,
do know, that whosoever, whether man or woman,
shall come unto the *king* **sovereign** into the inner court,
who is not called,
there is one *law* **edict** of his to *put* **deathify** him *to death*,
except **apart from** such to whom the *king* **sovereign**
shall *hold out* **extend** the golden *sceptre* **scion**,
that he may live:
but I have not been called
to come in unto the *king* **sovereign** these thirty days.
12 And they told to *Mordecai* **Mordekay**
Esther's **Ester's** words.
13 Then *Mordecai* **Mordekay**
commanded to answer Esther **said to respond to Ester**,
Think **Consider** not with *thyself* **thy soul**
that thou shalt escape in the *king's* **sovereign's** house,
more than all the *Jews* **Yah Hudiym**.

SOVEREIGNESS ESTER'S MISSION

14 For if **in hushing,**
thou *altogether holdest thy peace* **hushest** at this time,
then shall *there enlargement* **respite**
and *deliverance arise* **rescue stand**
to the *Jews* **Yah Hudiym** from another place;
but thou and thy father's house shall be destroyed:
and who knoweth whether
thou *art come to* **touchest** the *kingdom* **sovereigndom**
for *such* a time as this?
15 Then *Esther bade them* **Ester said to**
return *Mordecai* **Mordekay** this *answer*,
16 Go, gather *together* all the *Jews* **Yah Hudiym**
that are *present* **found** in Shushan, and fast ye for me,
and neither eat nor drink three days, night or day:
I also and my *maidens will* **lasses shall** fast likewise;
and *so will* **thus shall** I go in unto the *king* **sovereign**,
which is not according to the *law* **edict**:
and if I *perish* **destruct**, I *perish* **destruct**.
17 So *Mordecai went his way* **Mordekay passed**,
and *did* **worked** according to all
that *Esther* **Ester** had *commanded* **misvahed** him.

SOVEREIGNESS ESTER'S PETITION

5 Now it *came to pass* **became,** on the third day,
that *Esther* **Ester**
put on **enrobed** her *royal* **sovereigndom** *apparel*,
and stood in the inner court
of the *king's* **sovereign's** house,
over against the *king's* **sovereign's** house:
and the *king sat* **sovereign settled**
upon *his royal throne* **the throne of his sovereigndom**
in the *royal house* **house of the sovereigndom**,
over against the *gate* **portal** of the house.
2 And it was so,
when the *king* **sovereign**
saw *Esther* **Ester** the *queen* **sovereigness**
standing in the court,
that she *obtained* **bore charism** in his *sight* **eyes**:
and the *king held out* **sovereign extended** to *Esther* **Ester**
the golden *sceptre* **scion** that was in his hand.
So *Esther drew near* **Ester approached**,
and touched the top of the *sceptre* **scion**.
3 Then said the *king* **sovereign** unto her,
What *wilt thou* **to thee**, *queen Esther* **sovereigness Ester**?
and what is thy request?
it shall be even given thee
to the half of the *kingdom* **sovereigndom**.
4 And *Esther answered* **Ester said**,
If it *seem* **be** good unto the *king* **sovereign**,
let the *king* **sovereign** and Haman come this day
unto the banquet that I have *prepared* **worked** for him.
5 Then the *king* **sovereign** said,
Cause Haman to make haste,
that he may *do* **work** as *Esther* **Ester** hath *said* **worded**.
So the *king* **sovereign** and Haman came
to the banquet that *Esther* **Ester** had *prepared* **worked**.
6 And the *king* **sovereign** said unto *Esther* **Ester**
at the banquet of wine,
What is thy petition?
and it shall be *granted* **given** thee:
and what is thy request?
even to the half of the *kingdom* **sovereigndom**
it shall be *performed* **worked**.
7 Then answered *Esther* **Ester**, and said,
My petition and my request is;
8 If I have found *favour* **charism**
in the *sight* **eyes** of the *king* **sovereign**,
and if it *please* **be good with** the *king* **sovereign**
to *grant* **give** my petition,
and to *perform* **work** my request,
let the *king* **sovereign** and Haman come to the banquet
that I shall *prepare* **work** for them,
and I *will do* **shall work** to morrow
as the king hath said
according to the word of the sovereign.

HAMAN FILLED WITH FURY

9 Then went Haman forth that day
joyful **cheerful** and with a *glad* **good** heart:
but when Haman saw *Mordecai* **Mordekay**
in the *king's gate* **sovereign's portal**,
that he *stood* **arose** not *up*, nor *moved* **agitated** for him,
he was *full of indignation* **filled with fury**
against *Mordecai* **Mordekay**.
10 Nevertheless Haman refrained himself:
and when he came *home* **to his house**,
he sent and called for his *friends* **loved ones**,
and Zeresh his *wife* **woman**.
11 And Haman *told* **scribed** them
of the *glory* **honour** of his riches,
and the *multitude* **abundance** of his *children* **sons**,
and all *the things* **those**
wherein the *king* **sovereign** had *promoted* **greatened** him,
and how he had *advanced* **lifted** him
above the *princes* **governors** and servants
of the *king* **sovereign**.
12 Haman said moreover,
Yea, *Esther* **Ester** the *queen* **sovereigness**
did let no man come in with the *king* **sovereign**
unto the banquet that she had *prepared* **worked**
but myself;
and to morrow am I *invited* **called** unto her also
with the *king* **sovereign**.
13 Yet all this *availeth* **equateth** me *nothing* **naught**,
so long as **all the time**
that I see *Mordecai* **Mordekay** the *Jew* **Yah Hudiy**
sitting **settled** at the *king's gate* **sovereign's portal**.
14 Then said Zeresh his *wife* **woman**
and all his *friends* **loved ones** unto him,
Let a *gallows* **tree** be *made* **worked** of fifty cubits high,
and *to morrow* **in the morning**
speak **say** thou unto the *king* **sovereign**
that *Mordecai* **Mordekay** may be hanged thereon:
then go thou in *merrily* **cheerfully** with the *king* **sovereign**
unto the banquet.
And the *thing* **word well**—pleased **the face of** Haman;
and he caused the *gallows* **tree** to be *made* **worked**.

MORDEKAY HONOURED

6 On that night
could not the king sleep **the sovereign's sleep fled away**,
and he *commanded* **said** to bring the *book* **scroll**
of *records* **memorial** of the *chronicles* **words of the days**;
and they were *read* **called out**
before **at the face of** the *king* **sovereign**.
2 And it was found *written* **inscribed**,
that *Mordecai* **Mordekay**
had told of Bigthana and Teresh,
two of the *king's chamberlains* **sovereign's eunuchs**,

the *keepers* **guards** of the *door* **threshold**,
who sought to *lay* **send their** hand
on the *king Ahasuerus* **sovereign Achash Rosh**.
3 And the *king* **sovereign** said,
What *honour* **esteem** and *dignity* **greatness**
hath been *done* **worked** to *Mordecai* **Mordekay** for this?
Then said the *king's servants* **sovereign's lads**
that ministered unto him,
There is nothing done **No word hath been worked**
for him.
4 And the *king* **sovereign** said, Who is in the court?
Now Haman was come
into the outward court of the *king's* **sovereign's** house,
to *speak* **say** unto the *king* **sovereign**
to hang *Mordecai* **Mordekay** on the *gallows* **tree**
that he had prepared for him.
5 And the *king's servants* **sovereign's lads** said unto him,
Behold, Haman standeth in the court.
And the *king* **sovereign** said, Let him come in.
6 So Haman came in.
And the *king* **sovereign** said unto him,
What shall be *done* **worked** unto the man
whom the *king* **sovereign** delighteth to *honour* **esteem**?
Now Haman *thought* **said** in his heart,
To whom *would* **should** the *king* **sovereign** delight
to *do honour* **work esteem** more than to myself?
7 And Haman *answered* **said to** the *king* **sovereign**,
For the man
whom the *king* **sovereign** delighteth to *honour* **esteem**,
8 Let the *royal apparel* **robe of the sovereigndom**
be brought
which the *king useth to wear* **sovereign enrobeth**,
and the horse that the *king* **sovereign** rideth upon,
and the *crown royal* **diadem of the sovereigndom**
which is *set* **given** upon his head:
9 And let this *apparel* **robe** and horse
be *delivered* **given** to the hand of *one* **the man**
of the *king's* **sovereign's** most noble *princes* **governors**,
that they may *array* **enrobe** the man *withal*
whom the *king* **sovereign** delighteth to *honour* **esteem**,
and *bring him* **have him ride** on horseback
through the *street* **broadway** of the city,
and *proclaim before him* **call out at his face**,
Thus shall it be *done* **worked** to the man
whom the *king* **sovereign** delighteth to *honour* **esteem**.
10 Then the *king* **sovereign** said to Haman,
Make haste, *and* take the *apparel* **robe** and the horse,
as thou hast *said* **worded**,
and *do* **work** even so
to *Mordecai* **Mordekay** the *Jew* **Yah Hudiy**,
that *sitteth* **settleth** at the *king's gate* **sovereign's portal**:
let *nothing fail* **no word fall**
of all that thou hast *spoken* **worded**.
11 Then took Haman the *apparel* **robe** and the horse,
and *arrayed Mordecai* **enrobed Mordekay**,
and *brought him on horseback* **had him ride**
through the *street* **broadway** of the city,
and *proclaimed before him* **called out at his face**,
Thus shall it be *done* **worked** unto the man
whom the *king* **sovereign** delighteth to *honour* **esteem**.
12 And *Mordecai* **Mordekay**
came again **returned** to the *king's gate* **sovereign's portal**.
But Haman hasted to his house mourning,
and having his head covered.
13 And Haman *told* **scribed to** Zeresh his *wife* **woman**
and all his *friends* **loved ones**
every thing **all** that had befallen him.
Then said his wise men and Zeresh his *wife* **woman**
unto him,
If *Mordecai* **Mordekay**
be of the seed of the *Jews* **Yah Hudiym**,
before **at the face of** whom thou hast begun to fall,
thou shalt not prevail against him,
but **in falling,** shalt *surely* fall *before him* **at his face**.
14 And while they were yet *talking* **wording** with him,
came the king's chamberlains
the sovereign's eunuchs touched,
and hasted to bring Haman unto the banquet
that *Esther* **Ester** had *prepared* **worked**.

HAMAN HANGED

7 So the *king* **sovereign** and Haman
came to *banquet* **drink**
with *Esther* **Ester** the *queen* **sovereigness**.
2 And the *king* **sovereign** said again unto *Esther* **Ester**
on the second day at the banquet of wine,
What is thy petition, *queen Esther* **sovereigness Ester**?
and it shall be *granted* **given** thee:
and what is thy request?
and it shall be *performed* **worked**,
even to the half of the *kingdom* **sovereigndom**.
3 Then *Esther* **Ester** the *queen* **sovereigness**
answered and said,
If I have found *favour* **charism** in thy *sight* **eyes**,
O *king* **sovereign**,
and if it *please* **be good with** the *king* **sovereign**,
let my *life* **soul** be given me at my petition,
and my people at my request:
4 For we are sold, I and my people,
to be *destroyed* **desolated**,
to be *slain* **slaughtered**, and to *perish* **destruct**.
But if **Even though** we had been sold
for *bondmen* **servants** and *bondwomen* **maids**,
I had *held my tongue* **hushed**,
although the *enemy* **tribulator**
could not countervail **equated not**
the *king's* **sovereign's** damage.
5 Then *the king Ahasuerus* **sovereign Achash Rosh**
answered
and said unto *Esther* **Ester** the *queen* **sovereigness**,
Who is he, and where is he,
that durst presume in his heart **whose heart hath filled him**
to do so **thus to work**?
6 And *Esther* **Ester** said,
The *adversary* **tribulator** and enemy
is this *wicked* **evil** Haman.
Then Haman was *afraid before* **frightened at the face**
of the *king* **sovereign** and the *queen* **sovereigness**.
7 And the *king* **sovereign** arising from the banquet of wine
in his *wrath* **fury** went into the palace garden:
and Haman stood up
to *make request* **beseech** for his *life* **soul**
to *Esther* **Ester** the *queen* **sovereigness**;
for he saw that there was evil
determined **finished** against him by the *king* **sovereign**.
8 Then the *king* **sovereign**
returned out of the palace garden
into the *place* **house** of the banquet of wine;
and Haman was fallen upon the bed
whereon *Esther* **Ester** was.
Then said the *king* **sovereign**,
will **shall** he *force* **subdue** the *queen* **sovereigness**
also before me in the house?
As the word went out of *king's* **sovereign's** mouth,
they covered Haman's face.
9 And Harbonah, one of the *chamberlains* **eunuchs**,
said *before* **at the face of** the *king* **sovereign**,
Behold also, the *gallows* **tree** fifty cubits high,
which Haman had *made* **worked** for *Mordecai* **Mordekay**,
who had *spoken* **worded** good for the *king* **sovereign**,
standeth in the house of Haman.
Then the *king* **sovereign** said, Hang him thereon.
10 So they hanged Haman on the *gallows* **tree**
that he had prepared for *Mordecai* **Mordekay**.
Then was the *king's wrath* **sovereign's fury**
pacified **assuaged**.

MORDEKAY PROMOTED

8 On that day
did the *king Ahasuerus* **sovereign Achash Rosh**
give the house of Haman
the *Jews' enemy* **Yah Hudiym's tribulator**
unto *Esther* **Ester** the *queen* **sovereigness**.
And *Mordecai* **Mordekay**
came *before* **at the face of** the *king* **sovereign**;
for *Esther* **Ester** had told what he was unto her.
2 And the *king took* **sovereign twisted** off his *ring* **signet**,
which he had *taken* **passed** from Haman,
and gave it unto *Mordecai* **Mordekay**.
And *Esther* **Ester** set *Mordecai* **Mordekay**

over the house of Haman.
3 And *Esther spake yet again* **Ester added to word**
before **at the face of** the *king* **sovereign**,
and fell down at **the face of** his feet,
and besought **charism of** him with *tears* **weeping**
to *put away* **pass over** the *mischief* **evil**
of Haman the *Agagite* **Agagiy**,
and his *device* **fabrication** that he had *devised* **fabricated**
against the *Jews* **Yah Hudiym**.
4 Then the *king* **sovereign**
held out **extended** the golden *sceptre* **scion**
toward *Esther* **Ester**.
So *Esther* **Ester** arose,
and stood *before* **at the face of** the *king* **sovereign**,
5 And said, If it *please* **be good with** the *king* **sovereign**,
and if I have found *favour* **charism** in his *sight* **face**,
and the *thing seem right* **word prosper**
before **at the face of** the *king* **sovereign**,
and I be *pleasing* **goodly** in his eyes
let it be *written* **inscribed**
to *reverse* **return** the *letters* **scrolls**
devised by **the fabrication of** Haman
the son of *Hammedatha* **Medatha** the *Agagite* **Agagiy**,
which he *wrote* **inscribed**
to destroy the *Jews* **Yah Hudiym**
which are in all
the *king's provinces* **sovereign's jurisdictions**:
6 For how can I *endure to*
see the evil that shall *come unto* **find** my people?
or how can I *endure to*
see the destruction of my kindred?
7 Then *the king Ahasuerus* **sovereign Achash Rosh**
said unto *Esther* **Ester** the *queen* **sovereigness**
and to *Mordecai* **Mordekay** the *Jew* **Yah Hudiy**, Behold,
I have given *Esther* **Ester** the house of Haman,
and him they have hanged upon the *gallows* **tree**,
because he *laid* **extended** his hand
upon the *Jews* **Yah Hudiym**.
8 *Write* **Inscribe** ye also for the *Jews* **Yah Hudiym**,
as it *liketh you* **be good in your eyes**,
in the *king's* **sovereign's** name,
and seal it with the *king's ring* **sovereign's signet**:
for the *writing* **inscribing**
which is *written* **inscribed** in the *king's* **sovereign's** name,
and sealed with the *king's ring* **sovereign's signet**,
may no man *reverse* **return**.
9 Then were the *king's* **sovereign's** scribes
called at that time in the third month,
that is, the month Sivan,
on the three and twentieth *day* thereof;
and it was *written* **inscribed** according to all
that *Mordecai commanded* **Mordekay misvahed**
unto the *Jews* **Yah Hudiym**,
and to the *lieutenants* **satraps**, and the *deputies* **governors**
and *rulers* **governors** of the *provinces* **jurisdictions**
which are from *India* **Hodu** unto *Ethiopia* **Kush**,
an hundred twenty and seven *provinces* **jurisdictions**,
unto *every province* **jurisdiction by jurisdiction**
according to the *writing* **inscribing** thereof,
and unto *every* people **by people**
after their language,
and to the *Jews* **Yah Hudiym**
according to their *writing* **inscribings**,
and according to their *language* **tongue**.
10 And he *wrote* **inscribed**
in *the king Ahasuerus'* **sovereign Achash Rosh**'s name,
and sealed it with the *king's ring* **sovereign's signet**,
and sent *letters* **scrolls**
by *posts* **the hand of runners** on horseback,
and riders on *mules* **stallions**, *camels* **mules**,
and *young dromedaries* **sons of mares**:
11 Wherein the *king* **sovereign**
granted **gave** the *Jews* **Yah Hudiym**
which were in *every* city **by city**
to *gather themselves together* **congregate**,
and to stand for their *life* **soul**,
to *destroy* **desolate**, to *slay* **slaughter**,
and to *cause to perish* **destroy**,
all the *power* **virtue** of the people and province
that *would assault* **should besiege** them,
both little ones **toddlers** and women,
and *to take the spoil of them for a prey* **spoil their plunder**,
12 Upon one day in all the *provinces* **jurisdictions**
of *king Ahasuerus* **sovereign Achash Rosh**, *namely*,
upon the thirteenth *day* of the twelfth month,
which is the month Adar.
13 The *copy* **transcript** of the *writing* **inscribing**
for *a commandment* **an edict** to be given
in every province **jurisdiction by jurisdiction**
was *published* **exposed** unto all people,
and that the *Jews* **Yah Hudiym**
should be ready against that day
to avenge themselves on their enemies.
14 So the *posts* **runners**
that rode upon *mules* **stallions** and camels went *out*,
being hastened and *pressed on* **hastened**
by the *king's commandment* **sovereign's word**.
And the *decree* **edict** was given at Shushan the palace.
15 And *Mordecai* **Mordekay** went out
from the *presence* **face** of the *king* **sovereign**
in *royal apparel* **a robe of the sovereigndom**
of blue and white,
and with a great crown of gold,
and with a *garment* **robe**
of *fine linen* **bleached cotton** and purple:
and the city of Shushan
rejoiced **resounded** and *was glad* **cheered**.
16 The *Jews* **Yah Hudiym** had light,
and *gladness* **cheerfulness**,
and *joy* **rejoicing**, and *honour* **esteem**.
17 And *in every province* **jurisdiction by jurisdiction**,
and *in every* city **by city**,
whithersoever **whatever place**
the *king's commandment* **sovereign's word**
and his *decree came* **edict touched**,
the *Jews* **Yah Hudiym**
had *joy* **cheer** and *gladness* **rejoicing**,
a *feast* **banquet** and a good day.
And many of the people of the land
became Jews **Yah Hudahized**;
for the fear of the *Jews* **Yah Hudiym** fell upon them.

THE DOMINATION OF THE YAH HUDIYM

9 Now in the twelfth month, that is, the month Adar,
on the thirteenth day of the same,
when the *king's commandment* **sovereign's word**
and his *decree drew near* **edict touched**
to be *put in execution* **worked**,
in the day that the enemies of the *Jews* **Yah Hudiym**
hoped **expected** to *have power* **dominate** over them,
(though it was *turned to the contrary* **overturned**,
that the *Jews had rule* **Yah Hudiym dominated** over them
that hated them;)
2 The *Jews* **Yah Hudiym**
gathered themselves together **congregated** in their cities
throughout all the *provinces* **jurisdictions**
of *the king Ahasuerus* **sovereign Achash Rosh**,
to *lay* **send his** hand on such as sought their *hurt* **evil**:
and no man could *withstand them* **stand at their face**;
for the fear of them fell upon all people.
3 And all the *rulers* **governors**
of the *provinces* **jurisdictions**,
and the *lieutenants* **satraps**, and the *deputies* **governors**,
and *officers* **those that did the work**
of the *king* **sovereign**,
helped **lifted up** the *Jews* **Yah Hudiym**;
because the fear of *Mordecai* **Mordekay** fell upon them.
4 For *Mordecai* **Mordekay** was great
in the *king's* **sovereign's** house,
and his fame
went out throughout all the *provinces* **jurisdictions**:
for this man *Mordecai* **Mordekay**
waxed greater **walked** and *greater* **greatened**.
5 Thus the *Jews* **Yah Hudiym** smote all their enemies
with the stroke of the sword,
and slaughter, and destruction,
and *did* **worked**
what they would **according to their pleasure**
unto those that hated them.
6 And in Shushan the palace the *Jews* **Yah Hudiym**
slew **slaughtered** and destroyed five hundred men.

7 And Parshandatha, and Dalphon, and Aspatha,
8 And Poratha, and *Adalia* **Adalya**, and Aridatha,
9 And Parmashta, and Arisai, and *Aridai* **Ariday**,
and *Vajezatha* **Vayezatha**,
10 The ten sons of Haman
the son of *Hammedatha* **Medatha**,
the *enemy* **tribulator** of the *Jews* **Yah Hudiym**,
slew **slaughtered** they;
but on the *spoil* **plunder**
laid **extended** they not their hand.
11 On that day
the number of those that were *slain* **slaughtered**
in Shushan the palace
was brought *before* **at the face of** the *king* **sovereign**.
12 And the *king* **sovereign**
said unto *Esther* **Ester** the *queen* **sovereigness**,
The *Jews* **Yah Hudiym** have *slain* **slaughtered**
and destroyed five hundred men in Shushan the palace,
and the ten sons of Haman;
what have they *done* **worked** in the *rest* **survivors**
of the *king's provinces* **sovereign's jurisdictions**?
now what is thy petition?
and it shall be *granted* **given** thee:
or what is thy request *further* **again**?
and it shall be *done* **worked**.
13 Then said *Esther* **Ester**,
If it *please* **be good with** the *king* **sovereign**,
let it be *granted* **given**
to the *Jews* **Yah Hudiym** which are in Shushan
to *do* **work** to morrow also
according unto this day's *decree* **edict**,
and let Haman's ten sons
be hanged upon the *gallows* **tree**.
14 And the *king* **sovereign**
commanded **said** it so to be *done* **worked**:
and the *decree* **edict** was given at Shushan;
and they hanged Haman's ten sons.
15 For the *Jews* **Yah Hudiym** that were in Shushan
gathered themselves together **congregated**
on the fourteenth day also of the month Adar,
and *slew* **slaughtered** three hundred men at Shushan;
but on the *prey* **plunder**
they *laid* **extended** not their hand.
16 But the *other Jews* **Yah Hudiym survivors**
that were in the *king's provinces* **sovereign's jurisdictions**
gathered themselves together **congregated**,
and stood for their *lives* **souls**,
and *had rest* **rested** from their enemies,
and *slew* **slaughtered** of their *foes* **haters**
seventy and five thousand,
but they *laid* **extended** not their hands
on the *prey* **plunder**,
17 On the thirteenth day of the month Adar;
and on the fourteenth day of the same rested they,
and *made* **worked** it
a day of *feasting* **banqueting** and *gladness* **cheerfulness**.
18 But the *Jews* **Yah Hudiym** that were at Shushan
assembled together **congregated**
on the thirteenth *day* thereof,
and on the fourteenth thereof;
and on the fifteenth *day* of the same they rested,
and *made* **worked** it
a day of *feasting* **banqueting** and *gladness* **cheerfulness**.
19 Therefore the *Jews* **Yah Hudiym** of the *villages* **courts**,
that *dwelt* **settled**
in the *unwalled towns* **cities of the suburbs**,
made **worked** the fourteenth day of the month Adar
a day of gladness **cheerfulness** and *feasting* **banqueting**,
and a good day,
and of sending portions *one* **man** to *another* **friend**.

THE DAYS OF PURIM

20 And *Mordecai* **Mordekay**
wrote **inscribed** these *things* **words**,
and sent *letters* **scrolls** unto all the *Jews* **Yah Hudiym**
that were in all the *provinces* **jurisdictions**
of the *king Ahasuerus* **sovereign Achash Rosh**,
both nigh and far,
21 To *stablish* **raise** *this* among them,
that they should *keep* **work**
the fourteenth day of the month Adar,
and the fifteenth day of the same, *yearly* **year by year**,
22 As the days
wherein the *Jews* **Yah Hudiym**
rested from their enemies,
and the month which was turned unto them
from *sorrow* **grief** to *joy* **cheer**,
and from mourning into a good day:
that they should *make* **work** them
days of *feasting* **banqueting** and *joy* **cheer**,
and of sending portions *one* **man** to *another* **friend**,
and gifts to the *poor* **needy**.
23 And the *Jews* **Yah Hudiym**
undertook to *do* **work** as they had begun,
and as *Mordecai* **Mordekay** had *written* **inscribed**
unto them;
24 Because Haman
the son of *Hammedatha* **Medatha**, the *Agagite* **Agagiy**,
the *enemy* **tribulator** of all the *Jews* **Yah Hudiym**,
had *devised* **fabricated** against the *Jews* **Yah Hudiym**
to destroy them,
and had *cast* **felled** Pur, that is, the *lot* **pebble**,
to *consume* **agitate** them, and to destroy them;
25 But when *Esther* **Ester** came
before **at the face of** the *king* **sovereign**,
he *commanded* **said** by *letters* **scrolls**
that his *wicked device* **evil fabrication**,
which he *devised* **fabricated**
against the *Jews* **Yah Hudiym**,
should return upon his own head,
and that he and his sons should be hanged
on the *gallows* **tree**.
26 Wherefore they called these days Purim
after the name of Pur.
Therefore for all the words of this *letter* **epistle**,
and of that which they had seen
concerning *this matter* **thus**,
and which *had come* **touched** unto them,
27 The *Jews ordained* **Yah Hudiym arose**,
and took upon them, and upon their seed,
and upon all such as joined themselves unto them,
so as it should not *fail* **pass away**,
that they *would keep* **should work** these two days
according to their *writing* **inscribing**,
and according to their *appointed time* **appointment**
every year **by year**;
28 And that these days
should be remembered and *kept* **worked**
throughout every generation **by generation**,
every family **by family**,
every province **jurisdiction by jurisdiction**,
and every city **by city**;
and that these days of Purim should not *fail* **pass away**
from among the *Jews* **Yah Hudiym**,
nor the memorial of them
perish **be consumed** from their seed.
29 Then *Esther* **Ester** the *queen* **sovereigness**,
the daughter of *Abihail* **Abi Hail**,
and *Mordecai* **Mordekay** the *Jew* **Yah Hudiy**,
wrote **inscribed** with all *authority* **power**,
to *confirm* **raise** this second *letter* **epistle** of Purim.
30 And he sent the *letters* **scrolls**
unto all the *Jews* **Yah Hudiym**,
to the hundred twenty and seven *provinces* **jurisdictions**
of the *kingdom* **sovereigndom** of *Ahasuerus* **Achash Rosh**,
with words of *peace* **shalom** and truth,
31 To *confirm* **raise** these days of Purim
in their *times appointed* **appointment**,
according as *Mordecai* **Mordekay** the *Jew* **Yah Hudiy**
and *Esther* **Ester** the *queen* **sovereigness**
had *enjoined* **raised** them,
and as they had *decreed* **raised**
for *themselves* **their souls** and for their seed,
the *matters* **words** of the fastings and their cry.
32 And the *decree* **edict** of *Esther* **Ester**
confirmed **raised** these *matters* **words** of Purim;
and it was *written* **inscribed** in the *book* **scroll**.

THE GREATNESS OF MORDEKAY

10 And *the king Ahasuerus* **sovereign Achash Rosh**
laid a tribute **set a vassal** upon the land,
and upon the isles of the sea.

2 And all the *acts* **works** of his power and of his might,
and the *declaration* **sum**
of the greatness of *Mordecai* **Mordekay**,
whereunto the *king advanced* **sovereign greatened** him,
are they not *written* **inscribed** in the *book* **scroll**
of the *chronicles* **words of the days**
of the *kings* **sovereigns** of *Media* **Maday** and Persia?
3 For *Mordecai* **Mordekay** the *Jew* **Yah Hudiy**
was *next* **second**
unto *king Ahasuerus* **sovereign Achash Rosh**,
and great among the *Jews* **Yah Hudiym**,
and *accepted* **pleased**
of the *multitude* **abundance** of his brethren,
seeking the *wealth of* **goodness for** his people,
and *speaking peace* **wording shalom** to all his seed.

KEY TO INTERPRETING THE EXEGESES:
King James text is in regular type;
Text under exegeses is in oblique type;
Text of exegeses is in bold type.

1 There was a man in the land of *Uz* **Us**,
whose name was *Job* **Iyob**;
and that man was *perfect* **integrious** and *upright* **straight**,
and one that *feared God* **awed Elohim**,
and *eschewed* **turned aside from** evil.
2 And there were born unto him
seven sons and three daughters.
3 His *substance* **chattel** also
was seven thousand *sheep* **flocks**,
and three thousand camels,
and five hundred yoke of oxen,
and five hundred she *asses* **burros**,
and a *very* **mighty** great *household* **servantry**;
so that this man
was the greatest of all the men of the east.
4 And his sons went
and *feasted* **worked a banquet** in their houses,
every one **each man** his day;
and sent and called for their three sisters
to eat and to drink with them.
5 And it *was so* **became**,
when the days of *their feasting* **banqueting**
were gone about,
that *Job* **Iyob** sent and *sanctified* **hallowed** them,
and *rose up* **started** early in the morning,
and *offered burnt offerings* **holocausted holocausts**
according to the number of them all:
for *Job* **Iyob** said,
It may be that **Perhaps** my sons have sinned,
and cursed God **yet blessed Elohim** in their hearts.
Thus *did Job* **worked Iyob** continually.

SATAN'S FIRST CHALLENGE

6 *Now* there *was* **became** a day
when the sons of *God* **Elohim**
came to *present* **station** themselves
before the LORD **by Yah Veh**,
and Satan came also among them.
7 And *the LORD* **Yah Veh** said unto Satan,
Whence comest thou?
Then Satan answered *the LORD* **Yah Veh**, and said,
From *going* **flitting** to and fro in the earth,
and from walking *up* **forth** and *down* **back** in it.
8 And *the LORD* **Yah Veh** said unto Satan,
Hast thou *considered* **set thy heart**
on my servant *Job* **Iyob**,
that there is none like him in the earth,
a perfect **an integrious** and *an upright* **straight** man,
one that *feareth God* **aweth Elohim**,
and *escheweth* **turneth aside from** evil?
9 Then Satan answered *the LORD* **Yah Veh**, and said,
Doth *Job* **Iyob** fear *God for naught* **Elohim gratuitously**?
10 Hast not thou made an hedge about him,
and *about* **throughout** his house,
and *about* **throughout** all that he hath
on every side **all around**?
thou hast blessed the work of his hands,
and his *substance* **chattel**
is increased **breaketh forth** in the land.
11 But *put forth* **extend** thine hand *now* **I beseech**,
and touch all that he hath,
and he will curse **whether he shall bless** thee to thy face.
12 And *the LORD* **Yah Veh** said unto Satan, Behold,
all that he hath is in thy *power* **hand**;
only upon himself *put* **extend** not *forth* thine hand.
So Satan went forth
from the *presence* **face** of *the LORD* **Yah Veh**.

IYOB'S FIRST TEST

13 And there *was* **became** a day
when his sons and his daughters
were eating and drinking wine
in their *eldest* **firstborn** brother's house:
14 And there came *a messenger* **an angel** unto *Job* **Iyob**,
and said, The oxen were plowing,
and the *asses feeding* **she burros tending**
beside them **at their hands**:

15 And the Sabeans *fell upon* **felled** them,
and took them away;
yea, they have *slain* **smitten** the *servants* **lads**
with the *edge* **mouth** of the sword;
and I only am escaped alone to tell thee.
16 While he was yet *speaking* **wording**,
there came also another, and said,
The fire of *God* **Elohim** is fallen from *heaven* **the heavens**,
and hath burned up the *sheep* **flocks**,
and the *servants* **lads**, and consumed them;
and I only am escaped alone to tell thee.
17 While he was yet *speaking* **wording**,
there came also another, and said,
The *Chaldeans made* **Kesediym set** out three *bands* **heads**,
and *fell upon* **stripped** the camels,
and have *carried* **taken** them away, yea,
and *slain* **smitten** the servants
with the *edge* **mouth** of the sword;
and I only am escaped alone to tell thee.
18 While he was yet *speaking* **wording**,
there came also another, and said,
Thy sons and thy daughters
were eating and drinking wine
in their *eldest* **firstborn** brother's house:
19 And, behold,
there came a great wind from **across** the wilderness,
and *smote* **touched** the four corners of the house,
and it fell upon the *young men* **lads**, and they are dead;
and I only am escaped alone to tell thee.
20 Then *Job* **Iyob** arose, and *rent* **ripped** his mantle,
and *shaved* **sheared** his head,
and fell down upon the *ground* **earth**,
and *worshipped* **prostrated**.
21 And said,
Naked came I out of my mother's *womb* **belly**,
and naked shall I return thither:
the LORD **Yah Veh** gave,
and *the LORD* **Yah Veh** hath taken away;
blessed be the name of *the LORD* **Yah Veh**.
22 In all this *Job* **Iyob** sinned not,
nor *charged God* **attributed Elohim**
foolishly **with frivolity**.

SATAN'S SECOND CHALLENGE

2 Again there *was* **became** a day
when the sons of *God* **Elohim**
came to *present* **station** themselves
before the LORD **by Yah Veh**,
and Satan came also among them
to *present* **station** himself *before the LORD* **by Yah Veh**.
2 And *the LORD* **Yah Veh** said unto Satan,
From whence comest thou?
And Satan answered *the LORD* **Yah Veh**, and said,
From *going* **flitting** to and fro in the earth,
and from walking *up* **forth** and *down* **back** in it.
3 And *the LORD* **Yah Veh** said unto Satan,
Hast thou *considered* **set thy heart**
on my servant *Job* **Iyob**,
that there is none like him in the earth,
a perfect **an integrious** and *an upright* **straight** man,
one that *feareth God* **aweth Elohim**,
and *escheweth* **turneth aside from** evil?
and still he *holdeth fast* **upholdeth** his integrity,
although thou *movedst* **goadest** me *against him*,
to *destroy* **swallow** him *without cause* **gratuitously**.
4 And Satan answered *the LORD* **Yah Veh**, and said,
Skin for skin, yea,
all that a man hath *will* **shall** he give for his *life* **soul**.
5 But *put forth* **extend** thine hand *now* **I beseech**,
and touch his bone and his flesh,
and he will curse **whether he shall bless** thee to thy face.
6 And *the LORD* **Yah Veh** said unto Satan, Behold,
he is in thine hand; but *save* **guard** his *life* **soul**.

IYOB'S SECOND TEST

7 So went Satan forth
from the *presence* **face** of *the LORD* **Yah Veh**,
and smote *Job* **Iyob** with *sore boils* **evil ulcers**
from the sole of his foot unto his *crown* **scalp**.
8 And he took him a potsherd to scrape himself withal;
and he *sat down* **settled** among the ashes.
9 Then said his *wife* **woman** unto him,
Dost **Shalt** thou still *retain* **uphold** thine integrity?
curse God **bless Elohim**, and die.
10 But he said unto her, Thou *speakest* **wordest**
as one of the foolish *women speaketh* **wordeth**.
What? **Yea,**
shall we *receive* **take** good at the hand of *God* **Elohim**,
and shall we not *receive* **take** evil?
In all this *did not Job sin* **Iyob sinned not** with his lips.

IYOB'S THREE FRIENDS

11 *Now* when *Job's* **Iyob's** three friends
heard of all this evil that was come upon him,
they came *every one* **each man** from his own place;
Eliphaz **Eli Phaz** the *Temanite* **Temaniy**,
and Bildad the *Shuhite* **Shuachiy**,
and *Zophar* **Sophar** the *Naamathite* **Naamahiy**:
for they had *made an appointment* **congregated** together
to come to *mourn* **wag** with him
and to *comfort* **sigh with** him.
12 And when they lifted up their eyes afar off,
and *knew* **recognized** him not,
they lifted up their voice, and wept;
and they *rent every one* **ripped each man** his mantle,
and sprinkled dust upon their heads
toward *heaven* **the heavens**.
13 So they *sat down* **settled** with him upon the ground
seven days and seven nights,
and none *spake* **worded** a word unto him:
for they saw that *his grief* **the pain**
was *very* **mighty** great.

IYOB SPEAKS

3 After this opened *Job* **Iyob** his mouth,
and *cursed* **abased** his day.
2 And *Job spake* **Iyob answered**, and said,
3 Let the day *perish* **destruct** wherein I was born,
and the night in which it was said,
There is a *man* **mighty** child conceived.
4 Let that day be darkness;
let not *God regard* **Elohah require** it from above,
neither let the light shine upon it.
5 Let darkness and the shadow of death *stain* **redeem** it;
let a *cloud dwell* **cloudiness tabernacle** upon it;
let the *blackness* **eclipses** of the day *terrify* **frighten** it.
6 As for that night, let darkness *seize upon* **take** it;
let it not *be joined* **rejoice** unto the days of the year,
let it not come into the number of the *months* **moons**.
7 *Lo* **Behold**, let that night be *solitary* **sterile**,
let no *joyful voice* **shout** come therein.
8 Let them curse it that curse the day,
who are ready to
raise up their mourning **waken a leviathan**.
9 Let the stars of the *twilight thereof* **evening breeze**
be dark **darken**;
let it *look for* **await** light, but have none;
neither let it see the *dawning* **eyelids** of the *day* **dawn**:
10 Because it shut not *up*
the doors of my *mother's womb* **belly**,
nor hid *sorrow* **toil** from mine eyes.
11 Why died I not from the womb?
why did I not give up the ghost
— expire when I came out of the belly?
12 Why did the knees *prevent* **anticipate** me?
or why the breasts that I should suck?
13 For now should I have lain *still* **down**
and *been quiet* **rested**,
I should have slept: then had I been at rest,
14 With *kings* **sovereigns** and counsellors of the earth,
which built *desolate places* **parched areas** for themselves;
15 Or with *princes* **governors** that had gold,
who filled their houses with silver:
16 Or as an hidden *untimely birth* **miscarriage**
I had not been;
as infants which never saw light.
17 There the wicked cease from *troubling* **commotion**;
and there the *weary be at* **wearied of force** rest.
18 There the *prisoners rest* **bound relax** together;
they hear not the voice of the *oppressor* **exactor**.
19 The small and great are there;
and the servant is *free* **liberated** from his *master* **adoni**.
20 Wherefore is light given to him that is in misery,
and life unto the bitter *in* soul;

21 Which *long for* **await** death, but it *cometh* **be** not;
and dig for it more than for hid treasures;
22 Which *rejoice exceedingly* **cheer and twirl**,
and *are glad* **rejoice**,
when they can find the *grave* **tomb**?
23 *Why is light given to a man*
— To the mighty whose way is hid,
and whom *God* **Elohah** hath hedged in?
24 For my sighing cometh
before I eat **at the face of my bread**,
and my roarings are poured out like the waters.
25 For the *thing which I greatly feared* **dread I dreaded**
is come upon me,
and that which I *was afraid of* **feared** is come unto me.
26 I was not *in safety* **serenified**, neither had I rest,
neither *was I quiet* **rested I**; yet *trouble* **commotion** came.

ELI PHAZ ANSWERS

4 Then *Eliphaz* **Eli Phaz** the *Temanite* **Temaniy**
answered and said,
2 If we *assay to commune* **test a word** with thee,
wilt **shalt** thou *be grieved* **weary**?
but who can *withhold* **refrain** himself
from *speaking* **utterances**?
3 Behold, thou hast instructed many,
and thou hast strengthened the weak hands.
4 Thy *words* **utterances** have *upholden* **raised** him
that *was falling* **faltered**,
and thou hast strengthened the *feeble* **kneeling** knees.
5 But now it is come upon thee,
and thou *faintest* **weariest**;
it toucheth thee, and thou art *troubled* **terrified**.
6 Is not this thy *fear* **awe**, thy confidence, thy hope,
and the *uprightness* **integrity** of thy ways?
7 Remember, I pray thee,
who ever *perished* **destructed**, being innocent?
or where were the *righteous* **straight** cut off?
8 Even as I have seen,
they that plow *iniquity* **mischief**,
and *sow wickedness* **seed toil**,
reap the same **thus harvest**.
9 By the *blast* **breath** of *God* **Elohah**
they *perish* **destruct**,
and by the *breath* **spirit/wind** of his nostrils
are they *consumed* **finished off**.
10 The roaring of the lion,
and the voice of the *fierce* **roaring** lion,
and the teeth of the *young lions* **whelps**,
are *broken* **pulled**.
11 The old lion *perisheth* **destructeth**
for lack of **without** prey,
and the *stout* **roaring** lion's whelps
are *scattered abroad* **separated**.
12 Now a *thing* **word** was *secretly* **by stealth**
brought to me,
and mine ear *received a little* **took an inkling** *thereof*.
13 In *thoughts* **sentiments** from the visions of the night,
when deep sleep falleth on men,
14 *Fear came upon* **Dread confronted** me, and trembling,
which *made all* my **abundant** bones *to shake* **dreaded**.
15 Then a spirit passed before my face;
the hair of my flesh stood *up* **on end**:
16 It stood *still*,
but I could not *discern* **recognize** the *form* **visage** *thereof*:
an image **a manifestation** was before mine eyes,
there was silence, **Stillness!** and I heard a voice, *saying*,
17 Shall mortal man be more just than *God* **Elohah**?
shall *a man* **the mighty** be more pure
han his *maker* **Worker**?
18 Behold, he put no trust in his servants;
and his angels he *charged* **set** with *folly* **braggadocio**:
19 *How much less in them* **Yea, they**
that *dwell* **tabernacle** in houses of clay,
whose foundation is in the dust,
which are crushed *before* **at the face of** the moth*?*
20 They are *destroyed* **crushed** from morning to evening:
they *perish for ever* **destruct in perpetuity**
without *any regarding* **setting** it.
21 Doth not their *excellency* **remainder** which is in them
go away **pull stakes**?
they die, even without wisdom.

5 Call *now* **I beseech**,
if there be any that *will* **shall** answer thee;
and to which of the *saints wilt* **holy shalt** thou *turn* **face**?
2 For *wrath killeth* **vexation slaughtereth** the foolish *man*,
and envy *slayeth* **deathifieth** the *silly one* **enticed**.
3 I have seen the foolish taking root:
but suddenly I cursed his habitation **of rest**.
4 His children are far from *safety* **salvation**,
and they are crushed in the *gate* **portal**,
neither is there any to *deliver* **rescue** them.
5 Whose harvest the *hungry* **famished** eateth up,
and taketh it even *out of* **through** the thorns,
and the robber
swalloweth up **gulpeth** their *substance* **valuables**.
6 Although *affliction* **mischief**
cometh not forth of the dust,
neither *doth trouble* **toil**
spring **sprout** out of the *ground* **soil**;
7 Yet *man* **humanity** is born unto *trouble* **toil**,
as the *sparks* **sons of the burning coal lift to** fly *upward*.
8 **But** I *would* **should** seek unto *God* **El**,
and unto *God* **Elohim**
would **should** I *commit* **set** my *cause* **word**:
9 Which *doeth* **worketh** great *things*
and unsearchable **not to be probed**;
marvellous things **marvels** without number:
10 Who giveth rain upon the **face of the** earth,
and sendeth waters upon the *fields* **face of the outways**:
11 To set *up on high* **in the heights**
those that be low **the lowly**;
that *those which mourn* **the darkened**
may be *exalted to safety* **lifted unto salvation**.
12 He *disappointeth* **breaketh down**
the *devices* **fabrications** of the *crafty* **subtle,**
so that their hands
cannot perform **work not** their *enterprise* **substance**.
13 He *taketh* **captureth** the wise in their own craftiness:
and the counsel of the *froward* **twisters**
is *carried headlong* **hastened**.
14 They meet with darkness in the *daytime* **day**,
and grope in the noonday as in the night.
15 But he saveth the *poor* **needy** from the sword,
from their mouth,
and from the hand of the *mighty* **strong**.
16 So the poor *hath* **becometh** hope,
and *iniquity stoppeth* **wickedness shutteth** her mouth.
17 Behold, *happy* **blithe** is the man
whom *God correcteth* **Elohah reproveth**:
therefore *despise* **spurn** not thou
the *chastening* **discipline** of *the Almighty* **Shadday**:
18 For he *maketh sore* **paineth**, and bindeth *up*:
he *woundeth* **striketh**, and his hands *make whole* **heal**.
19 He shall *deliver* **rescue** thee in six *troubles* **tribulations**:
yea, in seven there shall no evil touch thee.
20 In famine he shall redeem thee from death:
and in war from the *power* **hand** of the sword.
21 Thou shalt be hid from the *scourge* **lash** of the tongue:
neither shalt thou *be afraid of destruction* **awe devastation**
when it cometh.
22 At *destruction* **devastation** and *famine* **hunger**
thou shalt laugh:
neither shalt thou *be afraid of* **awe**
the *beasts* **live beings** of the earth.
23 For *thou shalt be in league* **thy covenant shall be**
with the stones of the field:
and the beasts of the field
shall be at *peace* **shalom** with thee.
24 And thou shalt know that thy *tabernacle* **tent**
shall be in *peace* **shalom**;
and thou shalt visit thy habitation **of rest**,
and shalt not sin.
25 Thou shalt know also that thy seed shall be great,
and thine offspring as the *grass* **herbage** of the earth.
26 Thou shalt come to thy *grave* **tomb**
in *a full age* **maturity**,
like as a *shock of corn cometh* **heap ascendeth**
in his *season* **time**.
27 *Lo* **Behold** this,
we have *searched* **probed** it, so **be** it *is*;
hear it, and know thou it for thy good.

IYOB ANSWERS

6 But *Job* **Iyob** answered and said,
2 Oh that *my grief* **in weighing,**
my vexation were *throughly* weighed,
and my calamity *laid* **lifted** in the balances together!
3 For now it *would* **should** be heavier
than the sand of the sea:
therefore my words are *swallowed up* **gulped**.
4 For the arrows of *the Almighty* **Shadday** are within me,
the poison whereof drinketh up my spirit:
the terrors of *God* **Elohah**
do set themselves in array **line up** against me.
5 *Doth* **Shall** the wild *ass* **runner** bray
when he hath *grass* **sprouts**?
or *loweth* **belloweth** the ox over his fodder?
6 *Can that which is unsavoury* **Shall slime** be eaten
without salt?
or is there *any* taste in the *white* **slime** of an egg?
7 *The things* **Those** that my soul refused to touch
are as my *sorrowful meat* **bloody bread**.
8 *Oh* **Who giveth** that I might have my *request* **petition**;
and that *God* **Elohah**
would grant me the thing that I long for
should give me hope!
9 *Even that it would please God* **Though Elohah willeth**
to *destroy* **crush** me;
that he *would* **should** let loose his hand, and cut me off!
10 Then should *I yet have comfort* **yet my sighing be**; yea,
I would harden myself in sorrow **should jump with pangs**:
let him not spare;
for I have not concealed
the *words* **sayings** of the Holy One.
11 What is my *strength* **force**, that I should *hope* **await**?
and what is mine end,
that I should prolong my *life* **soul**?
12 Is my *strength* **force** the *strength* **force** of stones?
or is my flesh of *brass* **copper**?
13 Is not my help in me?
and is *wisdom* **substance** driven quite from me?
14 To him that *is afflicted* **melteth,**
pity **mercy** should be *shewed* from his friend;
but he forsaketh the *fear* **awe** of *the Almighty* **Shadday**.
15 My brethren have *dealt deceitfully* **covered over**
as a *brook* **wadi**,
and as the *stream* **reservoir** of *brooks* **wadies**
they pass away;
16 Which are *blackish* **darkened** by reason of the ice,
and wherein the snow is *hid* **concealed**:
17 What time they *wax warm* **dissipate**,
they *vanish* **are exterminated**:
when it is hot,
they are *consumed* **extinguished** out of their place.
18 The paths of their way are turned aside;
they *go* **ascend** to *nothing* **waste**, and *perish* **destruct**.
19 The *troops* **paths** of Tema looked,
the *companies* **caravans** of Sheba
waited for **awaited** them.
20 They were *confounded* **shamed**
because they had hoped;
they came thither, and *were ashamed* **blushed**.
21 For now ye are *nothing* **nought**;
ye see my casting down, and *are afraid* **awe**.
22 Did I say, Bring unto me?
or, *Give a reward for* **Bribe** me of your substance?
23 Or, *Deliver* **Rescue** me
from the *enemy's* hand **of the tribulator**?
or, Redeem me from the hand of the *mighty* **tyrant**?
24 Teach me, and I *will hold my tongue* **shall hush**:
and cause me to *understand* **discern**
wherein I have **inadvertently** erred.
25 How *forcible* **reinforcing**
are *right words* **sayings of straightness**!
but what doth your *arguing* **reproving** reprove?
26 Do ye *imagine* **fabricate**
to reprove *words* **utterances**,
and the *speeches* **sayings** of *one that is desperate* **a quitter**,
which are — as wind?
27 Yea, ye *overwhelm* **fell** the *fatherless* **orphan**,
and ye dig *a pit* for your friend.
28 Now therefore *be content, look upon* **will to face** me;
for it is evident unto *you* **your face** if I lie.
29 Return, I *pray* **beseech** you,
let it not be *iniquity* **wickedness**;
yea, return again, my *righteousness* **justness** is in it.
30 Is there *iniquity* **wickedness** in my tongue?
cannot my *taste* **palate**
discern *perverse things* **calamity**?

7 Is there not *an appointed time* **a hostility**
to man upon earth?
are *not* his days also like the days of an hireling?
2 As a servant *earnestly desireth* **gulpeth** the shadow,
and as an hireling
looketh **awaiteth** for *the reward of* his *work* **deeds**:
3 *So am I made to possess* **Thus have I inherited**
months **moons** of vanity,
and *wearisome nights* **nights of toil**
are *appointed* **numbered** to me.
4 When I lie down, I say, When shall I arise,
and the *night* **evening** be *gone* **flown**?
and I am *full* **satiated** of tossings to and fro
unto the *dawning of the day* **evening breeze**.
5 My flesh is *clothed* **enrobed**
with *worms* **maggots** and clods of dust;
my skin is *broken* **split**,
and *become loathsome* **dissipateth**.
6 My days are swifter than a *weaver's shuttle* **weaver**,
and are *spent* **finished off** without hope.
7 O remember that my life is *wind* **wind/spirit**:
mine eye shall *no more* **not return to** see good.
8 The eye of him that hath seen me
shall *see me no more* **not lurk**:
thine eyes are upon me, and I am not.
9 *As* the cloud *is consumed* **finisheth off**
and *vanisheth away* **goeth**:
so he that *goeth down* **descendeth** to *the grave* **sheol**
shall *come up no more* **ascend not again**.
10 He shall return *no more* **not again** to his house,
neither shall his place
know **recognize** him *any more* **again.**
11 Therefore I *will* **shall** not *refrain* **spare** my mouth;
I *will speak* **shall word**
in the *anguish* **tribulation** of my spirit;
I *will complain* **shall meditate**
in the bitterness of my soul.
12 Am I a sea, or a *whale* **monster**,
that thou settest a *watch* **guard** over me?
13 When I say,
My *bed* **bedstead** shall *comfort* **sigh for** me,
my *couch* **bed** shall *ease* **lift** my *complaint* **meditation**;
14 Then thou *scarest* **terrifiest** me with dreams,
and *terrifiest* **frightenest** me through visions:
15 So that my soul chooseth strangling,
and death rather than my *life* **bones**.
16 I *loathe* **spurn** it;
I *would* **shall** not live *alway* **eternally**:
let me *alone* **decease**; for my days are vanity.
17 What is man,
that thou shouldest *magnify* **greaten** him?
and that thou shouldest set thine heart upon him?
18 And that thou shouldest visit him every morning,
and *try* **proof** him every *moment* **blink**?
19 How long
wilt **shalt** thou not *depart* **look away** from me,
nor let me *alone* **loose** till I swallow down my *spittle* **spit**?
20 I have sinned; what shall I do unto thee,
O thou *preserver* **guardian** of *men* **humanity**?
why hast thou set me as a *mark* **target** against thee,
so that I am a burden to myself?
21 And why dost thou not
pardon **lift** my *transgression* **rebellion**,
and *take* **pass** away my *iniquity* **perversity**?
for now shall I *sleep* **lie** in the dust;
and thou shalt seek me *in the morning* **early**,
but I shall not be.

BILDAD ANSWERS

8 Then answered Bildad the *Shuhite* **Shuachiy**,
and said,
2 *How long* **Until when**
wilt **shalt** thou *speak* **utter** these *things*?
and how long shall the words — **the sayings of thy mouth**

be *like a strong* **much** wind?
3 Doth *God pervert* **El twist** judgment?
or doth *the Almighty* **Shadday**
pervert justice **twist justness**?
4 If thy children have sinned against him,
and he have *cast* **sent** them away
for **by the hand of** their *transgression* **rebellion**;
5 If thou *wouldest* **shouldest** seek unto *God* **El**
betimes **early**
and *make thy supplication* **seekest charism**
to the Almighty **of Shadday**;
6 If thou wert pure and *upright* **straight**;
surely now he *would* **should** awake for thee,
and make the habitation **of rest**
of thy *righteousness prosperous* **justness at shalom**.
7 Though thy beginning was *small* **little**,
yet thy *latter end* **finality** should *greatly* **mightily** increase.
8 For enquire, I *pray* **beseech** thee, of the *former* **first** age,
and prepare thyself
to the *search* **probing** of their fathers:
9 (For we are *but* of yesterday, and know *nothing* **naught**,
because our days upon earth are a shadow:)
10 Shall not they teach thee, and *tell* **say to** thee,
and utter *words* **utterances** out of their heart?
11 Can the rush *grow up* **rise** without mire?
can the *flag grow* **bulrush increase** without water?
12 Whilst it is yet in his *greenness* **unripeness**,
and not *cut down* **plucked**,
it withereth *before* **at the face of** any *other* herb.
13 So are the paths of all that forget *God* **El**;
and the *hypocrite's* **profaner's** hope shall *perish* **destruct**:
14 Whose hope shall be cut off,
and whose *trust* **confidence**
shall be a spider's *web* **house**.
15 He shall lean upon his house,
but it shall not stand:
he shall *hold* **strengthen** it *fast*,
but it shall not *endure* **arise**.
16 He is *green before* **moist at the face of** the sun,
and his *branch* **sprout** shooteth forth in his garden.
17 His roots are *wrapped* **entwined** about the heap,
and seeth the *place* **house** of stones.
18 If he *destroy him* **be swallowed** from his place,
then it shall deny him, *saying*, I have not seen thee.
19 Behold, this is the joy of his way,
and out of the *earth* **dust** shall others *grow* **sprout**.
20 Behold,
God will **El shall** not *cast away* **spurn**
a perfect man **the integrious**,
neither *will* **shall** he *help* **strengthen the hand**
of the *evil doers* **vilifiers**:
21 Till he fill thy mouth with laughing,
and thy lips with *rejoicing* **shouting**.
22 They that hate thee
shall be *clothed* **enrobed** with shame;
and the *dwelling place* **tent** of the wicked
shall come to nought.

IYOB ANSWERS

9 Then *Job* **Iyob** answered and said,
Truly I know it is so *of a truth*:
but how should man be *just* **justified** with *God* **El**?
3 If he *will* **desireth to** contend with him,
he cannot answer him one of a thousand.
4 He is wise in heart, and *mighty* **strong** in *strength* **force**:
who hath hardened *himself* against him,
and hath *prospered* **been at shalom**?
5 Which removeth the mountains, and they know not:
which overturneth them in his *anger* **wrath**.
6 Which shaketh the earth out of her place,
and the pillars thereof tremble.
7 Which *commandeth* **saith to** the sun, and it riseth not;
and sealeth up the stars.
8 Which alone spreadeth out the heavens,
and treadeth upon the *waves* **bamahs** of the sea.
9 Which *maketh Arcturus* **worketh Ash**, *Orion* **Kesil**,
and *Pleiades* **Kimah**, and the chambers of the south.
10 Which *doeth* **worketh** great *things*
past finding out **— unable to be probed**;
yea, and *wonders* **marvels** without number.
11 *Lo* **Behold**, he *goeth* **passeth** by me, and I see him not:
he passeth on also, but I *perceive* **discern** him not.
12 Behold, he *taketh away* **seizeth**,
who *can hinder* **turneth** him **back**?
who *will* **shall** say unto him, What *doest* **workest** thou?
13 If *God* **Elohah**
will **shall** not *withdraw* **turn back** his *anger* **wrath**,
the proud helpers *do stoop* **prostrate** under him.
14 How much less shall I answer him,
and choose out my words *to reason* with him?
15 Whom, though I were *righteous* **justified**,
yet *would* **should** I not answer,
but I *would make supplication* **should seek charism**
to **from** my judge.
16 If I had called, and he had answered me;
yet *would* **should** I not *believe* **trust**
that he had hearkened unto my voice.
17 For he *breaketh* **crusheth** me with a *tempest* **whirling**,
and *multiplieth* **aboundeth** my wounds
without cause **gratuitously**.
18 He *will* **shall** not *suffer* **give** me
to *take* **return** my *breath* **spirit to me**,
but *filleth* **satiateth** me with *bitterness* **bitternesses**.
19 If *I speak of strength* **of force**,
lo **behold**, he is strong:
and if of judgment,
who shall *set me a time to plead* **congregate to me**?
20 If I justify myself,
mine own mouth shall *condemn me* **judge me wicked**:
if *I say*, I am *perfect* **integrious**,
it shall also *prove me perverse* **pervert me**.
21 *Though I were perfect* **I am integrious**,
yet *would* **should** I not know my soul:
I would despise **should spurn** my life.
22 This is one *thing*, therefore I said it,
He *destroyeth* **finisheth off**
the *perfect* **integrious** and the wicked.
23 If the *scourge slay* **whip deathify** suddenly,
he *will laugh* **shall deride**
at the *trial* **testing** of the innocent.
24 The earth is given into the hand of the wicked:
he covereth the faces of the judges *thereof*;
if not, where, and who is he?
25 Now my days are swifter than a *post* **runner**:
they flee away, they see no good.
26 They are passed away as the *swift* ships **of longing**:
as the eagle that *hasteth to the prey* **pounceth for food**.
27 If I say, I *will* **shall** forget my *complaint* **meditation**,
I *will leave off* **shall forsake** my *heaviness* **face**,
and *comfort* **relax** *myself*:
28 I *am afraid of* **fear** all my *sorrows* **contortions**,
I know that thou
wilt **shalt** not *hold* **exonerate** me *innocent*.
29 If I be wicked, why then labour I in vain?
30 If I *wash* **bathe** myself with snow water,
and *make my hands never so clean*
cleanse my palms in purity;
31 Yet shalt thou *plunge* **dip** me in the *ditch* **pit of ruin**,
and mine own clothes shall abhor me.
32 For he is not a man, as I *am*,
that I should answer him,
and we should come together in judgment.
33 Neither is there any *daysman* **reprover** betwixt us,
that might *lay* **place** his hand upon us both.
34 Let him *take his rod away* **turn aside his scion** from me,
and let not his *fear terrify* **terror frighten** me:
35 Then *would* **should** I *speak* **word**,
and not *fear* **awe** him;
but it is not so with me.

10 My soul *is weary of my* **loatheth** life;
I *will* **shall** leave my *complaint* **meditation** upon myself;
I *will speak* **shall word** in the bitterness of my soul.
2 I *will* **shall** say unto *God* **Elohah**,
Do not condemn me **Judge me not wicked**;
shew me **let me know**
wherefore thou contendest with me.
3 Is it good unto thee that thou shouldest oppress,
that thou shouldest *despise* **spurn**
the *work* **labour** of *thine hands* **thy palms**,
and shine upon the counsel of the wicked?
4 Hast thou eyes of flesh? or seest thou as man seeth?

5 Are thy days as the days of man?
are thy years as *man's* days **of the mighty**,
6 That thou *enquirest* **seekest**
after *mine iniquity* **my perversity**,
and searchest after my sin?
7 *Thou knowest that*, **As to your knowledge**
I am not wicked;
and there is none
that can *deliver* **escape** out of thine hand.
8 Thine hands have *made* **formed** me
and *fashioned* **worked** me together round about;
yet thou *dost destroy* **swallowest** me.
9 Remember, I beseech thee,
that thou hast *made* **worked** me as the clay;
and *wilt* **shalt** thou *bring* **return** me into dust *again*?
10 Hast thou not poured me out as milk,
and curdled me like cheese?
11 Thou hast *clothed* **enrobed** me with skin and flesh,
and hast *fenced* **hedged** me with bones and sinews.
12 Thou hast *granted* **worked** me life and *favour* **mercy**,
and thy visitation hath *preserved* **guarded** my spirit.
13 And these *things* hast thou hid in thine heart:
I know that this is with thee.
14 If I sin, then thou *markest* **guardest** me,
and thou *wilt* **shalt** not *acquit* **exonerate** me
from mine iniquity.
15 If I be wicked, woe unto me;
and if I be *righteous* **justified**,
yet *will* **shall** I not lift *up* my head.
I am *full of confusion* **satiated with abasement**;
therefore see thou *mine affliction* **my humiliation**;
16 For it *increaseth* **riseth**.
Thou huntest me as a *fierce* **roaring** lion:
and *again* **turnest back;**
thou shewest thyself marvellous upon me.
17 Thou renewest thy witnesses against me,
and *increasest thine indignation* **aboundest thy vexation**
upon **with** me;
changes and *war* **hostility** are against me.
18 Wherefore then hast thou brought me forth
out of the womb?
Oh that I had *given up the ghost* **expired**,
and no eye had seen me!
19 *I should have been* **As not being**
as though I had not been **I have become**;
I should have been carried — **brought** from the *womb* **belly**
to the *grave* **tomb**.
20 Are not my days few?
cease *then, and let me alone* **set away from me**,
that I may *take comfort* **relax** a little,
21 Before I go *whence I shall* **and** not return,
even to the land of darkness and the shadow of death;
22 A land of darkness, as darkness *itself*;
and of the shadow of death, without any order,
and where the *light* **shining** is as darkness.

SOPHAR ANSWERS

11 Then answered
Zophar **Sophar** the *Naamathite* **Naamahiy**, and said,
2 Should not the *multitude* **abundance** of words
be answered?
and should a man full of *talk* **lips** be justified?
3 Should thy lies make men *hold their peace* **hush**?
and when thou *mockest* **deridest**,
shall no *man make thee ashamed* **one shame thee**?
4 For thou hast said, My doctrine is pure,
and I am *clean* **pure** in thine eyes.
5 But *oh that God would speak*
who giveth that Elohah should word,
and open his lips against thee;
6 And that he *would shew* **should tell** thee
the *secrets* **concealments** of wisdom,
that they are *double to that which is* **a double substance**!
Know that *God* **Elohah** exacteth of thee
less than thine iniquity deserveth **thy perversity**.
7 Canst thou by *searching* **probing** find out *God* **Elohah**?
canst thou find out
the *Almighty unto perfection* **conclusion of Shadday**?
8 It is as high as *heaven* **the heavens**;
what *canst* **doest** thou *do*?
deeper than *hell* **sheol**;
what *canst* **knowest** thou *know*?
9 The measure thereof is longer than the earth,
and broader than the sea.
10 If he *cut off* **pass by**, and shut up,
or *gather together* **congregate**,
then who *can hinder* **shall turn** him **back**?
11 For he knoweth vain men:
he seeth *wickedness* **mischief** *also*;
will he not then consider **shall no one discern** it?
12 For *vain* **empty** man *would be wise* **disheartening**,
though *man* **humanity** be born
like a wild *ass's* **runner's** colt.
13 If thou prepare thine heart,
and *stretch out thine hands* **spread thy palms** toward him;
14 If *iniquity* **mischief** be in thine hand,
put **remove** it far away,
and let not wickedness
dwell **tabernacle** in thy *tabernacles* **tents**.
15 For then shalt thou lift *up* thy face
without spot **apart from blemish**;
yea, thou shalt be *stedfast* **firmed**, and shalt not *fear* **awe**:
16 Because thou shalt forget thy *misery* **toil**,
and remember it as waters that pass away:
17 And *thine age* **transcience**
shall *be clearer than* **arise above** the noonday:
thou shalt *shine forth* **fly**, thou shalt be as the morning.
18 And thou shalt *be secure* **confide**,
because there is hope;
yea, thou shalt dig *about thee*,
and thou shalt *take thy rest in safety* **lie down confidently**.
19 Also thou shalt *lie down* **repose**,
and none shall *make* **tremble** thee *afraid*;
yea many shall *make suit unto thee* **stroke thy face**.
20 But the eyes of the wicked shall *fail* **be finished off**,
and *they shall not escape* **flight destructeth from them**,
and their hope shall be
as the *giving up* **expiration** of the *ghost* **soul**.

IYOB ANSWERS

12 And *Job* **Iyob** answered and said,
2 *No doubt* **Truly** but ye are the people,
and wisdom shall die with you.
3 *But* **Yea**,
I have *understanding as well* **such a heart** as you;
I am not *inferior to* **fallen lower than** you:
yea, who knoweth not such *things* as these?
4 I am as one *mocked* **ridiculed** of his *neighbour* **friend**,
who calleth upon *God* **Elohah**, and he answereth him:
the just *upright man* **integrious**
is *laughed to scorn* **ridiculed**.
5 He that *is ready to slip* **prepareth to waver** with his feet
is as a *lamp despised* **flambeau disrespected**
in the *thought* **thoughts** of him that *is at ease* **relaxeth**.
6 The *tabernacles* **tents** of *robbers* **ravagers**
prosper **serenify**,
and they that provoke *God* **El** are *secure* **confident**;
into whose hand *God* **Elohah** bringeth *abundantly*.
7 But ask *now* **I beseech** the *beasts* **animals**,
and they shall teach thee;
and the *fowls* **flyers** of the air,
and they shall tell thee:
8 Or *speak* **meditate** to the earth,
and it shall teach thee:
and the fishes of the sea
shall *declare* **scribe** unto thee.
9 Who knoweth not in all these
that the hand of *the LORD* **Yah Veh**
hath *wrought* **worked** this?
10 In whose hand is the soul of *every* **all** living *thing*,
and the *breath* **spirit** of all *mankind* **flesh of man**.
11 Doth not the ear *try words* **proof utterances**?
and the *mouth* **palate** taste his *meat* **food**?
12 With the *ancient* **aged** is wisdom;
and in length of days understanding.
13 With him is wisdom and *strength* **might**,
he hath counsel and understanding.
14 Behold, he breaketh down,
and it cannot be built *again*:
he shutteth up a man,
and there *can* be no opening.
15 Behold, he *withholdeth* **restraineth** the waters,

and they dry *up*:
also he sendeth them out,
and they overturn the earth.
16 With him is strength and *wisdom* **substance**:
the deceived **they that err inadvertently**
and *the deceiver* **they that cause to err inadvertently**
are his.
17 He *leadeth* **walketh** counsellors away *spoiled* **stripped**,
and maketh the judges *fools* **to halal**.
18 He looseth the bond of *kings* **sovereigns**,
and *girdeth* **bindeth** their loins with a girdle.
19 He *leadeth princes* **walketh priests**
away *spoiled* **stripped**,
and *overthroweth* **perverteth** the *mighty* **perrenial**.
20 He *removeth away* **turneth aside**
the *speech* **lip** of the *trusty* **trustworthy**,
and taketh away the *understanding* **taste** of the aged.
21 He poureth *contempt* **disrespect**
upon *princes* **volunteers**,
and *weakeneth* **looseth** the *strength* **girdle**
of the *mighty* **gatherers**.
22 He *discovereth deep things* **exposeth depths**
out of darkness,
and bringeth out to light the shadow of death.
23 He increaseth the *nations* **goyim**,
and destroyeth them:
he *enlargeth* **spreadeth** the *nations* **goyim**,
and *straiteneth* **leadeth** them *again*.
24 He *taketh away* **turneth aside** the heart
of the *chief* **head** of the people of the earth,
and causeth them to *wander* **staggar** in a *wilderness* **waste**
where there is no way.
25 They grope in the dark without light,
and he maketh them to stagger
like a drunken man **as intoxicated**.

13 *Lo* **Behold**, mine eye hath seen all this,
mine ear hath heard and *understood it* **discerned**.
2 *What ye know* **As to your knowledge**,
the same do I know also:
I am not *inferior to* **fallen lower than** you.
3 *Surely I would speak* **But I word**
to *the Almighty* **Shadday**,
and I desire to *reason with God* **reprove El**.
4 But ye are *forgers* **patchers** of *lies* **falsehoods**,
ye are all *physicians of no value* **worthless healers**.
5 *O that* **Who giveth, that in hushing**,
ye *would altogether hold your peace* **should hush**!
and it should be your wisdom.
6 Hear *now* **I beseech**, my *reasoning* **reproof**,
and hearken to the *pleadings* **defence** of my lips.
7 *Will* **Shall** ye *speak wickedly* **word wickedness**
for *God* **El**?
and *talk* **word** deceitfully for him?
8 *Will* **Shall** ye *accept his person* **lift his face**?
will **shall** ye contend for *God* **El**?
9 Is it good that he should *search* **probe** you *out*?
or as one *man* mocketh *another* **a man**,
do ye so mock **ye** him?
10 **In reproving,** He *will surely* **shall** reprove you,
if ye *do secretly accept persons* **covertly lift faces**.
11 Shall not his *excellency* **exalting**
make **frighten** you *afraid*?
and his dread fall upon you?
12 Your *remembrances* **memorials** are like unto ashes,
your *bodies* **backs** to *bodies* **backs** of clay.
13 *Hold your peace* **Hush**, let me alone,
that I may *speak* **word**,
and let *come on me what will* **whatever pass over me**.
14 Wherefore do I *take* **lift** my flesh in my teeth,
and *put* **set** my *life* **soul** in *mine hand* **my palm**?
15 *Though he slay* **Behold, he severeth** me,
yet *will I trust in him* **I shall not await**:
but I *will maintain* **shall reprove** mine own ways
before him **at his face**.
16 He also shall be my salvation:
for *an hypocrite* **a profaner**
shall not come *before him* **at this face**.
17 *Hear diligently my speech*
Hearken! Hear my utterances,
and my *declaration* **utterance** with your ears.
18 Behold *now* **I beseech**,
I have *ordered* **lined up** my *cause* **judgment**;
I know that I shall be justified.
19 Who is he that *will plead* **shall contend** with me?
for now, if I *hold my tongue* **hush**,
I shall *give up the ghost* **expire**.
20 Only *do* **work** not **these** two *things* unto me:
then *will* **shall** I not hide myself from *thee* **thy face**.
21 *Withdraw thine hand* **Remove thy palm** far from me:
and let not thy *dread make* **terror frighten** me *afraid*.
22 Then call thou, and I *will answer* **shall respond**:
or let me *speak* **word**, and answer thou me.
23 How many
are *mine iniquities* **my perversities** and sins?
make **have** me to know
my *transgression* **rebellion** and my sin.
24 Wherefore hidest thou thy face,
and *holdest* **fabricatest** me for thine enemy?
25 *Wilt* **Shalt** thou
break a leaf driven to and fro **terrify a dispersed leaf**?
and *wilt* **shalt** thou pursue the dry stubble?
26 For thou *writest bitter things* **inscribest bitternesses**
against me,
and makest me
to possess the *iniquities* **perversities** of my youth.
27 Thou *puttest* **settest** my feet also in the stocks,
and *lookest narrowly* **guardest** unto all my paths;
thou *settest a print* **engravest**
upon the *heels* **roots** of my feet.
28 And he, as *a rotten thing* **rotteness**,
consumeth **weareth out**,
as *a garment* **clothing** that is moth eaten.

14 *Man that is* **Humanity** born of a woman
is of few **be short of** days
and *full of trouble* **satiated with commotion**.
2 He cometh forth like a *flower* **blossom**,
and is *cut down* **clipped**:
he fleeth also as a shadow,
and *continueth* **standeth** not.
3 And dost thou open thine eyes upon such an one,
and bringest me into judgment with thee?
4 Who *can bring a clean thing* **shall give purity**
out of *an unclean* **foul**?
not one.
5 Seeing his days are *determined* **appointed**,
the number of his months are with thee,
thou hast *appointed* **worked** his *bounds* **statutes**
that he cannot pass;
6 *Turn* **Look away** from him, that he may *rest* **cease**,
till he shall *accomplish* **please**, as an hireling, his day.
7 For there is hope of a tree, if it be cut down,
that it *will sprout* **shall change** again,
and that the *tender branch* **sprout** *thereof*
will **shall** not cease.
8 Though the root *thereof wax old* **age** in the earth,
and the *stock* **stump** *thereof* die in the *ground* **dust**;
9 *Yet* through the scent of water it *will bud* **shall blossom**,
and *bring forth boughs* **work harvest** like a plant.
10 *But man* **The mighty** dieth, and *wasteth away* **decayeth**:
yea, *man giveth up the ghost* **humanity expireth**,
and where is he?
11 *As* the waters *fail* **gad about** from the sea,
and the flood *decayeth* **parcheth** and drieth *up*:
12 So man lieth down, and riseth not:
till the heavens be no more, they shall not awake,
nor *be raised* **waken** out of their sleep.
13 *O* **Who giveth**
that thou *wouldest* **shouldest** hide me in *the grave* **sheol**,
that thou *wouldest* **shouldest** keep me secret,
until thy wrath be *past* **turned**,
that thou *wouldest* **shouldest**
appoint **set** me a *set time* **statute**,
and remember me!
14 If *a man* **the mighty** die, shall he *live again* **enliven**?
all the days of my *appointed time* **hostility**
will **shall** I *wait* **await**,
till my change come.
15 Thou shalt call, and I *will* **shall** answer thee:
thou *wilt have a desire* **shalt yearn**
to **for** the work of thine hands.

16 For now thou *numberest* **scribest** my *steps* **paces**:
dost thou not *watch* **guard** over my sin?
17 My *transgression* **rebellion**
is sealed up in a *bag* **bundle**,
and thou *sewest up mine iniquity* **patchest my perversity**.
18 *And surely* **But** the mountain falling
cometh to nought **withereth**,
and the rock is removed out of his place.
19 The waters *wear* **pulverize** the stones:
thou *washest away* **overflowest**
the *things which grow out* **spontaneous growth**
of the dust of the earth;
and thou destroyest the hope of man.
20 Thou prevailest *for ever* **in perpetuity** against him,
and he passeth:
thou *changest* **alterest** his *countenance* **face**,
and sendest him away.
21 His sons *come to honour* **be honoured**,
and he knoweth it not;
and they are *brought low* **belittled**,
but he *perceiveth* **discerneth** it not of them.
22 But his flesh upon him shall *have* pain,
and his soul within him shall mourn.

Eli Phaz Answers

15 Then answered
Eliphaz **Eli Phaz** the *Temanite* **Temaniy**,
and said, Should *a* **the** wise *man*
utter vain **answer spirit/wind** knowledge,
and fill his belly with the *east wind* **easterly**?
3 Should he *reason* **reprove**
with *unprofitable talk* **useless words**?
or with *speeches* **utterances**
wherewith he *can do no good* **benefiteth not**?
4 Yea, thou *castest off fear* **breakest awe**,
and *restrainest prayer* **diminishest meditation**
before God **at the face of El**.
5 For thy mouth
uttereth thine iniquity **teacheth thy perversity**,
and thou choosest the tongue of the *crafty* **subtle**.
6 Thine own mouth *condemneth* **judgeth** thee **wicked**,
and not I:
yea, thine own lips *testify* **answer** against thee.
7 Art thou the first *man* **human** that was born?
or wast thou *made before* **whirled at the face of** the hills?
8 Hast thou heard
the *secret* **private counsel** of *God* **Elohah**?
and dost thou *restrain* **diminish** wisdom to thyself?
9 What knowest thou, that we know not?
what *understandest* **discernest** thou, which is not in us?
10 With us are both the *grayheaded* **grayed**
and *very* **the** aged *men*,
much elder **more advanced in days** than thy father.
11 Are the consolations of *God small* **El petty** with thee?
is there any *secret thing* **gentle word** with thee?
12 Why doth thine heart *carry* **take** thee away?
and what do thy eyes *wink* **twinkle** at,
13 That thou turnest thy spirit against *God* **El**,
and lettest *such words* **utterances** go out of thy mouth?
14 What is man, that he should be *clean* **purified**?
and he which is — born of a woman,
that he should be *righteous* **justified**?
15 Behold,
he *putteth no trust* **trusteth not** in his *saints* **holy**;
yea, the heavens are not clean in his *sight* **eyes**.
16 How much more *abominable* **abhorrent**
and *filthy* **muddled** is man,
which drinketh *iniquity* **wickedness** like water?
17 I *will* **shall** shew thee, hear me;
and that which I have seen I *will declare* **shall scribe**;
18 Which **the** wise *men* have told from their fathers,
and have not *hid* **concealed** it:
19 Unto whom alone the earth was given,
and no stranger passed among them.
20 The wicked *man*
travaileth with pain **writheth** all his days,
and the number of years
is hidden to the *oppressor* **tyrant**.
21 A *dreadful sound* **voice of dread** is in his ears:
in *prosperity* **shalom**
the *destroyer* **ravager** shall come upon him.
22 He *believeth* **trusteth** not
that he shall return out of darkness,
and he is *waited* **watched** for of the sword.
23 He wandereth abroad for bread, *saying*, Where is it?
he knoweth that the day of darkness
is *ready* **prepared** at his hand.
24 *Trouble* **Tribulation** and *anguish* **distress**
shall *make* **frighten** him *afraid*;
they shall prevail against him,
as a *king* **sovereign** ready to the *battle* **tumult**.
25 For he stretcheth out his hand against *God* **El**,
and *strengtheneth himself* **prevaileth mightily**
against *the Almighty* **Shadday**.
26 He runneth upon him, *even on* **upon** his neck,
upon the thick bosses of his *bucklers* **shields**:
27 Because he covereth his face with his *fatness* **fat**,
and *maketh collops of fat on* **worketh plump** his flanks.
28 And he *dwelleth* **tabernacleth** in *desolate* **cut off** cities,
and in houses which no man *inhabiteth* **settleth**,
which are ready to *become heaps* **heap**.
29 He shall not *be rich* **enrich**,
neither shall his *substance continue* **valuables arise**,
neither shall he
prolong **extend** the *perfection* **acquisitions** *thereof*
upon the earth.
30 He shall not *depart* **turn aside** out of darkness;
the flame shall *dry up* **wither** his *branches* **sprouts**,
and by the *breath* **wind/spirit** of his mouth
shall he *go away* **turn aside**.
31 Let not him that *is deceived* **strayeth** trust in vanity:
for vanity shall be his *recompence* **exchange**.
32 It shall *be accomplished* **not be fulfilled**
before **in** his *time* **day**,
and his *branch* **palm leaf** shall not *be* green.
33 He shall *shake off* **violate** his *unripe* **sour** grape
as the vine,
and shall cast *off* his *flower* **blossom**
as the olive.
34 For the *congregation* **witness** of *hypocrites* **profaners**
shall be *desolate* **sterile**,
and fire shall consume the *tabernacles* **tents** of bribery.
35 They conceive *mischief* **toil**,
and *bring forth vanity* **birth mischief**,
and their belly prepareth deceit.

Iyob Answers

16 Then *Job* **Iyob** answered and said,
2 I have heard many *such things* **of these**:
miserable comforters **sighers of toil** are ye all.
3 Shall *vain* words **of wind/spirit** have an end?
or what *emboldeneth* **reinforceth** thee
that thou answerest?
4 I also *could speak* **had worded** as ye *do*:
if **O that** your soul were in my soul's stead,
I could *heap up words* **charm utterances** against you,
and shake mine head at you.
5 But I *would* **should** strengthen you with my mouth,
and the moving of my lips
should *asswage your grief* **spare you**.
6 Though I *speak* **word**,
my *grief* **pain** is not *asswaged* **spared**:
and though I *forbear* **cease**, what *am I eased* **goes**?
7 But now he hath *made* **wearied** me *weary*:
thou hast *made desolate* **desolated**
all my *company* **witnesses**.
8 And thou hast *filled* **plucked** me *with wrinkles*,
which is **for** a witness *against me*:
and my *leanness* **emaciation** rising up in me
beareth witness **answereth** to my face.
9 He teareth me in his wrath, who *hateth* **opposeth** me:
he gnasheth upon me with his teeth;
mine enemy **my tribulator** sharpeneth his eyes
upon me.
10 They have gaped upon me with their mouth;
they have smitten me upon the cheek reproachfully;
they have *gathered themselves together* **fulfilled**
against me.
11 *God* **El** hath *delivered* **shut** me to the *ungodly* **pervert**,
and *turned* **hurled** me *over* into the hands of the wicked.
12 I was *at ease* **serene**, but he hath broken me *asunder*:
he hath also taken me by my neck,

and *shaken* **shattered** me *to pieces,*
and *set me up* **raised me** for his *mark* **target**.
13 His archers *compass* **surround** me *round about,*
he cleaveth my reins *asunder,*
and *doth* **spareth** not *spare;*
he poureth out my *gall* **bitters** upon the *ground* **earth**.
14 He *breaketh* **breacheth** me
with **at the face of** breach upon breach,
he runneth upon me like *a giant* **the mighty**.
15 I have sewed *sackcloth* **saq** upon my skin,
and *defiled* **exploited** my horn in the dust.
16 My face *is foul* **foameth** with weeping,
and on my eyelids is the shadow of death;
17 Not for *any injustice* **violence** in *mine hands* **my palms**:
also my prayer is pure.
18 O earth, cover not thou my blood,
and let my cry have no place.
19 Also now, behold,
my witness is in *heaven* **the heavens**,
and my *record is on high* **witness in the heights**.
20 My friends scorn me:
but mine eye *poureth out tears* **drippeth** unto *God* **Elohah**.
21 O that one might *plead* **reprove** for *a man* **the mighty**
with *God* **Elohah**
as a *man* **son of humanity** *pleadeth*
for his *neighbour* **friend**!
22 When *a few* years **of number** are come,
then I shall go the way whence I shall not return.
17 My *breath* **spirit** is *corrupt* **despoiled**,
my days are extinct,
the *graves* **tombs** are *ready* for me.
2 Are there not mockers with me?
and doth not mine eye
continue **stay** in their *provocation* **rebelling**?
3 *Lay down now* **Set, I beseech**,
put me in a surety **my pledge** with thee;
who is he that *will strike* **shall clap** hands with me?
4 For thou hast hid their heart
from *understanding* **comprehension**:
therefore shalt thou not exalt them.
5 He that *speaketh* **telleth**
flattery **smoothing it over** to his friends,
even the eyes of his children shall *fail* **finish off**.
6 He hath *made* **set** me also
a *byword* **proverb** of the people;
and aforetime **at the face of when** I was as *a tabret* **spit**.
7 Mine eye also is dim *by reason of sorrow* **of vexation**,
and all my *members are* **forms** as a shadow.
8 *Upright men* **The straight** shall be astonied at this,
and the innocent shall *stir up* **waken** himself
against the *hypocrite* **profaner**.
9 The *righteous* **just** also shall hold on his way,
and he that hath *clean* **pure** hands
in strengthening,
shall *be stronger and stronger* **strengthen**.
10 But as for you all,
do ye return **ye**, and come *now* **I beseech**:
for I *cannot find one* **find none** wise *man* among you.
11 My days are past,
my *purposes* **intrigues** are *broken off* **torn**,
even the *thoughts* **possessions** of my heart.
12 They *change* **set** the night into day:
the light is *short* **near**
because of **at the face of** the darkness.
13 If I *wait* **await**, *the grave* **sheol** is mine house:
I have *made* **spread** my bed in the darkness.
14 I have *said* **called** to *corruption* **the pit of ruin**,
Thou art my father:
to the *worm* **maggot**,
Thou art my mother, and my sister.
15 And where is now my hope?
as for my hope, who shall *see* **observe** it?
16 They shall *go down* **descend**
to the *bars* **veins** of *the pit* **sheol**,
when our rest together is in the dust.

BILDAD ANSWERS

18 Then answered Bildad the *Shuhite* **Shuachiy**,
and said,
2 *How long will it be* **Until when**
ere ye *make* **set** an end of *words* **utterances**?
mark **discern**, and afterwards we *will speak* **shall word**.
3 Wherefore are we
counted **machinated** as *beasts* **animals**,
and *reputed vile* **foul** in your *sight* **eyes**?
4 He teareth *himself* **his soul** in his *anger* **wrath**:
shall the earth be forsaken for thee?
and shall the rock be removed out of his place?
5 Yea, the light of the wicked
shall *be put out* **extinguish**,
and the *spark* **flame** of his fire
shall not *shine* **illuminate**.
6 The light shall *be dark* **darken** in his *tabernacle* **tent**,
and his *candle* **lamp**
shall *be put out* **extinguish** with him.
7 The *steps* **paces** of his strength
shall *be straitened* **constrict**,
and his own counsel shall cast him down.
8 For he is *cast* **sent** into a net by his own feet,
and he walketh upon a *snare* **netting**.
9 The *gin* **snare** shall *take* **hold** him by the heel,
and the robber shall prevail against him.
10 The *snare* **cord** is *laid* **hid** for him in the *ground* **earth**,
and a trap for him in the *way* **path**.
11 Terrors shall *make* **frighten** him *afraid*
on every side **round about**,
and shall *drive* **scatter** him to his feet.
12 His strength shall *be hungerbitten* **famish**,
and *destruction* **calamity** shall be *ready* **prepared**
at his side.
13 It shall devour the strength of his *skin* **veins**:
even the firstborn of death
shall devour his *strength* **veins**.
14 His confidence
shall be *rooted* **torn** out of his *tabernacle* **tent**,
and it shall *bring* **pace** him to the *king* **sovereign** of terrors.
15 It shall *dwell* **tabernacle** in his *tabernacle* **tent**,
because it is none of his **without him**:
brimstone **sulphur** shall be *scattered* **winnowed**
upon his habitation **of rest**.
16 His roots shall *be dried up* **wither** beneath,
and above shall his *branch* **harvest** be *cut off* **clipped**.
17 His *remembrance* **memorial**
shall *perish* **destruct** from the earth,
and he shall have no name
in the street **at the face of the outways**.
18 He shall be *driven* **exiled** from light into darkness,
and chased out of the world.
19 He shall neither have son nor *nephew* **posterity**
among his people,
nor *any remaining* **survivors** in his *dwellings* **sojournings**.
20 They that come after him shall be astonied at his day,
as *they that went before* **the ancients**
were *affrighted* **whirled away**.
21 Surely such
are the *dwellings* **tabernacles** of the wicked,
and this is the place of him that knoweth not *God* **El**.

IYOB ANSWERS

19 Then *Job* **Iyob** answered and said,
2 How long *will* **shall** ye *vex* **grieve** my soul,
and *break* **crush** me *in pieces* with *words* **utterances**?
3 These ten times have ye *reproached* **shamed** me:
ye are not ashamed **yet ye shame not**
that ye *make yourselves strange to* **injure** me.
4 And be it *indeed* **truly** that I have erred **inadvertently**,
mine error *remaineth* **stayeth** with myself.
5 If *indeed* **truly**
ye *will magnify yourselves* **shall greaten** against me,
and *plead* **reprove** against me my reproach:
6 Know now
that *God* **Elohah** hath *overthrown* **twisted** me,
and hath *compassed* **surrounded** me with his *net* **lair**.
7 Behold, I cry out of *wrong* **violence**,
but I am not *heard* **answered**:
I cry *aloud*, but there is no judgment.
8 He hath *fenced up* **walled in** my way that I cannot pass,
and he hath set darkness in my paths.
9 He hath stripped me of my *glory* **honour**,
and *taken* **turned aside** the crown from my head.
10 He hath *destroyed me* **pulled me down**
on every side **all around**,

and I am gone:
and mine hope hath he *removed* **plucked** like a tree.
11 He hath also kindled his wrath against me,
and he *counteth* **fabricated** me unto him
as one of his *enemies* **tribulators**.
12 His troops come together,
and raise *up* their way against me,
and encamp round about my *tabernacle* **tent**.
13 He hath *put* **removed** my brethren *far* from me,
and *mine acquaintance* **they whom I know**
are verily estranged from me.
14 My *kinsfolk* **neighbours**
have *failed* **deceased**,
and *my familiar friends* **they whom I know**
have forgotten me.
15 They that *dwell* **sojourn** in mine house, and my maids,
count **fabricate** me for a stranger:
I am an alien in their *sight* **eyes**.
16 I called my servant,
and he *gave me no answer* **answered me not**;
I *intreated him* **sought his charism** with my mouth.
17 My *breath* **spirit** is strange to my *wife* **woman**,
though I *intreated* **sought charism**
for the *children's sake of mine own body* **sons of my belly**.
18 Yea, *young children despised* **sucklings spurned** me;
I arose, and they *spake* **worded** against me.
19 All my *inward friends* **private councilmen** abhorred me:
and they whom I loved are turned against me.
20 My bone
cleaveth **adhereth** to my skin and to my flesh,
and I am escaped with the skin of my teeth.
21 *Have pity upon me* **Grant me charism**,
have pity upon me **grant me charism**, O ye my friends;
for the hand of *God* **Elohah** hath touched me.
22 Why do ye *persecute* **pursue** me as *God* **El**,
and are not satisfied with my flesh?
23 *Oh* **Who giveth**
that my *words* **utterances** were now *written* **inscribed**!
oh **who giveth** that they were *printed* **inscribed**
in a *book* **scroll**!
24 That they were *graven* **hewn** with an iron *pen* **stylus**
and lead in the rock *for ever* **eternally**!
25 For I know that my redeemer liveth,
and that he shall *stand* **arise** at the latter *day*
upon the *earth* **dust**:
26 And *though*
after my skin *worms destroy this body* **be stricken**,
yet in my flesh shall I see *God* **Elohah**:
27 Whom I shall see for myself,
and mine eyes shall *behold* **see**,
and not *another* **a stranger**;
though my reins be *consumed* **finished off**
within *me* **my bosom**.
28 But ye should say, Why *persecute* **pursue** we him,
seeing the root of the *matter* **word** is found in me?
29 *Be* **Dodge** ye *afraid* **at the face** of the sword:
for *wrath bringeth the punishments*
furious are the perversities of the sword,
that ye may know there is *a judgment* **the plea**.

SOPHAR ANSWERS

20 Then answered
Zophar **Sophar** the *Naamathite* **Naamahiy**, and said,
2 Therefore do my *thoughts* **sentiments**
cause me to *answer* **respond**,
and for this I *make haste* **hasten**.
3 I have heard the *check* **discipline** of my reproach,
and the spirit of my *understanding* **discernment**
causeth me to answer.
4 Knowest thou *not* this *of old* **eternally**,
since *man* **humanity** was placed upon earth,
5 That the *triumphing* **shout** of the wicked is short,
and the *joy* **cheer** of the *hypocrite* **profaner**
but for a *moment* **blink**?
6 Though his *excellency* **exaltation**
mount up **ascend** to the heavens,
and his head reach unto the **thick** clouds;
7 Yet he shall *perish for ever* **destruct in perpetuity**
like his own dung:
they which have seen him shall say, Where is he?
8 He shall fly *away* as a dream, and shall not be found:
yea, he shall be chased away as a vision of the night.
9 The eye also which *saw* **scanned** him
shall see him *no more* **not again**;
neither shall his place any more *behold* **observe** him.
10 His *children* **sons** shall seek to please the poor,
and his hands shall restore their *goods* **strength**.
11 His bones are full of *the sin of* his youth,
which shall lie down with him in the dust.
12 Though *wickedness* **evil**
be sweet **sweeteneth** in his mouth,
though he *hid* **concealeth** it under his tongue;
13 Though he spare it, and forsake it not;
but *keep* **withhold** it still within his *mouth* **palate**:
14 Yet his *meat* **bread** in his *bowels* **inwards** is turned,
it is the *gall* **venom** of asps within him.
15 He hath swallowed *down riches* **valuables**,
and he shall vomit them up *again*:
God **El** shall *cast* **dispossess** them out of his belly.
16 He shall suck the *poison* **rosh** of asps:
the *viper's* **hisser's** tongue shall *slay* **slaughter** him.
17 He shall not see the *rivers* **rivulets**, the floods,
the *brooks* **wadies** of honey and butter.
18 That which he laboured for shall he restore,
and shall not swallow *down*:
according to his *substance* **valuables**
thus shall the *restitution* **exchange** be,
and he shall not *rejoice therein* **leap for joy**.
19 Because he hath *oppressed* **crushed**
and hath forsaken the poor;
because he hath *violently taken away* **stripped** an house
which he builded not;
20 Surely he shall not *feel quietness* **know serenity**
in his belly,
he shall not *save* **rescue** of that which he desired.
21 There shall none of his *meat be left* **food survive**;
therefore **none** shall *no man look for* **writhe** his goods .
22 In the fulness of his *sufficiency* **gluttony**
he shall be *in straits* **constricted**:
every hand of the wicked shall come upon him.
23 When he is about to fill his belly,
God **He** shall *cast* **send** the *fury* **fuming** of his wrath
upon him,
and shall rain it upon him while he is eating.
24 He shall flee from the iron *weapon* **armour**,
and the bow of *steel* **copper**
shall *strike* **pass** him through.
25 It is drawn, and cometh out of the body;
yea, the *glittering* **lightning** sword cometh out of his gall:
terrors are upon him.
26 All darkness shall be hid in his *secret places* **hideouts**:
a fire not *blown* **puffed** shall consume him;
it shall go *ill* **evilly** with him
that *is left* **surviveth** in his *tabernacle* **tent**.
27 The *heaven* **heavens**
shall *reveal* **expose** his *iniquity* **perversity;**
and the earth shall rise *up* against him.
28 The *increase* **produce** of his house
shall *depart* **be exposed**,
and *his goods* shall flow away in the day of his wrath.
29 This is the *portion* **allotment**
of *a* wicked *man* **humanity** from *God* **Elohim**,
and the *heritage* **inheritance**
appointed unto him by God **of his sayings of El**.

IYOB ANSWERS

21 But *Job* **Iyob** answered and said,
2 *Hear diligently my speech*
In hearing, hear my utterances,
and let this be your consolations.
3 *Suffer* **Allow** me that I may *speak* **word**;
and after that I have *spoken* **worded**, *mock on* **deride**.
4 As for me,
is my *complaint* **meditation** to *man* **humanity**?
and if it were *so*,
why should not my spirit be *troubled* **curtailed**?
5 *Mark* **Face** me, and be astonished,
and *lay* **set** your hand upon your mouth.
6 Even when I remember I *am afraid* **terrify**,
and trembling taketh hold on my flesh.
7 Wherefore do the wicked live, *become old* **antiquate**,
yea, *are mighty* **prevail mightily** in *power* **valour**?

8 Their seed is established
in their sight with them **at their face**,
and their offspring *before* **at** their eyes.
9 Their houses are *safe* **at shalom** from *fear* **dread**,
neither is the *rod* **scion** of *God* **Elohah** upon them.
10 Their *bull gendereth* **ox passeth**,
and *faileth* **loatheth** not;
their *cow calveth* **heifer slippeth away**,
and *casteth* **aborteth** not her calf.
11 They send forth their *little ones* **sucklings** like a flock,
and their children dance.
12 They *take* **lift** the *timbrel* **tambourine** and harp,
and *rejoice* **cheer**
at the *sound* **voice** of the *organ* **woodwind**.
13 They *spend* **waste away**,
finishing off their days in *wealth* **good**,
and in a *moment* **blink**,
go down **descend** to *the grave* **sheol**.
14 *Therefore* they say unto *God* **El**, *Depart* **Turn** from us;
for we desire not the knowledge of thy ways.
15 What is *the Almighty* **Shadday**,
that we should serve him?
and what *profit* **benefit** should we have,
if we *pray* **intercede** unto him?
16 *Lo* **Behold**, their good is not in their hand:
the counsel of the wicked is far from me.
17 How oft is the *candle* **lamp** of the wicked
put out **extinguished**!
and *how oft* cometh their *destruction* **calamity** upon them!
God distributeth sorrows **He apportioneth pangs**
in his *anger* **wrath**.
18 They are as *stubble* **straw**
before **at the face of** the wind,
and as chaff
that the *storm carrieth away* **hurricane stealeth**.
19 *God* **Elohah**
layeth up his *iniquity* **punishment of mischief**
for his *children* **sons**:
he *rewardeth* **doth shalam** him, and he shall know it.
20 His eyes shall see his destruction,
and he shall drink
of the *wrath* **fury** of *the Almighty* **Shadday**.
21 For what *pleasure* **delight** hath he
in his house after him,
when the number of his months
is *cut off* **severed** in *the midst* **half**?
22 Shall any teach *God* **El** knowledge?
seeing he judgeth those that are *high* **lofted**.
23 One dieth in *his full strength* **the integrity of his bones**,
being wholly *at ease* **serene** and *quiet* **secure**.
24 His *breasts* **pails** are full of milk,
and his bones are moistened with marrow.
25 And another dieth in the bitterness of his soul,
and never eateth *with pleasure* **good**.
26 They shall lie *down alike* **together** in the dust,
and the *worms* **maggots** shall cover them.
27 Behold, I know your *thoughts* **fabrications**
and the *devices* **intrigues**
which ye *wrongfully imagine* **violate** against me.
28 For ye say,
Where is the house of the *prince* **volunteer**?
and where are the *dwelling places* **tents**
— the tabernacles of the wicked?
29 Have ye not asked them that *go* **pass** by the way?
and do ye not *know* **recognize** their *tokens* **signs**,
30 That the *wicked* **evil** is *reserved* **spared**
to the day of *destruction* **calamity**?
they shall be brought forth to the day of *wrath* **fury**.
31 Who shall *declare* **tell** his way to his face?
and who shall *repay* **shalam** him
for what he hath *done* **worked**?
32 Yet shall he be brought to the *grave* **tomb**,
and shall *remain* **watch** in the *tomb* **heap**.
33 The clods of the *valley* **wadi**
shall *be sweet* **sweeten** unto him,
and *every man* **all humanity** shall draw after him,
as there are innumerable *before him* **at his face**.
34 How then *comfort* **sigh** ye **over** me in vain,
seeing in your *answers* **responses**
there *remaineth falsehood* **surviveth treason**?

ELI PHAZ ANSWERS

22 Then *Eliphaz* **Eli Phaz** the *Temanite* **Temaniy**
answered and said,
2 *Can a man be profitable* **Be the mighty useful** unto God,
as he that *is wise* **comprehendeth**
may be *profitable* **useful** unto himself?
3 Is it any *pleasure* **delight** to *the Almighty* **Shadday**,
that thou art *righteous* **justified**?
or is it gain to him,
that thou makest thy ways *perfect* **integrious**?
4 *Will* **Shall** he reprove thee for *fear* **awe** of thee?
will **shall** he enter with thee into judgment?
5 Is not thy *wickedness* **evil** great?
and *thine iniquities infinite* **thy perversities endless**?
6 For thou hast taken a pledge from thy brother
for nought **gratuitously**,
and stripped the naked of their clothing.
7 Thou hast not given water
to the *weary* **languid** to drink,
and thou hast withholden bread
from the *hungry* **famished**.
8 But as for the *mighty* man **of arm**,
he had the earth;
and the *honourable man* **face of the exalted**
dwelt **settled** in it.
9 Thou hast sent widows away empty,
and the arms of the *fatherless* **orphan**
have been *broken* **crushed**.
10 Therefore snares are round about thee,
and sudden *fear troubleth* **dread terrifieth** thee;
11 Or darkness, that thou canst not see;
and abundance of waters cover thee.
12 Is not *God* **Elohah**
in the height of *heaven* **the heavens**?
and *behold* **see** the *height* **head** of the stars,
how high they are!
13 And thou sayest, How *doth God* **shall El** know?
can he judge through the *dark cloud* **dripping darkness**?
14 Thick clouds are a covering to him, that he seeth not;
and he walketh
in the *circuit* **circle** of *heaven* **the heavens**.
15 Hast thou *marked* **regarded** the *old* **eternal** way
which *wicked* **mischievous** men have trodden?
16 Which were *cut down* **plucked** out of time,
whose foundation was *overflown* **poured** with a flood:
17 Which said unto *God* **El**, *Depart* **Turn away** from us:
and what can *the Almighty* **Shadday** do for them?
18 Yet he filled their houses with good *things*:
but the counsel of the wicked is far from me.
19 The *righteous* **just** see it, and *are glad* **cheer**:
and the innocent *laugh* **deride** them *to scorn*.
20 Whereas our *substance* **opponent** is not cut *down* **off**,
but the *remnant* **remainder** of them the fire consumeth.
21 *Acquaint now thyself* **Be accustomed, I beseech,**
with him,
and be at *peace* **shalom**:
thereby good shall come unto thee.
22 Receive, I *pray* **beseech** thee,
the *law* **torah** from his mouth,
and *lay up* **set** his *words* **sayings** in thine heart.
23 If thou return to *the Almighty* **Shadday**,
thou shalt be built *up*,
thou shalt *put away iniquity* **remove wickedness**
far from thy *tabernacles* **tents**.
24 Then shalt thou *lay up gold* **set diggings** as dust,
and *the gold* of Ophir
as the *stones* **rocks** of the *brooks* **wadies**.
25 Yea, *the Almighty* **Shadday**
shall be thy *defence* **diggings**,
and thou shalt have *plenty* **strengths** of silver.
26 For then shalt thou have thy delight
in *the Almighty* **Shadday**,
and shalt lift *up* thy face unto *God* **Elohah**.
27 Thou shalt *make thy prayer* **intreat** unto him,
and he shall hear thee,
and thou shalt *pay* **shalam** thy vows.
28 Thou shalt also *decree a thing* **cut a saying**,
and it shall *be established* **arise** unto thee:
and the light shall *shine upon* **illuminate** thy ways.
29 When *men are cast down* **abased**,

then thou shalt say, There is *lifting up* **arrogance**;
and he shall save the *humble person* **downcast eye**.
30 He shall *deliver* **rescue** the island of the innocent:
and it *is delivered* **escapeth**
by the *pureness* **purity** of *thine hands* **thy palms**.

IYOB ANSWERS

23 Then *Job* **Iyob** answered and said,
2 Even to day
is my *complaint bitter* **meditation rebellious**:
my *stroke* **hand** is heavier than my *groaning* **sighing**.
3 *Oh* **Who giveth** that I knew where I might find him!
that I might come *even* to his *seat* **place**!
4 *I would order my cause* **O that I line up my judgment**
before him **at his face**,
and fill my mouth with *arguments* **reproofs**.
5 *I would* **O that I** know the *words* **utterances**
which he *would* **should** answer me,
and *understand* **discern**
what he *would* **should** say unto me.
6 *Will* **Shall** he *plead* **contend** against me
with his *great power* **abundant force**?
No; but he *would put strength* **should set it** in me.
7 There the *righteous* **straight**
might *dispute with* **reprove** him;
so should I be *delivered* **slipped away**
for ever **in perpetuity** from my judge.
8 Behold, I go *forward* **eastward**, but he is not there;
and backward, but I cannot *perceive* **discern** him:
9 On the left *hand*, where he *doth work* **worketh**,
but I cannot *behold him* **see**:
he *hideth* **shroudeth** himself on the right *hand*,
that I cannot see *him*:
10 But he knoweth the way *that I take* **of mine**:
when he hath *tried* **proofed** me,
I shall come forth as gold.
11 My foot hath held his steps,
his way have I *kept* **guarded**, and not *declined* **perverted**.
12 Neither have I gone back
from the *commandment* **misvah** of his lips;
I have *esteemed* **treasured**
the *words* **sayings** of his mouth
more than my *necessary food* **statutes**.
13 But he is in one mind, and who can turn him?
and what his soul desireth, even that he *doeth* **worketh**.
14 For he *performeth* **shall shalam**
the thing that is appointed for me **my statute**:
and many such *things* are with him.
15 Therefore am I *troubled* **terrified** at his *presence* **face**:
when I *consider* **discern**, I *am afraid of* **dread** him.
16 For *God maketh* **El tenderizeth** my heart *soft*,
and *the Almighty troubleth* **Shadday terrifieth** me:
17 Because I was not *cut off* **exterminated**
before **at the face of** the darkness,
neither hath he covered the darkness
from my face.

24 Why,
seeing times are not hidden from *the Almighty* **Shadday**,
do they that know him not see his days?
2 *Some remove* **They overtake** the *landmarks* **borders**;
they *violently take away flocks* **strip droves**,
and feed *thereof*.
3 They drive away the *ass* **she burro**
of the *fatherless* **orphan**,
they take the widow's ox for a pledge.
4 They *turn* **pervert** the needy out of the way:
the *poor* **humble** of the earth hide *themselves together*.
5 Behold, as wild *asses* **runners** in the *desert* **wilderness**,
go they forth to their *work* **deeds**;
rising *betimes* **early** for a prey:
the *wilderness yieldeth food* **plains for bread**
for them and for their *children* **lads**.
6 They *reap every one his corn* **harvest their fodder**
in the field:
and they *gather* **glean** the *vintage* **vineyard**
of the wicked.
7 They cause the naked
to *lodge* **stay overnight** without *clothing* **robe**,
that they have no covering in the cold.
8 They are *wet* **moist**
with the *showers* **floods** of the mountains,
and embrace the rock for want of a *shelter* **refuge**.
9 They *pluck* **strip** the *fatherless* **orphan** from the breast,
and take a pledge of the *poor* **humble**.
10 They cause him to go naked without *clothing* **robe**,
and they take away the *sheaf* **omer**
from the *hungry* **famished**;
11 Which *make* **press** oil *within* **between** their walls,
and tread their *winepresses* **troughs**, and *suffer* thirst.
12 Men groan from out of the city,
and the soul of the *wounded* **pierced** crieth out:
yet *God layeth* **Elohah setteth** not *folly* **frivolity** to them.
13 They are of those that rebel against the light;
they *know* **recognize** not the ways *thereof*,
nor *abide* **settle** in the paths *thereof*.
14 The murderer rising with the light
killeth **severeth** the *poor* **humble** and needy,
and in the night is as a thief.
15 The eye also of the adulterer
waiteth **guardeth** for the *twilight* **evening breeze**,
saying, No eye shall *see* **observe** me:
and *disguiseth* **setteth** his face **covertly**.
16 In the dark they dig through houses,
which they had *marked* **sealed** for themselves
in the *daytime* **day**:
they know not the light.
17 For the morning is to them
even **altogether** as the shadow of death:
if one *know* **recognize** them,
they are in the terrors of the shadow of death.
18 He is swift *as* **at the face of** the waters;
their *portion* **allotment** is *cursed* **abased** in the earth:
he *beholdeth* **faceth** not the way of the vineyards.
19 *Drought* **Parch** and heat
consume **strip** the snow waters:
so *doth the grave* **shall Sheol** those which have sinned.
20 The womb shall forget him;
the *worm* **maggot** shall *feed sweetly on* **suck** him;
he shall be no more remembered;
and wickedness shall be broken as a tree.
21 He *evil entreateth* **tendeth** the *barren* **sterile**
that beareth not:
and *doeth not good to* **well—pleaseth not** the widow.
22 He draweth also the mighty with his *power* **force**:
he riseth up, and no *man is sure of* **one trusteth** his life.
23 *Though it be given him to be in safety*
He giveth him confidence,
whereon he *resteth* **leaneth**;
yet his eyes are upon their ways.
24 They are exalted for a little *while*,
but are gone and *brought low* **subdued**;
they are *taken out of the way* **shut up** as all other,
and *cut off* **clipped** as the tops of the ears *of corn*.
25 And if it be not *so* now, who *will* **shall** make me a liar,
and *make* **set** my *speech* **utterances**
nothing worth **as nought**?

BILDAD ANSWERS

25 Then answered Bildad the *Shuhite* **Shuachiy**,
and said,
2 Dominion and *fear* **dread** are with him,
he *maketh peace* **worketh shalom**
in his *high places* **heights**.
3 Is there any number of his *armies* **troops**?
and upon whom doth not his light arise?
4 How then can man be justified with *God* **El**?
or how can he be *clean* **purified**,
that is born of a woman?
5 Behold even to the moon, and it shineth not;
yea, the stars are not pure in his *sight* **eyes**.
6 How much less man,
that is a worm **— a maggot**?
and the son of *men* **humanity**,
which is a worm **— a maggot**?

IYOB ANSWERS

26 But *Job* **Iyob** answered and said,
2 How hast thou helped him
that *is without power* **hath no force**?
how savest thou the arm
that hath no strength?
3 How hast thou counselled him that hath no wisdom?
and how hast thou

plentifully declared the thing as it is
abundantly made known his substance?
4 To whom hast thou *uttered words* **told utterances**?
and whose *spirit* **breath** came from thee?
5 *Dead things are formed from* **Ghosts writhe**
under the waters,
and *the inhabitants thereof dwell*
they who tabernacle there.
6 *Hell* **Sheol** is naked before him,
and *destruction* **Abaddon** hath no covering.
7 He stretcheth out the north over the *empty place* **waste**,
and hangeth the earth upon *nothing* **naught whatever**.
8 He *bindeth up* **tribulateth** the waters in his thick clouds;
and the cloud is not *rent* **split** under them.
9 He holdeth back the face of his throne,
and spreadeth his cloud upon it.
10 He hath *compassed* **circled the face of** the waters
with *bounds* **statutes**,
until the *day* **light** and *night* **dark**
come to an end **conclude**.
11 The pillars of *heaven tremble* **the heavens quake**
and *are astonished* **marvel** at his *reproof* **rebuke**.
12 He *divideth* **splitteth** the sea with his *power* **force**,
and by his *understanding* **discernment**
he *smiteth through* **striketh** the proud.
13 By his spirit he hath *garnished* **glorified** the heavens;
his hand hath *formed* **writhed**
the *crooked* **fugitive** serpent.
14 *Lo* **Behold**, these are *parts* **the end** of his ways:
but how *little a portion* **an inkling of a word**
is heard of him?
but the thunder of his *power* **might**
who *can understand* **discerneth**?

27 *Moreover Job* **Iyob**
continued **added to lift** his *parable* **proverb**, and said,
2 *As God* **El** liveth,
who hath *taken away* **turned aside** my judgment;
and *the Almighty* **Shadday**,
who hath *vexed* **embittered** my soul;
3 All the while my breath is in me,
and the spirit of *God* **Elohah** is in my nostrils;
4 My lips shall not *speak* **word** wickedness,
nor my tongue *utter* **mutter** deceit.
5 *God forbid* **Far be it** that I should justify you:
till I *die* **expire**
I *will* **shall** not *remove* **turn aside**
from mine integrity *from me*.
6 My *righteousness* **justness** I *hold fast* **uphold**,
and *will* **shall** not *let it go* **slacken**:
my heart shall not reproach me
so long as I live **all my days**.
7 Let mine enemy be as the wicked,
and he that riseth up against me
as the *unrighteous* **wicked**.
8 For what is the hope of the *hypocrite* **profaner**,
though he hath gained,
when *God taketh away* **Elohah extracteth** his soul?
9 *Will God* **Shall El** hear his cry
when *trouble* **tribulation** cometh upon him?
10 *Will* **Shall** he delight himself in *the Almighty* **Shadday**?
will **shall** he *always* **at all times** call upon *God* **Elohah**?
11 I *will* **shall** teach you by the hand of *God* **El**:
that which is with *the Almighty* **Shadday**
will **shall** I not conceal.
12 Behold, all ye yourselves have seen it;
why then are ye thus *altogether* **in being vain,** vain?
13 This is the *portion* **allotment**
of *a man* **wicked humanity**
with *God* **El**,
and the *heritage* **inheritance** of *oppressors* **tyrants**,
which they shall *receive* **take** of *the Almighty* **Shadday**.
14 If his *children be multiplied* **sons abound**,
it is for the sword:
and his offspring shall not be satisfied with bread.
15 *Those that remain of him* **His survivors**
shall be *buried* **entombed** in death:
and his widows shall not weep.
16 Though he heap *up* silver as the dust,
and prepare *raiment* **robes** as the clay;
17 He may prepare it, but the just shall *put it on* **enrobe**,
and the innocent shall *divide* **allot** the silver.
18 He buildeth his house as a moth,
and as a *booth* **sukkoth/brush arbor**
that the *keeper maketh* **guardian worketh**.
19 The rich man shall lie down,
but he shall not be gathered:
he openeth his eyes, and he is not.
20 Terrors *take hold on* **overtake** him as waters,
a *tempest* **hurricane** stealeth him away in the night.
21 The *east wind carrieth* **easterly lifteth** him *away*,
and he *departeth* **goeth**:
and *as a storm hurleth* **whirleth** him out of his place.
22 *For God* **And** shall cast upon him, and not spare:
in fleeing, he *would fain flee* **fleeth** out of his hand.
23 *Men* **They** shall clap their *hands* **palms** at him,
and shall hiss him out of his place.

28 Surely there is a *vein* **source** for the silver,
and a place for gold where they *fine* **refine** it.
2 Iron is taken out of the *earth* **dust**,
and *brass* **copper** is *molten* **poured** out of the stone.
3 He setteth an end to darkness,
and *searcheth out* **probeth** all *perfection* **conclusion**:
the stones of darkness, and the shadow of death.
4 The *flood* **wadi** breaketh out
from the *inhabitant* **sojourner**;
even the waters — forgotten of the foot:
they *are dried up* **languish**,
they *are gone* **drift** away from men.
5 *As for* the earth, out of it cometh bread:
and under it is turned up as it were fire.
6 The stones of it are the place of sapphires:
and it hath dust of gold.
7 There is a path which no *fowl* **swooper** knoweth,
and which the *vulture's* **hawk's** eye
hath not *seen* **scanned**:
8 The *lion's whelps* **sons of pride** have not trodden it,
nor the *fierce* **roaring** lion *passed by it* **attacked**.
9 He *putteth forth* **extendeth** his hand upon the *rock* **flint**;
he overturneth the mountains by the roots.
10 He *cutteth out* **splitteth** rivers among the rocks;
and his eye seeth *every precious thing* **all the esteemed**.
11 He bindeth the floods from *overflowing* **weeping**;
and the *thing that is hid* **concealed**
bringeth he forth to light.
12 But where shall wisdom be found?
and where is the place of *understanding* **discernment**?
13 Man knoweth not the *price thereof* **appraisal**;
neither is it found in the land of the living.
14 The *depth* **abyss** saith, *It is* not in me:
and the sea saith, *It is* not with me.
15 *It cannot be gotten for gold*
Gold shall not be given for it,
neither shall silver be weighed for the price *thereof*.
16 *It cannot be valued* **Nor balanced**
with the *gold* **ore** of Ophir,
with the *precious* **esteemed** onyx, or the sapphire.
17 The gold and the crystal
cannot equal **be not ranked with** it:
and the exchange of it **nor exchanged**
shall not be for *jewels* **instruments** of *fine* **pure** gold.
18 *No mention* **Nor remembered**
shall be *made of coral* **corals,** or *of* pearls:
for the *price* **sowing** of wisdom is above *rubies* **pearls**.
19 The topaz of *Ethiopia* **Kush**
shall not *equal* **be ranked with** it,
neither shall it be *valued* **balanced** with *pure gold* **ore**.
20 Whence then cometh wisdom?
and where is the place of *understanding* **discernment**?
21 Seeing it is *hid* **concealed** from the eyes of all living,
and *kept close* **hidden**
from the *fowls* **flyers** of the *air* **heavens**.
22 *Destruction* **Abaddon** and death say,
We have heard the fame *thereof* with our ears.
23 *God understandeth* **Elohim discerneth** the way *thereof*,
and he knoweth the place *thereof*.
24 For he looketh to the ends of the earth,
and seeth under the whole *heaven* **heavens**;
25 To *make* **work** the weight for the winds;
and he *weigheth* **gaugeth** the waters by measure.
26 When he *made* **worketh** a *decree* **statute** for the rain,

and a way for the lightning of the *thunder* **voice**:
27 Then did he see it, and *declare* **scribe** it;
he prepared it, yea, and *searched* **probed** it *out.*
28 And unto *man* **humanity** he said, Behold,
the *fear* **awe** of *the Lord* **Adonay**,
that is wisdom;
and to *depart* **turn aside** from evil
is *understanding* **discernment**.

29 *Moreover Job* **Iyob**
continued **lifted to add** his *parable* **proverb**, and said,
2 *Oh* **Who giveth** that I were
as in *months past* **ancient moons**,
as in the days when *God preserved* **Elohah guarded** me;
3 When his *candle shined* **lamp halaled** upon my head,
and when by his light I walked through darkness;
4 As I was in the days of *my youth* **winter**,
when the *secret* **private counsel** of *God* **Elohah**
was upon my *tabernacle* **tent**;
5 When *the Almighty* **Shadday** was yet with me,
when my *children* **lads** were **round** about me;
6 When I *washed* **bathed** my steps with butter,
and the rock poured me out *rivers* **rivulets** of oil;
7 When I went out to the *gate* **portal** through the city,
when I prepared my *seat* **settlement**
in the *street* **broadway**!
8 The *young men* **lads** saw me, and hid themselves:
and the aged arose, and stood up.
9 The *princes* **governors** refrained *talking* **uttering**,
and *laid* **set** their *hand* **palm** on their mouth.
10 The *nobles held* **eminent hid** their *peace* **voice**,
and their tongue *cleaved* **adhered**
to *the roof of* their *mouth* **palate**.
11 When the ear heard *me,*
then it *blessed* **called** me **blithesome**;
and when the eye saw me,
it gave witness to me:
12 Because I *delivered* **rescued** the *poor* **humble** that cried,
and the *fatherless* **orphan**,
and him that had *none to help him* **no helper**.
13 The blessing of him that was ready to *perish* **destruct**
came upon me:
and I caused the widow's heart to *sing for joy* **shout**.
14 *I put on righteousness* **enrobed justness**,
and it *clothed* **enrobed** me:
my judgment was as a *robe* **mantle** and a *diadem* **turban**.
15 I was eyes to the blind, and feet was I to the lame.
16 I was a father to the *poor* **needy**:
and the *cause* **contention** which I knew not
I searched out **probed**.
17 And I brake the *jaws* **molars** of the wicked,
and *plucked* **cast** the *spoil* **prey** out of his teeth.
18 Then I said, I shall *die* **expire** in my nest,
and *I shall multiply* **my days shall abound** as the sand.
19 My root was spread out by the waters,
and the dew
lay all night **stayed overnight** upon my *branch* **clippings**.
20 My *glory* **honour** was *fresh in* **new within** me,
and my bow was *renewed* **changed** in my hand.
21 Unto me *men gave ear* **they hearkened**, and waited,
and *kept silence* **hushed** at my counsel.
22 After my words they *spake* **reiterated** not *again;*
and my *speech* **utterances** dropped upon them.
23 And they waited for me as for the rain;
and they *opened* **gaped** their mouth *wide*
as for the *latter* **after** rain.
24 *If* I laughed on them, they *believed it* **trusted** not;
and the light of my *countenance* **face**
they *cast* **felled** not *down.*
25 I chose out their way, and *sat chief* **settled as head**,
and *dwelt* **tabernacled** as a *king* **sovereign**
in the *army* **troops**,
as one that *comforteth* **sigheth over** the mourners.

30 But now they that are *younger* **of fewer days** than I
have me in derision **ridicule me**,
whose fathers I *would* **should** have *disdained* **spurned**
to have set with the dogs of my flock.
2 Yea, *whereto might the strength* **what is the force**
of their hands *profit* **to** me,
in whom *old age was perished* **maturity destructed**?
3 For *want* **lack** and *famine* **hunger**
they were *solitary* **sterile**;
fleeing **gnawing** into the *wilderness* **parch**
in former time **of yesternight**
desolate **devastation** and *waste* **ruin**.
4 Who *cut up* **plucked** mallows by the *bushes* **shrubs**,
and juniper roots for their *meat* **bread**.
5 They were *driven forth* **exiled** from *among men* **the back**,
(they *cried* **shouted** after them as *after* a thief;)
6 To *dwell* **tabernacle**
in the *cliffs* **chasms** of the *valleys* **wadies**,
in caves **holes** of the *earth* **dust**, and *in* the rocks.
7 Among the *bushes* **shrubs** they brayed;
under the nettles they were *gathered together* **scraped**.
8 *They were children* **Sons** of fools,
yea, *children* **sons** of *base* **nameless** men:
they were viler than **ejected from** the earth.
9 And now am I their *song* **strummer**,
yea, I am their *byword* **utterance**.
10 They abhor me, they flee far from me,
and spare not to spit in my face.
11 Because he hath loosed my cord,
and *afflicted* **humbled** me,
they have also *let loose* **sent away**
the bridle *before me* **from my face**.
12 Upon my right *hand* rise the *youth* **offspring**;
they *push* **send** away my feet,
and they raise up against me
the ways of their destruction.
13 They *mar* **tear up** my path,
they *set forward* **benefit** my calamity,
they have no helper.
14 They came *upon me*
as a *wide breaking in of waters* **broad breach**:
in **under** the *desolation* **devastation**
they rolled themselves *upon me.*
15 Terrors are turned upon me:
they pursue my *soul* **reputation** as the wind:
and my *welfare* **salvation** passeth away as a **thick** cloud.
16 And now my soul is poured out upon me;
the days of *affliction* **humiliation**
have taken hold upon me.
17 My bones *are pierced* **penetrate** in me
in the night *season*:
and my *sinews take no rest* **gnawing lieth not down**.
18 By the great force *of my disease*
is my *garment changed* **robe disguised**:
it bindeth me about as the *collar* **mouth** of my coat.
19 He hath cast me into the *mire* **clay**,
and I am become like dust and ashes.
20 I cry unto thee,
and thou *dost not hear* **answerest** me **not**:
I stand up, and thou *regardest* **discernest** me not.
21 Thou *art become* **turnest** cruel to me:
with thy *strong* **mighty** hand
thou opposest *thyself against* me.
22 Thou liftest me up to the wind;
thou *causest me to ride upon it* **drivest me**,
and *dissolvest* **razest** my substance.
23 For I know
that thou *wilt bring* **shalt return** me to death,
and to the house *appointed* **of the congregation**
for all **of all the** living.
24 Howbeit he *will* **shall** not
stretch out **extend** his hand to the *grave* **prey**,
though they cry in his *destruction* **calamity**.
25 Did not I weep for him
that *was in trouble* **had a hard day**?
was not my soul grieved for the *poor* **needy**?
26 When I *looked for* **awaited** good,
then evil came *unto me*:
and when I waited for light,
there came darkness.
27 My *bowels* **inwards** boiled, and *rested* **hushed** not:
the days of *affliction* **humiliation**
prevented **anticipated** me.
28 I went *mourning* **darkened** without the *sun* **heat**:
I *stood up* **arose**, and I cried in the congregation.
29 I am a brother to *dragons* **monsters**,
and a *companion* **friend** to *owls* **daughters of the owl**.
30 My skin is black upon me,

and my bones are *burned* **scorched** with *heat* **parch.**
31 My harp also
is turned to **be into** mourning,
and my *organ* **woodwind**
into the voice of them that weep.

31 I *made* **cut** a covenant with mine eyes;
why then should I *think* **discern** upon a *maid* **virgin**?
2 For what *portion* **allotment** of *God* **Elohah**
is *there* from above?
and what inheritance of *the Almighty* **Shadday**
from *on high* **the heights**?
3 Is not *destruction* **calamity** to the wicked?
and a *strange punishment* **strangeness**
to the *workers* **doers** of *iniquity* **mischief**?
4 Doth not he see my ways,
and *count* **scribe** all my *steps* **paces**?
5 If I have walked with vanity,
or if my foot hath hasted to deceit;
6 Let me be weighed
in *an even* **a** balance **of justness**
that *God* **Elohah** may know mine integrity.
7 If my step hath *turned* **extended** out of the way,
and mine heart walked after mine eyes,
and if any *blot* **blemish**
hath *cleaved* **adhered** to *mine hands* **my palms**;
8 Then let me *sow* **seed**, and let another eat;
yea, let my offspring be rooted out.
9 If mine heart have been *deceived* **enticed** by a woman,
or *if* I have *laid wait* **lurked**
at my *neighbour's door* **friend's portal**;
10 Then let my *wife* **woman** grind unto another,
and let others *bow down upon* **kneel to** her.
11 For this is *an heinous crime* **intrigue**; yea,
it is an iniquity to be punished by the judges
a judicial perversity.
12 For it is a fire that consumeth to *destruction* **Abaddon**,
and *would* **should** root out all *mine increase* **my produce**.
13 If I *did despise* **spurned** the *cause* **judgment**
of my *manservant* **servant** or of my *maidservant* **maid**,
when they contended with me;
14 What then shall I *do* **work** when *God* **El** riseth *up*?
and when he visiteth, what shall I *answer* **respond** him?
15 Did not he that *made* **worked** me in the *womb* **belly**
make **work** him?
and did not one *fashion* **prepare** us in the womb?
16 If I have withheld the poor from their desire,
or have *caused* **finished off** the eyes of the widow *to fail*;
17 Or have eaten my morsel myself alone,
and the *fatherless* **orphan** hath not eaten *thereof*;
18 (For from my youth he *was brought* **grew** up with me,
as *with* a father,
and I have *guided* **led** her from my mother's *womb* **belly**;)
19 If I have seen any *perish* **destruct**
for want of *clothing* **robe**,
or *any poor* without covering **to the needy**;
20 If his loins have not blessed me,
and *if* he were not *warmed* **heated**
with the fleece of my *sheep* **lambs**;
21 If I have *lifted up* **shaken** my hand
against the *fatherless* **orphan**,
when I saw my help in the *gate* **portal**:
22 Then let *mine arm* **my shoulder**
fall from my shoulder blade,
and mine arm
be broken from the *bone* **stem**.
23 For *destruction* **calamity** from *God* **El**
was a *terror* **dread** to me,
and by reason of his *highness* **exalting**
I could not endure.
24 If I have *made* **set** gold my hope,
or have said to the *fine gold* **ore**, *Thou art* my confidence;
25 If I *rejoiced* **cheered**
because my *wealth was* **valuables were** great,
and because mine hand had *gotten* **found** much;
26 If I *beheld* **saw** the *sun* **light** when it *shined* **halaled**,
or the moon walking in *brightness* **esteem**;
27 And my heart
hath been *secretly enticed* **covertly duped**,
or my mouth hath kissed my hand:
28 This also were
an iniquity to be punished by the judge
a judicial perversity:
for I should have denied *the God that is* **El** above.
29 If I *rejoiced* **cheered**
at the *destruction* **calamity** of him that hated me,
or *lifted up myself* **wakened** when evil found him:
30 Neither have I *suffered* **given** my *mouth* **palate** to sin
by *wishing a curse* **asking an oath** to his soul.
31 If the men of my *tabernacle* **tent** said not,
Oh **Who giveth** that we had of his flesh!
we cannot be satisfied.
32 The *stranger* **sojourner**
did not lodge **stayed not overnight**
in the *street* **outways**:
but I opened my doors to the *traveller* **wayward**.
33 If I covered my *transgressions* **rebellions**
as *Adam* **humanity**,
by hiding mine *iniquity* **perversity** in my bosom:
34 Did I *fear* **dread** a great multitude,
or did the *contempt* **disrespect** of families terrify me,
that I *kept silence* **hushed**,
and went not out of the *door* **portal**?
35 *Oh* **Who giveth** that one *would* **should** hear me!
behold, my *desire* **mark** is,
that *the Almighty would* **Shadday should** answer me,
and that *mine adversary* **my man of contention**
had *written* **scribed** a *book* **scroll**.
36 Surely I *would take* **should lift** it upon my shoulder,
and *bind* **fasten** it as a crown to me.
37 I *would declare unto* **should tell** him
the number of my *steps* **paces**;
as *a prince would* **an eminent should** I go near unto him.
38 If my *land* **soil** cry against me,
or that the furrows *likewise thereof*
complain **weep together**;
39 If I have eaten the *fruits thereof* **produce**
without *money* **silver**,
or have caused the *owners thereof* **masters**
to *lose* **expire** their *life* **soul**:
40 Let *thistles* **thorns** grow instead of wheat,
and *cockle* **stinkweed** instead of barley.
The words of *Job* **Iyob**
are ended **be consummated**.

32 So these three men
ceased to answer Job **shabbathized from answering Iyob**,
because he was *righteous* **just** in his own eyes.

WRATH OF ELI HU IS KINDLED

2 Then was kindled the wrath of *Elihu* **Eli Hu**
the son of *Barachel* **Barach El** the *Buzite* **Buziy**,
of the *kindred* **family** of Ram:
against *Job* **Iyob** was his wrath kindled,
because he justified *himself* **his soul**
rather than *God* **Elohim**.
3 Also against his three friends was his wrath kindled,
because they had found no answer,
and *yet* had *condemned Job* **judged Iyob wicked**.
4 Now *Elihu* **Eli Hu**
had waited till *Job* **Iyob** had *spoken* **worded**,
because they were elder than he **by days**.
5 When *Elihu* **Eli Hu** saw that there was no answer
in the mouth of *these* three men,
then his wrath was kindled.
6 And *Elihu* **Eli Hu**,
the son of *Barachel* **Barach El** the *Buzite* **Buziy**
answered and said,
I am *young* **of few days**, and ye are *very old* **aged**;
wherefore I *was afraid* **feared**,
and *durst not* **awed**
to shew you *mine opinion* **my knowledge**.
7 I said, Days should *speak* **word**,
and *multitude* **abundance** of years
should *teach* **make known** wisdom.
8 *But* **Surely** there is a spirit in man:
and the *inspiration* **breath** of *the Almighty* **Shadday**
giveth them *understanding* **discernment**.
9 **The** Great *men* are not *always wise* **enwisened**:
neither do the aged *understand* **discern** judgment.
10 Therefore I said, Hearken to me;
I also *will* **shall** shew *mine opinion* **my knowledge**.
11 Behold, I *waited for* **awaited** your words;

I gave ear to your reasons,
whilst ye *searched out what to say* **probed utterances**.
12 Yea, I *attended* **discerned** unto you, and, behold,
there was none of you that *convinced Job* **reproved Iyob**,
or that answered his *words* **sayings**:
13 Lest ye should say, We have found out wisdom:
God thrusteth **El disperseth** him *down*, not man.
14 Now he hath not *directed* **arranged**
his *words* **utterances** against me:
neither *will I answer him* **shall I respond**
with **to** your *speeches* **sayings**.
15 They were *amazed* **dismayed**,
they answered no more:
they *left off speaking* **removed from uttering**.
16 When I *had waited* **awaited**,
(for they *spake* **worded** not,
but stood still, and answered no more;)
17 *I said*, I *will* **shall** answer also my *part* **allotment**,
I also *will* **shall** shew *mine opinion* **my knowledge**.
18 For I am full of *matter* **utterances**,
the spirit *within me* **of my belly**
constraineth **distresseth** me.
19 Behold,
my belly is as wine which hath no *vent* **opening**;
it is ready to burst **to split** like new *bottles* **skins**.
20 I *will speak* **shall word**, that I may *be refreshed* **respire**:
I *will* **shall** open my lips and answer.
21 Let me not, I *pray* **beseech** you,
accept any man's person **lift the face of humanity**,
neither *let me* give *flattering titles* **honorary degrees**
unto *man* **humanity**.
22 For I know not
to give *flattering titles* **honorary degrees**;
in so doing my *maker* **worker**
would soon take **should shortly lift** me *away*.

33 *Wherefore* **But**, *Job* **Iyob**, I *pray* **beseech** thee,
hear my *speeches* **utterances**,
and hearken to all my words.
2 Behold, *now* **I beseech**, I have opened my mouth,
my tongue hath *spoken* **worded** in my *mouth* **palate**.
3 My *words* **sayings**
shall be of the *uprightness* **straightness** of my heart:
and my lips shall utter knowledge *clearly* **purely**.
4 The spirit of *God* **El** hath *made* **worked** me,
and the breath of *the Almighty* **Shadday**
hath *given* **enlivened** me *life*.
5 If thou canst *answer me* **respond**,
set thy words in order before me **line up at my face**,
stand up **get set**.
6 Behold,
I am according to thy *wish* **mouth** in *God's* **El's** stead:
I also am formed out of the clay.
7 Behold, my terror shall not *make* **frighten** thee *afraid*,
neither shall my *hand* **burden** be heavy upon thee.
8 Surely thou hast *spoken* **said** in *mine hearing* **my ears**,
and I have heard the voice of thy *words* **utterances**,
saying,
9 I am *clean* **pure** without *transgression* **rebellion**,
I am *innocent* **covered**;
neither is there *iniquity* **perversity** in me.
10 Behold, he findeth *occasions* **alienations** against me,
he *counteth* **fabricateth** me for his enemy,
11 He *putteth* **setteth** my feet in the stocks,
he *marketh* **guardeth** all my paths.
12 Behold, in this thou art not *just* **justified**:
I *will* **shall** answer thee,
that *God* **Elohah** is greater than man.
13 Why dost thou strive against him?
for he *giveth* **answereth** not *account of*
any of his *matters* **words**.
14 For *God speaketh* **El wordeth** once, yea twice,
yet man perceiveth **he observeth** it not.
15 In a dream, in a vision of the night,
when deep sleep falleth upon men,
in *slumberings* **drowsiness** upon the bed;
16 Then he *openeth* **exposeth** the ears of men,
and sealeth their *instruction* **discipline**,
17 That he may *withdraw man* **turn humanity aside**
from his *purpose* **work**,
and *hide pride* **cover over arrogance**
from *man* **the mighty**.
18 He *keepeth back* **spareth** his soul from the pit **of ruin**,
and his life from *perishing* **passing** by the *sword* **spear**.
19 He is *chastened* **reproved** also
with *pain* **sorrow** upon his bed,
and the *multitude* **strife** of his bones
with strong pain **is perrenial**:
20 So that his life *abhorreth* **loatheth** bread,
and his soul *dainty meat* **food of desire**.
21 His flesh is *consumed away* **finished off**,
that it cannot be seen;
and his bones that were not seen
stick out **are exposed**.
22 Yea, his soul draweth near unto the *grave* **pit of ruin**,
and his life to the *destroyers* **deathifiers**.
23 If there be *a messenger* **an angel** with him,
an interpreter, one among a thousand,
to *shew unto man* **tell humanity**
his *uprightness* **straightness**:
24 Then *he is gracious* **granteth he charism** unto him,
and saith, *Deliver* **Rescue** him
from *going down* **descending** to the pit **of ruin**:
I have found *a ransom* **a koper/an atonement**.
25 His flesh shall be *fresher* **rejuvinated**
than a child's **as ladhood**:
he shall return to the days of his youth:
26 He shall *pray unto God* **intreat Elohah**,
and he *will be favourable unto* **shall please** him:
and he shall see his face with *joy* **shouting**:
for he *will render* **shall restore** unto man
his *righteousness* **justness**.
27 He *looketh upon* **observeth** men,
and if any say, I have sinned,
and perverted that which was *right* **straight**,
and it profited me not;
28 He *will deliver* **shall redeem** his soul
from *going* **passing** into the pit **of ruin**,
and his life shall see the light.
29 *Lo* **Behold**,
all these *things worketh God* **doeth El**
oftentimes **twice and thrice** with *man* **the mighty**,
30 To *bring back* **return** his soul from the pit **of ruin**,
to be enlightened with the light of the living.
31 Mark well, O *Job* **Iyob**, hearken unto me:
hold thy peace **hush**, and I *will speak* **shall word**.
32 If thou hast *any thing to say* **utterances**,
answer me **respond**:
speak **word**, for I desire to justify thee.
33 If not, hearken unto me:
hold thy peace **hush**,
and I shall teach thee wisdom.

34 *Furthermore Elihu* **Eli Hu** answered and said,
2 Hear my *words* **utterances**, O ye wise *men*;
and *give ear* **hearken** unto me,
ye that *have knowledge* **know**.
3 For the ear *trieth words* **proofeth utterances**,
as the *mouth* **palate** tasteth *meat* **to eat**.
4 Let us choose to us judgment:
let us know among ourselves what is good.
5 For *Job* **Iyob** hath said, I am *righteous* **justified**:
and *God* **El** hath *taken away* **turned aside** my judgment.
6 should I lie against my *right* **judgment**?
my *wound* **arrow** is incurable
without *transgression* **rebellion**.
7 What *man* **mighty** is like *Job* **Iyob**,
who drinketh up *scorning* **derision** like water?
8 Which *goeth* **caravaneth** in *company* **companionship**
with the *workers* **doers** of *iniquity* **mischief**,
and walketh with *wicked men* **men of wickedness**.
9 For he hath said,
It profiteth a man nothing **Useless for the mighty**
that he should *delight himself* **be pleased**
with *God* **Elohim**.
10 Therefore hearken unto me
ye men of *understanding* **heart**:
far be it from *God* **El**, that he should do wickedness;
and from *the Almighty* **Shadday**,
that he should *commit iniquity* **do wickedness**.
11 For the *work* **deeds** of *a man* **humanity**
shall he *render unto* **shalam** him,

and *cause every man to find* **present to every man**
according to his ways.
12 Yea, *surely* **truly,** *God will* **El shall** not do wickedly,
neither *will the Almighty* **shall Shadday**
pervert **twist** judgment.
13 Who hath given him a charge over the earth?
or who hath *disposed* **set** the whole world?
14 If he set his heart upon man,
if he gather unto himself his spirit and his breath;
15 All flesh shall *perish* **expire** together,
and *man* **humanity** shall *turn again* **return** unto dust.
16 If *now* thou hast *understanding* **discernment**, hear this:
hearken to the voice of my *words* **utterances**.
17 Shall even he that hateth *right govern* **judgment bind**?
and *wilt* **shalt** thou *condemn* **judge** him **wicked**
that is most just?
18 *Is it fit to say* **Sayest thou** to a *king* **sovereign**,
Thou art wicked **Beli Yaal**?
and to *princes* **volunteers**, *Ye are ungodly* **Wicked**?
19 *How much less to him* — that accepteth not
the *persons* **faces** of *princes* **governors**,
nor *regardeth* **recognizeth** the *rich* **opulent**
more than **the face of** the poor?
for they all are the work of his hands.
20 In a *moment* **blink** shall they die,
and the people shall *be troubled* **shake** at midnight,
and pass away:
and the mighty shall *be taken away* **turn aside**
without hand.
21 For his eyes are upon the ways of man,
and he seeth all his *goings* **paces**.
22 There is no darkness, nor shadow of death,
where the *workers* **doers** of *iniquity* **mischief**
may hide *themselves*.
23 For he *will* **shall** not *lay* **set** upon man more *than right*;
that he should *enter* **go** into judgment with *God* **El**.
24 He shall *break in pieces* **shatter the** mighty *men*
without number **unable to probe**,
and *set* **stand** others in their stead.
25 Therefore he *knoweth* **recognizeth** their *works* **acts**,
and he overturneth them in the night,
so that they are *destroyed* **crushed**.
26 He *striketh* **slappeth** them as wicked *men*
in the *open sight* **place** of *others* **seeing**;
27 Because they turned back from **after** him,
and *would* **comprehended** not *consider*
any of his ways:
28 So that they cause the cry of the poor
to come unto him,
and he heareth the cry of the *afflicted* **humble**.
29 When he *giveth quietness* **resteth**,
who then *can make trouble* **judgeth wicked**?
and when he hideth his face,
who then *can behold* **observeth** him?
whether *it be done* against a *nation* **goyim**,
or against *a man only* **humanity altogether**:
30 *That the hypocrite reign not*
From the reign of the profaner of humanity,
lest the people be ensnared.
31 Surely it is meet to be said unto *God* **El**,
I have borne *chastisement*,
I *will* **shall** not *offend any more* **despoil**:
32 **Except** That which I see not teach thou me:
if I have done *iniquity* **wickedness**,
I will do no more **never again**.
33 Should it be according to thy mind?
he *will recompense* **shalam** it,
whether thou refuse, or whether thou choose;
and not I:
therefore *speak* **word** what thou knowest.
34 Let men of understanding *tell me* **say**,
and let a wise *man* **mighty** hearken unto me.
35 *Job* **Iyob** hath *spoken* **worded**
without *knowledge* **comprehending**,
and his words were without wisdom.
36 My *desire* **longing** is that *Job* **Iyob**
may be *tried unto the end* **proofed in perpetuity**
because of his *answers* **responses**
for *wicked men* **men of mischief**.
37 For he addeth rebellion unto his sin,
he clappeth *his hands* among us,
and *multiplieth* **aboundeth** his *words* **sayings**
against *God* **El**.

35 *Elihu spake moreover* **Eli Hu answered**, and said,
2 *Thinkest* **Fabricatest** thou this to be *right* **judgment**,
that thou saidst,
My *righteousness* **justness** is more than *God's* **El's**?
3 For thou saidst,
What *advantage will* **use shall** it be unto thee?
and, What *profit* **benefit** shall I have,
if I be cleansed from my sin?
4 I *will answer* **shall respond** thee **utterances**,
and thy *companions* **friends** with thee.
5 Look unto the heavens, and see;
and *behold* **observe** the *clouds* **vapours**
which are *higher than thou* **heightened above thee**.
6 If thou sinnest, what *doest* **workest** thou against him?
or if thy *transgressions* **rebellions** be multiplied,
what doest thou unto him?
7 If thou be *righteous* **justified**, what givest thou him?
or what *receiveth* **taketh** he of thine hand?
8 Thy wickedness may *hurt* **be for** a man as thou *art*;
and thy *righteousness* **justness**
may profit **for** the son of *man* **humanity**.
9 By reason of the *multitude* **abundance** of oppressions
they *make the oppressed to cry* **cause crying**:
they cry out by reason of the arm of the *mighty* **great**.
10 But none saith,
Where is *God* **Elohah** my *maker* **Worker**,
who giveth *songs* **psalms** in the night;
11 Who teacheth us
more than the *beasts* **animals** of the earth,
and *maketh us wiser* **enwiseneth us more**
than the *fowls* **flyers** of *heaven* **the heavens**?
12 There they cry, but none *giveth answer* **answereth**,
because **at the face** of the *pride* **pomp** of evil *men*.
13 Surely *God will* **El shall** not hear vanity,
neither *will the Almighty regard* **shall Shadday observe** it.
14 Although thou sayest thou shalt not *see* **observe** him,
yet judgment is before him **the plea is at his face**;
therefore trust **writhe** thou in him.
15 But now, because it is not *so*,
he hath visited in his *anger* **wrath**;
yet he knoweth it not in *great extremity* **mighty stupidity**:
16 Therefore doth *Job open* **Iyob gasp** his mouth in vain;
he *multiplieth words* **weaveth utterances**
without knowledge.

36 *Elihu* **Eli Hu** also *proceeded* **added**, and said,
2 *Suffer me a little* **Stay around**,
and I *will* **shall** shew thee
that I have yet *to speak* **utterances**
on *God's* **Elohah's** behalf.
3 I *will fetch* **shall lift** my knowledge from afar,
and *will ascribe righteousness* **shall give justness**
to my Maker.
4 For truly my *words* **utterances** shall not be false:
he that is *perfect* **integrious** in knowledge is with thee.
5 Behold,
God **El** is mighty, and *despiseth* **spurneth** not *any*:
he is — mighty in *strength* **force** and *wisdom* **heart**.
6 He *preserveth* **enliveneth** not *the life of* the wicked:
but giveth *right* **judgment** to the *poor* **humble**.
7 He *withdraweth* **diminisheth** not his eyes
from the *righteous* **just**:
but with *kings are they* **sovereigns** on the throne;
yea, he *doth establish* **settleth** them *for ever* **in perpetuity**,
and they are exalted **lifted**.
8 And if they be bound in *fetters* **bonds**,
and be *holden* **captured** in cords of *affliction* **humiliation**;
9 Then he *sheweth* **telleth** them their *work* **deeds**,
and their *transgressions* **rebellions**
that they have *exceeded* **prevailed mightily**.
10 He *openeth* **exposeth** also their ear to discipline,
and *commandeth* **sayeth**
that they return from *iniquity* **mischief**.
11 If they *obey* **hearken** and serve him,
they shall *spend* **conclude** their days in *prosperity* **good**,
and their years in pleasures.
12 But if they *obey* **hearken** not,
they shall *perish* **pass away expired** by the *sword* **spear**,

and they shall die without knowledge.
13 But the *hypocrites* **profaners** in heart *heap up* **set** wrath:
they cry not when he bindeth them.
14 *They die* **Their soul dieth** in *youth* **ladhood**,
and their life
is among the *unclean* **hallowed whoremongers**.
15 He delivereth the poor in his *affliction* **humiliation**,
and *openeth* **exposeth** their ears in oppression.
16 Even so *would* **should** he have removed thee
out of the *strait* **mouth of the narrow**
into a *broad place* **broadness**,
where there is no *straitness* **narrowness under**;
and that which should *be set* **rest** on thy table
should be full of fatness.
17 But thou hast fulfilled the *judgment* **plea** of the wicked:
judgment **the plea** and *justice* **judgment**
take hold on thee **are upheld**.
18 Because there is *wrath* **fury**,
beware lest he *take* **goad** thee *away*
with *his stroke* **gluttony**:
then a great *ransom* **koper/atonement**
cannot deliver **shall not extend to** thee.
19 *Will* **Shall** he *esteem* **appraise** thy *riches* **opulence**?
no, not *gold* **mines**, nor all the forces of *strength* **force**.
20 *Desire* **Gulp** not the night,
when people *are cut off* **ascend** in their *place* **stead**.
21 *Take heed*, **On guard!** *regard* **face** not *iniquity* **mischief**:
for this hast thou chosen
rather than *affliction* **humiliation**.
22 Behold, *God exalteth* **El lofteth** by his *power* **force**:
who teacheth like him?
23 Who hath enjoined him his way?
or who can say,
Thou hast *wrought iniquity* **done wickedness**?
24 Remember that thou *magnify* **increase** his *work* **deeds**,
which men behold.
25 *Every man* **All humanity** may see it;
man may *behold it* **ascan** far off.
26 Behold, *God* **El** is *great* **exceedingly excellent**,
and we know him not,
neither can the number of his years
be *searched out* **probed**.
27 For he *maketh small* **diminisheth** the drops of water:
they *pour down* **refine** rain
according to **into** the *vapour thereof* **mist**:
28 Which the *clouds do drop* **vapours flow** and *distil* **drip**
upon *man* **humanity** abundantly.
29 Also can any *understand* **discern**
the spreadings of the **thick** clouds,
or the *noise* **clamorings**
of his *tabernacle* **sukkoth/brush arbor**?
30 Behold, he spreadeth his light upon it,
and covereth the *bottom* **roots** of the sea.
31 For by them *judgeth* **pleadeth** he
the cause of the people;
he giveth *meat* **food** in abundance.
32 With *clouds* **his two palms** he covereth the light;
and *commandeth* **misvaheth** it
not to shine by the cloud that cometh betwixt
and intercedeth.
33 The *noise thereof* **shouting**
sheweth **telleth** concerning *it* **him**,
the *cattle* **chattel** also *concerning*
and the *vapour* **holocaust**.
37 At this also my heart trembleth,
and is *moved* **loosed** out of his place.
2 **In hearing,**
Hear *attentively* the *noise* **commotion** of his voice,
and the *sound* **meditation** that goeth out of his mouth.
3 He *directeth* **releaseth** under the whole *heaven* **heavens**,
and his lightning unto the *ends* **wings** of the earth.
4 After it a voice roareth:
he thundereth with the voice of *his excellency* **pomp**;
and he *will* **shall** not *stay* **restrain** them
when his voice is heard.
5 *God* **El** thundereth marvellously with his voice;
great *things doeth* **worketh** he,
which we *cannot comprehend* **perceive not**.
6 For he saith to the snow, Be thou on the earth;
likewise to the *small* **downpour of** rain,
and to the *great* **downpour of** rain of his strength.
7 He sealeth up the hand of *every man* **all humanity**;
that all men may know his work.
8 Then the *beasts go into dens* **live beings lurk**,
and *remain* **tabernacle** in their *places* **habitations**.
9 Out of the *south* **chamber**
cometh the *whirlwind* **hurricane**:
and cold out of the *north* **scattering**.
10 By the breath of *God* **El** frost is given:
and the breadth of the waters is *straitened* **narrowed**.
11 Also by *watering* **showering**
he *wearieth* **overloadeth** the thick cloud:
he scattereth his *bright* **lightning** cloud:
12 And it is turned round about by his counsels:
that they may do
whatsoever he *commandeth* **misvaheth** them
upon the face of the world in the earth.
13 He causeth it to come,
whether for *correction* **a scion**,
or for his land, or for mercy.
14 Hearken unto this, O *Job* **Iyob**: stand *still*,
and *consider* **discern**
the *wondrous works* **marvels** of *God* **El**.
15 Dost thou know when *God disposed* **Elohah set** them,
and caused the light of his cloud to shine?
16 Dost thou know the balancings of the **thick** clouds,
the *wondrous works* **marvels** of him
which is *perfect* **integrious** in knowledge?
17 How thy *garments* **clothes** are *warm* **hot**,
when he *quieteth* **resteth** the earth
by the *south wind* **southerly**?
18 Hast thou with him
spread out **expanded** the *sky* **vapours**,
which is strong,
and as a *molten looking glass* **poured reflector**?
19 *Teach us* **Let us know** what *we* shall say unto him;
for we cannot *order our speech* **line up**
by reason of **at the face of the** darkness.
20 Shall it be *told* **scribed** him that I *speak* **word**?
if a man *speak* **say**, surely he shall be swallowed *up*.
21 And now *men* **they** see not the bright light
which is in the *clouds* **vapours**:
but the wind passeth, and *cleanseth* **purifieth** them.
22 *Fair weather* **Clear sky** cometh out of the north:
with *God* **Elohah** is *terrible* **awesome** majesty.
23 *Touching the Almighty* **Shadday**,
we cannot find him out:
he is **exceedingly** excellent
in *power* **force**, and in judgment,
and *in plenty of justice* **abundant in justness**:
he *will* **shall** not *afflict* **humble**.
24 Men do therefore fear him:
he *respecteth* **seeth** not any that are wise of heart.

YAH VEH ANSWERS IYOB

38 Then *the LORD* **Yah Veh**
answered *Job* **Iyob** out of the *whirlwind* **storm**, and said,
2 Who is this that darkeneth counsel
by *words* **utterances** without knowledge?
3 Gird up *now* **I beseech**, thy loins like a *man* **mighty**;
for I *will demand* **shall ask** of thee,
and *answer thou me* **let me know**.
4 Where wast thou
when I *laid the foundations of* **founded** the earth?
declare **tell**,
if thou *hast understanding* **knowest discernment**.
5 Who *hath laid* **set** the *measures* **measurements** *thereof*,
if thou knowest?
or who hath stretched the line upon it?
6 Whereupon are the foundations *thereof fastened* **sunk**?
or who *laid* **poured** the corner stone *thereof*;
7 When the morning stars *sang* **shouted** together,
and all the sons of *God* **Elohim** shouted *for joy*?
8 Or who *shut up* **hedged in** the sea with doors,
when it *brake forth* **gushed**,
as if it had **when it** issued out of the womb?
9 When I *made* **set** the cloud
the garment thereof **for a robe**,
and *thick* **dripping** darkness
a swaddling band for it **for a swathe**,
10 And brake up for it my *decreed place* **statute**,

and set bars and doors,
11 And said, Hitherto shalt thou come,
but *no further* **add not**:
and here shall *thy proud* **the pomp of thy** waves
be stayed **set**?
12 Hast thou *commanded* **misvahed** the morning
since thy days;
and caused the *dayspring* **dawn** to know his place;
13 That it might take hold of the *ends* **wings** of the earth,
that the wicked might be shaken out of it?
14 It is turned as clay to the seal;
and they *stand* **set** as a *garment* **robe**.
15 And from the wicked their light is withholden,
and the *high* **lofted** arm shall be broken.
16 Hast thou entered
into the *springs* **fountains** of the sea?
or hast thou walked
in the search of **probing** the *depth* **abyss**?
17 Have the *gates* **portals** of death
been *opened* **exposed** unto thee?
or hast thou seen
the *doors* **portals** of the shadow of death?
18 Hast thou *perceived* **discerned**
the *breadth* **broadness** of the earth?
declare **tell** if thou knowest it all.
19 Where is the way where light *dwelleth* **tabernacleth**?
and *as for* darkness, where is the place *thereof,*
20 That thou shouldest take it
to the *bound thereof* **border**,
and that thou shouldest *know* **discern** the paths
to the house *thereof*?
21 Knowest thou it, because thou wast then born?
or *because* the number of thy days is great?
22 Hast thou entered into the treasures of the snow?
or hast thou seen the treasures of the hail,
23 Which I have *reserved* **spared**
against the time of *trouble* **tribulation**,
against the day of battle and war?
24 *By what way* **Whence** is the light *parted* **allotted**,
which scattereth the *east wind* **easterly** upon the earth?
25 Who hath divided a *watercourse* **channel**
for the overflowing of waters,
or a way for the lightning of *thunder* **voices**;
26 To cause it to rain on the earth, where no man is;
on the wilderness, wherein there is no *man* **human**;
27 To satisfy the *desolate* **devastation**
and *waste ground* **ruin**;
and to cause the *bud* **source** of the *tender herb* **sprout**
to *spring forth* **sprout**?
28 Hath the rain a father?
or who hath begotten the drops of dew?
29 Out of whose *womb* **belly** came the ice?
and the *hoary frost* **hoarfrost** of *heaven* **the heavens**,
who hath gendered it?
30 The waters are hid as *with* a stone,
and the face of the *deep* **abyss** is *frozen* **captured**.
31 Canst thou bind
the *sweet influences* **bonds** of *Pleiades* **Kimah**,
or loose the *bands* **cords** of *Orion* **Kesil**?
32 Canst thou bring forth *Mazzaroth* **the constellations**
in *his season* **their time**?
or canst thou *guide Arcturus* **lead Ash** with his sons?
33 Knowest thou
the *ordinances* **statutes** of *heaven* **the heavens**?
canst thou set the dominion *thereof* in the earth?
34 Canst thou lift up thy voice to the **thick** clouds,
that abundance of waters may cover thee?
35 Canst thou send lightnings,
that they may go and say unto thee, Here we are?
36 Who hath put wisdom in the *inward parts* **reins**?
or who hath given *understanding* **discernment**
to the *heart* **observant**?
37 Who can *number* **scribe** the *clouds* **vapours** in wisdom?
or who can *stay* **lay down**
the bottles of *heaven* **the heavens**,
38 When the dust *groweth* **firmeth** into *hardness* **mire**,
and the clods *cleave fast together* **adhere**?
39 *Wilt* **Shalt** thou hunt the prey for the **roaring** lion?
or fill the *appetite* **life** of the *young lions* **whelps**,
40 When they *couch* **prostrate** in their *dens* **habitations**,
and *abide* **settle** in the *covert* **sukkoth/brush arbor**
to *lie in wait* **lurk**?
41 Who *provideth* **prepareth** for the raven his *food* **hunt**?
when his *young ones* **children** cry unto *God* **El**,
they *wander for lack of meat* **stray without food**.

39 Knowest thou the time
when the wild goats of the rock *bring forth* **birth**?
or canst thou *mark* **guard**
when the hinds *do calve* **writhe**?
2 Canst thou *number* **scribe** the *months* **moons**
that they fulfil?
or knowest thou the time when they *bring forth* **birth**?
3 They *bow themselves* **kneel**,
they *bring forth* **adhere to** their *young ones* **children**,
they *cast out* **send** their *sorrows* **pangs**.
4 Their *young ones* **sons** are *in good liking* **plump**,
they *grow up* **abound** with *corn* **grain**;
they go forth, and return not unto them.
5 Who hath *sent out* **released** the *wild ass* **runner**
free **liberated**?
or who hath loosed the bands of the *wild ass* **onager**?
6 Whose house I have *made* **set** the *wilderness* **plains**,
and the *barren land* **salty** his *dwellings* **tabernacles**.
7 He *scorneth* **ridiculeth** the multitude of the city,
neither *regardeth* **heareth** he
the *crying* **clamorings** of the *driver* **exactor**.
8 The *range* **gleanings** of the mountains is his pasture,
and he searcheth after *every* **all the** green *thing.*
9 *Will* **Willeth** the *unicorn be willing* **reem**
to serve thee,
or *abide* **stay overnight** by thy *crib* **manger**?
10 Canst thou bind the *unicorn* **reem**
with his band in the furrow?
or *will* **shall** he harrow the valleys after thee?
11 *Wilt* **Shalt** thou *trust* **confide in** him,
because his *strength* **force** is great?
or *wilt* **shalt** thou leave thy labour to him?
12 *Wilt* **Shalt** thou *believe* **trust** him,
that he *will bring home* **shall return** thy seed,
and gather it into thy *barn* **threshingfloor**?
13 *Gavest thou the goodly wings* **Or pinions**
unto the peacocks **to leap for joy**?
or *wings and feathers* **plumage** unto the *ostrich* **stork**?
14 Which leaveth her eggs in the earth,
and *warmeth* **heateth** them in dust,
15 And forgetteth that the foot may *crush* **squeeze** them,
or that the *wild beast* **field life** may *break* **trample** them.
16 She is hardened against her *young ones* **sons**,
as though they were not her's:
her labour is in vain without *fear* **dread**;
17 Because *God* **Elohah**
hath *deprived her of wisdom* **exacted wisdom of her**,
neither hath he *imparted* **allotted** to her
understanding **discernment**.
18 What time she *lifteth up herself* **flappeth**
on high **in the heights**,
she *scorneth* **ridiculeth** the horse and his rider.
19 Hast thou given the horse *strength* might?
hast thou *clothed* **enrobed** his neck with thunder?
20 Canst thou *make* **cause** him *afraid* **to quiver**
as a *grasshopper* **locust**?
the *glory* **majesty** of his nostrils is *terrible* **terror**.
21 He *paweth* **diggeth** in the valley,
and rejoiceth in his *strength* **force**:
he goeth on to *meet* **confront** the *armed men* **armour**.
22 He *mocketh at fear* **ridiculeth dread**,
and is not *affrighted* **dismayed**;
neither turneth he back from **the face of** the sword.
23 The quiver *rattleth* **whizzeth** against him,
the *glittering* **flaming** spear and the *shield* **dart**.
24 He swalloweth the *ground* **earth**
with *fierceness* **quaking** and *rage* **commotion**:
neither *believeth* **trusteth** he
that it is the *sound* **voice** of the trumpet.
25 He saith among the trumpets, *Ha, ha* **Aha**;
and he *smelleth* **scenteth** the *battle* **war** afar off,
the thunder of the *captains* **governors**, and the shouting.
26 *Doth* **Soareth** the hawk *fly*
by thy *wisdom* **discernment**,
and *stretch* **spread** her wings toward the south?

27 *Doth* **Goeth** the eagle
mount up at thy *command* **mouth,**
and make her nest on high?
28 She *dwelleth* **tabernacleth**
and *abideth* **stayeth overnight** on the rock,
upon the crag of the rock,
and the *strong place* **hunthold**.
29 From thence she *seeketh the prey* **exploreth for food**,
and her eyes *behold* **scan** afar off.
30 Her *young ones also* **chicks** suck up blood:
and where the *slain* **pierced** are, there is she.

40 Moreover
the LORD **Yah Veh** answered *Job* **Iyob**, and said,
2 Shall he that contendeth with *the Almighty* **Shadday**
instruct **reprove** him?
he that reproveth *God* **Elohah**, let him answer it.

IYOB ANSWERS YAH VEH

3 Then *Job* **Iyob** answered *the LORD* **Yah Veh**, and said,
4 Behold, I am *vile* **abased**;
what shall I *answer* **respond to** thee?
I *will lay mine* **shall set my** hand *upon* **unto** my mouth.
5 Once have I *spoken* **worded**;
but I *will* **shall** not answer:
yea, twice; but *I will proceed no further* **not again**.

YAH VEH ANSWERS IYOB

6 Then answered *the LORD* **Yah Veh** unto *Job* **Iyob**
out of the *whirlwind* **storm**, and said,
7 Gird up thy loins *now* **I beseech**, like a *man* **mighty**:
I *will demand* **shall ask** of thee,
and *declare thou unto me* **let me know**.
8 *Wilt* **Shalt** thou *also disannul* **break** my judgment?
wilt **shalt** thou *condemn* **judge** me **wicked**,
that thou mayest be *righteous* **justified**?
9 Hast thou an arm like *God* **El**?
or *canst* shalt thou thunder with a voice like him?
10 *Deck* **Adorn** thyself *now* **I beseech,**
with *majesty* **pomp** and *excellency* **loftiness**;
and *array* **enrobe** thyself
with *glory* **majesty** and *beauty* **honour**.
11 *Cast abroad* **Scatter** the *rage* **fury** of thy wrath:
and *behold* **see** every one that is *proud* **pompous**,
and abase him.
12 *Look on* **See** every one that is *proud* **pompous**,
and *bring him low* **subdue him**;
and *tread down* **trample** the wicked in their place.
13 Hide them in the dust together;
and bind their faces in *secret* **hiding**.
14 Then *will* **shall** I also confess unto thee
that thine own right *hand can* **shall** save thee.
15 Behold *now* **I beseech,**
behemoth, which I *made* **worked** with thee;
he eateth grass as an ox.
16 *Lo now* **Behold I beseech,**
his *strength* **force** is in his loins,
and his *force* **strength** is in the navel of his belly.
17 He *moveth* **bendeth** his tail like a cedar:
the sinews of his *stones* **testis**
are *wrapped together* **entwined**.
18 His bones
are as *strong pieces* **gatherings** of *brass* **copper**;
his bones
are like bars **as forgings** of iron.
19 He is the *chief* **beginning** of the ways of *God* **El**:
he that made him can make his sword to approach unto him
his Worker approacheth with his sword.
20 Surely the mountains
bring **bear** him *forth food* **produce**,
where all the *beasts* **live beings** of the field *play* **laugh**.
21 He lieth under the *shady trees* **lotuses**,
in the covert of the *reed* **stalk**, and *fens* **mire**.
22 The *shady trees* **lotuses** cover him with their shadow;
the willows of the *brook* **wadi**
compass **surround** him *about*.
23 Behold, he drinketh up a river, and hasteth not:
he *trusteth* **is confident**
that he can *draw up Jordan* **gush Yarden** into his mouth.
24 He taketh it with his eyes:
his *nose pierceth* **nostrils pierce** through snares.

41 Canst thou draw out leviathan with an hook?
or **drown** his tongue with a cord *which thou lettest down*?
2 Canst thou *put an hook* **set a rush** into his *nose* **nostrils**?
or bore his jaw through with a thorn?
3 *Will* **Shall** he *make many* **abound**
with supplications unto thee?
will **shall** he *speak soft words* **word tenderly** unto thee?
4 *Will* **Shall** he *make* **cut** a covenant with thee?
wilt **shalt** thou take him for a servant *for ever* **eternally**?
5 *Wilt* **Shalt** thou *play* **laugh** with him as with a bird?
or *wilt* **shalt** thou bind him for thy *maidens* **lasses**?
6 Shall *the* **his** companions
make a banquet of **market** him?
shall they *part* **halve** him among the merchants?
7 *Canst thou fill* **Fillest thou** his skin
with *barbed irons* **barbs**?
or his head with fish *spears* **harpoons**?
8 *Lay thine hand* **Set thy palm** upon him,
remember the *battle* **war**, *do no more* **add not**.
9 Behold, the hope of him *is in vain* **lieth**:
shall not one be cast down
even at the *sight* **visage** of him?
10 None is so fierce that *dare stir* **they waken** him *up*:
who then *is able to stand before me* **setteth at my face**?
11 Who *hath prevented* **anticipateth** me,
that I should *repay* **shalam** him?
whatsoever is under the whole *heaven* **heavens** is mine.
12 I *will* **shall** not *conceal* **hush as to** his *parts* **veins**,
nor **the word of** his *power* might,
nor **the beauty of** his *comely* proportion.
13 Who *can discover* **exposeth**
the face of his *garment* **robe**?
or who *can come* **cometh** to him with his double bridle?
14 Who *can open* **openeth** the doors of his face?
his teeth are *terrible* **a terror** round about.
15 His *scales* **strong shields** are his *pride* **pomp**,
shut up *together as with a close* **as a constricted** seal.
16 One *is so near to another* **approacheth one**,
that no *air can come* **wind/spirit cometh** between them.
17 They *are joined one* **adhere man** to *another* **brother**,
they stick together,
that they *cannot be sundered* **be not separated**.
18 By his *neesings* **sneezings** a light *doth shine* **halaleth**,
and his eyes are like the eyelids of the *morning* **dawn**.
19 Out of his mouth go *burning lamps* **flambeaus**,
and sparks of fire *leap out* **escape**.
20 Out of his nostrils goeth smoke,
as out of a *seething pot* **pressure cooker** or *caldron* **rush**.
21 His *breath kindleth* **soul inflameth** coals,
and a flame goeth out of his mouth.
22 In his neck *remaineth* **stayeth** strength,
and *sorrow is turned into joy before him*
languish leapeth at his face.
23 The flakes of his flesh *are joined together* **adhere**:
they are firm **firmed** in themselves;
they *cannot be moved* **totter not**.
24 His heart is *as firm* **firmed** as a stone; yea,
as hard **firmed** as a *piece* **slice** of the nether *millstone*.
25 *When he raiseth up himself* **From his lifting**,
the mighty *are afraid* **dodge him**:
by reason of breakings they purify themselves.
26 The sword of him that *layeth at* **overtaketh** him
cannot hold **riseth not**:
the spear, the *dart* **arrow**, nor the habergeon.
27 He *esteemeth* **fabricateth** iron as straw,
and *brass* **copper** as rotten *wood* **timber**.
28 The *arrow* **son of the bow** cannot make him flee:
slingstones are turned with him into stubble.
29 *Darts* **Clubs** are *counted* **fabricated** as stubble:
he laugheth at the *shaking* **quaking** of a *spear* **dart**.
30 *Sharp stones* **Pieces of potsherd** are under him:
he spreadeth *sharp pointed things* **ore** upon the mire.
31 He *maketh* **setteth** the deep to boil like a *pot* **caldron**:
he maketh the sea like a *pot of ointment* **spicy broth**.
32 He maketh a path to *shine* **enlighten** after him;
one would think **he fabricateth** the *deep* **abyss**
to be *hoary* **greyed**.
33 Upon *earth* **dust** there is not his like,
who is *made* **worked** without *fear* **terror**.
34 He *beholdeth* **seeth** all *high things* **the heights**:
he is *a king* **sovereign**
over all the *children* **sons** of pride.

IYOB ANSWERS YAH VEH

42 Then *Job* **Iyob** answered *the LORD* **Yah Veh**,
and said,
2 I know that thou *canst do every thing* **art able in all**,
and that no *thought* **intrigue**
can be withholden **shall be cut off** from thee.
3 Who is he that *hideth* **concealeth** counsel
without knowledge?
therefore have I *uttered* **told**
that I *understood* **discerned** not;
things too *wonderful* **marvellous** for me,
which I knew not.
4 Hear, I beseech thee, and I *will speak* **shall word**:
I *will demand* **shall ask** of thee,
and *declare thou unto me* **let me know**.
5 I have heard of thee by the hearing of the ear:
but now mine eye *seeth* **hath seen** thee.
6 Wherefore I *abhor myself* **spurn**,
and *repent* **sigh** in dust and ashes.

YAH VEH ANSWERS ELI PHAZ

7 And it *was so* **became**,
that after *the LORD* **Yah Veh**
had *spoken* **worded** these words unto *Job* **Iyob**,
the LORD **Yah Veh**
said to *Eliphaz* **Eli Phaz** the *Temanite* **Temaniy**,
My wrath is kindled against thee,
and against thy two friends:
for ye have not *spoken* **worded** of me
the thing that *is right* **which be established**,
as my servant *Job hath* **Iyob**.
8 Therefore take unto you now
seven bullocks and seven rams,
and go to my servant *Job* **Iyob**,
and *offer up* **holocaust** for yourselves
a *burnt offering* **holocaust**;
and my servant *Job* **Iyob** shall pray for you:
for him *will I accept* **shall I lift from his face**:
lest I deal **so as not to work** with you *after your* folly,
in that ye have not *spoken* **worded** of me
the thing **that** which is *right* **established**,
like my servant *Job* **Iyob**.
9 So *Eliphaz* **Eli Phaz** the *Temanite* **Temaniy**
and Bildad the *Shuhite* **Shuachiy**
and *Zophar* **Sophar** the *Naamathite* **Naamahiy** went,
and *did* **worked** according
as *the LORD commanded* **Yah Veh worded** them:
the LORD **Yah Veh**
also accepted Job **lifted the face of Iyob**.

YAH VEH DOUBLES IYOB'S SUBSTANCE

10 And *the LORD* **Yah Veh**
turned the captivity of *Job* **Iyob**,
when he prayed for his friends:
also *the LORD gave Job* **Yah Veh added to Iyob**
twice as much as he had *before* **faced**.
11 Then came there unto him all his brethren,
and all his sisters,
and all they
that had *been of his acquaintance* **known him before**,
and did eat bread with him in his house:
and they *bemoaned* **wagged with** him,
and *comforted* **sighed over** him
over all the evil
that *the LORD* **Yah Veh** had brought upon him:
every man also gave him *a piece of money* **one ingot**,
and every one *an earring* **one nosering** of gold.
12 So *the LORD* **Yah Veh**
blessed the *latter end* **finality** of *Job* **Iyob**
more than his beginning:
for he had fourteen thousand *sheep* **flocks**,
and six thousand camels,
and a thousand yoke of oxen,
and a thousand she *asses* **burros**.
13 He had also seven sons and three daughters.
14 And he called the name of the first, *Jemima* **Yemima**;
and the name of the second, Kezia;
and the name of the third, *Kerenhappuch* **Qeren Hap Puch**.
15 And in all the land
were no women found so *fair* **beautiful**
as the daughters of *Job* **Iyob**:
and their father gave them inheritance
among their brethren.
16 After this lived *Job* **Iyob** an hundred and forty years,
and saw his sons, and his sons' sons,
even four generations.
17 So *Job* **Iyob** died,
being *old* **aged** and *full* **satisfied** of days.

KEY TO INTERPRETING THE EXEGESES:
King James text is in regular type;
Text under exegeses is in oblique type;
Text of exegeses is in bold type.

BOOK I

1 *Blessed* **Blithe** is the man
that walketh not in the counsel of the *ungodly* **wicked**,
nor standeth in the way of sinners,
nor *sitteth* **settleth** in the *seat* **settlement** of the scornful.
2 But his delight is in the *law* **torah** of *the LORD* **Yah Veh**;
and in his *law* **torah** doth he meditate day and night.
3 And he shall be like a tree
planted **transplanted** by the *rivers* **rivulets** of water,
that *bringeth forth* **giveth** his fruit in his *season* **time**;
his leaf also shall not wither;
and whatsoever he *doeth* **worketh** shall prosper.
4 The *ungodly* **wicked** are not so:
but are like the chaff
which the wind *driveth away* **disperseth**.
5 Therefore the *ungodly* **wicked**
shall not *stand* **rise** in the judgment,
nor sinners
in the *congregation* **witness** of the *righteous* **just**.
6 For *the LORD* **Yah Veh**
knoweth the way of the *righteous* **just**:
but the way of the *ungodly* **wicked** shall *perish* **destruct**.

2 Why do the *heathen rage* **goyim conspire**,
and the *people* **nations**
imagine a vain thing **meditate vanity**?
2 The *kings* **sovereigns** of the earth
set **station** themselves,
and the *rulers take* **potentates set** counsel together,
against *the LORD* **Yah Veh**,
and against his anointed, *saying*,
3 Let us *break* **tear** their bands *asunder*,
and cast away their *cords* **ropes** from us.
4 He that *sitteth* **settleth** in the heavens shall laugh:
the Lord **Adonay** shall *have* **deride** them *in derision*.
5 Then shall he *speak* **word** unto them in his wrath,
and *vex* **terrify** them in his *sore displeasure* **fuming**.
6 Yet have I *set* **anointed** my *king* **sovereign**
upon my holy *hill of Zion* **mount Siyon**.
7 I *will declare* **shall scribe** the *decree* **statute**:
the LORD **Yah Veh** hath said unto me,
Thou art my *Son* **Ben°**; this day have I begotten thee.
°Ben: cp 2:12
8 Ask of me,
and I shall give thee the *heathen* **goyim**
for thine inheritance,
and the *uttermost parts* **finalities** of the earth
for thy possession.
9 Thou shalt *break* **shatter** them with a *rod* **scion** of iron;
thou shalt *dash* **splatter** them *in pieces*
like a potter's vessel **as a formed instrument**.
10 *Be wise* **Comprehend** now therefore,
O ye *kings* **sovereigns**:
be *instructed* **disciplined**, ye judges of the earth.
11 Serve *the LORD* **Yah Veh** with *fear* **awe**,
and *rejoice* **twirl** with trembling.
12 Kiss the *Son* **Bar°**, lest he be angry,
and ye *perish* **destruct** from the way,
when his wrath *is kindled* **burneth** but a little.
Blessed **Blithe** are all they
that *put their trust* **seek refuge** in him.
°Bar: cp 2:7

3 A Psalm of David,
when he fled from *Absalom* **the face of Abi Shalom**
his son.
1 *LORD* **Yah Veh**,
how are they increased that trouble me
how my tribulators abound by the myriads!
many are they that rise *up* against me.
2 Many there be which say of my soul,
There is no *help* **salvation** for him in *God* **Elohim**.
Selah.
3 But thou, O *LORD* **Yah Veh**, art a *shield* **buckler** for me;
my *glory* **honour**, and the lifter *up* of mine head.
4 I *cried* **called** unto *the LORD* **Yah Veh** with my voice,
and he *heard* **answered** me out of his holy *hill* **mountain**.
Selah.
5 I laid me down and slept; I awaked;
for *the LORD* **Yah Veh** sustained me.
6 I *will* **shall** not *be afraid* **awe**
of ten thousands **myriads** of people,
that have set *themselves* against me round about.
7 Arise, O *LORD* **Yah Veh**; save me, O my *God* **Elohim**:
for thou hast smitten all mine enemies
upon the cheek bone;
thou hast broken the teeth of the *ungodly* **wicked**.
8 Salvation *belongeth* unto *the LORD* **Yah Veh**:
thy blessing is upon thy people.
Selah.

4 To *the chief Musician* **His Eminence**,
on *Neginoth* **Strummer**,
A Psalm of David.
1 *Hear* **Answer** me when I call,
O *God* **Elohim** of my *righteousness* **justness**:
thou hast enlarged me
when I was in *distress* **tribulation**;
have mercy upon me **grant me charism**,
and hear my prayer.
2 O ye sons of men,
how long *will ye turn my glory* **shall my honour**
be into shame?
how long will **— shall** ye love vanity,
and seek after *leasing* **lies**?
Selah.
3 But know that *the LORD* **Yah Veh** hath set apart
him that is *godly* **mercied** for himself:
the LORD will **Yah Veh shall** hear when I call unto him.
4 *Stand in awe* **Quiver** and sin not:
commune **say** with your own heart upon your bed,
and be still.
Selah.
5 *Offer* **Sacrifice** the sacrifices of *righteousness* **justness**,
and *put your trust* **confide** in *the LORD* **Yah Veh**.
6 There be many that say,
Who *will shew us any* **shall let us see** good?
LORD **O Yah Veh**,
lift thou up the light of thy *countenance* **face** upon us.
7 Thou hast *put gladness* **given cheerfulness** in my heart,
more than in the time
that their *corn* **crop** and their *wine* **juice**
increased **abounded by the myriads**.
8 I *will both* **shall altogether**
lay me down in *peace* **shalom**, and sleep:
for thou, *LORD* **O Yah Veh**, only
makest me dwell in safety **settlest me confidently**.

5 To *the chief Musician* **His Eminence**,
upon *Nehiloth* **Flute**,
A Psalm of David.
1 *Give ear* **Hearken** to my *words* **sayings**,
O *LORD* **Yah Veh**,
consider **discern** my meditation.
2 Hearken unto the voice of my cry,
my *King* **Sovereign**, and my *God* **Elohim**:
for unto thee *will* **shall** I pray.
3 My voice shalt thou hear in the morning,
O *LORD* **Yah Veh**;
in the morning
will I direct my prayer **shall I arrange** unto thee,
and *will look up* **shall watch**.
4 For thou art not *a God* **an El**
that *hath pleasure* **delighteth** in wickedness:
neither shall evil *dwell* **sojourn** with thee.
5 *The foolish* **They that halal**
shall not *stand* **settle** in *thy sight* **thine eyes**:
thou hatest all *workers of iniquity* **doing mischief**.
6 Thou shalt destroy them that *speak leasing* **word lies**:
the LORD will **Yah Veh shall** abhor
the *bloody* **man of bloods** and *deceitful man* **deceit**.
7 But as for me, I *will* **shall** come into thy house
in the *multitude* **abundance** of thy mercy:
and in thy *fear will* **awe shall** I *worship* **prostrate**
toward thy holy *temple* **manse**.
8 Lead me, O *LORD* **Yah Veh**,

in thy *righteousness* **justness**
because of mine *enemies* **opponents**;
make **straighten** thy way *straight before* **at** my face.
9 For there is *no faithfulness* **nought established**
in their mouth;
their *inward part is very wickedness* **inwards are calamities**;
their throat is an open *sepulchre* **tomb**;
they *flatter* **smooth over** with their tongue.
10 *Destroy thou them* **They have guilted**, O *God* **Elohim**;
let them fall by their own counsels;
cast **drive** them out in the *multitude* **abundance**
of their *transgressions* **rebellions**;
for they have rebelled against thee.
11 But let all those that *put their trust* **seek refuge** in thee
rejoice **cheer**:
let them *ever* **eternally** shout *for joy*,
because thou *defendest* **coverest** them **over**:
let them also that love thy name
be joyful **jump for joy** in thee.
12 For thou, *LORD* **O Yah Veh**,
wilt **shalt** bless the *righteous* **just**;
with *favour* **pleasure**
wilt **shalt** thou *compass* **surround** him as *with* a shield.

6 To *the chief Musician* **His Eminence,**
on *Neginoth* **Strummer** upon *Sheminith* **Octave**,
A Psalm of David.
1 O *LORD* **Yah Veh**,
rebuke **reprove** me not in *thine anger* **thy wrath**,
neither *chasten* **discipline** me in thy *hot displeasure* **fury**.
2 *Have mercy upon me* **Grant me charism**,
O *LORD* **Yah Veh**;
for I *am weak* **languish**:
O *LORD* **Yah Veh**, heal me;
for my bones are *vexed* **terrified**.
3 My soul is also *sore vexed* **mighty terrified**:
but thou, O *LORD* **Yah Veh**, how long?
4 Return, O *LORD* **Yah Veh**, *deliver* **rescue** my soul:
oh save me for thy mercies' sake.
5 For in death
there is no *remembrance* **memorial** of thee:
in *the grave* **sheol**
who shall *give* **extend** thee *thanks* **hands**?
6 I am *weary* **belaboured** with my *groaning* **sighing**;
all the night make I my bed to swim;
I *water* **flow** my *couch* **bedstead** with my tears.
7 Mine eye is *consumed* **motheaten**
because of grief **in vexation**;
it *waxeth old* **antiquateth**
because of all *mine enemies* **my tribulators**.
8 *Depart* **Turn away** from me,
all ye *workers of iniquity* **doing mischief**;
for *the LORD* **Yah Veh**
hath heard the voice of my weeping.
9 *The LORD* **Yah Veh** hath heard my supplication;
the LORD will receive **Yah Veh shall take** my prayer.
10 Let all mine enemies *be ashamed* **shame**
and *sore vexed* **terrify mightily**:
let them return
and *be ashamed suddenly* **shame in a blink**.

7 *Shiggaion* **Lyric Poem** of David,
which he sang unto *the LORD* **Yah Veh**,
concerning the words of *Cush* **Kush**
the *Benjamite* **Ben Yaminiy**.
1 O *LORD* **Yah Veh** my *God* **Elohim**,
in thee *do I put my trust* **seek I refuge**:
save me from all them that *persecute* **pursue** me,
and *deliver* **rescue** me:
2 Lest he tear my soul like a lion,
rending **craunching** it *in pieces*,
while there is none to *deliver* **rescue**.
3 O *LORD* **Yah Veh** my *God* **Elohim**,
If I have *done* **worked** this;
if there be *iniquity* **wickedness** in my *hands* **palms**;
4 If I have *rewarded* **dealt** evil unto him
that was at *peace* **shalom** with me;
(yea, I have *delivered* **rescued** him
that *without cause* **vainly** is *mine enemy* **my tribulator**:)
5 Let the enemy *persecute* **pursue** my soul,
and *take it* **overtake**;
yea, let him tread down my life upon the earth,
and *lay* **tabernacle** mine honour in the dust.
Selah.
6 Arise, O *LORD* **Yah Veh**, in *thine anger* **thy wrath**,
lift up thyself
because of the *rage* **fury** of *mine enemies* **my tribulators**:
and awake for me *to* the judgment
that thou hast *commanded* **misvahed**.
7 *So* **Thus**
shall the *congregation* **witnesses** of the *people* **nations**
compass **surround** thee *about*:
for their sakes therefore
return thou *on high* **in the heights**.
8 *The LORD* **Yah Veh**
shall *judge* **plead the cause of** the people:
judge me, O *LORD* **Yah Veh**,
according to my *righteousness* **justness**,
and according to mine integrity that is in me.
9 *Oh* **I beseech**,
let the *wickedness* **evil** of the wicked
come to an end **cease**;
but establish the just:
for *the righteous God* **just Elohim**
trieth **proofeth** the hearts and reins.
10 My *defence* **buckler** is *of God* **upon Elohim**,
which saveth the *upright* **straight** in heart.
11 *God judgeth the righteous* **Elohim is a just judge**,
and *God is angry with the wicked* **El is enraged** every day.
12 If he turn not, he *will whet* **shall sharpen** his sword;
he hath bent his bow, and *made it ready* **prepared**.
13 He hath also prepared for him
the instruments of death;
he *ordaineth* **maketh** his arrows
against *the persecutors* **them who hotly pursue**.
14 Behold, he *travaileth* **despoileth** with *iniquity* **mischief**,
and hath conceived *mischief* **toil**,
and *brought forth* **hath birthed** falsehood.
15 He *made* **digged** a *pit* **well**, and digged it,
and is fallen into the *ditch which* **pit of ruin** he made.
16 His *mischief* **toil** shall return upon his own head,
and his *violent dealing* **violence**
shall *come down* **descend** upon his own *pate* **scalp**.
17 I *will praise the LORD* **shall extend hands to Yah Veh**
according to his righteousness:
and *will sing praise* **shall psalm**
to the name of *the LORD most high* **Yah Veh Elyon**.

8 To *the chief Musician* **His Eminence,** upon Gittith,
A Psalm of David.
1 O *LORD* **Yah Veh**, our *Lord* **Adonay**,
how *excellent* **mighty** is thy name in all the earth!
who hast *set* **given** thy *glory* **majesty** above the heavens.
2 Out of the mouth of *babes* **infants** and sucklings
hast thou *ordained* **founded** strength
because of *thine enemies* **thy tribulators**,
that thou mightest
still **shabbathize** the enemy and the avenger.
3 When I *consider* **see** thy heavens,
the work of thy fingers,
the moon and the stars,
which thou hast *ordained* **established**;
4 What is man,
that thou *art mindful of* **rememberest** him?
and the son of *man* **humanity**,
that thou visitest him?
5 For thou hast made him
a little *lower* **less** than *the angels* **Elohim**,
and hast crowned him
with *glory* **honour** and *honour* **majesty**.
6 Thou *madest* **hast** him to *have dominion* **reign**
over the works of thy hands;
thou hast put all *things* under his feet:
7 *All sheep* **Flocks** and oxen,
yea, and the *beasts* **animals** of the field;
8 The *fowl* **birds** of the *air* **heavens**,
and the fish of the sea,
and whatsoever passeth through the paths of the seas.
9 O *LORD* **Yah Veh** our *Lord* **Adonay**,
how excellent is thy name in all the earth!

9 To *the chief Musician* **His Eminence,**
upon *Muthlabben* **Muth Labben/Death of the Son,**
A Psalm of David.
1 I *will praise thee* **shall extend hands,** O *LORD* **Yah Veh,**
with my whole heart;
I *will shew forth* **shall scribe** all thy marvellous works.
2 I *will be glad* **shall cheer**
and *rejoice* **jump for joy** in thee:
I *will sing praise* **shall psalm** to thy name,
O thou *most High* **Elyon.**
3 When mine enemies are turned back,
they shall *fall* **falter**
and *perish* **destruct** at thy *presence* **face.**
4 For thou hast *maintained* **worked**
my *right* **judgment** and my *cause* **plea;**
thou *satest* **settlest** in the throne judging *right* **justness.**
5 Thou hast rebuked the *heathen* **goyim,**
thou hast destroyed the wicked,
thou hast *put out* **erased** their name
for ever **eternally** and *ever* **eternally.**
6 O thou enemy,
destructions **parched areas**
are *come to a perpetual end* **consumated in perpetuity:**
and thou hast *destroyed* **uprooted** cities;
their memorial *is perished* **destructeth** with them.
7 But *the LORD* **Yah Veh**
shall *endure for ever* **settle eternally:**
he hath prepared his throne for judgment.
8 And he shall judge the world in *righteousness* **justness,**
he shall *minister judgment* **plead the cause**
to **of** the *people* **nations** in *uprightness* **straightnesses.**
9 *The LORD* **Yah Veh**
also will **shall** be a *refuge* **secure loft** for the oppressed,
a *refuge* **secure loft** in times of *trouble* **tribulation.**
10 And they that know thy name
will put their trust **shall confide** in thee:
for thou, *LORD* **O Yah Veh,**
hast not forsaken them that seek thee.
11 *Sing praises* **Psalm** to *the LORD* **Yah Veh,**
which *dwelleth* **settleth** in *Zion* **Siyon:**
declare **tell** among the people his *doings* **exploits.**
12 When he *maketh inquisition* **searcheth** for blood,
he remembereth them:
he forgetteth not the cry of the humble.
13 *Have mercy upon me* **Grant me charism,**
O *LORD* **Yah Veh;**
consider **see** my *trouble* **humiliation**
which I suffer of them that hate me,
thou that liftest me *up* from the *gates* **portals** of death:
14 That I may *shew forth* **scribe** all thy *praise* **halal**
in the *gates* **portals** of the daughter of *Zion* **Siyon:**
I *will rejoice* **shall twirl** in thy salvation.
15 The *heathen* **goyim** are sunk down
in the pit **of ruin** that they *made* **worked:**
in the net which they hid
is their own foot *taken* **captured.**
16 *The LORD* **Yah Veh** is known
by the judgment which he *executeth* **worketh:**
the wicked is snared
in the *work* **deeds** of his own *hands* **palms.**
Higgaion **Meditation.**
Selah.
17 The wicked shall be turned into *hell* **sheol,**
and all the *nations* **goyim** that forget *God* **Elohim.**
18 For the needy
shall not *alway* be forgotten **in perpetuity:**
the *expectation* **hope** of the *poor* **humble**
shall not *perish for ever* **destruct eternally.**
19 Arise, O *LORD* **Yah Veh;**
let not man *prevail* **strengthen:**
let the *heathen* **goyim** be judged *in thy sight* **at thy face.**
20 Put them in *fear* **awe,** O *LORD* **Yah Veh:**
that the *nations* **goyim**
may know themselves to be but men.
Selah.

10 Why standest thou afar off, O *LORD* **Yah Veh?**
why *hidest* **concealest** thou thyself
in times of *trouble* **tribulation?**
2 The wicked in his *pride* **pomp**
doth persecute **hotly pursueth** the *poor* **humble:**
let them be *taken* **grabbed** in the *devices* **intrigue**
that they have *imagined* **machinated.**
3 For the wicked
boasteth **halaleth** of his *heart's* **soul's** desire,
and blesseth the *covetous* **greedy,**
whom *the LORD abhorreth* **Yah Veh scorneth.**
4 The wicked,
through *the pride of his countenance* **lifted nostrils,**
will **shall** not seek *after God:*
God **Elohim** is not in all his *thoughts* **intrigues.**
5 His ways *are always grievous* **writhe at all times;**
thy judgments are *far above* **in the heights**
out of his sight:
as for all his *enemies* **tribulators,** he puffeth at them.
6 He hath said in his heart, I shall not *be moved* **totter:**
generation to generation
for I shall never be in *adversity* **evil.**
7 His mouth is full of *cursing* **oaths**
and *deceit* **deceits** and fraud:
under his tongue is *mischief* **toil** and *vanity* **mischief.**
8 He *sitteth* **settleth**
in the *lurking places* **lurks** of the *villages* **courts:**
in the *secret places* **coverts**
doth he *murder* **slaughtereth** the innocent:
his eyes *are privily set* **hath he hid**
against **from** the *poor* **unfortunate.**
9 He *lieth in wait secretly* **lurketh in the coverts**
as a lion in his *den* **sukkoth/brush arbor:**
he *lieth in wait* **lurketh** to catch the *poor* **humble:**
he *doth catch* **catcheth** the *poor* **humble,**
when he draweth him into his net.
10 He *croucheth* **crusheth,**
and *humbleth* **prostrateth** *himself,*
that the *poor* **army of the unfortunates**
may fall by his *strong ones* **mighty.**
11 He hath said in his heart, *God* **El** hath forgotten:
he hideth his face;
he *will never* **shall not** see it **in perpetuity.**
12 Arise, O *LORD* **Yah Veh;**
O *God* **El,** lift up thine hand: forget not the humble.
13 Wherefore doth the wicked
contemn God **scorn Elohim?**
he hath said in his heart,
Thou *wilt* **shalt** not require it.
14 Thou hast seen it;
for thou *beholdest* **scannest**
mischief **toil** and *spite* **vexation,**
to *requite it with* **give into** thy hand:
the *poor* **unfortunate**
committeth himself **is left** unto thee;
thou art the helper of the *fatherless* **orphan.**
15 Break thou the arm of the wicked and the evil *man:*
seek out his wickedness till thou find none.
16 *The LORD* **Yah Veh** is *King* **Sovereign**
for ever **eternally** and *ever* **eternally:**
the *heathen are perished* **goyim destruct** out of his land.
17 *LORD* **O Yah Veh,**
thou hast heard the desire of the humble:
thou *wilt* **shalt** prepare their heart,
thou *wilt cause* **shalt hearken** thine ear *to hear:*
18 To judge the *fatherless* **orphan** and the oppressed,
that the man of the earth
may *no more oppress* **not terrify again.**

11 To *the chief Musician* **His Eminence,**
A Psalm of David.
1 In *the LORD put I my trust* **Yah Veh I seek refuge:**
how say ye to my soul,
Flee **Wander** as a bird to your mountain?
2 For, *lo* **behold,** the wicked bend their bow,
they *make ready* **prepare** their arrow
upon the *string* **cord,**
that they may *privily* **in darkness**
shoot at the *upright* **straight** in heart.
3 If the foundations *be destroyed* **demolish,**
what can the *righteous* **just** do?
4 *The LORD* **Yah Veh** is in his holy *temple* **manse,**
the LORD'S **Yah Veh's** throne is in *heaven* **the heavens:**

his eyes *behold* **see**, his eyelids *try* **proof**,
the *children* **sons** of *men* **humanity**.
5 *The LORD trieth* **Yah Veh proofeth** the *righteous* **just**:
but the wicked and him that loveth violence
his soul hateth.
6 Upon the wicked he shall rain snares,
fire and *brimstone* **sulphur**,
and *an horrible tempest* **a raging wind/spirit**:
this shall be the portion **— the allotment** of their cup.
7 For *the righteous LORD* **just Yah Veh**
loveth *righteousness* **justness**;
his *countenance* **face**
doth behold **seeth** the *upright* **straight**.

12 To *the chief Musician* **His Eminence**,
upon *Sheminith* **the Octave**,
A Psalm of David.
1 *Help* **Save**, *LORD* **O Yah Veh**;
for the *godly man ceaseth* **mercied have deceased**;
for the *faithful fail* **trustworthy have disappeared**
from among the *children* **sons** of *men* **humanity**.
2 They *speak* **word** every *one* **man**
vanity with his *neighbour* **friend**:
with *flattering* lips **that smooth it over**
and *with a double heart* **heart to heart**
do they *speak* **word**.
3 *The LORD* **Yah Veh** shall cut off
all *flattering* lips **that smooth it over**,
and the tongue
that *speaketh proud things* **wordeth greatnesses**:
4 Who have said,
With our tongue *will* **shall** we prevail **mightily**;
our lips are our own: who is *lord* **adoni** over us?
5 For the *oppression* **devastation** of the *poor* **humble**,
for the *sighing* **shrieking** of the needy,
now *will* **shall** I arise, saith *the LORD* **Yah Veh**;
I *will* **shall** set him in safety from him that puffeth at him.
6 The *words* **sayings** of *the LORD* **Yah Veh**
are pure *words* **sayings**:
as silver *tried* **refined** in a furnace of earth,
purified seven times **refined sevenfold**.
7 Thou shalt *keep* **guard** them, O *LORD* **Yah Veh**,
thou shalt *preserve them* **guard us** from this generation
for ever **eternally**.
8 The wicked walk *on every side* **round about**,
when the *vilest men* **violent sons of humanity**
are exalted.

13 To *the chief Musician* **His Eminence**,
A Psalm of David.
1 How long *wilt* **shalt** thou forget me, O *LORD* **Yah Veh**?
for ever **in perpetuity**?
how long *wilt* **shalt** thou hide thy face from me?
2 How long shall I *take* **set** counsel in my soul,
having *sorrow* **grief** in my heart daily?
how long shall mine enemy *be exalted* **loft** over me?
3 *Consider* **Look** and *hear* **answer** me,
O *LORD* **Yah Veh** my *God* **Elohim**:
lighten mine eyes, lest I sleep *the sleep of* **in** death;
4 Lest mine enemy say, I have prevailed against him;
and *those that trouble me rejoice* **my tribulators twirl**
when I *am moved* **totter**.
5 But I have *trusted* **confided** in thy mercy;
my heart shall *rejoice* **twirl** in thy salvation.
6 I *will* **shall** sing unto *the LORD* **Yah Veh**,
because he hath dealt *bountifully* with me.

14 To *the chief Musician* **His Eminence**,
A Psalm of David.
1 The fool hath said in his heart,
There is no God **Elohim is not**.
They *are corrupt* **have ruined**,
they have done *abominable works* **abhorrent exploits**,
there is none that *doeth* **worketh** good.
2 *The LORD* **Yah Veh**
looked down from *heaven* **the heavens**
upon the *children* **sons** of *men* **humanity**,
to see if there were any
that *did understand* **comprehend**,
and seek *God* **Elohim**.
3 They are all *gone* **turned** aside,
they are *all* together *become filthy* **muddled**:
there is none that *doeth* **worketh** good, no, not one.
4 Have all the *workers* **doers** of *iniquity* **mischief**
no knowledge **not known**?
who eat up my people as they eat bread,
and call not upon *the LORD* **Yah Veh**.
5 *There were they in great fear* **In dreading, they dreaded**:
for *God* **Elohim** is in the generation of the *righteous* **just**.
6 Ye have shamed the counsel of the *poor* **humble**,
because *the LORD* **Yah Veh** is his refuge.
7 *Oh* **Who giveth** that the salvation of *Israel* **Yisra El**
were *come* out of *Zion* **Siyon**!
when *the LORD* **Yah Veh**
bringeth back **returneth** the captivity of his people,
Jacob **Yaaqov** shall *rejoice* **twirl**,
and Israel **Yisra El** shall *be glad* **cheer**.

15 A Psalm of David.
1 *LORD* **Yah Veh**,
who shall *abide* **sojourn** in thy *tabernacle* **tent**?
who shall *dwell* **tabernacle** in thy holy *hill* **mountain**?
2 He that walketh *uprightly* **integriously**,
and *worketh righteousness* **doeth justness**,
and *speaketh* **wordeth** the truth in his heart.
3 He that *backbiteth* **steppeth** not with his tongue,
nor *doeth* **worketh** evil to his *neighbour* **friend**,
nor *taketh up* **lifteth** a reproach against his neighbour.
4 In whose eyes
a *vile person* **spurner** is *contemned* **despised**;
but he honoureth them that *fear the LORD* **awe Yah Veh**.
He that *sweareth* **oatheth** to *his own hurt* **vilify himself**,
and changeth not.
5 He that *putteth* **giveth** not *out* his *money* **silver** to usury,
nor taketh *reward* **bribe** against the innocent.
He that *doeth* **worketh** these *things*
shall *never be moved* **not totter eternally**.

16 *Michtam* **Poem** of David.
1 *Preserve* **Guard** me, O *God* **El**:
for in thee *do I put my trust* **I seek refuge**.
2 O my soul, thou hast said unto *the LORD* **Yah Veh**,
Thou art my *Lord* **Adonay**:
my goodness *extendeth* not to thee;
3 But to the *saints* **holy** that are in the earth,
and to the *excellent* **mighty**, in whom is all my delight.
4 Their *sorrows* **contortions** shall *be multiplied* **abound**
that hasten after another *god*:
their *drink offerings* **libations** of blood
will **shall** I not *offer* **libate**,
nor *take up* **lift** their names into my lips.
5 *The LORD* **Yah Veh** is the portion
of mine *inheritance* **allotment** and of my cup:
thou *maintainest* **upholdest** my *lot* **pebble**.
6 The lines are fallen unto me in *pleasant places* **pleasure**;
yea, I have a *goodly heritage* **glorious inheritance**.
7 I *will* **shall** bless *the LORD* **Yah Veh**
who hath *given* **counselled** me *counsel*:
my reins also *instruct* **discipline** me in the night *seasons*.
8 I have set *the LORD* **Yah Veh**
always **continually** before me:
because he is at my right *hand*,
I shall not *be moved* **totter**.
9 Therefore my heart *is glad* **cheereth**,
and my *glory rejoiceth* **honour twirleth**:
my flesh also shall *rest in hope* **tabernacle confidently**.
10 For thou *wilt* **shalt** not
leave **forsake** my soul in *hell* **sheol**;
neither *wilt* **shalt** thou *suffer* **give**
thine Holy **thy Mercied** One
to see *corruption* **the pit of ruin**.
11 Thou *wilt shew me* **shalt have me know** the path of life:
in **at** thy *presence* **face**
is *fulness of joy* **satisfying cheerfulness**;
at thy right *hand*
there are pleasures *for evermore* **in perpetuity**.

17 A Prayer of David.
1 Hear *the right* **justness**, O *LORD* **Yah Veh**,
attend **hearken** unto my *cry* **shouting**,

give ear **hearken** unto my prayer,
that goeth not out of feigned lips **of lips without deceit**.
2 Let my *sentence* **judgment**
come forth from thy *presence* **face**;
let thine eyes *behold* **see**
the things **those** that are *equal* **in straightnesses**.
3 Thou hast *proved* **proofed** mine heart;
thou hast visited me in the night;
thou hast *tried* **refined** me,
and shalt find *nothing* **naught**;
I *am purposed* **have plotted**
that my mouth shall not transgress.
4 Concerning the *works* **deeds** of *men* **humanity**,
by the word of thy lips
I have *kept* **guarded** me from the paths of the destroyer.
5 *Hold up* **Uphold** my *goings* **steps** in thy paths,
that my *footsteps slip* **steps totter** not.
6 I have called upon thee,
for thou *wilt hear* **shalt answer** me, O *God* **El**:
incline **extend** thine ear unto me,
and *hear* my *speech* **sayings**.
7 *Shew* **Distinguish** thy marvellous *lovingkindness* **mercy**,
O thou that savest by thy right *hand*
them which *put their trust in thee* **seek refuge**
from those that rise *up against them*.
8 *Keep* **Guard** me as the *apple* **pupil**
— the daughter of the eye,
hide me under the shadow of thy wings,
9 From **the face of** the wicked that *oppress* **ravage** me,
from my *deadly* **soul** enemies,
who *compass* **surround** me *about*.
10 They are *inclosed* **shut up** in their own fat:
with their mouth they *speak proudly* **word pompously**.
11 They have now *compassed* **surrounded** us
in our steps:
they have set their eyes
bowing down **extending** to the earth;
12 Like as a lion that *is greedy of* **yearneth for** his prey,
and as *it were a young lion* **a whelp**
lurking **settling** in *secret places* **coverts**.
13 Arise, O *LORD* **Yah Veh**,
disappoint him **anticipate his face**,
cast him down **have him kneel**:
deliver **slip away** my soul from the wicked,
which is thy sword:
14 From men which are thy hand, O *LORD* **Yah Veh**,
from **transcient** men *of the world*,
which have their *portion* **allotment** in this life,
and whose belly
thou fillest with thy *hid* **treasured** treasure:
they are full of children **their sons satiate**,
and leave the *rest of their substance* **remainder**
to their *babes* **infants**.
15 As for me,
I *will behold* **shall see** thy face in *righteousness* **justness**:
I shall be satisfied, when I awake,
with thy *likeness* **manifestation.**

18 To *the chief Musician* **His Eminence**,
A Psalm of David, the servant of *the LORD* **Yah Veh**,
who *spake* **worded** unto *the LORD* **Yah Veh**
the words of this song
in the day that *the LORD delivered* **Yah Veh rescued** him
from the *hand* **palm** of all his enemies,
and from the hand of *Saul* **Shaul**:
And he said,
1 I *will love* **shall mercy** thee,
O *LORD* **Yah Veh**, my strength.
2 *The LORD* **Yah Veh** is my rock,
and my *fortress* **stronghold**, and my *deliverer* **escape**;
my *God* **El**, my *strength* **rock**,
in whom I *will trust* **seek refuge**;
my buckler, and the horn of my salvation,
and my *high tower* **secure loft**.
3 I *will* **shall** call upon *the LORD* **Yah Veh**,
who is worthy to be praised **— the halaled**:
so shall I be saved from mine enemies.
4 The *sorrows* **cords** of death
compassed **surrounded** me,
and the *floods* **wadies** of *ungodly men* **Beli Yaal**
made me afraid **frightened me**.
5 The *sorrows* **cords** of *hell* **sheol**
compassed **surrounded** me *about*:
the snares of death *prevented* **anticipated** me.
6 In my *distress* **tribulation**
I called upon *the LORD* **Yah Veh**,
and cried unto my *God* **Elohim**:
he heard my voice out of his *temple* **manse**,
and my cry came *before him* **at his face**,
even into his ears.
7 Then the earth shook and *trembled* **quaked**;
the foundations also of the *hills* **mountains**
moved **quaked** and were shaken,
because he was *wroth* **inflamed**.
8 There *went up* **ascended** a smoke out of his nostrils,
and fire out of his mouth *devoured* **consumed**:
coals were *kindled* **burnt** by it.
9 He *bowed* **spread** the heavens also,
and *came down* **descended**:
and **dripping** darkness was under his feet.
10 And he rode upon a cherub, and *did fly* **flew**:
yea, he *did fly* **flew** upon the wings of the wind.
11 He *made* **set** darkness his *secret place* **covert**;
his *pavilion* **sukkoth/brush arbor** round about him
were dark waters
and thick clouds of *the skies* **vapours**.
12 At the *brightness* **brilliance** that was before him
his thick clouds passed, hail *stones* and coals of fire.
13 *The LORD* **Yah Veh** also thundered in the heavens,
and the Highest **Elyon** gave his voice;
hail *stones* and coals of fire.
14 Yea, he sent out his arrows, and scattered them;
and he shot out lightnings,
and *discomfited* **scattered** them.
15 Then the *channels* **reservoirs** of waters were seen,
and the foundations of the world
were *discovered* **exposed** at thy rebuke,
O *LORD* **Yah Veh**,
at the *blast* **breath**
of the *breath* **wind/spirit** of thy nostrils.
16 He sent from *above* **the heights**,
he took me, he drew me out of many waters.
17 He *delivered* **rescued** me from my strong enemy,
and from them which hated me:
for they were *too strong for me* **stronger than I**.
18 They *prevented* **anticipated** me
in the day of my calamity:
but *the LORD* **Yah Veh** was my *stay* **support**.
19 He brought me forth also into *a large place* **an expanse**;
he *delivered* **rescued** me, because he delighted in me.
20 *The LORD rewarded* **Yah Veh dealt** me
according to my *righteousness* **justness**;
according to the *cleanness* **purity** of my hands
hath he *recompensed* **returned to** me.
21 For I have *kept* **guarded**
the ways of *the LORD* **Yah Veh**,
and have not **done** wickedly
departed from **against** my *God* **Elohim**.
22 For all his judgments were before me,
and I did not *put away* **turn aside** his statutes from me.
23 I was also *upright* **integrious** before him,
and I *kept* **guarded** myself
from *mine iniquity* **my perversity**.
24 Therefore
hath *the LORD recompensed* **Yah Veh returned to** me
according to my *righteousness* **justness**,
according to the *cleanness* **purity** of my hands
in his *eyesight* **eyes**.
25 With the *merciful* **mercied,**
thou wilt shew thyself merciful;
with an *upright man* **integrious mighty,**
thou wilt shew thyself upright **integrious**;
26 With the pure,
thou wilt shew thyself pure **purified**;
and with the *froward* **pervert,**
thou wilt shew thyself froward **a wrestler**.
27 For thou *wilt* **shalt** save the *afflicted* **humble** people;
but *wilt bring down high looks* **shalt abase lofted eyes**.
28 For thou *wilt* **shalt** light my *candle* **lamp**:
the LORD **Yah Veh** my *God* **Elohim**

will enlighten **shall illuminate** my darkness.
29 For by thee I have run through a troop;
and by my *God* **Elohim** have I leaped over a wall.
30 *As for God* **EL**, his way is *perfect* **integrious**:
the *word* **saying** of *the LORD* **Yah Veh** is *tried* **refined**:
he is a buckler to all those that *trust* **seek refuge** in him.
31 For who is *God* **Elohah**
save the LORD **except Yah Veh**?
or who is a rock
save **except** our *God* **Elohim**?
32 *It is God that* **El** girdeth me with *strength* **valour**,
and *maketh* **giveth** my way *perfect* **integrious**.
33 He *maketh* **placeth** my feet *like* **as** hinds' *feet*,
and *setteth* **standeth** me upon my *high places* **bamahs**.
34 He teacheth my hands to war,
so that a bow of steel is *broken* **bent** by mine arms.
35 Thou hast also given me
the *shield* **buckler** of thy salvation:
and thy right *hand* hath holden me *up*,
and thy *gentleness* **humbleness**
hath made me *great* **abound**.
36 Thou hast enlarged my *steps* **paces** under me,
that my *feet did not slip* **ankles wavered not**.
37 I have pursued mine enemies, and overtaken them:
neither *did I turn again* **returned I**
till they were *consumed* **finished off**.
38 I have *wounded* **struck** them
that they were not able to rise:
they are fallen under my feet.
39 For thou hast girded me
with *strength* **valour** unto the *battle* **war**:
thou hast *subdued* **knuckled** under me
those that rose *up against me*.
40 Thou hast also given me the necks of mine enemies;
that I might *destroy* **exterminate** them that hate me.
41 They cried, but there was *none to save them* **no savior**:
even unto *the LORD* **Yah Veh**, but he answered them not.
42 Then *did I beat* **I pulverized** them *small* as the dust
before **at the face of** the wind:
I *did cast* **poured** them out
as the *dirt* **mire** in the *streets* **outways**.
43 Thou hast *delivered* **slipped** me **away**
from the strivings of the people;
and thou hast *made* **set** me
the head of the *heathen* **goyim**:
a people *whom* I have not known shall serve me.
44 *As soon as they hear of me* **At the hearing of the ear**,
they shall *obey* **hearken unto** me:
the **sons of** strangers
shall *submit themselves unto* **disavow** me.
45 The **sons of** strangers shall *fade away* **wither**,
and *be afraid* **tremble** out of their *close places* **borders**.
46 *The LORD* **Yah Veh** liveth; and blessed be my rock;
and let *the God* **Elohim** of my salvation be *exalted* **lofted**.
47 *It is God that avengeth me* **El giveth me vengeance**,
and subdueth the people under me.
48 He *delivereth me* **slippeth me away** from mine enemies:
yea, thou liftest me up above those that rise *up against me*:
thou hast *delivered* **rescued** me
from the *violent man* **man of violence**.
49 Therefore
will I give thanks **shall I extend hands** unto thee,
O *LORD* **Yah Veh**, among the *heathen* **goyim**,
and *sing praises* **psalm** unto thy name.
50 *Great deliverance giveth he* **He greateneth salvation**
to his *king* **sovereign**;
and *sheweth* **worketh** mercy to his anointed,
to David, and to his seed *for evermore* **eternally**.

19

To *the chief Musician* **His Eminence**,
A Psalm of David.
1 The heavens
declare **scribe** the *glory* **honour** of *God* **El**;
and the *firmament* **expanse**
sheweth **telleth** his handywork.
2 Day unto day *uttereth speech* **gusheth sayings**,
and night unto night sheweth knowledge.
3 There is no *speech* **saying** nor *language* **word**,
where their voice is not heard.
4 Their line is gone out through all the earth,
and their *words* **utterances** to the end of the world.
In them hath he set a *tabernacle* **tent** for the sun,
5 Which is as a *bridegroom* **groom**
coming out of his *chamber* **canopy**,
and rejoiceth as *a strong man* **the mighty**
to run *a race* **the path**.
6 His *going forth* **source**
is from the end of the *heaven* **heavens**,
and his circuit
unto the ends of it:
and there is *nothing* **naught** hid from the heat *thereof*.
7 The *law* **torah** of *the LORD* **Yah Veh**
is perfect,
converting **restoring** the soul:
the *testimony* **witness** of *the LORD* **Yah Veh**
is *sure* **trustworthy**,
making wise **enwisening** the *simple* **gullible**.
8 The *statutes* **precepts** of *the LORD* **Yah Veh**
are *right* **straight**,
rejoicing **cheering** the heart:
the *commandment* **misvah** of *the LORD* **Yah Veh**
is pure,
enlightening the eyes.
9 The *fear* **awe** of *the LORD* **Yah Veh**
is *clean* **pure**,
enduring for ever **standing eternally**:
the judgments of *the LORD* **Yah Veh**
are *true* **truth**;
and righteous **justified** altogether.
10 More to be desired *are they* than gold,
yea, than much *fine* **pure** gold:
sweeter also than honey
and **the droppings of** the honeycomb.
11 Moreover by them is thy servant *warned* **enlightened**:
and in *keeping of* **guarding** them
there is great *reward* **final result**.
12 Who *can understand* **discerneth**
is **inadvertent** errors?
cleanse **exonerate** thou me from *secret faults* **the hidden**.
13 *Keep back* **Spare** thy servant also
from *presumptuous sins* **arrogance**;
let them not *have dominion* **reign** over me:
then shall I be *upright* **integrious**,
and I shall be *innocent* **exonerated**
from the great *transgression* **rebellion**.
14 Let the *words* **sayings** of my mouth,
and the meditation of my heart,
be *acceptable in thy sight* **pleasing at thy face**,
O *LORD* **Yah Veh**, my *strength* **rock**, and my redeemer.

20

To *the chief Musician* **His Eminence**,
A Psalm of David.
1 *The LORD hear* **Yah Veh answereth** thee
in the day of *trouble* **tribulation**;
the name of *the God* **Elohim** of *Jacob* **Yaaqov**
defend **lofteth** thee;
2 *Send* **He sendeth** thee help from the *sanctuary* **holies**,
and *strengthen* **supporteth** thee out of *Zion* **Siyon**;
3 *Remember* **He remembereth** all thy offerings,
and *accept* **fatteneth** thy *burnt sacrifice* **holocausts**;
Selah.
4 *Grant* **He giveth** thee according to thine own heart,
and *fulfil* **fulfilleth** all thy counsel.
5 We *will rejoice* **shall shout** in thy salvation,
and in the name of our *God* **Elohim**
we *will set up* **shall raise** our banners:
the LORD **Yah Veh**
fulfil **fulfilleth** all thy *petitions* **requests**.
6 Now know I
that *the LORD* **Yah Veh** saveth his anointed;
he *will hear* **shall answer** him
from his holy *heaven* **heavens**
with the *saving strength* **might of salvation**
of his right *hand*.
7 Some *trust* in chariots, and some in horses:
but we *will* **shall** remember
the name of *the LORD* **Yah Veh** our *God* **Elohim**.
8 They *are brought down* **have knuckled under** and fallen:
but we are risen, and *stand upright* **restored**.
9 Save, *LORD* **O Yah Veh**:

let the *king hear* **sovereign answer** us
when **the day** we call.

21 To *the chief Musician* **His Eminence,**
A Psalm of David.
1 The *king* **sovereign** shall *joy* **cheer** in thy strength,
O *LORD* **Yah Veh**;
and in thy salvation
how *greatly* **mightily** shall he *rejoice* **twirl**!
2 Thou hast given him his heart's desire,
and hast not withholden the *request* **longing** of his lips.
Selah.
3 For thou *preventest* **anticipatest** him
with the blessings of goodness:
thou settest a crown of pure gold on his head.
4 He asked life of thee, and thou gavest it him,
even length of days *for ever* **eternally** and *ever* **eternally**.
5 His *glory* **honour** is great in thy salvation:
honour and majesty hast thou *laid* **placed** upon him.
6 For thou hast *made* **set** him
most blessed for ever **for blessings eternally**:
thou hast *made* **cheered** him
exceeding glad **with cheerfulness**
with thy *countenance* **face**.
7 For the *king* **sovereign**
trusteth **confideth** in *the LORD* **Yah Veh**,
and through the mercy of *the most High* **Elyon**
he shall not *be moved* **totter**.
8 Thine hand shall find out all thine enemies:
thy right *hand* shall find out those that hate thee.
9 Thou shalt *make* **set** them as a fiery oven
in the time *of thine anger* **at thy face**:
the LORD **Yah Veh** shall swallow them *up* in his wrath,
and the fire shall *devour* **consume** them.
10 Their fruit shalt thou destroy from the earth,
and their seed
from *among* the *children* **sons** of *men* **humanity**.
11 For they *intended* **extended** evil against thee:
they *imagined a mischievous device* **machinated intrigue**,
which they are not able *to perform*.
12 *Therefore shalt thou make them turn their back*
Thou shalt set their shoulder,
when thou shalt make ready thine arrows upon thy strings
thou shalt prepare thy cords
against the face of them.
13 Be thou *exalted* **lofted**, *LORD* **O Yah Veh**,
in thine own strength:
so *will* **shall** we sing and *praise* **psalm** thy *power* **might**.

22 To *the chief Musician* **His Eminence,**
upon Aijeleth Shahar **on the Hind of the Dawn**,
A Psalm of David.
1 My *God* **El**, my *God* **El**, why hast thou forsaken me?
why art thou — so far from *helping me* **my salvation**,
and from the words of my roaring?
2 O my *God* **Elohim**, I *cry* **call** in the *daytime* **day**,
but thou *hearest* **answerest** not;
and in the night *season*, and am not silent.
3 But thou art holy,
O thou that *inhabitest* **settlest**
in the *praises* **halals** of *Israel* **Yisra El**.
4 Our fathers *trusted* **confided** in thee:
they *trusted* **confided**,
and thou *didst deliver them* **slipped them away**.
5 They cried unto thee, and *were delivered* **escaped**:
they *trusted* **confided** in thee,
and *were not confounded* **shamed not**.
6 But I am a *worm* **maggot**, and no man;
a reproach of *men* **humanity**,
and despised of the people.
7 All they that see me *laugh* **deride** me *to scorn*:
they *shoot* **bust** out the lip, they shake the head, *saying,*
8 He *trusted* **rolled** on *the LORD* **Yah Veh**
that he *would deliver* **should rescue** him:
let him *deliver* **slip** him **away**, seeing he delighted in him.
9 But thou art he
that *took* **gushed** me out of the *womb* **belly**:
thou didst make me *hope* **confident**
when I was upon my mother's breasts.
10 I was cast upon thee from the womb:
thou art my *God* **El** from my mother's belly.
11 Be not far from me; for *trouble* **tribulation** is near;
for there is *none to help* **no helper**.
12 Many *bulls* **bullocks** have *compassed* **surrounded** me:
strong bulls **the mighty** of Bashan
have *beset* **surrounded** me *round*.
13 They gaped upon me with their mouths,
as a *ravening* **tearing** and a roaring lion.
14 I am poured out like water,
and all my bones are *out of joint* **separated**:
my heart is like wax;
it is melted in the midst of my *bowels* **inwards**.
15 My *strength* **force** is dried up like a potsherd;
and my tongue *cleaveth* **adhereth** to my *jaws* **prey**;
and thou hast *brought* **set** me into the dust of death.
16 For dogs have *compassed* **surrounded** me:
the *assembly* **witness** of *the wicked* **vilifiers**
have *inclosed* **surrounded** me:
they pierced **as a lion** my hands and my feet.
17 I may *tell* **scribe** all my bones:
they look and *stare* **see** upon me.
18 They *part* **allot** my *garments* **clothes** among them,
and *cast lots upon* **toss pebbles for** my *vesture* **robe**.
19 But be not thou far from me, O *LORD* **Yah Veh**:
O my *strength* **might**, haste thee to help me.
20 *Deliver* **Rescue** my soul from the sword;
my *darling* **only** from the *power* **hand** of the dog.
21 Save me from the lion's mouth:
for thou hast *heard* **answered** me
from the horns of the *unicorns* **reems**.
22 I *will declare* **shall scribe** thy name unto my brethren:
in the midst of the congregation
will I praise **shall I halal** thee.
23 Ye that *fear the LORD* **awe Yah Veh**, *praise* **halal** him;
all ye the seed of *Jacob* **Yaaqov**, *glorify* **honour** him;
and *fear* **dodge** him, all ye the seed of *Israel* **Yisra El**.
24 For he hath not despised nor *abhorred* **abominated**
the *affliction* **humbling** of the *afflicted* **humble**;
neither hath he hid his face from him;
but when he cried unto him, he heard.
25 My *praise* **halal** shall be of thee
in the great congregation:
I *will pay* **shall shalam** my vows
before them that *fear* **awe** him.
26 The *meek* **humble** shall eat and be satisfied:
they shall *praise the LORD* **halal Yah Veh** that seek him:
your heart shall live *for ever* **eternally**.
27 All the *ends* **finalities** of the world shall remember
and turn unto *the LORD* **Yah Veh**:
and all the *kindreds* **families** of the *nations* **goyim**
shall *worship before thee* **prostrate at thy face**.
28 For the *kingdom* **sovereigndom**
is *the LORD'S* **Yah Veh's**:
and he is the *governor* **sovereign**
among the *nations* **goyim**.
29 All *they that be* **the** fat upon earth
shall eat and *worship* **prostrate**:
all they that *go down* **descend** to the dust
shall *bow before him* **kneel at his face**:
and none *can keep alive* **shall enliven** his own soul.
30 A seed shall serve him;
it shall be *accounted* **ascribed** to *the Lord* **Adonay**
for a generation.
31 They shall come,
and shall *declare* **tell** his *righteousness* **justness**
unto a people that shall be born,
that he hath *done* **worked** *this*.

23 A Psalm of David.
1 *The LORD is my shepherd* **Yah Veh Raah**;
I shall not *want* **lack**.
2 He *maketh me to lie down* **reposeth me**
in *green pastures* **sprouting folds**:
he *leadeth* **guideth** me
beside the *still waters* **waters of rest**.
3 He restoreth my soul:
he leadeth me in the paths of *righteousness* **justness**
for his name's sake.
4 Yea, though I walk through the valley
of the shadow of death,

I *will fear* **shall awe** no evil:
for thou art with me;
thy *rod* **scion** and thy *staff* **crutch**
they *comfort* **sigh over** me.
5 Thou *preparest* **arrangest** a table *before me* **at my face**
in the presence of *mine enemies* **my tribulators**:
thou anointest my head with *oil* **ointment**;
my cup *runneth over* **satiateth**.
6 Surely goodness and mercy shall *follow* **pursue** me
all the days of my life:
and I *will dwell* **shall settle**
in the house of *the LORD* **Yah Veh**
for *ever* **a length of days**.

24 A Psalm of David.
1 The earth is *the LORD'S* **Yah Veh's**,
and the fulness *thereof*;
the world, and they that *dwell* **settle** therein.
2 For he hath founded it upon the seas,
and established it upon the *floods* **rivers**.
3 Who shall ascend
into the *hill* **mountain** of *the LORD* **Yah Veh**?
or who shall *stand* **rise** in his holy place?
4 He that hath *clean hands* **innocent palms**,
and a pure heart;
who hath not lifted up his soul unto vanity,
nor *sworn* **oathed** deceitfully.
5 He shall *receive* **lift** the blessing
from *the LORD* **Yah Veh**,
and *righteousness* **justness**
from *the God* **Elohim** of his salvation.
6 This is the generation of them that seek him,
that seek thy face, O *Jacob* **Yaaqov**.
Selah.
7 Lift up your heads, O ye *gates* **portals**;
and be ye lift up, ye *everlasting doors* **eternal portals**;
and the *King* **Sovereign** of *glory* **honour** shall come in.
8 Who is this *King* **Sovereign** of *glory* **honour**?
The LORD **Yah Veh** strong and mighty,
the LORD **Yah Veh** mighty in *battle* **war**.
9 Lift up your heads, O ye *gates* **portals**;
even lift them up, ye *everlasting doors* **eternal portals**;
and the *King* **Sovereign** of *glory* **honour** shall come in.
10 Who is this *King* **Sovereign** of *glory* **honour**?
The LORD of hosts **Yah Veh Sabaoth**,
he is the *King* **Sovereign** of *glory* **honour**.
Selah.

25 *A Psalm* of David.
1 Unto thee, O *LORD* **Yah Veh**, *do* I lift up my soul.
2 O my *God* **Elohim**, I *trust* **confide** in thee:
let me not *be ashamed* **shame**,
let not mine enemies *triumph* **jump for joy** over me.
3 Yea, let none that *wait on* **await** thee *be ashamed* **shame**:
let them *be ashamed* **shame**
which *transgress without cause* **deal vanity covertly**.
4 *Shew* **Have** me **know** thy ways, O *LORD* **Yah Veh**;
teach me thy paths.
5 *Lead* **Aim** me in thy truth, and teach me:
for thou art *the God* **Elohim** of my salvation;
on thee do I wait **I await thee** all the day.
6 Remember, O *LORD* **Yah Veh**,
thy tender mercies
and thy *loving kindnesses* **kind mercies**;
for they *have been ever of old* **be eternal**.
7 Remember not the sins of my youth,
nor my *transgressions* **rebellions**:
according to thy mercy
remember thou me for thy goodness' sake,
O *LORD* **Yah Veh**.
8 Good and *upright* **straight** is *the LORD* **Yah Veh**:
therefore *will* **shall** he teach sinners in the way.
9 The *meek will* **humble shall** he *guide* **aim** in judgment:
and the *meek will* **humble shall** he teach his way.
10 All the paths of *the LORD* **Yah Veh**
are mercy and truth
unto such as *keep* **guard** his covenant
and his *testimonies* **witnesses**.
11 For thy name's sake, O *LORD* **Yah Veh**,
pardon mine iniquity **forgive my perversity**; for it is great.
12 What man is he that *feareth the LORD* **aweth Yah Veh**?
him shall he teach in the way that he shall choose.
13 His soul shall *dwell at ease* **stay in goodness**;
and his seed shall *inherit* **possess** the earth.
14 The *secret* **private counsel** of *the LORD* **Yah Veh**
is with them that *fear* **awe** him;
and he *will shew* **shall have** them **know** his covenant.
15 Mine eyes
are *ever* **continually** toward *the LORD* **Yah Veh**;
for he shall pluck my feet out of the net.
16 *Turn thee unto* **Face** me,
and *have mercy upon me* **grant me charism**;
for I am *desolate* **alone** and *afflicted* **humble**.
17 The *troubles* **tribulations** of my heart are enlarged:
O bring thou me out of my distresses.
18 *Look upon mine affliction* **See my humiliation**
and my *pain* **toil**;
and *forgive* **lift** all my sins.
19 *Consider* **See** mine enemies;
for they *are many* **abound by the myriads**;
and they hate me with *cruel* hatred **of violence**.
20 O *keep* **guard** my soul, and *deliver* **rescue** me:
let me not *be ashamed* **shame**;
for I *put* **seek** my *trust* **refuge** in thee.
21 Let integrity and *uprightness* **straightness**
preserve **guard** me;
for I *wait on* **await** thee.
22 Redeem *Israel* **Yisra El**, O *God* **Elohim**,
out of all his *troubles* **tribulations**.

26 *A Psalm* of David.
1 Judge me, O *LORD* **Yah Veh**;
for I have walked in mine integrity:
I have *trusted also* **confided** in *the LORD* **Yah Veh**;
therefore I shall not *slide* **waver**.
2 *Examine* **Proof** me, O *LORD* **Yah Veh**,
and prove **proof** me; *try* **refine** my reins and my heart.
3 For thy *lovingkindness* **mercy** is before mine eyes:
and I have walked in thy truth.
4 I have not *sat* **settled** with vain *persons* **men**,
neither *will* **shall** I go in with *dissemblers* **imposters**.
5 I have hated the congregation of *evildoers* **vilifiers**;
and *will* **shall** not *sit* **settle** with the wicked.
6 I *will* **shall** wash *mine hands* **my palms** in innocency:
so will I compass **thus shall I surround**
thine **thy sacrifice** altar,
O *LORD* **Yah Veh**:
7 That I may *publish with* **have them hear**
the voice of *thanksgiving* **extended hands**,
and *tell* **scribe** of all thy wondrous works.
8 *LORD* **O Yah Veh**,
I have loved the habitation of thy house,
and the place
where thine honour dwelleth
of the tabernacle of thy honour.
9 Gather not my soul with sinners,
nor my life with *bloody* men **of blood**:
10 In whose hands is *mischief* **intrigue**,
and their right *hand* is full of bribes.
11 But as for me, I *will* **shall** walk in mine integrity:
redeem me, and *be merciful unto me* **grant me charism**.
12 My foot standeth *in an even place* **straight**:
in the congregations *will* **shall** I bless *the LORD* **Yah Veh**.

27 *A Psalm* of David.
1 *The LORD* **Yah Veh** is my light and my salvation;
whom shall I *fear* **dread**?
the LORD **Yah Veh** is the *strength* **stronghold** of my life;
of whom shall I *be afraid* **dread**?
2 When the *wicked* **vilifiers**,
even mine enemies **my tribulators**
and *my foes* **mine enemies**,
came upon me to eat up my flesh,
they stumbled and fell.
3 Though *an host* **a camp** should encamp against me,
my heart shall not *fear* **awe**:
though war should rise against me,
in this *will* **shall** I *be confident* **confide**.
4 *One thing* **This one**
have I *desired* **asked** of *the LORD* **Yah Veh**,

that *will* **shall** I seek after;
that I may *dwell* **settle** in the house of *the LORD* **Yah Veh**
all the days of my life,
to *behold* **see** the *beauty* **pleasantness**
of *the LORD* **Yah Veh**,
and to *enquire* **search** in his *temple* **manse**.
5 For in the *time* **day** of *trouble* **evil**
he shall hide me in his *pavilion* **sukkoth/brush arbor**:
in the *secret* **covert** of his *tabernacle* **tent**
shall he hide me;
he shall *set* **lift** me *up* upon a rock.
6 And now shall mine head be lifted *up*
above mine enemies round about me:
therefore *will I offer* **shall I sacrifice** in his *tabernacle* **tent**
sacrifices of *joy* **shouting**;
I *will* **shall** sing, yea,
I *will sing praises* **shall psalm** unto *the LORD* **Yah Veh**.
7 Hear, O *LORD* **Yah Veh**, when I *cry* **call** with my voice:
have mercy also upon me **grant me charism**,
and answer me.
8 *When thou saidst,* Seek ye my face;
my heart said unto thee,
Thy face, *LORD* **O Yah Veh**, *will* **shall** I seek.
9 Hide not thy face *far* from me;
put **pervert** not thy servant away in *anger* **wrath**:
thou hast been my help;
leave me not, neither forsake me,
O *God* **Elohim** of my salvation.
10 When my father and my mother forsake me,
then *the LORD will take* **Yah Veh shall gather** me *up*.
11 Teach me thy way, O *LORD* **Yah Veh**,
and lead me in a *plain* **straight** path,
because of mine enemies.
12 *Deliver* **Give** me not *over*
unto the *will* **soul** of *mine enemies* **my tribulators**:
for false witnesses are risen up against me,
and such as *breathe out cruelty* **exhale violence**.
13 *I had fainted,* unless I had *believed* **trusted**
to see the goodness of *the LORD* **Yah Veh**
in the land of the living.
14 *Wait on the LORD* **Await Yah Veh**:
be of good courage **prevail**,
and he shall strengthen thine heart:
wait, I say, on the LORD **yea, await Yah Veh**.

28 *A Psalm* of David.
1 Unto thee *will I cry* **shall I call**,
O *LORD* **Yah Veh** my rock;
be not silent **hush not** to me:
lest, if thou *be silent* **hush** to me,
I become like them
that *go down* **descend** into the *pit* **well**.
2 Hear the voice of my supplications,
when I cry unto thee,
when I lift *up* my hands
toward *thy holy oracle* **the pulpit of thy holies**.
3 Draw me not away with the wicked,
and with the *workers* **doers** of *iniquity* **mischief**,
which *speak peace* **word shalom**
to their *neighbours* **friends**,
but *mischief* **evil** is in their hearts.
4 Give them according to their deeds,
and according to the *wickedness* **evil**
of their *endeavours* **exploits**:
give them after the work of their hands;
render **return** to them *their desert* **as they dealt**.
5 Because they *regard* **discern** not
the *works* **deeds** of *the LORD* **Yah Veh**,
nor the *operation* **work** of his hands,
he shall *destroy* **demolish** them, and not build them *up*.
6 Blessed be *the LORD* **Yah Veh**,
because he hath heard the voice of my supplications.
7 *The LORD* **Yah Veh**
is my strength and my *shield* **buckler**;
my heart *trusted* **confided** in him, and I am helped:
therefore my heart *greatly rejoiceth* **jumpeth for joy**;
and with my song
will I praise **shall I extend hands unto** him.
8 *The LORD* **Yah Veh** is their strength,
and he is the *saving strength* **stronghold of salvations**
of his anointed.
9 Save thy people, and bless thine inheritance:
feed **befriend** them also,
and lift them up *for ever* **eternally**.

29 A Psalm of David.
1 Give unto *the LORD* **Yah Veh**,
O ye *mighty* **sons of El**,
give unto *the LORD* **Yah Veh**
glory **honour** and strength.
2 Give unto *the LORD* **Yah Veh**
the *glory due unto* **honour of** his name;
worship the LORD **prostrate to Yah Veh**
in the *beauty* **majesty** of *holiness* **his holies**.
3 The voice of *the LORD* **Yah Veh** is upon the waters:
the *God* **El** of *glory* **honour** thundereth:
the LORD **Yah Veh** is upon many waters.
4 The voice of *the LORD is powerful* **Yah Veh hath force**;
the voice of *the LORD is full of* **Yah Veh in** majesty.
5 The voice of *the LORD* **Yah Veh** breaketh the cedars;
yea, *the LORD* **Yah Veh** breaketh the cedars of Lebanon.
6 He maketh them also to *skip* **dance** like a calf;
Lebanon and *Sirion* **Shirion**
like a *young unicorn* **son of reems**.
7 The voice of *the LORD* **Yah Veh**
divideth **heweth** the flames of fire.
8 The voice of *the LORD* **Yah Veh**
shaketh **twirleth** the wilderness;
the LORD **Yah Veh**
shaketh **twirleth** the wilderness of *Kadesh* **Qadesh**.
9 The voice of *the LORD* **Yah Veh**
maketh **causeth** the hinds *to calve* **writhe**,
and *discovereth* **strippeth** the forests:
and in his *temple* **manse**
doth every one speak **all say** of his *glory* **honour**.
10 *The LORD sitteth* **Yah Veh settleth** upon the flood;
yea, *the LORD sitteth King* **Yah Veh settleth Sovereign**
for ever **eternally**.
11 *The LORD* **Yah Veh**
will **shall** give strength unto his people;
the LORD **Yah Veh**
will **shall** bless his people with *peace* **shalom**.

30 A Psalm and Song
at the *dedication* **hanukkah** of the house of David.
1 I *will extol* **shall exalt** thee, O *LORD* **Yah Veh**;
for thou hast *lifted* **bailed** me up,
and hast not made my *foes* **enemies**
to *rejoice* **cheer** over me.
2 O *LORD* **Yah Veh** my *God* **Elohim**,
I cried unto thee, and thou hast healed me.
3 O *LORD* **Yah Veh**,
thou hast *brought up* **ascended** my soul
from *the grave* **sheol**:
thou hast *kept me alive* **enlivened me**,
that I should not *go down* **descend** to the *pit* **well**.
4 *Sing* **Psalm** unto *the LORD* **Yah Veh**,
O ye *saints* **mercied** of his,
and *give thanks* **extend hands**
at the *remembrance* **memorial** of his holiness.
5 For his *anger endureth* **wrath is** but a *moment* **blink**;
in his *favour* **pleasure** is life:
weeping may *endure* **stay** for *a night* **an evening**,
but *joy cometh* **shouting** in the morning.
6 And in my *prosperity* **serenity** I said,
I shall *never be moved* **not totter eternally**.
7 *LORD* **O Yah Veh**, by thy *favour* **pleasure**
thou hast made my mountain
to stand *strong* **in strength**:
thou *didst hide* **hid** thy face, and I was *troubled* **terrified**.
8 I *cried* **called** to thee, O *LORD* **Yah Veh**;
and unto *the LORD* **Yah Veh**
I *made supplication* **sought charism**.
9 What *profit* **gain** is there in my blood,
when I *go down* **descend** to the pit **of ruin**?
Shall the dust *praise* **extend hands unto** thee?
shall it *declare* **tell** thy truth?
10 Hear, O *LORD* **Yah Veh**,
and *have mercy upon me* **grant me charism**:
LORD **O Yah Veh**, be thou my helper.

11 Thou hast turned for me
my *mourning* **chopping** into **round** dancing:
thou hast *put off* **loosed** my *sackcloth* **saq**,
and girded me with *gladness* **cheerfulness**;
12 To the end
that my *glory* **honour** may *sing praise* **psalm** to thee
and not *be silent* **hush**.
O *LORD* **Yah Veh** my *God* **Elohim**,
I *will give thanks* **shall extend hands** unto thee
for ever **eternally**.

31 To *the chief Musician* **His Eminence**,
A Psalm of David.
1 In thee, O *LORD* **Yah Veh**,
do I put my trust **I seek refuge**;
let me *never be ashamed* **not eternally shame**:
deliver **slip** me **away** in thy *righteousness* **justness**.
2 *Bow down* **Extend** thine ear to me;
deliver **rescue** me *speedily* **quickly**:
be thou my *strong* rock **of stronghold**,
for an house of *defence* **stronghold** to save me.
3 For thou art my rock and my *fortress* **stronghold**;
therefore for thy name's sake lead me, and guide me.
4 Pull me out of the net
that they have *laid privily* **hid** for me:
for thou art my *strength* **stronghold**.
5 Into thine hand I *commit* **oversee** my spirit:
thou hast redeemed me,
O *LORD God* **Yah Veh El** of truth.
6 I have hated them that regard *lying* **vain** vanities:
but I *trust* **confide** in *the LORD* **Yah Veh**.
7 I *will be glad* **shall cheer** and *rejoice* **twirl** in thy mercy:
for thou hast *considered* **seen** my *trouble* **humiliation**;
thou hast known my soul in *adversities* **tribulations**;
8 And hast not shut me up into the hand of the enemy:
thou hast *set* **stood** my feet in *a large room* **an expanse**.
9 *Have mercy upon me* **Grant me charism**,
O *LORD* **Yah Veh**,
for I am *in trouble* **tribulated**:
mine eye is *consumed* **motheaten** with *grief* **vexation**,
yea, my soul and my belly.
10 For my life is *spent* **finished off** with grief,
and my years with sighing:
my *strength faileth* **force faltereth**
because of *mine iniquity* **my perversity**,
and my bones are *consumed* **motheaten**.
11 I was a reproach
among all *mine enemies* **my tribulators**,
but *especially* **mightily**
among my *neighbours* **fellow tabernaclers**,
and a *fear* **dread** to *mine acquaintance* **those I know**:
they that did see me without fled from me.
12 I am forgotten
as *a dead man out of mind* **one dead of heart**:
I am like *a broken vessel* **an instrument that destructeth**.
13 For I have heard the slander of many:
fear was on every side **terror surrounded**:
while they *took* **set** counsel *together* against me,
they *devised* **intrigued** to take away my *life* **soul**.
14 But I *trusted* **confided** in thee, O *LORD* **Yah Veh**:
I said, Thou art my *God* **Elohim**.
15 My times are in thy hand:
deliver **rescue** me from the hand of mine enemies,
and from them that *persecute* **pursue** me.
16 *Make* **Light** thy face *to shine* upon thy servant:
save me for thy mercies' sake.
17 Let me not *be ashamed* **shame**, O *LORD* **Yah Veh**;
for I have called upon thee:
let the wicked *be ashamed* **shame**,
and let them *be silent* **hush** in *the grave* **sheol**.
18 Let the *lying* **false** lips be *put to silence* **muted**;
which *speak grievous things* **word impudence**
proudly **with pomp** and *contemptuously* **disrespect**
against the *righteous* **just**.
19 *Oh* how great is thy goodness,
which thou hast *laid up* **treasured**
for them that *fear* **awe** thee;
which thou hast *wrought* **done**
for them that *trust* **seek refuge** in thee
before the sons of *men* **humanity**!
20 Thou shalt hide them
in the *secret* **covert** of thy *presence* **face**
from the pride of man:
thou shalt *keep* **hide** them *secretly*
in a *pavilion* **sukkoth/brush arbor**
from the strife of tongues.
21 Blessed be *the LORD* **Yah Veh**:
for he hath shewed me his marvellous *kindness* **mercy**
in a *strong* city **with rampart**.
22 For I said in my haste,
I am cut off *from before* **in front of** thine eyes:
nevertheless **surely** thou heardest
the voice of my supplications
when I cried unto thee.
23 O love *the LORD* **Yah Veh**, all ye his *saints* **mercied**:
for the LORD **Yah Veh**
preserveth **guardeth** the *faithful* **trustworthy**,
and *plentifully rewardeth* **doth shalam**
the *proud doer* **pompous worker**.
24 *Be of good courage* **Prevail**,
and he shall strengthen your heart,
all ye that *hope in the LORD* **await Yah Veh**.

32 *A Psalm* of David, *Maschil* **On Comprehension**.
1 *Blessed* **Blithe** is he
whose *transgression* **rebellion** is *forgiven* **lifted**,
whose sin is covered.
2 *Blessed* **Blithe** is *the man* **humanity**
unto whom *the LORD* **Yah Veh**
imputeth **fabricateth** not *iniquity* **perversity**,
and in whose spirit there is no *guile* **deceit**.
3 When I *kept silence* **hushed**,
my bones *waxed old* **wore out**
through my roaring all the day long.
4 For day and night thy hand was heavy upon me:
my moisture is turned into the *drought* **parch** of summer.
Selah.
5 I *acknowledged* **made known**
my sin unto thee,
and *mine iniquity* **my perversity**
have I not *hid* **covered over**.
I said, I *will confess* **shall extend hands**
for my *transgressions* **rebellions** unto *the LORD* **Yah Veh**;
and thou *forgavest* **liftest** the *iniquity* **perversity** of my sin.
Selah.
6 For this shall every one that is *godly* **mercied**
pray unto thee in a time when thou mayest be found:
surely in the *floods* **overflowing** of great waters
they shall not *come nigh unto* **touch** him.
7 Thou art my *hiding place* **covert**;
thou shalt *preserve* **guard** me from *trouble* **tribulation**;
thou shalt *compass* **surround** me *about*
with *songs* **shouts** of *deliverance* **escape**.
Selah.
8 I *will instruct* **shall have** thee **discern**
and teach thee in the way which thou shalt go:
I *will guide* **shall counsel** thee with mine eye.
9 Be ye not as the horse, or as the mule,
which *have no understanding* **discern not**:
whose mouth must be *held in* **muzzled**
with bit and bridle,
lest they come near unto thee.
10 Many sorrows shall be to the wicked:
but he that *trusteth* **confideth** in *the LORD* **Yah Veh**,
mercy shall *compass* **surround** him *about*.
11 *Be glad* **Cheer** in *the LORD* **Yah Veh**,
and *rejoice* **twirl**, ye *righteous* **just**:
and shout *for joy*,
all ye that are *upright* **straight** in heart.

33 *Rejoice* **Shout** in *the LORD* **Yah Veh**,
O ye *righteous* **just**:
for *praise is comely for* **halal befitteth** the *upright* **straight**.
2 *Praise the LORD* **Extend hands to Yah Veh** with harp:
sing **psalm** unto him with the *psaltery* **bagpipe**
and *an instrument of ten strings* **decachord**.
3 Sing unto him a new song;
play skilfully **strum well—pleasingly**
with a *loud noise* **blast**.
4 For the word of *the LORD* **Yah Veh** is *right* **straight**;

and all his works *are done in truth* **trustworthy**.
5 He loveth *righteousness* **justness** and judgment:
the earth is full
of the *goodness* **mercy** of *the LORD* **Yah Veh**.
6 By the word of *the LORD* **Yah Veh**
were the heavens *made* **worked**;
and all the host of them
by the *breath* **spirit/wind** of his mouth.
7 He gathereth the waters of the sea
together as an heap:
he *layeth up the deep in storehouses*
giveth treasuries in the abyss.
8 Let all the earth *fear the LORD* **awe Yah Veh**:
let all *the inhabitants of* **that settle in** the world
stand in awe of **dodge** him.
9 For he *spake* **said**, and it *was done* **became**;
he *commanded* **misvahed**, and it stood *fast*.
10 *The LORD bringeth* **Yah Veh voideth**
the counsel of the *heathen* **goyim** *to nought*:
he *maketh* **anulleth**
the *devices* **fabrications** of the people *of none effect*.
11 The counsel of *the LORD* **Yah Veh**
standeth *for ever* **eternally**,
the *thoughts* **fabrications** of his heart
to all generations **generation to generation**.
12 *Blessed* **Blithe** is the *nation* **goyim**
whose *God* **Elohim** is *the LORD* **Yah Veh**;
and the people whom he hath chosen
for his own inheritance.
13 *The LORD* **Yah Veh** looketh from *heaven* **the heavens**;
he beholdeth all the sons of *men* **humanity**.
14 From the *place* **establishment**
of his *habitation* **settlement**
he *looketh* **peereth** upon all
the inhabitants of **that settled on** the earth.
15 He *fashioneth* **formeth** their hearts *alike* **together**;
he *considereth* **discerneth** all their works.
16 There is no *king* **sovereign** saved
by the *multitude* **abundance** of *an host* **valour**:
a **the** mighty *man* is not *delivered* **rescued**
by *much strength* **abundant force**.
17 An horse is *a vain thing* **falsehood** for *safety* **salvation**:
neither shall he *deliver* **rescue** *any*
by his great *strength* **valour**.
18 Behold, the eye of *the LORD* **Yah Veh**
is upon them that *fear* **awe** him,
upon them that *hope in* **await** his mercy;
19 To *deliver* **rescue** their soul from death,
and to *keep* **enliven** them *alive* in famine.
20 Our soul *waiteth for the LORD* **awaiteth Yah Veh**:
he is our help and our *shield* **buckler**.
21 For our heart shall *rejoice* **cheer** in him,
because we have *trusted* **confided** in his holy name.
22 Let thy mercy, O *LORD* **Yah Veh**, be upon us,
according as we *hope in* **await** thee.

34

A Psalm of David,
when he *changed* **altered** his *behaviour* **taste**
before Abimelech **at the face of Abi Melech**;
who *drove him away* **exiled him**, and he *departed* **went**.
1 I *will* **shall** bless *the LORD* **Yah Veh** at all times:
his *praise* **halal** shall continually be in my mouth.
2 My soul shall *make her boast* **halal**
in *the LORD* **Yah Veh**:
the humble shall hear *thereof*, and *be glad* **cheer**.
3 O *magnify the LORD* **greaten Yah Veh** with me,
and let us exalt his name together.
4 I sought *the LORD* **Yah Veh**, and he heard me,
and *delivered* **rescued** me from all my *fears* **terrors**.
5 They looked unto him, and *were lightened* **sparkled**:
and their faces *were* **blushed** not *ashamed*.
6 This *poor man cried* **humble one called**,
and *the LORD* **Yah Veh** heard *him*,
and saved him out of all his *troubles* **tribulations**.
7 The angel of *the LORD* **Yah Veh**
encampeth round about them that *fear* **awe** him,
and *delivereth* **rescueth** them.
8 O taste and see that *the LORD* **Yah Veh** is good:
blessed **blithe** is the *man* **mighty**
that *trusteth* **seeketh refuge** in him.
9 O *fear the LORD* **awe Yah Veh**, ye his *saints* **holy**:
for there is no *want* **lack** to them that *fear* **awe** him.
10 The *young lions do* **whelps** lack,
and *suffer hunger* **famish**:
but they that seek *the LORD* **Yah Veh**
shall not *want* **lack** any good *thing*.
11 Come, ye *children* **sons**, hearken unto me:
I *will* **shall** teach you the *fear* **awe** of *the LORD* **Yah Veh**.
12 What man is he that desireth life,
and loveth *many* days, that he may see good?
13 *Keep* **Guard** thy tongue from evil,
and thy lips from *speaking guile* **wording deceit**.
14 *Depart* **Turn away** from evil, and *do* **work** good;
seek *peace* **shalom**, and pursue it.
15 The eyes of *the LORD* **Yah Veh**
are upon the *righteous* **just**,
and his ears *are open* unto their cry.
16 The face of *the LORD* **Yah Veh**
is against them that *do* **work** evil,
to cut off *the remembrance of them* **their memorial**
from the earth.
17 *The righteous* **They** cry,
and *the LORD* **Yah Veh** heareth,
and *delivereth* **rescueth** them
out of all their *troubles* **tribulations**.
18 *The LORD* **Yah Veh** is nigh unto them
that are of a *broken* **crushed** heart;
and saveth such as be of a contrite spirit.
19 Many are the *afflictions* **evils** of the *righteous* **just**:
but *the LORD delivereth* **Yah Veh rescueth** him
out of them all.
20 He *keepeth* **guardeth** all his bones:
not one of them is broken.
21 Evil shall *slay* **deathify** the wicked:
and they that hate the *righteous* **just**
shall *be desolate* **have guilted**.
22 *The LORD* **Yah Veh**
redeemeth the soul of his servants:
and none of them that *trust* **seek refuge** in him
shall be desolate **hath guilted**.

35

A Psalm of David.
1 *Plead my cause* **Defend**, O *LORD* **Yah Veh**,
with them that *strive* **contend** with me:
fight against them that fight against me.
2 Take hold of *shield* **buckler** and *buckler* **shield**,
and *stand up* **arise** for mine help.
3 Draw out also the spear,
and *stop the way against* **shut up and confront** them
that *persecute* **pursue** me:
say unto my soul, I am thy salvation.
4 Let them *be confounded* **shame**
and *put to* shame **them** that seek after my soul:
let them *be turned back* **apostatize**
and *brought to confusion* **blush**
that *devise my hurt* **fabricate me evil**.
5 Let them be as chaff *before* **at the face of** the wind:
and **in overthrowing**,
let the angel of *the LORD chase* **Yah Veh overthrow** them.
6 Let their way be dark and slippery:
and let the angel of *the LORD* **Yah Veh**
persecute **pursue** them.
7 For *without cause* **gratuitously** have they hid for me
their net in a pit **of ruin**,
which *without cause* **gratuitously** they have digged
for my soul.
8 Let *destruction* **devastation** come upon him
at unawares **as he hath not known**;
and let his net that he hath hid *catch himself* **capture him**:
into that very *destruction* **devastation** let him fall.
9 And my soul
shall *be joyful* **twirl** in *the LORD* **Yah Veh**:
it shall rejoice in his salvation.
10 All my bones shall say, *LORD* **O Yah Veh**,
who is like unto thee,
which *deliverest* **rescuest** the *poor* **humble**
from him that is *too strong for him* **stronger than he**,
yea, the *poor* **humble** and the needy
from him that *spoileth* **strippeth** him?
11 *False witnesses* **Witnesses of violence** did rise up;

they *laid to my charge things* **asked me** that I knew not.
12 They *rewarded* **did shalam** me evil for good
to the *spoiling* **bereaving** of my soul.
13 But as for me,
when they were sick, my *clothing* **robe** was *sackcloth* **saq**:
I humbled my soul with fasting;
and my prayer returned into mine own bosom.
14 I *behaved myself* **walked**
as though he *had been* **be** my friend or brother:
I *bowed down heavily* **prostrated darkened**,
as one that mourneth for *his* **a** mother.
15 But in *mine adversity* **my limping**
they *rejoiced* **cheered**,
and gathered *themselves* together:
yea, the *abject* **smiters**
gathered *themselves together* against me,
and I knew it not;
they *did tear me* **ripped**, and *ceased* **hushed** not:
16 With *hypocritical* **profaners**,
mockers in feasts **jeerers at bakings**,
they gnashed upon me with their teeth.
17 *Lord* **Adonay**,
how long *wilt* **shalt** thou *look on* **see** me?
rescue **restore** my soul
from their *destructions* **devastations**,
my *darling* **only** from the *lions* **whelps**.
18 I *will give thee thanks* **shall extend hands to thee**
in the great congregation:
I *will praise* **shall halal** thee among *much* **mighty** people.
19 Let not them that are mine enemies
wrongfully rejoice **falsely cheer** over me:
neither let them wink — **blink** with the eye
that hate me *without a cause* **gratuitously**.
20 For they *speak* **word** not *peace* **shalom**:
but they *devise deceitful matters* **fabricate words of deceit**
against them that *are quiet* **rest** in the land.
21 Yea,
they *opened* **enlarged** their mouth *wide* against me,
and said, Aha, aha, our eye hath seen it.
22 *This* thou hast seen, O *LORD* **Yah Veh**:
keep **hush** not *silence*:
O *Lord* **Adonay**, be not far from me.
23 *Stir up thyself* **Waken**, and awake to my judgment,
even unto my *cause* **defence**,
my *God* **Elohim** and my *Lord* **Adonay**.
24 Judge me, O *LORD* **Yah Veh** my *God* **Elohim**,
according to thy *righteousness* **justness**;
and let them not *rejoice* **cheer** over me.
25 Let them not say in their hearts,
Ah, so would we have it: **Aha, aha, O soul!**
let them not say, We have swallowed him *up*.
26 Let them *be ashamed* **shame**
and *brought to confusion* **blush** together
that *rejoice* **cheer** at mine *hurt* **evil**:
let them be *clothed* **enrobed** with shame and dishonour
that *magnify themselves* **greaten** against me.
27 Let them shout *for joy*, and *be glad* **cheer**,
that *favour* **delight in** my *righteous cause* **justness**:
yea, let them say continually,
Let the LORD **Yah Veh** be *magnified* **greatened**,
which *hath pleasure* **delighteth**
in the *prosperity* **shalom** of his servant.
28 And my tongue shall *speak* **meditate**
of thy *righteousness* **justness**
and of thy *praise* **halal** all the day long.

36

To *the chief Musician* **His Eminence**,
A Psalm of David the servant of *the LORD* **Yah Veh**.
1 The *transgression* **rebellion** of the wicked
saith **doth oracle** within my heart,
that there is no *fear* **dread** of *God* **Elohim**
before his eyes.
2 For he *flattereth* **smootheth over** himself
in his own eyes,
until his *iniquity* **perversity** be found to be *hateful* **hated**.
3 The words of his mouth
are *iniquity* **mischief** and deceit:
he hath *left off to be wise* **ceased comprehending**,
and to *do good* **well—please**.
4 He *deviseth* **fabricateth** mischief upon his bed;
he setteth himself in a way that is not good;
he *abhorreth* **spurneth** not evil.
5 Thy mercy, O *LORD* **Yah Veh**, is in the heavens;
and thy *faithfulness* **trustworthiness**
reacheth unto the *clouds* **vapours**.
6 Thy *righteousness* **justness**
is like the *great mountains* **mountains of El**;
thy judgments are a great *deep* **abyss**:
O *LORD* **Yah Veh**,
thou *preservest man* **savest human** and *beast* **animal**.
7 How *excellent* **esteemed** is thy *lovingkindness* **mercy**,
O *God* **Elohim**!
therefore the *children* **sons** of *men* **humanity**
put their trust **seek refuge** under the shadow of thy wings.
8 They shall *be abundantly satisfied* **satiate**
with the fatness of thy house;
and thou shalt *make* **have** them drink
of the *river* **wadi** of thy pleasures.
9 For with thee is the fountain of life:
in thy light shall we see light.
10 O *continue* **draw out** thy *lovingkindness* **mercy**
unto them that know thee;
and thy *righteousness* **justness**
to the *upright* **straight** in heart.
11 Let not the foot of *pride* **pomp** come against me,
and let not the hand of the wicked *remove* **waver** me.
12 There are the *workers* **doers** of *iniquity* **mischief** fallen:
they are *cast down* **overthrown**,
and shall not be able to rise.

37

A Psalm of David.
1 *Fret* **Inflame** not *thyself*
because of *evildoers* **vilifiers**,
neither be thou envious
against the workers of *iniquity* **wickedness**.
2 For they shall *soon* **quickly** be *cut down* **clipped**
like the grass,
and wither as the green *herb* **sprout**.
3 *Trust* **Confide** in *the LORD* **Yah Veh**, and *do* **work** good;
so **thus** shalt thou *dwell* **tabernacle** in the land,
and *verily thou shalt be fed* **tend to trustworthiness**.
4 Delight thyself also in *the LORD* **Yah Veh**:
and he shall give thee the *desires* **requests** of thine heart.
5 *Commit* **Roll** thy way unto *the LORD* **Yah Veh**;
trust **confide** also in him;
and he shall *bring it to pass* **work it**.
6 And he shall bring forth
thy *righteousness* **justness** as the light,
and thy judgment as the noonday.
7 *Rest* **Be still** in *the LORD* **Yah Veh**,
and *wait patiently* **writhe** for him:
fret **inflame** not *thyself*
because of him who prospereth in his way,
because of the man
who *bringeth wicked devices to pass* **worketh intrigue**.
8 *Cease from anger* **Let go of wrath**,
and forsake *wrath* **fury**:
fret **inflame** not *thyself in any wise to do evil* **to vilify**.
9 For *evildoers* **vilifiers** shall be cut off:
but those that *wait upon the LORD* **await Yah Veh**,
they shall *inherit* **possess** the earth.
10 For yet a little *while*,
and the wicked shall not be:
yea, thou shalt *diligently consider* **discern** his place,
and it shall not be.
11 But the *meek* **humble** shall *inherit* **possess** the earth;
and shall delight themselves
in the abundance of *peace* **shalom**.
12 The wicked *plotteth* **intrigueth** against the just,
and gnasheth upon him with his teeth.
13 *The Lord* **Adonay** shall laugh at him:
for he seeth that his day is coming.
14 The wicked have drawn out the sword,
and have bent their bow,
to *cast down* **fell** the *poor* **humble** and needy,
and to *slay* **slaughter**
such as be of upright conversation **the straight of way**.
15 Their sword shall enter into their own heart,
and their bows shall be broken.
16 A little that *a righteous man* **the just** hath

is better than the *riches* **abundance** of many wicked.
17 For the arms of the wicked shall be broken:
but *the LORD* **Yah Veh** upholdeth the *righteous* **just**.
18 *The LORD* **Yah Veh**
knoweth the days of the *upright* **integrious**:
and their inheritance shall be *for ever* **eternal**.
19 They shall not *be ashamed* **shame** in the evil time:
and in the days of famine
they shall *be satisfied* **satiate**.
20 But the wicked shall *perish* **destruct**,
and the enemies of *the LORD* **Yah Veh**
shall be as the *fat* **esteem** of *lambs* **rams**:
they shall consume — **finished off**;
into smoke shall they *consume away* **be finished off**.
21 The wicked borroweth,
and *payeth* **doth** not **shalam** *again*:
but the *righteous* **just**
sheweth mercy **granteth charism**, and giveth.
22 For such as be blessed of him
shall *inherit* **possess** the earth;
and they that be *cursed* **abased** of him
shall be cut off.
23 The *steps* **paces** of *a good man* **the mighty**
are *ordered* **established** by *the LORD* **Yah Veh**:
and he delighteth in his way.
24 Though he fall, he shall not be *utterly* cast down:
for *the LORD* **Yah Veh** upholdeth him with his hand.
25 I have been *young* **a lad**, and *now am old* **have aged**;
yet have I not seen the *righteous* **just** forsaken,
nor his seed *begging* **seeking** bread.
26 He *is ever merciful* **ever granteth charism all days**,
and lendeth;
and his seed *is blessed* **shall be for blessings**.
27 *Depart* **Turn away** from evil, and *do* **work** good;
and *dwell for evermore* **tabernacle eternally**.
28 For *the LORD* **Yah Veh** loveth judgment,
and forsaketh not his *saints* **mercied**;
they are *preserved for ever* **guarded eternally**:
but the seed of the wicked shall be cut off.
29 The *righteous* **just** shall *inherit* **possess** the land,
and *dwell* **tabernacle** therein *for ever* **eternally**.
30 The mouth of the *righteous* **just**
speaketh **meditateth** wisdom,
and his tongue *talketh* **wordeth** of judgment.
31 The *law* **torah** of his *God* **Elohim** is in his heart;
none of his steps shall *slide* **waver**.
32 The wicked watcheth the *righteous* **just**,
and seeketh to *slay* **deathify** him.
33 *The LORD* **Yah Veh**
will **shall** not *leave* **forsake** him in his hand,
nor *condemn* **judge** him **wicked** when he is judged.
34 *Wait on the LORD* **Await Yah Veh**,
and *keep* **guard** his way,
and he shall exalt thee to *inherit* **possess** the land:
when the wicked are cut off, thou shalt see it.
35 I have seen the wicked *in great power* **tyrant**,
and spreading himself **stripped naked**
like a green *bay tree* **native**.
36 Yet he passed away, and, *lo* **behold**, he was not:
yea, I sought him, but he could not be found.
37 *Mark* **Regard** the *perfect man* **integrious**,
and *behold* **see** the *upright* **straight**:
for the *end* **finality** of that man is *peace* **shalom**.
38 But the *transgressors* **rebels**
shall be *destroyed* **desolated** together:
the *end* **finality** of the wicked shall be cut off.
39 But the salvation of the *righteous* **just**
is of *the LORD* **Yah Veh**:
he is their strength — **their stronghold**
in the time of *trouble* **tribulation**.
40 And *the LORD* **Yah Veh** shall help them,
and *deliver* **slip** them **away**:
he shall *deliver* **slip** them **away** from the wicked,
and save them, because they *trust* **seek refuge** in him.

38

A Psalm of David,
to bring to remembrance **remember**.
1 O *LORD* **Yah Veh**,
rebuke **reprove** me not in thy *wrath* **rage**:
neither *chasten* **discipline** me in thy *hot displeasure* **fury**.
2 For thine arrows *stick fast in* **penetrate** me,
and thy hand *presseth* **penetrateth** me *sore*.
3 There is no *soundness* **integrity** in my flesh
because **at the face** of *thine anger* **thy rage**;
neither is there any *rest* **shalom** in my bones
because **at the face** of my sin.
4 For *mine iniquities* **my perversities**
are *gone* **passed** over mine head:
as an heavy burden they are too heavy for me.
5 My wounds stink and *are corrupt* **dissolve**
because **at the face** of my *foolishness* **folly**.
6 I am *troubled* **bent**;
I am *bowed down greatly* **prostrated mightily**;
I go *mourning* **darkened** all the day long.
7 For my *loins* **flanks**
are filled with *loathsome disease* **scorching**:
and there is no soundness in my flesh.
8 I am *feeble* **exhausted** and *sore broken* **mighty crushed**:
I have roared
by reason of the *disquietness* **growling** of my heart.
9 *Lord* **Adonay**, all my desire is before thee;
and my *groaning* **sighing** is not hid from thee.
10 My heart *panteth* **palpitateth**,
my *strength faileth* **force forsaketh** me:
as for the light of mine eyes,
it also is *gone from* **not in** me.
11 My lovers and my friends
stand *aloof from* **against** my *sore* **plague**;
and my *kinsmen* **neighbours** stand afar off.
12 They also that seek after my *life* **soul**
lay snares for **snare** me:
and they that seek my *hurt* **evil**
speak mischievous things **word calamities**,
and *imagine* **meditate** deceits all the day long.
13 But I, as *a* deaf *man*, heard not;
and I was as a *dumb man* **mute**
that openeth not his mouth.
14 Thus I was as a man that heareth not,
and in whose mouth are no reproofs.
15 For in thee, O *LORD* **Yah Veh**, *do I hope* **I await**:
thou *wilt hear* **shalt answer**,
O *Lord* **Adonay** my *God* **Elohim**.
16 For I said, *Hear me*,
lest *otherwise* they should *rejoice* **cheer** over me:
when my foot *slippeth* **tottereth**,
they *magnify* **greaten** *themselves* against me.
17 For I am *ready* **prepared** to *halt* **limp**,
and my sorrow is continually before me.
18 For I *will declare mine iniquity* **shall tell my perversity**;
I will **shall** be *sorry* **concerned** for my sin.
19 But mine enemies *are lively* **enliven**,
and they are *strong* **mighty**:
and they that hate me *wrongfully* **falsely**
are multiplied **abound by the myriads**.
20 They also that *render* **shalam** evil for good
are *mine adversaries* **my satans**;
because I *follow the thing that is* **pursue** good.
21 Forsake me not, O *LORD* **Yah Veh**:
O my *God* **Elohim**, be not far from me.
22 *Make haste* **Hasten** to help me,
O *Lord* **Adonay** my salvation.

39

To *the chief Musician* **His Eminence**,
even to Juduthun **Yeduthun/A Laudatory**,
A Psalm of David.
1 I said, I *will take heed to* **shall guard** my ways,
that I sin not with my tongue:
I *will keep* **shall guard** my mouth with a *bridle* **muzzle**,
while the wicked is before me.
2 I was *dumb* **mute** with silence,
I *held my peace, even* **hushed** from good;
and my *sorrow* **pain** was *stirred* **troubled**.
3 My heart *was hot* **heated** within me,
while I *was musing* **meditated** the fire burned:
then *spake* **worded** I with my tongue,
4 *LORD* **O Yah Veh**, *make me to* **let me** know mine end,
and the measure of my days, what it is:
that I may know how *frail* **forsaken** I am.
5 Behold, thou hast *made* **given** my days
as *an handbreadth* **a palm span**;

and *mine age* **my transcience**
is as *nothing* **naught** before thee:
verily *every man at his best state* **all humanity**
is altogether **stationed in** vanity.
Selah.
6 Surely every man walketh in *a vain shew* **an image**:
surely they *are disquieted* **roar** in vain:
he heapeth *up riches,*
and knoweth not who shall gather *them.*
7 And now, *Lord* **O Adonay**, what *wait I for* **await I**?
my hope is in thee.
8 *Deliver* **Rescue** me from all my *transgressions* **rebellions**:
make **set** me not the reproach of the foolish.
9 I was *dumb* **mute**, I opened not my mouth;
because thou *didst* **worked** it.
10 *Remove* **Turn aside** thy *stroke away* **plague** from me:
I am *consumed* **finished off**
by the *blow* **choking** of thine hand.
11 When thou with *rebukes* **reproofs**
dost correct **disciplinest** man for *iniquity* **perversity**,
thou *makest* **dissolvest** his *beauty to consume away* **desire**
like a moth:
surely *every man* **all humanity** is vanity.
Selah.
12 Hear my prayer, O *LORD* **Yah Veh**,
and give ear **hearken** unto my cry;
hold not thy peace **hush not** at my tears:
for I am a *stranger* **sojourner** with thee,
and a sojourner **settler**, as all my fathers *were.*
13 O *spare* **look on** me, that I may *recover strength* **relax**,
before I go hence, and be no more.

40 To *the chief Musician* **His Eminence**,
A Psalm of David.
1 *I waited patiently for the LORD*
In awaiting, I awaited Yah Veh;
and he *inclined* **extended** unto me, and heard my cry.
2 He *brought* **ascended** me *up* also
out of *an horrible pit* **a roaring well**,
out of the miry *clay* **mire**,
and *set* **raised** my feet upon a rock,
and established my *goings* **steps**.
3 And he hath *put* **given** a new song in my mouth,
even praise **halal** unto our *God* **Elohim**:
many shall see it, and *fear* **awe**,
and shall *trust* **confide** in *the LORD* **Yah Veh**.
4 *Blessed* **Blithe** is that *man* **mighty**
that *maketh the LORD* **setteth Yah Veh**
his *trust* **confidant**,
and *respecteth* **faceth** not the proud,
nor *such as turn aside* **swerveth** to lies.
5 Many, O *LORD* **Yah Veh** my *God* **Elohim**,
are thy *wonderful works* **marvels**
which thou hast *done* **worked**,
and thy *thoughts* **fabrications**
which are to us—ward **toward us**:
they cannot be reckoned up in order
none can line them up unto thee:
if I *would declare* **should tell** and *speak* **word** *of them,*
they are *more* **mightier** than can be *numbered* **scribed**.
6 Sacrifice and offering thou didst not desire;
mine ears hast thou *opened* **pierced**:
burnt offering **holocaust** and *sin offering* **for sin**
hast thou not *required* **asked**.
7 Then said I, *Lo* **Behold**, I come:
in the *volume* **roll** of the *book* **scroll**
it is *written* **inscribed** of me,
8 I delight to *do* **work** thy *will* **pleasure**,
O my *God* **Elohim**:
yea, thy *law* **torah** is within my *heart* **inwards**.
9 I have *preached righteousness* **evangelized justness**
in the great congregation:
lo **behold**, I have not *refrained* **restrained** my lips,
O *LORD* **Yah Veh**, thou knowest.
10 I have not *hid* **covered** thy *righteousness* **justness**
within my heart;
I have *declared* **said**
thy *faithfulness* **trustworthiness** and thy salvation:
I have not concealed
thy *lovingkindness* **mercy** and thy truth
from the great congregation.
11 *Withhold* **Restrain** not thou
thy tender mercies from me,
O *LORD* **Yah Veh**:
let thy *lovingkindness* **mercy** and thy truth
continually *preserve* **guard** me.
12 For innumerable evils
have *compassed* **surrounded** me *about*:
mine iniquities **my perversities**
have *taken hold upon* **overtaken** me,
so that I am not able to *look up* **see**;
they are *more* **mightier** than the hairs of mine head:
therefore my heart *faileth* **forsaketh** me.
13 Be pleased, O *LORD* **Yah Veh**, to *deliver* **rescue** me:
O *LORD* **Yah Veh**, *make haste* **hasten** to help me.
14 Let them *be ashamed* **shame**
and *confounded* **blush** together
that seek after my soul to *destroy* **scrape** it **away**;
let them *be driven backward* **apostatize**
and *put to* shame
that *wish* **desire** me evil.
15 *Let them be desolate* **Desolate them**
for a reward **in the finality** of their shame
that say unto me, Aha, aha.
16 Let all those that seek thee
rejoice and *be glad* **cheer** in thee:
let such as love thy salvation say continually,
The LORD **Yah Veh** be *magnified* **greatened**.
17 But I am *poor* **humble** and needy;
yet *the Lord thinketh* **Adonay fabricateth** upon me:
thou art my help *and my deliverer* **who slippeth me away**;
make no tarrying **tarry not**, O my *God* **Elohim**.

41 To *the chief Musician* **His Eminence**,
A Psalm of David.
1 *Blessed* **Blithe** is he
that *considereth* **comprehendeth** the poor:
the LORD will deliver **Yah Veh shall rescue** him
in *time* **the day** of *trouble* **evil**.
2 *The LORD will preserve* **Yah Veh shall guard** him,
and *keep* **enliven** him *alive*;
and he shall be *blessed* **blithesome** upon the earth:
and thou *wilt* **shalt** not *deliver* **give** him
unto the *will* **soul** of his enemies.
3 *The LORD will strengthen* **Yah Veh shall support** him
upon the *bed* **bedstead** of *languishing* **bleeding**:
thou *wilt make all* **shalt turn** his bed in his sickness.
4 I said, *LORD* **O Yah Veh**,
be merciful unto me **grant me charism**:
heal my soul; for I have sinned against thee.
5 Mine enemies *speak* **say** evil of me,
When shall he die, *and* his name *perish* **destruct**?
6 And if he come to see me, he *speaketh* **wordeth** vanity:
his heart gathereth *iniquity* **mischief** to itself;
when he goeth *abroad* **without**, he *telleth* **wordeth** it.
7 All that hate me *whisper* **enchant** *together* against me:
against me do they *devise* **fabricate** my *hurt* **evil**.
8 *An evil disease* **A word of Beli Yaal**, *say they,*
cleaveth fast **is poured** unto him:
and now that he lieth
he shall rise *up no more* **never again**.
9 Yea, *mine own familiar friend* **my man of shalom**,
in whom I *trusted* **confided**,
which did eat of my bread,
hath *lifted up* **greatened** his heel against me.
10 But thou, O *LORD* **Yah Veh**,
be merciful unto me **grant me charism**, and raise me *up*,
that I may *requite* **shalam** them.
11 By this I know that thou *favourest* **delightest in** me,
because mine enemy
doth **shall** not *triumph* **blast** over me.
12 And as for me, thou upholdest me in mine integrity,
and *settest* **stationest** me before thy face
for ever **eternally**.
13 Blessed
be *the LORD God* **Yah Veh Elohim** of *Israel* **Yisra El**
from *everlasting* **eternity**, and to *everlasting* **eternity**.
Amen, and Amen.

42
To *the chief Musician* **His Eminence**,
Maschil **On Comprehension**,
for the sons of *Korah* **Qorach**.
1 As the hart
panteth **yearneth** after the water *brooks* **reservoirs**,
so *panteth* **yearneth** my soul after thee, O *God* **Elohim**.
2 My soul thirsteth for *God* **Elohim**, for the living *God* **El**:
when shall I come
and *appear before God* **be seen at the face of Elohim**?
3 My tears have been my *meat* **bread** day and night,
while they *continually* **all day** say unto me,
Where is thy *God* **Elohim**?
4 When I remember these *things*,
I pour out my soul in me:
for I had *gone* **passed on** with the multitude,
I *went* **walked gently** with them
to the house of *God* **Elohim**,
with the voice of *joy* **shouting**
and *praise* **extended hands**,
with a multitude that *kept holyday* **celebrated**.
5 Why *art thou cast down* **prostratest thou**, O my soul?
and *why art thou disquieted* **roarest thou** in me?
hope thou in God **await Elohim**:
for I shall yet *praise* **extend hands unto** him
for the *help* **salvation** of his *countenance* **face**.
6 O my *God* **Elohim**,
my soul *is cast down* **prostrateth** within me:
therefore *will* **shall** I remember thee
from the land of *Jordan* **Yarden**,
and of the *Hermonites* **Hermoniym**,
from the *hill Mizar* **little mountain**.
7 *Deep* **Abyss** calleth unto *deep* **abyss**
at the *noise waterspouts* **voice culverts**:
all thy *waves* **breakers** and thy *billows* **waves**
are gone **have passed** over me.
8 Yet *the LORD will command* **Yah Veh shall misvah**
his *lovingkindness* **mercy** in the *daytime* **day**,
and in the night his song shall be with me,
and my prayer unto *the God* **El** of my life.
9 I *will* **shall** say unto *God* **El** my rock,
Why hast thou forgotten me?
why go I *mourning* **darkened**
because of the oppression of the enemy?
10 *As with a sword* **murder** in my bones,
mine enemies **my tribulators** reproach me;
while **all day** they say *daily* unto me,
Where is thy *God* **Elohim**?
11 Why *art* **prostratest** thou *cast down*, O my soul?
and why *art* **roarest** thou *disquieted* within me?
hope thou in *God* **Elohim**:
for I shall *yet praise* **extend hands to** him,
who is the *health* **salvation** of my *countenance* **face**,
and my *God* **Elohim**.

43
Judge me, O *God* **Elohim**,
and *plead* **defend** my *cause* **defence**
against an *ungodly nation* **unmercied goyim**:
O *deliver me* **slip me away** from the
deceitful **man of deceits** and *unjust man* **wickedness**.
2 For thou art *the God* **Elohim** of my *strength* **stronghold**:
why dost thou cast me off?
why go I *mourning* **darkened**
because of the oppression of the enemy?
3 O send out thy light and thy truth: let them lead me;
let them bring me unto thy holy *hill* **mountain**,
and to thy tabernacles.
4 Then *will* **shall** I go
unto the **sacrifice** altar of *God* **Elohim**,
unto *God* **El**, *my exceeding joy* **the cheer of my twirling**:
yea, upon the harp
will I praise **shall I extend hands unto** thee,
O *God* **Elohim** my *God* **Elohim**.
5 Why *art* **prostratest** thou *cast down*, O my soul?
and why *art* **roarest** thou *disquieted* within me?
hope in God **await Elohim**:
for I shall yet *praise* **extend hands unto** him,
who is the *health* **salvation** of my *countenance* **face**,
and my *God* **Elohim**.

44
To *the chief Musician* **His Eminence**,
for the sons of *Korah* **Qorach**,
Maschil **On Comprehension**.
1 We have heard with our ears, O *God* **Elohim**,
our fathers have *told* **scribed** us,
what work **the deeds** thou didst in their days,
in the *times of old* **former days**.
2 How thou *drive out* **dispossessed** the *heathen* **goyim**
with thy hand,
and plantedst them;
how thou *didst afflict* **vilified** the *people* **nations**,
and *cast* **sent** them out.
3 For they *got* **possessed** not the land *in possession*
by their own sword,
neither did their own arm save them:
but thy right *hand*, and thine arm,
and the light of thy *countenance* **face**,
because thou hadst *a favour* **pleasure** unto them.
4 Thou art my *King* **Sovereign**, O *God* **Elohim**:
command deliverances **misvah salvations**
for *Jacob* **Yaaqov**.
5 Through thee
will **shall** we push down our *enemies* **tribulators**:
through thy name
will **shall** we *tread* **trample** them *under*
that rise up against us.
6 For I *will* **shall** not *trust* **confide** in my bow,
neither shall my sword save me.
7 But thou hast saved us from our *enemies* **tribulators**,
and hast *put* **shamed** them *to shame* that hated us.
8 In *God* **Elohim** we *boast* **halal** all the day long,
and *praise* **halal** thy name *for ever* **eternally**.
Selah.
9 *But* **Yea** thou hast cast off, and *put* **shamed** us *to shame*;
and goest not forth with our *armies* **hosts**.
10 Thou makest us to turn back
from the *enemy* **tribulator**:
and they which hate us spoil for themselves.
11 Thou hast given us
like sheep appointed **as a flock** for *meat* **food**;
and hast *scattered* **winnowed** us
among the *heathen* **goyim**.
12 Thou sellest thy people for nought,
and *dost not increase* **aboundest not**
thy wealth by their price.
13 Thou *makest* **settest** us a reproach
to our *neighbours* **fellow tabernaclers**,
a *scorn* **derision** and a *derision* **ridicule**
to them that are round about us.
14 Thou *makest* **settest** us a *byword* **proverb**
among the *heathen* **goyim**,
a shaking of the head among the *people* **nations**.
15 My *confusion* **shame** is *continually* **all day** before me,
and the shame of my face hath covered me,
16 For the voice of him
that reproacheth and blasphemeth;
by reason **at the face** of the enemy and avenger.
17 All this is come upon us;
yet have we not forgotten thee,
neither have we *dealt falsely* **falsified** in thy covenant.
18 Our heart is not *turned back* **apostatized**,
neither have our steps *declined* **stretched** from thy way;
19 Though thou hast *sore broken* **crushed** us
in the place of *dragons* **monsters**,
and covered us with the shadow of death.
20 If we have forgotten the name of our *God* **Elohim**,
or *stretched out* **spread** our *hands* **palms**
to a strange *god* **el**;
21 Shall not *God search* **Elohim probe** this *out*?
for he knoweth the *secrets* **concealments** of the heart.
22 Yea, for thy sake
are we *killed* **slaughtered** all the day long;
we are *counted* **machinated**
as *sheep* **flock** for the slaughter.
23 Awake, why sleepest thou, O *Lord* **Adonay**?
arise **awake**, cast us not off *for ever* **in perpetuity**.
24 Wherefore hidest thou thy face,
and forgettest
our *affliction* **humiliation** and our oppression?

25 For our soul *is bowed down* **sinketh** to the dust:
our belly *cleaveth* **adhereth** unto the earth.
26 Arise for our help,
and redeem us for thy mercies' sake.

45 To *the chief Musician* **His Eminence,**
upon *Shoshannim* **Trumpets,**
for the sons of *Korah* **Qorach,**
Maschil **On Comprehension,**
A Song of *loves* **the Beloved.**
1 My heart *is inditing* **bubbleth** a good *matter* **word**:
I speak of the things which I have made **say of my works**
touching **to** the *king* **sovereign**:
my tongue
is the *pen* **stylus** of a *ready writer* **skillful scribe.**
2 Thou art *fairer* **beautified**
than **above** the *children* **sons** of *men* **humanity**:
grace **charism** is poured into thy lips:
therefore *God* **Elohim** hath blessed thee
for ever **eternally**.
3 Gird thy sword upon thy *thigh* **flank**, O *most* mighty,
with thy glory and thy majesty.
4 And in thy majesty ride **thou;**
prosperously **prosper thou** because **of thy word** of truth
and *meekness* **humbleness** and *righteousness* **justness**;
and thy right *hand*
shall teach thee *terrible things* **awesomenesses**.
5 Thine arrows are *sharp* **pointened**
in the heart of the *king's* **sovereign's** enemies;
whereby the people fall under thee.
6 Thy throne, O *God* **Elohim**,
is *for ever* **eternally** and *ever* **eternally**:
the *sceptre* **scion** of thy *kingdom* **sovereigndom**
is a *right sceptre* **straight scion**.
7 Thou lovest *righteousness* **justness**,
and hatest wickedness:
therefore *God* **Elohim**,
thy *God* **Elohim**, hath anointed thee
with the *oil* **ointment** of *gladness* **rejoicing**
above thy *fellows* **companions**.
8 All thy *garments* **clothes**
smell of myrrh, and aloes, and cassia,
out of the ivory *palaces* **manses**,
whereby they **whose strummings**
have *made* **cheered** thee *glad*.
9 *Kings'* **Sovereigns'** daughters
were among thy *honourable women* **esteemed**:
upon thy right *hand*
did stand the *queen* **mistress** in *gold* **ore** of Ophir.
10 Hearken, O daughter, and *consider* **see**,
and *incline* **extend** thine ear;
forget *also* thine own people, and thy father's house;
11 *So* shall the *king greatly* **sovereign** desire thy beauty:
for he is thy *Lord* **adoni**;
and *worship* **prostrate** thou **to** him.
12 And the daughter of *Tyre* **Sor**
shall be there with *a gift* **an offering**;
even the rich among the people
shall *intreat* **stroke** thy *favour* **face**.
13 The *king's* **sovereign's** daughter
is all *glorious* **honourable** within:
her *clothing* **robe** is of *wrought gold* **gold brocade**.
14 She shall be brought unto the *king* **sovereign**
in *raiment of needlework* **embroidery**:
the virgins her *companions that follow* **friends behind** her
shall be brought unto thee.
15 With *gladness* **cheerfulness** and rejoicing
shall *they* be brought:
they shall enter into the *king's palace* **sovereign's manse**.
16 Instead of thy fathers, shall be thy *children* **sons**,
whom thou mayest
make princes **set governors** in all the earth.
17 I *will* **shall** make thy name to be remembered
in all generations **generation to generation**:
therefore shall the people *praise* **extend hands unto** thee
for ever **eternally** and *ever* **eternally**.

46 To *the chief Musician* **His Eminence,**
for the sons of *Korah* **Qorach,**
A Song *upon Alamoth* **for Virgins**.
1 *God* **Elohim** is our refuge and strength,
a *very present* **mighty found** help in *trouble* **tribulation**.
2 Therefore *will* **shall** not we *fear* **awe**,
though the earth *be removed* **changeth**,
and *though* the mountains *be carried* **totter**
into the *midst* **heart** of the *sea* **seas**;
3 *Though* the waters *thereof* roar and *be troubled* **foam**,
though the mountains *shake* **quake**
with the *swelling* **pomp** *thereof*.
Selah.
4 There is a river,
the streams whereof **whose rivulets**
shall *make glad* **cheer** the city of *God* **Elohim**,
the *holy place* **holies** of the tabernacles
of *the most High* **Elyon**.
5 *God* **Elohim** is in the midst of her;
she shall not *be moved* **totter**:
God **Elohim** shall help her,
and that right early **at the face of the morning**.
6 The *heathen raged* **goyim roared**,
the *kingdoms were moved* **sovereigndoms tottered**:
he *uttered* **gave** his voice, the earth melted.
7 *The LORD of hosts* **Yah Veh Sabaoth** is with us;
the *God* **Elohim** of *Jacob* **Yaaqov** is our *refuge* **secure loft**.
Selah.
8 Come,
behold **see** the *works* **deeds** of *the LORD* **Yah Veh**,
what desolations he hath *made* **set** in the earth.
9 He *maketh* **shabbathizeth** wars *to cease*
unto the end of the earth;
he breaketh the bow,
and *cutteth* **choppeth** the spear *in sunder*;
he burneth the *chariot* **wagon** in the fire.
10 *Be still* **Let go**, and know that I *am God* — **Elohim**:
I will **shall** be *exalted* **lofted** among the *heathen* **goyim**,
I will **shall** be *exalted* **lofted** in the earth.
11 *The LORD of hosts* **Yah Veh Sabaoth** is with us;
the God **Elohim** of *Jacob* **Yaaqov** is our *refuge* **secure loft**.
Selah.

47 To *the chief Musician* **His Eminence,**
A Psalm for the sons of *Korah* **Qorach.**
1 O clap your *hands* **palms**, all ye people;
shout unto *God* **Elohim**
with the voice of *triumph* **shouting**.
2 For *the LORD most high* **Yah Veh Elyon**
is *terrible* **awesome**;
he is a great *King* **Sovereign** over all the earth.
3 He shall subdue the people under us,
and the nations under our feet.
4 He shall choose our inheritance for us,
the *excellency* **pomp** of *Jacob* **Yaaqov** whom he loved.
Selah.
5 *God is gone up* **Elohim hath ascended** with a *shout* **blast**,
the LORD **Yah Veh** with the *sound* **voice** of a trumpet.
6 *Sing praises* **Psalm** to *God* **Elohim**,
sing praises **psalm**:
sing praises **psalm** unto our *King* **Sovereign**,
sing praises **psalm**.
7 For *God* **Elohim** is the *King* **Sovereign** of all the earth:
sing ye praises **psalm**
with understanding **comprehendingly**.
8 *God* **Elohim** reigneth over the *heathen* **goyim**:
God sitteth **Elohim settleth**
upon the throne of his holiness.
9 The *princes* **volunteers** of the people
are gathered *together*,
even the people of the *God* **Elohim** of Abraham:
for the *shields* **bucklers** of the earth
belong **be** unto *God* **Elohim**:
he is *greatly exalted* **mightily ascended**.

48 A Song and Psalm for the sons of *Korah* **Qorach**.
1 Great is *the LORD* **Yah Veh**,
and *greatly to be praised* **mightily halaled**
in the city of our *God* **Elohim**,
in the mountain of his holiness.
2 Beautiful for *situation* **elevation**,
the joy of the whole earth,
is mount *Zion* **Siyon**, on the *sides* **flanks** of the north,

the city of the great *King* **Sovereign**.
3 *God* **Elohim** is known in her *palaces* **citadels**
for a *refuge* **secure loft**.
4 For, *lo* **behold**,
the *kings were assembled* **sovereigns congregated**,
they passed by together.
5 They saw *it, and* so they marvelled;
they were *troubled* **terrified**, and hasted away.
6 *Fear* **Trembling** took hold upon them there,
and pain **pangs**, as of *a woman in travail* **birthing**.
7 Thou breakest the ships of Tarshish with an east wind.
8 As we have heard, so have we seen
in the city of *the LORD of hosts* **Yah Veh Sabaoth**,
in the city of our *God* **Elohim**:
God will **Elohim shall** establish it *for ever* **eternally**.
Selah.
9 We have *thought of* **compared** thy *lovingkindness* **mercy**,
O *God* **Elohim**, in the midst of thy *temple* **manse**.
10 According to thy name, O *God* **Elohim**,
so is thy *praise* **halal** unto the ends of the earth:
thy right *hand* is full of *righteousness* **justness**.
11 Let mount *Zion rejoice* **Siyon cheer**,
let the daughters of *Judah be glad* **Yah Hudah twirl**,
because of thy judgments.
12 *Walk about Zion* **Surround Siyon**,
and go round about **surround** her:
tell **scribe to** the towers *thereof.*
13 *Mark ye well* **Set your heart on** her *bulwarks* **trenches**,
consider **contemplate** her *palaces* **citadels**;
that ye may *tell* **scribe** it to the generation *following* **after**.
14 For this *God* **Elohim** is our *God* **Elohim**
for ever **eternally** and *ever* **eternally**:
he *will be our guide even unto* **shall drive us over** death.

49

To *the chief Musician* **His Eminence**,
A Psalm for the sons of *Korah* **Qorach**.
1 Hear this, all ye people;
give ear **hearken**,
all ye *inhabitants of* **transcients settled in** the world:
2 Both *low* **sons of humanity** and *high* **sons of man**,
rich and *poor* **needy**, together.
3 My mouth shall *speak* **word** of wisdom;
and the meditation of my heart
shall be of *understanding* **discernment**.
4 I *will* **shall** incline mine ear to a *parable* **proverb**:
I *will* **shall** open my *dark saying* **riddle** upon the harp.
5 Wherefore should I *fear* **awe** in the days of evil,
when the *iniquity* **perversity** of my heels
shall *compass* **surround** me *about*?
6 They that *trust* **confide** in their *wealth* **valuables**,
and *boast* **halal** themselves
in the *multitude* **abundance** of their riches;
7 *None of them can by any means*
In redeeming, no man shall redeem his brother,
nor give to *God* **Elohim**
a *ransom* **koper/an atonement** for him:
8 (For the redemption of their soul is *precious* **esteemed**,
and it ceaseth *for ever* **eternally**:)
9 That he should still live *for ever* **in perpetuity**,
and not see *corruption* **the pit of ruin**.
10 For he seeth that wise men die,
likewise **together**
the fool and the *brutish person perish* **stupid destruct**,
and leave their *wealth* **valuables** to others.
11 Their inward thought is,
that their houses shall *continue for ever* **be eternal**,
and their *dwelling places* **tabernacles**
to all generations **generation to generation**;
they call their *lands* **soil** after their own names.
12 *Nevertheless man being in honour abideth not*
Humanity stayeth not in esteem:
he is like the *beasts* **animals** that *perish* **decease**.
13 This their way is their folly:
yet their posterity
approve **is pleased with** their *sayings* **mouth**.
Selah.
14 *Like sheep* **As a flock**
they are *laid* **set** in *the grave* **sheol**;
death shall *feed on* **tend** them;
and the *upright* **straight**
shall *have dominion over* **subjugate** them in the morning;
and their *beauty* **form**
shall *consume* **wear out** in *the grave* **sheol**
from their *dwelling* **residence**.
15 But *God will* **Elohim shall** redeem my soul
from the *power* **hand** of *the grave* **sheol**:
for he shall *receive* **take** me.
Selah.
16 *Be not thou afraid* **Awe not**
when *one is made rich* **man enricheth**,
when the *glory* **honour** of his house
is increased **aboundeth**;
17 For when he dieth
he shall *carry nothing away* **take naught**:
his *glory* **honour** shall not descend after him.
18 Though while he lived he blessed his soul:
and *men will praise* **they shall extend hands unto** thee,
when thou *doest well to* **well—pleasest** thyself.
19 He shall go to the generation of his fathers;
they shall never see light **in perpetuity**.
20 *Man* **Humanity** that is in *honour* **esteem**,
and *understandeth* **discerneth** not,
is like the beasts that perish.

50

A Psalm of Asaph.
1 *The mighty God, even the LORD* **El — Elohim Yah Veh**
hath *spoken* **worded**,
and called the earth from the rising of the sun
unto the *going down* **entry** *thereof.*
2 Out of *Zion* **Siyon**, the perfection of beauty,
God **Elohim** hath shined.
3 Our *God* **Elohim** shall come,
and shall not *keep silence* **hush**:
a fire shall *devour before him* **consume at his face**,
and it shall *be very tempestuous* **whirl mightily**
round about him.
4 He shall call to the heavens from above,
and to the earth,
that he may *judge* **plead the cause of** his people.
5 Gather my *saints* **mercied** together unto me;
those that have *made* **cut** a covenant with me
by sacrifice.
6 And the heavens
shall *declare* **tell** his *righteousness* **justness**:
for *God* **Elohim** is judge himself.
Selah.
7 Hear, O my people, and I *will speak* **shall word**;
O *Israel* **Yisra El**,
and I *will testify* **shall witness** against thee:
I *am God* — **Elohim**, *even* thy *God* **Elohim**.
8 I *will* **shall** not reprove thee
for thy sacrifices or thy *burnt offerings* **holocausts**,
to have been continually before me.
9 I *will* **shall** take no bullock out of thy house,
nor he goats out of thy folds.
10 For every beast of the forest is mine,
and the *cattle* **animals** upon a thousand *hills* **mountains**.
11 I know all the *fowls* **flyers** of the mountains:
and the *wild beasts* **creatures** of the field
are mine **with me**.
12 If I *were hungry* **famished**,
I *would* **should** not *tell* **say to** thee:
for the world is mine, and the fulness *thereof.*
13 *Will* **Shall** I eat the flesh of *bulls* **the mighty**,
or drink the blood of **he** goats?
14 *Offer* **Sacrifice** unto *God* **Elohim**
thanksgiving **extended hands**;
and *pay* **shalam** thy vows unto *the most High* **Elyon**:
15 And call upon me in the day of *trouble* **tribulation**:
I *will deliver* **shall rescue** thee,
and thou shalt *glorify* **honour** me.
16 But unto the wicked *God* **Elohim** saith,
What hast thou to do to *declare* **scribe** my statutes,
or that thou shouldest *take* **lift** my covenant
in thy mouth?
17 Seeing thou hatest *instruction* **discipline**,
and castest my words behind thee.
18 When thou sawest a thief,
then thou *consentedst* **wast pleased** with him,
and hast *been partaker* **allotted** with adulterers.

19 Thou *givest* **extendest** thy mouth to evil,
and thy tongue *frameth* **contriveth** deceit.
20 Thou *sittest* **settlest**
and *speakest* **wordest** against thy brother;
thou *slanderest* **givest to trip up**
thine own mother's son.
21 These *things* hast thou *done* **worked**,
and I *kept silence* **hushed**;
thou *thoughtest* **equatest**
that I *was altogether such an one* **had become** as thyself:
but I *will* **shall** reprove thee,
and *set them in order before* **line them up at** thine eyes.
22 *Now* **I beseech,** *consider* **discern** this,
ye that forget *God* **Elohah**,
lest I tear *you* in pieces,
and there be none to *deliver* **rescue**.
23 Whoso *offereth praise* **sacrificeth extended hands**
glorifieth **honoureth** me:
and to him
that *ordereth his conversation aright* **setteth his way**
will I shew **shall I have see** the salvation of *God* **Elohim**.

51

To *the chief Musician* **His Eminence**,
A Psalm of David,
when Nathan the prophet came unto him,
after he had gone in to *Bath—sheba* **Bath Sheba**.
1 *Have mercy upon me* **Grant me charism**,
O *God* **Elohim**,
according to thy *lovingkindness* **mercy**:
according unto the *multitude* **abundance**
of thy tender mercies
blot **wipe** out my *transgressions* **rebellions**.
2 *Wash* **Launder** me *throughly* **aboundingly**
from *mine iniquity* **my perversity**,
and *cleanse* **purify** me from my sin.
3 For I *acknowledge* **know** my *transgressions* **rebellions**:
and my sin is *ever* **continually** before me.
4 Against thee, thee only, have I sinned,
and *done* **worked** this evil in *thy sight* **thine eyes**:
that thou mightest be justified
when thou *speakest* **wordest**,
and be *clear* **pure** when thou judgest.
5 Behold, I was *shapen* **writhed** in *iniquity* **perversity**;
and in sin did my mother conceive me.
6 Behold, thou desirest truth in the *inward parts* **reins**:
and in the hidden *part*
thou shalt *make* **have** me to know wisdom.
7 *Purge* **Purify** me with hyssop,
and I shall be *clean* **purified**:
wash **launder** me, and I shall be whiter than snow.
8 Make me to hear
joy **rejoicing** and *gladness* **cheerfulness**;
that the bones which thou hast *broken* **crushed**
may *rejoice* **twirl**.
9 Hide thy face from my sins,
and *blot* **wipe** out all *mine iniquities* **my perversities**.
10 Create in me a *clean* **pure** heart, O *God* **Elohim**;
and renew a *right* **steadfast** spirit within me.
11 Cast me not away from thy *presence* **face**;
and take not thy holy spirit from me.
12 Restore unto me the *joy* **rejoicing** of thy salvation;
and uphold me with thy free **voluntary** spirit.
13 Then *will* **shall** I teach *transgressors* **rebels** thy ways;
and sinners shall *be converted* **return** unto thee.
14 *Deliver* **Rescue** me from *bloodguiltiness* **bloods**,
O *God* **Elohim**, *thou God* **Elohim** of my salvation:
and my tongue
shall *sing aloud* **shout** of thy *righteousness* **justness**.
15 O *Lord* **Adonay**, open thou my lips;
and my mouth shall *shew forth* **tell** thy *praise* **halal**.
16 For thou desirest not sacrifice;
else *would* **should** I give it:
thou delightest not in *burnt offering* **holocaust**.
17 The sacrifices of *God* **Elohim** are a broken spirit:
a broken and a *contrite* **crushed** heart, O *God* **Elohim**,
thou *wilt* **shalt** not despise.
18 *Do good* **Well—please** in thy good pleasure
unto *Zion* **Siyon**:
build thou the walls of *Jerusalem* **Yeru Shalem**.
19 Then shalt thou *be pleased* **delight**
with **in** the sacrifices of *righteousness* **justness**,
with *burnt offering* **holocaust**,
and *whole burnt offering* **total holocaust**:
then shall they *offer* **holocaust** bullocks
upon *thine* **thy sacrifice** altar.

52

To *the chief Musician* **His Eminence**,
Maschil **On Comprehension**,
A Psalm of David,
when Doeg the *Edomite* **Edomiy** came and told *Saul* **Shaul**,
and said unto him,
David is come to the house of *Ahimelech* **Achi Melech**.
1 Why *boastest* **halalest** thou thyself in *mischief* **evil**,
O mighty *man?*
the *goodness* **mercy** of *God* **El**
endureth continually **is every day**.
2 The tongue *deviseth mischiefs* **fabricateth calamities**;
like a *sharp* **sharpened** razor, working deceitfully.
3 Thou lovest evil more than good;
and *lying* **falsehood**
rather than to *speak righteousness* **word justness**.
Selah.
4 Thou lovest all *devouring* **swallowing** words,
O thou deceitful tongue.
5 *God* **El** shall *likewise destroy* **pull** thee **down**
for ever **in perpetuity**,
he shall take thee away,
and *pluck* **uproot** thee out of thy *dwelling place* **tent**,
and *root* **uproot** thee out of the land of the living.
Selah.
6 The *righteous* **just** also shall see, and *fear* **awe**,
and shall laugh at him:
7 *Lo* **Behold**, *this is* the *man* **mighty**
that *made* **set** not *God* **Elohim** his *strength* **stronghold**;
but *trusted* **confided** in the abundance of his riches,
and strengthened himself in his *wickedness* **calamity**.
8 But I am like a green olive tree
in the house of *God* **Elohim**:
I *trust* **confide** in the mercy of *God* **Elohim**
for ever **eternally** and *ever* **eternally**.
9 I *will praise* **shall extend hands unto** thee
for ever **eternally**,
because thou hast *done* **worked** it:
and I *will wait on* **shall await** thy name;
for it is good before thy *saints* **mercied**.

53

To *the chief Musician* **His Eminence**,
upon *Mahalath* **Stroking**,
Maschil **On Comprehension**, *A Psalm* of David.
1 The fool hath said in his heart,
There is no *God* **Elohim**.
Corrupt are they **They have ruined**,
and have done
abominable iniquity **abhorrent wickedness**:
there is none that *doeth* **worketh** good.
2 *God* **Elohim** looked down from *heaven* **the heavens**
upon the *children* **sons** of *men* **humanity**,
to see if there were any that *did understand* **discerned**,
that *did* seek *God* **Elohim**.
3 Every one of them *is gone back* **hath apostatized**:
they are altogether *become filthy* **muddled**;
there is none that *doeth* **worketh** good, no, not one.
4 Have the *workers* **doers** of *iniquity* **mischief**
no knowledge **not known**?
who eat up my people as they eat bread:
they have not called upon *God* **Elohim**.
5 *There were they in great fear* **In dreading, they dreaded**,
where no *fear* **dread** was:
for *God* **Elohim** hath scattered the bones
of him that encampeth against thee:
thou hast *put* **shamed** them *to shame*,
because *God* **Elohim** hath *despised* **spurned** them.
6 *Oh* **Who giveth** that the salvation of *Israel* **Yisra El**
were come out of *Zion* **Siyon**!
When *God bringeth* **Elohim turneth** back
the captivity of his people,
Jacob **Yaaqov** shall *rejoice* **twirl**,
and *Israel* **Yisra El** shall *be glad* **cheer**.

54 To *the chief Musician* **His Eminence,**
on *Neginoth* **Strummer,**
Maschil **On Comprehension**, *A Psalm* of David,
when the *Ziphims* **Ziphiym** came and said to *Saul* **Shaul**,
Doth not David hide himself with us?
1 Save me, O *God* **Elohim**, by thy name,
and *judge me* **plead my cause** by thy *strength* **might**.
2 Hear my prayer, O *God* **Elohim**;
give ear **hearken** to the *words* **sayings** of my mouth.
3 For strangers are risen *up* against me,
and *oppressors* **tyrants** seek after my soul:
they have not set *God* **Elohim** before them.
Selah.
4 Behold, *God* **Elohim** is mine helper:
the Lord **Adonay** is with them that uphold my soul.
5 He shall *reward* **return** evil
unto mine *enemies* **opponents**:
cut **exterminate** them *off* in thy truth.
6 I *will freely* **shall voluntarily** sacrifice unto thee:
I *will praise* **shall extend hands unto** thy name,
O *LORD* **Yah Veh**;
for it is good.
7 For he hath *delivered* **rescued** me
out of all *trouble* **tribulation**:
and mine eye hath seen *his desire upon* mine enemies.

55 To *the chief Musician* **His Eminence,**
on *Neginoth* **Strummer,**
Maschil **A Discerning**, *A Psalm* of David.
1 Give ear to my prayer, O *God* **Elohim**;
and *hide* **conceal** not thyself from my supplication.
2 *Attend* **Hearken** unto me, and *hear me* **answer**:
I *mourn* **ramble on** in my *complaint* **meditation**,
and *make a noise* **quake**;
3 Because of the voice of the enemy,
because **at the face** of the oppression of the wicked:
for they *cast iniquity* **topple mischief** upon me,
and in wrath they *hate* **oppose** me.
4 My heart *is sore pained* **writheth** within me:
and the terrors of death are fallen upon me.
5 *Fearfulness* **Awe** and trembling are come upon me,
and horror hath *overwhelmed* **covered over** me.
6 And I said, Oh **who giveth**
that I had *wings* **pinions** like a dove!
for then *would* **should** I fly away,
and *be at rest* **tabernacle**.
7 *Lo* **Behold**, then *would* **should** I wander far off,
and *remain* **stay overnight** in the wilderness.
Selah.
8 I *would* **should** hasten my escape
from the *windy storm* **rushing wind** and *tempest* **storm**.
9 *Destroy* **Swallow**, O *Lord* **Adonay**,
and divide their tongues:
for I have seen violence and strife in the city.
10 Day and night
they *go about it upon* **surround** the walls *thereof*:
mischief also and *sorrow* **toil** are in the midst of it.
11 *Wickedness* **Calamity** is in the midst *thereof*:
deceit **fraud** and *guile* **deceit**
depart not from her *streets* **broadways**.
12 For it was not an enemy that reproached me;
then I could have borne it:
neither was it he that hated me
that *did magnify himself* **greatened** against me;
then I *would* **should** have hid myself from him:
13 But *it was* thou, a man mine equal, my *guide* **chiliarch**,
and mine acquaintance **whom I know**.
14 We *took sweet* **sweetened private** counsel together,
and walked unto the house of *God* **Elohim**
in *company* **conspiracy**.
15 Let *death seize upon* **desolations deceive** them,
and let them *go down quick* **descend alive**
into *hell* **sheol**:
for wickedness **evil** is in their *dwellings* **sojournings**,
and among them.
16 As for me, I *will* **shall** call upon *God* **Elohim**;
and *the LORD* **Yah Veh** shall save me.
17 Evening, and morning, and at noon,
will **shall** I *pray* **meditate**, and *cry aloud* **roar**:
and he shall hear my voice.
18 He hath *delivered* **redeemed** my soul in *peace* **shalom**
from the battle that was against me:
for there *were* **be** many with me.
19 *God* **El** shall hear, and *afflict* **answer** them,
even he that *abideth* **settleth** of *old* **antiquity**.
Selah.
Because they have no changes,
therefore they *fear* **awe** not *God* **Elohim**.
20 He hath *put forth* **extended** his hands
against such as be at *peace* **shalom** with him:
he hath *broken* **profaned** his covenant.
21 *The words of* his mouth
were smoother **was more tender** than butter,
but war was in his heart:
his words were softer than *oil* **ointment**,
yet were they *drawn swords* **openings**.
22 Cast *thy burden* **that which he giveth thee**
upon *the LORD* **Yah Veh**,
and he shall sustain thee:
he shall *never suffer* **not give** the *righteous* **just**
to *be moved* **totter eternally**.
23 But thou, O *God* **Elohim**,
shalt *bring* **descend** them *down*
into the *pit* **well** of *destruction* **the pit of ruin**:
bloody and deceitful men **men of bloods and deceit**
shall *not live out half* **halve** their days;
but I *will trust* **shall confide** in thee.

56 To *the chief Musician* **His Eminence,**
on *Jonath—elem—rechokim* **The Mute Distant Dove**,
Michtam **Poem** of David,
when the *Philistines* **Peleshethiym**
took hold of him in Gath.
1 *Be merciful unto me* **Grant me charism**, O *God* **Elohim**:
for man *would swallow* **should gulp** me *up*;
he fighting daily oppresseth me.
2 Mine *enemies* **opponents**
would **should** daily *swallow* **gulp** me *up*:
for they be many that fight against me,
O thou *most High* **Elyon**.
3 *What time I am afraid* **The day I awe**,
I *will trust* **shall confide** in thee.
4 In *God* **Elohim** I *will praise* **shall halal** his word,
in *God* **Elohim** I *have put my trust* **shall confide**;
I *will* **shall** not *fear* **awe**
what flesh *can do* **shall work** unto me.
5 Every day they *wrest* **contort** my words:
all their *thoughts* **fabrications** are against me for evil.
6 They *gather themselves together* **dodge**,
they hide *themselves*,
they *mark* **guard** my *steps* **heelprints**,
when they *wait for* **await** my soul.
7 Shall they escape by *iniquity* **mischief**?
in *thine anger cast down* **thy wrath descend** the people,
O *God* **Elohim**.
8 Thou *tellest* **scribest** my wanderings:
put **set** thou my tears into thy *bottle* **skin**:
are they not in thy *book* **scroll**?
9 *When I cry unto thee* **The day I call**,
then shall mine enemies turn back:
this I know; for *God* **Elohim** is for me.
10 In *God* **Elohim**
will I praise his **shall I halal the** word:
in *the LORD* **Yah Veh**
will I praise his **shall I halal the** word.
11 In *God have I put my trust* **Elohim I confide**:
I *will* **shall** not *be afraid* **awe**
what *man can do* **humanity shall work** unto me.
12 Thy vows are upon me, O *God* **Elohim**:
I *will render* **shall shalam**
praises **extended hands** unto thee.
13 For thou hast *delivered* **rescued** my soul from death:
wilt **shalt** not thou *deliver* my feet from falling,
that I may walk *before God* **at the face of Elohim**
in the light of the living?

57 To *the chief Musician* **His Eminence,**
Al—taschith **Al Tashcheth/Ruin Not**,
Michtam **Poem** of David,

when he fled from **the face of** *Saul* **Shaul** in the cave.
1 *Be merciful unto me* **Grant me charism**, O *God* **Elohim**,
be merciful unto me **grant me charism**:
for my soul *trusteth* **seeketh refuge** in thee:
yea, in the shadow of thy wings
will I make my **shall I seek** refuge,
until these calamities be overpast.
2 I *will cry* **shall call** unto *God most high* **Elohim Elyon**;
unto *God* **El**
that *performeth* **consumateth** all *things* for me.
3 He shall send from *heaven* **the heavens**,
and save me from the reproach of him
that *would* **should** swallow *me up* **after me**.
Selah.
God **Elohim** shall send *forth* his mercy and his truth.
4 My soul is among **roaring** lions:
and I lie even among them that are *set on fire* **inflamed**,
even the sons of *men* **humanity**,
whose teeth are spears and arrows,
and their tongue a sharp sword.
5 Be thou *exalted* **lofted**, O *God* **Elohim**,
above the heavens;
let thy glory be **thy honour**
above all the earth.
6 They have prepared a net for my steps;
my soul is bowed down:
they have digged a pit *before me* **at my face**,
into the midst whereof they are fallen *themselves*.
Selah.
7 My heart is *fixed* **prepared**, O *God* **Elohim**,
my heart is *fixed* **prepared**:
I *will* **shall** sing and *give praise* **psalm**.
8 Awake *up*, my *glory* **honour**;
awake, *psaltery* **bagpipe** and harp:
I *myself will* **shall** awake early.
9 I *will praise* **shall extend hands unto** thee,
O *Lord* **Adonay**, among the people:
I *will sing* **shall psalm** unto thee among the nations.
10 For thy mercy is great unto the heavens,
and thy truth unto the *clouds* **vapours**.
11 Be thou *exalted* **lofted**, O *God* **Elohim**,
above the heavens:
let thy glory be **thy honour**
above all the earth.

58

To *the chief Musician* **His Eminence**,
Al—taschith **Al Tashcheth/Ruin Not**,
Michtam **Poem** of David.
1 *Do* **Truly, word** ye *indeed speak righteousness* **justness**,
O *congregation* **mute**?
do ye judge uprightly **judge ye in straightnesses**,
O ye sons of *men* **humanity**?
2 Yea, in heart ye *work* **do** wickedness;
ye weigh the violence of your hands in the earth.
3 The wicked are estranged from the womb:
they *go astray* **stray**
as soon as they be born **from the belly**,
speaking **wording** lies.
4 Their poison is like the poison of a serpent:
they are like the deaf *adder* **asp**
that *stoppeth* **shutteth** her ear;
5 Which *will* **shall** not hearken to the voice of charmers,
charming *never* **charms** so wisely.
6 Break their teeth, O *God* **Elohim**, in their mouth:
break **pull** out the *great* **grinder** teeth
of the *young lions* **whelps**, O *LORD* **Yah Veh**.
7 Let them *melt away* **dissipate** as waters
which *run* **pass** continually:
when he *bendeth his bow to shoot* **aimeth** his arrows,
let them be as cut *in pieces* **off**.
8 As a snail *which melteth* **dissolveth**,
let *every one of* them pass away:
like the *untimely birth* **miscarriage** of a woman,
that they may not see the sun.
9 Before your *pots can feel* **caldrons discern** the thorns,
he shall *take* **whirl** them away *as with a whirlwind*,
both living **alive**, and *in his wrath* **fuming**.
10 The *righteous* **just** shall *rejoice* **cheer**
when he seeth the *vengeance* **avengement**:
he shall wash his *feet* **steps** in the blood of the wicked.
11 So that *a man* **humanity** shall say,
Verily there is a *reward* **fruit** for the *righteous* **just**:
verily he is *a God* **Elohim** that judgeth in the earth.

59

To *the chief Musician* **His Eminence**,
Al—taschith **Al Tashcheth/Ruin Not**,
Michtam **Poem** of David;
when *Saul* **Shaul** sent,
and they *watched* **guarded** the house to *kill* **deathify** him.
1 *Deliver* **Rescue** me from mine enemies,
O my *God* **Elohim**:
defend **loft** me from them that rise *up against me*.
2 *Deliver* **Rescue** me
from the *workers* **doers** of *iniquity* **mischief**,
and save me from *bloody men* **men of blood**.
3 For, *lo* **behold**, they *lie in wait* **lurk** for my soul:
the *mighty are gathered* **strong dodge** against me;
not for my *transgression* **rebellion**,
nor for my sin, O *LORD* **Yah Veh**.
4 They run and prepare themselves
without *my fault* **perversity**:
awake to *help* **meet** me, and *behold* **see**.
5 Thou therefore,
O *LORD God of hosts* **Yah Veh Elohim Sabaoth**,
the God **Elohim** of *Israel* **Yisra El**,
awake to visit all the *heathen* **goyim**:
be **grant** not *merciful* **charism**
to any *wicked transgressors* **who deal covertly**.
Selah.
6 They return at evening:
they *make a noise* **roar** like a dog,
and go round about the city.
7 Behold, they *belch* **gush** *out* with their mouth:
swords are in their lips: for who, *say they*, doth hear?
8 But thou, O *LORD* **Yah Veh**, shalt laugh at them;
thou shalt *have* **deride** all the *heathen in derision* **goyim**.
9 *Because of his strength* **O my Strength,**
will I wait upon **shall I regard** thee:
for *God* **Elohim** is my *defence* **secure loft**.
10 The *God* **Elohim** of my mercy
shall *prevent* **anticipate** me:
God **Elohim** shall *let* **have** me see *my desire upon*
mine *enemies* **opponents**.
11 *Slay* **Slaughter** them not, lest my people forget:
scatter **stagger** them by thy *power* **valour**;
and *bring* **topple** them *down*,
O *Lord* **Adonay** our *shield* **buckler**.
12 For the sin of their mouth and the words of their lips
let them even be *taken* **captured** in their *pride* **pomp**:
and for *cursing* **oathing** and *lying* **deception**
which they *speak* **scribe**.
13 *Consume* **Finish** them **off** in *wrath* **fury**,
consume **finish** them **off**, that they may not be:
and let them know
that *God ruleth* **Elohim reigneth** in *Jacob* **Yaaqov**
unto the *ends* **finality** of the earth.
Selah.
14 And at evening *let them* **they** return;
and let them make a noise **they roar** like a dog,
and go round about the city.
15 *Let them* **They** wander *up and down for meat* **to eat**,
and *grudge* **murmer** if they be not satisfied.
16 But I *will* **shall** sing of thy power;
yea, I *will sing aloud* **shall shout** of thy mercy
in the morning:
for thou hast been my *defence* **secure loft**
and *refuge* **retreat**
in the day of my *trouble* **tribulation**.
17 Unto thee, O my strength, *will* **shall** I sing:
for *God* **Elohim** is my *defence* **secure loft**,
and the God **Elohim** of my mercy.

60

To *the chief Musician* **His Eminence**,
upon *Shushan—eduth* **Trumpet of Witness**,
Michtam **Poem** of David,
when he strove with *Aram—naharaim* **Aram Naharaim**
and with *Aram—zobah* **Aram Sobah**,
when *Joab* **Yah Ab** returned,
and smote of Edom
in the *valley of salt* **Valley of Salt/Gay Melach**

twelve thousand.
1 O *God* **Elohim**, thou hast cast us off,
thou hast *scattered* **breached** us,
thou hast been *displeased* **angry**;
O *turn thyself* **return** to us *again*.
2 Thou hast *made* **quaked** the earth *to tremble*;
thou hast broken it:
heal the breaches *thereof*; for it *shaketh* **tottereth**.
3 Thou hast *shewed* **had** thy people
hard things **see hardship**:
thou hast made us to drink
the wine of *astonishment* **staggering**.
4 Thou hast given *a banner* **an ensign**
to them that *fear* **awe** thee,
that it may *be displayed* **flutter**
because **at the face** of *the truth* **trueness**.
Selah.
5 That thy beloved may be *delivered* **rescued**;
save with thy right *hand*, and *hear me* **answer**.
6 *God* **Elohim** hath spoken in his holiness;
I *will rejoice* **shall jump for joy**,
I *will divide* **shall allot** Shechem,
and *mete* **measure** out
the valley of *Succoth* **Sukkoth/Brush Arbors**.
7 *Gilead* **Gilad** is mine,
and *Manasseh* **Menash Sheh** is mine;
Ephraim **Ephrayim** also
is the *strength* **stronghold** of mine head;
Judah **Yah Hudah** is my *lawgiver* **statute setter**;
8 Moab is my *wash pot* **bath caldron**;
over Edom *will* **shall** I cast out my shoe:
Philistia **Pelesheth**, *triumph* **shout** thou because of me.
9 Who *will* **shall** bring me
into the *strong* city **with rampart**?
who *will* **shall** lead me into Edom?
10 *Wilt* **Shalt** not thou, O *God* **Elohim**,
which hadst cast us off?
and thou, O *God* **Elohim**,
which didst not go out with our *armies* **hosts**?
11 Give us help from *trouble* **tribulation**:
for vain is the *help* **salvation** of *man* **humanity**.
12 Through *God* **Elohim** we shall *do* **work** valiantly:
for he it is
that shall *tread down* **trample** our *enemies* **tribulators**.

61 To *the chief Musician* **His Eminence**,
upon *Neginah* **Strings**,
A Psalm of David.
1 Hear my *cry* **shouting**, O *God* **Elohim**;
attend **hearken** unto my prayer.
2 From the end of the earth
will I cry **shall I call** unto thee,
when my heart *is overwhelmed* **languisheth**:
lead me to the rock that is *higher* **loftier** than I.
3 For thou hast been a *shelter* **refuge** for me,
and a strong tower **a tower of strength**
from **the face of** the enemy.
4 I *will abide* **shall sojourn** in thy *tabernacle* **tent**
for ever **eternally**:
I *will trust* **shall seek refuge** in the covert of thy wings.
Selah.
5 For thou, O *God* **Elohim**, hast heard my vows:
thou hast given me the *heritage* **possession**
of those that *fear* **awe** thy name.
6 Thou *wilt prolong* **shalt add**
to the *king's life* **sovereign's days**:
and **to** his years
as many generations **generation to generation**.
7 He shall *abide before God* **settle at the face of Elohim**
for ever **eternally**:
O *prepare* **number** mercy and truth,
which may *preserve* **guard** him.
8 So *will I sing praise* **shall I psalm** unto thy name
for ever **eternally**,
that I may *daily perform* **day by day shalam** my vows.

62 To *the chief Musician* **His Eminence**,
to Jeduthun **Yeduthun/A Laudatory**, A Psalm of David.
1 Truly my soul *waiteth upon God* **is silent unto Elohim**:
from him *cometh* **be** my salvation.
2 He only is my rock and my salvation;
he is my defence **my secure loft**;
I shall not *be* **totter** greatly *moved*.
3 How long *will* **shall** ye
imagine mischief **assail** against a man?
ye shall be *slain* **murdered** all of you:
as a *bowing* **spread** wall *shall ye be*,
and as a tottering fence **— an overthrown wall**.
4 They only *consult* **counsel**
to *cast* **drive** him *down* from his *excellency* **exaltation**:
they *delight in lies* **lie to please**:
they bless with their mouth,
but they *curse* **abase** inwardly.
Selah.
5 My soul, *wait* **hush** thou only upon *God* **Elohim**;
for my *expectation* **hope** is from him.
6 He only is my rock and my salvation:
he is my defence **my secure loft**;
I shall not *be moved* **totter**.
7 In *God* **Elohim** is my salvation and my *glory* **honour**:
the rock of my strength, *and* my refuge,
is in *God* **Elohim**.
8 *Trust* **Confide** in him at all times;
ye people, pour out your heart *before him* **at his face**:
God **Elohim** is a refuge for us.
Selah.
9 Surely *men of low degree* **sons of humanity** are vanity,
and *men of high degree* **sons of men** are a lie:
to be *laid* **ascended** in the balance,
they are altogether *lighter than vanity* **vain**.
10 *Trust* **Confide** not in oppression,
and become not vain in robbery:
if *riches increase* **thy valuables flourish**,
set not your heart *upon them*.
11 *God* **Elohim** hath *spoken* **worded** once;
twice have I heard this;
that *power belongeth unto God* **strength be with Elohim**.
12 Also unto thee, O *Lord* **Adonay**, *belongeth* mercy:
for thou *renderest* **shalt shalam**
to *every man* **each** according to his work.

63 A Psalm of David,
when he was in the wilderness of *Judah* **Yah Hudah**.
1 O *God* **Elohim**, thou art my *God* **El**;
early *will* **shall** I seek thee:
my soul thirsteth for thee,
my flesh *longeth* **yearneth** for thee
in a *dry* **parched** and *thirsty* **languid** land,
where no **without** water *is*;
2 To see thy *power* **strength** and thy *glory* **honour**,
so as **thus** I have seen thee in the *sanctuary* **holies**.
3 Because thy *lovingkindness* **mercy** is better than life,
my lips shall *praise* **laud** thee.
4 Thus *will* **shall** I bless thee while I live:
I *will* **shall** lift *up* my *hands* **palms** in thy name.
5 My soul shall be satisfied
as *with* marrow and *fatness* **fat**;
and my mouth shall *praise* **halal** *thee*
with *joyful* **shouting** lips:
6 When I remember thee upon my bed,
and meditate on thee in the *night* watches.
7 Because thou hast been my help,
therefore in the shadow of thy wings
will I rejoice **shall I shout**.
8 My soul *followeth hard* **adhereth** after thee:
thy right *hand* upholdeth me.
9 But those that seek my soul, to *destroy it* **devastation**,
shall go into the *lower parts of the* **nethermost** earth.
10 They shall *fall* **flow** by **the hands of** the sword:
they shall *be a portion* **become an allotment** for foxes.
11 But the *king* **sovereign**
shall *rejoice* **cheer** in *God* **Elohim**;
every one that *sweareth* **oatheth** by him shall *glory* **halal**:
but the mouth of them that *speak lies* **word falsehoods**
shall be *stopped* **shut**.

64 To *the chief Musician* **His Eminence**,
A Psalm of David.
1 Hear my voice, O *God* **Elohim**,
in my *prayer* **meditation**:

preserve **guard** my life
from *fear* **dread** of the enemy.
2 Hide me
from the *secret* **private** counsel of the *wicked* **vilifiers**;
from the *insurrection* **conspiracy**
of the *workers* **doers** of *iniquity* **mischief**:
3 Who *whet* **pointen** their tongue like a sword,
and *bend their bows to shoot* **aim** their arrows,
even bitter words:
4 That they may shoot *in secret* **from the coverts**
at the *perfect* **integrious**:
suddenly *do* they shoot *at* him, and *fear* **awe** not.
5 They *encourage* **strengthen** themselves
in an evil *matter* **word**:
they *commune* **scribe** of *laying* **hiding** snares *privily*;
they say, Who shall see *them*?
6 They search out *iniquities* **wickednesses**;
in searching,
they *accomplish* **consumate** a *diligent* search:
both the inward *thought of every one of them* **man**
and the heart, is deep.
7 But *God* **Elohim** shall shoot at them with an arrow;
suddenly shall they be *wounded* **struck**.
8 So they shall *make* **trip upon** their own tongue
to fall upon themselve:
all that see them shall flee away.
9 And all *man* **humanity** shall *fear* **awe**,
and shall *declare* **tell** the *work* **deeds** of *God* **Elohim**;
for they shall
wisely consider of **comprehend** his *doing* **work**.
10 The *righteous* **just** shall *be glad* **cheer**
in *the LORD* **Yah Veh**,
and shall *trust* **seek refuge** in him;
and all the *upright* **straight** in heart shall *glory* **halal**.

65

To *the chief Musician* **His Eminence**,
A Psalm, *and* Song of David.
1 *Praise waiteth* **Halal is silent** for thee,
O *God* **Elohim**, in *Sion* **Siyon**:
and unto thee shall **they shalam** the vow *be performed*.
2 O thou that hearest prayer,
unto thee shall all flesh come.
3 *Iniquities* **Words of perversities**
prevail **mightily** against me:
as for our *transgressions* **rebellions**,
thou shalt *purge* **kapar/atone** them *away*.
4 *Blessed is the man* **Blithe be they** whom thou choosest,
and *causest to approach* **drawest nigh** *unto thee*,
that he may *dwell* **tabernacle** in thy courts:
we shall be satisfied with the goodness of thy house,
even of thy holy *temple* **manse**.
5 *By terrible things in righteousness* **In awesome justness**
wilt **shalt** thou answer us,
O *God* **Elohim** of our salvation;
who art the confidence of all the ends of the earth,
and of them that are afar off upon the sea:
6 Which by his *strength* **force**
setteth fast **establisheth** the mountains;
being girded with *power* **might**:
7 Which *stilleth* **laudeth** the *noise* **roaring** of the seas,
the *noise* **roaring** of their waves,
and the *tumult* **roar** of the *people* **nations**.
8 They also
that *dwell* **settle** in the *uttermost parts* **extremities**
are afraid **awe** at thy *tokens* **signs**:
thou makest the *outgoings* **risings**
of the morning and evening to *rejoice* **shout**.
9 Thou visitest the earth, and *waterest* **overflowest** it:
thou greatly enrichest it
with the *river* **rivulet** of *God* **Elohim**,
which is — full of water:
thou preparest them *corn* **crop**,
when thou hast so *provided* **prepared** for it.
10 Thou *waterest* **saturatest** the *ridges* **furrows**
thereof abundantly:
thou *settlest* **descendest in** the furrows *thereof*:
thou *makest* **dissolvest** it *soft* with showers:
thou blessest the *springing* **sprouting** *thereof*.
11 Thou crownest the year with thy goodness;
and thy *paths drop* **routes drip** fatness.
12 They *drop* **drip**
upon the *pastures* **folds** of the wilderness:
and the *little hills* **mountains**
rejoice on every side **are girt with twirling round about**.
13 The *pastures* **rams**
are *clothed* **enrobed** with flocks;
the valleys also
are *covered over* **shrouded** with *corn* **grain**;
they shout *for joy*, they *also* sing.

66

To *the chief Musician* **His Eminence**,
A Song *or* Psalm.
1 *Make a joyful noise* **Shout ye** unto *God* **Elohim**,
all ye *lands* **earth**:
2 *Sing* **Psalm** forth the honour of his name:
make **set** his *praise glorious* **halal honoured**.
3 Say unto *God* **Elohim**,
How *terrible art thou in* **awesome** thy works!
through the greatness of thy *power* **strength**
shall thine enemies *submit themselves* **emaciate** unto thee.
4 All the earth shall *worship* **prostrate unto** thee,
and shall *sing* **psalm** unto thee;
they shall *sing to* **psalm** thy name.
Selah.
5 Come and see the *works* **deeds** of *God* **Elohim**:
he is terrible in his doing **his awesome exploits**
toward the *children* **sons** of *men* **humanity**.
6 He turned the sea into dry *land*:
they *went* **passed** through the *flood* **river** on foot:
there did we *rejoice* **cheer** in him.
7 He *ruleth* **reigneth** by his *power* **might**
for ever **eternally**;
his eyes *behold* **watch** the *nations* **goyim**:
let not the *rebellious exalt* **revolters loft** themselves.
Selah.
8 O bless our *God* **Elohim**, ye people,
and *make* **have them hear**
the voice of his *praise* **halal** *to be heard*:
9 Which *holdeth* **setteth** our soul in life,
and *suffereth* **giveth** not our feet to *be moved* **topple**.
10 For thou, O *God* **Elohim**, hast *proved* **proofed** us:
thou hast *tried* **refined** us, as silver is *tried* **refined**.
11 Thou broughtest us into the *net* **stronghold**;
thou *laidst affliction* **settest oppression** upon our loins.
12 Thou hast caused men to ride over our heads;
we went through fire and *through* water:
but thou broughtest us out *into a wealthy place* **satiated**.
13 I *will* **shall** go into thy house
with *burnt offerings* **holocausts**:
I *will pay* **shall shalam** thee my vows,
14 Which my lips have *uttered* **gasped**,
and my mouth hath *spoken* **worded**,
when I was in *trouble* **tribulation**.
15 I *will offer* **shall holocaust** unto thee
burnt sacrifices **holocausts** of fatlings,
with the incense of rams;
I *will offer* **shall work** bullocks with **he** goats.
Selah.
16 Come and hear, all ye that *fear God* **awe Elohim**,
and I *will declare* **shall scribe**
what he hath *done* **worked** for my soul.
17 I *cried* **called** unto him with my mouth,
and he was *extolled with* **exalted under** my tongue.
18 If I *regard iniquity* **see mischief** in my heart,
the Lord will **Adonay shall** not hear me:
19 *But verily God* **Surely Elohim** hath heard *me*;
he hath *attended* **hearkened** to the voice of my prayer.
20 Blessed be *God* **Elohim**,
which hath not turned away my prayer,
nor his mercy from me.

67

To *the chief Musician* **His Eminence**,
on *Neginoth* **Strummer**,
A Psalm *or* Song.
1 *God be merciful* **Elohim grant charism** unto us,
and bless us;
and cause his face to *shine* **lighten** upon us;
Selah.
2 That thy way may be known upon earth,
thy *saving health* **salvation** among all *nations* **goyim**.

3 Let the people *praise* **extend hands unto** thee,
O *God* **Elohim**;
let all the people *praise* **extend hands unto** thee.
4 O let the nations *be glad* **cheer** and *sing for joy* **shout**:
for thou shalt judge the people *righteously* **straightly**,
and *govern* **lead** the nations upon earth.
Selah.
5 Let the people *praise* **extend hands unto** thee,
O *God* **Elohim**;
let all the people *praise* **extend hands unto** thee.
6 Then shall the earth *yield* **give** her *increase* **produce**;
and *God* **Elohim**,
even our own God **our Elohim**, shall bless us.
7 *God* **Elohim** shall bless us;
and all the *ends* **finality** of the earth shall *fear* **awe** him.

68 To *the chief Musician* **His Eminence**,
on *Neginoth* **Strummer**,
A Psalm *or* Song of David.
1 Let *God* **Elohim** arise, let his enemies be scattered:
let them also that hate him flee *before him* **from his face**.
2 As smoke is *driven away* **dispersed**, *so* drive them away:
as wax melteth *before* **at the face of** the fire,
so let the wicked *perish* **destruct**
at the *presence* **face** of *God* **Elohim**.
3 *But let the righteous be glad* **The just cheer**;
let them rejoice **they jump for joy**
before God **at the face of Elohim**:
yea, let them exceedingly **they cheerfully** rejoice.
4 Sing unto *God* **Elohim**, *sing praises* **psalm** to his name:
extol him that rideth upon the *heavens* **plains**
by his name *JAH* **Yah**,
and *rejoice before him* **jump for joy at his face**.
5 A father of the *fatherless* **orphan**,
and a *judge of* **pleader for** the widows,
is *God* **Elohim** in his holy habitation.
6 *God* **Elohim** setteth the *solitary* **lonely**
in *families* **households**:
he bringeth out those which are bound
with chains **into prosperity**:
but the *rebellious* **revolting**
dwell in a *dry land* **parch**.
7 O *God* **Elohim**,
when thou wentest forth
before **at the face of** thy people,
when thou *didst march* **pacest**
through the *wilderness* **desolation**;
Selah:
8 The earth *shook* **quaked**,
the heavens also dropped
at the *presence* **face** of *God* **Elohim**:
even Sinai itself was moved **thus also Sinay**
at the *presence* **face** of *God* **Elohim**,
the God **Elohim** of *Israel* **Ysra El**.
9 Thou, O *God* **Elohim**,
didst send a plentiful rain
hast shaken an abundant downpour,
whereby thou *didst confirm* **establishest** thine inheritance,
when it *was weary* **wearied**.
10 Thy *congregation hath dwelt therein* **lives have settled**:
thou, O *God* **Elohim**,
hast prepared of thy goodness for the *poor* **humble**.
11 *The Lord* **Adonay** gave the *word* **saying**:
great was the *company of those* **host**
that *published* **evangelized** it.
12 *Kings of armies did flee apace*
In fleeing, sovereigns of hosts fled:
and she *that tarried* **whose habitation of rest is** at home
divided **allotted** the spoil.
13 Though ye have *lien* **lain** among the *pots* **stalls**,
yet shall ye be as the
as wings of a dove covered with silver,
and her feathers **as pinions** with *yellow gold* **green ore**.
14 When *the Almighty* **Shadday**
scattered kings **spread sovereigns** in it,
it was *white as snow* **snowwhite** in Salmon.
15 The *hill* **mountain** of *God* **Elohim**
is as the *hill* **mountain** of Bashan;
an high hill **peaks of the mountain**
as the *hill* **mountain** of Bashan.
16 Why *leap* **stand** ye **guard**,
ye *high hills?* **peaks of the mountains**
this is the hill **— the mountain**
which God **Elohim** desireth to *dwell in;* **settle?**
yea, *the LORD will dwell* **Yah Veh shall tabernacle** in it
for ever **in perpetuity**.
17 The chariots of *God* **Elohim**
are *twenty thousand* **two myriads**,
even thousands of *angels* **reinforcements**:
the Lord **Adonay** is among them,
as in *Sinai* **Sinay**, in the *holy place* **holies**.
18 Thou hast ascended *on high* **the heights**,
thou hast *led captivity captive* **captured the captives**:
thou hast *received* **taken** gifts for *men* **humanity**;
yea, *for* the *rebellious* **revolters** also,
that *the LORD God* **Yah Elohim**
might *dwell among them* **tabernacle**.
19 Blessed be *the Lord* **Adonay**,
who *daily* **day by day** loadeth us *with benefits*,
even the God **— El** of our salvation.
Selah.
20 *He that is our God is the God of salvation*
El — our El of salvations;
and unto *GOD the Lord* **Yah Veh Adonay**
belong **be** the issues from death.
21 But *God* **Elohim**
shall *wound* **strike** the head of his enemies,
and the hairy scalp of such an one
as goeth on still in his *trespasses* **guilt**.
22 *The Lord* **Adonay** said,
I *will bring again* **shall return**
from Bashan,
I *will bring my people again* **shall return**
from the depths of the sea:
23 That thy foot may be *dipped* **stricken**
in the blood of thine enemies,
and the tongue of thy dogs in the same.
24 They have seen thy *goings* **ways**, O *God* **Elohim**;
even the *goings* **ways** of my *God* **El**, my *King* **Sovereign**,
in the *sanctuary* **holies**.
25 The singers *went before* **preceded**,
the *players on instruments followed* **strummers** after;
among them were the *damsels* **virgins**
playing with timbrels **tambourining**.
26 Bless ye *God* **Elohim** in the congregations,
even the Lord **Adonay**,
from the fountain of *Israel* **Yisra El**.
27 There is *little Benjamin* **insignificant Ben Yamin**
with their *ruler* **subjugator**,
the *princes* **governors** of *Judah* **Yah Hudah**
and their *council* **company**,
the *princes* **governors** of Zebulun,
and the *princes* **governors** of Naphtali.
28 Thy *God* **Elohim**
hath *commanded* **misvahed** thy strength:
strengthen, O *God* **Elohim**,
that which thou hast *wrought* **done** for us.
29 Because of thy *temple* **manse** at *Jerusalem* **Yeru Shalem**
shall *kings* **sovereigns** bring presents unto thee.
30 Rebuke the *company of spearmen* **live stalkers**,
the *multitude* **witnesses** of the *bulls* **mighty**,
with the calves of the people,
till every one submit himself **each prostrating**
with *pieces* **fragments** of silver:
scatter thou the people that delight in war.
31 *Princes* **Wealth** shall come out of *Egypt* **Misrayim**;
Ethiopia **Kush** shall *soon stretch out* **run** her hands
unto *God* **Elohim**.
32 Sing unto *God* **Elohim**,
ye *kingdoms* **sovereigndoms** of the earth;
O *sing praises* **psalm** unto *the Lord* **Adonay**;
Selah:
33 To him that rideth upon the heavens of **the** heavens,
which were of *old* **antiquity**;
lo **behold**, he *doth send out* **giveth** his voice,
and that a mighty voice **— a voice of strength**.
34 *Ascribe* **Give** ye strength unto *God* **Elohim**:
his *excellency* **pomp** is over *Israel* **Yisra El**,
and his strength is in the clouds.
35 *O God, thou art terrible* **Awesome, O Elohim**

out of thy *holy places* **hallowed refuge**:
the God of Israel **El of Yisra El** is he
that giveth strength and *power* **mights**
unto *his* **the** people.
Blessed be *God* **Elohim**.

69 To *the chief Musician* **His Eminence**,
upon *Shoshannim* **Trumpets**,
A Psalm of David.
1 Save me, O *God* **Elohim**;
for the waters are come in unto *my* **the** soul.
2 I sink in deep mire,
where there is no *standing* **foothold**:
I am come into *deep* **depths of** waters,
where the *floods* **streams** overflow me.
3 I am *weary* **belaboured** of my *crying* **calling**:
my throat is *dried* **scorched**:
mine eyes *fail* **are finished off**
while I *wait for* **await** my *God* **Elohim**.
4 They that hate me *without a cause* **gratuitously**
are more than the hairs of mine head
abound by the myriads:
they that *would destroy* **should exterminate** me,
being mine enemies *wrongfully* **of falseness**, are mighty:
then I restored that which I *took* **stripped** not *away*.
5 O *God* **Elohim**, thou knowest my *foolishness* **folly**;
and my *sins* **guiltinesses** are not *hid* **concealed** from thee.
6 Let not them that *wait on* **await** thee,
O *Lord GOD of hosts* **Adonay Yah Veh Sabaoth**,
be *ashamed* **shamed** for my sake:
let not those that seek thee
be confounded **shame** for my sake,
O *God* **Elohim** of *Israel* **Yisra El**.
7 Because for thy sake I have borne reproach;
shame hath covered my face.
8 I am become a stranger unto my brethren,
and *an alien* **a stranger** unto my mother's *children* **sons**.
9 For the zeal of thine house hath eaten me *up*;
and the reproaches of them that reproached thee
are fallen upon me.
10 When I wept,
and chastened my soul with fasting **in the fasting of my soul**,
that was to my reproach.
11 I *made sackcloth* **gave saq** also my *garment* **robe**;
and I became a proverb to them.
12 They that *sit* **settle** in the *gate* **portal**
speak **meditate** against me;
and I was the song
of *the drunkards* **them drinking intoxicants**.
13 But as for me,
my prayer is unto thee, O *LORD* **Yah Veh**,
in *an acceptable* **a pleasant** time:
O *God* **Elohim**,
in the *multitude* **abundance** of thy mercy *hear me* **answer**,
in the truth of thy salvation.
14 *Deliver* **Rescue** me out of the mire, and let me not sink:
let me be *delivered* **rescued** from them that hate me,
and out of the *deep* **depths of** waters.
15 Let not the *waterflood* **water streams** overflow me,
neither let the deep swallow me *up*,
and let not the *pit* **well** shut her mouth upon me.
16 *Hear me* **Answer**, O *LORD* **Yah Veh**;
for thy *lovingkindness* **mercy** is good:
turn unto **face** me
according to the *multitude* **abundance**
of thy tender mercies.
17 And hide not thy face from thy servant;
for I am *in trouble* **tribulated**:
hear **answer** me *speedily* **hastily**.
18 Draw nigh unto my soul, *and* redeem it:
deliver **redeem** me because of mine enemies.
19 Thou hast known my reproach,
and my shame, and my dishonour:
mine adversaries **my tribulators** are all before thee.
20 Reproach hath broken my heart;
and I am full of heaviness:
and I *looked for some* **awaited one** to *take pity* **wag**,
but there was none;
and for *comforters* **sighers**, but I found none.
21 They gave me also *gall for my meat* **rosh to chew**;
and in my thirst
they gave me *vinegar* **fermentation** to drink.
22 Let their table become a snare
before them **at their face**:
and *that which should have been* for their *welfare* **shalom**,
let it become a *trap* **snare**.
23 Let their eyes be darkened, that they see not;
and make their loins continually to *shake* **waver**.
24 Pour out *thine indignation* **thy rage** upon them,
and let thy *wrathful anger* **fuming wrath**
take hold of **overtake** them.
25 Let their *habitation be* **walls** desolate;
and let none *dwell* **settle** in their tents.
26 For they *persecute him* **pursue**
whom thou hast smitten;
and they *talk* **scribe** to the *grief* **sorrow**
of *those whom thou hast wounded* **thy pierced**.
27 *Add iniquity* **Give perversity**
unto **for** their *iniquity* **perversity**:
and let them not come into thy *righteousness* **justness**.
28 Let them be *blotted* **wiped** out
of *the book* **scroll** of the living,
and not be *written* **scribed** with the *righteous* **just**.
29 But I am *poor* **humble** and *sorrowful* **pained**:
let thy salvation, O *God* **Elohim**,
set me up on high **loft me**.
30 I *will praise* **shall halal** the name of *God* **Elohim**
with a song,
and *will magnify* **shall greaten** him
with *thanksgiving* **extended hands**.
31 This also shall **well**—please *the LORD* **Yah Veh**
better than an ox or bullock
that hath horns **horned** and *hoofs* **hoofed**.
32 The humble shall see *this*, and *be glad* **cheer**:
and your heart shall live that seek *God* **Elohim**.
33 For *the LORD* **Yah Veh** heareth the *poor* **needy**,
and despiseth not his *prisoners* **bound**.
34 Let the *heaven* **heavens** and earth *praise* **halal** him,
the seas, and *every thing* **all** that *moveth* **creepeth** *therein*.
35 For *God will* **Elohim shall** save *Zion* **Siyon**,
and *will* **shall** build the cities of *Judah* **Yah Hudah**:
that they may *dwell* **settle** there,
and *have* **possess** it *in possession*.
36 The seed also of his servants shall inherit it:
and they that love his name
shall *dwell* **tabernacle** *therein*.

70 To *the chief Musician* **His Eminence**,
A Psalm of David,
to *bring to remembrance* **remember**.
1 *Make haste*, O *God* **Elohim**, to *deliver* **rescue** me;
make haste **hasten** to help me, O *LORD* **Yah Veh**.
2 Let them *be ashamed* **shame** and *confounded* **blush**
that seek after my soul:
let them *be turned backward* **apostatize**,
and *put to confusion* **shame**,
that desire my *hurt* **evil**.
3 *Let them be turned back* **Return them**
for *a reward* **finality** of their shame that say, Aha, aha.
4 Let all those that seek thee
rejoice and *be glad* **cheer** in thee:
and let such as love thy salvation say continually,
Let God **Elohim** be *magnified* **greatened**.
5 But I am *poor* **humble** and needy:
make haste **hasten** unto me, O *God* **Elohim**:
thou art my help *and my deliverer* **who slippeth me away**;
O *LORD* **Yah Veh**, *make no tarrying* **tarry not**.

71 In thee, O *LORD* **Yah Veh**,
do I put my trust **I seek refuge**:
let me never be *put to confusion* **eternally shamed**.
2 *Deliver* **Rescue** me in thy *righteousness* **justness**,
and *cause me to escape* **slip me away**:
incline **extend** thine ear unto me, and save me.
3 Be thou my *strong* **rock — my** habitation,
whereunto I may continually resort:
thou hast *given commandment* **misvahed** to save me;
for thou art my rock and my *fortress* **stronghold**.
4 *Deliver me* **Slip me away**, O my *God* **Elohim**,
out of the *hand* **palm** of the wicked,

out of the hand
of the *unrighteous* **wicked** and *cruel* **embittered** *man.*
5 For thou art my hope, O *Lord GOD* **Adonay Yah Veh**:
thou art my *trust* **confidant** from my youth.
6 By thee have I been holden up from the *womb* **belly**:
thou art he
that *took* **cut** me out of my mother's *bowels* **inwards**:
my *praise* **halal** shall be continually of thee.
7 I am as *a wonder* **an omen** unto many;
but thou art my *strong* refuge **of strength**.
8 Let my mouth be filled with thy *praise* **halal**
and with thy *honour* **beauty** all the day.
9 Cast me not off in the time of old age;
forsake me not
when my *strength faileth* **force be finished off**.
10 For mine enemies *speak* **say** against me;
and they that *lay wait* **guard** for my soul
take counsel together,
11 Saying, *God* **Elohim** hath forsaken him:
persecute **pursue** and *take* **grab** him;
for there is none to *deliver him* **rescue**.
12 O *God* **Elohim**, be not far from me:
O my *God* **Elohim**, *make haste* **hasten** for my help.
13 Let them be *confounded* **shamed**
and *consumed* **finished off**
that are *adversaries* **satans** to my soul;
let them be covered with reproach and dishonour
that seek my *hurt* **evil**.
14 But I *will hope* **shall await** continually,
and *will yet praise* **shall halal** thee
more and more **increasingly**.
15 My mouth shall *shew forth* **scribe**
thy *righteousness* **justness** and thy salvation all the day;
for I know not the *numbers thereof* **scribing**.
16 I *will* **shall** go in the *strength* **might**
of *the Lord GOD* **Adonay Yah Veh**:
I *will make mention of* **shall remember**
thy *righteousness* **justness**, *even of* thine only.
17 O *God* **Elohim**, thou hast taught me from my youth:
and hitherto
have I *declared* **told** thy *wondrous works* **marvels**.
18 Now also when I am *old* **aged** and *greyheaded* **greyed**,
O *God* **Elohim**, forsake me not;
until I have *shewed thy strength* **told of thine arm**
unto *this* **a** generation,
and thy *power* **might** to every one that is to come.
19 Thy *righteousness* **justness** also, O *God* **Elohim**,
is *very high* **in the heights**,
who hast *done* **worked** great *things*:
O *God* **Elohim**, who is like unto thee!
20 Thou, which hast *shewed* me **see**
great and *sore troubles* **evil tribulations**,
shalt *quicken me again* **enliven me**,
and shalt *bring me up again* **ascend me**
from the *depths* **abysses** of the earth.
21 Thou shalt *increase* **abound** my greatness,
and *comfort* **surround** me *on every side* **and sigh**.
22 I *will* **shall** also *praise* **extend hands unto** thee
with the *psaltery* **instrument of bagpipe**,
even thy truth, O my *God* **Elohim**:
unto thee *will I sing* **shall I psalm** with the harp,
O thou Holy One of *Israel* **Yisra El**.
23 My lips shall *greatly rejoice* **shout**
when I *sing* **psalm** unto thee;
and my soul,
which thou hast redeemed.
24 My tongue also
shall *talk* **meditate** of thy *righteousness* **justness**
all the day long:
for they *are confounded* **shame**,
for they *are brought unto shame* **blush**,
that seek my *hurt* **evil**.

72

A Psalm for Solomon **For Shelomoh**.
1 Give the *king* **sovereign** thy judgments, O *God* **Elohim**,
and thy *righteousness* **justness**
unto the *king's* **sovereign's** son.
2 He shall *judge* **plead the cause of** thy people
with *righteousness* **justness**,
and thy *poor* **humble** with judgment.
3 The mountains shall *bring peace* **bear shalom**
to the people,
and the little hills, by *righteousness* **justness**.
4 He shall judge the *poor* **humble** of the people,
he shall save the *children* **sons** of the needy,
and shall *break in pieces* **crush** the oppressor.
5 They shall *fear* **awe** thee
as long as **at the face of** the sun and moon *endure*,
throughout all generations **generation to generation**.
6 He shall *come down* **descend** like rain
upon the mown *grass* **fleece**:
as showers that water the earth.
7 In his days shall the *righteous flourish* **just blossom**;
and abundance of *peace* **shalom**
so long as the moon endureth **until there be no moon**.
8 He shall *have dominion also* **subjugate** from sea to sea,
and from the river unto the *ends* **finalities** of the earth.
9 *They that dwell in the wilderness* **Desertdwellers**
shall *bow before him* **kneel at his face**;
and his enemies shall lick the dust.
10 The *kings* **sovereigns**
of Tarshish and of the *isles* **islands**
shall *bring presents* **return offerings**:
the *kings* **sovereigns** of Sheba and Seba
shall *offer gifts* **oblate their hire**.
11 Yea,
all *kings* **sovereigns** shall *fall down* **prostrate** before him:
all *nations* **goyim** shall serve him.
12 For he shall *deliver* **rescue** the needy when he crieth;
the *poor* **humble** also, and him that hath no helper.
13 He shall spare the poor and needy,
and shall save the souls of the needy.
14 He shall redeem their soul
from *deceit* **fraud** and violence:
and *precious* **esteemed** shall their blood be
in his *sight* **eyes**.
15 And he shall live,
and to him shall be given of the gold of Sheba:
prayer also shall be made for him **he shall be prayed for**
continually;
and daily **all day** shall he be *praised* **blessed**.
16 There shall be an *handful* **increase** of *corn* **grain**
in the earth upon the top of the mountains;
the fruit thereof shall *shake* **quake** like Lebanon:
and they of the city shall flourish
like *grass* **herbage** of the earth.
17 His name shall *endure for ever* **be eternal**:
his name shall be *continued as long as* **perpetuated**
at the face of the sun:
and *men* **they themselves** shall be blessed in him:
all *nations* **goyim** shall call him *blessed* **blithesome**.
18 Blessed be *the LORD God* **Yah Veh Elohim**,
the God **Elohim** of *Israel* **Yisra El**,
who *only doeth wondrous things* **alone worketh marvels**.
19 And blessed be his *glorious* **honoured** name
for ever **eternally**:
and let the whole earth be filled with his *glory* **honour**;
Amen, and Amen.
20 The prayers of David the son of *Jesse* **Yishay**
are *ended* **concluded**.

BOOK III

73

A Psalm of Asaph.
1 Truly *God* **Elohim** is good to *Israel* **Yisra El**,
even to such as are of a clean **to the pure of** heart.
2 But as for me, my feet were *almost gone* **spread**;
my steps had *well nigh slipped* **not poured**.
3 For I was envious at *the foolish* **them that halal**,
when I saw the *prosperity* **shalom** of the wicked.
4 For there are no bands in their death:
but their *strength* **might** is *firm* **fat**.
5 They are not in *trouble as other* **toil of** men;
neither are they *plagued* **touched** like *other men* **humans**.
6 Therefore *pride compasseth* **pomp choketh** them
about as a chain;
violence *covereth* **shroudeth** them
as a **masculine** garment.
7 Their eyes stand out with *fatness* **fat**:
they *have more than the heart could wish*
surpass the imagination of the heart.

8 They *are corrupt* **blaspheme,**
and *speak wickedly* **word evil** concerning oppression:
they *speak* **word** loftily.
9 They set their mouth against the heavens,
and their tongue walketh through the earth.
10 Therefore his people return hither:
and waters of *a full cup* **fulness** are wrung out to them.
11 And they say, How doth *God* **El** know?
and is there knowledge in *the most High* **Elyon**?
12 Behold, these are the *ungodly* **wicked,**
who *prosper in the world* **be eternally serene;**
they increase in *riches* **valuables.**
13 Verily I have *cleansed* **purified** my heart in vain,
and washed my *hands* **palms** in innocency.
14 For all the day long have I been *plagued* **touched,**
and *chastened every morning* **reproofed mornings.**
15 If I say, I *will speak* **shall scribe** thus;
behold, I should *offend* **deal covertly**
against **with** the generation of thy *children* **sons.**
16 When I *thought* **fabricated** to know this,
it was *too painful for me* **toilsome in mine eyes;**
17 Until I went
into the *sanctuary* **hallowed refuge** of *God* **El;**
then *understood* **discerned** I their *end* **finality.**
18 Surely thou didst set them in *slippery* **smooth** places:
thou castedst them down into *destruction* **ruins.**
19 How are they *brought* into desolation,
as in a *moment* **blink!**
in consuming, they are *utterly* consumed with terrors.
20 As a dream *when one awaketh* **upon awakening;**
so, O *Lord* **Adonay,** when thou awakest,
thou shalt despise their image.
21 Thus my heart *was grieved* **embittered**
and I was pricked in my reins.
22 So *foolish* **stupid** was I, and *ignorant* **knew not:**
I was as *a beast* **an animal** before thee.
23 Nevertheless I am continually with thee:
thou hast holden me by my right hand.
24 Thou shalt *guide* **lead** me with thy counsel,
and afterward *receive* **take** me to *glory* **honour.**
25 Whom have I in *heaven but thee* **the heavens?**
and there is none upon earth that I desire beside thee.
26 My flesh and my heart *faileth* **finisheth off:**
but *God* **Elohim** is the *strength* **rock** of my heart,
and my *portion for ever* **allotment eternally.**
27 For, *lo* **behold,**
they that are far from thee shall *perish* **destruct:**
thou hast *destroyed* **exterminated** all them
that *go a whoring* **whore** from thee.
28 But it is good for me to draw near to *God* **Elohim:**
I have put my *trust* **refuge**
in *the Lord GOD* **Adonay Yah Veh,**
that I may *declare* **scribe** all thy works.

74

Maschil **On Comprehension** of Asaph.
1 O *God* **Elohim,**
why hast thou cast us off *for ever* **in perpetuity?**
why doth *thine anger* **thy wrath** smoke
against the *sheep* **flock** of thy pasture?
2 Remember thy *congregation* **witness,**
which thou hast *purchased* **chattelized** of *old* **antiquity;**
the *rod* **scion** of thine inheritance,
which thou hast redeemed;
this mount *Zion* **Siyon,**
wherein thou hast *dwelt* **tabernacled.**
3 Lift up thy *feet* **steps**
unto the perpetual *desolations* **ruins;**
even all that the enemy hath *done wickedly* **vilified**
in the *sanctuary* **holies.**
4 *Thine enemies* **Thy tribulators** roar
in the midst of thy congregations;
they set up their ensigns for signs.
5 *A man was famous* **He was known**
according as he had lifted up axes upon the thick trees.
6 But now they *break down* **hammer**
the *carved work* **engravings** *thereof*
at once **together** with axes and **sledge** hammers.
7 They have *cast* **sent** fire
into thy *sanctuary* **hallowed refuge**
they have *defiled by casting down* **profaned**
the *dwelling place* **tabernacle** of thy name
to the *ground* **earth.**
8 They said in their hearts,
Let us *destroy* **oppress** them together:
they have burned *up*
all the *synagogues* **congregations** of *God* **El** in the land.
9 We see not our signs: there is no more any prophet:
neither is there among us
any that knoweth *how long* **until when.**
10 O *God* **Elohim,** *how long* **until when**
shall the *adversary* **tribulator** reproach?
shall the enemy *blaspheme* **scorn** thy name
for ever **in perpetuity?**
11 Why *withdrawest* **turnest** thou thy hand,
even thy right *hand?*
pluck **finish** it out of thy bosom.
12 For *God* **Elohim** is my *King* **Sovereign** of *old* **antiquity,**
working **doing** salvation in the midst of the earth.
13 Thou *didst divide* **brakest** the sea
by thy strength:
thou brakest the heads of the *dragons* **monsters**
in the waters.
14 Thou *brakest* **crushest** the heads of leviathan *in pieces,*
and gavest him *to be meat* **for food** to the people
inhabiting the wilderness **— the desertdwellers.**
15 Thou *didst cleave* **splittest**
the fountain and the *flood* **wadi:**
thou driedst up *mighty* **perrenial** rivers.
16 The day is thine, the night also is thine:
thou hast prepared the light and the sun.
17 Thou hast *set* **stationed** all the borders of the earth:
thou hast *made* **formed** summer and winter.
18 Remember this,
that the enemy hath reproached, O *LORD* **Yah Veh,**
and that the foolish people
have *blasphemed* **scorned** thy name.
19 O *deliver* **give** not the soul of thy turtledove
unto the *multitude of the wicked* **live beings:**
forget not the *congregation* **lives** of thy *poor* **humble**
for ever **in perpetuity.**
20 *Have respect* **Look** unto the covenant:
for the *dark places* **darknesses** of the earth
are full of the *habitations* **folds** of *cruelty* **violence.**
21 O let not the oppressed return *ashamed* **shamed:**
let the *poor* **humble** and needy *praise* **halal** thy name.
22 Arise, O *God* **Elohim,**
plead **defend** thine own *cause* **defence:**
remember *how the foolish man reproacheth thee daily*
your reproach of the fool all the day.
23 Forget not the voice of *thine enemies* **thy tribulators:**
the *tumult* **roaring** of those that rise *up against thee*
increaseth **ascendeth** continually.

75

To *the chief Musician* **His Eminence,**
Al—taschith **Al Taschcheth/Ruin Not,**
A Psalm *or* Song of Asaph.
1 Unto thee, O *God* **Elohim,**
do we give thanks **we extend hands,**
unto thee do we give thanks **we extend hands:**
for that thy name is near
thy *wondrous works declare* **marvels scribe.**
2 When I shall *receive* **take** the congregation
I *will* **shall** judge *uprightly* **in straightnesses.**
3 The earth
and all *the inhabitants thereof* **that settle therein**
are dissolved:
I *bear up* **gauge** the pillars of it.
Selah.
4 I said unto *the fools* **them that halal,**
Deal not foolishly **Halal not:**
and to the wicked, Lift not up the horn:
5 Lift not up your horn *on high* **to the heights:**
speak not with a stiff **or word with an impudent** neck.
6 For *promotion cometh* **the mount of exaltation**
is neither from the *east* **source,**
nor from *the west* **duskward,**
nor from the *south* **wilderness.**
7 But *God* **Elohim** is the judge:
he *putteth down* **abaseth** one,
and *setteth up* **exalteth** another.

8 For in the hand of *the LORD* **Yah Veh** there is a cup,
and the wine *is red* **foameth**; it is full of mixture;
and he poureth out *of the same* **thus**:
but the dregs *thereof,*
all the wicked of the earth
shall wring them out, and drink them.
9 But I *will declare for ever* **shall tell eternally**;
I will sing praises **I shall psalm**
to *the God* **Elohim** of *Jacob* **Yaaqov**.
10 All the horns of the wicked also *will* **shall** I cut off;
but the horns of the *righteous* **just** shall be exalted.

76 To *the chief Musician* **His Eminence,**
on *Neginoth* **Strummer**,
A Psalm *or* Song of Asaph.
1 In *Judah* **Yah Hudah** is *God* **Elohim** known:
his name is great in *Israel* **Yisra El**.
2 In Salem also *is* **are** his *tabernacle* **sukkoth/brush arbors**,
and his *dwelling place* **habitation** in *Zion* **Siyon**.
3 There brake he the *arrows* **burning flash** of the bow,
the *shield* **buckler**, and the sword, and the *battle* **war**.
Selah.
4 Thou art more *glorious* **lightened** and *excellent* **mighty**
than the mountains of prey.
5 The *stouthearted* **mighty of heart** are spoiled,
they have *slept* **slumbered** their sleep:
and none of the men of *might* **valour**
have found their hands.
6 At thy rebuke, O *God* **Elohim** of *Jacob* **Yaaqov**,
both the chariot and horse
are cast into a dead sleep **sleep soundly**.
7 Thou, *even* thou, art *to be feared* **awesome**:
and who may stand *in thy sight* **at the face of thine eyes**
when once thou art angry **since thy wrath**?
8 Thou didst cause *judgment* **their plea**
to be heard from *heaven* **the heavens**;
the earth *feared* **awed**, and *was still* **rested**,
9 When *God* **Elohim** arose to judgment,
to save all the *meek* **humble** of the earth.
Selah.
10 Surely the *wrath* **fury** of *man* **humanity**
shall *praise* **extend hands unto** thee:
the *remainder* **survivors** of *wrath* **fury**
shalt thou *restrain* **gird**.
11 Vow, and *pay* **shalam**
unto *the LORD* **Yah Veh** your *God* **Elohim**:
let all that be round about him bring presents
unto *him that ought to be feared* **the awesome one**.
12 He shall cut off the spirit of *princes* **the eminent**:
he is *terrible* **awesome**
to the *kings* **sovereigns** of the earth.

77 To *the chief Musician* **His Eminence,**
to Jeduthun **Yeduthun/A Laudatory**, A Psalm of Asaph.
1 I cried unto *God* **Elohim** with my voice,
even unto *God* **Elohim** with my voice;
and he *gave ear* **hearkened** unto me.
2 In the day of my *trouble* **tribulation**
I sought *the Lord* **Adonay**:
my *sore* **hand** ran in the night, and *ceased* **exhaled** not:
my soul refused to *be comforted* **sigh**.
3 I remembered *God* **Elohim**, and *was troubled* **roared**:
I *complained* **meditated**,
and my spirit *was overwhelmed* **languished**.
Selah.
4 Thou holdest mine *eyes waking* **eye guards**:
I am so *troubled* **agitated** that I cannot *speak* **word**.
5 I have *considered* **fabricated** the days of *old* **antiquity**,
the years of *ancient times* **eternity**.
6 I *call to remembrance* **remember** my *song* **strumming**
in the night:
I *commune* **meditate** with mine own heart:
and my spirit *made diligent search* **searched**.
7 *Will the Lord* **Shall Adonay** cast off *for ever* **eternally**?
and *will he be favourable no more*
shall he never again be pleased?
8 Is his mercy *clean gone for ever* **ceased in perpetuity**?
doth his *promise fail* **saying cease**
for evermore **generation to generation**?
9 Hath *God* **El** forgotten to *be gracious* **grant charism**?
hath he in *anger* **wrath** shut up his tender mercies?
Selah.
10 And I said, This is my *infirmity* **stroke**:
but I will remember
— the years of the right *hand* of *the most High* **Elyon**.
11 I *will* **shall** remember
the *works* **exploits** of *the LORD* **Yah**:
surely I *will* **shall** remember thy *wonders* **marvels**
of *old* **antiquity**.
12 I *will* **shall** meditate also of all thy *work* **deeds**,
and *talk* **meditate** of thy *doings* **exploits**.
13 Thy way, O *God* **Elohim**, is in the *sanctuary* **holies**:
who is so great *a God* **an El** as *our God* **Elohim**?
14 Thou art *the God* **El**
that *doest wonders* **workest marvels**:
thou hast *declared* **made known** thy strength
among the people.
15 Thou hast with thine arm redeemed thy people,
the sons of *Jacob* **Yaaqov** and *Joseph* **Yoseph**.
Selah.
16 The waters saw thee, O *God* **Elohim**,
the waters saw thee; they *were afraid* **writhed**:
the depths also *were troubled* **quaked**.
17 The **thick** clouds *poured out* **flooded** water:
the *skies sent out a sound* **vapours gave voice**:
thine arrows also went abroad.
18 The voice of thy thunder
was in the *heaven* **whirlwind**:
the lightnings lightened the world:
the earth *trembled* **quivered** and *shook* **quaked**.
19 Thy way is in the sea,
and thy path in the great waters,
and thy *footsteps* **heelprints** are not known.
20 Thou leddest thy people like a flock
by the hand of *Moses* **Mosheh** and *Aaron* **Aharon**.

78 *Maschil* **A Discerning** of Asaph.
1 *Give ear* **Hearken**, O my people, to my *law* **torah**:
incline **extend** your ears
to the *words* **sayings** of my mouth.
2 I *will* **shall** open my mouth in a *parable* **proverb**:
I *will utter dark sayings* **shall gush riddles** of *old* **antiquity**:
3 Which we have heard and known,
and our fathers have *told* **scribed unto** us.
4 We *will* **shall** not *hide* **conceal them**
from their *children* **sons**,
shewing **scribing** to the generation *to come* **after**
the *praises* **halals** of *the LORD* **Yah Veh**,
and his strength, and his *wonderful works* **marvels**
that he hath *done* **worked**.
5 For he *established* **raised** a *testimony* **witness**
in *Jacob* **Yaaqov**,
and *appointed* **set** a *law* **torah** in *Israel* **Yisra El**,
which he *commanded* **misvahed** our fathers,
that they should make them known to their *children* **sons**:
6 That the generation *to come* **after** might know them,
even the children which should — **the sons to** be born;
who should arise
and *declare* **scribe** them to their *children* **sons**:
7 That they might set their hope in *God* **Elohim**,
and not forget the works of *God* **El**,
but *keep* **guard** his *commandments* **misvoth**:
8 And might not be as their fathers,
a *stubborn* **revolting** and rebellious generation;
a generation that *set* **prepared** not their heart *aright*,
and whose spirit
was not *stedfast* **trustworthy** with *God* **El**.
9 The *children* **sons** of *Ephraim* **Ephrayim**,
being armed, *and carrying* **hurling** bows,
turned back in the day of battle.
10 They *kept* **guarded** not the covenant of *God* **Elohim**,
and refused to walk in his *law* **torah**;
11 And forgat his *works* **exploits**,
and his *wonders* **marvels** that he had *shewed* them **see**.
12 *Marvellous things did* **Marvels worked** he
in *the sight* **front** of their fathers,
in the land of *Egypt* **Misrayim**, in the field of *Zoan* **Soan**.
13 He *divided* **split** the sea,
and *caused* **passed** them *to pass* through;
and he *made* **stationed** the waters *to stand* as an heap.

14 In the *daytime* **day** also he led them with a cloud,
and all the night with a light of fire.
15 He *clave* **split** the rocks in the wilderness,
and gave them drink as out of the great *depths* **abysses**.
16 He brought *streams* **flows** also out of the rock,
and caused waters to *run down* **descend** like rivers.
17 And they sinned yet *more* **again** against him
by *provoking the most High* **rebelling against Elyon**
in the *wilderness* **parch**.
18 And they *tempted God* **tested El** in their heart
by asking *meat* **food** for their *lust* **soul**.
19 Yea, they *spake* **worded** against *God* **Elohim**;
they said,
Can God furnish **Arrangeth El** a table in the wilderness?
20 Behold, he smote the rock,
that the waters *gushed out* **flowed**,
and the *streams* **wadies** overflowed;
can he give **giveth he** bread also?
can he provide **prepareth he** flesh for his people?
21 Therefore *the LORD* **Yah Veh** heard this,
and was wroth:
so a fire was kindled against *Jacob* **Yaaqov**,
and *anger* **wrath**
also *came up* **ascended** against *Israel* **Yisra El**;
22 Because they *believed* **trusted** not in *God* **Elohim**,
and *trusted* **confided** not in his salvation:
23 Though he had
commanded **misvahed** the *clouds* **vapours** from above,
and opened the doors of *heaven* **the heavens**,
24 And had rained down manna upon them to eat,
and had given them
of the *corn* **crop** of *heaven* **the heavens**.
25 Man *did eat angels' food* **ate the bread of the mighty**:
he sent them *meat* **hunt** to *the full* **satiate**.
26 He *caused an east wind to blow* **plucked an easterly**
in the *heaven* **heavens**:
and by his *power* **strength**
he *brought in* **drove** the *south wind* **southerly**.
27 He rained flesh also upon them as dust,
and *feathered fowls* **winged flyers**
like as the sand of the sea:
28 And he *let it fall* **felled them** in the midst of their camp,
round about their *habitations* **tabernacles**.
29 So they did eat, and were *well filled* **mightily satiated**:
for he gave them their own desire;
30 They were not estranged from their *lust* **desire**.
But while their *meat* **food** was yet in their mouths,
31 The wrath of *God came* **Elohim ascended** upon them,
and *slew* **slaughtered** the fattest of them,
and *smote the chosen men* **caused the youths**
of *Israel* **Yisra El to kneel**.
32 For all this they sinned still,
and *believed* **trusted** not for his *wondrous works* **marvels**.
33 Therefore their days
did he consume **he finished off** in vanity,
and their years in *trouble* **terror**.
34 When he *slew* **slaughtered** them,
then they sought him:
and they returned
and *enquired* **sought** early after *God* **El**.
35 And they remembered
that *God* **Elohim** was their rock,
and *the high God* **El Elyon** their redeemer.
36 *Nevertheless* **But**
they *did flatter* **duped** him with their mouth,
and they lied unto him with their tongues.
37 For their heart was not *right* **established** with him,
neither were they *stedfast* **trustworthy** in his covenant.
38 But he, *being full of compassion* **the merciful**,
forgave **did kapar/atone** their *iniquity* **perversity**,
and *destroyed* **ruined** them not:
yea, many a time **and he abounded**
turned he his anger away **to turn his wrath**,
and *did not stir up all* **wakened not** his *wrath* **fury**.
39 For he remembered that they were *but* flesh;
a wind that passeth *away*,
and *cometh not again* **returneth not**.
40 How oft did they *provoke* **rebel against** him
in the wilderness,
and *grieve* **contort** him in the *desert* **desolation**!
41 Yea, they turned back and *tempted God* **tested El**,
and *limited* **branded** the Holy One of *Israel* **Yisra El**.
42 They remembered not his hand,
nor the day when he *delivered* **redeemed** them
from the *enemy* **tribulator**.
43 How he had *wrought* **set** his signs in *Egypt* **Misrayim**,
and his *wonders* **omens** in the field of *Zoan* **Soan**:
44 And had turned their rivers into blood;
and their *floods* **flows**, that they could not drink.
45 He sent *divers sorts of flies* **swarms** among them,
which devoured them;
and frogs, which *destroyed* **ruined** them.
46 He gave also
their *increase* **produce** unto the caterpiller,
and their labour unto the locust.
47 He *destroyed* **slaughtered** their vines with hail,
and their sycomore trees with *frost* **aphis**.
48 He *gave* **shut** up their *cattle also* **beasts** to the hail,
and their *flocks* **chattel**
to *hot thunderbolts* **burning flashes**.
49 He *cast* **sent** upon them
the fierceness of his *anger* **fuming wrath**,
wrath **fury**, and *indignation* **rage**, and *trouble* **tribulation**,
by sending evil angels *among them*.
50 He *made a way* **weighed a path** to his *anger* **wrath**;
he spared not their soul from death,
but *gave* **shut up** their life *over* to the pestilence;
51 And smote all the firstborn in *Egypt* **Misrayim**;
the *chief* **firstfruits** of their strength
in the *tabernacles* **tents** of Ham:
52 But made his own *people*
to *go forth* **pull stakes** like *sheep* **a flock**,
and *guided* **drove** them in the wilderness
like a *flock* **drove**.
53 And he led them on *safely* **confidently**,
so that they *feared* **dreaded** not:
but the sea *overwhelmed* **covered over** their enemies.
54 And he brought them
to the border of his *sanctuary* **holies**,
even to — this mountain,
which his right *hand* had *purchased* **chattelized**.
55 He *cast out* **exiled** the *heathen also* **goyim**
before them **from their face**,
and *divided* **felled** them an inheritance by line,
and made the *tribes* **scions** of *Israel* **Yisra El**
to dwell **tabernacle** in their tents.
56 Yet they *tempted* **tested** and *provoked* **rebelled**
the most high God **against Elohim Elyon**,
and *kept* **guarded** not his *testimonies* **witnesses**:
57 But *turned back* **apostatized**,
and dealt *unfaithfully* **covertly** like their fathers:
they were turned aside like a deceitful bow.
58 For they *provoked* **vexed** him *to anger*
with their *high places* **bamahs**,
and moved him to jealousy
with their *graven images* **sculptiles**.
59 When *God* **Elohim** heard this, he was wroth,
and *greatly abhorred Israel* **mightily spurned Yisra El**:
60 So that he forsook the tabernacle of Shiloh,
the tent
which he *placed* **tabernacled** among *men* **humanity**;
61 And *delivered* **gave** his strength into captivity,
and his *glory* **beauty** into the *enemy's* **tribulator's** hand.
62 He *gave* **shut up** his people *over* also unto the sword;
and *was wroth with* **passed over** his inheritance.
63 The fire consumed their *young men* **youths**;
and their *maidens* **virgins**
were not *given to marriage* **halaled**.
64 Their priests fell by the sword;
and their widows *made no lamentation* **wept not**.
65 Then *the Lord* **Adonay** awaked as *one* out of sleep,
and like *a* **the** mighty *man*
that shouteth *by reason* of wine.
66 And he smote his *enemies* **tribulators**
in the hinder parts **behind**:
he *put* **gave** them to *a perpetual* **an eternal** reproach.
67 Moreover
he *refused* **spurned** the *tabernacle* **tent** of *Joseph* **Yoseph**,
and chose not the *tribe* **scion** of *Ephraim* **Ephrayim**:
68 But chose the *tribe* **scion** of *Judah* **Yah Hudah**,

the mount *Zion* **Siyon** which he loved.
69 And he built his *sanctuary* **hallowed refuge**
like high palaces **lofty,**
like the earth
which he hath *established for ever* **founded eternally**.
70 He chose David also his servant,
and took him from the *sheepfolds* **flock folds**:
71 *From following the ewes* **After the sucklings**
great with young
he brought him to *feed Jacob* **tend Yaaqov** his people,
and *Israel* **Yisra El** his inheritance.
72 So he *fed* **tended** them
according to the integrity of his heart;
and *guided* **led** them
by the *skilfulness* **discernment** of his *hands* **palms**.

79 A Psalm of Asaph.
O *God* **Elohim**,
the *heathen* **goyim** are come into thine inheritance;
thy holy *temple* **manse** have they *defiled* **fouled**;
they have *laid Jerusalem* **set Yeru Shalem** on heaps.
2 The *dead bodies* **carcases** of thy servants
have they given *to be meat* **for food**
unto the *fowls* **flyers** of the *heaven* **heavens**,
the flesh of thy *saints* **mercied**
unto the *beasts* **live beings** of the earth.
3 Their blood have they *shed* **poured** like water
round about *Jerusalem* **Yeru Shalem**;
and there was none to *bury them* **entomb**.
4 We are become a reproach
to our *neighbours* **fellow tabernaclers**,
a *scorn* **derision** and *derision* **ridicule**
to them that are round about us.
5 How long, *LORD* **O Yah Veh**?
wilt **shalt** thou be angry *for ever* **in perpetuity**?
shall thy jealousy burn like fire?
6 Pour out thy *wrath* **fury**
upon the *heathen* **goyim**
that have not known thee,
and upon the *kingdoms* **sovereigndoms**
that have not called upon thy name.
7 For they have devoured *Jacob* **Yaaqov**,
and *laid waste* **desolated**
his *dwelling place* **habitation of rest**.
8 O remember not against us
former iniquities **first perversities**:
let thy tender mercies
speedily prevent **hastily anticipate** us:
for we are *brought very low* **mightily languished**.
9 Help us, O *God* **Elohim** of our salvation,
for the *glory* **word of the honour** of thy name:
and *deliver* **rescue** us,
and *purge away* **kapar/atone** our sins,
for thy name's sake.
10 Wherefore should the *heathen* **goyim** *say*,
Where is their *God* **Elohim**?
let him be known among the *heathen* **goyim** in our sight
by the *revenging* **vengeance** of the blood of thy servants
which is *shed* **poured**.
11 Let the *sighing* **shrieking** of the *prisoner* **bound**
come before thee **be at thy face**;
according to the greatness of *thy power* **thine arm**
preserve thou those that are appointed to die
let the sons of death remain;
12 And *render* **return**
unto our *neighbours* **fellow tabernaclers** sevenfold
into their bosom their reproach,
wherewith they have reproached thee, O *Lord* **Adonay**.
13 So we thy people and *sheep* **flock** of thy pasture
will give thee thanks **shall extend hands unto thee**
for ever **eternally**:
we *will shew forth* **shall scribe** thy *praise* **halal**
to all generations **generation to generation**.

80 To *the chief Musician* **His Eminence**,
upon *Sho—shannim—Eduth* **Trumpets of Witness**,
A Psalm of Asaph.
1 *Give ear* **Hearken**, O *Shepherd* **Raah** of *Israel* **Yisra El**,
thou that *leadest Joseph* **drivest Yoseph** like a flock;
thou that *dwellest* **settlest**
between **among** the *cherubims* **cherubim**,
shine forth.
2 *Before Ephraim* **At the face of Ephrayim**
and *Benjamin* **Ben Yamin** and *Manasseh* **Menash Sheh**
stir up **waken** thy *strength* **might**,
and come *and save us* **be our salvation**.
3 *Turn us again* **Return to us**, O *God* **Elohim**,
and cause thy face to *shine* **lighten**;
and we shall be saved.
4 O *LORD God of hosts* **Yah Veh Elohim Sabaoth**,
how long *wilt* **shalt** thou *be angry* **fume**
against the prayer of thy people?
5 Thou feedest them with the bread of tears;
and givest them **triple** tears to drink *in great measure*.
6 Thou *makest* **settest** us a strife unto our neighbours:
and our enemies *laugh* **deride** among themselves.
7 *Turn us again* **Return us**,
O *LORD God of hosts* **Yah Veh Elohim Sabaoth**,
and *cause* **lighten** thy face *to shine*;
and we shall be saved.
8 Thou hast *brought* **plucked** a vine
out of *Egypt* **Misrayim**:
thou hast *cast out* **exiled** the *heathen* **goyim**,
and planted it.
9 *Thou preparedst room before it*
In facing, thou hast faced,
and **in rooting,** didst cause it to *take deep* root,
and it filled the land.
10 The *hills* **mountains** were covered
with the shadow of it,
and the *boughs thereof* **branches**
were like the *goodly* cedars **of El**.
11 She sent out her *boughs* **harvest** unto the sea,
and her branches unto the river.
12 Why hast thou then
broken down **breached** her *hedges* **walls**,
so that all they which pass by the way *do* pluck her?
13 The *boar* **hog** out of the *wood* **forest**
doth waste **wasteth** it,
and the *wild beast* **creature** of the field
doth devour **tendeth** it.
14 Return, we beseech thee,
O *God of hosts* **Elohim Sabaoth**:
look down from *heaven* **the heavens**,
and *behold* **see**, and visit this vine;
15 And the *vineyard* **plant**
which thy right *hand* hath planted,
and the *branch* **son**
that thou *madest strong* **strengthened** for thyself.
16 *It is* — burned with fire, *it is* — cut down:
they *perish* **destruct**
at the rebuke of thy *countenance* **face**.
17 Let thy hand be upon the man of thy right *hand*,
upon the son of *men* **humanity**
whom thou *madest strong* **strengthened** for thyself.
18 So *will* **shall** not we go *back* **apostatize** from thee:
quicken **enliven** us, and we *will* **shall** call upon thy name.
19 *Turn us again* **Return us**,
O *LORD God of hosts* **Yah Veh Elohim Sabaoth**,
cause thy face to *shine* **lighten**; and we shall be saved.

81 To *the chief Musician* **His Eminence**,
upon Gittith, *A Psalm* of Asaph.
1 *Sing aloud* **Shout** unto *God* **Elohim**
our strength:
make a joyful noise **shout** unto *the God* **Elohim**
of *Jacob* **Yaaqov**.
2 *Take* **Lift** a psalm,
and *bring hither* **give** the *timbrel* **tambourine**,
the pleasant harp with the *psaltery* **bagpipe**.
3 *Blow up* **Blast** the trumpet in the new moon,
in the *time appointed* **full moon**,
on our *solemn feast* **celebration** day.
4 For this was a statute for *Israel* **Yisra El**,
and a *law* **judgment** of *the God* **Elohim** of *Jacob* **Yaaqov**.
5 This he *ordained* **set** in *Joseph* **Yoseph**
for a *testimony* **witness**,
when he went out through the land of *Egypt* **Misrayim**:
where I heard a *language* **lip** that I *understood* **knew** not.
6 I *removed* **turned aside** his shoulder

from the burden:
his *hands were delivered* **palms passed away**
from the *pots* **boilers**.
7 Thou calledst in *trouble* **tribulation**,
and I *delivered* **rescued** thee;
I answered thee in the *secret place* **covert** of thunder:
I *proved* **proofed** thee at the waters of *Meribah* **Strife**.
Selah.
8 Hear, O my people,
and I *will testify* **shall witness** unto thee:
O *Israel* **Yisra El**, if thou *wilt* **shalt** hearken unto me;
9 There shall no strange *god* **el** be in thee;
neither shalt thou *worship* **prostrate**
to any strange *god* **el**.
10 I *am the LORD* — **Yah Veh** thy *God* **Elohim**,
which *brought* **ascended** thee
out of the land of *Egypt* **Misrayim**:
open **enlarge** thy mouth *wide*, and I *will* **shall** fill it.
11 But my people *would* **willed**
to not hearken to my voice;
and *Israel would* **Yisra El had** none of me.
12 So I *gave* **sent** them *up*
unto *their own hearts' lust* **the warp of their heart**:
and they walked in their own counsels.
13 Oh that my people had hearkened unto me,
and *Israel* **Yisra El** had walked in my ways!
14 I should *soon* **shortly** have subdued their enemies,
and turned my hand against their *adversaries* **tribulators**.
15 The haters of *the LORD* **Yah Veh**
should have submitted themselves unto
emaciated before him:
but their time
should have *endured for ever* **become eternal**.
16 He should have fed them also
with the *finest* **fat** of the wheat:
and with honey out of the rock
should I have satisfied thee.

82

A Psalm of Asaph.
1 *God standeth* **Elohim stationeth**
in the *congregation* **witness** of *the mighty* **El**;
he judgeth among the *gods* **elohim**.
2 How long *will* **shall** *ye* judge *unjustly* **wickedly**,
and *accept* **lift** the *persons* **faces** of the wicked?
Selah.
3 *Defend* **Judge** the poor and *fatherless* **orphan**:
do justice to **justify**
the *afflicted* **humble** and *needy* **impoverished**.
4 *Deliver* **Slip away** the poor and needy:
rid **rescue** them out of the hand of the wicked.
5 They know not,
neither *will* **shall** they *understand* **discern**;
they walk on in darkness:
all the foundations of the earth *are out of course* **totter**.
6 I have said, Ye are *gods* **elohim**;
and all of you are *children* **sons** of *the most High* **Elyon**.
7 *But* ye shall **surely** die like *men* **humanity**,
and fall like one of the *princes* **governors**.
8 Arise, O *God* **Elohim**, judge the earth:
for thou shalt inherit all *nations* **goyim**.

83

A Song *or* Psalm of Asaph.
1 *Keep not thou silence* **Quiet not**, O *God* **Elohim**:
hold not thy peace **hush not**,
and be not still **rest not**, O *God* **El**.
2 For, *lo* **behold**, thine enemies *make a tumult* **roar**:
and they that hate thee have lifted up the head.
3 They have *taken crafty* **strategized private** counsel
against thy people,
and *consulted* **counseled**
against thy *hidden* **treasured** ones.
4 They have said, Come,
and let us cut them off from *being a nation* **the goyim**;
that the name of *Israel* **Yisra El**
may be no more *in remembrance* **remembered**.
5 For they have *consulted* **counseled** together
with one *consent* **heart**:
they *are confederate* **have cut a covenant** against thee:
6 The *tabernacles* **tents** of Edom,
and the *Ishmaelites* **Yishma Eliym**;
of Moab, and the *Hagarenes* **Hagariym**;
7 Gebal, and Ammon, and *Amalek* **Amaleq**;
the *Philistines* **Peleshethiym**
with the *inhabitants* **settlers** of *Tyre* **Sor**;
8 *Assur* **Ashshur** also is joined with them:
they have *holpen* **been an arm to** the *children* **sons** of Lot.
Selah.
9 *Do* **Work** unto them as unto *the Midianites* **Midyan**;
as *to* Sisera, as *to Jabin* **Yabiyn**,
at the *brook* **wadi** of *Kison* **Qishon**:
10 *Which perished* **desolated** at *Endor* **En Dor**:
they became as dung for the *earth* **soil**.
11 *Make* **Place** their *nobles* **volunteers** like Oreb,
and like *Zeeb* **Zebach**:
yea, all their *princes* **libations** as *Zebah* **Zebach**,
and as *Zalmunna* **Sal Munna**:
12 Who said,
Let us *take to ourselves* **possess**
the *houses* **folds** of *God in possession* **Elohim**.
13 O my *God* **Elohim**, *make* **place** them like a wheel;
as the stubble *before* **at the face of** the wind.
14 As the fire burneth a *wood* **forest**,
and as the flame *setteth* **inflameth** the mountains *on fire*;
15 So *persecute* **pursue** them with thy *tempest* **storm**,
and *make* **terrify** them *afraid* with thy *storm* **hurricane**.
16 Fill their faces with *shame* **abasement**;
that they may seek thy name, O *LORD* **Yah Veh**.
17 Let them *be confounded* **shame**
and *troubled for ever* **terrify eternally**;
yea, let them *be put to shame* **blush**, and *perish* **destruct**:
18 That *men* **they** may know that thou,
whose name alone is *JEHOVAH* **Yah Veh**,
art *the most high* **Elyon** over all the earth.

84

To *the chief Musician* **His Eminence,**
upon Gittith,
A Psalm for the sons of *Korah* **Qorach**.
1 How *amiable* **beloved** are thy tabernacles,
O *LORD of hosts* **Yah Veh Sabaoth**!
2 My soul *longeth* **yearneth**,
yea, even *fainteth* **finisheth off**
for the courts of *the LORD* **Yah Veh**:
my heart and my flesh
crieth out **shouteth** for the living *God* **El**.
3 Yea, the *sparrow* **bird** hath found an house,
and the swallow a nest for herself,
where she may *lay* **set** her *young* **chicks**,
even thine **thy sacrifice** altars,
O *LORD of hosts* **Yah Veh Sabaoth**,
my *King* **Sovereign**, *and* my *God* **Elohim**.
4 *Blessed* **Blithe** are they that *dwell* **settle** in thy house:
they *will be* **shall** still *praising* **halal** thee.
Selah.
5 *Blessed* **Blithe** is *the man* **humanity**
whose strength is in thee;
in whose heart are the *ways* **highways** of them.
6 Who passing through the valley of *Baca* **Weeping**
make **place** it a *well* **fountain**;
the **early** rain
also *filleth the pools* **covereth with blessings**.
7 They go from *strength* **valour** to *strength* **valour**,
every one of them in Zion appeareth before God
to be seen of Elohim in Siyon.
8 O *LORD God of hosts* **Yah Veh Elohim Sabaoth**,
hear my prayer:
give ear **hearken**, O *God* **Elohim** of *Jacob* **Yaaqov**.
Selah.
9 *Behold* **See**, O *God* **Elohim** our *shield* **buckler**,
and look upon the face of thine anointed.
10 For a day in thy courts is better than a thousand.
I *had rather* **choose to** be a *doorkeeper* **threshhold waiter**
in the house of my *God* **Elohim**,
than to *dwell* **twirl** in the tents of wickedness.
11 For *the LORD God* **Yah Veh Elohim**
is a sun and shield:
the LORD **Yah Veh**
will give grace **shall grant charism** and *glory* **honour**:
no good *thing will* **shall** he withhold
from them that walk *uprightly* **integriously**.
12 O *LORD of hosts* **Yah Veh Sabaoth**,

blessed **blithe** is the *man* **human**
that *trusteth* **confideth** in thee.

85 To *the chief Musician* **His Eminence**,
A Psalm for the sons of *Korah* **Qorach**.
1 *LORD* **Yah Veh**,
thou *hast been favourable* **art pleased** unto thy land:
thou hast brought back the captivity of *Jacob* **Yaaqov**.
2 Thou hast *forgiven* **lifted** the *iniquity* **perversity**
of thy people,
thou hast covered all their sin.
Selah.
3 Thou hast taken away all thy *wrath* **fury**:
thou hast turned *thyself*
from the *fierceness* **fuming** of *thine anger* **thy wrath**.
4 *Turn* **Return to** us, O *God* **Elohim** of our salvation,
and *cause thine anger to cease* **break thy vexation**
toward us.
5 *Wilt* **Shalt** thou be angry with us *for ever* **eternally**?
wilt **shalt** thou draw out thine anger
to all generations **generation to generation**?
6 *Wilt* **Shalt** thou not *revive us again* **return to enliven us**:
that thy people may *rejoice* **cheer** in thee?
7 *Shew us* **Let us see** thy mercy, O *LORD* **Yah Veh**,
and *grant* **give** us thy salvation.
8 I *will* **shall** hear
what *God the LORD will speak* **El Yah Veh shall word**:
for he *will speak peace* **shall word shalom**
unto his people, and to his *saints* **mercied**:
but let them not turn again to folly.
9 Surely his salvation is nigh them that *fear* **awe** him;
that *glory* **honour** may *dwell* **tabernacle** in our land.
10 Mercy and truth are met together;
righteousness **justness** and *peace* **shalom**
have kissed *each other*.
11 Truth shall *spring* **sprout** out of the earth;
and *righteousness* **justness** shall look *down*
from *heaven* **the heavens**.
12 Yea, *the LORD* **Yah Veh** shall give *that which is* good;
and our land shall yield her *increase* **produce**.
13 *Righteousness* **Justness** shall go *before him* **at his face**;
and shall set us in the way of his steps.

86 A Prayer of David.
1 *Bow down* **Extend** thine ear, O *LORD* **Yah Veh**,
hear **answer** me: for I am *poor* **humble** and needy.
2 *Preserve* **Guard** my soul; for I am *holy* **mercied**:
O thou my *God* **Elohim**,
save thy servant that *trusteth* **confideth** in thee.
3 *Be merciful unto me* **Grant me charism**, O *Lord* **Adonay**:
for I *cry* **call** unto thee *daily* **all day**.
4 *Rejoice* **Cheer** the soul of thy servant:
for unto thee, O *Lord* **Adonay**, do I lift *up* my soul.
5 For thou, *Lord* **O Adonay**,
art good, and *ready to forgive* **forgiving**;
and *plenteous* **abundant** in mercy
unto all them that call upon thee.
6 *Give ear* **Hearken**, O *LORD* **Yah Veh**, unto my prayer;
and *attend* **hearken** to the voice of my supplications.
7 In the day of my *trouble* **tribulation**
I *will* **shall** call upon thee:
for thou *wilt* **shalt** answer me.
8 Among the *gods* **elohim** there is none like unto thee,
O *Lord* **Adonay**;
neither are there any works like unto thy works
no works like thine.
9 All *nations* **goyim** whom thou hast *made* **worked**
shall come and *worship before thee* **prostrate at thy face**,
O *Lord* **Adonay**;
and shall *glorify* **honour** thy name.
10 For thou *art* great,
and *doest wondrous things* **workest marvels**:
thou art *God* **Elohim** alone.
11 Teach me thy way, O *LORD* **Yah Veh**;
I *will* **shall** walk in thy truth:
unite my heart to *fear* **awe** thy name.
12 I *will praise* **shall extend hands unto** thee,
O *Lord* **Adonay** my *God* **Elohim**, with all my heart:
and I *will glorify* **shall honour** thy name
for evermore **eternally**.
13 For great is thy mercy toward me:
and thou hast *delivered* **rescued** my soul
from the *lowest hell* **nethermost sheol**.
14 O *God* **Elohim**,
the *proud* **arrogant** are risen against me,
and the *assemblies* **witnesses** of *violent men* **tyrants**
have sought after my soul;
and have not set thee before them.
15 But thou, O *Lord* **Adonay**,
art *a God* **an El** full of *compassion* **mercy**,
and *gracious* **charismatic**, *longsuffering* **slow to wrath**,
and *plenteous* **abundant** in mercy and truth.
16 O *turn unto* **face** me,
and *have mercy upon me* **grant me charism**;
give thy strength unto thy servant,
and save the son of *thine handmaid* **thy maid**.
17 *Shew* **Work** me a *token* **sign** for good;
that they which hate me may see it,
and *be ashamed* **shame**:
because thou, *LORD* **O Yah Veh**,
hast *holpen* **helped** me, and *comforted* **sighed over** me.

87 A Psalm *or* Song for the sons of *Korah* **Qorach**.
1 His foundation is in the holy mountains.
2 *The LORD* **Yah Veh**
loveth the *gates* **portals** of *Zion* **Siyon**
more than all the *dwellings* **tabernacles** of *Jacob* **Yaaqov**.
3 *Glorious things* **Honours** are *spoken* **worded** of thee,
O city of *God* **Elohim**.
Selah.
4 I *will make mention of* **shall remember**
Rahab and *Babylon* **Babel**
to them that know me:
behold *Philistia* **Pelesheth**,
and *Tyre* **Sor**, with *Ethiopia* **Kush**;
this *man* was born there.
5 And of *Zion* **Siyon** it shall be said,
This **man** and that man was born in her:
and *the highest* **Elyon** himself shall establish her.
6 *The LORD* **Yah Veh** shall *count* **scribe**,
when he *writeth up* **charteth** the people,
that this *man* was born there.
Selah.
7 As well the singers
as the *players on instruments* **pluckers** shall be there:
all my *springs* **fountains** are in thee.

88 A Song *or* Psalm for the sons of *Korah* **Qorach**,
to *the chief Musician* **His Eminence**,
upon Mahalath Leannoth **on Stroking the Humbled**,
Maschil **On Comprehension** of Heman
the *Ezrahite* **Zerachiy**.
1 O *LORD God* **Yah Veh Elohim** of my salvation,
I have cried day and night before thee:
2 Let my prayer come *before thee* **at thy face**:
incline **extend** thine ear unto my *cry* **shouting**;
3 For my soul *is full of troubles* **satiateth with evil**:
and my life *draweth nigh* **toucheth** unto *the grave* **sheol**.
4 I am *counted* **fabricated** with them
that *go down* **descend** into the *pit* **well**:
I *am as a man* — **a mighty** that hath no *strength* **might**:
5 *Free* **Liberated** among the dead,
like the *slain* **pierced** that lie in the *grave* **tomb**,
whom thou rememberest no more:
and they are cut off from thy hand.
6 Thou hast *laid* **placed** me
in the *lowest pit* **nethermost well**,
in darkness, in the deeps.
7 Thy *wrath lieth hard* **fury proppeth** upon me,
and thou hast *afflicted* **humbled** me with all thy waves.
Selah.
8 Thou hast *put away* **far removed**
mine acquaintance far from me **them whom I know**;
thou hast *made* **placed** me
an *abomination* **abhorrence** unto them:
I am shut up — **restrained**, and I cannot come forth.
9 Mine eye *mourneth* **languisheth**
by reason of affliction **from humiliation**:
LORD **O Yah Veh**, I have called daily upon thee,
I have *stretched out* **spread** my *hands* **palms** unto thee.

10 *Wilt* **Shalt** thou *shew wonders* **work marvels**
to the dead?
shall the *dead* **ghosts** arise
and *praise* **extend hands unto** thee?
Selah.
11 Shall thy *lovingkindness* **mercy**
be *declared* **scribed** in the *grave* **tomb**?
or thy *faithfulness* **trustworthiness**
in *destruction* **Abaddon**?
12 Shall thy *wonders* **marvels** be known in the dark?
and thy *righteousness* **justness**
in the land of *forgetfulness* **oblivion**?
13 But unto thee have I cried, O *LORD* **Yah Veh**;
and in the morning
shall my prayer *prevent* **anticipate** thee.
14 *LORD* **O Yah Veh**, why castest thou off my soul?
why hidest thou thy face from me?
15 I am *afflicted* **humbled**
and ready to die — **expiring**
from my youth up **since ladhood**:
while I *suffer* **bear** thy terrors I am *distracted* **perplexed**.
16 Thy *fierce wrath goeth* **fuming passeth** over me;
thy terrors *have cut me off* **exterminate me**.
17 They *came round about* **surround** me *daily* **all day**
like water;
they *compassed me about* **surround me** together.
18 Lover and friend
hast thou *put far* **far removed** from me,
and *mine acquaintance* **they whom I know** into darkness.

89

Maschil **On Comprehension**
of Ethan the *Ezrahite* **Zerachiy**.
1 I *will* **shall** sing of the mercies of *the LORD* **Yah Veh**
for ever **eternally**:
with my mouth
will **shall** I make known thy *faithfulness* **trustworthiness**
to all generations **generation to generation**.
2 For I have said,
Mercy shall be built up *for ever* **eternally**:
thy *faithfulness* **trustworthiness**
shalt thou establish in the very heavens.
3 I have *made* **cut** a covenant with my chosen,
I have *sworn* **oathed** unto David my servant,
4 Thy seed *will* **shall** I establish *for ever* **eternally**,
and build up thy throne
to all generations **generation to generation**.
Selah.
5 And the heavens
shall *praise* **extend hands unto** thy *wonders* **marvels**,
O *LORD* **Yah Veh**:
thy *faithfulness* **trustworthiness** also
in the congregation of the *saints* **holy**.
6 For who in the *heaven* **vapours**
can **shall** be *compared* **ranked**
unto the LORD **with Yah Veh**?
who among the sons of *the mighty* **El**
can **shall** be likened unto *the LORD* **Yah Veh**?
7 *God* **El** is greatly to be *feared* **awed**
in the *assembly* **private counsel** of the *saints* **holy**,
and *to be had in reverence* **awed**
of **over** all them that are about him.
8 O *LORD God of hosts* **Yah Elohim Sabaoth**,
who is a *strong LORD* **powerful Yah** like unto thee?
or to thy *faithfulness* **trustworthiness** round about thee?
9 Thou *rulest* **reignest** the *raging* **rising** of the sea:
when the waves *thereof* arise, thou *stillest* **laudest** them.
10 Thou hast *broken* **crushed** Rahab *in pieces*,
as one that is *slain* **pierced**;
thou hast scattered thine enemies
with thy *strong* arm **of strength**.
11 The heavens are thine, the earth also is thine:
as for the world and the fulness *thereof*,
thou hast founded them.
12 The north and the *south* **right** thou hast created them:
Tabor and Hermon shall *rejoice* **shout** in thy name.
13 Thou hast *a mighty arm* **an arm of might**:
strong **strengthened** is thy hand,
and high **lofted** is thy right *hand*.
14 *Justice* **Justness** and judgment
are the *habitation* **establishment** of thy throne:
mercy and truth shall *go before* **anticipate** thy face.
15 *Blessed* **Blithe** is the people
that know the *joyful sound* **shout**:
they shall walk, O *LORD* **Yah Veh**,
in the light of thy *countenance* **face**.
16 In thy name shall they *rejoice* **twirl** all the day:
and in thy *righteousness* **justness**
shall they be *exalted* **lofted**.
17 For thou art the *glory* **beauty** of their strength:
and *in* **at** thy *favour* **pleasure**
our horn shall be *exalted* **lofted**.
18 For *the LORD* **Yah Veh** is our *defence* **buckler**;
and the Holy One of *Israel* **Yisra El** is our *king* **sovereign**.
19 Then thou *spakest* **wordest** in vision
to thy *holy* **mercied** one, and saidst,
I have *laid* **placed** help upon one that is mighty;
I have exalted one chosen out of the people.
20 I have found David my servant;
with my holy *oil* **ointment** have I anointed him:
21 With whom my hand shall be established:
mine arm also shall strengthen him.
22 The enemy shall not exact upon him;
nor the son of wickedness *afflict* **abase** him.
23 And I *will beat down* **shall crush** his *foes* **tribulators**
before **at** his face,
and *plague* **smite** them that hate him.
24 But my *faithfulness* **trustworthiness** and my mercy
shall be with him:
and in my name shall his horn be *exalted* **lofted**.
25 I *will* **shall** set his hand *also* in the sea,
and his right *hand* in the rivers.
26 He shall *cry* **call** unto me, Thou *art* — my father,
my *God* **El**, and the rock of my salvation.
27 Also I *will make* **shall give** him **to be** my firstborn,
higher than the kings **Elyon of the sovereigns** of the earth.
28 My mercy *will I keep* **shall I guard** for him
for evermore **eternally**,
and my covenant
shall *stand fast* **be trustworthy** with him.
29 His seed also *will I make* **shall I set**
to endure for ever **eternal**,
and his throne as the days of *heaven* **the heavens**.
30 If his *children* **sons** forsake my *law* **torah**,
and walk not in my judgments;
31 If they *break* **profane** my statutes,
and *keep* **guard** not my *commandments* **misvoth**;
32 Then *will* **shall** I visit their *transgression* **rebellion**
with the *rod* **scion**,
and their *iniquity* **perversity** with *stripes* **plagues**.
33 Nevertheless my *lovingkindness* **mercy**
will **shall** I not *utterly take from him* **void**,
nor *suffer* **falsify** my *faithfulness to fail* **trustworthiness**.
34 My covenant *will* **shall** I not *break* **profane**,
nor alter the *thing that is gone out* **proceedings** of my lips.
35 Once have I *sworn* **oathed** by my holiness
that I *will* **shall** not lie unto David.
36 His seed shall *endure for ever* **be eternal**,
and his throne as the sun before me.
37 It shall be established *for ever* **eternally** as the moon,
and as a *faithful* **trustworthy** witness
in *heaven* **the vapours**.
Selah.
38 But thou hast cast off and *abhorred* **spurned**,
thou hast *been wroth with* **passed over** thine anointed.
39 Thou hast *made void* **rejected**
the covenant of thy servant:
thou hast profaned his *crown* **separatism**
by casting it to the *ground* **earth**.
40 Thou hast *broken down* **breached** all his *hedges* **walls**;
thou hast *brought* **set** his *strong holds* **fortresses** to ruin.
41 All that pass by the way spoil him:
he is a reproach to his *neighbours* **fellow tabernaclers**.
42 Thou hast *set up* **exalted**
the right *hand* of his *adversaries* **tribulators**;
thou hast made all his enemies to *rejoice* **cheer**.
43 Thou hast also turned the *edge* **form** of his sword,
and hast not *made* **raised** him to *stand in the battle* **war**.
44 Thou hast *made* **shabbathized** his *glory to cease* **purity**,
and *cast* **precipitated** his throne
down to the *ground* **earth**.

45 The days of his youth hast thou *shortened* **curtailed**:
thou hast covered him with shame.
Selah.
46 How long, *LORD* **O Yah Veh**?
wilt **shalt** thou hide thyself *for ever* **in perpetuity**?
shall thy *wrath* **fury** burn like fire?
47 Remember how *short my time is* **transcient**:
wherefore hast thou
made **created** all *men* **sons of humanity** in vain?
48 What *man is he that* **mighty** liveth,
and shall not see death?
shall he *deliver* **rescue** his soul
from the hand of *the grave* **sheol**?
Selah.
49 *Lord* **Adonay**,
where are thy *former lovingkindnesses* **first mercies**,
which thou *swarest* **oathest** unto David
in thy *truth* **trustworthiness**?
50 Remember, *Lord* **Adonay**,
the reproach of thy servants;
how I *do* bear in my bosom *the reproach of*
all the *mighty* **great** people;
51 Wherewith thine enemies have reproached,
O *LORD* **Yah Veh**;
wherewith they have reproached
the *footsteps* **heelprints** of thine anointed.
52 Blessed be *the LORD for evermore* **Yah Veh eternally**.
Amen, and Amen.

BOOK IV

90 A Prayer of *Moses* **Mosheh**
the man of *God* **Elohim**.
1 *Lord* **Adonay**,
thou hast been our *dwelling place* **habitation**
in all generations **generation to generation**.
2 Before the mountains were *brought forth* **birthed**,
or ever thou *hadst formed* **writhed**
the earth and the world,
even from *everlasting* **eternity** to *everlasting* **eternity**,
thou *art God* — **El**.
3 Thou turnest man to *destruction* **be crushed**;
and sayest, Return, ye *children* **sons** of *men* **humanity**.
4 For a thousand years in thy *sight* **eyes**
are *but* as yesterday when it is past,
and as — a watch in the night.
5 Thou *carriest* **causest** them
away as with a flood **to be floodborne**;
they are as a sleep:
in the morning they are like grass
which *groweth up* **changeth**.
6 In the morning it flourisheth, and *groweth up* **changeth**;
in the evening it is cut *down*, and withereth.
7 For we are *consumed* **finished off**
by *thine anger* **thy wrath**,
and by thy *wrath* **fury** are we *troubled* **terrified**.
8 Thou hast set our *iniquities* **perversities** before thee,
our *secret sins* **concealed**
in the light of thy *countenance* **face**.
9 For all our days *are passed away* **have turned face**
in thy *wrath* **fury**:
we *spend* **finish off** our years
as a *tale that is told* **meditation**.
10 The days of our years
are *threescore years and ten* **seventy years**;
and if by *reason of strength* **might**
they be *fourscore* **eighty** years,
yet is their *strength* **pride**, *labour* **toil** and *sorrow* **mischief**;
for it is *soon cut off* **quickly passed over**,
and we fly away.
11 Who knoweth the *power* **strength**
of *thine anger* **thy wrath**?
even according to thy fear **as thy awe**, so *is* thy *wrath* **fury**.
12 So *teach us* **have us know** to number our days,
that we may apply our hearts unto wisdom.
13 Return, O *LORD* **Yah Veh**, how long?
and *let it repent thee* **sigh thou** concerning thy servants.
14 O satisfy us *early* **mornings** with thy mercy;
that we may *rejoice* **shout** and *be glad* **cheer** all our days.
15 *Make us glad* **Cheer us** according to the days
wherein thou hast *afflicted* **humbled** us,
and the years *wherein* we have seen evil.
16 Let thy *work appear* **deeds be seen** unto thy servants,
and thy *glory* **majesty** unto their *children* **sons**.
17 And let the *beauty* **pleasantness**
of *the LORD* **Yah Veh** our *God* **Elohim** be upon us:
and establish thou the work of our hands upon us;
yea, the work of our hands establish thou it.

91 He that *dwelleth* **settleth**
in the *secret place of the most High* **covert of Elyon**
shall *abide* **stay**
under the shadow of *the Almighty* **Shadday**.
2 I *will* **shall** say of *the LORD* **Yah Veh**,
He is my refuge and my *fortress* **stronghold**:
my *God* **Elohim**; in him *will I trust* **shall I confide**.
3 *Surely* he shall *deliver* **rescue** thee
from the snare of the *fowler* **snarer**,
and from the *noisome* **calamitous** pestilence.
4 He shall cover thee with his *feathers* **pinions**,
and under his wings shalt thou *trust* **seek refuge**:
his truth shall be thy shield and buckler.
5 Thou shalt not *be afraid* **awe**
for the *terror* **dread** by night;
nor for the arrow that flieth by day;
6 Nor for the pestilence that walketh in darkness;
nor for the *destruction* **ruin**
that *wasteth* **devastateth** at noonday.
7 A thousand shall fall at thy side,
and *ten thousand* **myriads** at thy right *hand*;
but it shall not *come nigh* **approach** thee.
8 Only with thine eyes shalt thou *behold* **look**
and see the *reward* **retribution** of the wicked.
9 Because thou hast *made the LORD* **set Yah Veh**,
which is my refuge, *even the most High* **Elyon**,
thy habitation;
10 There shall no evil *befall* **happen** thee,
neither shall any plague come nigh thy *dwelling* **tent**.
11 For he shall *give* **misvah** his angels *charge* over thee,
to *keep* **guard** thee in all thy ways.
12 They shall *bear* **lift** thee *up* in their *hands* **palms**,
lest thou *dash* **stub** thy foot against a stone.
13 Thou shalt tread upon the **roaring** lion and *adder* **asp**:
the *young lion* **whelp** and the *dragon* **monster**
shalt thou trample under feet.
14 Because he hath
set his love upon **attached himself to** me,
therefore *will I deliver* **shall I slip** him **away**:
I *will set* **shall loft** him *on high*,
because he hath known my name.
15 He shall call upon me, and I *will* **shall** answer him:
I *will* **shall** be with him in *trouble* **tribulation**;
I *will deliver* **shall rescue** him, and honour him.
16 With *long life will* **length of days shall** I satisfy him,
and *shew him* **let him see** my salvation.

92 A Psalm *or* Song
for the *sabbath* **shabbath** day.
1 It is *a good thing*
to *give thanks* **extend hands** unto *the LORD* **Yah Veh**,
and to *sing praises* **psalm** unto thy name,
O *most High* **Elyon**:
2 To *shew forth* **tell** thy *lovingkindness* **mercy**
in the morning,
and thy *faithfulness* **trustworthiness**
every night **in the nights**,
3 Upon *an instrument of ten strings* **the decachord**,
and upon the *psaltery* **bagpipe**;
upon the harp with a *solemn sound* **meditation**.
4 For thou, *LORD* **O Yah Veh**,
hast *made* **cheered** me *glad* through thy *work* **deeds**:
I *will triumph* **shall shout** in the works of thy hands.
5 O *LORD* **Yah Veh**, how *great* **greatened** are thy works!
and thy *thoughts* **fabrications**
are very deep **mightily deepened**.
6 A *brutish* **stupid** man knoweth not;
neither *doth* a fool *understand this* **discern**.
7 When the wicked *spring* **blossom** as the *grass* **herbage**,
and when all the *workers* **doers** of *iniquity* **mischief**
do flourish;
it is that they shall be *destroyed* **desolated**

for ever **eternally**:
8 But thou, *LORD* **O Yah Veh**,
art *most high for evermore* **in the heights eternally**.
9 For, *lo* **behold**, thine enemies, O *LORD* **Yah Veh**,
for, *lo* **behold**, thine enemies shall *perish* **destruct**;
all the *workers* **doers** of *iniquity* **mischief**
shall be *scattered* **separated**.
10 But my horn shalt thou exalt
like *the horn of an unicorn* **a reem**:
I shall be anointed with *fresh oil* **green ointment**.
11 Mine eye also shall *see* **look**
my desire on mine enemies **on my observers**,
and mine ears shall hear
my desire of the wicked **the vilifiers**
that rise up against me.
12 The *righteous* **just** shall *flourish* **blossom**
like the palm tree:
he shall *grow* **increase** like a cedar in Lebanon.
13 Those that be *planted* **transplanted**
in the house of *the LORD* **Yah Veh**
shall *flourish* **blossom** in the courts of our *God* **Elohim**.
14 They shall still *bring forth fruit* **germinate**
in *old age* **greyness**;
they shall be fat and *flourishing* **green**;
15 To *shew* **tell** that *the LORD* **Yah Veh** is *upright* **straight**:
he is — my rock,
and there is no *unrighteousness* **wickedness** in him.

93 *The LORD* **Yah Veh** reigneth,
he *is clothed* **hath enrobed** with *majesty* **pomp**;
the LORD is clothed **Yah Veh hath enrobed** with strength,
wherewith he hath girded himself:
the world also is stablished,
that it *cannot be moved* **totter not**.
2 Thy throne is established *of old* **since then**:
thou art from *everlasting* **eternity**.
3 The *floods* **rivers** have lifted *up*, O *LORD* **Yah Veh**,
the *floods* **rivers** have lifted *up* their voice;
the *floods* **rivers** lift *up* their waves.
4 *The LORD on high* **Yah Veh in the heights**
is mightier than the *noise* **voice** of many waters,
yea, than the mighty waves of the sea.
5 Thy *testimonies* **witnesses**
are *very sure* **mighty trustworthy**:
holiness *becometh* **befitteth** thine house,
O *LORD* **Yah Veh**, *for ever* **to length of days**.

94 *O LORD God, to whom vengeance belongeth*
O El of vengeance;
O God, to whom vengeance belongeth
O Yah Veh El of vengeance,
shew thyself **shine forth**.
2 Lift up thyself, thou judge of the earth:
render a reward **return a dealing** to the *proud* **pompous**.
3 *LORD* **O Yah Veh**, how long shall the wicked,
how long shall the wicked *triumph* **jump for joy**?
4 How long shall they *utter* **gush**
and *speak hard things* **word impudence**?
and all the *workers* **doers** of *iniquity* **mischief**
boast themselves **say**?
5 They *break in pieces* **crush** thy people,
O *LORD* **Yah Veh**,
and *afflict* **humble** thine *heritage* **inheritance**.
6 They *slay* **slaughter**
the widow and the *stranger* **sojourner**,
and murder the *fatherless* **orphan**.
7 Yet they say, *The LORD* **Yah Veh** shall not see,
neither shall *the God* **Elohim** of *Jacob* **Yaaqov**
regard **discern** *it*.
8 *Understand* **Discern**, ye *brutish* **stupid** among the people:
and *ye* fools, when *will* **shall** ye *be wise* **discern**?
9 He that planted the ear, shall he not hear?
he that formed the eye, shall he not *see* **scan**?
10 He that *chastiseth* **disciplineth** the *heathen* **goyim**,
shall not he *correct* **reprove**?
he that teacheth *man* **humanity** knowledge,
shall not he know?
11 *The LORD* **Yah Veh**
knoweth the *thoughts* **fabrications** of *man* **humanity**,
that they are vanity.
12 *Blessed is the man* **Blithe be the mighty**
whom thou *chastenest* **disciplinest**, O *LORD* **Yah**,
and teachest him out of thy *law* **torah**;
13 That thou mayest *give him* rest **him**
from the days of *adversity* **evil**,
until the pit **of ruin** be digged **for the wicked**.
14 For *the LORD* **Yah Veh**
will **shall** not *cast off* **abandon** his people,
neither *will* **shall** he forsake his inheritance.
15 But judgment shall return unto *righteousness* **justness**:
and all the *upright* **straight** in heart shall *follow* **be after** it.
16 Who *will* **shall** rise *up* for me
against the *evildoers* **vilifiers**?
or who *will stand up* **shall set** for me
against the *workers* **doers** of *iniquity* **mischief**?
17 Unless *the LORD* **Yah Veh** had been my help,
my soul had almost *dwelt* **tabernacled** in silence.
18 When I said, My foot *slippeth* **tottereth**;
thy mercy, O *LORD* **Yah Veh**, *held* **supported** me *up*.
19 In the *multitude* **abundance** of my thoughts within me
thy *comforts* **consolations** delight my soul.
20 Shall the throne of *iniquity* **calamity**
have fellowship **join** with thee,
which *frameth mischief* **formeth toil** by a *law* **statute**?
21 They *gather themselves together* **troop**
against the soul of the *righteous* **just**
and *condemn* **judge wicked** the innocent blood.
22 But *the LORD* **Yah Veh** is my *defence* **secure loft**;
and my *God* **Elohim** is the rock of my refuge.
23 And he shall *bring* **turn** upon them
their own *iniquity* **mischief**,
and shall *cut* **exterminate** them *off*
in their own *wickedness* **evil**:
yea, the LORD **Yah Veh** our *God* **Elohim**
shall *cut* **exterminate** them *off*.

95 O come, let us *sing* **shout**
unto *the LORD* **Yah Veh**:
let us *make a joyful noise* **shout**
to the rock of our salvation.
2 Let us *come before* **anticipate** his *presence* **face**
with *thanksgiving* **extended hands**,
and *make a joyful noise* **shout** unto him with psalms.
3 For *the LORD* **Yah Veh** is a great *God* **El**,
and a great *King* **Sovereign** above all *gods* **elohim**.
4 In his hand
are the *deep places* **innermost depths** of the earth:
the *strength* **strengths** of the *hills* **mountains**
is **are** his also.
5 The sea is his, and he *made* **worked** it:
and his hands formed the dry *land*.
6 O come, let us *worship* **prostrate** and *bow down* **kneel**:
let us kneel *before the LORD* **at the face of Yah Veh**
our *maker* **Worker**.
7 For he is our *God* **Elohim**;
and we are the people of his pasture,
and the *sheep* **flock** of his hand.
To day if ye *will* **shall** hear his voice,
8 Harden not your heart, as in the *provocation* **strife**,
and as in the day of *temptation* **testing** in the wilderness:
9 When your fathers *tempted* **tested** me,
proved **proofed** me, and saw my *work* **deeds**.
10 Forty years long
was I grieved with **loathed I** this generation, and said,
It is a people that *do err* **stray** in their heart,
and they have not known my ways:
11 Unto whom I *sware* **oathed** in my wrath
that they should not enter into my rest.

96 O sing unto *the LORD* **Yah Veh** a new song:
sing unto *the LORD* **Yah Veh**, all the earth.
2 Sing unto *the LORD* **Yah Veh**, bless his name;
shew forth **evangelize** his salvation from day to day.
3 *Declare* **Scribe** his *glory* **honour**
among the *heathen* **goyim**,
his *wonders* **marvels** among all people.
4 For *the LORD* **Yah Veh** is great,
and *greatly* **mightily** to be praised:
he is *to be feared* **awesome** above all *gods* **elohim**.
5 For all the *gods* **elohim** of the *nations* **people** are idols:

but *the LORD made* **Yah Veh worked** the heavens.
6 Honour and majesty are *before him* **at his face** :
strength and beauty are in his *sanctuary* **hallowed refuge**.
7 Give unto *the LORD* **Yah Veh**,
O ye *kindreds* **families** of the people,
give unto *the LORD* **Yah Veh**
glory **honour** and strength.
8 Give unto *the LORD* **Yah Veh**
the *glory due unto* **honour of** his name:
bring **lift** an offering, and come into his courts.
9 O *worship the LORD* **prostrate to Yah Veh**
in the *beauty* **majesty** of *holiness* **his holies**:
fear before him **writhe at his face**, all the earth.
10 Say among the *heathen* **goyim,**
that the LORD **Yah Veh** reigneth:
the world also shall be established
that it shall not *be moved* **totter**:
he shall *judge* **plead the cause of** the people
righteously **in straightnesses**.
11 Let the heavens *rejoice* **cheer**,
and let the earth *be glad* **twirl**;
let the sea *roar* **thunder**, and the fulness *thereof*.
12 Let the field *be joyful* **jump for joy**,
and all that is therein:
then shall all the trees of the *wood rejoice* **forest shout**.
13 *Before the LORD* **At the face of Yah Veh**:
for he cometh, for he cometh to judge the earth:
he shall judge the world with *righteousness* **justness**,
and the people with his *truth* **trustworthiness**.

97
The LORD **Yah Veh** reigneth;
let the earth *rejoice* **twirl**;
let the *multitude of isles* **great islands**
be glad thereof **cheer**.
2 Clouds and **dripping** darkness are round about him:
righteousness **justness** and judgment
are the *habitation* **establishment** of his throne.
3 A fire goeth *before* **at the face of** him,
and *burneth up* **inflameth** his *enemies* **tribulators**
round about.
4 His lightnings enlightened the world:
the earth saw, and *trembled* **writhed**.
5 The *hills* **mountains** melted like wax
at the *presence* **face** of *the LORD* **Yah Veh**,
at the *presence* **face**
of *the Lord* **Adonay** of the whole earth.
6 The heavens *declare* **tell** his *righteousness* **justness**,
and all the people see his *glory* **honour**.
7 *Confounded* **Shamed** be all they
that serve *graven images* **sculptiles**,
that *boast* **halal** themselves of idols:
worship **prostrate to** him, all ye *gods* **elohim**.
8 *Zion* **Siyon** heard, and *was glad* **cheered**;
and the daughters of *Judah rejoiced* **Yah Hudah twirled**
because of thy judgments, O *LORD* **Yah Veh**.
9 For thou, *LORD* **O Yah Veh**,
art *high* **Elyon** above all the earth:
thou art *exalted far* **ascended mightily**
above all *gods* **elohim**.
10 Ye that love *the LORD* **Yah Veh**, hate evil:
he *preserveth* **guardeth** the souls of his *saints* **mercied**;
he *delivereth* **rescueth** them
out of the hand of the wicked.
11 Light is *sown* **seeded** for the *righteous* **just**,
and *gladness* **cheerfulness** for the *upright* **straight** in heart.
12 *Rejoice in the LORD* **Cheer in Yah Veh**,
ye *righteous* **just**;
and *give thanks* **extend hands**
at the remembrance of his holiness.

98
A Psalm.
1 O sing unto *the LORD* **Yah Veh** a new song;
for he hath *done marvellous things* **worked marvels**:
his right *hand*, and his holy arm,
hath gotten him the victory **saveth**.
2 *The LORD* **Yah Veh** hath made known his salvation:
his *righteousness* **justness** hath he *openly shewed* **exposed**
in the *sight* **eyes** of the *heathen* **goyim**.
3 He hath remembered his mercy
and his *truth* **trustworthiness**
toward the house of *Israel* **Yisra El**:
all the *ends* **finalities** of the earth
have seen the salvation of our *God* **Elohim**.
4 *Make a joyful noise* **Shout** unto *the LORD* **Yah Veh**,
all the earth:
make a loud noise **break forth**,
and *rejoice* **shout**, and *sing praise* **psalm**.
5 *Sing* **Psalm** unto *the LORD* **Yah Veh** with the harp;
with the harp, and the voice of a psalm.
6 With trumpets and *sound* **voice** of *cornet* **trumpet**
make a joyful noise **shout**
before the LORD **at the face of Yah Veh**,
the *King* **Sovereign**.
7 Let the sea *roar* **thunder**, and the fulness *thereof*;
the world, and they that *dwell* **settle** *therein*.
8 Let the *floods* **rivers** clap their *hands* **palms**:
let the *hills be joyful* **mountains shout** together
9 *Before the LORD* **At the face of Yah Veh**;
for he cometh to judge the earth:
with *righteousness* **justness** shall he judge the world,
and the people *with equity* **in straightnesses**.

99
The LORD **Yah Veh** reigneth;
let the people *tremble* **quiver**;
he *sitteth* **settleth**
between the cherubims **on the cherubim**;
let the earth *be moved* **quake**.
2 *The LORD* **Yah Veh** is great in *Zion* **Siyon**;
and he is high above all the people.
3 Let them *praise* **extend hands**
unto thy great and *terrible* **awesome** name; *for* it is holy.
4 The *king's* **sovereign's** strength also loveth judgment;
thou *dost establish equity* **establishest straightnesses**,
thou *executest* **workest** judgment
and *righteousness* **justness** in *Jacob* **Yaaqov**.
5 Exalt ye *the LORD* **Yah Veh** our *God* **Elohim**,
and *worship* **prostrate** at *his footstool* **the stool of his feet**;
for he is holy.
6 *Moses* **Mosheh** and *Aaron* **Aharon**
among his priests,
and *Samuel* **Shemu El**
among them that call upon his name;
they called upon *the LORD* **Yah Veh**,
and he answered them.
7 He *spake* **worded** unto them
in the *cloudy* pillar **of cloud**:
they *kept* **guarded** his *testimonies* **witnesses**,
and the *ordinance* **statute** that he gave them.
8 Thou answeredst them,
O *LORD* **Yah Veh** our *God* **Elohim**:
thou wast *a God* **an El** that *forgavest* **bore** them,
though thou
tookest vengeance of **avenged** their *inventions* **exploits**.
9 Exalt *the LORD* **Yah Veh** our *God* **Elohim**,
and *worship* **prostrate** at his holy *hill* **mountain**;
for *the LORD* **Yah Veh** our *God* **Elohim** is holy.

100
A Psalm of *praise* **extended hands**.
1 *Make a joyful noise* **Shout** unto *the LORD* **Yah Veh**,
all ye *lands* **earth**.
2 Serve *the LORD* **Yah Veh** with *gladness* **cheerfulness**:
come *before* **at** his *presence* **face** with *singing* **shouting**.
3 Know ye that *the LORD* **Yah Veh** he is *God* **Elohim**:
it is he that hath made **he hath worked** us,
and not we ourselves;
we are his people, and the *sheep* **flock** of his pasture.
4 Enter into his *gates* **portals**
with *thanksgiving* **extended hands**,
and into his courts with *praise* **halal**:
be thankful **extend hands** unto him, *and* bless his name.
5 For *the LORD* **Yah Veh** is good;
his mercy is *everlasting* **eternal**;
and his *truth* **trustworthiness**
endureth to all generations **generation to generation**.

101
A Psalm of David.
1 I *will* **shall** sing of mercy and judgment:
unto thee, O *LORD* **Yah Veh**, *will I sing* **shall I psalm**.
2 I *will behave myself wisely* **shall discern**
in *a perfect* **an integrious** way.

O when *wilt* **shalt** thou come unto me?
I *will* **shall** walk within my house
with a perfect **in integrity of** heart.
3 *I will* **shall** set no *wicked thing* **word of Beli Yaal**
before mine eyes:
I hate the work of *them that turn aside* **swervers**;
it shall not *cleave* **adhere** to me.
4 A *froward* **perverted** heart
shall *depart* **turn aside** from me:
I *will* **shall** not know *a wicked person* **evil**.
5 Whoso *privily slandereth* **covertly tongue—lasheth**
his *neighbour* **friend**,
him *will I cut off* **shall I exterminate**:
him that hath an high look **a lofty eye**
and *a proud* **an enlarged** heart,
will not I suffer **I am not able**.
6 Mine eyes
shall be upon the *faithful* **trustworthy** of the land,
that they may *dwell* **settle** with me:
he that walketh in *a perfect* **an integrious** way,
he shall *serve* **minister to** me.
7 He that worketh deceit
shall not *dwell* **settle** within my house:
he that *telleth lies* **wordeth falsehoods**
shall not *tarry in my sight* **be established in my eyes**.
8 *I will early destroy* **Mornings I shall exterminate**
all the wicked of the land;
that I may cut off all *wicked doers* **the mischievous**
from the city of *the LORD* **Yah Veh**.

102

A Prayer of the *afflicted* **humble**,
when he *is overwhelmed* **languisheth**,
and poureth out his *complaint* **meditation**
before the LORD **at the face of Yah Veh**.
1 Hear my prayer, O *LORD* **Yah Veh**,
and let my cry come unto thee.
2 Hide not thy face from me
in the day *when* I am in *trouble* **tribulation**;
incline **extend** thine ear unto me:
in the day *when* I call answer me *speedily* **hastily**.
3 For my days are *consumed* **finished off** like smoke,
and my bones are *burned* **scorched**
as *an hearth* **a burning**.
4 My heart is smitten, and withered like *grass* **herbage**;
so that I forget to eat my bread.
5 By reason of the voice of my *groaning* **sighing**
my bones *cleave* **adhere** to my *skin* **flesh**.
6 I am like a pelican of the wilderness:
I am *like* **likened to** an owl of the *desert* **parched areas**.
7 I watch,
and am as a *sparrow* **bird** alone upon the *house top* **roof**.
8 Mine enemies reproach me all the day;
and they that *are mad against* **halaled** me
are sworn **have oathed** against me.
9 For I have eaten ashes like bread,
and *mingled* **mixed** my drink with weeping.
10 *Because* **At the face** of thine indignation
and thy *wrath* **rage**:
for thou hast lifted me up, and cast me down.
11 My days are like a shadow that *declineth* **spreadeth**;
and I am withered like *grass* **herbage**.
12 But thou, O *LORD* **Yah Veh**,
shall *endure for ever* **settle eternal**;
and thy *remembrance* **memorial**
unto all generations **generation to generation**.
13 Thou shalt arise,
and *have* **shall** mercy *upon Zion* **Siyon**:
for the time to *favour* **grant** her **charism**,
yea, the *set time* **season**, is come.
14 For thy servants
take pleasure **are pleased** in her stones,
and *favour* **grant charism unto** the dust *thereof*.
15 So the *heathen* **goyim**
shall *fear* **awe** the name of *the LORD* **Yah Veh**,
and all the *kings* **sovereigns** of the earth thy *glory* **honour**.
16 When *the LORD* **Yah Veh** shall build *up Zion* **Siyon**,
he shall *appear* **be seen** in his *glory* **honour**.
17 He *will regard* **shall face** the prayer
of the *destitute* **naked**,
and not despise their prayer.
18 This shall be *written* **inscribed**
for the generation *to come* **after**:
and the people which shall be created
shall *praise the LORD* **halal Yah**.
19 For he hath looked *down*
from the height of his *sanctuary* **holies**;
from *heaven* **the heavens**
did the LORD behold **Yah Veh scanned** the earth;
20 To hear the *groaning* **shrieking** of the *prisoner* **bound**;
to loose *those that are appointed to* **the sons of** death;
21 To *declare* **scribe**
the name of *the LORD* **Yah Veh** in *Zion* **Siyon**,
and his *praise* **halal** in *Jerusalem* **Yeru Shalem**;
22 When the people are gathered *together*,
and the *kingdoms* **sovereigndoms**,
to serve *the LORD* **Yah Veh**.
23 He *weakened* **humbled** my *strength* **force** in the way;
he *shortened* **curtailed** my days.
24 I said, O my *God* **El**,
take **ascend** me not *away* in the midst of my days:
thy years are
throughout all generations **generation to generation**.
25 *Of old* **At thy face**
hast thou *laid the foundation of* **founded** the earth:
and the heavens are the work of thy hands.
26 They shall *perish* **destruct**,
but thou shalt *endure* **stand**:
yea, all of them shall *wax old* **wear out**
like *a garment* **clothes**;
as a *vesture* **robe** shalt thou change them,
and they shall be changed:
27 But thou art the same,
and thy years shall *have no end* **not consumate**.
28 The *children* **sons** of thy servants
shall *continue* **tabernacle**,
and their seed shall be established
before thee **at thy face**.

103

A Psalm of David.
1 Bless *the LORD* **Yah Veh**, O my soul:
and all that is within me, *bless* his holy name.
2 Bless *the LORD* **Yah Veh**, O my soul,
and forget not all his *benefits* **dealings**:
3 Who forgiveth all *thine iniquities* **thy perversities**;
who healeth all thy *diseases* **sicknesses**;
4 Who redeemeth thy life from *destruction* **the pit of ruin**;
who crowneth thee with *lovingkindness* **mercy**
and tender mercies;
5 Who satisfieth thy mouth with good *things*;
so that thy youth is renewed like the eagle's.
6 *The LORD executeth* **Yah Veh worketh**
righteousness **justness** and judgment
for all that are oppressed.
7 He made known his ways unto *Moses* **Mosheh**,
his *acts* **exploits** unto the *children* **sons** of *Israel* **Yisra El**.
8 *The LORD* **Yah Veh** is merciful and *gracious* **charismatic**,
slow to *anger* **wrath**, and *plenteous* **abundant** in mercy.
9 He *will* **shall** not *always chide* **contend in perpetuity**:
neither *will* **shall** he *keep his anger* **guard**
for ever **eternally**.
10 He hath not *dealt* **worked** with us
after our sins;
nor *rewarded* **dealt with** us
according to our *iniquities* **perversities**.
11 For as the *heaven* **heavens**
is high **be lofted** above the earth,
so great is **thus prevaileth mightily** his mercy
toward them that *fear* **awe** him.
12 As far as the *east* **rising** is from the *west* **dusk**,
so far hath he removed
our *transgressions* **rebellions** from us.
13 Like as a father *pitieth* **mercieth** his *children* **sons**,
so the LORD **thus Yah Veh**
pitieth **mercieth** them that *fear* **awe** him.
14 For he knoweth our *frame* **form**;
he remembereth that we are dust.
15 *As for* — man, his days are as grass:
as a *flower* **blossom** of the field,
so he *flourisheth* **blossometh**.
16 For the wind passeth over it, and it is gone;

and the place *thereof* shall *know* **recognize** it no more.
17 But the mercy of *the LORD* **Yah Veh**
is from *everlasting* **eternity** to *everlasting* **eternity**
upon them that *fear* **awe** him,
and his *righteousness* **justness**
unto *children's children* **sons' sons**;
18 To such as *keep* **guard** his covenant,
and to those that remember his *commandments* **precepts**
to *do* **work** them.
19 *The LORD* **Yah Veh**
hath prepared his throne in the heavens;
and his *kingdom ruleth* **sovereigndom reigneth** over all.
20 Bless *the LORD* **Yah Veh**, ye his angels,
that excel **mighty** in *strength* **force**,
that *do* **work** his *commandments* **words**,
hearkening unto the voice of his word.
21 Bless ye *the LORD* **Yah Veh**, all *ye* his hosts;
ye ministers of his, that *do* **work** his pleasure.
22 Bless *the LORD* **Yah Veh**,
all his works in all places of his *dominion* **reign**:
bless *the LORD* **Yah Veh**, O my soul.

104 Bless *the LORD* **Yah Veh**, O my soul.
O *LORD* **Yah Veh** my *God* **Elohim**,
thou art *very great* **greatened mightily**;
thou art *clothed* **enrobed** with honour and majesty.
2 Who coverest *thyself* with light as with a *garment* **cloth**:
who stretchest *out* the heavens like a curtain:
3 Who *layeth* **felleth** the beams
of his *chambers* **upper room** in the waters:
who *maketh the* **setteth thick** clouds his chariot:
who walketh upon the wings of the wind:
4 Who *maketh* **worketh** his angels spirits;
his ministers a flaming fire:
5 Who *laid* **founded**
the *foundations* **establishments** of the earth,
that *it* **they** should not *be removed* **totter**
for ever **eternally and eternally**.
6 Thou coveredst it with the *deep* **abyss**
as *with a garment* **a robe**:
the waters stood above the mountains.
7 *At* **From** thy rebuke they fled;
at **from** the voice of thy thunder they hasted away.
8 They *go up* **ascend** by the mountains;
they *go down* **descend** by the valleys
unto the place which thou hast founded for them.
9 Thou hast set a *bound* **border**
that they may not pass over;
that they turn not again to cover the earth.
10 He sendeth the springs into the *valleys* **wadies**,
which *run* **pass** among the *hills* **mountains**.
11 They give drink to every *beast* **live being** of the field:
the wild *asses quench* **runners break** their thirst.
12 By them shall the *fowls* **flyers** of the *heaven* **heavens**
have their habitation **tabernacle**,
which *sing among* **give voice between** the branches.
13 He *watereth* **moisteneth** the *hills* **mountains**
from his *chambers* **upper room**:
the earth is satisfied with the fruit of thy works.
14 He causeth the grass to *grow* **sprout**
for the *cattle* **animals**,
and herb for the service of *man* **humanity**:
that he may bring forth *food* **bread** out of the earth;
15 And wine that *maketh glad* **cheereth** the heart of man,
and *oil* **ointment** to make his face to shine,
and bread which *strengtheneth* **supporteth** man's heart.
16 The trees of *the LORD* **Yah Veh** are *full of sap* **satiated**;
the cedars of Lebanon, which he hath planted;
17 Where the birds *make their nests* **nest**:
as for the stork, the *fir trees* **firs** are her house.
18 The high *hills* **mountains**
are a refuge for the wild goats;
and the rocks for the conies.
19 He *appointed* **worked** the moon for seasons:
the sun knoweth his *going down* **entry**.
20 Thou *makest* **settest** darkness, and it is night:
wherein
all the *beasts* **live beings** of the forest *do* creep *forth*.
21 The *young lions* **whelps** roar after their prey,
and seek their *meat* **food** from *God* **El**.
22 The sun ariseth, they gather themselves *together*,
and *lay them down* **crouch** in their *dens* **habitations**.
23 *Man* **Humanity** goeth forth unto his *work* **deeds**
and to his *labour* **service** until the evening.
24 O *LORD* **Yah Veh**,
how *manifold are* thy works **abound by the myriads**!
in wisdom hast thou *made* **worked** them all:
the earth is full of thy *riches* **chattel**.
25 So is this great and *wide* **broad hand of the** sea,
wherein are *things creeping* **creepers** innumerable,
both small and great *beasts* **live beings**.
26 There go the ships:
there is that leviathan,
whom thou hast *made* **formed** to *play* **laugh** *therein*.
27 These *wait* **expect** all upon thee;
that thou mayest give them their *meat* **food**
in due season **on time**.
28 That thou givest them,
they *gather* **gleen**:
thou openest thine hand,
they are *filled* **satiated** with good.
29 Thou hidest thy face, they are *troubled* **terrified**:
thou *takest away* **gatherest** their *breath* **spirit**,
they *die* **expire**, and return to their dust.
30 Thou sendest forth thy spirit, they are created:
and thou renewest the face of the *earth* **soil**.
31 The *glory* **honour** of *the LORD* **Yah Veh**
shall *endure for ever* **be eternal**:
the LORD **Yah Veh** shall *rejoice* **cheer** in his works.
32 He looketh on the earth, and it trembleth:
he toucheth the *hills* **mountains**, and they smoke.
33 I *will* **shall** sing unto *the LORD* **Yah Veh**
as long as I live **during my life**:
I *will sing praise* **shall psalm** to my *God* **Elohim**
while I *have my being* **still be**.
34 My meditation of him shall *be sweet* **please**:
I *will be glad* **shall cheer** in *the LORD* **Yah Veh**.
35 Let the sinners be consumed out of the earth,
and let the wicked be no more.
Bless thou *the LORD* **Yah Veh**, O my soul.
Praise ye the LORD **Halalu Yah**.

105 O *give thanks* **extend hands**
unto *the LORD* **Yah Veh**;
call upon his name:
make known his *deeds* **exploits** among the people.
2 Sing unto him, *sing psalms* **psalm** unto him:
talk **meditate** ye of all his *wondrous works* **marvels**.
3 *Glory* **Halal** ye in his holy name:
let the heart of them *rejoice* **cheer**
that seek *the LORD* **Yah Veh**.
4 Seek *the LORD* **Yah Veh**, and his strength:
seek his face *evermore* **continually**.
5 Remember his *marvellous works* **marvels**
that he hath *done* **worked**;
his *wonders* **omens**, and the judgments of his mouth;
6 O ye seed of Abraham his servant,
ye *children* **sons** of *Jacob* **Yaaqov** his chosen.
7 He is *the LORD* **Yah Veh** our *God* **Elohim**:
his judgments are in all the earth.
8 He hath remembered his covenant *for ever* **eternally**,
the word which he *commanded* **misvahed**
to a thousand generations.
9 Which *covenant he made* **he cut** with Abraham,
and his oath unto *Isaac* **Yischaq**;
10 And *confirmed* **stood** the same
unto *Jacob* **Yaaqov** for a *law* **statute**,
and to *Israel* **Yisra El** for an *everlasting* **eternal** covenant:
11 Saying,
Unto thee *will* **shall** I give the land of *Canaan* **Kenaan**,
the *lot* **cord** of your inheritance:
12 When they were *but a* few *men* in number;
yea, very few, and *strangers* **sojourned** in it.
13 When they went from one *nation* **goyim** to another,
from *one kingdom* **sovereigndom** to another people;
14 He *suffered* **allowed** no *man* **human**
to *do them* wrong **them**:
yea, he reproved *kings* **sovereigns** for their sakes;
15 *Saying*, Touch not mine anointed,
and *do* **vilify not** my prophets *no harm*.

16 *Moreover* he called for a famine upon the land:
he brake the whole *staff* **rod** of bread.
17 He sent a man *before them* **at their face**,
even Joseph **Yoseph**, who was sold for a servant:
18 Whose feet they *hurt* **humbled** with fetters:
he **his soul** was laid in iron:
19 Until the time that his word came:
the *word* **saying** of *the LORD tried* **Yah Veh refined** him.
20 The *king* **sovereign** sent and loosed him;
even the *ruler* **sovereign** of the people,
and *let him go free* **loosed him**.
21 He *made* **set** him *lord* **adoni** of his house,
and *ruler* **sovereign** of all his *substance* **chattel**:
22 To bind his *princes* **governors** at his *pleasure* **soul**;
and *teach* **enwisen** his *senators wisdom* **elders**.
23 *Israel* **Yisra El** also came into *Egypt* **Misrayim**;
and *Jacob* **Yaaqov** sojourned in the land of Ham.
24 And *he increased* his people
greatly **became mighty fruitbearing**;
and *made them stronger* **mightier**
than their *enemies* **tribulators**.
25 He turned their heart to hate his people,
to *deal subtilly with* **deceive** his servants.
26 He sent *Moses* **Mosheh** his servant;
and *Aaron* **Aharon** whom he had chosen.
27 They *shewed* **set words of** his signs among them,
and *wonders* **omens** in the land of Ham.
28 He sent darkness, and *made it dark* **it darkened**;
and they rebelled not against his word.
29 He turned their waters into blood,
and *slew* **deathified** their fish.
30 Their land
brought forth **teemed with** frogs *in abundance*,
in the chambers of their *kings* **sovereigns**.
31 He *spake* **said**,
and there came *divers sorts of flies* **swarms**,
and *lice* **stingers** in all their *coasts* **borders**.
32 He gave them hail for *rain* **downpour**,
and flaming fire in their land.
33 He smote their vines also and their fig trees;
and brake the trees of their *coasts* **borders**.
34 He *spake* **said**,
and the locusts came, and *caterpillers* **cankerworms**,
and that without number — **innumerable**,
35 And did eat up all the herbs in their land,
and devoured the fruit of their *ground* **soil**.
36 He smote also all the firstborn in their land,
the *chief* **firstfruits** of all their strength.
37 He brought them forth also with silver and gold:
and *there was* not one *feeble person* **faltered**
among their *tribes* **scions**.
38 *Egypt was glad* **Misrayim cheered** when they departed:
for the *fear* **dread** of them fell upon them.
39 He spread a cloud for a covering;
and fire to *give light* **lighten** in the night.
40 *The people* **They** asked, and he brought quails,
and satisfied them with the bread of *heaven* **the heavens**.
41 He opened the rock,
and the waters *gushed out* **flowed**;
they *ran* **walked** in the *dry places* **parch** like a river.
42 For he remembered his holy *promise* **word**,
and Abraham his servant.
43 And he brought forth his people *with joy* **rejoicing**,
and his chosen *with gladness* **shouting**:
44 And gave them the lands of the *heathen* **goyim**:
and they *inherited* **possessed**
the *labour* **toil** of the *people* **nations**;
45 That they might *observe* **guard** his statutes,
and *keep* **guard** his *laws* **torah**.
Praise ye the LORD **Halalu Yah**.

106 *Praise ye the LORD* **Halalu Yah**.
O *give thanks* **extend hands** unto *the LORD* **Yah Veh**;
for he is good:
for his mercy *endureth for ever* **is eternal**.
2 Who can utter the *mighty acts* **might**
of *the LORD* **Yah Veh**?
who can *shew forth* **hear** all his *praise* **halal**?
3 *Blessed* **Blithe** are they that *keep* **guard** judgment,
and he that *doeth righteousness* **worketh justness**
at all times.
4 Remember me, O *LORD* **Yah Veh**,
with the *favour that thou bearest* **pleasure**
unto **of** thy people:
O visit me with thy salvation;
5 That I may see the good of thy chosen,
that I may *rejoice* **cheer**
in the *gladness* **cheerfulness** of thy *nation* **goyim**,
that I may *glory* **halal** with thine inheritance.
6 We have sinned with our fathers,
we have *committed iniquity* **perverted**,
we have done wickedly.
7 Our fathers *understood* **comprehended** not
thy *wonders* **marvels** in *Egypt* **Misrayim**;
they remembered not
the *multitude* **abundance** of thy mercies;
but *provoked him* **rebelled** at the sea,
even at the *Red* **Reed** sea.
8 *Nevertheless* he saved them for his name's sake,
that he might make his *mighty power to be* **might** known.
9 He rebuked the *Red* **Reed** sea also,
and it *was dried up* **parched**:
so he *led* **walked** them through the *depths* **abysses**,
as through the wilderness.
10 And he saved them
from the hand of him that hated them,
and redeemed them from the hand of the enemy.
11 And the waters covered their *enemies* **tribulators**:
there was not one **none** of them *left* **remained**.
12 Then *believed* **trusted** they his words;
they sang his *praise* **halal**.
13 They *soon forgat* **hasted to forget** his works;
they waited not for his counsel:
14 But *lusted exceedingly* **in desiring**,
desired in the wilderness,
and *tempted God* **tested El** in the *desert* **desolation**.
15 And he gave them their *request* **petition**;
but sent *leanness* **emaciation** into their soul.
16 They envied *Moses* **Mosheh** also in the camp,
and *Aaron* **Aharon** the *saint* **holy** of *the LORD* **Yah Veh**.
17 The earth opened and swallowed *up* Dathan
and covered the *company* **witness** of *Abiram* **Abi Ram**.
18 And a fire *was kindled* **burnt** in their *company* **witness**;
the flame burned *up* the wicked.
19 They *made* **worked** a calf in Horeb,
and *worshipped* **prostrated to** the molten *image*.
20 Thus they changed their *glory* **honour**
into the *similitude* **pattern** of an ox
that eateth *grass* **herbage**.
21 They forgat *God* **El** their saviour,
which had *done* **worked** great *things* in *Egypt* **Misrayim**;
22 *Wondrous works* **Marvels** in the land of Ham,
and terrible things **awesomenesses** by the *Red* **Reed** sea.
23 *Therefore* he said
that he *would destroy* **should desolate** them,
had not Moses **unless Mosheh** his chosen
stood *before him* **at his face** in the breach,
to turn away his *wrath* **fury**,
lest he should *destroy* **ruin** *them*.
24 Yea, they *despised* **spurned** the *pleasant* land **of desire**,
they *believed* **trusted** not his word:
25 But *murmured* **rebelled** in their tents,
and hearkened not unto the voice of *the LORD* **Yah Veh**.
26 Therefore he lifted up his hand against them,
to *overthrow* **fell** them in the wilderness:
27 To *overthrow* **fell** their seed also
among the *nations* **goyim**,
and to *scatter* **winnow** them in the lands.
28 They joined *themselves also unto Baalpeor* **Baal Peor**,
and ate the sacrifices of the dead.
29 Thus they *provoked* **vexed** him *to anger*
with their *inventions* **exploits**:
and the plague brake in upon them.
30 Then stood up *Phinehas* **Pinechas**,
and *executed judgment* **prayed**:
and *so* the plague was *stayed* **restrained**.
31 And that was *counted* **fabricated** unto him
for *righteousness* **justness**
unto all generations **generation to generation**
for evermore **eternally**.

32 They *angered* **enraged** him also at the waters of strife,
so that it went *ill* **evilly** with *Moses* **Mosheh**
for their sakes:
33 Because they *provoked* **rebelled against** his spirit,
so that he *spake unadvisedly* **babbled** with his lips.
34 They *did not destroy* **desolated not** the *nations* **people**,
concerning whom
the LORD commanded **Yah Veh said to** them:
35 But were mingled among the *heathen* **goyim**,
and learned their works.
36 And they served their idols:
which were a snare unto them.
37 Yea, they sacrificed their sons and their daughters
unto *devils* **demons**,
38 And *shed* **poured** innocent blood,
even the blood of their sons and of their daughters,
whom they sacrificed unto the idols of *Canaan* **Kenaan**:
and the land was *polluted* **profaned** with blood.
39 Thus were they *defiled* **fouled** with their own works,
and *went a whoring* **whored**
with **in** their *own inventions* **exploits**.
40 Therefore was the wrath of *the LORD* **Yah Veh**
kindled against his people,
insomuch that he abhorred his own inheritance.
41 And he gave them into the hand of the *heathen* **goyim**;
and they that hated them *ruled* **reigned** over them.
42 Their enemies also oppressed them,
and they were *brought into subjection* **subdued**
under their hand.
43 Many times did he *deliver* **rescue** them;
but they *provoked him* **rebelled** with their counsel,
and were *brought low* **subdued** for their *iniquity* **perversity**.
44 *Nevertheless*
he *regarded* **saw** their *affliction* **tribulation**,
when he heard their *cry* **shouting**:
45 And he remembered for them his covenant,
and *repented* **sighed**
according to the *multitude* **abundance** of his mercies.
46 He *made* **gave** them also to be *pitied* **mercied**
at the face of all those
that *carried* **captured** them *captives*.
47 Save us, O *LORD* **Yah Veh** our *God* **Elohim**,
and gather us from among the *heathen* **goyim**,
to *give thanks* **extend hands** unto thy holy name,
and to *triumph* **laud** in thy *praise* **halal**.
48 Blessed
be *the LORD God* **Yah Veh Elohim** of *Israel* **Yisra El**
from *everlasting* **eternity** to *everlasting* **eternity**:
and let all the people say, Amen.
Praise ye the LORD **Halalu Yah**.

BOOK V

107

1 O *give thanks* **extend hands**
unto *the LORD* **Yah Veh**,
for he is good:
for his mercy *endureth for ever* **is eternal**.
2 Let the redeemed of *the LORD* **Yah Veh** say *so*,
whom he hath redeemed
from the hand of the *enemy* **tribulator**;
3 And gathered them out of the lands,
from the *east* **rising**, and from *the west* **duskward**,
from the north, and from *the south* **seaward**.
4 They *wandered* **strayed** in the wilderness
in a *solitary* way **of desolation**;
they found no city *to dwell in* **of settlement**.
5 *Hungry* **Famished** and thirsty,
their soul *fainted* **languished** in them.
6 Then they cried unto *the LORD* **Yah Veh**
in their *trouble* **tribulation**,
and he *delivered* **rescued** them out of their distresses.
7 And he *led* **aimed** them *forth* by the *right* **straight** way,
that they might go to a city of *habitation* **settlement**.
8 *Oh that men would praise the LORD*
Extend hands unto Yah Veh
for his *goodness* **mercy**,
and for his *wonderful works* **marvels**
to the *children* **sons** of *men* **humanity**!
9 For he satisfieth the *longing* **yearning** soul,
and filleth the *hungry* **famished** soul with goodness.
10 Such as *sit* **settle** in darkness
and in the shadow of death,
being bound in *affliction* **humiliation** and iron;
11 Because they rebelled
against the *words* **sayings** of *God* **El**,
and *contemned* **scorned** the counsel
of *the most High* **Elyon**:
12 *Therefore*
he *brought down* **subdued** their heart with *labour* **toil**;
they *fell down* **stumbled**,
and there was *none to help* **no helper**.
13 Then they cried unto *the LORD* **Yah Veh**
in their *trouble* **tribulation**,
and he saved them out of their distresses.
14 He brought them out of darkness
and the shadow of death,
and *brake* **tore** their bands in sunder.
15 *Oh that men would praise the LORD*
Extend hands unto Yah Veh
for his *goodness* **mercy**,
and for his *wonderful works* **marvels**
to the *children* **sons** of *men* **humanity**!
16 For he hath broken the *gates* **doors** of *brass* **copper**,
and cut the bars of iron *in sunder*.
17 Fools *because* **by way** of their *transgression* **rebellion**,
and *because* **by way** of their *iniquities* **perversities**,
are *afflicted* **humbled**.
18 Their soul abhorreth all manner of *meat* **food**;
and they *draw near* **touch**
unto the *gates* **portals** of death.
19 Then they cry unto *the LORD* **Yah Veh**
in their *trouble* **tribulation**,
and he saveth them out of their distresses.
20 He sent his word, and healed them,
and *delivered* **rescued** them
from their *destructions* **pitfalls**.
21 *Oh that men would praise the LORD*
Extend hands unto Yah Veh
for his *goodness* **mercy**,
and for his *wonderful works* **marvels**
to the *children* **sons** of *men* **humanity**!
22 And let them sacrifice the sacrifices
of *thanksgiving* **extended hands**,
and *declare* **scribe** his works with *rejoicing* **shouting**.
23 They that *go down* **descend** to the sea in ships,
that *do business* **work** in great waters;
24 These see the works of *the LORD* **Yah Veh**,
and his *wonders* **marvels** in the deep.
25 For he *commandeth* **sayeth**,
and *raiseth* **stayeth** the stormy wind,
which lifteth up the waves *thereof*.
26 They *mount up* **ascend** to the *heaven* **heavens**,
they *go down again* **descend** to the *depths* **abysses**:
their soul is melted because of *trouble* **evil**.
27 They *reel to and fro* **celebrate**,
and stagger like *a drunken man* **one intoxicated**,
and *are at their wit's end* **all their wisdom is swallowed**.
28 Then they cry unto *the LORD* **Yah Veh**
in their *trouble* **tribulation**,
and he bringeth them out of their distresses.
29 He *maketh* **raiseth** the storm *a calm* **to hush**,
so that the waves *thereof are still* **hush**.
30 Then *are* they *glad* **cheer**
because they *be quiet* **hush**;
so he *bringeth* **leadeth** them
unto *their desired* **the** haven **of their desire**.
31 *Oh that men would praise the LORD*
Extend hands unto Yah Veh
for his *goodness* **mercy**,
and for his *wonderful works* **marvels**
to the *children* **sons** of *men* **humanity**!
32 Let them exalt him *also*
in the congregation of the people,
and *praise* **halal** him
in the *assembly* **settlement** of the elders.
33 He *turneth* **setteth** rivers
into a wilderness,
and the *watersprings* **springs of waters**
into *dry ground* **thirst**;
34 A fruitful land into *barrenness* **salt**,
for the *wickedness* **evil** of them that *dwell* **settle** therein.

35 He *turneth* **setteth** the wilderness
into a *standing* **marsh of** water,
and *dry ground* **parched earth**
into *watersprings* **springs of waters**.
36 And there
he *maketh the hungry to dwell* **settleth the famished**,
that they may prepare a city for *habitation* **settlement**;
37 And *sow* **seed** the fields, and plant vineyards,
which may *yield* **work** fruits of *increase* **produce**.
38 He blesseth them also,
so that they *are multiplied greatly* **abound mightily**;
and *suffereth* **diminisheth** not
their *cattle* **animals** *to decrease*.
39 *Again,* they *are minished* **diminish**
and *brought low* **prostrate**
through *oppression* **restraint**,
affliction **evil**, and *sorrow* **grief**.
40 He poureth *contempt* **disrespect**
upon *princes* **volunteers**,
and causeth them to *wander* **stray** in the *wilderness* **waste**,
where there is no way.
41 Yet *setteth he the poor on high* **he lofteth the needy**
from affliction **after humiliation**,
and *maketh him* **setteth** families like a flock.
42 The *righteous* **straight** shall see it, and *rejoice* **cheer**:
and all *iniquity* **wickedness** shall *stop* **shut** her mouth.
43 Whoso is wise,
and *will observe* **shall guard** these *things*,
even they shall *understand* **discern**
the *lovingkindness* **mercy** of *the LORD* **Yah Veh**.

108

A Song *or* Psalm of David.
1 O *God* **Elohim**, my heart is *fixed* **prepared**;
I *will* **shall** sing and *give praise* **psalm**,
even with my *glory* **honour**.
2 Awake, *psaltery* **bagpipe** and harp:
I *myself will* **shall** awake early.
3 I *will praise* **shall extend hands unto** thee,
O *LORD* **Yah Veh**,
among the people:
and I *will sing praises* **shall psalm** unto thee
among the *nations* **people**.
4 For thy mercy is great above the heavens:
and thy truth *reacheth* unto the *clouds* **vapours**.
5 Be thou *exalted* **lofted**, O *God* **Elohim**,
above the heavens:
and thy *glory* **honour** above all the earth;
6 That thy beloved may be *delivered* **rescued**:
save with thy right *hand,* and answer me.
7 *God* **Elohim** hath *spoken* **worded** in his holiness;
I *will rejoice* **shall jump for joy**,
I *will divide* **shall allot** Shechem,
and mete out
the valley of *Succoth* **Sukkoth/Brush Arbors**.
8 *Gilead* **Galad** is mine; *Manasseh* **Menash Sheh** is mine;
Ephraim **Ephrayim** also
is the *strength* **stronghold** of mine head;
Judah **Yah Hudah** is my *lawgiver* **statute setter**;
9 Moab is my *wash pot* **bath caldron**;
over Edom *will* **shall** I cast out my shoe;
over *Philistia will* **Pelesheth shall** I triumph.
10 Who *will* **shall** bring me into the *strong* **fortressed** city?
who *will* **shall** lead me into Edom?
11 *Wilt* **Shalt** not thou, *O God* **Elohim**,
who hast cast us off?
and *wilt* **shalt** not thou, O *God* **Elohim**,
go *forth* with our hosts?
12 Give us help from *trouble* **tribulation**:
for vain is the *help* **salvation** of *man* **humanity**.
13 Through *God* **Elohim** we shall *do* **work** valiantly:
for he *it is that* shall tread down our *enemies* **tribulators**.

109

To *the chief Musician* **His Eminence**,
A Psalm of David.
1 *Hold not thy peace* **Hush not**,
O *God* **Elohim** of my *praise* **halal**;
2 For the mouth of *the wicked* **wickedness**
and the mouth of *the deceitful* **deceit**
are opened against me:
they have *spoken* **worded** against me
with a *lying* **false** tongue.
3 They *compassed about* **surrounded me**
also with words of hatred;
and fought against me *without a cause* **gratuitously**.
4 For my love they are my *adversaries* **satans**:
but I *give myself unto* — prayer.
5 And they have *rewarded* **set upon** me evil for good,
and hatred for my love.
6 Set thou a wicked *man* over him:
and let Satan stand at his right *hand*.
7 When he shall be judged,
let him be *condemned* **judged wicked**:
and let his prayer become sin.
8 Let his days be few;
and let another take his *office* **oversight**.
9 Let his *children* **sons** be *fatherless* **orphans**,
and his *wife* **woman** a widow.
10 *Let his children be continually vagabonds*
In wandering, let his sons wander,
and beg **ask**:
let them seek *their bread also*
out of their *desolate places* **parched areas**.
11 Let the *extortioner catch* **exactor snare** all that he hath;
and let the strangers *spoil* **plunder** his labour.
12 Let there be none to *extend* **draw out** mercy unto him:
neither let there be any to *favour* **grant charism**
to his *fatherless children* **orphans**.
13 Let his posterity be cut off;
and in the **another** generation *following*
let their name be *blotted* **wiped** out.
14 Let the *iniquity* **perversity** of his fathers
be remembered with *the LORD* **Yah Veh**;
and let not the sin of his mother be *blotted* **wiped** out.
15 Let them be before *the LORD* **Yah Veh** continually,
that he may cut off the *memory* **memorial** of them
from the earth.
16 Because
hat he remembered not to *shew* **work** mercy,
but *persecuted* **pursued** the *poor* **humble** and needy man,
that he might *even slay* **deathify**
the *broken* **dejected** in heart.
17 As he loved *cursing* **to abase**, so let it come unto him:
as he delighted not in blessing, so let it be far from him.
18 As he *clothed* **enrobed** himself with *cursing* **abasing**
like as with his *garment* **tailoring**,
so let it come into his *bowels* **inwards** like water,
and like *oil* **ointment** into his bones.
19 Let it be unto him
as the *garment* **clothes** which covereth him,
and for a girdle wherewith he is girded continually.
20 Let this be
the reward **for the deeds** of *mine adversaries* **my satans**
from *the LORD* **Yah Veh**,
and of them that *speak* **word** evil against my soul.
21 But *do* **work** thou for me,
O *GOD the Lord* **Yah Veh Adonay**, for thy name's sake:
because thy mercy is good, *deliver* **rescue** thou me.
22 For I am *poor* **humble** and needy,
and my heart is *wounded* **pierced** within me.
23 I am gone like the shadow when it *declineth* **spreadeth**:
I am *tossed up and down* **shaken** as the locust.
24 My knees *are weak* **falter** through fasting;
and my flesh *faileth* **emaciates** of *fatness* **ointment**.
25 I became also a reproach unto them:
when they looked upon **they see** me,
they *shaked* **shake** their heads.
26 Help me, O *LORD* **Yah Veh** my *God* **Elohim**:
O save me according to thy mercy:
27 That they may know that this is thy hand;
that thou, *LORD* **O Yah Veh**, hast *done* **worked** it.
28 Let them *curse* **abase**, but bless thou:
when they arise, let them *be ashamed* **shame**;
but let thy servant *rejoice* **cheer**.
29 Let *mine adversaries* **my satans**
be clothed **enrobe** with shame,
and let them cover themselves
with their own *confusion* **shame**, as with a mantle.
30 *I will greatly praise the LORD*
I shall mightily halal Yah Veh with my mouth;
yea, I *will praise* **shall extend hands unto** him

among the *multitude* **great**.
31 For he shall stand at the right *hand* of the *poor* **needy**,
to save him from those that *condemn* **judge** his soul.

110
A Psalm of David.
1 *The LORD said* **An oracle of Yah Veh**
unto my *Lord* **Adonay**,
Sit **Settle** thou at my right *hand*,
until I *make* **set** thine enemies
thy footstool **the stool of thy feet**.
2 *The LORD* **Yah Veh** shall send the rod of thy strength
out of *Zion* **Siyon**:
rule **subjugate** thou in the midst of thine enemies.
3 Thy people shall *be willing* **volunteer**
in the day of thy *power* **valour**,
in the *beauties* **majesties** of holiness
from the womb of the *morning* **dawn**:
thou hast the dew of thy *youth* **childhood**.
4 *The LORD hath sworn* **Yah Veh oathed**,
and *will* **shall** not *repent* **sigh**,
Thou art a priest *for ever* **eternally**
after the *order* **word** of *Melchizedek* **Malki Sedeq**.
5 *The Lord* **Adonay** at thy right *hand*
shall strike *through kings* **sovereigns**
in the day of his wrath.
6 He shall *judge among* **plead the cause**
of the *heathen* **goyim**,
he shall fill the places with the *dead* bodies;
he shall *wound* **strike** the heads
over *many countries* **the great land**.
7 He shall drink of the *brook* **wadi** in the way:
therefore shall he lift *up* the head.

111
Praise ye the LORD **Halalu Yah**.
I *will praise the LORD* **shall extend hands unto Yah Veh**
with my whole heart,
in the *assembly* **private counsel** of the *upright* **straight**,
and in the *congregation* **witness**.
2 The works of *the LORD* **Yah Veh** are great,
sought out of all them that *have pleasure* **delight** therein.
3 His *work* **deed** is honourable and *glorious* **majestic**:
and his *righteousness* **justness**
endureth for ever **standeth eternal**.
4 He hath *made* **worked** his *wonderful works* **marvels**
to be remembered — **a memorial**:
the LORD **Yah Veh** is *gracious* **charismatic**
and *full of compassion* **merciful**.
5 He hath given *meat* **prey**
unto them that *fear* **awe** him:
he *will ever* **shall eternally**
be mindful of **remember** his covenant.
6 He hath *shewed* **told** his people
the *power* **force** of his works,
that he may give them
the *heritage* **inheritance** of the *heathen* **goyim**.
7 The works of his hands are *verity* **truth** and judgment;
all his commandments are *sure* **trustworthy**.
8 They *stand fast* **sustain**
for ever **eternally** and *ever* **eternally**,
and are *done* **worked**
in truth and *uprightness* **straightness**.
9 He sent redemption unto his people:
he hath *commanded* **misvahed** his covenant
for ever **eternally**:
holy and *reverend* **awesome** is his name.
10 The *fear* **awe** of *the LORD* **Yah Veh**
is the beginning of wisdom:
a good *understanding* **comprehension**
have all they that *do his commandments* **work them**:
his *praise endureth for ever* **halal standeth eternal**.

112
Praise ye the LORD **Halalu Yah**.
Blessed is **Blithe be** the man
that *feareth the LORD* **aweth Yah Veh**,
that delighteth *greatly* **mightily**
in his *commandments* **misvoth**.
2 His seed shall be mighty upon earth:
the generation of the *upright* **straight** shall be blessed.
3 Wealth and riches shall be in his house:
and his *righteousness* **justness**
endureth for ever **standeth eternal**.
4 Unto the *upright* **straight**
there ariseth light in the darkness:
he is *gracious* **charismatic**,
and *full of compassion* **merciful**, and *righteous* **just**.
5 A good man *sheweth favour* **granteth charism**,
and lendeth:
he *will guide* **shall sustain** his *affairs* **words**
with *discretion* **judgment**.
6 Surely he shall not *be moved for ever* **totter eternally**:
the *righteous* **just**
shall be *in everlasting remembrance* **an eternal memorial**.
7 He shall not *be afraid of* **awe** evil *tidings* **reports**:
his heart is *fixed* **established**,
trusting **confiding** in *the LORD* **Yah Veh**.
8 His heart is *established* **sustained**,
he shall not *be afraid* **awe**,
until he see his *desire upon his enemies* **tribulators**.
9 He hath *dispersed* **scattered**,
he hath given to the *poor* **needy**;
his *righteousness* **justness**
endureth for ever **standeth eternal**;
his horn shall be *exalted* **lofted** with honour.
10 The wicked shall see it, and be *grieved* **vexed**;
he shall gnash with his teeth, and melt away:
the desire of the wicked shall *perish* **destruct**.

113
Praise ye the LORD **Halalu Yah**.
Praise **Halal**, O ye servants of *the LORD* **Yah Veh**,
praise **halal** the name of *the LORD* **Yah Veh**.
2 Blessed be the name of *the LORD* **Yah Veh**
from this time forth and *for evermore* **eternally**.
3 From the rising of the sun
unto the *going down* **entry** *of the same*
the LORD'S **Yah Veh's** name is to be *praised* **halaled**.
4 *The LORD is high* **Yah Veh be lofted**
above all *nations* **goyim**,
and his *glory* **honour**
above the heavens.
5 Who is like unto *the LORD* **Yah Veh** our *God* **Elohim**,
who *dwelleth on high* **lofteth in his settlement**,
6 Who *humbleth* **abaseth** *himself*
to *behold the things that are in heaven* **see in the heavens**,
and in the earth!
7 He raiseth *up* the poor out of the dust,
and lifteth the needy out of the dunghill;
8 That he may set him with *princes* **volunteers**,
even with the *princes* **volunteers** of his people.
9 He *maketh* **causeth** the *barren woman* **sterile**
to *keep* **settle** house,
and to be a *joyful* **cheerful** mother of *children* **sons**.
Praise ye the LORD **Halalu Yah**.

114
When *Israel* **Yisra El**
went out of *Egypt* **Misrayim**,
the house of *Jacob* **Yaaqov**
from a people *of strange language* **unintelligible**;
2 *Judah* **Yah Hudah** was his *sanctuary* **holies**,
and Israel **Yisra El** his *dominion* **reign**.
3 The sea saw it, and fled:
Jordan was driven **Yarden turned** back.
4 The mountains *skipped* **danced** like rams,
and the little hills like *lambs* **sons of flocks**.
5 What *ailed thee*, O thou sea, that thou fleddest?
thou *Jordan* **Yarden**, that thou *wast driven* **turnest** back?
6 Ye mountains, that ye *skipped* **danced** like rams;
and ye *little* hills, like *lambs* **sons of flocks**?
7 *Tremble* **Writhe**, thou earth,
at the *presence* **face** of *the Lord* **Adonay**,
at the *presence* **face** of *the God* **Elohah** of *Jacob* **Yaaqov**;
8 Which turned the rock into a *standing* **marsh** water,
the flint into a fountain of waters.

115
Not unto us, O *LORD* **Yah Veh**, not unto us,
but unto thy name give *glory* **honour**,
for thy mercy, and for thy truth's sake.
2 Wherefore should the *heathen* **goyim** say,
Where is *now* **I beseech,** their *God* **Elohim**?
3 But our *God* **Elohim** is in the heavens:
he hath *done* **worked**

whatsoever he hath *pleased* **desired**.
4 Their idols are silver and gold,
the work of *men's* **human** hands.
5 They have mouths, but they *speak* **word** not:
eyes have they, but they see not:
6 They have ears, but they hear not:
noses **nostrils** have they, but they *smell* **scent** not:
7 They have hands, but they *handle* **touch** not:
feet have they, but they walk not:
neither *speak* **mutter** they through their throat.
8 They that *make* **work** them are like unto them;
so is every one that *trusteth* **confideth** in them.
9 O *Israel* **Yisra El**,
trust **confide** thou in *the LORD* **Yah Veh**:
he is their help and their *shield* **buckler**.
10 O house of *Aaron* **Aharon**,
trust **confide** in *the LORD* **Yah Veh**:
he is their help and their *shield* **buckler**.
11 Ye that *fear the LORD* **awe Yah Veh**,
trust **confide** in *the LORD* **Yah Veh**:
he is their help and their *shield* **buckler**.
12 *The LORD* **Yah Veh** hath been mindful of us:
he *will* **shall** bless us;
he *will* **shall** bless the house of *Israel* **Yisra El**;
he *will* **shall** bless the house of *Aaron* **Aharon**.
13 He *will* **shall** bless them
that *fear the LORD* **awe Yah Veh**, *both* small and great.
14 *The LORD* **Yah Veh** shall increase you *more and more*,
you and your *children* **sons**.
15 Ye are blessed of *the LORD* **Yah Veh**
which *made heaven* **worked the heavens** and earth.
16 The *heaven* **heavens**,
even the heavens, are *the LORD'S* **Yah Veh's**:
but the earth
hath he given to the *children* **sons** of *men* **humanity**.
17 The dead *praise* **halal** not *the LORD* **Yah**,
neither any that *go down* **descend** into silence.
18 But we *will* **shall** bless *the LORD* **Yah**
from this time *forth* and *for evermore* **eternally**.
Praise the LORD **Halalu Yah**.

116

I love *the LORD* **Yah Veh**,
because he hath heard my voice and my supplications.
2 Because he hath *inclined* **extended** his ear unto me,
therefore
will **shall** I call *upon him as long as I live* **all my days**.
3 The *sorrows* **cords** of death
compassed **surrounded** me,
and the *pains of hell* **straits of sheol**
gat hold upon **found** me:
I found *trouble* **tribulation** and *sorrow* **grief**.
4 Then called I upon the name of *the LORD* **Yah Veh**;
O *LORD* **Yah Veh**, I beseech thee,
deliver **rescue** my soul.
5 *Gracious* **Charismatic** is *the LORD* **Yah Veh**,
and *righteous* **just**;
yea, our *God is merciful* **Elohim mercieth**.
6 *The LORD* **Yah Veh**
preserveth **guardeth** the *simple* **gullible**:
I *was brought low* **languished**, and he *helped* **saved** me.
7 Return unto thy rest, O my soul;
for *the LORD* **Yah Veh** hath dealt *bountifully* with thee.
8 For thou hast *delivered* **rescued** my soul from death,
mine eyes from tears,
and my feet from falling.
9 I *will* **shall** walk *before the LORD* **at the face of Yah Veh**
in the land of the living.
10 I *believed* **trusted**, therefore have I *spoken* **worded**:
I was *greatly afflicted* **mightily humbled**:
11 I said in my haste, All *men* **humans** are liars.
12 What shall I *render* **return** unto *the LORD* **Yah Veh**
for all his benefits toward me?
13 I *will take* **shall lift** the cup of salvation,
and call upon the name of *the LORD* **Yah Veh**.
14 I *will pay* **shall shalam** my vows
unto *the LORD* **Yah Veh**
now in the presence of all his people.
15 *Precious* **Esteemed**
in the *sight* **eyes** of *the LORD* **Yah Veh**
is the death of his *saints* **mercied**.
16 **I beseech,** *O LORD* **O Yah Veh**,
truly I *am* thy servant;
I *am* thy servant,
and the son of *thine handmaid* **thy maid**:
thou hast loosed my bonds.
17 I *will offer* **shall sacrifice** to thee
the sacrifice of *thanksgiving* **extended hands**,
and *will* **shall** call upon the name of *the LORD* **Yah Veh**.
18 I *will pay* **shall shalam** my vows
unto *the LORD* **Yah Veh**
now in the presence of all his people,
19 In the courts of *the LORD'S* **Yah Veh's** house,
in the midst of thee, O *Jerusalem* **Yeru Shalem**.
Praise ye the LORD **Halalu Yah**.

117

O *praise the LORD* **halal Yah Veh**,
all ye *nations* **goyim**:
praise **laud** him,
all ye *people* **nations**.
2 For his *merciful kindness* **mercy**
is great **prevaileth mightily** toward us:
and the truth of *the LORD* **Yah Veh**
endureth for ever **is eternal**.
Praise ye the LORD **Halalu Yah**.

118

O *give thanks* **extend hands**
unto *the LORD* **Yah Veh**;
for he is good:
because his mercy *endureth for ever* **is eternal**.
2 Let *Israel now* **Yisra El, I beseech,** say,
that his mercy *endureth for ever* **is eternal**.
3 Let the house of *Aaron now* **Aharon I beseech,** say,
that his mercy *endureth for ever* **is eternal**.
4 Let them, *now* **I beseech,**
that *fear the LORD* **awe Yah Veh** say,
that his mercy *endureth for ever* **is eternal**.
5 I called upon *the LORD* **Yah** in *distress* **the straits**:
the LORD **Yah** answered me,
and set me in a large place **from an expanse**.
6 *The LORD* **Yah Veh** is on my side;
I *will* **shall** not *fear* **awe**:
what *can man do* **shall humanity work** unto me?
7 *The LORD* **Yah Veh** taketh my part
with *them that help me* **my helpers**:
therefore shall I see *my desire upon* them that hate me.
8 *It is* better to *trust* **seek refuge** in *the LORD* **Yah Veh**
than to *put confidence* **confide** in *man* **humanity**.
9 *It is* better to *trust* **seek refuge** in *the LORD* **Yah Veh**
than to *put confidence* **confide** in *princes* **volunteers**.
10 All *nations compassed* **goyim surrounded** me *about*:
but in the name of *the LORD* **Yah Veh**
will I destroy **I shall cut** them **off**.
11 They *compassed* **surrounded** me *about*;
yea, they *compassed* **surrounded** me *about*:
but in the name of *the LORD* **Yah Veh**
I *will destroy* **shall cut** them **off**.
12 They *compassed* **surrounded** me *about* like bees:
they are *quenched* **extinguished** as the fire of thorns:
for in the name of *the LORD* **Yah Veh**
I *will destroy* **shall cut** them **off**.
13 **In overthrowing,**
Thou hast *thrust sore at me* **overthrown me**
that I might fall:
but *the LORD* **Yah Veh** helped me.
14 *The LORD* **Yah** is my strength and *song* **psalm**,
and is become my salvation.
15 The voice of *rejoicing* **shouting** and salvation
is in the *tabernacles* **tents** of the *righteous* **just**:
the right *hand* of *the LORD* **Yah Veh**
doeth **worketh** valiantly.
16 The right *hand* of *the LORD* **Yah Veh** is exalted:
the right *hand of the LORD* **Yah Veh**
doeth **worketh** valiantly.
17 I shall not die, but live,
and *declare* **scribe** the works of *the LORD* **Yah**.
18 **In disciplining,**
The LORD **Yah** hath *chastened* **disciplined** me *sore*:
but he hath not given me over unto death.
19 Open to me the *gates* **portals** of *righteousness* **justness**:
I *will* **shall** go into them,

and I *will praise the LORD* **shall extend hands unto Yah**:
20 This *gate* **portal** of *the LORD* **Yah Veh**,
into which the *righteous* **just** shall enter.
21 I *will praise* **shall extend hands unto** thee:
for thou hast *heard* **answered** me,
and art become my salvation.
22 The stone *which* the builders refused
is become the head *stone* of the corner.
23 This is *the LORD'S* **Yah Veh's** doing;
it is marvellous in our eyes.
24 This is the day
which the LORD **Yah Veh** hath *made* **worked**;
we *will rejoice* **shall twirl** and *be glad* **cheer** in it.
25 Save now° **I beseech**,
I beseech thee, O *LORD* **Yah Veh**:
O *LORD* **Yah Veh**, I beseech thee,
send now prosperity **prosper, I beseech**.
°Hoshia Nah
26 Blessed be he
that cometh in the name of *the LORD* **Yah Veh**:
we have blessed you
out of the house of *the LORD* **Yah Veh**.
27 *God* **El** is *the LORD* **Yah Veh**,
which hath *shewed us light* **enlightened us**:
bind the *sacrifice* **celebration** with *cords* **ropes**,
even unto the horns of the **sacrifice** altar.
28 Thou art my *God* **El**,
and I *will praise* **shall extend hands unto** thee:
thou art my *God* **Elohim**, I *will* **shall** exalt thee.
29 O *give thanks* **extend hands** unto *the LORD* **Yah Veh**;
for he is good:
for his mercy *endureth for ever* **is eternal**.

119

ALEPH.

1 *Blessed* **Blithed** are the *undefiled* **integrious** in the way,
who walk in the *law* **torah** of *the LORD* **Yah Veh**.
2 *Blessed* **Blithed** are they
that *keep* **guard** his *testimonies* **witnesses**,
and that seek him with the whole heart.
3 They also do no *iniquity* **wickedness**:
they walk in his ways.
4 Thou hast *commanded* **misvahed** *us*
to *keep* **guard** thy precepts *diligently* **mightily**.
5 O that my ways
were *directed* **prepared** to *keep* **guard** thy statutes!
6 Then shall I not *be ashamed* **shame**,
when I *have respect* **look**
unto all thy *commandments* **misvoth**.
7 I *will praise* **shall extend hands unto** thee
with *uprightness* **straightness** of heart,
when I shall have learned
thy *righteous judgments* **judgments of justness**.
8 I *will keep* **shall guard** thy statutes:
O forsake me not *utterly* **mightily**.

BETH.

9 Wherewithal shall a young man *cleanse* **purify** his way?
by *taking heed thereto* **guarding** according to thy word.
10 With my whole heart have I sought thee:
O let me not *wander* **err inadvertantly**
from thy *commandments* **misvoth**.
11 Thy *word* **sayings** have I *hid* **treasured** in mine heart,
that I might not sin against thee.
12 Blessed *art* thou, O *LORD* **Yah Veh**:
teach me thy statutes.
13 With my lips
have I *declared* **scribed** all the judgments of thy mouth.
14 I have rejoiced
in the way of thy *testimonies* **witnesses**,
as *much as in all riches* **over all wealth**.
15 I *will* **shall** meditate in thy precepts,
and *have respect* **scan** unto thy ways.
16 I *will* **shall** delight myself in thy statutes:
I *will* **shall** not forget thy word.

GIMEL.

17 Deal *bountifully* with thy servant,
that I may live, and *keep* **guard** thy word.
18 *Open* **Expose** thou mine eyes,
that I may behold *wondrous things* **marvels**
out of thy *law* **torah**.
19 I am a *stranger* **sojourner** in the earth:
hide not thy *commandments* **misvoth** from me.
20 My soul *breaketh* **crusheth** for the *longing* **desire**
that it hath unto thy judgments at all times.
21 Thou hast rebuked the *proud* **arrogant**
that are cursed,
which *do* err **inadvertently**
from thy *commandments* **misvoth**.
22 *Remove* **Roll away** from me
reproach and *contempt* **disrespect**;
for I have *kept* **guarded** thy *testimonies* **witnesses**.
23 *Princes* **Governors** also
did sit **settled** and *speak* **worded** against me:
but thy servant *did meditate* **meditated** in thy statutes.
24 Thy *testimonies* **witnesses** also are my delight
and my *counsellors* **councilmen**.

DALETH.

25 My soul *cleaveth* **adhereth** unto the dust:
quicken **enliven** thou me according to thy word.
26 I have *declared* **scribed** my ways,
and thou *heardest* **answerest** me:
teach me thy statutes.
27 *Make* **Have** me to *understand* **discern**
the way of thy precepts:
so shall I *talk* **meditate** of thy *wondrous works* **marvels**.
28 My soul *melteth* **drippeth** for *heaviness* **grief**:
strengthen **raise** thou me according unto thy word.
29 *Remove* **Turn aside** from me
the way of *lying* **falsehoods**:
and *grant me thy law graciously*
with thy torah grant me charism.
30 I have chosen the way of *truth* **trustworthiness**:
thy judgments have I *laid* **placed** *before me*.
31 I have *stuck* **adhered** unto thy *testimonies* **witnesses**:
O *LORD* **Yah Veh**, *put me not to* shame **me not**.
32 I *will* **shall** run the way of thy *commandments* **misvoth**,
when thou shalt enlarge my heart.

HE.

33 Teach me, O *LORD* **Yah Veh**, the way of thy statutes;
and I shall *keep* **guard** it unto the end.
34 *Give me understanding* **Have me discern**,
and I shall *keep* **guard** thy *law* **torah**;
yea, I shall *observe* **guard** it with my whole heart.
35 *Make* **Aim** me *to go*
in the path of thy *commandments* **misvoth**;
for therein do I delight.
36 *Incline* **Extend** my heart unto thy *testimonies* **witnesses**,
and not to *covetousness* **greed**.
37 *Turn away* **Pass** mine eyes
from *beholding* **seeing** vanity;
and *quicken* **enliven** thou me in thy way.
38 *Stablish* **Raise up** thy *word* **sayings** unto thy servant,
who *is devoted to thy fear* **aweth thee**.
39 *Turn away* **Pass** my reproach which I fear:
for thy judgments are good.
40 Behold, I have *longed* **desired** after thy precepts:
quicken **enliven** me in thy *righteousness* **justness**.

VAU.

41 Let thy mercies come also unto me,
O *LORD* **Yah Veh**,
even thy salvation, according to thy *word* **sayings**.
42 So shall I have *wherewith* **a word**
to answer him that reproacheth me:
for I *trust* **confide** in thy word.
43 And *take* **strip** not the word of truth
utterly **mightily** out of my mouth;
for I have *hoped in* **awaited** thy judgments.
44 So shall I *keep* **guard** thy *law* **torah** continually
for ever **eternally** and *ever* **eternally**.
45 And I *will* **shall** walk at *liberty* **large**:
for I seek thy precepts.
46 I *will speak* **shall word** of thy *testimonies* **witnesses**
also before *kings* **sovereigns**,
and *will* **shall** not *be ashamed* **shame**.
47 And I *will* **shall** delight myself
in thy *commandments* **misvoth**,

which I have loved.
48 My *hands* **palms** also
will **shall** I lift up unto thy *commandments* **misvoth**,
which I have loved;
and I *will* **shall** meditate in thy statutes.

ZAIN.
49 Remember the word unto thy servant,
upon which thou hast caused me to *hope* **await**.
50 This is my *comfort* **sighing** in my *affliction* **humiliation**:
for thy *word hath quickened* **sayings have enlivened** me.
51 The *proud* **arrogant**
have *had me greatly in derision* **mightily scorned me**:
yet have I not *declined* **stretched** from thy *law* **torah**.
52 I remembered thy judgments of *old* **eternity**,
O *LORD* **Yah Veh**;
and have *comforted* **sighed over** myself.
53 *Horror* **Raging** hath taken hold upon me
because of the wicked that forsake thy *law* **torah**.
54 Thy statutes have been my *songs* **psalms**
in the house of my *pilgrimage* **sojournings**.
55 I have remembered thy name, O *LORD* **Yah Veh**,
in the night,
and have *kept* **guarded** thy *law* **torah**.
56 This I had, because I *kept* **guarded** thy precepts.

CHETH.
57 *Thou art my portion*, O *LORD* **Yah Veh is my allotment**:
I have said that I *would keep* **should guard** thy words.
58 I *intreated* **stroked** thy *favour* **face** with my whole heart:
be merciful unto **grant** me **charism**
according to thy *word* **sayings**.
59 I *thought on* **fabricated** my ways,
and turned my feet unto thy *testimonies* **witnesses**.
60 I *made haste* **hastened**, and *delayed* **lingered** not
to *keep* **guard** thy *commandments* **misvoth**.
61 The *bands* **cords** of the wicked
have *robbed* **surrounded** me:
but I have not forgotten thy *law* **torah**.
62 At midnight I *will* **shall** rise
to *give thanks* **extend hands** unto thee
because of thy *righteous* judgments **of justness**.
63 I am a companion of all them that *fear* **awe** thee,
and of them that *keep* **guard** thy precepts.
64 The earth, O *LORD* **Yah Veh**, is full of thy mercy:
teach me thy statutes.

TETH.
65 Thou hast *dealt well* **worked good** with thy servant,
O *LORD* **Yah Veh**, according unto thy word.
66 Teach me good *judgment* **taste** and knowledge:
for I have *believed* **trusted** thy *commandments* **misvoth**.
67 Before I was *afflicted* **humbled**
I *went astray* **erred inadvertently**:
but now have I *kept* **guarded** thy *word* **sayings**.
68 Thou art good, and doest good;
teach me thy statutes.
69 The *proud* **arrogant**
have *forged a lie* **patched falsehood** against me:
but I *will keep* **shall guard** thy precepts
with my whole heart.
70 Their heart is *as fat as grease* **fattened**;
but I delight in thy *law* **torah**.
71 It is good for me that I have been *afflicted* **humbled**;
that I might learn thy statutes.
72 The *law* **torah** of thy mouth
is better unto me than thousands of gold and silver.

JOD.
73 Thy hands
have *made* **worked** me and *fashioned* **established** me:
give me understanding **have me discern**,
that I may learn thy *commandments* **misvoth**.
74 They that *fear* **awe** thee
will be glad **shall cheer** when they see me;
because I have *hoped in* **awaited** thy word.
75 I know, O *LORD* **Yah Veh**,
that thy judgments are *right* **justness**,
and that thou in *faithfulness* **trustworthiness**
hast *afflicted* **humbled** me.
76 Let, I pray thee,
thy *merciful kindness* **mercy** be for my *comfort* **sighing**,
according to thy *word* **sayings** unto thy servant.
77 Let thy tender mercies come unto me, that I may live:
for thy *law* **torah** is my delight.
78 Let the *proud be ashamed* **arrogant shame**;
for they
dealt perversely with me without a cause
twisted me falsely:
but I *will* **shall** meditate in thy precepts.
79 Let those that *fear* **awe** thee turn unto me,
and those that have known thy *testimonies* **witnesses**.
80 Let my heart be *sound* **integrious** in thy statutes;
that I *be* **shame** not *ashamed*.

CAPH.
81 My soul *fainteth* **is finished off** for thy salvation:
but I *hope in* **await** thy word.
82 Mine eyes *fail* **are finished off** for thy *word* **sayings**,
saying, When *wilt* **shalt** thou *comfort* **sigh over** me?
83 For I am become like a *bottle* **skin** in the smoke;
yet do I not forget thy statutes.
84 How many are the days of thy servant?
when *wilt* **shalt** thou *execute* **work** judgment
on them that *persecute* **pursue** me?
85 The *proud* **arrogant** have digged pits for me,
which are not after thy *law* **torah**.
86 All thy *commandments* **misvoth**
are *faithful* **trustworthy**:
they *persecute* **pursue** me *wrongfully* **falsely**;
help thou me.
87 They had almost *consumed* **finished** me **off**
upon earth;
but I forsook not thy precepts.
88 *Quicken* **Enliven** me after thy *lovingkindness* **mercy**;
so shall I *keep* **guard** the *testimony* **witness** of thy mouth.

LAMED.
89 *For ever* **Eternally**, O *LORD* **Yah Veh**,
thy word is *settled* **stationed** in *heaven* **the heavens**.
90 Thy *faithfulness* **trustworthiness**
is unto all generations **generation to generation**:
thou hast established the earth, and it *abideth* **standeth**.
91 They *continue* **stand** this day
according to *thine ordinances* **thy judgments**:
for all are thy servants.
92 Unless thy *law* **torah** had been my delights,
I should then have *perished* **destructed**
in *mine affliction* **my humiliation**.
93 I *will never* **shall eternally not** forget thy precepts:
for with them thou hast *quickened* **enlivened** me.
94 I am thine, save me: for I have sought thy precepts.
95 The wicked have *waited for* **awaited** me to destroy me:
but I *will consider* **shall discern** thy *testimonies* **witnesses**.
96 I have seen an end of all *perfection* **conclusion**:
but thy *commandment* **misvah** is *exceeding* **mighty** broad.

MEM.
97 O how love I thy *law* **torah**!
it is my meditation all the day.
98 *Thou through thy commandments* **Thy misvoth**
hast made me wiser **have enwisened me**
than **above** mine enemies:
for they are *ever* **eternally** with me.
99 I *have* **comprehend** more *understanding*
than all my teachers:
for thy *testimonies* **witnesses** are my meditation.
100 I *understand* **discern** more than the *ancients* **elders**,
because I *keep* **guard** thy precepts.
101 I have *refrained* **restrained** my feet
from every evil way,
that I might *keep* **guard** thy word.
102 I have not *departed* **turned aside**
from thy judgments:
for thou hast taught me.
103 How *sweet* **smooth** are thy *words* **sayings**
unto my *taste* **palate**!
yea, sweeter — than honey to my mouth!
104 Through thy precepts I *get understanding* **discern**:
therefore I hate every false way.

NUN.

105 Thy word is a lamp unto my feet,
and a light unto my path.
106 I have *sworn* **oathed**,
and I *will perform* **shall raise** it,
that I *will keep* **shall guard**
thy *righteous* judgments **of justness**.
107 I am *afflicted very much* **humbled mightily**:
quicken **enliven** me, O *LORD* **Yah Veh**,
according unto thy word.
108 *Accept* **Be pleased**, I beseech thee,
the *freewill offerings* **voluntaries** of my mouth,
O *LORD* **Yah Veh**, and teach me thy judgments.
109 My soul is continually in my *hand* **palm**:
yet do I not forget thy *law* **torah**.
110 The wicked have *laid* **given** a snare for me:
yet I *erred* **strayed** not from thy precepts.
111 Thy *testimonies* **witnesses**
have I *taken as an heritage for ever* **inherited eternally**:
for they are the rejoicing of my heart.
112 I have *inclined* **extended** mine heart
to *perform* **work** thy statutes *alway* **eternally**,
even unto the end.

SAMECH.

113 I hate *vain thought* **skeptics**:
but thy *law do* **torah** I love.
114 Thou art my *hiding place* **covert**
and my *shield* **buckler**:
I *hope in* **await** thy word.
115 *Depart* **Turn away** from me, ye *evildoers* **vilifiers**:
for I *will keep* **shall guard**
the *commandments* **misvoth** of my *God* **Elohim**.
116 Uphold me according unto thy *word* **sayings**,
that I may live:
and let me not *be ashamed* **shame**
of my *hope* **expectation**.
117 Hold thou me up, and I shall be *safe* **saved**:
and I *will have respect* **shall look**
unto thy statutes continually.
118 Thou hast *trodden down* **trampled** all them
that err **inadvertently** from thy statutes:
for their deceit is falsehood.
119 Thou *puttest away* **shabbathizest**
all the wicked of the earth like dross:
therefore I love thy *testimonies* **witnesses**.
120 My flesh *trembleth* **standeth on end**
for *fear* **dread** of thee;
and I *am afraid of* **awe** thy judgments.

AIN.

121 I have *done* **worked** judgment and *justice* **justness**:
leave me not to mine oppressors.
122 *Be surety* **Pledge** for thy servant for good:
let not the *proud* **arrogant** oppress me.
123 Mine eyes *fail* **are finished off** for thy salvation,
and for the *word* **sayings** of thy *righteousness* **justness**.
124 *Deal* **Work** with thy servant
according unto thy mercy,
and teach me thy statutes.
125 I am thy servant;
give **have** me *understanding* **discern**,
that I may know thy *testimonies* **witnesses**.
126 It is time *for thee, LORD* **O Yah Veh**, to work:
for they have *made void* **broken** thy *law* **torah**.
127 Therefore
I love thy *commandments* **misvoth** above gold;
yea, above *fine* **pure** gold.
128 Therefore I *esteem* **straighten** all thy precepts
concerning all things to be **all** right;
and I hate every false way.

PE.

129 Thy *testimonies* **witnesses** are *wonderful* **marvels**:
therefore *doth* my soul *keep* **guardeth** them.
130 The entrance of thy words giveth light;
it giveth understanding unto the simple
so that the gullible may discern.
131 I *opened* **gaped** my mouth, and *panted* **gulped**:
for I longed for thy *commandments* **misvoth**.
132 *Look thou upon* **Face** me,
and *be merciful unto me* **grant me charism**,
as thou usest to do **and judgment**
unto those that love thy name.
133 *Order* **Establish** my steps in thy *word* **sayings**:
and let not any *iniquity* **mischief**
have dominion over **dominate** me.
134 Deliver me from the oppression of *man* **humanity**:
so *will I keep* **shall I guard** thy precepts.
135 *Make* **Lighten** thy face *to shine* upon thy servant;
and teach me thy statutes.
136 *Rivers* **Rivulets** of waters
run down **descend** mine eyes,
because they *keep* **guard** not thy *law* **torah**.

TZADDI.

137 *Righteous* **Just** art thou, O *LORD* **Yah Veh**,
and *upright* **straight** are thy judgments.
138 Thy *testimonies* **witnesses**
that thou hast *commanded* **misvahed**
are *righteous* **justness**
and *very faithful* **mighty trustworthy**.
139 My zeal hath *consumed* **exterminated** me,
because
mine enemies **my tribulators** have forgotten thy words.
140 Thy *word* **saying** is *very pure* **mighty refined**:
therefore thy servant loveth it.
141 I am *small* **insignificant** and despised:
yet do not I forget thy precepts.
142 Thy *righteousness* **justness**
is an *everlasting righteousness* **eternal justness**,
and thy *law* **torah** is the truth.
143 *Trouble* **Tribulation** and *anguish* **distress**
have *taken hold on* **found** me:
yet thy *commandments* **misvoth** are my delights.
144 The *righteousness* **justness**
of thy *testimonies* **witnesses**
is *everlasting* **eternal**:
give me understanding **have me discern**, and I shall live.

KOPH.

145 I *cried* **called** with *my* whole heart;
hear me **answer**, O *LORD* **Yah Veh**:
I *will keep* **shall guard** thy statutes.
146 I *cried* **called** unto thee; save me,
and I shall *keep* **guard** thy *testimonies* **witnesses**.
147 I *prevented* **anticipated**
the *dawning of the morning* **evening breeze**, and cried:
I *hoped in* **awaited** thy word.
148 Mine eyes *prevent* **anticipate** the *night* watches,
that I might meditate in thy *word* **sayings**.
149 Hear my voice
according unto thy *lovingkindness* **mercy**:
O *LORD* **Yah Veh**,
quicken **enliven** me according to thy judgment.
150 They draw nigh
that *follow after mischief* **pursue intrigue**:
they are far from thy *law* **torah**.
151 Thou art near, O *LORD* **Yah Veh**;
and all thy *commandments* **misvoth** are truth.
152 *Concerning thy testimonies* **Thy witnesses**,
I have known of *old* **antiquity**
that thou hast founded them *for ever* **eternally**.

RESH.

153 *Consider mine affliction* **See my humiliation**,
and *deliver* **rescue** me:
for I do not forget thy *law* **torah**.
154 *Plead* **Defend** my *cause* **defence**, and deliver me:
quicken **enliven** me according to thy *word* **sayings**.
155 Salvation is far from the wicked:
for they seek not thy statutes.
156 Great are thy tender mercies, O *LORD* **Yah Veh**:
quicken **enliven** me according to thy judgments.
157 Many are my *persecutors* **pursuers**
and *mine enemies* **my tribulators**;
yet *do I not decline* **I stretch not**
from thy *testimonies* **witnesses**.
158 I *beheld* **saw them**

the transgressors **that deal covertly**,
and *was grieved* **loathed**;
because they *kept* **guarded** not thy *word* **sayings**.
159 *Consider* **See** how I love thy precepts:
quicken **enliven** me, O *LORD* **Yah Veh**,
according to thy *lovingkindness* **mercy**.
160 *Thy word is true from the beginning*
The sum of thy word is truth:
and every one of thy *righteous* judgments **of justness**
endureth for ever **is eternal**.

SCHIN.

161 *Princes* **Governors** have *persecuted* **pursued** me
without a cause **gratuitously**:
but my heart *standeth in awe of* **dreadeth** thy word.
162 I rejoice at thy *word* **sayings**,
as one that findeth great spoil.
163 I hate and abhor *lying* **falsehood**
but thy *law do* **torah** I love.
164 Seven times a day *do I praise* **I halal** thee
because of thy *righteous* judgments **of justness**.
165 Great *peace* **shalom**
have they which love thy *law* **torah**:
and *nothing shall offend them*
they have no stumblingblock.
166 *LORD* **O Yah Veh**,
I have *hoped for* **expected** thy salvation,
and *done* **worked** thy *commandments* **misvoth**.
167 My soul hath *kept* **guarded** thy *testimonies* **witnesses**;
and I love them *exceedingly* **mightily**.
168 I have *kept* **guarded**
thy precepts and thy *testimonies* **witnesses**:
for all my ways are before thee.

TAU.

169 Let my *cry* **shouting**
come near *before thee* **at thy face**,
O *LORD* **Yah Veh**:
give **have** me *understanding* **discern**
according to thy word.
170 Let my supplication come *before thee* **at thy face**:
deliver **rescue** me according to thy *word* **sayings**.
171 My lips shall *utter praise* **gush halal**,
when thou hast taught me thy statutes.
172 My tongue shall *speak* **answer** of thy *word* **sayings**:
for all thy *commandments* **misvoth**
are *righteousness* **justness**.
173 Let thine hand help me;
for I have chosen thy precepts.
174 I have *longed* **desired** for thy salvation,
O *LORD* **Yah Veh**;
and thy *law* **torah** is my delight.
175 Let my soul live, and it shall *praise* **halal** thee;
and let thy judgments help me.
176 I have *gone astray* **strayed** like a lost *sheep* **lamb**;
seek thy servant;
for I *do not* forget **not** thy *commandments* **misvoth**.

120

A Song of degrees.
1 In my *distress* **tribulation**
I *cried* **called** unto *the LORD* **Yah Veh**,
and he *heard* **answered** *me*.
2 *Deliver* **Rescue** my soul, O *LORD* **Yah Veh**,
from *lying* **false** lips, *and* from a deceitful tongue.
3 What shall be given unto thee?
or what shall be *done* **added** unto thee,
thou *false* **deceitful** tongue?
4 *Sharp* **Pointened** arrows of the mighty,
with coals of juniper.
5 Woe is me, that I sojourn in *Mesech* **Meshech**,
that I dwell in the tents of *Kedar* **Qedar**!
6 My soul hath *long dwelt* **greatly tabernacled**
with him that hateth *peace* **shalom**.
7 I am for *peace* **shalom**:
but when I *speak* **word**, they are for war.

121

A Song of degrees.
1 I *will* **shall** lift up mine eyes unto the *hills* **mountains**,
from whence cometh my help.
2 My help *cometh* from *the LORD* **Yah Veh**,
which *made heaven* **worked the heavens** and earth.
3 He *will* **shall** not *suffer* **give** thy foot to *be moved* **topple**:
he that *keepeth* **guardeth** thee *will* **shall** not slumber.
4 Behold, he that *keepeth Israel* **guardeth Yisra El**
shall neither slumber nor sleep.
5 *The LORD* **Yah Veh** is thy *keeper* **guard**:
the LORD **Yah Veh** is thy shade upon thy right hand.
6 The sun shall not smite thee by day,
nor the moon by night.
7 *The LORD* **Yah Veh**
shall *preserve* **guard** thee from all evil:
he shall *preserve* **guard** thy soul.
8 *The LORD* **Yah Veh**
shall *preserve* **guard** thy going out and thy coming in
from this time *forth*, and even *for evermore* **eternally**.

122

A Song of degrees of David.
1 I *was glad* **cheered** when they said unto me,
Let us go into the house of *the LORD* **Yah Veh**.
2 Our feet shall stand within thy *gates* **portals**,
O *Jerusalem* **Yeru Shalem**.
3 *Jerusalem* **Yeru Shalem** is builded
as a city *that is compact* **joined** together:
4 *Whither* **And there** the *tribes go up* **scions ascend**,
the *tribes* **scions** of *the LORD* **Yah**,
unto the *testimony* **witness** of *Israel* **Yisra El**,
to *give thanks* **extend hands**
unto the name of *the LORD* **Yah Veh**.
5 For there are *set* **settled** thrones of judgment,
the thrones of the house of David.
6 *Pray* **Ask** for the *peace* **shalom** of *Jerusalem* **Yeru Shalem**:
they shall *prosper* **be content** that love thee.
7 *Peace* **Shalom** be within thy *walls* **trenches**,
and *prosperity* **serenity** within thy *palaces* **citadels**.
8 For my brethren and *companions'* **friend's** sakes,
I *will now say* **shall beseech a word**,
Peace **Shalom** be within thee.
9 Because of the house
of the *LORD* **Yah Veh** our *God* **Elohim**
I *will* **shall** seek thy good.

123

A Song of degrees.
1 Unto thee lift I up mine eyes,
O thou that *dwellest* **settlest** in the heavens.
2 Behold, as the eyes of servants *look*
unto the hand of their *masters* **adonim**,
and as the eyes of a *maiden* **maid**
unto the hand of her *mistress* **lady**;
so our eyes
wait upon the LORD **unto Yah Veh** our *God* **Elohim**,
until that he *have mercy upon* **grant** us **charism**.
3 *Have mercy upon* **Grant** us **charism**,
O *LORD* **Yah Veh**,
have mercy upon **grant** us **charism**:
for we are *exceedingly filled* **abundantly satiated**
with *contempt* **disrespect**.
4 Our soul is *exceedingly filled* **abundantly satiated**
with the *scorning* **derision** of those that *are at ease* **relax**,
and with the *contempt* **disrespect** of the *proud* **pompous**.

124

A Song of degrees of David.
1 If it had not been *the LORD* **for Yah Veh**
who was on our side,
now **I beseech,** may *Israel* **Yisra El** say;
2 If it had not been *the LORD* **for Yah Veh**
who was on our side,
when *men* **humanity** rose *up* against us:
3 Then they had swallowed us *up quick* **alive**,
when their wrath was kindled against us:
4 Then the waters had *overwhelmed* **overflowed** us,
the *stream* **wadi** had *gone* **passed** over our soul:
5 Then the *proud* **overflowing** waters
had *gone* **passed** over our soul.
6 Blessed be *the LORD* **Yah Veh**,
who hath not given us as a prey to their teeth.
7 Our soul *is* escaped
as a bird out of the snare of the *fowlers* **ensnarers**:
the snare is broken, and we *are* escaped.
8 Our help is in the name of *the LORD* **Yah Veh**,
who *made heaven* **worked the heavens** and earth.

125
A Song of degrees.
1 They that *trust* **confide** in *the LORD* **Yah Veh**
shall be as mount *Zion* **Siyon**,
which *cannot be removed* **shall not totter**,
but *abideth for ever* **settleth eternally**.
2 As the mountains
are round about Jerusalem **surround Yeru Shalem**,
so *the LORD* **Yah Veh**
is round about **surroundeth** his people
from *henceforth* **this time** even *for ever* **eternally**.
3 For the *rod* **scion** of *the wicked* **wickedness**
shall not rest upon the *lot* **pebble** of the *righteous* **just**;
lest the *righteous* **just**
put forth **extend** their hands unto *iniquity* **wickedness**.
4 Do good, O *LORD* **Yah Veh**,
unto *those that be* **the** good,
and to *them that are upright* **the straight** in their hearts.
5 As for such as *turn aside* **pervert**
unto their *crooked ways* **crookednesses**,
the LORD **Yah Veh** shall *lead* **walk** them *forth*
with the *workers* **doers** of *iniquity* **mischief**:
but *peace* **shalom** shall be upon *Israel* **Yisra El**.

126
A Song of degrees.
1 When *the LORD turned again* **Yah Veh returned**
the *captivity* **returning** of *Zion* **Siyon**,
we were like them that dream.
2 Then was our mouth filled with laughter,
and our tongue with *singing* **shouting**:
then said they among the *heathen* **goyim**,
The LORD **Yah Veh**
hath *done great things* **worked greatly** for them.
3 *The LORD* **Yah Veh**
hath *done great things* **worked greatly** for us;
whereof we *are glad* **cheer**.
4 *Turn again* **Return** our captivity, O *LORD* **Yah Veh**,
as the *streams* **reservoirs** in the south.
5 They that *sow* **seed** in tears
shall *reap* **harvest** in *joy* **shouting**.
6 **In going,** He that goeth *forth* and weepeth,
bearing *precious* **sowing** seed,
shall doubtless come again with *rejoicing* **shouting**,
bringing **bearing** his sheaves *with him*.

127
A Song of degrees for *Solomon* **Shelomoh**.
1 Except *the LORD* **Yah Veh** build the house,
they *labour* **toil** in vain that build it:
except *the LORD keep* **Yah Veh guard** the city,
the *watchman waketh but* **guard guardeth** in vain.
2 It is vain for you to *rise up* **start** early,
to *sit up* **settle down** late,
to eat the bread of *sorrows* **contorting**:
for so he giveth his beloved sleep.
3 *Lo* **Behold**, *children* **sons** are an *heritage* **inheritance**
of *the LORD* **Yah Veh**:
and the fruit of the *womb* **belly** is his *reward* **hire**.
4 As arrows *are* in the hand of a mighty man;
so are *children* **sons** of the youth.
5 *Happy* **Blithe** is the *man* **mighty**
that hath his quiver full of them:
they shall not *be ashamed* **shame**,
but they shall *speak* **word**
with the enemies in the *gate* **portal**.

128
A Song of degrees.
1 *Blessed is* **Blithed be** every one
that *feareth the LORD* **aweth Yah Veh**;
that walketh in his ways.
2 For thou shalt eat the labour of *thine hands* **thy palms**:
happy **blithe** shalt thou be,
and it shall be *well* **good** with thee.
3 Thy *wife* **woman** shall be as a *fruitful* **fruitbearing** vine
by the *sides* **flanks** of thine house:
thy *children* **sons** like olive *plants* **transplants**
round about **surrounding** thy table.
4 Behold, that thus shall the *man* **mighty** be blessed
that *feareth the LORD* **aweth Yah Veh**.
5 *The LORD* **Yah Veh** shall bless thee out of *Zion* **Siyon**:
and thou shalt see the good of *Jerusalem* **Yeru Shalem**

all the days of thy life.
6 Yea, thou shalt see thy *children's children* **sons' sons**,
and *peace* **shalom** upon *Israel* **Yisra El**.

129
A Song of degrees.
1 *Many a time* **Greatly** have they *afflicted* **tribulated** me
from my youth,
may *Israel now* **Yisra El**, **I beseech,** say:
2 *Many a time* **Greatly** have they *afflicted* **tribulated** me
from my youth:
yet they have not prevailed against me.
3 The plowers plowed upon my back:
they *made long* **lengthened** their furrows.
4 *The LORD* **Yah Veh** is *righteous* **just**:
he hath *cut asunder* **chopped**
the *cords* **ropes** of the wicked.
5 Let them *all be confounded* **shame**
and *turned back* **apostatize**
that hate *Zion* **Siyon**.
6 Let them be as the grass upon the *house tops* **roofs**,
which withereth *afore it groweth up* **ere it is drawn**:
7 Wherewith the mower filleth not his *hand* **palm**;
nor he that bindeth *sheaves* his bosom.
8 Neither do they which *go* **pass** by say,
The blessing of *the LORD* **Yah Veh** be upon you:
we bless you in the name of *the LORD* **Yah Veh**.

130
A Song of degrees.
1 Out of the depths
have I *cried* **called** unto thee, O *LORD* **Yah Veh**.
2 *Lord* **Adonay**, hear my voice:
let thine ears *be attentive* **hearken**
to the voice of my supplications.
3 If thou, *LORD* **O Yah**,
shouldest *mark iniquities* **regard perversities**,
O *Lord* **Adonay**, who shall stand?
4 But there is forgiveness with thee,
that thou mayest be *feared* **awed**.
5 I *wait for the LORD* **await Yah Veh**,
my soul *doth wait* **awaiteth**,
and in his word *do I hope* **I await**.
6 My soul *waiteth for the Lord* **be for Adonay**
more than they that *watch* **guard** for the morning:
I say, more than — they that *watch* **guard** for the morning.
7 Let *Israel hope in the LORD* **Yisra El await Yah Veh**:
for with *the LORD* **Yah Veh** there is mercy,
and with him *is plenteous* **aboundeth** redemption.
8 And he shall redeem *Israel* **Yisra El**
from all his *iniquities* **perversities**.

131
A Song of degreesof David.
1 *LORD* **O Yah Veh**,
my heart is not *haughty* **lifted**, nor mine eyes *lofty* **lofted**:
neither *do I exercise myself* **walk I**
in *great matters* **greatness**,
or in *things too high for me* **marvels**.
2 Surely I have *behaved* **placed myself**
and *quieted myself* **hushed my soul**,
as a child that is weaned of his mother:
my soul is even as *a* weaned *child*.
3 Let *Israel hope in the LORD* **Yisra El await Yah Veh**
from *henceforth* **this time** and *for ever* **eternally**.

132
A Song of degrees.
1 *LORD* **O Yah Veh**,
remember David, and all his *afflictions* **humblings**:
2 How he *sware* **oathed** unto *the LORD* **Yah Veh**,
and vowed
unto the *mighty God* **Almighty** of *Jacob* **Yaaqov**;
3 Surely I *will* **shall** not come
into the *tabernacle* **tent** of my house,
nor *go up* **ascend** into *my bed* **the bedstead of my beds**;
4 I *will* **shall** not give sleep to mine eyes,
or *slumber* **drowsiness** to mine eyelids,
5 Until I find out a place for *the LORD* **Yah Veh**,
an habitation **tabernacles**
for the *mighty God* **Almighty** of *Jacob* **Yaaqov**.
6 *Lo* **Behold**, we heard of it at *Ephratah* **Ephrath**:
we found it in the fields of the *wood* **forest**.
7 We *will* **shall** go into his tabernacles:

we *will worship* **shall prostrate**
at *his footstool* **the stool of his feet.**
8 Arise, O *LORD* **Yah Veh**, into thy rest;
thou, and the ark of thy strength.
9 Let thy priests
be clothed **enrobe** with *righteousness* **justness**;
and let thy *saints* **mercied** shout *for joy*.
10 For thy servant David's sake
turn not away the face of thine anointed.
11 *The LORD* **Yah Veh** hath *sworn* **oathed** in truth
unto David;
he *will* **shall** not turn from it;
Of the fruit of thy *body* **belly**
will **shall** I set upon thy throne.
12 If thy *children will keep* **sons shall guard** my covenant
and my *testimony* **witness** that I shall teach them,
their *children* **sons** shall also *sit* **settle** upon thy throne
for evermore **eternally**.
13 For *the LORD* **Yah Veh** hath chosen *Zion* **Siyon**;
he hath desired it for his *habitation* **settlement**.
14 This is my rest *for ever* **eternally**:
here *will I dwell* **shall I settle**; for I have desired it.
15 **In blessing,**
I *will abundantly* **shall** bless her *provision* **hunt**:
I *will* **shall** satisfy her *poor* **needy** with bread.
16 I *will* **shall** also
clothe **enrobe** her priests with salvation:
and **in shouting,** her *saints* **mercied** shall shout
aloud for joy.
17 There *will I make* **shall I sprout** the horn of David
to bud:
I have *ordained* **arranged** a lamp for mine anointed.
18 His enemies *will I clothe* **shall I enrobe** with shame:
but upon himself shall his *crown* **separatism** flourish.

133

A Song of degrees of David.
1 Behold, how good and how pleasant *it is*
for brethren to *dwell* **settle** together in unity!
2 It is like the *precious* **good** ointment upon the head,
that ran down **descending** upon the beard,
even Aaron's **Aharon's** beard:
that *went down* **descended**
to the skirts of his *garments* **tailoring;**
3 As the dew of Hermon,
and as the dew
that descended upon the mountains of *Zion* **Siyon**:
for there *the LORD* **Yah Veh**
commanded **misvahed** the blessing,
even life for evermore **life eternal**.

134

A Song of degrees.
1 Behold, bless ye *the LORD* **Yah Veh**,
all *ye* servants of *the LORD* **Yah Veh**,
which by night stand in the house of *the LORD* **Yah Veh**.
2 Lift up your hands in the *sanctuary* **holies**,
and bless *the LORD* **Yah Veh**.
3 *The LORD* **Yah Veh**
that *made heaven* **worked the heavens** and earth
bless thee out of *Zion* **Siyon**.

135

Praise ye the LORD **Halalu Yah**.
Praise **Halal** ye the name of *the LORD* **Yah Veh**;
praise him **halal**, O ye servants of *the LORD* **Yah Veh**.
2 Ye that stand in the house of *the LORD* **Yah Veh**,
in the courts of the house of our *God* **Elohim**.
3 *Praise the LORD* **Halalu Yah**;
for *the LORD* **Yah Veh** is good:
sing praises **psalm** unto his name; for it is pleasant.
4 For *the LORD* **Yah**
hath chosen *Jacob* **Yaaqov** unto himself,
and Israel **Yisra El** for his peculiar treasure.
5 For I know that *the LORD* **Yah Veh** is great,
and that our *Lord* **Adonay** is above all *gods* **elohim**.
6 Whatsoever *the LORD pleased* **Yah Veh desired**,
that *did* **worked** he in *heaven* **the heavens**,
and in earth, in the seas, and all *deep places* **abysses**.
7 He causeth the vapours
to ascend from the ends of the earth;
he *maketh* **worketh** lightnings for the rain;
he bringeth the wind out of his treasuries.
8 Who smote the firstborn of *Egypt* **Misrayim**,
both of *man and beast* **human unto animal**.
9 Who sent *tokens* **signs** and *wonders* **omens**
into the midst of thee, O *Egypt* **Misrayim**,
upon *Pharaoh* **Paroh**, and upon all his servants.
10 Who smote great *nations* **goyim**,
and *slew* **slaughtered** mighty *kings* **sovereigns**;
11 *Sihon king* **Sichon sovereign** of the *Amorites* **Emoriy**,
and Og *king* **sovereign** of Bashan,
and all the *kingdoms* **sovereigndoms** of *Canaan* **Kenaan**:
12 And gave their land for an *heritage* **inheritance**,
an *heritage* **inheritance** unto *Israel* **Yisra El** his people.
13 Thy name, O *LORD* **Yah Veh**,
endureth for ever **is eternal**;
and thy memorial, O *LORD* **Yah Veh**,
throughout all generations **generation to generation**.
14 For *the LORD* **Yah Veh**
will judge **shall plead the cause of** his people,
and he *will repent himself* **shall sigh**
concerning his servants.
15 The idols of the *heathen* **goyim** are silver and gold,
the work of *men's* **human** hands.
16 They have mouths, but they *speak* **word** not;
eyes have they, but they see not;
17 They have ears, but they *hear* **hearken** not;
neither is there *any breath* **spirit/wind** in their mouths.
18 They that *make* **work** them are like unto them:
so is every one that *trusteth* **confideth** in them.
19 Bless *the LORD* **Yah Veh**, O house of *Israel* **Yisra El**:
bless *the LORD* **Yah Veh**, O house of *Aaron* **Aharon**:
20 Bless *the LORD* **Yah Veh**, O house of Levi:
ye that *fear the LORD* **awe Yah Veh**,
bless *the LORD* **Yah Veh**.
21 Blessed be *the LORD* **Yah Veh** out of *Zion* **Siyon**,
which *dwelleth* **tabernacleth** at *Jerusalem* **Yeru Shalem**.
Praise ye the LORD **Halalu Yah**.

136

O give thanks **extend hands**
unto *the LORD* **Yah Veh**;
for he is good:
for his mercy *endureth for ever* **is eternal**.
2 O *give thanks* **extend hands**
unto the *God* **Elohim** of *gods* **elohim**:
for his mercy *endureth for ever* **is eternal**.
3 O *give thanks* **extend hands**
to *the Lord* **Adonay** of *lords* **adonim**:
for his mercy *endureth for ever* **is eternal**.
4 To him who alone
doeth **worketh** great *wonders* **marvels**:
for his mercy *endureth for ever* **is eternal**.
5 To him that by *wisdom* **discernment**
made **worked** the heavens:
for his mercy *endureth for ever* **is eternal**.
6 To him
that *stretched out* **expandeth** the earth above the waters:
for his mercy *endureth for ever* **is eternal**.
7 To him that *made* **worked** great lights:
for his mercy *endureth for ever* **is eternal**:
8 The sun to *rule* **reign** by day:
for his mercy *endureth for ever* **is eternal**:
9 The moon and stars to *rule* **reign** by night:
for his mercy *endureth for ever* **is eternal**.
10 To him that smote *Egypt* **Misrayim** in their firstborn:
for his mercy *endureth for ever* **is eternal**:
11 And brought out *Israel* **Yisra El** from among them:
for his mercy *endureth for ever* **is eternal**:
12 With a strong hand, and with a stretched out arm:
for his mercy *endureth for ever* **is eternal**.
13 To him
which *divided* **cut** the *Red* **Reed** sea into *parts* **pieces**:
for his mercy *endureth for ever* **is eternal**:
14 And made *Israel* **Yisra El**
to pass through the midst of it:
for his mercy *endureth for ever* **is eternal**:
15 But *overthrew Pharaoh* **shook off Paroh**
and his *host* **valiant** in the *Red* **Reed** sea:
for his mercy *endureth for ever* **is eternal**.
16 To him
which *led* **walked** his people through the wilderness:
for his mercy *endureth for ever* **is eternal**.

17 To him which smote great *kings* **sovereigns**:
for his mercy *endureth for ever* **is eternal**:
18 And *slew famous kings* **slaughtered mighty sovereigns**:
for his mercy *endureth for ever* **is eternal**:
19 *Sihon king* **Sichon sovereign** of the *Amorites* **Emoriy**:
for his mercy *endureth for ever* **is eternal**:
20 And Og the *king* **sovereign** of Bashan:
for his mercy *endureth for ever* **is eternal**:
21 And gave their land for an *heritage* **inheritance**:
for his mercy *endureth for ever* **is eternal**:
22 Even an *heritage* **inheritance**
unto *Israel* **Yisra El** his servant:
for his mercy *endureth for ever* **is eternal**.
23 Who remembered us in our *low estate* **lowliness**:
for his mercy *endureth for ever* **is eternal**:
24 And hath *redeemed* **separated** us
from our *enemies* **tribulators**:
for his mercy *endureth for ever* **is eternal**.
25 Who giveth *food* **bread** to all flesh:
for his mercy *endureth for ever* **is eternal**.
26 O *give thanks* **extend hands**
unto *the God* **El** of *heaven* **the heavens**:
for his mercy *endureth for ever* **is eternal**.

137

By the rivers of *Babylon* **Babel**,
there we *sat down* **settled**,
yea, we wept, when we remembered *Zion* **Siyon**.
2 We hanged our harps upon the willows
in the midst *thereof*.
3 For there they that *carried* **captured** us *away captive*
required **asked** of us **the words of** a song;
and they that *wasted* **caused us to howl,**
required of us mirth **cheerfulness**, *saying*,
Sing us *one* of the songs of *Zion* **Siyon**.
4 How shall we sing *the LORD'S* **Yah Veh's** song
in a strange *land* **soil**?
5 If I forget thee, O *Jerusalem* **Yeru Shalem**,
let my right *hand* forget *her cunning*.
6 If I do not remember thee,
let my tongue
cleave to the roof of my mouth **adhere to my palate**;
if I *prefer* **ascend** not *Jerusalem* **Yeru Shalem**
above my *chief joy* **head cheerfulness**.
7 Remember, O *LORD* **Yah Veh**,
the *children* **sons** of Edom
in the day of *Jerusalem* **Yeru Shalem**;
who said, *Rase it* **Strip naked**, *rase it* **strip naked**,
even to the foundation *thereof*.
8 O daughter of *Babylon* **Babel**,
who art to be *destroyed* **ravaged**;
happy **blithe** shall he be,
that *rewardeth* **shall shalam** thee
as **the deeds** thou hast *served* **dealt** us.
9 *Happy* **Blithe** shall he be,
that taketh and *dasheth* **splattereth** thy *little ones* **infants**
against the *stones* **rocks**.

138

A Psalm of David.
1 I *will praise* **shall extend hands unto** thee
with my whole heart:
before *the gods* **Elohim/elohim,**
will I sing praise **shall I psalm** unto thee.
2 I *will worship* **shall prostrate**
toward thy holy *temple* **manse,**
and *praise* **extend hands unto** thy name
for thy *lovingkindness* **mercy** and for thy truth:
for thou hast *magnified* **greatened** thy *word* **saying**
above all thy name.
3 In the day when I *cried* **called** thou answeredst me,
and *strengthenedst* **encouragedst** me
with strength in my soul.
4 All the *kings* **sovereigns** of the earth
shall *praise* **extend hands unto** thee, O *LORD* **Yah Veh**,
when they hear the *words* **sayings** of thy mouth.
5 Yea, they shall sing in the ways of *the LORD* **Yah Veh**:
for great is the *glory* **honour** of *the LORD* **Yah Veh**.
6 Though *the LORD* **Yah Veh** be high,
yet *hath* he *respect* **seeth** unto the lowly:
but the *proud* **lofty** he knoweth afar off.
7 Though I walk in the midst of *trouble* **tribulation**,
thou *wilt revive* **shalt enliven** me:
thou shalt *stretch forth* **extend** thine hand
against the wrath of mine enemies,
and thy right *hand* shall save me.
8 *The LORD* **Yah Veh**
will perfect **shall consumate** that which concerneth me:
thy mercy, O *LORD* **Yah Veh**, *endureth for ever* **is eternal**:
forsake **slacken** not the works of thine own hands.

139

To *the chief Musician* **His Eminence**,
A Psalm of David.
1 O *LORD* **Yah Veh**,
thou hast *searched* **probed** me, and known *me*.
2 Thou knowest my *downsitting* **settling**
and mine uprising,
thou *understandest* **discernest**
my *thought* **intention** afar off.
3 Thou *compassest* **winnowest** my path
and my *lying down* **reposing**,
and art *acquainted with* **accustomed to** all my ways.
4 For there is not *a word* **an utterance** in my tongue,
but, lo **behold**, O *LORD* **Yah Veh**,
thou knowest it altogether.
5 Thou hast *beset* **besieged** me behind and before,
and *laid thine hand* **placed thy palm** upon me.
6 Such knowledge is too *wonderful* **marvellous** for me;
it is high **lofty**, *I cannot attain unto* **I am not able for** it.
7 Whither shall I go from thy spirit?
or whither shall I flee from thy *presence* **face**?
8 If I ascend *up* into *heaven* **the heavens,**
thou art there:
if I *make my bed in hell* **bed down in sheol**,
behold, thou *art there*.
9 If I *take* **lift** the wings of the *morning* **dawn**,
and *dwell* **tabernacle**
in the *uttermost parts* **finality** of the sea;
10 Even there shall thy hand lead me,
and thy right *hand* shall hold me.
11 If I say, Surely the darkness shall *cover* **crush** me;
even the night shall be light about me.
12 Yea, the darkness *hideth* **darkeneth** not from thee;
but the night *shineth* **enlighteneth** as the day:
the darkness and the light are both alike to thee
as the darkness, so the light.
13 For thou hast *possessed* **chattelized** my reins:
thou hast covered me in my mother's *womb* **belly**.
14 I *will praise* **shall extend hands unto** thee;
for I am
fearfully and wonderfully made **awesomely distinguished**:
marvellous are thy works;
and that my soul knoweth right well.
15 My *substance* **might** was not *hid* **concealed** from thee,
when I was *made in secret* **covertly worked**,
and *curiously wrought* **embroidered**
in the *lowest parts* **nethermost** of the earth.
16 Thine eyes did see my *substance* **embryo**,
yet being unperfect;
and in thy *book* **scroll**
all my members were written **were they inscribed**,
which in continuance were fashioned
in the days they were formed,
when *as yet there* was none *of* **among** them.
17 How *precious* **esteemed** also
are thy *thoughts* **intentions** unto me,
O *God* **El**!
how *great* **mighty** is the *sum* **head** of them!
18 If I should *count* **scribe** them,
they *are* **abound** more *in number* than the sand:
when I awake, I am still with thee.
19 Surely thou *wilt slay* **shalt severe** the wicked,
O *God* **Elohah**:
depart **turn aside** from me therefore,
ye *bloody* men **of blood**.
20 For they *speak* **say** against thee *wickedly* **intrigue**,
and thine enemies *take thy name* **be lifted** in *vain* **vanity**.
21 Do not I hate them, O *LORD* **Yah Veh**, that hate thee?
and *am not I grieved with those* **do I not loathe them**
that *rise up against* **resist** thee?
22 I hate them with *perfect* **conclusive** hatred:
I count them mine enemies.

23 *Search* **Probe** me, O *God* **El**, and know my heart:
try **proof** me, and know my thoughts:
24 And see
if there be *any wicked* **a contorting** way in me,
and lead me in the way *everlasting* **eternal**.

140 To *the chief Musician* **His Eminence**,
A Psalm of David.
1 *Deliver* **Rescue** me, O *LORD* **Yah Veh**,
from the evil *man* **humanity**:
preserve **guard** me from the *violent* man **of violence**;
2 Which *imagine mischiefs* **machinate evils** in their heart;
continually are **all day**
they *gathered* **sojourn** together *for* war.
3 They have *sharpened* **pointened** their tongues
like a serpent;
adders' **asp's** poison is under their lips.
Selah.
4 *Keep* **Guard** me, O *LORD* **Yah Veh**,
from the hands of the wicked;
preserve me from the *violent* man **of violence**;
who have *purposed* **machinated**
to overthrow my *goings* **steps**.
5 The *proud* **pompous**
have hid a *snare* **line** for me, and cords;
they have spread a net
by the *wayside* **hand of the route**;
they have set *gins* **snares** for me.
Selah.
6 I said unto *the LORD* **Yah Veh**, Thou art my *God* **El**:
hear **hearken unto** the voice of my supplications,
O *LORD* **Yah Veh**.
7 O *GOD the Lord* **Yah Veh Adonay**,
the strength of my salvation,
thou hast covered my head
in the day of *battle* **armament**.
8 *Grant* **Give** not, O *LORD* **Yah Veh**,
the desires of the wicked:
further **promote** not his *wicked device* **intrigue**;
lest they *exalt themselves* **be lofted**.
Selah.
9 As for the head of those
that *compass* **surround** me *about*,
let the *mischief* **toil** of their own lips cover them.
10 Let *burning coals fall* **coals topple** upon them:
let them be cast — **fell them** into the fire;
into deep pits, that they rise not *up again*.
11 Let *not an evil speaker* **no man of tongue**
be established in the earth:
evil shall hunt the *violent* man **of violence**
to overthrow him.
12 I know that *the LORD* **Yah Veh**
will maintain **shall work**
the *cause* **plea** of the *afflicted* **humble**,
and the right **judgment** of the *poor* **needy**.
13 Surely the *righteous* **just**
shall *give thanks* **extend hands** unto thy name:
the *upright* **straight** shall *dwell* **settle**
in thy presence **at thy face**.

141 A Psalm of David.
1 *LORD* **O Yah Veh**, I *cry* **call** unto thee:
make haste **hasten** unto me;
give ear **hearken** unto my voice,
when I *cry* **call** unto thee.
2 Let my prayer
be *set forth before thee* **prepared at thy face** as incense;
and the *lifting up* **burden** of my *hands* **palms**
as the evening *sacrifice* **offering**.
3 Set a *watch* **guard**, O *LORD* **Yah Veh**,
before my mouth;
keep **guard** the door of my lips.
4 *Incline* **Stretch** not my heart to any evil *thing* **word**,
to *practise* **exploit** wicked *works* **exploits**
with men that *work iniquity* **do mischief**:
and let me not eat of their *dainties* **delicacies**.
5 *Let the righteous smite me; it shall be a kindness*
The just hammer me in mercy:
and *let him* reprove me;
it shall be an *excellent oil* **ointment**,
which shall not break my head:
for yet my prayer also
shall be *in* **against** their *calamities* **evil**.
6 When their judges are *overthrown* **released**
in stony places **by the hands of the rocks**,
they shall hear my *words* **sayings**;
for they are *sweet* **pleasing**.
7 Our bones are scattered at *the grave's* **sheol's** mouth,
as when one *cutteth* **cleaveth** and *cleaveth wood* **splitteth**
upon the earth.
8 But mine eyes are unto thee,
O *GOD the Lord* **Yah Veh Adonay**:
in thee *is my trust* **I seek refuge**;
leave **strip** not my soul *destitute* **naked**.
9 *Keep* **Guard** me from the **hands of the** snares
which they have *laid* **ensnared** for me,
and the *gins* **snares**
of the *workers* **doers** of *iniquity* **mischief**.
10 Let the wicked fall into their own nets,
whilst that I *withal escape* **altogether pass on**.

142 *Maschil* **On Comprehension** of David:
A Prayer when he was in the cave.
1 I cried unto *the LORD* **Yah Veh** with my voice;
with my voice unto *the LORD* **Yah Veh**
did I make my supplication **sought I charism**.
2 I poured out my *complaint* **meditation**
before him **at his face**;
I shewed before him my trouble
I told my tribulation to his face.
3 When my spirit *was overwhelmed* **languished** within me,
then thou knewest my path.
In the way wherein I walked
have they *privily laid* **hid** a snare for me.
4 I looked *on my* **to the** right *hand*, and *beheld* **saw**,
but there was no *man* **one**
that *would know* **should recognize** me:
refuge failed **retreat destructed from** me;
no *man cared for* **one sought** my soul.
5 I cried unto thee, O *LORD* **Yah Veh**: I said,
Thou art my refuge and my *portion* **allotment**
in the land of the living.
6 *Attend* **Hearken** unto my *cry* **shouting**;
for I am *brought very low* **mightily languished**:
deliver **rescue** me from my *persecutors* **pursuers**;
for they are *stronger* **more strengthened** than I.
7 Bring my soul out of *prison* **the lockup**,
that I may *praise* **extend hands to** thy name:
the *righteous* **just** shall *compass* **surround** me *about*;
for thou shalt deal *bountifully* with me.

143 A Psalm of David.
1 Hear my prayer, O *LORD* **Yah Veh**,
give ear **hearken** to my supplications:
in thy *faithfulness* **trustworthiness** answer me,
and in thy *righteousness* **justness**.
2 And enter not into judgment with thy servant:
for *in* **at** thy *sight* **face** shall no *man* **one** living be justified.
3 For the enemy hath *persecuted* **pursued** my soul;
he hath *smitten* **crushed** my life *down* to the *ground* **earth**;
he hath *made me to dwell* **settled me** in darkness,
as those that have been *long* **eternally** dead.
4 *Therefore is*
my spirit *overwhelmed* **languisheth** within me;
my heart within me *is desolate* **desolateth**.
5 I remember the days of *old* **antiquity**;
I meditate on all thy *work* **deeds**;
I *muse* **meditate** on the work of thy hands.
6 I *stretch forth* **spread** my hands unto thee:
my soul
thirsteth after thee, as a thirsty land
is as a languid land for thee.
Selah.
7 *Hear* **Answer** me *speedily* **hastily**, O *LORD* **Yah Veh**:
my spirit *faileth* **finisheth off**:
hide not thy face from me,
lest I be like unto them
that *go down* **descend** into the *pit* **well**.
8 Cause me to hear thy *lovingkindness* **mercy**
in the morning;

for in thee do I *trust* **confide**:
cause me to know the way wherein I should walk;
for I lift up my soul unto thee.
9 *Deliver* **Rescue** me, O *LORD* **Yah Veh**,
from mine enemies:
I flee unto thee to hide me **Cover me with thyself**.
10 Teach me to *do* **work** thy *will* **pleasure**;
for thou art my *God* **Elohim**:
thy spirit is good;
lead me into the land of *uprightness* **straightness**.
11 *Quicken* **Enliven** me, O *LORD* **Yah Veh**,
for thy name's sake:
for thy *righteousness'* **justness'** sake
bring my soul out of *trouble* **tribulation**.
12 And of thy mercy cut off mine enemies,
and *destroy* **exterminate** all them
that *afflict* **tribulate** my soul:
for I am thy servant.

144

A Psalm of David.
1 Blessed be *the LORD* **Yah Veh** my *strength* **rock**
which teacheth my hands to war,
and my fingers to *fight* **war**:
2 My *goodness* **mercy**, and my *fortress* **stronghold**;
my *high tower* **secure loft**,
and my deliverer **who slippeth me away**;
my *shield* **buckler**, *and he* in whom I *trust* **seek refuge**;
who subdueth my people under me.
3 *LORD* **O Yah Veh**, what is *man* **humanity**,
that thou *takest knowledge of* **knowest** him!
or the son of man,
that thou *makest account of* **fabricatest** him!
4 *Man* **Humanity** is *like* **likened** to vanity:
his days are as a shadow that passeth away.
5 *Bow* **Spread** thy heavens, O *LORD* **Yah Veh**,
and *come down* **descend**:
touch the mountains, and they shall smoke.
6 *Cast forth* **Lightning the** lightning, and scatter them:
shoot out **send** thine arrows, and *destroy* **agitate** them.
7 Send thine hand from *above* **the heights**;
rid **tear** me **loose**,
and *deliver* **rescue** me out of great waters,
from the hand of strange *children* **sons**;
8 Whose mouth *speaketh* **wordeth** vanity,
and their right *hand* is a right *hand* of falsehood.
9 I *will* **shall** sing a new song unto thee, O *God* **Elohim**:
upon a *psaltery* **bagpipe**
and *an instrument of ten strings* **a decachord**
will I sing praises **shall I psalm** unto thee.
10 *It is he that*
— Who giveth salvation unto *kings* **sovereigns**:
who *delivereth* **releaseth** David his servant
from the *hurtful* **evil** sword.
11 *Rid* **Tear** me **loose**, and *deliver* **rescue** me
from the hand of strange *children* **sons**,
whose mouth *speaketh* **wordeth** vanity,
and their right *hand* is a right *hand* of falsehood:
12 That our sons
may be as plants grown up in their youth;
that our daughters
may be as **prominent** corner *stones* **pillars**,
polished after **carved in** the *similitude* **pattern**
of a *palace* **manse**:
13 That our *garners* **granaries** may be full,
affording all manner of store **producing species by species**:
that our *sheep* **flock**
may bring forth *thousands* **a thousandfold**
and *ten thousands* **abound by the myriads**
in our *streets* **outways**:
14 That our *oxen* **chiliarchs** may *be strong to labour* **bear**;
that there be no *breaking in* **breaching**, nor going out;
that there be no *complaining* **outcry**
in our *streets* **broadways**.
15 *Happy* **Blithe** is that people, that is *in such a case* **thus**:
yea, *happy* **blithe** is that people,
whose *God* **Elohim** is *the LORD* **Yah Veh**.

145

David's *Psalm of Praise* **Halal**.
1 I *will extol* **shall exalt** thee, my *God* **Elohim**,
O *king* **sovereign**;
and I *will* **shall** bless thy name
for ever **eternally** and *ever* **eternally**.
2 Every day *will* **shall** I bless thee;
and I *will praise* **shall halal** thy name
for ever **eternally** and *ever* **eternally**
3 Great is *the LORD* **Yah Veh**,
and *greatly* **mightily** to be *praised* **halaled**;
and his greatness is *unsearchable* **not to be probed**.
4 *One generation* **Generation to generation**
shall *praise* **laud** thy works *to another*,
and shall *declare* **tell** thy *mighty acts* **might**.
5 I *will speak* **shall meditate**
of the glorious honour of thy majesty,
and of thy *wondrous works* **marvellous words**.
6 And *men* shall *speak* **say**
of the *might* **strength** of thy *terrible* **awesome** acts:
and I *will declare* **shall scribe** thy greatness.
7 They shall *abundantly utter* **gush**
the *memory* **memorial** of thy great goodness,
and shall *sing* **shout** of thy *righteousness* **justness**.
8 *The LORD* **Yah Veh** is *gracious* **charismatic**,
and *full of compassion* **merciful**;
slow to *anger* **wrath**, and of great mercy.
9 *The LORD* **Yah Veh** is good to all:
and his tender mercies are over all his works.
10 All thy works shall *praise* **extend hands unto** thee,
O *LORD* **Yah Veh**;
and thy *saints* **mercied** shall bless thee.
11 They shall *speak* **say**
of the *glory* **honour** of thy *kingdom* **sovereigndom**,
and *talk* **word** of thy *power* might;
12 To make known to the sons of *men* **humanity**
his *mighty acts* **might**,
and the *glorious* **honour of** majesty of his kingdom.
13 Thy *kingdom* **sovereigndom**
is an *everlasting kingdom* **eternal sovereigndom**,
and thy *dominion* **reign**
endureth throughout all generations
generation to generation.
14 *The LORD* **Yah Veh** upholdeth all that fall,
and raiseth up all *those* that be bowed down.
15 The eyes of all *wait upon* **expect** thee;
and thou givest them
their *meat in due season* **food on time**.
16 Thou openest thine hand,
and satisfiest the *desire* **pleasure** of *every* **all** living *thing*.
17 *The LORD* **Yah Veh** is *righteous* **just** in all his ways,
and *holy* **mercied** in all his works.
18 *The LORD* **Yah Veh** is nigh
unto all them that call upon him,
to all that call upon him in truth.
19 He *will fulfil* **shall work** the *desire* **pleasure** of them
that *fear* **awe** him:
he also *will* **shall** hear their cry, and *will* **shall** save them.
20 *The LORD* **Yah Veh**
preserveth **guardeth** all them that love him:
but all the wicked *will* **shall** he *destroy* **desolate**.
21 My mouth shall *speak* **word**
the *praise* **halal** of *the LORD* **Yah Veh**:
and let all flesh bless his holy name
for ever **eternally** and *ever* **eternally**.

146

Praise ye the LORD **Halalu Yah**.
Praise the LORD **Halal Yah Veh**, O my soul.
2 *While I live* **In my life**
will I praise the LORD **I shall halal Yah Veh**:
I *will sing praises* **shall psalm** unto my *God* **Elohim**
while I *have any being* **be**.
3 *Put not your trust* **Confide not** in *princes* **volunteers**,
nor in the son of *man* **humanity**,
in whom there is no *help* **salvation**.
4 His *breath* **spirit** goeth forth,
he returneth to his *earth* **soil**;
in that very day his thoughts *perish* **destruct**.
5 *Happy is* **Blithe be** he
that hath *the God* **El** of *Jacob* **Yaaqov** for his help,
whose *hope* **expectation**
is in *the LORD* **Yah Veh** his *God* **Elohim**:
6 Which *made heaven* **worked the heavens**, and earth,
the sea, and all that therein is:

which *keepeth* **guardeth** truth *for ever* **eternally**:
7 Which *executeth* **worketh** judgment for the oppressed:
which giveth *food* **bread** to the *hungry* **famished**.
The LORD **Yah Veh** looseth the *prisoners* **bound**:
8 *The LORD* **Yah Veh** openeth *the eyes of* the blind:
the LORD **Yah Veh** raiseth them that are bowed down:
the LORD **Yah Veh** loveth the *righteous* **just**:
9 *The LORD* **Yah Veh**
preserveth **guardeth** the *strangers* **sojourners**;
he *relieveth* **restoreth** the *fatherless* **orphan** and widow:
but the way of the wicked
he *turneth upside down* **twisteth**.
10 *The LORD* **Yah Veh** shall reign *for ever* **eternally**,
even thy *God* **Elohim**, O *Zion* **Siyon**,
unto all generations **generation to generation**.
Praise ye the LORD **Halalu Yah**.

147

Praise ye the LORD **Halalu Yah**:
for it is good to *sing praises* **psalm** unto our *God* **Elohim**;
for it is pleasant;
and *praise is comely* **halal befitteth**.
2 *The LORD* **Yah Veh**
doth build up Jerusalem **buildeth Yeru Shalem**:
he gathereth *together*
the *outcasts* **overthrown** of *Israel* **Yisra El**.
3 He healeth the broken in heart,
and bindeth up their *wounds* **contortions**.
4 He *telleth* **numbereth** the number of the stars;
he calleth them all by their names.
5 Great is our *Lord* **Adonay**, and of great *power* **force**:
his *understanding is infinite* **discernments innumerable**.
6 *The LORD* **Yah Veh**
lifteth up **restoreth** the *meek* **humble**:
he *casteth* **abaseth** the wicked *down* to the *ground* **earth**.
7 *Sing unto the LORD* **Answer Yah Veh**
with *thanksgiving* **extended hands**;
sing praise **psalm** upon the harp unto our *God* **Elohim**:
8 Who covereth the *heaven* **heavens** with **thick** clouds,
who prepareth rain for the earth,
who *maketh* **sprouteth** grass *to grow*
upon the mountains.
9 He giveth to the *beast* **animal** his *food* **bread**,
and to the *young* **sons of** ravens which *cry* **call**.
10 He delighteth not in the *strength* **might** of the horse:
he taketh not pleasure in the legs of a man.
11 *The LORD* **Yah Veh** taketh pleasure
in them that *fear* **awe** him,
in those that *hope* **await** in his mercy.
12 *Praise the LORD* **Laud Yah Veh**,
O *Jerusalem* **Yeru Shalem**;
praise **halal** thy *God* **Elohim**, O *Zion* **Siyon**.
13 For he hath strengthened the bars
of thy *gates* **portals**;
he hath blessed thy *children* **sons** within thee.
14 He *maketh peace* **setteth shalom** in thy borders,
and *filleth* **satisfieth** thee with the *finest* **fat** of the wheat.
15 He sendeth forth his *commandment* **sayings**
upon earth:
his word runneth very *swiftly* **quickly**.
16 He giveth snow like wool:
he scattereth the hoarfrost like ashes.
17 He casteth forth his ice like morsels:
who can stand *before* **at the face of** his cold?
18 He sendeth out his word, and melteth them:
he causeth his wind to blow, and the waters flow.
19 He *sheweth* **telleth** his word unto *Jacob* **Yaaqov**,
his *statutes* **words** and his judgments unto *Israel* **Yisra El**.
20 He hath not *dealt* **worked** so with any *nation* **goyim**:
and as for his judgments, they have not known them.
Praise ye the LORD **Halalu Yah**.

148

Praise ye the LORD **Halalu Yah**.
Praise ye the LORD **Halal Yah Veh** from the heavens:
Praise **Halal** him in the heights.
2 *Praise* **Halal** ye him, all his angels:
praise **halal** ye him, all his hosts.
3 *Praise* **Halal** ye him, sun and moon:
praise **halal** him, all ye stars of light.
4 *Praise* **Halal** him, ye heavens of **the** heavens,
and ye waters that be above the heavens.
5 Let them *praise* **halal** the name of *the LORD* **Yah Veh**:
for he *commanded* **misvahed**, and they were created.
6 He hath also *stablished* **stood** them
for ever **eternally** and *ever* **eternally**:
he hath *made* **given** a *decree* **statute**
which shall not pass.
7 *Praise the LORD* **Halal Yah Veh** from the earth,
ye *dragons* **monsters**, and all *deeps* **abysses**:
8 Fire, and hail; snow, and *vapours* **smoke**;
stormy wind *fulfilling* **working** his word:
9 Mountains, and all hills; fruitful trees, and all cedars:
10 *Beasts* **Live beings**, and all *cattle* **animals**;
creeping things **creepers**, and *flying fowl* **birds of wing**:
11 *Kings* **Sovereigns** of the earth, and all *people* **nations**;
princes **governors**, and all judges of the earth:
12 Both *young men* **youths**, and maidens;
old men **aged**, and *children* **lads**:
13 Let them *praise* **halal** the name of *the LORD* **Yah Veh**:
for his name alone is *excellent* **lofted**;
his *glory* **majesty**
is above the earth and *heaven* **the heavens**.
14 He also exalteth the horn of his people,
the *praise* **halal** of all his *saints* **mercied**;
even of the *children* **sons** of *Israel* **Yisra El**,
a people near unto him.
Praise ye the LORD **Halalu Yah**.

149

Praise ye the LORD **Halalu Yah**.
Sing unto *the LORD* **Yah Veh** a new song,
and his *praise* **halal** in the congregation of *saints* **mercied**.
2 Let *Israel rejoice* **Yisra El cheer**
in him that *made* **worked** him:
let the *children* **sons** of *Zion* **Siyon**
be joyful **twirl** in their *King* **Sovereign**.
3 Let them *praise* **halal** his name in the **round** dance:
let them *sing praises* **psalm** unto him
with the *timbrel* **tambourine** and harp.
4 For *the LORD* **Yah Veh** taketh pleasure in his people:
he *will beautify* **shall adorn** the *meek* **humble**
with salvation.
5 Let the *saints* **mercied**
be joyful **jump for joy** in *glory* **honour**:
let them *sing aloud* **shout** upon their beds.
6 Let the *high praises of God* **exaltations of El**
be in their *mouth* **throat**,
and a *twoedged* sword **of teeth** in their hand;
7 To *execute* **work** vengeance upon the *heathen* **goyim**,
and *punishments* **reproofs** upon the *people* **nations**;
8 To bind their *kings* **sovereigns** with *chains* **bonds**,
and their *nobles* **honoured** with fetters of iron;
9 To *execute* **work** upon them
the judgment *written* **inscribed**:
this *honour* **majesty** have all his *saints* **mercied**.
Praise ye the LORD **Halalu Yah**.

150

Praise ye the LORD **Halalu Yah**.
Praise God **Halal El** in his *sanctuary* **holies**:
praise **halal** him
in the *firmament* **expanse** of his *power* **strength**.
2 *Praise* **Halal** him
for his *mighty acts* **might**:
praise **Halal** him
according to his *excellent* **abundant** greatness.
3 *Praise* **Halal** him
with the *sound* **blast** of the trumpet:
praise **halal** him
with the *psaltery* **bagpipe** and harp.
4 *Praise* **Halal** him
with the *timbrel* **tambourine** and **round** dance:
praise **halal** him
with *stringed instruments* **strummers**
and *organs* **woodwinds**.
5 *Praise* **Halal** him
upon the *loud* **hearkening** cymbals:
praise **halal** him
upon the *high sounding* **clanging** cymbals.
6 Let *every thing that hath breath* **all that breatheth**
praise the LORD **halal Yah**.
Praise ye the LORD **Halalu Yah**.

KEY TO INTERPRETING THE EXEGESES:
King James text is in regular type;
Text under exegeses is in oblique type;
Text of exegeses is in bold type.

1 The proverbs of *Solomon* **Shelomoh**
the son of David,
king **sovereign** of *Israel* **Yisra El**;
2 To know wisdom and *instruction* **discipline**;
to *perceive the words* **discern sayings**
of *understanding* **discernment**;
3 To *receive the instruction* **take discipline**
of *wisdom* **comprehending**, *justice* **justness**,
and judgment, and *equity* **straightnesses**;
4 To give *subtilty* **strategy** to the *simple* **gullible**,
to the *young man* **lad** knowledge and *discretion* **intrigue**.
5 *A* **The** wise *man will* **shall** hear,
and *will* **shall** increase *learning* **doctrine**;
and *a man of understanding* **the discerning**
shall *attain* **chattelize** unto wise counsels:
6 To *understand* **discern** a proverb,
and the *interpretation* **satire**;
the words of the wise, and their *dark sayings* **riddles**.
7 The *fear* **awe** of *the LORD* **Yah Veh**
is the beginning of knowledge:
but fools
despise **disrespect** wisdom and *instruction* **discipline**.
8 My son, hear the *instruction* **discipline** of thy father,
and *forsake* **abandon** not the *law* **torah** of thy mother:
9 For they shall be
an ornament **a wreath** of *grace* **charism** unto thy head,
and *chains about* **chokers around** thy *neck* **throat**.
10 My son, if sinners entice thee,
consent thou **shalt** not **will**.
11 If they say, Come with us,
let us *lay wait* **lurk** for blood,
let us *lurk privily* **hide out** for the innocent
without cause **gratuitously**:
12 Let us swallow them up alive as *the grave* **sheol**;
and *whole* **integrious**,
as those that *go down* **descend** into the *pit* **well**:
13 We shall find all *precious substance* **esteemed wealth**,
we shall fill our houses with spoil:
14 *Cast in* **Fell** thy *lot* **pebble** among us;
let us all have one *purse* **pouch**:
15 My son, walk not thou in the way with them;
refrain **withhold** thy foot from their path:
16 For their feet run to evil,
and *make haste* **hasten** to *shed* **pour** blood.
17 Surely *in vain* **gratuitously** the net is *spread* **winnowed**
in the *sight* **eye** of any *bird* **master of wing**.
18 And they *lay wait* **lurk** for their own blood;
they *lurk privily* **hide out** for their own *lives* **souls**.
19 So are the ways
of every one that is greedy of *gain* **greed**;
which taketh away
the *life* **soul** of *the owners thereof* **their masters**.
20 Wisdom *crieth without* **shouteth out**;
she *uttereth* **giveth** her voice in the *streets* **broadways**:
21 She *crieth* **calleth out**
in the *chief place* **top** of *concourse* **the roaring**,
in the *openings* **portals** of the *gates* **portals**:
in the city she *uttereth* **sayeth** her *words* **sayings**, *saying*,
22 How long, ye *simple ones* **gullible**,
will **shall** ye love *simplicity* **gullibility**?
and the scorners delight in their scorning,
and fools hate knowledge?
23 Turn you at my reproof:
behold, I *will pour out* **shall gush** my spirit unto you,
I *will* **shall** make known my words unto you.
24 Because I have called, and ye refused;
I have stretched out my hand,
and no *man regarded* **one hearkened**;
25 But ye have *set at nought* **loosed** all my counsel,
and *would* **willed** none of my reproof:
26 I also *will* **shall** laugh at your calamity;
I *will mock* **shall deride** when your *fear* **dread** cometh;
27 When your *fear* **dread**
cometh as *desolation* **devastation**,
and your *destruction* **calamity**
cometh as a *whirlwind* **hurricane**;
when *distress* **tribulation** and *anguish* **distress**
cometh upon you.
28 Then shall they call upon me,
but I *will* **shall** not answer;
they shall seek me early, but they shall not find me:
29 For that they hated knowledge,
and did not choose the *fear* **awe** of *the LORD* **Yah Veh**:
30 They *would* **willed** none of my counsel:
they *despised* **scorned** all my reproof.
31 Therefore shall they eat of the fruit of their own way,
and be *filled* **satiated** with their own *devices* **counsels**.
32 For the *turning away* **apostasy** of the *simple* **gullible**
shall *slay* **slaughter** them,
and the *prosperity* **serenity** of fools shall destroy them.
33 But whoso hearkeneth unto me
shall *dwell safely* **tabernacle confidently**,
and shall *be quiet* **relax** from *fear* **dread** of evil.

2 My son,
if thou *wilt receive* **shalt take** my *words* **sayings**,
and hide my *commandments* **misvoth** with thee;
2 So that thou *incline* **hearken** thine ear
unto wisdom,
and *apply* **extend** thine heart
to *understanding* **discernment**;
3 Yea, if thou *criest* **callest**
after *knowledge* **discernment**,
and *liftest up* **givest** thy voice
for *understanding* **discerning**;
4 If thou seekest her as silver,
and searchest for her as for hid treasures;
5 Then shalt thou *understand* **discern**
the *fear* **awe** of *the LORD* **Yah Veh**,
and find the knowledge of *God* **Elohim**.
6 For *the LORD* **Yah Veh** giveth wisdom:
out of his mouth
cometh knowledge and *understanding* **discernment**.
7 He *layeth up sound wisdom* **treasureth substance**
for the *righteous* **straight**:
he is a buckler to them that walk *uprightly* **integriously**.
8 He *keepeth* **guardeth** the paths of judgment,
and *preserveth* **guardeth** the way of his *saints* **mercied**.
9 Then shalt thou
understand righteousness **discern justness**,
and judgment, and *equity* **straightnesses**;
yea, every good *path* **route**.
10 When wisdom entereth into thine heart,
and knowledge *is pleasant unto* **pleaseth** thy soul;
11 *Discretion* **Intrigue** shall *preserve* **guard** thee,
understanding **discernment** shall *keep* **guard** thee:
12 To *deliver* **rescue** thee
from the way of *the* evil *man*,
from the man
that *speaketh froward things* **wordeth perversions**;
13 Who *leave* **forsake**
the paths of *uprightness* **straightness**,
to walk in the ways of darkness;
14 Who *rejoice* **cheer** to *do* **work** evil,
and *delight* **twirl**
in the *frowardness* **perversions** of *the wicked* **evil**;
15 Whose ways *are crooked* **pervert**,
and they froward — **pervert** in their *paths* **routes**:
16 To *deliver* **rescue** thee from the strange woman,
even from the stranger
which *flattereth* **smootheth over** with her *words* **sayings**;
17 Which forsaketh the *guide* **chiliarch** of her youth,
and forgetteth the covenant of her *God* **Elohim**.
18 For her house *inclineth* **sinketh** unto death,
and her *paths* **routes** unto *the dead* **ghosts**.
19 None that go unto her return *again*,
neither *take* **overtake** they *hold* of the paths of life.
20 That thou mayest walk in the way of good *men*,
and *keep* **guard** the paths of the *righteous* **just**.
21 For the *upright* **straight**
shall *dwell* **tabernacle** in the land,
and the *perfect* **integrious** shall remain in it.
22 But *the wicked* **they that deal covertly**
shall be cut off from the earth,
and the transgressors shall be *rooted* **uprooted** out of it.

3 My son, forget not my *law* **torah**;
but let thine heart
keep **guard** my *commandments* **misvoth**:
2 For length of days, and *long* **years of** life,
and *peace* **shalom**, shall they add to thee.
3 Let not mercy and truth forsake thee:
bind them about thy *neck* **throat**;
write **inscribe** them upon the *table* **slab** of thine heart:
4 So shalt thou find *favour* **charism**
and good *understanding* **comprehension**
in the *sight* **eye** of *God* **Elohim** and *man* **humanity**.
5 *Trust* **Confide** in *the LORD* **Yah Veh** with all thine heart;
and lean not unto thine own *understanding* **discernment**.
6 In all thy ways *acknowledge* **know** him,
and he shall *direct* **straighten** thy paths.
7 Be not wise in thine own eyes:
fear the LORD **awe Yah Veh**,
and *depart* **turn aside** from evil.
8 It shall be health to thy navel,
and *marrow* **moisture** to thy bones.
9 Honour *the LORD* **Yah Veh** with thy *substance* **wealth**,
and with the firstfruits of all *thine increase* **thy produce**:
So **Thus** shall thy *barns* **ingatherings**
be filled with *plenty* **sufficiency**,
and thy *presses* **troughs** shall *burst out* **break forth**
with *new wine* **juice**.
11 My son, *despise* **spurn** not
the *chastening* **discipline** of *the LORD* **Yah Veh**;
neither *be weary of* **abhor** his *correction* **reproof**:
12 For whom *the LORD* **Yah Veh** loveth
he *correcteth* **reproveth**;
even as a father the son
in whom he *delighteth* **be pleased**.
13 *Happy is* **Blithe be** the *man* **human**
that findeth wisdom,
and the *man* **human**
that *getteth understanding* **produceth discernment**.
14 For the merchandise of it
is better than the merchandise of silver,
and the *gain* **produce** thereof than *fine gold* **ore**.
15 She is more *precious* **esteemed** than *rubies* **pearls**:
and all *the things thou canst desire* **thy desires**
are not to be compared unto her.
16 Length of days is in her right *hand*;
and in her left *hand* riches and honour.
17 Her ways are ways of pleasantness,
and all her paths are *peace* **shalom**.
18 She is a tree of life
to them that *lay hold upon* **uphold** her:
and *happy is every one* **blithesome be they**
that *retaineth* **uphold** her.
19 *The LORD* **Yah Veh** by wisdom
hath founded the earth;
by *understanding* **discernment**
hath he established the heavens.
20 By his knowledge
the *depths* **abysses** are *broken up* **split**,
and the *clouds drop down* **vapours drip** the dew.
21 My son, let not them *depart* **pervert** from thine eyes:
keep sound wisdom **guard substance**
and *discretion* **intrigue**:
22 So shall they be life unto thy soul,
and *grace* **charism** to thy *neck* **throat**.
23 Then shalt thou walk in thy way *safely* **confidently**,
and thy foot shall not *stumble* **stub**.
24 When thou liest down,
thou shalt not *be afraid* **dread**:
yea, thou shalt lie down,
and thy sleep shall *be sweet* **please**.
25 *Be* **Awe** not *afraid of* sudden fear,
neither of the *desolation* **devastation** of the wicked,
when it cometh.
26 For *the LORD* **Yah Veh** shall be thy *confidence* **hope**,
and shall *keep* **guard** thy foot from *being taken* **capture**.
27 Withhold not good
from *them to whom it is due* **thy masters**,
when it is in the *power* **El** of thine hand to *do* **work** it.
28 Say not unto thy *neighbour* **friend**,
Go, and *come again* **return**,
and to morrow I *will* **shall** give;
when thou hast it by thee.
29 *Devise* **Inscribe** not evil against thy *neighbour* **friend**,
seeing he *dwelleth securely* **settleth confidently** by thee.
30 Strive not with *a man* **humanity**
without cause **gratuitously**,
if he have *done* **dealt** thee no *harm* **evil**.
31 Envy thou not the *oppressor* **man of violence**,
and choose none of his ways.
32 For *the froward* **he that perverteth**
is *abomination* **abhorrence** to *the LORD* **Yah Veh**:
but his *secret* **private counsel**
is with the *righteous* **straight**.
33 The curse of *the LORD* **Yah Veh**
is in the house of the wicked:
but he blesseth the habitation **of rest** of the just.
34 Surely he scorneth the scorners:
but he giveth *grace* **charism** unto the *lowly* **humble**.
35 The wise shall inherit *glory* **honour**:
but *shame* **abasement**
shall be the *promotion* **exaltation** of fools.

4 Hear, ye *children* **sons**,
the *instruction* **discipline** of a father,
and *attend* **hearken** to know *understanding* **discernment**.
2 For I give you good doctrine,
forsake ye not my *law* **torah**.
3 For I was my father's son,
tender and only *beloved*
in the sight **at the face** of my mother.
4 He taught me also, and said unto me,
Let thine heart *retain* **uphold** my words:
keep **guard** my *commandments* **misvoth**, and live.
5 *Get* **Chattelize** wisdom,
get understanding **chattelize discernment**:
forget it not;
neither *decline* **stretch**
from the *words* **sayings** of my mouth.
6 Forsake her not, and she shall *preserve* **guard** thee:
love her, and she shall *keep* **guard** thee.
7 Wisdom is the *principal thing* **firstfruits**;
therefore get **chattelize** wisdom:
and with all thy *getting* **chattelizing**
get understanding **chattelize discernment**.
8 Exalt her, and she shall *promote* **exalt** thee:
she shall bring thee to honour,
when thou dost embrace her.
9 She shall give to thine head
an ornament **a wreath** of *grace* **charism**:
with a crown of *glory* **beauty**
shall she *deliver to* **shield** thee.
10 Hear, O my son, and *receive* **take** my sayings;
and the years of thy life shall *be many* **abound**.
11 I have taught thee in the way of wisdom;
I have *led* **aimed** thee in *right paths* **routes of straightness**.
12 When thou goest,
thy *steps* **paces** shall not be straitened;
and when thou runnest, thou shalt not stumble.
13 *Take fast hold of instruction* **Uphold discipline**;
let her not go:
keep **guard** her; for she is thy life.
14 Enter not into the path of the wicked,
and go not **nor be blithesome** in the way of evil *men*.
15 Avoid it, pass not by it,
turn **deviate** from it, and pass away.
16 For they sleep not,
except they have *done mischief* **vilified**;
and their sleep is *taken away* **stripped**,
unless they cause some to *fall* **trip**.
17 For they eat the bread of wickedness,
and drink the wine of violence.
18 But the path of the just is as the *shining* **brilliant** light,
that *shineth* **goeth on and lighteneth** more and more
unto *the perfect* **establishing the** day.
19 The way of the wicked is as darkness:
they know not at what they stumble.
20 My son, *attend* **hearken** to my words;
incline **extend** thine ear unto my sayings.
21 Let them not *depart* **pervert** from thine eyes;
keep **guard** them in the midst of thine heart.

22 For they are life unto those that find them,
and *health* **healing** to all their flesh.
23 *Keep* **Guard** thy heart *with all diligence* **under guard**;
for out of it are the issues of life.
24 *Put away* **Turn aside** from thee
a *froward* **perverted** mouth,
and perverse lips *put* **remove** far from thee.
25 Let thine eyes look *right on* **straightforward**,
and let thine eyelids *look straight* **straighten** before thee.
26 *Ponder* **Weigh** the *path* **route** of thy feet,
and let all thy ways be established.
27 *Turn* **Stretch** not to the right *hand* nor to the left:
remove **turn aside** thy foot from evil.

5 My son, *attend* **hearken** unto my wisdom,
and bow **extend** thine ear
to my *understanding* **discernment**:
2 That thou mayest regard *discretion* **intrigue**,
and that thy lips may *keep* **guard** knowledge.
3 For the lips of a *strange woman* **stranger**
drop as an honeycomb,
and her *mouth* **palate** is smoother than *oil* **ointment**:
4 But her *end* **finality** is bitter as wormwood,
sharp as a *twoedged* sword **of mouths**.
5 Her feet *go down* **descend** to death;
her *steps* **paces** take hold on *hell* **sheol**.
6 Lest thou shouldest *ponder* **weigh** the path of life,
her *ways are moveable* **routes drift**,
that thou *canst* not know them.
7 Hear me now therefore, O ye *children* **sons**,
and *depart* **turn** not **aside**
from the *words* **sayings** of my mouth.
8 Remove thy way far from her,
and come not nigh the *door* **portal** of her house:
9 Lest thou give thine honour unto others,
and thy years unto the cruel:
10 Lest strangers be *filled* **satiated**
with thy *wealth* **produce**;
and thy *labours* **contorting** be in the house of a stranger;
11 And thou *mourn* **growl** at the *last* **finality**,
when thy flesh and thy *body* **meat**
are *consumed* **finished off**,
12 And say, How have I hated *instruction* **discipline**,
and my heart *despised* **scorned** reproof;
13 And have not obeyed the voice of my teachers,
nor *inclined* **extended** mine ear
to them that *instructed* **taught** me!
14 I was almost in all evil
in the midst of the congregation and *assembly* **witness**.
15 Drink waters out of thine own *cistern* **well**,
and *running waters* **flowings** out of thine own well.
16 Let thy fountains
be *dispersed abroad* **shattered in the outways**,
and *rivers* **rivulets** of waters
in the *streets* **broadways**.
17 Let them be only thine own,
and not strangers' with thee.
18 Let thy fountain be blessed:
and *rejoice* **cheer** with the *wife* **woman** of thy youth.
19 Let her be as the *loving* hind **of loves**
and *pleasant* roe **of charism**;
let her *breasts* **nipples** satisfy thee at all times;
and *be thou ravished* **err inadvertently**
always **continually** with her love.
20 And why *wilt* **shalt** thou, my son,
be ravished **err inadvertently**
with a *strange woman* **stranger**,
and embrace the bosom of a stranger?
21 For the ways of man
are before the eyes of *the LORD* **Yah Veh**,
and he *pondereth* **weigheth** all his *goings* **routes**.
22 His own *iniquities* **perversities**
shall *take* **capture** the wicked himself,
and he shall be *holden* **upheld** with the cords of his sins.
23 He shall die without *instruction* **discipline**;
and in the greatness of his folly
he shall *go astray* **err inadvertently**.

6 My son, if thou *be surety* **pledgest**
for thy friend,
if thou hast *stricken* **clapped** thy *hand* **palm**
with a stranger,
2 Thou art snared
with the *words* **sayings** of thy mouth,
thou art *taken* **captured**
with the *words* **sayings** of thy mouth.
3 *Do* **Work** this now, my son, and deliver thyself,
when thou art come into the *hand* **palm** of thy friend;
go, *humble thyself* **prostrate**,
and *make sure* **encourage** thy friend.
4 Give not sleep to thine eyes,
nor *slumber* **drowsiness** to thine eyelids.
5 Deliver thyself
as a *roe* **gazelle** from the hand *of the hunter*,
and as a bird from the hand of the *fowler* **snarer**.
6 Go to the ant, thou *sluggard* **sloth**;
consider **see** her ways, and *be wise* **enwisen**:
7 Which having no *guide* **commander**,
overseer **officer**, or *ruler* **sovereign**,
8 *Provideth* **Prepareth** her *meat* **bread** in the summer,
and *gathereth* **harvesteth** her food in the harvest.
9 How long *wilt* **shalt** thou *sleep* **lie down**,
O *sluggard* **sloth**?
when *wilt* **shalt** thou arise out of thy sleep?
10 *Yet* a little sleep, a little *slumber* **drowsiness**,
a little *folding* **clasping** of the hands to *sleep* **lie down**:
11 So shall thy poverty come
as one that *travelleth* **walketh**,
and thy *want* **lack** as *an armed* **a** man **with buckler**.
12 A *naughty person* **human Beli Yaal**,
a *wicked man* **man of mischief**,
walketh with a *froward* **perverted** mouth.
13 He *winketh* **blinketh** with his eyes,
he *speaketh* **uttereth** with his feet,
he *teacheth* **pointeth** with his fingers;
14 *Frowardness* **Perversion** is in his heart,
he *deviseth mischief* **inscribeth evil**
continually **at all times**;
he *soweth discord* **sendeth contention**.
15 Therefore shall his calamity come suddenly;
suddenly **in a blink** shall he be broken
without *remedy* **healing**.
16 These six *things*
doth the LORD hate **Yah Veh hateth**:
yea, seven
are an *abomination* **abhorrence** unto *him* **his soul**:
17 A *proud look* **lofty eye**, a *lying* **false** tongue,
and hands that *shed* **pour** innocent blood,
18 An heart that *deviseth* **inscribeth**
wicked imaginations **mischievous fabrications**,
feet that *be swift* **hasten** in running to *mischief* **evil**,
19 A false witness that *speaketh* **breatheth** lies,
and he that *soweth discord* **spreadeth contention**
among brethren.
20 My son,
keep **guard** thy father's *commandment* **misvah**,
and *forsake* **abandon** not the *law* **torah** of thy mother:
21 Bind them continually upon thine heart,
and *tie* **fasten** them about thy *neck* **throat**.
22 When thou goest, it shall lead thee;
when thou *sleepest* **liest down**, it shall *keep* **guard** thee;
and when thou awakest, it shall *talk* **meditate** with thee.
23 For the *commandment* **misvah** is a lamp;
and the *law* **torah** is light;
and reproofs of *instruction* **discipline** are the way of life:
24 To *keep* **guard** thee from the evil woman,
from the *flattery of the* tongue
of a *strange woman* **stranger that smoothes it over**.
25 *Lust* **Desire** not after her beauty in thine heart;
neither let her take thee with her eyelids.
26 *For by means of a whorish woman*
a man is brought to a piece of bread:
For as a woman whoreth for a round of bread,
and the adulteress **so a man's woman**
will **shall** hunt for the *precious life* **esteemed soul.**
27 Can a man take fire in his bosom,
and his clothes not be burned?
28 Can *one* **a man** go upon *hot* coals,
and his feet not *be burned* **blister**?
29 *So* **Thus** he

that goeth in to his *neighbour's wife* **friend's woman**;
whosoever toucheth her
shall not be *innocent* **exonerated**.
30 *Men do not* despise **not** a thief,
if he steal to *satisfy* **fill** his soul
when he *is hungry* **famisheth**;
31 But if he be found,
he shall *restore* **shalam** sevenfold;
he shall give all the *substance* **wealth** of his house.
32 But whoso *committeth adultery* **adulterizeth**
with a woman
lacketh *understanding* **heart**:
he that *doeth* **worketh** it *destroyeth* **ruineth** his own soul.
33 A *wound* **plague** and *dishonour* **abasement**
shall *he get* **find him**;
and his reproach shall not be wiped away.
34 For jealousy is the *rage* **fury** of *a man* **the mighty**:
therefore he *will* **shall** not spare
in the day of *vengeance* **avengement**.
35 He *will* **shall** not *regard* **lift the face**
of any *ransom* **koper/atonement**;
neither *will he rest content* **shall he will**
though thou *givest many gifts* **aboundest bribes**.

7 My son, *keep* **guard** my *words* **sayings**,
and *lay up* **treasure** my *commandment* **misvoth** with thee.
2 *Keep* **Guard** my *commandments* **misvoth**, and live;
and my *law* **torah** as the *apple* **pupil** of thine eye.
3 Bind them upon thy fingers,
write **inscribe** them upon the table of thine heart.
4 Say unto wisdom, Thou art my sister;
and call *understanding* **discernment** thy *kinswoman* **kin**:
5 That they may *keep* **guard** thee
from the strange woman,
from the stranger
which *flattereth* **smootheth over** with her *words* **sayings**.
6 For at the window of my house
I looked through my *casement* **lattice**,
7 And *beheld* **saw** among the *simple ones* **gullible**,
I discerned among the *youths* **sons**,
a *young man void of understanding* **lad lacking heart**,
8 Passing through the street *near* **beside** her corner;
and he *went* **paced** the way to her house,
9 In the *twilight* **evening breeze**,
in the evening **of the day**,
in the *black and dark night* **darkness of midnight**:
10 And, behold, there met him a woman
with the *attire* **masculine garment** of *an harlot* **a whore**,
and subtil of **with guarded** heart.
11 (She *is loud* **roareth** and *is stubborn* **revolteth**;
her feet *abide* **tabernacle** not in her house:
12 *Now is she without* **At this time in the outways**,
now in the streets **at that time in the broadways**,
and *lieth in wait at* **lurketh beside** every corner.)
13 So she *caught* **held** him, and kissed him,
and with *an impudent* **strengthened** face said unto him,
14 I have *peace offerings* **shelamim** with me;
this day *have I payed* my vows **be at shalom**.
15 Therefore came I forth to meet thee,
diligently to seek **seeking early** thy face,
and I have found thee.
16 I have *decked* **spread** my *bed* **bedstead**
with *coverings of tapestry* **spreads**,
with *carved works* **carvings**,
with *fine linen* **tapestry** of *Egypt* **Misrayim**.
17 I have *perfumed* **rubbed** my bed with myrrh,
aloes, and cinnamon.
18 Come, let us *take our fill of love* **satiate with loves**
until the morning:
let us *solace ourselves* **leap for joy** with loves.
19 For the *goodman* **man** is not at home,
he is gone a *long* **far** journey:
20 He hath taken a *bag* **bundle** of *money* **silver**
with him **in his hand**,
and *will* **shall** come home
at the day *appointed* **of the full moon**.
21 With her *much fair speech* **abundant doctrine**
she caused him to *yield* **stretch**,
with the *flattering* **smoothing over** of her lips
she *forced* **drove** him.
22 He goeth after her *straightway* **suddenly**,
as an ox goeth to the slaughter,
or as a fool
to the *correction* **discipline** of *the stocks* **tinklers**;
23 Till *a dart* **an arrow** strike through his liver;
as a bird hasteth to the snare,
and knoweth not that it is for his *life* **soul**.
24 Hearken unto me now therefore, O ye *children* **sons**,
and *attend* **hearken** to the *words* **sayings** of my mouth.
25 Let not thine heart *decline* **deviate** to her ways,
go **stray** not *astray* in her paths.
26 For she hath cast down many *wounded* **pierced**:
yea, many *strong men* **mighty**
have been *slain* **slaughtered** by her.
27 Her house is the way to *hell* **sheol**,
going down **descending** to the chambers of death.

8 Doth not wisdom *cry* **call**?
and *understanding put forth* **discernment give** her voice?
2 She standeth in the top of *high places* **the heights**,
by the way in the *places* **houses** of the paths.
3 She *crieth* **shouteth** at the *gates* **handle of the portals**,
at the *entry* **mouth** of the city,
at the *coming in* **entry** at the *doors* **portals**.
4 Unto you, O men, I call;
and my voice is to the sons of *man* **humanity**.
5 O ye *simple* **gullible**,
understand wisdom **discern strategy**:
and, ye fools,
be ye of *an understanding* **a discerning** heart.
6 Hear;
for I *will* **shall** speak of *excellent things* **eminence**;
and the opening of my lips
shall be *right things* **straightnesses**.
7 For my *mouth* **palate** shall *speak* **meditate** truth;
and wickedness is an *abomination* **abhorrence** to my lips.
8 All the *words* **sayings** of my mouth
are in *righteousness* **justness**;
there is *nothing froward* **naught twisted**
or *perverse* **perverted** in them.
9 They are all *plain* **straightforward**
to him that *understandeth* **discerneth**,
and *right* **straight** to them that find knowledge.
10 *Receive* **Take** my *instruction* **discipline**, and not silver;
and knowledge rather than choice *gold* **ore**.
11 For wisdom is better than *rubies* **pearls**;
and all *the things that may be desired* **those desires**
are not to be compared to it.
12 I wisdom dwell with *prudence* **strategy**,
and find out knowledge of *witty inventions* **intrigue**.
13 The *fear* **awe** of *the LORD* **Yah Veh** is to hate evil:
pride **pomp**, and *arrogancy* **pompousness**,
and the evil way,
and the *froward* mouth **of perversions**, do I hate.
14 Counsel is mine, and *sound wisdom* **substance**:
I am *understanding* **discernment**; I have *strength* **might**.
15 By me *kings* **sovereigns** reign,
and *princes* **potentates**
decree justice **set statutes of justness**.
16 By me *princes rule* **governors govern**,
and *nobles* **volunteers**, *even* all the judges of the earth.
17 I love them that love me;
and those that seek me early shall find me.
18 Riches and honour are with me;
yea, durable riches **expensive antiques**
and *righteousness* **justness**.
19 My fruit is better than *gold* **ore**,
yea, than *fine* **pure** gold;
and my *revenue* **produce** than choice silver.
20 I *lead* **walk** in the way of *righteousness* **justness**,
in the midst of the paths of judgment:
21 That I may cause *those that love me* **my lovers**
to inherit substance; and I *will* **shall** fill their treasures.
22 *The LORD possessed* **Yah Veh chattelized** me
in the beginning of his way,
before **in** his *works of old* **ancient deeds**.
23 I was *set up* **libated** from *everlasting* **eternity**,
from the *beginning* **top**,
or ever the earth was **from the antiquity of the earth**.
24 When there were no *depths* **abysses**,

I was *brought forth* **writhed**;
when there were no fountains
abounding **heavy** with water.
25 Before the mountains were *settled* **sunk**,
before **at the face of** the hills was I *brought forth* **writhed**:
26 While as yet he had not *made* **worked** the earth,
nor the *fields* **outways**,
nor the *highest part* **top** of the dust of the world.
27 When he prepared the heavens, I was there:
when he *set a compass* **engraved a circle**
upon the face of the *depth* **abyss**:
28 When he *established* **strengthened**
the *clouds* **vapours** above:
when he strengthened
the *fountains* **eyes** of the *deep* **abyss**:
29 When he *gave* **set** to the sea his *decree* **statute**,
that the waters
should not pass his *commandment* **mouth**:
when he *appointed* **prescribed**
the foundations of the earth:
30 Then I was *by* **beside** him, as one brought up *with him*:
and I was *daily* **day by day** his delight,
rejoicing always **laughing at all times**
before him **at his face**;
31 *Rejoicing* **Laughing**
in the *habitable part* **world** of his earth;
and my delights were with the sons of *men* **humanity**.
32 Now therefore hearken unto me, O ye *children* **sons**:
for *blessed* **blithe** are they that *keep* **guard** my ways.
33 Hear *instruction* **discipline**, and *be wise* **enwisen**,
and refuse it not.
34 *Blessed* **Blithe** is the *man* **human** that heareth me,
watching daily **guarding day by day** at my gates,
waiting at the posts of my *doors* **portals**.
35 For whoso findeth me findeth life,
and shall *obtain favour* **promote pleasure**
of *the LORD* **Yah Veh**.
36 But he that sinneth against me
wrongeth **violateth** his own soul:
all they that hate me love death.

9 Wisdom hath builded her house,
she hath hewn out her seven pillars:
2 She hath *killed* **slaughtered** her *beasts* **slaughter**;
she hath *mingled* **mixed** her wine;
she hath also *furnished* **arranged** her table.
3 She hath sent forth her *maidens* **lasses**:
she *crieth* **calleth**
upon the *highest places* **high arches** of the city,
4 Whoso is *simple* **gullible**, let him turn in hither:
as for him that wanteth understanding
whoever lacketh heart, she saith to him,
5 Come, eat of my bread,
and drink of the wine which I have *mingled* **mixed**.
6 Forsake the *foolish* **gullible**, and live;
and go **blithesome**
in the way of *understanding* **discernment**.
7 He that *reproveth* **disciplineth** a scorner
getteth **taketh** to himself *shame* **abasement**:
and he that *rebuketh a* **reproveth the** wicked *man*
getteth himself a blot **shall be blemished**.
8 Reprove not a scorner, lest he hate thee:
rebuke **reprove** a wise *man*, and he *will* **shall** love thee.
9 Give *instruction to a wise man* **to the wise**,
and he *will be yet wiser* **shall enwisen**:
teach a just man **let the just know**,
and he *will* **shall** increase in *learning* **doctrine**.
10 The *fear* **awe** of *the LORD* **Yah Veh**
is the beginning of wisdom:
and the knowledge of the holy
is *understanding* **discernment**.
11 For by me thy days shall *be multiplied* **abound**,
and the years of thy life shall *be increased* **increase**.
12 *If thou be wise* **In enwisening**,
thou shalt be *wise for thyself* **enwisened**:
but if thou scornest, thou alone shalt bear it.
13 A foolish woman *is clamorous* **roareth**:
she is simple — **gullible**, and knoweth *nothing* **not what**.
14 For she *sitteth* **settleth** at the *door* **portal** of her house,
on a *seat* **throne** in the *high places* **heights** of the city,
15 To call *passengers* **them who pass by the way**
who go right on **to straighten** their ways:
16 Whoso is *simple* **gullible**, let him turn in hither:
and *as for him that wanteth understanding*
whoever lacketh heart, she saith to him,
17 Stolen waters *are sweet* **sweeten**,
and *bread eaten in secret* **covert bread**
is pleasant **pleaseth**.
18 But he knoweth not that *the dead* **ghosts** are there;
and that her *guests* **called ones**
are in the depths of *hell* **sheol**.

10 The proverbs of *Solomon* **Shelomoh**.
A wise son *maketh a glad* **cheereth a** father:
but a foolish son is the *heaviness* **grief** of his mother.
2 Treasures of wickedness *profit nothing* **benefit naught**:
but *righteousness delivereth* **justness rescueth** from death.
3 *The LORD will* **Yah Veh shall** not *suffer* **allow**
the soul of the *righteous* **just** to famish:
but he *casteth away* **expelleth**
the *substance* **calamity** of the wicked.
4 He *becometh poor* **impoverisheth**
that *dealeth with a slack hand* **worketh a deceitful palm**:
but the hand of the *diligent* **decisive**
maketh rich **enricheth**.
5 He that *gathereth* **harvesteth** in summer
is a *wise* **comprehending** son:
but he that sleepeth **soundly** in harvest
is a son that *causeth shame* **shameth**.
6 Blessings are upon the head of the just:
but violence covereth the mouth of the wicked.
7 The *memory* **memorial** of the just
is *blessed* **for blessings**:
but the name of the wicked shall rot.
8 The wise in heart
will receive commandments **shall take misvoth**:
but a *prating* fool **of lips** shall fall.
9 He that walketh *uprightly* **integriously**
walketh *surely* **confidently**:
but he that perverteth his ways shall be known.
10 He that *winketh* **blinketh** with the eye
causeth sorrow **giveth contortion**:
but a *prating* fool **of lips** shall fall.
11 The mouth of *a righteous man* **the just**
is a *well* **fountain** of life:
but violence covereth the mouth of the wicked.
12 Hatred *stirreth up strifes* **waketh contentions**:
but love covereth all *sins* **rebellions**.
13 In the lips of him that *hath understanding* **discerneth**
wisdom is found:
but a *rod* **scion** is for the back of him
that *is void of understanding* **lacketh heart**.
14 **The** Wise *men lay up* **treasure** knowledge:
but the mouth of the *foolish* **fool** is near *destruction* **ruin**.
15 The *rich man's* wealth **of the rich**
is his *strong* city **of strength**:
the *destruction* **ruin** of the poor is their poverty.
16 The *labour* **deed** of the *righteous tendeth* **just be** to life:
the *fruit* **produce** of the wicked to sin.
17 He is in the way of life
that *keepeth instruction* **guardeth discipline**:
but he that *refuseth* **forsaketh** reproof *erreth* **strayeth**.
18 He that hideth hatred with *lying* **false** lips,
and he that uttereth a slander, is a fool.
19 In the *multitude* **abundance** of words
there wanteth not sin **rebellion ceaseth not**:
but he that *refraineth* **spareth** his lips
is wise **comprehendeth**.
20 The tongue of the just is as choice silver:
the heart of the wicked is little worth.
21 The lips of the *righteous feed* **just befriend** many:
but fools die for *want* **lack** of *wisdom* **heart**.
22 The blessing of *the LORD* **Yah Veh**,
it maketh rich **enricheth**,
and he addeth no *sorrow* **contorting** with it.
23 It is as *sport* **ridicule** to a fool
to do mischief **work intrigue**:
but a man of *understanding* **discernment** hath wisdom.
24 The *fear* **terror** of the wicked,
it shall come upon him:

but the desire of the *righteous* **just**
shall be *granted* **given**.
25 As the *whirlwind* **hurricane** passeth,
so *is* the wicked *no more* **be not**:
but the *righteous* **just** is an *everlasting* **eternal** foundation.
26 As vinegar to the teeth, and as smoke to the eyes,
so is the *sluggard* **sloth** to them that send him.
27 The *fear* **awe** of *the LORD* **Yah Veh**
prolongeth **addeth** days:
but the years of the wicked
shall be *shortened* **curtailed.**
28 The hope of the *righteous* **just**
shall be *gladness* **cheerfulness**:
but the *expectation* **hope** of the wicked
shall *perish* **destruct.**
29 The way of *the LORD* **Yah Veh**
is strength **be a stronghold** to the *upright* **integrious**:
but *destruction* **ruin**
shall be to the *workers* **doers** of *iniquity* **mischief**.
30 The *righteous* **just**
shall never *be removed* **totter eternally**:
but the wicked shall not *inhabit* **tabernacle on** the earth.
31 The mouth of the just
bringeth forth **germinateth** wisdom:
but the *froward* tongue **of perversions** shall be cut out.
32 The lips of the *righteous* **just**
know what *is acceptable* **pleaseth**:
but the mouth of the wicked
speaketh frowardness **perverteth**.

11 *A false balance* **Balances of deceit**
is abomination **are an abhorrence** to *the LORD* **Yah Veh**:
but a *just weight* **stone of shalom** is his *delight* **pleasure**.
2 *When pride* **Arrogance** cometh,
then cometh *shame* **abasement**:
but with the *lowly* **humble** is wisdom.
3 The integrity of the *upright* **straight**
shall *guide* **lead** them:
but the perverseness
of *transgressors* **them who deal covertly**
shall *destroy* **ravage** them.
4 *Riches profit* **Wealth benefiteth** not
in the day of *wrath* **fury**:
but *righteousness delivereth* **justness rescueth** from death.
5 The *righteousness* **justness** of the *perfect* **integrious**
shall *direct* **straighten** his way:
but the wicked shall fall by his own wickedness.
6 The *righteousness* **justness** of the *upright* **straight**
shall *deliver* **rescue** them:
but *transgressors* **they who deal covertly**
shall be *taken* **captured**
in their own *naughtiness* **calamity**.
7 When a wicked *man* **human** dieth,
his *expectation* **hope** shall *perish* **destruct**:
and the hope of *unjust men* **the mischievous**
perisheth **shall destruct**.
8 The *righteous* **just**
is *delivered* **rescued** out of *trouble* **tribulation**,
and the wicked cometh in his stead.
9 *An hypocrite* **A profaner** with his mouth
destroyeth **ruineth** his *neighbour* **friend**:
but through knowledge
shall the just be *delivered* **rescued.**
10 When it *goeth well* **be good** with the *righteous* **just**,
the city *rejoiceth* **jumpeth for joy**:
and when the wicked *perish* **destruct**, there is shouting.
11 By the blessing of the *upright* **straight**
the city is *exalted* **lofted**:
but it is *overthrown* **demolished**
by the mouth of the wicked.
12 *He that is void of wisdom* **Whoever lacketh heart**
despiseth **disrespecteth** his *neighbour* **friend**:
but a man of *understanding* **discernment**
holdeth his peace **husheth**.
13 A **walking** talebearer
revealeth secrets **exposeth private counsel**:
but he that is of a *faithful* **trustworthy** spirit
concealeth the *matter* **word**.
14 *Where no counsel is* **Without counsels**,
the people fall:
but in the *multitude* **abundance** of counsellors
there is *safety* **salvation**.
15 He that *is surety* **pledgeth** for a stranger
shall *smart for it* **shout evil**:
and he that hateth *suretiship* **to clap** is *sure* **confident**.
16 A *gracious* woman **of charism**
retaineth **upholdeth** honour:
and *strong men retain* **tyrants uphold** riches.
17 The merciful man *doeth good* **dealeth** to his own soul:
but he that is cruel troubleth his own flesh.
18 The wicked worketh a *deceitful work* **false deed**:
but to him that *soweth righteousness* **seedeth justness**
shall be a *sure reward* **hire of truth**.
19 As *righteousness tendeth* **justness** to life:
so he that pursueth evil *pursueth it* to his own death.
20 They that are of a *froward* **perverted** heart
are *abomination* **an abhorrence** to *the LORD* **Yah Veh**:
but *such as are upright* **the integrious** in their way
are his *delight* **pleasure**.
21 *Though* hand *join* in hand,
the *wicked* **evil** shall not be *unpunished* **exonerated**:
but the seed of the *righteous* **just**
shall *be delivered* **escape**.
22 As a *jewel* **nosering** of gold in a *swine's* **hog's** snout,
so is a *fair* **beautiful** woman
which *is without discretion* **turneth aside from taste**.
23 The desire of the *righteous* **just** is only good:
but the *expectation* **hope** of the wicked is *wrath* **fury**.
24 There is that scattereth, and yet increaseth;
and there is **one**
that *withholdeth more than is meet* **spareth straightness**,
but *it tendeth to poverty* **lacketh**.
25 The *liberal soul* **soul for blessings**
shall be *made fat* **fattened**:
and he that *watereth* **saturateth**
shall *be watered* **flow** also himself.
26 He that withholdeth *corn* **grain**,
the *people* **nations** shall *curse* **pierce** him:
but blessing shall be upon the head of him
that *selleth it* **marketeth kernels**.
27 He that *diligently* **early** seeketh good
procureth favour **seeketh pleasure**:
but he that seeketh *mischief* **evil**,
it shall come unto him.
28 He that *trusteth* **confideth** in his riches shall fall;
but the *righteous* **just**
shall *flourish* **blossom** as a *branch* **leaf**.
29 He that troubleth his own house
shall inherit the wind:
and the fool shall be servant to the wise of heart.
30 The fruit of the *righteous* **just** is a tree of life;
and he that *winneth* **taketh** souls is wise.
31 Behold,
the *righteous* **just** shall be *recompensed* **shalamed**
in the earth:
much more the wicked and the sinner.

12 Whoso loveth *instruction* **discipline**
loveth knowledge:
but he that hateth reproof is *brutish* **stupid**.
2 *A* **The** good *man*
obtaineth favour **produceth pleasure**
of *the LORD* **Yah Veh**:
but a man of *wicked devices* **intrigue**
will **shall** he *condemn* **judge wicked**.
3 A *man* **human** shall not be established by wickedness:
but the root of the *righteous* **just**
shall not *be moved* **totter**.
4 A virtuous woman is a crown to her *husband* **master**:
but she that *maketh ashamed* **shameth**
is as rottenness in his bones.
5 The *thoughts* **fabrications** of the *righteous* **just**
are *right* **justness**:
but the counsels of the wicked are deceit.
6 The words of the wicked
are to *lie in wait* **lurk** for blood:
but the mouth of the *upright* **straight**
shall *deliver* **rescue** them.
7 The wicked are *overthrown* **overturned**, and are not:
but the house of the *righteous* **just** shall stand.

8 A man shall be *commended* **halaled**
according to
his wisdom **the comprehension of his mouth**:
but he that is of a *perverse* **perverted** heart
shall be *despised* **disrespected**.
9 He that is *despised* **abased**, and hath a servant,
is better than he that honoureth himself,
and lacketh bread.
10 *A righteous man regardeth* **The just knoweth**
the *life* **soul** of his *beast* **animal**:
but the tender mercies of the wicked are cruel.
11 He that *tilleth* **serveth** his *land* **soil**
shall be satisfied with bread:
but he that *followeth vain persons* **pursueth vanities**
is void of understanding **lacketh heart**.
12 The wicked desireth the *net* **lair** of evil *men*:
but the root of the *righteous yieldeth fruit* **just giveth**.
13 The *wicked is snared* **snare of evil**
is by the *transgression* **rebellion** of *his* lips:
but the just shall come out of *trouble* **tribulation**.
14 A man shall be satisfied with good
by the fruit of his mouth:
and the *recompence* **dealing** of *a man's* **human** hands
shall *be rendered* **return** unto him.
15 The way of a fool is *right* **straight** in his own eyes:
but he that hearkeneth unto counsel is wise.
16 A fool's *wrath* **vexation** is *presently* known **in a day**:
but *a prudent man* **the subtle** covereth *shame* **abasement**.
17 He that *speaketh truth* **breatheth trustworthily**
sheweth forth righteousness **telleth justness**:
but a false witness deceit.
18 There is that *speaketh* **babbleth**
like the *piercings* **stabs** of a sword:
but the tongue of the wise is *health* **healing**.
19 The lip of truth shall be established *for ever* **eternally**:
but a *lying* **false** tongue is but for a *moment* **blink**.
20 Deceit is in the heart of them that *imagine* **inscribe** evil:
but to the counsellors of *peace* **shalom**
is *joy* **cheerfulness**.
21 There shall no *evil* **mischief** happen to the just:
but the wicked shall be filled with *mischief* **evil**.
22 *Lying* **False** lips
are *abomination* **abhorrence** to *the LORD* **Yah Veh**:
but they that *deal truly* **work trustworthily**
are his *delight* **pleasure**.
23 A *prudent man* **subtle human**
concealeth **covereth** knowledge:
but the heart of fools *proclaimeth foolishness* **calleth folly**.
24 The hand of the *diligent* **decisive** shall *bear rule* **reign**:
but the *slothful* **deceitful** shall be *under tribute* **a vassal**.
25 *Heaviness* **Concern** in the heart of man
maketh it stoop **prostrateth him**:
but a good word *maketh it glad* **cheereth**.
26 The *righteous* **just**
is more excellent than **exploreth** his *neighbour* **friend**:
but the way of the wicked seduceth them.
27 The *slothful man roasteth* **deceitful singeth** not
that which he took in hunting **his hunt**:
but the *substance* **wealth**
of a *diligent man* **decisive human**
is precious **esteemed**.
28 In the way of *righteousness* **justness** is life:
and in the pathway *thereof* there is no death.

13

A wise son
heareth his father's *instruction* **discipline**:
but a scorner heareth not rebuke.
2 A man shall eat good by the fruit of his mouth:
but the soul of the *transgressors* **covert**
shall eat **hath** violence.
3 He that *keepeth* **guardeth** his mouth
keepeth **guardeth** his *life* **soul**:
but he that *openeth wide* **spreadeth** his lips
shall have *destruction* **ruin**.
4 The soul of the *sluggard* **sloth** desireth,
and hath *nothing* **naught**:
but the soul of the *diligent* **decisive**
shall *be made fat* **fatten**.
5 *A righteous man hateth lying* **The just hate false** words:
but *a man is loathsome* **the wicked stink**,
and *cometh to shame* **blush**.
6 *Righteousness* **Justness**
keepeth him that is upright **guardeth the integrious**
in the way:
but wickedness *overthroweth* **perverteth** the sinner.
7 There is that *maketh* **enricheth** himself *rich*,
yet hath *nothing* **naught**:
there is that *maketh* **impoverisheth** himself *poor*,
yet hath great *riches* **wealth**.
8 The *ransom* **koper/atonement** of a man's *life* **soul**
are his riches:
but the *poor* **impoverished** heareth not rebuke.
9 The light of the *righteous rejoiceth* **just cheereth**:
but the lamp of the wicked shall be *put out* **extinguished**.
10 Only *by pride* **arrogance**
cometh contention **giveth strife**:
but with the *well advised* **counseled** is wisdom.
11 Wealth *gotten* by vanity shall *be diminished* **diminish**:
but he that gathereth by *labour* **hand**
shall *increase* **abound**.
12 Hope *deferred* **drawn out**
maketh **wearieth** the heart *sick*:
but when the desire cometh, it is a tree of life.
13 Whoso *despiseth* **disrespecteth** the word
shall be *destroyed* **despoiled**:
but he that *feareth* **aweth** the *commandment* **misvah**
shall *be rewarded* **shalam**.
14 The *law* **torah** of the wise is a fountain of life,
to *depart* **turn aside** from the snares of death.
15 Good *understanding* **comprehension**
giveth *favour* **charism**:
but the way of *transgressors* **the covert**
is *hard* **perrenial**.
16 *Every prudent man* **All the subtle**
dealeth **work** with knowledge:
but a fool *layeth open his* **spreadeth** folly.
17 A wicked *messenger* **angel** falleth into *mischief* **evil**:
but a *faithful* **trustworthy** ambassador is *health* **healing**.
18 Poverty and *shame* **abasement**
shall be to him
that *refuseth instruction* **avoideth discipline**:
but he that regardeth reproof shall be honoured.
19 The desire *accomplished* **that becometh**
is *sweet* **pleasant** to the soul:
but it is *abomination* **abhorrence** to fools
to *depart* **turn aside** from evil.
20 He that walketh with **the** wise *men*
shall be *wise* **enwisened**:
but *a companion of* **he that befriendeth** fools
shall be *destroyed* **blast**.
21 Evil pursueth sinners:
but *to the righteous good shall be repayed*
good is the shalam of the just.
22 *A* **The** good *man*
leaveth an inheritance to his children's children
hath his sons' sons to inherit:
and the *wealth* **valuables** of the sinner
is *laid up* **treasured** for the just.
23 *Much* **Abundant** food
is in the tillage of the *poor* **impoverished**:
but there is that is *destroyed* **scraped away**
for want of judgment.
24 He that spareth his *rod* **scion** hateth his son:
but he that loveth him
chasteneth **rising early disciplineth** him *betimes*.
25 The *righteous* **just** eateth to the satisfying of his soul:
but the belly of the wicked shall *want* **lack**.

14

Every wise woman buildeth her house:
but the foolish
plucketh it down **demolisheth** with her hands.
2 He that walketh in his *uprightness* **straightness**
feareth the LORD **aweth Yah Veh**:
but *he that is perverse* **the perverted** in his ways
despiseth him.
3 In the mouth of the *foolish* **fool** is a rod of *pride* **pomp**:
but the lips of the wise shall *preserve* **guard** them.
4 Where no oxen are, the *crib* **manger** is *clean* **empty**:
but *much increase* **abundant produce**
is by the *strength* **force** of the ox.

5 A *faithful* **trustworthy** witness *will* **shall** not lie:
but a false witness *will utter* **shall breathe** lies.
6 A scorner seeketh wisdom, and *findeth* it **is** not:
but knowledge is *easy* **swift**
unto him that *understandeth* **discerneth**.
7 Go from the *presence* **front** of a foolish man,
when thou perceivest not *in him* the lips of knowledge.
8 The wisdom of the *prudent* **subtle**
is to *understand* **discern** his way:
but the folly of fools is deceit.
9 Fools *make a mock* **scorn** at *sin* **guilt**:
but among the *righteous* **straight** there is *favour* **pleasure**.
10 The heart knoweth *his own* bitterness **of soul**;
and a stranger *doth* **mingleth** not *intermeddle*
with his *joy* **cheerfulness**.
11 The house of the wicked
shall be *overthrown* **desolated**:
but the *tabernacle* **tent** of the *upright* **straight**
shall *flourish* **blossom**.
12 There is a way which seemeth *right* **straight**
unto **at the face of** a man,
but the *end* **finality** *thereof* are the ways of death.
13 Even in laughter the heart *is sorrowful* **paineth**;
and the *end* **finality** of that *mirth* **cheerfulness**
is *heaviness* **grief**.
14 *The backslider* **Whoso apostatizeth** in heart
shall be *filled* **satiated** with his own ways:
and a good man *shall be satisfied from* **of** himself.
15 The *simple believeth* **gullible trusteth** every word:
but the *prudent man* **subtle**
looketh well to **discerneth** his *going* **step**.
16 *A* **The** wise *man feareth* **aweth**,
and *departeth* **turneth aside** from evil:
but the fool *rageth* **passeth on**, and is confident.
17 He that *is soon angry* **hath quick wrath**
dealeth foolishly **worketh folly**:
and a man of *wicked devices* **intrigue** is hated.
18 The *simple* **gullible** inherit folly:
but the *prudent* **subtle**
are *crowned* **surrounded** with knowledge.
19 The evil *bow before* **prostrate at the face of** the good;
and the wicked at the *gates* **portals** of the *righteous* **just**.
20 The *poor* **impoverished** is hated
even of his own *neighbour* **friend**:
but *the rich hath many friends*
many are they who love the rich.
21 He that *despiseth* **disrespecteth** his *neighbour* **friend**
sinneth:
but he that
hath mercy **granteth charism** on the *poor* **humble**,
happy **blithe** is he.
22 Do they not *err* **stray** that *devise* **inscribe** evil?
but mercy and truth shall be to them
that *devise* **inscribe** good.
23 In all *labour* **contorting** there is *profit* **advantage**:
but the *talk* **word** of the lips
tendeth **be** only to *penury* **lack**.
24 The crown of the wise is their riches:
but the *foolishness* **folly** of fools is folly.
25 A true witness *delivereth* **rescueth** souls:
but *a* **the** deceitful *witness speaketh* **breatheth** lies.
26 In the *fear* **awe** of *the LORD* **Yah Veh**
is strong confidence:
and his *children* **sons** shall have *a place of* refuge.
27 The *fear* **awe** of *the LORD* **Yah Veh** is a fountain of life,
to *depart* **turn aside** from the snares of death.
28 In the *multitude* **abundance** of people
is the *king's honour* **sovereign's majesty**:
but in the *want* **finality** of *people* **nations**
is the *destruction* **ruin** of the *prince* **potentate**.
29 He that is slow to wrath
is of great *understanding* **discernment**:
but he that is *hasty* **quick** of spirit exalteth folly.
30 A *sound* heart **of healing** is the life of the flesh:
but envy the rottenness of the bones.
31 He that oppresseth the poor
reproacheth his *Maker* **Worker**:
but he that honoureth him
hath mercy **granteth charism** on the *poor* **needy**.
32 The wicked
is *driven away* **overthrown** in his *wickedness* **evil**:
but the *righteous hath hope* **just seeketh refuge**
in his death.
33 Wisdom resteth in the heart of him
that *hath understanding* **discerneth**:
but that which is in the midst of fools is made known.
34 *Righteousness* **Justness** exalteth a *nation* **goyim**:
but sin is a *reproach* **shame** to *any people* **all nations**.
35 The *king's favour* **sovereign's pleasure**
is toward a *wise* **comprehending** servant:
but his *wrath* **outburst of passion**
is *against him* **one** that *causeth shame* **shameth**.

15 A *soft* **tender** answer turneth away *wrath* **fury**:
but *grievous* **contorting** words *stir up anger* **ascend wrath**.
2 The tongue of the wise
useth **well—pleaseth** knowledge *aright*:
but the mouth of fools
poureth out foolishness **gusheth folly**.
3 The eyes of *the LORD* **Yah Veh** are in every place,
beholding **watching** the evil and the good.
4 A *wholesome* **healing** tongue is a tree of life:
but perverseness therein is a breach in the spirit.
5 A fool
despiseth **scorneth** his father's *instruction* **discipline**:
but he that regardeth reproof *is prudent* **strategizeth**.
6 In the house of the *righteous* **just**
is much *treasure* **wealth**:
but in the revenues of the wicked is trouble.
7 The lips of the wise *disperse* **winnow** knowledge:
but the heart of the foolish *doeth* — not so.
8 The sacrifice of the wicked
is an *abomination* **abhorrence** to *the LORD* **Yah Veh**:
but the prayer of the *upright* **straight**
is his *delight* **pleasure**.
9 The way of the wicked
is an *abomination* **abhorrence** unto *the LORD* **Yah Veh**:
but he loveth him
that *followeth after righteousness* **pursueth justness**.
10 *Correction* **Discipline** is *grievous* **evil**
unto him that forsaketh the way:
and he that hateth reproof shall die.
11 *Hell* **Sheol** and *destruction* **abaddon**
are before *the LORD* **Yah Veh**:
how much more then
the hearts of the *children* **sons** of *men* **humanity**?
12 A scorner loveth not one that reproveth him:
neither *will* **shall** he go unto the wise.
13 A *merry* **cheerful** heart
maketh a cheerful countenance **well—pleaseth the face**:
but by *sorrow* **contortion** of the heart
the spirit is *broken* **stricken**.
14 The heart of him that *hath understanding* **discerneth**
seeketh knowledge:
but the *mouth* **face** of fools
feedeth on foolishness **befriendeth folly**.
15 All the days of the afflicted are evil:
but he that is of a merry heart
hath a continual *feast* **banquet**.
16 Better is little with the *fear* **awe** of *the LORD* **Yah Veh**
than great treasure *and trouble therewith* **with confusion**.
17 Better is a *dinner* **ration** of *herbs* **greens** where love is,
than a *stalled* **foddered** ox and hatred *therewith*.
18 A *wrathful* man **of fury**
stirreth up **throttleth** strife:
but he that is slow to *anger* **wrath**
appeaseth **resteth** strife.
19 The way of the *slothful man* **sloth**
is as an hedge of thorns:
but the way of the *righteous* **straight**
is *made plain* **raised**.
20 A wise son *maketh a glad* **cheereth a** father:
but a foolish *man* **human** despiseth his mother.
21 Folly is *joy* **cheerfulness**
to him that *is destitute of wisdom* **lacketh heart**:
but a man of *understanding* **discernment**
walketh *uprightly* **straightly**.
22 Without **private** counsel
purposes **fabrications** are *disappointed* **broken**:
but in the *multitude* **abundance** of counsellors

they *are established* **rise.**
23 A man hath *joy* **cheerfulness**
by the answer of his mouth:
and a word *spoken in due season* **in time**, how good is it!
24 The way of life is above to the *wise* **comprehending**,
that he may *depart* **turn aside**
from *hell beneath* **sheol downward**.
25 *The LORD will destroy* **Yah Veh shall uproot**
the house of the *proud* **pompous**:
but he *will establish* **shall station**
the border of the widow.
26 The *thoughts* **fabrications** of *the wicked* **evil**
are an *abomination* **abhorrence** to *the LORD* **Yah Veh**:
but the *words* **sayings** of the pure are pleasant *words.*
27 He that is greedy of *gain* **greed**
troubleth his own house;
but he that hateth gifts shall live.
28 The heart of the *righteous* **just**
studieth **meditateth** to answer:
but the mouth of the wicked
poureth out **gusheth** evil *things.*
29 *The LORD* **Yah Veh** is far from the wicked:
but he heareth the prayer of the *righteous* **just**.
30 The light of the eyes *rejoiceth* **cheereth** the heart:
and a good report *maketh* **fatteneth** the bones *fat.*
31 The ear that heareth the reproof of life
abideth **stayeth** among the wise.
32 He that *refuseth instruction* **avoideth discipline**
despiseth **spurneth** his own soul:
but he that heareth reproof getteth *understanding* **heart**.
33 The *fear* **awe** of *the LORD* **Yah Veh**
is the *instruction* **discipline** of wisdom;
and *before* **at the face of** honour is humility.

16 The *preparations* **arrangements** of the heart
in *man* **humanity**,
and the answer of the tongue,
is from *the LORD* **Yah Veh**.
2 All the ways of a man are *clean* **pure** in his own eyes;
but *the LORD weigheth* **Yah Veh gaugeth** the spirits.
3 *Commit* **Roll** thy works unto *the LORD* **Yah Veh**,
and thy *thoughts* **fabrications** shall be established.
4 *The LORD* **Yah Veh** hath made all *things*
for himself **to answer to him**:
yea, even the wicked for the day of evil.
5 Every one that is *proud* **lofty** in heart
is an *abomination* **abhorrence** to *the LORD* **Yah Veh**:
though hand join hand **hand by hand**,
he shall not be *unpunished* **exonerated**.
6 By mercy and truth
iniquity *is purged* **doth kapar/atone**:
and by the *fear* **awe** of *the LORD* **Yah Veh**
men depart **turn aside** from evil.
7 When a man's ways please *the LORD* **Yah Veh**,
he maketh even his enemies
to be at *peace* **shalom** *with him.*
8 Better is a little with *righteousness* **justness**
than great *revenues* **produce** without *right* **judgment**.
9 *A man's* **The human** heart
deviseth **fabricateth** his way:
but *the LORD* **Yah Veh**
directeth **establisheth** his *steps* **pace**.
10 *A divine sentence* **Divination**
is in the lips of the *king* **sovereign**:
his mouth *transgresseth* **treasoneth** not in judgment.
11 A just weight and balance are *the LORD'S* **Yah Veh's**:
all the *weights* **stones** of the *bag* **pouch** are his work.
12 It is an *abomination* **abhorrence**
to kings **for sovereigns** to *commit* **work** wickedness:
for the throne is established by *righteousness* **justness**.
13 *Righteous lips* **Lips of justness**
are the *delight* **pleasure** of *kings* **sovereigns**;
and they love him that *speaketh right* **wordeth straight**.
14 The *wrath* **fury** of a *king* **sovereign**
is as *messengers* **angels** of death:
but a wise man *will pacify it* **shall kapar/atone**.
15 In the light of the *king's countenance* **sovereign's face**
is life;
and his *favour* **pleasure**
is as a **thick** cloud of the *latter* **after** rain.

16 How much better *is it to get* **to chattelize** wisdom
than gold **above ore**!
and to *get understanding* **chattelize discernment**
rather to be chosen *than* **above** silver!
17 The highway of the *upright* **straight**
is to *depart* **turn aside** from evil:
he that *keepeth* **guardeth** his way
preserveth **guardeth** his soul.
18 *Pride* **Pomp**
goeth before destruction **faceth the breech**,
and *an haughty* **a lifted** spirit
before a fall **faceth the stumble**.
19 Better it is
to be *of an humble* **a lowly** spirit with the *lowly* **humble**,
than to *divide* **allot** the spoil with the *proud* **pompous**.
20 He that handleth
a *matter wisely* **word comprehendingly**
shall find good:
and whoso *trusteth* **confideth** in *the LORD* **Yah Veh**,
happy is he **O how blithe**.
21 The wise in heart shall be called *prudent* **discerning**:
and the sweetness of the lips
increaseth *learning* **doctrine**.
22 *Understanding* **Comprehension**
is a *wellspring* **fountain** of life
unto *him that hath it* **its master**:
but the *instruction* **discipline** of fools is folly.
23 The heart of the wise
teacheth **comprehendeth** his mouth,
and addeth *learning* **doctrine** to his lips.
24 Pleasant *words* **sayings** are as an honeycomb,
sweet to the soul, and *health* **healing** to the bones.
25 There is a way that seemeth *right* **straight**
unto **at the face of** a man,
but the *end thereof* **finality** are the ways of death.
26 *He that laboureth* **The soul of the toiler**
laboureth **toileth** for himself;
for his mouth craveth it of him.
27 *An ungodly man* **A man of Beli Yaal** diggeth up evil:
and in his lips there is as *a burning* **an inflamed** fire.
28 A *froward* man **of perversions** *soweth* **sendeth** strife:
and a whisperer separateth *chief friends* **chiliarchs**.
29 A *violent* man **of violence** enticeth his *neighbour* **friend**,
and *leadeth* **walketh** him into the way that is not good.
30 He shutteth his eyes
to *devise froward things* **fabricate perversions**:
moving **biting** his lips he *bringeth* **concludeth** evil *to pass.*
31 *The hoary head* **Greyness** is a crown of *glory* **beauty**,
if it be found in the way of *righteousness* **justness**.
32 He that is slow to *anger* **wrath**
is better than the mighty;
and he that *ruleth* **reigneth** his spirit
than he that *taketh* **captureth** a city.
33 The *lot* **pebble** is cast into the *lap* **bosom**;
but *the whole disposing* **all judgment** *thereof*
is of *the LORD* **Yah Veh**.

17 Better is a *dry* **parched** morsel,
and *quietness* **serenity** therewith,
than an house full of sacrifices with strife.
2 A *wise* **comprehending** servant
shall *have rule* **reign** over a son
that *causeth shame* **shameth**,
and shall *have part of* **be allotted** the inheritance
among the brethren.
3 The *fining pot* **crucible** is for silver,
and the furnace for gold:
but *the LORD trieth* **Yah Veh proofeth** the hearts.
4 A *wicked doer* **vilifier**
giveth heed **hearkeneth** to *false* lips **of mischief**;
and a *liar* **falsifier**
giveth ear **hearkeneth** to a *naughty* tongue **of calamity**.
5 Whoso *mocketh* **derideth** the *poor* **impoverished**
reproacheth his *Maker* **Worker**:
and he that *is glad* **cheereth** at calamities
shall not be *unpunished* **exonerated**.
6 *Children's children* **Sons' sons**
are the crown of *old men* **the aged**;
and the *glory* **beauty** of *children* **sons** are their fathers.
7 *Excellent speech* **A lip of rest**

becometh **befitteth** not a fool:
much less *do lying* **false** lips a *prince* **volunteer**.
8 A *gift* **bribe** is as a *precious* stone **of charism**
in the eyes of *him that hath it* **his master**:
whithersoever it *turneth* **faceth**,
it *prospereth* **comprehendeth**.
9 He that covereth a *transgression* **rebellion**
seeketh love;
but he that *repeateth* **reiterateth** a *matter* **word**
separateth *very* friends.
10 *A reproof entereth more* **Rebuke penetrateth**
into a *wise man* **discerner**
more than an hundred *stripes* **smitings**
into a fool.
11 *An evil man* **A rebel** seeketh *only rebellion* **evil**:
therefore a cruel *messenger* **angel**
shall be sent against him.
12 Let a bear *robbed* **bereaved** of her whelps meet a man,
rather than **but not** a fool in his folly.
13 Whoso *rewardeth* **returneth** evil for good,
evil shall not depart from his house.
14 The beginning of strife
is as when one *letteth* **busteth** out water:
therefore leave off contention,
before it be meddled with **ere it faceth a quarrel**.
15 He that justifieth the wicked,
and he that *condemneth* **judgeth wicked** the just,
even they both are *abomination* **abhorrence**
to *the LORD* **Yah Veh**.
16 Wherefore is there a price in the hand of a fool
to *get* **chattelize** wisdom,
seeing he hath no heart to it?
17 A friend loveth at all times,
and a brother is born for *adversity* **tribulation**.
18 A *man void of understanding* **human that lacketh heart**
striketh hands **clappeth palms**,
and becometh *surety* **a pledge**
in the presence **at the face** of his friend.
19 He loveth *transgression* **rebellion** that loveth strife:
and he that *exalteth* **lifteth** his *gate* **portal**
seeketh *destruction* **a breech**.
20 He that hath a *froward* **perverted** heart
findeth no good:
and he that hath a *perverse* **turned** tongue
falleth into *mischief* **evil**.
21 He that begetteth a fool
doeth it to his sorrow **hath grief**:
and the father of a fool hath no *joy* **cheer**.
22 A *merry* **cheerful** heart
doeth good **well—pleaseth** like a *medicine* **cure**:
but a *broken* **stricken** spirit drieth the bones.
23 *A* **The** wicked *man* taketh a *gift* **bribe** out of the bosom
to pervert the ways of judgment.
24 Wisdom *is before* **faceth** him
that *hath understanding* **discerneth**;
but the eyes of a fool are in the ends of the earth.
25 A foolish son is a *grief* **vexation** to his father,
and bitterness to her that bare him.
26 Also to *punish* **penalize** the just is not good,
nor to *strike princes* **smite volunteers**
for *equity* **straightness**.
27 He that *hath* **knoweth** knowledge
spareth his *words* **sayings**:
and a man of *understanding* **discernment**
is of *an excellent* **cool** spirit.
28 Even a fool, when he *holdeth his peace* **husheth**,
is *counted* **fabricated** wise:
and he that shutteth his lips
is esteemed a man of understanding **a discerner**.

18

Through desire a man,
having separated himself,
seeketh and *intermeddleth* **quarreleth**
with all *wisdom* **substance**.
2 A fool hath no delight in *understanding* **discernment**,
but that his heart may *discover* **expose** itself.
3 When the wicked cometh,
then cometh also *contempt* **disrespect**,
and with *ignominy* **abasement** reproach.
4 The words of a man's mouth are as deep waters,
and the *wellspring* **fountain** of wisdom
as a *flowing brook* **gushing wadi**.
5 It is not good
to *accept* **lift** the *person* **face** of the wicked,
to *overthrow* **pervert** the *righteous* **just** in judgment.
6 A fool's lips enter into contention,
and his mouth calleth for *strokes* **poundings**.
7 A fool's mouth is his *destruction* **ruin**,
and his lips are the snare of his soul.
8 The words of a *talebearer* **whisperer**
are as wounds **inflame**,
and they *go down* **descend**
into the *innermost parts* **chambers** of the belly.
9 He also that *is slothful* **slacketh** in his work
is brother to him that is a *great waster* **master of ruin**.
10 The name of *the LORD* **Yah Veh**
is a *strong* tower **of strength**:
the *righteous* **just** runneth into it, and is *safe* **lofted**.
11 The *rich man's* wealth **of the rich**
is his *strong* city **of strength**,
and as *an high* **a lofted** wall
in his own *conceit* **imagination**.
12 *Before destruction* **At the face of the breech**
the heart of man is *haughty* **lifted**,
and before **at the face of** honour is humility.
13 He that *answereth* **respondeth** a *matter* **word**
before he heareth it,
it is folly and shame unto him.
14 The spirit of a man
will **shall** sustain his *infirmity* **disease**;
but a *wounded* **stricken** spirit who can bear?
15 The heart of the *prudent* **discerning**
getteth **chattelizeth** knowledge;
and the ear of the wise seeketh knowledge.
16 *A man's gift* **The gift of a human**
maketh room for **enlargeth** him,
and *bringeth* **leadeth** him
before great men **at the face of the great**.
17 He that is first in **presenting** his own *cause* **defence**
seemeth **be** just;
but his *neighbour* **friend** cometh
and *searcheth* **probeth** him.
18 The *lot* **pebble**
causeth contentions to *cease* **shabbathize**,
and *parteth* **separateth** between the mighty.
19 A brother *offended* **rebelled against**
is harder to be won than a strong city **is as a city of strength**:
and their contentions are like the bars of a *castle* **citadel**.
20 A man's belly shall be satisfied
with the fruit of his mouth;
and with the *increase* **produce** of his lips
shall he be *filled* **satisfied**.
21 Death and life are in the *power* **hand** of the tongue:
and they that love it shall eat the fruit thereof.
22 Whoso findeth a *wife* **woman** findeth *a* good *thing*,
and *obtaineth favour* **produceth pleasure**
of *the LORD* **Yah Veh**.
23 The *poor* **impoverished**
useth intreaties **wordeth supplications**;
but the rich answereth *roughly* **strong**.
24 A man that hath friends must shew himself friendly:
and there is a *friend* **lover**
that *sticketh* **adhereth** closer than a brother.

19

Better *is the poor* **the impoverished**
that walketh in his integrity,
than *he that is perverse* **the perverted**
in *his* lips, and is a fool.
2 Also,
that the soul be without knowledge, it is not good;
and he that hasteth with his feet sinneth.
3 The *foolishness* **folly** of *man* **humanity**
perverteth his way:
and his heart *fretteth* **rageth** against *the LORD* **Yah Veh**.
4 Wealth *maketh* **addeth** many friends;
but the poor is separated from his *neighbour* **friend**.
5 A false witness shall not be *unpunished* **exonerated**,
and he that *speaketh* **breatheth** lies shall not escape.
6 Many *will intreat* **shall stroke** the *favour* **face**
of the *prince* **volunteer**:

and every man is a friend to *him that giveth* **a man of** gifts.
7 All the brethren of the *poor* **impoverished** do hate him:
how much more
do his *friends* **companions** go far from him?
he pursueth them with *words* **sayings**,
yet they are *wanting to him* **not**.
8 He that *getteth wisdom* **chattelizeth heart**
loveth his own soul:
he that *keepeth understanding* **guardeth discernment**
shall find good.
9 A false witness shall not be *unpunished* **exonerated**,
and he that *speaketh* **breatheth** lies shall *perish* **destruct**.
10 Delight is not *seemly* **befitting** for a fool;
much less for a servant
to *have rule* **reign** over *princes* **governors**.
11 The *discretion* **comprehension** of a *man* **human**
deferreth **prolongeth** his *anger* **wrath**;
and it is his *glory* **beauty**
to pass over a *transgression* **rebellion**.
12 The *king's wrath* **sovereign's rage**
is as the *roaring* **growling** of a *lion* **whelp**;
but his *favour* **pleasure** is as dew upon the *grass* **herbage**.
13 A foolish son is the calamity of his father:
and the contentions of a *wife* **woman**
are a continual *dropping* **dripping**.
14 House and *riches* **wealth**
are the inheritance of fathers:
and a *prudent wife* **comprehending woman**
is from *the LORD* **Yah Veh**.
15 *Slothfulness casteth* **Sloth falleth** into a deep sleep;
and *an idle* **a deceitful** soul shall *suffer hunger* **famish**.
16 He that *keepeth* **guardeth** the *commandment* **misvah**
keepeth **guardeth** his own soul;
but he that despiseth his ways shall die.
17 He that *hath pity* **granteth charism** upon the poor
lendeth unto *the LORD* **Yah Veh**;
and that which he hath *given* **dealt**
will he pay him again **shall he shalam**.
18 *Chasten* **Discipline** thy son while there is hope,
and *let* **lift** not thy soul *spare* for his *crying* **death**.
19 *A man* **One** of *great* **harsh** wrath
shall *suffer punishment* **bear the penalty**:
for if thou *deliver* **rescue** him, yet thou must do it again.
20 Hear counsel, and *receive instruction* **take discipline**,
that thou mayest *be wise* **enwisen**
in thy *latter end* **finality**.
21 There are many *devices* **fabrications** in a man's heart;
nevertheless the counsel of *the LORD* **Yah Veh**,
that shall *stand* **rise**.
22 The desire of a *man* **human** is his *kindness* **mercy**:
and *a poor man* **the impoverished**
is better than a *liar* **man of lies**.
23 The *fear* **awe** of *the LORD tendeth* **Yah Veh be** to life:
and he *that hath it* shall *abide* **stay** satisfied;
he shall not be visited with evil.
24 *A slothful man* **The sloth** hideth his hand in his bosom,
and *will* **shall** not
so much as bring **return** it to his mouth *again*.
25 Smite a scorner,
and the *simple will beware* **gullible shall strategize**:
and reprove one that *hath understanding* **discerneth**,
and he *will understand* **shall discern** knowledge.
26 He that *wasteth* **ravageth** his father,
and *chaseth* **fleeth** away his mother,
is a son that *causeth shame* **shameth**,
and *bringeth reproach* **blusheth**.
27 Cease, my son,
to hear the *instruction* **discipline**
that causeth to err **inadvertently**
from the *words* **sayings** of knowledge.
28 *An ungodly* **A** witness **of Beli Yaal** scorneth judgment:
and the mouth of the wicked
devoureth iniquity **swalloweth mischief**.
29 Judgments are prepared for scorners,
and *stripes* **poundings** for the back of fools.

20 Wine *is a mocker* **scorneth**,
strong drink is raging **intoxicant roareth**:
and whosoever *is deceived* **erreth inadvertently** *thereby*
is not *wise* **enwisened**.
2 The *fear* **terror** of a *king* **sovereign**
is as the *roaring* **growling** of a *lion* **whelp**:
whoso *provoketh* **enrageth** him *to anger*
sinneth against his own soul.
3 It is an honour for a man
to *cease* **shabbathize** from strife:
but every fool *will be meddling* **shall quarrel**.
4 The *sluggard* **sloth**
will **shall** not plow *by reason of the cold* **in winter**;
therefore shall he *beg* **ask** in harvest,
and have *nothing* **naught**.
5 Counsel in the heart of man is like deep water;
but a man of *understanding* **discernment**
will draw it out **shall bail**.
6 *Most men* **An abundance of humanity**
will proclaim every one **shall each call out**
his own *goodness* **mercy**:
but a *faithful* **trustworthy** man who can find?
7 The just *man* walketh in his integrity:
his *children* **sons** are *blessed* **blithe** after him.
8 A *king* **sovereign**
that *sitteth* **settleth** in the throne of *judgment* **pleading**
scattereth **winnoweth** *away* all evil with his eyes.
9 Who can say, I have *made* **purified** my heart *clean*,
I am *pure* **purified** from my sin?
10 *Divers weights* **A stone and a stone**,
and divers measures **an ephah and an ephah**,
yea, both of them
are *alike abomination* **abhorrence** to *the LORD* **Yah Veh**.
11 Even a *child* **lad**
is *known* **recognized** by his *doings* **exploits**,
whether his *work* **deeds** be pure,
and whether it be *right* **straight**.
12 The hearing ear, and the seeing eye,
the LORD **Yah Veh**
hath *made* **worked** even both of them.
13 Love not sleep,
lest thou *come to poverty* **be dispossessed**;
open thine eyes, and thou shalt be satisfied with bread.
14 *It is naught* **Evil,** *it is naught* **evil**!
saith the *buyer* **chattelizer**:
but when he *is gone his way* **hath gad about**,
then he *boasteth* **halaleth**.
15 There is gold,
and *a multitude* **an abundance** of *rubies* **pearls**:
but the lips of knowledge
are *a precious jewel* **an esteemed instrument**.
16 Take his *garment* **clothes**
that is *surety* **pledge** for a stranger:
and take a pledge of him
for a *strange woman* **stranger**.
17 Bread of *deceit* **falsehood** is *sweet* **pleasant** to a man;
but afterwards his mouth shall be filled with gravel.
18 Every *purpose* **fabrication** is established by counsel:
and with *good advice make* **counsels work** war.
19 He that goeth about as a talebearer
revealeth secrets **exposeth private counsel**:
therefore meddle not with him
that *flattereth* **enticeth** with his lips.
20 Whoso *curseth* **abaseth** his father or his mother,
his lamp shall be *put out* **extinguished**
in *obscure* **mid** darkness.
21 An inheritance
may be *gotten hastily* **obtained by avarice**
at the *beginning* **first**;
but the *end thereof* **finality** shall not be blessed.
22 Say not thou, I *will recompense* **shall shalam for** evil;
but wait on the LORD **await Yah Veh**,
and he shall save thee.
23 *Divers weights* **A stone and a stone**
are an *abomination* **abhorrence** unto *the LORD* **Yah Veh**;
and *a false balance is* **balances of deceit are** not good.
24 *Man's goings* **The paces of the mighty**
are of *the LORD* **Yah Veh**;
how can a *man then* **human**
understand **discern** his own way?
25 It is a snare to the *man* **human**
who *devoureth* **hastily cheweth** that which is holy,
and after vows to *make enquiry* **search**.
26 A wise *king* **sovereign**

scattereth **winnoweth** the wicked,
and *bringeth* **turneth** the wheel over them.
27 The *spirit* **breath** of *man* **humanity**
is the *candle* **lamp** of *the LORD* **Yah Veh**,
searching all the *inward parts* **chambers** of the belly.
28 Mercy and truth *preserve* **guard** the *king* **sovereign**:
and his throne is upholden by mercy.
29 The *glory* **beauty** of *young men* **youths**
is their *strength* **force**:
and the *beauty* **majesty** of *old men* **elders**
is the *grey head* **greyness**.
30 The *blueness* **lashes** of a wound
cleanseth away **purify** evil:
so *do stripes* **strokes** the inward parts of the belly.

21 The *king's* **sovereign's** heart
is in the hand of *the LORD* **Yah Veh**,
as the *rivers* **rivulets** of water:
he *turneth* **stretcheth** it whithersoever he *will* **desire**.
2 Every way of a man is *right* **straight** in his own eyes:
but *the LORD pondereth* **Yah Veh gaugeth** the hearts.
3 *To do* **Choose to work** justice and judgment
is more acceptable to the LORD **unto Yah Veh**
rather than sacrifice.
4 An high look, and a *proud* **broad** heart,
and the plowing of the wicked, is sin.
5 The *thoughts* **fabrications** of the *diligent* **decisive**
tend **be** only to *plenteousness* **advantage**;
but of every one that is hasty**,** only to want.
6 The *getting* **deeds** of treasures by a *lying* **false** tongue
is a vanity
tossed to and fro **dispersed** of them that seek death.
7 The *robbery* **devastation** of the wicked
shall *destroy* **cut** them;
because they refuse to *do* **work** judgment.
8 The way of **a guilty** man is *froward and strange* **perverse**:
but as for the pure, his *work* **deed** is *right* **straight**.
9 It is better to *dwell* **settle**
in a corner of the *housetop* **roof**,
than with a *brawling* **contentious** woman
in a *wide* **community** house.
10 The soul of the wicked desireth evil:
his *neighbour* **friend**
findeth **granteth** no *favour* **charism** in his eyes.
11 When the scorner is *punished* **penalized**,
the *simple is made wise* **gullible enwiseneth**:
and when the wise *is instructed* **comprehendeth**,
he *receiveth* **taketh** knowledge.
12 The *righteous man* **Just One**
wisely considereth **comprehendeth**
the house of the wicked:
but *God overthroweth* **perverteth** the wicked
for their *wickedness* **evil**.
13 Whoso *stoppeth* **shutteth** his ears
at the cry of the poor,
he also shall *cry* **call out** himself,
but shall not be *heard* **answered**.
14 A **covert** gift *in secret*
pacifieth anger **tameth wrath**:
and a *reward* **bribe** in the bosom strong *wrath* **fury**.
15 It is *joy* **cheerfulness** to the just to *do* **work** judgment:
but *destruction* **ruin** shall be
to the workers of *iniquity* **mischief**.
16 The *man* **human** that *wandereth* **strayeth**
out of the way of *understanding* **comprehension**
shall *remain* **rest** in the congregation of *the dead* **ghosts**.
17 He that loveth *pleasure* **cheerfulness**
shall be a *poor* man **of lack**:
he that loveth wine and *oil* **ointment**
shall not *be rich* **enrich**.
18 The wicked
shall be *a ransom* **a koper/an atonement**
for the *righteous* **just**,
and *the transgressor* **they who deal covertly**
for the *upright* **straight**.
19 It is better to *dwell* **settle** in the **land of the** wilderness,
than with a *contentious* **woman of contentions**
and *an angry woman* **vexations**.
20 There is treasure to be desired and *oil* **ointment**
in the *dwelling* **habitation of rest** of the wise;
but a foolish *man spendeth* **human swalloweth** it up.
21 He that *followeth* **pursueth**
after righteousness **justness** and mercy
findeth life, *righteousness* **justness**, and honour.
22 *A* **The** wise *man scaleth* **ascendeth**
the city of the mighty,
and *casteth down* **toppleth**
the strength of the confidence *thereof*.
23 Whoso *keepeth* **guardeth** his mouth and his tongue
keepeth **guardeth** his soul from *troubles* **tribulations**.
24 Proud and *haughty* **arrogant** scorner is his name,
who *dealeth* **worketh**
in proud wrath **the fury of arrogance**.
25 The desire of the *slothful killeth* **sloth deathifieth** him;
for his hands refuse to *labour* **work**.
26 *He coveteth greedily* **In desiring,**
he desireth all the day long:
but the *righteous* **just** giveth and spareth not.
27 The sacrifice of the wicked is *abomination* **abhorrence**:
how much more,
when he bringeth it with *a wicked mind* **intrigue**?
28 A *false* witness **of lies** shall *perish* **destruct**:
but the man that heareth
speaketh constantly **wordeth in perpetuity**.
29 A wicked man *hardeneth* **strengtheneth** his face:
but *as for the upright* **the straight**,
he *directeth* **establisheth** his way.
30 There is no wisdom nor *understanding* **discernment**
nor counsel against *the LORD* **Yah Veh**.
31 The horse is prepared against the day of *battle* **war**:
but *safety* **salvation** is of *the LORD* **Yah Veh**.

22 A *good* name
is rather to be chosen than great riches,
and *loving favour* **good charism**
rather than silver and gold.
2 The rich and *poor* **impoverished** meet together:
the LORD **Yah Veh** is the *maker* **Worker** of them all.
3 *A prudent man foreseeth* **The subtle seeth** the evil,
and hideth himself:
but the *simple* **gullible** pass on,
and are *punished* **penalized**.
4 *By* **The finality of** humility
and the *fear* **awe** of *the LORD* **Yah Veh**
are riches, and honour, and life.
5 Thorns and snares
are in the way of the *froward* **pervert**:
he that *doth keep* **guardeth** his soul
shall be far from them.
6 *Train up a child* **Hanukkah a lad by mouth**
in the way he should go **about his way**:
and when he *is old* **ageth**,
he *will* **shall** not *depart* **turn aside** from it.
7 The rich *ruleth* **reigneth** over the *poor* **impoverished**,
and the borrower is servant
to the *lender* **man that lendeth**.
8 He that *soweth iniquity* **seedeth wickedness**
shall *reap vanity* **harvest mischief**:
and the *rod* **scion** of his *anger* **fury**
shall *fail* **be finished off**.
9 He that hath a *bountiful* **good** eye shall be blessed;
for he giveth of his bread to the poor.
10 *Cast out* **Exile** the scorner, and contention shall go out;
yea, *strife* **pleading** and *reproach* **abasement**
shall *cease* **shabbathize**.
11 He that loveth pureness of heart,
for the *grace* **charism** of his lips
the *king* **sovereign** shall be his friend.
12 The eyes of *the LORD* **Yah Veh** preserve knowledge,
and he *overthroweth* **perverteth** the words
of *the transgressor* **them who deal covertly**.
13 The *slothful man* **sloth** saith,
There is a lion without, **A lion in the outways!**
I shall be *slain in* **murdered within** the *streets* **broadways**.
14 The mouth of *strange women* **strangers**
is a *deep pit* **chasm**:
he that *is abhorred of the LORD* **enrageth Yah Veh**
shall fall therein.
15 *Foolishness* **Folly** is bound in the heart of a *child* **lad**;
but the *rod* **scion** of *correction* **discipline**

shall *drive* **remove** it far from him.
16 He *that* oppresseth the poor
to *increase his riches* **abound**,
and he *that* giveth to the rich,
shall surely come to want **only to lack**.
17 *Bow down* **Extend** thine ear,
and hear the words of the wise,
and *apply* **set** thine heart unto my knowledge.
18 For it is a *pleasant thing* **pleasure**
if thou *keep* **guard** them within *thee* **thy belly**;
they shall *withal be fitted* **be established** in thy lips.
19 That thy *trust* **confidence**
may be in *the LORD* **Yah Veh**,
I have made known to thee this day, even to thee.
20 Have not I *written* **inscribed** to thee
excellent things **thrice** in counsels and knowledge,
21 That I might *make* **have** thee know
the *certainty* **truth** of the *words* **sayings** of truth;
that thou mightest *answer* **respond**
to the *words* **sayings** of truth
to them that send unto thee?
22 *Rob* **Strip** not the poor, because he is poor:
neither *oppress* **crush** the *afflicted* **humble**
in the *gate* **portal**:
23 For *the LORD* **Yah Veh**
will plead **shall defend** their *cause* **defence**,
and *spoil* **defraud** the soul
of those that *spoiled* **defrauded** them.
24 *Make no friendship* **Befriend not**
with an angry man **a master of fury**;
and with a furious man thou shalt not go:
25 Lest thou *learn* **be taught** his ways,
and *get* **take** a snare to thy soul.
26 Be not thou *one* of them that *strike hands* **clap palms**,
or of them that *are sureties* **pledge** for *debts* **loans**.
27 If thou hast *nothing* **naught** to *pay* **shalam**,
why should he take away thy bed from under thee?
28 Remove not the *ancient landmark* **eternal border**,
which thy fathers have *set* **worked**.
29 Seest thou a man *diligent* **skillful** in his *business* **work**?
he shall *stand before kings* **set at the face of sovereigns**;
he shall not *stand* **set**
before mean men **at the face of darkness**.

23 When thou *sittest* **settlest**
to eat with a *ruler* **sovereign**,
consider diligently **in discerning**,
discern what is *before thee* **at thy face**:
2 And *put* **set** a knife to thy throat,
if *thou be a man given to appetite* **thy soul be thy master**.
3 *Be not desirous* **Desire not** of his *dainties* **delicacies**:
for they are *deceitful meat* **a bread of lies**.
4 Labour not to *be rich* **enrich**:
cease from thine own *wisdom* **discernment**.
5 *Wilt* **Shalt** thou *set* **flit** thine eyes
upon that which is not?
for *riches certainly make themselves*
in working, they work wings;
they fly away as an eagle toward *heaven* **the heavens**.
6 Eat thou not the bread of *him that hath* an evil eye,
neither desire thou his *dainty meats* **delicacies**:
7 For as he *thinketh* **guardeth** in his *heart* **soul**, so is he:
Eat and drink, saith he to thee;
but his heart is not with thee.
8 The morsel which thou hast eaten
shalt thou dost vomit *up*,
and *lose* **ruin** thy *sweet* **pleasant** words.
9 *Speak* **Word** not in the ears of a fool:
for he *will despise* **shall disrespect**
the *wisdom* **comprehension** of thy *words* **utterances**.
10 Remove not the *old landmark* **eternal border**;
and enter not into the fields of the *fatherless* **orphan**:
11 For their redeemer is *mighty* **strong**;
he shall *plead* **defend** their *cause* **defence** with thee.
12 Apply thine heart unto *instruction* **discipline**,
and thine ears to the words of knowledge.
13 Withhold not *correction* **discipline** from the *child* **lad**:
for if thou beatest **when thou smittest** him
with the *rod* **scion**,
he shall not die.
14 Thou shalt *beat* **smite** him with the *rod* **scion**,
and shalt *deliver* **rescue** his soul from *hell* **sheol**.
15 My son, if thine heart *be wise* **enwisen**,
my heart shall *rejoice* **cheer**, even mine.
16 Yea, my reins shall rejoice,
when thy lips *speak right things* **word straightnesses**.
17 Let not thine heart envy sinners:
but *be thou in the fear of the LORD* **awe thou Yah Veh**
all the day long.
18 For surely there is *an end* **a finality**;
and thine *expectation* **hope** shall not be cut off.
19 Hear thou, my son, and *be wise* **enwisen**,
and *guide* **blithe** thine heart in the way.
20 Be not among *winebibbers* **wine carousers**;
among *riotous eaters* **gluttons** of flesh:
21 For the *drunkard* **carouser** and the glutton
shall *come to poverty* **be dispossessed**:
and drowsiness
shall *clothe a man* **enrobe** with *rags* **shreds**.
22 Hearken unto thy father that begat thee,
and *despise* **disrespect** not thy mother
when she *is old* **ageth**.
23 *Buy* **Chattelize** the truth, and sell it not;
also wisdom, and *instruction* **discipline**,
and *understanding* **discernment**.
24 The father of the *righteous* **just**
in twirling, shall *greatly rejoice* **twirl**:
and he that begetteth *a* **the** wise *child*
shall *have joy of* **cheer in** him.
25 Thy father and thy mother shall *be glad* **cheer**,
and she that bare thee shall *rejoice* **twirl**.
26 My son, give me thine heart,
and let thine eyes *observe* **guard** my ways.
27 For a whore is a deep *ditch* **chasm**;
and a *strange woman* **stranger** is a narrow *pit* **well**.
28 She also *lieth in wait* **lurketh** as *for a prey* **a robber**,
and increaseth *the transgressors* **them who deal covertly**
among *men* **humanity**.
29 Who hath woe? who hath *sorrow* **the will**?
who hath contentions? who hath *babbling* **meditation**?
who hath wounds *without cause* **gratuitously**?
who hath *redness* **flushness** of eyes?
30 They that *tarry long* **linger** at the wine;
they that go to *seek mixed wine* **probe cocktails**.
31 *Look* **See** not thou upon the wine
when it *is red* **hath reddened**,
when it giveth his *colour* **eye** in the *cup* **pouch**,
when it *moveth itself aright* **passeth in straightnesses**.
32 *At the last* **Finally** it biteth like a serpent,
and *stingeth* **woundeth** like *an adder* **a hisser**.
33 Thine eyes shall *behold* **see** strange women,
and thine heart
shall *utter perverse things* **word perversions**.
34 Yea, thou shalt be
as he that lieth down in the *midst* **heart** of the sea,
or as he that lieth upon the top of a mast.
35 They have *stricken* **smitten** me, *shalt thou say*,
and I was not sick;
they have *beaten* **hammered** me, and I *felt* **knew** it not:
when shall I awake?
I *will* **shall** seek it *yet* again **and again**.

24 Be not thou envious against evil men,
neither desire to be with them.
2 For their heart
studieth destruction **meditateth devastation**,
and their lips *talk* **word** of *mischief* **toil**.
3 Through wisdom is an house builded;
and by *understanding* **discernment** it is established:
4 And by knowledge shall the chambers be filled
with all *precious* **esteemed** and pleasant *riches* **wealth**.
5 *A* **The** wise *man is strong* **is a mighty in strength**;
yea, a man of knowledge
increaseth strength **strengtheneth force**.
6 For by *wise counsel* **counsels**
thou shalt *make* **work** thy war:
and in *multitude* **abundance** of counsellors
there is *safety* **salvation**.
7 Wisdom is too high for a fool:
he openeth not his mouth in the *gate* **portal**.

8 He that *deviseth* **fabricateth** to *do evil* **vilify**
shall be called a *mischievous person* **master of intrigue**.
9 The *thought* **intrigue** of *foolishness* **folly** is sin:
and the scorner
is an *abomination* **abhorrence** to *men* **humanity**.
10 If thou *faint* **slacken** in the day of *adversity* **tribulation**,
thy *strength* **force** is *small* **tribulated**.
11 If thou *forbear* **spare** to *deliver* **rescue**
them that are *drawn* **taken** unto death,
and those that
are ready to be slain **totter from the slaughter**;
12 If thou sayest, Behold, we knew it not;
doth not he that *pondereth* **gaugeth** the heart
consider **discern** it?
and he that *keepeth* **guardeth** thy soul,
doth not he know it?
and shall not he *render* **return**
to *every man* **all humanity**
according to his *works* **deeds**?
13 My son, eat thou honey, because it is good;
and the honeycomb, which is sweet to thy *taste* **palate**:
14 So shall the knowledge of wisdom be unto thy soul:
when thou hast found it,
then there shall be a *reward* **finality**,
and thy *expectation* **hope** shall not be cut off.
15 *Lay not wait* **Lurk not**, O wicked *man*,
against the *dwelling* **habitation of rest**
of the *righteous* **just**;
spoil **ravage** not his *resting place* **repose**:
16 For *a* **the** just *man* falleth seven *times*,
and riseth *up again*:
but the wicked shall fall into *mischief* **evil**.
17 *Rejoice* **Cheer** not when thine enemy falleth,
and let not thine heart *be glad* **twirl** when he stumbleth:
18 Lest *the LORD* **Yah Veh** see it,
and it *displease him* **vilify in his eye**,
and he turn away his wrath from him.
19 *Fret* **Inflame** not thyself
because of evil men **at vilifiers**,
neither be thou envious at the wicked:
20 For there shall be no *reward* **finality** to the evil *man*;
the *candle* **lamp** of the wicked
shall be *put out* **extinguished**.
21 My son,
fear **awe** thou *the LORD* **Yah Veh** and the *king* **sovereign**:
and meddle not with them
that *are given to change* **reiterate**:
22 For their calamity shall rise suddenly;
and who knoweth the *ruin* **calamity** of them both?
23 These *things* also *belong* **be** to the wise.
It is not good
to *have respect of persons* **recognize faces** in judgment.
24 He that saith unto the wicked, Thou art *righteous* **just**;
him shall the people *curse* **pierce**,
nations shall *abhor* **enrage at** him:
25 But *to* them that *rebuke* **reprove** him
shall be *delight* **pleased**,
and a good blessing shall come upon them.
26 *Every man* **He** shall kiss *his* **the** lips that
giveth a right answer **respond straight forward words**.
27 Prepare thy work *without* **in the outways**,
and *make it fit for thyself* **ready it** in the field;
and afterwards build thine house.
28 Be not a witness against thy *neighbour* **friend**
without cause **gratuitously**;
and *deceive* **entice** not with thy lips.
29 Say not, I *will do so* **shall work** to him
as he hath *done* **worked** to me:
I *will render* **shall return** to the man
according to his *work* **deeds**.
30 I *went* **passed** by the field of the *slothful* **man of sloth**,
and by the vineyard of the *man* **human**
void of understanding **that lacketh heart**;
31 And, *lo* **behold**,
it was all *grown over* **ascended** with *thorns* **thistles**,
and nettles had covered the face *thereof*,
and the stone wall *thereof* was broken down.
32 Then I saw, and *considered it* **set my heart** well:
I *looked upon it* **saw**,
and *received instruction* **took discipline**.
33 *Yet* a little sleep, a little *slumber* **drowsiness**,
a little *folding* **clasping** of the hands to *sleep* **lie down**:
34 So shall thy poverty come as one that travelleth;
and thy *want* **lack** as *an armed man* **a man with buckler**.

25

These are also proverbs of *Solomon* **Shelomoh**,
which the men of *Hezekiah* **Yechizqi Yah**,
king **sovereign** of *Judah* **Yah Hudah**
copied out **transcribed**.
2 It is the *glory* **honour** of *God* **Elohim**
to *conceal* **hide** a *thing* **word**:
but the honour of *kings* **sovereigns**
is to *search out* **probe** a *matter* **word**.
3 The *heaven* **heavens** for height,
and the earth for depth,
and the heart of *kings* **sovereigns**
is unsearchable **are not to be probed**.
4 *Take away* **Remove** the dross from the silver,
and there shall come forth
a vessel **an instrument** for *the finer* **refining**.
5 *Take away* **Remove** the wicked
from *before* **the face of** the *king* **sovereign**,
and his throne
shall be established in *righteousness* **justness**.
6 *Put* **Estéem** not *forth* thyself
in the presence **at the face** of the *king* **sovereign**,
and stand not in the place of great *men*:
7 For better it is that it be said unto thee,
Come up **Ascend** hither;
than that thou shouldest be *put lower* **abased**
in the presence **at the face** of the *prince* **volunteer**
whom thine eyes have seen.
8 Go not forth hastily to strive,
lest *thou know not what to do* **what thou workest**
in the *end thereof* **finality**,
when thy *neighbour* **friend**
hath *put thee to shame* **shamed thee?**
9 *Debate* **Defend** thy *cause* **defence**
with thy *neighbour himself* **friend**;
and *discover* **expose** not a *secret* **private counsel**
to another:
10 Lest he that heareth *it put thee to* shame **thee**,
and thine *infamy* **slander** turn not away.
11 A word *fitly spoken* **roundly worded**
is *like* apples of gold in *pictures* **imageries** of silver.
12 As *an earring* **a nosering** of gold,
and an ornament of *fine gold* **ore**,
so is a wise reprover upon an *obedient* **hearkening** ear.
13 As the cold of snow in the *time* **day** of harvest,
so is a *faithful messenger* **trustworthy ambassador**
to them that send him:
for he *refresheth* **restoreth** the soul
of his *masters* **adonim**.
14 *Whoso boasteth* **The man who halaleth** himself
of a false gift
is *like clouds* **vapour** and wind without *rain* **downpour**.
15 By long *forbearing* **wrath**
is a *prince persuaded* **commander enticed**,
and a *soft* **tender** tongue breaketh the bone.
16 Hast thou found honey?
eat so much as is sufficient for thee,
lest thou be *filled therewith* **satiated**, and vomit it.
17 *Withdraw* **Esteem** thy foot
from thy *neighbour's* **friend's** house;
lest he be *weary* **satiated** of thee, and *so* hate thee.
18 A man that *beareth* **answereth** false witness
against his *neighbour* **friend** is a *maul* **mallet**,
and a sword, and a *sharp* **pointened** arrow.
19 Confidence
in *an unfaithful man* **one who dealeth covertly**
in *time* **a day** of *trouble* **tribulation**
is *like* a broken tooth, and a **dislocated** foot *out of joint*.
20 As he that *taketh away a garment* **removeth clothes**
in **on a** cold *weather* **day**,
and as vinegar upon nitre,
so is he that singeth songs to an *heavy* **evil** heart.
21 If *thine enemy be hungry* **he that hateth thee famish**,
give him bread to eat;
and if he *be thirsty* **thirst**, give him water to drink:
22 For thou shalt *heap* **take** coals *of fire* upon his head,

and *the LORD* **Yah Veh** shall *reward* **shalam** thee.
23 The north wind
driveth away rain **whirleth the downpour**:
so doth an *angry countenance* **enraged face**
a *backbiting* **covert** tongue.
24 It is better to *dwell* **settle**
in the corner of the *housetop* **roof**,
than with a *brawling* **contentious** woman
and in a *wide* **community** house.
25 As cold waters to a *thirsty* **languid** soul,
so is good news from a far *country* **land**.
26 *A righteous man falling down* **The just tottering**
before **at the face of** the wicked
is as *a troubled* **an agitated** fountain,
and a *corrupt spring* **ruined fountain**.
27 It is not good to eat *much* **abundant** honey:
so for men to search **as one probing**
their own *glory* **honour**
is *not glory* **honour**.
28 *He that hath no rule* **The man without control**
over his own spirit
is *like* a city that is *broken down* **breached**,
and without walls.

26 As snow in summer, and as rain in harvest,
so honour is not *seemly* **befitting** for a fool.
2 As the bird by wandering, as the swallow by flying,
so *the curse causeless* **abasing**
shall not come **gratuitously**.
3 A whip for the horse,
a *bridle* **bit** for the *ass* **he burro**,
and a *rod* **scion** for the fool's back.
4 Answer not a fool according to his folly,
lest thou also be *like* **likened** unto him.
5 Answer a fool according to his folly,
lest he be wise in his own *conceit* **eyes**.
6 He that sendeth *a message* **word** by the hand of a fool
cutteth off the feet, and drinketh *damage* **violence**.
7 The legs of the lame *are not equal* **languish**:
so is a *parable* **proverb** in the mouth of fools.
8 As he that *bindeth* **bundleth** a stone
in a *sling* **stoneheap**,
so is he that giveth honour to a fool.
9 As a thorn *goeth up* **ascendeth**
into the hand of *a drunkard* **one intoxicated**,
so is a *parable* **proverb** in the mouths of fools.
10 *The great God that formed*
Great is the whirler of all *things;*
both rewardeth **he hireth** the fool,
and *rewardeth* **hireth** transgressors.
11 As a dog returneth to his vomit,
so a fool *returneth to* **repeateth** his folly.
12 Seest thou a man wise in his own *conceit* **eyes**?
there is more hope of a fool than of him.
13 The *slothful man* **sloth** saith,
There is a **A roaring** lion in the way;
a lion is in the *streets* **broadways**.
14 As the door turneth upon his hinges,
so *doth* the *slothful* **sloth** upon his bed.
15 The *slothful* **sloth** hideth his hand in his bosom;
it *grieveth* **wearieth** him
to *bring* **return** it *again* to his mouth.
16 The *sluggard* **sloth** is wiser in his own *conceit* **eyes**
than seven men that can *render a reason* **return taste**.
17 He that passeth by,
and meddleth with strife *belonging not to him* **not his**,
is *like* one that *taketh* **upholdeth** a dog by the ears.
18 As *a mad man* **the rabid**
who *casteth firebrands* **shooteth fiery darts**,
arrows, and death,
19 So is the man that deceiveth his *neighbour* **friend**,
and saith, Am not I *in sport* **laughing**?
20 Where *no wood* **the final timber** is,
there the fire goeth out:
so where there is no *talebearer* **whisperer**,
the strife *ceaseth* **subsideth**.
21 As coals *are to burning* **to** coals,
and *wood* **timber** to fire;
so is a contentious man to *kindle* **scorch** strife.
22 The words of a *talebearer* **whisperer**
are as wounds **inflame**,
and they *go down* **descend**
into the *innermost parts* **chambers** of the belly.
23 *Burning* **Inflamed** lips and *a wicked* **an evil** heart
are *like* a potsherd *covered* **overlaid** with silver dross.
24 He that hateth
dissembleth with **is recognized by** his lips,
and *layeth up* **placeth** deceit within him;
25 When *he speaketh fair* **his voice granteth charism**,
believe **trust** him not:
for there are seven *abominations* **abhorrences**
in his heart.
26 Whose hatred is covered by deceit,
his *wickedness* **evil** shall be *shewed* **exposed**
before the *whole* congregation.
27 Whoso diggeth a pit **of ruin** shall fall therein:
and he that rolleth a stone, it *will* **shall** return upon him.
28 A *lying* **false** tongue
hateth those that are *afflicted* **oppressed** by it;
and a *flattering* **smooth** mouth
worketh *ruin* **overthrow**.

27 *Boast* **Halal** not thyself
in the day of to morrow;
for thou knowest not what a day may *bring forth* **birth**.
2 Let another *man praise* **halal** thee,
and not thine own mouth;
a stranger, and not thine own lips.
3 A stone is heavy, and the sand weighty;
but a fool's *wrath* **vexation** is heavier than *them* both.
4 *Wrath* **Fury** is cruel,
and *anger is outrageous* **wrath overfloweth**;
but who is able to stand *before* **at the face of** envy?
5 *Open rebuke* **Exposed reproof**
is better than *secret* **hidden** love.
6 *Faithful* **Trustworthy** are the wounds of a *friend* **lover**;
but the kisses of *an enemy are deceitful* **haters abound**.
7 The *full* **satiated** soul
loatheth **trampleth** an honeycomb;
but to the *hungry* **famished** soul
every **all** bitter *thing* is sweet.
8 As a bird that wandereth from her nest,
so is a man that wandereth from his place.
9 *Ointment* **Oil** and *perfume* **incense**
rejoice **cheer** the heart:
so *doth* the sweetness of a man's friend
by *hearty* **soul** counsel.
10 Thine own friend, and thy father's friend, forsake not;
neither go into thy brother's house
in the day of thy calamity:
for better is a *neighbour* **fellow tabernacler** that is near
than a brother far off.
11 My son, *be wise* **enwisen**,
and *make* **cheer** my heart *glad*,
that I may *answer* **return a word**
to him that reproacheth me.
12 *A prudent man foreseeth* **The subtle seeth** the evil,
and hideth *himself;*
but the *simple* **gullible** pass on,
and are *punished* **penalized**.
13 Take his *garment* **clothes**
that *is surety* **pledgeth** for a stranger,
and *take a pledge of him* **pledge it**
for a *strange woman* **stranger**.
14 He that blesseth his friend with a *loud* **great** voice,
rising early in the morning,
it shall be *counted a curse* **fabricated an abasing** to him.
15 A continual *dropping* **dripping**
in a *very rainy* **torrential** day
and a contentious woman are alike.
16 Whosoever *hideth* **treasureth** her
hideth **treasureth** the wind,
and the ointment of his right *hand,*
which bewrayeth itself **calleth out.**
17 Iron sharpeneth iron;
so a man sharpeneth the *countenance* **face** of his friend.
18 Whoso *keepeth* **guardeth** the fig tree
shall eat the fruit *thereof*:
so he that *waiteth on* **guardeth** his *master* **adoni**
shall be honoured.

19 As in water face *answereth* to face,
so the heart of *man* **humanity** to *man* **humanity**.
20 *Hell* **As sheol** and *destruction* **abaddon**
are never *full* **satisfied;**
so the eyes of *man* **humanity** are never satisfied.
21 As the *fining pot* **crucible** for silver,
and the furnace for gold;
so is a man *to his praise* **by the halal of his mouth**.
22 Though thou shouldest *bray* **pestle** a fool
in a *mortar* **pestle**
among *wheat* **grits** with a pestle,
yet *will* **shall** not his *foolishness* **folly**
depart **turn aside** from him.
23 *Be thou diligent to know the state*
In knowing, know the face of thy flocks,
and look well **set thy heart** to thy *herds* **droves.**
24 For *riches are* **wealth be** not *for ever* **eternal**:
and doth the crown endure **nor the separatism**
to every generation? **generation to generation.**
25 The *hay appeareth* **grass exposeth**,
and the *tender grass sheweth itself* **sprout is seen**,
and herbs of the mountains are gathered.
26 The lambs are for thy *clothing* **robe**,
and the **he** goats are the price of the field.
27 And thou shalt have **doe** goats' milk enough
for thy *food* **bread**,
for the *food* **bread** of thy household,
and for the *maintenance for* **life of** thy *maidens* **lasses**.

28 The wicked flee when no *man* **one** pursueth:
but the *righteous* **just** are *bold* **confident** as a *lion* **whelp**.
2 For the *transgression* **rebellion** of a land
many are the *princes thereof* **governors**:
but *by* a *man of understanding* **human that discerneth**
and *knowledge* **knoweth such**
the state thereof shall be prolonged.
3 *A poor man* **An impoverished mighty**
that oppresseth the poor
is *like* a sweeping rain which leaveth no *food* **bread**.
4 They that forsake the *law* **torah**
praise **halal** the wicked:
but such as *keep* **guard** the *law* **torah**
contend with **throttle** them.
5 Evil men *understand* **discern** not judgment:
but they that seek *the LORD* **Yah Veh**
understand **discern** all *things*.
6 Better is the *poor* **impoverished**
that walketh in his *uprightness* **integrity**,
than he that *is perverse in* **perverteth** his ways,
though he be rich.
7 Whoso *keepeth* **guardeth** the *law* **torah**
is a *wise* **discerning** son:
but he that
is a companion of riotous men **befriendeth gluttons**
shameth his father.
8 He that by *usury* **interest** and *unjust gain* **bounty**
increaseth **aboundeth** his *substance* **wealth**,
he shall gather it for him
that *will pity* **shall grant charism unto** the poor.
9 He that turneth away his ear
from hearing the *law* **torah**,
even his prayer shall be *abomination* **abhorrence**.
10 Whoso causeth the *righteous* **straight**
to *go astray* **err inadvertently** in an evil way,
he shall fall *himself* into his own pit:
but the *upright* **integrious**
shall *have* **inherit the** good *things in possession*.
11 The rich man is wise in his own *conceit* **eyes**;
but the poor that *hath understanding* **discerneth**
searcheth him out.
12 When *righteous men do rejoice* **the just jump for joy,**
there is great *glory* **beauty**:
but when the wicked rise,
a man is hidden **humanity is searched**.
13 He that covereth his *sins* **rebellions**
shall not prosper:
but whoso *confesseth* **extendeth hands**
and forsaketh *them*
shall *have mercy* **be mercied.**
14 *Happy* **Blithe** is the *man* **human**
that *feareth alway* **continually dreadeth**:
but he that hardeneth his heart
shall fall into *mischief* **evil.**
15 As a *roaring* **growling** lion, and a ranging bear;
so is a wicked *ruler* **sovereign** over the poor people.
16 The *prince* **eminent**
that *wanteth understanding* **lacketh discernment**
is also a great oppressor:
but he that hateth *covetousness* **greed**
shall prolong his days.
17 A *man* **human** that *doeth violence* **violateth**
to the blood of *any person* **a soul**
shall flee to the *pit* **well;**
let no man *stay* **uphold** him.
18 Whoso walketh *uprightly* **integriously** shall be saved:
but he that *is perverse in* **perverteth** his ways
shall fall at once.
19 He that *tilleth* **serveth** his *land* **soil**
shall *have plenty of* **satiate with** bread:
but he that *followeth after vain persons* **pursueth vanity**
shall *have* **satiate with** poverty *enough*.
20 A *faithful* **trustworthy** man
shall abound with blessings:
but he that *maketh haste* **hasteth** to *be rich* **enrich**
shall not be *innocent* **exonerated.**
21 To *have respect of persons* **respect faces** is not good:
for for a *piece* **morsel** of bread
that *man will transgress* **mighty shall rebel.**
22 *He* **The man** that hasteth to *be rich* **have wealth**
hath an evil eye,
and *considereth* **perceiveth** not
that *poverty* **lack** shall come upon him.
23 He that *rebuketh a man* **reproveth humanity**
afterwards
shall find more favour
than he that *flattereth* **smootheth over** with the tongue.
24 Whoso *robbeth* **strippeth** his father or his mother,
and saith, It is no *transgression* **rebellion;**
the same is the companion of a *destroyer* **man ruiner**.
25 He that is of *a proud* **an enlarged** heart
stirreth up **throttleth** strife:
but he that *putteth his trust* **confideth**
in *the LORD* **Yah Veh**
shall be *made fat* **fattened**.
26 He that *trusteth* **confideth** in his own heart is a fool:
but whoso walketh *wisely* **in wisdom,**
he shall *be delivered* **escape**.
27 He that giveth unto the *poor* **impoverished**
shall not lack:
but he that *hideth* **concealeth** his eye
shall have many a curse.
28 When the wicked rise,
men **humans** hide themselves:
but when they *perish* **destruct**,
the *righteous increase* **just abound**.

29 *He, that being often reproved* **A man of reproofs**
hardeneth his **with hardened** neck,
shall *suddenly be destroyed* **break in a blink**,
and that without *remedy* **healing**.
2 When the *righteous are in authority* **just abound**,
the people *rejoice* **cheer**:
but when the wicked *beareth rule* **reign,**
the people *mourn* **sigh.**
3 *Whoso* **The man that** loveth wisdom
rejoiceth **cheereth** his father:
but he that
keepeth company with harlot **befriendeth whores**
spendeth **destroyeth** his *substance* **wealth**.
4 The *king* **sovereign** by judgment
establisheth **standeth** the land:
but *he* **the man** that receiveth *gifts* **exaltments**
overthroweth **demolisheth** it.
5 A *man* **mighty**
that *flattereth* **smootheth over** his *neighbour* **friend**
spreadeth a net for his *feet* **steps**.
6 In the *transgression* **rebellion** of an evil man
there is a snare:
but the *righteous* **just**
doth sing **shall shout** and *rejoice* **cheer**.

7 The *righteous* **just**
considereth **knoweth** the *cause* **plea** of the poor:
but the wicked *regardeth* **discerneth** not to know it.
8 Scornful men *bring* **puff on** a city *into a snare*:
but **the** wise *men* turn away wrath.
9 *If a* **A** wise man *contendeth* **judgeth** with a foolish man,
whether he *rage* **quiver** or *laugh* **ridicule**,
there is no rest.
10 The *bloodthirsty* **men of blood**
hate the *upright* **integrious**:
but the *just* **straight** seek his soul.
11 A fool uttereth all his *mind* **spirit**:
but *a* **the** wise *man keepeth it in till* **laudeth** afterwards.
12 If a *ruler* **sovereign** hearken to *lies* **false words**,
all his *servants* **ministers** are wicked.
13 The *poor* **impoverished** and the *deceitful* man **of frauds**
meet together:
the LORD **Yah Veh** lighteneth both their eyes.
14 The *king* **sovereign**
that *faithfully* judgeth the poor **in truth**,
his throne shall be established *for ever* **eternally**.
15 The *rod* **scion** and reproof give wisdom:
but a *child left to himself* **lad sent away**
bringeth **shameth** his mother *to shame.*
16 When the wicked *are multiplied* **abound**,
transgression increaseth **rebellion aboundeth**:
but the *righteous* **just** shall see their *fall* **ruin**.
17 *Correct* **Discipline** thy son, and he shall give thee rest;
yea, he shall give *delight* **delicately** unto thy soul.
18 Where there is no vision,
the people *perish* **be exposed**:
but he that *keepeth* **guardeth** the *law* **torah**,
happy **blithe** is he.
19 A servant
will **shall** not be *corrected* **disciplined** by words:
for though he *understand* **discern**
he *will* **shall** not answer.
20 Seest thou a man that is hasty in his words?
there is more hope of a fool than of him.
21 He that *delicately bringeth up* **pampereth** his servant
from a child **since ladhood**
shall have him become *his son* **successor**
at the *length* **finality**.
22 *An angry* **A** man **of wrath**
stirreth up **throttleth** strife,
and a *furious man* **master of fury**
aboundeth in *transgression* **rebellion**.
23 *A man's pride* **The pomp of humanity**
shall *bring* **abase** him *low*:
but honour shall uphold the *humble* **abased** in spirit.
24 Whoso *is partner* **allotteth** with a thief
hateth his own soul:
he heareth *cursing* **oaths**, and *bewrayeth* **telleth** it not.
25 The *fear* **trembling** of *man* **humanity**
bringeth **giveth** a snare:
but whoso
putteth his trust **confideth** in *the LORD* **Yah Veh**
shall be *safe* **lofted**.
26 Many seek the *ruler's favour* **sovereign's face**;
but *every* man's judgment
cometh **be** from *the LORD* **Yah Veh**.
27 *An unjust man* **A man of wickedness**
is an *abomination* **abhorrence** to the just:
and *he that is upright* **the straight** in the way
is *abomination* **abhorrence** to the wicked.

THE ORACLE OF AGUR

30 The words of Agur the son of *Jakeh* **Yaqeh**,
even the prophecy **burden**:
the *man spake* **oracle of a mighty** unto *Ithiel* **Ithi El**,
even unto *Ithiel* **Ithi El** and *Ucal* **Ukal**,
2 Surely I am more *brutish* **stupid** than *any* man,
and have not the *understanding* **discernment**
of *a man* **humanity**.
3 I neither learned wisdom,
nor *have* **know** the knowledge of the holy.

PROPHECY OF THE SON OF HUMANITY

4 Who hath ascended up into *heaven* **the heavens**,
or descended?
who hath gathered the wind in his fists?
who hath *bound* **narrowed** the waters in a *garment* **cloth**?
who hath *established* **raised**
all the *ends* **finalities** of the earth?
what is his name, and what is his son's name,
if thou *canst tell* **knowest**?
5 Every *word* **saying** of *God* **Elohah** is *pure* **refined**:
he is a *shield* **buckler**
unto them that *put their trust* **seek refuge** in him.
6 Add thou not unto his words,
lest he reprove thee, and thou be found a liar.
7 *Two things have I required* **These two ask I** of thee;
deny me **withhold** them not before I die:
8 Remove far from me vanity and **word of** lies:
give me neither poverty nor riches;
feed me with food convenient **tear my statute bread** for me:
9 Lest I *be full* **satiate**, and deny thee, and say,
Who is *the LORD* **Yah Veh**?
or lest I be *poor* **dispossessed**, and steal,
and take the name of my *God in vain* **Elohim**.
10 *Accuse* **Tongue—lash** not a servant
unto his *master* **adoni**,
lest he *curse* **abase** thee,
and thou *be found guilty* **hast guilted**.
11 There is a generation that *curseth* **abaseth** their father,
and *doth not bless* **blesseth not** their mother.
12 There is a generation that are pure in their own eyes,
and yet is **but** not washed from their *filthiness* **dung**.
13 There is a generation, O how lofty *are* their eyes!
and their eyelids *are* lifted *up*.
14 There is a generation, whose teeth are *as* swords,
and their *jaw teeth* **molars** *as* knives,
to devour the *poor* **humble** from off the earth,
and the needy from *among men* **humanity**.
15 The horseleach hath two daughters, *crying*, Give, give.
There are **These** three *things that* are never satisfied,
yea, four *things* say not, *It is* enough:
16 *The grave* **sheol**; and the *barren* **restrained** womb;
the earth that is not *filled* **satiated** with water;
and the fire that saith not, *It is* enough.
17 The eye that *mocketh at his* **derideth** father,
and *despiseth* **disrespecteth** to obey *his* mother,
the ravens of the *valley* **wadi** shall *pick* **bore** it *out*,
and the *young* **sons of** eagles shall eat it.
18 *There be* **These** three *things*
which are too *wonderful* **marvellous** for me,
yea, four which I know not:
19 The way of an eagle in the *air* **heavens**;
the way of a serpent upon a rock;
the way of a ship in the *midst* **heart** of the sea;
and the way of a *man* **mighty** with a *maid* **virgin**.
20 Such is the way of an adulterous woman;
she eateth, and wipeth her mouth,
and saith, I have done no *wickedness* **mischief**.
21 *For* **These** three *things* **quake** the earth *is disquieted*
and for four *which* it cannot bear:
22 For a servant when he reigneth;
and a fool when he is *filled* **satiated** with *meat* **bread**;
23 For *an odious woman* **she who hateth**
when she is married;
and *an handmaid* **a maid**
that *is heir to* **possesseth** her *mistress* **lady**.
24 *There be* **These** four *things*
which are little upon the earth,
but **in enwisening,**
they *are exceeding wise* **enwisen**:
25 The ants are a people not strong,
yet they prepare their *meat* **bread** in the summer;
26 The conies are *but a feeble folk* **not a mighty people**,
yet *make* **set** they their houses in the rocks;
27 The locusts have no *king* **sovereign**,
yet go they forth all of them by *bands* **ranks**;
28 The *spider taketh hold* **lizard grabbeth** with her hands,
and is in *kings' palaces* **sovereign's manses**.
29 *There be* **These** three *things which go well* **pace good**,
yea, four *are comely* **well—please** in going:
30 A lion *which is strongest* **mighty** among *beasts* **animals**,
and turneth not *away for any* **from the face**;
31 *A greyhound* **One girt in the loins**; an he goat also;
and a *king* **sovereign**, against whom there is no rising *up*.
32 If thou hast *done foolishly* **follied** in lifting *up* thyself,

or if thou hast *thought evil* **intrigued**,
lay thine hand upon thy mouth.
33 Surely the churning of milk
bringeth forth butter,
and the *wringing* **churning** of the *nose* **nostrils**
bringeth forth blood:
so the *forcing* **churning** of wrath
bringeth forth strife.

THE WORDS OF SOVEREIGN LEMU EL

31 The words of *king Lemuel* **sovereign Lemu El**,
the *prophecy* **burden**
that his mother *taught* **disciplined** him.
2 What, my *son* **bar**?
and what, the *son* **bar** of my *womb* **belly**?
and what, the *son* **bar** of my vows?
3 Give not thy *strength* **valour** unto women,
nor thy ways
to that which *destroyeth kings* **wipeth out sovereigns**.
4 It is not for *kings* **sovereigns**, O *Lemuel* **Lemu El**,
it is not for *kings* **sovereigns** to drink wine;
nor for *princes strong drink* **potentates intoxicants**:
5 Lest they drink, and forget the *law* **statute**,
and *pervert* **alter** the *judgment* **plea**
of any of the *afflicted* **sons of humiliation**.
6 Give *strong drink* **intoxicants**
unto him that is *ready* to *perish* **destruct**,
and wine
unto those that be *of heavy hearts* **bitter of soul**.
7 Let him drink, and forget his poverty,
and remember his *misery* **toil** no more.
8 Open thy mouth for the *dumb* **mute**
in the *cause* **plea** of all
such as are appointed to destruction — **sons of survivors**.
9 Open thy mouth, judge *righteously* **justness**,
and plead the cause of the *poor* **humble** and needy.
10 Who can find a virtuous woman?
for her price is far above *rubies* **pearls**.
11 The heart of her *husband* **master**
doth safely trust **confideth** in her,
so that he shall have no *need* **lack** of spoil.
12 She *will do* **shall deal** him good and not evil
all the days of her life.
13 She seeketh wool, and flax,
and worketh *willingly* **with delight** with her *hands* **palms**.
14 She is like the merchants' ships;
she bringeth her *food* **bread** from afar.
15 She riseth also while it is yet night,
and giveth *meat* **the prey** to her household,
and a *portion* **statute** to her *maidens* **lasses**.
16 She *considereth* **intrigueth** a field,
and *buyeth* **taketh** it:
with the fruit of her *hands* **palms**
she planteth a vineyard.
17 She girdeth her loins with strength,
and strengtheneth her arms.
18 She *perceiveth* **tasteth** that her merchandise is good:
her *candle* **lamp** goeth not out by night.
19 She *layeth* **extendeth** her hands to the spindle,
and her *hands hold* **palms uphold** the *distaff* **spindle**.
20 She *stretcheth out* **spreadeth** her *hand* **palm**
to the *poor* **humble**;
yea, she *reacheth forth* **extendeth** her hands
to the needy.
21 She *is* **aweth** not *afraid of* the snow
for her household:
for all her household are *clothed* **enrobed** with scarlet.
22 She *maketh* **worketh** herself
coverings of tapestry **spreads**;
her *clothing* **robe** is *silk* **fine linen** and purple.
23 Her *husband* **master** is known in the *gates* **portals**,
when he *sitteth* **settleth** among the elders of the land.
24 She *maketh fine linen* **worketh wraps**, and selleth *it*;
and *delivereth* **giveth** girdles unto the *merchant* **Kenaaniy**.
25 Strength and *honour* **majesty** are her *clothing* **robe**;
and she shall *rejoice in time to come* **laugh the day after**.
26 She openeth her mouth with wisdom;
and in her tongue is the *law* **torah** of *kindness* **mercy**.
27 She *looketh well to* **watcheth**
the ways of her household,
and eateth not the bread of *idleness* **sloth**.
28 Her *children* **sons** arise *up*,
and call her *blessed* **blithesome**;
her *husband* **master** *also*, and he *praiseth* **halaleth** her.
29 Many daughters have *done* **worked** virtuously,
but thou *excellest* **ascendest** them all.
30 *Favour is deceitful* **Charism is false**, and beauty is vain:
but a woman that *feareth the LORD* **aweth Yah Veh**,
she shall be *praised* **halaled**.
31 Give her of the fruit of her hands;
and let her own works
praise **halal** her in the *gates* **portals**.

THE CONGREGATIONER 1, 2

KEY TO INTERPRETING THE EXEGESES:
King James text is in regular type;
Text under exegeses is in oblique type;
Text of exegeses is in bold type.

THE WORDS OF THE CONGREGATIONER

1 The words of the *Preacher* **Congregationer**,
the son of David,
king **sovereign** in *Jerusalem* **Yeru Shalem**.
2 Vanity of vanities, saith the *Preacher* **Congregationer**,
vanity of vanities; all is vanity.
3 What *profit* **advantage** hath *a man* **humanity**
of all his *labour* **toil**
which he *taketh* **toileth** under the sun?
4 *One* generation passeth *away*,
and *another* generation cometh:
but the earth *abideth for ever* **standeth eternal**.
5 The sun also ariseth, and the sun goeth *down*,
and *hasteth* **swalloweth** to his place where he arose.
6 The wind goeth toward the south,
and turneth about unto the north;
it *whirleth* **goeth** about continually,
and the wind returneth again according to his circuits.
7 All the *rivers run* **wadies go** into the sea;
yet the sea is not full;
unto the place from whence the *rivers* **wadies** come,
thither they return *again* **to go**.
8 All *things are full of labour* **words belabour**;
man cannot *utter* **word** it:
the eye is not satisfied with seeing,
nor the ear filled with hearing.
9 *The thing hath been* **What hath became**,
it is that which shall *be* **become**;
and that which is done **What was worked**
is that which shall be *done* **worked**:
and there is *no* **naught** new *thing* under the sun.
10 Is there any *thing* **word** whereof it may be said,
See, this is new?
it hath been already *of old time* **eternally**,
which was *before us* **at our face**.
11 There is no *remembrance* **memorial**
of *former things* **firsts**;
neither shall there be any *remembrance* **memorial**
of *things that are to come* **lasts**
with those that shall *come after* **become**.
12 I the *Preacher* **Congregationer**
was *king* **sovereign** over *Israel* **Yisra El**
in *Jerusalem* **Yeru Shalem**.
13 And I gave my heart to seek
and *search out* **explore** by wisdom
concerning all *things that are done* **those worked**
under *heaven* **the heavens**:
this *sore travail* **evil drudgery** hath *God* **Elohim** given
to the sons of *man* **humanity**
to be *exercised* **humbled** therewith.
14 I have seen all the works
that are *done* **worked** under the sun;
and, behold, all is vanity and *vexation* **gnawing** of spirit.
15 That which is *crooked* **twisted**
cannot be *made straight* **straightened**:
and that which is *wanting* **lacking**
cannot be numbered.
16 I *communed* **worded** with mine own heart, saying,
Lo **Behold**, I *am come to great estate* **have greatened**,
and have *gotten* **increased** more wisdom
than all they *that have been before me* **at my face**
in *Jerusalem* **Yeru Shalem**:
yea, my heart *had* **hath seen**
great *experience of* wisdom and knowledge.
17 And I gave my heart to know wisdom,
and to know madness and folly:
I perceived that this also is *vexation* **gnawing** of spirit.
18 For in *much* **abundant** wisdom
is *much grief* **abundant vexation**:
and he that increaseth knowledge increaseth sorrow.

2 I said in mine heart, Go to, *now* **I beseech**,
I *will prove* **shall test** thee with *mirth* **cheerfulness**,
therefore enjoy pleasure **see good**:
and, behold, this also is vanity.
2 I said of laughter, *It is mad* **Halal**:
and of *mirth* **cheerfulness**, What *doeth* **worketh** it?
3 I *sought* **explored** in mine heart
to *give myself* **draw my flesh** unto wine,
yet *acquainting* **driving** mine heart with wisdom;
and to lay hold on folly,
till I might see what was that good
for the sons of *men* **humanity**,
which they should *do* **work** under the *heaven* **heavens**
all **the number of** the days of their life.
4 I *made me great* **greatened my** works;
I builded me houses; I planted me vineyards:
5 I *made* **worked** me gardens and orchards,
and I planted trees in them of all *kind of* fruits:
6 I *made* **worked** me pools of water,
to *water* **wet** therewith the *wood* **forest**
that *bringeth forth* **sprouteth** trees:
7 I *got me* **chattelized** servants and *maidens* **maids**,
and had *servants born in* **sons of** my house;
also I had *great possessions* **abundant chattel**
of *great and small cattle* **oxen and flocks**
above all that were in *Jerusalem* **Yeru Shalem**
before me **at my face**:
8 I gathered me also silver and gold,
and the peculiar treasure of *kings* **sovereigns**
and of the *provinces* **jurisdictions**:
I *gat* **worked** me
men singers **songsters** and *women singers* **songtresses**,
and the delights of the sons of *men* **humanity**,
as musical instruments, and that of all sorts
and mistresses of mistresses.
9 So I *was great* **greatened**,
and increased more than all
that were *before me* **at my face** in *Jerusalem* **Yeru Shalem**:
also my wisdom *remained* **stayed** with me.
10 And whatsoever mine eyes *desired* **asked**
I *kept* **set** not **aside** from them,
I withheld not my heart from any *joy* **cheerfulness**;
for my heart *rejoiced* **cheered** in all my *labour* **toil**:
and this was my *portion* **allotment** of all my *labour* **toil**.
11 Then I *looked on* **faced** all the works
that my hands had *wrought* **worked**,
and on the *labour* **toil**
that I had *laboured* **toiled** to *do* **work**: and, behold,
all was vanity and *vexation* **gnawing** of spirit,
and there was no *profit* **advantage** under the sun.
12 And I turned *myself* **my face** to *behold* **see** wisdom,
and madness, and folly:
for what can *the man* **humanity** do
that cometh after the *king* **sovereign**?
even that which hath been already *done* **worked**.
13 Then I saw that wisdom *excelleth* **advantageth over** folly,
as far as light *excelleth* **advantageth over** darkness.
14 The *wise man's* eyes **of the wise** are in his head;
but the fool walketh in darkness:
and I myself perceived also
that one *event* **happening** happeneth to them all.
15 Then said I in my heart,
As it happeneth to the fool, so it happeneth even to me;
and why was I then more *wise* **enwisened**?
Then I *said* **worded** in my heart, that this also is vanity.
16 For there is no *remembrance* **memorial** of the wise
more than of the fool *for ever* **eternally**;
seeing that which now is in **that already**
the days to come shall all be forgotten.
And how dieth the wise *man*? as the fool.
17 Therefore I hated life;
because the work that is *wrought* **worked** under the sun
is *grievous* **evil** unto me:
for all is vanity and *vexation* **gnawing** of spirit.
18 Yea, I hated all my *labour* **toil**
which I had *taken* **toiled** under the sun:
because I should leave it unto *the man* **humanity**
that shall be after me.
19 And who knoweth
whether he shall be *a* wise *man* or *a* fool?
yet shall he *have rule* **dominate** over all my *labour* **toil**
wherein I have *laboured* **toiled**,
and wherein I have s*hewed* **enwisened** myself *wise*

under the sun.
This is also vanity.
20 *Therefore I went about to cause*
I turned my heart **around**
to *despair of* **quit** all the *labour* **toil**
which I *took* **toiled** under the sun.
21 For there is a *man* **human**
whose *labour* **toil** is in wisdom,
and in knowledge, and in *equity* **prosperity**;
yet to a *man* **human** that hath not *laboured* **toiled** therein
shall he *leave* **give** it for his *portion* **allotment**.
This also is vanity and a great evil.
22 For what hath *man* **humanity** of all his *labour* **toil**,
and of the *vexation* **gnawing** of his heart,
wherein he hath *laboured* **toiled** under the sun?
23 For all his days are sorrows,
and his *travail grief* **drudgery vexation**;
yea, his heart *taketh* **lieth** not *rest* **down** in the night.
This is also vanity.
24 There is *nothing* **naught** better for a *man* **human**,
than that he should eat and drink,
and that he should *make* **delight** his soul
enjoy **to see** good in his *labour* **toil**.
This also I saw,
that it was from the hand of *God* **Elohim**.
25 For who can eat,
or who else can hasten *hereunto* **out**, more than I?
26 *For God giveth to a man* **Giving humanity**
that is good *in his sight* **at his face**
wisdom, and knowledge, and *joy* **cheerfulness**:
but to the sinner he giveth *travail* **drudgery**,
to gather and to heap *up*,
that he may give to him
that is good *before God* **at the face of Elohim**.
This also is vanity and *vexation* **gnawing** of spirit.

TIME

3 To *every thing* **all** there is a season,
and a time to every *purpose* **desire**
under the *heaven* **heavens**:
2 A time to *be born* **birth**,
and a time to die;
a time to plant,
and a time to *pluck up that which is* **uproot the** planted;
3 A time to *kill* **slaughter**,
and a time to heal;
a time to *break down* **breach**,
and a time to build *up;*
4 A time to weep,
and a time to laugh;
a time to *mourn* **chop**,
and a time to dance;
5 A time to cast away stones,
and a time to gather stones *together*;
a time to embrace,
and a time to *refrain* **be far** from embracing;
6 A time to *get* **seek**,
and a time to *lose* **destroy**;
a time to *keep* **guard**,
and a time to cast *away;*
7 A time to *rend* **rip**,
and a time to sew;
a time to *keep silence* **hush**,
and a time to *speak* **word**;
8 A time to love,
and a time to hate;
a time of war,
and a time of *peace* **shalom**.
9 What *profit* **advantage** hath he that worketh
in that wherein he *laboureth* **toileth**?
10 I have seen the *travail* **drudgery**,
which *God* **Elohim**
hath given to the sons of *men* **humanity**
to be *exercised in it* **humbled therein**.
11 He hath *made every thing* **worked all**
beautiful in his time:
also he hath *set the world* **given eternally** in their heart,
so that no *man* **human** can find out the work
that *God maketh* **Elohim worketh**
from the *beginning* **top** to the end.
12 I know that there is no good in them,
but *for a man to rejoice* **to cheer**,
and to *do* **work** good in his life.
13 And also
that *every man* **all humanity** should eat and drink,
and *enjoy* **see** the good of all his *labour* **toil**,
it is the gift of *God* **Elohim**.
14 I know that, whatsoever *God doeth* **Elohim worketh**,
it shall be *for ever* **eternal**:
nothing **naught** can be *put to it* **augmented**,
nor *any thing taken from it* **aught diminished**:
and *God doeth it,* **Elohim worketh**
that *men* **one** should *fear before him* **awe at his face**.
15 That which hath been *is now* **already is**;
and that which is to be *hath already been* **already was**;
and *God requireth* **Elohim seeketh**
that which is *past* **pursued**.
16 And moreover I saw under the sun
the place of judgment,
that wickedness was there;
and the place of *righteousness* **justness**,
that *iniquity* **wickedness** was there.
17 I said in mine heart,
God **Elohim** shall judge the *righteous* **just** and the wicked:
for there is a time there
for every *purpose* **desire** and for every work.
18 I said in mine heart
concerning the *estate* **word** of the sons of *men* **humanity**,
that *God* **Elohim** might *manifest* **purify** them,
and that they might see
that they themselves are *beasts* **animals**.
19 For that which
befalleth **happeneth to** the sons of *men* **humanity**
befalleth beasts **happeneth to animals**;
even *one thing befalleth* **this happeneth to** them:
as *the one* **this** dieth, so dieth *the other* **that**;
yea, they have all one *breath* **spirit**;
so that *a man* **humanity** hath no *preeminence* **advantage**
above *a beast* **an animal**:
for all is vanity.
20 All go unto one place;
all are of the dust, and all *turn* **return** to dust *again*.
21 Who knoweth the spirit of *man* **the son of humanity**
that *goeth* **ascendeth** upward,
and the spirit of the *beast* **animal**
that *goeth* **descendeth** downward to the earth?
22 Wherefore I *perceive* **see**
that there is *nothing* **naught** better,
than that a *man* **human**
should *rejoice* **cheer** in his own works;
for that is his *portion* **allotment**:
for who shall bring him to see what shall be after him?
4 So I returned,
and *considered* **saw** all the oppressions
that are *done* **worked** under the sun:
and behold the tears of *such as were* **the** oppressed,
and they had no *comforter* **one to sigh**;
and *on the side* **in the hand** of their oppressors
there was *power* **force**;
but they had no *comforter* **one to sigh**.
2 *Wherefore I praised* **I lauded** the dead
which are already dead
more than the living which *are* yet *alive* **live**.
3 Yea, better is he than both they,
which hath not yet been,
who hath not seen the evil work
that is *done* **worked** under the sun.
4 Again, I *considered* **saw** all *travail* **the toil**,
and *every right* **all the prosperity of** work,
that for this a man is envied of his *neighbour* **friend**.
This is also vanity and *vexation* **gnawing** of spirit.
5 The fool *foldeth* **embraceth** his hands *together*,
and eateth his own flesh.
6 Better is *an handful* **a palm full** with *quietness* **rest**,
than *both the hands* **fists** full with *travail* **toil**
and *vexation* **gnawing** of spirit.
7 Then I returned, and I saw vanity under the sun.

THE CONGREGATIONER 4—6

8 There is one *alone,* and there is *not a* **no** second;
yea, he hath neither *child* **son** nor brother:
yet is there no end of all his *labour* **toil**;
neither is his eye satisfied with riches;
neither *saith he,* For whom *do I labour* **toil I**,
and *bereave* **lack** my soul of good?
This is also vanity,
yea, it is *a sore travail* **an evil drudgery**.
9 Two are better than one;
because they have a good *reward* **hire** for their *labour* **toil**.
10 For if they fall,
the one *will lift up* **shall raise** his *fellow* **companion**:
but woe to him that is *alone* **one** when he falleth;
for he hath *not another* **no second** to *help* **raise** him *up.*
11 *Again* **Yea**, if two lie together, then they *have* heat:
but how can one be warm *alone*?
12 And if one prevail against him,
two shall withstand him;
and a *threefold cord* **triple thread** is not quickly *broken* **torn**.
13 Better is a poor and a wise child
than an *old* **aged** and foolish *king* **sovereign**,
who *will* **shall perceive** no more
be admonished **to be enlightened**.
14 For out of *prison* **the house of binding**
he cometh to reign;
whereas also
he that is born in his *kingdom* **sovereigndom**
becometh *poor* **impoverished**.
15 I *considered* **saw** all the living which walk under the sun,
with the second child that shall stand *up* in his stead.
16 There is no end of all the people,
even of all that have been *before them* **at their face**:
they also *that come after* **the final**
shall not *rejoice* **cheer** in him.
Surely this also is vanity and *vexation* **gnawing** of spirit.

5 *Keep* **Guard** thy foot
when thou goest to the house of *God* **Elohim**,
and be *more ready* **nearer** to hear,
than to give the sacrifice of fools:
for they *consider* **know** not that they *do* **work** evil.
2 *Be* **Terrify** not *rash* with thy mouth,
and let not thine heart *be hasty* **hasten**
to utter *any thing before God* **a word at the face of Elohim**:
for *God* **Elohim** is in *heaven* **the heavens**,
and thou upon earth:
therefore let thy words be few.
3 For a dream cometh
through **by** the *multitude* **abundance** of *business* **drudgery**;
and a fool's voice
is known by multitude **by the abundance** of words.
4 When thou vowest a vow unto *God* **Elohim**,
defer not to *pay* **shalam** it;
for he hath no *pleasure* **delight** in fools:
pay **shalam** that which thou hast vowed.
5 Better is it that thou shouldest not vow,
than that thou shouldest vow and not *pay* **shalam**.
6 *Suffer* **Give** not thy mouth to cause thy flesh to sin;
neither say thou *before* **at the face of** the angel,
that it was an **inadvertent** error:
wherefore should God be angry
why enrage Elohim at thy voice,
and *destroy* **despoil** the work of thine hands?
7 For in the *multitude* **abundance** of dreams
and many words there are also divers vanities
words and vanities abound:
but *fear* **awe** thou *God* **Elohim**.
8 If thou seest the oppression of the *poor* **impoverished**,
and *violent perverting* **stripping** of judgment
and *justice* **justness** in a *province* **jurisdiction**,
marvel not at the *matter* **desire**:
for he that is
higher than the highest **high above the high** regardeth;
and there be *higher than they* **the high above them**.
9 Moreover the *profit* **advantage** of the earth is for all:
the *king* **sovereign** *himself* is served by the field.
10 He that loveth silver shall not be satisfied with silver;
nor he that loveth abundance with *increase* **produce**:
this is also vanity.
11 When *goods increase* **good aboundeth**,
they *are increased* **abound by the myriads** that eat them:
and what *good* **prosperity** is there
to the *owners* **masters** *thereof,*
saving the beholding of them **except seeing** with their eyes?
12 The sleep of a *labouring man* **server** is sweet,
whether he eat little or *much* **abound**:
but the *abundance* **sufficiency** of the rich
will **shall** not *suffer* **allow** him to sleep.
13 There is *a sore* **an** evil **stroke**
which I have seen under the sun,
namely,
riches *kept* **guarded** for the *owners* **masters** *thereof*
to **for** their *hurt* **evil**.
14 But those riches *perish* **destruct** by evil *travail* **drudgery**:
and he begetteth a son,
and there is *nothing* **naught** in his hand.
15 As he came forth of his mother's *womb* **belly**,
naked shall he return to go as he came,
and shall *take nothing* **lift naught** of his *labour* **toil**,
which he may carry *away* in his hand.
16 And this also is *a sore* **an** evil **stroke**,
that *in all points* as he came, *so* **thus** shall he go:
and what *profit* **advantage** hath he
that hath *laboured* **toiled** for the *wind* **spirit/wind**?
17 All his days also he eateth in darkness,
and he *hath much sorrow* **aboundeth vexation**
and *wrath* **rage** with his sickness.
18 Behold that which I have seen:
it is good and *comely* **beautiful** *for one* to eat and to drink,
and to *enjoy* **see** the good of all his *labour* **toil**
that he *taketh* **toileth** under the sun
all **the number of** the days of his life,
which *God* **Elohim** giveth him:
for it is his *portion* **allotment**.
19 *Every man* **All humanity** also
to whom *God* **Elohim**
hath given riches and *wealth* **holdings**,
and *hath given him power* **dominance** to eat *thereof,*
and to *take* **bear** his *portion* **allotment**,
and to *rejoice* **cheer** in his *labour* **toil**;
this is the gift of *God* **Elohim**.
20 For he shall not *much* **abound**
to remember the days of his life;
because *God answereth* **Elohim humbleth** him
in the *joy* **cheerfulness** of his heart.

6 There is an evil which I have seen under the sun,
and it is *common* **abundant** among *men* **humanity**:
2 A man to whom *God* **Elohim** hath given riches,
wealth **holdings**, and honour,
so that he wanteth *nothing* **naught** for his soul
of all that he desireth,
yet *God* **Elohim** giveth him not
power **dominance** to eat *thereof,*
but a *stranger* **man** eateth it:
this is vanity, and it is an evil *disease* **sickness**.
3 If a man beget an hundred *children,*
and live many years,
so that the days of his years be many,
and his soul be not *filled* **satisfied** with good,
and also that he have no *burial* **tomb**;
I say,
that an untimely birth **a miscarriage** is better than he.
4 For he cometh in with vanity,
and *departeth* **goeth** in darkness,
and his name shall be covered with darkness.
5 Moreover he hath not seen the sun,
nor known *any thing* **aught**:
this hath more rest than the other.
6 *Yea,* **Even** though he live a thousand years
twice told **two times**,
yet hath he seen no good: do not all go to one place?
7 All the *labour* **toil** of *man* **humanity** is for his mouth,
and yet the *appetite* **soul** is not filled.
8 For what hath the wise more than the fool?
what hath the *poor* **humble**,
that knoweth to walk before the living?
9 Better is the *sight* **visage** of the eyes

than the *wandering* **walking** of the *desire* **soul**:
this is also vanity and *vexation* **gnawing** of spirit.
10 That which hath *been* **become**
is named **its name is** already **called**,
and it is known that it is *man* **humanity**:
neither may he *contend* **be able to plead his cause**
with him that is mightier than he.
11 Seeing there be *many things* **abounding words**
that *increase* **abound** vanity,
what is *man* **humanity** the *better* **more**?
12 For who knoweth
what is good for *man* **humanity** in *this* life,
all **the number of** the days of his *vain* life **of vanity**
which he *spendeth* **worketh** as a shadow?
for who can tell *a man* **humanity**
what shall be after him under the sun?

7 A *good* name is better than *precious* ointment;
and the day of death than the day of *one's* birth.
2 It is better to go to the house of mourning,
than to go to the house of *feasting* **banqueting**:
for that is the end of all *men* **humanity**;
and the living *will lay* **shall give** it to his heart.
3 *Sorrow* **Vexation** is better than laughter:
for by the *sadness* **evil** of the *countenance* **face**
the heart is *made better* **well—pleased**.
4 The heart of the wise
is in the house of mourning;
but the heart of fools
is in the house of *mirth* **cheerfulness**.
5 It is better to hear the rebuke of the wise,
than for a man to hear the song of fools.
6 For as the *crackling* **voice** of thorns under a *pot* **caldron**,
so is the laughter of the fool:
this also is vanity.
7 Surely oppression
maketh a wise man mad **causeth the wise to halal**;
and a gift destroyeth the heart.
8 Better is the *end of a thing* **final word**
than the beginning *thereof*:
and the *patient in* **long** spirit
is better than the *proud in* **lofty** spirit.
9 Be not hasty in thy spirit to be *angry* **vexed**:
for *anger* **vexation** resteth in the bosom of fools.
10 Say not thou, What *is the cause* **hath become**
that the *former* **first** days were better than these?
for thou dost not
enquire wisely **ask out of wisdom** concerning this.
11 Wisdom is good with an inheritance:
and *by it there is profit* **more** to them that see the sun.
12 For wisdom is a *defence* **shadow**,
and money **silver** is a *defence* **shadow**:
but the *excellency* **advantage** of knowledge is,
that wisdom
giveth life to them that have it **enliveneth its masters**.
13 *Consider* **See** the work of *God* **Elohim**:
for who can *make that straight* **straighten**,
which he hath *made crooked* **twisted**?
14 In the day of *prosperity* **good** be joyful,
but in the day of *adversity consider* **evil see**:
God **Elohim** also
hath *set* **worked** the one over against the other,
to the *end* **word**
that *man* **humanity** should find *nothing* **naught** after him.
15 All *things* have I seen in the days of my vanity:
there is a **the** just *man*
that *perisheth* **destructeth** in his *righteousness* **justness**,
and there is *a* **the** wicked *man*
that prolongeth *his life* in his *wickedness* **evil**.
16 Be not *righteous over much* **aboundingly just**;
neither *make thyself over wise* **more enwisened**:
why shouldest thou *destroy* **desolate** thyself?
17 Be not *over much* **aboundingly** wicked,
neither be thou foolish:
why shouldest thou die before thy time?
18 It is good that thou shouldest take hold of this;
yea, also from this *withdraw* **leave** not thine hand:
for he that *feareth God* **aweth Elohim**
shall come forth of them all.
19 Wisdom strengtheneth the wise
more than ten *mighty men* **potentates**
which are in the city.
20 For there is not a just *man* **human** upon earth,
that *doeth* **worketh** good, and sinneth not.
21 Also *take no heed* **give not thine heart**
unto all words that are *spoken* **worded**;
lest thou hear thy servant *curse* **abase** thee:
22 For oftentimes also thine own heart knoweth
that thou thyself likewise hast *cursed* **abased** others.
23 All this have I *proved* **tested** by wisdom:
I said, I *will be wise* **shall enwisen**;
but it was far from me.
24 That which is far off, and *exceeding* **deep** deep,
who can find it out?
25 I *applied* **turned** mine heart **around** to know,
and to *search* **explore**, and to seek out wisdom,
and the *reason of things* **machinations**,
and to know the wickedness of folly,
even of *foolishness* **folly** and madness:
26 And I find more bitter than death the woman,
whose heart is *snares* **lairs** and *nets* **devoted**,
and her hands as bands:
whoso *pleaseth God* **be good at the face of Elohim**
shall escape from her;
but the sinner shall be *taken* **captured** by her.
27 *Behold* **See**, this have I found,
saith the *preacher* **Congregationer**, *counting* one by one,
to find out the *account* **machinations**:
28 Which yet my soul seeketh, but I find not:
one *man* **human** among a thousand have I found;
but a woman among all those have I not found.
29 *Lo* **See**, this only have I found,
that *God* **Elohim**
hath *made man upright* **worked humanity straight**;
but they have sought out many *inventions* **machinations**.

8 Who is as the wise *man*?
and who knoweth the interpretation of a *thing* **word**?
a man's **human** wisdom
maketh **lighteneth** his face *to shine*,
and the *boldness* **strength** of his face shall be changed.
2 *I counsel thee to keep the king's commandment*
Guard the sovereign's mouth,
and that *in regard* **word** of the oath of *God* **Elohim**.
3 Be not hasty to go *out of his sight* **from his face**:
stand not in an evil *thing* **word**;
for he *doeth* **worketh** whatsoever *pleaseth him* **he desireth**.
4 Where the word of a *king* **sovereign** is,
there is *power* **dominion**:
and who may say unto him, What *doest* **workest** thou?
5 Whoso *keepeth* **guardeth** the *commandment* **misvah**
shall *feel* **know** no evil *thing* **word**:
and *a wise man's heart* **the heart of the wise**
discerneth **knoweth** both time and judgment.
6 Because to every *purpose* **desire**
there is time and judgment,
therefore the *misery* **evil** of *man* **humanity**
is great upon him.
7 For he knoweth not that which shall be:
for who can tell him when it shall be?
8 There is no *man* **human**
that *hath power* **is potentate** over the spirit
to *retain* **restrain** the spirit;
neither hath he power in the day of death:
and there is no *discharge* **shooting** in that war;
neither shall wickedness
deliver those that are given to it **rescue its masters**.
9 All this have I seen,
and *applied* **gave** my heart unto every work
that is *done* **worked** under the sun:
there is a time wherein
one man ruleth over another **human dominateth human**
to his own *hurt* **evil**.
10 And *so* **thus** I saw the wicked *buried* **entombed**,
who had come and gone from the place of the holy,
and they were forgotten in the city
where they had so *done* **worked**:
this is also vanity.

THE CONGREGATIONER 8—10

11 Because sentence against an evil work
is not *executed speedily* **quickly worked,**
therefore the heart of the sons of *men* **humanity**
is fully set in them to *do* **work** evil.
12 Though a sinner *do* **work** evil an hundred times,
and *his days* be prolonged,
yet surely I know that it shall be *well* **good** with them
that *fear God* **awe Elohim,**
which *fear before him* **awe at his face:**
13 But it shall not be *well* **good** with the wicked,
neither shall he prolong his days,
which are as a shadow;
because he *feareth* **aweth** not
before God **at the face of Elohim.**
14 There is a vanity
which is *done* **worked** upon the earth;
that there be **the** just *men,*
unto whom it *happeneth* **toucheth**
according to the work of the wicked;
again, there be **the** wicked *men,*
to whom it *happeneth* **toucheth**
according to the work of the *righteous* **just:**
I said that this also is vanity.
15 Then I *commended mirth* **lauded cheerfulness,**
because *a man* **humanity**
hath no better *thing* under the sun,
than to eat, and to drink, and to *be merry* **cheer:**
for that shall *abide* **join** with him of his *labour* **toil**
the days of his life,
which *God* **Elohim** giveth him under the sun.
16 When I *applied* **gave** mine heart to know wisdom,
and to see the *business* **drudgery**
that is *done* **worked** upon the earth:
(for also there is that neither day nor night
seeth sleep with his eyes:)
17 Then I *beheld* **saw** all the work of *God* **Elohim,**
that *a man* **humanity** cannot find out the work
that is *done* **worked** under the sun:
because though *a man labour* **humanity toil** to seek it out,
yet he shall not find it; yea farther;
though *a* **the** wise *man think to know it* **sayeth he knoweth,**
yet shall he not be able to find it.

9 For all this
I *considered* **gave** in my heart even to declare all this,
that the *righteous* **just,** and the wise,
and their *works* **service,**
are in the hand of *God* **Elohim:**
no *man* **human** knoweth either love or hatred
by all that *is before them* **at their face.**
2 All *things* come alike to all:
there is one *event* **happening** to the *righteous* **just,**
and to the wicked;
to the good and to the *clean* **pure,**
and to the *unclean* **foul;**
to him that sacrificeth, and to him that sacrificeth not:
as *is* the good, so *is* the sinner;
and he that *sweareth* **oatheth,**
as he that *feareth* **aweth** an oath.
3 This is an evil among all *things*
that are *done* **worked** under the sun,
that there is one event **one happening** unto all:
yea, also
the heart of the sons of *men* **humanity** is full of evil,
and *madness* **folly** is in their heart while they live,
and after that *they go to* — **unto** the dead.
4 For to him that is joined to all the living
there is *hope* **confidence:**
for a living dog is better than a dead lion.
5 For the living know that they shall die:
but the dead know *not any thing* **naught,**
neither have they any more a *reward* **hire;**
for *the memory of them* **their memorial** is forgotten.
6 Also their love, and their hatred, and their envy,
is *now perished* **already destructed;**
neither have they any more
a portion for ever **an allotment eternally**
in *any thing* **aught** that is *done* **worked** under the sun.
7 Go thy way, eat thy bread with *joy* **cheerfulness,**
and drink thy wine with a *merry* **good** heart;
for *God* **Elohim**
now accepteth **is already pleased in** thy works.
8 Let thy *garments* **clothes** be *always* **at all times** white;
and let thy head lack no ointment.
9 *Live joyfully* **See life**
with the *wife* **woman** whom thou lovest
all the days of the life of thy vanity,
which he hath given thee under the sun,
all the days of thy vanity:
for that is thy *portion* **allotment** in *this* life,
and in thy *labour* **toil**
which thou *takest* **toilest** under the sun.
10 Whatsoever thy hand findeth to *do* **work,**
do **work** it with thy might **force;**
for there is no work, nor *device* **machination,**
nor knowledge, nor wisdom,
in *the grave* **sheol,** whither thou goest.
11 I returned, and saw under the sun,
that the race is not to the swift,
nor the *battle* **war** to the *strong* **mighty,**
neither yet bread to the wise,
nor yet riches to *men of understanding* **the discerning,**
nor yet *favour to men of skill* **charism to the knowing;**
but time and *chance* **coincidence** happeneth to them all.
12 For *man* **humanity** also knoweth not his time:
as the fishes that are *taken* **held** in an evil *net* **lure,**
and as the birds that are *caught* **held** in the snare;
so are the sons of *men* **humanity** snared in an evil time,
when it falleth suddenly upon them.
13 This wisdom have I seen also under the sun,
and it *seemed* **be** great unto me:
14 There was a little city, and few men within it;
and there came a great *king* **sovereign** against it,
and *besieged* **surrounded** it,
and built great *bulwarks* **lairs** against it:
15 Now there was found in it a poor wise man,
and he by his wisdom *delivered* **rescued** the city;
yet no *man* **human** remembered that same poor man.
16 Then said I, Wisdom is better than *strength* **might:**
nevertheless the poor man's wisdom
the wisdom of the poor is despised,
and his words are not heard.
17 The words of **the** wise *men* are heard in *quiet* **rest**
more than the cry of him
that *ruleth* **reigneth** among fools.
18 Wisdom is better than *weapons* **instruments** of war:
but one sinner destroyeth *much* **abounding** good.

10 Dead flies
cause the ointment of the *apothecary* **perfumer**
to *send forth a stinking savour* **gush and stink:**
so *doth* a little folly
him that is in *reputation* **esteem** for wisdom and honour.
2 *A wise man's heart* **The heart of the wise**
is at his right *hand;*
but *a fool's heart* **the heart of a fool**
at his left.
3 Yea also, when he that is a fool walketh by the way,
his *wisdom* **heart** faileth *him,*
and he saith to every one that he is a fool.
4 If the spirit of the *ruler* **sovereign**
rise up **ascend** against thee,
leave not thy place;
for *yielding pacifieth* **healing alloweth** great *offences* **sins.**
5 There is an evil which I have seen under the sun,
as an **inadvertent** error
which proceedeth from **the face of** the *ruler* **potentate:**
6 Folly is *set* **given** in great *dignity* **heights,**
and the rich *sit* **settle** in *low place* **lowliness.**
7 I have seen servants upon horses,
and *princes* **governors**
walking as servants upon the earth.
8 He that diggeth a pit shall fall *into it* **therein;**
and whoso *breaketh an hedge* **breacheth a wall,**
a serpent shall bite him.
9 Whoso *removeth* **plucketh** stones
shall be *hurt* **contorted** therewith;
and he that *cleaveth wood* **splitteth timber**

shall be *endangered* **cut** thereby.
10 If the iron be *blunt* **dull**,
and he do not *whet* **sharpen** the *edge* **face**,
then must he
put to more strength **prevail mightily with valour:**
but wisdom *is profitable* **advantageth** to *direct* **prosper**.
11 Surely the serpent *will* **shall** bite without enchantment;
and a *babbler* **master of tongue**
is no better **advantageth not**.
12 The words of *a wise man's mouth* **the mouth of the wise**
are gracious **have charism**;
but the lips of a fool *will* **shall** swallow *up himself*.
13 The beginning of the words of his mouth
is *foolishness* **folly**:
and the *end* **finality** of his talk
is *mischievous* **evil** madness.
14 A fool also *is full of* **aboundeth** words:
a man **humanity** cannot tell what shall be;
and what shall be after him, who can tell him?
15 The *labour* **toil** of the foolish
wearieth every one of **belaboureth** them,
because he knoweth not how to go to the city.
16 Woe to thee, O land,
when thy *king* **sovereign** is a *child* **lad**,
and thy *princes* **governors** eat in the morning!
17 *Blessed* **Blithe** art thou, O land,
when thy *king* **sovereign** is the son of nobles,
and thy *princes* **governors** eat *in due season* **on time**,
for *strength* **might**, and not for *drunkenness* **drinking**!
18 By much *slothfulness* **sloth**
the *building decayeth* **framing subdueth**;
and through idleness of the hands
the house droppeth through.
19 *A feast* **Bread** is *made* **worked** for laughter,
and wine *maketh merry* **cheereth the life**:
but *money* **silver** answereth all *things*.
20 *Curse* **Abase** not the *king* **sovereign**,
no not *in thy thought* **knowingly**;
and *curse* **abase** not the rich in thy bedchamber:
for a *bird* **flyer** of the *air* **heavens**
shall carry the voice,
and *that which hath* **the master of** wings
shall tell the *matter* **word**.

11 *Cast* **Send** thy bread
upon the **face of the** waters:
for thou shalt find it after *many* **abundant** days.
2 Give *a portion* **an allotment** to seven, and also to eight;
for thou knowest not what evil shall be upon the earth.
3 If the **thick** clouds be full of *rain* **downpour**,
they *empty* **pour** *themselves* upon the earth:
and if the tree fall toward the south, or toward the north,
in the place where the tree falleth, there it shall be.
4 He that *observeth* **regardeth** the wind
shall not *sow* **seed**;
and he that *regardeth* **seeth** the **thick** clouds
shall not *reap* **harvest**.
5 As thou knowest not
what is the way of the *spirit* **wind/spirit**,
nor how the bones *do grow* in the *womb* **belly**
of her that is *with child* **full**:
even so thou knowest not the works of *God* **Elohim**
who *maketh* **worketh** all.
6 In the morning sow thy seed,
and in the evening *withhold* **leave** not thine hand:
for thou knowest not *whether* **which** shall prosper,
either this or that,
or whether they both shall be *alike* **one** good.
7 Truly the light is sweet,
and *a pleasant thing* **good** it is
for the eyes to *behold* **see** the sun:
8 But if *a man* **human** live *many* **and abound in** years,
and *rejoice* **cheer** in them all;
yet let him remember the days of darkness;
for they shall *be many* **abound**.
All that cometh is vanity.
9 *Rejoice* **Cheer**, O *young man* **youth**, in thy youth;
and let thy heart *cheer* **better** thee
in the days of thy youth,
and walk in the ways of thine heart,
and in the *sight* **visage** of thine eyes:
but know thou, that for all these *things*
God will **Elohim shall** bring thee into judgment.
10 *Therefore remove sorrow* **Turn vexation aside**
from thy heart,
and *put away* **pass** evil from thy flesh:
for childhood and *youth* **dawn** are vanity.

12 Remember now thy Creator
in the days of thy youth,
while the evil days come not,
nor the years *draw nigh* **touch**,
when thou shalt say, I have no *pleasure* **delight** in them;
2 While the sun, or the light, or the moon, or the stars,
be not darkened,
nor the **thick** clouds return after the *rain* **downpour**:
3 In the day when the *keepers* **guards** of the house
shall *tremble* **agitate**,
and the *strong* **valiant** men shall *bow themselves* **twist**,
and the grinders cease
because they are *few* **diminished**,
and those that look out of the windows be darkened,
4 And the doors shall be shut in the streets,
when the *sound* **voice** of the grinding is low,
and he shall rise *up* at the voice of the bird,
and all the daughters of *musick* **song**
shall *be brought low* **prostrate**;
5 Also when they shall *be afraid of* **awe** that which is high,
and *fears* **terrors** shall be in the way,
and the almond tree shall flourish,
and the *grasshopper* **locust** shall be a burden,
and desire shall *fail* **break down**:
because *man* **humanity**
goeth to his *long home* **eternal house**,
and the *mourners* **choppers**
go about **turn around** the streets:
6 Or ever the silver cord be *loosed* **removed**,
or the golden bowl be broken,
or the pitcher be broken at the fountain,
or the wheel *broken* **cracked** at the *cistern* **well**.
7 Then shall the dust return to the earth as it was:
and the spirit shall return unto *God* **Elohim** who gave it.
8 Vanity of vanities,
saith the *preacher* **Congregationer**;
all is vanity.
9 And moreover,
because the *preacher* **Congregationer** was *wise* **wiser**,
he still taught the people knowledge;
yea, he *gave good heed* **hearkened**, and *sought out* **probed**,
and set in order *many* **abounding** proverbs.
10 The *preacher* **Congregationer**
sought to find out *acceptable* words **of delight**:
and that which was *written* **inscribed**
was *upright* **straightness**, *even* — words of truth.
11 The words of the wise are as goads,
and as nails *fastened* **implanted**
by the masters of *assemblies* **gatherings**,
which are given from one *shepherd* **attendant**.
12 And *further* **moreover**, by these, my son,
be *admonished* **enlightened**:
of *making many books* **working abundant scrolls**
there is no end;
and *much* **abundant** study
is a weariness of **belaboureth** the flesh.
13 Let us hear the conclusion of the whole *matter* **word**:
Fear God **Awe Elohim**,
and *keep* **guard** his *commandments* **misvoth**:
for this is the whole *duty of man* **of humanity**.
14 For *God* **Elohim** shall bring every work into judgment,
with every *secret thing* **concealment**,
whether *it be* good, *or* whether *it be* evil.

KEY TO INTERPRETING THE EXEGESES:
King James text is in regular type;
Text under exegeses is in oblique type;
Text of exegeses is in bold type.

THE SONG OF SONGS
1 The song of songs, which is *Solomon's* **Shelomoh's**.

THE WOMAN SPEAKS
2 Let him kiss me with the kisses of his mouth:
for thy *love is* **loves are** better than wine.
3 Because of the *savour* **scent** of thy good ointments
thy name is as ointment poured forth,
therefore *do* the virgins love thee.
4 Draw me, we *will* **shall** run after thee:
the *king* **sovereign** hath brought me into his chambers:
we *will be glad* **shall cheer** and *rejoice* **twirl** in thee,
we *will* **shall** remember thy *love* **loves** more than wine:
the upright **they** love thee **in straightnesses**.
5 I am black, but comely,
O ye daughters of *Jerusalem* **Yeru Shalem**,
as the tents of *Kedar* **Qedar**,
as the curtains of *Solomon* **Shelomoh**.
6 *Look not upon* **See** me **not**, because I am black,
because the sun hath *looked upon* **tanned** me:
my mother's *children were angry with* **sons scorched** me;
they *made* **set** me the *keeper* **guard** of the vineyards;
but mine own vineyard have I not *kept* **guarded**.
7 Tell me, O thou whom my soul loveth,
where thou *feedest* **tendest**,
where thou *makest thy flock to rest* **resposest** at noon:
for why should I be as one that *turneth aside* **is veiled**
by the *flocks* **droves** of thy companions?

THE MAN RESPONDS
8 If thou know not,
O thou *fairest* **beautiful** among women,
go thy way forth by the *footsteps* **heelprints** of the flock,
and *feed* **tend** thy kids
beside the *shepherds' tents* **tabernacles of the tenders**.
9 I have compared thee, O my *love* **friend**,
to a *company of horses* **mare** in *Pharaoh's* **Paroh's** chariots.
10 Thy cheeks are comely with rows *of jewels*,
thy neck with *chains of gold* **beads**.
11 We *will make* **shall work** thee *borders* **rows** of gold
with *studs* **sequins** of silver.

THE WOMAN
12 While the *king sitteth at* **sovereign be in** his *table* **circle**,
my *spikenard* **nard**
sendeth forth **giveth** the *smell* **scent** *thereof*.
13 A bundle of myrrh is my well—beloved unto me;
he shall *lie all night* **stay overnight** betwixt my breasts.
14 My beloved is unto me as a cluster of camphire
in the vineyards of *Engedi* **En Gedi**.

THE MAN
15 Behold, thou art *fair* **beautiful**, my *love* **friend**;
behold, thou art *fair* **beautiful**; thou hast doves' eyes.

THE WOMAN
16 Behold, thou art *fair* **beautiful**, my beloved,
yea, pleasant:
also our *bed* **bedstead** is green.
17 The beams of our house are cedar,
and our *rafters* **troughs** of *fir* **firs**.

THE MAN
2 I am the rose of Sharon, *and* the lily of the valleys.
2 As the lily among thorns,
so is my *love* **friend** among the daughters.

THE WOMAN
3 As the apple tree among the trees of the *wood* **forest**,
so is my beloved among the sons.
I sat down under his shadow
with great delight **and delighted**,
and his fruit was sweet to my *taste* **palate**.
4 He brought me to the *banqueting* house **of wine**,
and his banner over me was love.
5 *Stay* **Sustain** me with *flagons* **cakes**,
comfort **spread** me with apples:
for I am *sick* **worn out** of love.
6 His left *hand* is under my head,
and his right *hand doth embrace* **embraceth** me.
7 I *charge* **oath** you,
O ye daughters of *Jerusalem* **Yeru Shalem**,
by the *roes* **gazelles**, and by the hinds of the field,
that ye *stir not up* **not waken**,
nor awake *my* **the** love, till he *please* **desireth**.
8 The voice of my beloved!
behold, he cometh leaping upon the mountains,
skipping upon the hills.
9 My beloved is *like a roe* **likened to a gazelle**
or a *young* **fawn** hart:
behold, he standeth behind our wall,
he *looketh* **peereth** forth at the windows,
shewing himself **flourishing** through the lattice.
10 My beloved *spake* **answered**, and said unto me,
Rise up **Arise**, my *love* **friend**, my *fair one* **beautiful**,
and come away.
11 For, *lo* **behold**, the winter *is past* **hath passed**,
the *rain is over* **downpour hath passed** and gone;
12 The *flowers appear* **blossoms be seen** on the earth;
the time of *the singing of birds* **psalming**
is come **hath touched**,
and the voice of the *turtle* **turtledove**
is heard in our land;
13 The fig tree *putteth forth* **ripeneth** her *green* **unripe** figs,
and the vines with the *tender grape* **blossom**
give *a good smell* **their scent**.
Arise, my *love* **friend**, my *fair one* **beautiful**,
and come away.
14 O my dove, that art in the clefts of the rock,
in the *secret places* **coverts** of the *stairs* **steep steps**,
let me see thy *countenance* **visage**,
let me hear thy voice;
for *sweet* **pleasant** is thy voice,
and thy *countenance is* **visage** comely.
15 Take **hold** us the foxes,
the little foxes, that *spoil* **despoil** the *vines* **vineyards**:
for our *vines* **vineyards** have *tender grapes* **blossoms**.
16 My beloved is mine, and I am his:
he *feedeth* **tendeth** among the lilies.
17 Until the day *break* **breathe**,
and the shadows flee away,
turn *around*, my beloved,
and be thou *like* **likened to** a *roe* **gazelle**
or a *young* **fawn** hart
upon the mountains of Bether.
3 By night on my bed
I sought him whom my soul loveth:
I sought him, but I found him not.
2 I *will* **shall** rise *now* **I beseech**,
and go about the city in the streets,
and in the broad ways
I *will* **shall** seek him whom my soul loveth:
I sought him, but I found him not.
3 The *watchmen* **guards** that *go about* **surround** the city
found me: *to whom I said*,
Saw ye him whom my soul loveth?
4 It was but a little that I passed from them,
but I found him whom my soul loveth:
I held him, and *would* **did** not let him go,
until I had brought him into my mother's house,
and into the chamber of her that conceived me.
5 I *charge* **oath** you,
O ye daughters of *Jerusalem* **Yeru Shalem**,
by the *roes* **gazelles**, and by the hinds of the field,
that ye stir not up, nor awake *my* **the** love,
till he *please* **desireth**.
6 Who is this
that *cometh* **ascendeth** out of the wilderness
like *pillars* **columns** of smoke,
perfumed **incensed** with myrrh and frankincense,
with all powders of the merchant?
7 Behold his bed, which is *Solomon's* **Shelomoh's**;
threescore valiant men are about **sixty mighty surround** it,
of the *valiant* **mighty** of *Israel* **Yisra El**.
8 They all hold swords, *being expert* **taught** in war:
every man hath his sword upon his *thigh* **flank**
because of *fear* **dread** in the night.
9 *King Solomon* **Sovereign Shelomoh**
made **worked** himself a *chariot* **palanquin**
of the *wood* **timber** of Lebanon.
10 He *made* **worked** the pillars *thereof* of silver,

the *bottom* **railings** *thereof* of gold,
the *covering of it* **saddle** of purple,
the midst *thereof* being paved with love,
for the daughters of *Jerusalem* **Yeru Shalem**.
11 Go forth, O ye daughters of *Zion* **Siyon**,
and *behold king Solomon* **see sovereign Shelomoh**
with the crown wherewith his mother crowned him
in the day of his *espousals* **wedding**,
and in the day of the *gladness* **cheerfulness** of his heart.

THE MAN

4 Behold, thou art *fair* **beautiful**, my *love* **friend**;
behold, thou art *fair* **beautiful**;
thou hast doves' eyes *within* **throughout** thy *locks* **veil**:
thy hair is as a *flock* **drove** of **doe** goats,
that *appear* **eat** from mount *Gilead* **Gilad**.
2 Thy teeth are like a
flock of sheep that are even shorn **clipped drove**,
which *came up* **ascended** from the *washing* **bathing**;
whereof every one *bear twins* **twinned**,
and none is *barren* **bereft** among them.
3 Thy lips are like a thread of scarlet,
and thy speech is comely:
thy temples are like a *piece* **slice** of a pomegranate
within **throughout** thy *locks* **veil**.
4 Thy neck is like the tower of David
builded for *an armoury* **arsenals**,
whereon there hang a thousand bucklers,
all shields of mighty men.
5 Thy two breasts
are like two *young roes that are* **fawn gazelle** twins,
which *feed* **tend** among the lilies.
6 Until the day *break* **breathe**,
and the shadows flee away,
I *will get* **shall walk** me to the mountain of myrrh,
and to the hill of frankincense.
7 Thou art all *fair* **beautiful**, my *love* **friend**;
there is no *spot* **blemish** in thee.
8 Come with me from Lebanon, *my spouse* **bride**,
with me from Lebanon:
look **observe** from the top of *Amana* **Amanah**,
from the top of Shenir and Hermon,
from the *lions' dens* **habitations of lions**,
from the mountains of the leopards.
9 Thou hast *ravished my heart* **disheartened me**,
my *sister, my spouse* **sister bride**;
thou hast *ravished my heart* **disheartened me**
with one of thine eyes,
with one *chain* **choker** of thy neck.
10 How *fair is* **beautified** thy *love* **loves**,
my *sister, my spouse* **sister bride**!
how much better is thy love than wine!
and the *smell* **scent** of thine ointments than all spices!
11 Thy lips, O *my spouse* **bride**,
drop as the honeycomb:
honey and milk are under thy tongue;
and the *smell* **scent** of thy *garments* **clothes**
is like the *smell* **scent** of Lebanon.
12 A garden inclosed is my *sister,*
my spouse **sister bride**;
a *spring shut up* **wave inclosed**,
a fountain sealed.
13 Thy *plants* **branches**
are *an orchard* **a paradise** of pomegranates,
with *pleasant* **precious** fruits;
camphire, with *spikenard* **nard**,
14 *Spikenard* **Nard** and saffron;
calamus **stalk** and cinnamon,
with all trees of frankincense;
myrrh and aloes, with all the *chief* **head** spices:
15 A fountain of gardens, a well of living waters,
and *streams* **flows** from Lebanon.

THE WOMAN

16 Awake, O *north wind* **northerly**;
and come, thou *south* **southerly**;
blow **puff** upon my garden,
that the spices *thereof* may flow out.
Let my beloved come into his garden
and eat his *pleasant* **precious** fruits.

THE MAN

5 I am come into my garden,
my *sister, my spouse* **sister bride**:
I have *gathered* **plucked** my myrrh with my spice;
I have eaten my *honeycomb* **honey of the forest**
with my honey;
I have drunk my wine with my milk: eat, O friends;
drink, *yea, drink abundantly* **and intoxicate**, O beloved.

THE WOMAN QUOTES THE MAN

2 I sleep, but my heart waketh:
it is the voice of my beloved that knocketh,
saying, Open to me, my sister, my *love* **friend**,
my dove, my *undefiled* **integrious**:
for my head is filled with *dew* **dewdrops**,
and my locks with the *drops* **dewdrops** of the night.
3 I have *put off* **stripped** my coat;
how shall I *put it on* **enrobe**?
I have washed my feet; how shall I *defile* **foul** them?

THE WOMAN SPEAKS FOR HERSELF

4 My beloved *put in* **extended** his hand by the hole
of the door,
and my *bowels were moved* **inwards roared** for him.
5 I rose up to open to my beloved;
and my hands *dropped with* **dripped** myrrh,
and my fingers with *sweet smelling* myrrh,
that passeth upon the *handles* **palms** of the lock.
6 I opened to my beloved;
but my beloved had withdrawn himself,
and *was gone* **had passed**:
my soul failed when he *spake* **worded**:
I sought him, but I *could not find* **found** him **not**;
I called him, but he *gave me no answer* **answered not**.
7 The *watchmen* **guards**
that *went about* **surrounded** the city found me,
they smote me, they wounded me;
the *keepers* **guards** of the walls
took away **lifted** my veil from me.
8 I *charge* **oath** you,
O daughters of *Jerusalem* **Yeru Shalem**,
if ye find my beloved,
that ye tell him, that I am *sick* **worn out** of love.

THE DAUGHTERS

9 What is thy beloved more than *another* beloved,
O thou *fairest* **beautiful** among women?
what is thy beloved more than *another* beloved,
that thou *dost so charge* **thus oathest** us?

THE WOMAN

10 My beloved is *white* **clear** and *ruddy* **red**,
the *chiefest* **bannerbearer** among *ten thousand* **myriads**.
11 His head is as *the most fine* **ore of pure** gold,
his locks are *bushy* **pendulous**, and black as a raven.
12 His eyes are as *the eyes of* doves
by the *rivers* **reservoirs** of waters,
washed **bathed** with milk, and *fitly* **in fulness** set.
13 His cheeks are as a *bed* **furrow** of spices,
as *sweet flowers* **towers of spices**:
his lips like lilies,
dropping sweet smelling **dripping passing** myrrh.
14 His hands are as gold rings *set* **filled** with the beryl:
his *belly is as bright* **inwards as fabricated** ivory
overlaid **covered** with sapphires.
15 His legs *are* as pillars of **white** marble,
set **founded** upon sockets of *fine* **pure** gold:
his *countenance is* **visage** as Lebanon,
excellent as the **as select** cedars.
16 His *mouth is most* **palate** sweet:
yea, he is altogether *lovely* **desirable**.
This is my beloved, and this is my friend,
O daughters of *Jerusalem* **Yeru Shalem**.

THE DAUGHTERS

6 Whither is thy beloved gone,
O thou *fairest* **beautiful** among women?
whither is thy beloved turned *aside* **his face**?
that we may seek him with thee.

THE WOMAN

2 My beloved *is gone down* **descended** into his garden,
to the *beds* **furrows** of spices,
to *feed in* **tend** the gardens, and to *gather* **gleen** lilies.
3 I am my beloved's, and my beloved is mine:
he *feedeth* **tendeth** among the lilies.

THE MAN

4 Thou art beautiful, O my *love* **friend**, as Tirzah,
comely as *Jerusalem* **Yeru Shalem**,
terrible **awesome** as *an army with banners* **bannerbearers**.
5 Turn away thine eyes from me,
for they have *overcome* **encouraged** me:
thy hair is as a *flock* **drove** of **doe** goats
that *appear* **eat** from *Gilead* **Gilad**.
6 Thy teeth are as a *flock* **drove** of *sheep* **ewes**
which *go up* **ascend** from the *washing* **bathing**,
whereof every one *beareth twins* **twinneth**,
and there is not one *barren* **bereft** among them.
7 As a *piece* **slice** of a pomegranate are thy temples
within **throughout** thy *locks* **veil**.
8 *There are threescore queens* **Sixty sovereignesses**,
and *fourscore* **eighty** concubines,
and virgins without number.
9 My dove, my *undefiled* **integrious** is *but* one;
she is the *only* one of her mother,
she is the *choice one* **pure** of her that bare her.

CONCERNING HER ADMIRERS

The daughters saw her,
and *blessed* **pronounced** her **blithesome**;
yea, the *queens* **sovereignesses** and the concubines,
and they *praised* **halaled** her.
10 Who is she that looketh forth as the *morning* **dawn**,
fair **beautiful** as the moon,
clear as the sun **pure as heat**,
and *terrible* **awesome**
as *an army with banners* **bannerbearers**.

THE WOMAN SPEAKS FOR HERSELF

11 I *went down* **descended** into the garden of nuts
to see the *fruits* **unripeness** of the *valley* **wadi**,
and to see whether the vine *flourished* **blossomed**
and the pomegranates budded.
12 Or ever I *was aware* **knew**,
my soul *made* **set** me
like the chariots of *Amminadib* **Ammi Nadib**.
13 Return, return, O *Shulamite* **Shulammith**;
return, return, that we may *look* **see** upon thee.
What *will* **shall** ye see in the Shulamite **Shulammith**?
As it were
the *company* **round dance** of *two armies* **Machanah.**

THE MAN

7 How *beautiful* **beautified**
are thy *feet* **steps** with shoes,
O *prince's* **volunteer's** daughter!
the *joints* **roundness** of thy *thighs* **flanks**
are like jewels **as ornaments**,
the work of the hands of *a cunning workman* **an expert**.
2 Thy navel *is like* **as** a round *goblet* **bowl**,
which *wanteth not liquor* **lacketh no cocktail**:
thy belly *is like* **as** an heap *of wheat*
set about **hedged** with lilies.
3 Thy two breasts *are like* **as** two *young roes* **fawn gazelles**
that are — twins.
4 Thy neck *is* as a tower of ivory;
thine eyes *like* **as** the fishpools in Heshbon,
by the *gate* **portal** of *Bath—rabbim* **Daughter of Rabbim:**
thy *nose* **nostrils** *is* as the tower of Lebanon
which *looketh* **watcheth**
toward Damascus **at the face of Dammeseq**.
5 Thine head upon thee *is like Carmel* **as an orchard**,
and the *hair* **thrum** of thine head *like* **as** purple;
the *king* **sovereign** is *held* **bound** in the *galleries* **curls**.
6 How *fair* **beautified** and how *pleasant* **pleasing** art thou,
O love, for delights!
7 This thy *stature* **height** is *like* **likened** to a palm tree,
and thy breasts to clusters *of grapes*.
8 I said, I *will go up* **shall ascend** to the palm tree,
I *will* **shall** take hold of the *boughs* **twigs** *thereof*:
now also thy breasts shall be as clusters of the vine,
and the *smell* **scent** of thy *nose like* **nostrils as** apples;
9 And *the roof of thy mouth* **thy palate**
like the best **as good** wine for my beloved,
that goeth *down sweetly* **in straightnesses**,
causing the lips of those that are asleep
to *speak* **tranquilly flow**.

THE WOMAN

10 I am my beloved's, and his desire is toward me.
11 Come, my beloved, let us go forth into the field;
let us *lodge* **stay overnight** in the villages.
12 Let us *get up* **start** early to the vineyards;
let us see if the vine *flourish* **blossom**,
whether the tender grape appear — **the blossom open**,
and the pomegranates bud forth:
there *will* **shall** I give thee my loves.
13 The mandrakes give a *smell* **scent**,
and at our *gates* **portals**
are all manner *of pleasant fruits* **preciousnesses**,
new and old, *which* I have *laid up* **treasured** for thee,
O my beloved.

8 O **who giveth** that thou wert as my brother,
that sucked the breasts of my mother!
when I should find thee *without* **in the outways**,
I *would* **should** kiss thee;
yea, I should not be *despised* **disrespected**.
2 I *would lead* **should drive** thee,
and bring thee into my mother's house,
who *would instruct* **should teach** me:
I *would cause* **should have** thee
to drink of *spiced* **perfumed** wine
of the **squeezed** juice of my pomegranate.
3 His left *hand* should be under my head,
and his right *hand* should embrace me.
4 I *charge* **oath** you,
O daughters of *Jerusalem* **Yeru Shalem**,
that ye *stir* not **waken** *up*,
nor awake *my* **the** love, until he *please* **desireth**.

THE DAUGHTERS

5 Who is this
that *cometh up* **ascendeth** from the wilderness,
leaning upon her beloved?

THE WOMAN

I *raised* **wakened** thee *up* under the apple tree:
there thy mother *brought* **pledged** thee *forth*:
there she *brought* **pledged** thee *forth* that bare thee.
6 Set me as a seal upon thine heart,
as a seal upon thine arm:
for love is strong as death;
jealousy is *cruel* **hard** as *the grave* **sheol**:
the *coals* **burning flashes** *thereof*
are *coals* **burning flashes** of fire,
which hath — a most vehement flame.
7 Many waters cannot quench love,
neither can the *floods drown* **rivers overflow** it:
if a man *would* **should** give
all the *substance* **wealth** of his house for love,
it would utterly be contemned
in disrespecting, he should be disrespected.

THE DAUGHTERS

8 We have a little sister, and she hath no breasts:
what shall we *do* **work** for our sister
in the day when she shall be *spoken* **worded** for?
9 If she be a wall,
we *will* **shall** build upon her a *palace* **wall** of silver:
and if she be a door,
we *will inclose* **shall besiege** her
with *boards* **a slab** of cedar.

THE WOMAN

10 I am a wall, and my breasts like towers:
then was I in his eyes as one that found *favour* **shalom**.
11 *Solomon* **Shelomoh**
had a vineyard at *Baalhamon* **Baal Hamon**;
he *let out* **gave** the vineyard unto *keepers* **guards**;
every one **each man** for the fruit *thereof*
was to bring a thousand *pieces of* silver.
12 My vineyard, which is mine, is *before me* **at my face**:
thou, O *Solomon* **Shelomoh**, *must have* **hast** a thousand,
and those that *keep* **guard** the fruit *thereof* two hundred.

THE MAN

13 Thou that *dwellest* **settlest** in the gardens,
the companions hearken to thy voice:
cause me to hear it.
14 *Make haste* **Flee**, my beloved,
and be thou *like* **likened** to a *roe* **gazelle**
or to a *young* **fawn** hart upon the mountains of spices.

KEY TO INTERPRETING THE EXEGESES:
King James text is in regular type;
Text under exegeses is in oblique type;
Text of exegeses is in bold type.

THE FIRST LAMENTATION

1 How *doth the city sit* **hath she settled** solitary,
that was full of **the city abounding with** people!
how *is* **hath** she become as a widow!
she that was great among the *nations* **goyim**,
and *princess* **governess** among the *provinces* **jurisdictions**,
how *is* **hath** she become *tributary* **a vassal**!
2 **In weeping,** She weepeth *sore* in the night,
and her tears are on her cheeks:
among all her lovers
she hath none to *comfort* **sigh over** her:
all her friends have dealt treacherously with her,
they are — become her enemies.
3 *Judah* **Yah Hudah** is *gone into captivity* **exiled**
because of *affliction* **humiliation**,
and because of *great* **abundant** servitude:
she *dwelleth* **settleth** among the *heathen* **goyim**,
she findeth no rest:
all her *persecutors* **pursuers** overtook her
between the straits.
4 The ways of *Zion do* **Siyon** mourn,
because none come
to the *solemn feasts* **congregation festivals**:
all her *gates* **portals** are desolate:
her priests sigh, her virgins *are afflicted* **grieve**,
and she is *in bitterness* **embittered**.
5 Her *adversaries* **tribulators**
are the chief **have become her heads**,
her enemies *prosper* **serenify**;
for *the LORD* **Yah Veh** hath *afflicted* **grieved** her
for the *multitude* **abundance**
of her *transgressions* **rebellions**:
her *children* **infants** are *gone into captivity* **captured**
before **at the face of** the *enemy* **tribulator**.
6 And from the daughter of *Zion* **Siyon**
all her *beauty* **majesty** is departed:
her *prince* **governors** are become like harts
that find no pasture,
and they are gone without *strength* **force**
before **at the face of** the pursuer.
7 *Jerusalem* **Yeru Shalem** remembered
in the days of her *affliction* **humiliation**
and of her *miseries* **persecutions**
all her *pleasant things* **desires**
that she had in the days of *old* **antiquity**,
when her people
fell into the hand of the *enemy* **tribulator**,
and *none did help her* **she had no helper**:
the *adversaries* **tribulators** saw her,
and *did mock at* **ridiculed** her *sabbaths* **shabbathisms**.
8 **In sinning,**
Jerusalem **Yeru Shalem** hath *grievously* sinned;
therefore she is removed:
all that honoured her *despise* **disesteem** her,
because they have seen her nakedness:
yea, she sigheth, and turneth backward.
9 Her *filthiness* **foulness** is in her *skirts* **hems**;
she remembereth not her *last end* **finality**;
therefore
she *came down wonderfully* **descended marvellously**:
she had *no comforter* **none to sigh**.
O *LORD* **Yah Veh**, *behold* **see** my *affliction* **humiliation**:
for the enemy hath *magnified* **greatened** *himself*.
10 The *adversary* **tribulator** hath spread out his hand
upon all her *pleasant things* **desires**:
for she hath seen
that the *heathen* **goyim** entered into her *sanctuary* **holies**,
whom thou didst command
that they should not enter into thy congregation.
11 All her people sigh, they seek bread;
they have given their *pleasant things* **desires** for *meat* **food**
to relieve the soul:
see, O *LORD* **Yah Veh**, and *consider* **look**;
for I am become *vile* **a glutton**.
12 Is it *nothing* **naught** to you,
all ye that pass by **the way**?
behold **look**,
and see if there be any sorrow like unto my sorrow,
which *is done* **be exploited** unto me,
wherewith *the LORD* **Yah Veh** hath afflicted me
in the day of his *fierce anger* **fuming wrath**.
13 From above **the heights**
hath he sent fire into my bones,
and it *prevaileth against* **subjugateth** them:
he hath spread a net for my feet,
he hath turned me back:
he hath *made* **given** me
desolate **desolation** and *faint* **bleeding** all the day.
14 The yoke of my *transgressions* **rebellions**
is bound by his hand:
they are *wreathed* **entwined**,
and *come up* **ascend** upon my neck:
he hath made my *strength* **force** to *fall* **falter**,
the Lord **Adonay**
hath *delivered* **given** me into their hands,
from whom — I am not able to rise *up*.
15 *The Lord* **Adonay**
hath *trodden under foot* **trampled** all my mighty *men*
in the midst of me:
he hath called *an assembly* **a congregation** against me
to *crush* **break** my young men:
the Lord **Adonay** hath trodden the virgin,
the daughter of *Judah* **Yah Hudah**,
as in a winepress **of virgins**.
16 For these *things* I weep;
mine eye, mine eye *runneth down* **cascadeth** with water,
because the *comforter* **sigher**
that should *relieve* **restore** my soul is far from me:
my *children* **sons** are desolate,
because the enemy prevailed **mightily**.
17 *Zion* **Siyon** spreadeth forth her hands,
and there is none to *comfort* **sigh over** her:
the LORD **Yah Veh** hath commanded
concerning *Jacob* **Yaaqov**,
that his *adversaries* **tribulators**
should be round about him:
Jerusalem **Yeru Shalem**
is *as a menstruous woman* **excluded among them**.
18 *The LORD* **Yah Veh** is *righteous* **just**;
for I have rebelled against his *commandment* **mouth**:
hear, I pray you, all people, and *behold* **see** my sorrow:
my virgins and my young men are gone into captivity.
19 I called for my *lovers* **beloveds**,
but they deceived me:
my priests and mine elders
gave up the ghost **expired** in the city,
while they sought *their meat* **food**
to *relieve* **restore** their souls.
20 *Behold* **See**, O *LORD* **Yah Veh**;
for I am *in distress* **tribulated**:
my *bowels are troubled* **inwards foam**;
mine heart is turned within me;
in rebelling, *for* I have *grievously* rebelled:
abroad **outwardly** the sword bereaveth,
at home there is as death.
21 They have heard that I sigh:
there is none to *comfort* **sigh over** me:
all mine enemies have heard of my *trouble* **evil**;
they *are glad* **rejoice** that thou hast *done* **worked** it:
thou *wilt* **shalt** bring the day that thou hast called,
and **so** they shall be *like* unto me.
22 Let all their *wickedness* **evil**
come *before thee* **at thy face**;
and *do* **exploit** unto them,
as thou hast *done* **exploited** unto me
for all my *transgressions* **rebellions**:
for my sighs are many, and my heart *is faint* **bleedeth**.

THE SECOND LAMENTATION

2 How hath *the Lord* **Adonay**
covered **overcast** the daughter of *Zion* **Siyon** with a cloud
in his *anger* **wrath**,
and cast down from *heaven* **the heavens** unto the earth
the beauty of *Israel* **Yisra El**,
and remembered not *his footstool* **the stool of his feet**
in the day of his *anger* **wrath**!

2 *The Lord* **Adonay** hath swallowed up
all the *habitations* **folds** of *Jacob* **Yaaqov**,
and hath not *pitied* **spared**:
he hath *thrown down* **demolished** in his *wrath* **fury**
the *strong holds* **fortresses**
of the daughter of *Judah* **Yah Hudah**;
he hath *brought* **touched** them down to the *ground* **earth**:
he hath *polluted* **profaned** the *kingdom* **sovereigndom**
and the *princes* **governors** *thereof.*
3 He hath cut off in his *fierce anger* **fuming wrath**
all the horn of *Israel* **Yisra El**:
he hath *drawn* **turned** back his right *hand*
from *before* **the face of** the enemy,
and he burned against *Jacob* **Yaaqov** like a flaming fire,
which *devoureth* **consumeth** round about.
4 He hath bent his bow like an enemy:
he *stood* **stationed** with his right *hand*
as *an adversary* **a tribulator**,
and *slew* **slaughtered** all
that were *pleasant* **a desire** to the eye
in the *tabernacle* **tent** of the daughter of *Zion* **Siyon**:
he poured out his fury like fire.
5 *The Lord* **Adonay** was as an enemy:
he hath swallowed *up Israel* **Yisra El**,
he hath swallowed *up* all her *palaces* **citadels**:
he hath *destroyed* **ruined** his *strong holds* **fortresses**,
and hath *increased* **abounded**
in the daughter of *Judah* **Yah Hudah**
mourning and *lamentation* **sighing**.
6 And he hath *violently taken away* **violated**
his *tabernacle* **sukkoth/brush arbor**
as *if it were of* a garden:
he hath *destroyed* **ruined**
his *places of the assembly* **seasons**:
the LORD **Yah Veh** hath caused
the *solemn feasts* **seasons** and *sabbaths* **shabbaths**
to be forgotten in *Zion* **Siyon**,
and hath *despised* **scorned**
in the *indignation* **rage** of his *anger* **wrath**
the *king* **sovereign** and the priest.
7 *The Lord* **Adonay** hath cast off his **sacrifice** altar,
he hath *abhorred* **rejected** his *sanctuary* **holies**,
he hath *given* **shut** up into the hand of the enemy
the walls of her *palaces* **citadels**;
they have *made a noise* **given voice**
in the house of *the LORD* **Yah Veh**,
as in the day of a *solemn feast* **season**.
8 *The LORD* **Yah Veh** hath *purposed* **machinated**
to *destroy* **ruin** the wall of the daughter of *Zion* **Siyon**:
he hath stretched out a line,
he hath not *withdrawn* **turned back** his hand
from *destroying* **swallowing**:
therefore
he made the *rampart* **trench** and the wall to lament;
they languished together.
9 Her *gates* **portals** are sunk into the *ground* **earth**;
he hath destroyed and broken her bars:
her *king* **sovereign** and her *princes* **governors**
are among the *Gentiles* **goyim**:
the *law* **torah** is *no more* **not**;
her prophets also
find no vision from *the LORD* **Yah Veh**.
10 The elders of the daughter of *Zion* **Siyon**
sit **settle** upon the *ground* **earth**, and *keep silence* **hush**:
they have *cast up* **ascended** dust upon their heads;
they have girded themselves with *sackcloth* **saq**:
the virgins of *Jerusalem* **Yeru Shalem**
hang down **lower** their heads to the *ground* **earth**.
11 Mine eyes *do fail* **are finished off** with tears,
my *bowels are troubled* **inwards foam**,
my liver is poured upon the earth,
for the *destruction* **breech** of the daughter of my people;
because the *children* **infants** and the sucklings
swoon **languish** in the *streets* **broadways** of the city.
12 They say to their mothers,
Where is *corn* **crop** and wine?
when they *swooned* **languished** as the *wounded* **pierced**
in the *streets* **broadways** of the city,
when their soul was poured out
into their mothers' bosom.
13 What *thing* shall I take to witness for thee?
what *thing* shall I liken to thee,
O daughter of *Jerusalem* **Yeru Shalem**?
what shall I *equal* **equate** to thee,
that I may *comfort* **sigh over** thee,
O virgin daughter of *Zion* **Siyon**?
for thy breach is great like the sea:
who *can* **shall** heal thee?
14 Thy prophets have seen *vain* **thy vanity**
and *foolish things for thee* **thy slime**:
and they have not
discovered thine iniquity **exposed thy perversity**,
to turn away thy captivity;
but have seen for thee *false* **vain** burdens
and *causes of banishment* **seductions**.
15 All that pass by **the way**
clap their *hands* **palms** at thee;
they hiss and wag their head
at the daughter of *Jerusalem* **Yeru Shalem**,
saying, Is this the city that *men call* **is said**
The perfection of **Total** beauty,
The joy of the whole earth?
16 All thine enemies
have *opened* **gasped** their mouth against thee:
they hiss and gnash the teeth:
they say, We have swallowed her *up*:
certainly **surely** this is the day that we *looked for* **awaited**;
we have found, we have seen *it*.
17 *The LORD* **Yah Veh**
hath *done* **worked** that which he had *devised* **intrigued**;
he hath *fulfilled* **cut** his *word* **saying**
that he had commanded in the days of *old* **antiquity**:
he hath *thrown down* **demolished**,
and hath not *pitied* **spared**:
and he hath caused thine enemy
to *rejoice* **cheer** over thee,
he hath *set* **lifted** *up* the horn
of *thine adversaries* **thy tribulators**.
18 Their heart cried unto *the Lord* **Adonay**,
O wall of the daughter of *Zion* **Siyon**,
let tears *run down* **cascade** like a *river* **wadi** day and night:
give thyself no *rest* **breather**;
let not the *apple* **daughter** of thine eye *cease* **be stilled**.
19 Arise, cry out in the night:
in the *beginning* **head** of the watches
pour out thine heart like water
before the face of *the Lord* **Adonay**:
lift up thy *hands* **palms** toward him
for the *life* **soul** of thy *young children* **infants**,
that *faint* **languish** for *hunger* **famine**
in the top of *every street* **all the outways**.
20 *Behold* **See**, O *LORD* **Yah Veh**, and *consider* **look**
to whom thou hast *done this* **exploited thus**.
Shall the women eat their fruit,
and children — **infants** of a **palm** span *long*?
shall the priest and the prophet be *slain* **slaughtered**
in the *sanctuary* **holies** of *the Lord* **Adonay**?
21 The *young* **lad** and the *old* **aged**
lie on the *ground* **earth** in the *streets* **outways**:
my virgins and my young men are fallen by the sword;
thou hast *slain* **slaughtered** them
in the day of *thine anger* **thy wrath**;
thou hast *killed* **slaughtered**, and not *pitied* **spared**.
22 Thou hast called as in a *solemn* day **of season**
my terrors round about,
so that in the day of *the LORD'S anger* **Yah Veh's wrath**
none escaped **there be no escapee** nor *remained* **survivor**:
those that I have
swaddled **palm spanned** and *brought up* **abounded**
hath mine enemy consumed.

THE THIRD LAMENTATION

3 I am the *man* **mighty**
that hath seen *affliction* **humiliation**
by the *rod* **scion** of his *wrath* **fury**.
2 He hath *led* **driven** me,
and *brought* **walked** me into darkness,
but not into **without** light.
3 Surely against me is he turned;
he turneth his hand *against me* all the day.

4 My flesh and my skin hath he *made old* **worn out**;
he hath broken my bones.
5 He hath builded against me,
and *compassed* **surrounded** me with *gall* **rosh** and travail.
6 He hath set me in dark places,
as *they that be* **the** dead of old.
7 He hath *hedged* **walled** me *about* **in**,
that I cannot get out:
he hath *made* **weighted** my *chain heavy* **copper**.
8 Also when I cry and shout, he shutteth out my prayer.
9 He hath *inclosed* **walled in** my ways with hewn *stone*,
he hath *made* **bent** my paths *crooked*.
10 He was unto me *as* a bear *lying in wait* **lurking**,
and as a lion in *secret places* **coverts**.
11 He hath turned aside my ways,
and *pulled me in pieces* **torn me**:
he hath *made* **set** me desolate.
12 He hath bent his bow,
and *set* **stationed** me as a *mark* **target** for the arrow.
13 He hath caused the *arrows* **sons** of his quiver
to enter into my reins.
14 I was a *derision* **ridicule** to all my people;
and their *song* **strumming** all the day.
15 He hath *filled* **satiated** me with *bitterness* **bitternesses**,
he hath *made me drunken* **satiated me** with wormwood.
16 He hath also *broken* **crushed** my teeth
with gravel *stones*,
he hath covered me with ashes.
17 And thou hast removed my soul
far off from *peace* **shalom**:
I forgat *prosperity* **good**.
18 And I said,
My *strength* **perpetuity** and my hope is perished
from *the LORD* **Yah Veh**:
19 Remembering mine *affliction* **humiliation**
and my *misery* **persecution**,
the wormwood and the *gall* **rosh**.
20 **In remembering,**
My soul *hath them still in remembrance* **remembereth**,
and *is humbled* **sinketh** in me.
21 This I *recall* **return** to my *mind* **heart**,
therefore *have I hope* **I await**.
22 It is of *the LORD'S* **Yah Veh's** mercies
that we are not consumed,
because his *compassions* **tender mercies**
fail not **never finish**.
23 *They are new every morning* **New by mornings**:
great is thy *faithfulness* **trustworthiness**.
24 *The LORD* **Yah Veh** is my *portion* **allotment**,
saith my soul;
therefore *will I hope in* **shall I await** him.
25 *The LORD* **Yah Veh** is good
unto them that *wait for* **await** him,
to the soul that seeketh him.
26 It is good *that a man should both hope* **to await**
and quietly wait for — **to silently await** the salvation
of *the LORD* **Yah Veh**.
27 It is good for a *man* **mighty**
that he bear the yoke of his youth.
28 He *sitteth* **settleth** alone and *keepeth silence* **husheth**,
because he hath borne it upon him.
29 He *putteth* **giveth** his mouth in the dust;
if so be there may be hope.
30 He giveth his cheek to him that smiteth him:
he is *filled full* **satiated** with reproach.
31 For *the Lord* **Adonay**
will **shall** not cast off *for ever* **eternally**:
32 But though he *cause grief* **grieve thee**,
yet *will* **shall** he *have compassion* **mercy**
according to the *multitude* **abundance** of his mercies.
33 For he *doth not afflict* **neither humbleth**
willingly **from his heart**
nor *grieve* **grieveth** the *children* **sons** of men.
34 To crush under his feet
all the *prisoners* **bound** of the earth.
35 To *turn aside* **pervert** the *right* **judgment**
of a *man* **mighty**
before the face of *the most High* **Elyon**,
36 To *subvert* **twist** a man in his *cause* **defence**,
the Lord approveth **Adonay seeth** not.
37 Who is he that saith, and it *cometh to pass* **becometh**,
when *the Lord* **Adonay** commandeth it not?
38 Out of the mouth of *the most High* **Elyon**
proceedeth not evil and good?
39 Wherefore doth a living *man* **human** complain,
a *man* **mighty** for *the punishment of* his sins?
40 Let us search and *try* **probe** our ways,
and *turn again* **return** to *the LORD* **Yah Veh**.
41 Let us lift up our heart with *our hands* **palms**
unto *God* **El** in the heavens.
42 We have transgressed and have rebelled:
thou hast not *pardoned* **forgiven**.
43 Thou hast covered with *anger* **wrath**,
and *persecuted* **pursued** us:
thou hast slain, thou hast not *pitied* **spared**.
44 Thou hast covered thyself with a cloud,
that our prayer should not pass through.
45 Thou hast *made* **set** us *as* the offscouring and refuse
in the midst of the people.
46 All our enemies
have *opened* **gasped** their mouths against us.
47 *Fear* **Dread** and a *snare* **pit** is come upon us,
desolation and *destruction* **breech**.
48 Mine eye *runneth down* **cascadeth**
with *rivers* **rivulets** of water
for the *destruction* **breech** of the daughter of my people.
49 Mine eye *trickleth down* **floweth**, and ceaseth not,
without any *intermission* **relaxation**.
50 Till *the LORD* **Yah Veh** look down,
and *behold* **see** from *heaven* **the heavens**.
51 Mine eye *affecteth mine heart* **exploiteth my soul**
because of all the daughters of my city.
52 **In hunting,** Mine enemies *chased* **hunted** me *sore*,
like a bird, *without cause* **gratuitously**.
53 They have *cut off* **exterminated** my life
in the *dungeon* **well**,
and *cast* **hand tossed** a stone upon me.
54 Waters *flowed over* **overflowed** mine head;
then I said, I am cut off.
55 I called upon thy name, O *LORD* **Yah Veh**,
out of the *low dungeon* **nether well**.
56 Thou hast heard my voice:
hide **conceal** not thine ear
at my *breathing* **respiration**, at my cry.
57 Thou drewest near in the day that I called upon thee:
thou saidst, *Fear* **Awe** not.
58 O *Lord* **Adonay**,
thou hast *pleaded* **defended**
the *causes* **defences** of my soul;
thou hast redeemed my life.
59 O *LORD* **Yah Veh**,
thou hast seen my *wrong* **writhing**:
judge thou my *cause* **judgment**.
60 Thou hast seen all their vengeance
and all their *imaginations* **machinations** against me.
61 Thou hast heard their reproach, O *LORD* **Yah Veh**,
and all their *imaginations* **machinations** against me;
62 The lips of those that rose *up* against me,
and their *device* **meditation** against me all the day.
63 *Behold* **Look at** their sitting *down*, and their rising *up*;
I am their *musick* **satire**.
64 *Render* **Return** unto them
a recompence **their dealings**,
O *LORD* **Yah Veh**, according to the work of their hands.
65 Give them *sorrow* **covering** of heart,
thy curse unto them.
66 Persecute and *destroy* **desolate** them in *anger* **wrath**
from under the heavens of *the LORD* **Yah Veh**.

THE FOURTH LAMENTATION

4 How is the gold *become dim* **faded**!
how is the most fine gold — **the good ore** changed!
the stones of the *sanctuary* **holies**
are poured out in the top of *every street* **all the outways**.
2 The *precious* **esteemed** sons of *Zion* **Siyon**,
comparable **balanced** to *fine* **pure** gold,
how are they *esteemed* **reckoned**
as *earthen pitchers* **pottery bottles**,
the work of the hands of the *potter* **former**!
3 Even the *sea monsters* *draw out* **strip** the breast,

they *give suck to* **suckle** their *young ones* **whelps**:
the daughter of my people is *become* cruel,
like the ostriches in the wilderness.
4 The tongue of the *sucking child* **suckling**
cleaveth to the roof of his mouth **adhereth to his palate**
for thirst:
the *young children* **infants** ask bread,
and no *man breaketh* **one spreadeth** it unto them.
5 They that did *feed* **eat** delicately
are *desolate* **desolated** in the *streets* **outways**:
they that were *brought up in* **entrusted with** scarlet
embrace dunghills.
6 For the *punishment of the iniquity* **perversity**
of the daughter of my people
is *greater than the punishment of* **greatened above**
the sin of Sodom,
that was *overthrown* **overturned** as in a *moment* **blink**,
and no hands *stayed on* **writhed over** her.
7 Her *Nazarites* **Separatists**
were *purer than* **purified as** snow,
they were **dazzling** whiter than milk,
they were more ruddy in body **their bones more reddened**
than *rubies* **pearls**,
their *polishing* **separatism** was of sapphire:
8 Their *visage* **form** is *blacker* **darker** than *a coal* **darkness**;
they are not *known* **recognized** in the *streets* **outways**:
their skin *cleaveth* **adhereth** to their bones;
it is withered, it is become like *a stick* **wood**.
9 They that be *slain* **pierced** with the sword
are better than they
that be *slain* **pierced** with *hunger* **famine**:
for these *pine* **flow** away,
stricken through **stabbed**
for *want of the fruits* **the produce** of the field.
10 The hands of the *pitiful* **mercied** women
have *sodden* **stewed** their own children:
they were their *meat* **chewing**
in the *destruction* **breech** of the daughter of my people.
11 *The LORD* **Yah Veh** hath accomplished his fury;
he hath poured out his fierce *anger* **wrath**,
and hath kindled a fire in *Zion* **Siyon**,
and it hath *devoured* **consumed** the foundations *thereof.*
12 The *kings* **sovereigns** of the earth,
and all *the inhabitants of* **that settled** the world,
would **should** not have *believed* **trusted**
that the *adversary* **tribulator** and the enemy
should have entered
into the *gates* **portals** of *Jerusalem* **Yeru Shalem**.
13 For the sins of her prophets,
and the *iniquities* **perversities** of her priests,
that have *shed* **poured** the blood of the just
in the midst of her,
14 They have wandered
as blind *men* in the *streets* **outways**,
they have polluted themselves with blood,
so that *men could not* **they are not able**
to touch their *garments* **robes**.
15 They *cried* **called** unto them,
Depart ye; **Turn aside!** *it is unclean;* **Foul!**
depart, depart **Turn aside! Turn aside!**
touch not: **Touch not!**
when they fled away and wandered,
they said among the *heathen* **goyim**,
They shall *no more* **never again** sojourn there.
16 The anger of *the LORD* **Yah Veh**
hath *divided* **allotted** them;
he *will no more regard* **shall never again scan** them:
they *respected* **bore** not the persons of the priests,
they *favoured* **granted** not **charism to** the elders.
17 As for us,
our eyes as yet *failed* **are finished off** for our vain help:
in our watching we have watched for a *nation* **goyim**
that could not save *us.*
18 They hunt our *steps* **paces**,
that we cannot go in our *streets* **broadways**:
our end is near, our days are fulfilled;
for our end is come.
19 Our *persecutors* **pursuers**
are swifter than the eagles of the *heaven* **heavens**:
they *hotly* pursued us upon the mountains,
they *laid wait* **lurked** for us in the wilderness.
20 The *breath* **spirit/wind** of our nostrils,
the anointed of *the LORD* **Yah Veh**,
was *taken* **captured** in their pits,
of whom we said,
Under his shadow
we shall live among the *heathen* **goyim**.
21 Rejoice and *be glad* **cheer**, O daughter of Edom,
that *dwellest* **settlest** in the land of *Uz* **Us**;
the cup also shall pass through unto thee:
thou shalt *be drunken* **intoxicate**,
and shalt *make* **strip** thyself naked.
22 *The punishment of thine iniquity* **Thy perversity**
is *accomplished* **consumated**, O daughter of *Zion* **Siyon**;
he *will* **shall** no more *carry* **exile** thee *away into captivity*:
he *will* **shall** visit *thine iniquity* **thy perversity**,
O daughter of Edom;
he *will discover* **shall expose** thy sins.

THE FIFTH LAMENTATION

5 Remember, O *LORD* **Yah Veh**,
what is come upon us:
consider **look**, and *behold* **see** our reproach.
2 Our inheritance is turned to strangers,
our houses to *aliens* **strangers**.
3 We are orphans and fatherless,
our mothers are as widows.
4 We have drunken our water for money;
our *wood* **timber** is *sold* **priced** unto us.
5 *Our necks are under persecution* **They pursue our necks**:
we labour, and *have no* rest **not**.
6 We have given the hand to the *Egyptians* **Misrayim**,
and to the Assyrians **to Ashshuriym**,
to be satisfied with bread.
7 Our fathers have sinned, and are not;
and we have borne their *iniquities* **perversities**.
8 Servants have *ruled* **reigned** over us:
there is none that *doth deliver* **separateth** us
out of their hand.
9 We gat our bread *with the peril of our lives* **by our souls**
because of the sword of the wilderness.
10 Our skin was *black* **shriveled** like an oven
because of the *terrible* **raging** famine.
11 They *ravished* **humbled** the women
in *Zion* **Siyon**,
and the *maids* **virgins**
in the cities of *Judah* **Yah Hudah**.
12 *Princes* **Governors** are hanged up by their hand:
the faces of elders were not *honoured* **esteemed**.
13 They *took* **lifted** the young men to grind,
and the *children* **lads**
fell **stumbled** under the *wood* **timber**.
14 The elders
have *ceased* **shabbathized** from the *gate* **portal**,
the young men from their *musick* **strumming**.
15 The joy of our heart *is ceased* **shabbathized**;
our **round** dance is turned into mourning.
16 The crown is fallen from our head:
woe unto us, that we have sinned!
17 For this our heart *is faint* **bleedeth**;
for these *things* our eyes *are dim* **darken**.
18 Because of the mountain of *Zion* **Siyon**,
which is desolate, the foxes walk upon it.
19 Thou, O *LORD* **Yah Veh**,
remainest for ever **settlest eternally**;
thy throne from generation to generation.
20 Wherefore dost thou forget us *for ever* **in perpetuity**,
and forsake us *so long* **for length of days of** time?
21 *Turn thou* **Return** us unto thee, O *LORD* **Yah Veh**,
and we shall *be turned* **return**;
renew our days as of *old* **antiquity**.
22 But **in spurning,**
thou hast *utterly rejected* **spurned** us;
thou art *very wroth* **mighty enraged** against us.

KEY TO INTERPRETING THE EXEGESES:
King James text is in regular type;
Text under exegeses is in oblique type;
Text of exegeses is in bold type.

THE VISIONS OF YESHA YAH

1 The vision of *Isaiah* **Yesha Yah** the son of *Amoz* **Amos**,
which he saw concerning
Judah **Yah Hudah** and *Jerusalem* **Yeru Shalem**
in the days of *Uzziah* **Uzzi Yah**, *Jotham* **Yah Tham**,
Ahaz **Ach Az**, and *Hezekiah* **Yechizq Yah**,
kings **sovereigns** of *Judah* **Yah Hudah**.
2 Hear, O heavens, and *give ear* **hearken**, O earth:
for *the LORD* **Yah Veh** hath *spoken* **worded**,
I have nourished and *brought up children* **raised sons**,
and they have rebelled against me.
3 The ox knoweth his *owner* **chatteler**,
and the *ass* **burro** his master's *crib* **manger**:
but *Israel* **Yisra El** doth not know,
my people doth not *consider* **discern**.
4 *Ah* **Ho** sinful *nation* **goyim**,
a people *laden* **heavy** with *iniquity* **perversity**,
a seed of *evildoers* **vilifiers**,
children **sons** that are *corrupters* **ruiners**:
they have forsaken *the LORD* **Yah Veh**,
they have *provoked* **scorned**
the Holy One of *Israel* **Yisra El** *unto anger*,
they are *gone away* **estranged** backward.
5 Why should ye be *stricken* **smitten** any more?
ye *will* **shall increase** revolt *more and more*:
the whole head is sick,
and the whole heart *faint* **bleedeth**.
6 From the sole of the foot even unto the head
there is no *soundness* **integrity** in it;
but wounds, and *bruises* **lashes**,
and *putrifying sores* **dripping wounds**:
they have not been *closed* **squeezed**, neither bound up,
neither *mollified* **tenderized** with ointment.
7 Your *country* **land** is desolate,
your cities are burned with fire:
your *land* **soil**, strangers devour it in your presence,
and it is desolate, as overthrown by strangers.
8 And the daughter of *Zion is left* **Siyon remaineth**
as a *cottage* **sukkoth/brush arbor** in a vineyard,
as a *lodge* **hammock**
in a *garden of cucumbers* **cucumber field**,
as a *besieged* **guarded** city.
9 *Except the LORD of hosts* **Unless Yah Veh Sabaoth**
had *left* **let remain** unto us
a very *small remnant* **few survivors**,
we should have been as *Sodom* **Sedom**,
and we should have been like unto *Gomorrah* **Amorah**.
10 Hear the word of *the LORD* **Yah Veh**,
ye *rulers* **commanders** of *Sodom* **Sedom**;
give ear **hearken** unto the *law* **torah** of our *God* **Elohim**,
ye people of *Gomorrah* **Amorah**.
11 *To what purpose* **Wherefore**
is the *multitude* **abundance** of your sacrifices unto me?
saith *the LORD* **Yah Veh**:
I am *full* **satiated**
of the *burnt—offerings* **holocausts** of rams,
and the fat of *fed beasts* **fatlings**;
and I delight not in the blood of bullocks,
or of lambs, or of he goats.
12 When ye come
to *appear before me* **be seen at my face**,
who hath *required* **besought** this at your hand,
to *tread* **trample** my courts?
13 *Bring* **Add** no more vain *oblations* **offerings**;
incense is an *abomination* **abhorrence** unto me;
the new moons and *sabbaths* **shabbaths**,
the calling of *assemblies* **convocations**,
I *cannot away with* **am unable**;
it is *iniquity* **mischief**,
even the *solemn meeting* **private assembly**.
14 Your new moons and your *appointed feasts* **seasons**
my soul hateth:
they are a *trouble* **burden** unto me;
I am weary to bear them.
15 And when ye spread forth your *hands* **palms**,
I *will hide* **shall conceal** mine eyes from you:
yea, when ye *make many* **abound** prayers,
I *will* **shall** not hear:
your hands are *full of* **filled with** blood.
16 *Wash* **Baptize** you, *make you clean* **purify you**;
put away **turn aside** the evil of your *doings* **exploitations**
from *before* **in front of** mine eyes;
cease to *do evil* **vilify**;
17 Learn to *do well* **well—please**;
seek judgment, *relieve* **blithe** the oppressed,
judge the *fatherless* **orphan**, plead for the widow.
18 Come *now* **I beseech**, and let us reason together,
saith *the LORD* **Yah Veh**:
though your sins be as scarlet,
they shall *be as white* **whiten** as snow;
though they be *red* **reddened** like crimson,
they shall be as wool.
19 If ye *be willing* **so** will and *obedient* **hearken**,
ye shall eat the good of the land:
20 But if ye refuse and rebel,
ye shall be devoured with the sword:
for the mouth of *the LORD* **Yah Veh**
hath *spoken it* **worded**.
21 How is the *faithful* **trustworthy** city
become an *harlot* **whore**!
it was full of judgment;
righteousness lodged **justness stayed overnight** in it;
but now murderers.
22 Thy silver is become dross,
thy *wine mixed* **potion diluted** with water:
23 Thy *princes are rebellious* **governors revolt**,
and — companions of thieves:
every one loveth *gifts* **bribes**,
and *followeth after rewards* **pursueth bribes**:
they judge not the *fatherless* **orphan**,
neither doth the *cause* **plea** of the widow
come unto them.
24 *Therefore saith the Lord, the LORD of hosts*
An oracle of Adonay Yah Veh Sabaoth,
the *mighty One* **Almighty** of *Israel* **Yisra El**,
Ah **Ho**, I *will ease me* **shall sigh**
of mine adversaries **over my tribulators**,
and avenge me of mine enemies:
25 And I *will* **shall** turn my hand upon thee,
and *purely purge* **in purity refine** away thy dross,
and *take away* **turn aside** all thy tin:
26 And I *will* **shall** restore thy judges as at the first,
and thy counsellors as at the beginning:
afterward thou shalt be called,
The city of *righteousness* **justness**,
the *faithful* **trustworthy** city.
27 *Zion* **Siyon** shall be redeemed with judgment,
and *her converts* **those of her that return**
with *righteousness* **justness**.
28 And the *destruction* **breaking**
of the *transgressors* **rebels**
and of the sinners shall be together,
and they that forsake *the LORD* **Yah Veh**
shall be *consumed* **finished off**.
29 For they shall *be ashamed* **shame**
of the **mighty** oaks which ye have desired,
and ye shall *be confounded* **blush**
for the gardens that ye have chosen.
30 For ye shall be as an oak whose leaf *fadeth* **withereth**,
and as a garden that hath no water.
31 And the *strong* **powerful** shall be as *tow* **tuft**,
and *the maker of it* **his deeds** as a spark,
and they shall both burn together,
and none shall quench *them*.

THE LAST DAYS

2 The word
that *Isaiah* **Yesha Yah** the son of *Amoz* **Amos**
saw concerning
Judah **Yah Hudah** and *Jerusalem* **Yeru Shalem**.
2 And it shall *come to pass* **become,** in the last days,
that the mountain
of the *LORD'S* house **of Yah Veh**
shall be established in the top of the mountains,
and shall be *exalted* **lifted** above the hills;
and all *nations* **goyim** shall flow unto it.
3 And many people shall go and say,

Come ye, and let us *go up* **ascend**
to the mountain of *the LORD* **Yah Veh**,
to the house of *the God* **Elohim** of *Jacob* **Yaaqov**;
and he *will* **shall** teach us of his ways,
and we *will* **shall** walk in his paths:
for out of *Zion* **Siyon** shall go forth the *law* **torah**,
and the word of *the LORD* **Yah Veh**
from *Jerusalem* **Yeru Shalem**.
4 And he shall judge among the *nations* **goyim**,
and shall *rebuke* **reprove** many people:
and they shall *beat* **forge** their swords into plowshares,
and their spears into *pruninghooks* **psalmpicks**:
nation **goyim** shall not lift *up* sword against *nation* **goyim**,
neither shall they learn war any more.
5 O house of *Jacob* **Yaaqov**, come ye,
and let us walk in the light of *the LORD* **Yah Veh**.
6 Therefore thou hast *forsaken* **abandoned** thy people
the house of *Jacob* **Yaaqov**,
because they *be replenished* **fulfilled** from the east,
and are *soothsayers* **cloudgazers**
like the *Philistines* **Peleshethiym**,
and they *please themselves* **clap**
in **with** the children of strangers.
7 Their land also is *full* **filled** of silver and gold,
neither is there any end of their treasures;
their land is also *full* **filled** of horses,
neither is there any end of their chariots:
8 Their land also is *full* **filled** of idols;
they *worship* **prostrate to** the work of their own hands,
that which their own fingers have *made* **worked**:
9 And *the mean man boweth down* **humanity prostrateth**,
and *the great man humbleth himself* **man abaseth**:
therefore *forgive* **lift** them not.
10 Enter into the rock, and hide thee in the dust,
for **at the face of** fear of *the LORD* **Yah Veh**,
and for the *glory* **majesty** of his *majesty* **pomp**.
11 The lofty *looks* **eyes** of *man* **humanity**
shall *be humbled* **abase**,
and the haughtiness of men shall *be bowed down* **prostrate**,
and *the LORD* **Yah Veh** alone
shall be exalted in that day.
12 For the day of *the LORD of hosts* **Yah Veh Sabaoth**
shall be upon
every one that is proud **all the pompous** and lofty,
and upon *every one* **all** that is lifted *up*;
and he shall be *brought low* **abased**:
13 And upon all the cedars of Lebanon,
that are high and lifted up,
and upon all the oaks of Bashan,
14 And upon all the high mountains,
and upon all the hills that are lifted *up*,
15 And upon every high tower,
and upon every *fenced* **fortified** wall,
16 And upon all the ships of Tarshish,
and upon all *pleasant pictures* **observations of desire**.
17 And the loftiness of *man* **humanity**
shall *be bowed down* **prostrate**,
and the haughtiness of men shall *be made low* **abase**:
and *the LORD* **Yah Veh** alone
shall be exalted in that day.
18 And the idols
he shall *utterly abolish* **totally pass away**.
19 And they shall go into the *holes* **caves** of the rocks,
and into the caves of the *earth* **dust**,
for **at the face of** fear of *the LORD* **Yah Veh**,
and for the *glory* **majesty** of his *majesty* **pomp**,
when he ariseth to *shake terribly* **terrify** the earth.
20 In that day *a man* **humanity**
shall cast his idols of silver, and his idols of gold,
which they *made each one* **worked** for himself
to *worship* **prostrate to**,
to the *moles* **burrowers** and to the bats;
21 To go into the *clefts* **crevices** of the rocks,
and into the *tops* **clefts** of the *ragged* rocks,
for **at the face of** fear of *the LORD* **Yah Veh**,
and for the *glory* **majesty** of his *majesty* **pomp**,
when he ariseth to *shake terribly* **terrify** the earth.
22 Cease ye from *man* **humanity**,
whose breath is in his nostrils:
for wherein is he to be *accounted of* **fabricated**?

JUDGMENT ON YERU SHALEM AND YAH HUDAH

3 For, behold,
the Lord, the LORD of hosts **Adonay Yah Veh Sabaoth**,
doth *take away* **turn aside**
from *Jerusalem* **Yeru Shalem** and from *Judah* **Yah Hudah**
the *stay* **support** and the *staff* **support**,
the whole *stay* **support** of bread,
and the whole *stay* **support** of water,
2 The mighty *man*, and the man of war,
the judge, and the prophet,
and the *prudent* **diviner**, and the *ancient* **aged**,
3 The *captain* **governor** of fifty,
and the *honourable man* **lifted face**,
and the counsellor,
and the *cunning artificer* **wise engraver**,
and the *eloquent* **discerning** orator.
4 And I *will* **shall** give
children **lads** to be their *princes* **governors**,
and *babes* **freaks** shall *rule* **reign** over them.
5 And the people shall be *oppressed* **exacted**,
every one by another **man upon man**,
and every one by his neighbour
even man upon his friend:
the *child* **lad** shall *behave himself proudly* **abuse**
against the *ancient* **aged**,
and the base against the honourable.
6 When a man shall *take hold of* **apprehend** his brother
of the house of his father, *saying*,
Thou hast clothing, be thou our *ruler* **commander**,
and let this *ruin* **stumblingblock** be under thy hand:
7 In that day shall he *swear* **lift his hand**,
saying, I *will* **shall** not be *an healer* **a binder**;
for in my house is neither bread nor clothing:
make **set** me not a *ruler* **commander** of the people.
8 For *Jerusalem is ruined* **Yeru Shalem hath faltered**,
and *Judah is* **Yah Hudah hath** fallen:
because their tongue and their *doings* **exploitations**
are against *the LORD* **Yah Veh**,
to *provoke* **rebel against** the eyes of his *glory* **honour**.
9 The *shew* **partiality** of their *countenance* **face**
doth *witness* **answer** against them;
and they *declare* **tell** their sin as *Sodom* **Sedom**,
they *hide* **conceal** it not.
Woe unto their soul!
for they have *rewarded* **dealt** evil unto themselves.
10 Say ye to the *righteous* **just**,
that it shall be *well with him* **for good**:
for they shall eat the fruit of their *doings* **exploitations**.
11 Woe unto the wicked! *it shall be ill with him* — **evil**:
for the *reward* **dealing** of his hands
shall be *given* **worked** him.
12 As for my people,
children **exploiters** are their *oppressors* **exactors**,
and women *rule* **reign** over them.
O my people, they which *lead* **blithe** thee
cause thee to *err* **stray**,
and *destroy* **swallow** the way of thy paths.
13 *The LORD standeth up* **Yah Veh stationeth** to plead,
and standeth to *judge* **plead the cause of** the people.
14 *The LORD will* **Yah Veh shall** enter into judgment
with the *ancients* **elders** of his people,
and the *princes* **governors** *thereof*:
for ye have *eaten up* **burnt** the vineyard;
the *spoil* **stripping** of the *poor* **humble** is in your houses.
15 What mean ye that ye *beat* **crush** my people *to pieces*,
and grind the faces of the *poor* **humble**?
saith the Lord GOD of hosts
an oracle of Adonay Yah Veh Sabaoth.
16 *Moreover the LORD* **Yah Veh** saith,
Because the daughters of *Zion* **Siyon** are *haughty* **lifted**,
and walk with stretched forth *necks* **throats**
and *wanton eyes* **ogling**,
walking and *mincing* **waddling** *as* they go,
and *making a* tinkling with their feet:
17 Therefore *the Lord* **Adonay**
will smite with a scab **shall scrape**
the *crown of the head* **scalp**
of the daughters of *Zion* **Siyon**,
and *the LORD* **Yah Veh**
will discover **shall strip naked**

their *secret parts* **pudenda**.
18 In that day
the Lord will take away **Adonay shall turn aside**
the bravery of their tinkling ornaments about their feet
their adornments of tinklers,
and *their cauls* **nets**,
and their *round tires like the moon* **ornaments**,
19 The *chains* **pendants**, and the bracelets,
and the *mufflers* **veils**,
20 The *bonnets* **tiaras**,
and the *ornaments of the legs* **anklets**,
and the *headbands* **bands**,
and the *tablets* **housings of the soul**,
and the *earrings* **amulets**,
21 The *rings* **signets**, and *nose jewels* **nostrilrings**,
22 The *changeable suits of apparel* **mantles**,
and the mantles,
and the *wimples* **cloaks**, and the *crisping pins* **pockets**,
23 The *glasses* **rolls**, and the *fine linen* **wraps**,
and the *hoods* **turbans**, and the vails.
24 And it shall *come to pass* **become**,
that instead of sweet *smell* **spice**
there shall be *stink* **putridity**;
and instead of a girdle
a *rent* **noose**;
and instead of *well set hair* **the work of the curler**
baldness;
and instead of a *stomacher* **festive mantle**
a *girding* **girdle** of *sackcloth* **saq**;
and burning **scarring** instead of beauty.
25 Thy men shall fall by the sword,
and thy *mighty* **might** in the war.
26 And her *gates lament* **portals shall mourn** and mourn;
and she being *desolate* **exonerated**
shall *sit* **settle** upon the *ground* **land**.

THE SPROUT OF YAH VEH

4 And in that day
seven women shall take hold of one man, saying,
We *will* **shall** eat our own bread,
and *wear* **enrobe** our own apparel:
only let us be called by thy name,
to *take away* **gather** our reproach.
2 In that day
shall the *branch* **sprout** of *the LORD* **Yah Veh**
be *beautiful* **splendid** and *glorious* **honourable**,
and the fruit of the earth
shall be *excellent* **for pomp** and *comely* **adornment**
for *them that are escaped* **the escapees** of *Israel* **Yisra El**.
3 And it shall *come to pass* **become**,
that he that *is left* **surviveth** in *Zion* **Siyon**,
and he that remaineth in *Jerusalem* **Yeru Shalem**,
shall be *called* **said** holy,
even every one
that is *written among the living* **inscribed for life**
in *Jerusalem* **Yeru Shalem**:
4 When *the Lord* **Adonay**
shall have *washed away* **baptized** the *filth* **dung**
of the daughters of *Zion* **Siyon**,
and shall have *purged* **cleansed**
the blood of *Jerusalem* **Yeru Shalem**
from the midst *thereof*
by the spirit of judgment, and by the spirit of burning.
5 And *the LORD will* **Yah Veh shall** create
upon every dwelling place of mount *Zion* **Siyon**,
and upon her *assemblies* **convocations**,
a cloud and smoke by day,
and the *shining* **brilliance** of a flaming fire by night:
for upon all the *glory* **honour** shall be a *defence* **canopy**.
6 And there shall be *a tabernacle* **sukkoth/brush arbors**
for a shadow in the *daytime* **day** from the heat,
and for a place of refuge,
and for a covert from *storm* **flood** and from rain.

SONG OF THE VINEYARD

5 *Now* **I beseech,**
will **shall** I sing to my *wellbeloved* **beloved**
a song of my beloved touching his vineyard.
My *wellbeloved* **beloved** hath a vineyard
in *a very fruitful hill* **the horn of the son of oil**:
2 And he *fenced* **walled** it,
and *gathered out* **stoned** the stones *thereof*,
and planted it with the *choicest vine* **choice**,
and built a tower in the midst of it,
and also made a *winepress* **trough** therein:
and he *looked* **awaited**
that it should *bring forth* **work** grapes,
and it *brought forth wild grapes* **worked stinkweeds**.
3 And now,
O *inhabitants* **settlers** of *Jerusalem* **Yeru Shalem**,
and men of *Judah* **Yah Hudah**,
judge, I *pray* **beseech** you,
betwixt me and my vineyard.
4 What could have been
done **worked** more to my vineyard,
that I have not *done* **worked** in it?
wherefore **why**, when I *looked* **awaited**
that it should *bring forth* **work** grapes,
brought it forth wild grapes **it worked stinkweeds**?
5 And now go to;
I *will tell* **shall make** you **know**
what I *will do* **shall work** to my vineyard:
I *will take away* **shall turn aside** the hedge *thereof*,
and it shall be *eaten up* **burnt**;
and *break down* **breach** the wall *thereof*,
and it shall be *trodden down* **trampled**:
6 And I *will lay it waste* **shall place it desolate**:
it shall not be *pruned* **plucked**, nor *digged* **hoed**;
but there shall *come up* **ascend** briers and thorns:
I *will* **shall** also *command* **misvah** the **thick** clouds
that they rain no rain upon it.
7 For the vineyard of *the LORD of hosts* **Yah Veh Sabaoth**
is the house of *Israel* **Yisra El**,
and the men of *Judah* **Yah Hudah**
his *pleasant* plant **of delights**:
and he *looked for* **awaited** judgment,
but behold oppression;
for *righteousness* **justness**,
but behold a cry.

HO AND JUDGMENT

8 *Woe* **Ho** unto them that *join* **touch** house to house,
that *lay* **approach** field to field,
till *there be no* **the final** place,
that they may be *placed* **settled** alone
in the midst of the earth!
9 In mine ears, *said the LORD of hosts* **Yah Veh Sabaoth**,
Of a truth **If not** many houses shall *be* **become** desolate,
even great and *fair* **good**, without *inhabitant* **settler**.
10 *Yea* **Assuredly**, ten acres of vineyard
shall *yield* **work** one bath,
and the seed of an *homer* **chomer**
shall *yield* **work** an ephah.
11 *Woe* **Ho** unto them
that *rise up* **start** early in the morning,
that they may *follow strong drink* **pursue intoxicants**;
that *continue until night* **linger in the evening breeze**,
till wine inflame them!
12 And the harp, and the *viol* **bagpipe**,
the *tabret* **tambourine**, and pipe, and wine,
are in their *feasts* **banquets**:
but they *regard* **scan** not
the *work* **deeds** of *the LORD* **Yah Veh**,
neither *consider* **see** the *operation* **work** of his hands.
13 Therefore my people are *gone into captivity* **exiled**,
because they have no knowledge:
and their honourable men are famished,
and their multitude *dried up* **parched** with thirst.
14 Therefore *hell* **sheol** hath enlarged *herself* **her soul**,
and *opened* **gaped** her mouth without *measure* **statute**:
and their glory, and their multitude,
and their *pomp* **uproar**,
and he that *rejoiceth* **jumpeth for joy**,
shall descend into it.
15 And *the mean man* **humanity**
shall *be brought down* **prostrate**,
and *the mighty* man shall *be humbled* **abase**,
and the eyes of the lofty shall *be humbled* **abase**:
16 But *the LORD of hosts* **Yah Veh Sabaoth**
shall be *exalted* **lifted** in judgment,
and *God* **El** that is holy
shall be *sanctified* **hallowed** in *righteousness* **justness**.
17 Then shall the lambs *feed* **graze**

after their *manner* **word**,
and the *waste places* **parched areas**
of the *fat ones* **fatlings**
shall *strangers* **sojourners** eat.
18 *Woe* **Ho** unto them that draw *iniquity* **perversity**
with cords of vanity,
and sin as it were with a *cart* **wagon** rope:
19 That say, Let him *make speed* **hasten**,
and hasten his work, that we may see it:
and let the counsel of the Holy One of *Israel* **Yisra El**
draw nigh **approach** and come, that we may know it!
20 *Woe* **Ho** unto them that *call* **say**
concerning evil good, and good evil;
that *put* **set** darkness for light, and light for darkness;
that *put* **set** bitter for sweet, and sweet for bitter!
21 *Woe* **Ho** unto them that are wise in their own eyes,
and *prudent* **discerning** in their *own sight* **face**!
22 *Woe* **Ho** unto them that are mighty to drink wine,
and men of *strength* **valour**
to *mingle strong drink* **mix intoxicants**:
23 Which justify the wicked for *reward* **a bribe**,
and *take away* **turn aside**
the *righteousness* **justness** of the *righteous* **just** from him!
24 Therefore as the **tongue of** fire devoureth the stubble,
and the flame *consumeth* **slacketh** the *chaff* **hay**,
so their root shall be as *rottenness* **putridity**,
and their blossom shall *go up* **ascend** as dust:
because they have *cast away* **spurned** the *law* **torah**
of *the LORD of hosts* **Yah Veh Sabaoth**,
and *despised* **scorned** the *word* **saying**
of the Holy One of *Israel* **Yisra El**.
25 Therefore is the *anger* **wrath** of *the LORD* **Yah Veh**
kindled against his people,
and he hath stretched forth his hand against them,
and hath smitten them:
and the hills *did tremble* **quaked**,
and their carcases were *torn* **sweepings**
in the midst of the *streets* **outways**.
For all this his *anger* **wrath** is not turned away,
but his hand is stretched out still.
26 And he *will* **shall** lift *up* an ensign
to the *nations* **goyim** from far,
and *will* **shall** hiss unto them from the end of the earth:
and, behold, they shall come *with speed* **quickly,** swiftly:
27 None shall *be weary* **languish** nor *stumble* **falter**
among them;
none shall slumber nor sleep;
neither shall the girdle of their loins be loosed,
nor the latchet of their shoes be *broken* **torn**:
28 Whose arrows are *sharp* **pointened**,
and all their bows bent,
their horses' hoofs shall be *counted* **fabricated** like flint,
and their *wheels* **whirlers** like a *whirlwind* **hurricane**:
29 Their roaring shall be like a **roaring** lion,
they shall roar like *young lions* **whelps**:
yea, they shall *roar* **growl**, and *lay* **take** hold of the prey,
and shall *carry* **slip** it away *safe*
and none shall *deliver it* **rescue**.
30 And in that day they shall *roar* **growl** against them
like the *roaring* **growling** of the sea:
and if one look unto the land,
behold darkness and *sorrow* **tribulation**,
and the light is darkened in the *heavens* **setting** *thereof.*

THE VISION OF YESHA YAH

6 In the year that *king Uzziah* **sovereign Uzzi Yah** died
I saw also *the Lord* **Adonay** sitting upon a throne,
high and lifted up,
and his *train* **drape** filled the *temple* **manse**.
2 Above it stood the *seraphims* **seraphim**:
each one had six wings — **six wings to one**;
with *twain* **two** he covered his face,
and with *twain* **two** he covered his feet,
and with *twain* **two** he *did fly* **flew**.
3 And one *cried* **called** unto another, and said,
Holy, holy, holy, *is the LORD of hosts* **Yah Veh Sabaoth**:
the whole earth is full of his glory.
4 And the *posts* **hinges** of the *door* **threshold**
moved **shook** at the voice of him that cried,
and the house was filled with smoke.
5 Then said I, Woe is me! for I am *undone* **mute**;
because I am a man of *unclean* **foul** lips,
and I *dwell* **settle** in the midst of a people
of *unclean* **fouled** lips:
for mine eyes have seen the *King* **Sovereign**,
the LORD of hosts **Yah Veh Sabaoth**.
6 Then flew one of the *seraphims* **seraphim** unto me,
having a *live coal* **hot stone** in his hand,
which he had taken with the tongs
from off the **sacrifice** altar:
7 And he *laid* **touched** it upon my mouth,
and said, *Lo* **Behold**, this hath touched thy lips;
and thine *iniquity* **perversity** is *taken away* **turned aside**,
and thy sin *purged* **kapared/atoned**.

THE COMMISSION OF YESHA YAH

8 Also I heard the voice of *the Lord* **Adonay**, saying,
Whom shall I send, and who *will* **shall** go for us?
Then said I, Here am I; send me.
9 And he said, Go, and *tell* **say to** this people,
In hearing, Hear ye *indeed*, but *understand* **discern** not;
and **in seeing,** see ye *indeed*, but *perceive* **know** not.
10 *Make* **Fatten** the heart of this people *fat*,
and *make* **burden** their ears *heavy*,
and *shut* **stroke** their eyes;
lest they see with their eyes, and hear with their ears,
and *understand* **discern** with their heart,
and convert, and be healed.
11 Then said I, *Lord* **Adonay**, how long?
And he *answered* **said**,
Until the cities be wasted without *inhabitant* **settler**,
and the houses without *man* **humanity**,
and the *land* **soil** be **wasted**
utterly desolate — **a desolation**,
12 And *the LORD* **Yah Veh**
have **far** removed *men far away* **humanity**,
and there be a great forsaking in the midst of the land.
13 But yet in it shall be a tenth, and it shall return,
and shall be *eaten* **burnt**:
as *a teil* **an oak** tree, and as an oak,
whose *substance* **stump** is in them,
when they cast *their leaves*:
so the holy seed shall be the *substance* **stumps** *thereof.*

WAR AGAINST YERU SHALEM

7 And it *came to pass* **became,**
in the days of *Ahaz* **Ach Az**,
the son of *Jotham* **Yah Tham**,
the son of *Uzziah* **Uzzi Yah**,
king **sovereign** of *Judah* **Yah Hudah**,
that *Rezin* **Resin** the *king* **sovereign** of *Syria* **Aram**,
and *Pekah* **Peqach** the son of *Remaliah* **Remal Yah**,
king **sovereign** of *Israel* **Yisra El**,
went up toward Jerusalem **ascended to Yeru Shalem**
to war against it, but could not *prevail* **fight** against it.
2 And it was told the house of David, saying,
Syria is confederate **Aram resteth**
with *Ephraim* **Ephrayim**.
And his heart *was moved* **shook**,
and the heart of his people,
as the trees of the *wood are moved* **forest shake**
with **at the face of** the wind.
3 Then said *the LORD* **Yah Veh** unto *Isaiah* **Yesha Yah**,
Go forth *now* **I beseech,** to meet *Ahaz* **Ach Az**,
thou, and *Shearjashub* **Shear Yashub** thy son,
at the end of the *conduit* **channel**
of the *upper* **most high** pool
in the highway of the fuller's field;
4 And say unto him, *Take heed* **On guard**,
and *be quiet* **rest**; *fear* **awe** not,
neither *be fainthearted* **tenderize thy heart**
for the two tails of these smoking *firebrands* **brands**,
for the *fierce anger* **fuming wrath**
of *Rezin* **Resin** with *Syria* **Aram**,
and of the son of *Remaliah* **Remal Yah**.
5 Because *Syria* **Aram**, *Ephraim* **Ephrayim**,
and the son of *Remaliah* **Remal Yah**,
have *taken* **counselled** evil *counsel* against thee, saying,
6 Let us *go up* **ascend** against *Judah* **Yah Hudah**,
and *vex* **loathe** it,
and let us *make a breach therein* **split it** for us,
and *set a king* **reign a sovereign** in the midst of it,
even the son of *Tabeal* **Tabe El**:

7 Thus saith *the Lord GOD* **Adonay Yah Veh**,
It shall not *stand* **rise**,
neither shall it *come to pass* **become**.
8 For the head of *Syria* **Aram** is *Damascus* **Dammeseq**,
and the head of *Damascus* **Dammeseq** is *Rezin* **Resin**;
and within *threescore* **sixty** and five years
shall *Ephraim* **Ephrayim** be broken,
that it be not **from** a people.
9 And the head of *Ephraim* **Ephrayim**
is *Samaria* **Shomeron**,
and the head of *Samaria* **Shomeron**
is *Remaliah's* **Remal Yah's** son.
If ye *will* **shall** not *believe* **trust**,
surely ye shall not be *established* **trustworthy**.

THE SIGN OF IMMANU EL

10 Moreover *the LORD* **Yah Veh**
spake again **added to word** unto *Ahaz* **Ach Az**, saying,
11 Ask thee a sign of *the LORD* **Yah Veh** thy *God* **Elohim**;
ask it either in *the depth* **deepening**,
or in *the height* **heightening** above.
12 But *Ahaz* **Ach Az** said, I *will* **shall** not ask,
neither *will I tempt the LORD* **shall I test Yah Veh**.
13 And he said, Hear ye now, O house of David;
Is it *a small thing* **petty** for you to weary men,
but *will* **shall** ye weary my *God* **Elohim** also?
14 Therefore *the Lord* **Adonay** himself
shall give you a sign;
Behold, a virgin shall conceive, and bear a son,
and shall call his name *Immanuel* **Immanu El**.
15 Butter and honey shall he eat,
that he may know to refuse the evil,
and choose the good.
16 For before the *child* **lad** shall know to refuse the evil,
and choose the good,
the *land* **soil** that thou abhorrest shall be forsaken
at the face of both her *kings* **sovereigns**.
17 *The LORD* **Yah Veh** shall bring upon thee,
and upon thy people, and upon thy father's house,
days that have not come,
from the day that *Ephraim* **Ephrayim**
departed **turned aside** from *Judah* **Yah Hudah**;
even the *king* **sovereign** of *Assyria* **Ashshur**.
18 And it shall *come to pass* **become,** in that day,
that *the LORD* **Yah Veh** shall hiss for the fly
that is in the *uttermost part* **end**
of the rivers of *Egypt* **Misrayim**,
and for the bee that is in the land of *Assyria* **Ashshur**.
19 And they shall come, and shall rest all of them
in the *desolate valleys* **wadies of desolations**,
and in the holes of the rocks,
and upon all thorns, and upon all *bushes* **pastures**.
20 In the same day shall *the Lord* **Adonay**
shave with a razor *that is hired* **the hireling**,
namely, by them beyond the river,
by the *king* **sovereign** of *Assyria* **Ashshur**,
the head, and the hair of the feet:
and it shall also *consume* **scrape away** the beard.
21 And it shall *come to pass* **become**, in that day,
that a man shall *nourish* **keep alive**
a young *cow* **heifer of the herd**, and two *sheep* **flock**;
22 And it shall *come to pass* **become**,
for the abundance of milk that they shall *give* **work**
he shall eat butter:
for butter and honey shall every one eat
that *is left* **remaineth** in the land.
23 And it shall *come to pass* **become**, in that day,
that every place shall be,
where there were
a thousand vines at a thousand silverlings,
it shall *even* be for briers and thorns.
24 With arrows and with bows shall *men* come thither;
because all the land shall become briers and thorns.
25 And on all hills
that shall be *digged* **hoed** with the *mattock* **hoe**,
there shall not come thither the fear of briers and thorns:
but it shall be for the sending forth of oxen,
and for the *treading* **trampling** of *lesser cattle* **lambs**.

THE FALL OF DAMMESEQ AND SHOMERON

8 *Moreover the LORD* **Yah Veh** said unto me,
Take thee a great roll,
and *write* **inscribe** in it with a man's *pen* **stylus**
concerning *Mahershalalhashbaz* **Mahers Halal Hash Baz**.
2 And I *took* **witnessed** unto me
faithful **trustworthy** witnesses to record,
Uriah **Uri Yah** the priest,
and *Zechariah* **Zechar Yah**
the son of *Jeberechiah* **Yeberech Yah**.
3 And I *went unto* **approached** the prophetess;
and she conceived, and bare a son.
Then said *the LORD* **Yah Veh** to me,
Call his name
Mahershalalhashbaz **Mahers Halal Hash Baz**.
4 For before the *child* **lad** shall have knowledge
to *cry* **call out**, My father, and my mother,
the *riches* **valuables** of *Damascus* **Dammeseq**
and the spoil of *Samaria* **Shomeron**
shall be *taken away before* **borne at the face**
of the *king* **sovereign** of *Assyria* **Ashshur**.
5 *The LORD* **Yah Veh**
spake also **added to word** unto me *again*, saying,
6 Forasmuch as this people
refuseth the waters of *Shiloah* **Shiloach**
that go *softly* **gently**, and *rejoice* **in joy**
in *Rezin* **Resin** and *Remaliah's* **Remal Yah's** son;
7 *Now* therefore, behold,
the Lord bringeth up **Adonay ascendeth** upon them
the waters of the river, *strong* **mighty** and many,
even the *king* **sovereign** of *Assyria* **Ashshur**,
and all his *glory* **honour**:
and he shall *come up* **ascend**
over all his *channels* **reservoirs**,
and go over all his banks:
8 And he shall pass through *Judah* **Yah Hudah**;
he shall overflow and *go* **pass** over,
he shall *reach even* **touch** to the neck;
and the stretching out of his wings
shall fill the breadth of thy land, O *Immanuel* **Immanu El**.
9 *Associate yourselves* **Be broken**, O ye people,
and ye shall be broken *in pieces*;
and *give ear* **hearken**, all ye of far *countries* **lands**:
gird *yourselves*, and ye shall be broken *in pieces*;
gird *yourselves*, and ye shall be broken *in pieces*.
10 **In counselling**, *Take* counsel *together*,
and it shall *come to nought* **break**;
speak **word** the word, and it shall not *stand* **rise**:
for *God* **El** is with us.
11 For *the LORD* **Yah Veh**
spake **said** thus to me with a strong hand,
and *instructed* **disciplined** me
that I should not walk in the way of this people, saying,
12 Say ye not, *A confederacy* **Conspiracy**,
to all them to whom this people shall say,
A confederacy **Conspiracy**;
neither *fear* **awe** ye their *fear* **awesomeness**,
nor be *afraid* **awed**.
13 *Sanctify* **Hallow**
the LORD of hosts **Yah Veh Sabaoth** himself;
and let him be your *fear* **awesomeness**,
and let him be your dread.
14 And he shall be for a *sanctuary* **holies**;
but for a stone of *stumbling* **stubbing**
and for a rock of offence
to both the houses of *Israel* **Yisra El**,
for a *gin* **snare** and for a snare
to the *inhabitants* **settlers** of *Jerusalem* **Yeru Shalem**.
15 And many among them shall *stumble* **falter**, and fall,
and be broken, and be snared, and *be taken* **captured**.
16 Bind up the *testimony* **witness**,
seal the *law* **torah** among my disciples.
17 And I *will wait upon the LORD* **shall await Yah Veh**,
that hideth his face from the house of *Jacob* **Yaaqov**,
and I *will look for* **shall await** him.
18 Behold, I and the children
whom *the LORD* **Yah Veh** hath given me
are for signs and for *wonders* **omens** in *Israel* **Yisra El**
from *the LORD of hosts* **Yah Veh Sabaoth**,
which *dwelleth* **tabernacleth** in mount *Zion* **Siyon**.
19 And when they shall say unto you,
Seek unto *them that have familiar spirits* **spiritists**,
and unto *wizards* **knowers**

that *peep* **chirp**, and that mutter:
should not a people seek unto their *God* **Elohim**?
for the living to the dead?
20 To the *law* **torah** and to the *testimony* **witness**:
if they *speak* **say** not according to this word,
it is because there is no *light* **dawn** in them.
21 And they shall pass through it,
hardly bestead **hardened** and *hungry* **famished**:
and it shall *come to pass* **become**,
that when they shall *be hungry* **famish**,
they shall *fret themselves* **enrage** and *curse* **abase**
their *king* **sovereign** and their *God* **Elohim**,
and *look* **face** upward.
22 And they shall look unto the earth;
and behold *trouble* **tribulation** and darkness,
dimness **darkness** of *anguish* **distress**;
and they shall be *driven* **expelled** to darkness.

A PROMISE OF LIGHT

9 Nevertheless the *dimness* **obscurity** shall not be such
as *was* in her *vexation* **narrowness**,
when at the first **time** he lightly afflicted
the land of Zebulun and the land of Naphtali,
and afterward *did more grievously afflict* **honoured** her
by the way of the sea, beyond *Jordan* **Yarden**,
in *Galilee* **Galiyl** of the *nations* **goyim**.
2 The people that walked in darkness
have seen a great light:
they that *dwell* **settle** in the land of the shadow of death,
upon them hath the light *shined* **illuminated**.
3 Thou hast *multiplied* **greatened** the *nation* **goyim**,
and not *increased* **greatened** the *joy* **cheerfulness**:
they *joy before thee* **cheer at thy face**
according to the *joy* **cheerfulness** in harvest,
and *as men rejoice* **twirl** when they *divide* **allot** the spoil.
4 For thou hast broken the yoke of his burden,
and the *staff* **rod** of his shoulder,
the *rod* **scion** of his *oppressor* **exactor**,
as in the day of *Midian* **Midyan**.
5 For every *battle* **boot** of the *warrior* **booted**
is with confused noise **quaketh,**
and garments rolled in blood;
but this shall be with burning *and* fuel of fire.

A CHILD IS BORN, A SON IS GIVEN

6 For unto us a child is born, unto us a son is given:
and the *government* **dominion**
shall be upon his shoulder:
and his name° shall be called
Wonderful **Marvelous**, Counsellor,
The mighty God **Mighty El**,
The everlasting **Eternal** Father,
The Prince **Governor** of *Peace* **Shalom**.

°singular

7 Of the increase
of his *government* **dominion** and *peace* **shalom**
there shall be no end,
upon the throne of David,
and upon his *kingdom* **sovereigndom**,
to *order* **establish** it, and to *establish* **support** it
with judgment and with *justice* **justness**
from henceforth even *for ever* **eternally**.
The zeal of *the LORD of hosts* **Yah Veh Sabaoth**
will perform **shall work** this.

THE WRATH OF YAH VEH

8 *The Lord* **Adonay** sent a word into *Jacob* **Yaaqov**,
and it hath *lighted* **fallen** upon *Israel* **Yisra El**.
9 And all the people shall know,
even Ephraim **Ephrayim**
and the *inhabitant* **settler** of *Samaria* **Shomeron**,
that say **saying**
in the *pride* **pomp** and *stoutness* **greatness** of heart,
10 The bricks are fallen down,
but we *will* **shall** build with hewn stones:
the sycomores are cut down,
but we *will* **shall** change them into cedars.
11 Therefore *the LORD* **Yah Veh**
shall *set up* **loft** the *adversaries* **tribulators** of *Rezin* **Resin**
against him,
and *join* **cover** his enemies *together*;
12 The *Syrians before* **Aramiym in front**,
and the *Philistines* **Peleshethiym** behind;
and they shall devour *Israel* **Yisra El** with open mouth.
For all this his *anger* **wrath** is not turned away,
but his hand is stretched out still.
13 For the people turneth not unto him that smiteth them,
neither do they seek
the LORD of hosts **Yah Veh Sabaoth**.
14 Therefore *the LORD* **Yah Veh**
will **shall** cut off from *Israel* **Yisra El**
head and tail, *branch* **palm leaf** and rush, in one day.
15 The *ancient* **elder** and *honourable* **lifted face**,
he is the head;
and the prophet that teacheth *lies* **falsehood**,
he is the tail.
16 For *the leaders of* this people **that blithe them**
cause them to *err* **stray**;
and they that are *led* **blithed** *of them*
are *destroyed* **swallowed**.
17 Therefore *the Lord* **Adonay**
shall *have no joy* **not cheer** in their *young men* **youths**,
neither shall *have* **he** mercy *on*
their *fatherless* **orphans** and widows:
for every one
is *an hypocrite* **a profaner** and *an evildoer* **a vilifier**,
and every mouth *speaketh* **wordeth** folly.
For all this his *anger* **wrath** is not turned away,
but his hand is stretched out still.
18 For wickedness burneth as the fire:
it shall devour the briers and thorns,
and shall kindle in the thickets of the forest,
and they shall *mount up* **spiral upward,**
like the *lifting up* **rising** of smoke.
19 Through the wrath
of *the LORD of hosts* **Yah Veh Sabaoth**
is the land *darkened* **burnt**,
and the people shall be as the fuel of the fire:
no man shall spare his brother.
20 And he shall *snatch* **cut** on the right *hand*,
and *be hungry* **famish**;
and he shall eat on the left *hand*,
and *they* shall not be satisfied:
they shall eat every man the flesh of his own arm:
21 *Manasseh* **Menash Sheh**, *Ephraim* **Ephrayim**;
and *Ephraim* **Ephrayim**, *Manasseh* **Menash Sheh**:
and they together shall be against *Judah* **Yah Hudah**.
For all this his *anger* **wrath** is not turned away,
but his hand is stretched out still.

HO TO THE SCRIBES

10 *Woe* **Ho** unto them that
decree unrighteous decrees **engrave statutes of mischief**,
and that *write grievousness* **inscribe toil**
which they have *prescribed* **incribed**;
2 To *turn aside* **pervert** the *needy* **poor**
from *judgment* **pleading their cause**,
and *to take away* **strip** the *right* **judgment**
from the *poor* **humble** of my people,
that widows may be their *prey* **spoil**,
and that they may *rob* **plunder** the *fatherless* **orphan**!
3 And what *will* **shall** ye *do* **work** in the day of visitation,
and in the *desolation* **devastation**
which shall come from far?
to whom *will* **shall** ye flee for help?
and where *will* **shall** ye leave your *glory* **honour**?
4 Without me
they shall *bow down* **kneel** under the *prisoners* **bound**,
and they shall fall under the *slain* **slaughtered**.
For all this his *anger* **wrath** is not turned away,
but his hand is stretched out still.
5 *O Assyrian* **Ho Ashshuri**,
the *rod* **scion** of *mine anger* **my wrath**,
and the *staff* **rod** in their hand
is *mine indignation* **my rage**.
6 I *will* **shall** send him
against *an hypocritical nation* **a goyim of profaners**,
and against the people of my wrath
will I give him a charge **shall I misvah him**,
to take the spoil, and to *take* **plunder** the *prey* **plunder**,
and to *tread them down* **set them for trampling**
like the *mire* **heap** of the *streets* **outways**.
7 Howbeit he *meaneth* **considereth** not so,
neither doth his heart *think* **fabricate** so;

but it is in his heart
to *destroy* **desolate** and cut off *nations* **goyim** not a few.
8 For he saith,
Are not my *princes* **governors**
altogether *kings* **sovereigns**?
9 Is not *Calno* **Kalneh** as *Carchemish* **Karchemish**?
is not Hamath as Arpad?
is not *Samaria* **Shomeron** as *Damascus* **Dammeseq**?
10 As my hand
hath found the *kingdoms* **sovereigndoms** of the idol,
and whose *graven images* **sculptiles** did excel them
of *Jerusalem* **Yeru Shalem** and *of Samaria* **Shomeron**;
11 Shall I not **work**, as I have *done* **worked**
unto *Samaria* **Shomeron** and her idols,
so *do* **work** to *Jerusalem* **Yeru Shalem** and her idols?
12 Wherefore it shall *come to pass* **become**,
that when *the Lord* **Adonay**
hath *performed* **clipped** his whole work
upon mount *Zion* **Siyon** and on *Jerusalem* **Yeru Shalem**,
I will punish **shall visit**
upon the fruit of the *stout* **greatness of** heart
of the *king* **sovereign** of *Assyria* **Ashshur**,
and the *glory* **adornment** of his *high looks* **haughty eyes**.
13 For he saith,
By the *strength* **force** of my hand I have *done* **worked** it,
and by my wisdom; for I *am prudent* **discern**:
and I have *removed* **turned aside**
the *bounds* **borders** of the people,
and have *robbed* **plundered** their treasures,
and I have *put* **brought** down the *inhabitants* **settlers**
like *a valiant man* **the mighty**:
14 And my hand hath found as a nest
the *riches* **valuables** of the people:
and as one gathereth eggs that are *left* **forsaken**,
have I gathered all the earth;
and there was none that *moved* **flapped** the wing,
or *opened* **gaped** the mouth, or *peeped* **chirped**.
15 Shall the ax boast itself
against him that heweth therewith?
or shall the *saw magnify* **rasp greaten** itself
against him that shaketh it?
as if the *rod* **scion** should shake itself
against them that lift it *up*,
or as if the *staff* **rod** should lift *up* itself,
as if it were no *wood* **timber**.
16 Therefore shall *the Lord* **Adonay**,
the Lord of hosts **Adonay Sabaoth**,
send among his *fat ones leanness* **fatness emaciation**;
and under his *glory* **honour**
he shall *kindle* **burn** a burning like the burning of a fire.
17 And the light of *Israel* **Yisra El** shall be for a fire,
and his Holy One for a flame:
and it shall burn and *devour* **consume**
his thorns and his briers in one day;
18 And shall *consume* **finish off**
the *glory* **honour** of his forest,
and of his *fruitful field* **orchard/Karmel**,
both soul and *body* **flesh**:
and they shall be as when
a standardbearer fainteth **an ensignbearer melteth**.
19 And the *rest* **survivors** of the trees of his forest
shall be *few* **numerable**,
that a *child* may *write* **lad inscribe** them.

THE SURVIVING ESCAPEES

20 And it shall *come to pass* **become** in that day,
that the *remnant* **survivors** of *Israel* **Yisra El**,
and *such as are escaped* **the escapees**
of the house of *Jacob* **Yaaqov**,
shall *no more again* **not add**
stay **to lean** upon him that smote them;
but shall *stay* **lean** upon *the LORD* **Yah Veh**,
the Holy One of *Israel* **Yisra El**, in truth.
21 The *remnant* **survivors** shall return,
even the *remnant* **survivors** of *Jacob* **Yaaqov**,
unto the mighty *God* **El**.
22 For though thy people *Israel* **Yisra El**
be as the sand of the sea,
yet a remnant **the survivors** of them shall return:
the consumption *decreed* **appointed**
shall overflow with *righteousness* **justness**.
23 For *the Lord GOD of hosts* **Adonay Yah Veh Sabaoth**
shall *make* **work** a *consumption* **final finish**,
even determined **appointed**, in the midst of all the land.
24 Therefore thus saith
the Lord GOD of hosts **Adonay Yah Veh Sabaoth**,
O my people that *dwellest* **settlest** in *Zion* **Siyon**,
be not afraid of **awe not** the *Assyrian* **Ashshuri**:
he shall smite thee with a *rod* **scion**,
and shall lift *up* his *staff* **rod** against thee,
after the *manner* **way** of *Egypt* **Misrayim**.
25 For yet a very little while,
and the *indignation* **rage** shall *cease* **conclude**,
and *mine anger* **my wrath**
in their *destruction* **consumption**.
26 And *the LORD of hosts* **Yah Veh Sabaoth**
shall *stir up* **waken** a *scourge* **whip** for him
according to the *slaughter* **striking** of *Midian* **Midyan**
at the rock of Oreb:
and as his rod was upon the sea,
so shall he lift it *up*
after the *manner* **way** of *Egypt* **Misrayim**.

THE OINTMENT DESPOILS THE YOKE

27 And it shall *come to pass* **become,** in that day,
that his burden shall *be taken away* **turn aside**
from off thy shoulder,
and his yoke from off thy neck,
and the yoke shall *be destroyed* **despoil**
because **at the face** of the *anointing* **ointment**.
28 He is come to *Aiath* **Ayath**, he is passed to Migron;
at Michmash
he *hath laid up* **mustereth** his *carriages* **instruments**:
29 They are *gone* **passed** over the passage:
they have taken up their lodging at Geba;
Ramah *is afraid* **trembleth**;
Gibeah **Gibah** of *Saul is fled* **Shaul fleeth**.
30 *Lift up* **Resound** thy voice,
O daughter of *Gallim* **heaps**:
cause it to be heard unto **hearken O** Laish,
O *poor* **humble** Anathoth.
31 Madmenah *is removed* **fleeth**;
the *inhabitants* **settlers** of *Gebim* **the way of the dugouts**
gather **withdraw** themselves *to flee*.
32 As yet shall he *remain* **stand** at Nob that day:
he shall shake his hand
against the mount of *the daughter of Zion* **Bath Siyon**,
the hill of *Jerusalem* **Yeru Shalem**.
33 Behold,
the Lord, the LORD of hosts **Adonay Yah Veh Sabaoth**,
shall lop the *bough* **foliage** with *terror* **violence**:
and the high ones of *stature* **height**
shall be *hewn* **cut** *down*,
and the *haughty* **lofty** shall be *humbled* **abased**.
34 And he shall *cut down* **strike** the thickets of the forest
with iron,
and Lebanon shall **have a mighty** fall *by a mighty one*.

THE BRANCH

11 And there shall come forth a rod
out of the *stem* **stump** of *Jesse* **Yishay**,
and a Branch shall *grow* **bear fruit** out of his roots:
cp Yesha Yah 11:10
2 And the spirit of *the LORD* **Yah Veh** shall rest upon him,
the spirit of wisdom and understanding,
the spirit of counsel and might,
the spirit of knowledge
and of the *fear* **awe** of *the LORD* **Yah Veh**;
3 And shall *make* **scent** him *of quick understanding*
in the *fear* **awe** of *the LORD* **Yah Veh**:
and he shall not judge after the sight of his eyes,
neither reprove after the hearing of his ears:
4 But with *righteousness* **justness** shall he judge the poor,
and reprove with *equity* **straightness**
for the *meek* **humble** of the earth:
and he shall smite the earth
with the *rod* **scion** of his mouth,
and with the *breath* **spirit** of his lips
shall he *slay* **execute** the wicked.
5 And *righteousness* **justness**
shall be the girdle of his loins,
and *faithfulness* **trustworthiness**
the girdle of his *reins* **loins**.

6 The wolf also shall *dwell* **sojourn** with the lamb,
and the leopard shall *lie down* **crouch** with the kid;
and the calf and the *young lion* **whelp**
and the fatling together;
and a little *child* **lad** shall *lead* **drive** them.
7 And the *cow* **heifer** and the bear shall *feed* **graze**;
their *young ones* **children** shall *lie down* **crouch** together:
and the lion shall eat straw like the ox.
8 And the *sucking child* **suckling**
shall *play* **stroke** on the hole of the asp,
and the weaned *child* shall *put* **stretch forth** his hand
on the *cockatrice' den* **hisser's hole**.
9 They shall not *hurt* **vilify** nor *destroy* **ruin**
in all my holy mountain:
for the earth shall *be full* **fill**
of the knowledge of *the LORD* **Yah Veh**,
as the waters cover the sea.
10 And in that day there shall be a root of *Jesse* **Yishay**,
which shall stand for an ensign of the people;
to it shall the *Gentiles* **goyim** seek:
and his rest shall be *glorious* **honourable**.

cp Yesha Yah 11:1

THE SURVIVORS RESTORED

11 And it shall *come to pass* **become**, in that day,
that the Lord **Adonay**
shall set his hand again *the second time* **secondly**
to *recover* **chattel** the *remnant* **survivors** of his people,
which shall *be left* **survive**,
from *Assyria* **Ashshur**, and from *Egypt* **Misrayim**,
and from Pathros, and from *Cush* **Kush**, and from Elam,
and from Shinar, and from Hamath,
and from the islands of the sea.
12 And he shall *set up* **lift** an ensign
for the *nations* **goyim**,
and shall *assemble* **gather**
the *outcasts* **overthrown** of *Israel* **Yisra El**,
and gather *together*
the *dispersed* **scattered** of *Judah* **Yah Hudah**
from the four *corners* **wings** of the earth.
13 The envy also of *Ephraim* **Ephrayim**
shall *depart* **turn aside**,
and the *adversaries* **tribulators** of *Judah* **Yah Hudah**
shall be cut off:
Ephraim **Ephrayim**
shall not envy *Judah* **Yah Hudah**,
and *Judah* **Yah Hudah**
shall not *vex Ephraim* **tribulate Ephrayim**.
14 But they shall fly
upon the shoulders of the *Philistines* **Peleshethiym**
toward the west **seaward**;
they shall *spoil* **plunder**
them **the sons** of the east together:
they shall *lay* **extend** their hand upon Edom and Moab;
and the *children* **sons** of Ammon
shall *obey* **hearken unto** them.
15 And *the LORD* **Yah Veh**
shall *utterly destroy* **devote**
the tongue of the *Egyptian* **Misrayim** sea;
and with *his mighty wind* **the strength of his wind/spirit**
shall he shake his hand over the river,
and shall smite it in the seven *streams* **wadies**,
and *make* **maketh** men *go over dryshod* **tread in shoes**.
16 And there shall be an highway
for the *remnant* **survivors** of his people,
which shall *be left* **survive**, from *Assyria* **Ashshur**;
like as it was to *Israel* **Yisra El**
in the day that he *came up* **ascended**
out of the land of *Egypt* **Misrayim**.

A PSALM OF EXTENDED HANDS

12 And in that day thou shalt say, O *LORD* **Yah Veh**,
I *will praise* **shall extend hands unto** thee:
though thou wast angry with me,
thine anger **thy wrath** is turned away,
and thou *comfortedst* **sighedst over** me.
2 Behold, *God* **El** is my salvation;
I *will trust* **shall confide**, and not *be afraid* **fear**:
for *the LORD JEHOVAH* **Yah Yah Veh**
is my strength and *my song* **psalm**;
he also is become my salvation.
3 Therefore with *joy* **rejoicing** shall ye *draw* **bail** water
out of the *wells* **fountains** of salvation.
4 And in that day shall ye say,
Praise the LORD **Extend hands unto Yah Veh**,
call upon his name,
declare his doings **make known his exploits**
among the people,
make mention **remember** that his name is exalted.
5 *Sing* **Psalm** unto *the LORD* **Yah Veh**;
for he hath *done excellent things* **worked pomp**:
this is known in all the earth.
6 *Cry out* **Resound** and shout,
thou *inhabitant* **settlers** of *Zion* **Siyon**:
for great is the Holy One of *Israel* **Yisra El**
in the midst of thee.

THE BURDEN OF BABEL

13 The burden of *Babylon* **Babel**,
which *Isaiah* **Yesha Yah** the son of *Amoz* **Amos** did see.
2 Lift ye up *a banner* **an ensign**
upon the *high* **barren** mountain,
exalt the voice unto them, shake the hand,
that they may go
into the *gates* **portals** of the *nobles* **volunteers**.
3 I have *commanded* **misvahed** my *sanctified ones* **hallowed**,
I have also called my mighty *ones*
for *mine anger* **my wrath**,
even them
that *rejoice* **jump for joy** in my *highness* **pomp**.
4 The *noise* **voice** of a multitude in the mountains,
like as **in the likeness** of a great people;
a tumultuous **an uproar of** noise
of the *kingdoms* **sovereigndoms** of *nations* **goyim**
gathered *together*:
the LORD of hosts **Yah Veh Sabaoth**
mustereth the host of the *battle* **war**.
5 They come from a far *country* **land**,
from the end of *heaven* **the heavens**,
even the LORD **Yah Veh**,
and the *weapons* **instruments** of his *indignation* **rage**,
to *destroy* **despoil** the whole land.
6 Howl ye;
for the day of *the LORD is at hand* **Yah Veh approacheth**;
it shall come as a *destruction* **ravage**
from *the Almighty* **Shadday**.
7 Therefore shall all hands *be faint* **slacken**,
and every man's heart shall melt:
8 And they shall *be afraid* **terrify**:
pangs **pains** and *sorrows* **pangs** shall take hold of them;
they shall *be in pain* **writhe**
as a woman *that travaileth* **birthing**:
they shall *be amazed* **marvel**
one at another **every man at friend**;
their faces shall be as flames.
9 Behold, the day of *the LORD* **Yah Veh** cometh,
cruel both with wrath and *fierce anger* **fuming wrath**,
to *lay* **set** the land desolate:
and he shall *destroy* **desolate** the sinners *thereof* out of it.
10 For the stars of *heaven* **the heavens**
and *the constellations thereof* **kesil**
shall not *give* **halal** their light:
the sun shall be darkened in his going forth,
and the moon
shall not *cause* **illuminate** her light *to shine*.
11 And I *will punish* **shall visit** the world for their evil,
and the wicked for their *iniquity* **perversity**;
and I *will* **shall** cause
the *arrogancy* **pomp** of the *proud* **arrogant**
to *cease* **shabbathize**,
and *will lay low* **shall abase**
the *haughtiness* **pomp** of the *terrible* **tyrant**.
12 I *will make* **shall esteem** a man
more precious than *fine* **pure** gold;
even a man — **humanity**
than the *golden wedge* **ore** of Ophir.
13 Therefore I *will shake* **shall quake** the heavens,
and the earth shall *remove* **quake** out of her place,
in the wrath of *the LORD of hosts* **Yah Veh Sabaoth**,
and in the day of his *fierce anger* **fuming wrath**.
14 And it shall be as the *chased roe* **driven gazelle**,
and as a *sheep* **flock**
that *no man taketh up* **none shall gather**:

they shall every man *turn to* **face** his own people,
and flee every *one* **man** into his own land.
15 Every one that is found shall be thrust through;
and every one that is *joined unto them* **scraped away**
shall fall by the sword.
16 Their *children* **sucklings** also
shall be *dashed to pieces* **splattered** before their eyes;
their houses shall be *spoiled* **plundered**,
and their *wives ravished* **women lain with and raped**.
17 Behold,
I *will stir up the Medes* **shall waken the Maday**
against them,
which shall not *regard* **fabricate** silver;
and as for gold, they shall not delight in it.
18 Their bows also
shall *dash* **splatter** the *young men* **lads** *to pieces*;
and they shall *have no pity on* **not mercy**
the fruit of the *womb* **belly**;
their eye shall not spare *children* **sons**.
19 And *Babylon* **Babel**,
the *glory* **splendour** of *kingdoms* **sovereigndoms**,
the *beauty* **adornment**
of the *Chaldees' excellency* **Kesediym's pomp**,
shall be as when *God* **Elohim**
overthrew *Sodom* **Sedom** and *Gomorrah* **Amorah**.
20 It shall never be *inhabited* **settled in perpetuity**,
neither shall it be *dwelt* **tabernacled** in
from generation to generation:
neither shall the *Arabian pitch* **Arabiy** tent there;
neither shall the *shepherds* **tenders**
make their fold **crouch** there.
21 But *wild beasts of the* desert **dwellers**
shall *lie* **crouch** there;
and their houses
shall be *full* **filled** of *doleful creatures* **howlers**;
and **daughters of the** owls shall *dwell* **tabernacle** there,
and *satyrs* **bucks** shall dance there.
22 And the *wild beasts of the islands* **island howlers**
shall *cry* **answer** in their *desolate houses* **abandonments**,
and *dragons* **monsters**
in their *pleasant palaces* **manses of luxury**:
and her time is near to come,
and her days shall not be *prolonged* **drawn out**.

YAH VEH MERCIES YAAQOV

14 For *the LORD* **Yah Veh**
will **shall** *have* mercy *on Jacob* **Yaaqov**,
and *will* **shall** yet choose *Israel* **Yisra El**,
and set them in their own *land* **soil**:
and the *strangers* **sojourners** shall be joined with them,
and they shall *cleave* **be scraped**
to the house of *Jacob* **Yaaqov**.
2 And the people shall take them,
and bring them to their place:
and the house of *Israel* **Yisra El** shall *possess* **inherit** them
in the *land* **soil** of *the LORD* **Yah Veh**
for servants and *handmaids* **maids**:
and they shall *take them captives,* **be captured**
whose captives they were **by their captors**;
and they shall *rule over* **subjugate**
their *oppressors* **exactors**.
3 And it shall *come to pass* **become,**
in the day that *the LORD* **Yah Veh**
shall *give thee* rest **thee** from thy *sorrow* **contortion**,
and from thy *fear* **quivering**,
and from the hard *bondage* **service**
wherein thou wast made to serve
which was served on thee,
4 That thou shalt *take up* **lift** this proverb
against the *king* **sovereign** of *Babylon* **Babel**, and say,
How hath the *oppressor ceased* **exactor shabbathized**!
the *golden city* **extortioners of gold**
ceased **shabbathized**!
5 *The LORD* **Yah Veh**
hath broken the *staff* **rod** of the wicked,
and the *sceptre* **scion** of the *rulers* **sovereigns**.
6 He who smote the people in wrath
with a *continual stroke* **stroke without revolt,**
he that *ruled* **subjugated** the *nations* **goyim**
in *anger* **wrath**
is persecuted, *and* none *hindereth* **spareth**.
7 The whole earth is at rest, *and is quiet* **resteth**:
they break forth into *singing* **shouting**.
8 Yea, the fir trees *rejoice* **cheer** at thee,
and the cedars of Lebanon, *saying,*
Since thou art laid down,
no *feller is come up* **cutter ascendeth** against us.
9 *Hell* **Sheol** from beneath *is moved* **quaketh** for thee
to meet thee at thy coming:
it *stirreth up* **wakeneth** the *dead* **ghost** for thee,
even all the *chief ones* **he goats** of the earth;
it hath raised up from their thrones
all the *kings* **sovereigns** of the *nations* **goyim**.
10 All they shall *speak* **answer** and say unto thee,
Art thou also *become weak* **worn** as we?
art thou become like unto us?
11 Thy pomp is brought down to *the grave* **sheol**,
and the *noise* **sound** of thy *viols* **bagpipes**:
the *worm* **maggot** is spread under thee,
and the *worms* **maggots** cover thee.

THE HALALED ONE

12 How art thou fallen from *heaven* **the heavens**,
O *Lucifer* **Halaled one**, son of the *morning* **dawn**!
how art thou cut down to the *ground* **earth**,
which didst *weaken* **vanquish** the *nations* **goyim**!
13 For thou hast said in thine heart,
I *will* **shall** ascend into *heaven* **the heavens**,
I *will* **shall** exalt my throne above the stars of *God* **El**:
I *will* **shall** sit also upon the mount of the congregation,
in the *sides* **flanks** of the north:
14 I *will* **shall** ascend
above the *heights* **bamahs** of the **thick** clouds;
I will be — like *the most High* **Elyon**.
15 Yet thou shalt be brought down to *hell* **sheol**,
to the *sides* **flanks** of the *pit* **well**.
16 They that see thee shall *narrowly look* **peer** upon thee,
and consider **discern** thee, *saying,*
Is this the man that *made* **quaked** the earth *to tremble,*
that *did shake kingdoms* **quaked sovereigndoms**;
17 That *made* **set** the world as a wilderness,
and *destroyed* **demolished** the cities *thereof*;
that opened not the house of his *prisoners* **bound**?
18 All the *kings* **sovereigns** of the *nations* **goyim**,
even all of them, lie in *glory* **honour**,
every *one* **man** in his own house.
cp Yahn 12:31, Loukas 10:18, Apocalypse 12:7—12
19 But thou art cast out of thy *grave* **tomb**
like an *abominable* **abhorrent** branch,
and as the *raiment* **robe**
of *those that are slain* **the slaughtered**,
thrust through **stabbed** with a sword,
that *go down* **descend** to the stones of the *pit* **well**;
as a carcase *trodden under feet* **trampled**.
20 Thou shalt not be *joined* **united** with them
in *burial* **the tomb**,
because thou hast *destroyed* **ruined** thy land,
and *slain* **slaughtered** thy people:
the seed of *evildoers* **vilifiers**
shall never **eternally** be *renowned* **called out**.
21 Prepare slaughter for his *children* **sons**
for the *iniquity* **perversity** of their fathers;
that they do not rise, nor possess the land,
nor fill the face of the world with cities.
22 For I *will* **shall** rise *up* against them,
saith the LORD of hosts **an oracle of Yah Veh Sabaoth**,
and cut off from *Babylon* **Babel** the name,
and *remnant* **survivors**, and *son* **offspring**,
and *nephew* **posterity**,
saith the LORD **an oracle of Yah Veh**.
23 I *will also make* **shall set** it a possession for the bittern,
and *pools* **marshes** of water:
and I *will* **shall** sweep it
with the *besom* **broom** of *destruction* **desolation**,
saith the LORD of hosts **an oracle of Yah Veh Sabaoth**.

THE BURDEN OF ASHSHUR

24 *The LORD of hosts* **Yah Veh Sabaoth**
hath *sworn* **oathed**, saying,
Surely as I have *thought* **considered**,
so shall it *come to pass* **become**;
and as I have *purposed* **counselled**,
so shall it *stand* **rise**:

25 That I *will* **shall** break the *Assyrian* **Ashshuri**
in my land,
and upon my mountains *tread* **trample** him *under foot*:
then shall his yoke *depart* **turn aside** from off them,
and his burden *depart* **turn aside** from off their shoulders.
26 This is the *purpose* **counsel**
that is *purposed* **counselled** upon the whole earth:
and this is the hand
that is stretched out upon all the *nations* **goyim**.
27 For *the LORD of hosts* **Yah Veh Sabaoth**
hath *purposed* **counselled**,
and who shall *disannul* **break it**?
and his hand is stretched out,
and who shall turn it back?

THE BURDEN OF PELESHETH

28 In the year that *king Ahaz* **sovereign Ach Az** died
was this burden.
29 *Rejoice* **Cheer** not thou, whole *Palestina* **Pelesheth**,
because the *rod* **scion** of him that smote thee is broken:
for out of the serpent's root
shall come forth a *cockatrice* **hisser**,
and his fruit shall be a *fiery* flying *serpent* **seraph**.
30 And the firstborn of the poor shall *feed* **graze**,
and the needy shall *lie down in safety* **crouch confidently**:
and I *will* **shall** kill thy root with famine,
and he shall *slay* **slaughter** thy *remnant* **survivors**.
31 Howl, O *gate* **portal**; cry, O city;
thou, whole *Palestina* **Pelesheth**, art dissolved:
for there shall come from the north a smoke,
and none shall be alone in his *appointed times* **seasons**.
32 What shall one then
answer the *messengers* **angels** of the *nation* **goyim**?
That *the LORD* **Yah Veh** hath founded *Zion* **Siyon**,
and the *poor* **humble** of his people
shall *trust* **seek refuge** in it.

THE BURDEN OF MOAB

15 The burden of Moab.
Because in the night
Ar of Moab is *laid waste* **ravaged**,
and *brought to silence* **rendered mute**;
because in the night
Kir **Qir** of Moab is *laid waste* **ravaged**,
and brought to silence **rendered mute**;
2 He *is gone up* **ascendeth** to *Bajith* **Bayith**, and to Dibon,
the *high places* **bamahs**, *to weep* **weeping**:
Moab shall howl over Nebo, and over Medeba:
on all their heads shall be baldness,
and every beard cut off.
3 In their *streets* **outways**
they shall gird *themselves* with sackcloth:
on *the tops of* their *houses* **roofs**,
and in their *streets* **broadways**,
every one shall howl,
descending into weeping abundantly.
4 And Heshbon shall cry, and *Elealeh* **El Aleh**:
their voice shall be heard *even* unto *Jahaz* **Yahsah**:
therefore the *armed soldiers* **equipped** of Moab
shall *cry out* **shout**;
his *life* **soul** shall *be grievous* **tremble** unto him.
5 My heart shall cry out for Moab;
his fugitives *shall flee* unto *Zoar* **Soar**,
an heifer of three *years old*:
for by the *mounting up* **ascent** of *Luhith* **Luchith**
with weeping shall they *go it up* **ascend**;
for in the way of *Horonaim* **Horonayim**
they shall *raise up* **waken** a cry of *destruction* **breaking**.
6 For the waters of Nimrim shall be *desolate* **desolations**:
for the hay is withered away,
the *grass faileth* **sprout finisheth**, there is no green *thing*.
7 Therefore the abundance they have *gotten* **worked**,
and that which they have *laid up* **mustered**,
shall they *carry* **bear** away
to the *brook* **wadi** of the willows.
8 For the cry is gone round about the borders of Moab;
the howling *thereof* unto *Eglaim* **Eglayim**,
and the howling *thereof* unto Beerelim.
9 For the waters of Dimon shall be *full* **filled** of blood:
for I *will bring more* **shall place additions** upon Dimon,
lions upon *him that escapeth* **the escapees** of Moab,
and upon the *remnant* **survivors** of the *land* **soil**.

JUSTICE UPON MOAB

16 Send ye the *lamb* **ram**
to the *ruler* **sovereign** of the land
from *Sela* **the rock** to the wilderness,
unto the mount of the daughter of *Zion* **Siyon**.
2 For it shall be, *that*,
as a *wandering bird* **flapping flyer**
cast **sent** out of the nest,
so the daughters of Moab
shall be at the *fords* **passages** of Arnon.
3 Take counsel, *execute judgment* **work justice**;
make **place** thy shadow
as the night in the midst of the *noonday* **noon**;
hide the *outcasts* **expelled**;
bewray **expose/expel** not him that *wandereth* **flappeth**.
4 Let mine *outcasts dwell* **expelled sojourn** with thee,
Moab; be thou a covert to them
from the face of the *spoiler* **ravager**:
for the *extortioner is at an end* **oppressor ceaseth**,
the *spoiler ceaseth* **ravage finisheth**,
the *oppressors* **tramplers** are consumed out of the land.
5 And in mercy shall the throne be established:
and he shall sit upon it in truth
in the *tabernacle* **tent** of David,
judging, and seeking judgment,
and hasting *righteousness* **justness**.
6 We have heard of the *pride* **pomp** of Moab;
he is *very proud* **mighty pompous**:
even of his *haughtiness* **pomp**,
and his *pride* **pomp**, and his wrath:
but his lies shall not be so.
7 Therefore shall Moab howl for Moab,
every one shall howl:
for the foundations of *Kirhareseth* **Qir Hareseth**
shall ye *mourn* **meditate**; surely they *are* **be** stricken.
8 For the fields of Heshbon languish,
and the vine of Sibmah:
the *lords* **masters** of the *heathen* **goyim**
have *broken down* **hammered**
the *principal plants* **grapevines** *thereof*,
they are *come* **touched** *even* unto *Jazer* **Yazer**,
they wandered through the wilderness:
her branches are *stretched out* **abandoned**,
they are *gone* **passed** over the sea.
9 Therefore I *will bewail* **shall weep**
with the weeping of *Jazer* **Yazer** the vine of Sibmah:
I *will water* **shall saturate** thee with my tears,
O Heshbon, and *Elealeh* **El Aleh**:
for the shouting for thy summer fruits
and for thy harvest is fallen.
10 And *gladness* **cheerfulness** is *taken away* **gathered up**,
and *joy* **twirling** out of the *plentiful field* **orchard/Karmel**;
and in the vineyards there shall be no *singing* **shouting**,
neither shall there be shouting:
the treaders shall tread out no wine
in *their presses* **troughs**;
I have made their *vintage* shouting to *cease* **shabbathize**.
11 Wherefore my *bowels* **inwards** shall *sound* **roar**
like an harp for Moab,
and mine *inward parts* **inwards**
for *Kirharesh* **Qir Hareseth**.
12 And it shall *come to pass* **become**,
when it is seen
that Moab is weary on the *high place* **bamah**,
that he shall come to his *sanctuary* **holies** to pray;
but he shall not prevail.
13 This is the word
that *the LORD* **Yah Veh** hath *spoken* **worded**
concerning Moab **ever** since *that time*.
14 But now *the LORD* **Yah Veh** hath *spoken* **worded**,
saying, Within three years, as the years of an hireling,
and the *glory* **honour** of Moab
shall be *contemned* **abased**,
with all that great multitude;
and the *remnant* **survivors**
shall be *very small and feeble* **not many**.

THE BURDEN OF DAMMESEQ

17 The burden of *Damascus* **Dammeseq**.
Behold,
Damascus **Dammeseq** is *taken away* **turned aside**

from being a city,
and it shall be a ruinous *heap* **ruin**.
2 The cities of Aroer are forsaken:
they shall be for *flocks* **droves**,
which shall *lie down* **crouch**,
and none shall *make* **cause** them *afraid* **to tremble**.
3 The fortress also
shall *cease* **shabbathize** from *Ephraim* **Ephrayim**,
and the *kingdom* **sovereigndom**
from *Damascus* **Dammeseq**,
and the *remnant* **survivors** of *Syria* **Aram**:
they shall be as the *glory* **honour**
of the *children* **sons** of *Israel* **Yisra El**,
saith the LORD of hosts **an oracle of Yah Veh Sabaoth**.
4 And in that day it shall *come to pass* **become**,
that the *glory* **honour** of *Jacob* **Yaaqov**
shall *be made thin* **languish**,
and the fatness of his flesh shall *wax lean* **emaciate**.
5 And it shall be
as when the *harvestman* **harvester**
gathereth the *corn* **stalks**,
and *reapeth* **harvesteth** the ears with his arm;
and it shall be
as he that gathereth ears in the valley of Rephaim.
6 Yet *gleaning grapes* **gleanings** shall *be left* **survive** in it,
as the shaking of an olive *tree*,
two or three berries
in the top of the uppermost *bough* **branch**,
four or five
in the *outmost fruitful branches* **fruitbearing twigs**
thereof,
saith the LORD God of Israel
an oracle of Yah Veh Elohim of Yisra El.
7 At that day
shall *a man* **humanity** look to his *Maker* **Worker**,
and his eyes
shall *have respect* **see** to the Holy One of *Israel* **Yisra El**.
8 And he shall not look to the **sacrifice** altars,
the work of his hands,
neither shall *respect* **see**
that which his fingers have *made* **worked**,
either the *groves* **asherah**, or the *images* **sun icons**.
9 In that day shall his *strong* **stronghold** cities
be as a forsaken *bough* **forest**, and an uppermost branch,
which they *left* **forsook**
because **at the face** of the *children* **sons** of *Israel* **Yisra El**:
and there shall be desolation.
10 Because thou hast forgotten
the God **Elohim** of thy salvation,
and hast not *been mindful of* **remembered**
the rock of thy *strength* **stronghold**,
therefore shalt thou plant pleasant plants,
and shalt *set* **seed** it with strange *slips* **twigs**:
11 In the day shalt thou *make* **hedge** thy plant *to grow*,
and in the morning shalt thou *make* **blossom** thy seed
to flourish:
but the harvest shall be a heap
in the day of grief and of desperate *sorrow* **pain**.
12 *Woe* **Ho** to the multitude of many people,
which *make a noise* **roar** like the *noise* **roar** of the seas;
and to the *rushing* **uproar** of nations,
that *make a rushing* **shall be wasted**
like the *rushing mighty* **wasting of many** waters!
13 The nations shall *rush* **roar**
like the *rushing* **roaring** of many waters:
but God shall rebuke them **and shall be rebuked**,
and they shall flee far off,
and shall be *chased* **pursued**
as the chaff of the mountains
before **at the face of** the wind,
and like a *rolling thing* **whirler**
before **at the face of** the *whirlwind* **hurricane**.
14 And behold at *eveningtide* **evening time**,
trouble **terror**;
and before the morning he is not.
This is the *portion* **allotment** of them that spoil us,
and the *lot* **pebble** of them that *rob* **plunder** us.

THE BURDEN OF KUSH

18 *Woe* **Ho** to the land *shadowing* **whirring** with wings,
which is beyond the rivers of *Ethiopia* **Kush**:
2 That sendeth ambassadors by the sea,
even in *vessels* **instruments** of bulrushes
upon the **face of the** waters, *saying*,
Go, ye swift *messengers* **angels**,
to a *nation scattered* **goyim drawn** and *peeled* **polished**,
to a people *terrible* **awesome**
from their beginning *hitherto* **and onward**;
a *nation meted out* **goyim lined up**
and *trodden down* **trampled**,
whose land the rivers have *spoiled* **split**!
3 All ye *inhabitants* **settlers** of the world,
and *dwellers* **tabernaclers** on the earth,
see ye, when he lifteth up an ensign on the mountains;
and when he *bloweth* **blasteth** a trumpet, hear ye.
4 For *so the LORD* **thus Yah Veh** said unto me,
I *will* **shall** *take my* rest,
and I *will consider* **shall scan** in my dwelling place
like a clear heat upon *herbs* **the light**,
and like a **thick** cloud of dew in the heat of harvest.
5 For, *afore* **at the face of** the harvest,
when the *bud* **blossom** is *perfect* **consumated**,
and the sour grape is ripening in the *flower* **blossom**,
he shall both
cut off the sprigs with *pruning hooks* **psalmpicks**,
and *take away* **turn aside**
and *cut down* **lop off** the *branches* **tendrils**.
6 They shall be left together
unto the *fowls* **swoopers** of the mountains,
and to the *beasts* **animals** of the earth:
and the *fowls* **swoopers** shall summer upon them,
and all the *beasts* **animals** of the earth
shall winter upon them.
7 In that time shall the present be brought
unto *the LORD of hosts* **Yah Veh Sabaoth**
of a people *scattered* **drawn** and *peeled* **polished**,
and from a people *terrible* **awesome**
from their beginning *hitherto* **and onward**;
a *nation* **goyim**
meted out **lined up** and *trodden under foot* **trampled**,
whose land the rivers have *spoiled* **split**,
to the place of the name
of *the LORD of hosts* **Yah Veh Sabaoth**,
the mount *Zion* **Siyon**.

THE BURDEN OF MISRAYIM

19 The burden of *Egypt* **Misrayim**.
Behold,
the LORD **Yah Veh** rideth upon a swift **thick** cloud,
and shall come into *Egypt* **Misrayim**:
and the idols of *Egypt* **Misrayim**
shall *be moved* **totter** at his *presence* **face**,
and the heart of *Egypt* **Misrayim**
shall melt in the midst of it.
2 And I *will set* **shall hedge** the *Egyptians* **Misrayim**
against the *Egyptians* **Misrayim**:
and they shall fight every *one* **man** against his brother,
and every one against his *neighbour* **friend**;
city against city,
and
kingdom **sovereigndom** against *kingdom* **sovereigndom**.
3 And the spirit of *Egypt* **Misrayim**
shall *fail* **evacuate** in the midst *thereof*;
and I *will destroy* **shall swallow up** the counsel *thereof*:
and they shall seek to the idols,
and to the *charmers* **spiritists**,
and to *them that have familiar spirits* **necromancers**,
and to the *wizards* **knowers**.
4 And the *Egyptians* **Misrayim**
will I give over **shall I shut**
into the hand of *a cruel lord* **hard adonim**;
and a *fierce king* **strong sovereign**
shall *rule* **reign** over them,
saith the Lord **an oracle of Adonay**,
the LORD of host **Yah Veh Sabaoth**.
5 And the waters shall *fail* **dry** from the sea,
and the river shall *be wasted* **parch**
and *dried up* **wither**.
6 And they shall turn the rivers far away;
and the *brooks* **rivers** of *defence* **rampart**
shall *be emptied* **languish** and *dried up* **parch**:
the *reeds* **stalks** and *flags* **reeds** shall wither.

7 The *paper reeds* **nakednesses** by the *brooks* **rivers**,
by the mouth of the *brooks* **rivers**,
and every *thing sown* **plant** by the *brooks* **rivers**,
shall wither, *be driven away* **disperse**, and be no more.
8 The fishers also shall mourn,
and all they that cast *angle* **hooks** into the *brooks* **rivers**
shall *lament* **mourn**,
and they that spread nets upon the **face of the** waters
shall languish.
9 *Moreover* they that *work* **serve** in *fine* **drawn** flax,
and they that weave *networks* **white linen**,
shall *be confounded* **shame**.
10 And they shall be *broken* **crushed**
in the purposes *thereof*,
all that *make sluices and ponds* **hire to work marshes**
for *fish* **souls**.
11 Surely the *princes* **governors** of *Zoan* **Soan** are fools,
the counsel of the wise counsellors of *Pharaoh* **Paroh**
is become brutish:
how say ye unto *Pharaoh* **Paroh**,
I am the son of the wise,
the son of ancient *kings* **sovereigns**?
12 Where are they? where are thy wise *men*?
and let them tell thee, *now* **I beseech**,
and let them know what
the LORD of hosts **Yah Veh Sabaoth**
hath *purposed* **counselled** upon *Egypt* **Misrayim**.
13 The *princes* **governors** of *Zoan* **Soan**
are become *fools* **folly**,
the *princes* **governors** of Noph are deceived;
they have also *seduced Egypt* **strayed Misrayim**,
even they that are the stay **the chiefs**
of the *tribes thereof* **scions.**
14 *The LORD* **Yah Veh** hath *mingled* **mixed**
a *perverse spirit* **spirit of perversities** in the midst *thereof*:
and they have caused *Egypt* **Misrayim** to *err* **stray**
in every work *thereof*,
as *a drunken man* **an intoxicated** staggereth in his vomit.
15 Neither shall there be *any* work for *Egypt* **Misrayim**,
which the head or tail, *branch* **palm leaf** or rush,
may *do* **work**.
16 In that day shall *Egypt* **Misrayim** be like unto women:
and it shall *be afraid* **tremble** and *fear* **fear**
because **at the face** of the *shaking* **waving** of the hand
of *the LORD of hosts* **Yah Veh Sabaoth**,
which he shaketh over it.
17 And the *land* **soil** of *Judah* **Yah Hudah**
shall be a terror unto *Egypt thereof* **Misrayim**,
every one that *maketh mention* **remembereth**
shall *be afraid* **fear** in himself,
because **at the face** of the counsel
of *the LORD of hosts* **Yah Veh Sabaoth**,
which he hath *determined* **counselled** against it.
18 In that day
shall five cities in the land of *Egypt* **Misrayim**
speak the *language* **lip** of *Canaan* **Kenaan**,
and *swear* **oath** to *the LORD of hosts* **Yah Veh Sabaoth**;
of one shall be *called* **said**,
The city of *destruction* **demolition**.
19 In that day shall there be
an **a sacrifice** altar to *the LORD* **Yah Veh**
in the midst of the land of *Egypt* **Misrayim**,
and a *pillar at* **monolith beside** the border *thereof*
to *the LORD* **Yah Veh**.
20 And it shall be for a sign and for a witness
unto *the LORD of hosts* **Yah Veh Sabaoth**
in the land of *Egypt* **Misrayim**:
for they shall cry unto *the LORD* **Yah Veh**
because **at the face** of the oppressors,
and he shall send them a saviour, *and a* great *one*,
and he shall *deliver* **rescue** them.
21 And *the LORD* **Yah Veh**
shall be known to *Egypt* **Misrayim**,
and the *Egyptians* **Misrayim**
shall know *the LORD* **Yah Veh** in that day,
and shall *do* **serve** sacrifice and *oblation* **offerings**;
yea, they shall vow a vow unto *the LORD* **Yah Veh**,
and *perform it* **shalam**.
22 And *the LORD* **Yah Veh** shall smite *Egypt* **Misrayim**:
he shall smite and heal it:
and they shall return *even* to *the LORD* **Yah Veh**,
and he shall be intreated of them, and shall heal them.
23 In that day shall there be a highway
out of *Egypt* **Misrayim** to *Assyria* **Ashshur**,
and the *Assyrian* **Ashshuri**
shall come into *Egypt* **Misrayim**,
and the *Egyptian* **Misrayim** into *Assyria* **Ashshur**,
and the *Egyptians* **Misrayim**
shall serve with the *Assyrians* **Ashshuri**.
24 In that day shall *Israel* **Yisra El** be the third
with *Egypt* **Misrayim** and with *Assyria* **Ashshur**,
even a blessing in the midst of the land:
25 Whom *the LORD of hosts* **Yah Veh Sabaoth**
shall bless, saying,
Blessed be *Egypt* **Misrayim** my people,
and *Assyria* **Ashshur** the work of my hands,
and *Israel* **Yisra El** mine inheritance.

THE BURDEN OF MISRAYIM AND KUSH

20 In the year that Tartan came unto Ashdod,
(when Sargon the *king* **sovereign** of *Assyria* **Ashshur**
sent him,)
and fought against Ashdod, and *took* **captured** it;
2 At the same time *spake the LORD* **worded Yah Veh**
by *Isaiah* **the hand of Yesha Yah** the son of *Amoz* **Amos**,
saying, Go and loose the sackcloth from off thy loins,
and *put* **pull** off thy shoe from thy foot.
And he *did* **worked** so,
walking naked and *barefoot* **unshod**.
3 And *the LORD* **Yah Veh** said,
Like as my servant *Isaiah* **Yesha Yah**
hath walked naked and *barefoot* **unshod** three years
for a sign and *wonder* **omen**
upon *Egypt* **Misrayim** and upon *Ethiopia* **Kush**;
4 So shall the *king* **sovereign** of *Assyria* **Ashshur**
lead **drive** away the *Egyptians* **Misrayim** prisoners,
and the *Ethiopians captives* **Kushi exiles**,
young **lads** and *old* **aged**, naked and *barefoot* **unshod**,
even with their buttocks *uncovered* **stripped**,
to the *shame* **nakedness** of *Egypt* **Misrayim**.
5 And they shall be *afraid* **dismayed** and *ashamed* **shamed**
of *Ethiopia* **Kush** their expectation,
and of *Egypt* **Misrayim** their *glory* **adornment**.
6 And the *inhabitant* **settler** of this *isle* **island**
shall say in that day,
Behold, *such* **thus** is our expectation,
whither we flee for help to be *delivered* **rescued**
from the king **at the face of the sovereign**
of *Assyria* **Ashshur**:
and how shall we escape?

THE BURDEN OF BABEL

21 The burden of the *desert* **wilderness** of the sea.
As *whirlwinds* **hurricanes** in the south pass through;
so it cometh from the *desert* **wilderness**,
from *a terrible* **an awesome** land.
2 A *grievous* **hard** vision is *declared* **told** unto me;
the *treacherous dealer* **coverter**
dealeth treacherously **coverteth**,
and the *spoiler spoileth* **ravager ravageth**.
Go up **Ascend**, O Elam: besiege, O *Media* **Maday**;
all the sighing *thereof* have I made to *cease* **shabbathize**.
3 Therefore are my loins filled with pain:
pangs have taken hold upon me,
as the pangs of a woman *that travaileth* **birthing**:
I *was bowed down* **twisted** at the hearing of it;
I *was dismayed* **terrified** at the seeing of it.
4 My heart *panted* **staggered**,
fearfulness **trembling** affrighted me:
the *night* **evening breeze** of my pleasure
hath he *turned* **set** into *fear* **trembling** unto me.
5 *Prepare* **Line up** the table, watch in the watchtower,
eat, drink:
arise, ye *princes* **governors**,
and anoint the *shield* **buckler**.
6 For thus hath *the Lord* **Adonay** said unto me,
Go, *set* **stand** a *watchman* **watcher**,
let him *declare* **tell** what he seeth.
7 And he saw a chariot
with a *couple* **pair** of *horsemen* **cavalry**,
a chariot of *asses* **burros**, *and* a chariot of camels;
and **in hearkening,** he hearkened

diligently with much heed:
8 And he *cried* **called out**, A lion:
My Lord **Adonay**,
I stand continually upon the watchtower
in the *daytime* **day**,
and I am *set* **stationed** in my *ward* **guard** whole nights:
9 And, behold, here cometh a chariot of men,
with a *couple* **pair** of *horsemen* **cavalry**.
And he answered and said,
Babylon **Babel** is fallen, is fallen;
and all the *graven images* **sculptiles** of her *gods* **elohim**
he hath broken unto the *ground* **earth**.
10 O my threshing,
and the *corn* **sons** of my *floor* **threshingfloor**:
that which I have heard
of *the LORD of hosts* **Yah Veh Sabaoth**,
the God **Elohim** of *Israel* **Yisra El**,
have I *declared* **told** unto you.

THE BURDEN OF DUMAH

11 The burden of Dumah.
He calleth to me out of Seir,
Watchman **Guard**, what of the night?
Watchman **Guard**, what of the night?
12 The *watchman* **guard** said,
The morning cometh, and also the night:
if ye *will* **shall** enquire, enquire ye: return, come.

THE BURDEN OF ARABIA

13 The burden upon Arabia.
In the forest in Arabia shall ye *lodge* **stay overnight**,
O ye *travelling companies* **caravans** of Dedanim.
14 The *inhabitants* **settlers** of the land of Tema
brought water to **confront** him that was thirsty,
they *prevented* **anticipated** with their bread him that fled.
15 For they fled from **the face of** the swords,
from **the face of** the drawn sword,
and from **the face of** the bent bow,
and from **the face of** the *grievousness* **heaviness** of war.
16 For thus hath *the Lord* **Adonay** said unto me,
Within a year, according to the years of an hireling,
and all the *glory* **honour** of *Kedar* **Qedar** shall *fail* **finish**:
17 And the *residue* **survivors**
of the number of *archers* **bows**,
the mighty *men* of the *children* **sons** of *Kedar* **Qedar**,
shall be diminished:
for *the LORD God* **Yah Veh Elohim** of *Israel* **Yisra El**
hath *spoken it* **worded**.

THE BURDEN OF GAY HIZZAYON

22 The burden of
the valley of vision **Gay Hizzayon/Valley of Vision**
What aileth thee now,
that thou art wholly *gone up* **ascended**
to the *housetops* **roofs**?
2 Thou that art full of *stirs* **clamors**,
a *tumultuous* **roaring** city,
a *joyous city* **city jumping for joy**:
thy *slain* **pierced** *men* are not slain with the sword,
nor dead in *battle* **war**.
3 All thy *rulers* **commanders** are fled together,
they are bound by the *archers* **bows**:
all that are found in thee are bound together,
which have fled from far.
4 Therefore said I, Look away from me;
I *will weep bitterly* **am embittered in weeping**,
labour **hasten** not to *comfort* **sigh over** me,
because of the *spoiling* **ravage**
of the daughter of my people.
5 For it is a day of *trouble* **confusion**,
and of *treading down* **trampling**, and of perplexity
by *the Lord GOD of hosts* **Adonay Yah Veh Sabaoth**
in *the valley of vision* **Gay Hizzayon/Valley of Vision**,
breaking down **digging** the walls,
and of crying to the mountains.
6 And Elam bare the quiver
with chariots of *men* **humanity** and *horsemen* **cavalry**,
and *Kir uncovered* **Qir stripped naked** the *shield* **buckler**.
7 And it shall *come to pass* **become**,
that thy choicest valleys shall be *full* **filled** of chariots,
and *the horsemen shall set themselves in array*
in placing, the cavalry shall place themselves
at the *gate* **portal**.
8 And he *discovered* **exposed**
the covering of *Judah* **Yah Hudah**,
and thou didst look in that day
to the armour of the house of the forest.
9 Ye have seen also
the *breaches* **fissures** of the city of David,
that they *are many* **abound by the myriads**:
and ye gathered together
the waters of the *lower* **nether** pool.
10 And ye have *numbered* **scribed**
the houses of *Jerusalem* **Yeru Shalem**,
and the houses have ye *broken* **pulled** down
to fortify the wall.
11 Ye *made* **worked** also a *ditch* **reservoir**
between the two walls for the water of the old pool:
but ye have not looked unto the *maker* **worker** *thereof*,
neither *had respect* **saw** unto him
that *fashioned* **formed** it *long ago* **in the distant past**.
12 And in that day
did the Lord GOD of hosts **Adonay Yah Veh Sabaoth**
call **called** to weeping, and to *mourning* **chopping**,
and to baldness, and to girding with sackcloth:
13 And behold *joy* **rejoicing** and *gladness* **cheerfulness**,
slaying **slaughtering** oxen,
and *killing sheep* **slaughtering flock**,
eating flesh, and drinking wine:
let us eat and drink; for to morrow we shall die.
14 And it was *revealed* **exposed** in mine ears
by *the LORD of hosts* **Yah Veh Sabaoth**,
Surely this *iniquity* **perversity**
shall not be *purged* **kapared/atoned** from you till ye die,
saith *the Lord GOD of hosts* **Adonay Yah Veh Sabaoth**.
15 Thus saith
the Lord GOD of hosts **Adonay Yah Veh Sabaoth**,
Go, get thee unto this *treasurer* **useful one**,
even unto Shebna, which is over the house, *and say*,
16 What hast thou here and whom hast thou here,
that thou hast hewed thee out a *sepulchre* **tomb** here,
as he that heweth him out a *sepulchre* **tomb** on high,
and *that graveth an habitation* **engraveth a tabernacle**
for himself in a rock?
17 Behold, *the LORD* **Yah Veh**
will carry thee away with a mighty captivity
in casting, shall cast thee, O mighty,
and *will surely* **in covering, shall** cover thee.
18 *He will surely violently turn and toss thee like a ball*
In whirling, he whirleth
he shall whirl thee as a whirler
into a *large country* **land large of hand**:
there shalt thou die,
and there the chariots of thy *glory* **honour**
shall be the *shame* **abasement**
of *thy lord's* **adoni's** house.
19 And I *will drive* **shall exile** thee from thy station,
and from thy *state* **function**
shall he *pull* **break** thee *down*.
20 And it shall *come to pass* **become**, in that day,
that I *will* **shall** call my servant *Eliakim* **El Yaqim**
the son of *Hilkiah* **Hilqi Yah**:
21 And I *will clothe* **shall enrobe** him with thy *robe* **coat**,
and strengthen him with thy girdle,
and I *will commit* **shall give** thy *government* **reign**
into his hand:
and he shall be a father
to the *inhabitants* **settlers** of *Jerusalem* **Yeru Shalem**,
and to the house of *Judah* **Yah Hudah**.
22 And the key of the house of David
will I lay **shall I give** upon his shoulder;
so he shall open, and none shall shut;
and he shall shut, and none shall open.
23 And I *will fasten* **shall stake** him
as a nail **stake** in a *sure* **trustworthy** place;
and he shall be for *a glorious* **an honourable** throne
to his father's house.
24 And they shall hang upon him
all the *glory* **honour** of his father's house,
the offspring and the *issue* **outcasts**,
all *vessels of small quantity* **lesser instruments**,
from the *vessels* **instruments** of *cups* **bowls**,
even to all the *vessels* **instruments** of *flagons* **bagpipes**.

25 In that day,
saith the LORD of hosts **an oracle of Yah Veh Sabaoth,**
shall the *nail* **stake**
that is *fastened* **staked** in the *sure* **trustworthy** place
be removed, and be cut down, and fall;
and the burden that was upon it shall be cut off:
for *the LORD* **Yah Veh** hath *spoken it* **worded.**

THE BURDEN OF SOR

23 The burden of *Tyre* **Sor.**
Howl, ye ships of Tarshish; for it is *laid waste* **ravaged,**
so that there is no house, no entering in:
from the land of *Chittim* **Kittim**
it is *revealed* **exposed** to them.
2 Be still, ye *inhabitants* **settlers** of the *isle* **island;**
thou whom the merchants of *Zidon* **Sidon,**
that pass over the sea, have *replenished* **fulfilled.**
3 And by great waters the seed of *Sihor* **Shichor,**
the harvest of the river, is her *revenue* **produce;**
and she is a *mart* **merchant** of *nations* **goyim.**
4 Be thou *ashamed* **shamed,** O *Zidon* **Sidon:**
for the sea hath *spoken* **said,**
even the *strength* **stronghold** of the sea, saying,
I *travail* **writhe** not, nor *bring forth* **birth** children,
neither do I nourish *up young men* **youths,**
nor *bring up* **raise** virgins.
5 As at the report concerning *Egypt* **Misrayim,**
so shall they *be sorely pained* **writhe**
at the report of *Tyre* **Sor.**
6 Pass ye over to Tarshish;
howl, ye *inhabitants* **settlers** of the *isle* **island.**
7 Is this your *joyous city* **city jumping for joy,**
whose antiquity is of ancient days?
her own feet shall *carry* **bear** her afar off to sojourn.
8 Who hath taken this counsel against *Tyre* **Sor,**
the *crowning city* **crown,**
whose merchants are *princes* **governors,**
whose *traffickers* **merchants**
are the honourable of the earth?
9 *The LORD of hosts* **Yah Veh Sabaoth**
hath *purposed* **counselled** it,
to *stain* **profane** the *pride* **pomp** of all *glory* **splendour,**
and to *bring into contempt* **abase**
all the honourable of the earth.
10 Pass through thy land as a river,
O daughter of Tarshish:
there is no more *strength* **girdle.**
11 He stretched out his hand over the sea,
he *shook* **quaked** the *kingdoms* **sovereigndoms:**
the LORD **Yah Veh**
hath *given a commandment* **misvahed**
against *the merchant city* **Kenaan,**
to *destroy* **desolate** the strong holds *thereof.*
12 And he said,
Thou shalt *no more rejoice* **not add to jump for joy,**
O thou oppressed virgin, daughter of *Zidon* **Sidon:**
arise, pass over to *Chittim* **Kittim;**
there also shalt thou *have no* **not** rest.
13 Behold the land of the *Chaldeans* **Kesediym;**
this people was not, *till* the *Assyrian* **Ashshuri** founded it
for *them that dwell in the wilderness* **the desert dwellers:**
they *set up* **raised** the towers *thereof,*
they *raised up* **stripped bare** the *palaces* **citadels** *thereof;*
and he *brought* **set** it to ruin.
14 Howl, ye ships of Tarshish:
for your *strength* **stronghold** is *laid waste* **ravaged.**
15 And it shall *come to pass* **become** in that day,
that *Tyre* **Sor** shall be forgotten seventy years,
according to the days of one *king* **sovereign:**
after the end of seventy years
shall *Tyre* **it be to Sor**
sing as an harlot **as the song of a whore.**
16 Take an harp, go about the city,
thou *harlot* **whore** that hast been forgotten;
make sweet melody **strum well—pleasingly,**
sing many songs **abound the song,**
that thou mayest be remembered.
17 And it shall *come to pass* **become**
after the end of seventy years,
that *the LORD will* **Yah Veh shall** visit *Tyre* **Sor,**
and she shall turn to her *hire* **payoff,**
and shall *commit fornication* **whore**
with all the *kingdoms* **sovereigndoms** of the *world* **earth**
upon the face of the *earth* **soil.**
18 And her merchandise and her *hire* **payoff**
shall be *holiness to the LORD* **holy to Yah Veh:**
it shall not be treasured nor *laid up* **hoarded;**
for her merchandise shall be for them
that *dwell before the LORD* **settle at the face of Yah Veh,**
to eat *sufficiently* **to satisfaction,**
and for *durable clothing* **antique covering.**

YAH VEH EVACUATES THE EARTH

24 Behold,
the LORD maketh **Yah Veh evacuateth** the earth *empty,*
and *maketh it waste* **wasteth it,**
and *turneth it upside* **twisteth it face** down,
and scattereth abroad the *inhabitants* **settlers** *thereof.*
2 And it shall be,
as with the people, so with the priest;
as with the servant, so with his *master* **adoni;**
as with the maid, so with her *mistress* **lady;**
as with the *buyer* **chatteler,** so with the seller;
as with the lender, so with the borrower;
as with the *taker of usury* **exactor,**
so with the *giver of usury* **exactor** to him.
3 **In evacuating,**
The land shall be *utterly emptied* **evacuated,**
and *utterly spoiled* **in plundering, shall be plundered:**
for *the LORD* **Yah Veh** hath *spoken* **worded** this word.
4 The earth mourneth and *fadeth away* **withereth,**
the world languisheth and *fadeth away* **withereth,**
the *haughty* **high** people of the earth *do* languish.
5 The earth also is *defiled* **profaned**
under the *inhabitants* **settlers** *thereof;*
because
they have *transgressed* **trespassed** the *laws* **torah,**
changed **passed over** the *ordinance* **statute,**
broken the *everlasting* **eternal** covenant.
6 Therefore hath the *curse* **oath** devoured the earth,
and *they that dwell* **the settlers** therein
are desolate **have guilted:**
therefore the *inhabitants* **settlers** of the earth
are *burned* **scorched,** and few men *left* **survive.**
7 The *new wine* **juice** mourneth, the vine languisheth,
all the *merryhearted do* **cheerful** sigh.
8 The *mirth* **joy** of *tabrets* **tambourines**
ceaseth **shabbathizeth,**
the *noise* **uproar** of them that *rejoice* **jump for joy**
endeth **ceaseth,**
the joy of the harp *ceaseth* **shabbathizeth.**
9 They shall not drink wine with a song;
strong drink shall *be bitter to* **embitter** them that drink it.
10 The city of *confusion* **waste** is broken down:
every house is shut up, that no man may come in.
11 There is *a crying* **an outcry** for wine
in the *streets* **outways;**
all *joy* **cheerfulness** is *darkened* **obscured,**
the *mirth* **joy** of the land is *gone* **exiled.**
12 In the city *is left* **surviveth** desolation,
and the *gate* **portal**
is *smitten* **crushed** with *destruction* **waste.**
13 When thus it shall be
in the midst of the land among the people,
there shall be as the shaking of an olive *tree,*
and as the *gleaning grapes* **gleanings**
when the *vintage* **crop** is *done* **finished.**
14 They shall lift up their voice,
they shall *sing* **shout**
for the *majesty* **pomp** of *the LORD* **Yah Veh,**
they shall *cry aloud* **resound** from the sea.
15 Wherefore *glorify* **honour** ye *the LORD* **Yah Veh**
in the *fires* **flames,**
even the name
of *the LORD God* **Yah Veh Elohim** of *Israel* **Yisra El**
in the *isles* **islands** of the sea.
16 From the uttermost *part* **wing** of the earth
have we heard songs,
even glory **splendour** to the *righteous* **just.**
But I said, My *leanness,* **emaciation!**
my *leanness,* **emaciation!** woe unto me!
the *treacherous dealers* **coverters**

have *dealt treacherously* **coverted**;
yea, the *treacherous dealers* **coverters**
have *dealt very treacherously* **coverted**.
17 Fear, and the pit, and the snare, are upon thee,
O *inhabitant* **settler** of the earth.
18 And it shall *come to pass* **become**,
that he who fleeth from the *noise* **voice** of the fear
shall fall into the pit;
and he that *cometh up* **ascendeth**
out of the midst of the pit
shall be *taken* **captured** in the snare:
for the windows from on high are open,
and the foundations of the earth *do shake* **quake**.
19 **In shattering,**
The earth is *utterly broken down* **shattered**,
In breaking,
the earth is *clean dissolved* **broken**,
In toppling,
the earth is *moved exceedingly* **toppled**.
20 **In staggering,**
The earth shall *reel to and fro* **stagger**
like a drunkard **as intoxicated**,
and shall *be removed* **sway** like a *cottage* **hammock**;
and the *transgression* **rebellion** *thereof*
shall be heavy upon it;
and it shall fall, and not rise *again*.
21 And it shall *come to pass* **become**, in that day,
that *the LORD* **Yah Veh** shall *punish* **visit**
upon the host of the high ones *that are* on high,
and the *kings* **sovereigns** of the *earth* **soil**
upon the *earth* **soil**.
22 And they shall
be gathered together **gather a gathering**,
as *prisoners* **bound** are gathered in the *pit* **well**,
and shall be shut up in the *prison* **lockup**,
and after many days shall they be visited.
23 Then the moon shall *be confounded* **blush**,
and the sun *ashamed* **shame**,
when *the LORD of hosts* **Yah Veh Sabaoth**
shall reign in mount *Zion* **Siyon**,
and in *Jerusalem* **Yeru Shalem**,
and before his *ancients gloriously* **elders honourably**.

THE EXALTMENT OF EXTENDED HANDS

25 O *LORD* **Yah Veh**, thou *art* my *God* **Elohim**;
I *will* **shall** exalt thee,
I *will praise* **shall extend hands unto** thy name;
for thou hast *done wonderful things* **worked marvels**;
thy counsels of *old* **the distant past**
are *faithfulness* **trustworthiness** and *truth* **amen**.
2 For thou hast *made* **set** of a city an heap;
of a *defenced* **fortified** city a ruin:
a *palace* **citadel** of strangers to be no city;
it shall *never* **eternally not** be built.
3 Therefore shall the strong people *glorify* **honour** thee,
the city of the *terrible nations* **tyrant goyim**
shall fear thee.
4 For thou hast been a *strength* **stronghold** to the poor,
a strength to the needy in his *distress* **tribulation**,
a refuge from the *storm* **flood**,
a shadow from the *heat* **parchedness**,
when the *blast* **wind** of the *terrible ones* **tyrants**
is as a *storm* **flood** against the wall.
5 Thou shalt *bring down* **subdue**
the *noise* **uproar** of strangers,
as the *heat* **parchedness** in a *dry place* **parch**;
even the heat with the shadow of a **thick** cloud:
the branch of the *terrible ones* **tyrants**
shall *be brought low* **answer**.
6 And in this mountain
shall *the LORD of hosts* **Yah Veh Sabaoth**
make **work** unto all people
a *feast* **banquet** of *fat things* **oil**,
a *feast* **banquet** of *wines on the lees* **dregs**,
of *fat things full of marrow* **marrowed oil**,
of *wines on the lees well refined* **filtered dregs**.
7 And he *will destroy* **shall swallow** in this mountain
the face of the *covering* **veil**
cast **veiled** over all people,
and the vail that is spread over all *nations* **goyim**.
8 He *will* **shall** swallow *up* death in *victory* **perpetuity**;
and *the Lord GOD* **Adonay Yah Veh**
will **shall** wipe away tears from off all faces;
and the rebuke of his people
shall he *take away* **turn aside** from off all the earth:
for *the LORD* **Yah Veh** hath *spoken it* **worded**.
9 And it shall be said in that day,
Lo **Behold**, this is our *God* **Elohim**;
we have *waited for* **awaited** him,
and he *will* **shall** save us:
this is *the LORD* **Yah Veh**;
we have *waited for* **awaited** him,
we *will be glad* **shall twirl** and *rejoice* **cheer**
in his salvation.
10 For in this mountain
shall the hand of *the LORD* **Yah Veh** rest,
and Moab shall be *trodden down* **threshed** under him,
even as straw is *trodden down* **threshed**
for **in the water of** the dunghill.
11 And he shall spread *forth* his hands
in the midst of them,
as he that swimmeth spreadeth forth *his hands* to swim:
and he shall *bring down* **abase** their *pride* **pomp**
together with the *spoils* **lurkings** of their hands.
12 And the fortress of the *high fort* **secure loft** of thy walls
shall he *bring down* **prostrate**, *lay low* **lower**,
and *bring* **touch** to the *ground* **earth**, *even* to the dust.

SONG OF THE LAND OF YAH HUDAH

26 In that day
shall this song be sung in the land of *Judah* **Yah Hudah**;
We have a strong city;
salvation *will God appoint* **shall he place**
for walls and *bulwarks* **trenches**.
2 Open ye the *gates* **portals**,
that the *righteous nation* **just goyim**
which *keepeth* **guardeth** the *truth* **trust** may enter in.
3 Thou *wilt keep* **shalt guard** him
in *perfect peace* **shalom shalom**,
whose *mind* **imagination** is *stayed* **propped** on thee:
because he *trusteth* **confideth** in thee.
4 *Trust* **Confide** ye
in *the LORD for ever* **Yah Veh eternally**:
for in *the LORD JEHOVAH* **Yah Yah Veh**
is *everlasting strength* **an eternal rock**:
5 For he *bringeth down* **prostrateth** them
that *dwell* **settle** on high;
the *lofty* **exalted** city, he *layeth it low* **lowereth**;
he *layeth it low* **lowereth**, *even* to the *ground* **earth**;
he *bringeth* **toucheth** it *even* to the dust.
6 The foot shall *tread* **trample** it *down*,
even the feet of the *poor* **humble**,
and the steps of the *needy* **poor**.
7 The way of the just is *uprightness* **straightness**:
thou, *most upright* **O straight**,
dost weigh the *path* **route** of the just.
8 Yea, in the way of thy judgments, O *LORD* **Yah Veh**,
have we *waited for* **awaited** thee;
the desire of our soul is to thy name,
and to the *remembrance* **memorial** of thee.
9 With my soul have I desired thee in the night;
yea, with my spirit within me *will* **shall** I seek thee early:
for when thy judgments are in the earth,
the *inhabitants* **settlers** of the world
will **shall** learn *righteousness* **justness**.
10 *Let favour be shewed* **Grant charism** to the wicked,
yet *will* **shall** he not learn *righteousness* **justness**:
in the land of *uprightness* **straightforwardness**
will **shall** he deal *unjustly* **wickedly**,
and *will* **shall** not *behold* **see**
the *majesty* **pomp** of *the LORD* **Yah Veh**.
11 *LORD* **Yah Veh**, *when* thy hand is lifted up,
they *will* **shall** not see:
but they shall see, and *be ashamed* **shame**
for their envy at the people;
yea, the fire of *thine enemies* **thy tribulators**
shall devour them.
12 *LORD* **Yah Veh**,
thou *wilt ordain peace* **shalt set shalom** for us:
for thou also hast *wrought* **made** all our works in us.
13 O *LORD* **Yah Veh** our *God* **Elohim**,
other lords **adonim** beside thee

have *had dominion over* **mastered** us:
but by thee only
will **shall** we *make mention of* **memorialize** thy name.
14 *They are* dead, they shall not live;
they are deceased **ghosts**, they shall not rise:
therefore hast thou visited and *destroyed* **desolated** them,
and *made* **destroyed**
all their *memory to perish* **memorial**.
15 Thou hast increased the *nation* **goyim**,
O *LORD* **Yah Veh**,
thou hast increased the *nation* **goyim**:
thou art *glorified* **honoured**:
thou hadst removed it far unto all the ends of the earth.
16 *LORD* **Yah Veh**,
in *trouble* **tribulation** have they visited thee,
they poured out *a prayer* **an enchantment**
when thy chastening *was* upon them.
17 *Like* **Such** as a woman *with child* **having conceived**,
that *draweth near the time of* **approacheth**
her *delivery* **begetting**,
is in pain **writheth**, *and* crieth out in her pangs;
so have we been *in thy sight* **at thy face**,
O *LORD* **Yah Veh**.
18 We have *been with child* **conceived**,
we have *been in pain* **writhed**,
we have *as it were brought forth* **begotten** wind;
we have not *wrought* **worked** any *deliverance* **salvation**
in the earth;
neither have the *inhabitants* **settlers** of the world fallen.
19 Thy dead *men* shall live,
together with my *dead body* **carcase** shall they arise.
Awake and *sing* **shout**, ye that *dwell* **tabernacle** in dust:
for thy dew is as the dew of herbs,
and the
earth shall cast out the dead **land of ghosts shall fall**.
20 Come, my people,
enter thou into thy chambers,
and shut thy doors about thee:
hide thyself *as it were* for a little *moment* **blink**,
until the *indignation be overpast* **rage passeth over**.
21 For, behold,
the LORD **Yah Veh** cometh out of his place
to *punish* **visit upon** the *inhabitants* **settlers** of the earth
for their *iniquity* **perversity**:
the earth also shall *disclose* **expose** her blood,
and shall no more cover her *slain* **slaughtered**.

THE DELIVERANCE OF YISRA EL

27 In that day *the LORD* **Yah Veh**
with his *sore* **hard** and great and strong sword
shall *punish* **visit**
upon leviathan the *piercing* **fugitive** serpent,
even leviathan that crooked serpent;
and he shall slay the *dragon* **monster** that is in the sea.
2 In that day *sing* **answer** ye unto her,
A vineyard of *red wine* **desire**.
3 I *the LORD do keep* **Yah Veh guard** it;
I *will water* **shall moisten** it every *moment* **blink**:
lest any *hurt* **visit upon** it,
I *will keep* **shall guard** it night and day.
4 Fury is not in me:
who would set the briers and thorns against me in battle
who shall give me briers — thorns in war?
I *would go* **should stride** through them,
I *would* **should** burn them together.
5 Or let him take hold of my *strength* **stronghold**,
that he may *make peace* **work shalom** with me;
and he shall *make peace* **work shalom** with me.
6 He shall cause them that come of *Jacob* **Yaaqov**
to *take* root:
Israel **Yisra El** shall blossom and bud,
and fill the face of the world with *fruit* **produce**.
7 Hath he smitten him, as he smote those that smote him?
or is he *slain* **slaughtered**
according to the slaughter of them
that are *slain* **slaughtered** by him?
8 In *measure* **seah**, when it *shooteth forth* **extendeth**,
thou *wilt debate* **shalt strive** with it:
he *stayeth* **removeth** his *rough* **hard** wind
in the day of the *east wind* **easterly**.
9 By this therefore
shall the *iniquity* **perversity** of *Jacob* **Yaaqov**
be *purged* **kapared/atoned**;
and this is all the fruit to *take away* **turn aside** his sin;
when he *maketh* **setteth** all the stones
of the **sacrifice** altar
as *chalkstones* **lime** that are *beaten in sunder* **shattered**,
the *groves* **asherah** and *images* **sun icons**
shall not *stand up* **rise**.
10 Yet the *defenced* **fortified** city shall be *desolate* **alone**,
and the habitation **of rest** *forsaken* **sent away**,
and left — **forsaken** like a wilderness:
there shall the calf *feed* **graze**,
and there shall he *lie down* **crouch**,
and *consume* **finish off** the *branches* **twigs** *thereof*.
11 When the *boughs* **harvests** *thereof* are withered,
they shall be broken off:
the women come, and *set* **light** them *on fire* **up**:
for it is a people of no understanding:
therefore he that *made* **worked** them
will **shall** not *have* mercy *on* them,
and he that formed them
will shew them no favour **shall grant them no charism**.
12 And it shall *come to pass* **become** in that day,
that *the LORD* **Yah Veh**
shall beat off from the *channel* **stream** of the river
unto the *stream* **wadi** of *Egypt* **Misrayim**,
and ye shall be gathered one by one,
O ye *children* **sons** of *Israel* **Yisra El**.
13 And it shall *come to pass* **become** in that day,
that the great trumpet shall *be blown* **blast**,
and they shall come
which were ready to perish **to those destructing**
in the land of *Assyria* **Ashshur**,
and the *outcasts* **expelled** in the land of *Egypt* **Misrayim**,
and shall *worship the LORD* **prostrate to Yah Veh**
in the holy mount at *Jerusalem* **Yeru Shalem**.

HO TO EPHRAYIM

28 *Woe* **Ho** to the crown of *pride* **pomp**,
to the *drunkards* **intoxicated** of *Ephraim* **Ephrayim**,
whose *glorious beauty* **adornment of splendour**
is a *fading flower* **withering blossom**,
which are on the head
of the *fat* valleys **of ointment**
of them that are *overcome* **hammered** with wine!
2 Behold, *the Lord* **Adonay** hath a mighty and strong one,
which as a tempest of hail
and a *destroying storm* **ruinous whirling**,
as a flood of *mighty* **many** waters overflowing,
shall *cast down* **set** to the earth with the hand.
3 The crown of *pride* **pomp**,
the *drunkards* **intoxicated** of *Ephraim* **Ephrayim**,
shall be *trodden* **trampled** under feet:
4 And the *glorious beauty* **adornment of splendour**,
which is on the head of the *fat* valley **of ointment**,
shall be a *fading flower* **withering blossom**,
and as the *hasty fruit* **firstfruits** before the summer;
which when he that *looketh* **seeth** upon it seeth,
while it is yet in his *hand* **palm**
he *eateth it up* **swalloweth**.
5 In that day shall *the LORD of hosts* **Yah Veh Sabaoth**
be for a crown of *glory* **splendour**,
and for a *diadem* **corona** of *beauty* **adornment**,
unto the *residue* **survivors** of his people,
6 And for a spirit of judgment
to him that sitteth in judgment,
and for *strength* **might** to them
that turn the *battle* **war** to the *gate* **portal**.
7 But they also have erred **inadvertently** through wine,
and through *strong drink* **intoxicants**
are out of the way **stagger**;
the priest and the prophet have erred **inadvertently**
through *strong drink* **intoxicants**,
they are swallowed *up* of wine,
they *are out of the way* **stagger**
through *strong drink* **intoxicants**;
they err **inadvertently** in *vision* **sight**,
they *stumble* **waver** in judgment.
8 For all tables are *full* **filled** of vomit and *filthiness* **dung**,
so that there is no place *clean*.
9 Whom shall he teach knowledge?

and whom shall he *make* **have**
to *understand doctrine* **discern the report**?
them that are weaned from the milk,
and *drawn* **weaned** from the breasts.
10 For *precept must be* **misvah** upon *precept* **misvah**,
precept **misvah** upon *precept* **misvah**;
line upon line, line upon line;
here a little, *and* there a little:
11 For with *stammering* **jeering** lips and another tongue
will **shall** he *speak* **word** to this people.
12 To whom he said, This is the rest *wherewith*
ye may *cause the weary to* rest **the languid**;
and this is the *refreshing* **rest**:
yet they *would* **willed to** not hear.
13 But the word of *the LORD* **Yah Veh** was unto them
precept **misvah** upon *precept* **misvah**,
precept **misvah** upon *precept* **misvah**;
line upon line, line upon line;
here a little, *and* there a little;
that they might go, and *fall* **falter** backward,
and be broken, and snared, and *taken* **captured**.
14 Wherefore hear the word of *the LORD* **Yah Veh**,
ye scornful men, that *rule* **reign over** this people
which is in *Jerusalem* **Yeru Shalem**.
15 Because ye have said,
We have *made* **cut** a covenant with death,
and with *hell* **sheol**
are we at agreement **worked we seers**;
when the overflowing *scourge* **whip** shall pass through,
it shall not come unto us:
for we have *made* **set** lies our refuge,
and under falsehood have we hid ourselves:
16 Therefore thus saith *the Lord GOD* **Adonay Yah Veh**,
Behold, I lay in *Zion* **Siyon** for a foundation a stone,
a *tried* **proofed** stone, a *precious* **esteemed** corner *stone*,
a *sure* **founded** foundation:
he that *believeth* **trusteth** shall not *make haste* **hasten**.
17 Judgment also *will I lay* **shall I set** to the line,
and *righteousness* **justness** to the *plummet* **plumb line**:
and the hail shall *sweep* **snatch** away the refuge of lies,
and the waters shall overflow the *hiding place* **covert**.
18 And your covenant with death
shall be *disannulled* **kapared/atoned**,
and your *agreement* **vision** with *hell* **sheol**
shall not *stand* **rise**;
when the overflowing *scourge* **whip** shall pass through,
then ye shall be *trodden down* **trampled** by it.
19 *From the time that it goeth forth*
As often as it passeth over
it shall take you:
for morning by morning shall it pass over,
by day and by night:
and it shall be *a vexation* **an agitation**
only to *understand* **discern** the report.
20 For the bed is shorter than
that a man can stretch himself on it **to extend thereon**:
and the covering narrower than
that he can wrap himself in it **to enfold therein**.
21 For *the LORD* **Yah Veh** shall rise *up*
as *in mount Perazim* **the mount of breaches**,
he shall *be wroth* **quiver**
as *in the valley of Gibeon* **Gay Gibon**,
that he may *do* **work** his work, his strange work;
and *bring to pass* **serve** his *act* **service**,
his strange *act* **service**.
22 Now therefore be ye not *mockers* **translators**,
lest your *bands* **bonds** be *made strong* **strengthened**:
for I have heard from
the Lord GOD of hosts **Adonay Yah Veh Sabaoth**
a *consumption* **final finish**,
even determined **appointed** upon the whole earth.
23 *Give ye ear* **Hearken ye**, and hear my voice;
hearken, and hear my *speech* **saying**.
24 Doth the *plowman* **plower** plow all day to sow?
doth he open
and *break the clods of his ground* **harrow his soil**?
25 When he hath *made plain* **equalized** the face *thereof*,
doth he not *cast abroad* **scatter** the *fitches* **fennelflowers**,
and scatter the cummin,
and *cast in the principal* **set the** wheat **in rows**
and the *appointed* **designated** barley
and the *rie* **spelt** in their *place* **border**?
26 For his *God* **Elohim**
doth *instruct* **discipline** him to *discretion* **judgment**,
and doth teach him.
27 For the *fitches* **fennelflowers**
are not threshed with a *threshing instrument* **sickle**,
neither is a *cart* **wagon** wheel
turned about upon the cummin;
but the *fitches* **fennelflowers**
are *beaten out* **threshed** with a *staff* **rod**,
and the cummin with a *rod* **scion**.
28 Bread *corn* is *bruised* **pulverized**;
because **in threshing**,
he *will* **shall** not *ever be threshing it* **thresh in perpetuity**,
nor *break* **crusheth** it with the wheel of his *cart* **wagon**,
nor *bruise* **pulverize** it with his *horsemen* **cavalry**.
29 This also cometh forth
from *the LORD of hosts* **Yah Veh Sabaoth**,
which is wonderful — **marvellous** in counsel,
and *excellent in working* **greatened in support**.

HO TO ARI EL

29 *Woe* **Ho** to *Ariel* **Ari El**,
to Ariel **Ari El** the city *where* David *dwelt* **encamped**!
add ye **scrape ye up** year to year;
let them *kill sacrifices* **strike celebrations**.
2 Yet I *will* **shall** distress *Ariel* **Ari El**,
and there shall be
heaviness **mourning** and *sorrow* **sighing**:
and it shall be unto me as *Ariel* **Ari El**.
3 And I *will camp* **shall encamp** against thee
round about **as a whirler**,
and *will lay siege* **shall besiege** against thee
with a *mount* **station**,
and I *will* **shall** raise *forts* **ramparts** against thee.
4 And thou shalt be *brought down* **abased**,
and shalt *speak* **word** out of the *ground* **earth**,
and thy *speech* **saying**
shall *be low* **prostrate** out of the dust,
and thy voice shall be,
as of *one that hath a familiar spirit* **a spiritist**,
out of the *ground* **earth**,
and thy *speech* **saying** shall *whisper* **chirp** out of the dust.
5 Moreover the multitude of thy strangers
shall be *like small dust* **as pulverized**,
and the multitude of the *terrible ones* **tyrants**
shall be as chaff that passeth away:
yea, it shall be *at an instant* **in a blink** suddenly.
6 Thou shalt be visited
of *the LORD of hosts* **Yah Veh Sabaoth**
with thunder, and with *earthquake* **quake**,
and great *noise* **voice**,
with *storm* **hurricane** and *tempest* **storm**,
and the flame of devouring fire.
7 And the multitude of all the *nations* **goyim**
that *fight* **host** against *Ariel* **Ari El**,
even all that *fight* **host** against her
and her *munition* **hunthold**,
and that distress her,
shall be as a dream of a night vision.
8 It shall even be
as when *an hungry man* **the famished** dreameth,
and, behold, he eateth;
but he awaketh, and his soul is empty:
or as when a thirsty man dreameth,
and, behold, he drinketh;
but he awaketh, and, behold, he is *faint* **languid**,
and his soul *hath appetite* **yearneth**:
so shall the multitude of all the *nations* **goyim** be,
that *fight* **host** against mount *Zion* **Siyon**.
9 *Stay yourselves* **Linger**, and *wonder* **marvel**;
cry ye out **stare**, *and cry* **stare**:
they *are drunken* **intoxicate**, but not with wine;
they stagger, but not with *strong drink* **intoxicants**.
10 For *the LORD* **Yah Veh**
hath *poured out* **libated** upon you
the spirit of *deep* **sound** sleep,
and hath *closed* **bound** your eyes:
the prophets and your *rulers* **heads**,
the seers hath he covered.

11 And the vision of all is become unto you
as the words of a *book* **scroll** that is sealed,
which *men deliver* **be given**
to one that *is learned* **knoweth the scroll**, saying,
Read **Call out** this, I *pray* **beseech** thee:
and he saith, I cannot; for it is sealed:
12 And the *book* **scroll** is *delivered* **given** to him
that *is not learned* **knoweth not the scroll**, saying,
Read **Call out** this, *I pray thee*:
and he saith, I *am not learned* **know not the scroll**.
13 *Wherefore the Lord* **Adonay** said,
Forasmuch
as this people draw near *me* with their mouth,
and with their lips *do* honour me,
but have removed their heart far from me,
and their fear toward me
is taught by the *precept* **misvah** of men:
14 Therefore, behold,
I *will proceed* **shall add**
to do a *marvellous work* **marvel** among this people,
even a work and a wonder **a marvellous marvel**:
for the wisdom of their wise *men*
shall *perish* **destruct**,
and the understanding of their *prudent men* **discerning**
shall be hid.
15 *Woe* **Ho** unto them that *seek deep* **deepen**
to hide their counsel from *the LORD* **Yah Veh**,
and their works *are* **become** in the dark,
and they say, Who seeth us? and who knoweth us?
16 Surely your turning *of things* upside down
shall be *esteemed* **fabricated**
as the *potter's clay* **former's morter**:
for shall the work say of him that *made* **worked** it,
He *made* **worked** me not?
or shall the *thing framed* **former**
say of *him that framed it* **the former**,
He *had no understanding* **discerned not**?
17 Is it not yet a very little while,
and Lebanon shall be turned
into *a fruitful field* **an orchard/Karmel**,
and the *fruitful field* **orchard/Karmel**
shall be *esteemed* **fabricated** as a forest?
18 And in that day
shall the deaf hear the words of the *book* **scroll**,
and the eyes of the blind
shall see out of *obscurity* **thick darkness**,
and out of darkness.
19 The *meek* **humble** also
shall increase *their joy* **cheerfulness**
in *the LORD* **Yah Veh**,
and *the poor among men* **needy humanity**
shall *rejoice* **twirl**
in the Holy One of *Israel* **Yisra El**.
20 For the *terrible one* **tyrant**
is brought to nought **ceaseth**,
and the scorner is *consumed* **finished off**,
and all that watch for *iniquity* **mischief** are cut off:
21 That *make a man* **cause humanity**
an offender for a **to sin in** word,
and *lay a snare for* **ensnare** him
that reproveth in the *gate* **portal**,
and *turn aside* **pervert** the just
for a *thing of nought* **waste**.
22 Therefore thus saith *the LORD* **Yah Veh**,
who redeemed Abraham
concerning the house of *Jacob* **Yaaqov**,
Jacob **Yaaqov** shall not now *be ashamed* **shame**,
neither shall his face now *wax* pale.
23 But when he seeth his children,
the work of mine hands, in the midst of him,
they shall *sanctify* **hallow** my name,
and *sanctify* **hallow** the Holy One of *Jacob* **Yaaqov**,
and shall *fear the God* **awe Elohim** of *Israel* **Yisra El**.
24 They also that *erred* **strayed** in spirit
shall *come to* **know** understanding,
and they that *murmured* **rebelled** shall learn doctrine.

HO TO THE REVOLTING SONS

30 *Woe* **Ho** to the *rebellious children* **revolting sons**,
saith the LORD **an oracle of Yah Veh**,
that *take* **work** counsel, but not of me;
and that *cover with a covering* **pour a pouring**,
but not of my spirit,
that they may *add* **scrape up** sin to sin:
2 That walk to *go down* **descend** into *Egypt* **Misrayim**,
and have not asked at my mouth;
to strengthen themselves
in the *strength* **stronghold** of *Pharaoh* **Paroh**,
and to *trust* **seek refuge** in the shadow of *Egypt* **Misrayim**!
3 Therefore
shall the *strength* **stronghold** of *Pharaoh* **Paroh**
be your shame,
and the trust in the shadow of *Egypt* **Misrayim**
your *confusion* **shame**.
4 For his *princes* **governors** were at *Zoan* **Soan**,
and his *ambassadors came to* **angels touched** Hanes.
5 They were all ashamed
of a people that *could not profit* **benefiteth** them **not**,
nor be an help nor *profit* **benefit**,
but a shame, and also a reproach.

THE BURDEN OF THE ANIMALS OF THE SOUTH

6 The burden of the *beasts* **animals** of the south:
into the land of *trouble* **tribulation** and *anguish* **distress**,
from whence *come* the *young* **roaring lion** and old lion,
the *viper* **hisser** and *fiery* flying *serpent* **seraph**,
they *will carry* **shall bear** their *riches* **valuables**
upon the shoulders of *young asses* **colts**,
and their treasures upon the *bunches* **humps** of camels,
to a people that shall not *profit* **benefit** them.
7 For the *Egyptians shall help in vain* **Misrayim be vanity**,
and *to no purpose* **shall help in vain**:
therefore have I *cried* **called** concerning this,
Their *strength* **pride** is to *sit still* **shabbathize**.
8 Now go, *write* **inscribe** it before them in a *table* **slab**,
and *note* **engrave** it in a *book* **scroll**,
that it may be for the *time to come* **latter day**
for ever **eternally** and *ever* **eternally**:
9 That this is a rebellious people,
lying children **deceptive sons**,
children **sons** that will **to** not hear
the *law* **torah** of *the LORD* **Yah Veh**:
10 Which say to the seers, See not;
and to the *prophets* **seers**,
Prophesy **See** not unto us
right things **straightforwardnesses**,
speak **word** unto us smooth *things*,
prophesy deceits **see delusions**:
11 *Get you* **Turn ye aside** out of the way,
turn aside **pervert** out of the path,
cause the Holy One of *Israel* **Yisra El**
to *cease* **shabbathize** from *before us* **our face**.
12 Wherefore thus saith the Holy One of *Israel* **Yisra El**,
Because ye *despise* **spurn** this word,
and *trust* **confide** in oppression and perverseness,
and *stay* **lean** thereon:
13 Therefore this *iniquity* **perversity** shall be to you
as a **falling** breach *ready to fall*,
swelling **bulging** out in a *high* **lofted** wall,
whose breaking cometh suddenly *at an instant* **in a blink**.
14 And he shall break it
as the breaking of the *potters' vessel* **former's bag**
that is *broken in pieces* **crushed**;
he shall not spare:
so that there shall not be found
in the *bursting* **fracture** of it
a *sherd* **potsherd** to take fire from the *hearth* **burning**,
or to *take* **strip** water *withal* out of the *pit* **dugout**.
15 For thus saith *the Lord GOD* **Adonay Yah Veh**,
the Holy One of *Israel* **Yisra El**;
In returning and rest shall ye be saved;
in *quietness* **resting** and in confidence
shall be your *strength* **might**:
and ye *would* **willed** not.
16 But ye said, No; for we *will* **shall** flee upon horses;
therefore shall ye flee:
and, We *will* **shall** ride upon the swift;
therefore shall they that pursue you be swift.
17 One thousand *shall flee*
at **the face of** the rebuke of one;
at **the face of** the rebuke of five shall ye flee:
till ye *be left* **remain** as a *beacon* **mast**

upon the top of a mountain,
and as an ensign on an hill.
18 And therefore *will the LORD* **shall Yah Veh** wait,
that he may *be gracious* **grant charism** unto you,
and therefore *will* **shall** he be exalted,
that he may *have* mercy *upon* you:
for *the LORD* **Yah Veh** is *a God* **an Elohim** of judgment:
blessed **blithesome** are all they that wait for him.
19 For the people shall *dwell* **settle** in *Zion* **Siyon**
at *Jerusalem* **Yeru Shalem**:
in weeping, thou shalt **not** weep *no more*:
in granting charism,
he *will be very gracious* **shall grant charism**
unto thee at the voice of thy cry;
when he shall hear it, he *will* **shall** answer thee.
20 And *though the Lord* **Adonay**
give **giveth** you the bread of *adversity* **tribulation**,
and the water of *affliction* **oppression**,
yet shall not thy teachers
be removed into a corner **withdraw** any more,
but thine eyes shall see thy teachers:
21 And thine ears shall hear a word behind thee,
saying, This is the way, walk ye in it,
when ye turn to the right *hand*,
and *when ye turn to* the left.
22 Ye shall *defile* **foul** also the *covering* **overlay**
of thy *graven images* **sculptiles** of silver,
and the *ornament* **ephod**
of thy *molten images* **moltings** of gold:
thou shalt cast them away as a menstruous cloth;
thou shalt say unto it, Get thee hence.
23 Then shall he give the rain of thy seed,
that thou shalt *sow* **seed** the *ground* **soil** withal;
and bread of the *increase* **produce** of the *earth* **soil**,
and it shall be fat and *plenteous* **fattened**:
in that day shall thy *cattle feed* **chattel graze**
in *large pastures* **enlarged meadows**.
24 The oxen likewise and the *young asses* **colts**
that *ear* **serve** the *ground* **soil**
shall eat *clean provender* **seasoned fodder**,
which hath been winnowed
with the *shovel* **winnowing fork**
and with the *fan* **winnowing basket**.
25 And there shall be upon every *high* **lifted** mountain,
and upon every high hill,
rivers **rivulets** and streams of waters
in the day of the great slaughter, when the towers fall.
26 Moreover the light of the moon
shall be as the light of the sun,
and the light of the sun shall be sevenfold,
as the light of seven days,
in the day that *the LORD* **Yah Veh**
bindeth up the breach of his people,
and healeth the stroke of their wound.
27 Behold,
the name of *the LORD* **Yah Veh** cometh from far,
burning with his *anger* **wrath**,
and the burden *thereof* is heavy:
his lips are *full of indignation* **filled with rage**,
and his tongue as a devouring fire:
28 And his *breath* **spirit**, as an overflowing *stream* **wadi**,
shall *reach to the midst of* **halve** the neck,
to sift the *nations* **goyim** with the sieve of vanity:
and there shall be a bridle in the jaws of the people,
causing them to *err* **stray**.
29 Ye shall have a song, as in the night
when a holy *solemnity* **celebration** is *kept* **hallowed**;
and *gladness* **cheerfulness** of heart,
as when one goeth with a pipe
to come into the mountain of *the LORD* **Yah Veh**,
to the *mighty One* **Rock** of *Israel* **Yisra El**.
30 And *the LORD* **Yah Veh** shall cause
his *glorious voice* **voice of majesty** to be heard,
and *shall shew the lighting down of his arm*
the resting of his arm shall be seen,
with the *indignation* **rage** of his *anger* **wrath**,
and *with* the flame of a devouring fire,
with scattering, and *tempest* **flood**, and hailstones.
31 For through the voice of *the LORD* **Yah Veh**
shall the *Assyrian* **Ashshuri** be beaten down,
which smote with a *rod* **scion**.
32 And in every *place* **passage**
where the *grounded staff* **founded rod** shall pass,
which *the LORD* **Yah Veh** shall *lay* **rest** upon him,
it shall be with *tabrets* **tambourines** and harps:
and in *battles* **wars** of *shaking* **waving**
will **shall** he fight with it.
33 For *Tophet* **Topheth**
is *ordained of old* **lined up from yesterday**;
yea, for the *king* **sovereign** it is prepared;
he hath *made it deep* **deepened** and *large* **enlarged**:
the *pile* **fuel pile** *thereof*
is fire and *much wood* **abounding timber**;
the breath of *the LORD* **Yah Veh**,
like a *stream* **wadi** of *brimstone* **sulphur**,
doth *kindle* **burn** it.

HO TO THEM THAT LOOK NOT UPON THE HOLY ONE

31 *Woe* **Ho** to them
that *go down to Egypt* **descend to Misrayim** for help;
and *stay* **lean** on horses, and *trust* **confide** in chariots,
because they are many;
and in *horsemen* **cavalry**,
because they are *very strong* **mightily mighty**;
but they look not unto the Holy One of *Israel* **Yisra El**,
neither seek *the LORD* **Yah Veh**!
2 Yet he also is wise, and *will* **shall** bring evil,
and *will* **shall** not *call back* **turn aside** his words:
but *will* **shall** arise
against the house of the *evildoers* **vilifiers**,
and against the help of them that work *iniquity* **mischief**.
3 Now the *Egyptians* **Misrayim**
are *men* **human** and not *God* **El**;
and their horses flesh, and not spirit.
When *the LORD* **Yah Veh** shall stretch out his hand,
both he that helpeth shall *fall* **falter**,
and he that is *holpen* **helped** shall fall *down*,
and they all shall *fail* **finish** together.
4 For thus hath *the LORD spoken* **Yah Veh said** unto me,
Like as the lion and the *young lion* **whelp**
roaring **meditating** on his prey,
when a *multitude* **fulness** of *shepherds* **tenders**
is called forth against him,
he *will* **shall** not *be afraid* **terrify** of their voice,
nor *abase* **humble** himself
for the *noise of them* **multitude**:
so shall *the LORD of hosts* **Yah Veh Sabaoth**
come down **descend** to fight for mount *Zion* **Siyon**,
and for the hill *thereof*.
5 As birds flying,
so *will the LORD of hosts* **shall Yah Veh Sabaoth**
defend Jerusalem **garrison Yeru Shalem**;
defending **garrisoning** also he *will* **shall** deliver it;
and passing over he *will preserve* **shall rescue** it.
6 Turn ye unto him
from whom the *children* **sons** of *Israel* **Yisra El**
have *deeply revolted* **deepened revolt**.
7 For in that day every man shall *cast away* **spurn**
his idols of silver, and his idols of gold,
which your own hands
have *made* **worked** unto you for a sin.
8 Then shall the *Assyrian* **Ashshuri** fall with the sword,
not of *a mighty* man;
and the sword, not of *a mean man* **humanity**,
shall devour him:
but he shall flee from **the face of** the sword,
and his *young men* **youths** shall be *discomfited* **vassals**.
9 And he shall pass over to his *strong hold* **rock**
for *fear* **terror**,
and his *princes* **governors**
shall *be afraid* **dismay** of the ensign,
saith the LORD **an oracle of Yah Veh**,
whose *fire* **flame** is in *Zion* **Siyon**,
and his furnace in *Jerusalem* **Yeru Shalem**.

THE REIGN OF JUSTNESS

32 Behold, a king shall reign in *righteousness* **justness**,
and *princes* **governors** shall *rule* **govern** in judgment.
2 And a man shall be
as *an hiding place* **a refuge** from the wind,
and a covert from the *tempest* **flood**;
as *rivers* **rivulets** of water in a *dry place* **parch**,

as the shadow of a *great* **heavy** rock
in a *weary* **languid** land.
3 And the eyes of them that see
shall not *be dim* **look away,**
and the ears of them that hear shall hearken.
4 The heart also of the *rash* **hasty**
shall *understand* **discern** knowledge,
and the tongue of the stammerers
shall *be ready* **hasten** to *speak plainly* **word clearly.**
5 The *vile person* **fool**
shall be no more called *liberal* **volunteer,**
nor the *churl* **crafty** said to be *bountiful* **opulent.**
6 For the *vile person* **fool**
will speak villany **shall word folly,**
and his heart *will* **shall** work *iniquity* **mischief,**
to *practise hypocrisy* **work profanity,**
and to *utter* **word** error against *the LORD* **Yah Veh,**
to *make empty* **pour out** the soul of the *hungry* **famished,**
and he *will* **shall** cause the drink of the thirsty to *fail* **lack.**
7 The instruments also of the *churl* **crafty** are evil:
he *deviseth wicked devices* **counselleth intrigue**
to *destroy* **despoil** the *poor* **humble**
with *lying words* **false sayings,**
even when the needy *speaketh right* **wordeth judgment.**
8 But the *liberal* **volunteer**
deviseth liberal things **counselleth voluntarily;**
and by *liberal things* **volunteering** shall he *stand* **rise.**

RELAXED WOMEN AND CONFIDENT DAUGHTERS

9 Rise up, ye women that are *at ease* **relaxed;**
hear my voice, ye *careless* **confident** daughters;
give ear **hearken** unto my *speech* **saying.**
10 Many days and years shall ye *be troubled* **quiver,**
ye *careless women* **confiding:**
for the *vintage* **crop** shall *fail* **finish off,**
the *gathering* **ingathering** shall not come.
11 Tremble, ye women that are *at ease* **relaxed;**
be troubled **quiver,** ye *careless ones* **confiding:**
strip you, and *make you* **strip** bare,
and gird sackcloth — **a girdle** upon *your* loins.
12 They shall *lament* **chop** for the *teats* **breasts,**
for the *pleasant fields* **fields of desire,**
for the *fruitful* **fruitbearing** vine.
13 Upon the *land* **soil** of my people
shall *come up* **ascend** thorns and briers;
yea, upon all the houses of joy
in the *joyous* city **of jumping for joy:**
14 Because the *palaces* **citadels**
shall be *forsaken* **abandoned;**
the multitude of the city shall be *left* **forsaken;**
the *forts* **mounds** and **lookout** towers
shall be for *dens for ever* **caves eternally,**
a joy of wild *asses* **runners,** a pasture of *flocks* **droves;**
15 Until the spirit be poured **out** upon us from on high,
and the wilderness be *a fruitful field* **an orchard/Karmel,**
and the *fruitful field* **orchard/Karmel**
be *counted* **fabricated** for a forest.
16 Then judgment
shall *dwell* **tabernacle** in the wilderness,
and *righteousness* **justness**
remain **settle** in the *fruitful field* **orchard/Karmel.**
17 And the work of *righteousness* **justness**
shall be *peace* **shalom;**
and the *effect* **service** of *righteousness* **justness**
quietness **resting** and *assurance* **confidence**
for ever **eternally.**
18 And my people shall *dwell* **settle**
in a *peaceable habitation* **habitation of shalom of rest,**
and in *sure dwellings* **confident tabernacles,**
and in *quiet* resting places **of relaxation;**
19 When it shall hail,
coming down **descending** on the forest;
and the city shall be *low* **lowered**
in a *low place* **lowland.**
20 *Blessed* **Blithesome** are ye
that *sow* **seed** beside all waters,
that send forth *thither* the feet of the ox and the *ass* **burro.**

HO TO THE RAVAGER

33 *Woe* **Ho** to thee that *spoilest* **ravagest,**
and thou wast not *spoiled* **ravaged;**
and dealest *treacherously* **covertly,**
and they dealt not *treacherously* **covertly** with thee!
when thou shalt *cease* **consumate** to *spoil* **ravage,**
thou shalt be *spoiled* **ravaged;**
and when thou shalt *make an* end
to deal *treacherously* **covertly,**
they shall deal *treacherously* **covertly** with thee.
2 O *LORD* **Yah Veh,** *be gracious* **grant charism** unto us;
we have *waited for* **awaited** thee:
be thou their arm *every morning* **mornings,**
our salvation also in the time of *trouble* **tribulation.**
3 At the *noise* **voice** of the *tumult* **multitude**
the people fled;
at *the lifting up of thyself* **thy exaltation**
the *nations* **goyim** were scattered.
4 And your spoil shall be gathered
like the *gathering* **ingathering** of the caterpiller:
as the running *to and fro* **about** of locusts
shall he *run* **yearn** upon them.
5 *The LORD* **Yah Veh** is exalted;
for he *dwelleth* **tabernacleth** on high:
he hath filled *Zion* **Siyon**
with judgment and *righteousness* **justness.**
6 And wisdom and knowledge
shall be the *stability* **trustworthiness** of thy times,
and *strength* **wealth** of salvation:
the *fear* **awe** of *the LORD* **Yah Veh** is his treasure.
7 Behold,
their *valiant ones* **heros** shall cry *without* **outwardly:**
the *ambassadors* **angels** of *peace* **shalom**
shall weep bitterly.
8 The highways lie *waste* **desolated,**
the *wayfaring man* **passer of the way**
ceaseth **shabbathizeth:**
he hath broken the covenant,
he hath *despised* **spurned** the cities,
he *regardeth* **fabricateth** no man.
9 The earth mourneth and languisheth:
Lebanon *is ashamed* **blusheth**
and *hewn down* **withereth:**
Sharon is like a *wilderness* **plain;**
and Bashan and *Carmel* **Karmel/orchard**
shake *off their fruits.*
10 Now *will* **shall** I rise, saith *the LORD* **Yah Veh;**
now *will* **shall** I be exalted; now *will* **shall** I lift *up* myself.
11 Ye shall conceive *chaff* **hay,**
ye shall *bring forth* **beget** stubble:
your *breath* **spirit,** as fire, shall devour you.
12 And the people
shall be as the *burnings* **calcinations** of lime:
as thorns cut up shall they be burned in the fire.
13 Hear, ye that are far off, what I have *done* **worked;**
and, ye that are near, acknowledge my might.
14 The sinners in *Zion are afraid* **Siyon fear;**
fearfulness **trembling**
hath *surprised* **holden** the *hypocrites* **profaners.**
Who among us shall *dwell* **sojourn**
with the devouring fire?
who among us shall *dwell* **sojourn**
with *everlasting* **eternal** burnings?
15 He that walketh *righteously* **in justness,**
and *speaketh uprightly* **wordeth straightly;**
he that *despiseth* **spurneth** the gain of oppressions,
that shaketh his *hands* **palms**
from *holding of* **upholding** bribes,
that *stoppeth* **shutteth** his ears from hearing of blood,
and *shutteth* **bindeth** his eyes from seeing evil;
16 He shall *dwell* **tabernacle** on high:
his *place of defence* **secure loft**
shall be the *munitions* **huntholds** of rocks:
bread shall be given him;
his waters shall be *sure* **trustworthy.**
17 Thine eyes shall see the *king* **sovereign** in his beauty:
they shall *behold* **see** the land that is very far off.
18 Thine heart shall meditate terror.
Where is the scribe? where is the *receiver* **weigher?**
where is he that *counted* **scribed** the towers?
19 Thou shalt not see *a fierce* **an obstinate** people,
a people of a deeper *speech* **lip**
than thou *canst perceive* **hearest;**
of a *stammering* **deriding** tongue,

that thou *canst* not understand.
20 *Look* **See** upon *Zion* **Siyon**,
the city of our *solemnities* **seasons**:
thine eyes shall see *Jerusalem* **Yeru Shalem**
a *quiet habitation* **habitation of rest and relaxation**,
a *tabernacle* **tent** that shall not *be taken down* **migrate**;
not one of the stakes *thereof*
shall *ever* be *removed* **pulled in perpetuity**,
neither shall any of the cords *thereof* be *broken* **torn**.
21 But there *the glorious LORD* **mighty Yah Veh**
will **shall** be unto us a place of
broad rivers and streams **rivers — rivers broad of hand**;
wherein shall go no *galley* **ships** with oars,
neither shall *gallant* **mighty** ship pass thereby.
22 For *the LORD* **Yah Veh** is our judge,
the LORD **Yah Veh** is our *lawgiver* **statute setter**,
the LORD **Yah Veh** is our *king* **sovereign**;
he *will* **shall** save us.
23 Thy *tacklings* **cords** are *loosed* **abandoned**;
they *could not well strengthen*
held not the base of their mast,
they *could not* spread **not** the sail:
then is the prey of a great spoil *divided* **allotted**;
the lame *take* **plunder** the *prey* **plunder**.
24 And the *inhabitant* **fellow tabernacler** shall not say,
I am sick:
the people that *dwell* **settle** therein
shall *be forgiven* **bear** their *iniquity* **perversity**.

YAH VEH JUDGES THE GOYIM

34 *Come near* **Approach**, ye *nations* **goyim**, to hear;
and hearken, ye *people* **nations**:
let the earth hear, and all *that is therein* **its fulness**;
the world,
and all *things that come forth of it* **its offspring**.
2 For the *indignation* **rage** of *the LORD* **Yah Veh**
is upon all *nations* **goyim**,
and his fury upon all their *armies* **hosts**:
he hath *utterly destroyed* **devoted** them,
he hath *delivered* **given** them to the slaughter.
3 Their *slain* **pierced** also shall be cast out,
and their stink
shall *come up* **ascend** out of their carcases,
and the mountains shall be melted with their blood.
4 And all the host of *heaven* **the heavens**
shall be dissolved,
and the heavens shall be rolled together as a scroll:
and all their host shall *fall down* **wither**,
as the leaf *falleth off* **withereth** from the vine,
and as a *fading fig* **withering** from the fig tree.
5 For my sword
shall be *bathed* **saturated** in *heaven* **the heavens**:
behold,
it shall *come down* **descend** upon *Idumea* **Edom**,
and upon the people of my *curse* **devotement**,
to judgment.
6 The sword of *the LORD* **Yah Veh** is filled with blood,
it is *made fat* **fattened** with *fatness* **fat**,
and with the blood of *lambs* **rams** and **he** goats,
with the fat of the kidneys of rams:
for *the LORD* **Yah Veh** hath a sacrifice in *Bozrah* **Bosrah**,
and a great slaughter in the land of *Idumea* **Edom**.
7 And the *unicorns* **reems**
shall *come down* **descend** with them,
and the bullocks with the *bulls* **mighty**;
and their land shall be *soaked* **saturated** with blood,
and their dust *made fat with fatness* **fatteneth with fat**.
8 For it is the day
of *the LORD'S vengeance* **Yah Veh's avengement**,
and the year of *recompences* **satisfactions**
for the *controversy* **strife** of *Zion* **Siyon**.
9 And the *streams* **wadies** *thereof*
shall be turned into *pitch* **asphalt**,
and the dust *thereof* into *brimstone* **sulphur**,
and the land *thereof* shall become burning *pitch* **asphalt**.
10 It shall not be quenched night nor day;
the smoke *thereof* shall *go up for ever* **ascend eternally**:
from generation to generation it shall lie *waste* **parched**;
none shall pass through *it for ever and ever* **in perpetuity**.
11 But the *cormorant* **pelican** and the bittern
shall possess it;
the owl also and the raven shall *dwell* **tabernacle** in it:
and he shall stretch *out* upon it
the line of *confusion* **waste**, and the stones of emptiness.
12 They shall call the nobles *thereof* to the kingdom,
but none shall be there,
and all her *princes* **governors** shall *be nothing* **decease**.
13 And thorns
shall *come up* **ascend** in her *palaces* **citadels**,
nettles **thistles** and *brambles* **thorns**
in the fortresses *thereof*:
and it shall be an habitation **of rest** of *dragons* **monsters**,
and a court for **daughters of the** owls.
14 The *wild beasts of the desert* **desert dwellers**
shall also meet
with the *wild beasts of the island* **island howlers**,
and the *satyr* **buck** shall *cry* **call** to his *fellow* **friend**;
the *screech owl* **night spectre** also shall rest there,
and find for herself a place of rest.
15 There shall *the great owl make her* **arrowsnake** nest,
and *lay* **escape**, and *hatch* **split**,
and *gather* **brood** under her shadow:
there shall the *vultures* **falcons** also be gathered,
every *one* **woman** with her *mate* **friend**.
16 Seek ye out of the *book* **scroll** of *the LORD* **Yah Veh**,
and *read* **call out**:
no one of these shall *fail* **lack**,
none **no woman** shall *want* **oversee** her mate:
for my mouth it hath *commanded* **misvahed**,
and his spirit it hath gathered them.
17 And he hath *cast* **felled** the *lot* **pebble** for them,
and his hand hath *divided* **allotted** it unto them by line:
they shall possess it *for ever* **eternally**,
from generation to generation
shall they *dwell* **tabernacle** therein.

THE WAY OF HOLINESS

35 The wilderness and the *solitary place* **parch**
shall *be glad* **rejoice** for them;
and the *desert* **plain** shall *rejoice* **twirl**,
and blossom as the rose.
2 **In blossoming,** It shall blossom *abundantly*,
and *rejoice* **twirl**
even with *joy* **twirling** and *singing* **shouting**:
the *glory* **honour** of Lebanon shall be given unto it,
the *excellency* **majesty**
of *Carmel* **Karmel/orchard** and Sharon,
they shall see the *glory* **honour** of *the LORD* **Yah Veh**,
and the *excellency* **majesty** of our *God* **Elohim**.
3 Strengthen ye the weak hands,
and *confirm* **strengthen** the *feeble* **faltering** knees.
4 Say to them that are of a *fearful* **hasty** heart,
Be strong, *fear* **awe** not:
behold, your *God* **Elohim!**
will come with vengeance **avengement shall come**,
even God with a recompence — **the dealing of Elohim**;
he *will* **shall** come and save you.
5 Then the eyes of the blind shall be opened,
and the ears of the deaf shall be unstopped.
6 Then shall the lame *man* leap as an hart,
and the tongue of the *dumb sing* **mute shout**:
for in the wilderness shall waters *break out* **split**,
and *streams* **wadies** in the *desert* **plain**.
7 And the *parched ground* **mirage**
shall become a *pool* **marsh**,
and the thirsty *land springs* **fountains** of water:
in the habitation **of rest** of *dragons* **monsters**,
where each lay **in its repose**,
shall be grass with *reeds* **stalks** and *rushes* **bulrushes**.
8 And an highway shall be there, and a way,
and it shall be called The way of holiness;
the *unclean* **foul** shall not pass over it;
but it shall be for those:
the wayfaring men **waywalkers**, though fools,
shall not err *therein*.
9 No lion shall be there,
nor any ravenous *beast* **live being**
shall *go up* **ascend** thereon,
it shall not be found there;
but the redeemed shall walk *there*:
10 And the *ransomed* **redeemed** of *the LORD* **Yah Veh**
shall return,

and come to *Zion* **Siyon** with *songs* **shouting**
and *everlasting joy* **eternal cheerfulness**
upon their heads:
they shall *obtain* **attain**
joy **rejoicing** and *gladness* **cheerfulness,**
and *sorrow* **grief** and sighing shall flee away.

SANCHERIB APPREHENDS YAH HUDAH

36 Now it *came to pass* **became,**
in the fourteenth year
of *king Hesekiah* **sovereign Yechizqi Yah,**
that Sennacherib **Sancherib,**
king **sovereign** of *Assyria* **Ashshur**
came up **ascended** against all the *defenced* **fortified** cities
of *Judah* **Yah Hudah**, and *took* **apprehended** them.
2 And the *king* **sovereign** of *Assyria* **Ashshur**
sent *Rabshakeh* **Rab Shaqeh**
from Lachish to *Jerusalem* **Yeru Shalem**
unto king *Hesekiah* **Yechizqi Yah**
heavy with *a great army* **valiant.**
And he stood
by the *conduit* **channel** of the *upper* **most high** pool
in the highway of the fuller's field.
3 Then came forth unto him *Eliakim* **El Yaqim,**
Hilkiah's **Hilqi Yah's** son, which was over the house,
and Shebna the scribe,
and *Joah* **Yah Ach**, Asaph's son,
the *recorder* **memorializer.**
4 And *Rabshakeh* **Rab Shaqeh** said unto them,
Say ye *now* **I beseech,** to *Hesekiah* **Yechizqi Yah,**
Thus saith the great *king* **sovereign,**
the *king* **sovereign** of *Assyria* **Ashshur,**
What confidence is this wherein thou *trustest* **confidest?**
5 I say, *sayest thou,*
(but *they are but vain* **only lip** words)
I have counsel and *strength* **might** for war:
now on whom *dost thou trust* **confidest thou,**
that thou rebellest against me?
6 *Lo* **Behold,** thou *trustest* **confidest**
in the *staff* **crutch** of this *broken reed* **crushed stalk,**
on *Egypt* **Misrayim;**
whereon if a man *lean* **prop,**
it *will* **shall** go into his *hand* **palm,** and pierce it:
so is *Pharaoh* **Paroh** *king* **sovereign** of *Egypt* **Misrayim**
to all that *trust* **confide** in him.
7 But if thou say to me,
We *trust* **confide** in *the LORD* **Yah Veh** our *God* **Elohim:**
is it not he,
whose *high places* **bamahs** and whose **sacrifice** altars
Hesekiah **Yechizqi Yah** hath *taken away* **turned aside,**
and said
to *Judah* **Yah Hudah** and to *Jerusalem* **Yeru Shalem,**
Ye shall *worship* **prostrate**
before **at the face of** this **sacrifice** altar?
8 Now therefore *give pledges* **pledge,** I *pray* **beseech** thee,
to my *master* **adoni**
the *king* **sovereign** of *Assyria* **Ashshur,**
and I *will* **shall** give thee two thousand horses,
if thou be able on thy part to *set* **give** riders upon them.
9 How then *wilt* **shalt** thou turn away the face
of one *captain* **governor**
of the *least* **lesser** of my *master's* **adoni's** servants,
and *put thy trust* **confide** on *Egypt* **Misrayim**
for chariots and for *horsemen* **cavalry?**
10 And am I now *come up* **ascended**
without *the LORD* **Yah Veh**
against this land to *destroy* **ruin** it?
the LORD **Yah Veh** said unto me,
Go up **Ascend** against this land, and *destroy* **ruin** it.
11 Then said
Eliakim **El Yaqim** and Shebna and *Joah* **Yah Ach**
unto *Rabshakeh* **Rab Shaqeh,**
Speak **Word,** I *pray* **beseech** thee,
unto thy servants in *the Syrian language* **Aramaic;**
for we *understand it* **hear:**
and *speak* **word** not to us
in *the Jews' language* **Yah Hudaic,**
in the ears of the people that are on the wall.
12 But *Rabshakeh* **Rab Shaqeh** said,
Hath my *master* **adoni** sent me to thy *master* **adoni**
and to thee to *speak* **word** these words?
hath he not *sent me* to the men that sit upon the wall,
that they may eat their own *dung* **excrements,**
and drink *their own piss* **the urine at their feet** with you?
13 Then *Rabshakeh* **Rab Shaqeh** stood,
and *cried* **called out** with a *loud* **great** voice
in *the Jews' language* **Yah Hudaic**, and said,
Hear ye the words of the great *king* **sovereign,**
the *king* **sovereign** of *Assyria* **Ashshur.**
14 Thus saith the *king* **sovereign,**
Let not *Hesekiah* **Yechizqi Yah** deceive you:
for he shall not be able to *deliver* **rescue** you.
15 Neither let *Hesekiah* **Yechizqi Yah**
make **have** you *trust* **confide** in *the LORD* **Yah Veh,**
saying,
The LORD will surely deliver
In rescuing, Yah Veh shall rescue us:
this city shall not be *delivered* **given**
into the hand of the *king* **sovereign** of *Assyria* **Ashshur.**
16 Hearken not to *Hesekiah* **Yechizqi Yah:**
for thus saith the *king* **sovereign** of *Assyria* **Ashshur,**
Make an agreement **Work** with me
by a present **a blessing,**
and come out to me:
and eat ye every *one* **man** of his vine,
and every *one* **man** of his fig tree,
and drink ye every *one* **man**
the waters of his own *cistern* **well;**
17 Until I come
and take you away to a land like your own land,
a land of *corn* **crop** and *wine* **juice,**
a land of bread and vineyards.
18 *Beware*
lest *Hesekiah persuade* **Yechizqi Yah goad** you,
saying, *the LORD will deliver* **Yah Veh shall rescue** us.
Hath any **man** of the *gods* **elohim** of the *nations* **goyim**
delivered **rescued** his land
out of the hand of the *king* **sovereign** of *Assyria* **Ashshur?**
19 Where are the *gods* **elohim** of Hamath and Arphad?
where are the *gods* **elohim** of *Sepharvaim* **Sepharvayim?**
and have they *delivered Samaria* **rescued Shomeron**
out of my hand?
20 Who are they
among all the *gods* **elohim** of these lands,
that have *delivered* **rescued** their land out of my hand,
that *the LORD* **Yah Veh**
should *deliver Jerusalem* **rescue Yeru Shalem**
out of my hand?
21 But they *held their peace* **hushed,**
and answered him not a word:
for the *king's commandment* **sovereign's misvah** was,
saying, Answer him not.
22 Then came *Eliakim* **El Yaqim,**
the son of *Hilkiah* **Hilqi Yah,**
that was over the household,
and Shebna the scribe,
and *Joah* **Yah Ach**, the son of Asaph,
the *recorder* **memorializer,**
to *Hesekiah* **Yechizqi Yah** with their clothes *rent* **ripped,**
and told him the words of *Rabshakeh* **Rab Shaqeh.**
37 And it *came to pass* **became,**
when *king Hesekiah* **sovereign Yechizqi Yah** heard it,
that he *rent* **ripped** his clothes,
and covered himself with *sackcloth* **saq,**
and went into the house of *the LORD* **Yah Veh.**
2 And he sent *Eliakim* **El Yaqim,**
who was over the household,
and Shebna the scribe,
and the elders of the priests covered with *sackcloth* **saq,**
unto *Isaiah* **Yesha Yah** the prophet
the son of *Amoz* **Amos.**
3 And they said unto him,
Thus saith *Hesekiah* **Yechizqi Yah,**
This day is a day of *trouble* **tribulation,**
and of rebuke, and of *blasphemy* **scorning:**
for the *children* **sons** are come to the *birth* **matrix,**
and there is not strength to *bring forth* **beget.**
4 It may be *the LORD* **Yah Veh** thy *God* **Elohim**
will **shall** hear the words of *Rabshakeh* **Rab Shaqeh,**
whom the *king* **sovereign** of *Assyria* **Ashshur**
his *master* **adoni**

hath sent to reproach the living *God* **Elohim**,
and *will* **shall** reprove the words
which *the LORD* **Yah Veh** thy *God* **Elohim** hath heard:
wherefore lift up thy prayer
for the *remnant* **survivors** that *is left* **survive**.
5 So the servants
of *king Hesekiah* **sovereign Yechizqi Yah**
came to *Isaiah* **Yesha Yah**.
6 And *Isaiah* **Yesha Yah** said unto them,
Thus shall ye say unto your *master* **adoni**,
Thus saith *the LORD* **Yah Veh**,
Be not afraid **Awe not at the face**
of the words that thou hast heard,
wherewith the *servants* **lads**
of the *king* **sovereign** of *Assyria* **Ashshur**
have blasphemed me.
7 Behold, I *will send a blast* **shall give a spirit** upon him,
and he shall hear a *rumour* **report**,
and return to his own land;
and I *will cause him to fall* **shall fell him**
by the sword in his own land.
8 So *Rabshakeh* **Rab Shaqeh** returned,
and found the *king* **sovereign** of *Assyria* **Ashshur**
warring **fighting** against Libnah:
for he had heard that he was departed from Lachish.
9 And he heard say concerning *Tirhakah* **Tirhaqah,**
king **sovereign** of *Ethiopia* **Kush**,
He is come forth to *make war* **fight** with thee.
And when he heard it,
he sent *messengers* **angels** to *Hesekiah* **Yechizqi Yah**,
saying,
10 Thus shall ye *speak* **say** to *Hesekiah* **Yechizqi Yah,**
king **sovereign** of *Judah* **Yah Hudah**, saying,
Let not thy *God* **Elohim**, in whom thou *trustest* **confidest**,
deceive thee, saying,
Jerusalem **Yeru Shalem** shall not be given
into the hand of the *king* **sovereign** of *Assyria* **Ashshur**.
11 Behold, thou hast heard
what the *kings* **sovereigns** of *Assyria* **Ashshur**
have *done* **worked** to all lands
by *destroying* **devoting** them *utterly*;
and shalt thou be *delivered* **rescued**?
12 Have the *gods* **elohim** of the *nations* **goyim**
delivered **rescued** them
which my fathers have *destroyed* **ruined**,
as Gozan, and Haran, and *Rezeph* **Reseph**,
and the *children* **sons** of Eden which were in Telassar?
13 Where is the *king* **sovereign** of Hamath,
and the *king* **sovereign** of Arphad,
and the *king* **sovereign**
of the city of *Sepharvaim* **Sepharvayim**,
Hena, and *Ivah* **Avvah**?
14 And *Hesekiah* **Yechizqi Yah**
received **took** the *letter* **scroll**
from the hand of the *messengers* **angels**,
and *read it* **called it out**:
and *Hesekiah went up* **Yechizqi Yah ascended**
unto the house of *the LORD* **Yah Veh**,
and spread it *before the LORD* **at the face of Yah Veh**.
15 And *Hesekiah* **Yechizqi Yah**
prayed unto *the LORD* **Yah Veh**, saying,
16 O *LORD of hosts* **Yah Veh Sabaoth**,
God **Elohim** of *Israel* **Yisra El**,
that *dwellest* **settlest**
between **upon** the *cherubims* **cherubim**,
thou *art the God* **Elohim**, *even* thou alone,
of all the *kingdoms* **sovereigndoms** of the earth:
thou hast *made heaven* **worked the heavens** and earth.
17 *Incline* **Extend** thine ear, O *LORD* **Yah Veh**, and hear;
open thine eyes, O *LORD* **Yah Veh**, and see:
and hear all the words of *Sennacherib* **Sancherib**,
which hath sent to reproach the living *God* **Elohim**.
18 *Of a truth* **Truly**, *LORD* **O Yah Veh**,
the *kings* **sovereigns** of *Assyria* **Ashshur**
have *laid waste* **parched** all the *nations* **lands**,
and their *countries* **lands**,
19 And have *cast* **given** their *gods* **elohim** into the fire:
for they were no *gods* **elohim**,
but the work of *men's* **human** hands,
wood **timber** and stone:
therefore they have destroyed them.
20 Now therefore, O *LORD* **Yah Veh** our *God* **Elohim**,
save us from his hand,
that all the kingdoms of the earth may know
that thou art *the LORD* **Yah Veh**, *even* thou only.
21 Then *Isaiah* **Yesha Yah** the son of *Amoz* **Amos**
sent unto *Hesekiah* **Yechizqi Yah**, saying,
Thus saith
the LORD God **Yah Veh Elohim** of *Israel* **Yisra El**,
Whereas thou hast prayed to me against
Sennacherib **Sancherib,**
king **sovereign** of *Assyria* **Ashshur**:
22 This is the word which *the LORD* **Yah Veh**
hath *spoken* **worded** concerning him;
The virgin, the daughter of *Zion* **Siyon**,
hath despised thee, *and laughed* **ridiculed** thee *to scorn*;
the daughter of *Jerusalem* **Yeru Shalem**
hath shaken her head *at* **behind** thee.
23 Whom hast thou reproached and blasphemed?
and against whom hast thou exalted thy voice,
and lifted up thine eyes on high?
even against the Holy One of *Israel* **Yisra El**.
24 By **the hand of** thy servants
hast thou reproached *the Lord* **Adonay**,
and hast said, By the *multitude* **abundance** of my chariots
am I *come up* **ascended** to the height of the mountains,
to the *sides* **flanks** of Lebanon;
and I *will* **shall** cut down
the *tall* **height of the** cedars *thereof*,
and the choice fir trees *thereof*:
and I *will* **shall** enter into the height of his *border* **edge**,
and the forest of his *Carmel* **Karmel/orchard**.
25 I have digged, and drunk water;
and with the sole of my *feet* **steps**
have I *dried up* **parched**
all the rivers of the *besieged places* **rampart**.
26 Hast thou not heard *long ago* **in the distant past**,
how I have *done* **worked** it;
and of ancient *times* **days**, that I have formed it?
now have I brought it to *pass* **become**,
that thou shouldest
be to lay waste *defenced* **fortified** cities
into *ruinous* **desolated** heaps.
27 Therefore their *inhabitants* **settlers**
were *of small power* **short handed**,
they were dismayed and *confounded* **shamed**:
they were as the *grass* **herbage** of the field,
and as the green *herb* **sprouts**,
as the grass on the *housetops* **roofs**,
and as *corn blasted* **the field**
before it be grown up **at the face of the stalks**.
28 But I know thy *abode* **sitting**,
and thy going out, and thy coming in,
and thy *rage* **quaking** against me.
29 Because thy *rage* **quaking** against me,
and thy *tumult* **uproar**,
is come up **ascendeth** into mine ears,
therefore
will I put **I shall set** my hook in thy *nose* **nostrils**,
and my *bridle* **bit** in thy lips,
and I *will* **shall** turn thee back
by the way by which thou camest.
30 And this shall be a sign unto thee,
Ye shall eat this year
such as groweth of itself **the spontaneous growth**;
and the second year
that which springeth of the same
the spontaneous growth:
and in the third year sow ye, and *reap* **harvest**,
and plant vineyards, and eat the fruit *thereof*.
31 And the *remnant* **escapees** that *is escaped* **survived**
of the house of *Judah* **Yah Hudah**
shall again take root downward,
and *bear* **work** fruit upward:
32 For out of *Jerusalem* **Yeru Shalem**
shall go forth *a remnant* **survivors**,
and *they that escape* **the escapees**
out of mount *Zion* **Siyon**:
the zeal of *the LORD of hosts* **Yah Veh Sabaoth**
shall *do* **work** this.

33 Therefore thus saith *the LORD* **Yah Veh**
concerning the *king* **sovereign** of *Assyria* **Ashshur**,
He shall not come into this city,
nor shoot an arrow there,
nor *come before it* **anticipate** with *shields* **buckler**,
nor *cast* **pour** a bank against it.
34 By the way that he came, by the same shall he return,
and shall not come into this city,
saith the LORD **an oracle of Yah Veh**.
35 For I *will defend* **shall garrison** this city to save it
for mine own sake, and for my servant David's sake.
36 Then the angel of *the LORD* **Yah Veh** went forth,
and smote in the camp of *the Assyrians* **Ashshur**
a hundred and *fourscore* **eighty** and five thousand:
and when they *arose* **started** early in the morning,
behold, they were all dead *corpses* **carcases**.
37 So *Sennacherib* **Sancherib,**
king **sovereign** of *Assyria* **Ashshur**
departed **pulled stakes**,
and went and returned, and *dwelt* **settled** at Nineveh.
38 And it *came to pass* **became**,
as he was *worshipping* **prostrating**
in the house of Nisroch his *god* **elohim**,
that *Adrammelech* **Adram Melech** and *Sharezer* **Shareser**
his sons smote him with the sword;
and they escaped into the land of *Armenia* **Ararat**:
and *Esarhaddon* **Esar Chaddon** his son
reigned in his stead.

THE HEALING OF YECHIZQI YAH

38 In those days
was *Hesekiah* **Yechizqi Yah** sick unto death.
And *Isaiah* **Yesha Yah** the prophet the son of *Amoz* **Amos**
came unto him, and said unto him,
Thus saith *the LORD* **Yah Veh**,
Set **Misvah concerning** thine house *in order*:
for thou shalt die, and not live.
2 Then *Hesekiah* **Yechizqi Yah**
turned his face toward the wall,
and prayed unto *the LORD* **Yah Veh**,
3 And said, Remember *now* **I beseech**,
O *LORD* **Yah Veh**, I beseech thee,
how I have walked *before thee* **at thy face** in truth
and with a *perfect* heart **of shalom**,
and have *done* **worked** that which is good
in thy *sight* **eyes**.
And *Hesekiah* **Yechizqi Yah**
wept *sore* **with great weeping**.
4 Then came the word of *the LORD* **Yah Veh**
to *Isaiah* **Yesha Yah**, saying,
5 Go, and say to *Hesekiah* **Yechizqi Yah**,
Thus saith *the LORD* **Yah Veh**,
the God **Elohim** of David thy father,
I have heard thy prayer, I have seen thy tears:
behold, I *will* **shall** add unto thy days fifteen years.
6 And I *will deliver* **shall rescue** thee and this city
out of the *hand* **palm**
of the *king* **sovereign** of *Assyria* **Ashshur**:
and I *will defend* **shall garrison** this city.
7 And this shall be a sign unto thee
from *the LORD* **Yah Veh**,
that *the LORD* **Yah Veh**
will do **shall work** this *thing* **word**
that he hath *spoken* **worded**;
8 Behold, I *will bring again* **shall turn back**
the shadow of the degrees,
which is *gone down* **descended**
in the sun dial of *Ahaz* **Ach Az**,
ten degrees backward.
So the sun *returned* **turned back** ten degrees,
by which degrees it was *gone down* **descended**.
9 The *writing* **inscribing** of *Hesekiah* **Yechizqi Yah,**
king **sovereign** of *Judah* **Yah Hudah**,
when he had been sick,
and *was recovered* **livened** of his sickness:
10 I said in the *cutting off* **severing** of my days,
I shall go to the *gates* **portals** of *the grave* **sheol**:
I am *deprived* **oversighted**
of the *residue* **remnant** of my years.
11 I said, I shall not see *the LORD* **Yah**,
even the LORD — **Yah**, in the land of the living:
I shall *behold man* **scan humanity** no more
with the *inhabitants* **settlers** of the *world* **deceased**.
12 *Mine age is departed*
My generation hath pulled stakes,
and is *removed* **exiled** from me
as a *shepherd's* **tender's** tent:
I have *cut off* **severed** like a weaver my life:
he *will cut me off* **shall clip me**
with pining sickness **from the thrum**:
from day *even* to night
wilt **shalt** thou *make an end of* **shalam** me.
13 I *reckoned* **equated** till morning, *that,*
as a lion, so *will* **shall** he break all my bones:
from day *even* to night
wilt **shalt** thou *make an end of* **shalam** me.
14 Like a *crane* **horse** or a swallow,
so did I chatter **thus I chirped**:
I *did mourn* **cooed** as a dove:
mine eyes *fail with looking upward* **languish on high**:
O *LORD* **Yah Veh**, I am oppressed;
undertake for me **be my pledge**.
15 What shall I *say* **word**?
he hath *both spoken* **said** unto me,
and himself hath *done* **worked** *it*:
I shall *go softly* **walk gently** all my years
in the bitterness of my soul.
16 *O Lord* **Adonay**, by these *things men live* **is life**,
and in all these *things* is the life of my spirit:
so *wilt* **shalt** thou *recover* **fatten** me,
and *make me to live* **enliven me**.
17 Behold,
for *peace* **shalom**
I *had great bitterness* **was bitterly embittered**:
but thou hast in *love* **being attached** to my soul
delivered it from the pit of *corruption* **ruin**:
for thou hast cast all my sins behind thy back.
18 For *the grave* **sheol**
cannot praise **extendeth not hands unto** thee,
death *can not celebrate* **halaleth** thee **not**:
they that *go down* **descend** into the *pit* **well**
cannot hope for **shall not expect** thy truth.
19 The living, the living,
he shall *praise* **extend hands unto** thee,
as I *do* this day:
the father to the *children* **sons**
shall make known thy truth.
20 *The LORD* **Yah Veh** was ready to save me:
therefore we *will sing* **shall strum**
my *songs to the stringed instruments* **strummings**
all the days of our life
in the house of *the LORD* **Yah Veh**.
21 For *Isaiah* **Yesha Yah** had said,
Let them *take* **bear** a lump of figs,
and *lay it for a plaister* **massage it** upon the *boil* **ulcer**,
and he shall *recover* **live**.
22 *Hesekiah* **Yechizqi Yah** also had said,
What is the sign that I shall *go up* **ascend**
to the house of *the LORD* **Yah Veh**?

THE VISITORS FROM BABEL

39 At that time *Merodachbaladan* **Merodach Bel Adoni**,
the son of *Baladan* **Bel Adoni**,
king **sovereign** of *Babylon* **Babel**,
sent *letters* **scrolls** and *a present* **an offering**
to *Hesekiah* **Yechizqi Yah**:
for he had heard that he had been sick,
and *was recovered* **strengthened**.
2 And *Hesekiah* **Yechizqi Yah**
was glad of **cheered over** them,
and *shewed* **had** them **see**
the house of his *precious things* **spicery**,
the silver, and the gold, and the spices,
and the *precious* **good** ointment,
and all the house of his *armour* **instruments**,
and all that was found in his treasures:
there was *nothing* **no word** in his house,
nor in all his *dominion* **reign**,
that *Hesekiah shewed* **Yechizqi Yah had** them not **see**.
3 Then came *Isaiah* **Yesha Yah** the prophet
unto *king Hesekiah* **sovereign Yechizqi Yah**,
and said unto him, What said these men?

and from whence came they unto thee?
And *Hesekiah* **Yechizqi Yah** said,
They are come from a far *country* **land** unto me,
even from *Babylon* **Babel**.
4 Then said he, What have they seen in thine house?
And *Hesekiah answered* **Yechizqi Yah said**,
All that is in mine house have they seen:
there is *nothing* **no word** among my treasures
that I *have not shewed them* **had them not see**.
5 Then said *Isaiah* **Yesha Yah** to *Hesekiah* **Yechizqi Yah**,
Hear the word of *the LORD of hosts* **Yah Veh Sabaoth**:
6 Behold, the days come, that all that is in thine house,
and that which thy fathers have *laid up in store* **treasured**
until this day,
shall be *carried* **borne** to *Babylon* **Babel**:
nothing **no word** shall *be left* **remain**,
saith *the LORD* **Yah Veh**.
7 And of thy sons that shall issue from thee,
which thou shalt beget, shall they take away;
and they shall be eunuchs in the *palace* **manse**
of the *king* **sovereign** of *Babylon* **Babel**.
8 Then said *Hesekiah* **Yechizqi Yah** to *Isaiah* **Yesha Yah**,
Good is the word of *the LORD* **Yah Veh**
which thou hast spoken.
He said *moreover*,
For there shall be *peace* **shalom** and truth in my days.

THE SIGH OF ELOHIM

40 *Comfort* **Sigh** ye, *comfort ye* **sigh ye over** my people,
saith your *God* **Elohim**.
2 *Speak ye comfortably to Jerusalem*
Word ye to the heart of Yeru Shalem,
and *cry* **call out** unto her,
that her *warfare* **hostility** is *accomplished* **fulfilled**,
that her *iniquity* **perversity** is *pardoned* **satisfied**:
for she hath *received* **taken**
of *the LORD'S* **Yah Veh's** hand double for all her sins.
3 The voice of him that crieth in the wilderness,
Prepare **Face** ye the way of *the LORD* **Yah Veh**,
make straight **straighten** in the *desert* **plain**
a highway for our *God* **Elohim**.
4 Every valley shall be *exalted* **lifted**,
and every mountain and hill shall be *made low* **lowered**:
and the crooked shall be *made straight* **straightened**,
and the *rough places plain* **ridges a plain valley**:
5 And the *glory* **honour** of *the LORD* **Yah Veh**
shall be *revealed* **exposed**,
and all flesh shall see it together:
for the mouth of *the LORD* **Yah Veh**
hath *spoken* **worded** it.
6 The voice said, *Cry* **Call out**.
And he said, What shall I *cry* **call out**?
All flesh is grass, and all the *goodliness* **mercy** *thereof*
is as the *flower* **blossom** of the field:
7 The grass withereth,
the *flower fadeth* **blossom withereth**:
because the spirit of *the LORD* **Yah Veh** bloweth upon it:
surely the people is grass.
8 The grass withereth,
the *flower fadeth* **blossom withereth**:
but the word of our *God* **Elohim**
shall *stand for ever* **rise eternally**.
9 O *Zion* **Siyon**, that *bringest good tidings* **evangelizest**,
get **ascend** thee *up* into the high mountain;
O *Jerusalem* **Yeru Shalem**,
that *bringest good tidings* **evangelizest**,
lift up thy voice with *strength* **force**;
lift *it up*, *be* **awe** not *afraid*;
say unto the cities of *Judah* **Yah Hudah**,
Behold your *God* **Elohim**!
10 Behold, *the Lord GOD* **Adonay Yah Veh**
will **shall** come with *strong hand* **strength**,
and his arm shall *rule* **reign** for him:
behold, his *reward* **hire** is with him,
and his *work before him* **deeds at his face**.
11 He shall *feed* **tend** his *flock* **drove**
like a *shepherd* **tender**:
he shall gather the lambs with his arm,
and *carry* **bear** them in his bosom,
and shall gently *lead* **guide**
those that *are with young* **suckle**.
12 Who hath measured the waters
in *the hollow of his hand* **his palm**,
and *meted out heaven* **gauged the heavens**
with the span,
and *comprehended* **contained** the dust of the earth
in a *measure* **tierce**,
and weighed the mountains in *scales* **weights**,
and the hills in a balance?
13 Who hath *directed* **gauged**
the Spirit of *the LORD* **Yah Veh**,
or being his *counsellor* **councilman**
hath *taught* **made known to** him?
14 With whom *took he counsel* **counselled he**,
and *who instructed* **had** him **discern**,
and taught him in the path of judgment,
and taught him knowledge,
and *shewed* **made known** to him
the way of *understanding* **discernment**?
15 Behold,
the *nations* **goyim** are as a drop of a *bucket* **pail**,
and are *counted* **fabricated**
as the *small dust* **powder** of the balance:
behold, he *taketh up* **lifteth** the *isles* **islands**
as *a very little thing* **pulverized**.
16 And Lebanon is not sufficient to burn,
nor the *beasts* **live beings** *thereof*
sufficient for a *burnt offering* **holocaust**.
17 All *nations* **goyim** before him are as *nothing* **nought**;
and they are *counted* **fabricated** to him
less than nothing **as deceased**, and *vanity* **waste**.
18 To whom then *will* **shall** ye liken *God* **El**?
or what likeness *will* **shall** ye *compare* **line up** unto him?
19 The *workman* **engraver**
melteth **poureth** a *graven image* **sculptile**,
and the *goldsmith* **refiner**
spreadeth it over **overlayeth** with gold,
and *casteth* **refineth** silver chains.
20 He that is so *impoverished* **cut off**
that he hath no *oblation* **exaltment**
chooseth a tree that *will* **shall** not rot;
he seeketh unto him a *cunning workman* **wise engraver**
to prepare a *graven image* **sculptile**,
that shall not *be moved* **topple**.
21 Have ye not known? have ye not heard?
hath it not been told you from the beginning?
have ye not *understood* **discerned**
from the foundations of the earth?
22 It is he that *sitteth* **settleth** upon the circle of the earth,
and the *inhabitants* **settlers** *thereof*
are as *grasshoppers* **locusts**;
that stretcheth out the heavens as a *curtain* **veil**,
and spreadeth them out as a tent to *dwell* **settle** in:
23 That *bringeth* **giveth** the *princes* **potentates**
to *nothing* **nought**;
he *maketh* **worketh** the judges of the earth
as *vanity* **waste**.
24 Yea, they shall not be planted;
yea, they shall not be *sown* **seeded**:
yea, their *stock* **stump** shall not *take* root in the earth:
and he shall also *blow* **puff** upon them,
and they shall wither,
and the *whirlwind* **storm**
shall *take* **bear** them away as stubble.
25 To whom then *will* **shall** ye liken me,
or *shall I be equal* **equate**? saith the Holy One.
26 Lift up your eyes on high,
and *behold* **see** who hath created these *things*,
that bringeth out their host by number:
he calleth them all by names
by the greatness of his *might* **strength**,
for that he is strong in *power* **force**;
not one faileth **no man lacketh**.
27 Why sayest thou, O *Jacob* **Yaaqov**,
and *speakest* **wordest**, O *Israel* **Yisra El**,
My way is hid from *the LORD* **Yah Veh**,
and my judgment is passed over from my *God* **Elohim**?
28 Hast thou not known? hast thou not heard,
that the *everlasting God* **eternal Elohim**,
the LORD **Yah Veh**, the Creator of the ends of the earth,
fainteth **wearieth** not, neither *is weary* **belaboureth**?

there is no *searching* **probing**
of his *understanding* **discernment**.
29 He giveth *power* **strength** to the *faint* **weary**;
and to them that have no *might* **strength**
he *increaseth strength* **aboundeth might**.
30 Even the *youths* **lads**
shall *faint* **weary** and *be weary* **belabour**,
and **in faltering,**
the *young men* **youths** shall *utterly fall* **falter**:
31 But they that *wait upon the LORD* **await Yah Veh**
shall *renew* **change** their *strength* **force**;
they shall *mount up* **ascend** with *wings* **pinions** as eagles;
they shall run, and not *be weary* **belabour**;
and they shall walk, and not *faint* **weary**.

THE FIRST AND THE FINAL

41 *Keep silence* **Hush** before me, O islands;
and let the *people* **nations**
renew **change** their *strength* **force**:
let them come near; then let them *speak* **word**:
let us *come near* **approach** together to judgment.
2 Who *raised up* **wakened** the *righteous man* **just**
from the *east* **rising**,
called him to his foot,
gave the *nations before him* **goyim at his face**,
and *made* **had** him *rule over kings* **subjugate sovereigns**?
he gave them as the dust to his sword,
and as *driven* **disbursed** stubble to his bow.
3 He pursued them, and passed *safely* **in shalom**;
even by the way that he had not gone with his feet.
4 Who hath *wrought* **made** and *done* **worked** it,
calling the generations from the beginning?
I *the LORD* **Yah Veh**, the first, and *with* the *last* **final**;
I am he.
5 The *isles* **islands** saw it, and *feared* **awed**;
the ends of the earth *were afraid* **trembled**,
drew near **approached**, and came.
6 They helped every *one* **man** his *neighbour* **friend**;
and *every one* said to his brother, *Be of good* courage.
7 So the *carpenter* **engraver**
encouraged **strengthened** the *goldsmith* **refiner**,
and he that smootheth with the hammer
him that *smote* **hammered** the anvil, saying,
It is *ready for the sodering* **good to be joined**:
and he *fastened* **strengthened** it with nails,
that it should not *be moved* **topple**.
8 But thou, *Israel* **Yisra El**, art my servant,
Jacob **Yaaqov** whom I have chosen,
the seed of Abraham my *friend* **beloved**.
9 Thou whom I have *taken* **strengthened**
from the ends of the earth,
and called thee from the *chief men* **nobles** *thereof*,
and said unto thee, Thou art my servant;
I have chosen thee, and not *cast* **spurned** thee *away*.
10 *Fear* **Awe** thou not; for I am with thee:
be not dismayed **look not around**;
for I am thy *God* **Elohim**:
I *will* **shall** strengthen thee; yea, I *will* **shall** help thee;
yea, I *will* **shall** uphold thee
with the right *hand* of my *righteousness* **justness**.
11 Behold,
all they that were *incensed* **inflamed** against thee
shall be *ashamed* **shamed** and confounded:
they shall be as *nothing* **nought**;
and *they that strive with thee* **the men of thy strife**
shall *perish* **destruct**.
12 Thou shalt seek them, and shalt not find them,
even them that contended **the men of contention**
with thee:
they **the men** that war against thee
shall be as *nothing* **deceased**, and as *a thing* of nought.
13 For I *the LORD* **Yah Veh** thy *God* **Elohim**
will **shall** hold thy right *hand*, saying unto thee,
Fear **Awe** not; I *will* **shall** help thee.
14 *Fear* **Awe** not, thou *worm Jacob* **maggot Yaaqov**,
and ye men of *Israel* **Yisra El**; I *will* **shall** help thee,
saith the LORD **an oracle of Yah Veh**,
and thy redeemer, the Holy One of *Israel* **Yisra El**.
15 Behold, I *will make* **shall set** thee
a new *sharp* **sickle** threshing *instrument* **sledge**
having **a master of** teeth:
thou shalt thresh the mountains,
and *beat* **pulverize** them *small*,
and shalt *make* **set** the hills as chaff.
16 Thou shalt *fan* **winnow** them,
and the wind shall *carry* **bear** them away,
and the *whirlwind* **storm** shall scatter them:
and thou shalt *rejoice* **twirl** in *the LORD* **Yah Veh**,
and *shalt glory* **shall halal** in the Holy One of *Israel* **Yisra El**.
17 When the *poor* **humble** and needy seek water,
and there is none,
and their tongue *faileth* **drieth** for thirst,
I *the LORD will hear* **Yah Veh shall answer** them,
I *the God* **Elohim** of *Israel* **Yisra El**
will **shall** not forsake them.
18 I *will* **shall** open rivers in *high places* **the barrens**,
and fountains in the midst of the valleys:
I *will make* **shall set** the wilderness
a *pool* **marsh** of water,
and the *dry land* **land of parch**
springs of water.
19 I *will plant* **shall give** in the wilderness the cedar,
the shittah tree, and the myrtle, and the oil tree;
I *will* **shall** set in the *desert* **plain** the fir tree,
and the *pine* **oak**, and the *box tree* **cedar** together:
20 That they may see, and know,
and *consider* **set**, and *understand* **comprehend** together,
that the hand of *the LORD* **Yah Veh**
hath *done* **worked** this,
and the Holy One of *Israel* **Yisra El** hath created it.
21 *Produce* **Approach with** your *cause* **plea**,
saith *the LORD* **Yah Veh**;
bring forth your *strong reasons* **mights**,
saith the *King* **Sovereign** of *Jacob* **Yaaqov**.
22 Let them bring *them* forth,
and *shew* **tell** us what shall happen:
let them *shew* **tell** the former *things*, what they be,
that we may *consider* **set our heart on** them,
and know the latter end of them;
or
declare us things for to come **let us hear of the coming**.
23 *Shew the things* **Tell of those**
that are to come *hereafter* **afterward**,
that we may know that ye are *gods* **elohim**:
yea, *do good* **well—please**, or *do evil* **vilify**,
that we may *be dismayed* **look around**,
and *behold* **see** it together.
24 Behold, ye are of *nothing* **nought**,
and your *work of nought* **deeds a hissing**:
an *abomination* **abhorrence** is he that chooseth you.
25 I have *raised up* **wakened** *one* from the north,
and he shall come:
from the rising of the sun shall he call upon my name:
and he shall come upon *princes* **prefects** as *upon* morter,
and as the *potter treadeth clay* **former trampleth mire**.
26 Who hath *declared* **told** from the beginning,
that we may know?
and *beforetime* **from the face**,
that we may say, *He is righteous* **Just**?
yea, there is none that *sheweth* **telleth**,
yea, there is none that *declareth* **hearkeneth**,
yea, there is none that heareth your *words* **sayings**.
27 *The first shall say to Zion* **First to Siyon**,
Behold, behold them:
and I *will* **shall** give to *Jerusalem* **Yeru Shalem**
one that *bringeth good tidings* **evangelizeth**.
28 For I *beheld* **saw**, and there was no man;
even among them, and there was no counsellor,
that, when I asked of them, could *answer a* **return** word.
29 Behold, they are all *vanity* **mischief**;
their works *are nothing* **ceased**:
their *molten images* **libations**
are wind and *confusion* **waste**.

THE SERVANT OF YAH VEH

42 Behold my servant, whom I uphold;
mine elect **my chosen**,
in whom my soul *delighteth* **is pleased**;
I have *put* **given** my spirit upon him:
he shall bring forth judgment to the *Gentiles* **goyim**.
2 He shall not cry, nor lift *up*,
nor cause his voice to be heard in the *street* **outway**.

3 A *bruised reed* **crushed stalk** shall he not break,
and the smoking flax shall he not quench:
he shall bring forth judgment unto truth.
4 He shall not *fail* **dim** nor *be discouraged* **crush**,
till he have set judgment in the earth:
and the *isles* **islands** shall *wait for* **await** his *law* **torah**.
5 Thus saith *God the LORD* **El Yah Veh**,
he that created the heavens, and stretched them out;
he that *spread forth* **expanded** the earth,
and *that which cometh out of it* **its offspring**;
he that giveth breath unto the people upon it,
and spirit to them that walk therein:
6 I *the LORD* **Yah Veh**
have called thee in *righteousness* **justness**,
and *will* **shall** hold thine hand,
and *will keep* **shall guard** thee,
and give thee for a covenant of the people,
for a light of the *Gentiles* **goyim**;
7 To open the blind eyes,
to bring out the *prisoners* **bound** from the *prison* **lock up**,
and them that sit in darkness out of the prison house.
8 I am *the LORD* **Yah Veh**: that is my name:
and my *glory will* **honour shall** I not give to another,
neither my *praise* **halal** to *graven images* **sculptiles**.
9 Behold,
the former *things are come to pass* **have become**,
and **the** new *things do I declare* **I tell**:
before they *spring forth* **sprout**
I *tell you* **let you hear** of them.

SING AND HALAL TO YAH VEH

10 Sing unto *the LORD* **Yah Veh** a new song,
and his *praise* **halal** from the end of the earth,
ye that *go down* **descend** to the sea,
and *all that is therein* **its fulness**;
the *isles* **islands**, and the *inhabitants* **settlers** *thereof*.
11 Let the wilderness and the cities *thereof*
lift *up their voice*,
the *villages* **courts** that *Kedar* **Qedar** doth *inhabit* **settle**:
let the *inhabitants* **settlers** of the rock *sing* **shout**,
let them shout from the top of the mountains.
12 Let them *give glory* **set honour**
unto *the LORD* **Yah Veh**,
and *declare* **tell** his *praise* **halal** in the islands.
13 *The LORD* **Yah Veh** shall go forth as *a* mighty *man*,
he shall *stir up* **waken** jealousy like a man of war:
he shall *cry* **shout**, yea, *roar* **whoop**;
he shall prevail **mightily** against his enemies.
14 I have *long time holden my peace* **eternally hushed**;
I have *been still* **hushed**, and refrained myself:
now will **shall** I *cry* **scream**
like a *travailing* **birthing** woman;
I *will destroy* **shall puff**
and *devour at once* **gulp altogether**.
15 I *will make waste* **shall parch the** mountains and hills,
and *dry up* **wither** all their herbs;
and I *will make* **shall set** the rivers islands,
and I *will dry up* **shall wither** the *pools* **marshes**.
16 And I *will bring* **shall carry** the blind
by a way that they knew not;
I *will lead* **shall tread** them
in paths that they have not known:
I *will make* **shall set** darkness light
before them **at their face**,
and crooked *things* straight.
These *things will* **words shall** I *do* **work** unto them,
and not forsake them.
17 They shall *be turned back* **apostatize backward**,
they shall *be greatly ashamed* **shamingly shame**,
that *trust* **confide** in *graven images* **sculptiles**,
that say to the *molten images* **moltens**,
Ye *are* our *gods* **elohim**.
18 Hear, ye deaf; and look, ye blind, that ye may see.
19 Who is blind, but my servant?
or deaf, as my *messenger* **angel** that I sent?
who is blind as he that is *perfect* **at shalom**
and blind as *the LORD'S* **Yah Veh's** servant?
20 Seeing *many things* **much**,
but thou *observest* **guardest** not;
opening the ears, but he heareth not.
21 *The LORD is well pleased* **Yah Veh delighteth**
for his *righteousness'* **justness'** sake;
he *will magnify* **shall greaten** the *law* **torah**,
and make it honourable **mightily**.
22 But this is a people
robbed **plundered** and *spoiled* **plundered**;
they are all of them **all their youths are** snared *in holes*,
and they are hid in prison houses:
they are for a *prey* **plunder**,
and none *delivereth* **rescueth**;
for a *spoil* **plunder**, and none saith, Restore.
23 Who among you
will give ear to **shall hearken unto** this?
who *will* **shall** hearken
and hear *for the time to come* **afterward**?
24 Who gave *Jacob* **Yaaqov** for a *spoil* **plunder**,
and *Israel* **Yisra El** to the *robbers* **plunderers**?
did not *the LORD* **Yah Veh**,
he against whom we have sinned?
for they *would* **willed to** not walk in his ways,
neither *were* **hearkened** they
obedient unto his *law* **torah**.
25 Therefore he hath poured upon him
the fury of his *anger* **wrath**,
and the strength of *battle* **war**:
and it hath *set* **inflamed** him on fire round about,
yet he knew not;
and it burned him, yet he *laid* **set** it not to heart.

YAH VEH, THE REDEEMER

43 But now thus saith *the LORD* **Yah Veh**
that created thee, O *Jacob* **Yaaqov**,
and he that formed thee, O *Israel* **Yisra El**,
Fear **Awe** not:
for I have redeemed thee,
I have called *thee by* thy name;
thou art mine.
2 When thou passest through the waters,
I *will* **shall** be with thee;
and through the rivers, they shall not overflow thee:
when thou walkest through the fire,
thou shalt not *be burned* **blister**;
neither shall the flame *kindle* **burn** upon thee.
3 For I am *the LORD* **Yah Veh** thy *God* **Elohim**,
the Holy One of *Israel* **Yisra El**, thy Saviour:
I gave *Egypt* **Misrayim** for thy *ransom* **koper/atonement**,
Ethiopia **Kush** and Seba for thee.
4 Since thou wast precious in my *sight* **eyes**,
thou hast been honourable, and I have loved thee:
therefore *will* **shall** I give *men* **humanity** for thee,
and *people* **nations** for thy *life* **soul**.
5 *Fear* **Awe** not: for I am with thee:
I *will* **shall** bring thy seed from the *east* **rising**,
and gather thee from the *west* **dusk**;
6 I *will* **shall** say to the north, Give up;
and to the south, *Keep* **Refrain** not *back*:
bring my sons from far,
and my daughters from the ends of the earth;
7 *Even* every one that is called by my name:
for I have created him for my *glory* **honour**,
I have formed him;
yea, I have *made* **worked** him.
8 Bring forth the blind people that have eyes,
and the deaf that have ears.
9 Let all the *nations* **goyim** be gathered *together*,
and let the *people be assembled* **nations gather**:
who among them can *declare* **tell** this,
and *shew us* **let us hear the** former *things*?
let them *bring* **give** forth their witnesses,
that they may be justified:
or let them hear, and say, *It is* truth.
10 Ye are my witnesses,
saith the LORD **an oracle of Yah Veh**,
and my servant whom I have chosen:
that ye may know and *believe* **trust** me,
and *understand* **discern** that I am he:
before me **at my face** there was no *God* **El** formed,
neither shall there be after me.
11 I, *even* I, *am the LORD* **Yah Veh**;
and *beside* **except** me there is no saviour.
12 I have *declared* **told**, and have saved,
and I have *shewed* **had thee hear**,

when there was *no* **nought** strange *god* among you:
therefore ye are my witnesses,
saith the LORD **an oracle of Yah Veh,**
that *I am God* **I — El.**
13 Yea, before the day *was* I am he;
and *there is* none *that* can *deliver* **rescue** out of my hand:
I *will work* **shall do,** and who shall *let it* **turn it back?**
14 Thus saith *the LORD* **Yah Veh,** your redeemer,
the Holy One of *Israel* **Yisra El;**
For your sake I have sent to *Babylon* **Babel,**
and have brought down all their *nobles* **fugitives,**
and the *Chaldeans* **Kesediym,**
whose *cry* **shouting** is in the ships.
15 I am *the LORD* **Yah Veh,** your Holy One,
the creator of *Israel* **Yisra El,** your *King* **Sovereign.**
16 Thus saith *the LORD* **Yah Veh,**
which *maketh* **giveth** a way in the sea,
and a path in the *mighty* **strong** waters;
17 Which bringeth forth the chariot and horse,
the *army* **valiant** and the *power* **strong;**
they shall lie down together, they shall not rise:
they are *extinct* **extinguished,**
they are quenched as *tow* **flax.**
18 Remember ye not the former *things,*
neither *consider* **discern** the *things of old* **ancient.**
19 Behold, I *will do* **shall work** a new *thing;*
now it shall *spring forth* **sprout;** shall ye not know it?
I *will* **shall** even *make* **set** a way in the wilderness,
and rivers in the *desert* **desolation.**
20 The *beast* **live being** of the field shall honour me,
the *dragons* **monsters** and the **daughters of the** owls:
because I give waters in the wilderness,
and rivers in the *desert* **desolation,**
to give drink to my people, my chosen.
21 This people have I formed for myself;
they shall *shew forth* **scribe** my *praise* **halal.**
22 But thou hast not called upon me,
O *Jacob* **Yaaqov;**
but thou hast been *weary* **belaboured** of me,
O *Israel* **Yisra El.**
23 Thou hast not brought me
the *small cattle* **lambs** of thy *burnt offering* **holocausts;**
neither hast thou honoured me with thy sacrifices.
I have not caused thee to serve with an offering,
nor *wearied* **belaboured** thee with incense.
24 Thou hast *bought* **chatteled** me
no sweet *cane* **stalk** with *money* **silver,**
neither hast thou *filled* **satiated** me
with the fat of thy sacrifices:
but thou hast *made* **caused** me
to serve with thy sins,
thou hast *wearied* **belaboured** me
with *thine iniquities* **thy perversities.**
25 I, *even* I, *am* he
that *blotteth* **wipeth** out thy *transgressions* **rebellions**
for mine own sake,
and *will* **shall** not remember thy sins.
26 *Put me in remembrance* **Remind me:**
let us plead together:
declare **scribe** thou, that thou mayest be justified.
27 Thy first father hath sinned,
and thy *teachers* **translators**
have *transgressed* **rebelled** against me.
28 Therefore I have profaned
the *princes* **governors** of the *sanctuary* **holies,**
and have given *Jacob* **Yaaqov** to the *curse* **devotement,**
and *Israel* **Yisra El** to *reproaches* **revilings.**

YISRA EL, YAH VEH'S CHOSEN

44 Yet now hear, O *Jacob* **Yaaqov** my servant;
and *Israel* **Yisra El,** whom I have chosen:
2 Thus saith *the LORD* **Yah Veh** that *made* **worked** thee,
and formed thee from the *womb* **belly,**
which *will* **shall** help thee;
Fear **Awe** not, O *Jacob* **Yaaqov,** my servant;
and thou, *Jesurun* **Yeshurun,** whom I have chosen.
3 For I *will* **shall** pour water upon him that is thirsty,
and *floods* **flows** upon the dry *ground:*
I *will* **shall** pour my spirit upon thy seed,
and my blessing upon thine offspring:
4 And they shall *spring up* **sprout**
as among **between** the grass,
as willows by the water *courses* **streams.**
5 One shall say, I am *the LORD'S* **Yah Veh's;**
and another shall call *himself*
by the name of *Jacob* **Yaaqov;**
and another shall *subscribe* **inscribe** with his hand
unto *the LORD* **Yah Veh,**
and *surname himself* **an honorary degree**
by the name of *Israel* **Yisra El.**
6 Thus saith *the LORD* **Yah Veh**
the *King* **Sovereign** of *Israel* **Yisra El,**
and his redeemer *the LORD of hosts* **Yah Veh Sabaoth;**
I am the first, and I am the *last* **final;**
and *beside* **except** me there is no *God* **Elohim.**
7 And who, as I, shall call, and shall *declare* **tell** it,
and *set it in order* **line it up** for me,
since I appointed **set** the *ancient* **original** people?
and *the things* **those** that are coming, and shall come,
let them *shew* **tell** unto them.
8 Fear ye not, neither *be afraid* **fear:**
have not I
told thee from that time **had thee hear ever since,**
and have *declared* **told** it? ye are even my witnesses.
Is there *a God beside* **an Elohah except** me?
yea, there is no *God* **rock;** I know not any.
9 They that *make* **form** a *graven image* **sculptile**
are all of them *vanity* **waste;**
and their *delectable things* **desires** shall not *profit* **benefit;**
and they are their own witnesses;
they see not, nor know;
that they may *be ashamed* **shame.**
10 Who hath formed *a god* **an el,**
or *molten* **poured** a *graven image* **sculptile**
that is *profitable* **beneficial** for *nothing* **nought?**
11 Behold,
all his *fellows* **companions** shall *be ashamed* **shame:**
and the *workmen* **engravers,** they are of *men* **humanity:**
let them all be gathered together, let them stand up;
yet they shall fear,
and they shall *be ashamed* **shame** together.
12 The *smith* **engraver of iron** with the *tongs* **axe**
both worketh in the coals,
and *fashioneth* **formeth** it with hammers,
and *worketh* **maketh** it
with the *strength* **force** of his arms:
yea, he is *hungry* **famished,**
and his *strength faileth* **force is not:**
he drinketh no water, and *is faint* **wearieth.**
13 The *carpenter* **engraver of timber**
stretcheth out his *rule* **line;**
he *marketh it out* **surveyeth** with a *line* **stylus;**
he *fitteth* **worketh** it with planes,
and he *marketh it out* **surveyeth** with the compass,
and *maketh* **worketh** it after the *figure* **pattern** of a man,
according to the *beauty* **adornment** of *a man* **humanity;**
that it may *remain* **settle** in the house.
14 He *heweth* **cuteth** him down cedars,
and taketh the cypress and the oak,
which he strengtheneth for himself
among the trees of the forest:
he planteth an ash,
and the *rain* **downpour** doth nourish it.
15 Then shall it be for *a man* **humanity** to burn:
for he *will* **shall** take *thereof,* and warm **heat** himself;
yea, he kindleth it, and baketh bread;
yea, he *maketh a god* **worketh an el,**
and *worshippeth it* **prostrateth;**
he maketh it a *graven image* **sculptile,**
and *falleth down* **prostrateth** thereto.
16 He burneth *part* **half** *thereof* in the fire;
with *part* **half** *thereof* he eateth flesh;
he roasteth roast, and is satisfied:
yea, he *warmeth* **heateth** *himself,*
and saith, Aha, I am *warm* **heated,**
I have seen the *fire* **flame:**
17 And the *residue* **survivors** *thereof*
he *maketh a god* **worketh an el,**
even his *graven image* **sculptile:**
he *falleth down* **prostrateth** unto it,
and worshippeth it **prostrateth,** and prayeth unto it,

and saith, *Deliver* **Rescue** me; for thou art my *god* **el**.
18 They have not known nor *understood* **discerned**:
for he hath *shut* **daubed** their eyes,
that they cannot see **from seeing**,
and their hearts,
that they cannot understand **from comprehending**.
19 And none *considereth in* **turneth to** his heart,
neither is there knowledge
nor *understanding* **discernment** to say,
I have burned *part of it* **half** in the fire;
yea, also I have baked bread upon the coals *thereof*;
I have roasted flesh, and eaten it:
and shall I *make* **work** the *residue* **remnant** *thereof*
an *abomination* **abhorrence**?
shall I *fall down* **prostrate** to the *stock* **product** of a tree?
20 He *feedeth* **grazeth** on ashes:
a *deceived* **mocked** heart
hath *turned* **perverted** him *aside*,
that he cannot *deliver* **rescue** his soul,
nor say, Is there not a *lie* **falsehood** in my right *hand*?
21 Remember these, O *Jacob* **Yaaqov** and *Israel* **Yisra El**;
for thou art my servant:
I have formed thee; thou art my servant:
O *Israel* **Yisra El**, thou shalt not be forgotten of me.
22 I have blotted out, as a thick cloud,
thy *transgressions* **rebellions**,
and, as a **thick** cloud, thy sins:
return unto me; for I have redeemed thee.
23 *Sing* **Shout**, O ye heavens;
for *the LORD* **Yah Veh** hath *done* **worked** it:
shout, ye *lower parts of the* **nethermost** earth:
break forth into *singing* **shouting**, ye mountains,
O forest, and every tree therein:
for *the LORD* **Yah Veh** hath redeemed *Jacob* **Yaaqov**,
and *glorified* **adorned** himself in *Israel* **Yisra El**.
24 Thus saith *the LORD* **Yah Veh**, thy redeemer,
and he that formed thee from the *womb* **belly**,
I am *the LORD* **Yah Veh** that *maketh* **worketh** all *things*;
that stretcheth forth the heavens alone;
that *spreadeth abroad* **expandeth** the earth by myself;
25 That *frustrateth* **breaketh**
the *tokens* **signs** of *the liars* **lies**,
and *maketh* **exposeth** diviners mad;
that turneth wise *men* backward,
and *maketh* **follieth** their knowledge *foolish*;
26 That *confirmeth* **raiseth** the word of his servant,
and *performeth* **doth shalam**
the counsel of his *messengers* **angels**;
that saith to *Jerusalem* **Yeru Shalem**,
Thou shalt be *inhabited* **settled**;
and to the cities of *Judah* **Yah Hudah**,
Ye shall be built,
and I *will* **shall** raise *up*
the *decayed places* **parched areas** *thereof*:
27 That saith to the *deep* **abyss**, *Be dry* **Parch**,
and I *will dry up* **shall wither** thy rivers:
28 That saith of *Cyrus* **Koresh**, *He is* my *shepherd* **tender**,
and shall *perform* **shalam** all my *pleasure* **delight**:
even saying to *Jerusalem* **Yeru Shalem**,
Thou shalt be built;
and to the *temple* **manse**,
Thy foundation shall be laid **Thou shalt be founded**.

YAH VEH'S ANOINTED

45 Thus saith *the LORD* **Yah Veh** to his anointed,
to *Cyrus* **Koresh**,
whose right *hand* I have *holden* **strengthened**,
to subdue *nations before him* **goyim at his face**;
and I *will* **shall** loose the loins of *kings* **sovereigns**,
in opening, to open
before him **at his face** the *two leaved gates* **doors**;
and the *gates* **portals** shall not be shut;
2 I *will* **shall** go *before thee* **at thy face**,
and *make the crooked places straight*
straighten the esteemed:
I *will* **shall** break in pieces the gates of *brass* **copper**,
and cut *in asunder* **apart** the bars of iron:
3 And I *will* **shall** give thee the treasures of darkness,
and hidden *riches* **treasures** of *secret places* **coverts**,
that thou mayest know that I, *the LORD* **Yah Veh**,
which call thee by thy name,
am *the God* **Elohim** of *Israel* **Yisra El**.
4 For *Jacob* **Yaaqov** my servant's sake,
and *Israel mine elect* **Yisra El my chosen**,
I have even called thee by thy name:
I have *surnamed thee* **given thee an honorary degree**,
though thou hast not known me.
5 *I am the LORD* **I — Yah Veh**, and there is none else,
there is no *God* **Elohim** beside me:
I girded thee, though thou hast not known me:
6 That they may know from the rising of the sun,
and from the *west* **dusk**,
that there is none *beside* **final except** me.
I am the LORD **I — Yah Veh**, and there is none else.
7 I form the light, and create darkness:
I *make peace* **work shalom**, and create evil:
I *the LORD do* **Yah Veh work** all these *things*.
8 *Drop down* **Drip**, ye heavens, from above,
and let the *skies* **vapours**
pour down righteousness **flow justness**:
let the earth open,
and let them *bring forth* **bear fruit of** salvation,
and let *righteousness spring up* **justness sprout** together;
I *the LORD* **Yah Veh** have created it.
9 *Woe* **Ho** unto him that striveth with his *Maker* **Former**!
Let the potsherd strive
with the potsherds of the *earth* **soil**.
Shall the *clay* **morter**
say to him that *fashioneth* **formeth** it,
What *makest* **workest** thou?
or thy *work* **deeds**, He hath no hands?
10 *Woe* **Ho** unto him that saith unto his father,
What begettest thou?
or to the woman,
What hast thou *brought forth* **whirled**?
11 Thus saith *the LORD* **Yah Veh**,
the Holy One of *Israel* **Yisra El**, and his *Maker* **Former**,
Ask me of *things* **those which are** to come
concerning my sons,
and concerning the *work* **deeds** of my hands
command **misvah** ye me.
12 I have *made* **worked** the earth,
and created *man* **humanity** upon it:
I, *even* my hands, have stretched out the heavens,
and all their host have I *commanded* **misvahed**.
13 I have *raised* **wakened** him *up*
in *righteousness* **justness**,
and I *will direct* **shall straighten** all his ways:
he shall build my city,
and he shall *let go* **send away** my *captives* **exiles**,
not for price nor *reward* **bribe**,
saith *the LORD of hosts* **Yah Veh Sabaoth**.
14 Thus saith *the LORD* **Yah Veh**,
The labour of *Egypt* **Misrayim**,
and merchandise
of *Ethiopia* **Kush** and of the *Sabeans* **Sebaiym**,
men of *stature* **measure**,
shall *come* **pass** over unto thee, and they shall be thine:
they shall come after thee;
in *chains* **bonds** they shall *come* **pass** over,
and they shall *fall down* **prostrate** unto thee,
they shall *make supplication* **pray** unto thee,
saying, Surely *God* **El** is in thee;
and there is none else, there is no God beside me
— final — Elohim.
15 *Verily* **Surely** thou art *a God* **an El** that hidest thyself,
O *God* **Elohim** of *Israel* **Yisra El**, the Saviour.
16 They shall be *ashamed* **shamed**, and also confounded,
all of them:
they shall go to *confusion* **shame** together
that are *makers* **engravers** of *idols* **molds**.
17 *But Israel* **Yisra El** shall be saved in *the LORD* **Yah Veh**
with an *everlasting* **eternal** salvation:
ye shall not be *ashamed* **shamed** nor confounded
world without end **unto the eternal ages**.
18 For thus saith *the LORD* **Yah Veh**
that created the heavens;
God **Elohim** himself
that formed the earth and *made* **worked** it;
he hath established it,
he created it not *in vain* **a waste**,

he formed it to be *inhabited* **settled**:
I am the LORD **I — Yah Veh**; and there is none else.
19 I have not *spoken in secret* **worded covertly**,
in a dark place of the earth:
I said not unto the seed of *Jacob* **Yaaqov**,
Seek ye me in *vain* **waste**:
I *the LORD speak righteousness* **Yah Veh word justness**,
I *declare things that are right* **tell it straight**.
20 *Assemble yourselves* **Gather** and come;
draw near together,
ye *that are escaped* **escapees** of the *nations* **goyim**:
they have no knowledge
that *set up* **bear**
the *wood* **timber** of their *graven image* **sculptile**,
and pray unto *a god* **an el** that cannot save.
21 Tell ye, and bring them near;
yea, let them *take* counsel together:
who hath *declared* **caused** this **to be heard**
from *ancient time* **antiquity**?
who hath told it from that time?
have not I *the LORD* **Yah Veh**?
and *there is no God else beside* **no Elohim except** me;
a just *God* **El** and a Saviour;
there is none *beside* **final except** me.
22 *Look unto* **Face** me, and be ye saved,
all the *ends* **finalities** of the earth:
for *I am God* **I — El**, and there is none else.
23 I have *sworn* **oathed** by myself,
the word is gone out of my mouth
in *righteousness* **justness**,
and shall not return,
That unto me every knee shall *bow* **kneel**,
every tongue shall *swear* **oath**.
Philippians 2:9—11
24 Surely, shall *one* **he** say,
in *the LORD* **Yah Veh**
have I *righteousness* **justness** and strength:
even to him shall *men* come;
and all that are *incensed* **inflamed** against him
shall *be ashamed* **shame**.
25 In *the LORD* **Yah Veh**
shall all the seed of *Israel* **Yisra El** be justified,
and shall *glory* **halal**.

THE IDOLS OF BABEL

46 Bel *boweth down* **kneeleth**, Nebo stoopeth,
their idols were upon the *beasts* **live beings**,
and upon the *cattle* **animals**:
your *carriages* **loads** were heavy loaden;
they are — a burden to the *weary beast* **languid**.
2 They stoop, they *bow down* **kneel** together;
they could not *deliver* **rescue** the burden,
but *themselves* **their souls** are gone into captivity.
3 Hearken unto me, O house of *Jacob* **Yaaqov**,
and all the *remnant* **survivors**
of the house of *Israel* **Yisra El**,
which are *borne by me* **laden** from the belly,
which are *carried* **borne** from the womb:
4 And even to your *old age* **agedness** I am he;
and *even* to *hoar hairs* **greyness**
will **shall** I *carry* **bear** *you*:
I have *made* **worked**, and I *will* **shall** bear;
even I *will carry* **shall bear**,
and *will deliver* **shall rescue** you.
5 To whom *will* **shall** ye liken me,
and *make me equal* **equate me**,
and *compare* **liken** me, that we may be like?
6 They *lavish* **scatter** gold out of the *bag* **pouch**,
and weigh silver in the *balance* **beam**,
and hire a *goldsmith* **refiner**;
and he *maketh* **worketh** it *a god* **an el**:
they *fall down* **prostrate**, yea, they *worship* **prostrate**.
7 They bear him upon the shoulder, they *carry* **bear** him,
and set him in his place, and he standeth;
from his place shall he not *remove* **depart**:
yea, one shall cry unto him, yet can he not answer,
nor save him out of his *trouble* **tribulation**.
8 Remember this, *and shew yourselves men* **be manly**:
bring it again to mind **restore heart**,
O ye *transgressors* **rebels**.
9 Remember the former *things of old* **from eternity**:
for *I am God* **I — El**, and there is none else;
I am God **I — Elohim**, *and there is none like me* — **final**,
10 *Declaring* **Telling** the end from the beginning,
and from *ancient times* **antiquity**
the things **former** that are not *yet done* **worked**,
saying, My counsel shall *stand* **rise**,
and I *will do* **shall work** all my *pleasure* **delight**:
11 Calling a *ravenous bird* **swooper** from the *east* **rising**,
the man that executeth my counsel
from a far *country* **land**:
yea, I have *spoken it* **worded**,
I *will* **shall** also bring it *to pass*;
I have *purposed* **formed** it, I *will* **shall** also *do* **work** it.
12 Hearken unto me, ye *stouthearted* **mighty hearted**,
that are far from *righteousness* **justness**:
13 I bring near my *righteousness* **justness**;
it shall not be far *off* **removed**,
and my salvation shall not *tarry* **delay**:
and I *will* **shall** place salvation in *Zion* **Siyon**
for *Israel my glory* **Yisra El mine adornment**.

THE FALL OF BABEL

47 *Come down* **Descend**, and sit in the dust,
O virgin daughter of *Babylon* **Babel**,
sit on the *ground* **earth**:
there is no throne,
O daughter of the *Chaldeans* **Kesediym**:
for thou shalt *no more* **not add**
to be called tender and delicate.
2 Take the millstones, and grind *meal* **flour**:
uncover **expose** thy *locks* **vail**,
make bare the leg **strip the train**,
uncover **expose** the *thigh* **leg**, pass over the rivers.
3 Thy nakedness shall be *uncovered* **exposed**,
yea, thy *shame* **reproach** shall be seen:
I *will* **shall** take *vengeance* **avengement**,
and I *will* **shall** not meet thee as a *man* **human**.
4 *As for* our redeemer,
the LORD of hosts **Yah Veh Sabaoth** is his name,
the Holy One of *Israel* **Yisra El**.
5 Sit thou silent, and get thee into darkness,
O daughter of the *Chaldeans* **Kesediym**:
for thou shalt no more be called,
The lady of *kingdoms* **sovereigndoms**.
6 I was *wroth* **enraged** with my people,
I have *polluted* **profaned** mine inheritance,
and given them into thine hand:
thou didst *shew* **set** them no *mercy* **mercies**;
upon the *ancient* **aged**
hast thou *very heavily laid* **made mighty heavy** thy yoke.
7 And thou saidst,
I shall be a lady *for ever* **eternally**:
so that thou didst not *lay* **set** these *things* to thy heart,
neither didst remember the latter end of it.
8 Therefore hear now this,
thou *that art given to pleasures* **voluptuous**,
that *dwellest carelessly* **settlest confidently**,
that sayest in thine heart,
I am, and none else beside me — **I final**;
I shall not sit *as* a widow,
neither shall I know *the loss of children* **bereavement**:
9 But these two *things* shall come to thee
in a *moment* **blink** in one day,
the loss of children **bereavement**, and widowhood:
they shall come upon thee in their *perfection* **integrity**
for the *multitude* **abundance** of thy sorceries,
and for the *great abundance* **mighty might**
of *thine enchantments* **thy charms**.
10 For thou hast *trusted* **confided** in thy *wickedness* **evil**:
thou hast said, None seeth me.
Thy wisdom and thy knowledge,
it hath *perverted* **turned** thee **away**;
and thou hast said in thine heart,
I am, and none else beside me **I— final**.
11 Therefore shall evil come upon thee;
thou shalt not know
from whence it riseth **the dawn thereof**:
and *mischief* **calamity** shall fall upon thee;
thou shalt not be able to *put it off* **kapar/atone it**:
and *desolation* **devastation**
shall come upon thee suddenly,

which thou shalt not know.
12 Stand *now* **I beseech,**
with *thine enchantments* **thy charms,**
and with the *multitude* **abundance** of thy sorceries,
wherein thou hast laboured from thy youth;
if so be thou shalt be able to *profit* **benefit,**
if so be thou mayest *prevail* **terrify.**
13 Thou art wearied
in the *multitude* **abundance** of thy counsels.
Let *now* **I beseech,**
the *astrologers* **horoscopists of the heavens,**
the *stargazers* **seers of stars,**
the *monthly prognosticators* **knowers of months,**
stand up, and save thee
from these *things* that shall come upon thee.
14 Behold, they shall be as stubble;
the fire shall burn them;
they shall not *deliver themselves* **rescue their souls**
from the *power* **hand** of the flame:
there shall not be a coal to *warm at* **heat,**
nor *fire* **flame** to sit before it.
15 Thus shall they be unto thee
with whom thou hast laboured,
even thy merchants, from thy youth:
they shall wander every *one to his quarter* **man beyond;**
none shall save thee **thou shalt have no saviour.**

THE HARDNESS OF YISRA EL

48 Hear ye this, O house of *Jacob* **Yaaqov,**
which are called by the name of *Israel* **Yisra El,**
and are come forth
out of the waters of *Judah* **Yah Hudah,**
which *swear* **oath** by the name of *the LORD* **Yah Veh,**
and *make mention of* **memorialize**
the God **Elohim** of *Israel* **Yisra El,**
but not in truth, nor in *righteousness* **justness.**
2 For they call themselves of the holy city,
and *stay* **prop** themselves
upon *the God* **Elohim** of *Israel* **Yisra El;**
The LORD of hosts **Yah Veh Sabaoth** is his name.
3 I have *declared* **told** the former *things*
from the beginning **ever since;**
and they went forth out of my mouth,
and I *shewed* **had** them **hear;**
I *did* **worked** them suddenly,
and they *came to pass* **became.**
4 Because I knew that thou art *obstinate* **hard,**
and thy neck is an iron sinew,
and thy *brow brass* **forehead copper;**
5 I have even *from the beginning* **ever since**
declared **told** it to thee;
before it *came to pass* **became,**
I shewed it **I had** thee **hear:**
lest thou shouldest say,
Mine idol hath *done* **worked** them,
and my *graven image* **sculptile,**
and my *molten image* **libation,**
hath *commanded* **misvahed** them.
6 Thou hast heard, see all this;
and *will* **shall** not ye *declare* **tell** it?
I have *shewed* **had** thee **hear** new *things* from this time,
even hidden things — **guarded,**
and thou didst not know them.
7 They are created now, and not from the beginning;
even before **at the face of** the day
when thou heardest them not;
lest thou shouldest say, Behold, I knew them.
8 Yea, thou heardest not; yea, thou knewest not;
yea, from that time that thine ear was not opened:
for I knew that **in dealing covertly,**
thou *wouldest* **shouldest** deal
very treacherously **covertly,**
and wast called a *transgressor* **rebel**
from the *womb* **belly.**
9 For my name's sake
will **shall** I *defer mine anger* **prolong my wrath,**
and for my *praise* **halal**
will **shall** I *refrain* **restrain** for thee,
that I cut thee not off.
10 Behold, I have refined thee, but not with silver;
I have chosen thee
in the furnace of *affliction* **humiliation.**
11 For mine own sake,
even for mine own sake, *will* **shall** I *do* **work** it:
for how should *my name be polluted* **it be profaned?**
and I *will* **shall** not give my *glory* **honour** unto another.
12 Hearken unto me,
O *Jacob* **Yaaqov** and *Israel* **Yisra El,** my called;
I am **I** —he; *I am the* **I** — first, I also *am the last* — **final.**
13 Mine hand also hath
laid the foundation of **founded** the earth,
and my right *hand* **palm** hath spanned the heavens:
when I call unto them, they stand up together.
14 All ye, *assemble yourselves* **gather,** and hear;
which among them hath *declared* **told** these *things?*
The LORD **Yah Veh** hath loved him:
he *will do* **shall work** his *pleasure* **delight**
on *Babylon* **Babel,**
and his arm shall be on the *Chaldeans* **Kesediym.**
15 I, *even* I, have *spoken* **worded;** yea, I have called him:
I have brought him,
and he shall *make* **prosper** his way *prosperous.*
16 *Come ye near* **Approach** unto me, hear ye this;
I have not *spoken in secret* **worded covertly**
from the beginning;
from the time that it was, there am I:
and now *the Lord GOD* **Adonay Yah Veh,** and his Spirit,
hath sent me.
17 Thus saith *the LORD* **Yah Veh,** thy Redeemer,
the Holy One of *Israel* **Yisra El;**
I am the LORD **I** — **Yah Veh** thy *God* **Elohim**
which teacheth thee to *profit* **benefit,**
which *leadeth* **aimeth** thee
by the way that thou shouldest *go.*
18 O that thou hadst hearkened
to my *commandments* **misvoth!**
then had thy *peace* **shalom** been as a river,
and thy *righteousness* **justness** as the waves of the sea:
19 Thy seed also had been as the sand,
and the offspring of thy *bowels* **inwards**
like the *gravel* **belly** *thereof;*
his name should not have been cut off
nor destroyed from *before me* **my face.**
20 Go ye forth of *Babylon* **Babel,**
flee ye from the *Chaldeans* **Kesediym,**
with a voice of *singing declare* **shouting tell** ye,
tell **have us hear** this, utter it *even* to the end of the earth;
say ye, *The LORD* **Yah Veh**
hath redeemed his servant *Jacob* **Yaaqov.**
21 And they thirsted not
when he *led* **carried** them
through the *deserts* **parched areas:**
he caused the waters to flow out of the rock for them:
he *clave* **split** the rock *also,*
and the waters *gushed out* **flowed.**
22 There is no *peace* **shalom,** saith *the LORD* **Yah Veh,**
unto the wicked.

THE SERVANT OF YAH VEH

49 *Listen* **Hearken,** O *isles* **islands,** unto me;
and hearken, ye *people* **nations,** from far;
The LORD **Yah Veh** hath called me from the *womb* **belly;**
from the *bowels* **inwards** of my mother
hath he *made mention of* **mentioned** my name.
2 And he hath *made* **set** my mouth like a sharp sword;
in the shadow of his hand hath he hid me,
and *made* **set** me a polished *shaft* **arrow;**
in his quiver hath he hid me;
3 And said unto me,
Thou art my servant, O *Israel* **Yisra El,**
in whom I *will* **shall** be *glorified* **adorned.**
4 Then I said, I have laboured in vain,
I have *spent* **finished off** my *strength* **force**
for *nought* **a waste,** and in vain:
yet surely my judgment is with *the LORD* **Yah Veh,**
and my *work* **deeds** with my *God* **Elohim.**
5 And now, saith *the LORD* **Yah Veh**
that formed me from the *womb* **belly** to be his servant,
to *bring Jacob again* **return Yaaqov** to him,
Though *Israel* **Yisra El** be not gathered,
yet shall I be *glorious* **honoured**
in the eyes of *the LORD* **Yah Veh,**

and my *God* **Elohim** shall be my strength.
6 And he said, It is *a light thing* **trifling**
that thou shouldest be my servant
to raise up the *tribes* **scions** of *Jacob* **Yaaqov**,
and to restore the *preserved* **guarded** of *Israel* **Yisra El**:
I *will* **shall** also give thee for a light to the *Gentiles* **goyim**,
that thou mayest be my salvation
unto the end of the earth.
7 Thus saith *the LORD* **Yah Veh**,
the Redeemer of *Israel* **Yisra El**, *and* his Holy One,
to *him whom man despiseth*
the despised in soul,
to *him whom the nation abhorreth*
the abhorrent of the goyim,
to a servant of *rulers* **sovereigns**,
Kings **Sovereigns** shall see and arise,
princes **governors** also shall *worship* **prostrate**,
because of *the LORD* **Yah Veh**
that is *faithful* **trustworthy**,
and the Holy One of *Israel* **Yisra El**,
and he shall choose thee.

THE RESTORATION OF YISRA EL

8 Thus saith *the LORD* **Yah Veh**,
In *an acceptable* **a** time **of pleasure**
have I *heard* **answered** thee,
and in a day of salvation have I helped thee:
and I *will preserve* **shall guard** thee,
and give thee for a covenant of the people,
to *establish* **raise** the earth,
to cause to inherit
the *desolate heritages* **desolated inheritances**;
9 That thou mayest say to the *prisoners* **bound**, Go forth;
to them that are in darkness, *Shew* **Expose** *yourselves*.
They shall *feed* **graze** in the ways,
and their pastures shall be in all *high places* **the barrens**.
10 They shall not *hunger* **famish** nor thirst;
neither shall *the heat* **glare** nor sun smite them:
for he that *hath mercy on* **mercieth** them
shall *lead* **drive** them,
even by the springs of water shall he guide them.
11 And I *will make* **shall set** all my mountains a way,
and my highways shall be exalted.
12 Behold, these shall come from far:
and, *lo* **behold**, these from the north
and from the *west* **seaward**;
and these from the land of Sinim.
13 *Sing* **Shout**, O heavens; and *be joyful* **twirl**, O earth;
and break forth into *singing* **shouting**, O mountains:
for *the LORD* **Yah Veh**
hath *comforted* **sighed over** his people,
and *will have* **shall** mercy
upon his afflicted **his humbled**.
14 But *Zion* **Siyon** said,
The LORD **Yah Veh** hath forsaken me,
and *my Lord* **Adonay** hath forgotten me.
15 Can a woman forget her *sucking child* **suckling**,
that she should not *have compassion on* **mercy**
the son of her *womb* **belly**?
yea, they may forget, yet *will* **shall** I not forget thee.
16 Behold,
I have *graven* **engraved** thee
upon the palms of my hands;
thy walls are continually before me.
17 Thy *children* **sons** shall *make haste* **hasten**;
thy *destroyers* **demolishers**
and they that *made* **parched** thee *waste*
shall go forth of thee.
18 Lift up thine eyes round about, and *behold* **see**:
all these gather *themselves together*, and come to thee.
As I live, *saith the LORD* **an oracle of Yah Veh**,
thou shalt surely *clothe* **enrobe** thee with them all,
as with an ornament,
and bind them *on thee*, as a bride *doeth*.
19 For thy *waste* **parched areas**
and thy *desolate places* **desolated**,
and the land of thy destruction,
shall even now be too *narrow* **restricted**
by reason of the *inhabitants* **settlers**,
and they that swallowed thee *up*
shall be far *away* **removed**.
20 *The children which thou shalt have,*
after thou hast lost the other,
The sons of thy bereavements
shall say again in thine ears,
The place is too *strait* **tribulated** for me:
give place to **approach** me that I may *dwell* **settle**.
21 Then shalt thou say in thine heart,
Who hath begotten me these,
seeing I have *lost my children* **aborted**,
and am *desolate* **sterile**,
a captive **an exile**, *and removing to and fro* **turned aside**?
and who hath *brought up* **nourished** these?
Behold, I *was left* alone **survived**;
these, where had they been?
22 Thus saith *the Lord GOD* **Adonay Yah Veh**,
Behold,
I *will* **shall** lift up mine hand to the *Gentiles* **goyim**,
and *set up* **lift** my *standard* **ensign** to the people:
and they shall bring thy sons in *their arms* **bosom**,
and thy daughters
shall be *carried* **borne** upon their shoulders.
23 And *kings* **sovereigns**
shall be thy *nursing fathers* **nurturers**,
and their *queens* **governesses**
thy *nursing mothers* **sucklers**:
they shall *bow down* **prostrate** to thee
with their *face* **nostrils** toward the earth,
and lick up the dust of thy feet;
and thou shalt know that *I am the LORD* **I — Yah Veh**:
for they shall not *be ashamed* **shame**
that *wait for* **await** me.
24 Shall the prey be taken from the mighty,
or the *lawful* **just** captive *delivered* **rescued**?
25 But thus saith *the LORD* **Yah Veh**,
Even the captives of the mighty shall be taken away,
and the prey of the *terrible* **tyrant**
shall be *delivered* **rescued**:
for I *will* **shall** contend with him
that contendeth with thee,
and I *will* **shall** save thy *children* **sons**.
26 And I *will* **shall** feed them that oppress thee
with their own flesh;
and they shall *be drunken* **intoxicate**
with their own blood,
as with *sweet wine* **squeezed juice**:
and all flesh shall know that I *the LORD* **Yah Veh**
am thy Saviour and thy Redeemer,
the *mighty* **Almighty** One of *Jacob* **Yaaqov**.

THE SIN OF YISRA EL

50 Thus saith *the LORD* **Yah Veh**,
Where is the *bill* **scroll** of your mother's divorcement,
whom I have *put* **sent** away?
or **to** which of my *creditors* **exactors**
is it to whom I have sold you?
Behold,
for your *iniquities* **perversities** have ye sold yourselves,
and for your *transgressions* **rebellions**
is your mother *put* **sent** away.
2 Wherefore, when I came, was there no man?
when I called, was there none to answer?
In shortening, Is my hand shortened *at all*,
that it cannot redeem?
or have I no *power* **force** to *deliver* **rescue**?
behold, at my rebuke I *dry up* **parch** the sea,
I *make* **set** the rivers a wilderness:
their fish stinketh, because there is no water,
and dieth for thirst.
3 I *clothe* **enrobe** the heavens with *blackness* **darkness**,
and I *make sackcloth* **set saq** their covering.

THE TONGUE OF THE DISCIPLED

4 *The Lord GOD* **Adonay Yah Veh**
hath given me the tongue of the *learned* **discipled**,
that I should know
how to *speak* **reinforce** a word *in season*
to *him that is* **the** weary:
he wakeneth morning by morning,
he wakeneth mine ear to hear as the *learned* **discipled**.
5 *The Lord GOD* **Adonay Yah Veh** hath opened mine ear,
and I was not rebellious,
neither *turned away back* **apostatized backward**.

A MESSIANIC PROPHECY

6 I gave my back to the smiters,
and my cheeks to them that *plucked off the hair* **balden**:
I hid not my face from shame and spitting.
7 For *the Lord GOD will* **Adonay Yah Veh shall** help me;
therefore shall I not be confounded:
therefore have I set my face like a flint,
and I know that I shall not *be ashamed* **shame**.
8 He is near that justifieth me;
who *will* **shall** contend with me?
let us stand together:
who is *mine adversary* **the master of my judgment**?
let him come near to me.
9 Behold,
the Lord GOD will **Adonay Yah Veh shall** help me;
who is he that shall *condemn* **declare** me **wicked**?
lo **behold**,
they all shall *wax old* **wear out** as *a garment* **clothes**;
the moth shall eat them *up*.
10 Who is among you that feareth *the LORD* **Yah Veh**,
that *obeyeth* **hearkeneth unto** the voice of his servant,
that walketh in darkness, and hath no *light* **brilliance**?
let him *trust* **confide** in the name of *the LORD* **Yah Veh**,
and *stay* **lean** upon his *God* **Elohim**.
11 Behold, all ye that kindle a fire,
that *compass yourselves about* **girt** with sparks:
walk in the *light* **flame** of your fire,
and in the sparks that ye have *kindled* **burnt**.
This shall ye have of mine hand;
ye shall lie down in *sorrow* **agony**.

SIYON'S ETERNAL SALVATION

51 Hearken to me,
ye that *follow after righteousness* **pursue justness**,
ye that seek *the LORD* **Yah Veh**:
look unto the rock whence ye are hewn,
and to the *hole* **quarry** of the *pit* **well**
whence ye are *digged* **bored out**.
2 Look unto Abraham your father,
and unto Sarah that *bare* **writhed** you:
for **one, I have** called him *alone*,
and blessed him, and *increased* **abounded** him.
3 For *the LORD* **Yah Veh**
shall *comfort Zion* **sigh over Siyon**:
he *will comfort* **shall sigh over**
all her *waste places* **parched areas**;
and he *will make* **shall set** her wilderness like Eden,
and her *desert* **plain**
like the garden of *the LORD* **Yah Veh**;
joy **rejoicing** and *gladness* **cheerfulness**
shall be found therein,
thanksgiving **extended hands**,
and the voice of *melody* **psalm**.
4 Hearken unto me, my people;
and *give ear* **hearken** unto me, O my nation:
for a *law* **torah** shall proceed from me,
and I *will make* **shall rest** my judgment *to rest*
for a light of the people.
5 My *righteousness* **justness** is near;
my salvation is gone forth,
and mine arms shall judge the people;
the *isles* **islands** shall *wait upon* **await** me,
and on mine arm shall they *trust* **wait**.
6 Lift up your eyes to the heavens,
and look upon the earth beneath:
for the heavens shall vanish away like smoke,
and the earth shall *wax old* **wear out**
like *a garment* **clothes**,
and they that *dwell* **settle** therein
shall die *in like manner* **as stingers**:
but my salvation shall be *for ever* **eternal**,
and my *righteousness* **justness**
shall not be *abolished* **broken down**.
7 Hearken unto me, ye that know *righteousness* **justness**,
the people in whose heart is my *law* **torah**;
fear **awe** ye not the reproach of men,
neither *be ye afraid* **terrify** of their revilings.
8 For the moth shall eat them *up* like *a garment* **clothes**,
and the *worm* **moth** shall eat them like wool:
but my *righteousness* **justness** shall be *for ever* **eternal**,
and my salvation from generation to generation.
9 Awake, awake, *put on* **enrobe** strength,
O arm of *the LORD* **Yah Veh**;
awake, as in the ancient days,
in the generations *of old* **eternal**.
Art thou not it that hath *cut Rahab* **hewn Rahab/pride**,
and *wounded* **pierced** the *dragon* **monster**?
10 Art thou not it which hath *dried* **parched** the sea,
the waters of the great *deep* **abyss**;
that hath *made* **set** the depths of the sea
a way for the *ransomed* **redeemed** to pass over?
11 Therefore
the redeemed of *the LORD* **Yah Veh** shall return,
and come with *singing* **shouting** unto *Zion* **Siyon**;
and *everlasting joy* **eternal cheerfulness**
shall be upon their head:
they shall *obtain* **attain**
gladness **rejoicing** and *joy* **cheerfulness**;
and sorrow **grief** and *mourning* **sighing** shall flee away.
12 I, *even* I, *am* he that *comforteth* **sigheth over** you:
who art thou,
that thou shouldest *be afraid of* **awe** a man that shall die,
and of the son of *man* **humanity**
which shall be *made* **given** as grass;
13 And forgettest *the LORD* **Yah Veh** thy *maker* **worker**,
that hath stretched forth the heavens,
and laid the foundations of the earth;
and hast feared continually every day
because **at the face** of the fury of the oppressor,
as if he were *ready* **prepared** to *destroy* **ruin**?
and where is the fury of the oppressor?
14 The *captive exile* **stroller** hasteneth
that he may be loosed,
and that he should not die in the pit **of ruin**,
nor that his bread should *fail* **lack**.
15 But *I am the LORD* **I — Yah Veh** thy *God* **Elohim**,
that *divided* **split** the sea, whose waves roared:
The LORD of hosts **Yah Veh Sabaoth** is his name.
16 And I have *put* **set** my words in thy mouth,
and I have covered thee in the shadow of mine hand,
that I may plant the heavens,
and lay the foundations of the earth,
and say unto *Zion* **Siyon**, Thou *art* my people.

THE CUP OF YAH VEH'S FURY

17 Awake, awake,
stand up **arise**, O *Jerusalem* **Yeru Shalem**,
which hast drunk at the hand of *the LORD* **Yah Veh**
the cup of his fury;
thou hast drunken
the *dregs* **chalice** of the cup of *trembling* **staggering**,
and wrung *them* out.
18 There is none to guide her
among all the sons whom she hath *brought forth* **borne**;
neither is there any that *taketh* **holdeth** her by the hand
of all the sons that she hath *brought up* **nourished**.
19 These two *things are come unto* **confront** thee;
who shall *be sorry for* **wag over** thee?
desolation **ravage**, and *destruction* **breaking**,
and the famine, and the sword:
by whom shall I *comfort* **sigh over** thee?
20 Thy sons have *fainted* **languished**,
they lie at the head of all the *streets* **outways**,
as *a wild bull* **an antelope** in a net:
they are full of the fury of *the LORD* **Yah Veh**,
the rebuke of thy *God* **Elohim**.
21 Therefore hear *now* **I beseech** this,
thou *afflicted* **humbled**,
and *drunken* **intoxicated**, but not with wine:
22 Thus saith thy *Lord the LORD* **Adonay Yah Veh**,
and thy *God* **Elohim**
that pleadeth the cause of his people,
Behold, I have taken out of thine hand
the cup of *trembling* **staggering**,
even the *dregs* **chalice** of the cup of my fury;
thou shalt *no more* **not add to** drink it again:
23 But I *will put* **shall set** it
into the hand of them that *afflict* **grieve** thee;
which have said to thy soul,
Bow down **Prostrate**, that we may *go* **pass** over:
and thou hast *laid* **set** thy *body* **back** as the *ground* **earth**,
and as the *street* **outway**, to them that *went* **passed** over.

SIYON REDEEMED

52 Awake, awake;
put on **enrobe** thy strength, O *Zion* **Siyon**;
put on **enrobe**
thy *beautiful garment* **clothes of adornment**,
O *Jerusalem* **Yeru Shalem**, the holy city:
for henceforth
there shall *no more* **not add to** come into thee
the uncircumcised and the *unclean* **foul**.
2 Shake thyself from the dust;
arise, *and* sit down, O *Jerusalem* **Yeru Shalem**:
loose thyself from the *bands* **bonds** of thy neck,
O captive daughter of *Zion* **Siyon**.
3 For thus saith *the LORD* **Yah Veh**,
Ye have sold yourselves *for nought* **gratuitously**;
and ye shall be redeemed without *money* **silver**.
4 For thus saith *the Lord GOD* **Adonay Yah Veh**,
My people *went down aforetime* **descended formerly**
into *Egypt* **Misrayim** to sojourn there;
and the *Assyrian* **Ashshuri** oppressed them
without cause **unceasingly**.
5 Now therefore, what have I here,
saith the LORD **an oracle of Yah Veh**,
that my people is taken away *for nought* **gratuitously**?
they that *rule* **reign** over them *make* **cause** them to howl,
saith the LORD **an oracle of Yah Veh**;
and my name
continually every day is *blasphemed* **scorned**.
6 Therefore my people shall know my name:
therefore *they shall know* in that day
that I *am* — he that doth speak: behold, *it is* I.

A MESSIANIC PROPHECY

7 How *beautiful* **befitting** upon the mountains
are the feet of him
that *bringeth good tidings* **evangelizeth**,
that *publisheth peace* **hearkeneth shalom**;
that *bringeth good tidings* **evangelizeth** of good,
that *publisheth* **hearkeneth** salvation;
that saith unto *Zion* **Siyon**, Thy *God* **Elohim** reigneth!
8 Thy *watchmen* **watchers** shall lift *up* the voice;
with the voice together shall they *sing* **shout**:
for they shall see eye to eye,
when *the LORD* **Yah Veh**
shall *bring again Zion* **return Siyon**.
9 Break forth into joy, *sing* **shout** together,
ye *waste places* **parched areas** of *Jerusalem* **Yeru Shalem**:
for *the LORD* **Yah Veh**
hath *comforted* **sighed over** his people,
he hath redeemed *Jerusalem* **Yeru Shalem**.
10 *The LORD* **Yah Veh**
hath *made bare* **stripped** his holy arm
in the eyes of all the *nations* **goyim**;
and all the *ends* **finalities** of the earth
shall see the salvation of our *God* **Elohim**.
11 *Depart* **Turn** ye *aside*, *depart* **turn** ye **aside**,
go ye out from thence,
touch *no unclean thing* **not the foul**;
go ye out of the midst of her;
be ye *clean* **purified**,
that bear the *vessels* **instruments** of *the LORD* **Yah Veh**.
12 For ye shall not go out with haste,
nor go by *flight* **retreat**:
for *the LORD* **Yah Veh**
will **shall** go *before you* **at thy face**;
and *the God* **Elohim** of *Israel* **Yisra El**
will be your rereward **shall gather you**.

A MESSIANIC PROPHECY

13 Behold, my servant shall *deal prudently* **comprehend**,
he shall be exalted and *extolled* **lifted**,
and be *very high* **mightily lifted**.
14 As many were astonied at thee;
his visage was so *marred more than any* **ruined by** man,
and his form *more than* **by** the sons of *men* **humanity**:
15 So shall he sprinkle many *nations* **goyim**;
the *kings* **sovereigns** shall shut their mouths at him:
for that which had not been *told* **scribed** them
shall they see;
and that which they had not heard
shall they *consider* **discern**.

53 Who hath *believed* **trusted** our report?
and to whom
is the arm of *the LORD revealed* **Yah Veh exposed**?
2 For he shall *grow up before him* **ascend at his face**
as a *tender plant* **sprout**,
and as a root out of *a dry ground* **parched earth**:
he hath no form nor *comeliness* **majesty**;
and when we shall see him,
there is no *beauty* **visage** that we should desire him.
3 He is despised and *rejected* **abandoned** of men;
a man of sorrows,
and *acquainted with grief* **knowing sickness**:
and we hid as it were our faces from him;
he was despised, and we *esteemed* **machinated** him not.
4 Surely he hath borne our *griefs* **sicknesses**,
and *carried* **borne** our sorrows:
yet we *did esteem* **machinated** him *stricken* **plagued**,
smitten of *God* **Elohim**, and *afflicted* **abased**.
5 But he was *wounded* **pierced**
for our *transgressions* **rebellions**,
he was bruised **crushed** for our *iniquities* **perversities**:
the chastisement of our *peace* **shalom** was upon him;
and with his *stripes* **lashes** we are healed.
6 All we like *sheep* **a flock** have *gone astray* **strayed**;
we have *turned* **faced** every *one* **man** to his own way;
and *the LORD* **Yah Veh** hath *laid* **met** on him
the *iniquity* **perversity** of us all.
7 *He was oppressed* **Of him they exacted**,
and he was *afflicted* **abased**,
yet he opened not his mouth:
he is brought as a lamb to the slaughter,
and as *a sheep* **an ewe**
before **at the face of** her shearers is *dumb* **muted**,
so he openeth not his mouth.
8 He was taken
from prison **by restraint** and *from* **by** judgment:
and who shall *declare* **meditate** his generation?
for he was cut off out of the land of the living:
for the *transgression* **rebellion** of my people
was *he stricken* **the plague upon him**.
9 And he *made* **gave** his *grave* **tomb** with the wicked,
and with the rich in his death;
because he had *done* **worked** no violence,
neither was *any* deceit in his mouth.
10 Yet it *pleased the LORD* **delighted Yah Veh**
to *bruise* **crush** him;
he hath *put* **stroked** him *to grief*:
when thou shalt *make* **set** his soul
an offering for sin **for the guilt**,
he shall see his seed, he shall prolong his days,
and the *pleasure* **delight** of *the LORD* **Yah Veh**
shall prosper in his hand.
11 He shall see of the *travail* **toil** of his soul,
and shall be satisfied:
by his knowledge
shall my *righteous* **just** servant justify many;
for he shall bear their *iniquities* **perversities**.
12 Therefore *will* **shall** I *divide* **allot** him *a portion*
with the great,
and he shall *divide* **allot** the spoil with the *strong* **mighty**;
because he hath poured out his soul unto death:
and he was numbered with the *transgressors* **rebels**;
and he bare the sin of many,
and *made intercession* **interceded**
for the *transgressors* **rebels**.

THE GLORY OF SIYON

54 *Sing* **Shout**, O *barren* **sterile**,
thou that *didst* **bore** not *bear*;
break forth into *singing* **shouting**, and *cry aloud* **resound**,
thou that *didst* **writhed** not *travail with child*:
for more are the *children* **sons** of the *desolate* **desolated**
than the *children* **sons** of the married *wife*,
saith *the LORD* **Yah Veh**.
2 Enlarge the place of thy tent,
and let them stretch forth the curtains
of *thine habitations* **thy tabernacles**:
spare not, lengthen thy cords, and strengthen thy stakes;
3 For thou shalt *break forth* **separate**
on the right *hand* and on the left;

and thy seed shall *inherit* **succeed** the *Gentiles* **goyim**,
and make **settle** the *desolate* **desolated** cities
to be inhabited.
4 *Fear* **Awe** not; for thou shalt not *be ashamed* **shame**:
neither be thou *confounded* **ashamed**;
for thou shalt not *be put to shame* **blush**:
for thou shalt forget the shame of thy youth,
and shalt not remember
the reproach of thy widowhood any more.
5 For thy *Maker* **Worker** is *thine husband* **thy master**;
the LORD of hosts **Yah Veh Sabaoth** is his name;
and thy Redeemer the Holy One of *Israel* **Yisra El**;
The *God* **Elohim** of the whole earth shall he be called.
6 For *the LORD* **Yah Veh** hath called thee
as a woman forsaken and *grieved* **contorted** in spirit,
and a *wife* **woman** of youth, when thou wast refused,
saith thy *God* **Elohim**.
7 For a small *moment* **blink** have I forsaken thee;
but with great mercies *will* **shall** I gather thee.
8 In *a little wrath* **an outburst of rage**
I hid my face from thee for a *moment* **blink**;
but with *everlasting kindness* **eternal mercy**
will I have mercy on **shall I mercy** thee,
saith *the LORD* **Yah Veh** thy Redeemer.
9 For this is as the waters of *Noah* **Noach** unto me:
for *as* I have *sworn* **oathed**
that the waters of *Noah* **Noach**
should no more *go* **pass** over the earth;
so have I *sworn* **oathed**
that I *would* **should** not be *wroth* **enraged** with thee,
nor rebuke thee.
10 For the mountains shall depart,
and the hills *be removed* **topple**;
but my *kindness* **mercy** shall not depart from thee,
neither shall the covenant of my *peace* **shalom**
be removed **topple**,
saith *the LORD* **Yah Veh**
that *hath mercy on* **mercieth** thee.
11 O thou *afflicted* **humbled**,
tossed with tempest **stormed**,
and not *comforted* **sighed over**,
behold, I *will lay* **shall crouch** thy stones
with *fair colours* **stribium**,
and lay thy foundations with sapphires.
12 And I *will make thy windows* **shall set thy sun**
of *agates* **rubies**,
and thy *gates* **portals** of *carbuncles* **carbuncle stones**,
and all thy borders of *pleasant* stones **of delight**.
13 And all thy *children* **sons**
shall be *taught* **discipled** of *the LORD* **Yah Veh**;
and great shall be the *peace* **shalom** of thy *children* **sons**.
14 In *righteousness* **justness**
shalt thou *be established* **establish thyself**:
thou shalt be far **removed** from oppression;
for thou shalt not *fear* **awe**:
and from *terror* **ruin**;
for it shall not *come near* **approach** thee.
15 Behold,
in sojourning, they shall *surely gather together* **sojourn**,
but not by me:
whosoever shall *gather together* **sojourn** against thee
shall fall for thy sake.
16 Behold, I have created the *smith* **engraver**
that *bloweth* **puffeth** the coals in the fire,
and that bringeth forth an instrument for his work;
and I have created the *waster* **ruiner** to *destroy* **ruin**.
17 No *weapon* **instrument** that is formed against thee
shall prosper;
and every tongue that shall rise against thee in judgment
thou shalt *condemn* **declare wicked**.
This is the *heritage* **inheritance**
of the servants of *the LORD* **Yah Veh**,
and their *righteousness* **justness** is of me,
saith the LORD **an oracle of Yah Veh**.

YAH VEH'S OPEN INVITATION

55 Ho, every one that thirsteth,
come ye to the waters,
and he that hath no *money* **silver**;
come ye, *buy* **market for kernels**, and eat;
yea, come, *buy* **market for kernels** wine and milk
without *money* **silver** and without price.
2 Wherefore do ye *spend money* **weigh silver**
for that which is not bread?
and your labour for that which satisfieth not?
in hearkening, hearken *diligently* unto me,
and eat ye that which is good,
and let your soul delight itself in fatness.
3 *Incline* **Extend** your ear, and come unto me:
hear, and your soul shall live;
and I *will make* **shall cut**
an *everlasting* **eternal** covenant with you,
even the *sure* **trustworthy** mercies of David.
4 Behold, I have given him *for* a witness
to the *people* **nations**,
a leader **eminent** and *commander* **misvaher**
to the *people* **nations**.
5 Behold,
thou shalt call a *nation* **goyim** that thou knowest not,
and *nations* **goyim** that knew not thee shall run unto thee
because of *the LORD* **Yah Veh** thy *God* **Elohim**,
and for the Holy One of *Israel* **Yisra El**;
for he hath *glorified* **adorned** thee.
6 Seek ye *the LORD* **Yah Veh** while he may be found,
call ye upon him while he is near:
7 Let the wicked forsake his way,
and the *unrighteous* man **of mischief**
his *thoughts* **fabrications**:
and let him return unto *the LORD* **Yah Veh**,
and he *will* **shall** *have* mercy *upon* him;
and to our *God* **Elohim**,
for he *will abundantly pardon* **shall abound to forgive**.
8 For my *thoughts* **fabrications**
are not your *thoughts* **fabrications**,
neither are your ways my ways,
saith the LORD **an oracle of Yah Veh**.
9 For *as* the heavens are higher than the earth,
so are my ways higher than your ways,
and my *thoughts* **fabrications**
than your *thoughts* **fabrications**.
10 For as the *rain cometh down* **downpour descendeth**,
and the snow from *heaven* **the heavens**,
and returneth not thither,
but *watereth* **saturateth** the earth,
and maketh it *bring forth* **beget** and *bud* **sprout**,
that it may give seed to the *sower* **seeder**,
and bread to the eater:
11 So shall my word be that goeth forth out of my mouth:
it shall not return unto me void,
but it shall *accomplish* **work** that which I *please* **desire**,
and it shall prosper *in the thing* whereto I sent it.
12 For ye shall go out with *joy* **cheerfulness**,
and be led forth with *peace* **shalom**:
the mountains and the hills shall break forth
before you **at thy face** into *singing* **shouting**,
and all the trees of the field shall clap their *hands* **palms**.
13 Instead of the thorn
shall *come up* **ascend** the fir tree,
and instead of the brier
shall *come up* **ascend** the myrtle tree:
and it shall be to *the LORD* **Yah Veh** for a name,
for an *everlasting* **eternal** sign that shall not be cut off.

SALVATION FOR ALL

56 Thus saith *the LORD* **Yah Veh**,
Keep **Guard** ye judgment, and *do justice* **work justness**:
for my salvation is near to come,
and my *righteousness* **justness** to be *revealed* **exposed**.
2 *Blessed* **Blithesome** is the man that *doeth* **worketh** this,
and the son of *man* **humanity** that layeth hold on it;
that *keepeth* **guardeth** the *sabbath* **shabbath**
from *polluting* **profaning** it,
and *keepeth* **guardeth** his hand
from *doing* **working** any evil.
3 Neither let the son of the stranger,
that hath joined himself to *the LORD* **Yah Veh**,
speak **say**, saying,
In separating,
The LORD **Yah Veh** hath *utterly* separated me
from his people:
neither let the eunuch say, Behold, I am a dry tree.
4 For thus saith *the LORD* **Yah Veh** unto the eunuchs

that *keep* **guard** my *sabbaths* **shabbaths**,
and choose *the things* **those** that *please* **delight** me,
and *take* hold *of* my covenant;
5 Even unto them
will **shall** I give in mine house and within my walls
a *place* **hand** and a name
better than of sons and of daughters:
I *will* **shall** give them an *everlasting* **eternal** name,
that shall not be cut off.
6 Also the sons of the stranger,
that join themselves to *the LORD* **Yah Veh**,
to *serve* **minister to** him,
and to love the name of *the LORD* **Yah Veh**,
to be his servants,
every one that *keepeth* **guardeth** the *sabbath* **shabbath**
from *polluting* **profaning** it,
and *taketh hold of* **holdeth** my covenant;
7 Even them *will* **shall** I bring to my holy mountain,
and *make* **cheer** them *joyful* in my house of prayer:
their *burnt offerings* **holocausts** and their sacrifices
shall be *accepted* **a pleasure**
upon *mine* **my sacrifice** altar;
for mine house shall be called
an house of **my** prayer for all people.
8 *The Lord GOD* **An oracle of Adonay Yah Veh**,
which gathereth
the *outcasts* **overthrown** of *Israel* **Yisra El** *saith*,
Yet *will* **shall** I gather *others* to him,
beside those that are gathered unto him.
9 All ye *beasts* **live beings** of the field, come to devour,
yea, all ye *beasts* **live beings** in the forest.
10 His *watchmen* **watchers** are blind:
they *are all ignorant* **know not**,
they are all *dumb* **mute** dogs, they cannot bark;
sleeping **dreaming**, lying down, loving to slumber.
11 Yea, they are *greedy* dogs **strong of soul**
which *can never have enough* **know not satisfaction**,
and they are *shepherds* **tenders**
that *cannot understand* **know not to discern**:
they all *look to* **face** their own way,
every *one* **man** for his gain, from his *quarter* **end**.
12 Come ye, *say they*, I *will fetch* **shall take** wine,
and we *will fill ourselves* **shall carouse**
with *strong drink* **intoxicants**;
and to morrow shall be as this day,
and *much more abundant* **a mighty great remainder**.

THE JUST DESTRUCT

57 The *righteous perisheth* **just destructeth**,
and no man *layeth* **setteth** it to heart:
and merciful men are *taken away* **gathered**,
none *considering* **discerning**
that the *righteous* **just** is *taken away* **gathered**
from **the face of** the evil *to come*.
2 He shall enter into *peace* **shalom**:
they shall rest in their beds,
each one walking in his *uprightness* **straightforwardness**.
3 But *draw near* **approach** hither,
ye sons of the *sorceress* **cloudgazer**,
the seed of the adulterer and the whore.
4 Against whom do ye *sport* **delight** yourselves?
against whom *make ye a wide* **enlarge ye the** mouth,
and *draw out* **lengthen** the tongue?
are ye not children of *transgression* **rebellion**,
a seed of falsehood,
5 *Enflaming yourselves* **Heating up** with *idols* **elohim**
under every green tree,
slaying **slaughtering** the children in the *valleys* **wadies**
under the *clifts* **clefts** of the rocks?
6 Among the *smooth stones* **smooth stones/allotment**
of the *stream* **wadi** is thy *portion* **allotment**;
they, they are thy *lot* **pebble**:
even to them hast thou poured a *drink offering* **libation**,
thou hast *offered a meat* **holocausted an** offering.
should I *receive comfort* **sigh** in these?
7 Upon a lofty and *high* **lifted** mountain
hast thou set thy bed:
even thither *wentest* **ascendest** thou *up*
to *offer* **sacrifice** sacrifice.
8 Behind the doors also and the posts
hast thou set up thy remembrance:
for thou hast *discovered* **exposed** thyself
to another than **from** me,
and art *gone up* **ascended**;
thou hast enlarged thy bed,
and *made* **cut** thee *a covenant* with them;
thou lovedst their bed where thou sawest it.
9 And thou *wentest* **strollest** to the *king* **sovereign**
with ointment,
and *didst increase* **abounded** thy perfumes,
and *didst send* **sent** thy *messengers* **ambassadors** far off,
and *didst debase* **debased** thyself *even* unto *hell* **sheol**.
10 Thou art *wearied* **belaboured**
in the greatness of thy way;
yet saidst thou not, *There is no hope* **I quit!**:
thou hast found the life of thine hand;
therefore thou wast not *grieved* **worn**.
11 And of whom
hast thou been *afraid* **concerned** or *feared* **awed**,
that thou hast lied, and hast not remembered me,
nor *laid* **set** it to thy heart?
have not I *held my peace even of old* **hushed eternally**,
and thou *fearest* **awest** me not?
12 I *will declare* **shall tell** thy *righteousness* **justness**,
and thy works;
for they shall not *profit* **benefit** thee.
13 When thou criest,
let thy *companies deliver* **throngs rescue** thee;
but the wind shall *carry* **bear** them all away;
vanity shall take them:
but he that *putteth his trust* **seeketh refuge** in me
shall *possess* **inherit** the land,
and shall inherit my holy mountain;
14 And shall say, *Cast ye* **Raise** up, *cast ye* **raise** up,
prepare **face** the way,
take up **lift** the stumblingblock
out of the way of my people.
15 For thus saith the high and *lofty* **lifted** One
that *inhabiteth* **tabernacleth** eternity,
whose name is Holy;
I *dwell* **tabernacle** in the high and holy *place*,
with him also
that is of a *contrite* **crushed** and *humble* **lowly** spirit,
to *revive* **enliven** the spirit of the *humble* **lowly**,
and to *revive* **enliven** the heart
of the *contrite* **crushed** *ones*.
16 For I *will* **shall** not contend *for ever* **eternally**,
neither *will* **shall** I be *always wroth* **perpetually enraged**:
for the spirit should *fail before me* **languish at my face**,
and the *souls* **breath** which I have *made* **worked**.
17 For the *iniquity* **perversity**
of his *covetousness* **greedy gain**
was I *wroth* **enraged**, and smote him:
I hid me, and was *wroth* **enraged**,
and he went on *frowardly* **apostate**
in the way of his heart.
18 I have seen his ways, and *will* **shall** heal him:
I *will lead* **shall guide** him also,
and *restore comforts* **shalam solaces** unto him
and to his mourners.
19 I create the fruit of the lips;
Peace **Shalom**, *peace* **shalom** to him that is far off,
and to him that is near, saith *the LORD* **Yah Veh**;
and I *will* **shall** heal him.
20 But the wicked are like the *troubled* **driven** sea,
when it cannot rest,
whose waters *cast up mire* **expel filth** and *dirt* **mire**.
21 There is no *peace* **shalom**, saith my *God* **Elohim**,
to the wicked.

ON FASTING

58 *Cry aloud* **Call out with the throat**, spare not,
lift up thy voice like a trumpet,
and *shew* **tell** my people their *transgression* **rebellion**,
and the house of *Jacob* **Yaaqov** their sins.
2 Yet they seek me *daily* **day by day**,
and delight to know my ways,
as a *nation* **goyim** that *did righteousness* **worked justness**,
and forsook not
the *ordinance* **judgment** of their *God* **Elohim**:
they ask of me
the *ordinances* **judgments** of *justice* **justness**;

they take delight in approaching to *God* **Elohim**.
3 Wherefore have we fasted, *say they*, and thou seest not?
wherefore have we *afflicted* **humbled** our soul,
and thou takest no knowledge?
Behold, in the day of your fast ye find *pleasure* **delight**,
and exact all your *labours* **contortions**.
4 Behold, ye fast for strife and *debate* **strive**,
and to smite with the fist of wickedness:
ye shall not fast as ye do this day,
to *make* **have** your voice to be heard on high.
5 Is it such a fast that I have chosen?
a day for *a man* **humanity** to *afflict* **humble** his soul?
is it to bow down his head as a bulrush,
and to spread *sackcloth* **saq** and ashes *under him*?
Wilt **Shalt** thou call this a fast,
and an acceptable **a** day **of pleasure**
to *the LORD* **Yah Veh**?
6 Is not this the fast that I have chosen?
to loose the bands of wickedness,
to undo the *heavy burdens* **bundles of the yoke pole**,
and to *let* **send away** the *oppressed* **crushed**
go free **liberated**,
and that ye *break* **tear** every yoke **pole**?
7 Is it not to *deal* **separate** thy bread
to the *hungry* **famished**,
and that thou bring
the *poor that are cast out* **humble outcasts** to thy house?
when thou seest the naked, that thou cover him;
and that thou *hide* **conceal** not thyself
from thine own flesh?
8 Then shall thy light
break forth **split** as the *morning* **dawn**,
and thine health
shall *spring forth speedily* **sprout quickly**:
and thy *righteousness* **justness**
shall go *before thee* **at thy face**;
the *glory* **honour** of *the LORD* **Yah Veh**
shall *be thy rereward* **gather thee up**.
9 Then shalt thou call,
and *the LORD* **Yah Veh** shall answer;
thou shalt cry, and he shall say, *Here I am* **Behold, I**.
If thou *take away* **turn aside** from the midst of thee
the yoke **pole**,
the *putting forth* **extending** of the finger,
and *speaking vanity* **wording mischief**;
10 And if thou *draw out* **produce** thy soul
to the *hungry* **famished**,
and satisfy the *afflicted* **humbled** soul;
then shall thy light rise in obscurity,
and thy darkness be as the noon *day*:
11 And *the LORD* **Yah Veh** shall guide thee continually,
and satisfy thy soul in *drought* **parches**,
and *make fat* **fatten** thy bones:
and thou shalt be like a *watered* **saturated** garden,
and like a spring of water, whose waters fail not.
12 And they that shall be of thee
shall build the *old waste places* **original parched areas**:
thou shalt raise *up* the foundations
of *many generations* **generation and generation**;
and thou shalt be called,
The *repairer* **waller** of the breach,
The restorer of paths to *dwell* **settle** *in*.
13 If thou turn away thy foot from the *sabbath* **shabbath**,
from *doing* **working** thy *pleasure* **delight** on my holy day;
and call the *sabbath* **shabbath** a *delight* **luxury**,
the holy of *the LORD* **Yah Veh**, honourable;
and shalt honour him,
not *doing* **working** thine own ways,
nor finding thine own *pleasure* **delight**,
nor *speaking* **wording** thine own words:
14 Then shalt thou delight thyself in *the LORD* **Yah Veh**;
and I *will* **shall** cause thee to ride
upon the *high places* **bamahs** of the earth,
and feed thee
with the *heritage* **inheritance** of *Jacob* **Yaaqov** thy father:
for the mouth of *the LORD* **Yah Veh**
hath *spoken it* **worded**.

ON SEPARATION FROM YAH VEH

59 Behold,
the LORD'S **Yah Veh's** hand is not shortened,
that it cannot save **from saving**;
neither his ear heavy, *that it cannot hear* **from hearing**:
2 But your *iniquities* **perversities** have separated
between you and **between** your *God* **Elohim**,
and your sins have hid his face from you,
that he *will* **shall** not hear.
3 For your *hands* **palms** are *defiled* **profaned** with blood,
and your fingers with *iniquity* **perversity**;
your lips have *spoken lies* **worded falsehoods**,
your tongue hath muttered *perverseness* **wickedness**.
4 None calleth for *justice* **justness**,
nor any pleadeth for *truth* **trustworthiness**:
they *trust* **confide** in *vanity* **waste**,
and *speak lies* **word vanity**;
they conceive *mischief* **toil**,
and bring forth *iniquity* **mischief**.
5 They *hatch cockatrice'* **split hisser's** eggs,
and weave the spider's web:
he that eateth of their eggs dieth,
and that which is crushed
breaketh out **splitteth** into a *viper* **hisser**.
6 Their webs shall not become *garments* **clothes**,
neither shall they cover themselves with their works:
their works are works of *iniquity* **mischief**,
and the *act* **deed** of violence is in their *hands* **palms**.
7 Their feet run to evil,
and they *make haste* **hasten** to *shed* **pour** innocent blood:
their *thoughts* **fabrications**
are *thoughts* **fabrications** of *iniquity* **mischief**;
wasting **ravage** and *destruction* **breaking**
are in their *paths* **highways**.
8 The way of *peace* **shalom** they know not;
and there is no judgment in their *goings* **route**:
they have made them *crooked* **perverted** paths:
whosoever *goeth* **treadeth** therein
shall not know *peace* **shalom**.
9 Therefore is judgment far **removed** from us,
neither doth *justice* **justness** overtake us:
we *wait for* **await** light, but behold obscurity;
for *brightness* **brilliancies**, but we walk in darkness.
10 We grope for the wall like the blind,
and we grope as if we had no eyes:
we *stumble* **falter** at noon *day*
as in the *night* **evening breeze**;
we are in *desolate places* **fertile fields** as dead *men*.
11 We roar all like bears,
and *mourn sore* **in cooing, coo** like doves:
we *look for* **await** judgment, but there is none;
for salvation, but it is far *off* **removed** from us.
12 For our *transgressions* **rebellions**
are multiplied **abound by the myriads** before thee,
and our sins *testify* **answer** against us:
for our *transgressions* **rebellions** are with us;
and as for our *iniquities* **perversities**, we know them;
13 In *transgressing* **rebelling** and lying
against *the LORD* **Yah Veh**,
and departing away from our *God* **Elohim**,
speaking **wording** oppression and revolt,
conceiving and *uttering* **muttering** from the heart
words of falsehood.
14 And judgment is *turned away* **removed** backward,
and *justice* **justness** standeth afar off:
for truth *is fallen* **faltereth** in the *street* **broadway**,
and *equity* **straightforwardness** cannot enter.
15 Yea, truth *faileth* **lacketh**;
and he that *departeth* **turneth aside** from evil
maketh himself a prey **is spoiled**:
and *the LORD saw it* **Yah Veh seeth**,
and it *displeased him* **be evil in his eyes**
that there *was* **be** no judgment.

THE REDEEMER

16 And he saw that there was no man,
and *wondered* **astonisheth** that there was no intercessor:
therefore his arm *brought salvation unto* **saved** him;
and his *righteousness* **justness**, it sustained him.
17 For he *put on righteousness* **enrobed justness**
as a *breastplate* **habergeon**,
and an helmet of salvation upon his head;
and he *put on* **enrobed**
the *garment* **clothes** of *vengeance* **avengement**

for *clothing* **robes,**
and was *clad* **covered** with zeal as a *cloke* **mantle.**
18 According to their *deeds* **dealings,**
accordingly he *will repay* **shall shalam,**
fury to his *adversaries* **tribulators,**
recompence **dealing** to his enemies;
to the islands
he *will repay recompence* **shall shalam.**
19 So shall they *fear* **awe** the name of *the LORD* **Yah Veh**
from the *west* **dusk,**
and his *glory* **honour** from the rising of the sun.
When the *enemy* **tribulator**
shall come in like a *flood* **river,**
the Spirit of *the LORD* **Yah Veh**
shall *lift up a standard against him* **cause him to flee.**
20 And the Redeemer shall come to *Zion* **Siyon,**
and unto them that turn
from *transgression* **rebellion** in *Jacob* **Yaaqov,**
saith the LORD **an oracle of Yah Veh.**
21 As for me,
this is my covenant with them, saith *the LORD* **Yah Veh;**
My spirit that is upon thee,
and my words which I have *put* **set** in thy mouth,
shall not depart out of thy mouth,
nor out of the mouth of thy seed,
nor out of the mouth of thy seed's seed,
saith *the LORD* **Yah Veh,**
from henceforth and *for ever* **eternally.**

THE HONOUR OF SIYON

60 Arise, *shine* **enlighten;** for thy light is come,
and the *glory* **honour** of *the LORD* **Yah Veh**
is risen upon thee.
2 For, behold, the darkness shall cover the earth,
and *gross* **dripping** darkness the *people* **nation:**
but *the LORD* **Yah Veh** shall arise upon thee,
and his *glory* **honour** shall be seen upon thee.
3 And the *Gentiles* **goyim** shall come to thy light,
and *kings* **sovereigns**
to the *brightness* **brilliance** of thy rising.
4 Lift up thine eyes round about, and see:
all they gather *themselves together,* they come to thee:
thy sons shall come from far,
and thy daughters shall *be nursed* **nurture** at thy side.
5 Then thou shalt *see* **awe,** and flow together,
and thine heart shall fear, and *be enlarged* **enlarge;**
because the abundance of the sea
shall be *converted* **turned over** unto thee,
the *forces* **valued** of the *Gentiles* **goyim**
shall come unto thee.
6 The *multitude* **throngs** of camels shall cover thee,
the dromedaries of *Midian* **Midyan** and Ephah;
all they from Sheba shall come:
they shall *bring* **bear** gold and incense;
and they shall *shew forth* **evangelize**
the *praises* **halals** of *the LORD* **Yah Veh.**
7 All the flocks of *Kedar* **Qedar**
shall *be gathered* **gather** together unto thee,
the rams of *Nebaioth* **Nebayoth** shall minister unto thee:
they shall *come up* **ascend** with *acceptance* **pleasure**
on *mine* **my sacrifice** altar,
and I *will glorify* **shall adorn** the house
of my *glory* **adornment.**
8 Who are these that fly as a cloud,
and as the doves to their windows?
9 Surely the *isles* **islands** shall *wait for* **await** me,
and the ships of Tarshish first, to bring thy sons from far,
their silver and their gold with them,
unto the name of *the LORD* **Yah Veh** thy *God* **Elohim,**
and to the Holy One of *Israel* **Yisra El,**
because he hath *glorified* **adorned** thee.
10 And the sons of strangers shall build up thy walls,
and their *kings* **sovereigns** shall minister unto thee:
for in my *wrath* **rage** I smote thee,
but in my *favour* **pleasure**
have I had mercy on **I mercied** thee.
11 Therefore thy *gates* **portals** shall be open continually;
they shall not be shut day nor night;
that men may bring unto thee
the forces of the *Gentiles* **goyim,**
and that their *kings* **sovereigns** may be *brought* **driven.**
12 For the *nation* **goyim** and *kingdom* **sovereigndom**
that *will* **shall** not serve thee shall *perish* **destruct;**
yea, those *nations* **goyim** shall be utterly *wasted* **parched.**
13 The *glory* **honour** of Lebanon shall come unto thee,
the fir tree, the *pine* **oak** tree, and the *box* **cedar** together,
to *beautify* **adorn** the place of my *sanctuary* **holies;**
and I *will make* **shall honour**
the place of my feet *glorious.*
14 The sons also of them that *afflicted* **humbled** thee
shall come *bending* **prostrating** unto thee;
and all they that *despised* **scorned** thee
shall *bow themselves down* **prostrate**
at the soles of thy feet;
and they shall call thee, The city of *the LORD* **Yah Veh,**
The *Zion* **Siyon** of the Holy One of *Israel* **Yisra El.**
15 *Whereas* **Instead** thou hast been forsaken and hated,
so that no man *went* **passed** through *thee,*
I *will make* **shall set** thee an eternal *excellency* **pomp,**
a joy of *many generations* **generation and generation.**
16 Thou shalt also suck the milk of the *Gentiles* **goyim,**
and shalt suck the breast of *kings* **sovereigns:**
and thou shalt know that I *the LORD* **Yah Veh**
am thy Saviour and thy Redeemer,
the *mighty* **Almighty** One of *Jacob* **Yaaqov.**
17 For *brass* **copper** I *will* **shall** bring gold,
and for iron I *will* **shall** bring silver,
and for *wood brass* **timber copper,** and for stones iron:
I *will* **shall** also *make* **set** thy *officers* **overseers**
peace **shalom,**
and thine exactors
righteousness **justness.**
18 Violence shall no more be heard
in thy land,
wasting **ravage** nor *destruction* **breaking**
within thy borders;
but thou shalt call thy walls Salvation,
and thy *gates Praise* **portals Halal.**
19 The sun shall be no more thy light by day;
neither for *brightness* **brilliance**
shall the moon *give light unto* **lighten** thee:
but *the LORD* **Yah Veh** shall be unto thee
an *everlasting* **eternal** light,
and thy *God* **Elohim** thy *glory* **adornment.**
20 Thy sun shall no more go down;
neither shall thy moon *withdraw itself* **be gathered:**
for *the LORD* **Yah Veh**
shall be thine *everlasting* **eternal** light,
and the days of thy mourning
shall be *ended* **at shalom.**
21 Thy people also shall be all *righteous* **just:**
they shall *inherit* **be successor of** the land
for ever **eternally,**
the branch of my planting, the work of my hands,
that I may be *glorified* **adorned.**
22 A little *one* shall become a thousand,
and a *small one a strong nation* **little a mighty goyim:**
I *the LORD will* **Yah Veh shall** hasten it in his time.

A MESSIANIC PROPHECY

61 The Spirit of *the Lord GOD* **Adonay Yah Veh**
is upon me;
because *the LORD* **Yah Veh** hath anointed me
to *preach good tidings* **evangelize** unto the *meek* **humble;**
he hath sent me to bind up the brokenhearted,
to *proclaim* **call out** liberty to the captives,
and *the opening of the prison to them that are bound*
in opening, an opening to the bound;
2 To *proclaim* **call out**
the *acceptable* year **of pleasure** of *the LORD* **Yah Veh,**
and the day of *vengeance* **avengement**
of our *God* **Elohim;**
to *comfort* **sigh over** all that mourn;
3 To *appoint* **set** unto them that mourn in *Zion* **Siyon,**
to give unto them *beauty* **adornment** for ashes,
the oil of *joy* **rejoicing** for mourning,
the *garment* **mantle** of *praise* **halal**
for the spirit of heaviness;
that they might be called
trees **mighty oaks** of *righteousness* **justness,**
the planting of *the LORD* **Yah Veh,**
that he might be glorified **to be adorned.**

4 And they shall build
the *old wastes* **original parched areas**,
they shall raise *up*
the former *desolations* **desolated areas**,
and they shall *repair* **renovate** the *waste* **parched** cities,
the *desolations* **desolated areas**
of *many generations* **generation and generation**.
5 And strangers shall stand and *feed* **tend** your flocks,
and the sons of the *alien* **stranger**
shall be your *plowmen* **cultivators** and your vinedressers.
6 But ye shall be *named* **called**
the Priests of *the LORD* **Yah Veh**:
men shall call **it shall be said of** you,
the Ministers of our *God* **Elohim**:
ye shall eat the *riches* **valuables** of the *Gentiles* **goyim**,
and in their *glory* **honour**
shall ye *boast* **change** yourselves.
7 For your shame *ye shall have* double;
and *for confusion* **shame**
they shall *rejoice* **shout** in their *portion* **allotment**:
therefore in their land they shall possess the double:
everlasting joy **eternal cheerfulness** shall be unto them.
8 For I *the LORD* **Yah Veh** love judgment,
I hate *robbery* **stripping** for *burnt offering* **holocaust**;
and I *will direct* **shall give** their *work* **deeds** in truth,
and I *will make* **shall cut** an *everlasting* **eternal** covenant
with them.
9 And their seed
shall be known among the *Gentiles* **goyim**,
and their offspring among the people:
all that see them shall acknowledge them,
that they *are* the seed
which *the LORD* **Yah Veh** hath blessed.
10 **In rejoicing,**
I *will* **shall** *greatly* rejoice in *the LORD* **Yah Veh**,
my soul shall *be joyful* **twirl** in my *God* **Elohim**;
for he hath *clothed* **enrobed** me
with the *garment* **clothes** of salvation,
he hath *covered* **clothed** me
with the *robe* **mantle** of *righteousness* **justness**,
as a bridegroom decketh *himself*
as a priest with ornaments,
and as a bride adorneth *herself*
with *her jewels* **instruments**.
11 For as the earth bringeth forth her *bud* **sprout**,
and as the garden
causeth the things that are sown in it to spring forth
sprouteth the seedling;
so *the Lord GOD* **Adonay Yah Veh**
will cause righteousness and praise to spring forth
shall sprout justness and halal
before all the *nations* **goyim**.

SIYON'S NEW HOME

62 For *Zion's* **Siyon's** sake
will **shall** I not *hold my peace* **hush**,
and for *Jerusalem's* **Yeru Shalem's** sake
I *will* **shall** not rest,
until the *righteousness* **justness** *thereof*
go forth as *brightness* **brilliance**,
and the salvation thereof
as a *lamp* **flambeau** that burneth.
2 And the *Gentiles* **goyim**
shall see thy *righteousness* **justness**,
and all *kings* **sovereigns** thy *glory* **honour**:
and thou shalt be called by a new name,
which the mouth of *the LORD* **Yah Veh**
shall *name* **appoint**.
3 Thou shalt also be a crown of *glory* **adornment**
in the *hand* **palm** of *the LORD* **Yah Veh**,
and a royal *diadem* **turban**
in the hand of thy *God* **Elohim**.
4 *Thou shalt no more be termed*
Neither shall it be said of you,
Forsaken;
neither shall **it be said of** thy land *any more be termed*,
Desolate:
but thou shalt be called *Hephzibah* **Hephsi Bah**,
and thy land *Beulah* **Beulah/Married**:
for *the LORD* **Yah Veh** delighteth in thee,
and thy land shall be *married* **Beulah/Married**.
5 For *as a young man* **youth** marrieth a virgin,
so shall thy sons marry thee:
and as the bridegroom *rejoiceth* **joyeth** over the bride,
so shall thy *God* **Elohim** rejoice over thee.
6 I have *set watchmen* **guards to oversee** upon thy walls,
O *Jerusalem* **Yeru Shalem**,
which shall *never hold their peace* **not hush continually**
day nor night:
ye that *make mention of the LORD* **remember Yah Veh**,
keep not *silence* **quiet**,
7 And give him no *rest* **quiet**, till he establish,
and till he *make Jerusalem* **set Yeru Shalem**
a *praise* **halal** in the earth.
8 *The LORD* **Yah Veh** hath *sworn* **oathed**
by his right *hand*, and by the arm of his strength,
Surely I *will* **shall** no more give thy *corn* **crop**
to be *meat* **food** for thine enemies;
and the sons of the stranger
shall not drink thy *wine* **juice**,
for the which thou hast laboured:
9 But they that have gathered it shall eat it,
and *praise the LORD* **halal Yah Veh**;
and they that have *brought it together* **gathered**
shall drink it in the courts of my *holiness* **holies**.
10 *Go* **Pass** through, *go* **pass** through the *gates* **portals**;
prepare **face** ye the way of the people;
cast **raise** up, *cast* **raise** up the highway;
gather out **stone** the stones;
lift up *a standard* **an ensign** for the people.
11 Behold, *the LORD* **Yah Veh** hath *proclaimed* **thee hear**
unto the end of the world,
Say ye to the daughter of *Zion* **Siyon**,
Behold, thy salvation cometh;
behold, his *reward* **hire** is with him,
and his *work before him* **deeds at his face**.
12 And they shall call them,
The holy people, The redeemed of *the LORD* **Yah Veh**:
and thou shalt be called,
Sought out, A city not forsaken.

THE DAY OF YAH VEH

63 Who is this that cometh from Edom,
with *dyed garment* **dazzling clothes** from Bozrah?
this that is *glorious* **esteemed** in his *apparel* **robe**,
travelling **strolling** in the greatness of his *strength* **force**?
I that speak in *righteousness* **justness**,
mighty **great** to save.
2 Wherefore art thou red in *thine apparel* **thy robe**,
and thy *garment* **clothes**
like him that treadeth in the winefat?
3 I have trodden the *winepress* **press** alone;
and of the people there was *none* **no man** with me:
for I *will* **shall** tread them in *mine anger* **my wrath**,
and trample them in my fury;
and their *blood* **squeezings**
shall be sprinkled upon my *garment* **clothes**,
and I *will stain* **shall profane** all my *raiment* **robe**.
4 For the day of *vengeance* **avengement** is in mine heart,
and the year of my redeemed is come.
5 And I looked, and there was none to help;
and I *wondered* **astonied** that there was none to uphold:
therefore mine own arm
brought salvation unto **hath saved** me;
and my fury, it upheld me.
6 And I *will tread down* **shall trample** the people
in mine anger,
and *make* **intoxicate** them *drunk*
in my fury,
and I *will* **shall** bring down their *strength* **squeezings**
to the earth.
7 I *will mention* **shall remember**
the *lovingkindnesses* **mercies** of *the LORD* **Yah Veh**,
and the *praises* **halals** of *the LORD* **Yah Veh**,
according to all
that *the LORD* **Yah Veh** hath *bestowed on* **dealt** us,
and the great goodness
toward the house of *Israel* **Yisra El**,
which he hath *bestowed* **dealt** on them
according to his mercies,
and according to the *multitude* **abundance**
of his *lovingkindnesses* **mercies**.

8 For he said, Surely they are my people,
children **sons** that *will* **shall** not *lie* **falsify**:
so he was their Saviour.
9 In all their *affliction* **tribulation**
he was *afflicted* **tribulated**,
and the angel of his *presence* **face** saved them:
in his love and in his *pity* **compassion**
he redeemed them;
and he bare them,
and *carried* **bore** them all the days of *old* **antiquity**.
10 But they rebelled, and *vexed* **contorted** his holy Spirit:
therefore he was turned to be their enemy,
and he fought against them.
11 Then he remembered the days of *old* **antiquity**,
Moses **Mosheh**, and his people, *saying,*
Where is he that *brought* **ascended** them *up* out of the sea
with the *shepherd* **tender** of his flock?
where is he that *put* **set** his holy Spirit within him?
12 That *led* **carried** them
by the right *hand* of *Moses* **Mosheh**
with his *glorious* arm **of adornment**,
dividing **splitting** the water *before them* **at their face**,
to *make* **work** himself an *everlasting* **eternal** name?
13 That *led* **carried** them through the *deep* **abyss**,
as an horse in the wilderness,
that they should not *stumble* **falter**?
14 As *a beast* **an animal**
goeth down **descendeth** into the valley,
the Spirit of *the LORD* **Yah Veh**
caused him to rest **rested him**:
so didst thou *lead* **drive** thy people,
to *make* **work** thyself
a *glorious name* **name of adornment**.
15 Look down from *heaven* **the heavens**,
and *behold* **see**
from the *habitation* **residence** of thy holiness
and of thy *glory* **adornment**:
where is thy zeal and thy *strength* **might**,
the *sounding* **roar**
of thy *bowels* **inwards** and of thy mercies toward me?
are they restrained?
16 *Doubtless* **Assuredly** thou art our father,
though Abraham *be ignorant of* **knew** us **not**,
and *Israel acknowledge* **Yisra El acknowledged** us not:
thou, O *LORD* **Yah Veh**, art our father, our redeemer;
thy name is from *everlasting* **eternity**.
17 O *LORD* **Yah Veh**,
why hast thou made us to *err* **stray** from thy ways,
and hardened our heart from thy *fear* **awe**?
Return for thy servants' sake,
the *tribes* **scions** of thine inheritance.
18 The people of thy holiness
have possessed it but a little while:
our *adversaries* **tribulators**
have *trodden down* **trampled** thy *sanctuary* **holies**.
19 We are thine:
thou *never barest rule* **hast not eternally reigned** over them;
they were not called by thy name.

A PRAYER FOR MERCY

64 Oh that thou
wouldest rend **shouldest rip** the heavens,
that thou *wouldest come down* **shouldest descend**,
that the mountains might *flow down* **quake**
at thy *presence* **face**,
2 As *when* the *melting* **brush** fire *burneth* **kindleth**,
the fire causeth the waters to boil,
to make thy name known to thine *adversaries* **tribulators**,
that the *nations* **goyim** may *tremble* **quiver**
at thy *presence* **face**!
3 When thou *didst terrible things* **worked awesomenesses**
which we *looked* **awaited** not *for*,
thou *camest down* **descendest**,
the mountains *flowed down* **quaked** at thy *presence* **face**.
4 For since *the beginning of the world* **eternity**
men have not **neither was it** heard,
nor perceived by the ear,
neither hath the eye seen, O *God* **Elohim**, beside thee,
what he hath *prepared* **worked** for him
that waiteth for him.
1 Corinthians 2:9, 10
5 Thou meetest him
that rejoiceth and worketh *righteousness* **justness**,
those that remember thee in thy ways:
behold, thou art *wroth* **enraged**; for we have sinned:
in those is *continuance* **eternity**, and we shall be saved.
6 But we are all as *an unclean thing* **foul**,
and all our *righteousnesses* **justnesses**
are as *filthy rags* **menstrual clothes**;
and we all *do fade* **wither** as a leaf;
and our *iniquities* **perversities**, like the wind,
have *taken* **borne** us away.
7 And there is none that calleth upon thy name,
that *stirreth up* **waketh** himself to take hold of thee:
for thou hast hid thy face from us,
and hast *consumed* **melted** us,
because **by the hand** of our *iniquities* **perversities**.
8 But now, O *LORD* **Yah Veh**, thou art our father;
we are the *clay* **morter**, and thou our *potter* **Former**;
and we all are the work of thy hand.
9 Be not *wroth very sore* **mightily enraged**,
O *LORD* **Yah Veh**,
neither remember *iniquity for ever* **perversity eternally**:
behold, *see* **look**, we beseech thee, we are all thy people.
10 Thy holy cities are a wilderness,
Zion **Siyon** is a wilderness,
Jerusalem **Yeru Shalem** a desolation.
11 Our *holy and our beautiful house*
holies of adornment,
where our fathers *praised* **halaled** thee,
is burned up with fire:
and all our *pleasant things* **desirables**
are *laid waste* **parched**.
12 *Wilt* **Shalt** thou refrain thyself for these *things*,
O *LORD* **Yah Veh**?
wilt **shalt** thou *hold thy peace* **hush**,
and *afflict* **humble** us *very sore* **mightily**?

JUDGMENT

65 I am sought of them that asked not *for me*;
I am found of them that sought me not:
I said, Behold me, behold me,
unto a *nation* **goyim** that was not called by my name.
2 I have spread out my hands all the day
unto a *rebellious* **revolting** people,
which walketh in a way that was not good,
after their own *thoughts* **fabrications**;
3 A people that *provoke* **vex** me *to anger*
continually to my face;
that sacrificeth in gardens,
and *burneth* incense upon altars of brick;
4 Which *remain* **settle** among the *graves* **tombs**,
and *lodge* **stay overnight** in the *monuments* **guards**,
which eat swine's flesh,
and *broth* **soup** of *abominable things* **stench**
is in their *vessels* **instruments**;
5 Which say, *Stand by thyself* **Approach**,
come not near to me;
for I am holier than thou **lest I hallow thee**.
These are a smoke in my *nose* **nostrils**,
a fire that burneth all the day.
6 Behold, it is *written before me* **inscribed at my face**:
I *will* **shall** not *keep silence* **hush**,
but *will recompense* **shall shalam**,
even *recompense* **shalam** into their bosom,
7 Your *iniquities* **perversities**,
and the *iniquities* **perversities** of your fathers together,
saith *the LORD* **Yah Veh**,
which have *burned incense* **incensed**
upon the mountains,
and *blasphemed* **reproached** me upon the hills:
therefore *will* **shall** I measure their former *work* **deeds**
into their bosom.

PRESERVATION

8 Thus saith *the LORD* **Yah Veh**,
As the *new wine* **juice** is found in the cluster,
and one saith, *Destroy* **Ruin** it not; for a blessing is in it:
so *will* **shall** I *do* **work** for my servants' sakes,
that I may not *destroy* **ruin** them all.
9 And I *will* **shall** bring forth a seed out of *Jacob* **Yaaqov**,
and out of *Judah* **Yah Hudah**
an inheritor **a possessor** of my mountains:

and *mine elect* **my chosen** shall *inherit it* **be successor**,
and my servants shall *dwell* **tabernacle** there.
10 And Sharon shall be a *fold* **habitation of rest** of flocks,
and *the valley of Achor* **Gaymek Achor**
a place for the herds to *lie down in* **repose**,
for my people that have sought me.
11 But ye are they that forsake *the LORD* **Yah Veh**,
that forget my holy mountain,
that *prepare* **line up** a table for *that troop* **Gad**,
and that *furnish the drink offering* **fulfill the cocktails**
unto *that number* **Fate**.
12 Therefore *will* **shall** I number you to the sword,
and ye shall all *bow down* **kneel** to the slaughter:
because when I called, ye *did not answer* **answered not**;
when I *spake* **worded**, ye *did not hear* **heard not**;
but *did* **worked** evil before mine eyes,
and *did choose* **chose** that wherein I delighted not.
13 Therefore thus saith *the Lord GOD* **Adonay Yah Veh**,
Behold, my servants shall eat,
but ye shall *be hungry* **famish**:
behold, my servants shall drink,
but ye shall *be thirsty* **thirst**:
behold, my servants shall *rejoice* **cheer**,
but ye shall *be ashamed* **shame**:
14 Behold,
my servants shall *sing* **shout** for *joy* **goodness** of heart,
but ye shall cry for *sorrow* **pain** of heart,
and shall howl for *vexation* **breaking** of spirit.
15 And ye shall leave your name
for *a curse* **an oath** unto my chosen:
for *the Lord GOD* **Adonay Yah Veh**
shall *slay* **deathify** thee,
and call his servants by another name:
16 That he who blesseth himself in the earth
shall bless himself in the *God* **Elohim** of *truth* **amen**;
and he that *sweareth* **oatheth** in the earth
shall *swear* **oath** by the *God* **Elohim** of *truth* **amen**;
because the former *troubles* **tribulations** are forgotten,
and because they are hid from mine eyes.

NEW HEAVENS, NEW EARTH

17 For, behold, I create new heavens and a new earth:
and the former shall not be remembered,
nor *come* **ascend** into *mind* **heart**.
18 But *be ye glad* **rejoice** and *rejoice* **twirl**
for ever **eternally**
in that which I create:
for, behold,
I create *Jerusalem* **Yeru Shalem** a *rejoicing* **twirling**,
and her people a joy.
19 And I *will rejoice* **shall twirl** in *Jerusalem* **Yeru Shalem**,
and *joy* **rejoice** in my people:
and the voice of weeping shall be no more heard in her,
nor the voice of crying.
20 There shall be no more thence
an infant **a suckling** of days,
nor an *old man* **elder** that hath not filled his days:
for the *child* **lad** shall die **a son of** an hundred years *old*;
but the sinner *being* **a son of** an hundred years *old*
shall be *accursed* **abased**.
21 And they shall build houses, and *inhabit* **settle** them;
and they shall plant vineyards, and eat the fruit of them.
22 They shall not build, and another *inhabit* **settle**;
they shall not plant, and another eat:
for as the days of a tree are the days of my people,
and *mine elect* **my chosen**
shall *long enjoy* **waste away** the work of their hands.
23 They shall not labour in vain,
nor *bring forth* **beget** for *trouble* **terror**;
for they are the seed
of the blessed of *the LORD* **Yah Veh**,
and their offspring with them.
24 And it shall *come to pass* **become**,
that before they call, I *will* **shall** answer;
and while they are yet speaking, I *will* **shall** hear.
25 The wolf and the lamb
shall *feed together* **graze as one**,
and the lion shall eat straw like the bullock:
and dust shall be the serpent's *meat* **bread**.
They shall not *hurt* **vilify** nor *destroy* **ruin**
in all my holy mountain, saith *the LORD* **Yah Veh**.

THE THRONE OF YAH VEH

66 Thus saith *the LORD* **Yah Veh**,
The *heaven is* **heavens are** my throne,
and the earth is *my footstool* **the stool of my feet**:
where is the house that ye build unto me?
and where is the place of my rest?
2 For all those *things* hath mine hand *made* **worked**,
and all those *things* have been,
saith the LORD **an oracle of Yah Veh**:
but to this man *will* **shall** I look,
even to him that is poor — **the humbled**
and *of a contrite* **smitten of** spirit,
and trembleth at my word.
3 *He that killeth* **Whoever slaughtereth** an ox
is as if he slew **smiteth** a man;
he that **whoever** sacrificeth a lamb,
as if he *cut off* **breaketh** a dog's neck;
he that offereth **whoever holocausteth**
an *oblation* **offering**,
as if he offered — swine's blood;
he that burneth **whoever memorializeth with** incense,
as if he blessed an idol **blesseth mischief**.
Yea, they have chosen their own ways,
and their soul delighteth in their abominations.
4 I also *will* **shall** choose their *delusions* **exploits**,
and *will* **shall** bring their *fears* **terrors** upon them;
because when I called, none *did answer* **answered**;
when I *spake* **worded**, they *did not hear* **heard not**:
but they *did* **worked** evil before mine eyes,
and chose that in which I delighted not.
5 Hear the word of *the LORD* **Yah Veh**,
ye that tremble at his word;
Your brethren that hated you,
that cast you out for my name's sake, said,
Let *the LORD* **Yah Veh** be *glorified* **honoured**:
but he shall *appear* **be seen** to your *joy* **cheerfulness**,
and they shall *be ashamed* **shame**.
6 A voice of *noise* **uproar** from the city,
a voice from the *temple* **manse**,
a voice of *the LORD* **Yah Veh**
that *rendereth recompence* **doth shalam**
to his enemies.
7 Before she *travailed* **writhed**, she *brought forth* **bore**;
before her *pain* **pangs** came,
she was *delivered* **rescued** of a *man* **male** child.
8 Who hath heard such *a thing*?
who hath seen such *things*?
shall the earth *be made to bring forth* **writhe** in one day?
or shall a *nation* **goyim** be born at *once* **one time**?
for *as soon* **even** as *Zion travailed* **Siyon writhed**,
she *brought forth* **bore** her *children* **sons**.
9 Shall I *bring* **break forth** to the birth,
and not cause to *bring forth* **beget**?
saith *the LORD* **Yah Veh**:
Shall I cause to *bring forth* **beget**,
and *shut the womb* **restrain**?
saith thy *God* **Elohim**.
10 Rejoice ye with *Jerusalem* **Yeru Shalem**,
and *be glad* **twirl** with her, all ye that love her:
rejoice for joy with her, all ye that mourn for her:
11 That ye may suck,
and be satisfied with the breasts of her consolations;
that ye may *milk* **suck** out,
and *be delighted* **delight**
with the *abundance* **full breast** of her *glory* **honour**.
12 For thus saith *the LORD* **Yah Veh**, Behold,
I *will* **shall** extend *peace* **shalom** to her
like a river,
and the *glory* **honour** of the *Gentiles* **goyim**
like a flowing *stream* **wadi**:
then shall ye suck, ye shall be borne upon her sides,
and be *dandled* **stroked** upon her knees.
13 As *one* **man**
whom his mother *comforteth* **sigheth over**,
so *will* **shall** I *comfort* **sigh over** you;
and ye shall be *comforted* **sighed over**
in *Jerusalem* **Yeru Shalem**.
14 And when ye see *this*, your heart shall rejoice,
and your bones shall *flourish* **blossom**
like *an herb* **a sprout**:

and the hand of *the LORD* **Yah Veh**
shall be known toward his servants,
and *his indignation* **rage** toward his enemies.
15 For, behold,
the LORD will **Yah Veh shall** come with fire,
and with his chariots like a *whirlwind* **hurricane**,
to *render* **turn** his *anger* **wrath** with fury,
and his rebuke with flames of fire.
16 For by fire and by his sword
will the LORD plead with **shall Yah Veh judge** all flesh:
and the *slain* **pierced** of *the LORD* **Yah Veh**
shall *be many* **abound by the myriads**.
17 They that *sanctify* **hallow** *themselves*,
and purify *themselves*
in the gardens behind *one tree* in the midst,
eating swine's flesh,
and the abomination, and the mouse,
shall be consumed together,
saith the LORD **an oracle of Yah Veh**.
18 For *I know* their works and their *thoughts* **fabrications**:
it shall come,
that I *will* **shall** gather all *nations* **goyim** and tongues;
and they shall come, and see my *glory* **honour**.
19 And I *will* **shall** set a sign among them,
and I *will* **shall** send
those that escape of them **the escapees**
unto the *nations* **goyim**,
to Tarshish, Pul, and Lud, that draw the bow,
to Tubal, and *Javan* **Yavan**, to the *isles* **islands** afar off,
that have not heard my fame,
neither have seen my *glory* **honour**;
and they shall *declare* **tell** my *glory* **honour**
among the *Gentiles* **goyim**.
20 And they shall bring all your brethren
for an offering unto *the LORD* **Yah Veh**
out of all *nations* **goyim**
upon horses, and in chariots, and in *litters* **palanquins**,
and upon mules, and upon *swift beasts* **prancers**,
to my holy mountain *Jerusalem* **Yeru Shalem**,
saith *the LORD* **Yah Veh**,
as the *children* **sons** of *Israel* **Yisra El**
bring an offering in a *clean vessel* **pure instrument**
into the house of *the LORD* **Yah Veh**.
21 And I *will* **shall** also take of them
for priests *and* for *Levites* **Leviym**,
saith *the LORD* **Yah Veh**.
22 For as the new heavens and the new earth,
which I *will make* **shall work**,
shall *remain before me* **stand at my face**,
saith the LORD **an oracle of Yah Veh**,
so shall your seed and your name *remain* **stand**.
23 And it shall *come to pass* **become**,
that from *one* new moon to *another* **new moon**,
and **enough**
from *one sabbath* **shabbath** to *another* **shabbath**,
shall all flesh come to *worship* **prostrate** before me,
saith *the LORD* **Yah Veh**.
24 And they shall go forth,
and *look upon* **see** the carcases of the men
that have *transgressed* **rebelled** against me:
for their *worm* **maggot** shall not die,
neither shall their fire be quenched;
and they shall be an abhorring unto all flesh.

KEY TO INTERPRETING THE EXEGESES:
King James text is in regular type;
Text under exegeses is in oblique type;
Text of exegeses is in bold type.

THE GENEALOGY OF YIRME YAH

1 The words of *Jeremiah* **Yirme Yah**
the son of *Hilkiah* **Hilqi Yah**,
of the priests that *were* in Anathoth
in the land of *Benjamin* **Ben Yamin**:
2 To whom the word of *the LORD* **Yah Veh** came
in the days of *Josiah* **Yoshi Yah**
the son of Amon *king* **sovereign** of *Judah* **Yah Hudah**,
in the thirteenth year of his reign.
3 It came also in the days of *Jehoiakim* **Yah Yaqim**
the son of *Josiah* **Yoshi Yah**,
king **sovereign** of *Judah* **Yah Hudah**,
unto the *end* **consumation**
of the eleventh year of *Zedekiah* **Sidqi Yah**
the son of *Josiah* **Yoshi Yah**,
king **sovereign** of *Judah* **Yah Hudah**,
unto the *carrying away* **exile**
of *Jerusalem captive* **Yeru Shalem** in the fifth month.

THE CALLING OF YIRME YAH

4 Then the word of *the LORD* **Yah Veh** came unto me,
saying,
5 Before I formed thee in the belly
I knew thee;
and before thou camest forth out of the womb
I *sanctified* **hallowed** thee,
and I *ordained* **gave** thee
a prophet unto the *nations* **goyim**.
6 Then said I, *Ah* **Aha**, *Lord GOD* **Adonay Yah Veh**!
behold, I *cannot speak* **know no word**:
for I am a *child* **lad**.
7 But *the LORD* **Yah Veh** said unto me,
Say not, I am a *child* **lad**:
for thou shalt go to all that I shall send thee,
and whatsoever I *command* **misvah** thee
thou shalt *speak* **word**.
8 *Be not afraid of* **Awe not** their faces:
for I am with thee to *deliver* **rescue** thee,
saith the LORD **an oracle of Yah Veh**.
9 Then *the LORD put forth* **Yah Veh extended** his hand,
and touched my mouth.
And *the LORD* **Yah Veh** said unto me,
Behold, I have *put* **given** my words in thy mouth.
10 See, I have this day set thee **overseer**
over the *nations* **goyim**
and over the *kingdoms* **sovereigndoms**,
to *root out* **uproot**, and to pull down, and to destroy,
and to *throw down* **demolish**, to build, and to plant.

THE ALMOND SPROUT

11 Moreover
the word of *the LORD* **Yah Veh** came unto me, saying,
Jeremiah **Yirme Yah**, what seest thou?
And I said, I see a *rod* **sprout** of an almond tree.
12 Then said *the LORD* **Yah Veh** unto me,
Thou hast *well seen* **well—pleased in seeing**:
for I *will hasten* **shall watch** my word to *perform* **work** it.

THE PRESSURE CALDRON

13 And the word of *the LORD* **Yah Veh**
came unto me *the second time* **secondly**, saying,
What seest thou?
And I said, I see a *seething pot* **pressure caldron**;
and the face thereof is *toward* **at the face of** the north.
14 *Then the LORD* **Yah Veh** said unto me,
Out of the north an evil shall *break forth* **loosen**
upon all the *inhabitants* **settlers** of the land.
15 For, *lo* **behold**, I *will* **shall** call all the families
of the *kingdoms* **sovereigndoms** of the north,
saith the LORD **an oracle of Yah Veh**;
and they shall come,
and they shall *set* **give** every *one* **man** his throne
at the *entering* **opening** of the *gates* **portals**
of *Jerusalem* **Yeru Shalem**,
and against all the walls *thereof* round about,
and against all the cities of *Judah* **Yah Hudah**.
16 And I *will utter* **shall word** my judgments against them
touching all their *wickedness* **evil**,
who have forsaken me,

and have *burned incense* **incensed**
unto other *gods* **elohim**,
and *worshipped* **prostrated**
unto the works of their own hands.
17 Thou therefore gird up thy loins, and arise,
and speak **word** unto them
all that I *command* **misvah** thee:
be not dismayed at their faces,
lest I *confound* **break** thee *before them* **at their face**.
18 For, behold,
I have *made* **given** thee this day a *defenced* **fortified** city,
and an iron pillar, and *brasen* **copper** walls
against the whole land,
against the *kings* **sovereigns** of *Judah* **Yah Hudah**,
against the *princes* **governors** *thereof*,
against the priests *thereof*,
and against the people of the land.
19 And they shall fight against thee;
but they shall not prevail against thee;
for I am with thee,
saith the LORD **an oracle of Yah Veh**,
to *deliver* **rescue** thee.

YISRA EL ABANDONS YAH VEH

2 Moreover
the word of *the LORD* **Yah Veh** came to me, saying,
2 Go and *cry* **call** in the ears of *Jerusalem* **Yeru Shalem**,
saying, Thus saith *the LORD* **Yah Veh**;
I remember thee, the *kindness* **mercy** of thy youth,
the love of *thine espousals* **thy bethrothals**,
when thou wentest after me in the wilderness,
in a land that was not *sown* **seeded**.
3 *Israel* **Yisra El** was holiness unto *the LORD* **Yah Veh**,
and the *firstfruits* **firstlings** of his *increase* **produce**:
all that devour him shall *offend* **guilt**;
evil shall come upon them, saith *the LORD* **Yah Veh**.
4 Hear ye the word of *the LORD* **Yah Veh**,
O house of *Jacob* **Yaaqov**,
and all the families of the house of *Israel* **Yisra El**:
5 Thus saith *the LORD* **Yah Veh**,
What *iniquity* **wickedness** have your fathers found in me,
that they are *gone* far **removed** from me,
and have walked after vanity, and are become vain?
6 Neither said they, Where is *the LORD* **Yah Veh**
that *brought* **ascended** us
up out of the land of *Egypt* **Misrayim**,
that *led* **carried** us through the wilderness,
through a land of *deserts* **plains** and of *pits* **chasms**,
through a land of *drought* **parch**,
and of the shadow of death,
through a land that no man passed through,
and where no *man dwelt* **human settled**?
7 And I brought you
into a *plentiful country* **land of orchards/Karmel**,
to eat the fruit *thereof* and the goodness *thereof*;
but when ye entered, ye *defiled* **fouled** my land,
and *made* **set** mine *heritage* **inheritance**
an *abomination* **abhorrence**.
8 The priests said not, Where is *the LORD* **Yah Veh**?
and they that *handle* **manipulate** the *law* **torah**
knew me not:
the *pastors* **tenders** also *transgressed* **rebelled** against me,
and the prophets prophesied by Baal,
and walked after *things* **those** that do not *profit* **benefit**.
9 Wherefore I *will* **shall** yet plead with you,
saith *the LORD* **Yah Veh**,
and with your *children's children* **sons' sons**
will **shall** I plead.
10 For pass over the *isles* **islands** of *Chittim* **Kittim**,
and see;
and send unto *Kedar* **Qedar**,
and *consider diligently* **discern mightily**,
and see if there be such *a thing*.
11 Hath a *nation* **goyim** changed their *gods* **elohim**,
which are yet no *gods* **elohim**?
but my people have changed their *glory* **honour**
for that which doth not *profit* **benefit**.
12 Be astonished, O ye heavens, at this,
and *be horribly afraid* **shutter**,
be ye *very desolate* **mightily parched**,
saith *the LORD* **Yah Veh**.
13 For my people have *committed* **worked** two evils;
they have forsaken me the fountain of living waters,
and hewed them out *cisterns* **wells**,
broken *cisterns* **wells**, that can hold no water.
14 Is *Israel* **Yisra El** a servant?
is he *a homeborn slave* **house born**?
why is he *spoiled* **a plunder**?
15 The *young lions* **whelps** roared upon him,
and yelled **gave their voice**,
and they *made* **placed** his land *waste* **desolate**:
his cities are burned without *inhabitant* **settler**.
16 Also the *children* **sons**
of Noph and *Tahapanes* **Tachpanches**
have *broken the crown of* **grazed** thy *head* **scalp**.
17 Hast thou not *procured* **worked** this unto thyself,
in that thou hast forsaken
the LORD **Yah Veh** thy *God* **Elohim**,
when he led **the time he carried** thee by the way?
18 And now what hast thou to do
in the way of *Egypt* **Misrayim**,
to drink the waters of *Sihor* **Shichor**?
or what hast thou to do in the way of *Assyria* **Ashshur**,
to drink the waters of the river?
19 Thine own *wickedness* **evil**
shall *correct* **discipline** thee,
and thy *backslidings* **apostasies** shall reprove thee:
know therefore and see that it is *an* evil *thing* and bitter,
that thou hast forsaken
the LORD **Yah Veh** thy *God* **Elohim**,
and that my fear is not in thee,
saith the Lord GOD of hosts
an oracle of Adonay Yah Veh Sabaoth.
20 For of *old* **eternal** time I have broken thy yoke,
and *burst* **torn** thy *bands* **bonds**;
and thou saidst, I *will* **shall** not *transgress* **serve**;
when upon every high hill and under every green tree
thou *wanderest* **strollest**, *playing the harlot* **whoring**.
21 Yet I had planted thee *a noble vine* — **choice**,
wholly a *right seed* **seed of truth**:
how then
art thou turned into the *degenerate* **twisted** plant
of a strange vine unto me?
22 For though thou *wash* **launder** thee with nitre,
and *take thee much* **abound thy** soap,
yet *thine iniquity* **thy perversity** is *marked* **inscribed**
before me **at my face**,
saith the Lord GOD **an oracle of Adonay Yah Veh**.
23 How canst thou say, I am not *polluted* **fouled**,
I have not gone after Baalim?
see thy way in the valley,
know what thou hast *done* **worked**:
thou art a swift dromedary
traversing **entangling** her ways;
24 A wild *ass used* **runner discipled** to the wilderness,
that *snuffeth up* **gulpeth** the wind
at *her pleasure* **the yearning of her soul**;
in her occasion who can turn her *away* **back**?
all they that seek her *will* **shall** not weary themselves;
in her month they shall find her.
25 Withhold thy foot from being unshod,
and thy throat from thirst:
but thou saidst, *There is no hope* **I quit!**: no;
for I have loved strangers, and after them *will* **shall** I go.
26 As the thief is *ashamed* **shamed** when he is found,
so is the house of *Israel ashamed* **Yisra El shamed**
they, their *kings* **sovereigns**, their *princes* **governors**,
and their priests, and their prophets.
27 Saying to a *stock* **tree**, Thou art my father;
and to a stone, Thou hast *brought me forth* **begotten me**:
for they have
turned **faced the nape of** their *back* **neck** unto me,
and not their face:
but in the time of their *trouble* **evil** they *will* **shall** say,
Arise, and save us.
28 But where are thy *gods* **elohim**
that thou hast *made* **worked** thee?
let them arise,
if they can save thee in the time of thy *trouble* **evil**:
for *according to* the number of thy cities
are thy *gods* **elohim**, O *Judah* **Yah Hudah**.

9 Wherefore *will* **shall** ye plead with me?
ye all have *transgressed* **rebelled** against me,
saith the LORD **an oracle of Yah Veh**.
0 In vain have I smitten your *children* **sons**;
they *received* **took** no *correction* **discipline**:
your own sword hath devoured your prophets,
like a *destroying* **ruining** lion.
1 O generation, see ye the word of *the LORD* **Yah Veh**.
Have I been a wilderness unto *Israel* **Yisra El**?
a land of darkness?
wherefore say my people, We *are lords* **ramble on**;
we *will* **shall** come no more unto thee?
32 Can a *maid* **virgin** forget her ornaments,
or a bride her *attire* **bands**?
yet my people have forgotten me days without number.
33 Why *trimmest* **well—pleasest** thou thy way
to seek love?
therefore hast thou also
taught the *wicked ones* **evil** thy ways.
34 Also in thy *skirts* **wings**
is found the blood of the souls
of the *poor* **needy** innocents:
I have not found it by *secret search* **digging**,
but upon all these.
35 Yet thou sayest, Because I am *innocent* **exonerated**,
surely his *anger* **wrath** shall turn from me.
Behold, I *will plead with* **shall judge** thee,
because thou sayest, I have not sinned.
36 Why gaddest thou about so *much* **mightily**
to change thy way?
thou also shalt be *ashamed* **shamed** of *Egypt* **Misrayim**,
as thou wast *ashamed* **shamed** of *Assyria* **Ashshur**.
37 Yea, thou shalt go forth from him,
and thine hands upon thine head:
for *the LORD* **Yah Veh**
hath *rejected* **spurned** thy confidences,
and thou shalt not prosper in them.

THE WHOREDOM OF YISRA EL

3 *They say* **Saying**,
If a man *put* **send** away his *wife* **woman**,
and she go from him, and become another man's,
shall he return unto her again?
in profaning,
shall not that land be *greatly polluted* **profaned**?
but thou hast *played the harlot* **whored**
with many *lovers* **friends**;
yet return *again* to me,
saith the LORD **an oracle of Yah Veh**.
2 Lift up thine eyes unto the *high places* **barrens**,
and see where thou hast not been
lien **lain** with **and raped**.
In the ways hast thou sat for them,
as the *Arabian* **Arabiy** in the wilderness;
and thou hast *polluted* **profaned** the land
with thy whoredoms
and with thy *wickedness* **evil**.
3 Therefore the showers have been withholden,
and there hath been no *latter* **after** rain;
and thou hadst a **woman's — a** whore's forehead,
thou refusedst to *be ashamed* **shame**.
4 *Wilt* **Shalt** thou not from this time *cry* **call** unto me,
My father,
thou art the *guide* **chiliarch** of my youth?
5 *Will* **Shall** he *reserve his anger for ever* **guard eternally**?
will **shall** he *keep it to the end* **guard in perpetuity**?
Behold, thou hast *spoken* **worded**
and *done* **worked** evil *things* as thou couldest.

THE UNTRUSTWORTHINESS OF YISRA EL

6 *The LORD* **Yah Veh** said also unto me
in the days of *Josiah* **Yoshi Yah**, the *king* **sovereign**,
Hast thou seen that which
backsliding Israel **apostate Yisra El** hath *done* **worked**?
she is gone up upon every high mountain
and under every green tree,
and there *hath played the harlot* **whored**.
7 And I said after she had *done* **worked** all these *things*,
Turn thou unto me. But she returned not.
And her *treacherous* **covert** sister *Judah* **Yah Hudah** saw it.
8 And I saw, when for all the causes
whereby *backsliding Israel* **apostate Yisra El**
committed adultery **adulterized**
I had *put* **sent** her away,
and given her a *bill* **scroll** of divorce;
yet her *treacherous* sister *Judah* **Yah Hudah**
who dealeth covertly *feared* **awed** not,
but went and *played the harlot* **whored** also.
9 And it *came to pass* **became,**
through the *lightness* **voice** of her whoredom,
that she *defiled* **profaned** the land,
and *committed adultery* **adulterized** with stones
and with *stocks* **timber**.
10 And yet for all this
her *treacherous* sister *Judah* **Yah Hudah**
who dealeth covertly
hath not turned unto me with her whole heart,
but *feignedly* **in falsehood**,
saith the LORD **an oracle of Yah Veh**.
11 And *the LORD* **Yah Veh** said unto me,
The *backsliding Israel* **apostate Yisra El**
hath justified *herself* **her soul**
more than *treacherous Judah*
Yah Hudah that dealeth covertly.
12 Go and *proclaim* **call out** these words
toward the north **northward**, and say,
Return, thou *backsliding Israel* **apostate Yisra El**,
saith the LORD **an oracle of Yah Veh**;
and I will **shall** not cause *mine anger* **my face**
to fall upon you: for I *am* merciful,
saith the LORD **an oracle of Yah Veh**,
and I will **shall** not *keep anger for ever* **guard eternally**.
13 Only acknowledge *thine iniquity* **thy perversity**,
that thou hast *transgressed* **rebelled**
against *the LORD* **Yah Veh** thy *God* **Elohim**,
and hast scattered thy ways to the strangers
under every green tree,
and ye have not *obeyed* **hearkened unto** my voice,
saith the LORD **an oracle of Yah Veh**.
14 Turn, O *backsliding children* **apostate sons**,
saith the LORD **an oracle of Yah Veh**;
for I am married unto you:
and I *will* **shall** take you one of a city,
and two of a family,
and I *will* **shall** bring you to *Zion* **Siyon**:
15 And I *will* **shall** give you *pastors* **tenders**
according to mine heart,
which shall *feed* **tend** you
with knowledge and *understanding* **comprehending**.
16 And it shall *come to pass* **become**,
when ye *be multiplied* **abound** and *increased* **bear fruit**
in the land, in those days,
saith the LORD **an oracle of Yah Veh**,
they shall say no more,
The ark of the covenant of *the LORD* **Yah Veh**:
neither shall it *come* **ascend** to *mind* **heart**:
neither shall they remember it;
neither shall they visit it;
neither shall that be *done* **worked** any more.
17 At that time they shall call *Jerusalem* **Yeru Shalem**
the throne of *the LORD* **Yah Veh**;
and all the *nations* **goyim**
shall *be gathered* **congregate** unto it,
to the name of *the LORD* **Yah Veh**,
to *Jerusalem* **Yeru Shalem**:
neither shall they walk any more
after the *imagination* **warp** of their evil heart.
18 In those days the house of *Judah* **Yah Hudah**
shall walk with the house of *Israel* **Yisra El**,
and they shall come together out of the land of the north
to the land that
I have given for an inheritance unto your fathers
your fathers shall inherit.
19 But I said,
How shall I *put* **place** thee among the *children* **sons**,
and give thee a *pleasant land* **land of desire**,
a *goodly heritage* **splendid inheritance**
of the hosts of *nations* **goyim**?
and I said, Thou shalt call me, My father;
and shalt not turn away from **after** me.
20 Surely as a *wife* **woman**
treacherously departeth **dealeth covertly**

from her *husband* **friend**,
so have ye dealt *treacherously* **covertly** with me,
O house of *Israel* **Yisra El**,
saith the LORD **an oracle of Yah Veh**.
21 A voice was heard upon the *high places* **barrens**,
weeping *and* supplications
of the *children* **sons** of *Israel* **Yisra El**:
for they have perverted their way,
and they have forgotten
the LORD **Yah Veh** their *God* **Elohim**.
22 Return, ye *backsliding children* **apostate sons**,
and I *will* **shall** heal your *backslidings* **apostasies**.
Behold, we come unto thee;
for thou art *the LORD* **Yah Veh** our *God* **Elohim**.
23 *Truly* **Surely** in *vain* **falsehood**
is salvation hoped for from the hills,
and from the multitude of mountains:
truly **surely** in *the LORD* **Yah Veh** our *God* **Elohim**
is the salvation of *Israel* **Yisra El**.
24 For shame hath devoured
the labour of our fathers from our youth;
their flocks and their herds,
their sons and their daughters.
25 We lie down in our shame,
and our confusion covereth us:
for we have sinned
against *the LORD* **Yah Veh** our *God* **Elohim**,
we and our fathers, from our youth even unto this day,
and have not *obeyed* **hearkened unto** the voice
of *the LORD* **Yah Veh** our *God* **Elohim**.

YAH VEH PLEADS WITH YISRA EL

4 If thou *wilt* **shalt** return, O *Israel* **Yisra El**,
saith the LORD **an oracle of Yah Veh**,
return unto me:
and if thou *wilt put away* **shalt turn aside**
thine abominations *out of my sight* **from my face**,
then shalt thou not *remove* **wander**.
2 And thou shalt *swear* **oath**, *The LORD* **Yah Veh** liveth,
in truth, in judgment, and in *righteousness* **justness**;
and the *nations* **goyim** shall bless themselves in him,
and in him shall they *glory* **halal**.
3 For thus saith *the LORD* **Yah Veh**
to the men
of *Judah* **Yah Hudah** and *Jerusalem* **Yeru Shalem**,
Break up **Till** your *fallow ground* **tillage**,
and *sow* **seed** not among thorns.
4 Circumcise yourselves to *the LORD* **Yah Veh**,
and *take away* **turn aside** the foreskins of your heart,
ye men of *Judah* **Yah Hudah**
and *inhabitants* **settlers** of *Jerusalem* **Yeru Shalem**:
lest my fury come forth like fire,
and burn that none can quench it,
because **at the face** of the evil
of your *doings* **exploitations**.

YAH VEH WARNS YISRA EL

5 *Declare* **Tell** ye in *Judah* **Yah Hudah**,
and *publish* **let it be heard** in *Jerusalem* **Yeru Shalem**;
and say, *Blow* **Blast** ye the trumpet in the land:
cry **call out**, *gather together* **fulfill**, and say,
Assemble yourselves **Gather**,
and let us go into the *defenced* **fortified** cities.
6 *Set up* **Lift** the *standard* **ensign** toward *Zion* **Siyon**:
retire **withdraw**, stay not:
for I *will* **shall** bring evil from the north,
and a great *destruction* **breaking**.
7 The lion is *come up* **ascended** from his thicket,
and the *destroyer* **ruiner** of the *Gentiles* **goyim**
is on his way;
he is gone forth from his place
to *make* **set** thy land desolate;
and thy cities shall *be laid waste* **set desolate**,
without *an inhabitant* **a settler**.
8 For this gird you with *sackcloth* **saq**,
lament **chop** and howl:
for the *fierce anger* **fuming wrath** of *the LORD* **Yah Veh**
is not turned back from us.
9 And it shall *come to pass* **become,** at that day,
saith the LORD **an oracle of Yah Veh**,
that the heart of the *king* **sovereign** shall *perish* **destruct**,
and the heart of the *princes* **governors**;
and the priests shall *be astonished* **astonish**,
and the prophets shall *wonder* **marvel**.
10 Then said I, *Ah* **Aha**, *Lord GOD* **Adonay Yah Veh**!
in deceiving, *surely* thou hast *greatly* deceived
this people and *Jerusalem* **Yeru Shalem**, saying,
Ye shall have *peace* **shalom**;
whereas the sword *reacheth* **toucheth** unto the soul.
11 At that time shall it be said to this people
and to *Jerusalem* **Yeru Shalem**,
A *dry* **clear** wind of the *high places* **barrens**
in the wilderness
toward the daughter of my people,
not to *fan* **winnow**, nor to *cleanse* **purify**,
12 *Even* a full wind *from those places*
shall come unto me:
now also
will **shall** I *give sentence* **word judgment** against them.
13 Behold, he shall *come up* **ascend** as clouds,
and his chariots shall be as a *whirlwind* **hurricane**:
his horses are swifter than eagles.
Woe unto us! for we are *spoiled* **ravaged**.
14 O *Jerusalem* **Yeru Shalem**,
wash **launder** thine heart from *wickedness* **evil**,
that thou mayest be saved.
How long **Until when**
shall thy *vain thoughts* **fabrications of mischief**
lodge **stay overnight** within thee?
15 For a voice *declareth* **telleth** from Dan,
and *publisheth affliction* **hearkeneth mischief**
from mount *Ephraim* **Ephrayim**.
16 *Make ye mention to* **Remind** the *nations* **goyim**;
behold,
publish **let it be heard** against *Jerusalem* **Yeru Shalem**,
that *watchers* **guards** come from a far *country* **land**,
and give out their voice
against the cities of *Judah* **Yah Hudah**.
17 As *keepers* **guards** of a field,
are they against her round about;
because she hath been rebellious against me,
saith the LORD **an oracle of Yah Veh**.
18 Thy way and thy *doings* **exploitations**
have *procured* **worked** these *things* unto thee;
this is thy *wickedness* **evil**,
because it is bitter, because it reacheth unto thine heart.
19 My *bowels* **inwards**, my *bowels* **inwards**!
I *am pained at my very* **writhe at the walls of my** heart;
my heart *maketh a noise* **roareth** in me;
I cannot *hold my peace* **hush**,
because thou hast heard, O my soul,
the *sound* **voice** of the trumpet, the *alarm* **blast** of war.
20 *Destruction* **Breaking** upon *destruction* **breaking**
is *cried* **called out**;
for the whole land is *spoiled* **ravaged**:
suddenly are my tents *spoiled* **ravaged**,
and my curtains in a *moment* **blink**.
21 How long shall I see the *standard* **ensign**,
and hear the *sound* **voice** of the trumpet?
22 For my people is foolish, they have not known me;
they are *sottish children* **foolish sons**,
and they *have none understanding* **discern not**:
they are wise to *do evil* **vilify**,
but to *do good* **well—please** they have no knowledge.
23 I *beheld* **saw** the earth, and, *lo* **behold**,
it was *without form* **a waste**, and *void* **empty**;
and the heavens, and they had no light.
24 I *beheld* **saw** the mountains,
and, *lo* **behold**, they *trembled* **quaked**,
and all the hills *moved lightly* **slightly**.
25 I *beheld* **saw**, and, *lo* **behold**,
there was no *man* **human**,
and all the *birds* **flyers** of the heavens were fled.
26 I *beheld* **saw**, and, *lo* **behold**,
the *fruitful place* **orchard/Karmel** was a wilderness,
and all the cities *thereof* were *broken* **pulled** down
at the *presence* **face** of *the LORD* **Yah Veh**,
and by his *fierce anger* **fuming wrath**.
27 For thus hath *the LORD* **Yah Veh** said,
The whole land shall be desolate;
yet *will* **shall** I not *make* **work** a *full end* **final finish**.
28 For this shall the earth mourn,

and the heavens above *be black* **darken**;
because I have *spoken* **worded** it,
I have *purposed* **intrigued** *it*,
and *will* **shall** not *repent* **sigh**,
neither *will* **shall** I turn back from it.
29 The whole city shall flee
for the *noise* **voice** of the *horsemen* **cavalry**
and *bowmen* **they that hurl the bow**;
they shall go into *thickets* **thick clouds**,
and *climb up* **ascend** upon the rocks:
every city shall be forsaken,
and not a man *dwell* **settle** therein.
30 And *when thou art spoiled* **thou, O ravaged**,
what *wilt* **shalt** thou *do* **work**?
Though thou *clothest* **enrobest** thyself
with *crimson* **scarlet**,
though thou *deckest* **adornest** thee
with ornaments of gold,
though thou *rentest* **rippest** thy *face* **eyes**
with *painting* **stibium**,
in vain shalt thou *make* **beautify** thyself *fair*;
thy lovers will despise
they who pant after thee shall spurn thee,
they *will* **shall** seek thy *life* **soul**.
31 For I have heard a voice
as of *a woman in travail* **stroking**,
and the *anguish* **tribulation** as of her
that *bringeth forth her first child* **bursteth the matrix**,
the voice of the daughter of *Zion* **Siyon**,
that *bewaileth herself* **sigheth**,
that spreadeth her *hands* **palms**, *saying*,
Woe is me *now* **I beseech**!
for my soul *is wearied* **languisheth** because of murderers.

THE SEARCH FOR THE MAN THAT WORKETH JUDGMENT

5 *Run ye to and fro* **Flit**
through the *streets* **outways** of *Jerusalem* **Yeru Shalem**,
and see *now* **I beseech**, and know,
and seek in the *broad places* **broadways** *thereof*,
if ye can find a man,
if there be any that *executeth* **worketh** judgment,
that seeketh *the truth* **trustworthiness**;
and I *will pardon it* **shall forgive**.
2 And though they say, *The LORD* **Yah Veh** liveth;
surely they *swear* **oath** falsely.
3 O *LORD* **Yah Veh**,
are not thine eyes upon *the truth* **trustworthiness**?
thou hast *stricken* **smitten** them,
but they have not *grieved* **writhed**;
thou hast *consumed* **finished** them **off**,
but they have refused to *receive* **take** correction:
they have *made* **toughened** their faces
harder than **as** a rock;
they have refused to return.
4 Therefore I said,
Surely these are poor; they are *foolish* **follied**:
for they know not the way of *the LORD* **Yah Veh**,
nor the judgment of their *God* **Elohim**.
5 I *will* **shall** get me unto the great *men*,
and *will speak* **shall word** unto them;
for they have known the way of *the LORD* **Yah Veh**,
and the judgment of their *God* **Elohim**:
but these have altogether broken the yoke,
and burst **torn** the bonds.
6 Wherefore a lion out of the forest shall *slay* **smite** them,
and a wolf of the *evenings* **plains** shall *spoil* **ravage** them,
a leopard shall watch over their cities:
every one that goeth out thence shall be torn *in pieces*:
because their *transgressions* **rebellions**
are many **abound by the myriads**,
and their *backslidings* **apostasies** are *increased* **mighty**.
7 How shall I *pardon* **forgive** thee for this?
thy *children* **sons** have forsaken me,
and *sworn* **oathed** by them that are no *gods* **elohim**:
when I had *fed* **oathed** them *to the full*,
they then *committed adultery* **adulterized**,
and *assembled themselves by troops* **trooped**
in the *harlots'* **whore** houses.
8 They *were* **wandered** as *fed* **nourished** horses
in the morning:
every *one neighed* **man sounded**
after his *neighbour's wife* **friend's woman**.
9 Shall I not visit for these *things*?
saith the LORD **an oracle of Yah Veh**:
and shall not my soul be avenged
on such a *nation* **goyim** as this?
10 *Go ye up* **Ascend ye** upon her *walls* **fortifications**
and *destroy* **ruin**;
but *make* **work** not a *full end* **final finish**:
take away **turn aside** her *battlements* **tendrils**;
for they are not *the LORD'S* **Yah Veh's**.
11 For the house of *Israel* **Yisra El**
and the house of *Judah* **Yah Hudah**
in dealing covertly,
have dealt *very treacherously* **covertly** against me,
saith the LORD **an oracle of Yah Veh**.
12 They have *belied the LORD* **disowned Yah Veh**,
and said, *It is* not he;
neither shall evil come upon us;
neither shall we see sword nor famine:
13 And the prophets shall become wind,
and the word is not in them:
thus shall it be *done* **worked** unto them.
14 Wherefore thus saith
the LORD God of hosts **Yah Veh Elohim Sabaoth**,
Because ye *speak* **word** this word, behold,
I *will make* **shall give** my words in thy mouth fire,
and this people *wood* **timber**, and it shall devour them.
15 *Lo* **Behold**,
I *will* **shall** bring a *nation* **goyim** upon you from far,
O house of *Israel* **Yisra El**,
saith the LORD **an oracle of Yah Veh**:
it is a *mighty nation* **perennial goyim**,
it is an *ancient nation* **eternal goyim**,
a *nation* **goyim** whose language thou knowest not,
neither *understandest* **hearest** what they *say* **word**.
16 Their quiver is as an open *sepulchre* **tomb**,
they are all mighty *men*.
17 And they shall eat *up* thine harvest, and thy bread,
which thy sons and thy daughters should eat:
they shall eat *up* thy flocks and thine herds:
they shall eat *up* thy vines and thy fig trees:
they shall impoverish thy *fenced* **fortified** cities,
wherein thou *trustedst* **confidedst**, with the sword.
18 Nevertheless in those days,
saith the LORD **an oracle of Yah Veh**,
I *will* **shall** not *make* **work** a *full end* **final finish** with you.
19 And it shall *come to pass* **become**, when ye shall say,
Wherefore *doeth* **worketh**
the LORD **Yah Veh** our *God* **Elohim**
all these *things* unto us?
then shalt thou *answer* **say to** them,
Like as ye have forsaken me,
and served strange *gods* **elohim** in your land,
so shall ye serve strangers in a land that is not yours.
20 *Declare* **Tell** this in the house of *Jacob* **Yaaqov**,
and *publish* **let it be heard** in *Judah* **Yah Hudah**, saying,
21 Hear *now* **I beseech**, this, O foolish people,
and without *understanding* **heart**;
which have eyes, and see not;
which have ears, and hear not:
22 *Fear* **Awe** ye not me?
saith the LORD **an oracle of Yah Veh**:
will **shall** ye not *tremble* **writhe** at my *presence* **face**,
which have *placed* **set** the sand
for the *bound* **border** of the sea
by *a perpetual decree* **an eternal statute**,
that it cannot pass it:
and though the waves *thereof toss themselves* **agitate**,
yet can they not prevail;
though they roar,
yet can they not pass over it?
23 But this people hath a revolting and a rebellious heart;
they are *revolted* **turned aside** and gone.
24 Neither say they in their heart,
Let us *now* **I beseech**,
fear the LORD **awe Yah Veh** our *God* **Elohim**,
that giveth *rain* **downpour**,
both the *former* **early** and the *latter* **after**,
in his *season* **time**:
he *reserveth* **guardeth** unto us

the *appointed* **statute** weeks of the harvest.
25 Your *iniquities* **perversities**
have *turned away these things* **perverted**,
and your sins have withholden good *things* from you.
26 For among my people are found wicked *men*:
they *lay wait* **observe**, as he that *setteth* **weaveth** snares;
they *set* **station** a *trap* **ruin**, they *catch* **captivate** men.
27 As a cage is full of *birds* **flyers**,
so are their houses full of deceit:
therefore they are *become great* **greatened**,
and *waxen rich* **enriched**.
28 They are *waxen fat* **fattened**, they shine:
yea, they overpass the *deeds* **words** of the *wicked* **evil**:
they *judge* **plead** not the cause,
the cause of the *fatherless* **orphan**, yet they prosper;
and the *right* **judgment** of the needy do they not judge.
29 Shall I not visit for these *things*?
saith the LORD **an oracle of Yah Veh**:
shall **I** not **avenge** my soul *be avenged*
on such a *nation* **goyim** as this?
30 A *wonderful* **desolation** and horrible *thing*
is *committed* **become** in the land;
31 The prophets prophesy falsely,
and the priests *bear rule* **subjugate** by their *means* **hands**;
and my people love *to have* it so:
and what *will* **shall** ye *do* **work** in the end *thereof*?

YERU SHALEM IS VISITED

6 O ye *children* **sons** of *Benjamin* **Ben Yamin**,
gather **withdraw** yourselves
to flee out of the midst of *Jerusalem* **Yeru Shalem**,
and *blow* **blast** the trumpet in *Tekoa* **Teqoa**,
and *set up* **lift** a *sign of fire* **burden**
in *Bethhaccerem* **Beth Hak Kerem**:
for evil *appeareth* **looketh** out of the north,
and great *destruction* **breaking**.
2 I have *likened* **severed** the daughter of *Zion* **Siyon**
to a *comely and delicate woman*
delicate habitation of rest.
3 The *shepherds* **tenders** with their *flocks* **droves**
shall come unto her;
they shall *pitch* **stake** their tents against her round about;
they shall *feed* **tend** every *one in* **man at** his *place* **hand**.
4 *Prepare* **Hallow** ye war against her;
arise, and let us *go up* **ascend** at noon.
Woe unto us! for the day *goeth* **faceth** away,
for the shadows of the evening are stretched out.
5 Arise, and let us *go* **ascend** by night,
and let us *destroy* **ruin** her *palaces* **citadels**.
6 For thus hath *the LORD of hosts* **Yah Veh Sabaoth** said,
Hew **Cut** ye down trees,
and *cast* **pour** a mount against *Jerusalem* **Yeru Shalem**:
this is the city to be visited;
she is wholly oppression in the midst of her.
7 As *a fountain casteth out her* **digging a well for** waters,
so she *casteth out* **diggeth** her *wickedness* **evil**:
violence and *spoil* **ravage** is heard in her;
before me **at my face** continually
is *grief* **sickness** and wounds.
8 Be thou instructed, O *Jerusalem* **Yeru Shalem**,
lest my soul depart from thee;
lest I *make* **set** thee desolate, a land not *inhabited* **settled**.
9 Thus saith *the LORD of hosts* **Yah Veh Sabaoth**,
They shall throughly glean
the *remnant* **survivors** of *Israel* **Yisra El** as a vine:
turn back thine hand
as a *grapegatherer* **clipper** into the baskets.
10 To whom shall I *speak* **word**,
and *give warning* **witness**, that they may hear?
behold,
their ear is uncircumcised, and they cannot hearken:
behold,
the word of *the LORD* **Yah Veh** is unto them a reproach;
they have no delight in it.
11 Therefore
I am *full* **filled** of the fury of *the LORD* **Yah Veh**;
I am weary *with holding in* **of containing**:
I *will* **shall** pour it out
upon the *children abroad* **suckling in the outways**,
and upon the *assembly* **private counsel**
of *young men* **youths** together:
for even the *husband* **man** with the *wife* **woman**
shall be *taken* **captured**,
the *aged* **elder** with him that is full of days.
12 And their houses shall be turned unto others,
with their fields and *wives* **women** together:
for I *will* **shall** stretch out my hand
upon the *inhabitants* **settlers** of the land,
saith the LORD **an oracle of Yah Veh**.
13 For from the least of them
even unto the greatest of them
every one
is given to covetousness **greedily gaineth to greedy gain**;
and from the prophet even unto the priest
every one *dealeth* **worketh** falsely.
14 They have healed also
the *hurt of the daughter* **breaking** of my people slightly,
saying, *Peace* **Shalom**, *peace* **shalom**;
when there is no *peace* **shalom**.
15 Were they *ashamed* **shamed** when they had
committed abomination **worked abhorrence**? nay,
they were not at all ashamed
in shaming, they shamed not,
neither *could they blush* **knew they to shame**:
therefore they shall fall among them that fall:
at the time that I visit them they shall *be cast down* **falter**,
saith *the LORD* **Yah Veh**.
16 Thus saith *the LORD* **Yah Veh**,
Stand ye in the ways, and see,
and ask for the *old* **eternal** paths, where is the good way,
and walk therein,
and ye shall find *rest* **a resting place** for your souls.
But they said, We *will* **shall** not walk *therein*.
17 Also I *set watchmen* **raise watchers** over you,
saying, Hearken to the *sound* **voice** of the trumpet.
But they said, We *will* **shall** not hearken.
18 Therefore hear, ye *nations* **goyim**,
and know, O *congregation* **witness**, what is among them.
19 Hear, O earth: behold,
I *will* **shall** bring evil upon this people,
even the fruit of their *thoughts* **fabrications**,
because they have not hearkened unto my words,
nor to my *law* **torah**, but *rejected* **spurned** it.
20 To what purpose cometh there to me
incense from Sheba,
and the *sweet cane* **good stalk** from a far *country* **land**?
your *burnt offerings* **holocausts**
are not *acceptable* **pleasing**,
nor your sacrifices *sweet* **pleasing** unto me.
21 Therefore thus saith *the LORD* **Yah Veh**, Behold,
I *will lay* **shall give** stumblingblocks before this people,
and the fathers and the sons together
shall *fall* **falter** upon them;
the *neighbour* **fellow tabernacler** and his friend
shall *perish* **destruct**.
22 Thus saith *the LORD* **Yah Veh**,
Behold, a people cometh from the north *country* **land**,
and a great *nation* **goyim** shall be *raised* **wakened**
from the *sides* **flanks** of the earth.
23 They shall lay hold on bow and *spear* **dart**;
they are cruel, and *have no mercy* **mercy not**;
their voice roareth like the sea;
and they ride upon horses,
set in array **lined up** as men for war against thee,
O daughter of *Zion* **Siyon**.
24 We have heard the fame *thereof*:
our hands *wax feeble* **slacken**:
anguish **tribulation** hath taken hold of us,
and pain **pang**, as of a woman *in travail* **birthing**.
25 Go not forth into the field, nor walk by the way;
for the sword of the enemy and *fear* **terror**
is *on every side* **round about**.
26 O daughter of my people,
gird thee with *sackcloth* **saq**, and wallow thyself in ashes:
make **work** thee mourning, as for an only son,
most *bitter lamentation* **chopping of bitterness**:
for the *spoiler* **ravager** shall suddenly come upon us.
27 I have *set* **given** thee for a tower
and a fortress among my people,
that thou mayest know and *try* **proof** their way.
28 They are all

grievous revolters **turned aside by revolters,**
walking with *slanders* **talebearers**:
they are *brass* **copper** and iron;
they are all *corrupters* **ruiners**.
29 The bellows are *burned* **scorched**,
the lead is consumed of the fire;
the *founder melteth* **refiner refineth** in vain:
for the *wicked* **evil** are not *plucked* **torn** away.
30 *Reprobate* **Refuse** silver
shall *men call them* **they be called**,
because *the LORD* **Yah Veh** hath *rejected* **refused** them.

MESSAGE AT THE HOUSE OF YAH VEH

7 The word that came to *Jeremiah* **Yirme Yah**
from *the LORD* **Yah Veh**, saying,
2 Stand in the *gate* **portal**
of the *LORD'S* house **of Yah Veh**,
and *proclaim* **call out** there this word, and say,
Hear the word of *the LORD* **Yah Veh**,
all *ye* of *Judah* **Yah Hudah**,
that enter in at these *gates* **portals**
to *worship the LORD* **prostrate before Yah Veh**.
3 Thus saith *the LORD of hosts* **Yah Veh Sabaoth**,
the *God* **Elohim** of *Israel* **Yisra El**,
Amend **Well—prepare** your ways
and your *doings* **exploits**,
and I *will* **shall** cause you
to *dwell* **tabernacle** in this place.
4 *Trust* **Confide** ye not in *lying* **false** words, saying,
The *temple* **manse** of *the LORD* **Yah Veh**,
The *temple* **manse** of *the LORD* **Yah Veh**,
The *temple* **manse** of *the LORD* **Yah Veh**,
are these.
5 For if **in well—preparing,**
ye *throughly amend* **well—prepare**
your ways and your *doings* **exploitations**;
if **in working,** ye *throughly execute* **work** judgment
between a man and his *neighbour* **friend**;
6 If ye oppress not the *stranger* **sojourner**,
the *fatherless* **orphan**, and the widow,
and *shed* **pour** not innocent blood in this place,
neither walk after other *gods* **elohim** to your *hurt* **evil**:
7 Then *will* **shall** I cause you
to *dwell* **tabernacle** in this place,
in the land that I gave to your fathers,
for ever **eternally** and *ever* **eternally**.
8 Behold, ye *trust* **confide** in *lying* **false** words,
that cannot *profit* **benefit**.
9 *Will* **Shall** ye steal, murder,
and *commit adultery* **adulterize**, and *swear* **oath** falsely,
and *burn* incense unto Baal,
and walk after other *gods* **elohim** whom ye know not;
10 And come and stand *before me* **at my face**
in this house, which is called by my name,
and say, We are *delivered* **rescued!**
to do **in order to work**
all these *abominations* **abhorrences**?
11 Is this house, which is called by my name,
become a *den* **cave** of *robbers* **tyrants** in your eyes?
Behold, even I have seen it,
saith the LORD **an oracle of Yah Veh**.
12 But go ye *now* **I beseech,**
unto my place which was in Shiloh,
where I *set* **tabernacle** my name at the first,
and see what I *did* **worked** to it
for the wickedness **at the face of the evil**
of my people *Israel* **Yisra El**.
13 And *now* **I beseech**,
because ye have *done* **worked** all these works,
saith the LORD **an oracle of Yah Veh**,
and I *spake* **worded** unto you,
rising up **starting** early and *speaking* **wording**,
but ye heard not;
and I called you, but ye answered not;
14 Therefore *will* **shall** I *do* **work** unto this house,
which is called by my name, wherein ye *trust* **confide**,
and unto the place
which I gave to you and to your fathers,
as I have *done* **worked** to Shiloh.
15 And I *will* **shall** cast you *out of* **from** my *sight* **face**,
as I have cast out all your brethren,
even the whole seed of *Ephraim* **Ephrayim**.
16 Therefore pray not thou for this people,
neither lift *up cry* **shout** nor prayer for them,
neither *make intercession* **intercede** to me:
for I *will* **shall** not hear thee.
17 Seest thou not what they *do* **work**
in the cities of *Judah* **Yah Hudah**
and in the *streets* **outways** of *Jerusalem* **Yeru Shalem**?
18 The *children* **sons** gather *wood* **timber**,
and the fathers *kindle* **burn** the fire,
and the women knead their dough,
to *make cakes* **work wafers**
to the *queen* **sovereigness** of *heaven* **the heavens**,
and to *pour out drink offerings* **libate libations**
unto other *gods* **elohim**,
that they may *provoke* **vex** me *to anger*.
19 Do they *provoke* **vex** me *to anger?*
saith the LORD **an oracle of Yah Veh**:
do they not provoke **and not** themselves
to the *confusion* **shame** of their own faces?
20 Therefore thus saith *the Lord GOD* **Adonay Yah Veh**;
Behold, *mine anger* **my wrath** and my fury
shall be poured out upon this place,
upon *man* **humanity**, and upon *beast* **animal**,
and upon the trees of the field,
and upon the fruit of the *ground* **soil**;
and it shall burn, and shall not be quenched.
21 Thus saith *the LORD of hosts* **Yah Veh Sabaoth**,
the *God* **Elohim** of *Israel* **Yisra El**;
Put **Scrape up** your *burnt offerings* **holocausts**
unto your sacrifices, and eat flesh.
22 For I *spake* **worded** not unto your fathers,
nor *commanded* **misvahed** them in the day
that I brought them out of the land of *Egypt* **Misrayim**,
concerning *burnt offerings* **holocausts** or sacrifices:
23 But this *thing commanded* **misvahed** I them,
saying, *Obey* **Hearken to** my voice,
and *I will be* **I AM** your *God* **Elohim**,
and ye *shall* be my people:
and walk ye
in all the ways that I have *commanded* **misvahed** you,
that it may *be well unto* **well—please** you.
24 But they hearkened not, nor *inclined* **extended** their ear,
but walked in the counsels
and in the *imagination* **warp** of their evil heart,
and went backward, and not *forward* **toward the face**.
25 Since the day that your fathers came forth
out of the land of *Egypt* **Misrayim** unto this day
I have even sent unto you all my servants the prophets,
daily *rising up* **starting** early and sending them:
26 Yet they hearkened not unto me,
nor *inclined* **extended** their ear, but hardened their neck:
they *did worse than* **vilified above** their fathers.
27 Therefore
thou shalt *speak* **word** all these words unto them;
but they *will* **shall** not hearken to thee:
thou shalt also call unto them;
but they *will* **shall** not answer thee.
28 But thou shalt say unto them,
This is a *nation* **goyim** that *obeyeth* **hearkeneth** not
unto the voice of *the LORD* **Yah Veh** their *God* **Elohim**,
nor *receiveth correction* **taketh discipline**:
truth is perished **trustworthiness destructeth**,
and is cut off from their mouth.
29 *Cut off thine hair* **Shear thy separatism**, *O Jerusalem*,
and cast it away,
and *take up* **lift** a lamentation on *high places* **the barrens**;
for *the LORD* **Yah Veh**
hath *rejected* **spurned** and *forsaken* **abandoned**
the generation of his wrath.
30 For the *children* **sons** of *Judah* **Yah Hudah**
have *done* **worked** evil in my *sight* **eyes**,
saith the LORD **an oracle of Yah Veh**:
they have set their abominations
in the house which is called by my name,
to *pollute* **foul** it.

THE BAMAHS OF TOPHETH

31 And they have built
the *high places* **bamahs** of *Tophet* **Topheth**,
which is in

the valley of the son of Hinnom
Gay Ben Hinnom/Valley of the Son of Burning,
to burn their sons and their daughters in the fire;
which I *commanded* **misvahed** *them* not,
neither *came* **ascended** it into my heart.
32 Therefore, behold, the days come,
saith the LORD **an oracle of Yah Veh**,
that it shall no more be *called* **said**, *Tophet* **Topheth**
nor *the valley of the son of Hinnom*
Gay Ben Hinnom/Valley of the Son of Burning,
but
the valley of slaughter **Gay Haregah/Valley of Slaughter**:
for they shall *bury* **entomb** in *Tophet* **Topheth**,
till there be no place.
33 And the carcases of this people shall be meat
for the *fowls* **flyers** of the *heaven* **heavens**,
and for the *beasts* **animals** of the earth;
and none shall *fray* **tremble** them away.
34 Then *will* **shall** I cause to *cease* **shabbathize**
from the cities of *Judah* **Yah Hudah**,
and from the *streets* **outways** of *Jerusalem* **Yeru Shalem**,
the voice of *mirth* **rejoicing**,
and the voice of *gladness* **cheerfulness**,
the voice of the bridegroom, and the voice of the bride:
for the land shall be *desolate* **parched**.

THE SIN OF YAH HUDAH

8 At that time,
saith the LORD **an oracle of Yah Veh**,
they shall bring out
the bones of the *kings* **sovereigns** of *Judah* **Yah Hudah**,
and the bones of his *princes* **governors**,
and the bones of the priests,
and the bones of the prophets,
and the bones
of the *inhabitants* **settlers** of *Jerusalem* **Yeru Shalem**,
out of their *graves* **tombs**:
2 And they shall spread them *before* **to** the sun,
and the moon, and all the host of *heaven* **the heavens**,
whom they have loved, and whom they have served,
and after whom they have walked,
and whom they have sought,
and **to** whom they have *worshipped* **prostrated**:
they shall not be gathered, nor be *buried* **entombed**;
they shall be for dung upon the face of the *earth* **soil**.
3 And death shall be chosen rather than life
by all the *residue of them* **survivors**
that *remain* **survive** of this evil family,
which *remain* **survive**
in all the places whither I have driven them,
saith the LORD of hosts **an oracle of Yah Veh Sabaoth**.
4 Moreover thou shalt say unto them,
Thus saith *the LORD* **Yah Veh**;
shall they fall, and not arise?
shall he turn away, and not return?
5 Why then is this people of *Jerusalem* **Yeru Shalem**
slidden **turned** back by a perpetual *backsliding* **apostasy**?
they *hold fast* **uphold** deceit, they refuse to return.
6 I hearkened and heard,
but they *spake* **worded** not aright:
no man *repented* **sighed for** him of his *wickedness* **evil**,
saying, What have I *done* **worked**?
every one turned to his *course* **race**,
as the horse *rusheth* **overfloweth** into the *battle* **war**.
7 Yea, the stork in the *heaven* **heavens**
knoweth her *appointed times* **seasons**;
and the *turtle* **turtledove**
and the *crane* **swallow** and the *swallow* **thrush**
observe **regard** the time of their coming;
but my people
know not the judgment of *the LORD* **Yah Veh**.
8 How do ye say, We are wise,
and the *law* **torah** of *the LORD* **Yah Veh** is with us?
Lo **Behold**,
certainly **surely** in *vain made* **falsehood worked** he it;
the *pen* **false stylus** of the scribes
is in vain **worketh falsehood**.
9 The wise *men* are ashamed,
they are dismayed and *taken* **captured**:
lo **behold**, they have *rejected* **spurned**
the word of *the LORD* **Yah Veh**;
and what wisdom is in them?
10 Therefore *will* **shall** I give their *wives* **women**
unto others,
and their fields
to them that shall *inherit them* **be their successors**:
for every one from the least even unto the greatest
is given to covetousness **greedily gaineth to greedy gain**,
from the prophet even unto the priest
every one *dealeth* **worketh** falsely.
11 For they have healed
the *hurt* **breaking** of the daughter of my people slightly,
saying, *Peace* **Shalom**, *peace* **shalom**;
when there is no *peace* **shalom**.
12 Were they ashamed when they had
committed abomination **worked abhorrence**?
nay **in shaming**,
they *were not at all ashamed* **shamed not**,
neither *could* **knew** they **to** blush:
therefore shall they fall among them that fall:
in the time of their visitation
they shall *be cast down* **falter**,
saith *the LORD* **Yah Veh**.
13 **In consuming**, I *will* **shall** *surely* consume them,
saith the LORD **an oracle of Yah Veh**:
there shall be no grapes on the vine,
nor figs on the fig tree,
and the leaf shall *fade* **wither**;
and *the things* **those** that I have given them
shall pass away from them.
14 Why do we sit *still? assemble yourselves* **gather**,
and let us enter into the *defenced* **fortified** cities,
and let us be *silent* **still** there:
for *the LORD* **Yah Veh** our *God* **Elohim**
hath *put* **hushed** us *to silence*,
and given us water of *gall* **rosh** to drink,
because we have sinned against *the LORD* **Yah Veh**.
15 We *looked for peace* **awaited shalom**,
but no good *came*;
and for a time of *health* **healing**,
and behold *trouble* **fright**!
16 The snorting of his horses was heard from Dan:
the whole land *trembled* **quaked** at the *sound* **voice**
of the neighing of his *strong ones* **mighty**;
for they are come, and have devoured the land,
and *all that is in it* **the fulness thereof**;
the city, and those that *dwell* **settle** therein.
17 For, behold,
I *will* **shall** send serpents, *cockatrices* **hissers**, among you,
which *will not be charmed* **shall have no charmer**,
and they shall bite you,
saith the LORD **an oracle of Yah Veh**.
18 *When I would comfort* **I should cheer** myself
against *sorrow* **grief**,
my heart *is faint* **bleedeth** in me.
19 Behold!
the voice of the *cry* **shout** of the daughter of my people
because of them
that dwell in a far country **in a land afar off**:
Is not *the LORD* **Yah Veh** in *Zion* **Siyon**?
is not her *king* **sovereign** in her?
Why have they *provoked* **vexed** me *to anger*
with their *graven images* **sculptiles**,
and with strange vanities?
20 The harvest is past, the summer is *ended* **concluded**,
and we are not saved.
21 For the *hurt* **breaking** of the daughter of my people
am I *hurt* **broken**; I am *black* **darkened**;
astonishment hath taken hold on **desolation holdeth** me.
22 Is there no balm in *Gilead* **Gilad**;
is there no *physician* **healer** there?
why *then* **assuredly** is not the health
of the daughter of my people *recovered* **ascended**?

A LAMENTATION OVER SIYON

9 *Oh* **Who giveth** that my head were waters,
and mine eyes a fountain of tears,
that I might weep day and night
for the *slain* **pierced** of the daughter of my people!
2 *Oh* **Who giveth** that I had in the wilderness
a lodging place of *wayfaring men* **caravans**;
that I might *leave* **forsake** my people, and go from them!

for they be all adulterers,
an **a private** assembly
of treacherous men **who deal covertly**.
3 And they bend their tongues like their bow
for *lies* **falsehood**:
but they *are* **prevail** not *valiant* **mightily**
for *the truth* **trustworthiness** upon the earth;
for they proceed from evil to evil, and they know not me,
saith the LORD **an oracle of Yah Veh**.
4 *Take ye heed* **On guard** every *one* **man**
of his *neighbour* **friend**,
and *trust* **confide** ye not in any brother:
for **in tripping the heel**,
every brother *will utterly supplant* **shall trip the heel**,
and every *neighbour* **friend**
will **shall** walk with *slanders* **talebearers**.
5 And they *will deceive* **shall mock** every *one* **man**
his *neighbour* **friend**,
and *will* **shall** not *speak* **word** the truth:
they have taught their tongue
to *speak lies* **word falsehoods**,
and weary themselves to *commit iniquity* **pervert**.
6 *Thine habitation is* **Thou settlest** in the midst of deceit;
through deceit they refuse to know me,
saith the LORD **an oracle of Yah Veh**.
7 Therefore thus saith
the LORD of hosts **Yah Veh Sabaoth**,
Behold, I *will melt* **shall refine** them, and *try* **proof** them;
for how shall I *do* **work**
for **at the face of** the daughter of my people?
8 Their tongue is *as an* **a slaughtering** arrow *shot out*;
it *speaketh* **wordeth** deceit:
one speaketh peaceably **wording shalom**
to his *neighbour* **friend** with his mouth,
but *in heart he layeth his wait* **setteth his inwards to lurk**.
9 Shall I not visit them for these *things*?
saith the LORD **an oracle of Yah Veh**:
shall not my soul be avenged
on such a *nation* **goyim** as this?
10 For the mountains
will I take up **shall I lift**
a weeping and *wailing* **lamentation**,
and for the *habitations* **folds** of the wilderness
a lamentation,
because they are burned *up*,
so that *none* **no man** can pass through *them*;
neither can men **nor** hear the voice of the *cattle* **chattel**;
both the *fowl* **flyer** of the heavens and the *beast* **animal**
are fled; they are gone.
11 And I *will make Jerusalem* **shall give Yeru Shalem**
to become heaps,
and a *den* **habitation** of *dragons* **monsters**;
and I *will make* **shall work** the cities of *Judah* **Yah Hudah**
desolate, without *an inhabitant* **settler**.
12 Who is the wise man,
that may *understand* **discern** this?
and who is he to whom
the mouth of *the LORD hath spoken* **Yah Veh worded**,
that he may *declare* **tell** it,
for what the land *perisheth* **destructeth**
and is burned *up* like a wilderness,
that none passeth through?
13 And *the LORD* **Yah Veh** saith,
Because they have forsaken my *law* **torah**
which I *set before them* **gave at their face**,
and have not *obeyed* **hearkened unto** my voice,
neither walked therein;
14 But have walked
after the *imagination* **warp** of their own heart,
and after Baalim,
which their fathers taught them:
15 Therefore
thus saith *the LORD of hosts* **Yah Veh Sabaoth**,
the God **Elohim** of *Israel* **Yisra El**;
Behold, I *will* **shall** feed them, *even* this people,
with wormwood,
and give them water of gall to drink.
16 I *will* **shall** scatter them also
among the *heathen* **goyim**,
whom neither they nor their fathers have known:
and I *will* **shall** send a sword after them,
till I have *consumed* **finished** them **off**.
17 Thus saith *the LORD of hosts* **Yah Veh Sabaoth**,
Consider **Discern** ye,
and call for the *mourning women* **lamenters**,
that they may come;
and send for *cunning women* **the wise**,
that they may come:
18 And let them *make haste* **hasten**,
and *take up* **lift** a *wailing* **lamentation** for us,
that our eyes may *run down* **drip** with tears,
and our eyelids *gush out* **flow** with waters.
19 For a voice of *wailing* **lamentation**
is heard out of *Zion* **Siyon**,
How are we *spoiled* **ravaged**!
we are *greatly confounded* **mightily shamed**,
because we have forsaken the land,
because our *dwellings* **tabernacles** have cast us out.
20 Yet hear the word of *the LORD* **Yah Veh**,
O ye women,
and let your ear *receive* **take** the word of his mouth,
and teach your daughters *wailing* **lamentation**,
and every *one* **woman** her *neighbour* **friend** lamentation.
21 For death is *come up* **ascended** into our windows,
and is entered into our palaces,
to cut off the *children* **sucklings**
from *without* **the outways**,
and the *young men* **youths** from the *streets* **broadways**.
22 *Speak, Thus* **Word thus**,
saith the LORD **an oracle of Yah Veh**,
Even the carcases of *men* **humanity**
shall fall as dung upon the *open* **face of the** field,
and as the *handful* **omer** after the *harvestman* **harvester**,
and none shall gather *them*.
23 Thus saith *the LORD* **Yah Veh**,
Let not the wise *man glory* **halal** in his wisdom,
neither let the mighty *man glory* **halal** in his might,
let not the rich *man glory* **halal** in his riches:
24 But let him that *glorieth glory* **halaleth halal** in this,
that he *understandeth* **comprehendeth** and knoweth me,
that *I am the LORD* **I — Yah Veh**
which *exercise lovingkindness* **work mercy**,
judgment, and *righteousness* **justness**, in the earth:
for in these *things* I delight,
saith the LORD **an oracle of Yah Veh**.
25 Behold, the days come,
saith the LORD **an oracle of Yah Veh**,
that I *will punish all* **shall visit upon** them
which are circumcised
with the uncircumcised **in the foreskin**;
26 *Egypt* **Misrayim**, and *Judah* **Yah Hudah**, and Edom,
and the *children* **sons** of Ammon, and Moab,
and all that *are in the utmost corners* **chop the edges**,
that *dwell* **settle** in the wilderness:
for all these *nations* **goyim** are uncircumcised,
and all the house of *Israel* **Yisra El**
are uncircumcised in the heart.

THE HANDIWORK OF ENGRAVERS

10 Hear ye the word
which *the LORD speaketh* **Yah Veh wordeth** unto you,
O house of *Israel* **Yisra El**:
2 Thus saith *the LORD* **Yah Veh**,
Learn not the way of the *heathen* **goyim**,
and be not dismayed at the signs of *heaven* **the heavens**;
for the *heathen* **goyim** are dismayed at them.
3 For the *customs* **statutes** of the people are vain:
for one cutteth a tree out of the forest,
the work of the hands of the *workman* **engraver**,
with the ax.
4 They *deck* **beautify** it with silver and with gold;
they *fasten* **strengthen** it with nails and with hammers,
that it *move* **wiggle** not.
5 They are *upright* **spun** as the palm tree,
but *speak* **word** not:
in bearing, they must *needs* be borne,
because they cannot *go* **pace**.
Be not *afraid* **awed** of them;
for they *cannot do evil* **vilify not**,
neither also is it in them to *do good* **well—please**.
6 Forasmuch as there is none like unto thee,

O *LORD* **Yah Veh**;
thou art great, and thy name is great in might.
7 Who *would* **should** not *fear* **awe** thee,
O *King* **Sovereign** of *nations* **goyim**?
for *to thee doth it appertain* **it becometh thee**:
forasmuch as among all the wise *men*
of the *nations* **goyim**,
and in all their *kingdoms* **sovereigndoms**,
there is none like unto thee.
8 But they are *altogether* brutish and foolish:
the *stock* **tree** is a *doctrine* **discipline** of vanities.
9 *Silver spread into plates* **Expanded silver**
is brought from Tarshish,
and gold from Uphaz,
the work of the *workman* **engraver**,
and of the hands of the *founder* **refiner**:
blue and purple is their *clothing* **robe**:
they are all the work of *cunning men* **wise**.
10 But *the LORD* **Yah Veh**
is the *true God* **Elohim of truth**,
he is the living *God* **Elohim**,
and *an everlasting king* **eternal sovereign**:
at his *wrath* **rage** the earth shall *tremble* **quake**,
and the *nations* **goyim**
shall not be able to abide his *indignation* **rage**.
11 Thus shall ye say unto them,
The *gods* **elah**
that have not made the heavens and the earth,
even they shall *perish* **destruct** from the earth,
and from under these heavens.
12 He hath *made* **worked** the earth by his *power* **force**,
he hath established the world by his wisdom,
and hath stretched out the heavens
by his *discretion* **discernment**.
13 When he *uttereth* **giveth** his voice,
there is a multitude of waters in the heavens,
and he causeth the vapours
to ascend from the ends of the earth;
he *maketh* **worketh** lightnings with rain,
and bringeth forth the wind out of his treasures.
14 *Every man* **All humanity** is brutish in *his* knowledge:
every *founder* **refiner**
is *confounded* **shamed** by the *graven image* **sculptile**:
for his *molten image* **libation** is falsehood,
and there is no *breath* **spirit** in them.
15 They are vanity, *and* the work of *errors* **frauds**:
in the time of their visitation they shall *perish* **destruct**.
16 The *portion* **allotment** of *Jacob* **Yaaqov**
is not like them:
for he is the former of all *things*;
and *Israel* **Yisra El** is the *rod* **scion** of his inheritance:
The LORD of hosts **Yah Veh Sabaoth** is his name.
17 Gather up thy *wares* **bundles** out of the land,
O *inhabitant* **settler** of the *fortress* **siege**.
18 For thus saith *the LORD* **Yah Veh**, Behold,
I *will* **shall** sling out the *inhabitants* **settlers** of the land
at *this once* **one time**,
and *will distress* **shall tribulate** them,
that they may *find it so* **be found out**.
19 Woe is me for my *hurt* **breaking**!
my wound *is grievous* **stroketh**;
but I said,
Truly **Surely** this is a *grief* **stroke**, and I must bear it.
20 My *tabernacle* **tent** is *spoiled* **ravaged**,
and all my cords are *broken* **torn**:
my *children* **sons** are gone forth of me, and they are not:
there is none to stretch forth my tent any more,
and to *set up* **raise** my curtains.
21 For the *pastors* **tenders** are become *brutish* **stupid**,
and have not sought *the LORD* **Yah Veh**:
therefore they shall not *prosper* **comprehend**,
and all their *flocks* **pastures** shall be scattered.
22 Behold, the *noise* **voice** of the *bruit* **report** is come,
and a great *commotion* **quake**
out of the north *country* **land**,
to *make* **set** the cities of *Judah* **Yah Hudah** desolate,
and a den **habitation** of *dragons* **monsters**.
23 O *LORD* **Yah Veh**,
I know that the way of *man* **humanity**
is not in *himself* **humanity**:
it is not in man
that walketh to *direct* **establish** his *steps* **paces**.
24 O *LORD* **Yah Veh**, correct me, but with judgment;
not in *thine anger* **thy wrath**,
lest thou *bring* **diminish** me *to nothing*.
25 Pour out thy fury
upon the *heathen* **goyim** that know thee not,
and upon the families that call not on thy name:
for they have eaten up *Jacob* **Yaaqov**, and devoured him,
and *consumed* **finished** him **off**,
and have *made* **desolated** his habitation *desolate* **of rest**.

THE BROKEN COVENANT

11 The word that came to *Jeremiah* **Yirme Yah**
from *the LORD* **Yah Veh**, saying,
2 Hear ye the words of this covenant,
and *speak* **word** unto the men of *Judah* **Yah Hudah**,
and to the *inhabitants* **settlers** of *Jerusalem* **Yeru Shalem**;
3 And say thou unto them,
Thus saith
the LORD God **Yah Veh Elohim** of *Israel* **Yisra El**;
Cursed be the man
that *obeyeth* **hearkeneth** not
unto the words of this covenant,
4 Which I *commanded* **misvahed** your fathers
in the day that I brought them forth
out of the land of *Egypt* **Misrayim**,
from the iron furnace, saying,
Obey **Hearken unto** my voice, and *do* **work** them,
according to all which I *command* **misvah** you:
so *shall* ye be my people,
and *I will be* **I AM** your *God* **Elohim**:
5 That I may *perform* **raise** the oath
which I have *sworn* **oathed** unto your fathers,
to give them a land flowing with milk and honey,
as it is this day.
Then answered I, and said,
So be it **Amen**, O *LORD* **Yah Veh**.
6 Then *the LORD* **Yah Veh** said unto me,
Proclaim **Call out** all these words
in the cities of *Judah* **Yah Hudah**,
and in the *streets* **outways** of *Jerusalem* **Yeru Shalem**,
saying,
Hear ye the words of this covenant, and *do* **work** them.
7 For **in witnessing,**
I *earnestly protested* **witnessed** unto your fathers
in the day that I *brought* **ascended** them *up*
out of the land of *Egypt* **Misrayim,**
even unto this day,
rising **starting** early and *protesting* **witnessing**,
saying, *Obey* **Hearken unto** my voice.
8 Yet they *obeyed* **hearkened** not,
nor *inclined* **extended** their ear,
but walked every *one* **man**
in the *imagination* **warp** of their evil heart:
therefore I *will* **shall** bring upon them
all the words of this covenant,
which I commanded **misvahed** them to *do* **work**:
but they *did* **worked** them not.
9 And *the LORD* **Yah Veh** said unto me,
A conspiracy is found
among the men of *Judah* **Yah Hudah**,
and among
the *inhabitants* **settlers** of *Jerusalem* **Yeru Shalem**.
10 They are turned back
to the *iniquities* **perversities** of their forefathers,
which refused to hear my words;
and they went after other *gods* **elohim** to serve them:
the house of *Israel* **Yisra El**
and the house of *Judah* **Yah Hudah**
have broken my covenant
which I *made* **cut** with their fathers.
11 Therefore thus saith *the LORD* **Yah Veh**,
Behold, I *will* **shall** bring evil upon them,
which they shall not be able to escape;
and though they shall cry unto me,
I *will* **shall** not hearken unto them.
12 Then shall the cities of *Judah* **Yah Hudah**
and *inhabitants* **settlers** of *Jerusalem* **Yeru Shalem** go
and cry unto the *gods* **elohim**
unto whom they *offer* incense:

but **in saving,** they shall not save them *at all*
in the time of their *trouble* **evil**.
13 For *according to* the number of thy cities
were thy *gods* **elohim**, O *Judah* **Yah Hudah**;
and *according to* the number
of the *streets* **outways** of *Jerusalem* **Yeru Shalem**
have ye set up **sacrifice** altars to *that* **the** shameful *thing,*
even **sacrifice** altars to *burn* incense unto Baal.
14 Therefore pray not thou for this people,
neither lift up a *cry* **shout** or prayer for them:
for I *will* **shall** not *hear them* **hearken**
in the time that they *cry* **call out** unto me
for their *trouble* **evil**.
15 What hath my beloved to do in mine house,
seeing
she hath *wrought lewdness* **worked intrigue** with many,
and the holy flesh is passed from thee?
when thou doest evil, then thou *rejoicest* **jumpest for joy**.
16 *The LORD* **Yah Veh** called thy name,
A green olive *tree, fair* **beautiful**,
and of *goodly* **formed** fruit:
with the *noise* **voice** of a great *tumult* **rush**
he hath kindled fire upon it,
and the branches of it are *broken* **shattered**.
17 For *the LORD of hosts* **Yah Veh Sabaoth**,
that planted thee,
hath *pronounced* **worded** evil against thee,
for **because of** the evil of the house of *Israel* **Yisra El**
and of the house of *Judah* **Yah Hudah**,
which they have *done* **worked** against themselves
to *provoke* **vex** me *to anger*
in *offering incense* **incensing** unto Baal.
18 And *the LORD* **Yah Veh**
hath given me knowledge of it, and I know it:
then thou
shewedst me **hadst me see** their *doings* **exploitations**.
19 But I was like a lamb or an *ox* **bullock**
that is brought to the slaughter;
and I knew not
that they had *devised devices* **fabricated fabrications**
against me, *saying,*
Let us *destroy* **ruin** the tree with the *fruit* **bread** *thereof,*
and let us cut him off from the land of the living,
that his name may be no more remembered.
20 But, O *LORD of hosts* **Yah Veh Sabaoth**,
that judgest *righteously* **justly**,
that *triest* **proofest** the reins and the heart,
let me see thy *vengeance* **avengement** on them:
for unto thee have I *revealed* **exposed** my *cause* **plea**.
21 Therefore thus saith *the LORD* **Yah Veh**
of the men of Anathoth, that seek thy *life* **soul**, saying,
Prophesy not in the name of *the LORD* **Yah Veh**,
that thou die not by our hand:
22 Therefore
thus saith *the LORD of hosts* **Yah Veh Sabaoth**,
Behold, I *will punish* **shall visit upon** them:
the *young men* **youths** shall die by the sword;
their sons and their daughters shall die by famine:
23 And there shall be no *remnant* **survivors** of them:
for I *will* **shall** bring evil upon the men of Anathoth,
even the year of their visitation.

THE PRAYER OF YIRME YAH

12 *Righteous* **Just** art thou, O *LORD* **Yah Veh**,
when I plead with thee:
yet let me *talk* **word** with thee of thy judgments:
Wherefore doth the way of the wicked prosper?
wherefore are all they *happy* **serene**
that **in dealing covertly,** deal *very treacherously* **covertly**?
2 Thou hast planted them, yea,
they have *taken root* **rooted**:
they grow, yea, they *bring forth* **work** fruit:
thou art near in their mouth, and far from their reins.
3 But thou, O *LORD* **Yah Veh**, knowest me:
thou hast seen me,
and *tried* **proofed** mine heart toward thee:
pull **tear** them out like *sheep* **flock** for the slaughter,
and *prepare* **hallow** them for the day of slaughter.
4 How long shall the land mourn,
and the herbs of every field wither,
for the *wickedness* **evil** of them that *dwell* **settle** therein?
the *beasts* **animals** are *consumed* **scraped away**,
and the *birds* **flyers**;
because they said, He shall not see our last end.
5 If thou hast run with *the footmen* **them on foot**,
and they have wearied thee,
then how canst thou *contend* **be inflamed** with horses?
and if in the land of *peace* **shalom**,
wherein thou *trustedst* **confidest**, *they wearied thee,*
then how *wilt* **shalt** thou *do* **work**
in the *swelling* **pomp** of *Jordan* **Yarden**?
6 For even thy brethren, and the house of thy father,
even they have dealt *treacherously* **covertly** with thee;
yea, they have called a multitude after thee:
believe **trust** them not,
though they *speak fair* **word good** words unto thee.
7 I have forsaken mine house,
I have *left* **abandoned** mine *heritage* **inheritance**;
I have given the *dearly beloved* **love** of my soul
into the *hand* **palm** of her enemies.
8 Mine *heritage* **inheritance** is unto me
as a lion in the forest;
it crieth out **giveth her voice** against me:
therefore have I hated it.
9 Mine *heritage* **inheritance** is unto me
as a speckled *bird* **swooper**,
the *birds* **swoopers** round about are against her;
come ye,
assemble **gather** all the *beasts* **live beings** of the field,
come *to devour* **for food**.
10 Many *pastors* **tenders**
have *destroyed* **ruined** my vineyard,
they have *trodden* **trampled** my *portion* **allotment**
under foot,
they have *made* **given the allotment**
of my *pleasant portion* **desire**
a desolate wilderness.
11 They have *made* **set** it desolate,
and being desolate it mourneth unto me;
the whole land is *made desolate* **desolated**,
because no man *layeth* **setteth** it to heart.
12 The *spoilers* **ravagers** are come
upon all *high places* **the barrens** through the wilderness:
for the sword of *the LORD* **Yah Veh** shall devour
from the *one* end of the land
even to the *other* end of the land:
no flesh shall have *peace* **shalom**.
13 They have sown wheat, but shall *reap* **harvest** thorns:
they have *put themselves to pain* **worn out**,
but shall not *profit* **benefit**:
and they shall *be ashamed* **shame**
of your *revenues* **produce**
because of the *fierce anger* **fuming wrath**
of *the LORD* **Yah Veh**.
14 Thus saith *the LORD* **Yah Veh**
against all mine evil *neighbours* **fellow tabernaclers**,
that touch the inheritance
which I have caused my people *Israel* **Yisra El** to inherit;
Behold,
I *will pluck* **shall uproot** them out of their *land* **soil**,
and *pluck out* **uproot** the house of *Judah* **Yah Hudah**
from among them.
15 And it shall *come to pass* **become**,
after that I have *plucked* **uprooted** them *out*
I *will* **shall** return, and *have* compassion *on* them,
and *will bring* **shall return** them *again*,
every man to his *heritage* **inheritance**,
and every man to his land.
16 And it shall *come to pass* **become**,
if they *will* **shall** diligently learn the ways of my people,
to *swear* **oath** by my name, *The LORD* **Yah Veh** liveth;
as they taught my people to *swear* **oath** by Baal;
then shall they be built in the midst of my people.
17 But if they *will* **shall** not *obey* **hearken**,
I will utterly pluck up **In uprooting, I shall uproot**
and destroy that *nation* **goyim**,
saith the LORD **an oracle of Yah Veh**.

THE FLAX GIRDLE

13 Thus saith *the LORD* **Yah Veh** unto me,
Go and *get* **chattel** thee a *linen* **flax** girdle,
and *put* **set** it upon thy loins, and put it not in water.

2 So I *got* **chatteled** a girdle
according to the word of *the LORD* **Yah Veh**,
and *put* **set** it on my loins.
3 And the word of *the LORD* **Yah Veh**
came unto me *the second time* **secondly**, saying,
4 Take the girdle that thou hast *got* **chatteled**,
which is upon thy loins,
and arise, go to Euphrates,
and hide it there in a hole of the rock.
5 So I went, and hid it by Euphrates,
as *the LORD commanded* **Yah Veh misvahed** me.
6 And it *came to pass* **became**,
after **at the end of** many days,
that *the LORD* **Yah Veh** said unto me,
Arise, go to Euphrates, and take the girdle from thence,
which I *commanded* **misvahed** thee to hide there.
7 Then I went to Euphrates, and digged,
and took the girdle from the place where I had hid it:
and, behold, the girdle was *marred* **ruined**,
it *was profitable* **prospered** for *nothing* **nought**.
8 Then the word of *the LORD* **Yah Veh** came unto me,
saying,
9 Thus saith *the LORD* **Yah Veh**,
After this manner *will I mar* **shall I ruin**
the *pride* **pomp** of *Judah* **Yah Hudah**,
and the great *pride* **pomp** of *Jerusalem* **Yeru Shalem**.
10 This evil people, which refuse to hear my words,
which walk in the *imagination* **warp** of their heart,
and walk after other *gods* **elohim**,
to serve them, and to *worship* **prostrate to** them,
shall *even* be as this girdle,
which *is good* **prospereth** for *nothing* **nought**.
11 For as the girdle
cleaveth **adhereth** to the loins of a man,
so have I caused to *cleave* **adhere** unto me
the whole house of *Israel* **Yisra El**
and the whole house of *Judah* **Yah Hudah**,
saith the LORD **an oracle of Yah Veh**;
that they might be unto me for a people, and for a name,
and for a *praise* **halal**, and for *a glory* **an adornment**:
but they *would not hear* **hearkened not**.

WINEBAGS

12 *Therefore* thou shalt *speak* **say** unto them this word;
Thus saith
the LORD God **Yah Veh Elohim** of *Israel* **Yisra El**,
Every *bottle* **bag** shall be filled with wine:
and they shall say unto thee,
In knowing, *Do we not certainly* know **we not**
that every *bottle* **bag** shall be filled with wine?
13 Then shalt thou say unto them,
Thus saith *the LORD* **Yah Veh**, Behold,
I *will* **shall** fill all the *inhabitants* **settlers** of this land,
even the *kings* **sovereigns** that sit upon David's throne,
and the priests, and the prophets,
and all the *inhabitants* **settlers** of *Jerusalem* **Yeru Shalem**,
with *drunkenness* **intoxication**.
14 And I *will dash* **shall shatter** them
one **man** against *another* **brother**,
even the fathers and the sons together,
saith the LORD **an oracle of Yah Veh**:
I *will* **shall** not *pity* **compassion**,
nor spare, nor *have* mercy,
but *destroy* **ruin** them.
15 Hear ye, and *give ear* **hearken**; be not *proud* **lifted**:
for *the LORD* **Yah Veh** hath *spoken* **worded**

THE THREAT OF EXILE

16 Give *glory* **honour**
to *the LORD* **Yah Veh** your *God* **Elohim**,
before he cause darkness,
and before your feet *stumble* **stub**
upon the *dark* **evening breeze of the** mountains,
and, while ye look for light,
he *turn* **set** it into the shadow of death,
and *make it gross* **place dripping** darkness.
17 But if ye *will* **shall** not hear it,
my soul shall weep in *secret places* **coverts**
for **at the face of** your *pride* **arrogance**;
and mine eye shall weep sore,
and *run down* **drip** with tears,
because the LORD'S flock **Yah Veh's drove**
is *carried away captive* **captured**.
18 Say unto the *king* **sovereign** and to the *queen* **lady**,
Humble yourselves **Abase**, sit down:
for your *principalities* **headships**
shall *come down* **descend**,
even the crown of your *glory* **adornment**.
19 The cities of the south shall be shut up,
and none shall open *them*:
Judah **Yah Hudah** shall be *carried away captive* **exiled** all of it,
it shall be *wholly carried away captive* **exiled in shalom**.
20 Lift up your eyes,
and *behold* **see** them that come from the north:
where is the *flock* **drove** that was given thee,
thy *beautiful* flock **of adornment**?
21 What *wilt* **shalt** thou say
when he shall *punish* **visit upon** thee?
for thou hast taught them to be *captains* **chiliarchs**,
and as chief over thee:
shall not *sorrows* **pangs** take thee,
as a woman *in travail* **birthing**?
22 And if thou say in thine heart,
Wherefore *come* **confront** these *things* upon me?
For the greatness of *thine iniquity* **thy perversity**
are thy *skirts discovered* **drapings exposed**,
and thy heels *made bare* **violated**.
23 Can the *Ethiopian change* **Kushiy overturn** his skin,
or the leopard his *spots* **streaks**?
then may ye also *do good* **be able to well—please**,
that are *accustomed* **discipled** to *do evil* **vilify**.
24 Therefore *will* **shall** I scatter them as the stubble
that passeth away by the wind of the wilderness.
25 This is thy *lot* **pebble**,
the portion of thy measures from me,
saith the LORD **an oracle of Yah Veh**;
because thou hast forgotten me,
and *trusted* **confided** in falsehood.
26 Therefore *will* **shall** I *discover* **strip** thy *skirts* **drapings**
upon thy face,
that thy *shame* **abasement** may *appear* **be seen**.
27 I have seen thine adulteries, and thy neighings,
the *lewdness* **intrigue** of thy whoredom,
and thine abominations on the hills in the fields.
Woe unto thee, O *Jerusalem* **Yeru Shalem**!
wilt **shalt** thou not be *made clean* **purified**?
when shall it once be **until when**?

DROUGHT, FAMINE, SWORD, AND PESTILENCE

14 The word of *the LORD* **Yah Veh**
that came to *Jeremiah* **Yirme Yah** concerning the dearth.
2 *Judah* **Yah Hudah** mourneth,
and the *gates* **portals** *thereof* languish;
they are *black* **darkened** unto the *ground* **earth**;
and the *cry* **outcry** of *Jerusalem* **Yeru Shalem**
is gone up **ascendeth**.
3 And their *nobles* **mighty**
have sent their little *ones* to the waters:
they came to the *pits* **dugouts**, and found no water;
they returned with their *vessels* **instruments** empty;
they were *ashamed* **shamed** and *confounded* **ashamed**,
and covered their heads.
4 Because the *ground* **soil** is *chapt* **broken**,
for there was no *rain* **downpour** in the earth,
the *plowmen* **cultivators** were *ashamed* **shamed**,
they covered their heads.
5 Yea, the hind also *calved* **birthed** in the field,
and forsook it, because there was no *grass* **sprout**.
6 And the wild *asses* **runners**
did stand in the *high places* **barrens**,
they *snuffed up* **gulped** the wind like *dragons* **monsters**;
their eyes *did fail* **finished off**,
because there was no *grass* **herbage**.
7 O *LORD* **Yah Veh**,
though our *iniquities* **perversities**
testify **answer** against us,
do **workest** thou it for thy name's sake:
for our *backslidings* **apostasies**
are many **abound by the myriads**;
we have sinned against thee.
8 O the *hope* **expectation** of *Israel* **Yisra El**,
the saviour *thereof* in time of *trouble* **tribulation**,
why shouldest thou be

as a *stranger* **sojourner** in the land,
and as a *wayfaring man* **caravan**
that *turneth aside* **stretcheth**
to *tarry for a night* **stay overnight**?
9 Why shouldest thou be
as a man *astonied* **dumbfounded**,
as a mighty *man* that cannot save?
yet thou, O *LORD* **Yah Veh**, art in the midst of us,
and we are called by thy name; leave us not.
10 Thus saith *the LORD* **Yah Veh** unto this people,
Thus have they loved to wander,
they have not *refrained* **spared** their feet,
therefore *the LORD* **Yah Veh**
doth not accept **is not pleased in** them;
he *will now* **shall, I beseech,**
remember their *iniquity* **perversity**, and visit their sins.
11 Then said *the LORD* **Yah Veh** unto me,
Pray not for this people for their good.
12 When they fast, I *will* **shall** not hear their *cry* **shout**;
and when they *offer burnt offering* **holocaust a holocaust**
and an *oblation* **offering,**
I will not accept them **they shall not please me**:
but I *will consume* **shall finish** them **off** by the sword,
and by the famine, and by the pestilence.
13 Then said I, *Ah* **Aha**, *Lord GOD* **Adonay Yah Veh**!
behold, the prophets say unto them,
Ye shall not see the sword, neither shall ye have famine;
but I *will* **shall** give you
assured peace **shalom of truth** in this place.
14 Then *the LORD* **Yah Veh** said unto me,
The prophets prophesy *lies* **falsehoods** in my name:
I sent them not, neither have I *commanded* **misvahed** them,
neither *spake* **worded** unto them:
they prophesy unto you a false vision and divination,
and *a thing of nought* **worthlessness**,
and the deceit of their heart.
15 Therefore thus saith *the LORD* **Yah Veh**
concerning the prophets that prophesy in my name,
and I sent them not,
yet they say, Sword and famine shall not be in this land;
By sword and famine shall those prophets be consumed.
16 And the people to whom they prophesy
shall be cast out
in the *streets* **outways** of *Jerusalem* **Yeru Shalem**
because **at the face** of the famine and the sword;
and they shall have none to *bury* **entomb** them,
them, their *wives* **women**,
nor their sons, nor their daughters:
for I *will* **shall** pour their *wickedness* **evil** upon them.
17 *Therefore* thou shalt say this word unto them;
Let mine eyes *run* **drip** with tears night and day,
and let them not cease:
for the virgin daughter of my people
is broken with a great *breach* **breaking**,
with a *very grievous blow* **mighty stroking stroke**.
18 If I go forth into the field, then behold**!**
the *slain* **pierced** with the sword!
and if I enter into the city, then behold**!**
them that are sick with **the sickness of** famine!
yea, both the prophet and the priest
go about **merchandise** into a land that they know not.
19 **In spurning,**
Hast thou *utterly rejected Judah* **spurned Yah Hudah**?
hath thy soul lothed *Zion* **Siyon**?
why hast thou smitten us, and there is no healing for us?
we *looked for peace* **awaited shalom**,
and there is no good;
and for the time of healing, and behold *trouble* **fright**!
20 We acknowledge, O *LORD* **Yah Veh**, our wickedness,
and the *iniquity* **perversity** of our fathers:
for we have sinned against thee.
21 Do not *abhor* **scorn** us, for thy name's sake,
do not disgrace the throne of thy *glory* **honour**:
remember, break not thy covenant with us.
22 Are there any among the vanities of the *Gentiles* **goyim**
that can cause *rain* **downpour**?
or can the heavens give showers?
art not thou he, O *LORD* **Yah Veh** our *God* **Elohim**?
therefore we *will wait upon* **shall await** thee:
for thou hast *made* **worked** all these *things*.

15 Then said *the LORD* **Yah Veh** unto me,
Though *Moses* **Mosheh** and *Samuel* **Shemu El**
stood *before me* **at my face,**
yet my *mind* **soul** could not be toward this people:
cast **send** them *out of my sight* **from my face,**
and let them go forth.
2 And it shall *come to pass* **become,**
if they say unto thee, Whither shall we go forth?
then thou shalt *tell* **say to** them,
Thus saith *the LORD* **Yah Veh**;
Such as are for death, to death;
and such as are for the sword, to the sword;
and such as are for the famine, to the famine;
and such as are for the captivity, to the captivity.
3 And I *will appoint over* **shall visit upon** them
four *kinds* **families**,
saith the LORD **an oracle of Yah Veh**:
the sword to *slay* **slaughter**, and the dogs to *tear* **drag**,
and the *fowls* **flyers** of the *heaven* **heavens**,
and the *beasts* **animals** of the earth,
to devour and *destroy* **ruin**.
4 And I *will cause* **shall give** them
to be removed **for an agitation**
into all *kingdoms* **sovereigndoms** of the earth,
because of *Manasseh* **Menash Sheh**
the son of *Hesekiah* **Yechizqi Yah,**
king **sovereign** of *Judah* **Yah Hudah**,
for that which he *did* **worked** in *Jerusalem* **Yeru Shalem**.
5 For who shall *have pity upon* **compassion** thee,
O *Jerusalem* **Yeru Shalem**?
or who shall *bemoan* **wag over** thee?
or who shall *go* **turn** aside
to ask *how thou doest* **of thy shalom**?
6 Thou hast *forsaken* **abandoned** me,
saith the LORD **an oracle of Yah Veh,**
thou art gone backward:
therefore *will* **shall** I stretch out my hand against thee,
and *destroy* **ruin** thee; I am weary with *repenting* **sighing**.
7 And I *will* **shall** fan them with a *fan* **winnowing basket**
in the *gates* **portals** of the land;
I *will* **shall** bereave them *of children*,
I *will* **shall** destroy my people
since they return not from their ways.
8 Their widows are *increased* **mighty** to me
above the sand of the seas:
I have brought upon them
against the mother of the *young men* **youths**
a *spoiler* **ravager** at *noonday* **noon**:
I have caused *him* to fall upon it suddenly,
and terrors upon the city.
9 She that hath borne seven languisheth:
she hath *given up* **expired** the *ghost* **soul**;
her sun is gone down while it was yet day**:**
she hath been
ashamed **shamed** and *confounded* **blushed**:
and the *residue* **survivors** of them
will I deliver **shall I give** to the sword
before **at the face of** their enemies,
saith the LORD **an oracle of Yah Veh.**
10 Woe is me, my mother,
that thou hast borne me a man of strife
and a man of contention to the whole earth!
I have neither lent on usury,
nor men have lent to me on usury;
yet every one of them doth *curse* **abase** me.
11 *The LORD* **Yah Veh** said,
Verily it shall be well with thy remnant
In releasing, I release you for good;
verily I will cause the enemy to entreat thee well
did I not intercede for thee with the enemy
in the time of evil
and in the time of *affliction.* **tribulation?**
12 *Shall iron break the northern iron*
Breaketh one iron — iron from the north
and the *steel* **copper**?
13 Thy *substance* **valuables** and thy treasures
will **shall** I give to the *spoil* **plunder** without price,
and that for all thy sins, even in all thy borders.
14 And I *will make* **shall cause** thee to pass

with thine enemies into a land which thou knowest not:
for a fire is kindled in *mine anger* **my wrath**,
which shall burn upon you.
15 O *LORD* **Yah Veh**, thou knowest:
remember me, and visit me,
and *revenge* **avenge** me of my *persecutors* **pursuers**;
take me not away
in *thy longsuffering* **the length of thy wrath**:
know that for thy sake
I have *suffered rebuke* **borne reproach**.
16 Thy words were found, and I did eat them;
and thy word was unto me
the *joy* **rejoicing** and *rejoicing* **cheerfulness**
of mine heart:
for I am called by thy name,
O *LORD God of hosts* **Yah Veh Elohim Sabaoth**.
17 I sat not in the *assembly* **private counsel**
of *the mockers* **them that ridicule**,
nor *rejoiced* **jumped for joy**;
I sat alone because of thy hand:
for thou hast filled me with *indignation* **rage**.
18 Why is my pain perpetual, and my wound incurable,
which refuseth to be healed?
Wilt **Shalt** thou be altogether unto me as a liar,
and as waters that *fail* **are not trustworthy**?
19 Therefore thus saith *the LORD* **Yah Veh**,
If thou return, then *will* **shall** I bring thee again,
and thou shalt stand *before me* **at my face**:
and if thou take forth the *precious* **esteemed**
from the *vile* **glutton**,
thou shalt be as my mouth:
let them return unto thee; but return not thou unto them.
20 And I *will make* **shall give** thee unto this people
a fenced *brasen* **copper** wall:
and they shall fight against thee,
but they shall not prevail against thee:
for I am with thee to save thee and to *deliver* **rescue** thee,
saith the LORD **an oracle of Yah Veh**.
21 And I *will deliver* **shall rescue** thee
out of the *hand* **palm** of the *wicked* **evil**,
and I *will* **shall** redeem thee
out of the hand of the *terrible* **tyrant**.

SWORD AND FAMINE

16 The word of *the LORD* **Yah Veh** came also unto me,
saying,
2 Thou shalt not take thee a *wife* **woman**,
neither shalt thou have sons or daughters in this place.
3 For thus saith *the LORD* **Yah Veh**
concerning the sons and concerning the daughters
that are born in this place,
and concerning their mothers that bare them,
and concerning their fathers that begat them in this land;
4 They shall die *of grievous* deaths **of sicknesses**;
they shall not be *lamented* **chopped after**;
neither shall they be *buried* **entombed**;
but they shall be as dung upon the face of the *earth* **soil**:
and they shall be *consumed* **finished off**
by the sword, and by famine;
and their carcases shall be meat
for the *fowls* **flyers** of *heaven* **the heavens**,
and for the *beasts* **animals** of the earth.
5 For thus saith *the LORD* **Yah Veh**,
Enter not into the house of **a feast of** mourning,
neither go to *lament* **chop** nor *bemoan* **wag over** them:
for I have *taken away* **gathered** my *peace* **shalom**
from this people,
saith the LORD **an oracle of Yah Veh**,
even *lovingkindness* **mercy** and mercies.
6 Both the great and the *small* **lesser** shall die in this land:
they shall not be *buried* **entombed**,
neither *shall men lament for them* **chopped over**,
nor *cut* **incise** themselves,
nor *make* **balden** themselves *bald* for them:
7 Neither shall *men tear* **they separate** *themselves*
for them in mourning,
to *comfort* **sigh over** them for the dead;
neither shall *men give* **they cause** them
the cup of consolation to drink
for their father or for their mother.
8 Thou shalt not *also* go
into the house of *feasting* **banquets**,
to sit with them to eat and to drink.
9 For thus saith *the LORD of hosts* **Yah Veh Sabaoth**,
the God **Elohim** of *Israel* **Yisra El**;
Behold,
I *will* **shall** cause to *cease* **shabbathize** out of this place
in your eyes, and in your days,
the voice of *mirth* **rejoicing**,
and the voice of *gladness* **cheerfulness**,
the voice of the bridegroom, and the voice of the bride.
10 And it shall *come to pass* **become**,
when thou shalt *shew* **tell** this people all these words,
and they shall say unto thee,
Wherefore hath *the LORD* **Yah Veh**
pronounced **worded** all this great evil against us?
or what is our *iniquity* **perversity**?
or what is our sin that we have *committed* **sinned** against
the LORD **Yah Veh** our *God* **Elohim**?
11 Then shalt thou say unto them,
Because your fathers have forsaken me,
saith the LORD **an oracle of Yah Veh**,
and have walked after other *gods* **elohim**,
and have served them,
and have *worshipped* **prostrated to** them,
and have forsaken me,
and have not *kept* **guarded** my *law* **torah**;
12 And **in working**,
ye have *done worse* **worked vilifying**
than **above** your fathers;
for, behold, ye walk every *one* **man**
after the *imagination* **warp** of his evil heart,
that they may not hearken unto me:
13 Therefore *will* **shall** I cast you out of this land
into a land that ye know not, neither ye nor your fathers;
and there shall ye serve other *gods* **elohim** day and night;
where I *will* **shall** not *shew* **give** you *favour* **charism**.
14 Therefore, behold, the days come,
saith the LORD **an oracle of Yah Veh**,
that it shall no more be said, *The LORD* **Yah Veh** liveth,
that *brought up* **ascended**
the *children* **sons** of *Israel* **Yisra El**
out of the land of *Egypt* **Misrayim**;
15 But, *The LORD* **Yah Veh** liveth,
that *brought up* **ascended** the *children* **sons** of *Israel* **Yisra El**
from the land of the north,
and from all the lands whither he had driven them:
and I *will bring* **shall return** them *again*
into their *land* **soil** that I gave unto their fathers.
16 Behold, I *will* **shall** send for many fishers,
saith the LORD **an oracle of Yah Veh**,
and they shall fish them;
and after *will* **shall** I send for many hunters,
and they shall hunt them from every mountain,
and from every hill, and out of the holes of the rocks.
17 For mine eyes are upon all their ways:
they are not hid from my face,
neither is their *iniquity* **perversity**
hid *from* **in front of** mine eyes.
18 And first I *will recompense* **shall shalam**
for their *iniquity* **perversity** and their sin double;
because they have *defiled* **profaned** my land,
they have filled mine inheritance
with the carcases of their *detestable* **abominations**
and *abominable things* **abhorrences**.
19 O *LORD* **Yah Veh**,
my strength, and my *fortress* **stronghold**,
and my *refuge* **retreat** in the day of *affliction* **tribulation**,
the *Gentiles* **goyim** shall come unto thee
from the *ends* **finalities** of the earth,
and shall say,
Surely our fathers have inherited *lies* **falsehoods**,
vanity, *and things* wherein there is no *profit* **benefit**.
20 Shall *a man make gods* **humanity work elohim**
unto himself,
and they *are no gods* **be no elohim**?
21 Therefore, behold,
I *will this once* **shall at this time** cause them to know,
I *will* **shall** cause them to know mine hand and my might;
and they shall know
that my name is *The LORD* **Yah Veh**.

THE SIN OF YAH HUDAH

17 The sin of *Judah* **Yah Hudah**
is *written* **engraved** with a *pen* **stylus** of iron,
and with the *point* **nail** of a *diamond* **brier**:
it is *graven* **engraved** upon the table of their heart,
and upon the horns of your **sacrifice** altars;
2 Whilst their *children* **sons**
remember their **sacrifice** altars and their *groves* **asherah**
by the green trees upon the high hills.
3 O my mountain in the field,
I *will* **shall** give
thy *substance* **valuables** and all thy treasures
to the *spoil* **plunder**,
and thy *high places* **bamahs** for sin,
throughout all thy borders.
4 *And thou,* even thyself,
shalt *discontinue* **release** from thine *heritage* **inheritance**
that I gave thee;
and I *will* **shall** cause thee to serve thine enemies
in the land which thou knowest not:
for ye have kindled a fire in *mine anger* **my wrath**,
which shall burn *for ever* **eternally**.
5 Thus saith *the LORD* **Yah Veh**;
Cursed be the *man* **mighty**
that *trusteth* **confideth** in *man* **humanity**,
and *maketh* **setteth** flesh his arm,
and whose heart
departeth **turneth aside** from *the LORD* **Yah Veh**.
6 For he shall be like the *heath* **naked** in the *desert* **plain**,
and shall not see when good cometh;
but shall *inhabit* **tabernacle**
in the *parched places* **scorches** in the wilderness,
in a salt land and not *inhabited* **settled**.
7 Blessed is the *man* **mighty**
that *trusteth* **confideth** in *the LORD* **Yah Veh**,
and whose *hope the LORD* **confidence Yah Veh** is.
8 For he shall be as a tree
planted **transplanted** by the waters,
and that *spreadeth out* **extendeth** her roots
by the *river* **stream**,
and shall not see when heat cometh,
but her leaf shall be green;
and shall not be *careful* **concerned**
in the year of drought,
neither shall *cease* **depart** from *yielding* **working** fruit.
9 The heart is *deceitful* **crooked** above all *things,*
and *desperately wicked* **incurable**:
who *can know* **knoweth** it?
10 I *the LORD search* **Yah Veh probe** the heart,
I try **proof** the reins,
even to give every man according to his ways,
and according to the fruit of his *doings* **exploitations**.
11 *As* the partridge *sitteth on eggs* **broodeth**,
and *hatcheth them* **begetteth** not;
so he that *getteth* **worketh** riches,
and not by *right* **judgment**,
shall *leave* **forsake** them in the *midst* **half** of his days,
and at his end shall be a fool.
12 A *glorious* **honourable** high throne from the beginning
is the place of our *sanctuary* **holies**.
13 O *LORD* **Yah Veh**,
the *hope* **expectation** of *Israel* **Yisra El**,
all that forsake thee shall *be ashamed* **shame**,
and they that *depart* **turn aside** from me
shall be *written* **inscribed** in the earth,
because they have forsaken *the LORD* **Yah Veh**,
the fountain of living waters.
14 Heal me, O *LORD* **Yah Veh**, and I shall be healed;
save me, and I shall be saved:
for thou art my *praise* **halal**.
15 Behold, they say unto me,
Where is the word of *the LORD* **Yah Veh**?
let it come *now* **I beseech**.
16 *As for me,* I have not hastened
from *being a pastor to follow* **tending after** thee:
neither have I desired the *woeful* **incurable** day;
thou knowest:
that which *came* **proceeded** out of my lips
was *right before thee* **straightforward at thy face**.
17 Be not a *terror* **ruin** unto me:
thou art my *hope* **refuge** in the day of evil.
18 Let them *be confounded* **shame**
that *persecute* **pursue** me,
but let not me *be confounded* **shame**:
let them *be dismayed* **dismay**,
but let not me *be dismayed* **dismay**:
bring upon them the day of evil,
and *destroy* **break** them
with double *destruction* **breaking**.

ON HALLOWING THE SHABBATH

19 Thus said *the LORD* **Yah Veh** unto me;
Go and stand in the *gate* **portal**
of the *children* **sons** of the people,
whereby the *kings* **sovereigns** of *Judah* **Yah Hudah**
come in, and by the which they go out,
and in all the *gates* **portals** of *Jerusalem* **Yeru Shalem**;
20 And say unto them,
Hear ye the word of *the LORD* **Yah Veh**,
ye *kings* **sovereigns** of *Judah* **Yah Hudah**,
and all *Judah* **Yah Hudah**,
and all the *inhabitants* **settlers** of *Jerusalem* **Yeru Shalem**,
that enter in by these *gates* **portals**:
21 Thus saith *the LORD* **Yah Veh**;
Take heed to yourselves **Guard your souls**,
and bear no burden on the *sabbath* **shabbath** day,
nor bring it in
by the *gates* **portals** of *Jerusalem* **Yeru Shalem**;
22 Neither carry forth a burden out of your houses
on the *sabbath* **shabbath** day,
neither *do* **work** ye any work,
but hallow ye the *sabbath* **shabbath** day,
as I *commanded* **misvahed** your fathers.
23 But they *obeyed* **hearkened** not,
neither *inclined* **extended** their ear,
but *made* **hardened** their neck *stiff,*
that they might not hear,
nor *receive instruction* **take discipline**.
24 And it shall *come to pass* **become**,
in hearkening, if ye *diligently hearken* **hearken** unto me,
saith the LORD **an oracle of Yah Veh**,
to bring in no burden
through the *gates* **portals** of this city
on the *sabbath* **shabbath** day,
but hallow the *sabbath* **shabbath** day,
to *do* **work** no work therein;
25 Then shall there enter into the *gates* **portals** of this city
kings **sovereigns** and *princes* **governors**
sitting upon the throne of David,
riding in chariots and on horses, they,
and their *princes* **governors**,
the men of *Judah* **Yah Hudah**,
and the *inhabitants* **settlers** of *Jerusalem* **Yeru Shalem**:
and this city shall *remain for ever* **settle eternally**.
26 And they shall come
from the cities of *Judah* **Yah Hudah**,
and *from the places* **round** about *Jerusalem* **Yeru Shalem**,
and from the land of *Benjamin* **Ben Yamin**,
and from the *plain* **lowland**, and from the mountains,
and from the south,
bringing *burnt offerings* **holocausts**, and sacrifices,
and *meat* offerings, and incense,
and bringing *sacrifices of praise* **extended hands**,
unto the house of *the LORD* **Yah Veh**.
27 But if ye *will* **shall** not hearken unto me
to hallow the *sabbath* **shabbath** day,
and not to bear a burden,
even entering in
at the *gates* **portals** of *Jerusalem* **Yeru Shalem**
on the *sabbath* **shabbath** day;
then *will* **shall** I kindle a fire in the *gates* **portals** *thereof,*
and it shall devour
the *palaces* **citadels** of *Jerusalem* **Yeru Shalem**,
and it shall not be quenched.

THE FORMER

18 The word which came to *Jeremiah* **Yirme Yah**
from *the LORD* **Yah Veh**, saying,
2 Arise,
and *go down* **descend** to the *potter's* **former's** house,
and there I *will* **shall** cause thee to hear my words.
3 Then I *went down* **descended**

to the *potter's* **former's** house, and, behold,
he *wrought* **worked** a work on the *wheels* **stones.**
4 And the *vessel* **instrument**
that he *made* **worked** of *clay* **morter**
was *marred* **ruined**
as morter in the hand of the *potter* **former**:
so he *made it again* **turned and worked**
another *vessel* **instrument**,
as seemed *good* **straight**
to the *potter* **former** to *make* **work** *it.*
5 Then the word of *the LORD* **Yah Veh** came to me,
saying,
6 O house of *Israel* **Yisra El**,
cannot I *do* **work** with you as this *potter* **former**?
saith the LORD **an oracle of Yah Veh**.
Behold,
as the *clay is* **morter** in the *potter's* **former's** hand,
so are ye in mine hand, O house of *Israel* **Yisra El**.
7 At what *instant* **blink** I shall *speak* **word**
concerning a *nation* **goyim**,
and concerning a *kingdom* **sovereigndom**,
to *pluck up* **uproot**, and to pull down, and to destroy it;
8 If that *nation* **goyim**,
against whom I have *pronounced* **worded**,
turn from their evil,
I *will repent* **shall sigh** of the evil
that I *thought* **fabricated** to *do* **work** unto them.
9 And at what *instant* **blink** I shall *speak* **word**
concerning a *nation* **goyim**, and concerning a kingdom,
to build and to plant it;
10 If it *do* **work** evil in my *sight* **eyes**,
that it *obey* **hearken** not **unto** my voice,
then I *will repent* **shall sigh** of the good,
wherewith I said
I *would benefit them* **should well—please**.
11 Now therefore *go to* **I beseech**,
speak to the men of *Judah* **Yah Hudah**,
and to the *inhabitants* **settlers** of *Jerusalem* **Yeru Shalem**,
saying, Thus saith *the LORD* **Yah Veh**;
Behold, I *frame* **form** evil against you,
and *devise* **fabricate** a *device* **fabrication** against you:
return ye *now* **I beseech**,
every *one* **man** from his evil way,
and *make* **well—please in** your ways
and your *doings good* **exploitations**.
12 And they said, *There is no hope* **I quit!**:
but we *will* **shall** walk after our own *devices* **fabrications**,
and *we will every one* **shall each man**
do **work** the *imagination* **warp** of his evil heart.
13 Therefore thus saith *the LORD* **Yah Veh**;
Ask ye *now* **I beseech**, among the *heathen* **goyim**,
who hath heard such *things*:
the virgin of *Israel* **Yisra El**
hath *done a very horrible thing* **worked mighty horribly**.
14 *Will a man leave* **Shall** the snow of Lebanon **cease**
which cometh from the rock of the field?
or shall the *cold* **strange cool** flowing waters
that come from another place be forsaken **be uprooted**?
15 Because my people hath forgotten me,
they have *burned incense* **incensed** to vanity,
and they have caused them
to *stumble* **falter** in their ways
from the *ancient* **eternal** paths,
to walk in paths, in a way not *cast* **raised** *up*;
16 To *make* **set** their land desolate,
and a perpetual **an eternal** hissing;
every one that passeth thereby
shall *be astonished* **astonish**, and wag his head.
17 I *will* **shall** scatter them as with an east wind
before **at the face of** the enemy;
I *will* **shall** shew them the *back* **neck**, and not the face,
in the day of their calamity.
18 Then said they,
Come and let us *devise devices* **fabricate fabrications**
against *Jeremiah* **Yirme Yah**;
for the *law* **torah** shall not *perish* **destruct** from the priest,
nor counsel from the wise,
nor the word from the prophet.
Come, and let us smite him with the tongue,
and let us not *give heed* **hearken**
to **unto** any of his words.
19 *Give heed* **Hearken** to me, O *LORD* **Yah Veh**,
and hearken to the voice of them that contend with me.
20 Shall evil *be recompensed* **shalam** for good?
for they have digged a *pit* **chasm** for my soul.
Remember that I stood *before thee* **at thy face**
to *speak* **word** good for them,
and to turn away thy *wrath* **fury** from them.
21 Therefore *deliver up* **give** their *children* **sons**
to the famine,
and pour **them** out *their blood*
by the *force* **hand** of the sword;
and let their *wives* **women** be bereaved *of their children*,
and be widows;
and let their men be *put to death* **slaughtered**;
let their *young men* **youths**
be *slain* **smitten** by the sword in *battle* **war**.
22 Let a cry be heard from their houses,
when thou shalt bring a troop suddenly upon them:
for they have digged a *pit* **chasm** to *take* **capture** me,
and hid snares for my feet.
23 Yet, *LORD* **Yah Veh**,
thou knowest all their counsel against me
to *slay* **execute** me:
forgive **kapar/atone** not their *iniquity* **perversity**,
neither *blot* **wipe** out their sin from thy *sight* **face**,
but let them *be overthrown before thee* **falter at thy face**;
deal **work** thus with them
in the time of *thine anger* **thy wrath**.

THE BROKEN INSTRUMENT

19 Thus saith *the LORD* **Yah Veh**,
Go and *get* **chattel**
a *potter's earthen* **former's potsherd** bottle,
and take of the *ancients* **elders** of the people,
and of the *ancients* **elders** of the priests;
2 And go forth unto
the valley of the son of Hinnom
Gay Ben Hinnom/Valley of the Son of Burning,
which is by the *entry* **opening**
of the *east gate* **potter's portal**,
and *proclaim* **call out** there
the words that I shall *tell* **word** thee,
3 And say, Hear ye the word of *the LORD* **Yah Veh**,
O *kings* **sovereigns** of *Judah* **Yah Hudah**,
and *inhabitants* **settlers** of *Jerusalem* **Yeru Shalem**;
Thus saith *the LORD of hosts* **Yah Veh Sabaoth**,
the God **Elohim** of *Israel* **Yisra El**;
Behold, I *will* **shall** bring evil upon this place,
the which whosoever heareth, his ears shall tingle.
4 Because they have forsaken me,
and have *estranged* **recognized** this place,
and have *burned incense* **incensed** in it
unto other *gods* **elohim**,
whom neither they nor their fathers have known,
nor the *kings* **sovereigns** of *Judah* **Yah Hudah**,
and have filled this place with the blood of innocents;
5 They have built also the *high places* **bamahs** of Baal,
to burn their sons with fire
for *burnt offerings* **holocausts** unto Baal,
which I *commanded* **misvahed** not, nor *spake* **worded** *it*,
neither *came* **ascended** it into my *mind* **heart**:
6 Therefore, behold, the days come,
saith the LORD **an oracle of Yah Veh**,
that this place shall no more be called *Tophet* **Topheth**,
nor *The valley of the son of Hinnom*
Gay Ben Hinnom/Valley of the Son of Burning,
but
the valley of slaughter **Gay Haregah/Valley of Slaughter**.
7 And I *will make void* **shall vacate**
the counsel of *Judah* **Yah Hudah**
and *Jerusalem* **Yeru Shalem** in this place;
and I *will* **shall** cause them to fall by the sword
before **at the face of** their enemies,
and by the hands of them that seek their *lives* **souls**:
and their carcases *will* **shall** I give to be *meat* **food**
for the *fowls* **flyers** of the *heaven* **heavens**,
and for the *beasts* **animals** of the earth.
8 And I *will make* **shall set** this city desolate,
and an hissing;
every one that passeth thereby

shall be astonished and hiss
because of all the *plagues* **wounds** *thereof.*
9 And I *will* **shall** cause them to *eat* **feed**
the flesh of their sons and the flesh of their daughters,
and they shall eat every *one* **man**
the flesh of his friend in the siege and *straitness* **distress**,
wherewith their enemies,
and they that seek their *lives* **souls**,
shall *straiten* **distress** them.
10 Then shalt thou break the bottle
in the *sight* **eyes** of the men that go with thee,
11 And shalt say unto them,
Thus saith *the LORD of hosts* **Yah Veh Sabaoth**;
Even so will **Thus shall** I break this people and this city,
as one breaketh a *potter's vessel* **former's instrument**,
that cannot be *made whole* **healed** again:
and they shall *bury* **entomb** them in *Tophet* **Topheth**,
till there be no place to *bury* **entomb**.
12 Thus *will I do* **shall I work** unto this place,
saith the LORD **an oracle of Yah Veh**,
and to the *inhabitants* **settlers** thereof,
and *even make* **give** this city as *Tophet* **Topheth**:
13 And the houses of *Jerusalem* **Yeru Shalem**,
and the houses
of the *kings* **sovereigns** of *Judah* **Yah Hudah**,
shall be *defiled* **fouled** as the place of *Tophet* **Topheth**,
because of all the houses upon whose roofs
they have *burned incense* **incensed**
unto all the host of *heaven* **the heavens**,
and have *poured out drink offerings* **libated libations**
unto other *gods* **elohim**.
14 Then came *Jeremiah* **Yirme Yah** from *Tophet* **Topheth**,
whither *the LORD* **Yah Veh** had sent him to prophesy;
and he stood in the court
of the *LORD'S house* **house of Yah Veh**;
and said to all the people,
15 Thus saith *the LORD of hosts* **Yah Veh Sabaoth**,
the God **Elohim** of *Israel* **Yisra El**; Behold,
I *will* **shall** bring upon this city and upon all her towns
all the evil that I have *pronounced* **worded** against it,
because they have hardened their necks,
that they might not hear my words.

YIRME YAH IS PERSECUTED

20 *Now Pashur* **Pashchur** the son of Immer the priest,
who was also *chief governor* **eminent overseer**
in the house of *the LORD* **Yah Veh**,
heard that *Jeremiah* **Yirme Yah**
prophesied these *things* **words**.
2 Then *Pashur* **Pashchur**
smote *Jeremiah* **Yirme Yah** the prophet,
and *put* **gave** him in the *stocks* **stockades** that were
in the **most** high *gate* **portal** of *Benjamin* **Ben Yamin**,
which was by the house of *the LORD* **Yah Veh**.
3 And it *came to pass* **became**, on the morrow,
that *Pashur* **Pashchur** brought forth *Jeremiah* **Yirme Yah**
out of the *stocks* **stockades**.
Then said *Jeremiah* **Yirme Yah** unto him,
The LORD **Yah Veh**
hath not called thy name *Pashur* **Pashchur**,
but *Magormissabib*
Magor Mis Sabib/Terror Round About.
4 For thus saith *the LORD* **Yah Veh**,
Behold, I *will make* **shall give** thee a terror to thyself,
and to all thy *friends* **loved ones**:
and they shall fall by the sword of their enemies,
and thine eyes shall *behold* **see** it:
and I *will* **shall** give all *Judah* **Yah Hudah**
into the hand of the *king* **sovereign** of *Babylon* **Babel**,
and he shall *carry* **exile** them *captive* into *Babylon* **Babel**,
and shall *slay* **smite** them with the sword.
5 *Moreover I will deliver* **I shall give**
all the *strength* **wealth** of this city,
and all the labours *thereof*,
and all the *precious* **esteemed** *things thereof*,
and all the treasures
of the *kings* **sovereigns** of *Judah* **Yah Hudah**
will **shall** I give into the hand of their enemies,
which shall *spoil* **plunder** them, and take them,
and carry them to *Babylon* **Babel**.
6 And thou, *Pashur* **Pashchur**,
and all that *dwell* **settle** in thine house
shall go into captivity:
and thou shalt come to *Babylon* **Babel**,
and there thou shalt die,
and shalt be *buried* **entombed** there,
thou, and all thy *friends* **loved ones**,
to whom thou hast prophesied *lies* **falsehoods**.

YIRME YAH'S COMPLAINT

7 O *LORD* **Yah Veh**,
thou hast *deceived* **deluded** me,
and I was *deceived* **deluded**;
thou art stronger than I, and hast prevailed:
I am *in derision* **ridiculed** daily,
every one *mocketh* **derideth** me.
8 For *since I spake* **I have worded enough,**
I *cried* **called** out, I cried violence and *spoil* **ravage**;
because the word of *the LORD* **Yah Veh**
was made a reproach unto me,
and a *derision* **ridicule**, daily.
9 Then I said, I *will* **shall** not *make* mention *of* him,
nor *speak* **word** any more in his name.
But *his word* **it** was in mine heart
as a burning fire *shut up* **restrained** in my bones,
and I was weary with *forbearing* **containing**,
and I *could not stay* **was not able**.
10 For I heard the *defaming* **slandering** of many,
fear on every side **terror round about**.
Report **Tell**, *say they*, and we *will report it* **shall tell.**
All my *familiars* **men of shalom**
watched for **guarded at** my *halting* **limping side**, *saying*,
Peradventure he *will* **shall** be *enticed* **deluded**,
and we shall prevail against him,
and we shall take our *revenge* **avengement** on him.
11 But *the LORD* **Yah Veh** is with me
as a mighty *terrible one* **tyrant**:
therefore my *persecutors* **pursuers** shall *stumble* **falter**,
and they shall not prevail:
they shall be *greatly ashamed* **mightily shamed**;
for they shall not *prosper* **comprehend**:
their *everlasting* **eternal** confusion
shall never be forgotten.
12 But, O *LORD of hosts* **Yah Veh Sabaoth**,
that *triest righteous* **proofest the just**,
and seest the reins and the heart,
let me see thy *vengeance* **avengement** on them:
for unto thee have I *opened* **exposed** my *cause* **plea**.
13 Sing unto *the LORD* **Yah Veh**,
praise **halal** ye *the LORD* **Yah Veh**:
for he hath *delivered* **rescued** the soul of the *poor* **needy**
from the hand of *evildoers* **vilifiers**.
14 Cursed be the day wherein I was born:
let not the day wherein my mother bare me be blessed.
15 Cursed be the man
who *brought tidings* **evangelized** to my father,
saying, A *man child* **male son** is born unto thee;
making **in cheering, cheering** him *very glad*.
16 And let that man be as the cities
which *the LORD overthrew* **Yah Veh turned against**,
and *repented* **sighed** not:
and let him hear the cry in the morning,
and the shouting at *noontide* **noon time**;
17 Because he *slew* **executed** me not from the womb;
or that my mother might have been my *grave* **tomb**,
and her womb *to be always* **eternally** great *with me*.
18 Wherefore came I forth out of the womb
to see *labour* **toil** and *sorrow* **grief**,
that my days
should be *consumed* **finished off** with shame?

YIRME YAH'S MESSAGE TO SIDQI YAH

21 The word which came unto *Jeremiah* **Yirme Yah**
from *the LORD* **Yah Veh**,
when *king Zedekiah* **sovereign Sidqi Yah** sent unto him
Pashur **Pashchur** the son of *Melchiah* **Malki Yah**,
and *Zephaniah* **Sephan Yah**
the son of *Maaseiah* **Maase Yah** the priest, saying,
2 Enquire, I *pray* **beseech** thee,
of *the LORD* **Yah Veh** for us;
for *Nebuchadrezzar* **Nebukadnets Tsar**
king **sovereign** of *Babylon* **Babel**
maketh war **fighteth** against us;

if so be that
the LORD will deal **Yah Veh shall work** with us
according to all his *wondrous* **marvellous** works,
that he may *go up* **ascend** from us.
3 Then said *Jeremiah* **Yirme Yah** unto them,
Thus shall ye say to *Zedekiah* **Sidqi Yah**:
4 Thus saith
the LORD God **Yah Veh Elohim** of *Israel* **Yisra El**;
Behold, I *will* **shall** turn back the *weapons* **vessels** of war
that are in your hands,
wherewith ye fight
against the *king* **sovereign** of *Babylon* **Babel**,
and against the *Chaldeans* **Kesediym**,
which besiege you without the walls,
and I *will assemble* **shall gather** them
into the midst of this city.
5 And I myself *will* **shall** fight against you
with an outstretched hand and with a strong arm,
even in *anger* **wrath**, and in fury, and in great *wrath* **rage**.
6 And I *will* **shall** smite the *inhabitants* **settlers** of this city,
both *man* **human** and *beast* **animal**:
they shall die of a great pestilence.
7 And afterward,
saith the LORD **an oracle of Yah Veh**,
I *will deliver Zedekiah* **shall give Sidqi Yah**,
king **sovereign** of *Judah* **Yah Hudah**,
and his servants, and the people,
and such as *are left* **survive** in this city
from the pestilence,
from the sword, and from the famine,
into the hand of *Nebuchadrezzar* **Nebukadnets Tsar**
king **sovereign** of *Babylon* **Babel**,
and into the hand of their enemies,
and into the hand of those that seek their *life* **soul**:
and he shall smite them
with the *edge* **mouth** of the sword;
he shall not spare them,
neither *have pity* **spare**, nor *have* mercy.
8 And unto this people thou shalt say,
Thus saith *the LORD* **Yah Veh**;
Behold, I *set before you* **give at thy face**
the way of life, and the way of death.
9 He that *abideth* **settleth** in this city
shall die by the sword,
and by the famine, and by the pestilence:
but he that goeth out,
and falleth to the *Chaldeans* **Kesediym** that besiege you,
he shall live,
and his *life* **soul** shall be unto him for a *prey* **spoil**.
10 For I have set my face against this city for evil,
and not for good,
saith the LORD **an oracle of Yah Veh**:
it shall be given into the hand
of the *king* **sovereign** of *Babylon* **Babel**,
and he shall burn it with fire.
11 And touching the house
of the *king* **sovereign** of *Judah* **Yah Hudah**, *say,*
Hear ye the word of *the LORD* **Yah Veh**;
12 O house of David, thus saith *the LORD* **Yah Veh**;
Execute judgment **Plead the cause** in the morning,
and *deliver him that is spoiled* **rescue the stripped**
out of the hand of the oppressor,
lest my fury go out like fire,
and burn that none can quench *it,*
because **at the face** of the evil of your *doings* **exploits**.
13 Behold, I am against thee,
O *inhabitant* **settler** of the valley, and rock of the plain,
saith the LORD **an oracle of Yah Veh**;
which say, Who shall *come down* **descend** against us?
or who shall enter into our habitations?
14 But I *will punish* **shall visit upon** you
according to the fruit of your *doings* **exploits**,
saith the LORD **an oracle of Yah Veh**:
and I *will* **shall** kindle a fire in the forest *thereof,*
and it shall devour all *things* round about it.

THE HOUSE OF YAH HUDAH'S JUDGMENT

22 Thus saith *the LORD* **Yah Veh**;
Go down **Descend** to the house
of the *king* **sovereign** of *Judah* **Yah Hudah**,
and *speak* **word** there this word,
2 And say, Hear the word of *the LORD* **Yah Veh**,
O *king* **sovereign** of *Judah* **Yah Hudah**,
that sittest upon the throne of David,
thou, and thy servants,
and thy people that enter in by these *gates* **portals**:
3 Thus saith *the LORD* **Yah Veh**;
Execute **Work** ye judgment and *righteousness* **justness**,
and *deliver* **rescue** the *spoiled* **stripped**
out of the hand of the oppressor:
and do no wrong,
do no violence to **violate not** the *stranger* **sojourner**,
the *fatherless* **orphan**, nor the widow,
neither *shed* **pour** innocent blood in this place.
4 For if **in working,** ye *do* **work** this *thing indeed* **word**,
then shall there enter in by the *gates* **portals** of this house
kings **sovereigns** sitting upon the throne of David,
riding in chariots and on horses,
he, and his servants, and his people.
5 But if ye *will* **shall** not hear these words,
I *swear* **oath** by myself,
saith the LORD **an oracle of Yah Veh**,
that this house shall become a *desolation* **parched area**.
6 For thus saith *the LORD* **Yah Veh** unto
the *king's* house **of the sovereign** of *Judah* **Yah Hudah**;
Thou art *Gilead* **Gilad** unto me,
and the head of Lebanon:
yet surely I *will make* **shall place** thee a wilderness,
and cities which are not *inhabited* **settled**.
7 And I *will prepare destroyers* **shall hallow ruiners**
against thee,
every *one* **man** with his *weapons* **instruments**:
and they shall cut down thy choice cedars,
and *cast* **fell** them into the fire.
8 And many *nations* **goyim** shall pass by this city,
and they shall say every man to his *neighbour* **friend**,
Wherefore hath *the LORD done* **Yah Veh worked** thus
unto this great city?
9 Then they shall *answer* **say**,
Because they have forsaken the covenant
of *the LORD* **Yah Veh** their *God* **Elohim**,
and *worshipped* **prostrated to** other *gods* **elohim**,
and served them.
10 Weep ye not for the dead,
neither *bemoan* **wag over** him:
but **in weeping,** weep *sore* for him that goeth away:
for he shall return no more,
nor see his native *country* **land**.
11 For thus saith *the LORD* **Yah Veh**
touching **as to** Shallum the son of *Josiah* **Yoshi Yah**,
king **sovereign** of *Judah* **Yah Hudah**,
which reigned instead of *Josiah* **Yoshi Yah** his father,
which went forth out of this place;
He shall not return thither any more:
12 But he shall die in the place
whither they have *led* **exiled** him *captive,*
and shall see this land no more.
13 *Woe* **Ho** unto him
that buildeth his house
by unrighteousness **without justness**,
and his *chambers* **upper rooms**
by wrong **without judgment**;
that useth his *neighbour's* **friend's** service
without wages **gratuitously**,
and giveth him not for his *work* **deeds**;
14 That saith,
I *will* **shall** build me a *wide* house **of measure**
and *large chambers* **breathtaking upper rooms**,
and *cutteth* **rippeth** him out windows;
and *it is* cieled with cedar,
and *painted* **anointed** with vermilion.
15 Shalt thou reign,
because thou *closest thyself* **art inflamed** in cedar?
did not thy father eat and drink,
and *do* **work** judgment and *justice* **justness**,
and then it was *well with him* **for his good**?
16 He *judged* **pleaded** the cause
of the *poor* **humble** and needy;
then it was *well with him* **for his good**:
was not this to know me?
saith the LORD **an oracle of Yah Veh**.

17 But thine eyes and thine heart
are not but for thy *covetousness* **greedy gain**,
and for to *shed* **pour** innocent blood, and for oppression,
and for *violence*, **race** to *do* **work** it.
18 Therefore thus saith *the LORD* **Yah Veh** concerning
Jehoiakim **Yah Yaqim** the son of *Josiah* **Yoshi Yah**,
king **sovereign** of *Judah* **Yah Hudah**;
They shall not *lament* **chop** for him,
saying, *Ah* **Ho** my brother! or, *Ah* **Ho** sister!
they shall not *lament* **chop** for him, *saying*,
Ah lord **Ho adoni**! or, *Ah* **Ho** his *glory* **majesty**!
19 He shall be *buried* **entombed**
with the *burial* **tomb** of *an ass* **a burro**,
drawn **dragged** and cast forth
beyond the *gates* **portals** of *Jerusalem* **Yeru Shalem**.
20 *Go up* **Ascend** to Lebanon, and cry;
and *lift up* **give** thy voice in Bashan,
and cry from *the passages* **Abirim**:
for all thy lovers are *destroyed* **broken**.
21 I *spake* **worded** unto thee in thy *prosperity* **serenity**;
but thou saidst, I *will* **shall** not hear.
This hath been thy *manner* **way** from thy youth,
that thou *obeyedst* **hearkenedst** not **unto** my voice.
22 The wind shall *eat up* **tend** all thy *pastors* **tenders**,
and thy lovers shall go into captivity:
surely then
shalt thou be *ashamed* **shamed** and confounded
for all thy *wickedness* **evil**.
23 O *inhabitant* **settler** of Lebanon,
that *makest thy nest* **nestest** in the cedars,
how *gracious* **charismatic** shalt thou be
when pangs come upon thee,
the *pain* **pang** as of a woman *in travail* **birthing**!
24 *As* I live, *saith the LORD* **an oracle of Yah Veh**,
though *Coniah* **Kon Yah** the son of *Jehoiakim* **Yah Yaqim**,
king **sovereign** of *Judah* **Yah Hudah**
were the *signet* **seal** upon my right hand,
yet *would* **should** I *pluck* **tear** thee thence;
25 And I *will* **shall** give thee
into the hand of them that seek thy *life* **soul**,
and into the hand of them whose face thou fearest,
even into the hand of *Nebuchadrezzar* **Nebukadnets Tsar**
king **sovereign** of *Babylon* **Babel**,
and into the hand of the *Chaldeans* **Kesediym**.
26 And I *will* **shall** cast thee out,
and thy mother that bare thee,
into another *country* **land**, where ye were not born;
and there shall ye die.
27 But to the land
whereunto they *desire* **lift their soul** to return,
thither shall they not return.
28 Is this man *Coniah* **Kon Yah**
a despised *broken* **splattered** idol?
is he a vessel **an instrument**
wherein is no *pleasure* **delight**?
wherefore are they cast out, he and his seed,
and are cast into a land which they know not?
29 O earth, earth, earth,
hear the word of *the LORD* **Yah Veh**.
30 Thus saith *the LORD* **Yah Veh**,
Write **Inscribe** ye this man *childless* **barren**,
a *man* **mighty** that shall not prosper in his days:
for no man of his seed shall prosper,
sitting upon the throne of David,
and *ruling* **reigning** any more in *Judah* **Yah Hudah**.

THE JUST SPROUT

23 *Woe be* **Ho** unto the *pastors* **tenders**
that destroy and scatter the *sheep* **flock** of my pasture!
saith the LORD **an oracle of Yah Veh**.
2 Therefore thus
saith *the LORD God* **Yah Veh Elohim** of *Israel* **Yisra El**
against the *pastors* **tenders** that *feed* **tend** my people;
Ye have scattered my flock, and driven them away,
and have not visited them:
behold,
I *will* **shall** visit upon you the evil of your *doings* **exploits**,
saith the LORD **an oracle of Yah Veh**.
3 And I *will* **shall** gather the *remnant* **survivors** of my flock
out of all *countries* **lands** whither I have driven them,
and *will bring* **shall return** them *again*
to their *folds* **habitations of rest**;
and they shall be *fruitful* **fruitbearing**
and *increase* **abound**.
4 And I *will set up shepherds* **shall raise tenders**
over them which shall *feed* **tend** them:
and they shall *fear* **awe** no more, nor be dismayed,
neither shall they be *lacking* **oversighted**,
saith the LORD **an oracle of Yah Veh**.
5 Behold, the days come,
saith the LORD **an oracle of Yah Veh**,
that I *will* **shall** raise unto David
a *righteous Branch* **just Sprout**,
and a *King* **Sovereign**
shall reign and *prosper* **comprehend**,
and shall *execute* **work** judgment and *justice* **justness**
in the earth.
6 In his days *Judah* **Yah Hudah** shall be saved,
and *Israel* **Yisra El** shall dwell *safely* **confidently**:
and this is his name whereby he shall be called,
THE LORD OUR RIGHTEOUSNESS
YAH VEH SIDQENUW.
7 Therefore, behold, the days come,
saith the LORD **an oracle of Yah Veh**,
that they shall no more say, *The LORD* **Yah Veh** liveth,
which *brought up* **ascended**
the *children* **sons** of *Israel* **Yisra El**
out of the land of *Egypt* **Misrayim**;
8 But, *The LORD* **Yah Veh** liveth,
which *brought up* **ascended** and which led
the seed of the house of *Israel* **Yisra El**
out of the north *country* **land**,
and from all *countries* **lands** whither I had driven them;
and they shall *dwell* **settle** in their own *land* **soil**.
9 Mine heart within me
is broken because of the prophets;
all my bones *shake* **flutter**;
I am like *a drunken* **an intoxicated** man,
and like a *man* **mighty**
whom wine hath *overcome* **overpassed**,
because **at the face** of *the LORD* **Yah Veh**,
and *because* **at the face** of the words of his holiness.
10 For the land is *full* **filled** of adulterers;
for *because* **at the face** of *swearing* **oathing**
the land mourneth;
the *pleasant places* **folds** of the wilderness
are *dried up* **withered**,
and their *course* **race** is evil,
and their *force* **might** is not right.
11 For both prophet and priest are profane;
yea, in my house have I found their *wickedness* **evil**,
saith the LORD **an oracle of Yah Veh**.
12 Wherefore their way shall be unto them
as slippery *ways* in the darkness:
they shall be *driven on* **overthrown**, and fall therein:
for I *will* **shall** bring evil upon them,
even the year of their visitation,
saith the LORD **an oracle of Yah Veh**.
13 And I have seen *folly* **frivolity**
in the prophets of *Samaria* **Shomeron**;
they prophesied in Baal,
and caused my people *Israel* **Yisra El** to *err* **stray**.
14 I have seen also
in the prophets of *Jerusalem* **Yeru Shalem**
an horrible thing **a horror**:
they *commit adultery* **adulterize**,
and walk in *lies* **falsehoods**:
they strengthen also the hands of *evildoers* **vilifiers**,
that *none* **no man** doth return from his *wickedness* **evil**;
they are all of them unto me as *Sodom* **Sedom**,
and the *inhabitants* **settlers** *thereof*
as *Gomorrah* **Amorah**.
15 Therefore
thus saith *the LORD of hosts* **Yah Veh Sabaoth**
concerning the prophets;
Behold, I *will* **shall** feed them with wormwood,
and make them drink the water of gall:
for from the prophets of *Jerusalem* **Yeru Shalem**
is profaneness gone forth into all the land.
16 Thus saith *the LORD of hosts* **Yah Veh Sabaoth**,
Hearken not

unto the words of the prophets that prophesy unto you:
they make you vain:
they *speak* **word** a vision of their own heart,
and not out of the mouth of *the LORD* **Yah Veh**.
17 They say *still* **saying** unto them that *despise* **scorn** me,
The LORD **Yah Veh** hath *said* **worded**,
Ye shall have *peace* **shalom**;
and they say unto every one
that walketh after the *imagination* **warp** of his own heart,
No evil shall come upon you.
18 For who hath stood
in the **private** counsel of *the LORD* **Yah Veh**,
and hath *perceived* **seen** and heard his word?
who hath *marked* **hearkened unto** his word, and heard it?
19 Behold,
a *whirlwind* **storm** of *the LORD* **Yah Veh**
is gone forth in fury,
even a *grievous whirlwind* **whirling storm**:
it shall *fall grievously* **whirl** upon the head of the wicked.
20 The *anger* **wrath** of *the LORD* **Yah Veh**
shall not return,
until he have *executed* **worked**,
and till he have *performed* **raised**
the *thoughts* **intrigue** of his heart:
in the latter days
ye shall *consider it perfectly* **discern with discernment**.
21 I have not sent these prophets, yet they ran:
I have not *spoken* **worded** to them, yet they prophesied.
22 But if they had stood in my **private** counsel,
and had caused my people to hear my words,
then they should have turned from their evil way,
and from the evil of their *doings* **exploits**.
23 Am I *a God at hand* **an Elohim nearby**,
saith the LORD **an oracle of Yah Veh**,
and not *a God* **an Elohim** afar off?
24 Can *any* **man** hide himself in *secret places* **coverts**
that I shall not see him?
saith the LORD **an oracle of Yah Veh**.
Do not I fill *heaven* **the heavens** and earth?
saith the LORD **an oracle of Yah Veh**.
25 I have heard what the prophets said,
that prophesy *lies* **falsehoods** in my name, saying,
I have dreamed, I have dreamed.
26 How long shall this be in the heart of the prophets
that prophesy *lies* **falsehoods**?
yea, *they are* prophets of the deceit of their own heart;
27 Which *think* **fabricate**
to cause my people to forget my name
by their dreams which they *tell* **scribe**
every man to his *neighbour* **friend**,
as their fathers have forgotten my name for Baal.
28 The prophet that hath a dream,
let him *tell* **scribe** a dream;
and he that hath my word,
let him *speak* **word** my word *faithfully* **in truth**.
What is the *chaff* **straw** to the *wheat* **grain**?
saith the LORD **an oracle of Yah Veh**.
29 Is not my word *like* **thus** as a fire?
saith the LORD **an oracle of Yah Veh**;
and like a hammer
that breaketh **shattereth** the rock *in pieces*?
30 Therefore, behold, I am against the prophets,
saith the LORD **an oracle of Yah Veh**,
that steal my words
every *one* **man** from his *neighbour* **friend**.
31 Behold, I am against the prophets,
saith the LORD **an oracle of Yah Veh**,
that *use* **take** their tongues, and say, *He saith.* **An oracle!**
32 Behold, I am against them that prophesy false dreams,
saith the LORD **an oracle of Yah Veh**,
and *do tell* **scribe** them,
and cause my people to *err* **stray** by their *lies* **falsehoods**,
and by their *lightness* **frothiness**;
yet I sent them not, nor *commanded* **misvahed** them:
therefore **in benefitting,** they shall not *profit* **benefit**
this people *at all*,
saith the LORD **an oracle of Yah Veh**.
33 And when this people, or the prophet, or a priest,
shall ask thee, saying,
What is the burden of *the LORD* **Yah Veh**?
thou shalt *then* say unto them, What burden?
I *will* **shall** even *forsake* **abandon** you,
saith the LORD **an oracle of Yah Veh**.
34 And as for the prophet, and the priest, and the people,
that shall say, The burden of *the LORD* **Yah Veh**,
I *will* **shall** even *punish* **visit**
upon that man and his house.
35 Thus shall ye say
every *one* **man** to his *neighbour* **friend**,
and every *one* **man** to his brother,
What hath *the LORD* **Yah Veh** answered?
and, What hath *the LORD spoken* **Yah Veh worded**?
36 And the burden of *the LORD* **Yah Veh**
shall ye *mention* **remember** no more:
for every man's word shall be his burden;
for ye have perverted the words of the living *God* **Elohim**,
of *the LORD of hosts* **Yah Veh Sabaoth** our *God* **Elohim**.
37 Thus shalt thou say to the prophet,
What hath *the LORD* **Yah Veh** answered thee?
and, What hath *the LORD spoken* **Yah Veh worded**?
38 But since ye say, The burden of *the LORD* **Yah Veh**;
therefore thus saith *the LORD* **Yah Veh**;
Because ye say this word,
The burden of *the LORD* **Yah Veh**,
and I have sent unto you, saying,
Ye shall not say, The burden of *the LORD* **Yah Veh**;
39 Therefore, behold, I, *even I*,
will utterly **in forgetting, shall** forget you,
and I *will forsake* **shall abandon** you,
and the city that I gave you and your fathers,
and cast you out of my presence **from my face**:
40 And I *will bring* **shall give**
an *everlasting* **eternal** reproach upon you,
and *a perpetual* **an eternal** shame,
which shall not be forgotten.

THE FIG BASKETS

24 *The LORD shewed me* **Yah Veh had me see**,
and, behold, two baskets of figs
were set before **congregated at the face of**
the *temple* **manse** of *the LORD* **Yah Veh**,
after that *Nebuchadrezzar* **Nebukadnets Tsar**
king **sovereign** of *Babylon* **Babel**
had *carried away captive Jeconiah* **exiled Yechon Yah**
the son of *Jehoiakim* **Yah Yaqim,**
king **sovereign** of *Judah* **Yah Hudah**,
and the *princes* **governors** of *Judah* **Yah Hudah**,
with the *carpenters* **engravers** and *smiths* **locksmiths**,
from *Jerusalem* **Yeru Shalem**,
and had brought them to *Babylon* **Babel**.
2 One basket had *very* **mighty** good figs,
even like the figs that are first ripe:
and the *other* **one** basket
had *very naughty* **mighty evil** figs,
which could not be eaten, they were so *bad* **evil**.
3 Then said *the LORD* **Yah Veh** unto me,
What seest thou, *Jeremiah* **Yirme Yah**?
And I said, Figs;
the good figs, *very* **mighty** good;
and the evil, *very* **mighty** evil,
that cannot be eaten, they are so evil.
4 Again the word of *the LORD* **Yah Veh** came unto me,
saying,
5 Thus saith *the LORD* **Yah Veh**,
the God **Elohim** of *Israel* **Yisra El**;
Like these good figs,
so *will* **shall** I acknowledge
them that are carried away captive of Judah
the exiles of Yah Hudah,
whom I have sent out of this place
into the land of the *Chaldeans* **Kesediym** for *their* good.
6 For I *will* **shall** set mine eyes upon them for good,
and I *will bring* **shall return** them *again* to this land:
and I *will* **shall** build them,
and not *pull them down* **break**;
and I *will* **shall** plant them,
and not *pluck them up* **uproot**.
7 And I *will* **shall** give them an heart to know me,
that *I am the LORD* **I — Yah Veh**:
and they *shall* be my people,
and *I will be* **I AM** their *God* **Elohim**:

for they shall return unto me with their whole heart.
8 And as the evil figs, which cannot be eaten,
they are so evil;
surely thus saith *the LORD* **Yah Veh**,
So *will* **shall** I give *Zedekiah* **Sidqi Yah**
the *king* **sovereign** of *Judah* **Yah Hudah**,
and his *princes* **governors**,
and the *residue* **survivors** of *Jerusalem* **Yeru Shalem**,
that *remain* **survive** in this land,
and them that *dwell* **settle** in the land of *Egypt* **Misrayim**:
9 And I *will deliver* **shall give** them
to be removed **for an agitation**
into all the *kingdoms* **sovereigndoms** of the earth
for *their hurt* **evil**,
to be — a reproach and a proverb,
a *taunt* **gibe** and *a curse* **an abasement**,
in all places whither I shall drive them.
10 And I *will* **shall** send the sword, the famine,
and the pestilence, among them,
till they be consumed from off the *land* **soil**
that I gave unto them and to their fathers.

THE SEVENTY YEAR CAPTIVITY

25 The word that came to *Jeremiah* **Yirme Yah**
concerning all the people of *Judah* **Yah Hudah**
in the fourth year of *Jehoiakim* **Yah Yaqim**
the son of *Josiah* **Yoshi Yah**
king **sovereign** of *Judah* **Yah Hudah**,
that was the first year of
Nebuchadrezzar **Nebukadnets Tsar**
king **sovereign** of *Babylon* **Babel**;
2 The which *Jeremiah* **Yirme Yah** the prophet
spake **worded** unto all the people of *Judah* **Yah Hudah**,
and to all the *inhabitants* **settlers**
of *Jerusalem* **Yeru Shalem**, saying,
3 From the thirteenth year of *Josiah* **Yoshi Yah**
the son of Amon *king* **sovereign** of *Judah* **Yah Hudah**,
even unto this day, that is the three and twentieth year,
the word of *the LORD* **Yah Veh** hath come unto me,
and I have *spoken* **worded** unto you,
rising **starting** early and *speaking* **wording**;
but ye have not hearkened.
4 And *the LORD* **Yah Veh** hath sent unto you
all his servants the prophets,
rising **starting** early and sending them;
but ye have not hearkened,
nor *inclined* **extended** your ear to hear.
5 *They said* **Saying,** Turn ye again *now* **I beseech,**
every *one* **man** from his evil way,
and from the evil of your *doings* **exploits**,
and *dwell* **settle** in the *land* **soil**
that *the LORD* **Yah Veh**
hath given unto you and to your fathers
for ever **eternally** and *ever* **eternally**:
6 And go not after other *gods* **elohim** to serve them,
and to *worship* **prostrate to** them,
and *provoke* **vex** me not *to anger*
with the works of your hands;
and I *will do you no hurt* **shall not vilify you**.
7 Yet ye have not hearkened unto me,
saith the LORD **an oracle of Yah Veh**;
that ye might *provoke* **vex** me *to anger*
with the works of your hands to your own *hurt* **evil**.
8 Therefore
thus saith *the LORD of hosts* **Yah Veh Sabaoth**;
Because ye have not heard my words,
9 Behold,
I *will* **shall** send and take all the families of the north,
saith the LORD **an oracle of Yah Veh**,
and *Nebuchadrezzar* **Nebukadnets Tsar**
king **sovereign** of *Babylon* **Babel**, my servant,
and *will* **shall** bring them against this land,
and against the *inhabitants* **settlers** *thereof*,
and against all these *nations* **goyim** round about,
and *will utterly destroy* **shall devote** them,
and *make* **set** them
an astonishment **a desolation**, and an hissing,
and *perpetual desolations* **eternal parched areas**.
10 *Moreover I will take* **I shall destroy** from them
the voice of *mirth* **rejoicing**,
and the voice of *gladness* **cheerfulness**,
the voice of the bridegroom, and the voice of the bride,
the *sound* **voice** of the millstones,
and the light of the *candle* **lamp**.
11 And this whole land
shall be a *desolation* **parched area**,
and *an astonishment* **a desolation**;
and these *nations* **goyim**
shall serve the *king* **sovereign** of *Babylon* **Babel**
seventy years.
12 And it shall *come to pass* **become**,
when seventy years are *accomplished* **fulfilled**,
that I *will punish* **shall visit**
upon the *king* **sovereign** of *Babylon* **Babel**,
and that *nation* **goyim**,
saith the LORD **an oracle of Yah Veh**,
for their *iniquity* **perversity**,
and the land of the *Chaldeans* **Kesediym**,
and *will make* **shall set** it *perpetual* **eternal** desolations.
13 And I *will* **shall** bring upon that land
all my words
which I have *pronounced against it* **worded**,
even all that is *written* **inscribed** in this *book* **scroll**,
which *Jeremiah* **Yirme Yah** hath prophesied
against all the *nations* **goyim**.
14 For many *nations* **goyim** and great *kings* **sovereigns**
shall serve themselves of them also:
and I *will recompense* **shall shalam** them
according to their deeds,
and according to the works of their own hands.
15 For thus saith
the LORD God **Yah Veh Elohim** of *Israel* **Yisra El**
unto me;
Take the wine cup of this fury at my hand,
and cause all the *nations* **goyim**, to whom I send thee,
to drink it.
16 And they shall drink,
and *be moved* **agitate**, and *be mad* **halal**,
because **at the face** of the sword
that I *will* **shall** send among them.
17 Then took I the cup at *the LORD'S* **Yah Veh's** hand,
and made all the *nations* **goyim** to drink,
unto whom *the LORD* **Yah Veh** had sent me:
18 *To wit, Jerusalem* **Yeru Shalem**,
and the cities of *Judah* **Yah Hudah**,
and the *kings* **sovereigns** *thereof*,
and the *princes* **governors** *thereof*,
to *make* **give** them a *desolation* **parched area**,
an astonishment **a desolation**,
an hissing, and *a curse* **an abasement**; as it is this day;
19 *Pharaoh king* **Paroh sovereign** of *Egypt* **Misrayim**,
and his servants, and his *princes* **governors**,
and all his people;
20 And all the *mingled people* **comingled**,
and all the *kings* **sovereigns** of the land of *Uz* **Us**,
and all the *kings* **sovereigns**
of the land of the *Philistines* **Peleshethiym**,
and *Ashkelon* **Ashqelon**, and Azzah, and *Ekron* **Eqron**,
and the *remnant* **survivors** of Ashdod,
21 Edom, and Moab, and the *children* **sons** of Ammon,
22 And all the *kings* **sovereigns** of *Tyrus* **Sor**,
and all the *kings* **sovereigns** of *Zidon* **Sidon**,
and the *kings* **sovereigns** of the *isles* **islands**
which are beyond the sea,
23 Dedan, and Tema, and Buz,
and all that *are in the utmost corners* **chop the edges**,
24 And all the *kings* **sovereigns** of Arabia,
and all the *kings* **sovereigns**
of the *mingled people* **comingled**
that *dwell* **tabernacle** in the *desert* **wilderness**,
25 And all the *kings* **sovereigns** of Zimri,
and all the *kings* **sovereigns** of Elam,
and all the *kings* **sovereigns** of the *Medes* **Maday**,
26 And all the *kings* **sovereigns** of the north,
far and near, *one* **man** with *another* **brother**,
and all the *kingdoms* **sovereigndoms** of the *world* **earth**,
which are upon the face of the *earth* **soil**:
and the *kings* **sovereigns** of Sheshach
shall drink after them.
27 *Therefore* thou shalt say unto them,
Thus saith *the LORD of hosts* **Yah Veh Sabaoth**,

the God **Elohim** of *Israel* **Yisra El**;
Drink ye, and *be drunken* **intoxicate**,
and *spue* **vomit**, and fall, and rise no more,
because **at the face** of the sword
which I *will* **shall** send among you.
28 And it shall be,
if they refuse to take the cup at thine hand to drink,
then shalt thou say unto them,
Thus saith *the LORD of hosts* **Yah Veh Sabaoth**;
In drinking, Ye shall *certainly* drink.
29 For, *lo* **behold**,
I begin to *bring evil on* **vilify** the city
which is called by my name,
and **in exonerating,**
should ye be *utterly unpunished* **exonerated**?
Ye shall not be unpunished:
for I *will* **shall** call for a sword
upon all the *inhabitants* **settlers** of the earth,
saith the LORD of hosts **an oracle of Yah Veh Sabaoth**.
30 Therefore prophesy thou against them all these words,
and say unto them,
The LORD **Yah Veh** shall roar from on high,
and *utter* **give** his voice from his holy habitation **of rest**;
in roaring,
he shall *mightily* roar upon his habitation **of rest**;
he shall *give a shout* **answer**,
as they that tread *the grapes*,
against all the *inhabitants* **settlers** of the earth.
31 *A noise* **An uproar**
shall come *even* to the ends of the earth;
for *the LORD* **Yah Veh**
hath a controversy with the *nations* **goyim**,
he *will plead with* **shall judge** all flesh;
he *will* **shall** give them that are wicked to the sword,
saith the LORD **an oracle of Yah Veh**.
32 Thus saith *the LORD of hosts* **Yah Veh Sabaoth**,
Behold, evil shall go forth
from *nation* **goyim** to *nation* **goyim**,
and a great *whirlwind* **storm** shall be *raised up* **wakened**
from the *coasts* **flanks** of the earth.
33 And the *slain* **pierced** of *the LORD* **Yah Veh**
shall be at that day from *one* end of the earth
even unto *the other* end of the earth:
they shall not be *lamented* **chopped over**,
neither gathered, nor *buried* **entombed**;
they shall be dung upon the *ground* **face of the soil**.
34 Howl, ye *shepherds* **tenders**, and cry;
and wallow yourselves *in the ashes*,
ye *principal* **mighty** of the flock:
for the days
of your slaughter and of your *dispersions* **scatterings**
are *accomplished* **fulfilled**;
and ye shall fall
like *a pleasant vessel* **an instrument of desire**.
35 And *the shepherds shall have no way to flee*
flight from the tenders shall destruct,
nor the principal of the flock to escape
and escape from the mighty of the flock.
36 A voice of the cry of the *shepherds* **tenders**,
and an howling of the *principal* **mighty** of the flock,
shall be heard:
for *the LORD* **Yah Veh**
hath *spoiled* **ravaged** their pasture.
37 And the *peaceable habitations* **folds of shalom**
are *cut down* **severed**
because **at the face** of the *fierce anger* **fuming wrath**
of *the LORD* **Yah Veh**.
38 He hath forsaken his *covert* **sukkoth/brush arbor**,
as the *lion* **whelp**:
for their land is desolate
because **at the face** of the *fierceness* **fuming**
of the oppressor,
and *because* **at the face** of his *fierce anger* **fuming wrath**.

WARNING TO THE CITIES OF YAH HUDAH

26 In the beginning
of the *reign* **sovereigndom** of *Jehoiakim* **Yah Yaqim**
the son of *Josiah* **Yoshi Yah,**
king **sovereign** of *Judah* **Yah Hudah**
came this word from *the LORD* **Yah Veh**, saying,
2 Thus saith *the LORD* **Yah Veh**;
Stand in the court
of the *LORD'S* house **of Yah Veh**,
and *speak* **word** unto all the cities of *Judah* **Yah Hudah**,
which come to *worship* **prostrate**
in the *LORD'S* house **of Yah Veh**,
all the words
that I *command* **misvah** thee to *speak* **word** unto them;
diminish not a word:
3 If so be they *will* **shall** hearken,
and turn every man from his evil way,
that I may *repent* **sigh** me of the evil,
which I *purpose* **fabricate** to *do* **work** unto them
because **at the face** of the evil of their *doings* **exploits**.
4 And thou shalt say unto them,
Thus saith *the LORD* **Yah Veh**;
If ye *will* **shall** not hearken to me,
to walk in my *law* **torah**,
which I have set *before you* **at thy face**,
5 To hearken to the words of my servants the prophets,
whom I sent unto you,
both rising up **starting** early, and sending *them*,
but ye have not hearkened;
6 Then *will I make* **shall I give** this house like Shiloh,
and *will make* **shall give** this city *a curse* **an abasement**
to all the *nations* **goyim** of the earth.
7 So the priests and the prophets and all the people
heard *Jeremiah* **Yirme Yah** speaking these words
in the house of *the LORD* **Yah Veh**.
8 *Now* it *came to pass* **became**,
when *Jeremiah* **Yirme Yah**
had *made an end of speaking* **finished wording** all that
the LORD **Yah Veh** had *commanded* **misvahed** him
to *speak* **word** unto all the people,
that the priests and the prophets and all the people
took **apprehended** him, saying,
In dying, Thou shalt *surely* die.
9 Why hast thou prophesied
in the name of *the LORD* **Yah Veh**, saying,
This house shall be like Shiloh,
and this city shall be *desolate* **parched**
without *an inhabitant* **a settler**?
And all the people
were gathered **congregated** against *Jeremiah* **Yirme Yah**
in the house of *the LORD* **Yah Veh**.
10 When the *princes* **governors** of *Judah* **Yah Hudah**
heard these *things* **words**,
then they *came up* **ascended**
from the *king's* **sovereign's** house
unto the house of *the LORD* **Yah Veh**,
and sat down in the *entry* **opening** of the new *gate* **portal**
of the *LORD'S* house **of Yah Veh**.
11 Then *spake* **said** the priests and the prophets
unto the *princes* **governors** and to all the people, saying,
This man *is worthy to die* **hath judgment of death**;
for he hath prophesied against this city,
as ye have heard with your ears.
12 Then *spake Jeremiah* **said Yirme Yah**
unto all the *princes* **governors** and to all the people,
saying, *The LORD* **Yah Veh** sent me to prophesy
against this house and against this city
all the words that ye have heard.
13 Therefore now
amend **well—prepare** your ways and your *doings* **exploits**,
and obey
the voice of *the LORD* **Yah Veh** your *God* **Elohim**;
and *the LORD will repent him* **Yah Veh shall sigh**
of the evil that he hath *pronounced* **worded** against you.
14 As for me, behold, I am in your hand:
do **work** with me as seemeth good
and *meet unto you* **straight in your eyes**.
15 But **in knowing,** know ye *for certain* **this**,
that if ye *put me to death* **deathify me**,
ye shall surely *bring* **give** innocent blood
upon yourselves, and upon this city,
and upon the *inhabitants* **settlers** *thereof*:
for of a truth *the LORD* **Yah Veh** hath sent me unto you
to *speak* **word** all these words in your ears.
16 Then said the *princes* **governors** and all the people
unto the priests and to the prophets;
This man

is not worthy to die **hath not judgment of death**:
for he hath *spoken* **worded** to us
in the name of *the LORD* **Yah Veh** our *God* **Elohim**.
17 Then rose up *certain* **men** of the elders of the land,
and *spake* **said**
to all the *assembly* **congregation** of the people, saying,
18 *Micah* **Michah Yah** the *Morasthite* **Moreshethiy**
prophesied in the days of *Hesekiah* **Yechizqi Yah,**
king **sovereign** of *Judah* **Yah Hudah**,
and *spake* **said** to all the people of *Judah* **Yah Hudah**,
saying, Thus saith *the LORD of hosts* **Yah Veh Sabaoth**;
Zion **Siyon** shall be plowed like a field,
and *Jerusalem* **Yeru Shalem** shall become heaps,
and the mountain of the house
as the *high places* **bamahs** of a forest.
19 Did *Hesekiah* **Yechizqi Yah**
king **sovereign** of *Judah* **Yah Hudah**
and all *Judah* **Yah Hudah**
put him at all to death **in deathifying, deathify him**?
did he not fear *the LORD* **Yah Veh**,
and *besought the LORD* **stroked the face of Yah Veh**,
and *the LORD repented him* **Yah Veh sighed** of the evil
which he had *pronounced* **worded** against them?
Thus might we *procure* **work** great evil against our souls.
20 And there was also a man
that prophesied in the name of *the LORD* **Yah Veh**,
Urijah **Uri Yah** the son of *Shemaiah* **Shema Yah**
of *Kirjathjearim* **Qiryath Arim**,
who prophesied against this city and against this land
according to all the words of *Jeremiah* **Yirme Yah**.
21 And when *Jehoiakim* **Yah Yaqim** the *king* **sovereign**,
with all his mighty *men*, and all the *princes* **governors**,
heard his words,
the *king* **sovereign** sought to *put* **deathify** him *to death*:
but when *Urijah* **Uri Yah** heard it,
he *was afraid* **awed**,
and fled, and went into *Egypt* **Misrayim**;
22 And *Jehoiakim* **Yah Yaqim** the *king* **sovereign**
sent men into *Egypt* **Misrayim**,
namely, *Elnathan* **El Nathan** the son of Achbor,
and *certain* men with him into *Egypt* **Misrayim**.
23 And they fetched forth *Urijah* **Uri Yah**
out of *Egypt* **Misrayim**,
and brought him
unto *Jehoiakim* **Yah Yaqim** the *king* **sovereign**;
who *slew* **smote** him with the sword,
and cast his *dead body* **carcase**
into the *graves* **tombs** of the *common* **sons of the** people.
24 Nevertheless the hand of Ahikam the son of Shaphan
was with *Jeremiah* **Yirme Yah**,
that they should not give him into the hand of the people
to put **deathify** him *to death*.

YAH HUDAH UNDER NEBUKADNETS TSAR

27 In the beginning
of the *reign* **sovereigndom** of *Jehoiakim* **Yah Yaqim**
the son of *Josiah* **Yoshi Yah,**
king **sovereign** of *Judah* **Yah Hudah**
came this word unto *Jeremiah* **Yirme Yah**
from *the LORD* **Yah Veh**, saying,
2 Thus saith *the LORD* **Yah Veh** to me;
Make **Work** thee bonds and *yokes* **yoke poles**,
and *put* **give** them upon thy neck,
3 And send them to the *king* **sovereign** of Edom,
and to the *king* **sovereign** of Moab,
and to the *king* **sovereign**
of the *Ammonites* **sons of Ammon**,
and to the *king* **sovereign** of *Tyrus* **Sor**,
and to the *king* **sovereign** of *Zidon* **Sidon**,
by the hand of the *messengers* **angels**
which come to *Jerusalem* **Yeru Shalem**
unto *Zedekiah* **Sidqi Yah,**
king **sovereign** of *Judah* **Yah Hudah**;
4 And *command* **misvah** them
to say **saying** unto their *masters* **adonim**,
Thus saith *the LORD of hosts* **Yah Veh Sabaoth**,
the God **Elohim** of *Israel* **Yisra El**;
Thus shall ye say unto your *masters* **adonim**;
5 I have *made* **worked** the earth,
the man **with humanity** and the *beast* **animal**
that are upon the *ground* **face of the earth**,
by my great *power* **strength** and by my outstretched arm,
and have given it unto whom
it *seemed meet unto me* **hath been straight in my eyes**.
6 And now have I given all these lands
into the hand of
Nebuchadnezzar **Nebukadnets Tsar**
king **sovereign** of *Babylon* **Babel**, my servant;
and the *beasts* **live beings** of the field
have I given him also to serve him.
7 And all *nations* **goyim** shall serve him,
and his son, and his son's son,
until the very time of his land come:
and then many *nations* **goyim** and great *kings* **sovereigns**
shall **cause him to** serve *themselves of him*.
8 And it shall *come to pass* **become**,
that the *nation* **goyim** and *kingdom* **sovereigndom**
which *will* **shall** not serve the same
Nebuchadnezzar **Nebukadnets Tsar**
king **sovereign** of *Babylon* **Babel**,
and that *will* **shall** not *put* **give** their neck
under the yoke of the *king* **sovereign** of *Babylon* **Babel**,
that *nation will I punish* **goyim shall I visit upon**,
saith the LORD **an oracle of Yah Veh**, with the sword,
and with the famine, and with the pestilence,
until I have consumed them by his hand.
9 Therefore hearken not ye to your prophets,
nor to your diviners, nor to your dreamers,
nor to your *enchanters* **cloudgazers**,
nor to your sorcerers,
which speak unto you, saying,
Ye shall not serve the *king* **sovereign** of *Babylon* **Babel**:
10 For they prophesy a *lie* **falsehood** unto you,
to remove you far from your *land* **soil**;
and that I should drive you out,
and ye should *perish* **destruct**.
11 But the *nations* **goyim** that bring their neck
under the yoke of the *king* **sovereign** of *Babylon* **Babel**,
and serve him,
those *will* **shall** I *let remain* **leave** still
in their own *land* **soil**,
saith the LORD **an oracle of Yah Veh**;
and they shall *till* **serve** it, and *dwell* **settle** therein.
12 I *spake* **worded** also
to *Zedekiah* **Sidqi Yah**
king **sovereign** of *Judah* **Yah Hudah**
according to all these words, saying,
Bring your necks
under the yoke of the *king* **sovereign** of *Babylon* **Babel**,
and serve him and his people, and live.
13 Why *will* **shall** ye die, thou and thy people,
by the sword, by the famine, and by the pestilence,
as *the LORD* **Yah Veh**
hath *spoken* **worded** against the *nation* **goyim**
that *will* **shall** not serve
the *king* **sovereign** of *Babylon* **Babel**?
14 Therefore hearken not unto the words of the prophets
that *speak* **say** unto you, saying,
Ye shall not serve the *king* **sovereign** of *Babylon* **Babel**:
for they prophesy a *lie* **falsehood** unto you.
15 For I have not sent them,
saith the LORD **an oracle of Yah Veh**,
yet they prophesy a *lie* **falsehood** in my name;
that I might drive you out,
and that ye might *perish* **destruct**,
ye, and the prophets that prophesy unto you.
16 Also I *spake* **worded**
to the priests and to all this people, saying,
Thus saith *the LORD* **Yah Veh**;
Hearken not to the words of your prophets
that prophesy unto you, saying, Behold,
the *vessels* **instruments**
of the *LORD'S* house **of Yah Veh**
shall now *shortly be brought again* **be quickly returned**
from *Babylon* **Babel**:
for they prophesy a *lie* **falsehood** unto you.
17 Hearken not unto them;
serve the *king* **sovereign** of *Babylon* **Babel**, and live:
wherefore should this city be *laid waste* **parched**?
18 But if they be prophets,

and if the word of *the LORD* **Yah Veh** be with them,
let them *now* **I beseech,** *make intercession* **intercede**
to *the LORD of hosts* **Yah Veh Sabaoth**,
that the *vessels* **instruments** which *are left* **remain**
in the house of *the LORD* **Yah Veh**,
and in the house
of the *king* **sovereign** of *Judah* **Yah Hudah**,
and at *Jerusalem* **Yeru Shalem**,
go not to *Babylon* **Babel**.
19 For thus saith *the LORD of hosts* **Yah Veh Sabaoth**
concerning the pillars,
and concerning the sea, and concerning the bases,
and concerning
the *residue* **rest** of the *vessels* **instruments**
that remain in this city,
20 Which *Nebuchadnezzar* **Nebukadnets Tsar**
king **sovereign** of *Babylon* **Babel** took not,
when he *carried away captive Jeconiah* **exiled Yechon Yah**
the son of *Jehoiakim* **Yah Yaqim**,
king **sovereign** of *Judah* **Yah Hudah**
from *Jerusalem* **Yeru Shalem** to *Babylon* **Babel**,
and all the nobles
of *Judah* **Yah Hudah** and *Jerusalem* **Yeru Shalem**;
21 Yea, thus saith *the LORD of hosts* **Yah Veh Sabaoth**,
the God **Elohim** of *Israel* **Yisra El**,
concerning the *vessels* **instruments**
that remain in the house of *the LORD* **Yah Veh**,
and in the house
of the *king* **sovereign** of *Judah* **Yah Hudah**
and of *Jerusalem* **Yeru Shalem**;
22 They shall be carried to *Babylon* **Babel**,
and there shall they be until the day that I visit them,
saith the LORD **an oracle of Yah Veh**;
then *will I bring them up* **shall I ascend them**,
and *restore* **return** them to this place.

HANAN YAH, THE PSEUDO PROPHET

28 And it *came to pass* **became,** the same year,
in the beginning of the *reign* **sovereigndom**
of *Zedekiah* **Sidqi Yah**
king **sovereign** of *Judah* **Yah Hudah**,
in the fourth year, *and* in the fifth month,
that Hananiah **Hanan Yah**
the son of *Azur* **Azzur** the prophet,
which was of *Gibeon* **Gibon**,
spake **said** unto me in the house of *the LORD* **Yah Veh**,
in the *presence* **eyes** of the priests and of all the people,
saying,
2 Thus *speaketh* **saith**
the LORD of hosts **Yah Veh Sabaoth**,
the God **Elohim** of *Israel* **Yisra El**, saying,
I have broken the yoke
of the *king* **sovereign** of *Babylon* **Babel**.
3 Within two *full* years **of days**
will I bring again **shall I restore** into this place
all the *vessels* **instruments**
of the *LORD'S* house **of Yah Veh**,
that *Nebuchadnezzar* **Nebukadnets Tsar**
king **sovereign** of *Babylon* **Babel**
took away from this place,
and carried them to *Babylon* **Babel**:
4 And I *will bring again* **shall restore** to this place
Jeconiah **Yechon Yah**
the son of *Jehoiakim* **Yah Yaqim**
king **sovereign** of *Judah* **Yah Hudah**,
with all the *captives* **exiles** of *Judah* **Yah Hudah**,
that went into *Babylon* **Babel**,
saith the LORD **an oracle of Yah Veh**:
for I *will* **shall** break the yoke
of the *king* **sovereign** of *Babylon* **Babel**.
5 Then the prophet *Jeremiah* **Yirme Yah**
said unto the prophet *Hananiah* **Hanan Yah**
in the *presence* **eyes** of the priests,
and in the *presence* **eyes** of all the people
that stood in the house of *the LORD* **Yah Veh**,
6 Even the prophet *Jeremiah* **Yirme Yah** said, Amen:
the LORD do **Yah Veh work** so:
the LORD perform **Yah Veh raise** thy words
which thou hast prophesied,
to *bring again* **return** the *vessels* **instruments**
of the *LORD'S* house **of Yah Veh**,
and all *that is carried away captive* **the exiles**,
from *Babylon* **Babel** into this place.
7 Nevertheless hear thou *now* **I beseech,**
this word that I *speak* **word** in thine ears,
and in the ears of all the people;
8 The prophets that have been *before me* **at my face**
and *before thee of old* **at thy face originally**
prophesied both against many *countries* **lands**,
and against great *kingdoms* **sovereigndoms**,
of war, and of evil, and of pestilence.
9 The prophet which prophesieth of *peace* **shalom**,
when the word of the prophet
shall *come to pass* **become**,
then shall the prophet be known,
that *the LORD* **Yah Veh** hath *truly* **in truth** sent him.
10 Then *Hananiah* **Hanan Yah** the prophet
took the yoke **pole**
from off the prophet *Jeremiah's* **Yirme Yah's** neck,
and brake it.
11 And *Hananiah* **Hanan Yah**
spake **said** in the *presence* **eyes** of all the people,
saying, Thus saith *the LORD* **Yah Veh**;
Even so *will* **shall** I break the yoke
of *Nebuchadnezzar* **Nebukadnets Tsar**
king **sovereign** of *Babylon* **Babel**
from the neck of all *nations* **goyim**
within the space of two *full* years **of days**.
And the prophet *Jeremiah* **Yirme Yah** went his way.
12 Then the word of *the LORD* **Yah Veh**
came unto *Jeremiah* **Yirme Yah** *the prophet*,
after that *Hananiah* **Hanan Yah** the prophet
had broken the yoke **pole** from off the neck
of the prophet *Jeremiah* **Yirme Yah**, saying,
13 Go and *tell Hananiah* **say to Hanan Yah**, saying,
Thus saith *the LORD* **Yah Veh**;
Thou hast broken the *yokes* **yoke poles** of *wood* **timber**;
but thou shalt *make* **work** for them
yokes **yoke poles** of iron.
14 For thus saith *the LORD of hosts* **Yah Veh Sabaoth**,
the God **Elohim** of *Israel* **Yisra El**;
I have *put* **given** a yoke of iron
upon the neck of all these *nations* **goyim**,
that they may serve
Nebuchadnezzar **Nebukadnets Tsar**
king **sovereign** of *Babylon* **Babel**;
and they shall serve him:
and I have given him
the *beasts* **live beings** of the field also.
15 Then said the prophet *Jeremiah* **Yirme Yah**
unto *Hananiah* **Hanan Yah** the prophet,
Hear *now Hananiah* **I beseech Hanan Yah**;
The LORD **Yah Veh** hath not sent thee;
but thou *makest* **causest** this people
to *trust* **confide** in a *lie* **falsehood**.
16 Therefore thus saith *the LORD* **Yah Veh**;
Behold, I *will cast* **shall send** thee
from off the face of the *earth* **soil**:
this year thou shalt die,
because thou hast *taught rebellion* **worded revolt**
against *the LORD* **Yah Veh**.
17 So *Hananiah* **Hanan Yah** the prophet
died the same year in the seventh month.

YIRME YAH'S SCROLL TO THE EXILES

29 *Now* these are the words of the *letter* **scroll**
that *Jeremiah* **Yirme Yah** the prophet
sent from *Jerusalem* **Yeru Shalem**
unto the *residue* **remnant** of the elders
which were *carried away captives* **exiled**,
and to the priests, and to the prophets,
and to all the people whom
Nebuchadnezzar **Nebukadnets Tsar**
king **sovereign** of *Babylon* **Babel**
had *carried away captive* **exiled**
from *Jerusalem* **Yeru Shalem** to *Babylon* **Babel**;
2 (After that *Jeconiah* **Yechon Yah** the *king* **sovereign**,
and the *queen* **lady**, and the eunuchs,
the *princes* **governors** of *Judah* **Yah Hudah**
and *Jerusalem* **Yeru Shalem**,
and the *carpenters* **engravers**, and the *smiths* **locksmiths**,
were departed from *Jerusalem* **Yeru Shalem**;)

3 By the hand of *Elasah* **El Asah** the son of Shaphan,
and *Gemariah* **Gemar Yah** the son of *Hilkiah* **Hilqi Yah**,
(whom *Zedekiah* **Sidqi Yah**
king **sovereign** of *Judah* **Yah Hudah**
sent unto *Babylon* **Babel**
to *Nebuchadnezzar* **Nebukadnets Tsar**
king **sovereign** of *Babylon* **Babel**) saying,
4 Thus saith *the LORD of hosts* **Yah Veh Sabaoth**,
the God **Elohim** of *Israel* **Yisra El**,
unto all that are *carried away captives* **exiled**,
whom I have caused to be *carried away* **exiled**
from *Jerusalem* **Yeru Shalem** unto *Babylon* **Babel**;
5 Build ye houses, and *dwell* **settle** *in them*;
and plant gardens, and eat the fruit of them;
6 Take ye *wives* **women**, and beget sons and daughters;
and take *wives* **women** for your sons,
and give your daughters to *husbands* **men**,
that they may bear sons and daughters;
that ye may *be increased* **abound** there,
and not *diminished* **diminish**.
7 And seek the *peace* **shalom** of the city
whither I have caused you
to be *carried away captives* **exiled**,
and pray unto *the LORD* **Yah Veh** for it:
for in *the peace* **shalom** *thereof*
shall ye have *peace* **shalom**.
8 For thus saith *the LORD of hosts* **Yah Veh Sabaoth**,
the God **Elohim** of *Israel* **Yisra El**;
Let not your prophets and your diviners,
that be in the midst of you, deceive you,
neither hearken to your dreams
which ye cause to be dreamed.
9 For they prophesy *falsely* **falsehood** unto you
in my name:
I have not sent them,
saith the LORD **an oracle of Yah Veh**.
10 For thus saith *the LORD* **Yah Veh**,
That *after* **according to my mouth**,
seventy years be *accomplished* **fulfilled**
at *Babylon* **Babel**,
I *will* **shall** visit you,
and *perform* **raise** my good word toward you,
in causing you to return to this place.
11 For I know the *thoughts* **fabrications**
that I *think* **fabricate** toward you,
saith the LORD **an oracle of Yah Veh**,
thoughts **fabrications** of *peace* **shalom**, and not of evil,
to give you an *expected* end **and hope**.
12 Then shall ye call upon me,
and ye shall go and pray unto me,
and I *will* **shall** hearken unto you.
13 And *ye* shall seek me, and find me,
when ye shall search for me with all your heart.
14 And I *will* **shall** be found of you,
saith the LORD **an oracle of Yah Veh**:
and I *will turn away* **shall restore** your captivity,
and I *will* **shall** gather you from all the *nations* **goyim**,
and from all the places whither I have driven you,
saith the LORD **an oracle of Yah Veh**;
and I *will bring* **shall return** you *again* into the place
whence I caused you to be *carried away captive* **exiled**.
15 Because ye have said, *The LORD* **Yah Veh**
hath raised us up prophets in *Babylon* **Babel**;
16 *Know that*
thus saith *the LORD* **Yah Veh** of the *king* **sovereign**
that *sitteth* **settleth** upon the throne of David,
and of all the people that *dwelleth* **settleth** in this city,
and of your brethren that are not gone forth with you
into *captivity* **exile**;
17 Thus saith *the LORD of hosts* **Yah Veh Sabaoth**;
Behold, I *will* **shall** send upon them the sword,
the famine, and the pestilence,
and *will make* **shall give** them like *vile* **putrified** figs,
that cannot be eaten, they are so evil.
18 And I *will persecute* **shall pursue after** them
with the sword, with the famine, and with the pestilence,
and *will deliver* **shall give** them
to be removed **for an agitation**
to all the *kingdoms* **sovereigndoms** of the earth,
to be a curse **for an oath**,
and *an astonishment* **a desolation**,
and an hissing, and a reproach,
among all the *nations* **goyim** whither I have driven them:
19 Because they have not hearkened to my words,
saith the LORD **an oracle of Yah Veh**,
which I sent unto them by my servants the prophets,
rising up **starting** early and sending them;
but ye *would not hear* **hearkened not**,
saith the LORD **an oracle of Yah Veh**.
20 Hear ye therefore the word of *the LORD* **Yah Veh**,
all ye *of the captivity* **exiles**,
whom I have sent
from *Jerusalem* **Yeru Shalem** to *Babylon* **Babel**:
21 Thus saith *the LORD of hosts* **Yah Veh Sabaoth**,
the God **Elohim** of *Israel* **Yisra El**,
of *Ahab* **Ach Ab** the son of *Kolaiah* **Kola Yah**,
and of *Zedekiah* **Sidqi Yah**
the son of *Maaseiah* **Maase Yah**,
which prophesy a *lie* **falsehood** unto you in my name;
Behold, I *will deliver* **shall give** them
into the hand of *Nebuchadrezzar* **Nebukadnets Tsar**
king **sovereign** of *Babylon* **Babel**,
and he shall *slay* **smite** them before your eyes;
22 And of them shall be taken up *a curse* **an abasement**
by all the *captivity* **exiles** of *Judah* **Yah Hudah**
which are in *Babylon* **Babel**, saying,
The LORD make **Yah Veh set** thee
like *Zedekiah* **Sidqi Yah** and like *Ahab* **Ach Ab**,
whom the *king* **sovereign** of *Babylon* **Babel**
roasted **scorched** in the fire;
23 Because they have *committed villany* **worked folly**
in *Israel* **Yisra El**,
and have *committed adultery* **adulterized**
with their *neighbour's wives* **friend's women**,
and have *spoken lying* **worded false** words in my name,
which I have not *commanded* **misvahed** them;
even I know, and am a witness,
saith the LORD **an oracle of Yah Veh**.
24 Thus shalt thou also *speak* **say**
to *Shemaiah* **Shema Yah**, the *Nehelamite* **Nechlamiy**,
saying,
25 Thus *speaketh* **saith**
the LORD of hosts **Yah Veh Sabaoth**,
the God **Elohim** of *Israel* **Yisra El**, saying,
Because thou hast sent *letters* **scrolls** in thy name
unto all the people that are at *Jerusalem* **Yeru Shalem**,
and to *Zephaniah* **Sephan Yah**
the son of *Maaseiah* **Maase Yah** the priest,
and to all the priests, saying,
26 *The LORD* **Yah Veh** hath *made* **given** thee priest
in the stead of *Jehoiada* **Yah Yada** the priest,
that ye should be *officers* **overseers**
in the house of *the LORD* **Yah Veh**,
for every man that is *mad* **insane**,
and *maketh himself a prophet* **prophesieth**,
that thou shouldest *put* **give** him
in prison **to the stockade**, and in the stocks.
27 Now therefore why hast thou not *reproved* **rebuked**
Jeremiah **Yirme Yah** of *Anathoth* **Anathothiy**,
which *maketh himself a prophet* **prophesieth** to you?
28 For therefore he sent unto us in *Babylon* **Babel**,
saying, This *captivity* is long:
build ye houses, and *dwell* **settle** *in them*;
and plant gardens, and eat the fruit of them.
29 And *Zephaniah* **Sephan Yah** the priest
read **called out** this *letter* **scroll**
in the ears of *Jeremiah* **Yirme Yah** the prophet.
30 Then came the word of *the LORD* **Yah Veh**
unto *Jeremiah* **Yirme Yah**, saying,
31 Send to all *them of the captivity* **the exiles**, saying,
Thus saith *the LORD* **Yah Veh**
concerning *Shemaiah* **Shema Yah**
the *Nehelamite* **Nechlamiy**;
Because that *Shemaiah* **Shema Yah**
hath prophesied unto you, and I sent him not,
and he caused you to *trust* **confide** in a *lie* **falsehood**:
32 Therefore thus saith *the LORD* **Yah Veh**;
Behold, I *will punish* **shall visit upon**
Shemaiah **Shema Yah** the *Nehelamite* **Nechlamiy**,
and his seed:

he shall not have a man
to *dwell* **settle** among this people;
neither shall he *behold* **see** the good
that I *will do* **shall work** for my people,
saith the LORD **an oracle of Yah Veh**;
because he hath *taught rebellion* **worded revolt**
against *the LORD* **Yah Veh**.

YISRA EL RESTORED

30 The word that came to *Jeremiah* **Yirme Yah**
from *the LORD* **Yah Veh**, saying,
2 Thus *speaketh* **saith**
the LORD God **Yah Veh Elohim** of *Israel* **Yisra El**, saying,
Write **Inscribe** thee all the words
that I have *spoken* **worded** unto thee in a *book* **scroll**.
3 For, *lo* **behold**, the days come,
saith the LORD **an oracle of Yah Veh**,
that I *will bring again* **shall restore**
the captivity of my people
Israel **Yisra El** and *Judah* **Yah Hudah**,
saith *the LORD* **Yah Veh**:
and I *will* **shall** cause them to return to the land
that I gave to their fathers, and they shall possess it.
4 And these are the words
that *the LORD spake* **Yah Veh worded**
concerning *Israel* **Yisra El**
and concerning *Judah* **Yah Hudah**.
5 For thus saith *the LORD* **Yah Veh**;
We have heard a voice of trembling,
of fear, and not of *peace* **shalom**.
6 Ask ye *now* **I beseech**,
and see whether
a *man doth travail with child* **male shall birth**?
wherefore do I see every *man* **mighty**
with his hands on his loins,
as a woman *in travail* **birthing**,
and all faces are turned into *paleness* **pale green**?
7 *Alas* **Ho**! for that day is great, so that none is like it:
it is even the time of *Jacob's trouble* **Yaaqov's tribulation**,
but he shall be saved out of it.
8 For it shall *come to pass* **become,** in that day,
saith the LORD of hosts **an oracle of Yah Veh Sabaoth**,
that I *will* **shall** break his yoke from off thy neck,
and *will burst* **shall tear** thy bonds,
and strangers shall no more
cause him to serve *themselves of him*:
9 But they shall serve
the LORD **Yah Veh** their *God* **Elohim**,
and David their *king* **sovereign**,
whom I *will* **shall** raise *up* unto them.
10 Therefore *fear* **awe** thou not,
O my servant *Jacob* **Yaaqov**,
saith the LORD **an oracle of Yah Veh**;
neither be dismayed, O *Israel* **Yisra El**: for, *lo* **behold**,
I *will save thee* **am thy saviour** from afar,
and thy seed from the land of their captivity;
and *Jacob* **Yaaqov** shall return,
and shall *be in* rest, and *be quiet* **relax**,
and none shall make him *afraid* **tremble**.
11 For I am with thee,
saith the LORD **an oracle of Yah Veh**,
to save thee:
though I *make a full end* **work a final finish**
of all *nations* **goyim** whither I have scattered thee,
yet I *will* **shall** not *make a full end* **work a final finish**
of thee:
but I *will correct* **shall discipline** thee
in *measure* **judgment**,
and *will not leave thee altogether unpunished.*
in exonerating, shall not exonerate thee
12 For thus saith *the LORD* **Yah Veh**,
Thy *bruise* **breech** is incurable,
and thy wound is *grievous* **worn**.
13 There is none to plead thy cause,
that thou mayest be *bound up* **bandaged**:
thou hast no *healing medicines* **bandage healers**.
14 All thy lovers have forgotten thee; they seek thee not;
for I have *wounded* **smitten** thee
with the wound of an enemy,
with the chastisement of a cruel one,
for the *multitude* **abundance**
of *thine iniquity* **thy perversity**;
because thy sins were *increased* **mighty**.
15 Why criest thou for *thine affliction* **thy breech**?
thy sorrow is incurable
for the *multitude* **abundance**
of *thine iniquity* **thy perversity**:
because thy sins were *increased* **mighty**,
I have *done* **worked** these *things* unto thee.
16 Therefore all they that devour thee shall be devoured;
and all *thine adversaries* **thy tribulators**,
every one of them, shall go into captivity;
and they that *spoil* **plunder** thee
shall be *a spoil* **plundered**,
and all that *prey upon* **plunder** thee
will **shall** I give for a *prey* **plunder**.
17 For I *will restore* **shall ascend** health unto thee,
and I *will* **shall** heal thee of thy wounds,
saith the LORD **an oracle of Yah Veh**;
because they called thee *an Outcast* **Expelled**, *saying,*
This is *Zion* **Siyon**, whom no man seeketh after.
18 Thus saith *the LORD* **Yah Veh**; Behold,
I *will bring again* **shall restore**
the captivity of *Jacob's* **Yaaqov's** tents,
and *have* **shall** mercy *on* his *dwellingplaces* **tabernacles**;
and the city shall be builded upon her own heap,
and the *palace* **citadel** shall *remain* **be settled**
after the *manner* **judgment** *thereof.*
19 And out of them
shall proceed *thanksgiving* **extended hands**
and the voice of them that *make merry* **ridicule**:
and I *will multiply* **shall abound** them,
and they shall not be *few* **diminished**;
I *will also glorify* **shall honour** them,
and they shall not be *small* **belittled**.
20 Their *children* **sons** also shall be as *aforetime* **formerly**,
and their *congregation* **witness**
shall be established *before me* **at my face**,
and I *will punish* **shall visit upon** all that oppress them.
21 And their *nobles* **mighty** shall be of themselves,
and their *governor* **sovereign**
shall proceed from the midst of them;
and I *will* **shall** cause him to *draw near* **approach**,
and he shall approach unto me:
for who is this
that *engaged* **pleased** his heart to approach unto me?
saith the LORD **an oracle of Yah Veh**.
22 And ye *shall* be my people,
and *I will be* **I AM** your *God* **Elohim**.
23 Behold, the *whirlwind* **storm** of *the LORD* **Yah Veh**
goeth forth with fury,
a continuing *whirlwind* **storm**:
it shall *fall with pain* **whirl** upon the head of the wicked.
24 The *fierce anger* **fuming wrath** of *the LORD* **Yah Veh**
shall not return,
until he hath *done* **worked** it,
and until he have *performed* **raised**
the *intents* **intrigue** of his heart:
in the latter days ye shall *consider* **discern** it.

YAH VEH'S ETERNAL LOVE

31 At the same time,
saith the LORD **an oracle of Yah Veh**,
will I **shall** be *the God* **Elohim**
of all the families of *Israel* **Yisra El**,
and they shall be my people.
2 Thus saith *the LORD* **Yah Veh**,
The people, *which were left* **the survivors** of the sword
found *grace* **charism** in the wilderness;
even Israel **Yisra El**, when I went to cause him to rest.
3 *The LORD* **Yah Veh**
hath *appeared* **been seen**
of old unto me **by me in the distance**, *saying,*
Yea, I have loved thee with an *everlasting* **eternal** love:
therefore with lovingkindness have I drawn thee.
4 Again I *will* **shall** build thee, and thou shalt be built,
O virgin of *Israel* **Yisra El**:
thou shalt again be adorned
with thy *tabrets* **tambourines**,
and shalt go forth in the *dances* **round dancing**
of them that *make merry* **entertain**.
5 Thou shalt yet plant vines

upon the mountains of *Samaria* **Shomeron**:
the planters shall plant,
and shall *eat* **profane** them *as common things*.
6 For there shall be a day,
that the *watchmen* **guards**
upon the mount *Ephraim* **Ephrayim** shall *cry* **call**,
Arise ye, and let us *go up* **ascend** to *Zion* **Siyon**
unto *the LORD* **Yah Veh** our *God* **Elohim.**
7 For thus saith *the LORD* **Yah Veh**;
Sing **Shout** with *gladness* **cheerfulness** for *Jacob* **Yaaqov**,
and *shout* **resound** among the chief of the *nations* **goyim**:
publish ye **let it be heard**, praise ye, and say,
O *LORD* **Yah Veh**, save thy people,
the *remnant* **survivors** of *Israel* **Yisra El**.
8 Behold,
I *will* **shall** bring them from the north *country* **land**,
and gather them from the *coasts* **flanks** of the *earth* **land**,
and with them the blind and the lame,
the woman with child
and her that *travaileth with child* **birtheth** together:
a great *company* **congregation** shall return thither.
9 They shall come with weeping,
and with supplications *will* **shall** I lead them:
I *will* **shall** cause them
to walk by the *rivers* **wadies** of waters in a straight way,
wherein they shall not *stumble* **falter**:
for I am a father to *Israel* **Yisra El**,
and *Ephraim* **Ephrayim** is my firstborn.
10 Hear the word of *the LORD* **Yah Veh**,
O ye *nations* **goyim**,
and *declare* **tell** it in the *isles* **islands** afar off, and say,
He that *scattered Israel* **winnowed Yisra El**
will **shall** gather him, and *keep* **guard** him,
as a *shepherd doth* **tender** his *flock* **drove**.
11 For *the LORD* **Yah Veh** hath redeemed *Jacob* **Yaaqov**,
and *ransomed* **redeemed** him
from the hand *of him* that was stronger than he.
12 Therefore they shall come
and *sing* **shout** in the height of *Zion* **Siyon**,
and shall flow together
to the goodness of *the LORD* **Yah Veh**,
for *wheat* **crop**, and for *wine* **juice**, and for oil,
and for the *young* **sons** of the flock and of the herd:
and their soul shall be as a *watered* **saturated** garden;
and they shall not
sorrow any more at all **add to languish**.
13 Then shall the virgin
rejoice **cheer** in the *dance* **round dancing**,
both *young men* **youths** and *old* **elders** together:
for I *will* **shall** turn their mourning into *joy* **rejoicing**,
and *will comfort* **shall sigh over** them,
and *make* **cheer** them *rejoice* from their *sorrow* **grief**.
14 And I *will* **shall**
satiate the soul of the priests with fatness,
and my people shall be satisfied with my goodness,
saith the LORD **an oracle of Yah Veh**.
15 Thus saith *the LORD* **Yah Veh**;
A voice was heard in Ramah,
lamentation, *and bitter* weeping **of bitterness**;
Rahel **Rachel** weeping for her *children* **sons**
refused to *be comforted* **sigh** for her *children* **sons**,
because they were not.
16 Thus saith *the LORD* **Yah Veh**;
Refrain **Withhold** thy voice from weeping,
and thine eyes from tears:
for *thy work shall be rewarded*
thou shalt have a hire for thy deeds,
saith the LORD **an oracle of Yah Veh**;
and they shall *come again* **turn back**
from the land of the enemy.
17 And there is hope in thine end,
saith the LORD **an oracle of Yah Veh**,
that thy *children* **sons**
shall *come again* **turn back** to their own border.
18 **In hearing,** I have *surely* heard *Ephraim* **Ephrayim**
bemoaning **wagging over** himself *thus;*
Thou hast chastised me, and I was *chastised* **disciplined**,
as a *bullock unaccustomed to the yoke* **calf not trained**:
turn thou me, and I shall be turned;
for thou art *the LORD* **Yah Veh** my *God* **Elohim**.
19 Surely after that I was turned, I *repented* **sighed**;
and after that I was instructed,
I *smote* **slapped** upon my *thigh* **flank**:
I was *ashamed* **shamed**, yea, even confounded,
because I did bear the reproach of my youth.
20 Is *Ephraim* **Ephrayim** my *dear* **esteemed** son?
is he a pleasant child — **a child of delights**?
for since I *spake* **worded sufficient** against him,
I do earnestly **In remembering, I** remember him still:
therefore my *bowels* **inwards** are troubled for him;
I will surely have mercy upon
In mercying, I shall mercy him,
saith the LORD **an oracle of Yah Veh**.
21 *Set thee up waymarks* **Station monuments**,
make **set** thee *high heaps* **pillars**:
set thine heart toward the highway,
even the way which thou wentest:
turn again, O virgin of *Israel* **Yisra El**,
turn again to these thy cities.
22 How long *wilt* **shalt** thou go about,
O thou *backsliding* **apostate** daughter?
for *the LORD* **Yah Veh**
hath created *a new thing* **newness** in the earth,
A *woman* **female** shall *compass* **surround** a *man* **mighty**.
23 Thus saith *the LORD of hosts* **Yah Veh Sabaoth**,
the God **Elohim** of *Israel* **Yisra El**;
As yet they shall *use* **say** this *speech* **word**
in the land of *Judah* **Yah Hudah** and in the cities *thereof,*
when I shall *bring again* **restore** their captivity;
The LORD **Yah Veh** bless thee,
O habitation **of rest** of *justice* **justness**,
and mountain of holiness.
24 And there shall *dwell* **settle** in *Judah* **Yah Hudah** itself,
and in all the cities *thereof* together,
husbandmen **cultivators**,
and they that go forth with *flocks* **droves**.
25 For I have satiated the *weary* **languid** soul,
and I have *replenished* **fulfilled**
every *sorrowful* **languishing** soul.
26 Upon this I awaked, and *beheld* **saw**;
and my sleep *was sweet unto* **pleased** me.
27 Behold, the days come,
saith the LORD **an oracle of Yah Veh**,
that I *will* **shall** sow the house of *Israel* **Yisra El**
and the house of *Judah* **Yah Hudah**
with the seed of *man* **humanity**,
and with the seed of *beast* **animal**.
28 And it shall *come to pass* **become**,
that like as I have watched over them,
to *pluck up* **uproot**, and to break down,
and to *throw down* **demolish**, and to destroy,
and to *afflict* **vilify**;
so *will* **shall** I watch over them, to build, and to plant,
saith the LORD **an oracle of Yah Veh**.
29 In those days they shall say no more,
The fathers have eaten a sour grape,
and the *children's* **sons's** teeth are *set on edge* **dull**.
30 But every *one* **man** shall die
for his own *iniquity* **perversity**:
every man **all humanity** that eateth the sour grape,
his teeth shall be *set on edge* **dulled**.

YAH VEH CUTS A NEW COVENANT

31 Behold, the days come,
saith the LORD **an oracle of Yah Veh**,
that I *will make* **shall cut** a new covenant
with the house of *Israel* **Yisra El**,
and with the house of *Judah* **Yah Hudah**:
32 Not according to the covenant
that I *made* **cut** with their fathers
in the day that I *took* **held** them by the hand
to bring them out of the land of *Egypt* **Misrayim**;
which my covenant they brake,
although I was *an husband* **a master** unto them,
saith the LORD **an oracle of Yah Veh**:
33 But this shall be the covenant
that I *will make* **shall cut** with the house of *Israel* **Yisra El**;
After those days,
saith the LORD **an oracle of Yah Veh**,
I *will put* **shall give** my *law* **torah**
in their *inward parts* **inwards**,

and *write* **inscribe** it in their hearts;
and *will* **shall** be their *God* **Elohim**,
and they shall be my people.
34 And they shall teach no more
every man his *neighbour* **friend**,
and every man his brother, saying,
Know *the LORD* **Yah Veh**:
for they shall all know me,
from the least of them unto the greatest of them,
saith the LORD **an oracle of Yah Veh**:
for I *will* **shall** forgive their *iniquity* **perversity**,
and I *will* **shall** remember their sin no more.
35 Thus saith *the LORD* **Yah Veh**,
which giveth the sun for a light by day,
and the *ordinances* **statutes** of the moon and of the stars
for a light by night,
which *divideth* **spliteth** the sea
when the waves *thereof* roar;
The LORD of hosts **Yah Veh Sabaoth** is his name:
36 If those *ordinances* **statutes**
depart from *before me* **my face**,
saith the LORD **an oracle of Yah Veh**,
then the seed of *Israel* **Yisra El** also
shall *cease* **shabbathizeth**
from being a *nation before me* **goyim at my face**
for ever **all the days**.
37 Thus saith *the LORD* **Yah Veh**;
If *heaven* **the heavens** above can be measured,
and the foundations of the earth
searched out beneath **probed downward**,
I *will* **shall** also
cast off **spurn** all the seed of *Israel* **Yisra El**
for all that they have *done* **worked**,
saith the LORD **an oracle of Yah Veh**.

THE NEW CITY

38 Behold, the days come,
saith the LORD **an oracle of Yah Veh**,
that the city shall be built to *the LORD* **Yah Veh**
from the tower of *Hananeel* **Hanan El**
unto the *gate* **portal** of the corner.
39 And the measuring line shall *yet* go forth
over against it upon the hill Gareb,
and shall compass about *to Goath* **Goah**.
40 And the whole valley of the *dead bodies* **carcases**,
and of the *ashes* **fat**,
and all the fields unto the *brook* **wadi** of *Kidron* **Qidron**,
unto the corner of the horse *gate* **portal**
toward the *east* **rising**,
shall be holy unto *the LORD* **Yah Veh**;
it shall not be *plucked up* **uprooted**,
nor thrown down any more *for ever* **eternally**.

YIRME YAH SHUT UP

32 The word that came to *Jeremiah* **Yirme Yah**
from *the LORD* **Yah Veh**
in the tenth year of *Zedekiah* **Sidqi Yah**
king **sovereign** of *Judah* **Yah Hudah**,
which **year** was the eighteenth year
of *Nebuchadrezzar* **Nebukadnets Tsar**.
2 For then the *king* **sovereign**
of *Babylon's army* **Babel's valiant**
besieged *Jerusalem* **Yeru Shalem**:
and *Jeremiah* **Yirme Yah** the prophet
was shut up in the court of the *prison* **target area**,
which was in
the *king* **sovereign** of *Judah's* **Yah Hudah's** house.
3 For *Zedekiah* **Sidqi Yah**
king **sovereign** of *Judah* **Yah Hudah**
had shut him up, saying,
Wherefore dost thou prophesy, *and say* **saying**,
Thus saith *the LORD* **Yah Veh**,
Behold, I *will* **shall** give this city
into the hand of the *king* **sovereign** of *Babylon* **Babel**,
and he shall *take* **capture** it;
4 And *Zedekiah* **Sidqi Yah**
king **sovereign** of *Judah* **Yah Hudah**
shall not escape
out of the hand of the *Chaldeans* **Kesediym**,
but **in giving,** shall *surely* be *delivered* **given**
into the hand of the *king* **sovereign** of *Babylon* **Babel**,
and shall *speak* **word** with him mouth to mouth,
and his eyes shall *behold* **see** his eyes;
5 And he shall *lead Zedekiah* **carry Sidqi Yah**
to *Babylon* **Babel**,
and there shall he be until I visit him,
saith the LORD **an oracle of Yah Veh**:
though ye fight with the *Chaldeans* **Kesediym**,
ye shall not prosper.

YIRME YAH CHATTELS A FIELD

6 And *Jeremiah* **Yirme Yah** said,
The word of *the LORD* **Yah Veh** came unto me, saying,
7 Behold,
Hanameel **Hanam El** the son of Shallum thine uncle
shall come unto thee, saying,
Buy **Chattel** thee my field that is in Anathoth:
for the *right* **judgment** of redemption
is thine to *buy* **chattel** it.
8 So *Hanameel* **Hanam El** mine uncle's son
came to me in the court of the *prison* **target area**
according to the word of *the LORD* **Yah Veh**,
and said unto me,
Buy **Chattel** my field, *I pray* **beseech** thee,
that is in Anathoth,
which is in the *country* **land** of *Benjamin* **Ben Yamin**:
for the *right* **judgment** of *inheritance* **possession** is thine,
and the redemption is thine; *buy* **chattel** it for thyself.
Then I knew
that this was the word of *the LORD* **Yah Veh**.
9 And I *bought* **chatteled** the field of *Hanameel* **Hanam El**
my uncle's son, that was in Anathoth,
and weighed him the *money* **silver**,
even seventeen shekels of silver.
10 And I *subscribed* **inscribed** the *evidence* **scroll**,
and sealed *it*, and *took* **witnessed** witnesses,
and weighed him the *money* **silver** in the balances.
11 So I took the *evidence* **scroll** of the *purchase* **chattel**,
both that which was sealed
according to the *law* **misvah** and *custom* **statute**,
and that which was *open* **exposed**:
12 And I gave the *evidence* **scroll** of the *purchase* **chattel**
unto Baruch the son of *Neriah* **Neri Yah**,
the son of *Maaseiah* **Machse Yah**,
in the *sight* **eyes** of *Hanameel* **Hanam El**
mine uncle's *son*,
and in the *presence* **eyes** of the witnesses
that *subscribed* **inscribed** the *book* **scroll**
of the *purchase* **chattel**,
before **in the eyes of** all the *Jews* **Yah Hudiym**
that sat in the court of the *prison* **target area**.
13 And I *charged* **misvahed** Baruch
before them **in their eyes**, saying,
14 Thus saith *the LORD of hosts* **Yah Veh Sabaoth**,
the God **Elohim** of *Israel* **Yisra El**;
Take these *evidences* **scrolls**,
this *evidence* **scroll** of the *purchase* **chattel**,
both which is sealed,
and this *evidence* **scroll** which is *open* **exposed**;
and *put* **give** them
in *an earthen vessel* **a potsherd instrument**,
that they may *continue* **stand** many days.
15 For thus saith *the LORD of hosts* **Yah Veh Sabaoth**,
the God **Elohim** of *Israel* **Yisra El**;
Houses and fields and vineyards
shall be *possessed* **chatteled** again in this land.
16 *Now when* **After** I had *delivered* **given**
the *evidence* **scroll** of the *purchase* **chattel**
unto Baruch the son of *Neriah* **Neri Yah**,
I prayed unto *the LORD* **Yah Veh**, saying,
17 *Ah Lord GOD* **Aha Adonay Yah Veh**! behold,
thou hast *made* **worked**
the *heaven* **heavens** and the earth
by thy great power and stretched out arm,
and there is *nothing* **no word**
too *hard* **marvellous** for thee:
18 Thou *shewest lovingkindness* **workest mercy**
unto thousands,
and *recompensest* **shalam**
iniquity **for the perversity** of the fathers
into the bosom of their *children* **sons** after them:
the Great, the Mighty *God* **El**,
the LORD of hosts **Yah Veh Sabaoth**, is his name,

19 Great in counsel, and *mighty* **great** in *work* **exploits**:
for thine eyes are open
upon all the ways of the sons of *men* **humanity**:
to give every *one* **man** according to his ways,
and according to the fruit of his *doings* **exploits**:
20 Which hast set signs and *wonders* **omens**
in the land of *Egypt* **Misrayim**, *even* unto this day,
and in *Israel* **Yisra El**, and among *other men* **humanity**;
and hast *made* **worked** thee a name, as at this day;
21 And hast brought forth thy people *Israel* **Yisra El**
out of the land of *Egypt* **Misrayim** with signs,
and with *wonders* **omens**,
and with a strong hand, and with a stretched out arm,
and with great *terror* **awesomeness**;
22 And hast given them this land,
which thou didst *swear* **oath** to their fathers to give them,
a land flowing with milk and honey;
23 And they came in, and possessed it;
but they *obeyed* **hearkened** not *unto* thy voice,
neither walked in thy *law* **torah**;
they have *done nothing* **not worked**
of all that thou *commandedst* **misvahedst** them
to *do* **work**:
therefore thou hast *caused* **confronted** all this evil
to come upon them:
24 Behold the mounts,
they are come unto the city to *take* **capture** it;
and the city
is given into the hand of the *Chaldeans* **Kesediym**,
that fight against it, *because* **at the face** of the sword,
and of the famine, and of the pestilence:
and what thou hast *spoken* **worded**
is *come to pass* **become**;
and, behold, thou seest it.
25 And thou hast said unto me,
O Lord GOD **Adonay Yah Veh**,
Buy **Chattel** thee the field for *money* **silver**,
and *take* **witness** witnesses;
for the city
is given into the hand of the *Chaldeans* **Kesediym**.

YAH VEH'S RESPONSE

26 Then came the word of *the LORD* **Yah Veh**
unto *Jeremiah* **Yirme Yah**, saying,
27 Behold,
I am the LORD **I — Yah Veh**, *the God* **Elohim** of all flesh:
is there any *thing* **word** too *hard* **marvellous** for me?
28 Therefore thus saith *the LORD* **Yah Veh**;
Behold,
I *will* **shall** give this city
into the hand of the *Chaldeans* **Kesediym**,
and into the hand of
Nebuchadrezzar **Nebukadnets Tsar**
king **sovereign** of *Babylon* **Babel**,
and he shall take it:
29 And the *Chaldeans* **Kesediym**,
that fight against this city,
shall come and *set* **kindle** fire on this city,
and burn it with the houses,
upon whose roofs
they have *offered incense* **incensed** unto Baal,
and *poured out drink offerings* **libated libations**
unto other *gods* **elohim**, to *provoke* **vex** me *to anger*.
30 For the *children* **sons** of *Israel* **Yisra El**
and the *children* **sons** of *Judah* **Yah Hudah**
have only *done* **worked** evil *before me* **in my eyes**
from their youth:
for the *children* **sons** of *Israel* **Yisra El**
have only *provoked* **vexed** me *to anger*
with the work of their hands,
saith the LORD **an oracle of Yah Veh**.
31 For this city hath been to me
as a provocation of *mine anger* **my wrath** and of my fury
from the day that they built it even unto this day;
that I should *remove it* **turn it aside** from before my face,
32 Because of all the evil
of the *children* **sons** of *Israel* **Yisra El**
and of the *children* **sons** of *Judah* **Yah Hudah**,
which they have *done* **worked**
to *provoke* **vex** me *to anger*,
they, their *kings* **sovereigns**,
their *princes* **governors**, their priests, and their prophets,
and the men of *Judah* **Yah Hudah**,
and the *inhabitants* **settlers** of *Jerusalem* **Yeru Shalem**.
33 And they have *turned* **faced** unto me the *back* **neck**,
and not the face:
though I taught them,
rising up **starting** early and teaching them,
yet they have not hearkened
to *receive instruction* **take discipline**.
34 But they set their abominations in the house,
which is called by my name, to *defile* **foul** it.
35 And they built the *high places* **bamahs** of Baal,
which are in
the valley of the son of Hinnom
Gay Ben Hinnom/Valley of the Son of Burning,
to cause their sons and their daughters
to pass through *the fire* unto Molech;
which I *commanded* **misvahed** them not,
neither *came* **ascended** it into my *mind* **heart**,
that they should *do* **work** this *abomination* **abhorrence**,
to cause *Judah* **Yah Hudah** to sin.
36 And now therefore thus saith *the LORD* **Yah Veh**,
the God **Elohim** of *Israel* **Yisra El**,
concerning this city, whereof ye say,
It shall be *delivered* **given** into the hand
of the *king* **sovereign** of *Babylon* **Babel**
by the sword, and by the famine, and by the pestilence;
37 Behold,
I *will* **shall** gather them out of all *countries* **lands**,
whither I have driven them in *mine anger* **my wrath**,
and in my fury, and in great *wrath* **rage**;
and I *will bring* **shall return** them *again* unto this place,
and I *will* **shall** cause them
to *dwell safely* **settle confidently**:
38 And they *shall* be my people,
and *I will be* **I AM** their *God* **Elohim**:
39 And I *will* **shall** give them one heart, and one way,
that they may *fear* **awe** me for ever,
for the good of them,
and of their *children* **sons** after them:
40 And I *will make* **shall cut**
an *everlasting* **eternal** covenant with them,
that I *will* **shall** not turn away from **after** them,
to *do* **well—please** them *good*;
but I *will put* **shall give** my fear in their hearts,
that they shall not *depart* **turn aside** from me.
41 Yea, I *will* **shall** rejoice over them to do them good,
and I *will* **shall** plant them in this land
assuredly **in truth**
with my whole heart and with my whole soul.
42 For thus saith *the LORD* **Yah Veh**;
Like as I have brought all this great evil upon this people,
so *will* **shall** I bring upon them all the good
that I have *promised* **worded** them.
43 And fields shall be *bought* **chatteled** in this land,
whereof ye say,
It is desolate without *man* **humanity** or *beast* **animal**;
it is given into the hand of the *Chaldeans* **Kesediym**.
44 Men shall *buy* **chattel** fields for *money* **silver**,
and *subscribe evidences* **inscribe scrolls**, and seal them,
and *take* **witness** witnesses
in the land of *Benjamin* **Ben Yamin**,
and *in the places* **round** about *Jerusalem* **Yeru Shalem**,
and in the cities of *Judah* **Yah Hudah**,
and in the cities of the mountains,
and in the cities of the *valley* **lowland**,
and in the cities of the south:
for I *will cause* **shall restore** their captivity *to return*,
saith the LORD **an oracle of Yah Veh**.

THE RESTORATION BY YAH VEH

33 Moreover the word of *the LORD* **Yah Veh**
came unto *Jeremiah* **Yirme Yah**
the second time **secondly**,
while he was yet *shut up* **restrained**
in the court of the *prison* **target area**, saying,
2 Thus saith *the LORD* **Yah Veh**
the *maker* **worker** *thereof*,
the LORD **Yah Veh** that formed it, to establish it;
the LORD **Yah Veh** is his name;
3 Call unto me, and I *will* **shall** answer thee,

and *shew* **tell** thee great and *mighty things* **fortified**,
which thou knowest not.
4 For thus saith *the LORD* **Yah Veh**,
the God **Elohim** of *Israel* **Yisra El**,
concerning the houses of this city,
and concerning the houses
of the *kings* **sovereigns** of *Judah* **Yah Hudah**,
which are *thrown* **pulled** down by the mounts,
and by the sword;
5 They come to fight with the *Chaldeans* **Kesediym**,
but it is to fill them
with the *dead bodies* **carcases** of *men* **humanity**,
whom I have *slain* **smitten**
in *mine anger* **my wrath** and in my fury,
and for all whose *wickedness* **evil**
I have hid my face from this city.
6 Behold,
I *will bring* **shall ascend** it health and *cure* **healing**,
and I *will cure* **shall heal** them,
and *will reveal* **shall expose** unto them
the abundance of *peace* **shalom** and truth.
7 And I *will cause* **shall restore**
the captivity of *Judah* **Yah Hudah**
and the captivity of *Israel* **Yisra El** *to return*,
and *will* **shall** build them, as at the first.
8 And I *will cleanse* **shall purify** them
from all their *iniquity* **perversity**,
whereby they have sinned against me;
and I *will pardon* **shall forgive**
all their *iniquities* **perversities**,
whereby they have sinned,
and whereby they have *transgressed* **rebelled** against me.
9 And it shall be to me a name of *joy* **rejoicing**,
a *praise* **halal** and an *honour* **adornment**
before all the *nations* **goyim** of the earth,
which shall hear all the good that I *do* **work** unto them:
and they shall fear and *tremble* **quiver**
for all the goodness and for all the *prosperity* **shalom**
that I *procure* **work** unto it.
10 Thus saith *the LORD* **Yah Veh**;
Again there shall be heard in this place,
which ye say shall be *desolate* **parched dry**
without *man* **humanity** and without *beast* **animal**,
even in the cities of *Judah* **Yah Hudah**,
and in the *streets* **outways** of *Jerusalem* **Yeru Shalem**,
that are *desolate* **desolated**, without *man* **humanity**,
and without *inhabitant* **settler**, and without *beast* **animal**,
11 The voice of *joy* **rejoicing**,
and the voice of *gladness* **cheerfulness**,
the voice of the bridegroom, and the voice of the bride,
the voice of them that shall say,
Praise **Extend hands**
the LORD of hosts **unto Yah Veh Sabaoth**:
for *the LORD* **Yah Veh** is good;
for his mercy *endureth for ever* **be eternal**:
and of them
that shall bring *the sacrifice of praise* **extended hands**
into the house of *the LORD* **Yah Veh**.
For I *will* **shall** cause to *return* **restore**
the captivity of the land, as at the first,
saith *the LORD* **Yah Veh**.
12 Thus saith *the LORD of hosts* **Yah Veh Sabaoth**;
Again in this place, which is *desolate* **parched dry**
without *man* **humanity** and without *beast* **animal**,
and in all the cities *thereof*,
shall be an habitation **of rest** of *shepherds* **tenders**
causing their flocks to *lie down* **crouch**.
13 In the cities of the mountains,
in the cities of the *vale* **lowland**,
and in the cities of the south,
and in the land of *Benjamin* **Ben Yamin**,
and in the places **round** about *Jerusalem* **Yeru Shalem**,
and in the cities of *Judah* **Yah Hudah**,
shall the flocks pass again
under the hands of him that telleth them,
saith *the LORD* **Yah Veh**.
14 Behold, the days come,
saith the LORD **an oracle of Yah Veh**,
that I *will perform* **shall raise** that good *thing* **word**
which I have *promised* **worded**
unto the house of *Israel* **Yisra El**
and to the house of *Judah* **Yah Hudah**.
15 In those days, and at that time,
will **shall** I cause
the *Branch* **Sprout** of *righteousness* **justness**
to *grow up* **sprout** unto David;
and he shall *execute* **work**
judgment and *righteousness* **justness** in the land.
16 In those days shall *Judah* **Yah Hudah** be saved,
and *Jerusalem* **Yeru Shalem**
shall *dwell safely* **tabernacle confidently**:
and this is the name wherewith she shall be called,
The LORD our righteousness **Yah Veh Sidqenuw**.
17 For thus saith *the LORD* **Yah Veh**;
David shall never *want* **cut** a man to sit upon the throne
of the house of *Israel* **Yisra El**;
18 Neither shall the priests the *Levites* **Leviym**
want **cut** a man *before me* **at my face**
to *offer burnt offerings* **holocaust holocausts**,
and to *kindle meat* **incense** offerings,
and to *do* **work** sacrifice continually.
19 And the word of *the LORD* **Yah Veh**
came unto *Jeremiah* **Yirme Yah**, saying,
20 Thus saith *the LORD* **Yah Veh**;
If ye can break my covenant of the day,
and my covenant of the night,
and that there should not be day and night
in *their season* **time**;
21 Then may also my covenant be broken
with David my servant,
that he should not have a son to reign upon his throne;
and with the *Levites* **Leviym** the priests, my ministers.
22 As the host of *heaven* **the heavens**
cannot be *numbered* **scribed**,
neither the sand of the sea measured:
so *will* **shall** I *multiply* **abound**
the seed of David my servant,
and the *Levites* **Leviym** that minister unto me.
23 Moreover the word of *the LORD* **Yah Veh**
came to *Jeremiah* **Yirme Yah**, saying,
24 *Considerest* **Seest** thou not
what this people have *spoken* **worded**, saying,
The two families which *the LORD* **Yah Veh** hath chosen,
he hath *even cast them off* **spurned**?
thus they have *despised* **scorned** my people,
that they should be no more a *nation* **goyim**
before them **at their face**.
25 Thus saith *the LORD* **Yah Veh**;
If my covenant be not with day and night,
and if I have not *appointed* **set** the *ordinances* **statutes**
of *heaven* **the heavens** and earth;
26 Then *will* **shall** I *cast away* **spurn**
the seed of *Jacob* **Yaaqov** and David my servant,
so that I *will* **shall** not take *any* of his seed
to be *rulers* **sovereigns** over the seed of Abraham,
Isaac **Yischaq**, and *Jacob* **Yaaqov**:
for I *will cause* **shall restore** their captivity *to return*,
and *have* **shall** mercy *on* them.

THE WORD AGAINST SIDQI YAH

34 The word which came unto *Jeremiah* **Yirme Yah**
from *the LORD* **Yah Veh**,
when *Nebuchadnezzar* **Nebukadnets Tsar**
king **sovereign** of *Babylon* **Babel**,
and all his *army* **valiant**,
and all the kingdoms of the earth
of *his dominion* **the reign of his hand**,
and all the people,
fought against *Jerusalem* **Yeru Shalem**,
and against all the cities *thereof*, saying,
2 Thus saith
the LORD **Yah Veh**, *the God* **Elohim** of *Israel* **Yisra El**;
Go and *speak* **say** to *Zedekiah* **Sidqi Yah**
king **sovereign** of *Judah* **Yah Hudah**,
and *tell* **say to** him, Thus saith *the LORD* **Yah Veh**;
Behold, I *will* **shall** give this city
into the hand of the *king* **sovereign** of *Babylon* **Babel**,
and he shall burn it with fire:
3 And thou shalt not escape out of his hand,
but **in apprehending,**
shalt *surely be taken* **be apprehended**,

and *delivered* **given** into his hand;
and thine eyes shall *behold* **see**
the eyes of the *king* **sovereign** of *Babylon* **Babel**,
and he shall *speak* **word** with thee mouth to mouth,
and thou shalt go to *Babylon* **Babel**.
4 Yet hear the word of *the LORD* **Yah Veh**,
O *Zedekiah* **Sidqi Yah**
king **sovereign** of *Judah* **Yah Hudah**;
Thus saith *the LORD* **Yah Veh** of thee,
Thou shalt not die by the sword:
5 *But* thou shalt die in *peace* **shalom**:
and with the *burnings* **cremations** of thy fathers,
the former *kings* **sovereigns**
which were *before thee* **at thy face**,
so shall they burn *odours* for thee;
and they *will lament* **shall chop for** thee, *saying*,
Ah lord **Ho adoni**!
for I have *pronounced* **worded** the word,
saith the LORD **an oracle of Yah Veh**.
6 Then *Jeremiah* **Yirme Yah** the prophet
spake **worded** all these words
unto *Zedekiah* **Sidqi Yah**
king **sovereign** of *Judah* **Yah Hudah**
in *Jerusalem* **Yeru Shalem**,
7 When the *king* **sovereign**
of *Babylon's army* **Babel's valiant**
fought against *Jerusalem* **Yeru Shalem**,
and against all the cities of *Judah* **Yah Hudah**
that *were left* **remained**,
against Lachish, and against *Azekah* **Azeqah**:
for these *defenced* **fortified** cities
remained of the cities of *Judah* **Yah Hudah**.
8 *This is* the word that came unto *Jeremiah* **Yirme Yah**
from *the LORD* **Yah Veh**,
after that the *king Zedekiah* **sovereign Sidqi Yah**
had *made* **cut** a covenant with all the people
which were at *Jerusalem* **Yeru Shalem**,
to *proclaim* **call out** liberty unto them;
9 That every man should let his *manservant* **servant**,
and every man his *maidservant* **maid**,
being an Hebrew or an Hebrewess,
go free **be sent away liberated**;
that none should serve himself of them,
to wit, of a *Jew* **Yah Hudahiy** his brother.
10 Now when all the *princes* **governors**,
and all the people,
which had entered into the covenant,
heard that every *one* **man**
should let his *manservant* **servant**,
and every *one* **man** his *maidservant* **maid**,
go *free* **liberated**,
that none should serve themselves of them any more,
then they *obeyed* **hearkened**, and *let* **sent** them *go* **away**.
11 But afterward they turned,
and caused the servants and the *handmaids* **maids**,
whom they had *let go free* **sent away liberated**, to return,
and brought them into subjection
for servants and for *handmaids* **maids**.
12 Therefore the word of *the LORD* **Yah Veh**
came to *Jeremiah* **Yirme Yah** from *the LORD* **Yah Veh**,
saying,
13 Thus saith *the LORD* **Yah Veh**,
the God **Elohim** of *Israel* **Yisra El**;
I *made* **cut** a covenant with your fathers
in the day that I brought them forth
out of the land of *Egypt* **Misrayim**,
out of the house of *bondmen* **servants**, saying,
14 At the end of seven years
let ye go **send ye away** every man his brother an Hebrew,
which hath been sold unto thee;
and when he hath served thee six years,
thou shalt *let him go free* **send him away liberated**
from thee:
but your fathers hearkened not unto me,
neither *inclined* **extended** their ear.
15 And ye were *now* **to day** turned,
and had *done right* **worked straight** in my *sight* **eyes**,
in *proclaiming* **calling out** liberty
every man to his *neighbour* **friend**;
and ye had *made* **cut** a covenant *before me* **at my face**
in the house which is called by my name:
16 But ye turned and *polluted* **profaned** my name,
and caused every man his servant,
and every man his *handmaid* **maid**,
whom he had *set at* **extended** liberty
at their *pleasure* **soul**,
to return, and brought them into subjection,
to be unto you for servants and for *handmaids* **maids**.
17 Therefore thus saith *the LORD* **Yah Veh**;
Ye have not hearkened unto me,
in *proclaiming* **calling out** liberty,
every *one* **man** to his brother,
and every man to his *neighbour* **friend**:
behold, I proclaim a liberty for you,
saith the LORD **an oracle of Yah Veh**,
to the sword, to the pestilence, and to the famine;
and I *will make* **shall give** you
to be removed **for an agitation**
into all the kingdoms of the earth.
18 And I *will* **shall** give the men
that have *transgressed* **tresspassed** my covenant,
which have not
performed **raised** the words of the covenant
which they had *made before me* **cut at my face**,
when they cut the calf in *twain* **two**,
and passed between the *parts* **sections** *thereof*,
19 The *princes* **governors** of *Judah* **Yah Hudah**,
and the *princes* **governors** of *Jerusalem* **Yeru Shalem**,
the eunuchs, and the priests,
and all the people of the land,
which passed between the *parts* **sections** of the calf;
20 I *will* **shall** even give them
into the hand of their enemies,
and into the hand of them that seek their *life* **soul**:
and their *dead bodies* **carcases** shall be for *meat* **food**
unto the *fowls* **flyers** of the *heaven* **heavens**,
and to the *beasts* **animals** of the earth.
21 And *Zedekiah* **Sidqi Yah**
king **sovereign** of *Judah* **Yah Hudah**
and his *princes* **governors**
will **shall** I give into the hand of their enemies,
and into the hand of them that seek their *life* **soul**,
and into the hand
of the *king* **sovereign** of *Babylon's army* **Babel's valiant**,
which are *gone up* **ascended** from you.
22 Behold, I *will command* **shall misvah**,
saith the LORD **an oracle of Yah Veh**,
and cause them to return to this city;
and they shall fight against it,
and *take* **capture** it, and burn it with fire:
and I *will make* **shall give** the cities of *Judah* **Yah Hudah**
a desolation without *an inhabitant* **a settler**.

THE OBEDIENCE OF THE HOUSE OF THE RECHABIYM

35 The word which came unto *Jeremiah* **Yirme Yah**
from *the LORD* **Yah Veh**
in the days of *Jehoiakim* **Yah Yaqim**
the son of *Josiah* **Yoshi Yah**
king **sovereign** of *Judah* **Yah Hudah**, saying,
2 Go unto the house of the *Rechabites* **Rechabiym**,
and *speak* **word** unto them,
and bring them into the house of *the LORD* **Yah Veh**,
into one of the chambers, and give them wine to drink.
3 Then I took *Jaazaniah* **Yaazan Yah**
the son of *Jeremiah* **Yirme Yah**,
the son of *Habaziniah* **Chabatz Tzan Yah**,
and his brethren, and all his sons,
and the whole house of the *Rechabites* **Rechabiym**;
4 And I brought them
into the house of *the LORD* **Yah Veh**,
into the chamber of the sons of Hanan,
the son of *Igdaliah* **Yigdal Yah**, a man of *God* **Elohim**,
which was *by* **beside** the chamber
of the *princes* **governors**,
which was above the chamber of *Maaseiah* **Maase Yah**
the son of Shallum,
the *keeper* **guard** of the *door* **threshold**:
5 And I *set before* **gave at the face of** the sons
of the house of the *Rechabites* **Rechabiym**
pots **bowls** full of wine, and cups,
and I said unto them, Drink ye wine.

6 But they said, We *will* **shall** drink no wine:
for *Jonadab* **Yah Nadab**
the son of Rechab our father
commanded **misvahed** us, saying, Ye shall drink no wine,
neither ye, nor your sons *for ever* **eternally**:
7 Neither shall ye build house,
nor *sow* **seed** seed, nor plant vineyard, nor have *any*:
but all your days ye shall *dwell* **settle** in tents;
that ye may live many days in the *land* **face of the soil**
where ye be *strangers* **sojourners**.
8 Thus have we *obeyed* **hearkened**
unto the voice of *Jonadab* **Yah Nadab**
the son of Rechab our father
in all that he hath *charged* **misvahed** us,
to drink no wine all our days,
we, our *wives* **women**, our sons, nor our daughters;
9 Nor to build houses for us to *dwell* **settle** in:
neither have we vineyard, nor field, nor seed:
10 But we have *dwelt* **settled** in tents,
and have *obeyed* **hearkened**,
and *done* **worked** according to all
that *Jonadab* **Yah Nadab** our father
commanded **misvahed** us.
11 But it *came to pass* **became**,
when *Nebuchadrezzar* **Nebukadnets Tsar**
king **sovereign** of *Babylon* **Babel**
came up **ascended** into the land, that we said,
Come, and let us go to *Jerusalem* **Yeru Shalem**
for fear **from the face** of the *army* **valiant**
of the *Chaldeans* **Kesediym**,
and *for fear* **from the face** of the *army* **valiant**
of the *Syrians* **Aramiym**:
so we *dwell* **settle** at *Jerusalem* **Yeru Shalem**.
12 Then came the word of *the LORD* **Yah Veh**
unto *Jeremiah* **Yirme Yah**, saying,
13 Thus saith *the LORD of hosts* **Yah Veh Sabaoth**,
the God **Elohim** of *Israel* **Yisra El**;
Go and *tell* **say to** the men of *Judah* **Yah Hudah**
and the *inhabitants* **settlers** of *Jerusalem* **Yeru Shalem**,
will **shall** ye not *receive instruction* **take discipline**
to hearken to my words?
saith the LORD **an oracle of Yah Veh**.
14 The words of *Jonadab* **Yah Nadab**
the son of Rechab,
that he *commanded* **misvahed** his sons not to drink wine,
are *performed* **raised**;
for unto this day they drink none,
but *obey* **hearken**
unto their father's *commandment* **misvah**:
notwithstanding I have *spoken* **worded** unto you
rising **starting** early and *speaking* **wording**;
but ye hearkened not unto me.
15 I have sent also unto you all my servants the prophets,
rising up **starting** early and sending them, saying,
Return ye *now* **I beseech,** every man from his evil way,
and *amend* **well—prepare** your *doings* **exploits**,
and go not after other *gods* **elohim** to serve them,
and ye shall *dwell* **settle** in the *land* **soil**
which I have given to you and to your fathers:
but ye have not *inclined* **extended** your ear,
nor hearkened unto me.
16 Because the sons of *Jonadab* **Yah Nadab**
the son of Rechab
have *performed* **raised** the *commandment* **misvah**
of their father,
which he *commanded* **misvahed** them;
but this people hath not hearkened unto me:
17 Therefore thus saith
the LORD God of hosts **Yah Veh Elohim Sabaoth**,
the God **Elohim** of *Israel* **Yisra El**;
Behold, I *will* **shall** bring upon *Judah* **Yah Hudah**
and upon all
the *inhabitants* **settlers** of *Jerusalem* **Yeru Shalem**
all the evil that I have *pronounced* **worded** against them:
because I have *spoken* **worded** unto them,
but they have not heard;
and I have called unto them,
but they have not answered.
18 And *Jeremiah* **Yirme Yah** said
unto the house of the *Rechabites* **Rechabiym**,
Thus saith *the LORD of hosts* **Yah Veh Sabaoth**,
the God **Elohim** of *Israel* **Yisra El**;
Because ye have *obeyed* **hearkened**
unto the *commandment* **misvah**
of *Jonadab* **Yah Nadab** your father,
and *kept* **guarded** all his *precepts* **misvoth**,
and *done* **worked** according unto all
that he hath *commanded* **misvahed** you:
19 Therefore thus saith
the LORD of hosts **Yah Veh Sabaoth**,
the God **Elohim** of *Israel* **Yisra El**;
Jonadab **Yah Nadab** the son of Rechab
shall not *want* **cut** a man to stand *before me* **at my face**
for ever **all days**.

YIRME YAH INSCRIBES A SCROLL

36 And it *came to pass* **became**,
in the fourth year of *Jehoiakim* **Yah Yaqim**
the son of *Josiah* **Yoshi Yah**
king **sovereign** of *Judah* **Yah Hudah**,
that this word came unto *Jeremiah* **Yirme Yah**
from *the LORD* **Yah Veh**, saying,
2 Take thee a roll of a *book* **scroll**,
and *write* **inscribe** therein
all the words that I have *spoken* **worded** unto thee
against *Israel* **Yisra El**, and against *Judah* **Yah Hudah**,
and against all the *nations* **goyim**,
from the day I *spake* **worded** unto thee,
from the days of *Josiah* **Yoshi Yah**, even unto this day.
3 *It may be that* **Perhaps** the house of *Judah* **Yah Hudah**
will **shall** hear all the evil
which I *purpose* **fabricate** to *do* **work** unto them;
that they may return every man from his evil way;
that I may forgive their *iniquity* **perversity** and their sin.
4 Then *Jeremiah* **Yirme Yah**
called Baruch the son of *Neriah* **Neri Yah**:
and Baruch *wrote* **inscribed**
from the mouth of *Jeremiah* **Yirme Yah**
all the words of *the LORD* **Yah Veh**,
which he had *spoken* **worded** him,
upon a roll of a *book* **scroll**.
5 And *Jeremiah* **Yirme Yah**
commanded **misvahed** Baruch, saying,
I am *shut up* **restrained**;
I cannot go into the house of *the LORD* **Yah Veh**:
6 Therefore go thou, and *read* **call out** in the roll,
which thou hast *written* **inscribed** from my mouth,
the words of *the LORD* **Yah Veh** in the ears of the people
in the *LORD'S* house **of Yah Veh**
upon the fasting day:
and also thou shalt *read* **call** them **out**
in the ears of all *Judah* **Yah Hudah**
that come out of their cities.
7 *It may be* **Perhaps** they *will present* **shall fell**
before the LORD **at the face of Yah Veh**
their supplication
and *will* **shall** return every *one* **man** from his evil way:
for great is the *anger* **wrath** and the fury
that *the LORD* **Yah Veh** hath *pronounced* **worded**
against this people.
8 And Baruch the son of *Neriah* **Neri Yah**
did **worked** according to all
that *Jeremiah* **Yirme Yah** the prophet
commanded **misvahed** him,
reading **calling out** in the *book* **scroll**
the words of *the LORD* **Yah Veh**
in the *LORD'S* house **of Yah Veh**.
9 And it *came to pass* **became**
in the fifth year of *Jehoiakim* **Yah Yaqim**
the son of *Josiah* **Yoshi Yah**
king **sovereign** of *Judah* **Yah Hudah**,
in the ninth month,
that they *proclaimed* **called** a fast
before the LORD **at the face of Yah Veh**
to all the people in *Jerusalem* **Yeru Shalem**,
and to all the people
that came from the cities of *Judah* **Yah Hudah**
unto *Jerusalem* **Yeru Shalem**.
10 Then *read* Baruch **called out** in the *book* **scroll**
the words of *Jeremiah* **Yirme Yah**
in the house of *the LORD* **Yah Veh**,

in the chamber of *Gemariah* **Gemar Yah**
the son of Shaphan the scribe,
in the *higher* **most high** court,
at the *entry* **opening** of the new *gate* **portal**
of the *LORD'S* house **of Yah Veh**,
in the ears of all the people.
11 When *Michaiah* **Michah Yah**
the son of *Gemariah* **Gemar Yah**, the son of Shaphan,
had heard out of the *book* **scroll**
all the words of *the LORD* **Yah Veh**,
12 Then he *went down* **descended**
into the *king's* **sovereign's** house,
into the scribe's chamber: and, *lo* **behold**,
all the *princes* **governors** sat there,
even Elishama **Eli Shama** the scribe,
and *Delaiah* **Dela Yah** the son of *Shemaiah* **Shema Yah**,
and *Elnathan* **El Nathan** the son of Achbor,
and *Gemariah* **Gemar Yah** the son of Shaphan,
and *Zedekiah* **Sidqi Yah** the son of *Hananiah* **Hanan Yah**,
and all the *princes* **governors**.
13 Then *Michaiah declared* **Michah Yah told** unto them
all the words that he had heard,
when Baruch *read* **called out** the *book* **scroll**
in the ears of the people.
14 Therefore all the *princes* **governors** sent
Jehudi **Yah Hudiy** the son of *Nethaniah* **Nethan Yah**,
the son of *Shelemiah* **Shelem Yah**,
the son of *Cushi* **Kushiy**, unto Baruch, saying,
Take in thine hand the roll
wherein thou hast *read* **called out**
in the ears of the people,
and come.
So Baruch the son of *Neriah* **Neri Yah**
took the roll in his hand, and came unto them.
15 And they said unto him,
Sit down *now* **I beseech**,
and *read it* **call it out** in our ears.
So Baruch *read it* **called it out** in their ears.
16 *Now* it *came to pass* **became**,
when they had heard all the words,
they *were afraid both one* **feared man** and *other* **friend**,
and said unto Baruch,
In telling, We *will* **shall** *surely* tell the *king* **sovereign**
of all these words.
17 And they asked Baruch, saying,
Tell us *now* **I beseech,** ,
How didst thou *write* **inscribe** all these words
at his mouth?
18 Then Baruch *answered* **said to** them,
He *pronounced* **called out** all these words unto me
with his mouth,
and I *wrote them* **inscribed** with ink in the *book* **scroll**.
19 Then said the *princes* **governors** unto Baruch,
Go, hide thee, thou and *Jeremiah* **Yirme Yah**;
and let no man know where ye be.

YAH YAQIM BURNS YIRME YAH'S SCROLL

20 And they went in to the *king* **sovereign** into the court,
but they *laid up* **oversaw** the roll
in the chamber of *Elishama* **Eli Shama** the scribe,
and told all the words in the ears of the *king* **sovereign**.
21 So the *king* **sovereign** sent *Jehudi* **Yah Hudiy**
to *fetch* **take** the roll:
and he took it
out of *Elishama* **Eli Shama** the scribe's chamber.
And *Jehudi read it* **Yah Hudiy called it out**
in the ears of the *king* **sovereign**,
and in the ears of all the *princes* **governors**
which stood beside the *king* **sovereign**.
22 *Now* the *king* **sovereign** sat in the winterhouse
in the ninth month:
and *there was a fire* on the hearth
a burning *before him* **at his face**.
23 And it *came to pass* **became,**
that when *Jehudi* **Yah Hudiy**
had *read* **called out** three or four leaves,
he *cut* **ripped** it with the *penknife* **scribe's knife**,
and cast it into the fire that was on the hearth,
until all the roll was consumed in the fire
that was on the hearth.
24 Yet they *were* **feared** not *afraid*,
nor *rent* **ripped** their *garments* **clothes**,
neither the *king* **sovereign**,
nor any of his servants that heard all these words.
25 Nevertheless *Elnathan* **El Nathan**
and *Delaiah* **Dela Yah** and *Gemariah* **Gemar Yah**
had *made intercession* **interceded** to the *king* **sovereign**
that he *would* **should** not burn the roll:
but he *would* **should** not hear them.
26 But the *king commanded* **sovereign misvahed**
Jerahmeel **Yerachme El** the son of *Hammelech* **Melech**,
and *Seraiah* **Sera Yah** the son of *Azriel* **Ezri El**,
and *Shelemiah* **Shelem Yah** the son of *Abdeel* **Abde El**,
to take Baruch the scribe
and *Jeremiah* **Yirme Yah** the prophet:
but *the LORD* **Yah Veh** hid them.

YIRME YAH INSCRIBES A SECOND SCROLL

27 Then the word of *the LORD* **Yah Veh**
came to *Jeremiah* **Yirme Yah**,
after that the *king* **sovereign** had burned the roll,
and the words which Baruch *wrote* **inscribed**
at the mouth of *Jeremiah* **Yirme Yah**, saying,
28 **Return,** Take thee *again* another roll,
and *write* **inscribe** in it
all the former words that were in the first roll,
which *Jehoiakim* **Yah Yaqim**
the *king* **sovereign** of *Judah* **Yah Hudah** hath burned.
29 And thou shalt say to *Jehoiakim king* **Yah Yaqim**
sovereign of *Judah* **Yah Hudah**,
Thus saith *the LORD* **Yah Veh**;
Thou hast burned this roll, saying,
Why hast thou *written* **inscribed** therein, saying,
In coming, The *king* **sovereign** of *Babylon* **Babel**
shall *certainly* come and *destroy* **ruin** this land,
and shall cause to *cease* **shabbathize** from thence
man **humanity** and *beast* **animal**?
30 Therefore thus saith *the LORD* **Yah Veh**
of *Jehoiakim* **Yah Yaqim**
king **sovereign** of *Judah* **Yah Hudah**;
He shall have none to sit upon the throne of David:
and his *dead body* **carcase** shall be cast out
in the day to the *heat* **parchedness**,
and in the night to the frost.
31 And I *will punish* **shall visit upon** him
and his seed and his servants for their *iniquity* **perversity**;
and I *will* **shall** bring upon them,
and upon
the *inhabitants* **settlers** of *Jerusalem* **Yeru Shalem**,
and upon the men of *Judah* **Yah Hudah**,
all the evil that I have *pronounced* **worded** against them;
but they hearkened not.
32 Then took *Jeremiah* **Yirme Yah** another roll,
and gave it to Baruch the scribe,
the son of *Neriah* **Neri Yah**;
who *wrote* **inscribed** therein
from the mouth of *Jeremiah* **Yirme Yah**
all the words of the *book* **scroll**
which *Jehoiakim* **Yah Yaqim**
king **sovereign** of *Judah* **Yah Hudah**
had burned in the fire:
and there were added besides unto them
many like words.

YIRME YAH IMPRISONED

37 And *king Zedekiah* **sovereign Sidqi Yah**
the son of *Josiah* **Yoshi Yah** reigned
instead of *Coniah* **Kon Yah**
the son of *Jehoiakim* **Yah Yaqim**,
whom *Nebuchadrezzar* **Nebukadnets Tsar**
king **sovereign** of *Babylon* **Babel**
made *king* **sovereign** in the land of *Judah* **Yah Hudah**.
2 But neither he,
nor his servants, nor the people of the land,
did hearken unto the words of *the LORD* **Yah Veh**,
which he *spake* **worded**
by **the hand of** the prophet *Jeremiah* **Yirme Yah**.
3 And *Zedekiah* **Sidqi Yah** the *king* **sovereign**
sent *Jehucal* **Yehuchal** the son of *Shelemiah* **Shelem Yah**
and *Zephaniah* **Sephan Yah**
the son of *Maaseiah* **Maase Yah** the priest
to the prophet *Jeremiah* **Yirme Yah**, saying,
Pray *now* **I beseech,**

unto *the LORD* **Yah Veh** our *God* **Elohim** for us.
4 *Now Jeremiah* **Yirme Yah**
came in and went out among the people:
for they had not *put* **given** him
into **the** prison **house**.
5 Then *Pharaoh's army* **Paroh's valiant**
was come forth out of *Egypt* **Misrayim**:
and when the *Chaldeans* **Kesediym**
that besieged *Jerusalem* **Yeru Shalem**
heard *tidings* **the report** of them,
they *departed* **ascended** from *Jerusalem* **Yeru Shalem**.
6 Then came the word of *the LORD* **Yah Veh**
unto the prophet *Jeremiah* **Yirme Yah**, saying,
7 Thus saith *the LORD* **Yah Veh**,
the God **Elohim** of *Israel* **Yisra El**;
Thus shall ye say
to the *king* **sovereign** of *Judah* **Yah Hudah**,
that sent you unto me to enquire of me;
Behold, *Pharaoh's army* **Paroh's valiant**,
which is come forth to help you,
shall return to *Egypt* **Misrayim** into their own land.
8 And the *Chaldeans* **Kesediym**
shall *come again* **return**, and fight against this city,
and *take* **capture** it, and burn it with fire.
9 Thus saith *the LORD* **Yah Veh**;
Deceive not *yourselves* **your souls**, saying,
The *Chaldeans* **Kesediym**
shall *surely depart* **walk and go** from us:
for they shall not *depart* **go**.
10 For though ye had smitten
the whole *army* **valiant** of the *Chaldeans* **Kesediym**
that fight against you,
and there *remained* **survived**
but wounded men among them,
yet should they rise up every man in his tent,
and burn this city with fire.
11 And it *came to pass* **became**,
that when the *army* **valiant** of the *Chaldeans* **Kesediym**
was broken up **ascended** from *Jerusalem* **Yeru Shalem**
for fear **from the face** of *Pharaoh's army* **Paroh's valiant**,
12 Then *Jeremiah* **Yirme Yah**
went forth out of *Jerusalem* **Yeru Shalem**
to go into the land of *Benjamin* **Ben Yamin**,
to *separate himself thence* **receive an allotment**
in the midst of the people.
13 And
when he was in the *gate* **portal** of *Benjamin* **Ben Yamin**,
a *captain* **master** of the *ward* **visitation** was there,
whose name was *Irijah* **Yiri Yah**,
the son of *Shelemiah* **Shelem Yah**,
the son of *Hananiah* **Hanan Yah**;
and he *took Jeremiah* **apprehended Yirme Yah**
the prophet, saying,
Thou fallest away to the *Chaldeans* **Kesediym**.
14 Then said *Jeremiah* **Yirme Yah**, *It is false* **Falsehood**;
I fall not away to the *Chaldeans* **Kesediym**.
But he hearkened not to him:
so *Irijah took Jeremiah* **Yiri Yah apprehended Yirme Yah**,
and brought him to the *princes* **governors**.
15 Wherefore the *princes* **governors**
were *wroth* **enraged** with *Jeremiah* **Yirme Yah**,
and smote him,
and *put* **gave** him in *prison* **the bond house**
in the house of *Jonathan* **Yah Nathan** the scribe:
for they had *made* **worked** that the prison **house**.
16 When *Jeremiah* **Yirme Yah** was entered
into the *dungeon* **well house**, and into the *cabins* **prisons**,
and *Jeremiah* **Yirme Yah**
had *remained* **settled** there many days;
17 Then *Zedekiah* **Sidqi Yah**, the *king* **sovereign**
sent, and took him out:
and the *king* **sovereign** asked him *secretly* **covertly**
in his house, and said,
Is there *any* word from *the LORD* **Yah Veh**?
And *Jeremiah* **Yirme Yah** said, There is:
for, said he, thou shalt be *delivered* **given**
into the hand of the *king* **sovereign** of *Babylon* **Babel**.
18 Moreover *Jeremiah* **Yirme Yah**
said unto *king Zedekiah* **sovereign Sidqi Yah**,
What have I *offended* **sinned** against thee,
or against thy servants, or against this people,
that ye have *put* **given** me *in* **unto the** prison **house**?
19 Where are *now* your prophets
which prophesied unto you, saying,
The *king* **sovereign** of *Babylon* **Babel**
shall not come against you, nor against this land?
20 Therefore hear now, I *pray* **beseech** thee,
O my *lord* **adoni** the *king* **sovereign**:
let my supplication, I *pray* **beseech** thee,
be accepted before thee **fall at thy face**;
that thou cause me not to return
to the house of *Jonathan* **Yah Nathan** the scribe,
lest I die there.
21 Then *Zedekiah* **Sidqi Yah**, the *king* **sovereign**
commanded **misvahed**
that they should *commit Jeremiah* **muster Yirme Yah**
into the court of the *prison* **target area**,
and that they should give him daily
a *piece* **round** of bread
out of the bakers' *street* **outway**,
until all the bread in the city were *spent* **consumed**.
Thus *Jeremiah remained* **Yirme Yah settled**
in the court of the *prison* **target area**.

YIRME YAH IN A PIT

38 Then *Shephatiah* **Shaphat Yah** the son of Mattan,
and *Gedaliah* **Gedal Yah** the son of *Pashur* **Pashchur**,
and *Jucal* **Yuchal** the son of *Shelemiah* **Shelem Yah**,
and *Pashur* **Pashchur** the son of *Malchiah* **Malki Yah**,
heard the words that *Jeremiah* **Yirme Yah**
had spoken unto all the people, saying,
2 Thus saith *the LORD* **Yah Veh**,
He that *remaineth* **settleth** in this city
shall die by the sword,
by the famine, and by the pestilence:
but he that goeth forth to the *Chaldeans* **Kesediym**
shall live;
for he shall have his *life* **soul** for a *prey* **spoil**,
and shall live.
3 Thus saith *the LORD* **Yah Veh**,
In giving, This city shall *surely* be given into the hand
of the *king* **sovereign** of *Babylon's army* **Babel's valiant**,
which shall *take* **capture** it.
4 Therefore
the *princes* **governors** said unto the *king* **sovereign**,
We beseech thee, let this man be *put to death* **deathified**:
for thus he *weakeneth* **slackeneth** the hands
of the men of war that *remain* **survive** in this city,
and the hands of all the people,
in *speaking* **wording** such words unto them:
for this man seeketh not
the *welfare* **shalom** of this people,
but the *hurt* **evil**.
5 Then *Zedekiah* **Sidqi Yah**, the *king* **sovereign** said,
Behold, he is in your hand:
for the *king* **sovereign** is not he
that can *do any thing* **word** against you.
6 Then took they *Jeremiah* **Yirme Yah**,
and cast him into the *dungeon* **well**
of *Malchiah* **Malki Yah** the son of *Hammelech* **Melech**,
that was in the court of the *prison* **target area**:
and they *let* **sent** down *Jeremiah* **Yirme Yah** with cords.
And in the *dungeon* **well** there was no water, but mire:
so *Jeremiah* **Yirme Yah** sunk in the mire.
7 *Now* when *Ebedmelech* **Ebed Melech**
the *Ethiopian* **Kushiy**, *one* **a man** of the eunuchs
which was in the *king's* **sovereign's** house,
heard that they had *put Jeremiah* **given Yirme Yah**
in the *dungeon* **well**;
the *king* **sovereign** then sitting
in the *gate* **portal** of *Benjamin* **Ben Yamin**;
8 *Ebedmelech* **Ebed Melech** went forth
out of the *king's* **sovereign's** house,
and *spake* **worded** to the *king* **sovereign**, saying,
9 **O** My *lord the king* **adoni sovereign**,
these men have *done evil* **vilified**
in all that they have *done* **worked**
to *Jeremiah* **Yirme Yah** the prophet,
whom they have cast into the *dungeon* **well**;
and he is like to die *for hunger* **at the face of famine**
in the place where he is:

for there is no more bread in the city.
10 Then the *king* **sovereign**
commanded Ebedmelech **misvahed Ebed Melech**
the *Ethiopian* **Kushiy**, saying,
Take from hence thirty men *with thee* **under thy hand**,
and *take up Jeremiah* **ascend Yirme Yah** the prophet
out of the *dungeon* **well**, before he die.
11 So *Ebedmelech* **Ebed Melech**
took the men *with him* **under his hand**,
and went into the house of the *king* **sovereign**
under the treasury,
and took thence *old cast clouts* **decayed rags**
and *old* **decayed** rotten rags,
and *let* **sent** them down by cords
into the *dungeon* **well** to *Jeremiah* **Yirme Yah**.
12 And *Ebedmelech* **Ebed Melech**, the *Ethiopian* **Kushiy**
said unto *Jeremiah* **Yirme Yah**,
Put now **Set I beseech**,
these *old cast clouts* **decayed rags** and rotten rags
under *thine armholes* **the elbow holes for thy hands**
under the cords.
And *Jeremiah did* **Yirme Yah worked** so.
13 So they drew up *Jeremiah* **Yirme Yah** with cords,
and *took* **ascended** him *up* out of the *dungeon* **well**:
and *Jeremiah remained* **Yirme Yah settled**
in the court of the *prison* **target area**.
14 Then *Zedekiah* **Sidqi Yah** the *king* **sovereign** sent,
and took *Jeremiah* **Yirme Yah** the prophet unto him
into the third entry
that is in the house of *the LORD* **Yah Veh**:
and the *king* **sovereign** said unto *Jeremiah* **Yirme Yah**,
I *will* **shall** ask thee a *thing* **word**;
hide nothing **conceal naught** from me.
15 Then *Jeremiah* **Yirme Yah**
said unto *Zedekiah* **Sidqi Yah**,
If I *declare it* **tell** unto thee,
in deathifying,
wilt **shalt** thou not *surely put me to death* **deathify me**?
and if I *give thee* counsel **thee**,
wilt **shalt** thou not hearken unto me?
16 So *Zedekiah* **Sidqi Yah** the *king* **sovereign**
sware secretly **oathed covertly** unto *Jeremiah* **Yirme Yah**,
saying, *As the LORD* **Yah Veh** liveth,
that *made* **worked** us this soul,
I *will* **shall** not *put* **deathify** thee *to death*,
neither *will* **shall** I give hee into the hand of these men
that seek thy *life* **soul**.
17 Then said *Jeremiah* **Yirme Yah**
unto *Zedekiah* **Sidqi Yah**,
Thus saith *the LORD* **Yah Veh**,
the God of hosts **Elohim Sabaoth**,
the God **Elohim** of *Israel* **Yisra El**;
If **in going forth,** thou *wilt assuredly* **shalt** go forth
unto the *king* **sovereign** of *Babylon's* **Babel's**
princes **governors**,
then thy soul shall live,
and this city shall not be burned with fire;
and thou shalt live, and thine house:
18 But if thou *wilt* **shalt** not go forth
to the *king* **sovereign** of *Babylon's* **Babel's**
princes **governors**,
then shall this city be given
into the hand of the *Chaldeans* **Kesediym**,
and they shall burn it with fire,
and thou shalt not escape out of their hand.
19 And *Zedekiah* **Sidqi Yah** the *king* **sovereign**
said unto *Jeremiah* **Yirme Yah**,
I am *afraid* **concerned** of the *Jews* **Yah Hudiym**
that are fallen to the *Chaldeans* **Kesediym**,
lest they *deliver* **give** me into their hand,
and they *mock* **exploit** me.
20 But *Jeremiah* **Yirme Yah** said,
They shall not *deliver* **give** thee.
Obey **Hear**, I beseech thee,
the voice of *the LORD* **Yah Veh**,
which I *speak* **word** unto thee:
so it shall *be well unto* **well—please** thee,
and thy soul shall live.
21 But if thou refuse to go forth,
this is the word
that *the LORD* **Yah Veh** hath *shewed* me **see**:
22 And, behold, all the women that *are left* **survive**
in the *king* **sovereign** of *Judah's* **Yah Hudah's** house
shall be brought forth
to the *king* **sovereign** of *Babylon's* **Babel's**
princes **governors**,
and those *women* shall say,
Thy *friends* **men of shalom** have *set* **goaded** thee *on*,
and have prevailed against thee:
thy feet are sunk in the mire,
and they are *turned away back* **apostatized backward**.
23 So they shall bring out all thy *wives* **women**
and thy *children* **sons** to the *Chaldeans* **Kesediym**:
and thou shalt not escape out of their hand,
but shalt be *taken* **apprehended**
by the hand of the *king* **sovereign** of *Babylon* **Babel**:
and thou shalt cause this city to be burned with fire.
24 Then said *Zedekiah* **Sidqi Yah**
unto *Jeremiah* **Yirme Yah**,
Let no man know of these words, and thou shalt not die.
25 But if the *princes* **governors** hear
that I have *talked* **worded** with thee,
and they come unto thee, and say unto thee,
Declare **Tell** unto us *now* **I beseech**,
what thou hast *said* **worded** unto the *king* **sovereign**,
hide it **conceal** not from us,
and we *will* **shall** not *put* **deathify** thee *to death*;
also what the *king said* **sovereign worded** unto thee:
26 Then thou shalt say unto them,
I presented my supplication
before **at the face of** the *king* **sovereign**,
that he *would* **should** not cause me
to return to *Jonathan's house* **the house of Yah Nathan**,
to die there.
27 Then came all the *princes* **governors**
unto *Jeremiah* **Yirme Yah**,
and asked him:
and he told them according to all these words
that the *king* **sovereign** had *commanded* **misvahed**.
So they *left off speaking with him* **hushed**;
for the *matter* **word** was not *perceived* **heard**.
28 So *Jeremiah* **Yirme Yah**
abode **settled** in the court of the *prison* **target area**
until the day
that *Jerusalem* **Yeru Shalem** was *taken* **captured**:
and he was there
when *Jerusalem* **Yeru Shalem** was *taken* **captured**.

YERU SHALEM CAPTURED

39 In the ninth year of *Zedekiah* **Sidqi Yah**
king **sovereign** of *Judah* **Yah Hudah**,
in the tenth month,
came *Nebuchadrezzar* **Nebukadnets Tsar**
king **sovereign** of *Babylon* **Babel**
and all his *army* **valiant** against *Jerusalem* **Yeru Shalem**,
and they besieged it.
2 And in the eleventh year of *Zedekiah* **Sidqi Yah**,
in the fourth month, the ninth *day* of the month,
the city was *broken up* **split**.
3 And all the *princes* **governors**
of the *king* **sovereign** of *Babylon* **Babel** came in,
and sat in the middle *gate* **portal**,
even *Nergalsharezer* **Nergal Shareser**,
Samgarnebo **Samgar Nebo**, Sarsechim,
Rabsaris **the rabbi eunuch**,
Nergalsharezer **Nergal Shareser**,
Rabmag **the rabbi magi**,
with all the *residue* **survivors** of the *princes* **governors**
of the *king* **sovereign** of *Babylon* **Babel**.
4 And it *came to pass* **became**,
that when *Zedekiah* **Sidqi Yah**
the *king* **sovereign** of *Judah* **Yah Hudah** saw them,
and all the men of war,
then they fled, and went forth out of the city by night,
by the way of the *king's* **sovereign's** garden,
by the *gate* **portal** betwixt the two walls:
and he went out the way of the plain.
5 But the *Chaldean's army* **Kesediym's valiant**
pursued after them,
and overtook *Zedekiah* **Sidqi Yah**
in the plains of *Jericho* **Yericho**:

and when they had taken him,
they *brought him up* **ascended him**
to *Nebuchadnezzar* **Nebukadnets Tsar**
king **sovereign** of *Babylon* **Babel**
to Riblah in the land of Hamath,
where he *gave* **worded** judgment upon him.
6 Then the *king* **sovereign** of *Babylon* **Babel**
slew **slaughtered** the sons of *Zedekiah* **Sidqi Yah**
in Riblah before his eyes:
also the *king* **sovereign** of *Babylon* **Babel**
slew **slaughtered** all the nobles of *Judah* **Yah Hudah**.
7 Moreover
he *put out Zedekiah's* **blinded Sidqi Yah's** eyes,
and bound him with *chains* **coppers**,
to carry him to *Babylon* **Babel**.
8 And the *Chaldeans* **Kesediym**
burned the *king's* **sovereign's** house,
and the houses of the people, with fire,
and brake down the walls of *Jerusalem* **Yeru Shalem**.
9 Then *Nebuzaradan* **Nebu Zaradan**
the *captain of the guard* **rabbi slaughterer**
carried away captive **exiled** into *Babylon* **Babel**
the remnant of the people
that *remained* **survived** in the city,
and those that fell away, that fell to him,
with the *rest* **remnant**
of the people that *remained* **survived**.
10 But *Nebuzaradan* **Nebu Zaradan**
the *captain of the guard* **rabbi slaughterer**
left **let survive** of the poor of the people,
which had *nothing* **naught**,
in the land of *Judah* **Yah Hudah**,
and gave them vineyards and **plowed** fields
at the same time **that same day**.

YIRME YAH SPARED

11 *Now Nebuchadrezzar* **Nebukadnets Tsar**
king **sovereign** of *Babylon* **Babel**
gave charge **misvahed** concerning *Jeremiah* **Yirme Yah**
to Nebuzaradan **by the hand of Nebu Zaradan**
the *captain of the guard* **rabbi slaughterer**, saying,
12 Take him, and *look well to* **set thine eyes unto** him,
and *do* **work** him no *harm* **evil**;
but *do* **work** unto him
even as he shall *say* **word** unto thee.
13 So *Nebuzaradan* **Nebu Zaradan**
the *captain of the guard* **rabbi slaughterer** sent,
and *Nebushasban* **Nebu Shazban**,
Rabsaris **the rabbi eunuch**,
and *Nergalsharezer* **Nergal Shareser**,
Rabmag **the rabbi magi**,
and all the *king* **sovereign**
of *Babylon's princes* **Babel's rabbis**;
14 Even they sent, and took *Jeremiah* **Yirme Yah**
out of the court of the *prison* **target area**,
and *committed* **gave** him unto *Gedaliah* **Gedal Yah**
the son of Ahikam the son of Shaphan,
that he should carry him home:
so he *dwelt* **settled** among the people.
15 *Now* the word of *the LORD* **Yah Veh**
came unto *Jeremiah* **Yirme Yah**,
while he was *shut up* **restrained**
in the court of the *prison* **guard area**, saying,
16 Go and *speak* **say**
to *Ebedmelech* **Ebed Melech** the *Ethiopian* **Kushiy**, saying,
Thus saith *the LORD of hosts* **Yah Veh Sabaoth**,
the God **Elohim** of *Israel* **Yisra El**; Behold,
I *will* **shall** bring my words upon this city for evil,
and not for good;
and they shall be *accomplished*
in that day *before thee* **at thy face**.
17 But I *will deliver* **shall rescue** thee in that day,
saith the LORD **an oracle of Yah Veh**:
and thou shalt not be given into the hand of the men
of whom thou *art afraid* **fearest to face**.
18 *For* **In rescuing,**
I *will surely deliver* **shall rescue** thee,
and thou shalt not fall by the sword,
but thy *life* **soul** shall be for a *prey* **spoil** unto thee:
because thou hast *put thy trust* **confided** in me,
saith the LORD **an oracle of Yah Veh**.

YIRME YAH RESCUED

40 The word that came to *Jeremiah* **Yirme Yah**
from *the LORD* **Yah Veh**,
after that *Nebuzaradan* **Nebu Zaradan**
the *captain of the guard* **rabbi slaughterer**
had *let him go* **sent him away** from Ramah,
when he had taken him being bound in *chains* **manacles**
among all *that were carried away captive* **the exiles**
of *Jerusalem* **Yeru Shalem** and *Judah* **Yah Hudah**,
which were *carried away captive* **exiled**
unto *Babylon* **Babel**.
2 And the *captain of the guard* **rabbi slaughterer**
took *Jeremiah* **Yirme Yah**, and said unto him,
The LORD **Yah Veh** thy *God* **Elohim**
hath *pronounced* **worded** this evil upon this place.
3 *Now the LORD* **Yah Veh** hath brought it,
and *done* **worked** according as he hath *said* **worded**:
because ye have sinned against *the LORD* **Yah Veh**,
and have not *obeyed* **hearkened unto** his voice,
therefore this *thing* is come upon you.
4 And now, behold, I loose thee this day
from the *chains* **manacles** which were upon thine hand.
If it seem good *unto thee* **in thine eyes**
to come with me into *Babylon* **Babel**, come;
and I *will look well* **shall set mine eyes** unto thee:
but if it seem *ill unto thee* **evil in thine eyes**
to come with me into *Babylon* **Babel**, *forbear* **cease**:
behold **see**, all the land is *before thee* **at thy face**:
whither it seemeth good
and *convenient for thee* **straight in thine eyes** to go,
thither go.
5 *Now* while he was not yet gone back, *he said*,
Go **Turn** back also to *Gedaliah* **Gedal Yah**
the son of Ahikam the son of Shaphan,
whom the *king* **sovereign** of *Babylon* **Babel**
hath made *governor* **overseer**
over the cities of *Judah* **Yah Hudah**,
and *dwell* **settle** with him among the people:
or go wheresoever it seemeth
convenient unto thee **straight in thine eyes** to go.
So the *captain of the guard* **rabbi slaughterer**
gave him *victuals* **rations** and a *reward* **load/burden**,
and *let* **sent** him *go* **away**.
6 Then went *Jeremiah* **Yirme Yah**
unto *Gedaliah* **Gedal Yah**
the son of Ahikam to *Mizpah* **Mispeh**;
and *dwelt* **settled** with him among the people
that *were left* **survived** in the land.
7 *Now* when all
the *captains* **governors** of the *forces* **valiant**
which were in the fields, *even* they and their men,
heard that the *king* **sovereign** of *Babylon* **Babel**
had made *Gedaliah* **Gedal Yah** the son of Ahikam
governor **overseer** in the land,
and had committed unto him men, and women,
and *children* **toddlers**, and of the poor of the land,
of them that were not
carried away captive **exiled** to *Babylon* **Babel**;
8 Then they came to *Gedaliah* **Gedal Yah**
to *Mizpah* **Mispeh**,
even *Ishmael* **Yishma El**
the son of *Nethaniah* **Nethan Yah**,
and *Johanan* **Yah Hanan** and *Jonathan* **Yah Nathan**
the sons of *Kareah* **Qareach**,
and *Seraiah* **Sera Yah** the son of *Tanhumeth* **Tachumeth**,
and the sons of *Ephai* **Ophay**
the *Netophathite* **Netophathiy**,
and *Jezaniah* **Yezan Yah**
the son of a *Maachathite* **Maachahiy**,
they and their men.
9 And *Gedaliah* **Gedal Yah**
the son of Ahikam the son of Shaphan
sware **oathed** unto them and to their men, saying,
Fear **Awe** not to serve the *Chaldeans* **Kesediym**:
dwell **settle** in the land,
and serve the *king* **sovereign** of *Babylon* **Babel**,
and it shall *be well with* **well—please** you.
10 As for me, behold,
I *will dwell* **shall settle** at *Mizpah* **Mispeh**,
to *serve the Chaldeans* **stand at the face of the Kesediym**,

which *will* **shall** come unto us:
but ye, gather ye wine, and summer fruits, and oil,
and *put* **set** them in your *vessels* **instruments**,
and *dwell* **settle** in your cities
that ye have *taken* **apprehended**.
11 Likewise
when all the *Jews* **Yah Hudiym** that were in Moab,
and among the *Ammonites* **sons of Ammon**,
and in Edom, and that were in all the *countries* **lands**,
heard that the *king* **sovereign** of *Babylon* **Babel**
had *left a remnant* **given survivors** of *Judah* **Yah Hudah**,
and that he had *set over* **oversee** them
Gedaliah **Gedal Yah**
the son of Ahikam the son of Shaphan;
12 Even all the *Jews* **Yah Hudiym**
returned out of all places whither they were driven,
and came to the land of *Judah* **Yah Hudah**,
to *Gedaliah* **Gedal Yah**, unto *Mizpah* **Mispeh**,
and gathered wine and summer fruits
very much **mighty abounding**.
13 Moreover
Johanan **Yah Hanan** the son of *Kareah* **Qareach**,
and all the *captains* **governors** of the *forces* **valiant**
that were in the fields,
came to *Gedaliah* **Gedal Yah** to *Mizpah* **Mispeh**,
14 And said unto him,
In knowing, Dost thou *certainly* know that Baalis
the *king* **sovereign** of the *Ammonites* **sons of Ammon**
hath sent *Ishmael* **Yishma El**
the son of *Nethaniah* **Nethan Yah**
to *slay thee* **smite thy soul**?
But *Gedaliah* **Gedal Yah** the son of Ahikam
believed **trusted** them not.
15 Then *Johanan* **Yah Hanan** the son of *Kareah* **Qareach**
spake **said** to *Gedaliah* **Gedal Yah** in *Mizpah* **Mispeh**
secretly **covertly** saying, Let me go, *I pray thee,*
and I *will slay Ishmael* **shall smite Yishma El**
the son of *Nethaniah* **Nethan Yah**,
and no man shall know it:
wherefore should he *slay thee* **smite thy soul**,
that all the *Jews* **Yah Hudiym**
which are gathered unto thee should be scattered,
and the *remnant* **survivors** in *Judah* **Yah Hudah**
perish **destruct**?
16 But *Gedaliah* **Gedal Yah** the son of Ahikam
said unto *Johanan* **Yah Hanan**
the son of *Kareah* **Qareach**,
Thou shalt not *do* **work** this *thing* **word**:
for thou *speakest* **wordest** falsely of *Ishmael* **Yishma El**.

GEDAL YAH IS EXECUTED

41 *Now* it *came to pass* **became** in the seventh month,
that Ishmael **Yishma El** the son of *Nethaniah* **Nethan Yah**
the son of *Elishama* **Eli Shama**,
of the seed *royal* **of the sovereigndom**,
and the *princes* **rabbis** of the *king* **sovereign**,
even ten men with him,
came unto *Gedaliah* **Gedal Yah** the son of Ahikam
to *Mizpah* **Mispeh**;
and there they did eat bread together in *Mizpah* **Mispeh**.
2 Then arose *Ishmael* **Yishma El**
the son of *Nethaniah* **Nethan Yah**,
and the ten men that were with him,
and smote *Gedaliah* **Gedal Yah**
the son of Ahikam the son of Shaphan with the sword,
and *slew* **executed** him,
whom the *king* **sovereign** of *Babylon* **Babel**
had made *governor* **overseer** over the land.
3 *Ishmael* **Yishma El** also *slew* **smote**
all the *Jews* **Yah Hudiym** that were with him,
even with *Gedaliah* **Gedal Yah**, at *Mizpah* **Mispeh**,
and the *Chaldeans* **Kesediym** that were found there,
and the men of war.
4 And it *came to pass* **became** the second day
after he had *slain Gedaliah* **executed Gedal Yah**,
and no man knew it,
5 That there came *certain* **men** from Shechem,
from Shiloh, and from *Samaria* **Shomeron**,
even fourscore **eighty** men, having their beards shaven,
and their clothes *rent* **ripped**,
and having *cut themselves* **incised**,
with offerings and incense in their hand,
to bring them to the house of *the LORD* **Yah Veh**.
6 And *Ishmael* **Yishma El**
the son of *Nethaniah* **Nethan Yah**
went forth from *Mizpah* **Mispeh** to meet them,
weeping *all along* **and walking** as he went:
and it *came to pass* **became**,
as he met them, he said unto them,
Come to *Gedaliah* **Gedal Yah** the son of Ahikam.
7 And it was so,
when they came into the midst of the city,
that *Ishmael* **Yishma El** the son of *Nethaniah* **Nethan Yah**
slew **slaughtered** them,
and cast them into the midst of the *pit* **well**,
he, and the men that were with him.
8 But ten men were found among them
that said unto *Ishmael* **Yishma El**, *Slay* **Execute** us not:
for we have **hidden** treasures in the field,
of wheat, and of barley, and of oil, and of honey.
So he *forbare* **ceased**,
and slew them not among their brethren.
9 Now the *pit* **well** wherein *Ishmael* **Yishma El**
had cast all the *dead bodies* **carcases** of the men,
whom he had *slain* **smitten**
because **under the hand** of *Gedaliah* **Gedal Yah**,
was it which Asa the *king* **sovereign** had *made* **worked**
for fear **at the face** of *Baasha* **Basha**
king **sovereign** of *Israel* **Yisra El**:
and Ishmael **Yishma El** the son of *Nethaniah* **Nethan Yah**
filled it with them that were *slain* **pierced**.
10 Then *Ishmael carried away captive* **Yishma El captured**
all the *residue* **survivors** of the people
that were in *Mizpah* **Mispeh**,
even the *king's* **sovereign's** daughters, and all the people
that *remained* **survived** in *Mizpah* **Mispeh**,
whom *Nebuzaradan* **Nebu Zaradan**
the *captain of the guard* **rabbi slaughterer**
had *committed* **mustered**
to *Gedaliah* **Gedal Yah** the son of Ahikam:
and *Ishmael* **Yishma El** the son of *Nethaniah* **Nethan Yah**
carried **captured** them *away captive*,
and *departed to go* **went to pass** over
to the *Ammonites* **sons of Ammon**.

YAH HANAN RESCUES THE PEOPLE

11 But when
Johanan **Yah Hanan** the son of *Kareah* **Qareach**,
and all the *captains* **governors** of the *forces* **valiant**
that were with him,
heard of all the evil
that *Ishmael* **Yishma El** the son of *Nethaniah* **Nethan Yah**
had *done* **worked**,
12 Then they took all the men,
and went to fight with *Ishmael* **Yishma El**
the son of *Nethaniah* **Nethan Yah**,
and found him
by the great waters that are in *Gibeon* **Gibon**.
13 Now it *came to pass* **became**, that when all the people
which were with *Ishmael* **Yishma El**
saw *Johanan* **Yah Hanan** the son of *Kareah* **Qareach**,
and all the *captains* **governors** of the *forces* **valiant**
that were with him, *then* they *were glad* **cheered**.
14 So all the people that *Ishmael* **Yishma El**
had *carried away captive* **captured** from *Mizpah* **Mispeh**
cast about **turned around** and returned, and went
unto *Johanan* **Yah Hanan** the son of *Kareah* **Qareach**.
15 But *Ishmael* **Yishma El**
the son of *Nethaniah* **Nethan Yah**
escaped from *Johanan* **the face of Yah Hanan**
with eight men,
and went to the *Ammonites* **sons of Ammon**.
16 Then took *Johanan* **Yah Hanan**
the son of *Kareah* **Qareach**,
and all the *captains* **governors** of the *forces* **valiant**
that were with him,
all the *remnant* **survivors** of the people
whom he had *recovered* **returned**
from *Ishmael* **Yishma El**
the son of *Nethaniah* **Nethan Yah**,
from *Mizpah* **Mispeh**,
after *that* he had *slain* **smitten**

Gedaliah **Gedal Yah** the son of Ahikam,
even mighty men of war,
and the women, and the children, and the eunuchs,
whom he had
brought again **returned** from *Gibeon* **Gibon**:
17 And they departed, and *dwelt* **settled**
in the *habitation* **inn** of *Chimham* **Kimham**,
which is *by Bethlehem* **beside Beth Lechem**,
to go to enter into *Egypt* **Misrayim**,
18 *Because* **At the face** of the *Chaldeans* **Kesediym**:
for they *were afraid of them* **awed at their face**,
because
Ishmael **Yishma El** the son of *Nethaniah* **Nethan Yah**
had *slain Gedaliah* **smitten Gedal Yah**
the son of Ahikam,
whom the *king* **sovereign** of *Babylon* **Babel**
made *governor* **overseer** in the land.

WARNING AGAINST APPROACHING MISRAYIM

42 Then all the *captains* **governors** of the *forces* **valiant**,
and *Johanan* **Yah Hanan** the son of *Kareah* **Qareach**,
and *Jezaniah* **Yezan Yah** the son of *Hoshaiah* **Hosha Yah**,
and all the people from the least even unto the greatest,
came near,
2 And said unto *Jeremiah* **Yirme Yah** the prophet,
Let, we beseech thee,
our supplication be accepted *before thee* **at thy face**,
and pray for us unto *the LORD* **Yah Veh** thy *God* **Elohim**,
even for all *this remnant* **these survivors**;
(for we *are left* **survived**
but a few of *many* **an abundance**,
as thine eyes *do behold* **see** us:)
3 That *the LORD* **Yah Veh** thy *God* **Elohim**
may *shew* **tell** us the way wherein we may walk,
and the *thing* **word** that we may *do* **work**.
4 Then *Jeremiah* **Yirme Yah** the prophet said unto them,
I have heard *you*; behold,
I *will* **shall** pray
unto *the LORD* **Yah Veh** your *God* **Elohim**
according to your words;
and it shall *come to pass* **become**,
that whatsoever *thing* **word**
the LORD **Yah Veh** shall answer you,
I *will declare* **shall tell** it unto you;
I *will keep nothing back* **shall withhold no word**
from you.
5 Then they said to *Jeremiah* **Yirme Yah**,
The LORD **Yah Veh** be *a true* **in truth**
and **a** faithful witness between us,
if we *do* **work** not even according to all *things* **the word**
for the which *the LORD* **Yah Veh** thy *God* **Elohim**
shall send thee to us.
6 Whether *it be* good, or whether *it be* evil,
we *will obey* **shall hearken unto** the voice
of *the LORD* **Yah Veh** our *God* **Elohim**,
to whom we send thee;
that it may *be well with* **well—please** us,
when we *obey* **hearken unto** the voice
of *the LORD* **Yah Veh** our *God* **Elohim**.
7 And it *came to pass after* **became at the end of** ten days,
that the word of *the LORD* **Yah Veh**
came unto *Jeremiah* **Yirme Yah**.
8 Then called he
Johanan **Yah Hanan** the son of *Kareah* **Qareach**,
and all the *captains* **governors** of the *forces* **valiant**
which were with him,
and all the people from the least even to the greatest,
9 And said unto them, Thus saith *the LORD* **Yah Veh**,
the God **Elohim** of *Israel* **Yisra El**,
unto whom ye sent me
to *present* **fell** your supplication *before him* **at his face**;
10 If ye *will still abide* **shall return and settle** in this land,
then *will* **shall** I build you, and not *pull* **break** you down,
and I *will* **shall** plant you, and not *pluck* **uproot** you *up*:
for I *repent me* **sigh** of the evil
that I have *done* **worked** unto you.
11 *Be* **Awe** not *afraid of*
the *king* **sovereign** of *Babylon* **Babel**,
of whom ye *are afraid* **fear at his face**;
be not *afraid* **awed** of him,
saith the LORD **an oracle of Yah Veh**:
for I am with you to save you,
and to *deliver* **rescue** you from his hand.
12 And I *will shew* **shall give** mercies unto you,
that he may *have* mercy *upon* you,
and *cause* **restore** you *to return* to your own *land* **soil**.
13 But if ye say,
We *will* **shall** not *dwell* **settle** in this land,
neither *obey* **hearken unto** the voice
of *the LORD* **Yah Veh** your *God* **Elohim**,
14 Saying, No;
but we *will* **shall** go into the land of *Egypt* **Misrayim**,
where we shall see no war,
nor hear the *sound* **voice** of the trumpet,
nor have hunger of bread;
and there *will* **shall** we *dwell* **settle**:
15 And now therefore
hear the word of *the LORD* **Yah Veh**,
ye *remnant* **survivors** of *Judah* **Yah Hudah**;
Thus saith *the LORD of hosts* **Yah Veh Sabaoth**,
the God **Elohim** of *Israel* **Yisra El**;
If **in setting**, ye *wholly* set your faces
to enter into *Egypt* **Misrayim**, and go to sojourn there;
16 Then it shall *come to pass* **become**,
that the sword, which ye feared,
shall overtake you there in the land of *Egypt* **Misrayim**,
and the famine, whereof ye were *afraid* **concerned**,
shall *follow close after* **adhereth to** you
there in *Egypt* **Misrayim**; and there ye shall die.
17 *So* shall it be with all the men that set their faces
to go into *Egypt* **Misrayim** to sojourn there;
they shall die by the sword,
by the famine, and by the pestilence:
and *none of them* **there** shall *remain* **be no survivors**
escape **or escapees**
from **the face of** the evil that I *will* **shall** bring upon them.
18 For thus saith *the LORD of hosts* **Yah Veh Sabaoth**,
the God **Elohim** of *Israel* **Yisra El**;
As *mine anger* **my wrath** and my fury
hath been poured forth
upon the *inhabitants* **settlers** of *Jerusalem* **Yeru Shalem**;
so shall my fury be poured forth upon you,
when ye shall enter into *Egypt* **Misrayim**:
and ye shall be an *execration* **oath**,
and *an astonishment* **a desolation**,
and *a curse* **an abasement**, and a reproach;
and ye shall see this place no more.
19 *The LORD* **Yah Veh** hath *said* **worded** concerning you,
O ye *remnant* **survivors** of *Judah* **Yah Hudah**;
Go ye not into *Egypt* **Misrayim**:
in knowing, know *certainly*
that I have *admonished* **witnessed to** you this day.
20 For *ye dissembled in* your *hearts* **souls have strayed**,
when ye sent me
unto *the LORD* **Yah Veh** your *God* **Elohim**, saying,
Pray for us unto *the LORD* **Yah Veh** our *God* **Elohim**;
and according unto all
that *the LORD* **Yah Veh** our *God* **Elohim** shall say,
so *declare* **tell** unto us, and we *will do* **shall work** it.
21 And *now* I have this day *declared* **told** it to you;
but ye have not *obeyed* **hearkened unto** the voice
of *the LORD* **Yah Veh** your *God* **Elohim**,
nor *any thing* **aught**
for the which he hath sent me unto you.
22 Now therefore **in knowing,**
know *certainly* that ye shall die by the sword,
by the famine, and by the pestilence,
in the place whither ye desire to go *and* to sojourn.

YIRME YAH'S WARNING

43 And it *came to pass* **became**,
that when *Jeremiah* **Yirme Yah**
had *made an end of speaking* **concluded wording**
unto all the people
all the words of *the LORD* **Yah Veh** their *God* **Elohim**,
for which *the LORD* **Yah Veh** their *God* **Elohim**
had sent him to them, *even* all these words,
2 Then *spake* **said**
Azariah **Azar Yah** the son of *Hoshaiah* **Hosha Yah**,
and *Johanan* **Yah Hanan** the son of *Kareah* **Qareach**,
and all the *proud* **arrogant** men,
saying unto *Jeremiah* **Yirme Yah**, Thou speakest falsely:

the LORD **Yah Veh** our *God* **Elohim** hath not sent thee,
to say **saying**,
Go not into *Egypt* **Misrayim** to sojourn there:
3 But Baruch the son of *Neriah* **Neri Yah**
setteth **goadeth** thee *on* against us,
for to *deliver* **give** us
into the hand of the *Chaldeans* **Kesediym**,
that they might put us to death,
and *carry us away captives* **exile us** into *Babylon* **Babel**.
4 So *Johanan* **Yah Hanan** the son of *Kareah* **Qareach**,
and all the *captains* **governors** of the *forces* **valiant**,
and all the people,
obeyed **hearkened** not
unto the voice of *the LORD* **Yah Veh**,
to *dwell* **settle** in the land of *Judah* **Yah Hudah**.
5 But *Johanan* **Yah Hanan** the son of *Kareah* **Qareach**,
and all the *captains* **governors** of the *forces* **valiant**,
took all the *remnant* **survivors** of *Judah* **Yah Hudah**,
that were returned from all *nations* **goyim**,
whither they had been driven,
to *dwell* **sojourn** in the land of *Judah* **Yah Hudah**;
6 *Even men* **Mighty**, and women, and *children* **toddlers**,
and the *king's* **sovereign's** daughters,
and every *person* **soul** that *Nebuzaradan* **Nebu Zaradan**
the *captain of the guard* **rabbi slaughterer**
had left with *Gedaliah* **Gedal Yah**
the son of Ahikam the son of Shaphan,
and *Jeremiah* **Yirme Yah** the prophet,
and Baruch the son of *Neriah* **Neri Yah**.
7 So they came into the land of *Egypt* **Misrayim**:
for they *obeyed* **hearkened** not
unto the voice of *the LORD* **Yah Veh**:
thus came they *even* to *Tahpanhes* **Tachpanches**.
8 Then came the word of *the LORD* **Yah Veh**
unto *Jeremiah* **Yirme Yah** in *Tahpanhes* **Tachpanches**,
saying,
9 Take great stones in thine hand,
and hide them in the *clay* **cement** in the brickkiln,
which is at the *entry* **portal** of *Pharaoh's* **Paroh's** house
in *Tahpanhes* **Tachpanches**,
in the *sight* **eyes** of the men *of Judah* **Yah Hudah**;
10 And say unto them,
Thus saith *the LORD of hosts* **Yah Veh Sabaoth**,
the God **Elohim** of *Israel* **Yisra El**;
Behold, I *will* **shall** send and take
Nebuchadrezzar **Nebukadnets Tsar**
the *king* **sovereign** of *Babylon* **Babel**, my servant,
and *will* **shall** set his throne
upon these stones that I have hid;
and he shall spread his *royal* **glory** pavilion over them.
11 And when he cometh,
he shall smite the land of *Egypt* **Misrayim**,
and deliver such as are for death to death;
and such as are for captivity to captivity;
and such as are for the sword to the sword.
12 And I *will* **shall** kindle a fire
in the houses of the *gods* **elohim** of *Egypt* **Misrayim**;
and he shall burn them,
and *carry* **capture** them *away captives*:
and he shall *array* **cover** himself
with the land of *Egypt* **Misrayim**,
as a *shepherd* **tender**
putteth on **covereth with** his *garment* **clothes**;
and he shall go forth from thence in *peace* **shalom**.
13 He shall break also
the *images* **monoliths** of *Bethshemesh* **Beth Shemesh**,
that is in the land of *Egypt* **Misrayim**;
and the houses
of the *gods* **elohim** of the *Egyptians* **Misrayim**
shall he burn with fire.

WARNING CONCERNING IDOLATRY

44 The word that came to *Jeremiah* **Yirme Yah**
concerning all the *Jews* **Yah Hudiym**
which *dwell* **settle** in the land of *Egypt* **Misrayim**,
which *dwell* **settle** at Migdol,
and at *Tahpanhes* **Tachpanches**, and at Noph,
and in the *country* **land** of Pathros, saying,
2 Thus saith *the LORD of hosts* **Yah Veh Sabaoth**,
the God **Elohim** of *Israel* **Yisra El**;
Ye have seen all the evil that I have brought
upon *Jerusalem* **Yeru Shalem**,
and upon all the cities of *Judah* **Yah Hudah**;
and, behold, this day they are a *desolation* **parch**,
and no man *dwelleth* **settleth** therein,
3 *Because* **At the face** of their *wickedness* **evil**
which they have *committed* **worked**
to *provoke* **vex** me *to anger*,
in that they went to *burn* incense,
and to serve other *gods* **elohim**, whom they knew not,
neither they, ye, nor your fathers.
4 Howbeit I sent unto you all my servants the prophets,
rising **starting** early and sending them, saying,
Oh **I beseech**, *do* **work** not
this *abominable thing* **word of abhorrence** that I hate.
5 But they hearkened not,
nor *inclined* **extended** their ear
to turn from their *wickedness* **evil**,
to *burn no* **not** incense unto other *gods* **elohim**.
6 Wherefore my fury and *mine anger* **my wrath**
was poured forth,
and was *kindled* **burnt** in the cities of *Judah* **Yah Hudah**
and in the *streets* **outways** of *Jerusalem* **Yeru Shalem**;
and they are *wasted* **parched** and desolate, as at this day.
7 Therefore now thus saith *the LORD* **Yah Veh**,
the God of hosts **Elohim Sabaoth**,
the God **Elohim** of *Israel* **Yisra El**;
Wherefore *commit* **work** ye this great evil
against your souls,
to cut off from you man and woman,
child **infant** and suckling,
out of *Judah* **the midst of Yah Hudah**,
to leave you **that in surviving,** none *to remain* **survive**;
8 In that ye *provoke* **vex** me *unto wrath*
with the works of your hands,
burning incense **incensing** unto other *gods* **elohim**
in the land of *Egypt* **Misrayim**,
whither ye be gone to *dwell* **sojourn**,
that ye might cut yourselves off,
and that ye might be
a curse **an abasement** and a reproach
among all the *nations* **goyim** of the earth?
9 Have ye forgotten the *wickedness* **evil** of your fathers,
and the *wickedness* **evil**
of the *kings* **sovereigns** of *Judah* **Yah Hudah**,
and the *wickedness* **evil** of their *wives* **women**,
and your own *wickedness* **evil**,
and the *wickedness* **evil** of your *wives* **women**,
which they have *committed* **worked**
in the land of *Judah* **Yah Hudah**,
and in the *streets* **outways** of *Jerusalem* **Yeru Shalem**?
10 They are not *humbled* **crushed** *even* unto this day,
neither have they *feared* **awed**,
nor walked in my *law* **torah**, nor in my statutes,
that I *set before you* **gave at your face**
and *before* **at the face of** your fathers.
11 Therefore
thus saith *the LORD of hosts* **Yah Veh Sabaoth**,
the God **Elohim** of *Israel* **Yisra El**;
Behold, I *will* **shall** set my face against you for evil,
and to cut off all *Judah* **Yah Hudah**.
12 And I *will* **shall** take
the *remnant* **survivors** of *Judah* **Yah Hudah**,
that have set their faces
to go into the land of *Egypt* **Misrayim** to sojourn there,
and they shall all be consumed,
and fall in the land of *Egypt* **Misrayim**;
they shall *even* be consumed
by the sword and by the famine:
they shall die, from the least even unto the greatest,
by the sword and by the famine:
and they shall be an *execration* **oath**,
and *an astonishment* **a desolation**,
and *a curse* **an abasement**, and a reproach.
13 For I *will punish* **shall visit upon** them
that *dwell* **settle** in the land of *Egypt* **Misrayim**,
as I have *punished Jerusalem* **visited upon Yeru Shalem**,
by the sword, by the famine, and by the pestilence:
14 So that none
of the *remnant* **survivors** of *Judah* **Yah Hudah**,
which are gone into the land of *Egypt* **Misrayim**

to sojourn there,
shall escape or remain — **escapees or survivors**
that they should return into the land of *Judah* **Yah Hudah**,
to the which they *have a desire* **lift their soul**
to return to *dwell* **settle** there:
for none shall return but such as shall escape.
15 Then all the men which knew that their *wives* **women**
had *burned incense* **incensed** unto other *gods* **elohim**,
and all the women that stood by,
a great *multitude* **congregation**,
even all the people that *dwelt* **settled**
in the land of *Egypt* **Misrayim**, in Pathros,
answered *Jeremiah* **Yirme Yah**, saying,
16 *As for* the word that thou hast *spoken* **worded**
unto us in the name of *the LORD* **Yah Veh**,
we *will* **shall** not hearken unto thee.
17 But **in working,** we *will certainly do* **shall work**
whatsoever *thing* goeth forth out of our own mouth,
to *burn* incense
unto the *queen* **sovereigness** of *heaven* **the heavens**,
and to *pour out drink offerings* **libate libations** unto her,
as we have *done* **worked**, we, and our fathers,
our *kings* **sovereigns**, and our *princes* **governors**,
in the cities of *Judah* **Yah Hudah**,
and in the *streets* **outways** of *Jerusalem* **Yeru Shalem**:
for then
had we plenty of victuals **were we satiated with bread**,
and were *well* **good**, and saw no evil.
18 But since we *left off to burn* **ceased to** incense
to the *queen* **sovereigness** of *heaven* **the heavens**,
and to *pour out drink offerings* **libate libations** unto her,
we have wanted all *things*,
and have been consumed
by the sword and by the famine.
19 And when we *burned incense* **incensed**
to the *queen* **sovereigness** of *heaven* **the heavens**,
and *poured out drink offerings* **libated libations** unto her,
did we *make* **work** her cakes to *worship* **idolize** her,
and *pour out drink offerings* **libate libations** unto her,
without our men?
20 Then *Jeremiah* **Yirme Yah** said unto all the people,
to the *men* mighty, and to the women,
and to all the people
which had *given* **answered** him *that answer* **word**,
saying,
21 The incense that ye *burned* **incensed**
in the cities of *Judah* **Yah Hudah**,
and in the *streets* **outways** of *Jerusalem* **Yeru Shalem**,
ye, and your fathers, your *kings* **sovereigns**,
and your *princes* **governors**, and the people of the land,
did not *the LORD* **Yah Veh** remember them,
and *came* **ascended** it not into his *mind* **heart**?
22 So that *the LORD* **Yah Veh** could no longer bear,
because **at the face** of the evil of your *doings* **exploits**,
and *because* **at the face** of the *abominations* **abhorrences**
which ye have *committed* **worked**;
therefore is your land a *desolation* **parched area**,
and *an astonishment* **a desolation**,
and *a curse* **an abasement**,
without *an inhabitant* **a settler**, as at this day.
23 *Because* **At the face of that**
ye have *burned incense* **incensed**,
and because ye have sinned against *the LORD* **Yah Veh**,
and have not
obeyed **hearkened unto** the voice of *the LORD* **Yah Veh**,
nor walked in his *law* **torah**, nor in his statutes,
nor in his *testimonies* **witnesses**;
therefore this evil *is happened unto* **confronteth** you,
as at this day.
24 *Moreover*
Jeremiah **Yirme Yah** said unto all the people,
and to all the women,
Hear the word of *the LORD* **Yah Veh**,
all *Judah* **Yah Hudah**
that are in the land of *Egypt* **Misrayim**:
25 Thus saith *the LORD of hosts* **Yah Veh Sabaoth**,
the God **Elohim** of *Israel* **Yisra El**, saying;
Ye and your *wives* **women**
have both *spoken* **worded** with your mouths,
and fulfilled with your hand, saying,
In working, We *will surely perform* **shall work** our vows
that we have vowed,
to *burn* incense
to the *queen* **sovereigness** of *heaven* **the heavens**,
and to *pour out drink offerings* **libate libations** unto her:
in raising, ye *will surely accomplish* **shall raise** your vows,
and **in working,** *surely perform* **ye shall work** your vows.
26 Therefore hear ye the word of *the LORD* **Yah Veh**,
all *Judah* **Yah Hudah**
that *dwell* **settle** in the land of *Egypt* **Misrayim**;
Behold, I have *sworn* **oathed** by my great name,
saith *the LORD* **Yah Veh**,
that my name shall no more be *named* **called out**
in the mouth of any man of *Judah* **Yah Hudah**
in all the land of *Egypt* **Misrayim**, saying,
The Lord GOD **Adonay Yah Veh** liveth.
27 Behold,
I *will* **shall** watch over them for evil, and not for good:
and all the men of *Judah* **Yah Hudah**
that are in the land of *Egypt* **Misrayim**
shall be consumed by the sword and by the famine,
until *there be an end of them* **the consumation**.
28 Yet a *small number* **number of men,**
that escape — **escapees of** the sword
shall return out of the land of *Egypt* **Misrayim**
into the land of *Judah* **Yah Hudah**,
and all the *remnant* **survivors** of *Judah* **Yah Hudah**,
that are gone into the land of *Egypt* **Misrayim**
to sojourn there,
shall know whose words shall *stand* **rise**, mine, or theirs.
29 And this shall be a sign unto you,
saith the LORD **an oracle of Yah Veh**,
that I *will punish* **shall visit upon** you in this place,
that ye may know that my words
in rising, shall *surely stand* **rise** against you for evil:
30 Thus saith *the LORD* **Yah Veh**;
Behold, I *will* **shall** give
Pharaohhophra **Paroh Hophra**
king **sovereign** of *Egypt* **Misrayim**
into the hand of his enemies,
and into the hand of them that seek his *life* **soul**;
as I gave *Zedekiah* **Sidqi Yah**
king **sovereign** of *Judah* **Yah Hudah**
into the hand of
Nebuchadrezzar **Nebukadnets Tsar**
king **sovereign** of *Babylon* **Babel**,
his enemy, and that sought his *life* **soul.**

MESSAGE TO BARUCH

45 The word that *Jeremiah* **Yirme Yah** the prophet
spake **worded**
unto Baruch the son of *Neriah* **Neri Yah**,
when he had *written* **inscribed** these words
in a *book* **scroll**
at the mouth of *Jeremiah* **Yirme Yah**,
in the fourth year of *Jehoiakim* **Yah Yaqim**
the son of *Josiah* **Yoshi Yah**
king **sovereign** of *Judah* **Yah Hudah**, saying,
2 Thus saith *the LORD* **Yah Veh**,
the God **Elohim** of *Israel* **Yisra El**,
unto thee, O Baruch:
3 Thou *didst say* **saidst**,
Woe is me *now* **I beseech**!
for *the LORD* **Yah Veh** hath added grief to my sorrow;
I *fainted* **belaboured** in my sighing, and I find no rest.
4 Thus shalt thou say unto him,
The LORD **Yah Veh** saith thus; Behold,
that which I have built
will **shall** I break down,
and that which I have planted
I *will pluck up* **shall uproot**,
even this whole land.
5 And seekest thou great *things* for thyself? seek *them* not:
for, behold, I *will* **shall** bring evil upon all flesh,
saith the LORD **an oracle of Yah Veh**:
but thy *life will* **soul shall** I give unto thee for a *prey* **spoil**
in all places whither thou goest.

MESSAGE AGAINST THE GOYIM

46 The word of *the LORD* **Yah Veh**
which came to *Jeremiah* **Yirme Yah** the prophet
against the *Gentiles* **goyim**;

MESSAGE AGAINST MISRAYIM

2 Against *Egypt* **Misrayim,**
against the *army* **valiant** of *Pharaohnecho* **Paroh Nechoh**
king **sovereign** of *Egypt* **Misrayim,**
which was by the river Euphrates
in *Carchemish* **Karchemish,**
which *Nebuchadrezzar* **Nebukadnets Tsar**
king **sovereign** of *Babylon* **Babel**
smote in the fourth year of *Jehoiakim* **Yah Yaqim**
the son of *Josiah* **Yoshi Yah**
king **sovereign** of *Judah* **Yah Hudah.**
3 *Order* **Line up** ye the buckler and shield,
and draw near to *battle* **war.**
4 *Harness* **Hitch** the horses;
and *get up* **ascend,** ye *horsemen* **cavalry,**
and stand forth with *your* helmets;
furbish **polish** the *spears* **javelins,**
and put on **enrobe** the brigandines.
5 Wherefore have I seen them *dismayed* **terrorized**
and *turned away back* **apostatized backward?**
and their mighty *ones are beaten down* **crushed,**
and are fled *apace* **to a retreat,** and *look* **face** not back:
for fear **terror** was round about,
saith the LORD **an oracle of Yah Veh.**
6 Let not the swift flee away,
nor the mighty *man* escape;
they shall stumble,
and *fall toward the north* **falter northward**
by **the hand of** the river Euphrates.
7 Who is this that *cometh up* **ascendeth** as a *flood* **river,**
whose waters are *moved* **agitated** as the rivers?
8 *Egypt riseth up* **Misrayim ascendeth** like a *flood* **river,**
and his waters are *moved* **agitated** like the rivers;
and he saith,
I *will go up* **shall ascend,** and *will* **shall** cover the earth;
I *will* **shall** destroy the city
and the *inhabitants* **settlers** *thereof.*
9 *Come up* **Ascend,** ye horses; *and rage* **halal,** ye chariots;
and let the mighty *men* come forth;
the *Ethiopians* **Kushies** and the *Libyans* **Puties,**
that *handle* **manipulate** the *shield* **buckler;**
and the *Lydians* **Ludiym,**
that *handle* **manipulate** and bend the bow.
10 For this is the day
of *the Lord GOD of hosts* **Adonay Yah Veh Sabaoth,**
a day of *vengeance* **avengement,**
that he may avenge him of his *adversaries* **tribulators:**
and the sword shall devour,
and it shall be satiate
and *made drunk* **satiate** with their blood:
for *the Lord GOD of hosts* **Adonay Yah Veh Sabaoth**
hath a sacrifice in the north *country* **land**
by the river Euphrates.
11 *Go up* **Ascend** into *Gilead* **Gilad,** and take balm,
O virgin, the daughter of *Egypt* **Misrayim:**
in vain shalt thou *use many medicines* **abound healers;**
for thou shalt not be *cured* **bandaged.**
12 The *nations* **goyim**
have heard of thy *shame* **abasement,**
and thy *cry* **outcry** hath filled the land:
for the mighty *man*
hath *stumbled* **faltered** against the mighty,
and they are fallen both together.
13 The word that *the LORD* **Yah Veh**
spake **worded** to *Jeremiah* **Yirme Yah** the prophet,
how *Nebuchadrezzar* **Nebukadnets Tsar**
king **sovereign** of *Babylon* **Babel**
should come and smite the land of *Egypt* **Misrayim.**
14 *Declare* **Tell** ye in *Egypt* **Misrayim,**
and *publish* **be it heard** in Migdol,
and *publish* **be it heard** in Noph
and in *Tahpanhes* **Tachpanches:**
say ye, Stand fast, and prepare thee;
for the sword shall devour round about thee.
15 Why are thy *valiant men* **mighty** swept away?
they stood not,
because *the LORD did drive* **Yah Veh exiled** them.
16 He *made many to fall* **hath abounded the falterer,**
yea, *one* **man** fell upon *another* **friend:**
and they said,
Arise, and let us *go again* **return** to our own people,
and to the land of our *nativity* **kindred,**
from **the face of** the oppressing sword.
17 They *did cry* **called out** there,
Pharaoh king **Paroh sovereign** of *Egypt* **Misrayim**
is but *a noise* **an uproar;**
he hath passed the *time appointed* **season.**
18 *As* I live, *saith* **an oracle of** the *King* **Sovereign,**
whose name is *the LORD of hosts* **Yah Veh Sabaoth,**
Surely as Tabor is among the mountains,
and as *Carmel* **Karmel/orchard** by the sea,
so shall he come.
19 O thou daughter *dwelling* **settling** in *Egypt* **Misrayim,**
furnish **work vessels for** thyself to go into *captivity* **exile:**
for Noph shall be *waste* **desolate** and *desolate* **burned**
without *an inhabitant* **a settler.**
20 *Egypt* **Misrayim** is like a very *fair* **beautiful** heifer,
but destruction **extermination** cometh;
it cometh out of the north.
21 Also her *hired men* **hirelings**
are in the midst of her like fatted *bullocks* **calves;**
for they also *are turned* **faced** back,
and are fled away together:
they did not stand,
because the day of their calamity was come upon them,
and the time of their visitation.
22 The voice *thereof* shall go like a serpent;
for they shall march with *an army* **the valiant,**
and come against her with axes,
as *hewers* **choppers** of *wood* **timber.**
23 They shall cut down her forest,
saith the LORD **an oracle of Yah Veh,**
though it cannot be *searched* **probed;**
because they *are more* **abound by the myriads**
than **above** the grasshoppers, and are innumerable.
24 The daughter of *Egypt* **Misrayim**
shall *be confounded* **shame;**
she shall be *delivered* **given**
into the hand of the people of the north.
25 *The LORD of hosts* **Yah Veh Sabaoth,**
the God **Elohim** of *Israel* **Yisra El,** saith;
Behold, I *will punish* **shall visit upon** the multitude of No,
and *Pharaoh* **Paroh,** and *Egypt* **Misrayim,**
with their *gods* **elohim,** and their *kings* **sovereigns;**
even *Pharaoh* **Paroh,**
and *all* them that *trust* **confide** in him:
26 And I *will deliver* **shall give** them
into the hand of those that seek their *lives* **souls,**
and into the hand of *Nebuchadrezzar* **Nebukadnets Tsar**
king **sovereign** of *Babylon* **Babel,**
and into the hand of his servants:
and afterward it shall be *inhabited* **tabernacled in,**
as in the **ancient** days *of old,*
saith the LORD **an oracle of Yah Veh.**
27 But *fear* **awe** not thou, O my servant *Jacob* **Yaaqov,**
and be not dismayed, O *Israel* **Yisra El:** for, behold,
I *will save thee* **shall be thy saviour** from afar off,
and thy seed from the land of their captivity;
and *Jacob* **Yaaqov** shall return,
and *be in* rest and *at ease* **relax,**
and none shall *make* **frighten** him *afraid.*
28 *Fear* **Awe** thou not, O *Jacob* **Yaaqov** my servant,
saith the LORD **an oracle of Yah Veh:**
for I am with thee;
for I *will make a full end* **shall work a final finish**
of all the *nations* **goyim** whither I have driven thee:
but I *will* **shall** not
make a full end **work a final finish** of thee,
but *correct* **discipline** thee in *measure* **judgment;**
yet *will I not leave thee wholly unpunished*
in exonerating, I shall not exonerate thee.

WORD AGAINST THE PELESHETHIYM

47 The word of *the LORD* **Yah Veh**
that came to *Jeremiah* **Yirme Yah** the prophet
against the *Philistines* **Peleshethiym,**
before that *Pharaoh* **Paroh** smote *Gaza* **Azzah.**
2 Thus saith *the LORD* **Yah Veh;** Behold,
waters *rise up* **ascend** out of the north,
and shall be an overflowing *flood* **wadi,**
and shall overflow the land,

and *all that is therein* **its fulness**;
the city, and them that *dwell* **settle** therein:
then *the men* **humanity** shall cry **out**,
and all the *inhabitants* **settlers** of the land shall howl.
3 At the *noise* **voice** of the stamping of the hoofs
of his *strong horses* **mighty**,
at the *rushing* **quake** of his chariots,
and at the *rumbling* **roar** of his wheels,
the fathers shall not *look* **face** back to *their children* **sons**
for *feebleness* **slackness** of hands;
4 Because of the day that cometh
to *spoil* **ravage** all the *Philistines* **Peleshethiym**,
and to cut off from *Tyrus* **Sor** and *Zidon* **Sidon**
every *helper* **survivor** that *remaineth* **helpeth**:
for *the LORD* **Yah Veh**
will spoil **shall ravage** the *Philistines* **Peleshethiym**,
the *remnant* **survivors**
of the *country* **island** of *Caphtor* **Kaphtor**.
5 Baldness is come upon *Gaza* **Azzah**;
Ashkelon is *cut off* **severed**
with the *remnant* **survivors** of their valley:
how long *wilt* **shalt** thou *cut* **incise** thyself?
6 *O* **Ho** thou sword of *the LORD* **Yah Veh**,
how long *will* **shall** it be ere thou *be quiet* **rest**?
put up thyself into **gather** thy *scabbard* **sheath**,
rest, and be still.
7 How can it *be quiet* **rest**,
seeing *the LORD* **Yah Veh**
hath *given it a charge* **misvahed** against Ashkelon,
and against the sea *shore* **haven**?
there hath he *appointed it* **congregated**.

MESSAGE AGAINST MOAB

48 Against Moab
thus saith *the LORD of hosts* **Yah Veh Sabaoth**,
the God **Elohim** of *Israel* **Yisra El**;
Woe **Ho** unto Nebo! for it is *spoiled* **ravaged**:
Kiriathaim **Qiryathaim**
is *confounded* **shamed** and *taken* **captured**:
Misgab **The secure loft**
is *confounded* **shamed** and dismayed.
2 There shall be no more *praise* **halal** of Moab:
in Heshbon they have *devised* **fabricated** evil against it;
come, and let us cut it off from *being a nation* **goyim**.
Also thou shalt be *cut down* **severed**, O Madmen;
the sword shall *pursue* **go after** thee.
3 A voice of crying shall be from Horonaim,
spoiling **ravage** and great *destruction* **breaking**.
4 Moab is *destroyed* **broken**;
her little *ones* have caused a cry to be heard.
5 For in the *going up* **ascent** of *Luhith* **Luchith**
in weeping, *continual* weeping shall *go up* **ascend**;
for in the *going down* **descent** of Horonaim
the *enemies* **tribulators**
have heard a cry of *destruction* **breaking**.
6 Flee, *save* **rescue** your *lives* **souls**,
and be like the *heath* **naked tree** in the wilderness.
7 For because thou hast *trusted* **confided**
in thy works and in thy treasures,
thou shalt also be *taken* **captured**:
and *Chemosh* **Kemosh** shall go forth into *captivity* **exile**
with his priests and his *princes* **governors** together.
8 And the *spoiler* **ravager** shall come upon every city,
and no city shall escape:
the valley also shall *perish* **destruct**,
and the plain shall *be destroyed* **desolate**,
as *the LORD* **Yah Veh** hath *spoken* **said**.
9 Give wings unto Moab, that it may flee and get away:
for the cities thereof shall be desolate,
without any to *dwell* **settle** therein.
10 Cursed be he
that *doeth* **worketh** the work of *the LORD* **Yah Veh**
deceitfully,
and cursed be he
that *keepeth back* **withholdeth** his sword from blood.
11 Moab hath *been at ease* **relaxed** from his youth,
and he hath *settled* **rested** on his *lees* **dregs**,
and hath not been *emptied* **poured out**
from *vessel* **instrument** to *vessel* **instrument**,
neither hath he gone into *captivity* **exile**:
therefore his taste *remained* **stood** in him,
and his scent is not changed.
12 Therefore, behold, the days come,
saith the LORD **an oracle of Yah Veh**,
that I *will* **shall** send unto him *wanderers* **strollers**,
that shall cause him to *wander* **stroll**,
and shall *empty* **pour out** his *vessels* **instruments**,
and *break* **shatter** their *bottles* **bags**.
13 And Moab
shall be *ashamed* **shamed** of *Chemosh* **Kemosh**,
as the house of *Israel was ashamed* **Yisra El shamed**
of *Bethel* **Beth El** their confidence.
14 How say ye,
We are mighty and *strong* **valiant** men for the war?
15 Moab is *spoiled* **ravaged**,
and *gone up out of* **ascended** her cities,
and his chosen *young men* **youths**
are *gone down* **descended** to the slaughter,
saith the King **an oracle of the Sovereign**,
whose name is *the LORD of hosts* **Yah Veh Sabaoth**.
16 The calamity of Moab is near to come,
and his *affliction* **evil** hasteth *fast* **mightily**.
17 All ye that are **round** about him,
bemoan **wag over** him;
and all ye that know his name, say,
How is the *strong staff* **rod of strength** broken,
and the *beautiful rod* **staff of adornment**!
18 Thou daughter that *dost inhabit* **settlest** Dibon,
come down **descend** from thy *glory* **honour**,
and *sit* **settle** in thirst;
for the *spoiler* **ravager** of Moab
shall *come* **ascend** upon thee,
and he shall *destroy* **ruin** thy *strong holds* **fortresses**.
19 O *inhabitant* **settler** of Aroer,
stand by the way, and *espy* **watch**;
ask him that fleeth, and her that escapeth,
and say, What is done?
20 Moab is *confounded* **shamed**; for it is broken down:
howl and cry;
tell ye it in Arnon, that Moab is *spoiled* **ravaged**,
21 And judgment is come upon the plain *country* **land**;
upon Holon,
and upon *Jahazah* **Yahsah**, and upon Mephaath,
22 And upon Dibon, and upon Nebo,
and upon *Bethdiblathaim* **Beth Diblathayim**,
23 And upon *Kiriathaim* **Qiryathaim**,
and upon *Bethgamul* **Beth Gamul**,
and upon *Bethmeon* **Beth Meon**,
24 And upon *Kerioth* **Qerioth**, and upon Bozrah,
and upon all the cities of the land of Moab, far or near.
25 The horn of Moab is cut off, and his arm is broken,
saith the LORD **an oracle of Yah Veh**.
26 *Make ye* **Intoxicate** him *drunken*:
for he *magnified* **greatened** *himself*
against *the LORD* **Yah Veh**:
Moab also shall *wallow* **slurp** in his vomit,
and he also shall be *in derision* **ridiculed**.
27 For was not *Israel* **Yisra El**
a *derision* **ridicule** unto thee?
was he found among thieves?
for since *thou spakest of him* **from thy sufficient words**,
thou *skippedst* **swayedst** for joy.
28 O ye that *dwell* **settle** in Moab,
leave the cities, and *dwell* **tabernacle** in the rock,
and be like the dove that *maketh her nest* **nesteth**
in the sides of the *hole's* **pit's** mouth.
29 We have heard the *pride* **pomp** of Moab,
(he is *exceeding proud* **mightily pompous**)
his *loftiness* **haughtiness**, and his *arrogancy* **pomp**,
and his *pride* **pomp**, and the haughtiness of his heart.
30 I know his wrath,
saith the LORD **an oracle of Yah Veh**;
but it shall not be so; his lies shall not so *effect* **work** it.
31 Therefore *will* **shall** I howl for Moab,
and I *will* **shall** cry out for all Moab;
mine heart shall mourn — **meditate**
for the men of *Kirheres* **Qir Hareseth**.
32 O vine of Sibmah, I *will* **shall** weep for thee
with the weeping of *Jazer* **Yazer**:
thy *plants* **tendrils** are *gone* **passed** over the sea,
they *reach even* **touch** to the sea of *Jazer* **Yazer**:

the *spoiler* **ravager** is fallen upon thy summer fruits
and upon thy *vintage* **crop**.
33 And *joy* **cheerfulness** and *gladness* **twirling**
is *taken* **gathered** from the *plentiful field* **orchard/Karmel**,
and from the land of Moab,
and I have caused wine to *fail* **shabbathize**
from the *winepresses* **troughs**:
none shall tread with shouting;
their shouting shall be no shouting.
34 From the cry of Heshbon *even* unto *Elealeh* **El Aleh**,
and *even* unto *Jahaz* **Yahsah**,
have they *uttered* **given** their voice,
from *Zoar* **Soar** *even* unto Horonaim,
as an heifer of three *years old*:
for the waters also of Nimrim
shall be *desolate* **desolations**.
35 *Moreover*
I *will* **shall** cause to *cease* **shabbathize** in Moab,
saith the LORD **an oracle of Yah Veh**,
him that *offereth* **holocausteth** in the *high places* **bamahs**,
and him that *burneth incense* **incenseth**
to his *gods* **elohim**.
36 Therefore
mine heart shall *sound* **roar** for Moab like pipes,
and mine heart shall *sound* **roar** like pipes
for the men of *Kirheres* **Qir Hareseth**:
because the riches that he hath *gotten* **worked**
are *perished* **destroyed**.
37 For every head shall *be bald* **balden**,
and every beard *clipped* **diminished**:
upon all the hands shall be *cuttings* **incisions**,
and upon the loins *sackcloth* **saq**.
38 There shall be *lamentation generally* **chopping for all**
upon all the *housetops* **roofs** of Moab,
and in the *streets* **broadways** *thereof*:
for I have broken Moab like *a vessel* **an instrument**
wherein is no pleasure,
saith the LORD **an oracle of Yah Veh**.
39 They shall howl, *saying,* How is it broken down!
how hath Moab *turned* **faced** the *back* **neck**
with shame **shamed**!
so shall Moab be a *derision* **ridicule** and a *dismaying* **ruin**
to all them **round** about him.
40 For thus saith *the LORD* **Yah Veh**;
Behold, he shall fly as an eagle,
and shall spread his wings over Moab.
41 *Kerioth* **Qerioth** is *taken* **captured**,
and the *strong holds* **huntholds**
are *surprised* **apprehended**,
and the mighty *men's* hearts in Moab at that day
shall be as the heart of a woman in her *pangs* **tribulating**.
42 And Moab shall *be destroyed* **desolate**
from *being* a people,
because he hath *magnified* **greatened** *himself*
against *the LORD* **Yah Veh**.
43 Fear, and the pit, and the snare,
shall be upon thee, O *inhabitant* **settler** of Moab,
saith the LORD **an oracle of Yah Veh**.
44 He that fleeth from the **face of** fear
shall fall into the pit;
and he that *getteth up* **ascendeth** out of the pit
shall be *taken* **captured** in the snare:
for I *will* **shall** bring upon it, *even* upon Moab,
the year of their visitation,
saith the LORD **an oracle of Yah Veh**.
45 They that fled stood under the shadow of Heshbon
because of the force:
but a fire shall come forth out of Heshbon,
and a flame from *the midst of Sihon* **within Sichon**,
and shall devour the *corner* **edge** of Moab,
and the *crown* **scalp**
of the *head* **sons** of *the tumultuous ones* **uproar**.
46 Woe be unto thee, O Moab!
the people of *Chemosh perisheth* **Kemosh destruct**:
for thy sons are taken **with the** captives,
and thy daughters *captives* **with the captivity**.
47 Yet *will* **shall** I *bring again* **return** the captivity of Moab
in the latter days,
saith the LORD **an oracle of Yah Veh**.
Thus far **This** is the judgment of Moab.

MESSAGE AGAINST THE SONS OF AMMON

49 Concerning the *Ammonites* **sons of Ammon**,
thus saith *the LORD* **Yah Veh**;
Hath *Israel* **Yisra El** no sons? hath he no *heir* **successor**?
why *then* doth their *king inherit* **sovereign succeed** Gad,
and his people *dwell* **settle** in his cities?
2 Therefore, behold, the days come,
saith the LORD **an oracle of Yah Veh**,
that I *will* **shall** cause *an alarm* **a blast** of war
to be heard in Rabbah of the *Ammonites* **sons of Ammon**;
and it shall be a desolate heap,
and her daughters shall be burned with fire:
then shall *Israel* **Yisra El** be *heir* **successor** unto them
that were his *heirs* **successors**,
saith *the LORD* **Yah Veh**.
3 Howl, O Heshbon, for *Ai* **Ay** is *spoiled* **ravaged**:
cry, ye daughters of Rabbah, gird you with *sackcloth* **saq**;
lament **chop**, and *run to and fro* **flit** by the *hedges* **walls**;
for their *king* **sovereign** shall go into *captivity* **exile**,
and his priests and his *princes* **governors** together.
4 Wherefore *gloriest* **halalest** thou in the valleys,
thy flowing valley, O *backsliding* **apostate** daughter?
that *trusted* **confided** in her treasures, *saying,*
Who shall come unto me?
5 Behold, I *will* **shall** bring a fear upon thee,
saith the Lord GOD of hosts
an oracle of Adonay Yah Veh Sabaoth,
from all those that be **round** about thee;
and ye shall be driven out every man
right forth **from his face**;
and none shall gather *up* him that wandereth.
6 And afterward
I *will bring again* **shall return** the captivity
of the *children* **sons** of Ammon,
saith the LORD **an oracle of Yah Veh**.

MESSAGE AGAINST EDOM

7 Concerning Edom,
thus saith *the LORD of hosts* **Yah Veh Sabaoth**;
Is wisdom no more in Teman?
is counsel *perished* **destroyed**
from the *prudent* **discerning**?
is their wisdom *vanished* **spread thin**?
8 Flee ye, *turn* **face** back, *dwell* **settle** deep,
O *inhabitants* **settlers** of Dedan;
for I *will* **shall** bring the calamity of *Esau* **Esav** upon him,
the time that I *will* **shall** visit him.
9 If *grapegatherers* **clippers** come to thee,
would **should** they not
leave some gleaning grapes **let gleanings remain**?
if thieves by night,
they *will destroy* **shall ruin** till they have enough.
10 But I have *made Esau bare* **stripped Esav**,
I have *uncovered* **exposed** his *secret places* **coverts**,
and he shall not be able to hide himself:
his seed is *spoiled* **ravaged**,
and his brethren, and his *neighbours* **fellow tabernaclers**,
and he is not.
11 Leave thy *fatherless children* **orphans**,
I *will preserve* **shall enliven** them *alive*;
and let thy widows *trust* **confide** in me.
12 For thus saith *the LORD* **Yah Veh**; Behold,
they whose judgment was not to drink of the cup
in drinking, have *assuredly* drunken;
and art thou he that **in exonerating,**
shall *altogether go unpunished* **be exonerated**?
thou shalt not *go unpunished* **be exonerated**,
but **in drinking,** thou shalt *surely* drink of it.
13 For I have *sworn* **oathed** by myself,
saith the LORD **an oracle of Yah Veh**,
that Bozrah shall become a desolation,
a reproach, a *waste* **parch**, and *a curse* **an abasement**;
and all the cities *thereof*
shall be *perpetual wastes* **eternal parched areas**.
14 I have heard a *rumour* **report** from *the LORD* **Yah Veh**,
and an ambassador is sent unto the *heathen* **goyim**,
saying, Gather ye together, and come against her,
and rise up to the *battle* **war**.
15 For, *lo* **behold**,
I *will make* **shall give** thee
small among the *heathen* **goyim**,

and despised among *men* **humanity**.
16 Thy *terribleness* **trembling** hath deceived thee,
and the *pride* **arrogance** of thine heart,
O thou that *dwellest* **tabernaclest** in the clefts of the rock,
that *holdest* **apprehendest** the height of the hill:
though thou shouldest *make* **heighten** thy nest
as high as the eagle,
I *will* **shall** bring thee down from thence,
saith the LORD **an oracle of Yah Veh**.
17 Also Edom shall be a desolation:
every one that *goeth* **passeth** by it shall be astonished,
and shall hiss at all the *plagues* **wounds** *thereof*.
18 As in the overthrow
of *Sodom* **Sedom** and *Gomorrah* **Amorah**
and the *neighbour cities* **nearby tabernacles** *thereof*,
saith *the LORD* **Yah Veh**,
no man shall *abide* **settle** there,
neither shall a son of *man dwell* **humanity sojourn** in it.
19 Behold, he shall *come up* **ascend** like a lion
from the *swelling* **pomp** of *Jordan* **Yarden**
against the habitation **of rest** of the *strong* **perrenial**:
but I *will suddenly* **shall in a blink**
make him run away from her:
and who is a chosen *man*,
that I may *appoint over* **oversee** her?
for who is like me?
and who *will appoint me the time* **shall congregate with me**?
and who is that *shepherd* **tender**
that *will* **shall** stand *before me* **at my face**?
20 Therefore hear the counsel of *the LORD* **Yah Veh**,
that he hath *taken* **counselled** against Edom;
and his *purposes* **fabrications**,
that he hath *purposed* **fabricated**
against the *inhabitants* **settlers** of Teman:
Surely the *least* **lesser** of the flock
shall *draw* **drag** them out:
surely he shall *make* **desolate**
their habitations *desolate* **of rest** with them.
21 The earth *is moved* **quaketh**
at the *noise* **voice** of their fall,
at the cry the *noise* **voice** *thereof*
was heard in the *Red* **Reed** sea.
22 Behold, he shall *come up* **ascend** and fly as the eagle,
and spread his wings over Bozrah:
and at that day shall the heart of the mighty *men* of Edom
be as the heart of a woman in her *pangs* **tribulating**.

MESSAGE AGAINST DAMMESEQ

23 Concerning *Damascus* **Dammeseq**.
Hamath is *confounded* **shamed**, and Arpad:
for they have heard evil *tidings* **reports**:
they are *fainthearted* **melted**;
there is *sorrow* **concern** on the sea;
it cannot *be quiet* **rest**.
24 *Damascus is waxed feeble* **Dammeseq slacketh**,
and *turneth* **faceth** *herself* to flee,
and *fear* **terror** hath *seized on* **holden** her:
anguish **tribulation** and *sorrows* **pangs** have taken her,
as a woman *in travail* **birthing**.
25 How is the city of *praise* **halal** not *left* **forsaken**,
the city of my joy!
26 Therefore her *young men* **youths**
shall fall in her *streets* **broadways**,
and all the men of war
shall be *cut off* **severed** in that day,
saith the LORD of hosts **an oracle of Yah Veh Sabaoth**.
27 And I *will* **shall** kindle a fire
in the wall of *Damascus* **Dammeseq**,
and it shall consume
the *palaces* **citadels** of *Benhadad* **Ben Hadad**.

MESSAGE AGAINST QEDAR AND HAZOR

28 Concerning *Kedar* **Qedar**,
and concerning the *kingdoms* **sovereigndoms** of Hazor,
which *Nebuchadrezzar* **Nebukadnets Tsar**
king **sovereign** of *Babylon* **Babel** shall smite,
thus saith *the LORD* **Yah Veh**;
Arise ye, *go up* **ascend** to *Kedar* **Qedar**,
and *spoil* **ravage** the *men* **sons** of the east.
29 Their tents and their flocks shall they take away:
they shall *take* **bear** to themselves their curtains,
and all their *vessels* **instruments**, and their camels;
and they shall *cry* **call out** unto them,
Fear **Terror** is *on every side* **round about**.
30 Flee, *get you far off* **bemoan mightily**,
dwell **settle** deep, O ye *inhabitants* **settlers** of Hazor,
saith the LORD **an oracle of Yah Veh**;
for *Nebuchadrezzar* **Nebukadnets Tsar**
king **sovereign** of *Babylon* **Babel**
hath *taken counsel* **counselled** against you,
and hath *conceived* **fabricated** a *purpose* **fabrication**
against you.
31 Arise,
get **ascend** you *up* unto the *wealthy nation* **serene goyim**,
that *dwelleth without care* **settleth confidently**,
saith the LORD **an oracle of Yah Veh**,
which have neither *gates* **doors** nor bars,
which *dwell* **tabernacle** alone.
32 And their camels shall be a *booty* **plunder**,
and the multitude of their *cattle* **chattel** a spoil:
and I *will scatter* **shall winnow** into all winds
them that *are in the utmost corners* **chop the edges**;
and I *will* **shall** bring their calamity from all sides *thereof*,
saith the LORD **an oracle of Yah Veh**.
33 And Hazor shall be
a *dwelling for dragons* **habitation of monsters**,
and a desolation *for ever* **eternally**:
there shall no man *abide* **settle** there,
nor *any* **a** son of *man dwell* **humanity sojourn** in it.

MESSAGE AGAINST ELAM

34 The word of *the LORD* **Yah Veh**
that came to *Jeremiah* **Yirme Yah** the prophet
against Elam in the beginning of the *reign* **sovereigndom**
of *Zedekiah* **Sidqi Yah**
king **sovereign** of *Judah* **Yah Hudah**, saying,
35 Thus saith *the LORD of hosts* **Yah Veh Sabaoth**;
Behold, I *will* **shall** break the bow of Elam,
the *chief* **beginning** of their might.
36 And upon Elam *will* **shall** I bring the four winds
from the four *quarters* **ends** of *heaven* **the heavens**,
and *will scatter* **shall winnow** them
toward all those winds;
and there shall be no *nation* **goyim**
whither the *outcasts* **expelled** of Elam shall not come.
37 For I *will* **shall** cause Elam to be dismayed
before **at the face of** their enemies,
and *before* **at the face of** them that seek their *life* **soul**:
and I *will* **shall** bring evil upon them,
even my *fierce anger* **fuming wrath**,
saith the LORD **an oracle of Yah Veh**;
and I *will* **shall** send the sword after them,
till I have *consumed* **finished** them **off**:
38 And I *will* **shall** set my throne in Elam,
and *will* **shall** destroy from thence
the *king* **sovereign** and the *princes* **governors**,
saith the LORD **an oracle of Yah Veh**.
39 But it shall *come to pass* **become**, in the latter days,
that I *will bring again* **shall return** the captivity of Elam,
saith the LORD **an oracle of Yah Veh**.

MESSAGE AGAINST BABEL

50 The word that *the LORD spake* **Yah Veh worded**
against *Babylon* **Babel**
and against the land of the *Chaldeans* **Kesediym**
by *Jeremiah* **the hand of Yirme Yah** the prophet.
2 *Declare* **Tell** ye among the *nations* **goyim**,
and *publish* **let it be heard**,
and *set up a standard* **lift an ensign**;
publish **let it be heard**, and conceal not:
say, *Babylon* **Babel** is *taken* **captured**,
Bel is *confounded* **shamed**,
Merodach is broken *in pieces*;
her idols are *confounded* **shamed**,
her *images* **idols** are broken *in pieces*.
3 For out of the north
there *cometh up* **ascendeth** a *nation* **goyim** against her,
which shall *make* **place** her land desolate,
and none shall *dwell* **settle** therein:
they shall *remove* **wander**, they shall depart,
both *man* **humanity** and *beast* **animal**.
4 In those days, and in that time,
saith the LORD **an oracle of Yah Veh**,
the *children* **sons** of *Israel* **Yisra El** shall come,

they and the *children* **sons** of *Judah* **Yah Hudah** together,
going and weeping: they shall go,
and seek *the LORD* **Yah Veh** their *God* **Elohim.**
5 They shall ask the way to *Zion* **Siyon**
with their faces thitherward, *saying,*
Come, and let us join ourselves to *the LORD* **Yah Veh**
in *a perpetual* **an eternal** covenant
that shall not be forgotten.
6 My people hath been lost *sheep* **flocks**
their *shepherds* **tenders**
have caused them to *go astray* **stray,**
they have *turned* **apostatized** them *away*
on the mountains:
they have gone from mountain to hill,
they have forgotten their *restingplace* **repose.**
7 All that found them have devoured them:
and their *adversaries* **tribulators** said,
We *offend* **have** not **guilted,**
because they have sinned against *the LORD* **Yah Veh,**
the habitation **of rest** of *justice* **justness,**
even *the LORD* **Yah Veh,**
the *hope* **expectation** of their fathers.
8 *Remove* **Wander** out of the midst of *Babylon* **Babel,**
and go forth out of the land of the *Chaldeans* **Kesediym,**
and be as the he goats *before* **at the face of** the flocks.
9 For, *lo* **behold,** I *will raise* **shall waken**
and cause to *come up* **ascend** against *Babylon* **Babel**
an assembly **a congregation** of great *nations* **goyim**
from the north *country* **land:**
and they shall *set themselves in array* **line up** against her;
from thence she shall be *taken* **captured:**
their arrows shall be as of a mighty *expert man* **discerner;**
none shall return in vain.
10 And *Chaldea* **Kesediym** shall be a spoil:
all that spoil her shall be satisfied,
saith the LORD **an oracle of Yah Veh.**
11 Because ye *were glad* **cheered,**
because ye *rejoiced* **jumped for joy,**
O ye *destroyers* **plunderers** of mine *heritage* **inheritance,**
because ye are grown fat as the heifer at grass,
and *bellow* **resound** as *bulls* **mighty;**
12 Your mother shall *be sore confounded* **mightily shame;**
she that bare you shall *be ashamed* **blush:**
behold, the hindermost of the *nations* **goyim**
shall be a wilderness,
a *dry land* **parch,** and a *desert* **plain.**
13 Because of the *wrath* **rage** of *the LORD* **Yah Veh**
it shall not be *inhabited* **settled,**
but it shall be wholly desolate:
every one that *goeth* **passeth** by *Babylon* **Babel**
shall be astonished, and hiss at all her *plagues* **wounds.**
14 *Put yourselves in array* **Line up** against *Babylon* **Babel**
round about:
all ye that bend the bow,
shoot **hand toss** at her, spare no arrows:
for she hath sinned against *the LORD* **Yah Veh.**
15 Shout against her round about:
she hath given her hand:
her foundations are fallen, her walls are thrown down:
for it is the *vengeance* **avengement**
of *the LORD* **Yah Veh:**
take vengeance **avenge** upon her;
as she hath *done* **worked,** *do* **work** unto her.
16 Cut off the *sower* **seeder** from *Babylon* **Babel,**
and him that *handleth* **manipulateth** the sickle
in the time of harvest:
for fear **at the face** of the oppressing sword
they shall *turn* **face** every *one* **man** to his people,
and they shall flee every *one* **man** to his own land.
17 *Israel* **Yisra El** is a scattered *sheep* **lamb;**
the lions have driven him away:
first
the *king* **sovereign** of *Assyria* **Ashshur**
hath devoured him;
and last
this *Nebuchadrezzar* **Nebukadnets Tsar**
king **sovereign** of *Babylon* **Babel**
hath *broken* **craunched** his bones.
18 Therefore thus saith
the LORD of hosts **Yah Veh Sabaoth,**
the God **Elohim** of *Israel* **Yisra El;**
Behold, I *will punish* **shall visit**
upon the *king* **sovereign** of *Babylon* **Babel** and his land,
as I have *punished* **visited**
upon the *king* **sovereign** of *Assyria* **Ashshur.**
19 And I *will bring Israel again* **shall turn Yisra El back**
to his habitation **of rest,**
and he shall *feed* **tend**
on *Carmel* **Karmel/orchard** and Bashan,
and his soul shall be satisfied
upon mount *Ephraim* **Ephrayim** and *Gilead* **Gilad.**
20 In those days, and in that time,
saith the LORD **an oracle of Yah Veh,**
the *iniquity* **perversity** of *Israel* **Yisra El**
shall be sought for,
and there shall be none;
and the sins of *Judah* **Yah Hudah,**
and they shall not be found:
for I *will pardon* **shall forgive** them
whom I *reserve* **let remain.**
21 *Go up* **Ascend**
against the land of *Merathaim* **Merathayim,**
even against it,
and against the *inhabitants* **settlers** of *Pekod* **Peqod:**
waste **parch** and *utterly destroy* **devote** after them,
saith the LORD **an oracle of Yah Veh,**
and *do* **work** according to all
that I have *commanded* **misvahed** thee.
22 A *sound* **voice** of *battle* **war** is in the land,
and of great *destruction* **breaking.**
23 How is the hammer of the whole earth
cut *asunder* **apart** and broken!
how is *Babylon* **Babel**
become a desolation among the *nations* **goyim!**
24 I have laid a snare for thee,
and thou art also *taken* **captured,** O *Babylon* **Babel,**
and thou *wast not aware* **knewest not:**
thou art found, and also *caught* **apprehended,**
because thou hast *striven* **throttled**
against *the LORD* **Yah Veh.**
25 *The LORD* **Yah Veh**
hath opened his *armoury* **treasury,**
and hath brought forth
the *weapons* **instruments** of his *indignation* **rage:**
for this is the work
of *the Lord GOD of hosts* **Adonay Yah Veh Sabaoth**
in the land of the *Chaldeans* **Kesediym.**
26 Come against her from the *utmost border* **end,**
open her *storehouses* **granaries:**
cast **raise** her *up* as heaps, and *destroy* **devote** her *utterly:*
let *nothing of her be left* **there be no survivors.**
27 *Slay* **Parch** all her bullocks;
let them *go down* **descend** to the slaughter:
woe **ho** unto them!
for their day is come, the time of their visitation.
28 The voice of them that flee and escape
out of the land of *Babylon* **Babel,**
to *declare* **tell** in *Zion* **Siyon** the *vengeance* **avengement**
of *the LORD* **Yah Veh** our *God* **Elohim,**
the *vengeance* **avengement** of his *temple* **manse.**
29 *Call together* **Hearken** the archers
against *Babylon* **Babel:**
all ye that bend the bow,
camp **encamp** against it round about;
let *none thereof escape* **there be no escapees:**
recompense **shalam to** her according to her *work* **deeds;**
according to all that she hath *done* **worked,**
do **work** unto her:
for she hath been proud against *the LORD* **Yah Veh,**
against the Holy One of *Israel* **Yisra El.**
30 Therefore shall her *young men* **youths**
fall in the *streets* **broadways,**
and all her men of war
shall be *cut off* **severed** in that day,
saith the LORD **an oracle of Yah Veh.**
31 Behold, I am against thee,
O *thou most proud* **arrogance,**
saith the Lord GOD of hosts
an oracle of Adonay Yah Veh Sabaoth:
for thy day is come, the time that I *will* **shall** visit thee.

32 And the *most proud* **arrogant**
shall *stumble* **falter** and fall,
and none shall raise him up:
and I *will* **shall** kindle a fire in his cities,
and it shall devour all round about him.
33 Thus saith *the LORD of hosts* **Yah Veh Sabaoth**;
The *children* **sons** of *Israel* **Yisra El**
and the *children* **sons** of *Judah* **Yah Hudah**
were oppressed together:
and all that *took* **captured** them *captives*
held them *fast*;
they refused to *let* **send** them *go* **away**.
34 Their Redeemer is strong;
the LORD of hosts **Yah Veh Sabaoth** is his name:
in pleading, he shall *throughly* plead their *cause* **plea**,
that he may *give* rest *to* the land,
and *disquiet* **quake**
the *inhabitants* **settlers** of *Babylon* **Babel**.
35 A sword is upon the *Chaldeans* **Kesediym**,
saith the LORD **an oracle of Yah Veh**,
and upon the *inhabitants* **settlers** of *Babylon* **Babel**,
and upon her *princes* **governors**, and upon her wise *men*.
36 A sword is upon *the liars* **their lies**;
and they shall *dote* **folly**:
a sword is upon her mighty *men*;
and they shall be dismayed.
37 A sword is upon their horses, and upon their chariots,
and upon all the *mingled people* **comingled**
that are in the midst of her;
and they shall become as women:
a sword is upon her treasures;
and they shall be *robbed* **plundered**.
38 A *drought* **parch** is upon her waters;
and they shall be dried up:
for it is the land of *graven images* **sculptiles**,
and they *are mad upon their idols* **halal bugaboos**.
39 Therefore the *wild beasts of the desert* **desert dwellers**
with the *wild beasts of the islands* **island howlers**
shall *dwell* **settle** there,
and the **daughters of the** owls shall *dwell* **settle** therein:
and it shall be no more *inhabited* **settled**
for ever **in perpetuity**;
neither shall it be *dwelt* **tabernacled** in
from generation to generation.
40 As *God* **Elohim**
overthrew *Sodom* **Sedom** and *Gomorrah* **Amorah**
and the *neighbour cities* **nearby tabernacles** *thereof*,
saith the LORD **an oracle of Yah Veh**;
so shall no man *abide* **settle** there,
neither shall any son of *man* **humanity**
dwell **sojourn** therein.
41 Behold, a people shall come from the north,
and a great *nation* **goyim**,
and many *kings* **sovereigns** shall be *raised up* **wakened**
from the *coasts* **flanks** of the earth.
42 They shall hold the bow and the *lance* **dart**:
they are cruel, and *will* **shall** not *shew* mercy:
their voice shall roar like the sea,
and they shall ride upon horses,
every one put in array — **lined up**,
like a man to the *battle* **war**,
against thee, O daughter of *Babylon* **Babel**.
43 The *king* **sovereign** of *Babylon* **Babel**
hath heard the report of them,
and his hands *waxed feeble* **slackened**:
anguish **tribulation** took hold of him,
and pangs as of a woman *in travail* **birthing**.
44 Behold, he shall *come up* **ascend** like a lion
from the *swelling* **pomp** of *Jordan* **Yarden**
unto the habitation **of rest** of the *strong* **perrenial**:
but I *will make* **shall cause** them *suddenly* **in a blink**
run away from her:
and who is *a* chosen *man*, that I may appoint over her?
for who is like me?
and who *will appoint* **shall congregate with** me *the time*?
and who is that *shepherd* **tender**
that *will* **shall** stand *before me* **at my face**?
45 Therefore hear ye the counsel of *the LORD* **Yah Veh**,
that he hath *taken* **counselled** against *Babylon* **Babel**;
and his *purposes* **fabrications**,
that he hath *purposed* **fabricated**
against the land of the *Chaldeans* **Kesediym**:
Surely the *least* **lesser** of the flock
shall *draw* **drag** them out:
surely he shall *make* **desolate**
their *habitation desolate* **habitation of rest** with them.
46 At the *noise* **voice**
of the *taking* **apprehending** of *Babylon* **Babel**
the earth is *moved* **quaked**,
and the cry is heard among the *nations* **goyim**.

THE JUDGMENT OF BABEL

51 Thus saith *the LORD* **Yah Veh**; Behold,
I *will raise up* **shall waken** against *Babylon* **Babel**,
and against them
that *dwell* **settle** in the *midst* **heart**
of them that rise *up against me*,
a *destroying* **ruinous** wind;
2 And *will* **shall** send unto *Babylon* **Babel**
fanners **strangers**,
that shall *fan* **winnow** her,
and shall *empty* **evacuate** her land:
for in the day of *trouble* **evil**
they shall be against her round about.
3 Against him that bendeth let the archer bend his bow,
and against him
that *lifteth himself up* **ascendeth** in his brigandine:
and spare ye not her *young men* **youths**;
destroy **devote** ye *utterly* all her host.
4 Thus the *slain* **pierced** shall fall
in the land of the *Chaldeans* **Kesediym**,
and they that are thrust through in her *streets* **outways**.
5 For *Israel* **Yisra El** hath not been *forsaken* **abandoned**,
nor *Judah* **Yah Hudah** of his *God* **Elohim**,
of *the LORD of hosts* **Yah Veh Sabaoth**;
though their land was filled with *sin* **guilt**
against the Holy One of *Israel* **Yisra El**.
6 Flee out of the midst of *Babylon* **Babel**,
and *deliver* **rescue** every man his soul:
be not *cut off* **severed** in her *iniquity* **perversity**;
for this is the time
of *the LORD'S vengeance* **Yah Veh's avengement**;
he *will render* **in dealing shalom,**
he shall deal shalom unto her *a recompence*.
7 *Babylon* **Babel** hath been a golden cup
in *the LORD'S* **Yah Veh's** hand,
that *made* **intoxicated** all the earth *drunken*:
the *nations* **goyim** have drunken of her wine;
therefore the *nations are mad* **goyim halal**.
8 *Babylon* **Babel** is suddenly fallen and *destroyed* **broken**:
howl for her;
take balm for her *pain* **sorrow**,
if so be she may be healed.
9 We *would* **should** have healed *Babylon* **Babel**,
but she is not healed:
forsake her,
and let us go every *one* **man** into his own *country* **land**:
for her judgment
reacheth **toucheth** unto *heaven* **the heavens**,
and is lifted up *even* to the *skies* **vapours**.
10 *The LORD* **Yah Veh**
hath brought forth our *righteousness* **justness**:
come, and let us *declare* **scribe** in *Zion* **Siyon**
the work of *the LORD* **Yah Veh** our *God* **Elohim**.
11 *Make bright* **Polish** the arrows; *gather* **fill** the shields:
the LORD **Yah Veh** hath *raised up* **wakened**
the spirit of the *kings* **sovereigns** of the *Medes* **Maday**:
for his *device* **intrigue** is against *Babylon* **Babel**,
to *destroy* **ruin** it;
because
it is the *vengeance* **avengement** of *the LORD* **Yah Veh**,
the *vengeance* **avengement** of his *temple* **manse**.
12 *Set up* **Lift** the *standard* **ensign**
upon the walls of *Babylon* **Babel**,
make **strengthen** the *watch strong* **guard**,
set up **raise** the *watchmen* **guards**,
prepare the *ambushes* **lurks**:
for *the LORD* **Yah Veh** hath both *devised* **intrigued**
and *done* **worked** that which he spake
against the *inhabitants* **settlers** of *Babylon* **Babel**.

Apocalypse 18:1—17

13 O thou that *dwellest* **tabernaclest** upon many waters,
abundant in treasures, thine end is come,
and the measure of thy *covetousness* **greedy gain**.
14 *The LORD of hosts* **Yah Veh Sabaoth**
hath *sworn* **oathed** by *himself* **his soul**, *saying,*
Surely I *will* **shall** fill thee with *men* **humanity**,
as with *caterpillers* **cankerworms**;
and they shall *lift up* **answer** a shout against thee.

THE FORCE OF YAH VEH

15 He hath *made* **worked** the earth by his *power* **force**,
he hath established the world by his wisdom,
and hath stretched out the *heaven* **heavens**
by his *understanding* **discernment**.
16 When he *uttereth* **giveth** his voice,
there is a multitude of waters in the heavens;
and he causeth the vapours
to ascend from the ends of the earth:
he *maketh* **worketh** lightnings with rain,
and bringeth forth the wind out of his treasures.
17 *Every man* **All humanity** is brutish by his knowledge;
every *founder* **refiner** is *confounded* **shamed**
by the *graven image* **sculptile**:
for his *molten image* **libation** is falsehood,
and there is no *breath* **spirit** in them.
18 They are vanity, the work of *errors* **frauds**:
in the time of their visitation they shall *perish* **destruct**.
19 The *portion* **allotment** of *Jacob* **Yaaqov**
is not like them;
for he is the former of all *things*:
and *Israel is* the rod of his inheritance:
the LORD of hosts **Yah Veh Sabaoth** is his name.
20 Thou art my *battle ax* **disintegrator**
and *weapons* **instruments** of war:
for with thee *will I break in pieces* **shall I shatter**
the *nations* **goyim**,
and with thee *will I destroy* **shall I ruin**
kingdoms **sovereigndoms**;
21 And with thee *will I break in pieces* **shall I shatter**
the horse and his rider;
and with thee *will I break in pieces* **shall I shatter**
the chariot and his rider;
22 With thee also *will I break in pieces* **shall I shatter**
man and woman;
and with thee *will I break in pieces* **shall I shatter**
old **aged** and *young* **lad**;
and with thee *will I break in pieces* **shall I shatter**
the *young man* **youth** and the *maid* **virgin**;
23 I *will* **shall** also *break in pieces with thee* **shatter**
the *shepherd* **tender** and his *flock* **tender drove**;
and with thee *will I break in pieces* **shall I shatter**
the *husbandman* **cultivator** and his yoke *of oxen*;
and with thee *will I break in pieces* **shall I shatter**
captains **governors** and *rulers* **prefects**.
24 And I *will render* **shall shalam** unto *Babylon* **Babel**
and to all the *inhabitants* **settlers** of *Chaldea* **Kesediym**
all their evil that they have *done* **worked** in *Zion* **Siyon**
in your *sight* **eyes**,
saith the LORD **an oracle of Yah Veh**.
25 Behold, I am against thee,
O *destroying mountain* **mountain of ruin**,
saith the LORD **an oracle of Yah Veh**,
which *destroyest* **ruinest** all the earth:
and I *will* **shall** stretch out mine hand upon thee,
and roll thee down from the rocks,
and *will make* **shall give** thee a *burnt* **burning** mountain.
26 And they shall not take of thee a stone for a corner,
nor a stone for foundations;
but thou shalt be desolate *for ever* **eternally**,
saith the LORD **an oracle of Yah Veh**.

Apocalypse 8:8,9

27 *Set* **Lift** ye *up a standard* **an ensign** in the land,
blow **blast** the trumpet among the *nations* **goyim**,
prepare **hallow** the *nations* **goyim** against her,
call together **hearken** against her
the *kingdoms* **sovereigndoms** of Ararat,
Minni, and *Ashchenaz* **Ashkenaz**;
appoint a captain **muster an officer** against her;
cause the horses to *come up* **ascend**
as the *rough caterpillers* **shaggy cankerworms**.
28 *Prepare* **Hallow** against her the *nations* **goyim**
with the *kings* **sovereigns** of the *Medes* **Maday**,
the *captains* **governors** *thereof,*
and all the *rulers* **prefects** *thereof,*
and all the land of his *dominion* **reign**.
29 And the land shall tremble and *sorrow* **writhe**:
for every *purpose* **fabrication** of *the LORD* **Yah Veh**
shall *be performed* **rise** against *Babylon* **Babel**,
to *make* **set** the land of *Babylon* **Babel**
a desolation without *an inhabitant* **a settler**.
30 The mighty *men* of *Babylon* **Babel**
have *forborn* **ceased** to fight,
they have *remained* **settled** in their *holds* **huntholds**:
their might hath *failed* **withered**; they became as women:
they have burned her *dwellingplaces* **tabernacles**;
her bars are broken.
31 *One post* **Runner** shall run to meet *another* **runner**,
and *one messenger* **teller** to meet *another* **teller**,
to *shew* **tell** the *king* **sovereign** of *Babylon* **Babel**
that his city is *taken* **captured** at *one* **the** end,
32 And that the passages are *stopped* **apprehended**,
and the *reeds* **marshes** they have burned with fire,
and the men of war are *affrighted* **terrified**.
33 For thus saith *the LORD of hosts* **Yah Veh Sabaoth**,
the God **Elohim** of *Israel* **Yisra El**;
The daughter of *Babylon* **Babel** is like a threshingfloor,
it is time to *thresh* **tread** her:
yet a little while, and the time of her harvest shall come.
34 *Nebuchadrezzar* **Nebukadnets Tsar**
the *king* **sovereign** of *Babylon* **Babel**
hath devoured me, he hath crushed me,
he hath *made* **set** me an empty *vessel* **instrument**,
he hath swallowed me up like a *dragon* **monster**,
he hath filled his belly with my *delicates* **pleasures**,
he hath *cast* **thrust** me *out* **away**.
35 *The violence done to me and to*
My violence, and that of my flesh
be upon *Babylon* **Babel**,
shall the *inhabitant* **settler** of *Zion* **Siyon** say;
and my blood
upon the *inhabitants* **settlers** of *Chaldea* **Kesediym**,
shall *Jerusalem* **Yeru Shalem** say.
36 Therefore thus saith *the LORD* **Yah Veh**;
Behold, I *will* **shall** plead thy *cause* **plea**,
and *take vengeance* **avenge avengement** for thee;
and I *will dry up* **shall parch** her sea,
and *make her springs* dry **her fountains**.
37 And *Babylon* shall **Babel** become heaps,
a *dwellingplace* **habitation** for *dragons* **monsters**,
an astonishment **a desolation**, and an hissing,
without *an inhabitant* **a settler**.
38 They shall roar together like *lions* **whelps**:
they shall *yell* **growl** as lions' whelps.
39 In their heat
I *will make* **shall place** their *feasts* **banquets**,
and I *will make* **shall intoxicate** them *drunken*,
that they may *rejoice* **jump for joy**,
and sleep *a perpetual* **an eternal** sleep, and not wake,
saith the LORD **an oracle of Yah Veh**.
40 I *will* **shall** bring them down
like *lambs* **rams** to the slaughter,
like rams with he goats.
41 How is Sheshach *taken* **captured**!
and how is the *praise* **halal** of the whole earth
surprised **apprehended**!
how is *Babylon* **Babel**
become *an astonishment* **a desolation**
among the *nations* **goyim**!
42 The sea is *come up* **ascended** upon *Babylon* **Babel**:
she is covered with the multitude of the waves *thereof.*
43 Her cities are a desolation,
a *dry* **parched** land, and a *wilderness* **plain**,
a land wherein no man *dwelleth* **settleth**,
neither doth *any* **a** son of *man* **humanity**
pass *thereby* **therein**.
44 And I *will punish* **shall visit upon** Bel
in *Babylon* **Babel**,
and I *will* **shall** bring forth out of his mouth
that which he hath swallowed *up*:
and the *nations* **goyim**
shall not flow together *any* more unto him:

yea, the wall of *Babylon* **Babel** shall fall.
45 My people, go ye out of the midst of her,
and *deliver* **rescue** ye every man his soul
from the *fierce anger* **fuming wrath**
of *the LORD* **Yah Veh.**
46 And lest your heart *faint* **be tenderized,**
and ye *fear* **awe** for the *rumour* **report**
that shall be heard in the land;
a *rumour* **report** shall *both* come *one* **in a** year,
and after that in *another* **a** year
shall *come a rumour* **the report,**
and violence in the land,
ruler **sovereign** against *ruler* **sovereign.**
47 Therefore, behold, the days come,
that I *will do judgment* **shall visit**
upon the *graven images* **sculptiles** of *Babylon* **Babel:**
and her whole land shall *be confounded* **shame,**
and all her *slain* **pierced** shall fall in the midst of her.
48 Then the *heaven* **heavens** and the earth,
and all that is therein,
shall *sing* **shout** for *Babylon* **Babel:**
for the *spoilers* **ravagers** shall come unto her
from the north,
saith the LORD **an oracle of Yah Veh.**
49 As *Babylon* **Babel**
hath caused the *slain* **pierced** of *Israel* **Yisra El** to fall,
so at *Babylon* **Babel**
shall fall the *slain* **pierced** of all the earth.
50 Ye that have escaped the sword,
go away, stand not still:
remember *the LORD* **Yah Veh** afar off,
and let *Jerusalem* **Yeru Shalem**
come **ascend** into your *mind* **heart.**
51 We are *confounded* **shamed,**
because we have heard reproach:
shame hath covered our faces:
for strangers are come into the *sanctuaries* **holies**
of the *LORD'S* house **of Yah Veh.**
52 Wherefore, behold, the days come,
saith the LORD **an oracle of Yah Veh,**
that I *will do judgment* **shall visit**
upon her *graven images* **sculptiles:**
and through all her land
the *wounded* **pierced** shall *groan* **shriek.**
53 Though *Babylon* **Babel**
should *mount up to heaven* **ascend to the heavens,**
and though she should fortify the height of her strength,
yet from me shall *spoilers* **ravagers** come unto her,
saith the LORD **an oracle of Yah Veh.**
54 A *sound* **voice** of a cry *cometh* from *Babylon* **Babel,**
and great *destruction* **breaking**
from the land of the *Chaldeans* **Kesediym:**
55 Because *the LORD* **Yah Veh**
hath *spoiled Babylon* **ravaged Babel,**
and destroyed out of her the great voice;
when her waves *do* roar like great waters,
a noise **an uproar** of their voice is *uttered* **given:**
56 Because the *spoiler* **ravager** is come upon her,
even upon *Babylon* **Babel,**
and her mighty *men* are *taken* **captured,**
every one of their bows is broken:
for *the LORD God* **Yah Veh El** of *recompences* **dealings**
in dealing shalom, shall *surely requite* **deal shalom.**
57 And I *will make drunk* **shall intoxicate**
her *princes* **governors,**
and her wise *men,* her *captains* **governors,**
and her *rulers* **prefects,** and her mighty *men:*
and they shall sleep *a perpetual* **an eternal** sleep,
and not wake,
saith the King **an oracle of the Sovereign,**
whose name is *the LORD of hosts* **Yah Veh Sabaoth.**
58 Thus saith *the LORD of hosts* **Yah Veh Sabaoth;**
The broad walls of *Babylon* **Babel**
in stripping bare, shall be *utterly broken* **stripped bare,**
and her high *gates* **portals** shall be burned with fire;
and the people shall labour *in vain* **vainly enough,**
and the *folk* **nations** in the fire **enough,**
and they shall be weary.
59 The word which *Jeremiah* **Yirme Yah** the prophet
commanded **misvahed**
Seraiah **Sera Yah** the son of *Neriah* **Neri Yah,**
the son of *Maaseiah* **Machse Yah,**
when he went with *Zedekiah* **Sidqi Yah**
the *king* **sovereign** of *Judah* **Yah Hudah**
into *Babylon* **Babel** in the fourth year of his reign.
And *this Seraiah* **Sera Yah**
was a *quiet prince* **restive governor.**
60 So *Jeremiah* **Yirme Yah**
wrote **inscribed** in *a book* **one scroll**
all the evil that should come upon *Babylon* **Babel,**
even all these words
that are *written* **inscribed** against *Babylon* **Babel.**
61 And *Jeremiah* **Yirme Yah** said to *Seraiah* **Sera Yah,**
When thou comest to *Babylon* **Babel,** and shalt see,
and shalt *read* **call out** all these words;
62 Then shalt thou say, O *LORD* **Yah Veh,**
thou hast *spoken* **worded** against this place, to cut it off,
that none shall *remain* **settle** in it,
neither *man* **humanity** nor *beast* **animal,**
but that it shall be desolate *for ever* **eternally.**
63 And it shall be,
when thou hast *made an end of* **finished**
reading **calling out** this *book* **scroll,**
that thou shalt bind a stone to it,
and cast it into the midst of Euphrates:
64 And thou shalt say,
Thus shall *Babylon sink* **Babel drown,**
and shall not rise
from **the face of** the evil that I *will* **shall** bring upon her:
and they shall be weary.
Thus far are the words of *Jeremiah* **Yirme Yah.**

THE FALL OF YERU SHALEM

52 *Zedekiah* **Sidqi Yah**
was **a son of** one and twenty years *old*
when he began to reign,
and he reigned eleven years in *Jerusalem* **Yeru Shalem.**
And his mother's name was Hamutal
the daughter of *Jeremiah* **Yirme Yah** of Libnah.
2 And he *did* **worked** that which was evil
in the eyes of *the LORD* **Yah Veh,**
according to all
that *Jehoiakim* **Yah Yaqim** had *done* **worked.**
3 For through the *anger* **wrath** of *the LORD* **Yah Veh**
it *came to pass* **became**
in *Jerusalem* **Yeru Shalem** and *Judah* **Yah Hudah,**
till he had cast them out from his *presence* **face,**
that *Zedekiah* **Sidqi Yah** rebelled
against the *king* **sovereign** of *Babylon* **Babel.**
4 And it *came to pass* **became**
in the ninth year of his reign,
in the tenth month, in the tenth *day* of the month,
that *Nebuchadrezzar* **Nebukadnets Tsar**
king **sovereign** of *Babylon* **Babel** came,
he and all his *army* **valiant,**
against *Jerusalem* **Yeru Shalem,**
and *pitched* **encamped** against it,
and built *forts* **battering towers** against it round about.
5 So the city was *besieged* **under siege**
unto the eleventh year
of *king Zedekiah* **sovereign Sidqi Yah.**
6 And in the fourth month, in the ninth *day* of the month,
the famine *was sore* **prevailed** in the city,
so that there was no bread for the people of the land.
7 Then the city was *broken up* **split,**
and all the men of war fled,
and went forth out of the city by night
by the way of the *gate* **portal** between the two walls,
which was by the *king's* **sovereign's** garden;
(*now* the *Chaldeans* **Kesediym**
were by the city round about:)
and they went by the way of the plain.
8 But the *army* **valiant** of the *Chaldeans* **Kesediym**
pursued after the *king* **sovereign,**
and overtook *Zedekiah* **Sidqi Yah**
in the plains of *Jericho* **Yericho;**
and all his *army* **valiant** was scattered from him.
9 Then they *took* **apprehended** the *king* **sovereign,**
and *carried* **ascended** him *up*
unto the *king* **sovereign** of *Babylon* **Babel**
to Riblah in the land of Hamath;

where he *gave* **worded** judgment upon him.
10 And the *king* **sovereign** of *Babylon* **Babel**
slew **slaughtered** the sons of *Zedekiah* **Sidqi Yah**
before his eyes:
he *slew* **slaughtered** also
all the *princes* **governors** of *Judah* **Yah Hudah** in Riblah.
11 Then he *put out* **blinded** the eyes
of *Zedekiah* **Sidqi Yah**;
and the *king* **sovereign** of *Babylon* **Babel**
bound him in *chains* **coppers**,
and carried him to *Babylon* **Babel**,
and *put* **gave** him in *prison* **the house of visitation**
till the day of his death.
12 *Now* in the fifth month, in the tenth *day* of the month,
which **year** was the nineteenth year
of *Nebuchadrezzar* **Nebukadnets Tsar**
king **sovereign** of *Babylon* **Babel**,
came *Nebuzaradan* **Nebu Zaradan**,
captain of the guard **rabbi slaughterer**,
which *served* **stood at the face**
of the *king* **sovereign** of *Babylon* **Babel**,
into *Jerusalem* **Yeru Shalem**,
13 And burned the house of *the LORD* **Yah Veh**,
and the *king's* **sovereign's** house;
and all the houses of *Jerusalem* **Yeru Shalem**,
and all the houses of the great *men*, burned he with fire:
14 And all the *army* **valiant** of the *Chaldeans* **Kesediym**,
that were with the *captain of the guard* **rabbi slaughterer**,
brake down all the walls of *Jerusalem* **Yeru Shalem**
round about.
15 Then *Nebuzaradan* **Nebu Zaradan**
the *captain of the guard* **rabbi slaughterer**
carried away captive **exiled**
certain of the poor of the people,
and the *residue* **remnant** of the people
that *remained* **survived** in the city,
and those that fell away,
that fell to the *king* **sovereign** of *Babylon* **Babel**,
and the *rest* **remnant** of the multitude.
16 But *Nebuzaradan* **Nebu Zaradan**
the *captain of the guard* **rabbi slaughterer**
left certain **let survive** of the poor of the land
for vinedressers and for *husbandmen* **plowers**.
17 Also the pillars of *brass* **copper**
that were in the house of *the LORD* **Yah Veh**,
and the bases, and the *brasen* **copper** sea
that was in the house of *the LORD* **Yah Veh**,
the *Chaldeans* **Kesediym** brake,
and *carried* **bore** all the *brass* **copper** of them
to *Babylon* **Babel**.
18 The caldrons also, and the shovels,
and the *snuffers* **tweezers**, and the *bowls* **sprinklers**,
and the *spoons* **hollow bowls**,
and all the *vessels* **instruments** of *brass* **copper**
wherewith they ministered, took they away.
19 And the basons, and the *firepans* **trays**,
and the *bowls* **sprinklers**, and the caldrons,
and the *candlesticks* **menorah**, and the spoons,
and the *cups* **exoneration basins**;
that which was of gold *in* gold,
and that which was of silver *in* silver,
took the *captain of the guard* **rabbi slaughterer** away.
20 The two pillars, one sea,
and twelve *brasen* **copper** bulls
that were under the bases,
which *king Solomon* **sovereign Shelomah**
had *made* **worked** in the house of *the LORD* **Yah Veh**:
the *brass* **copper** of all these *vessels* **instruments**
was without weight.
21 And *concerning* the pillars,
the height of one pillar was eighteen cubits
and a *fillet* **thread** of twelve cubits
did *compass* **surround** it;
and the thickness *thereof* was four fingers: *it was* hollow.
22 And a *chapiter* **cap** of *brass* **copper** was upon it;
and the height of one *chapiter* **cap** was five cubits,
with *network* **netting** and pomegranates
upon the *chapiters* **caps** round about, all of *brass* **copper**.
The second pillar also and the pomegranates
were like unto these.
23 And there were ninety and six pomegranates
on a *side* **wind**;
and all the pomegranates upon the *network* **netting**
were an hundred round about.
24 And the *captain of the guard* **rabbi slaughterer**
took *Seraiah* **Sera Yah** the chief priest,
and *Zephaniah* **Sephan Yah** the second priest,
and the three *keepers* **guards** of the *door* **threshold**:
25 He took also out of the city *an* **one** eunuch,
which had the charge **an overseer** of the men of war;
and seven men of them
that *were near* **saw** the *king's person* **sovereign's face**,
which were found in the city;
and the *principal* scribe **of the governor** of the host,
who *mustered* **hosted** the people of the land;
and *threescore* **sixty** men of the people of the land,
that were found in the midst of the city.
26 So *Nebuzaradan* **Nebu Zaradan**
the *captain of the guard* **rabbi slaughterer** took them,
and *brought* **carried** them
to the *king* **sovereign** of *Babylon* **Babel** to Riblah.
27 And the *king* **sovereign** of *Babylon* **Babel** smote them,
and *put* **deathified** them *to death* in Riblah
in the land of Hamath.
Thus *Judah* **Yah Hudah** was *carried away captive* **exiled**
out of his own *land* **soil**.
28 This is the people whom
Nebuchadrezzar **Nebukadnets Tsar**
carried away captive **exiled**:
in the seventh year
three thousand *Jews* and three and twenty **Yah Hudiym**:
29 In the eighteenth year
of *Nebuchadrezzar* **Nebukadnets Tsar**
he *carried away captive* **exiled**
from *Jerusalem* **Yeru Shalem**
eight hundred thirty and two *persons* **souls**:
30 In the three and twentieth year
of *Nebuchadrezzar* **Nebukadnets Tsar**
Nebuzaradan **Nebu Zaradan**
the *captain of the guard* **rabbi slaughterer**
carried away captive **exiled** of the *Jews* **Yah Hudiym**
seven hundred forty and five *persons* **souls**:
all the *persons* **souls** were four thousand and six hundred.
31 And it *came to pass* **became,**
in the seven and thirtieth year
of the *captivity* **exile** of *Jehoiachin* **Yah Yachin**
king **sovereign** of *Judah* **Yah Hudah**,
in the twelfth month,
in the five and twentieth *day* of the month,
that *Evilmerodach* **Evil Merodach**
king **sovereign** of *Babylon* **Babel**
in the *first* year of his *reign* **sovereigndom**
lifted up the head of *Jehoiachin* **Yah Yachin**
king **sovereign** of *Judah* **Yah Hudah**,
and brought him forth out of **the** prison **house**.
32 And *spake kindly* **worded good** unto him,
and *set* **gave** his throne
above the throne of the *kings* **sovereigns**
that were with him in *Babylon* **Babel**,
33 And changed his prison *garment* **clothes**:
and he did continually eat bread *before him* **at his face**
all the days of his life.
34 And for his *diet* **ration**,
there was a continual *diet* **ration** given him
of the *king* **sovereign** of *Babylon* **Babel**,
every day a *portion* **word** until the day of his death,
all the days of his life.

KEY TO INTERPRETING THE EXEGESES:
King James text is in regular type;
Text under exegeses is in oblique type;
Text of exegeses is in bold type.

THE VISIONS OF YECHEZQ EL

1 *Now* it *came to pass* **became,** in the thirtieth year,
in the fourth *month,* in the fifth *day* of the month,
as I was among the *captives* **exiles**
by the river of *Chebar* **Kebar,**
that the heavens were opened,
and I saw visions of *God* **Elohim.**
2 In the fifth *day* of the month,
which was the fifth year
of *king Jehoiachin's captivity* **sovereign Yah Yachin's exile,**
3 The word of *the LORD* **Yah Veh** came expressly
unto *Ezekiel* **Yechezq El** the priest, the son of Buzi,
in the land of the *Chaldeans* **Kesediym**
by the river *Chebar* **Kebar;**
and the hand of *the LORD* **Yah Veh** was there upon him.

OMENS

4 And I *looked* **saw,** and, behold,
a *whirlwind* **spirit/wind of storm** came out of the north,
a great cloud, and a fire *infolding* **overtaking** itself,
and a *brightness* **brilliance** was **round** about it,
and out of the midst *thereof*
as the *colour* **eyes** of *amber* **brilliant copper,**
out of the midst of the fire.

FOUR LIVE BEINGS

5 Also out of the midst *thereof*
came the likeness of four *living creatures* **live beings.**
And this was their *appearance* **visage;**
they **these** had the likeness of a *man* **human.**
6 And *every* one had four faces,
and *every* one had four wings.
7 And their feet were straight feet;
and the sole of their feet was like the sole of a calf's foot:
and they sparkled
like the *colour* **eye** of burnished *brass* **copper.**
8 And they had the hands of a *man* **human**
under their wings on their four *sides* **quarters;**
and they four had their faces and their wings.
9 Their wings were joined *one* **woman** to *another* **sister;**
they turned not when they went;
they went every *one straight* **man face** forward.
10 As for the likeness of their faces,
they four had the face of a *man* **human,**
and the face of a lion, on the right *side*:
and they four had the face of an ox on the left *side*;
they four also had the face of an eagle.
11 Thus were their faces:
and their wings *were stretched* **spread** upward;
two *wings of every one* **of each man**
were joined *one* **man** to *another* **man,**
and two covered their bodies.
12 And they went *every one* **each man**
straight **face** forward:
whither the spirit was to go, they went;
and they turned not when they went.
13 As for the likeness of the *living creatures* **live beings,**
their *appearance* **visage** was like burning coals of fire,
and like the *appearance* **visage** of *lamps* **flambeaus:**
it went up and down
among the *living creatures* **live beings;**
and the fire was *bright* **brilliant,**
and out of the fire went forth lightning.
14 And the *living creatures* **live beings** ran and returned
as the *appearance* **visage** of a flash *of lightning.*

THE WHEEL IN THE MIDST OF A WHEEL

15 *Now* as I *beheld* **saw** the *living creatures* **live beings,**
behold one wheel upon the earth
by the living creatures **beside the live beings,**
with his four faces.
16 The *appearance* **visage** of the wheels and their work
was like unto the *colour* **eye** of a beryl:
and they four had one likeness:
and their *appearance* **visage** and their work
was as it were a wheel in the *middle* **midst** of a wheel.
17 When they went,
they went upon their four *sides* **quarters:**
and they turned not when they went.
18 As for their *rings* **rims,**
they were so high that they were *dreadful* **awesome;**
and their *rings* **rims**
were full of eyes round about them four.
19 And when the *living creatures* **live beings** went,
the wheels went *by them* **beside:**
and when the *living creatures* **live beings**
were lifted *up* from the earth,
the wheels were lifted *up.*
20 Whithersoever the spirit was to go, they went,
thither was their spirit to go;
and the wheels were lifted *up*
over against **alongside** them:
for the spirit of the *living creature* **live being**
was in the wheels.
21 *When those went* **In their going,**
these went **they go;**
and when those stood **in their standing,**
these stood **they stand;**
and when those were **in their being** lifted *up*
from the earth,
the wheels *were* lifted *up over against* **alongside** them:
for the spirit of the *living creature* **live being**
was in the wheels.
22 And the likeness of the *firmament* **expanse**
upon the heads of the *living creature* **live being**
was as the *colour* **eye** of *the terrible* **awesome** crystal,
stretched forth over their heads above.
23 And under the *firmament* **expanse**
were their wings straight,
the one **woman** toward *the other* **sister:**
every one **each man** had two,
which covered *on this side* **here,**
and *every one* **each man** had two,
which covered *on that side* **there,**
their bodies.
24 And when they went,
I heard the *noise* **voice** of their wings,
like the *noise* **voice** of great waters,
as the voice of *the Almighty* **Shadday,**
the voice of *speech* **rushing,**
as the *noise* **voice** of *an host* **a camp:**
when they stood, they let down their wings.
25 And there was a voice from the *firmament* **expanse**
that was over their heads,
when they stood, and had let down their wings.

THE HONOUR THRONE

26 And above the *firmament* **expanse**
that was over their heads
was the likeness of a throne,
as the *appearance* **visage** of a sapphire stone:
and upon the likeness of the throne
was the likeness
as the *appearance* **visage** of a *man* **human**
above upon it.
27 And I saw as the *colour* **eye** of *amber* **brilliant copper,**
as the *appearance* **visage** of fire
round about *within it* **the housing,**
from the *appearance* **visage** of his loins
even upward,
and from the *appearance* **visage** of his loins
even downward,
I saw as it were the *appearance* **visage** of fire,
and it had *brightness* **brilliance** round about.
28 As the *appearance* **visage** of the bow
that is in the cloud in the day of *rain* **downpour,**
so was the *appearance* **visage** of the *brightness* **brilliance**
round about.
This was the *appearance* **visage** of the likeness
of the *glory* **honour** of *the LORD* **Yah Veh.**
And when I saw *it,* I fell upon my face,
and I heard a voice of one that spake.

THE CALL OF YECHEZQ EL

2 And he said unto me, Son of *man* **humanity,**
stand upon thy feet,
and I *will speak* **shall word** unto thee.
2 And the spirit entered into me
when he *spake* **worded** unto me,
and *set* **stood** me upon my feet,
that I heard him that spake unto me.

3 And he said unto me, Son of *man* **humanity**,
I send thee to the *children* **sons** of *Israel* **Yisra El**,
to a *rebellious nation* **rebelling goyim**
that hath rebelled against me:
they and their fathers
have *transgressed* **rebelled** against me,
even unto this *very* **same** day.
4 For they are *impudent children* **hard faced sons**
and *stiffhearted* **strong hearted**.
I *do* send thee unto them;
and thou shalt say unto them,
Thus saith *the Lord GOD* **Adonay Yah Veh**.
5 And they,
whether they *will* **shall** hear,
or whether they *will forbear* **shall desist**,
(for they are a rebellious house,)
yet shall know
that there hath been a prophet among them.
6 And thou, son of *man* **humanity**,
be not *afraid* **awed** of them,
neither be *afraid* **awed** of their words,
though *briers* **thistles** and *thorns* **prickles** be with thee,
and thou dost *dwell* **settle** among scorpions:
be not *afraid* **awed** of their words,
nor be dismayed at their *looks* **faces**,
though they be a rebellious house.
7 And thou shalt *speak* **word** my words unto them,
whether they *will* **shall** hear,
or whether they *will forbear* **shall desist**:
for they are most rebellious.
8 But thou, son of *man* **humanity**,
hear what I say unto thee;
Be not thou rebellious like that rebellious house:
open **gape** thy mouth, and eat that I give thee.
9 And when I *looked* **saw**, behold,
an hand was sent unto me;
and, *lo* **behold**, a roll of a *book* **scroll** was therein;
10 And he spread it *before me* **at my face**;
and it was *written within* **inscribed on the face**
and *without* **on the back**:
and there was *written* **inscribed** therein lamentations,
and *mourning* **meditations**, and woe.

THE COMMISSION OF YECHEZQ EL

3 *Moreover* he said unto me, Son of *man* **humanity**,
eat that thou findest; eat this roll,
and go *speak* **word** unto the house of *Israel* **Yisra El**.
2 So I opened my mouth,
and he *caused me to eat* **fed me** that roll.
3 And he said unto me, Son of *man* **humanity**,
cause **feed** thy belly *to eat*,
and fill thy *bowels* **inwards** with this roll that I give thee.
Then did I eat it;
and it was in my mouth as honey for sweetness.
4 And he said unto me, Son of *man* **humanity**,
go, get thee unto the house of *Israel* **Yisra El**,
and *speak* **word** with my words unto them.
Apocalypse 10:1—11
5 For thou art not sent to a people
of *a strange speech* **deep lip**
and of an *hard language* **heavy tongue**,
but to the house of *Israel* **Yisra El**;
6 Not to many people of a *strange speech* **deep lip**
and of an *hard language* **heavy tongue**,
whose words thou canst not *understand* **hear**.
Surely, had I sent thee to them,
they *would* **should** have hearkened unto thee.
7 But the house of *Israel* **Yisra El**
will **willeth to** not hearken unto thee;
for they *will* **willed to** not hearken unto me:
for all the house of *Israel* **Yisra El**
are *impudent* **strong foreheaded** and hardhearted.
8 Behold, I have *made* **given** thy face strong
against **alongside** their faces,
and thy forehead strong
against **along side** their foreheads.
9 As *an adamant harder* **a brier stronger** than flint
have I *made* **given** thy forehead:
fear **awe** them not,
neither be dismayed at their *looks* **faces**,
though they be a rebellious house.

10 *Moreover* he said unto me, Son of *man* **humanity**,
all my words that I shall *speak* **word** unto thee
receive **take** in thine heart, and hear with thine ears.
11 And go, get thee to them of the *captivity* **exile**,
unto the *children* **sons** of thy people,
and *speak* **word** unto them, and *tell* **say to** them,
Thus saith *the Lord GOD* **Adonay Yah Veh**;
whether they *will* **shall** hear,
or whether they *will forbear* **shall desist**.
12 Then the spirit *took* **bore** me *up*,
and I heard behind me a voice of a great *rushing* **quake**,
saying,
Blessed be the *glory* **honour** of *the LORD* **Yah Veh**
from his place.
13 *I heard* also the *noise* **voice** of the wings
of the *living creatures* **live beings**
that *touched one another* **kissed woman to sister**,
and the *noise* **voice** of the wheels
over against **alongside** them,
and a *noise* **voice** of a great *rushing* **quake**.
14 So the spirit lifted me *up*, and took me away,
and I went in bitterness, in the *heat* **fury** of my spirit;
but the hand of *the LORD* **Yah Veh**
was strong upon **strengthened** me.
15 Then I came to them of the *captivity* **exile**
at *Telabib* **Tel Aviv**,
that *dwelt* **settled** by the river of *Chebar* **Kebar**,
and I *sat* **settled** where they *sat* **settled**,
and *remained* **settled** there
astonished among them seven days.

YAH VEH'S WARNING CONCERNING NOT WARNING

16 And it *came to pass* **became**, at the end of seven days,
that the word of *the LORD* **Yah Veh** came unto me,
saying,
17 Son of *man* **humanity**,
I have *made* **given** thee a *watchman* **watcher**
unto the house of *Israel* **Yisra El**:
therefore hear the word at my mouth,
and *give* **enlighten** them *warning* from me.
18 *When I say* **In my saying** unto the wicked,
In dying, Thou shalt *surely* die;
and thou *givest* **enlightenest** him not *warning*,
nor *speakest* **wordest** to *warn* **enlighten** the wicked
from his wicked way,
to save his life **that he may live**;
the same wicked *man* shall die in his *iniquity* **perversity**;
but his blood *will* **shall** I *require* **seek** at thine hand.
19 Yet if thou *warn* **enlighten** the wicked,
and he turn not from his wickedness,
nor from his wicked way,
he shall die in his *iniquity* **perversity**;
but thou hast *delivered* **rescued** thy soul.
20 Again, When *a righteous man* **the just**
doth turn from his *righteousness* **justness**,
and *commit iniquity* **work wickedness**,
and I *lay* **give** a stumblingblock *before him* **at his face**,
he shall die:
because thou hast not *given* **enlightened** him *warning*,
he shall die in his sin,
and his *righteousness* **justness**
which he hath *done* **worked**
shall not be remembered;
but his blood *will* **shall** I *require* **seek** at thine hand.
21 Nevertheless
if thou *warn* **enlighten** the *righteous man* **just**,
that the *righteous* **just** sin not, and he doth not sin,
in living, he shall *surely* live,
because he is *warned* **enlightened**;
also thou hast *delivered* **rescued** thy soul.

YAH VEH REVEALS HIS HONOUR

22 And the hand of *the LORD* **Yah Veh**
was there upon me;
and he said unto me, Arise, go forth into the *plain* **valley**,
and *I will* **shall** there *talk* **word** with thee.
23 Then I arose, and went forth into the *plain* **valley**:
and, behold,
the *glory* **honour** of *the LORD* **Yah Veh** stood there,
as the *glory* **honour**
which I saw by the river of *Chebar* **Kebar**:
and I fell on my face.

24 Then the spirit entered into me,
and *set* **stood** me upon my feet,
and *spake* **worded** with me, and said unto me,
Go, shut thyself within thine house.
25 But thou, O son of *man* **humanity**, behold,
they shall *put bands* **give ropes** upon thee,
and shall bind thee with them,
and thou shalt not go out among them:
26 And I *will* **shall** make thy tongue
cleave **stick** to *the roof of* thy *mouth* **palate**,
that thou shalt be *dumb* **muted**,
and shalt not be to them a **man** reprover:
for they are a rebellious house.
27 But when I *speak* **word** with thee,
I *will* **shall** open thy mouth,
and thou shalt say unto them,
Thus saith *the Lord GOD* **Adonay Yah Veh**;
He that heareth, let him hear;
and he that *forbeareth* **desisteth**, let him *forbear* **desist**:
for they are a rebellious house.

THE SIEGE OF YERU SHALEM

4 Thou also, son of *man* **humanity**,
take thee a *tile* **brick**,
and *lay it before thee* **give it at thy face**,
and *pourtray* **engrave** upon it the city,
even Jerusalem **Yeru Shalem**:
2 And *lay* **give** siege against it,
and build a *fort* **battering tower** against it,
and *cast* **pour** a mount against it;
set **give** the camp also against it,
and set *battering* rams against it round about.
3 Moreover take thou unto thee an iron *pan* **griddle**,
and *set* **give** it for a wall of iron
between thee and **between** the city:
and *set* **establish** thy face against it,
and it shall be *besieged* **under siege**,
and thou shalt *lay* siege against it.
This shall be a sign to the house of *Israel* **Yisra El**.
4 Lie thou also upon thy left side,
and *lay* **set** the *iniquity* **perversity**
of the house of *Israel* **Yisra El** upon it:
according to the number of the days
that thou shalt lie upon it
thou shalt bear their *iniquity* **perversity**.
5 For I have *laid* **given** upon thee
the years of their *iniquity* **perversity**,
according to the number of the days,
three hundred and ninety days:
so shalt thou bear the *iniquity* **perversity**
of the house of *Israel* **Yisra El**.
6 And when thou hast *accomplished* **concluded** them,
lie *again* **secondly** on thy right side,
and thou shalt bear the *iniquity* **perversity**
of the house of *Judah* **Yah Hudah** forty days:
I have *appointed* **given** thee
each **a day for a year,** a day for a year.
7 Therefore thou shalt *set* **establish** thy face
toward the siege of *Jerusalem* **Yeru Shalem**,
and thine arm shall be *uncovered* **stripped**,
and thou shalt prophesy against it.
8 And, behold,
I *will lay bands* **shall give ropes** upon thee,
and thou shalt not turn thee
from *one* **thy** side to *another* **thy side**,
till thou hast *ended* **finished** the days of thy siege.
9 Take thou also unto thee wheat, and barley,
and beans, and lentiles, and millet, and *fitches* **spelt**,
and *put* **give** them in one *vessel* **instrument**,
and *make* **work** thee bread *thereof*,
according to the number of the days
that thou shalt lie upon thy side,
three hundred and ninety days shalt thou eat *thereof*.
10 And thy *meat* **food** which thou shalt eat
shall be by weight, twenty shekels a day:
from time to time shalt thou eat it.
11 Thou shalt drink water by measure,
the sixth *part* of an hin:
from time to time shalt thou drink.
12 And thou shalt eat it as barley *cakes* **ashcakes**,
and thou shalt bake it
with dung **balls**
that cometh out of man **of human excrement**,
in their *sight* **eyes**.
13 And *the LORD* **Yah Veh** said,
Even thus shall the *children* **sons** of *Israel* **Yisra El**
eat their *defiled* **fouled** bread among the *Gentiles* **goyim**,
whither I *will* **shall** drive them.
14 Then said I, *Ah Lord GOD* **Aha Adonay Yah Veh**!
behold, my soul hath not been *polluted* **fouled**:
for from my youth up even till now
have I not eaten of *that which dieth of itself* **a carcase**,
or *is* torn *in pieces*;
neither came there
abominable **stench** flesh into my mouth.
15 Then he said unto me, *Lo* **See**,
I have given thee *cow's* **cow** dung
for *man's dung* **human dung balls**,
and thou shalt *prepare* **work** thy bread therewith.
16 *Moreover* he said unto me, Son of *man* **humanity**,
behold, I *will* **shall** break the *staff* **rod** of bread
in *Jerusalem* **Yeru Shalem**:
and they shall eat bread by weight,
and with *care* **concern**;
and they shall drink water by measure,
and with astonishment:
17 That they may want bread and water,
and be astonied *one* **man** with *another* **brother**,
and *consume away* **dissolve** for their *iniquity* **perversity**.

THE DESOLATION OF YERU SHALEM

5 And thou, son of *man* **humanity**,
take thee a sharp *knife* **sword**, take thee a barber's razor,
and cause it to pass upon thine head and upon thy beard:
then take thee balances *to weigh* **for weights**,
and *divide the hair* **allot them**.
2 Thou shalt burn with *fire* **flame**
a third *part* in the midst of the city,
when the days of the siege are fulfilled:
and thou shalt take a third *part*,
and smite **round** about it with a *knife* **sword**:
and a third *part* thou shalt scatter in the wind;
and I *will* **shall** draw out a sword after them.
3 Thou shalt also take *thereof* a few in number,
and bind them in thy *skirts* **wings**.
4 Then take of them again,
and cast them into the midst of the fire,
and burn them in the fire;
for thereof shall a fire come forth
into all the house of *Israel* **Yisra El**.
5 Thus saith *the Lord GOD* **Adonay Yah Veh**;
This is *Jerusalem* **Yeru Shalem**:
I have set it
in the midst of the *nations* **goyim** and *countries* **lands**
that are round about her.
6 And she hath *changed* **rebelled against** my judgments
into wickedness more than the *nations* **goyim**,
and my statutes more than the *countries* **lands**
that are round about her:
for they have refused my judgments and my statutes,
they have not walked in them.
7 Therefore thus saith *the Lord GOD* **Adonay Yah Veh**;
Because ye multiplied more than the *nations* **goyim**
that are round about you,
and have not walked in my statutes,
neither have *kept* **worked** my judgments,
neither have *done* **worked** according to the judgments
of the *nations* **goyim** *that are* round about you;
8 Therefore thus saith *the Lord GOD* **Adonay Yah Veh**;
Behold, I, even I, am against thee,
and *will execute* **shall work** judgments
in the midst of thee
in the *sight* **eyes** of the *nations* **goyim**.
9 And I *will do* **shall work** in thee
that which I have not *done* **worked**,
and whereunto
I *will* **shall** not *do* **work** any more the like,
because of all thine *abominations* **abhorrences**.
10 Therefore the fathers shall eat the sons
in the midst of thee,
and the sons shall eat their fathers;
and I *will execute* **shall work** judgments in thee,

and the whole *remnant* **survivors** of thee
will I scatter **shall I winnow** into all the winds.
11 Wherefore, *as* I live,
saith the Lord GOD **an oracle of Adonay Yah Veh**;
Surely,
because thou hast *defiled* **fouled** my *sanctuary* **holies**
with all thy *detestable things* **abominations**,
and with all thine *abominations* **abhorrences**,
therefore *will* **shall** I also diminish thee;
neither shall mine eye spare,
neither *will I have any pity* **shall I compassion**.
12 A third *part* of thee shall die with the pestilence,
and with famine shall they be *consumed* **finished off**
in the midst of thee:
and a third *part* shall fall by the sword round about thee;
and I *will scatter* **shall winnow** a third *part*
into all the winds,
and I *will* **shall** draw out a sword after them.
13 Thus shall *mine anger* **my wrath**
be *accomplished* **finished off**,
and I *will* **shall** cause my fury to rest upon them,
and I *will be comforted* **shall be sighed over**:
and they shall know that I *the LORD* **Yah Veh**
have *spoken it* **worded** in my zeal,
when I have *accomplished* **finished off** my fury in them.
14 *Moreover* I *will make* **shall give** thee
waste **for a parched area**,
and a reproach among the *nations* **goyim**
that are round about thee,
in the *sight* **eyes** of all that pass by.
15 So it shall be a reproach and a *taunt* **revilement**,
an instruction **a discipline**
and *an astonishment* **a desolation**
unto the *nations* **goyim** *that are* round about thee,
when I shall *execute* **work** judgments in thee
in *anger* **wrath** and in fury
and in *furious rebukes* **reproofs of fury**.
I *the LORD* **Yah Veh** have *spoken it* **worded**.
16 When I shall send upon them
the evil arrows of famine,
which shall be for their *destruction* **ruin**,
and which I *will* **shall** send to *destroy* **ruin** you:
and I *will* **shall** increase the famine upon you,
and *will* **shall** break your *staff* **rod** of bread:
17 So *will* **shall** I send upon you
famine and evil *beasts* **live beings**,
and they shall bereave thee:
and pestilence and blood shall pass through thee;
and I *will* **shall** bring the sword upon thee.
I *the LORD* **Yah Veh** have *spoken it* **worded**.

A PROPHECY AGAINST THE MOUNTAINS OF YISRA EL

6 And the word of *the LORD* **Yah Veh** came unto me,
saying,
2 Son of *man* **humanity**,
set thy face toward the mountains of *Israel* **Yisra El**,
and prophesy against them,
3 And say, Ye mountains of *Israel* **Yisra El**,
hear the word of *the Lord GOD* **Adonay Yah Veh**;
Thus saith *the Lord GOD* **Adonay Yah Veh**
to the mountains, and to the hills,
to the *rivers* **reservoirs**, and to the valleys;
Behold, I, *even* I, *will* **shall** bring a sword upon you,
and I *will* **shall** destroy your *high places* **bamahs**.
4 And your **sacrifice** altars shall *be* desolate,
and your *images* **sun icons** shall be broken:
and I *will cast down* **shall fell** your *slain men* **pierced**
before **at the face of** your idols.
5 And I *will lay* **shall give** the *dead* carcases
of the *children* **sons** of *Israel* **Yisra El**
before **at the face of** their idols;
and I *will scatter* **shall winnow** your bones
round about your **sacrifice** altars.
6 In all your *dwellingplaces* **sites**
the cities shall be *laid waste* **parched**,
and the *high places* **bamahs** shall *be* desolate;
that your **sacrifice** altars may be *laid waste* **parched**
and *made desolate* **have guilted**,
and your idols may be broken and *cease* **shabbathize**,
and your *images* **sun icons** may be cut down,
and your works may be *abolished* **erased**.
7 And the *slain* **pierced** shall fall in the midst of you,
and ye shall know that *I am the LORD* **I — Yah Veh**.
8 Yet *will I leave a remnant* **shall I let some remain**,
that ye may have
some that shall escape **escapees of** the sword
among the *nations* **goyim**,
when ye shall be *scattered* **winnowed**
through the *countries* **lands**.
9 And *they that escape of you* **the escapees**
shall remember me among the *nations* **goyim**
whither they shall be *carried captives* **captured**,
because I am broken with their whorish heart,
which hath *departed* **turned aside** from me,
and with their eyes,
which *go a whoring* **whore** after their idols:
and they shall lothe *themselves*
for **at the face of** the evils
which they have *committed* **worked**
in all their *abominations* **abhorrences**.
10 And they shall know that *I am the LORD* **I — Yah Veh**,
and that I have not *said in vain* **worded gratuitously**
that I *would do* **should work** this evil unto them.
11 Thus saith *the Lord GOD* **Adonay Yah Veh**;
Smite with thine *hand* **palm**, and stamp with thy foot,
and say, *Alas* **Ach!**
for all the evil *abominations* **abhorrences**
of the house of *Israel* **Yisra El**!
for they shall fall by the sword,
by the famine, and by the pestilence.
12 He that is far off shall die of the pestilence;
and he that is near shall fall by the sword;
and he that *remaineth* **surviveth**
and is *besieged* **under guard**
shall die by the famine:
thus *will I accomplish* **shall I finish off** my fury upon them.
13 Then shall ye know that *I am the LORD* **I — Yah Veh**,
when their *slain men* **pierced** shall be among their idols
round about their **sacrifice** altars,
upon every high hill, in all the tops of the mountains,
and under every green tree, and under every thick oak,
the place where they
did offer sweet savour **gave a scent of rest**
to all their idols.
14 So *will* **shall** I stretch out my hand upon them,
and *make* **give** the land desolate,
yea, more *desolate* **desolation**
than the wilderness toward *Diblath* **Riblah**,
in all their *habitations* **sites**:
and they shall know that *I am the LORD* **I — Yah Veh**.

THE APPROACH OF THE END

7 Moreover
the word of *the LORD* **Yah Veh** came unto me, saying,
2 Also, thou son of *man* **humanity**,
thus saith *the Lord GOD* **Adonay Yah Veh**
unto the *land* **soil** of *Israel* **Yisra El**;
An end,
the end is come upon the four *corners* **wings** of the land.
3 Now is the end *come* upon thee,
and I *will* **shall** send *mine anger* **my wrath** upon thee,
and *will* **shall** judge thee according to thy ways,
and *will recompense* **shall give** upon thee
all thine *abominations* **abhorrences**.
4 And mine eye shall not spare thee,
neither *will I have pity* **shall I compassion**:
but I *will recompense* **shall give** thy ways upon thee,
and thine *abominations* **abhorrences**
shall be in the midst of thee:
and ye shall know that *I am the LORD* **I — Yah Veh**.
5 Thus saith *the Lord GOD* **Adonay Yah Veh**
An evil, *an only* **one** evil, behold, is come.
6 An end is come, the end is come:
it *watcheth* **waketh** for thee; behold, it is come.
7 The *morning* **corona** is come unto thee,
O thou that *dwellest* **settlest** in the land:
the time is come, the day of *trouble* **confusion** is near,
and not the *sounding again* **shouting** of the mountains.
8 Now *will* **shall** I *shortly* **soon** pour out my fury
upon thee,
and *accomplish mine anger* **finish off my wrath**
upon thee:

and I *will* **shall** judge thee according to thy ways,
and *will recompense* **shall give** thee
for all thine *abominations* **abhorrences**.
9 And mine eye shall not spare,
neither *will I have pity* **shall I compassion**:
I *will recompense* **shall give** thee according to thy ways
and thine *abominations* **abhorrences**
that are in the midst of thee;
and ye shall know
that *I am the LORD* **I — Yah Veh** that smiteth.
10 Behold the day, behold, it is come:
the *morning* **corona** is gone forth;
the rod hath blossomed, *pride* **arrogance** hath budded.
11 Violence is risen up into a rod of wickedness:
none of them shall *remain*, nor of their multitude,
nor of any of *theirs* **abundance:**
neither shall there be *wailing* **lamentation** for them.
12 The time is come, the day *draweth near* **toucheth**:
let not the *buyer rejoice* **chatteler cheer**,
nor the seller mourn:
for *wrath* **fuming** is upon all the multitude *thereof.*
13 For the seller shall not return to that which is sold,
although
they were yet alive **their life was among the living**:
for the vision is touching the whole multitude *thereof,*
which shall not return;
neither shall *any* **man** strengthen himself
in the *iniquity* **perversity** of his life.
14 They have *blown* **blast** the *trumpet* **blast**,
even to *make all ready* **prepare**;
but none goeth to the *battle* **war**:
for my *wrath* **fuming** is upon all the multitude *thereof.*
15 The sword is without,
and the pestilence and the famine within **the house**:
he that is in the field shall die with the sword;
and he that is in the city,
famine and pestilence shall devour him.
16 But *they that escape of them* **the escapees**
shall escape,
and shall be on the mountains like doves of the valleys,
all of them *mourning* **roaring**,
every *one* **man** for his *iniquity* **perversity**.
17 All hands shall *be feeble* **slacken**,
and all knees shall *be weak as water* **go watery**.
18 They shall *also* gird *themselves* with *sackcloth* **saq**,
and *horror* **trembling** shall cover them;
and shame shall be upon all faces,
and baldness upon all their heads.
19 They shall cast their silver in the *streets* **outways**,
and their gold shall be *removed* **excluded**:
their silver and their gold
shall not be able to *deliver* **rescue** them
in the day of the wrath of *the LORD* **Yah Veh**:
they shall not satisfy their souls,
neither fill their *bowels* **inwards**:
because it is the stumblingblock
of their *iniquity* **perversity**.
20 As for the *beauty* **splendour** of his ornament,
he set it in *majesty* **pomp**:
but they *made* **worked** the images
of their *abominations* **abhorrences**
and of their *detestable things* **abominations** therein:
therefore have I *set it far* **given to exclude it** from them.
21 And I *will* **shall** give it
into the hands of the strangers for a *prey* **plunder**,
and to the wicked of the earth for a spoil;
and they shall *pollute* **profane** it.
22 My face *will* **shall** I turn also from them,
and they shall *pollute* **profane** my *secret place* **hideout**:
for the *robbers* **tyrants** shall enter into it,
and *defile* **profane** it.
23 *Make* **Work** a chain:
for the land is *full* **filled**
of *bloody crimes* **judgments of blood**,
and the city is *full* **filled** of violence.
24 Wherefore
I *will* **shall** bring the *worst* **evil** of the *heathen* **goyim**,
and they shall possess their houses:
I *will* **shall** also make the pomp of the strong
to *cease* **shabbathize**;
and their *holy places* **hallowed**
shall be *defiled* **profaned**.
25 *Destruction* **Severence** cometh;
and they shall seek *peace* **shalom**,
and there shall be none.
26 *Mischief* **Calamity** shall come upon *mischief* **calamity**,
and *rumour* **report** shall *be* upon *rumour* **report**;
then shall they seek a vision of the prophet;
but the *law* **torah** shall *perish* **destruct** from the priest,
and counsel from the *ancients* **elders**.
27 The *king* **sovereign** shall mourn,
and the *prince* **hierarch**
shall be *clothed* **enrobed** with desolation,
and the hands of the people of the land
shall *be troubled* **terrify**:
I *will do* **shall work** unto them after their way,
and *according to* **after** their *deserts* **judgments**
will **shall** I judge them;
and they shall know that *I am the LORD* **I — Yah Veh.**

THE FIGURINE OF JEALOUSY

8 And it *came to pass* **became,** in the sixth year,
in the sixth *month,* in the fifth *day* of the month,
as I sat in mine house,
and the elders of *Judah* **Yah Hudah**
sat *before me* **at my face**,
that the hand of *the Lord GOD* **Adonay Yah Veh**
fell there upon me.
2 Then I *beheld* **saw**,
and *lo* **behold** a likeness as the *appearance* **visage** of fire:
from the *appearance* **visage** of his loins even downward,
fire;
and from his loins even upward,
as the *appearance* **visage** of *brightness* **brilliance**,
as the *colour* **eye** of *amber* **brilliant copper**.
Apocalypse 1:12—16
3 And he *put forth* **extended** the *form* **pattern** of an hand,
and took me by a *lock* **tassel** of mine head;
and the spirit lifted me up
between the earth and **between** the *heaven* **heavens**,
and brought me in the visions of *God* **Elohim**
to *Jerusalem* **Yeru Shalem**,
to the *door* **opening** of the inner *gate* **portal**
that *looketh toward the north* **faceth northward**;
where was the seat of the *image* **figurine** of jealousy,
which provoketh to jealousy.
4 And, behold,
the *glory* **honour** of *the God* **Elohim** of *Israel* **Yisra El**
was there,
according to the *vision* **visage**
that I saw in the *plain* **valley**.
5 Then said he unto me, Son of *man* **humanity**,
lift up thine eyes *now* **I beseech**,
the way *toward the north* **northward**.
So I lifted up mine eyes
the way *toward the north* **northward**,
and behold northward
at the *gate* **portal** of the **sacrifice** altar
this *image* **figurine** of jealousy in the entry.
6 He said *furthermore* unto me, Son of *man* **humanity**,
seest thou what they *do* **work**?
even the great *abominations* **abhorrences**
that the house of *Israel committeth* **Yisra El worketh** here,
that I should *go* far *off* **remove** from my *sanctuary* **holies**?
but turn thee yet again,
and thou shalt see greater abominations.
7 And he brought me to the *door* **portal** of the court;
and when I *looked* **saw**, behold *a* **one** hole in the wall.
8 Then said he unto me, Son of *man* **humanity**,
dig *now* **I beseech,** in the wall:
and when I had digged in the wall,
behold *a door* **one opening**.
9 And he said unto me, Go in,
and *behold* **see**
the *wicked abominations* **evil abhorrences**
that they *do* **work** here.
10 So I went in and saw; and behold
every *form* **pattern** of *creeping things* **creepers**,
and abominable *beasts* **animals**,
and all the idols of the house of *Israel* **Yisra El**,
pourtrayed **engraved** upon the wall

round about, **round about**.
11 And there stood *before* **at the face of** them
seventy men
of the *ancients* **elders** of the house of *Israel* **Yisra El**,
and in the midst of them
stood *Jaazaniah* **Yaazan Yah** the son of Shaphan,
with every man his censer in his hand;
and a *thick* **voluminous** cloud of incense
went up **ascended**.
12 Then said he unto me, Son of *man* **humanity**,
hast thou seen what the *ancients* **elders**
of the house of *Israel do* **Yisra El work** in the dark,
every man in the chambers of his imagery?
for they say, *The LORD* **Yah Veh** seeth us not;
the LORD **Yah Veh** hath forsaken the earth.
13 He said also unto me, Turn thee yet again,
and thou shalt see greater *abominations* **abhorrences**
that they *do* **work**.
14 Then he brought me
to the *door* **opening** of the *gate* **portal**
of the *LORD'S* house **of Yah Veh**
which was *toward the north* **northward**; and, behold,
there sat women weeping for Tammuz.
15 Then said he unto me,
Hast thou seen *this,* O son of *man* **humanity**?
turn thee yet again, and thou shalt see
greater *abominations* **abhorrences** than these.
16 And he brought me into the inner court
of the LORD'S house **of Yah Veh**, and, behold,
at the *door* **portal**
of the *temple* **manse** of *the LORD* **Yah Veh**,
between the porch and the **sacrifice** altar,
were about five and twenty men,
with their backs
toward the *temple* **manse** of *the LORD* **Yah Veh**,
and their faces *toward the east* **eastward**;
and they *worshipped* **prostrated to** the sun
toward the east **eastward**.
17 Then he said unto me,
Hast thou seen *this,* O son of *man* **humanity**?
Is it *a light thing* **trifling** to the house of *Judah* **Yah Hudah**
that they *commit* **work** the *abominations* **abhorrences**
which they *commit* **work** here?
for they have filled the land with violence,
and have returned to *provoke* **vex** me *to anger*:
and, *lo* **behold**,
they *put* **extend** the *branch* **twig** to their *nose* **nostrils**.
18 Therefore *will* **shall** I also *deal* **work** in fury:
mine eye shall not spare,
neither *will I have pity* **shall I compassion**:
and though they *cry* **call out** in mine ears
with a *loud* **great** voice, yet *will* **shall** I not hear them.

SLAUGHTER OF IDOLATERS

9 He *cried* **called out** also in mine ears
with a *loud* **great** voice, saying,
Cause them that have charge over the city
to *draw near* **approach**,
even every man
with his *destroying weapon* **instrument of ruin**
in his hand.
2 And, behold, six men came
from the way of the *higher gate* **most high portal**,
which *lieth toward the north* **faceth northward**,
and every man
a *slaughter weapon* **disintegrator instrument** in his hand;
and one man among them
was *clothed* **enrobed** with linen,
with a *writer's inkhorn* **scribe's inkwell**
by **upon** his *side* **loins**:
and they went in,
and stood beside the *brasen* **copper sacrifice** altar.
3 And the *glory* **honour**
of *the God* **Elohim** of *Israel* **Yisra El**
was gone up **ascended** from the cherub,
whereupon he was, to the threshold of the house.
And he called to the man *clothed* **enrobed** with linen,
which had the *writer's inkhorn* **scribe's inkwell**
by **upon** his *side* **loins**;
4 And *the LORD* **Yah Veh** said unto him,
Go **Pass** through the midst of the city,
through the midst of *Jerusalem* **Yeru Shalem**,
and *set* **tattoo** a *mark* **tattoo**
upon the foreheads of the men
that sigh and that *cry* **shriek**
for all the *abominations* **abhorrences**
that be *done* **worked** in the midst *thereof.*
5 And to the others he said in mine *hearing* **ears**,
Go **Pass** ye after him through the city, and smite:
let not your eye spare,
neither *have ye pity* **compassion**:
6 *Slay utterly* **Slaughter to ruin**
old **aged** and *young* **youth**,
both *maids* **virgins**, and *little children* **toddlers**,
and women:
but come not near any man
upon whom is the *mark* **tattoo**;
and begin at my *sanctuary* **holies**.
Then they began at the *ancient* **aged** men
which were *before* **at the face of** the house.
7 And he said unto them, *Defile* **Foul** the house,
and fill the courts with the *slain* **pierced**: go ye forth.
And they went forth, and *slew* **smote** in the city.
8 And it *came to pass* **became**,
while they were *slaying* **smiting** them,
and I *was left* **survived**,
that I fell upon my face, and cried, and said,
Ah Lord GOD **Aha Adonay Yah Veh**!
wilt **shalt** thou *destroy* **ruin**
all the *residue* **survivors** of *Israel* **Yisra El**
in thy pouring out of thy fury
upon *Jerusalem* **Yeru Shalem**?
9 Then said he unto me,
The *iniquity* **perversity**
of the house of *Israel* **Yisra El** and *Judah* **Yah Hudah**
is *exceeding* **mighty** great,
and the land is *full* **filled** of blood,
and the city *full* **filled** of *perverseness* **distortion**:
for they say, *The LORD* **Yah Veh** hath forsaken the earth,
and *the LORD* **Yah Veh** seeth not.
10 And as for me also, mine eye shall not spare,
neither *will I have pity* **shall I compassion**,
but I will recompense **I shall give** their way
upon their head.
11 And, behold, the man *clothed* **enrobed** with linen,
which had the *inkhorn by* **inkwell upon** his *side* **loins**,
reported the matter **returned word**, saying,
I have *done* **worked**
as thou hast *commanded* **misvahed** me.

THE HONOUR OF YAH VEH FILLS THE HOUSE

10 Then I *looked* **saw**, and, behold,
in the *firmament* **expanse**
that was above the head of the *cherubims* **cherubim**
there appeared over them as it were a sapphire stone,
as the *appearance* **visage** of the likeness of a throne.
2 And he *spake* **said** unto the man clothed with linen,
and said,
Go in between the wheels, *even* under the cherub,
and fill thine *hand* **fist** with coals of fire
from between the *cherubims* **cherubim**,
and scatter them over the city.
And he went in in my *sight* **eyes**.
3 *Now* the *cherubims* **cherubim**
stood on the right side of the house,
when the man went in;
and the cloud filled the inner court.
4 Then the *glory* **honour** of *the LORD* **Yah Veh**
went up **lifted** from the cherub,
and stood over the threshold of the house;
and the house was filled with the cloud,
and the court was *full* **filled** of the *brightness* **brilliance**
of the *LORD'S glory* **honour of Yah Veh**.
5 And the *sound* **voice**
of the *cherubims'* **cherubim's** wings
was heard *even* to the outer court,
as the voice of *the Almighty God* **El Shadday**
when he *speaketh* **wordeth**.
6 And it *came to pass* **became**,
that when he had *commanded* **misvahed**
the man *clothed* **enrobed** with linen, saying,
Take fire from between the wheels,

from between the *cherubims* **cherubim**;
then he went in, and stood beside the wheels.
7 And *one* cherub *stretched forth* **extended** his hand
from between the *cherubims* **cherubim**
unto the fire that was between the *cherubims* **cherubim**,
and *took* **lifted** *thereof*,
and *put* **gave** it into the *hands* **fists**
of *him* **the one** that was *clothed* **enrobed** with linen:
who took it, and went out.
8 And there *appeared* **was seen**
in the *cherubims* **cherubim**
the *form* **pattern** of a *man's* **human** hand
under their wings.

THE WHEEL IN THE MIDST OF A WHEEL

9 And when I *looked* **saw**, behold
the four wheels *by* **beside** the *cherubims* **cherubim**,
one wheel *by* **beside** one cherub,
and *another* **one** wheel *by another* **beside one** cherub:
and the *appearance* **visage** of the wheels
was as the *colour* **eye** of a beryl stone.
10 And as for their *appearances* **visages**,
they four had one likeness,
as if a wheel had been in the midst of a wheel.
11 When they went,
they went upon their four *sides* **quarters**;
they turned not as they went,
but to the place whither the head *looked* **faced**
they *followed* **went after** it;
they turned not as they went.
12 And their whole *body* **flesh**, and their backs,
and their hands, and their wings, and the wheels,
were full of eyes round about,
even the wheels that they four had.
13 As for the wheels,
it was *cried* **called out** unto them in my *hearing* **ears**,
O wheel.
14 And *every* **each** one had four faces:
the first face was the face of a cherub,
and the second face was the face of a *man* **human**,
and the third the face of a lion,
and the fourth the face of an eagle.
15 And the *cherubims* **cherubim** were lifted *up*.
This is the *living creature* **live being**
that I saw by the river of *Chebar* **Kebar**.
16 And when the *cherubims* **cherubim** went,
the wheels went *by* **beside** them:
and when the *cherubims* **cherubim** lifted *up* their wings
to *mount up* **lift** from the earth,
the same wheels also turned not from beside them.
17 When they stood, these stood;
and when they *were* lifted *up*,
these lifted *up* themselves *also*:
for the spirit of the *living creature* **live being** was in them.
18 Then the *glory* **honour** of *the LORD* **Yah Veh**
departed from off the threshold of the house,
and stood over the *cherubims* **cherubim**.
19 And the *cherubims* **cherubim** lifted *up* their wings,
and *mounted* **lifted** *up* from the earth in my *sight* **eyes**:
when they went out, the wheels also were beside them,
and *every one* **each** stood
at the *door* **opening** of the east *gate* **portal**
of the *LORD'S* house **of Yah Veh**;
and the *glory* **honour** of *the God* **Elohim** of *Israel* **Yisra El**
was over them above.
20 This is the *living creature* **live being** that I saw
under *the God* **Elohim** of *Israel* **Yisra El**
by the river of *Chebar* **Kebar**;
and I knew that they were the *cherubims* **cherubim**.
21 *Every* **Four,** *one* **each** had four faces *apiece*,
and *every one* **each** four wings;
and the likeness of the hands of a *man* **human**
was under their wings.
22 And the likeness of their faces
was the same faces
which I saw by the river of *Chebar* **Kebar**,
their *appearances* **visages** and themselves:
they went *every one straight* **each man face** forward.

JUDGMENT OF MEN WHO FABRICATE MISCHIEF

11 Moreover the spirit lifted me up,
and brought me unto the east *gate* **portal**
of the *LORD'S* house **of Yah Veh**,
which *looketh* **faceth** eastward: and behold!
at the *door* **opening** of the *gate* **portal**
five and twenty men;
among whom I saw
Jaazaniah **Yaazan Yah** the son of *Azur* **Azzur**,
and *Pelatiah* **Pelat Yah** the son of *Benaiah* **Bena Yah**,
princes **governors** of the people.
2 Then said he unto me, Son of *man* **humanity**,
these are the men that *devise* **fabricate** mischief,
and give wicked **counsellors evil** counsel in this city:
3 Which say, It is not near; let us build houses:
this *city* is the caldron, and we be the flesh.
4 Therefore prophesy against them,
prophesy, O son of *man* **humanity**.
5 And the Spirit of *the LORD* **Yah Veh** fell upon me,
and said unto me, Speak;
Thus saith *the LORD* **Yah Veh**;
Thus have ye said, O house of *Israel* **Yisra El**:
for I know the
things that come into your mind **degrees of your spirit**,
every one **each** of them.
6 Ye have *multiplied* **abounded** your *slain* **pierced**
in this city,
and ye have filled the *streets* **outways** *thereof*
with the *slain* **pierced**.
7 Therefore thus saith *the Lord GOD* **Adonay Yah Veh**;
Your *slain* **pierced**
whom ye have *laid* **set** in the midst of it,
they are the flesh, and this *city* is the caldron:
but I *will* **shall** bring you forth out of the midst of it.
8 Ye have *feared* **awed** the sword;
and I *will* **shall** bring a sword upon you,
saith the Lord GOD **an oracle of Adonay Yah Veh**.
9 And I *will* **shall** bring you out of the midst *thereof*,
and *deliver* **give** you into the hands of strangers,
and *will execute* **shall work** judgments among you.
10 Ye shall fall by the sword;
I *will* **shall** judge you in the border of *Israel* **Yisra El**;
and ye shall know that *I am the LORD* **I — Yah Veh**.
11 This *city* shall not be your caldron,
neither shall ye be *the* **for** flesh in the midst *thereof*;
but I *will* **shall** judge you in the border of *Israel* **Yisra El**:
12 And ye shall know that *I am the LORD* **I — Yah Veh**:
for ye have not walked in my statutes,
neither *executed* **worked** my judgments,
but have *done* **worked** after the *manners* **judgments**
of the *heathen* **goyim** that are round about you.
13 And it *came to pass* **became**, when I prophesied,
that *Pelatiah* **Pelat Yah**
the son of *Benaiah* **Bena Yah** died.
Then fell I down upon my face,
and cried with a loud voice, and said,
Ah Lord GOD **Aha Adonay Yah Veh**!
wilt **shalt** thou *make a full end* **work a final finish**
of the *remnant* **survivors** of *Israel* **Yisra El**?
14 Again the word of *the LORD* **Yah Veh** came unto me,
saying,
15 Son of *man* **humanity**, thy brethren,
even thy brethren, the men of thy *kindred* **redemption**,
and all the house of *Israel* **Yisra El** wholly,
are they unto whom
the *inhabitants* **settlers** of *Jerusalem* **Yeru Shalem**
have said,
Get you **Remove ye** far from *the LORD* **Yah Veh**:
unto us is this land given in possession.

WORD CONCERNING THE RESTORATION OF YISRA EL

16 Therefore say,
Thus saith *the Lord GOD* **Adonay Yah Veh**;
Although I have *cast* **removed** them far off
among the *heathen* **goyim**,
and although I have scattered them
among the *countries* **lands**,
yet *will* **shall** I be to them as a little *sanctuary* **holies**
in the *countries* **lands** where they shall come.
17 Therefore say,
Thus saith *the Lord GOD* **Adonay Yah Veh**;
I *will* **shall** even gather you from the people,
and assemble you out of the countries
where ye have been scattered,

and I *will* **shall** give you the *land* **soil** of *Israel* **Yisra El**.
18 And they shall come thither,
and they shall *take away* **turn aside**
all the *detestable things* **abominations** *thereof*
and all the *abominations* **abhorrences** *thereof*
from thence.
19 And I *will* **shall** give them one heart,
and I *will put* **shall give** a new spirit within you;
and I *will take* **shall turn aside** the *stony* heart **of stone**
out of their flesh,
and *will* **shall** give them an heart of flesh:
20 That they may walk in my statutes,
and *keep mine ordinances* **guard my judgments**,
and *do* **work** them:
and they *shall* be my people,
and *I will be* **I AM** their *God* **Elohim**.
21 But as for them whose heart walketh after the heart
of their *detestable things* **abominations**
and their *abominations* **abhorrences**,
I *will recompense* **shall give** their way
upon their own heads,
saith the Lord GOD **an oracle of Adonay Yah Veh**.
22 Then did the *cherubims* **cherubim** lift *up* their wings,
and the wheels beside them;
and the *glory* **honour** of *the God* **Elohim** of *Israel* **Yisra El**
was over them above.
23 And the *glory* **honour** of *the LORD* **Yah Veh**
went up **ascended** from the midst of the city,
and stood upon the mountain
which is *on the east side* **eastward** of the city.
24 Afterwards the spirit *took* **bore** me *up*,
and brought me in a vision by the Spirit of *God* **Elohim**
into *Chaldea* **Kesediym**, to them of the *captivity* **exile**.
So the vision that I had seen *went up* **ascended** from me.
25 Then I *spake* **worded** unto them of the *captivity* **exile**
all the *things* **words**
that *the LORD* **Yah Veh** had *shewed* me **see**.

YAH VEH'S WORD CONCERNING EXILE

12 The word of *the LORD* **Yah Veh** also came unto me,
saying,
2 Son of *man* **humanity**,
thou *dwellest* **settlest** in the midst of a rebellious house,
which have eyes to see, and see not;
they have ears to hear, and hear not:
for they are a rebellious house.
3 Therefore, thou son of *man* **humanity**,
prepare **work** thee *stuff* **instruments** for *removing* **exiling**,
and *remove* **exile** by day in their *sight* **eyes**;
and thou shalt *remove* **exile** from thy place
to another place in their *sight* **eyes**:
it may be **perhaps** they *will consider* **shall see**,
though they be a rebellious house.
4 Then shalt thou bring forth thy *stuff* **instruments**
by day in their *sight* **eyes**,
as *stuff* **instruments** for *removing* **exiling**:
and thou shalt go forth at even in their *sight* **eyes**,
as they that *go forth* **proceed** into *captivity* **exile**.
5 Dig thou through the wall in their *sight* **eyes**,
and carry out thereby.
6 In their *sight* **eyes** shalt thou bear it upon thy shoulders,
and carry it forth in the *twilight* **dusk**:
thou shalt cover thy face,
that thou see not the *ground* **earth**:
for I have *set* **given** thee for *a sign* **an omen**
unto the house of *Israel* **Yisra El**.
7 And I *did* **worked** so as I was *commanded* **misvahed**:
I brought forth my *stuff* **instruments** by day,
as *stuff* **instruments** for *captivity* **exile**,
and in the even
I digged through the wall with mine hand;
I brought it forth in the *twilight* **dusk**,
and I bare it upon my shoulder in their *sight* **eyes**.
8 And in the morning
came the word of *the LORD* **Yah Veh** unto me, saying,
9 Son of *man* **humanity**,
hath not the house of *Israel* **Yisra El**, the rebellious house,
said unto thee, What *dost* **workest** thou?
10 Say thou unto them,
Thus saith *the Lord GOD* **Adonay Yah Veh**;
This burden concerneth
the *prince* **hierarch** in *Jerusalem* **Yeru Shalem**,
and all the house of *Israel* **Yisra El**, that are among them.
11 Say, I am your *sign* **omen**:
like as I have *done* **worked**,
so shall it be *done* **worked** unto them:
in exiling, they shall *remove and go into captivity* **exile**.
12 And the *prince* **hierarch** that is among them
shall bear upon his shoulder in the *twilight* **dusk**,
and shall go forth:
they shall dig through the wall to carry out thereby:
he shall cover his face,
so that he see not the *ground* **earth** with his eyes.
13 My net also *will* **shall** I spread upon him,
and he shall be *taken* **apprehended** in my *snare* **lure**:
and I *will* **shall** bring him to *Babylon* **Babel**
to the land of the *Chaldeans* **Kesediym**;
yet shall he not see it, though he shall die there.
14 And I *will scatter* **shall winnow** toward every wind
all that are **round** about him to help him,
and all his bands;
and I *will* **shall** draw out the sword after them.
15 And they shall know that *I am the LORD* **I — Yah Veh**,
when I shall *scatter* **winnow** them
among the *nations* **goyim**,
and disperse them in the *countries* **lands**.
16 But I *will leave a few men* **shall let remain** of them
from the sword,
from the famine, and from the pestilence;
that they may *declare* **scribe**
all their *abominations* **abhorrences**
among the *heathen* **goyim** whither they come;
and they shall know that *I am the LORD* **I — Yah Veh**.
17 Moreover the word of *the LORD* **Yah Veh** came to me,
saying,
18 Son of *man* **humanity**, eat thy bread with quaking,
and drink thy water with *trembling* **quivering**
and with *carefulness* **concern**;
19 And say unto the people of the land,
Thus saith *the Lord GOD* **Adonay Yah Veh**
of the *inhabitants* **settlers** of *Jerusalem* **Yeru Shalem**,
and of the *land* **soil** of *Israel* **Yisra El**;
They shall eat their bread with *carefulness* **concern**,
and drink their water with astonishment,
that her land may be desolate
from *all that is therein* **the fulness thereof**,
because of the violence
of all them that *dwell* **settle** therein.
20 And the cities that are *inhabited* **settled**
shall be *laid waste* **parched**,
and the land shall be desolate;
and ye shall know that *I am the LORD* **I — Yah Veh**.
21 And the word of *the LORD* **Yah Veh** came unto me,
saying,
22 Son of *man* **humanity**,
what is that proverb that ye have
in the *land* **soil** of *Israel* **Yisra El**, saying,
The days are prolonged,
and every vision *faileth* **destroyed**?
23 Tell them therefore,
Thus saith *the Lord GOD* **Adonay Yah Veh**;
I *will make* **shall cause** this proverb to *cease* **shabbathize**,
and they shall no more *use* **proverbialize** it
as a proverb in *Israel* **Yisra El**;
but *say* **word** unto them,
The days *are at hand* **approach**,
and the *effect* **word** of every vision.
24 For there shall be no more any vain vision
nor *flattering* **smoothing** divination
within the house of *Israel* **Yisra El**.
25 For *I am the LORD* **I — Yah Veh**:
I *will speak* **shall word**,
and the word that I shall *speak* **word**
shall *come to pass* **work**;
it shall be no more *prolonged* **drawn out**:
for in your days, O rebellious house,
will I say **shall I word** the word,
and *will perform* **shall work** it,
saith the Lord GOD **an oracle of Adonay Yah Veh**.
26 Again the word of *the LORD* **Yah Veh** came to me,
saying,

27 Son of *man* **humanity**, behold,
they of the house of *Israel* **Yisra El** say,
The vision that he seeth is for many days *to come*,
and he prophesieth of the times that are far off.
28 Therefore say unto them,
Thus saith *the Lord GOD* **Adonay Yah Veh**;
There shall none of my words
be *prolonged* **drawn out** any more,
but the word which I have *spoken* **worded**
shall be *done* **worked**,
saith the Lord GOD **an oracle of Adonay Yah Veh.**

YAH VEH'S WORD CONCERNING PROPHETS

13 And the word of *the LORD* **Yah Veh** came unto me,
saying,
2 Son of *man* **humanity**,
prophesy against the prophets of *Israel* **Yisra El**
that prophesy,
and say thou unto them
that prophesy out of their own hearts,
Hear ye the word of *the LORD* **Yah Veh**;
3 Thus saith *the Lord GOD* **Adonay Yah Veh**;
Woe **Ho** unto the foolish prophets,
that *follow* **walk after** their own spirit,
and have seen *nothing* **naught**!
4 O *Israel* **Yisra El**,
thy prophets
are like the foxes in the *deserts* **parched areas**.
5 Ye have not *gone up* **ascended** into the *gaps* **breaches**,
neither *made up* **walled** the *hedge* **wall**
for the house of *Israel* **Yisra El** to stand in the *battle* **war**
in the day of *the LORD* **Yah Veh**.
6 They have seen vanity and lying divination, saying,
The LORD saith **An oracle of Yah Veh**:
and *the LORD* **Yah Veh** hath not sent them:
and they have *made others to hope* **hoped**
that they *would* **should** confirm the word.
7 Have ye not seen a vain vision,
and have ye not *spoken* **said** a lying divination,
whereas ye say **saying**,
The LORD saith it **An oracle of Yah Veh**;
albeit I have not *spoken* **worded**?
8 Therefore thus saith *the Lord GOD* **Adonay Yah Veh**;
Because ye have *spoken* **worded** vanity, and seen lies,
therefore, behold, I am against you,
saith the Lord GOD **an oracle of Adonay Yah Veh**.
9 And mine hand shall be upon the prophets
that see **seers of** vanity and *that divine* **diviners of** lies:
they shall not be
in the *assembly* **private counsel** of my people,
neither shall they be *written* **inscribed**
in the *writing* **inscribing** of the house of *Israel* **Yisra El**,
neither shall they enter into the *land* **soil** of *Israel* **Yisra El**;
and ye shall know
that I am *the Lord GOD* **Adonay Yah Veh**.
10 Because, even because they have seduced my people,
saying, *Peace* **Shalom**; and there was no *peace* **shalom**;
and one built up a wall, and, *lo* **behold**,
others daubed it with *untempered morter* **slime**:
11 Say unto them
which daub it with *untempered morter* **slime**,
that it shall fall:
there shall be an overflowing *shower* **downpour**;
and ye, O great hailstones, shall fall;
and a stormy wind shall *rend* **split** it.
12 *Lo* **Behold**, when the wall is fallen,
shall it not be said unto you,
Where is the daubing wherewith ye have daubed it?
13 Therefore thus saith *the Lord GOD* **Adonay Yah Veh**;
I *will* **shall** even *rend* **split** it with a stormy wind
in my fury;
and there shall be an overflowing *shower* **downpour**
in *mine anger* **my wrath**,
and great hailstones in my fury to *consume* **fully finish** it.
14 So *will I break down* **shall I demolish** the wall
that ye have daubed with *untempered morter* **slime**,
and bring it down **that it touch** to the *ground* **earth**,
so that the foundation *thereof*
shall be *discovered* **exposed**, and it shall fall,
and ye shall be *consumed* **finished off**
in the midst *thereof*:
and ye shall know that *I am the LORD* **I — Yah Veh**.
15 Thus *will I accomplish* **shall I finish off** my *wrath* **fury**
upon the wall,
and upon them
that have daubed it with *untempered morter* **slime**,
and *will* **shall** say unto you,
The wall is *no more* **not**, neither they that daubed it;
16 *To wit*, the prophets of *Israel* **Yisra El**
which prophesy concerning *Jerusalem* **Yeru Shalem**,
and which see **seers of** visions of *peace* **shalom** for her,
and there is no *peace* **shalom**,
saith the Lord GOD **an oracle of Adonay Yah Veh**.
17 Likewise, thou son of *man* **humanity**,
set thy face against the daughters of thy people,
which prophesy out of their own heart;
and prophesy thou against them,
18 And say, Thus saith *the Lord GOD* **Adonay Yah Veh**;
Woe to the women **Ho to them** that sew pillows
to all armholes **for all the elbow holes of my hands**,
and *make kerchiefs* **work vails**
upon the head of every *stature* **height**
to hunt souls!
will **shall** ye hunt the souls of my people,
and *will* **shall** ye *save* **let** the souls *alive* **live**
that come unto you?
19 And *will* **shall** ye *pollute* **profane** me
among my people
for *handfuls* **palmfuls** of barley
and for *pieces* **bits** of bread,
to *slay* **execute** the souls that should not die,
and to *save the souls alive* **enliven**
that should not live,
by your lying to my people that hear *your* lies?
20 Wherefore thus saith *the Lord GOD* **Adonay Yah Veh**;
Behold, I am against your pillows,
wherewith ye there hunt the souls
to *make them fly* **blossom**,
and I *will tear* **shall rip** them from your arms,
and *will let* **shall send away** the souls *go*,
even the souls that ye hunt to *make them fly* **blossom**.
21 Your *kerchiefs* **vails** also *will I tear* **shall I rip**,
and *deliver* **rescue** my people out of your hand,
and they shall be no more in your hand
to be *hunted* **lured**;
and ye shall know that *I am the LORD* **I — Yah Veh**.
22 Because with *lies* **falsehoods** ye have
made **pained** the heart of the *righteous sad* **just**,
whom I have not *made sad* **pained**;
and strengthened the hands of the *wicked* **evil**,
that he should not return from his wicked way,
by *promising* **enlivening** him *life*:
23 Therefore ye shall see no more vanity,
nor divine divinations:
for I *will deliver* **shall rescue** my people out of your hand:
and ye shall know that *I am the LORD* **I — Yah Veh**.

YAH VEH'S WORD CONCERNING IDOLATROUS ELDERS

14 Then came *certain* **men** of the elders of *Israel* **Yisra El**
unto me,
and sat *before me* **at my face**.
2 And the word of *the LORD* **Yah Veh** came unto me,
saying,
3 Son of *man* **humanity**,
these men have *set up* **ascended** their idols in their heart,
and *put* **gave** the stumblingblock of their *iniquity* **perversity**
before **at** their face:
should I be enquired of at all by them?
4 Therefore *speak* **word** unto them, and say unto them,
Thus saith *the Lord GOD* **Adonay Yah Veh**;
Every **Man by** man of the house of *Israel* **Yisra El**
that *setteth up* **ascendeth** his idols in his heart,
and *putteth* **setteth**
the stumblingblock of his *iniquity* **perversity**
before **at** his face,
and cometh to the prophet;
I *the LORD will* **Yah Veh shall** answer him that cometh
according to the *multitude* **abundance** of his idols;
5 That I may *take* **apprehend** the house of *Israel* **Yisra El**
in their own heart,
because they are all estranged from me
through their idols.

6 Therefore say unto the house of *Israel* **Yisra El**,
Thus saith *the Lord GOD* **Adonay Yah Veh**;
Repent **Turn**, *and* turn *yourselves* from your idols;
and turn *away* **from** your faces
from all your *abominations* **abhorrences**.
7 For *every one* **each man** of the house of *Israel* **Yisra El**,
or of the *stranger* **sojourner**
that sojourneth in *Israel* **Yisra El**,
which separateth himself from **after** me,
and *setteth up* **ascendeth** his idols in his heart,
and *putteth* **setteth**
the stumblingblock of his *iniquity* **perversity**
before **at** his face,
and cometh to a prophet
to enquire of him concerning me;
I *the LORD will* **Yah Veh shall** answer him by myself:
8 And I *will set* **shall give** my face against that man,
and *will make* **shall desolate** him a sign and a proverb,
and I *will* **shall** cut him off from the midst of my people;
and ye shall know that *I am the LORD* **I — Yah Veh**.
9 And if the prophet be *deceived* **deluded**
when he hath *spoken* **worded** a *thing* **word**,
I *the LORD* **Yah Veh**
have *deceived* **deluded** that prophet,
and I *will* **shall** stretch out my hand upon him,
and *will destroy* **shall desolate** him
from the midst of my people *Israel* **Yisra El**.
10 And they shall bear
the punishment of their iniquity **their perversity**:
the *punishment* **perversity** of the prophet
shall be even as the *punishment* **perversity**
of him that seeketh *unto him*;
11 That the house of *Israel* **Yisra El**
may *go* **stray** no more *astray* from me,
neither be *polluted* **fouled** any more
with all their *transgressions* **rebellions**;
but that they may be my people,
and I may be their *God* **Elohim**,
saith the Lord GOD **an oracle of Adonay Yah Veh**.
12 The word of *the LORD* **Yah Veh** came again to me,
saying,
13 Son of *man* **humanity**,
when the land sinneth against me
by *trespassing grievously* **treasoning a treason**,
then *will* **shall** I stretch out mine hand upon it,
and *will* **shall** break the *staff* **rod** of the bread *thereof*,
and *will* **shall** send famine upon it,
and *will* **shall** cut off
man **humanity** and *beast* **animal** from it:
14 Though these three men,
Noah **Noach**, *Daniel* **Dani El**, and *Job* **Iyob**, were in it,
they should *deliver but* **rescue** their own souls
by their *righteousness* **justness**,
saith the Lord GOD **an oracle of Adonay Yah Veh**.
15 If I cause *noisome beasts* **evil live beings**
to pass through the land,
and they *spoil* **bereave** *it*, so that it be desolate,
that no man may pass through
because **at the face** of the *beasts* **live beings**:
16 Though these three men were in **the midst of** it,
as I live,
saith the Lord GOD **an oracle of Adonay Yah Veh**,
they shall *deliver* **rescue** neither sons nor daughters;
they only shall be *delivered* **rescued**,
but the land shall be desolate.
17 Or *if* I bring a sword upon that land,
and say, Sword, *go* **pass** through the land;
so that I cut off *man* **humanity** and *beast* **animal** from it:
18 Though these three men were in **the midst of** it,
as I live,
saith the Lord GOD **an oracle of Adonay Yah Veh**,
they shall *deliver* **rescue** neither sons nor daughters,
but they only shall be *delivered* **rescued** themselves.
19 Or *if* I send a pestilence into that land,
and pour out my fury upon it in blood,
to cut off from it *man* **humanity** and *beast* **animal**:
20 Though *Noah* **Noach**, *Daniel* **Dani El**, and *Job* **Iyob**
were in **the midst of** it, *as* I live,
saith the Lord GOD **an oracle of Adonay Yah Veh**,
they shall *deliver* **rescue** neither son nor daughter;
they shall *but deliver* **rescue** their own souls
by their *righteousness* **justness**.
21 For thus saith *the Lord GOD* **Adonay Yah Veh**;
How much more
when I send my four *sore* **evil** judgments
upon *Jerusalem* **Yeru Shalem**,
the sword, and the famine,
and the *noisome beast* **evil live being**, and the pestilence,
to cut off from it *man* **humanity** and *beast* **animal**?
22 Yet, behold,
therein shall *be left a remnant* **remain escapees**
that shall be brought forth, *both* sons and daughters:
behold, they shall come forth unto you,
and ye shall see their way and their *doings* **exploits**:
and ye shall *be comforted* **sigh** concerning the evil
that I have brought upon *Jerusalem* **Yeru Shalem**,
even concerning all that I have brought upon it.
23 And they shall *comfort* **sigh over** you,
when ye see their ways and their *doings* **exploits**:
and ye shall know
that I have not *done without cause* **worked gratuitously**
all that I have *done* **worked** in it,
saith the Lord GOD **an oracle of Adonay Yah Veh**.

YAH VEH'S WORD CONCERNING THE CONSUMED VINE

15 And the word of *the LORD* **Yah Veh** came unto me,
saying,
2 Son of *man* **humanity**,
what is the vine tree more than any tree,
or than a branch which is
a twig among the trees of the forest?
3 shall *wood* **timber** be taken *thereof*
to *do* **work** any work?
or *will men take a pin of it* **shall a stake be taken**
to hang any *vessel* **instrument** thereon?
4 Behold, it is *cast* **given** into the fire for fuel;
the fire *devoureth* **consumeth** both the ends of it,
and the midst of it is *burned* **scorched**.
Is it meet **Shall it prosper** for *any* work?
5 Behold, when it was *whole* **integrious**,
it *was meet for* **worked** no work:
how much less shall it *be meet* **work** yet *for any* work,
when the fire hath devoured it,
and *it is burned* **scorched**?
6 Therefore thus saith *the Lord GOD* **Adonay Yah Veh**;
As the vine tree among the trees of the forest,
which I have given to the fire for fuel,
so *will* **shall** give
the *inhabitants* **settlers** of *Jerusalem* **Yeru Shalem**.
7 And I *will set* **shall give** my face against them;
they shall go out from *one* fire,
and *another* fire shall *devour* **consume** them;
and ye shall know that *I am the LORD* **I — Yah Veh**,
when I set my face against them.
8 And I *will make* **shall give** the land desolate,
because they have
committed **treasoned** a *trespass* **treason**,
saith the Lord GOD **an oracle of Adonay Yah Veh**.

YAH VEH'S WORD CONCERNING UNTRUSTING YERU SHALEM

16 Again the word of *the LORD* **Yah Veh** came unto me,
saying,
2 Son of *man* **humanity**, cause *Jerusalem* **Yeru Shalem**
to know her *abominations* **abhorrences**,
3 And say, Thus saith *the Lord GOD* **Adonay Yah Veh**
unto *Jerusalem* **Yeru Shalem**;
Thy *birth* **origin** and thy *nativity* **kindred**
is of the land of *Canaan* **Kenaan**;
thy father was an *Amorite* **Emoriy**,
and thy mother an *Hittite* **Hethiy**.
4 And as for thy *nativity* **kindred**,
in the day thou wast born thy navel was not cut,
neither wast thou *washed* **baptized** in water
to supple thee **for inspection**;
in salting, thou wast not salted *at all*,
nor swaddled at all **in swathing, thou wast not swathed**.
5 None eye pitied thee,
to *do any* **work one** of these unto thee,
to *have* compassion *upon* thee;
but thou wast cast out in the *open* **face of the** field,

to the lothing of thy *person* **soul**,
in the day that thou wast born.
6 And when I passed by thee,
and saw thee *polluted* **trampled** in thine own blood,
I said unto thee *when thou wast* in thy blood, Live;
yea, I said unto thee *when thou wast* in thy blood, Live.
7 I have *caused* **given** thee
to *multiply* **abound by the myriads**
as the *bud* **sprout** of the field,
and thou hast *increased* **abounded**
and *waxen great* **greatened**,
and thou art come
to *excellent* **an ornament of** ornaments:
thy breasts are fashioned,
and thine hair *is grown* **sprouted**,
whereas thou wast naked and *bare* **nude**.
8 *Now* when I passed by thee, and *looked upon* **saw** thee,
behold, thy time was the time of love;
and I spread my *skirt* **wing** over thee,
and covered thy nakedness:
yea, I *sware* **oathed** unto thee,
and entered into a covenant with thee,
saith the Lord GOD **an oracle of Adonay Yah Veh**,
and thou becamest mine.
9 Then *washed* **baptized** I thee with water;
yea, I throughly washed away thy blood from thee,
and I anointed thee with oil.
10 I *clothed* **enrobed** thee also
with *broidered work* **embroidery**,
and shod thee with badgers' skin,
and I *girded* **bound** thee *about* with *fine* **white** linen,
and I covered thee with silk.
11 I *decked* **adorned** thee also with ornaments,
and I *put bracelets* **gave clasps** upon thy hands,
and a chain on thy *neck* **throat**.
12 And I *put* **gave** a *jewel* **nosering**
on thy *forehead* **nostrils**,
and earrings in thine ears,
and a *beautiful* crown **of adornment**
upon thine head.
13 Thus wast thou *decked* **adorned** with gold and silver;
and thy *raiment* **robe** was of *fine* **white** linen,
and silk, and *broidered work* **embroidery**;
thou didst eat *fine* flour, and honey, and oil:
and thou wast *exceeding beautiful* **mightily beautified**,
and thou didst prosper into a *kingdom* **sovereigndom**.
14 And thy *renown* **name**
went forth among the *heathen* **goyim** for thy beauty:
for it was perfect through my *comeliness* **majesty**,
which I had *put* **set** upon thee,
saith the Lord GOD **an oracle of Adonay Yah Veh**.
15 But thou *didst trust* **confidedst** in thine own beauty,
and *playedst the harlot* **whored**
because of thy *renown* **name**,
and pouredst out thy *fornications* **whoredoms**
on every one that passed by; his it was.
16 And of thy *garment* **clothes** thou didst take,
and *deckedst* **workedst** thy *high places* **bamahs**
with *divers colours* **patches**,
and *playedst the harlot* **whored** thereupon:
the like things **it** shall not come, neither shall it be so.
17 Thou hast also taken
thy *fair jewels* **instruments of adornment**
of my gold and of my silver, which I had given thee,
and *madest* **workedst** to thyself images of *men* **males**,
and *didst commit whoredom* **whored** with them,
18 And tookest thy
broidered garment **clothes of embroidery**,
and coveredst them:
and thou hast *set* **given** mine oil and mine incense
before them **at their face**.
19 My meat also which I gave thee,
fine flour, and oil, and honey, *wherewith* I fed thee,
thou hast even *set it before them* **given at their face**
for a *sweet savour* **scent of rest**:
and thus it *was* **became**,
saith the Lord GOD **an oracle of Adonay Yah Veh**.
20 Moreover thou hast taken thy sons and thy daughters,
whom thou hast borne unto me,
and these hast thou sacrificed unto them to be devoured.
Is this of thy whoredoms a small matter,
21 That thou hast *slain* **slaughtered** my *children* **sons**,
and *delivered* **gave** them
to cause them to pass through *the fire* for them?
22 And in all thine *abominations* **abhorrences**
and thy whoredoms
thou hast not remembered the days of thy youth,
when thou wast naked and *bare* **nude**,
and wast *polluted* **trampled** in thy blood.
23 And it *came to pass* **became**,
after all thy *wickedness* **evil**,
(woe, woe unto thee!
saith the Lord GOD **an oracle of Adonay Yah Veh**;)
24 That thou hast also built unto thee
an *eminent place* **arch**,
and hast *made* **worked** thee *an high place* **a ramah**
in every *street* **broadway**.
25 Thou hast built thy *high place* **ramah**
at every head of the way,
and hast made thy beauty to be abhorred,
and hast *opened* **spread** thy feet
to every one that passed by,
and *multiplied* **abounded** thy whoredoms.
26 Thou hast also *committed fornication* **whored**
with the *Egyptians* **sons of Misrayim**
thy *neighbours* **fellow tabernaclers**, great of flesh;
and hast *increased* **abounded** thy whoredoms,
to *provoke* **vex** me *to anger*.
27 Behold,
therefore I have stretched out my hand over thee,
and have diminished thine *ordinary food* **statute**,
and *delivered* **gave** thee
unto the *will* **soul** of them that hate thee,
the daughters of the *Philistines* **Peleshethiym**,
which are ashamed of thy *lewd* way **of intrigue**.
28 Thou hast *played the whore* **whored** also
with the *Assyrians* **sons of Ashshur**,
because thou wast *unsatiable* **not satisfied**;
yea, thou hast *played the harlot* **whored** with them,
and yet couldest not be satisfied.
29 Thou hast *moreover*
multiplied **abounded** thy *fornication* **whoredom**
in the land of *Canaan* **Kenaan** unto *Chaldea* **Kesediym**;
and yet thou wast not satisfied herewith.
30 How weak is thine heart,
saith the Lord GOD **an oracle of Adonay Yah Veh**,
seeing thou *doest* **workest** all these *things*,
the work
of *an imperious* **a domineering** whorish woman;
31 In that thou buildest thine *eminent place* **arch**
in the head of every way,
and *makest thine high place* **workest thy ramah**
in every *street* **broadway**;
and hast not been as *an harlot* **a whore**,
in that thou *scornest hire* **ridiculest payoff**;
32 But as a *one* **woman**
that *commiteth adultery* **adulterizeth**,
which taketh strangers instead of her *husband* **man**!
33 They give *gifts* **payoffs** to all whores:
but thou givest thy *gifts* **payoffs** to all thy lovers,
and hirest them,
that they may come unto thee *on every side* **round about**
for thy whoredom.
34 And the contrary is in thee
from *other* women in thy whoredoms,
whereas none
followeth thee to commit whoredoms
whoreth after thee:
and in that thou givest a *reward* **payoff**,
and no *reward* **payoff** is given unto thee,
therefore thou art contrary.
35 Wherefore, O *harlot* **whore**,
hear the word of *the LORD* **Yah Veh**:
36 Thus saith *the Lord GOD* **Adonay Yah Veh**;
Because thy *filthiness* **copper** was poured out,
and thy nakedness *discovered* **exposed**
through thy whoredoms with thy lovers,
and with all the idols of thy *abominations* **abhorrences**,
and by the blood of thy *children* **sons**,
which thou didst give unto them;

37 Behold, therefore I *will* **shall** gather all thy lovers,
with whom thou hast *taken pleasure* **been pleased**,
and all *them* that thou hast loved,
with all *them* that thou hast hated;
I *will* **shall** even gather them round about against thee,
and *will discover* **shall expose** thy nakedness unto them,
that they may see all thy nakedness.
38 And I *will* **shall** judge thee,
as *women* **adulteresses**
that *break wedlock and shed* **pour** blood
are judged **have judgments**;
and I *will* **shall** give thee blood in fury and jealousy.
39 And I *will* **shall** also give thee into their hand,
and they shall throw down thine *eminent place* **arch**,
and shall *break* **pull** down thy *high places* **ramahs**:
they shall strip thee also of thy clothes,
and shall take thy *fair jewels* **instruments of adornment**,
and leave thee naked and *bare* **nude**.
40 They shall also
bring up **ascend** a *company* **congregation** against thee,
and they shall stone thee with stones,
and *thrust* **section** thee *through* with their swords.
41 And they shall burn thine houses with fire,
and *execute* **work** judgments upon thee
in the *sight* **eyes** of many women:
and I *will* **shall** cause thee
to *cease* **shabbathize** from *playing the harlot* **whoring**,
and thou also shalt give no *hire* **payoff** any more.
42 So *will I make* **shall I rest** my fury toward thee *to rest*,
and my jealousy shall *depart* **turn aside** from thee,
and I *will be quiet* **shall rest**,
and *will* **shall** be no more *angry* **vexed**.
43 Because
thou hast not remembered the days of thy youth,
but hast *fretted* me **quiver** in all these *things*;
behold,
therefore I also *will recompense* **shall give** thy way
upon thine head,
saith the Lord GOD **an oracle of Adonay Yah Veh**:
and thou shalt not *commit* **work** this *lewdness* **intrigue**
above all thine *abominations* **abhorrences**.
44 Behold, every one that *useth* **proverbializeth** proverbs
shall *use* **proverbialize** this proverb against thee,
saying, As is the mother, so is her daughter.
45 Thou art thy mother's daughter,
that lotheth her *husband* **man** and her *children* **sons**;
and thou art the sister of thy sisters,
which lothed their *husbands* **men** and their *children* **sons**:
your mother was an *Hittite* **Hethiy**,
and your father an *Amorite* **Emoriy**.
46 And thine *elder* **great** sister is *Samaria* **Shomeron**,
she and her daughters that *dwell* **settle** at thy left *hand*:
and thy younger sister,
that *dwelleth* **settleth** at thy right *hand*,
is *Sodom* **Sedom** and her daughters.
47 Yet hast thou not walked after their ways,
nor *done* **worked** after their *abominations* **abhorrences**:
but, *as if that were a very little thing* **lothed as belittled**,
thou wast *corrupted* **ruined** more than they
in all thy ways.
48 *As* I live,
saith the Lord GOD **an oracle of Adonay Yah Veh**,
Sodom **Sedom** thy sister hath not *done* **worked**,
she nor her daughters,
as thou hast *done* **worked**,
thou and thy daughters.
49 Behold, this was the *iniquity* **perversity**
of thy sister *Sodom* **Sedom**,
pride **pomp**, *fulness* **sufficiency** of bread,
and *abundance* **the serenity** of *idleness* **resting**
was in her and in her daughters,
neither did she strengthen the hand
of the *poor* **humble** and needy.
50 And they *were haughty* **lifted themselves**,
and *committed abomination* **worked abhorrence**
before me **at my face**:
therefore I took **turned** them *away* **aside** as I saw *good*.
51 Neither hath *Samaria* **Shomeron**
committed **sinned** half of thy sins;
but thou hast *multiplied* **abounded**
thine *abominations* **abhorrences** more than they,
and hast justified thy sisters
in all thine *abominations* **abhorrences**
which thou hast *done* **worked**.
52 Thou also, which hast judged thy sisters,
bear thine own shame for thy sins that thou hast
committed more *abominable* **abhorrent** than they:
they are more *righteous* **justified** than thou:
yea, be thou *confounded* **shamed** also,
and bear thy shame,
in that thou hast justified thy sisters.
53 When I shall *bring again* **return** their captivity,
the captivity of *Sodom* **Sedom**
and her daughters,
and the captivity of *Samaria* **Shomeron**
and her daughters,
then will I bring again **and** the captivity of thy captives
in the midst of them:
54 That thou mayest bear thine own shame,
and mayest be confounded
in all that thou hast *done* **worked**,
in that thou *art a comfort unto* **sighest over** them.
55 When thy sisters, *Sodom* **Sedom** and her daughters,
shall return to their former estate,
and *Samaria* **Shomeron** and her daughters
shall return to their former estate,
then thou and thy daughters
shall return to your former estate.
56 For thy sister *Sodom* **Sedom**
was not *mentioned* **reported** by thy mouth
in the day of thy *pride* **pomp**,
57 Before thy *wickedness* **evil** was *discovered* **exposed**,
as at the time of *thy* reproach
of the daughters of *Syria* **Aram**,
and all that are round about her,
the daughters of the *Philistines* **Peleshethiy**,
which despise thee round about.
58 Thou hast borne *thy lewdness* **thine intrigue**
and thine *abominations* **abhorrences**,
saith the LORD **an oracle of Yah Veh**.
59 For thus saith *the Lord GOD* **Adonay Yah Veh**;
I *will* **shall** even *deal* **work** with thee
as thou hast *done* **worked**,
which hast despised the oath in breaking the covenant.
60 *Nevertheless*
I *will* **shall** remember my covenant with thee
in the days of thy youth,
and I *will establish* **shall raise** unto thee
an *everlasting* **eternal** covenant.
61 Then thou shalt remember thy ways,
and *be ashamed* **shame**,
when thou shalt *receive* **take** thy sisters,
thine elder **thy greater** and thy younger:
and I *will* **shall** give them unto thee for daughters,
but not by thy covenant.
62 And I *will establish* **shall raise** my covenant with thee;
and thou shalt know that *I am the LORD* **I — Yah Veh**:
63 That thou mayest remember,
and *be confounded* **shame**,
and never open thy mouth any more
because **at the face** of thy shame,
when I am *pacified* **kapared/atoned** toward thee
for all that thou hast *done* **worked**,
saith the Lord GOD **an oracle of Adonay Yah Veh**.

TWO EAGLES AND A VINE

17 And the word of *the LORD* **Yah Veh**
came unto me, saying,
2 Son of *man* **humanity**, *put forth* **propound** a riddle,
and *speak* **proverbialize** a *parable* **proverb**
unto the house of *Israel* **Yisra El**;
3 And say, Thus saith *the Lord GOD* **Adonay Yah Veh**;
A great eagle with great wings,
longwinged **long pinioned**, full of *feathers* **plumage**,
which had divers colours **of embroidery**,
came unto Lebanon,
and took the *highest branch* **foliage** of the cedar:
4 He *cropped* **plucked** off
the top of his *young twigs* **sapplings**,
and carried it into a land of *traffick* **merchandise**;
he set it in *a city of merchants* **Kenaan**.

5 He took also of the seed of the land,
and *planted* **gave** it in a fruitful field;
he *placed* **took** it by great waters,
and set it as a willow tree.
6 And it *grew* **sprouted,**
and became a spreading vine of low *stature* **height,**
whose branches *turned toward* **faced** him,
and the roots *thereof* were under him:
so it became a vine, and *brought forth* **worked** branches,
and *shot forth sprigs* **extended foliage.**
7 There was also *another* **one** great eagle
with great wings and *many feathers* **much plumage:**
and, behold,
this vine *did bend* **bent** her roots toward him,
and *shot forth* **extended** her branches toward him,
that he might *water* **moisten** it
by the furrows of her plantation.
8 It was *planted* **transplanted**
in a good *soil* **field** by great waters,
that it might *bring forth* **work** branches,
and that it might bear fruit,
that it might be a *goodly* **mighty** vine.
9 Say thou, Thus saith *the Lord GOD* **Adonay Yah Veh;**
shall it prosper?
shall he not *pull up* **tear** the roots *thereof,*
and *cut* **lop** off the fruit *thereof,* that it wither?
it shall wither in all the *leaves* **prey** of her *spring* **sprout,**
even without great power or many people
to *pluck* **bear** it up by the roots *thereof.*
10 Yea, behold, being *planted* **transplanted,**
shall it prosper?
in withering, shall it not *utterly* wither,
when the east wind toucheth it?
it shall wither in the furrows *where it grew* **of the sprout.**
11 Moreover
the word of *the LORD* **Yah Veh** came unto me, saying,
12 Say *now* **I beseech,** to the rebellious house,
Know ye not what these *things mean* **be?**
tell *them,* Behold, the *king* **sovereign** of *Babylon* **Babel**
is come to *Jerusalem* **Yeru Shalem,**
and hath taken the *king* **sovereign** *thereof,*
and the *princes* **governors** *thereof,*
and led them with him to *Babylon* **Babel;**
13 And hath taken of the *king's* seed **of the kingdom,**
and *made* **cut** a covenant with him,
and hath taken an oath of him:
he hath also taken the mighty of the land:
14 That the *kingdom* might **sovereigndom** be *base* **lowly,**
that it might not lift itself *up,*
but that by *keeping* **guarding** of his covenant
it might stand.
15 But he rebelled against him
in sending his *ambassadors* **angels** into *Egypt* **Misrayim,**
that they might give him horses and much people.
shall he prosper?
shall he escape that *doeth* **worketh** such *things?*
or shall he break the covenant,
and be *delivered* **rescued?**
16 *As* I live,
saith the Lord GOD **an oracle of Adonay Yah Veh,**
surely in the place
where the king dwelleth **of the sovereign**
that *made* **caused** him *king* **to reign,**
whose oath he despised, and whose covenant he brake,
even with him in the midst of *Babylon* **Babel** he shall die.
17 Neither shall *Pharaoh* **Paroh**
with his *mighty army* **great valiant**
and great *company* **congregation**
make **work** for him in the war,
by *casting up* **pouring** mounts,
and building *forts* **battering towers,**
to cut off many *persons* **souls:**
18 Seeing he despised the oath by breaking the covenant,
when, *lo* **behold,** he had given his hand,
and hath *done* **worked** all these *things,*
he shall not escape.
19 Therefore thus saith *the Lord GOD* **Adonay Yah Veh;**
As I live, surely mine oath that he hath despised,
and my covenant that he hath broken,
even it *will I recompense* **shall I give** upon his own head.
20 And I *will* **shall** spread my net upon him,
and he shall be *taken* **apprehended** in my *snare* **lure,**
and I *will* **shall** bring him to *Babylon* **Babel,**
and *will* **shall** plead with him there
for his *trespass* **treason**
that he hath *trespassed* **treasoned** against me.
21 And all his fugitives with all his bands
shall fall by the sword,
and they that *remain* **survive**
shall be scattered toward all winds:
and ye shall know
that I *the LORD* **Yah Veh** have *spoken it* **worded.**
22 Thus saith *the Lord GOD* **Adonay Yah Veh;**
I *will* **shall** also take
of the *highest branch* **foliage** of the high cedar,
and *will set* **shall give** it;
I *will crop off* **shall pluck**
from the top of his *young twigs* **sprouts** a tender one,
and *will plant* **shall transplant** it
upon an high mountain and *eminent* **lofty:**
23 In the mountain of the height of *Israel* **Yisra El**
will I plant **shall I transplant** it:
and it shall *bring forth boughs* **bear branches,**
and *bear* **worketh** fruit, and be a *goodly* **mighty** cedar:
and under it
shall *dwell* **tabernacle** all *fowl* **bird** of every wing;
in the shadow of the branches *thereof*
shall they *dwell* **tabernacle.**
24 And all the trees of the field shall know
that I *the LORD* **Yah Veh**
have *brought down* **lowered** the high tree,
have *exalted* **heightened** the low tree,
have *dried up* **withered** the *green* **fresh** tree,
and have *made* **blossomed** the dry tree *to flourish:*
I *the LORD* **Yah Veh**
have *spoken* **worded** and have *done* **worked** it.

THE SINNING SOUL DIES

18 The word of *the LORD* **Yah Veh** came unto me again,
saying,
2 What mean ye, that ye *use* **proverbialize** this proverb
concerning the *land* **soil** of *Israel* **Yisra El,** saying,
The fathers have eaten sour grapes,
and the *children's* **sons'** teeth are *set on edge* **dull?**
3 *As* I live,
saith the Lord GOD **an oracle of Adonay Yah Veh,**
ye **it** shall not *have occasion* **become you** any more
to *use* **proverbialize** this proverb in *Israel* **Yisra El.**
4 Behold, all souls are mine;
as the soul of the father,
so also the soul of the son is mine:
the soul that sinneth, it shall die.

THE JUST MAN LIVES

5 But if a man be just,
and *do that which is lawful* **work judgment**
and *right* **justness,**
6 And hath not eaten upon the mountains,
neither hath lifted up his eyes
to the idols of the house of *Israel* **Yisra El,**
neither hath *defiled* **fouled**
his *neighbour's wife* **friend's woman,**
neither hath *come near* **approached**
to a menstruous **an excluded** woman,
7 And hath not oppressed *any* **man,**
but hath restored to the debtor his pledge,
in stripping, hath *spoiled none by violence* **not stripped,**
hath given his bread to the *hungry* **famished,**
and hath covered the naked with *a garment* **clothes;**
8 He that hath not given forth upon usury,
neither hath taken any *increase* **bounty,**
that hath *withdrawn* **turned** his hand
from *iniquity* **wickedness,**
hath *executed true* **worked** judgment **in truth**
between man and man,
9 Hath walked in my statutes,
and hath *kept* **guarded** my judgments,
to *deal truly* **work in truth;**
he is just, **in living,** he shall *surely* live,
saith the Lord GOD **an oracle of Adonay Yah Veh.**

THE TYRANT SON OF A JUST MAN DIES

10 If he beget a son that is a *robber* **tyrant**,
a *shedder* **pourer** of blood,
and that *doeth the like to any one of these things*
worketh these to one of his brothers besides,
11 And that *doeth* **worketh** not any of those *duties*,
but even hath eaten upon the mountains,
and *defiled* **fouled** his *neighbour's wife* **friend's woman**,
12 Hath oppressed the *poor* **humble** and needy,
in stripping, hath *spoiled by violence* **stripped**,
hath not restored the pledge,
and hath lifted up his eyes to the idols,
hath *committed abomination* **worked abhorrence**,
13 Hath given forth upon usury,
and hath taken *increase* **bounty**:
shall he then live? he shall not live:
he hath *done* **worked**
all these *abominations* **abhorrences**;
in dying, he shall *surely* die;
his blood shall be upon him.

THE JUST SON OF THE UNJUST FATHER LIVES

14 *Now, lo* **behold**, if he beget a son,
that seeth all his father's sins
which he hath *done* **worked**,
and *considereth* **seeth**, and *doeth* **worketh** not such like,
15 That hath not eaten upon the mountains,
neither hath lifted up his eyes
to the idols of the house of *Israel* **Yisra El**,
hath not *defiled* **fouled**
his *neighbour's wife* **friend's woman**,
16 Neither hath oppressed *any* **man**,
hath not withholden the pledge,
neither hath spoiled by violence
in stripping, hath not stripped,
but hath given his bread to the *hungry* **famished**,
and hath covered the naked with *a garment* **clothes**,
17 *That* hath *taken off* **turned** his hand
from the *poor* **humble**,
that hath not *received* **taken** usury nor *increase* **bounty**,
hath *executed* **worked** my judgments,
hath walked in my statutes;
he shall not die for the *iniquity* **perversity** of his father,
in living, he shall *surely* live.

THE UNJUST FATHER OF THE JUST SON DIES

18 *As* for his father,
because **in oppressing**, he *cruelly* oppressed,
spoiled **in stripping, stripped** his brother *by violence*,
and *did* **worked** that which is not good
among his people,
lo **behold**, even he shall die in his *iniquity* **perversity**.
19 Yet say ye, Why?
doth not the son bear the *iniquity* **perversity** of the father?
When the son hath *done* **worked**
that which is lawful **judgment** and *right* **justness**,
and hath *kept* **guarded** all my statutes,
and hath *done* **worked** them,
in living, he shall *surely* live.
20 The soul that sinneth, it shall die.
The son shall not bear
the *iniquity* **perversity** of the father,
neither shall the father bear
the *iniquity* **perversity** of the son:
the *righteousness* **justness** of the *righteous* **just**
shall be upon him,
and the wickedness of the wicked shall be upon him.

THE WICKED WHO TURNS TO JUSTNESS LIVES

21 But if the wicked *will* **shall** turn from all his sins
that he hath *committed* **worked**,
and *keep* **guard** all my statutes,
and *do that which is lawful* **work judgment**
and *right* **justness**,
in living, he shall *surely* live, he shall not die.
22 All his *transgressions* **rebellions**
that he hath *committed* **worked**,
they shall not be *mentioned* **remembered** unto him:
in his *righteousness* **justness** that he hath *done* **worked**
he shall live.
23 Have I any *pleasure* **desire** at all
that the wicked should die?
saith the Lord GOD **an oracle of Adonay Yah Veh**:
and not that he should return from his ways, and live?
24 But when the *righteous* **just**
turneth away from his *righteousness* **justness**,
and *committeth iniquity* **worketh wickedness**,
and *doeth* **worketh**
according to all the *abominations* **abhorrences**
that the wicked *man doeth* **worketh**,
shall he live?
All his *righteousness* **justness** that he hath *done* **worked**
shall not be *mentioned* **remembered**:
in his *trespass* **treason** that he hath *trespassed* **treasoned**,
and in his sin that he hath sinned, in them shall he die.

THE GAGE OF JUSTNESS

25 Yet ye say,
The way of *the Lord is not equal* **Adonay gaugeth not**.
Hear *now* **I beseech**, O house of *Israel* **Yisra El**;
Is not my way *equal* **gauged**?
are not your ways *unequal* **ungauged**?
26 When *a righteous man* **the just**
turneth away from his *righteousness* **justness**,
and *committeth iniquity* **worketh wickedness**,
and dieth in them;
for his *iniquity* **wickedness** that he hath *done* **worked**
shall he die.
27 Again, when the wicked *man* turneth away
from his wickedness that he hath *committed* **worked**,
and *doeth that which is lawful* **worketh judgment**
and *right* **justness**,
he shall save his soul alive **his soul shall live**.
28 Because he *considereth* **seeth**,
and turneth away from all his *transgressions* **rebellions**
that he hath *committed* **worked**,
in living, he shall *surely* live, he shall not die.
29 Yet saith the house of *Israel* **Yisra El**,
The way of *the Lord* **Adonay** is not *equal* **gauged**.
O house of *Israel* **Yisra El**,
are not my ways *equal* **gauged**?
are not your ways *unequal* **not gauged**?
30 Therefore I *will* **shall** judge you,
O house of *Israel* **Yisra El**,
every *one* **man** according to his ways,
saith the Lord GOD **an oracle of Adonay Yah Veh**.
Repent, and turn *yourselves*
from all your *transgressions* **rebellions**;
so *iniquity* **perversity**
shall not be your *ruin* **stumblingblock**.
31 Cast away from you all your *transgressions* **rebellions**,
whereby ye have *transgressed* **rebelled**;
and *make* **work** you a new heart and a new spirit:
for why *will* **shall** ye die, O house of *Israel* **Yisra El**?
32 For I have no *pleasure* **delight**
in the death of him that dieth,
saith the Lord GOD **an oracle of Adonay Yah Veh**:
wherefore turn *yourselves*, and live ye.

LAMENTATION

19 Moreover *take* **lift** thou *up* a lamentation
for the *princes* **hierarchs** of *Israel* **Yisra El**,
2 And say, What is thy mother? A **roaring** lioness:
she *lay down* **crouched** among lions,
she *nourished* **greatened** her whelps
among *young lions* **whelps**.
3 And she *brought up* **ascended** one of her whelps:
it became a *young lion* **whelp**,
and it learned to *catch the* prey;
it devoured *men* **humanity**.
4 The *nations* **goyim** also heard of him;
he was *taken* **apprehended** in their pit **of ruin**,
and they brought him with *chains* **hooks**
unto the land of *Egypt* **Misrayim**.
5 *Now* when she saw that she had waited,
and her hope was lost,
then she took *another* **one** of her whelps,
and *made* **set** him a *young lion* **whelp**.
6 And he went up and down among the lions,
he became a *young lion* **whelp**,
and learned to *catch the* prey,
and devoured *men* **humanity**.
7 And he knew their *desolate palaces* **abandonments**,
and he *laid waste* **parched** their cities;
and the land was desolate, and the fulness thereof,

by the *noise* **voice** of his roaring.
8 Then the *nations set* **goyim gave** against him
on every side **round about**
from the *provinces* **jurisdictions,**
and spread their net over him:
he was *taken* **apprehended** in their pit **of ruin.**
9 And they *put* **gave** him in *ward* **a cage** in *chains* **hooks,**
and brought him to the *king* **sovereign** of *Babylon* **Babel:**
they brought him into *holds* **huntholds,**
that his voice should no more be heard
upon the mountains of *Israel* **Yisra El.**
10 Thy mother is like a vine in thy blood,
planted **transplanted** by the waters:
she *was fruitful* **bore fruit** and *full of branches* **branched**
by reason of many waters.
11 And she had *strong* rods **of strength**
for the *sceptres* **scions** of them that *bare rule* **reigned,**
and her *stature* **height** was *exalted* **heightened**
among the *thick branches* **foliage,**
and she *appeared* **was seen** in her height
with the *multitude* **abundance** of her branches.
12 But she was *plucked up* **uprooted** in fury,
she was cast down to the *ground* **earth,**
and the east wind *dried up* **withered** her fruit:
her *strong* rods **of strength** were broken **off** and withered;
the fire consumed them.
13 And now she is *planted* **transplanted** in the wilderness,
in a *dry* **parched** and thirsty *ground* **earth.**
14 And fire is gone out of a rod of her branches,
which hath devoured her fruit,
so that she hath no *strong* rod **of strength**
to be a *sceptre* **scion** to *rule* **reign.**
This is a lamentation, and shall be for a lamentation.

THE ABHORRENCES OF YISRA EL

20 And it *came to pass* **became,** in the seventh year,
in the fifth *month,* the tenth *day* of the month,
that *certain* **men** of the elders of *Israel* **Yisra El**
came to enquire of *the LORD* **Yah Veh,**
and sat *before me* **at my face.**
2 Then came the word of *the LORD* **Yah Veh** unto me,
saying,
3 Son of *man* **humanity,**
speak **word** unto the elders of *Israel* **Yisra El,**
and say unto them,
Thus saith *the Lord GOD* **Adonay Yah Veh;**
Are ye come to enquire of me?
As I live,
saith the Lord GOD **an oracle of Adonay Yah Veh,**
I *will* **shall** not be enquired of by you.
4 *Wilt* **Shalt** thou judge them, son of *man* **humanity,**
wilt **shalt** thou judge them?
cause them to know
the *abominations* **abhorrences** of their fathers:
5 And say unto them,
Thus saith *the Lord GOD* **Adonay Yah Veh;**
In the day when I chose *Israel* **Yisra El,**
and lifted up mine hand
unto the seed of the house of *Jacob* **Yaaqov,**
and made myself known unto them
in the land of *Egypt* **Misrayim,**
when I lifted up mine hand unto them, saying,
I am the LORD **I — Yah Veh** your *God* **Elohim;**
6 In the day that I lifted up mine hand unto them,
to bring them forth of the land of *Egypt* **Misrayim**
into a land that I had *espied* **explored** for them,
flowing with milk and honey,
which is the *glory* **splendour** of all lands:
7 Then said I unto them,
Cast ye away every man the abominations of his eyes,
and *defile* **foul** not yourselves
with the idols of *Egypt* **Misrayim:**
I am the LORD **I — Yah Veh** your *God* **Elohim.**
8 But they rebelled against me,
and *would* **willed to** not hearken unto me:
they did not every man
cast away the abominations of their eyes,
neither did they forsake the idols of *Egypt* **Misrayim:**
then I said, I *will* **shall** pour out my fury upon them,
to *accomplish* **finish off** my *anger* **wrath** against them
in the midst of the land of *Egypt* **Misrayim.**
9 But I *wrought* **worked** for my name's sake,
that it should not be *polluted* **profaned**
before **in the eyes of** the *heathen* **goyim,**
among whom they were,
in whose *sight* **eyes** I made myself known unto them,
in bringing them forth out of the land of *Egypt* **Misrayim.**
10 Wherefore I caused them to go forth
out of the land of *Egypt* **Misrayim,**
and brought them into the wilderness.
11 And I gave them my statutes,
and *shewed* **caused** them **to know** my judgments,
which if a *man do* **human work,**
he shall even live in them.
12 Moreover also I gave them my *sabbaths* **shabbaths,**
to be a sign between me and them,
that they might know that *I am the LORD* **I — Yah Veh**
that *sanctify* **hallow** them.
13 But the house of *Israel* **Yisra El**
rebelled against me in the wilderness:
they walked not in my statutes,
and they *despised* **spurned** my judgments,
which if a *man do* **human work,**
he shall even live in them;
and my *sabbaths* **shabbaths**
they *greatly polluted* **mightily profaned:**
then I said,
I *would* **should** pour out my fury upon them
in the wilderness, to consume them.
14 But I *wrought* **worked** for my name's sake,
that it should not be *polluted* **profaned**
before **in the eyes of** the *heathen* **goyim,**
in whose *sight* **eyes** I brought them out.
15 Yet also
I lifted up my hand unto them in the wilderness,
that I *would* **should** not bring them into the land
which I had given them,
flowing with milk and honey,
which is the glory of all lands;
16 Because they *despised* **spurned** my judgments,
and walked not in my statutes,
but *polluted* **profaned** my *shabbaths* **shabbaths:**
for their heart went after their idols.
17 Nevertheless
mine eye spared them from *destroying* **ruining** them,
neither did I *make an end* **work a final finish**
of them in the wilderness.
18 But I said unto their *children* **sons** in the wilderness,
Walk ye not in the statutes of your fathers,
neither *observe* **guard** their judgments,
nor *defile* **foul** yourselves with their idols:
19 *I am the LORD* **I — Yah Veh** your *God* **Elohim;**
walk in my statutes,
and *keep* **guard** my judgments, and *do* **work** them;
20 And hallow my *sabbaths* **shabbaths;**
and they shall be a sign between me and **between** you,
that ye may know
that *I am the LORD* **I — Yah Veh** your *God* **Elohim.**
21 Notwithstanding the *children* **sons** rebelled against me:
they walked not in my statutes,
neither *kept* **guarded** my judgments to *do* **work** them,
which if a *man do* **human work,**
he shall even live in them;
they *polluted* **profaned** my *sabbaths* **shabbaths:**
then I said, I *would* **shall** pour out my fury upon them,
to accomplish my *anger* **wrath** against them
in the wilderness.
22 *Nevertheless I withdrew* **I turned back** mine hand,
and *wrought* **worked** for my name's sake,
that it should not be *polluted* **profaned**
in the *sight* **eyes** of the *heathen* **goyim,**
in whose *sight* **eyes** I brought them forth.
23 I lifted up mine hand unto them also in the wilderness,
that I *would* **should** scatter them
among the *heathen* **goyim,**
and *disperse* **winnow** them through the *countries* **lands;**
24 Because they had not *executed* **worked** my judgments,
but had despised my statutes,
and had *polluted* **profaned** my *sabbaths* **shabbaths,**
and their eyes were after their fathers' idols.
25 Wherefore I gave them also

statutes that were not good,
and judgments whereby they should not live;
26 And I *polluted* **fouled** them in their own *gifts* **offerings**,
in that they caused to pass through *the fire*
all that *openeth* **bursteth** the womb,
that I might *make them* desolate **them**,
to the end that
they might know that *I am the LORD* **I — Yah Veh**.
27 Therefore, son of *man* **humanity**,
speak **word** unto the house of *Israel* **Yisra El**,
and say unto them,
Thus saith *the Lord GOD* **Adonay Yah Veh**;
Yet in this your fathers have blasphemed me,
in that they have
committed **treasoned** a *trespass* **treason** against me.
28 For when I had brought them into the land,
for the which I lifted up mine hand to give it to them,
then they saw every high hill, and all the thick trees,
and they *offered* **sacrificed** there their sacrifices,
and there they *presented* **gave**
the *provocation* **vexation** of their *offering* **qorban**:
there also they *made* **set** their *sweet savour* **scent of rest**,
and *poured out* **libated** there
their *drink offerings* **libations**.
29 Then I said unto them,
What is the *high place* **bamah** whereunto ye go?
And the name *thereof* is called Bamah unto this day.

THE IDOLATRY OF THE HOUSE OF YISRA EL

30 Wherefore say unto the house of *Israel* **Yisra El**,
Thus saith *the Lord GOD* **Adonay Yah Veh**;
Are ye *polluted* **fouled**
after the *manner* **way** of your fathers?
and *commit ye whoredom* **whore ye**
after their abominations?
31 For when ye *offer* **bear** your *gifts* **offerings**,
when ye *make* **cause** your sons to pass through the fire,
ye *pollute* **foul** yourselves with all your idols,
even unto this day:
and shall I be enquired of by you,
O house of *Israel* **Yisra El**?
As I live,
saith the Lord GOD **an oracle of Adonay Yah Veh**,
I *will* **shall** not be enquired of by you.
32 And that
which *cometh* **ascendeth** into your *mind* **spirit**
shall not be at all,
that ye say, We *will* **shall** be as the *heathen* **goyim**,
as the families of the *countries* **lands**,
to *serve wood* **minister timber** and stone.

THE JUDGMENT AND RESTORATION OF YISRA EL

33 *As* I live,
saith the Lord GOD **an oracle of Adonay Yah Veh**,
surely with a *mighty* **strong** hand,
and with a stretched out arm,
and with fury poured out,
will I rule **shall I reign** over you:
34 And I *will* **shall** bring you out from the people,
and *will* **shall** gather you out of the *countries* **lands**
wherein ye are scattered,
with a *mighty* **strong** hand, and with a stretched out arm,
and with fury poured out.
35 And I *will* **shall** bring you
into the wilderness of the people,
and there *will* **shall** I plead with you face to face.
36 Like as I pleaded with your fathers
in the wilderness of the land of *Egypt* **Misrayim**,
so *will* **shall** I plead with you,
saith the Lord GOD **an oracle of Adonay Yah Veh**.
37 And I *will* **shall** cause you to pass under the *rod* **scion**,
and I *will* **shall** bring you into the bond of the covenant:
38 And I *will* **shall** purge out from among you the rebels,
and them that *transgress* **rebel** against me:
I *will* **shall** bring them forth
out of the *country* **land** where they sojourn,
and they shall not enter
into the *land* **soil** of *Israel* **Yisra El**:
and ye shall know that *I am the LORD* **I — Yah Veh**.
39 As for you, O house of *Israel* **Yisra El**,
thus saith *the Lord GOD* **Adonay Yah Veh**;
Go ye, serve ye every *one* **man** his idols,
and *hereafter also* **afterward**,
if ye *will* **shall** not hearken unto me:
but *pollute* **profane** ye my holy name no more
with your *gifts* **offerings**, and with your idols.
40 For in mine holy mountain,
in the mountain of the height of *Israel* **Yisra El**,
saith the Lord GOD **an oracle of Adonay Yah Veh**,
there shall all the house of *Israel* **Yisra El**,
all of them in the land, serve me:
there *will I accept* **shall I be pleased with** them,
and there *will* **shall** I require your *offerings* **exaltments**,
and the *firstfruits* **firstlings**
of your *oblations* **loads/burdens**,
with all your *holy things* **holies**.
41 I *will accept you* **shall be pleased**
with your *sweet savour* **scent of rest**,
when I bring you out from the people,
and gather you out of the *countries* **lands**
wherein ye have been scattered;
and I *will* **shall** be *sanctified* **hallowed** in you
before **in the eyes of** the *heathen* **goyim**.
42 And ye shall know that *I am the LORD* **I — Yah Veh**,
when I shall bring you into the *land* **soil** of *Israel* **Yisra El**,
into the *country* **land** for the which I lifted up mine hand
to give it to your fathers.
43 And there shall ye remember your ways,
and all your *doings* **exploits**,
wherein ye have been *defiled* **fouled**;
and ye shall lothe yourselves in your own *sight* **face**
for all your evils that ye have *committed* **worked**.
44 And ye shall know that *I am the LORD* **I — Yah Veh**,
when I have *wrought* **worked** with you
for my name's sake,
not according to your *wicked* **evil** ways,
nor according to your corrupt *doings* **exploits**,
O ye house of *Israel* **Yisra El**,
saith the Lord GOD **an oracle of Adonay Yah Veh**.

THE WORD OF YAH VEH CONCERNING THE SOUTH

45 Moreover
the word of *the LORD* **Yah Veh** came unto me, saying,
46 Son of *man* **humanity**,
set thy face *toward the south* **in the southerly way**,
and drop *thy word toward the south* **southward**,
and prophesy against the forest of the south field;
47 And say to the forest of the south,
Hear the word of *the LORD* **Yah Veh**;
Thus saith *the Lord GOD* **Adonay Yah Veh**;
Behold, I *will* **shall** kindle a fire in thee,
and it shall devour every *green* **fresh** tree in thee,
and every dry tree:
the flaming flame shall not be quenched,
and all faces from the south to the north
shall be *burned* **inflamed** *therein*.
48 And all flesh shall see
that I *the LORD* **Yah Veh** have *kindled* **burnt** it:
it shall not be quenched.
49 Then said I, *Ah Lord GOD* **Aha Adonay Yah Veh**!
they say of me,
Doth he not *speak parables* **proverbialize proverbs**?

YAH VEH'S WORD CONCERNING YISRA EL

21 And the word of *the LORD* **Yah Veh** came unto me,
saying,
2 Son of *man* **humanity**,
set thy face toward *Jerusalem* **Yeru Shalem**,
and drop *thy word* toward the *holy places* **holies**,
and prophesy against the *land* **soil** of *Israel* **Yisra El**,
3 And say to the *land* **soil** of *Israel* **Yisra El**,
Thus saith *the LORD* **Yah Veh**; Behold, I am against thee,
and *will* **shall** draw forth my sword out of his sheath,
and *will* **shall** cut off from thee
the *righteous* **just** and the wicked.
4 *Seeing then that I will* **Because I shall**
cut off from thee the *righteous* **just** and the wicked,
therefore shall my sword go forth out of his sheath
against all flesh from the south to the north:
5 That all flesh may know that I *the LORD* **Yah Veh**
have drawn forth my sword out of his sheath:
it shall not return any more.
6 Sigh therefore, thou son of *man* **humanity**,
with the breaking of thy loins;

and with bitterness sigh before their eyes.
7 And it shall be, when they say unto thee,
Wherefore sighest thou?
that thou shalt *answer* **say**, For the *tidings* **report**;
because it cometh:
and every heart shall melt,
and all hands shall *be feeble* **slacken**,
and every spirit shall *faint* **dim**,
and all knees shall be *weak* as water:
behold, it cometh, and shall be *brought to pass,*
saith the Lord GOD **an oracle of Adonay Yah Veh.**

YAH VEH'S WORD CONCERNING THE SWORD

8 Again the word of *the LORD* **Yah Veh** came unto me,
saying,
9 Son of *man* **humanity**, prophesy, and say,
Thus saith *the LORD* **Yah Veh**;
Say, A sword,
a sword is sharpened, and *also furbished* **polished**:
10 It is sharpened to *make a sore* **slaughter a** slaughter;
it is *furbished* **polished** *that it may glitter* **as lightning**:
should we then *make mirth* **rejoice**?
it *contemneth* **spurneth** the *rod* **scion** of my son,
as every tree.
11 And he hath given it to be *furbished* **polished**,
that it may be *handled* **manipulated by the palm**:
this sword is sharpened, and it is *furbished* **polished**,
to give it into the hand of the *slayer* **slaughterer**.
12 Cry and howl, son of *man* **humanity**:
for it shall be upon my people,
it shall be upon all the *princes* **hierarchs** of *Israel* **Yisra El**:
terrors by reason of **precipitation as to** the sword
shall be upon my people:
smite **slap** therefore upon thy *thigh* **flank**.
13 Because it is *a trial* **to proof**,
and what if *the sword contemn* **it spurneth**
even the *rod* **scion**?
it shall be no more,
saith the Lord GOD **an oracle of Adonay Yah Veh.**
14 Thou therefore, son of *man* **humanity**, prophesy,
and smite *thine hands* **thy palms** together,
and let the sword be doubled the third *time*,
the sword of the *slain* **pierced**:
it is the sword of the great *men* that are *slain* **pierced**,
which entereth into their privy **in their** chambers.
15 I have *set* **given** the *point* **brandish** of the sword
against all their *gates* **portals**,
that their heart may *faint* **melt**,
and their *ruins be multiplied* **stumblingblocks abound**:
ah **Ach**! it is made *bright* **lightning**,
it is wrapped up for the slaughter.
16 *Go thee one way or other,*
either **Unite** on the right *hand, or* **set** on the left,
whithersoever thy face *is set* **congregateth**.
17 I *will* **shall** also smite mine *hands* **palms** together,
and I *will* **shall** cause my fury to rest:
I *the LORD* **Yah Veh** have *said it* **worded**.
18 The word of *the LORD* **Yah Veh** came unto me again,
saying,
19 Also, thou son of *man* **humanity**,
appoint **set** thee two ways,
that the sword of the *king* **sovereign** of *Babylon* **Babel**
may come:
both *twain* **two** shall come forth out of one land:
and choose thou a *place* **hand**,
choose **cut** it at the head of the way to the city.
20 *Appoint* **Set** a way,
that the sword may come
to *Rabbath* **Rabbah** of the *Ammonites* **sons of Ammon**,
and to *Judah* **Yah Hudah** in *Jerusalem* **Yeru Shalem**
the *defenced* **fortified**.
21 For the *king* **sovereign** of *Babylon* **Babel**
stood at the *parting* **mother** of the way,
at the head of the two ways, to *use* **divine** divination:
he *made* **sharpened** his arrows *bright*,
he *consulted with images* **asked of teraphim**,
he *looked* **saw** in the liver.
22 At his right *hand*
was the divination for *Jerusalem* **Yeru Shalem**,
to *appoint captains* **set rams**,
to open the mouth in the *slaughter* **murder**,
to lift up the voice with shouting,
to *appoint battering* **set** rams against the *gates* **portals**,
to *cast* **pour** a mount, and to build a *fort* **battering tower**.
23 And it shall be unto them
as a *false* **vain** divination in their *sight* **eyes**,
to them that have *sworn* **oathed** oaths:
but he *will call to remembrance* **shall remember**
the *iniquity* **perversity**,
that they may be *taken* **apprehended**.
24 Therefore thus saith *the Lord GOD* **Adonay Yah Veh**;
Because ye have
made **memorialized** your *iniquity* **perversity**
to be remembered,
in that your *transgressions* **rebellions**
are *discovered* **exposed**,
so that in all your *doings* **exploits**
your sins *do appear* **be seen**;
because, *I say,*
that ye *are come to remembrance* **have memorialized**,
ye shall be *taken* **apprehended** with the *hand* **palm**.
25 And thou,
profane wicked *prince* **hierarch** of *Israel* **Yisra El**,
whose day is come,
when *iniquity* **the time of perversity**
have an end **shall be ended**,
26 Thus saith *the Lord GOD* **Adonay Yah Veh**;
Remove **Turn aside** the *diadem* **tiara**,
and *take* **lift** off the crown: this shall not be the same:
exalt **lift** him that is low, and abase him that is high.
27 *I will overturn* **Perverted**, *overturn* **perverted**,
overturn, **perverted!**
I set it: and it shall be no more,
until he come whose *right* **judgment** it is;
and I *will* **shall** give it *him*.
28 And thou, son of *man* **humanity**, prophesy and say,
Thus saith *the Lord GOD* **Adonay Yah Veh**
concerning the *Ammonites* **sons of Ammon**,
and concerning their reproach;
even say thou, The sword, the sword is *drawn* **loosed**:
for the slaughter it is *furbished* **polished**,
to consume because of the *glittering* **lightning**:
29 Whiles they see vanity unto thee,
whiles they divine a lie unto thee,
to *bring* **give** thee upon the necks
of them that are *slain* **pierced**,
of the wicked, whose day is come,
when **the time of** their *iniquity* **perversity**
shall *have an* end.
30 Shall I cause it to return into his sheath?
I *will* **shall** judge thee
in the place where thou wast created,
in the land of thy *nativity* **origin**.
31 And I *will* **shall** pour out mine *indignation* **rage**
upon thee,
I *will blow* **shall puff** against thee in the fire of my wrath,
and *deliver* **give** thee into the hand
of *brutish men* **men of burning**,
and *skilful* **engravers** to *destroy* **ruin**.
32 Thou shalt be for fuel to the fire;
thy blood shall be in the midst of the land;
thou shalt be no more remembered:
for I *the LORD* **Yah Veh** have *spoken it* **worded**.

YAH VEH'S WORD CONCERNING THE ABHORRENCES OF YISRA EL

22 Moreover
the word of *the LORD* **Yah Veh** came unto me, saying,
2 *Now,* thou son of *man* **humanity**,
wilt **shalt** thou judge,
wilt **shalt** thou judge the bloody city?
yea, thou shalt *shew* **make known to** her
all her *abominations* **abhorrences**.
3 *Then* say thou,
Thus saith *the Lord GOD* **Adonay Yah Veh**,
The city *sheddeth* **poureth** blood in the midst of it,
that her time may come,
and *maketh* **worketh** idols against herself
to *defile* **foul** herself.
4 Thou *art become guilty* **hast guilted**
in thy blood that thou hast *shed* **poured**;
and hast *defiled* **fouled** thyself

in thine idols which thou hast *made* **worked**;
and thou hast caused thy days to *draw near* **approach**,
and art come *even* unto thy years:
therefore have I *made* **given** thee
a reproach unto the *heathen* **goyim**,
and a *mocking* **ridicule** to all *countries* **lands**.
5 Those that be near, and those that be far from thee,
shall *mock* **ridicule** thee,
which art infamous **O polluted of name**
and much *vexed* **confused**.
6 Behold, the *princes* **hierarchs** of *Israel* **Yisra El**,
every *one* **man** were in thee
to their power to *shed* **pour** blood.
7 In thee have they *set light by* **abased** father and mother:
in the midst of thee
have they *dealt* **worked** by oppression
with the *stranger* **sojourner**:
in thee
have they vexed the *fatherless* **orphan** and the widow.
8 Thou hast despised mine *holy things* **holies**,
and hast profaned my *sabbaths* **shabbaths**.
9 In thee are men,
that carry tales **talebearers** to *shed* **pour** blood:
and in thee
they eat upon the mountains:
in the midst of thee
they *commit lewdness* **work intrigue**.
10 In thee
have they *discovered* **exposed** their fathers' nakedness:
in thee
have they *humbled* **debased** her
that was *set apart* **excluded** for *pollution* **foulness**.
11 And *one* **every man**
hath *committed abomination* **worked abhorrence**
with his *neighbour's wife* **friend's woman**;
and *another* **every man**
hath *lewdly defiled* **intriguingly fouled**
his daughter in law;
and *another* **every man** in thee
hath *humbled* **debased** his sister, his father's daughter.
12 In thee
have they taken *gifts* **bribes** to *shed* **pour** blood;
thou hast taken usury and *increase* **bounty**,
and thou hast greedily gained of thy *neighbours* **friends**
by extortion,
and hast forgotten me,
saith the Lord GOD **an oracle of Adonay Yah Veh**.
13 Behold, therefore I have smitten *mine hand* **my palm**
at thy *dishonest* **greedy** gain
which thou hast *made* **worked**,
and at thy blood which hath been in the midst of thee.
14 Can thine heart *endure* **stand**,
or can thine hands be strong,
in the days that I shall *deal* **work** with thee?
I *the LORD* **Yah Veh** have *spoken it* **worded**,
and *will do it* **shall work**.
15 And I *will scatter* **shall winnow** thee
among the *heathen* **goyim**,
and disperse thee in the *countries* **lands**,
and *will* **shall** consume thy *filthiness* **foulness** out of thee.
16 And thou shalt
take thine inheritance in **profane** thyself
in the *sight* **eyes** of the *heathen* **goyim**,
and thou shalt know that *I am the LORD* **I — Yah Veh**.
17 And the word of *the LORD* **Yah Veh** came unto me,
saying,
18 Son of *man* **humanity**,
the house of *Israel* **Yisra El** is to me become dross:
all they are *brass* **copper**, and tin, and iron, and lead,
in the midst of the furnace;
they are *even the dross* **drosses** of silver.
19 Therefore thus saith *the Lord GOD* **Adonay Yah Veh**;
Because ye are all become dross,
behold, therefore I *will* **shall** gather you
into the midst of *Jerusalem* **Yeru Shalem**.
20 *As* they gather silver, and *brass* **copper**,
and iron, and lead, and tin,
into the midst of the furnace,
to *blow* **puff** the fire upon it, to melt it;
so *will* **shall** I gather you
in *mine anger* **my wrath** and in my fury,
and I *will* **shall** leave you *there*, and melt you.
21 Yea, I *will* **shall** gather you,
and *blow* **puff** upon you in the fire of my wrath,
and ye shall be melted in the midst *thereof*.
22 As silver is melted in the midst of the furnace,
so shall ye be melted in the midst *thereof*;
and ye shall know that I *the LORD* **Yah Veh**
have poured out my fury upon you.
23 And the word of *the LORD* **Yah Veh** came unto me,
saying,
24 Son of *man* **humanity**, say unto her,
Thou art the land that is not *cleansed* **purified**,
nor rained upon in the day of *indignation* **rage**.
25 There is a conspiracy of her prophets
in the midst *thereof*,
like a roaring lion *ravening* **tearing** the prey;
they have devoured souls;
they have taken
the *treasure* **wealth** and *precious things* **esteemed**;
they have *made* **abounded** her *many* widows
in the midst *thereof*.
26 Her priests have violated my *law* **torah**,
and have profaned mine *holy things* **holies**:
they have *put no difference* **not separated**
between the holy and profane,
neither have they *shewed difference* **made known**
between the *unclean* **foul** and the *clean* **pure**,
and have *hid* **concealed** their eyes
from my *sabbaths* **shabbaths**,
and I am profaned among them.
27 Her *princes* **governors** in the midst *thereof*
are like wolves *ravening* **tearing** the prey,
to *shed* **pour** blood, *and* to destroy souls,
to *get dishonest* **greedily gain greedy** gain.
28 And her prophets
have daubed them with *untempered morter* **slime**,
seeing **seers of** vanity, and divining lies unto them,
saying, Thus saith *the Lord GOD* **Adonay Yah Veh**,
when *the LORD* **Yah Veh** hath not *spoken* **worded**.
29 The people of the land
have used oppression **in oppressing, have oppressed**,
and *exercised robbery* **in stripping, have stripped**,
and have vexed the *poor* **humble** and needy:
yea, they have oppressed the *stranger* **sojourner**
wrongfully **without judgment**.
30 And I sought for a man among them,
that should *make* **wall** up the *hedge* **wall**,
and stand in the *gap* **breach**
before me **at my face** for the land,
that I should not *destroy* **ruin** it: but I found none.
31 Therefore
have I poured out mine *indignation* **rage** upon them;
I have *consumed* **finished** them **off**
with the fire of my wrath:
their own way
have I *recompensed* **given** upon their heads,
saith the Lord GOD **an oracle of Adonay Yah Veh**.

WHORING IN MISRAYIM

23 The word of *the LORD* **Yah Veh** came again unto me,
saying,
2 Son of *man* **humanity**,
there were two women, the daughters of one mother:
3 And they *committed whoredoms* **whored**
in *Egypt* **Misrayim**;
they *committed whoredoms* **whored** in their youth:
there were their breasts *pressed* **pierced**,
and there they *bruised* **worked** the *teats* **nipples**
of their virginity.
4 And the names of them were
Aholah **Oholah** the *elder* **greater**,
and *Aholibah* **Oholi Bah** her sister:
and they were mine, and they bare sons and daughters.
Thus were their names;
Samaria is Aholah **Shomeron is Oholah**,
and *Jerusalem Aholibah* **Yeru Shalem Oholi Bah**.
5 And *Aholah* **Oholah**
played the harlot when she was mine **whored under me**;
and she *doted on* **panted after** her lovers,
on the *Assyrians* **Ashshuri** her neighbours,

6 Which were *clothed* **enrobed** with blue,
captains **governors** and *rulers* **prefects**,
all of them *desirable young men* **youths of desire**,
horsemen **cavalry** riding upon horses.
7 Thus she *committed* **gave** her whoredoms with them,
with all them
that were the chosen *men* **sons** of *Assyria* **Ashshur**,
and with all on whom she *doted* **panted after**:
with all their idols she *defiled* **fouled** herself.
8 Neither *left* **forsook** she her whoredoms
brought from *Egypt* **Misrayim**:
for in her youth they lay with her,
and they *bruised* **worked** the *breasts* **nipples**
of her virginity,
and poured their whoredom upon her.
9 Wherefore
I have *delivered* **given** her into the hand of her lovers,
into the hand of the *Assyrians* **sons of Ashshur**,
upon whom she *doted* **panted after**.
10 These *discovered* **exposed** her nakedness:
they took her sons and her daughters,
and *slew* **slaughtered** her with the sword:
and she became *famous* **a name** among women;
for they had *executed* **worked** judgment upon her.
11 And when her sister *Aholibah* **Oholi Bah** saw this,
she was more *corrupt* **ruined**
in her *inordinate love* **panting** than she,
and in her whoredoms
more than her sister in her whoredoms.
12 She *doted upon* **panted after**
the *Assyrians* **sons of Ashshur**
her neighbours, *captains* **governors** and *rulers* **prefects**
clothed **enrobed** most *gorgeously* **splendidly**,
horsemen **cavalry** riding upon horses,
all of them *desirable young men* **youths of desire**.
13 Then I saw that she was *defiled* **fouled**,
that they *took* **be** both one way,
14 And that she increased her whoredoms:
for when she saw
men *pourtrayed* **engraved** upon the wall,
the images of the *Chaldeans* **Kesediym**
pourtrayed **engraved** with vermilion,
15 *Girded* **Girdled** with girdles upon their loins,
exceeding in dyed attire upon their heads,
all of them *princes to look to* **tertiaries in visage**,
after the *manner* **likeness**
of the *Babylonians* **sons of Babel** of *Chaldea* **Kesediym**,
the land of their *nativity* **kindred**:
16 And *as soon as she saw them* **at the sight**
with **of** her eyes,
she *doted upon* **panted after** them,
and sent *messengers* **angels** unto them
into *Chaldea* **Kesediym**.
17 And the *Babylonians* **sons of Babel** came to her
into the bed of love,
and they *defiled* **fouled** her with their whoredom,
and she was *polluted* **fouled** with them,
and her *mind* **soul** was alienated from them.
18 So she *discovered* **exposed** her whoredoms,
and *discovered* **exposed** her nakedness:
then my *mind* **soul** was alienated from her,
like as my *mind* **soul** was alienated from her sister.
19 Yet she *multiplied* **abounded** her whoredoms,
in *calling to remembrance* **remembering**
the days of her youth,
wherein she had *played the harlot* **whored**
in the land of *Egypt* **Misrayim**.
20 For she *doted upon* **panted after**
their *paramours* **concubines**,
whose flesh is as the flesh of *asses* **burros**,
and whose *issue* **flux** is like the *issue* **flux** of horses.
21 Thus thou *calledst to remembrance* **visitest**
the *lewdness* **intrigue** of thy youth,
in *bruising* **working** thy *teats* **nipples**
by the *Egyptians* **Misrayim**
for the *paps* **breasts** of thy youth.
22 Therefore, O *Aholibah* **Oholi Bah**,
thus saith *the Lord GOD* **Adonay Yah Veh**; Behold,
I *will raise up* **shall waken** thy lovers against thee,
from whom thy *mind* **soul** is alienated,
and I *will* **shall** bring them against thee
on every side **round about**;
23 The *Babylonians* **sons of Babel**,
and all the *Chaldeans* **Kesediym**,
Pekod, and Shoa, and Koa,
and all the *Assyrians* **sons of Ashshur** with them:
all of them *desirable young men* **youths of desire**,
captains **governors** and *rulers* **prefects**,
great *lords* **tertiaries** and *renowned* **called out**,
all of them riding upon horses.
24 And they shall come against thee
with *chariots* **weapons**, *wagons* **chariots**, and wheels,
and with *an assembly* **a congregation** of people,
which shall set against thee
buckler **shield** and *shield* **buckler** and helmet
round about:
and I *will set* **shall give** judgment
before them **at their face**,
and they shall judge thee according to their judgments.
25 And I *will set* **shall give** my jealousy against thee,
and they shall *deal furiously* **work** with thee **in fury**:
they shall *take away* **turn aside**
thy *nose* **nostrils** and thine ears;
and thy *remnant* **posterity** shall fall by the sword:
they shall take thy sons and thy daughters;
and thy *residue* **posterity** shall be devoured by the fire.
26 They shall also strip thee out of thy clothes,
and take away thy *fair jewels* **instruments of adornment**.
27 Thus *will* **shall** I make thy *lewdness* **intrigue**
to *cease* **shabbathize** from thee,
and thy whoredom *brought*
from the land of *Egypt* **Misrayim**:
so that thou shalt not lift up thine eyes unto them,
nor remember *Egypt* **Misrayim** any more.
28 For thus saith *the Lord GOD* **Adonay Yah Veh**;
Behold, I *will deliver* **shall give** thee
into the hand *of* them whom thou hatest,
into the hand of them
from whom thy *mind* **soul** is alienated:
29 And they shall *deal* **work** with thee *hatefully* **in hatred**,
and shall take away all thy labour,
and shall *leave* **forsake** thee naked and bare:
and the nakedness of thy whoredoms
shall be *discovered* **exposed**,
both thy *lewdness* **intrigue** and thy whoredoms.
30 I *will do* **shall work** these *things* unto thee,
because thou hast *gone a whoring* **whored**
after the *heathen* **goyim**,
and because thou art *polluted* **fouled**
with their idols.
31 Thou hast walked in the way of thy sister;
therefore *will* **shall** I give her cup into thine hand.
32 Thus saith *the Lord GOD* **Adonay Yah Veh**;
Thou shalt drink of thy sister's cup deep and large:
thou shalt be *laughed to scorn* **ridiculed**
and *had in derision* **derided**;
it containeth *much* **an increase**.
33 Thou shalt be filled
with *drunkenness* **intoxication** and *sorrow* **grief**,
with the cup of *astonishment* **desolation** and desolation,
with the cup of thy sister *Samaria* **Shomeron**.
34 Thou shalt even drink it and suck it out,
and thou shalt *break* **craunch** the *sherds* **potsherds**
thereof,
and *pluck off* **tear** thine own breasts:
for I have *spoken it* **worded**,
saith the Lord GOD **an oracle of Adonay Yah Veh**.
35 Therefore thus saith *the Lord GOD* **Adonay Yah Veh**;
Because thou hast forgotten me,
and cast me behind thy back,
therefore bear thou also
thy *lewdness* **intrigue** and thy whoredoms.
36 *The LORD* **Yah Veh** said *moreover* unto me;
Son of *man* **humanity**,
wilt **shalt** thou judge
Aholah **Oholah** and *Aholibah* **Oholi Bah**?
yea,
declare **tell** unto them their *abominations* **abhorrences**;
37 That they have *committed adultery* **adulterized**,
and blood is in their hands,

and with their idols
have they *committed adultery* **adulterized**,
and have also caused their sons,
whom they bare unto me,
to pass for them through *the fire, to devour them* **for fuel**.
38 Moreover this they have *done* **worked** unto me:
they have *defiled* **fouled** my *sanctuary* **holies**
in the same day,
and have profaned my *sabbaths* **shabbaths**.
39 For when they had
slain **slaughtered** their *children* **sons** to their idols,
then they came the same day
into my *sanctuary* **holies** to profane it;
and, *lo* **behold**,
thus have they *done* **worked** in the midst of mine house.
40 And *furthermore* **also**,
that ye have sent for men to come from far,
unto whom *a messenger* **an angel** was sent;
and, *lo* **behold**, they came:
for whom thou *didst wash* **baptizedst** thyself,
paintedst thy eyes,
and *deckedst* **adornedst** thyself with ornaments,
41 And satest upon a stately bed,
and a table *prepared before it* **lined up at its face**,
whereupon thou hast set mine incense and mine oil.
42 And a voice of a **serene** multitude *being at ease*
was with her:
and with the men
of the *common sort* **abundance of humanity**
were brought *Sabeans* **Sabaiym/carousers**
from the wilderness,
which *put bracelets* **gave clasps** upon their hands,
and *beautiful* crowns **of adornment** upon their heads.
43 Then said I unto *her* **the one**
that was *old* **worn out** in adulteries,
Will **Shall** they now *commit whoredoms* **whore** with her,
and she with them?
44 Yet they went in unto her,
as they go in unto a woman
that *playeth the harlot* **whoreth**:
so went they in
unto *Aholah* **Oholah** and unto *Aholibah* **Oholi Bah**,
the *lewd* **intriguing** women.
45 And the *righteous* **just** men,
they shall judge them
after the *manner* **judgment** of adulteresses,
and after the *manner* **judgment**
of women that *shed* **pour** blood;
because they are adulteresses,
and blood is in their hands.
46 For thus saith *the Lord GOD* **Adonay Yah Veh**;
I *will bring up* **shall ascend** a *company* **congregation**
upon them,
and *will* **shall** give them to be removed
and *spoiled* **for plunder**.
47 And the *company* **congregation**
shall stone them with stones,
and *dispatch* **cut** them with their swords;
they shall *slay* **slaughter** their sons and their daughters,
and burn up their houses with fire.
48 Thus *will* **shall** I cause *lewdness* **intrigue**
to *cease* **shabbathize** out of the land,
that all women may be taught
not to *do* **work** after your *lewdness* **intrigue**.
49 And they shall
recompense **give** your *lewdness* **intrigue** upon you,
and ye shall bear the sins of your idols:
and ye shall know
that *I am the Lord GOD* **I — Adonay Yah Veh**.

THE CALDRON

24 Again in the ninth year,
in the tenth month, in the tenth *day* of the month,
the word of *the LORD* **Yah Veh** came unto me, saying,
2 Son of *man* **humanity**,
write **inscribe** thee the name of the day,
even of this same day:
the *king* **sovereign** of *Babylon* **Babel** *set* **propped** himself
against *Jerusalem* **Yeru Shalem** this same day.
3 And *utter* **proverbialize** a *parable* **proverb**
unto the rebellious house, and say unto them,
Thus saith *the Lord GOD* **Adonay Yah Veh**;
Set on a *pot* **caldron**, set it on,
and also pour water into it:
4 Gather the *pieces* **members** *thereof* into it,
even every good *piece* **member**,
the *thigh* **flank**, and the shoulder;
fill it with the choice bones.
5 Take the choice of the flock,
and *burn* **whirl** also the bones under it,
and *make it* **in boiling**, boil **it** well,
and let them seethe the bones *of it therein* **in its midst**.
6 Wherefore thus saith *the Lord GOD* **Adonay Yah Veh**;
Woe to the bloody city,
to the *pot* **caldron** whose scum is therein,
and whose scum is not gone out of it!
bring it out *piece* **member** by *piece* **member**;
let no *lot* **pebble** fall upon it.
7 For her blood is in the midst of her;
she set it upon the *top* **clearing** of a rock;
she poured it not upon the *ground* **earth**,
to cover it with dust;
8 That it might cause fury to *come up* **ascend**
to *take vengeance* **avenge avengement**;
I have *set* **given** her blood
upon the *top* **clearing** of a rock,
that it should not be covered.
9 Therefore thus saith *the Lord GOD* **Adonay Yah Veh**;
Woe to the bloody city!
I *will* **shall** even *make* **greaten** the pile for fire *great*.
10 *Heap on wood* **Abound the timber**,
kindle **inflame** the fire,
consume the flesh, and **in spicing,** spice it *well*,
and let the bones be *burned* **scorched**.
11 Then *set* **stand** it empty upon the coals *thereof*,
that the *brass* **copper** of it may be hot,
and may *burn* **scorch**,
and that the *filthiness* **foulness** of it
may be molten in *it* **its midst**,
that the scum of it may be consumed.
12 She hath wearied herself with *lies* **mischiefs**,
and her great scum went not forth out of her:
her scum shall be in the fire.
13 In thy *filthiness* **foulness** is *lewdness* **intrigue**:
because I have *purged* **purified** thee,
and thou wast not *purged* **purified**,
thou shalt not be *purged* **purified**
from thy *filthiness* **foulness** any more,
till I have caused my fury to rest upon thee.
14 I *the LORD* **Yah Veh** have *spoken it* **worded**:
it shall *come to pass* **become**, and I *will do* **shall work** it;
I *will* **shall** not *go back* **release**, neither *will* **shall** I spare,
neither *will* **shall** I *repent* **sigh**;
according to thy ways,
and according to thy *doings* **exploits**,
shall they judge thee,
saith the Lord GOD **an oracle of Adonay Yah Veh**.

THE DEATH OF YECHEZQ EL'S WOMAN

15 Also the word of *the LORD* **Yah Veh** came unto me,
saying,
16 Son of *man* **humanity**, behold,
I take away from thee the desire of thine eyes
with a *stroke* **plague**:
yet neither shalt thou *mourn* **chop** nor weep,
neither shall thy tears run *down*.
17 *Forbear to cry* **Hush thy shrieking**,
make **work** no mourning for the dead,
bind *the tire of thine head* **thy tiara** upon thee,
and *put on* **set** thy shoes upon thy feet,
and cover not thy *lips* **upper lip**,
and eat not the bread of men.
18 So I *spake* **worded** unto the people in the morning:
and at even my *wife* **woman** died;
and I *did* **worked** in the morning
as I was *commanded* **misvahed**.
19 And the people said unto me,
Wilt **Shalt** thou not tell us what these *things* are to us,
that thou *doest* **workest** *so*?
20 Then I *answered* **said to** them,
The word of *the LORD* **Yah Veh** came unto me, saying,
21 Speak unto the house of *Israel* **Yisra El**,

Thus saith *the Lord GOD* **Adonay Yah Veh**;
Behold, I *will* **shall** profane my *sanctuary* **holies**,
the *excellency* **pomp** of your strength,
the desire of your eyes,
and that which your soul *pitieth* **sympathizeth**;
and your sons and your daughters
whom ye have *left* **forsaken** shall fall by the sword.
22 And ye shall *do* **work** as I have *done* **worked**:
ye shall not cover your *lips* **upper lip**,
nor eat the bread of men.
23 And your *tires* **tiaras** shall be upon your heads,
and your shoes upon your feet:
ye shall not *mourn* **chop** nor weep;
but ye shall *pine away* **vanish**
for your *iniquities* **perversities**,
and *mourn one* **growl man** toward *another* **brother**.
24 Thus *Ezekiel* **Yechezq El** is unto you *a sign* **an omen**:
according to all that he hath *done* **worked,**
shall ye *do* **work**:
and when this cometh,
ye shall know that *I am the Lord GOD* **I — Adonay Yah Veh**.
25 Also, thou son of *man* **humanity**,
shall it not be in the day when I take from them
their *strength* **stronghold**,
the joy of their *glory* **adornment**, the desire of their eyes,
and *that whereupon they set*
the burden of their *minds* **souls**,
their sons and their daughters,
26 That *he that escapeth* **the escapees** in that day
shall come unto thee,
to cause thee to hear it with *thine* ears?
27 In that day shall thy mouth be opened
to *him which is escaped* **the escapees**,
and thou shalt *speak* **word**,
and be no more *dumb* **muted**:
and thou shalt be *a sign* **an omen** unto them;
and they shall know that *I am the LORD* **I — Yah Veh**.

YAH VEH'S WORD CONCERNING THE SONS OF AMMON

25 The word of *the LORD* **Yah Veh**
came again unto me, saying,
2 Son of *man* **humanity**,
set thy face against the *Ammonites* **sons of Ammon**,
and prophesy against them;
3 And say unto the *Ammonites* **sons of Ammon**,
Hear the word of *the Lord GOD* **Adonay Yah Veh**;
Thus saith *the Lord GOD* **Adonay Yah Veh**;
Because *thou saidst* **of thy saying**, Aha,
against my *sanctuary* **holies**,
when it was profaned;
and against the *land* **soil** of *Israel* **Yisra El**,
when it was *desolate* **desolated**;
and against the house of *Judah* **Yah Hudah**,
when they went into *captivity* **exile**;
4 Behold, therefore I *will deliver* **shall give** thee
to the *men* **sons** of the east for a possession,
and they shall set their *palaces* **walls** in thee,
and *make* **give** their *dwellings* **tabernacles** in thee:
they shall eat thy fruit, and they shall drink thy milk.
5 And I *will make* **shall give** Rabbah
a *stable* **habitation of rest** for camels,
and the *Ammonites* **sons of Ammon**
a *couching* **resting** place for flocks:
and ye shall know that *I am the LORD* **I — Yah Veh**.
6 For thus saith *the Lord GOD* **Adonay Yah Veh**;
Because thou hast clapped *thine hands* **the hand**,
and stamped with the *feet* **foot**,
and *rejoiced* **cheered** in *heart* **soul**
with all thy despite against the *land* **soil** of *Israel* **Yisra El**;
7 Behold,
therefore I *will* **shall** stretch out mine hand upon thee,
and *will deliver* **shall give** thee for *a spoil* **plunder**
to the *heathen* **goyim**;
and I *will* **shall** cut thee off from the people,
and I *will* **shall** cause thee
to *perish* **destruct** out of the countries:
I *will destroy* **shall desolate** thee;
and thou shalt know that *I am the LORD* **I — Yah Veh**.

YAH VEH'S WORD CONCERNING MOAB AND SEIR

8 Thus saith *the Lord GOD* **Adonay Yah Veh**;
Because *that* **of the saying of** Moab and Seir *do say*,
Behold,
the house of Judah **Yah Hudah**
is like unto all the *heathen* **goyim**;
9 Therefore, behold,
I *will* **shall** open the *side* **shoulder** of Moab
from the cities,
from his cities which are on his *frontiers* **edges**,
the *glory* **splendour** of the country,
Bethjeshimoth **Beth Ha Yeshimoth**,
Baalmeon **Baal Meon**, and *Kiriathaim* **Qiryathaim**,
10 Unto the *men* **sons** of the east
with the *Ammonites* **sons of Ammon**,
and *will* **shall** give them in possession,
that the *Ammonites* **sons of Ammon**
may not be remembered among the *nations* **goyim**.
11 And I *will execute* **shall work** judgments upon Moab;
and they shall know that *I am the LORD* **I — Yah Veh**.

YAH VEH'S WORD CONCERNING EDOM

12 Thus saith *the Lord GOD* **Adonay Yah Veh**;
Because that Edom hath *dealt* **worked**
against the house of *Judah* **Yah Hudah**
by *taking vengeance* **avenging avengement**,
and **in guilting,** hath *greatly offended* **guilted**,
and *revenged* **avenged** himself upon them;
13 Therefore thus saith *the Lord GOD* **Adonay Yah Veh**;
I *will* **shall** also stretch out mine hand upon Edom,
and *will* **shall** cut off
man **humanity** and *beast* **animal** from it;
and I *will make* **shall give** it *desolate* **parched**
from Teman;
and they of Dedan shall fall by the sword.
14 And I *will lay* **shall give** my *vengeance* **avengement**
upon Edom
by the hand of my people *Israel* **Yisra El**:
and they shall *do* **work** in Edom
according to *mine anger* **my wrath**
and according to my fury;
and they shall know my *vengeance* **avengement**,
saith the Lord GOD **an oracle of Adonay Yah Veh**.

YAH VEH'S WORD CONCERNING THE PELESHETHIYM

15 Thus saith *the Lord GOD* **Adonay Yah Veh**;
Because the *Philistines* **Peleshethiym**
have *dealt* **worked** by *revenge* **avengement**,
and have *taken vengeance* **avenged**
with a despiteful *heart* **soul**,
to *destroy* **ruin** it for the *old hatred* **eternal enmity**;
16 Therefore thus saith *the Lord GOD* **Adonay Yah Veh**;
Behold, I *will stretch out* **shall extend** mine hand
upon the *Philistines* **Peleshethiym**,
and I *will* **shall** cut off the *Cherethims* **Kerethiym**,
and destroy the *remnant* **survivors** of the sea *coast* **haven**.
17 And I *will execute* **shall work**
great vengeance **avengements**
upon them with *furious rebukes* **reproofs of fury**;
and they shall know that *I am the LORD* **I — Yah Veh**,
when I shall *lay my vengeance* **give my avengement**
upon them.

YAH VEH'S WORD CONCERNING SOR

26 And it *came to pass* **became,**
in the eleventh year, in the first *day* of the month,
that the word of *the LORD* **Yah Veh** came unto me,
saying,
2 Son of *man* **humanity**,
because that *Tyrus* **Sor**
hath said against *Jerusalem* **Yeru Shalem**, Aha,
she is broken
that was the gates — **the doors** of the people:
she is turned unto me:
I shall be *replenished* **fulfilled**,
now she is *laid waste* **parched**:
3 Therefore thus saith *the Lord GOD* **Adonay Yah Veh**;
Behold, I am against thee, O *Tyrus* **Sor**,
and *will* **shall** cause many *nations* **goyim**
to *come up* **ascend** against thee,
as the sea causeth his waves to *come up* **ascend**.
4 And they shall *destroy* **ruin** the walls of *Tyrus* **Sor**,
and break down her towers:
I *will* **shall** also scrape **off** her dust from her,
and *make* **give** her like the *top* **clearing** of a rock.
5 It shall be *a place* for the spreading of nets

in the midst of the sea:
for I have *spoken it* **worded**,
saith the Lord GOD **an oracle of Adonay Yah Veh**:
and it shall become a *spoil* **plunder** to the *nations* **goyim**.
6 And her daughters which are in the field
shall be *slain* **slaughtered** by the sword;
and they shall know that *I am the LORD* **I — Yah Veh**.
7 For thus saith *the Lord GOD* **Adonay Yah Veh**;
Behold, I *will* **shall** bring upon *Tyrus* **Sor**
Nebuchadrezzar **Nebukadnets Tsar**
king **sovereign** of *Babylon* **Babel**,
a *king* **sovereign** of *kings* **sovereigns**, from the north,
with horses, and with chariots,
and with *horsemen* **cavalry**,
and *companies* **congregations**, and much people.
8 He shall *slay* **slaughter** with the sword
thy daughters in the field:
and he shall *make* **give** a *fort* **battering tower**
against thee,
and *cast* **pour** a mount against thee,
and *lift up* **raise** the *buckler* **shield** against thee.
9 And he shall *set engines of war* **give battering rams**
against thy walls,
and with his *axes* **sword**
he shall *break* **pull** down thy towers.
10 By *reason of the abundance* **the throngs** of his horses
their dust shall cover thee:
thy walls shall *shake* **quake**
at the *noise* **voice** of the *horsemen* **cavalry**,
and of the wheels, and of the chariots,
when he shall enter into thy *gates* **portals**,
as *men enter* **entering** into a **split** city
wherein is made a breach.
11 With the hoofs of his horses
shall he *tread down* **trample** all thy *streets* **outways**:
he shall *slay* **slaughter** thy people by the sword,
and thy *strong garrisons* **monoliths of strength**
shall *go down* **lower** to the *ground* **earth**.
12 And they shall
make a spoil of **plunder** thy *riches* **valuables**,
and *make a prey of* **plunder** thy merchandise:
and they shall break down thy walls,
and *destroy* **pull down** thy pleasant houses:
and they shall *lay* **set** thy stones and thy timber
and thy dust in the midst of the water.
13 And I *will* **shall** cause the *noise* **roar** of thy songs
to *cease* **shabbathize**;
and the *sound* **voice** of thy harps shall be no more heard.
14 And I *will make* **shall give** thee
like the *top* **clearing** of a rock:
thou shalt be a place to spread nets upon;
thou shalt be built no more:
for I *the LORD* **Yah Veh** have *spoken it* **worded**,
saith the Lord GOD **an oracle of Adonay Yah Veh**.
15 Thus saith *the Lord GOD* **Adonay Yah Veh**
to *Tyrus* **Sor**;
shall not the *isles shake* **islands quake**
at the *sound* **voice** of thy *fall* **ruin**,
when the *wounded cry* **pierced shriek**,
when the slaughter is *made* **slaughtered**
in the midst of thee?
16 Then all the *princes* **hierarchs** of the sea
shall *come down* **descend** from their thrones,
and *lay away* **turn aside** their *robes* **mantles**,
and *put off* **strip**
their *broidered garments* **clothes of embroidery**:
they shall *clothe* **enrobe** themselves with trembling;
they shall sit upon the *ground* **earth**,
and shall tremble *at every moment* **in a blink**,
and be astonished at thee.
17 And they shall *take up* **lift** a lamentation for thee,
and say to thee, How art thou destroyed,
that wast *inhabited* **settled** of *seafaring men* **the seas**,
the renowned city, which wast strong in the sea,
she and her *inhabitants* **settlers**,
which *cause* **give** their terror
to be on all that *haunt* **settle** it!
18 Now shall the *isles* **islands** tremble
in the day of thy *fall* **ruin**;
yea, the *isles* **islands** that are in the sea
shall *be troubled* **terrify** at thy departure.
19 For thus saith *the Lord GOD* **Adonay Yah Veh**;
When I shall *make* **give** thee a *desolate* **parched** city,
like the cities that are not *inhabited* **settled**;
when I shall *bring up* **ascend** the *deep* **abyss** upon thee,
and great waters shall cover thee;
20 When I shall bring thee down
with them that descend into the *pit* **well**,
with the **original** people *of old time*,
and shall *set* **settle** thee
in the *low parts* **nethermost** of the earth,
in *places desolate of old* **the original parched areas**,
with them that *go down* **descend** to the *pit* **well**,
that thou be not *inhabited* **settled**;
and I shall *set glory* **give splendour**
in the land of the living;
21 I *will make* **shall give** thee *a terror* **terrors**,
and thou shalt be no more:
though thou be sought for,
yet shalt thou *never* **not eternally** be found again,
saith the Lord GOD **an oracle of Adonay Yah Veh**.

YAH VEH'S WORD CONCERNING THE LAMENTATION OF SOR

27 The word of *the LORD* **Yah Veh**
came again unto me, saying,
2 *Now*, thou son of *man* **humanity**,
take up **lift** a lamentation for *Tyrus* **Sor**;
3 And say unto *Tyrus* **Sor**,
O thou that *art situate* **settlest** at the entry of the sea,
which art a merchant of the people
for many *isles* **islands**,
Thus saith *the Lord GOD* **Adonay Yah Veh**;
O *Tyrus* **Sor**, thou hast said, I am of perfect beauty.
4 Thy borders are in the *midst* **heart** of the seas,
thy builders have perfected thy beauty.
5 They have made all thy *ship boards* **tables**
of fir trees of Senir:
they have taken cedars from Lebanon
to *make* **work** masts for thee.
6 Of the oaks of Bashan
have they *made* **worked** thine oars;
the *company* **daughters** of the *Ashurites* **Ashshuriym**
have *made* **worked** thy *benches* **boards** of ivory,
brought out of the *isles* **islands** of *Chittim* **Kittim**.
7 *Fine* **White** linen with *broidered work* **embroidery**
from *Egypt* **Misrayim**
was *that which thou spreadest forth* **thy spreadings**
to be thy sail;
blue and purple from the *isles* **islands** of *Elishah* **Eli Shah**
was that which covered thee.
8 The *inhabitants* **settlers** of *Zidon* **Sidon** and Arvad
were thy *mariners* **paddlers**:
thy wise *men*, O *Tyrus* **Sor**, that were in thee,
were thy *pilots* **sailers**.
9 The *ancients* **elders** of Gebal and the wise *men thereof*
were in thee thy *calkers* **breach holders**:
all the ships of the sea with their mariners were in thee
to *occupy* **pledge** thy merchandise.
10 They of Persia and of Lud and of *Phut* **Put**
were in thine *army* **valiant**, thy men of war:
they hanged the *shield* **buckler** and helmet in thee;
they *set* **gave** forth thy *comeliness* **majesty**.
11 The *men* **sons** of Arvad with thine *army* **valiant**
were upon thy walls round about,
and the *Gammadims* **warriors** were in thy towers:
they hanged their shields upon thy walls round about;
they have *made* **perfected** thy beauty *perfect*.
12 Tarshish was thy merchant
by reason **because** of the *multitude* **abundance**
of *all kind of riches* **wealth**;
with silver, iron, tin, and lead,
they *traded* **gave** in thy *fairs* **markets**.
13 *Javan* **Yavan**, Tubal, and Meshech,
they were thy merchants:
they *traded the persons* **gave the souls** of *men* **humanity**
and *vessels* **instruments** of *brass* **copper**
in **of** thy *market* **merchandise**.
Apocalypse 18:12, 13
14 They of the house of Togarmah
traded **gave** in thy *fairs* **markets**

with horses and *horsemen* **cavalry** and mules.
15 The *men* **sons** of Dedan were thy merchants;
many *isles* **islands** were the merchandise of thine hand:
they *brought thee for a present* **restored for their hire**
horns of ivory and *ebony* **ebonies**.
16 *Syria* **Aram** was thy merchant
by reason **because** of the *multitude* **abundance**
of *the wares of thy making* **thy works**:
they *occupied* **gave** in thy *fairs* **markets** with emeralds,
purple, and *broidered work* **embroidery**,
and *fine* **bleached** linen, and coral, and *agate* **rubies**.
17 *Judah* **Yah Hudah**, and the land of *Israel* **Yisra El**,
they were thy merchants:
they *traded* **gave** in thy *market* **merchandise**
wheat of Minnith, and Pannag,
and honey, and oil, and balm.
18 *Damascus* **Dammeseq** was thy merchant
in the *multitude* **abundance** of the wares of thy making,
for the *multitude* **abundance** of all *riches* **wealth**;
in the wine of Helbon, and white wool.
19 *Dan also* **Vedan** and *Javan* **Yavan**
going to and fro **gadding about**,
occupied **gave** in thy *fairs* **markets**:
bright iron, cassia, and *calamus* **stalks**,
were in thy *market* **merchandise**.
20 Dedan was thy merchant
in *precious* clothes **of liberation** for chariots.
21 Arabia, and all the *princes* **hierarchs** of *Kedar* **Qedar**,
they *occupied with thee* **merchandised**
in lambs, and rams, and **he** goats:
in these were *they thy* **the** merchants **of thy hand**.
22 The merchants of Sheba and Raamah,
they were thy merchants:
they *occupied* **gave** in thy *fairs* **markets**
with *chief of* all **head** spices,
and with all *precious* **esteemed** stones, and gold.
23 Haran, and *Canneh* **Kanneh**, and Eden,
the merchants of Sheba,
Asshur **Ashshur**, and *Chilmad* **Kilmad**,
were thy merchants.
24 These were thy merchants
in all sorts of things **of splendour**,
in blue *clothes* **robes**, and *broidered work* **embroidery**,
and in chests of rich *apparel* **damasks**,
bound with cords, and *made* of cedar,
among thy merchandise.
25 The ships of Tarshish
did sing of thee **strolled** in thy *market* **merchandise**:
and thou wast *replenished* **fulfilled**,
and *made very glorious* **mightily honoured**
in the *midst* **heart** of the seas.
26 Thy *rowers* **paddlers**
have brought thee into great waters:
the east wind
hath broken thee in the *midst* **heart** of the seas.
27 Thy *riches* **wealth**, and thy *fairs* **markets**,
thy merchandise,
thy mariners, and thy *pilots* **sailers**,
thy *calkers* **breach holders**,
and the *occupiers* **pledgers** of thy merchandise,
and all thy men of war, that are in thee,
and in all thy *company* **congregation**
which is in the *midst* **heart** of thee,
shall fall into the midst of the seas in the day of thy ruin.
28 The suburbs shall *shake* **quake**
at the *sound* **voice** of the cry of thy *pilots* **sailers**.
29 And all that *handle* **manipulate** the oar,
the mariners, and all the *pilots* **sailers** of the sea,
shall *come down* **descend** from their ships,
they shall stand upon the land;
30 And shall cause their voice to be heard against thee,
and shall cry bitterly,
and shall *cast up* **ascend** dust upon their heads,
they shall wallow themselves in the ashes:
31 And **in balding,** they shall
make themselves utterly bald **balden themselves** for thee,
and gird them with *sackcloth* **saq**,
and they shall weep for thee with bitterness of *heart* **soul**
and bitter *wailing* **chopping**.
32 And in their *wailing* **lamentation**
they shall *take up* **lift** a lamentation for thee,
and lament over thee, *saying*,
What *city* is like *Tyrus* **Sor**,
like the *destroyed* **severed** in the midst of the sea?
33 When thy *wares* **markets** went forth out of the seas,
thou *filledst* **satisfied** many people;
thou didst enrich the *kings* **sovereigns** of the earth
with the *multitude* **abundance** of thy *riches* **wealth**
and of thy merchandise.
34 In the time when thou shalt be broken by the seas
in the depths of the waters
thy merchandise and all thy *company* **congregation**
in the midst of thee shall fall.
35 All the *inhabitants* **settlers** of the *isles* **islands**
shall be astonished at thee,
and their *kings* **sovereigns**
shall *be sore afraid* **shudder with horror**,
they shall be *troubled* **irritated** in their *countenance* **face**.
36 The merchants among the people shall hiss at thee;
thou shalt be *a terror* **terrors**,
and *never shalt be any more* **shall not be eternally**.

YAH VEH'S WORD CONCERNING THE EMINENT OF SOR

28 The word of *the LORD* **Yah Veh**
came again unto me, saying,
2 Son of *man* **humanity**,
say unto the *prince* **eminent** of *Tyrus* **Sor**,
Thus saith *the Lord GOD* **Adonay Yah Veh**;
Because thine heart is *lifted up* **haughty**,
and thou hast said, I am *a God* **El**,
I sit in the seat of *God* **Elohim**,
in the *midst* **heart** of the seas;
yet thou art *a man* **human**, and not *God* **El**,
though thou *set* **give** thine heart
as the heart of *God* **Elohim**:
3 Behold, thou art wiser than *Daniel* **Dani El**;
there is *no secret* **nought shut up**
that they can *hide* **shade** from thee:
4 With thy wisdom
and with *thine understanding* **thy discernment**
thou hast *gotten* **worked** thee *riches* **valuables**,
and hast *gotten* **worked** gold and silver into thy treasures:
5 By *thy great* **the greatness of thy** wisdom
and by thy *traffick* **merchandise**
hast thou *increased* **abounded** thy *riches* **valuables**,
and thine heart is lifted *up*
because of thy *riches* **valuables**:
6 Therefore thus saith *the Lord GOD* **Adonay Yah Veh**;
Because thou hast *set* **given** thine heart
as the heart of *God* **Elohim**;
7 Behold, therefore I *will* **shall** bring strangers upon thee,
the *terrible* **tyrant** of the *nations* **goyim**:
and they shall draw their swords
against the beauty of thy wisdom,
and they shall *defile* **profane** thy *brightness* **splendour**.
8 They shall bring thee down to the pit **of ruin**,
and thou shalt die the deaths of them
that are *slain* **pierced** in the *midst* **heart** of the seas.
9 **In saying,**
Wilt **Shalt** thou *yet* say *before him* **at his face**
that slayeth thee, *I am God* **I — Elohim**?
but thou shalt be *a man* **human**, and no *God* **El** ,
in the hand of him that *slayeth* **slaughtereth** thee.
10 Thou shalt die the deaths of the uncircumcised
by the hand of strangers:
for I have *spoken it* **worded**,
saith the Lord GOD **an oracle of Adonay Yah Veh**.

YAH VEH'S WORD CONCERNING THE SOVEREIGN OF SOR

11 Moreover
the word of *the LORD* **Yah Veh** came unto me, saying,
12 Son of *man* **humanity**,
take up **lift** a lamentation
upon the *king* **sovereign** of *Tyrus* **Sor**, and say unto him,
Thus saith *the Lord GOD* **Adonay Yah Veh**;
Thou sealest up the *sum* **gauge**,
full of wisdom, and perfect in beauty.
13 Thou hast been in Eden the garden of *God* **Elohim**;
every *precious* **esteemed** stone was thy covering,
the sardius, topaz, and the diamond,
the beryl, the onyx, and the jasper,
the sapphire, the emerald, and the carbuncle, and gold:

the workmanship
of thy *tabrets* **tambourines** and of thy pipes
was prepared in thee in the day that thou wast created.
14 Thou art the *anointed* **overspreading** cherub
that covereth;
and I have *set* **given** thee *so*:
thou wast upon the holy mountain of *God* **Elohim**;
thou hast walked up and down
in the midst of the stones of fire.
15 Thou *wast perfect* **integrious** in thy ways
from the day that thou wast created,
till *iniquity* **wickedness** was found in thee.
16 By the *multitude* **abundance** of thy merchandise
they have filled the midst of thee with violence,
and thou hast sinned:
therefore I *will* **shall** cast thee as profane
out of the mountain of *God* **Elohim**:
and I *will* **shall** destroy thee, O covering cherub,
from the midst of the stones of fire.
17 Thine heart was *lifted up* **haughty**
because of thy beauty,
thou hast *corrupted* **ruined** thy wisdom
by reason of thy *brightness* **splendour**:
I *will* **shall** cast thee to the *ground* **earth**,
I *will lay* **shall give** thee
before kings **at the face of sovereigns**,
that they may *behold* **see** thee.
18 Thou hast *defiled* **profaned** thy *sanctuaries* **holies**
by the *multitude* **abundance**
of *thine iniquities* **thy perversities**,
by the *iniquity* **wickedness** of thy *traffick* **merchandise**;
therefore *will* **shall** I bring forth a fire
from the midst of thee,
it shall devour thee,
and I *will bring* **shall give** thee to ashes upon the earth
in the *sight* **eyes** of all them that *behold* **see** thee.
19 All they that know thee among the people
shall be astonished at thee:
thou shalt be *a terror* **terrors**,
and *never shalt thou be any more* **thou shalt not be**.

YAH VEH'S WORD CONCERNING SIDON

20 Again the word of *the LORD* **Yah Veh** came unto me,
saying,
21 Son of *man* **humanity**,
set thy face against *Zidon* **Sidon**, and prophesy against it,
22 And say, Thus saith *the Lord GOD* **Adonay Yah Veh**;
Behold, I am against thee, O *Zidon* **Sidon**;
and I *will* **shall** be *glorified* **honoured**
in the midst of thee:
and they shall know that *I am the LORD* **I — Yah Veh**,
when I shall have *executed* **worked** judgments in her,
and shall be *sanctified* **hallowed** in her.
23 For I *will* **shall** send into her pestilence,
and blood into her *streets* **outways**;
and the *wounded* **pierced**
shall be *judged* **felled** in the midst of her
by the sword upon her *on every side* **round about**;
and they shall know that *I am the LORD* **I — Yah Veh**.
24 And there shall be no more
a *pricking brier* **bitter prickle**
unto the house of *Israel* **Yisra El**,
nor *any grieving* **painful** thorn
of all that are round about them,
that despised them;
and they shall know
that I am *the Lord GOD* **Adonay Yah Veh**.
25 Thus saith *the Lord GOD* **Adonay Yah Veh**;
When I shall have gathered the house of *Israel* **Yisra El**
from the people among whom they are scattered,
and shall be *sanctified* **hallowed** in them
in the *sight* **eyes** of the *heathen* **goyim**,
then shall they *dwell* **settle** in their *land* **soil**
that I have given to my servant *Jacob* **Yaaqov**.
26 And they shall *dwell safely* **settle confidently** *therein*,
and shall build houses, and plant vineyards;
yea, they shall *dwell with confidence* **settle confidently**,
when I have *executed* **worked** judgments
upon all those that despise them round about them;
and they shall know
that *I am the LORD* **I — Yah Veh** their *God* **Elohim**.

YAH VEH'S WORD CONCERNING
THE SOVEREIGN OF MISRAYIM

29 In the tenth year,
in the tenth *month*, in the twelfth *day* of the month,
the word of *the LORD* **Yah Veh** came unto me, saying,
2 Son of *man* **humanity**,
set thy face against *Pharaoh* **Paroh**
king **sovereign** of *Egypt* **Misrayim**,
and prophesy against him,
and against all *Egypt* **Misrayim**:
3 *Speak* **Word**, and say,
Thus saith *the Lord GOD* **Adonay Yah Veh**;
Behold, I am against thee,
Pharaoh king **Paroh sovereign** of *Egypt* **Misrayim**,
the great *dragon* **monster**
that *lieth* **croucheth** in the midst of his rivers,
which hath said,
My river is mine own,
and I have *made* **worked** it for myself.
4 But I *will put* **shall give** hooks in thy jaws,
and I *will* **shall** cause the fish of thy rivers
to stick unto thy scales,
and I *will bring* **shall ascend** thee *up*
out of the midst of thy rivers,
and all the fish of thy rivers shall stick unto thy scales.
5 And I *will leave* **shall abandon** thee
thrown into the wilderness,
thee and all the fish of thy rivers:
that thou shalt fall upon the *open* **face of the** fields;
that thou shalt not be *brought* **gathered** together,
nor gathered:
I have given thee for *meat* **food**
to the *beasts* **live beings** of the *field* **earth**
and to the *fowls* **flyers** of the *heaven* **heavens**.
6 And all the *inhabitants* **settlers** of *Egypt* **Misrayim**
shall know that *I am the LORD* **I — Yah Veh**,
because they have been a *staff* **stalk** of *reed* **support**
to the house of *Israel* **Yisra El**.
7 When they *took hold of* **apprehended** thee
by thy *hand* **palm**,
thou didst *break* **crush**, and *rend* **split** all their shoulder:
and when they leaned upon thee, thou brakest,
and madest all their loins to *be at a stand* **shake**.
8 Therefore thus saith *the Lord GOD* **Adonay Yah Veh**;
Behold, I *will* **shall** bring a sword upon thee,
and cut off *man* **humanity** and *beast* **animal** out of thee.
9 And the land of *Egypt* **Misrayim**
shall be desolate and *waste* **parched**;
and they shall know that *I am the LORD* **I — Yah Veh**:
because he hath said,
The river is mine, and I have *made* **worked** it.
10 Behold,
therefore I am against thee, and against thy rivers,
and I *will make* **shall give** the land of *Egypt* **Misrayim**
utterly waste **in parching, parched** and desolate,
from the tower of *Syene* **Seven**
even unto the border of *Ethiopia* **Kush**.
11 No foot of *man* **humanity** shall pass through it,
nor foot of *beast* **animal** shall pass through it,
neither shall it be *inhabited* **settled** forty years.
12 And I *will make* **shall give** the land of *Egypt* **Misrayim**
desolate
in the midst of the *countries* **lands**
that are *desolate* **desolated**,
and her cities among the cities
that are *laid waste* **parched**
shall be desolate forty years:
and I *will* **shall** scatter the *Egyptians* **Misrayim**
among the *nations* **goyim**,
and *will disperse* **shall winnow** them
through the *countries* **lands**.
13 Yet thus saith *the Lord GOD* **Adonay Yah Veh**;
At the end of forty years
will **shall** I gather the *Egyptians* **Misrayim**
from the people whither they were scattered:
14 And I *will bring again* **shall return**
the captivity of *Egypt* **Misrayim**,
and *will* **shall** cause them to return
into the land of Pathros,
into the land of their *habitation* **origin**;

and they shall be there
a *base kingdom* **lowly sovereigndom**.
15 It shall be the *basest* **lowly**
of the *kingdoms* **sovereigndoms**;
neither shall it exalt itself any more
above the *nations* **goyim**:
for I *will* **shall** diminish them,
that they shall no more
rule over **subjugate** the *nations* **goyim**.
16 And it shall be no more
the confidence of the house of *Israel* **Yisra El**,
which *bringeth* **remembereth**
their *iniquity to remembrance* **perversity**,
when they shall *look* **face** after them:
but they shall know
that *I am the Lord GOD* **I — Adonay Yah Veh**.
17 And it *came to pass* **became,**
in the seven and twentieth year,
in the first *month*, in the first *day* of the month,
the word of *the LORD* **Yah Veh** came unto me, saying,
18 Son of *man* **humanity**,
Nebuchadrezzar **Nebukadnets Tsar**
king **sovereign** of *Babylon* **Babel**
caused his *army* **valiant**
to serve a great service against *Tyrus* **Sor**:
every head was *made bald* **baldened**,
and every shoulder was peeled:
yet had he no *wages* **hire**, nor his *army* **valiant**,
for *Tyrus* **Sor**, for the service that he had served against it:
19 Therefore thus saith *the Lord GOD* **Adonay Yah Veh**;
Behold, I *will* **shall** give the land of *Egypt* **Misrayim**
unto *Nebuchadrezzar* **Nebukadnets Tsar**
king **sovereign** of *Babylon* **Babel**;
and he shall *take* **lift** her multitude,
and *take* **spoil** her spoil,
and *take her prey* **plundereth her plunder**;
and it shall be the *wages* **hire** for his *army* **valiant**.
20 I have given him the land of *Egypt* **Misrayim**
for his *labour* **deeds** wherewith he served against it,
because they *wrought* **worked** for me,
saith the Lord GOD **an oracle of Adonay Yah Veh**.
21 In that day *will* **shall** I cause the horn
of the house of *Israel* **Yisra El** to *bud forth* **sprout**,
and I *will* **shall** give thee the opening of the mouth
in the midst of them;
and they shall know that *I am the LORD* **I — Yah Veh**.

YAH VEH'S WORD CONCERNING MISRAYIM

30 The word of *the LORD* **Yah Veh**
came again unto me, saying,
2 Son of *man* **humanity**, prophesy and say,
Thus saith *the Lord GOD* **Adonay Yah Veh**;
Howl ye, *Woe worth* **Hah** the day!
3 For the day is near,
even the day of *the LORD* **Yah Veh** is near, a cloudy day;
it shall be the time of the *heathen* **goyim**.
4 And the sword shall come upon *Egypt* **Misrayim**,
and great pain shall be in *Ethiopia* **Kush**,
when the *slain* **pierced** shall fall in *Egypt* **Misrayim**,
and they shall take away her multitude,
and her foundations shall be broken *down*.
5 *Ethiopia* **Kush**, and *Libya* **Put**, and *Lydia* **Lud**,
and all the *mingled people* **comingled**, and *Chub* **Kub**,
and the *men* **sons** of the land that is in *league* **covenant**,
shall fall with them by the sword.
6 Thus saith *the LORD* **Yah Veh**;
They also that uphold *Egypt* **Misrayim** shall fall;
and the *pride* **pomp** of her *power* **strength**
shall *come down* **topple**:
from the tower of *Syene* **Seven**
shall they fall in it by the sword,
saith the Lord GOD **an oracle of Adonay Yah Veh**.
7 And they shall *be* desolate
in the midst of the *countries* **lands**
that *are desolate* **desolated,**
and her cities
shall be in the midst of the cities that are wasted.
8 And they shall know that *I am the LORD* **I — Yah Veh**,
when I have *set* **given** a fire in *Egypt* **Misrayim**,
and when all her helpers shall be *destroyed* **broken**.
9 In that day shall *messengers* **angels**
go forth from *me* **my face** in ships
to make the *careless Ethiopians* **confident Kushies**
afraid **tremble**,
and great pain shall come upon them,
as in the day of *Egypt* **Misrayim**:
for, *lo* **behold**, it cometh.
10 Thus saith *the Lord GOD* **Adonay Yah Veh**;
I *will* **shall** also *make* **cause**
the multitude of *Egypt* **Misrayim** to *cease* **shabbathize**
by the hand of *Nebuchadrezzar* **Nebukadnets Tsar**
king **sovereign** of *Babylon* **Babel**.
11 He and his people with him,
the *terrible* **tyrant** of the *nations* **goyim**,
shall be brought to *destroy* **ruin** the land:
and they shall draw their swords against *Egypt* **Misrayim**,
and fill the land with the *slain* **pierced**.
12 And I *will make* **shall work** the rivers dry,
and sell the land into the hand of the *wicked* **evil**:
and I *will make* **shall desolate** the land *waste*,
and *all that is therein* **the fulness thereof**,
by the hand of strangers:
I *the LORD* **Yah Veh** have *spoken it* **worded**.
13 Thus saith *the Lord GOD* **Adonay Yah Veh**;
I *will* **shall** also destroy the idols,
and I *will* **shall** cause their *images* **idols**
to *cease* **shabbathize** out of Noph;
and there shall be no more
a *prince* **hierarch** of the land of *Egypt* **Misrayim**:
and I *will put* **shall give** a fear
in the land of *Egypt* **Misrayim**.
14 And *I will make Pathros* **I shall** desolate **Pathros**,
and *will set* **shall give** fire in *Zoan* **Soan**,
and *will execute* **shall work** judgments in No.
15 And I *will* **shall** pour my fury upon Sin,
the *strength* **stronghold** of *Egypt* **Misrayim**;
and I *will* **shall** cut off the multitude of No.
16 And I *will* **shall** set fire in *Egypt* **Misrayim**:
In writhing, Sin shall *have great pain* **writhe**,
and No shall be rent asunder,
and Noph shall have *distresses* **tribulations** daily.
17 The *young men* **youths** of *Aven* **mischief**
and of *Pibeseth* **Pi Beseth** shall fall by the sword:
and these cities shall go into captivity.
18 At *Tehaphnehes* **Tachpanches** also
the day shall be *darkened* **spared**,
when I shall break there
the *yokes* **yoke poles** of *Egypt* **Misrayim**:
and the pomp of her strength
shall *cease* **shabbathize** in her:
as for her, a cloud shall cover her,
and her daughters shall go into captivity.
19 Thus *will I execute* **shall I work** judgments
in *Egypt* **Misrayim**:
and they shall know that *I am the LORD* **I — Yah Veh**.
20 And it *came to pass* **became,** in the eleventh year,
in the first *month*, in the seventh *day* of the month,
that the word of *the LORD* **Yah Veh** came unto me,
saying,
21 Son of *man* **humanity**,
I have broken the arm of *Pharaoh* **Paroh**
king **sovereign** of *Egypt* **Misrayim**;
and, *lo* **behold**,
it shall *not be* **be not** bound *up*
to *be healed* **give to healers**,
to *put* **set** a *roller* **bandage** to bind it,
to *make* **strengthen** it *strong*
to *hold* **apprehend** the sword.
22 Therefore thus saith *the Lord GOD* **Adonay Yah Veh**;
Behold, I am against *Pharaoh* **Paroh**
king **sovereign** of *Egypt* **Misrayim**,
and *will* **shall** break his arms,
the strong, and that which was broken;
and I *will* **shall** cause the sword to fall out of his hand.
23 And I *will* **shall** scatter the *Egyptians* **Misrayim**
among the *nations* **goyim**,
and *will* **shall** disperse them through the *countries* **lands**.
24 And I *will* **shall** strengthen the arms
of the *king* **sovereign** of *Babylon* **Babel**,
and *put* **give** my sword in his hand:
but I *will* **shall** break *Pharaoh's* **Paroh's** arms,

and he shall groan *before him* **at his face**
with the groanings of a *deadly wounded* **pierced** man.
25 But I *will* **shall** strengthen the arms
of the *king* **sovereign** of *Babylon* **Babel**,
and the arms of *Pharaoh* **Paroh** shall fall down;
and they shall know that *I am the LORD* **I — Yah Veh**,
when I shall *put* **give** my sword
into the hand of the *king* **sovereign** of *Babylon* **Babel**,
and he shall *stretch* **extend** it out
upon the land of *Egypt* **Misrayim**.
26 And I *will* **shall** scatter the *Egyptians* **Misrayim**
among the *nations* **goyim**,
and *disperse* **winnow** them among the *countries* **lands**;
and they shall know that *I am the LORD* **I — Yah Veh**.

YAH VEH'S WORD CONCERNING PAROH

31 And it *came to pass* **became**, in the eleventh year,
in the third *month*, in the first *day* of the month,
that the word of *the LORD* **Yah Veh** came unto me,
saying,
2 Son of *man* **humanity**,
speak unto *Pharaoh* **Paroh**
king **sovereign** of *Egypt* **Misrayim**,
and to his multitude;
Whom art thou like in thy greatness?
3 Behold, the *Assyrian* **Ashshuri** was a cedar in Lebanon
with *fair* **beautiful** branches,
and with *a shadowing shroud* **an overshadowing forest**,
and of an high *stature* **height**;
and his *top* **foliage** was among the thick *boughs* **foliage**.
4 The waters *made* **greatened** him *great*,
the *deep set* **abyss lifted** him *up on high*
with her rivers *running* **passing** round about his plants,
and sent her *little rivers* **channels**
unto all the trees of the field.
5 Therefore his height was *exalted* **heightened**
above all the trees of the field,
and his *boughs* **twigs** were *multiplied* **greatened**,
and his *branches became long* **foliage lengthened**
because of the *multitude* **abundance** of waters,
when he *shot* **extended** forth.
6 All the *fowls* **flyers** of *heaven* **the heavens**
made their nests **nested** in his *boughs* **twigs**,
and under his *branches* **foliage**
did all the *beasts* **live beings** of the field
bring forth **begat** their young,
and under his shadow
dwelt **settled** all great *nations* **goyim**.
7 Thus was he *fair* **beautified** in his greatness,
in the length of his branches:
for his root was by great waters.
8 The cedars in the garden of *God* **Elohim**
could not *hide* **shade** him:
the fir trees were not like his *boughs* **twigs**,
and the chesnut trees were not like his *branches* **foliage**;
nor any tree in the garden of *God* **Elohim**
was like unto him in his beauty.
9 I have *made* **worked** him *fair* **beautiful**
by the *multitude* **abundance** of his branches:
so that all the trees of Eden,
that were in the garden of *God* **Elohim**, envied him.
10 Therefore thus saith *the Lord GOD* **Adonay Yah Veh**;
Because thou hast
lifted up thyself in **heightened thy** height,
and he hath *shot up* **given** his *top* **foliage**
among the thick *boughs* **foliage**,
and his heart is lifted *up* in his height;
11 I have therefore *delivered* **given** him
into the hand of the *mighty one* **el** of the *heathen* **goyim**;
in working, he shall *surely deal* **work** with him:
I have driven him out for his wickedness.
12 And strangers, the *terrible* **tyrants** of the *nations* **goyim**,
have cut him off, and have *left* **abandoned** him:
upon the mountains and in all the valleys
his branches are fallen,
and his *boughs* **foliage** are broken
by all the *rivers* **reservoirs** of the *land* **earth**;
and all the people of the earth
are *gone down* **descended** from his shadow,
and have *left* **abandoned** him.
13 Upon his ruin shall **tabernacle**
all the *fowls* **flyers** of the *heaven remain* **heavens**,
and all the *beasts* **live beings** of the field
shall be upon his *branches* **foliage**:
14 To the end that none of all the trees by the waters
exalt **heighten** themselves for their height,
neither *shoot up* **give** their *top* **foliage**
among the thick *boughs* **foliage**,
neither their *trees* **mighty oaks** stand up in their height,
all that drink water:
for they are all *delivered* **given** unto death,
to the *nether parts* **nethermost** of the earth,
in the midst of the *children* **sons** of *men* **humanity**,
with them that *go down* **descend** to the *pit* **well**.
15 Thus saith *the Lord GOD* **Adonay Yah Veh**;
In the day
when he *went down* **descended** to *the grave* **sheol**
I caused a mourning:
I covered the *deep* **abyss** for him,
and I *restrained* **withheld** the *floods* **rivers** *thereof*,
and the great waters were stayed:
and I caused Lebanon to *mourn* **darken** for him,
and all the trees of the field *fainted* **languished** for him.
16 I *made* **caused** the *nations* **goyim**
to *shake* **quake** at the *sound* **voice** of his *fall* **ruin**,
when I *cast* **brought** him down to *hell* **sheol**
with them that *descend* **descended** into the *pit* **well**:
and all the trees of Eden, the choice and best of Lebanon,
all that drink water, shall *be comforted* **sigh**
in the *nether parts* **nethermost** of the earth.
17 They also *went down* **descended** into *hell* **sheol**
with him
unto them that be *slain* **pierced** with the sword;
and they that *were* his arm,
that *dwelt* **settled** under his shadow
in the midst of the *heathen* **goyim**.
18 To whom art thou thus like in *glory* **honour**
and in greatness among the trees of Eden?
yet shalt thou be brought down with the trees of Eden
unto the *nether parts* **nethermost** of the earth:
thou shalt lie in the midst of the uncircumcised
with them that be *slain* **pierced** by the sword.
This is *Pharaoh* **Paroh** and all his multitude,
saith the Lord GOD **an oracle of Adonay Yah Veh**.

LAMENTATION AGAINST PAROH

32 And it *came to pass* **became**, in the twelfth year,
in the twelfth month, in the first *day* of the month,
that the word of *the LORD* **Yah Veh** came unto me,
saying,
2 Son of *man* **humanity**, *take up* **lift** a lamentation
for *Pharaoh king* **Paroh sovereign** of *Egypt* **Misrayim**,
and say unto him,
Thou art like a *young lion* **whelp** of the *nations* **goyim**,
and thou art as *a whale* **monsters** in the seas:
and thou camest forth with thy rivers,
and troubledst the waters with thy feet,
and fouledst their rivers.
3 Thus saith *the Lord GOD* **Adonay Yah Veh**;
I *will* **shall** therefore spread out my net over thee
with a *company* **congregation** of many people;
and they shall *bring* **ascend** thee *up* in my net.
4 Then *will I leave* **shall I abandon** thee upon the land,
I *will* **shall** cast thee forth upon the *open* **face of the** field,
and *will* **shall** cause
all the *fowls* **flyers** of the *heaven* **heavens**
to *remain* **tabernacle** upon thee,
and I *will fill* **shall satiate** the *beasts* **live beings**
of the whole earth with thee.
5 And I *will lay* **shall give** thy flesh upon the mountains,
and fill the valleys with thy *height* **carcase heaps**.
6 I *will* **shall** also *water* **wet** with thy blood
the land *wherein thou swimmest* **of thy swimming**,
even to the mountains;
and the *rivers* **reservoirs** shall be *full* **filled** of thee.
7 And when I shall put thee out,
I *will* **shall** cover the *heaven* **heavens**,
and *make* **darken** the stars *thereof dark*;
I *will* **shall** cover the sun with a cloud,
and the moon shall not *give her light* **lighten**.
8 All the *bright* lights
of the light of *heaven* **the heavens**

will I make dark **shall I darken** over thee,
and *set* **give** darkness upon thy land,
saith the Lord GOD **an oracle of Adonay Yah Veh.**
9 I *will* **shall** also vex the hearts of many people,
when I shall bring thy *destruction* **breaking**
among the *nations* **goyim,**
into the *countries* **lands** which thou hast not known.
10 Yea, I *will make* **shall cause** many people
amazed **to astonish** at thee,
and their *kings* **sovereigns**
shall *be horribly afraid* **shudder with horror** *for thee,*
when I shall *brandish* **flutter** my sword
before them **at their face;**
and they shall tremble *at every moment* **in a blink,**
every man for his own *life* **soul,** in the day of thy *fall* **ruin.**
11 For thus saith *the Lord GOD* **Adonay Yah Veh;**
The sword of the *king* **sovereign** of *Babylon* **Babel**
shall come upon thee.
12 By the swords of the mighty
will **shall** I cause thy multitude to fall,
the *terrible* **tyrants** of the *nations* **goyim,** all of them:
and they shall *spoil* **ravage** the pomp of *Egypt* **Misrayim,**
and all the multitude *thereof*
shall be *destroyed* **desolated.**
13 I *will* **shall** destroy also all the *beasts* **animals** *thereof*
from beside the great waters;
neither shall the foot of *man* **humanity**
trouble them any more,
nor the hoofs of *beasts* **animals** trouble them.
14 Then *will* **shall** I make their waters *deep* **drown,**
and cause their rivers to *run* **go** like oil,
saith the Lord GOD **an oracle of Adonay Yah Veh.**
15 When I shall *make* **give** the land of *Egypt* **Misrayim**
desolate,
and the *country* **land** hall be *destitute* **desolated**
of that whereof it was full **from the fulness thereof,**
when I shall smite all them that *dwell* **settle** therein,
then shall they know that *I am the LORD* **I — Yah Veh.**
16 This is the lamentation
wherewith they shall lament her:
the daughters of the *nations* **goyim** shall lament her:
they shall lament for her,
even for *Egypt* **Misrayim,** and for all her multitude,
saith the Lord GOD **an oracle of Adonay Yah Veh.**
17 It *came to pass* **became,**
also in the twelfth year, in the fifteenth *day* of the month,
that the word of *the LORD* **Yah Veh** came unto me,
saying,
18 Son of *man* **humanity,**
wail **lament** for the multitude of *Egypt* **Misrayim,**
and *cast* **bring** them down, *even* her,
and the daughters of the *famous nations* **mighty goyim,**
unto the *nether parts* **nethermost** of the earth,
with them that *go down* **descend** into the *pit* **well.**
19 *Whom dost thou pass in beauty?*
With whom hast thou been most pleasant?
go down **descend,**
and be thou laid with the uncircumcised.
20 They shall fall in the midst of them
that are *slain* **pierced** by the sword:
she is *delivered* **given** to the sword:
draw her and all her multitudes.
21 The *strong among* **el of** the mighty
shall *speak* **word** to him
out of the midst of *hell* **sheol** with them that help him:
they are *gone* **brought** down,
they lie uncircumcised, *slain* **pierced** by the sword.
22 *Asshur* **Ashshur** is there
and all her *company* **congregation:**
his *graves* **tombs** are **round** about him:
all of them *slain* **pierced,** fallen by the sword:
23 Whose *graves* **tombs** are *set* **given**
in the *sides* **flanks** of the *pit* **well,**
and her *company* **congregation**
is round about her *grave* **tomb:**
all of them *slain* **pierced,** fallen by the sword,
which *caused* **gave** terror in the land of the living.
24 There is Elam and all her multitude
round about her *grave* **tomb,**
all of them *slain* **pierced,** fallen by the sword,
which are *gone* **brought** down uncircumcised
into the *nether parts* **nethermost** of the earth,
which *caused* **gave** their terror in the land of the living;
yet have they borne their shame
with them that *go down* **descend** to the *pit* **well.**
25 They have *set* **given** her a bed
in the midst of the *slain* **pierced** with all her multitude:
her *graves* **tombs** are round about him:
all of them uncircumcised, *slain* **pierced** by the sword:
though their terror
was *caused* **given** in the land of the living,
yet have they borne their shame with them
that *go down* **descend** to the *pit* **well:**
he is *put* **given** in the midst of them that be *slain* **pierced.**
26 There is Meshech, Tubal,
and all her multitude:
her *graves* **tombs** are round about him:
all of them uncircumcised, *slain* **pierced** by the sword,
though they *caused* **gave** their terror
in the land of the living.
27 And they shall not lie with the mighty
that are fallen of the uncircumcised,
which are *gone down* **descended** to *hell* **sheol**
with their *weapons* **instruments** of war:
and they have *laid* **given** their swords under their heads,
but their *iniquities* **perversities** shall be upon their bones,
though they were the terror of the mighty
in the land of the living.
28 Yea,
thou shalt be broken in the midst of the uncircumcised,
and shalt lie with them
that are *slain* **pierced** with the sword.
29 There is Edom,
her *kings* **sovereigns,** and all her *princes* **hierarchs,**
which with their might are *laid* **given**
by them that were *slain* **pierced** by the sword:
they shall lie with the uncircumcised,
and with them that *go down* **descend** to the *pit* **well.**
30 There be the princes of the north,
all of them, and all the *Zidonians* **Sidonians,**
which are *gone* **brought** down with the *slain* **pierced;**
with their terror they are ashamed of their might;
and they lie uncircumcised
with them that be *slain* **pierced** by the sword,
and bear their shame
with them that *go down* **descend** to the *pit* **well.**
31 *Pharaoh* **Paroh** shall see them,
and shall *be comforted* **sigh** over all his multitude,
even Pharaoh **Paroh** and all his *army* **valiant**
slain **pierced** by the sword,
saith the Lord GOD **an oracle of Adonay Yah Veh.**
32 For I have *caused* **given** my terror
in the land of the living:
and he shall be laid in the midst of the uncircumcised
with them that are *slain* **pierced** with the sword,
even Pharaoh **Paroh** and all his multitude,
saith the Lord GOD **an oracle of Adonay Yah Veh.**

YECHEZQ EL, THE WATCHER

33 Again the word of *the LORD* **Yah Veh**
came unto me, saying,
2 Son of *man* **humanity,**
speak **word** to the *children* **sons** of thy people,
and say unto them,
When I bring the sword upon a land,
if the people of the land
take *a* **one** man of their *coasts* **edges,**
and *set* **give** him for their *watchman* **watcher:**
3 If when he seeth the sword come upon the land,
he *blow* **blast** the trumpet,
and *warn* **enlighten** the people;
4 Then in **hearkening,** whosoever *heareth* **hearkeneth**
the sound **unto the voice** of the trumpet,
and taketh not warning;
if the sword come, and take him away,
his blood shall be upon his own head.
5 He heard the *sound* **voice** of the trumpet,
and took not warning; his blood shall be upon him.
But he that taketh warning shall *deliver* **rescue** his soul.
6 But if the *watchman* **watcher** see the sword come,
and *blow* **blast** not the trumpet,

and the people be not warned; if the sword come,
and take *any person* **a soul** from among them,
he is taken away in his *iniquity* **perversity**;
but his blood *will* **shall** I require
at the *watchman's* **watcher's** hand.
7 So thou, O son of *man* **humanity**,
I have *set* **given** thee
a *watchman* **watcher** unto the house of *Israel* **Yisra El**;
therefore thou shalt hear the word at my mouth,
and *warn* **enlighten** them from me.
8 *When I say* **Saying** unto the wicked, O wicked *man*,
in dying, thou shalt *surely* die;
if thou dost not *speak* **word**
to *warn* **enlighten** the wicked from his way,
that wicked *man* shall die in his *iniquity* **perversity**;
but his blood *will I require* **shall I seek** at thine hand.
9 Nevertheless,
if thou *warn* **enlighten** the wicked of his way
to turn from it;
if he do not turn from his way,
he shall die in his *iniquity* **perversity**;
but thou hast *delivered* **rescued** thy soul.
10 Therefore, O thou son of *man* **humanity**,
speak **say** unto the house of *Israel* **Yisra El**;
Thus ye *speak* **say**, saying,
If our *transgressions* **rebellions** and our sins be upon us,
and we *pine away* **vanish** in them,
how should we then live?
11 Say unto them, *As* I live,
saith the Lord GOD **an oracle of Adonay Yah Veh**,
I have no *pleasure* **delight** in the death of the wicked;
but that the wicked turn from his way and live:
turn ye, turn ye from your evil ways;
for why *will* **shall** ye die, O house of *Israel* **Yisra El**?
12 Therefore, thou son of *man* **humanity**,
say unto the *children* **sons** of thy people,
The *righteousness* **justness** of the *righteous* **just**
shall not *deliver* **rescue** him
in the day of his *transgression* **rebellion**:
as for the wickedness of the wicked,
he shall not *fall* **falter** thereby
in the day that he turneth from his wickedness;
neither shall the *righteous* **just** be able to live
for his righteousness **by it** in the day that he sinneth.
13 When I shall say to the *righteous* **just**,
that **in living,** he shall *surely* live;
if he *trust* **confide** to his own *righteousness* **justness**,
and *commit iniquity* **work wickedness**,
all his *righteousnesses* **justnesses**
shall not be remembered;
but for his *iniquity* **wickedness**
that he hath *committed* **worked**, he shall die for it.
14 *Again, when I say* **Saying** unto the wicked,
In dying, Thou shalt *surely* die;
if he turn from his sin,
and *do that which is lawful* **work judgment**
and *right* **justness**;
15 If the wicked restore the pledge,
give again **shalam** that he had *robbed* **stripped**,
walk in the statutes of life,
without *committing iniquity* **working wickedness**;
in living, he shall *surely* live, he shall not die.
16 None of his sins that he hath *committed* **sinned**
shall be *mentioned* **remembered** unto him:
he hath *done* **worked**
that which is lawful **judgment** and *right* **justness**;
in living, he shall *surely* live.

THE WAY OF BALANCE

17 Yet the *children* **sons** of thy people say,
The way of *the Lord* **Adonay** is not *equal* **gauged**:
but as for them, their way is not *equal* **gauged**.
18 When the *righteous* **just**
turneth from his *righteousness* **justness**,
and *committeth iniquity* **worketh wickedness**,
he shall even die thereby.
19 But if the wicked turn from his wickedness,
and do that which is *lawful* **judgment** and *right* **justness**,
he shall live thereby.
20 Yet ye say,
The way of *the Lord* **Adonay** is not *equal* **gauged**.
O ye house of *Israel* **Yisra El**,
I *will* **shall** judge you every *one* **man** after his ways.

YERU SHALEM IS SMITTEN

21 And it *came to pass* **became,**
in the twelfth year of our *captivity* **exile**,
in the tenth *month*, in the fifth *day* of the month,
that one *that had escaped* **escapee**
out of *Jerusalem* **Yeru Shalem** came unto me, saying,
The city is smitten.
22 *Now* the hand of *the LORD* **Yah Veh**
was upon me in the evening,
afore he that was escaped came
at the face of the coming of the escapee;
and had opened my mouth,
until he came to me in the morning;
and my mouth was opened,
and I was no more *dumb* **mute**.
23 Then the word of *the LORD* **Yah Veh** came unto me,
saying,
24 Son of *man* **humanity**,
they that *inhabit* **settle** those *wastes* **parched areas**
of the *land* **soil** of *Israel* **Yisra El** *speak* **say**, saying,
Abraham was one,
and he *inherited* **was successor of** the land:
but we are many;
the land is given us for *inheritance* **possession**.
25 Wherefore say unto them,
Thus saith *the Lord GOD* **Adonay Yah Veh**;
Ye eat with the blood,
and lift up your eyes toward your idols,
and *shed* **pour** blood:
and shall ye possess the land?
26 Ye stand upon your sword,
ye work *abomination* **abhorrence**,
and ye *defiled* **fouled**
every *one* **man** his *neighbour's wife* **friend's woman**:
and shall ye possess the land?
27 Say thou thus unto them,
Thus saith *the Lord GOD* **Adonay Yah Veh**; *As* I live,
surely they that are in the *wastes* **parched areas**
shall fall by the sword,
and him that is in the *open* **face of the** field
will **shall** I give to the *beasts* **live beings** to be devoured,
and they that be in the *forts* **huntholds** and in the caves
shall die of the pestilence.
28 For I *will lay* **shall give** the land
most desolate **desolation and desolation**,
and the *pomp* **pomp** of her strength
shall *cease* **shabbathize**;
and the mountains of *Israel* **Yisra El** shall *be* desolate,
that none shall pass through.
29 Then shall they know that *I am the LORD* **I — Yah Veh**,
when I have *laid* **given** the land
most desolate **desolation and desolation**
because of all their *abominations* **abhorrences**
which they have *committed* **worked**.
30 Also, thou son of *man* **humanity**,
the *children* **sons** of thy people
still *are talking* **wording** against thee *by* **beside** the walls
and in the *doors* **portals** of the houses,
and *speak* **word** one to *another* **one**,
every *one* **man** to his brother, saying,
Come, I *pray* **beseech** you, and hear what is the word
that cometh forth from *the LORD* **Yah Veh**.
31 And they come unto thee
as the people *cometh* **entereth**,
and they sit *before thee* **at thy face** as my people,
and they hear thy words,
but they *will* **shall** not *do* **work** them:
for with their mouth they *shew much love* **work pantings**,
but their heart goeth after their *covetousness* **greedy gain**.
32 And, *lo* **behold**, thou art unto them
as a *very lovely* song **of pantings**
of one that hath a *pleasant* **beautiful** voice,
and can *play well* **strum goodly** on an instrument:
for they hear thy words, but they *do* **work** them not.
33 And when this *cometh to pass* **becometh**,
(*lo* **behold**, it *will come* **shall become**,)
then shall they know
that a prophet hath been among them.

YAH VEH'S WORD CONCERNING TENDERS

34 And the word of *the LORD* **Yah Veh**
came unto me, saying,
2 Son of *man* **humanity**,
prophesy against the *shepherds* **tenders** of *Israel* **Yisra El**,
prophesy, and say unto them,
Thus saith *the Lord GOD* **Adonay Yah Veh**
unto the *shepherds* **tenders**;
Woe be **Ho** to the *shepherds* **tenders** of *Israel* **Yisra El**
that *do feed* **tend** themselves!
should not the *shepherds feed* **tenders tend** the flocks?
3 Ye eat the fat, and ye *clothe* **enrobe** you with the wool,
ye *kill them that are fed* **sacrifice the fattened**:
but ye *feed* **tend** not the flock.
4 The *diseased* **worn** have ye not strengthened,
neither have ye healed that which was sick,
neither have ye bound up that which was broken,
neither have ye *brought again* **restored**
that which was *driven away* **expelled**,
neither have ye sought that which was lost;
but with *force* **severity** and with *cruelty* **tyranny**
have ye *ruled* **subjugated** them.
5 And they were scattered,
because there is no *shepherd* **tender**:
and they became *meat* **food**
to all the *beasts* **live beings** of the field,
when they were scattered.
6 My *sheep wandered* **flock erred inadvertently**
through all the mountains, and upon every high hill:
yea, my flock was scattered upon all the face of the earth,
and none did search or seek *after them.*
7 Therefore, ye *shepherds* **tenders**,
hear the word of *the LORD* **Yah Veh**;
8 *As* I live,
saith the Lord GOD **an oracle of Adonay Yah Veh**,
surely because my flock became a *prey* **plunder**,
and my flock became *meat* **food**
to every *beast* **live being** of the field,
because there was no *shepherd* **tender**,
neither did my *shepherds* **tenders** search for my flock,
but the *shepherds fed* **tenders tended** themselves,
and *fed* **tended** not my flock;
9 Therefore, O ye *shepherds* **tenders**,
hear the word of *the LORD* **Yah Veh**;
10 Thus saith *the Lord GOD* **Adonay Yah Veh**;
Behold, I am against the *shepherds* **tenders**;
and I *will* **shall** require my flock at their hand,
and cause them to *cease* **shabbathize**
from *feeding* **tending** the flock;
neither shall the *shepherds feed* **tenders tend** themselves
any more;
for I *will deliver* **shall rescue** my flock from their mouth,
that they may not be *meat* **food** for them.

THE TENDER OF YISRA EL

11 For thus saith *the Lord GOD* **Adonay Yah Veh**;
Behold, I, *even* I,
will **shall** both search my *sheep* **flock**,
and *seek* **search** them out.
12 As a *shepherd* **tender**
seeketh **searcheth** out his *flock* **drove**
in the day
that he is among his *sheep* **flock** that are scattered;
so *will I seek* **shall I search** out my *sheep* **flock**,
and *will deliver* **shall rescue** them
out of all places where they have been scattered
in the cloudy and *dark* day **of dripping darkness**.
13 And I *will* **shall** bring them out from the people,
and gather them from the *countries* **lands**,
and *will* **shall** bring them to their own *land* **soil**,
and *feed* **tend** them upon the mountains of *Israel* **Yisra El**
by the *rivers* **reservoirs**,
and in all the *inhabited places* **sites** of the *country* **land**.
14 I *will feed* **shall tend** them in a good pasture,
and upon the high mountains of *Israel* **Yisra El**
shall their *fold* **habitation of rest** be:
there shall they *lie* **crouch**
in a good *fold* **habitation of rest**,
and in a fat pasture shall they *feed* **graze**
upon the mountains of *Israel* **Yisra El**.
15 I *will feed* **shall tend** my flock,
and I *will* **shall** cause them to *lie down* **crouch**,
saith the Lord GOD **an oracle of Adonay Yah Veh**.
16 I *will* **shall** seek that which was lost,
and *bring again* **restore**
that which was *driven away* **expelled**,
and *will* **shall** bind up that which was broken,
and *will* **shall** strengthen that which was sick:
but I *will destroy* **shall desolate** the fat and the strong;
I *will feed* **shall tend** them with judgment.
17 And as for you, O my flock,
thus saith *the Lord GOD* **Adonay Yah Veh**;
Behold, I judge between *cattle* **lambs** and *cattle* **lambs**,
between the rams and the he goats.
18 *Seemeth it a small thing* **Be it belittling** unto you
to have *eaten up* **tended** the good pasture,
but ye must tread down **to have trampled** with your feet
the *residue* **remnant** of your pastures?
and to have drunk of the *deep* **pond** waters,
but ye must **to** foul *the residue* **that which remaineth**
with your feet?
19 And as for my flock,
they *eat* **tend** that
which ye have *trodden* **trampled** with your feet;
and they drink that
which ye have *fouled* **trampled** with your feet.
20 Therefore thus saith
the Lord GOD **Adonay Yah Veh** unto them;
Behold, I, *even* I,
will **shall** judge between the fat *cattle* **lambs**
and between the *lean cattle* **emaciated lambs**.
21 Because ye have *thrust* **shoved**
with side and with shoulder,
and *pushed* **butted** all the *diseased* **worn**
with your horns,
till ye have scattered them *abroad* **to the outways**;
22 Therefore *will* **shall** I save my flock,
and they shall no more be a *prey* **plunder**;
and I *will* **shall** judge
between *cattle* **lambs** and *cattle* **lambs**.
23 And I *will set up* **shall raise**
one *shepherd* **tender** over them,
and he shall *feed* **tend** them, *even* my servant David;
he shall *feed* **tend** them,
and he shall be their *shepherd* **tender**.
24 And I *the LORD* **Yah Veh**
will **shall** be their *God* **Elohim**,
and my servant David a *prince* **hierarch** among them;
I *the LORD* **Yah Veh** have *spoken it* **worded**.

YAH VEH CUTS A COVENANT OF SHALOM

25 And I *will make* **shall cut** with them
a covenant of *peace* **shalom**,
and *will* **shall** cause the evil *beasts* **live beings**
to *cease* **shabbathize** out of the land:
and they shall *dwell safely* **settle confidently**
in the wilderness,
and sleep in the *woods* **forests**.
26 And I *will make* **shall give** them
and *the places* round about my hill a blessing;
and I *will* **shall** cause the *shower* **downpour**
to *come down* **descend** in his *season* **time**;
there shall be *showers* **downpours** of blessing.
27 And the tree of the field shall *yield* **give** her fruit,
and the earth shall *yield* **give** her *increase* **produce**,
and they shall *be safe* **confide** in their *land* **soil**,
and shall know that *I am the LORD* **I — Yah Veh**,
when I have broken the *bands* **yoke poles** of their yoke,
and *delivered* **rescued** them
out of the hand of those that served themselves of them.
28 And they shall no more
be a *prey* **plunder** to the *heathen* **goyim**,
neither shall the *beast* **live being** of the land devour them;
but they shall *dwell safely* **settle confidently**,
and none shall *make* **terrify** them *afraid*.
29 And I *will* **shall** raise up for them
a plant of *renown* **name**,
and they shall be no more *consumed* **gathered**
with *hunger* **famine** in the land,
neither bear the shame of the *heathen* **goyim** any more.
30 Thus shall they know
that I *the LORD* **Yah Veh** their *God* **Elohim** am with them,

and *that* they, *even* the house of *Israel* **Yisra El**,
are my people,
saith the Lord GOD **an oracle of Adonay Yah Veh**.
31 And ye my flock, the flock of my pasture,
are *men* **human**,
and I *am* — your *God* **Elohim**,
saith the Lord GOD **an oracle of Adonay Yah Veh**.

YAH VEH'S WORD CONCERNING MOUNT SEIR

35 Moreover
the word of *the LORD* **Yah Veh** came unto me, saying,
2 Son of *man* **humanity**,
set thy face against mount Seir, and prophesy against it,
3 And say unto it,
Thus saith *the Lord GOD* **Adonay Yah Veh**;
Behold, O mount Seir, I am against thee,
and I *will stretch out* **shall extend** mine hand against thee,
and I *will make* **shall give** thee
most desolate **desolation and desolation**.
4 I *will lay* **shall set** thy cities *waste* **parched**,
and thou shalt be desolate,
and thou shalt know that *I am the LORD* **I — Yah Veh**.
5 Because thou hast had
a perpetual hatred **an eternal enmity**,
and hast *shed the blood of* **poured out**
the *children* **sons** of *Israel* **Yisra El**
by the *force* **hands** of the sword
in the time of their calamity,
in the time that their *iniquity* **perversity** had an end:
6 Therefore, *as* I live,
saith the Lord GOD **an oracle of Adonay Yah Veh**,
I *will prepare* **shall work** thee unto blood,
and blood shall pursue thee:
since thou hast not hated blood,
even blood shall pursue thee.
7 Thus *will I make* **shall I give** mount Seir
most desolate **desolation and desolation**,
and cut off from it
him that passeth out and him that returneth.
8 And I *will* **shall** fill his mountains
with his *slain men* **pierced**:
in thy hills, and in thy valleys,
and in all thy *rivers* **reservoirs**,
shall they fall that are *slain* **pierced** with the sword.
9 I *will make* **shall give** thee
perpetual **eternal** desolations,
and thy cities shall not *return* **be settled**:
and ye shall know that *I am the LORD* **I — Yah Veh**.
10 Because *thou hast said* **saying**,
These two *nations* **goyim** and these two *countries* **lands**
shall be mine, and we *will* **shall** possess it;
whereas *the LORD* **Yah Veh** was there:
11 Therefore, *as* I live,
saith the Lord GOD **an oracle of Adonay Yah Veh**,
I *will* **shall** even *do* **work**
according to *thine anger* **thy wrath**,
and according to thine envy
which thou hast *used* **worked**
out of thy hatred against them;
and I *will* **shall** make myself known among them,
when I have judged thee.
12 And thou shalt know that *I am the LORD* **I — Yah Veh**,
and that I have heard all thy *blasphemies* **scornings**
which thou hast *spoken* **said**
against the mountains of *Israel* **Yisra El**, saying,
They are *laid desolate* **desolated**,
they are given us *to consume* **for food**.
13 Thus with your mouth
ye have *boasted* **greatened** against me,
and have *multiplied* **abounded** your words against me:
I have heard them.
14 Thus saith *the Lord GOD* **Adonay Yah Veh**;
When the whole earth *rejoiceth* **cheereth**,
I *will make* **shall work** thee desolate.
15 As *thou didst rejoice* **thy cheerfulness**
at the inheritance of the house of *Israel* **Yisra El**,
because it was *desolate* **desolated**,
so *will I do* **shall I work** unto thee:
thou shalt be desolate,
O mount Seir, and all *Idumea* **Edom**, *even* all of it:
and they shall know that *I am the LORD* **I — Yah Veh**.

PROPHECY AGAINST THE MOUNTAINS OF YISRA EL

36 Also, thou son of *man* **humanity**,
prophesy unto the mountains of *Israel* **Yisra El**, and say,
Ye mountains of *Israel* **Yisra El**,
hear the word of *the LORD* **Yah Veh**:
2 Thus saith *the Lord GOD* **Adonay Yah Veh**;
Because the enemy hath said against you, Aha,
even the *ancient high places* **eternal bamahs**
are our's in possession:
3 Therefore prophesy and say,
Thus saith *the Lord GOD* **Adonay Yah Veh**;
Because they have *made* **desolated** you *desolate*,
and swallowed you *up on every side* **round about**,
that ye might be a possession
unto the *residue* **survivors** of the *heathen* **goyim**,
and ye are *taken up* **ascended**
in the lips of *talkers* **tongues**,
and are *an infamy* **a slander** of the people:
4 Therefore, ye mountains of *Israel* **Yisra El**,
hear the word of *the Lord GOD* **Adonay Yah Veh**;
Thus saith *the Lord GOD* **Adonay Yah Veh**
to the mountains, and to the hills,
to the *rivers* **reservoirs**, and to the valleys,
to the *desolate wastes* **desolated parches**,
and to the cities that are forsaken,
which became a *prey* **plunder** and derision
to the *residue* **survivors** of the *heathen* **goyim**
that are round about;
5 Therefore thus saith *the Lord GOD* **Adonay Yah Veh**;
Surely in the fire of my jealousy have I *spoken* **worded**
against the *residue* **survivors** of the *heathen* **goyim**,
and against all *Idumea* **Edom**,
which have *appointed* **given** my land
into their possession
with the *joy* **cheerfulness** of all their heart,
with despiteful *minds* **souls**,
to cast it out for a prey **a suburb to plunder**.
6 Prophesy therefore
concerning the *land* **soil** of *Israel* **Yisra El**,
and say unto the mountains, and to the hills,
to the *rivers* **reservoirs**, and to the valleys,
Thus saith *the Lord GOD* **Adonay Yah Veh**; Behold,
I have *spoken* **worded** in my jealousy and in my fury,
because ye have borne the shame of the *heathen* **goyim**:
7 Therefore thus saith *the Lord GOD* **Adonay Yah Veh**;
I have lifted up mine hand,
Surely the *heathen* **goyim** that are **round** about you,
they shall bear their shame.
8 But ye, O mountains of *Israel* **Yisra El**,
ye shall *shoot forth* **give** your branches,
and *yield* **bear** your fruit to my people of *Israel* **Yisra El**;
for they *are at hand* **approach** to come.
9 For, behold, I am for you,
and I *will turn* **shall face** unto you,
and ye shall be *tilled* **served** and *sown* **seeded**:
10 And I *will multiply men* **shall abound humanity**
upon you,
all the house of *Israel* **Yisra El**, *even* all of it:
and the cities shall be *inhabited* **settled**,
and the *wastes* **parched areas** shall be builded:
11 And I *will multiply* **shall abound** upon you
man **humanity** and *beast* **animal**;
and they shall *increase* **abound** and *bring* **bear** fruit:
and I *will* **shall** settle you after your *old* **former** estates,
and *will* **shall** do better unto you than at your beginnings:
and ye shall know that *I am the LORD* **I — Yah Veh**.
12 Yea, I *will* **shall** cause *men* **humanity**
to walk upon you,
even my people *Israel* **Yisra El**;
and they shall possess thee,
and thou shalt be their inheritance,
and thou shalt *no more henceforth* **not add**
to bereave them *of men*.
13 Thus saith *the Lord GOD* **Adonay Yah Veh**;
Because they say unto you,
Thou *land* devourest up *men* **humanity**,
and hast bereaved thy *nations* **goyim**:
14 Therefore thou shalt devour *men* **humanity** no more,
neither bereave thy *nations* **goyim** any more,
saith the Lord GOD **an oracle of Adonay Yah Veh**.

15 Neither *will* **shall** I cause *men* to hear in thee
the shame of the *heathen* **goyim** any more,
neither shalt thou
bear the reproach of the people any more,
neither shalt thou
cause thy *nations* **goyim** to *fall* **falter** any more,
saith the Lord GOD **an oracle of Adonay Yah Veh.**
16 Moreover
the word of *the LORD* **Yah Veh** came unto me, saying,
17 Son of *man* **humanity**,
when the house of *Israel* **Yisra El**
dwelt **settled** in their own *land* **soil**,
they *defiled* **fouled** it
by their own way and by their *doings* **exploits**:
their way was *before me* **at my face**
as the *uncleanness* **foulness**
of *a removed woman* **one excluded**.
18 Wherefore I poured my fury upon them
for the blood that they had *shed* **poured** upon the land,
and for their idols wherewith they had *polluted* **fouled** it:
19 And I scattered them among the *heathen* **goyim**,
and they were dispersed through the *countries* **lands**:
according to their way
and according to their *doings* **exploits** I judged them.
20 And when they entered unto the *heathen* **goyim**,
whither they went, they profaned my holy name,
when they said **saying** to them,
These are the people of *the LORD* **Yah Veh**,
and are gone forth out of his land.
21 But I *had pity for* **compassioned** mine holy name,
which the house of *Israel* **Yisra El** had profaned
among the *heathen* **goyim**, whither they went.
22 Therefore say unto the house of *Israel* **Yisra El**,
thus saith *the Lord GOD* **Adonay Yah Veh**;
I *do* **work** not this for your sakes,
O house of *Israel* **Yisra El**,
but for mine holy name's sake,
which ye have profaned among the *heathen* **goyim**,
whither ye went.
23 And I *will sanctify* **shall hallow** my great name,
which was profaned among the *heathen* **goyim**,
which ye have profaned in the midst of them;
and the *heathen* **goyim** shall know
that *I am the LORD* **I — Yah Veh**,
saith the Lord GOD **an oracle of Adonay Yah Veh**,
when I shall be *sanctified* **hallowed** in you
before their eyes.
24 For I *will* **shall** take you
from among the *heathen* **goyim**,
and gather you out of all *countries* **lands**,
and *will* **shall** bring you into your own *land* **soil**.
25 Then *will* **shall** I sprinkle *clean* **pure** water upon you,
and ye shall be *clean* **pure**:
from all your *filthiness* **foulness**, and from all your idols,
will I cleanse **shall I purify** you.
26 A new heart also *will* **shall** I give you,
and a new spirit *will I put* **shall I give** within you:
and I *will take away* **shall turn aside**
the stony heart out of your flesh,
and I *will* **shall** give you an heart of flesh.
27 And I *will put* **shall give** my spirit within you,
and *cause* **work** you to walk in my statutes,
and ye shall *keep* **guard** my judgments,
and *do* **work** them.
28 And ye shall *dwell* **settle**
in the land that I gave to your fathers;
and ye *shall* be my people,
and *I will be* **I AM** your *God* **Elohim**.
29 I *will* **shall** also save you
from all your *uncleannesses* **foulnesses**:
and I *will* **shall** call for the *corn* **crop**,
and *will increase* **shall abound** it,
and *lay* **give** no famine upon you.
30 And I *will multiply* **shall abound** the fruit of the tree,
and the *increase* **produce** of the field,
that ye shall *receive* **take** no more reproach of famine
among the *heathen* **goyim**.
31 Then shall ye remember your own evil ways,
and your *doings* **exploits** that were not good,
and shall lothe *yourselves in your own sight* **at your face**
for your *iniquities* **perversities**
and for your *abominations* **abhorrences**.
32 Not for your sakes *do* **work** I this,
saith the Lord GOD **an oracle of Adonay Yah Veh**,
be it known unto you:
be *ashamed* **shamed** and confounded for your own ways,
O house of *Israel* **Yisra El**.
33 Thus saith *the Lord GOD* **Adonay Yah Veh**;
In the day that I shall *have cleansed* **purify** you
from all your *iniquities* **perversities**
I *will* **shall** also cause *you* to *dwell* **settle** in the cities,
and the *wastes* **parched areas** shall be builded.
34 And the *desolate* **desolated** land shall be *tilled* **served**,
whereas it lay desolate
in the *sight* **eyes** of all that passed by.
35 And they shall say,
This land that was *desolate* **desolated**
is become like the garden of Eden;
and the *waste* **parched** and *desolate* **desolated**
and *ruined* **demolished** cities
are *become fenced* **fortified**, and are *inhabited* **settled**.
36 Then the *heathen* **goyim**
that *are left* **survive** round about you
shall know that I *the LORD* **Yah Veh**
build the *ruined places* **demolished**,
and plant that that was *desolate* **desolated**:
I *the LORD* **Yah Veh** have *spoken it* **worded**,
and I *will do* **shall work** it.
37 Thus saith *the Lord GOD* **Adonay Yah Veh**;
I will **shall** yet for this be enquired of
by the house of *Israel* **Yisra El**, to *do* **work** it for them;
I *will increase* **shall abound** them
with *men* **humanity** like a flock.
38 As the holy flock,
as the flock of *Jerusalem* **Yeru Shalem**
in her *solemn feasts* **seasons**;
so shall the *waste* **parched** cities
be filled with flocks of *men* **humanity**:
and they shall know that *I am the LORD* **I — Yah Veh.**

THE VISION OF THE VALLEY OF DRY BONES

37 The hand of *the LORD* **Yah Veh** was upon me,
and carried me out in the spirit of *the LORD* **Yah Veh**,
and *set* **rested** me *down* in the midst of the valley
which was full of bones,
2 And caused me to pass by them
round about **and round about**: and, behold,
there were very many in the *open* **face of the** valley;
and, *lo* **behold**, they were *very* **mighty** dry.
3 And he said unto me,
Son of *man* **humanity**, can these bones live?
And I *answered* **said**,
O Lord GOD **Adonay Yah Veh**, thou knowest.
4 Again he said unto me,
Prophesy upon these bones, and say unto them,
O ye dry bones, hear the word of *the LORD* **Yah Veh**.
5 Thus saith *the Lord GOD* **Adonay Yah Veh**
unto these bones;
Behold, I *will* **shall** cause *breath* **spirit** to enter into you,
and ye shall live:
6 And I *will lay* **shall give** sinews upon you,
and *will bring up* **shall ascend** flesh upon you,
and cover you with skin,
and *put breath* **give spirit** in you, and ye shall live;
and ye shall know that *I am the LORD* **I — Yah Veh**.
7 So I prophesied as I was *commanded* **misvahed**:
and as I prophesied, there was a *noise* **voice**,
and behold a *shaking* **quake**,
and the bones *came together* **approached**,
bone to his bone.
8 And when I *beheld* **saw**, *lo* **behold**,
the sinews and the flesh *came up* **ascended** upon them,
and the skin covered them above:
but there was no *breath* **spirit** in them.
9 Then said he unto me, Prophesy unto the *wind* **spirit**,
prophesy, son of *man* **humanity**,
and say to the *wind* **spirit**,
Thus saith *the Lord GOD* **Adonay Yah Veh**;
Come from the four *winds*, O *breath* **spirit**,
and *breathe* **puff** upon these *slain* **slaughtered**,
that they may live.

10 So I prophesied as he *commanded* **misvahed** me,
and the *breath* **spirit** came into them,
and they lived, and stood up upon their feet,
an exceeding great army **a mighty great valiant**.

THE INTERPRETATION

11 Then he said unto me, Son of *man* **humanity**,
these bones are the whole house of *Israel* **Yisra El**:
behold, they say,
Our bones are *dried* **withered**, and our hope is lost:
we are cut off for our parts.
12 Therefore prophesy and say unto them,
Thus saith *the Lord GOD* **Adonay Yah Veh**;
Behold, O my people,
I *will* **shall** open your *graves* **tombs**,
and cause you to *come up* **ascend**
out of your *graves* **tombs**,
and bring you into the *land* **soil** of *Israel* **Yisra El**.
13 And ye shall know that *I am the LORD* **I — Yah Veh**,
when I have opened your *graves* **tombs**, O my people,
and *brought* **ascended** you *up* out of your *graves* **tombs**,
14 And shall *put* **give** my spirit in you, and ye shall live,
and I shall *place* **set** you in your own *land* **soil**:
then shall ye know that I
the LORD **Yah Veh** have *spoken it* **worded**,
and *performed it* **worked**,
saith the LORD **an oracle of Yah Veh**.

YAH HUDAH AND YISRA EL BECOME ONE

15 The word of *the LORD* **Yah Veh** came again unto me,
saying,
16 Moreover, thou son of *man* **humanity**,
take thee one *stick* **tree**, and *write* **inscribe** upon it,
For *Judah* **Yah Hudah**,
and for the *children* **sons** of *Israel* **Yisra El**
his companions:
then take *another stick* **one tree**,
and *write* **inscribe** upon it,
For *Joseph* **Yoseph**, the *stick* **tree** of *Ephraim* **Ephrayim**
and for all the house of *Israel* **Yisra El** his companions:
17 And *join* **approach** them one to *another* **one**
into one *stick* **tree**;
and they shall become one in thine hand.
18 And when the *children* **sons** of thy people
shall *speak* **say** unto thee, saying,
wilt **shalt** thou not *shew* **tell** us
what *thou meanest by* these **be**?
19 *Speak* **Word** unto them,
Thus saith *the Lord GOD* **Adonay Yah Veh**;
Behold, I *will* **shall** take the *stick* **tree** of *Joseph* **Yoseph**,
which is in the hand of *Ephraim* **Ephrayim**,
and the *tribes* **scions** of *Israel* **Yisra El**
his *fellows* **companions**,
and *will put* **shall give** them with him,
even with the *stick* **tree** of *Judah* **Yah Hudah**,
and *make* **work** them one *stick* **tree**,
and they shall be one in mine hand.
20 And the *stick* **tree** whereon thou *writest* **inscribest**
shall be in thine hand before their eyes.
21 And *say* **word** unto them,
Thus saith *the Lord GOD* **Adonay Yah Veh**; Behold,
I *will* **shall** take the *children* **sons** of *Israel* **Yisra El**
from *among* **between** the *heathen* **goyim**,
whither they be gone,
and *will* **shall** gather them *on every side* **round about**,
and bring them into their own *land* **soil**:
22 And I *will make* **shall work** them one *nation* **goyim**
in the land upon the mountains of *Israel* **Yisra El**;
and one *king* **sovereign**
shall be *king* **sovereign** to them all:
and they shall be no more two *nations* **goyim**,
neither shall they be *divided* **halved**
into two *kingdoms* **sovereigndoms** any more *at all* **still**.
23 Neither shall they *defile* **foul** themselves
any more with their idols,
nor with their *detestable things* **abominations**,
nor with any of their *transgressions* **rebellions**:
but I *will* **shall** save them out of all their *dwellingplaces* **sites**,
wherein they have sinned,
and *will cleanse* **shall purify** them:
so *shall* they be my people,
and *I will be* **I AM** their *God* **Elohim**.

THE SOVEREIGNDOM OF DAVID

24 And David my servant
shall be *king* **sovereign** over them;
and they all shall have one *shepherd* **tender**:
they shall also walk in my judgments,
and *observe* **guard** my statutes, and *do* **work** them.
25 And they shall dwell in the land
that I have given unto *Jacob* **Yaaqov** my servant,
wherein your fathers have *dwelt* **settled**
and they shall *dwell* **settle** therein,
even they, and their *children* **sons**,
and their *children's children for ever* **sons' sons eternally**:
and my servant David
shall be their *prince for ever* **hierarch eternally**.

YAH VEH'S ETERNAL COVENANT

26 Moreover
I *will make* **shall cut** a covenant of *peace* **shalom**
with them;
it shall be an *everlasting* **eternal** covenant with them:
and I *will place* **shall give** them,
and *multiply* **abound** them,
and *will set* **shall give** my *sanctuary* **holies**
in the midst of them *for evermore* **eternally**.
27 My tabernacle also shall be with them:
yea, *I will be* **I AM** their *God* **Elohim**,
and they *shall* be my people.
28 And the *heathen* **goyim** shall know
that I *the LORD* **Yah Veh**
do sanctify Israel **hallow Yisra El**,
when my *sanctuary* **holies** shall be in the midst of them
for evermore **eternally**.

YAH VEH'S WORD CONCERNING GOG

38 And the word of *the LORD* **Yah Veh**
came unto me, saying,
2 Son of *man* **humanity**,
set thy face against Gog, the land of Magog,
the *chief prince* **Rosch hierarch**
of Meshech and Tubal,
and prophesy against him,
3 And say, Thus saith *the Lord GOD* **Adonay Yah Veh**;
Behold, I am against thee, O Gog,
the *chief prince* **Rosch hierarch**
of Meshech and Tubal:
4 And I *will* **shall** turn thee back,
and *put* **give** hooks into thy jaws,
and I *will* **shall** bring thee forth,
and all thine *army* **valiant**, horses and *horsemen* **cavalry**,
all of them *clothed* **enrobed**
with *all sorts of armour* **splendour**,
even a great *company* **congregation**
with *bucklers* **shields** and *shields* **bucklers**,
all of them *handling* **manipulating** swords:
5 Persia, *Ethiopia* **Kush**, and *Libya* **Put** with them;
all of them with *shield* **buckler** and helmet:
6 Gomer, and all his bands;
the house of Togarmah of the north *quarters* **flanks**,
and all his bands: and many people with thee.
7 Be thou prepared, and prepare for thyself,
thou, and all thy *company* **congregation**
that are *assembled* **congregated** unto thee,
and be thou a guard unto them.
8 After many days thou shalt be visited:
in the latter years thou shalt come into the land
that is *brought back* **restored** from the sword,
and is gathered out of many people,
against the mountains of *Israel* **Yisra El**,
which have been *always waste* **continually parched**:
but it is brought forth out of the *nations* **goyim**,
and they shall *dwell safely* **settle confidently** all of them.
9 Thou shalt ascend and *come* like a *storm* **devastation**,
thou shalt be like a cloud to cover the land,
thou, and all thy bands, and many people with thee.
10 Thus saith *the Lord GOD* **Adonay Yah Veh**;
It shall also *come to pass* **become**, that at the same time
shall *things come* **words ascend** into thy *mind* **heart**,
and thou shalt *think* **fabricate** an evil *thought* **fabrication**:
11 And thou shalt say,
I *will go up* **shall ascend**
to the land of *unwalled villages* **suburbs**;
I *will* **shall** go to them that *are at* rest,

that *dwell safely* **settle confidently**,
all of them *dwelling* **settling** without walls,
and having neither bars nor *gates* **doors**.
12 To *take* **spoil** a spoil,
and to *take a prey* **plunder a plunder**;
to turn thine hand
upon the *desolate places* **parched areas**
that are now inhabited,
and upon the people
that are gathered out of the *nations* **goyim**,
which have *gotten* **worked**
cattle **chattel** and *goods* **chattel**,
that *dwell in* **settle on** the *midst* **summit** of the land.
13 Sheba, and Dedan, and the merchants of Tarshish,
with all the *young lions* **whelps** *thereof*,
shall say unto thee, Art thou come to *take* **spoil** a spoil?
hast thou
gathered **congregated** thy *company* **congregation**
to *take* **plunder** a *prey* **plunder**?
to *carry* **bear** away silver and gold,
to take away *cattle* **chattel** and *goods* **chattel**,
to *take* **spoil** a great spoil?
14 Therefore, son of *man* **humanity**,
prophesy and say unto Gog,
Thus saith *the Lord GOD* **Adonay Yah Veh**;
In that day when my people of *Israel* **Yisra El**
dwelleth safely **settleth confidently**,
shalt thou not know it?
15 And thou shalt come
from thy place out of the north *parts* **flanks**,
thou, and many people with thee,
all of them riding upon horses,
a great *company* **congregation**,
and *a mighty army* **great valiant**:
16 And thou shalt *come up* **ascend**
against my people of *Israel* **Yisra El**,
as a cloud to cover the land;
it shall be in the latter days,
and I *will* **shall** bring thee against my land,
that the *heathen* **goyim** may know me
when I shall be *sanctified* **hallowed** in thee, O Gog,
before their eyes.
17 Thus saith *the Lord GOD* **Adonay Yah Veh**;
Art thou he
of whom I have *spoken* **worded** in *old* **ancient** time
by **the hand of** my servants the prophets of *Israel* **Yisra El**,
which prophesied in those days *many* years
that I *would* **should** bring thee against them?
18 And it shall *come to pass* **become,**
at the same time **in that day,**
when **the day** Gog shall come
against the *land* **soil** of *Israel* **Yisra El**,
saith the Lord GOD **an oracle of Adonay Yah Veh**,
that my fury shall *come up* **ascend** in my *face* **nostrils**.
19 For in my jealousy and in the fire of my wrath
have I *spoken* **worded**,
Surely in that day there shall be a great *shaking* **quake**
in the *land* **soil** of *Israel* **Yisra El**;
20 So that the fishes of the sea,
and the *fowls* **flyers** of the *heaven* **heavens**,
and the *beasts* **live beings** of the field,
and all *creeping things* **creepers**
that creep upon the *earth* **soil**,
and all the *men* **humans**
that are upon the face of the *earth* **soil**,
shall *shake* **quake** at my *presence* **face**,
and the mountains shall be *thrown down* **demolished**,
and the steep *places* **steps** shall fall,
and every wall shall fall to the *ground* **earth**.
21 And I *will* **shall** call for a sword against him
throughout all my mountains,
saith the Lord GOD **an oracle of Adonay Yah Veh**:
every man's sword shall be against his brother.
22 And I *will plead* **shall judge** against him
with pestilence and with blood;
and I *will* **shall** rain upon him, and upon his bands,
and upon the many people that are with him,
an overflowing *rain* **downpour**,
and great hailstones, fire, and *brimstone* **sulphur**.
23 Thus *will I magnify* **shall I greaten** myself,
and *sanctify* **hallow** myself;
and I *will* **shall** be known
in the eyes of many *nations* **goyim**,
and they shall know that *I am the LORD* **I — Yah Veh**.

39 Therefore, thou son of *man* **humanity**,
prophesy against Gog, and say,
Thus saith *the Lord GOD* **Adonay Yah Veh**;
Behold, I am against thee, O Gog,
the *chief prince* **Rosch hierarch**
of Meshech and Tubal:
2 And I *will* **shall** turn thee back,
and *leave but the sixth part of* **hexsect** thee,
and *will* **shall** cause thee to *come up* **ascend**
from the north *parts* **flanks**,
and *will* **shall** bring thee
upon the mountains of *Israel* **Yisra El**:
3 And I *will* **shall** smite thy bow out of thy left hand,
and *will* **shall** cause thine arrows
to fall out of thy right hand.
4 Thou shalt fall upon the mountains of *Israel* **Yisra El**,
thou, and all thy bands, and the people that is with thee:
I *will* **shall** give thee
unto the *ravenous* **swooper** birds of every *sort* **wing**,
and to the *beasts* **live beings** of the field
to be devoured **for food**.
5 Thou shalt fall upon the *open* **face of the** field:
for I have *spoken it* **worded**,
saith the Lord GOD **an oracle of Adonay Yah Veh**.
6 And I *will* **shall** send a fire on Magog,
and among them that *dwell carelessly* **settle confidently**
in the *isles* **islands**:
and they shall know that *I am the LORD* **I — Yah Veh**.
7 So *will* **shall** I make my holy name known
in the midst of my people *Israel* **Yisra El**;
and I *will* **shall** not
let them pollute **profane** my holy name any more:
and the *heathen* **goyim** shall know
that *I am the LORD* **I — Yah Veh**,
the Holy One in *Israel* **Yisra El**.
8 Behold, it *is* **hath** come, and it *is done* **hath become**,
saith the Lord GOD **an oracle of Adonay Yah Veh**;
this is the day whereof I have *spoken* **worded**.
9 And they that *dwell* **settle** in the cities of *Israel* **Yisra El**
shall go forth,
and shall *set on fire* **burn**
and burn the *weapons* **armament**,
both the *shields* **bucklers** and the *bucklers* **shields**,
the bows and the arrows,
and the handstaves, and the *spears* **javelins**,
and they shall burn them with fire seven years:
10 So that they shall
take **lift** no *wood* **timber** out of the field,
neither *cut down* **chop** any out of the forests;
for they shall burn the *weapons* **armaments** with fire:
and they shall spoil those that spoiled them,
and *rob* **plunder** those that *robbed* **plundered** them,
saith the Lord GOD **an oracle of Adonay Yah Veh**.
11 And it shall *come to pass* **become,** in that day,
that I *will* **shall** give unto Gog
a place there of *graves* **tombs** in *Israel* **Yisra El**,
the valley of *the passengers* **passersby**
on the east of the sea:
and it shall stop the *noses of the passengers* **passersby**:
and there shall they *bury* **entomb** Gog
and all his multitude:
and they shall call it
The *valley of Hamongog*
Valley of the Multitude of Gog/Gay Hamon Gog.
12 And seven months shall the house of *Israel* **Yisra El**
be burying of **entomb** them,
that they may *cleanse* **purify** the land.
13 Yea, all the people of the land shall *bury* **entomb** them;
and it shall be to them a *renown* **name**
the day that I shall be *glorified* **honoured**,
saith the Lord GOD **an oracle of Adonay Yah Veh**.
14 And they shall *sever out* **continually separate** men
of continual employment, passing through the land
to *bury* **entomb** with the *passengers* **the passersby**
those that remain upon the face of the earth,
to *cleanse* **purify** it:

after the end of seven months shall they *search* **probe**.
15 And the *passengers* **passersby**
that pass through the land,
when any seeth *a man's* **human** bone,
then shall he set *up a sign by* **a monument beside** it,
till the *buriers* **entombers** have *buried* **entombed** it
in the *valley of Hamongog*
Valley of the Multitude of Gog/Gay Hamon Gog.
16 And also the name of the city shall be Hamonah.
Thus shall they *cleanse* **purify** the land.
17 And, thou son of *man* **humanity**,
thus saith *the Lord GOD* **Adonay Yah Veh**;
Speak unto every *feathered fowl* **bird of wing**,
and to every *beast* **live being** of the field,
Assemble yourselves **Gather**, and come;
gather *yourselves on every side* **round about**
to my sacrifice that I *do* sacrifice for you,
even a great sacrifice
upon the mountains of *Israel* **Yisra El**,
that ye may eat flesh, and drink blood.
18 Ye shall eat the flesh of the mighty,
and drink the blood of the *princes* **hierarchs** of the earth,
of rams, of lambs, and of **he** goats, of bullocks,
all of them fatlings of Bashan.
19 And ye shall eat fat *till ye be full* **unto satiety**,
and drink blood till ye be *drunken* **intoxicated**,
of my sacrifice which I have sacrificed for you.
20 Thus ye shall be *filled* **satiated** at my table
with horses and chariots,
with mighty *men*, and with all men of war,
saith the Lord GOD **an oracle of Adonay Yah Veh**.
21 And I *will set* **shall give** my *glory* **honour**
among the *heathen* **goyim**,
and all the *heathen* **goyim** shall see my judgment
that I have *executed* **worked**,
and my hand that I have *laid* **set** upon them.
22 So the house of *Israel* **Yisra El** shall know
that *I am the LORD* **I — Yah Veh** their *God* **Elohim**
from that day and *forward* **beyond**.
23 And the *heathen* **goyim** shall know
that the house of *Israel* **Yisra El**
went into captivity **was exiled**
for their *iniquity* **perversity**:
because they *trespassed* **treasoned** against me,
therefore hid I my face from them,
and gave them
into the hand of their *enemies* **tribulators**:
so fell they all by the sword.
24 According to their *uncleanness* **foulness**
and according to their *transgressions* **rebellions**
have I *done* **worked** unto them,
and hid my face from them.

YAH VEH MERCIES YISRA EL

25 Therefore
thus saith *the Lord GOD* **Adonay Yah Veh**;
Now *will I bring again* **shall I return**
the captivity of *Jacob* **Yaaqov**,
and *have* mercy *upon* the whole house of *Israel* **Yisra El**,
and *will* **shall** be jealous for my holy name;
26 After that they have borne their shame,
and all their *trespasses* **treasons**
whereby they have *trespassed* **treasoned** against me,
when they *dwelt safely* **settled confidently**
in their *land* **soil**,
and none made them *afraid* **tremble**.
27 When I have *brought* **returned** them *again*
from the people,
and gathered them out of their enemies' lands,
and am *sanctified* **hallowed** in them
in the *sight* **eyes** of many *nations* **goyim**;
28 Then shall they know
that *I am the LORD* **I — Yah Veh** their *God* **Elohim**,
which caused them
to be *led into captivity* **exiled** among the *heathen* **goyim**:
but I have gathered them unto their own *land* **soil**,
and have *left* none of them **remain** any more there.
29 Neither *will* **shall** I hide my face any more from them:
for I have poured out my spirit
upon the house of *Israel* **Yisra El**,
saith the Lord GOD **an oracle of Adonay Yah Veh**.

THE HOUSE IS MEASURED

cp Apocalypse 11:1,2

40 In the five and twentieth year of our *captivity* **exile**,
in the beginning of the year,
in the tenth *day* of the month,
in the fourteenth year after that the city was smitten,
in the selfsame day
the hand of *the LORD* **Yah Veh** was upon me,
and brought me thither.
2 In the visions of *God* **Elohim**
brought he me into the land of *Israel* **Yisra El**,
and set **rested** me upon a *very* **mighty** high mountain,
by which was as the *frame* **building** of a city
on the south.
3 And he brought me thither, and, behold,
there was a man,
whose *appearance* **visage**
was like the *appearance* **visage** of *brass* **copper**,
with a line of flax in his hand,
and a measuring *reed* **stalk**;
and he stood in the *gate* **portal**.
4 And the man *said* **worded** unto me,
Son of *man* **humanity**,
behold **see** with thine eyes, and hear with thine ears,
and set thine heart
upon all that I shall *shew* **have** thee **see**;
for to the intent
that I might *shew* **have** them **see** unto thee
art thou brought hither:
declare **tell** all that thou seest
to the house of *Israel* **Yisra El**.
5 And behold a wall on the outside of the house
round about **and round about**,
and in the man's hand a measuring *reed* **stalk**
of six cubits *long* by the cubit
and *an hand breadth* **a palm span**:
so he measured the breadth of the building,
one *reed* **stalk**;
and the height, one *reed* **stalk**.
6 Then came he unto the *gate* **portal**
which *looketh toward the east* **faceth eastward**,
and *went up* **ascended** the *stairs* **steps** *thereof*,
and measured the threshold of the *gate* **portal**,
which was one *reed* **stalk** broad;
and the *other* **one** threshold *of the gate*,
which was one *reed* **stalk** broad.
7 And *every little* **each** chamber was one *reed* **stalk** long,
and one *reed* **stalk** broad;
and between the *little* chambers were five cubits;
and the threshold of the *gate* **portal**
by **beside** the porch of the *gate* **portal**
within **from the house** was one *reed* **stalk**.
8 He measured also the porch of the *gate* **portal**
within **from the house**, one *reed* **stalk**.
9 Then measured he the porch of the *gate* **portal**,
eight cubits;
and the *posts* **pilasters** *thereof*, two cubits;
and the porch of the *gate* **portal**
was inward **from the house**.
10 And the *little* chambers
of the *gate eastward* **portal of the way of the east**
were three *on this side* **here**, and three *on that side* **there**;
they three were of one measure:
and the *posts* **pilasters** had one measure
on this side **from here** and *on that side* **from there**.
11 And he measured
the breadth of the *entry* **opening** of the *gate* **portal**,
ten cubits;
and the length of the *gate* **portal**, thirteen cubits.
12 The *space* **border** *also*
before **at the face of** the *little* chambers
was one cubit *on this side* **from here**,
and the *space* **border**
was one cubit *on that side* **from there**:
and the *little* chambers
were six cubits *on this side* **from here**,
and six cubits *on that side* **from there**:.
13 He measured then the *gate* **portal**
from the roof of *one little* chamber to the roof *of another*:
the breadth was five and twenty cubits,

door **portal** against *door* **portal**.
14 He *made* **worked** also *posts* **pilasters**
of *threescore* **sixty** cubits,
even unto the *post* **pilaster** of the court
round about **and round about** the *gate* **portal**.
15 And from the face of the *gate* **portal** of the entrance
unto the face of the porch of the inner *gate* **portal**
were fifty cubits.
16 And there were *narrow* **shuttered** windows
to the *little* chambers,
and to their *posts* **pilasters** within the *gate* **portal**
round about **and round about**,
and likewise to the arches: and windows
were round about **and round about** *inward* **within**:
and upon each *post* **pilaster** were palm trees.

THE OUTWARD COURT

17 Then brought he me into the outward court,
and, *lo* **behold**, there were chambers,
and a pavement made for the court
round about **and round about**:
thirty chambers were upon the pavement.
18 And the pavement
by the *side* **shoulder** of the *gates* **portals**
over against **alongside** the length of the *gates* **portals**
was the *lower* **nether** pavement.
19 Then he measured the breadth
from the *forefront* **face** of the *lower gate* **nether portal**
unto the *forefront of* **face of** the inner court *without* **outward**,
an hundred cubits eastward and northward.

THE PORTAL AT THE FACE OF THE NORTHWARD WAY

20 And the *gate* **portal** of the outward court
that *looked toward* **faced** the *north* **northward way**
he measured the length *thereof*, and the breadth *thereof*.
21 And the *little* chambers *thereof*
were three *on this side* **from here**
and three *on that side* **from there**;
and the *posts* **pilasters** and the arches *thereof*
were after the measure of the first *gate* **portal**:
the length *thereof* was fifty cubits,
and the breadth five and twenty cubits.
22 And their windows, and their arches,
and their palm trees,
were after the measure of the *gate* **portal**
that *looketh toward* **faceth** the *east* **eastward way**;
and they *went up* **ascended** unto it by seven steps;
and the arches *thereof were before* **faced** them.
23 And the *gate* **portal** of the inner court
was over against the *gate* **portal**
toward the north **northward**,
and *toward the east* **eastward**;
and he measured from *gate* **portal** to *gate* **portal**
an hundred cubits.

THE PORTAL OF THE SOUTHWARD WAY

24 After that
he *brought* **carried** me *toward* the *south* **southward way**,
and behold a *gate* **portal**
toward the south **the southward way**:
and he measured the *posts* **pilasters** *thereof*
and the arches *thereof* according to these measures.
25 And there were windows in it and in the arches *thereof*
round about **and round about**, like those windows:
the length was fifty cubits,
and the breadth five and twenty cubits.
26 And there were seven steps *to go up to it* **of ascent**,
and the arches *thereof* were *before* **at the face of** them:
and it had palm trees,
one on this side **one from here**,
and *another on that side* **one from there**,
upon the *posts* **pilasters** *thereof*.
27 And there was a *gate* **portal** in the inner court
toward the south **the southward way**:
and he measured from *gate* **portal** to *gate* **portal**
toward the south **the southward way** an hundred cubits.

THE INNER COURT

28 And he brought me to the inner court
by the *south gate* **southward portal**
and he measured the *south gate* **southward portal**
according to these measures;
29 And the *little* chambers *thereof*,
and the *posts* **pilasters** *thereof*,
and the arches *thereof*, according to these measures:
and there were windows in it and in the arches *thereof*
round about **and round about**:
it was fifty cubits long, and five and twenty cubits broad.
30 And the arches round about **and round about**
were five and twenty cubits long, and five cubits broad.
31 And the arches *thereof*
were toward the *utter* **outer** court;
and palm trees were upon the *posts* **pilasters** *thereof*:
and the *going up to it* **ascent** had eight steps.
32 And he brought me into the inner court
toward **the way of** the east:
and he measured the *gate* **portal**
according to these measures.
33 And the *little* chambers *thereof*,
and the *posts* **pilasters** *thereof*, and the arches *thereof*,
were according to these measures:
and there were windows therein
and in the arches *thereof* round about **and round about**:
it was fifty cubits long, and five and twenty cubits broad.
34 And the arches *thereof* were toward the outward court;
and palm trees were upon the *posts* **pilasters** *thereof*,
on this side **from here**, and *on that side* **from there**:
and the *going up to it* **ascent** had eight steps.
35 And he brought me to the north *gate* **portal**,
and measured it according to these measures;
36 The *little* chambers *thereof*,
the *posts* **pilasters** *thereof*, and the arches *thereof*,
and the windows to it round about **and round about**:
the length was fifty cubits,
and the breadth five and twenty cubits.
37 And the *posts* **pilasters** *thereof*
were toward the utter court;
and palm trees were upon the *posts* **pilasters** *thereof*,
on this side **from here**, and *on that side* **from there**:
and the *going up to it* **ascent** had eight steps.

THE HOLOCAUST CHAMBERS

38 And the chambers and the *entries* **portals** *thereof*
were by the *posts* **pilasters** of the *gates* **portals**,
where they *washed* **cleansed**
the *burnt offering* **holocaust**.
39 And in the porch of the *gate* **portal**
were two tables *on this side* **from here**,
and two tables *on that side* **from there**,
to *slay* **slaughter** thereon the *burnt offering* **holocaust**
and *the sin offering* **that for the sin**
and *the trespass offering* **that for the guilt**.
40 And at the *side without* **shoulder outward**,
as one *goeth up* **ascendeth**
to the *entry* **opening** of the north *gate* **portal**,
were two tables;
and on the other *side* **shoulder**,
which was at the porch of the *gate* **portal**,
were two tables.
41 Four tables were *on this side* **from here**,
and four tables *on that side* **from there**,
by the *side* **shoulder** of the *gate* **portal**;
eight tables,
whereupon they *slew their sacrifices* **slaughtered**.
42 And the four tables were of hewn stone
for the *burnt offering* **holocaust**,
of *a* **one** cubit and an half long,
and *a* **one** cubit and an half broad,
and one cubit high:
whereupon also they *laid* **set** the instruments
wherewith they *slew* **slaughtered**
the *burnt offering* **holocaust** and the sacrifice.
43 And *within* **in the house** were hooks,
an hand broad **one palm span**,
fastened **established** round about **and round about**:
and upon the tables was the flesh of the *offering* **qorban**.

THE SINGERS' CHAMBERS

44 And *without* **outward** the inner *gate* **portal**
were the chambers of the singers in the inner court,
which was at the *side* **shoulder** of the north *gate* **portal**;
and their prospect **they faced**
was toward the south **the southward way**:
one at the *side* **shoulder** of the east *gate* **portal**
having the prospect **at the face**
toward the north **of the northward way**.

THE PRIESTS' CHAMBERS

45 And he *said* **worded** unto me,
This chamber,
whose prospect is toward the south
at the face of the southerly way,
is for the priests,
the *keepers* **guards** of the *charge* **guard** of the house.
46 And the chamber
whose prospect is toward the north
at the face of the northward
is for the priests,
the *keepers* **guards**
of the *charge* **guard** of the **sacrifice** altar:
these are the sons of *Zadok* **Sadoq**
among the sons of Levi,
which *come near to the LORD* **approach Yah Veh**
to minister unto him.
47 So he measured the court,
an hundred cubits long, and an hundred cubits broad,
foursquare **square**;
and the **sacrifice** altar
that was before **at the face of** the house.

THE HOUSE

48 And he brought me to the porch of the house,
and measured each *post* **pilaster** of the porch,
five cubits *on this side* **from here**,
and five cubits *on that side* **from there**:
and the breadth of the *gate* **portal**
was three cubits *on this side* **from here**,
and three cubits *on that side* **from there.**
49 The length of the porch was twenty cubits,
and the breadth eleven cubits,
and *he brought me by* the steps
whereby they *went up* **ascended** to it:
and there were pillars by the *posts* **pilasters**,
one on this side **one from here**,
and *another on that side* **one from there.**

THE MANSE

41 Afterward he brought me to the *temple* **manse**,
and measured the *posts* **pilasters**,
six cubits broad *on the one side* **from here**,
and six cubits broad *on the other side* **from there**,
which was the breadth of the *tabernacle* **tent**.
2 And the breadth of the *door* **opening** was ten cubits;
and the *sides* **shoulders** of the *door* **opening**
were five cubits *on the one side* **from here**,
and five cubits *on the other side* **from there**:
and he measured the length *thereof*, forty cubits:
and the breadth, twenty cubits.

THE HOLY OF HOLIES

3 Then went he *inward* **within**,
and measured the *post* **pilaster** of the *door* **opening**,
two cubits;
and the *door* **opening**, six cubits;
and the breadth of the *door* **opening**, seven cubits.
4 So he measured the length *thereof*, twenty cubits;
and the breadth, twenty cubits
before **at the face of** the *temple* **manse**:
and he said unto me,
This is the *most holy place* **holy of holies**.
5 After he measured the wall of the house, six cubits;
and the breadth of *every* side *chamber*, four cubits,
round about **and round about** the house
on every side **round about.**
6 And the *side chambers* **sides** were
three, one over another, and thirty in order
side by side thirty—three times;
and they entered into the wall which was of the house
for the *side chambers* **sides**
round about **and round about**,
that they might have hold,
but they had not **taken** hold in the wall of the house.
7 And there was an enlarging,
and a *winding* **spiraling** about
still upward **upward and upward**
to the *side chambers* **sides**:
for the *winding* **spiraling** about of the house
went *still upward* **upward and upward**
round about **and round about** the house:
therefore the breadth of the house
was *still upward* **upward and upward**,
and so *increased* **ascended**
from the *lowest* **nethermost** *chamber*
to the *highest* **most high** by the midst.
8 I saw also the height of the house
round about **and round about**:
the foundations of the *side chambers* **sides**
were a full *reed* **stalk** of six *great* **elbow** cubits.
9 The *thickness* **breadth** of the wall,
which was for the side *chamber without* **outward,**
was five cubits:
and that which was left was the *place* **house**
of the *side chambers that were within* **sides to the house.**
10 And between the chambers
was the *wideness* **breadth** of twenty cubits
round about **and round about** the house
on every side **round about.**
11 And the *doors* **openings** of the *side chambers* **sides**
were toward *the place* that **which** was left,
one *door* **opening**
toward **the way of** the north,
and *another door* **one opening**
toward the south **southerly**:
and the breadth of *the place* that **which** was left
was five cubits round about **and round about.**
12 *Now* the building
that was before **at the face**
of the *separate place* **separation**
at the *end toward the west* **edge of the way of the sea**
was seventy cubits broad;
and the wall of the building was five cubits *thick* **broad**
round about **and round about**,
and the length *thereof* ninety cubits.
13 So he measured the house, an hundred cubits long;
and the *separate place* **separation**, and the building,
with the walls *thereof*, an hundred cubits long;
14 Also the breadth of the face of the house,
and of the *separate place* **separation**
toward the east **eastward**,
an hundred cubits.
15 And he measured the length of the building
over against **at the face of** the *separate place* **separation**
which was behind it,
and the galleries *thereof*
on the one side **from here**
and *on the other side* **from there,**
an hundred cubits,
with the inner *temple* **manse**,
and the porches of the court;
16 The *door posts* **thresholds**,
and the *narrow* **shuttered** windows, and the galleries
round about **and round about** on their three *stories*,
over against the *door* **threshold**,
cieled with wood **with shingles of timber**
round about **and round about**,
and from the *ground* **earth** up to the windows,
and the windows were covered;
17 To that above the *door* **opening**,
even unto the inner house,
and *without* **outward**, and by all the wall
round about **and round about**
within **inward** and *without* **outward**, by measure.
18 And it was made
with *cherubims* **cherubim** and palm trees,
so that a palm tree was between a cherub and a cherub;
and *every* cherub had two faces;
19 So that the face of a *man* **human**
was toward the palm tree *on the one side* **from here**,
and the face of a *young lion* **whelp**
toward the palm tree *on the other side* **from there**:
it was made through all the house
round about **and round about.**
20 From the *ground* **earth** unto above the *door* **opening**
were *cherubims* **cherubim** and palm trees made,
and on the wall of the *temple* **manse**.
21 The posts of the *temple* **manse** were squared,
and the face of the *sanctuary* **holies**;
the *appearance of the one* **visage**
as the *appearance of the other* **visage.**
22 The **sacrifice** altar of *wood* **timber**

was three cubits high,
and the length *thereof* two cubits;
and the corners *thereof*, and the length *thereof*,
and the walls *thereof*, were of *wood* **timber**:
and he *said* **worded** unto me,
This is the table
that is *before the LORD* **at the face of Yah Veh**.
23 And the *temple* **manse** and the *sanctuary* **holies**
had two doors.
24 And the doors had two leaves *apiece*,
two *turning* **folding** leaves;
two *leaves* for the one door,
and two leaves for the other *door*.
25 And there were made on them,
on the doors of the *temple* **manse**,
cherubims **cherubim** and palm trees,
like as were made upon the walls;
and there were thick *planks* **timbers**
upon the face of the porch *without* **outward**.
26 And there were
narrow **shuttered** windows and palm trees
on the one side **from here**
and *on the other side* **from there**,
on the *sides* **shoulders** of the porch,
and *upon* the *side chambers* **sides** of the house,
and thick planks.

THE PRIESTS' CHAMBERS

42 Then he brought me forth into the *utter* **outer** court,
the *way toward the north* **northward way**:
and he brought me into the chamber
that was over against the *separate place* **separation**,
and which was before the building
toward the north **northward**.
2 *Before* **At the face of** the length of an hundred cubits
was the north *door* **opening**,
and the breadth was fifty cubits.
3 Over against the twenty *cubits*
which were for the inner court,
and over against the pavement
which was for the *utter* **outer** court,
was gallery *against* **at the face of** gallery
in *three stories* **tiers**.
4 And *before* **at the face of** the chambers
was a walk to ten cubits breadth inward,
a way of one cubit;
and their *doors toward the north* **openings northward**.
5 *Now* the *upper* **most high** chambers were shorter:
for the galleries *were higher* **contained** more than these,
than the *lower* **nether**,
and than the middlemost of the building.
6 For they were in *three stories* **tiers**,
but had not pillars as the pillars of the courts:
therefore *the building was straitened* **it was set**
more than the *lowest* **nethermost** and the middlemost
from the *ground* **earth**.
7 And the wall that was *without* **outward**
over against **alongside** the chambers,
toward the utter **the way of the outer** court
on the forepart **at the face** of the chambers,
the length *thereof* was fifty cubits.
8 For the length of the chambers
that were in the *utter* **outer** court was fifty cubits:
and, *lo* **behold**, *before* **at the face of** the *temple* **manse**
were an hundred cubits.
9 And from under these chambers
was the entry on the east *side*,
as one goeth into them from the *utter* **outer** court.
10 The chambers were in the *thickness* **breadth**
of the wall of the court
toward the east **to the eastward way**,
over against **at the face of** the *separate place* **separation**,
and *over against* **at the face of** the building.
11 And the way *before them* **at their face**
was like the *appearance* **visage** of the chambers
which were *toward the north* **to the northward way**,
as long as they, **as their length,**
and as broad as they **thus their breadth**:
and all their *goings out* **proceedings** were both
according to their *fashions* **judgments**,
and according to their *doors* **openings**.
12 And according to the *doors* **openings** of the chambers
that were *toward the south* **to the southward way**
was *a door* **an opening** in the head of the way,
even the way
directly before **turning at the face of** the wall
toward the east **to the eastward way**,
as one entereth into them.
13 Then said he unto me,
The *north* **northward** chambers
and the *south* **southward** chambers,
which are
before **at the face of** the *separate place* **separation**,
they be holy chambers,
where the priests that approach unto *the LORD* **Yah Veh**
shall eat the *most holy things* **holy of holies**:
there shall they *lay* **set**
the *most holy things* **holy of holies**,
and the *meat* offering,
and *the sin offering* **that for the sin**,
and *the trespass offering* **that for the guilt**;
for the place is holy.
14 When the priests enter therein,
then shall they not go out of the *holy place* **holies**
into the *utter* **outer** court,
but there they shall *lay* **set** their *garments* **clothes**
wherein they minister;
for they are holy;
and shall *put on* **enrobe** other *garments* **clothes**,
and shall approach to those *things*
which are for the people.

THE OUTWARD COURT IS MEASURED

15 *Now* when he had *made an end of* **finished**
measuring the inner house,
he brought me forth *toward* **the way of** the *gate* **portal**
whose prospect is toward **at the face**
of the *east* **eastward way**,
and measured it round about **and round about**.
16 He measured the east *side* **wind/spirit**
with the measuring *reed* **stalk**,
five *hundred reeds* **cubits of stalks**,
with the measuring *reed* **stalk**
round about **and round about**.
17 He measured the north *side* **wind/spirit**,
five hundred *reeds* **stalks**,
with the measuring *reed* **stalk**
round about **and round about**.
18 He measured the *south side* **southerly wind/spirit**,
five hundred *reeds* **stalks**, with the measuring *reed* **stalk**.
19 He turned about to the *west side* **seaward wind/spirit**,
and measured five hundred *reeds* **stalks**
with the measuring *reed* **stalk**.
20 He measured it by the four *sides* **winds/spirits**:
it had a wall round about **and round about**,
five hundred *reeds* long, and five hundred broad,
to *make a separation* **separate**
between the *sanctuary* **holies** and the profane *place*.

YAH VEH'S HONOUR FILLS THE HOUSE

43 Afterward he *brought* **carried** me to the *gate* **portal**,
even the *gate* **portal**
that *looketh toward* **faceth the way of** the east:
2 And, behold,
the *glory* **honour** of *the God* **Elohim** of *Israel* **Yisra El**
came from the way of the east:
and his voice was like a *noise* **voice** of many waters:
and the earth shined with his *glory* **honour**.
3 And it was according to the *appearance* **vision**
of the vision which I saw,
even according to the vision that I saw
when I came to *destroy* **ruin** the city:
and the visions were like the vision that I saw
by the river *Chebar* **Kebar**;
and I fell upon my face.
4 And the *glory* **honour** of *the LORD* **Yah Veh**
came into the house by the way of the *gate* **portal**
whose prospect is toward **at the face of the way**
of the east.
5 So the spirit *took* **bore** me *up*,
and brought me into the inner court; and, behold,
the *glory* **honour** of *the LORD* **Yah Veh** filled the house.
6 And I heard him speaking unto me out of the house;

and the man stood *by* **beside** me.
7 And he said unto me, Son of *man* **humanity**,
the place of my throne,
and the place of the soles of my feet,
where I *will dwell* **shall tabernacle**
in the midst of the *children* **sons** of *Israel* **Yisra El**
for ever **eternally**,
and my holy name,
shall the house of *Israel* **Yisra El** no more *defile* **foul**,
neither they, nor their *kings* **sovereigns**,
by their whoredom,
nor by the carcases of their *kings* **sovereigns**
in their *high places* **bamahs**.
8 In their *setting* **giving** of their threshold
by my thresholds,
and their post *by* **beside** my posts,
and the wall between me and **between** them,
they have even *defiled* **fouled** my holy name
by their *abominations* **abhorrences**
that they have *committed* **worked**:
wherefore I have *consumed* **finished** them **off**
in *mine anger* **my wrath**.
9 Now let them *put away* **far remove** their whoredom,
and the carcases of their *kings* **sovereigns**,
remove far from me,
and I *will dwell* **shall tabernacle** in the midst of them
for ever **eternally**.
10 Thou son of *man* **humanity**,
shew **tell** the house, to the house of *Israel* **Yisra El**,
that they may be ashamed
of their *iniquities* **perversities**:
and let them measure the *pattern* **gauge**.
11 And if they be ashamed
of all that they have *done* **worked**,
shew **make** them **know** the form of the house,
and the *fashion* **structure** *thereof*,
and the *goings out* **exits** *thereof*,
and the *comings in* **entrances** *thereof*,
and all the forms *thereof*,
and all the *ordinances* **statutes** *thereof*,
and all the forms *thereof*,
and all the *laws* **torah** *thereof*:
and *write it* **inscribe** in their *sight* **eyes**,
that they may *keep* **guard** the whole form *thereof*,
and all the *ordinances* **statutes** *thereof*,
and *do* **work** them.
12 This is the *law* **torah** of the house;
Upon the top of the mountain
the whole *limit* **border** *thereof*
round about **and round about**
shall be *most holy* **the holy of holies**.
Behold, this is the *law* **torah** of the house.

The Altar is Measured

13 And these are the measures of the **sacrifice** altar
after the cubits:
The cubit is a cubit and *an hand breadth* **palm span**;
even the *bottom* shall *be* **bosom** a cubit,
and the breadth a cubit,
and the border *thereof* by the *edge* **lip** *thereof*
round about shall be *a* **one** span:
and this shall be
the *higher place* **arch** of the **sacrifice** altar.
14 And from the *bottom upon* **bosom of** the *ground* **earth**
even to the *lower settle* **nether ledge**
shall be two cubits,
and the breadth one cubit;
and from the lesser *settle* **ledge**
even to the greater *settle* **ledge**
shall *be* four cubits,
and the breadth *one* cubit.
15 *So* **And** the altar shall be four cubits;
and from *the altar* **Ari El** and upward shall be four horns.
16 And *the altar* **Ari El** shall be twelve *cubits* long,
twelve broad, square in the four *squares* **quarters** *thereof*.
17 And the *settle* **ledge** shall be fourteen *cubits* long
and fourteen broad in the four *squares* **quarters** *thereof*;
and the border **round** about it shall be half a cubit;
and the *bottom thereof* **bosom**
shall be a cubit **round** about;
and his *stairs* **steps** shall *look toward* **face** the east.

The Ordinances of the Sacrifice Altar

18 And he said unto me, Son of *man* **humanity**,
thus saith *the Lord GOD* **Adonay Yah Veh**;
These are the ordinances of the **sacrifice** altar
in the day when they shall make it,
to *offer burnt offerings* **holocaust holocausts** thereon,
and to sprinkle blood thereon.
19 And thou shalt give to the priests
the *Levites* **Leviym** that be of the seed of *Zadok* **Sadoq**,
which approach unto me, to minister unto me,
saith the Lord GOD **an oracle of Adonay Yah Veh**,
a young **an ox son of a** bullock for *a sin offering* **the sin**.
20 And thou shalt take of the blood *thereof*,
and *put* **give** it on the four horns of it,
and on the four corners of the *settle* **ledge**,
and upon the border round about:
thus shalt thou cleanse and *purge* **kapar/atone** it.
21 Thou shalt take the bullock also
of *the sin offering* **that for the sin**,
and he shall burn it
in the *appointed* **specified** place of the house,
without the *sanctuary* **holies**.
22 And on the second day
thou shalt *offer a kid* **oblate a buck** of the **doe** goats
without blemish for a sin offering **integrious for the sin**;
and they shall cleanse the **sacrifice** altar,
as they *did cleanse it* **cleansed** with the bullock.
23 When thou hast *made an end of* **finished** cleansing it,
thou shalt *offer a young* **oblate an ox son of a** bullock,
without blemish **integrious**,
and a ram out of the flock, *without blemish* **integrious**.
24 And thou shalt *offer* **holocaust** them
before the LORD **at the face of Yah Veh**,
and the priests shall cast salt upon them,
and they shall *offer* **oblate** them *up*
for a *burnt offering* **holocaust** unto *the LORD* **Yah Veh**.
25 Seven days shalt thou *prepare* **work** every day
a goat for a sin offering **a buck for the sin**:
they shall also *prepare* **work**
a young **an ox son of a** bullock,
and a ram out of the flock, *without blemish* **integrious**.
26 Seven days shall they
purge **kapar/atone** the **sacrifice** altar and purify it;
and they shall *consecrate themselves* **fill their hands**.
27 And when these days are *expired* **finished**, it shall be,
that upon the eighth day, and *so forward* **beyond**,
the priests shall *make* **work**
your *burnt offerings* **holocausts** upon the **sacrifice** altar,
and your *peace offerings* **shelamim**;
and I *will accept* **shall be pleased with** you,
saith the Lord GOD **an oracle of Adonay Yah Veh**.

Yah Veh's Portal is Shut

44 Then he *brought* **turned** me back
the way of the *gate* **portal**
of the outward *sanctuary* **holies**
which *looketh* **faceth** toward the east; and it was shut.
2 Then said *the LORD* **Yah Veh** unto me;
This *gate* **portal** shall be shut, it shall not be opened,
and no man shall enter in by it;
because
the LORD **Yah Veh**, *the God* **Elohim** of *Israel* **Yisra El**,
hath entered in by it, therefore it shall be shut.
3 It is for the *prince* **hierarch**;
the prince, he shall sit in it to eat bread
before the LORD **at the face of Yah Veh**;
he shall enter by the way of the porch of that *gate* **portal**,
and shall go out by the way of the same.
4 Then brought he me the way of the north *gate* **portal**
before **at the face of** the house:
and I *looked* **saw**, and, behold,
the *glory* **honour** of *the LORD* **Yah Veh**
filled the house of *the LORD* **Yah Veh**:
and I fell upon my face.
5 And *the LORD* **Yah Veh** said unto me,
Son of *man* **humanity**, *mark well* **set thine heart**,
and *behold* **see** with thine eyes, and hear with thine ears
all that I say unto thee
concerning all the *ordinances* **statutes**
of the house of *the LORD* **Yah Veh**,
and all the *laws* **torah** *thereof*;

and *mark well* **set thy heart**
to the *entering in* **entrance** of the house,
with every *going forth* **exit** of the *sanctuary* **holies**.
6 And thou shalt say to the rebellious,
even to the house of *Israel* **Yisra El**,
Thus saith *the Lord GOD* **Adonay Yah Veh**;
O ye house of *Israel* **Yisra El**,
let it suffice you **Enough**
of all your *abominations* **abhorrences**,
7 In that ye have brought *into my sanctuary*
in sons of strangers,
uncircumcised in heart, and uncircumcised in flesh,
to be in my *sanctuary* **holies**, to *pollute* **profane** it,
even my house,
when ye *offer* **oblate** my bread, the fat and the blood,
and they have broken my covenant
because of **as to** all your *abominations* **abhorrences**.
8 And ye have not *kept* **guarded** the *charge* **guard**
of mine *holy things* **holies**:
but ye have set *keepers* **guards** of my *charge* **guard**
in my *sanctuary* **holies** for yourselves.
9 Thus saith *the Lord GOD* **Adonay Yah Veh**;
No **son of a** stranger,
uncircumcised in heart, nor uncircumcised in flesh,
shall enter into my *sanctuary* **holies**,
of any **son of a** stranger
that is among the *children* **sons** of *Israel* **Yisra El**.

THE IDOLATROUS LEVIYM

10 And the *Levites* **Leviym**
that *are gone away* far **removed** from me,
when *Israel went astray* **Yisra El strayed**,
which *went astray* **strayed** away from me after their idols;
they shall even bear their *iniquity* **perversity**.
11 Yet they shall be ministers in my *sanctuary* **holies**,
having charge at the *gates* **portals** of the house,
and ministering to the house:
they shall *slay* **slaughter** the *burnt offering* **holocaust**
and the sacrifice for the people,
and they shall stand *before* **at the face of** them
to minister unto them.
12 Because they ministered unto them
before **at the face of** their idols,
and *caused* **became to** the house of *Israel* **Yisra El**
to fall into iniquity **a stumblingblock of perversity**;
therefore have I lifted up mine hand against them,
saith the Lord GOD **an oracle of Adonay Yah Veh**,
and they shall bear their *iniquity* **perversity**.
13 And they shall not come near unto me,
to *do the office of a priest* **priest the priethood** unto me,
nor to come near to any of my *holy things* **holies**,
in the *most holy place* **holy of holies**:
but they shall bear their shame,
and their *abominations* **abhorrences**
which they have *committed* **worked**.
14 But I *will make* **shall give** them
keepers **guards** of the *charge* **guard** of the house,
for all the service *thereof*,
and for all that shall be *done* **worked** therein.

THE TRUSTWORTHY LEVIYM

15 But the priests the *Levites* **Leviym**,
the sons of *Zadok* **Sadoq**,
that *kept* **guarded**
the *charge* **guard** of my *sanctuary* **holies**
when the *children* **sons** of *Israel* **Yisra El**
went astray **strayed** from me,
they shall *come near to* **approach** me
to minister unto me,
and they shall stand *before me* **at my face**
to *offer* **oblate** unto me the fat and the blood,
saith the Lord GOD **an oracle of Adonay Yah Veh**:
16 They shall enter into my *sanctuary* **holies**,
and they shall *come near to* **approach** my table,
to minister unto me,
and they shall *keep* **guard** my *charge* **guard**.
17 And it shall *come to pass* **become**,
that when they enter in
at the *gates* **portals** of the inner court,
that they shall *be clothed* **enrobe**
with *linen garments* **flax clothes**;
and no wool shall *come* **ascend** upon them,
whiles they minister
in the *gates* **portals** of the inner court,
and *within* **the house**.
18 They shall have *linen bonnets* **flax tiaras**
upon their heads,
and shall have *linen* **flax** breeches upon their loins;
they shall not gird *themselves*
with any *thing that causeth sweat* **sweater**.
19 And when they go forth into the *utter* **outer** court,
even into the *utter* **outer** court to the people,
they shall *put off* **strip** their *garments* **clothes**
wherein they ministered,
and *lay* **leave** them in the holy chambers,
and they shall put on other *garments* **clothes**;
and they shall not *sanctify* **hallow** the people
with their *garments* **clothes**.
20 Neither shall they shave their heads,
nor *suffer* **extend** their locks *to grow long*;
they shall only *poll* **shear** their heads.
21 Neither shall any priest drink wine,
when they enter into the inner court.
22 Neither shall they take for their *wives* **women**
a widow,
nor her that is *put away* **expelled**:
but they shall take *maidens* **virgins**
of the seed of the house of *Israel* **Yisra El**,
or a widow
that *had a priest before* **was the widow of a priest**.
23 And they shall teach my people
the difference between *the* holy and **between** profane,
and cause them to *discern* **know**
between *the unclean* **foul** and *the clean* **between pure**.
24 And in controversy
they shall stand *in judgment* **and judge**;
and they shall judge *it* according to my judgments:
and they shall *keep* **guard** my *laws* **torah** and my statutes
in all *mine assemblies* **my congregations**;
and they shall hallow my *sabbaths* **shabbaths**.
25 And they shall come at no dead *person* **human**
to *defile* **foul** themselves:
but for father, or for mother, or for son, or for daughter,
for brother, or for sister that hath had no *husband* **man**,
they may *defile* **foul** *themselves*.
26 And after he is *cleansed* **purified**,
they shall *reckon* **scribe** unto him seven days.
27 And in the day that he goeth into the *sanctuary* **holies**,
unto the inner court, to minister in the *sanctuary* **holies**,
he shall *offer his sin offering* **oblate for his sin**,
saith the Lord GOD **an oracle of Adonay Yah Veh**.
28 And it shall be unto them for an inheritance:
I am their inheritance:
and ye shall give them no possession in *Israel* **Yisra El**:
I am their possession.
29 They shall eat the *meat* offering,
and *the sin offering* **that for the sin**,
and *the trespass offering* **that for the guilt**:
and every *dedicated thing* **devotement** in *Israel* **Yisra El**
shall be theirs.
30 And the *first* **firstlings** of all the firstfruits of all *things*,
and every *oblation* **exaltment** of all,
of *every sort* **all** of your *oblations* **exaltments**,
shall be the priest's:
ye shall also give unto the priest
the *first* **firstlings** of your dough,
that he may *cause* **rest** the blessing *to rest* in thine house.
31 The priests shall not eat
of any *thing that is dead of itself* **carcase**, or torn,
whether it be *fowl* **flyer** or *beast* **animal**.

FELLING THE LAND

45 *Moreover*, when ye shall
divide by lot **fell** the land for inheritance,
ye shall *offer* **lift** an *oblation* **exaltment**
unto *the LORD* **Yah Veh**,
an *holy portion* **holies** of the land:
the length
shall be the length of five and twenty thousand *reeds*,
and the breadth shall be ten thousand.
This shall be holy in all the borders *thereof* round about.
2 Of this there shall be for the *sanctuary* **holies**
five hundred *in length, with* **by** five hundred *in breadth*,

square round about;
and fifty cubits round about for the suburbs *thereof*.
3 And of this measure shalt thou measure
the length of five and twenty thousand,
and the breadth of ten thousand:
and in it shall be the *sanctuary* **holies**
and the *most holy place* **holy of holies**.
4 The *holy portion* **holies** of the land
shall be for the priests
the ministers of the *sanctuary* **holies**,
which shall *come near* **approach**
to minister unto *the LORD* **Yah Veh**:
and it shall be a place for their houses,
and an holy place for the sanctuary — **a holies**.
5 And the five and twenty thousand of length,
and the ten thousand of breadth,
shall *also* the *Levites* **Leviym**, the ministers of the house,
have for themselves,
for a possession for twenty chambers.
6 And ye shall *appoint* **give** the possession of the city
five thousand broad, and five and twenty thousand long,
over against **alongside** the *oblation* **exaltment**
of the *holy portion* **holies**:
it shall be for the whole house of *Israel* **Yisra El**.
7 And *a portion* **there** shall be for the *prince* **hierarch**
on the one side **from here**
and *on the other side* **from there**
of the *oblation* **exaltment** of the *holy portion* **holies**,
and of the possession of the city,
before the oblation **at the face of the exaltment**
of the *holy portion* **holies**,
and *before* **at the face of** the possession of the city,
from the *west side westward* **sea edge seaward**,
and from the east *side* **edge** eastward:
and the length shall be
over against **alongside** one of the *portions* **allotments**,
from the *west* **seaward** border unto the east border.
8 In the land shall be his possession in *Israel* **Yisra El**:
and my *princes* **hierarchs**
shall no more oppress my people;
and *the rest of* the land
shall they give to the house of *Israel* **Yisra El**
according to their *tribes* **scions**.

YAH VEH'S BALANCE SYSTEM

9 *Thus saith the Lord GOD*
An oracle of Adonay Yah Veh;
Let it suffice **Enough of** you,
O *princes* **hierarchs** of *Israel* **Yisra El**:
remove **turn aside** violence and *spoil* **ravage**,
and *execute* **work** judgment and *justice* **justness**,
take away **lift** your *exactions* **expulsions** from my people,
saith *the Lord GOD* **Adonay Yah Veh**.
10 *Ye shall have just balances* **Balances of justness**,
and a just ephah **an ephah of justness**,
and a just bath **a bath of justness**.
11 The ephah and the bath
shall be of one *measure* **gauge**,
that the bath may *contain* **bear**
the *tenth part* **tithe** of an *homer* **chomer**,
and the ephah the tenth *part* of an *homer* **chomer**:
the *measure* **quantity** *thereof* shall be
after the *homer* **chomer**.
12 And the shekel shall be twenty gerahs:
twenty shekels, five and twenty shekels, fifteen shekels,
shall be your maneh.

OFFERINGS

13 This is the *oblation* **exaltment** that ye shall *offer* **lift**;
the sixth *part* of an ephah of an *homer* **chomer** of wheat,
and ye shall give the sixth part of — **hexsect**
an ephah of an *homer* **chomer** of barley:
14 Concerning the *ordinance* **statute** of oil,
the bath of oil,
ye shall *offer* the *tenth part* **tithe** of a bath out of the cor,
which is an *homer* **chomer** of ten baths;
for ten baths are an *homer* **chomer**:
15 And one lamb out of the flock, out of two hundred,
out of the *fat pastures* **moist areas** of *Israel* **Yisra El**;
for *a meat* **an** offering,
and for a *burnt offering* **holocaust**,
and for *peace offerings* **shelamim**,
to *make reconciliation* **kapar/atone** for them,
saith the Lord GOD **an oracle of Adonay Yah Veh**.
16 All the people of the land
shall give this *oblation* **exaltment**
for the *prince* **hierarch** in *Israel* **Yisra El**.
17 And it shall be the *prince's part* **hierarch's**
to give burnt offerings **for holocausts**,
and *meat* offerings,
and *drink offerings* **libations**,
in the *feasts* **celebrations**,
and in the new moons, and in the *sabbaths* **shabbaths**,
in all *solemnities* **seasons** of the house of *Israel* **Yisra El**:
he shall *prepare the sin offering* **work that for the sin**,
and the *meat* offering, and the *burnt offering* **holocaust**,
and the *peace offerings* **shelamim**,
to *make reconciliation* **kapar/atone**
for the house of *Israel* **Yisra El**.
18 Thus saith *the Lord GOD* **Adonay Yah Veh**;
In the first *month*, in the first *day* of the month,
thou shalt take *a young* **an ox son of a** bullock,
without blemish **integrious**,
and cleanse the *sanctuary* **holies**:
19 And the priest shall take of the blood
of *the sin offering* **that for the sin**,
and *put* **give** it upon the posts of the house,
and upon the four corners
of the *settle* **ledge** of the **sacrifice** altar,
and upon the posts of the *gate* **portal** of the inner court.
20 And so thou shalt *do* **work**
the seventh *day* of the month
for every *one* **man** that erreth **inadvertently**,
and for *him that is simple* **the gullible**:
so shall ye *reconcile* **kapar/atone** the house.
21 In the first *month*, in the fourteenth day of the month,
ye shall have the *passover* **pasach**,
a *feast* **celebration** of *seven* **a week of** days;
unleavened bread **matsah** shall be eaten.
22 And upon that day shall the *prince* **hierarch**
prepare **work** for himself
and for all the people of the land
a bullock for *a sin offering* **the sin**.
23 And seven days of the *feast* **celebration**
he shall *prepare* **work** a *burnt offering* **holocaust**
to *the LORD* **Yah Veh**,
seven bullocks and seven rams
without blemish **integrious** daily the seven days;
and a *kid* **buck** of the **doe** goats daily
for *a sin offering* **the sin**.
24 And he shall *prepare a meat* **work an** offering
of an ephah for a bullock, and an ephah for a ram,
and an hin of oil for an ephah.
25 In the seventh *month*,
in the fifteenth day of the month,
shall he *do* **work** the like
in the *feast* **celebration** of the seven days,
according to the sin offering **as that for the sin**,
according to the burnt offering **so that for the holocaust**,
and according to the meat offering **as for the offering**,
and according to **so for** the oil.

THE OFFERINGS OF RULERS

46 Thus saith *the Lord GOD* **Adonay Yah Veh**;
The *gate* **portal** of the inner court
that *looketh* **faceth** toward the east
shall be shut the six *working days* **days of work**;
but on the *sabbath* **shabbath** it shall be opened,
and in the day of the new moon it shall be opened.
2 And the *prince* **hierarch** shall enter
by the way of the porch
of that *gate without* **portal outward**,
and shall stand by the post of the *gate* **portal**,
and the priests
shall *prepare* **work** his *burnt offering* **holocaust**
and his *peace offerings* **shelamim**,
and he shall *worship* **prostrate**
at the threshold of the *gate* **portal**:
then he shall go forth;
but the *gate* **portal** shall not be shut until the evening.
3 Likewise the people of the land shall *worship* **prostrate**
at the *door* **opening** of this *gate* **portal**
before the LORD **at the face of Yah Veh**

in the *sabbaths* **shabbaths** and in the new moons.
4 And the *burnt offering* **holocaust**
that the *prince* **hierarch** shall *offer* **oblate**
unto *the LORD* **Yah Veh** in the *sabbath* **shabbath** day
shall be six lambs *without blemish* **integrious**,
and a ram *without blemish* **integrious**.
5 And the *meat* offering shall be an ephah for a ram,
and the *meat* offering for the lambs
as he shall be *able to give* **the gift of his hand**,
and an hin of oil to an ephah.
6 And in the day of the new moon
it shall be *a young* **an ox son of a** bullock
without blemish **integrious**,
and six lambs, and a ram:
they shall be *without blemish* **integrious**.
7 And he shall *prepare a meat* **work an** offering,
an ephah for a bullock, and an ephah for a ram,
and for the lambs
according as his hand shall *attain unto* **attain**,
and an hin of oil to an ephah.
8 And when the *prince* **hierarch** shall enter,
he shall go in by the way of the porch of that *gate* **portal**,
and he shall go forth by the way *thereof*.
9 But when the people of the land
shall come *before the LORD* **at the face of Yah Veh**
in the *solemn feasts* **seasons**,
he that entereth in by the way of the north *gate* **portal**
to *worship* **prostrate**
shall go out by the way of the south *gate* **portal**;
and he that entereth by the way of the south *gate* **portal**
shall go forth by the way of the north *gate* **portal**:
he shall not return by the way of the *gate* **portal**
whereby he came in,
but shall go forth *over against* **opposite** it.
10 And the *prince* **hierarch** in the midst of them,
when they go in, shall go in;
and when they go forth, shall go forth.
11 And in the *feasts* **celebrations**
and in the *solemnities* **seasons**
the *meat* offering shall be an ephah to a bullock,
and an ephah to a ram,
and to the lambs as *he is able to give* **the gift of his hand**,
and an hin of oil to an ephah.
12 Now when the *prince* **hierarch**
shall *prepare* **work** a voluntary *burnt offering* **holocaust**
or *peace offerings voluntarily* **voluntary shelamim**
unto *the LORD* **Yah Veh**,
one **he** shall then open him the *gate* **portal**
that *looketh* **faceth** toward the east,
and he shall *prepare* **work** his *burnt offering* **holocaust**
and his *peace offerings* **shelamim**,
as he *did* **worked** on the *sabbath* **shabbath** day:
then he shall go forth;
and after his going forth
one **he** shall shut the *gate* **portal**.
13 Thou shalt daily *prepare* **work**
a *burnt offering* **holocaust** unto *the LORD* **Yah Veh**
of a lamb *of the first year* **a yearling son**
without blemish **integrious**:
thou shalt *prepare* **work** it
every morning **morning by morning**.
14 And thou shalt *prepare a meat* **work an** offering for it
every morning **morning by morning**,
the sixth *part* of an ephah,
and the third part of an hin of oil,
to *temper* **sprinkle** with the *fine* flour;
a meat **an** offering continually
by *a perpetual ordinance* **an eternal statute**
unto *the LORD* **Yah Veh**.
15 Thus shall they *prepare* **work** the lamb,
and the *meat* offering, and the oil,
every morning **morning by morning**
for a continual *burnt offering* **holocaust**.

RIGHTS OF INHERITANCE

16 Thus saith *the Lord GOD* **Adonay Yah Veh**;
If the *prince* **hierarch**
give a gift unto any **man** of his sons,
the inheritance *thereof* shall be his sons';
it shall be their possession by inheritance.
17 But if he give a gift of his inheritance
to one of his servants,
then it shall be his to the year of liberty;
after it shall return to the *prince* **hierarch**:
but his inheritance shall be his sons' for them.
18 Moreover the *prince* **hierarch**
shall not take of the people's inheritance by oppression,
to thrust them out of their possession;
but *he shall give* **that** his sons *inheritance* **shall inherit**
out of his own possession:
that my people be not scattered
every man from his possession.
19 After he brought me through the entry,
which was at the *side* **shoulder** of the *gate* **portal**,
into the holy chambers of the priests,
which *looketh toward the north* **faceth northward**:
and, behold, there was a place
on the two *sides westward* **flanks seaward**.

THE STEWING PLACE

20 Then said he unto me,
This is the place where the priests
shall *boil the trespass offering* **stew that for the guilt**
and *the sin offering* **that for the sin**,
where they shall bake the *meat* offering;
that they bear them not out into the *utter* **outer** court,
to *sanctify* **hallow** the people.
21 Then he brought me forth into the *utter* **outer** court,
and caused me to pass by the four corners of the court;
and, behold,
in every corner of the court there was a court
a court in the corner of a court,
a court in the corner of a court.
22 In the four corners of the court there were courts
joined **enclosed** of forty *cubits* long and thirty broad:
these four corners were of one measure.
23 And there was a row *of building* round about in them,
round about them four,
and it was made with *boiling places* **hearths**
under the *rows* **walls** round about.
24 Then said he unto me,
These are the *places* **houses** of them that *boil* **stew**,
where the ministers of the house
shall *boil* **stew** the sacrifice of the people.

WATERS ISSUE OUT FROM THE HOUSE

47 *Afterward he brought me again* **And he returned me**
unto the *door* **opening** of the house;
and, behold, waters issued out
from under the threshold of the house eastward:
for the *forefront* **face** of the house
stood toward the east **is eastward**,
and the waters *came down* **descended**
from under from the right *side* **shoulder** of the house,
at the south *side* of the **sacrifice** altar.
2 Then brought he me
out of the way of the *gate* **portal** northward,
and *led* **turned** me about the way *without* **outward**
unto the *utter gate* **outward portal**
by the way that *looketh* **faceth** eastward;
and, behold,
there *ran out* **poured** waters on the right *side* **shoulder**.

THE WATERS MEASURED

3 And when the man that had the line in his hand
went forth eastward,
he measured a thousand cubits,
and he *brought* **passed** me through the waters;
the waters were to the ankles.
4 Again he measured a thousand,
and *brought* **passed** me through the waters;
the waters were to the knees.
Again he measured a thousand,
and *brought* **passed** me through;
the waters were to the loins.
5 Afterward he measured a thousand;
and it was a *river* **wadi** that I could not pass over:
for the waters were risen, waters to swim in,
a *river* **wadi** that could not be passed over.
6 And he said unto me,
Son of *man* **humanity**, hast thou seen *this*?
Then he *brought* **carried** me,
and caused me to return to the *brink* **lip** of the *river* **wadi**.
7 *Now* when I had returned, behold,

at the *bank* **lip** of the *river* **wadi**
were *very* **mighty** many trees
on the one side **from here** and *on the other* **from there**.
8 Then said he unto me,
These waters issue out toward the east *country* **region**,
and *go down* **descend** into the *desert* **plain**,
and go into the sea:
which being brought forth into the sea,
the waters shall be healed.
9 And it shall *come to pass* **become**,
that every *thing* **soul** that liveth, which *moveth* **teemeth**,
whithersoever the *rivers* **wadies** shall come, shall live:
and there shall be a *very* **mighty** great multitude of fish,
because these waters shall come thither:
for they shall be healed;
and *every thing* **all** shall live
whither the *river* **wadi** cometh.
10 And it shall *come to pass* **become**,
that the fishers shall stand upon it
from *Engedi* **En Gedi** even unto *Eneglaim* **En Eglayim**;
they shall *be a place* **become** to spread forth nets;
their fish shall be *according to their kinds* **in species**,
as the fish of the great sea, *exceeding* **mighty** many.
11 But the *miry places* **mires** *thereof*
and the *marishes* **dugouts** *thereof* shall not be healed;
they shall be given to salt.
12 And by the *river* **wadi** upon the *bank* **lip** *thereof*,
on this side **from here** and *on that side* **from there**,
shall *grow* **ascend** all trees for *meat* **food**,
whose leaf shall not *fade* **wither**,
neither shall the fruit *thereof* be consumed:
it shall bring forth new fruit according to his months,
because their waters
they issued out of the *sanctuary* **holies**:
and the fruit *thereof* shall be for *meat* **food**,
and the leaf *thereof* for *medicine* **healing**.

THE BORDERS OF THE LAND

13 Thus saith *the Lord GOD* **Adonay Yah Veh**;
This shall be the border,
whereby ye shall inherit the land
according to the twelve *tribes* **scions** of *Israel* **Yisra El**:
Joseph **Yoseph** shall have *two portions* **boundaries**.
14 And ye shall inherit it,
one as well **man** as *another* **brother**:
concerning the which I lifted up mine hand
to give it unto your fathers:
and this land shall fall unto you for inheritance.
15 And this shall be the border of the land
toward the north *side* **edge**,
from the great sea,
the way of Hethlon, as men go to *Zedad* **Sedad**;
16 Hamath, Berothah, *Sibraim* **Sibrayim**,
which is between the border of *Damascus* **Dammeseq**
and **between** the border of Hamath;
Hazar—hatticon **Hasar Hat Tichon**,
which is by the *coast* **border** of Hauran.
17 And the border from the sea
shall be *Hazarenan* **Hasar Enon**,
the border of *Damascus* **Dammeseq**,
and the north northward, and the border of Hamath.
And this is the north *side* **edge**.
18 And the east *side* **edge**
ye shall measure *from* **between** Hauran,
and *from Damascus* **between Dammeseq**,
and *from Gilead* **between Gilad**,
and *from* **between** the land of *Israel* **Yisra El**
by *Jordan* **Yarden**,
from the border unto the east sea.
And this is the east *side* **edge**.
19 And the south *side* **edge** southward,
from Tamar
even to *the waters of strife* **Mayim Meribah**
in *Kadesh* **Qadesh**,
the *river* **wadi** to the great sea.
And this is the south *side* **edge** southward.
20 The *west side* **seaward edge** also
shall be the great sea from the border,
till a man come over against Hamath.
This is the *west side* **seaward edge**.
21 So shall ye *divide* **allot** this land unto you
according to the *tribes* **scions** of *Israel* **Yisra El**.
22 And it shall *come to pass* **become**,
that ye shall *divide it by lot* **fell it**
for an inheritance unto you,
and to the *strangers* **sojourners** that sojourn among you,
which shall beget *children* **sons** among you:
and they shall be unto you as *born in the country* **natives**
among the *children* **sons** of *Israel* **Yisra El**;
they shall *have* **fell an** inheritance with you
among the *tribes* **scions** of *Israel* **Yisra El**.
23 And it shall *come to pass* **become**,
that in what *tribe* **scion** the *stranger* **sojourner** sojourneth,
there shall ye give him his inheritance,
saith the Lord GOD **an oracle of Adonay Yah Veh**.

APPORTIONING THE LAND

48 *Now* these are the names of the *tribes* **scions**.
From the north end
to the *coast* **hand** of the way of Hethlon,
as one goeth to Hamath, *Hazarenan* **Hasar Enan**,
the border of *Damascus* **Dammeseq** northward,
to the *coast* **hand** of Hamath;
for these are his *sides* **edges** east and *west* **seaward**;
a portion for Dan, **one**.
2 And by the border of Dan,
from the east *side* **edge** unto the *west side* **seaward edge**,
a portion for Asher, **one**.
3 And by the border of Asher,
from the east side edge
even unto the *west side* **seaward edge**,
a portion for Naphtali, **one**.
4 And by the border of Naphtali,
from the east side edge unto the *west side* **seaward edge**,
a portion for *Menashsheh* **Menash Sheh, one**.
5 And by the border of *Manasseh* **Menash Sheh**,
from the east *side* **edge** unto the *side* **seaward edge**,
a portion for *Ephraim* **Ephrayim, one**.
6 And by the border of *Ephraim* **Ephrayim**,
from the east *side* **edge**
even unto the *west side* **seaward edge**,
a portion for Reu Ben, **one**.
7 And by the border of *Reuben* **Reu Ben**,
from the east *side* **edge** unto the *west side* **seaward edge**,
a portion for *Judah* **Yah Hudah, one**.

THE HALLOWED REFUGE

8 And by the border of *Judah* **Yah Hudah**,
from the east *side* **edge** unto the *west side* **seaward edge**,
shall be the *offering* **exaltment** which ye shall *offer* **lift**
of five and twenty thousand *reeds* in breadth,
and in length as one of the *other parts* **allotments**,
from the east *side* **edge** unto the *west side* **seaward edge**:
and the *sanctuary* **holies** shall be in the midst of it.
9 The *oblation* **exaltment**
that ye shall *offer* **lift** unto *the LORD* **Yah Veh**
shall be of five and twenty thousand in length,
and of ten thousand in breadth.
10 And for them, even for the priests,
shall be this holy *oblation* **exaltment**;
toward the north **northward**
five and twenty thousand *in length*,
and *toward the west* **seaward**
ten thousand in breadth,
and *toward the east* **eastward**
ten thousand in breadth,
and *toward the south* **southward**
five and twenty thousand in length:
and the *sanctuary* **holies** of *the LORD* **Yah Veh**
shall be in the midst *thereof*.
11 It shall be for the priests that are *sanctified* **hallowed**
of the sons of *Zadok* **Sadoq**;
which have *kept* **guarded** my *charge* **guard**,
which *went* **strayed** not *astray*
when
the *children* **sons** of *Israel went astray* **Yisra El strayed**,
as the *Levites went astray* **Leviym strayed**.
12 And this *oblation* **exaltment** of the land
that is *offered* **out of the exaltment**
shall be unto them a *thing most holy* **holy of holies**
by the border of the *Levites* **Leviym**.
13 And *over against* **alongside** the border of the priests
the *Levites* **Leviym** shall have

five and twenty thousand in length,
and ten thousand in breadth:
all the length shall be five and twenty thousand,
and the breadth ten thousand.
14 And they shall not sell of it, neither exchange,
nor *alienate* **pass away** the *firstfruits* **firstlings** of the land:
for it is holy unto *the LORD* **Yah Veh.**

THE COMMONS

15 And the five thousand,
that *are left* **remain** in the breadth
over against **at the face of** the five and twenty thousand,
shall be *a* profane *place* for the city,
for *dwelling* **sites**, and for suburbs:
and the city shall be in the midst *thereof.*
16 And these shall be the measures *thereof;*
the north *side* **edge** four thousand and five hundred,
and the south *side* **edge** four thousand and five hundred,
and on the east *side* **edge**
four thousand and five hundred,
and the *west side* **seaward edge**
four thousand and five hundred.
17 And the suburbs of the city shall be
toward the north **northward** two hundred and fifty,
and *toward the south* **southward** two hundred and fifty,
and *toward the east* **eastward** two hundred and fifty,
and *toward the west* **seaward** two hundred and fifty.
18 And *the residue* **that which remaineth**
in length *over against* **alongside**
the *oblation* **exaltment** of the *holy portion* **holies**
shall be ten thousand eastward,
and ten thousand *westward* **seaward**:
and it shall be *over against* **alongside**
the *oblation* **exaltment** of the *holy portion* **holies**;
and the *increase* **produce** *thereof*
shall be for *food* **bread** unto them that serve the city.
19 And they that serve the city
shall serve it out of all the *tribes* **scions** of *Israel* **Yisra El.**
20 All the *oblation* **exaltment** shall be
five and twenty thousand by five and twenty thousand:
ye shall *offer* **lift** the holy *oblation* **exaltment,**
foursquare **a fourth**, with the possession of the city.

THE HIERARCH'S AREA

21 And *the residue* **that which remaineth**
shall be for the *prince* **hierarch**,
on the one side **from here** and *on the other* **from there**
of the holy *oblation* **exaltment,**
and of the possession of the city,
over against **at the face of** the five and twenty thousand
of the *oblation* **exaltment**
toward the east **to the eastward** border,
and *westward* **seaward**
over against **at the face of** the five and twenty thousand
toward the west **to the seaward** border,
over against **alongside** the *portions* **allotments**
for the *prince* **hierarch**:
and it shall be the holy *oblation* **exaltment**;
and the *sanctuary* **holies** of the house
shall be in the midst *thereof.*
22 Moreover from the possession of the *Levites* **Leviym**,
and from the possession of the city,
being in the midst of that which is the *prince's* **hierarch's**,
between the border of *Judah* **Yah Hudah**
and the border of *Benjamin* **Ben Yamin**,
shall be for the *prince* **hierarch**.
23 As for the rest of the *tribes* **scions**,
from the east *side* **edge** unto the west *side* **edge**,
Benjamin shall have a portion **Ben Yamin, one.**
24 And by the border of *Benjamin* **Ben Yamin,**
from the east *side* **edge** unto the *west side* **seaward edge**,
Simeon shall have a portion **Shimon, one.**
25 And by the border of *Simeon* **Shimon**,
from the east *side* **edge** unto the *west side* **seaward edge**,
Issachar a portion **Yissachar, one.**
26 And by the border of *Issachar* **Yissachar**,
from the east *side* **edge** unto the *west side* **seaward edge**,
Zebulun *a portion*, **one.**
27 And by the border of Zebulun,
from the east *side* **edge** unto the *west side* **seaward edge**,
Gad, *a portion* **one.**
28 And by the border of Gad,
at the south side edge southward,
the border shall be even from Tamar
unto *the waters of strife* **Mayim Meribah**
in *Kadesh* **Qadesh**,
and to the *river* **wadi** toward the great sea.
29 This is the land which ye shall *divide by lot* **fell**
unto the *tribes* **scions** of *Israel* **Yisra El** for inheritance,
and these are their *portions* **allotments**,
saith the Lord GOD **an oracle of Adonay Yah Veh.**

THE EXITS

30 And these are the *goings out* **exits** of the city
on the north *side* **edge**,
four thousand and five hundred measures.
31 And the *gates* **portals** of the city
shall be after the names
of the *tribes* **scions** of *Israel* **Yisra El**:
three *gates* **portals** northward;
one *gate* **portal** of *Reuben* **Reu Ben,**
one *gate* **portal** of *Judah* **Yah Hudah,**
one *gate* **portal** of Levi.
32 And at the east *side* **edge**
four thousand and five hundred:
and three *gates* **portals**;
and one *gate* **portal** of *Joseph* **Yoseph,**
one *gate* **portal** of *Benjamin* **Ben Yamin,**
one *gate* **portal** of Dan.
33 And at the south *side* **edge**
four thousand and five hundred measures:
and three *gates* **portals**;
one *gate* **portal** of *Simeon* **Shimon,**
one *gate* **portal** of *Issachar* **Yissachar,**
one *gate* **portal** of Zebulun.
34 At the *west side* **seaward edge**
four thousand and five hundred,
with their three *gates* **portals**;
one *gate* **portal** of Gad,
one *gate* **portal** of Asher,
one *gate* **portal** of Naphtali.
35 It was round about eighteen thousand *measures*:
and the name of the city from that day shall be,
The LORD is there **Yah Veh Sham.**

KEY TO INTERPRETING THE EXEGESES:
King James text is in regular type;
Text under exegeses is in oblique type;
Text of exegeses is in bold type.

NEBUKADNETS TSAR BESEIGES YERU SHALEM

1 In the third year
of the *reign* **sovereigndom** of *Jehoiakim* **Yah Yaqim,**
king **sovereign** of *Judah* **Yah Hudah**
came *Nebuchadnezzar* **Nebukadnets Tsar**
king **sovereign** of *Babylon* **Babel**
unto *Jerusalem* **Yeru Shalem**, and besieged it.
2 And *the Lord* **Adonay** gave *Jehoiakim* **Yah Yaqim**
king **sovereign** of *Judah* **Yah Hudah** into his hand,
with part of the *vessels* **instruments**
of the house of *God* **Elohim:**
which he carried into the land of Shinar
to the house of his *god* **elohim**;
and he brought the *vessels* **instruments**
into the *treasure house* **treasury** of his *god* **elohim**.

NEBUKADNETS TSAR CHOOSES SONS OF YISRA EL FOR SERVICE

3 And the *king* **sovereign** *spake* **said** unto Ashpenaz
the *master* **rabbi** of his eunuchs,
that he should bring
certain of the *children* **sons** of *Israel* **Yisra El**,
and of the *king's* **sovereign's** seed,
and of the *princes* **nobles;**
4 Children in whom was no blemish,
but *well favoured* **good visaged,**
and *skilful* **comprehending** in all wisdom,
and *cunning* **knowing** in knowledge,
and *understanding science* **discerning knowledge,**
and such as had *ability* **force** in them
to stand in the *king's palace* **sovereign's manse,**
and whom they might teach
the *learning* **scrolls** and the tongue
of the *Chaldeans* **Kesediym.**
5 And the *king appointed* **sovereign numbered** them
a *daily provision* **day by day word**
of the *king's meat* **sovereign's delicacies,**
and of the wine which he drank:
so nourishing them three years,
that at the end *thereof*
they might stand *before* **at the face of** the *king* **sovereign.**
6 *Now* among these
were of the *children* **sons** of *Judah* **Yah Hudah,**
Daniel **Dani El,** *Hananiah* **Hanan Yah,**
Mishael **Misha El,** and *Azariah* **Azar Yah:**
7 Unto whom the *prince* **governor** of the eunuchs
gave **set** names:
for he *gave* **set** unto *Daniel* **Dani El**
the name of Belteshazzar **Belte Shats Tsar;**
and to *Hananiah* **Hanan Yah,** of Shadrach;
and to *Mishael* **Misha El,** of Meshach;
and to *Azariah* **Azar Yah,** of Abednego **Abed Nego.**
8 But *Daniel purposed* **Dani El set** in his heart
that he *would* **should** not *defile* **profane** *himself*
with the *portion* **delicacies** of the *king's meat* **sovereign,**
nor with the wine which he drank:
therefore he *requested* **besought**
of the *prince* **governor** of the eunuchs
that he might not *defile* **profane** *himself.*
9 *Now God* **Elohim** had *brought Daniel* **given Dani El**
into *favour* **mercy** and *tender love* **mercies**
with **at the face of** the *prince* **governor** of the eunuchs.
10 And the *prince* **governor** of the eunuchs
said unto *Daniel* **Dani El,**
I fear my *lord* **adoni** the *king* **sovereign,**
who hath
appointed **numbered** your *meat* **food** and your drink:
for why should he see your faces *worse liking* **enraged**
than the children which are of your *sort* **circle?**
then shall ye *make* **cause** me *endanger* **to owe** my head
to the *king* **sovereign.**
11 Then said *Daniel* **Dani El** to *Melzar* **the steward,**
whom the *prince* **governor** of the eunuchs
had *set over* **numbered**
Daniel **Dani El,** *Hananiah* **Hanan Yah,**
Mishael **Misha El,** and *Azariah* **Azar Yah,**
12 *Prove* **Test** thy servants, I beseech thee, ten days;
and let them give us *pulse* **herbs** to eat,
and water to drink.
13 Then let our *countenances* **visages**
be *looked upon* **seen** *before thee* **at thy face,**
and the *countenance* **visage** of the children that eat
of the *portion* **delicacies** of the *king's meat* **sovereign:**
and as thou seest, *deal* **work** with thy servants.
14 So he *consented* **hearkened** to them
in this *matter* **word,**
and *proved* **tested** them ten days.
15 And at the end of ten days their *countenances* **visages**
appeared fairer **were seen better** and fatter in flesh
than all the children which did eat
the *portion* **delicacies** of the *king's meat* **sovereign.**
16 Thus *Melzar* **the steward**
took away the portion of **lifted** their *meat* **delicacies,**
and the wine that they should drink;
and gave them *pulse* **herbs.**
17 As for these four children,
God **Elohim** gave them
knowledge and *skill* **comprehension**
in all *learning* **scrolls** and wisdom:
and *Daniel had understanding in* **Dani El discerned**
all visions and dreams.
18 *Now* at the end of the days
that the *king* **sovereign** had said he should bring them in,
then the *prince* **governor** of the eunuchs brought them in
before Nebuchadnezzar **at the face of Nebukadnets Tsar.**
19 And the *king communed* **sovereign worded** with them;
and among them all was found none
like *Daniel* **Dani El,** *Hananiah* **Hanan Yah,**
Mishael **Misha El,** and *Azariah* **Azar Yah:**
therefore stood they
before **at the face of** the *king* **sovereign.**
20 And in all *matters* **words** of wisdom
and *understanding* **of discernment,**
that the *king enquired* **sovereign besought** of them,
he found them ten *times* **hands** better than all
the *magicians* **horoscopists** and *astrologers* **enchanters**
that were in all his *realm* **sovereigndom.**
21 And *Daniel* **Dani El** continued
even unto the first year of *king Cyrus* **sovereign Koresh.**

DREAMS OF NEBUKADNETS TSAR

2 And in the second year of the *reign* **sovereigndom**
of *Nebuchadnezzar* **Nebukadnets Tsar,**
Nebuchadnezzar **Nebukadnets Tsar** dreamed dreams,
wherewith his spirit *was troubled* **agitated,**
and his sleep brake from him.
2 Then the *king commanded* **sovereign said** to call
the *magicians* **horoscopists,**
and the *astrologers* **enchanters,**
and the sorcerers, and the *Chaldeans* **Kesediym,**
for to *shew* **tell** the *king* **sovereign** his dreams.
So they came
and stood *before* **at the face of** the *king* **sovereign.**
3 And the *king* **sovereign** said unto them,
I have dreamed a dream,
and my spirit *was troubled* **agitated** to know the dream.
4 Then *spake* **worded** the *Chaldeans* **Kesediym**
to the *king* **sovereign** in *Syriack* **Aramaic,**
O *king* **sovereign,** live *for ever* **eternally:**
tell **say to** thy servants the dream,
and we *will* **shall** shew the interpretation.
5 The *king* **sovereign** answered
and said to the *Chaldeans* **Kesediym,**
The *thing* **utterance** is gone from me:
if ye *will* **shall** not make known unto me the dream,
with the interpretation *thereof,*
ye shall be *cut* **served** in pieces,
and your houses shall be *made* **set** a *dunghill* **cesspool.**
6 But if ye shew the dream, and the interpretation *thereof,*
ye shall *receive* **take in front** of me
gifts and *rewards* **largess** and great *honour* **esteem:**
therefore shew me the dream,
and the interpretation *thereof.*
7 They answered *again* **secondly** and said,
Let the *king tell* **sovereign say to** his servants the dream,
and we *will* **shall** shew the interpretation of it.
8 The *king* **sovereign** answered and said,
I know of certainty that ye *would* **should** gain the time,

because ye see the *thing* **utterance** is gone from me.
9 But if ye *will* **shall** not make known unto me the dream,
there is but — one decree for you:
for ye have prepared *lying* **false**
and *corrupt words* **ruinous utterances**
to *speak before* **say in front of** me,
till the time be changed:
therefore *tell* **say to** me the dream,
and I shall know
that ye can shew me the interpretation *thereof.*
10 The *Chaldeans* **Kesediym** answered
before **in front of** the *king* **sovereign**, and said,
There is not a man upon the *earth* **dry**
that can shew the *king's matter* **sovereign's utterance**:
therefore **because** there is no *king* **sovereign**,
lord **great**, nor *ruler* **dominator**,
that asked *such things* **utterances as these**
at any *magician* **horoscopist**,
or *astrologer* **enchanter**, or *Chaldean* **Kesediym.**
11 And it is *a rare thing* **an esteemed utterance**
that the *king requireth* **sovereign asketh**,
and there is none other that can shew it
before **in front of** the *king* **sovereign**,
except the *gods* **elahim**,
whose *dwelling* **whirling** is not with flesh.
12 *For this cause* **Therefore**
the *king was angry* **sovereign raged**
and **was** very *furious* **enraged**,
and *commanded* **said** to destroy
all the *wise men* **magi** of *Babylon* **Babel**.
13 And the decree *went forth* **emerged**
that the *wise men* **magi** should be *slain* **severed**;
and they *sought* **requested**
Daniel **Dani El** and his *fellows* **companions**
to be *slain* **severed**.
14 Then *Daniel answered* **Dani El responded**
with counsel and *wisdom* **taste**
to *Arioch* **Aryoch**the *captain* **great**
of the *king's guard* **slaughterers of the sovereign**,
which *was gone forth* **emerged**
to *slay* **sever** the *wise men* **magi** of *Babylon* **Babel**:
15 He answered and said to *Arioch* **Aryoch**
the *king's captain* **sovereign's dominator**,
Why is the decree *so hasty* **severe**
from the king **in front of the sovereign**?
Then *Arioch* **Aryoch**
made the *thing* **utterance** known to *Daniel* **Dani El**.
16 Then *Daniel went in* **Dani El entered**,
and *desired* **requested** of the *king* **sovereign**
that he *would* **should** give him *time* **an appointment**,
and that he *would* **should** shew the *king* **sovereign**
the interpretation.
17 Then *Daniel* **Dani El** went to his house,
and made the *thing* **utterance** known
to *Hananiah* **Hanan Yah**, *Mishael* **Misha El**,
and *Azariah* **Azar Yah**, his companions:
18 That they *would desire* **should request** mercies
of the God **in front of Elah** of *heaven* **the heavens**
concerning this *secret* **mystery**;
that *Daniel* **Dani El** and his *fellows* **companions**
should not *perish* **destruct** with the *rest* **remainder**
of the *wise men* **magi** of *Babylon* **Babel**.

DANI EL UNCOVERS THE MYSTERY

19 Then was the *secret revealed* **mystery exposed**
unto *Daniel* **Dani El** in a night vision.
Then *Daniel* **Dani El**
blessed *the God* **Elah** of *heaven* **the heavens**.
20 *Daniel* **Dani El** answered and said,
Blessed be the name of *God* **Elah**
for ever and ever **from eternity until eternity**:
for wisdom and might are his:
21 And he changeth the times and the seasons:
he *removeth kings* **passeth by sovereigns**,
and *setteth up kings* **raiseth sovereigns**:
he giveth wisdom unto the *wise* **magi**,
and *knowledge* **perception**
to them that know *understanding* **discernment**:
22 He *revealeth* **exposeth**
the *deep* **profound** and *secret things* **hidden**:
he knoweth what is in the darkness,
and the light *dwelleth with him* **he releaseth**.
23 I thank thee, and *praise* **laud** thee,
O thou *God* **Elah** of my fathers,
who hast given me wisdom and might,
and hast made known unto me now
what we *desired* **requested** of thee:
for thou hast *now* made known unto us
the *king's matter* **sovereign's utterance**.
24 Therefore
Daniel went in **Dani El entered** unto *Arioch* **Aryoch**,
whom the *king* **sovereign** had *ordained* **numbered**
to destroy the *wise men* **magi** of *Babylon* **Babel**:
he went and said thus unto him;
Destroy not the *wise men* **magi** of *Babylon* **Babel**:
bring **enter** me in *before* **front of** the *king* **sovereign**,
and I *will* **shall** shew unto the *king* **sovereign**
the interpretation.
25 Then *Arioch* **Aryoch** *brought in Daniel* **entered Dani El**
before **in front of** the *king in haste* **sovereign hastily**,
and said thus unto him,
I have found a *man* **mighty**
of the *captives* **sons of the exiles** of *Judah* **Yah Hudah**,
that *will* **shall** make known unto the *king* **sovereign**
the interpretation.
26 The *king* **sovereign** answered
and said to *Daniel* **Dani El**,
whose name was *Belteshazzar* **Belte Shats Tsar**,
Art thou able to make known unto me
the dream which I have seen,
and the interpretation *thereof?*
27 *Daniel* **Dani El** answered
in *the presence* **front** of the *king* **sovereign**, and said,
The *secret* **mystery**
which the *king* **sovereign** hath *demanded* **asked**
cannot the *wise men* **magi**, the *astrologers* **enchanters**,
the *magicians* **horoscopists**, the *soothsayers* **discerners**,
shew unto the *king* **sovereign**;
28 *But* **However**
there is *a God* **an Elah** in *heaven* **the heavens**
that *revealeth secrets* **exposeth mysteries**,
and maketh known
to *the king Nebuchadnezzar* **sovereign Nebukadnets Tsar**
what shall be the *latter* **final** days.
Thy dream, and the visions of thy head upon thy bed,
are these;
29 As for thee, O *king* **sovereign**,
thy thoughts **thine intentions**
came into thy mind **ascended** upon thy bed,
what should *come to pass hereafter* **become after this**:
and he that *revealeth secrets* **exposeth mysteries**
maketh known to thee what shall *come to pass* **become**.
30 But as for me,
this *secret* **mystery** is not *revealed* **exposed** to me
for *any* wisdom that I have **in me** *more* than any living,
but for *their sakes* **words** that shall make known
the interpretation to the *king* **sovereign**,
and that thou mightest know
the *thoughts* **intentions** of thy heart.

DANI EL RECALLS THE MYSTERY

31 Thou, O *king* **sovereign**, sawest,
and behold *a* **one** great image. — This great image,
whose *brightness* **cheerfulness** was excellent,
stood before **rose up in front of** thee;
and the *form thereof* **appearance** was *terrible* **terrifying**.
32 This image's head was of fine gold,
his breast and his arms of silver,
his *belly* **inwards** and his *thighs* **flanks** of *brass* **copper**,
33 His legs of iron,
his feet *part of* **from** iron and *part of* **from** clay.
34 Thou sawest till that a stone was cut out
without **not by** hands,
which *smote* **struck** the image
upon his feet *that were* of iron and clay,
and *brake* **pulverized** them *to pieces*.
35 Then was the iron, the clay, the *brass* **copper**,
the silver, and the gold,
broken to pieces together **pulverized as one**,
and became like the chaff of the summer threshingfloors;
and the wind *carried* **bore** them *away*,
that no place was found for them:

and the stone that *smote* **struck** the image
became a great *mountain* **rock**,
and filled the whole earth.

DANI EL INTERPRETS THE MYSTERY

36 This is the dream;
and we *will tell* **shall say** the interpretation *thereof*
before the king **in front of the sovereign**.
37 Thou, O *king* **sovereign**,
art a *king* **sovereign** of *kings* **sovereigns**:
for *the God* **Elah** of *heaven* **the heavens**
hath given thee a *kingdom* **sovereigndom**,
power, and *strength* **empowerment**, and *glory* **esteem**.
38 And *wheresoever* **everywhere**
the *children* **sons** of men *dwell* **whirl**,
the *beasts* **live beings** of the field
and the *fowls* **flyers** of the *heaven* **heavens**
hath he given into thine hand,
and hath made thee *ruler* **dominate** over them all.
Thou art this head of gold.
39 And *after thee* **in thy place**
shall arise another *kingdom* **sovereigndom**
inferior to thee **from thee of earth**,
and another third *kingdom* **sovereigndom**
of *brass* **copper**,
which shall *bear rule* **dominate** over all the earth.
40 And the fourth *kingdom* **sovereigndom**
shall be *strong* **mighty** as iron:
forasmuch **because that** as iron
breaketh in pieces **pulverizeth** and *subdueth* **crusheth**
all *things*:
and as iron that *breaketh* **shattereth** all these,
shall it *break in pieces* **pulverize** and *bruise* **shatter**.
41 And whereas thou sawest the feet and *toes* **digits**,
part of **from** potters' clay, and *part of* **from** iron,
the *kingdom* **sovereigndom** shall be divided;
but **from** there shall be in it of the strength of the iron,
forasmuch **because that** as thou sawest the iron
mixed **comingled** with miry clay.
42 And *as* the *toes* **digits** of the feet
were *part of* **from** iron, and *part of* **from** clay,
so the *kingdom* **sovereigndom** shall be
partly strong **from might**, and *partly* **from** broken.
43 And whereas thou sawest iron
mixed **comingled** with miry clay,
they shall *mingle themselves* **become comingled**
with the seed of men:
but they shall not *cleave one to another* **be this with that**,
even **behold** as iron is not *mixed* **comingled** with clay.
44 And in the days of these *kings* **sovereigns**
shall *the God* **Elah** of *heaven* **the heavens**
set up **raise** a *kingdom* **sovereigndom**,
which shall *never* **not** be *destroyed* **despoiled eternally**:
and the *kingdom* **sovereigndom**
shall not be left to other people,
but it shall *break in pieces* **pulverize** and consume
all these *kingdoms* **sovereigndoms**,
and it shall *stand for ever* **be raised eternally**.
45 *Forasmuch* **Because that** as thou sawest that the stone
was cut out of the *mountain without* **rock not by** hands,
and that it *brake in pieces* **pulverized** the iron,
the *brass* **copper**, the clay, the silver, and the gold;
the great *God* **Elah**
hath made known to the *king* **sovereign**
what shall *come to pass hereafter* **become after this**:
and the dream is certain,
and the iterpretation *thereof sure* **trustworthy**.

NEBUKADNETS TSAR PROMOTES DANI EL

46 Then
the king Nebuchadnezzar **sovereign Nebukadnets Tsar**
fell upon his face,
and *worshipped Daniel* **prostrated to Dani El**,
and *commanded* **said**
that they should *offer* **libate** an *oblation* **offering**
and *sweet odours* **savour of rest** unto him.
47 The *king* **sovereign** answered unto *Daniel* **Dani El**,
and said, *Of* **From** a truth *it is*,
that your *God* **Elah** is *a God* **an Elah** of *gods* **elahim**,
and a *Lord of kings* **master of sovereigns**,
and *a revealer* **an exposer** of *secrets* **mysteries**,
seeing **that** thou couldest *reveal* **expose** this *secret* **mystery**.
48 Then the *king* **sovereign**
made Daniel a great man **greatened Dani El**,
and gave him many great gifts,
and *made* **had** him *ruler* **dominate**
over the whole *province* **jurisdiction** of *Babylon* **Babel**,
and *chief* **great** of the *governors* **prefects**
over all the *wise men* **magi** of *Babylon* **Babel**.
49 Then *Daniel* **Dani El** requested of the *king* **sovereign**,
and he *set* **numbered**
Shadrach, Meshach, and *Abednego* **Abed Nego**,
over the *affairs* **service**
of the *province* **jurisdiction** of *Babylon* **Babel**:
but Daniel **and Dani El** *sat*
in the *gate* **portal** of the *king* **sovereign**.

NEBUKADNETS TSAR'S IMAGE OF GOLD

3 *NEBUCHADNEZZAR* **Nebukadnets Tsar**
the *king* **sovereign** made an image of gold,
whose height was *threescore* **sixty** cubits,
and the *breadth* **width** *thereof* six cubits:
he *set it up* **raised it** in the *plain* **valley** of Dura,
in the *province* **jurisdiction** of *Babylon* **Babel**.
2 Then *Nebuchadnezzar* **Nebukadnets Tsar**
the *king* **sovereign**
sent to gather together the *princes* **satraps**,
the *governors* **prefects**, and the *captains* **governors**,
the *judges* **mighty diviners**, the treasurers,
the *counsellors* **decreers**, the sherrifs,
and all the *rulers* **dominators**
of the *provinces* **jurisdictions**,
to come to the *dedication* **hanukkah** of the image
which *Nebuchadnezzar* **Nebukadnets Tsar**
the *king* **sovereign** had *set up* **raised**.
3 Then the *princes* **satraps**, the *governors* **prefects**,
and *captains* **governors**, the *judges* **mighty diviners**,
the treasurers, the counsellors, the sheriffs,
and all the *rulers* **dominators**
of the *provinces* **jurisdictions**
were gathered together
unto the *dedication* **hanukkah** of the image
that *Nebuchadnezzar* **Nebukadnets Tsar**
the *king* **sovereign** had *set up* **raised**;
and they *stood before* **rose in front of** the image
that *Nebuchadnezzar* **Nebukadnets Tsar**
had *set up* **raised**.
4 Then an *herald* **announcer**
cried aloud **called out with valour**,
To you *it is commanded* **they say**,
O people, nations, and *languages* **tongues**,
5 That at what time
ye hear the *sound* **voice** of the *cornet* **horn**,
flute, harp, sackbut, psaltery, *dulcimer* **symphonia**,
and all *kinds* **species** of *musick* **psalming**,
ye fall down and *worship* **prostrate to** the golden image
that *Nebuchadnezzar* **Nebukadnets Tsar**
the *king* **sovereign** hath *set up* **raised**:
6 And whoso
falleth not down and *worshippeth* **prostrateth**
shall the same *hour* **blink**
be *cast* **hurled** into the midst of a burning fiery furnace.
7 Therefore **then** at that *time* **appointment**,
when **that** all the people
heard the *sound* **voice** of the *cornet* **horn**,
flute, harp, sackbut, psaltery,
and all *kinds* **species** of *musick* **psalming**,
all the people, the nations, and the *languages* **tongues**,
fell down and *worshipped* **prostrated**
to the golden image
that *Nebuchadnezzar* **Nebukadnets Tsar**
the *king* **sovereign** had *set up* **raised**.
8 *Wherefore* **Therefore then** at that *time* **appointment**
certain Chaldeans came near **mighty Kesediym approached**,
and *accused* **chewed out** the *Jews* **Yah Hudiym**.
9 They *spake* **answered** and said to
the king Nebuchadnezzar **sovereign Nebukadnets Tsar**,
O *king* **sovereign**, live *for ever* **eternally**.
10 Thou, O *king* **sovereign**, has *made* **set** a decree,
that every man that shall hear
the *sound* **voice** of the *cornet* **horn**,
flute, harp, sackbut, psaltery, and *dulcimer* **symphonia**,
and all *kinds* **species** of *musick* **psalming**,

shall fall down and *worship* **prostrateth**
to the golden image:
11 And whoso
falleth not down and *worshippeth* **prostrateth**,
that he should be *cast* **hurled**
into the midst of a burning fiery furnace.
12 There are *certain Jews* **mighty Yah Hudiym**
whom thou has *set* **numbered** over the *affairs* **service**
of the *province* **jurisdiction** of *Babylon* **Babel**,
Shadrach, Meshach, and *Abednego* **Abed Nego**;
these *men* **mighty**, O *king* **sovereign**,
have not *regarded* **set their taste to** thee:
they serve not thy *gods* **elahim**,
nor *worship* **prostrate to** the golden image
which thou hast *set up* **raised**.
13 Then *Nebuchadnezzar* **Nebukadnets Tsar**
in *his rage* **quiver** and fury
commanded **said** to bring
Shadrach, Meshach, and *Abednego* **Abed Nego**.
Then they brought these *men* **mighty**
before **in front of** the *king* **sovereign**.
14 *Nebuchadnezzar* **Nebukadnets Tsar**
spake **answered** and said unto them,
Is it *true* **your intent**,
O Shadrach, Meshach, and *Abednego* **Abed Nego**,
do not ye serve my *gods* **elahim**,
nor *worship* **prostrate**
to the golden image which I have *set up* **raised**?
15 Now if ye be *ready* **prepared**
that at what time ye hear the sound of the *cornet* **horn**,
flute, harp, sackbut, psaltery, and *dulcimer* **symphonia**,
and all *kinds* **species** of *musick* **psalming**,
ye fall down and *worship* **prostrate**
to the image which I have made; *well*:
but if ye *worship* **prostrate** not,
ye shall be *cast* **hurled** the same *hour* **blink**
into the midst of a burning fiery furnace;
and who is that *God* **Elah**
that shall *deliver* **liberate** you out of my hands?
16 Shadrach, Meshach, and *Abednego* **Abed Nego**,
answered and said to the *king* **sovereign**,
O *Nebuchadnezzar* **Nebukadnets Tsar**,
we *are not careful to answer* **need not respond to** thee
in this *matter* **decision**.
17 If it be so, our *God* **Elah** whom we serve
is able to *deliver* **liberate** us
from the burning fiery furnace,
and he *will deliver* **shall liberate** us
out of **from** thine hand, O *king* **sovereign**.
18 But if not, be it known unto thee, O *king* **sovereign**,
that we *will* **shall** not serve thy *gods* **elahim**,
nor *worship* **prostrate to** the golden image
which thou has *set up* **raised**.
19 Then was *Nebuchadnezzar* **Nebukadnets Tsar**
full **filled** of fury,
and the *form* **image** of his *visage* **face**
was changed against
Shadrach, Meshach, and *Abednego* **Abed Nego**:
therefore he *spake* **answered**, and *commanded* **said**
that they should *heat* **kindle** the furnace
one seven times more than it was wont to be heated
seven above the usual kindling.
20 And he *commanded* **said**
to the most mighty *men* **mighty of valour**
that were *in* **among** his *army* **valiant**
to *bind* **shackle**
Shadrach, Meshach, and *Abednego* **Abed Nego**,
and to *cast* **hurl** them into the burning fiery furnace.
21 Then these *men* **mighty** were *bound* **shackled**
in their *coats* **mantles**, their *hosen* **undergarments**,
and their hats, and their *other garments* **robes**,
and were *cast* **hurled**
into the midst of the burning fiery furnace.
22 Therefore
because the *king's commandment* **sovereign's utterance**
was *urgent* **severe**,
and the furnace exceeding *hot* **kindled**,
the flame of the fire *slew* **severed** those *men* **mighty**
that took up Shadrach,
Meshach and *Abednego* **Abed Nego**.
23 And these three *men* **mighty**,
Shadrach, Meshach, and *Abednego* **Abed Nego**,
fell down *bound* **shackled**
into the midst of the burning fiery furnace.
24 Then *Nebuchadnezzar* **Nebukadnets Tsar**
the *king* **sovereign** *was astonied* **marvelled**,
and rose up *in haste* **hastily**,
and *spake* **answered**, *and said* **saying** unto his cousellors,
Did not we *cast* **hurl** three *men* **mighty** bound
into the midst of the fire?
They answered and said unto the *king* **sovereign**,
True **Certainly**, O *king* **sovereign**.
25 He answered and said,
Lo **Behold**, I see four *men loose* **mighty released**,
walking in the midst of the fire,
and they have no *hurt* **damage**;
and the *form* **appearance** of the fourth
is like the *Son* **Bar** of *God* **Elah**.
26 Then *Nebuchadnezzar* **Nebukadnets Tsar**
came near **approached** the *mouth* **portal**
of the burning fiery furnace,
and spake **answered**, and said,
Shadrach, Meshach, and *Abednego* **Abed Nego**,
ye servants of *the most high God* **Elyon Elah**,
come forth **emerge**, and come *hither*.
Then Shadrach, Meshach, and *Abednego* **Abed Nego**,
came forth of **emerged from** the midst of the fire.
27 And the *princes* **satraps**, *governors* **prefects**,
and *captains* **governors**,
and the *king's* **sovereign's** counsellors,
being gathered together, saw these *men* **mighty**,
upon whose bodies
the fire *had no power* **dominated not**,
nor was an hair of their head singed,
neither were their *coats* **mantles** changed,
nor the *smell* **scent** of fire had passed on them.
28 *Then Nebuchadnezzar* **Nebukadnets Tsar**
spake **answered**, and said,
Blessed be *the God* **Elah** of
Shadrach, Meshach, and *Abednego* **Abed Nego**,
who hath sent his angel
and *delivered* **liberated** his servants
that *trusted in* **attended** him,
and have changed the *king's word* **sovereign's utterance**,
and *yielded* **gave** their bodies,
that they might not serve nor *worship* **prostrate**
to any *god* **elah**, except their own *God* **Elah**.

NEBUKADNETS TSAR'S DECREE

29 *Therefore I make* **I set** a decree,
That every people, nation, and *language* **tongue**,
which *speak any thing amiss* **say misleadingly**
against *the God* **Elah** of
Shadrach, Meshach, and *Abednego* **Abed Nego**,
shall be *cut* **made** in pieces,
and their houses
shall be *made a dunghill* **equated to a cesspool**:
because **that** there is no other *God* **Elah**
that can *deliver after this sort* **rescue thus**.
30 Then the *king* **sovereign**
promoted **prospered**
Shadrach, Meshach, and *Abednego* **Abed Nego**,
in the *province* **jurisdiction** of *Babylon* **Babel**.

NEBUKADNETS TSAR'S PROCLAMATION

4 *NUBUCHADNEZZAR* **Nebukadnets Tsar**
the *king* **sovereign**,
unto all people, nations, and *languages* **tongues**,
that *dwell* **whirl** in all the earth;
Peace **Shalom** be *multiplied* **increased** unto you.
2 *I thought it good* **It was glorifying in front of me**
to shew the *signs* **omens** and *wonders* **marvels**
that the *high God* **Elyon Elah** hath *wrought* **done** toward me.
3 How great *are* his *signs* **omens**!
and how mighty *are* his *wonders* **marvels**!
his *kingdom* **sovereigndom**
is an *everlasting kingdom* **eternal sovereigndom**,
and his dominion is from generation to generation.

NEBUKADNETS TSAR'S DREAM OF THE TREE

4 I *Nebuchadnezzar* **Nebukadnets Tsar**
was at rest **serenized** in mine house,
and *flourishing* **green** in my *palace* **manse**:

5 I saw a dream which *made* **terrified** me *afraid,*
and the *thought* **conceptions** upon my bed
and the visions of my head *troubled* **terrified** me.
6 *Therefore made* I **set** a decree to *bring in* **enter**
all the *wise men* **magi** of *Babylon* **Babel**
before me **in front of me,**
that they might make known unto me
the interpretation of the dream.
7 Then *came in* **entered** the *magicians* **horoscopists,**
the *astrologers* **enchanters,** the *Chaldeans* **Kesediym,**
and the *soothsayers* **discerners:**
and I *told* **said** the dream *before* **in front of** them;
but they did not make known unto me
the interpretation *thereof.*
8 *But at the last* **Until finally**
Daniel **Dani El** came in *before* **in front of** me,
whose name was *Belteshazzar* **Belte Shats Tsar,**
according to the name of my *god* **elah,**
and in whom is the spirit of the holy *gods* **elahim:**
and *before* **in front of** him I *told* **said** the dream, *saying,*
9 O *Belteshazzar* **Belte Shats Tsar**
master **great** of the *magicians* **horoscopists,**
because I know
that the spirit of the holy *gods* **elahim** is in thee,
and no *secret troubleth* **mystery distresseth** thee,
tell **say to** me the visions of my dream that I have seen,
and the interpretation *thereof.*
10 Thus were the visions of mine head in my bed;
I saw, and behold a tree in the midst of the earth,
and the height *thereof* was great.
11 The tree *grew* **greatened,** and *was strong* **empowered,**
and the height *thereof*
reached **extended** unto *heaven* **the heavens,**
and the sight *thereof*
to the *end* **consummation** of all the earth:
12 The *leaves thereof were fair* **foliage was beautiful,**
and the fruit *thereof* much,
and in it was *meat* **food** for all:
the *beasts* **live beings** of the field
had shadow **shaded** under it,
and the *fowls* **birds** of the *heaven* **heavens**
dwelt **whirled** in the *boughs* **branches** *thereof,*
and all flesh was *fed* **nourished** of it.
13 I saw in the visions of my head upon my bed,
and, behold, a *watcher* **waker** and an holy one
came down **descended** from *heaven* **the heavens;**
14 He *cried aloud* **called out with valour,** and said thus,
Hew **Cut** down the tree, and *cut* **chop** off his branches,
shake off his *leaves* **foliage,** and scatter his fruit:
let the *beasts get away* **live beings flee** from under it,
and the *fowls* **birds** from his branches:
15 *Nevertheless* **However**
leave the stump of his roots in the earth,
even with a band of iron and *brass* **copper,**
in the *tender grass* **sprouts** of the field;
and let it be *wet* **dyed**
with the dew of *heaven* **the heavens,**
and *let* his portion *be* with the *beasts* **live beings**
in the *grass* **herbage** of the earth:
16 Let his heart be changed from man's,
and let a *beast's* **live being's** heart be given unto him;
and let seven times pass over him.
17 This *matter* **decision**
is by the decree of the *watchers* **wakers,**
and the *demand* **mandate**
by the *word* **edict** of the holy ones:
to the *intent* **word** that the living may know
that *the most High ruleth* **Elyon is dominator**
in the *kingdom* **sovereigndom** of men,
and giveth it to whomsoever he *will* **willeth,**
and *setteth up* **raiseth** over it the *basest* **lowliest** of men.
18 This dream
I *king Nebuchadnezzar* **sovereign Nebukadnets Tsar**
have seen.
Now thou, O *Belteshazzar* **Belte Shats Tsar,**
declare **say** the interpretation *thereof,*
forasmuch as **because that**
all the *wise men* **magi** of my *kingdom* **sovereigndom**
are not able to *make known unto me* **cause me to know**
the interpretation:
but thou art able;
for the spirit of the holy *gods* **elahim** is in thee.

DANI EL INTERPRETS THE DREAM OF THE TREE

19 Then *Daniel* **Dani El,**
whose name was *Belteshazzar* **Belte Shats Tsar,**
was *astonied* **astonished** for one *hour* **blink,**
and his *thoughts troubled* **intentions terrified** him.
The *king spake* **sovereign answered,** and said,
Belteshazzar **Belte Shats Tsar,**
let not the dream, or the interpretation *thereof,*
trouble **terrify** thee.
Belteshazzar **Belte Shats Tsar** answered and said,
My *lord* **master,** the dream be to them that hate thee,
and the interpretation *thereof* to thine enemies.
20 The tree that thou sawest,
which *grew* **greatened,** and *was strong* **empowered,**
whose height
reached **extended** unto the *heaven* **heavens,**
and the sight *thereof* to all the earth;
21 Whose *leaves were fair* **foliage was beautiful,**
and the fruit *thereof* much,
and in it was *meat* **food** for all;
under which
the *beasts* **live beings** of the field *dwelt* **whirled,**
and upon whose branches
the *fowls* **birds** of the *heaven* **heavens**
had their habitation **tabernacled:**
22 It is thou, O *king* **sovereign,**
that art *grown* **greatened**
and *become strong* **empowered:**
for thy greatness is *grown* **greatened,**
and *reacheth* **extendeth** unto *heaven* **the heavens,**
and thy dominion to the *end* **consummation** of the earth.
23 And whereas the *king* **sovereign**
saw a *watcher* **waker** and an holy one
coming down **descending** from *heaven* **the heavens,**
and saying,
Hew **Cut** the tree down, and *destroy* **despoil** it;
yet **however**
leave the stump of the roots *thereof* in the earth,
even with a band of iron and *brass* **copper,**
in the *tender grass* **sprouts** of the field;
and let it be *wet* **dyed**
with the dew of *heaven* **the heavens,**
and *let* his portion
be with the *beasts* **live beings** of the field,
till seven times pass over him;
24 This is the interpretation, O *king* **sovereign,**
and this is the decree of the *most High* **Elyon,**
which is *come* **happened**
upon my *lord* **master** the *king* **sovereign:**
25 That they shall *drive* **expel** thee from men,
and thy *dwelling* **whirling**
shall be with the *beasts* **live beings** of the field,
and they shall *make* **cause** thee
to *eat* **feed** on *grass* **herbage** as *oxen* **bulls,**
and they shall *wet* **dye** thee
with the dew of *heaven* **the heavens,**
and seven times shall pass over thee,
till thou know that *the most High* **Elyon**
ruleth **dominateth** in the *kingdom* **sovereigndom** of men,
and giveth it to whomsoever he *will* **willeth.**
26 And whereas they *commanded* **said**
to leave the stump of the tree roots;
thy *kingdom* **sovereigndom**
shall be *sure* **permanent** unto thee,
after **from** that thou shalt *have known* **know**
that the heavens *do rule* **dominate.**
27 *Wherefore* **Therefore,** O *king* **sovereign,**
let my *counsel* **ruling** be *acceptable* **glorifying** unto thee,
and break off thy sins by *righteousness* **justness,**
and *thine iniquities* **thy perverseness**
by *shewing mercy* **granting charism** to the *poor* **humble;**
if **whether** it may be
a lengthening of thy *tranquillity* **serenity.**

DANI EL'S INTERPRETATION FULFILLED

28 All this *came* **happened** upon
the king Nebuchadnezzar **sovereign Nebukadnets Tsar.**
29 At the end of twelve months
he walked in the *palace* **manse**

of the *kingdom* **sovereigndom** of *Babylon* **Babel**.
30 The *king spake* **sovereign answered**, and said,
Is not this great *Babylon* **Babel**, that I have built
for the house of the *kingdom* **sovereigndom**
by the *might* **empowerment** of my power,
and for the *honour* **esteem** of my majesty?
31 While the *word* **utterance**
was in the *king's* **sovereign's** mouth,
there fell a voice from *heaven* **the heavens**, *saying,*
O *king Nebuchadnezzar* **sovereign Nebukadnets Tsar**,
to thee *it is spoken* **they are saying**;
The *kingdom* **sovereigndom** is *departed* **passed**
from thee.
32 And they shall *drive* **expel** thee from men,
and thy *dwelling* **whirling**
shall be with the *beasts* **live beings** of the field:
they shall *make* **cause** thee
to *eat grass* **feed on herbage** as *oxen* **bulls**,
and seven times shall pass over thee,
until thou know
that the *most High ruleth* **Elyon is dominator**
in the *kingdom* **sovereigndom** of men,
and giveth it to whomsoever he *will* **willeth**.
33 The same *hour* **blink**
was the *thing fulfilled* **utterance consummated**
upon *Nebuchadnezzar* **Nebukadnets Tsar**:
and he was *driven* **expelled** from men,
and *did eat grass* **fed on herbage** as *oxen* **bulls**,
and his body was *wet* **dyed**
with the dew of *heaven* **the heavens**,
till his hairs were *grown* **greatened** like eagles' *feathers*,
and his nails like birds' *claws*.
34 And at the end of the days
I *Nebuchadnezzar* **Nebukadnets Tsar**
lifted up mine eyes unto *heaven* **the heavens**,
and *mine understanding* **perception** returned unto me,
and I blessed the *most High* **Elyon**,
and I *praised* **lauded** and *honoured* **esteemed** him
that liveth *for ever* **eternally**,
whose dominion is an *everlasting* **eternal** dominion,
and his *kingdom* **sovereigndom**
is from generation to generation:
35 And *the inhabitants of* **they that whirl on** the earth
are *reputed* **machinated** as *nothing* **nought**:
and he doeth *according to his will* **as he willeth**
in the army **among the valiant** of *heaven* **the heavens**,
and *among*
the inhabitants of **them that whirl on** the earth:
and none can tay his hand,
or say unto him, What doest thou?
36 At the same *time* **appointment**
my *reason* **perception** returned unto me;
and for the *glory* **esteem** of my *kingdom* **sovereigndom**,
mine *honour* **majesty** and *brightness* **cheerfulness**
returned unto me;
and my counsellors and my *lords sought* **nobles**
requested unto me;
and I was *established* **restored**
in my *kingdom* **sovereigndom**,
and excellent *majesty* **greatness** was added unto me.
37 Now I *Nebuchadnezzar* **Nebukadnets Tsar**
praise **laud** and *extol* **exalt** and *honour* **esteem**
the *King* **Sovereign** of *heaven* **the heavens**,
all whose *works* **acts** are truth,
and his ways *judgment* **plead cause**:
and those that walk in *pride* **arrogance**
he is able to abase.

BEL SHATS TSAR'S FEAST

5 *Belshazzar* **Bel Shats Tsar**, the *king* **sovereign**
made a great feast to a thousand of his *lords* **nobles**,
and drank *wine* **fermentation**
before **in front of** the thousand.
2 *Belshazzar* **Bel Shats Tsar**,
whiles he tasted the *wine* **fermentation**,
commanded **said** to bring the golden and silver vessels
which his father *Nebuchadnezzar* **Nebukadnets Tsar**
had *taken* **removed** out of the *temple* **manse**
which was in *Jerusalem* **Yeru Shalem**;
that the *king* **sovereign**, and his *princes* **nobles**,
his *wives* **mistresses**, and his concubines,
might drink *therein*.
3 Then they brought the golden vessels
that were *taken* **removed**
out of the *temple* **manse** of the house of *God* **Elah**
which was at *Jerusalem* **Yeru Shalem**;
and the *king* **sovereign**, and his *princes* **nobles**,
his wives, and his concubines, drank in them.
4 They drank *wine* **fermentation**,
and *praised* **lauded** the *gods* **elahim** of gold, and of silver,
of *brass* **copper**, of iron, of *wood* **timber**, and of stone.

THE SCRIBING ON THE WALL

5 In the same *hour* **blink**
came forth fingers **emerged digits** of a man's hand,
and *wrote* **inscribed**
over against **in front of** the *candlestick* **menorah**
upon the plaister of the wall
of the *king's palace* **sovereign's manse**:
and the *king* **sovereign** saw the *part* **palm** of the hand
that *wrote* **inscribed**.
6 Then the *king's countenance* **sovereign's cheerfulness**
was changed,
and his *thoughts troubled* **intentions terrified** him,
so that the *joints* **vertebrae** of his loins
were *loosed* **released**,
and his knees *smote* **knocked** one against another.
7 The *king cried aloud* **sovereign called out with valour**
to *bring in* **enter** the *astrologers* **enchanters**,
the *Chaldeans* **Kesediym**, and the *soothsayers* **discerners**.
And the *king spake* **sovereign answered**,
and said to the *wise men* **magi** of *Babylon* **Babel**,
Whosoever **Whatever man**
shall *read* **call out** this *writing* **inscribing**,
and shew me the interpretation *thereof*,
shall be *clothed* **enrobed** with *scarlet* **purple**,
and have a *chain* **necklace** of gold about his neck,
and shall be the third
ruler **to dominate** in the *kingdom* **sovereigndom**.
8 Then *came in* **entered**
all the *king's wise men* **sovereign's magi**:
but they could not *read* **call out** the *writing* **inscribing**,
nor make known to the *king* **sovereign**
the interpretation *thereof*.
9 Then was *king Belshazzar* **sovereign Bel Shats Tsar**
greatly *troubled* **terrified**,
and his *countenance* **cheerfulness** was changed in him,
and his *lords* **nobles** were *astonied* **perplexed**.
10 *Now* the *queen* **sovereigness**
by reason **because** of the *words* **utterances**
of the *king* **sovereign** and his *lords* **nobles**
came **entered** into the banquet house:
and the *queen spake* **sovereigness answered** and said,
O *king* **sovereign**, live *for ever* **eternally**:
let not *thy thoughts trouble* **thine intentions terrify** thee,
nor let thy *countenance* **cheerfulness** be changed:
11 There is a *man* **mighty** in thy *kingdom* **sovereigndom**,
in whom is the spirit of the holy *gods* **elahim**;
and in the days of thy father
light and *understanding* **comprehension** and wisdom,
like the wisdom of the *gods* **elahim**, was found in him;
whom
the king Nebuchadnezzar **sovereign Nebukadnets Tsar**
thy father, the *king* **sovereign**, *I say*, thy father,
made master **raised great** of the *magicians* **horoscopists**,
astrologers **enchanters**, *Chaldeans* **Kesediym**,
and *soothsayers* **discerners**;
12 *Forasmuch* **Because that** as an excellent spirit,
and *knowledge* **perception**,
and *understanding* **comprehension**,
interpreting of dreams,
and *shewing* **solving** of *hard sentences* **enigmas**,
and *dissolving* **unraveling** of *doubts* **riddles**,
were found in the same *Daniel* **Dani El**,
whom the *king named* **sovereign set the name**
Belteshazzar **Belte Shats Tsar**:
now let *Daniel* **Dani El** be called,
and he *will* **shall** shew the interpretation.
13 Then *was Daniel brought in* **Dani El entered**
before **in front of** the *king* **sovereign**.
And the *king* **sovereign**
spake **answered** and said unto *Daniel* **Dani El**,

Art thou that *Daniel* **Dani El**,
which art of the *children* **sons** of the *captivity* **exiles**
of *Judah* **Yah Hudah,**
whom the *king* **sovereign** my father
brought out of *Jewry* **Yah Hudah**?
14 I have even heard of thee,
that the spirit of *the gods* **elahim** is in thee,
and that light and *understanding* **comprehension**
and excellent wisdom is found in thee.
15 And now the *wise men* **magi,**
the *astrologers* **enchanters,**
have been *brought in before* **entered in front of** me,
that they should *read* **call out** this *writing* **inscribing,**
and make known unto me the interpretation *thereof*:
but they could not
shew the interpretation of the *thing* **utterance**:
16 And I have heard of thee,
that thou canst *make* **interpret** interpretations,
and *dissolve doubts* **unravel riddles**:
now if thou canst *read* **call out** the *writing* **inscribing,**
and make known to me the interpretation *thereof,*
thou shalt be *clothed* **enrobed** with *scarlet* **purple,**
and have a *chain* **necklace** of gold about thy neck,
and shalt be the third *ruler* **to dominate**
in the *kingdom* **sovereigndom.**

DANI EL INTERPRETS THE INSCRIBING

17 Then *Daniel* **Dani El** answered
and said *before* **in front of** the *king* **sovereign,**
Let thy gifts be to thyself,
and give thy *rewards* **largess** to another;
yet **however**
I will read **shall call out** the *writing* **inscribing**
unto the *king* **sovereign,**
and make known to him the interpretation.
18 O thou *king* **sovereign,**
the most high God **Elyon Elah**
gave *Nebuchadnezzar* **Nebukadnets Tsar** thy father
a *kingdom* **sovereigndom**, and *majesty* **greatness,**
and *glory* **esteem**, and *honour* **majesty:**
19 And *for the majesty* **from the greatness**
that he gave him,
all people, nations, and *languages* **tongues**
trembled **became agitated**
and *feared before* **terrified in front of** him:
whom he *would* **willed,** he *slew* **severed;**
and whom he *would* **willed,** he *kept alive* **let live;**
and whom he *would* **willed,** he *set up* **lifted;**
and whom he *would* **willed,** he *put down* **abased.**
20 But when his heart was lifted up,
and his *mind* **spirit**
hardened **empowered** in *pride* **seething,**
he was deposed from his *kingly* **sovereigndom** throne,
and they *took* **passed** his *glory* **esteem** from him:
21 And he was *driven* **expelled** from the sons of men;
and his heart
was *made like the beasts* **equated to live beings,**
and his *dwelling* **whirling**
was with the *wild asses* **onagers**:
they fed him with *grass like oxen* **herbage as bulls,**
and his body was *wet* **dyed**
with the dew of *heaven* **the heavens;**
till he knew that *the most high God* **Elyon Elah**
ruled **is dominator** in the *kingdom* **sovereigndom** of men,
and that he *appointeth* **raiseth** over it
whomsoever he *will* **willeth.**
22 And thou his *son* **bar**, O *Belshazzar* **Bel Shats Tsar,**
hast not *humbled* **abased** thine heart,
though **because that** thou knewest all this;
23 But hast lifted up thyself
against the *Lord* **Master** of *heaven* **the heavens;**
and they have brought the vessels of his house
before **in front of** thee,
and thou, and thy *lords* **nobles,**
thy *wives* **mistresses,** and thy concubines,
have drunk *wine* **fermentation** in them;
and thou hast *praised* **lauded** the *gods* **elahim** of silver,
and gold, of *brass* **copper**, iron, *wood* **timber**, and stone,
which see not, nor hear, nor know:
and *the God* **Elah** in whose hand thy breath is,
and whose are all thy ways,
hast thou not *glorified* **esteemed**:
24 Then was the *part* **palm** of the hand
sent *from* **in front of** him;
and this *writing* **inscribing** was *written* **signed.**
25 And this is the *writing* **inscribing**
that was *written* **signed,**
MENE **NUMBERED**, *MENE* **NUMBERED,**
TEKEL **BALANCED**, *UPHARSIN* **SPLIT.**
26 This is the interpretation of the *thing* **utterance**:
MENE **NUMBERED**;
God **Elah** hath numbered thy *kingdom* **sovereigndom,**
and *finished it* **dealt shalam.**
27 *TEKEL* **BALANCED**;
Thou art *weighed* **balanced** in the balances,
and art found *wanting* **deficient.**
28 *PERES* **SPLIT**;
Thy *kingdom* **sovereigndom** is *divided* **split,**
and given to the *Medes* **Maday** and Persians.
29 Then *commanded Belshazzar* **said Belte Shats Tsar,**
and they *clothed Daniel* **enrobed Dani El**
with *scarlet* **purple,**
and *put* a *chain* **necklace** of gold about his neck,
and *made a proclamation* **announced** concerning him,
that he should be the third *ruler* **dominator**
in the *kingdom* **sovereigndom.**
30 In that night was *Belshazzar* **Bel Shats Tsar,**
the *king* **sovereign** of the *Chaldeans* **Kesediym**
slain **severed.**
31 And *Darius* **Daryavesh** the *Median* **Maday**
took the *kingdom* **sovereigndom,**
being about threescore **a son of sixty** and two years *old.*

DARYAVESH RAISES ONE HUNDRED AND TWENTY SATRAPS

6 It *pleased Darius* **was glorifying in front of Daryavesh**
to *set* **raise** over the *kingdom* **sovereigndom**
an hundred and twenty *princes* **satraps,**
which should be over the whole *kingdom* **sovereigndom;**
2 And over these three *presidents* **eunuchs;**
of whom *Daniel* **Dani El** was first:
that *the princes* **these satraps**
might give *accounts* **decrees** unto them,
and the *king* **sovereign** should have no damage.
3 Then this *Daniel* **Dani El**
was preferred **became preminent**
above the *presidents* **eunuchs** and *princes* **satraps,**
because an excellent spirit was in him;
and the *king* **sovereign** thought to *set* **raise** him
over the whole *realm* **sovereigndom.**

DARYAVESH RAISES A BOND

4 Then the *presidents* **eunuchs** and *princes* **satraps**
sought to find *occasion* **pretext** against *Daniel* **Dani El**
concerning the *kingdom* **sovereigndom;**
but they could find
none occasion **no pretext** nor *fault* **ruining;**
forasmuch as **because that** he was *faithful* **trustworthy,**
neither was there any error or *fault* **ruining** found in him.
5 Then said these *men* **mighty,**
We shall not find any *occasion* **pretext**
against this *Daniel* **Dani El,**
except **therefore** we find it against him
concerning the *law* **decree** of his *God* **Elah.**
6 Then these *presidents* **eunuchs** and *princes* **satraps**
assembled together **conspired** to the *king* **sovereign,**
and said thus unto him,
King Darius **Sovereign Daryavesh**, live *for ever* **eternally.**
7 All the *presidents* **eunuchs**
of the *kingdom* **sovereigndom,**
the *governors* **prefects**, and the *princes* **satraps,**
the counsellors, and the *captains* **governors,**
have consulted together
to *establish* **raise up** a royal statute,
and to *make a firm a decree* **empower an edict,**
that whosoever shall *ask* **request** a *petition* **request**
of any *God* **Elah** or man *for* **until** thirty days,
save **except** of thee, O *king* **sovereign,**
he shall be *cast* **hurled** into the *den* **dugout** of lions.
8 Now, O *king* **sovereign**, *establish* **raise** the *decree* **bond,**
and sign the *writing* **inscribing**, that it be not changed,
according to the *law* **decree**
of the *Medes* **Maday** and Persians,
which *altereth* **passeth** not.

9 *Wherefore* **Therefore then**
king Darius **sovereign Daryavesh**
signed the *writing* **inscribing** and the *decree* **bond**.
10 Now when *Daniel* **Dani El** knew
that the *writing* **inscribing** was signed,
he *went* **entered** into his house;
and his windows being open in his *chamber* **upper room**
toward *Jerusalem* **Yeru Shalem**,
he kneeled upon his knees
three *times* **appointments** a day,
and prayed,
and *gave thanks* **extended hands**
before **in front of** his *God* **Elah**,
as he did *aforetime* **formerly**.
11 Then these *men assembled* **mighty conspired**,
and found *Daniel* **Dani El**
praying and making supplication **requesting charism**
before **in front of** his *God* **Elah**.
12 Then they *came near* **approached**,
and *spake before* **said in front of** the *king* **sovereign**
concerning the *king's decree* **sovereign's bond**;
Hast thou not signed a *decree* **bond**,
that every man that shall *ask a petition* **request**
of any *God* **Elah** or man *within* **until** thirty days,
save **except** of thee, O *king* **sovereign**,
shall be cast into the *den* **dugout** of lions?
The *king* **sovereign** answered and said,
The *thing* **utterance** is *true* **certain**,
according to the *law* **decree**
of the *Medes* **Maday** and Persians, which altereth not.
13 Then answered they
and said *before* **in front of** the *king* **sovereign**,
That *Daniel* **Dani El**, which is of the *children* **sons**
of the *captivity* **exile** of *Judah* **Yah Hudah**,
regardeth not **his taste to** thee, O *king* **sovereign**,
nor the decree that thou hast signed,
but *maketh* **requesteth** his *petition* **request**
three *times* **appointments** a day.
14 Then the *king* **sovereign**,
when he heard these *words* **utterances**,
was sore displeased **much stank** with himself,
and set his *heart* **anxiety** on *Daniel* **Dani El**
to *deliver* **liberate** him:
and he laboured till the *going down* **downing** of the sun
to *deliver* **rescue** him.
15 Then these *men* **mighty**
assembled **conspired** unto the *king* **sovereign**,
and said unto the *king* **sovereign**,
Know, O *king* **sovereign**,
that the *law* **decree** of the *Medes* **Maday** and Persians is,
That no *decree* **bond** nor *statute* **edict**
which the *king establisheth* **sovereign raiseth**
may be changed.

DANI EL IN THE DUGOUT

16 Then the *king commanded* **sovereign said**,
and they brought *Daniel* **Dani El**,
and *cast* **hurled** him into the *den* **dugout** of lions.
Now the *king spake* **sovereign answered**
and said unto *Daniel* **Dani El**,
Thy *God* **Elah**
whom thou servest *continually* **perpetually**,
he *will deliver* **shall liberate** thee.
17 And *a* **one** stone was brought,
and *laid* **set** upon the mouth of the *den* **dugout**;
and the *king* **sovereign** sealed it with his own signet,
and with the signet of his *lords* **nobles**;
that *the purpose* **his will** might not be changed
concerning *Daniel* **Dani El**.
18 Then the *king* **sovereign** went to his *palace* **manse**,
and *passed the night* **lodged overnight** fasting:
neither were instruments *of musick*
brought before **entered in front of** him:
and his sleep *went* **fled** from him.
19 Then the *king* **sovereign** arose
very early in the morning **in the splendour of dawn**,
and went *in haste* **hastily** unto the *den* **dugout** of lions.
20 And when he *came to* **approached** the *den* **dugout**,
he cried with a *lamentable* **contorting** voice
unto *Daniel* **Dani El**:
and the *king spake* **sovereign answered**
and said to *Daniel* **Dani El**,
O *Daniel* **Dani El**, servant of the living *God* **Elah**,
is thy *God* **Elah**, whom thou servest continually,
able to *deliver* **liberate** thee from the lions?

DANI EL LIBERATED FROM THE DUGOUT

21 Then *said Daniel* **uttered Dani El**
unto the *king* **sovereign**,
O *king* **sovereign**, live *for ever* **eternally**.
22 My *God* **Elah** hath sent his angel,
and hath shut the lions' mouths,
that they have not *hurt* **despoiled** me:
forasmuch as before **because that in front of** him
innocency **purity** was found in me;
and also *before* **in front of** thee,
O *king* **sovereign**, have I done no *hurt* **wickedness**.
23 Then was the *king* **sovereign**
exceeding *glad* **rejoiced** for him,
and *commanded* **said**
that they should take *Daniel up* **Dani El**
out of the *den* **dugout**.
So *Daniel* **Dani El** was taken *up* out of the *den* **dugout**,
and no *manner of hurt* **damage** was found upon him,
because he *believed* **trusted** in his *God* **Elah**.
24 And the *king commanded* **sovereign said**,
and they brought those *men* **mighty**
which had *accused Daniel* **chewed out Dani El**,
and they *cast* **hurled** them into the *den* **dugout** of lions,
them, their *children* **sons**, and their *wives* **women**;
and had the mastery of **until the lions dominated** them,
and *brake all* **pulverized** their bones *in pieces*
or ever they *came* **happened**
at the bottom of the *den* **dugout**.

DARYAVESH'S DECREE

25 Then *king Darius* **sovereign Daryavesh**
wrote **inscribed**
unto all people, nations, and *languages* **tongues**,
that *dwell* **twirl** in all the earth;
Peace **Shalom** be *multiplied* **increased** unto you.
26 I *make* **set in front of me** a decree,
That in every dominion of my *kingdom* **sovereigndom**
men *tremble* **become agitated** and *fear* **terrify**
before the God **in front of the Elah** of *Daniel* **Dani El**:
for he is the living *God* **Elah**,
and *stedfast for ever* **permanent eternally**,
and his *kingdom* **sovereigndom**
that which shall not be *destroyed* **despoiled**,
and his dominion shall be
even unto the *end* **consummation**.
27 He *delivereth* **liberateth** and rescueth,
and he *worketh signs* **doeth omens** and *wonders* **marvels**
in *heaven* **the heavens** and in earth,
who hath *delivered Daniel* **liberated Dani El**
from the *power* **hand** of the lions.
28 So this *Daniel* **Dani El** prospered
in the *reign* **sovereigndom** of *Darius* **Daryavesh**,
and
in the *reign* **sovereigndom** of *Cyrus* **Koresh** the Persian.

DANI EL'S DREAM OF FOUR LIVE BEINGS

7 In the first year
of *Belshazzar* **Bel Shats Tsar**
king **sovereign** of *Babylon* **Babel**
Daniel had **Dani El saw** a dream and visions of his head
upon his bed:
then he *wrote* **inscribed** the dream,
and *told* **said** the sum of the *matters* **utterances**.
2 *Daniel spake* **Dani El answered** and said,
I saw in my vision by night, and, behold,
the four winds of the *heaven* **heavens**
strove **rushed forth** upon the great sea.
3 And four great *beasts* **live beings**
came up **ascended** from the sea,
diverse **changed** one from another.
4 The first was like a lion, and had eagle's wings:
I *beheld* **saw** till the wings *thereof* were plucked,
and it was lifted up from the earth,
and *made stand* **raised** upon the feet as a man,
and a man's heart was given to it.
5 And behold another *beast* **live being**,
a second, like to a bear,
and it raised up itself on *one* **its** side,

and it had three ribs
in the mouth of it between the teeth of it:
and they said thus unto it, Arise, devour much flesh.
6 After this I *beheld* **saw**, and *lo* **behold** another,
like a leopard,
which had upon the back of it four wings of a *fowl* **flyer**;
the *beast* **live being** had also four heads;
and dominion was given to it.
7 After this I saw in the night visions,
and behold a fourth *beast* **live being**,
dreadful **terrifying** and *terrible* **burly**,
and *strong exceedingly* **exceedingly mighty**;
and it had great iron teeth:
it devoured and *brake in pieces* **pulverized**,
and *stamped* **trampled**
the *residue* **survivors** with the feet of it:
and it was *diverse* **changed**
from all the *beasts* **live beings**
that were *before* **in front of** it;
and it had ten horns.
8 I *considered* **was comprehending** the horns,
and, behold,
there *came up among* **ascended between** them
another little horn,
before **in front of** whom there were
three of the first horns *plucked up by the roots* **uprooted**:
and, behold, in this horn were eyes like the eyes of man,
and a mouth *speaking* **uttering** great *things*.

DANI EL SEES THE ANCIENT OF DAYS

9 I *beheld* **saw** till the thrones were *cast down* **hurled**,
and the Ancient of days did sit,
whose *garment* **robe** was white as snow,
and the hair of his head like the *pure* **clean** wool:
his throne was like the fiery flame,
and his wheels as *burning* **flaming** fire.
10 A fiery *stream issued* **river flowed**
and *came forth* **emerged** from *before* **in front of** him:
thousand thousands ministered unto him,
and ten thousand times ten thousand **a myriad myriads**
stood before **rose up in front of** him:
the judgment was set,
and the *books* **scrolls** were opened.
11 I *beheld* **saw** then
because of the voice of the great *words* **utterances**
which the horn *spake* **uttered**:
I *beheld even* **saw**
till the *beast* **live being** was *slain* **severed**,
and his body destroyed, and given to the burning flame.
12 *As concerning* the *rest* **survivors**
of the *beasts* **live beings**,
they had their dominion *taken* **pass** away:
yet their lives were *prolonged* **given**
for a season **until an appointment** and time.

DANI EL SEES THE SON OF MAN

13 I saw in the night visions, and, behold,
one like the *Son* **Bar** of man
came **coming** with the clouds of *heaven* **the heavens**,
and *came* **coming** to the Ancient of days,
and they *brought* **approached** him *near*
before **in front of** him.
14 And there was given him dominion,
and *glory* **esteem**, and a *kingdom* **sovereigndom**,
that all people, nations, and *languages* **tongues**,
should serve him:
his dominion is an *everlasting* **eternal** dominion,
which shall not pass away,
and his *kingdom* **sovereigndom**
that which shall not be *destroyed* **despoiled**.
15 I *Daniel* **Dani El** was grieved in my spirit
in the midst of my *body* **sheath**,
and the visions of my head *troubled* **terrified** me.

DANI EL INTERPRETS THE UTTERANCES

16 I *came near* **approached**
unto one of them that *stood by* **rose**,
and *asked* **requested of** him the *truth* **certainty** of all this.
So he *told* **said to** me, and made me know
the interpretation of the *things* **utterances**.
17 These great *beasts* **live beings**,
which are four, are four *kings* **sovereigns**,
which shall arise out of the earth.
18 But the *saints* **holy** of *the most High* **Elyon**
shall take the *kingdom* **sovereigndom**,
and *possess* **hold** the *kingdom* **sovereigndom**
for ever **eternally**,
even *for ever* **eternally** and *ever* **eternally**.
19 Then I *would* **willed to** know the *truth* **certainty**
of the fourth *beast* **live being**,
which was *diverse* **changed** from all the others,
exceeding *dreadful* **terrifying**,
whose teeth were of iron, and his nails of *brass* **copper**;
which devoured, *brake in pieces* **pulverized**,
and *stamped* **trampled** the *residue* **survivors** with his feet;
20 And of the ten horns that were in his head,
and of the other which *came up* **ascended**,
and *before* **in front of** whom three fell;
even of that horn that had eyes,
and a mouth that *spake* **uttered** very great *things*,
whose *look* **vision** was *more stout* **greater**
than his *fellows* **companions**.
21 I *beheld* **saw**,
and the same horn made war with the *saints* **holy**,
and prevailed against them;
22 *Until* the Ancient of days came,
and *judgment* **the pleading of the cause**
was given to the *saints* **holy** of *the most High* **Elyon**;
and the *time came* **appointment happened**
that the *saints* **holy**
possessed **held** the *kingdom* **sovereigndom**.
23 Thus he said, The fourth *beast* **live being**
shall be the fourth *kingdom* **sovereigndom** upon earth,
which shall be *diverse* **changed** from all kingdoms,
and shall devour the whole earth,
and shall tread it down, and *break* **pulverize** it *in pieces*.
24 And the ten horns out of this *kingdom* **sovereigndom**
are ten *kings* **sovereigns** that shall arise:
and another shall rise after them;
and he shall be *diverse* **changed** from the first,
and he shall *subdue* **abase** three *kings* **sovereigns**.
25 And he shall *speak great words* **utter utterances**
against **concerning** the *most High* **Elyon**,
and shall wear out the *saints* **holy** of *the most High* **Elyon**,
and *think* **willeth** to change
times **appointments** and *laws* **decrees**:
and they shall be given into his hand
until a time and times and the dividing of time.
26 But the *judgment* **pleaded cause** shall *sit* **set**,
and they shall *take* **pass** away his dominion,
to *consume* **desolate** and to destroy it
unto the *end* **consummation**.
27 And the *kingdom* **sovereigndom** and dominion,
and the greatness of the *kingdom* **sovereigndom**
under the whole *heaven* **heavens**,
shall be given to the people
of the *saints* **holy** of *the most High* **Elyon**,
whose *kingdom* **sovereigndom**
is an *everlasting kingdom* **eternal sovereigndom**,
and all dominions
shall serve and *obey* **hearken unto** him.
28 *Hitherto* **Until thus**
is the *end* **conclusion** of the *matter* **utterance**.
As for me Daniel **I, Dani El**,
my *cogitations* **intentions** much *troubled* **terrified** me,
and my *countenance* **cheerfulness** changed in me:
but I *kept* **guarded** the *matter* **utterance** in my heart.

DANI EL'S VISION OF THE RAM AND THE BUCK

8 In the third year of the *reign* **sovereigndom**
of *king Belshazzar* **sovereign Bel Shats Tsar**
a vision *appeared unto* **was seen by** me,
even unto me *Daniel* **Dani El**,
after that which *appeared unto* **was seen by** me
at the *first* **beginning**.
2 And I saw in a vision; and it *came to pass* **became**,
when I saw, that I was at Shushan in the palace,
which is in the *province* **jurisdiction** of Elam;
and I saw in a vision, and I was by the river of Ulai.
3 Then I lifted up mine eyes, and saw, and, behold,
there stood *before* **at the face of** the river
a **one** ram which had *two* horns:
and the *two* horns were high;
but one was higher than the *other* **second**,

and the higher *came up* **ascended** last.
4 I saw the ram *pushing westward* **butting seaward**,
and northward, and southward;
so that no *beasts* **live beings**
might stand *before him* **at his face**,
neither *was there any* that could *deliver* **rescue**
out of his hand;
but he *did* **worked** according to his *will* **pleasure**,
and *became great* **greatened**.
5 And as I *was considering* **discerned**, behold,
an he goat **a buck of the doe goats**
came from the *west* **dusk**
on the face of the whole earth,
and touched not the *ground* **earth**:
and the *goat* **buck** had a *notable* horn **of vision**
between his eyes.
6 And he came to the ram *that had two* **master of** horns,
which I had seen standing *before* **at the face of** the river,
and ran unto him in the fury of his *power* **force**.
7 And I saw him *come* **touch** close *unto* **beside** the ram,
and he was *moved with choler* **embittered** against him,
and smote the ram, and brake his two horns:
and there was no *power* **force** in the ram
to stand *before him* **at his face**,
but he cast him down to the *ground* **earth**,
and *stamped upon* **trampled** him:
and there was none
that could *deliver* **rescue** the ram out of his hand.
8 Therefore the *he goat* **buck of the doe goats**
waxed very great **greatened mightily**:
and when he was *strong* **mighted**,
the great horn was broken;
and for it *came up* **ascended** four *notable ones* **of vision**
toward the four winds of *heaven* **the heavens**.
9 And out of one of them came forth a little horn,
which *waxed exceeding great* **greatened exceedingly**,
toward the south, and toward the *east* **rising**,
and toward the *pleasant land* **splendour**.
10 And it *waxed great* **greatened**,
even to the host of *heaven* **the heavens**;
and it *cast down* **felled** *some* of the host and of the stars
to the *ground* **earth**,
and *stamped upon* **trampled** them.
11 Yea, he *magnified* **greatened** *himself*
even to the *prince* **governor** of the host,
and by him
the *daily sacrifice* **continual** was *taken away* **lifted**,
and the place of the *sanctuary* **holies** was cast down.
12 And an host was given him
against the *daily sacrifice* **continual**
by reason of *transgression* **rebellion**,
and it cast down the truth to the *ground* **earth**;
and it *practised* **worked**, and prospered.
13 Then I heard one *saint* **holy one** speaking,
and *another saint* **one holy one**
said unto *that certain saint* **such a one** which spake,
How long shall be the vision
concerning **of** the *daily sacrifice* **continual**,
and the *transgression* **rebellion** of *desolation* **desolating**,
to give both the *sanctuary* **holies** and the host
to be *trodden under foot* **trampled**?
14 And he said unto me,
Unto two thousand and three hundred
days **evening mornings**;
then shall the *sanctuary* **holies** be *cleansed* **justified**.

A MIGHTY INTERPRETS THE VISION

15 And it *came to pass* **became**,
when I, *even* I *Daniel* **Dani El**, had seen the vision,
and sought for *the meaning* **discernment**,
then, behold,
there stood before me
as the *appearance* **visage** of a *man* **mighty**.
16 And I heard a *man's* **human** voice
between *the banks of* Ulai,
which called, and said, *Gabriel* **Gabri El**,
make **cause** this *man* **one**
to *understand* **discern** the vision.
17 So he came *near* **beside** where I stood:
and when he came,
I *was afraid* **frightened**, and fell upon my face:
but he said unto me,
Understand **Discern**, O son of *man* **humanity**:
for at the time of the end shall be the vision.
18 *Now* as he was *speaking* **wording** with me,
I was *in a deep sleep* **sleeping soundly**
on my face toward the *ground* **earth**:
but he touched me, and *set* **stood** me *upright* **standing**.
19 And he said, Behold,
I *will make* **shall cause** thee **to** know
what shall be in the last end of the *indignation* **rage**:
for at the *time appointed* **season** the end shall be.
20 The ram which thou sawest
having two **master of** horns
are the *kings* **sovereigns** of *Media* **Maday** and Persia.
21 And the *rough goat* **buck buck**
is the *king* **sovereign** of *Grecia* **Yavan**:
and the great horn that is between his eyes
is the first *king* **sovereign**.
22 *Now* that being broken, whereas four stood up for it,
four *kingdoms* **sovereigndoms** shall stand *up*
out of the *nation* **goyim**, but not in his *power* **force**.
23 And in the *latter time* **finality**
of their *kingdom* **sovereigndom**,
when the *transgressors* **rebels**
are *come to the full* **consumated**,
a *king* **sovereign** of *fierce countenance* **strong face**,
and *understanding dark sentences* **discerning riddles**,
shall stand *up*.
24 And his *power* **force** shall be mighty,
but not by his own *power* **force**:
and he shall *destroy wonderfully* **ruin marvelously**,
and shall prosper, and *practise* **work**,
and shall *destroy* **ruin** the mighty
and the *holy people* **people of the holy one**.
25 And through his *policy* **comprehension** also
he shall cause *craft* **deceit** to prosper in his hand;
and he shall *magnify* **greaten** *himself* in his heart,
and by *peace* **serenity** shall *destroy* **ruin** many:
he shall also stand *up*
against the *Prince* **Governor** of *princes* **governors**;
but he shall be broken *without* **by a final** hand.
26 And the vision of the evening and the morning
which was *told* **said** is *true* **in truth**:
wherefore shut thou up the vision;
for it shall be for many days.
27 And I *Daniel* **Dani El**
fainted, and was **became** sick *certain* **for** days;
afterward I rose up,
and *did* **worked** the *king's business* **sovereign's work**;
and I was *astonished* **stunned** at the vision,
but none *understood* **discerned** it.

DANI EL DISCERNS THE SCROLL OF THE SEVENTY WEEKS

9 In the first year
of *Darius* **Daryavesh** the son of *Ahasuerus* **Achach Rosh**,
of the seed of the *Medes* **Maday**,
which *was made king* **reigned sovereign**
over the *realm* **sovereigndom**
of the *Chaldeans* **Kesediym**;
2 In the first year of his reign
I *Daniel understood* **Dani El discerned** by *books* **scrolls**
the number of the years,
whereof the word of *the LORD* **Yah Veh**
came to *Jeremiah* **Yirme Yah** the prophet,
that he *would accomplish* **should fulfill** seventy years
in the *desolations* **parched areas**
of *Jerusalem* **Yeru Shalem**.
3 And I *set* **gave** my face
unto *the Lord God* **Adonay Elohim**,
to seek by prayer and supplications,
with fasting, and *sackcloth* **saq**, and ashes:
4 And I prayed unto *the LORD* **Yah Veh** my *God* **Elohim**,
and *made* **extended** my *confession* **hands**, and said,
I beseech O *Lord* **Adonay**,
the great and *dreadful God* **awesome El**,
keeping **guarding** the covenant and mercy
to them that love him, and to them
that *keep* **guard** his *commandments* **misvoth**;
5 We have sinned,
and have *committed iniquity* **perverted**,
and have done wickedly, and have rebelled,

even by *departing* **turning aside**
from thy *precepts* **misvoth** and from thy judgments:
6 Neither have we hearkened
unto thy servants the prophets,
which *spake* **worded** in thy name
to our *kings* **sovereigns**,
our *princes* **governors**, and our fathers,
and to all the people of the land.
7 O *Lord* **Adonay**,
righteousness belongeth **justness** unto thee,
but unto us *confusion* **shame** of faces, as at this day;
to the men of *Judah* **Yah Hudah**,
and to the *inhabitants* **settlers** of *Jerusalem* **Yeru Shalem**,
and unto all *Israel* **Yisra El**,
that are near, and *that are* far off,
through all the *countries* **lands**
whither thou hast driven them,
because of their *trespass* **treason**
that they have *trespassed* **treasoned** against thee.
8 *O Lord* **Adonay**,
to us *belongeth confusion* **be shame** of face,
to our *kings* **sovereigns**, to our *princes* **governors**,
and to our fathers,
because we have sinned against thee.
9 To *the Lord* **Adonay** our *God* **Elohim**
belong **be** mercies and forgivenesses,
though we have rebelled against him;
10 Neither have we *obeyed* **hearkened unto** the voice
of *the LORD* **Yah Veh** our *God* **Elohim**,
to walk in his *laws* **torah**,
which he *set before us* **gave at our face**
by **the hand of** his servants the prophets.
11 Yea, all *Israel* **Yisra El**
have *transgressed* **trespassed** thy *law* **torah**,
even by *departing* **turning aside**,
that they might not *obey* **hearken unto** thy voice;
therefore the *curse* **oath** is poured upon us,
and the oath that is *written* **inscribed**
in the *law* **torah** of *Moses* **Mosheh**
the servant of *God* **Elohim**,
because we have sinned against him.
12 And he hath *confirmed* **raised** his words,
which he *spake* **worded** against us,
and against our judges that judged us,
by bringing upon us a great evil:
for under the whole *heaven* **heavens**
hath not been *done* **worked**
as hath been *done* **worked** upon *Jerusalem* **Yeru Shalem**.
13 As it is *written* **inscribed**
in the *law* **torah** of *Moses* **Mosheh**,
all this evil is come upon us:
yet *made* **stroked** we not *our prayer* **the face**
before the LORD **of Yah Veh** our *God* **Elohim**,
that we might turn from our *iniquities* **perversities**,
and *understand* **comprehend** thy truth.
14 Therefore
hath *the LORD* **Yah Veh** watched upon the evil,
and brought it upon us:
for *the LORD* **Yah Veh** our *God* **Elohim**
is *righteous* **just** in all his works which he *doeth* **worketh**:
for we *obeyed* **hearkened** not **unto** his voice.
15 And now, *O Lord* **Adonay** our *God* **Elohim**,
that hast brought thy people forth
out of the land of *Egypt* **Misrayim**
with a *mighty* **strong** hand,
and hast *gotten* **worked** thee *renown* **a name**,
as at this day;
we have sinned, we have done wickedly.
16 *O Lord* **Adonay**,
according to all thy *righteousness* **justness**,
I beseech thee,
let thine *anger* **wrath** and thy fury be turned away
from thy city *Jerusalem* **Yeru Shalem**, thy holy mountain:
because for our sins,
and for the *iniquities* **perversities** of our fathers,
Jerusalem **Yeru Shalem** and thy people
are *become* a reproach to all that are **round** about us.
17 Now therefore, O our *God* **Elohim**,
hear the prayer of thy servant, and his supplications,
and cause thy face to *shine* **lighten**
upon thy *sanctuary* **holies** that is desolate,
for *the Lord's* **Adonay's** sake.
18 O my *God* **Elohim**,
incline **extend** thine ear, and hear;
open thine eyes,
and *behold* **see** our *desolations* **desolated**,
and the city which is called by thy name:
for we do not *present* **fell** our supplications
before thee **at thy face**
for our *righteousnesses* **justnesses**,
but for thy great mercies.
19 *O Lord* **Adonay**, hear; *O Lord* **Adonay**, forgive;
O Lord **Adonay**, hearken and *do* **work**;
defer **delay** not, for thine own sake, *O* my *God* **Elohim**:
for thy city and thy people are called by thy name.
20 And whiles I was speaking, and praying,
and *confessing* **extending my hands for** my sin
and the sin of my people *Israel* **Yisra El**,
and *presenting* **felling** my supplication
before the LORD **at the face of Yah Veh** my *God* **Elohim**
for the holy mountain of my *God* **Elohim**;
21 Yea, whiles I was speaking in prayer,
even the man *Gabriel* **Gabri El**,
whom I had seen in the vision at the beginning,
being *caused to fly swiftly* **wearied in weariness**,
touched me
about the time of the evening *oblation* **offering**.
22 And *he informed me* **discerned**,
and *talked* **worded** with me, and said,
O *Daniel* **Dani El**,
I am now come forth to *give* **cause** thee
skill and understanding **to comprehend discernment**.
23 At the beginning of thy supplications
the *commandment* **word** came forth,
and I am come to *shew* **tell** *thee*;
for thou art *greatly beloved* **desired**:
therefore *understand* **discern** the *matter* **word**,
and *consider* **discern** the vision.
24 Seventy weeks are *determined* **cut** upon thy people
and upon thy holy city,
to *finish* **restrain** the *transgression* **rebellion**,
and to *make an end of* **seal up** sins,
and to *make reconciliation* **kapar/atone**
for *iniquity* **perversity**,
and to bring in *everlasting righteousness* **eternal justness**,
and to seal up the vision and *prophecy* **the prophet**,
and to anoint the *most Holy* **holy of holies**.
25 Know therefore and *understand* **comprehend**,
that from the
going forth **proceeding** of the *commandment* **word**
to restore and to build *Jerusalem* **Yeru Shalem**
unto the Messiah the *Prince* **Eminent** shall be
seven weeks, and *threescore* **sixty** and two weeks:
the *street* **broadway** shall be
built again **restored and rebuilt**,
and the *wall* **trench**,
even in *troublous* times **of distress**.
26 And after *threescore* **sixty** and two weeks
shall Messiah be cut off,
but not for himself:
and the people of the *prince* **eminent** that shall come
shall *destroy* **ruin** the city and the *sanctuary* **holies**;
and the end *thereof* shall be with *a flood* **an overflowing**,
and unto the end of the war
desolations are determined **desolating is appointed**.
27 And he shall *confirm* **prevail mightily**
the covenant with many *for* one week:
and in the *midst* **half** of the week
he shall cause the sacrifice and the *oblation* **offering**
to *cease* **shabbathize**,
and for the *overspreading* **wing** of abominations
he shall *make it* desolate **it**,
even until the *consummation* **final finish**,
and that *determined* **appointed**
shall be poured upon the *desolate* **desolated**.

DANI EL'S VISION OF ONE HUMAN AND MICHAH EL

10 In the third year of *Cyrus* **Koresh**
king **sovereign** of Persia
a *thing* **word** was *revealed* **exposed** unto *Daniel* **Dani El**,
whose name was called *Belteshazzar* **Belte Shats Tsar**;

and the *thing* **word** was *true* **in truth**,
but the *time appointed* **hostility** was *long* **great**:
and he *understood* **discerned** the *thing* **word**,
and had *understanding* **discernment** of the vision.
2 In those days I *Daniel* **Dani El**
was mourning three *full* weeks **of days**.
3 I ate no *pleasant* bread **of desire**,
neither came flesh nor wine in my mouth,
in anointing, neither did I anoint myself *at all*,
till three *whole* weeks **of days** were fulfilled.
4 And in the four and twentieth day of the first month,
as I was by the *side* **hand** of the great river,
which is *Hiddekel* **Hiddeqel**;
5 Then I lifted up mine eyes, and *looked* **saw**,
and behold *a certain* **one** man *clothed* **enrobed** in linen,
whose loins were girded with fine *gold* **ore** of Uphaz:
6 His body also was like the beryl,
and his face as the *appearance* **visage** of lightning,
and his eyes as *lamps* **flambeaus** of fire,
and his arms and his feet
like in *colour to polished brass* **eye as burnished copper**,
and the voice of his words like the voice of a multitude.
7 And I *Daniel* **Dani El** alone saw the vision:
for the men that were with me saw not the vision;
but **nevertheless**
a great *quaking* **trembling** fell upon them,
so that they fled to hide themselves.
8 Therefore I *was left* **remained** alone,
and saw this great vision,
and there remained no *strength* **force** in me:
for my *comeliness* **majesty** was turned in me
into *corruption* **ruin**,
and I retained no *strength* **force**.
9 Yet heard I the voice of his words:
and when I heard the voice of his words,
then was I *in a deep sleep* **sleeping soundly** on my face,
and my face toward the *ground* **earth**.
10 And, behold, an hand touched me,
which *set* **staggered** me upon my knees
and *upon* the palms of my hands.
11 And he said unto me,
O *Daniel* **Dani El**, a man *greatly beloved* **desired**,
understand **discern** the words
that I *speak* **word** unto thee,
and **in standing,** stand *upright*:
for unto thee am I now sent.
And when he had *spoken* **worded** this word unto me,
I stood trembling.
12 Then said he unto me, *Fear* **Awe** not, *Daniel* **Dani El**:
for from the first day
that thou didst *set* **give** thine heart to *understand* **discern**,
and to *chasten* **humble** thyself
before **at the face of** thy *God* **Elohim**,
thy words were heard, and I am come for thy words.
13 But the *prince* **governor**
of the *kingdom* **sovereigndom** of Persia
withstood **stood against** me one and twenty days:
but, *lo* **behold**, *Michael* **Michah El**,
one of the *chief princes* **head governors**,
came to help me;
and I remained there
with **beside** the *kings* **sovereigns** of Persia.
14 *Now* I am come
to *make* **cause** thee *understand* **to discern**
what shall befall thy people in the latter days:
for yet the vision is for *many* days.
15 And when he had *spoken* **worded** such words
unto me,
I *set* **gave** my face toward the *ground* **earth**,
and I became *dumb* **mute**.
16 And, behold, *one like the similitude* **a likeness**
of the sons of *men* **humanity** touched my lips:
then I opened my mouth, and *spake* **worded**,
and said unto him that stood before me,
O my *lord* **adoni**,
by the vision my *sorrows* **pangs** are turned upon me,
and I have retained no *strength* **force**.
17 For how can the servant of *this my lord* **my adoni**
talk with this my lord **word this with my adoni**?
for as for me, *straightway* **at this time**
there *remained* **stood** no *strength* **force** in me,
neither *is* **remained** there breath *left* in me.
18 Then there came again and touched me
one like the *appearance* **visage** of a *man* **human**,
and he strengthened me,
19 And said, O man *greatly beloved* **desired**,
fear **awe** not:
peace **shalom** be unto thee, be strong, yea, be strong.
And when he had *spoken* **worded** unto me,
I was strengthened, and said,
Let my *lord speak* **adoni word**;
for thou hast strengthened me.
20 Then said he,
Knowest thou wherefore I come unto thee?
and now *will* **shall** I return
to fight with the *prince* **governor** of Persia:
and when I am gone forth, *lo* **behold**,
the *prince* **governor** of *Grecia* **Yavan** shall come.
21 *But I will shew* **Nevertheless I shall tell** thee
that which is *noted* **signified**
in the *scripture* **inscribing** of truth:
and there is none that holdeth with me in these *things*,
but *Michael* **Michah El** your *prince* **governor**.

THE SOVEREIGNS OF THE NORTH AND THE SOUTH

11 Also I
in the first year of *Darius* **Daryavesh** the *Mede* **Maday**,
even I, I stood to *confirm* **strengthen him**
and to *strengthen him* **be his stronghold**.
2 And now *will I shew* **shall I tell** thee the truth.
Behold,
there shall stand *up* yet three *kings* **sovereigns** in Persia;
and the fourth shall be
far richer **enriched in greater riches** than they all:
and by his strength through his riches
he shall *stir up* **waken** all
against the *realm* **sovereigndom** of *Grecia* **Yavan**.
3 And a mighty *king* **sovereign** shall stand *up*,
that shall *rule* **reign** with great *dominion* **reign**,
and *do* **work** according to his *will* **pleasure**.
4 And when he shall stand *up*,
his *kingdom* **sovereigndom** shall be broken,
and shall be *divided* **halved**
toward the four winds of *heaven* **the heavens**;
and not to his posterity,
nor according to his *dominion* **reign**
which he *ruled* **reigned**:
for his *kingdom* **sovereigndom**
shall be *plucked up* **uprooted**,
even for others beside those.
5 And the *king* **sovereign** of the south shall be strong,
and *one* of his *princes* **governors**;
and he shall be strong above him,
and *have dominion* **reign**;
his *dominion* **reign** shall be a great *dominion* **reign**.
6 And in the end of years
they shall join *themselves together*;
for the *king's* **sovereign's** daughter of the south
shall come to the *king* **sovereign** of the north
to *make an agreement* **work a straightness**:
but she shall not retain the *power* **force** of the arm;
neither shall he stand, nor his arm:
but she shall be given up,
and they that brought her, and he that begat her,
and he that strengthened her in these times.
7 But out of a branch of her roots
shall *one* stand *up* in his *estate* **station**,
which shall come with *an army* **the valiant**,
and shall enter into the *fortress* **stronghold**
of the *king* **sovereign** of the north,
and shall *deal* **work** against them, and shall prevail:
8 And shall also carry captives into *Egypt* **Misrayim**
their *gods* **elohim**, with their *princes* **libations**,
and with their *precious vessels* **instruments of desire**
of silver and of gold;
and he shall *continue* **stand** more years
than the *king* **sovereign** of the north.
9 So the *king* **sovereign** of the south
shall come into his *kingdom* **sovereigndom**,
and shall return into his own *land* **soil**.
10 But his sons shall be *stirred up* **throttled**,

and shall *assemble* **gather**
a multitude of *great forces* **valiant**:
and **in coming,** *one* shall *certainly* come,
and overflow, and pass through:
then shall he return, and be *stirred up* **throttled**,
even to his *fortress* **stronghold**.
11 And the *king* **sovereign** of the south
shall be *moved with choler* **embittered**,
and shall come forth and fight with him,
even with the *king* **sovereign** of the north:
and he shall *set forth* **cause** a great multitude **to stand**;
but the multitude shall be given into his hand.
12 And when he hath *taken* **borne** away the multitude,
his heart shall be lifted *up*;
and he shall *cast down many ten thousands* **fell myriads**:
but he shall not be strengthened *by it*.
13 For the *king* **sovereign** of the north shall return,
and shall *set forth* **stand** a multitude
greater than the former,
and **in coming,** shall *certainly* come
after certain **at the end of times, even** years
with a great *army* **valiant**
and with much *riches* **acquisitions**.
14 And in those times there shall many stand *up*
against the *king* **sovereign** of the south:
also the *robbers* **sons of tyrants** of thy people
shall *exalt* **lift** themselves to *establish* **stand** the vision;
but they shall *fall* **falter**.
15 So the *king* **sovereign** of the north shall come,
and *cast up* **pour** a mount,
and *take* **capture** the most *fenced* **fortified** cities:
and the arms of the south shall not withstand,
neither his chosen people,
neither shall there be any *strength* **force** to withstand.
16 But he that cometh against him
shall *do* **work** according to his own *will* **pleasure**,
and none shall stand *before him* **at his face**:
and he shall stand in the *glorious* land **of splendour**,
which by his hand shall be *consumed* **fully finished**.
17 He shall also set his face to enter
with the *strength* **power**
of his whole *kingdom* **sovereigndom**,
and *upright ones* **straight** with him;
thus shall he *do* **work**:
and he shall give him the daughter of women,
corrupting **to ruin** her:
but she shall not stand *on his side*, neither be for him.
18 After this
shall he *turn* **set** his face unto the *isles* **islands**,
and shall take many:
but a *prince* **commander** for his own behalf
shall cause *the* **his** reproach *offered by him*
to *cease* **shabbathize**;
without his own reproach
he shall cause it to turn upon him.
19 Then he shall turn his face
toward the *fort* **stronghold** of his own land:
but he shall *stumble* **falter** and fall, and not be found.
20 Then shall stand *up* in his *estate* **station**
a raiser of **an exactor who passeth** taxes
in the *glory* **majesty** of the *kingdom* **sovereigndom**:
but within *few days* **one day**
he shall be *destroyed* **broken**,
neither in *anger* **wrath**, nor in *battle* **war**.
21 And in his *estate* **station**
shall stand *up a vile person* **a despised**,
to whom they shall not give
the *honour* **majesty** of the *kingdom* **sovereigndom**:
but he shall come in *peaceably* **serenity**,
and *obtain* **hold** the *kingdom* **sovereigndom**
by *flatteries* **soothings**.
22 And with the arms of *a flood* **an overflowing**
shall they be *overflown* **overflowed**
from *before him* **his face**,
and shall be broken;
yea, also the *prince* **eminent** of the covenant.
23 And after *the league made with* **joining** him
he shall work deceitfully:
for he shall *come up* **ascend**,
and shall become *strong* **mighty**
with a small *people* **goyim**.
24 He shall enter *peaceably* **in serenity**
even upon the *fattest places* **fatness**
of the *province* **jurisdiction**;
and he shall *do* **work** that
which his fathers have not *done* **worked**,
nor his fathers' fathers;
he shall scatter among them
the *prey* **plunder**, and spoil, and *riches* **acquisitions**:
yea, and he shall
forecast **fabricate** his *devices* **fabrications**
against the *strong holds* **fortresses**, even for a time.
25 And he shall *stir up* **waken**
his *power* **force** and his *courage* **heart**
against the *king* **sovereign** of the south
with a great *army* **valiant**;
and the *king* **sovereign** of the south
shall be *stirred up* **throttled** to *battle* **war**
with a *very* **mighty** great and mighty *army* **valiant**;
but he shall not stand:
for they shall *forecast devices* **fabricate fabrications**
against him.
26 Yea,
they that feed of *the portion of his meat* **his delicacies**
shall *destroy* **break** him,
and his *army* **valiant** shall overflow:
and many shall fall down *slain* **pierced**.
27 And both of these *kings'* **sovereign's** hearts
shall be to *do mischief* **vilify**,
and they shall *speak* **word** lies at one table;
but it shall not prosper:
for yet the end shall be at the *time appointed* **season**.
28 Then shall he return into his land
with great *riches* **acquisitions**;
and his heart shall be against the holy covenant;
and he shall *do exploits* **work**,
and return to his own land.
29 At the *time appointed* **season** he shall return,
and come toward the south;
but it shall not be as the former, or as the latter.
30 For the ships of *Chittim* **Kittim** shall come against him:
therefore he shall be *grieved* **dejected**, and return,
and *have indignation* **rage** against the holy covenant:
so shall he *do* **work**;
he shall even return,
and *have intelligence* **discern** with them
that forsake the holy covenant.
31 And arms shall stand on his part,
and they shall *pollute* **profane** the *sanctuary* **holies**
of *strength* **the stronghold**,
and shall *take away* **turn aside**
the *daily sacrifice* **continual**,
and they shall *place* **give** the abomination
that *maketh desolate* **desolateth**.
32 And such as *do wickedly* **declare wicked**
against the covenant
shall he *corrupt* **profane** by *flatteries* **soothings**:
but the people that *do* know their *God* **Elohim**
shall *be strong* **strengthen**, and *do exploits* **work**.
33 And they that *understand* **comprehend**
among **of** the people
shall *instruct many* **have many discern**:
yet they shall *fall* **falter** by the sword, and by flame,
by captivity, and by *spoil* **plunder**, *many* days.
34 *Now* when they shall *fall* **falter**,
they shall be *holpen* **helped** with a little help:
but many shall *cleave* **join** to them
with *flatteries* **soothings**.
35 And *some* of them *of understanding* **that comprehend**
shall *fall* **falter**,
to *try* **refine** them, and to purge,
and to *make* **whiten** them *white*,
even to the time of the end:
because it is yet for a *time appointed* **season**.
36 And the *king* **sovereign**
shall *do* **work** according to his *will* **pleasure**;
and he shall exalt himself,
and *magnify* **greaten** himself above every *god* **el**,
and shall *speak marvellous things* **word marvels**
against *the God* **El** of *Gods* **Elohim**,

and shall prosper
till the *indignation* **rage** be *accomplished* **concluded**:
for that that is *determined* **appointed**
shall be *done* **worked**.
37 Neither shall he *regard* **discern**
the *God* **Elohim** of his fathers, nor the desire of women,
nor *regard* **discern** any *god* **elohah**:
for he shall *magnify* **greaten** himself above all.
38 But in his *estate* **station**
shall he honour the *God* **Elohah** of *forces* **strongholds**
and *a god* **an elohah** whom his fathers knew not
shall he honour with gold, and silver,
and with *precious* **esteemed** stones,
and *pleasant things* **desires**.
39 Thus shall he *do* **work**
in the *most strong holds* **fortresses of strongholds**
with a strange *god* **elohah**,
whom he shall *acknowledge* **recognize**
and *increase* **abound** with *glory* **honour**:
and he shall cause them to *rule* **reign** over many,
and shall *divide* **allot** the *land* **soil** for *gain* **price**.
40 And at the time of the end
shall the *king* **sovereign** of the south *push* **but** at him:
and the *king* **sovereign** of the north shall come
against him like a whirlwind **and whirl him away**,
with chariots, and with *horsemen* **cavalry**,
and with many ships;
and he shall come into the *countries* **lands**,
and shall overflow and pass over.
41 He shall enter also
into the *glorious* land **of splendour**,
and many *countries* shall *be overthrown* **falter**:
but these shall escape out of his hand,
even Edom, and Moab,
and the *chief* **first** of the *children* **sons** of Ammon.
42 He shall *stretch forth* **extend** his hand also
upon the *countries* **lands**:
and the land of *Egypt* **Misrayim** shall not escape.
43 But he shall *have power* **reign**
over the **hidden** treasures of gold and of silver,
and over all
the *precious things* **desires** of *Egypt* **Misrayim**:
and the *Libyans* **Lubiym** and the *Ethiopians* **Kushiym**
shall be at his *steps* **paces**.
44 But *tidings* **reports**
out of the *east* **rising** and out of the north
shall *trouble* **terrify** him:
therefore he shall go forth with great fury
to *destroy* **desolate**,
and *utterly to make away* **to devote** many.
45 And he shall plant
the *tabernacles* **tents** of his *palace* **pavilion**
between the seas
in the *glorious* holy mountain **of splendour**;
yet he shall come to his end, and none shall help him.

THE TIME OF TRIBULATION

12 And at that time shall *Michael* **Michah El** stand up,
the great *prince* **governor**
which standeth for the *children* **sons** of thy people:
and there shall be a time of *trouble* **tribulation**,
such as never was since there was a *nation* **goyim**
even to that same time:
and at that time thy people shall *be delivered* **escape**,
every one that shall be found
written **inscribed** in the *book* **scroll**.

THE RESURRECTION

2 And **the** many *of them*
that sleep in the *dust of the earth* **soil of dust** shall awake,
some to *everlasting* **eternal** life,
and some to *shame* **reproach**
and *everlasting* **eternal** contempt.
3 And they that *be wise* **comprehend**
shall *shine* **have brilliancy**
as the *brightness* **brilliance** of the *firmament* **expanse**;
and they that *turn* **justify** many *to righteousness*
as the stars *for ever and ever* **eternally and eternally**.

THE SCROLL OF DANI EL SEALED

cp Apocalypse 22:10

4 But thou, O *Daniel* **Dani El**,
shut up the words, and seal the *book* **scroll**,
even to the time of the end:
many shall *run to and fro* **flit**,
and knowledge shall *be increased* **abound**.
5 Then I *Daniel looked* **Dani El saw**, and, behold,
there stood other two,
the one on this side of the *bank* **lip** of the river,
and the *other* **one** on that side of the *bank* **lip** of the river.
6 And *one* said to the man *clothed* **enrobed** in linen,
which was *upon* **above** the waters of the river,
How long **Until when** shall it be
to the end of these *wonders* **marvels**?
7 And I heard the man *clothed* **enrobed** in linen,
which was *upon* **above** the waters of the river,
when he *held* **lifted** *up* his right *hand* and his left *hand*
unto *heaven* **the heavens**,
and *sware* **oathed** by him that liveth *for ever* **eternally**
that it shall be
for a *time* **season**, *times* **seasons**, and an half;
and when he shall have *accomplished* **finished**
to scatter the *power* **hand** of the holy people,
all these *things* shall be finished.
8 And I heard, but I *understood* **discerned** not:
then said I, O my *Lord* **Adonay**,
what shall be the end of these *things*?
9 And he said, Go thy way, *Daniel* **Dani El**:
for the words are closed up and sealed
till the time of the end.
10 Many shall be purified,
and *made white* **whitened**, and *tried* **refined**;
but the wicked shall do wickedly:
and none of the wicked shall *understand* **discern**;
but the *wise* **enwisened**
shall *understand* **comprehendingly discern**.
11 And from the time that the *daily sacrifice* **continual**
shall be *taken away* **turned aside**,
and the abomination that *maketh desolate* **desolateth**
set up **be given**,
there shall be a thousand two hundred and ninety days.
12 *Blessed* **Blithesome** is he that waiteth,
and *cometh to* **toucheth**
the thousand three hundred and five and thirty days.
13 But go thou thy way till the end be:
for thou shalt rest,
and stand in thy *lot* **pebble** at the end of the days.

KEY TO INTERPRETING THE EXEGESES:
King James text is in regular type;
Text under exegeses is in oblique type;
Text of exegeses is in bold type.

YAH VEH'S WORD TO HOSHEA

1 The word of *the LORD* **Yah Veh**
that came unto *Hosea* **Hoshea**, the son of Beeri,
in the days of *Uzziah* **Uzzi Yah**, *Jotham* **Yah Tham**,
Ahaz **Ach Az**, and *Hesekiah* **Yechizqi Yah**,
kings **sovereigns** of *Judah* **Yah Hudah**,
and in the days of *Jeroboam* **Yarob Am**
the son of *Joash* **Yah Ash**,
king **sovereign** of *Israel* **Yisra El**.

HOSHEA MARRIES GOMER

2 The beginning
of the word of *the LORD* **Yah Veh** by *Hosea* **Hoshea**.
And *the LORD* **Yah Veh** said to *Hosea* **Hoshea**,
Go, take unto thee a *wife* **woman** of whoredoms
and children of whoredoms:
for the land hath *committed great whoredom* **whored**,
departing from *the LORD* **Yah Veh**.

GOMER BEARS YIZRE EL

3 So he went and took Gomer the daughter of Diblaim;
which conceived, and bare him a son.
4 And *the LORD* **Yah Veh** said unto him,
Call his name *Jezreel* **Yizre El**;
for yet a little *while*,
and I *will avenge* **shall visit** the blood of *Jezreel* **Yizre El**
upon the house of *Jehu* **Yah Hu**,
and *will* **shall** cause to *cease* **shabbathize**
the *kingdom* **sovereigndom** of the house of *Israel* **Yisra El**.
5 And it shall *come to pass* **become,** at that day,
that I *will* **shall** break the bow of *Israel* **Yisra El**
in the valley of *Jezreel* **Yizre El**.

GOMER BEARS LO RUCHAMAH

6 And she conceived again, and bare a daughter.
And *God* **he** said unto him,
Call her name *Lo—ruhamah* **Lo Ruchamah**:
for *I will no more have* **shall not add to** mercy *upon*
the house of *Israel* **Yisra El**;
but **in bearing,** I *will* **shall** *utterly take* **bear** them away.
7 But I *will have* **shall** mercy
upon the house of *Judah* **Yah Hudah**,
and *will* **shall** save them
by *the LORD* **Yah Veh** their *God* **Elohim**,
and *will* **shall** not save them by bow, nor by sword,
nor by *battle* **war**, by horses, nor by *horsemen* **cavalry**.

GOMER BEARS LO AMMI

8 *Now* when she had weaned *Lo—ruhamah* **Lo Ruchamah**,
she conceived, and bare a son.
9 Then said *God* **He**,
Call his name *Loammi* **Lo Ammi**:
for ye are not my people,
and I *will* **shall** not be *your God* **yours**.

FROM LO AMMI TO SONS OF EL

10 Yet the number of the *children* **sons** of *Israel* **Yisra El**
shall be as the sand of the sea,
which cannot be measured nor *numbered* **scribed**;
and it shall *come to pass* **become**,
that in the place where it was said unto them,
Ye are not my people **Lo Ammi**,
there it shall be said unto them,
Ye are the sons of the living *God* **El**.
11 Then shall the *children* **sons** of *Judah* **Yah Hudah**
and the *children* **sons** of *Israel* **Yisra El**
be gathered together,
and *appoint* **set** themselves one head,
and they shall *come up* **ascend** out of the land:
for great shall be the day of *Jezreel* **Yizre El**.

YAH VEH'S JUDGMENT

2 Say ye unto your brethren, *Ammi* **My people**;
and to your sisters, *Ruhamah* **Mercied**.
2 Plead with your mother, plead:
for she is not my *wife* **woman**,
neither am I her *husband* **man**:
let her *therefore put away* **turn aside** her whoredoms
out of her sight **from her face**,
and her adulteries from between her breasts;
3 Lest I strip her naked,
and set her as in the day that she was born,
and *make* **set** her as a wilderness,
and set her like a *dry* **parched** land,
and *slay* **deathify** her with thirst.
4 And I *will* **shall** not *have* mercy *upon* her *children* **sons**;
for they be the *children* **sons** of whoredoms.
5 For their mother hath *played the harlot* **whored**:
she that conceived them hath done shamefully:
for she said, I *will* **shall** go after my lovers,
that give me my bread and my water,
my wool and my flax, mine oil and my drink.
6 Therefore, behold,
I *will* **shall** hedge up thy way with thorns,
and *make* **wall** a wall, that she shall not find her paths.
7 And she shall *follow after* **pursue** her lovers,
but she shall not overtake them;
and she shall seek them,
but shall not find them:
then shall she say,
I *will* **shall** go and return to my first *husband* **man**;
for then was it better with me than *now* **at this time**.
8 For she did not know that I gave her *corn* **crop**,
and *wine* **juice**, and oil,
and *multiplied* **abounded** her silver and gold,
which they *prepared* **worked** for Baal.
9 Therefore *will* **shall** I return,
and take away my *corn* **crop** in the time *thereof*,
and my *wine* **juice** in the season *thereof*,
and *will recover* **shall rescue** my wool and my flax
given to cover her nakedness.
10 And now
will **shall** I *discover* **expose** her *lewdness* **vulva**
in the *sight* **eyes** of her lovers,
and *none* **no man**
shall *deliver* **rescue** her out of mine hand.
11 I *will* **shall** also
cause all her *mirth* **joy** to *cease* **shabbathize**,
her *feast days* **celebrations**, her new moons,
and her *sabbaths* **shabbaths**,
and all her *solemn feasts* **seasons**.
12 And I *will destroy* **shall desolate**
her vines and her fig trees,
whereof she hath said,
These are my *rewards* **payoffs**
that my lovers have given me:
and I *will make* **shall set** them a forest,
and the *beasts* **live beings** of the field shall eat them.
13 And I *will* **shall** visit upon her the days of Baalim,
wherein she *burned incense* **incensed** to them,
and she *decked* **adorned** herself
with her *earrings* **noserings** and her *jewels* **ornaments**,
and she went after her lovers, and forgat me,
saith the LORD **an oracle of Yah Veh**.

YAH VEH'S RESTORATION

14 Therefore, behold, I *will allure* **shall entice** her,
and *bring* **carry** her into the wilderness,
and *speak* **word** comfortably unto her.
15 And I *will* **shall** give her her vineyards from thence,
and *the valley of Achor* **Gaymek Achor**
for *a door* **an opening** of hope:
and she shall *sing* **answer** there,
as in the days of her youth,
and as in the day when she *came up* **ascended**
out of the land of *Egypt* **Misrayim**.
16 And it shall be at that day,
saith the LORD **an oracle of Yah Veh**,
that thou shalt call me *Ishi* **My man**;
and shalt call me no more *Baali* **My Baal**.
17 For I *will take away* **shall turn aside**
the names of Baalim out of her mouth,
and they shall no more be remembered by their name.
18 And in that day
will I make **shall I cut** a covenant for them
with the *beasts* **live beings** of the field
and with the *fowls* **flyers** of *heaven* **the heavens**,
and with the *creeping things* **creepers** of the *ground* **soil**:
and I *will* **shall** break the bow
and the sword and the *battle* **war** out of the earth,
and *will make* **shall cause** them
to lie down *safely* **confidently**.
19 And I *will* **shall** betroth thee unto me

for ever **eternally**;
yea, I *will* **shall** betroth thee unto me
in *righteousness* **justness**, and in judgment,
and in *lovingkindness* **mercy**, and in mercies.
20 I *will* **shall** even betroth thee unto me
in *faithfulness* **trustworthiness**:
and thou shalt know *the LORD* **Yah Veh**.
21 And it shall *come to pass* **become**, in that day,
I *will hear* **shall answer**,
saith the LORD **an oracle of Yah Veh**,
I *will hear* **shall answer** the heavens,
and they shall *hear* **answer** the earth;
22 And the earth shall *hear* **answer** the *corn* **crop**,
and the *wine* **juice**, and the oil;
and they shall *hear Jezreel* **answer Yizre El**.
23 And I *will* **shall** sow her unto me in the earth;
and I *will have mercy* **shall Mercy/Ruchamah**
upon her that had not obtained mercy
Not Mercied/Lo Ruchamah;
and I *will* **shall** say to
them which were not my people
Not My People/Lo Ammi,
Thou art my people **My People/Ammi**;
and they shall say, *Thou art my God* **My Elohim**.

HOSHEA'S RECONCILIATION

3 Then said *the LORD* **Yah Veh** unto me, Go yet,
love a woman beloved of her friend, yet an adulteress,
according to the love of *the LORD* **Yah Veh**
toward the *children* **sons** of *Israel* **Yisra El**,
who *look to* **face** other *gods* **elohim**,
and love *flagons* **cakes** of *wine* **grapes**.
2 So I bought her to me for fifteen *pieces of* silver,
and *for an homer* **a chomer** of barley,
and *an half homer* **a lethech** of barley:
3 And I said unto her,
Thou shalt *abide* **settle** for me many days;
thou shalt not *play the harlot* **whore**,
and thou shalt not be for another man:
so *will* **shall** I also be for thee.
4 For the *children* **sons** of *Israel* **Yisra El**
shall *abide* **settle** many days
without a king **with no sovereign**,
and *without a prince* **no governor**,
and without a **no** sacrifice,
and without an image **no monolith**,
and without an **no** ephod,
and without **no** teraphim:
5 Afterward
shall the *children* **sons** of *Israel* **Yisra El** return,
and seek *the LORD* **Yah Veh** their *God* **Elohim**,
and David their *king* **sovereign**;
and shall fear *the LORD* **Yah Veh** and his goodness
in the latter days.

YAH VEH'S CONTROVERSY

4 Hear the word of *the LORD* **Yah Veh**,
ye *children* **sons** of *Israel* **Yisra El**:
for *the LORD* **Yah Veh** hath a controversy
with the *inhabitants* **settlers** of the land,
because there is no truth, nor mercy,
nor knowledge of *God* **Elohim** in the land.
2 By *swearing* **oathing**, and lying, and *killing* **murder**,
and stealing, and *committing adultery* **adulterizing**,
they *break out* **separate**, and blood toucheth blood.
3 Therefore shall the land mourn,
and every one that *dwelleth* **settleth** therein
shall languish,
with the *beasts* **live beings** of the field,
and with the *fowls* **flyers** of *heaven* **the heavens**;
yea, the fishes of the sea also
shall be *taken away* **gathered**.
4 Yet let no man strive, nor reprove *another* **man**:
for thy people are as they that strive with the priest.
5 Therefore shalt thou *fall* **falter** in the day,
and the prophet also
shall *fall* **falter** with thee in the night,
and I *will destroy* **shall sever** thy mother.
6 My people are *destroyed* **severed** for lack of knowledge:
because thou hast *despised* **spurned** knowledge,
I *will* **shall** also *reject* **spurn** thee,
that thou shalt be no priest to me:
seeing
thou hast forgotten the *law* **torah** of thy *God* **Elohim**,
I *will* **shall** also forget thy *children* **sons**.
7 As *they were increased* **their abundance**,
so they sinned against me:
therefore *will* **shall** I change their *glory* **honour**
into *shame* **abasement**.
8 They eat up the sin of my people,
and they *set* **lift** their *heart* **soul**
on their *iniquity* **perversity**.
9 And there shall be, like people, like priest:
and I *will punish* **shall visit upon** them for their ways,
and *reward them* **return** their *doings* **exploits**.
10 For they shall eat,
and not *have enough* **be satisfied**:
they shall *commit whoredom* **whore**,
and shall not *increase* **break forth**:
because they have *left off* **forsaken**
to *take heed to the LORD* **guard unto Yah Veh**.
11 Whoredom and wine and *new wine* **juice**
take away the heart.
12 My people ask *counsel* at their *stocks* **trees**,
and their staff *declareth* **telleth** unto them:
for the spirit of whoredoms hath caused them to *err* **stray**,
and they have *gone a whoring* **whored**
from under their *God* **Elohim**.
13 They sacrifice upon the tops of the mountains,
and *burn* incense upon the hills,
under oaks and poplars and *elms* **terebinth**,
because the shadow *thereof* is good:
therefore your daughters shall *commit whoredom* **whore**,
and your *spouses* **brides**
shall *commit adultery* **adulterize**.
14 I *will* **shall** not *punish* **visit upon** your daughters
when they *commit whoredom* **whore**,
nor your *spouses* **brides**
when they *commit adultery* **adulterize**:
for themselves are separated with whores,
and they sacrifice with *harlots* **hallowed whores**:
therefore the people that *doth* **discerneth** not *understand*
shall fall.
15 Though thou, *Israel* **Yisra El**, *play the harlot* **whoreth**,
yet let not *Judah offend* **Yah Hudah become guilty**;
and come not ye unto Gilgal,
neither *go ye up to Bethaven* **ascend ye to Beth Aven**,
nor *swear* **oath**, *The LORD* **Yah Veh** liveth.
16 For *Israel slideth back* **Yisra El rebelleth**
as a *backsliding* **revolting** heifer:
now *the LORD will feed* **Yah Veh shall tend** them
as a lamb in *a large place* **an expanse**.
17 *Ephraim* **Ephrayim** is joined to idols:
let **leave** him alone.
18 Their *drink* **potion** is *sour* **turned**:
they have *committed whoredom* **whored** continually:
her *rulers* **bucklers** with *shame* **abasement** do love,
Give ye.
19 The wind hath bound her up in her wings,
and they shall be *ashamed* **shamed**
because of their sacrifices.

YAH VEH'S JUDGMENT AGAINST YISRA EL

5 Hear ye this, O priests;
and hearken, ye house of *Israel* **Yisra El**;
and *give ye ear* **hearken**, O house of the *king* **sovereign**;
for judgment is toward you,
because ye have been a snare on *Mizpah* **Mispeh**,
and a net spread upon Tabor.
2 And the *revolters* **deviates**
are profound to make **have deepened to** slaughter,
though I have been a *rebuker* **discipliner** of them all.
3 I know *Ephraim* **Ephrayim**,
and *Israel* **Yisra El** is not *hid* **concealed** from me:
for *now,* O *Ephraim* **Ephrayim**,
thou *committest whoredom* **whorest**,
and *Israel* **Yisra El** *is defiled* **fouleth**.
4 They *will* **shall** not *frame* **give** their *doings* **exploits**
to turn unto their *God* **Elohim**:
for the spirit of whoredoms is in the midst of them,
and they have not known *the LORD* **Yah Veh**.
5 And the *pride* **pomp** of *Israel* **Yisra El**
doth testify **answereth** to his face:

therefore shall *Israel* **Yisra El** and *Ephraim* **Ephrayim**
fall **falter** in their *iniquity* **perversity**;
Judah **Yah Hudah** also shall *fall* **falter** with them.
6 They shall go with their flocks and with their herds
to seek *the LORD* **Yah Veh**;
but they shall not find *him*;
he hath withdrawn himself from them.
7 They have dealt *treacherously* **covertly**
against *the LORD* **Yah Veh**:
for they have begotten strange *children* **sons**:
now shall a month devour them
with their *portions* **allotments**.
8 *Blow* **Blast** ye the *cornet* **trumpet** in *Gibeah* **Gibah**,
and the trumpet in Ramah:
cry aloud **shout** at *Bethaven* **the house of mischief**,
after thee, O *Benjamin* **Ben Yamin**.
9 *Ephraim* **Ephrayim** shall be desolate
in the day of rebuke:
among the *tribes* **scions** of *Israel* **Yisra El**
have I made known
that which shall *surely* be **trustworthy**.
10 The *princes* **governors** of *Judah* **Yah Hudah**
were like them that remove the *bound* **border**:
therefore I will **I shall** pour out my wrath
upon them like water.
11 *Ephraim* **Ephrayim**
is oppressed and *broken* **crushed** in judgment,
because he *willingly walked* **willed to walk**
after the *commandment* **misvah**.
12 Therefore *will* **shall** I be unto *Ephraim* **Ephrayim**
as a moth,
and to the house of *Judah* **Yah Hudah** as rottenness.
13 When *Ephraim* **Ephrayim** saw his sickness,
and *Judah* **Yah Hudah** saw his *wound* **sore**,
then went *Ephraim* **Ephrayim** to the *Assyrian* **Ashshuri**,
and sent to *king Jareb* **sovereign Yareb to plead**:
yet could he not heal you,
nor cure you of your *wound* **sore**.
14 For I *will* **shall** be unto *Ephraim* **Ephrayim**
as a **roaring** lion,
and as a *young lion* **whelp**
to the house of *Judah* **Yah Hudah**:
I, *even* I, *will* **shall** tear and go away;
I *will take* **shall bear** away,
and none shall rescue *him*.
15 I *will* **shall** go and return to my place,
till they acknowledge their *offence* **having guilted**,
and seek my face:
in their *affliction* **tribulation** they *will* **shall** seek me early.

YISRA EL'S CALL TO RETURN TO YAH VEH

6 Come, and let us return unto *the LORD* **Yah Veh**:
for he hath torn, and he *will* **shall** heal us;
he hath smitten, and he *will* **shall** bind us *up*.
2 After two days *will* he *revive* **shall enliven** us:
in the third day he *will* **shall** raise us *up*,
and we shall live *in his sight* **at his face**.
3 Then shall we know,
if we *follow on* **pursue** to know *the LORD* **Yah Veh**:
his *going forth* **proceeding**
is prepared as the *morning* **dawn**;
and he shall come unto us as the *rain* **downpour**,
as the *latter and former* **after** rain **poureth** unto the earth.

YAH VEH'S RESPONSE

4 O *Ephraim* **Ephrayim**, what shall I *do* **work** unto thee?
O *Judah* **Yah Hudah**, what shall I *do* **work** unto thee?
for your *goodness* **mercy** is as a morning cloud,
and as the early dew it goeth away.
5 Therefore have I hewed them by the prophets;
I have *slain* **slaughtered** them
by the *words* **sayings** of my mouth:
and thy judgments are as the light that goeth forth.
6 For I desired mercy, and not sacrifice;
and the knowledge of *God* **Elohim**
more than *burnt offerings* **holocausts**.
7 But they like *men* **humanity**
have *transgressed* **trespassed** the covenant:
there have they dealt *treacherously* **covertly** against me.
8 *Gilead* **Gilad**
is a city of them that *work iniquity* **do mischief**,
and *is polluted* **trippeth** with blood.
9 And as troops *of robbers wait for* **await** a man,
so the *company* **commune** of priests
murder in the way *by consent* **to** Shechem:
for they *commit lewdness* **work intrigue**
10 I have seen *an horrible thing* **horrific**
in the house of *Israel* **Yisra El**:
there is the whoredom of *Ephraim* **Ephrayim**,
Israel **Yisra El** is defiled.
11 Also, O *Judah* **Yah Hudah**,
he hath set an harvest for thee,
when I returned the captivity of my people.
7 When I *would* **should** have healed *Israel* **Yisra El**,
then the *iniquity* **perversity** of *Ephraim* **Ephrayim**
was discovered **exposed**,
and the *wickedness* **evil** of *Samaria* **Shomeron**:
for they *commit* **do** falsehood;
and the thief cometh in,
and the troop *of robbers*
spoileth without **strippeth in the outways**.
2 And they *consider* **say** not in their hearts
that I remember all their *wickedness* **evil**:
now their own *doings* **exploits**
have *beset* **surrounded** them *about*;
they are before my face.
3 They *make* **cheer**
the *king glad* **sovereign** with their *wickedness* **evil**,
and the *princes* **governors** with their *lies* **deceptions**.
4 They are all adulterers,
as an oven *heated* **burning** by the baker,
who *ceaseth* **shabbathizeth** from *raising* **waking**
after he hath kneaded the dough, until it be leavened.
5 In the day of our *king* **sovereign**
the *princes* **governors** have *made* **stroked** him *sick*
with *bottles of* wine **of fury**;
he *stretched* **drew** out his hand with scorners.
6 For they have *made ready* **approached;**
their heart *like* **is** an oven, whiles they *lie in wait* **lurk**:
their baker sleepeth all the night;
in the morning it burneth as a flaming fire.
7 They are all *hot* **heated** as an oven,
and have devoured their judges;
all their *kings* **sovereigns** are fallen:
there is none among them that calleth unto me.
8 *Ephraim* **Ephrayim**,
he hath *mixed himself* **mingled** among the people;
Ephraim **Ephrayim** is *a cake* **an ashcake** not turned.
9 Strangers have devoured his *strength* **force**,
and he knoweth it not:
yea, *gray hairs are* **greyness be** here and there upon him,
yet he knoweth not.
10 And the *pride* **pomp** of *Israel* **Yisra El**
testifieth **answereth** to his face:
and they do not return
to *the LORD* **Yah Veh** their *God* **Elohim**,
nor seek him for all this.
11 *Ephraim* **Ephrayim** also
is like a *silly* **deluded** dove without heart:
they call to *Egypt* **Misrayim**, they go to *Assyria* **Ashshur**.
12 When they shall go,
I *will* **shall** spread my net upon them;
I *will* **shall** bring them down
as the *fowls* **flyers** of the *heaven* **heavens**;
I *will chastise* **shall discipline** them,
as *their congregation hath heard*
reported to their witness.
13 Woe unto them! for they have fled from me:
destruction **ravage** unto them!
because they have *transgressed* **rebelled** against me:
though I have redeemed them,
yet they have *spoken* **worded** lies against me.
14 And they have not cried unto me with their heart,
when they howled upon their beds:
they *assemble* **sojourn** *themselves*
for *corn* **crop** and *wine* **juice**,
and they *rebel* **turn aside** against me.
15 Though I have
bound **disciplined** and strengthened their arms,
yet do they *imagine mischief* **fabricate evil** against me.
16 They return, but not to *the most High* **Elyon**:
they are like a deceitful bow:

their *princes* **governors** shall fall by the sword
for the rage of their tongue:
this shall be their derision
in the land of *Egypt* **Misrayim**.

8 Set the trumpet to thy *mouth* **palate**.
He shall come
as an eagle against the house of *the LORD* **Yah Veh**,
because they have *transgressed* **trespassed** my covenant,
and *trespassed* **rebelled** against my *law* **torah**.
2 *Israel* **Yisra El** shall cry unto me,
My *God* **Elohim**, we know thee.
3 *Israel* **Yisra El** hath cast off *the thing* that **which** is good:
the enemy shall pursue him.
4 They have set up *kings* **sovereigns**, but not by me:
they have *made princes* **dominated**, and I knew it not:
of their silver and their gold
have they *made* **worked** them idols,
that they may be cut off.
5 Thy calf, O *Samaria* **Shomeron**, hath cast *thee* off;
mine anger **my wrath** is kindled against them:
how long *will* **shall** it be
ere they *attain to* **be capable of** innocency?
6 For from *Israel* **Yisra El** was it also:
the *workman made* **engraver worked** it;
therefore it is not *God* **Elohim**:
but the calf of *Samaria* **Shomeron**
shall be *broken in pieces* **shattered**.
7 For they have *sown* **seeded** the wind,
and they shall *reap* **harvest** the *whirlwind* **hurricane**:
it hath no stalk:
the *bud* **sprout** shall *yield* **work** no *meal* **flour**:
if so be it *yield* **work**, the strangers shall swallow it *up*.
8 *Israel* **Yisra El** is swallowed *up*:
now shall they be among the *Gentiles* **goyim**
as *a vessel* **an instrument** wherein is no *pleasure* **delight**.
9 For they are *gone up* **ascended** to *Assyria* **Ashshur**,
a wild *ass* **runner** alone by himself:
Ephraim **Ephrayim** hath hired lovers.
10 Yea, though they have hired among the *nations* **goyim**,
now *will* **shall** I gather them,
and they shall *sorrow* **be pierced** a little
for the burden of the *king* **sovereign** of *princes* **governors**.
11 Because *Ephraim* **Ephrayim**
hath *made many* **abounded sacrifice** altars to sin,
sacrifice altars shall be unto him to sin.
12 I have *written* **inscribed** to him
the *great things* **myriads of greatnesses** of my *law* **torah**,
but they were *counted* **fabricated** as *a* strange *thing*.
13 They sacrifice flesh
for the sacrifices of *mine offerings* **my holocausts**,
and eat *it*;
but the LORD **Yah Veh**
accepteth them not **is not pleased with them**;
now *will* **shall** he remember their *iniquity* **perversity**,
and visit their sins:
they shall return to *Egypt* **Misrayim**.
14 For *Israel* **Yisra El** hath forgotten his *Maker* **Worker**,
and buildeth *temples* **manses**;
and *Judah* **Yah Hudah**
hath *multiplied fenced* **abounded fortified** cities:
but I *will* **shall** send a fire upon his cities,
and it shall devour the *palaces* **citadels** *thereof*.

9 *Rejoice* **Cheer** not, O *Israel* **Yisra El**,
for *joy* **twirling**, as *other* people:
for thou hast *gone a whoring* **whored**
from thy *God* **Elohim**,
thou hast loved a *reward* **payoff**
upon every *cornfloor* **crop threshingfloor**.
2 The *floor* **threshingfloor** and the *winepress* **trough**
shall not *feed* **tend** them,
and the *new wine* **juice** shall *fail* **deceive** in her.
3 They shall not *dwell* **settle**
in the *LORD'S* land **of Yah Veh**;
but *Ephraim* **Ephrayim** shall return to *Egypt* **Misrayim**,
and they shall eat *unclean things* **the foul**
in *Assyria* **Ashshur**.
4 They shall not *offer* **libate** wine *offerings*
to *the LORD* **Yah Veh**,
neither shall they *be pleasing unto* **please** him:
their sacrifices shall be unto them
as the bread of *mourners* **mischief**;
all that eat *thereof* shall be *polluted* **fouled**:
for their bread for their soul
shall not come into the house of *the LORD* **Yah Veh**.
5 What *will* **shall** ye *do* **work** in the *solemn* **season** day,
and in the day
of the *feast* **celebration** of *the LORD* **Yah Veh**?
6 For, *lo* **behold**,
they are gone because of *destruction* **ravage**:
Egypt **Misrayim** shall gather them *up*,
Memphis **Moph** shall *bury* **entomb** them:
the *pleasant places* **desirables** for their silver,
nettles **thistles** shall possess them:
thorns shall be in their *tabernacles* **tents**.
7 The days of visitation are come,
the days of *recompence* **satisfaction** are come;
Israel **Yisra El** shall know *it*:
the prophet is a fool,
the *spiritual* man **of the spirit** is *mad* **insane**,
for the *multitude* **abundance**
of *thine iniquity* **thy perversity**,
and the great *hatred* **enmity**.
8 The *watchman* **watcher** of *Ephraim* **Ephrayim**
was with my *God* **Elohim**:
but the prophet is a snare of a *fowler* **snarer**
in all his ways,
and *hatred* **enmity** in the house of his *God* **El**.
9 They have *deeply* **deepened,**
corrupted themselves **they have ruined**,
as in the days of *Gibeah* **Gibah**:
therefore he *will* **shall** remember their *iniquity* **perversity**,
he *will* **shall** visit their sins.
10 I found *Israel* **Yisra El** like grapes in the wilderness;
I saw your fathers
as the firstripe in the fig tree at her *first time* **beginning**:
but they went to *Baalpeor* **Baal Peor**,
and separated themselves unto *that* shame;
and their abominations were according as they loved.
11 *As for Ephraim* **Ephrayim**,
their *glory* **honour** shall fly *away* like a *bird* **flyer**,
from the *birth* **begetting**,
and from the *womb* **belly**, and from the conception.
12 Though they *bring up* **nourish** their *children* **sons**,
yet *will* **shall** I bereave them,
that there shall not be a *man left* **human**:
yea,
woe also to them when I *depart* **turn aside** from them!
13 *Ephraim* **Ephrayim**, as I saw *Tyrus* **Sor**,
is *planted* **transplanted**
in a *pleasant place* **habitation of rest**:
but *Ephraim* **Ephrayim** shall bring forth his *children* **sons**
to the *murderer* **slaughterer**.
14 Give them, O *LORD* **Yah Veh**:
what *wilt* **shalt** thou *give*?
give them
a miscarrying **an aborting** womb and dry breasts.
15 All their *wickedness* **evil** is in Gilgal:
for there I hated them:
for the *wickedness* **evil** of their *doings* **exploits**
I *will* **shall** drive them out of mine house,
I *will* **shall add not to** love them *no more*:
all their *princes* **governors** are revolters.
16 *Ephraim* **Ephrayim** is smitten,
their root is *dried up* **withered**,
they shall *bear* **work** no fruit:
yea, though they *bring forth* **beget**,
yet *will* **shall** I slay
even the *beloved fruit* **desire** of their *womb* **belly**.
17 My *God will cast* **Elohim shall spurn** them *away*,
because they *did not hearken* unto him:
and they shall be wanderers
among the *nations* **goyim**.

10 *Israel* **Yisra El** is an *empty* **evacuating** vine,
he *bringeth forth* **equateth** fruit unto himself:
according to the *multitude* **abundance** of his fruit
he hath *increased* **abounded** the **sacrifice** altars;
according to the goodness of his land
they have made goodly *images* **monoliths**.
2 Their heart is *divided* **allotted**;
now shall they

be found faulty **acknowledge having guilted**:
he shall break *down* **the neck of** their altars,
he shall *spoil* **ravage** their *images* **monoliths**.
3 For now they shall say, We have no *king* **sovereign**,
because we *feared* **awed** not *the LORD* **Yah Veh**;
what then should a *king do* **sovereign work a** to us?
4 They have *spoken* **worded** words,
swearing falsely **oathing vainly**
in *making* **cutting** a covenant:
thus judgment springeth *up*
as *hemlock* **rosh** in the furrows of the field.
5 The *inhabitants* **fellow tabernaclers**
of *Samaria* **Shomeron** shall *fear* **sojourn**
because of the *calves* **heifers** of *Bethaven* **Beth Aven**:
for the people *thereof* shall mourn over it,
and the *priests* **ascetics** *thereof* that *rejoiced* **twirled** on it,
for the *glory* **honour** *thereof*,
because it is *departed* **exiled** from it.
6 It shall be also *carried* **borne** unto *Assyria* **Ashshur**
for a oblation **an offering**
to *king Jareb* **sovereign Yareb to plead**:
Ephraim **Ephrayim**
shall *receive* **take** shame,
and *Israel* **Yisra El**
shall *be ashamed* **shame** of his own counsel.
7 As for *Samaria* **Shomeron**,
her *king* **sovereign** is *cut off* **severed**
as the *foam* **raging** upon the **face of the** water.
8 The *high places* **bamahs** also of Aven,
the sin of *Israel* **Yisra El**, shall be *destroyed* **desolated**:
the thorn and the thistle
shall *come up* **ascend** on their **sacrifice** altars;
and they shall say to the mountains, Cover us;
and to the hills, Fall on us.
9 O *Israel* **Yisra El**,
thou hast sinned from the days of *Gibeah* **Gibah**:
there they stood:
the *battle* **war** in *Gibeah* **Gibah**
against the *children* **sons** of *iniquity* **wickedness**
did not overtake them.
10 *It is in my desire* **I yearn**
that I should *chastise* **bind** them;
and the people shall *be gathered* **gather** against them,
when *they* **I** shall bind *themselves* **them**
in their two *furrows* **eyes**.
11 And *Ephraim* **Ephrayim** is as an heifer that is taught,
and loveth to *tread out the corn* **thresh**;
but I passed over upon her *fair* **good** neck:
I will make Ephraim **shall cause Ephrayim**
to *ride* **be ridden**;
Judah **Yah Hudah** shall plow,
and *Jacob* **Yaaqov** shall *break his clods* **harrow**.
12 Sow to yourselves in *righteousness* **justness**,
reap in **harvest to your mouth** mercy;
break up **till** your *fallow ground* **tillage**:
for it is time to seek *the LORD* **Yah Veh**,
till he come
and *rain righteousness* **pour justness** upon you.
13 Ye have plowed wickedness,
ye have *reaped iniquity* **harvested wickedness**;
ye have eaten the fruit of *lies* **deceptions**:
because thou didst *trust* **confide** in thy way,
in the *multitude* **abundance** of thy mighty *men*.
14 Therefore shall *a tumult* **an uproar** arise
among thy people,
and all thy fortresses shall be *spoiled* **ravaged**,
as Shalman *spoiled Betharbel* **ravaged Beth Arb El**
in the day of *battle* **war**:
the mother was *dashed in pieces* **splattered**
upon her *children* **sons**.
15 *So* **Thus** shall *Bethel do* **Beth El work** unto you
because **at the face of the evil**
of your *great wickedness* **evil**:
in *a morning* **the dawn**
shall the king of Israel utterly be cut off
in severing,
the sovereign of Yisra El shall be severed.

11 When *Israel* **Yisra El** was a *child* **lad**,
then I loved him,
and called my son out of *Egypt* **Misrayim**.
2 As they called them, so they went from *them* **their face**:
they sacrificed unto Baalim,
and *burned incense* **incensed** to *graven images* **sculptiles**.
3 I *taught Ephraim* **caused Ephrayim** also to *go* **tread**,
taking them by their arms;
but they knew not that I healed them.
4 I drew them with cords of a *man* **human**,
with *bands* **ropes** of love:
and I was to them
as they that *take off* **lift** the yoke on their jaws,
and I *laid meat* **extended** unto them **to eat**.
5 He shall not return into the land of *Egypt* **Misrayim**,
and the *Assyrian* **Ashshuri** shall be his *king* **sovereign**,
because they refused to return.
6 And the sword shall *abide* **whirl** on his cities,
and shall *consume* **finish off** his branches,
and devour *them*, because of their own counsels.
7 And my people
are *bent* **prone** to *backsliding from me* **apostasy**:
though they called them to *the most High* **Elyon**,
none at all *would* **should** exalt him.
8 How shall I give thee up, *Ephraim* **Ephrayim**?
how shall I *deliver* **buckler** thee, *Israel* **Yisra El**?
how shall I *make* **give** thee as Admah?
how shall I *set* **set** thee as *Zeboim* **Seboim**?
mine heart is turned within me,
my *repentings are kindled* **solaces yearn** together.
9 I *will* **shall** not *execute* **work**
the *fierceness* **fuming** of *mine anger* **my wrath**,
I *will* **shall** not return to *destroy Ephraim* **ruin Ephrayim**:
for *I am God* **I — El**, and not man;
the Holy One in the midst of thee:
and I *will* **shall** not enter into the city.
10 They shall walk after *the LORD* **Yah Veh**:
he shall roar like a lion:
when he shall roar,
then the *children* **sons** shall tremble
from the *west* **seaward**.
11 They shall tremble as a bird out of *Egypt* **Misrayim**,
and as a dove out of the land of *Assyria* **Ashshur**:
and I *will place* **shall settle** them in their houses,
saith the LORD **an oracle of Yah Veh**.
12 *Ephraim compasseth* **Ephrayim surroundeth** me *about*
with *lies* **deceptions**,
and the house of *Israel* **Yisra El** with deceit:
but *Judah yet ruleth* **Yah Hudah rambles on** with *God* **El**,
and is *faithful* **trustworthy** with the *saints* **holy**.

12 *Ephraim feedeth* **Ephrayim grazeth** on wind,
and *followeth after* **pursueth** the *east wind* **easterly**:
he daily increaseth **every day he aboundeth** lies
and *desolation* **ravage**;
and they *do make* **cut** a covenant
with the *Assyrians* **Ashshuri**,
and oil is *carried* **borne** into *Egypt* **Misrayim**.
2 *The LORD* **Yah Veh**
hath also a controversy with *Judah* **Yah Hudah**,
and *will punish Jacob* **shall visit upon Yaaqov**
according to his ways;
according to his *doings* **exploits**
will **shall** he *recompense* **return** him.
3 He *took* **tripped** his brother by the heel
in the *womb* **belly**,
and by his strength
he *had power* **prevailed** with *God* **Elohim**:
4 Yea, he *had power* **dominated** over the angel,
and prevailed:
he wept,
and *made supplication unto him* **was granted charism**:
he found him in *Bethel* **Beth El**,
and there he *spake* **worded** with us;
5 Even *the LORD God of hosts* **Yah Veh Elohim Sabaoth**;
the LORD **Yah Veh** is his memorial.
6 Therefore turn thou to thy *God* **Elohim**:
keep **guard** mercy and judgment,
and *wait on* **await** thy *God* **Elohim** continually.
7 He is *a merchant* **Kenaan**,
the balances of deceit are in his hand:
he loveth to oppress.
8 And *Ephraim* **Ephrayim** said,
Yet I am *become rich* **enriched**,

I have found me out *substance* **strength**:
in all my labours
they shall find none *iniquity* **perversity** in me
that were sin.
9 And I that am *the LORD* **Yah Veh** thy *God* **Elohim**
from the land of *Egypt* **Misrayim**
will **shall** yet *make* **cause** thee
to *dwell* **settle** in *tabernacles* **tents**,
as in the days of the *solemn feast* **seasons**.
10 I have also *spoken* **worded** by the prophets,
and I have *multiplied* **abounded** visions,
and used *similitudes* **comparisons**,
by the *ministry* **hand** of the prophets.
11 Is there *iniquity* **mischief** in *Gilead* **Gilad**?
surely they are vanity:
they sacrifice *bullocks* **oxen** in Gilgal;
yea, their **sacrifice** altars
are as heaps in the furrows of the fields.
12 And *Jacob* **Yaaqov**
fled into the *country* **field** of *Syria* **Aram**,
and *Israel* **Yisra El** served for a *wife* **woman**,
and for a *wife* **woman** he *kept sheep* **guarded**.
13 And by a prophet
the LORD brought Israel **Yah Veh ascended Yisra El**
out of *Egypt* **Misrayim**,
and by a prophet was he *preserved* **guarded**.
14 *Ephraim* **Ephrayim**
provoked **vexed** him *to anger*
most bitterly **with bitterness**:
therefore shall he *leave* **abandon** his blood upon him,
and his reproach
shall his *Lord return* **Adonay returneth** unto him.

13 When *Ephraim* **Ephrayim**
spake trembling **worded in terror**,
he *exalted* **lifted** himself in *Israel* **Yisra El**;
but when he *offended* **had guilted** in Baal, he died.
2 And now they **add to** sin *more and more*,
and have *made* **worked** them
molten images **moltens** of their silver,
and idols
according to their own *understanding* **discerning**,
all of it the work of the *craftsmen* **engravers**:
they say of them,
Let *the men* **humanity** that *sacrifice* **sacrificeth**
kiss the calves.
3 Therefore they shall be as the morning cloud
and as the early dew that passeth away,
as the chaff that is
driven with the whirlwind **stormed**
out of the *floor* **threshingfloor**,
and as the smoke out of the *chimney* **window**.
4 Yet *I am the LORD* **I — Yah Veh** thy *God* **Elohim**
from the land of *Egypt* **Misrayim**,
and thou shalt know no *god but* **elohim beside** me:
for there is no saviour *beside* **except** me.
5 I did know thee in the wilderness,
in the land of great *drought* **droughts**.
6 According to their pasture, so were they *filled* **satiated**;
they were *filled* **satiated**, and their heart was exalted;
therefore have they forgotten me.
7 Therefore I *will* **shall** be unto them as a **roaring** lion:
as a leopard by the way *will* **shall** I observe them:
8 I *will* **shall** meet them
as a bear that is bereaved *of her whelps*,
and *will rend* **shall rip** the *caul* **treasure** of their heart,
and there *will* **shall** I devour them like a **roaring** lion:
the wild *beast* **live being of the field** shall *tear* **split** them.
9 O *Israel* **Yisra El**, thou hast *destroyed* **ruined** thyself;
but in me is thine help.
10 *I will be thy king:* **Where is thy sovereign**
where is any other that may save **that saveth** thee
in all thy cities?
and thy judges of whom thou saidst,
Give me a *king* **sovereign** and *princes* **governors**?
11 I gave thee a *king* **sovereign** in *mine anger* **my wrath**,
and took him away in my wrath.
12 The *iniquity* **perversity** of *Ephraim* **Ephrayim**
is bound *up*; his sin is hid.
13 The *sorrows* **pangs** of a *travailing* **birthing** woman
shall come upon him: he is an unwise son;
for he should not stay
long in the place of the breaking forth
the time of the matrix
of *children* **sons**.
14 I *will* **shall** ransom them
from the *power* **hand** of *the grave* **sheol**;
I *will* **shall** redeem them from death:
O death, *I will be thy plagues* **where are thy pestilences**;
O *grave* **sheol**, *I will be thy destruction* **where is thy ruin**:
repentance **sighing** shall be hid from mine eyes.
I Corinthians 15:55
15 Though he *be fruitful* **bear fruit** among his brethren,
an east wind shall come,
the *wind* **wind/Spirit** of *the LORD* **Yah Veh**
shall *come up* **ascend** from the wilderness,
and his *spring* **fountain** shall *become dry* **shame**,
and his fountain shall *be dried up* **parch**:
he shall spoil the treasure
of all pleasant *vessels* **instruments**.
16 *Samaria* **Shomeron**
shall become desolate **hath guilted**;
for she hath rebelled against her *God* **Elohim**:
they shall fall by the sword:
their *infants* **sucklings**
shall be *dashed in pieces* **splattered**,
and their women *with child* **having conceived**
shall be *ripped up* **split**.

YAH VEH'S APPEAL TO YISRA EL

14 O *Israel* **Yisra El**,
return unto *the LORD* **Yah Veh** thy *God* **Elohim**;
for thou hast *fallen* **faltered**
by *thine iniquity* **thy perversity**.
2 Take with you words, and turn to *the LORD* **Yah Veh**:
say unto him, *Take away* **Bear** all *iniquity* **perversity**,
and *receive us graciously* **take goodly**:
so *will* **shall** we *render* **shalam**
the *calves* **bullocks** of our lips.
3 *Asshur* **Ashshur** shall not save us;
we *will* **shall** not ride upon horses:
neither *will* **shall** we say any more
to the work of our hands,
Ye are our gods **Our elohim**:
for in thee
the *fatherless findeth mercy* **orphan is mercied**.
4 I *will* **shall** heal their *backsliding* **apostasy**,
I *will* **shall** love them *freely* **voluntarily**:
for *mine anger* **my wrath** is turned away from him.
5 I *will* **shall** be as the dew unto *Israel* **Yisra El**:
he shall *grow* **blossom** as the lily,
and *cast forth* **smite** his roots as Lebanon.
6 His *branches* **sprouts** shall spread,
and his *beauty* **majesty** shall be as the olive *tree*,
and his *smell* **scent** as Lebanon.
7 They that *dwell* **settle** under his shadow shall return;
they shall *revive* **enliven** as the *corn* **crop**,
and *grow* **blossom** as the vine:
the *scent* **memorial** *thereof*
shall be as the wine of Lebanon.
8 *Ephraim shall say* **Ephrayim**,
What have I to do any more with idols?
I have *heard him* **answered**, and observed him:
I am like a green fir tree. From me is thy fruit found.
9 Who is wise,
and he shall *understand* **discern** these *things*?
prudent **discerning**, and he shall know them?
for the ways of *the LORD* **Yah Veh** are *right* **straight**,
and the just shall walk in them:
but the *transgressors* **rebels** shall *fall* **falter** therein.

KEY TO INTERPRETING THE EXEGESES:
King James text is in regular type;
Text under exegeses is in oblique type;
Text of exegeses is in bold type.

INTRODUCTION

1 The word of *the LORD* **Yah Veh**
that came to *Joel* **Yah El** the son of *Pethuel* **Pethu El**.
2 Hear this, ye *old men* **elders**,
and *give ear* **hearken**,
all ye *inhabitants* **settlers** of the land.
Hath this been in your days,
or even in the days of your fathers?

THE LAND IS DESOLATED

3 *Tell* **Scribe** ye your *children* **sons** of it,
and *let your children tell* **your sons** their *children* **sons**,
and their *children* **sons** another generation.
4 That which the palmerworm *hath left* **let remain**
hath the locust eaten;
and that which the locust *hath left* **let remain**
hath the cankerworm eaten;
and that which the cankerworm *hath left* **let remain**
hath the caterpiller eaten.
5 Awake, ye *drunkards* **intoxicated**, and weep;
and howl, all ye drinkers of wine,
because of the *new wine* **squeezed juice**;
for it is cut off from your mouth.
6 For a *nation* **goyim**
is come up **hath ascended** upon my land,
strong **mighty**, and without number,
whose teeth are the teeth of a lion,
and he hath the *cheek teeth* **molars**
of a *great* **roaring** lion.
7 He hath *laid* **set** my vine *waste* **desolate**,
and *barked* **chipped away** my fig tree:
in stripping, he hath *made* **stripped** it *clean bare*,
and cast it away;
the *branches* **tendrils** *thereof* are *made white* **whitened**.
8 Lament like a virgin girded with *sackcloth* **saq**
for the *husband* **master** of her youth.
9 The *meat* offering and the *drink offering* **libation**
is cut off from the house of *the LORD* **Yah Veh**;
the priests, the *LORD'S* ministers of **Yah Veh**, mourn.
10 The field is *wasted* **ravaged**, the *land* **soil** mourneth;
for the *corn is wasted* **crop ravageth**:
the *new wine is dried up* **juice withereth**,
the oil languisheth.
11 Be ye ashamed, O ye *husbandmen* **cultivators**;
howl, O ye vinedressers, for the wheat and for the barley;
because the harvest of the field is *perished* **destroyed**.
12 The vine *is dried up* **withereth**,
and the fig tree languisheth;
the pomegranate tree, the palm tree also,
and the apple tree,
even all the trees of the field, *are* withered:
because *joy* **rejoicing** is withered *away*
from the sons of *men* **humanity**.

CALL TO REPENTANCE

13 Gird *yourselves*, and *lament* **mourn**, ye priests:
howl, ye ministers of the **sacrifice** altar:
come, *lie all night* **stay overnight** in *sackcloth* **saq**,
ye ministers of my *God* **Elohim**:
for the *meat* offering and the *drink offering* **libation**
is withholden from the house of your *God* **Elohim**.
14 *Sanctify* **Hallow** ye a fast,
call a *solemn* **private** assembly,
gather the elders
and all the *inhabitants* **settlers** of the land
into the house of *the LORD* **Yah Veh** your *God* **El**,
and cry unto *the LORD* **Yah Veh**,

THE DAY OF YAH VEH

15 *Alas* **Aha** for the day!
for the day of *the LORD* **Yah Veh** is *at hand* **nearby**,
and as a *destruction* **ravage** from *the Almighty* **Shadday**
shall it come.
16 Is not the *meat* **food** cut off before our eyes,
yea, joy **cheerfulness** and *gladness* **twirling**
from the house of our *God* **Elohim**?
17 The *seed is rotten* **kernels rot** under their clods,
the *garners* **treasuries** *are laid* desolate,
the *barns* **granaries** are broken *down*;
for the *corn is withered* **crop withereth**.
18 How *do the beasts groan* **the animals sigh**!
the *herds* **droves** of cattle are perplexed,
because they have no pasture;
yea, the *flocks* **droves** of *sheep* **flocks**
are *made desolate* **guilted**.
19 O *LORD* **Yah Veh**, to thee *will I cry* **shall I call out**:
for the fire
hath devoured the *pastures* **folds** of the wilderness,
and the flame
hath *burned* **inflamed** all the trees of the field.
20 The *beasts* **animals** of the field
cry **yearn** also unto thee:
for the *rivers* **reservoirs** of waters
are dried up **withered**,
and the fire
hath devoured the *pastures* **folds** of the wilderness.
2 *Blow* **Blast** ye the trumpet in *Zion* **Siyon**,
and *sound an alarm* **shout** in my holy mountain:
let all the *inhabitants* **settlers** of the land *tremble* **quiver**:
for the day of *the LORD* **Yah Veh** cometh,
for it is *nigh at hand* **nearby**;
2 A day of **dripping** darkness and of *gloominess* **darkness**,
a day of clouds and of thick darkness,
as the *morning* **dawn** spread upon the mountains:
a great people and a *strong* **mighty**;
there hath not been *ever* **eternally** the like,
neither shall **add to** be *any more* after it,
even to the years
of *many generations* **generation and generation**.
3 A fire devoureth *before them* **at their face**;
and behind them a flame *burneth* **inflameth**:
the land is as the garden of Eden
before them **at their face**,
and behind them a desolate wilderness;
yea, and *nothing shall escape them*
there shall be no escapees.
4 The *appearance* **visage** of them
is as the *appearance* **visage** of horses;
and as *horsemen* **cavalry**, so shall they run.
5 Like the *noise* **voice** of chariots
on the tops of mountains
shall they *leap* **dance**,
like the *noise* **voice** of a flame of fire
that devoureth the stubble,
as a *strong* **mighty** people set in *battle* **war** array.
6 Before their face
the people shall *be much pained* **writhe**:
all faces shall gather *blackness* **flushness**.
7 They shall run like mighty *men*;
they shall *climb* **ascend** the wall like men of war;
and they shall march every *one* **man** on his ways,
and they shall not *break* **entangle** their *ranks* **paths**:
8 Neither shall *one* **man** thrust *another* **brother**;
they shall walk
every one **all the mighty** in *his path* **their highway**:
and when they fall upon the sword,
they shall not be *wounded* **cropped**. clipped, pruned
9 They shall run to and fro in the city;
they shall run upon the wall,
they shall *climb up* **ascend** upon the houses;
they shall enter in at the windows like a thief.
10 The earth shall quake *before them* **at their face**;
the heavens shall *tremble* **quake**:
the sun and the moon shall *be dark* **darken**,
and the stars
shall *withdraw* **gather** their *shining* **brilliance**:
11 And *the LORD* **Yah Veh** shall *utter* **give** his voice
before **at the face of** his *army* **valiant**:
for his camp is *very* **mighty** great:
for he is *strong* **mighty** that *executeth* **worketh** his word:
for the day of *the LORD* **Yah Veh** is great
and *very terrible* **mighty awesome**;
and who can *abide* **contain** it?
12 Therefore also now,
saith the LORD **an oracle of Yah Veh**,
turn ye *even* to me with all your heart,
and with fasting,
and with weeping, and with *mourning* **chopping**:
13 And *rend* **rip** your heart,

and not your *garments* **clothes**,
and turn unto *the LORD* **Yah Veh** your *God* **Elohim**:
for he is *gracious* **charismatic** and merciful,
slow to *anger* **wrath**, and of great *kindness* **mercy**,
and *repenteth him of* **he sigheth concerning** the evil.
14 Who knoweth *if he will return* — **he returneth**
and repent **yea, he sigheth**,
and *leave a blessing* **letteth a blessing remain**
behind him;
even a meat — **an** offering and a *drink offering* **libation**
unto *the LORD* **Yah Veh** your *God* **Elohim**?
15 *Blow* **Blast** the trumpet in *Zion* **Siyon**,
sanctify **hallow** a fast, call a *solemn* **private** assembly:
16 Gather the people, *sanctify* **hallow** the congregation,
assemble **gather** the elders,
gather the *children* **sucklings**,
and those that suck the breasts:
let the bridegroom go forth of his chamber,
and the bride out of her *closet* **canopy**.
17 Let the priests, the ministers of *the LORD* **Yah Veh**,
weep between the porch and the **sacrifice** altar,
and let them say, Spare thy people, O *LORD* **Yah Veh**,
and give not thine *heritage* **inheritance** to reproach,
that the *heathen* **goyim** should *rule* **reign** over them:
wherefore should they say among the people,
Where is their *God* **Elohim**?
18 Then *will the LORD* **shall Yah Veh**
be jealous for his land,
and *pity* **compassion** his people.
19 Yea, *the LORD will* **let Yah Veh** answer
and say unto his people,
Behold, I *will* **shall** send you *corn* **crop**,
and *wine* **juice**, and oil,
and ye shall be satisfied therewith:
and I *will* **shall** no more *make* **give** you a reproach
among the *heathen* **goyim**:
20 But I *will* **shall** remove far off from you
the northern *army*,
and *will* **shall** drive him
into a land *barren* **parched** and desolate,
with his face toward the east sea,
and his *hinder part* **end** toward the *utmost* **latter** sea,
and his stink shall *come up* **ascend**,
and his *ill savour* **stench** shall *come up* **ascend**,
because he hath *done great things* **greatened to work**.
21 *Fear* **Awe** not, O *land* **soil**;
be glad **twirl** and *rejoice* **cheer**:
for *the LORD* **Yah Veh**
will do great things **shall work greatly**.
22 *Be* **Awe** not *afraid*, ye *beasts* **animals** of the field:
for the *pastures* **folds** of the wilderness do spring,
for the tree beareth her fruit,
the fig tree and the vine
do yield **give** their *strength* **valuables**.
23 *Be glad* **Twirl** then, ye *children* **sons** of *Zion* **Siyon**,
and *rejoice* **cheer**
in *the LORD* **Yah Veh** your *God* **Elohim**:
for he hath given you
the *former rain moderately* **early pour in justness**,
and he *will* **shall** cause to *come* **bring** down for you
the *rain* **downpour**,
the *former* **early** rain, and the *latter* **after** rain
in the first *month*.
24 And the *floors* **threshingfloors**
shall be *full of wheat* **filled with grain**,
and the *fats* **troughs** shall overflow with *wine* **juice** and oil.
25 And I *will restore* **shall shalam** to you
the years that the locust hath eaten, the cankerworm,
and the caterpiller, and the palmerworm,
my great *army* **valiant** which I sent among you.
26 And ye shall eat *in plenty* **and consume**,
and be satisfied,
and *praise* **halal**
the name of *the LORD* **Yah Veh** your *God* **Elohim**,
that hath *dealt wondrously* **worked marvelously**
with you:
and my people shall never *be ashamed* **shame eternally**.
27 And ye shall know
that I am in the midst of *Israel* **Yisra El**,
and that *I am the LORD* **I — Yah Veh** your *God* **Elohim**,
and none else:
and my people
shall *never be ashamed* **not shame eternally**.

YAH VEH'S SPIRIT POURED UPON ALL FLESH

28 And it shall *come to pass* **become**, afterward,
that I *will* **shall** pour out my spirit upon all flesh;
and your sons and your daughters shall prophesy,
your *old men* **elders** shall dream dreams,
your *young men* **youths** shall see visions:
29 And also
upon the servants and upon the *handmaids* **maids**
in those days *will* **shall** I pour out my spirit.

SIGNS OF OMENS

30 And I *will shew wonders* **shall give omens**
in the heavens and in the earth,
blood, and fire, and *pillars* **columns** of smoke.
31 The sun shall be turned into darkness,
and the moon into blood,
before **at the face of the coming**
of the great and *terrible* **awesome**
day of *the LORD* **Yah Veh** *come*.
32 And it shall *come to pass* **become**,
that whosoever
shall call on the name of *the LORD* **Yah Veh**
shall be *delivered* **rescued**:
for in mount *Zion* **Siyon** and in *Jerusalem* **Yeru Shalem**
shall be *deliverance* **an escape**,
as *the LORD* **Yah Veh** hath said,
and in the *remnant* **survivors**
whom *the LORD* **Yah Veh** shall call.

THE GOYIM JUDGED

3 For, behold, in those days, and in that time,
when I shall *bring again* **return** the captivity
of *Judah* **Yah Hudah** and *Jerusalem* **Yeru Shalem**,
2 I *will* **shall** also gather all *nations* **goyim**,
and *will* **shall** bring them down
into *the valley of Jehoshaphat* **Gay Yah Shaphat**,
and *will* **shall** plead with them there
for my people and for my *heritage* **inheritance**
Israel **Yisra El**,
whom they have scattered among the *nations* **goyim**,
and *parted* **allotted** my land.
3 And they *have cast lots* **handle pebbles** for my people;
and have given a *boy* **child** for *an harlot* **a whore**,
and sold a *girl* **child** for wine, that they might drink.
4 Yea, and what have ye to do with me,
O *Tyre* **Sor**, and *Zidon* **Sidon**,
and all the *coasts* **regions** of *Palestine* **Pelesheth**?
will **shall** ye *render* **deal** me *a recompence* **shalam**?
and if ye *recompense* **deal** me,
swiftly and *speedily* **quickly**
will **shall** I return your *recompence* **dealing**
upon your own head;
5 Because ye have taken my silver and my gold,
and have carried into your *temples* **manses**
my goodly *pleasant things* **desirables**:
6 The *children also* **sons** of *Judah* **Yah Hudah**
and the *children* **sons** of *Jerusalem* **Yeru Shalem**
have ye sold unto the *Grecians* **sons of Yavaniy**,
that ye might remove them far from their border.
7 Behold, I *will raise* **shall waken** them
out of the place whither ye have sold them,
and *will* **shall** return your *recompence* **dealing**
upon your own head:
8 And I *will* **shall** sell your sons and your daughters
into the hand of the *children* **sons** of *Judah* **Yah Hudah**,
and they shall sell them to the *Sabeans* **Shebaiym**,
to a *people* **goyim** far off:
for *the LORD* **Yah Veh** hath *spoken* **worded** *it*.
9 *Proclaim ye* **Call ye out** this among the *Gentiles* **goyim**;
Prepare **Hallow** war, wake up the mighty *men*,
let all the men of war draw near;
let them *come up* **ascend**:
10 *Beat* **Forge** your plowshares into swords,
and your *pruninghooks* **psalmpicks** into *spears* **javelins**:
let the *weak* **vanquished** say, I am *strong* **mighty**.
11 *Assemble yourselves* **Hurry**,
and come, all ye *heathen* **goyim**,
and gather yourselves together round about:
thither cause thy mighty ones to *come down* **descend**,

O *LORD* **Yah Veh**.
12 Let the *heathen* **goyim** be wakened,
and *come up* **ascend**
to *the valley of Jehoshaphat* **Gay Yah Shaphat**:
for there *will* **shall** I sit
to judge all the *heathen* **goyim** round about.
13 *Put ye in* **Extend** the sickle,
for the harvest is *ripe* **ripened**:
come, *get you down* **descend ye**;
for the *press is full* **winepress filleth**,
the *fats* **troughs** overflow;
for their *wickedness* **evil** is great.
14 Multitudes, multitudes in the valley of decision:
for the day of *the LORD* **Yah Veh** is near
in the valley of decision.
15 The sun and the moon shall be darkened,
and the stars
shall *withdraw* **gather** their *shining* **brilliance**.
16 *The LORD* **Yah Veh** also shall roar out of *Zion* **Siyon**,
and *utter* **give** his voice from *Jerusalem* **Yeru Shalem**;
and the heavens and the earth shall *shake* **quake**:
but *the LORD* **Yah Veh**
will **shall** be the *hope* **refuge** of his people,
and the *strength* **stronghold**
of the *children* **sons** of *Israel* **Yisra El**.
17 So shall ye know
that *I am the LORD* **I — Yah Veh** your *God* **Elohim**
dwelling **tabernacling** in *Zion* **Siyon**, my holy mountain:
then shall *Jerusalem* **Yeru Shalem** be holy,
and there shall no strangers pass through her any more.
18 And it shall *come to pass* **become,** in that day,
that the mountains
shall *drop down new wine* **drip squeezed juice**,
and the hills shall *flow* **go** with milk,
and all the *rivers* **reservoirs** of *Judah* **Yah Hudah**
shall *flow* **go** with waters,
and a fountain shall *come* **go** forth
of the house of *the LORD* **Yah Veh**,
and shall *water* **wet** the *valley* **wadi** of Shittim.
19 *Egypt* **Misrayim** shall be a desolation,
and Edom shall be a desolate wilderness,
for the violence
against the *children* **sons** of *Judah* **Yah Hudah**,
because they have *shed* **poured** innocent blood
in their land.
20 But *Judah* **Yah Hudah**
shall *dwell for ever* **settle eternally**,
and *Jerusalem* **Yeru Shalem**
from generation to generation.
21 For I *will cleanse* **shall exonerate** their blood
that I have not *cleansed* **exonerated**:
for *the LORD* **Yah Veh**
dwelleth **tabernacleth** in *Zion* **Siyon**.

KEY TO INTERPRETING THE EXEGESES:
King James text is in regular type;
Text under exegeses is in oblique type;
Text of exegeses is in bold type.

INTRODUCTION

1 The words of Amos,
who was among the *herdmen* **branders** of *Tekoa* **Teqoa**,
which he saw concerning *Israel* **Yisra El**
in the days of *Uzziah* **Uzzi Yah**
king **sovereign** of *Judah* **Yah Hudah**,
and in the days of *Jeroboam* **Yarob Am**
the son of *Joash* **Yah Ash** *king* **sovereign** of *Israel* **Yisra El**,
two years *before* **at the face of** the *earthquake* **quake**.
2 And he said, *The LORD* **Yah Veh**
will **shall** roar from *Zion* **Siyon**,
and *utter* **give** his voice from *Jerusalem* **Yeru Shalem**;
and the *habitations* **folds** of the *shepherds* **tenders**
shall mourn,
and the top of *Carmel* **Karmel/orchard** shall wither.
3 Thus saith *the LORD* **Yah Veh**;
For three
transgressions **rebellions** of *Damascus* **Dammeseq**,
and for four,
I *will* **shall** not turn *away* **back** *the punishment thereof;*
because they have threshed *Gilead* **Gilad**
with *threshing instruments* **sickles** of iron:
4 But I *will* **shall** send a fire
into the house of *Hazael* **Haza El**,
which shall devour
the *palaces* **citadels** of *Benhadad* **Ben Hadad**.
5 I *will* **shall** break also the bar of *Damascus* **Dammeseq**,
and cut off the *inhabitant* **settler**
from the *plain* **valley** of Aven,
and him that *holdeth* **upholdeth** the sceptre
from the house of Eden:
and the people of *Syria* **Aram**
shall *go into captivity* **be exiled** unto *Kir* **Qir**,
saith *the LORD* **Yah Veh**.
6 Thus saith *the LORD* **Yah Veh**;
For three *transgressions* **rebellions** of *Gaza* **Azzah**,
and for four,
I *will* **shall** not turn *away* **back** *the punishment thereof;*
because they *carried away captive* **exiled**
the *whole captivity* **complete exiles**,
to *deliver* **shut** them up to Edom:
7 But I *will* **shall** send a fire on the wall of *Gaza* **Azzah**,
which shall devour the *palaces* **citadels** *thereof*:
8 And I *will* **shall** cut off the *inhabitant* **settler**
from Ashdod,
and him that *holdeth* **upholdeth** the *sceptre* **scion**
from Ashkelon,
and I *will* **shall** turn mine hand against *Ekron* **Eqron**:
and the *remnant* **survivors** of the *Philistines* **Peleshethiym**
shall *perish* **destruct**,
saith *the Lord GOD* **Adonay Yah Veh**.
9 Thus saith *the LORD* **Yah Veh**;
For three *transgressions* **rebellions** of*Tyrus* **Sor**,
and for four,
I *will* **shall** not turn *away* **back** *the punishment thereof;*
because they delivered *up*
the *whole captivity* **complete exiles** to Edom,
and remembered not the *brotherly* covenant **of brethren**:
10 But I *will* **shall** send a fire on the wall of *Tyrus* **Sor**,
which shall devour the *palaces* **citadels** *thereof.*
11 Thus saith *the LORD* **Yah Veh**;
For three *transgressions* **rebellions** of Edom,
and for four,
I *will* **shall** not turn *away* **back** *the punishment thereof;*
because he did pursue his brother with the sword,
and *did cast off all pity* **ruined mercies**,
and his *anger* **wrath** did tear *perpetually* **eternally**,
and he *kept* **guarded** his wrath *for ever* **in perpetuity**:
12 But I *will* **shall** send a fire upon Teman,
which shall devour the *palaces* **citadels** of Bozrah.
13 Thus saith *the LORD* **Yah Veh**;
For three *transgressions* **rebellions**
of the *children* **sons** of Ammon,
and for four,
I *will* **shall** not turn *away* **back** *the punishment thereof* ;
because they have

ripped up **split** the women with child of *Gilead* **Gilad**,
that they might enlarge their border:
14 But I *will* **shall** kindle a fire in the wall of Rabbah,
and it shall devour the *palaces* **citadels** *thereof*,
with *shouting* **shouts** in the day of *battle* **war**,
with a *tempest* **storm**
in the day of the *whirlwind* **hurricane**:
15 And their *king* **sovereign** shall go into *captivity* **exile**,
he and his *princes* **governors** together,
saith *the LORD* **Yah Veh**.

JUDGMENT ON YAH HUDAH AND YISRA EL

2 Thus saith *the LORD* **Yah Veh**;
For three *transgressions* **rebellions** of Moab,
and for four,
I *will* **shall** not turn *away* **back** *the punishment thereof*;
because he burned the bones
of the *king* **sovereign** of Edom into lime:
2 But I *will* **shall** send a fire upon Moab,
and it shall devour
the *palaces* **citadels** of *Kirioth* **Qerioth**:
and Moab shall die with *tumult* **an uproar**,
with *shouting* **shouts**,
and with the *sound* **voice** of the trumpet:
3 And I *will* **shall** cut off the judge from the midst *thereof*,
and *will slay* **shall slaughter**
all the *princes* **governors** *thereof* with him,
saith *the LORD* **Yah Veh**.
4 Thus saith *the LORD* **Yah Veh**;
For three *transgressions* **rebellions** of *Judah* **Yah Hudah**,
and for four,
I *will* **shall** not turn **back** *away the punishment thereof*;
because they have *despised* **spurned**
the *law* **torah** of *the LORD* **Yah Veh**,
and have not *kept* **guarded** his *commandments* **statutes**,
and their lies caused them to *err* **stray**,
after the which their fathers have walked:
5 But I *will* **shall** send a fire upon *Judah* **Yah Hudah**,
and it shall devour
the *palaces* **citadels** of *Jerusalem* **Yeru Shalem**.
6 Thus saith *the LORD* **Yah Veh**;
For three *transgressions* **rebellions** of *Israel* **Yisra El**,
and for four,
I *will* **shall** not turn *away* **back** *the punishment thereof*;
because they sold the *righteous* **just** for silver,
and the *poor* **needy** for a pair of shoes;
7 That *pant* **gulp** after the dust of the earth
on the head of the poor,
and *turn aside* **pervert** the way of the *meek* **humble**:
and a man and his father
will **shall** go in unto the *same maid* **lass**,
to profane my holy name:
8 And they *lay themselves down* **stretch out**
upon clothes laid to pledge
by **beside** every **sacrifice** altar,
and they drink the wine of the condemned
in the house of their *god* **elohim**.
9 Yet *destroyed* **desolated** I the *Amorite* **Emoriy**
before them **at their face**,
whose height was like the height of the cedars,
and he was *strong* **powerful** as the oaks;
yet I *destroyed* **desolated** his fruit from above,
and his roots from beneath.
10 Also I *brought* **ascended** you *up*
from the land of *Egypt* **Misrayim**,
and *led* **carried** you forty years through the wilderness,
to possess the land of the *Amorite* **Emoriy**.
11 And I raised up of your sons for prophets,
and of your *young men* **youths** for *Nazarites* **Separatists**.
Is it not even thus, O ye *children* **sons** of *Israel* **Yisra El**?
saith the LORD **an oracle of Yah Veh**.
12 But ye gave the *Nazarites* **Separatists** wine to drink;
and *commanded* **misvahed** the prophets, saying,
Prophesy not.
13 Behold, I am pressed under you,
as a *cart* **wagon** is pressed that is full of *sheaves* **omers**.
14 Therefore the flight shall *perish* **destruct** from the swift,
and the strong shall not strengthen his force,
neither shall the mighty *deliver himself* **rescue his soul**:
15 Neither shall he stand
that *handleth* **manipulateth** the bow;
and he that is swift of foot shall not *deliver* **rescue** *himself*:
neither shall he that rideth the horse
deliver himself **rescue his soul**.
16 And he that is *courageous* **strong of heart**
among the mighty
shall flee away naked in that day,
saith the LORD **an oracle of Yah Veh**.

YAH VEH'S WORD AGAINST THE SONS OF YISRA EL

3 Hear this word
that *the LORD* **Yah Veh** hath *spoken* **worded** against you,
O *children* **sons** of *Israel* **Yisra El**,
against the whole family which I *brought up* **ascended**
from the land of *Egypt* **Misrayim**, saying,
2 You only have I known of all the families of the *earth* **soil**:
therefore I *will punish* **shall visit upon** you
for all your *iniquities* **perversities**.
3 Can two walk together,
except they *be agreed* **congregate**?
4 *Will* **Shall** a lion roar in the forest,
when he hath no prey?
will a young lion cry **shall a whelp give voice**
out of his *den* **habitation**,
if **except** he have *taken nothing* **captured**?
5 *Can* **Falleth** a bird *fall* in a snare upon the earth,
where no *gin* **snare** is for him?
shall one *take up* **ascend** a snare from the *earth* **soil**,
and *have taken nothing at all*
if in capturing, it hath not captured?
6 Shall a trumpet *be blown* **blast** in the city,
and the people not *be afraid* **tremble**?
shall there be evil in a city,
and *the LORD* **Yah Veh** hath not *done* **worked** it?
7 Surely *the Lord GOD* **Adonay Yah Veh**
will do nothing **shall work no word**,
but he *revealeth* **exposeth** his *secret* **private counsel**
unto his servants the prophets.
8 The lion hath roared, who *will* **shall** not *fear* **awe**?
the Lord GOD **Adonay Yah Veh** hath *spoken* **worded**,
who *can but* **doth not** prophesy?
9 *Publish* **Let it be heard**
in the *palaces* **citadels** at Ashdod,
and in the *palaces* **citadels** in the land of *Egypt* **Misrayim**,
and say, Assemble yourselves
upon the mountains of *Samaria* **Shomeron**,
and *behold* **see** the great *tumults* **confusions**
in the midst *thereof*,
and the oppressed in the midst *thereof*.
10 For they know not
to *do right* **work straightforwardness**,
saith the LORD **an oracle of Yah Veh**,
who *store up* **treasure** violence and *robbery* **ravage**
in their *palaces* **citadels**.
11 Therefore thus saith *the Lord GOD* **Adonay Yah Veh**;
An adversary there shall *be* **A tribulator**
— even round about the land;
and he shall bring down thy strength from thee,
and thy *palaces* **citadels** shall be *spoiled* **plundered**.
12 Thus saith *the LORD* **Yah Veh**;
As the *shepherd* **tender**
taketh **rescueth** out of the mouth of the lion
two legs, or a piece of an ear;
so shall the *children* **sons** of *Israel* **Yisra El**
be *taken out* **rescued**
that *dwell* **settle** in *Samaria* **sShomeron**
in the *corner* **edge** of a bed,
and in *Damascus* **Dammeseq** in a *couch* **bedstead**.
13 Hear ye,
and *testify* **witness** in the house of *Jacob* **Yaaqov**,
saith the Lord GOD **an oracle of Adonay Yah Veh**,
the God of hosts **Elohim Sabaoth**,
14 That in the day that I shall visit
the *transgressions* **rebellions** of *Israel* **Yisra El** upon him
I *will* **shall** also visit the **sacrifice** altars of *Bethel* **Beth El**:
and the horns of the **sacrifice** altar shall be cut off,
and fall to the *ground* **earth**.
15 And I *will* **shall** smite the winter house
with the summer house;
and the houses of ivory shall *perish* **destruct**,
and the great houses shall *have an end* **be consummated**,
saith the LORD **an oracle of Yah Veh**.

YISRA EL IS UNREPENTANT

4 Hear this word, ye *kine* **heifers** of Bashan,
that are in the mountain of *Samaria* **Shomeron**,
which oppress the poor, which crush the needy,
which say to their *masters* **adonim**,
Bring, and let us drink.
2 *The Lord GOD* **Adonay Yah Veh**
hath *sworn* **oathed** by his holiness,
that, *lo* **behold**, the days shall come upon you,
that he *will take* **shall lift** you *away* with hooks,
and your posterity with fishhooks.
3 And ye shall go out at the breaches,
every cow at that which is before her **women in front**;
and ye shall cast them into the palace,
saith the LORD **an oracle of Yah Veh**.
4 Come to *Bethel* **Beth El**, and *transgress* **rebel**;
at Gilgal *multiply transgression* **abound rebellion**;
and bring your sacrifices *every* **at** morning,
and your tithes after three years **of days**:
5 And *offer a sacrifice of thanksgiving*
incense with extended hands
with *leaven* **fermentation**,
and *proclaim* **call out**
and *publish the free offerings*
let the voluntaries be heard:
for *this liketh you* **thus have ye loved**,
O ye *children* **sons** of *Israel* **Yisra El**,
saith the Lord GOD **an oracle of Adonay Yah Veh**.
6 And I also have given you
cleanness **innocency** of teeth in all your cities,
and *want* **lack** of bread in all your places:
yet have ye not returned unto me,
saith the LORD **an oracle of Yah Veh**.
7 And also
I have withholden the *rain* **downpour** from you,
when there were yet three months to the harvest:
and I caused it to rain upon one city,
and caused it not to rain upon *another* **one** city:
one *piece* **allotment** was rained upon,
and the *piece* **allotment** whereupon it rained not
withered.
8 So two or three cities wandered unto one city,
to drink water; but they were not satisfied:
yet have ye not returned unto me,
saith the LORD **an oracle of Yah Veh**.
9 I have smitten you with blasting and *mildew* **pale green**:
when your gardens and your vineyards
and your fig trees and your *olive trees* **olives**
increased **abounded**,
the palmerworm devoured *them*:
yet have ye not returned unto me,
saith the LORD **an oracle of Yah Veh**.
10 I have sent among you the pestilence
after the manner **by the way** of *Egypt* **Misrayim**:
your *young men* **youths**
have I *slain* **slaughtered** with the sword,
and have taken away your horses;
and I have *made* **caused** the stink of your camps
to *come up* **ascend** unto your nostrils:
yet have ye not returned unto me,
saith the LORD **an oracle of Yah Veh**.
11 I have *overthrown some of* **turned against** you,
as *God* **Elohim**
overthrew *Sodom* **Sedom** and *Gomorrah* **Amorah**,
and ye were as a *firebrand* **brand**
plucked **rescued** out of the burning:
yet have ye not returned unto me,
saith the LORD **an oracle of Yah Veh**.
12 Therefore thus *will I do* **shall I work** unto thee,
O *Israel* **Yisra El**:
and because I *will do* **shall work** this unto thee,
prepare to meet thy *God* **Elohim**, O *Israel* **Yisra El**.
13 For, *lo* **behold**,
he that formeth the mountains, and createth the wind,
and *declareth* **telleth** unto *man* **humanity**
what is his *thought* **meditation**,
that *maketh* **worketh** the *morning* **dawn** darkness,
and treadeth upon the *high places* **bamahs** of the earth,
The LORD, The God of hosts **Yah Veh Elohim Sabaoth**,
is his name.

YAH VEH'S LAMENTATION AGAINST YISRA EL

5 Hear ye this word which I *take up* **lift** against you,
even a lamentation, O house of *Israel* **Yisra El**.
2 The virgin of *Israel* **Yisra El** is fallen;
she shall *no more* **add not to** rise:
she is *forsaken* **abandoned** upon her *land* **soil**;
there is none to raise her up.
3 For thus saith *the Lord GOD* **Adonay Yah Veh**;
The city that went out by a thousand
shall *leave* **let remain** an hundred,
and that which went forth by an hundred
shall *leave* **let remain** ten,
to the house of *Israel* **Yisra El**.
4 For thus saith *the LORD* **Yah Veh**
unto the house of *Israel* **Yisra El**,
Seek ye me, and ye shall live:
5 But seek not *Bethel* **Beth El**, nor enter into Gilgal,
and pass not to *Beersheba* **Beer Sheba**:
for **in exiling**,
Gilgal shall *surely go into captivity* **be exiled**,
and *Bethel* **Beth El** shall come to *nought* **mischief**.
6 Seek *the LORD* **Yah Veh**, and *ye* shall live;
lest he *break out* **prosper** like fire
in the house of *Joseph* **Yoseph**,
and devour *it*,
and there be none to quench it in *Bethel* **Beth El**.
7 Ye who turn judgment to wormwood,
and leave off *righteousness* **justness** in the earth,
8 Seek him that *maketh the seven stars* **worketh Kimah**
and *Orion* **Kesil**,
and turneth the shadow of death into the morning,
and maketh the day dark with night:
that calleth for the waters of the sea,
and poureth them out upon the face of the earth:
The LORD **Yah Veh** is his name:
9 That *strengtheneth* **releaseth** the *spoiled* **ravaged**
against the strong,
so that the *spoiled* shall **ravaged**
come against the fortress.
10 They hate him
that *rebuketh* **reproveth** in the *gate* **portal**,
and they abhor him
that *speaketh uprightly* **wordeth integriously**.
11 Forasmuch therefore
as your *treading* **trampling** is upon the poor,
and ye take from him burdens of *wheat* **grain**:
ye have built houses of hewn stone,
but ye shall not *dwell* **settle** in them;
ye have planted *pleasant* vineyards **of desire**,
but ye shall not drink wine of them.
12 For I know
your *manifold transgressions* **great rebellions**
and your mighty sins:
they *afflict* **tribulate** the just,
they take a *bribe* **koper/atonement**,
and they *turn aside* **pervert** the *poor* **needy**
in the *gate* **portal** *from their right*.
13 Therefore the *prudent* **comprehending**
shall keep *silence* **still** in that time; for it is an evil time.
14 Seek good, and not evil, that ye may live:
and so
the LORD, the God of hosts **Yah Veh Elohim Sabaoth**,
shall be with you, as ye have *spoken* **said**.
15 Hate the evil, and love the good,
and *establish* **set** judgment in the *gate* **portal**:
it may be that **perhaps**
the LORD God of hosts **Yah Veh Elohim Sabaoth**
will be gracious **shall grant charism**
unto the *remnant* **survivors** of *Joseph* **Yoseph**.

THE DAY OF YAH VEH

16 Therefore
the LORD, the God of hosts, the Lord,
Yah Veh Elohim Sabaoth Adonay saith thus;
Wailing **Chopping** shall be in all streets;
and they shall say in all the *highways* **outways**,
Alas! alas! **Hah! Hah!**
and they shall call the *husbandman* **cultivator**
to mourning,
and such as *are skilful of* **know** lamentation
to *wailing* **chopping**.

17 And in all vineyards shall be *wailing* **chopping**:
for I *will* **shall** pass *through thee* **in your midst**,
saith *the LORD* **Yah Veh**.
18 *Woe* **Ho** unto you
that desire the day of *the LORD* **Yah Veh**!
to what end is it for you?
the day of *the LORD* **Yah Veh** is darkness, and not light.
19 As if a man did flee from **the face of** a lion,
and a bear met him;
or went into the house,
and *leaned* **propped** his hand on the wall,
and a serpent bit him.
20 Shall not the day of *the LORD* **Yah Veh**
be darkness, and not light?
even very dark, and no *brightness* **brilliance** in it?
21 I hate, I *despise* **spurn** your *feast days* **celebrations**,
and I *will* **shall** not *smell* **scent**
in your *solemn* **private** assemblies.
22 Though ye *offer* **holocaust** me
burnt offerings **holocausts**
and your *meat* offerings,
I *will* **shall** not *accept them* **be pleased**:
neither *will* **shall** I *regard* **scan**
the *peace offerings* **shelamim** of your *fat beasts* **fatlings**.
23 *Take* **Turn** thou *away* **aside** from me
the *noise* **roar** of thy songs;
for I *will* **shall** not hear
the *melody* **psalm** of thy *viols* **bagpipes**.
24 But let judgment *run down* **roll** as waters,
and *righteousness* **justness**
as a *mighty stream* **perennial wadi**.
25 Have ye *offered* **brought near** unto me
sacrifices and offerings in the wilderness forty years,
O house of *Israel* **Yisra El**?
26 But ye have borne the *tabernacle* **sukkoth/brush arbor**
of your *Moloch* **sovereign** and *Chiun* **Kiun** your images,
the star of your *god* **elohim**,
which ye *made* **worked** to yourselves.
27 Therefore
will **shall** I cause you to go into *captivity* **exile**
beyond *Damascus* **Dammeseq**,
saith *the LORD* **Yah Veh**,
whose name is *The God of hosts* **Elohim Sabaoth**.

HO TO THEM THAT RELAX IN SIYON

6 *Woe* **Ho** to them that *are at ease* **relax** in *Zion* **Siyon**,
and *trust* **confide** in the mountain of *Samaria* **Shomeron**,
which are *named* **appointed**
chief **firstlings** of the *nations* **goyim**,
to whom the house of *Israel* **Yisra El** came!
2 Pass ye unto *Calneh* **Kalneh**, and see;
and from thence go ye to Hamath the *great* **rabbi**:
then go down **descend** to Gath
of the *Philistines* **Peleshethiym**:
be they better than these *kingdoms* **sovereigndoms**?
or their border greater than your border?
3 Ye that *put far* **cast** away the evil day,
and cause the *seat* **settlement** of violence to come near;
4 That lie upon beds of ivory,
and stretch themselves upon their *couches* **bedsteads**,
and eat the *lambs* **rams** out of the flock,
and the calves out of the midst of the stall;
5 That *chant* **chatter**
to the *sound* **mouth** of the *viol* **bagpipe**,
and *invent* **fabricate** to themselves
instruments of *musick* **song**,
like David;
6 That drink wine in *bowls* **sprinklers**,
and anoint themselves with the *chief* **firstlings** ointments:
but they are not *grieved* **worn**
for the *affliction* **breaking** of *Joseph* **Yoseph**.
7 Therefore now shall they *go captive* **be exiled**
with the first that *go captive* **be exiled**,
and the *banquet* **feast of revelling**
of them that stretched themselves
shall be *removed* **turned aside**.
8 *The Lord GOD* **Adonay Yah Veh**
hath *sworn* **oathed** by *himself* **his soul**,
saith the LORD the God of hosts
an oracle of Yah Veh Elohim Sabaoth,
I *abhor* **loathe** the *excellency* **pomp** of *Jacob* **Yaaqov**,
and hate his *palaces* **citadels**:
therefore *will I deliver* **shall I shut** up the city
with *all that is therein* **the fulness thereof**.
9 And it shall *come to pass* **become**,
if there remain ten men in one house, that they shall die.
10 And *a man's* **his** uncle shall *take* **bear** him *up*,
and he that *burneth* **cremateth** him,
to bring out the bones out of the house,
and shall say unto him
that is by the *sides* **flanks** of the house,
Is there yet any with thee?
and he shall say, *No* **That's final**.
Then shall he say, *Hold thy tongue* **Hush**:
for we may not *make mention of* **memorialize**
the name of *the LORD* **Yah Veh**.
11 For, behold,
the LORD commandeth **Yah Veh misvaheth**,
and he *will* **shall** smite the great house
with *breaches* **dewdrops**,
and the little house with *clefts* **fissures**.
12 Shall horses run upon the rock?
will **shall** one plow *there* with oxen?
for ye have turned judgment into *gall* **rosh**,
and the fruit of *righteousness* **justness**
into *hemlock* **wormwood**:
13 Ye which *rejoice* **cheer** in a *thing* **word** of nought,
which say,
Have we not taken to us horns by our own strength?
14 But, behold,
I *will* **shall** raise *up* against you a *nation* **goyim**,
O house of *Israel* **Yisra El**,
saith the LORD the God of hosts
an oracle of Yah Veh Elohim Sabaoth;
and they shall afflict you from the entering in of Hemath
unto the *river* **wadi** of the *wilderness* **plain**.

WARNING VISIONS

7 Thus *hath the Lord GOD* **Adonay Yah Veh**
shewed unto me **hath me see**;
and, behold, he formed *grasshoppers* **grubbers**
in the beginning of the *shooting up* **ascending**
of the *latter* **after** growth;
and, *lo* **behold**, it was the latter growth
after the *king's mowings* **sovereign's shearings**.
2 And it *came to pass* **became**,
that when they had *made an end of* **finished** eating
the *grass* **herbage** of the land,
then I said, *O Lord GOD* **Adonay Yah Veh**,
forgive, I beseech thee:
by whom **how** shall *Jacob* **Yaaqov** arise? for he is small.
3 *The LORD repented* **Yah Veh sighed** for this:
It shall not be, saith *the LORD* **Yah Veh**.
4 Thus *hath the Lord GOD* **Adonay Yah Veh**
shewed unto me **hath me see**:
and, behold, *the Lord GOD* **Adonay Yah Veh**
called to contend by fire,
and it devoured the great *deep* **abyss**,
and did eat up *a part* **an allotment**.
5 Then said I, O *Lord GOD* **Adonay Yah Veh**,
cease, I beseech thee:
by whom **How** shall *Jacob* **Yaaqov** arise? for he is small.
6 *The LORD repented* **Yah Veh sighed** for this:
This also shall not be,
saith *the Lord GOD* **Adonay Yah Veh**.
7 Thus he *shewed* **hath** me **see**: and, behold,
the Lord stood **Adonay stationed** upon a wall
made by a plumbline, with a plumbline in his hand.
8 And *the LORD* **Yah Veh** said unto me,
Amos, what seest thou?
And I said, A plumbline.
Then said *the LORD* **Yah Veh Adonay**,
Behold, I *will* **shall** set a plumbline
in the midst of my people *Israel* **Yisra El**:
I *will* **shall** not *again* **add to** pass by them any more:
9 And the *high places* **bamahs** of *Isaac* **Yischaq**
shall be *desolate* **desolated**,
and the *sanctuaries* **holies** of *Israel* **Yisra El**
shall be *laid waste* **parched**;
and I *will* **shall** rise
against the house of *Jeroboam* **Yarob Am** with the sword.
10 Then *Amaziah* **Amas Yah** the priest of *Bethel* **Beth El**

sent to *Jeroboam* **Yarob Am**
king **sovereign** of *Israel* **Yisra El**, saying,
Amos hath conspired against thee
in the midst of the house of *Israel* **Yisra El**:
the land is not able to *bear* **contain** all his words.
11 For thus Amos saith,
Jeroboam **Yarob Am** shall die by the sword,
and **in exiling,**
Israel **Yisra El** shall *surely be led away captive* **be exiled**
out of their own *land* **soil**.
12 Also *Amaziah* **Amas Yah** said unto Amos,
O thou seer, go,
flee thee *away* into the land of *Judah* **Yah Hudah**,
and there eat bread, and prophesy there:
13 But **add not to** prophesy *not again*
any more at *Bethel* **Beth El**:
for it is the *king's chapel* **holies of the sovereigndom**,
and it is the *king's court* **house of the sovereign**.
14 Then answered Amos, and said to *Amaziah* **Amas Yah**,
I was no prophet, neither was I a prophet's son;
but I was an herdman,
and a *gatherer* **pincher** of *sycomore fruit* **sycomores**:
15 And *the LORD* **Yah Veh** took me
as I followed the flock,
and *the LORD* **Yah Veh** said unto me,
Go, prophesy unto my people *Israel* **Yisra El**.
16 Now therefore
hear thou the word of *the LORD* **Yah Veh**:
Thou sayest, Prophesy not against *Israel* **Yisra El**,
and *drop* **drip** not
thy word against the house of *Isaac* **Yischaq**.
17 Therefore thus saith *the LORD* **Yah Veh**;
Thy *wife* **woman** shall *be an harlot* **whore** in the city,
and thy sons and thy daughters shall fall by the sword,
and thy *land* **soil** shall be *divided* **allotted** by line;
and thou shalt die in a *polluted land* **foul soil**:
and **in exiling,**
Israel **Yisra El** shall *surely go into captivity* **be exiled**
forth of **from** his *land* **soil**.

THE BASKET OF SUMMER FRUIT

8 Thus *hath the Lord GOD* **Adonay Yah Veh**
shewed unto me **hath me see**:
and behold a basket of summer fruit.
2 And he said, Amos, what seest thou?
And I said, A basket of summer fruit.
Then said *the LORD* **Yah Veh** unto me,
The end is come upon my people of *Israel* **Yisra El**;
I *will* **shall** not *again* **add to** pass by them any more.
3 And the songs of the *temple* **manse**
shall be howlings in that day,
saith the Lord GOD **an oracle of Adonay Yah Veh**:
there shall be many *dead bodies* **carcases** in every place;
they shall cast them forth *with silence* **hushed**.
4 Hear this, O ye that *swallow up* **gulp** the needy,
even to make the *poor* **humble** of the land
to *fail* **shabbathize**,
5 Saying,
When *will* **shall be** the new moon *be gone* **passed**,
that we may *sell corn* **market for kernels**?
and the *sabbath* **shabbath**,
that we may *set forth wheat* **open grain**,
making **lessening** the ephah *small*,
and **greatening** the shekel *great*,
and *falsifying* **twisting** the balances by deceit?
6 That we may *buy* **chattel** the poor for silver,
and the needy for a pair of shoes;
yea, and *sell* **market for kernels**
the *refuse* **chaff** of the *wheat* **grain**?
7 *The LORD* **Yah Veh** hath *sworn* **oathed**
by the *excellency* **pomp** of *Jacob* **Yaaqov**,
Surely *I will never* **shall not in perpetuity**
forget any of their works.
8 shall not the land *tremble* **quake** for this,
and every one mourn that *dwelleth* **settleth** therein?
and it shall *rise up* **ascend** wholly as a *flood* **light**;
and it shall be *cast out* **expelled** and drowned,
as by the *flood* **river** of *Egypt* **Misrayim**.
9 And it shall *come to pass* **become,** in that day,
saith the Lord GOD **an oracle of Adonay Yah Veh**,
that I *will* **shall** cause the sun to go down at noon,
and I *will* **shall** darken the earth in the *clear* **light of** day:
10 And I *will* **shall** turn your *feasts* **celebrations**
into mourning,
and all your songs into lamentation;
and I *will bring up sackcloth* **shall ascend saq**
upon all loins,
and baldness upon every head;
and I *will make* **shall set** it
as the mourning of an only *son*,
and the end *thereof* as a bitter day.
11 Behold, the days come,
saith the Lord GOD **an oracle of Adonay Yah Veh**,
that I *will* **shall** send a famine in the land,
not a famine of bread, nor a thirst for water,
but of hearing the words of *the LORD* **Yah Veh**:
12 And they shall wander from sea to sea,
and from the north even to the *east* **rising**,
they shall *run to and fro* **flit**
to seek the word of *the LORD* **Yah Veh**,
and shall not find *it*.
13 In that day
shall the *fair* **beautiful** virgins and *young men* **youths**
faint **languish** for thirst.
14 They that *swear* **oath**
by the *sin* **guilt** of *Samaria* **Shomeron**,
and say, Thy *god* **elohim**, O Dan, liveth;
and, The *manner* **way** of *Beersheba* **Beer Sheba** liveth;
even they shall fall, and never rise *up* again.

YAH VEH'S JUDGMENT

9 I saw *the Lord* **Adonay**
standing **stationed** upon the **sacrifice** altar:
and he said, Smite the lintel of the door,
that the *posts* **thresholds** may *shake* **quake**:
and *cut* **crop** them in the head, all of them;
and I *will slay* **shall slaughter** the last of them
with the sword:
he that fleeth of them shall not flee away,
and *he that escapeth* **any escapee** of them
shall not be *delivered* **rescued**.
2 Though they dig into *hell* **sheol**,
thence shall mine hand take them;
though they *climb up* **ascend** to *heaven* **the heavens**,
thence *will* **shall** I bring them down:
3 And though they hide themselves
in the top of *Carmel* **Karmel/orchard**,
I *will* **shall** search and take them out thence;
and though they be hid from my *sight* **eyes**
in the *bottom* **floor** of the sea,
thence *will I command* **shall I misvah** the serpent,
and he shall bite them:
4 And though they go into captivity
before **at the face of** their enemies,
thence *will I command* **shall I misvah** the sword,
and it shall *slay* **slaughter** them:
and I *will* **shall** set mine eyes upon them for evil,
and not for good.
5 And *the Lord GOD of hosts* **Adonay Yah Veh Sabaoth**
is he that toucheth the land, and it shall melt,
and all that *dwell* **settle** therein shall mourn:
and it shall *rise up* **ascend** wholly like a *flood* **river**;
and shall be drowned,
as *by* the *flood* **river** of *Egypt* **Misrayim**.
6 It is he
that buildeth his *stories* **steps** in the *heaven* **heavens**,
and hath founded his *troop* **band** in the earth;
he that calleth for the waters of the sea,
and poureth them out upon the face of the earth:
The LORD **Yah Veh** is his name.
7 Are ye not
as *children* **sons** of the *Ethiopians* **Kushiym** unto me,
O *children* **sons** of *Israel* **Yisra El**?
saith the LORD **an oracle of Yah Veh**.
Have not I *brought up Israel* **ascended Yisra El**
out of the land of *Egypt* **Misrayim**?
and the *Philistines* **Peleshethiym** from *Caphtor* **Kaphtor**,
and the *Syrians* **Aramiym** from *Kir* **Qir**?
8 Behold, the eyes of *the Lord GOD* **Adonay Yah Veh**
are upon the sinful *kingdom* **sovereigndom**,
and I *will destroy* **shall desolate** it
from off the face of the *earth* **soil**;

saving **finally,** that **in desolating,**
I *will* **shall** not *utterly destroy* **desolate**
the house of *Jacob* **Yaaqov,**
saith the LORD **an oracle of Yah Veh.**
9 For, *lo* **behold,** I *will command* **shall misvah,**
and I *will sift* **shall shake** the house of *Israel* **Yisra El**
among all *nations* **goyim,**
like as *corn* is *sifted* **shaken** in a sieve,
yet shall not *the least grain* **a kernel** fall upon the earth.
10 All the sinners of my people shall die by the sword,
which say,
The evil shall not *overtake* **approach**
nor *prevent* **confront** us.

THE RESTORATION OF YISRA EL

11 In that day *will* **shall** I raise *up*
the *tabernacle* **sukkoth/brush arbor** of David
that is fallen,
and *close up* **wall** the breaches *thereof;*
and I *will* **shall** raise *up* his ruins,
and I *will* **shall** build it as in the **original** days *of old:*
12 That they may possess the *remnant* **survivors** of Edom,
and of all the *heathen* **goyim,**
which are called by my name,
saith the LORD **an oracle of Yah Veh**
that *doeth* **worketh** this.
13 Behold, the days come,
saith the LORD **an oracle of Yah Veh,**
that the *plowman* **plower**
shall *overtake* **approach** the *reaper* **harvester,**
and the treader of grapes him that *soweth* **draweth** seed;
and the mountains
shall *drop sweet wine* **drip squeezed juice,**
and all the hills shall melt.
14 And I *will bring again* **shall return**
the captivity of my people of *Israel* **Yisra El,**
and they shall build the *waste* **desolated** cities,
and *inhabit* **settle** them;
and they shall plant vineyards,
and drink the wine *thereof;*
they shall also *make* **work** gardens,
and eat the fruit of them.
15 And I *will* **shall** plant them upon their *land* **soil,**
and they shall no more
be *pulled up* **uprooted** out of their *land* **soil**
which I have given them,
saith *the LORD* **Yah Veh** thy *God* **Elohim.**

KEY TO INTERPRETING THE EXEGESES:
King James text is in regular type;
Text under exegeses is in oblique type;
Text of exegeses is in bold type.

THE VISION OF OBAD YAH CONCERNING EDOM

1 The vision of *Obadiah* **Obad Yah.**
Thus saith *the Lord GOD* **Adonay Yah Veh**
concerning Edom;
We have heard a *rumour* **report**
from *the LORD* **Yah Veh,**
and an ambassador is sent among the *heathen* **goyim,**
Arise ye, and let us rise up against her in *battle* **war.**
2 Behold,
I have *made* **given** thee small among the *heathen* **goyim:**
thou art *greatly* **mightily** despised.
3 The *pride* **arrogance** of thine heart hath deceived thee,
thou that *dwellest* **tabernaclest** in the clefts of the rock,
whose *habitation* **settlement** is high;
that saith in his heart,
Who shall bring me down to the *ground* **earth?**
4 Though thou *exalt* **heighten** *thyself* as the eagle,
and though thou set thy nest among the stars,
thence *will* **shall** I bring thee down,
saith the LORD **an oracle of Yah Veh.**
5 If thieves came to thee, if *robbers* **ravagers** by night,
(how art thou cut off!)
would **should** they not have stolen till they had enough?
if the *grapegatherers* **clippers** came to thee,
would **should** they not
leave some grapes **let remain gleanings?**
6 How *are the things of Esau* **Esav**
hath been searched *out!*
how are his *hidden things sought up* **treasures bulged!**
7 All the men of thy *confederacy* **covenant**
have *brought* **sent** thee *even* to the border:
the men that were at *peace* **shalom** with thee
have deceived thee, and prevailed against thee;
they that eat **set** thy bread *have laid* a wound under thee:
there is *none understanding* **no discernment** in him.
8 shall I not in that day,
saith the LORD **an oracle of Yah Veh,**
even destroy the wise *men* out of Edom,
and *understanding* **discernment**
out of the mount of *Esau* **Esav?**
9 And thy mighty *men,* O Teman, shall be dismayed,
to the end that every *one* **man** of the mount of *Esau* **Esav**
may be cut off by *slaughter* **severing.**
10 For thy violence against thy brother *Jacob* **Yaaqov**
shame shall cover thee,
and thou shalt be *cut off for ever* **severed eternally.**
11 In the day that thou stoodest on the other side,
in the day that the strangers
carried away captive **captured** his *forces* **valiant,**
and *foreigners* **strangers** entered into his *gates* **portals,**
and *cast lots* **handled pebbles**
upon *Jerusalem* **Yeru Shalem,**
even thou wast as one of them.
12 But thou shouldest not have *looked* **seen**
on the day of thy brother
in the day that he became a stranger;
neither shouldest thou have *rejoiced* **cheered**
over the *children* **sons** of *Judah* **Yah Hudah**
in the day of their *destruction* **destroying;**
neither shouldest thou
have *spoken proudly* **greatened thy mouth**
in the day of *distress* **tribulation.**
13 Thou shouldest not have entered
into the *gate* **portal** of my people
in the day of their calamity;
yea, thou shouldest not have *looked* **seen**
on their *affliction* **evil** in the day of their calamity,
nor have *laid hands* **extended** on their *substance* **valiant**
in the day of their calamity;
14 Neither shouldest thou have stood in the crossway,
to cut off those of his *that did escape* **escapees;**
neither shouldest thou have *delivered* **shut** up
those of his *that did remain* **survivors**
in the day of *distress* **tribulation.**
15 For the day of *the LORD* **Yah Veh**
is near upon all the *heathen* **goyim:**

as thou hast *done* **worked**,
it shall be *done* **worked** unto thee:
thy *reward* **dealing** shall return upon thine own head.
16 For as ye have drunk upon my holy mountain,
so shall all the *heathen* **goyim** drink continually,
yea, they shall drink, and they shall *swallow down* **gulp**,
and they shall be as though they had not been.
17 But upon mount *Zion* **Siyon**
shall be *deliverance* **an escape**,
and there shall be *holiness* **a holies**;
and the house of *Jacob* **Yaaqov**
shall possess their possessions.
18 And the house of *Jacob* **Yaaqov** shall be a fire,
and the house of *Joseph* **Yoseph** a flame,
and the house of *Esau* **Esav** for stubble,
and they shall *kindle* **inflame** in them, and devour them;
and there shall not be any *remaining* **survivors**
of the house of *Esau* **Esav**;
for *the LORD* **Yah Veh** hath *spoken it* **worded**.
19 And they of the south
shall possess the mount of *Esau* **Esav**;
and they of the *plain* **lowland**
the *Philistines* **Peleshethiym**:
and they shall possess the fields of *Ephraim* **Ephrayim**,
and the fields of *Samaria* **Shomeron**:
and *Benjamin* **Ben Yamin** shall possess *Gilead* **Gilad**.
20 And the *captivity* **exiles** of *this host* **the valiant**
of the *children* **sons** of *Israel* **Yisra El**
shall possess that of the *Canaanites* **Kenaaniym**,
even unto *Zarephath* **Sarephath**;
and the *captivity* **exiles** of *Jerusalem* **Yeru Shalem**,
which is in Sepharad,
shall possess the cities of the south.
21 And saviours
shall *come up* **ascend** on mount *Zion* **Siyon**
to judge the mount of *Esau* **Esav**;
and the *kingdom* **sovereigndom**
shall be *the LORD'S* **Yah Veh's**.

KEY TO INTERPRETING THE EXEGESES:
King James text is in regular type;
Text under exegeses is in oblique type;
Text of exegeses is in bold type.

YAH VEH'S WORD TO YONAH

1 *Now* the word of *the LORD* **Yah Veh**
came unto *Jonah* **Yonah** the son of *Amittai* **Amittay**,
saying,
2 Arise, go to Nineveh, that great city,
and *cry* **call out** against it;
for their *wickedness* **evil**
is come up before me **hath ascended at my face**.

YONAH FLEES FROM YAH VEH

3 But *Jonah* **Yonah** rose up to flee unto Tarshish
from the *presence* **face** of *the LORD* **Yah Veh**,
and *went down* **descended** to *Joppa* **Yapho**;
and he found a ship going to Tarshish:
so he *paid* **gave** the *fare* **hire** *thereof,*
and *went down* **descended** into it,
to go with them unto Tarshish
from the *presence* **face** of *the LORD* **Yah Veh**.
4 But *the LORD* **Yah Veh**
sent out **cast forth** a great wind into the sea,
and there was a *mighty tempest* **great storm** in the sea,
so that the ship was *like* **fabricated** to be broken.
5 Then the mariners were *afraid* **awed**,
and cried every man unto his *god* **elohim**,
and cast forth the *wares* **instruments** that were in the ship
into the sea, to lighten it of them.
But *Jonah was gone down* **Yonah descended**
into the *sides* **flanks** of the ship;
and he lay, and was *fast asleep* **sleeping soundly**.
6 So the *shipmaster came to* **great sailer approached** him,
and said unto him, What meanest thou, O **sound** sleeper?
arise, call upon thy *God* **Elohim**,
if so be that *God will think* **Elohim shall shine** upon us,
that we *perish* **destruct** not.
7 And they said every *one* **man** to his *fellow* **friend**,
Come, and let us *cast lots* **fell pebbles**,
that we may know
for whose cause **on whose account** this evil is upon us.
So they *cast lots* **felled pebbles**,
and the *lot* **pebble** fell upon *Jonah* **Yonah**.
8 Then said they unto him,
Tell us, we *pray* **beseech** thee,
for whose cause this evil is upon us;
What is *thine occupation* **thy work**?
and whence comest thou?
what is thy *country* **land**? and of what people art thou?
9 And he said unto them, I am an Hebrew;
and I fear *the LORD* **Yah Veh**,
the God **Elohim** of *heaven* **the heavens**,
which *hath made* **worked** the sea and the dry *land*.
10 Then were the men *exceedingly afraid* **greatly awed**,
and said unto him, Why hast thou *done* **worked** this?
For the men knew that he fled
from the *presence* **face** of *the LORD* **Yah Veh**,
because he had told them.
11 Then said they unto him,
What shall we *do* **work** unto thee,
that the sea may *be calm* **subside** unto us?
for the sea wrought, and *was tempestuous* **stormed**.

YONAH SWALLOWED BY A GREAT FISH

12 And he said unto them,
Take me up, and cast me forth into the sea;
so shall the sea *be calm* **subside** unto you:
for I know that *for* **on** my *sake* **account**
this great *tempest* **storm** is upon you.
13 Nevertheless the men *rowed* **paddled** hard
to *bring it* **return** to the *land* **dry**;
but they could not:
for the sea wrought,
and *was tempestuous* **stormed** against them.
14 Wherefore
they *cried* **called out** unto *the LORD* **Yah Veh**, and said,
We beseech thee, O *LORD* **Yah Veh**,
we beseech thee,
let us not *perish* **destruct** for this man's *life* **soul**,
and *lay* **give** not upon us innocent blood:
for thou, O *LORD* **Yah Veh**,

hast *done* **worked** as it *pleased* **delighted** thee.
15 So they *took up Jonah* **lifted Yonah**,
and cast him forth into the sea:
and the sea *ceased* **stood** from her raging.
16 Then the men
feared the LORD exceedingly **awed Yah Veh greatly**,
and *offered* **sacrificed** a sacrifice
unto *the LORD* **Yah Veh**,
and *made* **vowed** vows.
17 *Now the LORD* **Yah Veh**
had *prepared* **numbered** a great fish
to swallow up *Jonah* **Yonah**.
And *Jonah* **Yonah** was in the *belly* **inwards** of the fish
three days and three nights.

YONAH'S PRAYER, YAH VEH'S ANSWER

2 Then *Jonah* **Yonah**
prayed unto *the LORD* **Yah Veh** his *God* **Elohim**
out of the fish's *belly* **inwards**,
2 And said, I *cried* **called out**
by reason **because** of *mine affliction* **my tribulation**
unto *the LORD* **Yah Veh**,
and he *heard* **answered** me;
out of the belly of *hell* **sheol** cried I,
and thou heardest my voice.
3 For thou hadst cast me into the deep,
in the midst of the seas;
and the *floods* compassed **rivers surrounded** me *about*:
all thy *billows* **breakers** and thy waves passed over me.
4 Then I said,
I am *cast out of* **expelled from** thy *sight* **eyes**;
yet I *will* **shall** look again toward thy holy *temple* **manse**.
5 The waters *compassed* **surrounded** me *about*,
even to the soul:
the *depth closed* **abyss surrounded** me *round about*,
the *weeds* **reeds** were *wrapped* **bound** about my head.
6 I *went down* **descended**
to the *bottoms* **bases** of the mountains;
the earth with her bars was about me *for ever* **eternally**:
yet hast thou *brought up* **ascended** my life
from *corruption* **the pit of ruin**,
O *LORD* **Yah Veh** my *God* **Elohim**.
7 When my soul *fainted* **languished** within me
I remembered *the LORD* **Yah Veh**:
and my prayer came in unto thee,
into thine holy *temple* **manse**.
8 They that observe *lying* **vain** vanities
forsake their own mercy.
9 But I *will* **shall** sacrifice unto thee
with the voice of *thanksgiving* **extended hands**;
I *will pay* **shall shalam** that that I have vowed.
Salvation is of *the LORD* **Yah Veh**.
10 And *the LORD spake* **Yah Veh said** unto the fish,
and it vomited out *Jonah* **Yonah** upon the dry *land*.

YAH VEH'S SECOND WORD TO YONAH

3 And the word of *the LORD* **Yah Veh**
came unto *Jonah the second time* **Yonah secondly**,
saying,
2 Arise, go unto Nineveh, that great city,
and *preach* **call out** unto it
the *preaching* **calling out** that I *bid* **word** thee.
3 So *Jonah* **Yonah** arose, and went unto Nineveh,
according to the word of *the LORD* **Yah Veh**.
Now Nineveh was *an exceeding* **a** great city **of Elohim**
of three days' *journey* **walk**.
4 And *Jonah* **Yonah** began to enter into the city
a **one** day's *journey* **walk**,
and he *cried* **called out**, and said,
Yet forty days,
and Nineveh shall be *overthrown* **turned against**.
5 So the *people* **men** of Nineveh
believed God **trusted Elohim**,
and *proclaimed* **called out** a fast,
and *put on sackcloth* **enrobed saq**,
from the greatest of them even to the *least* **lesser** of them.
6 For word *came* **touched**
unto the *king* **sovereign** of Nineveh,
and he arose from his throne,
and he *laid* **passed** his *robe* **mighty mantle** from him,
and covered him with *sackcloth* **saq**, and sat in ashes.
7 And he caused it to be *proclaimed* **cried out**
and *published* **said** through Nineveh
by the *decree* **taste** of the *king* **sovereign** and his nobles,
saying,
Let neither *man* **humanity** nor *beast* **animal**, herd nor flock,
taste *any thing* **aught**:
let them not *feed* **graze**, nor drink water:
8 But let *man* **humanity** and *beast* **animal**
be covered with *sackcloth* **saq**,
and *cry mightily* **call out severely** unto *God* **Elohim**:
yea, let them turn every *one* **man** from his evil way,
and from the violence that is in their *hands* **palms**.
9 Who *can tell* **knoweth**
if *God will* **Elohim shall** turn and *repent* **sigh**,
and turn away from his *fierce anger* **fuming wrath**,
that we *perish* **destruct** not?
10 And *God* **Elohim** saw their works,
that they turned from their evil way;
and *God repented* **Elohim sighed** of the evil,
that he had *said* **worded**
that he *would do* **should work** unto them;
and he *did* **worked** it not.

YONAH'S ANGER, YAH VEH'S MERCY

4 But it *displeased Jonah exceedingly*
was greatly evil to Yonah,
and he was very angry.
2 And he prayed unto *the LORD* **Yah Veh**, and said,
I *pray* **beseech** thee, O *LORD* **Yah Veh**,
was not this my *saying* **word**,
when I was yet in my *country* **soil**?
Therefore I *fled before* **anticipated to flee** unto Tarshish:
for I knew that thou art a *gracious God* **charismatic El**,
and merciful, slow to anger, and of great *kindness* **mercy**,
and *repentest* **sighest** thee of the evil.
3 Therefore now, O *LORD* **Yah Veh**,
take, I beseech thee, my *life* **soul** from me;
for it is better for me to die than to live.
4 Then said *the LORD* **Yah Veh**,
Doest thou well—**please** to be *angry* **inflamed**?
5 So *Jonah* **Yonah** went out of the city,
and sat on the east *side* of the city,
and there *made* **worked** him
a *booth* **sukkoth/brush arbor**,
and sat under it in the shadow,
till he might see what *would* **should** become of the city.
6 And *the LORD God* **Yah Veh Elohim**
prepared **numbered** a gourd,
and *made* **caused** it
to *come up* **ascend** over *Jonah* **Yonah**,
that it might be a shadow over his head,
to *deliver* **rescue** him from his *grief* **evil**.
So Jonah was exceeding glad
In cheering, Yonah greatly cheered of the gourd.
7 But *God prepared* **Elohim numbered** a *worm* **maggot**
when the *morning rose* **dawn ascended**
the *next day* **morrow**,
and it smote the gourd that it withered.
8 And it *came to pass* **became**, when the sun did arise,
that *God* **Elohim**
prepared **numbered** a vehement east wind;
and the sun *beat* **smote** upon the head of *Jonah* **Yonah**,
that he *fainted* **languished**,
and *wished in himself* **asked of his soul** to die, and said,
It is better for me to die than to live.
9 And *God* **Elohim** said to *Jonah* **Yonah**,
Doest thou well—**please** to be *angry* **inflamed**
for the gourd?
And he said,
I *do* well—**please** to be *angry* **inflamed**, *even* unto death.
10 Then said *the LORD* **Yah Veh**,
Thou hast *had pity on* **spared** the gourd,
for the which thou hast not laboured,
neither *madest it grow* **nourished**;
which *came up in* **was a son of** a night,
and *perished in* **destructed a son of** a night:
11 And should not I spare Nineveh, that great city,
wherein *are more than* **abound**
sixscore thousand persons **twelve myriads of humanity**
that *cannot discern* **know not**
between their right *hand* and their left *hand*;
and *also much cattle* **many animals**?

KEY TO INTERPRETING THE EXEGESES:
King James text is in regular type;
Text under exegeses is in oblique type;
Text of exegeses is in bold type.

YAH VEH'S WORD AGAINST SHOMERON AND YERU SHALEM

1 The word of *the LORD* **Yah Veh**
that came to *Micah* **Michah** the *Morasthite* **Moreshethiy**
in the days of *Jotham* **Yah Tham,**
Ahaz **Ach Az,** and *Hesekiah* **Yechizqi Yah,**
kings **sovereigns** of *Judah* **Yah Hudah,**
which he saw concerning
Samaria **Shomeron** and *Jerusalem* **Yeru Shalem.**
2 Hear, all ye people;
hearken, O earth, and all **the fulness** *that* therein *is*:
and let *the Lord GOD be* **Adonay Yah Veh**
witness against you,
the Lord **Adonay** from his holy *temple* **manse.**
3 For, behold,
the LORD **Yah Veh** cometh forth out of his place,
and *will come down* **shall descend,**
and tread upon the *high places* **bamahs** of the earth.
4 And the mountains shall *be molten* **melt** under him,
and the valleys shall *be cleft* **split,**
as wax *before* **at the face of** the fire,
and as the waters
that are poured down a *steep place* **descent.**
5 For the *transgression* **rebellion** of *Jacob* **Yaaqov**
is all this,
and for the sins of the house of *Israel* **Yisra El.**
What is the *transgression* **rebellion** of *Jacob* **Yaaqov**?
is it not *Samaria* **Shomeron**?
and what
are the *high places* **bamahs** of *Judah* **Yah Hudah**?
are they not *Jerusalem* **Yeru Shalem**?
6 *Therefore* I *will make Samaria* **shall set Shomeron**
as an heap of the field,
and as plantings of a vineyard:
and I *will* **shall** pour down the stones *thereof*
into the valley,
and I *will discover* **shall expose** the foundations *thereof.*
7 And all the *graven images* **sculptiles** *thereof*
shall be *beaten to pieces* **crushed,**
and all the *hires* **payoffs** *thereof*
shall be burned with the fire,
and all the idols *thereof will I lay* **shall I set** desolate:
for she gathered it of the *hire* **payoff** of *an harlot* **a whore,**
and they shall return
to the *hire* **payoff** of *an harlot* **a whore.**
8 Therefore I *will wail* **shall chop** and howl,
I *will* **shall** go stripped and naked:
I *will make* **shall work** a *wailing* **chopping**
like the *dragons* **monsters,**
and mourning as the **daughters of the** owls.
9 For her wound is incurable;
for it is come unto *Judah* **Yah Hudah;**
he *is come* **toucheth** unto the *gate* **portal** of my people,
even to *Jerusalem* **Yeru Shalem.**
10 *Declare* **Tell** ye it not at Gath,
in weeping, weep ye not *at all*:
in the house of Aphrah
roll **in wallowing, wallow** thyself in the dust.
11 Pass ye away,
thou *inhabitant* **settler** of *Saphir* **Shaphir,**
having thy shame naked:
the *inhabitant* **settler** of *Zaanan* **Saanan** came not forth
in the *mourning* **chopping** of *Bethezel* **Beth Ha Esel;**
he shall *receive* **take** of you his standing.
12 For the *inhabitant* **settler** of Maroth
waited carefully for **awaited** good:
but evil *came down* **descended** from *the LORD* **Yah Veh**
unto the *gate* **portal** of *Jerusalem* **Yeru Shalem.**
13 O thou *inhabitant* **settler** of Lachish,
bind **yoke** the chariot to the *swift beast* **stallion:**
she is the beginning of the sin
to the daughter of *Zion* **Siyon:**
for the *transgressions* **rebellions** of *Israel* **Yisra El**
were found in thee.
14 Therefore shalt thou give presents
to *Moreshethgath* **Moresheth Gath:**
the houses of Achzib shall be a lie
to the *kings* **sovereigns** of *Israel* **Yisra El.**
15 Yet *will* **shall** I bring *an heir* **a successor** unto thee,
O *inhabitant* **settler** of Mareshah:
he shall come unto Adullam
the *glory* **honour** of *Israel* **Yisra El.**
16 *Make* **Balden** thee *bald,* and *poll* **shear** thee
for *thy delicate children* **the sons of thy delights;**
enlarge thy baldness as the eagle;
for they are *gone into captivity* **exiled** from thee.

2 *Woe* **Ho** to them
that *devise iniquity* **fabricate mischief,**
and *work* **do** evil upon their beds!
when the morning is light, they *practise* **work** it,
because it is in the *power* **el** of their hand.
2 And they *covet* **desire** fields,
and *take* **strip** them *by violence;*
and houses, and *take* **bear** them away:
so they oppress a *man* **mighty** and his house,
even a man and his *heritage* **inheritance.**
3 Therefore thus saith *the LORD* **Yah Veh;**
Behold, against this family *do I devise* **I fabricate** an evil,
from which ye shall not *remove* **depart** your necks;
neither shall *ye* go haughtily: for this time is evil.
4 In that day
shall one take *up* a *parable* **proverb** against you,
and lament with a *doleful* lamentation **of lamentations,**
and say, **In ravaging,** We be *utterly spoiled* **ravaged:**
he hath changed the *portion* **allotment** of my people:
how hath he *removed* **departed** it from me!
turning away **in restoring,**
he hath *divided* **allotted** our fields.
5 Therefore thou shalt have none
that shall cast a cord by *lot* **pebble**
in the congregation of *the LORD* **Yah Veh.**
6 *Prophesy* ye **drip** not,
say they to them that prophesy **they drip:**
they shall not *prophesy* **drip** to them,
that they shall not *take* **remove** shame.
7 *O thou that art named*
the house of *Jacob* **Yaaqov sayeth,**
is the spirit of *the LORD* **Yah Veh** straitened?
are these his *doings* **exploits**?
do not my words *do good to* **well—please** him
that walketh *uprightly* **straight**?
8 *Even of late* **From yesterday**
my people is risen up as an enemy:
ye *pull off* **strip** the *robe* **mighty mantle**
with the *garment* **clothes**
from them that pass by *securely* **confidently**
as men *averse* **returning** from war.
9 The women of my people have ye *cast out* **expelled**
from their *pleasant* houses **of delights;**
from their *children* **sucklings**
have ye taken away my *glory for ever* **majesty eternally.**
10 Arise ye, and depart; for this is not *your* rest:
because it is *polluted* **fouled,** it shall *destroy* **despoil** you,
even with a sore destruction — **a forceful despoiling.**
11 If a man walking in the spirit and falsehood do lie,
saying, I will prophesy **I shall drip** unto thee of wine
and of *strong drink* **intoxicants;**
he shall *even be the prophet of* **drip unto** this people.

YAH VEH GATHERS THE SURVIVORS OF YISRA EL

12 *I will surely assemble* **In gathering, I shall gather,**
O *Jacob* **Yaaqov,** all of thee;
I will surely gather **In gathering, I shall gather**
the *remnant* **survivors** of *Israel* **Yisra El;**
I *will put* **shall set** them together
as the *sheep* **flock** of *Bozrah* **the fold,**
as the *flock* **drove** in the midst of their fold:
they shall *make great noise* **quake**
by reason of *the multitude of men* **humanity.**
13 The *breaker* **separater** is *come up* **ascended**
before them **at their face:**
they have *broken up* **separated,**
and have passed through the *gate* **portal,**
and are gone out by it:
and their *king* **sovereign**
shall pass *before them* **at their face,**
and *the LORD* **Yah Veh** on the head of them.

YAH VEH'S WORD TO YAAQOV AND YISRA EL

3 And I said, Hear, I *pray* **beseech** you,
O heads of *Jacob* **Yaaqov**,
and ye *princes* **commanders**
of the house of *Israel* **Yisra El**;
Is it not for you to know judgment?
2 Who hate the good, and love the evil;
who *pluck off* **strip** their skin from off them,
and their flesh from off their bones;
3 Who also eat the flesh of my people,
and *flay* **strip** their skin from off them;
and they break their bones,
and *chop* **spread** them *in pieces*,
as for the *pot* **caldron**, and as flesh within the caldron.
4 Then shall they cry unto *the LORD* **Yah Veh**,
but he *will* **shall** not *hear* **answer** them:
he *will* **shall** even hide his face from them at that time,
as they have *behaved* **vilified** *themselves ill*
in their *doings* **exploits**.
5 Thus saith *the LORD* **Yah Veh** concerning the prophets
that *make* **cause** my people *err* **to stray**,
that bite with their teeth, and *cry* **call out**, *Peace* **Shalom**;
and he that *putteth* **giveth** not into their mouths,
they even *prepare* **hallow** war against him.
6 Therefore night shall be unto you,
that ye shall not have a vision;
and it shall be *dark* **darkness** unto you,
that ye shall not divine;
and the sun shall go down over the prophets,
and the day shall be *dark* **darkened** over them.
7 Then shall the seers *be ashamed* **shame**,
and the diviners *confounded* **blush**:
yea, they shall all cover their *lips* **upper lip**;
for there is no answer of *God* **Elohim**.
8 But *truly* I am *full* **filled** of *power* **force**
by the spirit of *the LORD* **Yah Veh**,
and of judgment, and of might,
to declare unto *Jacob* **Yaaqov** his *transgression* **rebellion**,
and to *Israel* **Yisra El** his sin.
9 Hear this, I *pray* **beseech** you,
ye heads of the house of *Jacob* **Yaaqov**,
and *princes* **commanders** of the house of *Israel* **Yisra El**,
that abhor judgment, and pervert all *equity* **straightness**.
10 They build up *Zion* **Siyon** with blood,
and *Jerusalem* **Yeru Shalem** with *iniquity* **wickedness**.
11 The heads *thereof* judge for *reward* **bribes**,
and the priests *thereof* teach for *hire* **price**,
and the prophets *thereof* divine for *money* **silver**:
yet *will* **shall** they lean upon *the LORD* **Yah Veh**,
and say **saying**, Is not *the LORD* **Yah Veh** among us?
none evil can come upon us.
12 Therefore shall *Zion* **Siyon** for your sake
be plowed *as* a field,
and *Jerusalem* **Yeru Shalem** shall become heaps,
and the mountain of the house
as the *high places* **bamahs** of the forest.

THE SOVEREIGNDOM OF THE FINAL DAYS

4 But in the *last* **final** days it shall *come to pass* **become**,
that the mountain of the house of *the LORD* **Yah Veh**
shall be established in the top of the mountains,
and it shall be *exalted* **lifted** above the hills;
and people shall flow unto it.
2 And many *nations* **goyim** shall come,
and say, Come, and let us *go up* **ascend**
to the mountain of *the LORD* **Yah Veh**,
and to the house of *the God* **Elohim** of *Jacob* **Yaaqov**;
and he *will* **shall** teach us of his ways,
and we *will* **shall** walk in his paths:
for the *law* **torah** shall go forth of *Zion* **Siyon**,
and the word of *the LORD* **Yah Veh**
from *Jerusalem* **Yeru Shalem**.
3 And he shall judge among many people,
and *rebuke strong nations* **reprove mighty goyim** afar off;
and they shall *beat* **forge** their swords into plowshares,
and their spears into *pruninghooks* **psalmpicks**:
nation **goyim** shall not lift *up* a sword
against *nation* **goyim**,
neither shall they learn war any more.
4 But they shall sit every man
under his vine and under his fig tree;
and none shall make them *afraid* **tremble**:
for the mouth of *the LORD of hosts* **Yah Veh Sabaoth**
hath *spoken it* **worded**.
5 For all people *will* **shall** walk
every *one* **man** in the name of his *god* **elohim**,
and we *will* **shall** walk
in the name of *the LORD* **Yah Veh** our *God* **Elohim**
for ever **eternally** and *ever* **eternally**.
6 In that day,
saith the LORD **an oracle of Yah Veh**,
will I assemble **shall I gather** her that *halteth* **limpeth**,
and I *will* **shall** gather her that is *driven out* **expelled**,
and her that I have *afflicted* **vilified**;
7 And I *will make* **shall set** her that *halted* **limpeth**
a *remnant* **survivor**,
and her that was cast far off
a *strong nation* **mighty goyim**:
and *the LORD* **Yah Veh** shall reign over them
in mount *Zion* **Siyon** from henceforth,
even *for ever* **eternally**.
8 And thou, O *tower of the flock* **Migdal Eder**,
the *strong hold* **mound** of the daughter of *Zion* **Siyon**,
unto thee shall it come, even the first *dominion* **reign**;
the *kingdom* **sovereigndom**
shall come to the daughter of *Jerusalem* **Yeru Shalem**.
9 Now why dost thou *cry out aloud* **shout a shout**?
is there no *king* **sovereign** in thee?
is thy counsellor *perished* **destroyed**?
for pangs *have taken* **hold** thee
as a woman *in travail* **birthing**.
10 *Be in pain* **Writhe**, and *labour to* bring forth,
O daughter of *Zion* **Siyon**,
like a woman *in travail* **birthing**:
for now shalt thou go forth out of the city,
and thou shalt *dwell* **tabernacle** in the field,
and thou shalt go *even* to *Babylon* **Babel**;
there shalt thou be *delivered* **rescued**;
there *the LORD* **Yah Veh** shall redeem thee
from the *hand* **palm** of thine enemies.
11 Now also
many *nations* **goyim** are gathered against thee,
that say, Let her be *defiled* **profaned**,
and let our eye *look* **see** upon *Zion* **Siyon**.
12 But they know not
the *thoughts* **fabrications** of *the LORD* **Yah Veh**,
neither *understand* **discern** they his counsel:
for he shall gather them
as the *sheaves* **omers** into the *floor* **threshingfloor**.
13 Arise and thresh, O daughter of *Zion* **Siyon**:
for I *will make* **shall set** thine horn iron,
and I *will make* **shall set** thy hoofs *brass* **copper**:
and thou shalt *beat in pieces* **pulverize** many people:
and I *will consecrate* **shall devote** their **greedy** gain
unto *the LORD* **Yah Veh**,
and their *substance* **valuables**
unto the *Lord* **Adonay** of the whole earth.

THE BIRTH OF THE ETERNAL DOMINATOR

5 Now *gather thyself in troops* **troop thou**,
O daughter of troops:
he hath *laid* **set** siege against us:
they shall smite the judge of *Israel* **Yisra El**
with a *rod* **scion** upon the cheek.
2 But thou, *Bethlehem Ephratah* **Beth Lechem Ephrath**,
though thou be
little among the thousands of *Judah* **Yah Hudah**,
yet out of thee shall he come forth unto me
that is to be *ruler* **sovereign** in *Israel* **Yisra El**;
whose *goings forth* **proceedings**
have been from *of old* **antiquity**,
from *everlasting* **days eternal**.
3 Therefore *will* **shall** he give them up,
until the time that she which *travaileth* **birtheth**
hath *brought forth* **begotten**:
then the remnant of his brethren
shall return unto the *children* **sons** of *Israel* **Yisra El**.
4 And he shall stand and *feed* **tend**
in the strength of *the LORD* **Yah Veh**,
in the *majesty* **pomp**
of the name of *the LORD* **Yah Veh** his *God* **Elohim**;
and they shall *abide* **settle**:

for now shall he *be great* **greaten**
unto the *ends* **finalities** of the earth.
5 And this *man* shall be the *peace* **shalom,**
when the *Assyrian* **Ashshuriy** shall come into our land:
and when he shall tread in our *palaces* **citadels**,
then shall we raise against him seven *shepherds* **tenders**,
and eight *principal men* **libated of humanity**.
6 And they shall *waste* **tend**
the land of *Assyria* **Ashshur** with the sword,
and the land of Nimrod
in the *entrances* **openings** *thereof*:
thus shall he *deliver* **rescue** us
from the *Assyrian* **Ashshuri**,
when he cometh into our land,
and when he treadeth within our borders.
7 And the *remnant* **survivors** of *Jacob* **Yaaqov**
shall be in the midst of many people
as a dew from *the LORD* **Yah Veh**,
as the showers upon the *grass* **herbage**,
that *tarrieth* **awaiteth** not for man,
nor waiteth for the sons of *men* **humanity**.
8 And the remnant of *Jacob* **Yaaqov**
shall be among the *Gentiles* **goyim**
in the midst of many people
as a lion among the *beasts* **animals** of the forest,
as a *young lion* **whelp**
among the *flocks* **droves** of *sheep* **flocks**:
who, if he *go* **pass** through,
both *treadeth down* **trampleth**, and teareth in pieces,
and none *can deliver* **rescueth**.
9 Thine hand shall be lifted *up*
upon *thine adversaries* **thy tribulators**,
and all thine enemies shall be cut off.
10 And it shall *come to pass* **become,** in that day,
saith the LORD **an oracle of Yah Veh**,
that I *will* **shall** cut off thy horses out of the midst of thee,
and I *will* **shall** destroy thy chariots:
11 And *will* **shall** cut off the cities of thy land,
and *throw down* **demolish** all thy *strong holds* **fortresses**:
12 And I *will* **shall** cut off *witchcrafts* **sorceries**
out of thine hand;
and thou shalt have no *more soothsayers* **cloudgazers**:
13 Thy *graven images* **sculptiles** also *will* **shall** I cut off,
and thy *standing images* **monoliths**
out of the midst of thee;
and thou shalt no more
worship **prostrate to** the work of thine hands.
14 And I *will pluck up* **shall uproot** thy *groves* **asherah**
out of the midst of thee:
so *will I destroy* **shall I desolate** thy cities.
15 And I *will execute vengeance* **shall work avengement**
in *anger* **wrath** and fury upon the *heathen* **goyim**,
such as they have not heard.

YAH VEH'S CONTROVERSY WITH YISRA EL

6 Hear ye *now* **I beseech,** what *the LORD* **Yah Veh** saith;
Arise, contend thou before the mountains,
and let the hills hear thy voice.
2 Hear ye, O mountains,
the *LORD'S* controversy **of Yah Veh**,
and ye *strong* **perennial** foundations of the earth:
for *the LORD* **Yah Veh**
hath a controversy with his people,
and he *will plead with Israel* **shall reprove Yisra El**.
3 O my people, what have I *done* **worked** unto thee?
and wherein have I wearied thee?
testify **answer** against me.
4 For I *brought* **ascended** thee *up*
out of the land of *Egypt* **Misrayim**,
and redeemed thee out of the house of servants;
and I sent *before thee* **at thy face**
Moses **Mosheh**, *Aaron* **Aharon**, and *Miriam* **Miryam**.
5 O my people, remember *now* **I beseech,**
what *Balak king* **Balaq sovereign** of Moab
consulted **counselled**,
and what Balaam the son of Beor answered him
from Shittim unto Gilgal;
that ye may know
the *righteousness* **justness** of *the LORD* **Yah Veh**.
6 Wherewith shall I
come before the LORD **confront Yah Veh**,
and bow myself before the high *God* **Elohim**?
shall I *come before* **confront** him
with *burnt offerings* **holocausts**,
with *calves of a year old* **yearling sons**?
7 *Will the LORD* **Shall Yah Veh** be pleased
with thousands of rams,
or with *ten thousands* **myriads** of *rivers* **wadies** of oil?
shall I give my firstborn for my *transgression* **rebellion**,
the fruit of my *body* **belly** for the sin of my soul?
8 He hath *shewed* **told** thee, O *man* **humanity**,
what is good;
and what doth *the LORD* **Yah Veh** require of thee,
but to *do justly* **work judgment**, and to love mercy,
and to walk humbly with thy *God* **Elohim**?
9 *The LORD'S* **Yah Veh's** voice
crieth **calleth out** unto the city,
and the *man of wisdom* **counsellor** shall see thy name:
hear ye the rod, and who hath *appointed* **congregated** it.
10 Are there yet the treasures of wickedness
in the house of the wicked,
and the *scant measure* **emaciated ephah**
that *is abominable* **enrageth**?
11 Shall I *count them pure* **purify them**
with the wicked balances,
and with the *bag* **pouch** of deceitful *weights* **stones**?
12 For the rich *men thereof* are *full* **filled** of violence,
and the *inhabitants* **settlers** *thereof*
have spoken *lies* **falsehoods,**
and their tongue is deceitful in their mouth.
13 Therefore also
will I make thee sick **shall I stroke thee** in smiting thee,
in *making* **desolating** thee *desolate* because of thy sins.
14 Thou shalt eat, but not be *satisfied* **satiated**;
and thy *casting down* **hunger**
shall be in the midst of thee;
and thou shalt *take hold* **remove**,
but shalt not *deliver* **escape**;
and that which *thou deliverest* **escapeth**
will **shall** I give up to the sword.
15 Thou shalt *sow* **seed**, but thou shalt not *reap* **harvest**;
thou shalt tread the olives,
but thou shalt not anoint thee with oil;
and *sweet wine* **juice**, but shalt not drink wine.
16 For the statutes of Omri are *kept* **guarded**,
and all the works of the house of *Ahab* **Ach Ab**,
and ye walk in their counsels;
that I should *make* **give** thee a desolation,
and the *inhabitants* **settlers** *thereof* an hissing:
therefore ye shall bear the reproach of my people.

WOE IS YISRA EL

7 Woe is me!
for I am as *when they have gathered* **the ingathering**
of the summer fruits,
as the *grapegleanings* **gleanings** of the *vintage* **crop**:
there is no cluster to eat:
my soul desired the *firstripe* **firstling** fruit.
2 The *good man* **merciful**
is *perished* **destructed** out of the earth:
and there is none *upright* **straight** among *men* **humanity**:
they all *lie in wait* **lurk** for blood;
they hunt every man his brother with a net.
3 That they may do evil
with both *hands earnestly* **palms well—pleasingly**,
the *prince* **governor** asketh,
and the judge *asketh for a reward* **for satisfaction**;
and the great *man*,
he uttereth his mischievous desire
wordeth the mischief of his soul:
so they *wrap* **pervert** it *up*.
4 The best of them is as a *brier* **thorn**:
the most upright is sharper
straighter than a thorn hedge:
the day of thy *watchmen* **watchers** and thy visitation
cometh;
now shall be their perplexity.
5 Trust ye not in a friend,
put **confide** ye not *confidence* in a *guide* **chiliarch**:
keep **guard** the *doors* **opening** of thy mouth
from her that lieth in thy bosom.
6 For the son *dishonoureth* **disgraceth** the father,

the daughter riseth *up* against her mother,
the daughter in law against her mother in law;
a man's enemies are the men of his own house.

THE SURVIVORS IN THE FINAL DAYS

7 Therefore
I *will look* **shall watch** unto *the LORD* **Yah Veh**;
I *will wait for the God* **shall await Elohim**
of my salvation:
my *God will* **Elohim shall** hear me.
8 *Rejoice* **Cheer** not against me, O mine enemy:
when I fall, I shall arise;
when I sit in darkness,
the LORD **Yah Veh** shall be a light unto me.
9 I *will* **shall** bear the *indignation* **rage**
of *the LORD* **Yah Veh**,
because I have sinned against him,
until he plead my *cause* **plea**,
and *execute* **work** judgment for me:
he *will* **shall** bring me forth to the light,
and I shall *behold* **see** his *righteousness* **justness**.
10 Then *she that is* mine enemy shall see *it*,
and shame shall cover her which said unto me,
Where is *the LORD* **Yah Veh** thy *God* **Elohim**?
mine eyes shall *behold* **see** her:
now shall she be *trodden down* **trampled**
as the mire of the *streets* **outways**.
11 In the day that thy walls are to be built,
in that day shall the *decree* **statute** be far removed.
12 In that day *also*
he shall come even to thee from *Assyria* **Ashshur**,
and from the *fortified* cities **of siege**,
and *from* the *fortress* **siege** even to the river,
and from sea to sea, and *from* mountain to mountain.
13 Notwithstanding the land shall be desolate
because of them that *dwell* **settle** therein,
for the fruit of their *doings* **exploits**.
14 *Feed* **Tend** thy people with thy *rod* **scion**,
the flock of thine *heritage* **inheritance**,
which *dwell solitarily* **tabernacle alone**
in the *wood* **forest**,
in the midst of *Carmel* **Karmel/orchard**:
let them *feed* **graze** in Bashan and *Gilead* **Gilad**,
as in the **original** days *of old*.
15 According to the days
of thy coming out of the land of *Egypt* **Misrayim**
will I shew unto him marvellous things
shall I have him see marvels.
16 The *nations* **goyim** shall see
and be *confounded* **shamed** at all their might:
they shall *lay* **set** their hand upon their mouth,
their ears shall *be deaf* **deafen**.
17 They shall lick the dust like a serpent,
they shall *move* **quiver** out of their *holes* **strongholds**
like *worms* **creepers** of the earth:
they shall *be afraid* **fear**
of the LORD **Yah Veh** our *God* **Elohim**,
and shall *fear* **awe** because of thee.
18 Who is *a God* **an El** like unto thee,
that *pardoneth iniquity* **beareth perversity**,
and passeth by the *transgression* **rebellion**
of the *remnant* **survivors** of his *heritage* **inheritance**?
he *retaineth* **holdeth** not his *anger* **wrath**
for ever **eternally**,
because he delighteth *in* mercy.
19 He *will* **shall** turn again,
he *will have compassion upon* **shall mercy** us;
he *will* **shall** subdue our *iniquities* **perversities**;
and thou *wilt* **shalt** cast all their sins
into the *depths* **deep** of the sea.
20 Thou *wilt perform* **shalt give** the truth to *Jacob* **Yaaqov**,
and the mercy to Abraham,
which thou hast *sworn* **oathed** unto our fathers
from the days of *old* **antiquity**.

KEY TO INTERPRETING THE EXEGESES:
King James text is in regular type;
Text under exegeses is in oblique type;
Text of exegeses is in bold type.

THE BURDEN OF NINEVEH

1 The burden of Nineveh.
The *book* **scroll** of the vision
of *Nahum* **Nachum** the *Elkoshite* **Elqoshiy**.
2 *God* **El** is jealous,
and *the LORD revengeth* **Yah Veh avengeth**;
the LORD revengeth **Yah Veh avengeth**,
and is *furious* **a master of fury**;
the LORD will take vengeance on **Yah Veh shall avenge**
his *adversaries* **tribulators**,
and he *reserveth wrath* **guardeth** for his enemies.
3 *The LORD* **Yah Veh** is slow to *anger* **wrath**,
and great in *power* **force**,
and **in exonerating,**
will **shall** not *at all acquit the wicked* **exonerate:**
the LORD **Yah Veh** hath his way
in the *whirlwind* **hurricane** and in the *storm* **whirling**,
and the clouds are the dust of his feet.
4 He rebuketh the sea, and *maketh it dry* **withereth**,
and drieth *up* all the rivers:
Bashan languisheth, and *Carmel* **Karmel/orchard**,
and the *flower* **blossom** of Lebanon languisheth.
5 The mountains quake at him, and the hills melt,
and the earth is *burned* **lifted** at his *presence* **face**,
yea, the world, and all that *dwell* **settle** therein.
6 Who can stand
before **at the face of** his *indignation* **rage**?
and who *can abide* **rise**
in the *fierceness* **fuming** of his *anger* **wrath**?
his fury is poured out like fire,
and the rocks are *thrown* **pulled** down by him.
7 *The LORD* **Yah Veh** is good,
a *strong hold* **strength** in the day of *trouble* **tribulation**;
and he knoweth them that *trust* **seek refuge** in him.
8 But with an *overrunning flood* **overpassing overflowing**
he *will make an utter end* **shall work a final finish**
of the place *thereof*,
and darkness shall pursue his enemies.
9 What do ye *imagine* **fabricate**
against *the LORD* **Yah Veh**?
he *will make an full end* **shall work a final finish:**
affliction **tribulation** shall not rise *up* the second *time*.
10 For while they be *folden together* **entwined** as thorns,
and while they *are drunken* **carouse** as *drunkards* **carousers**,
they shall be devoured as stubble fully dry.
11 There is one come out of thee,
that *imagineth* **fabricateth** evil against *the LORD* **Yah Veh**,
a *wicked counsellor* **counsellor of Beli Yaal**.
12 Thus saith *the LORD* **Yah Veh**;
Though they be *quiet* **at shalom**, and likewise many,
yet thus shall they be *cut down* **shorn**,
when he shall pass through.
Though I have *afflicted* **humbled** thee,
I *will afflict* **shall humble** thee no more.
13 For now *will* **shall** I break his yoke **pole** from off thee,
and *will burst* **shall tear** thy bonds *in sunder*.
14 And *the LORD* **Yah Veh**
hath *given a commandment* **misvahed** concerning thee,
that no more of thy name be *sown* **seeded**:
out of the house of thy *gods* **elohim**
will **shall** I cut off
the *graven image* **sculptile** and the molten *image*:
I *will make* **shall set** thy *grave* **tomb**;
for thou art *vile* **abased**.
15 Behold upon the mountains
the feet of him that *bringeth good tidings* **evangelizeth**,
that *publisheth peace* **hearkeneth shalom**!
O *Judah* **Yah Hudah**,
keep **celebrate** thy *solemn feasts* **celebrations**,
perform **shalam** thy vows:
for *the wicked* **Beli Yaal**
shall *no more* **not add to** pass through thee;
he is utterly cut off.

THE FALL OF NINEVEH

2 He that *dasheth in pieces* **shattereth**
is *come up* **ascended** before thy face:

keep **guard** the *munition* **rampart**, watch the way,
make **strengthen** thy loins *strong*,
fortify **strengthen** thy power mightily.
2 For *the LORD* **Yah Veh** hath turned away
the *excellency* **pomp** of *Jacob* **Yaaqov**,
as the *excellency* **pomp** of *Israel* **Yisra El**:
for the *emptiers* **evacuators**
have *emptied* **evacuated** them *out*,
and *marred* **ruined** their vine *branches* **twigs**.
3 The *shield* **buckler** of his mighty *men*
is *made red* **reddened**,
the valiant men are in **dyed** scarlet:
the chariots shall be **fiery**
with *flaming torches* **cleavers of fire**
in the day of his preparation,
and the fir trees shall be *terribly* shaken.
4 The chariots shall *rage* **halal** in the *streets* **outways**,
they shall *justle one against another* **prowl** in the broad ways:
they shall seem like torches **their visage as flambeaus**,
they shall run like the lightnings.
5 He shall *recount* **remember** his *worthies* **mighty**:
they shall *stumble* **falter** in their *walk* **way**;
they shall make haste to the wall *thereof*,
and the *defence* **covering** shall be prepared.
6 The gates of the rivers shall be opened,
and the *palace* **manse** shall be *dissolved* **melted**.
7 And *Huzzab* **she that was stationed**
shall be *led away captive* **exiled/exposed**,
she shall be *brought up* **ascended**,
and her maids shall *lead* **drive** her
as with the voice of doves,
tabering **tambourining** upon their *breasts* **hearts**.
8 But Nineveh is of *old* **days** like a pool of water:
yet they shall flee away.
Stand, stand, *shall they cry*; but none shall look back.
9 *Take* **Plunder** ye the *spoil of* silver,
take **plunder** the *spoil of* gold:
for there is none end of the *store* **structure** and *glory* **honour**
out of all the *pleasant furniture* **vessels of desire**.
10 She is empty, and void, and *waste* **wasted**:
and the heart melteth, and the knees *smite together* **knock**,
and much pain is in all loins,
and the faces of them all gather *blackness* **flushness**.
11 Where is the *dwelling* **habitation** of the lions,
and the *feedingplace* **pasture** of the *young lions* **whelps**,
where the lion, *even* the *old* **roaring** lion, walked,
and the lion's whelp,
and none *made* **trembleth** them *afraid*?
12 The lion did tear in pieces enough for his whelps,
and strangled for his lionesses,
and filled his holes with prey,
and his *dens* **habitations** with *ravin* **prey**.
13 Behold, I am against thee,
saith the LORD of hosts **an oracle of Yah Veh Sabaoth**,
and I *will* **shall** burn her chariots in the smoke,
and the sword shall devour thy *young lions* **whelps**:
and I *will* **shall** cut off thy prey from the earth,
and the voice of thy *messengers* **angels**
shall no more be heard.

HO TO NINEVEH

3 *Woe* **Ho** to the bloody city!
it is all full of *lies* **deceptions** and *robbery* **tyranny**;
the prey departeth not;
2 The *noise* **voice** of a whip,
and the *noise* **voice**
of the *rattling* **quake** of *the wheels* **a wheel**,
and of the pransing horses,
and of the *jumping* **dancing** chariots.
3 The horseman *lifteth up* **ascendeth** both
the *bright* **flame of the** sword
and the *glittering* **lightning** spear:
and there is *a multitude* **an abundance** of *slain* **pierced**,
and *a great number* **the heaviness** of carcases;
and there is none end of their corpses;
they *stumble* **falter** upon their corpses:
4 Because of the multitude of the whoredoms
of the *wellfavoured harlot* **whore of good charism**,
the *mistress* **baalah** of *witchcrafts* **sorceries**,
that selleth *nations* **goyim** through her whoredoms,
and families through her *witchcrafts* **sorceries**.
5 Behold, I am against thee,
saith the LORD of hosts **an oracle of Yah Veh Sabaoth**;
and I *will discover* **shall expose** thy *skirts* **drapings**
upon thy face,
and I *will shew the nations* **shall have the goyim see**
thy nakedness,
and the *kingdoms* **sovereigndoms**
thy *shame* **abasement**.
6 And I *will* **shall** cast
abominable filth **abominations** upon thee,
and *make* **wither** thee *vile*,
and *will* **shall** set thee as a *gazingstock* **spectacle**.
7 And it shall *come to pass* **become**,
that all they that *look upon* **see** thee shall flee from thee,
and say, Nineveh is *laid waste* **ravaged**:
who *will bemoan* **shall wag over** her?
whence shall I seek *comforters* **sighers** for thee?
8 *Art thou better* **Well—pleasest thou**
more than *populous No* **No Ammon**,
that *was situate* **settled** among the rivers,
that had the waters round about it,
whose *rampart* **trench** was the sea,
and her wall was from the sea?
9 *Ethiopia* **Kush** and *Egypt* **Misrayim**
were her *strength* **might**,
and *it was infinite* **there was no end**;
Put and *Lubim* **Lubiym** were thy helpers.
10 Yet was she *carried away* **exiled**,
she went into captivity:
her *young children* **sucklings** also
were *dashed in pieces* **splattered**
at the top of all the *streets* **outways**:
and they *cast lots* **handled pebbles**
for her honourable men,
and all her great *men* were *bound* **chained** in chains.
11 Thou also shalt be *drunken* **intoxicated**:
thou shalt be *hid* **concealed**,
thou also shalt seek *strength* **a stronghold**
because of the enemy.
12 All thy *strong holds* **fortresses**
shall be like fig trees with the *firstripe figs* **firstlings**:
if they be shaken,
they shall *even* fall into the mouth of the eater.
13 Behold, thy people in the midst of thee are women:
the gates of thy land
in opening,
shall be *set wide open* **opened** unto thine enemies:
the fire shall devour thy bars.
14 *Draw* **Bail** thee waters for the siege,
fortify **strengthen** thy *strong holds* **fortresses**:
go into *clay* **mire** and tread the morter,
make strong **strengthen** the brickkiln.
15 There shall the fire devour thee;
the sword shall cut thee off,
it shall eat thee *up* like the cankerworm:
make **multiply** thyself *many* as the cankerworm,
make **multiply** thyself *many* as the locusts.
16 Thou hast *multiplied* **abounded** thy merchants
above the stars of *heaven* **the heavens**:
the cankerworm *spoileth* **spreadeth**,
and *fleeth away* **flieth**.
17 Thy *crowned* **princes** are as the locusts,
and thy *captains* **officers**
as the *great grasshoppers* **grubbing grubbers**,
which *camp* **encamp** in the *hedges* **walls** in the cold day,
but when the sun ariseth they flee away,
and their place is not known where they are.
18 Thy *shepherds* **tenders** slumber,
O *king* **sovereign** of *Assyria* **Ashshur**:
thy *nobles* **mighty** shall *dwell in the dust* **tabernacle**:
thy people is scattered upon the mountains,
and *no man* **no one** gathereth *them*.
19 There is no healing of thy *bruise* **break**;
thy wound *is grievous* **worn**:
all that hear the *bruit* **report** of thee
shall clap the *hands* **palms** over thee:
for upon whom
hath not thy *wickedness* **evil** passed continually?

KEY TO INTERPRETING THE EXEGESES:
King James text is in regular type;
Text under exegeses is in oblique type;
Text of exegeses is in bold type.

HABAKKUK'S FIRST BURDEN

1 The burden which Habakkuk the prophet did see.
2 O *LORD* **Yah Veh**,
how long shall I cry, and thou *wilt* **shalt** not hear!
even cry out unto thee of violence,
and thou *wilt* **shalt** not save!
3 Why dost thou *shew me iniquity* **have me see mischief**,
and cause me to *behold grievance* **scan at toil**?
for *spoiling* **ravage** and violence are before me:
and there are that *raise up* **lift** strife and contention.
4 Therefore the *law* **torah** is *slacked* **exhausted**,
and judgment
doth never go forth **goeth not in perpetuity**:
for the wicked
doth compass about **surroundeth** the *righteous* **just**;
therefore *wrong* **twisted** judgment proceedeth.

YAH VEH'S RESPONSE

5 *Behold* **See** ye among the *heathen* **goyim**,
and *regard* **look**, and *wonder* **marvel** marvellously:
for I *will work a work* **shall do a deed** in your days
which ye *will* **shall** not *believe* **trust**,
though it be *told you* **scribed**.
6 For, *lo* **behold**, I raise *up* the *Chaldeans* **Kesediym**,
that bitter and hasty *nation* **goyim**,
which shall *march* **walk**
through the *breadth* **expanse** of the land,
to possess the *dwellingplaces* **tabernacles**
that are not theirs.
7 They are terrible and *dreadful* **awesome**:
their judgment and their *dignity* **exalting**
shall proceed of themselves.
8 Their horses also are swifter than the leopards,
and are *more fierce* **sharper** than the evening wolves:
and their *horsemen* **cavalry** shall spread themselves,
and their *horsemen* **cavalry** shall come from far;
they shall fly as the eagle that hasteth to eat.
9 They shall come all for violence:
their faces
shall *sup up as the east wind* **suck the easterly**,
and they shall gather the captivity as the sand.
10 And they shall *scoff at the kings* **ridicule sovereigns**,
and the *princes* **potentates**
shall be a *scorn* **laughingstock** unto them:
they shall *deride* **ridicule** every *strong hold* **fortress**;
for they shall heap dust, and *take* **capture** it.
11 Then shall his *mind* **spirit** change,
and he shall pass over, and *offend* **shall guilt**,
imputing this his *power* **force** unto his *god* **elohah**.

HABAKKUK'S SECOND BURDEN

12 Art thou not from *everlasting* **antiquity**,
O *LORD* **Yah Veh** my *God* **Elohim**, mine Holy One?
we shall not die.
O *LORD* **Yah Veh**,
thou hast *ordained* **set** them for judgment;
and, O *mighty God* **Rock**,
thou hast *established* **founded** them
for *correction* **reproving**.
13 Thou art of purer eyes than to *behold* **see** evil,
and canst not look on *iniquity* **toil**:
wherefore lookest thou
upon them that deal *treacherously* **covertly**,
and *holdest thy tongue* **hushest** when the wicked
devoureth the man that is **swallow him
that is** more **just** *righteous than he*?
14 And *makest men* **workest humanity**
as the fishes of the sea,
as the *creeping things* **creepers**,
that have no *ruler* **sovereign** over them?
15 They *take up* **ascend** all of them with the *angle* **hook**,
they catch them in their net,
and gather them in their drag **net**:
therefore they *rejoice* **cheer** and *are glad* **twirl**.
16 Therefore they sacrifice unto their net,
and *burn* incense unto their drag **net**;
because by them their *portion* **allotment** is fat,
and their *meat plenteous* **food fattened**.
17 shall they therefore *empty* **drag** their net,
and not spare continually
to *slay* **slaughter** the *nations* **goyim**?
2 I *will* **shall** stand upon my *watch* **guard**,
and set me upon the *tower* **rampart**,
and *will* **shall** watch to see
what he *will say* **shall word** unto me,
and what I shall *answer* **respond**
when I am reproved **upon my reproof**.

YAH VEH'S RESPONSE

2 And *the LORD* **Yah Veh** answered me, and said,
Write **Inscribe** the vision,
and *make it plain* **explain it** upon *tables* **slabs**,
that he may run that *readeth it* **calleth out**.
3 For the vision is yet for *an appointed time* **a season**,
but at the end it shall *speak* **breathe**, and not lie:
though it tarry, wait for it;
because **in coming**, it *will surely* **shall** come,
it *will* **shall** not *tarry* **delay**.
4 Behold,
his soul which is *lifted up* **swollen**
is not *upright* **straight** in him:
but the just shall live by his *faith* **trustworthiness**.
5 Yea also,
because he *transgresseth* **dealeth covertly** by wine,
he is *a proud man* **an arrogant mighty**,
neither *keepeth at home* **resteth in his habitation**,
who enlargeth his *desire* **soul** as *hell* **sheol**,
and is as death, and cannot be satisfied,
but gathereth unto him all *nations* **goyim**,
and *heapeth* **gathereth** unto him all people:
6 Shall not all these
take up a parable **lift a proverb** against him,
and a *taunting proverb* **satire riddle** against him, and say,
Woe **Ho** to him
that *increaseth* **aboundeth** that which is not his!
how long?
and to him that *ladeth* **heavieth** himself
with *thick clay* **heavy pledges**!
7 Shall they not rise *up suddenly* **in a blink**
that shall bite thee,
and awake that shall *vex* **agitate** thee,
and thou shalt be for *booties* **plunder** unto them?
8 Because thou hast spoiled many *nations* **goyim**,
all the remnant of the people shall spoil thee;
because of *men's* **human** blood,
and for the violence of the land,
of the city, and of all that *dwell* **settle** therein.
9 *Woe* **Ho** to him that *coveteth* **greedily gaineth**
an evil *covetousness* **greedy gain** to his house,
that he may set his nest on high,
that he may be *delivered* **rescued**
from the *power* **palm** of evil!
10 Thou hast *consulted* **counselled** shame to thy house
by *cutting* **scraping** off many people,
and hast sinned against thy soul.
11 For the stone shall cry out of the wall,
and the *beam* **crossbeam** out of the timber
shall answer *it*.
12 *Woe to him that buildeth a town with*
Ho to the builder of a city by blood,
and stablisheth a city by *iniquity* **wickedness**!
13 Behold,
is it not of *the LORD of hosts* **Yah Veh Sabaoth**
that the *people* **nations** shall labour
in the very **for sufficient** fire,
and the people shall weary themselves
for *very* **sufficient** vanity?
14 For the earth shall be filled with the knowledge
of the *glory* **honour** of *the LORD* **Yah Veh**,
as the waters cover the sea.
15 *Woe* **Ho** unto him
that giveth his *neighbour* **friend** drink,
that *puttest* **scrapest** thy *bottle* **skin** *to him*,
and *makest* **intoxicatest** him *drunken* also,
that thou mayest look on their *nakedness* **pudenda**!
16 Thou art *filled* **satiated**
with shame — **abasement** for *glory* **honour**:
drink thou also,
and *let thy foreskin be uncovered* **be uncircumcised**:

the cup of *the LORD'S* **Yah Veh's** right *hand*
shall be turned unto thee,
and *shameful spewing* **an abasement**
shall be on thy *glory* **honour**.
17 For the violence of Lebanon shall cover thee,
and the *spoil* **ravage** of *beasts* **animals**,
which *made* **terrified** them *afraid*
because of *men's* **human** blood,
and for the violence of the land,
of the city, and of all that dwell therein.
18 What profiteth the *graven image* **sculptile**
that the *maker* **former** *thereof* hath *graven* **sculpted** it;
the molten *image*, and a teacher of *lies* **falsehoods**,
that the *maker* **former** of his *work* **form**
trusteth **confideth** therein,
to *make dumb* **work mute** idols?
19 *Woe* **Ho** unto him
that saith to the *wood* **timber**, Awake;
to the *dumb* **silent** stone, *Arise* **Awake**, it shall teach!
Behold, it is *laid over* **manipulated** with gold and silver,
and there is no *breath* **spirit** at all in the midst of it.
20 But *the LORD* **Yah Veh** is in his holy *temple* **manse**:
let all the earth keep silence *before him* **at his face**.

HABAKKUK'S LYRIC POEM

3 A prayer of Habakkuk the prophet
upon Shigionoth **A Lyric Poem**.
2 O *LORD* **Yah Veh**, I have heard thy *speech* **report**,
and was *afraid* **awed**:
O *LORD* **Yah Veh**,
revive **enliven** thy *work* **deeds** in the midst of the years,
in the midst of the years make known;
in *wrath* **quivering** remember mercy.
3 *God* **Elohah** came from Teman,
and the Holy One from mount Paran.
Selah.
His *glory* **majesty** covered the heavens,
and the earth was *full of* **filled with** his *praise* **halal**.
4 And *his brightness* **brilliance** was as the light;
he had horns *coming* out of his hand:
and there was the hiding of his *power* **strength**.
5 *Before him* **At his face** went the pestilence,
and burning coals went forth at his feet.
6 He stood,
and *measured* **shook** the earth:
he *beheld* **saw**,
and *drove asunder* **loosed** the *nations* **goyim**;
and the *everlasting* **eternal** mountains were scattered,
the perpetual hills *did bow* **prostrated**:
his ways are everlasting.
7 I saw the tents of *Cushan* **Kushan** in *affliction* **mischief**:
and the curtains of the land of *Midian* **Midyan**
did tremble **quivered**.
8 Was *the LORD displeased* **Yah Veh inflamed**
against the rivers?
was *thine anger* **thy wrath** against the rivers?
was thy wrath against the sea,
that thou didst ride upon thine horses
and thy chariots of salvation?
9 **In exposing,** Thy bow was *made quite naked* **exposed**,
according to the oaths of the tribes **the rods oathed**,
even thy word **saying**.
Selah.
Thou *didst cleave* **splittest** the earth with rivers.
10 The mountains saw thee, and they *trembled* **writhed**:
the *overflowing* **flooding** of the water passed by:
the *deep uttered* **abyss gave** his voice,
and lifted *up* his hands on high.
11 The sun and moon
stood still in their *habitation* **residence**:
at the light of thine arrows they went,
and at the *shining* **brilliance** of thy glittering spear.
12 Thou *didst march* **paced** through the land
in *indignation* **rage**,
thou *didst thresh* **threshed** the *heathen* **goyim**
in *anger* **wrath**.
13 Thou wentest forth for the salvation of thy people,
even for salvation with *thine anointed* **thy Messiah**;
thou *woundedst* **struck** the head
out of the house of the wicked,
by *discovering* **stripping naked**
the foundation unto the neck.
Selah.
14 Thou *didst strike* **pierced** through with his *staves* **rods**
the head of his *villages* **suburbs**:
they *came out as a whirlwind* **stormed** to scatter me:
their *rejoicing* **jumping for joy**
was as to devour the *poor secretly* **humble covertly**.
15 Thou *didst walk* **treaded** through the sea
with thine horses,
through the heap of great waters.
16 When I heard, my belly *trembled* **quivered**;
my lips quivered at the voice:
rottenness entered into my bones,
and I *trembled* **quivered** in myself,
that I might rest in the day of *trouble* **tribulation**:
when he *cometh up* **ascendeth** unto the people,
he *will invade* **shall troop against** them with his troops.
17 Although the fig tree shall not blossom,
neither shall *fruit* **produce** be in the vines;
the labour of the olive shall *fail* **deceive**,
and the fields shall *yield* **work** no *meat* **food**;
the flock shall be cut off from the fold,
and there shall be no herd in the stalls:
18 Yet I *will rejoice* **shall jump for joy**
in *the LORD* **Yah Veh**,
I *will joy* **shall twirl** in *the God* **Elohim** of my salvation.
19 *The LORD God* **Yah Veh Adonay**
is my *strength* **valour**,
and he *will make* **shall set** my feet like hinds' *feet*,
and he *will make* **shall cause** me
to *walk* **tread** upon *mine high places* **my bamahs**.
To *the chief singer* **his eminence**
on my *stringed instruments* **strummers**.

KEY TO INTERPRETING THE EXEGESES:
King James text is in regular type;
Text under exegeses is in oblique type;
Text of exegeses is in bold type.

INTRODUCTION

1 The word of *the LORD* **Yah Veh**
which came unto *Zephaniah* **Sephan Yah**
the son of *Cushi* **Kushiy,**
the son of *Gedaliah* **Gedal Yah,**
the son of *Amariah* **Amar Yah,**
the son of *Hizkiah* **Yechizqi Yah,**
in the days of *Josiah* **Yoshi Yah** the son of Amon,
king **sovereign** of *Judah* **Yah Hudah.**

IMPENDING DOOM

2 *I will utterly consume* **In gathering, I shall gather** all *things*
from off the *land* **face of the soil,**
saith the LORD **an oracle of Yah Veh.**
3 *I will consume* **shall gather**
man **humanity** and *beast* **animal;**
I will consume **shall gather**
the *fowls* **flyers** of the *heaven* **heavens,**
and the fishes of the sea,
and the stumblingblocks with the wicked:
and I *will* **shall** cut off *man* **humanity**
from *off* **the face of** the *land* **soil,**
saith the LORD **an oracle of Yah Veh.**
4 I *will* **shall** also stretch out mine hand
upon *Judah* **Yah Hudah,**
and upon all
the *inhabitants* **settlers** of *Jerusalem* **Yeru Shalem;**
and I *will* **shall** cut off the *remnant* **survivors** of Baal
from this place,
and the name of the *Chemarims* **ascetics** with the priests;
5 And them that *worship* **prostrate**
to the host of *heaven* **the heavens** upon the *housetops* **roofs;**
and them that *worship* **prostrate**
and that *swear* **oath** by *the LORD* **Yah Veh,**
and that *swear* **oath** by Malcham;
6 And them that are *turned back* **apostatized**
from *the LORD* **Yah Veh;**
and *those* that have not sought *the LORD* **Yah Veh,**
nor enquired for him.
7 *Hold thy peace* **Hush**
at the *presence* **face** of *the Lord GOD* **Adonay Yah Veh:**
for the day of *the LORD* **Yah Veh** is *at hand* **nearby:**
for *the LORD* **Yah Veh** hath prepared a sacrifice,
he hath *bid* **hallowed** his *guests* **called out ones.**
8 And it shall *come to pass* **become,**
in the day of the *LORD'S* sacrifice **of Yah Veh,**
that I *will punish* **shall visit upon** the *princes* **governors,**
and the *king's children* **sovereign's sons,**
and all such
as are *clothed* **enrobed** with strange *apparel* **robes.**
9 In the same day also *will I punish* **shall I visit upon**
all those that leap on the threshold,
which fill their *masters'* **adoniym's** houses
with violence and deceit.
10 And it shall *come to pass* **become,** in that day,
saith the LORD **an oracle of Yah Veh,**
that there shall be the *noise* **voice** of a cry
from the fish *gate* **portal,**
and an howling from the second,
and a great *crashing* **breaking** from the hills.
11 Howl, ye *inhabitants* **settlers** of *Maktesh* **Machtesh,**
for all the *merchant* peoples **of Kenaan** are cut down;
all they that bear silver are *cut off* **severed.**
12 And it shall *come to pass* **become,** at that time,
that I *will* **shall** search *Jerusalem* **Yeru Shalem**
with *candles* **lamps,**
and *punish* **visit upon** the men
that are *settled* **curdled** on their *lees* **dregs:**
that say in their heart,
The LORD will **Yah Veh shall** not *do good* **well—please,**
neither *will* **shall** he *do evil* **vilify.**
13 Therefore
their *goods* **valuables** shall become a *booty* **plunder,**
and their houses a desolation:
they shall also build houses, but not *inhabit them* **settle;**
and they shall plant vineyards,
but not drink the wine *thereof.*

THE GREAT DAY OF YAH VEH

14 The great day of *the LORD* **Yah Veh** is near, *it is* near,
and hasteth *greatly* **mightily,**
even the voice of the day of *the LORD* **Yah Veh:**
the mighty *man* shall *cry* **whoop** there bitterly.
15 That day is a day of wrath,
a day of *trouble* **tribulation** and distress,
a day of *wasteness* **devastation** and *desolation* **ruin,**
a day of darkness and *gloominess* **darkness,**
a day of clouds and *thick* **dripping** darkness,
16 A day of the trumpet and *alarm* **blast**
against the *fenced* **fortified** cities,
and against the high *towers* **corners.**
17 And I *will bring distress upon men*
shall tribulate humanity,
that they shall walk like blind *men,*
because they have sinned against *the LORD* **Yah Veh:**
and their blood shall be poured out as dust,
and their *flesh* **eating** as the dung **ball.**
18 Neither their silver nor their gold
shall be able to *deliver* **rescue** them
in the day of *the LORD'S* **Yah Veh's** wrath;
but the whole land shall be devoured
by the fire of his jealousy:
for he shall *make* **work**
even a *speedy riddance* **hasty final finish**
of all them that *dwell* **settle** in the land.

YAH VEH'S CALL TO THE GOYIM

2 Gather yourselves *together,* yea, gather *together,*
O *nation* **goyim** not *desired* **yearned for;**
2 Before the *decree bring forth* **statute begetteth,**
before the day pass as the chaff,
before the *fierce anger* **fuming wrath**
of *the LORD* **Yah Veh** come upon you,
before the day
of the *LORD'S anger* **wrath of Yah Veh** come upon you.
3 Seek ye *the LORD* **Yah Veh,**
all ye *meek* **humble** of the earth,
which have *wrought* **done** his judgment;
seek *righteousness* **justness,** seek *meekness* **humility:**
it may be **perhaps** ye shall be hid
in the day of the *LORD'S anger* **wrath of Yah Veh.**
4 For *Gaza* **Azzah** shall be forsaken,
and Ashkelon a desolation:
they shall drive out Ashdod at the noon *day,*
and *Ekron* **Eqron** shall be *rooted up* **uprooted.**
5 *Woe* **Ho** unto the *inhabitants* **settlers**
of the sea *coast* **boundary,**
the *nation* **goyim** of the *Cherethites* **Kerethiym!**
the word of *the LORD* **Yah Veh** is against you;
O *Canaan* **Kenaan,**
the land of the *Philistines* **Peleshethiym,**
I *will* **shall** even destroy thee,
that there shall be no *inhabitant* **settler.**
6 And the sea *coast* **boundary**
shall be *dwellings* **habitations of rest**
and *cottages* **meadows** for *shepherds* **tenders,**
and *folds* **walls** for flocks.
7 And the *coast* **boundary** shall be
for the *remnant* **survivors**
of the house of *Judah* **Yah Hudah;**
they shall *feed* **graze** thereupon:
in the houses of Ashkelon
shall they *lie down* **crouch** in the evening:
for *the LORD* **Yah Veh** their *God* **Elohim**
shall visit them,
and turn away their captivity.
8 I have heard the reproach of Moab,
and the revilings of the *children* **sons** of Ammon,
whereby they have reproached my people,
and *magnified* **greatened** *themselves* against their border.
9 Therefore *as* I live,
saith the LORD of hosts **an oracle of Yah Veh Sabaoth,**
the God **Elohim** of *Israel* **Yisra El,**
Surely Moab shall be as *Sodom* **Sedom,**
and the *children* **sons** of Ammon as *Gomorrah* **Amorah,**
even the *breeding* **possession** of nettles, and saltpits,
and *a perpetual* **an eternal** desolation:
the *residue* **survivors** of my people
shall *spoil* **plunder** them,

and the remnant of my *people* **goyim**
shall *possess* **inherit** them.
10 This shall they have for their *pride* **pomp**,
because they have reproached
and *magnified* **greatened** *themselves* against the people
of *the LORD of hosts* **Yah Veh Sabaoth**.
11 *The LORD* **Yah Veh**
will **shall** be *terrible* **awesome** unto them:
for he *will famish* **shall emaciate**
all the *gods* **elohim** of the earth;
and *men* shall *worship* **prostrate to** him,
every *one* **man** from his place,
even all the *isles* **islands** of the *heathen* **goyim**.
12 Ye *Ethiopians* **Kushiym** also,
ye shall be *slain* **pierced** by my sword.
13 And he *will* **shall** stretch out his hand
against the north,
and destroy *Assyria* **Ashshur**;
and *will make* **shall set** Nineveh a desolation,
and *dry* **parch** like a wilderness.
14 And *flocks* **droves** shall *lie down* **crouch**
in the midst of her,
all the *beasts* **live beings** of the *nations* **goyim**:
both the *cormorant* **pelican** and the bittern
shall *lodge* **stay overnight** in the upper lintels of it;
their voice shall sing in the windows;
desolation **parch** shall be in the thresholds:
for he shall *uncover* **strip naked** the cedar work.
15 This is the *rejoicing* city of **jumping for joy**
that *dwelt carelessly* **settled confidently**,
that said in her heart, I *am*, and there is none beside me:
how is she become a desolation,
a **resting** place for *beasts to lie down in* **live beings**!
every one that passeth by her shall hiss,
and wag his hand.

HO TO YERU SHALEM

3 *Woe* **Ho** to her
that *is filthy* **rebelleth** and *polluted* **profaneth**,
to — the oppressing city!
2 She *obeyed* **hearkened** not **unto** the voice;
she *received* **took** not *correction* **discipline**;
she *trusted* **confided** not in *the LORD* **Yah Veh**;
she *drew* **approached** not *near to* her *God* **Elohim**.
3 Her *princes* **governors** within her are roaring lions;
her judges are evening wolves;
they *gnaw* **craunch** not *the bones*
till *the morrow* **morning**.
4 Her prophets are *light* **frothy**
and *treacherous persons* **covert men**:
her priests have *polluted* **profaned** the *sanctuary* **holies**,
they have *done violence to* **violated** the *law* **torah**.
5 The just *LORD* **Yah Veh** is in the midst *thereof*;
he *will* **shall** not *do iniquity* **work wickedness**:
every morning **by morning**
doth he bring **he giveth** his judgment to light,
he *faileth* **lacketh** not;
but the *unjust* **wicked** knoweth no shame.
6 I have cut off the *nations* **goyim**:
their *towers* **corners** are *desolate* **desolated**;
I *made* **parched** their *streets waste* **outways**,
that none passeth by:
their cities are destroyed,
so that there is no man,
that there is *none inhabitant* **no settler**.
7 I said, Surely thou *wilt fear* **shalt awe** me,
thou *wilt receive instruction* **shalt take discipline**;
so their *dwelling* **habitation** should not be cut off,
howsoever I punished **all that I visited upon** them:
but **surely** they rose early,
and *corrupted* **ruined** all their *doings* **exploits**.

THE JUDGMENT OF THE GOYIM

8 Therefore wait ye upon me,
saith the LORD **an oracle of Yah Veh**,
until the day that I rise *up* to the prey:
for my *determination* **judgment**
is to gather the *nations* **goyim**,
that I may *assemble* **gather** the *kingdoms* **sovereigndoms**,
to pour upon them *mine indignation* **my rage**,
even all my *fierce anger* **fuming wrath**:
for all the earth
shall be devoured with the fire of my jealousy.
9 For then *will* **shall** I turn to the people
a *pure language* **purified lip**,
that they may all
call upon the name of *the LORD* **Yah Veh**,
to serve him with one *consent* **shoulder**.
10 From beyond the rivers of *Ethiopia* **Kush**
my *suppliants* **entreaters**,
even the daughter of my *dispersed* **scattered**,
shall bring mine offering.
11 In that day shalt thou not be *ashamed* **shamed**
for all thy *doings* **exploits**,
wherein thou hast *transgressed* **rebelled** against me:
for then I *will take away* **shall turn aside**
out of the midst of thee
them that *rejoice* **jump for joy** in thy *pride* **pomp**,
and thou shalt *no more* **not add**
to be *haughty* **lifted**
because of my holy mountain.

THE SURVIVORS OF YISRA EL

12 I *will* **shall** also *leave* **let remain** in the midst of thee
an *afflicted* **humbled** and poor people,
and they shall *trust* **seek refuge**
in the name of *the LORD* **Yah Veh**.
13 The *remnant* **survivors** of *Israel* **Yisra El**
shall not *do iniquity* **work wickedness**,
nor *speak* **word** lies;
neither shall a deceitful tongue be found in their mouth:
for they shall *feed* **graze** and *lie down* **crouch**,
and none shall *make* **tremble** them *afraid*.
14 Sing, O daughter of *Zion* **Siyon**;
shout, O *Israel* **Yisra El**;
be glad **cheer** and *rejoice* **jump for joy** with all the heart,
O daughter of *Jerusalem* **Yeru Shalem**.
15 *The LORD* **Yah Veh**
hath *taken away* **turned aside** thy judgments,
he hath *cast out* **faced** thine enemy:
the *king* **sovereign** of *Israel* **Yisra El**,
even the LORD **Yah Veh**, is in the midst of thee:
thou shalt not see evil any more.
16 In that day it shall be said to *Jerusalem* **Yeru Shalem**,
Fear **Awe** thou not:
and to Zion **Siyon**,
Let not thine hands *be slack* **slacken**.
17 *The LORD* **Yah Veh** thy *God* **Elohim**
in the midst of thee is mighty;
he *will* **shall** save,
he *will* **shall** rejoice over thee with *joy* **cheerfulness**;
he *will rest* **shall hush** in his love,
he *will joy* **shall twirl** over thee with *singing* **shouting**.
18 I *will* **shall** gather *them that are sorrowful* **the grieved**
for the *solemn assembly* **congregation**, who are of thee,
to whom the reproach of it was a burden.
19 Behold, at that time
I *will undo* **shall work** all that *afflict* **humble** thee:
and I *will* **shall** save her that *halteth* **limpeth**,
and gather her that was *driven out* **expelled**;
and I *will get* **shall set** them
praise **for a halal** and *fame* **a name**
in every land
where they have been put to **of their** shame.
20 At that time *will* **shall** I bring you *again*,
even in the time that I gather you:
for I *will make* **shall give** you a name and a *praise* **halal**
among all people of the earth,
when I *turn back* **return** your captivity before your eyes,
saith *the LORD* **Yah Veh**.

KEY TO INTERPRETING THE EXEGESES:
King James text is in regular type;
Text under exegeses is in oblique type;
Text of exegeses is in bold type.

THE PEOPLE DISRUPT THE BUILDING OF THE HOUSE OF YAH VEH

1 In the second year of *Darius* **Daryavesh**
the *king* **sovereign**,
in the sixth month, in the first day of the month,
came the word of *the LORD* **Yah Veh**
by *Haggai* **the hand of Haggay** the prophet
unto *Zerubbabel* **Zerub Babel**
the son of *Shealtiel* **Shealti El**,
governor **captain** of *Judah* **Yah Hudah**,
and to *Joshua* **Yah Shua** the son of *Josedech* **Yah Sadaq**,
the *high* **great** priest, saying,
2 Thus *speaketh* **saith**
the LORD of hosts **Yah Veh Sabaoth**, saying,
This people say, The time is not come,
the time that the *LORD'S* house **of Yah Veh**
should be built.

YAH VEH'S DISCIPLINE FOR THE DISRUPTED WORK

3 Then came the word of *the LORD* **Yah Veh**
by **the hand of** *Haggai* **Haggay** the prophet, saying,
4 Is it time for you,
O ye, to *dwell* **settle** in your cieled houses,
and this house *lie waste* **parch**?
5 Now therefore
thus saith *the LORD of hosts* **Yah Veh Sabaoth**;
Consider **Set thy heart on** your ways.
6 Ye have sown *much* **aboundingly**,
and *bring* **brought** in little;
ye eat, but ye have *not enough* **no satisfaction**;
ye drink, but ye are not *filled with drink* **intoxicated**;
ye *clothe* **enrobe** you, but there is none *warm* **heated**;
and he that *earneth wages* **hireth**
earneth wages **hireth**
to put it into a *bag with holes* **pierced bundle**.
7 Thus saith *the LORD of hosts* **Yah Veh Sabaoth**;
Consider **Set thy heart on** your ways.
8 *Go up* **Ascend** to the mountain, and bring *wood* **timber**,
and build the house;
and I *will take pleasure* **shall be pleased** in it,
and I *will* **shall** be *glorified* **honoured**,
saith *the LORD* **Yah Veh**.
9 Ye *looked for much* **faced aboundingly**,
and, *lo* **behold**, it came to little;
and when ye brought it home, I *did blow* **puffed** upon it.
Why **Wherefore**?
saith the LORD of hosts **an oracle of Yah Veh Sabaoth**.
Because of mine house that is *waste* **parched**,
and ye run every man unto his own house.
10 Therefore the *heaven* **heavens** over you
is stayed from dew,
and the earth is stayed from her *fruit* **produce**.
11 And I called for a *drought* **parch** upon the land,
and upon the mountains, and upon the *corn* **crop**,
and upon the *new wine* **juice**, and upon the oil,
and upon that which the *ground* **soil** bringeth forth,
and upon *men* **humanity**, and upon *cattle* **animals**,
and upon all the labour of the *hands* **palms**.

THE WORK BEGUN AGAIN

12 Then *Zerubbabel* **Zerub Babel**
the son of *Shealtiel* **Shealti El**,
and *Joshua* **Yah Shua** the son of *Josedech* **Yah Sadaq**,
the *high* **great** priest,
with all the *remnant* **survivors** of the people,
obeyed **hearkened unto** the voice
of *the LORD* **Yah Veh** their *God* **Elohim**,
and the words of *Haggai* **Haggay** the prophet,
as *the LORD* **Yah Veh** their *God* **Elohim** had sent him,
and the people *did fear* **awed**
before the LORD **at the face of Yah Veh**.
13 Then *spake Haggai* **said Haggay**
the *LORD'S messenger* **angel of Yah Veh**
in the *LORD'S message* **evangelism of Yah Veh**
unto the people, saying,
I am with you,
saith the LORD **an oracle of Yah Veh**.
14 And *the LORD* **Yah Veh**
stirred up **wakened** the spirit of *Zerubbabel* **Zerub Babel**
the son of *Shealtiel* **Shealti El**,
governor of *Judah* **Yah Hudah**,
and the spirit of *Joshua* **Yah Shua**
the son of *Josedech* **Yah Sadaq**, the *high* **great** priest,
and the spirit of all the *remnant* **survivors** of the people;
and they came and *did* **worked** work
in the house of *the LORD of hosts* **Yah Veh Sabaoth**,
their *God* **Elohim**,
15 In the four and twentieth day of the sixth month,
in the second year
of *Darius* **Daryavesh** the *king* **sovereign**.

THE NEW HOUSE

2 In the seventh *month*,
in the one and twentieth *day* of the month,
came the word of *the LORD* **Yah Veh**
by **the hand of** the prophet *Haggai* **Haggay**, saying,
2 Speak now to *Zerubbabel* **Zerub Babel**
the son of *Shealtiel* **Shealti El**,
governor of *Judah* **Yah Hudah**,
and to *Joshua* **Yah Shua** the son of *Josedech* **Yah Sadaq**,
the *high* **great** priest,
and to the *residue* **survivors** of the people, saying,
3 Who *is left* **surviveth** among you
that saw this house in her first *glory* **honour**?
and how *do ye* see **ye** it now?
is it not in your eyes
in comparison of it **such** as *nothing* **nought**?
4 Yet now *be strong* **prevail**, O *Zerubbabel* **Zerub Babel**,
saith the LORD **an oracle of Yah Veh**;
and *be strong* **prevail**, O *Joshua* **Yah Shua**,
son of *Josedech* **Yah Sadaq**, the *high* **great** priest;
and *be strong* **prevail**, all ye people of the land,
saith the LORD **an oracle of Yah Veh**,
and work: for I am with you,
saith the LORD of hosts **an oracle of Yah Veh Sabaoth**:
5 According to the word that I *covenanted* **cut** with you
when ye came out of *Egypt* **Misrayim**,
so my spirit *remaineth* **standeth** among you:
fear **awe** ye not.
6 For thus saith *the LORD of hosts* **Yah Veh Sabaoth**;
Yet once, it is a little while,
and I *will shake* **shall quake** the heavens,
and the earth, and the sea,
and the *dry land* **parched areas**;
7 And I *will shake* **shall quake** all *nations* **goyim**,
and the desire of all *nations* **goyim** shall come:
and I *will* **shall** fill this house with *glory* **honour**,
saith *the LORD of hosts* **Yah Veh Sabaoth**.
8 The silver is mine, and the gold is mine,
saith the LORD of hosts **an oracle of Yah Veh Sabaoth**.
9 The *glory* **honour** of this latter house
shall be greater than of the former,
saith the LORD of hosts **an oracle of Yah Veh Sabaoth**:
and in this place *will* **shall** I give *peace* **shalom**,
saith *the LORD of hosts* **Yah Veh Sabaoth**.

THE TORAH CONCERNING THE HALLOWED

10 In the four and twentieth *day* of the ninth *month*,
in the second year of *Darius* **Daryavesh**,
came the word of *the LORD* **Yah Veh**
by *Haggai* **the hand of Haggay** the prophet, saying,
11 Thus saith *the LORD of hosts* **Yah Veh Sabaoth**;
Ask *now* **I beseech,** the priests *concerning* the *law* **torah**,
saying,
12 If *one* **a man** bear holy flesh
in the *skirt* **wing** of his *garment* **clothes**,
and with his *skirt do* **wing** touch bread,
or pottage, or wine, or oil, or any *meat* **food**,
shall it be *holy* **hallowed**?
And the priests answered and said, No.
13 Then said *Haggai* **Haggay**,
If *one that is unclean by a dead body* **a fouled dead soul**
touch any of these,
shall it be *unclean* **fouled**?
And the priests answered and said,
It shall be *unclean* **fouled**.
14 Then answered *Haggai* **Haggay**, and said,
So is this people,
and so is this *nation before me* **goyim at my face**,
saith the LORD **an oracle of Yah Veh**;

and so is every work of their hands;
and that which they *offer* **oblate** there is *unclean* **fouled**.
15 And *now* **I beseech**, I pray you,
consider **set thy heart** from this day and upward,
from before a stone was *laid* **set** upon a stone
in the *temple* **manse** of *the LORD* **Yah Veh**:
16 Since *those days were* **then**,
when one came to an heap of twenty *measures*,
there were *but* ten:
when one came to the *pressfat* **trough**
for to draw out fats **to strip** fifty *vessels* out of the press,
there were *but* twenty.
17 I smote you with blasting and with *mildew* **pale green**
and with hail in all the *labours* **works** of your hands;
yet ye turned not to me,
saith the LORD **an oracle of Yah Veh**.
18 *Consider now* **Set thy heart I beseech**,
from this day and upward,
from the four and twentieth day of the ninth *month*,
even from the day that the foundation
of *the LORD'S temple* **Yah Veh's manse**
was *laid* **founded**,
consider it **set thy heart**.
19 Is the seed yet in the *barn* **granary**?
yea, as yet the vine, and the fig tree,
and the pomegranate, and the olive tree,
hath not *brought forth* **borne**:
from this day *will* **shall** I bless *you*.
20 And *again* **secondly** the word of *the LORD* **Yah Veh**
came unto *Haggai* **Haggay**
in the four and twentieth *day* of the month, saying,
21 Speak to *Zerubbabel* **Zerub Babel**,
governor of *Judah* **Yah Hudah**, saying,
I *will shake* **shall quake** the heavens and the earth;
22 And I *will overthrow* **shall overturn** the throne
of *kingdoms* **sovereigndoms**,
and I *will destroy* **shall desolate** the strength
of the *kingdoms* **sovereigndoms** of the *heathen* **goyim**;
and I *will overthrow* **shall overturn** the chariots,
and *those that ride in them* **their riders**;
and the horses and their riders shall *come down* **topple**,
every *one* **man** by the sword of his brother.
23 In that day,
saith the LORD of hosts **an oracle of Yah Veh Sabaoth**,
will **shall** I take thee,
O *Zerubbabel* **Zerub Babel**, my servant,
the son of *Shealtiel* **Shealti El**,
saith the LORD **an oracle of Yah Veh**,
and *will make* **shall set** thee as a *signet* **seal**:
for I have chosen thee,
saith the LORD of hosts **an oracle of Yah Veh Sabaoth**.

KEY TO INTERPRETING THE EXEGESES:
King James text is in regular type;
Text under exegeses is in oblique type;
Text of exegeses is in bold type.

YAH VEH ENRAGED WITH THE FATHERS

1 In the eighth month,
in the second year of *Darius* **Daryavesh**,
came the word of *the LORD* **Yah Veh**
unto *Zechariah* **Zechar Yah**,
the son of *Berechiah* **Berech Yah**,
the son of Iddo the prophet, saying,
2 **In being enraged,**
The LORD **Yah Veh** hath been *sore displeased* **enraged**
with your fathers.
3 *Therefore* say thou unto them,
Thus saith *the LORD of hosts* **Yah Veh Sabaoth**;
Turn ye unto me,
saith *the LORD of hosts* **Yah Veh Sabaoth**,
and I *will* **shall** turn unto you,
saith the LORD of hosts **an oracle of Yah Veh Sabaoth**.
4 Be ye not as your fathers,
unto whom the former prophets have *cried* **called out**,
saying, Thus **saying thus:**
saith the LORD of hosts **an oracle of Yah Veh Sabaoth**;
Turn ye *now* **I beseech**, from your evil *ways* **exploits**,
and from your evil *doings* **exploits**:
but they *did* **heard** not *hear*,
nor *hearken* **hearkened** unto me,
saith the LORD **an oracle of Yah Veh**.
5 Your fathers, where are they?
and the prophets,
do they live for ever **live they eternally**?
6 But my words and my statutes,
which I *commanded* **misvahed** my servants the prophets,
did they **overtook** not *take hold of* your fathers?
and they returned and said,
Like as *the LORD of hosts* **Yah Veh Sabaoth**
thought **intrigued** to *do* **work** unto us,
according to our ways,
and *according to* our *doings* **exploits**,
so hath he *dealt* **worked** with us.

THE RIDER ON THE RED HORSE

7 Upon the four and twentieth day of the eleventh month,
which is the month *Sebat* **Shebat**,
in the second year of *Darius* **Daryavesh**,
came the word of *the LORD* **Yah Veh**
unto *Zechariah* **Zechar Yah**,
the son of *Berechiah* **Berech Yah**,
the son of Iddo the prophet, saying,
8 I saw by night,
and behold a man riding upon a red horse,
and he stood among the myrtle trees
that were in the *bottom* **shade**;
and behind him were there red horses,
speckled **bay**, and white.
9 Then said I, O my *lord* **adoni**, what are these?
And the angel that *talked* **worded** with me said unto me,
I *will shew thee* **shall have thee see** what these be.
10 And the man that stood among the myrtle trees
answered and said,
These are they whom *the LORD* **Yah Veh** hath sent
to walk to and fro through the earth.
11 And they answered the angel of *the LORD* **Yah Veh**
that stood among the myrtle trees, and said,
We have walked to and fro through the earth,
and, behold,
all the earth *sitteth still* **settleth**, and *is at rest* **resteth**.
12 Then the angel of *the LORD* **Yah Veh**
answered and said,
O *LORD of hosts* **Yah Veh Sabaoth**,
how long *wilt* **shalt** thou not
have mercy *on Jerusalem* **Yeru Shalem**
and *on* the cities of *Judah* **Yah Hudah**,
against which thou hast *had indignation* **been enraged**
these *threescore and ten* **seventy** years?
13 And *the LORD* **Yah Veh**
answered the angel that *talked* **worded** with me
with good words
and *comfortable words* **words of solaces**.
14 So the angel that *communed* **worded** with me

said unto me, *Cry* **Call** thou **out**, saying,
Thus saith *the LORD of hosts* **Yah Veh Sabaoth**;
I am jealous
for *Jerusalem* **Yeru Shalem** and for *Zion* **Siyon**
with a great jealousy.
15 And **in my enraging,**
I am *very sore displeased* **greatly enraged**
with the *heathen* **goyim** that *are at ease* **relax**:
for I was but a little *displeased* **enraged**,
and they helped *forward the affliction* **for the evil**.
16 Therefore thus saith *the LORD* **Yah Veh**;
I am returned to *Jerusalem* **Yeru Shalem** with mercies:
my house shall be built in it,
saith the LORD of hosts **an oracle of Yah Veh Sabaoth**,
and a line shall be stretched forth
upon *Jerusalem* **Yeru Shalem**.
17 *Cry yet* **Call out**, saying,
Thus saith *the LORD of hosts* **Yah Veh Sabaoth**;
My cities through *prosperity* **good**
shall yet be *spread abroad* **scattered**;
and *the LORD* **Yah Veh**
shall yet *comfort Zion* **sigh over Siyon**,
and shall yet choose *Jerusalem* **Yeru Shalem**.

THE FOUR HORNS

18 Then lifted I up mine eyes, and saw,
and behold four horns.
19 And I said unto the angel that *talked* **worded** with me,
What be these?
And he *answered* **said to** me,
These are the horns
which have *scattered Judah* **winnowed Yah Hudah**,
Israel **Yisra El**, and *Jerusalem* **Yeru Shalem**.

THE FOUR ENGRAVERS

20 And *the LORD* **Yah Veh**
shewed me **had me see** four *carpenters* **engravers**.
21 Then said I, What come these to *do* **work**?
And he spake, saying,
These are the horns
which have *scattered Judah* **winnowed Yah Hudah**,
so that no **mouth of** man *did lift up* **lifted** his head:
but these are come to *fray* **tremble** them,
to *cast out* **hand toss** the horns of the *Gentiles* **goyim**,
which lifted *up* their horn
over the land of *Judah* **Yah Hudah**
to *scatter* **winnow** it.

THE MAN WITH THE MEASURING LINE

2 I lifted up mine eyes again, and *looked* **saw**,
and behold a man with a measuring line in his hand.
2 Then said I, Whither goest thou?
And he said unto me,
To measure *Jerusalem* **Yeru Shalem**,
to see what is the breadth *thereof*,
and what is the length *thereof*.
3 And, behold,
the angel that *talked* **worded** with me went forth,
and another angel went out to meet him,
4 And said unto him, Run,
speak **word** to *this young man* **yonder lad**, saying,
Jerusalem **Yeru Shalem** shall be *inhabited* **settled**
as *towns without walls* **suburbs**
for the *multitude* **abundance** of *men* **humanity**
and *cattle therein* **animals in her midst**:
5 For I,
saith the LORD **an oracle of Yah Veh**,
will **shall** be unto her a wall of fire round about,
and *will* **shall** be the *glory* **honour** in the midst of her.
6 Ho, ho, *come forth*, and flee from the land of the north,
saith the LORD **an oracle of Yah Veh**:
for I have spread you abroad
as the four winds of the *heaven* **heavens**,
saith the LORD **an oracle of Yah Veh**.
7 *Deliver* **Rescue** thyself, *O Zion* **Ho Siyon**,
that *dwellest* **settlest** with the daughter of *Babylon* **Babel**.
8 For thus saith *the LORD of hosts* **Yah Veh Sabaoth**;
After the *glory* **honour** hath he sent me
unto the *nations* **goyim** which spoiled you:
for he that toucheth you
toucheth the *apple* **pupil** of his eye.
9 For, behold, I *will* **shall** shake mine hand upon them,
and they shall be a spoil to their servants:
and ye shall know
that *the LORD of hosts* **Yah Veh Sabaoth** hath sent me.
10 *Sing* **Shout** and *rejoice* **cheer**,
O daughter of *Zion* **Siyon**:
for, *lo* **behold**, I come,
and I *will dwell* **shall tabernacle** in the midst of thee,
saith the LORD **an oracle of Yah Veh**.
11 And many *nations* **goyim**
shall be joined to *the LORD* **Yah Veh** in that day,
and shall be my people:
and I *will* **shall** dwell in the midst of thee,
and thou shalt know
that *the LORD of hosts* **Yah Veh Sabaoth**
hath sent me unto thee.
12 And *the LORD* **Yah Veh** shall inherit *Judah* **Yah Hudah**
his *portion* **allotment** in the holy *land* **soil**,
and shall choose *Jerusalem* **Yeru Shalem** again.
13 *Be silent* **Hush**, O all flesh,
before the LORD **at the face of Yah Veh**:
for he *is raised up* **awaketh** out of his holy habitation.

YAH SHUA THE GREAT PRIEST

3 And he *shewed me* **had me see**
Joshua **Yah Shua** the *high* **great** priest
standing *before* **at the face of**
the angel of *the LORD* **Yah Veh**,
and Satan standing at his right *hand* to *resist* **oppose** him.
2 And *the LORD* **Yah Veh** said unto Satan,
The LORD **Yah Veh** rebuke thee, O Satan;
even *the LORD* **Yah Veh**
that hath chosen *Jerusalem* **Yeru Shalem**
rebuke thee:
is not this a brand *plucked* **rescued** out of the fire?
3 *Now Joshua* **Yah Shua**
was *clothed* **enrobed** with *filthy garments* **dungy clothes**,
and stood *before* **at the face of** the angel.
4 And he answered and *spake* **said**
unto those that stood *before him* **at his face**, saying,
Take away **Turn aside** the *filthy garments* **dungy clothes**
from him.
And unto him he said, *Behold* **See**,
I have caused *thine iniquity* **thy perversity**
to pass from thee,
and I *will clothe* **shall enrobe** thee
with change of *raiment* **mantles**.
5 And I said,
Let them set a *fair mitre* **pure turban** upon his head.
So they set a *fair mitre* **pure turban** upon his head,
and *clothed* **enrobed** him with *garments* **clothes**.
And the angel of *the LORD* **Yah Veh** stood by.
6 And the angel of *the LORD* **Yah Veh**
protested **witnessed** unto *Joshua* **Yah Shua**, saying,
7 Thus saith *the LORD of hosts* **Yah Veh Sabaoth**;
If thou *wilt* **shalt** walk in my ways,
and if thou *wilt keep* **shalt guard** my *charge* **guard**,
then thou shalt also *judge* **plead the cause in** my house,
and shalt also *keep* **guard** my courts,
and I *will* **shall** give thee places to walk
among these that stand by.

THE SPROUT

8 Hear *now* **I beseech**,
O *Joshua* **Yah Shua** the *high* **great** priest, thou,
and thy *fellows* **friends** that sit *before thee* **at thy face**:
for they are men *wondered at* **of omens**:
for, behold,
I *will* **shall** bring forth my servant the *BRANCH* **SPROUT**.
9 For behold the stone
that I have *laid* **given**
before Joshua **at the face of Yah Shua**;
upon one stone shall be seven eyes:
behold,
I *will* **shall** engrave the *graving* **engraving** *thereof*,
saith the LORD of hosts **an oracle of Yah Veh Sabaoth**,
and I *will remove* **shall depart**
the *iniquity* **perversity** of that land
in one day.
10 In that day,
saith the LORD of hosts **an oracle of Yah Veh Sabaoth**,
shall ye call every man his *neighbour* **friend**
under the vine and under the fig tree.

THE GOLDEN MENORAH, AND THE TWO OLIVES

4 And the angel that *talked* **worded** with me
came again **returned**, and waked me,
as a man that is wakened out of his sleep.
2 And said unto me, What seest thou?
And I said, I *have looked* **saw**, and behold,
a *candlestick* **menorah** all of gold,
with a bowl upon the top of it,
and his seven lamps thereon,
and seven *pipes* **tubes** to the seven lamps,
which are upon the top *thereof*:
3 And two *olive trees* **olives** by it,
one upon the right *side* of the bowl,
and *the other* **one** upon the left *side thereof*.
4 So I answered
and *spake* **said** to the angel that *talked* **worded** with me,
saying, What are these, my *lord* **Adonay**?
5 Then the angel that *talked* **worded** with me
answered and said unto me,
Knowest thou not what these be?
And I said, No, my *lord* **Adonay**.
6 Then he answered and *spake* **said** unto me, saying,
This is the word of *the LORD* **Yah Veh**
unto *Zerubbabel* **Zerub Babel**, saying,
Not by *might* **valour**, nor by *power* **force**,
but by my spirit,
saith *the LORD of hosts* **Yah Veh Sabaoth**.
7 Who art thou, O great mountain?
before Zerubbabel **at the face of Zerub Babel**
thou shalt become a plain:
and he shall bring forth the headstone *thereof*
with *shoutings* **clamors**,
crying, Grace, grace **Charism, charism** unto it.
8 Moreover
the word of *the LORD* **Yah Veh** came unto me, saying,
9 The hands of *Zerubbabel* **Zerub Babel**
have laid the foundation of this house;
his hands shall also *finish it* **clip**;
and thou shalt know
that *the LORD of hosts* **Yah Veh Sabaoth**
hath sent me unto you.
10 For who hath *despised* **disrespected**
the day of *small things* **the lesser**?
for they shall *rejoice* **cheer**,
and shall see the *plummet* **tin weight**
in the hand of *Zerubbabel* **Zerub Babel:**
with those seven;
they are the eyes of *the LORD* **Yah Veh**,
which *run to and fro* **flit** through the whole earth.
11 Then answered I, and said unto him,
What are these two *olive trees* **olives**
upon the right *side* of the *candlestick* **menorah**
and upon the left *side thereof*?
12 And I answered *again* **secondly**, and said unto him,
What be these two olive branches
which *through* **by the hand of** the two golden *pipes* **tubes**
empty **pour out** the golden *oil* out of themselves?
13 And he *answered* **said to** me *and said* **saying**,
Knowest thou not what these be?
And I said, No, my *lord* **Adonay**.
14 Then said he,
These are the two *anointed ones* **sons of oil**,
that stand by the *Lord* **Adonay** of the whole earth.

THE FLYING ROLL

5 Then I turned, and lifted up mine eyes,
and *looked* **saw**, and behold, a flying roll.
2 And he said unto me, What seest thou?
And I *answered* **said**, I see a flying roll;
the length *thereof* is twenty cubits,
and the breadth *thereof* ten cubits.
3 Then said he unto me,
This is the *curse* **oath**
that goeth forth over the face of the whole earth:
for every one that stealeth shall be *cut off* **exonerated**
as on this side *according to it* **thus**;
and every one that *sweareth* **oatheth**
shall be *cut off* **exonerated**
as on that side *according to it* **thus**.
4 I *will* **shall** bring it forth,
saith the LORD of hosts **an oracle of Yah Veh Sabaoth**,
and it shall enter into the house of the thief,
and into the house of him
that *sweareth* **oatheth** falsely by my name:
and it shall *remain* **stay overnight**
in the midst of his house,
and shall *consume* **finish** it **off**
with the timber *thereof* and the stones *thereof*.

THE EPHAH

5 Then the angel that *talked* **worded** with me went forth,
and said unto me, Lift *up now* thine eyes,
and see what is this that goeth forth.
6 And I said, What is it?
And he said, This is an ephah that goeth forth.
He said *moreover*,
This is their *resemblance* **eye** through all the earth.
7 And, behold, there was lifted up a *talent* **round** of lead:
and this is *a* **one** woman
that sitteth in the midst of the ephah.
8 And he said, This is wickedness.
And he cast it into the midst of the ephah;
and he cast the *weight* **stone** of lead
upon the mouth *thereof*.
9 Then lifted I up mine eyes,
and *looked* **saw**, and, behold,
there came out two women,
and the wind was in their wings;
for *they* **these** had wings like the wings of a stork:
and they lifted up the ephah
between the earth and the *heaven* **heavens**.
10 Then said I to the angel that *talked* **worded** with me,
Whither do these *bear* **carry** the ephah?
11 And he said unto me,
To build it an house in the land of Shinar:
and it shall be established,
and set there upon her own *base*.

THE FOUR CHARIOTS

6 And I turned, and lifted up mine eyes,
and *looked* **saw**, and, behold,
there came four chariots
out from between two mountains;
and the mountains were mountains of *brass* **copper**.
2 in the first chariot were red horses;
and in the second chariot *black* **dark** horses;
3 And in the third chariot white horses;
and in the fourth chariot grisled and *bay* **strong** horses.
4 Then I answered
and said unto the angel that *talked* **worded** with me,
What are these, my *lord* **Adonay**?
5 And the angel answered and said unto me,
These are the four *spirits* **spirits/winds** of the heavens,
which go forth
from standing before *the Lord* **Adonay** of all the earth.
6 The *black* **dark** horses which are therein
go forth into the north *country* **land**;
and the white go forth after them;
and the grisled go forth toward the south *country* **land**.
7 And the *bay* **strong** went forth,
and sought to go that **in walking,**
they might walk *to and fro* through the earth:
and he said, Get you hence,
in walking, walk *to and fro* through the earth.
So **in walking,** they walked *to and fro* through the earth.
8 Then cried he upon me, and *spake* **worded** unto me,
saying, *Behold* **See**,
these that go toward the north *country* **land**
have *quieted* **rested** my spirit in the north *country* **land**.

YAH SHUA IS CROWNED

9 And the word of *the LORD* **Yah Veh** came unto me,
saying,
10 Take of *them of the captivity* **the exile**,
even of *Heldai* **Helday**, of *Tobijah* **Tobi Yah**,
and of *Jedaiah* **Yeda Yah**,
which are come from *Babylon* **Babel**,
and come thou the same day,
and go into the house of *Josiah* **Yoshi Yah**
the son of *Zephaniah* **Sephan Yah**;
11 Then take silver and gold, and *make* **work** crowns,
and set them upon the head of *Joshua* **Yah Shua**
the son of *Josedech* **Yah Sadaq**, the *high* **great** priest;
12 And *speak* **say** unto him, saying,

Thus *speaketh the LORD of hosts* **saith Yah Veh Sabaoth**,
saying,
Behold the man whose name is The *BRANCH* **SPROUT**;
and he shall *grow up* **sprout** out of his place,
and he shall build
the *temple* **manse** of *the LORD* **Yah Veh**:
13 Even he
shall build the *temple* **manse** of *the LORD* **Yah Veh**;
and he shall bear the *glory* **majesty**,
and shall sit and *rule* **reign** upon his throne;
and he shall be a priest upon his throne:
and the counsel of *peace* **shalom**
shall be between them both.
14 And the crowns shall be to Helem,
and to *Tobijah* **Tobi Yah**, and to *Jedaiah* **Yeda Yah**,
and to Hen the son of *Zephaniah* **Sephan Yah**,
for a memorial
in the *temple* **manse** of *the LORD* **Yah Veh**.
15 And they that are far off shall come
and build in the *temple* **manse** of *the LORD* **Yah Veh**,
and ye shall know
that *the LORD of hosts* **Yah Veh Sabaoth**
hath sent me unto you.
And this shall *come to pass* **become**,
if **in hearkening,** ye *will diligently obey* **shall hearken**
unto the voice of *the LORD* **Yah Veh** your *God* **Elohim**.

CONCERNING FASTING

7 And it *came to pass* **became**,
in the fourth year of *king Darius* **sovereign Daryavesh**,
that the word of *the LORD* **Yah Veh**
came unto *Zechariah* **Zechar Yah**
in the fourth *day* of the ninth month,
even in *Chisleu* **Kislav**;
2 When they had sent unto the house of *God* **El**
Sherezer **Shareser** and *Regemmelech* **Regem Melech**,
and their men,
to *pray before the LORD* **stroke the face of Yah Veh**,
3 And to *speak* **say** unto the priests which were in
the house of *the LORD of hosts* **Yah Veh Sabaoth**,
and to the prophets, saying,
should I weep in the fifth month,
separating myself,
as I have *done* **worked** these so many years?
4 Then came the word
of *the LORD of hosts* **Yah Veh Sabaoth** unto me, saying,
5 Speak unto all the people of the land, and to the priests,
saying,
When ye fasted and *mourned* **chopped**
in the fifth and seventh *month*,
even those seventy years,
did ye at all fast **in fasting, fasted ye** unto me,
even to me?
6 And when ye *did eat* **ate**, and when ye *did drink* **drank**,
did not ye eat for yourselves **ate ye not**,
and *drink* **drank ye not** for *yourselves* **them**?
7 *Should ye not hear* **Are not these** the words
which *the LORD* **Yah Veh** hath *cried* **called out**
by **the hand of** the former prophets,
when *Jerusalem* **Yeru Shalem**
was *inhabited* **settled** and *in prosperity* **serene**,
and the cities *thereof* round about her,
when *men inhabited* **they settled** the south
and the *plain* **lowland**?
8 And the word of *the LORD* **Yah Veh**
came unto *Zechariah* **Zechar Yah**, saying,
9 Thus *speaketh* **saith**
the LORD of hosts **Yah Veh Sabaoth**, saying,
Execute true judgment **Judge judgment in truth**,
and *shew* **work** mercy and *compassions* **mercies**
every man to his brother:
10 And oppress not the widow, nor the *fatherless* **orphan**,
the *stranger* **sojourner**, nor the *poor* **humble**;
and let *none* **no man** of you *imagine* **fabricate** evil
against his brother in your heart.
11 But they refused to hearken,
and *pulled away the* **gave a revolting** shoulder,
and *stopped* **made heavy** their ears,
that they should not hear.
12 Yea, they *made* **set** their hearts
as *an adamant stone* **a brier**,
lest they should hear the *law* **torah**,
and the words
which *the LORD of hosts* **Yah Veh Sabaoth**
hath sent in his spirit by **the hand of** the former prophets:
therefore came a great *wrath* **rage**
from *the LORD of hosts* **Yah Veh Sabaoth**.
13 Therefore it is *come to pass* **become**,
that as he *cried* **called out**,
and they *would* **should** not hear;
so they *cried* **called out**,
and I *would* **should** not hear,
saith *the LORD of hosts* **Yah Veh Sabaoth**:
14 But I *scattered* **stormed** them *with a whirlwind*
among all the *nations* **goyim** whom they knew not.
Thus the land *was desolate* **desolated** after them,
that no *man* **one** passed through nor returned:
for they *laid the pleasant* **set the** land **of desire** desolate.

YAH VEH'S NEW RELATIONSHIP WITH YISRA EL

8 Again the word
of *the LORD of hosts* **Yah Veh Sabaoth**
came *to me*, saying,
2 Thus saith *the LORD of hosts* **Yah Veh Sabaoth**;
I was jealous for *Zion* **Siyon** with great jealousy,
and I was jealous for her with great fury.
3 Thus saith *the LORD* **Yah Veh**;
I am returned unto *Zion* **Siyon**,
and *will dwell* **shall tabernacle**
in the midst of *Jerusalem* **Yeru Shalem**:
and *Jerusalem* **Yeru Shalem** shall be called a city of truth;
and the mountain of *the LORD of hosts* **Yah Veh Sabaoth**
the holy mountain.
4 Thus saith *the LORD of hosts* **Yah Veh Sabaoth**;
There shall yet
old men **eldermen** and *old women* **elderwomen**
dwell **settle** in the *streets* **broadways**
of *Jerusalem* **Yeru Shalem**,
and every man with his *staff* **crutch** in his hand
for *very age* **abundance of days**.
5 And the *streets* **broadways** of the city
shall be *full* **filled** of boys and girls
playing in the *streets* **broadways** *thereof*.
6 Thus saith *the LORD of hosts* **Yah Veh Sabaoth**;
If it be marvellous
in the eyes of the *remnant* **survivors** of this people
in these days,
should it **not** also be marvellous in mine eyes?
saith the LORD of hosts **an oracle of Yah Veh Sabaoth**.
7 Thus saith *the LORD of hosts* **Yah Veh Sabaoth**;
Behold, I *will save* **am the saviour of** my people
from the *east country* **land of the rising**,
and from the *west country*
land of the entrance of the sun;
8 And I *will* **shall** bring them,
and they shall *dwell* **tabernacle**
in the midst of *Jerusalem* **Yeru Shalem**:
and they *shall* be my people,
and *I will be* **I AM** their *God* **Elohim**,
in truth and in *righteousness* **justness**.
9 Thus saith *the LORD of hosts* **Yah Veh Sabaoth**;
Let your hands be strong,
ye that hear in these days
these words by the mouth of the prophets,
which were in the day that the foundation
of the house of *the LORD of hosts* **Yah Veh Sabaoth**
was *laid* **founded**,
that the *temple* **manse** might be built.
10 For *before* **at the face of** these days
there was no hire for *man* **humanity**,
nor any hire for *beast* **animal**;
neither *was* there any *peace* **shalom** to him
that went out or came in
because of the *affliction* **tribulation**:
for I *set* **send** all *men* **humanity**
every *one* **man** against his *neighbour* **friend**.
11 But now
I *will* **shall** not be
unto the *residue* **survivors** of this people
as in the former days,
saith the LORD of hosts **an oracle of Yah Veh Sabaoth**.
12 For the seed shall be *prosperous* **at shalom**;

the vine shall give her fruit,
and the *ground* **earth** shall give her *increase* **produce**,
and the heavens shall give their dew;
and I *will* **shall** cause
the *remnant* **survivors** of this people
to possess all these *things*.
13 And it shall *come to pass* **become**,
that as ye were *a curse* **an abasement**
among the *heathen* **goyim**,
O house of *Judah* **Yah Hudah**,
and house of *Israel* **Yisra El**;
so *will* **shall** I save you, and ye shall be a blessing:
fear **awe** not, *but* let your hands be strong.
14 For thus saith *the LORD of hosts* **Yah Veh Sabaoth**;
As I *thought* **intrigued** to *punish* **vilify** you,
when your fathers *provoked* **enraged** me *to wrath*,
saith *the LORD of hosts* **Yah Veh Sabaoth**,
and I *repented* **sighed** not:
15 So *again* have I *thought* **turned back and intrigued**
in these days to *do well*—**please**
unto Jerusalem **Yeru Shalem**
and *to* the house of *Judah* **Yah Hudah**:
fear **awe** ye not.
16 These are the *things* **words** that ye shall *do* **work**;
Speak **Word** ye every man
the truth to his *neighbour* **friend**;
execute the judgment of truth **judge truth and judgment**
and peace **shalom** in your *gates* **portals**:
17 And let *none* **no man** of you
imagine **fabricate** evil in your hearts
against his *neighbour* **friend**;
and love no false oath:
for all these are *things* **those** that I hate,
saith the LORD **an oracle of Yah Veh**.
18 And the word of *the LORD of hosts* **Yah Veh Sabaoth**
came unto me, saying,
19 Thus saith *the LORD of hosts* **Yah Veh Sabaoth**;
The fast of the fourth *month*, and the fast of the fifth,
and the fast of the seventh, and the fast of the tenth,
shall be to the house of *Judah* **Yah Hudah**
joy **rejoicing** and *gladness* **cheerfulness**,
and *cheerful feasts* **good seasons**;
therefore love the truth and *peace* **shalom**.
20 Thus saith *the LORD of hosts* **Yah Veh Sabaoth**;
It shall yet come to pass,
that there shall **yet** come people,
and the *inhabitants* **settlers** of many cities:
21 And the *inhabitants* **settlers** of one *city*
shall go to *another* **one**, saying,
Let us go speedily
to *pray before the LORD* **stroke the face of Yah Veh**,
and to seek *the LORD of hosts* **Yah Veh Sabaoth**:
I *will* **shall** go also.
22 Yea, many people and *strong nations* **mighty goyim**
shall come to seek *the LORD of hosts* **Yah Veh Sabaoth**
in *Jerusalem* **Yeru Shalem**,
and to *pray before the LORD* **stroke the face of Yah Veh**.
23 Thus saith *the LORD of hosts* **Yah Veh Sabaoth**;
In those days it shall *come to pass* **become**,
that ten men shall take hold
out of all *languages* **tongues** of the *nations* **goyim**,
even shall take hold of the *skirt* **wing**
of *him that is a Jew* **a man Yah Hudiy**,
saying, We *will* **shall** go with you:
for we have heard that *God* **Elohim** is with you.

THE BURDEN OF YAH VEH

9 The burden of the word of *the LORD* **Yah Veh**
in the land of Hadrach,
and *Damascus* **Dammeseq** shall be the rest *thereof*:
when the eyes of *man* **humanity**,
as of all the *tribes* **scions** of *Israel* **Yisra El**,
shall be toward *the LORD* **Yah Veh**.
2 And Hamath also shall border thereby;
Tyrus **Sor**, and *Zidon* **Sidon**,
though it be *very wise* **mightily enwisened**.
3 And *Tyrus* **Sor**
did build **built** herself a *strong hold* **rampart**,
and heaped *up* silver as the dust,
and *fine gold* **ore** as the mire of the *streets* **outways**.
4 Behold, *the Lord will* **Adonay shall** cast her out,
and he *will* **shall** smite her *power* **valiant** in the sea;
and she shall be devoured with fire.
5 Ashkelon shall see *it*, and *fear* **awe**;
Gaza **Azzah** also shall see *it*,
and *be very sorrowful* **writhe mightily**, and *Ekron* **Eqron**;
for her expectation shall be ashamed;
and the *king* **sovereign**
shall *perish* **destruct** from *Gaza* **Azzah**,
and Ashkelon shall not be *inhabited* **settled**.
6 And a *bastard* **mongrel** shall *dwell* **settle** in Ashdod,
and I *will* **shall** cut off
the *pride* **pomp** of the *Philistines* **Peleshethiym**.
7 And I *will take away* **shall turn aside**
his blood out of his mouth,
and his abominations from between his teeth:
but he that *remaineth* **surviveth**,
even he, shall be for our *God* **Elohim**,
and he shall be
as a *governor* **chiliarch** in *Judah* **Yah Hudah**,
and *Ekron* **Eqron** as a *Jebusite* **Yebusiy**.
8 And I *will* **shall** encamp about mine house
because of the *army* **station**,
because of him that passeth by,
and because of him that returneth:
and no *oppressor* **exactor**
shall pass through them any more:
for now have I seen with mine eyes.

THE SAVING SOVEREIGN

9 *Rejoice greatly* **Twirl mightily**,
O daughter of *Zion* **Siyon**;
shout, O daughter of *Jerusalem* **Yeru Shalem**:
behold, thy *King* **Sovereign** cometh unto thee:
he is just, and *having salvation* **saving**;
lowly **humble**, and riding upon *an ass* **a burro**,
and upon a colt the *foal of an ass* **son of a she burro**.
10 And I *will* **shall** cut off
the chariot from *Ephraim* **Ephrayim**,
and the horse from *Jerusalem* **Yeru Shalem**,
and the *battle* **war** bow shall be cut off:
and he shall *speak peace* **word shalom**
unto the *heathen* **goyim**:
and his dominion shall be from sea *even* to sea,
and from the river *even* to the *ends* **finalities** of the earth.
11 As for thee also,
by the blood of thy covenant
I have sent forth thy prisoners
out of the *pit* **well** wherein is no water.
12 Turn you to the *strong hold* **fortress**,
ye prisoners of hope:
even to day *do I declare* **I tell**
that I *will render* **shall return** double unto thee;
13 When I have bent *Judah* **Yah Hudah** for me,
filled the bow with *Ephraim* **Ephrayim**,
and *raised up* **wakened** thy sons, O *Zion* **Siyon**,
against thy sons, O *Greece* **Yavan**,
and *made* **set** thee as the sword of a mighty *man*.
14 And *the LORD* **Yah Veh** shall be seen over them,
and his arrow shall go forth as the lightning:
and *the Lord GOD* **Adonay Yah Veh**
shall *blow* **blast** the trumpet,
and shall go with *whirlwinds* **storms** of the south.
15 *The LORD of hosts* **Yah Veh Sabaoth**
shall defend them;
and they shall devour, and subdue with sling stones;
and they shall drink, and make a noise as through wine;
and they shall be filled like *bowls* **sprinklers**,
and as the corners of the **sacrifice** altar.
16 And *the LORD* **Yah Veh** their *God* **Elohim**
shall save them in that day as the flock of his people:
for they shall be as the stones of *a crown* **separatism**,
lifted up **raised** as an ensign upon his *land* **soil**.
17 For how great is his goodness,
and how great is his beauty!
corn **crop**
shall make the *young men cheerful* **youths flourish**,
and *new wine* **juice** the *maids* **virgins**.

YAH VEH'S PROVISION

10 Ask ye of *the LORD* **Yah Veh** rain
in the time of the *latter* **after** rain;
so *the LORD* **Yah Veh**

shall *make bright clouds* **work lightnings,**
and give them *showers* **downpours** of *rain* **downpour,**
to every *one grass* **man herbage** in the field.
2 For the *idols* **teraphim**
have *spoken vanity* **worded mischief,**
and the diviners have seen a *lie* **falsehood,**
and have *told false* **worded vain** dreams;
they *comfort* **sigh** in vain:
therefore they went their way as a flock,
they *were troubled* **answered,**
because **that** there was no *shepherd* **tender.**
3 *Mine anger* **My wrath**
was kindled against the *shepherds* **tenders,**
and I *punished* **visited** the **he** goats:
for *the LORD of hosts* **Yah Veh Sabaoth**
hath visited his *flock* **drove**
the house of *Judah* **Yah Hudah,**
and hath *made* **set** them
as his *goodly* horse **of majesty** in the battle.
4 Out of him came forth the corner,
out of him the *nail* **stake,** out of him the battle bow,
out of him every *oppressor* **exactor** together.
5 And they shall be as mighty *men,*
which *tread down their enemies* **trample**
in the mire of the *streets* **outways** in the battle:
and they shall fight,
because *the LORD* **Yah Veh** is with them,
and the riders on horses shall be *confounded* **shamed.**
6 And *I will strengthen* **prevail mightily**
shall the house of *Judah* **Yah Hudah,**
and I *will* **shall** save the house of *Joseph* **Yoseph,**
and I *will bring them again to place* **shall resettle** them;
for I *have* mercy *upon* them:
and they shall be as though I had not cast them off:
for *I am the LORD* **I — Yah Veh** their *God* **Elohim,**
and *will hear* **shall answer** them.
7 And *they of Ephraim* **Ephrayim**
shall be like a mighty *man,*
and their heart shall *rejoice* **cheer** as through wine:
yea, their *children* **sons** shall see it, and *be glad* **cheer;**
their heart shall *rejoice* **twirl** in *the LORD* **Yah Veh.**
8 I *will* **shall** hiss for them, and gather them;
for I have redeemed them:
and they shall *increase* **abound**
as they have *increased* **abounded.**
9 And I *will sow* **shall seed** them among the people:
and they shall remember me *in far countries* **afar off;**
and they shall live with their *children* **sons,**
and turn again.
10 I *will bring* **shall return** them *again also*
out of the land of *Egypt* **Misrayim,**
and gather them out of *Assyria* **Ashshur;**
and I *will* **shall** bring them
into the land of *Gilead* **Gilad** and Lebanon;
and *place* shall not be found for them.
11 And he shall pass through the sea
with *affliction* **tribulation,**
and shall smite the waves in the sea,
and all the deeps of the river shall *dry up* **wither:**
and the *pride* **pomp** of *Assyria* **Ashshur**
shall be brought down,
and the *sceptre* **scion** of *Egypt* **Misrayim**
shall *depart away* **turn aside.**
12 And *I will strengthen them* **they shall prevail mightily**
in *the LORD* **Yah Veh;**
and they shall walk up and down in his name,
saith the LORD **an oracle of Yah Veh.**

THE RAVAGE OF LEBANON

11 Open thy doors, O Lebanon,
that the fire may *devour* **consume** thy cedars.
2 Howl, fir tree; for the cedar is fallen;
because the mighty are *spoiled* **ravaged:**
howl, O ye oaks of Bashan;
for the forest of the *vintage* **crop**
is come down **be toppled.**
3 There is a voice
of the howling of the *shepherds* **tenders;**
for their *glory is spoiled* **mighty be ravaged:**
a voice of the roaring of *young lions* **whelps;**
for the *pride* **pomp** of *Jordan* **Yarden**
is spoiled **be ravaged.**
4 Thus saith *the LORD* **Yah Veh** my *God* **Elohim;**
Feed **Tend** the flock of the slaughter;
5 Whose *possessors slay* **chattelers slaughter** them,
and *hold themselves not guilty* **have not guilted:**
and they that sell them say,
Blessed be *the LORD* **Yah Veh;** for I am *rich* **enriched:**
and their own *shepherds pity* **tenders spare** them not.
6 For I *will* **shall** no more
pity **spare** the *inhabitants* **settlers** of the land,
saith the LORD **an oracle of Yah Veh:**
but, *lo* **behold,**
I *will deliver the men* **shall present humanity**
every one **each man** into his *neighbour's* **friend's** hand,
and into the hand of his *king* **sovereign:**
and they shall *smite* **crush** the land,
and out of their hand I *will* **shall** not *deliver* **rescue** them.
7 And I *will feed* **shall tend** the flock of slaughter,
even you **thus,** O *poor* **humble** of the flock.
And I took unto me two staves;
the one I called *Beauty* **Pleasantness,**
and the *other* **one** I called Bands;
and I *fed* **tended** the flock.
8 Three *shepherds* **tenders** also
I *cut* **chopped** off in one month;
and my soul lothed them,
and their soul also *abhorred* **lothed** me.
9 Then said I, I *will* **shall** not *feed* **tend** you:
that that dieth, let it die;
and that that is to be cut off, let it be cut off;
and let *the rest* **them that survive**
eat every one **each woman eat** the flesh of *another* **sister.**
10 And I took my staff, *even Beauty* **Pleasantness,**
and cut it asunder,
that I might break my covenant
which I had *made* **cut** with all the people.
11 And it was broken in that day:
and so the *poor* **humble** of the flock
that *waited upon* **guarded** me
knew that it was the word of *the LORD* **Yah Veh.**
12 And I said unto them,
If *ye think* **it be** good **in thine eyes,**
give *me* my *price* **hire;**
and if not, *forbear* **cease.**
So they weighed for my *price* **hire** thirty *pieces of* silver.
13 And *the LORD* **Yah Veh** said unto me,
Cast it unto the *potter* **former:**
a *goodly price* **mighty estimation**
that I was *prised* **appraised** at of them.
And I took the thirty *pieces* of silver,
and cast them to the *potter* **former**
in the house of *the LORD* **Yah Veh.**
14 Then I cut asunder *mine other* **my second** staff,
even Bands,
that I might break the brotherhood
between *Judah* **Yah Hudah** and *Israel* **Yisra El.**
15 And *the LORD* **Yah Veh** said unto me,
Take unto thee yet
the instruments of a foolish *shepherd* **tender.**
16 For, *lo* **behold,**
I *will* **shall** raise up a *shepherd* **tender** in the land,
which shall not visit those that be cut off,
neither shall seek the *young one* **lad,**
nor heal that that is broken,
nor *feed* **sustain** that that *standeth still* **be stationed:**
but he shall eat the flesh of the fat,
and *tear* **craunch** their *claws in pieces* **hoofs.**
17 *Woe* **Ho** to the idol *shepherd* **tender**
that *leaveth* **forsaketh** the flock!
the sword shall be upon his arm, and upon his right eye:
his arm shall *be clean dried up* **wither,**
and **in dimming,**
his right eye shall be *utterly darkened* **dimmed.**

THE SIEGE OF YERU SHALEM

12 The burden of the word of *the LORD* **Yah Veh**
for *Israel* **Yisra El,**
saith the LORD **an oracle of Yah Veh,**
which stretcheth forth the heavens,
and layeth the foundation of the earth,
and formeth the spirit of *man* **humanity** within him.

2 Behold, I *will make Jerusalem* **shall set Yeru Shalem**
a *cup* **bason** of *trembling* **staggering**
unto all the people round about,
when they shall be in the siege
both against *Judah* **Yah Hudah**
and against *Jerusalem* **Yeru Shalem**.
3 And in that day
will I make Jerusalem **shall I set Yeru Shalem**
a *burdensome* stone **of burden** for all *people* **goyim**:
all that burden themselves with it
in incising, shall be *cut in pieces* **incised**,
though all the people of the earth
be gathered *together* against it.

THE LIBERATION OF YERU SHALEM

4 In that day,
saith the LORD **an oracle of Yah Veh**,
I *will* **shall** smite
every horse with *astonishment* **consternation**,
and his rider with *madness* **insanity**:
and I *will* **shall** open mine eyes
upon the house of *Judah* **Yah Hudah**,
and *will* **shall** smite
every horse of the people with blindness.
5 And the *governors* **chiliarchs** of *Judah* **Yah Hudah**
shall say in their heart,
The *inhabitants* **settlers** of *Jerusalem* **Yeru Shalem**
shall be my strength
in *the LORD of hosts* **Yah Veh Sabaoth** their *God* **Elohim**.
6 In that day *will* I *make* **shall I set**
the *governors* **chiliarchs** of *Judah* **Yah Hudah**
like an *hearth* **laver** of fire among the *wood* **timber**,
and like a *torch* **flambeau** of fire in *a sheaf* **an omer**;
and they shall devour all the people round about,
on the right *hand* and on the left:
and *Jerusalem* **Yeru Shalem**
shall be *inhabited* **settled** again in her own place,
even in *Jerusalem* **Yeru Shalem**.
7 *The LORD* **Yah Veh** also
shall save the tents of *Judah* **Yah Hudah** first,
that the *glory* **adornment** of the house of David
and the *glory* **adornment**
of the *inhabitants* **settlers** of *Jerusalem* **Yeru Shalem**
do not magnify themselves **greaten not**
against *Judah* **Yah Hudah**.
8 In that day shall *the LORD* **Yah Veh**
defend the *inhabitants* **settlers** of *Jerusalem* **Yeru Shalem**;
and he that *is feeble* **faltereth** among them at that day
shall be as David;
and the house of David shall be as *God* **Elohim**,
as the angel of *the LORD* **Yah Veh**
before **at the face of** them.
9 And it shall *come to pass* **become,** in that day,
that I *will* **shall** seek
to *destroy* **desolate** all the *nations* **goyim**
that come against *Jerusalem* **Yeru Shalem**.

THE SPIRIT OF CHARISM

10 And I *will* **shall** pour upon the house of David,
and upon
the *inhabitants* **settlers** of *Jerusalem* **Yeru Shalem**,
the spirit of *grace* **charism** and of supplications:
and they shall look upon me whom they have pierced,
and they shall *mourn* **chop** for him,
as one *mourneth* **choppeth** for his only *son,*
and shall be *in bitterness* **embittered** for him,
as one that is *in bitterness* **embittered** for his firstborn.

THE CHOPPING IN YERU SHALEM

11 In that day
shall there *be a great mourning* **greaten a chopping**
in *Jerusalem* **Yeru Shalem**,
as the *mourning* **chopping**
of *Hadadrimmon* **Hadad Rimmon**
in the valley of *Megiddon* **Megiddo**.
12 And the land shall *mourn* **chop**,
every family **families by families** apart;
the family of the house of David apart,
and their *wives* **women** apart;
the family of the house of Nathan apart,
and their *wives* **women** apart;
13 The family of the house of Levi apart,
and their *wives* **women** apart;
the family of *Shimei* **Shimiy** apart,
and their *wives* **women** apart;
14 All the families that *remain* **survive**,
every family **families by families** apart,
and their *wives* **women** apart.

THE FOUNTAIN FOR SIN AND FOR EXCLUSION

13 In that day there shall be a fountain opened
to the house of David
and to the *inhabitants* **settlers** of *Jerusalem* **Yeru Shalem**
for sin and for *uncleanness* **exclusion**.
2 And it shall *come to pass* **become,** in that day,
saith the LORD of hosts **an oracle of Yah Veh Sabaoth**,
that I *will* **shall** cut off the names of the idols
out of the land,
and they shall no more be remembered:
and also I *will* **shall** cause the prophets
and the *unclean* spirit **of foulness** to pass out of the land.
3 And it shall *come to pass* **become**,
that when any **man** shall yet prophesy,
then his father and his mother that begat him
shall say unto him, Thou shalt not live;
for thou *speakest lies* **wordest falsehoods**
in the name of *the LORD* **Yah Veh**:
and his father and his mother that begat him
shall thrust him through when he prophesieth.
4 And it shall *come to pass* **become,** in that day,
that the prophets shall *be ashamed* **shame**
every one **each man** of his vision,
when he hath prophesied;
neither shall they *wear* **enrobe**
a *rough garment* **mighty mantle of hair** to deceive:
5 But he shall say, I am no prophet,
I am *an husbandman* **a man that serveth the soil**;
for man taught me to keep cattle **a human chatteler**
from my youth.
6 And one shall say unto him,
What are these wounds in thine hands?
Then he shall *answer* **say,**
Those with which I was *wounded* **smitten**
in the house of my *friends* **beloved**.
7 Awake, O sword, against my *shepherd* **tender**,
and against the *man* **mighty** that is my *fellow* **friend**,
saith the LORD of hosts **an oracle of Yah Veh Sabaoth**:
smite the *shepherd* **tender**,
and the *sheep* **flock** shall be scattered:
and I *will* **shall** turn mine hand
upon the *little ones* **belittled**.
8 And it shall *come to pass* **become,** that in all the land,
saith the LORD **an oracle of Yah Veh**,
two *parts* **mouths** therein shall be cut off and *die* **expire**;
but the third shall *be left* **remain** therein.
9 And I *will* **shall** bring the third *part* through the fire,
and *will* **shall** refine them as silver is refined,
and *will try* **shall proof** them as gold is *tried* **proofed**:
they shall call on my name,
and I *will hear* **shall answer** them:
I *will* **shall** say, *It is my people* **My people**:
and they shall say,
The LORD is my God **Yah Veh, My Elohim**.

THE GATHERING OF THE GOYIM

14 Behold, the day of *the LORD* **Yah Veh** cometh,
and thy spoil
shall be *divided* **allotted** in the midst of thee.
2 For I *will* **shall** gather all *nations* **goyim**
against *Jerusalem* **Yeru Shalem** to battle;
and the city shall be *taken* **captured**,
and the houses *rifled* **plundered**,
and the women *ravished* **lain with and raped**;
and half of the city shall go forth into *captivity* **exile**,
and the *residue* **remnant** of the people
shall not be cut off from the city.
3 Then shall *the LORD* **Yah Veh** go forth,
and fight against those *nations* **goyim**,
as *when* **the day** he fought in the day of *battle* **war**.

THE RETURN OF YAH VEH

4 And his feet shall stand in that day
upon the mount of Olives,
which is before Jerusalem **at the face of Yeru Shalem**
on the *east* **rising**,
and the mount of Olives

shall *cleave* **split** in *the midst thereof* **half**
toward the east **eastward** and *toward the west* **seaward**,
and there shall be a *very* **mighty** great valley;
and half of the mountain
shall *remove toward the north* **depart northward**,
and half of it *toward the south* **southward**.
5 And ye shall flee to the valley of the mountains;
for the valley of the mountains
shall *reach* **touch** unto *Azal* **Asel**:
yea, ye shall flee, like as ye fled
from *before* **the face of** the *earthquake* **quake**
in the days of *Uzziah* **Uzzi Yah**
king **sovereign** of *Judah* **Yah Hudah**:
and *the LORD* **Yah Veh** my *God* **Elohim** shall come,
and all the *saints* **holy** with thee.
6 And it shall *come to pass* **become** in that day,
that the light shall not be *clear* **esteemed**,
nor *dark* **curdled**:
7 But it shall be one day
which shall be known to *the LORD* **Yah Veh**,
not day, nor night:
but it shall *come to pass* **become**,
that at evening time it shall be light.
8 And it shall be in that day,
that living waters
shall go out from *Jerusalem* **Yeru Shalem**;
half of them toward the *former* **ancient** sea,
and half of them toward the *hinder* **latter** sea:
in summer and in winter shall it be.
9 And *the LORD* **Yah Veh** shall be *king* **sovereign**
over all the earth:
in that day shall there be one *LORD* **Yah Veh**,
and his name one.
10 All the land shall be *turned* **surrounded** as a plain
from Geba to Rimmon south of *Jerusalem* **Yeru Shalem**:
and it shall be lifted *up*,
and *inhabited* **settled** in her place,
from *Benjamin's gate* **the portal of Ben Yamin**
unto the place of the first *gate* **portal**,
unto the corner *gate* **portal**,
and from the tower of *Hananeel* **Hanan El**
unto the *king's winepresses* **sovereign's troughs**.
11 And *men* shall *dwell* **settle** in it,
and there shall be no more *utter destruction* **devotement**;
but *Jerusalem* **Yeru Shalem**
shall be *safely inhabited* **confidently settled**.
12 And this shall be the plague
wherewith *the LORD* **Yah Veh**
will **shall** smite all the people
that have *fought* **hosted** against *Jerusalem* **Yeru Shalem**;
Their flesh shall *consume away* **dissolve**
while they stand upon their feet,
and their eyes shall *consume away* **dissolve**
in their holes,
and their tongue shall *consume away* **dissolve**
in their mouth.
13 And it shall *come to pass* **become** in that day,
that a great *tumult* **confusion** from *the LORD* **Yah Veh**
shall be among them;
and they shall lay hold *every one* **each man**
on the hand of his *neighbour* **friend**,
and his hand shall *rise up* **ascend**
against the hand of his *neighbour* **friend**.
14 And *Judah* **Yah Hudah** also
shall fight at *Jerusalem* **Yeru Shalem**;
and the *wealth* **valuables**
of all the *heathen* **goyim** round about
shall be gathered *together*,
gold, and silver, and *apparel* **clothes**,
in *great* **mighty** abundance.
15 And so shall be the plague of the horse,
of the mule, of the camel, and of the *ass* **burro**,
and of all the *beasts* **animals**
that shall be in these *tents* **camps**,
as this plague.
16 And it shall *come to pass* **become**,
that every one that *is left* **remaineth**
of all the *nations* **goyim**
which came against *Jerusalem* **Yeru Shalem**
shall *even go up from* **ascend sufficiently** year to year
to *worship* **prostrate to** the *King* **Sovereign**,
the LORD of hosts **Yah Veh Sabaoth**,
and to *keep* **celebrate** the *feast* **celebration**
of *tabernacles* **sukkoth/brush arbors**.
17 And it shall be,
that whoso *will* **shall** not *come up* **ascend**
of *all* the families of the earth
unto *Jerusalem* **Yeru Shalem**
to *worship* **prostrate to** the *King* **Sovereign**,
the LORD of hosts **Yah Veh Sabaoth**,
even upon them shall be no *rain* **downpour**.
18 And if the family of *Egypt go* **Misrayim ascend** not *up*,
and come not,
that have no rain; **then not on them**
there shall be the plague,
wherewith *the LORD* **Yah Veh**
will **shall** smite the *heathen* **goyim**
that *come* **ascend** not *up*
to *keep* **celebrate** the *feast* **celebration**
of *tabernacles* **sukkoth/brush arbors**.
19 This shall be
the punishment **for the sin** of *Egypt* **Misrayim**,
and *the punishment* **for the sin** of all *nations* **goyim**
that *come* **ascend** not *up*
to keep **celebrate** the *feast* **celebration**
of *tabernacles* **sukkoth/brush arbors**.
20 In that day shall there be
upon the *bells* **jinglers** of the horses,
HOLINESS UNTO *THE LORD* **YAH VEH**;
and the *pots* **caldrons**
in the *LORD'S* house **of Yah Veh**
shall be like the *bowls* **sprinklers**
before **at the face of** the **sacrifice** altar.
21 Yea, every *pot* **caldron**
in *Jerusalem* **Yeru Shalem** and in *Judah* **Yah Hudah**
shall be *holiness* **holy**
unto *the LORD of hosts* **Yah Veh Sabaoth**:
and all they that sacrifice shall come and take of them,
and *seethe* **stew** therein:
and in that day
there shall be no more the *Canaanite* **Kenaaniy**
in the house of *the LORD of hosts* **Yah Veh Sabaoth**.

KEY TO INTERPRETING THE EXEGESES:
King James text is in regular type;
Text under exegeses is in oblique type;
Text of exegeses is in bold type.

YAH VEH'S LOVE FOR YISRA EL

1 The burden of the word of *the LORD* **Yah Veh**
to *Israel* **Yisra El** by **the hand of** Malachi.
2 I have loved you,
saith the LORD **an oracle of Yah Veh.**
Yet ye say, Wherein hast thou loved us?
Was not *Esau Jacob's* **Esav Yaaqov's** brother?
saith *the LORD* **Yah Veh:**
yet I loved *Jacob* **Yaaqov,**
3 And I hated *Esau* **Esav,**
and *laid* **set** his mountains
and his *heritage* **inheritance** waste
for the *dragons* **monsters** of the wilderness.
4 Whereas Edom saith, We are impoverished,
but we *will* **shall** return
and build the *desolate places* **parched areas;**
thus saith *the LORD of hosts* **Yah Veh Sabaoth,**
They shall build, but I *will throw* **shall break** down;
and they shall call them, The border of wickedness,
and, The people against whom *the LORD* **Yah Veh**
hath indignation for ever **be enraged eternally.**
5 And your eyes shall see, and ye shall say,
The LORD will **Yah Veh shall** be *magnified* **greatened**
from the border of *Israel* **Yisra El.**

PRIESTS PROFANE THE SACRIFICE ALTAR

6 A son honoureth his father,
and a servant his *master* **adoni:**
if then I be a father, where is mine honour?
and if I be *a master* **an adoni,**
where is my *fear* **awesomeness?**
saith *the LORD of hosts* **Yah Veh Sabaoth** unto you,
O priests, that despise my name.
And ye say, Wherein have we despised thy name?
7 Ye *offer polluted* **bring profaned** bread
upon *mine* **my sacrifice** altar;
and ye say, Wherein have we *polluted* **profaned** thee?
In that ye say **Saying,**
The table of *the LORD* **Yah Veh**
is *contemptible* **despised.**
8 And if ye *offer* **bring near** the blind for sacrifice,
is it not evil?
and if ye *offer* **bring near** the lame and sick, is it not evil?
offer **oblate** it *now* **I beseech,** unto thy governor;
will **shall** he be pleased with thee,
or *accept* **lift** thy *person* **face?**
saith *the LORD of hosts* **Yah Veh Sabaoth.**
9 And now, I *pray* **beseech** you,
beseech God **stroke the face of El**
that he *will be gracious* **shall grant charism** unto us:
this hath been by your *means* **hand:**
will **shall** he *regard* **lift** your *persons* **faces?**
saith *the LORD of hosts* **Yah Veh Sabaoth.**
10 Who is there even among you
that *would* **should** shut the doors *for nought?*
neither do ye *kindle fire on mine* **light my sacrifice** altar
for nought **gratuitously.**
I have no *pleasure* **delight** in you,
saith *the LORD of hosts* **Yah Veh Sabaoth,**
neither *will I accept* **shall** an offering
at your hand **please me.**
11 For from the rising of the sun
even unto the *going down* **entry** of the same
my name shall be great among the *Gentiles* **goyim;**
and in every place
incense shall be *offered* **brought near** unto my name,
and a pure offering:
for my name shall be great among the *heathen* **goyim,**
saith *the LORD of hosts* **Yah Veh Sabaoth.**
12 But ye have profaned it, *in that ye say* **saying,**
The table of *the LORD* **Yah Veh** is *polluted* **profaned;**
and the fruit *thereof,*
even his *meat* **food,** is contemptible.
13 Ye said also, Behold, what *a weariness is it* **trouble!**
and ye have *snuffed* **puffed** at it,
saith *the LORD of hosts* **Yah Veh Sabaoth;**
and ye brought that which was *torn* **stripped,**
and the lame, and the sick;
thus ye brought an offering:
should *I accept* this of your hand **please?**
saith *the LORD* **Yah Veh.**
14 But cursed be the deceiver,
which hath in his *flock* **drove** a male,
and voweth, and sacrificeth
unto *the Lord corrupt thing* **Adonay** a **ruin:**
for I am a great *King* **Sovereign,**
saith *the LORD of hosts* **Yah Veh Sabaoth,**
and my name is *dreadful* **awesome**
among the *heathen* **goyim.**

A MISVAH FOR THE PRIESTS

2 And now, O ye priests,
this *commandment* **misvah** is for you.
2 If ye *will* **shall** not hear,
and if ye *will* **shall** not *lay* **set** it to heart,
to give *glory* **honour** unto my name,
saith *the LORD of hosts* **Yah Veh Sabaoth,**
I *will* **shall** even send a curse upon you,
and I *will* **shall** curse your blessings:
yea, I have cursed them already,
because ye *do not lay* **set** it **not** to heart.
3 Behold, I *will corrupt* **shall rebuke** your seed,
and *spread* **winnow** dung upon your faces,
even the dung of your *solemn feasts* **celebrations;**
and one shall *take* **bear** you away with it.
4 And ye shall know
that I have sent this *commandment* **misvah** unto you,
that my covenant might be with Levi,
saith *the LORD of hosts* **Yah Veh Sabaoth.**
5 My covenant was with him of life and *peace* **shalom;**
and I gave them to him for the *fear* **awesomeness**
wherewith he *feared* **awed** me,
and was *afraid before* **dismayed at the face of** my name.
6 The *law* **torah** of truth was in his mouth,
and *iniquity* **perversity** was not found in his lips:
he walked with me
in *peace* **shalom** and *equity* **straightness**
and *did turn* **turned** many away from iniquity.
7 For the priest's lips should *keep* **guard** knowledge,
and they should seek the *law* **torah** at his mouth:
for he is the *messenger* **angel**
of *the LORD of hosts* **Yah Veh Sabaoth.**
8 But ye are *departed* **turned aside** out of the way;
ye have caused many to *stumble* **falter** at the *law* **torah;**
ye have *corrupted* **ruined** the covenant of Levi,
saith *the LORD of hosts* **Yah Veh Sabaoth.**
9 Therefore have I also *made* **given** you
contemptible **despised** and *base* **lowly**
before all the people,
according as **your mouth**
ye have not *kept* **guarded** my ways,
but have *been partial* **lifted thy face**
in **against** the *law* **torah.**
10 Have we not all one father?
hath not one *God* **El** created us?
why *do we deal treacherously* **deal we covertly**
every man against his brother,
by profaning the covenant of our fathers?
11 *Judah* **Yah Hudah** hath dealt *treacherously* **covertly,**
and an *abomination is committed* **abhorrence be worked**
in *Israel* **Yisra El** and in *Jerusalem* **Yeru Shalem;**
for *Judah* **Yah Hudah** hath profaned
the holiness of *the LORD* **Yah Veh** which he loved,
and hath married the daughter of a strange *god* **el.**
12 *The LORD will* **Yah Veh shall** cut off the man
that *doeth* **worketh** this,
the master **him that waketh**
and *the scholar* **him that answereth,**
out of the *tabernacles* **tents** of *Jacob* **Yaaqov,**
and him that *offereth* **bringeth near** an offering
unto *the LORD of hosts* **Yah Veh Sabaoth.**
13 And this have ye done *again* **secondly,**
covering the **sacrifice** altar of *the LORD* **Yah Veh**
with tears, with weeping, and with *crying out* **shrieking,**
insomuch
that he *regardeth* **faceth** not the offering any more,
or *receiveth* **taketh** it with *good will* **pleasure**
at your hand.

14 Yet ye say, *Wherefore* **Why**?
Because *the LORD* **Yah Veh** hath *been witness* **witnessed**
between thee and **between** the *wife* **woman** of thy youth,
against whom thou hast dealt *treacherously* **covertly**:
yet is she thy companion,
and the *wife* **woman** of thy covenant.
15 And *did not he make* **worked he not** one?
Yet had he the *residue of the* spirit **of survival**.
And wherefore one?
That he might seek a *godly* seed **of Elohim**.
Therefore take heed to **Guard** your spirit,
and let none deal *treacherously* **covertly**
against the *wife* **woman** of his youth.
16 For *the LORD* **Yah Veh**,
the God **Elohim** of *Israel* **Yisra El**,
saith that he hateth *putting* **sending** away:
for one covereth violence with his *garment* **robe**,
saith *the LORD of hosts* **Yah Veh Sabaoth**:
therefore take heed to **guard** your spirit,
that ye deal not *treacherously* **covertly**.
17 Ye have *wearied the LORD* **belaboured Yah Veh**
with your words.
Yet ye say, Wherein have we *wearied* **belaboured** him?
When ye say **Saying**,
Every one that *doeth* **worketh** evil
is good in the *sight* **eyes** of *the LORD* **Yah Veh**,
and he delighteth in them;
or, Where is the *God* **Elohim** of judgment?

PROPHECY OF YAH VEH'S ANGEL, AND HIS ADONAY

3 Behold, I *will* **shall** send my *messenger* **angel**,
and he shall *prepare* **face** the way *before me* **at my face**:
and the *Lord* **Adonay**, whom ye seek,
shall suddenly come to his *temple* **manse**,
even the *messenger* **angel** of the covenant,
whom ye delight in:
behold, he shall come,
saith *the LORD of hosts* **Yah Veh Sabaoth**.
Matthaios 11:10, Markos 1:2, Loukas 7:27
2 But who may *abide* **sustain** the day of his coming?
and who shall stand when he *appeareth* **be seen**?
for he is like a refiner's fire, and like fullers' soap:
3 And he shall sit as a refiner and purifier of silver:
and he shall purify the sons of Levi,
and purge them as gold and silver,
that they may *offer* **bring near** unto *the LORD* **Yah Veh**
an offering in *righteousness* **justness**.
4 Then shall the offering
of *Judah* **Yah Hudah** and *Jerusalem* **Yeru Shalem**
be pleasant unto the LORD **please Yah Veh**,
as in the *days of old for ever* **original eternal days**,
and as in *former* **ancient** years.
5 And I *will come near to* **shall approach** you to judgment;
and I *will* **shall** be a *swift* **hasty** witness
against the sorcerers,
and against the adulterers,
and against false *swearers* **oathers**,
and against those
that oppress the hireling in his *wages* **hire**,
the widow, and the *fatherless* **orphan**,
and that *turn aside* **pervert** the *stranger* **sojourner**
from his right,
and *fear* **awe** not me,
saith *the LORD of hosts* **Yah Veh Sabaoth**.
6 For *I am the LORD* **I — Yah Veh**, I change not;
therefore ye sons of *Jacob* **Yaaqov**
are not *consumed* **finished off**.

TITHING

7 Even from the days of your fathers
ye are *gone away* **turned aside**
from *mine ordinances* **my statutes**,
and have not *kept* **guarded** them.
Return unto me, and I *will* **shall** return unto you,
saith *the LORD of hosts* **Yah Veh Sabaoth**.
But ye said, Wherein shall we return?
8 *Will a man rob God* **Shall a human defraud Elohim**?
Yet ye have *robbed* **defrauded** me.
But ye say, Wherein have we *robbed* **defrauded** thee?
In tithes and *offerings* **exaltments**.
9 Ye are cursed with a curse:
for ye have *robbed* **defrauded** me,
even this whole *nation* **goyim**.
10 Bring ye all the tithes into the *storehouse* **treasure house**,
that there may be *meat* **prey** in mine house,
and *prove* **proof** me *now* **I beseech,** herewith,
saith *the LORD of hosts* **Yah Veh Sabaoth**,
if I *will* **shall** not open you
the windows of *heaven* **the heavens**,
and pour you out a blessing,
that there shall not be *room* enough *to receive it*.
11 And I *will* **shall** rebuke the devourer for your sakes,
and he shall not *destroy* **ruin** the fruits of your *ground* **soil**;
neither shall your vine *cast* **abort** her fruit
before the time in the field,
saith *the LORD of hosts* **Yah Veh Sabaoth**.
12 And all *nations* shall **goyim** call you *blessed* **blithesome**:
for ye shall be a delightsome land,
saith *the LORD of hosts* **Yah Veh Sabaoth**.
13 Your words have *been stout* **prevailed** against me,
saith *the LORD* **Yah Veh**.
Yet ye say,
What have we *spoken so much* **worded** against thee?
14 Ye have said, It is vain to serve *God* **Elohim**:
and what *profit* **greedy gain** is it
that we have *kept* **guarded** his *ordinance* **guard**,
and that we have walked *mournfully* **darkly**
before the LORD of hosts **at the face of Yah Veh Sabaoth**?
15 And now we call the *proud* **arrogant** *happy* **blithesome**;
yea, they that work wickedness *are set up* **built**;
yea, they that *tempt God* **proof Elohim**
are even *delivered* **rescued**.

THE SCROLL OF REMEMBRANCE

16 Then they that *feared the LORD* **awed Yah Veh**
spake often one **worded man** to *another* **friend**:
and *the LORD* **Yah Veh** hearkened, and heard *it*,
and a *book* **scroll** of remembrance
was *written before him* **inscribed at his face**
for them that *feared the LORD* **awed Yah Veh**,
and that *thought upon* **fabricated** his name.
17 And they shall be mine,
saith *the LORD of hosts* **Yah Veh Sabaoth**,
in that day
when I *make up* **work** my *jewels* **peculiar treasure**;
and I *will* **shall** spare them,
as a man spareth his own son that serveth him.
18 Then shall ye return, and *discern* **see**
between the *righteous* **just** and the wicked,
between him that serveth *God* **Elohim**
and **between** him that serveth him not.

THE DAY OF YAH VEH

4 For, behold, the day cometh,
that shall *burn* **inflame** as an oven;
and all the *proud* **arrogant**,
yea, and all that *do* **work** wickedly, shall be stubble:
and the day that cometh shall burn them *up*,
saith *the LORD of hosts* **Yah Veh Sabaoth**,
that it shall leave them neither root nor branch.

THE SUN OF JUSTNESS

2 But unto you that fear my name
shall the Sun of *righteousness* **justness** arise
with healing in his wings;
and ye shall go forth, and grow up as calves of the stall.
3 And ye shall *tread down* **trample** the wicked;
for they shall be ashes under the soles of your feet
in the day that I shall *do* **work** *this*,
saith *the LORD of hosts* **Yah Veh Sabaoth**.
4 Remember ye
the *law* **torah** of *Moses* **Mosheh** my servant,
which I *commanded* **misvahed** unto him in Horeb
for all *Israel* **Yisra El**,
with the statutes and judgments.

ELI YAH THE PROPHET

5 Behold, I *will* **shall** send you *Elijah* **Eli Yah** the prophet
before **at the face of** the coming
of the great and *dreadful* **awesome** day of *the LORD* **Yah Veh**:
6 And he shall turn the heart of the fathers
to the *children* **sons**,
and the heart of the *children* **sons** to their fathers,
lest I come and smite the earth with a *curse* **devotement**.

KEY TO INTERPRETING THE EXEGESES
King James text is in regular type;
Text under exegeses is in oblique type;
Text of exegeses is in bold type.

GENESIS OF THE EVANGELISMS:
GENEALOGY OF THE WORD

1 In the beginning was the Word,
and the Word was with *God* **Elohim,**
and *the Word was God* **Elohim was the Word.**
2 The same was in the beginning with *God* **Elohim.**

THE WORD IS THE CREATOR

3 All *things were made by* **became through** him;
and *without* **apart from** him
was not any thing made **nought became**
that *was made* **became.**
4 In him was life;
and the life was the light of *men* **humanity.**
5 And the light *shineth* **manifesteth** in darkness;
and the darkness *comprehended* **overtook** it not.

BAPTIZER YAHN'S WITNESS

6 There *was* **became** a *man* **human**
sent **apostolized** from *God* **Elohim,**
whose name was *John* **Yahn.**
7 The same came *for a* **to** witness,
to *bear* witness *of* **concerning** the Light,
that all *men* through him might *believe* **trust.**
8 He was not that Light,
but was sent to *bear* witness *of* **concerning** that Light.
9 That *was the true Light,*
which lighteth every *man* **human**
that cometh into the *world* **cosmos.**
10 He was in the *world* **cosmos,**
and the *world was made by* **cosmos became through** him,
and the *world* **cosmos** knew him not.
11 He came unto his own,
and his own *received* **took** him not.

THE ELOHIM BIRTH

12 But as many as *received* **took** him,
to them gave he *power* **authority**
to become the *sons* **children** of *God* **Elohim,**
even to them that *believe on* **trust in** his name:
13 Which were born,
not of blood, nor of the will of the flesh,
nor of the will of man,
but of *God* **Elohim.**

THE WORD BECAME FLESH

14 And the Word *was made* **became** flesh,
and *dwelt* **tabernacled** among us,
(and we *beheld* **saw** his glory,
the glory as of the only begotten of the Father,)
full of *grace* **charism** and truth.
15 *John bare witness of* **Yahn witnessed concerning** him,
and cried, *saying* **wording,**
This was he of whom I *spake* **said,**
He that cometh after me
is preferred before **became ahead of** me:
for he was *before me* **first.**
16 And of his fulness have all we *received* **taken,**
and *grace* **charism** for *grace* **charism.**
17 For the *law* **torah** was given *by Moses* **through Mosheh,**
but *grace* **charism** and truth
came by Jesus Christ **became through Yah Shua Messiah.**
18 No *man* **one** hath seen *God* **Elohim**
at any time — **not ever,**
the only begotten Son, which is in the bosom of the Father,
he hath declared him.

BAPTIZER YAHN INTERROGATED

19 And this is the *record* **witness** of *John* **Yahn,**
when the *Jews* **Yah Hudiym**
sent **apostolized** priests and *Levites* **Leviym**
from *Jerusalem* **Yeru Shalem** to ask him, Who art thou?
20 And he *confessed* **professed,** and denied not;
but *confessed* **professed,** I am not the *Christ* **Messiah.**
21 And they asked him, What then? Art thou *Elias* **Eli Yah**?
And he *saith* **wordeth,** I am not.
Art thou that prophet?
And he answered, No.
22 Then said they unto him, Who art thou?
that we may give an answer to them that sent us.
What *sayest* **wordest** thou *of* **concerning** thyself?
23 He said,
I am the voice of one crying in the wilderness,
Make straight **Straighten** the way of *the Lord* **Yah Veh,**
exactly as said the prophet *Esaias* **Yesha Yah.**
Yesha Yah 40:3
24 And they which were *sent* **apostolized**
were of the Pharisees.
25 And they asked him, and said unto him,
Why baptizest thou then,
if thou be not *that Christ* **the Messiah,**
nor *Elias* **Eli Yah,** neither that prophet?
26 *John* **Yahn** answered them, *saying* **wording,**
I baptize in water:
but there standeth one among you, whom ye know not;
27 He it is, who coming after me
is preferred before **became ahead of** me,
whose shoe's *latchet* **thongs** I am not worthy to unloose.
28 These *things were done* **became**
in *Bethabara* **Beth Abara** beyond *Jordan* **Yarden,**
where *John* **Yahn** was baptizing.

THE WORD IS ELOHIM'S LAMB

29 The next day
John **Yahn** seeth *Jesus* **Yah Shua** coming unto him,
and *saith* **wordeth,** Behold the Lamb of *God* **Elohim,**
which taketh away the sin of the *world* **cosmos.**
30 This is he *of* **concerning** whom I said,
After me cometh a man
which *is preferred before* **became ahead of** me:
for he was *before me* **first.**
31 And I knew him not:
but that he should be *made* manifest to *Israel* **Yisra El,**
therefore am I come baptizing *with* **in** water.

THE WORD IS ELOHIM'S SON

32 And *John bare record* **Yahn witnessed,**
saying **wording,**
I saw the Spirit descending from heaven *like* **as** a dove,
and it abode upon him.
33 And I knew him not:
but he that sent me to baptize *with* **in** water,
the same said unto me,
Upon whom thou shalt see the Spirit descending,
and *remaining* **abiding** on him,
the same is he
which baptizeth *with* **in** the Holy *Ghost* **Spirit.**
34 And I saw, and *bare record* **witnessed**
that this is the Son of *God* **Elohim.**

YAH SHUA'S MINISTRY BEGINS

35 Again the next day after *John* **Yahn** stood,
and two of his disciples;
36 And looking *upon Jesus* **at Yah Shua** as he walked,
he *saith* **wordeth,** Behold the Lamb of *God* **Elohim**!
37 And the two disciples heard him speak,
and they followed *Jesus* **Yah Shua.**
38 Then *Jesus* **Yah Shua** turned, and saw them following,
and *saith* **wordeth** unto them, What seek ye?
They said unto him, Rabbi,
(which is to *say* **word,**
being *interpreted Master* **translated Doctor,**)
where *dwellest* **abidest** thou?
39 He *saith* **wordeth** unto them, Come and see.
They came and saw where he *dwelt* **abode,**
and abode with him that day:
for it was about the tenth hour.

THE WORD IS THE MESSIAH

40 One of the two which heard *John* **Yahn** speak,
and followed him, was *Andrew* **Andreas,**
Simon Peter's **Shimon Petros'** brother.
41 He first findeth his own brother *Simon* **Shimon,**
and *saith* **wordeth** unto him, We have found the Messias,
which is, being *interpreted* **translated,**
the *Christ* **Messiah.**
42 And he brought him to *Jesus* **Yah Shua.**
And when *Jesus beheld* **Yah Shua looked at** him, he said,
Thou art *Simon* **Shimon** the son of *Jona* **Yonah**:
thou shalt be called *Cephas* **Kepha,**
which is by *interpretation* **translation,** *a Stone* **Petros.**
43 The day following
Jesus would **Yah Shua willed to** go forth into *Galilee* **Galiyl,**
and findeth *Philip* **Philippos,**
and *saith* **wordeth** unto him, Follow me.

44 Now *Philip* **Philippos** was of *Bethsaida* **Beth Sayad**,
the city of *Andrew* **Andreas** and *Peter* **Petros**.
45 *Philip* **Philippos** findeth *Nathanael* **Nethan El**,
and *saith* **wordeth** unto him, We have found him,
of whom *Moses* **Mosheh** in the *law* **torah**,
and the prophets, *did write* **scribed**,
Jesus **Yah Shua** of Nazareth, the son of *Joseph* **Yoseph**.
46 And *Nathanael said* **Nethan El wordeth** unto him,
Can there any good *thing* come out of Nazareth?
Philip saith **Philippos wordeth** unto him, Come and see.
47 *Jesus* **Yah Shua** saw *Nathanael* **Nethan El**
coming to him,
and *saith of* **wordeth concerning** him,
Behold **truly** an *Israelite indeed* **Yisra Eliy**,
in whom is no *guile* **deception**!
48 *Nathanael saith* **Nethan El wordeth** unto him,
Whence knowest thou me?
Jesus **Yah Shua** answered and *said* **spake** unto him,
Before that *Philip called* **Philippos voiced out to** thee,
when thou wast under the fig tree, I saw thee.
49 *Nathanael* **Nethan El** answered
and *saith* **wordeth** unto him,
Rabbi, thou art the Son of *God* **Elohim**;
thou art the *King* **Sovereign** of *Israel* **Yisra El**.
50 *Jesus* **Yah Shua** answered and *said* **spake** unto him,
Because I said unto thee, I saw thee under the fig tree,
believest **trustest** thou?
thou shalt see greater *things* than these.
51 And he *saith* **wordeth** unto him,
Verily, verily I say **Amen! Amen! I word** unto you,
Hereafter **From now on** ye shall see heaven open,
and the angels of *God* **Elohim**
ascending and descending
upon the Son of *man* **humanity**.

YAH SHUA'S FIRST SIGN

2 And the third day there *was* **became** a marriage
in *Cana* **Qanah** of *Galilee* **Galiyl**
and the mother of *Jesus* **Yah Shua** was there:
2 And both *Jesus* **Yah Shua** was called, and his disciples,
to the marriage.
3 And when they *wanted* **lacked** wine,
the mother of *Jesus saith* **Yah Shua wordeth** unto him,
They have no wine.
4 *Jesus saith* **Yah Shua wordeth** unto her,
Woman, what have I to do with thee?
mine hour is not yet come.
5 His mother *saith* **wordeth** unto the *servants* **ministers**,
Whatsoever he *saith* **wordeth** unto you, do it.
6 And there were set there six waterpots of stone,
after the manner of the purifying of the *Jews* **Yah Hudiym**,
containing two or three *firkins apiece* **measures each**.
7 *Jesus saith* **Yah Shua wordeth** unto them,
Fill the waterpots with water.
And they filled them *up* to the brim.
8 And he *saith* **wordeth** unto them, *Draw out* **Bail** now,
and bear unto the *governor* **arch** of *the feast* **entertainment**.
And they bare it.
9 When the *ruler* **arch** of *the feast* **entertainment**
had tasted the water that *was made* **became** wine,
and knew not whence it was:
(but the *servants* **ministers**
which *drew* **bailed** the water knew;)
the *governor* **arch** of *the feast* **entertainment**
called **voiced out to** the bridegroom,
10 And *saith* **wordeth** unto him,
Every *man* **human** at the beginning
doth set forth good wine;
and when *men* **ever they** have *well drunk* **intoxicated**,
then *that which is worse* **the lesser**:
but thou hast *kept* **guarded** the good wine until now.
11 This beginning of *miracles* **signs**
did *Jesus* **Yah Shua** in *Cana* **Qanah** of *Galilee* **Galiyl**,
and manifested *forth* his glory;
and his disciples *believed on* **trusted in** him.

YAH SHUA CLEARS THE PRIESTAL PRECINCT

12 After this he *went down* **descended**
to *Capernaum* **Kaphar Nachum**,
he, and his mother, and his brethren, and his disciples:
and they *continued* **abode** there not many days.
13 And the *Jews' passover* **Yah Hudiy's pasach**
was *at hand* **nigh**,
and *Jesus* **Yah Shua**
went up **ascended** to *Jerusalem* **Yeru Shalem**.
14 And found in the *temple* **priestal precinct**
those that sold oxen and sheep and doves,
and the *changers of money* **coindealers** sitting:
15 And when he had made a *scourge* **whip**
of *small cords* **ropes**,
he *drove* **cast** them all out
of the *temple* **priestal precinct**,
and the sheep, and the oxen;
and poured out the *changers' money* **coindealer's coins**,
and *overthrew* **overturned** the tables;
16 And said unto them that sold doves,
Take these *things* hence;
make not my Father's house an house of merchandise.
17 And his disciples remembered
that it was *written* **scribed**,
The zeal of thine house hath *eaten* **devoured** me up.
Psalm 69:9

YAH SHUA PROPHESIES HIS DEATH AND RESURRECTION

18 Then answered the *Jews* **Yah Hudiym**
and said unto him,
What sign shewest thou unto us,
seeing that thou doest these *things*?
19 *Jesus* **Yah Shua** answered and said unto them,
Destroy **Release** this *temple* **nave**,
and in three days I *will* **shall** raise it up.
20 Then said the *Jews* **Yah Hudiym**,
Forty and six years was this *temple* **nave** in building,
and *wilt* **shalt** thou *rear* **raise** it up in three days?
21 But he *spake* **worded**
of **concerning** the *temple* **nave** of his body.
22 When therefore he was risen from the dead,
his disciples remembered
that he had *said* **worded** this unto them;
and they *believed* **trusted** the scripture,
and the word which *Jesus* **Yah Shua** had said.

THE PASACH CELEBRATION

23 Now when he was in *Jerusalem* **Yeru Shalem**
at the *passover* **pasach**, in the *feast day* **celebration**,
many *believed* **trusted** in his name,
when they saw the *miracles* **signs** which he did.
24 But *Jesus* **Yah Shua**
did not commit **entrusted not** himself unto them,
because he knew all *men*,
25 And needed not that any **one**
should *testify of man* **witness concerning humanity**:
for he knew what was in *man* **humanity**.

THE SPIRIT BIRTH

3 There was a *man* **human** of the Pharisees,
named Nicodemus,
a ruler **an arch** of the *Jews* **Yah Hudiym**:
2 The same came to *Jesus* **Yah Shua** by night,
and said unto him, Rabbi,
we know that thou art a *teacher* **doctor**
come from *God* **Elohim**:
for no *man* **one** can do these *miracles* **signs** that thou doest,
except God **unless Elohim** be with him.
3 *Jesus* **Yah Shua** answered and said unto him,
Verily, verily, I say **Amen! Amen! I word** unto thee,
Except a man **Unless one** be born *again* **above**,
he cannot see the *kingdom* **sovereigndom** of *God* **Elohim**.
4 Nicodemus *saith* **wordeth** unto him,
How can a *man* **human** be born when he is old?
can he enter the second time into his mother's womb,
and be born?
5 *Jesus* **Yah Shua** answered,
Verily, verily I say **Amen! Amen! I word** unto thee,
Except a man be **Unless one is** born
of water and of the Spirit
he cannot enter
into the *kingdom* **sovereigndom** of *God* **Elohim**.
6 That which is born of the flesh is flesh;
and that which is born of the Spirit is spirit.
7 Marvel not that I said unto thee,
Ye must be born *again* **above**.
8 The *wind bloweth* **Spirit puffeth**
where *it listeth* **he willeth**,
and thou hearest the *sound thereof* **voice of him**,

but *canst not tell* **knowest not**
whence it cometh, and whither it goeth:
so **thus** is every one that is born of the Spirit.
9 Nicodemus answered and said unto him,
How can these *things* be?
10 *Jesus* **Yah Shua** answered and said unto him,
Art thou a *master* **doctor** of *Israel* **Yisra El**,
and knowest not these *things*?
11 *Verily, verily I say* **Amen! Amen! I word** unto thee,
We speak that we do know,
and *testify* **witness** that we have seen;
and ye *receive* **take** not our witness.
12 If I have *told* **said to** you **of the** earthly *things*,
and ye *believe* **trust** not,
how shall ye *believe* **trust**,
if I *tell* **say to** you of **the** heavenly *things*?
13 And no *man* **one** hath ascended up to heaven,
but **except** he that *came down* **descended** from heaven,
even the Son of *man* **humanity** which is in heaven.

ETERNAL LIFE

14 And **exactly** as *Moses* **Mosheh**
lifted up **exalted** the serpent in the wilderness,
even *so* **thus**
must the Son of *man* **humanity** be *lifted up* **exalted**:
15 That whosoever *believeth* **trusteth** in him
should not *perish* **destruct**, but have eternal life.

Yahn 12:30—34

16 For *God so* **Elohim** loved the *world,* **cosmos thus:**
that he gave his only begotten Son,
that whosoever *believeth* **trusteth** in him
should not *perish* **destruct**
but have *everlasting* **eternal** life.
17 For *God* **Elohim**
sent **apostolized** not his Son into the *world* **cosmos**
to *condemn* **judge** the *world* **cosmos**;
but that the *world* **cosmos** through him might be saved.
18 He that *believeth on* **trusteth in** him
is not *condemned* **judged**:
but he that *believeth* **trusteth** not
is *condemned* **judged** already,
because he hath not *believed* **trusted** in the name
of the only begotten Son of *God* **Elohim**.
19 And this is the *condemnation* **judgment**,
that light is come into the *world* **cosmos**,
and men loved darkness rather than light,
because their *deeds* **works** were evil.
20 For every one that doeth evil hateth the light,
neither cometh to the light,
lest his *deeds* **works** should be reproved.
21 But he that doeth truth cometh to the light,
that his *deeds* **works** may be *made* manifest,
that they are *wrought* **worked** in *God* **Elohim**.

BAPTIZER YAHN'S FINAL WITNESS

22 After these *things*
came *Jesus* **Yah Shua** and his disciples
into the land of *Judaea* **Yah Hudah**;
and there he tarried with them, and baptized.
23 And *John* **Yahn** also was baptizing
in *Aenon* **Ainon** near to *Salim* **Shalem**,
because there was much water there:
and they came, and were baptized.
24 For *John* **Yahn**
was not yet cast into *prison* **the guardhouse**.
25 Then there *arose* **became** a question
between some of *John's* **Yahn's** disciples
and the *Jews* **Yah Hudiym** about purifying.
26 And they came unto *John* **Yahn**, and said unto him,
Rabbi, he that was with thee beyond *Jordan* **Yarden**,
to whom thou *barest witness* **witnessest**,
behold, the same baptizeth, and all *men* come to him.
27 *John* **Yahn** answered and said,
A man **Humanity** can *receive nothing* **take naught**,
except **unless** it be given him from heaven.
28 Ye yourselves *bear me witness* **witnessed**, that I said,
I am not the *Christ* **Messiah**,
but that I am *sent before* **apostolized ahead of** him.
29 He that hath the bride is the bridegroom:
but the friend of the bridegroom,
which standeth and heareth him,
rejoiceth greatly **cheereth cheer**
because of the bridegroom's voice:
this my joy therefore is fulfilled.
30 He must *increase* **grow**, but I must *decrease* **lessen**.
31 He that cometh from above is above all:
he that is of the earth is *earthly* **of the earth**,
and speaketh of the earth:
he that cometh from heaven is above all.
32 And what he hath seen and heard,
that he *testifieth* **witnesseth**;
and no *man receiveth* **one taketh** his *testimony* **witness**.
33 He that hath *received* **taken** his *testimony* **witness**
hath set to his seal that *God* **Elohim** is true.
34 For he whom *God* **Elohim** hath *sent* **apostolized**
speaketh the *words* **rhema** of *God* **Elohim**:
for *God* **Elohim** giveth not the Spirit by measure unto him.
35 The Father loveth the Son,
and hath given all *things* into his hand.
36 He that *believeth on* **trusteth in** the Son
hath *everlasting* **eternal** life:
and he that *believeth not* **distrusteth** the Son
shall not see life;
but the wrath of *God* **Elohim** abideth on him.

YAH SHUA GOES TO GALIYL

4 When therefore *the Lord* **Adonay** knew
how the Pharisees had heard
that *Jesus* **Yah Shua** made and baptized
many more disciples than *John* **Yahn**,
2 (Though *Jesus* **Yah Shua** himself baptized not,
but his disciples),
3 He left *Judaea* **Yah Hudah**,
and departed again into *Galilee* **Galiyl**

YAH SHUA AND THE SHOMERONIY

4 And he must *needs go* **pass** through *Samaria* **Shomeron**.
5 Then cometh he to a city of *Samaria* **Shomeron**,
which is *called* **worded** Sychar,
near to the *parcel of ground* **field**
that *Jacob* **Yaaqov** gave to his son *Joseph* **Yoseph**.
6 Now *Jacob's well* **Yaaqov's fountain** was there.
Jesus **Yah Shua** therefore,
being wearied with **belabored from** his journey,
sat thus on the well:
and it was about the sixth hour.
7 There cometh a woman of *Samaria* **Shomeron**
to *draw* **bail** water:
Jesus saith **Yah Shua wordeth** unto her, Give me to drink.
8 (For his disciples were gone away unto the city
to *buy meat* **market for nourishment**).
9 Then *saith* **wordeth** the woman
of Samaria **— a Shomeroniy** unto him,
How is it that thou, being a *Jew* **Yah Hudiy**,
askest drink of me,
which am a woman *of Samaria* **— a Shomeroniy**?
for the *Jews have no dealings* **Yah Hudiym associate not**
with the *Samaritans* **Shomeroniym**
10 *Jesus* **Yah Shua** answered and said unto her,
If thou knewest the *gift* **gratuity** of *God* **Elohim**,
and who it is that *saith* **wordeth** to thee,
Give me to drink;
thou *wouldest* **shouldest ever** have asked of him,
and he *would* **should ever** have given thee living water.
11 The woman *saith* **wordeth** unto him,
Sir **Adoni**, thou hast *nothing* **naught** to *draw* **bail** *with*,
and the well is deep:
from whence then hast thou that living water?
12 Art thou greater than our father *Jacob* **Yaaqov**,
which gave us the well, and drank thereof himself,
and his *children* **sons**, and his *cattle* **stock**?
13 *Jesus* **Yah Shua** answered and said unto her,
Whosoever drinketh of this water shall thirst again:
14 But whosoever drinketh of the water
that I shall give him
shall never **ever** thirst **unto the eons**;
but the water that I shall give him
shall be in him a *well* **fountain** of water
springing up into *everlasting* **eternal** life.
15 The woman *saith* **wordeth** unto him,
Sir **Adoni**, give me this water, that I thirst not,
neither come hither to *draw* **bail**.
16 *Jesus saith* **Yah Shua wordeth** unto her,
Go, *call* **voice out to** thy *husband* **man**, and come hither.

17 The woman answered and said,
I have no *husband* **man**.
Jesus said **Yah Shua worded** unto her,
Thou hast well *said* **spoken**, I have no *husband* **man**:
18 For thou hast had five *husbands* **men**;
and he whom thou now hast is not thy *husband* **man**:
in that *saidst* **spakest** thou truly.
19 The woman *saith* **wordeth** unto him,
Sir **Adoni**, I perceive that thou art a prophet.
20 Our fathers worshipped in this mountain;
and ye *say* **word**, that in *Jerusalem* **Yeru Shalem**
is the place where men *ought* **need** to worship.
21 *Jesus saith* **Yah Shua wordeth** unto her,
Woman, *believe* **trust** me, the hour cometh,
when ye shall neither in this mountain,
nor yet at *Jerusalem* **Yeru Shalem**, worship the Father.
22 Ye worship ye know not what:
we know what we worship:
for salvation is of the *Jews* **Yah Hudiym**.
23 But the hour cometh, and now is,
when the true worshippers
shall worship the Father in spirit and in truth:
for the Father seeketh such to worship him.
24 *God* **Elohim** is a Spirit:
and they that worship him
must worship him in spirit and in truth.
25 The woman *saith* **wordeth** unto him,
I know that Messias cometh,
which is *called Christ* **worded Messiah**:
when **ever** he is come,
he *will tell us* **shall evangelize** all *things* **us**.
26 *Jesus saith* **Yah Shua wordeth** unto her,
I that speak **I AM speaketh** unto thee *am he*.
27 And upon this came his disciples,
and marvelled that he *talked* **spake** with the woman:
yet **indeed** no *man* **one** said, What seekest thou?
or, Why *talkest* **speakest** thou with her?
28 The woman then *left* **forsook** her waterpot,
and went her way into the city,
and *saith* **wordeth** to the men,
29 Come, see a *man* **human**,
which told me *all things that* — **as much as** ever I did:
is not this the *Christ* **Messiah**?
30 Then they went out of the city, and came unto him.

YAH SHUA'S FOOD

31 In *the mean while* **between**
his disciples *prayed* **asked** him,
saying **wording**, *Master* **Rabbi**, eat.
32 But he said unto them,
I have *meat* **food** to eat that ye know not of.
33 Therefore *said* **worded** the disciples one to another,
Hath any *man* **one** brought him *ought* to eat?
34 *Jesus saith* **Yah Shua wordeth** unto them,
My *meat* **food** is to do the will of him that sent me,
and to *finish* **complete** his work.
35 *Say* **Word** not ye, There are yet four months,
and then cometh harvest?
behold, I *say* **word** unto you,
Lift up your eyes, and *look on* **see** the *fields* **regions**;
for they are white already to harvest.
36 And he that *reapeth* **harvesteth**
receiveth wages **taketh reward**,
and gathereth fruit unto life eternal:
that both he that soweth and he that *reapeth* **harvesteth**
may *rejoice* **cheer** together.
37 *And* **For** herein is that *saying* **word** true,
One soweth, and another *reapeth* **harvesteth**.
38 I *sent* **apostolized** you
to *reap* **harvest** that whereon ye bestowed no labour:
other men **others** laboured,
and ye are entered into their labours.
39 And many of the *Samaritans* **Shomeroniym** of that city
believed on **trusted in** him
for the *saying* **word** of the woman,
which *testified* **witnessed**,
He *told me all that* **said to me — as much as** ever I did.

YAH SHUA AND THE SHOMERONIYM

40 So when the *Samaritans* **Shomeroniym**
were come unto him,
they *besought* **asked** him
that he *would tarry* **should abide** with them:
and he abode there two days.
41 And many more *believed* **trusted**
because of his own word;
42 And *said* **worded** unto the woman,
Now we *believe* **trust**, not because of thy *saying* **speech**:
for we have heard him ourselves,
and know that this is *indeed* **truly** the *Christ* **Messiah**,
the Saviour of the *world* **cosmos**.
43 Now after two days he departed thence,
and went into *Galilee* **Galiyl**.
44 For *Jesus* **Yah Shua** himself *testified* **witnessed**,
that a prophet hath no honour
in his own *country* **fatherland**.
45 Then when he was come into *Galilee* **Galiyl**,
the *Galilaeans* **Galiliy** received him,
having seen all *the things* that he did
at *Jerusalem* **Yeru Shalem** at the *feast* **celebration**:
for they also went unto the *feast* **celebration**.

YAH SHUA'S SECOND SIGN

46 So *Jesus* **Yah Shua** came again
into *Cana* **Qanah** of *Galilee* **Galiyl**,
where he made the water wine.
And there was a *certain nobleman* **sovereign**,
whose son was *sick* **frail** at *Capernaum* **Kaphar Nachum**.
47 When he heard that *Jesus* **Yah Shua**
was come out of *Judaea* **Yah Hudah** into *Galilee* **Galiyl**,
he went unto him,
and *besought* **asked** him
that he *would come down* **should descend**, and heal his son:
for he was *at the point of death* **about to die**.
48 Then said *Jesus* **Yah Shua** unto him,
Except **Unless** ye see signs and *wonders* **omens**,
ye *will* **shall** not *believe* **trust**.
49 The *nobleman saith* **sovereign wordeth** unto him,
Sir **Adoni**, *come down* **descend** ere my child die.
50 *Jesus saith* **Yah Shua wordeth** unto him,
Go thy way; thy son liveth.
And the *man believed* **human trusted** the word
that *Jesus* **Yah Shua** had *spoken* **said** unto him,
and he went his way.
51 And as he was *now going down* **already descending**,
his servants met him,
and *told* **evangelized** him *saying* **wording**,
Thy *son* **lad** liveth.
52 Then enquired he of them
the hour *when* **in which** he began to amend.
And they said unto him,
Yesterday at the seventh hour the fever left him.
53 So the father knew that it was at the same hour,
in the which *Jesus* **Yah Shua** said unto him,
Thy son liveth:
and himself *believed* **trusted**, and his whole house.
54 This is again
the second *miracle* **sign** that *Jesus* **Yah Shua** did,
when he was come out of *Judaea* **Yah Hudah**
into *Galilee* **Galiyl**.

YAH SHUA HEALS ON THE SHABBATH

5 After this
there was a *feast* **celebration** of the *Jews* **Yah Hudiym**;
and *Jesus* **Yah Shua**
went up **ascended** to *Jerusalem* **Yeru Shalem**.
2 Now there is at *Jerusalem* **Yeru Shalem**
by the sheep *market* **gate** a pool,
which is called in *the Hebrew tongue* **Hebraic**
Bethesda **Beth Hesed**,
having five *porches* **porticos**.
3 In these lay a *great* **vast** multitude of *impotent folk* **frail**,
of blind, *halt* **lame**, withered,
waiting for the moving of the water.
4 For an angel *went down* **descended** at a certain season
into the pool, and *troubled* **agitated** the water:
whosoever then first
after the *troubling* **agitating** of the water
stepped in **entered**
was made **became** whole of whatsoever disease he had.
5 And a *certain man* **human** was there,
which had *an infirmity* **a fraility** thirty and eight years.
6 When *Jesus* **Yah Shua** saw him lie,
and knew that he had been

now a long **already a vast** time in that case,
he *saith* **wordeth** unto him,
Wilt **Willest** thou *be made* **become** whole?
7 The *impotent man* **frail** answered him,
Sir **Adoni**, I have no *man* **human**,
when **whenever** the water is troubled,
to put me into the pool:
but while I am coming,
another *steppeth down* **descendeth** before me.
8 *Jesus saith* **Yah Shua wordeth** unto him,
Rise, take up thy *bed* **pad**, and walk.
9 And *immediately* **straightway**
the *man was made* **human became** whole,
and took up his *bed* **pad**, and walked:
and *on* **in** the same day was the *sabbath* **shabbath**.
10 The *Jews* **Yah Hudiym** therefore
said **worded** unto him that was cured,
It is the *sabbath day* **shabbath**:
it is not *lawful* **allowed** for thee to carry thy *bed* **pad**.
11 He answered them, He that made me whole,
the same said unto me, Take up thy *bed* **pad**, and walk.
12 Then asked they him,
What *man* **human** is that which said unto thee,
Take up thy *bed* **pad**, and walk?
13 And he that was healed *wist* **knew** not who it was:
for *Jesus* **Yah Shua** had conveyed himself away,
a multitude being in that place.
14 Afterward *Jesus* **Yah Shua**
findeth him in the *temple* **priestal precinct**,
and said unto him,
Behold, thou art *made* **become** whole:
sin no more,
lest *a* **somewhat** worse *thing come* **become** unto thee.
15 The *man* **human** departed,
and *told* **evangelized** the *Jews* **Yah Hudiym**
that it was *Jesus* **Yah Shua**, which had made him whole.
16 And therefore
did the *Jews* **Yah Hudiym** persecute *Jesus* **Yah Shua**,
and sought to *slay* **slaughter** him,
because he had done these *things*
on **in** the *sabbath day* **shabbath**.
17 But *Jesus* **Yah Shua** answered them,
My Father worketh hitherto, and I work.
18 Therefore the *Jews* **Yah Hudiym**
sought the more to *kill* **slaughter** him,
because he not only
had *broken* **released** the *sabbath* **shabbath**,
but *said* **worded** also that *God* **Elohim** was his Father,
making himself equal with *God* **Elohim**.
Philippians 2:5—8
19 Then answered *Jesus* **Yah Shua** and said unto them,
Verily, verily I say **Amen! Amen! I word** unto you,
The Son can do *nothing* **naught** of himself,
but what he seeth the Father do:
for what *things* soever he doeth,
these also doeth the Son likewise.
20 For the Father *loveth* **befriendeth** the Son,
and sheweth him all *things* that himself doeth:
and he *will* **shall** shew him greater works than these,
that ye may marvel.
21 For **exactly** as the Father raiseth *up* the dead,
and *quickeneth* **enliveneth** them;
even *so* **thus** the Son *quickeneth* **enliveneth**
whom he *will* **willeth**.
22 For the Father judgeth no *man* **one**,
but hath *committed* **given** all judgment unto the Son:
23 That all men should honour the Son,
even **exactly** as they honour the Father.
He that honoureth not the Son
honoureth not the Father which hath sent him.
24 *Verily, verily I say* **Amen! Amen! I word** unto you,
He that heareth my word,
and *believeth on* **trusteth** him that sent me,
hath *everlasting* **eternal** life,
and shall not come into *condemnation* **judgment**;
but is *passed* **departed** from death unto life.
25 *Verily, verily, I say* **Amen! Amen! I word** unto you,
The hour is coming, and now is,
when the dead
shall hear the voice of the Son of *God* **Elohim**:
and they that hear shall live.
26 For as the Father hath life in himself;
so **thus** hath he given to the Son to have life in himself;
27 And hath given him authority
to *execute* **do** judgment also,
because he is the Son of *man* **humanity**.

THE TWO RESURRECTIONS

28 Marvel not at this:
for the hour is coming, in the which
all that are in the *graves* **tombs** shall hear his voice,
29 And shall *come forth* **proceed**;
they that have done good,
unto the resurrection of life;
and they that have done evil,
unto the resurrection of *damnation* **judgment**.
30 I can of mine own self do *nothing* **naught**:
exactly as I hear, I judge: and my judgment is just;
because I seek not mine own will,
but the will of the Father which hath sent me.
31 If I *bear* witness *of* **concerning** myself,
my witness is not true.
32 There is another
that *beareth witness of* **witnesseth concerning** me;
and I know that the witness
which he witnesseth *of* **concerning** me is true.
33 Ye *sent* **apostolized** unto *John* **Yahn**,
and he *bare witness* **witnessed** unto the truth.
34 But I *receive* **take** not *testimony* **witness**
from *man* **humanity**:
but these *things I say* **I word**, that ye might be saved.
35 He was a burning and a *shining light* **manifest candle**:
and ye *were willing* **willed** for *a season* **an hour**
to *rejoice* **jump for joy** in his light.
36 But I have greater witness than that of *John* **Yahn**:
for the works
which the Father hath given me to *finish* **complete**,
the same works that I do, *bear* witness *of* **concerning** me,
that the Father hath *sent* **apostolized** me.
37 And the Father himself, which hath sent me,
hath *borne witness of* **witnessed concerning** me.
Ye have neither heard his voice *at any time* — **not ever**,
nor seen his *shape* **semblance**.
38 And ye have not his word abiding in you:
for whom he hath *sent* **apostolized**,him ye *believe* **trust** not.
39 Search the scriptures;
for in them ye think ye have eternal life:
and they are they which *testify of* **witness concerning** me.
40 And ye will **to** not come to me, that ye might have life.
41 I *receive* **take** not *honour* **glory** from *men* **humanity**.
42 But I know you,
that ye have not the love of *God* **Elohim** in you.
43 I am come in my Father's name,
and ye *receive* **take** me not:
if another shall come in his own name,
him ye *will receive* **shall take**.
44 How can ye *believe* **trust**,
which *receive honour* **take glory** one of another,
and seek not the *honour* **glory**
that cometh from *God* **Elohim** only?
45 Do not think that I *will* **shall** accuse you to the Father:
there is one that accuseth you,
even *Moses* **Mosheh**, in whom ye *trust* **hope**.
46 For had ye *believed Moses* **trusted Mosheh**,
ye *would* **should** have *believed* **trusted** me;
for he *wrote of* **scribed concerning** me.
47 But if ye *believe* **trust** not his *writings* **scribings**,
how shall ye *believe* **trust** my *words* **rhema**?

YAH SHUA FEEDS FIVE THOUSAND

6 After these *things*
Jesus **Yah Shua** went over the sea of *Galilee* **Galiyl**,
which is the sea of Tiberias.
2 And a *great* **vast** multitude followed him,
because they saw his *miracles* **signs**
which he did on them that were *diseased* **frail**.
3 And *Jesus* **Yah Shua** went up into a mountain,
and there he sat with his disciples.
4 And the *passover* **pasach**,
a *feast* **celebration** of the *Jews* **Yah Hudiym**, was nigh.
5 When *Jesus* **Yah Shua** then lifted up his eyes,
and saw a *great company* **vast multitude** come unto him,

he *saith* **wordeth** unto *Philip* **Philippos**,
Whence shall we *buy* **market** bread, that these may eat?
6 And this he *said* **worded** to *prove* **test** him:
for he himself knew what he *would* **should** do.
7 *Philip* **Philippos** answered him,
Two hundred *pennyworth* **denarion** of bread
is not sufficient for them,
that *every one* **each** of them may take a little.
8 One of his disciples, *Andrew* **Andreas**,
Simon Peter's **Shimon Petros'** brother
saith **wordeth** unto him,
9 There is a *lad* **child** here,
which hath five barley *loaves* **breads**,
and two small *fishes* **broilings**:
but what are they *among* **unto** so many?
10 And *Jesus* **Yah Shua** said,
Make the *men sit down* **humans repose**.
Now there was much *grass* **herbage** in the place.
So the men *sat down* **reposed**
in number about five thousand.
11 And *Jesus* **Yah Shua** took the *loaves* **breads**;
and when he had *given thanks* **eucharistized**,
he distributed to the disciples,
and the disciples to them that *were set down* **reposed**;
and likewise of the *fishes* **broilings**
as much as they *would* **willed**.
12 When they were filled,
he *said* **worded** unto his disciples,
Gather *up* **together** the fragments that *remain* **superabound**,
that *nothing be lost* **naught destruct**.
13 Therefore they gathered them together,
and filled twelve baskets
with the fragments of the five barley *loaves* **breads**,
which *remained* **superabounded** over and above
unto them that had eaten.
14 Then those men,
when they had seen the *miracle* **sign**
that *Jesus* **Yah Shua** did, *said* **worded**,
This is *of a truth* **truly** that prophet
that should come into the *world* **cosmos**.
15 When *Jesus* **Yah Shua** therefore *perceived* **knew**
that they *would* **should** come and *take* **seize** him *by force*,
to make him *a king* **sovereign**,
he departed again into a mountain himself alone.
16 And when *even was now come* **evening became**,
his disciples *went down* **descended** unto the sea,
17 And *entered* **embarked** into a *ship* **sailer**,
and went over the sea
toward Capernaum **unto Kaphar Nachum**.
And it *was now* **had already become** dark,
and *Jesus* **Yah Shua** was not come to them.
18 And the sea *arose* **was roused**
by *reason* **the puffing** of a *great* **mega** wind *that blew*.

YAH SHUA WALKS ON THE SEA

19 So when they *had rowed* **were driven**
about five and twenty or thirty *furlongs* **stadia**,
they see *Jesus* **Yah Shua** walking on the sea,
and *drawing* **becoming** nigh unto the *ship* **sailer**:
and they were *afraid* **awestricken**.
20 But he *saith* **wordeth** unto them,
It is I **I AM**; be not *afraid* **awed**.
21 Then they *willingly received* **willed to take** him
into the *ship* **sailer**:
and *immediately* **straightway** the *ship* **sailer**
was **became** at the land *whither* **into which** they went.
22 The day following, when the *people* **multitude**
which stood on the other side of the sea
saw that there was none other *boat* **skiff** there,
save **except** that one
whereinto his disciples *were entered* **embarked**,
and that *Jesus* **Yah Shua**
went not with his disciples into the *boat* **skiff**,
but that his disciples were gone away alone;
23 (Howbeit there came other *boats* **skiffs** from Tiberias
nigh unto the place where they did eat bread,
after that
the Lord **Adonay** had *given thanks* **eucharistized**:)
24 When the *people* **multitude** therefore saw
that *Jesus* **Yah Shua** was not there, neither his disciples,
they also *took shipping* **embarked into sailers**,
and came to *Capernaum* **Kaphar Nachum**,
seeking for *Jesus* **Yah Shua**.
25 And when they had found him
on the other side of the sea,
they said unto him, Rabbi,
when *camest* **becamest** thou hither?
26 *Jesus* **Yah Shua** answered them and said,
Verily, verily, I say **Amen! Amen! I word** unto you,
Ye seek me, not because ye saw the *miracles* **signs**,
but because ye did eat of the *loaves* **breads**,
and were *filled* **fed**.
27 *Labour* **Work** not for the *meat* **food**
which *perisheth* **destructeth**,
but for that *meat* **food**
which *endureth* **abideth** unto *everlasting* **eternal** life,
which the Son of *man* **humanity** shall give unto you:
for him hath *God* **Elohim** the Father sealed.
28 Then said they unto him, What shall we do,
that we might work the works of *God* **Elohim**?
29 *Jesus* **Yah Shua** answered and said unto them,
This is the work of *God* **Elohim**,
that ye *believe on* **trust in** him
whom he hath *sent* **apostolized**.
30 They said therefore unto him,
What sign *shewest* **doest** thou then,
that we may see, and *believe* **trust** thee?
what *dost* **workest** thou *work*?
31 Our fathers did eat manna in the *desert* **wilderness**;
exactly as it is *written* **scribed**,
He gave them bread from heaven to eat.
Nechem Yah 9:5
32 Then *Jesus* **Yah Shua** said unto them,
Verily, verily I say **Amen! Amen! I word** unto you,
Moses **Mosheh** gave you not that bread from heaven;
but my Father giveth you the true bread from heaven.
33 For the bread of *God* **Elohim**
is he which *cometh down* **descendeth** from heaven,
and giveth life unto the *world* **cosmos**.
34 Then said they unto him, *Lord* **Adonay**,
evermore give us this bread.

YAH SHUA, THE LIVING BREAD

35 And *Jesus* **Yah Shua** said unto them,
I am **I AM** the bread of life:
he that cometh to me shall never hunger;
and he that *believeth on* **trusteth in** me
shall never — **not ever** thirst.
36 But I said unto you,
That ye also have seen me, and *believe* **trust** not.
37 All that the Father giveth me shall come to me;
and him that cometh to me
I *will in no wise cast out* **shall never eject**.
38 For I *came down* **descended** from heaven,
not to do mine own will, but the will of him that sent me.
39 And this is the Father's will which hath sent me,
that of all which he hath given me
I should lose *nothing* **naught thereof**,
but should raise it *up* again at the *last* **final** day.
40 And this is the will of him that sent me,
that every one which seeth the Son,
and *believeth on* **trusteth in** him,
may have *everlasting* **eternal** life:
and I *will* **shall** raise him *up* at the *last* **final** day.
41 The *Jews* **Yah Hudiym** then murmured
at **concerning** him,
because he said,
I am **I AM** the bread
which *came down* **descended** from heaven.
42 And they *said* **worded**, Is not this *Jesus* **Yah Shua**,
the son of *Joseph* **Yoseph**,
whose father and mother we know?
how is it then that he *saith* **wordeth**,
I *came down* **descended** from heaven?
43 *Jesus* **Yah Shua** therefore
answered and said unto them,
Murmur not *among yourselves* **with one another**.
44 No *man* **one** can come to me,
except **unless** the Father which hath sent me draw him:
and I *will* **shall** raise him *up* at the *last* **final** day.
45 It is *written* **scribed** in the prophets,
And they shall be all *taught* **doctrinated** of *God* **Elohim**.

Every *man* **one** therefore that hath heard,
and hath learned of the Father, cometh unto me.
Yesha Yah 54:13
46 Not that any *man* **one** hath seen the Father,
save **except** he which is of *God* **Elohim**,
he hath seen the Father.
47 *Verily, verily I say* **Amen! Amen! I word** unto you,
He that *believeth on* **trusteth in** me
hath *everlasting* **eternal** life.
48 *I am* **I AM** that bread of life.
49 Your fathers did eat manna in the wilderness,
and are dead.
50 This is the bread
which *cometh down* **descendeth** from heaven,
that *a man* **anyone** may eat thereof, and not die.
51 *I am* **I AM** the living bread
which *came down* **descended** from heaven:
if any *man* **one** eat of this bread,
he shall live *for ever* **unto the eons**:
and the bread that I *will* **shall** give is my flesh,
which I *will* **shall** give for the life of the *world* **cosmos**.
52 The *Jews* **Yah Hudiym** therefore
strove among *themselves* **one another**, *saying* **wording**,
How can this man give us his flesh to eat?
53 Then *Jesus* **Yah Shua** said unto them,
Verily, verily I say **Amen! Amen! I word** unto you,
Except **Unless** ye eat the flesh of the Son of *man* **humanity**,
and drink his blood, ye have no life in you.
54 Whoso eateth my flesh, and drinketh my blood,
hath eternal life;
and I *will* **shall** raise him *up* at the *last* **final** day.
55 For my flesh is *meat indeed* **truly food**,
and my blood is **truly** drink *indeed*.
56 He that eateth my flesh, and drinketh my blood,
dwelleth **abideth** in me, and I in him.
57 **Exactly** As the living Father hath *sent* **apostolized** me,
and I live *by* **through** the Father:
so he that eateth me, even he shall live *by* **through** me.
58 This is that bread
which *came down* **descended** from heaven:
not **exactly** as your fathers did eat manna, and are dead:
he that eateth of this bread
shall live *for ever* **unto the eons**.
59 These *things* said he in the synagogue,
as he *taught* **doctrinated** in *Capernaum* **Kaphar Nachum**.
60 Many therefore of his disciples,
when they had heard this, said,
This is an hard *saying* **word**; who can hear it?
61 When *Jesus* **Yah Shua** knew in himself
that his disciples murmured *at* **concerning** it,
he said unto them, Doth this *offend* **scandalize** you?
62 What and if ye shall see the Son of *man* **humanity**
ascend *up* where he was before?
63 It is the spirit that *quickeneth* **enliveneth**;
the flesh *profiteth nothing* **benefiteth naught**:
the *words* **rhema** that I speak unto you,
they are spirit, and they are life.
64 But there are some of you that *believe* **trust** not.
For *Jesus* **Yah Shua** knew from the beginning
who they were that *believed* **trusted** not,
and who should betray him.
65 And he *said* **worded**, Therefore said I unto you,
that no *man* **one** can come unto me,
except **unless** it were given unto him of my Father.
66 From that time many of his disciples went back,
and walked no more with him.

PETROS' WITNESS

67 Then said *Jesus* **Yah Shua** unto the twelve,
will ye also go away?
68 Then *Simon Peter* **Shimon Petros** answered him,
Lord **Adonay**, to whom shall we go?
thou hast the *words* **rhema** of eternal life.
69 And we *believe* **trust** and *are sure* **know**
that thou art *that Christ* **the Messiah**,
the Son of the living *God* **Elohim**.
70 *Jesus* **Yah Shua** answered them,
Have not I chosen you twelve,
and one of you is *a devil* **Diabolos**?
71 He *spake* **worded**
of *Judas Iscariot* **Yah Hudah the urbanite**
the son of *Simon* **Shimon**:
for he it was that should betray him,
being one of the twelve.

7 After these *things*
Jesus **Yah Shua** walked in *Galilee* **Galiyl**:
for he *would* **willed to** not walk in *Jewry* **Yah Hudah**,
because the *Jews* **Yah Hudiym**
sought to *kill* **slaughter** him.

THE TABERNACLE STAKING CELEBRATION
(SUKKOTH/BRUSH ARBORS)

2 Now the *Jews' feast* **Yah Hudiy's celebration**
of *tabernacles* **tabernacle staking** was *at hand* **nigh**.
3 His brethren therefore said unto him,
Depart hence, and go into *Judaea* **Yah Hudah**,
that thy disciples also may see the works that thou doest.
4 For there is no *man* **one**
that doeth *any thing* **aught** in secret,
and he himself seeketh to be known *openly* **boldly**.
If thou do these *things*,
shew **manifest** thyself to the *world* **cosmos**.
5 For neither did his brethren *believe* **trust** in him.
6 Then *Jesus said* **Yah Shua worded** unto them,
My *time* **season** is not yet *come* **here**:
but your *time* **season** is alway *ready* **prepared**.
7 The *world* **cosmos** cannot hate you;
but me it hateth,
because I *testify of* **witness concerning** it,
that the works thereof are evil.
8 *Go* **Ascend** ye *up* unto this *feast* **celebration**:
I *go* **ascend** not *up* yet unto this *feast* **celebration**:
for my *time* **season** is not yet *full come* **fulfilled**.
9 When he had said these words unto them,
he abode still in *Galilee* **Galiyl**.
10 But when his brethren were *gone up* **ascended**,
then *went* **ascended** he also *up*
unto the *feast* **celebration**,
not *openly* **manifestly**, but as it were in secret.
11 Then the *Jews* **Yah Hudiym**
sought him at the *feast* **celebration**,
and *said* **worded**, Where is he?
12 And there was much murmuring
among the *people* **multitude** concerning him:
for **indeed** some *said* **worded**, He is a good man:
others *said* **spake**, Nay;
but he *deceiveth* **seduceth** the *people* **multitude**.
13 *Howbeit* **Yet indeed**
no *man* **one** spake *openly of* **boldly about** him
for *fear* **awe** of the *Jews* **Yah Hudiym**.
14 *Now about* **Already** the midst of the *feast* **celebration**
Jesus went up **Yah Shua ascended**
into the *temple* **priestal precinct**, and *taught* **doctrinated**.
15 And the *Jews* **Yah Hudiym** marvelled, *saying* **wording**,
How knoweth this *man letters* **one scribings**,
having never learned?
16 *Jesus* **Yah Shua** answered them, and said,
My doctrine is not mine, but his that sent me.
17 If any *man will* **one willeth to** do his will,
he shall know *of* **concerning** the doctrine,
whether it be of *God* **Elohim**,
or whether I speak of myself.
18 He that speaketh of himself seeketh his own glory:
but he that seeketh his glory that sent him,
the same is true,
and no *unrighteousness* **unjustness** is in him.
19 Did not *Moses* **Mosheh** give you the *law* **torah**,
and yet none of you *keepeth* **doeth** the *law* **torah**?
Why *go* **seek** ye *about* to *kill* **slaughter** me?
20 The *people* **multitude** answered and said,
Thou hast a *devil* **demon**:
who *goeth about* **seeketh** to *kill* **slaughter** thee?
21 *Jesus* **Yah Shua** answered and said unto them,
I have done one work, and ye all marvel.
22 *Moses* **Mosheh** therefore gave unto you circumcision;
(not because it is of *Moses* **Mosheh**, but of the fathers;)
and ye on the *sabbath day* **shabbath**
circumcise a *man* **human**.
23 If a *man* **human** on the *sabbath day* **shabbath**
receive **taketh** circumcision,
that the *law* **torah** of *Moses* **Mosheh**
should not be *broken* **released**;

are ye *angry* **choleric** at me,
because I have made a *man every whit* **human** whole
on the *sabbath day* **shabbath**?
24 Judge not according to *the appearance* **visage**,
but judge *righteous* **just** judgment.
25 Then *said* **worded**
some of *them of Jerusalem* **the Yeru Shalemiym**,
Is not this he, whom they seek to *kill* **slaughter**?
26 But, *lo* **behold**, he speaketh boldly,
and they *say nothing* **word naught** unto him.
Do the *rulers* **archs** know *indeed* **truly**
that this is **truly** the *very Christ* **Messiah**?
27 *Howbeit* **Yet** we know this *man* **one** whence he is:
but when *Christ* **ever the Messiah** cometh,
no *man* **one** knoweth whence he is.

YAH SHUA DOCTRINATES IN THE PRIESTAL PRECINCT

28 Then cried *Jesus* **Yah Shua**
in the *temple* **priestal precinct** as he *taught* **doctrinated**,
saying **wording**, Ye both know me,
and ye know whence *I am* **I AM**:
and I am not come of myself,
but he that *sent* **apostolized** me is true,
whom ye know not.
29 But I know him: for *I am from him* **of him, I AM**,
and he hath sent me.
30 Then they sought to *take* **seize** him:
but no *man* **one** laid hands on him,
because his hour was not yet come.
31 And many of the *people* **multitude**
believed on **trusted in** him, and *said* **worded**,
When *Christ* **ever the Messiah** cometh,
will **shall** he do **many** more *miracles* **signs** than these
which this *man* **one** hath done?
32 The Pharisees heard that the *people* **multitude**
murmured *such things* **these** concerning him;
and the Pharisees and the *chief* **arch** priests
sent officers **apostolized attendants** to *take* **seize** him.
33 Then said *Jesus* **Yah Shua** unto them,
Yet a little *while* **time** am I with you,
and then I go unto him that sent me.
34 Ye shall seek me, and shall not find me:
and where I am, thither ye cannot come.
35 Then said the *Jews* **Yah Hudiym** among themselves,
Whither *will* **shall** he go, that we shall not find him?
will **shall** he go unto the *dispersed* **Diaspora**
among the *Gentiles* **Hellenes**,
and *teach* **doctrinate** the *Gentiles* **Hellenes**?
36 What *manner of saying* **word** is this that he said,
Ye shall seek me, and shall not find me:
and where I am, thither ye cannot come?

YAH SHUA'S INVITATION TO TAKE THE HOLY SPIRIT

37 In the *last* **final** day,
that *great* **mega** day of the *feast* **celebration**,
Jesus **Yah Shua** stood and cried, *saying* **wording**,
If any *man* **one** thirst, let him come unto me, and drink.
38 He that *believeth on* **trusteth in** me,
exactly as the scripture hath said,
out of his belly shall flow *rivers* **streams** of living water.
39 (But this *spake* **said** he *of* **concerning** the Spirit,
which they that *believe on* **trust in** him should *receive* **take**:
for the Holy *Ghost* **Spirit** was not yet *given*;
because that *Jesus* **Yah Shua** was not yet glorified.)
40 Many of the *people* **multitude** therefore,
when they heard this *saying* **word**, *said* **worded**,
Of a truth **Truly** this is the Prophet.
41 Others *said* **worded**, This is the *Christ* **Messiah**.
But some *said* **worded**,
shall *Christ* **the Messiah** come out of *Galilee* **Galiyl**?
42 Hath not **indeed** the scripture said,
That *Christ* **the Messiah**
cometh of the *seed* **sperma** of David,
and out of the *town* **village** of *Bethlehem* **Beth Lechem**,
where David was?
Michah 5:2
43 So there *was* **became** a *division* **schism**
among the *people* **multitude** because of him.
44 And some of them
would have taken **willed to seize** him;
but no *man* **one** laid hands on him.
45 Then came the *officers* **attendants**
to the *chief* **arch** priests and Pharisees;
and they said unto them, Why have ye not brought him?
46 The *officers* **attendants** answered,
Never **ever** *man* spake **a human** like this *man* **human**.
47 Then answered them the Pharisees,
Are ye also *deceived* **seduced**?
48 Have any of the *rulers* **archs** or of the Pharisees
believed on **trusted in** him?
49 But this *people* **multitude**
who knoweth not the *law* **torah** are cursed.
50 Nicodemus *saith* **wordeth** unto them,
(he that came to *Jesus* **Yah Shua** by night,
being one of them,)
51 Doth our *law* **torah** judge any *man* **human**,
before **unless** it **first** hear him, and know what he doeth?
52 They answered and said unto him,
Art thou also of *Galilee* **Galiyl**?
Search, and *look* **see**:
for out of *Galilee* **Galiyl** ariseth no prophet.
53 And *every man* **each** went unto his own house.

8 *Jesus* **But Yah Shua** went unto the mount of Olives.

THE ADULTERESS

2 And *early in the morning* **at dawn**
he came again into the *temple* **priestal precinct**,
and all the people came unto him;
and he sat down, and *taught* **doctrinated** them.
3 And the scribes and Pharisees brought unto him
a woman *taken* **overtaken** in adultery;
and when they had set her in the midst,
4 They *say* **word** unto him, *Master* **Doctor**,
this woman was *taken* **overtaken** in adultery,
in the very act.
5 Now *Moses* **Mosheh** in the *law* **torah**
commanded **misvahed** us, that such should be stoned:
but what *sayest* **wordest** thou?
6 This they *said* **worded**, *tempting* **testing** him,
that they might have to accuse him.
But *Jesus* **Yah Shua** stooped down,
and with his finger *wrote on* **scribed in** the ground,
as though he heard them not.
7 So when they *continued* **abode** asking him,
he *lifted up* **unbent** himself, and said unto them,
He that is *without sin* **sinless** among you,
let him first cast a stone at her.
8 And again he stooped down,
and *wrote on* **scribed in** the ground.
9 And they which heard it,
being *convicted* **reproved** by their own conscience,
went out one by one,
beginning *at* **from** the *eldest* **elders**, even unto the *last* **final**:
and *Jesus* **Yah Shua** was left alone,
and the woman standing in the midst.
10 When *Jesus* **Yah Shua** had *lifted up* **unbent** himself,
and saw *none but* **no one except** the woman,
he said unto her, Woman,
where are those thine accusers?
hath no *man* **one** condemned thee?
11 She said, no *man* **one**, *Lord* **Adonay**.
And *Jesus* **Yah Shua** said unto her,
Neither do I condemn thee: go, and sin no more.
12 Then spake *Jesus* **Yah Shua** again unto them,
saying **wording**,
I am **I AM** the light of the *world* **cosmos**:
he that followeth me shall not walk in darkness,
but shall have the light of life.
13 The Pharisees therefore said unto him,
Thou *bearest record of* **witnessest concerning** thyself;
thy *record* **witness** is not true.
14 *Jesus* **Yah Shua** answered and said unto them,
Though I *bear record of* **witness concerning** myself,
yet my *record* **witness** is true:
for I know whence I came, and whither I go;
but ye *cannot tell* **know not** whence I come,
and whither I go.
15 Ye judge after the flesh; I judge no *man* **one**.
16 And yet if I judge, my judgment is true:
for I am not alone, but I and the Father that sent me.
17 It is also *written* **scribed** in your *law* **torah**,

that the *testimony* **witness** of two *men* **humans** is true.
18 *I am one that bear witness of*
I AM witnesseth concerning myself,
and the Father that sent me
beareth witness of **witnesseth concerning** me.
19 Then *said* **worded** they unto him, Where is thy Father?
Jesus **Yah Shua** answered,
Ye neither know me, nor my Father:
if ye had known me,
ye should have known my Father also.
20 These *words* **rhema**
spake *Jesus* **Yah Shua** in the treasury,
as he *taught* **doctrinated** in the *temple* **priestal precinct**
and no *man laid hands on* **one seized** him;
for his hour was not yet come.
21 Then said *Jesus* **Yah Shua** again unto them,
I go my way,
and ye shall seek me, and shall die in your sins:
whither I go, ye cannot come.
22 Then *said* **worded** the *Jews* **Yah Hudiym**,
will **shall** he *kill* **slaughter** himself?
because he *saith* **wordeth**, Whither I go, ye cannot come.
23 And he said unto them,
Ye are from beneath; I am from above:
ye are of this *world* **cosmos**;
I am not of this *world* **cosmos**.
24 I said therefore unto you, that ye shall die in your sins:
for if ye *believe* **trust** not that *I am he* **I AM**,
ye shall die in your sins.
25 Then *said* **worded** they unto him, Who art thou?
And *Jesus* **Yah Shua** saith unto them,
Even the same
that I *said* **spake** unto you from the beginning.
26 I have *many things* **much** to *say* **speak** and to judge
of **concerning** you:
but he that sent me is true;
and I *speak* **word** to the *world* **cosmos**
those *things* which I have heard of him.
27 They *understood* **knew** not
that he *spake* **worded** to them of the Father.

TRUTH LIBERATES

28 Then said *Jesus* **Yah Shua** unto them,
When **ever** ye have
lifted up **exalted** the Son of *man* **humanity**,
then shall ye know that *I am he* **I AM**,
and that I do *nothing* **naught** of myself;
but **exactly** as my Father hath *taught* **doctrinated** me,
I speak these *things*.
29 And he that sent me is with me:
the Father hath not *left* **forsaken** me alone;
for I do always those *things* that please him.
30 As he spake these words,
many *believed on* **trusted in** him.
31 Then *said Jesus* **worded Yah Shua**
to those *Jews* **Yah Hudiym** which *believed on* **trusted in** him,
If ye *continue* **abide** in my word,
then are ye **truly** my disciples *indeed*;
32 And ye shall know the truth,
and the truth shall *make* **liberate** you *free*.
33 They answered him, We be Abraham's *seed* **sperma**,
and were never — **not ever**
in bondage **servient** to any *man* **one**:
how *sayest* **wordest** thou, Ye shall be *made free* **liberated**?
34 *Jesus* **Yah Shua** answered them,
Verily, verily I say **Amen! Amen! I word** unto you,
Whosoever *committeth* **doeth** sin is the servant of sin.
35 And the servant abideth not in the house
for ever **unto the eons**:
but the Son abideth *for ever* **unto the eons**.
36 If the Son therefore shall *make* **liberate** you *free*,
ye shall be *free* **liberated** indeed.
37 I know that ye are Abraham's *seed* **sperma**;
but ye seek to *kill* **slaughter** me,
because my word hath no place in you.
38 I speak that which I have seen with my Father:
and ye do that which ye have seen with your father.
39 They answered and said unto him,
Abraham is our father.
Jesus saith **Yah Shua wordeth** unto them,
If ye were Abraham's children,
ye *would* **should** do the works of Abraham.
40 But now ye seek to *kill* **slaughter** me,
a *man* **human** that hath *told you* **spoken** the truth,
which I have heard of *God* **Elohim**: this did not Abraham.
41 Ye do the *deeds* **works** of your father.
Then said they to him,
We be not born of *fornication* **whoredom**;
we have one Father, even *God* **Elohim**.
42 *Jesus* **Yah Shua** said unto them,
If *God* **Elohim** were your Father,
ye *would* **should** love me:
for I proceeded forth and came from *God* **Elohim**;
neither came I of myself, but he *sent* **apostolized** me.
43 Why do ye not *understand* **know** my speech?
even because ye cannot hear my word.
44 Ye are of your father *the devil* **Diabolos**,
and the *lusts* **pantings** of your father ye will **to** do.
He was a murderer from the beginning,
and *abode* **stood** not in the truth,
because there is no truth in him.
When **ever** he speaketh a lie, he speaketh of his own:
for he is a liar, and the father of it.
45 And because I *tell* **word** you the truth,
ye *believe* **trust** me not.
46 Which of you *convinceth* **reproveth** me *of* **for** sin?
And if I *say* **word** the truth,
why do ye not *believe* **trust** me?
47 He that is of *God* **Elohim**
heareth *God's words* **the rhema of Elohim**:
ye therefore hear them not,
because ye are not of *God* **Elohim**.
48 Then answered the *Jews* **Yah Hudiym**,
and said unto him,
Say **Word** we not well
that thou art a *Samaritan* **Shomeroniy**,
and hast a *devil* **demon**?
49 *Jesus* **Yah Shua** answered, I have not a *devil* **demon**;
but I honour my Father, and ye *do* dishonour me.
50 And I seek not mine own glory:
there is one that seeketh and judgeth.
51 *Verily, verily, I say* **Amen! Amen! I word** unto you,
If any *man keep* **one guard** my *saying* **word**,
he shall never see death **unto the eons**.
52 Then said the *Jews* **Yah Hudiym** unto him,
Now we know that thou hast a *devil* **demon**.
Abraham is dead, and the prophets;
and thou *sayest* **wordest**,
If *a man keep* **any one guard** my *saying* **word**,
he shall never taste of death **unto the eons**.
53 Art thou greater than our father Abraham,
which is dead? and the prophets are dead:
whom makest thou thyself?
54 *Jesus* **Yah Shua** answered, If I *honour* **glorify** myself,
my *honour* **glory** is *nothing* **naught**:
it is my Father that *honoureth* **glorifieth** me;
of whom ye *say* **word**, that he is your *God* **Elohim**:
55 Yet ye have not known him; but I know him:
and if I should say, I know him not,
I shall be a liar like unto you:
but I know him, and *keep* **guard** his *saying* **word**.
56 Your father Abraham
rejoiced **jumped for joy** to see my day:
and he saw it, and *was glad* **cheered**.

YAH SHUA, THE ETERNAL I AM

57 Then said the *Jews* **Yah Hudiym** unto him,
Thou art not yet fifty years *old*,
and hast thou seen Abraham?
58 *Jesus* **Yah Shua** said unto them,
Verily, verily I say **Amen! Amen! I word** unto you,
Before Abraham *was* **became**, *I am* **I AM**.
59 Then took they *up* stones to cast at him:
but *Jesus hid* **Yah Shua secreted** himself,
and went out of the *temple* **priestal precinct**,
going **passing** through the midst of them,
and *so* **thus** passed by.

YAH SHUA HEALS ONE BORN BLIND

9 And as *Jesus* **Yah Shua** passed by,
he saw a *man* **human** which was blind from his birth.
2 And his disciples asked him, *saying* **wording**,
Master **Rabbi**, who did sin,

this man, or his parents, that he was born blind?
3 *Jesus* **Yah Shua** answered,
Neither hath this man sinned, nor his parents:
but that the works of *God* **Elohim**
should be *made* manifest in him.
4 I must work the works of him that sent me,
while it is day:
the night cometh, when no *man* **one** can work.
5 *As long as* **Whenever** I am in the *world* **cosmos**,
I am **I AM** the light of the *world* **cosmos**.
6 When he had thus *spoken* **said**,
he spat on the ground, and made clay of the spittle,
and he *anointed* **supplied** the eyes of the blind *man*
with the clay,
7 And said unto him, Go,
wash in the pool of *Siloam* **Shiloach**,
(which is by *interpretation* **translation**, *Sent* **Apostolized**.)
He went his way therefore,
and washed, and came seeing.
8 The neighbours therefore,
and they which before had seen him that he was blind,
said **worded**, Is not this he that sat and begged?
9 Some *said* **worded**, This is he:
others *said*, He is like him:
but he *said* **worded**, I am *he*.
10 Therefore *said* **worded** they unto him,
How were thine eyes opened?
11 He answered and said,
A *man* **human** that is *called Jesus* **worded Yah Shua**
made clay,
and *anointed* **supplied** mine eyes, and said unto me,
Go to the pool of *Siloam* **Shiloach**, and wash:
and I went and washed, and I *received sight* **saw**.
12 Then said they unto him, Where is he?
He *said* **worded**, I know not.
13 They brought to the Pharisees
him that *aforetime* **once** was blind.
14 And it was the *sabbath day* **shabbath**
when *Jesus* **Yah Shua** made the clay,
and opened his eyes.
15 Then again the Pharisees also asked him
how he *had received his sight* **saw**.
He said unto them, He put clay upon mine eyes,
and I washed, and *do* see.
16 Therefore *said* **worded** some of the Pharisees,
This *man* **human** is not of *God* **Elohim**,
because he *keepeth* **guardeth** not the *sabbath day* **shabbath**.
Others *said* **worded**,
How can a *man* **human** that is a sinner
do such *miracles* **signs**?
And there was a *division* **schism** among them.
17 They *say* **word** unto the blind man again,
What *sayest* **wordest** thou *of* **concerning** him,
that he hath opened thine eyes?
He said, He is a prophet.
18 But the *Jews* **Yah Hudiym** did not *believe* **trust**
concerning him,
that he had been blind, and *received his sight* **saw**,
until they *called* **voiced out**
to the parents of him that *had received his sight* **saw**.
19 And they asked them, *saying* **wording**,
Is this your son, who ye *say* **speak** was born blind?
how then doth he now see?
20 His parents answered them and said,
We know that this is our son, and that he was born blind:
21 But by what means he now seeth, we know not;
or who hath opened his eyes, we know not:
he is *of age* **mature**; ask him:
he shall speak *for* **concerning** himself.
22 These words *spake* **said** his parents,
because they *feared* **awed** the *Jews* **Yah Hudiym**:
for the *Jews* **Yah Hudiym** had *agreed* **covenanted** already,
that if any *man* **one**
did confess **professed** that he was *Christ* **Messiah**,
he should be *put out of the synagogue* **ex—synagogued**.
23 Therefore said his parents,
He is *of age* **mature**; ask him.
24 *Then again* **Of a second time**
called **voiced** they **out to** the *man* **human** that was blind,
and said unto him, Give *God* **Elohim** the *praise* **glory**:
we know that this *man* **human** is a sinner.
25 He answered and said,
Whether he be a sinner or no, I know not:
one *thing* I know, that, whereas I was blind, now I see.
26 Then said they to him again, What did he to thee?
how opened he thine eyes?
27 He answered them, I have *told* **said to** you already,
and ye did not hear:
wherefore *would* **will** ye **to** hear it again?
will ye also **to** be his disciples?
28 Then they *reviled* **abused** him, and said,
Thou art his disciple;
but we are *Moses'* **Mosheh's** disciples.
29 We know that *God* **Elohim** spake unto *Moses* **Mosheh**:
as for this *fellow*, we know not from whence he is.
30 The *man* **human** answered and said unto them,
Why **Indeed** herein is a *marvellous thing* **marvel**,
that ye know not from whence he is,
and yet he hath opened mine eyes.
31 Now we know that *God* **Elohim** heareth not sinners:
but if any *man* be *a worshipper of God* **Elohim—revering**,
and doeth his will, him he heareth.
32 *Since the world began* **From the first eon**
was it not heard
that any *man* **one** opened the eyes
of one that was born blind.
33 **Except** If this man were *not* of *God* **Elohim**,
he could do *nothing* **naught**.
34 They answered and said unto him,
Thou wast altogether born in sins,
and dost thou *teach* **doctrinate** us?
And they *cast him out* **ejected him**.

YAH SHUA, ELOHIM'S SON

35 *Jesus* **Yah Shua** heard
that they had *cast* **ejected** him *out*;
and when he had found him, he said unto him,
Dost thou *believe on* **trust in** the Son of *God* **Elohim**?
36 He answered and said, Who is he, *Lord* **Adoni**,
that I might *believe on* **trust in** him?
37 And *Jesus* **Yah Shua** said unto him,
Thou hast both seen him,
and it *is* **be** he that *talketh* **speaketh** with thee.
38 And he said, *Lord* **Adonay**, I *believe* **trust**.
And he worshipped him.
39 And *Jesus* **Yah Shua** said,
For **In** judgment I am come into this *world* **cosmos**,
that they which see not might see;
and that they which see might be *made* blind.
40 And some of the Pharisees which were with him
heard these words,
and said unto him, Are we blind also?
41 *Jesus* **Yah Shua** said unto them,
If ye were blind, ye should have no sin:
but now ye *say* **word**, We see;
therefore your sin *remaineth* **abideth**.

YAH SHUA THE GOOD SHEPHERD

10 *Verily, verily, I say* **Amen! Amen! I word** unto you,
He that entereth not *by* **through** the *door* **portal**
into the sheepfold,
but *climbeth up* **ascendeth** some other way,
the same is a thief and a robber.
2 But he that entereth in *by* **through** the *door* **portal**
is the shepherd of the sheep.
3 To him the *porter* **portalguard** openeth;
and the sheep hear his voice:
and he calleth his own sheep by name,
and leadeth them out.
4 And when **ever** he putteth forth his own sheep,
he goeth *before* **ahead of** them,
and the sheep follow him: for they know his voice.
5 And *a stranger will* **another shall** they not follow,
but *will* **shall** flee from him:
for they know not the voice of *strangers* **another**.
6 This parable spake *Jesus* **Yah Shua** unto them:
but they *understood* **knew** not
what *things* they were which he *spake* **told** unto them.

YAH SHUA THE PORTAL

7 Then said *Jesus* **Yah Shua** unto them again,
Verily, verily, I say **Amen! Amen! I word**, unto you,
I am **I AM** the *door* **portal** of the sheep.

8 All *that* — **As many as** ever came before me
are thieves and robbers:
but the sheep did not hear them.
9 *I am* **I AM** the *door* **portal**:
by **through** me if any *man* **one** enter in,
he shall be saved,
and shall go in and out, and find pasture.
10 The thief cometh not, *but for* **except** to *steal* **thieve**,
and to *kill* **sacrifice**, and to destroy:
I am come that they might have life,
and that they might have it
more abundantly **superabundantly**.

THE GOOD SHEPHERD PLACES HIS SOUL

11 *I am* **I AM** the good shepherd:
the good shepherd
giveth **placeth** his *life* **soul** for the sheep.
12 But he that is an hireling, and not **being** the shepherd,
whose own the sheep are not, seeth the wolf coming,
and *leaveth* **forsaketh** the sheep, and fleeth:
and the wolf *catcheth* **seizeth** them,
and scattereth the sheep.
13 The hireling fleeth, because he is an hireling,
and *careth* **concerneth** not for the sheep.
14 *I am* **I AM** the good shepherd, and know my sheep,
and am known of mine.
15 **Exactly** As the Father knoweth me,
even so know I the Father:
and I *lay down* **place** my *life* **soul** for the sheep.

OTHER SHEEP, ANOTHER COURTYARD:
ONE SHEPHERDDOM, ONE SHEPHERD

16 And other sheep I have,
which are not of this *fold* **courtyard**:
them also I must bring, and they shall hear my voice;
and there shall be one *fold* **shepherddom**,
and one shepherd.
17 Therefore doth my Father love me,
because I *lay down* **place** my *life* **soul**,
that I might take it again.
18 No *man* **one** taketh it from me,
but I *lay* **place** it *down* of myself.
I have *power* **authority** to *lay it down* **place**,
and I have *power* **authority** to take it again.
This *commandment* **misvah**
have I *received* **taken** of my Father.
19 There *was* **became** a *division* **schism**
therefore again
among the *Jews* **Yah Hudiym** for these *sayings* **words**.
20 And many of them *said* **worded**,
He hath a *devil* **demon**, and *is mad* **raveth**;
why hear ye him?
21 Others *said* **worded**,
These are not the *words* **rhema**
of *him that hath a devil* **one demonized**.
Can a *devil* **demon** open the eyes of the blind?

YAH SHUA, THE MESSIAH

22 And it *was* **became** at *Jerusalem* **Yeru Shalem**
the *feast of the dedication* **hanukkah**,
and it was *winter* **the downpour**.
23 And *Jesus* **Yah Shua**
walked in the *temple* **priestal precinct**
in *Solomon's porch* **Shelomoh's portico**.
24 Then *came* the *Jews* **Yah Hudiym**
round about **surrounded him**, and *said* **worded** unto him,
How long **Until when**
dost thou *make us to doubt* **lift our soul in suspense**?
If thou be the *Christ* **Messiah**, *tell* **say to** us *plainly* **boldly**.

YAH SHUA AND FATHER ARE ONE

25 *Jesus* **Yah Shua** answered them,
I *told* **said to** you, and ye *believed* **trusted** not:
the works that I do in my Father's name,
they *bear* witness *of* **concerning** me.
26 But ye *believe* **trust** not,
because ye are not of my sheep,
exactly as I said unto you.
27 My sheep hear my voice, and I know them,
and they follow me:
28 And I give unto them eternal life;
and they shall never *perish* **destruct unto the eons**,
neither shall any *man* **one**
pluck **seize** them out of my hand.
29 My Father, which gave them me, is greater than all;
and no *man* **one**
is able to *pluck* **seize** them out of my Father's hand.
30 I and *my* **the** Father are one.

YAH SHUA ACCUSED OF BLASPHEMY

31 Then the *Jews took up* **Yah Hudiym bore** stones again
to stone him.
32 *Jesus* **Yah Shua** answered them,
Many good works have I shewed you from my Father;
for which of those works do ye stone me?
33 The *Jews* **Yah Hudiym** answered him, *saying* **wording**,
For a good work we stone thee not; but for blasphemy;
and because that thou, being *a man* **human**,
makest thyself *God* **Elohim**.
34 *Jesus* **Yah Shua** answered them,
Is it not *written* **scribed** in your *law* **torah**,
I said, Ye are *gods* **elohim**?
Psalm 82:6
35 If he called them *gods* **elohim**,
unto whom the word of *God came* **Elohim became**,
and the scripture cannot be *broken* **released**;
36 *Say* **Word** ye of him,
whom the Father hath *sanctified* **hallowed**,
and *sent* **apostolized** into the *world* **cosmos**,
Thou blasphemest;
because I said, *I am* **I AM** the Son of *God* **Elohim**?
37 If I do not the works of my Father,
believe **trust** me not.
38 But if I do, though ye *believe* **trust** not me,
believe **trust** the works:
that ye may know, and *believe* **trust**,
that the Father is in me, and I in him.
39 Therefore they sought again to *take* **seize** him:
but he escaped out of their hand,
40 And went away again *beyond Jordan* **over Yarden**
into the place where *John* **Yahn** at first baptized;
and there he abode.
41 And many resorted unto him, and *said* **worded**,
Indeed, *John* **Yahn** did no *miracle* **sign**:
but all *things* that *John spake of* **Yahn said about** this man
were true.
42 And many *believed on* **trusted in** him there.

EL AZAR DIES

11 Now *a certain man* **someone** was *sick* **frail**,
named Lazarus — **El Azar**, of *Bethany* **Beth Ania**,
the town of *Mary* **Miryam** and her sister Martha.
2 (It was that *Mary* **Miryam**
which anointed *the Lord* **Adonay** with *ointment* **myrrh**,
and *wiped* **squeezedried** his feet with her hair,
whose brother *Lazarus* **El Azar** was *sick* **frail**.)
3 Therefore his sisters *sent* **apostolized** unto him,
saying **wording**, *Lord* **Adonay**, behold,
he whom thou *lovest* **befriendest** is *sick* **frail**.
4 When *Jesus* **Yah Shua** heard that, he said,
This *sickness* **frailty** is not unto death,
but for the glory of *God* **Elohim**,
that the Son of *God* **Elohim** might be glorified thereby.
5 Now *Jesus* **Yah Shua** loved Martha,
and her sister, and *Lazarus* **El Azar**.
6 When he had heard therefore that he was *sick* **frail**,
he abode two days still in the same place where he was.
7 Then after that *saith* **wordeth** he to his disciples,
Let us go into *Judaea* **Yah Hudah** again.
8 His disciples *say* **word** unto him, *Master* **Rabbi**,
the *Jews of late* **Yah Hudiym now** sought to stone thee;
and goest thou thither again?
9 *Jesus* **Yah Shua** answered,
Are there **indeed** not twelve hours in the day?
If any *man* **one** walk in the day, he stumbleth not,
because he seeth the light of this *world* **cosmos**.
10 But if a man walk in the night, he stumbleth,
because there is no light in him.
11 These *things* said he:
and after that he *saith* **wordeth** unto them,
Our friend *Lazarus* **El Azar** sleepeth;
but I go, that I may awake him out of sleep.
12 Then said his disciples,
Lord **Adonay**, if he sleep, he shall *do well* **be saved**.
13 Howbeit *Jesus* **Yah Shua**
spake of **said concerning** his death:

but they thought that he had *spoken* **worded**
of taking of rest **about sleeping** in *sleep* **slumber**.
14 Then said *Jesus* **Yah Shua** unto them *plainly* **boldly**,
Lazarus **El Azar** is dead.
15 And I am glad for your sakes that I was not there,
to the intent **that** ye may *believe* **trust**;
nevertheless **yet** let us go unto him.
16 Then said *Thomas* **Taom**,
which is *called Didymus* **worded Twin**,
unto his *fellowdisciples* **co—disciples**,
Let us also go, that we may die with him.
17 Then when *Jesus* **Yah Shua** came,
he found
that he had lain in the *grave* **tomb** four days already.
18 Now *Bethany* **Beth Ania**
was nigh unto *Jerusalem* **Yeru Shalem**,
about fifteen *furlongs* **stadia** off:
19 And many of the *Jews* **Yah Hudiym**
came to **them around** Martha and *Mary* **Miryam**,
to *comfort* **console** them concerning their brother.
20 Then Martha,
as soon as she heard that *Jesus* **Yah Shua** was coming,
went and met him:
but *Mary* **Miryam** sat still in the house.
21 Then said Martha unto *Jesus* **Yah Shua**, *Lord* **Adonay**,
if thou hadst been here, my brother had not died.
22 But I know, that even now,
whatsoever **— as much as ever**
thou *wilt* **shalt** ask of *God* **Elohim**,
God will **Elohim shall** give it thee.
23 *Jesus saith* **Yah Shua wordeth** unto her,
Thy brother shall rise *again*.
24 Martha *saith* **wordeth** unto him,
I know that he shall rise *again*
in the resurrection at the *last* **final** day.

YAH SHUA, THE RESSURECTION AND THE LIFE

25 *Jesus* **Yah Shua** said unto her,
I am **I AM** the resurrection, and the life:
he that *believeth* **trusteth** in me,
though he were dead, yet shall he live:
26 And whosoever liveth and *believeth* **trusteth** in me
shall never die **unto the eons**.
Believest **Trustest** thou this?
27 She *saith* **wordeth** unto him, Yea, *Lord* **Adonay**:
I believe **trust** that thou art the *Christ* **Messiah**,
the Son of *God* **Elohim**,
which should come into the *world* **cosmos**.
28 And when she had so said, she went her way,
and *called Mary* **voiced out to Miryam** her sister secretly,
saying, The *Master* **Doctor** is *come* **here**
and *calleth for* **voiceth out to** thee.
29 As soon as she heard that,
she arose quickly, and came unto him.
30 Now *Jesus* **Yah Shua** was not yet come into the town,
but was in that place where Martha met him.
31 The *Jews* **Yah Hudiym** then
which were with her in the house,
and *comforted* **consoled** her,
when they saw *Mary* **Miryam**,
that she rose *up hastily* **quickly** and went out,
followed her, *saying* **wording**,
She goeth unto the *grave* **tomb** to weep there.
32 Then when *Mary* **Miryam** was come
where *Jesus* **Yah Shua** was, and saw him,
she fell down *at* **to** his feet, *saying* **wording** unto him,
Lord **Adonay**, if thou hadst been here,
my brother had not died.
33 When *Jesus* **Yah Shua** therefore saw her weeping,
and the *Jews* **Yah Hudiym** also weeping
which came with her,
he *groaned* **sighed** in the spirit, and was troubled.
34 And said, Where have ye *laid* **placed** him?
They *said* **worded** unto him, *Lord* **Adonay**, come and see.
35 *Jesus* **Yah Shua** wept.
36 Then *said* **worded** the *Jews* **Yah Hudiym**,
Behold how he *loved* **befriended** him!
37 And some of them said,
Could not this man, which opened the eyes of the blind,
have caused that even this man should not have died?
38 *Jesus* **Yah Shua** therefore again
groaning **sighing** in himself cometh to the *grave* **tomb**.
It was a *cave* **grotto**, and a stone lay upon it.
39 *Jesus said* **Yah Shua worded**, Take ye away the stone.
Martha, the sister of him that was dead,
saith **wordeth** unto him,
Lord **Adonay**, *by this time* **already** he stinketh:
for he hath been dead four days.
40 *Jesus saith* **Yah Shua wordeth** unto her,
Said I not unto thee, that,
if thou *wouldest believe* **shouldest trust**,
thou shouldest see the glory of *God* **Elohim**?
41 Then they took away the stone
from the place where the dead was laid.
And *Jesus* **Yah Shua** lifted *up* his eyes, and said,
Father, I *thank* **eucharistize** thee that thou hast heard me.
42 And I knew that thou hearest me always:
but because of the *people* **multitude** which stand by
I said it, that they may *believe* **trust**
that thou hast *sent* **apostolized** me.
43 And when he thus had *spoken* **said**,
he cried with a *loud* **mega** voice,
Lazarus **El Azar**, come forth.
44 And he that was dead came forth,
bound hand and foot with *graveclothes* **swathes**:
and his face was bound about with a *napkin* **sudarium**.
Jesus saith **Yah Shua wordeth** unto them,
Loose **Release** him, and let him go.
45 Then many of the *Jews* **Yah Hudiym**
which came to *Mary* **Miryam**,
and had seen *the thing* **that** which *Jesus* **Yah Shua** did,
believed on **trusted in** him.
46 But some of them went their ways to the Pharisees,
and *told* **said to** them
what *things Jesus* **Yah Shua** had done.
47 Then gathered the *chief* **arch** priests and the Pharisees
a *council* **sanhedrim**,
and *said* **worded**, What do we?
for this *man* **human** doeth many *miracles* **signs**.
48 If we *let* **allow** him thus *alone*,
all men will believe on **everyone shall trust in** him:
and the Romans shall come
and take away both our place and *nation* **goyim**.
49 And one of them, *named* Caiaphas,
being the *high* **arch** priest that same year,
said unto them, Ye know *nothing at all* **not aught**,
50 Nor *consider* **reason**
that it is *expedient* **benefical** for us,
that one *man* **human** should die for the people,
and that the whole *nation perish* **goyim destruct** not.
51 And this *spake* **said** he not of himself:
but being *high* **arch** priest that year,
he prophesied
that *Jesus* **Yah Shua** should die for that *nation* **goyim**;
52 And not for that *nation* **goyim** only,
but that also he should gather together in one
the children of *God* **Elohim** that were scattered abroad.
53 Then from that day forth they took counsel together
for to *put him to death* **slaughter** him.
54 *Jesus* **Yah Shua** therefore
walked no more *openly* **boldly**
among the *Jews* **Yah Hudiym**;
but went thence
unto a *country* **region** near to the wilderness,
into a city *called Ephraim* **worded Ephrayim**,
and there *continued* **tarried** with his disciples.
55 And the *Jews' passover* **Yah Hudiy's pasach**
was nigh at hand:
and many *went out* **ascended**
of the country up **from the region**
to *Jerusalem* **Yeru Shalem**
before the *passover* **pasach**, to *purify* **hallow** themselves.
56 Then sought they for *Jesus* **Yah Shua**,
and *spake among themselves* **worded with each other**,
as they stood in the *temple* **priestal precinct**,
What think ye,
that he *will* **shall** not come to the *feast* **celebration**?
57 Now both the *chief* **arch** priests and the Pharisees
had given a *commandment* **misvah**,
that, if any *man* **one** knew where he were,
he should *shew* **disclose** it, that they might *take* **seize** him.

MIRYAM ANOINTS YAH SHUA

12 Then *Jesus* **Yah Shua**
six days before the *passover* **pasach**
came to *Bethany* **Beth Ania**, where *Lazarus* **El Azar** was,
which had been dead, whom he raised from the dead.
2 There they made him a supper;
and Martha *served* **ministered**:
but *Lazarus* **El Azar** was one of them
that *sat at the table* **reposed** with him.
3 Then took *Mary* **Miryam**
a *pound* **litra** of *ointment* **myrrh** of *spikenard* **nard**,
very costly **trustworthy and vastly precious**,
and anointed the feet of *Jesus* **Yah Shua**,
and *wiped* **squeezedried** his feet with her hair:
and the house was filled
with the *odour* **fragrance** of the *ointment* **myrrh**.
4 Then *saith* **wordeth** one of his disciples,
Judas Iscariot **Yah Hudah the urbanite**,
Simon's **Shimon's** son, which should betray him,
5 Why was not this *ointment* **myrrh** sold
for three hundred *pence* **denarion**, and given to the poor?
6 This he said,
not that he *cared* **was concerned** for the poor;
but because he was a thief, and had the bag,
and bare what was put therein.
7 Then said *Jesus* **Yah Shua**, *Let* **Allow** her *alone*:
against **unto** the day of my *burying* **embalming**
hath she *kept* **guarded** this.
8 For the poor always ye have with you;
but me ye have not always.
9 Much *people* **multitude** of the *Jews* **Yah Hudiym**
therefore knew that he was there:
and they came not for *Jesus'* **Yah Shua's** sake only,
but that they might see *Lazarus* **El Azar** also,
whom he had raised from the dead.
10 But the *chief* **arch** priests *consulted* **counseled**
that they might
put Lazarus **slaughter El Azar** also *to death*;
11 Because that *by reason* **because** of him
many of the *Jews* **Yah Hudiym** went away,
and *believed on Jesus* **trusted in Yah Shua**.

YAH SHUA'S TRIUMPHAL ENTRY

12 On the next day much *people* **multitude**
that were come to the *feast* **celebration**,
when they heard that *Jesus* **Yah Shua**
was coming to *Jerusalem* **Yeru Shalem**
13 Took branches of *palm trees* **phoinix**,
and went forth to meet him,
and cried, *Hosanna:* **Hoshia Na!**
Blessed is **Eulogized**
be the *King* **Sovereign** of *Israel* **Yisra El**
that cometh in the name of *the Lord* **Yah Veh**.
14 And *Jesus* **Yah Shua**,
when he had found a *young ass* **burrito**, sat thereon;
exactly as *it is written* **scribed**,
15 *Fear* **Awe** not, daughter of *Sion* **Siyon**:
behold, thy *King* **Sovereign** cometh,
sitting on *an ass's* **a burro's** colt.
Psalm 118:25, 26; Zechar Yah 9:9
16 These *things understood* **knew** not his disciples
at the first:
but when *Jesus* **Yah Shua** was glorified,
then remembered they
that these *things* were *written* **scribed** of him,
and that they had done these *things* unto him.
17 The *people* **multitude** therefore that was with him
when he *called Lazarus* **voiced out to El Azar**
out of his *grave* **tomb**, and raised him from the dead,
bare record **witnessed**.
18 For this cause the *people* **multitude** also met him,
for that they heard that he had done this *miracle* **sign**.
19 The Pharisees therefore said among themselves,
Perceive **See** ye how ye *prevail nothing* **benefit naught**?
behold, the *world* **cosmos** is gone after him.

HELLENES WILL TO SEE YAH SHUA

20 And there were *certain Greeks* **some Hellenes**
among **of** them that *came up* **ascended** to worship
at the *feast* **celebration**:
21 *The same* **These** came therefore to *Philip* **Philippos**,
which was of *Bethsaida* **Beth Sayad,** *Galilee* **Galiyl**,
and *desired* **asked** him, *saying* **wording**,
Sir Lord **Adoni**, we *would* **will to** see *Jesus* **Yah Shua**.
22 *Philip* **Philippos** cometh
and *telleth Andrew* **wordeth to Andreas**:
and again *Andrew* **Andreas** and *Philip* **Philippos**
tell Jesus **word to Yah Shua**.

YAH SHUA PROPHESIES HIS DEATH AND GLORIFICATION

23 And *Jesus* **Yah Shua** answered them, *saying* **wording**,
The hour is come,
that the Son of *man* **humanity** should be glorified.
24 *Verily, verily, I say* **Amen! Amen! I word** unto you,
Except **Unless** a *corn* **kernal** of *wheat* **grain**
fall into the ground and die, it abideth alone:
but if it die, it bringeth forth much fruit.
25 He that *loveth* **befriendeth** his *life* **soul** shall lose it;
and he that hateth his *life* **soul** in this *world* **cosmos**
shall *keep* **guard** it unto life eternal.
26 If any *man serve* **one minister to** me,
let him follow me;
and where I am, there shall also my *servant* **minister** be:
if any *man serve* **one minister to** me,
him *will* **shall** my Father honour.
27 Now is my soul troubled; and what shall I say?
Father, save me from this hour**:?**
but for this cause came I unto this hour.
28 Father, glorify thy name.
Then came there a voice from heaven, saying,
I have both glorified *it*, and *will* **shall** glorify *it* again.
29 The *people* **multitude** therefore,
that stood by, and heard it,
said **worded** that *it thundered* **thunder became**:
others *said* **worded**, An angel spake to him.

THE COSMOS ARCH EJECTED:
YAH SHUA EXALTED

30 *Jesus* **Yah Shua** answered and said,
This voice *came* **became** not because of me,
but for your sakes.
31 Now is the judgment of this *world* **cosmos**:
now shall the *prince* **arch** of this *world* **cosmos**
be *cast out* **ejected**.
32 And I, if I be *lifted up* **exalted** from the earth,
will **shall** draw all men unto me.
33 This he *said* **worded**,
signifying what death he should die.
Loukas 10:18, Revelation 12:7—12
34 The *people* **multitude** answered him,
We have heard out of the *law* **torah**
that *Christ* **the Messiah** abideth *forever* **unto the eons**:
and how *sayest* **wordest** thou,
The Son of *man* **humanity** must be *lifted up* **exalted**?
who is this Son of *man* **humanity**?
35 Then *Jesus* **Yah Shua** said unto them,
Yet a little *while* **time** is the light with you.
Walk while ye have the light,
lest darkness *come upon* **overtake** you:
for he that walketh in darkness
knoweth not whither he goeth.
36 While ye have light, *believe* **trust** in the light,
that ye may be the *children* **sons** of light.
These *things* spake *Jesus* **Yah Shua**, and departed,
and *did hide* **secreted** himself from them.
37 But though he had done so many *miracles* **signs**
before **in front of** them,
yet they *believed* **trusted** not *on* **in** him:
38 That the *saying* **word** of *Esaias* **Yesha Yah** the prophet
might be fulfilled, which he *spake* **said**,
Lord, who hath *believed* **trusted** our report?
and to whom hath the arm of *the Lord* **Yah Veh**
been *revealed* **unveiled**?
Yesha Yah 53:1
39 Therefore they could not *believe* **trust**,
because that *Esaias* **Yesha Yah** said again,
40 He hath blinded their eyes,
and *hardened* **petrified** their heart;
that they should not see with their eyes,
nor *understand* **comprehend** with their heart,
and *be converted* **turn around**, and I should heal them.
41 These *things* said *Esaias* **Yesha Yah**,
when he saw his glory, and spake *of* **concerning** him.
Yesha Yah 6:1

42 *Nevertheless* **Yet indeed,**
among the chief rulers **even of the archs** also
many *believed on* **trusted in** him;
but because of the Pharisees
they did not *confess* **profess** him,
lest they should be
put out of the synagogue **ex—synagogued**:
43 For they loved the *praise* **glory** of *men* **humanity**
more than the *praise* **glory** of *God* **Elohim**.
44 *Jesus* **Yah Shua** cried and said,
He that *believeth on* **trusteth in** me,
believeth not on **trusteth not in** me,
but *on* **in** him that sent me.
45 And he that seeth me seeth him that sent me.
46 I am come a light into the *world* **cosmos**,
that whosoever *believeth on* **trusteth in** me
should not abide in darkness.
47 And if any *man* **one** hear my *words* **rhema**,
and *believe* **trust** not,
I judge him not:
for I came not to judge the *world* **cosmos**,
but to save the *world* **cosmos**.
48 He that *rejecteth* **setteth** me **aside**,
and *receiveth* **taketh** not my *words* **rhema**,
hath one that judgeth him:
the word that I have spoken,
the same shall judge him in the *last* **final** day.
49 For I have not spoken of myself;
but the Father which sent me,
he gave me a *commandment* **misvah**,
what I should say, and what I should speak.
50 And I know that his *commandment* **misvah**
is life *everlasting* **eternal**:
whatsoever I speak therefore,
even **exactly** as the Father said unto me, *so* **thus** I speak.

YAH SHUA'S FINAL NIGHT: THE FINAL SUPPER

13 Now before
the *feast* **celebration** of the *passover* **pasach**,
when *Jesus* **Yah Shua** knew that his hour was come
that he should depart out of this *world* **cosmos**
unto the Father,
having loved his own which were in the *world* **cosmos**,
he loved them unto the *end* **completion**.

YAH SHUA PURIFIES THE DISCIPLES' FEET

2 And supper *being ended* **having become**,
the devil **Diabolos** having *now* **already** put into the heart
of *Judas Iscariot* **Yah Hudah the urbanite**,
Simon's **Shimon's** son, to betray him;
3 *Jesus* **Yah Shua,** knowing that the Father
had given all *things* into his hands,
and that he was come from *God* **Elohim**,
and went to *God* **Elohim**;
4 He riseth from supper,
and *laid aside* **placed** his *garments* **clothing**;
and took a *towel* **linen**, and girded himself.
5 *After that* **Then** he poureth water into a bason,
and began to wash the disciples' feet,
and to *wipe* **squeezedry** them
with the *towel* **linen** wherewith he was girded.
6 Then cometh he to *Simon Peter* **Shimon Petros**:
and *Peter saith* **Petros wordeth** unto him,
Lord **Adonay**, dost thou wash my feet?
7 *Jesus* **Yah Shua** answered and said unto him,
What I do thou knowest not now;
but thou shalt know *hereafter* **after this**.
8 *Peter saith* **Petros wordeth** unto him,
Thou shalt never wash my feet **unto the eons**.
Jesus **Yah Shua** answered him,
If I wash thee not, thou hast no part with me.
9 *Simon Peter saith* **Shimon Petros wordeth** unto him,
Lord **Adonay**, not my feet only,
but also my hands and my head.
10 *Jesus saith* **Yah Shua wordeth** to him,
He that is *washed* **bathed**
needeth not *save* **except** to wash his feet,
but is *clean* **pure** every whit:
and ye are *clean* **pure**, but **indeed** not all.
11 For he knew who should betray him;
Therefore said he, Ye are not all *clean* **pure**.
12 So after he had washed their feet,
and had taken his *garments* **clothing**,
and *was set down* **reposed** again,
he said unto them, Know ye what I have done to you?
13 Ye *call* **voice out to** me
Master **Doctor** and *Lord* **Adonay**:
and ye *say* **word** well; for *so I am* **I AM**.
14 If I then, your *Lord* **Adonay** and *Master* **Doctor**,
have washed your feet;
ye also *ought* **are indebted** to wash one another's feet.
15 For I have given you an example,
that ye should do **exactly** as I have done to you.
16 *Verily, verily, I say* **Amen! Amen! I word** unto you,
The servant is not greater than his lord;
neither he that is *sent* **apostolized**
greater than he that sent him.
17 If ye know these *things*,
happy **blessed** are ye if ye do them.
18 I *speak* **word** not *of* **concerning** you all:
I know whom I have chosen:
but that the scripture may be fulfilled,
He that eateth bread with me
hath lifted *up* his heel against me.
Psalm 41:9
19 Now I *tell* **word to** you *before* **ere** it *come* **becometh**,
that, when **ever** it *is come to pass* **becometh**,
ye may *believe* **trust** that *I am he* **I AM**.
20 *Verily, verily, I say* **Amen! Amen! I word** unto you,
He that *receiveth* **taketh** whomsoever I send
receiveth **taketh** me;
and he that *receiveth* **taketh** me
receiveth **taketh** him that sent me.
21 When *Jesus* **Yah Shua** had thus said,
he was troubled in spirit, and *testified* **witnessed**,
and said,
Verily, verily, I say **Amen! Amen! I word** unto you,
that one of you shall betray me.
22 Then the disciples looked one on another,
doubting of **perplexed about** whom he *spake* **worded**.
23 Now there was *leaning* **reposing**
on Jesus' **in Yah Shua's** bosom
one of his disciples, whom *Jesus* **Yah Shua** loved.
24 *Simon Peter* **Shimon Petros** therefore beckoned to him,
that he should ask who it should be
of **concerning** whom he *spake* **worded**.
25 He then *lying* **falling** on *Jesus' breast* **Yah Shua's chest**
saith **wordeth** unto him, *Lord* **Adonay**, who is it?
26 *Jesus* **Yah Shua** answered, He it is,
to whom I shall give a *sop* **morsel**,
when I have *dipped* **baptized** it.
And when he had *dipped* **baptized** the *sop* **morsel**,
he gave it to *Judas Iscariot* **Yah Hudah the urbanite**
the son of *Simon* **Shimon**.

SATAN ENTERS YAH HUDAH

27 And after the *sop* **morsel** Satan entered into him.
Then *said Jesus* **worded Yah Shua** unto him,
That thou doest, do quickly.
28 Now no *man at the table* **one reposing**
knew for what *intent* he *spake* **said** this unto him.
29 For some *of them* thought,
because *Judas* **Yah Hudah** had the bag,
that *Jesus* **Yah Shua** had *said* **worded** unto him,
Buy **Market for** those *things* that we have need of
against **unto** the *feast* **celebration**;
or, that he should give *something* **somewhat** to the poor.
30 He then having *received* **taken** the *sop* **morsel**
went *immediately* **straightway** out: and it was night.
31 Therefore, when he was gone out,
Jesus said **Yah Shua worded**,
Now is the Son of *man* **humanity** glorified,
and *God* **Elohim** is glorified in him.
32 If *God* **Elohim** be glorified in him,
God **Elohim** shall also glorify him in himself,
and shall straightway glorify him.
33 Little children, yet a little while I am with you.
Ye shall seek me:
and **exactly** as I said unto the *Jews* **Yah Hudiym**,
Whither I go, ye cannot come;
so now I say **I also word** to you.

A NEW MISVAH

34 A new *commandment* **misvah** I give unto you,
That ye love one another;
exactly as I have loved you,
that ye also love one another.
35 By this shall *all men* **everyone** know
that ye are my disciples,
if ye have love *one to* **in one** another.
36 *Simon Peter said* **Shimon Petros worded** unto him,
Lord **Adonay**, whither goest thou?
Jesus **Yah Shua** answered him,
Whither I go, thou canst not follow me now;
but thou shalt follow me afterwards.
37 *Peter said* **Petros worded** unto him,
Lord **Adonay**, why cannot I follow thee now?
I *will lay down* **shall place** my *life* **soul** for thy sake.
38 *Jesus* **Yah Shua** answered him,
Wilt **Shalt** thou *lay down* **place** thy *life* **soul** for my sake?
Verily, verily, I say **Amen! Amen! I word** unto thee,
The *cock* **rooster** shall not *crow* **voice**,
till thou hast **utterly** denied me thrice.

YAH SHUA PROMISES HIS PAROUSIA

14 Let not your heart be troubled:
ye *believe* **trust** in *God* **Elohim**, *believe* **trust** also in me.
2 In my Father's house are many *mansions* **abodes**:
if it were not so, I *would* **should** have *told* **said to** you.
I *go* **depart** to prepare a place for you.
3 And if I *go* **depart** and prepare a place for you,
I *will* **shall** come again,
and *receive* **take** you unto myself;
that where I am, there ye may be also.
4 And whither I go ye know, and the way ye know.
5 *Thomas saith* **Taom wordeth** unto him, *Lord* **Adoni**,
we know not whither thou goest;
and how can we know the way?
6 *Jesus saith* **Yah Shua wordeth** unto him,
I am **I AM** the way, the truth, and the life:
no *man* **one** cometh unto the Father, *but* **except** by me.
7 If ye had known me,
ye should have known my Father also:
and from henceforth ye know him, and have seen him.
8 *Philip saith* **Philippos wordeth** unto him,
Lord **Adoni**, shew us the Father,
and it *sufficeth* **satisfieth** us.
9 *Jesus saith* **Yah Shua wordeth** unto him,
Have I been so long time with you,
and yet hast thou not known me, *Philip* **Philippos**?
he that hath seen me hath seen the Father;
and how *sayest* **wordest** thou then, Shew us the Father?
10 *Believest* **trustest** thou not that I am in the Father,
and the Father in me?
the *words* **rhema** that I speak unto you
I speak not of myself:
but the Father that *dwelleth* **abideth** in me,
he doeth the works.
11 *Believe* **Trust** me that I *am* in the Father,
and the Father in me:
or else believe **but if not trust** me
for the very works' sake.
12 *Verily, verily, I say* **Amen! Amen! I word** unto you,
He that *believeth on* **trusteth in** me,
the works that I do shall he do also;
and greater works than these shall he do;
because I go unto my Father.
13 And whatsoever ye shall ask in my name,
that *will* **shall** I do,
that the Father may be glorified in the Son.
14 *If* **Whatever** ye shall ask *any thing* in my name,
I *will* **shall** do it.
15 If ye love me,
keep **guard** my *commandments* **misvoth**.

YAH SHUA PROMISES THE PARACLETE

16 And I *will pray* **shall ask** the Father,
and he shall give you another *Comforter* **Paraclete**,
that he may abide with you *for ever* **unto the eons**;
17 Even the Spirit of truth;
whom the *world* **cosmos** cannot *receive* **take**,
because it seeth him not, neither knoweth him:
but ye know him;
for he *dwelleth* **abideth** with you, and shall be in you.
18 I *will* **shall** not *leave* **forsake** you *comfortless* **orphaned**:
I *will* **shall** come to you.
19 Yet a little *while*,
and the *world* **cosmos** seeth me no more;
but ye see me: because I live, ye shall live also.
20 At that day ye shall know that I am in my Father,
and ye in me, and I in you.
21 He that hath my *commandments* **misvoth**,
and *keepeth* **guardeth** them, he it is that loveth me:
and he that loveth me shall be loved of my Father,
and I *will* **shall** love him,
and *will* **shall** manifest myself to him.
22 *Judas saith* **Yah Hudah wordeth** unto him,
not *Iscariot* **the urbanite**,
Lord **Adonay**, how *is* **be** it
that thou *wilt* **art about to** manifest thyself unto us,
and **indeed** not unto the *world* **cosmos**?
23 *Jesus* **Yah Shua** answered and said unto him,
If *a man* **anyone** love me,
he *will keep* **shall guard** my words:
and my Father *will* **shall** love him,
and we *will* **shall** come unto him,
and make our abode with him.
24 He that loveth me not
keepeth **guardeth** not my *sayings* **words**:
and the word which ye hear is not mine,
but the Father's which sent me.
25 These *things* have I spoken unto you,
being yet present **abiding** with you.
26 But the *Comforter* **Paraclete**,
which is the Holy *Ghost* **Spirit**,
whom the Father *will* **shall** send in my name,
he shall *teach* **doctrinate** you all *things*,
and *bring all things to your remembrance* **remind you**,
whatsoever I have said unto you.

YAH SHUA BESTOWS HIS UNITY

27 *Peace* **Shalom** I *leave* **release** with you,
my *peace* **shalom** I give unto you:
not **exactly** as the *world* **cosmos** giveth, give I unto you.
Let not your heart be troubled,
neither let it *be afraid* **coward**.
28 Ye have heard how I said unto you,
I go away, and come again unto you.
If ye loved me, ye *would rejoice* **should cheer**,
because I said, I go unto the Father:
for my Father is greater than I.
29 And now I have *told* **said to** you
before **ere** it *come to pass* **become**,
that, when **ever** it *is come to pass* **becometh**,
ye might *believe* **trust**.
30 Hereafter I *will* **shall** not *talk* **speak** much with you:
for the *prince* **arch** of this *world* **cosmos** cometh,
and hath *nothing* **naught** in me.
31 But that the *world* **cosmos** may know
that I love the Father;
and **exactly** as the Father
gave **misvahed** me *commandment*,
even *so* **thus** I do.
Arise, let us go hence.

ABIDING IN THE VINE

15 *I am* **I AM** the true vine,
and my Father is the *husbandman* **cultivator**.
2 Every branch in me that beareth not fruit
he taketh away:
and every branch that beareth fruit,
he *purgeth* **purifieth** it,
that it may *bring forth* **bear much** more fruit.
3 *Now* **Already** ye are *clean* **pure** through the word
which I have spoken unto you.
4 **Exactly** as the branch cannot bear fruit of itself,
except **unless** it abide in the vine;
no more **thus neither** can ye,
except **unless** ye abide in me.
5 *I am* **I AM** the vine, ye are the branches:
He that abideth in me, and I in him,
the same *bringeth forth* **beareth** much fruit:
for *without* **apart from** me ye can do *nothing* **naught**.
6 If *a man* **anyone** abide not in me,
he is cast forth as a branch, and is withered;
and men gather them **together**,

and cast them into the fire, and they are burned.
7 If ye abide in me, and my *words* **rhema** abide in you,
ye shall ask what ye will, and it shall be *done* unto you.
8 Herein is my Father glorified, that ye bear much fruit;
so shall ye be my disciples.
9 **Exactly** As the Father hath loved me,
so have I loved you:
continue **abide** ye in my love.
10 If ye *keep* **guard** my *commandments* **misvoth**,
ye shall abide in my love;
even **exactly** as I have *kept* **guarded**
my Father's *commandments* **misvoth**,
and abide in his love.
11 These *things* have I spoken unto you,
that my *joy* **cheer** might *remain* **abide** in you,
and that your *joy* **cheer** might be full.
12 This is my *commandment* **misvah**,
That ye love one another, **exactly** as I have loved you.
13 Greater love hath no *man* **one** than this,
that *a man lay down* **one place** his *life* **soul**
for his friends.
14 Ye are my friends, if ye do
whatsoever **as much as ever** I *command* **misvah** you.

THE NEW RELATIONSHIP

15 Henceforth I *call* **word** you not servants;
for the servant knoweth not what his lord doeth:
but I have *called* **said** you friends;
for all *things* that I have heard of my Father
I have made known unto you.
16 Ye have not chosen me, but I have chosen you,
and *ordained* **have set** you,
that ye should go and *bring forth* **bear** fruit,
and that your fruit should *remain* **abide**:
that whatsoever ye shall ask of the Father in my name,
he may give it you.
17 These *things* I *command* **misvah** you,
that ye love one another.
18 If the *world* **cosmos** hate you,
ye know that it hated me *before it hated you* **first**.
19 If ye were of the *world* **cosmos**,
the *world* **cosmos**
would love **should ever befriend** his own:
but because ye are not of the *world* **cosmos**,
but I have chosen you out of the *world* **cosmos**,
Therefore the *world* **cosmos** hateth you.
20 Remember the word that I said unto you,
The servant is not greater than his lord.
If they have persecuted me,
they *will* **shall** also persecute you;
if they have *kept* **guarded** my *saying* **word**,
they *will keep* **shall guard** yours also.
21 But all these *things*
will **shall** they do unto you for my name's sake,
because they know not him that sent me.
22 *If I had not* **Except I had** come and spoken unto them,
they had not had sin:
but now they have no *cloak* **pretext** for their sin.
23 He that hateth me hateth my Father also.
24 *If* **Except** I had *not* done among them
the works which none other man did,
they had not had sin:
but now have they both seen and hated
both me and my Father.
25 But this *cometh to pass* **becometh**,
that the word might be fulfilled
that is *written* **scribed** in their *law* **torah**,
They hated me *without a cause* **gratuitously**.
Psalms 35:19, 69:4
26 But when **ever** the *Comforter* **Paraclete** is come,
whom I *will* **shall** send unto you from the Father,
even the Spirit of truth,
which proceedeth from the Father,
he shall *testify of* **witness concerning** me:
27 And ye also shall *bear* witness,
because ye have been with me from the beginning.

EX—SYNOGOGUING AND MARTYRDOM

16 These *things* have I spoken unto you,
that ye should not be *offended* **scandalized**.
2 They shall *put* **ex—synogogue** you *out of the synagogues*:
yea, **yet** the *time* **hour** cometh,
that whosoever *killeth* **slaughtereth** you *will* **shall** think
that he *doeth God service* **offereth Elohim liturgy**.
3 And these *things will* **shall** they do unto you,
because they have not known the Father, nor me.
4 But these *things* have I *told* **spoken unto** you,
that when **ever** the *time* **hour** shall *come* **become**,
ye may remember that I told you of them.
And these *things* I said not unto you
at **from** the beginning,
because I was with you.
5 But now I go my way to him that sent me;
and none of you asketh me, Whither goest thou?
6 But because I have *said* **spoken** these *things* unto you,
sorrow hath filled your heart **full**.

THE MINISTRY OF THE PARACLETE

7 *Nevertheless I tell* **Yet I word** you the truth;
It is *expedient* **beneficial** for you that I go away:
for if I go not away,
the *Comforter will* **Paraclete shall** not come unto you;
but if I depart, I *will* **shall** send him unto you.
8 And when he is come,
he *will* **shall** reprove the *world* **cosmos**
of **concerning** sin,
and *of righteousness* **concerning justness**,
and *of* **concerning** judgment:
9 *Of sin* **Concerning sin indeed**,
because they *believe* **trust** not *on* **in** me;
10 *Of righteousness* **Concerning justness**,
because I go to my Father, and ye see me no more;
11 *Of* **Concerning** judgment,
because the *prince* **arch** of this *world* **cosmos** is judged.
12 I have yet *many things* **much** to *say* **word** unto you,
but ye cannot bear them now.
13 Howbeit when **ever** he, the Spirit of truth, is come,
he *will* **shall** guide you into all truth:
for he shall not speak of himself;
but whatsoever he shall hear, that shall he speak:
and he *will shew* **shall evangelize** you
things **those** to come.
14 He shall glorify me:
for he shall *receive* **take** of mine,
and shall *shew* **evangelize** it unto you.

YAH SHUA PROPHESIES HIS DEATH, RESURRECTION, AND PAROUSIA

15 All *things that* — **as much as** the Father hath are mine:
Therefore said I, that he shall take of mine,
and shall *shew* **evangelize** it unto you.
16 A little *while*, and ye shall not see me:
and again, a little *while*, and ye shall see me,
because I go to the Father.
17 Then said some of his disciples
among themselves **to one another**,
What is this that he *saith* **wordeth** unto us,
A little *while*, and ye shall not see me:
and again, a little *while*, and ye shall see me:
and, Because I go to the Father?
18 They *said* **worded** therefore,
What is this that he *saith* **wordeth**, A little *while*?
we *cannot tell* **know not** what he *saith* **wordeth**.
19 Now *Jesus* **Yah Shua** knew
that they *were desirous* **willed** to ask him,
and said unto them,
Do ye enquire **Seek ye**
among yourselves **with one another**
of **concerning** that I said,
A little *while*, and ye shall not see me:
and again, a little *while*, and ye shall see me?
20 *Verily, verily, I say* **Amen! Amen! I word** unto you,
That ye shall weep and lament,
but the *world* **cosmos** shall *rejoice* **cheer**:
and ye shall be sorrowful,
but your sorrow shall *be turned into joy* **become cheer**.
21 A woman when **ever** she *is in travail* **births**
hath sorrow,
because her hour is come:
but *as soon as* **whenever**
she *is delivered of* **beareth** the child,
she remembereth no more the anguish,
for *joy* **cheer**
that a *man* **human** is born into the *world* **cosmos**.

22 And **indeed** ye now therefore have sorrow:
but I *will* **shall** see you again,
and your heart shall *rejoice* **cheer**,
and your *joy* **cheer** no *man* **one** taketh from you.
23 And in that day ye shall ask me *nothing* **naught**.
Verily, verily, I say **Amen! Amen! I word** unto you,
Whatsoever **As much as ever**
ye shall ask the Father in my name,
he *will* **shall** give it you.
24 Hitherto have ye asked *nothing* **naught** in my name:
ask, and ye shall *receive* **take**
that your *joy* **cheer** may be *full* **fulfilled**.
25 These *things* have I spoken unto you in proverbs:
but the *time* **hour** cometh,
when I shall no more speak unto you in proverbs,
but I shall *shew* **evangelize** you *plainly* **boldly**
of **concerning** the Father.
26 At that day ye shall ask in my name:
and I *say* **word** not unto you,
that I *will pray* **shall ask** the Father for you:
27 For the Father himself *loveth* **befriendeth** you,
because ye have *loved* **befriended** me,
and have *believed* **trusted**
that I came out from *God* **Elohim**.
28 I came forth from the Father,
and am come into the *world* **cosmos**:
again, I leave the *world* **cosmos**, and go to the Father.
29 His disciples *said* **worded** unto him,
Lo **Behold**, now speakest thou *plainly* **boldly**,
and *speakest* **wordest** no proverb.
30 Now *are* we *sure* **know**
that thou knowest all *things*,
and needest not that any *man* should ask thee:
by **in** this we *believe* **trust**
that thou camest forth from *God* **Elohim**.
31 *Jesus* **Yah Shua** answered them,
Do ye now *believe* **trust**?
32 Behold, the hour cometh, yea, is now come,
that ye shall be scattered, *every man* **each** to his own,
and shall *leave* **forsake** me alone:
and yet I am not alone, because the Father is with me.
33 These *things* I have spoken unto you
that in me ye might have *peace* **shalom**.
In the *world* **cosmos** ye shall have tribulation:
but *be of good cheer;* **Courage**!
I have *overcome* **triumphed over** the *world* **cosmos**.

YAH SHUA'S PRAYER TO THE FATHER

17 These words spake *Jesus* **Yah Shua**,
and lifted *up* his eyes to heaven, and said,
Father, the hour is come; glorify thy Son,
that thy Son also may glorify thee:
2 **Exactly** As thou hast given him *power* **authority**
over all flesh,
that he should give eternal life
to as many as thou hast given him.
3 And this is life eternal,
that they might know thee the only true *God* **Elohim**,
and *Jesus Christ* **Yah Shua Messiah**,
whom thou hast *sent* **apostolized**.
4 I have glorified thee on the earth:
I have *finished* **completed** the work
which thou gavest me to do.
5 And now, O Father, glorify thou me with thine own self
with the glory which I had with thee
before the *world* **cosmos** was.
6 I have manifested thy name unto *the men* **humanity**
which thou gavest me out of the *world* **cosmos**:
thine they were, and thou gavest them me;
and they have *kept* **guarded** thy word.
7 Now they have known that all *things*
whatsoever **— as much as ever** thou hast given me
are of thee.
8 For I have given unto them
the *words* **rhema** which thou gavest me;
and they have *received* **taken** them,
and have known *surely* **truly** that I came out from thee,
and they have *believed* **trusted**
that thou didst *send* **apostolize** me.
9 I *pray* **ask** for them: I *pray* **ask** not for the *world* **cosmos**,
but for them which thou hast given me;
for they are thine.
10 And all mine are thine, and thine are mine;
and I am glorified in them.
11 And now I am no more in the *world* **cosmos**,
but these are in the *world* **cosmos**, and I come to thee.
Holy Father, *keep through* **guard in** thine own name
those whom thou hast given me,
that they may be one, **exactly** as we *are*.
12 While I was with them in the *world* **cosmos**,
I *kept* **guarded** them in thy name:
those that thou gavest me I have *kept* **guarded**,
and none of them is lost,
but **except** the son of *perdition* **destruction**;
that the scripture might be fulfilled.
13 And now come I to thee;
and these *things* I speak in the *world* **cosmos**,
that they might have my *joy* **cheer** fulfilled in themselves.
14 I have given them thy word;
and the *world* **cosmos** hath hated them,
because they are not of the *world* **cosmos**,
even **exactly** as I am not of the *world* **cosmos**.
15 I *pray* **ask** not
that thou shouldest take them out of the *world* **cosmos**,
but that thou shouldest *keep* **guard** them from the evil.
16 They are not of the *world* **cosmos**,
even **exactly** as I am not of the *world* **cosmos**.
17 *Sanctify* **Hallow** them *through* **in** thy truth:
thy word is truth.
18 **Exactly** As thou hast *sent* **apostolized** me
into the *world* **cosmos**,
even so have I also sent them into the *world* **cosmos**.
19 And for their sakes I *sanctify* **hallow** myself,
that they also might be *sanctified* **hallowed**
through **in** the truth.

YAH SHUA'S PRAYER FOR FUTURE TRUSTERS

20 Neither *pray* **ask** I for these *alone* **only**,
but for them also
which shall *believe on* **trust in** me through their word;
21 That they all may be one;
exactly as thou, Father, *art* in me, and I in thee,
that they also may be one in us:
that the *world* **cosmos** may *believe* **trust**
that thou hast *sent* **apostolized** me.
22 And the glory which thou gavest me
I have given them;
that they may be one, even **exactly** as we are one:
23 I in them, and thou in me,
that they may be *made perfect* **completed** in one;
and that the *world* **cosmos** may know
that thou hast *sent* **apostolized** me,
and hast loved them, as thou hast loved me.
24 Father, I will that they also, whom thou hast given me,
be with me where I am;
that they may *behold* **see** my glory,
which thou hast given me:
for thou lovedst me
before the foundation of the *world* **cosmos**.
25 O *righteous* **just** Father,
the *world* **cosmos** hath not known thee:
but I have known thee,
and these have known
that thou hast *sent* **apostolized** me.
26 And I have declared unto them thy name,
and *will* **shall** declare it:
that the love wherewith thou hast loved me
may be in them,
and I in them.

YAH SHUA IN THE GARDEN

18 When *Jesus* **Yah Shua** had *spoken* **said** these words,
he went forth with his disciples
over the brook *Cedron* **Qidron**, where was a garden,
into the which he entered, and his disciples.
2 And *Judas* **Yah Hudah** also, which betrayed him,
knew the place:
for *Jesus ofttimes* **Yah Shua often**
resorted **gathered together** thither with his disciples.

YAH HUDAH BETRAYS YAH SHUA

3 *Judas* **Yah Hudah** then,
having *received* **taken**
a *band of men* **squad** and *officers* **attendants**

from the *chief* **arch** priests and Pharisees,
cometh thither
with lanterns and *torches* **lamps** and weapons.
4 *Jesus* **Yah Shua** therefore,
knowing all *things* that should come upon him,
went forth, and said unto them, Whom seek ye?
5 They answered him,
Jesus of Nazareth **Yah Shua the Nazarene**.
Jesus saith **Yah Shua wordeth** unto them, *I am he* **I AM**.
And *Judas* **Yah Hudah** also, which betrayed him,
stood with them.
6 As soon then as he had said unto them, *I am he* **I AM**,
they went backward, and fell to unto the ground.
7 Then asked he them again, Whom seek ye?
And they said, *Jesus of Nazareth* **Yah Shua the Nazarene**.
8 *Jesus* **Yah Shua** answered,
I have *told* **said to** you that *I am he* **I AM**:
if therefore ye seek me, *let* **release** these **to** go their way:
9 That the *saying* might **word** be fulfilled,
which he *spake* **said**,
Of them which thou gavest me have I lost none.
10 Then *Simon Peter* **Shimon Petros** having a sword
drew it, and smote the *high* **arch** priest's servant,
and *cut off* **amputated** his right ear **lobe**.
The servant's name was *Malchus* **Melech**.
11 Then said *Jesus* **Yah Shua** unto *Peter* **Petros**,
Put *up* thy sword into the sheath:
the cup which my Father hath given me,
shall I not drink it?

YAH SHUA ARRESTED

12 Then the *band* **squad** and the *captain* **chiliarch**
and *officers* **attendants** of the *Jews* **Yah Hudiym**
took *Jesus* **Yah Shua**, and bound him,
13 And led him away to *Annas* **Hanan Yah** first;
for he was father in law to Caiaphas,
which was the *high* **arch** priest that same year.
14 Now Caiaphas was he,
which *gave counsel to* **counseled** the *Jews* **Yah Hudiym**,
that it was *expedient* **beneficial**
that one *man* **human** should *die* **be destroyed**
for the people.

PETROS' FIRST DENIAL

15 And *Simon Peter* **Shimon Petros** followed *Jesus* **Yah Shua**,
and so did another disciple:
that disciple
was *known unto* **acquainted with** the *high* **arch** priest,
and went in with *Jesus* **Yah Shua**
into the palace of the *high* **arch** priest.
16 But *Peter* **Petros** stood at the *door* **portal** without.
Then went out that other disciple,
which was *known* **acquainted**
unto **with** the *high* **arch** priest,
and *spake* **said** unto *her that kept the door* **the portalguard**,
and brought in *Peter* **Petros**.
17 Then *saith* **wordeth** the *damsel* **lass**
that kept the door — **the portalguard** unto *Peter* **Petros**,
Art not thou also one of this *man's* **human's** disciples?
He *saith* **wordeth**, *I am not* **Not I**.
18 And the servants and *officers* **attendants** stood there,
who had made a fire of coals; for it was cold:
and they warmed themselves:
and *Peter* **Petros** stood with them, and warmed himself.

YAH SHUA'S WITNESS

19 The *high* **arch** priest then asked *Jesus* **Yah Shua**
of **concerning** his disciples,
and *of* **concerning** his doctrine.
20 *Jesus* **Yah Shua** answered him,
I spake *openly* **boldly** to the *world* **cosmos**;
I ever taught in the synagogue,
and in the *temple* **priestal precinct**,
whither the *Jews* **Yah Hudiym**
always *resort* **come together on all sides**;
and in secret have I *said nothing* **spoken naught**.
21 Why askest thou me? ask them which heard me,
what I have *said* **spoken** unto them:
behold, they know what I said.
22 And when he had thus *spoken* **said**,
one of the *officers which stood by* **attendants present**
struck Jesus with the palm of his hand
gave Yah Shua a slap, saying,
Answerest thou the *high* **arch** priest *so* **thus**?
23 *Jesus* **Yah Shua** answered him,
If I have spoken *evil* **evily**,
bear witness *of* **concerning** the evil:
but if well, why *smitest* **floggest** thou me?
24 Now *Annas* **Hanan Yah** had *sent* **apostolized** him
bound unto Caiaphas the *high* **arch** priest.

PETROS' SECOND DENIAL

25 And *Simon Peter* **Shimon Petros**
stood and warmed himself.
They said therefore unto him,
Art not thou also one of his disciples?
He denied it, and said, *I am not* **Not I**.

PETROS' THIRD DENIAL

26 One of the servants of the *high* **arch** priest,
being his *kinsman* **kin**
whose ear *Peter cut off* **Petros amputated**,
saith **wordeth**, Did not I see thee in the garden with him?
27 *Peter* **Petros** then denied again:
and *immediately* **straightway** the *cock crew* **rooster voiced**.

YAH SHUA'S TRIAL

28 Then led they *Jesus* **Yah Shua** from Caiaphas
unto the *hall of judgment* **praetorium**:
and it was early **morning**;
and they themselves
went not into the *judgment hall* **praetorium**,
lest they should be defiled;
but that they might eat the *passover* **pasach**.
29 *Pilate* **Pilatos** then went out unto them, and said,
What accusation bring ye against this *man* **human**?
30 They answered and said unto him,
If **Unless** he were *not a malefactor* **an evildoer**,
we *would* **should** not have delivered him *up* unto thee.
31 Then said *Pilate* **Pilatos** unto them, Take ye him,
and judge him according to your *law* **torah**.
The *Jews* **Yah Hudiym** therefore said unto him,
It is not *lawful* **allowed** for us
to *put any man to death* **slaughter anyone**:
32 That the *saying* **word** of *Jesus* **Yah Shua**
might be fulfilled, which he *spake* **said**,
signifying what death he *should* **is about to** die.
33 Then *Pilate* **Pilatos**
entered into the *judgment hall* **praetorium** again,
and *called Jesus* **voiced out to Yah Shua**,
and said unto him,
Art thou the *King* **Sovereign** of the *Jews* **Yah Hudiym**?
34 *Jesus* **Yah Shua** answered him,
Sayest **Wordest** thou this *thing* of thyself,
or did others *tell* **say** it **to** thee *of* **concerning** me?
35 *Pilate* **Pilatos** answered, Am I a *Jew* **Yah Hudiy**?
Thine own *nation* **goyim** and the *chief* **arch** priests
have delivered thee unto me: what hast thou done?
36 *Jesus* **Yah Shua** answered,
My *kingdom* **sovereigndom** is not of this *world* **cosmos**:
if my *kingdom* **sovereigndom** were of this *world* **cosmos**,
then *would* **should** my *servants fight* **attendants agonize**,
that I should not be delivered to the *Jews* **Yah Hudiym**:
but now is my *kingdom* **sovereigndom** not from hence.
37 *Pilate* **Pilatos** therefore said unto him,
Art thou a *king* **sovereign** then?
Jesus **Yah Shua** answered,
Thou *sayest* **wordest** that I am a *king* **sovereign**.
To this end was I born,
and *for* **to** this cause came I into the *world* **cosmos**,
that I should *bear* witness unto the truth.
Every one that is of the truth heareth my voice.
38 *Pilate saith* **Pilatos wordeth** unto him, What is truth?
And when he had said this,
he went out again unto the *Jews* **Yah Hudiym**,
and *saith* **wordeth** unto them,
I find in him no *fault* **cause** at all.
39 But ye have a custom,
that I should release unto you
one at the *passover* **pasach**:
will **shall** ye therefore that I release unto you
the *King* **Sovereign** of the *Jews* **Yah Hudiym**?

YAH HUDIYM DEMAND YAH SHUA

40 Then cried they all again, *saying* **wording**,
Not this man, but *Barabbas* **Bar Abbas**.
Now *Barabbas* **Bar Abbas** was a robber.

YAH SHUA WREATHED

19 Then *Pilate* **Pilatos** therefore took *Jesus* **Yah Shua**,
and scourged him.
2 And the *soldiers* **warriors**
platted **braided** a *crown* **wreath** of thorns,
and put it on his head,
and they *put on* **arrayed** him *a* **in** purple *robe* **clothing**,
3 And *said* **worded**, *Hail* **Cheers**,
King **Sovereign** of the *Jews* **Yah Hudiym**!
and they *smote him with their hands* **gave him a slap**.
4 *Pilate* **Pilatos** therefore went forth again,
and *saith* **wordeth** unto them, Behold,
I bring him forth to you,
that ye may know that I find no *fault* **cause** in him.
5 Then came *Jesus* **Yah Shua** forth,
wearing **bearing** the *crown* **wreath** of thorns,
and the purple *robe* **clothing**.
And *Pilate saith* **Pilatos wordeth** unto them,
Behold the *man* **human**!
6 When the *chief* **arch** priests therefore
and *officers* **attendants** saw him,
they cried out, *saying* **wording**,
Crucify him, crucify him. **Stake! Stake!**
Pilate saith **Pilatos wordeth** unto them,
Take ye him, and *crucify him* **stake**:
for I find no *fault* **cause** in him.
7 The *Jews* **Yah Hudiym** answered him,
We have a *law* **torah**,
and by our *law* **torah** he *ought* **is indebted** to die,
because he made himself the Son of *God* **Elohim**.
8 When *Pilate* **Pilatos** therefore heard that *saying* **word**,
he was the more *afraid* **awestricken**;
9 And went again into the *judgment hall* **praetorium**,
and *saith* **wordeth** unto *Jesus* **Yah Shua**,
Whence art thou?
But *Jesus* **Yah Shua** gave him no answer.
10 Then *saith Pilate* **wordeth Pilatos** unto him,
Speakest thou not unto me?
knowest thou not
that I have *power* **authority** to *crucify* **stake** thee,
and have *power* **authority** to release thee?
11 *Jesus* **Yah Shua** answered,
Thou couldest have no *power* **authority** at all against me,
except it were given thee from above:
Therefore he that delivered me unto thee
hath the greater sin.
12 And from thenceforth
Pilate **Pilatos** sought to release him:
but the *Jews* **Yah Hudiym** cried out, *saying* **wording**,
If thou *let this man go* **release this one,**
thou art not *Caesar's* **the kaisar's** friend:
whosoever maketh himself a *king* **sovereign**
speaketh against Caesar **contradicteth the kaisar**.
13 When *Pilate* **Pilatos** therefore heard that *saying*,
he brought *Jesus* **Yah Shua** forth,
and sat down in the *judgment seat* **bamah**
in a place that is *called* **worded** the Pavement,
but in *the Hebrew* **Hebraic**, Gabbatha.
14 And it was the preparation of the *passover* **pasach**,
and about the sixth hour:
and he *saith* **wordeth** unto the *Jews* **Yah Hudiym**,
Behold your *king* **sovereign**!
15 But they cried out,
Away *with him*, away *with him*, *crucify* **stake** him.
Pilate saith **Pilatos wordeth** unto them,
shall I crucify your King **Stake your Sovereign**?
The *chief* **arch** priests answered,
We have no *king but Caesar* **sovereign except the kaisar**.

YAH SHUA IS STAKED

16 Then delivered he him therefore unto them
to be *crucified* **staked**.
And they took *Jesus* **Yah Shua**, and led him away.
17 And he bearing his *cross* **stake** went forth into a place
called **worded** the place of a *skull* **cranium**,
which is *called* **worded** in *the Hebrew* **Hebraic,**
Golgotha **Golgoleth**:
18 Where they *crucified* **staked** him,
and two other with him, on either side one,
and *Jesus* **Yah Shua** in the *midst* **middle**.
19 And *Pilate wrote* **Pilatos scribed** a title,
and put it on the *cross* **stake**.
And the *writing* **scribing** was
JESUS OF NAZARETH **YAH SHUA THE NAZARENE**
THE *KING* **SOVEREIGN** OF THE *JEWS* **YAH HUDIYM**.
20 This title then read many of the *Jews* **Yah Hudiym**:
for the place where *Jesus* **Yah Shua** was *crucified* **staked**
was nigh to the city:
and it was *written* **scribed** in *Hebrew* **Hebraic,**
and *Greek* **Hellenic**, and *Latin* **Romaic**.
21 Then *said* **worded**
the *chief* **arch** priests of the *Jews* **Yah Hudiym**
to *Pilate* **Pilatos**, *Write* **Scribe** not,
The *King* **Sovereign** of the *Jews* **Yah Hudiym**;
but that he said,
I am *King* **Sovereign** of the *Jews* **Yah Hudiym**.
22 *Pilate* **Pilatos** answered,
What I have *written* **scribed** I have *written* **scribed**.

WARRIORS GAMBLE OVER YAH SHUA'S GARMENTS

23 Then the *soldiers* **warriors**,
when they had *crucified Jesus* **staked Yah Shua**,
took his *garments* **clothing**, and made four parts,
to *every soldier* **each warrior** a part;
and also his *coat* **tunic**:
now the *coat* **tunic** was *without seam* **seamless**,
woven from the top.
24 They said therefore among *themselves* **each other**,
Let us not *rend* **split** it, but cast lots for it,
whose it shall be:
that the scripture might be fulfilled, which *saith* **wordeth**,
They *parted* **divided** my *raiment* **garment** among them,
and for my *vesture* **garments** they *did* cast lots.
These *things* **indeed** therefore the *soldiers* **warriors** did.
Psalm 22:18

YAH SHUA PRESENTS HIS MOTHER TO YAHN

25 Now there stood by the *cross* **stake** of *Jesus* **Yah Shua**
his mother, and his mother's sister,
Mary the wife of Cleophas **Miryam of Clopas**,
and *Mary* **Miryam the** Magdalene.
26 When *Jesus* **Yah Shua** therefore saw his mother,
and the disciple *standing by* **present**, whom he loved,
he *saith* **wordeth** unto his mother,
Woman, behold thy son!
27 Then *saith* **wordeth** he to the disciple,
Behold thy mother!
And from that hour
that disciple took her unto his own home.

YAH SHUA THIRSTS

28 After this, *Jesus* **Yah Shua** knowing that all *things*
were *now accomplished* **already completed**,
that the scripture might be *fulfilled* **completed**,
saith **wordeth**, I thirst.
29 Now there was set a vessel full of vinegar:
and they filled a spunge with vinegar,
and put it upon hyssop,
and *put* **offered** it to his mouth.
30 When *Jesus* **Yah Shua** therefore
had *received* **taken** the vinegar,
he said, It is finished°:
and he *bowed* **reclined** his head,
and *gave up the ghost* **surrendered his spirit**.
°see SUMMARY, SHALAM

PROPHESIES FULFILLED

31 The *Jews* **Yah Hudiym** therefore,
because it was the preparation,
that the bodies should not *remain* **abide**
upon the *cross* **stake** on the *sabbath day* **shabbath**,
(for that *sabbath day* **shabbath** was *an high* **a mega** day,)
besought Pilate **asked Pilatos**
that their legs might be broken,
and that they might be taken away.
32 Then came the *soldiers* **warriors**,
and **indeed** brake the legs of the first,
and of the other which was *crucified* **staked** with him.
33 But when they came to *Jesus* **Yah Shua**,
and saw that he was dead already,
they brake not his legs:
34 But one of the *soldiers* **warriors** with a spear
pierced his side,
and *forthwith* **straightway**
came there out blood and water.

35 And he that saw it *bare record* **witnessed**,
and his *record* **witness** is true:
and he knoweth that he *saith* **wordeth** true,
that ye might *believe* **trust**.
36 For these *things were done* **became**,
that the scripture should be fulfilled,
A **No** bone of him shall *not be broken* **be shattered**.
37 And again another scripture *saith* **wordeth**,
They shall *look on* **see unto** him whom they pierced.
Psalm 34:20, Zechar Yah 12:10

YAH SHUA'S BODY TAKEN

38 And after this *Joseph* **Yoseph** of *Arimathaea* **Ramah**,
being a disciple of *Jesus* **Yah Shua**,
but secretly for *fear* **awe** of the *Jews* **Yah Hudiym**,
besought Pilate **asked Pilatos**
that he might take *away* the body of *Jesus* **Yah Shua**:
and *Pilate gave* **Pilatos permitted** him *leave*.
He came therefore, and took the body of *Jesus* **Yah Shua**.
39 And there came also Nicodemus,
which at the first came to *Jesus* **Yah Shua** by night,
and brought a mixture of myrrh and aloes,
about an hundred *pound weight* **litra**.
40 Then took they the body of *Jesus* **Yah Shua**,
and *wound* **bound** it in linen clothes
with the *spices* **aromatics**,
exactly as the *manner* **custom** of the *Jews* **Yah Hudiym**
is to *bury* **embalm**.

YAH SHUA IS ENTOMBED

41 Now in the place where he was *crucified* **staked**
there was a garden;
and in the garden a new *sepulchre* **tomb**,
wherein
was never man yet laid **no one had ever been placed**.
42 There *laid* **placed** they *Jesus* **Yah Shua** therefore
because of the *Jews'* **Yah Hudiy** preparation day;
for the *sepulchre* **tomb** was nigh at hand.

YAH SHUA DISENTOMBED

20 **On** The first *day* of the *week* **shabbaths**
cometh *Mary* **Miryam the** Magdalene
in the early **morning**, when it was yet dark,
unto the *sepulchre* **tomb**,
and seeth the stone taken away from the *sepulchre* **tomb**.
2 Then she runneth,
and cometh to *Simon Peter* **Shimon Petros**,
and to the other disciple,
whom *Jesus loved* **Yah Shua befriended**,
and *saith* **wordeth** unto them,
They have taken away *the Lord* **Adonay**
out of the *sepulchre* **tomb**,
and we know not where they have *laid* **placed** him.
3 *Peter* **Petros** therefore went forth,
and that other disciple,
and came to the *sepulchre* **tomb**.
4 So they ran both together:
and the other disciple did outrun *Peter* **Petros**,
and came first to the *sepulchre* **tomb**.
5 And he stooping down, and looking in,
saw the linen clothes lying; yet **indeed** went he not in.
6 Then cometh *Simon Peter* **Shimon Petros** following him,
and went into the *sepulchre* **tomb**,
and seeth the linen clothes lie,
7 And the *napkin* **sudarium**, that was about his head,
not lying with the linen clothes,
but wrapped together in a place *by itself* **apart**.
8 Then went in also that other disciple,
which came first to the *sepulchre* **tomb**,
and he saw, and *believed* **trusted**.
9 For as yet they knew not the scripture,
that he must rise *again* from the dead.
10 Then the disciples went away again
unto their own home.

THE RESURRECTED YAH SHUA APPEARS TO MIRYAM

11 But *Mary* **Miryam** stood without
at the *sepulchre* **tomb** weeping:
and as she wept,
she stooped down, *and looked* into the *sepulchre* **tomb**,
12 And seeth two angels in white sitting,
the one at the head, and the other at the feet,
where the body of *Jesus* **Yah Shua** had lain.
13 And they *say* **word** unto her,
Woman, why weepest thou?
She *saith* **wordeth** unto them,
Because they have taken away my *Lord* **Adonay**,
and I know not where they have *laid* **placed** him.
14 And when she had thus said,
she turned herself back,
and saw *Jesus* **Yah Shua** standing,
and knew not that it was *Jesus* **Yah Shua**.
15 *Jesus saith* **Yah Shua wordeth** unto her,
Woman, why weepest thou? whom seekest thou?
She, *supposing* **thinking** him to be the gardener,
saith **wordeth** unto him,
Sir Lord **Adoni**, if thou have borne him hence,
tell me where thou hast *laid* **placed** him,
and I *will* **shall** take him away.
16 *Jesus saith* **Yah Shua wordeth** unto her, *Mary* **Miryam**.
She turned herself, and *saith* **wordeth** unto him, Rabboni;
which is to *say* **word**, *Master* **Doctor**.
17 *Jesus saith* **Yah Shua wordeth** unto her, Touch me not;
for I am not yet ascended to my Father:
but go to my brethren, and say unto them,
I ascend unto my Father, and your Father;
and to my *God* **Elohim**, and your *God* **Elohim**.
18 *Mary* **Miryam the** Magdalene came
and *told* **evangelized** the disciples
that she had seen *the Lord* **Adonay**,
and that he had *spoken* **said** these *things* unto her.

THE RESURRECTED YAH SHUA APPEARS TO TEN DISCIPLES

19 Then the same day at evening,
being the first *day* of the *week* **shabbaths**,
when the *doors* **portals** were shut
where the disciples were assembled
for *fear* **awe** of the *Jews* **Yah Hudiym**,
came *Jesus* **Yah Shua** and stood in the midst,
and *saith* **wordeth** unto them,
Peace **Shalom** *be* unto you.
20 And when he had so said,
he shewed unto them his hands and his side.
Then *were* the disciples *glad* **cheered**,
when they saw *the Lord* **Adonay**.
21 Then said *Jesus* **Yah Shua** to them again,
Peace **Shalom** *be* unto you:
exactly as my Father hath *sent* **apostolized** me,
even so send I you.

THE RESURRECTED YAH SHUA BESTOWS THE HOLY SPIRIT

22 And when he had said this,
he *breathed on* **puffed into** them,
and *saith* **wordeth** unto them,
Receive **Take** ye the Holy *Ghost* **Spirit**:
23 Whosesoever sins ye *remit* **release**,
they are *remitted* **released** unto them;
and whosesoever sins ye *retain* **hold**,
they are *retained* **held**.

TAOM APPEARS

24 But *Thomas* **Taom**,
one of the twelve, *called Didymus* **worded Twin**,
was not with them when *Jesus* **Yah Shua** came.
25 The other disciples therefore *said* **worded** unto him,
We have seen *the Lord* **Adonay**.
But he said unto them,
Except **Unless** I shall see in his hands
the *print* **imprint** of the nails,
and put my finger into the *print* **imprint** of the nails,
and thrust my hand into his side,
I *will* **shall** not *believe* **trust**.

THE RESURRECTED YAH SHUA APPEARS TO ELEVEN DISCIPLES

26 And after eight days again his disciples were within,
and *Thomas* **Taom** with them:
then came *Jesus* **Yah Shua**, the *doors* **portals** being shut,
and stood in the midst, and said,
Peace **Shalom** *be* unto you.
27 Then *saith* **wordeth** he to *Thomas* **Taom**,
Reach **Bear** hither thy finger,
and *behold* **see** my hands;
and *reach* **bear** hither thy hand,
and thrust it into my side:
and be not *faithless* **trustless**, but *believing* **trusting**.

TAOM'S WITNESS TO YAH SHUA'S DEITY

28 And *Thomas* **Taom** answered and said unto him,
My *Lord* **Adonay** and my *God* **Elohim**.
29 *Jesus saith* **Yah Shua wordeth** unto him,
Thomas **Taom**,
because thou hast seen me, thou hast *believed* **trusted**:
blessed are they that have not seen,
and yet have *believed* **trusted**.
30 And many other signs *truly* **indeed** did *Jesus* **Yah Shua**
in the *presence* **sight** of his disciples,
which are not *written* **scribed** in this *book* **scroll**:
31 But these are *written* **scribed**,
that ye might *believe* **trust**
that *Jesus* **Yah Shua** is the *Christ* **Messiah**,
the Son of *God* **Elohim**;
and that *believing* **trusting**
ye might have life *through* **in** his name.

THE RESURRECTED YAH MANIFESTS HIMSELF AGAIN

21 After these *things*
Jesus shewed **Yah Shua manifested** himself again
to the disciples at the sea of Tiberias;
and *on this wise shewed* **thus manifested** he himself.
2 There were together *Simon Peter* **Shimon Petros**,
and *Thomas called Didymus* **Taom worded Twin**,
and *Nathanael* **Nethan El** of *Cana* **Qanah** in *Galilee* **Galiyl**,
and the sons of Zebedee, and two other of his disciples.
3 *Simon Peter saith* **Shimon Petros wordeth** unto them,
I go a fishing.
They *say* **word** unto him, We also *go* **come** with thee.
They went forth, and *entered* **ascended**
into a *ship immediately* **sailer straightway**;
and that night they caught *nothing* **naught**.

CASTING THE NET

4 *But when the* **Yet early** morning
was now come **having already become**,
Jesus **Yah Shua** stood on the shore:
but the disciples knew not that it was *Jesus* **Yah Shua**.
5 Then *Jesus saith* **Yah Shua wordeth** unto them,
Children, have ye any *meat* **eats**?
They answered him, No.
6 And he said unto them,
Cast the net on the right *side* **part** of the *ship* **sailer**,
and *ye* shall find.
They cast therefore,
and now they were not able to draw it
for the multitude of fishes.
7 Therefore that disciple whom *Jesus* **Yah Shua** loved
saith **wordeth** unto *Peter* **Petros**, It is *the Lord* **Adonay**.
Now when *Simon Peter* **Shimon Petros** heard
that it was *the Lord* **Adonay**,
he girt his fisher's *coat* **outer enduement** unto him,
(for he was naked,)
and did cast himself into the sea.
8 And the other disciples came in a *little ship* **skiff**;
(for they were not far from land,
but as it were two hundred cubits,)
dragging the net with fishes.
9 As soon then as they were come to land,
they saw a fire of coals there,
and *fish* **broilings** laid thereon, and bread.
10 *Jesus saith* **Yah Shua wordeth** unto them,
Bring of the *fish* **broilings** which ye have now caught.
11 *Simon Peter went up* **Shimon Petros ascended**,
and drew the net to land full of *great* **mega** fishes,
an hundred and fifty and three:
and for all there were so many,
yet was not the net *broken* **split**.
12 *Jesus saith* **Yah Shua wordeth** unto them,
Come and dine.
And none of the disciples durst ask him, Who art thou?
knowing that it was *the Lord* **Adonay**.
13 *Jesus* **Yah Shua** then cometh, and taketh bread,
and giveth them, and *fish* **broilings** likewise.
14 This is *now* **already** the third time
that *Jesus* **Yah Shua** shewed himself to his disciples,
after that he was risen from the dead.

LOVE VS BEFRIEND

15 So when they had dined,
Jesus **Yah Shua**
saith **wordeth** to *Simon Peter* **Shimon Petros**,
Simon **Shimon**, son of *Jonas* **Yonah**,
lovest thou me **much** more than these?
He *saith* **wordeth** unto him, Yea, *Lord* **Adonay**;
thou knowest that I *love* **befriend** thee.
He *saith* **wordeth** unto him, Feed my lambs.
16 He *saith* **wordeth** to him again the second time,
Simon **Shimon**, son of *Jonas* **Yonah**, lovest thou me?
He *saith* **wordeth** unto him, Yea, *Lord* **Adonay**;
thou knowest that I *love* **befriend** thee.
He *saith* **wordeth** unto him, *Feed* **Shepherd** my sheep.
17 He *saith* **wordeth** unto him the third time,
Simon **Shimon**, son of *Jonas* **Yonah**,
lovest **befriendest** thou me?
Peter **Petros** was *grieved* **sorrowed**
because he said unto him the third time,
Lovest **Befriendest** thou me?
And he said unto him, *Lord* **Adonay**,
thou knowest all *things*;
thou knowest that I *love* **befriend** thee.
Jesus saith **Yah Shua wordeth** unto him, Feed my sheep.

YAH SHUA PROPHESIES PETROS' MARTYRDOM

18 *Verily, verily, I say* **Amen! Amen! I word** unto thee,
When thou wast young, thou girdedst thyself,
and walkedst whither thou *wouldest* **willest**:
but when **ever** thou shalt *be old* **senesce**,
thou shalt *stretch forth* **extend** thy hands,
and another shall gird thee,
and *carry* **bear** thee whither thou *wouldest* **willest** not.
19 This *spake* **said** he,
signifying by what death he should glorify *God* **Elohim**.
And when he had *spoken* **said** this,
he *saith* **wordeth** unto him, Follow me.
20 Then *Peter* **Petros**, turning *about* **around**,
seeth the disciple whom *Jesus* **Yah Shua** loved following;
which also leaned **who had reposed**
on his *breast* **chest** at supper, and said,
Lord **Adonay**, which is he that betrayeth thee?
Yahn 13:21—25
21 *Peter* **Petros** seeing him
saith **wordeth** to *Jesus* **Yah Shua**,
Lord **Adonay**, and what *shall this man do* **about this one**?
22 *Jesus saith* **Yah Shua wordeth** unto him,
If I will that he *tarry* **abide** till I come,
what is that to thee?
follow thou me.
23 Then went this *saying abroad* **word**
among **unto** the brethren,
that that disciple should not die:
yet *Jesus* **Yah Shua** said not unto him,
He shall not die;
but, If I will that he *tarry* **abide** till I come,
what is that to thee?

CONCLUSION

24 This is the disciple
which *testifieth of* **witnesseth about** these *things*,
and wrote these *things*:
and we know that his *testimony* **witness** is true.
25 And there are also many *other things* **others**
which Jesus — **as much as Yah Shua** did,
the which, if they should be *written* **scribed** every one,
I suppose that even the *world* **cosmos** itself
could not contain the *books* **scrolls**
that should be *written* **scribed**.
Amen.

KEY TO INTERPRETING THE EXEGESES
King James text is in regular type;
Text under exegeses is in oblique type;
Text of exegeses is in bold type.

YAH SHUA'S GENESIS

1 The *book* **scroll** of the *generation* **genesis**
of *Jesus Christ* **Yah Shua Messiah**,
the son of David, the son of Abraham.

FOURTEEN GENERATIONS: ABRAHAM TO DAVID

2 Abraham begat *Isaac* **Yischaq**;
and *Isaac* **Yischaq** begat *Jacob* **Yaaqov**;
and *Jacob* **Yaaqov**
begat *Judas* **Yah Hudah** and his brethren;
3 And *Judas* **Yah Hudah**
begat *Phares* **Peres** and *Zara* **Zerach**
of *Thamar* **Tamar**;
and *Phares* **Peres** begat *Esrom* **Hesron**;
and *Esrom* **Hesron** begat *Aram* **Ram**;
4 And *Aram* **Ram** begat *Aminadab* **Ammi Nadab**;
and *Aminadab* **Ammi Nadab** begat *Naasson* **Nachshon**;
and *Naasson* **Nachshon** begat Salmon;
5 And Salmon begat *Booz* **Boaz** of Rachab;
and *Booz* **Boaz** begat Obed of Ruth;
and Obed begat *Jesse* **Yishay**;
6 And *Jesse* **Yishay** begat David the *king* **sovereign**;

FOURTEEN GENERATIONS: TO THE BABEL EXILE

and David the *king* **sovereign** begat *Solomon* **Shelomoh**
of her that had been the wife of Urias **of Uri Yah's**;
7 And Solomon **Shelomoh** begat *Roboam* **Rechab Am**;
and *Roboam* **Rechab Am** begat *Abia* **Abi Yah**;
and *Abia* **Abi Yah** begat Asa;
8 And Asa begat *Josaphat* **Yah Shaphat**;
and *Josaphat* **Yah Shaphat** begat *Joram* **Yoram**;
and *Joram* **Yoram** begat *Ozias* **Uzzi Yah**;
9 And *Ozias* **Uzzi Yah** begat *Joatham* **Yah Tham**;
and *Joatham* **Yah Tham** begat Achaz;
and Achaz begat *Ezekias* **Yechizq Yah**;
10 And *Ezekias* **Yechizq Yah**
begat *Manasses* **Menash sheh**;
and *Manasses* **Menash Sheh** begat Amon;
and Amon begat *Josias* **Yoshi Yah**;
11 And *Josias* **Yoshi Yah**
begat *Jechonias* **Yechon Yah** and his brethren,
about the time
they were *carried away* **exiled** to *Babylon* **Babel**:

FOURTEEN GENERATIONS: TO THE MESSIAH

12 And after they were *brought* **exiled** to *Babylon* **Babel**,
Jechonias **Yechon Yah** begat *Salathiel* **Shealti El**;
and *Salathiel* **Shealti El** begat *Zorobabel* **Zerub Babel**;
13 And *Zorobabel* **Zerub Babel** begat *Abiud* **Abi Hud**;
and *Abiud* **Abi Hud** begat *Eliakim* **El Yaqim**;
and *Eliakim* **El Yaqim** begat *Azor* **Azzur**;
14 And *Azor* **Azzur** begat *Sadoc* **Sadoq**;
and *Sadoc* **Sadoq** begat *Achim* **Yah Qim**;
and *Achim* **Yah Qim** begat *Eliud* **Eli Ud**;
15 And *Eliud* **Eli Ud** begat *Eleazar* **El Azar**;
and *Eleazar* **El Azar** begat *Matthan* **Mattan**;
and *Matthan* **Mattan** begat *Jacob* **Yaaqov**;
16 And *Jacob* **Yaaqov** begat *Joseph* **Yoseph**
the *husband* **man** of *Mary* **Miryam**,
of whom was born *Jesus* **Yah Shua**,
who is *called Christ* **worded Messiah**.

FORTY—TWO GENERATIONS: SUMMARY

17 So all the generations from Abraham to David
are fourteen generations;
and from David
until the *carrying away* **exile** into *Babylon* **Babel**
are fourteen generations;
and from the *carrying away* **exile** into *Babylon* **Babel**
unto *Christ* **the Messiah**
are fourteen generations.

YAH SHUA MESSIAH IS BEGOTTEN BY THE HOLY SPIRIT

18 Now the birth of *Jesus Christ* **Yah Shua Messiah**
was *on this wise* **thus**:
When *as* **indeed** his mother *Mary* **Miryam**
was espoused to *Joseph* **Yoseph**,
before they came together,
she was found *with child* **having in womb**
of the Holy *Ghost* **Spirit**.
19 Then *Joseph* **Yoseph** her *husband* **man**,
being *a just man*,
and *not willing to* **having willed to not**
make her a publick example **expose her**,
was minded **had willed** to *put* **release** her *away*
privily **secretly**.
20 But while he *thought* **pondered** on these *things*,
behold, the angel of *the Lord* **Yah Veh**
appeared **manifested** unto him in a dream,
saying **wording**, *Joseph* **Yoseph**, thou son of David,
fear **awe** not to take unto thee
Mary **Miryam** thy *wife* **woman**:
for that which is *conceived* **begotten** in her
is of the Holy *Ghost* **Spirit**.
21 And she shall *bring forth* **birth** a son,
and thou shalt call his name *Jesus* **Yah Shua**:
for he shall save his people from their sins.

YAH SHUA MESSIAH IS VIRGIN BORN

22 Now all this *was done* **became**,
that it might be fulfilled
which was *spoken of the Lord* **rhetorized by Yah Veh**
by **through** the prophet, *saying* **wording**,
23 Behold, a virgin shall *be with child* **have in womb**,
and shall *bring forth* **birth** a son,
and they shall call his name *Emmanuel* **Immanu El**,
which *being interpreted* is **translated**,
God **Elohim** with us.
Yesha Yah 7:14
24 Then *Joseph being raised* **Yoseph, rousing** from sleep
did as the angel of *the Lord* **Yah Veh**
had *bidden* **ordered** him,
and took unto him his *wife* **woman**:
25 And knew her not
till she had *brought forth* **birthed** her firstborn son:
and he called his name *Jesus* **Yah Shua**.

THE VISIT OF THE MAGI

2 Now when *Jesus* **Yah Shua** was born
in *Bethlehem* **Beth Lechem** of *Judaea* **Yah Hudah**
in the days of Herod the *king* **sovereign**, behold,
there came *wise men* **magi**
from the *east* **rising** to *Jerusalem* **Yeru Shalem**,
2 *Saying* **Wording**,
Where is he
that is born *king* **sovereign** of the *Jews* **Yah Hudiym**?
for we have seen his star in the *east* **rising**,
and are come to worship him.
3 When Herod the *king* **sovereign** had heard these *things*,
he was troubled and all *Jerusalem* **Yeru Shalem** with him.
4 And when he had gathered all the *chief* **arch** priests
and scribes of the people together,
he *demanded* **inquired** of them
where *Christ* **the Messiah** should be born.
5 And they said unto him,
In *Bethlehem* **Beth Lechem** of *Judaea* **Yah Hudah**:
for thus it is *written by* **scribed through** the prophet,
6 And thou *Bethlehem* **Beth Lechem**,
in the land of *Juda* **Yah Hudah**,
art not the least
among the *princes* **governors** of *Juda* **Yah Hudah**:
for out of thee shall come a Governor,
that shall *rule* **shepherd** my people *Israel* **Yisra El**.
Michah 5:2
7 Then Herod,
when he had *privily* **secretly** called the *wise men* **magi**,
enquired of them *diligently* **precisely**
what time the star *appeared* **manifested**.
8 And he sent them to *Bethlehem* **Beth Lechem**, and said,
Go and *search diligently* **investigate precisely**
for the young child;
and when ye have found him,
bring me word again **evangelize me**,
that I may come and worship him also.
9 When they had heard the *king* **sovereign**, they departed;
and, *lo* **behold**, the star,
which they saw in the *east* **rising**, went before them,
till it came and stood over where the young child was.
10 When they saw the star, they *rejoiced* **cheered**
with exceeding great joy **an extremely mega cheer**.
11 And when they were come into the house,
they saw the young child with *Mary* **Miryam** his mother,
and fell down, and worshipped him:

and when they had opened their treasures,
they *presented* **offered** unto him *gifts* **oblations**;
gold, and frankincense, and myrrh.
12 And being *warned of God* **oracled** in a dream
that they should not return to Herod,
they departed into their own *country* **region**
through another way.

YOSEPH, MIRYAM, AND YAH SHUA FLEE TO MISRAYIM

13 And when they were departed, behold,
the angel of *the Lord appeareth* **Yah Veh manifesteth**
to *Joseph* **Yoseph** in a dream, *saying* **wording**,
Arise, and take the young child and his mother,
and flee into *Egypt* **Misrayim**,
and be thou there until I *bring* **say to** thee *word*:
for Herod *will* **shall** seek the young child to destroy him.
14 When he arose,
he took the young child and his mother by night,
and departed into *Egypt* **Misrayim**:
15 And was there until the death of Herod:
that it might be fulfilled which was *spoken* **rhetorized**
of *the Lord by* **Yah Veh through** the prophet,
saying **wording**,
Out of *Egypt* **Misrayim** have I called my son.
Hoshea 11:1
16 Then Herod,
when he saw that he was mocked of the *wise men* **magi**,
was *exceeding wroth* **extremely furious**,
and *sent forth* **apostolized**,
and *slew* **took out** all the *children* **lads**
that were in *Bethlehem* **Beth Lechem**,
and in all the *coasts* **boundaries** *thereof*,
from two years *old* and under,
according to the time
which he had *diligently* **precisely** enquired
of the *wise men* **magi**.
17 Then was fulfilled that which was
spoken **rhetorized** by *Jeremy* **Yirme Yah** the prophet,
saying **wording**,
18 In *Rama* **Ramah** was there a voice heard,
lamentation, and weeping,
and *great mourning* **much grieving**,
Rachel weeping for her children,
and *would* **willed to** not be comforted,
because they are not.
Yirme Yah 31:5

YOSEPH, MIRYAM, AND YAH SHUA GO TO NAZARETH

19 But when Herod was dead,
behold, an angel of *the Lord* **Yah Veh**
appeareth **manifesteth** in a dream
to *Joseph* **Yoseph** in *Egypt* **Misrayim**,
20 *Saying* **Wording**, Arise,
and take the young child and his mother,
and go into the land of *Israel* **Yisra El**:
for they *are dead* **have died**
which sought the young child's *life* **soul**.
21 And he arose,
and took the young child and his mother,
and came into the land of *Israel* **Yisra El**.
22 But when he heard
that Archelaus did reign in *Judaea* **Yah Hudah**
in the room of **for** his father Herod,
he was *afraid* **awestricken** to go thither:
notwithstanding,
being *warned of God* **oracled** in a dream,
he *turned aside* **departed** into the parts of *Galilee* **Galiyl**:
23 And he came and *dwelt* **settled**
in a city *called* **worded** Nazareth:
that it might be fulfilled
which was *spoken by* **rhetorized through** the prophets,
He shall be called a Nazarene.
cp Yesha Yah 11:1

BAPTIZER YAHN PREACHES REPENTANCE

3 In those days came *John* **Yahn** the *Baptist* **Baptizer**,
preaching in the wilderness of *Judaea* **Yah Hudah**,
2 And *saying* **wording**, Repent ye:
for the *kingdom* **sovereigndom** of *heaven* **the heavens**
is at hand **approacheth**.
3 For this is he that was *spoken* **rhetorized**
of **by** the prophet *Esaias* **Yesha Yah**, *saying* **wording**,
The voice of one crying in the wilderness,
Prepare ye the way of *the Lord* **Yah Veh**,
make his paths straight.
Yesha Yah 40:3
4 And the same *John* **Yahn**
had his *raiment* **enduement** of camel's hair,
and a leathern girdle about his loins;
and his *meat* **nourishment** was locusts and wild honey.
5 Then *went out* **proceeded** to him
Jerusalem **Yeru Shalem**, and all *Judaea* **Yah Hudah**,
and all the region round about *Jordan* **Yarden**,
6 And were baptized of him in *Jordan* **Yarden**,
confessing their sins.

BAPTIZER YAHN DERIDES THE PHARISEES AND SADOQIYM

7 But when he saw
many of the Pharisees and *Sadducees* **Sadoqiym**
come to his baptism,
he said unto them, O *generation* **progeny** of vipers,
who hath *warned* **exemplified** you
to flee from the wrath *to come* **about to be**?
8 *Bring forth* **Produce** therefore
fruits *meet* **worthy** for repentance:
9 And think not to *say* **word** within yourselves,
We have Abraham to our father:
for I *say* **word** unto you,
that *God* **Elohim** is able of these stones
to raise *up* children unto Abraham.
10 And *now* **already** also
the axe is laid unto the root of the trees:
therefore every tree
which *bringeth* **produceth** not *forth* good fruit
is *hewn down* **exscinded**, and cast into the fire.
11 I indeed baptize you *with* **in** water unto repentance:
but he that cometh after me is mightier than I,
whose shoes I am not *worthy* **adequate** to bear:
he shall baptize you
with **in** the Holy *Ghost* **Spirit**, and *with* fire:
12 Whose **winnowing** fan is in his hand,
and he *will* **shall** throughly purge his **threshing** floor,
and gather **together** his *wheat* **grain**
into the *garner* **granary**;
but he *will* **shall** burn *up* the chaff
with unquenchable fire.

BAPTIZER YAHN BAPTIZES YAH SHUA

13 Then cometh *Jesus* **Yah Shua**
from *Galilee* **Galiyl** to *Jordan* **Yarden** unto *John* **Yahn**,
to be baptized of him.
14 But *John* **Yahn** forbad him, *saying* **wording**,
I have need to be baptized of thee,
and comest thou to me?
15 And *Jesus* **Yah Shua** answering said unto him,
Suffer **Allow** it to be so now:
for thus it *becometh* **befitteth** us
to fulfil all *righteousness* **justness**.
Then he *suffered* **allowed** him.
16 And *Jesus* **Yah Shua**, when he was baptized,
went up **ascended** straightway out of the water:
and, *lo* **behold**, the heavens were opened unto him,
and he saw the Spirit of *God* **Elohim**
descending *like* **as** a dove,
and lighting upon him:
17 And *lo* **behold**, a voice from *heaven* **the heavens**,
saying **wording**, This is my beloved Son,
in **of** whom I *am well pleased* **well—approve**.

YAH SHUA TESTED BY DIABOLOS

4 Then was *Jesus led up* **Yah Shua brought** of the spirit
into the wilderness
to be *tempted* **tested** of *the devil* **Diabolos**.
2 And when he had fasted forty days and forty nights,
he was afterward an hungred.
3 And when the *tempter* **tester** came to him, he said,
If thou be the Son of *God* **Elohim**,
command **say** that these stones *be made* **become** bread.
4 But he answered and said, It is *written* **scribed**,
man **Humanity** shall not live by bread alone,
but by every *word* **rhema**
that proceedeth *out of* **through** the mouth of *God* **Yah Veh**.
Deuteronomy 8:3
5 Then *the devil* **Diabolos**
taketh him *up* into the holy city,
and setteth him

on a *pinnacle* **wing** of the *temple* **priestal precinct**,
6 And *saith* **wordeth** unto him,
If thou be the Son of *God* **Elohim**, cast thyself down:
for it is *written* **scribed**,
He shall *give* **misvah** his angels *charge* concerning thee:
and in their hands they shall bear thee *up*,
lest *at any time* **ever** thou dash thy foot against a stone.
Psalm 91:11, 12
7 *Jesus* **Yah Shua** said unto him,
It is *written* **scribed** again,
Thou shalt not *tempt* **test**
the Lord **Yah Veh** thy *God* **Elohim**.
Deuteronomy 6:16
8 Again, *the devil* **Diabolos** taketh him *up*
into an *exceeding* **extremely** high mountain,
and sheweth him
all the *kingdoms* **sovereigndoms** of the *world* **cosmos**,
and the glory of them;
9 And *saith* **wordeth** unto him,
All these *things will* **shall** I give thee,
if thou *wilt* **shalt** fall down and worship me.
10 Then *saith Jesus* **wordeth Yah Shua** unto him,
Get thee hence **Go**, Satan: for it is *written* **scribed**,
Thou shalt worship *the Lord* **Yah Veh** thy *God* **Elohim**,
and him only shalt thou *serve* **liturgize**.
Deuteronomy 6:13, 10:20
11 Then *the devil leaveth* **Diabolos forsaketh** him,
and, behold, angels came and ministered unto him.
12 Now when *Jesus* **Yah Shua** had heard
that *John* **Yahn** was *cast into prison* **betrayed**,
he departed into *Galilee* **Galiyl**;
13 And leaving Nazareth, he came
and *dwelt* **settled** in *Capernaum* **Kaphar Nachum**,
which is *upon* **at** the *sea coast* **seaside**,
in the *borders* **boundaries**
of *Zabulon* **Zebulun** and *Nephthalim* **Naphtali**:
14 That it might be fulfilled which was *spoken* **rhetorized**
by Essias **through Yesha Yah** the prophet,
saying **wording**,
15 The land of *Zabulon* **Zebulun**,
and the land of *Nephthalim* **Naphtali**,
by the way of the sea, beyond *Jordan* **Yarden**,
Galilee **Galiyl** of the *Gentiles* **goyim**;
16 The people which sat in darkness
saw *great* **a mega** light;
and to them which sat in the region and shadow of death
light is *sprung up* **risen**.
Yesha Yah 9:1, 2

YAH SHUA PREACHES REPENTANCE

17 From that time *Jesus* **Yah Shua** began to preach,
and to *say* **word**, Repent:
for the *kingdom* **sovereigndom** of *heaven* **the heavens**
is at hand **approacheth**.

YAH SHUA CALLS PETROS AND ANDREAS

18 And *Jesus* **Yah Shua**,
walking by the sea of *Galilee* **Galiyl**,
saw two brethren,
Simon called Peter **Shimon worded Petros**,
and *Andrew* **Andreas** his brother,
casting a net into the sea: for they were fishers.
19 And he *saith* **wordeth** unto them,
Follow **Come after** me,
and I *will* **shall** make you fishers of *men* **humanity**.
20 And they straightway *left* **forsook** their nets,
and followed him.

YAH SHUA CALLS YAAQOVOS AND YAHN

21 And *going on* **advancing** from thence,
he saw other two brethren,
James **Yaaqovos** *the son* of *Zebedee* **Zabdi**,
and *John* **Yahn** his brother,
in a *ship* **sailer** with *Zebedee* **Zabdi** their father,
mending **preparing** their nets; and he called them.
22 And they *immediately* **straightway**
left **forsook** the *ship* **sailer** and their father,
and followed him.
23 And *Jesus* **Yah Shua** went about all *Galilee* **Galiyl**,
teaching **doctrinating** in their synagogues,
and preaching
the *gospel* **evangelism** of the *kingdom* **sovereigndom**,
and *healing all manner of sickness* **curing every disease**
and *all manner of disease* **every debility**
among the people.
24 And his fame went *throughout* **into** all Syria:
and they *brought* **offered** unto him
all *sick people* **that were ill**
that were *taken* **held** with divers diseases and torments,
and those which were *possessed with devils* **demonized**,
and those which were lunatick,
and those that *had the palsy* **were paralyzed**;
and he *healed* **cured** them.
25 And there followed him
great **vast** multitudes of people from *Galilee* **Galiyl**,
and from Decapolis, and from *Jerusalem* **Yeru Shalem**,
and from *Judaea* **Yah Hudah**,
and from beyond *Jordan* **Yarden**.

YAH SHUA'S MOUNTAIN MESSAGE: THE BEATITUDES

5 And seeing the multitudes,
he *went up* **ascended** into a mountain:
and when he was set, his disciples came unto him:
2 And he opened his mouth,
and *taught* **doctrined** them, *saying* **wording**,
3 Blessed are the poor in spirit:
for theirs
is the *kingdom* **sovereigndom** of *heaven* **the heavens**.
4 Blessed are they that mourn:
for they shall be comforted.
5 Blessed are the meek:
for they shall inherit the earth.
6 Blessed are they
which do hunger and thirst after *righteousness* **justness**:
for they shall be filled.
7 Blessed are the merciful:
for they shall obtain mercy.
8 Blessed are the pure in heart:
for they shall see *God* **Elohim**.
9 Blessed are *the peacemakers* **they who shalam**:
for they shall be called the *children* **sons** of *God* **Elohim**.
10 Blessed are they
which are persecuted for *righteousness'* **justness'** sake:
for theirs
is the *kingdom* **sovereigndom** of *heaven* **the heavens**.
11 Blessed are ye,
When **ever** men shall *revile* **reproach** you,
and persecute you,
and shall say
all manner of **every** evil **rhema** against you falsely,
for my sake.
12 *Rejoice* **Cheer**, and *be exceeding glad* **jump for joy**:
for *great* **vast** is your reward in *heaven* **the heavens**:
for *so* **thus** persecuted they the prophets
which were before you.

THE TRUSTER'S POSITION

13 Ye are the salt of the earth:
but **except** if the salt have *lost his savour* **become insipid**,
wherewith **wherein** shall it be salted?
it is thenceforth *good* **not able** for *nothing* **naught**,
but to be cast out,
and to be *trodden under foot* **trampled** of *men* **humanity**.
14 Ye are the light of the *world* **cosmos**.
A city that is set on *an hill* **a mountain**
cannot be *hid* **secreted**.
15 Neither do men *light* **burn** a candle,
and put it under a *bushel* **measure**,
but **rather** on a *candlestick* **menorah**;
and it *giveth light* **radiateth** unto all that are in the house.
16 Let your light *so shine* **thus radiate**
before men **in front of humanity**,
that they may see your good works,
and glorify your Father which is in *heaven* **the heavens**.

YAH SHUA FULFILLS THE TORAH

17 *Think* **Presume** not that I am come
to *destroy* **disintegrate** the *law* **torah**, or the prophets:
I am not come to *destroy* **disintegrate**, *but* **rather** to fulfil.
18 For *verily I say* **Amen! I word** unto you,
Till heaven and earth pass,
one *jot* **iota** or one tittle
shall *in no wise* **not no way** pass from the *law* **torah**,
till all *be fulfilled* **becometh**.
19 Whosoever therefore shall *break* **release**

one of these least *commandments* **misvoth**,
and shall *teach men so* **doctrinate humanity thus**,
he shall be called the least
in the *kingdom* **sovereigndom** of *heaven* **the heavens**:
but whosoever shall do and *teach* **doctrinate** them,
the same shall be called *great* **mega**
in the *kingdom* **sovereigndom** of *heaven* **the heavens**.
20 For I *say* **word** unto you,
That *except* **unless** your *righteousness* **justness**
shall *exceed the righteousness* **superabound much more**
of **than** the scribes and Pharisees,
ye shall *in no case* **no way** enter
into the *kingdom* **sovereigndom** of *heaven* **the heavens**.

YAH SHUA'S VALUE SYSTEM: MURDER, RAGE, SLANDER

21 Ye have heard that it was *said* **rhetorized**
of them of old time **by the ancients**,
Thou shalt not *kill* **murder**;
and whosoever shall *kill* **murder**
shall be *in danger of* **subject to** the judgment:
22 But I *say* **word** unto you,
That *whosoever* **everyone**
who is *angry* **wroth** with his brother
without a cause **in vain**
shall be *in danger of* **subject to** the judgment:
and whosoever shall say to his brother, *Raca* **Req**,
shall be *in danger of* **subject to** the *council* **sanhedrim**:
but whosoever shall say, *Thou* fool,
shall be *in danger of* **subject to**
hell **Gay Hinnom/the Valley of Burning** fire.

ON FORGIVING

23 Therefore if thou *bring* **offer** thy *gift* **oblation**
to **at** the **sacrifice** altar,
and there rememberest
that thy brother hath *ought* **somewhat** against thee;
24 *Leave* **Release** there thy *gift* **oblation**
before **in front of** the **sacrifice** altar,
and go thy way;
first be reconciled to thy brother,
and then come and offer thy *gift* **oblation**.

ON SETTLING OUT OF COURT

25 Agree with thine adversary quickly,
whiles thou art in the way with him;
lest *at any time* **ever**
the adversary deliver thee to the judge,
and the judge deliver thee to the *officer* **attendant**,
and thou be cast into *prison* **a guardhouse**.
26 *Verily I say* **Amen! I word** unto thee,
Thou shalt *by no means* **not no way** come out thence,
till thou hast *paid* **given back**
the *uttermost farthing* **final quarter**.

ON ADULTERIZING

27 Ye have heard that it was *said* **rhetorized**
by *them of old time* **the ancients**,
Thou shalt not commit adultery **adulterize not**:
Exodus 20:14, Deuteronomy 5:18
28 But I *say* **word** unto you,
That *whosoever looketh on* **all who observe** a woman
to *lust* **pant** after her
hath *committed adultery* **adulterized** with her
already in his heart.

ON AVOIDING GAY HINNOM/THE VALLEY OF BURNING

29 And if thy right eye *offend* **scandalize** thee,
pluck it out, and cast it from thee:
for it is *profitable* **beneficial** for thee
that one of thy members should *perish* **destruct**,
and not that thy whole body should be cast
into *hell* **Gay Hinnom/the valley of burning**.
30 And if thy right hand *offend* **scandalize** thee,
cut **exscind** it *off*, and cast it from thee:
for it is *profitable* **beneficial** for thee
that one of thy members should *perish* **destruct**,
and not that thy whole body should be cast
into *hell* **Gay Hinnom/the Valley of Burning**.

ON DIVORCE

31 It hath been *said* **rhetorized**,
Whosoever shall *put away* **release** his *wife* **woman**,
let him give her a *writing* **scroll** of *divorcement* **apostasy**:
Deuteronomy 24:1
32 But I *say* **word** unto you,
That whosoever shall *put away* **release** his *wife* **woman**,
saving **except**
for the *cause* **word** of *fornication* **whoredom**,
causeth her to *commit adultery* **adulterize**:
and whosoever shall marry her that is *divorced* **released**,
committeth adultery **adulterizeth**.

ON OATHING

33 Again, ye have heard that it hath been *said* **rhetorized**
by *them of old time* **the ancients**,
Thou shalt not *forswear thyself* **oath**,
but shalt *perform* **give back** unto *the Lord* **Yah Veh**
thine oaths:
Leviticus 19:12, Numbers 30:2, Deuteronomy 23:21
34 But I *say* **word** unto you, *Swear* **Oath** not at all;
neither *by heaven* **at the heavens**;
for it is *God's* **Elohim's** throne:
35 Nor *by* **at** the earth; for it is his footstool:
neither *by Jerusalem* **unto Yeru Shalem**;
for it is the city of the *great king* **mega sovereign**.
36 Neither shalt thou *swear by* **oath at** thy head,
because thou canst not make one hair white or black.
37 But let your *communication* **word** be,
Yea, yea; Nay, nay:
for whatsoever is more **superabundant** than these
cometh **is** of evil.

ON RETALIATION

38 Ye have heard that it hath been *said* **rhetorized**,
An eye for an eye, and a tooth for a tooth:
Exodus 21:22—27, Leviticus 24:19, 20, Deuteronomy 19:21
39 But I *say* **word** unto you, That ye resist not evil:
but whosoever shall *smite* **slap** thee on thy right cheek,
turn to him the other also.
40 And if any man
will sue thee at the law **willeth to have thee judged**,
and take away thy *coat* **tunic**,
let him have **release** thy *cloak* **garment** also.
41 And whosoever shall compel thee to go a mile,
go with him twain.
42 Give to him that asketh thee,
and from him that *would* **willeth to** borrow of thee
turn not thou away.

ON LOVING YOUR ENEMY

43 Ye have heard that it hath been *said* **rhetorized**,
Thou shalt love thy neighbour, and hate thine enemy.
Leviticus 19:18, Psalm 139:21, 22
44 But I *say* **word** unto you, Love your enemies,
bless **eulogize** them that curse you,
do good to them that hate you,
and pray for them which *despitefully use* **threaten** you,
and persecute you;
45 That ye may be the *children* **sons** of your Father
which is in *heaven* **the heavens**:
for he maketh his sun to rise on the evil and on the good,
and *sendeth rain* **raineth** on the just and on the unjust.
46 For if ye love them which love you,
what reward have ye?
do not **indeed**
even the *publicans* **customs agents** the same?
47 And if ye salute your brethren only,
what do ye *more than others* **so superabundantly**?
do not **indeed**
even the *publicans so* **customs agents thus**?
48 Be ye therefore *perfect* **complete**,
even **exactly**
as your Father which is in *heaven* **the heavens**
is *perfect* **complete**.

ON DOING MERCIES

6 *Take* heed that ye do not your *alms* **mercies**
before men **in front of humanity**,
to be *seen* **observed** of them:
otherwise **but if not** ye have no reward of your Father
which is in *heaven* **the heavens**.
2 Therefore when **ever** thou doest *thine alms* **thy mercies**,
do not *sound a* trumpet *before* **ahead of** thee,
exactly as the hypocrites do
in the synagogues and in the streets,
that they may have glory of *men* **humanity**.
Verily I say **Amen! I word** unto you,

They have their reward.
3 But when thou doest *alms* **mercies**,
let not thy left *hand* know what thy right *hand* doeth:
4 That *thine alms* **thy mercies** may be in secret:
and thy Father which *seeth* **observeth** in secret
himself shall *reward* **give** thee *openly* **manifestly**.

ON PRAYER

5 And when **ever** thou prayest,
thou shalt not be **exactly** as the hypocrites *are*:
for they *love* **befriend** to pray standing in the synagogues
and in the corners of the *streets* **broadways**,
that they may be *seen of men* **manifest to humanity**.
Verily I say **Amen! I word** unto you,
They have their reward.
6 But thou, when **ever** thou prayest,
enter into thy *closet* **pantry**,
and when thou hast shut thy *door* **portal**,
pray to thy Father which is in secret;
and thy Father which *seeth* **observeth** in secret
shall *reward* **give** thee *openly* **manifestly**.
7 But when ye pray, use not vain repetitions,
exactly as the *heathen* **goyim** *do*:
for they think that they shall be heard
for their *much speaking* **polylogy**.
8 Be not ye therefore like unto them:
for your Father knoweth what *things* ye have need of,
before ye ask him.

A PRAYER EXAMPLE

9 *After this manner* therefore pray ye **thus**:
Our Father which art in *heaven* **the heavens**,
Hallowed be thy name.
10 Thy *kingdom* **sovereigndom** come.
Thy will *be done* **become** in earth, as it is in heaven.
11 Give us this day our *daily* bread **of subsistance**.
12 And forgive us our debts, as we forgive our debtors.
13 And *lead* **bring** us not into *temptation* **testing**,
but *deliver* **rescue** us from evil:
For thine is the *kingdom* **sovereigndom**,
and the *power* **dynamis**, and the glory,
for ever **unto the eons**. Amen.

ON FORGIVING

14 For if ye forgive
men **humanity** their *trespasses* **backslidings**,
your heavenly Father *will* **shall** also forgive you:
15 But *if* **unless** ye forgive *not men* **humanity**
their *trespasses* **backslidings**,
neither *will* **shall** your Father
forgive your *trespasses* **backslidings**.

ON FASTING

16 Moreover when **ever** ye fast,
be not, **exactly** as the hypocrites,
of a sad countenance — **sullen**:
for they *disfigure* **camouflage** their faces,
that they may *appear* **manifest** unto *men* **humanity** to fast.
Verily I say **Amen! I word** unto you,
They have their reward.
17 But thou, when thou fastest,
anoint thine head, and wash thy face;
18 That thou *appear* **manifest** not unto *men* **humanity** to fast,
but unto thy Father which is in secret:
and thy Father, which *seeth* **observeth** in secret,
shall reward thee *openly* **manifestly**.

ON TREASURING TREASURES

19 *Lay* **Treasure** not *up* for yourselves
treasures upon earth,
where moth and rust *doth corrupt* **dissolve**,
and where thieves break through and steal:
20 But *lay up* **treasure** for yourselves treasures in heaven,
where neither moth nor rust *doth corrupt* **dissolveth**,
and where thieves do not break through nor steal:
21 For where your treasure is,
there *will* **shall** your heart be also.

ON THE EYE

22 The *light* **candle** of the body is the eye:
if therefore thine eye be *single* **clear**,
thy whole body shall be *full of light* **brightly lighted**.
23 But if thine eye be evil,
thy whole body shall be *full of darkness* **dark**.
If therefore the light that is in thee be darkness,
how *great* **vast** is that darkness!

ON SERVING TWO ADONIM

24 No *man* **one** can serve two *masters* **adonim**:
for either he *will* **shall** hate the one,
and love the other;
or else he *will hold to* **shall uphold** the one,
and *despise* **disesteem** the other.
Ye cannot serve *God* **Elohim** and mammon.
25 Therefore I *say* **word** unto you,
Take no thought **Be not anxious** for your *life* **soul**,
what ye shall eat, or what ye shall drink;
nor yet for your body, what ye shall *put on* **endue**.
Is not **indeed**
the *life* **soul much** more than *meat* **nourishment**,
and the body than *raiment* **enduement**?
26 *Behold* **Look at** the *fowls* **flyers** of the *air* **heaven**:
for they sow not, neither do they *reap* **harvest**,
nor gather **together** into *barns* **granaries**;
yet your heavenly Father *feedeth* **nourisheth** them.
Are ye not *much better* **more surpassing** than they?
27 Which of you by *taking thought* **anxiety**
can add one cubit unto his *stature* **maturity**?
28 And why *take ye thought* **be ye anxious**
for *raiment* **enduement**?
Consider the lilies of the field, how they grow;
they *toil* **labour** not, neither do they spin:
29 And yet I *say* **word** unto you,
That even *Solomon* **Shelomoh** in all his glory
was not arrayed *like* **as** one of these.
30 Wherefore, if *God so* **Elohim**
thus clothe the *grass* **herbage** of the field,
which to day is, and to morrow is cast into the oven,
shall he not much more *clothe* you,
O ye of little *faith* **trust**?
31 Therefore *take no thought* **be not anxious**,
saying **wording**,
What shall we eat? or, What shall we drink?
or, Wherewithal shall we be *clothed* **arrayed**?
32 (For after all these *things* do the *Gentiles* **goyim** seek:)
for your heavenly Father knoweth
that ye have need of all these *things*.

YAH SHUA'S PROVISION

33 But seek ye first
the *kingdom* **sovereigndom** of *God* **Elohim**,
and his *righteousness* **justness**;
and all these *things* shall be added unto you.
34 *Take* therefore
no thought **be not anxious** for the morrow:
for the morrow
shall *take thought for the things* **be anxious** of itself.
Sufficient unto the day is the *evil* **malice** thereof.

ON JUDGING

7 Judge not, that ye be not judged.
2 For *with* **in** what judgment ye judge, ye shall be judged:
and *with* **in** what measure ye *mete* **measure**,
it shall be *measured* **remeasured** to you *again*.

ON TWIGS AND BEAMS

3 And why *beholdest* **lookest** thou **at** the *mote* **twig**
that is in thy brother's eye,
but *considerest* **perceivest** not the beam
that is in thine own eye?
4 Or how *wilt* **shalt** thou say to thy brother,
Let **Allow** me
pull out **to eject** the *mote* **twig** out of thine eye;
and, behold, a beam is in thine own eye?
5 Thou hypocrite,
first *cast out* **eject** the beam out of thine own eye;
and then shalt thou see clearly
to *cast out* **eject** the *mote* **twig** out of thy brother's eye.

ON GIVING, ASKING, SEEKING, AND KNOCKING

6 Give not that which is holy unto the *dogs* **hounds**,
neither cast ye your pearls *before* **in front of** swine,
lest **ever** they trample them *under* **at** their feet,
and turn again and *rend* **tear** you.
7 Ask, and it shall be given you;
seek, and ye shall find;
knock, and it shall be opened unto you:
8 For every one that asketh *receiveth* **taketh**;
and he that seeketh findeth;
and to him that knocketh it shall be opened.
9 Or what *man* **human** is there of you,

whom if his son ask bread, *will* **shall** he give him a stone?
10 Or if he ask a fish, *will* **shall** he give him a serpent?
11 If ye then, being evil,
know how to give good gifts unto your children,
how much more
shall your Father which is in *heaven* **the heavens**
give good *things* to them that ask him?

THE GOLDEN RULE

12 Therefore all
things whatsoever ye would — **as much as ever ye** will
that *men* **humanity** should do to you,
do ye even *so* **thus** to them:
for this is the *law* **torah** and the prophets.

ON GATES

13 Enter ye in *at* **through** the *strait* **narrow** gate:
for wide is the gate,
and broad is the way,
that leadeth to destruction,
and many there be which *go in thereat* **enter therein**:
14 Because *strait* **narrow** is the gate,
and *narrow* **tribulated** is the way,
which leadeth unto life,
and few there be that find it.

ON PSEUDO PROPHETS

15 *Beware* **Take heed** of *false* **pseudo** prophets,
which come to you in sheep's *clothing* **enduement**,
but inwardly they are *ravening* **rapacious** wolves.
16 Ye shall know them by their fruits.
Do men gather grapes of thorns, or figs of *thistles* **briers**?
17 Even *so* **thus** every good tree
bringeth forth **produceth** good fruit;
but a *corrupt* **putrefied** tree
bringeth forth **produceth** evil fruit.
18 A good tree
cannot *bring forth* **produce** evil fruit,
neither can a *corrupt* **putrefied** tree
bring forth **produce** good fruit.
19 Every tree that *bringeth* **produceth** not *forth* good fruit
is *hewn down* **exscinded**, and cast into the fire.
20 *Wherefore* **So then** by their fruits ye shall know them.

ON PSEUDO PROFESSORS

21 Not every one that *saith* **wordeth** unto me,
Lord **Adonay**, *Lord* **Adonay**,
shall enter into
the *kingdom* **sovereigndom** of *heaven* **the heavens**;
but he that doeth the will of my Father
which is in *heaven* **the heavens**.
22 Many *will* **shall** say to me in that day,
Lord **Adonay**, *Lord* **Adonay**,
have we not prophesied in thy name?
and in thy name *have cast out devils* **ejected demons**?
and in thy name done many *wonderful works* **dynamis**?
23 And then *will* **shall** I profess unto them,
I never **ever** knew you:
depart from me, ye that *work iniquity* **violate the torah**.

ON BUILDING

24 Therefore *whosoever* **everyone**
who heareth these *sayings* **words** of mine,
and doeth them,
I *will* **shall** liken him unto a *wise* **thoughtful** man,
which built his house upon a rock:
25 And the rain descended, and the *floods* **streams** came,
and the winds *blew* **puffed**, and beat upon that house;
and it fell not: for it was founded upon a rock.
26 And every one that heareth these sayings of mine,
and doeth them not,
shall be likened unto a foolish man,
which built his house upon the sand:
27 And the rain descended, and the *floods* **streams** came,
and the winds *blew* **puffed**,
and *beat* **dashed** upon that house;
and it fell: and *great* **mega** was the *fall* **downfall** of it.
28 And it *came to pass* **became**,
when *Jesus* **Yah Shua**
had *ended* **completed** these *sayings* **words**,
the *people* **multitude** were astonished at his doctrine:
29 For he *taught* **doctrinated** them
as *one* having authority,
and not as the scribes.

YAH SHUA CLEANSES A LEPER

8 When he
was come down **descended** from the mountain,
great **vast** multitudes followed him.
2 And, behold, there came a leper and worshipped him,
saying **wording**, *Lord* **Adonay**, if thou wilt,
thou canst *make* **purify** me *clean*.
3 And *Jesus put forth* **Yah Shua extended** his hand
and touched him, *saying* **wording**,
I will; be thou *clean* **pure**.
And *immediately* **straightway**
his leprosy was *cleansed* **purified**.
4 And *Jesus saith* **Yah Shua wordeth** unto him,
See thou *tell* **say to** no *man* **one**;
but go thy way, shew thyself to the priest,
and offer the *gift* **oblation**
that *Moses commanded* **Mosheh ordered**,
for a *testimony* **witness** unto them.

YAH SHUA HEALS A PARALYTIC

5 And when *Jesus* **Yah Shua**
was entered into *Capernaum* **Kaphar Nachum**,
there came unto him a centurion, beseeching him,
6 And *saying* **wording**, *Lord* **Adonay**,
my *servant* **lad** lieth at home *sick of the palsy* **paralyzed**,
grievously tormented **excessively tortured**.
7 And *Jesus saith* **Yah Shua wordeth** unto him,
I *will* **shall** come and *heal* *will* **shall cure** him.
8 The centurion answered and said, *Lord* **Adonay**,
I am not *worthy* **adequate**
that thou shouldest *come* **enter** under my *roof* **thatch**:
but *speak* **say** the word only,
and my *servant* **lad** shall be healed.
9 For I am a *man* **human** under authority,
having *soldiers* **warriors** under me:
and I *say* **word** to this man, Go, and he goeth;
and to another, Come, and he cometh;
and to my servant, Do this, and he doeth *it*.
10 When *Jesus* **Yah Shua** heard it, he marvelled,
and said to them that followed,
Verily I say **Amen! I word** unto you,
I have not found so *great faith* **much trust**,
no, not in *Israel* **Yisra El**.
11 And I *say* **word** unto you,
That many shall come
from the *east* **rising** and *west* **the lowering**,
and shall *sit down* **recline** with Abraham,
and *Isaac* **Yischaq**, and *Jacob* **Yaaqov**,
in the *kingdom* **sovereigndom** of *heaven* **the heavens**.
12 But the *children* **sons** of the *kingdom* **sovereigndom**
shall be *cast out* **ejected** into outer darkness:
there shall be weeping and gnashing of teeth.
13 And *Jesus* **Yah Shua** said unto the centurion,
Go thy way;
and as thou hast *believed* **trusted**,
so be it *done* unto thee.
And his servant lad was healed in the selfsame hour.

YAH SHUA ALLEVIATES A FEVER

14 And when *Jesus* **Yah Shua**
was come into *Peter's* **Petros'** house,
he saw his *wife's mother* **mother in law** laid,
and *sick of a fever* **fevered**.
15 And he touched her hand,
and the fever *left* **forsook** her:
and she arose, and ministered unto them.

YAH SHUA EJECTS DEMONIZED SPIRITS

16 When *the even was come* **evening became**,
they *brought* **offered** unto him
many that were *possessed with devils* **demonized**:
and he *cast out* **ejected** the spirits with his word,
and *healed* **cured** all that were *sick* **ill**:
17 That it might be fulfilled which was *spoken* **rhetorized**
by Esaias **through Yesha Yah** the prophet,
saying **wording**,
Himself took our *infirmities* **frailities**,
and bare our *sicknesses* **diseases**.
Yesha Yah 53:4

ON FOLLOWING YAH SHUA

18 Now when *Jesus* **Yah Shua**
saw *great* **vast** multitudes about him,

he *gave commandment* **summoned**
to depart unto the other side.
19 And a certain scribe came, and said unto him,
Master **Doctor**,
I *will* **shall** follow thee whithersoever thou goest.
20 And *Jesus saith* **Yah Shua wordeth** unto him,
The foxes have *holes* **burrows**,
and the *birds* **flyers** of the *air* **heaven** have nests;
but the Son of *man* **humanity**
hath not where to *lay* **recline** his head.
21 And another of his disciples said unto him,
Lord **Adonay**, *suffer* **permit** me first
to go and *bury* **entomb** my father.
22 But *Jesus* **Yah Shua** said unto him, Follow me;
and *let* **allow** the dead *bury* **to entomb** their dead.

YAH SHUA REBUKES THE WINDS AND THE SEA

23 And when he *was entered* **embarked** into a *ship* **sailer**,
his disciples followed him.
24 And, behold,
there *arose* **became** a *great tempest* **mega quake**
in the sea,
insomuch that
the *ship* **sailer** was *covered with* **veiled by** the waves:
but he was asleep.
25 And his disciples came to him, and *awoke* **roused** him,
saying **wording**, *Lord* **Adonay**, save us:
we *perish* **destruct**.
26 And he *saith* **wordeth** unto them,
Why are ye *fearful* **cowardly**, O ye of little *faith* **trust**?
Then he arose, and rebuked the winds and the sea;
and there *was* **became** a *great* **mega** calm.
27 But the *men* **humans** marvelled, *saying* **wording**,
What manner of man is this,
that even the winds and the sea obey him!

YAH SHUA EJECTS DEMONS

28 And when he was come to the other side
into the *country* **region** of the *Gergesenes* **Girgashiym**,
there met him two *possessed with devils* **demonized**,
coming out of the tombs,
exceeding fierce **extremely furious**,
so that no *man* **one** might **be able**
to pass *by* **through** that way.
29 And, behold, they cried out, *saying* **wording**,
What have we to do with thee, *Jesus* **Yah Shua**,
thou Son of *God* **Elohim**?
art thou come hither
to *torment* **torture** us before the *time* **season**?
30 And there was *a good way* **afar** off from them
an herd **a drove** of many swine feeding.
31 So the *devils* **demons** besought him, *saying* **wording**,
If thou *cast* **eject** us *out*,
suffer **allow** us to go away into the *herd* **drove** of swine.
32 And he said unto them, Go.
And when they were come out,
they went into the *herd* **drove** of swine:
and, behold, the whole *herd* **drove** of swine
ran violently down a *steep place* **cliff** into the sea,
and *perished* **died** in the waters.
33 And they that *kept* **fed** them fled,
and went their ways into the city,
and *told every thing* **evangelized all**,
and what was befallen
to the *possessed of the devils* **demonized**.
34 And, behold,
the whole city came out to meet *Jesus* **Yah Shua**:
and when they saw him,
they besought him that he *would* **should** depart
out of their *coasts* **boundaries**.
9 And he *entered* **embarked** into a *ship* **sailer**,
and passed over, and came into his own city.

YAH SHUA HEALS A PARALYTIC

2 And, behold, they *brought* **offered** to him
a *man sick of the palsy* **paralytic**, lying on a bed:
and *Jesus* **Yah Shua** seeing their *faith* **trust**
said unto the *sick of the palsy* **paralytic**;
Son, be of good cheer **Courage, child**;
thy sins be forgiven thee.

SCRIBES ACCUSE YAH SHUA OF BLASPHEMY

3 And, behold,
certain **some** of the scribes said within themselves,
This *man* blasphemeth.
4 And *Jesus* **Yah Shua**,
knowing their *thoughts* **deliberations** said,
Wherefore *think* **ponder** ye evil in your hearts?
5 For whether is easier, to say, Thy sins be forgiven thee;
or to say, Arise, and walk?
6 But that ye may know that the Son of *man* **humanity**
hath *power* **authority** on earth to forgive sins,
(then *saith* **wordeth** he to the *sick of the palsy* **paralytic**,)
Arise, take *up* thy bed, and go unto thine house.
7 And he arose, and departed to his house.
8 But when the multitudes saw it,
they marvelled, and glorified *God* **Elohim**,
which had given such *power* **authority**
unto *men* **humanity**.

MATTHAIOS FOLLOWS YAH SHUA

9 And as *Jesus* **Yah Shua** passed forth from thence,
he saw a *man* **human**
named Matthew **worded Matthaios**,
sitting at the *receipt of* custom:
and he *saith* **wordeth** unto him, Follow me.
And he arose, and followed him.

PHARISEES QUESTION THE DISCIPLES

10 And it *came to pass* **became**,
as *Jesus sat at meat* **Yah Shua reposed** in the house,
behold, many *publicans* **customs agents** and sinners
came and *sat down* **reposed** with him and his disciples.
11 And when the Pharisees saw it,
they said unto his disciples,
Why eateth your *Master* **Doctor**
with *publicans* **customs agents** and sinners?
12 But when *Jesus* **Yah Shua** heard that,
he said unto them,
They that be *whole* **able** need not a *physician* **healer**,
but they that are *sick* **ill**.
13 But go ye and learn what that *meaneth* **be**,
I will *have* mercy, and not sacrifice:
for I am not come to call the *righteous* **just**,
but sinners to repentance.
14 Then came to him the disciples of *John* **Yahn**,
saying **wording**,
Why do we and the Pharisees fast *oft* **much**,
but thy disciples fast not?
15 And *Jesus* **Yah Shua** said unto them,
Can the *children* **sons** of the bridechamber mourn,
as long as the bridegroom is with them?
but the days *will* **shall** come,
When **ever** the bridegroom shall be taken from them,
and then shall they fast.

THE PARABLE OF GARMENTS

16 No *man* **one**
putteth a *piece* **patch** of *new* **unfulled** cloth
unto an old garment,
for that *which is put in to fill it up* **fulness**
taketh from the garment,
and the *rent is made* **split becometh** worse.

THE PARABLE OF SKINS

17 Neither do men put new wine into old *bottles* **skins**:
else **but if not** the *bottles break* **skins burst**,
and the wine *runneth* **poureth** out,
and the *bottles perish* **skins destruct**:
but they put new wine into new *bottles* **skins**,
and both are preserved.

AN ARCH'S DEAD DAUGHTER

18 While he spake these *things* unto them, behold,
there came *a certain ruler* **an arch**, and worshipped him,
saying **wording**, My daughter is even now dead:
but come and *lay* **put** thy hand upon her,
and she shall live.
19 And *Jesus* **Yah Shua** arose, and followed him,
and so did his disciples.

YAH SHUA HEALS A HEMORRHAGE

20 And, behold, a woman,
which *was diseased with an issue of blood* **hemorrhaged**
twelve years, came behind him,
and touched the *hem* **edge** of his garment:
21 For she *said* **worded** within herself,
If I may *but* **only** touch his garment,
I shall be *whole* **saved**.
22 But *Jesus* **Yah Shua** turned *him about* **around**,

and when he saw her, he said,
Daughter, *be of good comfort* **courage**;
thy *faith* **trust** hath *made* **saved** thee *whole*.
And the woman was *made whole* **saved** from that hour.

YAH SHUA RESURRECTS THE ARCH'S DAUGHTER

23 And when *Jesus* **Yah Shua**
came into the *ruler's* **arch's** house,
and saw the *minstrels* **flutists**
and the *people making a noise* **multitude tumulting**,
24 He *said* **worded** unto them, *Give place* **Depart**:
for the *maid* **maiden** is not dead, but sleepeth.
And they *laughed* **ridiculed** him *to scorn*.
25 But when the *people* **multitude**
were put forth **was ejected**,
he *went in* **entered**,
and *took* **overpowered** her by the hand,
and the *maid* **maiden** arose.
26 And the fame hereof went abroad into all that land.

YAH SHUA OPENS BLIND EYES

27 And when *Jesus departed* **Yah Shua passed** thence,
two blind men followed him,
crying, and *saying* **wording**,
Thou son of David, *have* mercy *on* us.
28 And when he was come into the house,
the blind men came to him:
and *Jesus saith* **Yah Shua wordeth** unto them,
Believe **Trust** ye that I am able to do this?
They *said* **worded** unto him, Yea, *Lord* **Adonay**.
29 Then touched he their eyes, *saying* **wording**,
According to your *faith* **trust** be it unto you.
30 And their eyes were opened;
and *Jesus* **Yah Shua**
straitly charged **sternly enjoined** them, *saying* **wording**,
See that no *man* **one** know it.
31 But they, when they were departed,
spread abroad his fame **reported about him**
in all that *country* **land**.

YAH SHUA EJECTS A DEMON

32 As they went out, behold,
they *brought* **offered** to him a *dumb man* **mute human**
possessed with a devil **demonized**.
33 And when the *devil* **demon** was *cast out* **ejected**,
the *dumb* **mute** spake:
and the multitudes marvelled, *saying* **wording**,
It was never *so seen* **ever thus manifested**
in *Israel* **Yisra El**.
34 But the Pharisees *said* **worded**,
He *casteth out devils* **ejecteth demons**
through **in** the *prince* **arch** of *the devils* **demons**.

YAH SHUA HAS A SYMPATHETIC SPLEEN

35 And *Jesus* **Yah Shua**
went about all the cities and villages,
teaching **doctrinating** in their synagogues,
and preaching
the *gospel* **evangelism** of the *kingdom* **sovereigndom**,
and *healing* **curing** every *sickness* **disease**
and every *disease* **debility** among the people.
36 But when he saw the multitudes,
he *was moved with compassion* **had a sympathetic spleen**
on **for** them, because they fainted,
and were *scattered abroad* **tossed about**,
as sheep having no shepherd.
37 Then *saith* **wordeth** he unto his disciples,
The harvest *truly* **indeed** is *plenteous* **vast**,
but the *labourers* **workers** are few;
38 *Pray* **Petition** ye therefore
the Lord **Adonay** of the harvest,
that he *will send* **shall cast** forth *labourers* **workers**
into his harvest.

YAH SHUA AUTHORIZES HIS TWELVE DISCIPLES

10 And when he had called unto him
his twelve disciples,
he gave them *power* **authority**
against *unclean* **impure** spirits,
so as to *cast* **eject** them *out*,
and to *heal all manner of sickness* **cure every disease**
and *all manner of disease* **every debility**.

THE NAMES OF THE TWELVE APOSTLES

2 Now the names of the twelve apostles are these;
The first, *Simon* **Shimon**,
who is *called Peter* **worded Petros**,
and *Andrew* **Andreas** his brother;
James **Yaaqovos** *the son* of *Zebedee* **Zabdi**,
and *John* **Yahn** his brother;
3 *Philip* **Philippos**, and *Bartholomew* **Bar Talmay**;
Thomas **Taom**,
and *Matthew* **Matthaios** the *publican* **customs agent**;
James **Yaaqovos** *the son* of *Alphaeus* **Heleph**,
and Lebbaeus, *whose surname was* **called** Thaddaeus;
4 *Simon* **Shimon** the *Canaanite* **Kenaaniy**,
and *Judas Iscariot* **Yah Hudah the urbanite**,
who also betrayed him.

YAH SHUA APOSTOLIZES HIS APOSTLES

5 These twelve *Jesus sent forth* **Yah Shua apostolized**,
and *commanded* **evangelized** them, *saying* **wording**,
Go not into the way of the *Gentiles* **goyim**,
and into any city of the *Samaritans* **Shomeroniym**
enter ye not:
6 But go rather
to the lost sheep of the house of *Israel* **Yisra El**.
7 And as ye go, preach, *saying* **wording**,
The *kingdom* **sovereigndom** of *heaven* **the heavens**
is at hand **approacheth**.
8 *Heal* **Cure** the *sick* **frail**, *cleanse* **purify** the lepers,
raise the dead, *cast out devils* **eject demons**:
freely **gratuitously** ye have *received* **taken**,
freely **gratuitously** give.

THE APOSTLE'S POSSESSIONS

9 *Provide* **Acquire** neither gold, nor silver,
nor *brass* **copper** in your *purses* **girdles**,
10 Nor *scrip for your journey* **wallet in the way**,
neither two *coats* **tunics**, neither shoes,
nor yet *staves* **rods**:
for the *workman* **worker**
is worthy of his *meat* **nourishment**.

THE APOSTLE'S HOME

11 And into whatsoever city or *town* **village**
ye shall enter,
enquire **interrogate** who in it is worthy;
and there abide till ye go thence.
12 And when ye *come* **enter** into an house, salute it.
13 And if **indeed** the house be worthy,
let your *peace* **shalom** come upon it:
but if it be not worthy,
let your *peace return* **shalom turn again** to you.
14 And *whosoever* **if they** shall not receive you,
nor hear your words,
when ye depart out of that house or city,
shake off the dust of your feet.
15 *Verily I say* **Amen! I word** unto you,
It shall be more tolerable
for the land of *Sodom* **Sedom** and *Gomorrha* **Amorah**
in the day of judgment, than for that city.
16 Behold, I *send* **apostolize** you *forth*
as sheep in the midst of wolves:
be ye therefore *wise* **thoughtful** as serpents,
and *harmless* **unadulterated** as doves.

YAH SHUA PROPHESIES BETRAYAL

17 But *beware of men* **heed humanity**:
for they *will deliver* **shall betray** you
up to the *councils* **sanhedrim**,
and they *will* **shall** scourge you in their synagogues;
18 And *ye* shall be brought
before governors and *kings* **sovereigns** for my sake,
for **in** a *testimony* **witness** against them
and the *Gentiles* **goyim**.
19 But when **ever** they *deliver* **betray** you *up*,
take no thought **be not anxious**
how or what ye shall speak:
for it shall be given you in that same hour
what ye shall speak.
20 For it is not ye that speak,
but the Spirit of your Father which speaketh in you.

YAH SHUA PROPHESIES FAMILY TRAITORS

21 And the brother shall *deliver up* **betray** the brother
to death,
and the father the child:
and the children shall *rise up against* **attack** their parents,
and cause them to be *put to death* **deathified**.
22 And ye shall be hated of all *men* for my name's sake:

but he that *endureth* **abideth** to the *end* **completion**
shall be saved.
23 But when **ever** they persecute you in this city,
flee ye into another:
for *verily I say* **Amen! I word** unto you,
Ye shall not **no way**
have *gone over* **completed** the cities of *Israel* **Yisra El**
till **ever** the Son of *man* **humanity** be come.

ON SERVICE RANKS

24 The disciple is not above his *master* **doctor**,
nor the servant above his *Lord* **Adoni**.
25 It is enough for the disciple
that he be as his *master* **doctor**,
and the servant as his *Lord* **Adoni**.
If they have called the *master of the house* **housedespotes**
Beelzebub **Baal Zebub**,
how much more shall they *call* them of his household?
26 *Fear* **Awe** them not therefore:
for *there is nothing covered* **naught that shall be veiled**,
that shall not be *revealed* **unveiled**;
and *hid* **secret**, that shall not be known.
27 What I *tell* **word to** you in darkness,
that *speak* **say** ye in light:
and what ye hear in the ear,
that preach ye upon the housetops.
28 And *fear* **awe** not them which *kill* **slaughter** the body,
but are not able to *kill* **slaughter** the soul:
but rather *fear* **awe** him
which is able to destroy both soul and body
in *hell* **Gay Hinnom/the valley of burning**.
29 Are not **indeed** two sparrows
sold for *a farthing* **an assarion**?
and **not** one of them shall *not* fall on the ground
without your Father.
30 But the very hairs of your head are all numbered.
31 *Fear* **Awe** ye not therefore,
ye *are of more value than* **surpass** many sparrows.

ON HOMOLOGIZING

32 **All** — Whosoever therefore shall *confess* **profess** me
before men **in front of humanity**,
him *will* **shall** I *confess* **profess** also
before **in front of** my Father
which is in *heaven* **the heavens**.
33 But whosoever shall deny me
before men **in front of humanity**,
him *will* **shall** I also deny *before* **in front of** my Father
which is in *heaven* **the heavens**.
34 *Think* **Presume** not
that I am come to *send peace* **put shalom** on earth:
I came not to *send peace* **put shalom**, but a sword.
35 For I am come
to *set a man at variance* **alienate a human**
against his father,
and the daughter against her mother,
and the *daughter in law* **bride** against her mother in law.
36 And a *man's* **human's** foes
shall be they of his own household.
37 He that *loveth* **befriendeth** father or mother
more than me
is not worthy of me:
and he that *loveth* **befriendeth** son or daughter
more than me
is not worthy of me.
38 And he that taketh not his *cross* **stake**,
and followeth after me,
is not worthy of me.

ON THE SOUL

39 He that findeth his *life* **soul** shall lose it:
and he that loseth his *life* **soul** for my sake shall find it.
40 He that receiveth you receiveth me,
and he that receiveth me
receiveth him that *sent* **apostolized** me.
41 He that receiveth a prophet in the name of a prophet
shall *receive* **take** a prophet's reward;
and he that receiveth *a righteous man* **the just**
in the name of *a righteous man* **the just**
shall *receive a righteous man's* **take the just's** reward.
42 And whosoever shall give to drink
unto one of these little ones
a cup of cold *water* only in the name of a disciple,
verily I say **Amen! I word** unto you,
he shall *in no wise* **not no way** lose his reward.

BAPTIZER YAHN IN PRISON

11 And it *came to pass* **became**,
when *Jesus* **Yah Shua** had *made an end* **completed**
of commanding **ordaining** his twelve disciples,
he departed thence
to *teach* **doctrinate** and to preach in their cities.
2 Now when *John* **Yahn** had heard in the prison
the works of *Christ* **the Messiah**,
he sent two of his disciples,
3 And said unto him, Art thou he that should come,
or *do* **await** we *look for* another?
4 *Jesus* **Yah Shua** answered and said unto them,
Go and *shew John again* **evangelize Yahn**
those *things* which ye do hear and *see* **observe**:
5 The blind *receive their sight* **see**, and the lame walk,
the lepers are *cleansed* **purified**, and the *deaf* **mute** hear,
the dead are raised *up*,
and the poor
have the gospel preached to them **are evangelized**.
6 And blessed is he,
whosoever shall not be *offended* **scandalized** in me.

YAH SHUA'S WITNESS CONCERNING BAPTIZER YAHN

7 And as they departed,
Jesus **Yah Shua** began to *say* **word** unto the multitudes
concerning *John* **Yahn**,
What went ye out into the wilderness to *see* **observe**?
A reed shaken *with* **by** the wind?
8 But what went ye out for to see?
A *man* **human**
clothed in *soft raiment* **effeminate garment**?
behold, they that *wear soft clothing* **bear the effeminate**
are in *kings'* **sovereign's** houses.
9 But what went ye out for to see? A prophet?
yea, I *say* **word** unto you,
and more **superabundantly** than a prophet.
10 For this is he,
of **concerning** whom it is *written* **scribed**,
Behold, I *send* **apostolize** my *messenger* **angel**
before **in front of** thy face,
which shall prepare thy way before thee.
Yesha Yah 40:3, Malachi 3:1
11 *Verily I say* **Amen! I word** unto you,
Among them that are born of women
there hath not risen
a greater than *John* **Yahn** the *Baptist* **Baptizer**:
notwithstanding he that is least
in the *kingdom* **sovereigndom** of *heaven* **the heavens**
is greater than he.
12 And from the days of *John* **Yahn** the *Baptist* **Baptizer**
until now
the *kingdom* **sovereigndom** of *heaven* **the heavens**
suffereth violence **is taken by force**,
and the *violent* **enforcers** take it *by force*.
13 For all the prophets and the *law* **torah**
prophesied until *John* **Yahn**.
14 And if ye will **to** receive it,
this is *Elias* **Eli Yah**, which was *for* **about** to come.
15 He that hath ears to hear, let him hear.
16 But whereunto shall I liken this generation?
It is like unto children sitting in the markets,
and calling unto their *fellows* **comrades**,
17 And *saying* **wording**,
We have *piped* **fluted** unto you,
and ye have not danced;
we have *mourned* **lamented** unto you,
and ye have not *lamented* **chopped**.
18 For *John* **Yahn** came neither eating nor drinking,
and they *say* **word**,
He hath a *devil* **demon**.
19 The Son of *man* **humanity** came eating and drinking,
and they *say* **word**, Behold,
a *man gluttonous* **human glutton**, and a winebibber,
a friend of *publicans* **customs agents** and sinners.
But wisdom is justified of her children.

YAH SHUA REPROACHES THE CITIES

20 Then began he to *upbraid* **reproach** the cities
wherein most of his *mighty works* **dynamis**
were done **became**,

because they repented not:
21 Woe unto thee, Chorazin!
woe unto thee, *Bethsaida* **Beth Sayad**!
for if the *mighty works* **dynamis**,
which *were done* **became** in you,
had *been done* **become** in *Tyre* **Sor** and Sidon,
they *would* **should** have repented long ago
in *sackcloth* **saq** and ashes.
22 *But I say* **Moreover I word** unto you,
It shall be more tolerable for *Tyre* **Sor** and Sidon
at **in** the day of judgment, than for you.
23 And thou, *Capernaum* **Kaphar Nachum**,
which art exalted unto **the** heaven,
shalt be brought down to *hell* **hades**:
for if the *mighty works* **dynamis**,
which *have been done* **became** in thee,
had *been done* **become** in *Sodom* **Sedom**,
it *would* **should** have *remained* **abode** until this day.
24 *But I say* **Moreover I word** unto you,
That it shall be more tolerable
for the land of *Sodom* **Sedom** in the day of judgment,
than for thee.

YAH SHUA HOMOLOGIZES THE FATHER

25 At that *time* **season**,
Jesus **Yah Shua** answered and said,
I *thank* **confess** thee, O Father,
Lord **Adonay** of **the** heaven and **the** earth,
because thou hast *hid* **secreted** these *things*
from the wise and *prudent* **comprehending**,
and hast *revealed* **unveiled** them unto babes.
26 *Even so* **Yea**, Father:
for *so* **thus** it *seemeth good* **was well—approved**
in *thy sight* **front of thee**.
27 All *things* are delivered unto me of my Father:
and no *man* **one** knoweth the Son, *but* **except** the Father;
neither knoweth any *man* **one** the Father,
save **except** the Son,
and he to whomsoever
the Son *will reveal* **shall unveil** him.

YAH SHUA'S INVITATION TO REST

28 Come unto me,
all ye that labour and are *heavy laden* **overburdened**,
and I *will give you* **shall** rest **you**.
29 Take my yoke upon you, and learn of me;
for I am meek and *lowly* **humble** in heart:
and *ye* shall find rest unto your souls.
30 For my yoke is *easy* **kind**, and my burden is light.

YAH SHUA IS ADONAY OF THE SHABBATH

12 At that *time* **season**
Jesus **Yah Shua** went on the *sabbath day* **shabbath**
through the *corn* **spores**;
and his disciples were an hungred,
and began to pluck the *ears of corn* **cobs** and to eat.
2 But when the Pharisees saw it, they said unto him,
Behold,
thy disciples do that which is not *lawful* **allowed** to do
upon **in** the *sabbath day* **shabbath**.
3 But he said unto them,
Have ye not read what David did,
when he was an hungred, and they that were with him;
4 How he entered into the house of *God* **Elohim**,
and did eat the *shewbread* **prothesis bread**,
which was not *lawful* **allowed** for him to eat,
neither for them which were with him,
but **except** only for the priests?
5 Or have ye not read in the *law* **torah**,
how that on the *sabbath days* **shabbaths**
the priests in the *temple* **priestal precinct**
profane the *sabbath* **shabbath**,
and are *blameless* **unaccused**?
6 But I *say* **word** unto you,
That *in this place is one greater than the temple*
a greater than the priestal precinct is here.
7 But if ye had known what this *meaneth* **be**,
I will *have* mercy, and not sacrifice,
ye *would* **should** not
have *condemned* **adjudged** the *guiltless* **unaccused**.
8 For the Son of *man* **humanity** is *Lord* **Adonay**
even of the *sabbath day* **shabbath**.

Hoshea 6:6

YAH SHUA HEALS ON THE SHABBATH

9 And when he was departed thence,
he went into their synagogue:
10 And, behold,
there was a *man* **human** which had his hand withered.
And they asked him, *saying* **wording**,
Is it *lawful* **allowed**
to *heal* **cure** on the *sabbath days* **shabbaths**?
that they might accuse him.
11 And he said unto them,
What *man* **human** shall there be *among* **of** you,
that shall have one sheep,
and if it fall into a *pit* **cistern**
on the *sabbath day* **shabbaths**,
will **shall** he not *lay hold on* **indeed, overpower** it,
and lift it out?
12 How much then
is a man better than **a human surpasseth** a sheep?
Wherefore it is *lawful* **allowable** to do well
on the *sabbath days* **shabbaths**.
13 Then *saith* **wordeth** he to the *man* **human**,
Stretch forth **Extend** thine hand.
And he *stretched* **extended** it *forth*;
and it was restored whole, like as the other.
14 Then the Pharisees went out,
and *held a* **took** council against him,
how they might destroy him.

YAH SHUA CURES THE MULTITUDES

15 But when *Jesus* **Yah Shua** knew it,
he withdrew himself from thence:
and *great* **vast** multitudes followed him,
and he *healed* **cured** them all;
16 And *charged* **admonished** them
that they should not make him *known* **manifest**:
17 That it might be fulfilled which was *spoken* **rhetorized**
by Esaias **through Yesha Yah** the prophet,
saying **wording**,
18 Behold my *servant* **lad**, whom I have chosen;
my beloved,
in **of** whom my soul *is well pleased* **well—approveth**:
I will **shall** put my spirit upon him,
and he shall shew judgment to the *Gentiles* **goyim**.
19 He shall not strive, nor cry;
neither shall any *man* **one** hear his voice
in the *streets* **broadways**.
20 A *bruised* **crushed** reed shall he not break,
and smoking *flax* **linen** shall he not quench,
till he send forth judgment unto *victory* **triumph**.
21 And in his name shall the *Gentiles trust* **goyim hope**.

Yesha Yah 42:1—4

22 Then was *brought* **offered** unto him
one *possessed with a devil* **demonized**,
blind, and *dumb* **mute**:
and he *healed* **cured** him,
insomuch that
the blind and *dumb* **mute** both spake and *saw* **observed**.
23 And all the *people* **multitude** were *amazed* **astounded**,
and *said* **worded**, Is not this the son of David?

PHARISEES BLASPHEME THE HOLY SPIRIT

24 *But* **Except** when the Pharisees heard it, they said,
This *fellow* doth not *cast out devils* **eject demons**,
but by Beelzebub **except in Baal Zebub**
the *prince* **arch** of the *devils* **demons**.
25 And *Jesus* **Yah Shua** knew their *thoughts* **deliberations**,
and said unto them,
Every *kingdom* **sovereigndom** divided against itself
is brought to desolation **shall desolate**;
and every city or house divided against itself
shall not stand:
26 And if Satan *cast out* **eject** Satan,
he *is divided* **divideth** against himself;
how shall then his *kingdom* **sovereigndom** stand?
27 And if I *by Beelzebub* **in Baal Zebub**
cast out devils **eject demons**,
by **in** whom do your *children cast* **sons eject** them *out*?
Therefore they shall be your judges.
28 But if I *cast out devils* **eject demons**
by **in** the Spirit of *God* **Elohim**,
then the *kingdom* **sovereigndom** of *God* **Elohim**
is come unto **has arrived upon** you.

how can **any** *one* enter into a strong man's house,
and *spoil* **plunder** his *goods* **vessels**,
except **unless** he first bind the strong man?
and then he *will spoil* **shall plunder** his house.
30 He that is not with me is against me;
and he that gathereth not with me scattereth *abroad*.

THE UNFORGIVEN SIN

31 Wherefore I *say* **word** unto you,
All manner of **Every** sin and blasphemy
shall be forgiven unto *men* **humanity**:
but the blasphemy *against* **of** the Holy *Ghost* **Spirit**
shall not be forgiven unto *men* **humanity**.
32 And whosoever *speaketh* **sayeth** a word
against the Son of *man* **humanity**,
it shall be forgiven him:
but whosoever *speaketh* **sayeth**
against the Holy *Ghost* **Spirit**,
it shall not be forgiven him,
neither in this *world* **eon**,
neither in the *world to come* **about to be**.
33 Either make the tree good, and his fruit good;
or else make the tree *corrupt* **putrefied**,
and his fruit *corrupt* **putrefied**:
for the tree is known by his fruit.

YAH SHUA DENOUNCES THE SCRIBES AND PHARISEES

34 O *generation* **progeny** of vipers,
how can ye, being evil, speak good *things*?
for out of the **super** abundance of the heart
the mouth speaketh.
35 A good *man* **human**
out of the good treasure of the heart
bringeth forth good things **ejecteth good**:
and an evil *man* **human** out of the evil treasure
bringeth forth evil things **ejecteth evil**.
36 But I *say* **word** unto you,
That every idle *word* **rhema**
that *men* **humanity** shall speak,
they shall *give account* **render word**
thereof **concerning it**
in the day of judgment.
37 For by thy words thou shalt be justified,
and by thy words thou shalt be *condemned* **adjudged**.

YAH SHUA PROPHESIES HIS DEATH AND RESURRECTION

38 Then *certain* **some** of the scribes and of the Pharisees
answered, *saying* **wording**, *Master* **Doctor**,
we *would* **will to** see a sign from thee.
39 *But* **Except** he answered and said unto them,
An evil and adulterous generation seeketh after a sign;
and there shall no sign be given to it,
but **except** the sign of the prophet *Jonas* **Yonah**:
40 For **exactly** as *Jonas* **Yonah**
was three days and three nights
in the *whale's* **monster's** belly;
so **thus** shall the Son of *man* **humanity**
be three days and three nights in the heart of the earth.

YAH SHUA PROPHESIES CONDEMNATION

41 *The men of Nineveh* **Men — Nineviy**
shall rise in judgment with this generation,
and shall condemn it:
because they repented
at **unto** the preaching of *Jonas* **Yonah**; and, behold,
a greater **much more** than *Jonas* **Yonah** is here.
42 The *queen* **sovereigness** of the south
shall rise *up* in the judgment with this generation,
and shall condemn it:
for she came
from the *uttermost parts* **extremities** of the earth
to hear the wisdom of *Solomon* **Shelomoh**; and, behold,
a greater **much more** than *Solomon* **Shelomoh** is here.

ON IMPURE SPIRITS

43 When **ever** the *unclean* **impure** spirit
is gone out of a *man* **human**,
he *walketh* **passeth** through *dry* **waterless** places,
seeking rest, and findeth none.
44 Then he *saith* **wordeth**,
I *will* **shall** return into my house from whence I came *out*;
and when he is come,
he findeth it empty, swept, and *garnished* **adorned**.
45 Then goeth he,
and taketh with himself seven other spirits
more *wicked* **evil** than himself,
and they enter in and *dwell* **settle** there:
and the *last* **final** state of that *man* **human**
is **becometh** worse than the first.
Even *so* **thus**
shall it be also unto this *wicked* **evil** generation.

ON RELATIONSHIP WITH YAH SHUA

46 While he yet *talked* **spoke** to the *people* **multitudes**,
behold, his mother and his brethren stood without,
desiring **seeking** to speak with him.
47 Then **some** one said unto him, Behold,
thy mother and thy brethren stand without,
desiring **seeking** to speak with thee.
48 But he answered and said unto him that told him,
Who is my mother? and who are my brethren?
49 And he *stretched forth* **extended** his hand
toward his disciples, and said,
Behold my mother and my brethren!
50 For whosoever shall do the will of my Father
which is in *heaven* **the heavens**,
the same is my brother, and sister, and mother.

THE PARABLES OF THE SOVEREIGNDOM

13 The same day went *Jesus* **Yah Shua** out of the house,
and sat by the sea side.
2 And *great* **vast** multitudes
were gathered together unto him,
so that he *went* **embarked** into a *ship* **sailer**, and sat;
and the whole multitude stood on the shore.

THE SOWER PARABLE

3 And he spake *many things* **much** unto them in parables,
saying **wording**, Behold, a sower went forth to sow;
4 And *when he sowed* **in his sowing**,
some *seeds* **indeed** fell by the way side,
and the *fowls* **flyers** came and devoured them *up*:
5 *Some* **Others** fell upon *stony places* **rocky**,
where they had not much *earth* **soil**:
and *forthwith* **straightway** they sprung *up*,
because they had no *deepness* **depth** of *earth* **soil**:
6 And when the sun *was up* **rose**, they were scorched;
and because they had no root, they withered *away*.
7 And *some* **others** fell among thorns;
and the thorns *sprung up* **ascended**, and choked them:
8 But other fell into good *ground* **soil**,
and *brought forth* **gave** fruit,
some **indeed** an hundredfold,
some sixtyfold, some thirtyfold.
9 Who hath ears to hear, let him hear.

WHY PARABLES?

10 And the disciples came, and said unto him,
Why speakest thou unto them in parables?
11 He answered and said unto them,
Because it is given unto you to know the mysteries
of the *kingdom* **sovereigndom** of *heaven* **the heavens**,
but to them it is not given.
12 For whosoever hath, to him shall be given,
and he shall *have more abundance* **superabound**:
but whosoever hath not,
from him shall be taken away even that he hath.
13 Therefore speak I to them in parables:
because **in observing,** they *seeing see* **observe** not;
and hearing they hear not,
neither do they *understand* **comprehend**.
14 And in them
is fulfilled the prophecy of *Esaias* **Yesha Yah**,
which *saith* **wordeth**, By hearing ye shall hear,
and shall *not understand* **not no way comprehend**;
and *seeing* **observing,** ye shall *see* **observe**,
and shall not **no way** perceive:
15 For this people's heart is *waxed gross* **calloused**,
and their ears are dull of hearing,
and their eyes they have *closed* **shut**;
lest *at any time* **ever** they should see with their eyes
and hear with their ears,
and should *understand* **comprehend** with their heart,
and should *be converted* **turn around**,
and I should heal them.

Yesha Yah 6:9,10

16 But blessed are your eyes, for they *see* **observe**:
and your ears, for they hear.
17 For *verily I say* **Amen! I word** unto you,
That many prophets and *righteous men* **just**
have *desired* **panted**
to *see* **observe** those *things* which ye see,
and have not seen them;
and to hear those *things* which ye hear,
and have not heard them.
18 Hear ye therefore the parable of the sower.

THE PARABLE EXPLAINED

19 When any one
heareth the word of the *kingdom* **sovereigndom**,
and *understandeth* **comprehendeth** it not,
then cometh the *wicked* **evil** one,
and *catcheth away* **seizeth** that
which was sown in his heart.
This is he
which *received seed* **was sown** by the way side.
20 But he that *received the seed* **was sown**
into the *stony places* **rocky**,
the same is he that heareth the word,
and *anon* **straightway** with *joy receiveth* **cheer taketh** it;
21 Yet hath he not root in himself,
but *dureth for a while* **is temporary**:
for when tribulation or persecution *ariseth* **become**
because of the word,
by and by **straightway** he is *offended* **scandalized**.
22 He also
that *received seed among* **was sown in** the thorns
is he that heareth the word;
and the *care* **anxiety** of this *world* **eon**,
and the deceitfulness of riches,
choke **strangle** the word, and he becometh unfruitful.
23 But he
that *received seed* **was sown** into the good *ground* **soil**
is he that heareth the word,
and *understandeth it* **comprehendeth**;
which *also* **now** beareth fruit,
and *bringeth forth* **produceth**,
some **indeed** an hundredfold, some sixty, some thirty.

DARNEL AND SPERMA PARABLE

24 Another parable *put* **set** he forth unto them,
saying **wording**,
The *kingdom* **sovereigndom** of *heaven* **the heavens**
is likened unto a *man* **human**
which sowed good *seed* **sperma** in his field:
25 But while *men* **humanity** slept,
his enemy came
and sowed *tares* **darnel** among the *wheat* **grain**,
and went his way.
26 But when the *blade was sprung up* **herbage sprouted**,
and *brought forth* **produced** fruit,
then *appeared* **manifested the** *tares* **darnel** also.
27 So the servants of the *householder* **housedespotes**
came and said unto him, *Sir Lord* **Adoni**,
didst not **indeed** thou sow good *seed* **sperma** in thy field?
from whence then hath it *tares* **darnel**?
28 He said unto them,
An enemy — **a human** hath done this.
The servants said unto him,
Wilt thou then that we go and gather them *up*?
29 But he said, Nay;
lest while **ever** ye gather *up* the *tares* **darnel**,
ye *root up* **uproot** also the *wheat* **grain**
with them **simultaneously**.
30 *Let* **Allow** both grow together until the harvest:
and in the *time* **season** of harvest
I *will* **shall** say to the *reapers* **harvesters**,
Gather ye together first the *tares* **darnel**,
and bind them in bundles to burn them:
but gather **together** the *wheat* **grain**
into my *barn* **granary**.

THE MUSTARD KERNEL PARABLE

31 Another parable *put* **set** he forth unto them,
saying **wording**,
The *kingdom* **sovereigndom** of *heaven* **the heavens**
is like to a *grain* **kernal** of mustard *seed*,
which a *man* **human** took, and sowed in his field:
32 Which indeed is the least of all *seeds* **spermas**:
but when **ever** it is grown,
it is the greatest among herbs, and becometh a tree,
so that the *birds* **flyers** of the *air* **heavens**
come and *lodge* **nest** in the branches thereof.

THE FERMENTATION PARABLE

33 Another parable spake he unto them;
The *kingdom* **sovereigndom** of *heaven* **the heavens**
is like unto *leaven* **fermentation**, which a woman took,
and hid in three *measures* **seahs** of *meal* **flour**,
till the whole was *leavened* **fermented**.

THE PURPOSE OF PARABLES

34 All these *things* spake *Jesus* **Yah Shua**
unto the multitude in parables;
and *without* **apart from** a parable
spake he not unto them:
35 That it might be fulfilled
which was *spoken by* **rhetorized through** the prophet,
saying **wording**, I *will* **shall** open my mouth in parables;
I *will* **shall** utter *things* **those**
which have been *kept secret* **secreted**
from the foundation of the world cosmos.
Psalm 78:2

THE DARNEL AND SPERMA PARABLE EXPLAINED

36 Then *Jesus sent* **Yah Shua relased** the multitude *away*,
and went into the house:
and his disciples came unto him, *saying* **wording**,
Declare unto us the parable of the *tares* **darnel** of the field.
37 He answered and said unto them,
He that soweth the good *seed* **sperma**
is the Son of *man* **humanity**;
38 The field is the *world* **cosmos**;
the good *seed* **sperma**
are the *children* **sons** of the *kingdom* **sovereigndom**;
but the *tares* **darnel**
are the *children* **sons** of the *wicked one* **evil**;
39 The enemy that sowed them is *the devil* **Diabolos**;
the harvest is the *end* **completion** of the *world* **eon**;
and the *reapers* **harvesters** are the angels.
40 **Exactly** As therefore the *tares* **darnel** are gathered
and burned in the fire;
so **thus** shall it be
in the *end* **completion** of this *world* **eon**.
41 The Son of *man* **humanity**
shall *send forth* **apostolize** his angels,
and they shall gather out of his *kingdom* **sovereigndom**
all *things* **those** that *offend* **scandalize**,
and them which *do iniquity* **violate the torah**;
42 And shall cast them into a furnace of fire:
there shall be wailing and gnashing of teeth.
43 Then shall the *righteous* **just**
shine forth **resplend** as the sun
in the *kingdom* **sovereigndom** of their Father.
Who hath ears to hear, let him hear.
Apocalypse 14:14—20

THE SECRETED TREASURE PARABLE

44 Again,
the *kingdom* **sovereigndom** of *heaven* **the heavens**
is like unto treasure *hid* **secreted** in a field;
the which when a *man* **human** hath found,
he *hideth* **secreteth**,
and for *joy* **cheer** thereof
goeth and selleth all *that* — **as much as** he hath,
and *buyeth* **marketeth** that field.

THE PRECIOUS PEARL PARABLE

45 Again,
the *kingdom* **sovereigndom** of *heaven* **the heavens**
is like unto a *merchant man* **human merchant**,
seeking goodly pearls:
46 Who, when he had found one pearl
of great price **vastly precious**,
went and sold all *that* — **as much as** he had,
and *bought* **marketed** it.

THE NET PARABLE

47 Again,
the *kingdom* **sovereigndom** of *heaven* **the heavens**
is like unto a net, that was cast into the sea,
and gathered **together** of every *kind* **genos**:
48 Which, when it was full, they drew to shore,
and sat down, and gathered the good into vessels,
but cast the *bad* **putrefied** away.

THE COMPLETION OF THE EON

49 *So* **Thus** shall it be
at the *end* **completion** of the *world* **eon**:
the angels shall come forth,
and *sever* **set apart** the *wicked* **evil** from among the just,
50 And shall cast them into the furnace of fire:
there shall be wailing and gnashing of teeth.
51 *Jesus saith* **Yah Shua wordeth** unto them,
Have ye *understood* **comprehended** all these *things*?
They *say* **word** unto him, Yea, *Lord* **Adonay**.

THE HOUSEDESPOTES PARABLE

52 Then said he unto them,
Therefore every scribe which is *instructed* **discipled**
unto the *kingdom* **sovereigndom** of *heaven* **the heavens**
is like unto
a *man that is an householder* **human housedespotes**,
which *bringeth forth* **ejecteth** out of his treasure
things new and old.

YAH SHUA REJECTED IN HIS FATHERLAND

53 And it *came to pass* **became**,
that when *Jesus* **Yah Shua**
had *finished* **completed** these parables,
he departed thence.
54 And when he was come
into his *own country* **fatherland**,
he *taught* **doctrinated** them in their synagogue,
insomuch that they were astonished, and *said* **worded**,
Whence hath this man this wisdom,
and these *mighty works* **dynamis**?
55 Is not this the carpenter's son?
is not his mother *called Mary* **indeed worded Miryam**?
and his brethren, *James* **Yaaqovos**, and *Joses* **Yoses**,
and *Simon* **Shimon**, and *Judas* **Yah Hudah**?
56 And his sisters, are they not **indeed** all with us?
Whence then hath this man all these *things*?
57 And they were *offended* **scandalized** in him.
But *Jesus* **Yah Shua** said unto them,
A prophet is not *without honour* **dishonoured**,
save **except** in his own *country* **fatherland**,
and in his own house.
58 And he did not many *mighty works* **dynamis** there
because of their *unbelief* **trustlessness**.

BAPTIZER YAHN IS BEHEADED

14 At that *time* **season**
Herod the tetrarch heard of the fame of *Jesus* **Yah Shua**,
2 And said unto his *servants* **lads**,
This is *John* **Yahn** the *Baptist* **Baptizer**;
he is risen from the dead;
and *therefore* **because of this**
mighty works **dynamis**
do shew forth themselves **energizeth** in him.
3 For Herod had *laid hold on John* **overpowered Yahn**,
and bound him,
and put him in *prison* **a guardhouse** for Herodias' sake,
his brother *Philip's wife* **Philippos' woman**.
4 For *John said* **Yahn worded** unto him,
It is not *lawful* **allowed** for thee to have her.
5 And when he *would* **willed**
to have *put* **slaughtered** him *to death*,
he *feared* **awed** the multitude,
because they *counted* **regarded** him as a prophet.
6 But when Herod's birthday was *kept* **brought**,
the daughter of Herodias
danced *before them* **in their midst**,
and pleased Herod.
7 Whereupon he *promised* **professed** with an oath
to give her whatsoever she *would* **should** ask.
8 And she,
being *before instructed* **previously instigated**
of **by** her mother, said,
Give me here *John Baptist's* **Yahn the Baptizer's** head
in **on** a *charger* **platter**.
9 And the *king was sorry* **sovereign sorrowed**:
nevertheless for the oath's sake,
and them which *sat* **reposed** with him *at meat*,
he *commanded* **summoned** it to be given her.
10 And he sent,
and beheaded *John* **Yahn** in the *prison* **guardhouse**.
11 And his head was brought *in* **on** a *charger* **platter**,
and given to the *damsel* **maiden**:
and she brought it to her mother.
12 And his disciples came,
and took *up* the body, and *buried* **entombed** it,
and went and *told Jesus* **evangelized Yah Shua**.
13 When *Jesus* **Yah Shua** heard of it,
he departed thence *by ship* **in a sailer**
into a *desert* **desolate** place *apart* **privately**:
and when the *people* **multitude** had heard thereof,
they followed him on foot out of the cities.
14 And *Jesus* **Yah Shua** went forth,
and saw a great vast multitude,
and
was moved with compassion **had a sympathetic spleen**
toward them,
and he *healed* **cured** their *sick* **infirm**.

YAH SHUA FEEDS FIVE THOUSAND

15 And when it *was* **became** evening,
his disciples came to him, *saying* **wording**,
This is a *desert* **desolate** place,
and the *time* **hour** is *now* **already** past;
send **release** *the* multitude *away*,
that they may go into the villages,
and *buy* **market** themselves *victuals* **food**.
16 But *Jesus* **Yah Shua** said unto them,
They need not depart; give ye them to eat.
17 And they *say* **word** unto him,
We have here *but* **except only** five *loaves* **breads**,
and two fishes.
18 He said, Bring them hither to me.
19 And he *commanded* **summoned** the multitude
to *sit down* **recline** on the *grass* **herbage**,
and took the five *loaves* **breads**, and the two fishes,
and looking *up* to *the* heaven,
he *blessed* **eulogized**, and brake,
and gave the *loaves* **breads** to his disciples,
and the disciples to the multitude.
20 And they did all eat, and were filled:
and they took *up*
of the fragments that *remained* **superabounded**
twelve baskets full.
21 And they that had eaten
were about five thousand men,
beside **apart from** women and children.
22 And straightway *Jesus* **Yah Shua**
constrained **compelled** his disciples
to *get* **embark** into a *ship* **sailer**,
and to go before him unto the other side,
while he *sent* **released** the multitudes *away*.

YAH SHUA WALKS ON THE SEA

23 And when he had *sent* **released** the multitudes *away*,
he *went up* **ascended** into a mountain
apart **privately** to pray:
and when the evening *was come* **became**,
he was there alone.
24 But the *ship* **sailer**
was *now* **already** in the midst of the sea,
tossed with **tortured by** waves:
for the wind was contrary.
25 And in the fourth *watch* **guard** of the night
Jesus **Yah Shua** went unto them, walking on the sea.
26 And when the disciples saw him walking on the sea,
they were troubled, *saying* **wording**,
It is a *spirit* **phantasm**;
and they cried out for *fear* **awe**.
27 But straightway *Jesus* **Yah Shua** spake unto them,
saying **wording**, *Be of good cheer;* **Courage!**
it is I **I AM**; *be not afraid* **Awe not**.

PETROS WALKS ON THE SEA

28 And *Peter* **Petros** answered him and said,
Lord **Adonay**, if it be thou,
bid **summon** me come unto thee on the water.
29 And he said, Come.
And when *Peter* **Petros**
was come down **descended** out of the *ship* **sailer**,
he walked on the water, to go to *Jesus* **Yah Shua**.
30 But when he saw **observed** the wind
boisterous **mighty**,
he *was afraid* **awed**;
and beginning to *sink* **submerge**, he cried,
saying **wording**, *Lord* **Adonay**, save me.

31 And *immediately* **straightway**
Jesus stretched forth **Yah Shua extended** his hand,
and *caught* **took hold of** him,
and *said* **worded** unto him, O thou of little *faith* **trust**,
wherefore **where unto** didst thou doubt?
32 And when they *were* **had**
come **embarked** into the *ship* **sailer**,
the wind *ceased* **relaxed**.
33 Then they that were in the *ship* **sailer**
came and worshipped him, *saying* **wording**,
Of a truth **Truly** thou art the Son of *God* **Elohim**.
34 And when they were gone over,
they came into the land of *Gennesaret* **Kinneroth**.
35 And when the men of that place
had knowledge of him,
they *sent out* **apostolized**
into all that country round about,
and *brought* **offered** unto him all that were *diseased* **ill**;
36 And besought him
that they might only touch the *hem* **edge** of his garment:
and as many as touched
were *made perfectly whole* **saved**.

MISVAH VS TRADITION

15 Then came to *Jesus* **Yah Shua** scribes and Pharisees,
which were of *Jerusalem* **Yeru Shalem**, *saying* **wording**,
2 Why do thy disciples
transgress the tradition of the elders?
for they wash not their hands when **ever** they eat bread.
3 But he answered and said unto them,
Why do ye also
transgress the *commandment* **misvah** of *God* **Elohim**
by **for** your tradition?
4 For *God commanded* **Elohim misvahed**,
saying **wording**, Honour thy father and mother:
and, He that *curseth* **vilifieth** father or mother,
let him die the death.
5 But ye *say* **word**,
Whosoever shall say to his father or his mother,
It is a gift **An oblation**,
by whatsoever
thou mightest be *profited* **benefited** by me;
6 And **in no way** honour not his father or his mother,
he shall be free.
Thus have ye *made* **invalidated**
the *commandment* **misvah** of *God* **Elohim** *of none effect*
by **for** your tradition.
Exodus 20:12, 21:17
7 Ye hypocrites,
well did *Esaias* **Yesha Yah** prophesy *of* **concerning** you,
saying **wording**,
This people
draweth nigh unto **approacheth** me with their mouth,
and honoureth me with their lips;
but their heart is far from me.
9 But in vain they do *worship* **venerate** me,
teaching **doctrinating** for doctrines
the *commandments* **misvoth** of *men* **humanity**.
Yesha Yah 29:13
10 And he called the multitude, and said unto them,
Hear, and *understand* **comprehend**:
11 Not that which *goeth* **entereth** into the mouth
defileth **profaneth** a *man* **human**;
but that which *cometh* **proceedeth** out of the mouth,
this *defileth* **profaneth** a *man* **human**.
12 Then came his disciples, and said unto him,
Knowest thou
that the Pharisees were *offended* **scandalized**,
after they heard this *saying* **word**?
13 But he answered and said,
Every plant, which my heavenly Father hath not planted,
shall be *rooted up* **uprooted**.
14 *Let* **Allow** them *alone*:
they be blind *leaders* **guides** of the blind.
And if the blind *lead* **guide** the blind,
both shall fall into the *ditch* **cistern**.
15 Then answered *Peter* **Petros** and said unto him,
Declare unto us this parable.

ENTERING THE MOUTH VS PROCEEDING FROM THE MOUTH

16 And *Jesus* **Yah Shua** said,
Are ye also yet
without understanding **noncomprehending**?
17 Do not ye yet *understand* **comprehend**,
that *whatsoever* **all that** entereth in at the mouth
goeth **passeth** into the belly,
and is *cast out* **ejected** into the *draught* **privy**?
18 But those *things* which proceed out of the mouth
come forth from the heart;
and they *defile* **profane** the *man* **human**.

FROM THE HEART VS FROM THE MOUTH

19 For out of the heart proceed evil *thoughts* **reasonings**,
murders, adulteries, *fornications* **whoredoms**,
thefts, *false* **pseudo** witness, blasphemies:
20 These are *the things* **those**
which *defile* **profane** a *man* **human**:
but to eat with unwashen hands
defileth **profaneth** not a *man* **human**.

YAH SHUA EJECTS A DEMON

21 Then *Jesus* **Yah Shua** went thence,
and departed into the *coasts* **parts** of *Tyre* **Sor** and Sidon.
22 And, behold, a woman *of Canaan* **— a Kenaaniy**
came out of the same *coasts* **boundaries**,
and cried unto him, *saying* **wording**,
Have mercy on **Mercy** me, O *Lord* **Adonay**,
thou son of David;
my daughter
is *grievously vexed with a devil* **evilly demonized**.
23 But he answered her not a word.
And his disciples came and *besought* **asked** him,
saying **wording**, *Send her away* **Release her**;
for she crieth after us.
24 But he answered and said, I am not *sent* **apostolized**
but **except only** unto the lost sheep
of the house of *Israel* **Yisra El**.
25 Then came she and worshipped him, *saying* **wording**,
Lord **Adonay**, help me.
26 But he answered and said,
It is not *meet* **good** to take the children's bread,
and to cast it to *dogs* **puppies**.
27 And she said, *Truth* **Yea**, *Lord* **Adonay**:
yet **indeed** the *dogs* **puppies** eat of the crumbs
which fall from their *masters' Lord* **Adoni's** table.
28 Then *Jesus* **Yah Shua** answered and said unto her,
O woman, *great* **mega** is thy *faith* **trust**:
be it unto thee even as thou *wilt* **willest**.
And her daughter was made whole from that very hour.

YAH SHUA CURES THE MULTITUDES

29 And *Jesus* **Yah Shua** departed from thence,
and came nigh unto the sea of *Galilee* **Galiyl**;
and *went up* **ascended** into a mountain,
and sat down there.
30 And *great* **vast** multitudes came unto him,
having with them those that were lame,
blind, *dumb* **mute**, maimed, and many others,
and *cast* **tossed** them *down* at *Jesus'* **Yah Shua**'s feet;
and he *healed* **cured** them:
31 Insomuch that the multitude *wondered* **marvelled**,
when they *saw* **observed** the *dumb* **mute** to speak,
the maimed to be whole, the lame to walk,
and the blind to *see* **observe**:
and they glorified the *God* **Elohim** of *Israel* **Yisra El**.

YAH SHUA FEEDS FOUR THOUSAND

32 Then *Jesus* **Yah Shua** called his disciples unto him,
and said, I have *compassion* **a sympathetic spleen**
on the multitude,
because they *continue* **already abide** with me
now three days,
and have *nothing* **naught** to eat:
and I will **to** not *send* **release** them *away* fasting,
lest **ever** they faint in the way.
33 And his disciples *say* **word** unto him,
Whence should we have so much bread
in the wilderness, as to fill so *great* **vast** a multitude?
34 And *Jesus saith* **Yah Shua wordeth** unto them,
How many *loaves* **breads** have ye?
And they said, Seven, and a few *little fishes* **fishling**.
35 And he *commanded* **summoned** the multitude
to *sit down* **repose** on the *ground* **soil**.
36 And he took the seven *loaves* **breads** and the fishes,
and *gave thanks* **eucharistized**,
and brake them, and gave to his disciples,

37 And they did all eat, and were filled:
and they took *up* of the *broken meat* **fragments**
that *was left* **superabounded** seven baskets full.
38 And they that did eat were four thousand men,
beside **apart from** women and children.
39 And he *sent away* **released** the multitude,
and *took ship* **embarked into a sailer**,
and came into the *coasts* **boundaries** of Magdala.

YAH SHUA REBUKES THE PHARISEES AND THE SADOQIYM

16 The Pharisees also with the *Sadducees* **Sadoqiym** came,
and *tempting* **testing,** *desired* **asked** him
that he *would* **should** shew them a sign from **the** heaven.
2 He answered and said unto them,
When it *is* **becometh** evening,
ye *say* **word**, *It will be* fair weather:
for the *sky* **heaven** is *red* **fiery**.
3 And in the early morning,
It will be foul weather **Downpour** to day:
for the *sky* **heaven** is *red* **fiery** and *lowring* **gloomy**.
O ye hypocrites,
ye can **indeed know**
to discern the face of the *sky* **heaven**;
but can ye not *discern* the signs of the *times* **seasons**?
4 *A wicked* **An evil** and adulterous generation
seeketh after a sign;
and there shall no sign be given unto it,
but **except** the sign of the prophet *Jonas* **Yonah**.
And he left them, and departed.

YAH SHUA INTERPRETS THE FERMENTATION PARABLE

5 And when his disciples were come to the other side,
they had forgotten to take bread.
6 Then *Jesus* **Yah Shua** said unto them,
Take heed **See** and *beware of* **heed**
the *leaven* **fermentation**
of the Pharisees and of the *Sadducees* **Sadoqiym**.
7 And they reasoned among themselves, *saying* **wording**,
It is because we have taken no bread.
8 *Which when Jesus perceived* **Yah Shua knowing**,
he said unto them, O ye of little *faith* **trust**,
why reason ye among yourselves,
because ye have *brought* **taken** no bread?
9 Do ye not yet *understand* **comprehend**,
neither remember
the five *loaves* **breads** of the five thousand,
and how many baskets ye took *up*?
10 Neither the seven *loaves* **breads** of the four thousand,
and how many baskets ye took *up*?
11 How is it that ye do not *understand* **comprehend**
that I *spake* **said** it not to you concerning bread,
that ye should *beware of* **heed** the *leaven* **fermentation**
of the Pharisees and of the *Sadducees* **Sadoqiym**?
12 Then *understood* **comprehended** they
how that he *bade* **said to** them not
beware of **heed** the *leaven* **fermentation** of bread,
but of the doctrine
of the Pharisees and of the *Sadducees* **Sadoqiym**.

OPINIONS CONCERNING YAH SHUA

13 When *Jesus* **Yah Shua** came into the *coasts* **parts**
of *Caesarea Philippi* **Kaisaria Philippos**,
he asked his disciples, *saying* **wording**,
Whom do *men say* **humanity word**
that I the Son of *man* **humanity** am?
14 And they said,
Some **indeed,**
say that thou art John **Yahn** the *Baptist* **Baptizer**:
some Elias **others, Eli Yah**;
and others, *Jeremias* **Yirme Yah**,
or one of the prophets.

PETROS' WITNESS CONCERNING YAH SHUA

15 He *saith* **wordeth** unto them,
But whom *say* **word** ye that I am?
16 And *Simon Peter* **Shimon Petros** answered and said,
Thou art the *Christ* **Messiah**,
the Son of the living *God* **Elohim**.
17 And *Jesus* **Yah Shua** answered and said unto him,
Blessed art thou, *Simon Barjona* **Shimon Bar Yonah**:
for flesh and blood
hath not *revealed* **unveiled** it unto thee,
but my Father which is in *heaven* **the heavens**.
18 And I *say* **word** also unto thee,
That thou art *Peter* **Petros**,
and upon this rock I *will* **shall** build my *church* **ecclesia**;
and the gates of *hell* **hades**
shall not *prevail against* **overpower** it.
19 And I *will* **shall** give unto thee the keys
of the *kingdom* **sovereigndom** of *heaven* **the heavens**:
and whatsoever thou shalt bind on earth
shall be bound in *heaven* **the heavens**:
and whatsoever thou shalt *loose* **release** on earth
shall be *loosed* **released** in *heaven* **the heavens**.
20 Then charged he his disciples
that they should *tell* **say to** no *man* **one**
that he was *Jesus* **Yah Shua** the *Christ* **Messiah**.

YAH SHUA PROPHESIES HIS DEATH AND RESURRECTION

21 From that time forth
began *Jesus* **Yah Shua** to shew unto his disciples,
how that he must go unto *Jerusalem* **Yeru Shalem**,
and suffer *many things* **much**
of the elders and *chief* **arch** priests and scribes,
and be *killed* **slaughtered**,
and be raised again the third day.
22 Then *Peter* **Petros** took him,
and began to rebuke him, *saying* **wording**,
Be it far from **Kapur/Atone unto** thee, *Lord* **Adonay**:
this shall not **no way** be unto thee.
23 But he turned, and said unto *Peter* **Petros**,
Get **Go** thee behind me, Satan:
thou art *an offence* **a scandal** unto me:
for thou *savourest* **mindest** not
the things **those** that be of *God* **Elohim**,
but those that be of *men* **humanity**.
24 Then said *Jesus* **Yah Shua** unto his disciples,
If any *man will* **willeth to** come after me,
let him **utterly** deny himself,
and take *up* his *cross* **stake**, and follow me.

LOSE THE SOUL TO FIND THE SOUL

25 For whosoever *will* **willeth to** save his *life* **soul**
shall lose it:
and whosoever *will* **shall** lose his *life* **soul** for my sake
shall find it.
26 For what is a *man profited* **human benefited**,
if he shall gain the whole *world* **cosmos**,
and lose his own soul?
or what shall a *man* **human** give in exchange for his soul?
27 For the Son of *man* **humanity** shall come
in the glory of his Father with his angels;
and then he shall *reward every man* **give each**
according to his *works* **acts**.
28 *Verily I say* **Amen! I word** unto you,
There be some standing here,
which shall not **no way** taste of death,
till they see the Son of *man* **humanity**
coming in his *kingdom* **sovereigndom**.

YAH SHUA'S METAMORPHOSIS

17 And after six days *Jesus* **Yah Shua** taketh *Peter* **Petros**,
James **Yaaqovos**, and *John* **Yahn** his brother,
and bringeth them *up* into an high mountain
apart **privately**,
2 And was *transfigured* **metamorphosed**
before **in front of** them:
and his face *did shine* **radiated** as the sun,
and his *raiment was* **garment became** white as the light.
3 And, behold, there appeared unto them
Moses **Mosheh** and *Elias* **Eli Yah** talking with him.
4 Then answered *Peter* **Petros**,
and said unto *Jesus* **Yah Shua**,
Lord **Adonay**, it is good for us to be here:
if thou *wilt* **willest**, let us make here three tabernacles;
one for thee,
and one for *Moses* **Mosheh**, and one for *Elias* **Eli Yah**.
5 While he yet spake, behold,
a *bright* **brightly lighted** cloud overshadowed them:
and behold a voice out of the cloud,
which said **wording**, This is my beloved Son,
in **of** whom I *am well pleased* **well—approve**;
hear ye him.
6 And when the disciples heard it, they fell on their face,
and were *sore afraid* **extremely awestricken**.

7 And *Jesus* **Yah Shua** came and touched them,
and said, Arise, and be not *afraid* **awestricken**.
8 And when they had lifted *up* their eyes,
they saw no *man* **one**, *save Jesus* **except Yah Shua** only.
9 And as they *came down* **descended** from the mountain,
Jesus charged **Yah Shua misvahed** them, *saying* **wording**,
Tell **Say** the vision to no *man* **one**,
until the Son of *man* **humanity**
be risen *again* from the dead.

YAHN THE BAPTIZER IS THE ELI YAH TO COME

10 And his disciples asked him, *saying* **wording**,
Why then *say* **word** the scribes
that *Elias* **Eli Yah** must first come?
11 And *Jesus* **Yah Shua** answered and said unto them,
Elias truly **Eli Yah indeed** shall *first* come **first**,
and restore all *things*.
12 But I *say* **word** unto you,
That *Elias* **Eli Yah** is come already,
and they knew him not,
but have done *unto* **in** him
whatsoever **as much as** they *listed* **willed**.
Likewise **Thus** shall also
the Son of *man* **humanity** suffer of them.
13 Then the disciples *understood* **comprehended**
that he *spake* **said** unto them
of John **concerning Yahn** the *Baptist* **Baptizer**.

YAH SHUA REBUKES A DEMON

14 And when they were come to the multitude,
there came to him a *certain man* **human**,
kneeling *down* to him, and *saying* **wording**,
15 *Lord* **Adonay**, *have* mercy *on* my son:
for he is lunatick, and *sore vexed* **suffereth evilly**:
for *ofttimes* **often** he falleth into the fire,
and *oft* **often** into the water.
16 And I *brought* **offered** him to thy disciples,
and they could not cure him.
17 Then *Jesus* **Yah Shua** answered and said,
O *faithless* **trustless**
and *perverse* **thoroughly perverted** generation,
how long **until when** shall I be with you?
how long **until when** shall I *suffer* **tolerate** you?
bring him hither to me.
18 And *Jesus* **Yah Shua** rebuked the *devil* **demon**;
and he departed out of him:
and the *child* **lad** was cured from that very hour.
19 Then came the disciples to *Jesus* **Yah Shua**
apart **privately**, and said,
Why could not we *cast* **eject** him *out*?
20 And *Jesus* **Yah Shua** said unto them,
Because of your *unbelief* **trustlessness**:
for verily I say **Amen! I word** unto you,
If ye have *faith* **trust** as a *grain* **kernal** of mustard *seed*,
ye shall say unto this mountain,
Remove **Depart** hence to yonder place;
and it shall *remove* **depart**;
and *nothing* **naught** shall be impossible unto you.
21 Howbeit this *kind goeth* **genos proceedeth** not *out*
but by **except in** prayer and fasting.

YAH SHUA PROPHESIES HIS DEATH AND RESURRECTION

22 And while they *abode* **remained** in *Galilee* **Galiyl**,
Jesus **Yah Shua** said unto them,
The Son of *man* **humanity**
shall be betrayed into the hands of *men* **humanity**:
23 And they shall *kill* **slaughter** him,
and the third day he shall *be raised again* **rise**.
And they were *exceeding sorry* **extremely sorrowed**.

ON THE DOUBLE DRACHMA

24 And when they were come
to *Capernaum* **Kaphar Nachum**,
they that *received* **took**
tribute money **the double drachma**
came to *Peter* **Petros**, and said,
Doth not your *master* **doctor**
pay tribute **complete the double drachma**?
25 He *saith* **wordeth**, Yes.
And when he *was come* **had entered** into the house,
Jesus prevented **Yah Shua anticipated** him,
saying **wording**, What thinkest thou, *Simon* **Shimon**?
of whom do the *kings* **sovereigns** of the earth
take *custom* **completion** or tribute?
of their own *children* **sons**, or of *strangers* **others**?
26 *Peter saith* **Petros wordeth** unto him,
Of *strangers* **others**.
Jesus **Yah Shua** saith unto him,
Then are the *children free* **sons liberated**.
27 Notwithstanding,
lest we should *offend* **scandalize** them,
go thou to the sea, and cast an hook,
and take *up* the fish that first *cometh up* **ascendeth**;
and when thou hast opened his mouth,
thou shalt find a *piece of money* **stater**:
that take, and give unto them for me and thee.

THE GREATEST IN THE SOVEREIGNDOM OF THE HEAVENS

18 At the same *time* **hour**
came the disciples unto *Jesus* **Yah Shua**, *saying* **wording**,
Who **then** is the greatest
in the *kingdom* **sovereigndom** of *heaven* **the heavens**?
2 And *Jesus* **Yah Shua** called a little child unto him,
and set him in the midst of them,
3 And said, *verily I say* **Amen! I word** unto you,
Except **Unless** ye be *converted* **turned around**,
and become as little children,
ye shall not **no way** enter
into the *kingdom* **sovereigndom** of *heaven* **the heavens**.
4 Whosoever therefore
shall humble himself as this little child,
the same is greatest
in the *kingdom* **sovereigndom** of *heaven* **the heavens**.
5 And whoso shall receive one such little child in my name
receiveth me.
6 But whoso shall *offend* **scandalize**
one of these little ones which *believe* **trust** in me,
it were *better* **beneficial** for him
that a millstone **turned by a burro**
were hanged about his neck,
and that he were *drowned* **submerged**
in the depth of the sea.
7 Woe unto the *world* **cosmos**
because of *offences* **scandals**!
for it *must needs* be **necessary** that *offences* **scandals** come;
but **however** woe to that *man* **human**
by whom the *offence* **scandal** cometh!

ON AVOIDING SCANDALIZINGS

8 Wherefore
if thy hand or thy foot *offend* **scandalize** thee,
cut **exscind** them *off*, and cast them from thee:
it is *better* **well** for thee
to enter into life *halt* **lame** or maimed,
rather than having two hands or two feet
to be cast into *everlasting* **eternal** fire.
9 And if thine eye *offend* **scandalize** thee,
pluck it out, and cast it from thee:
it is *better* **well** for thee
to enter into life *with one eye one* **one—eyed**,
rather than having two eyes to be cast
into *hell* **Gay Hinnom/the Valley of Burning** fire.
10 *Take heed* **See** that ye *despise* **disesteem** not
one of these little ones;
for I say word unto you,
That in *heaven* **the heavens**
their angels *do always* **through all time**
behold **see** the face of my Father
which is in *heaven* **the heavens**.
11 For the Son of *man* **humanity**
is come to save that which was lost.

THE WANDERING SHEEP PARABLE

12 How think ye?
if *a man have* **any human become** an hundred sheep,
and one of them *be gone astray* **wander**,
doth he not *leave* **forsake** the ninety and nine,
and goeth into the mountains,
and seeketh that which *is gone astray* **wandereth**?
13 And if so be that he find it,
verily I say **Amen! I word** unto you,
he *rejoiceth* **cheereth** more of that *sheep*,
than of the ninety and nine
which *went* **wandered** not *astray*.
14 Even *so* **thus** it is not the will **in front** of your Father
which is in *heaven* **the heavens**,
that one of these little ones should *perish* **be lost**.

A SINNING BROTHER

15 Moreover
if thy brother shall *trespass against* **sin unto** thee,
go and *tell* **reprove** him *his fault*
between thee and him alone:
if he shall hear thee, thou hast gained thy brother.
16 But if he *will* **shall** not hear thee,
then take with thee one or two more,
that in the mouth of two or three witnesses
every *word* **rhema** may be established.
17 And if he shall *neglect* **refuse** to hear them,
tell **say** it unto the *church* **ecclesia**:
but if he *neglect* **refuse** to hear the *church* **ecclesia**,
let him be unto thee
exactly as *an heathen man* **the goyim**
and a *publican* **customs agent**.

ON BINDING AND RELEASING

18 *Verily I say* **Amen! I word** unto you,
Whatsoever **As much as ever**
ye shall bind on earth
shall be bound in **the** heaven:
and *whatsoever* **as much as ever**
ye shall *loose* **release** on earth
shall be *loosed* **released** in **the** heaven.

ON SYMPHONIZING TRUST

19 Again I *say* **word** unto you,
That if two of you shall *agree* **symphonize** on earth
as touching **concerning** any *thing* **matter**
that they shall ask,
it shall *be done* **become** for them of my Father
which is in *heaven* **the heavens**.
20 For where
two or three are gathered together in my name,
there am I in the midst of them.

THE FORGIVENESS PARABLE

21 Then came *Peter* **Petros** to him, and said,
Lord **Adonay**,
how oft shall my brother sin *against* **unto** me,
and I forgive him? till seven times?
22 *Jesus saith* **Yah Shua wordeth** unto him,
I *say* **word** not unto thee, Until seven times:
but, Until seventy times seven.
23 Therefore
is the *kingdom* **sovereigndom** of *heaven* **the heavens**
likened unto a *certain king* **human sovereign**,
which *would* **willed**
to *take account* **reckon word** of his servants.
24 And when he had begun to reckon,
one was brought unto him,
which owed him **a debtor of**
ten thousand talents **a myriad talent weights**.
25 But forasmuch as he had not to *pay* **give**,
his *Lord commanded* **adoni summoned** him to be sold,
and his *wife* **woman**, and children,
and all *that* — **as much as** he had,
and *payment to be made* **given back**.
26 The servant therefore fell down,
and worshipped him, *saying* **wording**, *Lord* **Adoni**,
have patience with me, and I *will pay* **shall give** thee all.
27 Then the *lord* **adoni** of that servant
was moved with compassion **had a sympathetic spleen**,
and *loosed* **released** him, and forgave him the debt.
28 But the same servant went out,
and found one of his *fellowservants* **co—servants**,
which *owed him* **was indebted**
an hundred *pence* **denarion**:
and he *laid hands on* **overpowered** him,
and *took* **strangled** him *by the throat, saying* **wording**,
Pay **Give** me *that thou owest* **thy debt**.
29 And his *fellowservant* **co—servant**
fell *down at* **to** his feet,
and besought him, *saying* **wording**,
Have patience with me, and I *will pay* **shall give** thee all.
30 And he *would* **willed** not:
but went and cast him into *prison* **a guardhouse**,
till he should *pay* **give** the debt.
31 So when his *fellowservants* **co—servants** saw
what *was done* **had become**,
they were *very sorry* **extremely sorrowed**,
and came and told unto their *lord* **adoni**
all that *was done* **had become**.
32 Then his *lord* **adoni**, after that he had called him,
said **worded** unto him, O thou *wicked* **evil** servant,
I forgave thee all that debt,
because thou *desiredst* **besoughtest** me:
33 Shouldest not thou also
have *had compassion on* **mercied**
thy *fellowservant* **co—servant**,
even as I *had pity on* **mercied** thee?
34 And his *lord* **adoni** was wroth,
and delivered him to the *tormentors* **torturers**,
till he should *pay* **give**
all that was *due* **indebted** unto him.
35 *So* **Thus** likewise
shall my *heavenly* Father **in the heavenlies**
do also unto you,
if ye from your hearts
forgive not *every one* **each** his brother
their *trespasses* **backslidings**.

19

And it *came to pass* **became**,
that when *Jesus* **Yah Shua**
had *finished* **completed** these *sayings* **words**,
he departed from *Galilee* **Galiyl**,
and came into the *coasts* **boundaries**
of *Judaea* **Yah Hudah** beyond *Jordan* **Yarden**;
2 And *great* **vast** multitudes followed him;
and he *healed* **cured** them there.

ON RELEASING A WOMAN

3 The Pharisees also came unto him,
tempting **testing** him, and *saying* **wording** unto him,
Is it *lawful* **allowed** for a *man* **human**
to *put away* **release** his *wife* **woman** for every cause?
4 And he answered and said unto them,
Have ye not read,
that he which *made* **created** *them* at the beginning
made **created** them male and female,
5 And said, For this cause
a *man* **human** shall leave father and mother,
and shall *cleave* **adhere** to his *wife* **woman**:
and they twain shall be one flesh?
6 Wherefore they are no more twain, but one flesh.
What therefore
God **Elohim** hath *joined together* **co—yoked**,
let not *man put asunder* **humanity separate**.
7 They *say* **word** unto him,
Why did *Moses* **Mosheh** then *command* **misvah**
to give a *writing* **scroll** of *divorcement* **apostasy**,
and to *put* **release** her *away*?
8 He *saith* **wordeth** unto them, *Moses* **Mosheh**,
because of *the hardness of* your *hearts* **hardheartedness**,
suffered **permitted** you
to *put away* **release** your *wives* **women**:
but from the beginning it *was* **became** not *so* **thus**.
9 And I *say* **word** unto you,
Whosoever shall *put away* **release** his *wife* **woman**,
except it be for *fornication* **whoredom**,
and shall marry another,
committeth adultery **adulterizeth**:
and whoso marrieth her which is *put away* **released**,
doth commit adultery **adulterizeth**.
10 His disciples *say* **word** unto him,
If the case of the *man* **human**
be *so* **thus** with his *wife* **woman**,
it is not *good* **beneficial** to marry.
11 But he said unto them,
All *men* cannot *receive* **accept** this *saying* **word**,
save **rather** they to whom it is given.

ON EUNUCHS

12 For there are some eunuchs,
which were *so* **thus** born
from their mother's womb:
and there are some eunuchs,
which were *made eunuchs* **eunuchized**
of *men* **humanity**:
and there be eunuchs,
which have *made* **eunuchized** themselves *eunuchs*
for the
kingdom **sovereigndom** of *heaven's* **the heavens'** sake.
He that is able to *receive* **accept** it,
let him *receive* **accept** it.

YAH SHUA RECEIVES LITTLE CHILDREN

13 Then were there *brought* **offered** unto him
little children,
that he should put his hands on them, and pray:
and the disciples rebuked them.
14 But *Jesus* **Yah Shua** said, *Suffer* **Allow** little children,
and forbid them not, to come unto me:
for of such
is the *kingdom* **sovereigndom** of *heaven* **the heavens**.
15 And he *laid* **put** his hands on them,
and departed thence.

ON ETERNAL LIFE

16 And, behold, one came and said unto him,
Good *Master* **Doctor**, what good *thing* shall I do,
that I may have eternal life?
17 And he said unto him,
Why *callest* **wordest** thou me good?
there is none good *but* **except** one,
that is, God **Elohim**:
but if thou *wilt* **willest to** enter into life,
keep **guard** the *commandments* **misvoth**.
18 He *saith* **wordeth** unto him, Which?
Jesus **Yah Shua** said,
Thou shalt *do no* **not** murder,
Thou shalt not *commit adultery* **adulterize**,
Thou shalt not steal,
Thou shalt not *bear false* **pseudo** witness,
19 Honour thy father and thy mother:
and, Thou shalt love thy neighbour as thyself.
20 The *young man said* **youth worded** unto him,
All these *things* have I *kept* **guarded** from my youth *up*:
what lack I yet?
21 *Jesus* **Yah Shua** said unto him,
If thou *wilt* **willest to** be *perfect* **complete**,
go and sell that thou hast, and give to the poor,
and thou shalt have treasure in the heaven:
and come and follow me.
22 But when the *young man* **youth**
heard that *saying* **word**,
he went away sorrowful:
for he had *great* **vast** possessions.

THE RICH AND THE SOVEREIGNDOM

23 Then said *Jesus* **Yah Shua** unto his disciples,
Verily I say **Amen! I word** unto you,
That a rich man shall *hardly* **with difficulty** enter
into the *kingdom* **sovereigndom** of *heaven* **the heavens**.
24 And again I *say* **word** unto you,
It is easier for a *camel* **rope°**
to *go* **pass** through the eye of a needle,
than for a rich man to enter
into the *kingdom* **sovereigndom** of *God* **Elohim**.

°rope: see Lamsa

25 When his disciples heard it,
they were *exceedingly amazed* **extremely astonished**,
saying **wording**, Who then can be saved?
26 But *Jesus beheld* **Yah Shua looked at** them,
and said unto them,
With *men* **humanity** this is impossible;
but with *God* **Elohim** all *things* are possible.

THE COST OF DISCIPLESHIP

27 Then answered *Peter* **Petros** and said unto him,
Behold, we have forsaken all, and followed thee;
so then what shall we have *therefore*?
28 And *Jesus* **Yah Shua** said unto them,
Verily I say **Amen! I word** unto you,
That ye which have followed me,
in the *regeneration* **regenesis,**
when **ever** the Son of *man* **humanity**
shall sit in the throne of his glory,
ye also shall sit upon twelve thrones,
judging the twelve *tribes* **scions** of *Israel* **Yisra El**.
29 And every one that hath forsaken houses,
or brethren, or sisters, or father, or mother,
or *wife* **woman**, or children, or lands,
for my name's sake,
shall *receive* **take** an hundredfold,
and shall inherit *everlasting* **eternal** life.
30 But many that are first shall be *last* **final**;
and the *last* **final** shall be first.

THE PARABLE OF THE VINEYARD WORKERS

20 For the *kingdom* **sovereigndom** of *heaven* **the heavens**
is like unto a *man* **human**
that is an *householder* **housedespotes**,
which went out **simultaneously** early in the morning
to hire *labourers* **workers** into his vineyard.
2 And when he had *agreed* **symphonized**
with the *labourers* **workers** for a *penny* **denarion** a day,
he *sent* **apostolized** them into his vineyard.
3 And he went out about the third hour,
and saw others standing idle in the *marketplace* **market**,
4 And said unto them; Go ye also into the vineyard,
and whatsoever is *right* **just** I *will* **shall** give you.
And they went their way.
5 Again he went out about the sixth and ninth hour,
and did likewise.
6 And about the eleventh hour he went out,
and found others standing idle,
and *saith* **wordeth** unto them,
Why stand ye here all the day idle?
7 They *say* **word** unto him,
Because no *man* **one** hath hired us.
He *saith* **wordeth** unto them,
Go ye also into the vineyard;
and whatsoever is *right* **just**, that shall ye *receive* **take**.
8 So when even *was come* **became**,
the *lord* **adoni** of the vineyard
saith **wordeth** unto his *steward* **manager**,
Call the *labourers* **workers**, and give them their hire,
beginning from the *last* **final** unto the first.
9 And when they came
that were hired about the eleventh hour,
they *received every man* **each took** a *penny* **denarion**.
10 But when the first came, they *supposed* **presumed**
that they should have *received* **taken much** more;
and they likewise
received every man **each took** a *penny* **denarion**.
11 And when they had *received* **taken** it,
they murmured
against the *goodman of the house* **housedespotes**,
12 *saying* **wording**,
These *last* **final** have *wrought* **produced** but one hour,
and thou hast made them equal unto us,
which have borne the burden and heat of the day.
13 But he answered one of them, and said,
Friend **Comrade**, I *do* **injure** thee *no wrong* **not**:
didst not thou *agree* **indeed symphonize** with me
for a *penny* **denarion**?
14 Take that thine is, and go thy way:
I *will* give unto this *last* **final**, even as unto thee.
15 Is it not *lawful* **allowed** for me
to do what I will with mine own?
Is thine eye evil, because I am good?
16 *So* **Thus** the *last* **final** shall be first,
and the first *last* **final**:
for many be called, but few *chosen* **selected**.

YAH SHUA PROPHESIES HIS DEATH AND RESURRECTION

17 And *Jesus* **Yah Shua**
going up **ascending** to *Jerusalem* **Yeru Shalem**
took the twelve disciples *apart* **privately** in the way,
and said unto them,
18 Behold, we *go up* **ascend** to *Jerusalem* **Yeru Shalem**;
and the Son of *man* **humanity** shall be betrayed
unto the *chief* **arch** priests and unto the scribes,
and they shall condemn him to death,
19 And shall *deliver* **betray** him to the *Gentiles* **goyim**
to mock, and to scourge, and to *crucify* **stake** him:
and the third day he shall rise *again*.

ON PRIORITY POSITIONS

20 Then came to him
the mother of *Zebedee's children* **Zabdi's sons**
with her sons, worshipping him,
and *desiring a certain thing* **asking somewhat** of him.
21 And he said unto her, What *wilt* **willest** thou?
She *saith* **wordeth** unto him,
Grant **Say** that these my two sons may sit,
the one *on* **by** thy right *hand*,
and the *other on* **one by** the left,
in thy *kingdom* **sovereigndom**.

22 But *Jesus* **Yah Shua** answered and said,
Ye know not what ye ask.
Are ye able to drink of the cup
that I shall drink of,
and *to be* baptized with the baptism
that I am baptized with?
They *say* **word** unto him, We are able.
23 And he *saith* **wordeth** unto them,
Ye shall drink indeed of my cup,
and be baptized
with the baptism that I am baptized with:
but to sit *on* **by** my right *hand*, and *on* **by** my left,
is not mine to give,
but it shall be given to them
for whom it is prepared of by my Father.

THE TEN INDIGNANT DISCIPLES

24 And when the ten heard it,
they were *moved with indignation* **indignified**
against **concerning** the two brethren.
25 But *Jesus* **Yah Shua** called them unto him, and said,
Ye know that the *princes* **archs** of the *Gentiles* **goyim**
exercise dominion over **overlord** them,
and they that are *great* **mega**
exercise authority upon **authorize over** them.
26 But it shall not be *so* **thus** among you:
but whosoever *will* **willeth**
to be *great* **mega** among you,
let him be your minister;
27 And whosoever *will* **willeth**
to be *chief* **first** among you,
let him be your servant:
28 *Even* **Exactly** as the Son of *man* **humanity**
came not to be ministered unto, but to minister,
and to give his *life* **soul** a *ransom* **redemption** for many.

YAH SHUA HEALS TWO BLIND

29 And as they *departed* **proceeded** from *Jericho* **Yericho**,
a *great* **vast** multitude followed him.
30 And, behold, two blind men sitting by the way side,
when they heard that *Jesus* **Yah Shua** passed by,
cried out, *saying* **wording**, *Have mercy on* **Mercy** us,
O *Lord* **Adonay**, thou son of David.
31 And the multitude rebuked them,
because **that** they should *hold their peace* **hush**:
but they cried the more, *saying* **wording**,
Have mercy on **Mercy** us,
O *Lord* **Adonay**, thou son of David.
32 And *Jesus* **Yah Shua** stood still,
and *called* **voiced out to** them, and said,
What will ye that I shall do unto you?
33 They *say* **word** unto him, *Lord* **Adonay**,
that our eyes may be opened.
34 So *Jesus* **Yah Shua**
had *compassion* **a sympathetic spleen** on them,
and touched their eyes:
and *immediately* **straightway**
their eyes *received sight* **saw**,
and they followed him.

YAH SHUA'S TRIUMPHAL ENTRY

21 And when they
drew nigh **approached** unto *Jerusalem* **Yeru Shalem**,
and were come to *Bethphage* **Beth Pag**,
unto the mount of Olives,
then *sent Jesus* **Yah Shua apostolized** two disciples,
2 *Saying* **Wording** unto them,
Go into the village over against you,
and straightway ye shall find *an ass* **a burro** tied,
and a colt with her:
loose **release** them, and bring them unto me.
3 And if any *man* **one** say ought unto you,
ye shall say, *the Lord* **Adonay** hath need of them;
and straightway he *will send* **shall apostolize** them.
4 All this *was done* **became**, that it might be fulfilled
which was *spoken by* **rhetorized through** the prophet,
saying **wording**,
5 *Tell* **Say** ye the daughter of *Sion* **Siyon**,
Behold, thy *king* **sovereign** cometh unto thee,
meek, and *sitting* **mounted** upon *an ass* **a burro**,
and a colt the *foal* **son** of *an ass* **a burro**.
Zechar Yah 9:9

6 And the disciples went, and did **exactly**
as *Jesus commanded* **Yah Shua ordered** them,
7 And brought the *ass* **burro**, and the colt,
and put on them their *clothes* **garments**,
and they set him thereon.
8 And *a very great* **many of the** multitude
spread their garments in the way;
others cut down branches from the trees,
and *strawed* **spread** them in the way.
9 And the multitudes that went before, and that followed,
cried, *saying* **wording**,
Hosanna **Hoshia Na** to the son of David:
Blessed **Eulogized** is he
that cometh in the name of *the Lord* **Yah Veh**;
Hosanna **Hoshia Na** in the *highest* **highests**.
Psalm 118:25, 26
10 And when he
was come **had entered** into *Jerusalem* **Yeru Shalem**,
all the city *was moved* **quaked**, *saying* **wording**,
Who is this?
11 And the multitude *said* **worded**,
This is *Jesus* **Yah Shua**
the prophet of Nazareth of *Galilee* **Galiyl**.

YAH SHUA CLEANSES THE PRIESTAL PRECINCT

12 And *Jesus went into* **Yah Shua entered**
the *temple* **priestal precinct** of *God* **Elohim**,
and *cast out* **ejected** all them that sold and *bought* **marketed**
in the *temple* **priestal precinct**,
and *overthrew* **upset** the tables
of the *moneychangers* **coindealers**,
and the *seats* **cathedras** of them that sold doves,
13 And *said* **worded** unto them, It is *written* **scribed**,
My house shall be called the house of prayer;
but ye have made it a *den* **grotto** of *thieves* **robbers**.
Yesha Yah 56:7

YAH SHUA CURES THE BLIND AND THE LAME

14 And the blind and the lame
came to him in the *temple* **priestal precinct**;
and he *healed* **cured** them.
15 And when the *chief* **arch** priests and scribes
saw the *wonderful things* **marvels** that he did,
and the *children* **lads**
crying in the *temple* **priestal precinct**,
and *saying* **wording**,
Hosanna **Hoshia Na** to the son of David;
they *were sore displeased* **indignified**,
Psalm 118:25, 26
16 And said unto him, Hearest thou what these *say* **word**?
And *Jesus saith* **Yah Shua wordeth** unto them, Yea;
have ye never ever read,
out of the mouth of babes and *sucklings* **nipplers**
thou hast *perfected praise* **prepared halal**?
Psalm 8:2
17 And he left them,
and went out of the city into *Bethany* **Beth Ania**;
and he *lodged* **camped** there.

YAH SHUA CURSES THE FIG TREE

18 Now in the **early** morning as he returned into the city,
he hungered.
19 And when he saw a fig tree in the way, he came to it,
and found *nothing* **naught** thereon,
but **except** leaves only,
and *said* **worded** unto it,
Let no fruit *grow on* **become from** thee
henceforward for ever **unto the eons**.
And *presently* **immediately** the fig tree withered away.
20 And when the disciples saw it,
they marvelled, *saying* **wording**,
How *soon is* **immediately** the fig tree withered away!
21 *Jesus* **Yah Shua** answered and said unto them,
Verily I say **Amen! I word** unto you,
If ye have *faith* **trust**, and doubt not,
ye shall not only do this *which is done* to the fig tree,
but also if ye shall say unto this mountain,
Be thou removed, and be thou cast into the sea;
it shall be *done*.
22 And all *things*,
whatsoever — **as much as ever** ye shall ask in prayer,
believing **trusting**, ye shall *receive* **take**.

ARCH PRIESTS AND PEOPLE'S PRESBYTERS QUESTION YAH SHUA'S AUTHORITY

23 And when he was come
into the *temple* **priestal precinct**,
the *chief* **arch** priests and the elders of the people
came unto him as he was *teaching* **doctrinating**,
and *said* **worded**,
By **In** what authority doest thou these *things*?
and who gave thee this authority?
24 And *Jesus* **Yah Shua** answered and said unto them,
I also *will* **shall** ask you one *thing* **word**,
which if ye tell me,
I *in like wise will tell* **shall also say to** you
by **in** what authority I do these *things*.
25 The baptism of *John* **Yahn**, whence was it?
from **of the** heaven, or of *men* **humanity**?
And they reasoned with themselves, *saying* **speaking**,
If we shall say, *From* **Of the** heaven;
he *will* **shall** say unto us,
Why did ye not then *believe* **trust** him?
26 But if we shall say, Of *men* **humanity**;
we *fear* **awe** the *people* **multitudes**;
for all *hold John* **regard Yahn** as a prophet.
27 And they answered *Jesus* **Yah Shua**, and said,
We *cannot tell* **know not**.
And he said unto them,
Neither *tell* **word** I you
by **in** what authority I do these *things*.

THE PARABLE OF THE TWO CHILDREN

28 But what think ye?
A *certain man* **human** had two *sons* **children**;
and he came to the first, and said,
Son **Child**, go work to day in my vineyard.
29 He answered and said, I will not:
but afterward he *repented* **regretted**, and went.
30 And he came to the second, and said likewise.
And he answered and said, I go, *sir* **adoni**: and went not.
31 Whether of them twain did the will of his father?
They *say* **word** unto him, The first.
Jesus saith **Yah Shua speaketh** unto them,
Verily I say **Amen! I word** unto you,
That
the *publicans* **customs agents** and the *harlots* **whores**
go into the *kingdom* **sovereigndom** of *God* **Elohim**
before **preceding** you.
32 For *John* **Yahn** came unto you
in the way of *righteousness* **justness**,
and ye *believed* **trusted** him not:
but the *publicans* **customs agents** and the *harlots* **whores**
believed **trusted** him:
and ye, when ye had seen it,
repented **regretted** not afterward,
that ye might *believe* **trust** him.

THE PARABLE OF THE VINEYARD

33 Hear another parable:
There was a *certain householder* **human housedespotes**,
which planted a vineyard, and hedged it round about,
and digged a *winepress* **trough** in it, and built a tower,
and *let* **leased** it out to *husbandmen* **cultivators**,
and went *into a far country* **abroad**:
34 And when the *time* **season** of the fruit
drew near **approached**,
he *sent* **apostolized** his servants
to the *husbandmen* **cultivators**,
that they might *receive* **take** the fruits of it.
35 And the *husbandmen* **cultivators** took his servants
and *beat* **indeed flogged** one,
and *killed* **slaughtered** another, and stoned another.
36 Again, he *sent* **apostolized** other servants
much more than the first:
and they did unto them likewise.
37 But *last of all* **afterward**
he *sent* **apostolized** unto them his son, *saying* **wording**,
They *will reverence* **shall respect** my son.
38 But when the *husbandmen* **cultivators** saw the son,
they said among themselves, This is the heir;
come, let us *kill* **slaughter** him,
and let us seize on his inheritance.
39 And they *caught* **took** him,
and *cast* **ejected** him out of the vineyard,
and *slew* **slaughtered** him.
40 When the *lord* **adoni** therefore of the vineyard cometh,
what *will* **shall** he do
unto those *husbandmen* **cultivators**?
41 They *say* **word** unto him,
He *will miserably* **shall evilly** destroy
those *wicked* **evil** men,
and *will let out* **shall lease** his vineyard
unto other *husbandmen* **cultivators**,
which shall *render* **give** him the fruits in their seasons.
42 *Jesus saith* **Yah Shua wordeth** unto them,
Did ye never **ever** read in the scriptures,
The stone which the builders *rejected* **disapproved**,
the same is become the head of the corner:
this is *the Lord's doing* **Yah Veh's becoming**,
and it is marvellous in our eyes?
Psalm 118:22, 23
43 Therefore *say* **word** I unto you,
The *kingdom* **sovereigndom** of *God* **Elohim**
shall be taken from you,
and given to a *nation* **goyim**
bringing forth **producing** the fruits thereof.
44 And whosoever shall fall on this stone
shall be *broken* **crushed**:
but on whomsoever it shall fall,
it will grind him to powder **shall be pulverized**.
Yesha Yah 8:14
45 And when the *chief* **arch** priests and Pharisees
had heard his parables,
they *perceived* **knew**
that he *spake of* **worded concerning** them.
46 But when they sought to lay hands on him,
they *feared* **awed** the multitude,
because they *took* **regarded** him *for* **as** a prophet.

THE PARABLE OF THE MARRIAGE FEAST

22 And *Jesus* **Yah Shua** answered
and *spake* **said** unto them again by parables,
and said **wording**,
2 The *kingdom* **sovereigndom** of *heaven* **the heavens**
is like unto a *certain king* **human sovereign**,
which made a marriage for his son,
3 And *sent forth* **apostolized** his servants
to call them that were bidden to the *wedding* **marriage**:
and they *would* **willed to** not come.
4 Again, he *sent forth* **apostolized** other servants,
saying **wording**, Tell them which are bidden,
Behold, I have prepared my dinner:
my *oxen* **bulls** and my fatlings are *killed* **sacrificed**,
and all *things* are *ready* **prepared**:
come unto the marriage.
5 But they *made light of* **disregarded** it,
and went their ways,
one **indeed** to his *farm* **field**, another to his merchandise:
6 And the *remnant took* **rest overpowered** his servants,
and *entreated* **insulted** them *spitefully*,
and *slew* **slaughtered** them.
7 But when the *king* **sovereign** heard thereof,
he was wroth:
and he sent forth his *armies* **warriors**,
and destroyed those murderers, and burned *up* their city.
8 Then *saith* **wordeth** he to his servants,
The *wedding* **marriage** is *ready* **indeed prepared**,
but they which were bidden were not worthy.
9 Go ye therefore into the highways,
and as many as **ever** ye shall find, bid to the marriage.
10 So those servants went out into the highways,
and gathered together all as many as they found,
both *bad* **evil** and good:
and the *wedding* **marriage** was *furnished* **filled**
with *guests* **those reposing**.
11 And when the *king came in* **sovereign entered**
to *see the guests* **observe those reposing**,
he saw there a *man* **human** which had not *on* **endued**
a *wedding garment* **marriage enduement**:
12 And he *saith* **wordeth** unto him, *Friend* **Comrade**,
how *camest* **enterest** thou in hither
not having a *wedding garment* **marriage enduement**?
And he was *speechless* **muzzled**.
13 Then said the *king* **sovereign** to the *servants* **ministers**,
Bind him hand and foot, and take him away,

and *cast* **eject** him into outer darkness,
there shall be weeping and gnashing of teeth.
14 For many are called, but few are *chosen* **selected**.

THE HERODIANS TEST YAH SHUA

15 Then went the Pharisees, and took counsel
how they might *entangle* **ensnare** him in *his talk* **word**.
16 And they *sent out* **apostolized** unto him
their disciples with the Herodians, *saying* **wording**,
Master **Doctor**, we know that thou art true,
and *teachest* **doctrinatest** the way of *God* **Elohim** in truth,
neither *carest* **concernest** thou for any *man* **one**:
for thou *regardest* **lookest** not
on the *person* **face** of *men* **humanity**.
17 *Tell* **Say to** us therefore, What thinkest thou?
Is it *lawful* **allowed** to give tribute unto *Caesar* **the Kaisar**,
or not?
18 But *Jesus* **Yah Shua**
perceived **knew** their *wickedness* **evil**, and said,
Why *tempt* **test** ye me, ye hypocrites?
19 Shew me the tribute *money* **coin**.
And they *brought* **offered** unto him a *penny* **denarion**.
20 And he *saith* **wordeth** unto them,
Whose is this *image* **icon** and *superscription* **epigraph**?
21 They *say* **word** unto him, *Caesar's* **The Kaisar's**.
Then *saith* **wordeth** he unto them,
Render **Give** therefore
unto Caesar the things which are Caesar's
the Kaisar's to the Kaisar;
and *unto God the things that are God's*
Elohim's to Elohim.
22 When they had heard these *words*, they marvelled,
and *left* **forsook** him, and went their way.

THE SADOQIYM TEST YAH SHUA

23 The same day came to him the *Sadducees* **Sadoqiym**,
which *say* **word** that there is no resurrection,
and asked him,
24 *Saying* **Wording**, *Master* **Doctor**,
Moses **Mosheh** said,
If *a man* **one** die, having no children,
his brother shall marry his *wife* **woman**,
and raise *up seed* **sperma** unto his brother.
25 Now there were with us seven brethren:
and the first, when he had married *a wife, deceased* **died**,
and, having no *issue* **sperma**,
left **forsook** his *wife* **woman** unto his brother:
26 Likewise the second also,
and the third, unto the seventh.
27 And *last of all* **afterward** the woman died also.
Genesis 38:8—10
28 Therefore in the resurrection
whose *wife* **woman** shall she be of the seven?
for they all had her.
29 *Jesus* **Yah Shua** answered and said unto them,
Ye *do err* **wander**, not knowing the scriptures,
nor the *power* **dynamis** of *God* **Elohim**.
30 For in the resurrection they neither marry,
nor are *given in marriage* **married off**,
but are as the angels of *God* **Elohim** in **the** heaven.
31 But
as touching **concerning** the resurrection of the dead,
have ye not read
that which was *spoken* **rhetorized** unto you
by *God* **Elohim**, *saying* **wording**,
32 *I am* **I AM** the *God* **Elohim** of Abraham,
and the *God* **Elohim** of *Isaac* **Yischaq**,
and the *God* **Elohim** of *Jacob* **Yaaqov**?
God **Elohim** is not the *God* **Elohim** of the dead,
but of the living.
33 And when the multitude heard this,
they were astonished at his doctrine.
Exodus 3:6

THE PHARISEES TEST YAH SHUA

34 But when the Pharisees had heard that he had
put **muzzled** the *Sadducees* **Sadoqiym** *to silence*,
they were gathered together.
35 Then one of them, *which was a lawyer* **a torahist**,
asked him a question,
tempting **testing** him, and *saying* **wording**,
36 *Master* **Doctor**,
which is the *great commandment* **mega misvah**
in the *law* **torah**?
37 *Jesus* **Yah Shua** said unto him,
Thou shalt love *the Lord* **Yah Veh** thy *God* **Elohim**
with **in** all thy heart,
and *with* **in** all thy soul, and *with* **in** all thy mind.
38 This is the first and *great commandment* **mega misvah**.
39 And the second is like unto it,
Thou shalt love thy neighbour as thyself.
40 *On* **In** these two *commandments* **misvoth**
hang all the *law* **torah** and the prophets.
Deuteronomy 6:5, Leviticus 19:18

YAH SHUA TESTS THE PHARISEES

41 While the Pharisees were gathered together,
Jesus **Yah Shua** asked them,
42 *Saying* **Wording**,
What think ye *of Christ* **concerning the Messiah**?
whose son is he?
They *say* **word** unto him, *The son* of David.
43 He *saith* **wordeth** unto them,
How then doth David in spirit call him *Lord* **Adonay**,
saying **wording**,
44 *The LORD said* **An oracle of Yah Veh**
unto my *Lord* **Adonay**,
Sit thou *on* **by** my right *hand*,
till I *make* **place** thine enemies thy footstool?
45 If David then call him *Lord* **Adonay**, how is he his son?
Psalm 110:1
46 And no *man* **one** was able to answer him a word,
neither durst any *man* **one** from that day forth
ask him any more questions.

THE PHARISEES' PSEUDO RELIGION

23 Then spake *Jesus* **Yah Shua**
to the multitude, and to his disciples,
2 *Saying* **Wording**,
The scribes and the Pharisees
sit in *Moses' seat* **Mosheh's cathedra**:
3 All *therefore whatsoever* **— as much as ever**
they *bid you observe* **say to you to guard**,
that *observe* **guard** and do;
but do not ye after their works:
for they *say* **word**, and do not.
4 For they bind heavy burdens
and *grievous to be borne* **oppressive**,
and *put* **place** them on *men's* **humanity's** shoulders;
but they themselves will **to** not *move* **wag** them
with one of their fingers.
5 But all their works they do
for to be *seen* **observed** of *men* **humanity**:
they *make broad* **broaden** their phylacteries,
and *enlarge* **magnify** the *borders* **edges** of their garments,
6 And *love* **befriend**
the *uppermost rooms* **preeminent resposings**
at *feasts* **suppers**,
and the *chief seats* **preeminent cathedras**
in the synagogues,
7 And *greetings* **salutations** in the markets,
and to be called of *men* **humanity**, Rabbi, Rabbi.

HONORARY TITLES RESERVED FOR DEITY

8 But be not ye called Rabbi:
for one is your Rabbi, even *Christ* **the Messiah**;
and all ye are brethren.
9 And call no man your father upon the earth:
for one is your Father, which is in *heaven* **the heavens**.
10 Neither be ye called *masters* **tutors**:
for one is your *Master* **tutor**, even *Christ* **the Messiah**.
11 But he that is greatest among you
shall be your *servant* **minister**.
12 And whosoever shall exalt himself
shall be *abased* **humbled**;
and he that shall humble himself shall be exalted.

YAH SHUA DENOUNCES THE PHARISEES

13 But woe unto you, scribes and Pharisees, hypocrites!
for ye shut *up*
the *kingdom* **sovereigndom** of *heaven* **the heavens**
against men **in front of humanity**:
for ye neither *go* **enter** in *yourselves*,
neither *suffer* **allow** ye them that are entering to go in.
14 Woe unto you, scribes and Pharisees, hypocrites!
for ye devour widows' houses,
and for a *pretence* **pretext** make *long* **far out** prayer:

therefore **because of this** ye shall *receive* **take**
the *greater damnation* **superabundant judgment**.
15 Woe unto you, scribes and Pharisees, hypocrites!
for ye *compass* **go about the** sea and *land* **the dry**
to make one proselyte,
and when **ever** he *is made* **becometh**,
ye make him *twofold more* **double**
the child of *hell* **Gay Hinnom/the Valley of Burning**
than yourselves.
16 Woe unto you, ye blind guides, which *say* **word**,
Whosoever shall *swear* **oath**
by **in** the *temple* **nave**,
it is *nothing* **naught**;
but whosoever shall *swear* **oath**
by **in** the gold of the *temple* **nave**,
he is a debtor!
17 Ye fools and blind: for whether is greater,
the gold,
or the *temple* **nave** that *sanctifieth* **halloweth** the gold?
18 And, Whosoever shall *swear* **oath**
by **in** the **sacrifice** altar,
it is *nothing* **naught**;
but whosoever *sweareth* **oatheth**
by **in** the *gift* **oblation** that is upon it,
he is *guilty* **a debtor**.
19 Ye fools and blind: for whether is greater,
the *gift* **oblation**,
or the **sacrifice** altar
that *sanctifieth* **halloweth** the *gift* **oblation**?
20 Whoso therefore shall *swear* **oath**
by **in** the **sacrifice** altar,
sweareth by **oatheth in** it, and *by* **in** all *things* thereon.
21 And whoso shall *swear* **oath**
by **in** the *temple* **nave**,
sweareth by **oatheth in** it,
and *by* **in** him that *dwelleth* **settleth** therein.
22 And he that shall *swear* **oath**
by **in the** heaven,
sweareth by **oatheth in** the throne of *God* **Elohim**,
and *by* **in** him that sitteth thereon.
23 Woe unto you, scribes and Pharisees, hypocrites!
for ye pay tithe of mint and anise and *cummin* **kammon**,
and have *omitted* **forsaken**
the weightier matters of the *law* **torah**,
judgment, mercy, and *faith* **the trust**:
these *ought* **needed** ye to have done,
and not to *leave the other* **forsake those** undone.
24 Ye blind guides,
which strain at a gnat, and swallow a camel.
25 Woe unto you, scribes and Pharisees, hypocrites!
for ye *make clean* **purify**
the *outside of the cup* **cup outwardly** and *of* the platter,
but *within* **inwardly**
they are full of *extortion* **plunder** and *excess* **unrestraint**.
26 Thou blind Pharisee,
cleanse **purify** first
that which is within the **inward** cup and platter,
that *the outside* **outwardly**
of them **they** may be *clean* **purified** also.
27 Woe unto you, scribes and Pharisees, hypocrites!
for ye are like unto
whited sepulchres **whitewashed tombs**, which indeed
appear **manifest** beautiful *outward* **outwardly**,
but are *within* **inwardly** full of dead *men's* bones,
and of all *uncleanness* **impurity**.
28 Even *so* **thus indeed** ye also
outwardly appear *righteous* **manifest just** unto *men* **humanity**,
but *within* **inwardly** ye are full of hypocrisy
and *iniquity* **violate the torah**.
29 Woe unto you, scribes and Pharisees, hypocrites!
because ye build the tombs of the prophets,
and *garnish* **adorn**
the *sepulchres* **tombs** of the *righteous* **just**,
30 And *say* **word**,
If we had been in the days of our fathers,
we *would* **should** not have been
partakers **communicants** with them
in the blood of the prophets.
31 Wherefore ye be witnesses unto yourselves,
that ye are the *children* **sons** of them
which *killed* **murdered** the prophets.
32 *Fill ye up* **Fulfill** then the measure of your fathers.
33 Ye serpents, ye *generation* **progeny** of vipers,
how can ye *escape* **flee** the *damnation* **judgment**
of *hell* **Gay Hinnom/the Valley of Burning**?
34 Wherefore, behold,
I *send* **apostolize** unto you prophets,
and wise men, and scribes:
and some of them
ye shall *kill* **slaughter** and *crucify* **stake**;
and some of them shall ye scourge in your synagogues,
and persecute them from city to city:
35 That upon you may come all the *righteous* **just** blood
shed **poured** upon the earth,
from the blood of *righteous* **just** Abel
unto the blood of *Zacharias* **Zechar Yah**
son of *Barachias* **Berech Yah**,
whom ye *slew* **murdered**
between the *temple* **nave** and the **sacrifice** altar.
36 *Verily I say* **Amen! I word** unto you,
All these *things* shall come upon this generation.

YAH SHUA LAMENTS OVER YERU SHALEM

37 O *Jerusalem, Jerusalem* **Yeru Shalem, Yeru Shalem**,
thou that *killest* **slaughterest** the prophets,
and stonest them which are *sent* **apostolized** unto thee,
how often *would* have **I willed**
gathered **to gather** thy children together,
even *as* **in the manner**
a hen gathereth her *chickens* **young** under her wings,
and ye *would* **willed** not!
38 Behold, your house is *left* **forsaken** unto you desolate.
39 For I *say* **word** unto you,
Ye shall not **no way** see me henceforth,
till ye shall say, *Blessed* **Eulogized** is he
that cometh in the name of *the Lord* **Yah Veh**.

YAH SHUA PROPHESIES DISINTEGRATION OF THE PRIESTAL PRECINCT

24 And *Jesus* **Yah Shua** went out,
and departed from the *temple* **priestal precinct**:
and his disciples came to him for to shew him
the *buildings* **edifices** of the *temple* **priestal precinct**.
2 And *Jesus* **Yah Shua** said unto them,
See ye not all these *things*?
verily I say **Amen! I word** unto you,
There shall not **no way** be *left* **allowed** here
one stone upon another,
that shall not **no way** be *thrown down* **disintegrated**.

YAH SHUA'S MOUN TOF OLIVES SPEECH

3 And as he sat upon the mount of Olives,
the disciples came unto him privately,
saying **wording**, Tell us,
when shall these *things* be?
and what shall be the sign of thy *coming* **parousia**,
and of the *end* **completion** of the *world* **eon**?
4 And *Jesus* **Yah Shua** answered and said unto them,
Take heed that no man **Look, lest anyone** deceive you.
5 For many shall come in my name, *saying* **wording**,
I am Christ **I AM the Messiah**;
and shall *deceive* **seduce** many.
6 And ye shall **be about**
to hear of wars and rumours of wars:
see that ye *be* not *troubled* **lament**:
for all these *things* must *come to pass* **become**,
but the *end* **completion** is not yet.
7 For *nation* **goyim**
shall rise against *nation* **goyim**,
and *kingdom* **sovereigndom**
against *kingdom* **sovereigndom**:
and there shall be famines, and pestilences,
and *earthquakes* **quakes**, in divers places.
8 All these are the beginning of *sorrows* **travail**.
9 Then shall they *deliver* **betray** you *up*
to be afflicted **unto affliction**,
and shall *kill* **slaughter** you:
and ye shall be hated of all *nations* **goyim**
for my name's sake.
10 And then shall many be *offended* **scandalized**,
and shall betray one another, and shall hate one another.
11 And many *false* **pseudo** prophets shall rise,
and shall *deceive* **seduce** many.

12 And because
iniquity **torah violations** shall *abound* **multiply**,
the love of many shall *wax* **breathe** cold.
13 But he
that shall *endure* **abide** unto the *end* **completion**,
the same shall be saved.
14 And this
gospel **evangelism** of the *kingdom* **sovereigndom**
shall be preached in all the world
for **in** a witness unto all *nations* **goyim**;
and then shall the *end* **completion** come.

THE GREAT TRIBULATION

15 When **ever** ye therefore
shall see the abomination of desolation,
spoken of **rhetorized**
by Daniel **through Dani El** the prophet,
stand in the holy place,
(whoso readeth, let him *understand* **comprehend**:)
16 Then let them which be in *Judaea* **Yah Hudah**
flee into the mountains:
17 Let him which is on the housetop
not *come down* **descend**
to take *any thing* **somewhat** out of his house:
18 Neither let him which is in the field
return back to take his *clothes* **garments**.
19 And woe unto them that *are with child* **have in womb**,
and to them that *give suck* **nipple** in those days!
20 But pray ye that your flight
be not in the *winter* **downpour**,
neither *on* **in** the *sabbath day* **shabbath**:
21 For then shall be *great* **mega** tribulation,
such as *was* **became** not
since **from** the beginning of the *world* **cosmos**
to *this time* **now**,
no, nor *ever* shall **no way** be.
22 And except those days should be shortened,
there should **not** no flesh **ever** be saved:
but **except** for the *elect's* **select's** sake
those days shall be shortened.
Dani El 9:27, 11:31, 12:11
23 Then if any *man* **one** shall say unto you,
lo **Behold**, *here is Christ* **here — the Messiah**, or there;
believe it **trust** not.
24 For there shall arise *false Christs* **pseudo messiahs**,
and *false* **pseudo** prophets,
and shall *shew* **give**
great **mega** signs and *wonders* **omens**;
insomuch that, if it *were* possible,
they shall *deceive* **seduce** the very *elect* **select**.
25 Behold, I have *told you before* **foretold you**.
26 Wherefore if they shall say unto you,
Behold, he is in the *desert* **wilderness**;
go not forth:
behold, he is in the *secret chambers* **pantry**;
believe it **trust** not.

YAH SHUA'S PAROUSIA

27 For **exactly**
as the lightning cometh out of the *east* **rising**,
and *shineth* **manifesteth** even unto the *west* **lowering**;
so **thus** shall also
the *coming* **parousia** of the Son of *man* **humanity** be.
28 For wheresoever the carcase is,
there *will* **shall** the eagles be gathered together.

POST—TRIBULATION OMENS

29 *Immediately* **Straightway**
after the tribulation of those days
shall the sun be darkened,
and the moon shall not give her *light* **brilliance**,
and the stars shall fall from *heaven* **the heavens**,
and the *powers* **dynamis** of the heavens shall be shaken:

THE PAROUSIA

30 And then shall *appear* **manifest**
the sign of the Son of *man* **humanity** in **the** heaven:
and then
shall all the *tribes* **scions** of the earth *mourn* **chop**,
and they shall see the Son of *man* **humanity**
coming in the clouds of **the** heaven
with *power* **dynamis** and *great* **vast** glory.
31 And he shall *send* **apostolize** his angels
with a *great sound* **mega voice** of a trumpet,
and they shall gather together
his *elect* **select** from the four winds,
from *one end* **the extremities** of *heaven* **the heavens**
to *the other* **their extremities**.

PRE—PAROUSIA SIGNS

32 Now learn a parable of the fig tree;
When **ever** his branch *is yet* **becometh already** tender,
and *putteth forth* **sprouteth** leaves,
ye know that *summer* **warmth** is nigh:
33 *So* **Thus** likewise ye,
when **ever** ye shall see all these *things*,
know that it is near, even at the *doors* **portals**.
34 *Verily I say* **Amen!** I word unto you,
This generation shall not **no way** pass,
till all these *things* be fulfilled.
35 **The** heaven and earth shall pass *away*,
but my words shall not **no way** pass *away*.
36 But *of* **concerning** that day and hour
knoweth no *man* **one**,
no, not the angels of *heaven* **the heavens**,
but **except** my Father only.
37 But **exactly** as the days of *Noe* **Noach** were,
so **thus** shall also
the *coming* **parousia** of the Son of *man* **humanity** be.
38 For **exactly** as in the days *that were*
before the *flood* **cataclysm**
they were eating and drinking,
marrying and *giving in marriage* **marrying off**,
until the day that *Noe* **Noach** entered into the ark,
39 And knew not until the *flood* **cataclysm** came,
and took them all away;
so **thus** shall also
the *coming* **parousia** of the Son of *man* **humanity** be.
40 Then shall two be in the field;
the one shall be taken,
and the *other left* **one be forsaken**.
41 Two *women* shall be grinding *at* **in** the mill;
the one shall be taken,
and the *other left* **one be forsaken**.
42 Watch therefore:
for ye know not what hour
your *Lord doth come* **Adonay cometh**.
43 But know this,
that if the *goodman of the house* **housedespotes**
had known
in what *watch* **guard** the thief *would* **should** come,
he *would* **should** have watched,
and *would* **should** not have *suffered* **allowed** his house
to be broken *up* **through**.
44 Therefore be ye also *ready* **prepared**:
for in such an hour as ye think not
the Son of *man* **humanity** cometh.
45 Who then
is a *faithful* **trustworthy** and *wise* **thoughtful** servant,
whom his *lord* **adoni**
hath *made* **seated** ruler over his *household* **therapy**,
to give them *meat* **nourishment** in due season?
46 Blessed is that servant, whom his *lord* **adoni**
when he cometh shall find *so* **thus** doing.
47 *Verily I say* **Amen! I word** unto you,
That he shall *make* **seat** him *ruler*
over all his *goods* **holdings**.
48 But and if that evil servant shall say in his heart,
My *lord delayeth* **adoni taketh** his **time** coming;
49 And shall begin
to *smite* **strike** his *fellowservants* **co—servants**,
and to eat and drink with the *drunken* **intoxicated**;
50 the *lord* **adoni** of that servant shall come
in a day when he *looketh* **expecteth** not *for him*,
and in an hour that he *is not aware of* **knoweth not**,
51 And shall *cut* **dichotomize** him *asunder*,
and *appoint him* **place** his portion with the hypocrites:
there shall be weeping and gnashing of teeth.

THE PARABLE OF THE TEN VIRGINS

25 Then
shall the *kingdom* **sovereigndom** of *heaven* **the heavens**
be likened unto ten virgins, which took their lamps,
and went forth to meet the bridegroom.
2 And five of them were *wise* **thoughtful**,
and five were foolish.

3 They that were foolish took their lamps,
and took no **olive** oil with them:
4 But the *wise* **thoughtful**
took **olive** oil in their vessels with their lamps.
5 While the bridegroom *tarried* **took his time**,
they all slumbered and slept.
6 And at midnight there *was* **became** a cry *made*,
Behold, the bridegroom cometh; go ye out to meet him.
7 Then all those virgins arose,
and *trimmed* **adorned** their lamps.
8 And the foolish said unto the *wise* **thoughtful**,
Give us of your **olive** oil;
for our lamps are *gone out* **quenched**.
9 But the *wise* **thoughtful** answered,
saying **wording**, Not so;
lest **ever** there be not *enough* **sufficient** for us and you:
but go ye rather to them that sell,
and *buy* **market** for yourselves.
10 And while they went to *buy* **market**,
the bridegroom came;
and they that were *ready* **prepared**
went in **entered** with him to the marriage:
and the *door* **portal** was shut.
11 Afterward came also the *other* **rest of the** virgins,
saying **wording**, *Lord* **Adoni**, *Lord* **Adoni**, open to us.
12 But he answered and said,
Verily I say **Amen! I word** unto you,
I know you not.
13 Watch therefore,
for ye know neither the day nor the hour
wherein the Son of *man* **humanity** cometh.

THE INVESTMENT TEST

14 For *the kingdom of heaven is* **exactly** as a *man* **human**
travelling into a far country **going abroad**,
who called his own servants,
and delivered unto them his *goods* **holdings**.
15 And unto one **indeed**
he gave five *talents* **talent weights**,
to another two, and to another one;
to *every man* **each**
according to his several *ability* **dynamis**;
and straightway *took his journey* **went abroad**.
16 Then he that had *received* **taken**
the five *talents* **talent weights**
went and *traded with* **worked in** the same,
and *made them* **produced**
other five *talents* **talent weights**.
17 And likewise he that had *received* two,
he also gained other two.
18 But he that had *received* **taken** one
went and digged in the *earth* **soil**,
and *hid* **secreted** his *lord's money* **adoni's silver**.
19 After a *long* **vast** time
the *lord* **adoni** of those servants cometh,
and reckoneth **words** with them.
20 And so he that had *received* **taken**
five *talents* **talent weights**
came and *brought* **offered**
other five *talents* **talent weights**,
saying **wording**, *Lord* **Adoni**,
thou deliveredst unto me five *talents* **talent weights**:
behold, I have gained beside them
five *talents more* **other talent weights**.
21 His *lord* **adoni** said unto him,
Well done, thou good and *faithful* **trustworthy** servant:
thou hast been *faithful* **trustworthy**
over *a few things* **little**,
I *will make* **shall seat** thee *ruler* over *many things* **much**:
enter thou into the *joy* **cheer** of thy *lord* **adoni**.
22 He also that had *received* **taken** two
talents **talent weights** came and said, *Lord* **Adoni**,
thou deliveredst unto me two *talents* **talent weights**:
behold, I have gained two other *talents* **talent weights**
beside them.
23 His *lord* **adoni** said unto him,
Well done, good and *faithful* **trustworthy** servant;
thou hast been *faithful* **trustworthy**
over *a few things* **little**,
I *will make* **shall seat** thee *ruler* over *many things* **much**:
enter thou into the *joy* **cheer** of thy *lord* **adoni**.
24 Then he which had *received* **taken**
the one *talent* **talent weight**
came and said, *Lord* **Adoni**,
I knew thee that thou art an hard *man* **human**,
reaping **harvesting** where thou hast not sown,
and gathering **together**
where thou hast not *strawed* **scattered**:
25 And I was *afraid* **awestricken**,
and went and *hid* **secreted** thy talent **weight**
in the *earth* **soil**:
lo **behold**, there thou hast that is thine.
26 His *lord* **adoni** answered and said unto him,
Thou *wicked* **evil** and slothful servant,
thou knewest that I *reap* **harvest** where I sowed not,
and gather **together** where I have not *strawed* **scattered**:
27 Thou *oughtest* **neededst** therefore
to have put my *money* **silver** to the exchangers,
and then at my coming
I should have received mine own with *usury* **interest**.
28 Take therefore the talent **weight** from him,
and give it unto him
which hath ten *talents* **talent weights**.
29 For unto every one that hath shall be given,
and he shall have **super** abundance:
but from him that hath not
shall be taken away even that which he hath.
30 And *cast* **eject** ye the *unprofitable* **useless** servant
into outer darkness:
there shall be weeping and gnashing of teeth.

YAH SHUA TESTS THE GOYIM

31 When **ever** the Son of *man* **humanity**
shall come in his glory, and all the holy angels with him,
then shall he sit upon the throne of his glory:
32 And *before* **in front of** him
shall be gathered all *nations* **goyim**:
and he shall *separate* **set apart** them one from another,
exactly as a shepherd
divideth **setteth apart** his sheep from the goats:
33 And he **indeed** shall set the sheep *on* **by** his right *hand*,
but the goats *on* **by** the left.
34 Then shall the *king* **sovereign** say
unto them *on* **by** his right *hand*,
Come, ye *blessed* **eulogized** of my Father,
inherit the *kingdom* **sovereigndom** prepared for you
from the foundation of the *world* **cosmos**:
35 For I was an hungred, and ye gave me *meat* **eats**:
I was thirsty, and ye gave me drink:
I was a stranger, and ye *took* **gathered** me in:
36 Naked, and ye *clothed* **arrayed** me:
I was *sick* **frail**, and ye visited me:
I was in *prison* **a guardhouse**, and ye came unto me.
37 Then shall the *righteous* **just** answer him,
saying **wording**, *Lord* **Adonay**,
when saw we thee an hungred, and *fed* **nourished** thee?
or thirsty, and gave thee drink?
38 When saw we thee a stranger,
and *took* **gathered** thee in?
or naked, and *clothed* **arrayed** thee?
39 Or when saw we thee *sick* **frail**,
or in *prison* **a guardhouse**,
and came unto thee?
40 And the *king* **sovereign** shall answer
and say unto them,
Verily I say **Amen! I word** unto you,
Inasmuch as ye have done it
unto one of the least of these my brethren,
ye have done it unto me.
41 Then shall he say also unto them *on* **by** the left *hand*,
Depart from me, ye cursed, into *everlasting* **eternal** fire,
prepared for *the devil* **Diabolos** and his angels:
42 For I was an hungred, and ye gave me no *meat* **eats**:
I was thirsty, and ye gave me no drink:
43 I was a stranger, and ye *took* **gathered** me not in:
naked, and ye *clothed* **arrayed** me not:
sick **frail**, and in *prison* **a guardhouse**,
and ye visited me not.
44 Then shall they also answer him, *saying* **wording**,
Lord **Adonay**,
when saw we thee an hungred, or athirst, or a stranger,
or naked, or *sick* **frail**, or in *prison* **a guardhouse**,

and did not minister unto thee?
45 Then shall he answer them, *saying* **wording**,
Verily I say **Amen! I word** unto you,
Inasmuch as ye did it not to one of the least of these,
ye did it not to me.
46 And these shall go away
into *everlasting* **eternal** punishment:
but the *righteous* **just** into life eternal.

YAH SHUA PROPHESIES HIS STAKING

26 And it *came to pass* **became**,
when *Jesus* **Yah Shua**
had *finished* **completed** all these *sayings* **words**,
he said unto his disciples,
2 Ye know that after two days
is the feast of the passover **becometh the pasach**,
and the Son of *man* **humanity**
is betrayed to be *crucified* **staked**.

THE PLOT TO SLAUGHTER YAH SHUA

3 Then assembled together the *chief* **arch** priests,
and the scribes, and the elders of the people,
unto the *palace* **courtyard** of the *high* **arch** priest,
who was *called* **worded** Caiaphas,
4 And *consulted* **counseled together**
that they might *take Jesus* **overpower Yah Shua**
by *subtilty* **deception**,
and *kill* **slaughter** him.
5 But they *said* **worded**,
Not *on* **in** the *feast day* **celebration**,
lest there be *an uproar* **a tumult** among the people.

A WOMAN ANOINTS YAH SHUA

6 Now when *Jesus* **Yah Shua**
was **became** in *Bethany* **Beth Ania**,
in the house of *Simon* **Shimon** the leper,
7 There came unto him a woman having an alabaster *box*
of very precious *ointment* **myrrh**,
and poured it on his head, as he *sat at meat* **reposed**.
8 But when his disciples saw it,
they *had indignation* **indignified**, *saying* **wording**,
To what purpose is this *waste* **destruction**?
9 For this *ointment* **myrrh** might have been sold for much,
and given to the poor.
10 *When Jesus understood* it **But Yah Shua knowing**,
he said unto them,
Why *trouble* **belabour and embarrass** ye the woman?
for she hath *wrought* **worked** a good work *upon* **unto** me.
11 For ye have the poor always with you;
but me ye have not always.
12 For in that she hath
poured this *ointment* **myrrh** on my body,
she did it *for* **unto** my *burial* **embalming**.
13 *Verily I say* **Amen! I word** unto you,
Wheresoever this *gospel* **evangelism** shall be preached
in the whole *world* **cosmos**,
there shall also this, that this woman hath done,
be *told for* **spoken unto** a memorial of her.

YAH HUDAH SEEKS A BRIBE

14 Then one of the twelve,
called Judas Iscariot **worded Yah Hudah the urbanite**,
went unto the *chief* **arch** priests,
15 And said unto them,
What will ye **to** give me,
and I *will* **shall** deliver him unto you?
And they covenanted with him for thirty *pieces of* silver.
16 And from that time
he sought opportunity to betray him.

YAH SHUA'S FINAL PASACH

17 Now the first day
of the *feast of unleavened bread* **matsah**
the disciples came to *Jesus* **Yah Shua**,
saying **wording** unto him,
Where *wilt* **willest** thou that we prepare for thee
to eat the *passover* **pasach**?
18 And he said, Go into the city to *such a man* **so and so**,
and say unto him, The *Master saith* **Doctor wordeth**,
My *time* **season** is *at hand* **nigh**;
I *will keep* **shall do** the *passover* **pasach** at thy house
with my disciples.
19 And the disciples did
as *Jesus* **Yah Shua** had *appointed* **ordered** them;
and they *made ready* **prepared** the *passover* **pasach**.
20 Now when *the even was come* **evening became**,
he *sat down* **reposed** with the twelve.
21 And as they did eat, he said,
Verily I say **Amen! I word** unto you,
that one of you shall betray me.
22 And they were *exceeding* **extremely** sorrowful,
and began *every one* **each** of them to *say* **word** unto him,
Lord **Adonay**, is it I?
23 And he answered and said,
He that *dippeth* **baptizeth** his hand with me in the dish,
the same shall betray me.
24 The Son of *man* **humanity indeed** goeth
exactly as it is *written of* **scribed concerning** him:
but woe unto that *man* **human**
by **through** whom the Son of *man* **humanity** is betrayed!
it had been good for that *man* **human**
if he had not been born.
25 Then *Judas* **Yah Hudah**, which betrayed him,
answered and said, *Master* **Rabbi**, is it I?
He *said* **worded** unto him, Thou hast said.

YAH SHUA'S FINAL EUCHARIST

26 And as they were eating, *Jesus* **Yah Shua** took bread,
and *blessed* it **eulogized** and brake it,
and gave it to the disciples, and said,
Take, eat; this is my body.
27 And he took the cup, and *gave thanks* **eucharistized**,
and gave it to them, *saying* **wording**, Drink ye all of it;
28 For this is my blood of the new *testament* **covenant**,
which is *shed* **poured** for many
for **unto** the *remission* **forgiveness** of sins.
29 But I *say* **word** unto you,
I *will* **shall** not **no way** drink henceforth
of this *fruit* **produce** of the vine,
until that day when I drink it new with you
in my Father's *kingdom* **sovereigndom**.
30 And when they had *sung an hymn* **hymned**,
they went out into the mount of Olives.
31 Then *saith Jesus* **wordeth Yah Shua** unto them,
All ye shall be *offended because of* **scandalized in** me
this night:
for it is *written* **scribed**, I *will* **shall** smite the shepherd,
and the sheep of the *flock* **shepherddom**
shall be scattered *abroad*.
32 But after I am risen *again*,
I *will* **shall** go before you into *Galilee* **Galiyl**.
Zechar Yah 13:7
33 *Peter* **Petros** answered and said unto him,
Though all *men* shall be *offended* **scandalized**
because of **in** thee,
yet *will* **shall** I never **ever** be *offended* **scandalized**.
34 *Jesus* **Yah Shua** said unto him,
Verily I say **Amen! I word** unto thee,
That this night, before the *cock crow* **rooster voiceth**,
thou shalt **utterly** deny me thrice.
35 *Peter said* **Petros worded** unto him,
Though I should **And if I must** die with thee,
yet will **shall** I not **ever utterly** deny thee.
Likewise also said all the disciples.

YAH SHUA IN GATH SHEMEN

36 Then cometh *Jesus* **Yah Shua** with them
unto a *place* **parcel**
called Gethsemane **worded Gath Shemen**,
and *saith* **wordeth** unto the disciples,
Sit ye here, while I go and pray yonder.
37 And he took with him *Peter* **Petros**
and the two sons of *Zebedee* **Zabdi**,
and began to be sorrowful and *very heavy* **to heave**.
38 Then *saith* **wordeth** he unto them,
My soul is exceeding sorrowful, even unto death:
tarry **abide** ye here, and watch with me.
39 And he *went a little farther* **proceeded**,
and fell on his face, and prayed, *saying* **wording**,
O my Father, if it be possible, let this cup pass from me:
nevertheless **however** not as I will,
but as thou *wilt* **willest**.
40 And he cometh unto the disciples,
and findeth them asleep,
and *saith* **wordeth** unto *Peter* **Petros**,
What **Thus**, could ye not watch with me one hour?
41 Watch and pray,

that ye enter not into *temptation* **testing**:
the spirit indeed is *willing* **eager**,
but the flesh is *weak* **frail**.
42 He went away again the second time, and prayed,
saying **wording**, O my Father,
if this cup may *not* pass **not** away from me,
except **unless** I drink it,
thy *will* **shall** be *done*.
43 And he came and found them asleep again:
for their eyes were heavy.
44 And he left them, and went away again,
and prayed the third time, saying the same words.
45 Then cometh he to his disciples,
and *saith* **wordeth** unto them,
Sleep *on now* **henceforth**, and *take your* rest:
behold, the hour *is at hand* **approacheth**,
and the Son of *man* **humanity**
is betrayed into the hands of sinners.
46 Rise, let us be going: behold,
he *is at hand* **approacheth** that *doth betray* **betrayeth** me.

YAH SHUA'S BETRAYAL AND ARREST

47 And while he yet spake, *lo* **behold**,
Judas **Yah Hudah**, one of the twelve, came,
and with him
a *great* **vast** multitude with swords and staves,
from the *chief* **arch** priests and elders of the people.
48 Now he that betrayed him gave them a sign,
saying **wording**, Whomsoever I shall kiss, that same is he:
hold **overpower** him *fast*.
49 And *forthwith* **straightway** he came to *Jesus* **Yah Shua**,
and said, *Hail* **Cheers**, *master* **Rabbi**;
and **ardently** kissed him.
50 And *Jesus* **Yah Shua** said unto him,
Friend **Comrade**, wherefore art thou *come* **here**?
Then came they, and laid hands on *Jesus* **Yah Shua**
and *took* **overpowered** him.
51 And, behold,
one of them which were with *Jesus* **Yah Shua**
stretched out **extended** his hand,
and *drew* **withdrew** his sword,
and *struck* **smote** a servant of the *high* **arch** priest's,
and *smote off* **removed** his ear **lobe**.
52 Then *said Jesus* **worded Yah Shua** unto him,
Put *up* again thy sword into his place:
for all they that take the sword
shall *perish with* **destruct in** the sword.
53 Thinkest thou
that I cannot now *pray to* **beseech** my Father,
and he shall presently give me
much more than twelve legions of angels?
54 But how then shall the scriptures be fulfilled,
that thus it must be?
55 In that same hour
said *Jesus* **Yah Shua** to the multitudes,
Are ye come out as against a *thief* **robber**
with swords and staves for to take me?
I sat daily with you
teaching **doctrinating** in the *temple* **priestal precinct**,
and ye *laid no hold on* **overpowered** me **not**.
56 But all this *was done* **became**,
that the scriptures of the prophets might be fulfilled.
Then all the disciples forsook him, and fled.

YAH SHUA FACES THE ARCH PRIEST

57 And they that had
laid hold on Jesus **overpowered Yah Shua**
led him away to Caiaphas the *high* **arch** priest,
where the scribes and the elders
were assembled **together**.
58 But *Peter* **Petros** followed him **from** afar *off*
unto the *high* **arch** priest's *palace* **courtyard**,
and *went in* **entered inside**,
and sat with the *servants* **attendants**,
to see the *end* **completion**.
59 Now the *chief* **arch** priests, and elders,
and all the *council* **sanhedrim**,
sought *false* **pseudo** witness against *Jesus* **Yah Shua**,
to *put* **deathify** him *to death*;
60 But found none:
yea, though many *false* **pseudo** witnesses came,
yet found they none.
At the last **Afterward** came two *false* **pseudo** witnesses,
61 And said, This *fellow* said,
I am able
to *destroy* **disintegrate** the *temple* **nave** of *God* **Elohim**,
and to build it *in* **through** three days.
62 And the *high* **arch** priest arose, and said unto him,
Answerest thou *nothing* **naught**?
what is it which these witness against thee?
63 But *Jesus held his peace* **Yah Shua hushed**.
And the *high* **arch** priest answered and said unto him,
I *adjure* **exorcise** thee by the living *God* **Elohim**,
that thou *tell* **say to** us
whether thou be the *Christ* **Messiah**,
the Son of *God* **Elohim**.
64 *Jesus saith* **Yah Shua wordeth** unto him,
Thou hast said:
nevertheless **moreover** I *say* **word** unto you,
Hereafter **From now on**
shall ye see the Son of *man* **humanity**
sitting *on* **by** the right *hand* of *power* **the dynamis**,
and coming in the clouds of **the** heaven.
65 Then the *high* **arch** priest *rent* **ripped** his clothes,
saying **wording**, He hath *spoken blasphemy* **blasphemed**;
what further need have we of witnesses?
behold, now ye have heard his blasphemy.
66 What think ye?
They answered and said, He is *guilty of* **subject to** death.
67 Then did they spit in his face,
and *buffeted* **punched** him;
and others *smote* **slapped** him
with the palms of their hands,
68 *Saying* **Wording**,
Prophesy unto us, thou *Christ* **Messiah**,
Who is he that smote thee?

PETROS' FIRST DENIAL

69 Now *Peter* **Petros** sat without in the *palace* **courtyard**:
and a *damsel* **lass** came unto him, *saying* **wording**,
Thou also wast with *Jesus* **Yah Shua** of *Galilee* **Galiyl**.
70 But he denied *before them* **in front of all**,
saying **wording**, I know not what thou *sayest* **speakest**.

PETROS' SECOND DENIAL

71 And when he was gone out into the *porch* **gate**,
another *maid* saw him,
and *said* **worded** unto them that were there,
This *fellow*
was also with *Jesus of Nazareth* **Yah Shua the Nazarene**.
72 And again he denied with an oath,
I *do not* know **not** the *man* **human**.

PETROS' THIRD DENIAL

73 And after a while came unto him they that stood by,
and said to *Peter* **Petros**,
Surely **Truly** thou also art one of them;
for thy speech *bewrayeth* **maketh** thee **evident**.
74 Then began he to curse and to *swear* **anathematize**,
saying, I know not the *man* **human**.
And *immediately* **straightway**
the *cock crew* **rooster voiced**.
75 And *Peter* **Petros** remembered
the *word* **rhema** of *Jesus* **Yah Shua**, which said unto him,
Before the *cock crow* **rooster voiceth**,
thou shalt **utterly** deny me thrice.
And he went out, and wept bitterly.

YAH SHUA FACES PILATOS

27 When the **early** morning *was come* **became**,
all the *chief* **arch** priests and elders of the people
took counsel against *Jesus* **Yah Shua**
to *put* **deathify** him *to death*:
2 And when they had bound him, they led him away,
and delivered him to Pontius *Pilate* **Pilatos** the governor.

YAH HUDAH'S REGRET

3 Then *Judas* **Yah Hudah**, which had betrayed him,
when he saw that he was condemned,
repented himself **regretted**,
and brought again the thirty *pieces of* silver
to the *chief* **arch** priests and elders,
4 *Saying* **Wording**, I have sinned
in that I have betrayed *the innocent* **guiltless** blood.
And they said, What is that to us? see thou to that.
5 And he *cast down* **tossed** the *pieces of* silver
in the *temple* **nave**,

and departed, and went and *hanged* **strangled** himself.
6 And the *chief* **arch** priests took the silver *pieces*,
and said, It is not *lawful for* **allowed**
to put them into the *treasury* **qurban**,
because it is the price of blood.
7 And they took counsel,
and *bought with* **marketed of** them the potter's field,
to *bury* **entomb** strangers in.
8 Wherefore that field was called,
The field of blood, unto this day.
9 Then was fulfilled that which was *spoken* **rhetorized**
by Jeremy **through Yirme Yah** the prophet,
saying **wording**, And they took the thirty *pieces of* silver,
the price of him that was *valued* **priced**,
whom they of the *children* **sons** of *Israel* **Yisra El**
did value **priced**;
10 And gave them *for* **unto** the potter's field,
exactly as *the Lord appointed* **Yah Veh ordered** me.
cp Zechar Yah 11:12,13
11 And *Jesus* **Yah Shua**
stood *before* **in front of** the governor:
and the governor asked him, *saying* **wording**,
Art thou the *king* **sovereign** of the *Jews* **Yah Hudiym**?
And *Jesus* **Yah Shua** said unto him,
Thou *sayest* **wordest**.
12 And *when he was* **in his being** accused
of the *chief* **arch** priests and elders,
he answered *nothing* **naught**.
13 Then *said Pilate* **worded Pilatos** unto him,
Hearest thou not
how *many things* **much** they witness against thee?
14 And he answered him
to never a word **not even a rhema**;
insomuch that the governor marvelled *greatly* **extremely**.
15 Now at that *feast* **celebration**
the governor was *wont* **accustomed**
to release unto the *people* **multitude** a prisoner,
whom they *would* **willed**.
16 And they had then *a notable* **an eminent** prisoner,
called Barabbas **worded Bar Abbas**.
17 Therefore when they were gathered together,
Pilate **Pilatos** said unto them,
Whom *will* **shall** ye that I release unto you?
Barabbas **Bar Abbas**,
or *Jesus* **Yah Shua**
which is *called Christ* **worded Messiah**?
18 For he knew
that for envy they had delivered him.
19 When he was set down on the *judgment seat* **bamah**,
his *wife sent* **woman apostolized** unto him,
saying **wording**,
Have thou *nothing* **naught** to do with that just man:
for I have suffered *many things* **much** this day in a dream
because of him.
20 But the *chief* **arch** priests and elders
persuaded **convinced** the multitude
that they should ask *Barabbas* **Bar Abbas**,
and destroy *Jesus* **Yah Shua**.
21 The governor answered and said unto them,
Whether of the twain *will* **shall** ye that I release unto you?
They said, *Barabbas* **Bar Abbas**.
22 *Pilate saith* **Pilatos wordeth** unto them,
What shall I do then with *Jesus* **Yah Shua**
which is *called Christ* **worded Messiah**?
They all *say* **word** unto him, *Let him be crucified* **Stake**.
23 And the governor said,
Why **Indeed**, what evil hath he done?
But they cried out *the more* **superabundantly**,
saying **wording**, *Let him be crucified* **Stake**.
24 When *Pilate* **Pilatos** saw
that he could *prevail nothing* **not benefit naught**,
but that rather a *tumult was made* **riot became**,
he took water,
and washed his hands before the multitude,
saying **wording**,
I am *innocent* **guiltless** of the blood of this just person:
see ye to it.
25 Then answered all the people, and said,
His blood be on us, and on our children.

BAR ABBAS RELEASED, YAH SHUA BETRAYED

26 Then released he *Barabbas* **Bar Abbas** unto them:
and when he had *scourged Jesus* **whipped Yah Shua**,
he *delivered* **betrayed** him to be *crucified* **staked**.
27 Then the *soldiers* **warriors** of the governor
took *Jesus* **Yah Shua** into the *common hall* **praetorium**,
and gathered **together** unto him
the whole *band* **squad** of soldiers.
28 And they stripped him, and put on him a scarlet robe.
29 And when they had
platted **braided** a *crown* **wreath** of thorns,
they put it upon his head, and a reed in his right *hand*:
and they *bowed the knee before* **kneeled in front of** him,
and mocked him, *saying* **wording**, *Hail* **Cheers**,
king **sovereign** of the *Jews* **Yah Hudiym**!
30 And they spit upon him, and took the reed,
and *smote* **struck** him on the head.
31 And after that they had mocked him,
they *took* **stripped** the robe *off* from him,
and *put* **endued** his own *raiment* **garment** on him,
and led him away to *crucify* **stake** him.
32 And as they came out,
they found a *man of Cyrene* **human — a Cyrenian**,
Simon **Shimon** by name:
him they compelled to bear his *cross* **stake**.
33 And when they were come unto a place
called Golgotha **worded Golgoleth**,
that is to *say* **word**, *a place of a skull* **cranium place**,
34 They gave him vinegar to drink
mingled with *gall* **choler**:
and when he had tasted thereof,
he *would* **willed to** not drink.

YAH SHUA IS STAKED

35 And they *crucified* **staked** him,
and *parted* **divided** his garments, casting lots:
that it might be fulfilled
which was *spoken* **rhetorized** by the prophet,
They *parted* **divided** my garments among them,
and upon my *vesture did* **garment** they cast lots.
Psalm 22:18
36 And sitting down they *watched* **guarded** him there;
37 And *set up over* **put above** his head
his accusation *written* **scribed**,
THIS IS *JESUS* **YAH SHUA**
THE *KING* **SOVEREIGN** OF THE *JEWS* **YAH HUDIYM**.
38 Then were there two *thieves* **robbers**
crucified **staked** with him,
one *on* **by** the right *hand*, and *another on* **one by** the left.
39 And they that passed by *reviled* **blasphemed** him,
wagging their heads,
40 And *saying* **wording**,
Thou that *destroyest* **disintegratest** the *temple* **nave**,
and buildest it in three days, save thyself.
If thou be the Son of *God* **Elohim**,
come down **descend** from the *cross* **stake**.
41 Likewise also the *chief* **arch** priests mocking him,
with the scribes and elders, *said* **worded**,
42 He saved others; himself he cannot save.
If he be the *king* **sovereign** of *Israel* **Yisra El**,
let him now *come down* **descend** from the *cross* **stake**,
and we *will believe* **shall trust in** him.
43 He *trusted* **confided** in *God* **Elohim**;
let him *deliver* **rescue** him now,
if he *will have him* **willeth**:
for he said, I am the Son of *God* **Elohim**.
44 The thieves also,
which were *crucified* **staked** with him,
cast the same in his teeth **reproached him**.
45 Now from the sixth hour
there *was* **became** darkness over all the *land* **earth**
unto the ninth hour.
46 And about the ninth hour
Jesus **Yah Shua** cried with a *loud* **mega** voice,
saying **wording**,
Eli, Eli, lama sabachthani?
that is *to say*,
My *God* **Elohim**, my *God* **Elohim**,
why hast thou forsaken me?
Psalm 22:1

47 Some of them that stood there,
when they heard that, *said* **worded**,
This *man calleth for Elias* **voiceth out to Eli Yah**.
48 And straightway one of them ran, and took a spunge,
and filled it with vinegar, and put it on a reed,
and gave him to drink.
49 The rest *said* **worded**, *Let be* **Allow**,
let us see
whether *Elias will* **Eli Yah shall** come to save him.
50 *Jesus* **Yah Shua**,
when he had cried again with a *loud* **mega** voice,
yielded up the ghost **released his spirit**.

MATERIAL AND PHYSICAL REACTIONS

51 And, behold,
the veil of the *temple* **nave** was *rent* **split** in twain
from *the top to the bottom* **above down**;
and the earth *did quake* **quaked**, and the rocks *rent* **split**;
52 And the *graves* **tombs** *were* opened;
and many bodies of the *saints* **holy** which slept arose,
53 And came out of the *graves* **tombs**
after his *resurrection* **rising**,
and *went* **entered** into the holy city,
and *appeared* **manifested** unto many.
54 Now when the centurion,
and they that were with him,
watching Jesus **guarding Yah Shua**,
saw the *earthquake* **quake**,
and those *things* that *were done* **became**,
they *feared greatly* **awed extremely**, *saying* **wording**,
Truly this was the Son of *God* **Elohim**.
55 And many women were there
beholding **observing from** afar *off*,
which followed *Jesus* **Yah Shua** from *Galilee* **Galiyl**,
ministering unto him:
56 Among which was *Mary* **Miryam the** Magdalene,
and *Mary* **Miryam**
the mother of *James* **Yaaqovos** and *Joses* **Yoses**,
and the mother of *Zebedee's children* **Zabdi's sons**.

YAH SHUA IS ENTOMBED

57 When *the even was come* **evening became**,
there came a rich *man* **human** of *Arimathaea* **Ramah**,
named *Joseph* **Yoseph**,
who also himself
was *Jesus' disciple* **discipled by Yah Shua**:
58 He went to *Pilate* **Pilatos**,
and *begged* **asked** the body of *Jesus* **Yah Shua**.
Then *Pilate* **Pilatos**
commanded **summoned** the body to be *delivered* **given**.
59 And when *Joseph* **Yoseph** had taken the body,
he *wrapped* **entwined** it in *a clean* **pure** linen *cloth*,
60 And laid it in his own new tomb,
which he had *hewn* **quarried** out in the rock:
and he rolled a *great* **mega** stone
to the *door* **portal** of the *sepulchre* **tomb**,
and departed.
61 And there was *Mary* **Miryam the** Magdalene,
and the other *Mary* **Miryam**,
sitting over against the *sepulchre* **tomb**.

THE TOMB IS SEALED AND GUARDED

62 Now the next day,
that followed **after** the day of the preparation,
the *chief* **arch** priests and Pharisees
came **gathered** together unto *Pilate* **Pilatos**,
63 *saying* **wording**, *Sir* **Adoni**,
we remember that that *deceiver* **seducer** said,
while he was yet alive,
After three days I *will* **shall** rise *again*.
64 *Command* **Summon** therefore
that the *sepulchre* **tomb** be *made sure* **secured**
until the third day,
lest **ever** his disciples come by night, and steal him away,
and say unto the people, He is risen from the dead:
so the *last error* **final deception**
shall be worse than the first.
65 *Pilate* **Pilatos** said unto them,
Ye have a *watch* **custodian**:
go your way, *make* **secure** it *as sure* as ye *can* **know**.
66 So they went,
and *made the sepulchre sure* **secured the tomb**,
sealing the stone, and setting a *watch* **custodian**.

YAH SHUA IS RESURRECTED

28 In the *end* **eve** of the *sabbath* **shabbaths**,
as it began to dawn
toward **unto** the first *day* of the *week* **shabbaths**,
came *Mary* **Miryam the** Magdalene
and the other *Mary* **Miryam**
to *see* **observe** the *sepulchre* **tomb**.
2 And, behold,
there *was a great earthquake* **became a mega quake**:
for the angel of *the Lord* **Yah Veh**
descended from **the** heaven,
and came and rolled back the stone from the *door* **portal**,
and sat upon it.
3 His countenance was *like* **as** lightning,
and his *raiment* **enduement** white as snow:
4 And for *fear* **awe** of him
the *keepers did shake* **guards quaked**,
and became as dead *men*
5 And the angel answered and said unto the women,
Fear not ye **Be ye not awestricken**:
for I know that ye seek *Jesus* **Yah Shua**,
which was *crucified* **staked**.
6 He is not here: for he is risen, **exactly** as he said.
Come, see the place where *the Lord* **Adonay** lay.
7 And go quickly,
and *tell* **say to** his disciples that he is risen from the dead;
and, behold, he goeth before you into *Galilee* **Galiyl**;
there shall ye see him:
lo **behold**, I have *told* **said to** you.
8 And they departed quickly from the *sepulchre* **tomb**
with *fear* **awe** and *great joy* **mega cheer**;
and did run to *bring* **evangelize** his disciples *word*.
9 And as they went to *tell* **evangelize** his disciples,
behold, *Jesus* **Yah Shua** met them, *saying* **wording**,
All hail **Cheers**.
And they came and *held* **overpowered** him by the feet,
and worshipped him.
10 Then *said Jesus* **worded Yah Shua** unto them,
Be **Awe** not *afraid*:
go *tell* **evangelize** my brethren
that they go into *Galilee* **Galiyl**,
and there shall they see me.

WARRIORS ARE BRIBED TO DENY THE RESURRECTION

11 Now when they were going, behold,
some of the *watch* **custodians** came into the city,
and *shewed* **evangelized** unto the *chief* **arch** priests
all *the things* **those** that *were done* **became**.
12 And when they were assembled with the elders,
and had taken counsel,
they gave *large money* **ample silver**
unto the *soldiers* **warriors**,
13 *saying* **wording**, Say ye,
His disciples came by night,
and stole him away while we slept.
14 And if *this come to the governor's ears* **the governor hear**,
we *will persuade* **shall convince** him,
and secure you **without making you anxious**.
15 So they took the *money* **silver**,
and did as they were *taught* **doctrinated**:
and this *saying* **word** is commonly reported
among the *Jews* **Yah Hudiym** until this day.
16 Then the eleven disciples
went away into *Galilee* **Galiyl**, into a mountain
where *Jesus* **Yah Shua** had *appointed* **ordained** them.
17 And when they saw him, they worshipped him:
but some doubted.

YAH SHUA'S FINAL MISVAH

18 And *Jesus* **Yah Shua** came and spake unto them,
saying **wording**, All *power* **authority** is given unto me
in heaven and in earth.
19 Go ye therefore, and *teach* **disciple** all *nations* **goyim**,
baptizing them in the name° of the Father,
and of the Son, and of the Holy *Ghost* **Spirit**:
20 *Teaching* **Doctrinating** them to *observe* **guard**
all *things whatsoever* — **as much as ever**
I have *commanded* **misvahed** you:
and, *lo* **behold**, I am with you *alway* **all days**,
even unto the *end* **completion** of the *world* **eon**.
Amen.

°name: Exodus 3:3—15, Yesha Yah 42:8, Yahn 8:58

KEY TO INTERPRETING THE EXEGESES
King James text is in regular type;
Text under exegeses is in oblique type;
Text of exegeses is in bold type.

YAH SHUA MESSIAH, THE SON OF ELOHIM

1 The beginning of the *gospel* **evangelism**
of *Jesus Christ* **Yah Shua Messiah**, the Son of *God* **Elohim**;

YAHN THE BAPTIZER

2 As it is *written* **scribed** in the prophets, Behold,
I *send* **apostolize** my *messenger* **angel** before thy face,
which shall prepare thy way *before* **in front of** thee.
3 The voice of one crying in the wilderness,
Prepare ye the way of *the Lord* **Yah Veh**,
make his paths straight.
Malachi 3:1, Yesha Yah 40:3
4 *John did baptize* **Yahn became baptizing** in the wilderness,
and *preach* **preaching** the baptism of repentance
for the *remission* **forgiveness** of sins.
5 And there *went out* **proceeded** unto him
all the *land* **region** of *Judaea* **Yah Hudah**,
and *they of Jerusalem* **the Yeru Shalemiym**,
and were all baptized of him
in the *river* **stream** of *Jordan* **Yarden**,
confessing **homologizing** their sins.
6 And *John* **Yahn** was *clothed* **endued** with camel's hair,
and with a girdle of *a skin* **leather** about his loins;
and he did eat locusts and wild honey;
7 And preached, *saying* **wording**,
There cometh one mightier than I after me,
the *latchet* **thongs** of whose shoes
I am not worthy to stoop down and *unloose* **release**.
8 I indeed have baptized you *with* **in** water:
but he shall baptize you *with* **in** the Holy *Ghost* **Spirit**.

YAHN BAPTIZES YAH SHUA

9 And it *came to pass* **became** in those days,
that *Jesus* **Yah Shua**
came from Nazareth of *Galilee* **Galiyl**,
and was baptized of *John* **Yahn** in *Jordan* **Yarden**.

HOLY SPIRIT DESCENDS ON YAH SHUA

10 And straightway
coming up **ascending** out of the water,
he saw the heavens *opened* **split**,
and the Spirit *like* **as** a dove descending upon him:
11 And there *came* **became** a voice
from *heaven* **the heavens**, *saying*,
Thou art my beloved Son,
in whom I *am well pleased* **well—approve**.

YAH SHUA TESTED BY SATAN

12 And immediately
the spirit *driveth* **casteth** him into the wilderness.
13 And he was there in the wilderness forty days,
tempted **tested** of Satan; and was with the wild beasts;
and the angels ministered unto him.

YAH SHUA PREACHES THE SOVEREIGNDOM OF ELOHIM

14 Now after that *John* **Yahn** was *put in prison* **betrayed**,
Jesus **Yah Shua** came into *Galilee* **Galiyl**,
preaching the *gospel* **evangelism**
of the *kingdom* **sovereigndom** of *God* **Elohim**,
15 And *saying* **wording**, The *time* **season** is fulfilled,
and the *kingdom* **sovereigndom** of *God* **Elohim**
is at hand **approacheth**:
repent ye, and *believe* **trust in** the *gospel* **evangelism**.
16 Now as he walked by the sea of *Galilee* **Galiyl**,
he saw *Simon* **Shimon** and *Andrews* **Andreas** his brother
casting a net into the sea: for they were fishers.
17 And *Jesus* **Yah Shua** said unto them, Come ye after me,
and I *will* **shall** make you
to become fishers of *men* **humanity**.
18 And straightway they forsook their nets,
and followed him.
19 And when he had
gone a little farther **advanced** thence,
he saw *James* **Yaaqovos** *the son* of *Zebedee* **Zabdi**,
and *John* **Yahn** his brother,
who also were in the *ship* **sailer**
mending **preparing** their nets.
20 And straightway he called them:
and they *left* **forsook** their father *Zebedee* **Zabdi**
in the *ship* **sailer**
with the *hired servants* **hirelings**, and went after him.

YAH SHUA DOCTRINATES IN THE SYNAGOGUE

21 And they *went into* **entered**
Capernaum **Kaphar Nachum**;
and straightway on the *sabbath day* **shabbaths**
he entered into the synagogue, and *taught* **doctrinated**.
22 And they were astonished at his doctrine:
for he *taught* **doctrinated** them as one that had authority,
and not as the scribes.

YAH SHUA REBUKES AN IMPURE SPIRIT

23 And there was in their synagogue
a *man* **human** with an *unclean* **impure** spirit;
and he *cried out* **screamed**,
24 *saying* **wording**, *Let us alone* **Aha!**;
what have we to do with thee,
thou *Jesus of Nazareth* **Yah Shua the Nazarene**?
art thou come to destroy us?
I know thee who thou art, the Holy One of *God* **Elohim**.
25 And *Jesus* **Yah Shua** rebuked him, *saying* **wording**,
Hold thy peace **Be muzzled**, and come out of him.
26 And when the *unclean* **impure** spirit
had *torn* **convulsed** him,
and cried with a *loud* **mega** voice, he came out of him.
27 And they were all *amazed* **astonished**,
insomuch that
they *questioned* **disputed** among themselves,
saying **wording**,
What *thing* is this? what new doctrine is this?
for with authority *commandeth* **ordereth** he
even the *unclean* **impure** spirits,
and they *do* obey him.
28 And immediately his fame spread abroad
throughout **into** all the region round about *Galilee* **Galiyl**.

YAH SHUA CURES SHIMON'S MOTHER IN LAW

29 And *forthwith* **straightway**,
when they were come out of the synagogue
they entered
into the house of *Simon* **Shimon** and *Andrew* **Andreas**,
with *James* **Yaaqovos** and *John* **Yahn**.
30 But *Simon's wife's mother* **Shimon's mother in law**
lay *sick of a fever* **fevered**,
and *anon* **straightway** they *tell* **word to** him *of* **about** her.
31 And he came and *took* **overpowered** her by the hand,
and lifted her *up*;
and *immediately* **straightway** the fever *left* **forsook** her,
and she ministered unto them.

YAH SHUA CASTS OUT DEMONS AND CURES

32 And *at even* **become evening**, when the sun *did* set,
they brought unto him all that were *diseased* **ill**,
and them that were *possessed with devils* **demonized**.
33 And all the city
was gathered together at the *door* **portal**.
34 And he *healed* **cured** many
that were *sick* **ill** of divers diseases,
and cast out many *devils* **demons**;
and *suffered* **allowed** not the *devils* **demons** to speak,
because they knew him.

YAH SHUA PRAYS AND PREACHES

35 And in the **early** morning,
rising *up a great* **an extreme** while before day,
he went out, and departed into a *solitary* **desolate** place,
and there prayed.
36 And *Simon* **Shimon** and they that were with him
followed after him.
37 And when they had found him,
they *said* **worded** unto him, All *men* seek for thee.
38 And he *said* **worded** unto them,
Let us go into the *next towns* **nearby villages**,
that I may preach there also: for therefore came I forth.
39 And he preached in their synagogues
throughout **in** all *Galilee* **Galiyl**,
and cast out *devils* **demons**.

YAH SHUA PURIFIES A LEPER

40 And there came a leper to him, beseeching him,
and kneeling down to him,
and *saying* **wording** unto him,
If thou *wilt* **willest**, thou canst *make* **purify** me *clean*.
41 And *Jesus* **Yah Shua**,
moved with *compassion* **sympathetic spleen**,
put forth **extended** his hand, and touched him,
and *saith* **wordeth** unto him,

I will; be thou *clean* **purified**.
42 And as soon as he had *spoken* **said**,
immediately **straightway** the leprosy departed from him,
and he was *cleansed* **purified**.
43 And he *straitly charged* **sternly enjoined** him,
and *forthwith sent* **straightway cast** him *away* **forth**;
44 And *saith* **wordeth** unto him,
See thou say *nothing* **naught** to any *man* **one**:
but go thy way, shew thyself to the priest,
and offer for thy *cleansing* **purifying**
those *things* which *Moses commanded* **Mosheh ordered**,
for **in** a *testimony* **witness** unto them.
45 But he went out, and began to *publish* **preach** it much,
and to *blaze abroad* **report** the *matter* **word**,
insomuch that *Jesus* **Yah Shua**
could no more *openly* **manifestly** enter into the city,
but was without in *desert* **desolate** places:
and they came to him from every quarter.

YAH SHUA CURES A PARALYTIC

2 And again
he entered into *Capernaum* **Kaphar Nachum**
after some days;
and it was *noised* **heard** that he was in the house.
2 And straightway many were gathered together,
insomuch
that there was no **more** room to *receive* **place** them,
no, not *so much as* **even** about the *door* **portal**:
and he *preached* **spoke** the word unto them.
3 And they come unto him,
bringing one *sick of the palsy* **paralyzed**,
which was borne of four.
4 And when they could not come nigh unto him
for the *press* **multitude**,
they uncovered the *roof* **thatch** where he was:
and when they had broken it *up*,
they *let down* **lowered** the *bed* **pad**
wherein the *sick of the palsy* **paralyzed** lay.
5 When *Jesus* **Yah Shua** saw their *faith* **trust**,
he *said* **worded** unto the *sick of the palsy* **paralyzed**,
Son, **Child**, thy sins be forgiven thee.
6 But there were *certain* **some** of the scribes sitting there,
and reasoning in their hearts,
7 Why doth this man thus speak blasphemies?
who can forgive sins *but God only* **except one — Elohim**?
Yesha Yah 43:25
8 And *immediately* **straightway**
when Jesus perceived **Yah Shua knowing** in his spirit
that they *so* **thus** reasoned within themselves,
he said unto them,
Why reason ye these *things* in your hearts?
9 Whether is it easier to say
to the *sick of the palsy* **paralyzed**,
Thy sins be forgiven thee;
or to say,
Arise, and take *up* thy *bed* **pad**, and walk?
10 But that ye may know that the Son of *man* **humanity**
hath *power* **authority** on earth to forgive sins,
(he *saith* **wordeth** to the *sick of the palsy* **paralyzed**,)
11 I *say* **word** unto thee, Arise,
and take *up* thy *bed* **pad**,
and go thy way into thine house.
12 And *immediately* **straightway** he arose,
took *up* the *bed* **pad**,
and went forth *before* **in front of** them all;
insomuch that they were all *amazed* **astounded**,
and glorified *God* **Elohim**, *saying* **wording**,
We never **ever** saw it *on this fashion* **thus**.

LEVI FOLLOWS YAH SHUA

13 And he went forth again by the sea side;
and all the multitude *resorted* **came** unto him,
and he *taught* **doctrinated** them.
14 And as he passed by,
he saw Levi *the son* of *Alphaeus* **Heleph**
sitting at the *receipt of custom* **customs**,
and *said* **worded** unto him, Follow me.
And he arose and followed him.

YAH SHUA REPOSES WITH CUSTOMS AGENTS AND SINNERS

15 And it *came to pass* **became**, that,
as *Jesus sat at meat* **Yah Shua reposed** in his house,
many *publicans* **customs agents** and sinners
sat **reposed** also together
with *Jesus* **Yah Shua** and his disciples:
for there were many, and they followed him.
16 And when the scribes and Pharisees
saw him eat with *publicans* **customs agents** and sinners,
they *said* **worded** unto his disciples,
How is it that he eateth and drinketh
with *publicans* **customs agents** and sinners?
17 When *Jesus* **Yah Shua** heard it,
he *saith* **wordeth** unto them,
They that are *whole* **able**
have no need of the *physician* **healer**,
but they that are *sick* **ill**:
I came not to call the *righteous* **just**,
but sinners to repentance.

ON FASTING

18 And the disciples of *John* **Yahn** and of the Pharisees
used to fast:
and they come and *say* **word** unto him,
Why do the disciples of *John* **Yahn** and of the Pharisees
fast,
but thy disciples fast not?
19 And *Jesus* **Yah Shua** said unto them,
Can the *children* **sons** of the bridechamber fast,
while **during the time** the bridegroom is with them?
as long **time** as they have the bridegroom with them,
they cannot fast.
20 But the days *will* **shall** come,
when the bridegroom shall be taken away from them,
and then shall they fast in those days.

ON PATCHING

21 No *man* **one**
also seweth a piece of *new* **unfulled** cloth
on an old garment:
else **but if not** the *new piece that filled it up* **fullness**
taketh away from the old,
and the *rent is made* **split becometh** worse.

NEW WINE, NEW SKINS

22 And no *man* **one**
putteth new wine into old *bottles* **skins**:
else **but if not** the new wine doth burst the *bottles* **skins**,
and the wine is *spilled* **poured**,
and the *bottles will be marred* **skins shall destruct**:
but new wine must be put into new *bottles* **skins**.

YAH SHUA, ADONAY OF THE SHABBATH

23 And it *came to pass* **became**,
that he *went* **passed** through the *corn fields* **spores**
on the *sabbath day* **shabbaths**;
and his disciples began, as they *went* **made their way**,
to pluck *the ears of corn*.
24 And the Pharisees *said* **worded** unto him, Behold,
why do they on the *sabbath day* **shabbaths**
that which is not *lawful* **allowed**?
25 And he *said* **worded** unto them,
Have ye never **ever** read what David did,
when he had need, and was an hungred,
he, and they that were with him?
26 How he *went into* **entered** the house of *God* **Elohim**
in the days of *Abiathar* **Abi Athar** the *high* **arch** priest,
and did eat the *shewbread* **prothesis bread**,
which is not *lawful* **allowed** to eat
but **except** for the priests,
and gave also to them which were with him?
Leviticus 24:5—9
27 And he *said* **worded** unto them,
The *sabbath* **shabbaths**
was made **became** for *man* **humanity**,
and not *man* **humanity** for the *sabbath* **shabbaths**:
28 Therefore the Son of *man* **humanity**
is *Lord* **Adonay** also of the *sabbath* **shabbath**.

YAH SHUA CURES ON THE SHABBATH

3 And he entered again into the synagogue;
and there was a *man* **human** there
which had a withered hand.
2 And they *watched* **observed** him,
whether he *would heal* **should cure** him
on the *sabbath day* **shabbaths**;
that they might accuse him.
3 And he *saith* **wordeth**

unto the *man* **human** which had the withered hand,
Stand *forth* **in our midst**.
4 And he *saith* **wordeth** unto them,
Is it *lawful* **allowed** to do good
on the *sabbath days* **shabbaths**,
or to do evil?
to save *life* **soul**, or to *kill* **slaughter**?
But they *held their peace* **hushed**.
5 And when he had looked round about on them
with *anger* **wrath**,
being grieved for the *hardness* **petrifaction** of their hearts,
he *saith* **wordeth** unto the *man* **human**,
Stretch forth **Extend** thine hand.
And he *stretched it out* **extended**:
and his hand was restored whole as the other.
6 And the Pharisees went forth,
and straightway
took **made** counsel with the Herodians against him,
how they might destroy him.
7 But *Jesus* **Yah Shua**
withdrew himself with his disciples
to the sea:
and a *great* **vast** multitude from *Galilee* **Galiyl**
followed him,
and from *Judaea* **Yah Hudah**,
8 And from *Jerusalem* **Yeru Shalem**,
and from *Idumaea* **Edom**,
and from beyond *Jordan* **Yarden**;
and they about *Tyre* **Sor** and Sidon,
a *great* **vast** multitude,
when they had heard
what great things **as much as** he did,
came unto him.
9 And he *spake* **said** to his disciples,
that a *small ship* **skiff** should wait on him
because of the multitude,
lest they should *throng* **tribulate** him.
10 For he had *healed* **cured** many;
insomuch
that they *pressed* **fell** upon him for to touch him,
as many as had *plagues* **scourges**.
11 And *unclean* **impure** spirits,
when they *saw* **observed** him,
fell down **prostrated** before him,
and cried, *saying* **wording**,
Thou art the Son of *God* **Elohim**.
12 And he *straitly charged* **admonished** them
that they should not make him *known* **manifest**.

YAH SHUA ORDAINS THE TWELVE

13 And he *goeth up* **ascendeth** into a mountain,
and calleth unto him whom he *would* **willed**:
and they *came* **went** unto him.
14 And he ordained twelve,
that they should be with him,
and that he might *send* **apostolize** them *forth* to preach,
15 And to have *power* **authority**
to *heal sicknesses* **cure diseases**,
and to cast out *devils* **demons**:
16 And *Simon* **to Shimon**
he *surnamed Peter* **added the name Petros**;
17 And *James the son of Zebedee* **Yaaqovos of Zabdi**,
and *John* **Yahn** the brother of *James* **Yaaqovos**;
and he *surnamed them* **added the names**
Boanerges **Ben Regaz**,
which is, The sons of thunder:
18 And *Andrew* **Andreas**, and *Philip* **Philippos**,
and *Bartholomew* **Bar Talmay**, and *Matthew* **Matthaios**,
and *Thomas* **Taom**,
and *James the son* **Yaaqovos** of *Alphaeus* **Heleph**,
and Thaddaeus,
and *Simon* **Shimon** the *Canaanite* **Kenaaniy**,
19 And *Judas Iscariot* **Yah Hudah the urbanite**,
which also betrayed him:
and they went into an house.
20 And the multitude cometh together again,
so that they could not so much as **even** eat bread.
21 And when his friends heard of it,
they went out to *lay hold on* **overpower** him:
for they *said* **worded**, He is *beside himself* **astounded**.

YAH SHUA ACCUSED OF HAVING BAAL ZEBUB

22 And the scribes
which came down from *Jerusalem* **Yeru Shalem**
said **spake**, He hath *Beelzebub* **Baal Zebub**,
and *by* **in** the *prince* **arch** of *the devils* **demons**
casteth he out *devils* **demons**.
23 And he called them unto him,
and *said* **worded** unto them in parables,
How can Satan cast out Satan?
24 And if a *kingdom* **sovereigndom**
be divided against itself,
that *kingdom* **sovereigndom** cannot stand.
25 And if a house be divided against itself,
that house cannot stand.
26 And if Satan rise *up* against himself, and be divided,
he cannot stand, but hath *an end* **a completion**.
27 No *man* **one** can enter
into *a strong man's* **the** house **of the mighty**,
and *spoil* **throughly plunder** his *goods* **vessels**,
except **unless**
he *will* **shall** first bind the *strong man* **mighty**;
and then he *will spoil* **shall throughly plunder** his house.

THE UNFORGIVEN SIN

28 *Verily I say* **Amen! I word** unto you,
All sins shall be forgiven unto the sons of *men* **humanity**,
and blasphemies
wherewith soever **as much as ever** they shall blaspheme:
29 But he that shall blaspheme against the Holy *Ghost* **Spirit**
hath never forgiveness **unto the eons**,
but is *in danger of* **subject to** eternal *damnation* **judgment**.
30 Because they *said* **worded**,
He hath an *unclean* **impure** spirit.

MOTHER AND BRETHREN SEEK YAH SHUA

31 There came then his brethren and his mother,
and, standing without,
sent **apostolized** unto him, *calling* **voicing out to** him.
32 And the multitude sat about him,
and they said unto him, Behold,
thy mother and thy brethren without seek for thee.
33 And he answered them, *saying* **wording**,
Who is my mother, or my brethren?
34 And he looked round about
on them which sat about him,
and *said* **worded**, Behold my mother and my brethren!
35 For whosoever shall do the will of *God* **Elohim**,
the same **this** is my brother, and my sister, and mother.
4 And he began again
to *teach* **doctrinate** by the sea side:
and there was gathered **together** unto him
a *great* **vast** multitude,
so that he *entered* **embarked** into a *ship* **sailer**,
and sat in the sea;
and the whole multitude was by the sea on the land.
2 And he taught **doctrinated** them
many things by **much in** parables,
and *said* **worded** unto them in his doctrine,

THE PARABLE OF THE SOWER

3 Hearken; Behold, there went out a sower to sow:
4 And it *came to pass* **became**, *as he sowed* **in his sowing**,
some **indeed** fell by the way side,
and the *fowls* **flyers** of the *air* **heaven**
came and devoured it *up*.
5 And *some* **others** fell on *stony ground* **rocky**,
where it had not much *earth* **soil**;
and *immediately* **straightway** it sprang *up*,
because it had no depth of *earth* **soil**:
6 But when the sun was *up* **risen**, it was scorched;
and because it had no root, it withered away.
7 And *some* **others** fell among thorns,
and the thorns *grew up* **ascended**,
and *choked* **strangled** it,
and it *yielded* **gave** no fruit.
8 And other fell on good *ground* **soil**,
and *did yield* **gave** fruit
that *sprang up* **ascended** and *increased* **grew**;
and brought forth, *some* **one** thirty,
and *some* **one** sixty, and *some* **one** an hundred.
9 And he *said* **worded** unto them,
He that hath ears to hear, let him hear.

THE PURPOSE OF PARABLES

10 And when he *was* **became** alone,
they that were about him with the twelve
asked of him the parable.
11 And he *said* **worded** unto them,
Unto you it is given to know the mystery
of the *kingdom* **sovereigndom** of *God* **Elohim**:
but unto them that are without,
all these *things are done* **become** in parables:
12 That *seeing* **observing** they may *see* **observe**,
and not perceive;
and hearing they may hear,
and not *understand* **comprehend**;
lest *at any time* **ever**
they should *be converted* **turn around**,
and their sins should *be* forgiven them.
Yesha Yah 6:9, 10

THE PARABLE OF THE SOWER INTERPRETED

13 And he *said* **worded** unto them,
Know ye not this parable?
and how then *will* **shall** *ye* know **ye** all parables?
14 The sower soweth the word.
15 And these are they by the way side,
where the word is sown;
but when they have heard,
Satan cometh *immediately* **straightway**,
and taketh away the word that was sown in their hearts.
16 And these are they likewise
which are sown on *stony ground* **rocky**;
who, when they have heard the word,
immediately **straightway**
receive **take** it with *gladness* **cheer**;
17 And have no root in themselves,
and so endure *but for a time* **temporarily**:
afterward **then**,
when *affliction* **tribulation** or persecution
ariseth **becometh** for the word's sake,
immediately **straightway** they are *offended* **scandalized**.
18 And these are they which are sown among thorns;
such as hear the word,
19 And the *cares* **anxieties** of this *world* **eon**,
and the deceitfulness of riches,
and the *lusts of other things* **remaining pantings**
entering in,
choke **strangle** the word, and it becometh unfruitful.
20 And these are they
which are sown on good *ground* **soil**;
such as hear the word, and receive it,
and *bring forth* **bear** fruit, *some* **one** thirtyfold,
some **one** sixty, and *some* **one** an hundred.

THE PARABLE OF THE CANDLE

21 And he *said* **worded** unto them,
Is a candle brought to be put under a *bushel* **measure**,
or under a bed?
and not *to be set* **put** on a *candlestick* **menorah**?
22 For there is *nothing hid* **naught secreted**,
which shall not **lest it shall** be manifested;
neither *was any thing* **hath ought**
kept secret **become secreted**,
but that it should *come abroad* **become manifested**.
23 If any *man* **one** have ears to hear, let him hear.
24 And he *said* **worded** unto them,
Take heed **Observe** what ye hear:
with **in** what measure ye *mete* **measure**,
it shall be measured to you:
and unto you that hear shall *more* be *given* **added**.
25 For he that hath, to him shall be given:
and he that hath not,
from him shall be taken even that which he hath.

SPORE SEASON AND HARVEST

26 And he *said* **worded**, *So* **Even thus**
is the *kingdom* **sovereigndom** of *God* **Elohim**,
as if a *man* **human**
should cast *seed* **spores** into the *ground* **soil**;
27 And should sleep, and rise night and day,
and the *seed* **spores** should *spring* **sprout** and grow *up*,
he knoweth not how.
28 For the earth *bringeth forth* **beareth** fruit
of herself **automatically**;
first the *blade* **herbage**, then the *ear* **kernel**,
after that the full *corn* **grain** in the *ear* **kernel**.
29 But when the fruit is *brought forth* **delivered**,
immediately **straightway**
he *putteth in* **apostolizeth** the sickle,
because the harvest is *come* **here**.

THE PARABLE OF THE MUSTARD KERNEL

30 And he *said* **worded**, Whereunto shall we liken
the *kingdom* **sovereigndom** of *God* **Elohim**?
or with what *comparison* **parable**
shall we *compare it* **cast along side**?
31 It is like a *grain* **kernel** of mustard *seed*,
which, when it is sown in the earth,
is less than all the *seeds* **sperma** that be in the earth:
32 But when it is sown, it *groweth up* **ascendeth**,
and becometh greater than all herbs,
and *shooteth out great* **produceth more mega** branches;
so that the *fowls* **flyers** of the *air* **heaven**
may *lodge* **nest** under the shadow of it.

YAH SHUA EXPLAINS THE PARABLES

33 And with many such parables
spake he the word unto them,
exactly as they were able to hear it.
34 But *without* **apart from** a parable
spake he not unto them:
and when they were alone,
he *expounded* **explained** all *things* to his disciples.

YAH SHUA STILLS THE MEGA WHIRLWIND

35 And the same day,
when the *even was come* **evening became**,
he *saith* **wordeth** unto them,
Let us pass *over* **through** unto the other side.
36 And when they had *sent away* **released** the multitude,
they took him even as he was in the *ship* **sailer**.
And there were also with him other *little ships* **skiffs**.
37 And there *arose* **became**
a *great storm of wind* **mega whirlwind**,
and the waves beat into the *ship* **sailer**,
so that it was *now* **already** full.
38 And he was in the *hinder part of the ship* **stern**,
asleep on a pillow:
and they *awake* **rouse** him, and *say* **word** unto him,
Master **Doctor**, *carest* **art** thou not **concerned**
that we *perish* **destruct**?
39 And he arose, and rebuked the wind,
and said unto the sea, *Peace* **Hush**, *be still* **muzzle**.
And the wind *ceased* **relaxed**,
and there *was a great* **became a mega** calm.
40 And he said unto them,
Why are ye *so fearful* **thus cowardly**?
how is it that ye have no *faith* **trust**?
41 And they *feared exceedingly* **awed a mega awe**,
and *said* **worded** one to another,
What *manner of man* **then** is this,
that even the wind and the sea obey him?

YAH SHUA EJECTS AN IMPURE SPIRIT OF DEMONS

5 And they came over unto the other side of the sea,
into the *country* **region** of the Gadarenes.
2 And when he was come out of the *ship* **sailer**,
immediately **straightway** there met him out of the tombs
a *man* **human** with an *unclean* **impure** spirit,
3 Who had his *dwelling* **settlement** among the tombs;
and no *man* **one** could bind him,
no, *not* **neither** with *chains* **fetters**:
4 Because that he had been often bound
with *fetters* **shackles** and *chains* **fetters**,
and the *chains* **fetters**
had been *plucked asunder* **drawn apart** by him,
and the *fetters broken in pieces* **shackles shattered**:
neither could any *man* **one** tame him.
5 And *always* **continually**, night and day,
he was in the mountains, and in the tombs,
crying, and cutting himself with stones.
6 But when he saw *Jesus* **Yah Shua from** afar *off*,
he ran and worshipped him,
7 And cried with a *loud* **mega** voice, and said,
What have I to do with thee, *Jesus* **Yah Shua**,
thou Son of *the most high God* **El Elyon**?
I *adjure* **oath** thee by *God* **Elohim**,
that thou *torment* **torture** me not.
8 For he *said* **worded** unto him,

Come out of the *man* **human**, thou *unclean* **impure** spirit.
9 And he asked him, What is thy name?
And he answered, *saying* **wording**,
My name is Legion: for we are many.
10 And he besought him much
that he *would* **should** not *send* **apostolize** them *away*
out of the *country* **region**.
11 Now there was there nigh unto the mountains
a *great herd* **mega drove** of swine feeding.
12 And all the *devils* **demons** besought him,
saying **wording**,
Send us into the swine, that we may enter into them.
13 And *forthwith* **straightway**
Jesus gave **Yah Shua permitted** them *leave*.
And the *unclean* **impure** spirits went out,
and entered into the swine:
and the *herd* **drove** ran violently down a *steep place* **cliff**
into the sea,
(they were about two thousand;)
and were *choked* **strangled** in the sea.
14 And they that fed the swine fled,
and *told* **evangelized** it in the city,
and in the *country* **field**.
And they went out to see what it was
that *was done* **had become**.
15 And they come to *Jesus* **Yah Shua**,
and *see* **observe** him
that was *possessed with the devil* **demonized**,
and had the legion,
sitting, and clothed, and *in his right mind* **sound minded**:
and they were *afraid* **awestricken**.
16 And they that saw it
told **declared** them how it *befell* **became** to him
that was *possessed with the devil* **demonized**,
and also concerning the swine.
17 And they began to *pray* **beseech** him
to depart out of their *coasts* **boundries**.
18 And when he *was come* **embarked** into the *ship* **sailer**,
he that had been *possessed with the devil* **demonized**
prayed **besought** him that he might be with him.
19 Howbeit *Jesus suffered* **Yah Shua allowed** him not,
but *saith* **wordeth** unto him, Go home to thy friends,
and *tell* **evangelize** them
how great things the Lord **as much as Adonay**
hath done for thee,
and hath *had compassion on* **mercied** thee.
20 And he departed,
and began to *publish* **preach** in Decapolis
how great things Jesus **as much as Yah Shua**
had done for him:
and all *men* did marvel.

YAIR'S DAUGHTERLING IN HER FINAL EXTREMITY

21 And when *Jesus* **Yah Shua**
was passed *over* **through** again by *ship* **sailer**
unto the other side,
much people **vast multitudes** gathered unto him:
and he was nigh unto the sea.
22 And, behold, there cometh
one of the *rulers of the synagogue* **synagogue archs**,
Jairus **Yair** by name;
and when he saw him, he fell at his feet,
23 And besought him *greatly* **much**, *saying* **wording**,
My *little daughter* **daughterling**
lieth at the point of death **is in her final extremity**:
I pray thee, come and *lay* **put** thy hands on her,
that she may be *healed* **saved**; and she shall live.
24 And *Jesus* **Yah Shua** went with him;
and *much people* **vast multitudes** followed him,
and thronged him.

YAH SHUA HEALS A FLUX

25 And a *certain* woman,
which had *an issue* **a flux** of blood twelve years,
26 And had suffered *many things* **much**
by many *physicians* **healers**,
and had spent all that she had,
and *was nothing bettered* **benefited naught**,
but rather grew worse,
27 When she had heard *of Jesus* **about Yah Shua**,
came in the *press* **multitude** behind,
and touched his garment.
28 For she *said* **worded**,
If I may touch but his clothes, I shall be *whole* **saved**.
29 And straightway
the fountain of her blood was dried *up*;
and she *felt* **knew** in her body
that she was healed of that *plague* **scourge**.
30 And *Jesus immediately* **Yah Shua straightway**
knowing in himself
that *virtue* **dynamis** had gone out of him,
turned him about in the *press* **multitude**,
and *said* **worded**, Who touched my clothes?
31 And his disciples *said* **worded** unto him,
Thou *seest* **observest** the multitude thronging thee,
and *sayest* **wordest** thou, Who touched me?
32 And he looked round about
to see her that had done this *thing*.
33 But the woman *fearing* **awing** and trembling,
knowing what *was done* **became** in her,
came and *fell down* **prostrated** before him,
and *told* **said to** him all the truth.
34 And he said unto her, Daughter,
thy *faith* **trust** hath *made* **saved** thee *whole*;
go in *peace* **shalom**, and be whole of thy *plague* **scourge**.

YAIR'S DAUGHTERLING ARISES

35 While he yet spake,
there came
from the *ruler* **arch** of the *synagogue's house* **synagogue**
certain which said **wording**, Thy daughter is dead:
why *troublest* **harrassest** thou the *Master* **Doctor**
any further?
36 *As soon as Jesus* **Straightway when Yah Shua**
heard the word that was spoken,
he *saith* **wordeth** unto the *ruler* **arch** of the synagogue,
Be **Awe** not *afraid*, only *believe* **trust**.
37 And he *suffered* **allowed**
no *man* **one** to follow **with** him,
save Peter **except Petros**, and *James* **Yaaqovos**,
and *John* **Yahn** the brother of *James* **Yaaqovos.**
38 And he cometh to the house
of the *ruler* **arch** of the *synagogue* **synagogue**,
and *seeth* **observeth** the tumult,
and them that wept and *wailed greatly* **halooed much**.
39 And when he *was come in* **entered**,
he *saith* **wordeth** unto them,
Why make ye this *ado* **tumult**, and weep?
the *damsel* **child** is not dead, but sleepeth.

YAIR'S DAUGHTERLING LIVES

40 And they *laughed* **ridiculed** him *to scorn*.
But when he had *put* **cast** them all out,
he taketh the father and the mother of the *damsel* **child**,
and them that were with him,
and entereth in
where the *damsel was lying* **child reposed**.
41 And he *took* **overpowered** the *damsel* **child**
by the hand,
and *said* **wordeth** unto her, *Talitha cumi* **Taleh quwm**;
which is, being *interpreted* **translated**,
Damsel **Maiden**, I *say* **word** unto thee, arise.
42 And straightway the *damsel* **maiden** arose,
and walked;
for she was of the age of twelve years.
And they were *astonished* **astounded**
with a *great astonishment* **mega ecstasis**.
43 And he charged them *straitly* **much**
that no *man* **one** should know it;
and *commanded* **said**
that something should be given her to eat.

YAH SHUA DISHONOURED IN HIS FATHERLAND

6 And he went out from thence,
and came into his *own country* **fatherland**;
and his disciples follow him.
2 And when the *sabbath day* **shabbath**
was come **became**,
he began to *teach* **doctrinate** in the synagogue:
and many hearing him were astonished, *saying* **wording**,
From whence hath this man these *things*?
and what wisdom is this which is given unto him,
that even such *mighty works* **dynamis**
are *wrought* **become** by his hands?
3 Is not this the carpenter, the son of *Mary* **Miryam**,

the brother of *James* **Yaaqovos**, and *Joses* **Yoses**,
and of *Juda* **Yah Hudah**, and *Simon* **Shimon**?
and are not his sisters here with us?
And they were *offended* **scandalized** at him.
4 But *Jesus said* **Yah Shua worded** unto them,
A prophet is not *without honour* **dishonoured**,
but **except** in his *own country* **fatherland**,
and among his own kin, and in his own house.
5 And he could there do no *mighty work* **dynamis**,
save **except** that
he *laid* **put** his hands upon a few sick folk,
and *healed* **cured** them.
6 And he marvelled
because of their *unbelief* **trustlessness**.
And he went round about the villages,
teaching **doctrinating**.

THE TWELVE ARE AUTHORIZED OVER DEMONS

7 And he called unto him the twelve,
and began to *send* **apostolize** them *forth* by two and two;
and gave them *power* **authority**
over *unclean* **impure** spirits;
8 And *commanded* **evangelized** them
that they should take *nothing* **naught**
for their *journey* **way**,
save **except** a *staff* **rod** only;
no *scrip* **wallet**, no bread,
no *money* **copper** in their *purse* **girdle**:
9 But be *shod* **tied** with sandals;
and not *put on* **endue** two *coats* **tunics**.
10 And he *said* **worded** unto them,
In what place soever ye enter into an house,
there abide till ye depart from that place.
11 And *whosoever shall not*
as many as ever shall neither receive you,
nor hear you,
when ye depart thence, shake off the dust under your feet
for a *testimony* **witness** against them.
Verily I say **Amen! I word** unto you,
It shall be more tolerable
for *Sodom* **Sedom** and *Gomorrha* **Amorah**
in the day of judgment,
than for that city.
12 And they went out,
and preached that men should repent.
13 And they cast out many *devils* **demons**,
and anointed with **olive** oil many that were sick,
and *healed* **cured** them.

HEROD FEARS YAHN THE BAPTIZER

14 And *king* **sovereign** Herod heard of him;
(for his name *was* **became** spread *abroad* **manifestly**:)
and he *said* **worded**,
That *John* **Yahn** the *Baptist* **Baptizer**
was risen from the dead,
and therefore *mighty works* **dynamis**
do shew forth themselves **energizeth** in him.
15 Others *said* **worded**, That it is *Elias* **Eli Yah**.
And others *said* **worded**, That it is a prophet,
or as one of the prophets.
16 But when Herod heard thereof, he said,
It **This** is *John* **Yahn**, whom I beheaded:
he is risen from the dead.
17 For Herod himself had *sent forth* **apostolized**
and *laid hold upon John* **overpowered Yahn**,
and bound him in *prison* **the guardhouse**
for Herodias' sake,
his brother *Philip's wife* **Philippos' woman**:
for he had married her.
18 For *John* **Yahn** had *said* **worded** unto Herod,
It is not *lawful* **allowed** for thee
to have thy brother's *wife* **woman**.
19 Therefore
Herodias *had a quarrel against* **begrudged** him,
and *would* **willed to** have *killed* **slaughtered** him;
but she could not:
20 For Herod *feared John* **awed Yahn**,
knowing that he was a just man and an holy,
and *observed* **regarded** him;
and when he heard him, he did *many things* **much**,
and heard him *gladly* **with pleasure**.

HEROD'S BIRTHDAY SUPPER

21 And when *a convenient* **an opportune** day
was come **became**,
that Herod on his birthday
made **prepared** a supper to his *lords* **magistrates**,
high captains **chiliarchs**,
and *chief estates* **preeminent** of *Galilee* **Galiyl**;
22 And when the daughter of the said Herodias
came in **entered**, and danced,
and pleased Herod and them that *sat* **reposed** with him,
the *king* **sovereign** said unto the *damsel* **maiden**,
Ask of me whatsoever thou *wilt* **willest**,
and I *will* **shall** give it thee.
23 And he *sware* **oathed** unto her,
Whatsoever thou shalt ask of me, I *will* **shall** give it thee,
unto the half of my *kingdom* **sovereigndom**.
24 And she went forth, and said unto her mother,
What shall I ask?
And she said,
The head of *John* **Yahn** the *Baptist* **Baptizer**.
25 And she *came in* **entered** straightway
with *haste* **diligence**
unto the *king* **sovereign** and asked, *saying* **wording**,
I will that thou give me
by and by in **immediately on** a *charger* **platter**
the head of *John* **Yahn** the *Baptist* **Baptizer**.
26 And the *king* **sovereign**
was exceeding sorry **became extremely sorrowful**;
yet for his oath's sake,
and for their sakes which *sat* **reposed** with him,
he *would* **willed to** not *reject her* **set her aside**.

HEROD HAS YAHN THE BAPTIZER BEHEADED

27 And *immediately* **straightway**
the *king* **sovereign**
sent an executioner **apostolized a speculator**,
and *commanded* **ordered** his head to be brought:
and he went
and beheaded him in the *prison* **guardhouse**,
28 And brought his head *in* **on** a *charger* **platter**,
and gave it to the *damsel* **maiden**:
and the *damsel* **maiden** gave it to her mother.
29 And when his disciples heard of it,
they came and took *up* his *corpse* **carcase**,
and *laid* **placed** it in a tomb.

APOSTLES EVANGELIZE TO YAH SHUA

30 And the apostles
gathered themselves together unto *Jesus* **Yah Shua**,
and *told* **evangelized** him all *things*,
both *what* **as much as** they had done,
and *what* **as much as** they had *taught* **doctrinated**.
31 And he said unto them,
Come ye yourselves apart into a *desert* **desolate** place,
and rest a *while* **little**:
for there were many coming and going,
and they had no *leisure* **opportunity** so much as to eat.
32 And they departed into a *desert* **desolate** place
by *ship* **sailer** privately.
33 And the *people* **multitude** saw them *departing* **going**,
and many knew him,
and *ran afoot* **crushed together** thither out of all cities,
and *outwent* **preceded** them,
and came together unto him.

YAH SHUA FEEDS FIVE THOUSAND

34 And *Jesus* **Yah Shua**, when he came out,
saw *much people* **vast multitudes**,
and
was moved with compassion **had a sympathetic spleen**
toward them,
because they were as sheep not having a shepherd:
and he began
to *teach* **doctrinate** them *many things* **much**.
35 And when the *day* **hour**
was now far **became already much** spent,
his disciples came unto him, and *said* **worded**,
This is a *desert* **desolate** place,
and *now* **already** the *time* **hour** is *far* **much** passed:
36 *Send* **Release** them *away*,
that they may go
into the *country round about* **surrounding fields**,

and into the villages, and *buy* **market** themselves bread:
for they have *nothing* **naught** to eat.
37 He answered and said unto them, Give ye them to eat.
And they *say* **word** unto him,
shall we go and *buy* **market**
two hundred *pennyworth* **denarion** of bread,
and give them to eat?
38 He *saith* **wordeth** unto them,
How many *loaves* **breads** have ye? go and see.
And when they knew, they *say* **word**,
Five, and two fishes.
39 And he *commanded* **ordered** them
to make all *sit down* **recline**
by companies **symposium by symposium**
upon the green *grass* **herbage**.
40 And they *sat down in ranks* **reposed row by row**,
by hundreds, and by fifties.
41 And when he had taken
the five *loaves* **breads** and the two fishes,
he looked *up* to the heaven,
and *blessed* **eulogized**, and brake the *loaves* **breads**,
and gave them to his disciples to set *before* **by** them;
and the two fishes divided he among them all.
42 And they did all eat, and were *filled* **fed**.
43 And they took *up* twelve baskets full of the fragments,
and of the fishes.
44 And they that did eat of the *loaves* **breads**
were about five thousand men.

YAH SHUA WALKS ON THE SEA

45 And straightway
he *constrained* **compelled** his disciples
to *get* **embark** into the *ship* **sailer**,
and to go to the other side
before unto *Bethsaida* **Beth Sayad**,
while he *sent away* **released** the *people* **multitudes**.
46 And when he had *sent* **bid** them *away* **farewell**,
he departed into a mountain to pray.
47 And when *even was come* **evening became**,
the *ship* **sailer** was in the midst of the sea,
and he alone on the land.
48 And he saw them *toiling* **torturing** in rowing;
for the wind was contrary unto them:
and about the fourth *watch* **guard** of the night
he cometh unto them, walking upon the sea,
and *would* **willed to** have passed by them.
49 But when they saw him walking upon the sea,
they *supposed* **thought** it had been a *spirit* it **phantasm**,
and *cried out* **screamed**:
50 For they all saw him, and were troubled.
And *immediately* **straightway** he *talked* **spoke** with them,
and *saith* **wordeth** unto them,
Be of good cheer: it is I; **Courage! I AM!**
be not afraid **Awe not**.
51 And he *went up* **ascended** unto them
into the *ship* **sailer**;
and the wind *ceased* **relaxed**:
and they were *sore amazed* **astounded** in themselves
beyond measure **very superabundantly**,
and *wondered* **marvelled**.
52 For they *considered* **comprehended** not
the miracle of the loaves **about the breads**:
for their heart was *hardened* **petrified**.

YAH SHUA SAVES AT KINNORETH

53 And when they had passed over,
they came into the land of *Gennesaret* **Kinneroth**,
and *drew to the shore* **moored**.
54 And when they were come out of the *ship* **sailer**,
straightway they knew him,
55 And ran through that whole region round about,
and began to carry about in *beds* **pads**
those that were *sick* **ill**,
where they heard he was.
56 And whithersoever he entered,
into villages, or cities, or *country* **fields**,
they *laid* **placed** the *sick* **frail** in the *streets* **markets**,
and besought him that they might touch
if it were but the *border* **edge** of his garment:
and as many as touched him
were *made whole* **ever saved**.

YAH SHUA ADMONISHES THE PHARISEES

7 Then *came* **gathered** together unto him the Pharisees,
and *certain* **some** of the scribes,
which came from *Jerusalem* **Yeru Shalem**.
2 And when they saw some of his disciples eat bread
with *defiled* **profane**,
that is *to say*, with unwashen hands,
they found fault.
3 For the Pharisees, and all the *Jews* **Yah Hudiym**,
except **unless** they wash their hands *oft* **to the fist**,
eat not,
holding **empowering** the tradition of the elders.
4 And when they come from the market,
except **unless** they *wash* **baptize**, they eat not.
And many other *things* there be,
which they have received to *hold* **empower**,
as the *washing* **baptism** of cups, and pots,
brasen vessels **copperware**, and of *tables* **beds**.
5 Then the Pharisees and scribes asked him,
Why walk not thy disciples
according to the tradition of the elders,
but eat bread with unwashen hands?
6 He answered and said unto them,
Well hath *Esaias* **Yesha Yah** prophesied
of **concerning** you hypocrites,
as it is *written* **scribed**,
This people honoureth me with their lips,
but their heart is far from me.
7 Howbeit in vain do they *worship* **venerate** me,
teaching **doctrinating** for doctrines
the *commandments* **misvoth** of *men* **humanity**.
Yesha Yah 29:13
8 For *laying aside* **forsaking**
the *commandment* **misvoth** of *God* **Elohim**,
ye *hold* **empower** the tradition of *men* **humanity**,
as the *washing* **baptism** of pots and cups:
and many other such like *things* ye do.
9 And he *said* **worded** unto them,
Full well ye *reject* **set aside**
the *commandment* **misvah** of *God* **Elohim**,
that ye may *keep* **guard** your own tradition.
10 For *Moses* **Mosheh** said,
Honour thy father and thy mother;
and, Whoso *curseth* **vilifieth** father or mother,
let him die the death:
Exodus 20:12, 21:17, Leviticus 20:9
11 But ye *say* **word**,
If a *man* **human** shall say to his father or mother,
It is Corban **Qurban**,
that is to say **which is**, *a gift* **Oblation**,
by whatsoever
thou mightest be *profited* **benefited** by *me*;
he shall be free.
12 And ye *suffer* **allow** him no more
to do ought for his father or his mother;
13 *Making* **Invalidating** the word of *God* **Elohim**
of none effect
through your tradition,
which ye have *delivered* **betrayed**:
and many such like *things* do ye.

ENTERING IN VS PROCEEDING OUT

14 And when he had called all the *people* **multitude**
unto him, he *said* **worded** unto them,
Hearken unto me *every one* **all** of you,
and *understand* **comprehend**:
15 There is *nothing* **naught** from without a *man* **human**,
that entering into him can *defile* **profane** him:
but *the things* **those** which *come* **proceed** out of him,
those are they that *defile* **profane** the *man* **human**.
16 If any man have ears to hear, let him hear.
17 And when he was entered into the house
from the *people* **multitude**,
his disciples asked him concerning the parable.
18 And he *saith* **wordeth** unto them,
Are ye *so* **thus**
without understanding **uncomprehending** also?
Do ye not *perceive* **comprehend**,
that *whatsoever thing* **all that** from without
entereth **into** the *man* **human**,

it cannot *defile* **profane** him;
19 Because it entereth not into his heart,
but into the belly,
and *goeth out* **proceedeth** into the *draught* **privy**,
purging **purifying** all *meats* **food**?
20 And he *said* **worded**,
That which *cometh* **departeth** out of the *man* **human**,
that *defileth* **profaneth** the *man* **human**.
21 For from within, out of the heart of *men* **humanity**,
proceed evil thoughts, adulteries,
fornications **whoredoms**, murders,
22 Thefts, *covetousness* **avarices**,
wickedness **evils**, deceit, lasciviousness,
an evil eye **maliciousness**, blasphemy,
pride, *foolishness* **thoughtlessness**:
23 All these *evil things* **maliciousnesses**
come **proceed** from within,
and *defile* **profane** the *man* **human**.

YAH SHUA CASTS OUT A DEMON

24 And from thence he arose,
and went into the borders of *Tyre* **Sor** and Sidon,
and entered into an house,
and *would have* **willed that** no *man* **one** know it:
but he could not be hid.
25 For a *certain* woman,
whose *young daughter* **daughterling**
had an *unclean* **impure** spirit,
heard *of* **concerning** him,
and came and *fell* **prostrated** at his feet:
26 The woman was a *Greek* **Hellenist**,
a *Syrophenician* **Syriaiy** by *nation* **genos**;
and she *besought* **asked** him
that he *would* **should** cast forth the *devil* **demon**
out of her daughter.
27 But *Jesus* **Yah Shua** said unto her,
Let **Allow** the children first be *filled* **fed**:
for it is not *meet* **good** to take the children's bread,
and to cast it unto the *dogs* **puppies**.
28 And she answered and *said* **worded** unto him,
Yes, *Lord* **Adonay**:
yet **indeed** the *dogs* **puppies** under the table
eat of the children's crumbs.
29 And he said unto her, For this *saying* **word** go thy way;
the *devil* **demon** is gone out of thy daughter.
30 And when she was come to her house,
she found the *devil* **demon** gone out,
and her daughter *laid* **put** upon the bed.
31 And again, departing from the *coasts* **boundries**
of *Tyre* **Sor** and Sidon,
he came unto the sea of *Galilee* **Galiyl**,
through the midst of the *coasts* **boundries** of Decapolis.

YAH SHUA HEALS A TONGUETIED MUTE

32 And they bring unto him one that was *deaf* **mute**,
and *had an impediment in his speech*
could hardly speak;
and they beseech him to put his hand upon him.
33 And he took him aside from the multitude,
and put his fingers into his ears,
and he spit, and touched his tongue;
34 And looking *up* to the heaven, he sighed,
and *saith* **wordeth** unto him, Ephphatha,
that is, Be opened.
35 And straightway his ears were opened,
and the *string* **bond** of his tongue was *loosed* **released**,
and he spake *plain* **straightforwardly**.
36 And he charged them
that they should *tell no man* **say to no one**:
but *the more* **as much as** he charged them,
so much the more *a great deal* **superabundantly**
they *published it* **preached**;
37 And were
beyond measure **superabundantly** astonished,
saying **wording**, He hath done all *things* well:
he maketh both the *deaf* **mute** to hear,
and the *dumb* **speechless** to speak.

YAH SHUA FEEDS FOUR THOUSAND

8 In those days the multitude being very great,
and having *nothing* **naught** to eat,
Jesus **Yah Shua** called his disciples unto him,
and *saith* **wordeth** unto them,
2 I have *compassion* **a sympathetic spleen**
on the multitude,
because
they have *now been* **already abode** with me three days,
and have *nothing* **naught** to eat:
3 And if I *send* **release** them *away* fasting
to their own houses,
they *will* **shall** faint by the way:
for *divers* **some** of them came from far.
4 And his disciples answered him,
From whence can *a man satisfy* **anyone fill** these men
with bread here in the wilderness?
5 And he asked them, How many *loaves* **breads** have ye?
And they said, Seven.
6 And he *commanded* **evangelized** the *people* **multitude**
to *sit down* **repose** on the *ground* **soil**:
and he took the seven *loaves* **breads**,
and *gave thanks* **eucharistized** and brake,
and gave to his disciples to set *before* **by** them;
and they did set them
before **forth to** the *people* **multitude**.
7 And they had a few small fishes:
and he *blessed* **eulogized**,
and *commanded* **said** to set them also *before them* **forth**.
8 So they did eat, and were *filled* **fed**:
and they took *up* of the
broken meat that was left **superabundant fragments**,
seven baskets.
9 And they that had eaten were about four thousand:
and he *sent* **released** them *away*.
10 And straightway
he *entered* **embarked** into a *ship* **sailer**
with his disciples,
and came into the parts of Dalmanutha.

THE PHARISEES SEEK A SIGN

11 And the Pharisees came forth,
and began to *question* **dispute** with him,
seeking of him a sign from **the** heaven,
tempting **testing** him.
12 And he sighed deeply in his spirit, and *saith* **wordeth**,
Why doth this generation seek after a sign?
Verily I say **Amen! I word** unto you,
There shall no sign be given unto this generation.

YAH SHUA INTERPRETS THE PARABLE OF THE FERMENTATION

13 And he *left* **released** them,
and *entering* **embarking** into the *ship* **sailer** again
departed to the other side.
14 Now the disciples had forgotten to take bread,
neither had they in the *ship* **sailer** with them
more than **except** one *loaf* **bead**.
15 And he charged them, *saying* **wording**, *Take heed* **See**,
beware **observe** of the *leaven* **fermentation**
of the Pharisees,
and of the *leaven* **fermentation** of Herod.
16 And they reasoned among *themselves* **one another**,
saying **wording**, because we have no bread.
17 And when *Jesus* **Yah Shua** knew it,
he *saith* **wordeth** unto them,
Why reason ye, because ye have no bread?
perceive **comprehend** ye not yet,
neither *understand* **comprehend?**
have ye your heart yet *hardened* **petrified**?
18 Having eyes, *see* **observe** ye not?
and having ears, hear ye not? and do ye not remember?
19 When I brake the five *loaves* **breads**
among five thousand,
how many baskets full of fragments took ye *up*?
They *say* **word** unto him, Twelve.
20 And when the seven among four thousand,
how many baskets full of fragments took ye *up*?
And they said, Seven.
21 And he *said* **worded** unto them,
How is it that ye do not *understand* **comprehend**?

YAH SHUA HEALS A BLIND

22 And he cometh to *Bethsaida* **Beth Sayad**;
and they bring a blind *man* unto him,
and besought him to touch him.
23 And he took the blind *man* by the hand,
and led him out of the *town* **village**;
and when he had spit on his eyes,

and put his hands upon him,
he asked him if he *saw* **observed** ought.
24 And he looked *up*, and *said* **worded**,
I *see men* **observe humans** as trees, walking.
25 *After that* **Then** he put his hands again upon his eyes,
and made him look *up*: and he was restored,
and *saw every man* **looked at everyone** clearly.
26 And he *sent* **apostolized** him *away* to his house,
saying **wording**, Neither *go into* **enter** the *town* **village**,
nor *tell* **say** it to any in the *town* **village**.

PETROS' WITNESS CONCERNING YAH SHUA

27 And *Jesus* **Yah Shua** went out, and his disciples,
into the *towns* **villages**
of *Caesarea Philippi* **Kaisaria Philippos**:
and *by* **on** the way he asked his disciples,
saying **wording** unto them,
Whom do *men say that I am* **humanity speak me to be**?
28 And they answered, *John* **Yahn** the *Baptist* **Baptizer**;
but *some* **others** say, *Elias* **Eli Yah**;
and others, One of the prophets.
29 And he *saith* **wordeth** unto them,
But whom *say ye that I am* **word ye me to be**?
And *Peter* **Petros** answereth and *saith* **wordeth** unto him,
Thou art the *Christ* **Messiah**.
30 And he *charged* **admonished** them
that they should *tell* **word** no *man of* **one about** him.

YAH SHUA PROPHESIES HIS DEATH AND RESURRECTION

31 And he began to *teach* **doctrinate** them,
that the Son of *man* **humanity**
must suffer *many things* **much**,
and be *rejected* **disapproved** of the elders,
and of the *chief priests,* **archpriests** and scribes,
and be *killed* **slaughtered**, and after three days rise again.
32 And he spake that *saying openly* **word boldly**.
And *Peter* **Petros** took him, and began to rebuke him.
33 But when he had turned about
and *looked on* **saw** his disciples,
he rebuked *Peter* **Petros**, *saying* **wording**,
Get thee behind me, Satan:
for thou *savourest* **mindest** not
the things **those** that be of *God* **Elohim**,
but *the things* **those** that be of *men* **humanity**.

ON LOSING THE SOUL TO SAVE THE SOUL

34 And when he had called the *people* **multitude**
unto him with his disciples also, he said unto them,
Whosoever come after me, let him deny himself,
and take *up* his *cross* **stake**, and follow me.
35 For whosoever *will* **willeth to** save his *life* **soul**
shall lose it;
but whosoever shall lose his *life* **soul** for my sake
and the *gospel's* **evangelism's**,
the **this** same shall save it.
36 For what shall it *profit* **benefit** a *man* **human**,
if he shall gain the whole *world* **cosmos**,
and lose his own soul?
37 Or what shall a *man* **human** give
in exchange for his soul?
38 Whosoever *therefore* **indeed**
shall be ashamed of me and of my words
in this adulterous and sinful generation;
of him also shall the Son of *man* **humanity** be ashamed,
when he cometh
in the glory of his Father with the holy angels.

YAH SHUA'S METAMORPHOSIS

9 And he *said* **worded** unto them,
Verily I say **Amen! I word** unto you,
That there be some of them that stand here,
which shall not taste of death,
till they have seen
the *kingdom* **sovereigndom** of *God* **Elohim**
come *with power* **in dynamis**.
2 And after six days *Jesus* **Yah Shua** taketh with him
Peter **Petros**, and *James* **Yaaqovos**, and *John* **Yahn**,
and *leadeth* **bringeth** them *up* into an high mountain
apart by themselves **alone**:
and he was *transfigured* **metamorphosed**
before **in front of** them.
3 And his raiment became *shining* **gleaming**,
exceeding **very** white as snow;
so as no fuller on earth can white them.
4 And there appeared unto them
Elias **Eli Yah** with *Moses* **Mosheh**:
and they were talking with *Jesus* **Yah Shua**.
5 And *Peter* **Petros** answered
and *said* **worded** to *Jesus* **Yah Shua**,
Master **Rabbi**, it is good for us to be here:
and let us make three tabernacles;
one for thee,
and one for *Moses* **Mosheh**, and one for *Elias* **Eli Yah**.
6 For he *wist* **knew** not what to *say* **speak**;
for they were *sore afraid* **utterly frightened**.
7 And there *was* **became** a cloud
that overshadowed them:
and a voice came out of the cloud, *saying* **wording**,
This is my beloved Son: hear him.
8 And suddenly, when they had looked round about,
they saw no *man* **one** any more,
save Jesus **but Yah Shua** only with themselves.
9 And as they came down from the mountain,
he charged them
that they should *tell* **declare to** no *man* **one**
what *things* they had seen,
till **except when** the Son of *man* **humanity**
were risen from the dead.
10 And they *kept* **empowered** that *saying* **word**
with themselves,
questioning one with another **disputing**
what the rising from the dead should mean.
11 And they asked him, *saying* **wording**,
Why *say* **word** the scribes
that *Elias* **Eli Yah** must first come?
12 And he answered and *told* **said to** them,
Elias verily **Eli Yah indeed** cometh first,
and restoreth all *things*;
and how it is *written* **scribed**
of the Son of *man* **humanity**,
that he must suffer *many things* **much**,
and be set at nought.
13 But I *say* **word** unto you,
That *Elias* **Eli Yah** is indeed come,
and they have done unto him
whatsoever **as much as** they *listed* **willed**,
exactly as it is *written* **scribed** of him.
Malachi 4:5, 6

YAH SHUA CASTS OUT A DEMON

14 And when he came to his disciples,
he saw a *great* **vast** multitude about them,
and the scribes *questioning* **disputing** with them.
15 And straightway all the *people* **multitude**,
when they *beheld* **saw** him,
were *greatly amazed* **utterly astonished**,
and running to him saluted him.
16 And he asked the scribes,
What *question* **dispute** ye with them?
17 And one of the multitude answered and said,
Master **Doctor**, I have brought unto thee my son,
which hath a *dumb* **speechless** spirit;
18 And wheresoever he *taketh* **overtaketh** him,
he teareth him:
and he foameth, and gnasheth with his teeth,
and *pineth* **withereth** away:
and I spake to thy disciples that they should cast him out;
and they could not.
19 He answereth him, and *saith* **wordeth**,
O *faithless* **trustless** generation,
how long **until when** shall I be with you?
how long **until when** shall I *suffer* **tolerate** you?
bring him unto me.
20 And they brought him unto him:
and when he saw him,
straightway the spirit *tare* **convulsed** him;
and he fell on the *ground* **soil**, and wallowed foaming.
21 And he asked his father,
How *long is it ago* **much time**
since this *came unto* **became** him?
And he said, *Of a child* **Since childhood**.
22 And *ofttimes* **often** it hath cast him into the fire,
and into the waters, to destroy him:
but if thou canst do *any thing* **aught**,
have *compassion* **a sympathetic spleen** on us,

and help us.
23 *Jesus* **Yah Shua** said unto him,
If thou canst *believe* **trust**,
all *things* are possible to him that *believeth* **trusteth**.
24 And straightway the father of the child cried out,
and *said* **worded** with tears, *Lord* **Adonay**, I *believe* **trust**;
help thou *mine unbelief* **my trustlessness**.
25 When *Jesus* **Yah Shua** saw
that the *people* **multitude** came running together,
he rebuked the *foul* **impure** spirit,
saying **wording** unto him,
Thou *dumb* **speechless** and deaf spirit,
I *charge* **order** thee,
come out of him, and enter no more into him.
26 And *the spirit* **having** cried,
and *rent* **having convulsed** him *sore* **much**,
and came out of him: and he *was* **became** as one dead;
insomuch that many *said* **worded**, He is dead.
27 But *Jesus* **Yah Shua**
took **overpowered** him by the hand,
and lifted him *up*; and he arose.
28 And when he was come into the house,
his disciples asked him privately,
Why could not we cast him out?
29 And he said unto them,
This *kind* **genos** can come forth by *nothing* **naught**,
but **except** by prayer and fasting.

Yah Shua Prophesies His Death and Resurrection

30 And they departed thence,
and passed through *Galilee* **Galiyl**;
and he *would* **willed**
not that any man **that no one** should know it.
31 For he *taught* **doctrinated** his disciples,
and *said* **worded** unto them,
The Son of *man* **humanity**
is *delivered* **betrayed** into the hands of men,
and they shall *kill* **slaughter** him;
and after that he is *killed* **slaughtered**,
he shall rise the third day.
32 But they *understood* **knew** not that *saying* **rhema**,
and were *afraid* **awestricken** to ask him.

The First are Final

33 And he came to *Capernaum* **Kaphar Nachum**:
and *being* **becoming** in the house he asked them,
What was it that ye *disputed* **reasoned** among yourselves
by **on** the way?
34 But they *held their peace* **hushed**:
for *by* **on** the way they had *disputed* **reasoned**
among *themselves* **one another**,
who should be the greatest.
35 And he sat down, and *called* **voiced out to** the twelve,
and *saith* **wordeth** unto them,
If any *man desire* **one willeth** to be first,
the same shall be *last* **final** of all,
and *servant* **minister** of all.
36 And he took a child, and set him in the midst of them:
and when he had taken him in his arms,
he said unto them,
37 Whosoever shall receive one of such children
in my name,
receiveth me:
and whosoever shall receive me,
receiveth not me, but him that *sent* **apostolized** me.
38 And *John* **Yahn** answered him, *saying* **wording**,
Master **Doctor**,
we saw one casting out *devils* **demons** in thy name,
and he followeth not us:
and we forbad him, because he followeth not us.
39 But *Jesus* **Yah Shua** said, Forbid him not:
for there is no *man* **one**
which shall do *a miracle* **dynamis** in my name,
that can *lightly speak evil of* **quickly vilify** me.
40 For he that is not against us is on our part.

Never Scandalize

41 For whosoever shall give you a cup of water to drink
in my name,
because ye belong to *Christ* **Messiah**,
verily I say **Amen! I word** unto you,
he shall not lose his reward.
42 And whosoever shall *offend* **scandalize**
one of these little ones that *believe* **trust** in me,
it is *better* **good** for him
that a millstone were hanged *about* **around** his neck,
and he were cast into the sea.

Amputate When Necessary

43 And if thy hand *offend* **scandalize** thee,
cut it off **amputate**:
it is *better* **good** for thee to enter into life maimed,
than having two hands to go into
hell **Gay Hinnom/the valley of burning**,
into the fire *that never shall be quenched* **unquenchable**:
44 Where their *worm* **maggot** dieth not,
and the fire is not quenched.
45 And if thy foot *offend* **scandalize** thee,
cut it off **amputate**:
it is *better* **good** for thee to enter *halt* **lame** into life,
than having two feet to be cast into
hell **Gay Hinnom/the valley of burning**,
into the fire *that never shall be quenched* **unquenchable**:
46 Where their *worm* **maggot** dieth not,
and the fire is not quenched.
47 And if thine eye *offend* **scandalize** thee,
pluck **cast** it out:
it is *better* **good** for thee
to enter into the *kingdom* **sovereigndom** of *God* **Elohim**
with one eye **one—eyed**,
than having two eyes to be cast into
hell **Gay Hinnom/the valley of burning** fire:
48 Where their *worm* **maggot** dieth not,
and the fire is not quenched.
49 For every one shall be salted with fire,
and every sacrifice shall be salted with salt.
50 Salt is good:
but if the salt *have lost his saltness* **become saltless**,
wherewith *will* **shall** ye season it?
Have salt in yourselves,
and *have peace* **shalam** one with another.

Marriage and Divorce

10 And he arose from thence,
and cometh into the *coasts* **boundaries**
of *Judaea* **Yah Hudah**
by the *farther* **other** side of *Jordan* **Yarden**:
and the *people resort* **multitude go** unto him again;
and, as he was *wont* **accustomed**,
he *taught* **doctrinated** them again.
2 And the Pharisees came to him, and asked him,
Is it *lawful* **allowed**
for a man to *put away* **release** his *wife* **woman**?
tempting **testing** him.
3 And he answered and said unto them,
What did *Moses command* **Mosheh misvah** you?
4 And they said, *Moses suffered* **Mosheh permitted**
to *write* **scribe** a *bill* **scroll** of *divorcement* **apostasy**,
and to *put* **release** her *away*.
5 And *Jesus* **Yah Shua** answered and said unto them,
For *the hardness of* your *heart* **hardheartedness**
he *wrote* **scribed** you this *precept* **misvah**.
6 But from the beginning of the creation
God **Elohim** made them male and female.
7 For this cause
shall a *man* **human** leave his father and mother,
and *cleave* **adhere** to his *wife* **woman**;
8 And they twain shall be one flesh:
so then they are no more twain, but one flesh.
9 What therefore
God **Elohim** hath *joined together* **co—yoked**,
let not *man put asunder* **humanity separate**.
10 And in the house his disciples asked him again
of **concerning** the same matter.
11 And he *saith* **wordeth** unto them,
Whosoever shall *put away* **release** his *wife* **woman**
and marry another,
committeth adultery **adulterizeth** against her.
12 And if a woman shall *put away* **release** her man,
and be married to another,
she *committeth adultery* **adulterizeth**.

Yah Shua Eulogizes Young Children

13 And they *brought* **offered** young children to him,
that he should touch them:
and his disciples rebuked those

that *brought* **offered** them.
14 But when *Jesus* **Yah Shua** saw it,
he *was much displeased* **indignified**, and said unto them,
Suffer **Allow** the little children to come unto me,
and forbid them not:
for of such is the *kingdom* **sovereigndom** of *God* **Elohim**.
15 *Verily I say* **Amen! I word** unto you,
Whosoever shall not receive
the *kingdom* **sovereigndom** of *God* **Elohim** as a little child,
he shall not enter therein.
16 And he took them *up* in his arms,
put his hands upon them, and *blessed* **eulogized** them.

WEALTHY BUT LOST

17 And when he *was gone forth* **departed** into the way,
there came one running, and kneeled to him,
and asked him, Good *Master* **Doctor**,
what shall I do that I may inherit eternal life?
18 And *Jesus* **Yah Shua** said unto him,
Why *callest* **wordest** thou me good?
there is none good *but* **except** one, *that is, God* **Elohim**.
19 Thou knowest the *commandments* **misvoth**,
Do not commit adultery **adulterize not**,
Do not kill **murder not**,
Do not steal **not**,
Do not bear false **pseudo** witness **not**,
Defraud not,
Honour thy father and mother.
20 And he answered and said unto him, *Master* **Doctor**,
all these have I *observed* **guarded** from my youth.
21 Then *Jesus* **Yah Shua**
beholding **looking at** him loved him,
and said unto him, One *thing* thou lackest:
go thy way, sell *whatsoever* **as much as** thou hast,
and give to the poor,
and thou shalt have treasure in heaven:
and come, take *up* the *cross* **stake**, and follow me.
22 And he was *sad* **gloomy** at that *saying* **word**,
and went away *grieved* **sorrowed**:
for he had *great* **vast** possessions.

YAH SHUA AND RICHES

23 And *Jesus* **Yah Shua** looked round about,
and *saith* **wordeth** unto his disciples,
How *hardly* **difficultly** shall they that have riches
enter into the *kingdom* **sovereigndom** of *God* **Elohim**!
24 And the disciples were astonished at his words.
But *Jesus* **Yah Shua** answereth again,
and *saith* **wordeth** unto them,
Children, how *hard* **difficult** is it
for them that *trust* **confide** in riches
to enter into the *kingdom* **sovereigndom** of *God* **Elohim**!
25 It is easier for a *camel* **rope°**
to *go* **pass** through the eye of a needle,
than for a rich man
to enter into the *kingdom* **sovereigndom** of *God* **Elohim**.

°see Lamsa

26 And they were astonished
out of measure **superabundantly**,
saying **wording** among themselves,
Who then can be saved?
27 And *Jesus* **Yah Shua** looking upon them *saith* **wordeth**,
With *men* **humanity** it is impossible,
but not with *God* **Elohim**:
for with *God* **Elohim** all *things* are possible.
28 Then *Peter* **Petros** began to *say* **word** unto him,
Lo **Behold**,
we have *left* **forsaken** all, and have followed thee.
29 And *Jesus* **Yah Shua** answered and said,
Verily I say **Amen! I word** unto you,
There is no *man* **one** that hath *left* **forsaken** house,
or brethren, or sisters, or father, or mother,
or *wife* **woman**, or children, or *lands* **fields**,
for my sake, and the *gospel's* **evangelism's**,
30 But he shall *receive* **take** an hundredfold
now in this *time* **season**,
houses,
and brethren, and sisters, and mothers, and children,
and *lands* **fields**, with persecutions;
and in the *world* **eons** to come eternal life.
31 But many that are first shall be *last* **final**;
and the *last* **final** first.

YAH SHUA PROPHESIES HIS DEATH AND RESURRECTION

32 And they were in the way
going up **ascending** to *Jerusalem* **Yeru Shalem**;
and *Jesus* **Yah Shua** went before them:
and they were *amazed* **astonished**;
and as they followed, they were *afraid* **awestricken**.
And he took again the twelve,
and began to *tell* **word to** them
what *things* should **be about to** happen unto him,
33 *Saying,* Behold,
we *go up* **ascend** to *Jerusalem* **Yeru Shalem**;
and the Son of *man* **humanity** shall be *delivered* **betrayed**
unto the *chief priests*, **archpriests** and unto the scribes;
and they shall condemn him to death,
and shall *deliver* **betray** him to the *Gentiles* **goyim**:
34 And they shall mock him, and shall scourge him,
and shall spit upon him, and shall *kill* **slaughter** him:
and the third day he shall rise again.

YAAQOVOS' AND YAHN'S SELFISH WILL

35 And *James* **Yaaqovos** and *John* **Yahn**,
the sons of *Zebedee* **Zabdi**,
come unto him, *saying* **wording**, *Master,* **Doctor**,
we *would* **will** that thou shouldest do for us
whatsoever we shall *desire* **ask**.
36 And he said unto them,
What *would* **will** ye that I should do for you?
37 They said unto him,
Grant **Give** unto us that we may sit,
one *on* **by** thy right *hand*,
and *the other on* **one by** thy left *hand*,
in thy glory.
38 But *Jesus* **Yah Shua** said unto them,
Ye know not what ye ask:
can ye drink of the cup that I drink *of*?
and be baptized
with the baptism that I am baptized *with*?
39 And they said unto him, We can.
And *Jesus* **Yah Shua** said unto them,
Ye shall indeed drink of the cup that I drink of;
and *with* the baptism that I am baptized *withal*
shall ye be baptized:
40 But to sit *on* **by** my right *hand* and *on* **by** my left *hand*
is not mine to give;
but it shall be given to them for whom it is prepared.
41 And when the ten heard it,
they began to *be much displeased* **indignify**
with James **about Yaaqovos** and *Yahn* **Yahn**.
42 But *Jesus* **Yah Shua** called them to him,
and *saith* **wordeth** unto them,
Ye know that they which are *accounted* **thought**
to rule over the *Gentiles* **goyim**
exercise lordship over **overlord** them;
and their *great* **mega** ones
exercise authority upon **authorize over** them.
43 But *so* **thus** shall it not be among you:
but whosoever *will* **willeth to** be *great* **mega** among you,
shall be your minister:
44 And whosoever of you *will* **willeth**
to be *the chiefest* **first**,
shall be servant of all.
45 For even the Son of *man* **humanity**
came not to be ministered unto,
but to minister,
and to give his *life* **soul** a *ransom* **redemption** for many.

YAH SHUA RESTORES BAR TAME'S SIGHT

46 And they came to *Jericho* **Yericho**:
and as he *went* **departed** out of *Jericho* **Yericho**
with his disciples
and *a great number of people* **an ample multitude**,
blind *Bartimaeus* **Bar Tame**, the son of *Timaeus* **Tame**,
sat by the *highway side* **wayside** begging.
47 And when he heard
that it was *Jesus of Nazareth* **Yah Shua the Nazarene**,
he began to cry out, and *say* **word**,
Jesus **Yah Shua**, thou son of David, *have* mercy *on* me.
48 And many *charged* **rebuked** him
that he should *hold his peace* **hush**:
but he cried the more *a great deal* **vastly**,
Thou son of David, *have* mercy *on* me.
49 And *Jesus* **Yah Shua** stood still,

and *commanded him to be called* **said, Voice out to him.**
And they *call* **voiced out to** the blind man,
saying **wording** unto him,
Be of good comfort **Courage**, rise;
he *calleth* **voiceth out to** thee.
50 And he, casting away his garment,
rose, and came to *Jesus* **Yah Shua**.
51 And *Jesus* **Yah Shua** answered
and *said* **worded** unto him,
What *wilt* **willest** thou that I should do unto thee?
The blind man said unto him,
Lord **Rabboni**, that I might *receive my sight* **see**.
52 And *Jesus* **Yah Shua** said unto him, Go thy way;
thy *faith* **trust** hath *made* **saved** thee *whole*.
And *immediately* **straightway** he *received his sight* **saw**,
and followed *Jesus* **Yah Shua** in the way.

YAH SHUA'S TRIUMPHANT ENTRY

11 And when they
came nigh to Jerusalem **approached Yeru Shalem**,
unto *Bethphage* **Beth Pag** and *Bethany* **Beth Ania**,
at the mount of Olives,
he *sendeth forth* **apostolizeth** two of his disciples,
2 And *saith* **wordeth** unto them,
Go your way into the village *over against* **in front of** you:
and *as soon* **straightway** as ye be entered into it,
ye shall find a colt tied, whereon never *man* **human** sat;
loose **release** him, and bring him.
3 And if any *man* **one** say unto you, Why do ye this?
say ye that *the Lord* **Adonay** hath need of him;
and straightway he *will send* **shall apostolize** him hither.
4 And they went their way,
and found the colt tied by the *door* **portal** without
in a place where two ways met;
and they *loose* **release** him.
5 And *certain* **some** of them that stood there
said **worded** unto them,
What do ye, *loosing* **releasing** the colt?
6 And they said unto them
even as *Jesus* **Yah Shua** had *commanded* **misvahed**:
and they *let* **released** them *go*.
7 And they brought the colt to *Jesus* **Yah Shua**,
and cast their garments on him; and he sat upon him.
8 And many spread their garments in the way:
and others
cut down branches **chopped spreadings** off the trees,
and *strawed* **spread** them in the way.
9 And they that went before, and they that followed,
cried, *saying* **wording**, *Hosanna* **Hoshia Na**;
Blessed is **Eulogized be** he
that cometh in the name of *the Lord* **Yah Veh**:
10 *Blessed* **Eulogized**
be the *kingdom* **sovereigndom** of our father David,
that cometh in the name of *the Lord* **Yah Veh**:
Hosanna **Hoshia Na** in the *highest* **highests**.
Psalm 118:25, 26
11 And *Jesus* **Yah Shua**
entered into *Jerusalem* **Yeru Shalem**,
and into the *temple* **priestal precinct**:
and when he had looked round about upon all *things*,
and *now the eventide was come*
already being the evening hour,
he went out unto *Bethany* **Beth Ania** with the twelve.

YAH SHUA CURSES THE BARREN FIG TREE

12 And on the morrow,
when they were come from *Bethany* **Beth Ania**,
he was hungry:
13 And seeing a fig tree afar off having leaves, he came,
if *haply* **then** he might find *any thing* **somewhat** thereon:
and when he came to it,
he found *nothing but* **naught except** leaves;
for the *time* **season** of figs was not yet.
14 And *Jesus* **Yah Shua** answered and said unto it,
no *man* **one** eat fruit of thee *hereafter* **any more**
for ever **unto the eons**.
And his disciples heard it.

YAH SHUA CLEANSES THE PRIESTAL PRECINCT

15 And they come to *Jerusalem* **Yeru Shalem**:
and *Jesus* **Yah Shua**
went into the *temple* **priestal precinct**,
and began to cast out
them that sold and *bought* **marketed**
in the *temple* **priestal precinct**,
and overthrew the tables
of the *moneychangers* **coindealers**,
and the *seats* **cathedras** of them that sold doves;
16 And *would not suffer that any man* **allowed no one**
should carry **to bear** any vessel
through the *temple* **priestal precinct**.
17 And he *taught* **doctrinated**, *saying* **wording** unto them,
Is it not *written* **scribed**,
My house shall be called of all *nations* **goyim**
the house of prayer?
but ye have made it a *den* **grotto** of *thieves* **robbers**.
Yesha Yah 56:7, Yirme Yah 7:11
18 And the scribes and *chief priests* **archpriests** eard it,
and sought how they might destroy him:
for they *feared* **awed** him, because all the *people* **multitude**
was astonished at his doctrine.
19 And when *even was come* **evening became**,
he *went* **departed** out of the city.

THE CURSED TREE WITHERED

20 And in the **early** morning, as they passed by,
they saw the fig tree dried *up* from the roots.
21 And *Peter* **Petros**
calling to remembrance **remembering**,
saith **wordeth** unto him, *Master* **Rabbi**, behold,
the fig tree which thou cursedst is withered away.

MOUNTAIN MOVING TRUST

22 And *Jesus* **Yah Shua** answering
saith **wordeth** unto them,
Have faith **Be trusting** in *God* **Elohim**.
23 For *verily I say* **Amen! I word** unto you,
That whosoever shall say unto this mountain,
Be thou removed, and be thou cast into the sea;
and shall not doubt in his heart,
but shall *believe* **trust**
that those *things* which he *saith* **wordeth**
shall *come to pass* **become**;
he shall have whatsoever he saith.
24 Therefore I *say* **word** unto you,
What things soever ye desire
All — as much as ever you ask,
when ye pray, *believe* **trust** that ye *receive* **take** them,
and ye shall have them.

FORGIVE, FORGIVEN

25 And when ye stand praying,
forgive, if ye have ought against any:
that your Father also which is in *heaven* **the heavens**
may forgive you your *trespasses* **backslidings**.
26 But if ye do not forgive,
neither *will* **shall** your Father
which is in *heaven* **the heavens**
forgive your *trespasses* **backslidings**.

YAH SHUA'S AUTHORITY IS CHALLENGED

27 And they come again to *Jerusalem* **Yeru Shalem**:
and as he was walking in the *temple* **priestal precinct**,
there come to him the *chief priests*,**archpriests**
and the scribes, and the elders,
28 And *say* **word** unto him,
By **In** what authority doest thou these *things*?
and who gave thee this authority to do these *things*?
29 And *Jesus* **Yah Shua** answered and said unto them,
I *will* **shall** also ask of you one *question* **word**,
and answer me, and I *will tell* **shall say to** you
by **in** what authority I do these *things*.
30 The baptism of *John* **Yahn**,
was it from heaven, or of *men* **humanity**? answer me.
31 And they *reasoned* **reckoned** with themselves,
saying **wording**, If we shall say, From heaven;
he *will* **shall** say, Why then did ye not *believe* **trust** him?
32 But if we shall say, Of *men* **humanity**;
they *feared* **awed** the people:
for all *men counted John* **regarded Yahn**,
that he was a prophet indeed.
33 And they answered
and *said* **worded** unto *Jesus* **Yah Shua**,
We *cannot tell* **know not**.
And *Jesus* **Yah Shua** answering *saith* **wordeth** unto them,
Neither *do I tell* **word I to** you
by **in** what authority I do these *things*.

THE PARABLE OF THE VINEYARD

12 And he began to *speak* **word** unto them
by **in** parables.
A *certain man* **human** planted a vineyard,
and set an hedge about it,
and digged a *place for the winefat* **winevat**,
and built a tower,
and *let* **leased** it *out* to *husbandmen* **cultivators**,
and went *into a far country* **abroad**.
2 And at the season
he *sent* **apostolized** to the *husbandmen* **cultivators**
a servant,
that he might *receive* **take**
from the *husbandmen* **cultivators**
of the fruit of the vineyard.
3 And they *caught* **took** him, and *beat* **flogged** him,
and *sent* **apostolized** him away empty.
4 And again he *sent* **apostolized** unto them
another servant;
and at him they cast stones,
and *wounded* **struck** him in the head,
and *sent* **apostolized** him away
shamefully **dishonourably** handled.
5 And again he *sent* **apostolized** another;
and him they *killed* **slaughtered**, and many others;
beating **indeed flogging** some,
and *killing* **slaughtering** some.
6 Having yet therefore one son, his wellbeloved,
he *sent* **apostolized** him also *last* **finally** unto them,
saying **wording**,
They *will reverence* **shall respect** my son.
7 But those *husbandmen* **cultivators**
said among themselves,
This is the heir; come, let us *kill* **slaughter** him,
and the inheritance shall be ours.
8 And they took him, and *killed* **slaughtered** him,
and cast him out of the vineyard.
9 What shall therefore *the Lord* **Adoni** of the vineyard do?
he *will* **shall** come
and destroy the *husbandmen* **cultivators**,
and *will* **shall** give the vineyard unto others.
10 And have ye not read this scripture;
The stone which the builders *rejected* **disapproved**
is become the head of the corner:
11 This was *the Lord's doing* **Yah Veh's becoming**,
and it is marvellous in our eyes?
Psalm 118:22, 23

ATTEMPTS TO SEIZE YAH SHUA

12 And they sought to *lay hold on* **overpower** him,
but *feared* **awed** the *people* **multitude**:
for they knew
that he had *spoken* **said** the parable against them:
and they *left* **forsook** him, and went their way.
13 And they *send* **apostolized** unto him
certain **some** of the Pharisees and of the Herodians,
to catch him in his words.
14 And when they were come, they *say* **word** unto him,
Master **Doctor**, we know that thou art true,
and *carest for* **concerned about** no *man* **one**:
for thou *regardest* **observest** not
the *person* **face** of *men* **humanity**,
but *teachest* **doctrinatest** the way of *God* **Elohim** in truth:
Is it *lawful* **allowed**
to give tribute to *Caesar* **the Kaisar**, or not?
15 shall we give, or shall we not give?
But he, knowing their hypocrisy, said unto them,
Why *tempt* **test** ye me?
bring me a *penny* **denarion**, that I may see it.
16 And they brought it. And he *saith* **wordeth** unto them,
Whose is this *image* **icon** and *superscription* **epigraph**?
And they said unto him, *Caesar's* **The kaisar's**.
17 And *Jesus* **Yah Shua** answering said unto them,
Render to Caesar the things that are Caesar's
Give the Kaisar's to the Kaisar,
and to God the things that are God's
and Elohim's to Elohim.
And they marvelled at him.

YAH SHUA ASKED CONCERNING THE RESURRECTION

18 Then come unto him the *Sadducees* **Sadoqiym**,
which *say* **word** there is no resurrection;
and they asked him, *saying* **wording**,
19 *Master* **Doctor**, *Moses wrote* **Mosheh scribed** unto us,
If *a man's* **one's** brother die,
and leave his *wife behind him* **woman**,
and leave no children,
that his brother should take his *wife* **woman**,
and raise *up seed* **sperma** unto his brother.
20 Now there were seven brethren:
and the first took a *wife* **woman**,
and dying left no *seed* **sperma**.
21 And the second took her, and died,
neither left he any *seed* **sperma**: and the third likewise.
22 And the seven *had* **took** her, and left no *seed* **sperma**:
last of all **finally** the woman died also.
23 In the resurrection therefore, when they shall rise,
whose *wife* **woman** shall she be of them?
for the seven had her to *wife* **woman**.
24 And *Jesus* **Yah Shua** answering said unto them,
Do ye not therefore *err* **wander**,
because ye know not the scriptures,
neither the *power* **dynamis** of *God* **Elohim**?
25 For when they shall rise from the dead,
they neither marry, nor are *given in marriage* **married off**;
but are as the angels which are in *heaven* **the heavens**.
26 And *as touching* **concerning** the dead, that they rise:
have ye not read in the *book* **scroll** of *Moses* **Mosheh**,
how in the *bush God spake* **brier Elohim said** unto him,
saying **wording**, I am the *God* **Elohim** of Abraham,
and the *God* **Elohim** of *Isaac* **Yischaq**,
and the *God* **Elohim** of *Jacob* **Yaaqov**?
27 He is not the *God* **Elohim** of the dead,
but the *God* **Elohim** of the living:
ye therefore do *greatly err* **vastly wander**.

THE GREATEST MISVAH

28 And one of the scribes came,
and having heard them *reasoning* **disputing** together,
and perceiving that he had answered them well,
asked him,
Which is the first *commandment* **misvah** of all?
29 And *Jesus* **Yah Shua** answered him,
The first of all the *commandments* **misvoth** is,
Hear, O *Israel* **Yisra El**;
the Lord **Yah Veh** our *God* **Elohim** is one *Lord* **Yah Veh**:
30 And thou shalt love *the Lord* **Yah Veh** thy *God* **Elohim**
with all thy heart, and with all thy soul,
and with all thy mind, and with all thy strength:
this is the first *commandment* **misvah**.
31 And the second is like, *namely this*,
Thou shalt love thy neighbour as thyself.
There is none other *commandment* **misvah**
greater than these.
Deuteronomy 6:4, 5, Leviticus 19:8
32 And the scribe said unto him,
Well, *Master* **Doctor**, thou hast said the truth:
for there is one *God* **Elohim**;
and there is none other but he:
33 And to love him with all the heart,
and with all the *understanding* **comprehension**,
and with all the soul, and with all the strength,
and to love his neighbour as himself,
is **much** more than all
whole *burnt offerings* **holocausts** and sacrifices.
34 And when *Jesus* **Yah Shua** saw
that he answered *discreetly* **mindfully**, he said unto him,
Thou art not far
from the *kingdom* **sovereigndom** of *God* **Elohim**.
And no *man* **one** after that durst ask him any question.

YAH SHUA ASKS THE PHARISEES

35 And *Jesus* **Yah Shua** answered and *said* **worded**,
while he *taught* **doctrinated**
in the *temple* **priestal precinct**,
How *say* **word** the scribes
that *Christ* **the Messiah** is the son of David?
36 For David himself said *by* **in** the Holy *Ghost* **Spirit**,
the LORD said **An oracle of Yah Veh**
to my *Lord* **Adonay**,
Sit thou *on* **by** my right *hand*,
till I *make* **establish** thine enemies
thy footstool **the stool of thy feet**
37 David therefore himself

calleth **wordeth** him *Lord* **Adonay**;
and whence is he then his son?
And the *common people* **vast multitude**
heard him gladly.
Psalm 110:1
38 And he *said* **worded** unto them in his doctrine,
Beware of **Observe** the scribes,
which *love* **will** to *go* **walk** in *long clothing* **stoles**,
and *love* salutations in the *marketplaces* **markets**,
39 And the *chief seats* **preeminent cathedras**
in the synagogues,
and the *uppermost rooms* **preeminent reposings**
at *feasts* **suppers**:
40 Which devour widows' houses,
and for a *pretence* **pretext** make *long* **far out** prayers:
these shall *receive* **take**
greater damnation **superabundant judgment**.

WIDOW'S OFFERING

41 And *Jesus* **Yah Shua**
sat *over against* **in front of** the treasury,
and *beheld* **observed** how the *people* **multitude**
cast *money* **copper** into the treasury:
and many that were rich cast in much.
42 And there came a *certain* poor widow,
and she *threw* **put** in two *mites* **leptons**,
which *make* **be** a *farthing* **quarter**.
43 And he called unto him his disciples,
and *saith* **wordeth** unto them,
Verily I say **Amen! I word** unto you,
That this poor widow hath cast **much** more in,
than all they which have cast into the treasury:
44 For all they did cast in of their *abundance* **surplus**;
but she of her *want* **lack** did cast in all
that — **as much as** she had,
even all her *living* **subsistence**.

YAH SHUA'S MOUNT OF OLIVES MESSAGE

13 And as he *went* **departed**
out of the *temple* **priestal precinct**,
one of his disciples *saith* **wordeth** unto him,
Master **Doctor**, *see* **behold** what manner of stones
and what *buildings* **edifices** are here!
2 And *Jesus* **Yah Shua** answering said unto him,
Seest **Observest** thou these *great buildings* **mega edifices**?
there shall not be *left* **allowed** one stone upon another,
that shall not be *thrown down* **disintegrated**.
3 And as he sat upon the mount of Olives
over against **in front of** the *temple* **priestal precinct**,
Peter **Petros** and *James* **Yaaqovos**
and *John* **Yahn** and *Andrew* **Andreas** asked him privately,
4 *Tell* **Say to** us, when shall these *things* be?
and what *shall be the* sign when all these *things*
shall be *fulfilled* **complete**?
5 And *Jesus* **Yah Shua** answering them began to *say* **word**,
Take heed **Observe,** lest any *man deceive* **one seduce** you:
6 For many shall come in my name,
saying **wording**, *I am Christ* **I AM**;
and shall *deceive* **seduce** many.
7 And when ye shall hear of wars and rumours of wars,
be **lament** ye not *troubled*:
for such *things* must *needs* be;
but the *end* **completion** shall not be yet.
8 For *nation* **goyim** shall rise against *nation* **goyim**,
and *kingdom* **sovereigndom**
against *kingdom* **sovereigndom**:
and there shall be *earthquakes* **quakes** in divers places,
and there shall be famines and troubles:
these are the beginnings of *sorrows* **travails**.
9 But *take heed* **observe** to yourselves:
for they shall *deliver* **betray** you
up to *councils* **sanhedrim**;
and in the synagogues ye shall be *beaten* **flogged**:
and ye shall be *brought* **set**
before *rulers* **governors** and *kings* **sovereigns** for my sake,
for a *testimony* **witness** against them.
10 And the *gospel* **evangelism**
must first be *published* **preached**
among all *nations* **goyim**.
11 But when they shall lead you,
and *deliver* **betray** you *up*,
take no thought beforehand **have no preanxiety**
what ye shall speak,
neither *do ye premeditate* **preanticipate**:
but whatsoever shall be given you in that hour,
that speak ye:
for it is not ye that speak, but the Holy *Ghost* **Spirit**.
12 Now the brother shall betray the brother to death,
and the father the *son* **child**;
and children shall rise *up* against their parents,
and shall cause them to be *put to death* **deathified**.
13 And ye shall be hated of all *men* for my name's sake:
but he that shall *endure* **abide** unto the *end* **completion**,
the **this** same shall be saved.

TRIBULATION

14 But when ye shall see the abomination of desolation,
spoken of **rhetorized** by *Daniel* **Dani El** the prophet,
standing where it *ought* **must** not,
(let him that readeth *understand* **comprehend**,)
then let them that be in *Judaea* **Yah Hudah**
flee to the mountains:
15 And let him that is on the housetop
not go down into the house,
neither enter therein, to take any thing out of his house:
16 And let him that is in the field
not turn back again for to take *up* his garment.
17 But woe to them that *are with child* **have in womb**,
and to them that *give suck* **nipple** in those days!
18 And pray ye that your flight
be not in the *winter* **downpour**.
19 For in those days shall be *affliction* **tribulation**,
such as *was* **became** not from the beginning
of the creation which *God* **Elohim** created
unto *this time* **now**, neither shall be.
20 And except **only**
that *the Lord* **Adonay** had shortened those days,
no flesh should be saved:
but for the *elect's* **select's** sake,
whom he hath *chosen* **selected**,
he hath shortened the days.
21 And then if any *man* **one** shall say to you,
Lo **Behold**, here *is Christ* **the Messiah**;
or, *lo* **nehold**, *he is* there;
believe **trust** him not:
22 For *false Christs* **pseudo messiahs**
and *false* **pseudo** prophets shall rise,
and shall *shew* **give** signs and *wonders* **omens**,
to seduce, if it were possible, even the *elect* **select**.
23 But *take ye heed* **observe**: behold,
I have foretold you all *things*.

POST—TRIBULATION

24 But in those days, after that tribulation,
the sun shall *be darkened* **darken**,
and the moon shall not give her *light* **brilliance**,
25 And the stars of *the* heaven shall fall,
and the *powers* **dynamis** that are in *heaven* **the heavens**
shall be shaken.
26 And then shall they see the Son of *man* **humanity**
coming in the clouds
with *great power* **vast dynamis** and glory.
27 And then shall he *send* **apostolize** his angels,
and shall gather together his *elect* **select**
from the four winds,
from the *uttermost part* **extremity** of the earth
to the *uttermost part* **extremity** of heaven.

THE FIG TREE PARABLE

28 Now learn a parable of the fig tree;
When her branch *is yet* **becometh already** tender,
and *putteth forth* **sprouteth** leaves,
ye know that summer is near:
29 *So* **Thus also** ye *in like manner*,
when ye shall see these *things come to pass* **become**,
know that it is nigh, even at the *doors* **portals**.
30 *Verily I say* **Amen! I word** unto you,
that this generation shall not pass,
till all these *things be done* **become**.
31 Heaven and earth shall pass *away*:
but my words shall not pass.
32 But *of* **concerning** that day and that hour
knoweth no *man* **one**,
no, not the angels which are in heaven, neither the Son,
but **except** the Father.

WATCH

33 *Take ye heed* **Observe**, watch and pray:
for ye know not when the *time* **season** is.
34 For *the Son of man is* as a *man* **human**
taking a far journey **having gone abroad**,
who *left* **forsook** his house,
and gave authority to his servants,
and to *every man* **each** his work,
and *commanded* **misvahed** the *porter* **portalguard** to watch.
35 Watch ye therefore:
for ye know not
when the *master* **adoni** of the house cometh,
at even, or at midnight,
or at the *cockcrowing* **roostervoice**,
or in the *early* morning:
36 Lest coming suddenly he find you sleeping.
37 And what I *say* **word** unto you I *say* **word** unto all,
Watch.
14 After two days was the *feast of the passover* **pasach**,
and *of unleavened bread* **the matsah**:
and the *chief priests* **archpriests** and the scribes sought
how they might *take* **overpower** him by *craft* **deception**,
and *put him to death* **slaughter him**.
2 But they *said* **worded**, Not on the *feast day* **celebration**,
lest **ever** there be *an uproar* **a tumult** of the people.

YAH SHUA IS ANOINTED

3 And being in *Bethany* **Beth Ania**
in the house of *Simon* **Shimon** the leper,
as he *sat at meat* **reposed**,
there came a woman having an alabaster *box*
of *ointment* **myrrh** of *spikenard* **nard**,
very precious **vastly trustworthy**;
and she *brake* **crushed** the *box* **alabaster**,
and poured it on his head.
4 And there were some
that *had indignation* **indignified** within themselves,
and *said* **worded**,
Why *was* **became** this *waste* **destruction**
of the *ointment made* **myrrh**?
5 For it might have been sold
for more than three hundred *pence* **denarion**,
and have been given to the poor.
And they *murmured* **sighed** against her.
6 And *Jesus* **Yah Shua** said,
Let **Allow** her *alone*; why *trouble* **embarrass** ye her?
she hath *wrought* **worked** a good work on me.
7 For ye have the poor with you always,
and whensoever ye will ye may do them *good* **well**:
but me ye have not always.
8 She hath done what she could:
she *is come aforehand* **hath anticipated**
to *anoint* **myrrh** my body to the *burying* **embalming**.
9 *Verily I say* **Amen! I word** unto you,
Wheresoever this *gospel* **evangelism** shall be preached
throughout the whole *world* **cosmos**,
this also that she hath done
shall be spoken of for a memorial of her.

YAH HUDAH PLANS TO BETRAY YAH SHUA

10 And *Judas Iscariot* **Yah Hudah the urbanite**,
one of the twelve,
went unto the *chief priests*, **archpriests**
to betray him unto them.
11 And when they heard it, they *were glad* **cheered**,
and *promised* **pre—evangelized** to give him *money* **silver**.
And he sought how
he might *conveniently* **opportunely** betray him.

PASACH PREPARATION

12 And the first day of *unleavened bread* **matsah**,
when they *killed* **sacrificed** the *passover* **pasach**,
his disciples *said* **worded** unto him,
Where wilt thou that we go and prepare
that thou mayest eat the *passover* **pasach**?
13 And he *sendeth forth* **apostolizeth** two of his disciples,
and *saith* **wordeth** unto them, Go ye into the city,
and there shall meet you
a *man* **human** bearing a pitcher of water: follow him.
14 And wheresoever he shall *go in* **enter**,
say ye to the *goodman of the house* **housedespotes**,
The *Master saith* **Doctor wordeth**,
Where is the *guestchamber* **lodge**,
where I shall eat the *passover* **pasach** with my disciples?
15 And he *will* **shall** shew you
a *large* **mega** upper room
furnished **spread** and prepared:
there *make ready* **prepare** for us.
16 And his disciples went forth, and came into the city,
and found **exactly** as he had said unto them:
and they *made ready* **prepared** the *passover* **pasach**.

YAH SHUA PROPHESIES HIS BETRAYAL

17 And *in the* **become** evening
he cometh with the twelve.
18 And as they *sat* **reposed** and did eat,
Jesus **Yah Shua** said,
Verily I say **Amen! I word** unto you,
One of you which eateth with me shall betray me.
19 And they began to be sorrowful,
and to *say* **word** unto him one by one, *Is it* I?
and another said, *Is it* I?
20 And he answered and said unto them,
It is one of the twelve,
that *dippeth* **baptizeth** with me in the dish.
21 The Son of *man* **humanity** indeed goeth,
exactly as it is *written of* **scribed concerning** him:
but woe to that *man* **human**
by whom the Son of *man* **humanity** is betrayed!
good were it for that *man* **human**
if he had never been born.

YAH SHUA'S FINAL PASACH

22 And as they did eat, *Jesus* **Yah Shua** took bread,
and *blessed* **eulogized**, and brake it, and gave to them,
and said, Take, eat: this is my body.
23 And he took the cup,
and when he had *given thanks* **eucharistized**,
he gave it to them:
and they all drank of it.
24 And he said unto them,
This is my blood of the new *testament* **covenant**,
which is *shed* **poured** for many.
25 *Verily I say* **Amen! I word** unto you,
I *will* **shall** drink no more of the *fruit* **produce** of the vine,
until that day that I drink it new
in the *kingdom* **sovereigndom** of *God* **Elohim**.
26 And when they had *sung an hymn* **hymned**,
they went out into the mount of Olives.

YAH SHUA PROPHESIES SCANDALIZING

27 And *Jesus saith* **Yah Shua wordeth** unto them,
All ye shall be *offended* **scandalized**
because of **in** me this night:
for it is *written* **scribed**,
I *will* **shall** smite the shepherd,
and the sheep shall be scattered.
28 But after that I am risen,
I *will* **shall** go before you into *Galilee* **Galiyl**.

Zechar Yah 13:7

YAH SHUA PROPHESIES PETROS' DENIALS

29 But *Peter* **Petros** said unto him,
Although all shall be *offended* **scandalized**,
yet *will* **shall** not I.
30 And *Jesus saith* **Yah Shua wordeth** unto him,
Verily I say **Amen! I word** unto thee,
That this day, even in this night,
before the *cock crow* **rooster voiceth** twice,
thou shalt deny me thrice.
31 But he *spake* **worded**
the more *vehemently* **superabundantly**,
If I *should* **must** die with thee,
I *will* **shall** not **never ever** deny thee *in any wise*.
Likewise also *said* **worded** they all.

YAH SHUA IN GATH SHEMEN

32 And they came to a *place* **parcel**
which was named *Gethsemane* **Geth Shemen**:
and he *saith* **wordeth** to his disciples,
Sit ye here, while I shall pray.
33 And he taketh with him *Peter* **Petros**
and *James* **Yaaqovos** and *John* **Yahn**,
and began to *be sore amazed* **utterly astonish**,
and to *be very heavy* **distress**;
34 And *saith* **wordeth** unto them,
My soul is exceeding sorrowful unto death:
tarry **abide** ye here, and watch.

YAH SHUA'S FIRST GATH SHEMEN PRAYER

35 And he *went forward* **proceeded** a little,
and fell on the *ground* **soil**, and prayed that,
if it were possible, the hour might pass from him.
36 And he *said* **worded**, Abba, Father,
all *things* are possible unto thee;
take away this cup from me:
nevertheless **yet** not what I will, but what thou *wilt*.
37 And he cometh, and findeth them sleeping,
and *saith* **wordeth** unto *Peter* **Petros**,
Simon **Shimon**, sleepest thou?
couldest not thou watch one hour?
38 Watch ye and pray,
lest ye enter into *temptation* **testing**.
The spirit *truly* **indeed** is *ready* **eager**, but the flesh is *weak* **frail**.

YAH SHUA'S SECOND GATH SHEMEN PRAYER

39 And again he went away, and prayed,
and *spake* **said** the same words.
40 And when he returned, he found them asleep again,
(for their eyes were heavy,)
neither *wist* **knew** they what to answer him.

YAH SHUA'S THIRD GATH SHEMEN PRAYER

41 And he cometh the third time,
and *saith* **wordeth** unto them,
Sleep *on now* **henceforth**, and *take your* rest:
it is enough, the hour is come;
behold, the Son of *man* **humanity**
is betrayed into the hands of sinners.
42 Rise *up*, let us go; *lo* **behold**,
he that betrayeth me *is at hand* **approacheth**.

YAH HUDAH BETRAYS YAH SHUA

43 And *immediately* **straightway**, while he yet spake,
cometh *Judas* **Yah Hudah**, **being** one of the twelve,
and with him
a *great* **vast** multitude with swords and staves,
from the *chief priests* **archpriests** and the scribes
and the elders.
44 And he that betrayed him
had given them a *token* **signal**, *saying* **wording**,
Whomsoever I shall kiss, that same is he;
take **overpower** him, and lead him away *safely* **securely**.
45 And as soon as he was come,
he goeth straightway to him,
and *saith* **speaketh**, *Master, master* **Rabbi, rabbi**;
and **ardently** kissed him.
46 And they laid their hands on him,
and *took* **overpowered** him.
47 And one of them *that stood by* **present** drew a sword,
and smote a servant of the *high priest*,**archpriest**
and *cut off* **removed** his ear **lobe**.
48 And *Jesus* **Yah Shua** answered and said unto them,
Are ye come out, as against a *thief* **robber**,
with swords and with staves to take me?
49 I was daily with you in the *temple* **priestal precinct**
teaching **doctrinating**, and ye *took* **overpowered** me not:
but **to fulfill** the scriptures *must be fulfilled*.
50 And they all forsook him, and fled.
51 And there followed him a *certain young man* **youth**,
having a linen cloth cast about his naked body
who arrayed his nakedness in linen;
and the *young men* **youths**
laid hold on **overpowered** him:
52 And he left the linen *cloth*, and fled from them naked.
53 And they led *Jesus* **Yah Shua** *away*
to the *high priest*:**archpriest**
and with him were *assembled* **come together**
all the *chief priests* **archpriests** and the elders
and the scribes.
54 And *Peter* **Petros** followed him afar off,
even into the *palace* **courtyard** of the *high priest*:**archpriest**
and he sat with the *servants* **attendants**,
and warmed himself at the fire.
55 And the *chief priests* **archpriests**
and all the *council* **sanhedrim**
sought for witness against *Jesus* **Yah Shua**
to *put* **deathify** him *to death*; and found none.

YAH SHUA'S TRIAL

56 For many
bare false witness **pseudo—witnessed** against him,
but their witness *agreed not together* **was not equal**.
57 And there arose *certain* **some**,
and *bare false witness* **pseudo—witnessed** against him,
saying **wording**,
58 We heard him *say* **word**,
I *will destroy* **shall disintegrate**
this *temple that is made with hands* **handmade nave**,
and *within* **by** three days I *will* **shall** build another
made without hands **not handmade**.
59 But neither *so* **thus**
did **was** their witness *agree together* **equal**.
60 And the *high priest* **archpriest** stood *up* in the midst,
and asked *Jesus* **Yah Shua**, *saying* **wording**,
Answerest thou *nothing* **naught**?
what is it which these witness against thee?
61 But he *held his peace* **hushed**,
and answered *nothing* **naught**.
Again the *high priest* **archpriest** asked him,
and *said* **worded** unto him,
Art thou the *Christ* **Messiah**, the Son of the *Blessed* **Eulogized**?

YAH SHUA AFFIRMS HIS DEITY

62 And *Jesus* **Yah Shua** said, *I am* **I AM**:
and ye shall see the Son of *man* **humanity**
sitting *on* **by** the right *hand* of *power* **the dynamis**,
and coming in the clouds of heaven.
63 Then the *high priest* **archpriest**
rent **ripped** his *clothes* **tunic**,
and *saith* **wordeth**, What need we any further witnesses?
64 Ye have heard the blasphemy:
what *think* **manifesteth to** ye?
And they all condemned him
to be *guilty of* **subject to** death.
65 And some began to spit on him,
and to cover his face, and to *buffet* **punch** him,
and to *say* **word** unto him, Prophesy:
and the *servants* **attendants**
did strike him with the palms of their hands **slapped him.**

PETROS' FIRST DENIAL

66 And as *Peter* **Petros** was beneath
in the *palace* **courtyard**,
there cometh
one of the *maids* **lasses** of the *high priest*:**archpriest**
67 And when she saw *Peter* **Petros** warming himself,
she looked upon him, and *said* **worded**,
And thou also
wast with *Jesus of Nazareth* **Yah Shua the Nazarene**.
68 But he denied, *saying* **wording**,
I know not,
neither understand I what thou *sayest* **wordest**.
And he went out into the *porch* **forecourt**;
and the *cock called* **rooster voiced**.

PETROS' SECOND DENIAL

69 And a *maid* **lass** saw him again,
and began to *say* **word** to them *that stood by* **present**,
This is one of them.
70 And he denied it again.

PETROS' THIRD DENIAL

And a little after,
they that stood by **those present**
said **worded** again to *Peter* **Petros**,
Surely **Truly** thou art one of them:
for thou art a *Galilaean* **Galiliy**,
and thy speech *agreeth* **homologizeth** *thereto*.
71 But he began to *curse* **anathemetize**
and to *swear* **oath**, *saying*,
I know not this *man* **human** of whom ye *speak* **word**.
72 And the second time the *cock crew* **rooster voiced**.
And *Peter called to mind* **Petros remembered**
the *word* **rhema** that *Jesus* **Yah Shua** said unto him,
Before the *cock crow* **rooster voiceth** twice,
thou shalt **utterly** deny me thrice.
And when he thought thereon, he wept.

YAH SHUA BETRAYED TO PILATOS

15 And straightway in the **early** morning
the *chief priests* **archpriests** *held* **made** a consultation
with the elders and scribes
and the whole *council* **sanhedrim**,
and bound *Jesus* **Yah Shua**, and *carried* **bore** him away,
and delivered him to *Pilate* **Pilatos**.
2 And *Pilate* **Pilatos** asked him,
Art thou the *King* **Sovereign** of the *Jews* **Yah Hudiym**?

And he answering said unto them,
Thou *sayest* **wordest** it.
3 And the *chief priests* **archpriests**
accused him of *many things* **much**:
but he answered *nothing* **naught**.
4 And *Pilate* **Pilatos** asked him again, *saying* **wording**,
Answerest thou *nothing* **naught**? behold,
how *many things* **much** they witness against thee.
5 But *Jesus* **Yah Shua** yet answered *nothing* **naught**;
so that *Pilate* **Pilatos** marvelled.
6 Now at that *feast* **celebration**
he released unto them one prisoner,
whomsoever they *desired* **asked**.
7 And there was one *named Barabbas* **worded Bar Abbas**,
which lay bound with them
that had *made insurrection* **co—rioted** with him,
who had *committed* **done** murder in the *insurrection* **riot**.
8 And the multitude crying *aloud* began to *desire* **ask** him
to do **exactly** as he had even done unto them.
9 But *Pilate* **Pilatos** answered them, *saying* **wording**,
will ye that I release unto you
the *King* **Sovereign** of the *Jews* **Yah Hudiym**?
10 For he knew that the *chief priests* **archpriests**
had *delivered* **betrayed** him for envy.
11 But the *chief priests* **archpriests**
moved **excited** the *people* **multitude**,
that he should rather release *Barabbas* **Bar Abbas**
unto them.
12 And *Pilate* **Pilatos** answered and said again unto them,
What will ye then that I shall do unto him
whom ye *call* **word**
the *king* **sovereign** of the *Jews* **Yah Hudiym**?
13 And they cried out again, *Crucify him.* **Stake!**
14 Then *Pilate said* **Pilatos worded** unto them,
Why **Indeed**, what evil hath he done?
And they cried out
the more *exceedingly* **superabundantly**,
Crucify him. **Stake!**
15 And so *Pilate* **Pilatos**,
willing to *content* **satisfy** the *people* **multitude**,
released *Barabbas* **Bar Abbas** unto them,
and *delivered Jesus* **betrayed Yah Shua**,
when he had *scourged* **whipped** him,
to be *crucified* **staked**.
16 And the *soldiers* **warriors** led him away
into the *hall* **courtyard**, *called* **which is the** Praetorium;
and they call together the whole *band* **squad**.
17 And they *clothed* **endued** him with purple,
and *platted* **braided** a *crown* **wreath** of thorns,
and put it about his head,
18 And began to salute him,
Hail **Cheers**, *King* **Sovereign** of the *Jews* **Yah Hudiym**!
19 And they *smote* **struck** him on the head with a reed,
and *did* spit upon him,
and *bowing* **placing** their knees worshipped him.
20 And when they had mocked him,
they *took off* **stripped** the purple from him,
and *put* **endued** his own clothes on him,
and led him out to *crucify* **stake** him.
21 And they compel one *Simon* **Shimon** a Cyrenian,
who passed by, coming out of the *country* **field**,
the father of Alexander and Rufus, to bear his *cross* **stake**.
22 And they bring him
unto the place *Golgotha* **Gulgoleth**,
which is, *being interpreted* **translated**,
The place of a skull **Cranium Place**.
23 And they gave him to drink
wine *mingled* with **tincture of** myrrh:
but he *received* **took** it not.

YAH SHUA IS STAKED

24 And when they had *crucified* **staked** him,
they *parted* **divided** his garments,
casting lots upon them, what every man should take.
25 And it was the third hour,
and they *crucified* **staked** him.
26 And the *superscription* **epigraph** of his accusation
was *written over* **epigraphed**,
THE *KING* **SOVEREIGN** OF THE *JEWS* **YAH HUDIYM**.
27 And with him they *crucify* **stake** two *thieves* **robbers**;
the one *on* **by** his right *hand*,
and the *other on* **one by** his left.
28 And the scripture was fulfilled, which *saith* **wordeth**,
And he was *numbered* **reckoned**
with the *transgressors* **torah violators**.
Yesha Yah 53:9, 12
29 And they that passed by *railed on* **blasphemed** him,
wagging their heads, and *saying* **wording**, *Ah* **Aha**,
thou that *destroyest* **disintegratest** the *temple* **nave**,
and buildest it in three days,
30 Save thyself, and come down from the *cross* **stake**.
31 Likewise also the *chief priests* **archpriests** mocking
said **worded** among *themselves* **one another**
with the scribes,
He saved others; himself he cannot save.
32 *Let Christ* **The Messiah!**
the *King* **Sovereign** of *Israel* **Yisra El!**
Let him descend now from the *cross* **stake**,
that we may see and *believe* **trust**.
And they that were *crucified* **staked** with him
reviled **reproached** him.
33 And when the sixth hour *was come* **became**,
there *was* **became** darkness over the whole *land* **earth**
until the ninth hour.
34 And at the ninth hour
Jesus **Yah Shua** cried with a *loud* **mega** voice,
saying **wording**, Eloi, Eloi, lama sabachthani?
which is, *being interpreted* **translated**,
My *God* **Elohim**, my *God* **Elohim**,
why hast thou forsaken me?
Psalm 22:1
35 And some of them *that stood by* **present**,
when they heard it, *said* **worded**, Behold,
he *calleth Elias* **voiceth out to Eli Yah**.
36 And one ran and filled a spunge full of vinegar,
and put it on a reed, and gave him to drink,
saying **wording**, *Let alone* **Allow**;
let us see whether *Elias will* **Eli Yah shall** come
to take him down.
37 And *Jesus* **Yah Shua**
cried with a loud **released a mega** voice,
and *gave up the ghost* **expired**.

REACTIONS: MATERIAL AND PHYSICAL

38 And the veil of the *temple* **nave** was *rent* **split** in twain
from *the top* **above** to *the bottom* **below**.
39 And when the centurion,
which *stood over against* **was present opposite** him,
saw that he *so* **thus** cried out,
and *gave up the ghost* **expired**, he said,
Truly this *man* **human** was the Son of *God* **Elohim**.
40 There were also women *looking on* **observing** afar off:
among whom was *Mary* **Miryam the** Magdalene,
and *Mary* **Miryam** the mother
of *James* **Yaaqovos** the less and of *Joses* **Yoses**,
and *Salome* **Shalome**;
41 (Who also, when he was in *Galilee* **Galiyl**,
followed him, and ministered unto him;)
and many other women
which *came up* **ascended** with him
unto *Jerusalem* **Yeru Shalem**.

YAH SHUA IS ENTOMBED

42 And *now* **already** when the even *was come* **became**,
because it was the preparation,
that is, the *day before the sabbath* **foreshabbath**,
43 *Joseph* **Yoseph** of *Arimathaea* **Rahmah**,
an honourable **a respected** counsellor,
which also *waited for* **awaited**
the *kingdom* **sovereigndom** of *God* **Elohim**, came,
and *went in boldly* **dared go in** unto *Pilate* **Pilatos**,
and *craved* **asked for** the body of *Jesus* **Yah Shua**.
44 And *Pilate* **Pilatos** marvelled if he were already dead:
and calling unto him the centurion,
he asked him whether he had been *any while* **long** dead.
45 And when he knew it of the centurion,
he *gave* **granted** the body to *Joseph* **Yoseph**.
46 And he bought *fine* linen, and took him down,
and wrapped him in the linen,
and laid him in a *sepulchre* **tomb**
which was hewn out of a rock,
and rolled a stone
unto the *door* **portal** of the *sepulchre* **tomb**.

47 And *Mary* **Miryam the** Magdalene
and *Mary* **Miryam** the mother of *Joses* **Yoses**
beheld **observed** where he was *laid* **placed.**

YAH SHUA IS RESURRECTED

16 And when the *sabbath* **shabbath** was past,
Mary **Miryam the** Magdalene,
and *Mary* **Miryam** the mother of *James* **Yaaqovos**,
and *Salome* **Shalome,**
had bought *sweet spices* **aromatics**,
that they might come and anoint him.
2 And very early in the morning
the first *day* of the *week* **shabbaths**,
they came unto the *sepulchre* **tomb**
at the rising of the sun.
3 And they *said* **worded** among themselves,
Who shall roll us away the stone
from the *door* **portal** of the *sepulchre* **tomb**?
4 And when they looked,
they *saw* **observed** that the stone was rolled away:
for it was *very great* **extremely mega.**
5 And entering into the *sepulchre* **tomb**,
they saw a *young man* **youth** sitting *on* **by** the right *side*,
clothed **arrayed** in a *long* white *garment* **stole**;
and they were *affrighted* **utterly astonished.**
6 And he *saith* **wordeth** unto them,
Be not *affrighted* **utterly astonished**:
Ye seek *Jesus of Nazareth* **Yah Shua the Nazarene**,
which was *crucified* **staked**:
he is risen; he is not here:
behold, the place where they *laid* **placed** him.
7 But go your way,
tell **say to** his disciples and *Peter* **Petros**
that he goeth before you into *Galilee* **Galiyl**:
there shall ye see him, **exactly** as he said unto you.
8 And they went out quickly,
and fled from the *sepulchre* **tomb**;
for they trembled
and *were amazed* **ecstasis overtook them**:
neither said they *any thing* **aught** to any *man* **one**;
for they were *afraid* **awestricken**.
9 Now when *Jesus* **Yah Shua** was risen early
the morning of the first *day* of the *week* **shabbaths,**
he *appeared* **manifested** first to *Mary* **Miryam the** Magdalene,
out of whom he had cast seven *devils* **demons**.
10 And she went
and *told* **evangelized** them that had been with him,
as they mourned and wept.
11 And they, when they had heard that he was alive,
and had been *seen* **observed** of her,
believed not **distrusted**.
12 After that he appeared in another form
unto two of them,
as they walked, and went into the *country* **field**.
13 And they went and *told* **evangelized** it
unto *the residue* **those remaining**:
neither *believed* **trusted** they them.
14 Afterward he appeared unto the eleven
as they *sat* **reposed** at meat,
and *upbraided them with* **reproached**
their *unbelief* **trustlessness**
and *hardness of heart* **hard—heartedness**,
because they *believed* **trusted** not them
which had *seen* **observed** him after he was risen.

YAH SHUA APOSTOLIZES THE TRUSTING

15 And he said unto them,
Go ye into all the *world* **cosmos**,
and preach the *gospel* **evangelism**
to *every creature* **all creation**.
16 He that *believeth* **trusteth** and is baptized
shall be saved;
but he that *believeth not* **distrusteth**
shall be *damned* **condemned**.

SIGNS FOLLOW THE TRUSTERS

17 And these signs shall follow them that *believe* **trust**;
In my name shall they cast out *devils* **demons**;
they shall speak with new tongues;
18 They shall take *up* serpents;
and if they drink *any* **aught** deadly *thing*,
it shall not *hurt* **injure** them;
they shall lay hands on the sick,
and they shall *recover* **be well.**

Loukas 10:19, 20

YAH SHUA IS TAKEN

19 *So* **But indeed** then
after *the Lord* **Adonay** had spoken unto them,
he was *received* **taken** *up* into heaven,
and sat *on* **by** the right *hand* of *God* **Elohim.**

SIGNS CONFIRM THE WORD

20 And they went forth, and preached every where,
the Lord working with them **Adonay co—working,**
and confirming the word *with* **by** signs following.
Amen.

KEY TO INTERPRETING THE EXEGESES
King James text is in regular type;
Text under exegeses is in oblique type;
Text of exegeses is in bold type.

INTRODUCTION
1 *Forasmuch as* **Since indeed**
many have taken in hand to set forth in order
a declaration *of* **about** those *things* **matters**
which are *most surely believed* **fully borne** among us,
2 Even as they delivered them unto us,
which from the beginning
were eyewitnesses **saw for ourselves**,
and *ministers* **became attendants** of the word;
3 *It seemed good to me* **I thought** also,
having *had perfect understanding* **followed precisely**
of all *things* from *the very first* **above**,
to *write* **scribe** unto thee in *order* **sequence**,
most *excellent Theophilus* **powerful Theo Philus**,
4 That thou mightest know
the certainty of those *things* **words**,
wherein **about which**
thou hast been *instructed* **catechized**.

YAHN THE BAPTIZER'S BIRTH FORETOLD
5 There *was* **became** in the days of Herod,
the *king* **sovereign** of *Judaea* **Yah Hudah**,
a *certain* priest named *Zacharias* **Zechar Yah**,
of the course of *Abia* **Abi Yah**:
and his *wife* **woman**
was of the daughters of *Aaron* **Aharon**,
and her name was *Elisabeth* **Eli Sheba**.
6 And they were both *righteous* **just**
before God **in the sight of Elohim**,
walking in all
the *commandments* **misvoth** and *ordinances* **judgments**
of *the Lord* **Yah Veh** blameless.
7 And they had no child,
because that Elisabeth **as Eli Sheba** was *barren* **sterile**,
and they both were
now well stricken in years **advanced in days**.
8 And it *came to pass* **became**,
that while he
executed the priest's office **priested** before *God* **Elohim**
in the order of his course,
9 According
to the custom of the *priest's office* **priesthood**,
his lot was to *burn* incense
when he *went* **entered**
into the *temple* **nave** of *the Lord* **Yah Veh**.
10 And the whole multitude of the people
were praying without at the *time* **hour** of incense.
11 And there appeared unto him
an angel of *the Lord* **Yah Veh**
standing *on* **by** the right *side*
of the **sacrifice** altar of incense.
12 And when *Zacharias* **Zechar Yah** saw him,
he was troubled, and *fear* **awe** fell upon him.
13 But the angel said unto him,
Fear **Awe** not, *Zacharias* **Zechar Yah**:
for thy *prayer* **petition** is heard;
and thy *wife Elisabeth* **woman Eli Sheba**
shall bear thee a son,
and thou shalt call his name *John* **Yahn**.
14 And *thou shalt have joy* **he shall be thy cheer**
and *gladness* **thy jumping for joy**;
and many shall *rejoice* **cheer** at his birth.
15 For he shall be *great* **mega**
in the sight of *the Lord* **Yah Veh**,
and shall not **no way** drink
neither wine nor *strong drink* **intoxicants**;
and he shall be filled **full** with the Holy *Ghost* **Spirit**,
even from his mother's womb.
16 And many of the *children* **sons** of *Israel* **Yisra El**
shall he turn to *the Lord* **Yah Veh** their *God* **Elohim**.
17 And he shall *go before* **precede** him
in the spirit and *power* **dynamis** of *Elias* **Eli Yah**
to turn the hearts of the fathers to the children,
and the *disobedient* **distrusting**
to the *wisdom* **thought** of the just;
to *make ready* **prepare** a people
prepared for *the Lord* **Yah Veh**.
18 And *Zacharias* **Zechar Yah** said unto the angel,
Whereby shall I know this? for I am *an old man* **elderly**,
and my *wife* **woman**
well stricken **advanced** in *years* **days**.
19 And the angel answering said unto him,
I am *Gabriel* **Gabri El**,
that stand in the *presence* **sight** of *God* **Elohim**;
and am *sent* **apostolized** to speak unto thee,
and to *shew* **evangelize** thee *these glad tidings*.
20 And, behold, thou shalt be *dumb* **hushed**,
and not able to speak,
until the day that these *things* shall be *performed*,
because thou *believest* **trustest** not my words,
which shall be fulfilled in their season.
21 And the people
waited for Zacharias **awaited Zechar Yah**,
and marvelled that he *tarried so long* **took his time**
in the *temple* **nave**.
22 And when he came out,
he could not speak unto them:
and they *perceived* **knew**
that he had seen a vision in the *temple* **nave**:
for he *beckoned* **nodded** unto them,
and *remained speechless* **continually abode mute**.
23 And it *came to pass* **became**, that,
as soon as the days of his *ministration* **liturgy**
were *accomplished* **fulfilled**,
he departed to his own house.
24 And after those days
his *wife Elisabeth* **woman Eli Sheba** conceived,
and *hid* **concealed** herself five months, *saying* **wording**,
25 Thus hath *the Lord dealt* **Yah Veh done** with me
in the days wherein he *looked on* **regarded** me,
to *take away* **remove** my reproach among *men* **humanity**.

YAH SHUA'S BIRTH FORETOLD
26 And in the sixth month the angel *Gabriel* **Gabri El**
was *sent* **apostolized** from *God* **Elohim**
unto a city of *Galilee* **Galiyl**, named Nazareth,
27 To a virgin
espoused to a man whose name was *Joseph* **Yoseph**,
of the house of David;
and the virgin's name was *Mary* **Miryam**.
28 And the angel *came in* **entered** unto her, and said,
Hail **Cheers**,
thou that art *highly favoured* **endued with charism**,
the Lord is **Yah Veh be** with thee:
blessed **eulogized** art thou among women.
29 And when she saw him,
she was troubled at his *saying* **word**,
and *cast in her mind* **reasoned**
what manner of salutation this should be.
30 And the angel said unto her,
Fear **Awe** not, *Mary* **Miryam**:
for thou hast found *favour* **charism** with *God* **Elohim**.
31 And, behold, thou shalt conceive in thy womb,
and *bring forth* **birth** a son,
and shalt call his name *Jesus* **Yah Shua**.
32 He shall be *great* **mega**,
and shall be called the Son of *the Highest* **Elyon**:
and *the Lord God* **Yah Veh Elohim**
shall give unto him the throne of his father David:
33 And he shall reign over the house of *Jacob* **Yaaqov**
for ever **unto the eons**;
and of his *kingdom* **sovereigndom**
there shall be no *end* **completion**.
34 Then said *Mary* **Miryam** unto the angel,
How shall this be, *seeing* **since** I know not a man?
35 And the angel answered and said unto her,
The Holy *Ghost* **Spirit** shall come upon thee,
and the *power* **dynamis** of *the Highest* **Elyon**
shall overshadow thee:
therefore also that holy *thing*
which *shall be born of thee* **thou shalt bear**
shall be called the Son of *God* **Elohim**.
36 And, behold, thy cousin *Elisabeth* **Eli Sheba**,
she hath also conceived a son in her *old age* **senescence**:
and this is the sixth month with her,
who was called *barren* **sterile**.
37 For with *God* **Elohim**
nothing **no rhema** shall be impossible.

38 And *Mary* **Miryam** said,
Behold the *handmaid* **maiden** of *the Lord* **Yah Veh**;
be it unto me according to thy *word* **rhema**.
And the angel departed from her.

MIRYAM VISITS ELI SHEBA

39 And *Mary* **Miryam** arose in those days,
and went into the *hill country* **mountains**
with *haste* **diligence**,
into a city of *Juda* **Yah Hudah**;
40 And entered into the house of *Zacharias* **Zechar Yah**,
and saluted *Elisabeth* **Eli Sheba**.

THE SONG OF ELI SHEBA

41 And it *came to pass* **became**, that,
when *Elisabeth* **Eli Sheba**
heard the salutation of *Mary* **Miryam**,
the *babe* **infant** leaped in her womb;
and *Elisabeth* **Eli Sheba** was filled **full**
with the Holy *Ghost* **Spirit**:
42 And she *spake out* **exclaimed** with a *loud* **mega** voice,
and said,
Blessed **Eulogized** art thou among women,
and *blessed* **eulogized** is the fruit of thy womb.
43 And whence is this to me,
that the mother of my *Lord* **Adonay** should come to me?
44 For, *lo* **behold**,
as soon as the voice of thy salutation
sounded **became** in mine ears,
the *babe* **infant** leaped in my womb **and jumped** for joy.
45 And blessed is she that *believed* **trusted**:
for there shall be a *performance* **completion**
of those *things* which were *told* **spoken to** her
from *the Lord* **Yah Veh**.

THE SONG OF MIRYAM

46 And *Mary* **Miryam** said,
My soul *doth magnify the Lord* **magnifieth Yah Veh**,
47 And my spirit *hath rejoiced* **jumpeth for joy**
in *God* **Elohim** my Saviour.
48 For he hath *regarded* **looked upon**
the *low estate* **humiliation**
of his *handmaiden* **maiden**:
for, behold, from *henceforth* **now on**
all generations shall call me blessed.
49 For he that is *mighty* **able**
hath *done to* **dealt with** me *great things* **magnificently**;
and holy is his name.
50 And his mercy is on them that *fear* **awe** him
from generation to generation.
51 He hath *shewed strength* **dealt power** with his arm;
he hath scattered the proud
in the *imagination* **mind** of their hearts.
52 He hath put down the *mighty* **dynasties**
from their *seats* **thrones**,
and exalted *them of low degree* **the humble**.
53 He hath filled the hungry with good *things*;
and the rich he hath *sent* **apostolized forth** empty *away*.
54 He hath *holpen* **supported**
his *servant Israel* **lad Yisra El**,
in remembrance of his **to remember** mercy;
55 **Exactly** As he spake to our fathers,
to Abraham,
and to his *seed for ever* **sperma unto the eons**.
56 And *Mary* **Miryam** abode with her about three months,
and returned to her own house.

THE BIRTH OF YAHN THE BAPTIZER

57 Now *Elisabeth's full* **Eli Sheba's** time *came* **fulfilled**
that she should *be delivered* **birth**;
and she *brought forth* **bore** a son.
58 And her *neighbours* **fellow settlers**
and her *cousins* **kindred** heard how *the Lord* **Yah Veh**
had *shewed great mercy upon* **magnified** her;
and they rejoiced with her.
59 And it *came to pass* **became**,
that on the eighth day they came to circumcise the child;
and they called him *Zacharias* **Zechar Yah**,
after the name of his father.
60 And his mother answered and said, *Not so* **Indeed not**;
but he shall be called *John* **Yahn**.
61 And they said unto her,
There is none of thy kindred that is called by this name.
62 And they *made signs* **nodded** to his father,
how he *would* **willed to** have him called.
63 And he asked for a *writing table* **tablet**,
and *wrote* **scribed**, *saying* **wording**,
His name is *John* **Yahn**.
And they marvelled all.
64 And his mouth was opened immediately,
and his tongue loosed, and he spake,
and *praised God* **eulogized Elohim**.
65 And *fear came* **awe became** on all
that *dwelt* **settled** round about them:
and all these *sayings* **rhema**
were *noised abroad* **thoroughly told** throughout
all the *hill country* **mountains** of *Judaea* **Yah Hudah**.
66 And all they that heard them
laid **placed** them *up* in their hearts, *saying* **wording**,
What *manner of child* **then** shall this **child** be!
And the hand of *the Lord* **Yah Veh** was with him.

THE PROPHECY OF ZECHAR YAH

67 And his father *Zacharias* **Zechar Yah**
was filled **full** with the Holy *Ghost* **Spirit**,
and prophesied, *saying* **wording**,
68 *Blessed* **Eulogized**
be *the Lord God* **Yah Veh Elohim** of *Israel* **Yisra El**;
for he hath visited
and *redeemed* **dealt redemption to** his people,
69 And hath raised *up* an horn of salvation for us
in the house of his *servant* **lad** David;
70 **Exactly** As he spake
by **through** the mouth of his holy prophets,
which have been *since* **from** the *world began* **eons**:
71 That we should *be saved* **have salvation**
from our enemies,
and from the hand of all that hate us;
72 To *perform the* **deal** mercy
promised to **with our** fathers,
and to remember his holy covenant;
73 The oath which he *sware* **oathed**
to our father Abraham,
74 That he *would grant* **should give** unto us,
that we being *delivered* **rescued**
out of the hand of our enemies
might *serve* **liturgize** him *without fear* **fearlessly**,
75 In *holiness* **mercy** and *righteousness* **justness**
before him **in his sight**, all the days of our life.
76 And thou, child,
shalt be called the prophet of *the Highest* **Elyon**:
for thou shalt *go before* **precede**
the face of *the Lord* **Adonay**
to prepare his ways;
77 To give knowledge of salvation unto his people
by **in** the *remission* **forgiveness** of their sins,
78 Through the *tender* **spleen of** mercy
of our *God* **Elohim**;
whereby the *dayspring* **rising** from on high
hath visited us,
79 To *give light to* **appear upon** them that sit in darkness
and in the shadow of death,
to *guide* **direct** our feet into the way of *peace* **shalom**.
80 And the child grew,
and *waxed strong* **empowered** in spirit,
and was in the *deserts* **wildernesses**
till the day of his *shewing* **exhibiting** unto *Israel* **Yisra El**.

THE BIRTH OF YAH SHUA

2 And it *came to pass* **became** in those days,
that there went out a *decree* **dogma**
from *Caesar* **Kaisar** Augustus
that all the world should be *taxed* **registered**.
2 (And this *taxing was* **registration** first *made* **became**
when Cyrenius was governor of Syria.)
3 And all went to *be taxed* **register**,
every one **each** into his own city.
4 And *Joseph* **Yoseph** also *went up* **ascended**
from *Galilee* **Galiyl**, out of the city of Nazareth,
into *Judaea* **Yah Hudah**, unto the city of David,
which is called *Bethlehem* **Beth Lechem**;
(because he was
of the house and *lineage* **patriarchy** of David:)
5 To *be taxed* **register** with *Mary* **Miryam**
his espoused *wife* **woman**,
being great with child **swelling within**.

6 And so it *was* **became**, that, while they were there,
the days were *accomplished* **fulfilled**
that she should *be delivered* **birth**.
7 And she *brought forth* **birthed** her firstborn son,
and *wrapped* **swathed** him *in swaddling clothes*,
and *laid* **reclined** him in a manger;
because there was no *room* **place** for them
in the *inn* **lodge**.
8 And there were in the same *country* **region**
shepherds abiding in the field,
keeping watch **guarding the guard**
over their *flock* **shepherddom** by night.
9 And, *lo* **behold**, the angel of *the Lord* **Yah Veh**
came upon **stood over** them,
and the glory of *the Lord* **Yah Veh**
shone round about **haloed** them:
and they *were sore afraid* **awed a mega awe**.
10 And the angel said unto them, *Fear* **Awe** not:
for, behold,
I *bring you good tidings* **evangelize to you**
of *great joy* **mega cheer**,
which shall be to all people.
11 For unto you is born this day in the city of David
a Saviour,
which is *Christ the Lord* **Messiah Adonay**.
12 And this shall be a sign unto you;
Ye shall find the *babe* **infant**
wrapped in swaddling clothes **swathed**,
lying in a manger.
13 And suddenly there *was* **became** with the angel
a multitude of the heavenly host
praising God **halaling Elohim**, and *saying* **wording**,
14 Glory to *God* **Elohim** in the *highest* **highests**,
and on earth *peace* **shalom**,
good will **well—approval** toward *men* **humanity**.
15 And it *came to pass* **became**,
as the angels were gone away from them into heaven,
the humans — the shepherds said one to another,
Let us now *go* **pass through**
even unto Bethlehem **as far as Beth Lechem**,
and see this *thing* **rhema**
which *is come to pass* **hath become**,
which *the Lord* **Yah Veh** hath made known unto us.
16 And they came with haste,
and found *Mary* **Miryam**, and *Joseph* **Yoseph**,
and the *babe* **infant** lying in a manger.
17 And when they had seen it,
they *made known abroad* **broadcasted** the *saying* **rhema**
which was *told* **spoken to** them concerning this child.
18 And all they that heard it
wondered at **marvelled about** those *things*
which were *told* **spoken to** them by the shepherds.
19 But *Mary* **Miryam**
kept **preserved** all these *things* **rhema**,
and *pondered* **considered** them in her heart.
20 And the shepherds returned,
glorifying and *praising God* **halaling Elohim**
for all *the things* **those**
that they had heard and seen,
exactly as it was *told* **spoken** unto them.

THE PRESENTATION OF YAH SHUA

21 And when eight days were *accomplished* **fulfilled**
for the circumcising of the child,
his name was called *Jesus* **Yah Shua**,
which was so *named* **called** of the angel
before he was conceived in the womb.
22 And when the days of her *purification* **purifying**
according to the *law* **torah** of *Moses* **Mosheh**
were *accomplished* **fulfilled**,
they brought him to *Jerusalem* **Yeru Shalem**,
to present him to *the Lord* **Yah Veh**;
23 (**Exactly** As *it is written* **scribed**
in the *law* **torah** of *the Lord* **Yah Veh**,
Every male that openeth the *womb* **matrix**
shall be called holy *to the Lord* **unto Yah Veh**;)
24 And to *offer* **give** a sacrifice
according to that which is said
in the *law* **torah** of *the Lord* **Yah Veh**,
A *pair* **yoke** of turtledoves,
or two *young pigeons* **youngling doves**.
25 And, behold,
there was a *man* **human** in *Jerusalem* **Yeru Shalem**,
whose name was *Simeon* **Shimon**;
and *the same man* **this human**
was just and *devout* **well—received**,
waiting for **awaiting** the consolation of *Israel* **Yisra El**:
and the Holy *Ghost* **Spirit** was upon him.
26 And it was *revealed* **oracled** unto him
by the Holy *Ghost* **Spirit**,
that he should not see death,
before he had seen *the Lord's Christ* **Yah Veh's Messiah**.
27 And he came *by* **in** the Spirit
into the *temple* **priestal precinct**:
and when the parents
brought in **introduced** the child *Jesus* **Yah Shua**,
to do for him
after the custom **as accustomed** of the *law* **torah**,
28 Then *took* **received** he him *up* in his arms,
and *blessed God* **eulogized Elohim**, and said,
29 *Lord* **Despotes**,
now *lettest* **release** thou thy servant *depart*
in *peace* **shalom**,
according to thy *word* **rhema**:
30 For mine eyes have seen thy salvation,
31 Which thou hast prepared
before the face of all people;
32 A light *to lighten* **of apocalypse to** the *Gentiles* **goyim**,
and the glory of thy people *Israel* **Yisra El**.
33 And *Joseph* **Yoseph** and his mother
marvelled at those *things*
which were spoken *of* **concerning** him.
34 And *Simeon blessed* **Shimon eulogized** them,
and said unto *Mary* **Miryam** his mother,
Behold, this *child* is set
for the *fall* **downfall** and *rising again* **resurrection**
of many in *Israel* **Yisra El**;
and for a sign
which shall be *spoken against* **contradicted**;
35 (Yea, a *sword* **sabre**
shall *pierce* **pass** through thy own soul also,)
that the *thoughts* **reasonings** of many hearts
may be *revealed* **unveiled**.
36 And there was one *Anna* **Hannah**, a prophetess,
the daughter of *Phanuel* **Peni El**,
of the *tribe* **scion** of *Aser* **Asher**:
she was *of great age* **advanced in many days**,
and had lived with *an husband* **a man**
seven years from her virginity;
37 And she was a widow
of about *fourscore* **eighty** and four years,
which departed not from the *temple* **priestal precinct**,
but *served God* **liturgized Elohim**
with fastings and *prayers* **petitions** night and day.
38 And she *coming in* **standing by** that *instant* **hour**
gave thanks **homologized** likewise unto *the Lord* **Adonay**,
and spake *of* **concerning** him to all them
that *looked for* **awaited** redemption
in *Jerusalem* **Yeru Shalem**.
39 And when they had *performed* **completed** all *things*
according to the *law* **torah** of *the Lord* **Yah Veh**,
they returned into *Galilee* **Galiyl**,
to their own city Nazareth.
40 And the child grew,
and *waxed strong* **empowered** in spirit,
filled with wisdom:
and the *grace* **charism** of *God* **Elohim** was upon him.

YAH SHUA'S LADHOOD MINISTRY

41 Now his parents
went to *Jerusalem* **Yeru Shalem** every year
at the *feast* **celebration** of the *passover* **pasach**.
42 And when he *was* **became** twelve years *old*,
they *went up* **ascended** to *Jerusalem* **Yeru Shalem**
after the custom of the *feast* **celebration**.
43 And when they had *fulfilled* **completed** the days,
as they returned,
the *child Jesus* **lad Yah Shua**
tarried **abode** behind in *Jerusalem* **Yeru Shalem**;
and *Joseph* **Yoseph** and his mother knew not of it.
44 But they, *supposing* **presuming** him
to have been in the *company* **caravan**,

went **had come** a day's journey;
and they sought him
among their *kinsfolk* **kin** and acquaintance.
45 And when they found him not,
they *turned back again* **returned**
to *Jerusalem* **Yeru Shalem**, seeking him.
46 And it *came to pass* **became**, that after three days
they found him in the *temple* **priestal precinct**,
sitting in the midst of the doctors,
both hearing them, and asking them *questions*.
47 And all that heard him were *astonished* **astounded**
at his *understanding* **comprehension** and answers.
48 And when they saw him,
they were *amazed* **astonished**:
and his mother said unto him, *Son* **Child**,
why hast thou thus dealt with us? behold,
thy father and I have sought thee *sorrowing* **grieving**.
49 And he said unto them, How is it that ye sought me?
wist **knew** ye not
that I must be about my Father's business?
50 And they *understood* **comprehended** not
the *saying* **rhema** which he spake unto them.
51 And he *went down* **descended** with them,
and came to Nazareth,
and *was subject* **subjugated** unto them:
but **and** his mother
thoroughly kept all these *sayings* **rhemas** in her heart.
52 And *Jesus increased* **Yah Shua advanced**
in wisdom and *stature* **maturity**,
and in *favour* **charism**
with *God* **Elohim** and *man* **humanity**.

YAHN THE BAPTIZER FULFILLS PROPHECY

3 Now in the fifteenth year
of the *reign* **governing** of *Tiberius Caesar* **Kaisar Tiberius**,
Pontius *Pilate* **Pilatos**
being governor of *Judaea* **Yah Hudah**,
and Herod being tetrarch of *Galilee* **Galiyl**,
and his brother *Philip* **Phillipos**
being tetrarch of *Ituraea* **Yetur**
and of the region of Trachonitis,
and Lysanias the tetrarch of Abilene,
2 *Annas* **Hanan Yah** and Caiaphas
being the *high priests* **archpriests**,
the *word* **rhema** of *God* **Elohim**
came **became** unto *John* **Yahn**
the son of *Zacharias* **Zechar Yah** in the wilderness.
3 And he came into all the *country* **region**
round about *Jordan* **Yarden**,
preaching the baptism of repentance
for the *remission* **forgiveness** of sins;
4 As *it is written* **scribed** in the *book* **scroll**
of the words of *Esaias* **Yesha Yah** the prophet,
saying **wording**,
The voice of one crying in the wilderness,
Prepare ye the way of *the Lord* **Yah Veh**,
make his paths straight.
5 Every valley shall be filled,
and every mountain and hill
shall be *brought low* **humbled**;
and the crooked shall be made into straight,
and the *rough* **jagged** ways shall be made **into** smooth;
6 And all flesh shall see the salvation of *God* **Elohim**.
Yesha Yah 40:3—5
7 Then *said* **worded** he to the multitude
that *came forth* **proceeded** to be baptized of him,
O *generation* **progeny** of vipers,
who hath *warned* **exemplified** you
to flee from the wrath *to come* **about to be**?
8 *Bring forth* **Produce** therefore
fruits worthy of repentance,
and begin not to *say* **word** within yourselves,
We have Abraham to our father:
for I *say* **word** unto you,
That *God* **Elohim** is able of these stones
to raise *up* children unto Abraham.
9 And *now* **already** also
the axe is laid unto the root of the trees:
every tree therefore
which *bringeth* **produceth** not *forth* good fruit
is *hewn down* **exscinded**, and cast into the fire.
10 And the *people* **multitude** asked him, *saying* **wording**,
What shall we do then?
11 He answereth and *saith* **wordeth** unto them,
He that hath two *coats* **tunics**,
let him impart to him that hath none;
and he that hath *meat* **food**, let him do likewise.
12 Then came also *publicans* **customs agents**
to be baptized,
and said unto him, *Master* **Doctor**, what shall we do?
13 And he said unto them,
Exact no more
than that which is *appointed* **ordained** you.
14 And the *soldiers* **warriors** likewise
demanded **asked** of him,
saying **wording**, And what shall we do?
And he said unto them,
Do violence to **Intimidate** no *man* **one**,
neither *accuse any falsely* **sycophant**;
and be *content* **satisfied** with your wages.
15 And as the people *were in expectation* **awaited**,
and all men *mused* **reasoned** in their hearts
of John **about Yahn**,
whether **lest ever** he *were* **be** the *Christ* **Messiah**, *or not;*
16 *John* **Yahn** answered, *saying* **wording** unto them all,
I indeed baptize you *with* **in** water;
but one mightier than I cometh,
the latchet of whose shoes
I am not *worthy* **adequate** to unloose:
he shall baptize you *with* **in** the Holy *Ghost* **Spirit**
and *with* **in** fire:
17 Whose **winnowing** fan is in his hand,
and he *will* **shall** throughly purge his **threshing** floor,
and *will* **shall** gather the *wheat* **grain**
into his *garner* **granary**;
but the chaff he *will* **shall** burn with fire unquenchable.
18 And *many* **much** other *things* **indeed**
in his *exhortation* **beseeching**
preached **evangelized** he unto the people.
19 But Herod the tetrarch,
being *reproved* **rebuked** by him *for* **concerning** Herodias
his brother *Philip's wife* **Phillipos' woman**,
and *for* **concerning** all the evils which Herod had done,
20 Added yet this above all,
that he *shut up John* **locked Yahn**
in *prison* **the guardhouse**.

THE BAPTISM OF YAH SHUA

21 Now when all the people were baptized,
it *came to pass* **became**,
that *Jesus* **Yah Shua** also being baptized, and praying,
the heaven was opened,
22 And the Holy *Ghost* **Spirit** descended
in a bodily *shape like* **semblance as** a dove upon him,
and a voice *came* **became** from heaven,
which *said* **worded**,
Thou art my beloved Son;
in thee I *am well pleased* **well—approve**.

THE GENEALOGY OF YAH SHUA

23 And *Jesus* **Yah Shua** himself
began to be about thirty years *of age*,
being (as was *supposed* **presumed**)
the son of *Joseph* **Yoseph**,
which was the son of Heli **of Eli**,
24 *Which was the son* of Matthat,
which was the son of Levi,
which was the son of Melchi **of Melech**,
which was the son of Janna **of Yanah**,
which was the son of Joseph **of Yoseph**,
25 *Which was the son of Mattathias* **of Mattith Yah**,
which was the son of Amos,
which was the son of Naum **of Nachum**,
which was the son of Esli,
which was the son of Nagge **of Nogah**,
26 *Which was the son* of Maath,
which was the son of Mattathias **of Mattith Yah**,
which was the son of Semei **of Shimi**,
which was the son of Joseph **of Yoseph**,
which was the son of Juda **of Yah Hudah**,
27 *Which was the son of Joanna* **of Yah Hanna**,
which was the son of Rhesa **of Rapha Yah**,
which was the son of Zorobabel **of Zerbub Babel**,

which was the son of Salathiel **of Shealti El**,
which was the son of Neri **of Neri Yah**,
28 *Which was the son of Melchi* **of Melech**,
which was the son of Addi,
which was the son of Cosam **of Qesem**,
which was the son of Elmodam **of Almodad**,
which was the son of Er,
29 *Which was the son of Jose* **of Yoses**,
which was the son of Eliezer **of Eli Ezer**,
which was the son of Jorim **of Yorim**,
which was the son of Matthat,
which was the son of Levi,
30 *Which was the son of Simeon* **of Shimon**,
which was the son of Juda **of Yah Hudah**,
which was the son of Joseph **of Yoseph**,
which was the son of Jonan,
which was the son of Eliakim **of El Yaqim**,
31 *Which was the son* of Melea,
which was the son of Menan **of Maina**,
which was the son of Mattatha,
which was the son of Nathan,
which was the son of David,
32 *Which was the son of Jesse* **of Yishay**,
which was the son of Obed,
which was the son of Booz,
which was the son of Salmon,
which was the son of Naasson **of Nachshon**,
33 *Which was the son of Aminadab* **of Ammi Nadab**,
which was the son of Aram **of Ram**,
which was the son of Esrom **of Hesron**,
which was the son of Phares **of Peres**,
which was the son of Juda **of Yah Hudah**,
34 *Which was the son of Jacob* **of Yaaqov**,
which was the son of Isaac **of Yischaq**,
which was the son of Abraham,
which was the son of Thara **of Terach**,
which was the son of Nachor,
35 *Which was the son of Saruch* **of Serug**,
which was the son of Ragau **of Reu**,
which was the son of Phalec **of Peleg**,
which was the son of Heber **of Eber**,
which was the son of Sala **of Shalach**,
36 *Which was the son of Cainan* **of Qeynan**,
which was the son of Arphaxad **of Arpachshad**,
which was the son of Sem **of Shem**,
which was the son of Noe **of Noach**,
which was the son of Lamech **of Lemech**,
37 *Which was the son of Mathusala* **of Methu Shelach**,
which was the son of Enoch **of Hanoch**,
which was the son of Jared **of Yered**,
which was the son of Maleleel **of Ma Halal El**,
which was the son of Cainan **of Qayin**,
38 *Which was the son of Enos* **of Enosh**,
which was the son of Seth **of Sheth**,
which was the son of Adam,
which was the son of God **of Elohim**.

THE TESTING OF YAH SHUA

4 And *Jesus* **Yah Shua**
being full of the Holy *Ghost* **Spirit**
returned from *Jordan* **Yarden**,
and was led by the Spirit into the wilderness,
2 Being forty days *tempted* **tested** of *the devil* **Diabolos**.
And in those days he *did eat nothing* **ate naught**:
and when they were *ended* **complete**,
he afterward hungered.
3 And *the devil* **Diabolos** said unto him,
If thou be the Son of *God* **Elohim**,
command **say** this stone that it *be made* **become** bread.
4 And *Jesus* **Yah Shua** answered him, *saying* **wording**,
It is *written* **scribed**,
That *man* **humanity** shall not live by bread alone,
but by every *word* **rhema** of *God* **Yah Veh**.
Deuteronomy 8:3
5 And *the devil* **Diabolos**,
taking **bringing** him *up* into an high mountain,
shewed unto him
all the *kingdoms* **sovereigndoms** of the world
in a moment of time.
6 And *the devil* **Diabolos** said unto him,
All this *power will* **authority shall** I give thee,
and the glory of them:
for that is delivered unto me;
and to whomsoever I *will* **shall** I give it.
7 If thou therefore *wilt* **shalt** worship *me* **in my sight**,
all shall be thine.
8 And *Jesus* **Yah Shua** answered and said unto him,
Get thee behind me, Satan:
for it is *written* **scribed**,
Thou shalt worship *the Lord* **Yah Veh** thy *God* **Elohim**,
and him only shalt thou *serve* **liturgize**.
Deuteronomy 6:13, 10:20
9 And he brought him to *Jerusalem* **Yeru Shalem**,
and *set* **stood** him
on a *pinnacle* **wing** of the *temple* **priestal precinct**,
and said unto him,
If thou be the Son of *God* **Elohim**,
cast thyself down from hence:
10 For it is *written* **scribed**,
He shall *give* **misvah** his angels
charge over **concerning** thee,
to *keep* **thoroughly guard** thee:
11 And in their hands they shall *bear* **lift** thee *up*,
lest *at any time* **ever** thou dash thy foot against a stone.
Psalm 91:11, 12
12 And *Jesus* **Yah Shua** answering said unto him, It is said,
Thou shalt not *tempt* **test**
the Lord **Yah Veh** thy *God* **Elohim**.
Deuteronomy 6:16
13 And when *the devil* **Diabolos**
had *ended* **completed** all the *temptation* **testing**,
he departed from him for a season.

YAH SHUA'S MINISTRY

14 And *Jesus* **Yah Shua** returned
in the *power* **dynamis** of the Spirit into *Galilee* **Galiyl**:
and there went out a fame *of* **concerning** him
through all the region round about.
15 And he *taught* **doctrinated** in their synagogues,
being glorified of all.
16 And he came to Nazareth,
where he had been *brought up* **nurtured**:
and, as his custom was,
he *went* **entered** into the synagogue
on the *sabbath* day **of the shabbaths**,
and *stood up for* **rose** to read.
17 And there was *delivered* **given** unto him
the *book* **scroll** of the prophet *Esaias* **Yesha Yah**.
And when he had *opened* **unfurled** the *book* **scroll**,
he found the place where it was *written* **scribed**,
18 The Spirit of *the Lord* **Yah Veh** is upon me,
because he hath anointed me
to *preach the gospel to* **evangelize** the poor;
he hath *sent* **apostolized** me
to heal the *brokenhearted* **crushed in heart**,
to preach *deliverance* **forgiveness** to the captives,
and *recovering of* sight to the blind,
to set at liberty **apostolize** them that are *bruised* **crushed in forgiveness**,
19 To preach the acceptable year of *the Lord* **Yah Veh**.
Yesha Yah 61:1, 2
20 And he *closed* **furled** the *book* **scroll**,
and he gave it *again* **back** to the *minister* **attendant**,
and sat down.
And the eyes of all them that were in the synagogue
were fastened on **stared at** him.
21 And he began to *say* **word** unto them,
This day is this scripture fulfilled in your ears.
22 And all *bare him witness* **witnessed**,
and *wondered* **marvelled**
at the *gracious* words **of charism**
which proceeded out of his mouth.
And they *said* **worded**, Is not this *Joseph's* **Yoseph's** son?
23 And he said unto them,
Ye *will surely* **shall most certainly** say unto me
this *proverb* **parable**,
Physician **Healer**, *heal* **cure** thyself:
whatsoever **as much as** we have heard
done **become** in *Capernaum* **Kaphar Nachum**,
do also here in thy *country* **fatherland**.
24 And he said, *Verily I say* **Amen! I word** unto you,
No prophet is *accepted* **acceptable**

in his own *country* **fatherland**.
25 But I *tell* **word** you of a truth,
many widows were in *Israel* **Yisra El**
in the days of *Elias* **Eli Yah**,
when the heaven was shut *up*
three years and six months,
when *great* **mega** famine
was **became** throughout all the land;
26 But unto none of them was *Elias* **Eli Yah** sent,
save **except** unto *Sarepta* **Sarephath**, a city of Sidon,
unto a woman that was a widow.
27 And many lepers were in *Israel* **Yisra El**
in the time of Eliseus **with Eli Shua** the prophet;
and none of them was *cleansed* **purified**,
saving **except** Naaman the *Syrian* **Syriaiy**.
28 And all they in the synagogue,
when they heard these *things*,
were filled **full** with *wrath* **fury**,
29 And rose *up*, and *thrust* **cast** him out of the city,
and led him unto the brow of the *hill* **mountain**
whereon their city was built,
that they might cast him down *headlong*.
30 But he passing through the midst of them
went his way,
31 And came down to *Capernaum* **Kaphar Nachum**,
a city of *Galilee* **Galiyl**,
and *taught* **doctrinated** them
on the *sabbath days* **shabbaths**.
32 And they were astonished at his doctrine:
for his word was *with power* **in authority**.

YAH SHUA ORDERS AN IMPURE DEMON

33 And in the synagogue there was a *man* **human**,
which had a spirit of an *unclean devil* **impure demon**,
and *cried out* **screamed** with a *loud* **mega** voice,
34 *saying* **wording**, *Let us alone;* **Aha!**
what have we to do with thee,
thou *Jesus of Nazareth* **Yah Shua — Nazarene**?
art thou come to destroy us?
I know thee who thou art; the Holy *One* of *God* **Elohim**.
35 And *Jesus* **Yah Shua** rebuked him, *saying* **wording**,
Hold thy peace **Be muzzled**, and come out of him.
And when the *devil* **demon**
had *thrown* **tossed** him in the midst,
he came out of him, and hurt him not.
36 And they *were* all *amazed* **became astonished**,
and *spake* **talked** among *themselves* **one another**,
saying **wording**, What a word is this!
for *with* **in** authority and *power* **dynamis**
he *commandeth* **ordereth** the *unclean* **impure** spirits,
and they come out.
37 And the *fame of* **echo concerning** him
went out **proceeded** into every place
of the *country* **region** round about.

YAH SHUA CURES SHIMON'S MOTHER IN LAW

38 And he arose out of the synagogue,
and entered into *Simon's* **Shimon's** house.
And *Simon's wife's* **Shimon's** mother **in law**
was *taken with* **overtaken by** a *great* **mega** fever;
and they *besought* **asked** him *for* **concerning** her.
39 And he stood over her, and rebuked the fever;
and it *left* **forsook** her:
and immediately she arose and ministered unto them.
40 Now when the sun was *setting* **lowering**,
all *they that* **— as many as** had any *sick* **frail**
with divers diseases
brought them unto him;
and he *laid* **put** his hands on *every* **each** one of them,
and *healed* **cured** them.
41 And *devils* **demons** also came out of many,
crying out, and *saying* **wording**,
Thou art *Christ* **the Messiah** the Son of *God* **Elohim**.
And he rebuking them
suffered **allowed** them not to speak:
for they knew that he was *Christ* **the Messiah**.
42 And when it *was* **became** day,
he departed and went into a *desert* **desolate** place:
and the *people* **multitude** sought him,
and came unto him,
and *stayed* **held** him,
that he should not depart from them.
43 And he said unto them,
I must *preach* **evangelize**
the *kingdom* **sovereigndom** of *God* **Elohim**
to other cities also:
for therefore am I *sent* **apostolized**.
44 And he preached in the synagogues of *Galilee* **Galiyl**.

YAH SHUA'S FIRST DISCIPLES

5 And it *came to pass* **became**, that,
as the *people pressed* **multitude imposed** upon him
to hear the word of *God* **Elohim**,
he stood by the lake of *Gennesaret* **Kinneroth**,
2 And saw two *ships* **sailers** standing by the lake:
but the *fishermen* **fishers**
were gone out of **had turned from** them,
and were rinsing their nets.
3 And he *entered* **embarked** into one of the *ships* **sailers**,
which was *Simon's* **Shimon's**,
and *prayed* **asked** him
that he *would thrust* **should launch** out a little
from the land.
And he sat down,
and *taught* **doctrinated** the *people* **multitude**
out of the *ship* **sailer**.
4 Now when he had *left* **paused** speaking,
he said unto *Simon* **Shimon**,
Launch out into the *deep* **depths**,
and *let down* **lower** your nets for a *draught* **catch**.
5 And *Simon* **Shimon** answering said unto him,
Master **Rabbi**,
we have *toiled* **laboured through** all the night,
and have taken *nothing* **naught**:
nevertheless at thy *word* **rhema**
I *will let down* **shall lower** the net.
6 And when they had this done,
they inclosed a *great* **vast** multitude of fishes:
and their net *brake* **ripped**.
7 And they *beckoned* **nodded** unto their partners,
which were in the other *ship* **sailer**,
that they should come and *help* **take** them.
And they came, and filled **full** both the *ships* **sailers**,
so that they began to sink.
8 When *Simon Peter* **Shimon Petros** saw it,
he *fell down* **prostrated** at *Jesus'* **Yah Shua's** knees,
saying **wording**, Depart from me;
for I am a sinful man, O *Lord* **Adonay**.
9 For *he was astonished* **astonishment enveloped him**,
and all that were with him,
at the *draught* **catch** of the fishes which they had taken:
10 And *so was* **likewise** also
James **Yaaqovos**, and *John* **Yahn**,
the sons of *Zebedee* **Zabdi**,
which were *partners* **partakers** with *Simon* **Shimon**.
And *Jesus* **Yah Shua** said unto *Simon* **Shimon**,
Fear **Awe** not;
from *henceforth* **now on**
thou shalt *catch men* **capture live humans**.
11 And when they had
brought **moored** their *ships* **sailers** to land,
they forsook all, and followed him.

YAH SHUA PURIFIES A LEPER

12 And it *came to pass* **became**,
when he was in a *certain* city, behold,
a man full of leprosy:
who seeing *Jesus* **Yah Shua** fell on his face,
and *besought* **petitioned** him, *saying,* **wording**,
Lord **Adonay**, if thou *wilt* **willest**,
thou canst *make* **purify** me *clean*.
13 And he *put forth* **extended** his hand, and touched him,
saying, I will: be thou *clean* **purified**.
And *immediately* **straightway**
the leprosy departed from him.
14 And he *charged* **evangelized** him
to *tell* **say to** no *man* **one**:
but go, and shew thyself to the priest,
and offer for thy *cleansing* **purifying**,
according **exactly** as *Moses* **Mosheh** commanded,
for a *testimony* **witness** unto them.
15 But so much the more
went there a fame abroad of him
word about him passed through:

and *great* **vast** multitudes came together to hear,
and to be *healed* **cured** by him
of their *infirmities* **frailties.**
16 And he withdrew himself into the wilderness,
and prayed.

YAH SHUA HEALS A PARALYTIC

17 And it *came to pass on a certain* **became one** day,
as he was *teaching* **doctrinating**,
that there were Pharisees and doctors of the *law* **torah**
sitting by,
which were come out
of every *town* **village** of *Galilee* **Galiyl**,
and *Judaea* **Yah Hudah**, and *Jerusalem* **Yeru Shalem**:
and the *power* **dynamis** of *the Lord* **Adonay**
was *present* to heal them.
18 And, behold, men brought in a bed
a *man* **human** which was *taken with a palsy* **paralyzed**:
and they sought *means* to bring him in,
and to *lay* **place** him *before him* **in his sight**.
19 And when they could not find
by **through** what way they might bring him in
because of the multitude,
they *went up* **ascended** on the housetop,
and let him down through the tiling
with his *couch* **recliner**
into the midst *before Jesus* **in front of Yah Shua**.
20 And when he saw their *faith* **trust**, he said unto him,
man **human**, thy sins are forgiven thee.
21 And the scribes and the Pharisees began to reason,
saying **wording**,
Who is this which speaketh blasphemies?
Who can forgive sins, *but God* **except Elohim** alone?
22 But *when Jesus* **Yah Shua,**
perceived **knowing** their *thoughts* **reasonings**,
he answering said unto them,
What reason ye in your hearts?
23 Whether is easier, to say, Thy sins be forgiven thee;
or to say, Rise *up* and walk?
24 But that ye may know that the Son of *man* **humanity**
hath *power* **authority** upon earth to forgive sins,
(he said unto the *sick of the palsy* **paralyzed**,)
I *say* **word** unto thee, Arise,
and take *up* thy *couch* **recliner**, and go into thine house.
25 And immediately he rose *up before them* **in their sight**,
and took *up* that whereon he lay,
and departed to his own house, glorifying *God* **Elohim**.
26 And they were all *amazed* **overtaken by ecstasis**,
and they glorified *God* **Elohim**,
and were filled **full** with *fear* **awe**, *saying* **wording**,
We have seen *strange things* **paradoxes** to day.

YAH SHUA CALLS LEVI

27 And after these *things* he went forth,
and saw a *publican* **customs agent**, named Levi,
sitting at the *receipt of custom* **customs**:
and he said unto him, Follow me.
28 And he left all, rose *up*, and followed him.
29 And Levi made him a *great* **mega** feast
in his own house:
and there was a *great company* **vast multitude**
of *publicans* **customs agents** and of others
that *sat down* **reposed** with them.
30 But their scribes and Pharisees
murmured against his disciples,
saying **wording**, Why do ye eat and drink
with *publicans* **customs agents** and sinners?
31 And *Jesus* **Yah Shua** answering said unto them,
They that are whole need not a *physician* **healer**;
but they that are *sick* **ill**.
32 I came not to call the *righteous* **just**,
but sinners to repentance.

YAH SHUA ON FASTING

33 And they said unto him,
Why do the disciples of *John* **Yahn**
fast *often* **frequently**, and make *prayers* **petitions**,
and likewise *the disciples of* the Pharisees;
but thine eat and drink?
34 And he said unto them,
Can ye make the *children* **sons** of the bridechamber fast,
while the bridegroom is with them?
35 But the days *will* **shall** come,
when **ever** the bridegroom
shall be *taken away* **removed** from them,
and then shall they fast in those days.
36 And he *spake* **worded** also a parable unto them;
no *man* **one** putteth a *piece* **patch** of a new garment
upon an old;
if otherwise **but if not**,
then both the new *maketh a rent* **splitteth**,
and the *piece that was taken* **patch** out of the new
agreeth **symphonizeth** not with the old.
37 And no *man* **one** putteth new wine
into old *bottles* **skins**;
else **but if not**
the new wine *will* **shall** burst the *bottles* **skins**,
and *be spilled* **pour forth**,
and the *bottles* **skins** shall *perish* **destruct**.
38 But new wine must be put into new *bottles* **skins**;
and both are preserved.
39 No *man* **one** also having drunk old *wine*
straightway desireth **willeth** new:
for he *saith* **wordeth**, The old is *better* **useful**.

YAH SHUA IS ADONAY OF THE SHABBATH

6 And it *came to pass* **became**
on the second *sabbath after the first* **first shabbath**,
that he went through the *corn fields* **spores**;
and his disciples plucked the *ears of corn* **kernels**,
and did eat, rubbing them in their hands.
2 And *certain* **some** of the Pharisees said unto them,
Why do ye that which is not *lawful* **allowed** to do
on the *sabbath days* **shabbaths**?
3 And *Jesus* **Yah Shua** answering them said,
Have ye not read so much as this, what David did,
when himself was an hungred,
and they which were with him;
4 How he *went* **entered** into the house of *God* **Elohim**,
and did take and eat the *shewbread* **prothesis bread**,
and gave also to them that were with him;
which it is not *lawful* **allowed** to eat
but **except** for the priests alone?
1 Shemu El 21:6

YAH SHUA RESTORES A WITHERED HAND

5 And he *said* **worded** unto them,
That the Son of *man* **humanity**
is *Lord* **Adonay** also of the *sabbath* **shabbath**.
6 And it *came to pass* **became**
also on another *sabbath* **shabbath**,
that he entered into the synagogue
and *taught* **doctrinated**:
and there was a *man* **human**
whose right hand was withered.
7 And the scribes and Pharisees *watched* **observed** him,
whether he *would heal* **should cure**
on the *sabbath day* **shabbath**;
that they might find an accusation against him.
8 But he knew their *thoughts* **reasonings**,
and said to the *man* **human**
which had the withered hand,
Rise *up*, and stand *forth* in the midst.
And he arose and stood *forth*.
9 Then said *Jesus* **Yah Shua** unto them,
I *will* **shall** ask you one *thing*;
Is it *lawful* **allowed** on the *sabbath days* **shabbaths**
to do good, or to do evil?
to save *life* **soul**, or to destroy *it*?
10 And looking round about upon them all,
he said unto the *man* **human**,
Stretch forth **Extend** thy hand.
And he did *so* **thus**:
and his hand was restored whole as the other.
11 And they were filled **full** with *madness* **mindlessness**;
and *communed* **talked thoroughly** one with another
what they might do to *Jesus* **Yah Shua**.

YAH SHUA SELECTS TWELVE APOSTLES

12 And it *came to pass* **became** in those days,
that he went out into a mountain to pray,
and continued all night in prayer to *God* **Elohim**.
13 And when it *was* **became** day,
he called unto him his disciples:
and of them he *chose* **selected** twelve,
whom also he named apostles;

14 *Simon* **Shimon**, (whom he also named *Peter* **Petros**,)
and *Andrew* **Andreas** his brother,
James **Yaaqovos** and *John* **Yahn**,
Philip **Phillipos** and *Bartholomew* **Bar Talmay**,
15 *Matthew* **Matthaios** and *Thomas* **Taom**,
James **Yaaqovos** the son of *Alphaeus* **Heleph**,
and *Simon* **Shimon** called *Zelotes* **the Zealot**,
16 And *Judas* **Yah Hudah** *the brother* of *James* **Yaaqovos**,
and *Judas Iscariot* **Yah Hudah the urbanite**,
which also *was* **became** the traitor.
17 And he *came down* **descended** with them,
and stood *in the plain* **on a level place**,
and the *company* **multitude** of his disciples,
and a *great* **vast** multitude of people
out of all *Judaea* **Yah Hudah** and *Jerusalem* **Yeru Shalem**,
and from the sea coast of *Tyre* **Sor** and Sidon,
which came to hear him,
and to be healed of their diseases;
18 And they that were vexed
with unclean **by impure** spirits:
and they were *healed* **cured**.
19 And the whole multitude sought to touch him:
for there went *virtue* **dynamis** out of him,
and healed them all.

THE BEATITUDES

20 And he lifted *up* his eyes on his disciples,
and *said* **worded**,
Blessed, *be ye* **the** poor:
for yours is the *kingdom* **sovereigndom** of *God* **Elohim**.
21 Blessed, *are ye* that hunger now: for ye shall be filled.
Blessed, *are ye* that weep now: for ye shall laugh.
22 Blessed are ye,
when **ever** *men* **humanity** shall hate you,
and when **ever** they shall *separate* **set** you **apart**
from their company,
and shall reproach you, and cast out your name as evil,
for the Son of *man's* **humanity's** sake.
23 *Rejoice* **Cheer** ye in that day, and leap for joy:
for, behold, your reward is *great* **vast** in heaven:
for in the like manner did their fathers unto the prophets.

THE WOES

24 But woe unto you that are rich!
for ye have received your consolation **in full**.
25 Woe unto you that are full! for ye shall hunger.
Woe unto you that laugh now!
for ye shall mourn and weep.
26 Woe unto you,
when **ever** all *men* **humanity** shall *speak* **say** well of you!
for *so* **in like manner**
did their fathers to the *false* **pseudo** prophets.

YAH SHUA ON LOVING ENEMIES

27 But I *say* **word** unto you which hear,
Love your enemies,
do *good* **well** to them which hate you,
28 *Bless* **Eulogize** them that curse you,
and pray for them which *despitefully use* **threaten** you.
29 And unto him
that *smiteth* **striketh** thee on the *one* cheek
offer **present** also the other;
and him that taketh away thy *cloak* **garment**
forbid not *to take* thy *coat* **tunic** also.
30 Give to every man that asketh of thee;
and of him that taketh away thy goods
ask them **demand** not *again*.
31 And **exactly** as ye *would* will
that *men* **humanity** should do to you,
do ye also to them likewise.
32 For if ye love them which love you,
what *thank have ye* **charism is yours**?
for sinners also love those that love them.
33 And if ye do good to them which do good to you,
what *thank have ye* **charism is yours**?
for sinners also do even the same.
34 And if ye lend to them
of whom ye hope to *receive* **take**,
what *thank have ye* **charism is yours**?
for sinners also lend to sinners,
to *receive as much again* **take equal**.
35 But love ye your enemies, and do good, and lend,
hoping for *nothing* **naught** again;
and your reward shall be *great* **vast**,
and ye shall be the *children* **sons** of *the Highest* **Elyon**:
for he is kind
unto the *unthankful* **uneucharistic** and to the evil.
36 Be ye therefore *merciful* **compassionate**
exactly as your Father also is *merciful* **compassionate**.

YAH SHUA ON JUDGING OTHERS

37 Judge not, and ye shall not **no way** be judged:
condemn not, and ye shall not **no way** be condemned:
forgive, and ye shall be forgiven:
38 Give, and it shall be given unto you;
good measure, *pressed down* **packed**,
and shaken *together*, and *running over* **overflowing**,
shall men give into your bosom.
For with the same measure that ye *mete withal* **measure**
it shall be *measured* **remeasured** to you *again*.
39 And he *spake* **said** a parable unto them,
Can the blind *lead* **guide** the blind?
shall they not **indeed** both fall into the *ditch* **cistern**?
40 The disciple is not above his *master* **doctor**:
but every one that is *perfect* **prepared**
shall be as his *master* **doctor**.
41 And why *beholdest* **seest** thou the *mote* **twig**
that is in thy brother's eye,
but perceivest not the beam that is in thine own eye?
42 Either how canst thou *say* **word** to thy brother,
Brother, *let* **allow** me
pull **cast** out the *mote* **twig** that is in thine eye,
when thou thyself
beholdest **seest** not the beam that is in thine own eye?
Thou hypocrite,
cast out first the beam out of thine own eye,
and then shalt thou see clearly
to *pull* **cast** *out* the *mote* **twig** that is in thy brother's eye.

YAH SHUA ON TREES AND FRUIT

43 For a good tree
bringeth **produceth** not *forth corrupt* **putrefied** fruit;
neither doth a *corrupt* **putrefied** tree
bring forth **produce** good fruit.
44 For *every* **each** tree is known by his own fruit.
For of thorns men do not gather figs,
nor of a *bramble bush* **brier**
gather **dry** they grapes.
45 A good *man* **human**
out of the good treasure of his heart
bringeth forth **produceth** that which is good;
and an evil *man* **human**
out of the evil treasure of his heart
bringeth forth **produceth** that which is evil:
for of the **super** abundance of the heart
his mouth speaketh.
46 And why call ye me, *Lord* **Adonay**, *Lord* **Adonay**,
and do not *the things* **that** which I *say* **word**?

YAH SHUA ON FOUNDATIONS

47 Whosoever cometh to me,
and heareth my *sayings* **words**, and doeth them,
I *will shew* **shall exemplify** you to whom he is like:
48 He is like a *man* **human** which built an house,
and digged deep,
and *laid* **placed** the foundation on a rock:
and when the flood *arose* **became**,
the stream *beat vehemently* **burst** upon that house,
and could not shake it: for it was founded upon a rock.
49 But he that heareth, and doeth not,
is like a *man* **human**
that *without* **apart from** a foundation
built an house upon the earth;
against **upon** which
the stream *did beat vehemently* **burst**,
and *immediately* **straightway** it fell;
and the *ruin* **fragmentation** of that house
was great **became mega**.

YAH SHUA HEALS THE CENTURION'S SERVANT

7 Now *when* **since** he had
ended **fulfilled** all his *sayings* **rhema**
in the *audience* **hearing** of the people,
he entered into *Capernaum* **Kaphar Nachum**.
2 And a *certain* centurion's servant,
who was *dear* **honourable** unto him,
was *sick* **ill**, and *ready* **about** to die.

3 And when he heard *of Jesus* **concerning Yah Shua**,
he *sent* **apostolized** unto him
the elders of the *Jews* **Yah Hudiym**,
beseeching **asking** him
that he *would* **should** come and *heal* **save** his servant.
4 And when they came to *Jesus* **Yah Shua**,
they besought him *instantly* **diligently**, *saying* **wording**,
That he was worthy for whom he should *do* **cause** this:
5 For he loveth our *nation* **goyim**,
and he hath built us a synagogue.
6 Then *Jesus* **Yah Shua** went with them.
And when he was *now* **already** not far from the house,
the centurion sent friends to him,
saying **wording** unto him,
Lord **Adonay**, *trouble* **harass** not thyself
for I am not *worthy* **adequate**
that thou shouldest enter under my *roof* **thatch**:
7 Wherefore neither *thought* **deemed** I myself worthy
to come unto thee:
but say in a word, and my *servant* **lad** shall be healed.
8 For I also am a *man* **human**
set **ordained** under authority,
having under me *soldiers* **warriors**,
and I *say* **word** unto this one, Go, and he goeth;
and to another, Come, and he cometh;
and to my servant, Do this, and he doeth *it*.
9 When *Jesus* **Yah Shua** heard these *things*,
he marvelled at him,
and turned him about,
and said unto the *people* **multitude** that followed him,
I *say* **word** unto you,
I have not found so *great faith* **much trust**,
no, not **even** in *Israel* **Yisra El**.
10 And they that were sent, returning to the house,
found the servant whole that had been *sick* **frail**.

YAH SHUA RAISES A WIDOW'S SON

11 And it *came to pass the day after* **became next**,
that he went into a city called Nain;
and *many* **enough** of his disciples went with him,
and much *people* **multitude**.
12 Now when he
came nigh to **approached** the gate of the city, behold,
there was a dead man carried out,
the only **begotten** son of his mother,
and she was a widow:
and *much people* **enough multitude** of the city
was with her.
13 And when *the Lord* **Adonay** saw her,
he had *compassion* **a sympathetic spleen** on her,
and said unto her, Weep not.
14 And he came and touched the *bier* **coffin**:
and they that bare him stood *still*.
And he said, *Young man* **Youth**,
I *say* **word** unto thee, Arise.
15 And he that was dead sat *up*, and began to speak.
And he *delivered* **gave** him to his mother.
16 And *there came a fear on* **an awe overtook** all:
and they glorified *God* **Elohim**, *saying* **wording**,
That a *great* **mega** prophet is risen *up* among us;
and, That *God* **Elohim** hath visited his people.
17 And this *rumour of* **word concerning** him
went forth throughout all *Judaea* **Yah Hudah**,
and throughout all the region round about.

BAPTIZER YAHN ENQUIRES OF YAH SHUA

18 And the disciples of *John* **Yahn**
shewed **evangelized** him *of* **about** all these *things*.
19 And *John* **Yahn** calling unto him two of his disciples
sent them to *Jesus* **Yah Shua**, *saying* **wording**,
Art thou he that should come?
or *look* **await** we *for* another?
20 When the men were come unto him, they said,
John Baptist **Yahn the baptizer**
hath *sent* **apostolized** us unto thee, *saying* **wording**,
Art thou he that should come?
or *look* **await** we *for* another?
21 And in that same hour he cured many
of their *infirmities* **diseases** and *plagues* **scourges**,
and of evil spirits;
and unto many *that were* blind
he *gave sight* **granted charism to see**.
22 Then *Jesus* **Yah Shua** answering said unto them,
Go your way, and *tell John* **evangelize Yahn**
what *things* ye have seen and heard;
how that the blind see, the lame walk,
the lepers *are cleansed* **purified**, the *deaf* **mute** hear,
the dead *are* raised,
to **and** the poor *the gospel is preached* **evangelized**.
23 And blessed is he, whosoever
shall not be offended **— unless you be scandalized** in me.
24 And when the *messengers* **angels** of *John* **Yahn**
were departed,
he began to *speak* **word** unto the *people* **multitude**
concerning *John* **Yahn**,
What went ye out into the wilderness for to see?
A reed shaken *with* **by** the wind?
25 But what went ye out for to see?
A *man* **human**
clothed in *soft raiment* **effeminate garment**?
Behold, they which are
gorgeously apparelled **gloriously garmented**,
and *live delicately* **indulgent**,
are in *kings' courts* **sovereign's palaces**.
26 But what went ye out for to see? A prophet?
Yea, I *say* **word** unto you,
and *much* **superabundantly** more than a prophet.
27 This is he, *of* **concerning** whom it is *written* **scribed**,
Behold,
I *send* **apostolize** my *messenger* **angel** before thy face,
which shall prepare thy way *before* **in front of** thee.
28 For I *say* **word** unto you,
Among those that are born of women
there is not a greater prophet
than *John* **Yahn** the *Baptist* **Baptizer**:
but he that is least
in the *kingdom* **sovereigndom** of *God* **Elohim**
is greater than he.
29 And all the people that heard him,
and the *publicans* **customs agents**, justified *God* **Elohim**,
being baptized with the baptism of *John* **Yahn**.
30 But the Pharisees and *lawyers* **torahists**
rejected **set aside** the counsel of *God* **Elohim**
against themselves,
being not baptized of him.
31 And *the Lord* **Adonay** said,
Whereunto then
shall I liken *the men* **humanity** of this generation?
and to what are they like?
32 They are like unto children
sitting in the *marketplace* **market**,
and calling one to another, and *saying* **wording**,
We have *piped* **fluted** unto you,
and ye have not danced;
we have *mourned* **lamented** to you,
and ye have not wept.
33 For *John* **Yahn** the *Baptist* **Baptizer** came
neither eating bread nor drinking wine;
and ye *say* **word**, He hath a *devil* **demon**.
34 The Son of *man* **humanity** is come eating and drinking;
and ye *say* **word**, Behold,
a gluttonous *man* **human**, and a winebibber,
a friend of *publicans* **customs agents** and sinners!
35 But wisdom is justified of all her children.

A WOMAN SINNER ANOINTS YAH SHUA

36 And one of the Pharisees
desired **asked** him that he *would* **should** eat with him.
And he *went into* **entered** the Pharisee's house,
and *sat down to meat* **reclined**.
37 And, behold, a woman in the city, which was a sinner,
when she knew that *Jesus* **Yah Shua**
sat at meat **reposed** in the Pharisee's house,
brought **provided** an alabaster *box* of *ointment* **myrrh**,
38 And stood at his feet behind him weeping,
and began to *wash* **moisten** his feet with tears,
and *did wipe* **squeezedried** them
with the hairs of her head,
and **ardently** kissed his feet,
and anointed them with the *ointment* **myrrh**.
39 Now when the Pharisee which had *bidden* **called** him
saw it,
he spake within himself, *saying* **wording**,

This *man,* if he were a prophet,
would **should** have known who
and what manner of woman this is that toucheth him:
for she is a sinner.

YAH SHUA ON LENDERS

40 And *Jesus* **Yah Shua** answering said unto him,
Simon **Shimon**, I have somewhat to say unto thee.
And he saith, *Master* **Doctor**, say on.
41 There was a *certain creditor* **lender**
which had two debtors:
the one *owed* **was indebted**
five hundred *pence* **denarion**,
and the other fifty.
42 And when they had *nothing* **naught** to *pay* **give back**,
he *frankly forgave* **granted** them both **charism**.
Tell me **Say** therefore,
which of them *will* **shall** love him most?
43 *Simon* **Shimon** answered and said,
I *suppose* **perceive** that he,
to whom he *forgave* **granted** most **charism**.
And he said unto him,
Thou hast *rightly* **straightforwardly** judged.
44 And he turned to the woman,
and said unto *Simon* **Shimon**,
Seest thou this woman?
I entered into thine house,
thou gavest me no water for my feet:
but she hath *washed* **moistened** my feet with tears,
and *wiped them* **squeezedried** with the hairs of her head.
45 Thou gavest me no kiss:
but this *woman* **one** since *the time I came in* **I entered**
hath not ceased to **ardently** kiss my feet.
46 My head with **olive** oil thou didst not anoint:
but this *woman* **one**
hath anointed my feet with *ointment* **myrrh**.
47 *Wherefore* **For this cause** I *say* **word** unto thee,
Her sins, which are many, are forgiven;
for she loved much:
but to whom little is forgiven, *the same* loveth little.
48 And he said unto her, Thy sins are forgiven.
49 And they that *sat at meat* **reposed** with him
began to *say* **word** within themselves,
Who is this that forgiveth sins also?
50 And he said to the woman,
Thy *faith* **trust** hath saved thee; go in *peace* **shalom**.

8 And it *came to pass afterward* **became in sequence**,
that he *went throughout* **passed through**
every city and village,
preaching and *shewing the glad tidings of* **evangelizing**
the *kingdom* **sovereigndom** of *God* **Elohim**:
and the twelve were with him,
2 And *certain* **some** women,
which had been *healed* **cured**
of evil spirits and *infirmities* **frailties**,
Mary **Miryam** called Magdalene,
out of whom went seven *devils* **demons**,
3 And *Joanna* **Yah Hanna** the *wife* **woman** of Chuza
Herod's *steward* **manager**,
and *Susanna* **Shoshanna**, and many others,
which ministered unto him of their *substance* **holdings**.

YAH SHUA ON THE SOWER

4 And when much *people* **multitude**
were gathered together,
and *were come* **journeyed** to him out of every city,
he *spake by* **said through** a parable:
5 A sower went out to sow his *seed* **spore**:
and as he sowed, some **indeed** fell by the way side;
and it was *trodden down* **trampled**,
and the *fowls* **flyers** of the *air* **heavens** devoured it.
6 And *some* **others** fell upon a rock;
and as soon as it *was sprung up* **sprouted**,
it withered *away,* because it *lacked* **had no** moisture.
7 And *some* **others** fell among thorns;
and the thorns *sprang up* **sprouted** with it, and choked it.
8 And other fell on good *ground* **earth**,
and *sprang up* **sprouted**
and *bare* **produced** fruit an hundredfold.
And when he had *said* **worded** these *things,*
he *cried* **voiced out**,
He that hath ears to hear, let him hear.
9 And his disciples asked him, *saying* **wording**,
What might this parable be?
10 And he said,
Unto you it is given to know the mysteries
of the *kingdom* **sovereigndom** of *God* **Elohim**:
but to *others* **the rest** in parables;
that seeing they might not see,
and hearing they might not *understand* **comprehend**.
11 Now the parable is this:
The *seed* **spore** is the word of *God* **Elohim**.
12 Those by the way side are they that hear;
then cometh *the devil* **Diabolos**,
and taketh away the word out of their hearts,
lest they should *believe* **trust** and be saved.
13 They on the rock *are they,*
which, when **ever** they hear,
receive the word with *joy* **cheer**;
and these have no root,
which for a *while believe* **season trust**,
and in *time* **season** of *temptation* **testing** fall away.
14 And that which fell among thorns are they,
which, when they have heard, go forth,
and are *choked* **strangled**
with cares **by anxieties** and riches and pleasures
of *this life* **existence**,
and bring no fruit to *perfection* **completion**.
15 But that on the *good ground* **beautiful earth** are they,
which in *an honest* **a beautiful** and good heart,
having heard the word, *keep it* **hold on**,
and *bring forth* **bear** fruit *with patience* **by endurance**.

YAH SHUA ON CANDLES

16 No *man* **one**, when he hath lighted a candle,
covereth **veileth** it with a vessel,
or putteth it under a bed;
but *setteth* **putteth** it on a *candlestick* **menorah**,
that they which enter in may see the light.
17 For *nothing* **naught** is *secret* **secreted**,
that shall not be *made* manifest;
neither *any thing hid* **secreted**,
that shall not be known
and *come abroad* **be manifest**.
18 *Take heed* **See** therefore how ye hear:
for whosoever hath, to him shall be given;
and whosoever hath not, from him shall be taken
even that which he *seemeth to have* **thinketh he hath**.
19 Then came to him his mother and his brethren,
and could not *come* **get** at him for the *press* **multitude**.
20 And it was *told* **evangelized** him
by certain which said **wording**,
Thy mother and thy brethren stand without,
desiring **willing** to see thee.
21 And he answered and said unto them,
My mother and my brethren
are these which hear the word of *God* **Elohim**, and do it.

YAH SHUA REBUKES THE WIND

22 Now it *came to pass on a certain* **became one** day,
that he *went* **embarked** into a *ship* **sailer**
with his disciples:
and he said unto them, Let us *go over* **pass through**
unto the other side of the lake.
And they *launched forth* **embarked**.
23 But as they sailed he fell asleep:
and there *came down* **descended**
a *storm of wind* **whirlwind** on the lake;
and they were filled **full** *with water,*
and were in *jeopardy* **peril**.
24 And they came to him, and *awoke* **roused** him,
saying **wording**, *Master, master* **Rabbi, rabbi**,
we *perish* **destruct**.
Then he arose, and rebuked the wind
and the *raging* **surging** of the water:
and they *ceased* **paused**, and there *was* **became** a calm.
25 And he said unto them, Where is your *faith* **trust**?
And they *being afraid wondered* **awing, marvelled**,
saying **wording** one to another,
What manner of man **Who then** is this!
for he *commandeth* **ordereth** even the winds and water,
and they obey him.

YAH SHUA EVANGELIZES TO IMPURE SPIRITS

26 And they *arrived* **sailed**
at **down to** the *country* **region** of the Gadarenes,
which is *over against Galilee* **opposite Galiyl**.
27 And when he went forth to land,
there met him out of the city a *certain* man,
which had *devils long* **demons enough** time,
and *ware no clothes* **not clothed in a garment**,
neither abode in any house, but in the tombs.
28 When he saw *Jesus* **Yah Shua**, he *cried out* **screamed**,
and *fell down* **prostrated** before him,
and with a *loud* **mega** voice said,
What have I to do with thee, *Jesus* **Yah Shua**,
thou Son of *God most high* **El Elyon**?
I *beseech* **petition** thee, *torment* **torture** me not.
29 (For he had *commanded* **evangelized**
the *unclean* **impure** spirit to come out of the *man* **human**.
For oftentimes it had caught him:
and he was *kept* **guarded**
bound with *chains* **fetters** and in *fetters* **shackles**;
and he *brake* **ripped** the *bands* **bonds**,
and was driven of the *devil* **demon** into the wilderness.)
30 And *Jesus* **Yah Shua** asked him, *saying* **wording**,
What is thy name?
And he said, Legion:
because many *devils* **demons** were entered into him.
31 And they besought him
that he *would* **should** not *command* **order** them
to go out into the *deep* **abyss**.
32 And there was there
an *herd* **a drove** of *many* **ample** swine
feeding **grazing** on the mountain:
and they besought him
that he *would suffer* **should allow** them
to enter into them.
And he *suffered* **allowed** them.
33 Then went the *devils* **demons** out of the *man* **human**,
and entered into the swine:
and the *herd* **drove** ran violently down a *steep place* **cliff**
into the lake, and were choked.
34 When they that *fed* **grazed** them
saw what *was done* **had become**,
they fled, and went and *told* **evangelized** it
in the city and in the *country* **field**.
35 Then they went out to see
what *was done* **had become**;
and came to *Jesus* **Yah Shua**,
and found the *man* **human**,
out of whom the *devils* **demons** were departed,
sitting at the feet of *Jesus* **Yah Shua**,
clothed, and *in his right mind* **sound minded**:
and they were *afraid* **awestricken**.
36 They also which saw it *told* **evangelized** them
by what means **how**
he that was *possessed of the devils* **demonized**
was *healed* **saved**.
37 Then the whole multitude
of the *country* **region** of the Gadarenes round about
besought **asked** him to depart from them;
for they were *taken* **held** with *great fear* **mega awe**:
and he *went up* **embarked** into the *ship* **sailer**,
and returned *back again*.
38 Now the man
out of whom the *devils* **demons** were departed
besought **petitioned** him that he might be with him:
but *Jesus sent* **Yah Shua released** him *away*,
saying **wording**,
39 Return to thine own house,
and *shew how great things* **declare as great as**
God **Elohim** hath done unto thee.
And he went his way,
and *published* **preached** throughout the whole city
how great *things Jesus* **Yah Shua** had done unto him.
40 And it *came to pass* **became**, that,
when *Jesus* **Yah Shua** *was* returned,
the *people gladly* **multitude** received him:
for they were all *waiting for* **awaiting** him.

YAIR'S DYING DAUGHTER

41 And, behold, there came a man named *Jairus* **Yair**,
and he was *a ruler* **an arch** of the synagogue:
and he fell down at *Jesus'* **Yah Shua's** feet,
and besought him
that he *would come into* **should enter** his house:
42 For he had one only *begotten* daughter,
about twelve years *of age,* and she *lay a* **was** dying.
But as he went
the *people thronged* **multitude strangled** him.

WOMAN TOUCHES YAH SHUA

43 And a woman
having **an** *issue* **a flux** of blood twelve years,
which had spent all her *living* **subsistence**
upon *physicians* **healers**,
neither could be *healed* **cured** of any,
44 Came behind him,
and touched the *border* **edge** of his garment:
and immediately her *issue* **flux** of blood *stanched* **stood**.
45 And *Jesus* **Yah Shua** said, Who touched me?
When all denied,
Peter **Petros** and they that were with him said,
Master **Rabbi**,
the multitude *throng* **hold** thee and press thee,
and *sayest* **wordest** thou, Who touched me?
46 And *Jesus* **Yah Shua** said,
Somebody **Someone** hath touched me:
for I *perceive* **know**
that *virtue* **dynamis** is gone out of me.
47 And when the woman saw that she was not hid,
she came trembling,
and *falling down* **prostrating** before him,
she *declared* **evangelized** unto him
before **in sight of** all the people
for what cause she had touched him,
and how she was healed immediately.
48 And he said unto her, Daughter,
be of good comfort **Courage**:
thy *faith* **trust** hath *made* **saved** thee *whole*;
go in *peace* **shalom**.

YAIR'S DAUGHTER DIES

49 While he yet spake, there cometh one
from the *ruler of the synagogue's house* **synagogue arch**,
saying **wording** to him, Thy daughter is dead;
trouble **harass** not the *Master* **Doctor**.
50 But when *Jesus* **Yah Shua** heard *it,*
he answered him, *saying* **wording**, *Fear* **Awe** not:
believe **trust** only, and she shall be *made whole* **saved**.
51 And when he *came* **entered** into the house,
he *suffered* **allowed** no *man* **one** to *go in* **enter**,
save Peter **except Petros**,
and *James* **Yaaqovos**, and *John* **Yahn**,
and the father and the mother of the *maiden* **lass**.
52 And all wept, and *bewailed* **chopped over** her:
but he said, Weep not; she is not dead, but sleepeth.
53 And they *laughed* **ridiculed** him *to scorn*,
knowing that she was dead.

YAH SHUA RAISES YAIR'S DAUGHTER

54 And he *put* **cast** them all out,
and *took* **overpowered** her by the hand,
and *called* **voiced out**, *saying* **wording**, *Maid* **Lass**, arise.
55 And her spirit *came again* **returned**,
and she arose straightway:
and he *commanded* **ordained** to give her *meat* **eats**.
56 And her parents were *astonished* **astounded**:
but he *charged* **evangelized** them
that they should *tell* **say to** no *man* **one**
what *was done* **had become**.

YAH SHUA APOSTOLIZES THE TWELVE

9 Then he called his twelve disciples together,
and gave them *power* **dynamis** and authority
over all *devils* **demons**, and to cure diseases.
2 And he *sent* **apostolized** them
to preach the *kingdom* **sovereigndom** of *God* **Elohim**,
and to heal the *sick* **frail**.
3 And he said unto them,
Take *nothing* **naught** for your journey,
neither *staves* **rod**, nor *scrip* **wallet**,
neither bread, neither *money* **silver**;
neither have two *coats apiece* **tunics each**.
4 And whatsoever house ye enter into,
there abide, and thence depart.
5 And *whosoever will* **as many as ever** not receive you,

when ye go out of that city,
shake off the very dust from your feet
for a *testimony* **witness** against them.
6 And they departed,
and *went* **passed** through the *towns* **villages**,
preaching the gospel **evangelizing**,
and healing every where.
7 Now Herod the tetrarch
heard of all that *was done* **had become** by him:
and he was **thoroughly** perplexed,
because that it was *said* **worded** of some,
that *John* **Yahn** was risen from the dead;
8 And of some, that *Elias* **Eli Yah** had *appeared;***manifested**
and of others,
that one of the *old* **ancient** prophets was risen *again.*
9 And Herod said, *John* **Yahn** have I beheaded:
but who is this, *of* **concerning** whom I hear such *things?*
And he *desired* **sought** to see him.

YAH SHUA FEEDS FIVE THOUSAND

10 And the apostles, when they were returned,
told **declared to** him *all that* **as much as** they had done.
And he took them,
and *went aside* **withdrew** privately
into a *desert* **desolate** place
belonging to the city called *Bethsaida* **Beth Sayad**.
11 And the *people* **multitude**,
when they knew it, followed him:
and he received them,
and spake unto them *of* **concerning**
the *kingdom* **sovereigndom** of *God* **Elohim**,
and healed them that had need of *healing* **therapy**.
12 And when the day began to *wear away* **recline**,
then came the twelve, and said unto him,
Send **Release** the multitude *away*,
that they may go
into the *towns* **villages** and *country* **fields** round about,
and lodge, and *get victuals* **find food**:
for we are here in a *desert* **desolate** place.
13 But he said unto them, Give ye them to eat.
And they said,
We have no more but five *loaves* **breads** and two fishes;
except **unless** we should go
and buy *meat* **food** for all this people.
14 For they were about five thousand men.
And he said to his disciples,
Make **Have** them *sit down* **recline** by fifties
in a company.
15 And they did so,
and *made* **had** them all *sit down* **recline**.
16 Then he took the five *loaves* **breads** and the two fishes,
and looking *up* to heaven, he *blessed* **eulogized** them,
and brake,
and gave to the disciples to set *before* **by** the multitude.
17 And they did eat, and were all filled:
and there was taken *up*
of fragments that *remained* **superabounded** to them
twelve baskets.

PETROS' PROFESSION OF YAH SHUA

18 And it *came to pass* **became**,
as he was alone praying, his disciples were with him:
and he asked them, *saying* **wording**,
Whom say the *people* **multitude** that I am?
19 They answering said, *John* **Yahn** the *Baptist* **baptizer**;
but *some say* **others**, *Elias* **Eli Yah**;
and others *say*,
that one of the *old* **ancient** prophets is risen *again.*
20 He said unto them, But whom *say* **word** ye that I am?
Peter **Petros** answering said,
The *Christ* **Messiah** of *God* **Elohim**.
21 And he straitly *charged* **admonished** them,
and *commanded* **evangelized** them
to *tell no man that thing* **say that to no one**;
22 Saying,
The Son of *man* **humanity** must suffer *many things* **much**,
and be *rejected* **disapproved** of the elders
and *chief* **arch** priests and scribes,
and be *slain* **slaughtered**, and be raised the third day.
23 And he *said* **worded** to them all,
If any *man will* **one willeth to** come after me,
let him deny himself,
and take *up* his *cross* **stake** daily, and follow me.
24 For whosoever *will* **willeth to** save his *life* **soul**
shall lose it:
but whosoever *will* **shall** lose his *life* **soul** for my sake,
the same shall save it.
25 For what is a *man advantaged* **human benefited**,
if he gain the whole *world* **cosmos**,
and lose himself, or be *cast away* **lost**?
26 For whosoever
shall be ashamed of me and of my words,
of him shall the Son of *man* **humanity** be ashamed,
when **ever** he shall come in his own glory,
and in his Father's, and of the holy angels.
27 But I *tell* **word to** you *of a truth* **truly**,
there be some standing here,
which shall not **no way** taste of death,
till they see the *kingdom* **sovereigndom** of *God* **Elohim**.

YAH SHUA'S METAMORPHOSIS

28 And it *came to pass* **became**
about *an* eight days after these *sayings* **words**,
he took *Peter* **Petros** and *John* **Yahn** and *James* **Yaaqovos**,
and *went up* **ascended** into a mountain to pray.
29 And as he prayed,
the *fashion* **semblance** of his *countenance* **face**
was altered **became another**,
and his *raiment* **garment**
was white and *glistering* **effulgent**.
30 And, behold, there talked with him two men,
which were *Moses* **Mosheh** and *Elias* **Eli Yah**:
31 Who appeared in glory,
and *spake* **worded** of his *decease* **exodus**
which he *should accomplish* **was about to fulfill**
at *Jerusalem* **Yeru Shalem**.
32 But *Peter* **Petros** and they that were with him
were *heavy* **burdened** with sleep:
and when they were **thoroughly** awake,
they saw his glory,
and the two men that stood with him.
33 And it *came to pass* **became**,
as they departed from him,
Peter **Petros** said unto *Jesus* **Yah Shua**,
Master **Rabbi**, it is good for us to be here:
and let us make three tabernacles;
one for thee,
and one for *Moses* **Mosheh**, and one for *Elias* **Eli Yah**:
not knowing what he *said* **worded**.
34 While he *thus spake* **worded these**,
there *came* **became** a cloud, and overshadowed them:
and they *feared* **awed** as they entered into the cloud.
35 And there *came* **became** a voice out of the cloud,
saying **wording**, This is my beloved Son: hear him.
36 And when the voice *was past* **had become**,
Jesus **Yah Shua** was found alone.
And they *kept it close* **hushed**,
and *told* **evangelized to** no *man* **one** in those days
any of those *things* which they had seen.

YAH SHUA REBUKES AN IMPURE SPIRIT

37 And it *came to pass* **became**, that on the next day,
when they were come down from the *hill* **mountain**,
much *people* **multitude** met him.
38 And, behold,
a man of the *company* **multitude** cried out,
saying **wording**, *Master* **Doctor**, I *beseech* **petition** thee,
look upon my son: for he is mine only *child* **begotten**.
39 And, *lo* **behold**,
a spirit taketh him, and he suddenly crieth out;
and it *teareth* **convulseth** him
that he foameth again **with frothing**,
and *bruising* **crushing** him hardly departeth from him.
40 And I *besought* **petitioned** thy disciples
to cast him out; and they could not.
41 And *Jesus* **Yah Shua** answering said,
O *faithless* **trustless**
and *perverse* **thoroughly perverted** generation,
how long **until when** shall I be with you,
and *suffer* **tolerate** you?
Bring thy son hither.
42 And as he was yet a coming,
the *devil threw* **demon burst** him *down*,
and *tare* **convulsed** him.

And *Jesus* **Yah Shua** rebuked the *unclean* **impure** spirit,
and healed the *child* **lad**,
and *delivered* **gave** him *again* **back** to his father.
43 And they were all *amazed* **astonished**
at the *mighty power* **majesty** of *God* **Elohim**.
But while they *wondered* **marvelled** every one
at all *things* which *Jesus* **Yah Shua** did,
he said unto his disciples,
44 *Let* **Place** these *sayings sink down* **words**
into your ears:
for the Son of *man* **humanity**
shall be delivered **is about to be betrayed**
into the hands of *men* **humanity**.
45 But they *understood* **knew** not this *saying* **rhema**,
and it was hid from them, that they perceived it not:
and they *feared* **awed** to ask him
of **about** that *saying* **rhema**.

ON BEING THE GREATEST

46 Then there *arose* **entered** a reasoning among them,
which of them should **ever** be greatest.
47 And *Jesus* **Yah Shua**,
perceiving the *thought* **reasoning** of their heart,
took **hold of** a child, and *set* **stood** him by him,
48 And said unto them,
Whosoever shall receive this child in my name
receiveth me:
and whosoever shall receive me
receiveth him that *sent* **apostolized** me:
for he that is least among you all,
the same shall be *great* **mega**.
49 And *John* **Yahn** answered and said, *Master* **Rabbi**,
we saw one casting out *devils* **demons** in thy name;
and we forbad him, because he followeth not with us.
50 And *Jesus* **Yah Shua** said unto him,
Forbid him not: for he that is not against us is for us.

SHOMERONIYM RECEIVE NOT YAH SHUA

51 And it *came to pass* **became**,
when the *time was come* **day fulfilled**
that he should be *received up* **taken**,
he *stedfastly set* **established** his face
to go to *Jerusalem* **Yeru Shalem**,
52 And *sent messengers* **apostolized angels**
before his face:
and they went,
and entered into a village of the *Samaritans* **Shomeroniym**
so as to *make ready* **prepare** for him.
53 And they did not receive him,
because his face was as though
he *would* **should** go to *Jerusalem* **Yeru Shalem**.
54 And when his disciples
James **Yaaqovos** and *John* **Yahn** saw this, they said,
Lord **Adonay**, *wilt* **willest** thou that we *command* **tell** fire
to *come down* **descend** from heaven,
and consume them, even as *Elias* **Eli Yah** did?
55 But he turned, and rebuked them, and said,
Ye know not what manner of spirit ye are of.
56 For the Son of *man* **humanity** is not come
to destroy *men's lives* **the souls of humanity**,
but to save them.
And they went to another village.

ON PRIORITIES

57 And it *came to pass* **became**, that,
as they went in the way,
a certain man **one** said unto him,
Lord **Adonay**,
I *will* **shall** follow thee whithersoever thou goest.
58 And *Jesus* **Yah Shua** said unto him,
Foxes have *holes* **burrows**,
and *birds* **flyers** of the *air* **heavens** have nests;
but the Son of *man* **humanity**
hath not where to *lay* **recline** his head.
59 And he said unto another, Follow me.
But he said, *Lord* **Adonay**,
suffer **allow** me first to go and *bury* **entomb** my father.
60 *Jesus* **Yah Shua** said unto him,
Let **Allow** the dead *bury* **to entomb** their dead:
but go thou and *preach* **evangelize**
the *kingdom* **sovereigndom** of *God* **Elohim**.
61 And another also said, *Lord* **Adonay**,
I *will* **shall** follow thee;
but *let* **allow** me first go bid them *farewell* **bye bye**,
which are at home at my house.
62 And *Jesus* **Yah Shua** said unto him, no *man* **one**,
having put his hand to the plough, and looking back,
is **well** fit for the *kingdom* **sovereigndom** of *God* **Elohim**.

YAH SHUA APOSTOLIZES THE SEVENTY

10 After these *things*
the Lord appointed **Adonay designated**
other seventy also,
and *sent* **apostolized** them *two and two* **by twos**
before his face into every city and place,
whither he himself *would* **was about to** come.
2 Therefore *said* **worded** he unto them,
The harvest *truly* **indeed** is *great* **vast**,
but the *labourers are* **workers** few:
pray **petition** ye therefore *the Lord* **Adonay** of the harvest,
that he *would* **should**
send **cast** forth *labourers* **workers** into his harvest.
3 Go *your ways*: behold,
I *send* **apostolize** you *forth* as lambs among wolves.
4 *Carry* **Bear** neither *purse* **pouch**,
nor *scrip* **wallet**, nor shoes:
and salute no *man* **one** by the way.
5 And into whatsoever house ye enter,
first *say* **word**, *Peace* **Shalom** be to this house.
6 And if **indeed** the son of *peace* **shalom** be there,
your *peace* **shalom** shall *rest* **repose** upon it:
but if not, it shall *turn* **return** to you *again*.
7 And in the same house *remain* **abide**,
eating and drinking such *things* as they give:
for the *labourer* **worker** is worthy of his hire.
Go **Depart** not from house to house.
8 And into whatsoever city ye enter,
and they receive you,
eat such *things* as are set *before* **by** you:
9 And *heal* **cure** the *sick* **frail** that are therein,
and *say* **word** unto them,
The *kingdom* **sovereigndom** of *God* **Elohim**
is come nigh unto **approacheth** you.
10 But into whatsoever city ye enter,
and they receive you not,
go your ways out into the *streets* **broadways** of the same,
and say,
11 Even the very dust of your city,
which *cleaveth on* **adhereth to** us,
we *do wipe* **scrape** off against you:
notwithstanding be ye sure of **however know** this,
that the *kingdom* **sovereigndom** of *God* **Elohim**
is come nigh unto **hath approached** you.
12 But I *say* **word** unto you,
that it shall be more tolerable in that day
for *Sodom* **Sedom**, than for that city.
13 Woe unto thee, Chorazin!
woe unto thee, *Bethsaida* **Beth Sayad**!
for if the *mighty works* **dynamis**
had *been done* **become** in *Tyre* **Sor** and Sidon,
which have *been done* **become** in you,
they had *a great while* **long** ago repented,
sitting in *sackcloth* **saq** and ashes.
14 But it shall be more tolerable
for *Tyre* **Sor** and Sidon at the judgment, than for you.
15 And thou, *Capernaum* **Kaphar Nachum**,
which art exalted to heaven,
shalt be *thrust* **brought** down *to hell* **hades**.
16 He that heareth you heareth me;
and he that *despiseth* **setteth** you **aside**
despiseth **setteth** me **aside**;
and he that *despiseth* **setteth** me **aside**
despiseth **setteth aside** him that *sent* **apostolized** me.

THE SEVENTY REPORT TO YAH SHUA

17 And the seventy returned again with *joy* **cheer**,
saying **wording**, *Lord* **Adonay**,
even the *devils are subject* **demons subjugate** unto us
through **by** thy name.
18 And he said unto them,
I *beheld* **observed** Satan as lightning fall from heaven.
Yahn 12:31, 32, Apocalypse 12:9
19 Behold, I give unto you *power* **authority**
to *tread* **trample** on serpents and scorpions,
and over all the *power* **dynamis** of the enemy:

and *nothing* **naught**
shall *by any means hurt* **no way injure** you.
20 *Notwithstanding* **However** in this *rejoice* **cheer** not,
that the spirits *are subject* **subjugate** unto you;
but rather *rejoice* **cheer**,
because your names are *written* **scribed** in heaven.
21 In that hour
Jesus rejoiced **Yah Shua jumped for joy** in spirit,
and said, I *thank* **avow** thee, O Father,
Lord **Adonay** of heaven and earth,
that thou hast *hid* **secreted** these *things*
from the wise and *prudent* **comprehending**,
and hast *revealed* **unveiled** them unto babes:
even so **yea**, Father;
for *so* **thus** it *seemed good* **became well—approved**
in *thy sight* **front of thee**.
22 All *things* are delivered to me of my Father:
and no *man* **one** knoweth who the Son is,
but **except** the Father;
and who the Father is, *but* **except** the Son,
and he to *whom* **whomever**
the Son *will* **willeth** to *reveal* **unveil** him.
23 And he turned him unto his disciples,
and said privately,
Blessed are the eyes which see *the things* **those** that ye see:
24 For I *tell* **word unto** you,
that many prophets and *kings* **sovereigns**
have *desired* **willed** to see those *things* which ye see,
and have not seen *them*;
and to hear those *things* which ye hear,
and have not heard *them*.

YAH SHUA ON TRUE NEIGHBOURSHIP

25 And, behold, a *certain lawyer stood up* **torahist rose**,
and *tempted* **tested** him, *saying* **wording**,
Master **Doctor**, what shall I do to inherit eternal life?
26 He said unto him,
What is *written* **scribed** in the *law* **torah**? how readest thou?
27 And he answering said,
Thou shalt love *the Lord* **Yah Veh** thy *God* **Elohim**
with all thy heart, and with all thy soul,
and with all thy *strength* **might**, and with all thy mind;
and thy neighbour as thyself.
28 And he said unto him,
Thou hast answered *right* **straightforwardly**:
this do, and thou shalt live.
29 But he, *willing* **having willed** to justify himself,
said unto *Jesus* **Yah Shua**, And who is my neighbour?
30 And *Jesus answering* **Yah Shua perceiving** said,
A *certain man went down* **human descended**
from *Jerusalem* **Yeru Shalem** to *Jericho* **Yericho**,
and fell among *thieves* **robbers**,
which stripped him of his raiment,
and *wounded* **plagued** him,
and departed, *leaving* **forsaking** him half dead.
31 And by *chance* **coincidence**,
there *came down* **descended** a *certain* priest that way:
and when he saw him,
he passed by *on the other side* **opposite**.
32 And likewise a *Levite* **Leviy**,
when he *was* **became** at the place,
came and *looked on him* **saw**,
and passed by *on the other side* **opposite**.
33 But a *certain Samaritan* **Shomeroniy**, as he journeyed,
came where he was: and when he saw him,
he had *compassion* **a sympathetic spleen** on him,
34 And went to him, and bound *up* his *wounds* **trauma**,
pouring in **olive** oil and wine,
and *set* **mounted** him on his own *beast* **animal**,
and brought him to an inn, and took care of him.
35 And on the morrow when he departed,
he *took* **cast** out two *pence* **denarion**,
and gave them to the *host* **innkeeper**, and said unto him,
Take care of him; and whatsoever thou spendest more,
when I come again, I *will repay* **shall give back to** thee.
36 Which now of these three, thinkest thou,
was **became** neighbour
unto him that fell among the *thieves* **robbers**?
37 And he said, He that *shewed* **dealt** mercy *on* **with** him.
Then said *Jesus* **Yah Shua** unto him,
Go, and do thou likewise.

YAH SHUA ON MINISTRY VS WORSHIP

38 Now it *came to pass* **became**, as they went,
that he entered into a *certain* village:
and a *certain* woman named Martha
received him into her house.
39 And she had a sister called *Mary* **Miryam**,
which also sat at *Jesus'* **Yah Shua**'s feet,
and heard his word.
40 But Martha was cumbered
about much *serving* **ministry**,
and *came to* **stood by** him, and said,
Lord **Adonay**, *dost* **art** thou not *care* **concerned**
that my sister hath left me to *serve* **minister** alone?
bid her **say** therefore that she help me.
41 And *Jesus* **Yah Shua** answered and said unto her,
Martha, Martha,
thou art *careful* **anxious** and troubled
about *many things* **much**:
42 But one *thing* is needful:
and *Mary* **Miryam** hath *chosen* **selected** that good part,
which shall not be *taken away* **removed** from her.

YAH SHUA'S PATTERN FOR PRAYER

11 And it *came to pass* **became**, that,
as he was praying in a *certain* place,
when he ceased, one of his disciples said unto him,
Lord **Adonay**, *teach* **doctrinate** us to pray,
exactly as *John* **Yahn** also
taught **doctrinated** his disciples.
2 And he said unto them,
when **ever** ye pray, *say* **word**,
Our Father which art in *heaven* **the heavens**,
Hallowed be thy name.
Thy *kingdom* **sovereigndom** come.
Thy will *be done* **become**, as in heaven, so in earth.
3 Give us *day by day* **daily** our *daily* **subsistence** bread.
4 And forgive us our sins;
for we also forgive every one that is indebted to us.
And *lead* **bear** us not into *temptation* **testing**;
but *deliver* **rescue** us from evil.

YAH SHUA ON PERSISTENCE

5 And he said unto them,
Which of you shall have a friend,
and shall go unto him at midnight, and say unto him,
Friend, lend me three *loaves* **breads**;
6 *For* **Since** a friend of mine in his journey is come to me,
and I have *nothing* **naught** to set *before* **by** him?
7 And he from within shall answer and say,
Trouble **Embarrass** me not:
the *door* **portal** is *now* **already** shut,
and my children are **lying** with me *in bed*;
I cannot rise and give thee.
8 I *say* **word** unto you,
Though he *will* **shall** not rise and give him,
because he is his friend,
yet **indeed** because of his *importunity* **impudence**
he *will* **shall** rise and give him as many as he needeth.
9 And I *say* **word** unto you,
Ask, and it shall be given you;
seek, and ye shall find;
knock, and it shall be opened unto you.
10 For every one that asketh *receiveth* **taketh**;
and he that seeketh findeth;
and to him that knocketh it shall be opened.
11 If a son shall ask bread of any of you that is a father,
will **shall** he give a stone?
or if *he ask* a fish,
will **shall** he for a fish give him a serpent?
12 Or if he shall ask an egg,
will **shall** he *offer* **give** him a scorpion?
13 If ye then, being evil,
know how to give good gifts unto your children:
how much more shall your heavenly Father
give the Holy Spirit to them that ask him?

YAH SHUA CASTS OUT A DEMON

14 And he was casting out a *devil* **demon**,
and it was *dumb* **mute**.
And it *came to pass* **became**,
when the *devil* **demon** was gone out,
the *dumb* **mute** spake;
and the *people wondered* **multitude marvelled**.

YAH SHUA ACCUSED OF BLASPHEMY

15 But some of them said,
He casteth out *devils* **demons**
through Beelzebub **by Baal Zebub**
the *chief* **arch** of the *devils* **demons**.
16 And others, *tempting* **testing** him,
sought of him a sign from heaven.
17 But he, knowing their thoughts, said unto them,
Every *kingdom* **sovereigndom** divided against itself
is brought to desolation **desolateth**;
and a house *divided* against a house falleth.
18 If Satan also *be divided* **divideth** against himself,
how shall his *kingdom* **sovereigndom** stand?
because ye *say* **word** that I cast out *devils* **demons**
through Beelzebub **by Baal Zebub**.
19 And if I by *Beelzebub* **Baal Zebub**
cast out *devils* **demons**,
by whom do your sons cast them out?
therefore shall they be your judges.
20 But if I *with* **by** the finger of *God* **Elohim**
cast out *devils* **demons**,
no doubt **then** the *kingdom* **sovereigndom** of *God* **Elohim**
is come **hath arrived** upon you.
21 When **ever** *a strong man* **the mighty** armed
keepeth **guardeth** his *palace* **courtyard**,
his *goods* **holdings** are in *peace* **shalom**:
22 But when a *stronger* **mightier** than he
shall come upon him,
and *overcome* **triumph over** him,
he taketh from him all his *armour* **panoply**
wherein he *trusted* **confided**,
and *divideth* **distributeth** his *spoils* **booty**.
23 He that is not with me is against me:
and he that gathereth not with me scattereth.
24 When **ever** the *unclean* **impure** spirit
is gone out of a *man* **human**,
he *walketh* **passeth** through *dry* **waterless** places,
seeking *rest* **repose**;
and finding none, he *saith* **wordeth**,
I *will* **shall** return unto my house whence I came out.
25 And when he cometh,
he findeth it swept and *garnished* **adorned**.
26 Then goeth he, and taketh to him seven other spirits
more *wicked* **evil** than himself;
and they enter in, and *dwell* **settle** there:
and the *last state* **finality** of that *man* **human**
is **becometh** worse than the first.
27 And it *came to pass* **became**,
as he *spake* **worded** these *things*,
a *certain* woman of the *company* **multitude**
lifted *up* her voice, and said unto him,
Blessed is the womb that bare thee,
and the *paps* **breasts** which thou hast *sucked* **nippled**.
28 But he said, *Yea* **Yet then** rather,
blessed are they that hear the word of *God* **Elohim**,
and *keep* **guard** it.

THE SIGN OF YONAH

29 And when the *people* **multitude**
were gathered thick together **thronged**,
he began to *say* **word**, This is an evil generation:
they seek a sign; and there shall no sign be given it,
but **except** the sign of *Jonas* **Yonah** the prophet.
30 For **exactly** as *Jonas* **Yonah**
was **became** a sign unto the *Ninevites* **Nineviym**,
so **thus** shall also the Son of *man* **humanity**
be to this generation.
31 The *queen* **sovereigness** of the south
shall rise *up* in the judgment
with the men of this generation,
and condemn them:
for she came from the *utmost parts* **extremities** of the earth
to hear the wisdom of *Solomon* **Sholomoh**;
and, behold,
a greater **much more** than *Solomon* **Sholomoh** is here.
32 The men of *Nineve* **Nineveh**
shall rise *up* in the judgment with this generation,
and shall condemn it:
for they repented at the preaching of *Jonas* **Yonah**;
and, behold,
a greater **much more** than *Jonas* **Yonah** is here.

YAH SHUA ON CANDLES AND MENORAH

33 No *man* **one**, when he hath lighted a candle,
putteth it in a secret place,
neither under a *bushel* **measure**,
but on a *candlestick* **menorah**,
that they which *come in* **enter**
may see the *light* **brilliance**.
34 The *light* **candle** of the body is the eye:
therefore when **ever** thine eye is *single* **clear**,
thy whole body also is *full of light* **brightly lighted**;
but when *thine eye is* evil,
thy body also is *full of darkness* **dark**.
35 *Take heed* **Scope out** therefore
that the light which is in thee be not darkness.
36 If thy whole body therefore
be *full of light* **brightly lighted**, having no part dark,
the whole shall be *full of light* **brightly lighted**,
as when **ever** the *bright shining* **lightning** of a candle
doth give **lighteth** thee *light*.

YAH SHUA ON THE SIX WOES

37 And as he spake,
a *certain* Pharisee *besought* **asked** him to dine with him:
and he *went in* **entered**, and *sat down to meat* **reposed**.
38 And when the Pharisee saw it, he marvelled
that he had not first *washed* **baptized** before dinner.
39 And *the Lord* **Adonay** said unto him,
Now *do* ye Pharisees
make clean the outside of **purify outward**
the cup and the platter;
but your inward *part*
is full of *ravening* **plunder** and wickedness.
40 *Ye fools* **Thoughtless**,
did not he that made that which is *without* **outward**
make that which is *within* **inward** also?
41 But rather give *alms* **mercies**
of *such things as ye have* **your inner self**;
and, behold, all *things* are *clean* **pure** unto you.
42 But woe unto you, Pharisees!
for ye tithe mint and rue and all *manner of* herbs,
and pass over judgment and the love of *God* **Elohim**:
these *ought* **must** ye to have done,
and not to *leave* **forsake** the other *undone*.
43 Woe unto you, Pharisees!
for ye love the *uppermost seats* **preeminent cathedras**
in the synagogues,
and *greetings* **salutations** in the markets.
44 Woe unto you, scribes and Pharisees, hypocrites!
for ye are as *graves which appear not* **covered tombs**,
and the *men* **humans** that walk over *them*
are not aware of them **know it not**.
45 Then answered one of the *lawyers* **torahists**,
and *said* **worded** unto him, *Master* **Doctor**,
thus *saying* **wording,** thou *reproachest* **insultest** us also.
46 And he said, Woe unto you also, ye *lawyers* **torahists**!
for ye *lade men* **overburden humanity**
with **oppressive** burdens *grievous to be borne*,
and ye yourselves touch not the burdens
with one of your fingers.
47 Woe unto you!
for ye build the *sepulchres* **tombs** of the prophets,
and your fathers *killed* **slaughtered** them.
48 *Truly* **Then** ye *bear* witness that ye *allow* **well—approve**
the *deeds* **works** of your fathers:
for they indeed *killed* **slaughtered** them,
and ye build their *sepulchres* **tombs**.
49 Therefore also said the wisdom of *God* **Elohim**,
I *will send* **shall apostolize** them prophets and apostles,
and *some* of them
they shall *slay* **slaughter** and persecute:
50 That the blood of all the prophets,
which was shed **poured forth**
from the foundation of the *world* **cosmos**,
may be required of this generation;
51 From the blood of Abel
unto the blood of *Zacharias* **Zechar Yah**
which *perished* **destructed**
between the **sacrifice** altar and the *temple* **house**:
Verily I say **Yea I word** unto you,
It shall be required of this generation.
52 Woe unto you, *lawyers* **torahists**!

for ye have taken away the key of knowledge:
ye entered not in yourselves,
and them that were entering in ye *hindered* **forbad**.
53 And as he *said* **worded** these *things* unto them,
the scribes and the Pharisees
began to *urge* **begrudge** him *vehemently* **excessively**,
and to provoke him
to *speak of many things* **instruct about much**:
54 *Laying wait* **Lurking** for him,
and seeking to *catch* **hunt** something out of his mouth,
that they might accuse him.

YAH SHUA ON HYPOCRISY

12 In the mean time,
when there were gathered together
an innumerable **a** multitude of *people* **myriads**,
insomuch that they *trode* **trampled** one upon another,
he began to *say* **word** unto his disciples first of all,
Beware **Heed** ye **yourselves**
of the *leaven* **fermentation** of the Pharisees
which is hypocrisy.
2 For there is *nothing* **naught**
covered **altogether concealed**,
that shall not be *revealed* **unveiled**;
neither *hid* **secreted**, that shall not be known.
3 Therefore
whatsoever **as much as** ye have spoken in darkness
shall be heard in the light;
and that which ye have spoken
in the ear in *closets* **pantries**
shall be *proclaimed* **preached** upon the housetops.
4 And I *say* **word** unto you my friends,
Be **Awe** not *afraid of* them that *kill* **slaughter** the body,
and after that have no more **superabundantly**
that they can do.
5 But I *will forewarn* **shall exemplify** you
whom ye shall *fear* **awe**:
Fear **Awe** him, which after he hath *killed* **slaughtered,**
hath *power* **authority**
to cast into *hell* **Gay Hinnom/the valley of burning**;
yea, I *say* **word** unto you, *Fear* **Awe** him.
6 Are not **indeed**
five sparrows sold for two *farthings* **assarions**,
and not one of them is forgotten
before God **in the sight of Elohim**?
7 But even the very hairs of your head are all numbered.
Fear **Awe** not therefore:
ye *are of more value than* **thoroughly surpass**
many sparrows.
8 Also I *say* **word** unto you,
Whosoever shall *confess* **profess** me
before men **in front of humanity**,
him shall the Son of *man* **humanity** also *confess* **profess**
before **in front of** the angels of *God* **Elohim**:
9 But he that denieth me *before men* **in sight of humanity**
shall be denied *before* **in sight**
of the angels of *God* **Elohim**.
10 And whosoever shall *speak* **say** a word
against the Son of *man* **humanity**,
it shall be forgiven him:
but unto him
that blasphemeth against the Holy *Ghost* **Spirit**
it shall not be forgiven.
11 And when **ever** they *bring* **offer** you
unto the synagogues,
and unto *magistrates* **hierarchies**, and *powers* **authorities**,
take ye no thought **be ye not anxious**
how or what *thing* ye shall answer,
or what ye shall *say* **plead**:
12 For the Holy *Ghost* **Spirit** shall *teach* **doctrinate** you
in the same hour what ye *ought to* **must** say.

YAH SHUA ON AVARICE

13 And one of the *company* **multitude** said unto him,
Master **Doctor**, *speak* **say** to my brother,
that he divide the inheritance with me.
14 And he said unto him, *man* **human**,
who *made* **seated** me a judge or a divider over you?
15 And he said unto them,
Take heed **See**,
and *beware of covetousness* **guard against avarice**:
for *a man's* **one's** life
consisteth **be** not in the **super** abundance
of *the things which he possesseth* **his holdings**.
16 And he *spake* **worded** a parable unto them,
saying **speaking**,
The *ground* **region** of a *certain* rich *man* **human**
brought forth plentifully **bore well**:
17 And he *thought* **reasoned** within himself,
saying **wording**, What shall I do,
because I have no room
where to *bestow* **gather** my fruits?
18 And he said, This *will* **shall** I do:
I *will* **shall** pull down my *barns* **granaries**,
and build greater;
and there *will* **shall** I *bestow* **gather**
all my *fruits* **produce** and my goods.
19 And I *will* **shall** say to my soul,
Soul, thou hast much goods laid *up* for many years;
take thine ease **rest**, eat, drink, and *be merry* **rejoice**.
20 But *God* **Elohim** said unto him, *Thou fool* **Thoughtless**,
this night thy soul shall be required of thee:
then whose shall those *things* be,
which thou hast *provided* **prepared**?
21 *So* **Thus** is he
that *layeth up treasure* **treasureth** for himself,
and is not rich toward *God* **Elohim**.

YAH SHUA ON ANXIETY FOR THE SOUL

22 And he said unto his disciples,
Therefore I *say* **word** unto you,
Take no thought **Be not anxious** for your *life* **soul**,
what ye shall eat;
neither for the body, what ye shall *put on* **endue**.
23 The *life* **soul** is more than *meat* **nourishment**,
and the body *is more* than *raiment* **enduement**.
24 *Consider* **Perceive** the ravens:
for they neither sow nor *reap* **harvest**;
which neither have *storehouse* **pantry** nor *barn* **granary**;
and *God feedeth* **Elohim nourisheth** them:
how much more
are ye *better than* ye **thoroughly surpass** the *fowls* **flyers**?
25 And which of you *with taking thought* **by anxiety**
can add to his stature one cubit?
26 If ye then be not able to do that *thing* which is least,
why *take* **be** ye *thought* **anxious** for the rest?
27 *Consider* **Perceive** the lilies how they grow:
they *toil* **labour** not, they spin not;
and yet I *say* **word** unto you,
that *Solomon* **Sholomoh** in all his glory
was not arrayed like one of these.
28 If then *God so* **Elohim thus** clothe the *grass* **herbage**,
which is to day in the field,
and to morrow is cast into the oven;
how much more *will he clothe* you,
O ye of little *faith* **trust**?
29 And seek not ye what ye shall eat,
or what ye shall drink,
neither be ye *of doubtful mind* **in suspense**.
30 For all these *things*
do the *nations* **goyim** of the *world* **cosmos** seek after:
and your Father knoweth
that ye have need of these *things*.
31 But rather
seek ye the *kingdom* **sovereigndom** of *God* **Elohim**;
and all these *things* shall be added unto you.
32 *Fear* **Awe** not, little *flock* **shepherddom**;
for *it is your Father's good pleasure*
your Father well—approveth
to give you the *kingdom* **sovereigndom**.
33 Sell *that ye have* **your holdings**,
and give *alms* **mercies**;
provide **make** yourselves *bags* **pouches**
which *wax* **antiquate** not *old*,
a treasure in the heavens *that faileth not* **inexhaustible**,
where no thief approacheth, neither moth corrupteth.
34 For where your treasure is,
there *will* **shall** your heart be also.

YAH SHUA ON PREPAREDNESS

35 Let your loins be girded about,
and *your lights* **candles** burning;
36 And ye yourselves
like unto *men* **humanity**

that *wait for* **await** their *Lord* **Adonay**,
when he *will return* **shall depart** from the *wedding* **marriage**;
that when he cometh and knocketh,
they may open unto him *immediately* **straightway**.
37 Blessed are those servants, whom *the Lord* **Adonay**
when he cometh shall find watching:
Verily I say **Amen! I word** unto you,
that he shall gird himself,
and *make* **recline** them *to sit down to meat*,
and *will come forth* **shall pass by**
and *serve* **minister to** them.
38 And if he shall come in the second *watch* **guard**,
or come in the third *watch* **guard**,
and find them *so* **thus**, blessed are those servants.
39 And this know,
that if the *goodman of the house* **housedespotes**
had known what hour the thief *would* **should** come,
he *would* **should** have watched,
and not have *suffered* **allowed**
his house to be broken through.
40 Be ye therefore *ready* **prepared** also:
for the Son of *man* **humanity**
cometh at an hour when ye think not.
41 Then *Peter* **Petros** said unto him, *Lord* **Adonay**,
speakest **wordest** thou this parable unto us,
or even to all?
42 And *the Lord* **Adonay** said,
Who then is that *faithful* **trustworthy**
and *wise steward* **thoughtful administrator**,
whom his *lord* **adoni**
shall *make ruler* **seat** over his *household* **therapy**,
to give them their *portion* **measure** of *meat* **grain**
in due season?
43 Blessed is that servant,
whom his *lord* **adoni** when he cometh
shall find *so* **thus** doing.
44 *Of a truth I say* **Truly I word** unto you,
that he *will make* **shall seat** him *ruler*
over all *that he hath* **his holdings**.
45 But and if that servant say in his heart,
My *lord delayeth* **adoni taketh** his **time in** coming;
and shall begin to *beat* **strike**
the *menservants* **lads** and *maidens* **lasses**,
and to eat and drink, and to *be drunken* **intoxicate**;
46 The *lord* **adoni** of that servant *will* **shall** come in a day
when he *looketh not for* **awaiteth** him **not**,
and at an hour
when **which** he *is not aware* **knoweth not**,
and *will cut him in sunder* **shall dichotomize him**,
and *will appoint him* **shall place** his portion
with the *unbelievers* **trustless**.
47 And that servant, which knew his *lord's* **adoni's** will,
and prepared not *himself*,
neither did according to his will,
shall be *beaten with many stripes* **flogged often**.
48 But he that knew not,
and *did commit things* **dealt** worthy of *stripes* **plagues**,
shall be *beaten with few stripes* **flogged little**.
For unto whomsoever much is given,
of him shall be much *required* **sought**:
and to whom men have *committed* **set forth** much,
of him they *will* **shall** ask *the more* **superabundantly**.

YAH SHUA ON UNITY VS DIVISION

49 I am come to *send* **cast** fire on the earth;
and what will I, if it be already *kindled* **lit**?
50 But I have a baptism to be baptized with;
and how am I *straitened* **held**
till it be *accomplished* **completed**!
51 *Suppose* **Think** ye
that I am come to give *peace* **shalom** on earth?
I *tell* **word unto** you, *Nay* **Indeed not**; but rather division:
52 For from henceforth
there shall be five in one house divided,
three against two, and two against three.
53 The father shall be divided against the son,
and the son against the father;
the mother against the daughter,
and the daughter against the mother;
the mother in law against her *daughter in law* **bride**,
and the *daughter in law* **bride** against her mother in law.

YAH SHUA ON PROOFING THE SEASON

54 And he *said* **worded** also to the *people* **multitude**,
when **ever** ye see a cloud rise out of the *west* **lowering**,
straightway ye *say* **word**,
There cometh a *shower* **thunderstorm**;
and *so* **thus** it *is* **becometh**.
55 And when **ever**
ye see the south wind blow **the southerly puffeth**,
ye *say* **word**, There *will* **shall** be *heat* **a scorch**;
and it *cometh to pass* **becometh**.
56 *Ye* hypocrites, ye *can discern* **know to proof**
the face of the *sky* **heavens** and of the earth;
but how is it
that ye *do not discern* **proof not** this *time* **season**?
57 Yea, and why even of yourselves
judge ye not what is *right* **just**?
58 When **indeed** thou goest with thine adversary
to the *magistrate* **arch**,
as thou art *in* **on** the way,
give *diligence* **work**
that thou mayest be *delivered* **released** from him;
lest **ever** he *hale* **drag** thee to the judge,
and the judge deliver thee to the officer,
and the officer cast thee into *prison* **the guardhouse**.
59 I *tell* **word unto** thee,
thou shalt not **no way** depart thence,
till thou hast *paid* **given back**
the *very last mite* **final flake**.

YAH SHUA ON REPENTANCE

13 There were present at that season
some that *told* **evangelized** him
of **about** the *Galilaeans* **Galiliym**,
whose blood
Pilate **Pilatos** had mingled with their sacrifices.
2 And *Jesus* **Yah Shua** answering said unto them,
Suppose **Think** ye that these *Galilaeans* **Galiliym**
were **became** sinners above all the *Galilaeans* **Galiliym**,
because they suffered such *things*?
3 I *tell* **word unto** you, *Nay* **Indeed not**:
but, *except* **unless** ye repent,
ye shall all likewise *perish* **destruct**.
4 Or those eighteen,
upon whom the tower in *Siloam* **Shiloach** fell,
and *slew* **slaughtered** them,
think ye that they *were sinners* **became indebted**
above all *men* **humanity**
that *dwelt* **settled** in *Jerusalem* **Yeru Shalem**?
5 I *tell* **word unto** you, *Nay* **Indeed not**:
but *except* **unless** ye repent,
ye shall all likewise *perish* **destruct**.

YAH SHUA ON THE FIG TREE

6 He *spake* **worded** also this parable;
A certain man **Someone** had a fig tree
planted in his vineyard;
and he came and sought fruit thereon, and found none.
7 Then said he unto the dresser of his vineyard, Behold,
these three years I come seeking fruit on this fig tree,
and find none:
cut **exscind** it *down*;
why *cumbereth it* **inactivate** the *ground* **earth**?
8 And he answering *said* **worded** unto him,
Lord **Adoni**, *let* **allow** it *alone* this year also,
till I shall dig about it, and *dung it* **cast in manure**:
9 And if it *bear* **indeed produce** fruit, *well*:
and if not,
then after that thou shalt cut it down
be about to exscind it.

YAH SHUA CURES ON THE SHABBATH

10 And he was *teaching* **doctrinating**
in one of the synagogues on the *sabbath* **shabbaths**.
11 And, behold, there was a woman
which had a spirit of *infirmity* **frailty** eighteen years,
and was *bowed* **bent** together,
and *could in no wise* **was completely unable**
lift up **to unbend** *herself*.
12 And when *Jesus* **Yah Shua** saw her,
he called *her to him*, and said unto her, Woman,
thou art *loosed* **released** from thine *infirmity* **frailty**.
13 And he *laid* **put** his hands on her:
and immediately she *was made straight* **straightened**,

and glorified *God* **Elohim**.
14 And the *ruler of the* synagogue **arch**
answered *with indignation* **indignifying**,
because that *Jesus* **Yah Shua**
had *healed* **cured** on the *sabbath day* **shabbath**,
and *said* **worded** unto the *people* **multitude**,
There are six days in which men *ought to* **must** work:
in them therefore come and be *healed* **cured**,
and not on the *sabbath day* **shabbath**.
15 *The Lord* **Adonay** then answered him, and said,
Thou hypocrite,
doth not each one of you on the *sabbath* **shabbath**
loose his ox or his *ass* **burro** from the *stall* **manger**,
and lead him away to *watering* **moisten**?
16 And *ought* **must** not this woman,
being a daughter of Abraham, whom Satan hath bound,
lo **behold**, these eighteen years,
be loosed from this bond on the *sabbath* **shabbath** day?
17 And when he had *said* **worded** these *things*,
all his adversaries *were ashamed* **shamed**:
and all the *people rejoiced* **multitude cheered**
for all the *glorious things* **glories**
that *were done* **became** by him.

Yah Shua on the Sovereigndom of Elohim: The Mustard Kernel

18 Then *said* **worded** he, Unto what
is the *kingdom* **sovereigndom** of *God* **Elohim** like?
and whereunto shall I *resemble* **liken** it?
19 It is like a *grain of* mustard *seed* **kernel**,
which a *man* **human** took, and cast into his garden;
and it grew, and *waxed* **became** a *great* **mega** tree;
and the *fowls* **flyers** of the *air* **heavens**
lodged **nested** in the branches of it.

The Fermentation

20 And again he said, Whereunto shall I liken
the *kingdom* **sovereigndom** of *God* **Elohim**?
21 It is like *leaven* **fermentation**,
which a woman took
and hid in three *measures* **seahs** of *meal* **flour**,
till the whole *was leavened* **fermented**.
22 And he went through the cities and villages,
teaching **doctrinating**,
and *journeying* **making his way**
toward *Jerusalem* **Yeru Shalem**.

The Narrow Gate

23 Then said one unto him,
Lord **Adonay**, are there few that be saved?
And he said unto them,
24 *Strive* **Agonize** to enter *in*
at **through** the *strait* **narrow** gate:
for many, I *say* **word** unto you, *will* **shall** seek to enter in,
and shall not be able.
25 *When once the master of the house is risen up*
From whenever the housedespotes riseth,
and hath *shut to* **locked** the *door* **portal**,
and ye begin to stand without,
and to knock at the *door* **portal**, *saying* **wording**,
Lord **Adonay**, *Lord* **Adonay**, open unto us;
and he shall answer and say unto you,
I know you not whence ye are:
26 Then shall ye begin to *say* **word**,
We have eaten and drunk in thy *presence* **sight**,
and thou hast *taught* **doctrinated**
in our *streets* **broadways**.
27 But he shall say, I *tell* **word unto** you,
I know you not whence ye are;
depart from me, all ye workers of *iniquity* **injustice**.
28 There shall be weeping and gnashing of teeth,
when **ever** ye shall see Abraham, and *Isaac* **Yischaq**,
and *Jacob* **Yaaqov**, and all the prophets,
in the *kingdom* **sovereigndom** of *God* **Elohim**,
and you yourselves thrust out.
29 And they shall come
from the *east* **rising**, and *from* the *west* **lowering**,
and from the north, and *from* the south,
and shall *sit down* **recline**
in the *kingdom* **sovereigndom** of *God* **Elohim**.
30 And, behold,
there are *last* **final** which shall be first,
and there are first which shall be *last* **final**.

Yah Shua's Response to Herod

31 The same day
there came *certain* **some** of the Pharisees,
saying **wording** unto him,
Get thee out, and depart hence:
for Herod *will kill* **willeth to slaughter** thee.
32 And he said unto them, Go ye, and *tell* **say to** that fox,
Behold, I cast out *devils* **demons**,
and I *do cures* **fully complete healings**
to day and to morrow,
and the third *day* I shall be *perfected* **completed**.
33 *Nevertheless* **However** I must walk to day,
and to morrow, and *the day following* **after**:
for it *cannot* be **not acceptable** that a prophet
perish **destruct** out of *Jerusalem* **Yeru Shalem**.

Yah Shua's Concern over Yeru Shalem

34 O *Jerusalem, Jerusalem* **Yeru Shalem, Yeru Shalem**,
which *killest* **slaughterest** the prophets,
and stonest them that are *sent* **apostolized** unto thee;
how often *would* I **willed**
to have gathered thy children together,
in manner as a hen *doth gather*
her *brood* **young** under *her* wings,
and ye *would* **willed** not!
35 Behold, your house is *left* **forsaken** unto you desolate:
and *Verily I say* **Amen! I word** unto you,
Ye shall not **no way** see me,
until *the time* **it** come when ye shall say,
Blessed **Eulogized** is he
that cometh in the name of *the Lord* **Yah Veh**.

Yah Shua Heals on the Shabbath

14 And it *came to pass* **became**,
as he *went* **came** into the house
of one of the *chief* **arch** Pharisees
to eat bread on the *sabbath day* **shabbath**,
that they *watched* **observed** him.
2 And, behold,
there was a *certain man before* **human in front of** him
which had the dropsy — **dropsical**.
3 And *Jesus* **Yah Shua** answering
spake **said** unto the *lawyers* **torahists** and Pharisees,
saying **wording**, Is it *lawful* **allowed**
to *heal* **cure** on the *sabbath day* **shabbath**?
4 And they *held their peace* **quieted**.
And he took **hold of** him,
and healed him, and *let* **released** him *go*;
5 And answered them, saying,
Which of you
shall have *an ass* **a burro** or an ox fallen into a pit,
and *will* **shall** not straightway *pull* **draw** him *out*
on the *sabbath* **shabbath** day?
6 And they could not *answer* **contradict** him *again*
as to these *things*.

Yah Shua on Position

7 And he *put forth* **worded** a parable
to those which were *bidden* **called**,
when he marked **heeding** how they *chose out* **selected**
the *chief rooms* **preeminent recliners**;
saying **wording** unto them.
8 when **ever** thou art *bidden* **called**
of any *man* **one** to a *wedding* **marriage**,
sit **recline** not *down* in the highest room;
lest **ever** a more honourable *man* than thou
be *bidden* **called** of him;
9 And he that *bade* **called** thee
and him come and say to thee,
Give this *man* **one** place;
and thou begin with shame
to *take* **hold on to** the *lowest room* **final place**.
10 But thou art *bidden* **called**,
go and *sit down* **repose** in the *lowest room* **final place**;
that when **ever** he that *bade* **called** thee cometh,
he may say unto thee, Friend, *go up* **ascend** higher:
then shalt thou have *worship* **glory**
in the *presence* **sight** of them
that *sit at meat* **repose** with thee.
11 For whosoever exalteth himself
shall be *abased* **humbled**;
and he that humbleth himself
shall be exalted.

12 Then *said* **worded** he also to him that *bade* **called** him,
when **ever** thou makest a dinner or a supper,
call **voice** not **out to** thy friends, nor thy brethren,
neither thy *kinsmen* **kin**, nor thy rich neighbours;
lest **ever** they also *bid* **call** thee *again* **back**,
and a recompence *be made* **become** thee.
13 But when **ever** thou makest a feast,
call the poor, the maimed, the lame, the blind:
14 And thou shalt be blessed;
for they cannot recompense thee:
for thou shalt be recompensed
at the resurrection of the just.

YAH SHUA ON THE MEGA SUPPER

15 And when one of them
that *sat at meat* **reposed** with him heard these *things*,
he said unto him,
Blessed is he that shall eat bread
in the *kingdom* **sovereigndom** of *God* **Elohim**.
16 Then said he unto him,
A *certain man* **human** made a *great* **mega** supper,
and *bade* **called** many:
17 And *sent* **apostolized** his servant at supper *time* **hour**
to say to them that were *bidden* **called**,
Come; for all *things* are *now ready* **already prepared**.
18 And they all *with one consent*
began to *make excuse* **beg off**.
The first said unto him,
I have bought a *piece of ground* **field**,
and I *must needs* **need** go and see it:
I *pray* **ask** thee have me *excused* **beg off**.
19 And another said,
I have bought five yoke of oxen, and I go to prove them:
I *pray* **ask** thee have me *excused* **beg off**.
20 And another said,
I have married a *wife* **woman**,
and therefore I cannot come.
21 So that servant came,
and *shewed* **evangelized** his *lord* **adoni** these *things*.
Then the *master of the house* **housedespotes**
being *angry* **wroth** said to his servant,
Go out quickly
into the *streets* **broadways** and *lanes* **streets** of the city,
and bring in hither the poor, and the maimed,
and the *halt* **lame**, and the blind.
22 And the servant said, *Lord* **Adoni**,
it is *done* **become** as thou hast *commanded* **ordered**,
and yet there is *room* **place**.
23 And the *lord* **adoni** said unto the servant,
Go out into the *highways* **ways** and hedges,
and compel them to *come in* **enter**,
that my house may be filled.
24 For I *say* **word** unto you,
That none of those men which were *bidden* **called**
shall taste of my supper.

YAH SHUA ON DISCIPLESHIP

25 And there went *great* **vast** multitudes with him:
and he turned, and said unto them,
26 If any *man* come to me,
and hate not his father, and mother, and *wife* **woman**,
and children, and brethren, and sisters,
yea, and **even** his own *life* **soul** *also*,
he cannot be my disciple.
27 And whosoever *doth* **shall** not bear his *cross* **stake**,
and come after me, cannot be my disciple.

THE TOWER

28 For which of you,
intending **having willed** to build a tower,
indeed sitteth not down first,
and *counteth* **computeth** the *cost* **expense**,
whether he have *sufficient to finish it* **for the finishing**?
29 Lest *haply* **ever**,
after he hath *laid* **placed** the foundation,
and is not able to *finish* **fully complete** it,
all that *behold* **observe** it begin to mock him,
30 *saying* **wording**, This *man* **human** began to build,
and was not able to *finish* **fully complete**.

SHALOM TREATY

31 Or what *king* **sovereign**,
going to *make* **encounter** war
against another *king* **sovereign**,
indeed sitteth not down first,
and *consulteth* **counseleth**
whether he be able *with* **by** ten thousand
to meet him that cometh against him
with twenty thousand?
32 *Or else* **But if not**,
while the other is yet *a great way* **afar** off,
he *sendeth an ambassage* **apostolizeth a presbytry**
and *desireth conditions of peace* **asketh for shalom**.
33 So *likewise* **then**, whosoever he be of you
that *forsaketh* **biddeth** not **bye bye**
all that he hath **to all his holdings**,
he cannot be my disciple.

YAH SHUA ON INSIPID SALT

34 Salt is good:
but if the salt have *lost his savour* **become insipid**,
wherewith shall it be seasoned?
35 It is neither **well** fit for the *land* **earth**,
nor yet for *the dunghill* **manure**; but men cast it *out*.
He that hath ears to hear, let him hear.

YAH SHUA ON THE LOST SHEEP

15 Then *drew near* **approached** unto him
all the *publicans* **customs agents** and sinners
for to hear him.
2 And the Pharisees and scribes murmured,
saying **wording**,
This *man receiveth* **one awaiteth** sinners,
and eateth with them.
3 And he *spake* **worded** this parable unto them,
saying **speaking**,
4 What *man* **human** of you, having an hundred sheep,
if he lose one of them,
doth not leave the ninety and nine in the wilderness,
and go after that which is lost, until he find it?
5 And when he hath found it,
he *layeth* **putteth** it on his shoulders, *rejoicing* **cheering**.
6 And when he cometh home,
he calleth together his friends and neighbours,
saying **wording** unto them, Rejoice with me;
for I have found my sheep which was lost.
7 I *say* **word** unto you,
that likewise *joy* **cheer** shall be in heaven
over one sinner that repenteth,
more than over ninety and nine just persons,
which need no repentance.

YAH SHUA ON THE LOST DRACHMA

8 Either what woman
having ten *pieces of silver* **drachmas**,
if she lose one *piece* **drachma**,
doth not **indeed** light a candle, and sweep the house,
and seek *diligently* **carefully** till she find it?
9 And when she hath found it,
she calleth her friends and her neighbours together,
saying **wording**, Rejoice with me;
for I have found the *piece* **drachma** which I had lost.
10 Likewise, I *say* **word** unto you,
there *is joy* **shall be cheer**
in the *presence* **sight** of the angels of *God* **Elohim**
over one sinner that repenteth.

YAH SHUA ON THE LOST SON

11 And he said, A *certain man* **human** had two sons:
12 And the younger of them said to his father,
Father, give me the portion of *goods* **substance**
that *falleth to* **is laid up for** me.
And he *divided* **distributed** unto them
his *living* **subsistence**.
13 And not many days after
the younger son gathered all together,
and *took his journey* **went abroad**
into a *far country* **distant region**,
and there *wasted* **squandered** his substance
with *riotous* **dissipative** living.
14 And when he had spent all,
there *arose* **became** a mighty famine in that *land* **region**;
and he began to *be in want* **lack**.
15 And he went
and joined himself to a citizen of that *country* **region**;
and he sent him into his fields to *feed* **graze** swine.
16 And he *would fain have filled* **panted to fill** his belly
with the *husks* **pods** that the swine did eat:

and no *man* **one** gave unto him.
17 And when he came to himself, he said,
How many *hired servants* **hirelings** of my father's
have bread *enough and to spare* **super abundant**,
and I *perish* **destruct** with *hunger* **famine**!
18 I *will* **shall** arise and go to my father,
and *will* **shall** say unto him,
Father, I have sinned against heaven,
and *before thee* **in thy sight**,
19 And am no more worthy to be called thy son:
make me as one of thy *hired servants* **hirelings**.
20 And he arose, and came to his father.
But when he was yet *a great way* **afar** off,
his father saw him,
and had *compassion* **a sympathetic spleen**,
and ran, and fell on his neck, and **ardently** kissed him.
21 And the son said unto him, Father,
I have sinned against heaven, and in thy sight,
and am no more worthy to be called thy son.
22 But the father said to his servants,
Bring forth the *best robe* **preeminent stole**,
and *put it on* **endue** him;
and *put* **give** a **finger** ring on his hand,
and shoes on his feet:
23 And bring hither the fatted calf, and *kill it* **sacrifice**;
and let us eat, and *be merry* **rejoice**:
24 For this my son was dead, and *is alive again* **reliveth**;
he was lost, and is found.
And they began to *be merry* **rejoice**.
25 Now his elder son was in the field:
and as he came and *drew nigh to* **approached** the house,
he heard *musick* **symphony** and *dancing* **chorus**.
26 And he called one of the *servants* **lads**,
and asked what these *things meant* **be**.
27 And he said unto him, Thy brother is come;
and thy father hath *killed* **sacrificed** the fatted calf,
because he hath *received* **taken** him safe and sound.
28 And he was *angry* **wroth**,
and *would* **willed to** not *go in* **enter**:
therefore came his father out,
and *intreated* **consoled** him.
29 And he answering said to his father,
Lo **Behold**, *these* **so** many years do I serve thee,
neither transgressed I at any time
never ever have I passed over
thy *commandment* **misvah**:
and yet thou never **ever** gavest me a *kid* **goat**,
that I might *make merry* **rejoice** with my friends:
30 But as soon as this thy son was come,
which hath devoured thy *living* **subsistence**
with *harlots* **whores**,
thou hast *killed* **sacrificed** for him the fatted calf.
31 And he said unto him, *Son* **Child**,
thou art ever with me, and all that I have is thine.
32 It was *meet* **necessary**
that we should *make merry* **rejoice**, and *be glad* **cheer**:
for this thy brother was dead, and *is alive again* **reliveth**;
and was lost, and is found.

YAH SHUA ON THE THOUGHTFUL ADMINISTRATOR

16 And he *said* **worded** also unto his disciples,
There was a *certain* rich *man* **human**,
which had *a steward* **an administrator**;
and *the same* **this one** was accused unto him
that he had *wasted* **squandered** his *goods* **holdings**.
2 And he *called* **voiced out to** him, and said unto him,
How is it that I hear this *of* **concerning** thee?
give *an account* **back word**
of thy *stewardship* **administration**;
for thou mayest **not still** be *no longer*
steward **administrator**.
3 Then the *steward* **administrator** said within himself,
What shall I do?
for my *lord taketh away* **adoni removeth** from me
the *stewardship* **administration**:
I cannot dig; to beg I am ashamed.
4 I *am resolved* **know** what to do,
that, when **ever** I am
put out of **removed from** the *stewardship* **administration**,
they may receive me into their houses.
5 So he called *every* **each** one
of his *lord's* **adoni's** debtors unto him,
and *said* **worded** unto the first,
How much *owest* **art** thou **indebted** unto my *lord* **adoni**?
6 And he said, An hundred *measures* **baths** of **olive** oil.
And he said unto him, *Take* **Receive** thy *bill* **scribing**,
and sit down quickly, and *write* **scribe** fifty.
7 Then said he to another,
And how much *owest* **art** thou **indebted**?
And he said, An hundred *measures* **kors** of *wheat* **grain**.
And he *said* **worded** unto him,
Take **Receive** thy *bill* **scribing**,
and *write fourscore* **scribe eighty**.
8 And *the Lord* **Adonay**
commended **halaled** the unjust *steward* **administrator**,
because he had done *wisely* **thoughtfully**:
for the *children* **sons** of this *world* **eon** are
in their generation
wiser **more thoughtful** than the *children* **sons** of light.
9 And I *say* **word** unto you,
Make to yourselves
friends of the mammon of *unrighteousness* **injustice**;
that, when **ever** ye fail,
they may receive you
into *everlasting habitations* **eternal tabernacles**.
10 He that is *faithful* **trustworthy** in that which is least
is *faithful* **trustworthy** also in much:
and he that is unjust in the least
is unjust also in much.
11 If therefore
ye have not *been faithful* **become trustworthy**
in the *unrighteous* **unjust** mammon,
who *will commit to your trust* **shall entrust you**
to **with** the true?
12 And if ye have not *been faithful* **become trustworthy**
in that which is *another man's* **another's**,
who shall give you that which is your own?
13 No *servant* **housekeeper**
can serve two *masters* **adonim**:
for either he *will* **shall** hate the one,
and love the other;
or else he *will hold to* **shall uphold** the one,
and *despise* **disesteem** the other.
Ye cannot serve *God* **Elohim** and mammon.
14 And the Pharisees also,
who *were covetous* **befriended silver**,
heard all these *things*:
and they *derided* **sneered at** him.
15 And he said unto them,
Ye are they which justify yourselves
before men **in the sight of humanity**;
but *God* **Elohim** knoweth your hearts:
for that
which is *highly esteemed* **high** among *men* **humanity**
is abomination in the sight of *God* **Elohim**.

YAH SHUA ON THE TORAH AND THE PROPHETS

16 The *law* **torah** and the prophets were until *John* **Yahn**:
since *that time* **then**
the *kingdom* **sovereigndom** of *God* **Elohim**
is *preached* **evangelized**,
and every man *presseth* **forceth** into it.
17 And it is easier for heaven and earth to pass,
than one tittle of the *law* **torah** to *fail* **fall**.
18 Whosoever *putteth away* **releaseth** his *wife* **woman**,
and marrieth another, *committeth adultery* **adulterizeth**:
and whosoever marrieth her
that is *put away* **released** from her *husband* **man**
committed adultery **adulterizeth**.

YAH SHUA ON THE RICH HUMAN AND EL AZAR

19 There was a *certain* rich *man* **human**,
which was clothed in purple and *fine* **white** linen,
and *fared sumptuously* **rejoiced radiantly**
every day **daily**:
20 And there was a *certain* beggar
named *Lazarus* **El Azar**,
which was *laid* **cast** at his gate, *full of sores* **ulcerous**,
21 And *desiring* **panting** to be *fed* **filled** with the crumbs
which fell from the rich man's table:
moreover **but even** the dogs came
and licked his *sores* **ulcers**.
22 And it *came to pass* **became**, that the beggar died,

and was *carried* **borne away** by the angels
into Abraham's bosom:
the rich man also died, and was *buried* **entombed**;
23 And in *hell* **hades** he lift *up* his eyes, being in torments,
and seeth Abraham afar off,
and *Lazarus* **El Azar** in his bosom.
24 And he *cried* **voiced out** and said, Father Abraham,
have mercy *on* me, and send *Lazarus* **El Azar**,
that he may *dip* **baptize** the tip of his finger in water,
and cool my tongue;
for I am *tormented* **grieved** in this flame.
25 But Abraham said, *Son* **Child**,
remember that thou in thy life *time*
receivedst **took** thy good *things*,
and likewise *Lazarus* **El Azar** evil *things*:
but now he is *comforted* **consoled**,
and thou art *tormented* **grieved**.
26 And beside all this, between us and you
there is a *great gulf fixed* **mega chasm established**:
so that they which *would* **will to** pass **through**
from hence to you cannot;
neither can they pass **through** to us,
that would come from thence.
27 Then he said, I *pray* **ask** thee therefore, father,
that thou *wouldest* **shouldest** send him
to my father's house:
28 For I have five brethren;
that he may *testify* **throroughly witness** unto them,
lest they also come into this place of torment.
29 Abraham *saith* **wordeth** unto him,
They have *Moses* **Mosheh** and the prophets;
let them hear them.
30 And he said, *Nay* **Indeed not**, father Abraham:
but if one went unto them from the dead,
they *will* **shall** repent.
31 And he said unto him,
If they hear not *Moses* **Mosheh** and the prophets,
neither *will* **shall** they be *persuaded* **convinced**,
though **not even if** one rose from the dead.

YAH SHUA ON SCANDALS

17 Then said he unto the disciples,
It is impossible
but that offences will **that scandals shall not** come:
but woe *unto him*, through whom they come!
2 It were *better* **more advantageous** for him
that **if** a millstone **turned by a burro**
were hanged about his neck,
and he *cast* **tossed** into the sea,
than that he should *offend* **scandalize**
one of these little ones.
3 Take heed to yourselves:
If thy brother *trespass* **sin** against thee, rebuke him;
and if he repent, forgive him.
4 And if he *trespass* **sin** against thee seven times in a day,
and seven times in a day turn again to thee,
saying **wording**, I repent;
thou shalt forgive him.
5 And the apostles said unto *the Lord* **Adonay**,
Increase **Add to** our *faith* **trust**.
6 And *the Lord* **Adonay** said,
If ye had *faith* **trust** as a *grain of* mustard *seed* **kernel**,
ye might *say* **word** unto this sycamine *tree*,
Be thou *plucked up by the root* **uprooted**,
and be thou planted in the sea;
and it should obey you.
7 But which of you,
having a servant plowing or *feeding cattle* **shepherding**,
will **shall** say unto him *by and by* **straightway**,
when he *is come* **entereth** from the field,
Go, *and sit down to meat* **pass near and repose**?
8 *And will* **But indeed, shall he** not *rather* say unto him,
Make ready **Prepare** wherewith I may sup,
and gird thyself,
and *serve* **minister to** me, till I have eaten and drunken;
and *afterward* **after these** thou shalt eat and drink?
9 *Doth he thank* **Hath he charism for** that servant
because he did *the things* **those**
that were *commanded* **ordained** of him?
I *trow* **think** not.
10 So likewise ye,
when **ever** ye shall have done all those *things*
which are *commanded* **ordained** you,
say **word**, We are *unprofitable* **useless** servants:
we have done that
which *was our duty* **we were indebted** to do.

YAH SHUA HEALS TEN LEPERS

11 And it *came to pass* **became**,
as he went to *Jerusalem* **Yeru Shalem**,
that he passed through
the midst of *Samaria* **Shomeron** and *Galilee* **Galiyl**.
12 And as he entered into a *certain* village,
there met him ten men that were lepers,
which stood afar off:
13 And they lifted *up* their voices, and *said* **worded**,
Jesus **Yah Shua**, *Master* **Rabbi**, *have* mercy *on* us.
14 And when he saw them, he said unto them,
Go shew yourselves unto the priests.
And it *came to pass* **became**, that,
as they went, they were *cleansed* **purified**.
15 And one of them, when he saw that he was healed,
turned back **returned**,
and with a *loud* **mega** voice glorified *God* **Elohim**,
16 And fell down on his face at his feet,
giving **eucharistizing** him *thanks*:
and he was a *Samaritan* **Shomeroniy**.
17 And *Jesus* **Yah Shua** answering said,
Were there not **indeed** ten *cleansed* **purified**?
but where are the nine?
18 There are not found
that returned to give glory to *God* **Elohim**,
save **except** this *stranger* **alien**.
19 And he said unto him, Arise, go thy way:
thy *faith* **trust** hath *made* **saved** thee *whole*.

YAH SHUA ON THE SOVEREIGNDOM OF ELOHIM

20 And when he was *demanded* **asked** of the Pharisees,
when the *kingdom* **sovereigndom** of *God* **Elohim**
should come,
he answered them and said,
The *kingdom* **sovereigndom** of *God* **Elohim**
cometh not with observation:
21 Neither shall they say,
Lo **Behold** here! or, *Lo* **Behold** there! for, behold,
the *kingdom* **sovereigndom** of *God* **Elohim** is within you.
22 And he said unto the disciples,
The days *will* **shall** come,
when ye shall *desire* **pant**
to see one of the days of the Son of *man* **humanity**,
and ye shall not see it.
23 And they shall say to you,
See **Behold** here; or, *see* **behold** there:
go not after *them*, nor *follow* **pursue** them.
24 For **exactly** as the lightning,
that *lighteneth* **lightningeth**
out of the one part under heaven,
shineth **radiateth** unto the other part under heaven;
so shall also the Son of *man* **humanity** be in his day.
25 But first must he suffer *many things* **much**,
and be *rejected* **dissapproved** of this generation.
26 And **exactly** as it *was* **became**
in the days of *Noe* **Noach**,
so shall it be also
in the days of the Son of *man* **humanity**.
27 They did eat, they drank, they married *wives*,
they *were given in marriage* **married off**,
until the day that *Noe* **Noach** entered into the ark,
and the *flood* **cataclysm** came, and destroyed them all.
28 Likewise also as it *was* **became** in the days of Lot;
they *did eat* **ate**, they drank,
they bought, they sold, they planted, they builded;
29 But the same day that Lot went out of *Sodom* **Sedom**
it rained fire and *brimstone* **sulphur** from heaven,
and destroyed *them* all.
30 *Even thus* **In like manner**
shall it be in the day
when the Son of *man* **humanity** is *revealed* **unveiled**.
31 In that day,
he which shall be upon the housetop,
and his *stuff* **vessels** in the house,
let him not *come down* **descend** to take it away:
and he that is in the field,

let him likewise not return *back*.
32 Remember Lot's *wife* **woman**.
33 Whosoever shall seek to save his *life* **soul**
shall lose it;
and whosoever shall lose *his life* **it**
shall preserve it.
34 I *tell* **word to** you, in that night
there shall be two *men* in one bed;
the one shall be taken,
and the other shall be *left* **forsaken**.
35 Two *women* shall be grinding together;
the one shall be taken, and the other *left* **forsaken**.
36 Two *men* shall be in the field;
the one shall be taken, and the other *left* **forsaken**.
37 And they answered and *said* **worded** unto him,
Where, *Lord* **Adonay**?
And he said unto them, Wheresoever the body is,
thither will **there shall** the eagles be gathered together.

YAH SHUA ON THE JUDGE AND THE WIDOW

18 And he *spake* **worded** a parable unto them
to this end,
that men *ought always to* **must ever** pray,
and not *to faint* **weary**;
2 *Saying* **Wording**,
There was in a city a judge,
which *feared* **awed** not *God* **Elohim**,
neither *regarded man* **respected humanity**:
3 And there was a widow in that city;
and she came unto him, *saying* **wording**,
Avenge me of mine adversary.
4 And he *would* **willed** not **to** for a *while* **time**:
but *afterward* **after these** he said within himself,
Though I *fear* **awe** not *God* **Elohim**,
nor *regard man* **respect humanity**;
5 Yet **indeed**
because this widow *troubleth* **embarrasseth** me,
I *will* **shall** avenge her,
lest by her *continual* coming **unto the completion**
she *weary* **subdue** me.
6 And *the Lord* **Adonay** said,
Hear what the unjust judge *saith* **wordeth**.
7 And shall not *God* **Elohim no way**
avenge his own *elect* **select**,
which cry day and night unto him,
though he *bear long* **be patient** with them?
8 I *tell* **word unto** you
that he *will* **shall** avenge them *speedily* **with quickness**.
Nevertheless **However**
when the Son of *man* **humanity** cometh,
shall he find *faith* **trust** on the earth?
9 And he *spake* **said** this parable unto *certain* **some**
which *trusted* **confided** in themselves
that they were *righteous* **just**,
and *despised others* **belittled the rest**:

YAH SHUA ON THE PHARISEE AND THE CUSTOMS AGENT

10 Two *men went up* **humans ascended**
into the *temple* **priestal precinct** to pray;
the one a Pharisee,
and the other a *publican* **customs agent**.
11 The Pharisee stood
and prayed *thus* **these** with himself,
God **Elohim**, I *thank* **eucharistize** thee,
that I am not **exactly**
as *other men are* **the rest of humanity**,
extortioners **plunderers**, unjust, adulterers,
or even as this *publican* **customs agent**.
12 I fast twice *in* **on** the *week* **shabbath**,
I *give tithes of* **tithe** all *that* **— as much as** I possess.
13 And the *publican* **customs agent**, standing afar off,
would **willed to** not **even** lift *up* so much as his eyes
unto heaven,
but *smote* **struck** upon his *breast* **chest**, *saying* **wording**,
God be merciful to **Elohim, kapur/atone for** me a sinner.
14 I *tell* **word unto** you,
this *man went down* **one descended** to his house justified
rather than the other:
for every one that exalteth himself
shall be *abased* **humbled**;
and he that humbleth himself
shall be exalted.

YAH SHUA ON INFANTS

15 And they *brought unto* **offered** him also infants,
that he *would* **should** touch them:
but when his disciples saw it, they rebuked them.
16 But *Jesus* **Yah Shua** called them *unto him*, and said,
Suffer **Allow** little children to come unto me,
and forbid them not:
for of such is the *kingdom* **sovereigndom** of *God* **Elohim**.
17 *Verily I say* **Amen! I word** unto you,
Whosoever *shall not* **— unless you**
receive the *kingdom* **sovereigndom** of *God* **Elohim**
as a little child
shall *in no wise enter* **no way entereth** therein.

YAH SHUA ON ETERNAL LIFE

18 And *a certain ruler* **an arch** asked him,
saying **wording**, Good *Master* **Doctor**,
what shall I do to inherit eternal life?
19 And *Jesus* **Yah Shua** said unto him,
Why *callest* **wordest** thou me good?
none is good, *save* **except** one, *that is*, *God* **Elohim**.
20 Thou knowest the *commandments* **misvoth**,
Do not commit adultery **adulterize**,
Do not kill **murder not**,
Do not **s**teal **not**,
Do not bear false **pseudo** witness **not**,
Honour thy father and thy mother.
21 And he said,
All these have I *kept* **guarded** from my youth *up*.
22 Now when *Jesus* **Yah Shua** heard these *things*,
he said unto him, Yet lackest thou one *thing*:
sell all *that* **— as much as** thou hast,
and distribute unto the poor,
and thou shalt have treasure in heaven:
and come, follow me.
23 And when he heard *this* **these**,
he *was very* **became exceeding** sorrowful:
for he was *very* **extremely** rich.
24 And when *Jesus* **Yah Shua** saw
that he *was very* **became exceeding** sorrowful, he said,
How *hardly* shall **difficultly** they that have riches
enter into the *kingdom* **sovereigndom** of *God* **Elohim**!
25 For it is easier for a *camel* **rope**°
to *go* **enter** through a needle's eye,
than for *a* **the** rich *man*
to enter into the *kingdom* **sovereigndom** of *God* **Elohim**.
°see Lamsa
26 And they that heard it said, Who then can be saved?
27 And he said,
The things **Those** which are impossible with *men* **humanity**
are possible with *God* **Elohim**.
28 Then *Peter* **Petros** said,
Lo **Behold**, we have *left* **forsaken** all, and followed thee.
29 And he said unto them,
Verily I say **Amen! I word** unto you,
There is no *man* **one** that hath *left* **forsaken** house,
or parents, or brethren, or *wife* **woman**, or children,
for the *kingdom* **sovereigndom** of *God's* **Elohim's** sake,
30 Who shall not **no way**
receive manifold **take much** more
in this present *time* **season**,
and in the *world* **eon** to come life *everlasting* **eternal**.

YAH SHUA PROPHECIES HIS DEATH AND RESURRECTION

31 Then he took unto him the twelve, and said unto them,
Behold, we *go up* **ascend** to *Jerusalem* **Yeru Shalem**,
and all *things* that are *written* **scribed**
by **through** the prophets
concerning the Son of *man* **humanity**
shall be *accomplished* **completed**.
32 For he shall be *delivered* **betrayed**
unto the *Gentiles* **goyim**,
and shall be mocked, and *spitefully entreated* **insulted**,
and spitted on:
33 And they shall scourge him,
and *put* **slaughter** him *to death*:
and the third day he shall rise *again*.
34 And they *understood* **comprehended**
none of these *things*:
and this *saying* **rhema** was *hid* **secreted** from them,
neither knew they
the things **those** which were *spoken* **worded**.

YAH SHUA HEALS SOMEONE BLIND

35 And it *came to pass* **became**,
that as he *was come nigh* **approached**
unto *Jericho* **Yericho**,
a *certain* blind *man* **one** sat by the way side begging:
36 And hearing the multitude *pass by* **going through**,
he asked what it meant.
37 And they *told* **evangelized** him,
that *Jesus of Nazareth* **Yah Shua the Nazarene**
passeth by.
38 And he cried, *saying* **wording**,
Jesus **Yah Shua**, *thou* son of David, *have* mercy *on* me.
39 And they which went before rebuked him,
that he should *hold his peace* **hush**:
but he cried so much the more,
Thou son of David, *have* mercy *on* me.
40 And *Jesus* **Yah Shua** stood,
and *commanded* **summoned** him to be brought unto him:
and when he *was come near* **approached**, he asked him,
41 *Saying* **Wording**,
What *wilt* **willest** thou that I shall do unto thee?
And he said, *Lord* **Adonay**,
that I may *receive my sight* **see**.
42 And *Jesus* **Yah Shua** said unto him,
Receive thy sight **See**: thy *faith* **trust** hath saved thee.
43 And immediately he *received his sight* **saw**,
and followed him, glorifying *God* **Elohim**:
and all the people, when they saw it,
gave *praise* **halal** unto *God* **Elohim**.

SALVATION COMES TO HOUSE OF ZAKKAY

19 And *Jesus* **Yah Shua**
entered and passed through *Jericho* **Yericho**.
2 And, behold, *there was* a man
named Zacchaeus **by name called Zakkay**,
which was the
chief among the publicans **arch customs agent**,
and he was rich.
3 And he sought to see *Jesus* **Yah Shua** who he was;
and could not for the *press* **multitude**,
because he was little of stature.
4 And he ran *before* **in front**,
and *climbed up* **ascended** into a sycomore *tree*
to see him:
for he was **about** to pass *that way* **through**.
5 And when *Jesus* **Yah Shua** came to the place,
he looked *up*, and saw him, and said unto him,
Zacchaeus **Zakkay**,
make haste **hasten**, and *come down* **descend**;
for to day I must abide at thy house.
6 And he *made haste* **hastened**,
and *came down* **descended**,
and received him *joyfully* **cheerfully**.
7 And when they saw it, they all murmured,
saying **wording**,
That he *was gone* **entered** to *be guest* **lodge**
with a man that is a sinner.
8 And *Zacchaeus* **Zakkay** stood,
and said unto *the Lord* **Adonay**:
Behold, *Lord* **Adonay**,
the half of my *goods* **holdings** I give to the poor;
and if I have *taken any thing* **sycophanted ought**
from any *man* **one** *by false accusation*,
I *restore* **give back to** him fourfold.
9 And *Jesus* **Yah Shua** said unto him,
This day is salvation *come to* **become** this house,
forsomuch as he also is a son of Abraham.
10 For the Son of *man* **humanity**
is come to seek and to save that which was lost.

YAH SHUA ON THE TEN MINAS

11 And as they heard these *things*,
he added and *spake* **said** a parable,
because he was nigh to *Jerusalem* **Yeru Shalem**,
and because they thought
that the *kingdom* **sovereigndom** of *God* **Elohim**
should immediately **was about to** appear.
12 He said therefore,
A *certain nobleman* **well born human**
went into a far *country* **region**
to *receive* **take** for himself a *kingdom* **sovereigndom**,
and to return.
13 And he called his ten servants,
and *delivered* **gave** them ten *pounds* **minas**,
and said unto them, *Occupy* **Barter** till I come.
14 But his citizens hated him,
and *sent* **apostolized** a *message* **presbytery** after him,
saying **wording**,
We *will* **shall** not have this *man* to reign over us.
15 And it *came to pass* **became**,
that when he *was returned* **came back**,
having *received* **taken** the *kingdom* **sovereigndom**,
then he *commanded* **said to voice out**
these servants to be called unto him,
to whom he had given the *money* **silver**,
that he might know
how much *every man* **each**
had *gained by trading* **thoroughly applied himself**.
16 Then came the first, *saying* **wording**, *Lord* **Adoni**,
thy *pound* **mina** hath *gained* **acquired** ten *pounds* **minas**.
17 And he said unto him, Well **done**, thou good servant:
because thou hast *been faithful* **become trustworthy**
in *very little* **the least**,
have thou authority over ten cities.
18 And the second came, *saying* **wording**, *Lord* **Adoni**,
thy *pound* **mina**
hath *gained* **produced** five *pounds* **minas**.
19 And he said likewise to him,
Be thou also over five cities.
20 And another came, *saying* **wording**,
Lord **Adoni**, behold, *here is* thy *pound* **mina**,
which I have *kept* **laid** *up* in a *napkin* **sudarium**:
21 For I *feared* **awed** thee,
because thou art an austere *man* **human**:
thou takest *up* that thou *layedst* **placedst** not *down*,
and *reapest* **harvestest**
that thou *didst* **sowest** not *sow*.
22 And he *saith* **wordeth** unto him,
Out of thine own mouth *will* **shall** I judge thee,
thou wicked **evil** servant.
Thou knewest that I was an austere *man* **human**,
taking *up* that I *laid* **placed** not *down*,
and *reaping* **harvesting** that I *did* **sowed** not *sow*:
23 *Wherefore* **Why** then
gavest not thou my *money* **silver** into the *bank* **table**,
that at my coming
I might have *required* **exacted** mine own
with *usury* **interest**?
24 And he said unto them that stood by,
Take from him the *pound* **mina**,
and give it to him that hath ten *pounds* **minas**.
25 (And they said unto him, *Lord* **Adoni**,
he hath ten *pounds* **minas**.)
26 For I *say* **word** unto you,
That unto every one which hath
shall be given;
and from him that hath not,
even that he hath shall be taken away from him.
27 But those mine enemies,
which *would* **willed** not that I should reign over them,
bring hither,
and *slay* **slaughter** them *before* **in front of** me.

YAH SHUA ENTERS YERU SHALEM

28 And when he had *thus spoken* **said these**,
he went *before* **ahead**,
ascending *up* to *Jerusalem* **Yeru Shalem**.
29 And it *came to pass* **became**,
when he *was come nigh* **approached**
to Bethpage **Beth Pag** and *Bethany* **Beth Ania**,
at the mount called *the mount* of Olives,
he *sent* **apostolized** two of his disciples,
30 Saying,
Go ye into the village *over against* **opposite** you;
in the which at your entering ye shall find a colt tied,
whereon yet never *man* **human ever** sat:
loose *him*, and bring him *hither*.
31 And if any *man* **one** ask you, Why do ye loose *him*?
thus shall *ye* say unto him,
Because *the Lord* **Adonay** hath need of him.
32 And they that were *sent* **apostolized** went their way,
and found even as he had said unto them.
33 And as they were loosing the colt,

the *owners* **adonim** *thereof* said unto them,
Why loose ye the colt?
34 And they said, *the Lord* **Adonay** hath need of him.
35 And they brought him to *Jesus* **Yah Shua**:
and they *cast* **tossed** their garments upon the colt,
and they *set Jesus* **mounted Yah Shua** thereon.
36 And as he went,
they spread their *clothes* **garments** in the way.
37 And when he *was come nigh* **approached**,
even **already** at the descent of the mount of Olives,
the whole multitude of the disciples
began to *rejoice* **cheer**
and *praise God* **halal Elohim** with a *loud* **mega** voice
for all the *mighty works* **dynamis** that they had seen;
38 *saying* **wording**,
Blessed **Eulogized** be the *King* **Sovereign**
that cometh in the name of *the Lord* **Yah Veh**:
peace **shalom** in heaven,
and glory in the *highest* **highests**.
Psalm 118:25, 26
39 And some of the Pharisees from among the multitude
said unto him, *Master* **Doctor**, rebuke thy disciples.
40 And he answered and said unto them,
I *tell* **word unto** you that,
if these should *hold their peace* **hush**,
the stones *would* **should** immediately cry out.
41 And when he *was come near* **approached**,
he *beheld* **saw** the city, and wept over it,
42 *Saying* **Wording**, If thou hadst known, even thou,
at least **yet indeed** in this thy day,
the things **these**
which *belong unto* **shall be for** thy *peace* **shalom**!
but now they are *hid* **secreted** from thine eyes.
43 For the days shall come upon thee,
that thine enemies
shall *cast* **envelop** a *trench* **palisade** about thee,
and *compass* **surround** thee *round*,
and *keep* **hold** thee in on every side,
44 And shall *lay* **raze** thee *even with the ground*,
and thy children within thee;
and they shall not *leave* **allow** in thee
one stone upon *another* **stone**;
because **for that** thou knewest not
the *time* **season** of thy visitation.

YAH SHUA ENTERS THE PRIESTAL PRECINCT

45 And he *went* **entered** into the *temple* **priestal precinct**,
and began to cast out them that sold therein,
and them that bought;
46 *Saying* **Wording** unto them,
It is *written* **scribed**, My house is the house of prayer:
but ye have made it a *den* **grotto** of *thieves* **robbers**.
47 And he *taught* **doctrinated** daily
in the *temple* **priestal precinct**.
But the *chief* **arch** priests and the scribes
and the *chief* **preeminent** of the people
sought to destroy him,
48 And could not find what they might do:
for all the people
were very attentive to hear him
heard him with suspense.

YAH SHUA'S AUTHORITY QUESTIONED

20 And it *came to pass* **became**,
that on one of those days,
as he *taught* **doctrinated** the people
in the *temple* **priestal precinct**,
and *preached the gospel* **evangelized**,
the *chief* **arch** priests and the scribes
came upon **stood by** him with the elders,
2 And *spake* **said** unto him, *saying* **wording**,
Tell **Say to** us, by what authority doest thou these *things*?
or who is he that gave thee this authority?
3 And he answered and said unto them,
I *will* **shall** also ask you one *thing* **word**;
and *answer* **say to** me:
4 The baptism of *John* **Yahn**,
was it from heaven, or of *men* **humanity**?
5 And they *reasoned* **reckoned** with themselves,
saying **wording**, If we shall say, From heaven;
he *will* **shall** say, Why then *believed* **trusted** ye him not?
6 But and if we say, Of *men* **humanity**;
all the people *will* **shall** stone us:
for they be *persuaded* **convinced**
that *John* **Yahn** was a prophet.
7 And they answered,
that they *could* **knew** not *tell* whence it was.
8 And *Jesus* **Yah Shua** said unto them,
Neither *tell* **word** I you
by what authority I do these *things*.

YAH SHUA ON THE CULTIVATORS

9 Then began he to *speak* **word** to the people this parable;
A *certain man* **human** planted a vineyard,
and *let* **leased** it *forth* to *husbandmen* **cultivators**,
and went *into a far country* **abroad**
for *a long* **an ample** time.
10 And at the season he *sent* **apostolized** a servant
to the *husbandmen* **cultivators**,
that they should give him of the fruit of the vineyard:
but the *husbandmen beat* **cultivators flogged** him,
and *sent* **apostolized** him *away* **forth** empty.
11 And again he *sent* **added to send** another servant:
and they *beat* **flogged** him also,
and *entreated* **dishonoured** him *shamefully*,
and *sent* **apostolized** him *away* **forth** empty.
12 And again he *sent* **added to send** a third:
and they *wounded* **traumatized** him also,
and cast him out.
13 Then said the *lord* **adoni** of the vineyard,
What shall I do?
I *will* **shall** send my beloved son:
it may be **perhaps** they *will reverence* **shall respect** him
when they see him.
14 But when the *husbandmen* **cultivators** saw him,
they reasoned among themselves, *saying* **wording**,
This is the heir: come, let us *kill* **slaughter** him,
that the inheritance may be ours.
15 So they cast him out of the vineyard,
and *killed* **slaughtered** him.
What therefore
shall the *lord* **adoni** of the vineyard do unto them?
16 He shall come
and destroy these *husbandmen* **cultivators**,
and shall give the vineyard to others.
And when they heard it, they said,
God forbid **May it not become**.
17 And he *beheld* **looked at** them, and said,
What is this then that is *written* **scribed**,
The stone which the builders *rejected* **dissapproved**,
the same **this** is become the head of the corner?
18 Whosoever shall fall upon that stone
shall be *broken* **crushed**;
but on whomsoever it shall fall,
it will grind him to powder **shall be pulverized**.
Psalm 118:22, 23
19 And the *chief* **arch** priests and the scribes
the same hour sought to lay hands on him;
and they *feared* **awed** the people:
for they *perceived* **knew**
that he had *spoken* **said** this parable against them.

YAH SHUA ON TRIBUTE

20 And they *watched* **observed** him,
and *sent forth spies* **apostolized liars in waiting**,
which should *feign* **hypocrize** themselves just men,
that they might take hold of his words,
that so they might *deliver* **betray** him
unto the *power* **hierarchy** and authority of the governor.
21 And they asked him, *saying* **wording**, *Master* **Doctor**,
we know that thou *sayest* **wordest**
and *teachest rightly* **doctrinatest straightforwardly**,
neither *acceptest* **takest** thou the *person of any* **face**,
but *teachest* **doctrinatest** the way of *God* **Elohim**
truly **in truth**:
22 Is it *lawful* **allowed** for us
to give tribute unto *Caesar* **the Kaisar**, or no?
23 But he perceived their *craftiness* **cunning**,
and said unto them, Why *tempt* **test** ye me?
24 Shew me a *penny* **denarion**.
Whose *image* **icon** and *superscription* **epigraph** hath it?
They answered and said, *Caesar's* **The Kaisar's**.
25 And he said unto them,
Render **Give back** therefore

unto Caesar the things which be Caesar's
the Kaisar's to the Kaisar,
and unto God the things which be God's
and Elohim's to Elohim.
26 And they could not
take hold of his *words* **rhema** before the people:
and they marvelled at his answer,
and *held their peace* **hushed**.

YAH SHUA ON MARRIAGE IN THE RESURRECTION

27 Then came *to him*
certain **some** of the *Sadducees* **Sadoqiym**,
which *deny* **contradict** that there is any resurrection;
and they asked him,
28 *Saying* **Wording**, *Master* **Doctor**,
Moses wrote **Mosheh scribed** unto us,
If any *man's* **one's** brother die, having a *wife* **woman**,
and he die *without children* **childless**,
that his brother should take his *wife* **woman**,
and raise *up seed* **sperma** unto his brother.
29 There were therefore seven brethren:
and the first took a *wife* **woman**,
and died *without children* **childless**.
30 And the second took her to *wife* **woman**,
and he died childless.
31 And the third took her;
and in like manner the seven also:
and they left no children, and died.
32 *Last of all* **Afterward** the woman died also.
33 Therefore in the resurrection
whose *wife of them is* **woman becometh** she?
for seven had her to *wife* **woman**.
34 And *Jesus* **Yah Shua** answering said unto them,
The *children* **sons** of this *world* **eon** marry,
and are *given in marriage* **married off**:
35 But they which shall be accounted worthy
to obtain that *world* **eon**,
and the resurrection from the dead,
neither marry, nor are *given in marriage* **married off**:
36 Neither **indeed** can they **even** die *any more*:
for they are equal unto the angels;
and are the *children* **sons** of *God* **Elohim**,
being the *children* **sons** of the resurrection.
37 Now that the dead are raised,
even *Moses shewed* **Mosheh disclosed** at the *bush* **brier**,
when he *calleth the Lord* **wordeth Yah Veh**
the *God* **Elohim** of Abraham,
and the *God* **Elohim** of *Isaac* **Yischaq**,
and the *God* **Elohim** of *Jacob* **Yaaqov**.
Exodus 3:1—6
38 For he is not a *God* **Elohim** of the dead,
but of the living: for all live unto him.
39 Then *certain* **some** of the scribes answering said,
Master **Doctor**, thou hast well said.
40 And *after that* **yet**
they durst not ask him any question at all.

YAH SHUA ON THE MESSIAH

41 And he said unto them,
How *say* **word** they that *Christ* **the Messiah** is David's son?
42 And David himself
saith **wordeth** in the *book* **scroll** of Psalms,
the LORD said **an oracle of Yah Veh**
unto my *Lord* **Adonay**,
Sit thou *on* **by** my right *hand*,
43 Till I *make* **place** thine enemies thy footstool.
Psalm 110:1
44 David therefore calleth him *Lord* **Adonay**,
how is he then his son?
45 Then in the *audience* **hearing** of all the people
he said unto his disciples,
46 *Beware of* **Heed** the scribes,
which *desire* **will** to walk in *long robes* **stoles**,
and *love greetings* **befriend salutations** in the markets,
and the *highest seats* **preeminent cathedras**
in the synagogues,
and the *chief rooms* **preeminent recliners**
at *feasts* **suppers**;
47 Which devour widows' houses,
and for a *shew* **pretext** make *long* **far out** prayers:
the same **these** shall *receive* **take**
greater damnation **more superabundant judgment**.

YAH SHUA ON THE WIDOW'S TWO FLAKES

21 And he looked *up*, and saw the rich *men*
casting their *gifts* **oblations** into the treasury.
2 And he saw also a *certain* **needy** poor widow
casting in thither two *mites* **flakes**.
3 And he said, *Of a truth I say* **Truly I word** unto you,
that this poor widow hath cast in more than they all:
4 For all these have of their **super** abundance
cast in unto the *offerings* **oblations** of *God* **Elohim**:
but she of her *penury* **lack**
hath cast in all the *living* **subsistence** that she had.

YAH SHUA ON THE COMPLETION OF THE EON

5 And as some *spake* **worded**
of **about** the *temple* **priestal precinct**,
how it was adorned with goodly stones and *gifts* **votives**,
he said,
6 As for these *things* which ye *behold* **observe**,
the days *will* **shall** come,
in the which there shall not be *left* **allowed**
one stone upon *another* **stone**,
that shall not be *thrown down* **disintegrated**.
7 And they asked him, *Saying* **Wording**, *Master* **Doctor**,
but **so** when shall these *things* be?
and what sign *will* **shall** there be
when **ever** these *things* shall *come to pass* **become**?
8 And he said,
Take heed **See** that ye be not *deceived* **seduced**:
for many shall come in my name, *saying* **wording**,
I am Christ **I AM**;
and the *time draweth near* **season approacheth**:
go ye not therefore after them.
9 But when **ever** ye shall hear
of wars and *commotions* **instabilities**,
be not terrified:
for these *things* must first *come to pass* **become**;
but the *end* **completion** is not *by and by* **straightway**.
10 Then *said* **worded** he unto them,
Nation **Goyim** shall rise against *nation* **goyim**,
and *kingdom* **sovereigndom**
against *kingdom* **sovereigndom**:
11 And *great earthquakes* **mega quakes**
shall be in divers places,
and famines, and pestilences;
and *fearful sights* **awesomenesses** and *great* **mega** signs
shall there be from heaven.
12 But before all these,
they shall lay their hands on you, and persecute you,
delivering **betraying** you *up* to the synagogues,
and into *prisons* **guardhouses**,
being brought before
kings **sovereigns** and *rulers* **governors**
for my name's sake.
13 And it shall turn to you for a *testimony* **witness**.
14 *Settle* **Place** it therefore in your hearts,
not to *meditate before* **premeditate**
what ye shall *answer* **plead**:
15 For I *will* **shall** give you a mouth and wisdom,
which all your adversaries
shall not be able to *gainsay* **refute** nor *resist* **withstand**.
16 And ye shall be betrayed both by parents,
and brethren, and *kinsfolks* **kin**, and friends;
and some of you
shall they *cause to be put to death* **deathify**.
17 And ye shall be hated of all men for my name's sake.
18 But there shall not **no way**
an hair of your head *perish* **destruct**.
19 In your *patience* **endurance** possess ye your souls.
20 And when **ever** ye shall see *Jerusalem* **Yeru Shalem**
compassed with armies **surrounded by warriors**,
then know
that the desolation thereof *is nigh* **approacheth**.
21 Then let them which are in *Judaea* **Yah Hudah**
flee to the mountains;
and let them which are in the midst of it depart *out*;
and let not them that are in the *countries* **regions**
enter *thereinto*.
22 For these be the days of vengeance,
that all *things* which are *written* **scribed** may be fulfilled.
23 But woe unto them that *are with child* **have in womb**,
and to them that *give suck* **nipple**, in those days!

for there shall be *great distress* **mega need**
in **upon** the *land* **earth**, and wrath upon this people.
24 And they shall fall by the edge of the sword,
and shall be *led away captive* **captured**
into all *nations* **goyim**:
and *Jerusalem* **Yeru Shalem**
shall be *trodden down* **trampled** of the *Gentiles* **goyim**,
until the *times* **seasons** of the *Gentiles* **goyim** be fulfilled.
25 And there shall be signs in the sun,
and in the moon, and in the stars;
and upon the earth *distress* **oppression** of *nations* **goyim**,
with perplexity;
the sea **surging** and *the waves roaring* **echoing**;
26 *Men's hearts failing them* **Humanity breathing cold**
for *fear* **awe**,
and for *looking after* **awaiting** those *things*
which are coming on the *earth* **world**:
for the *powers* **dynamis** of heaven shall be shaken.
Yesha Yah 13:9—13

YAH SHUA ON THE PAROUSIA OF THE SON OF HUMANITY

27 And then shall they see the Son of *man* **humanity**
coming in a cloud
with *power* **dynamis** and *great* **vast** glory.
28 And when these *things* begin to *come to pass* **become**,
then *look up* **unbend**, and lift *up* your heads;
for your redemption draweth nigh.
29 And he *spake* **said** to them a parable;
Behold **See** the fig tree, and all the trees;
30 when **ever** they now *shoot* **put** forth,
ye see and know of your own selves
that *summer* **warmth** is *now* **already** nigh *at hand.*
31 So likewise ye,
when **ever** ye see these *things come to pass* **become**,
know ye that the *kingdom* **sovereigndom** of *God* **Elohim**
is nigh *at hand.*
32 *Verily I say* **Amen! I word** unto you,
This generation shall not **no way** pass away,
till all *be fulfilled* **becometh**.
33 Heaven and earth shall pass away:
but my words shall not **no way** pass away.
34 And *take* heed to yourselves,
lest *at any time* **ever**
your hearts be *overcharged* **burdened**
with *surfeiting* **hangovers**, and *drunkenness* **intoxication**,
and *cares* **anxieties** of *this life* **existence**,
and so that day *come upon* **stand by** you unawares.
35 For as a snare shall it come on all them
that *dwell* **sit** on the face of the whole earth.
36 *Watch ye* **Stay awake** therefore,
and *pray always* **petition in every season**,
that ye may be accounted worthy
to escape all these *things*
that shall *come* **are about** to *pass* **become**,
and to stand before the Son of *man* **humanity**.
37 And in the day *time* he was *teaching* **doctrinating**
in the *temple* **priestal precinct**;
and at night he went out, and *abode* **camped**
in the mount that is called *the mount* of Olives.
38 And all the people came
early in the morning **at dawn** to him
in the *temple* **priestal precinct**, for to hear him.

SATAN ENTERS YAH HUDAH THE URBANITE

22 Nowthe *feast* **celebration** of *unleavened bread* **matsah**
drew nigh **approached**,
which is *called* **worded** the *Passover* **pasach**.
2 And the *chief* **arch** priests and scribes
sought how they might *kill* **take** him **out**;
for they *feared* **awed** the people.
3 Then entered Satan into
Judas surnamed Iscariot **Yah Hudah called the urbanite**,
being of the number of the twelve.
4 And he went his way,
and *communed* **talked**
with the *chief* **arch** priests and *captains* **strategoi**,
how he might betray him unto them.
5 And they *were glad* **cheered**,
and covenanted to give him *money* **silver**.
6 And he *promised* **avowed**,
and sought opportunity to betray him unto them
in the absence of **away from** the multitude.

YAH SHUA'S FINAL PASACH

7 Then came the day of *unleavened bread* **matsah**,
when the *passover* **pasach** must be *killed* **sacrificed**.
8 And he *sent Peter* **apostolized Petros** and *John* **Yahn**,
saying,
Go and prepare us the *passover* **pasach**, that we may eat.
9 And they said unto him,
Where *wilt* **willest** thou that we prepare?
10 And he said unto them, Behold,
when ye are entered into the city,
there shall a *man* **human** meet you,
bearing a pitcher of water;
follow him into the house where he entereth *in.*
11 And ye shall say
unto the *goodman of the house* **housedespotes**,
The *Master saith* **Doctor wordeth** unto thee,
Where is the *guestchamber* **lodge**,
where I shall eat the *passover* **pasach** with my disciples?
12 And he shall shew you
a *large* **mega** upper room *furnished* **spread**:
there *make ready* **prepare**.
13 And they went,
and found **exactly** as he had said unto them:
and they *made ready* **prepared** the *passover* **pasach**.
14 And when the hour *was come* **had become**,
he *sat down* **reposed**, and the twelve apostles with him.
15 And he said unto them,
With *desire* **panting** I have *desired* **panted**
to eat this *passover* **pasach** with you before I suffer:
16 For I *say* **word** unto you,
I *will* **shall** not *any more* **no way** eat thereof,
until it be fulfilled
in the *kingdom* **sovereigndom** of *God* **Elohim**.
17 And he *took* **received** the cup,
and *gave thanks* **eucharistized**, and said,
Take this, and divide it among yourselves:
18 For I *say* **word** unto you,
I *will* **shall** not **no way**
drink of the *fruit* **produce** of the vine,
until the *kingdom* **sovereigndom** of *God* **Elohim**
shall come.
19 And he took bread, and *gave thanks* **eucharistized**,
and brake it, and gave unto them, *saying* **wording**,
This is my body which is given for you:
this do in remembrance of me.
20 Likewise also the cup after *supper* **supping**,
saying **wording**,
This cup is the new *testament* **covenant** in my blood,
which is *shed* **poured forth** for you.
21 But, behold,
the hand of him that betrayeth me
is with me on the table.
22 And *truly* **indeed** the Son of *man* **humanity** goeth,
as *it was determined* **decreed**:
but woe unto that *man* **human**
by **through** whom he is betrayed!
23 And they began to *enquire* **dispute** among themselves,
which of them it was
that should *do* **be about to transact** this *thing.*
24 And there *was* **became** also a strife among them,
which of them should be *accounted* **thought** the greatest.
25 And he said unto them,
The *kings* **Sovereigns** of the *Gentiles* **goyim**
exercise lordship over **overlord** them;
and they
that *exercise authority upon* **authorize over** them
are called *benefactors* **well—workers**.
26 But ye shall not be so:
but he that is greatest among you,
let him be as the younger;
and he that *is chief* **governeth**,
as he that *doth serve* **ministereth**.
27 For whether is greater,
he that *sitteth at meat* **reposeth**,
or he that *serveth* **ministereth**?
is not **indeed** he that *sitteth at meat* **reposeth**?
but I am among you as he that *serveth* **ministereth**.
28 Ye are they which have continued **to abide** with me
in my *temptations* **testings**.
29 And I *appoint* **covenant** unto you

a *kingdom* **sovereigndom**,
exactly as my Father
hath *appointed* **covenanted** unto me;
30 That ye may eat and drink at my table
in my *kingdom* **sovereigndom**,
and sit on thrones
judging the twelve *tribes* **scions** of *Israel* **Yisra El**.
31 And *the Lord* **Adonay** said,
Simon, Simon **Shimon, Shimon**, behold,
Satan hath *desired to have* **demanded** you,
that he may sift you as *wheat* **grain**:
32 But I have *prayed* **petitioned** for thee,
that thy *faith* **trust** fail not:
and *when* **once** thou art *converted* **turned around**,
strengthen **establish** thy brethren.
33 And he said unto him, *Lord* **Adonay**,
I am *ready* **prepared** to go with thee,
both into *prison* **the guardhouse**, and to death.
34 And he said, I *tell* **word unto** thee, *Peter* **Petros**,
the *cock* **rooster** shall not **no way**
crow **voice out** this day,
before that thou shalt thrice deny that thou knowest me.
35 And he said unto them,
When I *sent* **apostolized** you without *purse* **pouch**,
and *scrip* **wallet**, and shoes,
lacked ye *any thing* **somewhat**?
And they said, *nothing* **naught**.
36 Then said he unto them, But now,
he that hath a *purse* **pouch**, let him take it,
and likewise his *scrip* **wallet**:
and he that hath no sword,
let him sell his garment, and buy one.
37 For I *say* **word** unto you,
that *is written* **scribed**
must yet be *accomplished* **completed** in me,
And he was reckoned
among **with** the *transgressors* **untorahed**:
for *the things* **those** concerning me
have *an end* **a completion**.
Yesha Yah 53:2
38 And they said, *Lord* **Adonay**, behold,
here are two swords.
And he said unto them, It is enough.

YAH SHUA'S PRAYERS ON THE MOUNT OF OLIVES

39 And he came out, and went,
as *he was wont* **his custom**, to the mount of Olives;
and his disciples also followed him.
40 And when he *was* **became** at the place,
he said unto them,
Pray that ye enter not into *temptation* **testing**.
41 And he was withdrawn from them about a stone's cast,
and *kneeled down* **placed his knees**, and prayed,
42 *Saying* **Wording**, Father,
if thou *be willing* **willest**, remove this cup from me:
nevertheless **however** not my will,
but thine, *be done* **become**.
43 And there appeared an angel unto him from heaven,
strengthening **invigorating** him.
44 And *being* **becoming** in an agony
he prayed more *earnestly* **intently**:
and his sweat *was* **became** as *it were*
great *drops* **clots** of blood
falling down to **descending upon** the *ground* **earth**.
45 And when he rose *up* from prayer,
and was come to his disciples,
he found them sleeping for sorrow,
46 And said unto them, Why sleep ye?
rise and pray, lest ye enter into *temptation* **testing**.

YAH SHUA'S ARREST

47 And while he yet spake, behold a multitude,
and he that was *called Judas* **worded Yah Hudah**,
one of the twelve, *went before* **preceded** them,
and *drew near* **approached** unto *Jesus* **Yah Shua** to kiss him.
48 But *Jesus* **Yah Shua** said unto him, *Judas* **Yah Hudah**,
betrayest thou the Son of *man* **humanity** with a kiss?
49 When they which were about him
saw what *would follow* **should become**,
they said unto him, *Lord* **Adonay**,
shall *we* smite with the sword?
50 And one of them
smote the servant of the *high* **arch** priest,
and *cut off* **removed** his right ear.
51 And *Jesus* **Yah Shua** answered and said,
Suffer **Allow** ye thus far.
And he touched his ear **lobe**, and healed him.
52 Then *Jesus* **Yah Shua** said unto the *chief* **arch** priests,
and *captains* **strategoi** of the *temple* **priestal precinct**,
and the elders, which were come to him,
Be ye come out,
as against a *thief* **robber**, with swords and staves?
53 When I was daily with you
in the *temple* **priestal precinct**,
ye *stretched forth* **extended** no hands against me:
but this is your hour,
and the *power* **authority** of darkness.

PETROS' THREE DENIALS OF YAH SHUA

54 Then took they him, and led him,
and brought him into the *high* **arch** priest's house.
And *Peter* **Petros** followed afar off.
55 And when they had *kindled* **lighted** a fire
in the midst of the *hall* **courtyard**,
and were set down together,
Peter **Petros** sat down among them.

PETROS' FIRST DENIAL

56 But a *certain maid beheld* **lass saw** him
as he sat by the *fire* **light**,
and *earnestly looked upon* **stared at** him, and said,
This *man* **one** was also with him.
57 And he denied him, *saying* **wording**,
Woman, I know him not.

PETROS' SECOND DENIAL

58 And after a little *while* another saw him, and said,
Thou art also of them.
And *Peter* **Petros** said, *man* **human**, *I am not* **Not I**.

PETROS' THIRD DENIAL

59 And *about the space of* one hour *after* **having passed**
another *confidently* **thoroughly** affirmed, *saying* **wording**,
Of a truth this *fellow* **one** also was with him:
for he is a *Galilaean* **Galiliy**.
60 And *Peter* **Petros** said, *Man* **Human**,
I know not what thou *sayest* **wordest**.
And immediately, while he yet spake,
the *cock crew* **rooster voiced out**.
61 And *the Lord* **Adonay** turned,
and looked upon *Peter* **Petros**.
And *Peter* **Petros**
remembered the word of *the Lord* **Adonay**,
how he had said unto him,
Before the *cock crow* **rooster voice out**,
thou shalt deny me thrice.
62 And *Peter* **Petros** went out, and wept bitterly.

YAH SHUA IS BLASPHEMED

63 And the men that held *Jesus* **Yah Shua** mocked him,
and *smote* **flogged** him.
64 And when they had *blindfolded* **entirely covered** him,
they struck him on the face, and asked him,
saying **wording**, Prophesy, who is it that smote thee?
65 And *many other things* **much more** blasphemously
spake **worded** they against him.

YAH SHUA BEFORE THE SANHEDRIM

66 And as soon as it *was* **became** day,
the elders of the people and the *chief* **arch** priests
and the scribes *came* **gathered** together,
and *led* **brought** him into their *council* **sanhedrim**,
saying **wording**,
67 *Art thou the Christ?* **If thou be the Messiah**
Tell **Say to** us.
And he said unto them, If I *tell* **say to** you,
ye *will* **shall** not **no way** *believe* **trust**:
68 And if I also ask you,
ye *will* **shall** not **no way** answer me,
nor *let* **release** me *go*.
69 *Hereafter shall* **From now on**
the Son of *man sit on* **humanity shall sit by** the right *hand*
of the *power* **dynamis** of *God* **Elohim**.
70 Then said they all,
Art thou then the Son of *God* **Elohim**?
And he said unto them, Ye *say* **word** that *I am* **I AM**.
71 And they said, What need we *any further* **still** witness?
for we ourselves have heard of his own mouth.

YAH SHUA BEFORE PILATOS

23 And the whole multitude of them arose,
and led him unto *Pilate* **Pilatos**.
2 And they began to accuse him, *saying* **wording**,
We found this *fellow* perverting the *nation* **goyim**,
and forbidding to give tribute to *Caesar* **the Kaisar**,
saying **wording**
that he himself is *Christ a King* **Messiah Sovereign**.
3 And *Pilate* **Pilatos** asked him, *saying* **wording**,
Art thou the *King* **Sovereign** of the *Jews* **Yah Hudiym**?
And he answered him and said,
Thou *sayest it* **hast worded**.
4 Then said *Pilate* **Pilatos** to the *chief* **arch** priests
and to the *people* **multitude**,
I find no *fault* **cause** in this *man* **human**.
5 And they were the more *fierce* **insistent**,
saying **wording**, He stirreth *up* the people,
teaching **doctrinating** throughout all *Jewry* **Yah Hudah**,
beginning from *Galilee* **Galiyl** to *this place* **here**.
6 When *Pilate* **Pilatos** heard of *Galilee* **Galiyl**,
he asked whether the *man* **human**
were **be** a *Galilaean* **Galiliy**.

YAH SHUA BEFORE HEROD

7 And as soon as he knew that he
belonged unto **is from** Herod's *jurisdiction* **authority**,
he *sent* **resent** him to Herod,
who himself also was at *Jerusalem* **Yeru Shalem**
at that time **in those days**.
8 And when Herod saw *Jesus* **Yah Shua**,
he was *exceeding glad* **extremely cheerful**:
for he *was desirous* **had willed** to see him
of **for** *a* long *season*,
because he had heard *many things of* **much about** him;
and he hoped to have seen some *miracle* **sign**
done **become** by him.
9 Then he *questioned with* **asked** him
in *many* **enough** words;
but he answered him *nothing* **naught**.
10 And the *chief* **arch** priests and scribes stood
and *vehemently* **vigorously** accused him.
11 And Herod with his *men of war* **warriors**
set **belittled** him *at nought*, and mocked him,
and arrayed him in *a gorgeous robe* **radiant apparel**,
and *sent* **resent** him *again* to *Pilate* **Pilatos**.
12 And the same day *Pilate* **Pilatos** and Herod
were made **became** friends *together* **with one another**:
for *before* **previously**
they were at enmity between themselves.

PILATOS WILLS TO RELEASE YAH SHUA

13 And *Pilate* **Pilatos**,
when he had called together the *chief* **arch** priests
and the *rulers* **archs** and the people,
14 Said unto them,
Ye have *brought* **offered** this *man* **human** unto me,
as one that *perverteth* **turneth away** the people:
and, behold, I,
having examined him *before you* **in your sight**,
have found no *fault* **cause** in this *man* **human**
touching **of** those *things* whereof ye accuse him:
15 *No, nor yet* **But not even** Herod:
for I *sent* **resent** you to him; and, *lo* **behold**,
nothing **naught** worthy of death
is *done unto* **transacted by** him.
16 I *will* **shall** therefore *chastise* **discipline** him,
and release *him*.
17 (For of necessity
he must release one unto them at the *feast* **celebration**.)
18 And *they* **the whole multitude**
cried out all at once **screamed simultaneously**,
saying **wording**, *Away with* **Take** this *man* **one**,
and release unto us *Barabbas* **Bar Abbas**:
19 (Who for a *certain sedition* **riot**
made **having become** in the city, and for murder,
was cast into *prison* **the guardhouse**.)
20 *Pilate* **Pilatos** therefore,
willing **having willed** to release *Jesus* **Yah Shua**,
spake again to them.
21 But they *cried* **shouted out**, *saying* **wording**,
Crucify him, crucify him. **Stake! Stake him!**
22 And he said unto them the third time,
Why **Indeed**, what evil hath he done?
I have found no cause of death in him:
I *will* **shall** therefore
chastise **discipline** him and *let* **release** him *go*.
23 And they *were instant* **imposed** with *loud* **mega** voices,
requiring **asking** that he might be *crucified* **staked**.
And the voices of them
and of the *chief* **arch** priests *prevailed* **overpowered**.
24 And *Pilate gave sentence* **Pilatos adjudged**
that it should be as they required.
25 And he released unto them
him that for *sedition* **riot** and murder
was cast into *prison* **the guardhouse**,
whom they had *desired* **asked**;
but he *delivered Jesus* **betrayed Yah Shua**
to their will **as they willed**.

SHIMON BEARS YAH SHUA'S STAKE

26 And as they led him away,
they *laid* **took** hold upon *one Simon* **Shimon**, a Cyrenian,
coming out of the *country* **field**,
and on him they *laid* **put** the *cross* **stake**,
that he might bear it after *Jesus* **Yah Shua**.
27 And there followed him
a *great company* **vast multitude** of people,
and of women,
which also *bewailed* **chopped** and lamented him.
28 But *Jesus* **Yah Shua** turning unto them said,
Daughters of *Jerusalem* **Yeru Shalem**, weep not for me,
but **however** weep for yourselves, and for your children.
29 For, behold, the days are coming,
in the which they shall say, Blessed are the *barren* **sterile**,
and the wombs that never bare,
and the *paps* **breasts** which never *gave suck* **nippled**.
30 Then shall they begin to *say* **word** to the mountains,
Fall on us;
and to the hills, *Cover* **Vail** us.
31 For if they do these *things*
in a *green tree* **watered staff**,
what shall *be done* **become** in the dry?
32 And there were also two other,
malefactors **evilworkers**,
led with him to be *put to death* **taken out**.

YAH SHUA IS STAKED

33 And when they were come to the place,
which is called *Calvary* **Cranium**,
there they *crucified* **staked** him,
and the *malefactors* **evilworkers**,
one *on* **indeed by** the right *hand*,
and the other *on* **by** the left.
34 Then *said Jesus* **worded Yah Shua**,
Father, forgive them; for they know not what they do.
And they *parted* **divided** his *raiment* **garment**,
and cast lots.
35 And the people stood *beholding* **observing**.
And the *rulers* **archs** also with them *derided him* **sneered**,
saying **wording**, He saved others; let him save himself,
if he be *Christ* **the Messiah**,
the *chosen* **selected** of *God* **Elohim**.
36 And the *soldiers* **warriors** also mocked him,
coming to him, and offering him vinegar,
37 And *saying* **wording**,
If thou be the *King* **Sovereign** of the *Jews* **Yah Hudiym**,
save thyself.
38 And *a superscription* **an epigraph**
also was *written* **scribed** over him
in *letters* **scribings** of *Greek* **Hellenic**,
and *Latin* **Romaic**, and *Hebrew* **Hebraic**,
THIS IS THE *KING* **SOVEREIGN**
OF THE *JEWS* **YAH HUDIYM**.
39 And one of the *malefactors* **evilworkers**
which were hanged
railed on **blasphemed** him, *saying* **wording**,
If thou be *Christ* **the Messiah**, save thyself and us.
40 But the other answering rebuked him,
saying **wording**, Dost not thou *fear God* **awe Elohim**,
seeing thou art in the same *condemnation* **judgment**?
41 And we indeed justly;
for we *receive the due reward* **take that worthy**
of our *deeds* **transactions**:
but this *man* **one**

hath *done nothing amiss* **transacted naught inordinate**.
42 And he *said* **worded** unto *Jesus* **Yah Shua**,
Lord **Adonay**, remember me
when **ever** thou comest into thy *kingdom* **sovereigndom**.
43 And *Jesus* **Yah Shua** said unto him,
Verily I say **Amen! I word** unto thee,
To day shalt thou be with me in paradise.

YAH SHUA EXPIRES

44 And it was about the sixth hour,
and there *was* **became** a darkness over all the earth
until the ninth hour.
45 And the sun was darkened,
and the veil of the *temple* **nave**
was *rent* **split** in the midst.
46 And when *Jesus* **Yah Shua**
had *cried* **voiced** with a *loud* **mega** voice, he said,
Father, into thy hands I *commend* **set forth** my spirit:
and having said thus, he *gave up the ghost* **expired**.
47 Now when the centurion
saw what *was done* **had become**,
he glorified *God* **Elohim**, *saying* **wording**,
Certainly **Indeed** this was a *righteous man* **just human**.
48 And all the *people* **multitude**
that *came* **convened** together to that *sight* **observation**,
beholding the things **observing these**
which *were done* **had become**,
smote **struck** their *breasts* **chests**, and returned.
49 And all his acquaintance,
and the women that followed him from *Galilee* **Galiyl**,
stood afar off, *beholding* **seeing** these *things*.

YAH SHUA ENTOMBED

50 And, behold, there was a man named *Joseph* **Yoseph**,
being a counsellor; *and he was* a good man, and *a* just:
51 (The same had not *consented* **agreed**
to the counsel and *deed* **acts** of them;)
he was of *Arimathaea* **Rahmah**,
a city of the *Jews* **Yah Hudiym**:
who also himself *waited for* **awaited**
the *kingdom* **sovereigndom** of *God* **Elohim**.
52 This *man* **one** went unto *Pilate* **Pilatos**,
and *begged* **asked** the body of *Jesus* **Yah Shua**.
53 And he took it down, and wrapped it in linen,
and *laid* **placed** it in a *sepulchre* **tomb**
that was *hewn in stone* **quarried from rock**,
wherein *never man before was* **no one yet had** laid.
54 And that day was the preparation,
and the *sabbath drew on* **shabbath dawned**.
55 And the women also,
which came with him from *Galilee* **Galiyl**,
followed after, and *beheld* **saw** the *sepulchre* **tomb**,
and how his body was *laid* **placed**.
56 And they returned,
and prepared *spices* **aromatics** and *ointments* **myrrh**;
and *rested* **indeed quieted** the *sabbath day* **shabbath**
according to the *commandment* **misvah**.

YAH SHUA'S RESURRECTION

24 Now upon the first *day* of the *week* **shabbaths**,
very early **deep** in the morning,
they came unto the *sepulchre* **tomb**,
bringing the *spices* **aromatics** which they had prepared,
and *certain others* **some** with them.
2 And they found the stone
rolled away from the *sepulchre* **tomb**.
3 And they entered in,
and found not the body
of *the Lord Jesus* **Adonay Yah Shua**.
4 And it *came to pass* **became**,
as they were *much* **thoroughly** perplexed thereabout,
behold, two men stood by them
in *shining garments* **flashing apparel**:
5 And as they *were afraid* **became awestricken**
and *bowed down* **reclined** their faces to the earth,
they said unto them,
Why seek ye the living *among* **with** the dead?
6 He is not here, but is risen:
remember how he spake unto you
when he was yet in *Galilee* **Galiyl**,
7 *Saying* **Wording**, The Son of *man* **humanity**
must be *delivered* **betrayed**
into the hands of sinful *men* **humanity**,
and be *crucified* **staked**, and the third day rise *again*.
8 And they remembered his *words* **rhema**,
9 And returned from the *sepulchre* **tomb**,
and *told* **evangelized** all these *things* unto the eleven,
and to all the rest.
10 It was *Mary* **Miryam the** Magdalene
and *Joanna* **Yah Hanna**,
and *Mary* **Miryam** *the mother* of *James* **Yaaqovos**,
and *other women* **the rest** that were with them,
which *told* **worded** these *things* unto the apostles.
11 And their *words* **rhema**
seemed to them **manifested in their sight** as *idle tales* **gab**,
and they *believed* **distrusted** them *not*.
12 Then arose *Peter* **Petros**,
and ran unto the *sepulchre* **tomb**;
and stooping down,
he *beheld* **saw** the linen clothes laid *by themselves* **alone**,
and departed, *wondering* **marvelling** in himself
at that which *was come to pass* **had become**.

ON THE WAY TO EMMAUS

13 And, behold, two of them went that same day
to a village *called* **named** Emmaus,
which was from *Jerusalem* **Yeru Shalem**
about *threescore furlongs* **sixty stadia**.
14 And they *talked* **homologized** together
of **about** all these *things* which had happened.
15 And it *came to pass* **became**, that,
while they *communed* **homologized**
together **with one another** and *reasoned* **disputed**,
Jesus **Yah Shua** himself *drew near* **approached**,
and went with them.
16 But their eyes were *holden* **overpowered**
that they should not know him.
17 And he said unto them,
What manner of *communications* **words** are these
that ye *have one to* **cast one against** another,
as ye walk, and are *sad* **sullen**?
18 And the one of them, whose name was Cleopas,
answering said unto him,
Art **Hast** thou only
a stranger **settled** in *Jerusalem* **Yeru Shalem**,
and hast not known *the things* **those**
which *are come to pass* **have become** there
in these days?
19 And he said unto them, What *things*?
And they said unto him,
Concerning *Jesus of Nazareth* **Yah Shua the Nazarene**,
which *was* **became a man** — a prophet
mighty **able** in *deed* **work** and word
before *God* **Elohim** and all the people:
20 And how the *chief* **arch** priests and our rulers **archs**
delivered him to be *condemned* **judged** to death,
and have *crucified* **staked** him.
21 But we *trusted* **hoped** that it had been he
which *should have redeemed Israel*
was about to redeem Yisra El:
and beside all this **but yet indeed**, to day is the third day
since these *things were done* **have become**.
22 *Yea, and certain* **Yet some** women also
of our company *made* **astounded** us *astonished*,
which *were early* **became at dawn**
at the *sepulchre* **tomb**;
23 And when they found not his body, they came,
saying **wording**,
that they had also seen a vision of angels,
which *said* **worded** that he was alive.
24 And *certain* **some** of them which were with us
went to the *sepulchre* **tomb**,
and found it even so as the women had said:
but him they saw not.
25 Then he said unto them, O *fools* **mindless**,
and slow of heart
to *believe* **trust** all that the prophets have spoken:
26 **Indeed,**
Ought **needed** not *Christ* **the Messiah**
to have suffered these *things*,
and to enter into his glory?
27 And beginning at *Moses* **Mosheh** and all the prophets,
he *expounded* **translated** unto them
in all the scriptures *the things* **those** concerning himself.

28 And they *drew nigh* **approached** unto the village,
whither they went:
and he *made as though* **had preplanned**
he would have gone **to go** further.
29 But they constrained him, *saying* **wording**,
Abide with us: for it is toward evening,
and the day *is far spent* **reclineth**.
And he *went in* **entered** to *tarry* **abide** with them.

THE INTERRUPTED EUCHARIST

30 And it *came to pass* **became**,
as he *sat at meat* **reclined** with them,
he took bread, and *blessed* **eulogized** it,
and brake, and gave to them.
31 And their eyes were opened, and they knew him;
and he *vanished out of their sight* **became invisible**.
32 And they said one to another,
Did not **indeed** our heart burn within us,
while he *talked* **spoke** with us by the way,
and while he opened to us the scriptures?
33 And they rose *up* the same hour,
and returned to *Jerusalem* **Yeru Shalem**,
and found the eleven gathered together,
and them that were with them,
34 *Saying* **Wording**, *the Lord* **Adonay** is risen indeed,
and hath appeared to *Simon* **Shimon**.
35 And they *told* **declared**
what things were done **of those in the way**,
and how he was known of them in breaking of bread.

YAH SHUA STANDS MIDST THE DISCIPLES

36 And as they thus spake,
Jesus **Yah Shua** himself stood in the midst of them,
and *saith* **wordeth** unto them,
Peace **Shalom** *be* unto you.
37 But they *were* **became** terrified
and *affrighted* **awestricken**,
and *supposed* **thought**
that they had *seen* **observed** a spirit.
38 And he said unto them, Why are ye troubled?
and why do thoughts *arise* **ascend** in your hearts?
39 *Behold* **See** my hands and my feet, *that it is I myself* **I AM**:
handle **touch** me, and see;
for a spirit hath not flesh and bones,
exactly as ye *see* **observe** me have.
40 And when he had thus *spoken* **said**,
he shewed them his hands and his feet.
41 And while they yet *believed not* **distrusted**
for *joy* **cheer**,
and *wondered* **marvelled**,
he said unto them, Have ye here any *meat* **food**?
42 And they gave him a *piece* **portion** of a broiled fish,
and of an honeycomb.
43 And he took it, and did eat *before them* **in their sight**.
44 And he said unto them,
These are the words which I spake unto you,
while I was yet with you, that all *things* must be fulfilled,
which were *written* **scribed**
in the *law* **torah** of *Moses* **Mosheh**,
and in the prophets, and in the psalms, concerning me.
45 Then opened he their *understanding* **mind**,
that they might *understand* **comprehend** the scriptures,
46 And said unto them, Thus it is *written* **scribed**,
and thus it
behoved Christ **was necessary for the Messiah** to suffer,
and to rise from the dead the third day:
47 And that repentance and *remission* **forgiveness** of sins
should be preached in his name
among all *nations* **goyim**,
beginning at *Jerusalem* **Yeru Shalem**.
48 And ye are witnesses of these *things*.
49 And, behold,
I *send* **apostolize**
the *promise* **pre—evangelism** of my Father upon you:
but *tarry* **sit** ye **down**
in the city of *Jerusalem* **Yeru Shalem**,
until ye be endued with *power* **dynamis** from on high.

YAH SHUA BORNE INTO HEAVEN

50 And he led them out as far as to *Bethany* **Beth Ania**,
and he lifted *up* his hands, and *blessed* **eulogized** them.
51 And it *came to pass* **became**,
while he blessed **in his eulogizing** them,
he *was parted* **passed** from them,
and *carried up* **was borne** into heaven.
52 And they worshipped him,
and returned to *Jerusalem* **Yeru Shalem**
with *great joy* **mega cheer**:
53 And were continually in the *temple* **priestal precinct**,
praising **halaling** and *blessing God* **eulogizing Elohim**.
Amen.

KEY TO INTERPRETING THE EXEGESES
King James text is in regular type;
Text under exegeses is in oblique type;
Text of exegeses is in bold type.

INTRODUCTION

1 **Indeed,**
The *former treatise* **first word** have I made,
O *Theophilus* **Theo Philos,**
of **concerning** all that *Jesus* **Yah Shua**
began both to do and *teach* **doctrinate,**
2 Until the day in which he was taken *up*,
after that he through the Holy *Ghost* **Spirit**
had *given commandments* **misvahed** unto the apostles
whom he had *chosen* **selected:**
3 To whom also he *shewed* **presented** himself alive
after his *passion* **suffering** by many *infallible* proofs,
being seen of them **through** forty days,
and *speaking of the things* **wording about those**
pertaining to **of**
the *kingdom* **sovereigndom** of *God* **Elohim:**
4 And, being *assembled* **thronged** together with them,
commanded **evangelized** them
that they should not
depart **separate** from *Jerusalem* **Yeru Shalem,**
but *wait for* **await**
the *promise* **pre—evangelism** of the Father,
which, saith he, ye have heard of me.
5 For *John truly* **Yahn indeed** baptized *with* **in** water;
but ye shall be baptized *with* **in** the Holy *Ghost* **Spirit**
not many days *hence* **after this.**
6 When **indeed** they therefore were come together,
they asked of him, *saying* **wording,** *Lord* **Adonay,**
wilt **shalt** thou at this time restore *again*
the *kingdom* **sovereigndom** to *Israel* **Yisra El?**
7 And he said unto them,
It is not for you to know the times or the seasons,
which the Father hath put in his own *power* **authority.**
8 But ye shall *receive power* **take dynamis,**
after that the Holy *Ghost* **Spirit** is come upon you:
and *ye* shall be witnesses unto me
both in *Jerusalem* **Yeru Shalem,**
and in all *Judaea* **Yah Hudah,**
and in *Samaria* **Shomeron,**
and unto the *uttermost part* **finality** of the earth.

YAH SHUA'S ASCENSION

9 And when he had *spoken* **said** these *things*,
while they *beheld* **looked,** he was *taken up* **lifted;**
and a cloud *received* **took** him out of their *sight* **eyes.**

PROPHECY OF THE PAROUSIA

10 And *while* **as** they *looked stedfastly* **stared**
toward **into** heaven as he went *up*,
behold, two men stood by them in white apparel;
11 Which also said, Ye men *of Galilee* **— Galiliym,**
why stand ye *gazing* **looking** *up* into heaven?
this same *Jesus* **Yah Shua,**
which is taken *up* from you into heaven,
shall *so* **thus** come in like manner
as ye have *seen* **observed** him go into heaven.

THE UPPER LOFT

12 Then returned they unto *Jerusalem* **Yeru Shalem**
from the mount called *Olivet* **Olive Orchard,**
which is *from Jerusalem* **near Yeru Shalem**
a *sabbath day's* **shabbath** journey.
13 And when they *were come in* **entered,**
they *went up* **ascended** into an upper *room* **loft,**
where abode both *Peter* **Petros,** and *James* **Yaaqovos,**
and *John* **Yahn** and *Andrew* **Andreas,**
Philip **Philippos,** and *Thomas* **Taom,**
Bartholomew **Bar Talmay,** and *Matthew* **Matthaios,**
and *James* **Yaaqovos** *the son* of *Alphaeus* **Heleph,**
and *Simon Zelotes* **Shimon the Zealot,**
and *Judas* **Yah Hudah** *the brother* of *James* **Yaaqovos.**
14 These all continued *with one accord* **in unanimity**
in prayer and *supplication* **petition,** with the women,
and Mary **Miryam** the mother of *Jesus* **Yah Shua,**
and with his brethren.

MATTHIAS REPLACES YAH HUDAH

15 And in those days
Peter stood up **Petros rose** in the midst of the disciples,
and said,
(the *number* **multitude** of names *together* **in one**
were about an hundred and twenty,)
16 Men and brethren,
this scripture must *needs have been* **be** fulfilled,
which the Holy *Ghost* **Spirit**
by **through** the mouth of David
spake before **foretold**
concerning Judas **about Yah Hudah,**
which *was* **became** guide
to them that took *Jesus* **Yah Shua.**
17 For he was *numbered* **reckoned** with us,
and *had obtained part* **was allotted his lot**
of this ministry.
18 *Now* **Then indeed**
this *man purchased* **one acquired** a *field* **parcel**
with **from** the reward of iniquity;
and *falling* **becoming** headlong,
he *burst asunder* **cracked open** in the *midst* **middle,**
and all his *bowels gushed out* **spleen poured forth.**
19 And it *was* **became** known
unto all *the dwellers* **settled** at *Jerusalem* **Yeru Shalem;**
insomuch as **so** that field is called
in their *proper tongue* **own dialect,**
Aceldama, **Heleq Dam,**
that is to say, The *field* **parcel** of blood.
20 For it is *written* **scribed** in the *book* **scroll** of Psalms,
Let his *habitation be* **hut become** desolate,
and let no *man dwell* **one settle** therein:
and his *bishoprick* **episcopate** let another take.
21 *Wherefore* **Therefore**
of these men which have *companied* **come** with us
all the time that *the Lord Jesus* **Adonay Yah Shua**
went in **entered** and *out* **exited** among us,
22 Beginning from the baptism of *John* **Yahn,**
unto that same day that he was taken *up* from us,
must one *be ordained to be* **become** a witness with us
of his resurrection.
23 And they *appointed* **set** two,
Joseph **Yoseph** called *Barsabas* **Bar Sabah,**
who was *surnamed* **called** Justus,
and Matthias.
24 And they prayed, and said, Thou, *Lord* **Adonay,**
which knowest the hearts of all men **all heart—knowing,**
shew whether of these two
the one thou hast *chosen* **selected,**
25 That he may take *part* **his lot**
of this ministry and apostleship,
from which *Judas* **Yah Hudah**
by transgression fell **transgressed,**
that he might go to his own place.
26 And they gave forth their lots;
and the lot fell upon Matthias;
and he was *numbered* **enrolled** with the eleven apostles.

THE DAY OF PENTECOST

2 And *when* **in** the day of Pentecost
was fully come **being fulfilled,**
they were all *with one accord* **in unanimity** in one place.
2 And suddenly
there *came a sound* **became an echo** from heaven
as of a *rushing mighty wind* **bearing forceful puff,**
and it filled **full** all the house where they were sitting.
3 And there appeared unto them
cloven **divided** tongues like as of fire,
and it sat upon each *one* of them.
4 And they were all filled **full** with the Holy *Ghost* **Spirit,**
and began to speak with other tongues,
exactly as the Spirit gave them utterance.
5 And there were
dwelling **settling** at *Jerusalem* **Yeru Shalem**
Jews **Yah Hudiym,** *devout* **well—received** men,
out of every *nation* **goyim** under heaven.
6 Now when this *was noised* **voice became** abroad,
the multitude came together,
and were *confounded* **confused,**
because that *every man* **each**
heard them speak in his own *language* **dialect.**
7 And they were all *amazed* **astounded** and marvelled,
saying **wording** one to another, Behold,
are not all these which speak *Galilaeans* **Galiliym?**
8 And how hear we

every man **each** in our own *tongue* **dialect**,
wherein we were born?
9 Parthians, and *Medes* **Maday**, and *Elamites* **Elamiym**,
and *the dwellers* **they who settled** in Mesopotamia,
and in *Judaea* **Yah Hudah**, and Cappadocia,
in Pontus, and Asia,
10 Phrygia, and Pamphylia, in *Egypt* **Misrayim**,
and in the parts of Libya about Cyrene,
and *strangers of Rome* **the Romans residing there**,
Jews **Yah Hudiym** and proselytes,
11 Cretes and *Arabians* **Arabs**,
we do hear them speak in our tongues
the *wonderful works* **magnificence** of *God* **Elohim**.
12 And they were all *amazed* **astounded**,
and were *in doubt* **thoroughly perplexed**,
saying **wording** one to another,
What *meaneth* **willeth** this **to be**?
13 Others *mocking said* **jeering worded**,
These men are full of new sweet wine.

PETROS' FIRST MESSAGE

14 But *Peter* **Petros**, standing *up* with the eleven,
lifted *up* his voice, and *said* **uttered** unto them,
Ye men of Judaea **Men — Yah Hudiym**,
and all ye that *dwell* **settle** at *Jerusalem* **Yeru Shalem**,
be this known unto you,
and hearken to my *words* **rhema**:

YAH EL'S PROPHECY FULFILLED

15 For these are not *drunken* **intoxicated**,
as ye *suppose* **perceive**,
seeing **indeed** it is but the third hour of the day.
16 But this is that which was *spoken* **said**
by **through** the prophet *Joel* **Yah El**;
17 And it shall *come to pass* **become** in the *last* **final** days,
saith God **wordeth Elohim**,
I *will* **shall** pour *out* **forth** of my Spirit upon all flesh:
and your sons and your daughters shall prophesy,
and your *young men* **youths** shall see visions,
and your *old men* **elders** shall dream dreams:
18 And **yet indeed**
on my servants and on my *hand maidens* **maids**
I *will* **shall** pour *out* **forth** in those days of my Spirit;
and they shall prophesy:
19 And I *will shew* **shall give**
wonders **omens** in **the** heaven above,
and signs in the earth *beneath* **below**;
blood, and fire, and vapour of smoke:
20 The sun shall be turned into darkness,
and the moon into blood,
before the *great* **mega** and *notable* **epiphanous**
day of *the Lord* **Yah Veh** come:
21 And it shall *come to pass* **become**,
that whosoever
shall call on the name of *the Lord* **Yah Veh**
shall be saved.
Yah El 2:31, 32

YAH SHUA IS ADONAY AND MESSIAH

22 *Ye men of Israel* **Men — Yisra Eliym**, hear these words;
Jesus of Nazareth **Yah Shua the Nazarene**,
a man *approved* **shown** of *God* **Elohim** among you
by *miracles* **dynamis** and *wonders* **omens** and signs,
which *God* **Elohim** did *by* **through** him
in the midst of you,
exactly as ye yourselves also know:
23 Him, being *delivered* **given over**
by the *determinate* **decreed** counsel
and *foreknowledge* **prognosis** of *God* **Elohim**,
ye have taken,
and *by wicked* **through untorahed** hands
have *crucified* **staked** and *slain* **taken out**:
24 Whom *God* **Elohim** hath raised *up*,
having loosed the *pains* **travail** of death:
because **as** it was not possible
that he should be *holden of* **overpowered by** it.

DAVID'S PROPHECY FULFILLED

25 For David *speaketh concerning* **wordeth unto** him,
I foresaw *the Lord always* **Yah Veh through all time**
before **in sight of** my face,
for he is *on* **by** my right *hand*,
that I should not be *moved* **shaken**:
26 Therefore did my heart rejoice,
and my tongue *was glad* **jumped for joy**;
moreover **yet** also my flesh shall *rest* **nest** in hope:
27 Because thou
wilt **shalt** not leave my soul in *hell* **hades**,
neither *wilt* **shalt** thou
suffer thine Holy One **give thy Merciful**
to see corruption.
28 Thou hast made known to me the ways of life;
thou shalt *make* **fill** me full of *joy* **rejoicing**
with thy *countenance* **face**.
Psalm 16:8—11
29 Men and brethren,
let **allow** me *freely speak* **to boldly say** unto you
of **concerning** the patriarch David,
that he is both dead and *buried* **entombed**,
and his *sepulchre* **tomb** is with us unto this day.
30 Therefore being a prophet,
and knowing that *God* **Elohim**
had *sworn with* **oathed** an oath to him,
that of the fruit of his loins, according to the flesh,
he *would* **should** raise *up Christ* **the Messiah**
to sit on his throne;
31 He *seeing* **foreseeing** this *before*
spake of the resurrection of *Christ* **the Messiah**,
that his soul was not left in *hell* **hades**,
neither his flesh did see corruption.
32 This *Jesus* **Yah Shua** hath *God* **Elohim** raised *up*,
whereof we all are witnesses.
33 Therefore
being by the right *hand* of *God* **Elohim** exalted,
and having *received* **taken** of the Father
the *promise* **pre—evangelism** of the Holy *Ghost* **Spirit**,
he hath *shed* **poured** forth this,
which ye now see and hear.
34 For David is not ascended into the heavens:
but he *saith* himself **wordeth**,
the LORD said **An oracle of Yah Veh**
unto my *Lord* **Adonay**,
Sit thou *on* **by** my right *hand*,
35 Until I *make* **place** thy *foes* **enemies**
thy footstool **the stool of they feet**.
Psalm 110:1
36 Therefore let all the house of *Israel* **Yisra El**
know *assuredly* **certainly**,
that *God* **Elohim** hath made the same *Jesus* **Yah Shua**,
whom ye have *crucified* **staked**,
both *Lord* **Adonay** and *Christ* **Messiah**.

ON TAKING THE GRATUITY OF THE HOLY SPIRIT

37 Now when they heard this,
they were *pricked* **pierced** in their heart,
and said unto *Peter* **Petros** and to the rest of the apostles,
Men and brethren, what shall we do?
38 Then *Peter* **Petros** said unto them,
Repent, and be baptized *every one* **each** of you
in the name of *Jesus Christ* **Yah Shua Messiah**
for **unto** the *remission* **forgiveness** of sins,
and ye shall *receive* **take**
the *gift* **gratuity** of the Holy *Ghost* **Spirit**.
39 For the *promise* **pre—evangelism** is unto you,
and to your children, and to all that are afar off,
even as many
as *the Lord* **Yah Veh** our *God* **Elohim** shall call.
Yah El 2:32
40 And with many other words
did he *testify* **witness** and *exhort* **beseech**,
saying **wording**,
Save yourselves **Be ye saved**
from this *untoward* **crooked** generation.

THE FIRST ECCLESIA

41 Then **indeed**
they that *gladly* **with pleasure** received his word
were baptized:
and *the same* **that** day there were added *unto them*
about three thousand souls.
42 And they continued stedfastly
in the apostles' doctrine and *fellowship* **communion**,
and in breaking of bread, and in prayers.
43 And *fear came* **awe became** upon every soul:
and many *wonders* **omens** and signs
were done by **became through** the apostles.

44 And all that *believed* **trusted** were *together* **in one,**
and had all *things* common;
45 And sold their possessions and goods,
and *parted* **divided** them to all *men,*
as every *man* **one** had need.
46 And they,
continuing daily *with one accord* **in unanimity**
in the *temple* **priestal precinct,**
and breaking bread from house to house
did eat **partook** their *meat* **nourishment**
with gladness **in jumping for joy**
and *singleness* **simplicity** of heart,
47 *Praising God* **Halaling Elohim,**
and having *favour* **charism** with all the people.
And *the Lord* **Adonay** added to the *church* **ecclesia** daily
such as should be saved.

THE DAY OF PENTECOST: PETROS' FIRST SIGN

3 Now *Peter* **Petros** and *John* **Yahn**
went up together **ascended themselves**
into the *temple* **priestal precinct** at the hour of prayer,
being the ninth *hour.*
2 And a *certain* man
being lame from his mother's womb was *carried* **borne,**
whom they *laid* **placed** daily
at the *gate* **portal** of the *temple* **priestal precinct**
which is *called* **worded** Beautiful,
to ask *alms* **mercies** of them
that entered into the *temple* **priestal precinct;**
3 Who seeing *Peter* **Petros** and *John* **Yahn**
about to *go* **enter** into the *temple* **priestal precinct**
asked *an alms* **mercies.**
4 And *Peter* **Petros,**
fastening **staring** his eyes upon him with *John* **Yahn,**
said, Look on us.
5 And he *gave heed unto* **heeded** them,
expecting **awaiting** to *receive* **take** something of them.
6 Then *Peter* **Petros** said, Silver and gold have I none;
but such as I have give I thee:
In the name of
Jesus Christ of Nazareth **Yah Shua Messiah the Nazarene**
rise *up* and walk.
7 And he *took* **seized** him by the right hand,
and *lifted* **raised** him *up*:
and immediately his feet and *ancle bones* **sockets**
received strength **solidified.**
8 And he leaping *up* stood, and walked,
and entered with them into the *temple* **priestal precinct,**
walking, and leaping, and *praising God* **halaling Elohim.**
9 And all the people saw him walking
and *praising God* **halaling Elohim:**
10 And they knew that it was he
which sat for *alms* **mercies**
at the Beautiful gate of the *temple* **priestal precinct:**
and they were filled **full**
with *wonder* **astonishment** and *amazement* **ecstasis**
at that which had happened unto him.
11 And as the lame man which was healed
held Peter **overpowered Petros** and *John* **Yahn,**
all the people *ran* **rushed** together unto them
in the *porch* **portico** that is called *Solomon's* **Sholomoh's,**
greatly wondering **utterly astonished.**

PETROS' SECOND MESSAGE

12 And when *Peter* **Petros** saw it,
he answered unto the people,
Ye men of Israel **Men — Yisra Eliym,** why marvel ye at this?
or why *look ye so earnestly on* **stare at** us,
as though by our own
power **dynamis** or *holiness* **reverence**
we had *made this man* **caused him** to walk?
13 The *God* **Elohim** of Abraham,
and of *Isaac* **Yischaq,** and of *Jacob* **Yaaqov,**
the *God* **Elohim** of our fathers,
hath glorified his *Son Jesus* **Lad Yah Shua;**
whom ye delivered *up,*
and denied him in the *presence* **face** of *Pilate* **Pilatos,**
when he *was determined* **had judged**
to *let* **release** him *go.*
14 But ye denied the Holy *One* and the Just,
and *desired* **asked a man** — a murderer
to be granted **charism** unto you;
15 And *killed* **slaughtered** the *Prince* **Hierarch** of life,
whom *God* **Elohim** hath raised from the dead;
whereof we are witnesses.
16 And his name *through faith* **by trust** in his name
hath *made* **solidified** this man *strong,*
whom ye *see* **observe** and know:
yea, the *faith* **trust** which is *by* **through** him
hath given him
this *perfect soundness* **complete wholeness**
in the presence of you all.
17 And now, brethren,
I *wot* **perceive** that through *ignorance* **unknowingness**
ye *did* **transacted** it,
exactly as *did* also your *rulers* **archs.**
18 But those *things,*
which *God before* **Elohim** had *shewed* **pre—evangelized**
by **through** the mouth of all his prophets,
that *Christ* **the Messiah** should suffer,
he hath *so* **thus** fulfilled.
19 Repent ye therefore, and *be converted* **turn around,**
that **unto wiping out** your sins *may be blotted out,*
when the *times* **seasons** of refreshing shall come
from the *presence* **face** of *the Lord* **Yah Veh.**
20 And he shall
send Jesus Christ **apostolize Yah Shua Messiah,**
which *before* **previously** was preached unto you:
21 Whom **indeed** the heaven must receive
until the times of *restitution* **restoration** of all *things,*
which *God* **Elohim** hath spoken
by **through** the mouth of all his holy prophets
since **from** the *world began* **eons.**
22 For *Moses truly* **Mosheh indeed** said unto the fathers,
A prophet shall *the Lord* **Yah Veh** your *God* **Elohim**
raise *up* unto you of your brethren, like unto me;
him shall ye hear in all *things*
whatsoever — **as much as** he shall *say* **speak** unto you.
Deuteronomy 18:15, 19
23 And it shall *come to pass* **become,** that every soul,
which *will* **shall** not hear that prophet,
shall be **utterly** destroyed from *among* the people.
24 Yea, and all the prophets from *Samuel* **Shemu El**
and those that follow *after* **in sequence,**
as many as have spoken,
have likewise *foretold* **pre—evangelized** of these days.
25 Ye are the *children* **sons** of the prophets,
and of the covenant
which *God made* **Elohim covenanted** with our fathers,
saying **wording** unto Abraham,
And in thy *seed* **sperma**
shall all the *kindreds* **patriarchies** of the earth
be *blessed* **eulogized.**
26 Unto you first, *God* **Elohim,**
having raised *up* his *Son Jesus* **Lad Yah Shua,**
sent **apostolized** him to *bless* **eulogize** you,
in turning away *every one* **each** of you
from his *iniquities* **evils.**

THE FIRST PERSECUTION

4 And as they spake unto the people,
the priests, and the *captain* **strategos**
of the *temple* **priestal precinct,**
and the *Sadducees* **Sadoqiym,** *came upon* **stood by** them,
2 Being grieved
that **because** they *taught* **doctrinated** the people,
and *preached through Jesus* **evangelized in Yah Shua**
the resurrection from the dead.
3 And they laid hands on them,
and put them in *hold* **guard** unto the *next day* **morrow:**
for it was *now eventide* **already evening.**
4 Howbeit
many of them which heard the word *believed* **trusted;**
and the number of the men
was **became** about five thousand.

PETROS' THIRD MESSAGE

5 And it *came to pass* **became** on the morrow,
that their *rulers* **archs,** and elders, and scribes,
6 And *Annas* **Hanan Yah** the *high* **arch** priest,
and Caiaphas, and *John* **Yahn,** and Alexander,
and as many as were of the *kindred* **genos**
of the *high* **arch** priest,
were gathered together at *Jerusalem* **Yeru Shalem.**

7 And when they had set them in the midst, they asked,
By **In** what *power* **dynamis**, or *by* **in** what name,
have ye done this?
8 Then *Peter* **Petros**, filled **full** with the Holy *Ghost* **Spirit**,
said unto them,
Ye *rulers* **archs** of the people, and elders of *Israel* **Yisra El**,
9 If we this day be examined of the good *deed* **work**
done to the *impotent man* **frail human**,
by what *means he* **this one** is *made whole* **saved**;
10 Be it known unto you all,
and to all the people of *Israel* **Yisra El**,
that *by* **in** the name of
Jesus Christ of Nazareth **Yah Shua Messiah the Nazarene**,
whom ye *crucified* **staked**,
whom *God* **Elohim** raised from the dead,
even by **in** him doth this *man* **one** stand
here before you **in your sight** whole.
11 This is the stone
which was *set at nought* **belittled** of you builders,
which is become **unto** the head of the corner.
12 Neither is there salvation in any other:
for there is *none other* **not another** name under heaven
given *among men* **by humanity**,
whereby we must be saved.
13 Now when they *saw* **observed**
the boldness of *Peter* **Petros** and *John* **Yahn**,
and *perceived* **overtook** that they were
unlearned **unlettered** and *ignorant* **unlearned**
men **humans**,
they marvelled;
and they *took knowledge of them* **knew**,
that they had been with *Jesus* **Yah Shua**.
14 And *beholding* **seeing** the *man* **human**
which was *healed* **cured** standing with them,
they could *say nothing against* **not refute** it.
15 But when they had *commanded* **summoned** them
to *go aside* **get** out of the *council* **sanhedrim**,
they *conferred* **considered**
among *themselves* **one another**,
16 *Saying* **Wording**,
What shall we do to these *men* **humans**?
for that indeed a *notable miracle* **known sign**
hath *been done by* **become through** them
is manifest to all them
that *dwell* **settle** in *Jerusalem* **Yeru Shalem**;
and we cannot deny it.
17 But that it spread no *further* **more** among the people,
let us *straitly* **threateningly** threaten them,
that they speak *henceforth* **no more** to no *man* **human**
in this name.
18 And they called them,
and *commanded* **evangelized** them
not to *speak* **utter** at all
nor *teach* **doctrinate** in the name of *Jesus* **Yah Shua**.
19 But *Peter* **Petros** and *John* **Yahn**
answered and said unto them,
Whether it be *right* **just** in the sight of *God* **Elohim**
to hearken unto you *more* **rather** than unto *God* **Elohim**,
judge ye.
20 For we cannot but speak
the things **those** which we have seen and heard.
21 So when they had further threatened them,
they *let* **released** them *go*,
finding *nothing* **naught** how they might punish them,
because of the people:
for all *men* glorified *God* **Elohim**
for **over** that which *was done* **became**.
22 For the *man* **human**
was *above* **more than** forty years *old*,
on whom this *miracle* **sign** of healing
was shewed **had become**.

MESSIANISTS FILLED WITH THE HOLY SPIRIT

23 And being *let go* **released**,
they *went* **came** to their own *company*,
and *reported all that* **evangelized as much as**
the *chief* **arch** priests and elders had said unto them.
24 And when they heard that,
they lifted *up* their voice to *God* **Elohim**
with one accord **in unanimity**, and said,
Lord **Despotes**, thou art *God* **Elohim**,
which hast made heaven, and earth, and the sea,
and all that in them is:
25 Who *by* **through** the mouth of thy *servant* **lad** David
hast said, Why did the *heathen rage* **goyim snort**
and the people *imagine* **premeditate in** vain *things*?
26 The *kings* **sovereigns** of the earth stood *up*,
and the *rulers* **archs** were gathered together
against *the Lord* **Yah Veh**, and against his *Christ* **Messiah**.
Psalm 2:1, 2
27 For of a truth against thy holy *child Jesus* **lad Yah Shua**,
whom thou hast anointed,
both Herod, and Pontius *Pilate* **Pilatos**,
with the *Gentiles* **goyim**, and the people of *Israel* **Yisra El**,
were gathered together,
28 For to do
whatsoever **as much as** thy hand and thy counsel
determined before **predetermined** to *be done* **become**.
29 And now, *Lord* **Yah Veh**,
behold **regard** their threatenings:
and *grant* **give** unto thy servants,
that with all boldness they may speak thy word,
30 By *stretching forth* **extending** thine hand to heal;
and that signs and *wonders* **omens** may *be done* **become**
by **through** the name
of thy holy *child Jesus* **lad Yah Shua**.
31 And when they had *prayed* **petitioned**,
the place was shaken
where they were assembled together;
and they were all filled **full** with the Holy *Ghost* **Spirit**,
and they spake the word of *God* **Elohim** with boldness.

TRUSTERS SHARE THEIR HOLDINGS

32 And the multitude of them that *believed* **trusted**
were of one heart and of one soul:
neither *said* **worded** any of them
that ought of *the things which he possessed* **his holdings**
was his own;
but they had all *things* common.
33 And with *great power* **mega dynamis**
gave the apostles witness
of the resurrection of *the Lord Jesus* **Adonay Yah Shua**:
and *great grace* **mega charism** was upon them all.
34 **Indeed** Neither was there any among them that lacked:
for as many as were possessors of *lands* **parcels** or houses
sold them,
and brought the prices of *the things* **those** that were sold,
35 And *laid* **placed** them *down* at the apostles' feet:
and *distribution was made* **distributed**
unto *every man* **each**
according as he had need **as any needed**.
36 And *Joses* **Yoses**,
who by the apostles
was *surnamed Barnabas* **called Bar Nabi**,
(which is, being *interpreted* **translated**
The son of consolation,)
a *Levite* **Leviy**,
and *of the country of Cyprus* **by genos — a Cypriy**,
37 Having *land* **a field**, sold it,
and brought the *money* **riches**,
and *laid* **placed** it at the apostles' feet.

HANAN YAH AND SAPPHIRA LIE TO THE HOLY SPIRIT

5 But a *certain* man named *Ananias* **Hanan Yah**,
with Sapphira his *wife* **woman**, sold a possession,
2 And kept back *part* of the price,
his *wife* **woman** also being *privy to it* **aware**,
and brought a *certain* part,
and *laid* **placed** it at the apostles' feet.
3 But *Peter* **Petros** said, *Ananias* **Hanan Yah**,
why hath Satan filled **full** thine heart
to lie to the Holy *Ghost* **Spirit**,
and to keep back *part* of the price of the *land* **parcel**?
4 *Whiles it remained* **In abiding**,
was **abode** it not **indeed** thine *own*?
and after it was sold,
was it not in thine own *power* **authority**?
why hast thou *conceived* **placed** this *thing* **matter**
in thine heart?
thou hast not lied unto *men* **humanity**,
but unto *God* **Elohim**.
5 And *Ananias* **Hanan Yah** hearing these words fell down,
and *gave up the ghost* **expired**:

and *great fear* **mega awe**
came **became** on all them that heard these *things.*
6 And the *young men* **youths** arose,
wound **enshrouded** him *up,*
and *carried* **brought** him *out* **forth,**
and *buried* **entombed** him.
7 And it *was* **became**
about the *space* **interval** of three hours after,
when his *wife* **woman,**
not knowing what *was done* **had become,**
came in **entered.**
8 And *Peter* **Petros** answered unto her, *Tell* **Say to** me
whether ye *sold* **gave** *up* the *land* **parcel** for so much?
And she said, Yea, for so much.
9 Then *Peter* **Petros** said unto her,
How is it that ye have *agreed together* **symphonized**
to *tempt* **test** the Spirit of *the Lord* **Yah Veh**?
behold, the feet of them
which have *buried* **entombed** thy *husband* **man**
are at the *door* **portal,**
and shall *carry* **bring** thee *out* **forth.**
10 Then fell she down *straightway* **immediately**
at his feet,
and *yielded up the ghost* **expired**:
and the *young men came in* **youths entered,**
and found her dead, and, *carrying* **bringing** her forth,
buried **entombed** her by her *husband* **man.**
11 And *great fear* **mega awe**
came **became** upon all the *church* **ecclesia,**
and upon *as many as* **all who** heard these *things.*

SIGNS AND OMENS

12 And *by* **through** the hands of the apostles
were many signs and *wonders* **omens**
wrought **become** among the people;
(and they were all *with one accord* **in unanimity**
in *Solomon's porch* **Sholomoh's portico.**
13 And of the rest durst no *man* **one** join himself to them:
but the people magnified them.
14 And *believers* **they who trusted**
were the more added to *the Lord* **Adonay,**
multitudes both of men and women.)
15 *Insomuch* **So** that they brought forth the *sick* **frail**
into the *streets* **broadways,**
and *laid* **placed** them on beds and *couches* **pads,**
that *at the least* **if even** the shadow of Peter
passing by **coming** might overshadow some of them.
16 There came also a multitude
out of the cities round about
unto *Jerusalem* **Yeru Shalem,**
bringing *sick* **frail** folks,
and them which were vexed
with unclean **by impure** spirits:
and they were *healed every one* **all cured.**

THE SECOND PERSECUTION

17 Then the *high* **arch** priest rose *up,*
and all they that were with him,
(which is the *sect* **heresy** of the *Sadducees* **Sadoqiym,**)
and were filled **full** with *indignation* **zeal,**
18 And laid their hands on the apostles,
and put them in the *common* **public** prison.
19 But the angel of *the Lord* **Yah Veh**
by **through the** night
opened the *prison doors* **guardhouse portals,**
and *brought* **led** them forth, and said,
20 Go, stand and speak in the *temple* **priestal precinct**
to the people,
all the *words* **rhema** of this life.
21 And when they heard that,
they entered into the *temple early* **priestal precinct**
in the morning **by dawn,** and *taught* **doctrinated.**
But the *high* **arch** priest came,
and they that were with him,
and called the *council* **sanhedrim** together,
and all the *senate* **ancients**
of the *children* **sons** of *Israel* **Yisra El,**
and *sent* **apostolized** to the prison to have them brought.
22 But when the *officers* **attendants** came,
and found them not in the *prison* **guardhouse,**
they returned and *told* **evangelized,**
23 *Saying* **Wording,**
The prison *truly* **indeed** found we shut
with all safety **in security,**
and the *keepers* **guards** standing without
before the *doors* **portals:**
but when we had opened, we found no *man* **one** within.
24 Now when the *high* priest and the *captain* **strategos**
of the *temple* **priestal precinct**
and the *chief* **arch** priests heard these *things* **words,**
they *doubted of* **were thoroughly perplexed about** them
whereunto **whatever** this *would grow* **should be.**
25 Then came one and *told* **evangelized** them,
saying **wording,** Behold,
the men whom ye put in *prison* **guardhouse**
are standing in the *temple* **priestal precinct,**
teaching **doctrinating** the people.
26 Then went
the *captain* **strategos** with the *officers* **attendants,**
and brought them without violence:
for they *feared* **awed** the people,
lest **that** they should *have been* **not be** stoned.
27 And when they had brought them,
they set them *before* **in** the *council* **sanhedrim:**
and the *high* **arch** priest asked them,
28 *Saying,* **Wording,**
In evanglizing,
Did not we *straitly command* **evangelize** you
that ye should not *teach* **doctrinate** in this name?
and, behold,
ye have filled *Jerusalem* **Yeru Shalem full**
with your doctrine,
and *intend* will to bring
this *man's* **human's** blood upon us.
29 Then *Peter* **Petros** and the other apostles
answered and said,
We *ought to* **must first** obey *God* **Elohim**
rather than *men* **humanity.**
30 The *God* **Elohim** of our fathers
raised *up Jesus* **Yah Shua,**
whom ye *slew* **thoroughly handled**
and hanged on a *tree* **staff.**
31 Him hath *God* **Elohim** exalted *with* **by** his right *hand*
to be a *Prince* **Hierarch** and *a* Savior,
for to give repentance to *Israel* **Yisra El,**
and forgiveness of sins.
32 And we are his witnesses of these *things* **rhema;**
and so is also the Holy *Ghost* **Spirit,**
whom *God* **Elohim** hath given to them
that **first** obey him.
33 When they heard *that,* they *were* cut° *to the heart,*
and *took counsel* **counseled** to *slay* **take** them **out.**
°as in cutting an oath or a covenant
34 Then *stood there up* **rose** one
in the *council* **sanhedrim,** a Pharisee,
named *Gamaliel* **Gamli El,** a doctor of the *law* **torah,**
had in reputation **honoured** among all the people,
and *commanded* **summoned**
to *put* **make** the apostles *forth* **out** a little space;
35 And said unto them, *Ye men of Israel* **Men — Yisra Eliym,**
take heed to yourselves
what ye *intend* **are about** to *do* **transact**
as *touching* **to** these *men* **humans.**
36 For before these days rose *up* Theudas,
boasting **wording** himself to be *somebody* **someone;**
to whom a number of men, about four hundred,
joined themselves:
who was *slain* **taken out;**
and all, as many as obeyed him,
were scattered **dissolved,** and *brought to* **became** nought.
37 After this man
rose *up Judas of Galilee* **Yah Hudah — a Galiliy**
in the days of the *taxing* **registration,**
and drew away much people after him:
he also *perished* **destructed;**
and all, *even* as many as obeyed him,
were dispersed **scattered.**
38 And now I *say* **word** unto you,
Refrain **Depart** from these *men* **humans,**
and let them alone:
for if this counsel or this work be of *men* **humanity,**
it *will come to nought* **shall disintegrate:**

39 But if it be of *God* **Elohim,**
ye cannot *overthrow* **disintegrate** it;
lest *haply* **ever** ye be found
even to *fight against God* **be Elohim—opponents.**
40 And *to him they agreed* **he convinced them:**
and when they had called the apostles,
and *beaten* **flogged** them,
they *commanded* **evangelized**
that they should not speak in the name of *Jesus* **Yah Shua,**
and *let* **released** them *go.*
41 *And* **Therefore indeed** they departed
from the *presence* **face** of the *council* **sanhedrim,**
rejoicing **cheering** that they were counted worthy
to *suffer shame* **be dishonoured** for his name.
42 And daily in the *temple* **priestal precinct,**
and in every house,
they *ceased* **paused** not
to *teach* **doctrinate** and *preach* **evangelize**
Jesus Christ **Yah Shua the Messiah.**

THE MINISTRY OF TABLES

6 And in those days,
when the number of the disciples was multiplied,
there *arose* **became** a murmuring
of the *Grecians* **Hellenists** against the Hebrews,
because their widows were *neglected* **overlooked**
in the daily *ministration* **ministry.**
2 Then the twelve
called the multitude of the disciples unto them,
and said, It is not *reason* **pleasing**
that we should leave the word of *God* **Elohim,**
and *serve* **minister** tables.
3 *Wherefore* **Therefore,** brethren,
look ye **scope** out *among you*
seven men of *honest report* **witness,**
full of the Holy *Ghost* **Spirit** and wisdom,
whom we may *appoint* **seat** over this *business* **need.**
4 But we *will* **shall**
give ourselves continually to **continue in** prayer,
and to the ministry of the word.
5 And the *saying pleased* **word was pleasing**
in sight of the whole multitude:
and they *chose Stephan* **selected Stephanos,**
a man full of *faith* **trust** and of the Holy *Ghost* **Spirit,**
and *Philip* **Philippos,** and Prochorus, and Nicanor,
and Timon, and Parmenas,
and Nicolas a proselyte *of Antioch* **— an Antiochan:**
6 Whom they set *before* **in the sight of** the apostles:
and when they had prayed,
they *laid* **put** their hands on them.
7 And the word of *God increased* **Elohim grew;**
and the number of the disciples multiplied
in *Jerusalem greatly* **Yeru Shalem extremely;**
and a *great company* **vast multitude** of the priests
were obedient to the faith **obeyed the trust.**

THIRD PERSECUTION

8 And *Stephen* **Stephanos,**
full of *faith* **trust** and *power* **dynamis,**
did *great wonders* **mega omens** and *miracles* **signs**
among the people.
9 Then there arose *certain* **some** of the synagogue,
which is *called the synagogue of the* **worded** Libertines,
and Cyrenians, and Alexandrians,
and of them of Cilicia and of Asia,
disputing with *Stephen* **Stephanos.**
10 And they were not able to *resist* **withstand**
the wisdom and the spirit by which he spake.
11 Then they *suborned* **instigated** men,
which *said* **worded,**
We have heard him speak blasphemous *words* **rhema**
against Moses **unto Mosheh,** and *against God* **Elohim.**
12 And they *stirred up* **excited** the people,
and the elders, and the scribes,
and *came upon* **stood by** him, and caught him,
and brought him to the *council* **sanhedrim,**
13 And set *up false* **pseudo** witnesses, which *said* **worded,**
This *man ceaseth* **human pauseth** not
to speak blasphemous *words* **rhema**
against this holy place, and the *law* **torah:**
14 For we have heard him *say* **word,**
that this *Jesus of Nazareth* **Yah Shua the Nazarene**
shall *destroy* **disintegrate** this place,
and shall change the customs
which *Moses* **Mosheh** delivered us.
15 And all that sat in the *council* **sanhedrim,**
looking stedfastly on **staring unto** him,
saw his face as it had been the face of an angel.

STEPHANOS' MESSAGE

7 Then said the *high* **arch** priest,
Are these *things so* **then thus?**
2 And he said, Men, brethren, and fathers, hearken;
The *God* **Elohim** of glory
appeared unto our father Abraham,
when he was in Mesopotamia,
before he *dwelt* **settled** in Haran,
3 And said unto him, Get thee out of thy *country* **land,**
and from thy kindred,
and come into the land which I shall shew thee.
4 Then came he
out of the land of the *Chaldaeans* **Kesediym,**
and *dwelt* **settled** in Haran:
and from thence, *when* **after** his father was dead,
he *removed* **exiled** him into this land,
wherein ye now *dwell* **settle.**
5 And he gave him none inheritance in it,
no, not *so much as to set his foot on* **even a foot bamah:**
yet he *promised* **pre—evangelized**
that he *would* **should** give it to him
for **unto** a possession,
and to his *seed* **sperma** after him,
when *as yet* he had no child.
6 And *God* **Elohim** spake *on this wise* **thus,**
That his *seed* **sperma**
should *sojourn* **be a settler** in *a strange* **another's** land;
and that they should bring them into *bondage* **servitude,**
and *entreat* **vilify** them *evil* four hundred years.
7 And the *nation* **goyim**
to whom **lest ever** they shall be *in bondage* **servient**
will **shall** I judge, said *God* **Elohim:**
and after that shall they come forth,
and *serve* **liturgize** me in this place.
8 And he gave him the covenant of circumcision:
and *so Abraham* **thus** begat *Isaac* **Yischaq,**
and circumcised him the eighth day;
and *Isaac* **Yischaq,** *begat Jacob* **Yaaqov;**
and *Jacob* **Yaaqov,** *begat* the twelve patriarchs.
9 And the patriarchs, *moved* with *envy* **zeal,**
sold Joseph **gave Yoseph** into *Egypt* **Misrayim:**
but *God* **Elohim** was with him,
10 And *delivered* **released** him
out of all his *afflictions* **tribulations,**
and gave him *favour* **charism** and wisdom
in the sight of *Pharaoh* **Paroh**
king **sovereign** of *Egypt* **Misrayim;**
and he *made* **seated** him governor
over *Egypt* **Misrayim** and all his house.
11 Now there came a *dearth* **famine**
over all the land
of *Egypt* **Misrayim** and *Chanaan* **Kenaan,**
and *great affliction* **mega tribulation:**
and our fathers found no *sustenance* **forage.**
12 But when *Jacob* **Yaaqov** heard
that there was *corn* **grain** in *Egypt* **Misrayim,**
he *sent out* **apostolized forth** our fathers first.
13 And at the second *time*
Joseph was made **Yoseph became** known to his brethren;
and *Joseph's kindred* **Yoseph's genos**
was *made known* **manifest** unto *Pharaoh* **Paroh.**
14 Then *sent Joseph* **apostolized Yoseph,**
and called his father *Jacob* **Yaaqov** to him,
and all his kindred,
threescore and fifteen **seventy and five** souls.
15 So *Jacob* **Yaaqov**
went down **descended** into *Egypt* **Misrayim,** and died,
he, and our fathers,
16 And were *carried over* **transplaced**
into *Sychem* **Shechem**
and *laid* **placed** in the *sepulchre* **tomb**
that Abraham bought for a *sum* **price** of *money* **silver**
of the sons of *Emmor* **Hamor**
the father of *Sychem* **Shechem.**

17 But *when* **exactly** **as** the time
of the *promise drew nigh* **pre—evangelism approached**,
which *God* **Elohim** had *sworn* **oathed** to Abraham,
the people grew and multiplied in *Egypt* **Misrayim**,
18 Till another *king* **sovereign** arose,
which knew not *Joseph* **Yoseph**.
19 *The same dealt subtilly* **This one sophisticated**
with our *kindred* **genos**,
and *evil entreated* **vilified** our fathers,
so that they
cast out **exposed** their *young children* **infants**,
to the end **that** they might not live.
20 In which *time Moses* **season Mosheh** was born,
and was exceeding *fair* **urbane** to *God* **Elohim**,
and *nourished up* **nurtured** in his father's house
three months:
21 And when he was *cast out* **exposed**,
Pharaoh's **Paroh's** daughter took him *up*,
and *nourished* **nurtured** him *for* **as** her own son.
22 And *Moses* **Mosheh** was *learned* **disciplined**
in all the wisdom of the *Egyptians* **Misrayim**,
and was *mighty* **able** in words and in *deeds* **works**.
23 And when *he was full*
forty years *old* **time was fulfilled**,
it *came into* **ascended upon** his heart
to visit his brethren the *children* **sons** of *Israel* **Yisra El**.
24 And seeing one of them *suffer wrong* **injured**,
he defended him,
and *avenged* **dealt vengeance for** him
that was *oppressed* **worn down**,
and smote the *Egyptian* **Misrayim**:
25 For he *supposed* **presumed** his brethren
would **should** have *understood* **comprehended**
how that *God by* **Elohim through** his hand
would deliver **should give** them **salvation**:
but they *understood* **comprehended** not.
26 And the next day
he *shewed himself* **appeared** unto them as they strove,
and *would* **should** have set them at *one* **shalom** again,
saying, *Sirs* **Men**, ye are brethren;
why *do* **injure** ye *wrong* one to another?
27 But he that *did* **injured** his neighbour *wrong*
thrust **shoved** him away, saying,
Who *made* **seated** thee
a ruler **an arch** and *a* judge over us?
28 *Wilt* **Willest** thou *kill me* **to take me out**
as **in the manner** thou *diddest* **tookest out**
the *Egyptian* **Misrayim** yesterday?
29 Then fled *Moses* **Mosheh** at this *saying* **word**,
and *was* **became** a *stranger* **settler**
in the land of *Madian* **Midyan**,
where he begat two sons.
30 And when forty years were *expired* **fulfilled**,
there appeared to him
in the wilderness of mount *Sina* **Sinay**
an angel of *the Lord* **Yah Veh**
in a flame of fire in a *bush* **brier**.
31 When *Moses* **Mosheh** saw it,
he *wondered* **marvelled** at the *sight* **vision**:
and as he drew near to *behold* **perceive** it,
the voice of *the Lord came* **Yah Veh became** unto him,
32 *Saying, I am the God* **I — Elohim** of thy fathers,
the God **Elohim** of Abraham,
and *the God* **Elohim** of *Isaac* **Yischaq**,
and *the God* **Elohim** of *Jacob* **Yaaqov**.
Then *Moses trembled* **Mosheh became trembling**,
and durst not *behold* **perceive**.
33 Then said *the Lord* **Yah Veh** to him,
Put off **Loose** thy shoes from thy feet:
for the place *where* **whereon** thou standest
is holy *ground* **land**.
34 *I have seen* **In seeing**,
I have seen the *affliction* **vilification** of my people
which is in *Egypt* **Misrayim**,
and I have heard their *groaning* **sighing**,
and am *come down* **descended** to *deliver* **release** them.
And now come,
I *will send* **shall apostolize** thee into *Egypt* **Misrayim**.
35 This *Moses* **Mosheh** whom they *refused* **denied**,
saying,

Who *made* **seated** thee *a ruler* **an arch** and *a* judge?
the same did *God send* **Elohim apostolize**
to be a ruler **arch** and *a deliverer* **redeemer**
by the hand of the angel
which appeared to him in the bush **brier**.
Exodus 3:2—6
36 *He brought* **This one led** them out,
after that he had *shewed wonders* **made omens** and signs
in the land of *Egypt* **Misrayim**, and in the *Red* **Reed** sea,
and in the wilderness forty years.
37 This is that *Moses* **Mosheh**,
which said unto the *children* **sons** of *Israel* **Yisra El**,
A prophet shall *the Lord* **Yah Veh** your *God* **Elohim**
raise *up* unto you of your brethren, like unto me;
him shall ye hear **ye him**.
Deuteronomy 18:15, 18, 19
38 This is he,
that *was* **became** in the *church* **ecclesia** in the wilderness
with the angel which spake to him
in the mount *Sina* **Sinay**, and with our fathers:
who received the *lively* **living** oracles to give unto us:
39 To whom our fathers *would* **willed**
to not *obey* **become obedient**,
but *thrust* **shoved** him **away** from them,
and in their hearts
turned back *again* into *Egypt* **Misrayim**,
40 Saying unto *Aaron* **Aharon**,
Make us *gods* **elohim** to *go before* **precede** us:
for *as for* this *Moses* **Mosheh**,
which *brought* **led** us out of the land of *Egypt* **Misrayim**,
we *wot* **know** not what is become of him.
41 And they made a calf in those days,
and *offered* **brought** sacrifice unto the idol,
and rejoiced in the works of their own hands.
42 Then *God* **Elohim** turned,
and *gave* **surrendered** them *up*
to *worship* **liturgize** the host of heaven;
exactly as it is *written* **scribed**
in the *book* **scroll** of the prophets,
O ye house of *Israel* **Yisra El**,
have ye offered to me
slain beasts **slaughters** and sacrifices
by the space of forty years in the wilderness?
43 Yea, ye took *up* the tabernacle of *Moloch* **Molech**,
and the star of your god *Remphan* **Kiyun**,
figures **types** which ye made to worship them:
and I *will carry* **shall exile** you *away*
beyond *Babylon* **Babel**.
44 Our fathers
had the tabernacle of witness in the wilderness,
exactly as he had *appointed* **ordained**,
speaking unto *Moses* **Mosheh**, that he should make it
according to the *fashion* **type** that he had seen.
45 Which also our fathers
that came after **having in succession received**
brought in with *Jesus* **Yah Shua°**
into the possession of the *Gentiles* **goyim**,
whom *God drave out* **Elohim expelled**
before **from** the face of our fathers,
unto the days of David;
46 Who found *favour* **charism**
before God **in the sight of Elohim**,
and *desired* **asked** to find a tabernacle
for the *God* **Elohim** of *Jacob* **Yaaqov**.

°Yah Shua: Mosheh's successor

47 But *Solomon* **Sholomoh** built him an house.
48 *Howbeit the most High dwelleth* **Yet Elyon settleth** not
in *temples made with hands* **handmade naves**;
exactly as *saith* **wordeth** the prophet,
49 Heaven is my throne, and earth is my footstool:
what house *will* **shall** ye build me?
saith the Lord **wordeth Yah Veh**:
or what is the place of my *rest* **shabbath**?
Yesha Yah 66:1, 2
50 Hath not **indeed** my hand made all these *things*?
51 Ye *stiffnecked* **hardnaped**
and *uncircumcised* **noncircumcised** in heart and ears,
ye *do always resist* **ever oppose** the Holy *Ghost* **Spirit**:
as your fathers did, so do ye.
52 Which of the prophets

have not your fathers persecuted?
and they have *slain* **slaughtered** them
which *shewed before* **pre—evangelized**
of **concerning** the coming of the Just *One*;
of whom ye have *been* **become** now
the *betrayers* **traitors** and murderers:
53 Who have *received* **taken** the *law* **torah**
by **unto** the *disposition* **ordinance** of angels,
and have not *kept* **guarded** it.

STEPHANOS IS STONED

54 When they heard these *things*,
they were cut to the heart,
and they gnashed on him with their teeth.
55 But he, being full of the Holy *Ghost* **Spirit**,
looked up stedfastly **stared** into heaven,
and saw the glory of *God* **Elohim**,
and *Jesus* **Yah Shua**
standing *on* **by** the right *hand* of *God* **Elohim**,
56 And said, Behold, I *see* **observe** the heavens opened,
and the Son of *man* **humanity**
standing *on* **by** the right *hand* of *God* **Elohim**.
57 Then they cried out with a *loud* **mega** voice,
and *stopped* **held** their ears,
and ran **violently** upon him
with one accord **in unanimity**,
58 And cast him out of the city, and stoned him:
and the witnesses *laid* **put** down their *clothes* **garments**
at *a young man's feet* **the feet of a youth**,
whose name was Saul **called Shaul**.
59 And they stoned *Stephen* **Stephanos**,
calling upon *God* **Elohim**, and *saying* **wording**,
Lord Jesus **Adonay Yah Shua**, receive my spirit.
60 And he *kneeled down* **placed his knees**,
and cried with a *loud* **mega** voice,
Lord **Adonay**, *lay* **set** not this sin to their charge.
And when he had said this, he fell asleep.

FOURTH PERSECUTION

8 And *Saul* **Shaul** was *consenting* **well—approving**
unto his death **his taking out**.
And at that *time* **day**
there *was a great* **became a mega** persecution
against **upon** the *church* **ecclesia**
which was at Jerusalem **in Yeru Shalem**;
and they were all *scattered abroad* **thoroughly dispersed**
throughout the regions
of *Judaea* **Yah Hudah** and *Samaria* **Shomeron**,
except the apostles.
2 And *devout* **well—received** men
carried *Stephen* **Stephanos** *to his burial*,
and made *great lamentation* **mega chopping** over him.
3 As for *Saul* **Shaul**,
he *made havock of* **ravaged** the *church* **ecclesia**,
entering into every house,
and *haling* **dragging** men and women
committed **delivered** them to *prison* **the guardhouse**.
4 Therefore **indeed**
they that were *scattered abroad* **thoroughly dispersed**
went every where **passed through**
preaching **evangelizing** the word.

PHILIPPOS DOES SIGNS

5 Then *Philip* **Philippos**
went down to the city of *Samaria* **Shomeron**,
and preached *Christ* **the Messiah** unto them.
6 And the *people with one accord* **multitude in unanimity**
gave heed unto **heeded** those *things*
which *Philip spake* **Philippos worded**,
hearing and seeing the *miracles* **signs** which he did.
7 For *unclean* **impure** spirits,
crying with *loud* **mega** voice,
came out of many that were possessed with them:
and many *taken with palsies* **paralyzed**,
and *that were* lame, were *healed* **cured**.
8 And there *was great joy* **became mega cheer**
in that city.
9 But there was a *certain* man,
called Simon **named Shimon**,
which *beforetime* **previously** in the same city
used sorcery,
and *bewitched* **astounded**
the *people* **goyim** of *Samaria* **Shomeron**,
giving out **wording** that himself
was some *great* **mega** one:
10 To whom they all *gave heed* **heeded**,
from the least to the *greatest* **mega**, *saying* **wording**,
This *man* **one**
is the *great power* **mega dynamis** of *God* **Elohim**.
11 And to him they *had regard* **heeded**,
because that of long time
he had *bewitched* **astounded** them
with *sorceries* **magicing**.
12 But when they *believed Philip* **trusted Philippos**
preaching the things **evangelizing those**
concerning the *kingdom* **sovereigndom** of *God* **Elohim**,
and the name of *Jesus Christ* **Yah Shua Messiah**,
they were baptized, both men and women.
13 Then *Simon* **Shimon** himself *believed* **trusted** also:
and when he was baptized,
he continued with *Philip* **Philippos**,
and *wondered* **was astounded**,
beholding **observing**
the *miracles* **dynamis** and **mega** signs
which *were done* **became**.
14 Now when the apostles
which were at *Jerusalem* **Yeru Shalem**
heard that *Samaria* **Shomeron**
had received the word of *God* **Elohim**,
they *sent* **apostolized** unto them
Peter **Petros** and *John* **Yahn**:
15 Who, when they *were come down* **descended**,
prayed *for* **concerning** them,
that they might *receive* **take** the Holy *Ghost* **Spirit**:
16 (For as yet he was fallen upon none of them:
only they were baptized
in the name of *the Lord Jesus* **Adonay Yah Shua**.)
17 Then *laid* **put** they their hands on them,
and they *received* **took** the Holy *Ghost* **Spirit**.
18 And when *Simon saw* **Shimon observed**
that through laying on of the apostles' hands
the Holy *Ghost* **Spirit** was given,
he offered them *money* **riches**,
19 *Saying* **Wording**, Give me also this *power* **authority**,
that on whomsoever I *lay* **put** hands,
he may *receive* **take** the Holy *Ghost* **Spirit**.
20 But *Peter* **Petros** said unto him,
Thy *money* **silver**
perish with thee **be unto thy destruction**,
because thou hast *thought* **presumed**
that the *gift* **gratuity** of *God* **Elohim**
may be *purchased with money* **acquired through riches**.
21 Thou hast neither part nor lot in this *matter* **word**:
for thy heart is not *right* **straight**
in the sight of *God* **Elohim**.
22 Repent therefore of this thy *wickedness* **malice**,
and *pray God* **petition Elohim**,
if *perhaps* **then** the *thought* **mind** of thine heart
may be forgiven thee.
23 For I *perceive* **see**
that thou art in the *gall* **choler** of bitterness,
and in the bond of iniquity.
24 Then answered *Simon* **Shimon**, and said,
Pray **Petition** ye to *the Lord* **Adonay** for me,
that none of these *things* which ye have *spoken* **said**
come upon me.
25 *And* **Therefore indeed** they,
when they had *testified* **witnessed**
and *preached* **spoken** the word of *the Lord* **Adonay**,
returned to *Jerusalem* **Yeru Shalem**,
and *preached the gospel* **evangelized**
in many villages of the *Samaritans* **Shomeroniym**.

PHILIPPOS AND THE ETHIOPIAN

26 And the angel of *the Lord* **Yah Veh**
spake unto *Philip* **Philippos**, *saying* **wording**,
Arise, and go toward the *south* **midday**
unto the way
that *goeth down* **descendeth** from *Jerusalem* **Yeru Shalem**
unto *Gaza* **Azzah**, which is *desert* **desolate**.
27 And he arose and went: and, behold,
a man *of Ethiopia* — **an Ethiopian**,
an eunuch *of great authority* — **a dynast** under Candace
queen **sovereigness** of the Ethiopians,

who had the charge of all her treasure,
and had come to *Jerusalem* **Yeru Shalem** for to worship,
28 Was returning, and sitting *in* **upon** his chariot
read *Esaias* **Yesha Yah** the prophet.
29 Then the Spirit said unto *Philip* **Philippos**,
Go near, and join thyself to this chariot.
30 And *Philip* **Philippos** ran *thither to him*,
and heard him read the prophet *Esaias* **Yesha Yah**,
and said, **Yet indeed,**
Understandest **Knowest** thou **then** what thou readest?
31 And he said, **Indeed,** How can I,
except **unless** some *man* **one** should guide me?
And he *desired Philip* **besought Philippos**
that he *would come up* **should ascend** and sit with him.
32 The *place* **passage** of the scripture which he read
was this,
He was led as a sheep to the slaughter;
and *like* **as** a lamb *dumb* **voiceless** before his shearer,
so **thus** opened he not his mouth:
33 In his humiliation his judgment was taken away:
and who shall declare his generation?
for his life is taken from the earth.
Yesha Yah 53:7, 8
34 And the eunuch answered *Philip* **Philippos**,
and said, I *pray* **petition** thee,
of **concerning** whom *speaketh* **wordeth** the prophet this?
of **concerning** himself, or *of* **concerning** some other *man*?
35 Then *Philip* **Philippos** opened his mouth,
and began *at* **from** the same scripture,
and preached unto him *Jesus* **Yah Shua**.
36 And as they went on their way,
they came unto a *certain* water:
and the eunuch said, *See* **Behold**, *here is* water;
what *doth hinder* **forbiddeth** me to be baptized?
37 And *Philip* **Philippos** said,
If thou *believest with* **trustest from** all thine heart,
thou *mayest* **art allowed**.
And he answered and said,
I *believe* **trust** that *Jesus Christ* **Yah Shua Messiah**
is the Son of *God* **Elohim**.
38 And he *commanded* **summoned** the chariot
to stand *still*:
and they *went down* **descended** both into the water,
both *Philip* **Philippos** and the eunuch;
and he baptized him.
39 And when they *were come up* **ascended**
out of the water,
the Spirit of *the Lord* **Yah Veh**
caught away Philip **seized Philippos**,
that the eunuch saw him no more:
and **indeed** he went on his way *rejoicing* **cheering**.
40 But *Philip* **Philippos** was found at *Azotus* **Ashdod**:
and passing through
he *preached* **evangelized** in all the cities,
till he came to *Caesarea* **Kaisaria**.

YAH SHUA CONFRONTS SHAUL

9 And *Saul* **Shaul**,
yet breathing out threatenings and *slaughter* **murder**
against **unto** the disciples of *the Lord* **Adonay**,
went unto the *high* **arch** priest,
2 And *desired* **asked** of him *letters* **epistles**
to *Damascus* **Dammeseq** to the synagogues,
that if he found any **being** of this way,
whether they were men or women,
he might bring them bound unto *Jerusalem* **Yeru Shalem**.
3 And as he *journeyed* **went**,
he came near Damascus
it became that he approached Dammeseq:
and suddenly
there shined round about him **he was enveloped**
in a light from heaven:
4 And he fell to the earth,
and heard a voice *saying* **wording** unto him,
Saul, Saul **Shaul, Shaul**, why persecutest thou me?
5 And he said, Who art thou, *Lord* **Adonay**?
And *the Lord* **Adonay** said,
I am Jesus **I AM Yah Shua** whom thou persecutest:
it is hard for thee to *kick* **heel** against the *pricks* **stings**.
6 And he trembling and astonished said, *Lord* **Adonay**,
what *wilt* **willest** thou have me to do?
And *the Lord* **Adonay** *said* unto him,
Arise, and *go into* **enter** the city,
and it shall be *told* **spoken** thee what thou must do.
7 And the men which journeyed with him
stood *speechless* **nodding**,
indeed hearing a voice,
but *seeing* **observing** no *man* **one**.
8 And *Saul* **Shaul** arose from the earth;
and when his eyes were opened, he saw no *man* **one**:
but they **hand** led him *by the hand*,
and brought him into *Damascus* **Dammeseq**.
9 And he was three days *without sight* **not seeing**,
and neither did eat nor drink.
10 And there was a *certain* disciple
at *Damascus* **Dammeseq**,
named *Ananias* **Hanan Yah**;
and to him said *the Lord* **Adonay** in a vision,
Ananias **Hanan Yah**.
And he said, Behold, *I am here, Lord* **I — Adonay**.
11 And *the Lord* **Adonay** said unto him, Arise,
and go into the street which is called Straight,
and *enquire* **seek** in the house of *Judas* **Yah Hudah**
for one *called Saul* **named Shaul**, *of Tarsus* **— a Tarsiy**:
for, behold, he prayeth,
12 And hath seen in a vision
a man named *Ananias coming in* **Hanan Yah entering**,
and putting his hand on him,
that he might *receive his sight* **see**.
13 Then *Ananias* **Hanan Yah** answered, *Lord* **Adonay**,
I have heard by many *of* **concerning** this man,
how much evil **as many evils as** he hath done
to thy *saints* **holy** at *Jerusalem* **Yeru Shalem**:
14 And here he hath authority from the *chief* **arch** priests
to bind all that call on thy name.
15 But *the Lord* **Adonay** said unto him, Go thy way:
for he is a *chosen* **selected** vessel unto me,
to bear my name
before **in the sight of** the *Gentiles* **goyim**,
and *kings* **sovereigns**,
and the *children* **sons** of *Israel* **Yisra El**:
16 For I *will shew* **shall exemplify** him
how great things **as much as** he must suffer
for my name's sake.

SHAUL FILLED FULL WITH THE HOLY SPIRIT

17 And *Ananias* **Hanan Yah** went *his way*,
and entered into the house;
and putting his hands on him said, Brother *Saul* **Shaul**,
the Lord **Adonay**, even *Jesus* **Yah Shua**,
that appeared unto thee in the way as thou camest,
hath *sent* **apostolized** me,
that thou mightest *receive thy sight* **see**,
and be filled **full** with the Holy *Ghost* **Spirit**.
18 And *immediately* **straightway** there fell from his eyes
as *it had been scales* **were leperous flakes**:
and **immediately** he *received sight forthwith* **saw**,
and arose, and was baptized.
19 And when he had *received meat* **taken nourishment**,
he was *strengthened* **invigorated**.
Then *was Saul certain* **Shaul became some** days
with the disciples which were at *Damascus* **Dammeseq**.

SHAUL PREACHES THE MESSIAH

20 And straightway
he preached *Christ* **the Messiah** in the synagogues,
that he is the Son of *God* **Elohim**.
21 But all that heard him were *amazed* **astounded**,
and *said* **worded**;
Is not this he that *destroyed* **ravaged** them
which called on this name in *Jerusalem* **Yeru Shalem**,
and came hither *for that intent*,
that he might bring them bound
unto the *chief* **arch** priests?
22 But *Saul* **Shaul**
increased the more in strength **became dynamic**,
and *confounded* **confused** the *Jews* **Yah Hudiym**
which *dwelt at Damascus* **settled in Dammeseq**,
proving **concluding** that this is *very Christ* **the Messiah**.
23 And after that many days were fulfilled,
the *Jews took counsel* **Yah Hudiym counseled**
to *kill* **take** him **out**:
24 But their *laying await* **plotting**

was known of *Saul* **Shaul**.
And they *watched* **observed** the gates day and night
to *kill* **take** him **out**.
25 Then the disciples took him by night,
and *let* **lowered** him *down by* **through** the wall
in a basket.

SHAUL IN YERU SHALEM

26 And when *Saul* **Shaul**
was come to *Jerusalem* **Yeru Shalem**,
he *assayed* **tried** to join himself to the disciples:
but they *were* all *afraid of* **awed** him,
and *believed* **trusted** not that he was a disciple.
27 But *Barnabas* **Bar Nabi** took him,
and brought him to the apostles,
and declared unto them
how he had seen *the Lord* **Adonay** in the way,
and that he had spoken to him,
and how he had *preached boldly* **boldness**
at *Damascus* **Dammeseq**
in the name of *Jesus* **Yah Shua**.
28 And he was with them
coming in **entering** and *going out* **departing**
at *Jerusalem* **Yeru Shalem**.
29 And he spake *boldly* **having boldness**
in the name of *the Lord Jesus* **Adonay Yah Shua**,
and disputed against the *Grecians* **Hellenists**:
but they *went about* **took in hand**
to *slay him* **take him out**.

SHAUL IN TARSUS

30 Which when the brethren knew,
they brought him down to *Caesarea* **Kaisaria**,
and *sent* **apostolized** him forth to Tarsus.
31 *Then* **Therefore indeed**
had the *churches rest* **ecclesiae shalom**
throughout all *Judaea* **Yah Hudah**
and *Galilee* **Galiyl** and *Samaria* **Shomeron**,
and were *edified* **built** *up*;
and walking in the *fear* **awe** of *the Lord* **Yah Veh**,
and in the *comfort* **consolation** of the Holy *Ghost* **Spirit**,
were multiplied.

PETROS HEALS A PARALYTIC

32 And it *came to pass* **became**,
as *Peter* **Petros** passed throughout *all quarters*,
he came down also to the *saints* **holy**
which *dwelt* **settled** at *Lydda* **Lod**.
33 And there
he found a *certain man* **human** named Aeneas,
which had *kept* **lain upon** his *bed* **pad** eight years,
and was *sick of the palsy* **paralyzed**.
34 And *Peter* **Petros** said unto him, Aeneas,
Jesus Christ **Yah Shua the Messiah**
maketh **healeth** thee *whole*:
arise, and *make thy bed* **extend**.
And he arose *immediately* **straightway**.
35 And all that *dwelt* **settled**
at *Lydda* **Lod** and *Saron* **Sharon** saw him,
and turned to *the Lord* **Adonay**.

PETROS RAISES ONE DEAD

36 Now there was at *Joppa* **Yapho**
a *certain* disciple° named Tabitha,
which by *interpretation* **translation**
is *called Dorcas* **worded Gazelle**:
this *woman* **one**
was full of good works and *almsdeeds* **mercies**
which she did.

°feminine: a female disciple.

37 And it *came to pass* **became** in those days,
that she was *sick* **frail**, and died:
whom when they had *washed* **bathed**,
they *laid* **placed** her in an upper *chamber* **loft**.
38 And *forasmuch* **being**
as Lydda **that Lod** was nigh to *Joppa* **Yapho**,
and the disciples had heard that *Peter* **Petros** was there,
they *sent* **apostolized** unto him two men,
desiring **beseeching** him
that he *would* **should** not *delay* **hesitate**
to *come* **pass through** to them.
39 Then *Peter* **Petros** arose and went with them.
When he was come,
they brought him into the upper *chamber* **loft**:
and all the widows stood by him weeping,
and shewing the *coats* **tunics** and garments
which Dorcas **— as many as Gazelle** made,
while she was with them.
40 But *Peter put* **Petros cast** them all *forth* **out**,
and *kneeled down* **placed his knees**, and prayed;
and turning him to the body said, Tabitha, arise.
And she opened her eyes:
and when she saw *Peter* **Petros**, she sat *up*.
41 And he gave her his hand, and *lifted* **raised** her *up*,
and when he had called the *saints* **holy** and widows,
presented her alive.
42 And it *was* **became** known
throughout all *Joppa* **Yapho**;
and many *believed* **trusted** in *the Lord* **Adonay**.
43 And it *came to pass* **became**,
that he *tarried* **abode** many days in *Joppa* **Yapho**
with one *Simon* **Shimon** a tanner.

CORNELIUS' VISION

10 There was a *certain* man in *Caesarea* **Kaisaria**
called **named** Cornelius,
a centurion of the *band* **squad** called *the* Italian *band*,
2 A *devout* **well revered** man,
and one that *feared God* **awed Elohim** with all his house,
which *gave much alms* **did many mercies** to the people,
and *prayed* **petitioned** to *God alway* **Elohim continually**.
3 He saw in a vision *evidently* **manifestly**
about the ninth hour of the day
an angel of *God* **Elohim** *coming in* **entering** to him,
and saying unto him, Cornelius.
4 And when he *looked on* **stared at** him,
he *was afraid* **became awestricken**, and said,
What is it, *Lord* **Adonay**?
And he said unto him,
Thy prayers and *thine alms* **thy mercies**
are *come up for* **ascended unto** a memorial
before God **in the sight of Elohim**.
5 And now send men to *Joppa* **Yapho**,
and *call for one Simon* **summon Shimon**,
whose surname is Peter **who is called Petros**:
6 He lodgeth with one *Simon* **Shimon** a tanner,
whose house is by the sea side:
he shall *tell* **speak to** thee what thou *oughtest to* **must** do.
7 And when the angel which spake unto Cornelius
was departed,
he called two of his *household servants* **housekeepers**,
and a *devout soldier* **well—revered warrior**
of them that waited on him *continually*;
8 And when he had declared all these *things* unto them,
he *sent* **apostolized** them to *Joppa* **Yapho**.

PETROS' VISION

9 On the morrow,
as they *went on their journey* **journeyed**,
and *drew nigh unto* **approached** the city,
Peter **Petros**
went up **ascended** upon the housetop to pray
about the sixth hour:
10 And he became *very* **intensely** hungry,
and *would* **willed to** have *eaten* **tasted**:
but while they *made ready* **prepared**,
he fell into a trance **an ecstasis fell upon him**,
11 And *saw* **observed** heaven opened,
and a *certain* vessel descending upon him,
as *it had been a great sheet* **— a mega linen**
knit **bound** at the four *corners* **beginnings**,
and let down to the earth:
12 Wherein were all *manner*
of fourfooted beasts **quadrepeds** of the earth,
and *wild* beasts, and *creeping things* **creepers**,
and *fowls* **flyers** of the *air* **heavens**.
13 And there *came* **became** a voice to him,
Rise, *Peter* **Petros**; *kill* **sacrifice**, and eat.
14 But *Peter* **Petros** said, *Not so* **No way**, *Lord* **Adonay**;
for I have never **ever** eaten *any thing* **ought**
that is *common* **profane** or *unclean* **impure**.
15 And *the voice spake unto him again the second time*
a second voice to him,
What *God* **Elohim** hath *cleansed* **purified**,
that call not thou common **thou shalt not profane**.
16 This *was done* **became** thrice:

and the vessel was *received up* **taken** again into heaven.
17 Now while *Peter* **Petros**
doubted **was thoroughly perplexed** in himself
what this vision which he had seen should *mean* **ever be**,
behold,
the men which were *sent* **apostolized** from Cornelius
had *made enquiry* **thoroughly interrogated**
for *Simon's* **Shimon's** house,
and stood *before* **by** the gate,
18 And called, and asked whether *Simon* **Shimon**,
which was surnamed Peter **called Petros**,
were lodged there.
19 While *Peter thought* **Petros pondered**
on **about** the vision,
the Spirit said unto him, Behold, three men seek thee.
20 Arise therefore, and *get thee down* **descend**,
and go with them, doubting *nothing* **naught**:
for **because** I have *sent* **apostolized** them.
21 Then *Peter went down* **Petros descended** to the men
which were *sent* **apostolized** unto him from Cornelius;
and said, Behold, I am he whom ye seek:
what is the cause wherefore ye are *come* **present**?
22 And they said, Cornelius the centurion,
a just man, and one that *feareth God* **aweth Elohim**,
and *of good report* **well witnessed**
among **by** all the *nation* **goyim** of the *Jews* **Yah Hudiym**,
was *warned from God* **oracled** by an holy angel
to *send for* **summon** thee into his house,
and to hear *words* **rhema** of thee.
23 Then *called* **invited** he them *in*, and lodged them.
And on the morrow *Peter* **Petros** went away with them,
and *certain* **some** brethren from *Joppa* **Yapho**
accompanied **came with** him.
24 And the morrow after
they entered into *Caesarea* **Kaisaria**.
And Cornelius *waited for* **awaited** them,
and he had called together
his kinsmen and *near* **dependant** friends.
25 And as *Peter was coming in* **Petros became entering**,
Cornelius met him,
and fell down at his feet, and worshipped him.
26 But *Peter took* **Petros raised** him *up*, *saying* **wording**,
Stand up **Arise**; I myself also am a *man* **human**.
27 And as he *talked* **conversed** with him,
he *went in* **entered**,
and found many that were come together.
28 And he said unto them,
Ye *know* **understand** how that it is *an unlawful thing* **illicit**
for a man *that is a Jew* — **a Yah Hudiy**
to *keep company* **join**,
or come unto one of another *nation* **scion**;
but *God* **Elohim** hath shewed me
that I should not *call* **word** any *man* **human**
common **profane** or *unclean* **impure**.
29 Therefore came I *unto you*
without gainsaying **unquestioningly**,
as soon as I was *sent for* **summoned**:
I ask therefore
for what *intent* **word** ye have *sent for* **summoned** me?
30 And Cornelius said,
For Four days *ago* I was fasting until this hour;
and at the ninth hour I prayed in my house, and, behold,
a man stood *before me* **in my sight**
in *bright clothing* **radiant apparel**,
31 And said, Cornelius, thy prayer is heard,
and *thine alms* **thy mercies**
are *had in remembrance* **remembered**
in the sight of *God* **Elohim**.
32 Send therefore to *Joppa* **Yapho**,
and call *hither Simon* **Shimon**,
whose surname is Peter **called Petros**;
he is lodged in the house of *one Simon* **Shimon**
a tanner by the sea side:
who, when he cometh, shall speak unto thee.
33 Immediately therefore I sent to thee;
and thou hast well done that thou art come.
Now therefore are we all here present
before God **in the sight of Elohim**,
to hear all *things* **those**
that are commanded thee of *God* **Elohim**.

PETROS' FOURTH MESSAGE

34 Then *Peter* **Petros** opened his mouth, and said,
Of a truth I *perceive* **overtake**
that *God* **Elohim** is *no respecter of persons* **not partial**:
35 But in every *nation* **goyim**, he that *feareth* **aweth** him,
and worketh *righteousness* **justness**,
is *accepted* **acceptable** with him.
36 The word which *God sent* **Elohim apostolized**
unto the *children* **sons** of *Israel* **Yisra El**,
preaching peace **evangelizing shalom**
by Jesus Christ **through Yah Shua Messiah**:
(he is *Lord* **Adonay** of all:)
37 That *word* **rhema**, *I say*, ye know,
which *was published* **became**
throughout all *Judaea* **Yah Hudah**,
and began from *Galilee* **Galiyl**,
after the baptism which *John* **Yahn** preached;
38 How *God* **Elohim**
anointed *Jesus of Nazareth* **Yah Shua the Nazarene**
with the Holy *Ghost* **Spirit** and with *power* **dynamis**:
who *went about* **passed through**
doing good **working well**,
and healing all
that were *oppressed* **overpowered** of *the devil* **Diabolos**;
for *God* **Elohim** was with him.
39 And we are witnesses of all *things* which he did
both in the *land* **region** of the *Jews* **Yah Hudiym**,
and in *Jerusalem* **Yeru Shalem**;
whom they *slew* **took out** and hanged on a *tree* **staff**:
40 Him *God* **Elohim** raised *up* the third day,
and *shewed* **gave** him *openly* **to become manifest**;
41 Not to all the people,
but unto witnesses
chosen before **preselected** of *God* **Elohim**,
even to us,
who did eat and drink with him
after he rose from the dead.
42 And he *commanded* **evangelized** us
to preach unto the people,
and to *testify* **witness** that it is he
which was *ordained* **decreed** of *God* **Elohim**
to be the Judge of *quick* **living** and dead.
43 To him give all the prophets witness,
that through his name
whosoever *believeth* **trusteth** in him
shall *receive remission* **take forgiveness** of sins.

HOLY SPIRIT POURED ON THE GOYIM

44 While *Peter* **Petros** yet spake these *words* **rhema**,
the Holy *Ghost* **Spirit** fell
on all them which heard the word.
45 And they of the circumcision which *believed* **trusted**
were *astonished* **astounded**,
as many as came with *Peter* **Petros**,
because that on the *Gentiles* **goyim** also
was poured out the *gift* **gratuity** of the Holy *Ghost* **Spirit**.
46 For they heard them speak with tongues,
and magnify *God* **Elohim**.
Then answered *Peter* **Petros**,
47 Can any *man* **one** forbid water,
that these should not be baptized,
which have *received* **taken** the Holy *Ghost* **Spirit**
exactly as well as we?
48 And he commanded them to be baptized
in the name of *the Lord* **Adonay**.
Then *prayed* **asked** they him
to *tarry certain* **abide some** days.

CORNELIUS' VISION: PETROS RELATES HIS VISION

11 And the apostles and brethren
that were in *Judaea* **Yah Hudah**
heard that the *Gentiles* **goyim**
had also received the word of *God* **Elohim**.
2 And when *Peter* **Petros**
was come up **ascended** to *Jerusalem* **Yeru Shalem**,
they that were of the circumcision contended with him,
3 *Saying* **Wording**,
Thou *wentest in* **enterest** to men uncircumcised,
and didst eat with them.
4 But *Peter* **Petros**
rehearsed the matter from the beginning **began**,
and expounded it *by order* **in sequence** unto them,

saying **wording**,
5 I was in the city of *Joppa* **Yapho** praying:
and in *a trance* **an ecstasis** I saw a vision,
A *certain* vessel descend,
as *it had been a great sheet* **a mega linen**,
let down from heaven by four *corners* **beginnings**;
and it came *even* to me:
6 *Upon* **Unto** the which
when I had *fastened mine eyes* **stared**,
I *considered* **perceived**,
and saw *fourfooted beasts* **quadrepeds** of the earth,
and *wild* beasts, and *creeping things* **creepers**,
and *fowls* **flyers** of the *air* **heavens**.
7 And I heard a voice *saying* **wording** unto me,
Arise, *Peter* **Petros**; *slay* **sacrifice** and eat.
8 But I said, *Not so* **No way**, *Lord* **Adonay**:
for *nothing common* **naught profane** or *unclean* **impure**
hath *at any time* **ever** entered into my mouth.
9 But the voice answered me *again* **twice** from heaven,
What *God* **Elohim** hath *cleansed* **purified**,
that *call not* common **profane thou not**.
10 And this *was done three times* **became thrice**:
and all were drawn *up* again into heaven.
11 And, behold, immediately there were three men
already *come unto* **standing by** the house
where **wherein** I was,
sent **apostolized** from *Caesarea* **Kaisaria** unto me.
12 And the Spirit *bade* **said for** me *go* **to come** with them,
nothing **naught** doubting.
Moreover
these six brethren *accompanied* **came with** me,
and we entered into the man's house:
13 And he *shewed* **evangelized** us
how he had seen an angel in his house,
which stood and said unto him,
Send **Apostolize** men to *Joppa* **Yapho**,
and *call for Simon* **summon Shimon**,
whose surname is Peter **called Petros**;
14 Who shall *tell* **speak rhemas to** thee *words*,
whereby thou and all thy house shall be saved.
15 And as I began to speak,
the Holy *Ghost* **Spirit** fell on them,
exactly as on us at the beginning.
16 Then remembered I
the *words* **rhema** of *the Lord* **Adonay**,
how that he *said* **worded**,
John **Yahn** indeed baptized *with* **in** water;
but ye shall be baptized *with* **in** the Holy *Ghost* **Spirit**.
17 *Forasmuch* **If** then *as*
God **Elohim** gave them the *like gift* **equal gratuity**
as he did unto us, who *believed* **trusted**
on *the Lord Jesus Christ* **Adonay Yah Shua Messiah**;
what was I, that I could *withstand God* **forbid Elohim**?
18 When they heard these *things*,
they *held their peace* **quieted**,
and glorified *God* **Elohim**, *saying* **wording**,
Then **yet indeed**
hath *God* **Elohim** also to the *Gentiles* **goyim**
granted **given** repentance unto life.

FIRST MESSIANISTS

19 *Now* **Therefore indeed**
they which were *scattered abroad* **thoroughly dispersed**
upon **by** the *persecution* **tribulation**
that *arose about Stephen* **became after Stephanos**
travelled as far as Phenice **passed through unto Phoinix**,
and Cyprus, and Antioch,
preaching **speaking** the word to none
but unto the *Jews* **Yah Hudiym** only.
20 And some of them
were men of Cyprus — **Cypriots** and *Cyrene* **Cyrenians**,
which, when they *were come to* **entered** Antioch,
spake unto the *Grecians* **Hellenists**,
preaching the Lord Jesus **evangelizing Adonay Yah Shua**.
21 And the hand of *the Lord* **Adonay** was with them:
and a *great* **vast** number *believed* **trusted**,
and turned unto *the Lord* **Adonay**.
22 Then *tidings of* **word about** these *things*
came **was heard** unto the ears of the *church* **ecclesia**
which was in *Jerusalem* **Yeru Shalem**:
and they *sent forth Barnabas* **apostolized Bar Nabi**,
that he should *go as far as* **pass through unto** Antioch.
23 Who, when he came,
and had seen the *grace* **charism** of *God* **Elohim**,
was glad **cheered**, and *exhorted* **besought** them all,
that with *purpose* **prothesis** of heart
they *would cleave unto the Lord* **should abide in Adonay**.
24 For he was a good man,
and full of the Holy *Ghost* **Spirit** and of *faith* **trust**:
and much *people* **multitude**
was added unto *the Lord* **Adonay**.
25 Then departed *Barnabas* **Bar Nabi** to Tarsus,
for to seek *Saul* **Shaul**:
26 And when he had found him,
he brought him unto Antioch.
And it *came to pass* **became**, that a whole year
they assembled themselves *with* **in** the *church* **ecclesia**,
and *taught* **doctrinated** much *people* **multitude**.
And the disciples were *called Christians* **oracled Messianists**
first in Antioch.
27 And in these days came prophets
from *Jerusalem* **Yeru Shalem** unto Antioch.
28 And there *stood up* **rose** one of them
named *Agabus* **Hagab**,
and signified *by* **through** the Spirit
that there *should* **was about to** be
great dearth **a mega** *throughout* **famine upon** all the world:
which *came to pass* **became**
in the days of Claudius Caesar **under Kaisar Claudius**.
29 Then the disciples, *every man* **each one**
according to his ability **exactly as each prospered**,
determined **decreed for ministry**
to send *relief* unto the brethren
which *dwelt* **settled** in *Judaea* **Yah Hudah**:
30 Which also they did,
and *sent* **apostolized** it to the elders
by **through** the hands
of *Barnabas* **Bar Nabi** and *Saul* **Shaul**.

FIFTH PERSECUTION

12 Now about that *time* **season**
Herod the *king* **sovereign** stretched forth his hands
to *vex certain* **vilify some** of the *church* **ecclesia**.
2 And he *killed James* **took out Yaaqovos**
the brother of *John* **Yahn** with the sword.
3 And because he saw it pleased the *Jews* **Yah Hudiym**,
he *proceeded further* **added** to take *Peter* **Petros** also.
(Then were the days of *unleavened bread* **matsah**.)
4 And when he had *apprehended* **seized** him,
he put him in *prison* **the guardhouse**,
and delivered him
to four quaternions of *soldiers* **warriors**
to *keep* **guard** him;
intending **having willed** after *Easter* **pasach**
to bring him forth to the people.
5 *Peter* **Petros** therefore **indeed**
was *kept* **guarded** in *prison* **the guardhouse**:
but prayer *was made without ceasing* **became intense**
of the *church* **ecclesia** unto *God* **Elohim** for him.
6 And when Herod
would have brought **was about to bring** him forth,
the *same* night
Peter **Petros** was sleeping between two *soldiers* **warriors**,
bound with two *chains* **fetters**:
and the *keepers* **guards** before the *door* **portal**
kept **guarded** the *prison* **guardhouse**.
7 And, behold,
the angel of *the Lord came upon him* **Yah Veh stood by**,
and a light *shined* **radiated** in the *prison* **dwelling**:
and he smote *Peter* **Petros** on the side,
and raised him *up*, *saying* **wording**, Arise *up* quickly.
And his *chains* **fetters** fell *off* from his hands.
8 And the angel said unto him,
Gird thyself, and bind on thy sandals.
And *so* **thus** he did.
And he *saith* **wordeth** unto him,
Cast **Array** thy garment *about thee*, and follow me.
9 And he went out, and followed him;
and *wist* **knew** not that it was true
which *was done by* **became through** the angel;
but thought he saw a vision.
10 When they *were past* **had passed through**

the first and the second *ward* **guardhouse**,
they came unto the iron gate
that *leadeth* **beareth** unto the city;
which opened to them *of his own accord* **automatically**:
and they went out,
and *passed on* **proceeded** through one street;
and *forthwith* **straightway** the angel departed from him.
11 And when *Peter was come* **Petros became** to himself,
he said, Now I know *of a surety* **truly**,
that *the Lord* **Yah Veh** hath *sent* **apostolized** his angel,
and hath *delivered* **released** me out of the hand of Herod,
and from all the expectation
of the people of the *Jews* **Yah Hudiym**.
12 And when he had *considered the thing* **awared**,
he came to the house of *Mary* **Miryam**
the mother of *John* **Yahn**,
whose surname was Mark **who was called Markos**;
where many were gathered together praying.
13 And as *Peter* **Petros**
knocked at the *door* **portal** of the gate,
a *damsel* **lass** came to *hearken* **obey**, named Rhoda.
14 And when she knew *Peter's* **Petros'** voice,
she opened not the gate for *gladness* **cheer**,
but *ran in* **hastened**,
and *told* **evangelized**
how Peter **that Petros** stood before the gate.
15 And they *said* **worded** unto her, Thou *art mad* **ravest**.
But she *constantly* **thoroughly** affirmed
that it was *even so* **thus**.
Then said they, It is his angel.
16 But *Peter continued* **Petros abode** knocking:
and when they had opened *the door*, and saw him,
they were *astonished* **astounded**.
17 But he, *beckoning* **signaling** unto them with the hand
to *hold their peace* **hush**,
declared unto them how *the Lord* **Yah Veh**
had *brought* **led** him out of the *prison* **guardhouse**.
And he said,
Go *shew* **evangelize** these *things* unto *James* **Yaaqovos**,
and to the brethren.
And he departed, and went into another place.
18 Now as *soon as it was* **it became** day,
there was no small *stir* **trouble**
among the *soldiers* **warriors**,
what was become of *Peter* **Petros**.
19 And when Herod had sought for him,
and found him not,
he examined the *keepers* **guards**,
and *commanded* **summoned** that they
should be *put to death* **led away**.
And he went down from *Judaea* **Yah Hudah**
to *Caesarea* **Kaisaria**, and there *abode* **tarried**.

HEROD IS MAGGOT EATEN

20 And Herod was *highly displeased* **exasperated**
with *them of Tyre* **the Soriym** and *Sidon* **the Sidoniym**:
but they *came* **presented themselves**
with one accord **in unanimity** to him,
and, having *made* **convinced** Blastus
the king's chamberlain their friend
who was over the sovereign's bedchamber,
desired peace **asked for shalom**;
because their *country* **region**
was nourished by the *king's* **sovereign's** country.
21 And upon *a set* **an ordered** day Herod,
arrayed **endued** in *royal* **sovereign** apparel,
sat upon his *throne* **bamah**,
and *made an oration unto* **addressed** them.
22 And the *people gave a shout* **public shouted**, *saying*,
It is the voice of a god, and not of a *man* **human**.
23 And immediately
the angel of *the Lord* **Yah Veh** smote him,
because he gave not *God* **Elohim** the glory:
and he *was* **became** eaten of *worms* **maggots**,
and *gave up the ghost* **expired**.
24 But the word of *God* **Elohim** grew and multiplied.
25 And *Barnabas* **Bar Nabi** and *Saul* **Shaul**
returned from *Jerusalem* **Yeru Shalem**,
when they had fulfilled their ministry,
and took with them *John* **Yahn**,
whose surname was Mark **who was called Markos**.

SHAUL AND BAR NABI ARE SET APART

13 Now there were in the *church* **ecclesia**
that was at Antioch
certain **some** prophets and *teachers* **doctors**;
as *Barnabas* **Bar Nabi** and *Simeon* **Shimon**
that was called Niger,
and *Lucius of Cyrene* — **Loukios a Cyrenian**, and Manaen,
which had been *brought up* **nursed**
with Herod the tetrarch,
and *Saul* **Shaul**.
2 As they *ministered* **liturgized** to *the Lord* **Adonay**,
and fasted,
the Holy *Ghost* **Spirit** said,
Separate me **Now set apart**
Barnabas **Bar Nabi** and *Saul* **Shaul**
for **unto** the work whereunto I have called them.

SHAUL'S AND BAR NABI'S FIRST JOURNEY

3 *And when they had* **Then having** fasted and prayed,
and *laid* **put** their hands on them,
they *sent* **released** them *away*.
4 *So* **Therefore indeed** they,
being *sent forth* **dispatched** by the Holy *Ghost* **Spirit**,
departed **went down** unto Seleucia;
and from thence they sailed to Cyprus.
5 And when they *were* **became** at Salamis,
they *preached* **evangelized** the word of *God* **Elohim**
in the synagogues of the *Jews* **Yah Hudiym**:
and they had also *John* **Yahn**
to **as** their *minister* **attendant**.
6 And when they had *gone* **passed** through the isle
unto Paphos,
they found a *certain sorcerer* **magi**,
a *false* **pseudo** prophet, a *Jew* **Yah Hudiy**,
whose name was *Bar—Jesus* **Bar Yah Shua**:
7 Which was with the *deputy* **proconsul** of the country,
Sergius *Paulus* **Paulos**,
a *prudent* man **of comprehension**;
who called for *Barnabas* **Bar Nabi** and *Saul* **Shaul**,
and *desired* **sought** to hear the word of *God* **Elohim**.
8 But Elymas the *sorcerer* **magi**
(for *so* **thus** is his name by *interpretation* **translation**)
withstood them,
seeking to *turn away* **thoroughly pervert**
the *deputy* **proconsul** from the *faith* **trust**.

SHAUL IS PAULOS

9 Then *Saul* **Shaul**, (who also is called *Paul* **Paulos**,)
filled **full** with the Holy *Ghost* **Spirit**,
set his eyes on **stared unto** him.
10 And said,
O full of all *subtilty* **deceit** and all *mischief* **malignity**,
thou *child* **son** of *the devil* **Diabolos**,
thou enemy of all *righteousness* **justness**,
wilt **shalt** thou not *cease* **pause**
to pervert **from thoroughly perverting**
the *right* **straight** ways of *the Lord* **Yah Veh**?
11 And now, behold,
the hand of *the Lord* **Adonay** is upon thee,
and thou shalt be blind,
not seeing the sun *for* **until** a season.
And immediately
there fell on him a *mist* **dimness** and a darkness;
and he went about seeking some
to **hand** lead him *by the hand*.
12 Then the *deputy* **proconsul**,
when he saw what *was done* **became**, *believed* **trusted**,
being astonished at the doctrine of *the Lord* **Adonay**.
13 Now when *Paul* **Paulos**
and *his company* **those around him**
loosed **embarked** from Paphos,
they came to Perga in Pamphylia:
and *John* **Yahn** departing from them
returned to *Jerusalem* **Jeru Shalem**.

PAULOS' SYNAGOGUE MESSAGE

14 But when they *departed* **passed through** from Perga,
they came to Antioch in Pisidia,
and *went* **entered** into the synagogue
on the *sabbath* **shabbath** day, and sat *down*.
15 And after
the reading of the *law* **torah** and the prophets
the *rulers of the* synagogue **archs**

sent **apostolized** unto them, *saying* **wording,**
Ye men and brethren,
if ye have any word of *exhortation* **consolation**
for the people, *say* **word on.**
16 Then *Paul stood up* **Paulos arose**
and *beckoning* **signaling** with his hand said,
Men *of Israel* — **Yisra Eliym,**
and ye that *fear God* **awe Elohim,**
give audience **hearken.**
17 The *God* **Elohim** of this people of *Israel* **Yisra El**
chose **selected** our fathers,
and exalted the people
when they dwelt as strangers **in their settling**
in the land of *Egypt* **Misrayim,**
and with an high arm *brought* **led** he them out of it.
18 And about the time of forty years
suffered **endured** he their manners in the wilderness.
19 And when he had
destroyed **taken out** seven *nations* **goyim**
in the land of *Chanaan* **Kenaan,**
he *divided* **allotted** their land to them *by lot.*
20 And after that he gave unto them judges
about the space of four hundred and fifty years,
until *Samuel* **Shemu El** the prophet.
21 And *afterward* **from thence**
they *desired* **asked** a *king* **sovereign:**
and *God* **Elohim** gave unto them *Saul* **Shaul**
the son of *Cis* **Qish,**
a man of the *tribe* **scion** of *Benjamin* **Ben Yamin,**
by the space of forty years.
22 And when he had removed him,
he raised *up* unto them David to be their *king* **sovereign;**
to whom also he *gave their testimony* **witnessed,**
and said, I have found David *the son* of *Jesse* **Yishay,**
a man after mine own heart,
which shall *fulfil* **do** all my will.
23 Of this man's *seed* **sperma** hath *God* **Elohim**
according to his *promise* **pre—evangelism**
raised unto *Israel* **Yisra El** a Saviour, *Jesus* **Yah Shua:**
24 When *John* **Yahn** had *first* **previously** preached
before **facing** his *coming* **entrance**
the baptism of repentance
to all the people of *Israel* **Yisra El.**
25 And as *John* **Yahn** fulfilled his *course* **race,**
he *said* **worded,**
Whom *think* **surmise** ye that I am? *I am not he* **not I AM.**
But, behold, there cometh one after me,
whose shoes of his feet I am not worthy to loose.
26 Men and brethren,
children **sons** of the *stock* **genos** of Abraham,
and whosoever among you *feareth God* **aweth Elohim,**
to you is the word of this salvation *sent* **apostolized.**
27 For they that *dwell* **settle** at *Jerusalem* **Yeru Shalem,**
and their *rulers* **archs,** because they knew him not,
nor yet the voices of the prophets
which are read every *sabbath day* **shabbath,**
they have fulfilled *them in condemning him* **by judging.**
28 And though they found no cause of death *in him,*
yet *desired* **asked** they *Pilate* **Pilatos**
that he should be *slain* **taken out.**
29 And when they had *fulfilled* **completed** all
that was *written of* **scribed concerning** him,
they took him down from the *tree* **staff,**
and *laid* **placed** him in a *sepulchre* **tomb.**
30 But *God* **Elohim** raised him from the dead:
31 And he was seen many days of them
which *came up* **ascended together** with him
from *Galilee* **Galiyl** to *Jerusalem* **Yeru Shalem,**
who are his witnesses unto the people.
32 And we *declare* **evangelize** unto you *glad tidings,*
how that the *promise* **pre—evangelism**
which *was made* **became** unto the fathers,
33 *God* **Elohim** hath fulfilled *the same* **this**
unto us their children,
in that he hath raised *up Jesus again* **Yah Shua;**
as it is also *written* **scribed** in the second psalm,
Thou art my Son, this day have I begotten thee.
Psalm 2:7
34 And as concerning
that he raised him *up* from the dead,
now *no more* **not about** to return to corruption,
he said *on this wise* **thus,**
I *will* **shall** give you
the *sure mercies* **trustworthy mercifuls** of David.
35 Wherefore he *saith* **wordeth** also in another *psalm,*
Thou shalt not *suffer thine Holy One* **give thy Merciful**
to see corruption.
Psalm 16:10
36 For **indeed** David,
after he had *served* **tended** his own generation
by the *will* **counsel** of *God* **Elohim,** fell on sleep,
and was *laid* **added** unto his fathers, and saw corruption:
37 But he, whom *God* **Elohim** raised *again,*
saw no corruption.
38 Be it known unto you therefore, men and brethren,
that through this man
is *preached* **evangelized** unto you the forgiveness of sins:
39 And *at* **in** him all that *believe* **trust**
are justified from all *things,*
from which ye could not be justified
at **in** the *law* **torah** of *Moses* **Mosheh.**
40 *Beware* **Look** therefore, lest that come upon you,
which is *spoken of* **said** in the prophets;
41 *Behold* **See,** ye despisers,
and *wonder* **marvel,** and *perish* **disappear:**
for I work a work in your days,
a work which ye shall
in no wise believe **not no way trust,**
though a man **even if one** declare it unto you.
42 And when the *Jews* **Yah Hudiym**
were gone **departed** out of the synagogue,
the *Gentiles besought* **goyim entreated**
that these *words* **rhema**
might be *preached* **spoken** to them
the next *sabbath* **shabbath.**
43 Now when the *congregation* **synagogue**
was *broken up* **released,**
many of the *Jews* **Yah Hudiym**
and *religious* **venerating** proselytes
followed *Paul* **Paulos** and *Barnabas* **Bar Nabi:**
who, speaking to them,
persuaded **convinced** them to *continue* **abide**
in the *grace* **charism** of *God* **Elohim.**
44 And the *next sabbath day* **coming shabbath**
came almost **nearly** the whole city **gathered** together
to hear the word of *God* **Elohim.**
45 But when the *Jews* **Yah Hudiym** saw the multitudes,
they were filled **full** with *envy* **zeal,**
and *spake against* **contradicted** those *things*
which were *spoken* **worded** by *Paul* **Paulos,**
by contradicting and blaspheming.

PAULOS AND BAR NABI TURN TO THE GOYIM

46 Then *Paul* **Paulos** and *Barnabas* **Bar Nabi**
waxed bold **emboldened,** and said,
It was necessary that the word of *God* **Elohim**
should first *have been* **be** spoken to you:
but *seeing* **since** ye *put* **shove** it from you,
and judge yourselves unworthy of *everlasting* **eternal** life,
lo **behold,** we turn to the *Gentiles* **goyim.**
47 For *so* **thus**
hath *the Lord commanded* **Yah Veh misvahed** us, *saying,*
I have *set* **placed** thee to be a light of the *Gentiles* **goyim,**
that thou shouldest be *for* **unto** salvation
unto the *ends* **finality** of the earth.
48 And when the *Gentiles* **goyim** heard this,
they *were glad* **cheered,**
and glorified the word of *the Lord* **Adonay:**
and as many as were ordained to eternal life
believed **trusted.**
49 And the word of *the Lord* **Adonay**
was *published* **borne** throughout all the region.
50 But the *Jews stirred up* **Yah Hudiym enraged**
the *devout* **venerating** and *honourable* **well—respected**
women,
and the *chief* **preeminent** men of the city,
and *raised* **roused** *up* persecution
against Paul **upon Paulos** and *Barnabas* **Bar Nabi,**
and *expelled* **cast** them out of their *coasts* **boundaries.**
51 But they shook off the dust of their feet
against **upon** them,

and came unto Iconium.
52 And the disciples were filled **full** with *joy* **cheer**,
and with the Holy *Ghost* **Spirit.**

MINISTRY IN THE ICONIUM SYNAGOGUE

14 And it *came to pass* **became** in Iconium,
that they *went* **entered** both together
into the synagogue of the *Jews* **Yah Hudiym**,
and *so* **thus** spake, **so** that a *great* **vast** multitude
both of the *Jews* **Yah Hudiym**
and also of the *Greeks believed* **Hellenists trusted.**
2 But the *unbelieving Jews* **distrusting Yah Hudiym**
stirred up **roused** the *Gentiles* **goyim**,
and *made* **vilified** their *minds evil affected* **souls**
against the brethren.
3 Long time therefore *abode* **indeed tarried** they
speaking boldly **having boldness** in *the Lord* **Adonay**,
which *gave testimony* **witnessed**
unto the word of his *grace* **charism**,
and *granted* **gave** signs and *wonders* **omens**
to *be done by* **become through** their hands.
4 But the multitude of the city was *divided* **schismed**:
and **indeed** part held with the *Jews* **Yah Hudiym**,
and part with the apostles.

MINISTRY IN LYCAONIA

5 And when
there *was an assault made* **became a violent impulse**
both of the *Gentiles* **goyim**,
and also of the *Jews* **Yah Hudiym** with their *rulers* **archs**,
to *use* **insult** them *despitefully*, and to stone them,
6 They were ware of it, and fled unto Lystra and Derbe,
cities of Lycaonia,
and unto the region *that lieth* round about:
7 And there they *preached the gospel* **evangelized.**

PAULOS HEALS ONE LAME

8 And there sat a *certain* man at Lystra,
impotent in his feet,
being *a cripple* **lame** from his mother's womb,
who never **ever** had walked:
9 *The same* **This one** heard *Paul* **Paulos** speak:
who *stedfastly beholding* **staring at** him,
and perceiving that he had *faith* **trust** to be *healed* **saved**,
10 Said with a *loud* **mega** voice,
Stand upright **Arise straight** on thy feet.
And he leaped and walked.
11 And when the *people* **multitude** saw
what *Paul* **Paulos** had done,
they lifted *up* their voices,
saying **wording** in *the speech of Lycaonia* **Lycaoniy**,
The *gods* **elohim** are *come down* **descended** to us
in the likeness of *men* **humanity**.
12 And **indeed**
they called *Barnabas* **Bar Nabi**, *Jupiter* **Zeus**;
and *Paul* **Paulos**, *Mercurius* **Hermes**,
because **since** he was
the *chief speaker* **governor of words**.
13 Then the priest of *Jupiter* **Zeus**,
which was before their city,
brought *oxen* **bulls** and *garlands* **wreaths** unto the gates,
and *would have done* **willed to** sacrifice
with the *people* **multitude**.
14 Which when the apostles,
Barnabas **Bar Nabi** and *Paul* **Paulos**, heard of,
they *rent* **ripped** their *clothes* **garments**,
and *ran in among* **leaped unto** the *people* **multitude**,
crying out,
15 And *saying* **wording**,
Sirs **Men**, why do ye these *things*?
We also are *men* **humans** of like passions with you,
and *preach* **evangelize** unto you
that ye should turn from these vanities
unto the living *God* **Elohim**,
which made heaven, and earth, and the sea,
and all *things* that are therein:
16 Who in *times past* **generations departed**
suffered **allowed** all *nations* **goyim**
to walk in their own ways.
17 *Nevertheless* **Though** he left not himself
without witness **unwitnessed**,
in that he did good,
and gave us rain from heaven, and fruitful seasons,
filling our hearts
with *food* **nourishment** and *gladness* **rejoicing**.
18 And *with* **wording** these *sayings*
scarce **with difficulty**
restrained **shabbathized** they the *people* **multitude**,
that they had not *done sacrifice* **sacrificed** unto them.

PAULOS STONED

19 And there came *thither certain Jews* **some Yah Hudiym**
from Antioch and Iconium,
who *persuaded* **convinced** the *people* **multitude**,
and having stoned *Paul* **Paulos**,
drew **dragged** him out of the city,
supposing **presuming** he had *been dead* **died**.
See: 2 Corinthians 12:1—3
20 Howbeit,
as the disciples *stood round about* **surrounded** him,
he rose *up*, and *came* **entered** into the city:
and **on** the *next day* **morrow**
he departed with *Barnabas* **Bar Nabi** to Derbe.
21 And when they had *preached the gospel* **evangelized**
to that city,
and had *taught* **discipled** many,
they returned *again* to Lystra,
and to Iconium, and Antioch,
22 *Confirming* **Establishing** the souls of the disciples,
and *exhorting* **beseeching** them
to *continue* **remain** in the *faith* **trust**,
and that we must through much tribulation
enter into the *kingdom* **sovereigndom** of *God* **Elohim**.

ECCLESIA ELDERS

23 And when they had *ordained* **voted** them elders
in every *church* **ecclesia**,
and had prayed with fasting,
they *commended* **set** them **forth** to *the Lord* **Adonay**,
on **in** whom they *believed* **trusted.**
24 And after they had passed throughout Pisidia,
they came to Pamphylia.
25 And when they had *preached* **spoken** the word
in Perga,
they *went down* **descended** into Attalia:
26 And thence sailed to Antioch,
from whence they had been *recommended* **delivered**
to the *grace* **charism** of *God* **Elohim**
for **unto** the work which they fulfilled.
27 And when they were come,
and had gathered the *church* **ecclesia** together,
they *rehearsed* **evangelized**
all that God **as much as Elohim** had done with them,
and how he had opened the *door* **portal** of *faith* **trust**
unto the *Gentiles* **goyim**.
28 And there they *abode long* **tarried no little** time
with the disciples.

YAH HUDIYM DOCTRINATE CUSTOM OF MOSHEH

15 And *certain* **some** men
which came down from *Judaea* **Yah Hudah**
taught **doctrinated** the brethren, and said,
Except **Unless** ye be circumcised
after the *manner* **custom** of *Moses* **Mosheh**,
ye cannot be saved.

PAULOS AND BAR NABI ASCEND TO YERU SHALEM

2 When therefore *Paul* **Paulos** and *Barnabas* **Bar Nabi**
had no small *dissension* **riot** and disputation
become with them,
they *determined* **ordained**
that *Paul* **Paulos** and *Barnabas* **Bar Nabi**,
and *certain* **some** other *of them*
should *go up* **ascend** to *Jerusalem* **Yeru Shalem**
unto the apostles and elders about this question.
3 And **therefore indeed**
being *brought on their way* **forwarded**
by the *church* **ecclesia**,
they passed through
Phenice **Phoinix** and *Samaria* **Shomeron**,
declaring
the *conversion* **turning around** of the *Gentiles* **goyim**:
and they caused *great joy* **mega cheer**
unto all the brethren.
4 And when they were come to *Jerusalem* **Yeru Shalem**,
they were received of the *church* **ecclesia**,
and of the apostles and elders,

and they *declared* **evangelized**
all things that God **as much as Elohim**
had done with them.
5 But there rose *up*
certain **some** of the *sect* **heresy** of the Pharisees
which *believed* **trusted**, *saying* **wording**,
That it was *needful* **necessary** to circumcise them,
and to *command* **evangelize** them
to *keep* **guard** the *law* **torah** of *Moses* **Mosheh**.
6 And the apostles and elders *came* **assembled** together
for to *consider of* **know about** this *matter* **word**.

PETROS' MESSAGE

7 And when there had *been* **become**
much *disputing* **disputation**,
Peter **Petros** rose *up*, and said unto them,
Men and brethren,
ye *know* **understand** how
that *a good while ago* **from ancient days**
God made choice **Elohim selected** among us,
that the *Gentiles by* **goyim through** my mouth
should hear the word of the *gospel* **evangelism**,
and *believe* **trust**.
8 And *God* **Elohim**,
which knoweth the hearts **all heart—knowing**,
bare them witness,
giving them the Holy *Ghost* **Spirit**,
even **exactly** as *he did* unto us;
9 And *put no difference* **distinguished not**
between us and them,
purifying their hearts by *faith* **trust**.
10 Now therefore why *tempt* **test** ye *God* **Elohim**,
to put a yoke upon the neck of the disciples,
which neither our fathers nor we were able to bear?
11 But we *believe* **trust**
that through the *grace* **charism**
of *the Lord Jesus Christ* **Adonay Yah Shua Messiah**
we shall be saved, *even* **in manner** as they.

PAULOS' AND BAR NABI'S WITNESS

12 Then all the multitude *kept silence* **hushed**,
and *gave audience* **hearkened**
to *Barnabas* **Bar Nabi** and *Paul* **Paulos**,
declaring
what miracles **as many signs** and *wonders* **omens**
God **Elohim** had *wrought* **done**
among the *Gentiles by* **goyim through** them.

YAAQOVOS' WITNESS

13 And after they had *held their peace* **hushed**,
James **Yaaqovos** answered, *saying* **wording**,
Men and brethren, hearken unto me:
14 *Simeon* **Shimon** hath declared
how God **exactly as Elohim** at the first
did visit the *Gentiles* **goyim**,
to take out of them a people *for* **unto** his name.
15 And to this
agree **symphonize** the words of the prophets;
exactly as it *is written* **scribed**,
16 After this I *will* **shall** return,
and *will build again* **shall rebuild**
the tabernacle of David,
which is fallen *down*;
and I *will build again* **shall rebuild**
the *ruins* **diggings** *thereof*,
and I *will* **shall** set it *up*:
17 That the *residue* **rest** of *men* **humanity**
might seek after *the Lord* **Yah Veh**,
and all the *Gentiles* **goyim**,
upon whom my name is called,
saith the Lord **wordeth Yah Veh**,
who doeth all these *things*.
Amos 9:11, 12
18 Known unto *God* **Elohim**
are all his works from the *beginning of the world* **eons**.
19 Wherefore *my sentence is* **I judge**,
that we *trouble not* **harrass** them **no further**,
which from among the *Gentiles* **goyim**
are turned to *God* **Elohim**:
20 But that we *write* **epistolize** unto them,
that they abstain from pollutions of idols,
and from *fornication* **whoredom**,
and from *things* **strangled**, and from blood.
21 For *Moses* **Mosheh**
of old time **from ancient generations**
hath in every city them that preach him,
being read in the synagogues
every *sabbath day* **shabbath**.
22 Then *pleased it* the apostles and elders **thought well**
with the whole *church* **ecclesia**,
to send *chosen* **select** men of their own company
to Antioch
with *Paul* **Paulos** and *Barnabas* **Bar Nabi**; *namely*,
Juda surnamed Barsabas **Yah Hudah called Bar Sabah**,
and Silas, *chief* **governing** men among the brethren:
23 And they *wrote letters by* **scribed through** them
after this manner **thus**;
The apostles and elders and brethren *send greeting*
unto the brethren which are of the *Gentiles* **goyim**
in Antioch and Syria and Cilicia, **Cheers**.
24 *Forasmuch* **Since** as we have heard,
that *certain* **some** which went out from us
have troubled you with words,
subverting **upsetting** your souls, *saying* **wording**,
Ye must be circumcised,
and, *keep* **Guard** the *law:* **torah!**
to whom we gave no such *commandment* **charge**:
25 *It seemed good unto us* **We thought well**,
being assembled **having become**
with one accord **in unanimity**,
to send *chosen* **select** men unto you
with our beloved *Barnabas* **Bar Nabi** and *Paul* **Paulos**,
26 *Men* **Humans**
that have *hazarded* **surrendered** their *lives* **souls**
for the name
of our *Lord Jesus Christ* **Adonay Yah Shua Messiah**.
27 We have *sent* **apostolized** therefore
Judas **Yah Hudah** and Silas,
who shall also *tell* **evangelize** you the same *things*
by mouth **through word**.
28 For *it seemed good to*
the Holy *Ghost* **Spirit**, and *to us*, **we thought well**
to *lay* **put** upon you no *greater* **more** burden
than **except** these necessary *things*;
29 That ye abstain
from *meats offered to idols* **idol sacrifices**,
and from blood, and from *things* strangled,
and from *fornication* **whoredom**:
from which if ye keep yourselves,
ye shall *do* **transact** well.
Fare ye well.
30 *So* **Therefore indeed**
when they were *dismissed* **released**,
they came to Antioch:
and when they had gathered the multitude together,
they *delivered* **gave over** the epistle:
31 Which when they had read,
they *rejoiced for* **cheered over** the consolation.
32 And *Judas* **Yah Hudah** and Silas,
being prophets also themselves,
exhorted **besought** the brethren
with **through** many words,
and *confirmed* **established** them.
33 And after they *tarried there a space* **had done time**,
they were *let go* **released** in *peace* **shalom**
from the brethren unto the apostles.
34 Notwithstanding
it pleased Silas **thought well** to abide there still.

PAULOS' SECOND JOURNEY

35 *Paul* **Paulos** also and *Barnabas* **Bar Nabi**
continued **tarried** in Antioch,
teaching **doctrinating** and *preaching* **evangelizing**
the word of *the Lord* **Adonay**, with many others also.
36 And some days after
Paul **Paulos** said unto *Barnabas* **Bar Nabi**,
Let us *go again* **now turn around**
and visit our brethren in every city
where **wherein** we have *preached* **evangelized**
the word of *the Lord* **Adonay**,
and see — how they do.
37 And *Barnabas determined* **Bar Nabi counseled**
to take with them *John* **Yahn**,
whose surname was Mark **who was called Markos**.

PAULOS AND BAR NABI SEPARATE

38 But *Paul thought not good* **Paulos deemed unworthy**
to take him with them,
who departed from them from Pamphylia,
and *went* **came** not with them to the work.
39 And *the contention was so sharp* **an agitation became**
between them,
so that they *departed asunder* **separated**
one from the other:
and so *Barnabas* **Bar Nabi** took *Mark* **Markos**,
and sailed unto Cyprus;
40 And *Paul chose* **Paulos selected** Silas, and departed,
being *recommended* **surrendered** by the brethren
unto the *grace* **charism** of *God* **Elohim**.
41 And he *went* **passed** through Syria and Cilicia,
confirming the *churches* **ecclesiae**.

TIMO THEOS JOINS PAULOS

16 Then *came* **arrived** he *to* **in** Derbe and Lystra:
and, behold, a *certain* disciple was there,
named *Timotheus* **Timo Theos**,
the son of a *certain* woman,
which was a Jewess, and believed
a trustworthy Yah Hudiy;
but his father was *a Greek* **Hellene**:
2 Which was *well reported* **witnessed** of
by the brethren that were at Lystra and Iconium.
3 *Him would Paul have* **Paulos willed him**
to go forth with him;
and took and circumcised him
because of the *Jews* **Yah Hudiym**
which were in those *quarters* **places**:
for they knew all that his father was a *Greek* **Hellene**.
4 And as they went through the cities,
they delivered them the *decrees* **dogmas**
for to *keep* **guard**,
that were *ordained* **judged** of the apostles and elders
which were at *Jerusalem* **Yeru Shalem**.
5 *And so* **Therefore indeed** were the *churches* **ecclesiae**
established **solidified** in the *faith* **trust**,
and *increased* **superabounded** in number daily.

PAULOS' VISION

6 Now when they had gone throughout Phrygia
and the **Galatian** region *of Galatia*,
and were forbidden of the Holy *Ghost* **Spirit**
to *preach* **speak** the word in Asia,
7 After they were come to Mysia,
they *assayed* **tested** to go into Bithynia:
but the Spirit *suffered* **allowed** them not.
8 And they passing by Mysia
came down **descended** to Troas.
9 And a vision appeared to *Paul* **Paulos**
in **through** the night;
There stood a man *of Macedonia* — **a Macedonian**
and prayed **who besought** him, *saying* **wording**,
Come over **Pass through** into Macedonia, and help us.
10 And after he had seen the vision,
immediately **straightway**
we *endeavoured* **sought** to go into Macedonia,
assuredly gathering **concluding**
that *the Lord* **Adonay** had called us
for to *preach the gospel* **evangelize** unto them.
11 Therefore *loosing* **embarking** from Troas,
we came *with a straight course* **straightly** to Samothracia,
and *the* next *day* to Neapolis;

ON TO PHILIPPI

12 And from thence to Philippi,
which is the *chief* **preeminent** city
of that part of Macedonia, and a colony:
and we were in that city
abiding certain **tarrying some** days.
13 And on the *sabbath* **day of the shabbaths**
we went out of the city by a *river* **stream** side,
where prayer was *wont* **presumed** to be made;
and we sat down, and spake unto the women
which *resorted thither* **came together**.
14 And a *certain* woman named Lydia,
a seller of purple, of the city of Thyatira,
which *worshipped God* **venerated Elohim**, heard us:
whose heart *the Lord* **Adonay** opened,
that she *attended* **heeded** unto the *things* **those**
which were spoken of by *Paul* **Paulos**.
15 And when she was baptized, and her household,
she *besought* **entreated** us, *saying* **wording**,
If ye have judged me
to be *faithful* **trustworthy** to *the Lord* **Adonay**,
come **enter** into my house, and abide *there*.
And she constrained us.

PAULOS EVANGELIZES OUT A SPIRIT OF PYTHON

16 And it *came to pass* **became**, as we went to prayer,
a *certain damsel* **lass**
possessed with **having** a spirit of *divination* **Python**
met us,
which *brought* **presented** her *masters* **adonim**
much *gain* **work** by soothsaying:
17 The same followed *Paul* **Paulos** and us,
and cried, *saying* **wording**,
These *men* **humans**
are the servants of *the most high God* **El Elyon**,
which *shew* **evangelize** unto us the way of salvation.
18 And this did she many days.
But *Paul* **Paulos**, being grieved,
turned and said to the spirit,
I *command* **evangelize** thee
in the name of *Jesus Christ* **Yah Shua Messiah**
to come out of her.
And he came out the same hour.
19 And when her *masters* **adonim** saw
that the *hope* **hopes** of their *gains was* **work were** gone,
they *caught Paul* **took Paulos** and Silas,
and drew them into the *marketplace* **market**
unto the *rulers* **archs**,
20 And brought them to the *magistrates* **strategoi**, saying,
These *men, being Jews* **humans — Yah Hudiym**,
do exceedingly trouble **utterly disturb** our city,
21 And *teach* **evangelize** customs,
which are not *lawful* **allowed** for us to receive,
neither to *observe* **do**, being Romans.
22 And the multitude *rose up* **stood** together against them:
and the *magistrates* **strategoi**
rent **tore** off their *clothes* **garments**,
and *commanded* **summoned** to *beat* **bastinado** them.

PAULOS AND SILAS UNDER GUARD

23 And when they had
laid **put** many *stripes* **plagues** upon them,
they cast them into *prison* **the guardhouse**,
charging **evangelizing** the *jailor* **prison guard**
to *keep* **guard** them *safely* **securely**:
24 Who,
having *received* **taken** such *a charge* **an evangelism**,
thrust **cast** them into the inner *prison* **guardhouse**,
and *made* **secured** their feet *fast* in the *stocks* **staves**.
25 And at midnight *Paul* **Paulos** and Silas prayed,
and *sang praises* **hymned** unto *God* **Elohim**:
and the prisoners heard them.

MEGA QUAKE SHAKES THE PRISON

26 And suddenly
there *was* **became** a *great earthquake* **mega quake**,
so that the foundations of the prison were shaken:
and immediately all the *doors* **portals** were opened,
and every one's bands were loosed.
27 And the *keeper* **guard** of the prison
awaking out of his sleep **becoming awake**,
and seeing the *prison doors* **guardhouse portals** open,
he drew out his sword,
and *would have killed* **was about to take** himself **out**,
supposing **presuming**
that the prisoners had *been fled* **escaped**.
28 But *Paul cried* **Paulos called** with a *loud* **mega** voice
saying **wording**, *Do* **Transact** thyself no *harm* **evil**:
for we are all here.
29 Then he *called* **asked** for a light,
and *sprang in* **leaped**, and *came* **became** trembling,
and *fell down* **prostrated** before *Paul* **Paulos** and Silas,
30 And brought them out, and said,
Sirs **Adonim**, what must I do to be saved?
31 And they said, *Believe* **Trust**
on *the Lord Jesus Christ* **Adonay Yah Shua Messiah**,
and thou shalt be saved, and thy house.
32 And they spake unto him
the word of *the Lord* **Adonay**,

and to all that were in his house.
33 And he took them **in** the same hour of the night,
and *washed* **bathed** their *stripes* **plagues**;
and was baptized, he and all his,
straightway **immediately**.
34 And when he had brought them into his house,
he set *meat before them* **forth a table**,
and *rejoiced* **jumped for joy**,
believing **trusting** in *God* **Elohim** with all his house.
35 And when it *was* **became** day,
the *magistrates* **strategoi**
sent **apostolized** the *serjeants* **staff bearers**,
saying **wording**, *Let* **Release** those *men go* **humans**.
36 And the *keeper of the prison* **prison guard**
told **evangelized** this *saying* **word** to *Paul* **Paulos**,
The *magistrates* **strategoi** have sent to *let* **release** you *go*:
now therefore depart, and go in *peace* **shalom**.
37 But *Paul* **Paulos** said unto them,
They have *beaten* **flogged** us *openly* **publicly**
uncondemned **unsentenced**,
being *Romans* **Roman humans**,
and have cast us into *prison* **the guardhouse**;
and now do they *thrust* **cast** us out *privily* **secretly**?
nay *verily* **indeed**;
but let them come themselves and *fetch* **lead** us out.
38 And the *serjeants* **staff bearers**
told **evangelized** these *words* **rhema**
unto the *magistrates* **strategoi**:
and they *feared* **awed**,
when they heard that they were Romans.
39 And they came and *besought* **entreated** them,
and led them out,
and *desired* **asked** them to depart out of the city.
40 And they went out of the *prison* **guardhouse**,
and entered *into the house of* **unto** Lydia:
and when they had seen the brethren,
they *comforted* **consoled** them, and departed.

ON TO THESSALONIKEE

17 Now when they had passed through
Amphipolis and Apollonia,
they came to *Thessalonica* **Thessalonikee**,
where was a synagogue of the *Jews* **Yah Hudiym**:
2 And *Paul* **Paulos**, as his *manner* **custom** *was*,
went **entered** in unto them,
and three *sabbath days* **shabbaths**
reasoned with them out of the scriptures,
3 Opening and *alleging* **setting forth**,
that *Christ* **the Messiah** must needs have suffered,
and risen *again* from the dead;
and that this *Jesus* **Yah Shua**,
whom I *preach* **evangelize** unto you,
is *Christ* **the Messiah**.
4 And some of them *believed* **confided**,
and *consorted* **associated** with *Paul* **Paulos** and Silas;
and of the *devout Greeks* **venerating Hellenes**
a *great* **vast** multitude,
and of the *chief* **preeminent** women not a few.
5 But the
Jews which believed not **distrusting Yah Hudiym**,
moved with envy **being zealous**,
took unto them *certain lewd fellows* **some evil men**
of the baser sort — **forum debaters**,
and *gathered* **assembled** a *company* **multitude**,
and *set all* **tumulted** the city *on an uproar*,
and *assaulted* **stood by** the house of Jason,
and sought to bring them out to the *people* **public**.
6 And when they found them not,
they *drew* **dragged** Jason and *certain* **some** brethren
unto the *rulers of the city* **politarchees**, crying,
These that have *turned* **roused** the world *upside down*
are *come hither* **present** also; Whom Jason hath received:
and these all *do* **transact** contrary
to the *decrees* **dogmas** of *Caesar* **the Kaisar**,
saying **wording** that there is another *king* **sovereign**,
one Jesus **Yah Shua**.
8 And they *troubled* **agitated** the *people* **multitude**
and the *rulers of the city* **politarchees**,
when they heard these *things*.
9 And when they had taken *security* **sufficient** of Jason,
and of the *other* **rest**, they *let them go* **released them**.

ON TO BEREA

10 And the brethren *immediately* **straightway**
sent away Paul **dispatched Paulos** and Silas
by **through** night unto Berea:
who coming *thither*
went into the synagogue of the *Jews* **Yah Hudiym**.
11 These were more *noble* **wellborn**
than those in *Thessalonica* **Thessalonikee**,
in that they received the word
with all *readiness of mind* **eagerness**,
and *searched* **examined** the scriptures daily,
whether those *things were so* **be thus**.
12 Therefore **indeed** many of them *believed* **trusted**;
also of *honourable* **well—respected** women
which were *Greeks* **Hellenists**, and of men, not a few.
13 But when
the *Jews* **Yah Hudiym** of *Thessalonica* **Thessalonikee**
had knowledge that the word of *God* **Elohim**
was *preached* **evangelized** of *Paul* **Paulos** at Berea,
they came *thither* **there** *also*,
and *stirred* **shook** *up* the *people* **multitude**.
14 And then *immediately* **straightway**
the brethren *sent away Paul* **apostolized Paulos forth**
to go as *it were to* **upon** the sea:
but Silas and *Timotheus* **Timo Theos** abode there still.

ON TO ATHENS

15 And they that *conducted Paul* **seated Paulos**
brought him unto Athens:
and *receiving* **taking** a *commandment* **misvah**
unto Silas and *Timotheus* **Timo Theos**
for to come to him *with all speed* **most quickly**,
they departed.
16 Now while *Paul* **Paulos**
waited for **awaited** them at Athens,
his spirit *was stirred* **agitated** in him,
when he *saw* **observed** the city
wholly given to idolatry **being downright idolatrous**.
17 Therefore **indeed**
disputed **reasoned** he in the synagogue
with the *Jews* **Yah Hudiym**,
and with the *devout* **venerating** persons,
and in the market daily with them that met with him.
18 Then *certain* **some** philosophers of the Epicureans,
and of the Stoicks, encountered him.
And some *said* **spake**,
What *will* **willeth** this *babbler say* **spermalogist to word**?
other some, He *seemeth* **thinketh well**
to be *a setter forth* **an evangelizer**
of strange *gods* **demons**:
because he *preached* **evangelized** unto them
Jesus **Yah Shua**, and the resurrection.
19 And they took him, and brought him unto Areopagus,
saying **wording**,
May **Can** we know what this new doctrine,
whereof thou speakest, is?
20 For thou *bringest* **bearest**
certain **somewhat** strange *things* to our *ears* **hearing**:
we *would* **will to** know therefore
what these *things* will **to** mean.
21 (For all the Athenians and strangers
which were **residing** there
spent their time **leisured** in *nothing else* **none other**,
but either to *tell* **word**, or to hear some new *thing*.)

PAULOS' AREOPAGUS MESSAGE

22 Then *Paul* **Paulos**
stood in the midst of *Mars' hill* **Areopagus**,
and said, *Ye men of Athens* **Men — Athenians**,
I *perceive* **observe** that in all *things*
ye are *too superstitious* **demon—dreaders**.
23 For as I passed *by* **through**,
and *beheld* **considered**
your *devotions* **objects of reverence**,
I found *an altar with this inscription* **a bamah epigraphed**,
TO THE UNKNOWN *GOD* **EL**
Whom therefore
ye *ignorantly worship* **unknowingly revere**,
him *declare* **evangelize** I unto you.
24 *God* **Elohim** that made the *world* **cosmos**
and all *things* therein,
seeing that he is Lord **this one being Adonay**

of heaven and earth,
dwelleth **settleth** not
in *temples made with hands* **handmade naves**;
25 Neither is *worshipped* **cured**
with men's **by human hands**
as though he needed *any thing* **aught**,
seeing he giveth to all life,
and *breath* **puffing**, and all *things*;
26 And hath made of one blood
all *nations* **goyim** of *men* **humanity**
for to *dwell* **settle** on all the face of the earth,
and hath *determined* **decreed** the times
before appointed **and prearranged the seasons**,
and the *bounds* **boundaries**
of their *habitation* **settlement**;
27 That they should seek *the Lord* **Yah Veh**,
if *haply* **then indeed** they might *feel after* **touch** him,
and find him,
though he be not far from *every* **each** one of us:
Yesha Yah 55:6
28 For in him we live, and *move* **stir**,
and *have our being* **be**;
as *certain* **some** also of your own poets have said,
For we are also his *offspring* **genos**.
29 *Forasmuch then* **Therefore**
as we are **being** the *offspring* **genos** of *God* **Elohim**,
we *ought* **are indebted** not to *think* **presume**
that the *Godhead* **Elohimness**
is **be** like unto gold, or silver, or stone,
graven **etched** by *art* **techniques**
and *man's device* **human deliberation**.
30 *And* **Therefore indeed**
the times of this *ignorance* **unknowingness**
God winked at **Elohim overlooked**;
but now *commandeth* **evangelizeth** all *men* **humanity**
every where to repent:
31 Because he hath *appointed* **set** a day,
in the which he *will* **shall be about to** judge the world
in *righteousness* **justness**
by that man whom he hath *ordained* **decreed**;
whereof he hath given assurance **having presented trust**
unto all *men*,
in that he hath raised him from the dead.
32 And when they heard of the resurrection of the dead,
some *mocked* **indeed jeered**: and others said,
We *will* **shall** hear thee again *of* **concerning** this *matter*.
33 *So Paul* **Thus Paulos** departed from among them.
34 Howbeit *certain* **some** men *clave unto* **joined** him,
and *believed* **trusted**:
among the which was
Dionysius the *Areopagite* **Areopagiy**,
and a woman named Damaris, and others with them.

ON TO CORINTH

18 After these *things*
Paul departed **Paulos separated** from Athens,
and came to Corinth;
2 And found a *certain Jew* **Yah Hudiy** named Aquila,
born in Pontos **a Pontican by genos**,
lately **recently** come from Italy,
with his *wife* **woman** Priscilla;
(because that Claudius had *commanded* **ordained**
all *Jews* **Yah Hudiym** to *depart* **separate** from Rome):
and came unto them.
3 And because he was *of the same craft* **a fellow artisan**,
he abode with them, and *wrought* **worked**:
for by their *occupation* **art**
they were *tentmakers* **tabernaclemakers**.
4 And he reasoned in the synagogue
every *sabbath* **shabbath**,
and *persuaded* **convinced**
the *Jews* **Yah Hudiym** and the *Greeks* **Hellenes**.
5 And when Silas and *Timotheus* **Timo Theos**
were come **down** from Macedonia,
Paul **Paulos** was *pressed* **held** in the spirit,
and *testified* **witnessed** to the *Jews* **Yah Hudiym**
that *Jesus* **Yah Shua** was *Christ* **the Messiah**.
6 And when they opposed themselves,
and blasphemed,
he shook his *raiment* **garment**, and said unto them,
Your blood be upon your own heads; I am *clean* **pure**;
from *henceforth* **now on**
I *will* **shall** go unto the *Gentiles* **goyim**.
7 And he departed thence,
and *entered into* **came to**
a certain man's **someone's** house, named Justus,
one that *worshipped God* **venerated Elohim**,
whose house joined *hard to* the synagogue.
8 And Crispus, the *chief ruler* **arch** of the synagogue,
believed **trusted** on *the Lord* **Adonay** with all his house;
and many of the Corinthians hearing *believed* **trusted**,
and were baptized.
9 Then *spake the Lord* **said Adonay** to *Paul* **Paulos**
in the night *by* **through** a vision,
Be **Awe** not *afraid*, but speak,
and *hold* **hush** not *thy peace*:
10 *For I am* **Because I AM** with thee,
and no *man* **one** shall *set* **put** on thee to *hurt* **vilify** thee:
for **because** I have much people in this city.
11 And he *continued* **sat** there a year and six months,
teaching **doctrinating** the word of *God* **Elohim**
among them.
12 And when Gallio was the *deputy* **proconsul** of Achaia,
the *Jews made insurrection* **Yah Hudiym rushed**
with one accord **in unanimity** against *Paul* **Paulos**,
and brought him to the *judgment seat* **bamah**,
13 *Saying* **Wording**, This *fellow* **one** persuadeth men
to *worship God* **venerate Elohim**
contrary to the *law* **torah**.
14 And when *Paul* **Paulos** was now
about to open his mouth,
Gallio said unto the *Jews* **Yah Hudiym**,
Therefore indeed,
If it were *a* **some** matter of *wrong* **injustice**
or *wicked lewdness* **evil villany**, O ye *Jews* **Yah Hudiym**,
reason would **according to word,**
that I should *bear with* **tolerate** you:
15 But if it be a question *of* **concerning** words and names,
and of your *law* **torah**, look ye to it;
for I will *be no* **to not be** judge of *such matters* **these**.
16 And he *drave* **dismissed** them
from the *judgment seat* **bamah**.
17 Then all the *Greeks* **Hellenes** took Sosthenes,
the *chief ruler* **arch** of the synagogue,
and *beat* **struck** him
before **in front of** the *judgment seat* **bamah**.
And Gallio *cared* **concerned himself**
for none of those *things*.

PAULOS' VOW

18 And *Paul after this tarried there* **Paulos abode** yet
a *good while* **long day**,
and then *took his leave of* **bade bye bye to** the brethren,
and sailed thence into Syria,
and with him Priscilla and Aquila;
having shorn his head in Cenchrea: for he had a vow.
19 And he *came to* **arrived in** Ephesus,
and left them there:
but he himself entered into the synagogue,
and reasoned with the *Jews* **Yah Hudiym**.
20 When they *desired* **asked** him
to *tarry longer* **abide more** time with them,
he consented not;
21 But bade them *farewell* **bye bye**, saying,
I must *by all means* **most certainly**
keep **do** this *feast* **celebration**
that cometh in *Jerusalem* **Yeru Shalem**:
but I *will* **shall** return again unto you,
if *God will* **Elohim willeth**.
And he *sailed* **embarked** from Ephesus.
22 And when he had
landed at Caesarea **come down to Kaisaria**,
and *gone up* **ascended**, and saluted the *church* **ecclesia**,
he *went down* **descended** to Antioch.
23 And after he had *spent* **done** some time there,
he departed,
and *went over* **passed through**
all the *country of Galatia* **Galatian region** and Phrygia
in *order* **sequence**,
strengthening **establishing** all the disciples.

APOLLOS IN EPHESUS

24 And a *certain Jew* **Yah Hudiy** named Apollos,
born at Alexandria **— an Alexandrian by genos**,
an *eloquent* **orator** man,
and *mighty* **able** in the scriptures,
came to **arrived in** Ephesus.
25 This *man* **one** was *instructed* **catechized**
in the way of *the Lord* **Adonay**;
and being *fervent* **zealous** in *the* spirit,
he spake and *taught diligently* **doctrinated exactly**
the things of the Lord **concerning Adonay**,
knowing **understanding** only the baptism of *John* **Yahn**.
26 And he began to *speak boldly* **have boldness**
in the synagogue:
whom when Aquila and Priscilla had heard,
they took him *unto them*, and expounded unto him
the way of *God* **Elohim** more *perfectly* **exactly**.
27 And when he *was disposed* **had willed**
to pass **through** into Achaia,
the brethren *wrote* **scribed**,
exhorting **encouraging** the disciples to receive him:
who, when he was come, *helped* **considered** them much
which had *believed* **trusted** through *grace* **charism**:
28 For he *mightily* **vigorously**
convinced **overwhelmed** the *Jews* **Yah Hudiym**,
and that publickly,
shewing *by* **through** the scriptures
that *Jesus* **Yah Shua** was *Christ* **the Messiah**.

PAULOS AT EPHESUS

19 And it *came to pass* **became**, that,
while Apollos was at Corinth,
Paul **Paulos** having passed through the upper *coasts* **parts**
came to Ephesus:
and finding *certain* **some** disciples,
2 He said unto them,
Have ye *received* **taken** the Holy *Ghost* **Spirit**
since ye *believed* **trusted**?
And they said unto him,
We have not *so much as* **even** heard
whether there be any Holy *Ghost* **Spirit**.
3 And he said unto them,
Unto what then were ye baptized?
And they said, Unto *John*'s **Yahn's** baptism.
4 Then said *Paul* **Paulos**,
John verily **Yahn indeed**
baptized *with* the baptism of repentance,
saying **wording** unto the people,
that they should *believe on* **trust in** him
which should come after him,
that is, *on Christ Jesus* **in the Messiah Yah Shua**.
5 When they heard *this*,
they were baptized
in the name of *the Lord Jesus* **Adonay Yah Shua**.
6 And when *Paul* **Paulos**
had *laid* **put** his hands upon them,
the Holy *Ghost* **Spirit** came on them;
and they spake with tongues, and prophesied.
7 And all the men were about twelve.
8 And he *went* **entered** into the synagogue,
and spake boldly **having boldness**
for the space of **unto** three months,
disputing **reasoning** and *persuading* **convincing**
the things
concerning the *kingdom* **sovereigndom** of *God* **Elohim**.
9 But when *divers* **some** were hardened,
and *believed not* **distrusted**,
but *spake evil of* **vilified** that way
before **in the sight of** the multitude,
he departed from them,
and *separated* **set apart** the disciples,
disputing **dialoguing** daily in the school of one Tyrannus.
10 And this *continued* **became**
by the space of **unto** two years;
so that all they which *dwelt* **settled** in Asia
heard the word of *the Lord Jesus* **Adonay Yah Shua**,
both *Jews* **Yah Hudiym** and *Greeks* **Hellenes**.

ELOHIM'S DYNAMIS THROUGH PAULOS

11 And *God* **Elohim**
wrought special miracles **did no ordinary dynamis**
by **through** the hands of *Paul* **Paulos**:
12 So that from his *body* **skin**
were brought unto the *sick* **frail**
handkerchiefs **sudarium** or aprons,
and the diseases *departed* **released** from them,
and the evil spirits went out of them.
13 Then *certain* **some** of the
vagabond Jews **Yah Hudiym wandering around**,
exorcists,
took *upon them* **in hand**
to *call* **name** over them which had evil spirits
the name of *the Lord Jesus* **Adonay Yah Shua**,
saying **wording**, We *adjure* **oath** you by *Jesus* **Yah Shua**
whom *Paul* **Paulos** preacheth.
14 And there were **some** seven sons of *one* Sceva,
a *Jew* **Yah Hudiy**, and *chief of the priests* **archpriest**,
which did so.
15 And the evil spirit answered and said,
Jesus **Yah Shua** I know,
and *Paul* **Paulos** I *know* **understand**;
but who are ye?
16 And the *man* **human** in whom the evil spirit was
leaped on them,
and *overcame* **overlorded** them,
and prevailed against them,
so that they *fled* **escaped** out of that house
naked and *wounded* **traumatized**.
17 And this *was* **became** known
to all the *Jews* **Yah Hudiym** and *Greeks* **Hellenes**
also *dwelling* **settling** at Ephesus;
and *fear* **awe** fell on them all,
and the name of *the Lord Jesus* **Adonay Yah Shua**
was magnified.
18 And many that *believed* **trusted** came,
and *confessed* **avowed**,
and *shewed* **evangelized** their *deeds* **acts**.
19 Many of them also
which *used curious arts* **transacted magic**
brought their *books* **scrolls** together,
and burned them *before* **in the sight of** all *men*:
and they *counted* **reckoned** the price of them,
and found it *fifty thousand pieces* **five myriads** of silver.
20 *So mightily* **Thus powerfully**
grew the word of *God* **Elohim** and prevailed.
21 After these *things* were *ended* **fulfilled**,
Paul purposed **Paulos placed** in the spirit,
when he had passed through Macedonia and Achaia,
to go to *Jerusalem* **Yeru Shalem**, saying,
After I have *been* **become** there, I must also see Rome.
22 So he *sent* **apostolized** into Macedonia
two of them that ministered unto him,
Timotheus **Timo Theos** and Erastus;
but he himself stayed in Asia for a *season* **time**.

TROUBLE OF THE SILVERSMITHS

23 And *the same time* **at that season**
there *arose* **became** no small *stir* **trouble**
about **concerning** that way.
24 For *a certain man* **someone** named Demetrius,
a silversmith,
which made silver *shrines* **naves** for *Diana* **Artemis**,
brought **presented** no small *gain* **work**
unto the *craftsmen* **technicians**;
25 Whom he *called* **gathered** together
with the *workmen* **workers**
of like **concerning such** occupation, and said,
Sirs **Men**, ye *know* **understand** that by this *craft* **work**
we *have our wealth* **prosper**.
26 Moreover ye *see* **observe** and hear,
that not alone at Ephesus,
but *almost* **throughout** nearly all Asia,
this *Paul* **Paulos** hath *persuaded* **convinced**
and *turned away* **removed** much *people* **multitude**,
saying **wording** that they be no *gods* **elohim**,
which *are made with* **become through** hands:
27 So that not only this our *craft* **part**
is **come** in *danger* **peril**
to *be set at nought* **come to disrepute**;
but also that the *temple* **priestal precinct**
of the *great* **mega** goddess *Diana* **Artemis**
should be *despised* **reckoned unto naught**,
and her *magnificence* **majesty**

should be destroyed **be about to be taken down,**
whom all Asia and the world *worshippeth* **venerateth.**
28 And when they heard these *sayings,*
they *were* **became** full of *wrath* **fury,**
and cried out, *saying* **wording,**
Great is Diana **Mega — Artemis** of the Ephesians.
29 And the whole city was filled **full** with confusion:
and having caught Gaius and Aristarchus,
men *of Macedonia* — **Macedonians,**
Paul's companions in travel **Paulos' co—travellers,**
they *rushed with one accord* **ran violently in unanimity**
into the theatre.
30 And when *Paul would have* **Paulos had willed**
entered **to enter** in unto the *people* **public,**
the disciples *suffered* **allowed** him not.
31 And *certain* **some** of the *chief of Asia* **Asiarchs,**
which were his friends, sent unto him,
desiring **entreating** him
that he *would* **should** not *adventure* **give** himself
into the theatre.
32 *Some* **Others indeed** therefore cried one *thing,*
and some another:
for the *assembly* **ecclesia** was confused:
and the more part knew not
wherefore **for what cause** they were come together.
33 And they *drew* **having previously instigated** Alexander
out of the multitude,
the *Jews* **Yah Hudiym** putting him forward.
And Alexander *beckoned* **signaled** with the hand,
and *would* **willed to** have *made his defence* **pleaded**
unto the *people* **public.**
34 But when they knew that he was *a Jew* **Yah Hudiy,**
all with one voice **there became from all**
about the space of **unto** two hours cried out,
Great is Diana **Mega — Artemis** of the Ephesians.
35 And when the *townclerk* **scribe**
had *appeased* **quieted** the *people* **multitude,**
he said, *Ye* men *of Ephesus* — **Ephesians, indeed,**
what *man* **human** is there that knoweth not
how that the city of the Ephesians
is a *worshipper* **nave sweeper**
of the *great* **mega** goddess *Diana* **Artemis,**
and of the *image which fell down from Jupiter* **meteorite?**
36 Seeing then that these *things* **being so**
cannot be spoken against,
ye *ought to* **must** be quiet,
and to *do nothing rashly* **transact naught precipitously.**
37 For ye have brought hither these men,
which are neither
robbers **strippers** of *churches* **priestal precincts,**
nor yet blasphemers of your goddess.
38 *Wherefore* **Therefore indeed,** if Demetrius,
and the *technicians* **artisans** which are with him,
have a *matter* **word** against any man,
the law is open **let them lead a forum debate,**
and there are *deputies* **proconsuls:**
let them *implead* **accuse** one another.
39 But if ye *enquire any thing* **seek aught**
concerning any other matters,
it shall be *determined* **resolved**
in a lawful assembly **by the ecclesia under the torah.**
40 For we are in *danger* **peril**
to be *called in question* **accused**
for **about** this day's *uproar* **riot,**
there being no cause *whereby* **concerning which**
we *may* **can** give *an account* **word**
of this *concourse* **coalition.**
41 And when he had *thus spoken* **said these**
he *dismissed* **released** the *assembly* **ecclesia.**

ON TO MACEDONIA AND HELLAS

20 And after the *uproar was ceased* **tumult paused,**
Paul **Paulos** called unto him the disciples,
and *embraced* **saluted** *them,*
and departed for to go into Macedonia.
2 And when he had
gone over **passed through** those parts,
and had *given* **besought** them
much exhortation **with many words,**
he came into *Greece* **Hellas,**
3 And *there abode* **did** three months.
And when
the Jews laid wait
there became a plotting by the Yah Hudiym
for him,
as he was about to *sail* **embark** into Syria,
he purposed **his decision became**
to return through Macedonia.
4 And there *accompanied* **followed** him into Asia
Sopater *of Berea* — **a Berean;**
and of the *Thessalonians* **Thessalonikeus,**
Aristarchus and Secundus;
and Gaius *of Derbe* **a Derbean,**
and *Timotheus* **Timo Theos;**
and *of Asia* **Asians,** Tychicus and Trophimus.
5 These *going before* **who preceded,**
tarried **abode** for us at Troas.

ON TO TROAS

6 And we sailed away from Philippi
after the days of *unleavened bread* **matsah,**
and came unto them to Troas in five days;
where we *abode* **tarried** seven days.
7 And upon the first *day* of the *week* **shabbath,**
when the disciples *came* **assembled** together
to break bread,
Paul preached **Paulos reasoned** unto them,
ready **about** to depart on the morrow;
and *continued* **stretched** his *speech* **words**
until midnight.
8 And there were many *lights* **lamps**
in the upper *chamber* **loft,**
where they were gathered together.
9 And there sat in a window
a certain young man **youth** named Eutychus,
being fallen **brought down** into a deep sleep:
and as *Paul was long preaching* **Paulos reasoned much,**
he *sunk* **was brought** down *with* **by** sleep,
and fell down from the third loft, and was taken *up* dead.
10 And *Paul went down* **Paulos descended,**
and fell on him,
and embracing him said,
Trouble **Tumult** not yourselves; for his *life* **soul** is in him.
11 When he therefore *was come up* **ascended** again,
and had broken bread, and *eaten* **tasted,**
and *talked a long while* **homologized at length,**
even till *break of day* **dawn,** *so* **thus** he departed.
12 And they brought the *young man* **lad** alive,
and were not a *little comforted* **slight measure consoled.**

ON TO MILETUS

13 And we *went before* **proceeded** to *ship* **the sailer,**
and *sailed* **embarked** unto Assos,
there intending **thence about** to take in *Paul* **Paulos:**
for *so* **thus** had he *appointed* **ordained,**
minding himself **about** to go afoot.
14 And when he *met with* **encountered** us at Assos,
we took him in, and came to Mitylene.
15 And we sailed thence, and *came the* **arrived** next *day*
over against **cast along side opposite** Hios;
and *the next day* **regarding another,** we arrived at Samos,
and *tarried* **abode** at Trogyllium;
and *the* next *day* we came to Miletus.
16 For *Paul* **Paulos**
had *determined* **judged** to sail by Ephesus,
because he would **that it** not **become**
spend the **that he waste** time in Asia:
for he hasted, if it were possible for him,
to be at *Jerusalem* **Yeru Shalem** the day of Pentecost.

PAULOS AND THE EPHESIAN ELDERS

17 And from Miletus he sent to Ephesus,
and called the elders of the *church* **ecclesia.**
18 And when they were come to him, he said unto them,
Ye *know* **understand,**
from the first day
that I came **from which I embarked** into Asia,
after what manner I have *been* **become** with you
at all *seasons* **times,**
19 Serving *the Lord* **Adonay**
with all *humility of mind* **humblemindedness,**
and with many tears, and *temptations* **testings,**
which *befell* **happened to** me
by the *lying in wait* **plotting** of the *Jews* **Yah Hudiym:**

20 And how I *kept back nothing* **withheld naught**
that was *profitable unto you* **beneficial,**
but have shewed **that I have not evangelized unto** you,
and have *taught* **doctrinated** you publickly,
and from house to house,
21 *Testifying* **Witnessing** both to the *Jews* **Yah Hudiym**,
and also to the *Greeks* **Hellenes**,
repentance *toward God* **unto Elohim**,
and *faith toward* **trust unto**
our *Lord Jesus Christ* **Adonay Yah Shua Messiah**.
22 And now, behold,
I go bound in the spirit unto *Jerusalem* **Yeru Shalem**,
not knowing *the things* **those**
that shall *befall* **meet** me there:
23 *Save* **Except** that the Holy *Ghost* **Spirit**
witnesseth in every city,
saying **wording** that bonds and *afflictions* **tribulations**
abide me.
24 But none of these *things* **words** move me,
neither *count* **regard** I my *life* **soul**
dear **precious** unto myself,
so that I might *finish* **complete** my *course* **race**
with *joy* **cheer**,
and the ministry, which I have *received* **taken**
of *the Lord Jesus* **Adonay Yah Shua**,
to *testify* **witness** the *gospel* **evangelism**
of the *grace* **charism** of *God* **Elohim**.
25 And now, behold, I know that ye all,
among whom I have *gone* **passed through**
preaching the *kingdom* **sovereigndom** of *God* **Elohim**,
shall see my face no more.
26 Wherefore
I *take you to record* **witness to you in** this day,
that I am pure from the blood of all *men*.
27 For I have not *shunned* **withheld**
to *declare* **evangelize** unto you
all the **whole** counsel of *God* **Elohim**.
28 *Take* heed therefore unto yourselves,
and to all the *flock* **shepherddom**,
over the which the Holy *Ghost* **Spirit**
hath *made* **placed** you *overseers* **episcopates**,
to *feed* **shepherd** the *church* **ecclesia** of *God* **Elohim**,
which he hath *purchased* **acquired**
with **through** his own blood.
29 For I know this, that after my departing
shall *grievous* **burdenous** wolves
enter in *among* **unto** you,
not sparing the *flock* **shepherddom**.
30 Also of your own selves shall men arise,
speaking *perverse things* **thorough perversions**,
to draw away disciples after them.
31 Therefore watch, and remember,
that *by the space of* **for** three years I *ceased* **paused** not
to *warn every* **remind each** one night and day with tears.
32 And now, brethren,
I *commend you* **set you forth** to *God* **Elohim**,
and to the word of his *grace* **charism**,
which is able to build you *up*,
and to give you an inheritance among all
them which are sanctified **the hallowed**.
33 I have *coveted* **panted after** no *man's* **one's** silver,
or gold, or *apparel* **garment**.
34 Yea, ye yourselves know,
that these hands
have *ministered* **tended** unto my necessities,
and to them that were with me.
35 I have *shewed you* **exemplified** all *things*,
how that *so* **thus** labouring
ye ought to support the *weak* **frail**,
and to remember
the words of *the Lord Jesus* **Adonay Yah Shua**,
how he said,
It is more blessed to give than to *receive* **take**.
36 And when he had *thus spoken* **said these**,
he *kneeled down* **placed his knees**,
and prayed with them all.
37 And *they all wept sore* **there became much weeping**,
and fell on *Paul's* **Paulos'** neck, and **ardently** kissed him,
38 *Sorrowing most of all* **Grieving especially**
for **over** the words which he *spake* **said**,
that they *should see* **were about to observe** his face
no more.
And they *accompanied* **forwarded** him
unto the *ship* **sailer**.

On to Sor

21 And it *came to pass* **became**,
that after we *were gotten* **withdrew** from them,
and had *launched* **embarked**,
we came *with a straight course* **straightly** unto Coos,
and *the day following* **next** unto Rhodes,
and from thence unto Patara:
2 And finding a *ship* **sailer**
sailing over **passing through** unto *Phenicia* **Phoinix**,
we went aboard, and set forth
in embarking, we embarked.
3 Now when *we had discovered* Cyprus **appeared**,
we left it on the left *hand*, and sailed into Syria,
and *landed* **moored** at *Tyre* **Sor**:
for there the *ship* **sailer** was to unlade her burden.

Disciples Warn Paulos

4 And finding disciples,
we *tarried* **abode** there seven days:
who *said* **worded** to *Paul* **Paulos** through the Spirit,
that he should not
go up **ascend** to *Jerusalem* **Yeru Shalem**.
5 And when **it became**
that we had *accomplished* **completed** those days,
we departed and went our way;
and they all *brought* **forwarded** us *on our way*,
with *wives* **women** and children,
till we were out of the city:
and we *kneeled down* **placed our knees** on the shore,
and prayed.
6 And when we had
taken our leave **saluted** one *of* another,
we *took ship* **embarked into a sailer**;
and they returned *home* **to their own** again.
7 And when we had *finished* **accomplished**
our *course* **sailing** from *Tyre* **Sor**,
we *came to* **arrived at** Ptolemais,
and saluted the brethren, and abode with them one day.
8 And *the next day*
we that were *of Paul's company* **around Paulos** departed,
and came unto *Caesarea* **Kaisaria**:
and we entered
into the house of *Philip* **Philippos** the evangelist,
which was one **being** of the seven; and abode with him.
9 And *the same man* **this one** had four daughters,
virgins, which did prophesy.

Hagab Warns Paulos

10 And as we *tarried there* **abode** many days,
there came down from *Judaea* **Yah Hudah**
a certain prophet, named *Agabus* **Hagab**.
11 And when he was come unto us,
he took *Paul's* **Paulos'** girdle,
and bound his own hands and feet, and said,
Thus *saith* **wordeth** the Holy *Ghost* **Spirit**.
So **Thus**
shall the *Jews* **Yah Hudiym** at *Jerusalem* **Yeru Shalem**
bind the man that owneth this girdle,
and shall *deliver* **betray** him
into the hands of the *Gentiles* **goyim**.
12 And when we heard these *things*,
both we, and they of that place,
besought **entreated** him
not to *go up* **ascend** to *Jerusalem* **Yeru Shalem**.

On to Yeru Shalem

13 Then *Paul* **Paulos** answered,
What *mean* **do** ye to weep
and to *break* **crumble** mine heart?
for I am *ready* **prepared** not to be bound only,
but also to die at *Jerusalem* **Yeru Shalem**
for the name of *the Lord Jesus* **Adonay Yah Shua**.
14 And *when* **he**,
would not be persuaded **not being convinced**,
we *ceased* **quieted**, saying,
The will of *the Lord be done* **Adonay become**.
15 And after those days we *took up our carriages* **packed**,
and *went up* **ascended** to *Jerusalem* **Yeru Shalem**.
16 There went with us also

certain **some** of the disciples of *Caesarea* **Kaisaria**,
and brought with them one Mnason of Cyprus,
an *old* **ancient** disciple, with whom we should lodge.
17 And when we
were come to Jerusalem **became at Yeru Shalem**,
the brethren received us *gladly* **with pleasure**.

PAULOS' VOW

18 And *the day following* **next**
Paul went **Paulos entered in** with us
unto *James* **Yaaqovos**;
and all the elders were *present* **come**.
19 And when he had saluted them,
he declared *particularly* **each, one by one**
what *things God* **Elohim** had *wrought* **done**
among the *Gentiles by* **goyim through** his ministry.
20 And when they heard it,
they glorified *the Lord* **Adonay**,
and said unto him, Thou *seest* **observest**, brother,
how many *thousands* **myriads** of *Jews* **Yah Hudiym**
there are which *believe* **trust**;
and they are all *zealous* **zealots** of the *law* **torah**:
21 And they are *informed of* **catechized about** thee,
that thou *teachest* **doctrinatest** all the *Jews* **Yah Hudiym**
which are among the *Gentiles* **goyim**
to *forsake Moses* **apostatize from Mosheh**,
saying **wording**
that they ought not to circumcise their children,
neither to walk after the customs.
22 What is it therefore?
the multitude must *needs* **most certainly** come together:
for they *will* **shall** hear that thou art come.
23 Do therefore this that we *say* **word** to thee:
We have four men which have a vow on them;
24 Them take, and *purify* **hallow** thyself with them,
and be *at charges with* **spent by** them,
that they may shave their heads:
and all may know that those *things*,
whereof they were *informed* **catechized**
concerning **about** thee,
are *nothing* **naught**;
but that thou thyself also *walkest orderly* **marchest**,
and *keepest* **guardest** the *law* **torah**.
25 *As touching* **Concerning** the *Gentiles* **goyim**
which *believe* **trust**,
we have *written* **epistolized** and *concluded* **judged**
that they *observe no* **guard none** such *thing*,
save only **except** that they *keep* **guard** themselves
from *things offered to idols* **idol sacrifices**,
and from blood, and from strangled,
and from *fornication* **whoredom**.
26 Then *Paul* **Paulos** took the men,
and the *next* day **after**
purifying **hallowing** himself with them
entered into the *temple* **priestal precinct**,
to *signify* **evangelize** the accomplishment
of the days of *purification* **hallowing**,
until that an offering should be offered
for *every* **each** one of them.

YAH HUDIYM SEIZE PAULOS

27 And when the seven days
were *almost ended* **about to be complete**,
the *Jews* **Yah Hudiym** which were of Asia,
when they *saw* **observed** him
in the *temple* **priestal precinct**,
stirred up all **confused** the *people* **whole multitude**,
and laid hands on him,
28 Crying out, Men *of Israel* — **Yisra Eliym**, help:
This is the *man* **human**,
that *teacheth all men* **doctrinateth everyone** every where
against the people, and the *law* **torah**, and this place:
and *further* **even** brought *Greeks* **Hellenes**
also into the *temple* **priestal precinct**,
and hath *polluted* **profaned** this holy place.
29 (For they had seen *before* **previously**
with him in the city Trophimus an Ephesian,
whom they *supposed* **presumed** that *Paul* **Paulos**
had brought into the *temple* **priestal precinct**.)
30 And all the city was *moved* **stirred**,
and the people *ran* **became rushing** together:
and they took *Paul* **Paulos**,
and drew him out of the *temple* **priestal precinct**:
and *forthwith* **straightway** the *doors* **portals** were shut.
31 And as they *went about* **sought** to *kill* **slaughter** him,
tidings came **reports ascended**
unto the *chief captain* **chiliarch** of the *band* **squad**,
that all *Jerusalem* **Yeru Shalem**
was *in an uproar* **confused**.
32 Who immediately
took *soldiers* **warriors** and centurions,
and ran down unto them:
and when they saw
the *chief captain* **chiliarch** and the *soldiers* **warriors**,
they *left beating of Paul* **paused striking Paulos**.
33 Then the *chief captain* **chiliarch**
came near **approached**, and took him,
and *commanded* **summoned** him
to be bound with two *chains* **fetters**;
and *demanded* **asked** who he was,
and what he had done.
34 And *some* **others** cried one *thing*,
some another, among the multitude:
and when he could not know the certainty
for **because of** the tumult,
he *commanded* **summoned** him
to be *carried* **brought** into the *castle* **encampment**.
35 And when he *came* **became** upon the stairs,
so it was **it so happened**,
that he was borne of the *soldiers* **warriors**
for the violence of the *people* **multitude**.
36 For the multitude of the people followed after,
crying, Away with him.

PAULOS PLEADS TO SPEAK

37 And as *Paul* **Paulos**
was **about** to be *led* **brought** into the *castle* **encampment**,
he *said* **worded** unto the *chief captain* **chiliarch**,
may *I* **Am I allowed to** speak **somewhat** unto thee?
Who said, *Canst* **Knowest** thou *speak Greek* **Hellenic**?
38 Art not thou **then** that *Egyptian* **Misrayim**,
which before these days *madest an uproar* **roused**,
and leddest out into the wilderness
four thousand men that were *murderers* **assassins**?
39 But *Paul* **Paulos** said, I am **indeed** a *man* **human**
which am a Jew — **a Yah Hudiy**
of Tarsus, a city in — **a Tarsiy of** Cilicia,
a citizen of no *mean* **ignoble** city:
and, I *beseech* **petition** thee,
suffer **allow** me to speak unto the people.

PAULOS PLEADS TO THE PEOPLE

40 And when he had *given* **allowed** him *licence*,
Paul **Paulos** stood on the stairs,
and *beckoned* **signaled** with the hand unto the people.
And when there *was made* **became**
a *great silence* **vast hush**,
he *spake unto* **addressed** them
in the Hebrew *tongue* **dialect**, *saying* **wording**,

22 Men, brethren, and fathers,
hear ye my *defence which I make* **pleading**
now unto you.
2 (And when they heard that he *spake* **addressed**
in the Hebrew *tongue* **dialect** to them,
they *kept* **presented** the more *silence* **quiet**: and he saith,)
3 I am *verily* **indeed** a man
which am a Jew — **a Yah Hudiy**,
born in Tarsus, *a city in* Cilicia,
yet *brought up* **nurtured** in this city
at the feet of *Gamaliel* **Gamli El**,
and *taught* **disciplined** according to
the *perfect manner* **exactness**
of the *law* **torah** of the fathers,
and *was zealous* **being a zealot** toward *God* **Elohim**,
exactly as ye all are this day.
4 And I persecuted this way unto the death,
binding and *delivering* **betraying** into prisons
both men and women.
5 As also the *high* **arch** priest doth *bear me* witness **me**,
and all the *estate of the elders* **presbytry**:
from whom also
I received *letters* **epistles** unto the brethren,
and went to *Damascus* **Dammeseq**
to bring them which were there bound

unto *Jerusalem* **Yeru Shalem**,
for to be *punished* **dishonoured**.
6 And it *came to pass* **became**, that,
as I *made my journey* **went**,
and *was come nigh* **approached**
unto Damascus **Dammeseq**
about *noon* **midday**, suddenly
there shone from heaven a great light round about me
I was enveloped in much light from heaven.
7 And I fell unto the ground,
and heard a voice *saying* **wording** unto me,
Saul, Saul **Shaul, Shaul**, why persecutest thou me?
8 And I answered, Who art thou, *Lord* **Adonay**?
And he said unto me,
I am Jesus of Nazareth **I AM Yah Shua the Nazarene**,
whom thou persecutest.
9 And they that were with me
saw **observed** indeed the light,
and *were afraid* **became awestricken**;
but they heard not the voice of him that spake to me.
10 And I said, What shall I do, *Lord* **Adonay**?
And *the Lord* **Adonay** said unto me, Arise,
and go into *Damascus* **Dammeseq**;
and there it shall be *told* **spoken to** thee
of **concerning** all *things* which are *appointed* **ordained**
for thee to do.
11 And when I could not *see* **look**
for the glory of that light,
being **hand** led *by the hand* of them that were with me,
I came into *Damascus* **Dammeseq**.
12 And one *Ananias* **Hanan Yah**,
a *devout* **well—revered** man according to the *law* **torah**,
having a good report **well witnessed**
of all the *Jews* **Yah Hudiym**
which *dwelt* **settled** there,
13 Came unto me, and stood **by**, and said unto me,
Brother *Saul* **Shaul**, *receive thy sight* **see**.
And the same hour I *looked up upon* **saw unto** him.
14 And he said,
The *God* **Elohim** of our fathers
hath *chosen* **preselected** thee,
that thou shouldest know his will, and see that Just *One*,
and shouldest hear the voice of his mouth.
15 For thou shalt be his witness unto all *men* **humanity**
of what thou hast seen and heard.
16 And now *why tarriest thou* **what art thou about to do**?
arise, and be baptized, and *wash away* **bathe** thy sins,
calling on the name of *the Lord* **Adonay**.
17 And it *came to pass* **became**, that,
when I *was come again* **returned**
to *Jerusalem* **Yeru Shalem**,
even while I prayed in the *temple* **priestal precinct**,
I *was* **became** in *a trance* **an ecstasis**;
18 And saw him *saying* **wording** unto me,
Make haste **Hasten**,
and get thee quickly out of *Jerusalem* **Yeru Shalem**:
for **because** they *will* **shall** not receive
thy *testimony* **witness** concerning me.
19 And I said, *Lord* **Adonay**,
they *know* **understand** that I imprisoned and *beat* **flogged**
in every synagogue
them that *believed* **trusted** on thee:
20 And when the blood of thy *martyr* **witness**
Stephen **Stephanos** was *shed* **poured forth**,
I also was standing by,
and consenting unto his *death* **taking out**,
and *kept* **guarded** the *raiment* **garment**
of them that *slew* **took** him **out**.
21 And he said unto me, Depart:
for I *will send* **shall apostolize** thee
far hence unto the *Gentiles* **goyim**.
22 And they *gave him audience unto* **heard** this word,
and then lifted *up* their voices, and *said* **worded**,
Away with such *a fellow* from the earth:
for it is not *fit* **becoming** that he should live.
23 And as they cried out,
and *cast off* **tossed** their *clothes* **garments**,
and *threw* **cast** dust into the air,
24 The *chief captain* **chiliarch**
commanded **summoned** him
to be brought into the *castle* **encampment**,
and *bade that he should be examined* **said to test him**
by scourging;
that he might know *wherefore* **for what cause**
they *cried so* **shouted thus** against him.
25 And as they *bound* **stretched** him with thongs,
Paul **Paulos** said unto the centurion that stood by,
Is it lawful for you **Are you allowed**
to scourge a *man that is* **human** — a Roman,
and *uncondemned* **unsentenced**?
26 When the centurion heard that,
he went and *told* **evangelized** the *chief captain* **chiliarch**,
saying **wording**,
Take heed **See** what thou *doest* **art about to do**:
for this *man* **human** is a Roman.
27 Then the *chief captain* **chiliarch** came,
and said unto him,
Tell **Word unto** me, art thou a Roman?
He said, Yea.
28 And the *chief captain* **chiliarch** answered,
With a *great* **vast** sum
obtained **acquired** I this *freedom* **citizenship**.
And *Paul* **Paulos** said, But I *was free born* — **born**.
29 Then straightway they departed from him
which *should have examined* **were about to test** him:
and the *chief captain* **chiliarch** also
was *afraid* **awestricken**,
after he knew **knowing** that he was a Roman,
and because he had bound him.

PAULOS PLEADS TO THE SANHEDRIM

30 On the morrow,
because he *would* **willed**
to have known **the certainty**
wherefore he was accused of the *Jews* **Yah Hudiym**,
he loosed him from his *bands* **bonds**,
and *commanded* **summoned** the *chief* **arch** priests
and all their *council* **sanhedrim** to *appear* **come**,
and brought *Paul* **Paulos** down,
and set him *before* **unto** them.

23

And *Paul* **Paulos**,
earnestly beholding **staring at** the *council* **sanhedrim**,
said, Men and brethren,
I have *lived* **citizenized** in all good conscience
before *God* **Elohim** until this day.
2 And the *high* **arch** priest *Ananias* **Hanan Yah**
commanded **ordered** them that stood by him
to *smite* **strike** him on the mouth.
3 Then said *Paul* **Paulos** unto him,
God shall smite **Elohim is about to strike** thee,
thou *whited* **whitewashed** wall:
for sittest thou to judge me after the *law* **torah**,
and *commandest* **summonest** me to be *smitten* **stricken**
contrary to the *law* **torah**?
4 And they that stood by said,
Revilest **Abusest** thou *God's high* **Elohim's arch** priest?
5 Then said *Paul* **Paulos**, I *wist* **knew** not, brethren,
that he was the *high* **arch** priest:
for it is *written* **scribed**,
Thou shalt not *speak* **say** evil
of the *ruler* **arch** of thy people.
6 But when *Paul perceived* **Paulos knew**
that the one part were *Sadducees* **Sadoqiym**,
and the other Pharisees,
he cried out in the *council* **sanhedrim**,
Men and brethren, I am a Pharisee, the son of a Pharisee:
of **concerning** the hope and resurrection of the dead
I am *called in question* **judged**.
7 And when he had so *said* **spoken**,
there *arose* **became** a *dissension* **riot**
between the Pharisees and the *Sadducees* **Sadoqiym**:
and the multitude was *divided* **schismed**.
8 For the *Sadducees say* **Sadoqiym indeed word**
that there is no resurrection, neither angel, nor spirit:
but the Pharisees *confess* **profess** both.
9 And there *arose* **became** a *great* **mega** cry:
and the scribes that were of the Pharisees' part arose,
and *strove* **fought fiercely**, *saying* **wording**,
We find no evil in this *man* **human**:
but if a spirit or an angel hath spoken to him,
let us not *fight against God* **be Elohim—resisters**.

10 And when there *arose* **became**
a great dissension **vast riot**,
the *chief captain* **chiliarch**,
fearing lest *Paul* **Paulos** should *have been* **be**
pulled in pieces **thoroughly drawn apart** of them,
commanded **summoned** the *soldiers* **warriors**
to *go down* **descend**,
and to *take* **seize** him *by force* from among them,
and to bring him into the *castle* **encampment**.

ADONAY ENCOURAGES PAULOS

11 And the **next** night *following*
the Lord **Adonay** stood by him,
and said, *Be of good cheer* **Courage**, *Paul* **Paulos**:
for as thou hast *testified of* **witnessed about** me
in *Jerusalem* **Yeru Shalem**,
so **thus** must thou bear witness also at Rome.

THE YAH HUDIYM COALITION

12 And when it *was* **became** day,
certain **some** of the *Jews* **Yah Hudiym**
banded together **made a coalition**,
and *bound* **anathematized** themselves *under a curse*,
saying **wording**
that they *would* **should** neither eat nor drink
till they had *killed Paul* **slaughtered Paulos**.
13 And they were more than forty
which had made this conspiracy.
14 And they came to the *chief* **arch** priests and elders,
and said, We have *bound* **anathematized** ourselves
under a great *curse* **anathema**,
that we *will eat nothing* **shall taste naught**
until we have *slain Paul* **slaughtered Paulos**.
15 Now therefore ye with the *council* **sanhedrim**
signify **manifest** to the *chief captain* **chiliarch**
that he bring him down unto you to morrow,
as though ye *would enquire something* **should know**
more *perfectly concerning* **exactly about** him:
and we, *or ever he come near* **before he approacheth**,
are *ready* **prepared** to *kill* **take** him **out**.
16 And when *Paul's* **Paulos'** sister's son
heard of their *lying in wait* **lurking**,
he *went* **came** and entered into the *castle* **encampment**,
and *told Paul* **evangelized to Paulos**.
17 Then *Paul* **Paulos**
called one of the centurions unto him, and said,
Bring this *young man* **youth**
unto the *chief captain* **chiliarch**:
for he hath *a certain thing* **somewhat**
to *tell* **evangelize to** him.
18 *So* **Therefore indeed** he took him,
and brought him to the *chief captain* **chiliarch**, and said,
Paul **Paulos** the prisoner called me unto him,
and *prayed* **asked** me
to bring this *young man* **youth** unto thee,
who hath *something* **somewhat** to *say* **speak to** thee.
19 Then the *chief captain* **chiliarch** took him by the hand,
and *went with him aside* **withdrew** privately,
and asked him,
What is that thou hast to *tell* **evangelize to** me?
20 And he said, The *Jews* **Yah Hudiym**
have *agreed* **covenanted** to *desire* **ask** thee
that thou *wouldest* **shouldest** bring down *Paul* **Paulos**
to morrow into the *council* **sanhedrim**,
as though they *would* **should** enquire somewhat of him
more *perfectly* **exactly**.
21 *But do not thou yield unto them*
Therefore let them not convince you:
for there *lie in wait* **lurk** for him
of them more than forty men,
which have *bound* **anathematized** themselves
with an oath,
that they *will* **shall** neither eat nor drink
till they have *killed* **taken** him **out**:
and now are they *ready* **prepared**,
looking for a promise **awaiting a pre—evangelism**
from thee.
22 *So* **Therefore indeed** the *chief captain* **chiliarch**
then *let* **released** the *young man depart* **youth**,
and charged **evangelized him**,
See thou *tell* **divulge to** no *man* **one**
that thou hast *shewed* **manifested** these *things* to me.

ON TO KAISARIA

23 And he called *unto him* two centurions, saying,
Make ready **Prepare** two hundred *soldiers* **warriors**
to go to *Caesarea* **Kaisaria**,
and horsemen *threescore and ten* **seventy**,
and *spearmen* **right receivers** two hundred,
at **from** the third hour of the night;
24 And *provide* **present** them *beasts* **animals**,
that they may *set Paul on* **mount Paulos**,
and bring him safe unto *Felix* **Phelix** the governor.
25 And he *wrote a letter* **scribed an epistle**
after this manner **containing this type**:
26 Claudius Lysias
unto the most *excellent* **powerful** governor *Felix* **Phelix;**
sendeth greeting **Cheers**:
27 This man was taken of the *Jews* **Yah Hudiym**,
and *should have been killed* **was about to be taken out**
of them:
then *came* I **stood by** with *an army* **warriors**,
and *rescued* **released** him,
having *understood* **learned** that he was a Roman.
28 And when I *would* **willed to** have known the cause
wherefore they accused him,
I brought him forth into their *council* **sanhedrim**:
29 Whom I *perceived* **found** to be accused of questions
of **about** their *law* **torah**,
but to have *nothing laid to his charge* **no accusation**
worthy of death or of bonds.
30 And when it was *told me* **disclosed**
how that the *Jews* **Yah Hudiym**
laid wait **plotted** for the man,
I sent *straightway* **immediately** to thee,
and *gave commandment* **evangelized** to his accusers
also to *say before* **word unto** thee
what they had against him.
Farewell.
31 *Then* **Therefore indeed** the *soldiers* **warriors**,
as it was *commanded* **ordained** them, took *Paul* **Paulos**,
and brought him *by* **through** night to Antipatris.
32 On the morrow
they *left* **allowed** the *horsemen* **cavalry** to go with him,
and returned to the *castle* **encampment**:
33 Who, when they *came to Caesarea* **entered Kaisaria**,
and *delivered* **gave over** the epistle to the governor,
presented *Paul* **Paulos** also before him.
34 And when the governor had read *the letter*,
he asked of what province he was.
And when he *understood that he was* **asked,** of Cilicia;
35 I *will* **shall** hear thee **patiently**, said he,
when thine accusers are also come.
And he *commanded* **summoned** him to be *kept* **guarded**
in Herod's *judgment hall* **praetorium**.

TERTULLUS' ACCUSATION AGAINST PAULOS

24 And after five days
Ananias **Hanan Yah** the *high* **arch** priest
descended with the elders,
and with *a certain* **some** orator named Tertullus,
who *informed* **manifested to** the governor
against *Paul* **Paulos**.
2 And when he was called *forth*,
Tertullus began to accuse him, *saying* **wording**,
Seeing that *by* **through** thee
we *enjoy great quietness* **have obtained much shalom**,
and that very worthy deeds
are *done* **become** unto this *nation* **goyim**
by thy *providence* **provision**,
3 We *accept* **receive** it *always* **every way**,
and *in all places* **everywhere**,
most *noble Felix* **powerful Phelix**,
with all *thankfulness* **eucharist**.
4 Notwithstanding,
that I *be not further tedious unto* **hinder** thee **no more**,
I *pray* **beseech** thee
that thou *wouldest* **shouldest** hear us
of thy *clemency a few words* **gentleness concisely**.
5 For we have found this man *a* pestilent *fellow*,
and *a mover of sedition* **stirring riot**
among all the *Jews* **Yah Hudiym** throughout the world,
and a *ringleader* **prime officer**
of the *sect* **heresy** of the Nazarenes:

6 Who also hath *gone about* **tested**
to profane the *temple* **priestal precinct**:
whom we *took* **overpowered**,
and *would* **willed to** have judged
according to our *law* **torah**.
7 But the *chief captain* **chiliarch** Lysias
came upon us **passed by**,
and with *great* **much** violence
took him away out of our hands,
8 *commanding* **summoning** his accusers
to come unto thee:
by examining of whom thyself
mayest take knowledge **canst know**
of **about** all these *things*,
whereof we accuse him.
9 And the *Jews* **Yah Hudiym**
also *assented* **covenanted**,
saying **professing** that these *things* were *so* **thus**.

PAULOS PLEADS TO PHELIX

10 Then *Paul* **Paulos**,
after that the governor had *beckoned* **nodded** unto him
to *speak* **word**, answered,
Forasmuch as I *know* **understand** that thou
hast been of many years a judge unto this *nation* **goyim**,
I do the more cheerfully *answer* **plead**
for **concerning** myself:
11 Because that thou *mayest understand* **canst know**,
that there are yet *but* **no more than** twelve days
since I went up **from my ascending**
to *Jerusalem* **Yeru Shalem** for to worship.
12 And they neither
found me in the *temple* **priestal precinct**
disputing **reasoning** with any *man* **one**,
neither *raising up* **making** the *people* **multitude conspire**,
neither in the synagogues, nor in the city:
13 Neither can they *prove the things* **present those**
whereof **about which** they now accuse me.
14 But this I *confess* **profess** unto thee,
that after the way which they *call* **word** heresy,
so worship **thus liturgize** I the *God* **Elohim** of my fathers,
believing **trusting** all *things* which are *written* **scribed**
in the *law* **torah** and in the prophets:
15 And have hope *toward God* **in Elohim**,
which they themselves also *allow* **await**,
that there *shall* **is about to** be a resurrection of the dead,
both of the just and unjust.
16 And *herein do* **in this** I exercise myself,
to have *always* **continually** a conscience void to offence
toward *God* **Elohim**, and *toward men* **humanity**.
17 Now *after* **through** many years
I came to *bring alms* **do mercies** to my *nation* **goyim**,
and offerings.
18 Whereupon *certain Jews* **some Yah Hudiym** from Asia
found me *purified* **hallowed**
in the *temple* **priestal precinct**,
neither with multitude, nor with tumult.
19 Who *ought* **need** to have been here
before **present by** thee,
and *object* **accuse**, if they had ought against me.
20 Or else let these same here say,
if they have found any *evil doing* **injustice** in me,
while I stood *before* **by** the *council* **sanhedrim**,
21 *Except it be for* **Other than about** this one voice,
that I cried standing among them,
Touching **Concerning** the resurrection of the dead
I am *called in question* **judged** by you this day.
22 And when *Felix* **Phelix** heard these *things*,
having more *perfect* **exact** knowledge
of **concerning** that way,
he *deferred* **delayed** them, and said,
When Lysias the *chief captain* **chiliarch**
shall *come down* **descend**,
I *will* **shall** know
the uttermost of your matter **exactly as to you**.
23 And he *commanded* **ordained** a centurion
to *keep Paul* **guard Paulos**,
and to let him have *liberty* **relaxation**,
and that he should forbid none of his *acquaintance* **own**
to *minister* **tend** or come unto him.

PAULOS' WITNESS TO PHELIX

24 And after *certain* **some** days,
when *Felix* **Phelix** came
with his *wife* **woman** Drusilla,
which was **being** a *Jewess* **Yah Hudiy**,
he *sent for Paul* **summoned Paulos**,
and heard him
concerning the *faith* **trust** in *Christ* **the Messiah**.
25 And as he reasoned
of righteousness **concerning justness**,
temperance **self—control**,
and **the** judgment *to come* **about to be**,
Felix trembled **Phelix became awestricken**
and answered,
Go thy way for *this time* **now**;
when I *have a convenient* **partake a** season,
I *will* **shall** call for thee.
26 He hoped *also* **simultaneously** that *money* **riches**
should *have been* **be** given him of *Paul* **Paulos**,
that he might loose him:
wherefore he *sent for* **summoned** him the oftener,
and *communed* **homologized** with him.
27 But after two years **being fulfilled**
Porcius Festus **Porkios Phestus**
came into Felix' room **succeeded Phelix**:
and *Felix* **Phelix**,
willing **having willed**
to *shew the Jews* **lay on the Yah Hudiym**
a *pleasure* **charism**,
left *Paul* **Paulos** bound.

YAH HUDIYM SEEK TO SUMMON PAULOS

25 *Now* **Therefore** when *Festus* **Phestus**
was come **embarked** into the province,
after three days
he ascended from *Caesarea* **Kaisaria**
to *Jerusalem* **Yeru Shalem**.
2 Then the *high* **arch** priest
and the *chief* **preeminent** of the *Jews* **Yah Hudiym**
informed **manifested** him against *Paul* **Paulos**,
and *besought* **entreated** him,
3 And *desired favour* **asked charism** against him,
that he *would send for* **should summon** him
to *Jerusalem* **Yeru Shalem**,
laying wait **lurking** in the way to *kill* **take him out**.
4 *But Festus* **Therefore indeed Phestus** answered,
that *Paul* **Paulos** should be *kept* **guarded**
at *Caesarea* **Kaisaria**,
and that he himself
would **was about to** depart *shortly* **quickly** *thither*.
5 Let them therefore, said he, which among you are able,
go down with me, and accuse this man,
if there be any wickedness in him.
6 And when he had tarried among them
more than ten days,
he *went down* **descended** unto *Caesarea* **Kaisaria**;
and *the next day* **on the morrow**
sitting on the *judgment seat* **bamah**
commanded Paul **summoned Paulos** to be brought.
7 And when he was come,
the *Jews* **Yah Hudiym** which *came down* **descended**
from *Jerusalem* **Yeru Shalem** stood round about,
and *laid* **brought** many
and *grievous complaints* **burdenous accusations**
against *Paul* **Paulos**,
which they could not *prove* **show**.
8 While he *answered* **pleaded** for himself,
Neither
against **unto** the *law* **torah** of the *Jews* **Yah Hudiym**,
neither *against* **unto** the *temple* **priestal precinct**,
nor yet *against Caesar* **unto the Kaisar**
have I *offended any thing at all* **sinned somewhat**.
9 But *Festus* **Phestus**,
willing **having willed**
to *do* **lay** the *Jews* **Yah Hudiym** a *pleasure* **charism**,
answered *Paul* **Paulos**, and said,
Wilt **Willest** thou
go up **ascend** to *Jerusalem* **Yeru Shalem**,
and there be judged
of **concerning** these *things before* **by** me?

PAULOS CALLS ON THE KAISAR

10 Then said *Paul* **Paulos,**
I stand at *Caesar's judgment seat* **the Kaisar's bamah,**
where I *ought to* **must** be judged:
to the *Jews* **Yah Hudiym**
have I *done no wrong* **not injured,**
as thou very well knowest.
11 For **indeed** if I *be an offender* **have injured,**
or have *committed any thing* **transacted somewhat**
worthy of death,
I *refuse* **shun** not to die:
but if there be none of these *things*
whereof these accuse me,
no *man may deliver* **one can grant charism of** me
unto them.
I *appeal unto Caesar* **call upon the Kaisar.**
12 Then *Festus* **Phestus,**
when he had *conferred* **talked** with the council,
answered,
Hast thou appealed unto *Caesar* **the Kaisar**?
unto *Caesar* **the Kaisar** shalt thou go.
13 And *after certain* **some** days **having past,**
king **sovereign** Agrippa and Bernice
came unto Caesarea **arrived in Kaisaria**
to salute *Festus* **Phestus.**
14 And when they had *been* **tarried** there many days,
Festus declared Paul's **Phestus propounded Paulos'** cause
unto the *king* **sovereign,** *saying* **wording,**
There is *a certain* **some** man
left *in bonds* **prisoner** by *Felix* **Phelix:**
15 About whom,
when I *was at Jerusalem* **became in Yeru Shalem,**
the *chief* **arch** priests and the elders
of the *Jews informed me* **Yah Hudiym manifested,**
desiring **asking** to have judgment against him.
16 To whom I answered,
It is not the *manner* **custom** of the Romans
to *deliver* **grant charism over** any *man* **human**
to die **unto destruction,**
before that he which is accused
have the accusers face to face,
and *have licence to answer for himself* **take his pleading**
concerning *the crime laid against him* **his accusation.**
17 Therefore, when they were come hither,
without any **making no** delay on the morrow
I sat on the *judgment seat* **bamah,**
and *commanded* **summoned** the man to be brought forth.
18 *Against* **Concerning** whom
when the accusers stood *up,*
they brought none accusation
of such *things* as I *supposed* **surmised:**
19 But had *certain* **some** questions against him
of **concerning** their own *superstition* **demondreading,**
and *of* **about** one *Jesus* **Yah Shua,** which was dead,
whom *Paul affirmed* **Paulos professed** to be alive.
20 And *because I doubted* **being perplexed**
of such manner of **about these** questions,
I *asked him* **worded,**
whether he *would* **willed**
to go to *Jerusalem* **Yeru Shalem,**
and there be judged *of* **concerning** these matters.
21 But when *Paul* **Paulos**
had *appealed* **called** to be *reserved* **guarded**
unto the *hearing* **diagnosis** of *Augustus* **Sebastos,**
I *commanded* **summoned** him to be kept
till I might send him to *Caesar* **the Kaisar.**
22 Then Agrippa said unto *Festus* **Phestus,**
I *would* also **will to** hear the *man* **human** myself.
To morrow, said he, thou shalt hear him.
23 *And* **Then** on the morrow,
when Agrippa was come, and Bernice,
with *great pomp* **much fantasy,**
and was entered into the place of hearing,
with the *chief captains* **chiliarchs,**
and *principal* **eminent** men of the city,
at *Festus' commandment* **Phestus' summons**
Paul **Paulos** was brought forth.
24 And *Festus* **Phestus** said, *King* **Sovereign** Agrippa,
and all men which are *here* present *with us* **together,**
ye *see* **observe** this man,
about whom all the multitude of the *Jews* **Yah Hudiym**
have *dealt* **interceded** with me,
both at *Jerusalem* **Yeru Shalem,** and also here,
crying that he *ought* **must** not *to* live any longer.
25 But when I *found* **overtook**
that he had *committed nothing* **transacted naught**
worthy of death,
and that he himself
hath *appealed* **called** to *Augustus* **Sebastos,**
I have *determined* **judged** to send him.
26 *Of* **About** whom
I have *no certain thing* **nought** to *write* **scribe**
unto my *lord* **adoni.**
Wherefore I have brought him forth *before* **by** you,
and specially *before* **by** thee, O *king* **sovereign** Agrippa,
that, *after* examination *had* **having become,**
I might have somewhat to *write* **scribe.**
27 For *it seemeth to me unreasonable*
I thought it irrational to send a prisoner,
and not withal to signify the *crimes* **accusations**
laid against him.

PAULOS PLEADS TO AGRIPPA

26 Then Agrippa said unto *Paul* **Paulos,**
Thou art *permitted* **allowed** to *speak* **word** for thyself.
Then *Paul stretched forth* **Paulos extended** the hand,
and *answered* **pleaded** for himself:
2 I *think* **deem** myself *happy* **blessed,**
king **Sovereign** Agrippa,
because I *shall answer* **am about to plead** for myself
this day
before **by** thee *touching* **concerning** all *the things*
whereof I am accused of the *Jews* **Yah Hudiym:**
3 Especially because I know thee
to be *expert* **knowledgeable** in all customs and questions
which are among the *Jews* **Yah Hudiym:**
wherefore I *beseech* **petition** thee to hear me patiently.
4 **Therefore indeed**
My *manner of life* **existence** from my youth,
which *was at the first* **became from the beginning**
among mine own *nation* **goyim**
at *Jerusalem* **Yeru Shalem,**
know all the *Jews* **Yah Hudiym;**
5 Which *knew* **foreknew** me from *the beginning* **above,**
if they *would testify* **willed to witness,**
that after the most *straitest sect* **exact heresy**
of our *religion* **ceremonials** I lived a Pharisee.
6 And now I stand and am judged
for **unto** the hope of the *promise* **pre—evangelism**
made of God **that became by Elohim,** unto our fathers:
7 Unto which *promise* our twelve *tribes* **scions,**
instantly serving God **intently liturgizing** day and night,
hope to *come* **arrive.**
For **Concerning** which *hope's sake* **hope,**
king **Sovereign** Agrippa,
I am accused of the *Jews* **Yah Hudiym.**
8 Why should it be *thought* **judged**
a thing incredible **trustless** with you,
that God **if Elohim** should raise the dead?
9 I *verily* **therefore indeed** thought with myself,
that I *ought to do many things* **must transact much**
contrary to the name
of *Jesus of Nazareth* **Yah Shua the Nazarene.**
10 Which *thing* I also did in *Jerusalem* **Yeru Shalem:**
and many of the *saints* **holy**
did I *shut up* **lock down** in *prison* **the guardhouse,**
having *received* **taken** authority
from the *chief* **arch** priests;
and when they were *put to death* **taken out,**
I *gave my voice* **brought down my pebble** against them.
11 And I *punished* **dishonoured** them oft
in every synagogue,
and compelled them to blaspheme;
and *being exceedingly mad* **raving superabundantly**
against them,
I persecuted them even unto *strange* **outlying** cities.
12 Whereupon as I went to *Damascus* **Dammeseq**
with authority and *commission* **permisssion**
from the *chief* **arch** priests,
13 At midday, O *king* **sovereign,**
I saw in the way a light from heaven,

above the *brightness* **radiance** of the sun,
shining round about **haloing** me
and them which *journeyed* **went** with me.
14 And when we were all fallen **down** to the earth,
I heard a voice speaking unto me,
and *saying* **wording** in the Hebrew *tongue* **dialect**,
Saul, Saul **Shaul, Shaul**, why persecutest thou me?
it is hard for thee to *kick* **heel** against the *pricks* **stings**.
15 And I said, Who art thou, *Lord* **Adonay**?
And he said,
I am Jesus **I AM Yah Shua** whom thou persecutest.
16 But rise, and stand upon thy feet:
for I have appeared unto thee *for this purpose* **unto this**,
to *make* **preselect** thee
a minister **an attendant** and a witness
both of these *things* which thou hast seen,
and of those *things*
in the which I *will* **shall** appear unto thee;
17 *Delivering* **Releasing** thee from the people,
and from the *Gentiles* **goyim**,
unto whom now I *send* **apostolize** thee,
18 To open their eyes,
and to turn them from darkness to light,
and *from* the *power* **authority** of Satan
unto *God* **Elohim**,
that they may *receive* **take** forgiveness of sins,
and *inheritance* **their lot** among them
which are *sanctified* **hallowed** by *faith* **trust** that is in me.
19 Whereupon, O *king* **Sovereign** Agrippa,
I *was* **became** not *disobedient* **distrusting**
unto the heavenly vision:
20 But *shewed* **evangelized** first
unto them of *Damascus* **Dammeseq**,
and at *Jerusalem* **Yeru Shalem**,
and *throughout* **into** all the *coasts* **regions**
of *Judaea* **Yah Hudah**,
and *then* to the *Gentiles* **goyim**,
that they should repent and turn to *God* **Elohim**,
and *do* **transact** works *meet for* **worthy of** repentance.
21 For these causes the *Jews caught* **Yah Hudiym took** me
in the *temple* **priestal precinct**,
and *went about* **tried** to *kill* **thoroughly handle** me.
22 Having therefore obtained help of *God* **Elohim**,
I *continue* **stand** unto this day,
witnessing both to *small* **little** and *great* **mega**,
saying **wording** none other *things*
than **except** those which the prophets and *Moses* **Mosheh**
did say should come **spoke of are about to become**:
23 *That Christ* **Whether the Messiah** should suffer,
and *that* **whether** he should be the first
that should rise from **the resurrection of** the dead,
and *should shew* **about to evangelize** light
unto the people, and to the *Gentiles* **goyim**.
24 And as he *thus spake* **pleaded these** for himself,
Festus **Phestus** said with a *loud* **mega** voice,
Paul **Paulos**, thou *art beside thyself* **ravest**;
much *learning* **scribing** doth make thee *mad* **maniacal**.
25 But he said, I am not *mad* **raving**,
most *noble Festus* **powerful Phestus**;
but *speak forth* **utter** the *words* **rhema** of truth
and *soberness* **soundmindedness**.
26 For the *king* **sovereign**
knoweth of **understandeth about** these *things*,
before whom also I speak *freely* **having boldness**:
for I am *persuaded* **convinced**
that none of these *things* are hidden from him;
for this *thing* was not *done* **transacted** in a corner.
27 *King* **Sovereign** Agrippa,
believest **trustest** thou the prophets?
I know that thou *believest* **trustest**.
28 Then Agrippa said unto *Paul* **Paulos**,
Almost **In a little** thou *persuadest* **convincest** me
to *be* **become** a *Christian* **Messianist**.
29 And *Paul* **Paulos** said,
I *would* **should vow** to *God* **Elohim**,
that not only thou, but also all that hear me this day,
were both almost **become both in little**,
and *altogether* **in much**
such as **what sort** I am, except these bonds.
30 And when he had *thus spoken* **said these**,
the *king* **sovereign** rose *up*,
and the governor, and Bernice,
and they that sat with them:
31 And when they *were gone aside* **had withdrawn**,
they *talked between themselves* **spake to one another**,
saying **wording**,
This *man doeth nothing* **human transacteth naught**
worthy of death or of bonds.
32 Then said Agrippa unto *Festus* **Phestus**,
This *man might* **human could** have been
set at liberty **released**,
if he had not appealed **except that he called**
unto *Caesar* **the Kaisar**.

ON TO ROME

27 And when it was *determined* **judged**
that we should sail into Italy,
they delivered *Paul* **Paulos**
and *certain* **some** other prisoners unto one named Julius,
a centurion of *Augustus' band* **the venerable squad**.
2 And *entering* **embarking**
into a *ship* **sailer** of Adramyttium,
we *launched* **embarked**,
meaning **about** to sail by the *coasts* **places** of Asia;
one Aristarchus,
a Macedonian of *Thessalonica* — **Thessalonikee**
being with us.
3 And *the next day* **on another**
we *touched at* **moored in** Sidon.
And Julius
courteously entreated Paul **supplied philantrophy to Paulos**,
and *gave him liberty* **allowed him** to go unto his friends
to *refresh himself* **obtain their care**.
4 And when we had *launched* **embarked** from thence,
we sailed under Cyprus,
because the winds were contrary.
5 And when we had sailed
over **through** the *sea* **deep** of Cilicia and Pamphylia,
we came **down** to Myra, *a city* of *Lycia* **Loukia**.
6 And there the centurion
found a *ship* **sailer** of Alexandria sailing into Italy;
and he *put* **embarked** us *therein*.
7 And when we had sailed slowly many days,
and *scarce* **with difficulty**
were come **became** over against Cnidus,
the wind not *suffering* **allowing** us,
we sailed under Crete, over against Salmone;
8 And, *hardly passing it* **with difficulty sailing by**,
came unto a place which is called
The fair havens **Good Harbor**;
nigh whereunto was the city of Lasea.
9 Now *when* much time *was spent* **being past**,
and *when* sailing *was now* **already being** dangerous,
because the fast was *now* already past,
Paul admonished **Paulos advised** them,
10 And *said* **worded** unto them, *Sirs* **Men**,
I *perceive* **observe** that this *voyage* **sailing**
will **is about to** be
with *hurt* **hubris** and much *damage* **loss**,
not only of the lading and *ship* **sailer**,
but also of our *lives* **souls**.
11 Nevertheless the centurion
believed the master **had confidence of the pilot**
and the *owner of the* ship **captain**,
more **rather** than those *things*
which were *spoken* **worded** by *Paul* **Paulos**.
12 And *because* the *haven* **harbor**
was not commodious **being inconvenient** to winter in,
the more part
advised to depart **placed counsel to embark** thence *also*,
if *by any means* **somehow**
they *might attain to Phenice* **could arrive in Phoinix**,
and there to winter;
which is an haven — **a harbor** of Crete,
and *lieth* **looketh**
toward the south west and north west.
13 And when the *south wind* **southerly**
blew softly **puffed gently**,
supposing **thinking** that they had
obtained **empowered** their *purpose* **prothesis**,
loosing thence, they sailed close by Crete.

THE STORM ON THE WAY
14 But not *long* **much** after
there *arose* **cast** against it a tempestuous wind,
called Euroclydon.
15 And when the *ship* **sailer** was caught,
and could not *bear up into* **eye against** the wind,
we *let her drive* **gave her up and were borne away.**
16 And *running under a certain* **sailing past some** island
which is called Clauda,
we *had much work* **were, with difficulty,**
to come by the boat **able to become masters of the skiff**:
17 Which when they had taken *up,*
they used helps, undergirding the *ship* **sailer**;
and, *fearing* **awing**
lest they should fall into the quicksands,
strake **lowered** sail, and *so* **thus** were *driven* **borne.**
18 And we being *exceedingly* **extremely tempest** tossed
with a tempest,
the next *day* they *lightened the ship* **made an ejection**;
19 And the third *day*
we *cast* **tossed** out with our own hands
the tackling of the *ship* **sailer**.
20 And when neither sun nor stars
in many days appeared,
and no small *tempest* **downpour** lay on us,
all hope that we should be saved
was *then* **finally** taken away.
21 But *after long abstinence* **there being much fasting**
Paul **Paulos then** stood forth in the midst of them,
and said, *Sirs* **O Men,**
ye **indeed**
should **needed to** have *hearkened unto* **first obeyed** me,
and not have *loosed* **embarked** from Crete,
and to have gained this *harm* **hubris** and loss.
22 And now I *exhort* **advise** you
to *be of good cheer* **cheer up**:
for there shall be no loss
of *any man's life among* **soul of** you,
but **except** of the *ship* **sailer.**
23 For there stood by me this night
the angel of *God* **Elohim,**
whose I am, and whom I *serve* **liturgize,**
24 *Saying* **Wording,** *Fear* **Awe** not, *Paul* **Paulos**;
thou must be *brought* **presented**
before *Caesar* **the Kaisar**:
and, *lo* **behold,**
God **Elohim** hath *given* **granted** thee **charism**
of all them that sail with thee.
25 Wherefore, *sirs* **men**, *be of good cheer* **cheer up**:
for I *believe God* **trust Elohim,**
that it shall be *even* **thus**
as it was told **in the manner it was spoken unto** me.
26 Howbeit
we must *be cast upon a certain island* **fall unto some isle.**
27 But when the fourteenth night *was come* **became,**
as we were *driven up and down* **borne** in Adria,
about midnight
the *shipmen deemed* **sailer crew surmised**
that they drew near to some *country* **region**;
28 And sounded, and found it twenty fathoms:
and when they had *gone* **passed through** a little further,
they sounded again, and found it fifteen fathoms.
29 Then *fearing* **awing** lest **somehow**
we should have fallen *upon rocks* **unto jagged places,**
they *cast* **tossed** four anchors out of the stern,
and *wished for the* **vowed that it become** day.
30 And as the *shipmen* **sailer crew**
were about to flee out of the *ship* **sailer,**
when they had *let down* **lowered** the *boat* **skiff**
into the sea,
under *colour* **pretext** as though
they *would have cast* **were about to extend** anchors
out of the *foreship* **prow,**
31 *Paul* **Paulos**
said to the centurion and to the *soldiers* **warriors,**
Except **Unless** these abide in the *ship* **sailer,**
ye cannot be saved.
32 Then the *soldiers* **warriors**
cut off the ropes of the *boat* **skiff,**
and let her fall off.
33 And *while* **until** the day was *coming on* **about to be,**
Paul besought **Paulos entreated** them all
to *take meat* **partake nourishment**, *saying* **wording,**
This day is the fourteenth day
that ye have *tarried* **awaited**
and *continued* **thoroughy completed** fasting,
having taken *nothing* **naught.**
34 Wherefore I *pray* **beseech** you
to take *some meat* **nourishment**:
for this is for your *health* **salvation**:
for there shall not an hair fall
from the head of any of you.
35 And when he had *thus spoken* **said these,**
he took bread,
and *gave thanks* **eucharistized** to *God* **Elohim**
in *presence* **sight** of them all:
and when he had broken it, he began to eat.
36 Then *were* **became** they all *of good cheer* **cheered up,**
and they also took *some meat* **nourishment.**
37 And we were in all in the *ship* **sailer**
two hundred
threescore and sixteen **and seventy and six** souls.
38 And when they had
eaten enough **gluttonized nourishment,**
they lightened the *ship* **sailer,**
and cast out the *wheat* **grain** into the sea.
39 And when it *was* **became** day, they knew not the land:
but they *discovered a certain creek* **perceived some bay**
with a shore,
into the which they *were minded* **had counseled,**
if it were possible, to *thrust in* **propel** the *ship* **sailer.**
40 And when they had taken *up* the anchors,
they *committed themselves* **let** unto the sea,
and **simultaneously** loosed the rudder *bands* **tiller,**
and *hoised up* **lifted** the *mainsail* **foresail**
to the *wind* **puffing,**
and *made toward* **held unto** shore.
41 And falling into a place *where* **of the** two seas *met,*
they ran the ship aground;
and the *forepart* **prow indeed** stuck *fast* **tight,**
and *remained* **abode** unmoveable,
but the *hinder part* **stern** was *broken* **loosed**
with **by** the violence of the waves.
42 And the *soldiers'* **warriors'** counsel
was **became** to *kill* **slaughter** the prisoners,
lest any of them should swim out, and *escape* **flee.**
43 But the centurion,
willing **having willed** to save *Paul* **Paulos,**
kept **forbad** them from their *purpose* **counsel**;
and *commanded* **summoned** that they which could swim
should cast *themselves* first *into the sea,*
and *get* **depart** to land:
44 And the rest, some **indeed** on boards,
and some on *broken pieces* **some** of the *ship* **sailer.**
And *so* **thus** it *came to pass* **became,**
that they *escaped all safe* **were saved** to land.

SAVED AT MELITA ISLAND
28 And when they were *escaped* **saved,**
then they knew that the island was called Melita.
2 And the *barbarous people* **barbarians**
shewed **presented** us
no *little kindness* **ordinary philantrophy**:
for they *kindled* **lit** a fire, and received us every one,
because of the *present* rain **standing by,**
and because of the cold.

VIPER SEIZES PAULOS' HAND
3 And when *Paul* **Paulos**
had *gathered* **tied** a *bundle* **multitude** of *sticks* **kindling,**
and *laid* **put** them on the fire,
there came a viper out of the heat,
and *fastened on* **seized** his hand.
4 And when the barbarians
saw the *venomous* beast hang *on* **from** his hand,
they *said* **worded** among *themselves* **one another,**
No doubt **Most certainly** this *man* **human** is a murderer,
whom, though he *hath escaped* **be saved from** the sea,
yet *vengeance suffereth* **judgment alloweth** not to live.
5 *And* **Therefore indeed**
he shook off the beast into the fire,
and *felt* **suffered** no *harm* **evil.**

6 Howbeit they *looked* **watched**
when he should *have swollen* **ought to be inflamed**,
or fallen down dead suddenly:
but after they had *looked a great while* **awaited much**,
and *saw no harm* **observed nought inordinate**
come to **become** him,
they changed their minds,
and *said* **worded** that he was *a god* **an El**.

PAULOS HEALS PUBLIUS' FATHER

7 In *the same quarters* **about those places**
were *possessions* **parcels**
of the *chief* **preeminent** man of the island,
whose name was Publius; who *received* **entertained** us,
and lodged us three days courteously.
8 And it *came to pass* **became**,
that the father of Publius *lay sick of* **was held by** a fever
and of *a bloody flux* **dysentery**:
to whom *Paul* **Paulos** entered in, and prayed,
and *laid* **put** his hands on him, and healed him.
9 *So* **Therefore** when this *was done* **became**,
others also **the rest**,
which had *diseases* **frailties** in the island,
came, and were *healed* **cured**:
10 Who also honoured us with many honours;
and when we *departed* **embarked**,
they *laded* **put** us with such *things*
as were *necessary* **needed**.
11 And after three months
we *departed* **embarked** in a *ship* **sailer** of Alexandria,
which had wintered in the isle,
whose sign was *Castor and Pollux* **Dioscuri**.
12 And *landing* **mooring** at Syracuse,
we *tarried* **abode** there three days.
13 And from thence
we *fetched a compass* **wandered around**,
and *came to* **arrived in** Rhegium:
and after one day
the *south wind blew up* **southerly sprung**,
and we came *the* next *day* to Puteoli:
14 Where we found brethren,
and were *desired* **besought**
to *tarry with* **abide among** them seven days:
and *so* **thus** we went *toward* **unto** Rome.
15 And from thence,
when the brethren heard *of* **concerning** us,
they came to meet us as far as Appii forum,
and The three taverns:
whom when *Paul* **Paulos** saw,
he *thanked God* **eucharistized Elohim**, and took courage.

PAULOS COMES TO ROME

16 And when we came to Rome,
the centurion delivered the prisoners
to the *captain of the guard* **arch warrior**:
but *Paul* **Paulos**
was *suffered* **allowed** to *dwell* **abide** by himself
with a *soldier* **warrior** that *kept* **guarded** him.

PAULOS WITNESSES TO THE YAH HUDIYM

17 And it *came to pass* **became**, that after three days
Paul **Paulos** called the *chief* **preeminent**
of the *Jews* **Yah Hudiym** together:
and when they were come together,
he *said* **worded** unto them, Men and brethren,
though I have *committed nothing* **done naught**
against the people, or customs of our fathers,
yet was I delivered prisoner from *Jerusalem* **Yeru Shalem**
into the hands of the Romans.
18 Who, when they had examined me,
would have let me go **had willed to release me**,
because there was no cause of death in me.
19 But when the *Jews* **Yah Hudiym**
spake against it **contradicted**,
I was *constrained* **compelled**
to *appeal* **call** unto *Caesar* **the Kaisar**;
not that I had *ought* **somewhat**
to accuse my *nation of* **goyim**.
20 *For* **Through** this cause therefore
have I *called for* **besought** you,
to see you, and to speak with you:
because **indeed**,
that for **sake of** the hope of *Israel* **Yisra El**
I am bound with this chain **this fetter is hung around me**.
21 And they said unto him,
We neither received *letters* **scribings**
out of *Judaea* **Yah Hudah**
concerning thee,
neither any of the brethren
that came *shewed* **evangelized**
or spake any *harm of* **evil concerning** thee.
22 But we desire to hear of thee what thou thinkest:
for **indeed** as concerning this *sect* **heresy**,
we know that every where
it is *spoken against* **contradicted**.
23 And when they had *appointed* **ordained** him a day,
there came many to him into his lodging;
to whom he expounded and *testified* **witnessed**
the *kingdom* **sovereigndom** of *God* **Elohim**,
persuading **convincing** them concerning *Jesus* **Yah Shua**,
both out of the *law* **torah** of *Moses* **Mosheh**,
and out of the prophets, from **early** morning till evening.
24 And some *believed* **indeed confided**
the things **in those** which were *spoken* **worded**,
and some *believed not* **distrusted**.

PAULOS TURNS FROM THE YAH HUDIYM

25 And *when they agreed not* **disagreeing**
among themselves **with one another**,
they *departed* **released**,
after that *Paul* **Paulos** had spoken one *word* **rhema**,
Well spake the Holy *Ghost* **Spirit**
by Esaias **through Yesha Yah** the prophet
unto our fathers,
26 *Saying* **Wording**, Go unto this people, and say,
Hearing ye shall hear,
and shall not *understand* **no way comprehend**;
and seeing ye shall see, and not *perceive* **no way see**:
27 For the heart of this people is *waxed gross* **calloused**,
and their ears *are dull* **burdensome** of hearing,
and their eyes have they *closed* **shut**;
lest **ever** they should see with their eyes,
and hear with their ears,
and *understand* **comprehend** with their heart,
and should *be converted* **turn around**,
and I should heal them.
Yesha Yah 6:9,10

ELOHIM'S SALVATION APOSTOLIZED TO THE GOYIM

28 Be it known therefore unto you,
that the salvation of *God* **Elohim**
is *sent* **apostolized** unto the *Gentiles* **goyim**,
and that they *will* **shall** hear it.
29 And when he had said these words,
the *Jews* **Yah Hudiym** departed,
and had *great reasoning* **much disputation**
among themselves.

PAULOS PREACHES AND DOCTRINATES THE SOVEREIGNDOM OF ELOHIM AND ADONAY YAH SHUA MESSIAH

30 And *Paul dwelt* **Paulos abode** two whole years
in his own *hired house* **rental**,
and received all that *came in* **entered** unto him,
31 Preaching the *kingdom* **sovereigndom** of *God* **Elohim**,
and *teaching* **doctrinating** those *things*
which concern
the Lord Jesus Christ **Adonay Yah Shua Messiah**,
with all *confidence* **boldness**,
no man forbidding him **unhindered**.

KEY TO INTERPRETING THE EXEGESES:
King James text is in regular type;
Text under exegeses is in oblique type;
Text of exegeses is in bold type.

SALUTATION

1
Paul **Paulos,**
a servant of *Jesus Christ* **Yah Shua Messiah,**
a called *to be an* apostle,
separated **set apart**
unto the *gospel* **evangelism** of *God* **Elohim,**
2 (Which he had *promised afore* **pre—evangelized**
by **through** his prophets in the holy scriptures,)
3 Concerning his Son *Jesus Christ* **Yah Shua Messiah**
our *Lord* **Adonay,**
which *was made* **became** of the *seed* **sperma** of David
according to the flesh;
4 And *declared to be* **decreed** the Son of *God* **Elohim**
with power **in dynamis,**
according to the spirit of holiness,
by the resurrection from the dead:
5 *By* **Through** whom
we have *received grace* **taken charism** and apostleship,
for **unto** obedience *to* **of** the *faith* **trust**
among all *nations* **goyim**, for his name:
6 Among whom are ye also
the called of *Jesus Christ* **Yah Shua Messiah:**
7 To all that be in Rome,
beloved of *God* **Elohim,** called *to be saints* **holy:**
Grace **Charism** to you and *peace* **shalom**
from *God* **Elohim** our Father,
and *the Lord Jesus Christ* **Adonay Yah Shua Messiah.**
8 First **indeed,** I *thank* **eucharistize** my *God* **Elohim**
through *Jesus Christ* **Yah Shua Messiah** for you all,
that your *faith* **trust** is *spoken of* **evangelized**
throughout **in** the whole *world* **cosmos.**

PAULOS DESIRES TO VISIT ROME

9 For *God* **Elohim** is my witness,
whom I *serve with* **liturgize in** my spirit
in the *gospel* **evangelism** of his Son,
that without ceasing **as unceasingly**
I make *mention* **remembrance** of you
always in my prayers;
10 *Making request* **Petitioning,**
if *by any means now at length* **somehow ever**
I might *have a prosperous journey* **prosper**
by **in** the will of *God* **Elohim** to come unto you.

SPIRITUAL CHARISMA

11 For I *long* **yearn** to see you,
that I may impart unto you some spiritual *gift* **charisma,**
to *the end ye may be established* **establish you;**
12 That is, that I may be *comforted* **consoled** together
with **in** you
by **through** the *mutual faith* **trust in one another**
both of you and me **— yours and mine.**
13 Now I *would* **will**
not have you ignorant **that you not be unknowing,** brethren,
that *oftentimes* **often**
I *purposed* **predetermined** to come unto you,
(but was *let* **forbidden** hitherto,)
that I might have some fruit among you also,
even **exactly** as among *other Gentiles* **the rest of the goyim.**
14 I am debtor
both to the *Greeks* **Hellenes,** and to the Barbarians;
both to the wise, and to the *unwise* **mindless.**
15 *So* **Thus,** as much as in me is,
I am *ready* **eager** to *preach the gospel* **evangelize**
to you that are at Rome also.

THE DYNAMIS OF THE EVANGELISM

16 For I am not ashamed
of the *gospel* **evangelism** of *Christ* **Messiah:**
for it is the *power* **dynamis** of *God* **Elohim** unto salvation
to every one that *believeth* **trusteth;**
both to the *Jew* **Yah Hudiy** first,
and also to the *Greek* **Hellene.**
17 For therein
is the *righteousness* **justness** of *God revealed* **Elohim unveiled**
from *faith* **trust** to *faith* **trust:**
exactly as *it is written* **scribed,**
The just shall live by *faith* **trust.**
Habakkuk 2:4

IRREVERENCE AND INJUSTICE

18 For the wrath of *God* **Elohim**
is *revealed* **unveiled** from heaven
against all *ungodliness* **irreverence**
and *unrighteousness* **injustice** of *men* **humanity,**
who hold the truth in *unrighteousness* **injustice;**
19 Because that which may be known of *God* **Elohim**
is manifest in them;
for *God* **Elohim** hath *shewed* **manifested** it unto them.
20 For *the invisible things of him* **his invisibles**
from the creation of the *world* **cosmos** are clearly seen,
being *understood* **comprehended**
by *the things that are made* **his doings,**
even **both** his eternal *power* **dynamis**
and *Godhead* **Divinity;**
so that they are *without excuse* **inexcusable:**
21 Because that, when they knew *God* **Elohim,**
they glorified him not as *God* **Elohim,**
neither *were thankful* **eucharistized;**
but became vain in their *imaginations* **reasonings,**
and their *foolish* **uncomprehending** heart was darkened.
22 Professing themselves to be wise,
they became fools,
23 And changed the glory
of the uncorruptible *God* **Elohim**
into an *image* **icon**
made like **likened** to corruptible *man* **humanity,**
and to *birds* **flyers,** and *fourfooted beasts* **quadrupeds,**
and *creeping things* **creepers.**
24 Wherefore *God* **Elohim** also
gave **surrendered** them *up* to *uncleanness* **impurity**
through **in** the *lusts* **pantings** of their own hearts,
to dishonour their own bodies
between **among** themselves:
25 Who *changed* **exchanged** the truth of *God* **Elohim**
into a lie,
and *worshipped* **venerated** and *served* **liturgized**
the creature *more than* **beyond** the Creator,
who is *blessed for ever* **eulogized unto the eons.**
Amen.

HOMOSEXUALITY

26 For this cause
God gave **Elohim surrendered** them *up*
unto *vile affections* **dishonourable passions:**
for *even* **both** their *women* **females**
did change **exchanged** the *natural use* **physical function**
into that which is against nature:
27 And likewise also the *men* **males,**
leaving **forsaking** the *natural use* **physical function**
of the *woman* **female,**
burned **inflamed** in their *lust* **craving** one toward another;
men with men **males among males**
working *that which is unseemly* **misbehaviour,**
and *receiving in* **taking unto** themselves
that *recompence* **retribution** of their *error* **seduction**
which was *meet* **necessary.**
28 And *even* **exactly** as they did not *like* **approve**
to *retain God* **regard Elohim** in *their* knowledge,
God gave **Elohim surrendered** them *over*
to a *reprobate* **disapproved** mind,
to do those *things* which are not *convenient* **becoming;**
29 Being filled with all *unrighteousness* **injustice,**
fornication **whoredom,** *wickedness* **evil,**
covetousness **avarice,** maliciousness;
full of envy, murder, *debate* **contention,**
deceit, *malignity* **mischievousness;** whisperers,
30 *Backbiters* **Slanderers,** *haters of God* **Elohim—haters,**
despiteful **insulters,** proud, *boasters* **braggarts,**
inventors of evil *things,*
disobedient **distrusting** to parents,
31 *Without understanding* **Uncomprehending,**
covenantbreakers **uncovenanted,**
without natural affection **selfish,**
implacable **disagreeable,** unmerciful:
32 Who knowing the judgment of *God* **Elohim,**
that they which *commit* **transact** such *things*
are worthy of death,
not only do the same,
but *have pleasure in* **think well of** them
that *do* **transact** them.

ELOHIM'S JUST JUDGMENT

2 Therefore thou art inexcusable, O *man* **humanity**,
whosoever thou art that judgest:
for wherein thou judgest another,
thou condemnest thyself;
for thou that judgest *doest* **transactest** the same *things.*
2 But we *are sure* **perceive**
that the judgment of *God* **Elohim** is according to truth
against them which *commit* **transact** such *things.*
3 And *thinkest* **reckonest** thou this, O *man* **humanity**,
that judgest them which *do* **transact** such *things,*
and doest the same,
that thou shalt escape the judgment of *God* **Elohim**?
4 Or *despisest* **disesteemest** thou
the riches of his *goodness* **kindness**
and *forbearance* **tolerance** and *longsuffering* **patience**;
not knowing that the *goodness* **kindness** of *God* **Elohim**
leadeth thee to repentance?
5 But after thy hardness and *impenitent* **unrepentant** heart
treasurest up unto thyself wrath
against **in** the day of wrath and *revelation* **apocalypse**
of the *righteous* **just** judgment of *God* **Elohim**;
6 Who *will render* **shall give back** to *every man* **each**
according to his *deeds* **works**:
7 To them who **indeed**
by *patient continuance* **endurance**
in *well doing* **good works**
seek for glory and honour
and *immortality* **incorruptibility**, eternal life:
8 But unto them that are *contentious* **rivalrous**,
and *do not obey* **indeed distrust** the truth,
but obey *unrighteousness* **injustice**,
indignation **fury**, and wrath,
9 Tribulation and *anguish* **distress**,
upon every soul of *man doeth* **humanity**
that worketh evil,
both of the *Jew* **Yah Hudiy** first,
and also of the *Gentile* **Hellene**;
10 But glory, honour, and *peace* **shalom**,
to every *man* **one** that worketh good,
both to the *Jew* **Yah Hudiy** first,
and also to the *Gentile* **Hellene**:
11 For there is no *respect of persons* **partiality**
with *God* **Elohim**.
12 For as many as have sinned without *law* **torah**
shall also *perish* **destruct** without *law* **torah**:
and as many as have sinned in *the law* **torah**
shall be judged *by the law* **through torah**;
13 (For not the hearers of the *law* **torah**
are just *before God* **with Elohim**,
but the doers of the *law* **torah** shall be justified.
14 For when the *Gentiles* **goyim**,
which have not the *law* **torah**,
do by nature *the things* **those** contained in the *law* **torah**,
these, having not the *law* **torah**,
are a *law* **torah** unto themselves:
15 Which *shew* **indicate** the work of the *law* **torah**
written **scribed** in their hearts,
their conscience also *bearing witness* **co—witnessing**,
and their *thoughts* **logic** *the mean while* accusing
or else *excusing* **pleading between** one another;)
16 In the day when *God* **Elohim**
shall judge the secrets of *men* **humanity**
by Jesus Christ **through Yah Shua Messiah**
according to my *gospel* **evangelism**.

THE YAH HUDIY AND THE TORAH

17 Behold, thou art *called a Jew* **named Yah Hudiy**,
and *restest* **reposest** in the *law* **torah**,
and makest thy boast *of God* **in Elohim**,
18 And knowest his will,
and approvest *the things* **those**
that *are more excellent* **thoroughly surpass**,
being *instructed* **catechized** out of the *law* **torah**;
19 And art confident
that thou thyself art a guide of the blind,
a light of them which are in darkness,
20 *An instructor* **A pedagogue** of the *foolish* **thoughtless**,
a *teacher* **doctor** of babes,
which hast the form of knowledge and of the truth
in the *law* **torah**.
21 Thou therefore which *teachest* **doctrinatest** another,
teachest **doctrinatest** thou not thyself?
thou that preachest, *a man should not steal* **Steal not**,
dost thou steal **stealest thou**?
22 Thou that *sayest* **wordest**,
a man should not commit adultery **Thou shalt not adulterize**,
dost thou *commit adultery* **adulterize**?
thou that abhorrest idols,
dost thou *commit sacrilege* **strip priestal precincts**?
23 Thou that makest thy boast *of the law* **in torah**,
through *breaking* **transgressing** the *law* **torah**
dishonourest thou *God* **Elohim**?
24 For the name of *God* **Elohim**
is blasphemed among the *Gentiles* **goyim** through you,
exactly as *it is written* **scribed**.
25 For circumcision *verily profiteth* **indeed benefiteth**,
if **ever** thou *keep* **transact** the *law* **torah**:
but if **ever** thou *be a breaker of* **transgress** the *law* **torah**,
thy circumcision is *made* **become** uncircumcision.
26 Therefore if **ever** the uncircumcision
keep **guard** the *righteousness* **judgment** of the *law* **torah**,
shall not **indeed** his uncircumcision
be *counted for* **reckoned unto** circumcision?
27 And shall not uncircumcision which is by nature,
if it *fulfil* **complete** the *law* **torah**, judge thee,
who *by* **through** the *letter* **scribing** and circumcision
dost transgress the *law* **torah**?
28 For he is not *a Jew* **Yah Hudiy**,
which is one *outwardly* **in manifestation**;
neither *is that* circumcision,
which is *outward* **in manifestation** in the flesh:
29 But he is *a Jew* **Yah Hudiy**,
which is one *inwardly* **in the secrets**;
and circumcision is that of the heart, in the spirit,
and not in the *letter* **scribing**;
whose *praise* **halal** is not of *men* **humanity**,
but of *God* **Elohim**.

THE SUPERABUNDANCE OF THE YAH HUDIY

3 What *advantage* **superabundance** then
hath the *Jew* **Yah Hudiy**?
or what *profit* **benefit** *is there* of circumcision?
2 Much every *way* **manner**: *chiefly* **first indeed**,
because that unto them
were *committed* **entrusted** the oracles of *God* **Elohim**.
3 For what if some *did not believe* **distrusted**?
shall their *unbelief* **distrust**
make the faith of God without effect
inactivate the trust of Elohim?
4 *God forbid* **So be it not**:
yea, let *God* **Elohim** be true,
but every *man* **human** a liar;
exactly as *it is written* **scribed**,
That **ever** thou mightest be justified in thy *sayings* **words**,
and mightest *overcome* **triumph**
when thou art **in being** judged.
Psalm 51:4

OUR UNJUSTNESS

5 But if our *unrighteousness* **unjustness**
commend the *righteousness* **justness** of *God* **Elohim**,
what shall we say?
Is *God unrighteous* **Elohim unjust**
who *taketh vengeance* **bringeth wrath**?
(I *speak* **word** as a *man* **human**)
6 *God forbid* **So be it not**:
for then **otherwise** how
shall *God* **Elohim** judge the *world* **cosmos**?
7 For if the truth of *God* **Elohim**
hath more abounded through **superaboundeth in** my lie
unto his glory;
why yet am I also judged as a sinner?
8 And not *rather,*
(**exactly** as we be *slanderously reported* **blasphemed**,
and **exactly** as some *affirm* **say** that we *say* **word**,)
Let us do evil, that good may come?
whose *damnation* **judgment** is just.
9 What then? *are* **excel** we *better than they?*
No, *in no wise* **most certainly not**:
for we have *before proved* **previously accused**
both *Jews* **Yah Hudiym** and *Gentiles* **Hellenes**,
that they are all under sin;

10 **Exactly** As *it is written* **scribed,**
There is none *righteous* **just**, *no,* not **even** one:
11 There is none that *understandeth* **comprehendeth**,
there is none that seeketh after *God* **Elohim**.
12 They are all *gone out of the way* **deviated**,
they are *together* **simultaneously**
become unprofitable **useless**;
there is none that doeth *good* **kindness**, *no,* not **even** one.
Psalm 14:1—3
13 Their *throat* **larynx** is an open *sepulchre* **tomb**;
with their tongues they have *used deceit* **deceived**;
the *poison* **venom** of asps is under their lips:
14 Whose mouth is full of cursing and bitterness:
15 Their feet are *swift* **sharp** to *shed* **pour** blood:
16 *Destruction* **Crushing** and misery are in their ways:
17 And the way of *peace* **shalom** have they not known:
18 There is no *fear* **awe** of *God* **Elohim** before their eyes.
Psalms 5:9, 10:7, 36:1, 140:3, Yesha Yah 59:7,8
19 Now we know that
what things soever **as much as**
the *law saith* **torah wordeth**,
it *saith* **speaketh** to them who are *under* **in** the *law* **torah**:
that every mouth may be *stopped* **sealed**,
and all the *world* **cosmos**
may become *guilty* **under judgment** before *God* **Elohim**.
20 *Therefore* **Because**
by the *deeds* **works** of the *law* **torah**
there shall *no* **not any** flesh be justified in his sight:
for *by* **through** the *law* **torah** is the knowledge of sin.

JUSTNESS THROUGH TRUST

21 But now the *righteousness* **justness** of *God* **Elohim**
without **apart from** the *law* **torah** is manifested,
being witnessed by the *law* **torah** and the prophets;
22 Even the *righteousness* **justness** of *God* **Elohim**
which is by faith **through trust**
of *Jesus Christ* **Yah Shua Messiah**
unto all and upon all them that *believe* **trust**:
for there is no *difference* **distinction**:
23 For all have sinned,
and *come short of* **failed** the glory of *God* **Elohim**;
24 Being justified *freely* **gratuitously** by his *grace* **charism**
through the redemption
that is in *Christ Jesus* **Messiah Yah Shua**:
25 Whom *God* **Elohim** hath *set forth* **predetermined**
to be a *propitiation* **kapporeth**
through *faith* **trust** in his blood,
to *declare* **indicate** his *righteousness* **justness**
for the *remission* **passing over** of sins
that *are past* **have previously transpired**,
through **in** the *forbearance* **tolerance** of *God* **Elohim**;
26 To *declare, I say* **indicate**,
at this time **in this present season**
unto his *righteousness* **justness**:
that he might be just,
and *the justifier of* **justifying** him
which believeth **by trust** in *Jesus* **Yah Shua**.
27 Where is boasting then? It is excluded.
By **Through** what *law* **torah**? of works?
Nay **indeed**: but *by* **through** the *law* **torah** of *faith* **trust**.
28 Therefore we *conclude* **reckon**
that a *man* **human** is justified by *faith* **trust**
without **apart from** the *deeds* **works** of the *law* **torah**.
29 **Or** Is he the *God* **Elohim**
of the *Jews* **Yah Hudiym** only?
is he **indeed** not also of the *Gentiles* **goyim**?
Yes **Yea**, of the *Gentiles* **goyim** also:
30 *Seeing* **Since** it is one *God* **Elohim**,
which shall justify the circumcision by *faith* **trust**,
and uncircumcision through *faith* **trust**.
31 Do we then *make void* **inactivate** the *law* **torah**
through *faith* **trust**?
God forbid **So be it not**:
yea **rather**, we *establish* **set** *the law* **torah**.

ABRAHAM'S JUSTNESS

4 What shall we say then that Abraham our father,
as pertaining to the flesh, hath found?
2 For if Abraham were justified by works,
he hath whereof to *glory* **boast**;
but not *before God* **toward Elohim**.
3 For what *saith* **wordeth** the scripture?
Abraham *believed God* **trusted Elohim**,
and it was *counted* **reckoned** unto him
for righteousness **unto justness**.
Genesis 15:6
4 Now to him that worketh
is the reward not reckoned of *grace* **charism**, but of debt.
5 But to him that worketh not,
but *believeth* **trusteth** on him
that justifieth the *ungodly* **irreverent**,
his *faith* **trust**
is *counted for righteousness* **reckoned unto justness**.
6 *Even* **Exactly** as David also *describeth* **wordeth**
the blessedness of *the man* **humanity**,
unto whom
God imputeth righteousness **Elohim reckoneth justness**
without **apart from** works,
7 *Saying,* Blessed are they
whose *iniquities* **torah violations** are forgiven,
and whose sins are covered.
8 Blessed is the man to whom
the Lord will **Adonay shall** not **no way** *impute* **reckon** sin.
Psalm 32:1, 2

JUSTNESS VS ORDINANCES

9 *Cometh* this blessedness then
upon the circumcision *only,*
or upon the uncircumcision also?
for we *say* **word**
that *faith* **trust** was reckoned to Abraham
for righteousness **unto justness**.
10 How was it then reckoned?
when he was **being** in circumcision,
or in uncircumcision?
Not in circumcision, but in uncircumcision.
11 And he *received* **took** the sign of circumcision,
a seal of the *righteousness* **justness**
of the *faith* **trust** which he had
yet **through** being *uncircumcised* **in uncircumcision**:
that he might be **unto his being** the father
of all them that *believe* **trust**,
though *they be not circumcised* **being in uncircumcision**;
that righteousness **unto justness**
might be imputed **being reckoned** unto them also:
12 And the father of circumcision
to them who are not of the circumcision only,
but who also *walk* **march** in the *steps* **tracks**
of that *faith* **trust** of our father Abraham,
which he had
being *yet uncircumcised* **in uncircumcision**.

JUSTIFICATION VS THE TORAH

13 For the *promise* **pre—evangelism**,
that he should be the heir of the *world* **cosmos**,
was not to Abraham, or to his *seed* **sperma**,
through the *law* **torah**,
but through the *righteousness* **justness** of *faith* **trust**.
14 For if they which are of the *law* **torah** be heirs,
faith **trust** is *made void* **voided**,
and the *promise* **pre—evangelism**
made of none effect **inactivated**:
15 *Because* **Indeed** the *law* **torah** worketh wrath:
for where no *law* **torah** is, there is no transgression.

JUSTNESS THROUGH TRUST BY CHARISM

16 Therefore it is *of faith* **through trust**,
that it might be by *grace* **charism**;
to the end **unto** the *promise* **pre—evangelism**
might be sure **being stedfast** to all the *seed* **sperma**;
not to that only which is of the *law* **torah**,
but to that also which is of the *faith* **trust** of Abraham;
who is the father of us all,
17 **(Exactly** As *it is written* **scribed**,
I have *made* **placed** thee a father of many *nations* **goyim**,)
before **in front of** him whom he *believed* **trusted**,
even God **Elohim**,
who *quickeneth* **enliveneth** the dead,
and calleth those *things which be not* **not being**
as *though they were* **being**.
18 Who against hope *believed* **trusted** in hope,
that he might become the father of many *nations* **goyim**;
according to that which was *spoken* **said**,
So **Thus** shall thy *seed* **sperma** be.
Genesis 15:5, 17:5

19 And being not *weak* **frail** in *faith* **the trust**,
he considered not his own body
now dead **already deadened**,
when he was about an **being some** hundred years old,
neither yet
the *deadness* **necrosis** of Sarah's *womb* **matrix**:
20 He *staggered* **doubted** not
at **unto** the *promise* **pre—evangelism** of *God* **Elohim**
through *unbelief* **trustlessness**;
but was *strong* **dynamized** in *faith* **trust**,
giving glory to *God* **Elohim**;
21 And being fully *persuaded* **assured** that,
what he had *promised* **pre—evangelized**,
he was able also to *perform* **do**.
22 And therefore it was *imputed* **reckoned** to him
for righteousness **unto justness**.
23 Now it was not *written* **scribed** for his sake alone,
that it was *imputed* **reckoned** to him;
24 But for us also,
to whom it shall be *imputed* **reckoned**,
if we *believe* **trust** on him
that raised up *Jesus* **Yah Shua** our *Lord* **Adonay**
from the dead;
25 Who was delivered for our *offences* **downfalls**,
and was raised again for our justification.

THE RESULT OF JUSTNESS

5 Therefore *being* **having been** justified by *faith* **trust**,
we have *peace* **shalom** with *God* **Elohim**
through our *Lord Jesus Christ* **Adonay Yah Shua Messiah**:
2 *By* **Through** whom also we have access
by **trust** *faith* into this *grace* **charism** wherein we stand,
and *rejoice* **boast** in hope of the glory of *God* **Elohim**.
3 And not only *so*, but we *glory* **boast** in tribulations also:
knowing that tribulation worketh *patience* **endurance**;
4 And *patience* **endurance**, *experience* **proof**;
and *experience* **proof**, hope:
5 And hope *maketh* **shameth** not *ashamed*;
because the love of *God* **Elohim**
is *shed abroad* **poured forth** in our hearts
by **through** the Holy *Ghost* **Spirit** which is given unto us.
6 For *when we were yet without strength* **we being frail**,
in due time **season**
Christ **Messiah** died for the *ungodly* **irreverent**.
7 For *scarcely* **difficultly**
for *a righteous man will one* **the just shall some** die:
yet peradventure **indeed perhaps**
for *a good man* **the good**
some *would* **should** even dare to die.
8 But *God* **Elohim** commendeth his love *toward* **unto** us,
in that, *while* we *were* **being** yet sinners,
Christ **Messiah** died for us.
9 Much more then,
being now **having been** justified *by* **in** his blood,
we shall be saved from wrath through him.
10 For if, *when we were* **being** enemies,
we were reconciled to *God* **Elohim**
by **through** the death of his Son,
much more, being reconciled,
we shall be saved *by* **in** his life.
11 And not only *so*,
but we also *joy* **boast** in *God* **Elohim**
through our *Lord Jesus Christ* **Adonay Yah Shua Messiah**,
by **through** whom we have now
received **taken** the *atonement* **reconciliation**.

THE ORIGIN OF SIN

12 Wherefore,
exactly as *by* **through** one *man* **human**
sin entered into the *world* **cosmos**,
and death *by* **through** sin;
and *so* **thus** death passed *upon* **unto** all *men* **humanity**,
for that all have sinned:
13 (For until the *law* **torah** sin was in the *world* **cosmos**:
but sin is not *imputed* **reckoned**
when there *is* **being** no *law* **torah**.
14 *Nevertheless* **Rather**
death reigned from Adam to *Moses* **Mosheh**,
even over them that had not sinned
after the *similitude* **likeness** of Adam's transgression,
who is the *figure* **type** of *him* **the one**
that was **about** to *come* **be**.

JUSTIFICATION AND LIFE THROUGH YAH SHUA MESSIAH

15 But not as the *offence* **downfall**,
so **thus** also is the *free gift* **charisma**.
For if through the *offence* **downfall** of one many be dead,
much more the *grace* **charism** of *God* **Elohim**,
and the *gift by grace* **gratuity in charism**,
which is by one *man* **human**,
Jesus Christ **Yah Shua Messiah**
hath *abounded* **superabounded** unto many.
16 And not as *it was by* **through** one that sinned,
so is the *gift* **gratuity**:
for the judgment **indeed** was by one
to condemnation,
but the *free gift* **charisma** is of many *offences* **downfalls**
unto justification.
17 For if by one man's *offence* **downfall**
death reigned *by* **through** one;
much more they which *receive* **take**
abundance **a superabundance** of *grace* **charism**
and of the *gift* **gratuity** of *righteousness* **justness**
shall reign in life *by* **through** one,
Jesus Christ **Yah Shua Messiah**.)
18 Therefore as *by the offence of* **through** one
judgment came upon **downfall unto** all *men* **humanity**
be to condemnation;
even *so* **thus** *by the righteousness of* **through** one
the free gift **justification**
came upon all men **unto all humanity**
be unto justification of life.
19 For **exactly** as
by **through** one *man's* **human's** disobedience
many were *made* **seated** sinners,
so by **thus through** the obedience of one
shall many be *made righteous* **seated just**.
20 Moreover the *law* **torah surreptitiously** entered,
that the *offence* **downfall** might *abound* **superabound**.
But where sin *abounded* **superabounded**,
grace **charism**
did much more abound **exceedingly superabounded**:
21 That **exactly** as sin hath reigned *unto* **in** death,
even *so* **thus** might *grace* **charism** reign
through *righteousness* **justness** unto eternal life
by Jesus Christ **through Yah Shua Messiah** our *Lord* **Adonay**.

DEAD TO SIN, ALIVE IN THE MESSIAH

6 What shall we say then?
shall we *continue* **abide** in sin,
that *grace* **charism** may *abound* **superabound**?
2 *God forbid* **So be it not**.
How shall we that are dead to sin,
still live *any longer* therein?
3 **Or** Know ye not, that so many of us
as were baptized into *Jesus Christ* **Yah Shua Messiah**
were baptized into his death?
4 Therefore we are *buried* **co—buried** with him
by **through** baptism into death:
that *like* **exactly** as *Christ* **Messiah**
was raised *up* from the dead
by **through** the glory of the Father,
even *so* **thus** we also should walk in newness of life.
5 For if we have been *planted together* **co—planted**
in the likeness of his death,
we shall be also
in the likeness **rather** of his resurrection:
6 Knowing this,
that our old *man* **humanity**
is *crucified with him* **co—staked**,
that the body of sin might be *destroyed* **inactivated**,
so that *henceforth* we should *not* **no longer** serve sin.
7 For he that is dead is *freed* **justified** from sin.
8 Now if we be dead with *Christ* **Messiah**,
we *believe* **trust** that we shall also *live* **co—live** with him:
9 Knowing that *Christ* **Messiah** being raised from the dead
dieth *no more* **not still**;
death *hath no more dominion over*
shall not still overlord him.
10 For in that he died, he died unto sin once:
but in that he liveth, he liveth unto *God* **Elohim**.
11 *Likewise* **Thus** reckon ye also yourselves
to be dead indeed unto sin, but alive unto *God* **Elohim**
through **in** *Jesus Christ* **Yah Shua Messiah** our *Lord* **Adonay**.

PRESENT YOUR MEMBERS AS WEAPONS OF JUSTNESS

12 Let not sin therefore reign in your mortal body,
that ye should obey it in the *lusts* **pantings** *thereof.*
13 Neither *yield* **present** ye your members
as *instruments* **weapons** of *unrighteousness* **injustice**
unto sin:
but yield yourselves unto *God* **Elohim**,
as *those that are* alive from the dead,
and your members
as *instruments* **weapons** of *righteousness* **justness**
unto *God* **Elohim**.
14 For sin shall not *have dominion over* **overlord** you:
for ye are not under the *law* **torah**,
but under *grace* **charism**.
15 What then? shall we sin,
because we are not under the *law* **torah**,
but under *grace* **charism**?
God forbid **So be it not**.
16 Know ye not, that to whom ye yield yourselves
servants *to obey* **unto obedience**,
his servants ye are to whom ye obey;
whether **either indeed** of sin unto death,
or of obedience unto *righteousness* **justness**?
17 But *God be thanked* **charism to Elohim**,
that ye were the servants of sin,
but ye have obeyed from the heart
that *form* **type** of doctrine
which was **wherein ye were** delivered *you.*
18 Being then *made free* **liberated** from sin,
ye became
the servants of righteousness **subservient to justness**.
19 I *speak after the manner of men* **word as a human**
because of the *infirmity* **frailty** of your flesh:
for **exactly** as ye have *yielded* **presented** your members
servants to *uncleanness* **impurity**
and to *iniquity* **torah violations**
unto *iniquity* **torah violations**;
even *so* **thus** now *yield* **present** your members
servants to *righteousness* **justness** unto holiness.
20 For when ye were the servants of sin,
ye were *free* **liberated** from *righteousness* **justness**.
21 What fruit had ye then
in those *things* whereof ye are now ashamed?
for the *end* **completion** of those *things* is death.
22 But now being *made free* **liberated** from sin,
and become *servants* **subservient** to *God* **Elohim**,
ye have your fruit unto holiness,
and the *end* **completion,** *everlasting* **eternal** life.
23 For the wages of sin is death;
but the *gift* **charisma** of *God* **Elohim** is eternal life
through Jesus **in Yah Shua Messiah** our *Lord* **Adonay**.

ANALOGY OF MARRIAGE

7 **Or** Know ye not, brethren,
(for I speak to them that know the *law* **torah**,)
how that the *law* **torah**
hath dominion over a man **overlordeth a human**
as long **time** as he liveth?
2 For the woman *which hath an husband* **under man**
is bound by the *law* **torah** to her *husband* **man**
so long as he liveth;
but if **ever** the *husband* **man** be dead,
she is *loosed* **inactivated**
from the *law* **torah** of her *husband* **man**.
3 *So then* **Therefore** if **ever**,
while her *husband* **man** liveth
she *be married to another man* **becometh another man's**,
she shall be *called* **oracled as** an adulteress:
but if *her husband* **ever her man** be dead,
she is *free* **liberated** from that *law* **torah**;
so that she is no adulteress,
though she *be married to* **become** another *man* **man's**.
4 *Wherefore* **So then**, my brethren,
ye also are *become dead* **deathified** to the *law* **torah**
by **through** the body of *Christ* **the Messiah**;
that ye should be *married to another* **another's**,
even to him who is raised from the dead,
that we should *bring forth* **bear** fruit unto *God* **Elohim**.
5 For when we were in the flesh,
the *motions* **sufferings** of sins,
which were *by* **through** the *law* **torah**,
did work **energized** in our members
to *bring forth* **bear** fruit unto death.
6 But now
we are *delivered* **inactivated** from the *law* **torah**,
that being dead wherein we were held;
so that we should serve in newness of spirit,
and not in the *oldness* **antiquity** of the *letter* **scribing**.
7 What shall we say then? Is the *law* **torah** sin?
God forbid **So be it not**.
Nay **Rather**, I had not known sin,
but by **except through** the *law* **torah**:
for I had not known *lust* **panting**,
except the *law* **torah** had *said* **worded**,
Thou shalt not *covet* **pant**.
8 But sin, taking *occasion* **opportunity**
by **through** the *commandment* **misvah**,
wrought **worked** in me
all *manner of concupiscence* **panting**.
For *without* **apart from** the *law* **torah**
sin was dead.
9 For I was alive
without **apart from** the *law once* **torah formerly**:
but when the *commandment* **misvah** came,
sin *revived* **relived**, and I died.
10 And the *commandment* **misvah**,
which was ordained to **unto life**,
I found *to be* **this** unto death.
11 For sin, taking *occasion* **opportunity**
by **through** the *commandment* **misvah**,
deceived **seduced** me,
and *by* **through** it *slew* **slaughtered** me.
12 *Wherefore* **So then indeed** the *law* **torah** is holy,
and the *commandment* **misvah** holy, and just, and good.

TWO NATURES UNDER THE TORAH

13 Was then that which is good
made **become** death unto me?
God forbid **So be it not**.
But sin, that it might *appear* **be manifest as** sin,
working death in me *by* **through** that which is good;
that sin *by* **through** the *commandment* **misvah**
might become exceeding sinful.
14 For we know that the *law* **torah** is spiritual:
but I am *carnal* **fleshly**, sold under sin.
15 For that which I *do* **work,** I *allow* **know** not:
for what I *would* **will**, that *do* **transact** I not;
but what I hate, that do I.
16 If then I do that which I *would* not **will**,
I *consent unto* **assent with** the *law* **torah** that it is good.
17 Now then it is *no more* **not still** I that *do* **work** it,
but sin that dwelleth in me.
18 For I know that in me (that is, in my flesh,)
dwelleth no good *thing*:
for to will is present with me;
but *how to perform* **to work** that which is good
I find not.
19 For the good that I *would* **will,** I do not:
but the evil which I *would* not **will**, that I *do* **transact**.
20 Now if I do that I *would* not will,
it is *no more* **not still** I that *do* **work** it,
but sin that dwelleth in me.
21 I find then *a law* **the torah**, that,
when I *would* **will to** do good, evil is present with me.
22 For I delight in the *law* **torah** of *God* **Elohim**
after the inward *man* **human**:
23 But I see another *law* **torah** in my members,
warring against the *law* **torah** of my mind,
and *bringing* **capturing** me *into captivity*
to the *law* **torah** of sin *which is* **being** in my members.
24 *O wretched man that I am* **Miserable human — I**!
who shall *deliver* **rescue** me from the body of this death?
25 I *thank God* **eucharistize Elohim**
through *Jesus Christ* **Yah Shua Messiah** our *Lord* **Adonay**.
So **Therefore** then with the mind
I myself **indeed** serve the *law* **torah** of *God* **Elohim**;
but with the flesh the *law* **torah** of sin.

THE TORAH OF THE SPIRIT; LIFE IN THE MESSIAH

8 There is therefore now no condemnation to them
which are in *Christ Jesus* **Messiah Yah Shua**,
who walk not after the flesh, but after the Spirit°.

°not in mss; but see 8:4

2 For the *law* **torah** of the Spirit of life
in *Christ Jesus* **Messiah Yah Shua**
hath *made* **liberated** me *free*
from the *law* **torah** of sin and death.
3 For *what the law could not do*
the torah, in being incapable,
in that it was *weak* **frail** through the flesh,
God **Elohim** sending his own Son
in the likeness of *sinful flesh* **the flesh of sin**, and for sin,
condemned sin in the flesh:
4 That the *righteousness* **judgment** of the *law* **torah**
might be fulfilled in us,
who walk not after the flesh, but after the Spirit.

In Flesh vs In Spirit

5 For they *that are* **being** after the flesh
do mind the things **think** of the flesh;
but they that are after the Spirit
the things **those** of the Spirit.
6 For *to be carnally minded* **the thought of the flesh**
is death;
but *to be spiritually minded* **the thought of the spirit**
is life and *peace* **shalom**.
7 Because the *carnal mind* **thought of the flesh**
is enmity *against God* **unto Elohim**:
for it is not *subject* **subjugated**
to the *law* **torah** of *God* **Elohim**,
neither indeed can be.
8 So then they *that are in the* **being in** flesh
cannot please *God* **Elohim**.
9 But ye are not in *the* flesh, but in *the* Spirit,
if *so be that* **ever** the Spirit of *God* **Elohim** dwell in you.
Now if *any man* **one**
have not the Spirit of *Christ* **Messiah**,
he is none of his.
10 And if *Christ* **Messiah** be in you,
the body is **indeed** dead because of sin;
but the Spirit is life because of *righteousness* **justness**.
11 But if the Spirit of him
that raised up *Jesus* **Yah Shua** from the dead
dwell in you,
he that raised up *Christ* **Messiah** from the dead
shall also *quicken* **enliven** your mortal bodies
by **through** his Spirit that dwelleth in you.
12 Therefore **then**, brethren, we are debtors,
not to the flesh, to live after the flesh.
13 For if ye live after the flesh, ye shall **be about to** die:
but if ye through the Spirit
do mortify **deathify** the *deeds* **functions** of the body,
ye shall live.
14 For as many as are led by the Spirit of *God* **Elohim**,
they are the sons of *God* **Elohim**.

The Spirit of Sonship

15 For ye have not *received* **taken**
the spirit of *bondage* **servitude** again to *fear* **awe**;
but ye have *received* **taken** the Spirit of *adoption* **sonship**,
whereby **wherein** we cry, Abba, Father.
16 The *Spirit itself* **selfsame Spirit**
beareth witness **co—witnesseth** with our spirit,
that we are the children of *God* **Elohim**:
17 And if children, then heirs; heirs of *God* **Elohim**,
and *joint—heirs* **co—heirs indeed** with *Christ* **Messiah**;
if *so be that* **ever** we *suffer with him* **co—suffer**,
that we may be also *glorified together* **co—glorified**.
18 For I reckon
that the sufferings of this present *time* **season**
are not worthy *to be compared* with the glory
which shall **about to** be *revealed* **unveiled** in us.
19 For the *earnest expectation* **intense anticipation**
of the creature
waiteth for **awaiteth** the *manifestation* **apocalypse**
of the sons of *God* **Elohim**.
20 For the creature
was *made subject* **subjugated** to vanity,
not *willingly* **voluntarily**,
but *by reason of* **through** him
who *hath subjected the same* **subjugated** in hope,
21 Because the creature itself also
shall be *delivered* **liberated**
from the *bondage* **servitude** of corruption
into the *glorious* liberty **of the glory**
of the children of *God* **Elohim**.
22 For we know that the whole creation
groaneth **co—sigheth** and *travaileth* **co—travaileth**
in pain *together* until now.
23 And not only *they*, but ourselves also,
which have the *firstfruits* **firstlings** of the Spirit,
even we ourselves *groan within* **sigh among** ourselves,
waiting for **awaiting** the *adoption* **sonship**,
to wit, the redemption of our body.
24 For we are saved by hope:
but hope that is seen is not hope:
for what *a man* **one** seeth,
why *doth* **shall** he yet hope *for?*
25 But if we hope for that we see not,
then *do* we
with patience wait for it **through endurance await.**

The Intercessory Ministry of the Holy Spirit

26 Likewise the Spirit also *helpeth* **co—helpeth**
our *infirmities* **frailties**:
for we know not what *we* should pray for
according as we *ought* **must**:
but the Spirit *itself*
maketh intercession **intercedeth exceedingly** for us
with *groanings which cannot be uttered* **unutterable sighs.**
27 And he that searcheth the hearts
knoweth what is the *mind* **thought** of the Spirit,
because he *maketh intercession* **intercedeth**
for the *saints* **holy**
according to the will of *God* **Elohim**.
28 And we know that all *things*
work together for **co—work unto** good
to them that love *God* **Elohim**,
to them *who are* **being** the called
according to his *purpose* **prothesis**.

The Sequence of Elohim's Protection

29 For whom he *did foreknow* **foreknew**,
he also *did predestinate* **predetermined**
to be conformed to the *image* **icon** of his Son,
that he might *be* **unto his being**
the firstborn among many brethren.
30 Moreover
whom he *did predestinate* **predetermined**,
them he also called:
and whom he called, them he also justified:
and whom he justified, them he also glorified.

Nine Questions

31 What shall we then say to these *things?*
If *God* **Elohim** be for us, who can be against us?
32 He that **yet indeed** spared not his own Son,
but delivered him up for us all,
how **indeed** shall he not with him also
freely give us all things **grant us charism with all**?
33 Who shall *lay any thing to the charge of* **accuse**
God's elect **Elohim's select**?
It is God that justifieth. **Elohim that justifieth?**
34 Who is he that condemneth?
It is Christ **Messiah** that died,
yea rather, that is risen again,
who is even at the right *hand* of *God* **Elohim**,
who also *maketh intercession for us.* **intercedeth for us?**
35 Who shall separate us
from the love of *Christ* **the Messiah**?
shall tribulation, or distress, or persecution,
or famine, or nakedness, or peril, or sword?
36 **Exactly** As *it is written* **scribed**,
For thy sake we are *killed* **deathified** all the day long;
we are *accounted* **reckoned** as sheep for the slaughter.
37 *Nay* **Rather**, in all these *things*
we are *more than conquerors* **exceedingly triumphant**
through him that loved us.
Psalm 44:22
38 For I am *persuaded* **convinced**,
that neither death, nor life, nor angels,
nor *principalities* **hierarchies**, nor *powers* **dynamis**,
nor *things* **the** present,
nor *things to come* **the about to be**,
39 Nor height, nor depth, nor any other *creature* **creation**,
shall be able to separate us from the love of *God* **Elohim**,
which is in
Christ Jesus **Messiah Yah Shua** our *Lord* **Adonay**.

ELOHIM'S SELECTION OF YISRA EL
9 I *say* **word** the truth in *Christ* **Messiah**, I lie not,
my conscience also *bearing me witness* **co—witnessing**
in the Holy *Ghost* **Spirit**,
2 That I have *great heaviness* **mega sorrow**
and *continual sorrow* **unceasing grief** in my heart.
3 For I *could wish* **had vowed** that
myself were *accursed* **anathema** from *Christ* **the Messiah**
for my brethren, my *kinsmen* **kin** according to the flesh:
4 Who are *Israelites* **Yisra Elym**;
to whom pertaineth **whose is** the *adoption* **sonship**,
and the glory, and the covenants,
and the *giving* **setting** of the *law* **torah**,
and the *service of God* **liturgy**,
and the *promises* **pre—evangelisms**;
5 Whose are the fathers,
and of whom as concerning the flesh
Christ **the Messiah** came, *who is* **being** over all,
God blessed for ever **Elohim eulogized unto the eons**.
Amen.
6 Not **such** as though the word of *God* **Elohim**
hath *taken none effect* **failed**.
For they are not all *Israel* **Yisra El**,
which are of *Israel* **Yisra El**:
7 Neither, because they are the *seed* **sperma** of Abraham,
are they all children:
but, In *Isaac* **Yischaq** shall thy *seed* **sperma** be called.
Genesis 21:12
8 That is, They which are the children of the flesh,
these are not the children of *God* **Elohim**:
but the children of the *promise* **pre—evangelism**
are *counted for* **reckoned unto** the *seed* **sperma**.
9 For this is the word of *promise* **pre—evangelism**,
At this *time will* **season shall** I come,
and Sarah shall have a son.
Genesis 18:10
10 And not only this;
but when *Rebecca* **Rebekah**
also had *conceived* **coition** by one,
even by our father *Isaac* **Yischaq**;
11 (For *the children* being not yet born,
neither having *done* **transacted** any good or evil,
that the *purpose* **prothesis** of *God* **Elohim**
according to *election* **selection** might *stand* **abide**,
not of works, but of him that calleth;)
12 It was *said* **rhetorized** unto her,
The *elder* **greater** shall serve the *younger* **lesser**.
Genesis 25:23
13 **Exactly** As *it is written* **scribed**,
Jacob **Yaaqov** have I loved, but *Esau* **Esav** have I hated.
Malachi 1:2, 3
14 What shall we say then?
Is there unrighteousness **Injustice** with *God* **Elohim**?
God forbid **So be it not**.
15 For he *saith* **wordeth** to *Moses* **Mosheh**,
I will have mercy on whom I will have mercy
I shall mercy whomever I shall mercy,
and I will have compassion
on whom I will have compassion
and I shall compassion whomever I shall compassion.
16 *So* **Therefore** then it is not of him that willeth,
nor of him that runneth,
but of *God* **Elohim** that *sheweth mercy* **mercieth**.
17 For the scripture *saith* **wordeth** unto *Pharaoh* **Paroh**,
Even *for* **unto** this *same purpose* have I raised thee up,
that I might *shew* **indicate** my *power* **dynamis** in thee,
and that my name might be *declared* **evangelized**
throughout **in** all the earth.
Hoshea 1:10
18 Therefore **then,**
hath he mercy on whom he will have mercy
he mercieth whom he willeth,
and whom he *will* **willeth** he hardeneth.
19 Thou *wilt* **shalt** say then unto me,
Why doth he yet *find fault* **blame**?
For who hath *resisted* **withstood** his *will* **counsel**?
20 *Nay but* **Yet then**, O *man* **humanity**,
who art thou
that *repliest against God* **contradictest Elohim**?
shall the *thing formed it* **molded**
say to him that *formed* **molded** ,
Why hast thou made me thus?
21 **Or** Hath not the potter *power* **authority** over the clay,
of the same lump
to make one vessel **indeed** unto honour,
and another unto dishonour?
22 *What* **And** if *God* **Elohim**,
willing **willeth** to *shew* **indicate** his wrath,
and to make his *power* **ability** known,
endured with **bore in** much *longsuffering* **patience**
the vessels of wrath *fitted to* **prepared unto** destruction:
23 And that he might make known the riches of his glory
on the vessels of mercy,
which he had *afore* **previously** prepared unto glory,
24 Even us, whom he hath called,
not of the *Jews* **Yah Hudiym** only,
but also of the *Gentiles* **goyim**?
25 As he *saith* **wordeth** also in *Osee* **Hoshea**,
I *will* **shall** call them my people,
which were not my people;
and her beloved,
which was not beloved.
26 And it shall *come to pass* **become**,
that in the place where it was *said* **rhetorized** unto them,
Ye are not my people;
there shall they be called
the *children* **sons** of the living *God* **Elohim**.
Hoshea 1:10
27 *Esaias* **Yesha Yah** also crieth
concerning Israel **in behalf of Yisra El**,
Though **Even if** the number
of the *children* **sons** of *Israel* **Yisra El**
be as the sand of the sea,
a remnant shall be saved:
28 For he *will finish* **shall complete** the *work* **word**,
and cut it short in *righteousness* **justness**:
because a short *work* **word**
will the Lord **shall Yah Veh** make upon the earth.
Yesha Yah 10:22, 23
29 And **exactly** as *Esaias said before* **Yesha Yah foretold**,
Except the Lord of **Unless Yah Veh** Sabaoth
had left *us* **behind** a *seed* **sperma**,
we had *been* **ever become** as *Sodoma* **Sedom**,
and *been made like* **ever likened**
unto Gomorrha **as Amorah**.

JUSTNESS BY TRUST
30 What shall we say then?
That the *Gentiles* **goyim**,
which *followed* **pursued** not *after righteousness* **justness**,
have *attained to righteousness* **overtaken justness**,
even the *righteousness* **justness** which is *of faith* **by trust**.
31 But *Israel* **Yisra El**, which *followed after* **pursued**
the *law* **torah** of *righteousness* **justness**,
hath not attained
to the *law* **torah** of *righteousness* **justness**.
32 *Wherefore* **Why**?
Because *they sought it* not by *faith* **trust**,
but as *it were* by the works of the *law* **torah**.
For they stumbled at that stumblingstone;
33 **Exactly** As *it is written* **scribed**,
Behold, I *lay* **place** in *Sion* **Siyon** a stumblingstone
and rock of *offence* **scandal**:
and whosoever *believeth* **trusteth** on him
shall not *be ashamed* **shame**.
Psalm 118:22, Yesha Yah 8:14, 28:16

YISRA EL LACKING TRUST
10 Brethren, **indeed,**
my heart's desire **the well approving of my heart**
and *prayer* **petition** to *God* **Elohim** for *Israel* **Yisra El** is,
that they might be saved **unto their salvation.**
2 For I *bear them record* **witness**
that they have a zeal of *God* **Elohim**,
but not according to knowledge.
3 For they being *ignorant* **unknowing**
of *God's righteousness* **Elohim's justness**,
and *going about* **seeking**
to *establish* **set** their own *righteousness* **justness**,
have not *submitted* **subjugated** themselves
unto the *righteousness* **justness** of *God* **Elohim**.
4 For *Christ* **Messiah**

is the *end* **completion** of the *law* **torah**
for righteousness **unto justness**
to every one that *believeth* **trusteth.**
5 For *Moses describeth* **Mosheh scribed**
the righteousness **of the justness** which is of the *law* **torah**,
That the *man* **human** which doeth those *things*
shall live *by* **in** them.
Leviticus 18:5
6 But the *righteousness* **justness** *which is* of *faith* **trust**
speaketh on this wise **wordeth thus**,
Say not in thine heart, Who shall ascend into heaven?
(that is, to bring *Christ* **Messiah** down *from above*:)
7 Or, Who shall descend into the *deep* **abyss**?
(that is, to bring up *Christ* **Messiah** *again* from the dead.)
8 But what *saith* **wordeth** it?
The *word* **rhema** is nigh thee,
even in thy mouth, and in thy heart:
that is, the *word* **rhema** of *faith* **trust**, which we preach;
Deuteronomy 30:12—14
9 That if **ever** thou shalt *confess with* **profess in** thy mouth
the Lord Jesus **Adonay Yah Shua**,
and shalt *believe* **trust** in thine heart
that *God* **Elohim** hath raised him from the dead,
thou shalt be saved.
10 For with the heart
man believeth **trust is** unto *righteousness* **justness**;
and with the mouth
confession **profession** is *made* unto salvation.
11 For the scripture *saith* **wordeth**,
Whosoever *believeth* **trusteth** on him
shall not *be ashamed* **shame**.
Yesha Yah 29:16, 49:23
12 For there is no *difference* **distinction**
between *the Jew* **both Yah Hudiy** and *the Greek* **Hellene**:
for the same *Lord* **Adonay** over all
is rich unto all that call upon him.
13 For whosoever
shall call upon the name of *the Lord* **Yah Veh**
shall be saved.
Yah El 2:32
14 How then shall they call on him
in whom they have not *believed* **trusted**?
and how shall they *believe* **trust** in him
of whom they have not heard?
and how shall they hear *without* **apart from** a preacher?
15 And how shall they preach,
except **unless** they be *sent* **apostolized**?
exactly as *it is written* **scribed,**
How beautiful are the feet of them
that *preach the gospel of peace* **evangelize shalom**,
and *bring glad tidings of* **evangelize** good *things*!
Yesha Yah 52:7, Nachum 1:15
16 But they have not all obeyed the *gospel* **evangelism**.
For *Esaias saith* **Yesha Yah wordeth**, *Lord* **Yah Veh**,
who hath *believed* **trusted** our *report* **hearing**?
Yesha Yah 53:1
17 So then *faith* **trust** *cometh* by hearing,
and hearing by the *word* **rhema** of *God* **Elohim**.
18 But I *say* **word**, Have they not heard?
Yes verily **Yet then**, their sound went into all the earth,
and their *words* **rhema**
unto the *ends* **extremities** of the world.
Psalm 19:4
19 But I *say* **word,** Did not *Israel* **Yisra El** know?
First *Moses saith* **Mosheh wordeth**,
I *will provoke* **shall incite** you to jealousy
by *them that are no people* **a nongoyim**,
and by *a foolish nation* **an uncomprehending goyim**
I *will anger* **shall enrage** you.
Deuteronomy 32:21
20 But *Esaias* **Yesha Yah** is very *bold* **courageous**,
and *saith* **wordeth**, I was found of them
that sought me not;
I *was made* **became** manifest unto them
that asked not after me.
21 But to *Israel* **Yisra El** he *saith* **wordeth**,
All day long I have *stretched forth* **extended** my hands
unto a *disobedient* **distrusting**
and *gainsaying* **contradicting** people.
Yesha Yah 42:6, 7, 65:1, 2

11

I *say* **word** then,
Hath *God cast* **Elohim shoved** away his people?
God forbid **So be it not.**
For I also am an *Israelite* **Yisra Eliy**,
of the *seed* **sperma** of Abraham,
of the *tribe* **scion** of *Benjamin* **Ben Yamin**.
2 *God* **Elohim** hath not *cast* **shoved** away his people
which he foreknew.
Wot **Or perceive** ye not
what the scripture *saith of Elias* **wordeth in Eli Yah**?
how he *maketh intercession* **intercedeth** to *God* **Elohim**
against *Israel saying* **Yisra El wording**,
3 *Lord* **Yah Veh**,
they have *killed* **slaughtered** thy prophets,
and digged down thine **sacrifice** altars;
and I **also** am *left* **behind** alone,
and they seek my *life* **soul**.
1 Sovereigns 19:10, 14
4 But what *saith* **wordeth**
the *answer of God* **oracle** unto him?
I have *reserved* **left** to myself seven thousand men,
who have not bowed the knee to *the image of* Baal.
1 Sovereigns 19:18
5 Even *so* **thus** then at this present *time* **season** also
there is a remnant
according to the *election* **selection** of *grace* **charism.**
6 And if by *grace* **charism,**
then is it *no more* **not still** of works:
otherwise *grace* **charism**
is *no more grace* **not still charism**.
But if *it be* of works,
then it is *no more grace* **not still charism**:
otherwise work is *no more* **not still** work.
7 What then?
Israel **Yisra El** hath not obtained
that which he seeketh for;
but the *election* **selection** hath obtained it,
and the rest were *blinded* **petrified.**
8 (*According* **Exactly** as *it is written* **scribed**,
God **Elohim** hath given them
the spirit of *slumber* **insensitivity**,
eyes that they should not see,
and ears that they should not hear;) unto this day **today**.
Yesha Yah 29:10
9 And David *saith* **wordeth**,
Let their table be *made* **into** a snare,
and **into** a *trap* **prey**,
and **into** a *stumblingblock* **scandal**,
and **into** a recompence unto them:
10 Let their eyes be darkened, that they may not see,
and bow down their back *alway* **continually**.
Psalm 69:22
11 I *say* **word** then,
Have they stumbled that they should fall?
God forbid **So be it not**:
but *rather* through their *fall* **downfall**
salvation is *come* unto the *Gentiles* **goyim**,
for to *provoke* **incite** them to jealousy.
12 Now if the *fall* **downfall** of them
be the riches of the *world* **cosmos**,
and the diminishing of them
the riches of the *Gentiles* **goyim**;
how much more their fulness?
13 For I *speak* **word** to you *Gentiles* **goyim**,
inasmuch **indeed**
as I am the apostle of the *Gentiles* **goyim**,
I *magnify mine office* **glorify my ministry**:
14 If *by any means* **somehow** I may *provoke* **incite**
to emulation them which are my flesh **to jealousy**,
and might save some of them.
15 For if the casting away of them
be the reconciling of the *world* **cosmos**,
what shall the *receiving* **reception** of them be,
but **except** life from the dead?
16 For if the *firstfruit* **firstlings** be holy,
the lump is also *holy*:
and if the root be holy, so are the branches.
17 And if some of the branches be *broken off* **exscinded**,
and thou, being a wild olive *tree*,

wert graffed in among them **were ingrafted**,
and with them
partakest **becamest co—partaker** of the root
and fatness of the *olive tree* **olives**;
18 *Boast* **Exult** not against the branches.
But if thou *boast* **exult**,
thou bearest not the root, but the root thee.
19 Thou *wilt* **shalt** say then,
The branches were *broken off* **exscinded**,
that I might be *graffed in* **ingrafted**.
20 Well;
because of *unbelief* **trustlessness**
they were *broken off* **exscinded**,
and thou standest by *faith* **trust**.
Be not highminded, but *fear* **awe**:
21 For if *God* **Elohim** spared not the natural branches,
take heed lest **somehow** he *also* spare not thee.
22 *Behold* **Perceive** therefore
the *goodness* **kindness** and severity of *God* **Elohim**:
on them which fell, **indeed** severity;
but toward thee, *goodness* **kindness**,
if **ever** thou *continue* **abide** in his *goodness* **kindness**:
otherwise thou also shalt be *cut off* **exscinded**.
23 And they also,
if **unless ever** they abide *not still* in *unbelief* **trustlessness**,
shall be *graffed in* **ingrafted**:
for *God* **Elohim** is able to *graff* **ingraft** them *in* again.
24 For if thou wert *cut* **exscinded** out of the olive *tree*
which is wild by nature,
and wert *graffed contrary to* **ingrafted against** nature
into a good olive *tree*:
how much more shall these, which be the natural *branches*,
be *graffed* **ingrafted** into their own *olive tree* **olives**?
25 For I *would* **will** not, brethren,
that ye should be *ignorant* **unknowing** of this mystery,
lest ye should
be wise in your own conceits **think beyond yourselves**;
that *blindness in* **petrifaction by** part
is happened to Israel **became unto Yisra El**,
until the fulness of the *Gentiles be come in* **goyim enter**.
26 And *so* **thus** all *Israel* **Yisra El** shall be saved:
exactly as *it is written* **scribed**,
There shall come out of *Sion* **Siyon** the *Deliverer* **Rescuer**,
and shall turn away *ungodliness* **irreverence**
from *Jacob* **Yaaqov**:
27 For this is my covenant unto them,
when I shall *take away* **remove** their sins.
Psalm 14:7, Yesha Yah 59:20
28 As concerning the *gospel* **evangelism**,
they are **indeed** enemies for your sakes:
but as touching the *election* **selection**,
they are beloved for the fathers' sakes.
29 For the *gifts* **charismata** and calling of *God* **Elohim**
are *without repentance* **irrevocable**.
30 For **exactly** as ye *in times past* **formerly**
have not believed God **distrusted Elohim**,
yet *have* now *obtained mercy* **be mercied**
through their *unbelief* **distrust**:
31 Even *so* **thus**
have these also now *not believed* **distrusted**,
that through your mercy
they also may *obtain mercy* **be mercied**.
32 For *God* **Elohim**
hath *concluded* **locked** them all **together**
in *unbelief* **distrust**,
that he might *have* mercy *upon* **them** all.
33 O the depth of the riches
both of the wisdom and knowledge of *God* **Elohim**!
how *unsearchable* **unexplorable** are his judgments,
and his ways *past finding out* **untraceable**!
34 For who hath known
the *mind* **Spirit** of *the Lord* **Yah Veh**?
or who hath *been* **become** his counsellor?
35 Or who hath first given to him,
and it shall be recompensed unto him *again*?
36 For of him, and through him, and *to* **unto** him,
are all *things*:
to whom be glory *for ever* **unto the eons**.
Amen.
Yesha Yah 40:13

THE HOLY METAMORPHOSIS

12

I beseech you therefore, brethren,
by **through** the *mercies* **compassions** of *God* **Elohim**,
that ye present your bodies a living sacrifice,
holy, *acceptable* **well—pleasing** unto *God* **Elohim**,
which is your *reasonable service* **logical liturgy**.
2 And be not *conformed* **configured** to this *world* **eon**:
but be ye *transformed* **metamorphosed**
by the renewing of your mind,
that ye may prove what is that good,
and *acceptable* **well—pleasing**,
and *perfect* **complete**, will of *God* **Elohim**.

THE CHARISMATA

3 For I *say* **word**, through the *grace* **charism** given unto me,
to every *man that is* **one being** among you,
not to *think of himself* **superexalt**
more *highly* than he *ought to think* **need superexalt**;
but to think *soberly* **unto being soundminded**,
according as *God* **Elohim** hath *dealt* **imparted**
to *every man* **each** the measure of *faith* **trust**.
Philippians 2:1—8
4 For **exactly** as we have many members in one body,
and all members have not the same *office* **function**:
5 *So* **Thus** we, *being* many, are one body in *Christ* **Messiah**,
and *every one* **each** members one of another.
6 Having then *gifts* **charismata**
differing **thoroughly excelling**
according to the *grace* **charism** that is given to us,
whether prophecy,
let us prophesy according to the proportion of *faith* **trust**;
7 *Or* **Whether** ministry,
let us wait on our ministering **in ministering**:
or he that teacheth **whether doctrinating**
on teaching **in doctrine**;
8 *Or he that exhorteth* **Whether consoling**,
on exhortation **in consolation**:
he that giveth **or imparting**,
let him do it with simplicity **in liberality**;
he that ruleth **or presiding**,
with **in** diligence;
he that sheweth mercy **or mercying**,
with cheerfulness **in hilarity**.
I Corinthians 12:1—11
9 Let love be *without dissimulation* **unhypocritical**.
Abhor *that which is* evil;
cleave **adhere** to *that which is* good.
10 *Be kindly* **Cherish**
affectioned **befriending** one to another
with brotherly love **in befriending**;
in honour preferring one another;
11 Not slothful in *business* **diligence**;
fervent **zealous** in spirit;
serving *the Lord* **Adonay in season**;
12 *Rejoicing* **Cheering** in hope;
patient **abiding** in tribulation;
continuing instant in prayer;
13 *Distributing* **Imparting**
to the *necessity* **needs** of *saints* **the holy**;
given to hospitality **pursuing the befriending of strangers**.
14 *Bless* **Eulogize** them which persecute you:
bless **eulogize**, and curse not.
15 *Rejoice* **Cheer** with them that *do rejoice* **cheer**,
and weep with them that weep.
16 Be of the same *mind* **thought** one toward another.
Mind **Think** not *high things* **highly**,
but *condescend to men of low estate*
lead with the humble.
Be not wise in your own conceits
Think not beyond yourselves.
17 *Recompense* **Give back** to no *man* **one** evil for evil.
Provide *things honest* **good**
in the sight of all *men* **humanity**.
18 If it be possible, as much as *lieth in* **be of** you,
live peaceably **shalam** with all *men* **humanity**.
19 Dearly beloved, avenge not yourselves,
but *rather* give place unto wrath:
for it is *written* **scribed**, Vengeance is mine;
I *will repay* **shall recompense**,
saith the Lord **wordeth Yah Veh**.
Deuteronomy 32:35

20 Therefore if **ever** thine enemy hunger, **force** feed him;
if **ever** he thirst, give him drink:
for in so doing
thou shalt heap coals of fire on his head.
21 *Be not overcome of evil* **Let not evil triumph over you**,
but *overcome evil with* **triumph over evil in** good.
Proverbs 25:21, 22

ALL AUTHORITY IS ELOHIM—ORDAINED

13 Let every soul *be subject* **subjugate**
unto the *higher powers* **superior authorities**.
For there is no *power* **authority**
but **except** of *God* **Elohim**:
the *powers* **authorities** that be
are ordained of *God* **Elohim**.
2 **So that** Whosoever *therefore*
resisteth **withstandeth** the *power* **authority**,
resisteth **opposeth** the ordinance of *God* **Elohim**:
and they that *resist* **withstand**
shall *receive* **take** to themselves *damnation* **judgment**.
3 For *rulers* **archs** are not *a terror* **an awe** to good works,
but to the evil.
Wilt **Willest** thou then not be *afraid* **awestricken**
of the *power* **authority**?
do that which is good,
and thou shalt have *praise* **halal** of the same:
4 For he is the minister of *God* **Elohim** to thee for good.
But if **ever** thou do that which is evil, be *afraid* **awed**;
for he beareth not the sword in vain:
for he is the minister of *God* **Elohim**,
a revenger to execute **the avenger unto** wrath
upon him that *doeth* **transacteth** evil.
5 Wherefore
ye must *needs be subject* **necessarily subjugate**,
not only for wrath, but also for conscience sake.
6 For for this cause *pay* **complete** ye tribute also:
for they are *God's ministers* **Elohim's liturgists**,
attending continually **continuing**
upon **unto** this *very thing*.
7 *Render* **Give back** therefore to all their dues:
tribute to whom tribute is due
to whom tribute, tribute;
custom to whom custom
to whom completion, completion;
fear to whom fear
to whom awe, awe;
honour to whom honour
to whom honour, honour.
8 *Owe no man any thing* **Be indebted to no one**,
but **except** to love one another:
for he that loveth another hath fulfilled the *law* **torah**.
9 For this,
Thou shalt not *commit adultery* **adulterize**,
Thou shalt not *kill* **murder**,
Thou shalt not steal,
Thou shalt not *bear false* **pseudo** witness,
Thou shalt not *covet* **pant**;
and if *there be* any other *commandment* **misvah**,
it is *briefly comprehended* **summed up**
in this *saying* **word**, namely,
Thou shalt love thy neighbour as thyself.
10 Love worketh no *ill* **evil** to his neighbour:
therefore love is the fulfilling of the *law* **torah**.
Exodus 20:13—17, Leviticus 19:18
11 And that, knowing the *time* **season**,
that *now* **already** it is *high time* **the hour**
to *awake* **rise** out of sleep:
for now is our salvation nearer
than when we *believed* **trusted**.
12 The night is *far spent* **advanced**,
the day *is at hand* **approacheth**:
let us therefore *cast* **put** off the works of darkness,
and let us *put on* **endue** the *armour* **weapon** of light.
13 Let us walk *honestly* **decorously**, as in the day;
not in *rioting* **carousing** and *drunkenness* **intoxication**,
not in *chambering* **coition** and *wantonness* **lechery**,
not in *strife* **contention** and *envying* **zeal**.
14 But *put* **endue** ye *on*
the Lord Jesus Christ **Adonay Yah Shua Messiah**,
and make not provision for the flesh
to *fulfil the lusts thereof* **do its pantings**.

THE FRAIL IN THE TRUST

14 Him that is *weak* **frail** in the *faith* **trust**
receive **take ye unto yourselves**,
but not to *doubtful disputations* **discern reasonings**.
2 For **indeed** one *believeth* **trusteth**
that he may eat all *things*:
another, who is *weak* **frail**, eateth herbs.
3 Let not him that eateth
despise **belittle** him that eateth not;
and let not him which eateth not
judge him that eateth:
for *God* **Elohim** hath *received* **taken** him **unto himself**.
4 Who art thou that judgest
another man's servant **another's housekeeper**?
to his own *master* **adoni** he standeth **firm** or falleth.
Yea, he shall *be holden up* **stand**:
for *God* **Elohim** is able to *make him* stand **him**.
5 One man *esteemeth* **judgeth** one day above another:
another *esteemeth* **judgeth** every day *alike*.
Let *every man* **each** be fully *persuaded* **assured**
in his own mind.
6 He that *regardeth* **thinketh of** the day,
regardeth **thinketh** it unto *the Lord* **Adonay**;
and he that *regardeth* **thinketh** not the day,
to *the Lord* **Adonay** he *doth not regard it* **thinketh not**.
He that eateth, eateth to *the Lord* **Adonay**,
for he *giveth God thanks* **eucharistizeth Elohim**;
and he that eateth not, to *the Lord* **Adonay** he eateth not,
and *giveth God thanks* **eucharistizeth Elohim**.
7 For none of us liveth to himself,
and no *man* **one** dieth to himself.
8 For *whether* **if ever** we live,
we live unto *the Lord* **Adonay**;
and *whether* **if ever** we die,
we die unto *the Lord* **Adonay**:
whether **if ever** we live therefore,
or **if ever we** die, we are *the Lord's* **Adonay's**.
9 For to this end *Christ* **Messiah**
both died, and rose, and *revived* **relived**,
that he might
be Lord both of **overlord** the dead and living.

JUDGING AND JUSTNESS

10 But why dost thou judge thy brother?
or why dost thou *set at nought* **belittle** thy brother?
for we shall all stand
before **by** the *judgment seat* **bamah** of *Christ* **the Messiah**.
11 For it is *written* **scribed**,
As I live, *saith the Lord* **wordeth Yah Veh**,
every knee shall bow to me,
and every tongue shall *confess* **avow** to *God* **Elohim**.
Yesha Yah 45:23, Philippians 2:10, 12
So **Therefore** then *every one* **each** of us
shall give *account of* **word concerning** himself
to *God* **Elohim**.
13 Let us *not* **no longer** therefore
judge one another *any more*:
but judge this rather,
that no *man* **one** put a *stumblingblock* **stumbling**
or *an occasion to fall* **a scandal** in his brother's way.
14 I know, and am *persuaded* **convinced**
by the Lord Jesus **in Adonay Yah Shua**,
that there is *nothing unclean* **naught profane**
of **through** itself:
but **except** to him that *esteemeth* **reckoneth**
any thing **somewhat** to be *unclean* **profane**,
to him it is *unclean* **profane**.
15 But if thy brother
be *grieved with thy meat* **sorrowed through food**,
now walkest thou not *charitably* **still longer in love**.
Destroy not him with thy *meat* **food**,
for whom *Christ* **Messiah** died.
16 Let not then your good be *evil spoken of* **blasphemed**:
17 For the *kingdom* **sovereigndom** of *God* **Elohim**
is not *meat* **eat** and drink;
but *righteousness* **justness**, and *peace* **shalom**,
and *joy* **cheer** in the Holy *Ghost* **Spirit**.
18 For he that in these *things* serveth *Christ* **the Messiah**
is *acceptable* **well—pleasing** to *God* **Elohim**,
and approved of *men* **humanity**.
19 Let us therefore *follow after* **then pursue**

the things **those** which make for *peace* **shalom,**
and *things* **those** wherewith one may edify another.
20 For *meat* **sake of food**
destroy **disintegrate** not the work of *God* **Elohim.**
All *things* indeed are pure;
but it is evil for that *man* **human**
who eateth *with offence* **through stumbling.**
21 It is good neither to eat *flesh* **meat,** nor to drink wine,
nor *any thing* **aught**
whereby **wherein** thy brother stumbleth,
or is *offended* **scandalized,** or is *made weak* **frailed.**
22 Hast thou *faith* **trust?**
have it to thyself *before God* **in sight of Elohim.**
Happy **Blessed** is he
that *condemneth* **judgeth** not himself
in that *thing* which he *alloweth* **approveth.**
23 And he that doubteth
is *damned* **condemned** if **ever** he eat,
because *he eateth* **it is** not of *faith* **trust:**
for whatsoever is not of *faith* **trust** is sin.

ON PLEASING SELF

15 We then that are *strong* **able**
ought **are indebted**
to bear the *infirmities* **frailties** of the *weak* **impotent,**
and not to please ourselves.
2 **Indeed** Let *every one* **each** of us please his neighbour
for **unto** *his* good to edification.
3 For even *Christ* **the Messiah** pleased not himself;
but, **exactly** as *it is written* **scribed,**
The reproaches of them that reproached thee fell on me.
4 For *whatsoever things* **as much as**
were *written aforetime* **preinscribed,**
were *written for* **preinscribed unto** our *learning* **doctrine,**
that we through *patience* **endurance**
and *comfort* **consolation** of the scriptures
might have hope.
5 Now the *God* **Elohim**
of *patience* **endurance** and consolation
grant you to be likeminded **give you like thoughts**
one *toward* **among** another
according to *Christ Jesus* **Messiah Yah Shua:**
6 That ye may with *one mind* **unanimity** and one mouth
glorify *God* **Elohim,**
even the Father
of our *Lord Jesus Christ* **Adonay Yah Shua Messiah.**
7 Wherefore *receive ye* **take unto yourselves** one another,
exactly as *Christ* **the Messiah**
also *received* **took** us to the glory of *God* **Elohim.**
8 Now I *say* **word** that *Jesus Christ* **Yah Shua Messiah**
was **became** a minister of the circumcision
for the truth of *God* **Elohim,**
to confirm **unto establishing**
the *promises made* **pre—evangelisms** unto the fathers:
9 And that the *Gentiles* **goyim** might
glorify *God* **Elohim** for his mercy;
exactly as *it is written* **scribed,**
For this cause
I *will confess* **shall avow** to thee
among the *Gentiles* **goyim,**
and *sing* **psalm** unto thy name.
10 And again he *saith* **wordeth,**
Rejoice, ye *Gentiles* **goyim,** with his people.
11 And again,
Praise the Lord **Halalu Yah,** all ye *Gentiles* **goyim;**
and *laud* **halal** him, all ye people.
12 And again, *Esaias saith* **Yesha Yah wordeth,**
There shall be a root of *Jesse* **Yishay,**
and he that shall rise
to *reign* **rule** over the *Gentiles* **goyim;**
in him shall the *Gentiles trust* **goyim hope.**
Psalm 18:49, 117:1, Yesha Yah11:1,10, 42:6, 7
13 Now the *God* **Elohim** of hope fill you **full**
with all *joy* **cheer** and *peace* **shalom**
in *believing* **trusting,**
that ye may *abound* **superabound** in hope,
through **in** the *power* **dynamis** of the Holy *Ghost* **Spirit.**
14 And I myself also
am *persuaded of* **convinced concerning** you,
my brethren, that ye also *are* **be** full of goodness,
filled **full** with all knowledge,
able also to *admonish* **remind** one another.
15 Nevertheless, brethren,
I have *written* **scribed** the more boldly unto you
in some sort **partly,**
as putting you in mind **of re—reminding you,**
because of the *grace* **charism**
that is given to me of *God* **Elohim,**
16 That I should be the *minister* **liturgist**
of *Jesus Christ* **Yah Shua Messiah** to the *Gentiles* **goyim,**
ministering **priesting**
the *gospel* **evangelism** of *God* **Elohim,**
that the offering up of the *Gentiles* **goyim**
might be *acceptable* **wellreceived,**
being *sanctified* **hallowed** by the Holy *Ghost* **Spirit.**
17 I have therefore *whereof I may glory* **boasting**
through Jesus Christ **in Yah Shua Messiah**
in those things which pertain to God **toward Elohim.**
18 For I *will* **shall** not dare to speak of any of those *things*
which *Christ* **Messiah** hath not *wrought* **worked** by me,
to make the *Gentiles* **goyim** obedient,
by word and *deed* **work,**
19 *Through mighty* **In dynamis**
of signs and *wonders* **omens,**
by **in** the *power* **dynamis** of the Spirit of *God* **Elohim;**
so that from *Jerusalem* **Yeru Shalem** and round about
unto Illyricum,
I have *fully preached* **fulfilled**
the *gospel* **evangelism** of *Christ* **the Messiah.**
20 Yea, *so* **thus** have I *strived* **befriendingly esteemed**
to *preach the gospel* **evangelize,**
not where *Christ* **Messiah** was named,
lest I should build
upon *another man's* **another's** foundation:
21 But **exactly** as it is *written* **scribed,**
To **Concerning** whom
he was **they that were** not *spoken of* **evangelized,**
they shall see:
and they that have not heard
shall *understand* **comprehend.**
Yesha Yah 52:15

PAULOS' TRAVEL PLANS

22 *For which cause* **Therefore** also
I have been much hindered from coming to you.
23 But now having no more place in these *parts* **climes,**
and having *a great desire* **an intense yearning**
these many years to come unto you;
24 *Whensoever* **If ever**
I *take my journey* **depart** into *Spain* **Spania,**
I *will* **shall** come to you:
for I *trust* **hope** to *see* **observe** you
in my *journey* **going through,**
and to be
brought on my way thitherward **forwarded** by you,
if **ever** first
I be *somewhat* **partly** filled *with your company* **by you.**
25 But now I go unto *Jerusalem* **Yeru Shalem**
to minister unto the *saints* **holy.**
26 For it hath *pleased* **well—approved**
them of Macedonia and Achaia
to make a *certain contribution* **communion**
for **unto** the poor *saints* **holy**
which are at Jerusalem **in Yeru Shalem.**
27 *It hath pleased them verily* **They indeed well—approved;**
and their debtors they are.
For if the *Gentiles* **goyim**
have *been made partakers* **communed**
of their *spiritual things* **spirituals,**
their duty is also **they are indebted**
to *minister* **liturgize** unto them in *carnal things* **fleshlies.**
28 When therefore I have *performed* **fully completed** this,
and have sealed to them this fruit,
I *will come by* **shall depart through** you
into *Spain* **Spania.**
29 And I am sure that, when I come unto you,
I shall come in the fulness of the *blessing* **eulogy**
of the *gospel* **evangelism** of *Christ* **the Messiah.**
30 Now I beseech you, brethren,
for the *Lord Jesus Christ's sake,*
sake of our Adonay Yah Shua Messiah
and for the love of the Spirit,

that ye *strive together* **co—strive** with me
in *your* prayers to *God* **Elohim** for me;
31 That I may be *delivered* **rescued** from them
that *do not believe* **distrust** in *Judaea* **Yah Hudah**;
and that my *service* **ministry**
which I have for Jerusalem **unto Yeru Shalem**
may be *accepted* **wellreceived** of the *saints* **holy**;
32 That I may come unto you *with joy* **in cheer**
by **through** the will of *God* **Elohim**,
and may with you be refreshed.
33 Now the *God* **Elohim** of *peace* **shalom** be with you all.
Amen.

PAULOS SALUTES THE HOLY

16 I commend unto you Phebe our sister,
which is **being** a *servant* **minister**
of the *church which is at* **ecclesia in** Cenchrea:
2 That ye *receive* **await** her in *the Lord* **Adonay**,
as becometh saints **worthily of the holy**,
and that ye *assist* **stand by** her
in whatsoever *business* **matter** she **ever** hath need of you:
for she hath *been* **become**
a *succourer* **patroness** of many,
and of myself also.
3 *Greet* **Salute** Priscilla and Aquila
my helpers **co—workers** in *Christ Jesus* **Messiah Yah Shua**:
4 Who have for my *life* **soul** laid down their own necks:
unto whom not only I *give thanks* **eucharistize**,
but also all the *churches* **ecclesiae** of the *Gentiles* **goyim**.
5 Likewise *greet* the *church* **ecclesia** that is in their house.
Salute my *wellbeloved* **beloved** Epaenetus,
who is the *firstfruits* **firstlings** of Achaia
unto *Christ* **Messiah**.
6 *Greet Mary* **Salute Miryam**,
who *bestowed* **laboured** much *labour on* **unto** us.
7 Salute Andronicus and Junia, my *kinsmen* **kin**,
and my *fellowprisoners* **co—captives**,
who are *of note* **eminent** among the apostles,
who also *were* **became** in *Christ* **Messiah** before me.
8 *Greet* **Salute** Amplias my beloved in *the Lord* **Adonay**.
9 Salute *Urbane* **Urbanos**,
our *helper* **co—worker** in *Christ* **Messiah**,
and Stachys my beloved.
10 Salute Apelles approved in *Christ* **Messiah**.
Salute them which are of Aristobulus' *household*.
11 Salute Herodion my *kinsmen* **kindred**.
Greet **Salute** them *that be of the household* of Narcissus,
which are **being** in *the Lord* **Adonay**.
12 Salute Tryphena and Tryphosa,
who labour in *the Lord* **Adonay**.
Salute the beloved Persis,
which laboured much in *the Lord* **Adonay**.
13 Salute Rufus *chosen* **selected** in *the Lord* **Adonay**,
and his mother and mine.
14 Salute Asyncritus, Phlegon, Hermas, Patrobas, Hermes,
and the brethren which are with them.
15 Salute Philologus, and Julia,
Nereus, and his sister, and Olympas,
and all the *saints* **holy** which are with them.
16 Salute one another *with* **in** an holy kiss.
The *churches* **ecclesiae** of *Christ* **the Messiah** salute you.

PAULOS WARNS THE HOLY

17 Now I beseech you, brethren,
mark **scope** them
which cause divisions and *offences* **scandals**
contrary to **against** the doctrine which ye have learned;
and *avoid* **deviate from** them.
18 For they that are such serve not
our *Lord Jesus Christ* **Adonay Yah Shua Messiah**,
but their own belly;
and *by good* **through kind** words
and *fair speeches* **eulogy**
deceive **seduce** the hearts of the simple.
19 For your obedience
is *come abroad* **spread forth** unto all *men*.
I *am glad* **cheer** therefore on your behalf:
but yet **indeed** *I would have* **I will that** you **be** wise
unto that which is good,
and *simple concerning* **unadulterated unto** evil.
20 And the *God* **Elohim** of *peace* **shalom**
shall *bruise* **crush** Satan under your feet
shortly **in quickness.**
The *grace* **charism**
of our *Lord Jesus Christ* **Adonay Yah Shua Messiah**
be with you.
Amen.

SALUTES OF THE MINISTERS

21 *Timotheus* **Timo Theos** my *workfellow* **co—worker**,
and Lucius, and Jason, and Sosipater,
my *kinsmen* **kindred**, salute you.
22 I Tertius, who *wrote* **scribed** this epistle,
salute you in *the Lord* **Adonay**.
23 Gaius mine *mine host* **my stranger**,
and of the whole *church* **ecclesia**, saluteth you.
Erastus the *chamberlain* **administrator** of the city
saluteth you,
and Quartus a brother.
24 The *grace* **charism**
of our *Lord Jesus Christ* **Adonay Yah Shua Messiah**
be with you all.
Amen.

DOXOLOGY

25 Now to him that is *of power* **able** to stablish you
according to my *gospel* **evangelism**,
and the preaching of *Jesus Christ* **Yah Shua Messiah**,
according to the *revelation* **apocalypse** of the mystery,
which was *kept secret* **hushed**
since *the world began* **eternal time**,
26 But now is *made manifest* **manifested**,
and *by the* **through prophetic** scriptures *of the prophets*,
according to the *commandment* **order**
of the *everlasting God* **eternal Elohim**,
made known to all *nations* **goyim**
for **unto** the obedience of *faith* **trust**:
27 To *God* **Elohim** only wise,
be glory through *Jesus Christ* **Yah Shua Messiah**
for ever **unto the eons**.
Amen.

KEY TO INTERPRETING THE EXEGESES:
King James text is in regular type;
Text under exegeses is in oblique type;
Text of exegeses is in bold type.

SALUTATION

1 *Paul* **Paulos**, *called to be an* **a called** apostle
of *Jesus Christ* **Yah Shua Messiah**
through the will of *God* **Elohim**,
and Sosthenes our brother,
2 Unto the *church* **ecclesia** of *God* **Elohim**
which is at **being in** Corinth,
to them that are *sanctified* **hallowed**
in *Christ Jesus* **Messiah Yah Shua**,
called *to be saints* **holy**,
with all that in every place call upon the name
of *Jesus Christ* **Yah Shua Messiah** our *Lord* **Adonay**,
both their's and our's:
3 *Grace be* **Charism** unto you, and *peace* **shalom**,
from *God* **Elohim** our Father,
and *from*
the Lord Jesus Christ **Adonay Yah Shua Messiah**.

CHARISM AND CHARISMA

4 I *thank* **eucharistize** my *God* **Elohim** always
on your behalf **concerning you**,
for the *grace* **charism** of *God* **Elohim** which is given you
by Jesus Christ **in Yah Shua Messiah**;
5 That in *every thing* **all** ye are enriched *by* **in** him,
in all *utterance* **word**, and *in* all knowledge;
6 *Even* **Exactly** as
the *testimony* **witness** of *Christ* **the Messiah**
was *confirmed* **established** in you:
7 So that ye *come behind* **fail** in no *gift* **charisma**;
waiting for **awaiting** the *coming* **apocalypse**
of our *Lord Jesus Christ* **Adonay Yah Shua Messiah**:
8 Who shall also *confirm* **establish** you
unto the *end* **completion**,
that ye may be blameless — **unaccusable**
in the day
of our *Lord Jesus Christ* **Adonay Yah Shua Messiah**.
9 *God* **Elohim** is *faithful* **trustworthy**,
by **through** whom ye were called
unto the *fellowship* **communion** of his Son
Jesus Christ **Yah Shua Messiah** our *Lord* **Adonay**.

SCHISMS IN THE ECCLESIA

10 Now I beseech you, brethren, *by* **through** the name
of our *Lord Jesus Christ* **Adonay Yah Shua Messiah**,
that ye all *speak* **word** the same *thing*,
and that there be no *divisions* **schisms** among you;
but that ye be *perfectly joined together* **prepared**
in the same mind and in the same *judgment* **opinion**.
11 For it hath been *declared* **evidenced** unto me
of **concerning** you, my brethren,
by them which are *of the house* of Chloe,
that there are contentions among you.
12 Now this I *say* **word**,
that *every one* **each** of you *saith* **wordeth**,
I am **indeed** of *Paul* **Paulos**; and I of Apollos;
and I of *Cephas* **Kepha**; and I of *Christ* **Messiah**.
13 Is *Christ* **the Messiah** divided?
was *Paul crucified* **Paulos staked** for you?
or were ye baptized in the name of *Paul* **Paulos**?
14 I *thank God* **eucharistize Elohim**
that I baptized none of you,
but **except** Crispus and Gaius;
15 Lest any should say
that I had baptized in *mine own* **my** name.
16 And I baptized also the household of Stephanas:
besides **finally**,
I know not *whether* **if** I baptized any other.
17 For *Christ sent* **Messiah apostolized** me not to baptize,
but to *preach the gospel* **evangelize**:
not *with* **in** wisdom of words,
lest the *cross* **stake** of *Christ* **the Messiah**
should be *made of none effect* **voided**.
18 For the *preaching* **word** of the *cross* **stake**
is to them that *perish* **destruct indeed** foolishness;
but unto us which are saved
it is the *power* **dynamis** of *God* **Elohim**.
19 For it is *written* **scribed**,
I *will* **shall** destroy the wisdom of the wise,
and *will bring to nothing* **shall set aside**
the *understanding* **comprehension**
of the *prudent* **comprending**.
Yesha Yah 29:14
20 Where is the wise? where is the scribe?
where is the disputer of this *world* **eon**?
hath not *God* **Elohim indeed**
made foolish **follied** the wisdom of this *world* **cosmos**?
21 For *after that* **since** in the wisdom of *God* **Elohim**
the *world by* **cosmos through** wisdom
knew not *God* **Elohim**,
it pleased God **Elohim well—approved**
by **that through** the foolishness of preaching
to save them that *believe* **trust**.
22 *For* **Since** the *Jews require* **Yah Hudiym ask** a sign,
and the *Greeks* **Hellenes** seek after wisdom:
23 But we preach *Christ crucified* **Messiah staked**,
unto the *Jews* **Yah Hudiym**
indeed a *stumblingblock* **scandal**,
and unto the *Greeks* **Hellens** foolishness;
24 But unto them which are called,
both *Jews* **Yah Hudiym** and *Greeks* **Hellenes**,
Christ **Messiah** the *power* **dynamis** of *God* **Elohim**,
and the wisdom of *God* **Elohim**.
25 Because the foolishness of *God* **Elohim**
is wiser than *men* **humanity**;
and the *weakness* **frailty** of *God* **Elohim**
is *stronger* **mightier** than *men* **humanity.**
26 For ye see your calling, brethren,
how that not many wise *men* after the flesh,
not many *mighty* **able**, not many *noble* **wellborne**,
are called:
27 But *God* **Elohim** hath *chosen* **selected**
the foolish *things* of the *world* **cosmos**
to *confound* **shame** the wise;
and *God* **Elohim** hath *chosen* **selected**
the *weak things* **frailties** of the *world* **cosmos**
to *confound* **shame** the *things which are* mighty;
28 And *base things* **the ignoble** of the *world* **cosmos**,
and *things which are despised* **the belittled**,
hath *God chosen* **Elohim selected**,
yea, and *things which are not* **those not being**,
to *bring to nought* **inactivate**
things that are **those being**:
29 That no flesh should *glory* **boast** in his *presence* **sight**.
30 But of him are ye in *Christ Jesus* **Messiah Yah Shua**,
who of *God* **Elohim** is *made* **become** unto us
wisdom, and *righteousness* **justness**,
and *sanctification* **holiness**, and redemption:
31 That, *according* **exactly** as *it is written* **scribed**,
He that *glorieth* **boasteth**,
let him *glory* **boast** in *the Lord* **Yah Veh**.
Yirme Yah 9:23, 24

PAULOS EVANGELIZES THE MESSIAH

2 And I **also**, brethren, when I came to you,
came not with excellency of *speech* **word** or of wisdom,
declaring **evangelizing** unto you
the *testimony* **witness** of *God* **Elohim**.
2 For I *determined* **judged**
not to know *any thing* **aught** among you,
save Jesus Christ **except Yah Shua Messiah**,
and him *crucified* **staked**.
3 And I *was* **became** with you in *weakness* **frailty**,
and in *fear* **awe**, and in much trembling.
4 And my *speech* **word** and my preaching
was not *with enticing* **in persuasive** words
of *man's* **human** wisdom,
but in *demonstration* **manifestation** of the Spirit
and of *power* **dynamis**:
5 That your *faith* **trust** should not *stand* **be**
in the wisdom of *men* **humanity**,
but in the *power* **dynamis** of *God* **Elohim**.
6 Howbeit we speak wisdom
among them that are *perfect* **complete**:
yet not the wisdom of this *world* **eon**,
nor of the *princes* **archs** of this *world* **eon**,
that *come to nought* **inactivate**:
7 But we speak the wisdom of *God* **Elohim** in a mystery,
even the hidden wisdom — **the secreted**,
which *God ordained* **Elohim predetermined**

before the *world* **eons** unto our glory:
8 Which none of the *princes* **archs** of this *world* **eon**
knew:
for **if** — had they known *it*, they *would* **should** not **ever**
have *crucified* **staked** the *Lord* **Adonay** of glory.

THE SECRETED MYSTERY SECRETED

9 But **exactly** as *it is written* **scribed**,
Eye hath not seen, nor ear heard,
neither have *entered* **ascended**
into the heart of *man* **humanity**,
the things **those** which *God* **Elohim** hath prepared
for them that love him.

THE SECRETED MYSTERY UNVEILED

10 But *God* **Elohim** hath *revealed* **unveiled** *them* unto us
by **through** his Spirit:
for the Spirit searcheth all *things*,
yea, the *deep things* **depths** of *God* **Elohim**.
11 For what *man* **human**
knoweth *the things* **those** of a *man* **human**,
save **except** the spirit of *man* **humanity** which is in him?
even *so the things* **thus those** of *God* **Elohim**
knoweth no *man* **one**,
but **except** the Spirit of *God* **Elohim**.
12 Now we have *received* **taken**,
not the spirit of the *world* **cosmos**,
but the spirit which is of *God* **Elohim**;
that we might know *the things* **those**
that are *freely given* **granted charism** to us
of *God* **Elohim**.
13 Which *things* also we speak, not in the words
which *man's* **human** wisdom *teacheth* **doctrinateth**,
but **in** which the Holy *Ghost* **Spirit** *teacheth* **doctrinateth**;
comparing **co—judging** spiritual *things* with spiritual.
14 But the *natural man* **soulical human**
receiveth not *the things* **those** of the Spirit of *God* **Elohim**:
for they are foolishness unto him:
neither can he know them,
because they are spiritually *discerned* **judged**.
15 But he that is spiritual **indeed** judgeth all *things*,
yet he himself is judged of no *man* **one**.
16 For who hath known the mind of *the Lord* **Adonay**,
that he may *instruct* **coalesce** him?
But we have the mind of *Christ* **Messiah**.

SPIRITUAL VS FLESHLY

3 And I, brethren,
could not speak unto you as unto spiritual,
but as unto *carnal* **fleshly**,
even as unto babes in *Christ* **Messiah**.
2 I have *fed* **given** you *with* milk **to drink**,
and not *with meat* **food**:
for *hitherto* ye were not **yet** able *to bear it*,
but neither yet now are ye able.
3 For ye are yet *carnal* **fleshly**:
for whereas there is among you *envying* **zeal**,
and *strife* **contention**, and divisions,
are ye not *carnal* **indeed fleshly**
and walk as *men* **humanity**?
4 For while one *saith* **wordeth**,
I **indeed** am of *Paul* **Paulos**; and another, I *am* of Apollos;
are ye not *carnal* **indeed fleshly**?
5 Who then is *Paul* **Paulos**, and who is Apollos,
but ministers *by* **through** whom ye *believed* **trusted**,
even as the *Lord* **Adonay** gave to *every man* **each**?
6 I have planted, Apollos *watered* **irrigated**;
but *God gave the increase* **Elohim grew**.
7 So then neither is he that planteth *any thing* **aught**,
neither he that *watereth* **irrigateth**;
but *God* **Elohim** that *giveth the increase* **groweth**.
8 Now he that planteth and he that *watereth* **irrigateth**
are one:
and *every man* **each** shall *receive* **take** his own reward
according to his own labour.
9 For we are *labourers together* **co—workers**
with *God* **Elohim**:
ye are God's husbandry — **Elohim's cultivation**,
ye are God's building — **Elohim's edifice**.
10 According to the *grace* **charism** of *God* **Elohim**
which is given unto me,
as a wise *masterbuilder* **architect**,
I have *laid* **placed** the foundation,
and another buildeth thereon.
But let *every man take heed* **each see**
how he buildeth thereupon.
11 For other foundation can no *man lay* **one place**
than that is laid,
which is *Jesus Christ* **Yah Shua Messiah**.
12 Now if any *man* **one** build upon this foundation
gold, silver, precious stones,
wood **timber**, *hay* **herbage**, stubble;
13 *Every man's* **Each one's** work
shall be *made* manifest:
for the day shall *declare* **evidence** it,
because it shall be *revealed by* **unveiled in** fire;
and the fire shall *try every man's* **proof each one's** work
of what sort it is.
14 If any *man's* **one's** work abide
which he hath built thereupon,
he shall *receive* **take** a reward.
15 If any *man's* **one's** work shall be burned,
he shall *suffer* **have** loss:
but he himself shall be saved;
yet *so* **thus** as *by* **through** fire.

ELOHIM'S HOLY NAVE

16 Know ye not
that ye are the *temple* **nave** of *God* **Elohim**,
and that the Spirit of *God* **Elohim** dwelleth in you?
17 If any *man defile* **one corrupt**
the *temple* **nave** of *God* **Elohim**,
him shall *God* **Elohim** destroy;
for the *temple* **nave** of *God* **Elohim** is holy,
which *temple* ye are.
18 Let no *man deceive* **one seduce** himself.
If any *man* **one** among you
seemeth **thinketh** to be wise in this *world* **eon**,
let him become a fool, that he may *be* **become** wise.
19 For the wisdom of this *world* **cosmos**
is foolishness with *God* **Elohim**.
For it is *written* **scribed**,
He *taketh* **graspeth** the wise
in their own *craftiness* **cunning**.
20 And again, *The Lord* **Yah Veh** knoweth
the *thoughts* **reasonings** of the wise, that they are vain.
Iyob 5:13, Psalm 94:11, 20
21 *Therefore* **So then**
let no *man glory* **one boast** in *men* **humanity**.
For all *things* are your's;
22 Whether *Paul* **Paulos**, *or* **whether** Apollos,
or Cephas **whether Kepha**, *or* **whether** the *world* **cosmos**,
or **whether** life, *or* **whether** death,
or things **whether the** present,
or things to come **whether the about to be**;
all are your's;
23 And ye are *Christ's* **Messiah's**;
and *Christ* **Messiah** is *God's* **Elohim's**.

THE MINISTRY

4 Let *a man so account of us* **humanity reckon us thus**,
as *of the ministers* **attendants** of *Christ* **Messiah**,
and *stewards* **administrators**
of the mysteries of *God* **Elohim**.
2 *Moreover* **Finally**
it is *required* **sought** in *stewards* **administrators**,
that *a man* **each** be found *faithful* **trustworthy**.
3 But with me it is *a very small thing* **insignificant**
that I should be judged of you,
or of *man's judgment* **humanity's day**:
yea **yet**, I judge not mine *own* self.
4 For I *know nothing by myself* **am aware of naught**;
yet am I not *hereby* **herein** justified:
but he that judgeth me is *the Lord* **Adonay**.
5 *Therefore* **So then**
judge *nothing* **naught** before the *time* **season**,
until **ever** *the Lord* **Adonay** come,
who both *will bring to* **shall** light **up**
the *hidden things* **secrets** of darkness,
and *will make* **shall** manifest the counsels of the hearts:
and then shall *every man* **each**
have praise **become the halal** of *God* **Elohim**.
6 And these *things*, brethren,
I have *in a figure transferred* **transfigured** to myself
and to Apollos for your sakes;

that ye might learn in us not to think *of men*
above **beyond** that which is *written* **scribed**,
that no **lest** one of you be puffed up
for one against another.
7 For who *maketh* **distinguisheth** thee
to differ from another?
and what hast thou
that thou *didst* **hast** not *receive* **taken**?
now if thou *didst receive it* **hast taken**,
why *dost thou glory* **boastest thou**,
as if thou hadst not *received it* **taken**?
8 *Now* **Already** ye *are full* **have gluttonized**,
now **already** ye *are rich* **have enriched**,
ye have reigned as *kings* **sovereigns**
without **apart from** us:
and **yet indeed,**
I would to God **O that** ye *did reign* **had reigned**,
that we also might *reign* **co—reign** with you.
9 For I think that *God* **Elohim**
hath *set forth* **manifested** us the apostles last,
as *it were appointed* **doomed** to death:
for we *are made* **become** a spectacle
unto the *world* **cosmos**,
and to angels, and to *men* **humanity**.
10 We are fools for *Christ's* **Messiah's** sake,
but ye *are wise* **thoughtful** in *Christ* **Messiah**;
we *are weak* **frail**, but ye *are strong* **mighty**;
ye *are honourable* **glorious**,
but we *are despised* **dishonoured**.
11 Even unto this present hour we both hunger, and thirst,
and are naked, and are *buffeted* **punched**,
and *have no certain dwellingplace* **unsettled**;
12 And labour, working with our own hands:
being reviled **abused**, *we bless* **eulogize**;
being persecuted, we *suffer* **tolerate** *it*:
13 *Being defamed* **Blasphemed**, we **comfort**:
we are *made* **become**
as the *filth* **offscouring** of the *world* **cosmos**,
and are the *offscouring* **offscrapings** of all *things*
unto this day **until now**.
14 I *write* **scribe** not these *things* to shame you,
but as my beloved *sons* **children**, I *warn* **remind** *you*.
15 For *though* **even if** ye have
ten thousand instructers **a myriad pedagogues**
in *Christ* **Messiah**,
yet *have ye* not many fathers:
for in *Christ Jesus* **Messiah Yah Shua**
I have begotten you through the *gospel* **evangelism**.
16 Wherefore I beseech you,
be ye *followers* **mimickers** of me.
17 For this cause
have I sent unto you *Timotheus* **Timo Theos**,
who is my beloved *son* **child**,
and *faithful* **trustworthy** in *the Lord* **Adonay**,
who shall *bring* **remind** you
into remembrance of my ways
which be in *Christ* **Messiah**,
exactly as I *teach* **doctrinate** every where
in every *church* **ecclesia**.
18 Now some are puffed up,
as though I *would* **should** not come to you.
19 But I *will* **shall** come to you *shortly* **quickly**,
if *the Lord will* **ever Adonay willeth**,
and *will* **shall** know,
not the *speech* **word** of them which are puffed up,
but the *power* **dynamis**.
20 For the *kingdom* **sovereigndom** of *God* **Elohim**
is not in word, but in *power* **dynamis**.
21 What will ye?
shall I come unto you with a rod,
or in love, and *in the* **a** spirit of meekness?

PAULOS REBUKES WHOREDOM

5 *It is reported commonly* **I actually hear**
that there is fornication **of whoredom** among you,
and such *fornication* **whoredom**
as is not *so much as* **even** named
among the *Gentiles* **goyim**,
that one should have his father's *wife* **woman**.
2 And ye are puffed up,
and have not **indeed** rather mourned,
that he that hath done this *deed* **work**
might be taken away from among you.
3 For I *verily* **indeed**,
as absent in body, but present in spirit,
have judged already, as though I were present,
concerning him that hath *so done this deed* **thus worked**,
4 In the name
of our *Lord Jesus Christ* **Adonay Yah Shua Messiah**,
when ye are gathered together, and my spirit,
with the *power* **dynamis**
of our *Lord Jesus Christ* **Adonay Yah Shua Messiah**,
5 To deliver such an one unto Satan
for **unto** the *destruction* **ruin** of the flesh,
that the spirit may be saved
in the day of the *Lord Jesus* **Adonay Yah Shua**.
6 Your *glorying* **boasting** is not good.
Know ye not that a little *leaven* **fermentation**
leaveneth **fermenteth** the whole lump?
7 Purge out therefore the old *leaven* **fermentation**,
that ye may be a new lump,
exactly as ye are *unleavened* **as matsah**.
For even *Christ* **Messiah** our *passover* **pasach**
is sacrificed for us:
8 *Therefore* **So then** let us *keep the feast* **celebrate**,
not *with* **in** old *leaven* **fermentation**,
neither *with* **in** the *leaven* **fermentation**
of malice and *wickedness* **evil**;
but *with* **in** the *unleavened bread* **matsah**
of sincerity and truth.
9 I *wrote* **scribed** unto you in an epistle
not to *company* **co—mingle**
with *fornicators* **whoremongers**:
10 Yet **most certainly** not *altogether*
with the *fornicators* **whoremongers** of this *world* **cosmos**,
or with the *covetous* **avaricious**,
or *extortioners* **plunderers**, or with idolaters;
for then must ye needs **otherwise be ye indebted**
to go out of the *world* **cosmos**.
11 But now I have *written* **scribed** unto you
not to *keep company* **co—mingle**,
if **ever** any *man* **one** that is *called a* **named** brother
be **either** a *fornicator* **whoremonger**,
or *covetous* **avaricious**, or an idolater,
or *a railer* **an abuser**, or *a drunkard* **an intoxicator**,
or *an extortioner* **a plunderer**;
with such an one *no not* **never** to eat.
12 For what have I to do
to judge them also that are without?
do not ye **indeed** judge them that are within?
13 But them that are without *God* **Elohim** judgeth.
Therefore *put* **take** away from among yourselves
that *wicked person* **evil**.

ON THE HOLY SUING THE HOLY

6 Dare any of you,
having a matter *against* **toward** another,
go to law **have judgment** before the unjust,
and not **indeed** before the *saints* **holy**?
2 *Do* **Know** ye not *know*
that the *saints* **holy** shall judge the *world* **cosmos**?
and if the *world* **cosmos** shall be judged *by* **in** you,
are ye unworthy to judge the *smallest matters* **lesser**?
3 Know ye not that we shall judge angels?
how much more
things that pertain to **those of** this *life* **existence**?
4 If **ever indeed** then ye have judgments
of *things pertaining to this life* **this existence**,
set them to judge
who are *least esteemed* **belittled** in the *church* **ecclesia**.
5 I *speak* **word** to *your* shame **you**.
Is it *so* **thus**,
that there *is not a* **be no** wise *man* among you?
no, not **even** one
that shall be able to *judge* **discern**
between **among** his brethren?
6 But brother *goeth to law* **be judged** with brother,
and that *before* **by** the *unbelievers* **trustless**.
7 *Now* **Already indeed** therefore
there is *utterly* **actually** a fault among you,
because ye *go to law one* **have judgment**
with *another* **your own**.

Why *do* **be** ye not rather *take wrong* **injured**?
why *do* **indeed be** ye not rather
suffer yourselves to be defrauded **cheated**?
8 *Nay* **Rather**, ye *do wrong* **injure**, and *defraud* **cheat**,
and that your brethren.
9 **Or** Know ye not
that the *unrighteous* **unjust** shall not inherit
the *kingdom* **sovereigndom** of *God* **Elohim**?
Be not *deceived* **seduced**:
neither *fornicators* **whoremongers**, nor idolaters,
nor adulterers, nor effeminate,
nor *abusers of themselves with mankind* **homosexuals**,
10 Nor thieves, nor *covetous* **avaricious**,
nor *drunkards* **intoxicators**, nor *revilers* **abusers**,
nor *extortioners* **plunderers**,
shall inherit the *kingdom* **sovereigndom** of *God* **Elohim**.
11 And *such* **these** were some of you:
but ye are *washed* **bathed**,
but ye are *sanctified* **hallowed**,
but ye are justified
in the name of *the Lord Jesus* **Adonay Yah Shua**,
and *by* **in** the Spirit of our *God* **Elohim**.
12 All *things* are *lawful unto* **allowed** me,
but all *things* are not *expedient* **beneficial**:
all *things* are *lawful for* **allowed** me,
but I *will* **shall** not be *brought*
under the *power* **authority** of any.
13 *Meats* **Food** for the belly, and the belly for *meats* **food**:
but *God* **Elohim** shall *destroy* **inactivate** both
it **this** and them.
Now the body is not for *fornication* **whoredom**,
but for *the Lord* **Adonay**;
and *the Lord* **Adonay** for the body.
14 And *God* **Elohim** hath both raised up *the Lord* **Adonay**,
and *will* **shall** also raise *up* us
by **through** his *own power* **dynamis**.
15 Know ye not
that your bodies are the members of *Christ* **Messiah**?
shall I then take the members of *Christ* **the Messiah**,
and make them the members of *an harlot* **a whore**?
God forbid **So be it not**.
16 *What?* **Or** know ye not
that he which is joined to *an harlot* **a whore** is one body?
for two, saith he, shall be **into** one flesh.
Genesis 2:24
17 But he that is joined unto *the Lord* **Adonay**
is one spirit.
18 Flee *fornication* **whoredom**.
Every sin *that a man* **if ever a human** doeth
is without the body;
but he that *committeth fornication* **whoreth**
sinneth *against* **unto** his own body.
19 *What?* **Or** know ye not that your body
is the *temple* **nave** of the Holy *Ghost* **Spirit**
which is in you,
which ye have of *God* **Elohim**, and ye are not your own?
20 For ye are bought with a price:
therefore **then** glorify *God* **Elohim** in your body,
and in your spirit, which are *God's* **Elohim's**.

On Intimate Relationships

7 Now concerning *the things* **those**
whereof **about which** ye *wrote* **scribed** unto me:
It is good for a *man* **human** not to touch a woman.
2 Nevertheless,
to avoid fornication **because of whoredom**,
let *every man* **each** have his own *wife* **woman**,
and let *every woman* **each** have her own *husband* **man**.
3 *Let the husband render*
The man is indebted to give back
unto the *wife due benevolence* **woman wellmindedness**:
and likewise also the *wife* **woman**
unto the *husband* **man**.
4 The *wife* **woman**
hath not *power* **authority** of her own body,
but the *husband* **man**:
and likewise also the *husband* **man**
hath not *power* **authority** of his own body,
but the *wife* **woman**.
5 *Defraud* **Cheat** ye not one the other,
except *it be* **somehow ever**
with consent **by symphonizing** for a *time* **season**,
that ye may *give yourselves* **have leisure**
to **for** fasting and prayer; and come together again,
that **lest** Satan *tempt* **test** you *not*
for your *incontinency* **restraint**.
6 But I *speak* **word** this by *permission* **experience**,
and not *of commandment* **by order**.
7 For I *would* **will**
that all *men were* **humanity be** even as I myself.
But *every man* **each**
hath his *proper gift* **own charisma** of *God* **Elohim**,
one *after this manner* **indeed thus**,
and another *after that* **thus**.
8 I *say* **word** therefore to the unmarried and widows,
It is good for them if **ever** they abide even as I.
9 But if they cannot *contain* **control themselves**,
let them marry:
for it is better to marry than *to burn* **be fiery**.
10 And unto the married I *command* **evangelize**,
yet not I, but *the Lord* **Adonay**,
Let not the *wife depart* **woman separate**
from her *husband* **man**:
11 But and if she *depart* **ever separate**,
let her *remain* **abide** unmarried
or be reconciled to her *husband* **man**:
and let not the *husband* **man**
put away **forsake** his *wife* **woman**.
12 But to the rest *speak* **word** I, not *the Lord* **Adonay**:
If any brother hath a *wife* **woman**
that believeth not — **trustless**,
and she *be pleased* **think well** to dwell with him,
let him not *put her away* **forsake her**.
13 And the woman which hath *an husband* **a man**
that believeth not — **trustless**,
and if he *be pleased* **think well** to dwell with her,
let her not *leave* **forsake** him.
14 For the *unbelieving husband* **trustless man**
is *sanctified by* **hallowed in** the *wife* **woman**,
and the *unbelieving wife* **trustless woman**
is *sanctified by* **hallowed in** the *husband* **man**:
else **then** were your children *unclean* **impure**;
but now are they holy.
15 But if the *unbelieving depart* **trustless separate**,
let him *depart* **separate**.
A brother or a sister is not *under bondage* **subservient**
in such *cases*:
but *God* **Elohim** hath called us to *peace* **shalom**.
16 For what knowest thou, O *wife* **woman**,
whether thou shalt save thy *husband* **man**?
or how knowest thou, O man,
whether thou shalt save thy *wife* **woman**?
17 *But* **Except** as *God* **Elohim**
hath *distributed* **imparted** to *every man* **each**,
as *the Lord* **Adonay** hath called *every one* **to each**,
so **thus** let him walk.
And *so* **thus** ordain I in all *churches* **ecclesiae**.

Circumcision, Decircumcision, Uncircumcision

18 Is any *man* called being circumcised?
let him not *become uncircumcised* **decircumcise**.
Is any called in uncircumcision?
let him not *be circumcised* **circumcise**.
19 Circumcision is *nothing* **naught**,
and uncircumcision is *nothing* **naught**,
but the *keeping* **guarding**
of the *commandments* **misvoth** of *God* **Elohim**.
20 Let *every man* **each** abide in *the same* **that** calling
wherein he was called.
21 Art thou called *being* a servant?
care **concern** not *for it*:
but if thou mayest be *made free* **able to be liberated**,
use it rather.
22 For he that is called in *the Lord* **Adonay**,
being a servant,
is *the Lord's freeman* **Adonay's liberated**:
likewise also he that is called,
being free **liberated**, is *Christ's* **Messiah's** servant.
23 Ye are bought with a price;
be not ye the servants of *men* **humanity**.
24 Brethren, let *every man* **each**, wherein he is called,
therein abide with *God* **Elohim**.

ON VIRGINS

25 Now concerning virgins
I have no *commandment of the Lord* **order from Adonay**:
yet I give my *judgment* **opinion**,
as one that hath *obtained mercy* **been mercied**
of *the Lord* **Adonay** to be *faithful* **trustworthy**.
26 *I suppose* **presume** therefore
that this is good for the present *distress* **necessity**,
I say, that it is good for a *man so* **human thus** to be.
27 Art thou bound unto a *wife* **woman**?
seek not to be loosed.
Art thou loosed from a *wife* **woman**?
seek not a *wife* **woman**.
28 But and if **ever** thou marry, thou hast not sinned;
and if **ever** a virgin marry, she hath not sinned.
Nevertheless
such shall have *trouble* **tribulation** in the flesh:
but I spare you.
29 But this I say, brethren,
the *time* **season** is *short* **shortened**:
it remaineth **finally**,
that both they that have *wives* **women**
be as though they had none;
30 And they that weep, as though they wept not;
and they that *rejoice* **cheer**,
as though they *rejoiced* **cheered** not;
and they that buy, as though they *possessed* **held** not;
31 And they that use this *world* **cosmos**,
as not abusing *it*:
for the *fashion* **configuration** of this *world* **cosmos**
passeth away.
32 But I *would* **will**
have you without carefulness **that you be unanxious**.
He that is unmarried *careth* **is anxious**
for *the things that belong to the Lord* **that of Adonay**,
how he may please *the Lord* **Adonay**:
33 But he that is married *careth* **is anxious**
for *the things that are* **that** of the *world* **cosmos**,
how he may please his *wife* **woman**.
34 There is difference *also*
between a *wife* **woman** and a virgin.
The unmarried woman *careth* **is anxious**
for *the things* **that** of *the Lord* **Adonay**,
that she may be holy both in body and in spirit:
but she that is married *careth* **is anxious**
for *the things* **that** of the *world* **cosmos**,
how she may please her *husband* **man**.
35 And this I *speak* **word** for your own *profit* **benefit**;
not that I may *cast a snare* **lay a noose** upon you,
but for that which is *comely* **honourable**,
and that ye may *attend* **with a view**
upon *the Lord* **Adonay**
without distraction **to undistracted devotion**.
36 But if any *man think* **one presume**
that he *behaveth himself uncomely* **misbehaveth**
toward his virgin,
if **ever** she *pass the flower of her age* **be beyond her acme**,
and *need so require* **thus becometh indebted**,
let him do what he *will* **willeth**, he sinneth not:
let them marry.
37 Nevertheless
he that standeth *stedfast* **grounded** in his heart,
having no *necessity* **distress**,
but hath *power over* **authority concerning** his own will,
and hath so *decreed* **judged** in his heart
that he *will keep* **shall guard** his virgin, doeth well.
38 So then he that
giveth her in marriage **marrieth her off**
doeth well;
but he that
giveth her not in marriage **marrieth her not off**
doeth better.
39 The *wife* **woman** is bound by the *law* **torah**
as long **time** as her *husband* **man** liveth;
but if **ever** her *husband be dead* **man sleep**,
she is *at liberty* **liberated** to be married to whom she will;
only in the *Lord* **Adonay**.
40 But *she is happier* **blessed be she**
if **ever** she *so* **thus** abide, after my *judgment* **opinion**:
and I think also that I have the Spirit of *God* **Elohim**.

ON IDOL SACRIFICES

8 Now *as touching* **concerning**
things offered unto idols **idol sacrifices**,
we know that we all have knowledge.
Knowledge puffeth up, but *charity* **love** edifieth.
2 And if any *man* **one** think,
that he knoweth *any thing* **aught**,
he knoweth *nothing* **naught** yet
exactly as he *ought* **needeth** to know.
3 But if any *man* **one** love *God* **Elohim**,
the same **this** is known of him.
4 As concerning therefore the eating of *those things*
that are offered in sacrifice unto idols **idol sacrifices**,
we know that an idol
is *nothing* **naught** in the *world* **cosmos**,
and that there is none other *God but* **Elohim except** one.
5 For *though* **if ever** there be **those**
that are *called gods* **worded elohim**,
whether in heaven or in earth,
(**exactly** as there be *gods* **elohim** many,
and *lords* **adoniym** many,)
6 But to us, *there is but* one *God* **Elohim**, the Father,
of whom *are* all *things* **be**, and we in him;
and one *Lord Jesus Christ* **Adonay Yah Shua Messiah**,
by **through** whom *are* all *things* **be**,
and we *by* **through** him.
7 *Howbeit* **Yet**
there is not in every *man* **one** that knowledge:
for some with conscience of the idol
unto this hour **until now** eat it
as *a thing offered unto* an idol **sacrifice**;
and their conscience being *weak* **frail** is *defiled* **stained**.
8 But *meat* **food**
commendeth **presenteth** us not to *God* **Elohim**:
for neither, if **ever** we eat,
are we the better **do we superabound**;
neither, if **ever** we eat not, *are we the worse* **do we lack**.
9 But *take heed* **see**,
lest *by any means* **somehow**
this *liberty* **authority** of your's
become a *stumblingblock* **stumbling**
to them that are *weak* **frail**.
10 For if **ever** any *man* **one**
see thee which hast knowledge
sit at meat **repose** in *the idol's temple* **an idolion**,
shall not **indeed** the conscience of him
which is weak **being frail**
be *emboldened* **edified** to eat
those things which are offered to idols **idol sacrifices**;
11 And through thy knowledge
shall the *weak* **frail** brother *perish* **destruct**,
for whom *Christ* **Messiah** died?
12 But when ye sin *so against* **thus unto** the brethren,
and *wound* **strike** their *weak* **frail** conscience,
ye sin *against Christ* **unto Messiah**.
13 Wherefore,
if *meat make* **food scandalize** my brother *to offend*,
I will **shall no way** eat no *flesh* **meat**
while **unto** the *world standeth* **eons**,
lest I *make* **scandalize** my brother *to offend*.

THE AUTHORITY OF THE HOLY

9 Am I not an apostle? am I not *free* **liberated**?
have I not **indeed** seen
Jesus Christ **Yah Shua Messiah** our *Lord* **Adonay**?
are not ye my work in *the Lord* **Adonay**?
2 If I be not an apostle unto others,
yet *doubtless* **indeed** I am to you:
for the seal of mine apostleship
are ye in *the Lord* **Adonay**.
3 *Mine answer* **My pleading**
to them that *do examine* **judge** me is this,
4 Have we not *power* **authority** to eat and to drink?
5 Have we not *power* **authority** to lead about a sister,
a *wife* **woman**, as well as *other* **the rest of the** apostles,
and *as* the brethren of the *Lord* **Adonay**,
and *Cephas* **Kepha**?
6 Or I only and *Barnabas* **Bar Nabi**,
have not we *power* **authority**
to *forbear working* **not work**?
7 Who *goeth a warfare any time* **ever warreth**

at his own *charges* **wages**?
who planteth a vineyard,
and eateth not of the fruit thereof?
or who *feedeth* **shepherdeth** a *flock* **shepherddom**,
and eateth not of the milk of the *flock* **shepherddom**?
8 *Say* **Speak** I these *things* as a *man* **human**?
or *saith* **indeed wordeth** not the *law* **torah** the same also?
9 For it is *written* **scribed**
in the *law* **torah** of *Moses* **Mosheh**,
Thou shalt not muzzle the mouth of the ox
that treadeth out the corn.
Doth God take care for **Concerneth Elohim with** oxen?
Deuteronomy 25:4
10 Or *saith* **wordeth** he it
altogether **most certainly** for our sakes?
For our sakes, *no doubt* **indeed**,
this is *written* **scribed**:
that he that ploweth *should* **is indebt to** plow in hope;
and that he that thresheth in hope
should *be partaker* **partake** of his hope.
11 If we have sown unto you *spiritual things* **spirituals**,
is it *a great thing* **so mega**
if we shall *reap* **harvest** your *carnal things* **fleshlies**?
12 If others
be partakers **partake** of this *power* **authority** over you,
are not we rather?
Nevertheless **Yet** we have not used this *power* **authority**;
but *suffer* **endure** all *things*,
lest we should **somehow** hinder
the *gospel* **evangelism** of *Christ* **the Messiah**.
13 *Do* **Know** ye not *know* that they
which *minister about holy things* **work the priestal**
live **eat** of the *things of the temple* **priestal precinct**?
and they which wait *at* **on** the **sacrifice** altar
are *partakers* **co—partakers** with the **sacrifice** altar?
14 Even *so* **thus** hath the *Lord* **Adonay** ordained
that they which *preach* **evangelize** the *gospel* **evangelism**
should live of the *gospel* **evangelism**.
15 But I have used none of these *things*:
neither have I *written* **scribed** these *things*,
that it should **thus** be *so done unto* **in** me:
for it were *better* **good** for me to die,
rather than that any *man* **one**
should *make my glorying* void **my boasting**.
16 For *though I preach the gospel* **even if I evangelize**,
I have *nothing* **naught** to *glory of* **boast**:
for necessity is laid upon me; yea, woe *is* unto me,
if **ever** I *preach* **evangelize** not *the gospel*!
17 For if I *do* **transact** this *thing willingly* **voluntarily**,
I have a reward:
but if *against my will* **involuntarily**,
a dispensation of the gospel **an administration**
is *committed* **entrusted** unto me.

THE REWARD OF THE HOLY

18 What is my reward then?
Verily that, when I *preach the gospel* **evangelize**,
I *may make* **place**
the *gospel* **evangelism** of *Christ* **the Messiah**
without charge,
that I abuse not my *power* **authority**
in the *gospel* **evangelism**.
19 For though I be *free* **liberated** from all *men*,
yet *have I made myself servant* **I am subservient** unto all,
that I might gain the more.
20 And unto the *Jews* **Yah Hudiym**,
I became as a *Jew* **Yah Hudiy**,
that I might gain the *Jews* **Yah Hudiym**;
to them that are under *the law* **torah**,
as under *the law* **torah**,
that I might gain them that are under *the law* **torah**;
21 To them that are *without law* **untorahed**,
as *without law* **untorahed**,
(being not *without law* **untorahed** to *God* **Elohim**,
but *under the law* **entorahed** to *Christ* **Messiah**,)
that I might gain them that are *without law* **untorahed**.
22 To the *weak* **frail** became I as *weak* **frail**,
that I might gain the *weak* **frail**:
I am *made all things to all men* **become all to all**,
that I might *by all means* **most certainly** save some.
23 And this I do for the *gospel's* **evangelism's** sake,
that I might be *partaker thereof with you* **a co—partaker**.
24 Know ye not that they which run in a *race* **stadium**
indeed run all,
but one *receiveth* **taketh** the *prize* **umpirage**?
So run **Run thus**, that ye may *obtain* **overtake**.
25 And *every man* **everyone**
that *striveth* **agonizeth** for the mastery
is *temperate* **self—controlled** in all *things*.
Now **Therefore** they *do it* **indeed**,
to *obtain* **take** a corruptible *crown* **wreath**;
but we an incorruptible.
26 I therefore *so* run **thus**, not as uncertainly;
so fight I **I fistfight thus**,
not as one that *beateth* **floggeth** the air:
27 But I *keep under* **subdue** my body,
and bring it into *subjection* **servitude**:
lest that *by any means* **somehow**,
when I have preached to others,
I myself should *be a castaway* **become disapproved**.

WARNINGS AGAINST IDOLATRY

10 Moreover, brethren,
I *would* **will** not that ye should be *ignorant* **unknowing**,
how that all our fathers were under the cloud,
and all passed through the sea;
2 And were all baptized unto *Moses* **Mosheh**
in the cloud and in the sea;
3 And did all eat the same spiritual *meat* **food**;
4 And did all drink the same spiritual drink:
for they drank of that spiritual Rock that followed them:
and that Rock was *Christ* **the Messiah**.
5 But *with* **in** many of them
God was not well pleased **Elohim well approved not**:
for they were *overthrown* **scattered** in the wilderness.
6 Now these *things were* **became** our *examples* **types**,
to the intent **that** we should not *lust* **pant** after evil *things*,
exactly as they *also lusted* **panted**.
7 Neither be ye idolaters,
exactly as were some of them;
as *it is written* **scribed**,
The people sat down to eat and drink,
and rose up to *play* **ridicule**.
Exodus 32:6
8 Neither let us *commit fornication* **whore**,
exactly as some of them *committed* **whored**,
and fell in one day three and twenty thousand.
9 Neither let us *tempt Christ* **test the Messiah**,
exactly as some of them also *tempted* **tested**,
and were destroyed of serpents.
10 Neither murmur ye,
exactly as some of them also murmured,
and were destroyed of the destroyer.
11 Now all these *things* happened unto them
for *ensamples* **types**:
and they are *written* **scribed**
for our *admonition* **reminding**,
upon **unto** whom the *ends* **completion** of the *world* **eons**
are come **has arrived**.
12 *Wherefore* **So then** let him that thinketh he standeth
take heed **see** lest he fall.

ON TESTING

13 There hath no *temptation* **testing** taken you
but **except** such as is *common to man* **human**:
but *God* **Elohim** is *faithful* **trustworthy**,
who *will* **shall** not *suffer* **allow** you to be *tempted* **tested**
above that ye are able **beyond your ability**;
but *will* **shall** with the *temptation* **testing**
also make *a way to escape* **an exit**,
that ye may be able to *bear* **endure** *it*.
14 Wherefore, my *dearly* beloved, flee from idolatry.
15 I *speak* **word** as *to wise men* **unto the thoughtful**;
judge ye what I say.

ON COMMUNION

16 The cup of *blessing* **eulogy** which we *bless* **eulogize**,
is it not **indeed**
the communion of the blood of *Christ* **the Messiah**?
The bread which we break,
is it not **indeed**
the communion of the body of *Christ* **the Messiah**?
17 For we being many are one bread, *and* one body:
for we *are* all *partakers* **partake** of that one bread.

18 *Behold Israel* **See Yisra El** after the flesh:
are not **indeed** they which eat of the sacrifices
partakers **communicants** of the **sacrifice** altar?
19 What say I then?
that the idol is *any thing* **somewhat**,
or that
which is offered in sacrifice to idols **an idol sacrifice**
is *any thing* **somewhat**?
20 But *I say,*
that *the things* **those** which the *Gentiles* **goyim** sacrifice,
they sacrifice to *devils* **demons**, and not to *God* **Elohim**:
and I *would* **will** not that ye
should have fellowships **become communicants**
with *devils* **demons**.
21 Ye cannot drink the cup of *the Lord* **Adonay**,
and the cup of *devils* **demons**:
ye cannot *be partakers* **partake**
of the *Lord's* table **of Yah Veh**,
and of the table of *devils* **demons**.
Malachi 1:7

ON CONSCIENCE

22 *Do* **Or, incite** we *provoke the Lord* **Adonay** to jealousy?
are we *stronger* **mightier** than he?
23 All *things* are *lawful for* **allowed** me,
but all *things* are not *expedient* **beneficial**:
all *things* are *lawful for* **allowed** me,
but all *things* edify not.
24 Let no *man* **one** seek his own,
but *every man* **each** another's *wealth*.
25 Whatsoever is sold in the shambles, *that* eat,
asking no question **not judging** for conscience sake:
26 For the earth is *the Lord's* **Yah Veh's**,
and the fulness thereof.
Psalm 24:1
27 If any of *them that believe not* **the trustless**
bid **call** you *to a feast,*
and ye *be disposed* **will** to go;
whatsoever is set *before* **by** you, eat,
asking no question **not judging** for conscience sake.
28 But if **ever** any *man* **one** say unto you,
This is *offered in sacrifice unto idols* **an idol sacrifice**,
eat not for his sake that *shewed* **disclosed** it,
and for conscience sake:
for the earth is *the Lord* **Yah Veh's**,
and the fulness thereof:
Psalm 24:1
29 Conscience, I *say* **word**,
not **indeed** thine own, but of the other:
for why is my liberty
judged of *another man's* **another's** conscience?
30 For if I by *grace be a partaker* **charism partake**,
why am I *evil spoken of* **blasphemed**
for that for which I *give thanks* **eucharistize**?
31 Whether therefore ye eat, *or* **whether ye** drink,
or **whether** whatsoever ye do,
do all to the glory of *God* **Elohim**.
32 *Give none offence* **Become inoffensive**,
neither to the *Jews* **Yah Hudiym**,
nor to the *Gentiles* **Hellene**,
nor **and** to the *church* **ecclesia** of *God* **Elohim**:
33 Even as I please all *men* in all *things,*
not seeking mine own *profit* **benefit**,
but *the profit* of many, that they may be saved.

ON RELATIONSHIPS

11 Be ye *followers* **mimickers** of me,
even **exactly** as I also *am* of *Christ* **Messiah**.
2 Now I *praise* **halal** you, brethren,
that ye remember me in all *things,*
and *keep* **hold** the *ordinances* **traditions**,
exactly as I delivered them to you.
3 But I *would have* **will that** you know,
that the head of every man is *Christ* **the Messiah**;
and the head of the woman is the man;
and the head of *Christ* **Messiah** is *God* **Elohim**.
4 Every man praying or prophesying,
having his head *covered* **veiled**,
dishonoureth **shameth** his head.
5 But every woman that prayeth or prophesieth
with her head *uncovered* **unveiled**
dishonoureth **shameth** her head:
for that is even all one as if she were shaven.
6 For if the woman be not *covered* **veiled**,
let her also be shorn:
but if it be a shame for a woman to be shorn or shaven,
let her be *covered* **veiled**.
7 For a man indeed
ought **is indebted** not to *cover* **veil** his head,
forasmuch **being** as he is the *image* **icon**
and glory of *God* **Elohim**:
but the woman is the glory of the man.
8 For the man is not of the woman:
but the woman of the man.
9 Neither **indeed** was the man created for the woman;
but the woman for the man.
10 For this cause *ought* the woman **is indebted**
to have *power* **authority** on her head
because of the angels.
11 *Nevertheless* **However**
neither is the man *without* **apart from** the woman,
neither the woman *without* **apart from** the man,
in *the Lord* **Adonay**.
12 For **exactly** as the woman is of the man,
even *so* **thus** is the man also *by* **through** the woman;
but all *things* of *God* **Elohim**.

ON TRESSES

13 Judge in yourselves: is it *comely* **befitting**
that a woman pray unto *God* **Elohim**
uncovered **unveiled**?
14 **Or** Doth not even nature itself *teach* **doctrinate** you,
that, if **ever** a man have *long hair* **tresses**,
it is a *shame* **dishonour** unto him?
15 But if **ever** a woman have *long hair* **tresses**,
it is a glory to her:
for *her hair is* **tresses are** given her for a *covering* **mantle**.
16 But if any *man* **one**
seem **thinketh** to be *contentious* **quarrelsome**,
we have no such custom,
neither the *churches* **ecclesiae** of *God* **Elohim**.

ON THE EUCHARIST

17 Now in this that I *declare unto you* **evangelize**,
I *praise* **halal** you not,
that ye come together not *for* **unto** the better,
but *for* **unto** the worse.
18 For **indeed** first of all,
when ye come together in the *church* **ecclesia**,
I hear that there be *divisions* **schisms** among you;
and I *partly believe* **somewhat trust** it.
19 For there must be also heresies among you,
that they which are approved
may *be made* **become** manifest among you.
20 When ye come together therefore into one place,
this is not to eat *the Lord's* **Adonay's** supper.
21 For in eating
every one taketh before other **each anticipateth**
his own supper:
and **indeed** one is hungry,
and another is *drunken* **intoxicated**.
22 *What?* **Indeed!**
have ye not houses to eat and to drink in?
or *despise* **disesteem** ye
the *church* **ecclesia** of *God* **Elohim**,
and shame them that have not?
What shall I say to you? shall I *praise* **halal** you in this?
I *praise* **halal** *you* not.

THE SEQUENCE OF THE EUCHARIST

23 For I have *received* **taken** of *the Lord* **Adonay**
that which also I delivered unto you,
That *the Lord Jesus* **Adonay Yah Shua**
in the *same* night in which he was betrayed
took bread:
24 And when he had *given thanks* **eucharistized**,
he brake it, and said,
Take, eat: this is my body, which is broken for you:
this do in remembrance of me.
25 After the same manner also *he took* the cup,
when he had supped **after supping**, *saying* **wording**,
This cup is the new *testament* **covenant** in my blood:
this do ye, as oft as **ever** ye drink it,
in remembrance of me.
26 For as often as **ever** ye eat this bread,

and drink this cup,
ye do *shew the Lord's* **evangelize Adonay's** death
till **ever** he come.
27 *Wherefore* **So then** whosoever shall eat this bread,
and **or** drink this cup of *the Lord* **Adonay**, unworthily,
shall be *guilty of* **subject**
to the body and blood of *the Lord* **Adonay**.
28 But let a *man examine* **human proof** himself,
and *so* **thus** let him eat of that bread,
and drink of that cup.
29 For he that eateth and drinketh unworthily,
eateth and drinketh *damnation* **judgment** to himself,
not discerning *the Lord's* **Adonay's** body.
30 For this cause
many are *weak* **frail** and *sickly* **infirm** among you,
and many sleep.
31 For if we *would judge* **should discern** ourselves,
we should not **ever** be judged.
32 But when we are judged,
we are *chastened* **disciplined** of *the Lord* **Adonay**,
that we should not be condemned
with the *world* **cosmos**.
33 *Wherefore* **So then**, my brethren,
when ye come together to eat,
tarry **await** one *for* another.
34 And if any *man* hunger, let him eat at home;
that ye come not together unto *condemnation* **judgment**.
And the rest *will* **shall** I *set in order* **ordain**
when **as ever** I come.

ON SPIRITUALS

12 Now concerning *spiritual gifts* **spirituals**, brethren,
I *would* **will** not have you *ignorant* **unknowing**.
2 Ye know that ye were *Gentiles* **goyim**,
carried away **led** unto these *dumb* **voiceless** idols,
even as ye were **ever** led.
3 Wherefore I *give* **make known to** you *to understand*,
that no *man* **one** speaking *by* **in** the Spirit of *God* **Elohim**
calleth Jesus accursed **wordeth, Yah Shua anathema**:
and that no *man* **one** can say,
that Jesus is the Lord **Adonay Yah Shua**,
but by **except in** the Holy *Ghost* **Spirit**.

DISTINCTIONS OF CHARISMATA MINISTRIES, AND ENERGIZINGS

4 Now there are *diversities* **distinctions**
of *gifts* **charismata**,
but the same Spirit.
5 And there are *differences* **distinctions**
of *administrations* **ministries**,
but the same *Lord* **Adonay**.
6 And there are *diversities* **distinctions**
of *operations* **energizings**,
but it is the same *God* **Elohim**
which *worketh* **energizeth** all in all.

DISTRIBUTIONS OF SPIRITUALS

7 But the manifestation of the Spirit
is given to *every man* **each** to *profit withal* **benefit**.
8 For **indeed** to one is given *by* **through** the Spirit
the word of wisdom;
to another the word of knowledge
by **in** the same Spirit;
9 To another *faith* **trust**
by **in** the same Spirit;
to another the *gifts* **charismata** of *healing* **healings**
by **in** the same Spirit;
10 To another
the *working* **energizings** of *miracles* **dynamis**;
to another prophecy;
to another *discerning* **discernments** of spirits;
to another *divers kinds* **genos** of tongues;
to another the *interpretation* **translation** of tongues:
11 But all these
worketh **energizeth** that one and the selfsame Spirit,
dividing **distributing** to *every man* **each his own**
severally **exactly** as he *will* **willeth**.

Romans 12:3—8

THE BODY OF THE MESSIAH

12 For **exactly** as the body is one,
and hath many members,
and all the members of that one body,
being many, are one body:
so **thus** also *is Christ* **the Messiah**.
13 For *by* **in** one Spirit are we all baptized into one body,
whether *we be Jews* **Yah Hudiym**,
or Gentiles **whether Hellenes**,
whether *we be bond or free* **servant, whether liberated**;
and have been all made to drink into one Spirit.

ONE BODY, MANY MEMBERS

14 For the body is not one member, but many.
15 If **ever** the foot shall say,
Because I am not the hand, I am not of the body;
is it therefore not of the body?
16 And if **ever** the ear shall say,
Because I am not the eye, I am not of the body;
is it therefore not of the body?
17 If the whole body were an eye,
where were the hearing?
If the whole were hearing,
where were the smelling?
18 But now hath *God* **Elohim** set the members
every one **each** of them in the body,
exactly as *it hath pleased him* **he hath willed**.
19 And if they were all one member,
where were the body?
20 But now are they many members **indeed**,
yet but one body.
21 And the eye cannot say unto the hand,
I have no need of thee:
nor again the head to the feet,
I have no need of you.
22 *Nay* **Rather**, much more those members of the body,
which *seem* **we think** to be *more feeble* **frail**,
are necessary:
23 And those *members* of the body,
which we think to be *less honourable* **dishonourable**,
upon these
we *bestow more abundant* **place superabundant** honour;
and our *uncomely parts* **misbehavors**
have *more abundant comeliness* **superabundant honour**.
24 For our *comely parts* **honourables** have no need:
but *God* **Elohim** hath *tempered* **co—mingled** the body
together,
having given *more abundant* **superabundant** honour
to that *part* which lacked.
25 That there should be no schism in the body;
but that the members
should have the same *care* **anxiety** one for another.
26 And whether one member suffer,
all the members *suffer with it* **co—suffer**;
or **whether** one member be *honoured* **glorified**,
all the members *rejoice with it* **co—rejoice**.
27 Now ye are the body of *Christ* **Messiah**,
and members in particular.

THE CHARISMATA IN THE ECCLESIA

28 And *God* **Elohim indeed**
hath set some in the *church* **ecclesia**,
first apostles,
secondarily prophets, thirdly *teachers* **doctors**,
after that miracles **then dynamis**,
then *gifts* **charismata** of healings,
helps **supports**, *governments* **pilots**,
diversities **genos** of tongues.
29 Are all apostles? are all prophets?
are all *teachers* **doctors**?
are **have** all *workers of miracles* **dynamis**?
30 Have all the *gifts* **charismata** of *healing* **healings**?
do all speak with tongues? do all *interpret* **translate**?
31 But *covet earnestly* **be zealous**
for the *best gifts* **better charismata**:
and yet shew I unto you a more excellent way.

THE WAY OF LOVE

13 *Though* **Even if** I speak
with the tongues of *men* **humans** and of angels,
and have not *charity* **love**,
I am become *as sounding brass* **echoing copper**,
or a *tinkling* **hallooing** cymbal.
2 And *though* **even if** I have *the gift of* prophecy,
and *understand* **perceive** all mysteries,
and all knowledge;
and *though* **even if** I have all *faith* **trust**,
so that I *could* remove mountains,

and have not *charity* **love**, I am *nothing* **naught**.
3 And *though* **even if**
I *bestow* **force feed** all my *goods* **holdings**
to feed the poor **upon others**,
and *though* **even if**
I *give* **surrender** my body to be burned,
and have not *charity* **love**,
it *profiteth* **benefiteth** me *nothing* **naught**.
4 *Charity suffereth long* **Love is patient**, and is kind;
charity envieth not **love is never jealous**;
charity vaunteth not itself **love never brags**,
is not puffed up **never puffs**,
5 *Doth not behave itself unseemly* **Never misbehaves**,
seeketh not her own **never self—seeking**,
is not easily provoked **never easily agitated**,
thinketh no **never reckoneth** evil;
6 *Rejoiceth not in iniquity* **Never cheereth in injustice**,
but *rejoiceth* **co—cheereth** in the truth;
7 *Beareth* **Endureth** all *things*,
believeth **trusteth** all *things*,
hopeth all *things*,
endureth **abideth** all *things*.
8 *Charity* **Love** never **ever** faileth:
but whether *there be* prophecies,
they shall *fail* **inactivate**;
whether *there be* tongues,
they shall *cease* **pause**;
whether *there be* knowledge,
it shall *vanish away* **inactivate**.
9 For we know *in* **by** part, and we prophesy *in* **by** part.
10 But when *that which is perfect* **the complete** is come,
then that which is *in* **by** part
shall be *done away* **inactivated**.
11 When I was a *child* **baby**,
I spake as a *child* **baby**,
I *understood* **thought** as a *child* **baby**,
I *thought* **reckoned** as a *child* **baby**:
but when I became a man,
I *put away childish things* **inactivated the babyish**.
12 For now we see through a *glass* **mirror**,
darkly **obscurely**;
but then face to face:
now I know *in* **by** part;
but then shall I know *even* **exactly** as also I am known.
13 And now abideth *faith* **trust**, hope, *charity* **love**,
these three;
but the greatest of these is *charity* **love**.

ON PROPHECY, TONGUES, AND TRANSLATION

14 *Follow after charity* **Pursue love**,
and *desire spiritual gifts* **be zealous for spirituals**,
but rather that ye may prophesy.
2 For he that speaketh in *an unknown°* **a** tongue
speaketh not unto *men* **humanity**, but unto *God* **Elohim**:
for no *man understandeth* **one heareth** him;
howbeit in the spirit he speaketh mysteries.
°unknown tongues are unknown in Scripture
3 But he that prophesieth
speaketh unto *men* **humanity** to edification,
and *exhortation* **beseeching**, and *comfort* **consolation**.
4 He that speaketh in *an unknown* **a** tongue
edifieth himself;
but he that prophesieth edifieth the *church* **ecclesia**.
5 I *would* **will** that ye all spake with tongues
but rather that ye prophesied:
for greater is he that prophesieth
than he that speaketh with tongues,
except **unless** he *interpret* **translate**,
that the *church* **ecclesia** may *receive* **take** edifying.
6 Now, brethren,
even if I come unto you speaking with tongues,
what shall I *profit* **benefit** you,
except **unless** I shall speak to you
either *by revelation* **in apocalypse**, or *by* **in** knowledge,
or *by* **in** prophesying, or *by* **in** doctrine?
7 *And even* **Yet still**,
things without life **the soulless** giving *sound* **voice**,
whether *pipe* **flute** or *harp* **cither**,
except **unless** they give a distinction in the sounds,
how shall it be known
what is *piped* **fluted** or *harped* **cithered**?
8 For if **ever** the trumpet give an uncertain *sound* **voice**,
who shall prepare himself to *the battle* **war**?
9 *So* **Thus** likewise ye,
except **unless** ye *utter by* **give through** the tongue
words *easy to be* **well** understood,
how shall it be known what is spoken?
for ye shall speak into the air.
10 There are, *it may be* **if perhaps**,
so many *kinds* **genos** of voices in the *world* **cosmos**,
and none of them is *without signification* **voiceless**.
11 Therefore *if* **unless ever** I know *not*
the *meaning* **dynamis** of the voice,
I shall be unto him that speaketh a barbarian,
and he that speaketh shall be a barbarian unto me.
12 Even *so ye* **thus**,
forasmuch as **since** ye are zealous of *spiritual gifts* **spirits**,
seek that ye may *excel* **superabound**
to the edifying of the *church* **ecclesia**.
13 Wherefore
let him that speaketh in *an unknown* **a** tongue
pray that he may *interpret* **translate**.
14 For if **ever** I pray in *an unknown* **a** tongue,
my spirit prayeth,
but my *understanding* **mind** is unfruitful.
15 What *is* **be** it then?
I *will* **shall** pray with the spirit,
and I *will* **shall** pray with the *understanding* **mind** also:
I *will sing* **shall psalm** with the spirit,
and I *will sing* **shall psalm**
with the *understanding* **mind** also.
16 *Else when* **Unless if**
thou shalt *bless* **eulogize** with the spirit,
how shall he
that *occupieth* **filleth** the *room* **place** of the unlearned say
Amen at thy *giving of thanks* **eucharist**,
seeing **since** he *understandeth* **perceiveth** not
what thou *sayest* **wordest**?
17 For thou *verily* **indeed**
givest thanks **eucharistizest** well,
but the other is not edified.
18 I *thank* **eucharistize** my *God* **Elohim**,
I speak with tongues more than ye all:
19 Yet in the *church* **ecclesia**
I *had rather* **will to** speak five words
with **through** my *understanding* **mind**,
that *by my voice* I might *teach* **catechize** others also,
than *ten thousand* **a myriad** words
in *an unknown* **a** tongue.
20 Brethren,
be not children in *understanding* **thought**:
howbeit **rather** in malice be ye *children* **babies**,
but in *understanding* **thought** be *men* **complete**.
21 In the *law* **torah** it is *written* **scribed**,
With men of **In** other tongues and **in** other lips
will I speak unto this people;
and yet *for all that will* **thus shall** they not hear me,
saith the Lord **wordeth Yah Veh**.
Yesha Yah 28:11, 12, Deuteronomy 28:49
22 *Wherefore* **So then** tongues are *for* **unto** a sign,
not to them that *believe* **trust**,
but to *them that believe not* **the trustless**:
but prophesying
serveth **is** not for *them that believe not* **the trustless**,
but for them which *believe* **trust**.
23 If **ever** therefore the whole *church* **ecclesia**
be come together into one place,
and all speak with tongues,
and there *come in those that are* **enter the** unlearned,
or *unbelievers* **trustless**,
will **shall** they not say that ye *are mad* **rave**?
24 But if **ever** all prophesy,
and there *come in* **enter**
one that believeth not **a trustless**,
or *one* **an** unlearned,
he is *convinced* **reproved** of all, he is judged of all:
25 And thus are the secrets of his heart
made **become** manifest;
and *so* **thus** falling down on his face
he *will* **shall** worship *God* **Elohim**,
and *report* **evangelize**

that *God* **Elohim** is in you *of a truth* **indeed**.
26 How is it then, brethren? when ye come together,
every one **each** of you hath a psalm, hath a doctrine,
hath a tongue, hath *a revelation* **an apocalypse**,
hath *an interpretation* **a translation**.
Let all *things* be *done* unto edifying.

RULES FOR SPEAKING IN A TONGUE

27 If **also** any *man* **one** speak in *an unknown* **a** tongue,
let it be by two, or at the most by three,
and that by *course* **part**; and let one *interpret* **translate**.
28 But *if there* **unless ever there** be
no interpreter **a translator**,
let him *keep silence* **hush** in the *church* **ecclesia**;
and let him speak to himself, and to *God* **Elohim**.

RULES FOR PROPHETS AND DISCERNERS

29 Let the prophets speak two or three,
and let the other *judge* **discern**.
30 If *any thing* **ever aught** be *revealed* **unveiled**
to another that sitteth by,
let the first *hold his peace* **hush**.
31 For ye may **can** all prophesy one by one,
that all may learn,
and all may be *comforted* **consoled**.
32 And the spirits of the prophets
are subject **subjugate** to the prophets.
33 For *God* **Elohim**
is not *the author* of *confusion* **instability**,
but of *peace* **shalom**,
as in all *churches* **ecclesiae** of the *saints* **holy**.
34 Let your women *keep silence* **hush**
in the *churches* **ecclesiae**:
for it is not *permitted* **allowed** unto them to speak;
but they are *commanded*
to *be under obedience* **subjugate**,
exactly as also *saith* **wordeth** the *law* **torah**.
35 And if they will **to** learn *any thing* **somewhat**,
let them ask their *husbands* **own men** at home:
for it is a shame
for women to speak in the *church* **ecclesia**.
36 *What?*
Or came the word of *God* **Elohim** out from you?
or *came it* **has it arrived** unto you only?
37 If any man think himself to be a prophet, or spiritual,
let him acknowledge that
the things **those** that I *write* **scribe** unto you
are the *commandments* **misvoth** of the *Lord* **Adonay**.
38 But if any *man* **one** be *ignorant* **unknowing**,
let him be *ignorant* **unknowing**.
39 *Wherefore* **So then**, brethren,
covet **be zealous** to prophesy,
and forbid not to speak with tongues.
40 Let all *things be done decently* **become decorous**
and in order.

THE EVANGELISM DEFINED

15 Moreover, brethren,
I *declare* **make known** unto you *the gospel* **evangelism**
which I *preached* **evangelized** unto you,
which also ye have *received* **taken**,
and wherein ye stand;
2 *By* **Through** which also ye are saved,
if ye *keep in memory what* **hold the word**
I *preached* **evangelized** unto you,
unless **except lest** ye have *believed* **trusted** in vain.
3 For I delivered unto you **in the** first
of all that which I also *received* **had taken**,
how that *Christ* **Messiah** died for our sins
according to the scriptures;
4 And that he was buried,
and that he rose *again* the third day
according to the scriptures:
5 And that he was seen of *Cephas* **Kepha**,
then of the twelve:
6 *After that* **Then**,
he was seen of above five hundred brethren at once;
of whom the *greater part remain* **most abide**
unto *this present* **now**,
but some are fallen asleep.
7 *After that* **Then**, he was seen of *James* **Yaaqovos**;
then of all the apostles.
8 And last of all he was seen of me also,
just as though as of one *born out of due time* **miscarried**.
9 For I am the least of the apostles,
that am not *meet* **adequate** to be called an apostle,
because I persecuted the *church* **ecclesia** of *God* **Elohim**.
10 But by the *grace* **charism** of *God* **Elohim**
I am what I am:
and his *grace* **charism**
which was bestowed upon **unto** me
was **became** not in vain;
but I laboured
more *abundantly* **superabundantly** than they all:
yet not I,
but the *grace* **charism** of *God* **Elohim**
which was with me.
11 Therefore whether *it were* I, *or* **whether** they,
so **thus** we preach, and *so* **thus** ye *believed* **trusted**.

THE RESURRECTION, ESSENTIAL TO THE TRUST

12 Now if *Christ* **Messiah** be preached
that he rose from the dead,
how *say* **word** some among you
that there is no resurrection of the dead?
13 But if there be no resurrection of the dead,
then is *Christ* **Messiah** not risen:
14 And if *Christ* **Messiah** be not risen,
then is our preaching vain,
and your *faith* **trust** is also vain.
15 Yea,
and we are found *false* **pseudo** witnesses of *God* **Elohim**;
because we have *testified* **witnessed** of *God* **Elohim**
that he raised up *Christ* **the Messiah**:
whom he raised not up,
if *so* **ever then** be that the dead rise not.
16 For if the dead rise not,
then is not *Christ* **Messiah** raised:
17 And if *Christ* **Messiah** be not raised,
your *faith* **trust** is vain; ye are yet in your sins.
18 Then they also
which are fallen asleep in *Christ* **Messiah**
are *perished* **destroyed**.
19 If in this life only we have hope in *Christ* **Messiah**,
we are of all *men* **humanity**
most miserable **least mercied**.

THE SEQUENCE OF THE RESURRECTION

20 But now is *Christ* **Messiah** risen from the dead,
and become the *firstfruits* **firstlings** of them that slept.
21 For since *by man* **through humanity,**
came death,
by man **through humanity,**
came also the resurrection of the dead.
22 For **exactly** as in Adam all die,
even *so* **thus** in *Christ* **the Messiah**
shall all be *made alive* **enlivened**.
23 But *every man* **each** in his own order:
Christ **Messiah** the *firstfruits* **firstlings**;
afterward **then** they that are *Christ's* **Messiah's**
at his *coming* **parousia**.
24 Then *cometh* the *end* **completion**,
when he shall have delivered *up*
the *kingdom* **sovereigndom** to *God* **Elohim**,
even the Father;
when he shall have *put down* **inactivated**
all *rule* **hierarchies** and all authority and *power* **dynamis**.
25 For he must reign,
till **whenever** he hath put all enemies under his feet.
26 The *last* **final** enemy
that shall be *destroyed* **inactivated**
is death.
27 For he hath *put* **subjugated** all *things* under his feet.
But when he saith
all *things* are *put under him* **subjugated**,
it is *manifest* **evident** that he is excepted,
which *did put* **subjugated** all *things* under him.
28 And when all *things*
shall be *subdued* **subjugated** unto him,
then shall the Son also himself
be *subject* **subjugated** unto him
that *put* **subjugated** all *things* under him,
that *God* **Elohim** may be all in all.
29 Else what shall they do
which are baptized for the dead,

if the dead rise not at all?
why are they then baptized for the dead?
30 And why stand we in *jeopardy* **peril** every hour?
31 *I protest by your rejoicing*
which I have in Christ Jesus our Lord,
I die daily
boasting in what I have
in Messiah Yah Shua our Adonay.
32 If after the manner of *men* **humanity**
I *have fought* **strove** with beasts at Ephesus,
what *advantageth* **benefiteth** it me, if the dead rise not?
let us eat and drink; for to morrow we die.
33 Be not *deceived* **seduced**:
evil *communications* **homilies**
corrupt *good manners* **kind habits.**
34 *Awake to righteousness* **Sober up justly**, and sin not;
for some *have not the knowledge* **are unknowing**
of *God* **Elohim**:
I *speak* **word** this to *your* shame **you**.

THE MANNER OF THE RESURRECTION

35 But some *man will* **shall** say,
How are the dead raised *up*?
and, with what body do they come?
36 Thou *fool* **thoughtless**,
that which thou sowest is not *quickened* **enlivened**,
except **unless** it die:
37 And that which thou sowest,
thou sowest not that body that shall be,
but *bare grain* **naked kernel**,
it may chance **if perhaps** of *wheat* **grain**,
or of some *other grain* **of the rest**:
38 But *God* **Elohim** giveth it a body
exactly as *it hath pleased him* **he hath willed**,
and to *every seed* **each sperma** his own body.
39 All flesh is not the same flesh:
but there is **indeed** one *kind of* flesh of *men* **humanity**,
another flesh of *beasts* **animals**,
another of fishes,
and another of *birds* **flyers**.
40 *There are* also *celestial* **heavenly** bodies,
and bodies *terrestrial* **earthly**:
but the glory of the *celestial* **heavenlies**
is *one* **indeed another,**
and the *glory of the terrestrial* **earthly**
is another.
41 *There is* one glory of the sun,
and another glory of the moon,
and another glory of the stars:
for *one* star
differeth from another **thoroughly surpasseth** star
in glory.
42 *So* **Thus** also is the resurrection of the dead.
It is sown in corruption;
it is raised in incorruption:
43 *It is* sown in dishonour;
it is raised in glory:
it is sown in *weakness* **frailty**;
it is raised in *power* **dynamis**:
44 *It is* sown a *natural* **soulical** body;
it is raised a spiritual body.
There is a *natural* **soulical** body,
and there is a spiritual body.
45 And *so* **thus** it is *written* **scribed**,
The first *man* **human** Adam
was made **became into** a living soul;
the *last* **final** Adam
was made a quickening **into an enlivening** spirit.
46 *Howbeit* **Rather** that was not first which is spiritual,
but that which is *natural* **soulical**;
and *afterward* **then** that which is spiritual.
47 The first *man* **human** is of the earth, *earthy* **dust**;
the second *man* **human** is *the Lord* **Adonay** from heaven.
48 **Such** As is the *earthy* **dust**,
such are they also that are *earthy* **dust**:
and **such** as is the *heavenly* **heavenlies**,
such are they also that are *heavenly* **heavenlies.**
49 And **exactly**
as we have borne the *image* **icon** of the *earthy* **dust**,
we shall also
bear the *image* **icon** of the *heavenly* **heavenlies**.
50 Now this I say, brethren, that flesh and blood
cannot inherit
the *kingdom* **sovereigndom** of *God* **Elohim**;
neither doth *corruption* **corruptibility**
inherit *incorruption* **incorruptibility.**

THE MYSTERY OF THE RESURRECTION

51 Behold, I *shew* **word** you a mystery;
Indeed, We shall not all sleep,
but we shall all be changed,
52 In a moment, in the *twinkling* **atom** of an eye,
at **in** the *last* **final** trump:
for *the trumpet* **indeed it** shall *sound* **trump**,
and the dead shall be raised incorruptible,
and we shall be changed.
53 For this corruptible
must *put on incorruption* **endue incorruptibility**,
and this mortal must *put on immortality* **endue athanasia**.
54 So when this corruptible
shall have *put on incorruption* **endued incorruptibility**,
and this mortal
shall have *put on immortality* **endued athanasia**,
then shall be *brought to pass* the *saying* **word**
that is *written* **scribed**,
Death is swallowed up in *victory* **triumph**.
Yesha Yah 25:8
55 O death, where is thy sting?
O *grave* **hades**, where is thy *victory* **triumph**?
56 The sting of death is sin;
and the *strength* **dynamis** of sin is the *law* **torah**.
57 But *thanks* **charism** be to *God* **Elohim**,
which giveth us the *victory* **triumph**
through our *Lord Jesus Christ* **Adonay Yah Shua Messiah**.
58 *Therefore* **So then**, my beloved brethren,
be ye *stedfast* **grounded**, unmoveable,
always *abounding* **superabounding**
in the work of *the Lord* **Adonay**,
forasmuch as ye know **knowing**
that your labour is not in vain in *the Lord* **Adonay**.

ON CONTRIBUTIONS

16 Now concerning the *collection* **contribution**
for **to** the *saints* **holy**,
exactly as I have *given order* **ordained**
to the *churches* **ecclesiae** of Galatia,
even *so* **thus** do ye.
2 Upon the first *day* of the *week* **shabbaths**
let *every one* **each** of you *lay* **place** by him *in store*,
as God hath **treasuring up as ever he** prospered *him*,
that there be no *gatherings* **contributions** when I come.
3 And when I come,
whomsoever ye shall approve
by **through** your *letters* **epistles**,
them *will* **shall** I send
to *bring* **bear away** your *liberality* **charism**
unto *Jerusalem* **Yeru Shalem**.
4 And if **ever** it be *meet* **worthy** that I go also,
they shall go with me.

PAULOS' TRAVEL PLANS

5 Now I *will* **shall** come unto you,
when I shall pass through Macedonia:
for I *do* pass through Macedonia.
6 And *it* may *be that* **perhaps** I *will* **shall** abide **nearby**,
yea, and winter with you,
that ye may *bring* **forward** me *on my journey*
whithersoever I go.
7 For I *will* **have willed to** not see you now *by* **in** the way;
but I *trust* **hope**
to *tarry a while* **abide some time** with you,
if *the Lord permit* **ever Adonay allow**.
8 But I *will tarry at* **shall abide in** Ephesus until Pentecost.
9 For a *great door* **mega portal** and *effectual* **energized**
is opened unto me,
and *there are* many adversaries.
10 Now if **ever** Timotheus come,
see that he may be with you *without fear* **fearless**:
for he worketh the work of *the Lord* **Adonay**, as I also *do*.
11 Let no *man* **one** therefore *despise* **belittle** him:
but *conduct* **forward** him *forth* in *peace* **shalom**,
that he may come unto me:
for I *look for* **await** him with the brethren.
12 *As touching our* **Concerning** brother Apollos,

I *greatly desired* **besought** him **much**
to come unto you with the brethren:
but *his will was* **he willed most certainly**
not *at all* to come *at this time* **now**;
but he *will* **shall** come
when he shall have *convenient time* **opportunity**.

ADMONITIONS AND SALUTES

13 Watch ye, stand *fast* **firm** in the *faith* **trust**,
quit you like men **manly**, *be strong* **powerful**.
14 Let all *your things be done with charity* **be in love**.
15 I beseech you, brethren,
(ye know the house of Stephanas,
that it is the *firstfruits* **firstlings** of Achaia,
and that they have *addicted* **ordained** themselves
to the ministry of the *saints* **holy**,)
16 That ye *submit* **subjugate** yourselves *unto* **under** such,
and to every one that *helpeth with us* **co—worketh**,
and laboureth.
17 I *am glad of* **cheer over** the *coming* **appearing**
of Stephanas and *Fortunatus* **Phortunatos** and Achaicus:
for that which was lacking on your part
they have *supplied* **fulfilled**.
18 For they have refreshed my spirit and your's:
therefore acknowledge ye them that are such.
19 The *churches* **ecclesiae** of Asia salute you.
Aquila and Priscilla salute you much in *the Lord* **Adonay**,
with the *church* **ecclesia** that is in their house.
20 All the brethren *greet* **salute** you.
Greet ye one another *with* **in** an holy kiss.
21 The salutation of *me Paul* **Paulos** with mine own hand.
22 If any *man love* **one befriend** not
the Lord Jesus Christ **Adonay Yah Shua Messiah**,
let him be Anathema Maranatha.
23 The *grace* **charism**
of our *Lord Jesus Christ* **Adonay Yah Shua Messiah**
be with you.
24 My love be with you all
in *Christ Jesus* **Messiah Yah Shua**.
Amen.

KEY TO INTERPRETING THE EXEGESES:
King James text is in regular type;
Text under exegeses is in oblique type;
Text of exegeses is in bold type.

SALUTATION

1 *Paul* **Paulos**,
an apostle of *Jesus Christ* **Yah Shua Messiah**
by **through** the will of *God* **Elohim**,
and *Timothy* **Timo Theos** *our* brother,
unto the *church* **ecclesia** of *God* **Elohim**
which is at **being in** Corinth,
with all the *saints which are* **holy being** in all Achaia:
2 *Grace be* **Charism** to you and *peace* **shalom**
from *God* **Elohim** our Father,
and *from*
the Lord Jesus Christ **Adonay Yah Shua Messiah**.
3 *Blessed* **Eulogized** be *God* **Elohim**, even the Father
of our *Lord Jesus Christ* **Adonay Yah Shua Messiah**,
the Father of *mercies* **compassions**,
and the *God* **Elohim** of all *comfort* **consolation**;
4 Who *comforteth* **consoleth** us in all our tribulation,
that we may be able to *comfort* **console** them
which are in any *trouble* **tribulation**,
by **through** the *comfort* **consolation** wherewith
we ourselves are *comforted* **consoled** of *God* **Elohim**.
5 For **exactly** as the sufferings of *Christ* **the Messiah**
abound **superabound** in us,
so **thus** our consolation also
aboundeth by Christ **superaboundeth through Messiah**.
6 And whether we be *afflicted* **tribulated**,
it is for your consolation and salvation,
which *is effectual* **energizeth** in the enduring
of the same sufferings which we also suffer:
or whether we be *comforted* **consoled**,
it is for your consolation and salvation.
7 And our hope of you is stedfast,
knowing, that **exactly**
as ye are *partakers* **communicants** of the sufferings,
so **thus** shall ye be also of the consolation.
8 For we *would* **will** not, brethren,
have you *ignorant* **unknowing** of our *trouble* **tribulation**
which *came to* **became** us in Asia,
that we were
pressed out of measure **excessively burdened**,
above strength **beyond dynamis**,
insomuch that we despaired even of *life* **living**:
9 But we had the sentence of death in ourselves,
that we should not *trust* **confide** in ourselves,
but in *God* **Elohim** which raiseth the dead:
10 Who *delivered* **rescued** us from so great a death,
and *doth deliver* **rescueth**:
in whom we *trust* **hope**
that he *will* **shall** yet *deliver* **rescue** *us*;
11 Ye also *helping together* **co—working**
by *prayer* **petition** for us,
that for the *gift bestowed upon* **charisma unto** us
by the means of many *persons* **faces**
thanks may be *given by* **eucharistized through** many
on our behalf.
12 For our *rejoicing* **boasting** is this,
the *testimony* **witness** of our conscience,
that *in simplicity* **with liberality**
and *Godly* sincerity **of Elohim**,
not *with* **in** fleshly wisdom,
but *by* **in** the *grace* **charism** of *God* **Elohim**,
we have had our *conversation* **behaviour**
in the *world* **cosmos**,
and more *abundantly* **superabundantly**
to you—ward **toward you**.
13 For we *write* **scribe** none other *things* unto you,
than **rather** what ye read or acknowledge;
and I *trust* **hope** ye shall acknowledge
even to the *end* **completion**;
14 **Exactly** As also ye have acknowledged us *in* **by** part,
that we are your *rejoicing* **boasting**,
even **exactly** as ye also are our's
in the day of *the Lord Jesus* **Adonay Yah Shua**.

PAULOS' ALTERED TRAVEL PLANS

15 And in this confidence
I *was minded* **had willed** to come unto you before,

that ye might have a second *benefit* **charism**;
16 And to pass *by* **through** you into Macedonia,
and to come again out of Macedonia unto you,
and of you to be *brought on my way* **forwarded**
toward Judaea **unto Yah Hudah**.

ELOHIM'S YEA

17 When I therefore was thus *minded* **counseled**,
did I **then** use *lightness* **levity**?
or *the things* **those** that I *purpose* **counsel**,
do I *purpose* **counsel** according to the flesh,
that with me there should be yea yea, and nay nay?
18 But as *God* **Elohim** is *true* **trustworthy**,
our word toward you *was* **became** not yea and nay.
19 For the Son of *God* **Elohim**,
Jesus Christ **Yah Shua Messiah**,
who was preached among you *by* **through** us,
even by **through** me
and Silvanus and *Timotheus* **Timo Theos**,
was **became** not yea and nay,
but in him *was* **became** yea.
20 For *all* **as many as** the *promises* **pre—evangelisms**
of *God* **Elohim** in him are yea, and in him Amen,
unto the glory of *God by* **Elohim through** us.
21 Now he which stablisheth us with you
in *Christ* **Messiah**,
and hath anointed us, is *God* **Elohim**;
22 Who hath also sealed us,
and given the *earnest* **pledge** of the Spirit in our hearts.
23 Moreover I call *God* **Elohim**
for a *record* **witness** upon my soul,
that to spare you I came *not as yet* **no more** unto Corinth.
24 Not for that we
have dominion over **overlord** your *faith* **trust**,
but are *helpers* **co—workers** of your *joy* **cheer**:
for by *faith* **trust** ye stand.

2 But I *determined* **judged** this with myself,
that I *would* **should** not come again to you
in *heaviness* **sorrow**.
2 For if I *make you sorry* **sorrow you**,
who is he then that *maketh* **rejoiceth** me *glad*,
but the same **except that**
which is *made sorry* **sorrowed** by me?
3 And I *wrote* **scribed** this same unto you,
lest, when I came,
I should have sorrow *from them*
of whom I *ought to rejoice* **need cheer**;
having confidence in you all,
that my *joy is the joy* **cheer be** of you all.
4 For out of much *affliction* **tribulation**
and *anguish* **oppression** of heart
I *wrote* **scribed** unto you *with* **through** many tears;
not that ye should *be grieved* **sorrow**,
but that ye might know the love which I have
more *abundantly* **superabundantly** unto you.

ON FORGIVING THE OFFENDER

5 But if any have *caused grief* **sorrowed**,
he hath not *grieved* **sorrowed** me, but *in* **by** part:
that I may not *overcharge* **overburden** you all.
6 Sufficient to such a man
is this *punishment* **disesteeming**,
which was *inflicted* of many.
7 So that contrariwise ye *ought* rather
to forgive him **grant charism**, and *comfort* **console** him,
lest *perhaps* **somehow**
such a one should be swallowed *up*
with *overmuch* **superabundant** sorrow.
8 Wherefore I beseech you
that ye *would* **should** confirm your love *toward* **unto** him.
9 For to this *end* also did I *write* **scribe**,
that I might know the proof of you,
whether ye be obedient in all *things*.
10 To whom ye
forgive any thing **somewhat grant charism**,
I *forgive* also:
for if I *forgave any thing* **somewhat granted charism**,
to whom I *forgave it* **granted charism**,
for your sakes *forgave I it*
in the *person* **face** of *Christ* **Messiah**;
11 Lest Satan should *get an advantage of* **defraud** us:
for we are not *ignorant* **unknowing**
of his *devices* **comprehensions**.
12 Furthermore, when I came to Troas
to *preach Christ's gospel* **evangelize the Messiah**,
and a *door* **portal** was opened unto me
of the Lord **in Adonay**,
13 I had no *rest* **relaxation** in my spirit,
because I found not Titus my brother:
but *taking my leave of* **bidding** them **bye bye**,
I went from thence into Macedonia.

THE TRIUMPHANT IN THE MESSIAH

14 Now *thanks* **charism** be unto *God* **Elohim**,
which always causeth us
to triumph in *Christ* **the Messiah**,
and *maketh manifest* **manifesteth** the *savour* **fragrance**
of his knowledge *by* **through** us in every place.
15 For we are unto *God* **Elohim**
a *sweet savour* **good fragrance** of *Christ* **Messiah**,
in them that are saved, and in them that *perish* **destruct**:
16 To the one **indeed**
we are the *savour* **fragrance** of death unto death;
and to the other the *savour* **fragrance** of life unto life.
And who is *sufficient* **adequate** for these *things*?
17 For we are not as many,
which *corrupt* **huckster** the word of *God* **Elohim**:
but as of sincerity, but as of *God* **Elohim**,
in the sight of *God* **Elohim** speak we in *Christ* **Messiah**.

SCRIBINGS OF THE HEART

3 Do we begin again to commend ourselves?
or need we **except that we need**, as some *others*,
epistles of commendation to you,
or *letters of* commendation from you?
2 Ye are our epistle *written* **inscribed** in our hearts,
known and read of all *men* **humanity**:
3 *Forasmuch as ye are manifestly declared* **Manifested**
to be the epistle of *Christ* **Messiah** ministered by us,
written **inscribed** not with ink,
but with the Spirit of the living *God* **Elohim**;
not in *tables* **slabs** of stone,
but in fleshy *tables* **slabs** of the heart.
4 And such *trust* **confidence** have we
through *Christ to God—ward* **the Messiah toward Elohim**:
5 Not that we are *sufficient* **adequate** of ourselves
to *think any thing* **reckon somewhat** as of ourselves;
but our *sufficiency* **adequacy** is of *God* **Elohim**;
6 Who also hath *made* **enabled** us *able*
ministers of the new *testament* **covenant**;
not of the *letter* **scribing**, but of the spirit:
for the *letter killeth* **scribing slaughtereth**,
but the spirit *giveth life* **enliveneth**.
7 But if the *ministration* **ministry** of death,
written and **inscribings** engraven in stones,
was glorious **became in glory**,
so that the *children* **sons** of *Israel* **Yisra El**
could not *stedfastly behold* **stare**
unto the face of *Moses* **Mosheh**
for the glory of his *countenance* **face**;
which *glory* was to be *done away* **inactivated**:
8 How **indeed**
shall not the *ministration* **ministry** of the spirit
be rather *glorious* **in glory**?
9 For if the *ministration* **ministry** of condemnation
be glory,
much more *doth*
the *ministration* **ministry** of *righteousness* **justness**
exceed **superaboundeth** in glory.
10 For even that which was *made glorious* **glorified**
had no glory in this *respect* **part**,
by reason **because** of the glory that excelleth.
11 For if that which is *done away* **inactivated**
was *glorious* **through glory**,
much more that which *remaineth* **abideth**
is glorious **be in glory**.

THE INACTIVATED COVENANT

12 Seeing then that we have such hope,
we use *great plainness* **much boldness** of speech:
13 And not **exactly** as *Moses* **Mosheh**,
which put a vail over his face,
that the *children* **sons** of *Israel* **Yisra El**
could not *stedfastly look* **stare** to the *end* **completion**
of that which is *abolished* **inactivated**:

14 But their *minds* **comprehensions**
were *blinded* **petrified**:
for until this day *remaineth* **abideth** the same
vail untaken away — **not unveiled**
in the reading of the old *testament* **covenant**;
which *vail* is *done away* **inactivated** in *Christ* **Messiah**.
15 But even unto this day, when *Moses* **Mosheh** is read,
the vail is **laid** upon their heart.
16 Nevertheless
when **ever** it shall turn to *the Lord* **Yah Veh**,
the vail shall be taken away.
Exodus 34:34
17 Now *the Lord* **Adonay** is that Spirit:
and where the Spirit of *the Lord* **Yah Veh** is,
there is liberty.
18 But we all, with *open* **unveiled** face
beholding as in a glass **reflecting**
the glory of *the Lord* **Yah Veh**,
are *changed* **metamorphosed** into the same *image* **icon**
from glory to glory,
even **exactly** as by the Spirit of *the Lord* **Yah Veh**.
Exodus 16:7

THE LIGHT FROM THE DARK

4 Therefore seeing we have this ministry,
exactly as we have *received mercy* **been mercied**,
we *faint* **weary** not;
2 But have *renounced* **disowned**
the *hidden things* **secrets** of *dishonesty* **shame**,
not walking in *craftiness* **cunningness**,
nor handling the word of *God* **Elohim** deceitfully;
but by manifestation of the truth commending ourselves
to every *man's* **human's** conscience
in the sight of *God* **Elohim**.
3 But if our *gospel* **evangelism** be *hid* **veiled**,
it is *hid to* **veiled among** them that are lost:
4 In whom the *God* **Elohim** of this *world* **eon**
hath blinded the *minds* **comprehensions**
of *them which believe not* **the trustless**,
lest the light of the
glorious gospel **evangelism of the glory**
of *Christ* **the Messiah**,
who is the *image* **icon** of *God* **Elohim**,
should *shine* **radiate** unto them.
5 For we preach not ourselves,
but *Christ Jesus the Lord* **Messiah Yah Shua Adonay**;
and ourselves your servants for *Jesus'* **Yah Shua's** sake.
6 For *God* **Elohim**,
who *commanded* **said** the light
to shine **radiate** out of darkness,
hath *shined* **radiated** in our hearts,
to give the light **for the radiancy**
of the knowledge of the glory of *God* **Elohim**
in the face of *Jesus Christ* **Yah Shua Messiah**.

ON CLAY VESSELS

7 But we have this treasure in *earthen* **clay** vessels,
that the excellency of the *power* **dynamis**
may be of *God* **Elohim**, and not of us.
8 We are *troubled on every side* **tribulated in all**,
yet not distressed;
we are perplexed, but not in despair;
9 Persecuted, but not forsaken;
cast down, but not destroyed;
10 Always *bearing* **carrying** about in the body
the *dying* **necrosis** of *the Lord Jesus* **Adonay Yah Shua**,
that the life also of *Jesus* **Yah Shua**
might be *made* manifest in our body.
11 For we which live are *alway* **ever** delivered unto death
for *Jesus'* **Yah Shua's** sake,
that the life also of *Jesus* **Yah Shua**
might be *made* manifest in our mortal flesh.
12 So then **indeed** death *worketh* **energizeth** in us,
but life in you.

THE SPIRIT OF TRUST

13 We having the same spirit of *faith* **the trust**,
according as *it is written* **scribed**,
I *believed* **trusted**, and therefore have I spoken;
we also *believe* **trust**, and therefore speak;
Psalm 116:10
14 Knowing that
he which raised *up the Lord Jesus* **Adonay Yah Shua**
shall raise *up* us also by *Jesus* **Yah Shua**,
and shall present us with you.
15 For all *things* **these** are for your sakes,
that the *abundant grace* **superabundant charism**
might through the *thanksgiving* **eucharist** of many
redound **superabound** to the glory of *God* **Elohim**.
16 *For which cause* **Therefore**, we *faint* **weary** not;
but though our outward *man perish* **humanity corrupt**,
yet the inward *man* is renewed day by day.
17 For our light *affliction* **tribulation**,
which is *but for a moment* **momentary**,
worketh for us
a far more **an exceeding unto** exceeding
and eternal *weight* **burden** of glory;
18 While we *look* **scope** not at the *things which are* seen,
but at the *things which are* not seen:
for the *things which are* seen are temporal;
but the *things which are* not seen are eternal.

HOUSES, TENTS, AND EDIFICES

5 For we know
that if **ever** our earthly house of this tabernacle
were dissolved **disintegrate**,
we have *a building* **an edifice** of *God* **Elohim**,
an house not *made with hands* **handmade**,
eternal in the heavens.
2 For in this we *groan* **sigh**,
earnestly desiring **yearning** to be *clothed upon* **endued**
with our house which is from heaven:
3 If *so be that* **indeed** being *clothed* **endued**
we shall not be found naked.

AT HOME, AWAY FROM HOME

4 For we *that are* **being** in this tabernacle *do groan* **sigh**,
being burdened:
not for that we would **since we will to not**
be *unclothed* **stripped**,
but *clothed upon* **endued**,
that *mortality* **the mortal** might be swallowed *up* of life.
5 Now he that hath *wrought* **worked** us
for the selfsame *thing* is *God* **Elohim**,
who also hath given unto us
the *earnest* **pledge** of the Spirit.
6 Therefore we are always *confident* **encouraged**,
knowing that, whilst we are at home in the body,
we are *absent* **away from home** from *the Lord* **Adonay**:
7 (For we walk *by faith* **through trust**,
not *by sight* **through semblance**:)
8 We are *confident* **encouraged**, *I say*,
and *willing* **well—approve** rather
to be *absent* **away from home** from the body,
and to be *present* **at home** with *the Lord* **Adonay**.
9 Wherefore we *labour* **befriendingly esteem**, that,
whether *present* **at home**,
or absent **whether away from home**,
we may be *accepted of* **well—pleasing unto** him.
10 For we must all *appear* **manifest**
before the judgment seat **in front of the bamah**
of *Christ* **the Messiah**;
that *every one* **each** may receive
the things done in **through** his body,
according to **toward** that he hath *done* **transacted**,
whether *it be* good, *or bad* **whether evil**.

ALL HAVE DIED

11 Knowing therefore the *terror* **awe** of *the Lord* **Adonay**,
we *persuade men* **convince humanity**;
but we are *made* manifest unto *God* **Elohim**;
and I *trust* **hope** also
are *made* manifest in your consciences.
12 For we commend not ourselves again unto you,
but give you *occasion* **opportunity**
to *glory* **boast** on our behalf,
that ye may have somewhat *to answer* **toward** them
which *glory* **boast** in *appearance* **face**, and not in heart.
13 For whether we be *beside ourselves* **astounded**,
it is to *God* **Elohim**:
or whether we be *sober* **soundminded**,
it is for your cause.
14 For the love of *Christ* **the Messiah**
constraineth **holdeth** us **together**;
because we thus judge,
that if one died for all, then were all dead:

15 And *that* he died for all,
that they which live
should *not henceforth* **no longer** live unto themselves,
but unto him which died for them, and rose *again.*

THE RECONCILIATION MINISTRY

16 *Wherefore* **So then**
henceforth know we no *man* **one** after the flesh:
yea, though we have known *Christ* **Messiah**
after the flesh,
yet **from** now *henceforth* **on**
know we him *no more* **not still**.
17 *Therefore* **So then** if any *man* **one** be in *Christ* **Messiah**,
he is a new *creature* **creation**:
old things are **the archaic has** passed *away*;
behold, all *things are* become new.
18 And all *things are* of *God* **Elohim**,
who hath reconciled us to himself
by Jesus Christ **through Yah Shua Messiah**,
and hath given to us the ministry of reconciliation;
19 *To wit* **How**, that *God* **Elohim** was in *Christ* **Messiah**,
reconciling the *world* **cosmos** unto himself,
not *imputing* **reckoning**
their *trespasses* **backslidings** unto them;
and hath *committed unto* **placed in** us
the word of reconciliation.
20 *Now then* **Therefore**
we are *ambassadors* **presbyters** for *Christ* **Messiah**,
as *though God* **Elohim**
did beseech you by **beseeching through** us:
we *pray* **petition** *you* in *Christ's* **Messiah's** stead,
be ye reconciled to *God* **Elohim**.
21 For he hath made him
to be sin for us **sin in our behalf**,
who knew no sin;
that we might *be made* **become**
the *righteousness* **justness** of *God* **Elohim** in him.

THE DAY OF SALVATION IS NOW!

6 We then, *as workers together with him* **co—working**,
beseech you also
that ye receive not the *grace* **charism** of *God* **Elohim**
in vain.
2 (For he *saith* **wordeth**,
I have heard thee
in *a time accepted* **an acceptable season**,
and in the day of salvation
have I *succoured* **helped** thee:
behold, now is the *accepted* **wellreceived** time;
behold, now is the day of salvation.)
3 Giving no *offence* **stumbling** in *any thing* **aught**,
that the ministry be not *blamed* **blemished**:
4 But in all *things approving* **commending** ourselves
as the ministers of *God* **Elohim**,
in *much patience* **many endurances**,
in *afflictions* **tribulations**,
in *necessities* **compulsions**, in distresses,
5 In stripes, in *imprisonments* **guardhouses**,
in *tumults* **instabilities**, in labours,
in watchings, in fastings;
6 *By pureness* **In holiness**, *by* **in** knowledge,
by longsuffering **in patience**, *by* **in** kindness,
by **in** the Holy *Ghost* **Spirit**,
by **in** love *unfeigned* **unpretentious**,
7 *By* **In** the word of truth,
by **in** the *power* **dynamis** of *God* **Elohim**,
by **through** the *armour* **weapon** of *righteousness* **justness**
on **by** the right *hand* and *on* **by** the left,
8 *By honour* **Through glory** and dishonour,
by evil report **through defamation**
and *good report* **euphony**:
as *deceivers* **seducers**, and *yet* true;
9 As unknown, and *yet* well known;
as dying, and, behold, we live;
as *chastened* **disciplined**, and not *killed* **deathified**;
10 As *sorrowful* **sorrowed**,
yet *alway rejoicing* **ever cheering**;
as poor, yet *making* **enriching** many *rich*;
as having *nothing* **naught**,
and *yet possessing* **holding** all *things*.
11 O ye Corinthians, our mouth is open unto you,
our heart is *enlarged* **broadened**.
12 Ye are not *straitened* **distressed** in us,
but ye are *straitened* **distressed**
in your own *bowels* **spleens**.
13 Now for a *recompence* **retribution** in the same,
(I *speak* **word** as unto *my* children,)
be ye also *enlarged* **broadened**.

ON UNEQUAL YOKES

14 Be ye not unequally yoked *together*
with *unbelievers* **the trustless**:
for what *fellowship* **partaking** hath *righteousness* **justness**
with *unrighteousness* **torah violations**?
and what communion hath light with darkness?
15 And what *concord* **symphony**
hath *Christ* **Messiah** with *Belial* **Beli Yaal**?
or what part hath *he that believeth* **the trusting**
with *an infidel* **the trustless**?
16 And what *agreement* **togetherness**
hath the *temple* **nave** of *God* **Elohim** with idols?
for ye are the *temple* **nave** of the living *God* **Elohim**;
exactly as *God* **Elohim** hath said,
I *will dwell in* **shall indwell** them,
and walk *in* **among** them;
and I *will* **shall** be their *God* **Elohim**,
and they shall be my people.
Leviticus 26:12, Yirme Yah 31:33,
Yechezq El 36:28, Zechar Yah 13:9

THE CALL TO BE SET APART

17 Wherefore come out from among them,
and be ye *separate* **set apart**,
saith the Lord **wordeth Yah Veh**,
and touch not the *unclean thing* **impure**;
and I *will* **shall also** receive you,
18 And *will* **shall** be
a Father unto you, **Father**,
and ye shall be *my* **unto me**, sons and daughters,
saith the Lord Almighty **wordeth Yah Veh Sabaoth**.
Yesha Yah 52:11, Yirme Yah 31:9

THE CALL TO PURIFY

7 Having therefore these *promises* **pre—evangelisms**,
dearly beloved, let us *cleanse* **purify** ourselves
from all *filthiness* **staining** of the flesh and spirit,
perfecting **fully completing** holiness
in the *fear* **awe** of *God* **Elohim**.
2 *Receive* **Accept** us;
we have *wronged* **injured** no *man* **one**,
we have corrupted no *man* **one**,
we have defrauded no *man* **one**.
3 I *speak* **word** not this
to condemn you **for condemnation**:
for I have *said before* **foretold**,
that ye are in our hearts
to *die* **co—die** and *live with you* **co—live**.
4 *Great* **Much** is my boldness of speech toward you,
great **much** is my *glorying* **boasting** of you:
I am filled **full** with *comfort* **consolation**,
I am *exceeding* **exceedingly**
joyful **superabundantly cheerful** in all our tribulation.
5 For, when we were come into Macedonia,
our flesh had no *rest* **relaxation**,
but we were *troubled on every side* **tribulated in all**;
without *were fightings* **strifes**, within *were fears* **awes**.
6 *Nevertheless God* **Yet Elohim**,
that *comforteth* **consoleth**
those that are cast down **the humbled**,
comforted **consoled** us
by **in** the *coming* **appearing** of Titus;
7 And not *by* **in** his *coming* **appearing** only,
but *by* **in** the consolation
wherewith he was *comforted* **consoled** in you,
when he *told* **evangelized** us
your *earnest desire* **yearning**,
your *mourning* **grieving**,
your *fervent mind* **zeal** toward me;
so that I *rejoiced* **cheered** the more.

SORROW TOWARD ELOHIM, REPENTANCE TO SALVATION

8 For though I *made* **sorrowed** you *sorry*
with a letter **in an epistle**,
I *do not repent* **regret not**, though I did *repent* **regret**:
for I *perceive* **see** that *the same* **this** epistle
hath *made* **sorrowed** you *sorry*,

though *it were* but for *a season* **an hour**.
9 Now I *rejoice* **cheer**,
not that ye were *made sorry* **sorrowed**,
but that ye sorrowed *to* **unto** repentance:
for ye *were made sorry* **sorrowed**
after a Godly manner **toward Elohim**,
that ye might *receive damage* **have no loss** by us
in nothing.
10 For *Godly* sorrow **toward Elohim**
worketh repentance to salvation
not to be repented of **unrequitable:**
but the sorrow of the *world* **cosmos** worketh death.
11 For behold this selfsame *thing*,
that ye sorrowed *after a Godly sort* **toward Elohim**,
what carefulness **how much diligence**
it *wrought* **worked** in you,
yea, what clearing of yourselves **rather, pleading**,
yea, what **rather,** indignation,
yea, what fear **rather, awe**,
yea, what vehement desire **rather, yearning**,
yea, what **rather,** zeal,
yea, what revenge **rather, vengeance**!
In all *things* **these**
ye have *approved* **commended** yourselves
to be *clear* **hallowed** in this matter.
12 *Wherefore* **Therefore**,
though I *wrote* **scribed** unto you,
I did it not for his *cause* **sake**
that had *done the wrong* **injured**,
nor for his *cause* **sake**
that *suffered wrong* **was injured**,
but **for sake** that our *care* **diligence** for you
in the sight of *God* **Elohim**
might *appear* **manifest** unto you.
13 Therefore we were
comforted **consoled** in your *comfort* **consolation**:
yea, and *exceedingly* the more **superabundantly**
joyed **cheered** we for the *joy* **cheer** of Titus,
because his spirit was refreshed by you all.
14 For if I have boasted *any thing* **somewhat** to him
of you,
I am not ashamed;
but as we spake all *things* to you in truth,
even *so* **thus** our boasting, *which I made* before Titus,
is found **becometh** a truth.
15 And his *inward affection* **spleen**
is more *abundant toward* **superabundant unto** you,
whilst he remembereth the obedience of you all,
how with *fear* **awe** and trembling ye received him.
16 I *rejoice* **cheer** therefore
that I *have confidence* **be encouraged**
in you in all *things*.

ON CONTRIBUTIONS

8 Moreover, brethren,
we *do you to wit* **make known to you**
of the *grace* **charism** of *God* **Elohim**
bestowed **given**
on **in** the *churches* **ecclesiae** of Macedonia;
2 How that in
a great trial **much proofing** of *affliction* **tribulation**
the *abundance* **superabundance** of their *joy* **cheer**
and their deep poverty
abounded **superabounded**
unto the riches of their liberality.
3 For to their *power* **dynamis**, I *bear record* **witness**,
yea, and beyond their *power* **dynamis**,
they *were willing* **volunteered** of themselves.
4 *Praying* **Petitioning** us with much *intreaty* **beseeching**
that we *would* **should** receive the *gift* **charism**,
and *take upon us* the *fellowship* **communion**
of the ministering **and ministry** to the *saints* **holy**.
5 And *this they did*, not **exactly** as we hoped,
but first gave their own selves to the *Lord* **Adonay**,
and unto us *by* **through** the will of *God* **Elohim**.
6 *Insomuch that we desired* **Unto my beseeching** Titus,
that **exactly** as he had begun **before**,
so **thus** he *would* **should** also *finish* **fully complete** in you
the same grace **this charism** also.
7 *Therefore* **Rather**,
exactly as ye *abound* **superabound** in *every thing* **all**,
in faith **trust**, and *utterance* **word**, and knowledge,
and *in* all diligence, and *in* your love to us,
see that ye *abound* **superabound**
in this *grace* **charism** also.
8 *I speak* **word,** not by *commandment* **order**,
but *by occasion of* **through** the *forwardness* **diligence**
of others,
and to prove the *sincerity* **genuineness** of your love.
9 For ye know the *grace* **charism**
of our *Lord Jesus Christ* **Adonay Yah Shua Messiah**,
that, *though he was* **being** rich,
yet for your sakes he became *poor* **impoverished**,
that ye through his poverty might be *rich* **enriched**.
10 And herein I give *my advice* **opinion**:
for this is *expedient* **beneficial** for you,
who have begun before, not only to do,
but also to *be forward* **will, from** a year *ago*.
11 Now therefore *perform* **fully complete** the doing of it;
that **exactly** as there was *a readiness* **an eagerness** to will,
so there may be a performance
thus to fully complete also
out of that which ye have.
12 For if there be
first a willing mind **set forth an eagerness**,
it is *accepted* **wellreceived**
according to *that a man* **whatever anyone** hath,
and not according to that he hath not.
13 *For I mean* not that *other men* **others** be *eased* **relaxed**,
and ye *burdened* **tribulated**:
14 But by an equality,
that *now at* **in** this *time* **present season**
your abundance
may be *a supply for* **unto** their *want* **lack**,
that their *abundance* **superabundance** also
may be *a supply for* **unto** your want:
that there may be equality:
15 **Exactly** As *it is written* **scribed**,
He that had *gathered* much
had nothing over **superabounded not**;
and he that had *gathered* little had no *lack* **less**.
Exodus 16:18
16 But *thanks* **charism** be to *God* **Elohim**,
which *put* **gave** the same *earnest care* **diligence**
into the heart of Titus for you.
17 For indeed
he *accepted* **received** the *exhortation* **consolation**;
but being more *forward* **diligent**,
of his own accord he **he voluntarily** went unto you.
18 And we have sent with him the brother,
whose *praise* **halal** is in the *gospel* **evangelism**
throughout all the *churches* **ecclesiae**;
19 And not that only,
but who was also *chosen* **voted** of the *churches* **ecclesiae**
to travel with us with this *grace* **charism**,
which is *administered* **ministered** by us
to the glory of the same *Lord* **Adonay**,
and *declaration* of your *ready mind* **eagerness**:
20 *Avoiding* **Abstaining** this,
that no man **lest anyone** should *blame* **blemish** us
in this *abundance* **stoutness**
which is *administered in this* **ministered** by us:
21 Providing for *honest things* **good**,
not only in the sight of *the Lord* **Adonay**,
but also in the sight of *men* **humanity**.
22 And we have sent with them our brother,
whom we have *oftentimes* **often** proved
being diligent in *many things* **much**,
but now much more diligent,
upon *the great* **much** confidence
which I have in **unto** you.
23 Whether *any do enquire* of Titus,
he is my
partner **communicant** and *fellowhelper* **co—worker**
concerning **unto** you:
or **whether** our brethren *be enquired of*,
they are
the *messengers* **apostles** of the *churches* **ecclesiae**,
and the glory of *Christ* **Messiah**.

24 *Wherefore shew* **Therefore indicate** ye to them,
and *before* **unto the face of** the *churches* **ecclesiae**,
unto the *proof* **indication** of your love,
and of our boasting on your behalf.

THE ZEAL OF GIVING

9 *For as* **Indeed,** *touching* **concerning**
the *ministering* **ministry** to the *saints* **holy**,
it is superfluous for me to *write* **scribe** to you:
2 For I know *the forwardness of* your *mind* **eagerness**,
for which I boast of you
to *them of Macedonia* **the Macedonians**,
that Achaia was *ready* **prepared** a year ago;
and your zeal hath provoked *very* many.
3 Yet have I sent the brethren,
lest our boasting of you should be in vain
in this *behalf* **part**;
that, **exactly** as I *said* **worded**,
ye may be *ready* **prepared**:
4 Lest *haply* **somehow**
if *they of Macedonia* **ever the Macedonians**
come with me,
and find you unprepared,
we (that we *say* **word** not, ye)
should be ashamed in this same confident boasting.
5 Therefore I *thought* **deemed** it necessary
to *exhort* **beseech** the brethren,
that they *would go before* **should precede** unto you,
and *make up beforehand* **pre—prepare**
your *bounty* **eulogy**,
whereof ye had *notice before* **been pre—evangelized**,
that the same might be *ready* **prepared thus**,
as a *matter of bounty* **eulogy**,
and not **exactly** as of *covetousness* **avarice**.
6 But this *I say*, He which soweth sparingly
shall *reap* **harvest** also sparingly;
and he which soweth *bountifully* **unto eulogy**
shall *reap also bountifully* **harvest unto eulogy**.
7 *Every man according* **Each exactly**
as he *purposeth* **prefereth** in his heart, *so let him give*;
not *grudgingly* **of sorrow**, or of *necessity* **compulsion**:
for *God* **Elohim** loveth a *cheerful* **hilarious** giver.
8 And *God* **Elohim** is able to make all *grace* **charism**
abound toward **superabound unto** you;
that ye,
always having all *sufficiency* **self—contentment**
in all *things*,
may *abound to* **superabound unto** every good work:
9 (**Exactly** As *it is written* **scribed**,
He hath *dispersed* **scattered** abroad;
he hath given to the *poor* **toiling**:
his *righteousness* **justness**
remaineth for ever **abideth unto the eons**.
Psalm 112:9
10 Now he
that *ministereth seed* **contributeth sperma** to the sower
both *minister* **supply** bread *for your food* **unto eating**,
and multiply your *seed sown* **spores**,
and *increase* **grow** the *fruits* **produce**
of your *righteousness* **justness**;)
11 Being enriched
in every thing to **unto** all *bountifulness* **liberality**,
which *causeth* **worketh** through us
thanksgiving **eucharist** to *God* **Elohim**.
12 For the *administration* **ministry** of this *service* **liturgy**
not only *supplieth* **fully furnisheth**
the *want* **lack** of the *saints* **holy**,
but is *abundant* **superabundant** also
by **through** many *thanksgivings* **eucharists**
unto *God* **Elohim**;
13 Whiles *by* **through** the *experiment* **proofing**
of this *ministration* **ministry**
they glorify *God* **Elohim** for your professed subjection
unto the *gospel* **evangelism** of *Christ* **the Messiah**,
and for your liberal *distribution* **communion** unto them,
and unto all *men*;
14 And by their *prayer* **petition** for you,
which *long* **yearn** after you
for the exceeding *grace* **charism** of *God* **Elohim** in you.
15 *Thanks* **Charism** be unto *God* **Elohim**
for his *unspeakable gift* **indescribable gratuity**.

PAULOS' WITNESS TO HIS MINISTRY

10 Now I *Paul* **Paulos** myself beseech you
by **through** the meekness and gentleness
of *Christ* **the Messiah**,
who **indeed** in *presence* **face**
am *base* **humble** among you,
but being absent
am *bold toward* **courageous unto** you:
2 But I *beseech* **petition** you,
that I may not be *bold* **courageous** when I am present
with that confidence,
wherewith I *think* **reckon** to be bold against some,
which *think of* **reckon** us
as if we walked according to the flesh.
3 For though we walk in the flesh,
we do not war after the flesh:
4 (For the weapons of our warfare are not *carnal* **fleshly**,
but *mighty* **able** through *God* **Elohim**
to the pulling down of *strong holds* **fortresses**;)
5 Casting down *imaginations* **logic**,
and every *high thing* **exaltation**
that exalteth itself against the knowledge of *God* **Elohim**,
and *bringing into captivity* **capturing**
every *thought* **comprehension**
to the obedience of *Christ* **the Messiah**;
6 And having in *a readiness* **preparedness**
to *revenge* **avenge** all disobedience,
when your obedience is fulfilled.
7 Do ye look *on things*
after the outward appearance **according to face**?
If any *man trust to* **one has confidence in** himself
that he is *Christ's* **Messiah's**,
let him of himself *think* **reckon** this again,
that, **exactly** as he is *Christ's* **Messiah's**,
even *so* **thus** are we *Christ's* **Messiah's**.
8 For *though* **even if** I should boast
somewhat more **superabundantly**
of **concerning** our authority,
which the *Lord* **Adonay** hath given us
for **unto** edification,
and not *for your destruction* **to pull you down**,
I should not *be ashamed* **shame**:
9 That I may not *seem* **be thought of**
as *if I would terrify* **ever I should utterly frighten** you
by letters **through epistles**.
10 For his *letters* **epistles indeed**, say they,
are *weighty* **burdenous** and *powerful* **mighty**;
but his *bodily presence* **body appearance** is *weak* **frail**,
and his *speech contemptible* **word belittling**.
11 Let such an one *think* **reckon** this, that,
such as we are in word *by letters* **through epistles**
when we are absent,
such *will* **shall** *we* be also in *deed* **work**
when we are present.
12 For we dare not
make **compare** ourselves *of the number*,
or *compare* **co—judge** ourselves
with some that commend themselves:
but they measuring themselves
by **in** themselves,
and *comparing* **co—judging** themselves
among themselves,
are **comprehend** not *wise*.
13 But we *will* **shall indeed** not boast
of things without our measure **immeasurably**,
but according to the measure of the *rule* **canon**
which *God* **Elohim** hath *distributed* **imparted** to us,
a measure to reach even unto you.
14 For we *stretch* **overextend** not ourselves
beyond our measure,
as though we reached not unto you:
for we *are come as far as* **have arrived** to you also
in *preaching* the *gospel* **evangelism**
of *Christ* **the Messiah**:
15 Not boasting *of things*
without our measure **immeasurably**,
that is, of other men's **in other's** labours;
but having hope,
when your *faith* **trust** is *increased* **grown**,
that we shall be *enlarged* **magnified** by you

according to our *rule* **canon**
abundantly **unto superabundance,**
16 To *preach the gospel* **evangelize**
in the regions beyond you,
and not **prepare** to boast in *another man's* **another's**
line of things made ready to our hand **canon.**
17 But he that *glorieth* **boasteth,**
let him *glory* **boast** in *the Lord* **Yah Veh.**
Yirme Yah 9:24
18 For not he that commendeth himself is approved,
but whom *the Lord* **Yah Veh** commendeth.
11 *Would to God* **O that** ye *could bear with* **tolerate me**
a little in my *folly* **thoughtlessness:**
and *indeed bear with* **yet tolerate** me.
2 For I am *jealous* **zealous** over you
with *Godly jealousy* **the zeal of Elohim:**
for I have *espoused* **betrothed** you to one *husband* **man,**
that I may present *you as a chaste* **hallowed** virgin
to *Christ* **the Messiah.**
3 But I *fear* **awe,** lest *by any means* **somehow,**
as the serpent *beguiled Eve* **seduced Havvah**
through **in** his *subtilty* **cunning,**
so **thus** your *minds* **comprehensions** should be corrupted
from the *simplicity* **liberality** that is in *Christ* **the Messiah.**
4 For **indeed** if he that cometh
preacheth another *Jesus* **Yah Shua,**
whom we have not preached,
or if ye *receive* **take** another spirit,
which ye have not *received* **taken,**
or another *gospel* **evangelism,**
which ye have not *accepted* **received,**
ye might *well bear with him* **have tolerated well.**
5 For I *suppose* **reckon** I *was not a whit* **failed in naught**
behind **beyond**
the *very chiefest* **extremely superior** apostles.
6 But though I be *rude* **unlearned** in *speech* **word,**
yet not in knowledge;
but **in all** we have been *throughly made* manifest
among **unto** you in all *things.*
7 **Or** Have I *committed an offence* **sinned**
in *abasing* **humbling** myself that ye might be exalted,
because I have *preached* **evangelized** to you
the *gospel* **evangelism** of *God freely* **Elohim gratuitously?**
8 I *robbed* **stripped** other *churches* **ecclesiae,**
taking wages *of them,*
to do you service **for your ministry.**
9 And when I was present with you, and wanted,
I was *chargeable* **insensitive** to no *man* **one:**
for that which was lacking to me
the brethren which came from Macedonia
supplied **fully furnished:**
and in all *things* I have *kept* **guarded** myself
from being burdensome **burdenless** unto you,
and so *will* **shall** I *keep* **guard** myself.
10 As the truth of *Christ* **Messiah** is in me,
no man shall *stop* **seal** me *of* **unto** this boasting
in the *regions* **climes** of Achaia.
11 *Wherefore* **Why?** because I love you not?
God **Elohim** knoweth.
12 But what I do, *that I will do* **I do,**
that I may *cut off occasion* **exscind opportunity**
from them which *desire occasion* **will for opportunity;**
that wherein they *glory* **boast,**
they may be found *even* **exactly** as we.

ON PSEUDO APOSTLES

13 For such are *false* **pseudo** apostles, deceitful workers,
transforming **transfiguring** themselves
into the apostles of *Christ* **Messiah.**
14 And no marvel; for Satan himself
is *transformed* **transfigured** into an angel of light.
15 Therefore it is *no great thing* **not mega**
if his ministers also be *transformed* **transfigured**
as the ministers of *righteousness* **justness;**
whose *end* **completion**
shall be according to their works.

PAULOS' SUFFERINGS

16 I *say* **word** again,
Let no *man* **one** think me *a fool* **to be thoughtless;**
if *otherwise, yet as a fool* **even as thoughtless** receive me,
that I **also** may boast myself a little.
17 That which I speak,
I speak *it* not after the *Lord* **Adonay,**
but as *it were foolishly* **in thoughtlessness,**
in this confidence of boasting.
18 *Seeing that* **Since** many *glory* **boast** after the flesh,
I *will glory* **shall boast** also.
19 For ye *suffer fools* **tolerate the thoughtless**
gladly **with pleasure,**
seeing ye *yourselves are wise* **being thoughtful.**
20 For ye *suffer* **tolerate,**
if *a man bring* **anyone enslave** you *into bondage,*
if *a man* **anyone** devour *you,*
if *a man* **anyone** take *of you,*
if *a man* **anyone** exalt himself,
if *a man smite* **anyone flog** you on the face.
21 I *speak as* **word** concerning *reproach* **dishonour,**
as though we had been *weak* **frail.**
Howbeit whereinsoever any is bold,
(I *speak foolishly* **word in thoughtlessness,)**
I am bold also.

APOSTLES VS PSEUDO APOSTLES

22 Are they Hebrews? *so am* I **also.**
Are they *Israelites* **Yisra Elym?** *so am* I **also.**
Are they the *seed* **sperma** of Abraham? *so am* I **also.**
23 Are they ministers of *Christ* **Messiah?**
(I speak *as a fool* **insanely)** I *am* more;
in labours more *abundant* **superabundant,**
in stripes *above measure* **excessively,**
in *prisons more frequent* **guardhouses superabundant,**
in deaths oft.
24 Of the *Jews* **Yah Hudiym**
five times *received* **took** I forty *stripes* save one.
25 Thrice *was I beaten with rods* **bastinadoed,**
once *was I* stoned,
thrice *I suffered shipwreck* **shipwrecked,**
a night and a day *I have been* **done** in the deep;
26 *In* journeyings often, *in* perils of *waters* **streams,**
in perils of robbers,
in perils by *mine own countrymen* **my genos,**
in perils by the *heathen* **goyim,** *in* perils in the city,
in perils in the wilderness, *in* perils in the sea,
in perils *among false* **of pseudo** brethren;
27 In *weariness* **labours** and *painfulness* **toil,**
in watchings often, in *hunger* **famine** and thirst,
in fastings often, in cold and nakedness.
28 *Beside those things* **Apart from those**
that are *without* **excepted,**
that which *cometh* **conspireth** upon me daily,
the *care* **anxieties** of all the *churches* **ecclesiae.**
29 Who is *weak* **frail,** and I am not *weak* **frail?**
who is *offended* **scandalized,** and I *burn* not **fiery?**
30 If I must *needs glory* **boast,**
I *will glory* **shall boast** of *the things* **those**
which concern *mine infirmities* **my frailties.**
31 The *God* **Elohim** and Father
of our *Lord Jesus Christ* **Adonay Yah Shua Messiah,**
which is blessed **being eulogized**
for evermore **unto the eons,**
knoweth that I lie not.
32 In *Damascus* **Dammeseq**
the *governor* **ethnarch** under Aretas the *king* **sovereign**
kept the city of the *Damascenes* **Dammeseqim**
with a garrison,
desirous **having willed** to *apprehend* **seize** me:
33 And through a window in a *basket* **wicker**
was I *let down by* **lowered through** the wall,
and escaped his hands.

PAULOS IN PARADISE

12 It is not *expedient* **beneficial** for me
doubtless **now** to *glory* **boast.**
I **indeed** will come to visions and *revelations* **apocalypses**
of the *Lord* **Adonay.**
2 I knew a *man* **human** in *Christ* **Messiah**
above fourteen years ago,
(whether in *the* body, I *cannot tell* **know not;**
or whether out of the body, I *cannot tell* **know not:**
God **Elohim** knoweth;)
such an one *caught up to* **seized unto** the third heaven.
3 And I knew such a *man* **human,**
(whether in *the* body, *or* **whether** out of the body,

I *cannot tell* **know not**: *God* **Elohim** knoweth;)
4 How that he was *caught up* **seized** into paradise,
and heard *unspeakable words* **inexpressable rhema**,
which it is not *lawful* **allowed**
for a *man* **human** to *utter* **speak**.
5 Of such an one *will I glory* **shall I boast**:
yet of myself I *will* **shall** not *glory* **boast**,
but **except** in *mine infirmities* **my frailties**.
6 For *though* **even if** I *would desire* **willed** to *glory* **boast**,
I shall not be *a fool* **thoughtless**;
for I *will* **shall** say the truth: but *now I forbear* **I spare**,
lest any *man* **one** should *think of* **reckon unto** me
above that which he seeth me *to be*,
or that he heareth **somewhat** of me.

PAULOS' THORN

7 And lest I should be **superciliously** exalted
above measure
through the *abundance* **excellence**
of the *revelations* **apocalypses**,
there was given to me a thorn in the flesh,
the messenger **an angel** of Satan to *buffet* **punch** me,
lest I should be **superciliously** exalted *above measure*.
Numbers 33:55, Yah Shua 23:13, Judges 2:3,
Yechezq El 28:24, Nachum 1:10
8 For this *thing* I besought the *Lord* **Adonay** thrice,
that it might depart from me.
9 And he said unto me,
My *grace* **charism** is sufficient for thee:
for my *strength* **dynamis**
is *made perfect* **completed** in *weakness* **frailty**.
Most gladly **With pleasure** therefore
will **shall** I rather *glory* **boast** in my *infirmities* **frailties**,
that the *power* **dynamis** of *Christ* **the Messiah**
may *rest* **tabernacle** upon me.
10 Therefore I *take pleasure* **well—approve**
in *infirmities* **frailties**, in *reproaches* **hubris**,
in *necessities* **compulsions**, in persecutions,
in distresses for *Christ's* **Messiah's** sake:
for when I am *weak* **frail**, then am I *strong* **able**.
11 I am become *a fool* **thoughtless** in *glorying* **boasting**;
ye have compelled me:
for I *ought to have been commended of you* **was indebted**:
for in *nothing* **naught** am I behind
the *very chiefest* **extremely superior** apostles,
though I be *nothing* **naught**.
12 *Truly* **Indeed** the signs of an apostle
were *wrought among* **worked in** you
in all *patience* **endurance**,
in signs, and *wonders* **omens**, and *mighty deeds* **dynamis**.
13 For what is it wherein ye were *inferior* **slighted**
to *other churches* **the rest of the ecclesiae**,
except it be
that I myself was not *burdensome* **insensitive** to you?
forgive me this wrong
grant me charism for this injustice.

PAULOS PREPARES A THIRD VISIT

14 Behold,
the third time I *am ready* **have prepared** to come to you;
and I *will* **shall** not be *burdensome* **insensitive** to you:
for I seek not your's but you:
for the children *ought not* **are not indebted**
to *lay* **treasure** *up* for the parents,
but the parents for the children.
15 And I *will very gladly* **shall with pleasure** spend
and be *spent for you* **expended for your souls**;
though the more *abundantly* **superabundantly** I love you,
the less I be loved.
16 But be it so, I did not *burden* **load** you **down**:
nevertheless **rather**, being *crafty* **cunning**,
I *caught* **took** you with *guile* **deceit**.
17 Did I *make a gain of* **defraud** you
by **through** any of them
whom I *sent* **apostolized** unto you?
18 I *desired* **besought** Titus,
and with him I *sent* **apostolized** a brother.
Did Titus *make a gain of* **defraud** you?
walked we not in the same spirit?
walked we — not in the same *steps* **tracks**?

PAULOS WARNS THE ECCLESIA

19 Again,
think ye that we *excuse ourselves* **plead** unto you?
we speak
before God **in sight of Elohim** in *Christ* **Messiah**:
but *we* do all *things, dearly* beloved, for your edifying.
20 For I *fear* **awe**, lest **somehow**, when I come,
I shall not find you such as I *would* **had willed**,
and that I shall be found unto you
such as ye *would* **had** not **willed**:
lest **somehow** there be *debates* **contentions**,
envyings **zeals**, *wraths* **furies**, *strifes* **rivalries**,
backbitings **slanders**, whisperings,
swellings **puffings up**, *tumults*, **instabilities**:
21 *And* lest, when I come again,
my *God will* **Elohim shall** humble me *among* **unto** you,
and that I shall *bewail* **mourn** many
which have sinned *already* **previously**,
and have not repented of the *uncleanness* **impurity**
and *fornication* **whoredom** and *lasciviousness* **lechery**
which they have *committed* **transacted**.

13 This is the third *time* I am coming to you.
In the mouth of two or three witnesses
shall every *word be established* **rhema stand**.
2 I *told you before* **foresaid**, and *foretell you* **forespeak**,
as if I were present, the second time;
and being absent now:
I *write* **scribe** to them
which *heretofore* **previously** have sinned,
and to all *other* **the rest**,
that, if **ever** I come again, I *will* **shall** not spare:
3 Since ye seek a proof of *Christ* **Messiah** speaking in me,
which *to you—ward* **unto you** is not *weak* **frail**,
but is *mighty* **dynamic** in you.
4 For *though* **if indeed**
he was *crucified through weakness* **staked by frailty**,
yet he liveth by the *power* **dynamis** of *God* **Elohim**.
For we also are *weak* **frail** in him,
but we shall live with him
by the *power* **dynamis** of *God toward* **Elohim unto** you.
5 *Examine* **Test** yourselves,
whether ye be in the *faith* **trust**; prove your own selves.
Or Know ye not your own selves,
how that *Jesus Christ* **Yah Shua Messiah** is in you,
except **somehow**
ye be *reprobates* **somewhat disapproved**?
6 But I *trust* **hope** that ye shall know
that we are not *reprobates* **disapproved**.
7 Now I *pray* **vow** to *God* **Elohim** that ye do no evil;
not that we should *appear* **manifest** approved,
but that ye should do that which is *honest* **good**,
though we be as *reprobates* **disapproved**.
8 For we can do *nothing* **naught** against the truth,
but for the truth.
9 For we *are glad* **cheer**,
when we are *weak* **frail**, and ye are *strong* **able**:
and this also we *wish* **vow**, *even* your perfection.
10 Therefore I *write* **scribe** these *things* being absent,
lest being present I should use *sharpness* **severity**,
according to the *power* **authority**
which *the Lord* **Adonay** hath given me to edification,
and not to *destruction* **pull you down**.

SALUTE AND DOXOLOGY

11 Finally, brethren, *farewell* **Cheers**.
Be *perfect* **prepared**, be of good comfort,
be of one mind **think the same**, *live in peace* **shalam**;
and the *God* **Elohim** of love and *peace* **shalom**
shall be with you.
12 *Greet* **Salute** one another *with* **in** an holy kiss.
13 All the *saints* **holy** salute you.
14 The *grace* **charism**
of *the Lord Jesus Christ* **Adonay Yah Shua Messiah**,
and the love of *God* **Elohim**,
and the communion of the Holy *Ghost* **Spirit**,
be with you all.
Amen.

KEY TO INTERPRETING THE EXEGESES:
King James text is in regular type;
Text under exegeses is in oblique type;
Text of exegeses is in bold type.

SALUTATION

1 *Paul* **Paulos**, an apostle,
(not of *men* **humanity**, neither *by man* **through humanity**,
but *by Jesus Christ* **through Yah Shua Messiah**,
and *God* **Elohim** the Father,
who raised him from the dead;)
2 And all the brethren which are with me,
unto the *churches* **ecclesiae** of Galatia:
3 *Grace be* **Charism** to you and *peace* **shalom**
from *God* **Elohim** the Father,
and *from*
our *Lord Jesus Christ* **Adonay Yah Shua Messiah**,
4 Who gave himself for our sins,
that he might *deliver* **release** us
from this present evil *world* **eon**,
according to the will of *God* **Elohim** and our Father:
5 To whom be glory
for ever and ever **unto the eons of the eons**.
Amen.

ONE EVANGELISM

6 I marvel that ye are
so soon removed **thus quickly transplaced**
from him that called you
into the *grace* **charism** of *Christ* **Messiah**
unto another *gospel* **evangelism**:
7 Which is not another;
but **except** there be some that trouble you,
and *would pervert* **will to overturn**
the *gospel* **evangelism** of *Christ* **the Messiah**.
8 But *though* **if ever** we, or an angel from heaven,
preach **evangelize** any other *gospel* unto you
than that which we have *preached* **evangelized** unto you,
let him be *accursed* **anathema**.
9 As we *said before* **foretold**, so *say* **word** I now again,
If any *man preach* **one evangelize** any other *gospel*
unto you than that ye have *received* **taken**,
let him be *accursed* **anathema**.
10 For do I now *persuade men* **convince humanity**,
or *God* **Elohim**?
or do I seek to please *men* **humanity**?
for if I yet pleased *men* **humanity**,
I should not **ever** be the servant of *Christ* **Messiah**.

PAULOS' APOCALYPSE

11 But I *certify* **make known to** you, brethren,
that the *gospel* **evangelism**
which was *preached of* **evangelized by** me
is not after *man* **humanity**.
12 For I neither *received* **took** it of *man* **humanity**,
neither was I *taught it* **doctrinated**,
but *by* **through** the *revelation* **apocalypse**
of *Jesus Christ* **Yah Shua Messiah**.
13 For ye have heard of my
conversation in time past **former behaviour**
in *the Jews' religion* **Yah Hudahism**,
how that *beyond measure* **excessively**
I persecuted the *church* **ecclesia** of *God* **Elohim**,
and *wasted* **ravaged** it:
14 And *profited* **advanced**
in *the Jews' religion* **Yah Hudahism**
above many my *equals* **contemporaries**
in mine own *nation* **genos**,
being more *exceedingly* **superabundantly**
zealous **a zealot** of the traditions of my *fathers* **patriarchs**.
15 But when *it pleased God* **Elohim well—approved**,
who *separated me* **set me apart** from my mother's womb,
and called me *by* **through** his *grace* **charism**,
16 To *reveal* **unveil** his Son in me,
that I might *preach* **evangelize** him
among the *heathen* **goyim**;
immediately **straightway** I *conferred* **counselled**
not with flesh and blood:
17 Neither *went* **ascended** I *up* to *Jerusalem* **Yeru Shalem**
to them which were apostles before me;
but I *went* **departed** into Arabia,
and returned again unto *Damascus* **Dammeseq**.
18 Then after three years
I *went up* **ascended** to *Jerusalem* **Yeru Shalem**
to *see Peter* **inquire of Petros**,
and abode with him fifteen days.
19 But other of the apostles saw I none,
save James the Lord's **except Yaaqovos Adonay's** brother.
20 Now *the things* **that** which I *write* **scribe** unto you,
behold, *before God* **in sight of Elohim**, I lie not.
21 *Afterwards* **Then**
I came into the *regions* **climes** of Syria and Cilicia;
22 And was unknown by face
unto the *churches* **ecclesiae** of *Judaea* **Yah Hudah**
which were in *Christ* **Messiah**:
23 But they had heard only,
That he which persecuted us *in times past* **formerly**
now *preacheth* **evangelizeth** the *faith* **trust**
which once he *destroyed* **ravaged**.
24 And they glorified *God* **Elohim** in me.

THE BROTHERS APPROVE PAULOS

2 Then **through** fourteen years *after*
I *went up* **ascended** again to *Jerusalem* **Yeru Shalem**
with *Barnabas* **Bar Nabi**, and took Titus with me also.
2 And I *went up* **ascended** by *revelation* **apocalypse**,
and *communicated* **propounded** unto them
that *gospel* **evangelism**
which I preach among the *Gentiles* **goyim**,
but privately to them
which were *of reputation* **well thought of**,
lest *by any means* **somehow** I should run, or had run,
in vain.
3 But neither Titus, who was with me,
being a *Greek* **Hellene**,
was compelled to be circumcised:
4 And that because of *false* **pseudo** brethren
unawares brought **surreptitiously smuggled** in,
who *came in privily* **surreptitiously entered**
to spy out our liberty
which we have in *Christ Jesus* **Messiah Yah Shua**,
that they might *bring* **enslave** us *into bondage*:
5 To whom we *gave place* **yielded** by subjection,
no, not for an hour;
that the truth of the *gospel* **evangelism**
might *continue* **continually abide** with you.
6 But of these
who *seemed* **were thought** to be somewhat,
(*whatsoever* **what sort** they **formerly** were,
it *maketh no matter* **mattereth not** to me:
God **Elohim**
accepteth **taketh** no *man's person* **human's face**:)
for they who *seemed* **were thought**
to be *somewhat in conference* **counsellors**
added *nothing* **naught** to me:
7 But contrariwise,
when they saw that *the gospel of* the uncircumcision
was *committed* **entrusted** unto me,
exactly as *the gospel of* the circumcision
was unto *Peter* **Petros**;
8 (For he that *wrought effectually* **energized**
in *Peter* **Petros** to the apostleship of the circumcision,
the same *was mighty* **energized**
in me *toward* **unto** the *Gentiles* **goyim**:)
9 And when *James* **Yaaqovos**,
Cephas **Kepha**, and *John* **Yahn**,
who *seemed* **were thought** to be pillars,
perceived **knew** the *grace* **charism**
that was given unto me,
they gave to me and *Barnabas* **Bar Nabi**
the *right hands* **rights** of *fellowship* **communion**;
that we should go unto the heathen **— we unto the goyim**,
and they unto the circumcision.
10 Only *they would* that we should remember the poor;
the same which I also was *forward* **diligent** to do.

PAULOS WITHSTANDS PETROS

11 But when *Peter* **Petros** was come to Antioch,
I withstood him to the face,
because he was to be *blamed* **condemned**.
12 For before that
certain **some** came from *James* **Yaaqovos**,
he did eat with the *Gentiles* **goyim**:
but when they were come,
he withdrew and *separated* **set** himself **apart**,

fearing **awestricken of** them
which were of the circumcision.
13 And the *other Jews* **rest of the Yah Hudiym**
dissembled **hypocrized** likewise with him;
insomuch **so as** that *Barnabas* **Bar Nabi** also
was *carried* **led** away with their *dissimulation* **hypocrisy**.
14 But when I saw that they
walked **were** not *uprightly* **straightfooted**
according to **unto** the truth of the *gospel* **evangelism**,
I said unto *Peter before* **Petros in front of** them all,
If thou, being *a Jew* **Yah Hudiy**,
livest *after the manner of Gentiles* **goyishly**,
and not *as do the Jews* **Yah Hudahaically**,
why compellest thou the *Gentiles* **goyim**
to *live as do the Jews* **Yah Hudahize**?
15 We who are *Jews* **Yah Hudiym** by nature,
and not sinners of the *Gentiles* **goyim**,
16 Knowing that *a man* **humanity** is not justified
by the works of the *law* **torah**,
but *by the faith* **only through trust**
of Jesus Christ **from Yah Shua Messiah**,
even we have *believed* **trusted**
in *Jesus Christ* **Yah Shua Messiah**
that we might be justified
by the *faith of Christ* **trust from Messiah**,
and not by the works of the *law* **torah**:
for **because** by the works of the *law* **torah**
shall no flesh be justified.
17 But if,
while we seek to be justified *by Christ* **in Messiah**,
we ourselves also are found sinners,
is *therefore Christ* **then Messiah** the minister of sin?
God forbid **So be it not**.
18 For if I build again
the things **those** which I *destroyed* **disintegrated**,
I *make* **constitute** myself a transgressor.
19 For I through the *law* **torah** am dead to the *law* **torah**,
that I might live unto *God* **Elohim**.
20 I *am* **have been**
crucified **co—staked** with *Christ* **Messiah**:
nevertheless I live;
yet not **no longer** I, but *Christ* **Messiah** liveth in me:
and the life which I now live in the flesh
I live *by* **in** the *faith* **trust** of the Son of *God* **Elohim**,
who loved me, and *gave* **surrendered** himself for me.
21 I do not *frustrate* **set aside**
the *grace* **charism** of *God* **Elohim**:
for if *righteousness* **justness**
come by **be through** the *law* **torah**,
then *Christ* **Messiah** is dead *in vain* **for naught**.

ON TAKING THE HOLY SPIRIT

3 O *foolish* **mindless** Galatians,
who hath *bewitched* **fascinated** you,
that ye should not obey the truth,
before whose eyes *Jesus Christ* **Yah Shua Messiah**
hath been *evidently set forth* **preinscribed**,
crucified **staked** among you?
2 This only *would* **will I to** learn of you,
Received **Took** ye the Spirit
by the works of the *law* **torah**,
or by the hearing of *faith* **trust**?
3 Are ye *so foolish* **thus mindless**?
having begun in the Spirit,
are ye now *made perfect* **fully completed** by the flesh?
4 Have ye suffered so *many things* **much** in vain?
if *it be yet* **indeed** in vain.
5 He therefore that *ministereth* **supplieth** to you the Spirit,
and *worketh miracles* **energizeth dynamis** among you,
doeth he it by the works of the *law* **torah**,
or by the hearing of *faith* **trust**?

ELOHIM'S COVENANT WITH ABRAHAM

6 Even as Abraham *believed God* **trusted Elohim**,
and it was *accounted* **reckoned** to him
for righteousness **unto justness**.
7 Know ye therefore that they which are of *faith* **trust**,
the same **these** are the *children* **sons** of Abraham.
8 And the scripture, foreseeing that *God* **Elohim**
would **should** justify the *heathen* **goyim**
through faith **by trust**,
preached before the gospel **pre—evangelized**
unto Abraham, *saying*,
In thee shall all *nations* **goyim** be *blessed* **eulogized**.
9 So then they which be of *faith* **trust**
are blessed with *faithful* **trustworthy** Abraham.
Genesis 12:1—3

THE WORKS OF THE TORAH VS THE CURSE OF THE TORAH

10 For as many as are of the works of the *law* **torah**
are under the curse:
for it is *written* **scribed**,
Cursed is every one
that *continueth* **abideth** not in all *things*
which are *written* **scribed**
in the *book* **scroll** of the *law* **torah** to do them.
11 But that no *man* **one** is justified
by **in** the *law* **torah** *in the sight of God* **by Elohim**,
it is evident:
for, The just shall live by *faith* **trust**.
12 And the *law* **torah** is not of *faith* **trust**:
but, The *man* **human** that doeth them shall live in them.
Deuteronomy 27:6, Habakkuk 2:4, Leviticus 18:5

MESSIAH'S MARKETING FROM THE TORAH'S CURSE

13 *Christ* **Messiah** hath *redeemed* **marketed** us
from the curse of the *law* **torah**,
being made **having become** a curse for us:
for it is *written* **scribed**,
Cursed is every one that hangeth on a *tree* **staff**:
14 That the blessing of Abraham
might *come on* **become unto** the *Gentiles* **goyim**
through Jesus Christ **in Yah Shua Messiah**;
that we might *receive* **take**
the *promise* **pre—evangelism** of the Spirit
through *faith* **trust**.
Deuteronomy 21:23
15 Brethren,
I *speak* **word** after the manner of *men* **humanity**;
Though it be but a man's **Yet still, a human** covenant,
yet if it be **being** confirmed,
no *man disannulleth* **one setteth aside**, or addeth thereto.
16 Now to Abraham and his *seed* **sperma**
were the *promises made* **pre—evangelisms rhetorized**.
He *saith* **wordeth** not, And to *seeds* **spermas**, as of many;
but as of one, And to thy *seed* **sperma**,
which is *Christ* **Messiah**.
Genesis 13:15, 25:5, 6
17 And this I *say* **word**, *that* the covenant,
that was *confirmed before of God* **pre—ratified by Elohim**
in *Christ* **Messiah**,
the *law* **torah**,
which *was* **became** four hundred and thirty years after,
cannot *disannul* **invalidate**,
that it should
make the promise of none effect
inactivate the pre—evangelism.
18 For if the inheritance be *of the law* **by torah**,
it is *no more of promise* **not still by pre—evangelism**:
but *God gave it* **Elohim granted charism** to Abraham
by promise **through pre—evangelism**.
19 *Wherefore* **Why** then *serveth* the *law* **torah**?
It was added because of transgressions,
till the *seed* **sperma** should come
to whom the *promise* **pre—evangelism** was made;
and it was ordained *by* **through** angels
in the hand of a mediator.
20 Now a mediator is not *a mediator* of one,
but *God* **Elohim** is one.
21 Is the *law* **torah** then
against the *promises* **pre—evangelisms** of *God* **Elohim**?
God forbid **So be it not**:
for if there had been a *law* **torah** given
which *could have given life* **was able to enliven**,
verily righteousness **indeed justness**
should have been by the *law* **torah**.
22 But the scripture
hath *concluded* **locked** all **together** under sin,
that the *promise* **pre—evangelism**
by *faith of Jesus Christ* **trust from Yah Shua Messiah**
might be given to them that *believe* **trust**.
23 But before *faith* **the trust** came,
we were *kept* **garrisoned** under the *law* **torah**,

shut up **locked together** unto the *faith* **trust**
which should afterwards be *revealed* **unveiled**.
24 *Wherefore* **So then** the *law* **torah**
was **became** our *schoolmaster* **pedagogue**
to bring us unto Christ **unto Messiah**,
that we might be justified by *faith* **trust**.
25 But after that *faith* **the trust** is come,
we are *no longer* **not still**
under a *schoolmaster* **pedagogue**.
26 For ye are all the *children* **sons** of *God* **Elohim**
by faith **through the trust**
in *Christ Jesus* **Messiah Yah Shua**.
27 For as many of you
as have been baptized into *Christ* **Messiah**
have *put on Christ* **endued Messiah**.
28 There is neither *Jew* **Yah Hudiy** nor *Greek* **Hellene**,
there is neither bond nor *free* **liberated**,
there is neither male nor female:
for ye are all one in *Christ Jesus* **Messiah Yah Shua**.
29 And if ye be *Christ's* **Messiah's**,
then are ye Abraham's *seed* **sperma**,
and heirs according to the *promise* **pre—evangelism**.

FROM SERVANT TO SONSHIP

4 Now I *say* **word**, That the heir,
as long **time** as he is a *child* **baby**,
differeth nothing from **surpasseth not** a servant,
though he be lord **being adoni** of all;
2 But is under
tutors **managers** and *governors* **administrators**
until the *time appointed* **preappointment** of the father.
3 Even *so* **thus** we, when we were *children* **babies**,
were *in bondage* **subservient**
under the elements of the *world* **cosmos**:
4 But when the fulness of the time was come,
God sent forth **Elohim apostolized** his Son,
made **become** of a woman,
made **become** under the *law* **torah**,
5 To *redeem* **market** them that were under the *law* **torah**,
that we might *receive* **take** the *adoption of sons* **sonship**.
6 And because ye are sons,
God **Elohim**
hath *sent forth* **apostolized** the Spirit of his Son
into your hearts, crying, Abba, Father.
7 *Wherefore* **So then** thou art *no more* **not still** a servant,
but a son;
and if a son,
then an heir of *God* **Elohim** through *Christ* **Messiah**.

CONCERNING SERVITUDE

8 *Howbeit* **Rather indeed** then,
when ye knew not *God* **Elohim**,
ye *did service* **were in servitude** unto them
which by nature are no *gods* **elohim**.
9 But now, after that ye have known *God* **Elohim**,
or rather are known of *God* **Elohim**,
how turn ye **around** again
to the *weak* **frail** and *beggarly* **poor** elements,
whereunto ye *desire again* **uppermostly** will
to be in *bondage* **servitude**?
10 Ye observe days, and months,
and *times* **seasons**, and years.
11 I am *afraid* **awestricken** of you,
lest **somehow** I have
bestowed upon you labour **laboured unto you** in vain.
12 Brethren, I *beseech* **petition** you, *be* **become** as I *am*;
for I *am* **also** as ye *are*:
ye have not injured me at all.
13 Ye know how through *infirmity* **frailty** of the flesh
I *preached the gospel* **pre—evangelized** unto you
at the first.
14 And my *temptation* **testing** which was in my flesh
ye *despised* **belittled** not, nor *rejected* **spit out**;
but received me as an angel of *God* **Elohim**,
even as Christ Jesus **Messiah Yah Shua**.

THE GALATIANS PERPLEX PAULOS

15 Where is then the blessedness ye spake of?
for I *bear you record* **witness**, that, if *it had been* possible,
ye *would have plucked out* **had extracted**
your own eyes,
and *have* **had ever** given them to me.
16 **So then,** Am I *therefore* become your enemy,
because I *tell you the truth* **be true**?
17 They *zealously affect* **are zealous over** you,
but not well;
yea **rather**, they *would* **will to** exclude you,
that ye might *affect* **be zealous over** them.
18 But it is good to be *zealously affected* **zealous**
always *in a* **over** good *thing*,
and not only *when I am* **in my being** present with you.
19 My little children, of whom I travail in birth again
until *Christ* **Messiah** be formed in you,
20 I *desire* **will** to be present with you now,
and to change my voice;
for I *stand in doubt of* **am perplexed in** you.

ALLEGORY OF HAGAR AND SARAH

21 *Tell* **Word to** me,
ye that *desire* **will** to be under the *law* **torah**,
do ye not hear the *law* **torah**?
22 For it is *written* **scribed**, that Abraham had two sons,
the one by *a bondmaid* **the lass**,
the other by *a freewoman* **the liberated**.
23 But **indeed** he *who was* of the *bondwoman* **lass**
was born after the flesh;
but he of the *freewoman* **liberated**
was by promise **through pre—evangelism**.
24 Which *things are an allegory* **are allegorized**:
for these are the two covenants;
the one **indeed** from the mount *Sinai* **Sinay**,
which *gendereth* **birtheth** to *bondage* **servitude**,
which is *Agar* **Hagar**.
25 For this *Agar* **Hagar** is mount *Sinai* **Sinay** in Arabia,
and *answereth* **correspondeth**
to Jerusalem **with Yeru Shalem**
which now is,
and is in *bondage* **servitude** with her children.
26 But *Jerusalem which is* **the Yeru Shalem** above
is *free* **liberated**,
which is the mother of us all.
27 For it is *written* **scribed**,
Rejoice, thou *barren* **sterile** that bearest not;
break forth and cry, thou that travailest not:
for *the desolate hath many more children*
many are the children of the desolate
rather than she which hath *an husband* **a man**.
Yesha Yah 54:1
28 Now we, brethren, as *Isaac* **Yischaq** was,
are the children of *promise* **pre—evangelism**.
29 But **exactly** as then he that was born after the flesh
persecuted him *that was born* after the Spirit,
even *so it is* **thus** now.
30 *Nevertheless* **Rather,** what *saith* **wordeth** the scripture?
Cast out the *bondwoman* **lass** and her son:
for the son of the *bondwoman* **lass**
shall not *be heir* **no way inherit**
with the son of the *freewoman* **liberated**.
Genesis 21:9, 10
31 So then, brethren,
we are not children of the *bondwoman* **lass**,
but of the *free* **liberated**.

THE LIBERTY OF THE LIBERATED

5 Stand *fast* **firm** therefore in the liberty
wherewith *Christ* **Messiah** hath *made us free* **liberated us**,
and be not *entangled* **begrudged** again
with the yoke of *bondage* **servitude**.

THE SERVITUDE OF SERVANTS

2 Behold, I *Paul say* **Paulos word** unto you,
that if **ever** ye be circumcised,
Christ **Messiah** shall *profit* **benefit** you *nothing* **naught**.
3 For I *testify* **witness** again
to every *man* **human** that is circumcised,
that he is a debtor to do the whole *law* **torah**.
4 *Christ is become of no effect unto you*
Ye are inactivated from the Messiah,
whosoever of you are justified *by* **in** the *law* **torah**;
ye are fallen from *grace* **charism**.

THE HOPE OF THE HOLY

5 For we through the Spirit *wait for* **await** the hope
of *righteousness* **justness** by *faith* **trust**.
6 For in *Jesus Christ* **Yah Shua Messiah**

neither circumcision *availeth any thing* **is of any ability**,
nor uncircumcision;
but *faith* **trust**
which *worketh by* **energizeth through** love.

THE TORAH FULFILLED IN LOVE

7 Ye did run well;
who did hinder you that ye should not obey the truth?
8 This *persuasion* **confidence**
cometh **is** not of him that calleth you.
9 A little *leaven* **fermentation**
leaveneth **fermenteth** the whole lump.
10 I have confidence in you *through the Lord* **in Adonay**,
that ye *will be none* **shall not think** otherwise *minded*:
but he that troubleth you shall bear his judgment,
whosoever he be.
11 And I, brethren, if I yet preach circumcision,
why do I yet suffer persecution?
then is the *offence* **scandal** of the *cross* **stake**
ceased **inactivated**.
12 *I would* **O that** they were even *cut off* **amputated**
which *trouble* **rouse you**.
13 For, brethren, ye have been called unto liberty;
only *use* not liberty
for an occasion **unto an opportunity** to the flesh,
but *by* **through** love serve one another.
14 For *all* the *law* **whole torah** is fulfilled in one word,
even in this; Thou shalt love thy neighbour as thyself.
Leviticus 19:18
15 But if ye bite and devour one another,
take heed **see** that ye be not consumed one of another.

THE IN SPIRIT WALK

16 This I *say* **word** then, Walk in *the* Spirit,
and ye shall not **no way**
fulfil **complete** the *lust* **panting** of the flesh.
17 For the flesh *lusteth* **panteth** against the Spirit,
and the Spirit against the flesh:
and these are contrary
the one to the other **to one another**:
so that ye cannot do *the things* **those**
that ye *would* **ever will**.
18 But if ye be *led of the Spirit* **Spirit led**,
ye are not under the *law* **torah**.

THE MANY WORKS OF THE FLESH

19 Now the works of the flesh are manifest,
which are *these*;
Adultery, *fornication* **whoredom**,
uncleanness **impurity**, *lasciviousness* **lechery**,
20 Idolatry, *witchcraft* **pharmacy**, *hatred* **enmity**,
variance **contention**, *emulations* **zeals**, *wrath* **fury**,
strife **rivalry**, *seditions* **divisions**, heresies,
21 Envyings, murders, *drunkenness* **intoxication**,
revellings **carousings**, and such like:
of the which I *tell you before* **forespeak**,
exactly as I have also *told you in time past* **foretold**,
that they which *do* **transact** such *things*
shall not inherit
the *kingdom* **sovereigndom** of *God* **Elohim**.

THE SINGULAR FRUIT OF THE SPIRIT

22 But the fruit of the Spirit is love, *joy* **cheer**,
peace **shalom**, *longsuffering* **patience**,
gentleness **kindness**, goodness, *faith* **trust**,
23 Meekness, *temperance* **self—control**:
against such there is no *law* **torah**.
24 And they that *are Christ's* **be the Messiah's**
have *crucified* **staked** the flesh
with the *affections* **passions** and *lusts* **pantings**.
25 If we live in *the* Spirit,
let us also *walk* **march** in *the* Spirit.
26 Let us not be *desirous of vain glory* **vainglorious**,
provoking **irritating** one another, envying one another.

THE MINISTRY OF RESTORATION

6 Brethren,
if **ever** a *man* **human** be overtaken in *a fault* **backsliding**,
ye which are spiritual,
restore **prepare** such an one in the spirit of meekness;
considering **scoping** thyself,
lest thou also be *tempted* **tested**.
2 Bear ye one another's burdens,
and *so* **thus** fulfil the *law* **torah** of *Christ* **the Messiah**.
3 For if *a man* **some one**
think himself to be *something* **somewhat**,
when he is nothing **being no one**,
he *deceiveth* **deludeth** himself.
4 But let *every man* **each** prove his own work,
and then
shall he have *rejoicing* **boasting** in himself alone,
and not in another.
5 For *every man* **each** shall bear his own burden.
6 Let him that is *taught* **catechized** in the word
communicate **impart** unto him that *teacheth* **catechizeth**
in all good *things*.
7 Be not *deceived* **seduced**;
God **Elohim** is not *mocked* **snubbed**:
for whatsoever a *man* **human** soweth,
that shall he also *reap* **harvest**.
8 For he that soweth to his flesh
shall of the flesh *reap* **harvest** corruption;
but he that soweth to the Spirit
shall of the Spirit *reap* **harvest** life *everlasting* **eternal**.
9 And let us not be weary in *well* doing **good**:
for in *due* **our own** season we shall *reap* **harvest**,
if we *faint* **weaken** not.
10 As we have therefore *opportunity* **season**,
let us *do* **work** good unto all *men*,
especially unto them
who are of the household of *faith* **the trust**.

PAULOS' BOASTING

11 Ye see how *large a letter* **great a scribing**
I have *written* **scribed** unto you with mine own hand.
12 As many as *desire* **will** to make a fair shew in the flesh,
they *constrain* **compel** you to be circumcised;
only lest they should suffer persecution
for the *cross* **stake** of *Christ* **the Messiah**.
13 For neither they themselves who are circumcised
keep **guard** the *law* **torah**;
but *desire* **will** to have you circumcised,
that they may *glory* **boast** in your flesh.
14 *But God forbid* **So be it not** that I should *glory* **boast**,
save **except** in the *cross* **stake**
of our *Lord Jesus Christ* **Adonay Yah Shua Messiah**,
by **through** whom
the *world* **cosmos** is *crucified* **staked** unto me,
and I **also** unto the *world* **cosmos**.
15 For in *Christ Jesus* **Messiah Yah Shua**
neither circumcision *availeth any thing* **is of any ability**,
nor uncircumcision,
but a new *creature* **creation**.
16 And as many as *walk* **march**
according to **by** this *rule* **canon**,
peace **shalom** be on them, and mercy,
and upon the *Israel* **Yisra El** of *God* **Elohim**.
17 From henceforth
let no *man trouble* **one belabour to embarrass** me:
for I bear in my body
the *marks* **stigmas** of the *Lord Jesus* **Adonay Yah Shua**.
18 Brethren, the *grace* **charism**
of our *Lord Jesus Christ* **Adonay Yah Shua Messiah**
be with your spirit.
Amen.

KEY TO INTERPRETING THE EXEGESES:
King James text is in regular type;
Text under exegeses is in oblique type;
Text of exegeses is in bold type.

SALUTATION

1 *Paul* **Paulos,**
an apostle of *Jesus Christ* **Yah Shua Messiah**
by **through** the will of *God* **Elohim,**
to the *saints which are at* **holy being in** Ephesus,
and to the *faithful* **trustworthy**
in *Christ Jesus* **Messiah Yah Shua:**
2 *Grace be* **Charism** to you, and *peace* **shalom,**
from *God* **Elohim** our Father,
and *from*
the Lord Jesus Christ **Adonay Yah Shua Messiah.**
3 Blessed be the *God* **Elohim** and Father
of our *Lord Jesus Christ* **Adonay Yah Shua Messiah,**
who hath blessed us *with* **in** all spiritual blessings
in *heavenly places* **the heavenlies** in *Christ* **Messiah:**
4 *According* **Exactly** as he hath *chosen* **selected** us in him
before the foundation of the *world* **cosmos,**
that we should be holy and *without blame* **unblemished**
before him **in his sight** in love:
5 Having *predestinated* **predetermined** us
unto *the adoption of children* **sonship**
by Jesus Christ **through Yah Shua Messiah** to himself,
according to the *good pleasure* **well—approval** of his will,
6 To the *praise* **halal** of the glory of his *grace* **charism,**
wherein he hath
made us accepted **endued us with charism**
in the beloved.
7 In whom we have redemption through his blood,
the forgiveness of *sins* **backslidings,**
according to the riches of his *grace* **charism;**
8 Wherein
he hath *abounded toward* **superabounded unto** us
in all wisdom and *prudence* **thought;**
9 Having made known unto us the mystery of his will,
according to his *good pleasure* **well—approval**
which he hath *purposed* **predetermined** in himself:
10 That in the *dispensation* **administration**
of the fulness of *times* **seasons**
he might *gather together in one* **sum up** all *things*
in *Christ* **the Messiah,**
both which are in *heaven* **the heavens,**
and which are on earth; *even* in him:
11 In whom also
we have *obtained an inheritance* **inherited,**
being *predestinated* **predetermined**
according to the *purpose* **prothesis** of him
who *worketh* **energizeth** all *things*
after the counsel of his own will:
12 *That we should be* **Unto our being**
to the *praise* **halal** of his glory,
who *first trusted* **forehoped** in *Christ* **the Messiah.**
13 In whom ye also *trusted,*
after that ye heard the word of truth,
the *gospel* **evangelism** of your salvation:
in whom also, *after that ye believed* **having trusted,**
ye were sealed
with that holy Spirit of *promise* **pre—evangelism,**
14 Which is the *earnest* **pledge** of our inheritance
until **unto** the redemption
of the *purchased possession* **acquisition,**
unto the *praise* **halal** of his glory.

THE SPIRIT OF WISDOM AND APOCALYPSE

15 Wherefore I also, after I heard of your *faith* **trust**
in the *Lord Jesus* **Adonay Yah Shua,**
and love unto all the *saints* **holy,**
16 *Cease* **Pause** not to *give thanks* **eucharistize** for you,
making *mention* **rememberance** of you in my prayers;
17 That the *God* **Elohim**
of our *Lord Jesus Christ* **Adonay Yah Shua Messiah,**
the Father of glory,
may give unto you
the spirit of wisdom and *revelation* **apocalypse**
in the knowledge of him:
18 The eyes of your *understanding* **mind**
being enlightened;
that ye may know **unto knowing**
what is the hope of his calling,
and what the riches of the glory of his inheritance
in the *saints* **holy,**
19 And what is the exceeding *greatness* **magnitude**
of his *power* **dynamis**
to us—ward **unto us** who *believe* **trust,**
according to the *working* **energizing**
of his mighty *power* might,
20 Which he *wrought* **energized** in *Christ* **the Messiah,**
when he raised him from the dead,
and *set* **sat** him *at* **by** his *own* right *hand*
in the *heavenly places* **heavenlies,**
21 Far above
all *principality* **hierarchies,** and *power* **authority,**
and might **dynamis,** and *dominion* **lordship,**
and every name that is named,
not only in this *world* **eon,**
but also in that which is to come:
22 And hath *put* **subjugated** all *things* under his feet,
and gave him *to be* the head over all *things*
to the *church* **ecclesia,**
23 Which is his body,
the fulness of him that filleth **full** all in all.

SALVATION BY CHARISM THROUGH THE TRUST

2 And you *hath he quickened,*
who were **being** dead in *trespasses* **backslidings** and sins;
2 Wherein *in time past* **formerly** ye walked
according to the *course* **eon** of this *world* **cosmos,**
according to the *prince* **arch**
of the *power* **authority** of the air,
the spirit that now *worketh* **energizeth**
in the *children* **sons** of *disobedience* **distrust:**
3 Among whom also
we all had our *conversation* **behaviour**
in times past **ever** in the *lusts* **pantings** of our flesh,
fulfilling **doing** the *desires* **will**
of the flesh and of the mind;
and were by nature the children of wrath,
even as *others* **the rest.**
4 But *God* **Elohim,** *who is* **being** rich in mercy,
for his *great* **vast** love wherewith he loved us,
5 Even *when we were* **being** dead in *sins* **backslidings,**
hath *quickened us together* **co—enlivened us**
with *Christ* **the Messiah,**
(by *grace* **charism** ye are saved;)
6 And hath *raised* **co—raised** us *up together,*
and *made us sit together* **co—seated us**
in *heavenly places* **the heavenlies**
in *Christ Jesus* **Messiah Yah Shua:**
7 That in the *ages* **eons** to come
he might *shew* **indicate**
the exceeding riches of his *grace* **charism**
in his kindness toward us
through Christ Jesus **in Messiah Yah Shua.**
8 For by *grace* **charism** are ye saved
through *faith* **the trust;**
and that not of yourselves:
it is the *gift* **oblation** of *God* **Elohim:**
9 Not of works, lest any *man* **one** should boast.
10 For we are his *workmanship* **doing,**
created in *Christ Jesus* **Messiah Yah Shua**
unto good works,
which *God* **Elohim**
hath *before ordained* **previously prepared**
that we should walk in them.

SHALOM THROUGH THE BLOOD OF MESSIAH

11 Wherefore remember,
that ye *being in time past* **ever**
Gentiles **goyim** in the flesh,
who are *called* **worded** Uncircumcision
by that which is *called* **worded** the Circumcision
in the flesh *made by hands* **handmade;**
12 That at that *time* **season**
ye were *without Christ* **apart from Messiah,**
being *aliens* **alienated**
from the *commonwealth* **citizenship** of *Israel* **Yisra El,**
and strangers
from the covenants of *promise* **the pre—evangelism,**
having no hope,
and *without God* **atheist** in the *world* **cosmos:**

13 But now in *Christ Jesus* **Messiah Yah Shua**
ye *who sometimes were* **formerly being** far off
are made **have become** nigh
by the blood of *Christ* **the Messiah**.
14 For he is our *peace* **shalom**, who hath made both one,
and hath *broken down* **loosed**
the middle *wall* **hedge** of partition *between us*;
15 Having *abolished* **inactivated** in his flesh the enmity,
even the *law* **torah** of *commandments* **misvoth**
contained in *ordinances* **dogmas**;
for to make in **that through** himself
of twain **created the two into** one new *man* **human**,
so making *peace* **shalom**;
16 And that he might **fully** reconcile
both unto *God* **Elohim**
in one body *by* **through** the *cross* **stake**,
having *slain* **slaughtered** the enmity *thereby* **therein**:
17 And came and *preached peace* **evangelized shalom**
to you which were afar off,
and to them that were nigh.
18 For through him we both have access *by* **in** one Spirit
unto the Father.

THE NEW HOLY NAVE

19 Now therefore
ye are no more strangers and *foreigners* **settlers**,
but *fellowcitizens* **co—citizens** with the *saints* **holy**,
and of the household of *God* **Elohim**;
20 And are built upon the foundation
of the apostles and prophets,
Jesus Christ **Yah Shua Messiah** himself
being the chief corner *stone*;
21 In whom all the
building fitly framed together **edifice co—joined**
groweth unto an holy *temple* **nave** in *the Lord* **Adonay**:
22 In whom ye also are *builded together* **co—settled**
for an habitation **unto a settlement** of *God* **Elohim**
through the **in** Spirit.

THE APOCALYPSE OF THE MYSTERY OF THE ECCLESIA

3 For this cause I *Paul* **Paulos**,
the prisoner of *Jesus Christ* **Yah Shua Messiah**
for you *Gentiles* **goyim**,
2 If **indeed** ye have heard
of the *dispensation* **administration**
of the *grace* **charism** of *God* **Elohim**
which is given me *to you—ward* **unto you**:
3 How that by *revelation* **apocalypse**
he made known unto me the mystery;
(**exactly** as I *wrote afore* **preinscribed** in few words,
4 *Whereby* **Whereunto**, when ye read,
ye may *understand* **be able to comprehend**
my *knowledge* **comprehension**
in the mystery of *Christ* **the Messiah**)
5 Which in other *ages* **generations**
was not made known unto the sons of *men* **humanity**,
as it is now *revealed* **unveiled**
unto his holy apostles and prophets *by the* **in** Spirit;
6 That the *Gentiles* **goyim** should be *fellowheirs* **co—heirs**,
and *of the same body* **co—bodied**,
and *partakers* **co—partakers** of his *promise* **pre—evangelism**
in *Christ by* **the Messiah through** the *gospel* **evangelism**:
7 Whereof I *was made* **became** a minister,
according to the *gift* **gratuity**
of the *grace* **charism** of *God* **Elohim**
given unto me
by the *effectual working* **energizing**
of his *power* **dynamis**.
8 Unto me,
who am less than the least of all *saints* **the holy**,
is this *grace* **charism** given,
that I should *preach* **evangelize**
among the *Gentiles* **goyim**
the *unsearchable* **untraceable** riches
of *Christ* **the Messiah**;
9 And to *make* **enlighten** all *men* **to** see
what is the *fellowship* **communion** of the mystery,
which from the *beginning of the world* **eons**
hath been *hid* **secreted** in *God* **Elohim**,
who created all *things*
by Jesus Christ **through Yah Shua Messiah**:
10 *To the intent* that now
unto the *principalities* **hierarchies** and *powers* **authorities**
in *heavenly places* **the heavenlies**
might be known *by* **through** the *church* **ecclesia**
the *manifold* **multifarious** wisdom of *God* **Elohim**,
11 According to the *eternal purpose* **prothesis of the eons**
which he *purposed* **made**
in *Christ Jesus* **Messiah Yah Shua** our *Lord* **Adonay**:
12 In whom we have boldness and access
with **in** confidence
by **through** the *faith of* **trust from** him.
13 Wherefore I *desire* **ask** that ye *faint* **weary** not
at my tribulations for you, which is your glory.

PAULOS' PRAYER FOR LOVE

14 For this cause I bow my knees unto the Father
of our *Lord Jesus Christ* **Adonay Yah Shua Messiah**,
15 Of whom the whole *family* **patriarchy**
in *heaven* **the heavens** and earth is named,
16 That he *would grant* **should give** you,
according to the riches of his glory,
to be *strengthened* **empowered** with *might* **dynamis**
by **through** his Spirit in the inner *man* **human**;
17 That *Christ* **the Messiah** may dwell in your hearts
by faith **through the trust**;
that ye, being rooted and *grounded* **founded** in love,
18 May be able to comprehend with all *saints* **the holy**
what is the breadth, and length, and depth, and height;
19 And to know the love of *Christ* **the Messiah**,
which *passeth* **exceedeth** knowledge,
that ye might be filled **full**
with **unto** all the fulness of *God* **Elohim**.

DOXOLOGY

20 Now unto him
that is able to do *exceeding abundantly* **superabundantly**
above all that we ask or *think* **comprehend**,
according to the *power* **dynamis**
that *worketh* **energizeth** in us,
21 Unto him be glory in the *church* **ecclesia**
by *Christ Jesus* **Messiah Yah Shua**
throughout **unto** all *ages* **generations**,
world without end **eon of the eons.**
Amen.

THE UNITY OF THE SPIRIT

4 I therefore, the prisoner *of the Lord* **in Adonay**,
beseech you that ye walk worthy
of the *vocation* **calling** wherewith ye are called,
2 With all *lowliness* **humblemindedness** and meekness,
with *longsuffering* **patience**,
forbearing **tolerating** one another in love;
3 *Endeavouring* **Diligent**
to *keep* **guard** the unity of the Spirit
in the bond of *peace* **shalom**.
4 *There is* one body, and one Spirit,
even **exactly** as ye are called in one hope of your calling;
5 One *Lord* **Adonay**, one *faith* **trust**, one baptism,
6 One *God* **Elohim** and Father of all,
who is above all, and through all, and in you all.

THE DESCENSION AND ASCENSION OF THE MESSIAH

7 But unto *every* **each** one of us is given *grace* **charism**
according to the measure of the *gift* **gratuity**
of *Christ* **the Messiah**.
8 Wherefore he *saith* **wordeth**,
When he ascended *up* on high,
he led captivity captive,
and gave gifts unto *men* **humanity**.
Psalm 68:18
9 (Now that he ascended,
what is it *but* **except** that he also descended first
into the *lower* **substrata** parts of the earth?
10 He that descended
is the same also that ascended *up* far above all heavens,
that he might *fill* **fulfill** all *things*.)

THE FOURFOLD MINISTRY

11 And he gave some **indeed**, apostles;
and some, prophets; and some, evangelists;
and some, *pastors* **shepherds** and *teachers* **doctors**;
12 For the perfecting of the *saints* **holy**,
for **unto** the work of the ministry,
for **unto** the edifying of the body of *Christ* **the Messiah**:
13 Till we all *come* **attain**
in **unto** the unity of the *faith* **trust**,

and of the knowledge of the Son of *God* **Elohim**,
unto a *perfect* **complete** man,
unto the measure of the *stature* **maturity**
of the fulness of *Christ* **the Messiah**:
14 That we *henceforth*
be no *more children* **longer babies**,
tossed to and fro **surging**, and carried about
with every wind of doctrine,
by **in** the *sleight* **dice** of men, and **in** cunning *craftiness*,
whereby they lie in wait to deceive
with their methods of seduction;
15 But *speaking the truth* **being true** in love,
may grow up into him in all *things*,
which is the head, *even Christ* **the Messiah**:
16 From whom the whole body
fitly joined together **co—joined** and *compacted* **coalesced**
by **through** that which every joint *supplieth* **contributeth**,
according to the *effectual working* **energizing**
in the measure of *every* **each single** part,
maketh *increase* **growth** of the body
unto the edifying of itself in love.

THE UNHOLY LIFE

17 This I *say* **word** therefore,
and *testify* **witness** in the *Lord* **Adonay**,
that ye *henceforth* walk *not* **no longer**
exactly as *other Gentiles walk* **the rest of the goyim**,
in the vanity of their mind,
18 Having the *understanding* **mind** darkened,
being alienated from the life of *God* **Elohim**
through the *ignorance* **unknowingness**
that is **being** in them,
because of **through** the *blindness* **petrifaction** of their heart:
19 Who being *past feeling* **apathetic**
have *given* **surrendered** themselves *over*
unto *lasciviousness* **lechery**,
to work **unto working** all *uncleanness* **impurity**
with greediness **in avarice**.

THE HOLY LIFE

20 But ye have not *so* **thus** learned *Christ* **the Messiah**;
21 If *so be that* **indeed** ye have heard him,
and have been *taught by* **doctrinated in** him,
exactly as the truth is in *Jesus* **Yah Shua**:
22 That ye put off
concerning the *former conversation* **previous behaviour**
the old *man* **humanity**,
which is corrupt
according to the *deceitful lusts* **pantings of delusion**;
23 And be renewed in the spirit of your mind;
24 And that ye *put on* **endue** the new *man* **humanity**,
which after *God* **Elohim**
is created in *righteousness* **justness**
and true *holiness* **mercy**.
25 Wherefore putting away lying,
let each speak *every man* truth with his neighbour:
for we are members one of another.

ADMONITIONS TO THE HOLY

26 Be ye *angry* **wroth**, and sin not:
let not the sun go down upon your *wrath* **rage**:
27 Neither give place to *the devil* **Diabolos**.
28 Let him that stole steal no more:
but rather let him labour,
working with his hands *the thing* **that** which is good,
that he may have
to *give* **impart** to him that *needeth* **hath need**.
29 Let no *corrupt communication* **putrefied word**
proceed out of your mouth,
but *that which is* **if any be** good
to the *use of* edifying **of that which is needed**,
that it may *minister grace* **give charism** unto the hearers.
30 And *grieve* **sorrow** not the holy Spirit of *God* **Elohim**,
whereby **in whom** ye are sealed
unto the day of redemption.
31 Let all bitterness, and *wrath* **fury**, and anger,
and *clamour* **crying out**, and *evil speaking* **blasphemy**,
be *put* **taken** away from you, with all malice:
32 And be ye kind one to another,
tenderhearted **tenderspleened**,
forgiving one another **granting charism to yourselves**,
even **exactly** as *God for Christ's sake* **Elohim in Messiah**
hath *forgiven* **granted charism to** you.

ON WALKING HOLY

5 Be ye therefore *followers* **mimickers** of *God* **Elohim**,
as *dear* **beloved** children;
2 And walk in love,
exactly as *Christ* **Messiah** also hath loved us,
and hath *given* **surrendered** himself for us
an offering and a sacrifice to *God* **Elohim**
for **unto** a
sweetsmelling savour **well fragranced fragrance**.
3 But *fornication* **whoredom**,
and all *uncleanness* **impurity**, or *covetousness* **avarice**,
let it not **no way** be *once* named among you,
exactly as *becometh saints* **befitteth the holy**;
4 Neither *filthiness* **shamefulness**,
nor *foolish talking* **morology**, nor *jesting* **repartee**,
which are not *convenient* **proper**:
but rather *giving of thanks* **eucharistize**.
5 For this ye know,
that no whoremonger, nor *unclean* **impure** person,
nor *covetous man* **avaricious**, who is an idolater,
hath any inheritance in the *kingdom* **sovereigndom**
of *Christ* **the Messiah** and of *God* **Elohim**.
6 Let no *man deceive* **one delude** you with vain words:
for *because of* **through** these *things*
cometh the wrath of *God* **Elohim**
upon the *children* **sons** of *disobedience* **distrust**.
7 Be not ye therefore
partakers with them **co—partakers**.
8 For ye were *sometimes* **formerly** darkness,
but now are *ye* light in *the Lord* **Adonay**:
walk as children of light:
9 (For the fruit of the Spirit is in all goodness
and *righteousness* **justness** and truth;)
10 Proving what is *acceptable* **well—pleasing**
unto *the Lord* **Adonay**.
11 And *have no fellowship* **co—partake not**
with the unfruitful works of darkness,
but rather reprove them.
12 For it is a shame even to *speak* **word** of those *things*
which *are done of* **become by** them in secret.
13 But all *things* that are reproved
are *made* manifest by the light:
for whatsoever doth *make* manifest is light.
14 Wherefore he *saith* **wordeth**,
Awake **Arise** thou that sleepest, and arise from the dead,
and *Christ* **the Messiah** shall *give* **illuminate** thee *light*.
15 See then *that* **how precisely** ye walk *circumspectly*,
not as *fools* **unwise**, but as wise,
16 *Redeeming* **Marketing** the *time* **season**,
because the days are evil.
17 Wherefore be ye not *unwise* **thoughtless**,
but *understanding* **comprehending**
what the will of *the Lord* **Adonay** is.
18 And be not *drunk* **intoxicated** with wine,
wherein is *excess* **dissipation**;
but be filled *with the* **full in** Spirit;
19 Speaking to yourselves in psalms and hymns
and spiritual *songs* **odes**,
singing and *making melody* **psalming** in your heart
to *the Lord* **Adonay**;
20 *Giving thanks* **Eucharistizing** always for all *things*
unto *God* **Elohim** and the Father in the name
of our *Lord Jesus Christ* **Adonay Yah Shua Messiah**;

ON SUBJUGATING SELVES

21 *Submitting* **Subjugating** yourselves one to another
in the *fear* **awe** of *God* **Elohim**.
22 *Wives* **Women**,
submit **subjugate** yourselves
unto your own *husbands* **men**,
as unto *the Lord* **Adonay**.
23 For the *husband* **man** is the head of the *wife* **woman**,
even as *Christ* **the Messiah**
is the head of the *church* **ecclesia**:
and he is the saviour of the body.
24 *Therefore* **Rather**,
exactly as the *church* **ecclesia**
is *subject* **subjugated** unto *Christ* **the Messiah**,
so let the wives be **even thus the women**
to their own *husbands* **men** in *every thing* **all**.
25 *Husbands* **Men**,

love your *wives* **women**,
even **exactly** as *Christ* **the Messiah**
also loved the *church* **ecclesia**,
and *gave* **surrendered** himself for it;
26 That he might *sanctify* **hallow** and *cleanse* **purify** it
with the *washing* **bathing** of water *by* **in** the *word* **rhema**,
27 That he might present it to himself
a glorious *church* **ecclesia**,
not having *spot* **stain**, or wrinkle, or any such *thing*;
but that it should be holy
and *without blemish* **unblemished**.
28 *So ought* **Thus are** men **indebted**
to love their *wives* **women** as their own bodies.
He that loveth his *wife* **woman** loveth himself.
29 For no *man* **one** ever yet hated his own flesh;
but *nourisheth* **nurtureth** and cherisheth it,
even **exactly** as *the Lord* **Adonay** the *church* **ecclesia**:
30 For we are members of his body,
of his flesh, and of his bones.
31 For this cause
shall a *man* **human** leave his father and mother,
and shall *be joined* **adhere** unto his *wife* **woman**,
and they two shall be **into** one flesh.
32 This is a *great* **mega** mystery:
but I *speak* **word**
concerning Christ **as to Messiah** and the *church* **ecclesia**.
33 *Nevertheless* **Moreover,**
let *every one* **each** of you *in particular so* **one by one**
thus love his *wife* **woman** even as himself;
and the *wife* **woman** see
that she *reverence* **awe** her *husband* **man**.

6 Children,
obey your parents in the *Lord* **Adonay**:
for this is *right* **just**.
2 Honour thy father and mother;
which is the first *commandment* **misvah**
with promise **in pre—evangelism**;
3 That it may be well with thee,
and thou *mayest live long* **shall be long lived**
on the earth.
Exodus 20:12
4 And, ye fathers,
provoke **enrage** not your children *to wrath*:
but *bring* **nurture** them *up* in the *nurture* **discipline**
and admonition of *the Lord* **Adonay**.
5 Servants,
be obedient to **obey** them that are *your masters* **adonim**
according to the flesh,
with *fear* **awe** and trembling,
in *singleness* **liberality** of your heart,
as unto *Christ* **the Messiah**;
6 Not with eyeservice, as *menpleasers* **humanitypleasers**;
but as the servants of *Christ* **the Messiah**,
doing the will of *God* **Elohim** from the *heart* **soul**;
7 With good will *doing service* **in servitude**,
as to the *Lord* **Adonay**, and not to *men* **humanity**:
8 Knowing that whatsoever good *thing*
any man **each** doeth,
the same shall he receive of *the Lord* **Adonay**,
whether *he be bond* **servant**, *or free* **whether liberated**.
9 And, ye *masters* **adoniym**,
do the same *things* unto them,
forbearing **leaving off** threatening:
knowing that your *Master* **Adonay**
also is in *heaven* **the heavens**;
neither is there *respect of persons* **partiality** with him.
10 Finally, my brethren,
be *strong* **dynamized** in *the Lord* **Adonay**,
and in the power of his might.

THE PANOPLY OF ELOHIM

11 *Put on* **Endue**
the whole *armour* **panoply** of *God* **Elohim**,
that ye may be able to stand
against the *wiles* **methods** of *the devil* **Diabolos**.
12 For we *wrestle* **quiver** not against flesh and blood,
but against *principalities* **hierarchies**,
against *powers* **authorities**,
against the *rulers* **cosmic powers**
of the darkness of this *world* **eon**,
against spiritual *wickedness* **evil**
in *high places* **the heavenlies**.
13 Wherefore take unto you
the whole *armour* **panoply** of *God* **Elohim**,
that ye may be able to withstand in the evil day,
and having *done* **worked** all, to stand.
14 Stand therefore,
having your loins girt about *with* **in** truth,
and having *on* **endued**
the breastplate of *righteousness* **justness**;
15 And your feet *shod with* **bound in** the preparation
of the *gospel* **evangelism** of *peace* **shalom**;
16 Above all, taking the shield of *faith* **the trust**,
wherewith **wherein** ye shall be able to quench
all the fiery *darts* **missiles** of the *wicked* **evil**.
17 And *take* **receive** the helmet of salvation,
and the sword of the Spirit,
which is the *word* **rhema** of *God* **Elohim**:
18 **In** Praying *always with* **in all seasons**
through all prayer and *supplication* **petition** in *the* Spirit,
and watching thereunto *with* **in** all perseverance
and *supplication* **petition** for all *saints* **the holy**;
19 And for me,
that *utterance* **word** may be given unto me,
that I may *open* **in opening** my mouth *boldly* **in boldness**,
to make known the mystery of the *gospel* **evangelism**,
20 For which I am
an ambassador **a presbyter** in *bonds* **fetters**:
that therein I may *speak boldly* **be bold**,
as I ought to **and** speak **as I must.**
21 But that ye also may know my affairs,
and how I *do* **transact**,
Tychicus, a beloved brother
and *faithful* **trustworthy** minister in *the Lord* **Adonay**,
shall make known to you all *things*:
22 Whom I have sent unto you
for **unto** the same purpose,
that ye might know **about** our affairs,
and that he might *comfort* **console** your hearts.

BENEDICTION

23 *Peace* **Shalom** *be* to the brethren,
and love with *faith* **trust**,
from *God* **Elohim** the Father
and *the Lord Jesus Christ* **Adonay Yah Shua Messiah**.
24 *Grace* **Charism** be with all them
that love our *Lord Jesus Christ* **Adonay Yah Shua Messiah**
in *sincerity* **incorruptibility**.
Amen.

KEY TO INTERPRETING THE EXEGESES:
King James text is in regular type;
Text under exegeses is in oblique type;
Text of exegeses is in bold type.

SALUTATION

1 *Paul* **Paulos** and *Timotheus* **Timo Theos**,
the servants of *Jesus Christ* **Yah Shua Messiah**,
to all the *saints* **holy** in *Christ Jesus* **Messiah Yah Shua**
which are at **being in** Philippi,
with the *bishops* **episcopates** and *deacons* **ministers**:
2 *Grace* **Charism** *be* unto you, and *peace* **shalom**,
from *God* **Elohim** our Father,
and *from*
the Lord Jesus Christ **Adonay Yah Shua Messiah**.

PAULOS' EUCHARIST FOR THE HOLY

3 I *thank* **eucharistize** my *God* **Elohim**
upon every remembrance of you,
4 Always in every *prayer* **petition** of mine for you
all *making request* **petitioning** with *joy* **cheer**,
5 For your *fellowship* **communion**
in the *gospel* **evangelism**
from the first day until now;
6 *Being* confident of this *very thing*,
that he which hath begun a good work in you
will perform **shall fully complete** it
until the day of *Jesus Christ* **Yah Shua Messiah**:
7 *Even* **Exactly** as it is *meet* **just**
for me to think this of you all,
because I have you in my heart;
inasmuch as **being** both in my bonds,
and in the
defence **pleading** and *confirmation* **establishment**
of the *gospel* **evangelism**,
ye all are *partakers* **co—partakers** of my *grace* **charism**.
8 For *God* **Elohim** is my *record* **witness**,
how *greatly I long* **I yearn** after you all
in the *bowels* **spleen** of *Jesus Christ* **Yah Shua Messiah**.
9 And this I pray,
that your love may *abound* **superabound**
yet more and more
in knowledge and in all *judgment* **perception**;
10 That ye may approve *things* **those** that are excellent;
that ye may be sincere and *without offence* **inoffensive**
till **unto** the day of *Christ* **Messiah**;
11 Being filled **full**
with the fruits of *righteousness* **justness**,
which are *by Jesus Christ* **through Yah Shua Messiah**,
unto the glory and *praise* **halal** of *God* **Elohim**.

LIFE IS IN MESSIAH

12 But I *would ye should understand* **will that ye know**,
brethren,
that *the things* **those**
which happened unto **concerning** me
have *fallen out rather* **come**
unto the *furtherance* **advancement**
of the *gospel* **evangelism**;
13 So that my bonds in *Christ* **Messiah**
are **become** manifest in all the *palace* **praetorium**,
and *in* **to** all *other places* **the rest**;
14 And many of the brethren in *the Lord* **Adonay**,
waxing confident **convinced** by my bonds,
are *much more* **superabundantly** bold
to speak the word *without fear* **fearlessly**.
15 Some indeed preach *Christ* **the Messiah**
even *of* **through** envy and *strife* **contention**;
and some also *of good will* **through well—approval**:
16 The one *preach Christ* **indeed evangelize Messiah**
of contention **from rivalry**, not *sincerely* **holily**,
supposing to *add affliction* **bring tribulation** to my bonds:
17 But the other of love, knowing that I am set
for the defence **unto the pleading**
of the *gospel* **evangelism**.
18 What *then* **indeed**?
notwithstanding **moreover**, every *way* **manner**,
whether in *pretence* **pretext**, *or* **whether** in truth,
Christ **Messiah** is *preached* **evangelized**;
and I therein *do rejoice* **rather cheer**,
yea, and *will rejoice* **shall cheer on**.
19 For I know that this shall turn to my salvation
through your *prayer* **petition**,
and the *supply* **contribution**
of the Spirit of *Jesus Christ* **Yah Shua Messiah**,
20 According
to my *earnest expectation* **intense anticipation**
and *my* hope,
that in *nothing* **naught** I shall be ashamed,
but that *with* **in** all boldness, as always,
so now also
Christ **Messiah** shall be magnified in my body,
whether *it be by* **through** life,
or by **whether through** death.
21 For to me to live is *Christ* **Messiah**,
and to die is gain.
22 But if I live in *the* flesh,
this is the fruit of my *labour* **work**:
yet what I shall choose I *wot* **know** not.
23 For I am *in a strait betwixt* **overtaken by** two,
having a *desire* **panting** to depart,
and to be with *Christ* **Messiah**;
which is *far* **rather much** better:
24 Nevertheless to abide in the flesh
is *more needful* **necessary** for you.
25 And having this confidence,
I know that I shall abide
and *continue* **remain** with you all
for **unto** your *furtherance* **advancement**
and *joy* **cheer** of *faith* **the trust**;
26 That your *rejoicing* **boasting**
may *be more abundant* **superabound**
in *Jesus Christ for* **Yah Shua Messiah in** me
by **through** my coming to you again.
27 Only *let your conversation be* **citizenize**
as *it becometh* **worthy**
of the *gospel* **evangelism** of *Christ* **the Messiah**:
that whether I come and see you,
or else be **whether** absent,
I may hear *of* **about** your affairs,
that ye stand *fast* **firm** in one spirit, with one *mind* **soul**,
striving together **co—striving**
for the *faith* **trust** of the *gospel* **evangelism**;
28 And in *nothing* **naught** terrified by your adversaries:
which is to them **indeed**
an *evident token* **indication** of *perdition* **destruction**,
but to you of salvation, and that of *God* **Elohim**.
29 For unto you *it is given* **is charism granted**
in the behalf of *Christ* **Messiah**,
not only to *believe* **trust** on him,
but also to suffer for his sake;
30 Having the same *conflict* **agony**
which **such as** ye saw in me, and now hear to be in me.

ON HUMBLING OF SELF

2 If *there be* therefore any consolation in *Christ* **Messiah**,
if any *comfort* **consolation** of love,
if any *fellowship* **communion** of the Spirit,
if any *bowels* **spleens** and *mercies* **compassions**,
2 Fulfil ye my *joy* **cheer**,
that ye be *likeminded* **of the same thought**,
having the same love,
being of one accord **co—souled**,
of one *mind* **thought**.
3 Let *nothing* **naught** be done
through *strife* **rivalry** or vainglory;
but in *lowliness of mind* **humblemindedness**
let each esteem other *better than* **superior to** themselves.
4 *Look* **Scope** not *every man* **each**
on **of** his own *things* **self**,
but *every man* **each** also on *the things* **those** of others.

MESSIAH'S HUMBLING OF SELF

5 **Indeed** Let this *mind* **thought** be in you,
which was also in *Christ Jesus* **Messiah Yah Shua**:
6 Who, being in the form of *God* **Elohim**,
thought **deemed** it not *robbery* **usurpation**
to be equal with *God* **Elohim**:
7 But *made* **voided** himself *of no reputation*,
and took *upon him* the form of a servant,
and *was made* **became** in the likeness of *men* **humanity**:
8 And being found in *fashion* **configuration**
as a *man* **human**,
he humbled himself, and became obedient unto death,
even the death of the *cross* **stake**.

MESSIAH'S EXALTATION

9 Wherefore,
God **Elohim** also hath *highly* **supremely** exalted him,
and *given* **granted** him **charism**
— a name *which is* above every name:
10 That *at* **in** the name of *Jesus* **Yah Shua**
every knee should bow,
of *things in heaven* **the heavenlies**,
and *things in earth* **earthly**,
and *things under the earth* **subterranean**;
11 And that every tongue should *confess* **avow**
that *Jesus Christ* **Yah Shua Messiah** is *Lord* **Adonay**,
to the glory of *God* **Elohim** the Father.
Yesha Yah 45:22,23

ON WORKING OUT SALVATION

12 *Wherefore* **So then**, my beloved,
exactly as ye have always obeyed,
not as in my presence only,
but now much more in my *absence* **being away**,
work out your own salvation
with *fear* **awe** and trembling.
Ephesians 2:8—10
13 For it is *God* **Elohim** which *worketh* **energizeth** in you
both to will and to *do* **energize**
of his *good pleasure* **well—approval**.
14 Do all *things without* **apart from** murmurings
and *disputings* **reasonings**:
15 That ye may be blameless
and *harmless* **unadulterated**,
the *sons* **children** of *God* **Elohim**,
without rebuke **unblemished**,
in the midst
of a crooked and *perverse nation* **perverted generation**,
among whom ye *shine* **manifest**
as lights in the *world* **cosmos**;
16 Holding forth the word of life;
that I may rejoice **unto boasting**
in **unto** the day of *Christ* **Messiah**,
that I have not run in vain, neither laboured in vain.
17 *Yea* **Rather**, and if I be *offered* **libated**
upon the sacrifice and service of your *faith* **trust**,
I *joy* **cheer**, and *rejoice* **co—rejoice** with you all.
18 For the same cause also do ye *joy* **cheer**,
and *rejoice with me* **co—rejoice**.

PAULOS SENDS TIMO THEOS AND EPAPHRODITUS

19 But I *trust* **hope** in the *Lord Jesus* **Adonay Yah Shua**
to send *Timotheus shortly* **Timo Theos quickly** unto you,
that I also may be *of good comfort* **wellsouled**,
when I know **about** your state.
20 For I have no *man likeminded* **one like—souled**,
who *will naturally care* **is genuinely concerned**
for **about** your state.
21 For all seek their own,
not *the things* **those**
which are *Jesus Christ's* **Yah Shua Messiah's**.
22 But ye know the proof of him,
that, as a *son* **child** with the father,
he hath served with me in the *gospel* **evangelism**.
23 Him **indeed** therefore
I hope to send *presently* **immediately**,
so soon as **ever** I shall see
about how it *will* **shall** go with me.
24 But I *trust* **confide** in *the Lord* **Adonay**
that I also myself shall come shortly.
25 Yet I *supposed* **deemed** it necessary
to send to you Epaphroditus,
my brother, and *companion in labour* **co—worker**,
and *fellowsoldier* **co—warrior**,
but your *messenger* **apostle**,
and he that ministered to my *wants* **need**.
26 *For* **Since** he *longed* **yearned** after you all,
and was *full of heaviness* **distressed**,
because that ye had heard that he had been *sick* **frail**.
27 For indeed he was *sick nigh unto* **frail close by** death:
but *God had mercy on* **Elohim mercied** him;
and not on him only, but on me also,
lest I should have sorrow upon sorrow.
28 I sent him therefore *the more carefully* **diligently**,
that, when ye see him again, ye may *rejoice* **cheer**,
and that I **also** may be *the less sorrowful* **ungrieving**.
29 Receive him therefore in *the Lord* **Adonay**
with all *gladness* **cheer**;
and hold such *in reputation* **honourable**:
30 Because for the work of *Christ* **Messiah**
he *was nigh* **approached** unto death,
not regarding **hazarding** his *life* **soul**,
to *supply* **fill full** your lack of *service* **liturgy** toward me.

WARNINGS

3 Finally, my brethren, *rejoice* **cheer** in the *Lord* **Adonay**.
To *write* **scribe** the same *things* to you,
to me indeed is not *grievous* **slothful**,
but for you it is *safe* **certain**.
2 *Beware of* **See to the** dogs,
beware of **see to the** evil workers,
beware of the concision **see to the incisors**.
3 For we are the circumcision,
which *worship God* **liturgize Elohim** in *the* spirit,
and *rejoice* **boast** in *Christ Jesus* **Messiah Yah Shua**,
and have no confidence in the flesh.
4 Though I might also have confidence in the flesh.
If any other man thinketh that he hath whereof
he might *trust* **confide** in the flesh, I more:
5 Circumcised the eighth day,
of the *stock* **genos** of *Israel* **Yisra El**,
of the *tribe* **scion** of *Benjamin* **Ben Yamin**,
an Hebrew of the Hebrews;
as touching the *law* **torah**, a Pharisee;
6 Concerning zeal, persecuting the *church* **ecclesia**;
touching the *righteousness* **justness**
which is in the law **in torah**, **become** blameless.
7 But *what things* **those that** were gain to me,
those I *counted* **deemed** loss for *Christ* **the Messiah**.
8 *Yea doubtless* **Rather yet then**,
and I *count* **deem** all *things but* loss
for the *excellency* **superiority** of the knowledge
of *Christ Jesus* **Messiah Yah Shua** my *Lord* **Adonay**:
for whom I have *suffered the loss of* **lost** all *things*,
and *do count* **deem** them
but dung **to be hound dog droppings**,
that I may *win Christ* **gain Messiah**,
9 And be found in him,
not having mine own *righteousness* **justness**,
which is of the *law* **torah**,
but that which is through *the faith* **trust**
of Christ **from Messiah**,
the *righteousness* **justness** which is *of God* **from Elohim**
by *faith* **the trust**:
10 That I may know him,
and the *power* **dynamis** of his resurrection,
and the *fellowship* **communion** of his sufferings,
being *made conformable* **conformed** unto his death;
11 If *by any means* **somehow**
I might attain unto the resurrection of the dead.
12 Not *as though* **that** I had already *attained* **taken**,
either **or** were already *perfect* **complete**:
but I *follow* **pursue** *after*,
if that I may apprehend
that for which also I am apprehended
of *Christ Jesus* **Messiah Yah Shua**.
13 Brethren,
I *count* **reckon** not myself to have apprehended:
but this one *thing I do*,
forgetting those *things* **indeed** which are behind,
and reaching forth
unto those *things* which are *before* **ahead**,
14 I *press* **pursue** toward the *mark* **scope**
for **unto** the *prize* **umpirage** of the *high* **upper** calling
of *God* **Elohim** in *Christ Jesus* **Messiah Yah Shua**.
15 Let us therefore, as many as be *perfect* **complete**,
be **think** thus *minded*:
and if in *any thing* **ought** ye *be* **think** otherwise *minded*,
God **Elohim** shall *reveal* **unveil** even this unto you.
16 *Nevertheless* **Moreover**,
whereto we have *already* attained,
let us *walk* **march** by the same *rule* **canon**,
let us *mind* **think** the same *thing*.
17 Brethren,
be *followers together* **co—mimickers** of me,
and *mark* **scope out** them which walk *so* **thus**
exactly as ye have us for *an ensample* **a type**.

18 (For many walk,
of whom I have *told* **worded to** you often,
and now *tell* **word to** you even weeping,
that they are the enemies
of the *cross* **stake** of *Christ* **the Messiah**:
19 Whose *end* **completion** is destruction,
whose *God* **elohim** is their belly,
and *whose glory is* **who glory** in their shame,
who *mind* **think** earthly *things*.)

ON HEAVENLY CITIZENSHIP

20 For our *conversation* **citizenship**
is **exists** in *heaven* **the heavens**;
from whence also we *look for* **await** the Saviour,
the Lord Jesus Christ **Adonay Yah Shua Messiah**:
21 Who shall *change* **transfigure**
our *vile* body **of humiliation**,
that it may *be fashioned* **become conformed**
like unto his glorious **to the** body **of his glory**,
according to the *working* **energizing** whereby he is able
even to *subdue* **subjugate** all *things* unto himself.

CHEER IN ADONAY ALWAY

4 *Therefore* **So then,**
my brethren *dearly* beloved and *longed* **yearned** for,
my *joy* **cheer** and *crown* **wreath**,
so **thus** stand *fast* **firm** in *the Lord* **Adonay**,
my dearly beloved.
2 I beseech Euodias, and beseech Syntyche,
that they be of the same *mind* **thought**
in *the Lord* **Adonay**.
3 And I *intreat* **ask** thee also,
true yokefellow **genuine colleague**,
help **uphold** those women
which *laboured with me* **co—strived**
in the *gospel* **evangelism**,
with Clement also,
and *with others* **the rest**
of my *fellowlabourers* **co—workers**,
whose names are in the *book* **scroll** of life.
4 *Rejoice* **Cheer** in *the Lord* **Adonay** alway:
and again I say, *Rejoice* **Cheer**.
5 Let your *moderation* **gentleness**
be known unto all *men* **humanity**.
The Lord **Adonay** is *at hand* **nigh**.
6 Be *careful* **anxious** for *nothing* **naught**;
but in *every thing* **all** by prayer and *supplication* **petition**
with *thanksgiving* **eucharist**
let your requests be *made* known unto *God* **Elohim**.
7 And the *peace* **shalom** of *God* **Elohim**,
which *passeth all understanding* **surpasses the mind**,
shall *keep* **garrison**
your hearts and *minds* **comprehensions**
through Christ Jesus **in Messiah Yah Shua**.
8 Finally, brethren,
whatsoever things **as much as** are true,
whatsoever things **as much as** are *honest* **venerate**,
whatsoever things **as much as** are just,
whatsoever things **as much as** are *pure* **hallowed**,
whatsoever things **as much as** are *lovely* **friendly**,
whatsoever things **as much as** are
of good report **euphonious**;
if *there be* any virtue, and if *there be* any *praise* **halal**,
think on **reckon** these *things*.
9 Those *things*, which ye have both learned,
and *received* **taken**, and heard, and seen in me,
do **transact**:
and the *God* **Elohim** of *peace* **shalom** shall be with you.

PAULOS' CHEER IN ADONAY

10 But I *rejoiced* **cheered** in the *Lord* **Adonay**
greatly **magnificently**,
that now *at the last* **again** your *care* **thought** of me
hath *flourished again* **reflourished**;
wherein ye were also *careful* **thoughtful**,
but *ye lacked opportunity* **inopportune**.
11 Not that I *speak* **word** in respect of *want* **lack**:
for I have learned, in whatsoever state I am,
therewith to be *content* **selfcontent**.
12 I know both how to be *abased* **humble**,
and I know how to *abound* **superabound**:
every where and in all *things* **and in all**
I am *instructed* **initiated**
both to be *full* **filled** and to be hungry,
both to *abound* **superabound** and to *suffer need* **lack**.
13 *I can do all things* **am mighty enough**
through Christ **in Messiah**
which *strengtheneth* **dynamizeth** me.
14 *Notwithstanding* **Moreover** ye have well done,
that ye *did communicate* **co—partook**
with **of** my *affliction* **tribulation**.
15 Now ye Philippians know also,
that in the beginning of the *gospel* **evangelism**,
when I departed from Macedonia,
no *church communicated with* **ecclesia imparted to** me
as concerning **unto the word**
of giving and *receiving* **taking**,
but **except** ye only.
16 For even in *Thessalonica* **Thessalonikee**
ye sent once and *again* **twice** unto my *necessity* **need**.
17 Not because I *desire* **seek** a gift:
but I *desire* **seek** fruit that may *abound* **superabound**
to your *account* **word**.
18 But I have all, and *abound* **superabound**:
I am **filled** full,
having received of Epaphroditus
the things which were sent **those** from you,
an odour of a sweet smell **a wellfragranced fragrance**,
a sacrifice acceptable, well—pleasing to *God* **Elohim**.
19 But my *God* **Elohim** shall *supply* **fill full** all your need
according to his riches in glory
by Christ Jesus **in Messiah Yah Shua**.

SALUTES AND BENEDICTIONS

20 Now unto *God* **Elohim** and our Father be glory
for ever and ever **unto the eons of the eons**.
Amen.
21 Salute *every saint* **all the holy**
in *Christ Jesus* **Messiah Yah Shua**.
The brethren which are with me *greet* **salute** you.
22 All the *saints* **holy** salute you,
chiefly **especially**
they that are of *Caesar's* **the Kaisar's** household.
23 The *grace* **charism**
of our *Lord Jesus Christ* **Adonay Yah Shua Messiah**
be with you all.
Amen.

KEY TO INTERPRETING THE EXEGESES:
King James text is in regular type;
Text under exegeses is in oblique type;
Text of exegeses is in bold type.

SALUTATION

1 *Paul* **Paulos**,
an apostle of *Jesus Christ* **Yah Shua Messiah**
by **through** the will of *God* **Elohim**,
and *Timotheus* **Timo Theos** our brother,
2 To the *saints* **holy** and *faithful* **trustworthy** brethren
in *Christ* **Messiah** which are at Colosse:
Grace be **Charism** unto you, and *peace* **shalom**,
from *God* **Elohim** our Father
and *the Lord Jesus Christ* **Adonay Yah Shua Messiah**.

EUCHARIST TO ELOHIM

3 We *give thanks to God* **eucharistize Elohim**
and the Father of our
Lord Jesus Christ **Adonay Yah Shua Messiah**,
praying always for you,
4 Since we heard
of your *faith* **trust** in *Christ Jesus* **Messiah Yah Shua**,
and of the love which ye have to all the *saints* **holy**,
5 For the hope which is laid up for you
in *heaven* **the heavens**,
whereof ye heard *before* **previously**
in the word of the truth of the *gospel* **evangelism**;
6 Which is *come* **present** unto you,
exactly as it is in all the *world* **cosmos**;
and *bringeth forth* **beareth** fruit,
exactly as *it doth* also in you,
since **from** the day ye heard *of it*,
and knew the *grace* **charism** of *God* **Elohim** in truth:
7 **Exactly** As ye also learned of Epaphras
our *dear fellowservant* **beloved co—servant**,
who is for you
a *faithful* **trustworthy** minister of *Christ* **the Messiah**;
8 Who also *declared* **evidenced** unto us
your love in *the* Spirit.

PRAYER FOR KNOWLEDGE OF MESSIAH'S WILL

9 For this cause we also, *since* **from** the day we heard *it*,
do **pause** not *cease* to pray for you,
and to *desire* **ask** that ye might be filled **full**
with the knowledge of his will in all wisdom
and spiritual *understanding* **comprehension**;
10 That ye might walk worthy of *the Lord* **Adonay**
unto all pleasing,
being fruitful **fruitbearing** in every good work,
and *increasing* **growing** in the knowledge of *God* **Elohim**;
11 *Strengthened with* **Dynamized in** all *might* **power**,
according to *his glorious* **the** power **of his glory**,
unto all *patience* **endurance** and *longsuffering* **patience**
with *joyfulness* **cheer**;
12 *Giving thanks* **Eucharistizing** unto the Father,
which hath *made* **enabled** us *meet* to *be partakers* **impart**
of the inheritance of the *saints* **holy** in light:
13 Who hath *delivered* **rescued** us
from the *power* **authority** of darkness,
and hath *translated* **removed** us
into the *kingdom* **sovereigndom**
of *his dear Son* **the Son of his love**:

YAH SHUA, REDEEMER

14 In whom we have redemption through his blood,
even the forgiveness of sins:

YAH SHUA, ICON OF ELOHIM

15 Who is the *image* **icon** of the invisible *God* **Elohim**,
the firstborn of *every creature* **all creation**:

YAH SHUA, CREATOR

16 For *by* **in** him were all *things* created,
that are in *heaven* **the heavens**,
and that are *in* **upon the** earth,
visible and invisible,
whether *they be* thrones,
or dominions **whether lordships**,
or principalities **whether hierarchies**,
or powers **whether authorities**:
all *things* were created *by* **through** him,
and *for* **unto** him:
17 And he is before all *things*,
and *by* **in** him all *things* consist.
18 And he is the head of the body, the *church* **ecclesia**:
who is the beginning, the firstborn from the dead;
that in all *things* he might *have* **be** the preeminence.
19 *For it pleased the Father that*
For in him *should* all fulness **is well—approved to** dwell;
Colossians 2:9
20 And, *having made peace* **did shalam**
through the blood of his *cross* **stake**,
by **through** him to **fully** reconcile all *things* unto himself;
by **through** him, *I say*,
whether *they be things in* upon the earth,
or things in heaven **whether in the heavens**.
21 And you,
that were sometime **being formerly** alienated
and enemies in *your* mind *by wicked* **in evil** works,
yet now hath he **fully** reconciled
22 In the body of his flesh through death,
to present you holy and *unblameable* **unblemished**
and *unreproveable* **unaccusable** in his sight:
23 If **indeed** ye *continue* **abide** in the *faith* **trust**
grounded **founded** and *settled* **grounded**,
and *be not moved away* **not transported**
from the hope of the *gospel* **evangelism**,
which ye have heard,
and which was preached *to every creature* **in all creation**
which is under heaven;
whereof I *Paul am made* **Paulos became** a minister;
24 Who now *rejoice* **cheer** in my sufferings for you,
and *fill up* **supplement** that which *is behind* **lacketh**
of the *afflictions* **tribulations** of *Christ* **the Messiah**
in my flesh
for his body's sake, which is the *church* **ecclesia**:
25 Whereof I *am made* **became** a minister,
according
to the *dispensation* **administration** of *God* **Elohim**
which is given to me *for* **unto** you,
to fulfil the word of *God* **Elohim**;
26 *Even* the mystery which hath been *hid* **secreted**
from *ages* **the eons** and from **the** generations,
but now is *made* manifest to his *saints* **holy**:
27 To whom *God would* **Elohim willeth to** make known
what is the riches of the glory of this mystery
among the *Gentiles* **goyim**;
which is *Christ* **Messiah** in you, the hope of glory:
28 Whom we *preach* **evangelize**,
warning every man **reminding all humanity**,
and *teaching every man* **doctrinating all humanity**
in all wisdom;
that we may present *every man* **all humanity**
perfect **complete** in *Christ Jesus* **Messiah Yah Shua**:
29 Whereunto I also labour,
striving **agonizing** according to his *working* **energizing**,
which *worketh* **energizeth dynamis** in me *mightily*.

2 For I *would* **will** that ye knew
what great conflict **how much agony** I have for you,
and *for* them at Laodicea,
and *for* as many as have not seen my face in the flesh;
2 That their hearts might be *comforted* **consoled**,
being *knit together* **coalesced** in love,
and unto all riches of the full *assurance* **bearance**
of *understanding* **comprehension**,
to the *acknowledgement* **knowledge**
of the mystery of *God* **Elohim**,
and of the Father, and of *Christ* **the Messiah**;
3 In whom are *hid* **secreted**
all the treasures of wisdom and knowledge.
4 And this I *say* **word**,
lest any *man* **one** should *beguile* **delude** you
with enticing **in persuasive** words.
5 For though I be absent in the flesh,
yet am I with you in *the* spirit,
joying **cheering** and *beholding* **seeing** your order,
and the *stedfastness* **solidity**
of your *faith* **trust** in *Christ* **Messiah**.
6 As ye have therefore *received* **taken**
Christ Jesus the Lord **the Messiah Yah Shua Adonay**,
so walk ye in him:
7 Rooted and built up in him,
and stablished in the *faith* **trust**,
exactly as ye have been *taught* **doctrinated**,
abounding **superabounding** therein

with thanksgiving **in eucharist**.
8 *Beware* **See to it** lest any *man spoil* **one seduce** you
through philosophy and vain *deceit* **delusion**,
after the tradition of *men* **humanity**,
after the *rudiments* **elements** of the *world* **cosmos**,
and not after *Christ* **Messiah**.

MESSIAH, THE FULNESS OF DEITY

9 For in him
dwelleth all the fulness of *the Godhead* **Deity** bodily.
Colossians 1:19
10 And ye are *complete* **fulfilled** in him,
which is the head
of all *principality* **hierarchy** and *power* **authority**:
11 In whom also
ye are circumcised with the circumcision
made without hands **not handmade**,
in *putting off* **stripping** the body of the sins of the flesh
by **in** the circumcision of *Christ* **the Messiah**:
12 *Buried with him* **Co—buried** in baptism,
wherein also
ye are *risen with him* **co—raised** through the *faith* **trust**
of the *operation* **energizing** of *God* **Elohim**,
who hath raised him from the dead.
13 And you, being dead in your *sins* **backslidings**
and the uncircumcision of your flesh,
hath he *quickened together with him* **co—enlivened**,
having *forgiven* **granted** you **charism**
all trespasses **for all your backslidings**;
14 *Blotting* **Wiping** out
the *handwriting* **handscribing** of *ordinances* **dogmas**
that was against us,
which was *contrary* **opposed** to us,
and took it out of the *way* **midst**,
nailing **spiking** it to his *cross* **stake**;
15 *And* having *spoiled* **stripped**
principalities **hierarchies** and *powers* **authorities**,
he *made a shew of* **exposed** them *openly* **boldly**,
triumphing over them in it.

WARNINGS

16 Let no *man* **one** therefore judge you
in *meat* **food**, or in drink,
or in *respect of an holyday* **apportioning a celebration**,
or of the new moon, or of the *sabbath days* **shabbaths**:
17 Which are a shadow
of *things to come* **the about to be**;
but the body is of *Christ* **the Messiah**.
18 Let no *man beguile* **one defraud** you
of your reward in a voluntary **of doing his will**
humility **in humblemindedness**
and *worshipping* **ceremonials** of angels,
intruding into those *things* which he hath not seen,
vainly puffed up by *his fleshly* **the** mind **of his flesh**,
19 And not *holding* **empowering** the Head,
from which *all* the **whole** body
by **through** joints and *bands* **bonds**
having *nourishment ministered* **been supplied**,
and *knit together* **co—alesced**,
increaseth **groweth**
with the *increase* **growth** of *God* **Elohim**.
20 *Wherefore* **Therefore**
if ye be dead with *Christ* **the Messiah**
from the *rudiments* **elements** of the *world* **cosmos**,
why, as though living in the *world* **cosmos**,
are ye *subject to ordinances* **dogmatized**,
21 (Touch not; taste not; *handle* **finger** not;
22 Which all are to perish with the *using* **consuming**;)
after the *commandments* **misvoth** and doctrines
of *men* **humanity**?
23 Which *things* have indeed a *shew* **word** of wisdom
in will *worship* **ceremony**,
and *humility* **humblemindedness**,
and neglecting of the body;
not in any honour to the *satisfying* **gratifying** of the flesh.

ON THE HOLY LIFE

3 If ye then be *risen* **co—raised** with *Christ* **the Messiah**,
seek those *things* which are above,
where *Christ* **the Messiah** sitteth
on **by** the right *hand* of *God* **Elohim**.
2 Set your *affection on things* **thought** above,
not *on things on* **upon** the earth.
3 For ye are dead,
and your life is *hid* **secreted** with *Christ* **the Messiah**
in *God* **Elohim**.
4 When *Christ* **ever the Messiah**, *who is* our life,
shall *appear* **be manifested**,
then shall ye also *appear* **be manifested**
with him in glory.

STRIPPING THE OLD HUMANITY

5 *Mortify* **Deaden** therefore
your members which are upon the earth;
fornication **whoredom**, *uncleanness* **impurity**,
inordinate affection **passion**, evil *concupiscence* **panting**,
and *covetousness* **avarice**, which is idolatry:
6 *For* **Through** which *things' sake*
the wrath of *God* **Elohim**
cometh on the *children* **sons** of *disobedience* **distrust**:
7 In the which ye also walked *some time* **formerly**,
when ye lived in them.
8 But now ye also put off all these;
anger **wrath**, *wrath* **fury**, malice, blasphemy,
filthy communication **shameful words** out of your mouth.
9 Lie not one to another,
seeing that ye have
put off **stripped** the old *man* **humanity**
with his *deeds* **functions**;
10 And have *put on* **endued** the new *man*,
which is renewed in knowledge
after the *image* **icon** of him that created him:
11 Where there is neither
Greek **Hellene** nor *Jew* **Yah Hudiy**,
circumcision nor uncircumcision, Barbarian, Scythian,
bond **servant** nor *free* **liberated**:
but *Christ* **Messiah** is all, and in all.

ENDUING THE NEW HUMANITY

12 *Put on* **Endue** therefore,
as the *elect* **select** of *God* **Elohim**, holy and beloved,
bowels **spleens** of *mercies* **compassions**, kindness,
humbleness of mind **humblemindedness**,
meekness, *longsuffering* **patience**;
13 *Forbearing* **Tolerating** one another,
and *forgiving* **granting** one another **charism**,
if **ever** any *man* **one** have *a quarrel* **blame** against any:
even **exactly** as *Christ* **the Messiah**
forgave you **hath granted you charism**,
so **thus** also *do* ye.
14 And above all these, *things put on charity* **love**,
which is the bond of *perfectness* **completion**.
15 And let the *peace* **shalom** of *God* **Elohim**
rule **umpire** in your hearts,
to the which also ye are called in one body;
and be ye *thankful* **eucharistic**.
16 Let the word of *Christ* **the Messiah**
dwell in **indwell** you richly in all wisdom;
teaching **doctrinating** and *admonishing* **reminding**
one another **yourselves**
in psalms and hymns and spiritual *songs* **odes**,
singing *with grace* **in charism** in your hearts
to *the Lord* **Adonay**.
17 And whatsoever ye **ever** do in word or *deed* **in work**,
do all in the name of *the Lord Jesus* **Adonay Yah Shua**,
giving thanks **eucharistizing**
to *God* **Elohim** and the Father
by **through** him.
18 *Wives* **Women**,
submit **subjugate** yourselves
unto your own *husbands* **men**,
as *it is fit* **proper** in *the Lord* **Adonay**.
19 *Husbands* **Men**,
love *your wives* **the women**,
and be not *bitter* **embittered** against them.
20 Children,
obey *your* **the** parents in all *things*:
for this is well pleasing unto the *Lord* **Adonay**.
21 Fathers,
provoke **excite** not your children *to anger*,
lest they be *discouraged* **apathetic**.
22 Servants,
obey in all *things*
your *masters* **adoniym** according to the flesh;
not *with* **in** eyeservice, as *menpleasers* **humanitypleasers**;

but in *singleness* **liberality** of heart,
fearing God **awing Elohim**:
23 And whatsoever ye do,
do it heartily **work from the soul**, as to *the Lord* **Adonay**,
and not unto *men* **humanity**;
24 Knowing that of *the Lord* **Adonay**
ye shall *receive* **take** the *reward* **recompense**
of the inheritance:
for ye serve *the Lord Christ* **Adonay Messiah**.
25 But he that *doeth wrong* **injureth**
shall receive for the *wrong* **injury**
which he hath done:
and there is no *respect of persons* **partiality**.

4 *Masters* **Adoniym**,
give **present** unto *your* servants
that which is just and equal;
knowing that
ye also have *a Master Lord* **an Adonay**
in *heaven* **the heavens**.
2 Continue in prayer,
and watch in the same *with thanksgiving* **in eucharist**;
3 *Withal* **Simultaneously** praying also for us,
that *God would* **Elohim should** open unto us
a door **an opening/a portal** of *utterance* **the word**,
to speak the mystery of *Christ* **the Messiah**,
for which I am also in bonds:
4 That I may *make it* manifest, as I *ought to* **must** speak.
5 Walk in wisdom toward them that are without,
redeeming **marketing** the *time* **season**.
6 Let your *speech* **word** be alway *with grace* **in charism**,
seasoned with salt,
that ye may know
how ye *ought to* **must** answer *every man* **each one**.

FINAL SALUTES

7 All my state
shall Tychicus *declare* **maketh known** unto you,
who is a beloved brother,
and a *faithful* **trustworthy** minister
and *fellowservant* **co—servant** in *the Lord* **Adonay**:
8 Whom I have sent unto you
for **unto** the same *purpose*,
that he might know **about** your estate,
and *comfort* **console** your hearts;
9 With Onesimus,
a *faithful* **trustworthy** and beloved brother,
who is *one* of you.
They shall make known unto you
all *things* which are *done* here.
10 Aristarchus my *fellowprisoner* **co—captive** saluteth you,
and *Marcus* **Markos**,
sister's son **cousin** to *Barnabas* **Bar Nabi**,
(*touching* **about** whom
ye *received commandments* **took misvoth**:
if **ever** he come unto you, receive him;)
11 And *Jesus* **Yah Shua**, which is *called* **worded** Justus,
who are **being** of the circumcision.
These only are my *fellowworkers* **co—workers**
unto the *kingdom* **sovereigndom** of *God* **Elohim**,
which have *been* **become**
a *comfort* **consolation** unto me.
12 Epaphras, who is *one* of you,
a servant of *Christ* **Messiah**, saluteth you,
always *labouring fervently* **agonizing** for you in prayers,
that ye may stand
perfect **complete** and *complete* **fulfilled**
in all the will of *God* **Elohim**.
13 For I *bear* **witness of** him *record*,
that he hath a *great* **vast** zeal for you,
and them *that are* in Laodicea, and them in Hierapolis.
14 *Luke* **Loukas**, the beloved *physician* **healer**,
and Demas, *greet* **salute** you.
15 Salute the brethren which are in Laodicea,
and Nymphas,
and the *church* **ecclesia** which is in his house.
16 And when **ever** this epistle is read among you,
cause that it be read also
in the *church* **ecclesia** of the Laodiceans;
and that ye likewise read *the epistle* **that** from Laodicea.
17 And say to Archippus, *Take heed* **See** to the ministry
which thou hast *received* **taken** in *the Lord* **Adonay**,
that thou fulfil it.
18 The salutation by the hand of me *Paul* **Paulos**.
Remember my bonds.
Grace **Charism** be with you.
Amen.

1 THESSALONIKEUS 1—3

KEY TO INTERPRETING THE EXEGESES:
King James text is in regular type;
Text under exegeses is in oblique type;
Text of exegeses is in bold type.

SALUTATION

1 *Paul* **Paulos**, and Silvanus, and *Timotheus* **Timo Theos**,
unto the *church* **ecclesia**
of *the Thessalonians* **Thessalonikeus**
which is in God the **in Elohim** Father
and *in the Lord Jesus Christ* **Adonay Yah Shua Messiah**:
Grace be **Charism** unto you, and *peace* **shalom**,
from *God* **Elohim** our Father,
and *the Lord Jesus Christ* **Adonay Yah Shua Messiah**.

PAULOS' EUCHARIST

2 We *give thanks* **eucharistize** to *God* **Elohim**
always for you all,
making *mention* **rememberance** of you in our prayers;
3 Remembering *without ceasing* **unceasingly**
your work of *faith* **trust**,
and labour of love, and *patience* **endurance** of hope
in our *Lord Jesus Christ* **Adonay Yah Shua Messiah**,
in *the sight* **front** of *God* **Elohim** and our Father;
4 Knowing, brethren beloved,
your *election of God* **selection by Elohim**.
5 For our *gospel came* **evangelism became** not unto you
in word only,
but also in *power* **dynamis**, and in the Holy *Ghost* **Spirit**,
and in much *assurance* **fullbearance**;
exactly as ye know what manner of men
we *were* **became** among you for your sake.
6 And ye became *followers* **mimickers** of us,
and of *the Lord* **Adonay**,
having received the word in much *affliction* **tribulation**,
with *joy* **cheer** of the Holy *Ghost* **Spirit**.
7 So that ye *were ensamples* **became types**
to all that *believe* **trust** in Macedonia and Achaia.
8 For from you *sounded out* **echoed forth**
the word of *the Lord* **Adonay**
not only in Macedonia and Achaia,
but also in every place
your *faith to God–ward* **trust toward Elohim**
is *spread abroad* **gone forth**;
so that we need not to speak *any thing* **aught**.
9 For they themselves *shew* **evangelize** of us
what manner of *entering in* **entrance** we had unto you,
and how ye turned **around** to *God* **Elohim** from idols
to serve the living and true *God* **Elohim**;
10 And to *wait for* **await** his Son
from *heaven* **the heavens**,
whom he raised from the dead, *even Jesus* **Yah Shua**,
which *delivered* **rescued** us from the wrath to come.

THE MINISTRY OF THESSALONIKEUS

2 For yourselves, brethren,
know our entrance in unto you,
that it *was* **became** not in vain:
2 But even after that we had suffered *before* **previously**,
and were *shamefully entreated* **insulted**,
exactly as ye know, at Philippi,
we were bold in our *God* **Elohim** to speak unto you
the *gospel* **evangelism** of *God* **Elohim**
with **in** much *contention* **agony**.
3 For our *exhortation* **consolation**
was not of *deceit* **seduction**,
nor of *uncleanness* **impurity**, nor in *guile* **deceit**:
4 But **exactly** as we were *allowed* **proofed** of *God* **Elohim**
to be *put in trust* **entrusted** with the *gospel* **evangelism**,
even so **thus** we speak;
not as pleasing *men* **humanity**,
but *God* **Elohim**, which *trieth* **proofeth** our hearts.
5 For neither *at any time* **ever**
used **became** we *flattering* **in fawning** words,
exactly as ye know,
nor **in** a *cloke* **pretext** of *covetousness* **avarice**;
God is witness **Elohim witnesseth**:
6 Nor of *men* **humanity** sought we glory,
neither of you, nor *yet* of others,
when we *might* **could** have been burdensome,
as the apostles of *Christ* **Messiah**.
7 But we *were* **became** gentle among you,
even as a nurse **ever** cherisheth her children:
8 *So being affectionately desirous* **Thus yearning** of you,
we *were willing* **well—approved**
to have imparted unto you,
not the *gospel* **evangelism** of *God* **Elohim** only,
but also our own souls,
because ye *were dear* **became beloved** unto us.
9 For ye remember, brethren, our labour and *travail* **toil**:
for *labouring* **working** night and day,
because **that** we *would* **should** not
be chargeable unto **overburden** any of you,
we preached unto you
the *gospel* **evangelism** of *God* **Elohim**.
10 Ye are witnesses, and *God* **Elohim** *also*,
how *holily* **mercifully** and justly and unblameably
we *behaved ourselves* **became**
among you that *believe* **trust**:
11 **Exactly** As ye know
how we *exhorted* **besought** and *comforted* **consoled**,
and *charged every* **witnessed each** one of you,
as a father *doth* his children,
12 That ye *would* **should witness**
to walk worthy of *God* **Elohim**,
who hath called you
unto his *kingdom* **sovereigndom** and glory.
13 For this cause also *thank* **eucharistize** we *God* **Elohim**
without ceasing **unceasingly**,
because, when ye *received* **took** the word of *God* **Elohim**
which ye heard of us,
ye received it not as the word of *men* **humanity**,
but **exactly** as it **truly** is *in truth*, the word of *God* **Elohim**,
which *effectually worketh* **energizeth** also in you
that *believe* **trust**.
14 For ye, brethren, became *followers* **mimickers**
of the *churches* **ecclesiae** of *God* **Elohim**
which **being** in *Judaea* **Yah Hudah**
are in Christ Jesus **being in Messiah Yah Shua**:
for ye also have suffered **in** like **manner** *things*
of **by** your own *countrymen* **co—scions**,
even **exactly** as they have of the *Jews* **Yah Hudiym**:
15 Who both *killed* **slaughtered**
the Lord Jesus **Adonay Yah Shua**, and their own prophets,
and have persecuted us;
and they please not *God* **Elohim**,
and are contrary to all *men* **humanity**:
16 Forbidding us to speak to the *Gentiles* **goyim**
that they might be saved, to fill *up* **full** their sins alway:
for the wrath *is come* **arrived** upon them
to *the uttermost* **completion**.
17 But we, brethren,
being *taken* **orphaned away** from *you* **your face**
for a *short time in presence* **season of an hour**,
not in heart,
endeavoured the more abundantly
being more superabundantly diligent
to see your face *with great desire* **in much panting**.
18 Wherefore
we *would have* **had willed to** come unto you,
even **indeed** I *Paul* **Paulos**,
once and *again* **twice**; but Satan hindered us.
19 For what is our hope, or *joy* **cheer**,
or *crown* **wreath** of *rejoicing* **boasting**?
Are **Or** not **indeed** even ye in *the presence* **front**
of our *Lord Jesus Christ* **Adonay Yah Shua Messiah**
at his *coming* **parousia**?
20 For ye are our glory and *joy* **cheer**.

THE HOLINESS OF THE TRUSTER

3 Wherefore when we could no longer *forbear* **endure**,
we *thought it good* **well—approved**
to be left at Athens alone;
2 And sent *Timotheus* **Timo Theos**, our brother,
and minister of *God* **Elohim**,
and our *fellowlabourer* **co—worker**
in the *gospel* **evangelism** of *Christ* **the Messiah**,
to establish you, and to *comfort* **console** you
concerning your *faith* **trust**:
3 That no *man* **one** should be *moved* **shaken**
by **in** these *afflictions* **tribulations**:
for yourselves know that we are *appointed* **set** thereunto.

1 THESSALONIKEUS 3—5

4 For verily, when we were with you,
we *told you before* **forespoke**
that we should *suffer tribulation* **be tribulated**;
even **exactly** as it *came to pass* **became**, and ye know.
5 For this cause,
when **even** I could no longer *forbear* **endure**,
I sent to know your *faith* **trust**,
lest *by some means* **somehow**
the *tempter* **tester** have *tempted* **tested** you,
and our labour be *in vain* **void**.
6 But now when *Timotheus* **Timo Theos**
came from you unto us,
and *brought us good tidings* **evangelized**
of your *faith* **trust** and *charity* **love**,
and that ye have good remembrance of us always,
desiring greatly **yearning** to see us,
exactly as we also *to see* you:
7 Therefore, brethren,
we were *comforted* **consoled** over you
in all our *affliction* **tribulation** and *distress* **necessity**
by **through** your *faith* **trust**:
8 For now we live,
if **ever** ye stand *fast* **firm** in *the Lord* **Adonay**.
9 For what *thanks* **eucharist**
can we *render* **recompense** to *God* **Elohim** *again* for you,
for all the *joy* **cheer** wherewith we *joy* **cheer** for your sakes
before **in front of** our *God* **Elohim**;
10 Night and day
praying exceedingly **petitioning superabundantly**
that we might see your face,
and might prepare
that which is lacking in your *faith* **trust**?
11 Now *God* **Elohim** himself and our Father,
and our *Lord Jesus Christ* **Adonay Yah Shua Messiah**,
direct our way unto you.
12 And *the Lord* **Adonay** make you to
increase **superabound** and *abound* **superabound**
in love one *toward* **unto** another,
and *toward* **unto** all *men*,
even **exactly** as we *do toward* **unto** you:
13 *To the end* **That** he may stablish your hearts
unblameable **unaccusable** in holiness
before God **in front of Elohim**, even our Father,
at the *coming* **parousia**
of our *Lord Jesus Christ* **Adonay Yah Shua Messiah**
with all his *saints* **holy**.

HOLINESS OVER IMMORALITY

4 *Furthermore* **Finally** then we beseech you, brethren,
and *exhort* **beseech**
you *by the Lord Jesus* **in Adonay Yah Shua**,
that **exactly** as ye have *received* **taken** of us
how ye *ought to* **must** walk and to please *God* **Elohim**,
so **that** ye *would abound* **should superabound**
more and more.
2 For ye know
what *commandments* **evangelisms** we gave you
by the Lord Jesus **through Adonay Yah Shua**.
3 For this is the will of *God* **Elohim**,
even your *sanctification* **holiness**,
that ye should abstain from *fornication* **whoredom**:
4 That *every* **each** one of you should know
how to *possess* **acquire** his vessel
in *sanctification* **holiness** and honour;
5 Not in the *lust* **passion** of *concupiscence* **panting**,
even **exactly** as the *Gentiles* **goyim**
which know not *God* **Elohim**:
6 That no *man go beyond* **one overstep**
and defraud his brother in any matter:
because that *the Lord* **Adonay**
is the avenger *of* **concerning** all such,
exactly as we also have *forewarned* **foretold** you
and *testified* **witnessed**.
7 For *God* **Elohim** hath not called us
unto *uncleanness* **impurity**, but *unto* **in** holiness.
8 He therefore that *despiseth* **setteth aside**,
despiseth **setteth aside** not *man* **humanity**,
but *God* **Elohim**, who hath also given unto us his holy Spirit.
9 But *as touching* **concerning**
brotherly love **befriending brethren**
ye need not that I *write* **scribe** unto you:
for ye yourselves are *taught of God* **Elohim—doctrinated**
to love one another.
10 And indeed ye do it *toward* **unto** all the brethren
which are in all Macedonia:
but we beseech you, brethren,
that ye *increase* **superabound** more and more;
11 And that ye *study* **befriend esteeming** to be quiet,
and to *do* **transact** your own business,
and to work with your own hands,
exactly as we *commanded* **evangelized** you;
12 That ye may walk *honestly* **respectably**
toward them that are without,
and that ye may *have lack of nothing* **need naught**.

THE HOPE OF THE RESURRECTION

13 But I *would* **will that you** not
have you to be ignorant **be unknowing**, brethren,
concerning them which are asleep,
that ye sorrow not,
even **exactly** as *others* **the rest** which have no hope.
14 For if we *believe* **trust**
that *Jesus* **Yah Shua** died and rose *again*,
even so **thus** them also
which sleep *in Jesus* **through Yah Shua**
will God **shall Elohim** bring with him.
15 For this we *say* **word** unto you
by **in** the word of *the Lord* **Adonay**,
that we which are alive and *remain* **survive**
unto the coming of *the Lord* **Adonay**
shall not *prevent* **no way precede** them which are asleep.
16 For *the Lord* **Adonay** himself
shall descend from heaven
with **in** a *shout* **summons**,
with **in** the voice of the archangel,
and *with* **in** the trump of *God* **Elohim**:
and the dead in *Christ* **Messiah** shall rise first:
17 Then we which are alive and *remain* **survive**
shall be *caught up together* **seized simultaneously**
with them in the clouds,
to meet *the Lord* **Adonay** in the air:
and *so* **thus** shall we ever be with *the Lord* **Adonay**.
18 *Wherefore* **So then**
comfort one another *with* **in** these words.

1 Corinthians 15:35—38

THE DAY OF ADONAY

5 But *of* **concerning** the times and the seasons,
brethren, ye have no need that I *write* **scribe** unto you.
2 For yourselves know *perfectly* **precisely**
that the day of *the Lord* **Adonay**
so **thus** cometh as a thief in the night.
3 For when **ever** they shall *say* **word**,
peace **shalom** and *safety* **security**;
then *sudden destruction* **unexpected ruin**
cometh upon **standeth over** them,
exactly as travail
upon a woman *with child* **having in womb**;
and they shall not **no way** escape.
4 But ye, brethren, are not in darkness,
that that day should overtake you as a thief.
5 Ye are all the *children* **sons** of light,
and the *children* **sons** of the day:
we are not of the night, nor of darkness.
6 Therefore let us not sleep, as *do others* **the rest**;
but let us watch and be sober.
7 For they that sleep sleep in the night;
and they that *be drunken* **intoxicate**
are drunken **intoxicate** in the night.
8 But let us, *who are* **being** of the day, be sober,
putting on **enduing** the breastplate of *faith* **trust** and love;
and for an helmet, the hope of salvation.
9 For *God* **Elohim** hath not *appointed* **placed** us to wrath,
but to *obtain* **acquire** salvation *by* **through**
our *Lord Jesus Christ* **Adonay Yah Shua Messiah**,
10 Who died for us,
that, whether we *wake* **watch**,
or **whether we** sleep,
we should live *together* **simultaneously** with him.

1 THESSALONIKEUS 5

11 Wherefore
comfort yourselves together **console one another**,
and edify one another, even as also ye do.

FINAL INSTRUCTIONS

12 And we *beseech* **ask** you, brethren,
to know them which labour among you,
and *are* **preside** over you in *the Lord* **Adonay**,
and *admonish* **remind** you;
13 And to esteem them
very highly **more superabundantly** in love
for their work's sake.
And be at peace **Shalam** among yourselves.
14 Now we *exhort* **beseech** you, brethren,
warn **remind** them that are *unruly* **disorderly**,
comfort **console** the *feebleminded* **timidsouled**,
support the *weak* **frail**, be patient toward all *men*.
15 See that *none* **not any one**
render **give back** evil for evil unto any *man* **one**;
but ever *follow* **pursue** that which is good,
both *among yourselves* **unto one another**,
and to *all men* **every one**.
16 *Rejoice evermore* **Cheer always**.
17 Pray *without ceasing* **unceasingly**.
18 In *every thing give thanks* **all eucharistize**:
for this is the will of *God* **Elohim**
in *Christ Jesus concerning* **Messiah Yah Shua unto** you.
19 Quench not the Spirit.
20 *Despise* **Belittle** not prophesyings.
21 *Prove* **Proof** all *things*; hold fast that which is good.
22 Abstain from all *appearance* **semblance** of evil.

TRIUNE HUMANITY

23 And the *very God* **selfsame Elohim** of *peace* **shalom**
sanctify **hallow** you *wholly* **completely**;
and *I pray God* your whole spirit and soul and body
be *preserved* **guarded** blameless
unto **in** the *coming* **parousia**
of our *Lord Jesus Christ* **Adonay Yah Shua Messiah**.
24 *Faithful* **Trustworthy** is he that calleth you,
who also *will* **shall** do it.
25 Brethren, pray for us.

FINAL SALUTES AND BENEDICTION

26 *Greet* **Salute** all the brethren *with* **in** an holy kiss.
27 *I charge* **oath** you by *the Lord* **Adonay**
that this epistle be read unto all the holy brethren.
28 The *grace* **charism**
of our *Lord Jesus Christ* **Adonay Yah Shua Messiah**
be with you.
Amen.

2 THESSALONIKEUS 1, 2

KEY TO INTERPRETING THE EXEGESES:
King James text is in regular type;
Text under exegeses is in oblique type;
Text of exegeses is in bold type.

SALUTATION

1 *Paul* **Paulos**, and Silvanus, and *Timotheus* **Timo Theos**,
unto the *church* **ecclesia**
of *the Thessalonians* **Thessalonikeus**
in *God* **Elohim** our Father
and *the Lord Jesus Christ* **Adonay Yah Shua Messiah**:
2 *Grace* **Charism** unto you, and *peace* **shalom**,
from *God* **Elohim** our Father
and *the Lord Jesus Christ* **Adonay Yah Shua Messiah**.

PAULOS' EUCHARIST

3 We are *bound* **indebted**
to *thank God* **eucharistize Elohim** always for you,
brethren,
exactly as it is *meet* **worthy**,
because that your *faith* **trust**
groweth exceedingly **increaseth greatly**,
and the *charity* **love** of *every* **each** one of you all
toward each other *aboundeth* **superaboundeth**;
4 So that we ourselves *glory* **boast** in you
in the *churches* **ecclesiae** of *God* **Elohim**
for your *patience* **endurance** and *faith* **trust**
in all your persecutions and tribulations that ye endure:
5 Which is *a manifest token* **an indication**
of the *righteous* **just** judgment of *God* **Elohim**,
that ye may be counted worthy
of the *kingdom* **sovereigndom** of *God* **Elohim**,
for which ye also suffer:
6 *Seeing it is a righteous thing* **If ever it be just**
with *God* **Elohim**
to recompense tribulation
to them that *trouble* **tribulate** you;
7 And to you who are *troubled* **tribulated,**
rest **relax** with us,
when the Lord Jesus shall be revealed
in the apocalypse of Adonay Yah Shua from heaven,
with his *mighty* angels **of dynamis**,
8 In flaming fire *taking* **giving** vengeance
on them that know not *God* **Elohim**,
and that obey not the *gospel* **evangelism**
of our *Lord Jesus Christ* **Adonay Yah Shua Messiah**:
9 Who shall be *punished* **penalized in judgment**
with *everlasting destruction* **eternal ruin**
from the *presence* **face** of *the Lord* **Adonay**,
and from the glory of his *power* **might**;
10 *When* **Whenever** he shall come
to be glorified in his *saints* **holy**,
and to be *admired* **marvelled**
in all them that *believe* **trust**
(because our *testimony* **witness** among you
was *believed* **trusted**) in that day.
11 *Wherefore* **Unto which** also we pray always for you,
that our *God* **Elohim**
would count **should deem** you worthy of this calling,
and fulfil all the *good pleasure* **well—approval**
of *his* goodness,
and the work of *faith with power* **trust in dynamis**:
12 That the name
of our *Lord Jesus Christ* **Adonay Yah Shua Messiah**
may be glorified in you, and ye in him,
according to the *grace* **charism** of our *God* **Elohim**
and *the Lord Jesus Christ* **Adonay Yah Shua Messiah**.

THE TORAH VIOLATOR

2 Now we *beseech* **ask** you, brethren,
by the *coming* **parousia**
of our *Lord Jesus Christ* **Adonay Yah Shua Messiah**,
and by our *gathering* **synagoguing** together unto him,
2 That ye be not *soon* **quickly** shaken *in* **of** mind,
or *be troubled* **lament**,
neither *by* **through** spirit, nor *by* **through** word,
nor *by letter* **through epistle** as from us,
as that the day of *Christ* **the Messiah** is *at hand* **present**.
3 Let no *man deceive* **one seduce** you
by **in** any *means* **manner**:
for that day shall not come **because**,

2 THESSALONIKEUS 2, 3

except **unless** there come
a falling away **an apostatizing** first,
and that *man* **human** of sin be *revealed* **unveiled**,
the son of *perdition* **destruction**;
4 **The adversary,** Who,
opposeth and exalteth **superciliously exalting** himself
above all that is *called God* **worded Elohim**,
or that is *worshipped* **venerated**;
so that he, as *God* **Elohim**,
sitteth in the *temple* **nave** of *God* **Elohim**,
shewing himself that he is *God* **Elohim**.
5 Remember ye not, that, *when I was* yet **being** with you,
I *told you* **worded** these *things* **unto you**?
6 And now ye know what *withholdeth* **holdeth back**
that he might be revealed **unto his being unveiled**
in his *time* **season**.
7 For the mystery of *iniquity* **torah violations**
doth already *work* **energizeth**:
only he *who now letteth will let* **holdeth back**
until he be *taken* out of *the way* **your midst**.
8 And then shall that *Wicked* **torah violator**
be *revealed* **unveiled**,
whom *the Lord* **Adonay** shall consume
with the spirit of his mouth,
and shall *destroy* **inactivate**
with the *brightness* **epiphany** of his *coming* **parousia**:
9 *Even him,* whose *coming* **parousia**
is after the *working* **energizing** of Satan
with **in** all *power* **dynamis**
and signs and lying *wonders* **omens**,
10 And *with* **in** all *deceivableness* **delusion**
of *unrighteousness* **injustice** in them that *perish* **destruct**;
because **for** they received not the love of the truth,
that they might be **unto their being** saved.
11 And for this cause *God* **Elohim** shall send them
strong delusion **an energized seduction**,
that they should *believe* **trust** a lie:
12 That they all might be *damned* **judged**
who *believed* **trusted** not the truth,
but *had pleasure* **well-approved**
in unrighteousness **injustice**.
13 But we are *bound* **indebted** to *give thanks* **eucharistize**
alway to *God* **Elohim** for you,
brethren beloved of *the Lord* **Adonay**,
because *God* **Elohim** hath from the beginning
chosen you to salvation
through sanctification **in holiness** of the Spirit
and *belief* **trust** of the truth:
14 Whereunto he called you
by **through** our *gospel* **evangelism**,
to the *obtaining* **acquiring** of the glory
of our *Lord Jesus Christ* **Adonay Yah Shua Messiah**.
15 Therefore, brethren, stand *fast* **firm**,
and *hold* **empower** the traditions
which ye have been *taught* **doctrinated**,
whether *by* **through** word,
or **whether through** our epistle.
16 Now our
Lord Jesus Christ **Adonay Yah Shua Messiah** himself,
and *God* **Elohim**, even our Father, which hath loved us,
and hath given us *everlasting* **eternal** consolation
and good hope *through grace* **in charism**,
17 *Comfort* **Console** your hearts,
and stablish you in every good word and work.

PAULOS' PETITION FOR PRAYER

3 Finally, brethren, pray for us,
that the word of *the Lord* **Adona**
may *have free course* **run**,
and be glorified, even as *it is* with you:
2 And that we may be *delivered* **rescued** from
unreasonable **inordinate** and *wicked men* **evil humanity**:
for all *men* have not *faith* **trust**.
3 But *the Lord* **Adonay** is *faithful* **trustworthy**,
who shall *stablish* **establish** you,
and *keep* **guard** you from evil.
4 And we have confidence in *the Lord* **Adonay**
touching **toward** you,
that ye both do and *will* **shall** do *the things*
that which we *command* **evangelize** you.
5 And *the Lord* **Adonay** direct your hearts
into the love of *God* **Elohim**,
and into the *patient waiting* **endurance**
for Christ **of the Messiah**.
6 Now we *command* **evangelize** you, brethren,
in the name
of our *Lord Jesus Christ* **Adonay Yah Shua Messiah**,
that ye *withdraw yourselves* **abstain**
from every brother that walketh disorderly,
and not after the tradition which he *received* **took** of us.
7 For yourselves know
how ye *ought to follow* **must mimic** us:
for we behaved not ourselves disorderly among you;
8 Neither did we eat any *man's* **one's** bread for nought;
but *wrought* **working**
with **in** labour and *travail* **toil** night and day,
that we might not *be chargeable to* **overburden**
any of you:
9 Not because we have not *power* **authority**,
but to *make* **give** ourselves *an ensample* **a type** unto you
to *follow* **mimic** us.
10 For even when we were with you,
this we *commanded* **evangelized** you,
that if any *would* **willeth to** not work,
neither *should he* **let him** eat.
11 For we hear
that there are some which walk among you disorderly,
working not at all **not even working**,
but *are busybodies* **overworking**.
12 Now them that are such
we *command* **evangelize** and *exhort* **beseech**
by **through**
our *Lord Jesus Christ* **Adonay Yah Shua Messiah**,
that with quietness they work, and eat their own bread.
13 But ye, brethren, be not weary in *well* doing **good**.
14 And if any *man* **one**
obey not our word *by* **through** this epistle,
note **signify** that man,
and *have no company* **co—mingle not** with him,
that he may *be ashamed* **shame**.
15 Yet *count him* **deem** not as an enemy,
but *admonish him* **remind** as a brother.

BENEDICTION

16 Now *the Lord* **Adonay** of *peace* **shalom** himself
give you *peace* **shalom**
always by **through** all *means* **in any manner**.
The Lord **Adonay** be with you all.
17 The salutation of *Paul* **Paulos** with mine own hand,
which is the *token* **sign** in every epistle:
so **thus** I *write* **scribe**.
18 The *grace* **charism**
of our *Lord Jesus Christ* **Adonay Yah Shua Messiah**
be with you all.
Amen.

KEY TO INTERPRETING THE EXEGESES:
King James text is in regular type;
Text under exegeses is in oblique type;
Text of exegeses is in bold type.

SALUTATION

1 *Paul* **Paulos,**
an apostle of *Jesus Christ* **Yah Shua Messiah**
by the *commandment* **order** of *God* **Elohim** our Saviour,
and *Lord Jesus Christ* **Adonay Yah Shua Messiah,**
which is our hope;
2 Unto *Timothy* **Timo Theos,**
my *own son* **genuine child** in *the faith* **trust**:
Grace **Charism,** mercy, and *peace* **shalom,**
from *God* **Elohim** our Father
and *Jesus Christ* **Yah Shua Messiah** our *Lord* **Adonay.**

PAULOS' BESEECHES TIMO THEOS

3 **Exactly** As I besought thee to abide still at Ephesus,
when I went into Macedonia,
that thou mightest *charge* **evangelize** some
that they
teach no other doctrine **not doctrinate otherwise,**
4 Neither *give* heed *to fables* **myths**
and *endless* **unending** genealogies,
which *minister* **cause** questions,
rather than *Godly edifying* **administration of Elohim**
which is in *faith* **trust**: *so do.*
5 Now the *end* **completion**
of the *commandment* **evangelism**
is *charity* **love** out of a pure heart,
and *of* a good conscience,
and *of faith unfeigned* **trust unhypocritical**:
6 From which some having *swerved* **misaimed,**
have turned aside unto *vain jangling* **mataeology;**
7 *Desiring* **Having willed**
to be *teachers* **doctors** of the *law* **torah;**
understanding **comprehending**
neither what they *say* **word,**
nor *whereof* **about which** they **thoroughly** affirm.
8 But we know that the *law* **torah** is good,
if *a man* **ever anyone** use it *lawfully* **torahically;**
9 Knowing this, that the *law* **torah**
is not *made* **set** for *a righteous man* **the just,**
but for the
lawless **torah violator** and *disobedient* **insubordinate,**
for the *ungodly* **irreverent** and for sinners,
for *unholy* **unmercied** and profane,
for *murderers of fathers* **patriciders**
and *murderers of mothers* **matriciders,** for manslayers,
10 For whoremongers,
for *them that defile themselves with mankind* **homosexuals,**
for *menstealers* **men subduers,**
for liars, for *perjured persons* **perjurers,**
and if there be any other *thing*
that is *contrary* **adverse** to sound doctrine;
11 According to
the *glorious gospel* **evangelism of the glory**
of the blessed *God* **Elohim,**
which was *committed to my trust* **entrusted to me.**

PAULOS' PERSONAL WITNESS

12 And I *thank* **have charism**
Christ Jesus **to Messiah Yah Shua** our *Lord* **Adonay,**
who hath *enabled* **dynamized** me,
for that he *counted* **deemed** me *faithful* **trustworthy,**
putting me into the ministry;
13 *Who was before* **Previously being** a blasphemer,
and a persecutor, and *injurious* **insulter**:
but I *obtained mercy* **was mercied,**
because I did it *ignorantly* **unknowingly**
in *unbelief* **trustlessness.**
14 And the *grace* **charism** of our *Lord* **Adonay**
was *exceeding abundant* **superabundant**
with *faith* **trust** and love
which is in *Christ Jesus* **Messiah Yah Shua.**
15 This is a *faithful saying* **trustworthy word,**
and worthy of all acceptation,
that *Christ Jesus* **Messiah Yah Shua**
came into the *world* **cosmos** to save sinners;
of whom I am *chief* **first.**
16 *Howbeit* **Yet** for this cause
I *obtained mercy* **was mercied,**
that in me first *Jesus Christ* **Yah Shua Messiah**
might *shew forth* **indicate** all *longsuffering* **patience,**
for a *pattern* **prototype** to them
which should hereafter *believe* **trust** on him
to life *everlasting* **eternal.**

BENEDICTION

17 Now unto the *King eternal* **Sovereign of the eons,**
immortal **incorruptible,** invisible,
the only wise *God* **Elohim,**
be honour and glory
for ever and ever **unto the eons of the eons.**
Amen.

PAULOS' MANDATE

18 This *charge* **evangelism** I *commit* **set forth** unto thee,
son Timothy **child Timo Theos,**
according to the prophecies
which *went before on* **preceded upon** thee,
that thou *by* **in** them mightest war a good warfare;
19 Holding *faith* **trust,** and a good conscience;
which some having *put* **shoved** away
concerning *faith* **the trust**
have *made shipwreck* **shipwrecked**:
20 Of whom is Hymenaeus and Alexander;
whom I have delivered unto Satan,
that they may *learn* **discipline them** not to blaspheme.

ON PETITIONS, PRAYERS, INTERCESSIONS, AND EUCHARISTS

2 I *exhort* **beseech** therefore, that, first of all,
supplications **petitions,** prayers, intercessions,
and *giving of thanks* **eucharists,**
be made for all *men* **humanity;**
2 For *kings* **sovereigns,**
and for all *that are* **being** in *authority* **supremacy;**
that we may *lead* **pass through**
a *quiet* **tranquil** and *peaceable life* **quiet existence**
in all *Godliness* **reverence** and *honesty* **veneration.**
3 For this is good and acceptable
in the sight of *God* **Elohim** our Saviour;
4 Who *will* **willeth**
have **that** all *men* **humanity** to be saved,
and to come unto the knowledge of the truth.
5 For there is one *God* **Elohim,** and one mediator
between *God* **Elohim** and *men* **humanity,**
the *man Christ Jesus* **human Messiah Yah Shua;**
6 Who gave himself a *ransom* **redemption** for all,
to be *testified* **witnessed** in *due* **his own** time.
7 Whereunto I am *ordained* **placed** a preacher,
and an apostle,
(I *speak* **word** the truth in *Christ* **Messiah,** and lie not;)
a *teacher* **doctor** of the *Gentiles* **goyim**
in *faith* **trust** and *verity* **truth.**

ON COSMIC MANNERS AND COSTUME

8 I *will* therefore **will**
that men pray **in** every *where* **place,**
lifting up *holy* hands **of mercy,**
without **apart from** wrath and *doubting* **reasoning.**
9 In like manner also, that women adorn themselves
in *modest apparel* **cosmic costume,**
with *shamefacedness* **awe**
and *sobriety* **soundmindedness;**
not *with broided* **in braided** hair, or gold, or pearls,
or *costly array* **vastly precious garments;**
10 But (which *becometh* **befitteth** women
professing Godliness **pre—evangelizing Elohim—reverence)**
with **through** good works.
11 Let the woman learn in *silence* **quietness**
with **in** all subjection.
12 But I *suffer* **permit** not a woman to *teach* **doctrinate,**
nor to *usurp authority over* **dominate** the man,
but to be in *silence* **quietness.**
13 For Adam was first *formed* **molded,** then *Eve* **Havvah.**
14 And Adam was not *deceived* **deluded,**
but the woman being *deceived* **deluded**
was **became** in the transgression.
15 Notwithstanding
she shall be saved *in* **through** childbearing,
if **ever** they *continue* **abide** in *faith* **trust** and *charity* **love**
and holiness with *sobriety* **soundmindedness.**

ON THE EPISCOPATE

3 This is a *true saying* **trustworthy word**,
If *a man* **anyone**
desire **reach for** the *office of a bishop* **episcopate**,
he *desireth* **panteth after** a good work.
2 *A bishop* **An episcopate** then
must be *blameless* **unapprehendable**,
the *husband* **man** of one *wife* **woman**, *vigilant* **sober**,
sober **soundminded**, *of good behaviour* **cosmic**,
given to hospitality **befriend strangers**, *apt to teach* **didactic**;
3 *Not given to wine* **No winesop**, no striker,
not *greedy of filthy lucre* **avaricious**; but *patient* **gentle**,
not a brawler **amicable**, *not covetous* **unavaricious**;
4 One that *ruleth* **presideth** well **over** his own house,
having his children in subjection
with all *gravity* **veneration**;
5 (For if *a man* **one** know not
how to *rule* **preside over** his own house,
how shall he take care
of the *church* **ecclesia** of *God* **Elohim**?)
6 Not a *novice* **neophyte**,
lest being *lifted up with pride* **inflated**
he fall into the *condemnation* **judgment**
of *the devil* **Diabolos**.
7 Moreover he must have a good *report* **witness**
of them which are without;
lest he fall into reproach
and the snare of *the devil* **Diabolos**.

ON MINISTERS

8 Likewise *must the deacons* **ministers** be *grave* **venerant**,
not *doubletongued* **doubleworded**,
not *given to* **heeding** much wine,
not *greedy of filthy lucre* **avaricious**;
9 Holding the mystery of the *faith* **trust**
in a pure conscience.
10 And let these also first be proved;
then let them *use the office of a deacon* **minister**,
being *found blameless* **unimpeachable**.
11 *Even so* **Likewise**
must their *wives* **women** be *grave* **venerant**,
not *slanderers* **diabolic**, sober,
faithful **trustworthy** in all *things*.
12 Let the *deacons* **ministers**
be the *husbands* **men** of one *wife* **woman**,
ruling **presiding over** their children
and their own houses well.
13 For they that
have used the office of a deacon **minister** well
purchase **acquire** to themselves a good degree,
and *great* **vast** boldness in the *faith* **trust**
which is in *Christ Jesus* **Messiah Yah Shua**.
14 These *things write* **scribe** I unto thee,
hoping to come unto thee *shortly* **very quickly**:
15 But if **ever** I *tarry long* **delay**,
that thou mayest know
how thou *oughtest to* **must** behave thyself
in the house of *God* **El**,
which is the *church* **ecclesia** of the living *God* **Elohim**,
the pillar and ground of the truth.

PAULOS' MEGA PROFESSION

16 And *without controversy* **professedly**
great **mega** is the mystery of *Godliness* **reverence**:
God **Elohim** *was* manifest in *the* flesh,
justified in *the* Spirit, seen of angels,
preached *unto* **in** the *Gentiles* **goyim**,
believed on **trusted** in the *world* **cosmos**,
received up **taken** into glory.

PAULOS' PROPHESIES APOSTACY

4 Now the Spirit
speaketh expressly **wordeth rhetorically**,
that in the latter *times* **seasons**
some shall depart from the *faith* **trust**,
giving heed to **heeding** seducing spirits,
and doctrines of *devils* **demons**;
2 *Speaking lies* **Pseudologists** in hypocrisy;
having their conscience
seared with a hot iron **cauterized**;
3 Forbidding to marry,
and commanding to abstain from *meats* **food**,
which *God* **Elohim** hath created
to be *received* **partaken** with *thanksgiving* **eucharist**
of them which believe **by the trustworthy**
and **which** know the truth.
4 For every creature of *God* **Elohim** is good,
and *nothing* **naught** to be *refused* **cast away**,
if it be *received* **taken** with *thanksgiving* **eucharist**:
5 For it is *sanctified* **hallowed**
by **through** the word of *God* **Elohim**
and *prayer* **intercession**.

ON BEING A GOOD MINISTER

6 *If thou put* **Lay these before** the brethren
in remembrance of these things,
thou shalt be a good minister
of *Jesus Christ* **Yah Shua Messiah**,
nourished up **nurtured** in the words of *faith* **the trust**
and of good doctrine,
whereunto thou hast *attained* **closely followed**.
7 But *refuse* **shun**
profane and *old wives' fables* **anile myths**,
and exercise thyself *rather* unto *Godliness* **reverence**.
8 For bodily exercise *profiteth* **benefiteth** little:
but *Godliness is profitable* **reverence is** unto all *things*,
having *promise* **pre—evangelism** of the life that now is,
and of that which is to come.
9 This is a *faithful saying* **trustworthy word**
and worthy of all acceptation.
10 For *therefore* **thereunto**
we both labour and suffer reproach,
because we *trust* **hope** in the living *God* **Elohim**,
who is the Saviour of all *men* **humanity**,
specially of *those that believe* **the trustworthy**.
11 **Evangelize** These *things command*
and *teach* **doctrinate**.
12 Let no *man despise* **one disesteem** thy youth;
but be thou *an example* **a type**
of the *believers* **trustworthy**,
in word, in *conversation* **behaviour**, in *charity* **love**,
in spirit, in *faith* **trust**, in purity.
13 Till I come, *give attendance* **heed** to reading,
to *exhortation* **consolation**, to doctrine.

DISREGARD NOT THE CHARISMA

14 *Neglect* **Disregard** not the *gift* **charisma** that is in thee,
which was given thee *by* **through** prophecy,
with the laying on of the hands of the presbytery.
15 Meditate upon these *things*;
give thyself wholly to **be in** them;
that thy *profiting* **advancement**
may *appear to* **be manifest among** all.
16 *Take* heed unto thyself, and unto the doctrine;
continue **abide** in them:
for in doing this thou shalt both save thyself,
and them that hear thee.

ON ELDERS AND WIDOWS

5 Rebuke not an elder°,
but *intreat him* **beseech** as a father;
and the younger *men* as brethren;
2 The elder°° *women* as mothers;
the younger as sisters, *with* **in** all purity.
°masculine, °°feminine
3 Honour widows that are widows indeed.
4 But if any widow
have children or *nephews* **descendants**,
let them learn first *to shew piety* **reverence**
at **in his own** home,
and to *requite* **give back recompense**
to their *parents* **progenitors**:
for that is good and acceptable
before God **in sight of Elohim**.
5 Now she that is a widow indeed, and *desolate* **alone**,
trusteth **hopeth** in *God* **Elohim**,
and *continueth* **abideth**
in *supplications* **petitions** and prayers
night and day.
6 But she that *liveth in pleasure* **luxuriateth**
is dead while she liveth.
7 And **evangelize** these *things give in charge*,
that they may be *blameless* **unapprehendable**.
8 But if any provide not for his own,
and specially for those of his own house,
he hath denied the *faith* **trust**,

and is worse than *an infidel* **the trustless.**
9 Let not a widow be *taken into the number* **enrolled**
under threescore **at less than sixty** years *old,*
having *been* **become** the *wife* **woman** of one man,
10 *Well reported of for* **Witnessed in** good works;
if she have *brought up* **fostered** children,
if she have lodged strangers,
if she have washed the *saints'* feet **of the holy,**
if she have relieved the *afflicted* **tribulated,**
if she have diligently followed every good work.
11 But the younger widows *refuse* **shun:**
for when **ever** they *have begun to wax wanton* **sensualize**
against *Christ* **Messiah,** they will **to** marry;
12 Having *damnation* **judgment,**
because they have *cast off* **set aside** their first *faith* **trust.**
13 And *withal* **simultaneously** they learn to be idle,
wandering about *from house to house* **the houses;**
and not only idle,
but *tattlers* **babblers** also and *busybodies* **overworking,**
speaking *things* **that** which they *ought* **must** not.
14 I will therefore that the younger *women* marry,
bear children, *guide the house* **be housedespotes,**
give none *occasion* **opportunity**
to **cause** the adversary to speak *reproachfully* **abusively.**
15 For some are already turned aside after Satan.
16 If any *man* **trustworthy°**
or *woman that believeth* **trustworthy°°**
have widows, let them relieve them,
and let not the *church* **ecclesia** be *charged* **burdened;**
that it may relieve them that are widows indeed.
°masculine; °°feminine
17 Let the elders that *rule* **preside** well
be *counted* **deemed** worthy of double honour,
especially they who labour in the word and doctrine.
18 For the scripture *saith* **wordeth,**
Thou shalt not muzzle the ox that treadeth *out the corn.*
And, The *labourer* **worker** is worthy of his reward.
Deuteronomy 25:4, Loukas 10:7

ON RESOLVING ACCUSATIONS

19 Against an elder receive not an accusation,
but **unless except** before two or three witnesses.
20 Them that sin *rebuke before* **reprove in sight of** all,
that *others* **the rest** also may *fear* **awe.**
21 I *charge* **witness** thee *before God* **in sight of Elohim,**
and *the Lord Jesus Christ* **Adonay Yah Shua Messiah,**
and the *elect* **select** angels,
that thou *observe* **guard** these *things*
without preferring one before another
apart from prejudging,
doing *nothing* **naught** by *partiality* **prejudice.**
22 *Lay* **Place** hands suddenly on no *man* **one,**
neither *be partaker* **partake** of *other men's* **another's** sins:
keep **guard** thyself *pure* **hallowed.**
23 Drink no longer water,
but use a little wine for thy stomach's sake
and *thine often infirmities* **thy frequent frailties.**
24 Some *men's* **human's** sins
are *open beforehand* **preevident,**
going before **preceding** to judgment;
and some *men* they follow after.
25 Likewise also the good works *of some*
are *manifest beforehand* **preevidenced;**
and they that *are* **have** otherwise
cannot be *hid* **secreted.**

6 Let as many servants as are under the yoke
count **deem** their own *masters* **despotes**
worthy of all honour,
that the name of *God* **Elohim** and *his* doctrine
be not blasphemed.
2 And they
that have *believing masters* **trustworthy despotes,**
let them not *despise* **disesteem** them,
because they are brethren;
but rather *do them service* **in servitude,**
because they are *faithful* **trustworthy** and beloved,
partakers **supporters** of the *benefit* **good work.**
These *things teach* **doctrinate** and *exhort* **beseech.**

ON PSEUDO DOCTRINE

3 If any *man teach* **one doctrinate** otherwise,
and *consent* **cometh** not to *wholesome* **sound** words,
even the words
of our *Lord Jesus Christ* **Adonay Yah Shua Messiah,**
and to the doctrine
which is according to *Godliness* **reverence;**
4 He is *proud* **inflated,** knowing *nothing* **naught,**
but *doting* **is diseased** about questions
and *strifes of words* **logomachy,**
whereof *cometh* **becometh** envy, *strife* **contention,**
railings **blasphemies,** evil surmisings,
5 *Perverse disputings of men* **Human diatribes**
of corrupt minds,
and *destitute* **deprived** of the truth,
supposing **presuming**
that gain is Godliness **reverence to be gain:**
from such *withdraw thyself* **depart.**
6 But *Godliness* **reverence**
with *contentment* **selfcontentment**
is *great* **mega** gain.
7 For we brought *nothing* **naught** into this *world* **cosmos,**
and it is *certain* **evident**
we can *carry nothing out* **bring naught forth.**
8 And having *food* **sustenance** and *raiment* **covering**
let us be therewith *content* **satisfied.**
9 But they that will **to** be rich
fall into *temptation* **testing** and a snare,
and into many
foolish **mindless** and *hurtful lusts* **injurious pantings,**
which *drown men* **sink humanity**
in *destruction* **ruin** and *perdition* **destruction.**
10 For *the love of money* **befriending silver**
is the root of all evil:
which while some *coveted after* **reached for,**
they have *erred* **strayed** from the *faith* **trust,**
and pierced themselves through
with many *sorrows* **griefs.**
11 But thou, O *man* **humanity** of *God* **Elohim,**
flee these *things;*
and *follow after righteousness* **pursue justness,**
Godliness **reverence,** *faith* **trust,** love,
patience **endurance,** meekness.
12 *Fight* **Agonize** the good *fight* **agony** of *faith* **the trust,**
lay **take** hold on eternal life,
whereunto thou art also called,
and hast professed a good profession
before **in sight of** many witnesses.
13 I *give* **evangelize** thee *charge*
in the sight of *God* **Elohim,**
who *quickeneth* **enliveneth** all *things,*
and *before Christ Jesus* **Messiah Yah Shua,**
who before Pontius *Pilate* **Pilatos**
witnessed a good *confession* **profession;**
14 That thou *keep* **guard** this *commandment* **misvah**
without spot **unstained,**
unrebukeable **unapprehendable,**
until the *appearing* **epiphany**
of our *Lord Jesus Christ* **Adonay Yah Shua Messiah:**
15 Which in his *times* **seasons** he shall shew,
who is the blessed and only *Potentate* **Dynast,**
the *King* **Sovereign** of *kings* **reigners,**
and *Lord* **Adonay** of *lords* **adoniym;**
16 Who only hath *immortality* **athanasia,**
dwelling in the **unapproachable** light
which no man can approach unto;
whom no *man* **human** hath seen, nor can see:
to whom be honour and power *everlasting* **eternal.**
Amen.

ON WARNING THE RICH

17 *Charge* **Evangelize** them that are rich in this *world* **eon,**
that they be not highminded,
nor *trust* **hope** in uncertain riches,
but in the living *God* **Elohim,**
who *giveth* **presenteth** us richly all *things* to enjoy;
18 That they *do* **work** good,
that they be rich in good works,
ready to distribute **to share well,**
willing to communicate **to commune;**
19 *Laying up in store* **Treasuring** for themselves
a good foundation
against the time to come **unto the about to be,**
that they may *lay* **take** hold on eternal life.

FINAL MANDATE AND BENEDICTION

20 O *Timothy* **Timo Theos,**
keep **guard** that
which is *committed to thy trust* **laid by thee,**
avoiding **turning aside**
from profane and vain *babblings* **voices,**
and *oppositions* **the antithesis**
of *science falsely so called* **pseudonymed knowledge**:
21 Which some *professing* **pre—evangelizing**
have *erred* **misaimed** concerning the *faith* **trust**.
Grace **Charism** be with thee.
Amen.

KEY TO INTERPRETING THE EXEGESES:
King James text is in regular type;
Text under exegeses is in oblique type;
Text of exegeses is in bold type.

SALUTATION

1 *Paul* **Paulos,**
an apostle of *Jesus Christ* **Yah Shua Messiah**
by **through** the will of *God* **Elohim,**
according to the *promise* **pre—evangelism** of life
which is in *Christ Jesus* **Messiah Yah Shua,**
2 To *Timothy* **Timo Theos,** *my dearly* beloved *son* **child**:
Grace **Charism**, mercy, and *peace* **shalom,**
from *God* **Elohim** the Father
and *Christ Jesus* **Messiah Yah Shua** our *Lord* **Adonay.**
3 I *thank God* **have charism to Elohim,**
whom I *serve* **liturgize** from my *forefathers* **progenitors**
with **in** pure conscience,
that *without ceasing* **unceasingly**
I have remembrance *of* **concerning** thee
in my *prayers* **petitions** night and day;
4 *Greatly desiring* **Yearning** to see thee,
being mindful of **remembering** thy tears,
that I may be filled **full** with *joy* **cheer;**
5 *When I call to* **Taking** remembrance
the *unfeigned faith* **unhypocritical trust** that is in thee,
which *dwelt* first *in* **indwelt**
thy *grandmother* **mammy** Lois, and thy mother Eunice;
and I am *persuaded* **convinced** that in thee also.
6 *Wherefore* **For which cause**
I *put* **remind** thee *in remembrance*
that thou *stir up* **refire** the *gift* **charisma** of *God* **Elohim,**
which is in thee
by **through** the *putting* **laying** on of my hands.
7 For *God* **Elohim** hath not given us
the spirit of *fear* **cowardice;**
but of *power* **dynamis**, and of love, and of a sound mind.
8 Be not thou therefore ashamed
of the *testimony* **witness** of our *Lord* **Adonay,**
nor of me his prisoner:
but be thou *partaker of the afflictions* **a co—sufferer**
of the *gospel* **evangelism**
according to the *power* **dynamis** of *God* **Elohim;**
9 Who hath saved us, and called us with an holy calling,
not according to our works,
but according to
his own *purpose* **prothesis** and *grace* **charism,**
which was given us in *Christ Jesus* **Messiah Yah Shua**
before *the world began* **eternal time,**
10 But is now *made* manifest
by **through** the *appearing* **epiphany**
of our Saviour *Jesus Christ* **Yah Shua Messiah,**
who hath *abolished* **indeed inactivated** death,
and hath *brought* **enlightened** life and immortality *to light*
through the *gospel* **evangelism**:
11 Whereunto I am *appointed* **placed**
a preacher, and an apostle,
and a *teacher* **doctor** of the *Gentiles* **goyim.**
12 For the which cause I also suffer these *things*:
nevertheless **yet** I am not ashamed:
for I know whom I have *believed* **trusted,**
and am *persuaded* **convinced**
that he is able to *keep* **guard**
that which I have *committed* **surrendered** unto him
against **unto** that day.
13 Hold fast the *form* **prototype** of sound words,
which thou hast heard of me,
in *faith* **trust** and love
which is in *Christ Jesus* **Messiah Yah Shua.**
14 That good *thing*
which was *committed unto* **laid by** thee
keep by **guard through** the Holy *Ghost* **Spirit**
which *dwelleth in* **indwelleth** us.
15 This thou knowest,
that all they which are in Asia be turned away from me;
of whom are Phygellus and Hermogenes.
16 *The Lord* **Adonay** give mercy
unto the house of Onesiphorus;
for he oft refreshed me,
and was not ashamed of my *chain* **fetter**:
17 But, when he *was* **became** in Rome,

he sought me out very diligently, and found me.
18 *The Lord grant* **Adonay give** unto him
that he may find mercy of *the Lord* **Adonay** in that day:
and in *how many things* **as much as**
he ministered unto me at Ephesus,
thou knowest *very well* **better**.

ON ENDURING HARDSHIP

2 Thou therefore, my son,
be *strong* **dynamized** in the *grace* **charism**
that is in *Christ Jesus* **Messiah Yah Shua**.
2 And *the things* **those** that thou hast heard of me
among **through** many witnesses,
the same commit **set** thou **forth**
to *faithful men* **trustworthy humanity**,
who shall be *able* **ample** to *teach* **doctrinate** others also.
3 Thou therefore endure *hardness* **hardship**,
as a good *soldier* **warrior**
of *Jesus Christ* **Yah Shua Messiah**.
4 No *man* **one** that warreth entangleth himself
with the *affairs* **transactions** of *this life* **existence**;
that he may please him
who hath *chosen* **enlisted** him *to be a soldier*.
5 And if *a man* **ever anyone**
also strive **contend** for masteries,
yet is he not *crowned* **wreathed**,
except **unless** he *strive lawfully* **contend torahically**.
6 The *husbandman that laboureth must be first partaker*
cultivator must labor before partaking of the fruits.
7 *Consider* **Comprehend** what I *say* **word**;
and *the Lord* **indeed Adonay** give thee
understanding **comprehension** in all *things*.
8 Remember that *Jesus Christ* **Yah Shua Messiah**
of the *seed* **sperma** of David was raised from the dead
according to my *gospel* **evangelism**:
9 Wherein I *suffer trouble* **endure hardship**,
as an evil *doer* **worker**, *even* unto bonds;
but the word of *God* **Elohim** is not bound.
10 Therefore I endure all *things*
for the *elect's* **select's** sakes,
that they may also obtain the salvation
which is in *Christ Jesus* **Messiah Yah Shua**
with eternal glory.
11 It is a *faithful saying* **trustworthy word**:
For if we *be dead with him* **co—die**,
we shall also *live with him* **co—live**:
12 If we *suffer* **endure**,
we shall also *reign with him* **co—reign**:
if we deny *him*, he also *will* **shall** deny us:
13 If we *believe not* **distrust**,
yet he abideth *faithful* **trustworthy**:
he cannot deny himself.
14 Of these *things put* **remind** them *in remembrance*,
charging **witnessing**
them before the Lord **in the sight of Adonay**
that they *strive* **logomachize** not about words to no profit,
but to the *subverting* **catastrophe** of the hearers.
15 *Study* **Be diligent** to *shew* **present** thyself
approved unto *God* **Elohim**,
a *workman* **worker**,
that needeth not to be ashamed **unashamed**,
rightly dividing **straightcutting** the word of truth.
16 But *shun* **stand aloof**
from profane and vain *babblings* **voices**:
for they *will increase* **shall advance**
unto more *ungodliness* **irreverence**.
17 And their word *will eat* **shall pasture**
as *doth* a *canker* **gangrene**:
of whom is Hymenaeus and Philetus;
18 Who concerning the truth have *erred* **misaimed**,
saying **wording**
that the resurrection *is past* **hath** already **become**;
and *overthrow* **overturn** the *faith* **trust** of some.
19 *Nevertheless* **But yet indeed**
the foundation of *God* **Elohim** standeth *sure* **solid**,
having this seal,
The Lord **Adonay Yah Veh** knoweth them that *are* **be** his.
And,
Let every one that nameth the name of *Christ* **Messiah**
depart from *iniquity* **injustice**.
Nachum 1:7, Yahn 10:14
20 But in a *great* **mega** house
there are not only vessels of gold and of silver,
but also of wood and of *earth* **clay**;
and some **indeed** to honour, and some to dishonour.
21 If *a man* **ever anyone** therefore
purge himself from these,
he shall be a vessel unto honour,
sanctified **hallowed**,
and *meet for the master's use* **useful to the despotes**,
and prepared unto every good work.
22 Flee also youthful *lusts* **pantings**:
but *follow righteousness* **pursue justness**,
faith **trust**, *charity* **love**, *peace* **shalom**,
with them that call on *the Lord* **Adonay**
out of a pure heart.
23 But foolish and *unlearned* **undisciplined** questions
avoid **shun**,
knowing that they *do gender* **birth** strifes.
24 And the servant of *the Lord* **Adonay** must not strive;
but be gentle unto all *men*,
apt to teach **didactic**, *patient* **enduring evil**,
25 In meekness
instructing **disciplining** those that oppose themselves;
if God peradventure **lestever Elohim**
will **shall** give them repentance
to the *acknowledging* **knowledge** of the truth;
26 And that they may *recover themselves* **sober up**
out of the snare of *the devil* **Diabolos**,
who are *taken captive* **captured alive** by him
at **unto** his will.

THE FINAL APOSTACY

3 This know also, that in the *last* **final** days
perilous times **furious seasons**
shall *come* **become present**.
2 For *men* **humanity** shall **be**
lovers of their own selves **befriending themselves**,
covetous **befriending silver**, *boasters* **braggarts**, proud,
blasphemers, *disobedient* **distrusting** to parents,
unthankful **uneucharistic**, *unholy* **unmercied**,
3 *Without natural affection* **Selfish**,
trucebreakers **disagreeable**, *false accusers* **diabolic**,
incontinent **uncontrollable**, *fierce* **savage**,
despisers of those that are good **unfriendly**,
4 Traitors, *heady* **precipitous**, *highminded* **inflated**,
lovers of **befriending** pleasures
more than *lovers of God* **befriending Elohim**;
5 Having a form of *Godliness* **reverence**,
but denying the *power* **dynamis** thereof:
from such turn away.
6 For of this sort are they which creep into houses,
and *lead captive silly* **captivate little** women
laden **heaped** with sins,
led away with divers *lusts* **pantings**,
7 *Ever* **Always** learning,
and never able to come to the knowledge of the truth.
8 Now *as* **in the manner**
Jannes and Jambres withstood *Moses* **Mosheh**,
so **thus** do these also *resist* **withstand** the truth:
men **humans** of corrupt minds,
reprobate **disapproved** concerning the *faith* **trust**.
9 But they shall *proceed* **advance** no *further* **more**:
for their *folly* **mindlessness**
shall be *manifest* **exposed** unto all *men*,
as their's also *was* **became**.

PAULOS' FINAL MANDATE

10 But thou hast
fully known **closely followed** my doctrine,
manner of life **the lifestyle**, *purpose* **the prothesis**,
faith **the trust**, *longsuffering* **the patience**,
charity **the love**, *patience* **the endurance**,
11 **the** Persecutions, *afflictions* **the sufferings**,
which came unto **such as became** me
at Antioch, at Iconium, at Lystra;
what **manner** persecutions I endured:
but out of *them* all
the Lord delivered **Adonay rescued** me.
12 Yea, and all that will **to** live *Godly* **reverently**
in *Christ Jesus* **Messiah Yah Shua** shall suffer persecution.
13 But evil *men* **humanity** and *seducers* **enchanters**
shall *wax worse and* **advance** worse,

deceiving **seducing**, and *being deceive*d **seduced**.
14 But *continue* **abide** thou in *the things* **those**
which thou hast learned
and hast been *assured of* **entrusted with**,
knowing of whom thou hast learned *them;*
15 And that from *a child* **infancy**
thou hast known the *holy scriptures* **priestal scribings**,
which are able to *make* **enwisen** thee *wise*
unto salvation through *faith* **trust**
which is in *Christ Jesus* **Messiah Yah Shua**.

ALL SCRIPTURE IS ELOHIM—SPIRITED

16 All scripture
is *given by inspiration of God* **Elohim—spirited**,
and is *profitable* **beneficial** for doctrine,
for *reproof* **proof**, for *correction* **setting straight**,
for *instruction* **discipline** in *righteousness* **justness**:
17 That the *man* **human** of *God* **Elohim**
may be *perfect* **equipped**,
thoroughly *furnished* **completed** unto all good works.
4 I *charge thee* **witness** therefore
before God **in sight of Elohim**,
and *the Lord Jesus Christ* **Adonay Yah Shua Messiah**,
who shall judge the *quick* **living** and the dead
at his *appearing* **epiphany**
and his *kingdom* **sovereigndom**;
2 Preach the word;
be instant in season **stand by opportunely**,
out of season **inopportunely**;
reprove, rebuke,
exhort *with* **in** all *longsuffering* **patience** and doctrine.
3 For the *time will come* **season shall be**
when they *will* **shall** not *endure* **tolerate** sound doctrine;
but after their own *lusts* **pantings**
shall they heap to themselves *teachers* **doctors**,
having itching ears **tickling their hearing**;
4 And they shall **indeed**
turn away *their ears* from **hearing** the truth,
and shall *be turned* **turn** unto *fables* **myths.**
5 But *watch* **be** thou **sober** in all *things*,
endure *afflictions* **hardship**, do the work of an evangelist,
make full proof of **fully bear** thy ministry.

PAULOS' DEPARTURE

6 For I am now ready to be *offered* **libated**,
and the *time* **season** of my departure
is at hand **standeth by**.
7 I have *fought* **agonized** a good *fight* **agony**,
I have *finished* **completed** my *course* **race**,
I have *kept* **guarded** the *faith* **trust**:
8 Henceforth there is laid up for me
a *crown* **wreath** of *righteousness* **justness**,
which *the Lord* **Adonay**, the *righteous* **just** judge,
shall give me *at* **in** that day:
and not to me only,
but unto all them also that love his *appearing* **epiphany**.
9 *Do thy diligence* **Be diligent**
to come *shortly* **quickly** unto me:
10 For Demas hath forsaken me,
having loved this present *world* **eon**,
and is departed unto *Thessalonica* **Thessalonikee**;
Crescens to Galatia, Titus unto Dalmatia.
11 Only *Luke* **Loukas** is with me.
Take *Mark* **Markos**, and bring him with thee:
for he is *profitable* **useful** to me *for* **unto** the ministry.
12 And Tychicus have I *sent* **apostolized** to Ephesus.
13 The cloak that I left at Troas with Carpus,
when thou comest, bring *with thee*,
and the *books* **scrolls**, *but* especially the parchments.

ON BEING ON GUARD

14 Alexander the coppersmith
did **indicated** me much evil:
the Lord reward **Adonay give back to** him
according to his works:
15 Of whom *be* **guard** thou *ware* also;
for he hath *greatly* **extremely** withstood our words.
16 *At* **In** my first *answer* **pleading**
no *man stood* **one convened** with me,
but all *men* forsook me:
I pray God
that it may **it** not be *laid* **reckoned** to *their charge* **them**.
17 Notwithstanding *the Lord* **Adonay** stood *with* **by** me,
and *strengthened* **dynamized** me;
that *by* **through** me
the preaching might be fully *known* **borne**,
and that all the *Gentiles* **goyim** might hear:
and I was *delivered* **rescued** out of the mouth of the lion.
18 And *the Lord* **Adonay** shall *deliver* **rescue** me
from every evil work,
and *will preserve* **shall save** me unto his
heavenly kingdom **sovereigndom of the heavenlies**:
to whom be glory
for ever and ever **unto the eons of the eons**.
Amen.

SALUTES AND BENEDICTION

19 Salute Prisca and Aquila,
and the household of Onesiphorus.
20 Erastus abode at Corinth:
but Trophimus have I left at *Miletum sick* **Miletus frail**.
21 *Do thy diligence* **Be diligent**
to come before *winter* **the downpour**.
Eubulus *greeteth* **saluteth** thee,
and Pudens, and Linus, and Claudia, and all the brethren.
22 *The Lord Jesus Christ* **Adonay Yah Shua Messiah**
be with thy spirit.
Grace **Charism** be with you.
Amen.

KEY TO INTERPRETING THE EXEGESES:
King James text is in regular type;
Text under exegeses is in oblique type;
Text of exegeses is in bold type.

SALUTATION

1 *Paul* **Paulos**, a servant of *God* **Elohim**,
and an apostle of *Jesus Christ* **Yah Shua Messiah**,
according to the *faith* **trust**
of *God's elect* **Elohim's select**,
and the *acknowledging* **knowledge** of the truth
which is after *Godliness* **reverence**;
2 In hope of eternal life, which *God* **Elohim**,
that cannot lie **the nonpseudo**
promised **pre—evangelized**
before *the world began* **eternal times**;
3 But hath in *due times* **his own seasons**
manifested his word *through* **in** preaching,
which is *committed* **entrusted** unto me
according to the *commandment* **order**
of *God* **Elohim** our Saviour;
4 To Titus, *mine own son* **genuine child**
after the **according to** common *faith* **trust**:
Grace **Charism**, mercy, and *peace* **shalom**,
from *God* **Elohim** the Father
and *the Lord Jesus Christ* **Adonay Yah Shua Messiah**
our Saviour.

ON SEATING OFFICERS

5 For this cause left I thee in Crete,
that thou shouldest *set in order the things* **arrange those**
that are *wanting* **lacking**,
and *ordain* **seat** elders in every city,
as I had *appointed* **ordained** thee:
6 If any be *blameless* **unaccusable**,
the *husband* **man** of one *wife* **woman**,
having *faithful* **trustworthy** children
not *accused* **under accusation** of *riot* **dissipation**
or *unruly* **insubordination**.
7 For *a bishop* **an episcopate**
must be *blameless* **unaccusable**,
as the *steward* **administrator** of *God* **Elohim**;
not *selfwilled* **selfpleasing**, not *soon angry* **wrathful**,
not given to wine **no winesop**, no striker,
not *given to filthy lucre* **avaricious**;
8 But *a lover of hospitality* **befriending strangers**,
a lover of good men **befriending good**,
sober **soundminded**,
just, *holy* **merciful**, *temperate* **self—controlled**;
9 *Holding fast* **Upholding** the *faithful* **trustworthy** word
as he hath been taught **of doctrine**,
that he may be able *by* **in** sound doctrine
both to *exhort* **beseech** and *to convince* **reprove**
the *gainsayers* **contradicters**.

ON EXPOSING INSUBORDINATES

10 For there are many
unruly and vain talkers **insubordinate mataeologists**
and *deceivers* **thought deluders**,
specially they of the circumcision:
11 Whose mouths must be stopped,
who *subvert* **overturn** whole houses,
teaching things **doctrinating** which they *ought* **must** not,
for *filthy lucre's* sake **shameful gain**.
12 One of themselves, *even* a prophet of their own, said,
The Cretians are *alway* **ever** liars,
evil beasts, *slow bellies* **idle wombs**.
13 This witness is true.
Wherefore **For which cause**
rebuke **reprove** them *sharply* **severely**,
that they may be sound in the *faith* **trust**;
14 Not giving heed to *Jewish fables* **Yah Hudahaic myths**,
and *commandments* **misvoth** of *men* **humanity**,
that turn from the truth.
15 Unto the pure **indeed** all *things* are pure:
but unto them that are defiled and *unbelieving* **trustless**
is *nothing* **naught** pure;
but even their mind and conscience is defiled.
16 They profess that they know *God* **Elohim**;
but in works they deny *him*,
being abominable, and *disobedient* **distrusting**,
and unto every good work *reprobate* **disapproved**.

ON SOUND DOCTRINE

2 But speak thou *the things* **those**
which *become* **befit** sound doctrine:
2 That the *aged men* **elders**° be sober, *grave* **venerant**,
temperate **soundminded**, sound in *faith* **the trust**,
in *charity* **love**, in *patience* **endurance**.
3 The *aged women* **elders**°° likewise,
that they be in behaviour as becometh holiness
in priestly demeanor,
not *false accusers* **diabolic**,
not *given* **subservient** to much wine,
teachers of **doctrinating** good *things*;
°masculine; °°feminine
4 That *they may teach* the young *women*
to **may** be *sober* **soundminded**,
to love **befriend** their *husbands* **men**,
to love **befriend** their children,
5 *To be discreet* **Soundminded**, *chaste* **hallowed**,
keepers at home **home guards**, good,
obedient **subjugated** to their own *husbands* **men**,
that the word of *God* **Elohim** be not blasphemed.
6 Young *men* likewise
exhort **beseech** to be *sober* **sound** minded.
7 *In* **Concerning** all *things*
shewing **present** thyself a *pattern* **type** of good works:
in doctrine
shewing uncorruptness **presenting incorruption**,
gravity **veneration**, *sincerity* **incorruptibility**,
8 *Sound speech* **Faultless words**
that cannot be condemned;
that he that is of the contrary part
may *be ashamed* **shame**,
having no evil *thing* to *say of* **word about** you.
9 *Exhort* servants to *be obedient* **subjugate**
unto their own *masters* **despotes**,
and to *please* **well—please** them *well* in all *things*;
not *answering again* **contradicting**;
10 Not *purloining* **embezzling**,
but *shewing* **indicating** all good *fidelity* **trust**;
that they may adorn the doctrine
of *God* **Elohim** our Saviour in all *things*.

ON THE SALVATIONAL CHARISM

11 For the *grace* **salvational charism**
of *God that bringeth salvation* **Elohim**
hath appeared to all *men* **humanity**,
12 *Teaching* **Disciplining** us that,
denying *ungodliness* **irreverence**
and *worldly lusts* **cosmic pantings**,
we should live *soberly* **soundmindedly**, *righteously* **justly**,
and *Godly* **reverently**, in this present *world* **eon**;
13 *Looking for* **Awaiting** that blessed hope,
and the *glorious appearing* **epiphany of the glory**
of the *great God* **mega Elohim**
and our Saviour *Jesus Christ* **Yah Shua Messiah**;
14 Who gave himself for us,
that he might redeem us
from all *iniquity* **torah violations**,
and purify unto himself a peculiar people,
zealous of **zealots in** good works.
15 These *things* speak, and *exhort* **beseech**,
and *rebuke* **reprove** with all *authority* **order**.
Let no *man despise* **one disesteem** thee.
3 *Put* **Remind** them *in mind* to *be subject* **subjugate**
to *principalities* **hierarchies** and *powers* **authorities**,
to obey magistrates,
to be *ready* **prepared** to every good work,
2 To *speak evil of* **blaspheme** no *man* **one**,
to be *no brawlers* **amicable**, *but* gentle,
shewing **indicating** all meekness unto all *men* **humanity**.
3 For we ourselves also were sometimes *foolish* **mindless**,
disobedient **distrusting**, *deceived* **seduced**,
serving divers *lusts* **pantings** and pleasures,
living **passing through** in malice and envy,
hateful, *and* hating one another.
4 But *after that* **when** the kindness and *love* **philanthropy**
of *God* **Elohim** our Saviour *toward man* appeared,
5 Not by works *of righteousness* **in justness**
which we have done,
but according to his mercy he saved us,

by **through** the *washing* **bathing**
of *regeneration* **regenesis**,
and renewing of the Holy *Ghost* **Spirit**;
6 Which he *shed* **poured forth** on us *abundantly* **richly**
through *Jesus Christ* **Yah Shua Messiah** our Saviour;
7 That *being* **having been** justified by his *grace* **charism**,
we should *be made* **become** heirs
according to the hope of eternal life.
8 This is a *faithful saying* **trustworthy word**,
and these *things* I will
that thou affirm *constantly* **thoroughly**,
that they which have *believed* **trusted** in *God* **Elohim**
might be *careful* **thoughtful**
to *maintain* **preside over** good works.
These *things* are good and *profitable* **beneficial**
unto *men* **humanity**.
9 But *avoid* **stand aloof from** foolish questions,
and genealogies, and contentions,
and *strivings about the law* **strifes of torahists**;
for they are *unprofitable* **unbeneficial** and vain.
10 A *man* **human** that is an heretick
after the first and second admonition *reject* **shun**;
11 Knowing that he that is such is *subverted* **perverted**,
and sinneth,
being *condemned of himself* **self—condemned**.

PERSONAL INSTRUCTIONS

12 When **ever** I shall send
Artemas unto thee, or Tychicus,
be diligent to come unto me to Nicopolis:
for I have *determined* **judged** there to winter.
13 *Bring* **Forward** Zenas the *lawyer* **torahist**
and Apollos *on their journey* diligently,
that *nothing* **naught** be *wanting* **lacking** unto them.
14 And let our's also learn to *maintain* **preside**
over good works *for* **unto** necessary *uses* **needs**,
that they be not unfruitful.

SALUTES AND BENEDICTION

15 All that are with me salute thee.
Greet **Salute** them that *love* **befriend** us in *the faith* **trust**.
Grace **Charism** be with you all.
Amen.

PHILEMON

KEY TO INTERPRETING THE EXEGESES:
King James text is in regular type;
Text under exegeses is in oblique type;
Text of exegeses is in bold type.

SALUTATION

1 *Paul* **Paulos**,
a prisoner of *Jesus Christ* **Yah Shua Messiah**,
and *Timothy* **Timo Theos** our brother,
unto Philemon our *dearly* beloved,
and *fellowlabourer* **co—worker**,
2 And to *our* beloved Apphia,
and Archippus our *fellowsoldier* **co—warrior**,
and to the *church* **ecclesia** in thy house:
3 *Grace* **Charism** to you, and *peace* **shalom**,
from *God* **Elohim** our Father
and *the Lord Jesus Christ* **Adonay Yah Shua Messiah**.
4 I *thank* **eucharistize** my *God* **Elohim**,
making *mention* **rememberance** of thee
always in my prayers,
5 Hearing of thy love and *faith* **trust**,
which thou hast toward *the Lord Jesus* **Adonay Yah Shua**,
and *toward* **unto** all *saints* **the holy**;
6 That the *communication* **communion** of thy *faith* **trust**
may become *effectual* **energized**
by the *acknowledging* **knowledge**
of *every* **all the** good *thing* which is in you
in *Christ Jesus* **Messiah Yah Shua**.
7 For we have
great joy **vast charism** and consolation in thy love,
because the *bowels* **spleens** of the *saints* **holy**
are *refreshed by* **rested through** thee, brother.
8 Wherefore, though
I might *be* **have** much *bold* **boldness** in *Christ* **Messiah**
to *enjoin* **order** thee
to do that which is *convenient* **proper**,
9 Yet for love's sake I rather beseech *thee*,
being such an one as *Paul* **Paulos** the *aged* **elder**,
and now also a prisoner
of *Jesus Christ* **Yah Shua Messiah**.
10 I beseech thee *for* **concerning** my *son* **child** Onesimus,
whom I have begotten in my bonds:
11 Which in time past was to thee *unprofitable* **useless**,
but now *profitable* **useful** to thee and to me:
12 Whom I have sent again:
thou therefore *receive* **take** him **unto you**,
that is, mine own *bowels* **spleen**:
13 Whom I *would have* **had willed**
retained **to hold back** with me,
that in thy stead he might have ministered unto me
in the bonds of the *gospel* **evangelism**:
14 But *without* **apart from** thy *mind* **decision**,
would I **will to** do *nothing* **naught**;
that thy *benefit* **good** should not be
as it were of necessity,
but *willingly* **voluntarily**.
15 For perhaps
he therefore *departed* **separated** for *a season* **an hour**,
that thou shouldest *receive* **have** him *for ever* **eternally**;
16 *Not now* **No longer** as a servant, but above a servant,
a brother beloved,
specially to me, but how much more unto thee,
both in the flesh, and in *the Lord* **Adonay**?
17 If thou *count* **regard** me therefore
a *partner* **communicant**,
receive **take** him **unto you** as myself.
18 If he hath *wronged thee* **injured**,
or *oweth thee* **is indebted** ought,
put **reckon** that *on mine account* **to me**;
19 I *Paul* **Paulos**
have *written it* **scribed** with mine own hand,
I *will repay it* **shall fully satisfy the penalty**:
albeit I *do* **word** not *say* to thee
how thou *owest* **art indebted** unto me
even thine own self *besides*.
20 Yea, brother,
let me have *joy* **benefit** of thee in *the Lord* **Adonay**:
refresh **rest** my *bowels* **spleen** in *the Lord* **Adonay**.
21 *Having confidence* **Being convinced**
in **of** thy obedience
I *wrote* **scribed** unto thee,
knowing that thou
wilt **shalt** also do more than I *say* **word**.
22 But *withal* **simultaneously** prepare me also a lodging:
for I *trust* **hope** that through your prayers
I shall be *given* **granted charism** unto you.

SALUTE AND BENEDICTION

23 There salute thee Epaphras,
my *fellowprisoner* **co—captive**
in *Christ Jesus* **Messiah Yah Shua**;
24 *Marcus* **Markos**, Aristarchus, Demas, *Lucas* **Loukas**,
my *fellowlabourers* **co—workers**.
25 The *grace* **charism**
of our *Lord Jesus Christ* **Adonay Yah Shua Messiah**
be with your spirit.
Amen.

KEY TO INTERPRETING THE EXEGESES:
King James text is in regular type;
Text under exegeses is in oblique type;
Text of exegeses is in bold type.

ELOHIM'S SON IS ELOHIM'S ESSENCE

1 *God, who at sundry times* **In many portions**
and in *divers* **many** manners,
spake in time past **Elohim, having spoken long ago**
unto the fathers *by* **in** the prophets,
2 Hath in these *last* **final** days
spoken unto us *by his* **in** Son,
whom he hath *appointed* **placed** heir of all *things*,
by **through** whom also he made the *worlds* **eons**;
3 Who being the *brightness* **effulgence** of *his* glory,
and the *express image* **character** of his *person* **essence**,
and *upholding* **bearing** all *things*
by the *word* **rhema** of his *power* **dynamis**,
when he had *by* **through** himself
purged **purified** our sins,
sat down *on* **in** the right *hand* of the Majesty on high;

THE SON, BETTER THAN THE ANGELS

4 Being *made* so much better than the angels,
inasmuch as he hath *by inheritance obtained* **inherited**
a more excellent name than they.
5 For unto which of the angels said he *at any time* **ever**,
Thou art my Son, this day have I begotten thee?
And again,
I *will* **shall** be to him**,** *a* Father,
and he shall be to me**,** *a* Son?
Psalm 2:7, 2 Shemu El 7:14
6 And again, when **ever** he bringeth *in*
the *firstbegotten* **firstborn** into the world,
he *saith* **wordeth**,
And let all the angels of *God* **Elohim** worship him.
Deuteronomy 32:43
7 And *of* **indeed unto** the angels he *saith* **wordeth**,
Who maketh his angels spirits,
and his *ministers* **liturgists** a flame of fire.
Psalm 104:4
8 But unto the Son *he saith*, Thy throne, O *God* **Elohim**,
is *for ever and ever* **unto the eons of the eons**:
a *sceptre* **scion** of *righteousness* **straightness**
is the *sceptre* **scion** of thy *kingdom* **sovereigndom**.
9 Thou hast loved *righteousness* **justness**,
and hated *iniquity* **torah violations**;
therefore *God* **Elohim**, *even* thy *God* **Elohim**,
hath anointed thee
with the **olive** oil of *gladness* **jumping for joy**
above thy *fellows* **partners**.
Psalm 45:6, 7
10 And, Thou, *Lord* **Adonay**, in the beginning
hast *laid the foundation of* **founded** the earth;
and the heavens are the works of thine hands:
11 They shall *perish* **destruct**;
but thou *remainest* **continually abidest**;
and they all shall *wax old* **antiquate** as doth a garment;
12 And as a *vesture* **mantle** shalt thou *fold* **coil** them *up*,
and they shall be changed:
but thou art the same, and thy years shall not fail.
Psalm 102:25—27
13 But to which of the angels said he *at any time* **ever**,
Sit *on* **by** my right *hand*,
until **ever** I *make* **place** thine enemies thy footstool?
Psalm 110:1
14 Are they not all *ministering* **indeed liturgizing** spirits,
sent forth **apostolized** to minister for them
who shall *be heirs of* **inherit** salvation?

2 Therefore we *ought* **must**
to give the more earnest **more superabundantly** heed
to the things **those** which we have heard,
lest *at any time* **ever** we should *let them slip* **float away**.
2 For if the word spoken *by* **through** angels
was **became** stedfast,
and every transgression and disobedience
received **took** a just recompence *of reward*;
3 How shall we escape,
if we *neglect* **ever** so *great* **vast** salvation;
which *at the first began* **in the beginning was taken**
to be spoken by the Lord **and told through Adonay**,
and was *confirmed* **established** unto us
by them that heard *him*;
4 *God* **Elohim** also *bearing them witness* **co—witnessing**,
both with signs and *wonders* **omens**,
and with divers *miracles* **dynamis**,
and *gifts* **impartations** of the Holy *Ghost* **Spirit**,
according to his own will?
5 For unto the angels hath he not
put in subjection **subjugated** the world to come,
whereof we speak.

THE SON LOWERED AND WREATHED

6 But *one in a certain place* **someone somewhere**
testified **witnessed**, *saying* **wording**,
What is *man* **humanity**,
that thou *art mindful of* **rememberest** him?
or the son of *man* **humanity**, that thou visitest him?
7 Thou *madest* **hast lowered** him
a little lower **somewhat less** than the angels°;
thou *crownedst* **hast wreathed** him
with glory and honour,
and *didst set* **seated** him over the works of thy hands:
8 Thou hast *put* **subjugated** all *things in subjection*
under his feet.
For in that he *put* **subjugated** all *in subjection* under him,
he *left nothing* **allowed naught**
that is not put under **unsubjugated to** him.
But now we see not yet
all *things put* **subjugated** under him.
9 But we see *Jesus* **Yah Shua**,
who was *made a little lower* **lowered somewhat less**
than the angels°
for the suffering of death,
crowned **wreathed** with glory and honour;
that he by the *grace* **charism** of *God* **Elohim**
should taste death for every man.
°cp Psalm 8:4—6
10 For it *became* **befitted** him,
for whom *are all things* **the all is**,
and *by whom are all things* **through whom the all be**,
in bringing many sons unto glory,
to *make* **complete**
the *captain* **hierarch** of their salvation *perfect*
through sufferings.
11 For both he that *sanctifieth* **halloweth**
and they who are *sanctified* **hallowed** are all of one:
for which cause he is not ashamed to call them brethren,
12 *Saying* **Wording**,
I *will declare* **shall evangelize** thy name
unto my brethren,
in the midst of the *church* **ecclesia**
will I sing praise **shall I hymn** unto thee.
Psalm 22:22
13 And again, I *will put my trust* **shall confide** in him.
And again, Behold I**,**
and the children which *God* **Elohim** hath given me.
Yesha Yah 8:17
14 *Forasmuch* **Since** then
as the children are partakers of flesh and blood,
he also himself likewise *took part* **partook** of the same;
that through death he might *destroy* **inactivate** him
that had the power of death, that is, *the devil* **Diabolos**;
15 And *deliver* **release** them
who **as many as** through *fear* **awe** of death
were **through** all their lifetime
subject to *bondage* **servitude**.
16 For *verily* **doubtless indeed**
he took not *on him the nature* **hold** of angels;
but he took *on him* **hold of** the *seed* **sperma** of Abraham.
Yesha Yah 41:9
17 Wherefore
in all *things it behooved him* **he was indebted**
to be *made like* **likened** unto his brethren,
that he might *be* **become**
a merciful and *faithful high priest* **trustworthy archpriest**
in things pertaining to God **unto Elohim**,
to *make reconciliation* **kapur/atone**
for the sins of the people.
18 For in that he himself hath suffered
being *tempted* **tested**,
he is able to *succour* **help** them
that are *tempted* **tested**.

THE SON, BETTER THAN MOSHEH

3 Wherefore, holy brethren,
partakers of the *heavenly* calling **of the heavenlies**,
consider
the Apostle and *High priest* **Archpriest** of our profession,
Christ Jesus **Messiah Yah Shua**;
2 *Who was faithful* **Being trustworthy** to him
that *appointed* **dealt with** him,
as also *Moses* **Mosheh** *was faithful* in all his house.
Numbers 12:7
3 For this *man* **one** was *counted* **deemed** worthy
of more glory than *Moses* **Mosheh**,
inasmuch as he who hath *builded* **prepared** the house
hath **the** more honour *than the house*.
Zechar Yah 6:12, 13
4 For every house is *builded* **prepared** by some *man* **one**;
but he that *built* **prepared** all *things* is *God* **Elohim**.
5 And *Moses verily* **Mosheh indeed**
was *faithful* **trustworthy** in all his house,
as a *servant* **therapist**,
for **unto** a *testimony* **witness**
of those *things* which were to be spoken *after*;
Numbers 12:7
6 But *Christ* **Messiah** as a son over his own house;
whose house are we,
if **ever** we hold *fast* **down** the *confidence* **boldness**
and the *rejoicing* **boasting** of the hope
firm **stedfast** unto the *end* **completion**.
7 Wherefore
(**exactly** as the Holy *Ghost* **Spirit** *saith* **wordeth**,
To day if **ever** ye *will* **shall** hear his voice,
8 Harden not your hearts, as in the provocation,
in the day of *temptation* **testing** in the wilderness:
9 *When* **Where** your fathers *tempted* **tested** me,
proved me, and saw my works forty years.
10 Wherefore
I was *grieved* **perturbed** with that generation, and said,
They *do alway err* **ever wander** in their heart;
and they have not known my ways.
11 So I *sware* **oathed** in my wrath,
If They shall *not* enter into my *rest* **shabbath**.)
Psalm 95:7—11
12 *Take heed* **See**, brethren,
lest there **ever** be in any of you
an evil heart of *unbelief* **trustlessness**,
in departing from the living *God* **Elohim**.
13 But *exhort one another* **console yourselves**
daily **each day**,
while **as long as** it is called To day;
lest any of you be hardened
through the *deceitfulness* **delusion** of sin.
14 For we are *made* **become**
partakers of *Christ* **the Messiah**,
if **ever** we hold **down** the beginning of our confidence
stedfast unto the *end* **completion**;
15 *While it is said* **In having worded**,
To day if **ever** ye *will* **shall** hear his voice,
harden not your hearts, as in the provocation.
Psalm 95:7,8
16 For some, when they had heard, did provoke:
howbeit **yet** not all
that came out of *Egypt* **Misrayim**
by Moses **through Mosheh**.
17 But with whom was he *grieved* **perturbed** forty years?
was it not **indeed** with them that had sinned,
whose carcases fell in the wilderness?
18 And to whom *sware* **oathed** he
that they should not enter into his *rest* **shabbath**,
but **except** to them that *believed not* **distrusted**?
19 So we see that they could not enter in
because of *unbelief* **trustlessness**.

ELOHIM'S SHABBATH

4 Let us therefore *fear* **awe**, lest **ever**,
a *promise* **pre—evangelism** being left *us*
of entering into his *rest* **shabbath**,
any of you should *seem* **think**
to *come short of it* **fall behind**.
2 For *unto us was the gospel preached*
we were evangelized,
as well as unto them **exactly as they**:
but the word *preached* **heard** did not *profit* **benefit** them,
not being *mixed* **co—mingled** with *faith* **the trust**
in them that heard it.
3 For we which have *believed* **trusted**
do enter into *rest* **shabbath**,
exactly as he said,
As I have *sworn* **oathed** in my wrath,
if they shall enter into my *rest* **shabbath**:
although the works *were finished* **had been**
from the foundation of the *world* **cosmos**.
Psalm 95:1
4 For he *spake in a certain place* **said somewhere**
of **about** the seventh *day on this wise* **thus**,
And *God* **Elohim**
did rest in **shabbathized** the seventh day
from all his works.
5 And in this *place* again,
If they shall enter into my *rest* **shabbath**.
6 *Seeing* **Since** therefore it remaineth
that some must enter therein,
and they to whom
it was *first preached* **previously evangelized**
entered not in because of *unbelief* **trustlessness**:
7 Again, he *limiteth* **decreed** a *certain* day,
saying **wording** in David, To day, after so long a time;
exactly as it is said,
To day if **ever** ye *will* **shall** hear his voice,
harden not your hearts.
Psalm 95:7, 8
8 For if *Jesus* **Yah Shua**°
had *given* **shabbathized** them *rest*,
then *would* **should** he not *afterward* **ever after**
have spoken *of* **about** another day.
°Yah Shua, Mosheh's successor
9 There remaineth therefore
a *rest* **shabbatism** to the people of *God* **Elohim**.
10 For he that is entered into his *rest* **shabbath**,
he also hath *ceased* **shabbathized** from his own works,
exactly as *God* **Elohim** *did* from his.
11 *Let us labour* **Be diligent** therefore
to enter into that *rest* **shabbath**,
lest any *man* **one** fall
after **in** the same example of *unbelief* **trustlessness**.
12 For the word of *God* **Elohim** is *quick* **living**,
and *powerful* **energized**,
and sharper than any *twoedged* **doublemouthed** sword,
piercing even **thoroughly penetrating**
to the *dividing asunder* **parting** of soul and spirit,
and of the joints and marrow,
and is a discerner
of the *thoughts* **deliberation** and *intents* **mind**
of the heart.
Yesha Yah 49:2
13 Neither is there any *creature* **creation**
that is not manifest in his sight:
but all *things* are naked and *opened* **exposed**
unto the eyes of him with whom we have *to do* **word**.
Proverbs 15:11

THE SON, OUR MEGA ARCHPRIEST

14 Seeing then
that we have a *great high priest* **mega archpriest**
that is passed into the heavens,
Jesus **Yah Shua** the Son of *God* **Elohim**,
let us *hold fast* **empower** our profession.
15 For we have not an *high priest* **archpriest**
which cannot *be touched* **sympathize**
with *the feeling of* our *infirmities* **frailties**;
but was in all points *tempted* **tested**
like as we are **according to our likeness**,
yet without **apart from** sin.
Hoshea 11:8
16 Let us therefore come boldly
unto the throne of *grace* **charism**,
that we may *obtain* **take** mercy,
and find *grace* **charism** to **opportunely** help
in time of need.
5 For every *high priest* **archpriest**
taken from among *men* **humanity**
is *ordained* **seated** for *men* **humanity**
in things pertaining to God **unto Elohim**,

that he may offer
both *gifts* **offerings** and sacrifices for sins:
2 Who can *have* compassion
on the ignorant **unknowing,**
and *on them that are out of the way* **the wandering;**
for that **since** he himself also
is *compassed* **surrounded** with *infirmity* **frailty.**
3 And *by reason hereof* **through these**
he *ought* **was indebted,**
exactly as for the people, *so* **thus** also for himself,
to offer for sins.
4 And no *man* **one** taketh this honour unto himself,
but **except** he that is called of *God* **Elohim,**
exactly as *was Aaron* **Aharon.**
Exodus 28:1, Numbers 16:40
5 *So* **Thus** also *Christ* **the Messiah** glorified not himself
to *be made* **become** an *high priest;* **archpriest**
but he that *said* **spake** unto him,
Thou art my Son, to day have I begotten thee.
6 **Exactly** As he *saith* **wordeth** also
in another place **elsewhere,**
Thou art a priest *for ever* **unto the eons**
after the order of *Melchisedec* **Malki Sedeq.**
Psalm 2:7, 110:4
7 Who in the days of his flesh, when he had offered up
prayers **petitions** and *supplications* **entreaties,**
with *strong* **mighty** crying and tears
unto him that was able to save him from death,
and was heard *in that he feared* **by his revering;**
Psalm 19:9
8 Though *he were* **being** a Son, yet learned he obedience
by *the things* **those** which he suffered;
9 And being *made perfect* **completed,**
he became the *author* **causer** of eternal salvation
unto all them that obey him;
10 *Called* **Addressed** of *God* **Elohim**
an *high priest* **archpriest**
after the order of *Melchisedec* **Malki Sedeq.**
11 *Of* **About** whom
we have many *things* **words** to *say* **word,**
and *hard* **untranslatable** to *be uttered* **speak,**
seeing **since** ye *are dull* **be sluggish** of hearing.

ON BECOMING DOCTORS

12 For when for the time
ye *ought* **are indebted** to be *teachers* **doctors,**
ye have need that one *teach* **doctrinate** you again
which be the first principles **the beginning elements**
of the oracles of *God* **Elohim;**
and are become such as have need of milk,
and not of *strong meat* **solid nourishment.**
13 For every one that *useth* **partaketh** milk
is *unskilful* **untested**
in the word of *righteousness* **justness:**
for he is a babe.
14 But *strong meat* **solid nourishment**
belongeth to **is for** them that are *of full age* **complete,**
even those who *by reason of use* **through habit**
have their *senses* **perceptions** exercised
to discern both good and evil.

ON BEARING ON TO COMPLETION

6 Therefore
leaving **forsaking** the *principles* **beginnings**
of the *doctrine* **word** of *Christ* **the Messiah,**
let us *go* **bear** on unto *perfection* **completion;**
not *laying* **casting down** again
the foundation of repentance from dead works,
and of *faith* **trust** toward *God* **Elohim,**
2 Of the doctrine of baptisms, and of laying on of hands,
and of resurrection of the dead, and of eternal judgment.
3 And this *will* **shall** we do,
if *God permit* **ever Elohim allow.**

ON FALLING AWAY

4 For it is impossible
for those who were once enlightened,
and have tasted
of the *heavenly gift* **gratuity of the heavenlies,**
and *were made* **became**
partakers of the Holy *Ghost* **Spirit,**
5 And have tasted the good *word* **rhema** of *God* **Elohim,**
and the *powers* **dynamis** of the *world* **eon** to come,
6 If they shall fall away,
to renew them again unto repentance;
seeing they *crucify* **restake** to themselves
the Son of *God* **Elohim** *afresh,*
and *put* **expose** him *to an open shame.*
7 For the earth
which drinketh in the rain that cometh oft upon it,
and bringeth forth *herbs meet* **botany wellfit** for them
by **through** whom it is *dressed* **cultivated,**
receiveth **partaketh** blessing from *God* **Elohim:**
Psalm 65:10
8 But that which *beareth* **bringeth forth** thorns and briers
is *rejected* **disapproved,** and is nigh unto cursing;
whose *end* **completion** is *to be burned* **unto scorching.**
9 But, beloved, we are *persuaded* **convinced**
of better *things of* **concerning** you,
and *things that accompany* **regarding** salvation,
though we thus speak.
10 For *God* **Elohim** is not *unrighteous* **unjust**
to forget your work and labour of love,
which ye have *shewed toward* **indicated unto** his name,
in that ye have ministered to the *saints* **holy,**
and do minister.
11 And we *desire* **pant** that *every* **each** *one* of you
do shew **indicate** the same diligence
to the full *assurance of hope* **bearance**
unto the *end* **completion:**
12 That ye be not *slothful* **sluggish,**
but *followers* **mimickers** of them
who through *faith* **trust** and patience
inherit the *promises* **pre—evangelisms.**
13 For when *God* **Elohim**
made promise to **pre—evangelized** Abraham,
because **since** he could *swear* **oath** by no greater,
he *sware* **oathed** by himself,
14 *Saying* **Wording,** Surely blessing I *will* **shall** bless thee,
and multiplying I *will* **shall** multiply thee.
15 And *so* **thus,** *after he had patiently endured* **being patient,**
he obtained the *promise* **pre—evangelism.**
16 For *men verily* **humanity indeed**
swear **oath** by the greater:
and an oath *for confirmation is to them* **establisheth**
an *end* **extremity** of all *strife* **controversy.**
17 Wherein *God* **Elohim,**
willing **having willed** more *abundantly* **superabundantly**
to shew unto the heirs of *promise* **pre—evangelism**
the immutability of his counsel,
confirmed it by an oath:
18 That *by* **through** two immutable *things* **matters,**
in which it was impossible for *God* **Elohim** to lie,
we might have a *strong* **mighty** consolation,
who have fled for refuge
to *lay hold upon* **empower** the hope set before us:
19 Which *hope* we have as an anchor of the soul,
both *sure* **certain** and stedfast,
and which entereth into that within the veil;

THE SON, OUR ARCHPRIEST UNTO THE EONS

20 *Whither* **Where** the forerunner is for us entered,
even Jesus **Yah Shua,**
made **having become** an *high priest* **archpriest**
for ever **unto the eons**
after the order of *Melchisedec* **Malki Sedeq.**
7 For this *Melchisedec* **Malki Sedeq,**
king **sovereign** of *Salem* **Shalem,**
priest of *the most high God* **El Elyon,**
who met **with** Abraham returning
from the *slaughter* **chopping** of the *kings* **sovereigns,**
and blessed him;
2 To whom also Abraham
gave **imparted** a *tenth part* **tithe** of all;
first *being by interpretation* **indeed translated**
King **Sovereign** of *righteousness* **justness,**
and *after that* **then** also
King **Sovereign** of *Salem* **Shalem,**
which is, *King* **Sovereign** of *peace* **shalom;**
3 *Without father* **Unfathered,**
without mother **unmothered,**
without descent **ungenealogized,**
having neither beginning of days
nor *end* **completion** of life;

but *made like* **likenessed** unto the Son of *God* **Elohim**;
abideth a priest *continually* **unto perpetuity**.
4 Now *consider* **observe**
how great this man was **his greatness**,
unto whom even the patriarch Abraham gave
the *tenth* **tithe from the top** of the *spoils* **heap**.
5 And *verily* **indeed** they that are of the sons of Levi,
who *receive* **take** the office of the priesthood,
have a *commandment* **misvah** to take tithes of the people
according to the *law* **torah**, that is, of their brethren,
though they come out of the loins of Abraham:
6 But he
whose descent is not counted from them
who is not genealogized
received tithes of **was tithed by** Abraham,
and blessed him that had the *promises* **pre—evangelisms**.
Genesis 14:20, Numbers 18:21
7 And *without* **apart from** all *contradiction* **controversy**
the *less* **lesser** is blessed of the better.
8 And here **indeed**
men **humanity** that die *receive* **take** tithes;
but there he *receiveth them*,
of whom it is witnessed that he liveth.
9 And as *I may so say* **saith the saying**,
Levi also, who *receiveth* **taketh** tithes,
payed tithes in **tithed through** Abraham.
10 For he was yet in the loins of his father,
when *Melchisedec* **Malki Sedeq** met **with** him.
11 If **indeed** therefore *perfection* **completion**
were *by* **through** the Levitical priesthood,
(for under it the people *received* **set** the *law* **torah**,)
what *further* need **yet** was there
that another priest should rise
after the order of *Melchisedec* **Malki Sedeq**,
and not be *called* **worded**
after the order of *Aaron* **Aharon**?
12 For the priesthood being *changed* **transplaced**,
there *is made* **becometh** of necessity
a *change* **transplacing** also of the *law* **torah**.
13 For he of whom these *things* are *spoken* **worded**
pertaineth to another tribe **another scion partaketh**,
of which no *man gave attendance* **one heeded**
at the **sacrifice** altar.
14 For it *is evident* **hath been preevidenced**
that our *Lord sprang* **Adonay rose** out of *Juda* **Yah Hudah**;
of **unto** which *tribe* **scion**
Moses **Mosheh** spake *nothing* **naught**
concerning priesthood.
Genesis 49:8, 10
15 And it is yet *far more* **more superabundantly** evident:
for that **if** after the *similitude* **likeness**
of *Melchisedec* **Malki Sedeq** there ariseth another priest,
16 Who *is made* **becometh**, not after the *law* **torah**
of a *carnal commandment* **fleshly misvah**,
but after the *power* **dynamis** of an *endless* **endless** life.
17 For he *testifieth* **witnesseth that**,
Thou art a priest *for ever* **unto the eons**
after the order of *Melchisedec* **Malki Sedeq**.
Psalm 110:4
18 For **indeed**
there *is verily* **becometh** a *disannulling* **putting away**
of the *commandment going before* **preceding misvah**
for **because of** the *weakness* **frailty**
and *unprofitableness* **unbeneficialness** thereof.
19 For the *law* **torah**
made nothing perfect **completed naught**,
but the *bringing in* **introduction** of a better hope *did*;
by the **through** which
we *draw nigh* **approach** unto *God* **Elohim**.
20 And inasmuch as not *without* **apart from** an oath
he was made priest:
21 (For those priests *were made* **had indeed become**
without **apart from** an oath;
but this with an oath
by **through** him that *said* **worded** unto him,
The Lord sware **Yah Veh oathed**
and *will* **shall** not *repent* **regret**,
Thou art a priest *for ever* **unto the eons**
after the order of *Melchisedec* **Malki Sedeq**:)
Psalm 110:4
22 By so much *was Jesus* **hath Yah Shua**
made a surety **become a pledge**
of a better *testament* **covenant**.
23 And they *truly were* **indeed became** many priests,
because they were *not suffered* **forbidden**
to *continue* **abide nearby** by reason of death:
24 But this *man* **one**,
because he *continueth ever* **abideth unto the eons**,
hath an *unchangeable* **inviolable** priesthood.
25 Wherefore he is able also
to save them *to the uttermost* **completely**
that come unto *God by* **Elohim through** him,
seeing he ever *liveth* **living**
to *make intercession* **intercede** for them.
26 For such an *high priest became* **archpriest befitted** us,
who is holy **merciful**, *harmless* **innocent**,
undefiled **unpolluted**, *separate* **separated** from sinners,
and *made* **become** higher than the heavens;
27 Who *needeth not daily* **hath no day by day neccessity**,
exactly as those *high priests*, **archpriest** *s* to offer up sacrifice,
first for his own sins, and then for the people's:
for this he did once, when he offered up himself.
28 For the *law maketh men* **torah seateth humans**
high priests which have infirmity **archpriests having frailty**;
but the word of the oath,
which was since **after** the *law* **torah**,
maketh the **completeth a** Son,
who is consecrated for evermore **unto the eons**.

THE SON, OUR ARCHPRIEST

8 Now of *the things* **those**
which we have *spoken* **worded,** this is the sum:
We have such an *high priest*,**archpriest**
who is *set* **seated** on the right *hand* of the throne
of the Majesty in the heavens;
2 A *minister* **liturgist** of the *sanctuary* **Holies**,
and of the true tabernacle,
which *the Lord pitched* **Yah Veh staked**,
and not *man* **humanity**.
3 For every *high priest* ,**archpriest**
is *ordained* to offer *gifts* **gratuities** and sacrifices:
wherefore it is of necessity
that this man have somewhat also to offer.
4 For **indeed** if he were on earth,
he should not *be* **ever been** a priest,
seeing that there are **there being** priests
that offer *gifts* **offerings** according to the *law* **torah**:
5 Who *serve* **liturgize** unto the example and shadow
of *heavenly things* **the heavenlies**,
as Moses was admonished of God
exactly as oracled to Mosheh
when he was about
to *make* **fully complete** the tabernacle:
for, See, *saith he*,
that thou make all *things* according to the *pattern* **type**
shewed to thee in the mount.
Exodus 25:40
6 But now
hath he obtained a more excellent *ministry* **liturgy**,
by how much **inasmuch as** also
he is the mediator of a better covenant,
which was established
upon better *promises* **pre—evangelisms**.
7 For if that first *covenant* had been *faultless* **blameless**,
then should no place have been sought for the second.
Exodus 3:8, 19:5
8 For *finding fault with* **blaming** them, he *saith* **wordeth**,
Behold, the days come, *saith the Lord* **wordeth Yah Veh**,
when I *will make* **shall complete** a new covenant
with the house of *Israel* **Yisra El**
and with the house of *Judah* **Yah Hudah**:
9 Not according to the covenant
that I made with their fathers
in the day when I *took them by the* **held their** hand
to lead them out of the land of *Egypt* **Misrayim**;
because they *continued* **abode** not in my covenant,
and I *regarded* **also disregarded** them *not*,
saith the Lord **wordeth Yah Veh**.
10 For this is the covenant that I *will make* **shall covenant**
with the house of *Israel* **Yisra El** after those days,
saith the Lord **wordeth Yah Veh**;

I *will put* **shall give** my *laws* **torah** into their mind,
and *write* **epigraph** them in their hearts:
and I *will* **shall** be to them, *a God* **Elohim**,
and they shall be to me, *a* people:
11 And they shall not **no way**
teach every man **doctrinate each** his neighbour,
and *every man* **each** his brother,
saying **wording**, Know *the Lord* **Yah Veh**:
for all shall know me, from the least to the *greatest* **mega**.
12 For I *will be merciful to* **shall kapur/atone**
their *unrighteousness* **injustice**,
and their sins and their *iniquities* **torah violations**
will I **shall I not no way still** remember *no more*.
Yirme Yah 31:31—34
13 In that he *saith* **wordeth**, A new *covenant*,
he hath *made the first old* **antiquated the first**.
Now that
which *decayeth* **antiquateth** and *waxeth old* **senesceth**
is *ready* **nigh** to *vanish away* **disappearing**.

THE COSMIC HOLY TABERNACLE

9 *Then verily* **But indeed** the first *covenant* **tabernacle**
had also
ordinances **judgments** of *divine service* **ministration**,
and a *worldly sanctuary* **cosmic Holies**.
2 For there was a tabernacle *made* **prepared**;
the first, wherein was the *candlestick* **menorah**,
and the table, and the *shewbread* **prothesis bread**;
which is *called* **worded** the *sanctuary* **Holies**.
Exodus 25:30
3 And after the second veil, the tabernacle
which is *called* **worded** the *Holiest of all* **Holy of Holies**;
4 Which had the golden *censer* **incenser**,
and the ark of the covenant
overlaid round **covered** about **on every side** with gold,
wherein was the golden *pot* **jar** that had manna,
and *Aaron's rod* **Aharon's scion** that *budded* **sprouted**,
and the *tables* **slabs** of the covenant;
Exodus 16:33, 25:10, 34:29, Leviticus 16:12,
Numbers 17:10, Deuteronomy 10:2, 5
5 And over it the *cherubims* **cherubim** of glory
shadowing the *mercyseat* **kapporeth**;
of **about** which we cannot now *speak* **word**
particularly **according to its parts**.
6 Now when these *things* were thus *ordained* **prepared**,
the priests **indeed**
went always into **continually entered** the first tabernacle,
accomplishing **fully completing**
the *service of God* **liturgy**.
7 But into the second
went the *high priest* **,archpriest** alone once every year,
not *without* **apart from** blood,
which he offered for himself,
and *for* **the** *errors* **unknowingnesses** of the people:
8 The Holy *Ghost* **Spirit** this *signifying* **evidencing**,
that the way into the *holiest of all* **Holies**
was not yet *made* manifest,
while as the first tabernacle was yet standing:
9 Which was a *figure* **parable**
for the time **unto that season** then present,
in which were offered both *gifts* **gratuities** and sacrifices,
that could not *make* **complete** him
that *did the service perfect* **liturgized**,
as pertaining to the conscience;
10 *Which stood* only *in meats* **upon food** and drinks,
and *divers washings* **more excellent baptisms**,
and *carnal ordinances* **judgments of flesh**,
imposed *on them* until
the *time* **season** of *reformation* **thorough straightening**.
11 But *Christ* **Messiah** being come,
an *high priest* **archpriest** of **the coming** good *things to come*,
by **through** a greater
and *more perfect* **complete** tabernacle,
not *made with hands* **handmade**,
that is *to say*, not of this *building* **creation**;
12 Neither *by* **through** the blood of goats and calves,
but *by* **through** his own blood
he entered in once into the *holy place* **Holies**,
having *obtained* **found** eternal redemption *for us*.
13 For if the blood of bulls and of goats,
and the ashes of an heifer sprinkling the *unclean* **profane**,
sanctifieth **halloweth** to the purifying of the flesh:
14 How much more shall the blood of *Christ* **the Messiah**,
who through the eternal Spirit offered himself
without spot **unblemished** to *God* **Elohim**,
purge **purify** your conscience from dead works
to *serve* **liturgize** the living *God* **Elohim**?
15 *And for this cause* **Through which**
he is the mediator of the new *testament* **covenant**,
that *by means of* **having become by** death,
for **unto** the redemption of the transgressions
that were under the first *testament* **covenant**,
they which are called
might *receive* **take** the *promise* **pre—evangelism**
of eternal inheritance.
16 For where a *testament* **covenant** is,
there must also of necessity
be **brought** the death of the *testator* **covenantor**.
17 For a *testament* **covenant** is *of force* **stedfast**
after men are dead **upon death**:
otherwise it is *of no strength* **not mighty enough** at all
while the *testator* **covenantor** liveth.
18 Whereupon neither
the first *testament* was *dedicated* **hanukkahed**
without **apart from** blood.
19 For when *Moses* **Mosheh**
had spoken every *precept* **misvah**
to all the people according to the *law* **torah**,
he took the blood of calves and of goats,
with water, and scarlet wool, and hyssop,
and sprinkled both the *book* **selfsame scroll**,
and all the people,
20 *Saying* **Wording**,
This is the blood of the *testament* **covenant**
which *God* **Yah Veh** hath *enjoined* **misvahed** unto you.
21 *Moreover* **Likewise** he sprinkled with blood
both the tabernacle,
and all the vessels of the *ministry* **liturgy**.
Exodus 24:8, 29:12, 36, Leviticus 14:16
22 And *almost* **nearly** all *things* are,
by **according to** the *law* **torah**,
purged with **purified in** blood;
and *without shedding* **apart from pouring** of blood
is no remission **becometh no forgiveness**.
23 It was therefore necessary **indeed**
that the *patterns of things* **examples** in the heavens
should be purified with these;
but the *heavenly things* **heavenlies** themselves
with better sacrifices than these.
24 For *Christ* **the Messiah** is not entered
into the *holy places made with hands* **handmade Holies**,
which are the figures **antitypes** of the true;
but into heaven itself,
now to *appear* **manifest**
in the *presence* **face** of *God* **Elohim** for us:
25 Nor yet that he should offer himself often,
exactly as the *high pries* **tarchpriest**
entereth into the *holy place* **Holies** every year
with **in** blood of others;
26 *For then* **Otherwise** must he often have suffered
since the foundation of the *world* **cosmos**:
but now once in the *end* **completion** of the *world* **eon**
hath he *appeared* **been manifest** to put away sin
by **through** the sacrifice of himself.
27 And **inasmuch** as it is *appointed* **laid out**
unto *men* **humanity** once to die,
but after this the judgment:
28 *So Christ* **Thus the Messiah** was *once* offered **once**
to *bear* **offer up** the sins of many;
and unto them that *look for* **await** him
shall he *appear* **be seen** the second *time*
without **apart from** sin unto salvation.

THE YEAR BY YEAR SACRIFICES UNDER THE TORAH

10 For the *law* **torah** having a shadow
of **the coming** good *things to come*,
and not the very *image* **icon** of the *things* **substance**,
can never **ever** with those sacrifices
which they offered year by year *continually* **in perpetuity**
make the comers thereunto perfect
complete them who come.
2 *For then* **Otherwise**

would **should** they not
have *ceased* **ever paused** to be offered?
because that
the *worshippers* **liturgizers** once *purged* **purified**
should have **not still** had *no more* conscience of sins.
3 But in those *sacrifices*
there is a remembrance *again made* of sins every year.
4 For it is *not possible* **impossible**
that the blood of bulls and of goats
should *take away* **remove** sins.
5 Wherefore when he cometh into the *world* **cosmos**,
he *saith* **wordeth**,
Sacrifice and offering thou *wouldest* **willest** not,
but a body hast thou prepared me:
6 In *burnt offerings* **holocausts** and *sacrifices* for sin
thou hast *had no pleasure* **not thought well**.
7 Then said I, *Lo* **Behold**, I come
(in the *volume* **heading** of the *book* **scroll**
it is *written of* **scribed concerning** me,)
to do thy will, O *God* **Elohim**.
8 Above when he *said* **worded**,
Sacrifice and offering
and *burnt offerings* **holocausts** and *offering* for sin
thou *wouldest* **willest** not,
neither hadst *pleasure therein* **thought well**;
which are offered by the *law* **torah**;
Psalm 40:6—8
9 Then said he, *Lo* **Behold**,
I come to do thy will, O *God* **Elohim**.
He taketh away the first,
that he may *establish* **set** the second.
10 *By the* **In** which will we are *sanctified* **hallowed**
through the offering
of the body of *Jesus Christ* **Yah Shua Messiah**
once *for all*.
11 And every priest **indeed** standeth daily
ministering **liturgizing** and offering
oftentimes the same sacrifices **often**,
which can never **ever** take away sins:

THE SON'S SACRIFICE — ONCE

12 But this *man* **one**,
after he had offered one sacrifice for sins
for ever **in perpetuity**,
sat down *on* **in** the right *hand* of *God* **Elohim**;
13 From henceforth *expecting* **awaiting**
till his enemies be *made* **placed** his footstool.
Psalm 110:1
14 For by one offering
he hath *perfected for ever* **completed in perpetuity**
them that are *sanctified* **hallowed**.
15 *Whereof* the Holy *Ghost* **Spirit** also
is a witness **witnesseth** to us:
for after that he had *said before* **foretold**,
16 This is the covenant
that I *will make* **shall covenant** with them
after those days,
saith the Lord **wordeth Yah Veh**,
I *will put* **shall give** my *laws* **torah** into their hearts,
and in their minds *will I write* **shall I epigraph** them;
17 And their sins and *iniquities* **torah violations**
will I **shall I not no way still** remember *no more*.
Yirme Yah 31:33, 34
18 Now where *remission* **forgiveness** of these is,
there is *no more* **not still** offering for sin.
19 Having therefore, brethren,
boldness to enter into the *holiest* **Holies**
by **in** the blood of *Jesus* **Yah Shua**,
20 By a *new* **freshly slaughtered** and living way,
which he hath *consecrated* **hanukkahed** for us,
through the veil, that is *to say*, his flesh;
21 And having *an high* **a mega** priest
over the house of *God* **El**;
22 Let us *draw* **come** near with a true heart
in full *assurance* **bearance** of *faith* **trust**,
having our hearts sprinkled from an evil conscience,
and our bodies *washed* **bathed** with pure water.
23 Let us hold *fast* **down** the profession of *our faith* **hope**
without wavering **unwaveringly**;
(for he is *faithful* **trustworthy**
that *promised* **pre—evangelized**;)
24 And let us consider one another
to *provoke* **agitate** unto love and to good works:
25 Not forsaking
the *assembling* **synagoguing** of ourselves together,
exactly as the *manner* **custom** of some is;
but *exhorting one another* **consoling**:
and so much the more,
as **long as** ye see the day approaching.

ON SINNING VOLUNTARILY

26 For if we sin *wilfully* **voluntarily**
after that
we have *received* **taken** the knowledge of the truth,
there remaineth *no more* **not still** sacrifice for sins,
27 But
a certain fearful looking for **an awesome expectation**
of judgment and *fiery indignation* **zeal of fire**,
which shall *devour* **eat** the *adversaries* **opposers**.
28 *He* **Anyone** that
despised Moses' law **set aside Mosheh's torah**
died *without mercy* **apart from compassion**
under two or three witnesses:
29 Of how much *sorer* **worse** punishment,
suppose **think** ye,
shall he be *thought* **deemed** worthy,
who hath *trodden under foot* **trampled down**
the Son of *God* **Elohim**,
and hath *counted* **deemed** the blood of the covenant,
wherewith **wherein** he was *sanctified* **hallowed**,
an unholy thing **profane**,
and hath *done despite unto* **insulted**
the Spirit of *grace* **charism**?
30 For we know him that hath said,
Vengeance *belongeth* unto me, I *will* **shall** recompense,
saith the Lord **wordeth Yah Veh**.
And again, *The Lord* **Yah Veh** shall judge his people.
Deuteronomy 32:35, 36
31 *It is a fearful thing* **How awesome**
to fall into the hands of the living *God* **Elohim**.
32 But *call to remembrance* **remember**
the *former* **previous** days, in which,
after ye were illuminated **having been enlightened**,
ye endured
a *great fight* **vast contention** of *afflictions* **sufferings**;
33 Partly **indeed**,
whilst ye were made a gazingstock **being theatricized**
both by reproaches and *afflictions* **tribulations**;
and partly,
whilst ye became *companions* **communicants**
of them that *were so used* **thus behaved**.
34 For ye
had compassion of **sympathized with** me in my bonds,
and *took joyfully* **received with cheer**
the *spoiling* **plunder** of your *goods* **holdings**,
knowing in yourselves that ye have in heaven
a better and *an enduring substance* **abiding holdings**.
35 Cast not away therefore your *confidence* **boldness**,
which hath *great* **mega** recompence *of reward*.
36 For ye have need of *patience* **endurance**, that,
after ye have **having** done the will of *God* **Elohim**,
ye might receive the *promise* **pre—evangelism**.
37 For yet a little *while* — **as much as — as long as**,
and he that shall come, *will* **shall** come,
and *will* **shall** not *tarry* **take his time**.
38 Now the just shall live by *faith* **trust**:
but if **ever** any *man draw back* **one withdraw**,
my soul shall *have no pleasure* **not think well** in him.
Habakkuk 2:3, 4
39 But we are not of them
who *draw back* **withdraw** unto *perdition* **destruction**;
but of them that *believe* **trust**
to **unto** the *saving* **acquiring** of the soul.

TRUST

11 Now *faith* **trust**
is the substance of *things hoped for* **our hoping**,
the *evidence* **proof** of *things* **those** not seen.
2 For *by* **in** it the elders *obtained a good report* **witnessed**.
3 Through *faith* **trust** we *understand* **comprehend**
that the *worlds* **eons** were *framed* **prepared**
by the *word* **rhema** of *God* **Elohim**,
so that **unto this**;

things **those** which are seen
were **became** not *made*
of *things* **those** which *do appear* **manifested.**
4 By *faith* **trust** Abel offered unto *God* **Elohim**
a *more excellent* **much better** sacrifice than *Cain* **Qayin,**
by **through** which he *obtained witness* **witnessed**
that he was righteous **to being just,**
God testifying **Elohim witnessing** of his *gifts* **gratuities:**
and *by* **through** it he being dead yet speaketh.
5 By *faith Enoch* **trust Hanoch** was *translated* **transplaced**
that he should not see death;
and was not found,
because *God* **Elohim** had *translated* **transplaced** him:
for before his *translation* **transplacing**
he had this *testimony* **witness,**
that he *pleased God* **well—pleased Elohim.**
6 But *without faith* **apart from trust**
it is impossible to *please him* **well—please:**
for he that cometh to *God* **Elohim**
must *believe* **trust** that he is,
and that he *is a rewarder* **becometh a recompenser**
of them that *diligently* seek him.
7 By *faith Noah* **trust Noach,**
being warned of God **oracled**
of things **concerning those** not seen as yet,
moved with *fear* **reverence,**
prepared an ark to the *saving* **salvation** of his house;
by the **through** which he condemned the *world* **cosmos,**
and became heir of the *righteousness* **justness**
which is by *faith* **trust.**
8 By *faith* **trust** Abraham,
when he was called to go out into a place
which he *should after receive* **was about to take**
for **unto** an inheritance, obeyed;
and he went out, not knowing whither he went.
9 By *faith* **trust**
he *sojourned* **settled**
in the land of *promise* **pre—evangelism,**
as in *a strange country* **another's,**
dwelling **settling** in tabernacles
with *Isaac* **Yischaq** and *Jacob* **Yaaqov,**
the heirs with him **co—heirs**
of the same *promise* **pre—evangelism:**
10 For he *looked for* **awaited** a city
which hath foundations,
whose *builder* **artificer** and *maker* **public worker**
is *God* **Elohim.**
11 Through *faith* **trust** also Sara **herself**
received strength **took dynamis** to conceive *seed* **sperma,**
and *was delivered of a child* **birthed**
when she was
past age **beyond the season of maturescence,**
because **since** she *judged* **deemed** him
faithful **trustworthy** who had *promised* **pre—evangelized.**
12 Therefore *sprang* **birthed** there even of one,
and him as good as dead,
so many **exactly** as the stars of the sky in multitude,
and as the sand which is by the sea shore innumerable.
13 These all died in *faith* **trust,**
not having *received* **taken** the *promises* **pre—evangelisms,**
but having seen them afar *off,*
and were *persuaded of them* **convinced,**
and *embraced them* **saluted,** and *confessed* **professed**
that they were strangers and pilgrims on the earth.
14 For they that *say* **word** such *things*
declare plainly **manifest**
that they seek a *country* **fatherland.**
15 And *truly* **indeed,**
if they had *been mindful of that country* **remembered**
from whence they came *out,*
they might have **ever** had *opportunity* **season**
to have returned.
16 But now they *desire* **reach for** a better *country,*
that is, an *heavenly* **heavenlies:**
wherefore *God* **Elohim**
is not ashamed to be called their *God* **Elohim:**
for he hath prepared for them a city.
17 By *faith* **trust** Abraham,
when he was *tried* **tested,** offered *up Isaac* **Yischaq:**
and he that had received the *promises* **pre—evangelisms**
offered *up* his only begotten *son,*
18 *Of* **Unto** whom it was *said* **spoken,**
That in *Isaac* **Yischaq** shall thy *seed* **sperma** be called:
19 *Accounting* **Reckoning** that *God* **Elohim**
was able to raise *him up,* even from the dead;
from whence also he received him in a *figure* **parable.**
20 By *faith* **trust**
Isaac **Yischaq** blessed *Jacob* **Yaaqov** and *Esau* **Esav**
concerning *things* **those** to come.
21 By *faith Jacob* **trust Yaaqov,** when he was a dying,
blessed *both* **each of** the sons of *Joseph* **Yoseph;**
and worshipped,
leaning upon the *top* **tip** of his *staff* **scion.**
22 By *faith Joseph* **trust Yoseph,** when he died,
made mention **remembered**
of **concerning** the *departing* **exodus**
of the *children* **sons** of *Israel* **Yisra El;**
and *gave commandment* **misvahed** concerning his bones.
23 By *faith Moses* **trust Mosheh,** when he was born,
was *hid* **secreted** three months of his *parents* **fathers,**
because they saw he was *a proper* **an urbane** child;
and they were not *afraid* **awestricken**
of the *king's commandment* **sovereign's ordinance.**
24 By *faith Moses* **trust Mosheh,**
when he *was come to years* **became mega,**
refused **denied** to be *called* **worded,**
the son of *Pharaoh's* **Paroh's** daughter;
25 Choosing rather to *suffer affliction* **co—suffer**
with the people of *God* **Elohim,**
than to *enjoy* the *pleasures* **temporary enjoyment**
of sin *for a season;*
26 Esteeming the reproach of *Christ* **the Messiah**
greater riches than the treasures in *Egypt* **Misrayim:**
for he *had respect* **looked away** unto the recompence
of the reward.
27 By *faith* **trust** he forsook *Egypt* **Misrayim,**
not *fearing* **awestricken**
by the *wrath* **fury** of the *king* **sovereign:**
for he *endured* **persevered,**
as seeing him who is invisible.
28 Through *faith* **trust** he *kept* **did** the *passover* **pasach,**
and the *sprinkling* **pouring** of blood,
lest he that destroyed the firstborn
should *touch* **finger** them.
29 By *faith* **trust**
they passed through the *Red* **Reed** sea
as *by* **through** dry *land:*
which the *Egyptians* **Misrayim**
assaying to do **taking on to test**
were *drowned* **swallowed.**
30 By *faith* **trust** the walls of Jericho fell *down,*
after they were *compassed about* **surrounded** seven days.
31 By *faith* **trust Rachab** the *harlot Rahab* **whore**
perished **co—destructed** not
with them that *believed not* **distrusted,**
when she had received the spies with *peace* **shalom.**
32 And what shall I *more say* **still word?**
for the time *would* **should** fail me
to *tell of Gedeon* **declare about Gidon,**
and *of Barak* **Baraq also,** and *of Samson* **Shimshon,**
and *of Jephthae* **Yipthach;** *of* David also,
and *Samuel* **Shemu El,** and *of* the prophets:
33 Who through *faith* **trust**
subdued *kingdoms* **sovereigndoms,**
wrought righteousness **worked justness,**
obtained *promises* **pre—evangelisms,**
stopped **sealed** the mouths of lions.
34 Quenched the *violence* **dynamis** of fire,
escaped **fled** the edge of the sword,
out of *weakness* **frailty** were *made strong* **empowered,**
waxed valiant **became mighty** in *fight* **war,**
turned to flight **put down** the *armies* **encampments**
of the aliens **others.**
35 Women *received* **took** their dead
raised to life again **by resurrection:**
and others were tortured,
not *accepting deliverance* **receiving redemption;**
that they might obtain a better resurrection:
36 And others *had trial of cruel* **took testings**
of mockings and scourgings, yea,

moreover **yet** of bonds and *imprisonment* **guardhouses**:
37 They were stoned,
they were sawn *asunder* **apart**,
were *tempted* **tested**,
were slain with **deathified in murder by** the sword:
they wandered about in sheepskins and goatskins;
being destitute **falling behind**,
afflicted **tribulated**, *tormented* **vilified**;
38 (Of whom the *world* **cosmos** was not worthy:)
they wandered
in *deserts* **wildernesses**, and *in* mountains,
and *in dens* **grottos** and *caves* **caverns** of the earth.
39 And these all,
having *obtained a good report* **witnessed**
through *faith* **the trust**,
received not the *promise* **pre—evangelism**:
40 *God* **Elohim**
having **previously** provided some better *thing* for us,
that they *without* **apart from** us
should not be *made perfect* **completed**.

FROM THE CLOUD OF WITNESSES TO YAH SHUA

12 *Wherefore* **Therefore**
seeing we also are *compassed about* **surrounded**
with so *great* **vast** a cloud of witnesses,
let us *lay aside* **put away** every weight,
and the sin which doth so easily beset *us*,
and let us run *with patience* **through endurance**
the *race* **contest** that is set before us,
2 *Looking* **Considering** unto *Jesus* **Yah Shua**
the *author* **hierarch** and *finisher* **completer**
of *our faith* **the trust**;
who for the *joy* **cheer** that was set before him
endured the *cross* **stake**,
despising **disesteeming** the shame,
and is *set down at* **seated**
in the right *hand* of the throne of *God* **Elohim**.

THE PURPOSE OF THE DISCIPLINE OF YAH VEH

3 For consider him
that endured such *contradiction* **controversy**
of **by** sinners *against* **unto** himself,
lest ye be wearied and *faint* **weakened**
in your *minds* **souls**.
4 Ye have not yet *resisted* **withstood** unto blood,
striving against **antagonizing with** sin.
5 And ye *have forgotten* **are utterly oblivious**
to the *exhortation* **consolation**
which *speaketh* **reasoneth** unto you
as unto *children* **sons**,
My son, *despise* **disregard** not thou
the *chastening* **discipline** of *the Lord* **Yah Veh**,
nor *faint* **weaken**
when thou art *rebuked of* **reproved by** him:
6 For whom *the Lord* **Yah Veh** loveth
he *chasteneth* **disciplineth**,
and scourgeth every son whom he receiveth.
Proverbs 3:11, 12
7 If ye endure *chastening* **discipline**,
God dealeth with **Elohim offereth** you as with sons;
for what son is he
whom the father *chasteneth* **disciplineth** not?
8 But if ye be *without chastisement* **apart from discipline**,
whereof all *are* **become** partakers,
then are ye bastards, and not sons.
9 *Furthermore* **Then indeed**
we have had fathers of our flesh
which *corrected* **disciplined** us,
and we *gave* **respected** them *reverence*:
shall we not much rather
be in subjection **subjugate** unto the Father of spirits,
and live?
10 For they *verily* **indeed** for a few days
chastened us **disciplined**
after their *own pleasure* **wellthinking**;
but he for *our profit* **benefit**,
that we might *be partakers* **partake** of his holiness.
11 Now **indeed** no *chastening* **discipline** for the present
seemeth **is thought** to be *joyous* **cheerful**,
but *grievous* **sorrowful**:
nevertheless afterward it *yieldeth* **giveth back**
the *peaceable* **shalom**
of the fruit of *righteousness* **justness**
unto them which are exercised *thereby* **through it**.
12 Wherefore *lift up* **straighten** the **limping** hands
which hang down,
and the *feeble* **paralyzed** knees;
13 And make straight *paths* **tracks** for your feet,
lest that which is lame be turned *out of the way* **aside**;
but let it rather be healed.
14 *Follow peace* **Pursue shalom** with all *men*,
and holiness,
without **apart from** which
no *man* **one** shall see *the Lord* **Adonay**:
15 *Looking diligently* **Overseeing**
lest any *man fail* **one fall behind**
of the *grace* **charism** of *God* **Elohim**;
lest any root of bitterness *springing up* **sprouting**,
trouble **harass** you,
and *thereby* **through this** many be defiled;
16 Lest there be any *fornicator* **whoremonger**,
or *profane person* **profaner**,
as *Esau* **Esav**, who for one morsel of *meat* **food**
sold **gave up** his *birthright* **firstrights**.
17 For ye know *how* that *afterward* **thereafter**,
when he *would* **willed to** have inherited the blessing,
he was *rejected* **disapproved**:
for he found no place of repentance,
though he sought it *carefully* with tears.

SINAY VS SIYON

18 For ye are not come
unto the mount that might be touched,
and that burned with fire,
nor unto *blackness* **clouds of gloom**,
and darkness, and tempest,
19 And the *sound* **echo** of a trumpet,
and the voice of *words* **rhemas**;
which *voice* they that heard, *intreated* **shunned**,
that the word
should not be *spoken* **added** to them any more:
20 (For they could not *endure* **bear**
that which was *commanded* **charged**,
And if *so much as* **ever**
a beast *touch* **finger** the mountain,
it shall be stoned,
or *thrust* **pierced** through with a *dart* **missile**:
21 And **thus**
so terrible **awesome** was the *sight* **manifestation**,
that *Moses* **Mosheh** said,
I *exceedingly fear* **am utterly frightened**
and *quake* **trembling**:)
Exodus 19:12, 20:18, 19
22 But ye are come unto mount *Sion* **Siyon**,
and unto the city of the living *God* **Elohim**,
the *heavenly Jerusalem* **Yeru Shalem of the heavenlies**,
and to *an innumerable company* **myriads** of angels,
23 To the *general assembly* **whole gathering**
and *church* **ecclesia** of the firstborn,
which are *written* **registered** in *heaven* **the heavens**,
and to *God* **Elohim** the Judge of all,
and to the spirits of **the** just *men*
made perfect **having been completed**,
24 And to *Jesus* **Yah Shua**
the mediator of the new covenant,
and to the blood of sprinkling,
that speaketh better *things* than *that of* Abel.
25 See that ye *refuse* **shun** not him that speaketh.
For if they *escaped* **fled** not
who *refused* **shunned** him that *spake* **oracled** on earth,
much more shall *not* we *escape*,
if we turn away from him
that speaketh from heaven **of the heavens**:
26 Whose voice then shook the earth:
but now he hath *promised* **pre—evangelized**,
saying **wording**,
Yet once more I *shake* **quake** not the earth only,
but also heaven.
27 And this *word*, Yet once more,
signifieth **evidenceth** the *removing* **transplacing**
of those *things* that are **shaken**,
as of *things* **those** that are made,
that those *things* which cannot be shaken

may *remain* **abide**.
28 Wherefore we
receiving **taking** a *kingdom* **sovereigndom**
which cannot be moved **unmovable**,
let us have *grace* **charism**,
whereby **through which** we may *serve* **minister**
God acceptably **to Elohim well—pleasingly**
with *reverence* **awe** and *Godly fear* **reverence**:
29 For our *God* **Elohim** is a consuming fire.

CONCLUSION

13 Let *brotherly love* **befriending the brethren**
continue **abide**.
2 Be not forgetful to *entertain* **befriend** strangers:
for *thereby* **through this**
some have *entertained* **lodged** angels *unawares* **in hiding**.
3 Remember them that are *in bonds* **bound**,
as *bound with them* **being co—bound**;
and them which *suffer adversity* **are vilified**,
as being yourselves also in the body.
4 Marriage is honourable in all,
and the *bed undefiled* **coition unpolluted**:
but whoremongers and adulterers
God will **Elohim shall** judge.
5 Let your *conversation* **manner**
be *without covetousness* **unavaricious**;
and be *content* **satisfied** with
such things as ye have **the present**:
for he hath said,
I *will* **shall** never **no way** *leave* **let loose of** thee,
nor **no way** forsake thee.
6 So that we may *boldly say* **courageously word**,
The Lord **Yah Veh** is my helper,
and I *will* **shall** not *fear* **be awestricken**
by what *man* **humanity** shall do unto me.
Psalm 118:6
7 Remember them which *have the rule over* **govern** you,
who have spoken unto you the word of *God* **Elohim**:
whose *faith follow* **trust mimic**,
considering the *end* **outcome**
of their *conversation* **behaviour**.
8 *Jesus Christ* **Yah Shua Messiah** the same yesterday,
and to day, and *for ever* **unto the eons**.
9 Be not carried about with divers and strange doctrines.
For it is a good *thing*
that the heart be established with *grace* **charism**;
not with *meats* **foods**,
which have not *profited* **benefited** them
that have *been occupied* **walked** therein.
10 We have *an* **a sacrifice** altar,
whereof they have no *right* **authority** to eat
which *serve* **minister** the tabernacle.
11 For the bodies of those *beasts* **live beings**,
whose blood is brought into the *sanctuary* **Holies**
by **through** the *high pries* **tarchpriest** for sin,
are burned without the *camp* **encampment**.
12 Wherefore *Jesus* **Yah Shua** also,
that he might *sanctify* **hallow** the people
with **through** his own blood, suffered without the gate.
13 Let us go forth therefore unto him
without the *camp* **encampment**,
bearing his reproach.
14 For here have we no *continuing* **abiding** city,
but we seek one to come.
15 *By* **Through** him therefore
let us offer the sacrifice of *praise* **halal** to *God* **Elohim**
continually, that is,
the fruit of *our* lips *giving thanks to* **professing** his name.
16 But to do good and *to communicate* **communion**
forget not:
for with such sacrifices *God* **Elohim** is well pleased.
17 Obey them that *have the rule over* **govern** you,
and submit yourselves:
for they watch for your souls,
as they that must give *account* **word**,
that they may do it with *joy* **cheer**,
and not *with grief* **sighing**:
for that is *unprofitable* **disadvantageous** for you.
18 Pray for us:
for we *trust* **are confident**
that we have a good conscience,
in all *things* willing to *live honestly* **behave well**.
19 But I beseech you *the rather* **superabundantly**
to do this,
that I may be restored to you *the sooner* **very quickly**.
20 Now the *God* **Elohim** of *peace* **shalom**,
that brought *again* from the dead
our *Lord Jesus* **Adonay Yah Shua**,
that *great* **mega** shepherd of the sheep,
through **in** the blood of the *everlasting* **eternal** covenant,
21 *Make* **Prepare** you *perfect* in every good work
to do his will,
working **doing** in you
that which is well—pleasing in his sight,
through *Jesus Christ* **Yah Shua Messiah**;
to whom be glory
for ever and ever **unto the eons of the eons**.
Amen.
22 And I beseech you, brethren,
suffer **tolerate** the word of *exhortation* **consolation**:
for I have *written a letter* **epistolized** unto you
in **through** few words.
23 Know ye
that *our* brother Timothy is *set at liberty* **released**;
with whom, if **ever** he come *shortly* **very quickly**,
I *will* **shall** see you.

SALUTES AND BENEDICTION

24 Salute all them that *have the rule over* **govern** you,
and all the *saints* **holy**.
They of Italy salute you.
25 *Grace* **Charism** be with you all.
Amen.

KEY TO INTERPRETING THE EXEGESES:
King James text is in regular type;
Text under exegeses is in oblique type;
Text of exegeses is in bold type.

SALUTATION

1 *James* **Yaaqovos,**
a servant of *God* **Elohim**
and of *the Lord Jesus Christ* **Adonay Yah Shua Messiah,**
to the twelve *tribes* **scions**
which are scattered abroad **of the diaspora,**
greeting **Cheers.**

TRUST AND TESTINGS

2 My brethren,
count **deem** it all *joy* **cheer**
when ye fall into divers *temptations* **testings;**
3 Knowing *this,*
that the *trying* **proofing** of your *faith* **trust**
worketh *patience* **endurance.**
4 But let *patience* **endurance**
have *her perfect* **complete** work,
that ye may be *perfect* **complete** and *entire* **whole,**
wanting nothing **lacking naught.**
5 If any of you lack wisdom, let him ask of *God* **Elohim,**
that giveth to all *men* liberally,
and *upbraideth* **reproacheth** not;
and it shall be given him.
6 But let him ask in *faith* **trust,**
nothing wavering **doubting naught.**
For he that *wavereth* **doubteth**
is like **resembleth** a *wave* **surge** of the sea
driven with the wind **windtossed** and tossed.
7 For let not that *man think* **human suppose**
that he shall *receive any thing* **take aught**
of the *Lord* **Adonay.**
8 A double *minded* **souled** man
is unstable in all his ways.
9 Let the brother of *low degree* **humbleness**
rejoice **boast** in *that he is exalted* **his exaltation:**
10 But the rich,
in *that he is made low* **his humiliation:**
because as the *flower* **blossom** of the *grass* **herbage**
he shall pass away.
11 For the sun is no sooner risen
with a *burning heat* **scorch,**
but it withereth the grass,
and the *flower* **blossom** thereof falleth,
and the *grace* **befittingness** of *the fashion of it* **its face**
perisheth **destructeth:**
so **thus** also
shall the rich *man* fade away in his ways.
12 Blessed is the man that endureth *temptation* **testing:**
for when he is tried **because, having become approved,**
he shall *receive* **take** the *crown* **wreath** of life,
which *the Lord* **Adonay** hath *promised* **pre—evangelized**
to them that love him.
13 Let no *man say* **one word** when he is *tempted* **tested,**
Because I am *tempted* **tested** of *God* **Elohim:**
for *God* **Elohim**
cannot **shall not** be *tempted* **tested** with evil,
neither *tempteth* **testeth** he any *man* **one:**
14 But *every man* **each** is *tempted* **tested,**
when he is *drawn away* **enticed** of his own *lust* **panting,**
and *enticed* **entrapped.**
15 Then when *lust* **panting** hath conceived,
it *bringeth forth* **birtheth** sin:
and sin, when it is *finished* **complete,**
bringeth forth **breedeth** death.
16 *Do* **Wander** not *err,* my beloved brethren.
17 Every good *gift* **gratuity**
and every *perfect gift* **complete gratuity** is from above,
and *cometh down* **descendeth** from the Father of lights,
with whom is no *variableness* **changeableness,**
neither shadow of turning.
18 Of his own will
begat **bred** he us with the word of truth,
that we should be
a *kind of a firstfruits* **firstlings** of his creatures.
19 *Wherefore* **So then,** my beloved brethren,
let every *man* **human** be *swift* **quick** to hear,
slow to speak, slow to wrath:
20 For the wrath of man
worketh not the *righteousness* **justness** of *God* **Elohim.**
21 Wherefore *lay apart* **put away** all *filthiness* **foulness**
and *superfluity* **superabundance** of *naughtiness* **malice,**
and receive *with* **in** meekness
the *engrafted* **implanted** word,
which is able to save your souls.
22 But be ye doers of the word,
and not hearers only,
deceiving **deluding** your own selves.
23 *For* **Because** if any be a hearer of the word,
and not a doer,
he *is like unto* **resembles** a man
beholding **perceiving** his *natural* **genetic** face
in a *glass* **mirror:**
24 For he *beholdeth* **perceiveth** himself,
and goeth *his way,*
and straightway forgetteth what manner *of man* he was.
25 But whoso looketh
into the *perfect law* **complete torah** of liberty,
and *continueth* **abideth** *therein,*
he being not a forgetful hearer,
but a doer of the work,
this *man* **one** shall be blessed in his *deed* **doing.**
26 If any *man* **one** among you
seem **think** to be *religious* **ceremonious,**
and bridleth not his tongue,
but *deceiveth* **deludeth** his own heart,
this man's *religion* **ceremony** is vain.
27 Pure *religion* **ceremony** and *undefiled* **unpolluted**
before God **with Elohim** and the Father is this,
To *visit* **scope out** the *fatherless* **orphans** and widows
in their *affliction* **tribulation,**
and to keep **guard** himself *unspotted* **unstained**
from the *world* **cosmos.**

THE TEST OF PARTIALITY

2 My brethren,
have not the *faith* **trust** of our
Lord Jesus Christ, the Lord **Adonay Yah Shua Messiah**
of glory
with respect of persons **in partiality.**
2 For if **ever** there come unto your *assembly* **synagogue**
a man *with a gold ring* **goldringed,**
in *goodly* **radiant** apparel,
and there come in also
a poor man in *vile raiment* **foul apparel;**
3 And ye *have respect to* **look upon** him
that *weareth* **beareth** the *gay clothing* **radiant apparel,**
and say unto him, Sit thou here *in a good place* **well;**
and say to the poor, Stand thou there,
or sit here under my footstool:
4 Are ye not then *partial* **discerning** in yourselves,
and are become judges of evil *thoughts* **reasonings?**
5 Hearken, my beloved brethren,
Hath not *God* **Elohim**
chosen **selected** the poor of this *world* **cosmos**
rich in *faith* **trust,**
and heirs of the *kingdom* **sovereigndom**
which he hath *promised* **pre—evangelized**
to them that love him?
6 But ye have *despised* **dishonoured** the poor.
Do not **the** rich *men oppress* **overpower** you,
and *draw* **drag** you *before* **unto** the judgment *seats?*
7 Do not they blaspheme that *worthy* **good** name
by the which ye are called?
8 If **yet indeed**
ye *fulfil* **complete** the *royal law* **sovereign torah**
according to the scripture,
Thou shalt love thy neighbour as thyself,
ye do well:
9 But if ye have *respect to persons* **partiality,**
ye *commit* **work** sin,
and are *convinced* **reproved** of the *law* **torah**
as transgressors.
10 For whosoever shall *keep* **guard** the whole *law* **torah,**
and yet *offend* **stumble** in one *point,*
he *is guilty of* **becometh subject to** all.
11 For he that said, Do not *commit adultery* **adulterize,**
said also, Do not *kill* **murder.**
Now if thou *commit no adultery* **dost not adulterize,**

yet if thou *kill* **murder**,
thou art become a transgressor of the *law* **torah**.
12 *So* **Thus** speak ye, and *so* **thus** do,
as they that shall be judged
by **through** the *law* **torah** of liberty.
13 For he shall have judgment *without mercy* **unmercied**,
that hath *shewed* **dealt** no mercy;
and mercy *rejoiceth* **exulteth** against judgment.
14 What *doth it profit* **benefit**, my brethren,
though a man say **if ever one word**
he hath *faith* **the trust**, and have not works?
can *faith* **the trust** save him?
15 If **ever** a brother or sister be naked,
and *destitute of* **lack** daily *food* **nourishment**,
16 And one of you say unto them,
Depart **Go** in *peace* **shalom**, be ye warmed and filled;
notwithstanding ye give them not
those *things* which are needful to the body;
what *doth* **benefiteth** it *profit*?
17 Even *so faith* **thus trust**, if **ever** it hath not works,
by itself is dead, *being alone*.
18 *Yea, a man* may *say* **Yet one sayeth**,
Thou hast *faith* **trust**, and I **also** have works:
shew me thy *faith without* **trust by** thy works,
and I *will* **shall also** shew thee my *faith* **trust** by my works°.
°This sentence is a play on emphasis.
19 Thou *believest* **trustest** that there is one *God* **Elohim**;
thou doest well:
the *devils* **demons** also *believe* **trust**,
and *tremble* **shudder**.
20 But *wilt* **willest** thou know, O vain *man* **human**,
that *faith without* **the trust apart from** works is dead?
21 Was not Abraham our father justified by works,
when he had offered *Isaac* **Yischaq** his son
upon the **sacrifice** altar?
22 Seest thou *how faith* **that the trust**
wrought **co—worked** with his works,
and by works
was *faith made perfect* **the trust completed**?
23 And the scripture was fulfilled which *saith* **wordeth**,
Abraham *believed God* **trusted Elohim**,
and it was *imputed* **reckoned** unto him
for righteousness **unto justness**:
and he was called the Friend of *God* **Elohim**.
24 Ye see *then how* **therefore**
that by works a *man* **human** is justified,
and not by *faith* **trust** only.
25 Likewise also
was not *Rahab* **Rachab** the *harlot* **whore**
justified by works,
when she had received the *messengers* **angels**,
and had sent them out another way?
26 For **exactly** as the body *without* **apart from** the spirit
is dead,
so faith without **thus the trust apart from** works
is dead also.

TESTING THE TONGUE

3 My brethren, be not many *masters* **doctors**,
knowing that
we shall *receive* **take** the greater condemnation.
2 For *in many things we offend all* **we all stumble much**.
If any *man offend* **one stumble** not in word,
the same **this one** is a *perfect* **complete** man,
and able also to bridle the whole body.
3 Behold, we put bits in the horses' mouths,
that they may obey us;
and we turn about their whole body.
4 Behold also the *ships* **sailers**,
which *though they be* **being** so great,
and *are* driven of *fierce* **hard** winds,
yet are they turned about
with **by** a very *small helm* **short rudder**,
whithersoever the **violent impulse**
governor listeth **of the straightener willeth**.
5 Even *so* **thus** the tongue is a little member,
and boasteth *great things* **mega**.
Behold, how *great a matter* **much forest**
a little fire *kindleth* **lighteth**!
6 And the tongue is a fire,
a *world* **cosmos** of *iniquity* **injustice**:
so **thus** is the tongue **seated** among our members,
that it *defileth* **staineth** the whole body,
and *setteth on fire* **inflameth**
the *course* **track** of *nature* **genetics**;
and it is *set on fire* **inflamed**
of hell **by Gay Hinnom/the Valley of Burning**.
7 For *every kind* **all nature, both** of beasts,
and of *birds* **fliers**, *and* **both** of *serpents* **creepers**,
and of *things* **those** in the sea, is tamed,
and hath been tamed of *mankind* **human nature**:
8 But the tongue can no *man* **human** tame;
it is an *unruly* **unrestrainable** evil
full of *deadly poison* **death bearing venom**.
9 *Therewith bless* **Therein eulogize** we *God* **Elohim**,
even the Father;
and *therewith* **therein** curse we *men* **humanity**,
which *are made* **be**
after the *similitude* **likeness** of *God* **Elohim**.
10 Out of the same mouth
proceedeth blessing **cometh eulogy** and cursing.
My brethren,
these *things ought not so to* **need not thus** be.
11 Doth a fountain send *forth* at the same *place* **cavern**
sweet *water* and bitter?
12 Can the fig tree, my brethren,
bear olive berries **make olives**?
either a vine, figs?
so can **thus** no fountain
maketh both *yield* salt water and fresh.
13 Who is *a* wise *man*
and *endued with knowledge* **understanding** among you?
let him shew out of a good *conversation* **behaviour**
his works *with* **in** meekness of wisdom.
14 But if ye
have bitter *envying* **zeal** and strife in your hearts,
glory **exult** not, and lie not against the truth.
15 This wisdom descendeth not from above,
but is earthly, *sensual* **soulical**, *devilish* **demonic**.
16 For where *envying* **zeal** and strife is,
there is *confusion* **instability** and every evil *work* **matter**.
17 But the wisdom that is from above
is first *pure* **indeed hallowed**,
then *peaceable* **at shalom**, gentle,
and easy to be intreated **agreeable**,
full of mercy and good fruits, *without partiality* **impartial**,
and *without hypocrisy* **unhypocritical**.
18 And the fruit of *righteousness* **justness**
is sown in *peace* **shalom**
of **by** them that make *peace* **shalom**.

ON SUBJUGATING AND RESISTING

4 *From* whence
come **be** wars and *fightings* **strifes** among you?
come **be they** not hence,
even of your *lust* **pleasures** that war in your members?
2 Ye *lust* **pant**, and have not:
ye *kill* **murder**,
and *desire to have* **are jealous**, and cannot obtain:
ye *fight* **strive** and war,
yet ye have not, because ye ask not.
3 Ye ask, and *receive* **take** not,
because ye ask *amiss* **evily**,
that ye may *consume* **spend** it
upon **in** your *lusts* **pleasures**.
4 Ye adulterers and adulteresses,
know ye not that the friendship of the *world* **cosmos**
is enmity with *God* **Elohim**?
whosoever therefore
will **willeth to** be a friend of the *world* **cosmos**
is *the* **seated an** enemy of *God* **Elohim**.
5 *Do ye* **Or** think **ye**
that the scripture *saith* **wordeth** in vain,
The spirit that dwelleth in us *lusteth* **yearneth** to envy?
6 But he giveth *more grace* **greater charism**.
Wherefore he *saith* **wordeth**,
God resisteth **Elohim opposeth** the proud,
but giveth *grace* **charism** unto the humble.
7 *Submit* **Subjugate** yourselves therefore to *God* **Elohim**.
Resist *the devil* **Diabolos**, and he *will* **shall** flee from you.
8 *Draw nigh to God* **Approach Elohim**,
and he *will draw nigh to* **shall approach** you.

Cleanse **Purify** your hands, *ye* sinners;
and *purify* **hallow** your hearts, *ye* double *minded* **souled**.
9 Be *afflicted* **miserable**, and mourn, and weep:
let your laughter be *turned* **overturned** to mourning,
and your *joy* **cheer** to *heaviness* **sadness**.
10 Humble yourselves in the sight of *the Lord* **Yah Veh**,
and he shall *lift* **exalt** you *up*.
11 *Speak* **Slander** not *evil* one *of* another, brethren.
He that *speaketh evil of* **slandereth** his brother,
and judgeth his brother,
speaketh evil of **slandereth** the *law* **torah**,
and judgeth the *law* **torah**:
but if thou judge the *law* **torah**,
thou art not a doer of the *law* **torah**, but a judge.
12 There is one *lawgiver* **torahsetter**,
who is able to save and to destroy:
who art thou that judgest another?
13 *Go to* **Come** now, ye that *say* **word**,
To day or to morrow we *will* **shall** go into such a city,
and *continue* **deal** there *a* **one** year,
and *buy and sell* **merchandise**, and get gain:
14 Whereas ye *know* **understand** not
what shall be on the morrow.
For what is your life? It is *even* **indeed** a vapour,
that *appeareth* **manifesteth** for a little *time*,
and then *vanisheth away* **disappeareth**.
15 For that ye *ought to say* **word**,
If *the Lord will* **ever Adonay willeth**,
we shall live, and do this, or that.
16 But now ye *rejoice* **boast** in your boastings:
all such *rejoicing* **boasting** is evil.
17 Therefore to him that knoweth to do good,
and doeth *it* not, to him it is sin.

ON TREASURING TREASURES

5 *Go to* **Come** now, ye rich *men*,
weep and howl for your miseries
that shall come upon you.
2 Your riches *are corrupted* **have putrefied**,
and your garments *are* **become** motheaten.
3 Your gold and silver *is cankered* **rusteth**;
and the rust of them
shall be **unto** a witness against you,
and shall eat your flesh as *it were* fire.
Ye have *heaped treasure* **treasured** *together*
for **in** the *last* **final** days.
4 Behold, the hire of the *labourers* **workers**
who have *reaped down* **ingathered** your *fields* **regions**,
of which *is of* you *kept back by fraud* **cheated**, crieth:
and the cries of them which have *reaped* **harvested**
are entered into the ears
of *the Lord of sabaoth* **Yah Veh Sabaoth**.
5 Ye *have lived in pleasure* **indulged** on the earth,
and *been wanton* **luxuriated**;
ye *have* nourished your hearts, as in a day of slaughter.
6 Ye *have* condemned and *killed* **murdered** the just;
and he *doth* **opposeth you** not *resist you*.

ON THE PAROUSIA

7 Be patient therefore, brethren,
unto the *coming* **parousia** of *the Lord* **Adonay**.
Behold, the *husbandman* **cultivator**
waiteth for **awaiteth** the precious fruit of the earth,
and hath long patience for it,
until **ever** he *receive* **take**
the *early* **morning** and *latter* **evening** rain.
8 Be ye also patient; stablish your hearts:
for **because** the *coming* **parousia** of the *Lord* **Adonay**
draweth nigh **approacheth**.
9 *Grudge* **Sigh** not one against another, brethren,
lest ye be condemned:
behold, the judge standeth before the *door* **portal**.
10 Take, my brethren, the prophets,
who have spoken in the name of *the Lord* **Yah Veh**,
for an example of *suffering affliction* **injurious hardship**,
and of patience.
11 Behold, we count them *happy* **blessed** which endure.
Ye have heard of the *patience* **endurance** of *Job* **Iyob**,
and have seen the *end* **completion** of *the Lord* **Yah Veh**;
that the *Lord* **Adonay** is *very pitiful* **large spleened**,
and *of tender mercy* **compassionate**.
12 But *above* **before** all *things*, my brethren,
swear **oath** not, neither by heaven, neither by the earth,
neither by any other oath:
but let your yea be yea; and *your* nay, nay;
lest ye fall into *condemnation* **hypocrisy**.

THE VOW OF TRUST

13 Is any among you *afflicted* **enduring hardship**?
let him pray.
Is any *merry* **cheerful**? let him *sing psalms* **psalm**.
14 Is any *sick* **frail** among you?
let him call for the elders of the *church* **ecclesia**;
and let them pray over him,
anointing him with **olive** oil
in the name of *the Lord* **Adonay**:
15 And the *prayer* **vow** of *faith* **the trust**
shall save the *sick* **wearied**,
and *the Lord* **Adonay** shall raise him up;
and if **ever** he have *committed* **done** sins,
they shall be forgiven him.
16 Confess your *faults* **backslidings** one to another,
and *pray* **vow** one for another, that ye may be healed.
The *effectual fervent prayer* **energized petition**
of *a righteous man* **the just**
availeth much **is mighty enough**.
17 *Elias* **Eli Yah** was a *man* **human**
subject to like passions **likepassioned** as we *are*,
and he prayed *earnestly* **a prayer** that it might not rain:
and it rained not on the earth
by the space of three years and six months.
18 And he prayed again, and the heaven gave rain,
and the earth *brought forth* **sprouted** her fruit.
19 Brethren,
if **ever** any *of* **among** you *do err* **wander** from the truth,
and one *convert* **turn** him **around**;
20 Let him know,
that he which *converteth* **turneth** the sinner **around**
from the *error* **wandering** of his way
shall save a soul from death,
and shall *hide* **vail** a multitude of sins.

KEY TO INTERPRETING THE EXEGESES:
King James text is in regular type;
Text under exegeses is in oblique type;
Text of exegeses is in bold type.

SALUTATION

1 *Peter* **Petros,**
an apostle of *Jesus Christ* **Yah Shua Messiah,**
to the *strangers scattered* **pilgrim diaspora**
throughout Pontus, Galatia,
Cappadocia, Asia, and Bithynia,
2 *Elect* **Select** according to the *foreknowledge* **prognosis**
of *God* **Elohim** the Father,
through sanctification of the **in holiness of** Spirit,
unto obedience and sprinkling of the blood
of *Jesus Christ* **Yah Shua Messiah:**
Grace **Charism** unto you,
and *peace* **shalom,** be multiplied.

THE LIVING HOPE

3 *Blessed* **Eulogized** be the *God* **Elohim** and Father
of our *Lord Jesus Christ* **Adonay Yah Shua Messiah,**
which according to his *abundant* **vast** mercy
hath *begotten* **rebirthed** us *again* unto a *lively* **living** hope
by the resurrection of *Jesus Christ* **Yah Shua Messiah**
from the dead,
4 To an inheritance
incorruptible, and *undefiled* **unpolluted,**
and that fadeth not away **— amaranthine,**
reserved in heaven for **guarded in the heavens unto** you,
5 Who are *kept* **garrisoned**
by **in** the *power* **dynamis** of *God* **Elohim**
through *faith* **trust** unto salvation
ready **prepared** to be *revealed* **unveiled**
in the *last time* **final season.**
6 Wherein ye *greatly rejoice* **jump for joy,**
though now for a *season* **little,** if need be,
ye are *in heaviness* **sorrowed**
through manifold temptations **in divers testings:**
7 That the *trial* **proofing** of your *faith* **trust,**
being much more precious
than of gold that *perisheth* **destructeth,**
though it be *tried with* **proofed through** fire,
might be found unto *praise* **halal** and honour and glory
at the *appearing* **apocalypse**
of *Jesus Christ* **Yah Shua Messiah:**
8 Whom having not seen, ye love;
in whom, though now ye see him not,
yet *believing* **trusting,** ye *rejoice* **jump for joy**
with *joy unspeakable* **inexpressible cheer**
9 and *full of glory* **glorified:**
Receiving the *end* **completion** of your *faith* **trust,**
even the salvation of *your* souls.
10 *Of* **Concerning** which salvation
the prophets have inquired
and *searched diligently* **investigated,**
who prophesied *of* **concerning** the *grace* **charism**
that should come unto you:
11 Searching **unto** what,
or *what manner of time* **which season**
the Spirit of *Christ* **Messiah** which was in them
did signify **evidenced,**
when it *testified beforehand* **prewitnessed**
the sufferings *of Christ* **unto Messiah,**
and the *glory that should follow* **glories after these.**
12 Unto whom it was *revealed* **unveiled,**
that not unto themselves, but unto us
they did minister *the things* **those,**
which are now *reported* **evangelized** unto you
by **through** them that have
preached the gospel **evangelized** unto you
with **in** the Holy *Ghost* **Spirit,**
sent down **apostolized** from heaven;
which *things* the angels *desire* **pant**
to *look* **stoop down** into.
13 Wherefore gird up the loins of your mind, be sober,
and hope to the *end* **completion**
for the *grace* **charism** that is to be brought unto you
at the *revelation* **apocalypse**
of *Jesus Christ* **Yah Shua Messiah;**
14 As obedient children,
not *fashioning* **configuring** yourselves
according to the *former lusts* **previous pantings**
in your *ignorance* **unknowingness:**
15 But as he which hath called you is holy,
so be ye holy in all *manner of conversation* **behaviour;**
16 Because *it is written* **scribed,**
Be ye holy; *for* **because** I am holy.
17 And if ye call on the Father,
who without respect of persons
judgeth according to *every man's* **each's** work,
pass **behave** the time of your *sojourning here* **settling**
in *fear* **awe:**
18 *Forasmuch as ye know* **Knowing** that ye were not
redeemed with *corruptible things* **corruptibles,**
as silver *and* **or** gold,
from your vain
conversation received by tradition from your fathers
patriarchal traditions;
19 But with the precious blood of *Christ* **Messiah,**
as of a lamb
without blemish **unblemished**
and *without spot* **unstained:**
20 Who *verily* **indeed** was *foreordained* **foreknown**
before the foundation of the *world* **cosmos,**
but was manifest in these *last* **final** times for you,
21 Who *by* **through** him *do believe* **trust** in *God* **Elohim,**
that raised him up from the dead, and gave him glory;
so that your *faith* **trust** and hope might be in *God* **Elohim.**
22 Seeing ye have *purified* **hallowed** your souls
in obeying the truth through the Spirit
unto *unfeigned love* **unhypocritical befriending**
of the brethren,
see that *ye* love one another *with* **from** a pure heart
fervently **intensely:**
23 Being *born again* **rebirthed,**
not of corruptible *seed* **spore,** but of incorruptible,
by **through** the word of *God* **Elohim,**
which liveth and abideth *for ever* **unto the eons.**
24 *For* **Because** all flesh is as *grass* **herbage,**
and all the glory of *man* **humanity**
as the *flower* **blossom** of *grass* **herbage.**
The *grass* **herbage** withereth,
and the *flower* **blossom** thereof falleth away:
25 But the *word* **rhema** of *the Lord* **Yah Veh**
endureth for ever **abideth unto the eons.**
And this is the *word* **rhema**
which by the gospel is preached **evangelized** unto you.

AS NEWBORN INFANTS

2 *Wherefore* **Therefore**
laying aside **putting away** all malice,
and all *guile* **deceit,** and hypocrisies,
and envies, and all *evil speakings* **slanders,**
2 As newborn *babes* **infants,**
desire **yearn for**
the *sincere* **undeceitful** milk of *the word* **logic,**
that ye may grow *thereby* **therein:**
3 If *so be* **ever** ye have tasted
that *the Lord* **Yah Veh** is *gracious* **kind.**
Psalm 34:8

AS LIVING STONES

4 To whom coming, *as unto* a living stone,
disallowed **disapproved** indeed *of men* **by humanity,**
but *chosen of God* **select with Elohim,**
and precious **honourable,**
5 Ye also, as *lively* **living** stones,
are built up a spiritual house, an holy priesthood,
to offer up spiritual sacrifices,
acceptable **wellreceived** to *God* **Elohim**
by Jesus Christ **through Yah Shua Messiah.**
6 Wherefore also it is contained in the scripture,
Behold, I *lay* **place** in *Sion* **Siyon** a chief corner stone,
elect **select,** *precious* **honourable:**
and he that *believeth* **trusteth** on him
shall not **no way** be *confounded* **shamed.**
7 Unto you therefore which *believe* **trust,** he is precious:
but unto them which *be disobedient* **distrust,**
the stone which the builders *disallowed* **disapproved,**
the same **this one**
is made **became** the head of the corner,
8 And a stone of stumbling, and a rock of *offence* **scandal,**
even to them which stumble at the word,

being disobedient **who distrust**:
whereunto also they were *appointed* **set**.
9 But ye are a *chosen generation* **select genos**,
a *royal* **sovereign** priesthood, an holy *nation* **goyim**,
a peculiar *people* **acquisition unto himself**;
that ye should
shew forth **evangelize** the *praises* **virtue** of him
who hath called you out of darkness
into his marvellous light;
10 Which in time past were not a people,
but are now the people of *God* **Elohim**:
which had not *obtained mercy* **been mercied**,
but now *have obtained mercy* **be mercied**.
11 *Dearly* beloved,
I beseech you as *strangers* **settlers** and pilgrims,
abstain from fleshly *lusts* **pantings**,
which war against the soul;
12 Having your *conversation honest* **behaviour good**
among the *Gentiles* **goyim**:
that, *whereas* **in that which**
they *speak against* **slander** you as evildoers,
they may by *your* good works,
which they shall *behold* **observe**,
glorify *God* **Elohim** in the day of visitation.

ON SUBJUGATING TO GOVERNMENTS

13 *Submit* **Subjugate** yourselves **therefore**
to every *ordinance of man* **creation of humanity**
for the *Lord's* sake **of Adonay**:
whether it be to the *king* **sovereign**, as supreme;
14 *Or* **Whether** unto governors,
as unto them that are sent *by* **through** him **indeed**
for the punishment of **unto avenging** evildoers,
and for the *praise* **halal** of them that do *well* **good**.
15 *For so* **Because thus** is the will of *God* **Elohim**,
that with *well doing* **doing good**
ye may *put to silence* **muzzle**
the *ignorance* **unknowingness**
of *foolish men* **thoughtless humanity**:
16 As *free* **liberated**,
and not *using your* **regarding** liberty
for a cloke **as a covering** of *maliciousness* **malice**,
but as the servants of *God* **Elohim**.
17 Honour all *men*. Love the brotherhood.
Fear God **Awe Elohim**. Honour the *king* **sovereign**.
18 *Servants* **Housekeepers**,
be subject **subjugate** to *your masters* **despotes**
with **in** all *fear* **awe**;
not only to the good and gentle,
but also to the *froward* **crooked**.
19 For this is *thankworthy* **charism**,
if *a man* **one** for conscience toward *God* **Elohim**
endure *grief* **sorrow**, suffering *wrongfully* **unjustly**.
20 For what *glory* **fame** is it,
if, when ye be *buffeted* **punched** for your *faults* **sinning**,
ye shall *take it patiently* **endure**?
but if, when ye do *well* **good**, and suffer *for it*,
ye *take it patiently* **endure**,
this is *acceptable* **charism** with *God* **Elohim**.
21 For even *hereunto* **unto this** were ye called:
because *Christ* **Messiah** also suffered for us,
leaving **behind** us an example,
that ye should follow his *steps* **tracks**.
22 Who did no sin,
neither was *guile* **deceit** found in his mouth:
23 Who, when he was *reviled* **abused**,
reviled not again **replied unabusively**;
when he suffered, he threatened not;
but *committed* **surrendered** himself to him
that judgeth *righteously* **justly**:
24 Who his own self
bare **took up** our sins in his own body on the *tree* **staff**,
that we, being dead to sins,
should live unto *righteousness* **justness**:
by whose *stripes* **bruises** ye were healed.
25 For ye were as **wandering** sheep *going astray*;
but are now returned
unto the Shepherd and *Bishop* **Episcopate** of your souls.

ON SUBJUGATING IN RELATIONSHIPS

3 Likewise, *ye wives* **women**,
be in subjection **subjugate yourselves**
to your own *husbands* **men**;
that, if any *obey not* **one distrust** the word,
they also may without the word be *won* **gained**
by **through** the *conversation* **behaviour**
of the *wives* **women**;
2 While they *behold* **observe**
your *chaste conversation* **hallowed behaviour**
coupled with fear **in awe**.
3 Whose *adorning* **cosmos**
let it not be
that outward *adorning of plaiting* **braiding** the hair,
and of *wearing* **wrapping around** of gold,
or of *putting on of apparel* **enduing garments**;
4 But *let it be the hidden man* **the secret human**
of the heart,
in that which is *not corruptible* **incorruptible**,
even the ornament — of a meek and quiet spirit,
which is in the sight of *God* **Elohim**
of great price **vastly precious**.
5 For after this manner in the old time
the holy women also,
who *trusted* **hoped** in *God* **Elohim**, adorned themselves,
being in subjection **subjugating**
unto their own *husbands* **men**;
6 *Even* as *Sara* **Sarah** obeyed Abraham,
calling him *lord* **adoni**:
whose *daughters* **children** ye *are* **became**,
as long as ye do *well* **good**,
and are not *afraid with* **awestricken of** any *amazement* **terror**.
7 Likewise, *ye husbands* **men**,
dwell with them **co—settle** according to knowledge,
giving **bestowing** honour *unto the wife*,
as unto the *weaker* **frailer** vessel,
and as being *heirs together* **co—heirs**
of the *grace* **charism** of life;
that your prayers be not *hindered* **excsinded**.
8 *Finally* **In completion**,
be ye all *of one mind* **likeminded**,
having compassion **sympathetic** one of another,
love **befriending** as brethren,
be pitiful **tenderspleened**, *be courteous* **friendly minded**:
9 Not *rendering* **giving back** evil for evil,
or *railing* **abuse** for *railing* **abuse**:
but contrariwise *blessing* **eulogize**;
knowing that ye are *thereunto* called **unto this**,
that ye should inherit a *blessing* **eulogy**.
10 For he that *will* **willeth to** love life, and see good days,
let him *refrain* **pause** his tongue from evil,
and his lips that they speak no *guile* **deceit**:
11 Let him *eschew* **deviate from** evil, and do good;
let him seek *peace* **shalom**, and *ensue* **pursue** it.
12 *For* **Because** the eyes of *the Lord* **Yah Veh**
are over the *righteous* **just**,
and his ears *are open* unto their *prayers* **petitions**:
but the face of *the Lord* **Yah Veh**
is against them that do evil.
13 And who is he that *will harm* **shall vilify** you,
if **ever** ye be *followers* **mimickers**
of that which is good?
14 But and if ye suffer for *righteousness'* **justness'** sake,
happy are ye **blessed**:
and be not *afraid* **awestricken**
of their *terror* **awesomeness**,
neither be troubled;
15 But *sanctify the Lord God°* **hallow Yah Veh Elohim°**
in your hearts:
and be *ready always* **ever prepared**
to *give an answer* **plead** to every *man* **one**
that asketh you a *reason* **word**
of **concerning** the hope that is in you
with meekness and *fear* **awe**:

°some mss: Adonay Messiah

16 Having a good conscience; that,
whereas **in that which** they *speak evil of* **slander** you,
as of evildoers, they may *be ashamed* **shame**
that *falsely accuse* **threaten**
your good *conversation* **behaviour** in *Christ* **Messiah**.
17 For it is better,
if *the will of God be* so **Elohim so willeth**,
that ye suffer for *well* doing **good**, than for *evil* doing **evil**.

18 *For Christ* **Because Messiah** also
hath once suffered for sins,
the just for the unjust,
that he might bring us to *God* **Elohim,**
being put to death **indeed deathified** in the flesh,
but *quickened* **enlivened** by the Spirit:
19 *By* **In** which also he went and preached
unto the spirits in *prison* **the guardhouse**;
20 Which sometime *were disobedient* **distrusted**,
when once the *longsuffering* **patience** of *God* **Elohim**
waited **awaited** in the days of *Noah* **Noach**,
while the ark was a preparing,
wherein few, that is,
eight souls were saved *by* **through** water.
21 The *like figure* **antitype** whereunto *even* baptism
doth also now *save* **saveth** us
(not the *putting away* **laying aside** of the filth of the flesh,
but the *answer* **question** of a good conscience
toward God **unto Elohim**,)
by **through** the resurrection
of *Jesus Christ* **Yah Shua Messiah**:
22 Who is gone into heaven,
and is *on* **in** the right *hand* of *God* **Elohim**;
angels and authorities and *powers* **dynamis**
being made subject **subjugated** unto him.

ON SUBJUGATING TO THE MESSIAH

4 Forasmuch then
as *Christ* **Messiah** hath suffered for us in the flesh,
arm yourselves **be weaponed** likewise
with the same mind:
for **because** he that hath suffered in the flesh
hath *ceased* **paused** from sin;
2 That he no longer should *live* **exist**
the rest of his **remaining** time in the flesh
to the *lusts* **pantings** of *men* **humanity**,
but to the will of *God* **Elohim**.
3 For the **passing** time *past* of our *life* **existence**
may suffice us
to have *wrought* **worked** the will of the *Gentiles* **goyim**,
when we walked in *lasciviousness* **lechery**,
lusts **pantings**, *excess of wine* **vinolent**,
revellings **carousings**, *banquetings* **drinking bouts**,
and *abominable* **illicit** idolatries:
4 Wherein they think it strange
that ye *run* **rush** not *with them*
to *the same excess* **their effusion** of *riot* **dissipation**,
speaking evil of you **blaspheming**:
5 Who shall give *account* **back word** to him
that *is ready* **hath prepared**
to judge the *quick* **living** and the dead.
6 For *for* **unto** this *cause*
was the gospel preached also to them that are dead
were the dead evangelized,
that they might **indeed** be judged
according to *men* **humanity** in *the* flesh,
but live according to *God* **Elohim** in *the* spirit.
7 But the *end* **completion** of all *things*
is at hand **approacheth**:
be ye therefore *sober* **sound**, and watch unto prayer.
8 And *above* **before** all *things*
have *fervent charity among* **intense love unto** yourselves:
for charity **because love**
shall *cover* **vail** the multitude of sins.
9 *Use hospitality* **Befriend strangers** one to another
without *grudging* **murmuring**.
10 **Exactly** As *every man* **each**
hath *received* **taken** the *gift* **charisma**,
even so minister the same *one to another* **unto yourselves**,
as good *stewards* **administrators**
of the *manifold grace* **divers charism** of *God* **Elohim**.
11 If any *man* **one** speak,
let him speak as the oracles of *God* **Elohim**;
if any *man* **one** minister,
let him do it as of the *ability* might
which *God giveth* **Elohim supplieth**:
that *God* **Elohim** in all *things* may be glorified
through *Jesus Christ* **Yah Shua Messiah**,
to whom be *praise* **glory** and dominion
for ever and ever **unto the eons of the eons**.
Amen.

ON TESTINGS OF FIRE

12 Beloved, *think* **may** it not **be** strange
concerning the *fiery trial* **firing in you**
which is to *try* **test** you,
as though *some* **somewhat** strange *thing*
happened unto you:
13 But *rejoice* **cheer**,
inasmuch **according** as ye are partakers
of *Christ's* **Messiah's** sufferings;
that, *when his glory shall be revealed*
at the apocalypse of his glory,
ye may *be glad* also **cheer**,
with *exceeding* **jumping for** joy.
14 If ye be reproached *for* **in** the name of *Christ* **Messiah**,
happy are ye **blessed**;
for **because** the spirit of glory and of *God* **Elohim**
resteth upon you:
on their part he is *evil spoken of* **indeed blasphemed**,
but on your part he is glorified.
15 *But* **Indeed**
let *none* **not any** of you suffer as a murderer,
or as a thief, or as an evildoer,
or as
a busybody in other men's matters **overseeing others**.
16 Yet if *any man suffer* as a *Christian* **Messianist**,
let him not be ashamed;
but let him glorify *God on* **Elohim in** this *behalf* **part**.
17 *For the time is come* **Because this is the season**
that judgment must begin
at **from** the house of *God* **El**:
and if *it* first *begin at* **from** us,
what shall the *end* **completion** be
of them that *obey not* **distrust**
the *gospel* **evangelism** of *God* **Elohim**?
18 And if the *righteous scarcely* **just difficultly** be saved,
where shall the *ungodly* **irreverent** and the sinner
appear **be manifest**?
19 *Wherefore* **So then**
let them that suffer according to the will of *God* **Elohim**
commit the keeping of **commend** their **own** souls *to him*
in *well* doing **good**,
as unto a *faithful* **trustworthy** Creator.

ON SHEPHERDING THE SHEPHERDDOM

5 The elders which are among you I *exhort* **beseech**,
who am also an elder — **a co—elder**,
and a witness of the sufferings of *Christ* **Messiah**,
and also a partaker of the glory
that shall be *revealed* **unveiled**:
2 *Feed* **Shepherd** the *flock* **shepherddom** of *God* **Elohim**
which is among you,
taking the oversight thereof **overseeing**,
not by *constraint* **compulsion**, but *willingly* **voluntarily**;
not for *filthy lucre* **avarice**, but *of a ready mind* **eagerly**;
3 Neither as *being lords over* **overlording**
God heritage **the inheritance**,
but *being ensamples* **becoming types**
to the *flock* **shepherddom**.
4 And when the *chief* **Arch** Shepherd
shall *appear* **manifest**,
ye shall receive a *crown* **wreath** of glory
that fadeth not away — **amaranthine**.
5 Likewise, *ye* younger,
submit **subjugate** yourselves unto the elder.
Yea, all *of you be subject* **subjugate** one to another,
and be *clothed* **enrobed**
with *humility* **humblemindedness**:
for God resisteth **because Elohim opposeth** the proud,
and giveth *grace* **charism** to the humble.
6 Humble yourselves therefore
under the *mighty* **powerful** hand of *God* **Elohim**,
that he may exalt you in *due time* **season**:
7 *Casting* **Tossing** all your *care* **anxiety** upon him;
for **because** he *careth for* **is concerned about** you.
8 Be sober, *be vigilant* **watch**;
because your adversary *the devil* **Diabolos**,
as a roaring lion,
walketh about, seeking whom he may *devour* **swallow**:
9 Whom *resist stedfast* **withstand solid** in the *faith* **trust**,
knowing that the same *afflictions* **sufferings**
are *accomplished* **completed**

in your *brethren* **brotherhood**
that are in the *world* **cosmos.**
10 But the *God* **Elohim** of all *grace* **charism,**
who hath called us unto his eternal glory
by Christ Jesus **in Messiah Yah Shua,**
after that ye have suffered a *while* **little,**
make **prepare** you *perfect,* stablish,
strengthen **invigorate**, *settle you***found.**
11 To him be glory and dominion
for ever and ever **unto the eons of the eons.**
Amen.

FINAL SALUTES

12 *By* **Through** Silvanus,
a *faithful* **trustworthy** brother unto you,
as I *suppose* **reckon,**
I have *written briefly* **scribed through few words,**
exhorting **beseeching,** and *testifying* **witnessing**
that this is the true *grace* **charism** of *God* **Elohim**
wherein ye stand.
13 *The church that is at Babylon* **They in Babel,**
elected together with you **the co—select,** saluteth you;
and *so doth Marcus* **Markos** my son.
14 *Greet* **Salute** ye one another with a kiss of *charity* **love.**
Peace **Shalom** *be* with you all
that are in *Christ Jesus* **Messiah Yah Shua.**
Amen.

KEY TO INTERPRETING THE EXEGESES:
King James text is in regular type;
Text under exegeses is in oblique type;
Text of exegeses is in bold type.

SALUTATION

1 *Simon Peter* **Shimon Petros,**
a servant and an apostle of *Jesus Christ* **Yah Shua Messiah,**
to them that *have obtained* **were allotted**
like **equally** precious *faith* **trust** with us
through **in** the *righteousness* **justness** of *God* **Elohim**
and our Saviour *Jesus Christ* **Yah Shua Messiah:**
2 *Grace* **Charism** and *peace* **shalom**
be multiplied unto you
through **in** the knowledge of *God* **Elohim,**
and of *Jesus* **Yah Shua** our *Lord* **Adonay,**
3 According as his *divine power* **elohimic dynamis**
hath *given* **granted** unto us all *things*
that pertain unto life and *Godliness* **reverence,**
through the knowledge of him
that hath called us *to* **through** glory and virtue:
4 *Whereby* **Through which** are given unto us
exceeding great **magnificent**
and precious *promises* **pre—evangelisms:**
that *by* **through** these
ye might be partakers of the *divine* **elohimic** nature,
having escaped the corruption
that is in the *world through lust* **cosmos in pantings.**
5 And beside this, *giving* **bringing in** all diligence,
add to **supply in** your *faith* **trust,** virtue;
and *to* **in** virtue, knowledge;
6 And *to* **in** knowledge, *temperance* **self—control;**
and *to temperance* **in self—control,** *patience* **endurance;**
and *to patience* **in endurance,** *Godliness* **reverence.**
7 And *to Godliness* **in reverence,**
brotherly kindness **befriending brethren;**
and *to brotherly kindness* **in befriending brethren,**
charity **love.**
8 For *if these things be* **these being** in you,
and *abound* **superabounding,**
they *make* **seat** you
that ye shall neither be *barren* **idle** nor unfruitful
in the knowledge
of our *Lord Jesus Christ* **Adonay Yah Shua Messiah.**
9 *But* **Indeed** he
that lacketh **to whom** these *things* **are not present**
is blind, and *cannot see afar off* **blinketh,**
and hath *forgotten* **taken forgetfulness**
that he was purged **of the purifying**
from his *old* sins **of long ago.**
10 Wherefore the rather, brethren, give diligence
to make your calling and *election sure* **selection stedfast:**
for *if ye do* **doing** these *things,*
ye shall *never fall* **not ever no way stumble:**
11 For *so* **thus** an entrance
shall be *ministered* **supplied** unto you *abundantly* **richly**
into the *everlasting kingdom* **eternal sovereigndom**
of our *Lord* **Adonay** and Saviour
Jesus Christ **Yah Shua Messiah.**
12 Wherefore I *will* **shall** not *be negligent* **disregard**
to *put* **ever remind** you *always in remembrance*
of **concerning** these *things,*
though ye know *them,*
and be established in the present truth.

PETROS' FINAL EVANGELISM

13 Yea, I *think* **deem** it *meet* **just,**
as long as I am in this tabernacle,
to *stir* **rouse** you *up*
by putting **in reminding** you *in remembrance;*
14 Knowing that *shortly* **quickly**
I must put off this **be the laying aside** of my tabernacle,
even **exactly** as
our *Lord Jesus Christ* **Adonay Yah Shua Messiah**
hath *shewed* **evidenced** me.
Yahn 21:18, 19
15 Moreover I *will endeavour* **shall be diligent**
that ye may *be able* **regard** after my *decease* **exodus**
to *have* **do** these *things always* **ever** in remembrance.
16 For we have not followed
cunningly devised fables **sophisticated myths,**
when we made known unto you

the *power* **dynamis** and *coming* **parousia**
of our *Lord Jesus Christ* **Adonay Yah Shua Messiah**,
but *were eyewitnesses* **became spectators** of his majesty.
17 For he *received* **hath taken**
from *God* **Elohim** the Father
honour and glory,
when there *came* **was brought** such a voice to him
from the *excellent* **majestic** glory,
This is my beloved Son,
in **of** whom I *am well pleased* **well—approve**.
18 And this voice
which *came* **was brought** from heaven we heard,
when we were **being** with him in the holy mount.

ON SCRIPTURE PROPHECY

19 We have also a *more sure* **stedfast** word of prophecy;
whereunto ye do well that ye take heed,
as unto a light that *shineth* **manifesteth**
in *a dark* **an obscure place**,
until the day **thoroughly** dawn,
and the day *star* **phospherescence** arise in your hearts:
20 Knowing this first,
that *no* **not any** prophecy of the scripture
is **becometh** of
any private interpretation **personal explanation**.
21 For the prophecy
came not in old time **was not ever brought**
by the will of *man* **humanity**:
but holy *men* **humanity** of *God* **Elohim** spake
as they were moved **borne** by the Holy *Ghost* **Spirit**.

ON PSEUDO PROPHETS AND PSEUDO DOCTORS

2 But there *were false* **became pseudo** prophets
also among the people,
even as there shall be *false teachers* **pseudo doctors**
among you,
who *privily* shall *bring in* **surreptitiously introduce**
damnable **destructive** heresies,
even denying the *Lord* **Despotes**
that *bought* **marketed** them,
and bring upon themselves *swift* **quick** destruction.
2 And many
shall follow their *pernicious* **destructive** ways;
by reason of **through** whom the way of truth
shall be *evil spoken of* **blasphemed**.
3 And *through covetousness* **in avarice**
shall they with *feigned* **fabricated** words
make merchandise *of* you:
whose judgment now of *a long time* **old**
lingereth **idleth** not,
and their *damnation* **destruction** slumbereth not.
4 For if *God* **Elohim** spared not the angels that sinned,
but *cast* **incarcerated** them *down to hell* **in Tartaros**,
and delivered them into *chains* **caverns** of darkness,
to be *reserved* **guarded** unto judgment;
5 And spared not the *old world* **ancient cosmos**,
but *saved Noah* **guarded Noach** the eighth *person*,
a preacher of *righteousness* **justness**,
bringing in the *flood* **cataclysm**
upon the *world* **cosmos** of the *ungodly* **irreverent**;
6 And *turning* **incinerating**
the cities of *Sodom* **Sedom** and *Gomorrha* **Amorah**
into ashes
condemned them with *an overthrow* **a catastrophe**,
making **setting** them an ensample unto those
that *after should* **were about to** live *ungodly* **irreverently**;
7 And *delivered* **rescued** just Lot,
vexed **worn down**
with **by** the *filthy conversation* **lecherous behaviour**
of the *wicked* **illicit**:
8 (For that *righteous* **just** man dwelling among them,
in seeing and hearing,
vexed **tortured** his *righteous* **just** soul *from* day *to* **by** day
with their *unlawful deeds* **untorahed works**;)
9 *The Lord* **Yah Veh** knoweth how
to *deliver* **rescue** the *godly* **wellrevering**
out of *temptations* **testings**,
and to *reserve* **guard** the unjust unto the day of judgment
to be punished:
10 But *chiefly* **especially** them that walk after the flesh
in the *lust* **panting** of *uncleanness* **defilement**,
and *despise government* **disesteem lordship**.
Presumptuous are they **Audacious**,
selfwilled **selfpleasing**,
they *are not afraid* **tremble not**
to *speak evil of dignities* **blaspheme glories**.
11 Whereas angels,
which are **being** greater
in *power* **might** and *might* **dynamis**,
bring *not railing accusation* **no blasphemous judgment**
against them *before the Lord* **with Yah Veh**.
12 But these,
as *natural brute beasts* **physical irrational live beings**,
made **born**
to be *taken* **captured** and *destroyed* **corrupted**,
speak evil of the things **blaspheme those**
that they understand not **in which they are unknowing**;
and shall *utterly perish* **corrupt** in their own corruption;
13 And shall receive
the reward of *unrighteousness* **injustice**,
as they that *count* **deem** it pleasure
to *riot* **indulge** in the day time.
Spots they are **Stains** and blemishes,
sporting **reveling** themselves
with **in** their own *deceivings* **delusions**
while they *feast* **revel** with you;
14 Having eyes full of adultery,
and *that cannot cease* **restless** from sin;
beguiling **entrapping** unstable souls:
an heart they have exercised
with *covetous practices* **avarice**;
cursed children **of curse**:
15 Which have forsaken the *right* **straight** way,
and *are gone astray* **wander**,
following the way
of *Balaam* **Bilam** *the son* of *Bosor* **Beor**,
who loved
the *wages* **rewards** of *unrighteousness* **injustice**;
16 But *was rebuked* **had reproof**
for his *iniquity* **own torah violations**:
the *dumb ass* **voiceless burro**
speaking with man's **uttering in a human** voice
forbad the *madness* **insanity** of the prophet.
17 These are *wells without water* **waterless fountains**,
clouds
that are *carried with* **driven by** a *tempest* **whirlwind**;
to whom the mist of darkness
is *reserved for ever* **guarded unto the eons**.
18 For when they
speak great swelling words **utter overbulgings** of vanity,
they *allure* **entrap** through the *lusts* **pantings** of the flesh,
through much wantonness **lechery**,
those that *were clean* **indeed** escaped from them
who *live* **remain** in *error* **seduction**.
19 While they *promise them* **pre—evangelize** liberty,
they themselves *are* **being** the servants of corruption:
for of whom *a man* **anyone** is *overcome* **slighted**,
of the same **by this** is he *brought in bondage* **subservient**.
20 For if after they have escaped
the *pollutions* **defilements** of the *world* **cosmos**
through the knowledge of *the Lord* **Adonay** and Saviour
Jesus Christ **Yah Shua Messiah**,
they are again entangled *therein* **by these**,
and *overcome* **slighted**,
the latter end is **their finality becometh** worse with them
than the *beginning* **first**.
21 For it had been better for them
not to have known the way of *righteousness* **justness**,
than, after they have known it,
to turn **again** from the holy *commandment* **misvah**
delivered unto them.
22 But it is happened unto them
according to the true proverb,
The dog *is turned* **returneth** to his own vomit *again*;
and the *sow* **hog** that *was washed* **bathed**
to her wallowing in the mire.

ON THE FINAL DAYS

3 This second epistle, beloved,
I *now write* **already scribe** unto you;
in *both* which I *stir up* **rouse** your *pure* **sincere** minds
by way of **in** remembrance:
2 That ye may *be mindful of* **remember** the *words* **rhemas**

which were *spoken before* **foresaid** by the holy prophets,
and of the *commandment* **misvah**
of us the apostles of *the Lord* **Adonay** and Saviour:
3 Knowing this first,
that there shall come in the *last* **final** days
scoffers **mockers**,
walking after their own *lusts* **pantings**,
4 And *saying* **wording**,
Where is the *promise* **pre—evangelism**
of his *coming* **parousia**?
for **from** since the fathers fell asleep,
all *things continue as they were* **continually abide thus**
as from the beginning of the creation.
5 *For* **From** this
they *willingly are ignorant of* will **to hide**,
that by the word of *God* **Elohim** the heavens were of old,
and the earth standing out of the water
and *in* **through** the water:
6 *Whereby* **Through which**
the *world* **cosmos** that then was,
being *overflowed* **flooded** with water,
perished **destructed**:
7 But the heavens and the earth, which are now,
by the same word are *kept in store* **treasured**,
reserved **guarded** unto fire
against **unto**
the day of judgment and *perdition* **destruction**
of *ungodly men* **irreverent humanity**.
8 But, beloved,
be not ignorant of this one thing **hide not from this**,
that one day is with *the Lord* **Yah Veh**
as a thousand years,
and a thousand years as one day.
9 *The Lord* **Yah Veh** is not slack
concerning his *promise* **pre—evangelism**,
as some *men count* **deem** slackness;
but is *longsuffering to us—ward* **patient unto us**,
not willing that any should *perish* **destruct**,
but that all should *come* **pass** to repentance.

THE DAY OF YAH VEH

10 But the day of *the Lord will* **Yah Veh shall** come
as a thief in the night;
in the which the heavens
shall pass away with a *great noise* **whir**,
and the elements **being causticized,**
shall *melt with fervent heat* **let loose**,
the earth also and the works that are therein
shall be burned *up*.
11 *Seeing then that* **Therefore** all these,
things shall be dissolved **having let loose**,
what manner *of persons ought ye to* **ye must** be
in *all* holy *conversation* **behaviour**
and *godliness* **reverence**,
12 *Looking for* **Awaiting** and hasting
unto the *coming* **parousia** of the day of *God* **Elohim**,
wherein **through which** the heavens being on fire
shall be *dissolved* **loosed**,
and the elements **being causticized,**
shall melt *with fervent heat* **down**?
13 Nevertheless we,
according to his *promise* **pre—evangelism**,
look for **await** new heavens and a new earth,
wherein dwelleth *righteousness* **justness**.
14 Wherefore, beloved,
seeing that ye *look for such things* **await these**,
be diligent that ye may be found of him in *peace* **shalom**,
without spot **unstained**, and *blameless* **unblemished**.
15 And *account* **deem** that the *longsuffering* **patience**
of our *Lord* **Adonay** is salvation;
even **exactly** as our beloved brother *Paul* **Paulos** also
according to the wisdom given unto him
hath *written* **scribed** unto you;
16 As also in all his epistles,
speaking in them *of* **concerning** these *things*;
in which are some *things*
hard to be understood **incomprehensible**,
which they that are unlearned and unstable *wrest* **twist**,
as *they do* also the *other* **rest of the** scriptures,
unto their own destruction.
17 Ye therefore, beloved,
seeing ye *know* **foreknow** these *things before*,
beware **guard** lest ye also,
being led away
with the *error* **seduction** of the *wicked* **illicit**,
fall from your own stedfastness.
18 But grow in *grace* **charism**,
and in the knowledge of our *Lord* **Adonay** and Saviour
Jesus Christ **Yah Shua Messiah**.
To him be glory
both now and *for ever* **unto the day of the eons**.
Amen.

KEY TO INTERPRETING THE EXEGESES:
King James text is in regular type;
Text under exegeses is in oblique type;
Text of exegeses is in bold type.

SALUTATION

1 *Jude* **Yah Hudah**,
the servant of *Jesus Christ* **Yah Shua Messiah**,
and brother of *James* **Yaaqovos**,
to them that are *sanctified* **hallowed**
by God **in Elohim** the Father,
and *preserved* **guarded** in *Jesus Christ* **Yah Shua Messiah**,
and called:
2 Mercy unto you,
and *peace* **shalom**, and love, be multiplied.

ON AGONIZING FOR THE TRUST

3 Beloved,
when I *gave* **made** all diligence to *write* **scribe** unto you
of **concerning** the common salvation,
it was needful for me **I had need** to *write* **scribe** unto you,
and *exhort* **beseech** you that ye should earnestly
contend **agonize** for the *faith* **trust**
which was once delivered unto the *saints* **holy**.
4 For *there are certain men* **some humans have**
crept **surreptitiously sneaked** in *unawares* **alongside**,
who were *before of old* **long ago**
ordained **preinscribed** to this *condemnation* **judgment**,
ungodly men **irreverent**,
turning **transplacing**
the *grace* **charism** of our *God* **Elohim**
into *lasciviousness* **lechery**,
and denying the only *Lord God* **Despotes Elohim**,
and our *Lord Jesus Christ* **Adonay Yah Shua Messiah**.

EXAMPLES OF PAST JUDGMENTS

5 I *will* therefore
put you in remembrance **shall remind you**,
though ye once knew this,
how that *the Lord* **Yah Veh**,
having saved the people
out of the land of *Egypt* **Misrayim**,
afterward **secondly** destroyed them
that *believed* **trusted** not.
6 And the angels
which *kept* **guarded** not their *first estate* **own hierarchy**,
but left their own *habitation* **house**,
he hath *reserved* **guarded**
in *everlasting chains* **eternal bonds** under *darkness* **gloom**
unto the judgment of the *great* **mega** day.
7 Even as *Sodom* **Sedom** and *Gomorrha* **Amorah**,
and the cities about them in like manner,
giving themselves over to fornication **whoring**,
and going after *strange* **other** flesh,
are set forth for an example,
suffering **enduring** the *vengeance* **judgment**
of eternal fire.
8 *Likewise* **Yet indeed** also these *filthy* dreamers
defile the flesh, *despise dominion* **set aside lordship**,
and *speak evil of dignities* **blaspheme glories**.
9 Yet *Michael* **Michah El** the archangel,
when *contending* **dialoguing** with *the devil* **Diabolos**
he *disputed* **reasoned** about the body of Moses,
durst not bring **up** *against him*
a *railing accusation* **blasphemy**,
but said, *The Lord* **Yah Veh** rebuke thee.
10 But these *speak evil* **blaspheme**
of those *things which* **indeed, as much as** they know not:
but *what* **as much as** they *know* **understand**
naturally **physically**,
as *brute beasts* **irrational live beings**,
in those *things* they corrupt themselves.
11 Woe unto them!
for **because** they have gone in the way of *Cain* **Qayin**,
and *ran greedily* **rushed**
after the *error* **seduction** of *Balaam* **Bilam** for reward,
and *perished* **destructed**
in the *gainsaying* **controversy** of *Core* **Korach**.
12 These are *spots* **reefs** in your *feasts of charity* **love**,
when they *feast* **revel** with you,
feeding **shepherding** themselves *without fear* **fearlessly**:
waterless clouds *they are without water*,
carried about of winds;
autumnal trees *whose fruit withereth*,
without fruit **unfruitful**, twice dead,
plucked up by the roots **uprooted**;
13 Raging waves of the sea,
foaming **frothing** out their own shame;
wandering **planetary** stars,
to whom is *reserved* **guarded**
the blackness of *darkness* **gloom**
for ever **unto the eons**.
14 And *Enoch* **Hanoch** also, the seventh from Adam,
prophesied of these, *saying* **wording**,
Behold, *the Lord* **Yah Veh** cometh
with ten thousands of his saints **among his holy myriads**,
15 To *execute* **deal** judgment upon all,
and to *convince* **convict** all
that are *ungodly* **irreverent among them**
of **concerning** all their *ungodly deeds* **irreverent works**
which they have *ungodly committed* **irreverently done**,
and *of* **concerning** all their *hard speeches* **hardnesses**
which *ungodly* **irreverent** sinners
have spoken against him.
16 These are murmurers, *complainers* **fatalists**,
walking after their own *lusts* **pantings**;
and their mouth
speaketh *great swelling words* **overbulgings**,
having men's persons in admiration **marveling over faces**
because of *advantage* **benefit**.

REMEMBERING THE RHEMAS

17 But, beloved, remember ye the *words* **rhemas**
which were *spoken before* **foresaid** of the apostles
of our *Lord Jesus Christ* **Adonay Yah Shua Messiah**;
18 How that they *told* **worded to you**
there should be mockers in the *last* **final** time,
who should walk after their own
ungodly lusts **irreverent pantings**.
19 These be they
who *separate themselves* **set boundaries**,
sensual **soulical**, having not the Spirit.
20 But ye, beloved,
building up yourselves on your most holy *faith* **trust**,
praying in the Holy *Ghost* **Spirit**,
21 *Keep* **Guard** yourselves in the love of *God* **Elohim**,
looking for **awaiting** the mercy
of our *Lord Jesus Christ* **Adonay Yah Shua Messiah**
unto eternal life.
22 And *of* some *have compassion* **indeed mercy**,
making a difference **discerning**:
23 And others save *with fear* **in awe**,
pulling **seizing** them out of the fire;
hating even the *garment* **tunic**
spotted **stained** by the flesh.

BENEDICTION

24 Now unto him that is able
to *keep* **guard** you *from falling* **unstumbling**,
and to *present* **stand** you *faultless* **unblemished**
before the presence **in sight** of his glory
with exceeding **in jumping for** joy,
25 To the only wise *God* **Elohim** our Saviour,
be glory and majesty,
dominion **power** and *power* **authority**,
both now and *ever* **unto all eons**.
Amen.

KEY TO INTERPRETING THE EXEGESES:
King James text is in regular type;
Text under exegeses is in oblique type;
Text of exegeses is in bold type.

THE WORD OF LIFE

1 That which was from the beginning,
which we have heard,
which we have seen with our eyes,
which we have *looked upon* **observed**,
and our hands have *handled* **touched**,
of **concerning** the Word of life;
2 (For the life was manifested,
and we have seen it, and *bear* witness,
and *shew* **evangelize** unto you that eternal life,
which was with the Father, and was manifested unto us;)
3 That which we have seen and heard
declare **evangelize** we unto you,
that ye also may have *fellowship* **communion** with us:
and truly our *fellowship* **communion** is with the Father,
and with his Son *Jesus Christ* **Yah Shua Messiah**.
4 And these *things write* **scribe** we unto you,
that your *joy* may **cheer** be **filled** full.
5 This then is the *message* **pre—evangelism**
which we have heard of him,
and *declare* **evangelize** unto you,
that *God* **Elohim** is light, and in him is no darkness at all.
6 If **ever** we say that we have
fellowship **communion** with him,
and walk in darkness, we lie, and do not the truth:
7 But if **ever** we walk in the light, as he is in the light,
we have *fellowship* **communion** one with another,
and the blood of *Jesus Christ* **Yah Shua Messiah** his Son
cleanseth **purifieth** us from all sin.
8 If **ever** we say that we have no sin,
we *deceive* **seduce** ourselves, and the truth is not in us.
9 If **ever** we *confess* **profess** our sins,
he is *faithful* **trustworthy** and just to forgive us our sins,
and to *cleanse* **purify** us
from all *unrighteousness* **injustice**.
10 If **ever** we say that we have not sinned,
we make him a liar, and his word is not in us.

YAH SHUA MESSIAH, THE PARACLETE

2 My little children,
these *things write* **scribe** I unto you, that ye sin not.
And if **ever** any *man* **one** sin,
we have *an advocate* **a Paraclete** with the Father,
Jesus Christ **Yah Shua Messiah** the *righteous* **just**:
2 And he is the *propitiation* **kopur/atonement** for our sins:
and not for ours only,
but also for *the sins of* the whole *world* **cosmos**.
3 And *hereby* **in this** we *do* know
that we *know* **have known** him,
if **ever** we *keep* **guard** his *commandments* **misvoth**.
4 He that *saith* **wordeth**, I *know* **have known** him,
and *keepeth* **guardeth** not his *commandments* **misvoth**,
is a liar, and the truth is not in him.
5 But whoso *keepeth* **ever guardeth** his word,
in him *verily* **truly** is the love of *God* **Elohim**
perfected **completed**:
hereby **in this** know we that we are in him.
6 He that *saith* **wordeth** he abideth in him
ought **is indebted** himself also *so* **thus** to walk,
even **exactly** as he walked.
7 Brethren,
I *write* **scribe** no new *commandment* **misvah** unto you,
but an old *commandment* **misvah**
which ye had from the beginning.
The old *commandment* **misvah** is the word
which ye have heard from the beginning.
8 Again,
a new *commandment* **misvah** I *write* **scribe** unto you,
which *thing* is true in him and in you:
because the darkness *is past* **passeth away**,
and the true light *now shineth* **already manifesteth**.
9 He that *saith* **wordeth that** he is in the light,
and hateth his brother, is in darkness even until now.
10 He that loveth his brother abideth in the light,
and there is
none occasion of stumbling **no scandal** in him.
11 But he that hateth his brother is in darkness,
and walketh in darkness,
and knoweth not whither he goeth,
because *that* darkness hath blinded his eyes.
12 I *write* **scribe** unto you, little children,
because your sins are forgiven you for his name's sake.
13 I *write* **scribe** unto you, fathers,
because ye have known him that is from the beginning.
I *write* **scribe** unto you, *young men* **youths**,
because ye have
overcome **triumphed over** the *wicked* **evil** one.
I *write* **scribe** unto you, little children,
because ye have known the Father.
14 I have *written* **scribed** unto you, fathers,
because ye have known him that is from the beginning.
I have *written* **scribed** unto you, *young men* **youths**,
because ye are *strong* **mighty**,
and the word of *God* **Elohim** abideth in you,
and ye have *overcome* **triumphed**
over the *wicked* **evil** one.

ON LOVING THE COSMOS

15 Love not the *world* **cosmos**,
neither *the things* **those** that are in the *world* **cosmos**.
If **ever** any *man* **one** love the *world* **cosmos**,
the love of the Father is not in him.
16 *For* **Because** all that is in the *world* **cosmos**,
the *lust* **panting** of the flesh,
and the *lust* **panting** of the eyes,
and the pride of *life* **existence**,
is not of the Father, but is of the *world* **cosmos**.
17 And the *world* **cosmos** passeth away,
and the *lust* **panting** thereof:
but he that doeth the will of *God* **Elohim**
abideth *for ever* **unto the eons**.

THE ANTIMESSIAH

18 Little children, it is the *last time* **final hour**:
and **exactly** as ye have heard
that *antichrist* **the antimessiah** shall come,
even now
are there many *antichrists* **antimessiahs have become**;
whereby we know that it is the *last time* **final hour**.
2 Yahn 7
19 They went out from us, but they were not of us;
for if they had been of us,
they *would no doubt* **should** have
continued **ever abode** with us:
but *they went out*,
that they might *be made* manifest
that they were not all of us.
20 But ye have an *unction* **anointing** from the Holy One,
and ye know all *things*.
21 I have not *written* **scribed** unto you
because ye know not the truth,
but because ye know it,
and that *no* **not any** lie is of the truth.
22 Who is a liar *but* **except** he that denieth
that *Jesus* **Yah Shua** is the *Christ* **Messiah**?
He is antichrist **This one is the antimessiah**,
that denieth the Father and the Son.
2 Yahn 7
23 Whosoever denieth the Son,
the same hath not the Father:
[but] he that acknowledgeth the Son hath the Father also.
24 Let that therefore abide in you,
which ye have heard from the beginning.
If **ever** that which ye have heard from the beginning
shall *remain* **abide** in you,
ye also shall *continue* **abide** in the Son, and in the Father.
25 And this is the *promise* **pre—evangelism**
that he hath *promised* **pre—evangelized** to us,
even — eternal life.
26 These *things* have I *written* **scribed** unto you
concerning them that seduce you.
27 But the anointing which ye have *received* **taken** of him
abideth in you,
and ye need not that any *man teach* **one doctrinate** you:
but as the same anointing
teacheth **doctrinateth** you *of* **concerning** all *things*,
and is truth, and is no lie,
and *even* **exactly** as it hath *taught* **doctrinated** you,
ye shall abide in him.

28 And now, little children, abide in him;
that, when he shall *appear* **manifest**,
we may have *confidence* **boldness**,
and not be ashamed before him at his *coming* **parousia**.
29 If **ever** ye know that he is *righteous* **just**,
ye know that every one that doeth *righteousness* **justness**
is born of him.

THE LOVE OF THE FATHER

3 *Behold* **Perceive**,
what manner of love
the Father hath *bestowed upon* **given** us,
that we should be called
the *sons* **children** of *God* **Elohim**:
therefore **for this** the *world* **cosmos** knoweth us not,
because it knew him not.
2 Beloved, now are we the *sons* **children** of *God* **Elohim**,
and it *doth* **be** not yet *appear* **manifest**
what we shall be;
but we know that,
when **if ever** he shall *appear* **be manifest**,
we shall be like him;
for **because** we shall see him **exactly** as he is.
3 And every *man* **one** that hath this hope in him
purifieth **halloweth** himself,
even **exactly** as he is *pure* **hallowed**.
4 Whosoever *committeth* **doeth** sin
transgresseth **violateth** also the *law* **torah**:
for sin is the *transgression* **violation** of the *law* **torah**.
5 And ye know that he was manifested
to take away our sins;
and in him is no sin.
6 Whosoever abideth in him sinneth not:
whosoever sinneth hath not seen him,
neither known him.
7 Little children, let no *man deceive* **one seduce** you:
he that doeth *righteousness* **justness** is *righteous* **just**,
even **exactly** as he is *righteous* **just**.
8 He that *committeth* **doeth** sin is of *the devil* **Diabolos**;
for the devil **because Diabolos**
sinneth from the beginning.
For **Unto** this *purpose*
the Son of *God* **Elohim** was manifested,
that he might *destroy* **let loose**
the works of *the devil* **Diabolos**.
9 Whosoever is born of *God* **Elohim** doth not *commit* sin;
for **because** his *seed remaineth* **sperma abideth** in him:
and he cannot sin, because he is born of *God* **Elohim**.
10 In this the children of *God* **Elohim** are manifest,
and the children of *the devil* **Diabolos**:
whosoever doeth not *righteousness* **justness**
is not of *God* **Elohim**,
neither he that loveth not his brother.

ON LOVING ONE ANOTHER

11 *For* **Because** this is the *message* **evangelism**
that ye heard from the beginning,
that we should love one another.
12 Not **exactly** as *Cain* **Qayin**,
who was of that *wicked* **evil** one,
and *slew* **slaughtered** his brother.
And *wherefore slew* **for what cause slaughtered** he him?
Because his own works were evil,
and his brother's *righteous* **just**.
13 Marvel not, my brethren,
if the *world* **cosmos** hate you.
14 We know
that we have *passed* **departed** from death unto life,
because we love the brethren.
He that loveth not his brother abideth in death.
15 Whosoever hateth his brother is a murderer:
and ye know that *no* **not any** murderer
hath eternal life abiding in him.
16 *Hereby perceive we* **In this have we known** the love
of God,
because he *laid down* **placed** his *life* **soul** for us:
and we *ought* **are indebted**
to *lay down* **place** our *lives* **souls** for the brethren.
17 But *whoso* **whoever**
hath this *world's good* **cosmos' subsistence**,
and *seeth* **observeth** his brother have need,
and shutteth up his *bowels of compassion* **spleen**
from him,
how *dwelleth* **abideth** the love of *God* **Elohim** in him?
18 My little children, let us not love in word,
neither in tongue; but in *deed* **work** and in truth.
19 And *hereby* **in this** we know that we are of the truth,
and shall *assure* **confide** our hearts
before **in front of** him.
20 *For* **Because** if **ever** our heart condemn us,
God **Elohim** is greater than our heart,
and knoweth all *things*.
21 Beloved, if **ever** our heart condemn us not,
then have we *confidence* **boldness** toward *God* **Elohim**.
22 And *whatsoever* **if ever** we ask,
we *receive* **take** of him,
because we *keep* **guard** his *commandments* **misvoth**,
and do those *things* that are pleasing in his sight.
23 And this is his *commandment* **misvah**,
That we should *believe on* **trust**
the name of his Son *Jesus Christ* **Yah Shua Messiah**,
and love one another,
exactly as he gave us *commandment* **misvah**.
24 And he
that *keepeth* **guardeth** his *commandments* **misvoth**
dwelleth **abideth** in him, and he in him.
And *hereby* **in this** we know that he abideth in us,
by the Spirit which he hath given us.

ON THE ANTIMESSIAH

4 Beloved, *believe* **trust** not every spirit,
but *try* **proof** the spirits
whether they *are* **be** of *God* **Elohim**:
because many *false* **pseudo** prophets
are gone out into the *world* **cosmos**.
2 *Hereby* **In this** know ye the Spirit of *God* **Elohim**:
Every spirit that *confesseth* **professeth**
that *Jesus Christ* **Yah Shua Messiah** is come in the flesh
is of *God* **Elohim**:
3 And every spirit that *confesseth* **professeth** not
that *Jesus Christ* **Yah Shua Messiah** is come in the flesh
is not of *God* **Elohim**:
and this is that *spirit* of *antichrist* **the antimessiah**,
whereof ye have heard that it should come;
and even now already is it in the *world* **cosmos**. 2 Yahn 7
4 Ye are of *God* **Elohim**, little children,
and have *overcome* **triumphed over** them:
because greater is he that is in you,
than he that is in the *world* **cosmos**.
5 They are of the *world* **cosmos**:
therefore **for this** speak they of the *world* **cosmos**,
and the *world* **cosmos** heareth them.
6 We are of *God* **Elohim**:
he that knoweth *God* **Elohim** heareth us;
he that is not of *God* **Elohim** heareth not us.
Hereby **By this** know we the spirit of truth,
and the spirit of *error* **seduction**.

ELOHIM IS LOVE

7 Beloved, let us love one another:
for **because** love is of *God* **Elohim**;
and every one that loveth is born of *God* **Elohim**,
and knoweth *God* **Elohim**.
8 He that loveth not
knoweth not God **hath not known Elohim**;
for God **because Elohim** is love.
9 In this was manifested
the love of *God toward* **Elohim in** us,
because that *God* **Elohim**
sent **apostolized** his only begotten Son
into the *world* **cosmos**,
that we might live through him.
10 *Herein* **In this** is love,
not that we loved *God* **Elohim**, but that he loved us,
and *sent* **apostolized** his Son
to be the *propitiation* **kopur/atonement** for our sins.
11 Beloved, if *God so* **Elohim thus** loved us,
we *ought* **are indebted** also to love one another.
12 No *man* **one** hath *seen God* **observed Elohim**
at any time — **not ever**.
If **ever** we love one another,
God dwelleth **Elohim abideth** in us,
and his love is *perfected* **completed** in us.

13 *Hereby* **In this** know we
that we *dwell* **abide** in him, and he in us,
because he hath given us of his Spirit.
14 And we have *seen* **observed** and *do testify* **witness**
that the Father *sent* **apostolized** the Son
to be the Saviour of the *world* **cosmos**.
15 Whosoever shall *confess* **profess**
that *Jesus* **Yah Shua** is the Son of *God* **Elohim**,
God dwelleth **Elohim abideth** in him,
and he in *God* **Elohim**.
16 And we have known and *believed* **trusted** the love
that *God* **Elohim** hath *to* **in us**.
God **Elohim** is love;
and he that *dwelleth* **abideth** in love
dwelleth **abideth** in *God* **Elohim**, and *God* **Elohim** in him.
17 *Herein* **In this** is our love *made perfect* **completed**,
that we may have boldness in the day of judgment:
because **exactly** as he is, so are we in this *world* **cosmos**.
18 There is no *fear* **awe** in love;
but *perfect* **complete** love casteth out *fear* **awe**:
because *fear* **awe** hath *torment* **punishment**.
He that *feareth* **aweth**
is not *made perfect* **completed** in love.
19 We love him, because he first loved us.
20 If *a man* **ever one** say, **Because** I love *God* **Elohim**,
and hateth his brother, he is a liar:
for he that loveth not his brother whom he hath seen,
how can he love *God* **Elohim** whom he hath not seen?
21 And this *commandment* **misvah** have we from him,
That he who loveth *God* **Elohim** love his brother also.

TRIUMPHING OVER THE COSMOS

5 Whosoever *believeth* **trusteth**
that *Jesus* **Yah Shua** is the *Christ* **Messiah**
is born of *God* **Elohim**:
and every one that loveth him that begat
loveth him also that is begotten of him.
2 *By* **In** this we know
that we love the children of *God* **Elohim**,
when we love *God* **Elohim**,
and *keep* **guard** his *commandments* **misvoth**.
3 For this is the love of *God* **Elohim**,
that we *keep* **guard** his *commandments* **misvoth**:
and his *commandments* **misvoth** are not grievous.
4 *For* **Because** whatsoever is born of *God* **Elohim**
overcometh **triumpheth over** the *world* **cosmos**:
and this is the *victory* **triumph**
that *overcometh* **triumpheth over** the *world* **cosmos**,
even our *faith* **trust**.
5 Who is he
that *overcometh* **triumpheth over** the *world* **cosmos**,
but **except** he that *believeth* **trusteth**
that *Jesus* **Yah Shua** is the Son of *God* **Elohim**?
6 This is he that came *by* **through** water and blood,
even Jesus Christ — **Yah Shua Messiah**;
not *by* **in** water only, but *by* **in** water and blood.
And *it is* the Spirit *that beareth witness* **witnesseth**,
because the Spirit is truth.
7 *For* **Because** there are three
that *bear record* **witness** in heaven,
the Father, the Word, and the Holy *Ghost* **Spirit**:
and these three are one.
8 And there are three that *bear* witness in earth,
the Spirit, and the water, and the blood:
and these three *agree* **are** in one.
9 If we *receive* **take** the witness of *men* **humanity**,
the witness of *God* **Elohim** is greater:
for **because** this is the witness of *God* **Elohim**
which he hath *testified of* **witnessed concerning** his Son.
10 He that *believeth* **trusteth** on the Son of *God* **Elohim**
hath the witness in himself:
he that *believeth* **trusteth** not *God* **Elohim**
hath made him a liar;
because he *believeth* **trusteth** not **in** the *record* **witness**
that *God gave of* **Elohim witnessed concerning** his Son.
11 And this is the *record* **witness**,
that *God* **Elohim** hath given to us eternal life,
and this life is in his Son.
12 He that hath the Son hath life;
and he that hath not the Son of *God* **Elohim** hath not life.
13 These *things* have I *written* **scribed** unto you
that *believe on* **trust**
in the name of the Son of *God* **Elohim**;
that ye may know that ye have eternal life,
and that ye may *believe* **trust**
on **in** the name of the Son of *God* **Elohim**.
14 And this is the *confidence* **boldness**
that we have *in* **toward** him, that,
if — **whatever** we ask *any thing* according to his will,
he heareth us:
15 And if **ever** we know that he hear us,
whatsoever we ask,
we know that we have the *petitions* **requests**
that we *desired* **asked** of him.
16 If **ever** any *man* **one**
see his brother sin a sin which is not unto death,
he shall ask,
and he shall give him life
for them that sin not unto death.
There is a sin unto death:
I do not *say* **word** that he shall *pray* **ask** for it.
17 All *unrighteousness* **injustice** is sin:
and there is a sin not unto death.
18 We know that
whosoever is born of *God* **Elohim** sinneth not;
but he that is begotten of *God* **Elohim**
keepeth **guardeth** himself,
and that *wicked* **evil** one toucheth him not.
19 And we know that we are of *God* **Elohim**,
and the whole *world* **cosmos**
lieth in *wickedness* **the evil one**.
20 And we know that the Son of *God* **Elohim** is come,
and hath given us *an understanding* **a mind**,
that we may know him that is true,
and we are in him that is true,
even in his Son *Jesus Christ* **Yah Shua Messiah**.
This is the true *God* **Elohim**, and eternal life.
21 Little children, *keep* **guard** yourselves from idols.
Amen.

KEY TO INTERPRETING THE EXEGESES:
King James text is in regular type;
Text under exegeses is in oblique type;
Text of exegeses is in bold type.

SALUTATION

1 The elder unto the *elect* **select** lady° and her children,
whom I love in the truth;
°lady: feminine of adoni
and not I only,
but also all they that have known the truth;
2 *For the truth's sake* **Because of the truth,**
which *dwelleth* **abideth** in us,
and shall be with us *for ever* **unto the eons.**
3 *Grace* **Charism** shall be with you,
mercy, *and peace* **shalom,**
from *God* **Elohim** the Father,
and from
the Lord Jesus Christ **Adonay Yah Shua Messiah,**
the Son of the Father, in truth and love.
4 I *rejoiced greatly* **cheered extremely**
that I found of thy children walking in truth,
exactly as we have *received* **taken**
a *commandment* **misvah** from the Father.
5 And now I beseech thee, lady,
not as though I *wrote* **scribed**
a new *commandment* **misvah** unto thee,
but that which we had from the beginning,
that we love one another.
6 And this is love,
that we walk after his *commandments* **misvoth.**
This is the *commandment* **misvah,**
That, **exactly** as ye have heard from the beginning,
ye should walk in it.

ON THE ANTIMESSIAH

7 *For* **Because** many *deceivers* **seducers**
are entered into the *world* **cosmos,**
who *confess* **profess** not
that *Jesus Christ* **Yah Shua Messiah** is come in the flesh.
This is *a deceiver* **the seducer**
and *an antichrist* **the antimessiah.**
1 Yahn 2:18, 22, 4:3
8 Look to yourselves,
that we lose not those *things* which we have wrought,
but that we *receive* **take** a full reward.
9 Whosoever transgresseth,
and abideth not in the doctrine of *Christ* **the Messiah,**
hath not *God* **Elohim.**
He that abideth in the doctrine of *Christ* **the Messiah,**
he hath both the Father and the Son.
10 If there come any unto you,
and bring not this doctrine,
receive **take** him not into your house,
neither *bid him God speed* **word to him, Cheers!:**
11 For he that *biddeth* **wordeth to** him,
God speed **Cheers!**
is partaker **partaketh** of his evil *deeds* **works.**

FINAL SALUTE

12 Having *many things* **much** to *write* **scribe** unto you,
I *would* **willed** not
write with paper **through sheet** and ink:
but I *trust* **hope** to come unto you,
and speak *face* **mouth** to *face* **mouth,**
that our *joy* **cheer** may be *filled* **full.**
13 The children of thy *elect* **select** sister *greet* **salute** thee.
Amen.

KEY TO INTERPRETING THE EXEGESES:
King James text is in regular type;
Text under exegeses is in oblique type;
Text of exegeses is in bold type.

SALUTATION

1 The elder unto the *wellbeloved* **beloved** Gaius,
whom I love in the truth.
2 Beloved, I *wish above* **vow concerning** all *things*
that thou mayest prosper and be *in health* **whole,**
even **exactly** as thy soul prospereth.
3 For I *rejoiced greatly* **cheered extremely,**
when the brethren came
and *testified* **witnessed** of the truth that is in thee,
even as thou walkest in the truth.
4 I have no greater *joy* **cheer than these,**
than to hear that my children walk in truth.

ON BEING TRUSTWORTHY

5 Beloved, thou *dost faithfully* **dealest trustworthily**
whatsoever **if ever** thou *dost* **workest**
to the brethren, and to strangers;
6 Which have *borne witness* **witnessed** of thy *charity* **love**
before **in the sight of** the *church* **ecclesia:**
whom if thou *bring* forward *on their journey*
after a godly sort **worthily of Elohim,**
thou shalt do well:
7 *Because* **Indeed** that for his name's sake they went forth,
taking *nothing* **naught** of the *Gentiles* **goyim.**
8 We therefore *ought* **are indebted** to *receive* **take** such,
that we might *be fellowhelpers* **become co—workers**
to the truth.
9 I *wrote* **scribed** unto the *church* **ecclesia:**
but Diotrephes,
who *loveth* **befriendeth**
to have the preeminence among them,
receiveth us not.
10 Wherefore, if **ever** I come,
I *will* **shall** remember his *deeds* **works** which he doeth,
prating **babbling** against us with *malicious* **evil** words:
and not *content therewith* **satisfied by these,**
neither doth he himself receive the brethren,
and forbiddeth them that *would* **will,**
and casteth them out of the *church* **ecclesia.**
11 Beloved, *follow* **mimic** not that which is evil,
but that which is good.
He that doeth good is of *God* **Elohim:**
but he that doeth evil hath not seen *God* **Elohim.**
12 Demetrius *hath good report* **is witnessed** of all *men,*
and of the truth itself:
yea, and we *also bear record* **witness;**
and ye know that our *record* **witness** is true.

FINAL SALUTE

13 I had *many things* **much** to *write* **scribe,**
but I *will* **shall** not *with* **through** ink and *pen* **reed**
write **scribe** unto thee:
14 But I *trust* **hope** I shall *shortly* **straightway** see thee,
and we shall speak *face* **mouth** to *face* **mouth.**
Peace **Shalom** *be* to thee. *Our* friends salute thee.
Greet **Salute** the friends by name.

KEY TO INTERPRETING THE EXEGESES:
King James text is in regular type;
Text under exegeses is in oblique type;
Text of exegeses is in bold type.

PROLOGUE

1 The *Revelation* **Apocalypse**
of *Jesus Christ* **Yah Shua Messiah**,
which *God* **Elohim** gave unto him,
to shew unto his servants *things* **those**
which must *shortly come to pass* **quickly become**;
and he *sent* **apostolized** and signified it
by **through** his angel
unto his servant *John* **Yahn**:
2 Who *bare record* **witnessed** of the word of *God* **Elohim**,
and of the *testimony* **witness**
of *Jesus Christ* **Yah Shua Messiah**,
and of all *things* that he saw.

THE FIRST BEATITUDE

3 Blessed is he that readeth,
and they that hear the words of this prophecy,
and *keep* **guard** those *things*
which are *written* **scribed** therein:
for the *time* **season** is *at hand* **near**.

SALUTATION FROM THE TRIUNE ELOHIM

4 *John* **Yahn** to the seven *churches* **ecclesiae**
which are in Asia:
Grace be **Charism** unto you, and *peace* **shalom**,
from him
which is, and which was, and which is to come
who is, and who was, and who is coming;
and from the seven Spirits
which are before **in sight of** his throne;
5 And from *Jesus Christ* **Yah Shua Messiah**,
who is the *faithful* **trustworthy** witness,
and the *first begotten* **firstborn** of the dead,
and the *prince* **arch** of the *kings* **sovereigns** of the earth.
Unto him that loved us,
and *washed* **bathed** us from our sins in his own blood,
6 And hath made us *kings* **sovereigns** and priests
unto *God* **Elohim** and his Father;
to him be glory and *dominion* **power**
for ever and ever **unto the eons of the eons**.
Amen.
7 Behold, he cometh with clouds;
and every eye shall see him,
and they *also* which pierced him:
and all *kindreds* **scions** of the earth
shall *wail* **chop** because of him.
Even so **Yea**, Amen.
8 *I am Alpha and Omega* **I AM the A and the Ω**,
the beginning and the *ending* **completion**,
saith the Lord **wordeth Yah Veh**,
which is, and which was, and which is to come
who is, and who was, and who is coming,
the Almighty **Sabaoth**.

THE SEVEN SCRIBINGS

9 I *John* **Yahn**, *who* also *am* your brother,
and *companion* **co—partaker** in tribulation,
and in the
kingdom **sovereigndom** and *patience* **endurance**
of *Jesus Christ* **Yah Shua Messiah**,
was **became** in the isle that is called Patmos,
for the word of *God* **Elohim**,
and for the *testimony* **witness**
of *Jesus Christ* **Yah Shua Messiah**.
10 I *was* **became** in *the* Spirit
on the Lord's **in Adonay's** day,
and heard behind me a *great* **mega** voice,
as of a trumpet,
11 *Saying* **Wording**,
I am Alpha and Omega **I AM the A and the Ω**,
the first and the *last* **final**:
and, What thou seest, *write* **scribe** in a *book* **scroll**,
and send it unto the seven *churches* **ecclesiae**
which are in Asia;
unto Ephesus, and unto Smyrna, and unto Pergamos,
and unto Thyatira, and unto Sardis,
and unto Philadelphia, and unto Laodicea.
12 And I turned **again** to see the voice that spake with me.
And *being turned* **turning again**,
I saw seven golden *candlesticks* **menorah**;
13 And in the midst of the seven *candlesticks* **menorah**
one like unto the Son of *man* **humanity**,
clothed with a garment down **endued** to the foot,
and girt *about* **to** the *paps* **breasts**
with a golden girdle.
14 His head and *his* hairs were white *like* **as** wool,
as white as snow;
and his eyes *were* as a flame of fire;
15 And his feet like *unto fine brass* **brilliant copper**,
as *if they burned* **fired** in a furnace;
and his voice as the *sound* **voice** of many waters.
16 And he had in his right hand seven stars:
and out of his mouth *went* **proceeded**
a sharp *twoedged sword* **double—mouthed sabre**:
and his *countenance* **visage**
was as the sun *shineth* **manifesteth** in his *strength* **dynamis**.
17 And when I saw him, I fell *at* **toward** his feet as dead.
And he *laid* **placed** his right hand upon me,
saying **wording** unto me, *Fear* **Awe** not;
I am **I AM** the first and the *last* **final**:
18 *I am* — he that liveth, and *was* **became** dead;
and, behold, I am alive *for evermore* **unto the eons**,
Amen;
and have the keys of *hell* **hades** and of death.
19 *Write the things* **Scribe those** which thou hast seen,
and *the things* **those** which are,
and *the things which shall* **those about to** be
hereafter **after these**;
20 The mystery of the seven stars
which thou sawest *in* **on** my right *hand*,
and the seven golden *candlesticks* **menorah**.
The seven stars
are the angels of the seven *churches* **ecclesiae**:
and the seven *candlesticks* **menorah** which thou sawest
are the seven *churches* **ecclesiae**.

THE FIRST SCRIBING

2 Unto the angel
of the *church* **ecclesia** of *Ephesus* **Ephesians**
write **scribe**;
These *things saith* **wordeth** he
that *holdeth* **empowereth** the seven stars
in his right *hand*,
who walketh in the midst
of the seven golden *candlesticks* **menorah**;
2 I know thy works, and thy labour,
and thy *patience* **endurance**,
and *how* **that** thou canst not bear them which are evil:
and thou hast *tried* **tested** them
which *say they are* **profess to be** apostles, and are not,
and hast found them *liars* **pseudos**:
3 And hast borne, and hast *patience* **endurance**,
and *for my name's sake* **because of my name**
hast laboured, and hast not *fainted* **wearied**.
4 *Nevertheless* **Yet** I have *somewhat* against thee,
because thou hast *left* **forsaken** thy first love.
5 Remember therefore from whence thou art fallen,
and repent, and do the first works;
or else I will **if not I shall** come unto thee quickly,
and *will remove* **shall stir** thy *candlestick* **menorah**
out of his place,
except **unless** thou repent.
6 But this thou hast,
that thou hatest the *deeds* **works** of the Nicolaitanes,
which I also hate.
7 He that hath an ear,
let him hear what the Spirit *saith* **wordeth**
unto the *churches* **ecclesiae**;
To him that *overcometh* **triumpheth**
will **shall** I give to eat of the *tree* **staff** of life,
which is in the midst of the paradise of *God* **Elohim**.

THE SECOND SCRIBING

8 And unto the angel
of the *church in Smyrna* **ecclesia of Smyrnians**
write **scribe**;
These *things saith* **wordeth** the first and the *last* **final**,
which *was* **became** dead, and is alive;
9 I know thy works, and tribulation,

and poverty, (but thou art rich)
and *I know* the blasphemy of them
which *say they* **word themselves**
are Jews **to be Yah Hudiym,**
and are not, but *are* the synagogue of Satan.
10 *Fear* **Awe** none of those *things*
which thou *shalt* **art about to** suffer: behold,
the devil shall **Diabolos is about to** cast *some of* you
into *prison* **the guardhouse**,
that ye may be *tried* **tested**;
and ye shall have tribulation ten days:
be thou *faithful* **trustworthy** unto death,
and I *will* **shall** give thee a *crown* **wreath** of life.
11 He that hath an ear,
let him hear what the Spirit *saith* **wordeth**
unto the *churches* **ecclesiae**;
He that *overcometh* **triumpheth**
shall not **no way** be *hurt* **injured** of the second death.

THE THIRD SCRIBING

12 And to the angel
of the *church* **ecclesia** in Pergamos
write **scribe**;
These *things saith* **wordeth** he
which hath the sharp
sword with two edges **double—mouthed sabre**;
13 I know thy works, and where thou *dwellest* **settlest**,
even where Satan's *seat* **throne** is:
and thou *holdest fast* **empowerest** my name,
and hast not denied my *faith* **trust**,
even in those days wherein Antipas
was my *faithful martyr* **trustworthy witness**,
who was *slain* **slaughtered** among you,
where Satan *dwelleth* **settleth**.
14 But I have a few *things* against thee,
because thou hast there
them that *hold* **empower** the doctrine of *Balaam* **Bilam**,
who *taught Balac* **doctrinated in Balaq**
to cast a *stumblingblock* **scandal**
before **in the sight of** the *children* **sons** of *Israel* **Yisra El**,
to eat *things sacrificed unto idols* **idol sacrifices**,
and to *commit fornication* **whore**.
15 *So* **Thus** hast thou also them
that *hold* **empower** the doctrine of the Nicolaitanes,
which *thing* I hate.
16 Repent;
or else I will **if not I shall** come unto thee quickly,
and *will fight against* **shall war with** them
with **in** the *sword* **sabre** of my mouth.
17 He that hath an ear,
let him hear what the Spirit *saith* **wordeth**
unto the *churches* **ecclesiae**;
To him that *overcometh* **triumpheth**
will **shall** I give to eat of the *hidden* **secreted** manna,
and *will* **shall** give him a white *stone* **pebble**,
and in the *stone* **pebble** a new name *written* **scribed**,
which no *man* **one** knoweth
saving **except** he that *receiveth* **taketh** it.

THE FOURTH SCRIBING

18 And unto the angel
of the *church* **ecclesia** in Thyatira
write **scribe**;
These *things saith* **wordeth** the Son of *God* **Elohim**,
who hath his eyes *like unto* **as** a flame of fire,
and his feet *are like fine brass* **as brilliant copper**;
19 I know thy works, and *charity* **love**,
and *service* **ministry**, and *faith* **trust**,
and thy *patience* **endurance**, and thy works;
and the *last to be* **final** more than the first.
20 *Notwithstanding* **Yet** I have a few *things* against thee,
because thou *sufferest* **allowest**
that woman *Jezebel* **Iy Zebel**,
which *calleth* **wordeth** herself a prophetess,
to *teach* **doctrinate** and to seduce my servants
to *commit fornication* **whore**,
and to eat *things sacrificed unto idols* **idol sacrifices**.
21 And I gave her *space* **time** to repent
of her *fornication* **whoredom**;
and she repented not.
22 Behold, I *will* **shall** cast her into a bed,
and them that *commit adultery* **adulterize** with her
into great tribulation,
except **unless** they repent of their *deeds* **works**.
23 And I *will kill* **shall slaughter** her children
with **in** death;
and all the *churches* **ecclesiae** shall know
that I am he **for I AM:**
which searcheth the reins and hearts:
and I *will* **shall** give unto *every one* **each** of you
according to your works.
24 But unto you I *say* **word**, and unto the rest in Thyatira,
as many as have not this doctrine,
and which have not known the depths of Satan,
as they *speak* **word**;
I *will* **shall** put upon you none other burden.
25 But that which ye have *already*
hold fast **empower** till **ever** I come.
26 And he that *overcometh* **triumpheth**,
and *keepeth* **guardeth** my works
unto the *end* **completion**,
to him
will **shall** I give *power* **authority** over the *nations* **goyim**:
27 And he shall *rule* **shepherd** them
with **in** a *rod* **scion** of iron;
as the vessels of a potter
shall they be *broken to shivers* **shattered**:
even as I *received* **also have taken** of my Father.
28 And I *will* **shall** give him the morning star.
29 He that hath an ear,
let him hear what the Spirit *saith* **wordeth**
unto the *churches* **ecclesiae**.

THE FIFTH SCRIBING

3 And unto the angel
of the *church* **ecclesia** in Sardis *write* **scribe**;
These *things saith* **wordeth** he
that hath the seven Spirits of *God* **Elohim**,
and the seven stars;
I know thy works,
that thou hast a name that thou livest, and art dead.
2 Be watchful,
and *strengthen* **establish** the *things which remain* **rest**,
that are *ready* **about** to die:
for I have not found thy works *perfect* **fulfilled**
before God **in the sight of Elohim**.
3 Remember therefore
how thou hast *received* **taken** and heard,
and *hold fast* **guard**, and repent.
If **ever** therefore thou shalt not watch,
I *will* **shall** come on thee as a thief,
and thou shalt not **no way** know
what hour I *will* **shall** come upon thee.
4 Thou hast a few names even in Sardis
which have not *defiled* **stained** their garments;
and they shall walk with me in white:
for **because** they are worthy.
5 He that *overcometh* **triumpheth**,
the same shall be *clothed* **arrayed**
in white *raiment* **garments**;
and I *will* **shall** not **no way**
blot out **erase** his name
out of the *book* **scroll** of life,
but I *will* **shall** confess his name
before **in sight of** my Father,
and *before* **in sight of** his angels.
6 He that hath an ear,
let him hear what the Spirit *saith* **wordeth**
unto the *churches* **ecclesiae**.

THE SIXTH SCRIBING

7 And to the angel
of the *church* **ecclesia** in Philadelphia *write* **scribe**;
These *things saith he that is* **wordeth the** holy,
he that is **the** true, *he* that hath the key of David,
he that openeth, and no *man* **one** shutteth;
and shutteth, and no *man* **one** openeth;
8 I know thy works: behold,
I have *set before thee* **given in thy sight**
an open *door* **portal**,
and no *man* **one** can shut it:
for **because** thou hast a little *strength* **dynamis**,
and hast *kept* **guarded** my word,
and hast not denied my name.

9 Behold,
I *will make* **shall give** them of the synagogue of Satan,
which *say they* **word themselves**
are Jews **to be Yah Hudiym**,
and are not, but *do* lie;
behold, I *will* **shall** make them to come and worship
before **in sight of** thy feet,
and to know that I have loved thee.
10 Because
thou hast *kept* **guarded** the word of my patience,
I also *will keep* **shall guard** thee
from the hour of *temptation* **testing**,
which shall **about to** come upon all the world,
to *try* **test** them that *dwell* **settle** upon the earth.
11 Behold, I come quickly:
hold **empower** that *fast* which thou hast,
that no *man* **one** take thy *crown* **wreath**.
12 Him that *overcometh* **triumpheth**
will **shall** I make a pillar
in the *temple* **nave** of my *God* **Elohim**,
and he shall *go no more* **not no way still go** out:
and I *will write* **shall scribe** upon him
the name of my *God* **Elohim**,
and the name of the city of my *God* **Elohim**,
which is **the** new *Jerusalem* **Yeru Shalem**,
which *cometh down* **descendeth** out of heaven
from my *God* **Elohim**:
and *I will write upon him* my new name.
13 He that hath an ear,
let him hear what the Spirit *saith* **wordeth**
unto the *churches* **ecclesiae**.

THE SEVENTH SCRIBING

14 And unto the angel
of the *church* **ecclesia** of the Laodiceans
write **scribe**;
These *things saith* **wordeth** the Amen,
the *faithful* **trustworthy** and true witness,
the beginning of the creation of *God* **Elohim**;
15 I know thy works, that thou art neither cold nor hot:
I would **O that** thou wert cold or hot.
16 *So* **Thus** then because thou art lukewarm,
and neither cold nor hot,
I *will spue* **am about to vomit** thee out of my mouth.
17 Because thou *sayest* **wordest**,
Because I am rich,
and *increased with goods* **enriched**,
and have need of *nothing* **naught**;
and knowest not that thou art *wretched* **miserable**,
and *miserable* **least mercied**,
and poor, and blind, and naked:
18 I counsel thee to *buy* **market** of me
gold *tried in* **fired by** the fire,
that thou mayest be *rich* **enriched**;
and white *raiment* **garments**,
that thou mayest be *clothed* **arrayed**,
and that the shame of thy nakedness
do not *appear* **be manifested**;
and anoint thine eyes with *eyesalve* **poultice**,
that thou mayest see.
19 As many as **ever** I *love* **befriend**,
I *rebuke* **reprove** and *chasten* **discipline**:
be zealous therefore, and repent.
20 Behold, I stand at the *door* **portal**, and knock:
if **ever** any *man* **one** hear my voice,
and open the *door* **portal**,
I *will* **shall** come in to him,
and *will* **shall** sup with him, and he with me.
21 To him that *overcometh* **triumpheth**
will **shall** I *grant* **give** to sit with me in my throne,
even as **also** *overcame* **triumphed**,
and am *set down* **seated** with my Father in his throne.
22 He that hath an ear,
let him hear what the Spirit *saith* **wordeth**
unto the *churches* **ecclesiae**.

IN SPIRIT, IN HEAVEN

4 After *this I looked* **these I perceived**,
and, behold, a *door was* **portal** opened in heaven:
and the first voice which I heard
was as *it were* of a trumpet *talking* **speaking** with me;
which said **wording**, *Come up* **Ascend** hither,
and I *will* **shall** shew thee *things*
those which must be *hereafter* **after these°**.
°some mss place **after these** at the beginning of verse 2
2 **(After these)** And *immediately* **straightway**
I *was in the* **became in** spirit: and, behold,
a throne *was* set in heaven, and one sat on the throne.
3 And he that sat was *to look upon* **in vision**
like a jasper and a *sardine* **sardius** stone:
and there was a rainbow
round about **surrounding** the throne,
in *sight* **vision** like unto an emerald.
4 And *round about* **surrounding** the throne
were four and twenty *seats* **thrones**:
and upon the *seats* **thrones**
I saw four and twenty elders sitting,
clothed **arrayed** in white *raiment* **garments**;
and they had on their heads *crowns* **wreaths** of gold.
5 And out of the throne
proceeded lightnings and thunderings and voices:
and *there were* seven lamps of fire
burning *before* **in sight of** the throne,
which are the seven Spirits of *God* **Elohim**.
6 And *before* **in sight of** the throne
there was a sea of glass like *unto crystal* **crystaline**:
and in the midst of the throne,
and *round about* **surrounding** the throne,
were four *beasts* **live beings** full of eyes
before **in front** and *behind* **in back**.
7 And the first *beast* **live being** was like a lion,
and the second *beast* **live being** like a calf,
and the third *beast* **live being**
had a face as a *man* **human**,
and the fourth *beast* **live being** was like a flying eagle.
8 And the four *beasts had* **live beings were**
each *of them* **surrounded with** six wings *about him*;
and *they were* full of eyes within:
and they **have no** rest *not* day and night,
saying **wording**, Holy, holy, holy,
Lord God Almighty **Yah Veh El Sabaoth**,
which was, and is, and is to come
who was, and who is, and who is coming.
Yesha Yah 6:3
9 And when those *beasts* **live beings**
give glory and honour and *thanks* **eucharist**
to him that sat on the throne,
who liveth *for ever and ever* **unto the eons of the eons**,
10 The four and twenty elders shall fall *down*
before **in sight of** him that sat on the throne,
and worship him that liveth
for ever and ever **unto the eons of the eons**,
and cast their *crowns* **wreaths**
before **in sight of** the throne,
saying **wording**,
11 Thou art worthy, O *Lord* **Yah Veh**,
to *receive* **take** glory and honour and *power* **dynamis**:
for **because** thou hast created all *things*,
and for thy *pleasure* **will** they are and were created.

THE SEVEN SEALED SCROLL

5 And I saw *in* **on** the right *hand* of him
that sat on the throne
a *book* **scroll**
written **scribed** within and *on the backside* **in back**,
sealed with seven seals.
2 And I saw a strong angel
proclaiming **preaching** with a *loud* **mega** voice,
Who is worthy to open the *book* **scroll**,
and to loose the seals thereof?
3 And no *man* **one** in heaven,
nor in earth, neither under the earth,
was able to open the *book* **scroll**, neither to look thereon.
4 And I wept much,
because no *man* **one** was found worthy
to open and to read the *book* **scroll**,
neither to look thereon.
5 And one of the elders *saith* **wordeth** unto me,
Weep not: behold,
the Lion **being** of the *tribe* **scion** of *Juda* **Yah Hudah**,
the Root of David,
hath *prevailed* **triumphed** to open the *book* **scroll**,

and to loose the seven seals thereof.
6 And I *beheld* **perceived**, and, *lo* **behold**,
in the midst of the throne
and of the four *beasts* **live beings**,
and in the midst of the elders,
stood a Lamb **standing**
as *it had* **having** been *slain* **slaughtered**,
having seven horns and seven eyes,
which are the seven Spirits of *God* **Elohim**
sent forth **apostolized** into all the earth.
7 And he came and took the *book* **scroll**
out of the right *hand* of him that sat upon the throne.
8 And when he had taken the *book* **scroll**,
the four *beasts* **live beings** and four and twenty elders
fell down *before* **in sight of** the Lamb,
having *every one* **each** of them *harps* **cithers**,
and golden *vials* **phials** full of *odours* **incense**,
which are the prayers of *saints* **the holy**.
9 And they sung a new *song* **ode**, *saying* **wording**,
Thou art worthy to take the *book* **scroll**,
and to open the seals thereof:
for **because** thou wast *slain* **slaughtered**,
and hast *redeemed* **marketed** us to *God* **Elohim**
by thy blood
out of every *kindred* **scion**, and tongue,
and people, and *nation* **goyim**;
10 And hast made us unto our *God* **Elohim**
kings **sovereigns** and priests:
and we shall reign on the earth.
11 And I *beheld* **perceived**,
and I heard the voice of many angels
round about **surrounding** the throne
and the *beasts* **live beings** and the elders:
and the number of them was
ten thousand **a myriad** times *ten thousand* **a myriad**,
and thousands of thousands;
12 *Saying* **Wording** with a *loud* **mega** voice,
Worthy is the Lamb that was *slain* **slaughtered**
to *receive power* **take dynamis**, and riches, and wisdom,
and *strength* might, and honour,
and glory, and *blessing* **eulogy**.
13 And every creature *which is* **being** in heaven,
and *on* **in** the earth, and under the earth,
and *such as are in* **upon** the sea,
and all *that are* **being** in them,
heard I *saying* **wording**,
Blessing **Eulogy**, and honour, and glory, and power,
be unto him that sitteth upon the throne,
and unto the Lamb
for ever and ever **unto the eons of the eons**.
14 And the four *beasts said* **live beings worded**,
Amen.
And the four and twenty elders
fell down and worshipped him that liveth
for ever and ever **unto the eons of the eons**.

THE FIRST SEAL

6 And I saw when the Lamb opened one of the seals,
and I heard, as *it were* the *noise* **voice** of thunder,
one of the four *beasts saying* **live beings wording**,
Come and see.
2 And I saw, and behold a white horse:
and he that sat on him had a bow;
and a *crown* **wreath** was given unto him:
and he went forth *conquering* **triumphing**,
and to *conquer* **triumph**.

THE SECOND SEAL

3 And when he had opened the second seal,
I heard the second *beast say* **live being wording**,
Come and see.
4 And there went out another horse *that was red* — **fiery**:
and *power* was given to him that sat thereon
to take *peace* **shalom** from the earth,
and that they should *kill* **slaughter** one another:
and there was given unto him a *great* **mega** sword.

THE THIRD SEAL

5 And when he had opened the third seal,
I heard the third *beast say* **live being wording**,
Come and see.
And I *beheld* **perceived**, and *lo* **behold** a black horse;
and he that sat on him
had a *pair of balances* **yoke** in his hand.
6 And I heard a voice
in the midst of the four *beasts say* **live beings wording**,
A *measure* **choinix** of *wheat* **grain**
for a *penny* **denarion**,
and three *measures* **choinixes** of barley
for a *penny* **denarion**;
and *see* thou *hurt* **injure** not the **olive** oil and the wine.

THE FOURTH SEAL

7 And when he had opened the fourth seal,
I heard the voice of the fourth *beast* **live being**
say **wording**,
Come and see.
8 And I *looked* **perceived**, and behold a *pale* **green** horse:
and his name that sat on him was Death,
and *Hell* **Hades** followed with him.
And *power* **authority** was given unto them
over the fourth part of the earth,
to *kill with sword* **slaughter in sabre**,
and *with hunger* **in famine**,
and *with* **in** death, and *with* **by** the beasts of the earth.

THE FIFTH SEAL

9 And when he had opened the fifth seal,
I saw under the **sacrifice** altar the souls of them
that were *slain* **slaughtered** for the word of *God* **Elohim**,
and for the *testimony* **witness** which they held:
10 And they cried with a *loud* **mega** voice,
saying **wording**,
How long **Until when**, O *Lord* **Despotes**,
the holy and **the** true,
dost thou not judge and avenge our blood
on **from** them that *dwell* **settle** on the earth?
11 And white *robes* **stoles**
were given unto *every one* **each** of them;
and it was *said* **rhetorized** unto them,
that they should rest yet for a little *season* **time**,
until their *fellowservants* **co—servants** also
and their brethren,
that should be killed **about to be slaughtered**
as they *were*,
should be fulfilled.

THE SIXTH SEAL

12 And I *beheld* **perceived**
when he had opened the sixth seal,
and, *lo* **behold**,
there *was a great earthquake* **became a mega quake**;
and the sun became black as *sackcloth* **saq** of hair,
and the moon became as blood;
13 And the stars of heaven fell unto the earth,
even as a fig tree casteth her *untimely figs* **unripened**,
when she is *shaken* **quaked** of a *mighty* **mega** wind.
14 And the heaven *departed* **separated**
as a scroll when it is *rolled together* **coiled**;
and every mountain and island
were *moved* **stirred** out of their places.
15 And the *kings* **sovereigns** of the earth,
and the *great men* **magistrates**, and the rich *men*,
and the *chief captains* **chiliarchs**,
and the *mighty men* **able**,
and every *bondman* **servant**,
and every *free man* **liberated**,
hid **secreted** themselves in the *dens* **grottos**
and in the rocks of the mountains;
16 And *said* **worded** to the mountains and rocks,
Fall on us,
and *hide* **secrete** us
from the face of him that sitteth on the throne,
and from the wrath of the Lamb:
17 *For* **Because** the *great* **mega** day of his wrath is come;
and who shall be able to stand?

ONE HUNDRED FORTY—FOUR THOUSAND SEALED

7 And after these *things* I saw four angels
standing on the four corners of the earth,
holding **overpowering** the four winds of the earth,
that the wind should not *blow* **puff** on the earth,
nor on the sea, nor on any tree.
2 And I saw another angel
ascending from the *east* **rising of the sun**,
having the seal of the living *God* **Elohim**:
and he cried with a *loud* **mega** voice to the four angels,

to whom it was given to *hurt* **injure** the earth and the sea,
3 *Saying* **Wording**, *Hurt* **Injure** not the earth,
neither the sea, nor the trees,
till we have sealed the servants of our *God* **Elohim**
in their foreheads.
4 And I heard the number *of them which were* sealed:
and there were — sealed
an hundred *and* forty *and* four thousand
of all the *tribes* **scions**
of the *children* **sons** of *Israel* **Yisra El**.
5 Of the *tribe* **scion** of *Juda* **Yah Hudah**
were sealed twelve thousand.
Of the *tribe* **scion** of *Reuben* **Reu Ben**
were sealed twelve thousand.
Of the *tribe* **scion** of Gad
were sealed twelve thousand.
6 Of the *tribe* **scion** of *Aser* **Asher**
were sealed twelve thousand.
Of the *tribe* **scion** of *Nepthalim* **Naphtali**
were sealed twelve thousand.
Of the *tribe* **scion** of *Manasses* **Menash Sheh**
were sealed twelve thousand.
7 Of the *tribe* **scion** of *Simeon* **Shimon**
were sealed twelve thousand.
Of the *tribe* **scion** of Levi
were sealed twelve thousand.
Of the *tribe* **scion** of *Issachar* **Yissachar**
were sealed twelve thousand.
8 Of the *tribe* **scion** of *Zabulon* **Zebulun**
were sealed twelve thousand.
Of the *tribe* **scion** of *Joseph* **Yoseph**
were sealed twelve thousand.
Of the *tribe* **scion** of *Benjamin* **Ben Yamin**
were sealed twelve thousand.

THE MULTITUDE FROM MEGA TRIBULATION

9 After *this* **these** I *beheld* **perceived**, and, *lo* **behold**,
a *great* **vast** multitude, which no *man* **one** could number,
of all *nations* **goyim**, and *kindreds* **scions**,
and *people* **peoples**, and tongues,
stood before **standing in sight of** the throne,
and *before* **in sight of** the Lamb,
clothed **arrayed** with white *robes* **stoles**,
and *palms* **phoinix** in their hands;
10 And cried with a *loud* **mega** voice, *saying* **wording**,
Salvation to our *God* **Elohim**
which sitteth upon the throne,
and unto the Lamb.
11 And all the angels stood
round about **surrounding** the throne,
and *about* the elders and the four *beasts* **live beings**,
and fell *before* **in sight of** the throne on their faces,
and worshipped *God* **Elohim**,
12 *Saying* **Wording**, Amen: *Blessing* **Eulogy**,
and glory, and wisdom, and *thanksgiving* **eucharist**,
and honour, and *power* **dynamis**, and might,
be unto our *God* **Elohim**
for ever and ever **unto the eons of the eons**.
Amen.
13 And one of the elders answered,
saying **wording** unto me,
What are these which are arrayed in white *robes* **stoles**?
and whence came they?
14 And I said unto him, *Sir* **Adonay**, thou knowest.
And he said to me,
These are they which came out of *great* **mega** tribulation,
and have *washed* **flowed** their *robes* **stoles**,
and *made them white* **whitened their stoles**
in the blood of the Lamb.
15 *Therefore* **For this**
are they *before* **in sight of** the throne of *God* **Elohim**
and *serve* **liturgize** *him* day and night in his *temple* **nave**:
and he that sitteth on the throne
shall *dwell* **tabernacle** among them.
16 They shall **not still** hunger *no more*,
neither **still** thirst *any more*;
neither shall the sun *light* **fall** on them
nor any *heat* **scorch**.
17 *For* **Because** the Lamb
which is in the midst of the throne
shall *feed* **shepherd** them,
and shall *lead* **guide** them unto living fountains of waters:
and *God* **Elohim** shall wipe *away*
all tears from their eyes.

THE SEVENTH SEAL

8 And when he had opened the seventh seal,
there *was silence* **became a hush** in heaven
about **as** the space of half an hour.

THE SEVEN TRUMPETS

2 And I saw the seven angels
which stood *before God* **in sight of Elohim**;
and to them were given seven trumpets.
3 And another angel came and stood at the **sacrifice** altar,
having a golden *censer* **frankincenser**;
and there was given unto him much incense,
that he should *offer* **give** it
with the prayers of all *saints* **the holy**
upon the golden **sacrifice** altar
which was *before* **in sight of** the throne.
4 And the smoke of the incense,
which came with the prayers of the *saints* **holy**,
ascended *up before God* **in sight of Elohim**
out of the angel's hand.
5 And the angel took the *censer* **frankincenser**,
and filled it *with* **out of the** fire of the **sacrifice** altar,
and cast *it into* **unto** the earth:
and there *were* **became** voices, and thunderings,
and lightnings, and *an earthquake* **a quake**.
6 And the seven angels which had the seven trumpets
prepared themselves to *sound* **trumpet**.

THE FIRST TRUMPET

7 The first angel *sounded* **trumpeted**,
and there *followed* **became** hail and fire
mingled with blood,
and they were cast *upon* **unto** the earth:
and the third part of trees was burnt up,
and all green *grass* **herbage** was burnt up.

THE SECOND TRUMPET

8 And the second angel *sounded* **trumpeted**,
and as *it were a great* **a mega** mountain burning with fire
was cast into the sea:
and the third part of the sea became blood;
9 And the third part of the creatures
which were in the sea, and had *life* **soul**, died;
and the third part of the *ships* **sailers**
were destroyed **corrupted**.

THE THIRD TRUMPET

10 And the third angel *sounded* **trumpeted**,
and there fell a *great* **mega** star from heaven,
burning as *it were* a lamp,
and it fell upon the third part of the *rivers* **streams**,
and upon the fountains of waters:
11 And the name of the star
is *called Wormwood* **worded Absinthe**:
and the third part of the waters
became *wormwood* **absinthe**;
and *many men* **much humanity** died of the waters,
because they were *made bitter* **embittered**.

THE FOURTH TRUMPET

12 And the fourth angel *sounded* **trumpeted**,
and the third part of the sun was *smitten* **deformed**,
and the third part of the moon,
and the third part of the stars;
so as **that** the third part of them was darkened,
and the day *shone* **manifested** not for a third part of it,
and the night likewise.

THE THREE WOES

13 And I *beheld* **perceived**, and heard *an* **one** angel
flying *through the midst of heaven* **in midheaven**,
saying **wording** with a *loud* **mega** voice,
Woe, woe, woe,
to *the inhabiters of* **them who settle on** the earth
by *reason of the other* **the rest of the** voices
of the trumpet of the three angels,
which are yet to sound **about to trumpet**!

THE FIFTH TRUMPET

9 And the fifth angel *sounded* **trumpeted**,
and I saw a star fall from heaven unto the earth:
and to him was given
the key of the *bottomless* pit **of the abyss**.

2 And he opened the *bottomless* pit **of the abyss**;
and there *arose* **ascended** a smoke out of the pit,
as the smoke of a *great* **mega** furnace;
and the sun and the air were darkened
by reason of **from** the smoke of the pit.
3 And there came out of the smoke
locusts *upon* **unto** the earth:
and unto them was given *power* **authority**,
as the scorpions of the earth have *power* **authority**.
4 And it was *commanded* **rhetorized to** them
that they should not *hurt* **injure**
the *grass* **herbage** of the earth,
neither any green *thing,* neither any tree;
but **except** only those *men* **humans** which have not
the seal of *God* **Elohim** in their foreheads.
5 And to them it was given
that they should not *kill* **slaughter** them,
but that they should be *tormented* **tortured** five months:
and their *torment* **torture**
was as the *torment* **torture** of a scorpion,
when he *striketh* **smiteth** a *man* **human**.
6 And in those days shall *men* **humanity** seek death,
and shall not find it;
and shall *desire* **pant** to die, and death shall flee from them.
7 And the *shapes* **likenesses** of the locusts
were like unto horses prepared unto *battle* **war**;
and on their heads
were as *it were crowns* **wreaths** like gold,
and their faces *were* as the faces of *men* **humans**.
8 And they had hair as the hair of women,
and their teeth *were as the teeth of* **as** lions.
9 And they had breastplates,
as *it were* breastplates of iron;
and the *sound* **voice** of their wings
was as the *sound* **voice** of chariots of many horses
running to *battle* **war**.
10 And they had tails like unto scorpions,
and there were stings in their tails:
and their *power* **authority**
was to *hurt men* **injure humanity** five months.
11 And they had a *king* **sovereign** over them,
which is — the angel of the *bottomless pit* **abyss**,
whose name in *the Hebrew tongue* **Hebraic**
is Abaddon,
but in *the Greek tongue* **Hellenic**
hath his name Apollyon.
12 One woe is *past* **gone**; *and,* behold,
there come two woes *more hereafter* **yet after these**.

THE SIXTH TRUMPET

13 And the sixth angel *sounded* **trumpeted**,
and I heard *a* **one** voice
from the four horns of the golden **sacrifice** altar
which is *before God* **in sight of Elohim**,
14 *Saying* **Wording** to the sixth angel
which had the trumpet,
Loose the four angels which are bound
in the *great river* **mega stream** Euphrates.
15 And the four angels were loosed,
which were prepared
for **unto** an hour, and a day, and a month, and a year,
for to *slay* **slaughter** the third *part* of *men* **humanity**.
16 And the number
of the *army* **warriors** of the horsemen were
two *hundred thousand thousand* **myriads of myriads**:
and I heard the number of them.
17 And thus I saw the horses in the vision,
and them that sat on them,
having breastplates *of fire* **fiery**, and *of jacinth* **jacinthine**,
and *brimstone* **sulphurous**:
and the heads of the horses *were* as the heads of lions;
and out of their mouths *issued* **proceeded** fire
and smoke and *brimstone* **sulphur**.
18 By these three
was the third part of *men killed* **humanity slaughtered**,
by the fire, and by the smoke,
and by the *brimstone* **sulphur**,
which *issued* **proceeded** out of their mouths.
19 For their *power* **authority** is in their mouth,
and in their tails:
for their tails *were* like unto serpents, and had heads,
and *with* **in** them they do *hurt* **injure**.

cp Apocalypse 16:12—14

20 And the rest of the *men* **humanity**
which were not *killed by* **slaughtered in** these plagues
yet repented not of the works of their hands,
that they should not worship *devils* **demons**,
and idols of gold, and silver, and *brass* **copper**,
and stone, and of wood:
which neither can see, nor hear, nor walk:
21 Neither repented they of their murders,
nor of their *sorceries* **pharmacies**,
nor of their *fornication* **whoredoms**,
nor of their *thefts* **thieveries**.

THE OPEN SCROLLETTE

10 And I saw another mighty angel
come down **descend** from heaven,
clothed **arrayed** with a cloud:
and a rainbow *was* upon his head,
and his face *was* as *it were* the sun,
and his feet as pillars of fire:
2 And he had in his hand a *little book* **scrollette** open:
and he set his right foot upon the sea,
and his left *foot* on the earth,
3 And cried with a *loud* **mega** voice,
exactly as *when* a lion roareth:
and when he had cried,
seven thunders *uttered* **spake in** their **own** voices.
4 And when the seven thunders
had uttered **spake in** their **own** voices,
I was about to *write* **scribe**:
and I heard a voice from heaven *saying* **wording** unto me,
Seal up those *things*
which the seven thunders *uttered* **spake**,
and *write* **scribe** them not.
5 And the angel
which I saw stand upon the sea and upon the earth
lifted up his hand to heaven,
6 And *sware by* **oathed in** him that liveth
for ever and ever **unto the eons of the eons**,
who created heaven,
and *the things that* **those** therein *are,*
and the earth, and *the things that* **those** therein *are,*
and the sea, and *the things which are* **those** therein,
that there should be time° *no longer* **not still**:

°Hellene: chronos

7 But in the days of the voice of the seventh angel,
when he shall *begin to sound* **be about to trumpet**,
the mystery of *God* **Elohim** should be *finished* **complete**,
as he hath *declared* **evangelized**
to his **own** servants the prophets.
8 And the voice which I heard from heaven
spake *unto* **with** me again, and *said* **worded**,
Go *and* take the *little book* **scrollette**
which is open in the hand of the angel
which standeth upon the sea and upon the earth.
9 And I went unto the angel, and *said* **worded** unto him,
Give me the *little book* **scrollette**.
And he *said* **worded** unto me, Take it, and *eat* **devour** it *up;*
and it shall *make* **embitter** thy belly *bitter,*
but it shall be in thy mouth sweet as honey.
10 And I took the *little book* **scrollette**
out of the angel's hand,
and *ate* **devoured** it *up;*
and it was in my mouth sweet as honey:
and as soon as I had eaten it,
my belly *was bitter* **embittered**.
11 And he *said* **worded** unto me,
Thou must prophesy again before many peoples,
and *nations* **goyim**, and tongues, and *kings* **sovereigns**.

THE NAVE MEASURED

11 And there was given me a reed like unto a *rod* **scion**:
and the angel stood, *saying* **wording**,
Rise, and measure the *temple* **nave** of *God* **Elohim**,
and the **sacrifice** altar, and them that worship therein.
2 But the *court* **courtyard**
which is without the *temple* **nave**
leave **cast** out, and measure it not;
for **because** it is given unto the *Gentiles* **goyim**:
and the holy city shall they *tread under foot* **trample**
forty *and* two months.

THE TWO WITNESSES

3 And I *will* **shall** give *power* unto my two witnesses,
and they shall prophesy
a thousand two hundred *and threescore* **sixty** days,
clothed **arrayed** in *sackcloth* **saq**.
4 These are the two *olive trees* **olives**,
and the two *candlesticks* **menorah**
standing *before* **in sight of** the *God* **Elohim** of the earth.
Zechar Yah 4:2—6, 11—14
5 And if any *man will hurt* **one willeth to injure** them,
fire proceedeth out of their mouth,
and devoureth their enemies:
and if any *man will hurt* **one willeth to injure** them,
he must *in this manner* **thus** be *killed* **slaughtered**.
cp 11:13
6 These have *power* **authority** to shut heaven,
that *it rain not* **the rain not rain**
in the days of their prophecy:
and have *power* **authority** over waters
to turn them to blood,
and to smite the earth with all plagues,
as often as **ever** they will.
7 And when they shall have
finished **completed** their *testimony* **witness**,
the beast that ascendeth out of the *bottomless pit* **abyss**
shall make war *against* **with** them,
and shall *overcome* **triumph over** them,
and *kill* **slaughter** them.
8 And their *dead bodies* **carcasses**
shall *lie in* **be on** the *street* **broadway**
of the *great city* **megalopolis**,
which spiritually is called
Sodom **Sedom** and *Egypt* **Misrayim**,
where also our *Lord* **Adonay** was *crucified* **staked**.
9 And they of the people and *kindreds* **scions**
and tongues and *nations* **goyim**
shall see their *dead bodies* **carcasses**
three days and an half,
and shall not *suffer* **allow** their *dead bodies* **carcasses**
to be put in *graves* **tombs**.
10 And they that *dwell* **settle** upon the earth
shall *rejoice* **cheer** over them, and *make merry* **rejoice**,
and shall send *gifts* **honorariums** one to another;
because these two prophets *tormented* **tortured** them
that *dwelt* **settled** on the earth.
11 And after three days and an half
the spirit of life from *God* **Elohim** entered into them,
and they stood upon their feet;
and *great fear* **mega awe**
fell upon them which *saw* **observed** them.
12 And they heard a *great* **mega** voice from heaven
saying **wording** unto them, *Come up* **Ascend** hither.
And they ascended *up* to heaven in a cloud;
and their enemies *beheld* **observed** them.
13 And *the same* **in that** hour
was there **became** a *great earthquake* **mega quake**,
and the tenth part of the city fell,
and in the *earthquake* **quake**
were *slain of men* **slaughtered**
seven thousand **names of humanity**:
and the *remnant* **rest**
were affrighted **became awestricken**,
and gave glory to the *God* **Elohim** of heaven.
cp 11:5
14 The second woe is *past* **gone**;
and, behold, the third woe cometh quickly.

THE SEVENTH TRUMPET

15 And the seventh angel *sounded* **trumpeted**;
and there *were great* **became mega** voices in heaven,
saying **wording**,
The *kingdoms* **sovereigndom** of this *world* **cosmos**
are become *the kingdoms* of *our Lord* **Yah Veh**,
and of his *Christ* **the Messiah**;
and he shall reign
for ever and ever **unto the eons of the eons**.
16 And the four and twenty elders,
which sat *before God* **in sight of Elohim**
on their *seats* **thrones**,
fell upon their faces, and worshipped *God* **Elohim**,
17 *Saying* **Wording**, We *give* **eucharistize** thee *thanks*,
O Lord God Almighty **Yah Veh El Sabaoth**,
which art, and wast, and art to come
who is, and who was, and who is coming;
because thou hast taken to thee
thy *great power* **mega dynamis**, and hast reigned.
18 And the *nations* **goyim** were *angry* **wroth**,
and thy wrath is come,
and the *time* **season** of the dead,
that they should be judged,
and that thou shouldest give reward
unto thy servants the prophets,
and to the *saints* **holy**,
and them that *fear* **awe** thy name,
small **minute** and *great* **mega**;
and shouldest destroy them which destroy the earth.
19 And the *temple* **nave** of *God* **Elohim**
was opened in heaven,
and there was seen in his *temple* **nave**
the ark of his *testament* **covenant**:
and there *were* **became** lightnings,
and voices, and thunderings,
and *an earthquake* **a quake**, and *great* **mega** hail.

THE PANORAMA OF SIGNS AND EVENTS

THE WOMAN

12 And there appeared
a *great wonder* **mega sign** in heaven;
a woman *clothed* **arrayed** with the sun,
and the moon under her feet,
and upon her head a *crown* **wreath** of twelve stars:
2 And she *being with child* **having in womb** cried,
travailing *in birth*,
and *pained* **tortured** to *be delivered* **birth**.

THE DRAGON

3 And there appeared another *wonder* **sign** in heaven;
and behold a *great red* **mega fiery** dragon,
having seven heads and ten horns,
and seven *crowns* **diadems** upon his heads.
4 And his tail
drew **dragged** the third part of the stars of heaven,
and did cast them to the earth:
and the dragon stood *before* **in sight of** the woman
which was ready **about** to *be delivered* **birth**,
for to devour her child
as soon as *it was born* **she birthed**.

THE MALE SON

5 And she *brought forth* **birthed** a *man child* **male son**,
who was **about** to *rule* **shepherd** all *nations* **goyim**
with **in** a *rod* **scion** of iron:
and her child was *caught* **seized** *up* unto *God* **Elohim**,
and *to* his throne.
6 And the woman fled into the wilderness,
where she hath a place prepared of *God* **Elohim**,
that they should *feed* **nourish** her there
a thousand two hundred *and threescore* **sixty** days.

WAR IN HEAVEN

7 And there *was* **became** war in heaven:
Michael **Michah El** and his angels
fought **warred** against the dragon;
and the dragon *fought* **warred** and his angels,
8 And *prevailed* **was** not **mighty enough**;
neither was their place **still** found *any more* in heaven.
9 And the *great* **mega** dragon was cast out,
that *old* **ancient** serpent,
called *the Devil* **Diabolos**, and Satan,
which *deceiveth* **seduceth** the whole world:
he was cast out *into* **unto** the earth,
and his angels were cast out with him.

VICTORY IN HEAVEN

10 And I heard a *loud* **mega** voice
saying **wording** in heaven,
Now *is come* **becometh** salvation, and *strength* **dynamis**,
and the *kingdom* **sovereigndom** of our *God* **Elohim**,
and the *power* **authority** of his *Christ* **the Messiah**:
for **because** the accuser of our brethren is cast down,
which accused them *before* **in sight of** our *God* **Elohim**
day and night.
11 And they *overcame* **triumphed over** him
by **through** the blood of the Lamb,
and *by* **through** the word of their *testimony* **witness**;

and they loved not their *lives* **souls** unto the death.
12 *Therefore* **For this** rejoice, ye heavens,
and ye that *dwell* **tabernacle** in them.
Woe to the *inhabiters* **settlers** of the earth and of the sea!
for the devil **because Diabolos**
is come down **descended** unto you,
having *great wrath* **mega fury,**
because he knoweth
that he hath but a *short time* **little season.**
Yahn 12:31, 32, Loukas 10:18

DRAGON PURSUES THE WOMAN

13 And when the dragon saw
that he was cast unto the earth,
he *persecuted* **pursued** the woman
which *brought forth* **birthed** the *man child* **male.**
14 And to the woman
were given two wings of a *great* **mega** eagle,
that she might fly into the wilderness, into her place,
where she is nourished
for a time, and times, and half a time,
from the face of the serpent.
15 And the serpent cast out of his mouth
water as a *flood* **stream** after the woman,
that he might cause her
to be *carried away of the flood* **streamborne.**
16 And the earth helped the woman,
and the earth opened her mouth,
and swallowed *up* the *flood* **stream**
which the dragon cast out of his mouth.

DRAGON WARS WITH THE WOMAN'S SPERMA

17 And the dragon was wroth with the woman,
and went to make war
with the *remnant* **rest** of her *seed* **sperma,**
which *keep* **guard**
the *commandments* **misvoth** of *God* **Elohim,**
and have
the *testimony* **witness** of *Jesus Christ* **Yah Shua Messiah.**

THE BEAST FROM THE SEA

13 And I stood upon the sand of the sea,
and saw a beast *rise up* **ascend** out of the sea,
having seven heads and ten horns,
and upon his horns ten *crowns* **diadems,**
and upon his heads the name of blasphemy.
2 And the beast which I saw
was like unto a *leopard* **panther,**
and his feet were as *the feet* of a bear,
and his mouth as the mouth of a lion:
and the dragon gave him his *power* **dynamis,**
and his *seat* **throne,** and *great* **mega** authority.
3 And I saw one of his heads
as *it were wounded* **slaughtered** to death;
and his *deadly wound* **death plague** was *healed* **cured:**
and all the *world* **earth**
wondered **marvelled** after the beast.
4 And they worshipped the dragon
which gave *power* **authority** unto the beast:
and they worshipped the beast, *saying* **wording,**
Who is like unto the beast?
who is able to *make* war with him?

THE BEAST WARS WITH THE HOLY

5 And there was given unto him a mouth
speaking *great things* **mega** and blasphemies;
and *power* **authority** was given unto him
to *continue* **deal** forty *and* two months.
6 And he opened his mouth in blasphemy
against *God* **Elohim,**
to blaspheme his name, and his tabernacle,
and them that *dwell* **tabernacle** in heaven.
7 And it was given unto him
to make war with the *saints* **holy,**
and to *overcome* **triumph over** them:
and *power* **authority** was given him
over all *kindreds* **scions,** and tongues, and *nations* **goyim.**
8 And all that *dwell* **settle** upon the earth
shall worship him,
whose names are not *written* **scribed**
in the *book* **scroll** of life of the Lamb
slain **slaughtered**
from the foundation of the *world* **cosmos.**
9 If any *man* **one** have an ear, let him hear.
10 *He that leadeth*
If anyone gathereth together into captivity
shall go into captivity **goeth:**
he that killeth with
if anyone slaughtereth at the sword,
must be killed with **at** the sword **is slaughtered.**
Here is the *patience* **endurance**
and the *faith* **trust** of the *saints* **holy.**

THE BEAST FROM THE EARTH

11 And I *beheld* **perceived** another beast
coming up **ascending** out of the earth;
and he had two horns like a lamb,
and he spake as a dragon.
12 And he *exerciseth* **dealeth** all the *power* **authority**
of the first beast *before* **in sight of** him,
and causeth the earth
and them which *dwell* **settle** therein
to worship the first beast,
whose *deadly wound* **death plague** was *healed* **cured.**
13 And he doeth *great wonders* **mega signs,**
so that he maketh fire *come down* **descend** from heaven
on **to** the earth in sight of *men* **humanity,**
14 And *deceiveth* **seduceth** them
that *dwell* **settle** on the earth
by the means of **through** those *miracles* **signs**
which he *had power* **was given** to do
in sight of the beast;
saying **wording** to them that *dwell* **settle** on the earth,
that they should make an *image* **icon** to the beast,
which had the *wound* **plague** by a sword,
and *did live* **lived.**
15 And he *had power* **was given**
to give life unto the *image* **icon** of the beast,
that the *image* **icon** of the beast should both speak,
and cause that as many as **ever**
would **should** not worship the *image* **icon** of the beast
should be *killed* **slaughtered.**

THE TATTOO OF THE BEAST

16 And he causeth all, both *small* **minute** and *great* **mega,**
rich and poor, *free* **liberated** and *bond* **servant,**
to *receive* **give them** a *mark* **tattoo** in their right hand,
or in their foreheads:
17 And that no *man* **one**
might *buy* **be able to market** or sell,
save **except** he that had the *mark* **tattoo,**
or the name of the beast, or the number of his name.

THE NUMBER OF THE BEAST

18 Here is wisdom.
Let him that hath *understanding* **a mind**
count **compute** the number of the beast:
for it is the number of a *man* **human;**
and his number is Six hundred *threescore* **sixty** *and* six.

THE SEVEN VISIONS

THE FIRST VISION

14 And I *looked* **perceived,** and, *lo* **behold,**
a Lamb *stood* **standing** on the mount *Sion* **Siyon,**
and with him an hundred forty *and* four thousand,
having his Father's name
written **scribed** in their foreheads.
2 And I heard a voice from heaven,
as the voice of many waters,
and as the voice of a *great* **mega** thunder:
and I heard the voice of *harpers* **citherists**
harping with **cithering at** their *harps* **cithers:**
3 And they sung as *it were* a new *song* **ode**
before **in sight of** the throne,
and *before* **in sight of** the four *beasts* **live beings,**
and the elders:
and no *man* **one** could learn that *song* **ode**
but **except** the hundred *and* forty *and* four thousand,
which were *redeemed* **marketed** from the earth.
4 These are they
which were not *defiled* **stained** with women;
for they are virgins.
These are they
which follow the Lamb whithersoever he goeth.
These were *redeemed* **marketed**
from among *men* **humanity,**
being the *firstfruits* **firstlings**

unto *God* **Elohim** and to the Lamb.
5 And in their mouth was found no *guile* **deceit**:
for they are *without fault* **unblemished**
before the throne of *God* **Elohim**.

THE SECOND VISION

6 And I saw another angel
fly in *the midst of heaven* **midheaven**,
having the *everlasting gospel* **eternal evangelism**
to *preach* **evangelize** unto them
that *dwell* **settle** on the earth,
and to every *nation* **goyim**, and *kindred* **scion**,
and tongue, and people,
7 *Saying with* **Wording in** a *loud* **mega** voice,
Fear God **Awe Elohim**, and give glory to him;
for **because** the hour of his judgment is come:
and worship him
that made heaven, and earth, and the sea,
and the fountains of waters.

THE THIRD VISION

8 And there followed another angel, *saying* **wording**,
Babylon **Babel** is fallen, is fallen,
that *great city* **megalopolis**,
because she *made* **gave** all *nations* **goyim** drink
of the wine of the *wrath* **fury**
of her *fornication* **whoredom**.

THE FOURTH VISION

9 And the third angel followed them,
saying with **speaking in** a *loud* **mega** voice,
If any *man* **one** worship the beast and his *image* **icon**,
and *receive* **take** his *mark* **tattoo** in his forehead,
or in his hand,
10 The same shall drink
of the wine of the *wrath* **fury** of *God* **Elohim**,
which is *poured out without mixture* **mingled undiluted**
into the cup of his *indignation* **wrath**;
and he shall be *tormented* **tortured**
with **in** fire and *brimstone* **sulphur**
in *the presence* **sight** of the holy angels,
and in *the presence* **sight** of the Lamb:
11 And the smoke of their *torment* **torture** ascendeth *up*
for ever and ever **unto the eons of the eons**:
and they have no rest day nor night,
who worship the beast and his *image* **icon**,
and *whosoever* **if any**
receiveth **taketh** the *mark* **tattoo** of his name.
12 Here is the *patience* **endurance** of the *saints* **holy**:
here are they that *keep* **guard**
the *commandments* **misvoth** of *God* **Elohim**,
and the *faith* **trust** of *Jesus* **Yah Shua**.

THE FIFTH VISION

THE SECOND BEATITUDE

13 And I heard a voice from heaven
saying **wording** unto me, *Write* **Scribe**,
Blessed are the dead
which die in *the Lord* **Yah Veh** from henceforth:
Yea, *saith* **wordeth** the Spirit,
that they may rest from their labours;
and their works do follow **with** them.

THE SIXTH VISION

THE HARVEST BY ONE LIKE UNTO THE SON OF HUMANITY

14 And I *looked* **perceived**, and behold, a white cloud,
and upon the cloud
one sat like unto the Son of *man* **humanity**,
having on his head a golden *crown* **wreath**,
and in his hand a sharp sickle.
15 And another angel came out of the *temple* **nave**,
crying *with* **in** a *loud* **mega** voice
to him that sat on the cloud,
Thrust **Send** in thy sickle, and *reap* **harvest**:
for **because** the *time* **hour** is come
for thee to *reap* **harvest**;
for **because** the harvest of the earth is *ripe* **dried**.
16 And he that sat on the cloud
thrust **cast** in his sickle on the earth;
and the earth was *reaped* **harvested**.

THE SEVENTH VISION

THE HARVEST BY THE ANGEL

17 And another angel came out of the *temple* **nave**
which is in heaven,
he also having a sharp sickle.
18 And another angel came out from the **sacrifice** altar,
which had *power* **authority** over fire;
and *cried* **voiced** with a *loud* **mega** cry
to him that had the sharp sickle, *saying* **speaking**,
Thrust **Send** in thy sharp sickle,
and *gather* **dry** the clusters *of the vine* of the earth;
for **because** her grapes are *fully ripe* **matured**.
19 And the angel *thrust* **cast** in his sickle into the earth,
and *gathered* **dried** the vine of the earth,
and cast it into the *great winepress* **mega trough**
of the *wrath* **fury** of *God* **Elohim**.
20 And the *winepress* **trough** was *trodden* **trampled**
without the city,
and blood came out of the *winepress* **trough**,
even unto the horse bridles,
by the space of **up to**
a thousand *and* six hundred *furlongs* **stadia**.

THE SEVEN FINAL PLAGUES

15 And I saw another sign in heaven,
great **mega** and marvellous,
seven angels having the seven *last* **final** plagues;
for **because** in them
is *filled up* **completed** the *wrath* **fury** of *God* **Elohim**.
2 And I saw as *it were* a sea of glass mingled with fire:
and them that had *gotten the victory* **triumphed**
over **from** the beast,
and *over* **from** his *image* **icon**,
and *over* **from** his *mark* **tattoo**,
and *over* **from** the number of his name,
stand on the sea of glass,
having the *harps* **cithers** of *God* **Elohim**.
3 And they sing the *song* **ode** of *Moses* **Mosheh**
the servant of *God* **Elohim**,
and the *song* **ode** of the Lamb,
saying **wording**,
Great **Mega** and marvellous are thy works,
Lord God Almighty **Yah Veh El Sabaoth**;
just and true are thy ways,
thou *King* **Sovereign** of *saints* **the holy**.
4 Who shall not *fear* **no way awe** thee, O *Lord* **Yah Veh**,
and glorify thy name?
for **because** thou only art *holy* **merciful**:
for **because** all *nations* **goyim** shall come
and worship *before thee* **in thy sight**;
for **because** thy judgments are *made* manifest.
5 And after *that* **these** I *looked* **perceived**, and, behold,
the *temple* **nave** of the tabernacle
of the *testimony* **witness** in heaven was opened:
6 And the seven angels came out of the *temple* **nave**,
having the seven plagues,
clothed **endued** in pure and *white* **radiant** linen,
and *having their breasts girded* **girt about the chest**
with golden girdles.
7 And one of the four *beasts* **live beings**
gave unto the seven angels seven golden *vials* **phials**
full of the *wrath* **fury** of *God* **Elohim**,
who liveth *for ever and ever* **unto the eons of the eons**.
8 And the *temple* **nave** was filled with smoke
from the glory of *God* **Elohim**,
and from his *power* **dynamis**;
and no *man* **one** was able to enter into the *temple* **nave**,
till the seven plagues of the seven angels
were *fulfilled* **completed**.
16 And I heard a *great* **mega** voice out of the *temple* **nave**
saying **wording** to the seven angels,
Go *your ways*,
and pour out the *vials* **phials**
of the *wrath* **fury** of *God* **Elohim**
upon **unto** the earth.

THE FIRST PLAGUE

2 And the first went, and poured out his *vial* **phial**
upon the earth;
and there *fell* **became**
a noisome and grievous sore **an evil ulcer**
upon the men **unto humanity**
which had the *mark* **tattoo** of the beast,
and *upon* them which worshipped his *image* **icon**.

THE SECOND PLAGUE

3 And the second angel poured out his *vial* **phial**
upon **into** the sea;
and it became as the blood of a dead *man*:
and every living soul died in the sea.

THE THIRD PLAGUE

4 And the third angel poured out his *vial* **phial**
upon **into** the *rivers* **streams** and **into** fountains of waters;
and they became blood.
5 And I heard the angel of the waters *say* **wording**,
Thou art *righteous* **just**, O *Lord* **Yah Veh**,
which art, and wast, and shalt be°
who is, and who was°,
because thou hast judged *thus* **these**.
°most mss omit, *and shalt be*
6 *For* **Because** they have *shed* **poured**
the blood of *saints* **the holy** and prophets,
and thou hast given them blood to drink;
for they are worthy.
7 And I heard another out of the **sacrifice** altar
say **wording**,
Even so **Yea**, *Lord God Almighty* **Yah Veh El Sabaoth**,
true and *righteous* **just** are thy judgments.

THE FOURTH PLAGUE

8 And the fourth angel poured out his *vial* **phial**
upon the sun;
and *power* **it** was given unto him
to scorch *men with* **humanity in** fire.
9 And *men* **humanity**
were scorched with *great heat* **mega scorch**,
and blasphemed the name of *God* **Elohim**,
which hath *power* **authority** over these plagues:
and they repented not to give him glory.

THE FIFTH PLAGUE

10 And the fifth angel poured out his *vial* **phial**
upon the *seat* **throne** of the beast;
and his *kingdom* **sovereigndom**
was full of darkness **became darkened**;
and they gnawed their tongues *for* **from** pain,
11 And blasphemed the *God* **Elohim** of heaven
because of **from** their pains and **from** their *sores* **ulcers**,
and repented not of their *deeds* **works**.

THE SIXTH PLAGUE

12 And the sixth angel poured out his *vial* **phial**
upon the *great river* **mega stream** Euphrates;
and the water thereof was dried up,
that the way of the *kings* **sovereigns**
of the *east* **rising of the sun** might be prepared.
13 And I saw three *unclean* **impure** spirits like frogs
come out of the mouth of the dragon,
and out of the mouth of the beast,
and out of the mouth of the *false* **pseudo** prophet.
14 For they are the spirits of *devils* **demons**,
working miracles **doing signs**,
which *go forth* **proceed** unto the *kings* **sovereigns**
of the earth and of the whole world,
to gather them to the *battle* **war**
of that *great* **mega** day of *God Almighty* **El Sabaoth**.

THE THIRD BEATITUDE

15 Behold, I come as a thief.
Blessed is he that watcheth,
and *keepeth* **guardeth** his garments,
lest he walk naked,
and they see his *shame* **misbehaviour**.
16 And he gathered them together into a place
called in *the Hebrew tongue* **Hebraic,**
Armageddon **Har Megiddo**.

THE SEVENTH PLAGUE

17 And the seventh angel poured out his *vial* **phial**
into the air;
and there came a *great* **mega** voice
out of the *temple* **nave** of heaven, from the throne,
saying **wording**, It *is done* **hath become**.
18 And there *were* **became** voices,
and thunders, and lightnings;
and there *was* **became** a *great earthquake* **mega quake**,
such as was not *since men* **from when humanity**
were **became** upon the earth,
so *mighty an earthquake* **vast a quake**,
and so great **thus mega**.
19 And the *great city* **megalopolis**
was divided **became** into three parts,
and the cities of the *nations* **goyim** fell:
and *great Babylon* **mega Babel**
came in remembrance **was remembered**
before God **in sight of Elohim**,
to give unto her the cup of the wine
of the *fierceness* **fury** of his wrath.
20 And every island fled away,
and the mountains were not found.
21 And there *fell* **descended** upon *men* **humanity**
a *great* **mega** hail out of heaven,
every stone about the weight of a talent
as a talentweight:
and *men* **humanity** blasphemed *God* **Elohim**
because of **from** the plague of the hail;
for **because** the plague thereof
was *exceeding great* **extremely mega**.

THE MEGA WHORE

17 And there came one of the seven angels
which had the seven *vials* **phials**,
and *talked* **spake** with me, *saying* **wording** unto me,
Come hither; I *will* **shall** shew unto thee the judgment
of the *great* **mega** whore that sitteth upon many waters:
2 With whom the *kings* **sovereigns** of the earth
have *committed fornication* **whored**,
and *the inhabitants of* **they who settled on** the earth
have *been made drunk* **intoxicated**
with **from** the wine of her *fornication* **whoredom**.
3 So he *carried* **bore** me away in *the* spirit
into the wilderness:
and I saw a woman sit upon a scarlet *coloured* beast,
full of names of blasphemy,
having seven heads and ten horns.
4 And the woman was arrayed
in purple and scarlet *colour*,
and *decked* **gilded**
with gold and precious stones and pearls,
having a golden cup in her hand full of abominations
and *filthiness* **impurity** of her *fornication* **whoredom**:
5 And upon her forehead was a name *written* **scribed**,
MYSTERY,
BABYLON **BABEL** THE *GREAT* **MEGA**,
THE MOTHER OF *HARLOTS* **WHORES**
AND ABOMINATIONS OF THE EARTH.
6 And I saw the woman
drunken with **intoxicated from** the blood
of the *saints* **holy**,
and *with* **from** the blood
of the *martyrs* **witnesses** of *Jesus* **Yah Shua**:
and when I saw her,
I *wondered with great admiration*
marvelled a mega marvel.

THE MYSTERY OF THE WOMAN AND THE BEAST FROM THE SEA

7 And the angel said unto me,
Wherefore didst **Why marvellest** thou *marvel*?
I *will tell* **shall say** thee the mystery of the woman,
and of the beast that *carrieth* **beareth** her,
which hath the seven heads and ten horns.
8 The beast that thou sawest
was, and is not;
and *shall* **is about to** ascend
out of the *bottomless pit* **abyss**,
and go into *perdition* **destruction**:
and they that *dwell* **settle** on the earth
shall *wonder* **marvel**,
whose names were not *written* **scribed**
in the *book* **scroll** of life
from the foundation of the *world* **cosmos**,
when they *behold* **see** the beast
that was, and is not, *and yet* **though** is.
9 And here is the mind which hath wisdom.
The seven heads are seven mountains,
on which **whereon** the woman sitteth.
10 And there are seven *kings* **sovereigns**:
five are fallen,
and one is,
and the other is not yet come;
and when he cometh,

he must *continue* **abide** a *short space* **little**.
11 And the beast that was, and is not,
even he is the eighth, and is of the seven,
and goeth into *perdition* **destruction**.
12 And the ten horns which thou sawest
are ten *kings* **sovereigns**,
which have *received* **taken** no *kingdom* **sovereigndom**
as yet;
but *receive power* **take authority** as *kings* **sovereigns**
one hour with the beast.
13 These have one *mind* **opinion**,
and shall *give* **distribute** their *power* **own dynamis**
and *strength* **authority** unto the beast.
14 These shall *make* war with the Lamb,
and the Lamb shall *overcome* **triumph over** them:
for **because** he is *Lord* **Adonay** of *lords* **adoniym**,
and *King* **Sovereign** *of kings* **sovereigns**:
and they that are with him are called,
and *chosen* **select**, and *faithful* **trustworthy**.
15 And he *saith* **wordeth** unto me,
The waters which thou sawest, where the whore sitteth,
are peoples, and multitudes,
and *nations* **goyim**, and tongues.
16 And the ten horns which thou sawest upon the beast,
these shall hate the whore,
and shall make her desolate and naked,
and shall eat her flesh, and burn her *with* **in** fire.
17 For *God hath put* **Elohim gave** in their hearts
to *fulfil* **deal** his *will* **opinion**,
and to *agree* **deal one opinion**,
and give their *kingdom* **sovereigndom** unto the beast,
until the *words* **rhemas** of *God* **Elohim**
shall be *fulfilled* **completed**.
18 And the woman which thou sawest
is that *great city* **megalopolis**,
which reigneth **having sovereigndom**
over the *kings* **sovereigns** of the earth.

BABEL IS FALLEN, IS FALLEN

18 And after these *things*
I saw another angel *come down* **descend** from heaven,
having *great power* **mega authority**;
and the earth was lightened *with* **by** his glory.
2 And he cried *mightily* **in might**
with a *strong* **mega** voice, *saying* **wording**,
Babylon **Babel** the *great* **mega** is fallen, is fallen,
and is become the *habitation* **settlement** of *devils* **demons**,
and the *hold* **guardhouse** of every *foul* **impure** spirit,
and a *cage* **guardhouse**
of every *unclean* **impure** and hateful *bird* **fowl**.
3 *For* **Because** all *nations* **goyim** have drunk of the wine
of the *wrath* **fury** of her *fornication* **whoredom**,
and the *kings* **sovereigns** of the earth
have *committed fornication* **whored** with her,
and the merchants of the earth are *waxed rich* **enriched**
through **from** the *abundance* **dynamis**
of her *delicacies* **luxuries**.
4 And I heard another voice from heaven,
saying **wording**, Come out of her, my people,
that ye be not *partakers* **co—partakers** of her sins,
and that ye *receive* **take** not of her plagues.
5 *For* **Because** her sins
have *reached* **followed** unto heaven,
and *God* **Elohim** hath remembered her *iniquities* **injustices**.
6 *Reward* **Give** her **back**
even as she *rewarded* **gave back to** you,
and double unto her double according to her works:
in the cup which she hath *filled* **fill mingled**
to her double.
7 *How* **As** much **as** she hath glorified herself,
and *lived deliciously* **luxuriated**,
so much *torment* **torture** and *sorrow* **mourning** give her:
for **because** she *saith* **wordeth** in her heart,
I sit a *queen* **sovereigness**, and am no widow,
and shall **no way** see no *sorrow* **mourning**.
8 *Therefore* **For this** shall her plagues come in one day,
death, and *sorrow* **mourning**, and famine;
and she shall be utterly *burned with* **burnt in** fire:
for strong **because mighty**
is *the Lord God* **Yah Veh Elohim**
who judgeth her.

SOVEREIGNS WEEP OVER BABEL'S FALL

9 And the *kings* **sovereigns** of the earth,
who have *committed fornication* **whored**
and *lived deliciously* **luxuriated** with her,
shall *bewail* **weep for** her, and *lament for* **chop over** her,
when they shall see the smoke of her *burning* **firing**,
10 Standing **from** afar *off*
for the *fear* **awe** of her *torment* **torture**, *saying* **wording**,
Alas **Woe**,
alas **woe** that *great city Babylon* **megalopolis Babel**,
that mighty city!
for **because** in one hour is thy judgment come.

MERCHANTS WEEP OVER BABEL'S FALL

11 And the merchants of the earth
shall weep and mourn over her;
for **because** no *man* **one**
buyeth their merchandise **marketeth her wares**
any **no** more:
12 The *merchandise* **wares** of gold, and silver,
and precious stones, and of pearls,
and *fine* **white** linen, and purple, and silk, and scarlet,
and all *thyine wood* **incense timber**,
and all *manner* vessels of *ivory* **elephantine**,
and all *manner* vessels of most precious *wood* **timber**,
and of *brass* **copper**, and iron, and marble,
13 And cinnamon, and *odours* **incense**,
and *ointments* **myrrh**, and frankincense,
and wine, and **olive** oil,
and fine flour, and *wheat* **grain**,
and *beasts* **animals**, and sheep, and horses, and chariots,
and *slaves* **bodies**, and souls of *men* **humanity**.
14 And the *fruits* **evening hour**
that thy soul lusted after **of thy soul's panting**
are *departed* **gone** from thee,
and all *things which were dainty* **the greasy**
and *goodly* **radiant** are *departed* **gone** from thee,
and thou shalt find them no more *at all* **no way**.
15 The merchants of these *things*,
which were *made rich* **enriched** by her,
shall stand **from** afar *off*
for the *fear* **awe** of her *torment* **torture**,
weeping and *wailing* **mourning**,
16 And *saying* **wording**,
Alas **Woe**,
alas **woe** that *great city* **megalopolis**,
that was *clothed* **arrayed** in *fine* **white** linen,
and purple, and scarlet,
and *decked with* **gilded in** gold,
and precious stones, and pearls!

PILOTS, PASSENGERS AND SAILERS CRY OVER BABEL'S FALL

17 *For* **Because** in one hour
so *great* **vast** riches is *come to nought* **desolated**.
And every *shipmaster* **pilot**,
and all the *company* **homogeneous crowd**
in *ships* **sailers**,
and *sailors* **ship crew**, and as many as *trade* **work** by sea,
stood **from** afar *off*,
18 And cried
when they saw the smoke of her *burning* **firing**,
saying **wording**,
What *city* is like unto this *great city* **megalopolis**!
19 And they cast dust on their heads, and cried,
weeping and *wailing* **mourning**, *saying* **wording**,
Alas **Woe**,
alas **woe** that *great city* **megalopolis**,
wherein were *made rich* **enriched**
all that had *ships* **sailers** in the sea
by reason of **from** her *costliness* **preciousness**!
for **because** in one hour is she *made desolate* **desolated**.
20 Rejoice over her, *thou* heaven,
and ye holy apostles and prophets;
for God **because Elohim**
hath *avenged you on* **judged your judgment of** her.
21 And *a* **one** mighty angel took up a stone
like a great **as a mega** millstone, and cast it into the sea,
saying **wording**, Thus with violence
shall that *great city Babylon* **megalopolis Babel**
be *thrown down* **cast**,
and shall **not no way**
still be found *no more at all*.

22 And the voice of *harpers* **citherists**, and musicians,
and of *pipers* **flutists**, and trumpeters,
shall **not no way still** be heard *no more at all* in thee;
and *no craftsman* **any technician**,
of whatsoever *craft he be* **technique**,
shall **not no way still** be found *any more* in thee;
and the *sound* **voice** of a millstone
shall **not no way still** be heard *no more at all* in thee;
23 And the light of a candle
shall **not no way still** *shine no more at all* **manifest** in thee;
and the voice of the bridegroom and of the bride
shall **not no way still** be heard *no more at all* in thee:
for **because** thy merchants
were the *great men* **magistrates** of the earth;
for by **because in** thy *sorceries* **pharmacies**
were all *nations deceived* **goyim seduced**.
24 And in her was found the blood of prophets,
and of *saints* **the holy**,
and of all that were *slain* **slaughtered** upon the earth.

THE FOUR HALALU YAH'S FROM HEAVEN

19 And after these *things* I heard a *great* **mega** voice
of *much people* **many multitudes** in heaven,
saying **wording**, *Alleluia* **Halalu Yah**;
Salvation, and glory, and honour, and *power* **dynamis**,
unto *the Lord* **Yah Veh** our *God* **Elohim**:
2 *For* **Because** true and *righteous* **just** are his judgments:
for **because** he hath judged the *great* **mega** whore,
which *did corrupt* **corrupted** the earth
with **in** her *fornication* **whoredom**,
and hath avenged the blood of his servants *at*
from her hand.
3 And *again* **secondly** they said, *Alleluia* **Halalu Yah**.
And her smoke *rose up* **ascended**
for ever and ever **unto the eons of the eons**.
4 And the four and twenty elders
and the four *beasts* **live beings** fell *down*
and worshipped *God* **Elohim** that sat on the throne,
saying **wording**, Amen; *Alleluia* **Halalu Yah**.
5 And a voice came out of the throne, *saying* **wording**,
Praise **Halal** our *God* **Elohim**, all ye his servants,
and ye that *fear* **awe** him,
both *small* **minute** and *great* **mega**.
6 And I heard
as *it were* the voice of a *great* **vast** multitude,
and as the voice of many waters,
and as the voice of mighty thunderings,
saying **wording**, *Alleluia* **Halalu Yah**:
for **because**
the Lord God omnipotent **Yah Veh El Sabaoth** reigneth.

THE MARRIAGE OF THE LAMB IS COME

7 Let us *be glad* **cheer** and *rejoice* **jump for joy**,
and give *honour* **glory** to him:
for **because** the marriage of the Lamb is come,
and his *wife* **woman** hath *made* **prepared** herself *ready*.
8 And to her was *granted* **given**
that she should be arrayed in *fine* **white** linen,
clean **pure** and *white* **radiant**:
for the *fine* **white** linen
is the *righteousness* **justification** of *saints* **the holy**.

THE FOURTH BEATITUDE

9 And he *saith* **wordeth** unto me, *Write* **Scribe**,
Blessed are they
which are called unto the marriage supper of the Lamb.
And he *saith* **wordeth** unto me,
These are the true *sayings* **words** of *God* **Elohim**.
10 And I fell *at* **in front of** his feet to worship him.
And he *said* **worded** unto me, See *thou do it* not:
I am thy *fellowservant* **co—servant**,
and of thy brethren
that have the *testimony* **witness** of *Jesus* **Yah Shua**:
worship *God* **Elohim**:
for the *testimony* **witness** of *Jesus* **Yah Shua**
is the spirit of prophecy.

THE SOVEREIGN OF SOVEREIGNS, ADONAY OF ADONIYM, AND WARRIORS IN HEAVEN SMITE THE GOYIM

11 And I saw heaven opened, and behold, a white horse;
and he that sat upon him
was called *faithful* **Trustworthy** and True,
and in *righteousness* **justness**
he *doth judge* **judgeth** and *make war* **warreth**.
12 His eyes were as a flame of fire,
and on his head were many *crowns* **diadems**;
and he had a name *written* **scribed**,
that no man knew, *but* **except** he himself.
13 And he was *clothed* **arrayed** with a *vesture* **garment**
dipped **baptized** in blood:
and his name is called The Word of *God* **Elohim**.
14 And the *armies which were* **warriors** in heaven
followed him upon white horses,
clothed **endued** in *fine* **white** linen,
white and *clean* **pure**.
15 And out of his mouth
goeth **proceedeth** a sharp *sword* **sabre**,
that *with* **in** it he should smite the *nations* **goyim**:
and he shall *rule* **shepherd** them
with **in** a *rod* **scion** of iron:
and he *treadeth* **trampleth** the *winepress* **wine trough**
of the *fierceness* **fury** and wrath
of *Almighty God* **El Sabaoth**.
16 And he hath on his *vesture* **garment** and on his thigh
a name *written* **scribed**,
KING **SOVEREIGN** OF *KINGS* **SOVEREIGNS**,
AND *LORD* **ADONAY** OF *LORDS* **ADONIYM**.

THE SUPPER OF THE MEGA ELOHIM

17 And I saw *an* **one** angel standing in the sun;
and he cried with a *loud* **mega** voice,
saying **wording**
to all the fowls that fly in *the midst of heaven* **midheaven**,
Come and gather yourselves together
unto the supper of the *great God* **mega Elohim**;
18 That ye may eat the flesh of *kings* **sovereigns**,
and the flesh of *captains* **chiliarchs**,
and the flesh of mighty *men*,
and the flesh of horses, and of them that sit on them,
and the flesh of all *men*,
both free **liberated** and *bond* **servant**,
both small **minute** and *great* **mega**.
19 And I saw the beast,
and the *kings* **sovereigns** of the earth,
and their *armies* **warriors**, gathered together to make war
against **with** him that sat on the horse,
and *against* **with** his *army* **warriors**.

BEAST AND PSEUDO PROPHET CAST INTO THE LAKE OF FIRE

20 And the beast was *taken* **seized**,
and with him the *false* **pseudo** prophet
that *wrought miracles before him* **did signs in his sight**,
with **in** which he *deceived* **seduced** them
that had *received* **taken** the *mark* **tattoo** of the beast,
and them that worshipped his *image* **icon**.
These *both* **two** were cast alive
into a lake of fire burning *with brimstone* **in sulphur**.

THE REST ARE SLAUGHTERED

21 And the *remnant* **rest** were *slain* **slaughtered**
with **at** the *sword* **sabre** of him
that sat upon the horse,
which *sword* proceeded out of his mouth:
and all the fowls were filled *with* **from** their flesh.

SATAN IS BOUND

20 And I saw an angel
come down **descending** from heaven,
having the key of the *bottomless pit* **abyss**
and a *great chain* **mega fetter** in his hand.
2 And he *laid hold on* **overpowered** the dragon,
that *old* **ancient** serpent,
which is *the Devil* **Diabolos**, and Satan,
and bound him a thousand years,
3 And cast him into the *bottomless pit* **abyss**,
and shut him up, and *set a seal upon* **sealed** him,
that he should **not no way**
deceive **still seduce** the *nations* **goyim** *no more*,
till the thousand years should be *fulfilled* **completed**:
and after *that* **these**
he must be loosed a little *season* **time**.

THE AXED SOULS REIGN WITH MESSIAH

4 And I saw thrones, and they sat upon them,
and judgment was given unto them:
and *I saw* the souls of them that were *beheaded* **axed**
for the witness of *Jesus* **Yah Shua**,
and for the word of *God* **Elohim**,
and which had not worshipped the beast,

neither his *image* **icon,**
neither had *received* **taken** his *mark* **tattoo**
upon their foreheads, or in their hands;
and they lived and reigned with *Christ* **Messiah**
a thousand years.

THE FIRST RESURRECTION

5 But the rest of the dead *lived* **relived** not *again*
until the thousand years
were finished **shall be completed.**
This is the first resurrection.

THE FIFTH BEATITUDE

6 Blessed and holy
is he that hath part in the first resurrection:
on such **over these**
the second death hath no *power* **authority,**
but they shall be priests
of *God* **Elohim** and of *Christ* **Messiah,**
and shall reign with him a thousand years.

SATAN IS LOOSED

7 And when the thousand years are *expired* **completed,**
Satan shall be loosed out of his *prison* **guardhouse,**
8 And shall go *out* to *deceive* **seduce** the *nations* **goyim**
which are in the four *quarters* **corners** of the earth,
Gog, and Magog, to gather them together to *battle* **war**:
the number of whom *is* as the sand of the sea.
9 And they *went up* **ascended** on the breadth of the earth,
and *compassed* **surrounded**
the *camp* **encampment** of the *saints about* **holy,**
and the beloved city:
and fire *came down* **descended** from *God* **Elohim**
out of heaven, and devoured them.

THE SENTENCE OF DIABOLOS

10 And *the devil* **Diabolos** that *deceived* **seduced** them
was cast into the lake of fire and *brimstone* **sulphur,**
where the beast and the *false* **pseudo** prophet are,
and shall be *tormented* **tortured** day and night
for ever and ever **unto the eons of the eons.**

THE JUDGMENT OF THE EARTH AND THE HEAVEN

11 And I saw a *great* **mega** white throne,
and him that sat on it,
from whose face the earth and the heaven fled away;
and there was found no place for them.

THE JUDGMENT OF THE HOLY

12 And I saw the dead, *small* **minute** and *great* **mega,**
stand *before God* **in sight of Elohim;**
and the *books* **scrolls** were opened:
and another *book* **scroll** was opened,
which is *the book* of life:
and the dead were judged out of those *things*
which were written **scribed** in the *books* **scrolls,**
according to their works.

THE JUDGMENT OF THE UNHOLY

13 And the sea gave up the dead which were in it;
and death and *hell* **hades**
delivered **gave** up the dead which were in them:
and they were judged
every man **each** according to their works.

THE SENTENCE OF DEATH AND HADES

14 And death and *hell* **hades**
were cast into the lake of fire.
This is the second death.

THE SENTENCE OF THE UNHOLY

15 And *whosoever* **if any** was not found
written **scribed** in the *book* **scroll** of life
was cast into the lake of fire.

THE NEW HEAVEN AND THE NEW EARTH

21 And I saw a new heaven and a new earth:
for the first heaven and the first earth were passed away;
and there was *no more* **not still a** sea.

THE NEW YERU SHALEM

2 And I *John* **Yahn** saw the holy city,
new *Jerusalem* **Yeru Shalem,**
coming down **descending** from *God* **Elohim**
out of heaven,
prepared as a bride adorned for her *husband* **man.**

ELOHIM'S NEW RELATIONSHIP WITH THE HOLY

3 And I heard a *great* **mega** voice out of heaven
saying **wording,** Behold,
the tabernacle of *God* **Elohim** is with *men* **humanity,**
and he *will dwell* **shall tabernacle** with them,
and they shall be his *people* **peoples,**
and *God* **Elohim** himself shall be with them,
and be — their *God* **Elohim.**
4 And *God* **Elohim**
shall wipe *away* all tears from their eyes;
and there shall *be no more* **not still be** death,
neither sorrow, nor crying,
neither shall there **no way still** be *any more* pain:
for **because** the *former things* **first** are *passed away* **gone.**
5 And he that sat upon the throne said,
Behold, I make all *things* new.
And he *said* **worded** unto me, *Write* **Scribe**:
for **because** these words are true and *faithful* **trustworthy.**
6 And he said unto me, It *is done* **hath become.**
I am Alpha and Omega **I AM the A and the Ω,**
the beginning and the *end* **completion.**
I *will* **shall** give unto him that is athirst
of the fountain of the water of life *freely* **gratuitously.**
7 He that *overcometh* **triumpheth**
shall inherit all *things*
and I *will* **shall** be *his* **to him,** *God* **Elohim,**
and he shall be *my* **to me,** son.

ELOHIM'S SEVERED RELATIONSHIP WITH THE UNHOLY

8 But the *fearful* **cowardly,** and *unbelieving* **trustless,**
and the abominable, and murderers, and whoremongers,
and *sorcerers* **pharmaceutists,** and idolaters,
and all *liars* **pseudos,**
shall have their part in the lake
which burneth with fire and *brimstone* **sulphur**:
which is the second death.

THE BRIDE

9 And there came unto me one of the seven angels
which had the seven *vials* **phials**
full of the seven *last* **final** plagues,
and *talked* **spake** with me, *saying* **wording,** Come hither,
I *will* **shall** shew thee the bride, the Lamb's *wife* **woman.**

THE NEW YERU SHALEM

10 And he *carried* **bore** me away in *the* spirit
to a *great* **mega** and high mountain,
and shewed me that *great city* **megalopolis,**
the holy *Jerusalem* **Yeru Shalem,**
descending out of heaven from *God* **Elohim,**
11 Having the glory of *God* **Elohim**:
and her light *was* like unto a stone most precious,
even like **as** a jasper stone, *clear as crystal* **crystaline;**
12 And had a wall *great* **mega** and high,
and had twelve gates, and at the gates twelve angels,
and names *written thereon* **epigraphed,**
which are *the names* of the twelve *tribes* **scions**
of the *children* **sons** of *Israel* **Yisra El**:
13 *On* **By** the *east* **rising** three gates;
on **by** the north three gates;
on **by** the south three gates;
and *on* **by** the *west* **lowering** three gates.
14 And the wall of the city had twelve foundations,
and in them
the names of the twelve apostles of the Lamb.

THE NEW YERU SHALEM'S MEASUREMENTS

15 And he that *talked* **spake** with me
had a golden reed to measure the city,
and the gates thereof, and the wall thereof.
16 And the city lieth foursquare,
and the length is as *large* **long** as the breadth:
and he measured the city with the reed,
twelve thousand *furlongs* **stadia.**
The length and the breadth and the height of it are equal.
17 And he measured the wall thereof,
an hundred *and* forty *and* four cubits,
according to the measure of a *man* **human,**
that **which** is, of the angel.

THE NEW YERU SHALEM'S MATERIALS

18 And the *building* **structure** of the wall of it
was *of* jasper:
and the city *was* pure gold, like unto *clear* **pure** glass.
19 And the foundations of the wall *of the city*
were garnished **adorned**
with all *manner of* precious stones.
The first foundation *was* jasper; the second, sapphire;
the third, *a* chalcedony; the fourth, *an* emerald;
20 The fifth, sardonyx; the sixth, sardius;

the seventh, chrysolyte; the eighth, beryl;
the ninth, *a* topaz; the tenth, *a* chrysoprasus;
the eleventh, *a* jacinth; the twelfth, *an* amethyst.
21 And the twelve gates were twelve pearls:
every several **each one** gate was of one pearl:
and the *street* **broadway** of the city was pure gold,
as *it were transparent* **diaphanous** glass.

THE NEW YERU SHALEM'S OMISSIONS

22 And I saw no *temple* **nave** therein:
for *the Lord God Almighty* **Yah Veh El Sabaoth**
and the Lamb are the *temple* **nave** of it.
23 And the city had no need of the sun,
neither of the moon, to *shine* **manifest** in it:
for the glory of *God did lighten* **Elohim lightened** it,
and the Lamb is the *light* **candle** thereof.
24 And the *nations* **goyim** of them which are saved
shall walk in the light of it:
and the *kings* **sovereigns** of the earth
do bring their glory and honour into it.
25 And the gates of it
shall not **no way** be shut *at all* by day:
for there shall be no night there.
26 And they shall bring the glory and honour
of the *nations* **goyim** into it.
27 And there shall *in* **not** no *wise* **way** enter into it
any thing **aught** that *defileth* **profaneth**,
neither *whatsoever worketh* **doeth** abomination,
or *maketh a lie* **lieth**:
but **except** they which are *written* **scribed**
in the Lamb's *book* **scroll** of life.

THE NEW YERU SHALEM'S THRONE, STREAM, AND STAFF OF LIFE

22 And he shewed me a pure *river* **stream**
of water of life,
clear **radiant** as *crystal* **crystaline**,
proceeding out of the throne
of *God* **Elohim** and of the Lamb.
2 In the midst of the *street* **broadway** of it,
and *on either side* **hence and hence** of the *river* **stream**,
was there the *tree* **staff** of life,
which *bare* **dealt** twelve *manner of* fruits,
and *yielded* **gave up** her fruit *every* **each single** month:
and the leaves of the *tree* **staff**
were for **unto** the *healing* **therapy** of the *nations* **goyim**.
3 And there shall **not still**
be *no more curse* **any anathema**:
but the throne of *God* **Elohim** and of the Lamb
shall be in it;
and his servants shall *serve* **liturgize** him:
4 And they shall see his face;
and his name shall be in their foreheads.
5 And there shall be no night there;
and they need no candle, neither light of the sun;
for the Lord God **because Yah Veh Elohim**
giveth **lighteth** them *light*:
and they shall reign
for ever and ever **unto the eons of the eons**.

SUMMATION

6 And he said unto me,
These *sayings* **words** are *faithful* **trustworthy** and true:
and *the Lord God* **Yah Veh Elohim** of the holy prophets
sent **apostolized** his angel
to shew unto his servants *the things* **those**
which must *shortly be done* **quickly become**.

THE SIXTH BEATITUDE

7 Behold, I come quickly:
blessed is he that *keepeth* **guardeth** the *sayings* **words**
of the prophecy of this *book* **scroll**.
8 And I *John* **Yahn** saw these *things*, and heard *them*.
And when I had heard and seen,
I fell down to worship
before **in front of** the feet of the angel
which shewed me these *things*.
9 Then *saith* **wordeth** he unto me, See *thou do it* not:
for I am thy *fellowservant* **co—servant**,
and of thy brethren the prophets,
and of them
which *keep* **guard** the *sayings* **words** of this *book* **scroll**:
worship *God* **Elohim**.
10 And he *saith* **wordeth** unto me,
Seal not the *sayings* **words**
of the prophecy of this *book* **scroll**:
for **because** the *time* **season** is *at hand* **near**.
11 He that *is unjust* **injureth**, let him *be unjust* **injure** still:
and he which *is filthy* **fouleth**, let him *be filthy* **foul** still:
and he that is *righteous* **just**,
let him *be righteous* **justify** still:
and he that is holy, let him be *holy* **hallowed** still.
12 And, behold, I come quickly;
and my reward is with me,
to give *every man* **up to each**
according as his work shall be.
13 *I am Alpha and Omega* **I AM the A and the Ω**,
the beginning and the *end* **completion**,
the first and the *last* **final**.

THE SEVENTH BEATITUDE

14 Blessed are they that do his *commandments* **misvoth**,
that they may have *right* **authority** to the *tree* **staff** of life,
and may enter in through the gates into the city.
15 For without are dogs, and *sorcerers* **pharmaceutists**,
and whoremongers, and murderers, and idolaters,
and whosoever *loveth* **befriendeth** and maketh a lie.

EPILOGUE

THE FINAL AFFIRMATION OF AUTHOR AND AUTHORSHIP

16 I *Jesus* **Yah Shua** have sent mine angel
to *testify* **witness** unto you
these in the *churches* **ecclesiae**.
I am **I AM** the root and the *offspring* **genos** of David,
and the *bright* **radiant** and *morning* **dawning** star.

THE FINAL INVITATION

17 And the Spirit and the bride *say* **word**, Come.
And let him that heareth**, let him** say, Come.
And let him that is athirst come.
And whosoever *will* **willeth**,
let him take the water of life *freely* **gratuitously**.

THE FINAL WARNING

18 For I *testify* **co—witness** unto every *man* **one**
that heareth the words of the prophecy
of this *book* **scroll**,
If **ever** any *man* **one** shall *add* **place** unto these *things*,
God **Elohim** shall *add* **place** unto him
the plagues that are *written* **scribed** in this *book* **scroll**:
19 And if **ever** any *man* **one** shall *take away* **remove**
from the words of the *book* **scroll** of this prophecy,
God **Elohim** shall *take away* **remove** his part
out of the *book* **scroll** of life, and out of the holy city,
and *from the things* **those**
which are written **scribed** in this *book* **scroll**.

THE FINAL PROMISE AND PRAYER

20 He which *testifieth* **witnesseth** these *things*
saith **wordeth**,
Surely **Yea**, I come quickly.
Amen.
Even so **Yea**, come, *Lord Jesus* **Adonay Yah Shua**.

THE FINAL BENEDICTION

21 The *grace* **charism**
of our *Lord Jesus Christ* **Adonay Yah Shua Messiah**
be with you all.
Amen.

FORWARD

This is a precious season in the annals of time – the hush preceding the parousia – when so many Messianists are eager to more fully understand the Scriptures. And never was it more easy to accomplish.

All Messianists ought to be ever grateful for the Authorized King James Version – for it brought to the English speaking world one of the most trustworthy versions of Scripture.

The greatest help to its fuller comprehension was the work of James Strong, when he prepared his Exhaustive Concordance – and his remarkable numbering system – all without the help of modern technological advances.

And now in this, our day, so many of the old standard research works are being republished keyed to Strong's Concordance.

Some of the most important and helpful are:

Theological Wordbook of the Old Testament,

The Englishman's Hebrew and Chaldee Concordance of the Old Testament by Wigram,

The Englishman's Greek Concordance of the New Testament by Wigram,

Vine's Expository Dictionary of Biblical Words,

and of course, the works on which these others are based,

Strong's Exhaustive Concordance, Complete and Unabridged Edition.

Note: Many of these volumes are still being offered without Strong's numbering system; and even Strong's Concordance is being offered in condensed versions. Insist on unabridged editions keyed to Strong. They'll expand your ministry in the span of life Elohim has granted you, and save you countless hours.

These five volumes together with an Authorized King James Version are all you will ever need to thoroughly research Scripture for yourself – even though English is your only language.

FORMAT:

All words are keyed to Strong's Concordance numbers, thus:

Old Covenant numbers and words are within braces, thus: {0000 Transliterated Hebrew, Arami Word};

New Covenant numbers and words are within brackets, thus: [0000 Transliterated Hellenic Word].

Any words not covered in the LEXICON may be researched by following the guidelines in Strong's Concordance.

Words within parenthesis, thus: (word) which follow the word being defined, may at times be omitted. At times it is necessary to place words within parenthesis to verbalize a noun.

PARTS OF SPEECH:

In most Versions, parts of speech have been altered to suit the translator. Where a manuscript would say, I shall rest you, the translators say, I shall give you rest – thus altering rest from a verb to a noun. Another similar example, I shall mercy you, the translators say, I shall shew you mercy.

The *exeGeses* adheres to the manuscripts.

Auxiliary verbs are not in the manuscripts. For further study, **see** may; **see** shall; **see** will.

TRANSLATION versus **TRANSLITERATION**:

Translating is transcribing a word from one **language** to another:

Transliterating is transcribing a word from one **alphabet** to another.

A number of words are treated as **transliterations**, even though they are imperfect; this may be due to alphabetic differences (c, ch, k, ts, z), or prefixes, and suffixes; yet they are offered to draw your attention to the association between languages.

Also included from time to time are words to enhance your understanding:

see draws your attention to a related word;

cp draws your attention to compare a contrasting word;

read draws your attention to a related Scripture;

note: draws your attention to a matter worth noting.

SUMMARY is a grouping of words of similar and/or contrasting root or subject matter. For example, tabernacle, temple, and tent are used interchangeably in most versions; the definition and distinction of each is thoroughly discussed under the following format:

- **SUMMARY:**
- **TABERNACLE, TEMPLE, TENT:**
- **tabernacle** followed by the study.
- **temple** followed by the study.
- **tent** followed by the study.

The word SUMMARY, and all the words of the SUMMARY are preceded by the sign •.

A thorough study of each of the subjects under **SUMMARY** will not only enlighten you on the various subjects, but give you insight into the understanding of what Scripture doctrinates.

May your spirit be as enriched as you read and research the unsearchable riches of Elohim's Holy Word.

A

A and Ω *title* [1 alpha] [5598 omega] the first and final letters of the Hellene alphabet; a title that Adonay Yah Shua ascribes to Himself.
ab, abba, father *transliterated noun* {1 ab} {2 ab} [5 abba] [3962 pater] **ab** is Hebrew for father; **abba** is a Hellenic transliteration; **pater** is the Hellenic translation.
Abaddon *transliterated name, noun* {10 abaddoh} {11 abaddon} [3 abaddon] Destroyer; destruction; **cp** Apollyon.
abandon *adjective* {2310 chadel} destitute.
abandon, allow, leave, let, set *verb* {3240 yanach} {5203 natash} to abandon; to allow to be; to allow to be set.
abandon, cease, decease, desist *verb* {2308 chadal} to be lacking; to stop.
abandon, release *verb* {8281 sharah} to free.
abase, abate, belittle, slight, swift, trifle *verb* {6819 tsaar} {6985 qat} {7034 qalah} {7043 qalal} to belittle in contempt; to make light of; to lessen.
abase, lower *verb* {8213 shaphel} {8214 shephal} to humiliate.
abasement, abasing *noun* {7022 qiyqalown} {7036 qalown} {7045 qelalah} an intense disgrace.
abate, abase, belittle, slight, swift, trifle *verb* {6819 tsaar} {6985 qat} {7034 qalah} {7043 qalal} to belittle in contempt; to make light of; to lessen.
abate, lack *verb* {2637 chacer} to lack, to lessen; spoken of the prophecy of the Messiah having become flesh; **read** Psalm 8:5.
Abde El *transliterated name* {5655 abdeel} Serving El.
Abdi El *transliterated name* {5661 abdiel} Servant of El.
Abel *transliterated name* {59 abel} Meadow.
Abel *transliterated name* {1893 hebel} [6 abel] son of Adam.
Abel Beth Maachah *transliterated name* {62 abelbethmaachah} Meadow of the House of Piercing.
Abel Hash Shittim *transliterated name* {63 abelhashshittim} Meadow of the Shittim; **see** Shittim.
Abel Keramim *transliterated name* {64 abelkeramim} Meadow of the Vineyards.
Abel Maim *transliterated name* {66 abelmayim} Meadow of the Waters.
Abel Mecholah *transliterated name* {65 abelmecholah} Meadow of the Round Dance.
Abel Misrayim *transliterated name* {67 abelmitsrayim} Meadow of Misrayim; **see** Misrayim.
abhor *verb* {6973 quts} in the sense of cutting off from.
abhor, abhorrent *verb* {8581 taab} to shrink from with horror; to loathe.
abhorrence *noun* {8441 toebah} an extreme loathing, especially to idolatry.
Abi *transliterated name* {21 abi} Father.
Abi Albon *transliterated name* {45 abialbon} Father Valiant.
Abi Asaph *transliterated name* {23 abiasaph} {43 ebjasaph} Father Gatherer.
Abi Athar *transliterated name* {54 ebyathar} [8 abiathar] Father of the Remains.
Abi Dah *transliterated name* {28 abida} Father Knoweth.
Abi Dan *transliterated name* {27 abidan} Father Judge.
Abi El *transliterated name* {22 abiel} Father El.
Abi Ezer *transliterated name* {44 abiezer} Father of Help.
Abi Gail *transliterated name* {26 abigail} Father of Joy.
Abi Gibon *transliterated name* {25 abigibon} Father of Gibon (Hill).
Abi Ha Ezri *transliterated name* {33 abihaezri} Father of Help;

cp Abi Ezer.
Abi Hail *transliterated name* {32 abihail} Father of Valour.
Abi Hu *transliterated name* {30 abihu} Father of Him.
Abi Hud *transliterated name* {31 abihud} [10 abioud] Father of Majesty.
Abi Mael *transliterated name* {39 abimael} Father Mael; meaning of Mael uncertain.
Abi Melech *transliterated name* {40 abimelech} Father Sovereign.
Abi Nadab *transliterated name* {41 abinadab} Father Volunteer.
Abi Ner *transliterated name* {74 abiner} Father Lamp.
Abi Noam *transliterated name* {42 abinoam} Father of Pleasantness.
Abi Ram *transliterated name* {48 abiram} Father Lofty.
Abi Shag *transliterated name* {49 abishag} Father of Error.
Abi Shai *transliterated name* {52 abishai} Father of Presents.
Abi Shalom *transliterated name* {53 abishalom} Father of Shalom; **see** shalom.
Abi Shua *transliterated name* {50 abishua} Father of Opulence.
Abi Shur *transliterated name* {51 abishur} Father of the Wall.
Abi Tal *transliterated name* {37 abital} Father of Dew.
Abi Tub *transliterated name* {36 abitub} Father of Goodness.
Abi Yah *transliterated name* {29 abiyah} [7 abia] Father Yah.
Abi Yam *transliterated name* {38 abiyam} Father of the Sea.
Abib *transliterated name*, **unripe** *adjective* {3, 4 eb} {24 abib} an unripened or tender produce; a month of the Hebrew calender; also a syllable in the name of the city, Tel Abib.
abide *verb* [1265 diameno] [1696 emmeno] [1961 epimeno] [2650 katameno] [3306 meno] [3887 parameno] [4357 prosmeno] [5278 hupomeno] the root, *meno*, with its various prefixes, carries various connotations; from remaining in a place, to having a oneship with Adonay Yah Shua; **read** Yahn 15:.
Abilene *transliterated name* [9 abilene] possibly, Of Abel.
able, can, enable, prevail *verb* {3201 yakol} {3202 yekel} {3546 kehal} [1410 dunamai] [2427 hikanoo] the dynamis to do; **see** dynamis.
abode *noun* [3438 mone] a staying, residence; the noun of abide; only in Yahn 14:2, 23.
abominable *adjective* [947 bdeluktos] stinky; loathsome; idolatrous.
abominate *verb* {8262 shaqats} [948 bdelussomai] to stink; to loathe.
abomination *noun* {8251 shiqquts} {8263 sheqets} [946 bdelugma] a stink; a loathing; especially in the nostrils of Elohim; usually refers to idols.
abort, bereave, bereft *verb* {7921 shakol} to miscarry or suffer abortion; to deprive of; to be deprived of.
abound by the myriads *verb* {7231 rabab} to increase innumerably; **see** myriad.
abound *verb* {6280 athar} to increase; to be adundant.
abound, greaten *verb* {7235 rabah} {7236 rebah} to increase; to be greatened, in any dimension.
above, up, upper *adverb* [507 ano] upward; the top.
above, upper, uppermost *adjective* [509 anothen] [510 anoterikos] [511 anoteron] from above; the source of the rebirth; **read** Yahn 3:1–8.
Abraham *transliterated name* {85 abraham} [11 abraam] Father of a Multitude; Abram's name after Yah Veh changed it.
Abram *transliterated name* {87 abram} Father Lofty; Abraham's name before Yah Veh changed it.
abroad (gone) *adverb* [590 apodemos] absent from one's own people.
abroad (went) *verb* [589 apodemeo] to go away from one's own people.
absent *adjective* [548 apeimi] away.
absinthe, wormwood *transliterated noun* {3939 laanah} [894 apsinthos] a bitter plant.
abstinence, private assembly *noun* {6116 atsereth} a sacrifice of self–restraint; **see** restraint.
abundance *noun* {6283 athereth} an ample supply.
abundance *noun* {8635 tarbuth} a greatening, in any dimension.
abundance, greatness, greatnesses *noun* {1420 gedullah} {1433 godel} {7230 rob} {7238 rebu} increase; magnitude; mighty acts.
abundance, throng *noun* {8229 shiphah} plenty; a crowd.
abundant, great, greater *adjective* {1419 gadol} {7227, 7229 rab} {7260 rabrab} {7690 saggiy} plentiful; large; older.
abuse, encourage *verb* {7292 rahab} in the sense of urging; of pressuring.
abusive *adjective* [486 antiloidoreo] to rail in reply.
abyss *noun* {6683 tsulah} {8415 tehom} [12 abussos] a deep, depthless chasm; sometimes refers to sheol and hades.
accusation, cause *noun* [156 aita] [157 aitiama] [158 aition] as asked; as inquired into.
accustomed *verb* [1480 ethizo] [1486 etho] to accustom; customary; usage.
accustomed, use, used, useful *verb* {5532 cakan} to be familiar by use; to be serviceable to.
Ach Ab *transliterated name* {256 achab} Brother (Friend) of His Father.
Ach Archel *transliterated name* {316 acharchel} Behind the Intrenchment.
Ach Ban *transliterated name* {257 achban} Brother of Discerning.
Ach Rach *transliterated name* {315 achrach} After His Brother.
Ach Umay *transliterated name* {267 achuwmay} Brother of Water.
Ach Zay *transliterated name* {273 achzay} Possessor.
Achasbay *transliterated name* {308 achacbay} uncertain derivative.
achashtariy *transliterated noun* {326 achashtariy} courier; a designation, rather than a name.
Achashverosh *transliterated name* {325 achashverowsh} the title of a Persian sovereign.
Achaz *transliterated name* {271 achaz} [881 akaz] Possessor.
Achaz Yah *transliterated name* {274 achazyah} Possessed of Yah.
Acher *transliterated name* {313 acher} Next, Other.
Achi *transliterated name* {278 echiy} {277 achiy} Brotherly.
Achi Am *transliterated name* {279 achiyam} Brother of the Mother.
Achi Ezer *transliterated name* {295 achiezer} Brother of Help.
Achi Hud *transliterated name* {282 achihud} Brother of Majesty; **cp** Achi Hud {284}.
Achi Hud *transliterated name* {284 achichud} Brother of Propounding; **cp** Achi Hud {282}.
Achi Lud *transliterated name* {286 achilud} Brother of Birth.
Achi Maas *transliterated name* {290 achiymaats} Brother of Closure.
Achi Man *transliterated name* {289 achiman} Brother of a Portion.
Achi Melech *transliterated name* {288 achimelech} Brother of the Sovereign.
Achi Moth *transliterated name* {287 achimoth} Brother of Death.
Achi Nadab *transliterated name* {292 achinadab} Brother Volunteer.
Achi Noam *transliterated name* {293 achinoam} Brother of Pleasantness.
Achi Qam *transliterated name* {296 achiyqam} Brother of Rising.
Achi Ra *transliterated name* {299 achira} Brother of Evil.
Achi Ram *transliterated name* {297 achiram} Brother Lofty.
Achi Ramiy *transliterated name* {298 achiyramiy} Of Achi Ram.
Achi Samach *transliterated name* {294 achisamach} Brother Upholder.
Achi Shachar *transliterated name* {300 achiyshachar} Brother of the Dawn.
Achi Shar *transliterated name* {301 achishar} Brother Songster.
Achi Thophel *transliterated name* {302 achithophel} Brother of Slime.
Achi Tub *transliterated name* {285 achitub} Brother of Goodness.
Achi Yah *transliterated name* {281 achiyah} Brother of Yah.
Achlab *transliterated name* {303 achlab} Fatness.
Achlay *transliterated name* {304 achlay} O That.
Achoach *transliterated name* {265 achowach} Brotherly.
Achoachiy *transliterated name* {266 achowchiy} Of Achoach.
Achuz Zam *transliterated name* {275 achuzzam} Possession.
Achuz Zath *transliterated name* {276 achuzzath} Possession.
Achyan *transliterated name* {291 achyan} Brotherly.
Achyo *transliterated name* {283 achyow} Brotherly.
acknowledge, know *verb* [1921 epiginosko] to recognize; to become acquainted with.
acquaintance *noun* {4378 makkar} one who is recognized.
acquaintance, known *noun* [1110 gnostos] one who is known by another.
acquire *verb* {5239 nalah} to gain; **see** acquisition.
acquire *verb* {7408 rakash} to acquire; to lay up.
acquisition *noun* {4512 minleh} that which is acquired; that which is gained.
acquisition *noun* {7399 rekush} that which is acquired; that which is layed up.

acre, pair, team, yoke *noun* {6776 tsemed} two, as joined; an acre, as a day's task for one yoke.
acts *noun* {4566, 4567 mabad} in the sense of deeds.
acts, function *noun* [4234 praxis] something done; a deed.
ad infinitum *adjective* {6783 tsmithuth} without limit.
Adalya *transliterated name* {118 adalya} of Persian derivative; a son of Haman.
Adam *transliterated name* {121 adam} [76 adam] Human; the first human; **see** human, humanity.
adam *transliterated noun* {120 adam} ruddy, human, humanity.
Adbe El *transliterated name* {110 adbeel} Lanquished of El.
add, again, augment, increase *verb* {3254 yacaph} to add to; to repeat.
Addar *transliterated name* {146 addar} Mighty.
Addi *transliterated name* {5716 adiy} [78 addi] Ornamental; **see** ornaments.
adhere *verb* {6821 tsaphad} to stick.
adhere, captivate, capture *verb* {3920 lachad} {3921 leked} [259 halosis] to catch; to cause to stick.
adhere, join, stick *verb* {1692 dabaq} {1693 debaq} [4347 proskollao] to join one's self to closely, stick to; to remain attached.
adhering *adjective* {1695 dabeq} joining closely; devoting.
Adi El *transliterated name* {5717 adiel} Ornament of El.
Adithayim *dual transliterated name* {5723 adiythayim} Double Prey.
adjudge *verb* [1948 epikrino] to decide or determine.
Adlay *transliterated name* {5724 adlay} the meaning uncertain.
Admatha *transliterated name* {133 admatha} a Persian nobleman.
administration *noun* [3622 oikonomia] management; oversight.
administrator *noun* [3621 oikonomeo] [3623 oikonomos] overseer; manager.
admonish, rebuke *verb* [2008 epitimao] to charge sharply.
Adonay, adoni, adonim *transliterated titles* {113 adoni, *plural* adonim} {*intensive plural* 136 adonay} [2960 kuriakos] [2961 kuriuo] [2962 kurios] Lord; one who has authority, whether deity, sovereign, landlord, slavelord, or a woman's man; in their original consonantal form, Adonay and adoni were one and the same, the vowels being added in the Masoretic Text between 600 and 800 A.D.; the Masoretic text also attempted to distinguish deity by using the intensive, plural Adonay; their fallibility is most evident in Psalm 110:1; and this error was also continued in the New Covenant; and we, in our fallibility, have attempted to correctly distinguish between Adonay, adoni, and adonim; **see** Gesenius, Theological Wordbook of the Old Testament; **cp** Yah Veh.
Adoni Bezeq *transliterated name* {137 adonibezeq} Adoni of Bezeq (in Pelesheth).
Adoni Qam *transliterated name* {140 adoniqam} Adoni of Rising.
Adoni Ram *transliterated name* {141 adoniyram} {151 adoram} Adoni Lofty.
Adoni Sedeq *transliterated name* {139 adonitsedeq} Adoni of Justness; **see** Sadoq.
Adoni Yah *transliterated name* {138 adoniyah} Adoni of Yah.
Adorayim *dual transliterated name* {115 adowrayim} Double Mound.
adorn *verb* {6286 paar} to embellish.
adornment *noun* {8597 tiphareth} ornament.
adornment, ornament, tiara *noun* {6287 peer} an embellishment; a tiara, as an adornment.
Adram Melech *transliterated name* {152 adrammelech} Mighty Sovereign.
Adri El *transliterated name* {5741 adriel} Drove of El.
Adullam *transliterated name* {5725 adullam} the meaning uncertain; a place in Pelesheth.
Adullamiy *transliterated name* {5726 adullamiy} Of Adullam.
adulterer *noun* [3432 moikos] male who commits sexual infidelity.
adulterer, adulteress *verbal noun* {5003 naaph} (adulterer) male and (adulteress) female who commit sexual infidelity.
adulteries *plural noun* {5004 niuph} {5005 naaphuph} sexual infidelities.
adulterize *verb* {5003 naaph} [3429 moikaomai] [3431 moikuo] to commit sexual infidelity.
adulterous *adjective* **adulteress** *noun* [3428 moikalis] given to sexual infidelity; a female who adulterizes.
adultery *noun* [3430 moikia] sexual infidelity.
advantage *noun* {3504 yithrown} {4195 mothar} gain.
adversary *noun* [476 antidikos] *plural noun* [480 antikimai] an opponent.
advocate *noun* {1781, 1782 dayan} one who pleads in behalf of another; **see** plead (for).
afar, far, distant past *adjective* {7350 rachoq} {7352 rachiq} {7369 racheq} remote; in time, or distance.
aftergrowth *noun* {3954 leqesh} a second growth or crop; metaphorically, development.
afterrain *noun* {4456 malqosh} the spring rain.
again, augment, increase, add *verb* {3254 yacaph} to repeat; to add to.
Age *transliterated name* {89 age} uncertain derivative.
age (old) *noun* {*plural* 2208 zaqun} {2209 ziqnah} old age.
age *noun* {2207 zoqen} old age.
age *verb* {2204 zaqen} to become old; **see** beard; **see** elder.
aged, elder *noun* {2205 zaqen} {3453 yashish} {3486 yasheh} one who is aged; an elder of a family or congregation.
agitate *verb* {2000 hamam} {2111, 2112 zuwa} {6470 paam} to disturb; to cause commotion.
agitation *noun* {2113 zevaah} commotion; disturbance.
agonize against *verb* [464 antagonizomai] literally, to antagonize; to struggle against.
agonize *verb* [75 agonizomai] to struggle; to contend.
agony, contest *noun* [73 agon] [74 agonia] a struggle; a contest.
Agrippas *transliterated name* [67 agrippas] Wild Horse Tamer.
Aha *interjection* [1436 ea] let it be.
Aha *interjection* {1889 heach} [3758 oua] an exclamation.
Aha *transliterated interjection* {162 ahahh} an exclamation; in most places used with Adonay Yah Veh.
Aharon *transliterated name* {175 aharon} [2 aaron] the meaning uncertain; the brother of Mosheh.
Achan *transliterated name* {5912 achan} Troublesome.
Achar *transliterated name* {5917 achar} Troublesome.
Achbor *transliterated name* {5907 achbowr} possibly, Mouse.
Achish *transliterated name* {397 achiysh} of uncertain derivative.
Akkad *transliterated name* {390 akkad} Fortress.
Akko *transliterated name* {5910 akkow} Hemmed In.
Akor *transliterated name* {5911 akowr} Troubled.
Achsah *transliterated name* {5915 achsah} Tinkler.
Achshaph *transliterated name* {407 achshaph} Sorcery.
Achzib *transliterated name* {392 achziyb} Deceitful.
Al Taschcheth *transliterated name* {516 altashcheth} Destroyeth Not.
alabaster *transliterated noun* [211 alabastron] the name of a stone; a container made of alabaster.
Alemeth *transliterated name* {5964 alemeth} Covering.
algumim *transliterated plural noun* {418 algummim} sticks of algum wood.
alien *noun* [241 allogenees] of other genes; foreigner; stranger.
alienate *verb* [526 apallotrioo] to estrange.
alienate *verb* [1369 dichazo] to make apart; to set against another.
alienate *verb* {5361 naqa} to feel aversion.
alienation *noun* {8569 tenuwah} enmity.
alight, drive *verb* {6795 tsanach} to come down; to cause to descend; to drive down.
Allam Melech *transliterated name* {487 allammelech} Oak of the Sovereign.
allegorize *transliterated verb* [238 allegoreo] to present as an allegory, as a veiled presentation.
Allon Bachuth *transliterated name* {439 allownbachuwth} Oak of Weeping.
allot, smooth it over *verb* {2505 chalaq} literally, to smooth; as tossing smooth pebbles to allot lands, inheritances; smoothing over as through flattery.
allotment, portion, smooth *noun* {2506 cheleq} {2508 chalaq} {2511 challaq} {2513 chelqah} {2515 chaluqqah} {4255 machleqah} {4256 machaloqeth} {4521 menath} smoothness of tongue; usually an inheritance allotted by pebble.
allow *verb* [1832 exesti] to permit; often mistranslated lawful, but is unrelated to law.
allow, forgive, forsake, leave, release, *verb* [863 aphieemi] to send forth.
allow, give *verb* {5414 nathan} {5415 nethan} literally, to give; to give permission.
allow, leave, let, set, abandon *verb* {3240 yanach} {5203 natash} to allow to be; to allow to be set; to abandon.
Almighty *title* {46 abiyr} a title of Elohim; **cp** Shadday; **see** mighty.

Almodad *transliterated name* {486 almodad} [1678 elmodam] Wizard.
almond *noun* {8247 shaqed} the tree or nut, as the earliest in bloom.
almond shaped *adjective* {8246 shaqed} shaped like almonds.
almugim *transliterated plural noun* {484 almuggiym} sticks of almugim wood.
aloes *transliterated noun* [250 aloe] a gum.
altar (sacrifice) *noun* {4056 madbach} {4196 mizbeach} [2379 thusiasterion] a furniture on which sacrifices are sacrificed; the Hebrew is from the root of the verb, sacrifice {2076 zabach}; **see** sacrifice.
alter, change, double, duplicate, fold, reiterate, repeat *verb* {8132 shana} {8133 shena} {8138 shanah} to reinforce by folding, by doubling; may include disguise, camouflage.
altogether, together, unitedly *adverb* {3162 yachad} as one; **see** unite.
Alvah, Alyah *transliterated name* {5933 alvah, alyah} Wickedness.
Alvan, Alyan *transliterated name* {5935 alvan, alyan} Ascended.
always *adverb* [3842 pantote] at all times.
Am Ram *transliterated name* {6019 amram} High People.
Am Ramiy *transliterated name* {6020 amramiy} Of Am Ram.
Amaleq *transliterated name* {6002 amaleq} the meaning uncertain; Of Esav.
Amaleqiy *transliterated name* {6003 amaleqiy} Of Amaleq.
Amanah *transliterated name* {548, 549 amanah} Amenable; Trustworthy; from the root, amen.
Amar Yah *transliterated name* {568 amaryah} Saying of Yah.
amaranthine *transliterated noun* [262 amarantinos] [263 amarantos] an imaginary flower that is unfading in character.
Amas Yah *transliterated name* {558 amatsyah} Strength of Yah.
Amas Yah *transliterated name* {6007 amacyah} Burden of Yah.
Amasay *transliterated name* {6022 amasay} Burdensome.
Amashsay *transliterated name* {6023 amashcay} possibly, Burdensome.
ambassador *title* **pang** *noun* {6735 tsir} an ambassador, as a representative; a pang, as writhing.
ambassage *verb* {6737 tsayar} to send an ambassador.
amen *transliterated noun, interjection* {543 amen} {544 omen} [281 amen] trustworthy; worthy of trust; from the Hebrew and Arami root {539, 540 aman} meaning trust; one of two words which transliterates into every language.
amen, amenable, trust *transliterated verb* {539, 540 aman} to confirm; to confide in.
amethyst *transliterated noun* [271 amethustos] a stone as an anti–intoxicant.
amicable *adjective* [269 amachos] without strife.
Amittay *transliterated name* {573 amittay} Truly.
Ammi El *transliterated name* {5988 ammiel} People of El.
Ammi Hud *transliterated name* {5989 ammihud} {5991 ammichur} People of Majesty.
Ammi Nadab *transliterated name* {5992 amminadab} {5993 amminadib} [284 aminadab] People of Volunteers.
Ammi Shadday *transliterated name* {5996 ammishadday} People of Shadday (Elohim, as the Almighty).
Ammi Zabad *transliterated name* {5990 ammiyzabad} People of Endowment.
Ammon *transliterated name* {5983 ammown} People; Inbred.
Ammoniy *transliterated name* {5984 ammowniy} Of Ammon.
Ammoniyth *transliterated name* {5985 ammowniyth} a female Ammoniy.
Amnon *transliterated name* {550 amnon} Trustworthy; from the root of amen.
Amon *transliterated name* {526 amon} [300 amon] Trained.
among, inward, middle, midst, within *noun* {7130 qereb} {8432 tavek} the nearest part; the center.
Amoq *transliterated name* {5987 amowq} Deep.
Amorah *transliterated name* {6017 amorah} [1116 gomorrha] Bind; Heap.
Amos *transliterated name* {531 amots} [301 amos] Strong.
Amos *transliterated name* {5986 amos} Burdened.
Amsi *transliterated name* {557 amtsiy} Strong.
Ana Yah *transliterated name* {6043 anayah} Answer of Yah.
Anacharath *transliterated name* {588 anacharath} Snorting.
Anam Melech *transliterated name* {6048 anammelech} Answer of Melech.
Anan Yah *transliterated name* {6055 ananyah} Overclouding of Yah.
Anaq *transliterated name* {6061 anaq} Choker.
Anaqiym *transliterated name* {6062 anaqiym} Of Anaq.
anathema *transliterated noun* [331 anathema] [2652 katanathema] a curse.
anathematize *verb* [332 anathematizo] [2653 katanathematizo] to bind by a curse.
Anathoth *plural transliterated name* {6068 anathowth} Answers.
Anathothi Yah *transliterated name* {6070 anthothiyah} Answers of Yah.
Anathothiy *transliterated name* {6069 anthothiy} Of Anathoth.
Ancient *title* {6268 attiq} the enduring one.
ancient(s), east, eastern *adjective* {6930 qadmon} {6931 qadmoniy} anterior.
ancient, antiquity, east, easterly, eastern, eastward, formerly, preceding *noun* {6921 qadim} {6924 qedem} {6925 qodam} {6926 qidmah} {6927 qadmah} literally, the forefront; from the front.
ancients *plural noun* {6917 qadumim} of antiquity.
ancients, archaic (the) *transliterated noun, adjective* [744 arkaios] that has been from the beginning; original; primeval.
Andreas *transliterated noun* [406 andreas] Manly.
angel *transliterated noun* {4397, 4398 malak} [32 angelos] messenger; an angel may be a messenger of Satan, of humanity, or of Elohim; angels are ministering spirits; this does not imply that they are either embodied or disembodied; the angel of Yah Veh in the Old Covenant is an embodied manifestation of Elohim, and may well have been Adonay Yah Shua; Yahn the Baptizer was the angel prophesied in the Old Covenant, and manifested in the New Covenant.
angels (equal to) *adjective* [2465 isangelos] like angels; angelic.
Ani Am *transliterated name* {593 aniyam} Mourning of People.
anile *adjective* [1126 graodees] old womanish.
animal *noun* {929 behemah} [2934 kteenos] a domesticated live possession; **see** behemoth; **cp** beast.
anise *noun* [432 aneethon] a seed used for flavoring.
ankles *dual noun* {7166 qarcol} the joints connecting the feet and legs.
anklet, march *noun* {685 etsadah} {6807 tseadah} a pacing; an ornament of that which paces; an ankle chain.
announce *verb* {3745 keraz} to proclaim.
announcer *noun* {3744 karoz} a proclaimer.
annul, disallow, discourage *verb* {5106 nuw} to refuse; dissuade.
anoint, libate, pour *verb* {4886 mashach} {5258 nacak} {5260 necak} {5480 cuwk} {8210 shaphach} [218 alipho] [4689 spendomai] [5548 chrio] symbolic of setting apart by libating (pouring on) of oil; of pouring a molten image.
anointed *noun* **Messiah** *transliterated title* {4899 mashiach} [5547 christos] anointed; Messiah is a transliteration of the Hebrew mashiach, and a translation of the Hellene Christos; Yah Shua Messiah is the Anointed of Yah Veh; **see** Messias; **note:** the *exeGeses* indicates whenever Messiah is preceded by the article, as in "the Messiah".
anointed, libated *noun* {5257 necik} symbolic of one set apart by libating (pouring on) oil.
anointing flask *noun* {610 acuwk} a container to hold anointing oil.
anointing *noun* {4888 moshchah} [5545 chrisma] a spiritual enduement; a chrism; **cp** charism.
anointing oil *noun* {4887 meshach} oil used for anointing; **see** anoint.
answer *noun* {4617 maaneh} response.
answer *verb* {6030, 6032 anah} to respond truthfully, as in witnessing.
ant *noun* {5244 nemalah} from its bisected appearance.
antelope *noun* {8377 tow} named after the white stripe on its cheek.
anticipate, confront, precede *verb* {6923 qadam} to front; **cp** east.
antimessiah *noun* [500 antikristos] one that opposes the Messiah; **cp** pseudo messiah.
Antipas *transliterated noun* [493 antipas] Stepfather.
antiquate, remove, transcribe *verb* {6275 athaq} that which has aged; to take away; to take down, as in transcribing.
antiquated, weaned *adjective* {6267 attiq} that which has endured; removed.
antique *adjective* {6266 athiq} {6276 atheq} that which has endured.
antiquity, east, easterly, eastern, eastward, formerly, preceding, ancient *noun* {6921 qadim} {6924 qedem} {6925

from the front.
antithesis *transliterated noun* [477 antithesis] an opposing thesis.
antitype *transliterated noun* [499 antitupon] the representation of a type.
Antothi Yah *transliterated name* {6070 antothiyah} Answers of Yah.
anus *noun* {6574 parshedon} the lower oriface of the alimentary canal.
anvil, step, support, time *noun* {6471 paamah} anvil, as a support; support, as a pedestal or column in a structure; a "stepper", as a supporter of the body; time, as an occasion or occurrence – but not as measured time.
anxiety *noun* [3308 merimna] excessive care or attention.
anxious *verb* [3309 merimnao] to be troubled with cares; to care for.
apart (from) *adverb* [5565 koris] separate; without making use.
apathetic (become) *verb* [120 athumeo] to become discouraged.
apathetic *adjective* [524 apalgeo] to become apathetic; to cease to feel pain or grief.
Apharesiym *plural transliterated name* {670 apharecay} Of a region in Ashshur.
Apharsechiy *transliterated name* {671 apharcechay} Of an Ashshur tribe.
Apheq, Aphiq *transliterated name* {663 apheq, aphiyq} Fortress.
Apheqah *transliterated name* {664 apheqah} Fortress.
Aphiach *transliterated name* {647 aphiyach} Puff.
aphis *noun* {2602 chanamal} a plant louse.
apocalypse *transliterated noun* [602 apokalupsis] a revelation, usually of the future; unveiling.
Apollos *transliterated name* [625 apollos] a sun deity.
Apollyon *transliterated name* [623 apolluon] Destroyer; the Hellene is a translation of the Hebrew Abaddon; **see** Abaddon.
apostasy *noun* {4878 meshubah} [647 apostasion] renunciation of a trust once held; renunciation of a marriage.
apostate *noun* {7726 shobab} {7628 shebiy} one who has turned from.
apostatize *verb* {5472 cuwg} [646 apostasia] renouncing a trust once held; renouncing a marriage.
apostle *noun* [652 apostolos] one who is commissioned; all apostles are disciples, but not all disciples are apostles; of his disciples, Yah Shua selected twelve to be his apostles; **cp** disciple.
apostleship *noun* [651 apostolee] the commission of the commissioned.
apostolize *verb* [649 apostello] [1821 exapostello] [4882 sunapostello] to commission as an apostle; **see** send.
Appayim *dual transliterated name* {649 appayim} Two Nostrils.
appear, look *verb* {8259 shaqaph} [398 anaphainoman] to become apparent; to gaze; **see** manifest.
appearance *noun* {7299 rave} aspect; from the root of {7200 raah} to see.
apple (tree) *noun* {8598 tappuach} the fruit or the tree.
appoint, bore, pierce *verb* {5344 naqab} to point out; to thrust or make a hole through.
appoint, number *verb* {4483 menah} {4484 mene} {4487 manah} to enumerate.
appointed *adjective* {2163 zahman} set; as in the setting of a time.
appointment *noun* {2165, 2166 zeman} a set period, usually of a specific time; **cp** time.
appraisal, arrangement *noun* {6187 erek} that which is lined up in a row for evaluation.
appraise, apprize, arrange, array, line up, rank *verb* {6186 arak} to line up in a row; to put in order.
approach *adjective* {7131 qareb} {7132 qerabah} used verbally; to bring near.
approach, bring near, oblate *verb* {7126 qarab} {7127 qereb} to draw near; to bring near; to offer for worship.
approve, prove, reprove *verb* {3198 yakach} [1381 dokimazo] to prove; to accept or reject the proving.
approved *adjective* [1384 dokimos] accepted; proved.
Aqan *transliterated name* {6130 aqan} Tortuous.
Aqqub *transliterated name* {6126 aqquwb} Restrained.
Aquila *transliterated name* [207 akulas] Eagle.
Arab *transliterated name* {694 arab} [690 araps] Lurker.
Arabahiy *transliterated name* {6164 arbathiy} Of (Beth Ha) Arabah.
Arabia *transliterated name* {6152 arab} [688 arabia] Sterile.
Arabiy *transliterated name* {6163 arabiy} Of Arabia.
Arach *transliterated name* {733 arach} Caravaning.
Aram *transliterated name* {758 aram} Highland.
Aram Naharaim *transliterated name* {763 aramnaharayim} Aram of the Two Rivers (Tigris, Euphrates).
Aramaic *transliterated adverb* {762 aramiyth} Of Aram.
Aramiy, Aramiym *transliterated name* {761 arammiy} {*plural* 761 arammiym} Of Aram.
Ararat *transliterated name* {780 ararat} the meaning uncertain.
Aravnah *transliterated name* {728 aravnah} Strong.
arch *transliterated noun* [758 archon] chief, as being first in rank or power.
arch, back, bow, brow, rim *noun* {1354 gab} that which is bowed, curved; also the top or rim.
archaic (the), ancient(s) *transliterated noun, adjective* [744 arkaios] that which has been from the beginning; original; primeval.
archangel *transliterated noun* [743 archangelos] a hierarch angel; **see** hierarch; **see** angel.
Archippus *transliterated name* [751 archippos] an arch (ruler) of the horse.
architect *transliterated noun* [753 architekton] a chief constructor; **cp** Creator.
archpriest *noun* [748 archieratikos] [749 archiereus] an arch priest.
archshepherd *noun* [750 archipoimeen] an arch shepherd.
Areli, Areliy *transliterated name* {692 areliy} Heroic; Of Areli.
Areopagus *transliterated name* [697 arios pagos] a compound name of Ares (a deity of war), and a stake (as a place to stake a tent).
Ari El *transliterated name* {739, 740, 741 ariel} Lion of El.
Ariday *transliterated name* {742 ariyday} the meaning uncertain; a son of Haman.
arise, arose, raise, rise, rose, rouse *verb* {6965, 6966 qum}[450 anisteemi] [1453 egiro] to stand forth; to rise; to be stirred up, awakened.
ark *noun* [2787 kibotos] a box; the Hellene refers to all arks; including Mosheh's coffin, Noach's ark, and the ark of the covenant.
ark *noun* {727 aron} a box of Yah Veh Elohim; a burial box; most often used of the ark of the covenant.
ark *noun* {8392 tebah} Noach's floating box.
Archiy *transliterated name* {757 archiy} Of Erech.
arm, foreleg *noun* {2220 zeroah} [1023 brakion] arm (human), foreleg (animal); denoting force, strength.
armament, armor, armory, arms *noun* {5402 nesheq} military equipment; arsenal.
Arodiy *transliterated name* {722 arowdiy} Of Arod.
Aroer *transliterated name* {6177 aroer} Naked.
Aroeriy *transliterated name* {6200 aroeriy} Of Aroer.
aromas *plural noun* {5561 samim} those that have an aroma.
arose, raise, rise, rose, rouse, arise *verb* {6965, 6966 qum}[450 anisteemi] [1453 egiro] to stand forth; to rise; to be stirred up, awakened.
Arpachshad *transliterated name* {775 arpachshad} [742 arphaxad] the meaning uncertain; a son of Noach.
arrange *verb* [392 anatassomai] to ordain; to line up in order.
arrange, array, line up, rank, appraise, apprize *verb* {6186 arak} to line up in a row; to put in order.
arrange, fail, hoe, lack *verb* {5737 adar} to arrange a vineyard, as in hoeing; to miss having.
arrangement, appraisal *noun* {6187 erek} that which is lined up in a row for evaluation.
arrangement, formation, rank *noun* {4633 maarak} {4634 maarakah} {4635 maareketh} an arrangment (physical or mental).
array, line up, rank, appraise, apprize, arrange *verb* {6186 arak} to line up in a row; to put in order.
arrogance *noun* {2087 zadon} presumptuous; haughtiness.
arrogant *adjective* {2086 zed} presumptuous; haughty.
arrow, quarry *noun* {4551 macca} a missle, as projecting; a quarry, in which stones are ejected.
arrowsnake *noun* {7091 qippoz} as darting after its prey.
Arsa *transliterated name* {777 artsa} Earthiness.
arsenals *plural noun* {8530 talpiah} tall towers.
Artach Shashta *transliterated title* {783 artachshasta} a title of Persian sovereigns.
Artemis *transliterated name* [735 aretemis] a Hellene goddess; mistranslated Dianna.
Arubboth *plural transliterated name* {700 arubbowth} Windows.
Aryeh *transliterated name* {745 aryeh} Lion.

Aryoch *transliterated name* {746 aryowch} the meaning uncertain; the name of two Babeliy.
as to what *participle* {3964 ma} concerning.
Asa *transliterated name* {609 asa} [760 asa] name of a sovereign.
Asa Yah *transliterated name* {6222 asayah} Worked (Worker) of Yah.
Asah El *transliterated name* {6214 asahel} Worked (Worker) of El.
Asal Yah *transliterated name* {683 atsalyahuw} Set Aside of Yah.
Asar El *transliterated name* {840 asarel} Blithed of El.
Asar Elah *transliterated name* {841 asarelah} Blithed of El.
ascend *verb* {5266 nacaq} {5559 celiq} [305 anabaino] [424 anerkomai] [4320 prosanabaino] to move upward; to go up; **cp** descend; **cp** descent.
ascend, holocaust, mount, regurgitate *verb* {5927, 5928 alah} to ascend, as a mountain; to mount an animal; to regurgitate food; to ascend a holocaust; **see** holocaust, *noun.*
ascent *noun* {4608 maaleh} a way, or steps of going up.
ascent, holocaust *noun* {5930 olah} an ascent to a higher area; an offering that has been holocausted; **see** holocaust, *verb.*
ascetics *plural noun* {3649 kamar} ones who withdraw to a solitary life.
Asel *transliterated name* {682 atsel} Set Aside.
Ash *transliterated name* {5906 ash} a constellation.
ashamed *adjective* [153 aiskunomai] [1870 epaiskunomai] humiliated; disgraced.
ashcake *noun* {5692 uggah} a round cake.
Ashchur *transliterated name* {806 ashchuwr} Dark.
Ashdod *transliterated name* {795 ashdod} [108 azotos] Ravager.
Ashdodiy *transliterated name* {796 ashdowdiy} Of Ashdod.
Ashdoth Pisgah *transliterated name* {798 ashdowthhappicgah} Springs of Pisgah.
Asher *transliterated name* {836 asher} [768 aseer] Blithesome.
Asherah *transliterated name* {842 asherah} a Phoenician goddess.
asherah, asherim *transliterated noun* {842 asherah, *plural* asherim} a wooden cultic altar or memorial.
Asheriy *transliterated name* {843 asheriy} Of Asher.
Ashkenaz *transliterated name* {813 ashkenaz} the meaning uncertain.
Ashqelon *transliterated name* {831 ashqelown} Weighing.
Ashqeloniy *transliterated name* {832 eshqelowniy} Of Ashqelon.
Ashshur *transliterated name* {804 ashshur} Blithesome.
Ashshuriy *transliterated name* {805 ashshuwriy} Of Ashshur.
Ashtaroth *plural transliterated name* {6252 ashtaroth} Phoenician gods of riches; also a place.
Ashtaroth Qarnaim *plural dual transliterated name* {6255 ashterothqarnayim} Ashtaroth of the Double Horns; **see** Ashtaroth.
Ashtarothiy *transliterated name* {6254 ashterathiy} Of Ashtaroth.
Ashtoreth *transliterated name* {6253 ashtoreth} Phoenician goddess of riches.
Asi El *transliterated name* {6221 asiel} Worked of El.
Asia *transliterated noun* [773 asia] thought to mean Asia Minor, the western shore of Asia.
Asians *transliterated noun* [774 asianos] of Asia.
Asiarch *transliterated noun* [775 asiarches] an arch of Asia.
ask, lend, loan *verb* {7592 shael} {7593 sheel} [154 aiteo] to inquire; to request or demand.
Asmon *transliterated name* {6111 atsmon} Bone–like.
asp *noun* {6620 pethen} [785 aspis] as a twister.
asphalt *noun* {2203 zepheth} as softened by the sun.
Asri El *transliterated name* {844 asriel} Blithed of El.
Asri Eliy *transliterated name* {845 asrieliy} Of Asri El.
assarion *transliterated noun* [787 assarion] a Roman coin.
assembly *noun* {3862 lahaqah} a gathering.
assessment *noun* {4371 mekec} a remuneration based on an enumeration (census); **see** evaluation.
assuage *verb* {7918 shakak} to appease; to allay fears.
astonish, desolate, stun *verb* {8074 shamem} {8075 shemam} to stun, as in to stupefy or devastate; to lay waste.
astonishment *noun* {8078 shimmamon} stun; **see** astonish.
Atha Yah *transliterated name* {6265 athayah} Reinforced of Yah.
Athach *transliterated name* {6269 athach} Lodging.
Athal Yah *transliterated name* {6271 athalyah} Constricted of Yah.
athanasia *transliterated noun* [110 athanasia] deathlessness.
Atharim *plural transliterated name* {871 atharim} Stepping Places.
athiest *noun* [112 atheos] without God.
Athlay *transliterated name* {6270 athlay} Constringent.
atom *transliterated noun* [823 atomos] minute; indivisible.
Atroth Beth Yah Ab *transliterated name* {5854 atrowthaddar} Crowns of the House of Yah Ab.
attach *verb* {2836 chashaq} to join; material to material; person to person.
attach, contrive, join *verb* {6775 tsamad} to link; to gird; mentally, to contrive.
attachments *plural noun* {2838 chashuq} rods connecting the posts or pillars.
attain, overtake, reach *verb* {5381 nasag} to attain by reaching for.
Attay *transliterated name* {6262 attay} Timely.
attend *verb* {7365 rechats} to tend at the bathing or baptizing.
attend, befriend, graze, tend *verb* {7462 raah} [5256 hupeereteo] to tend a flock or to pasture; to befriend, by attending to; to cause a flock to graze; **see** attendant; **see** Yah Veh Raah.
attendant *noun* [5257 hupeeretos] one who tends.
atonement *noun* **see kopur/atonement.**
audience, guard, hearing *noun* {4928 mishmaath} an audience; also obedience; a subject.
auditorium *noun* [201 akroateerion] a place of hearing.
aught, ought, naught, nought *noun* {3972 meumah} [3361 me] [3762 oudeis, oudemia, ouden] nil; several words, and combinations of words are used to indicate nil; these include the double negative, not aught, which the *exeGeses* renders as naught; most versions use the word, thing, which indicates an object; the *exeGeses* avoids thing; thing, as an object is not implied; **note:** ought is correctly aught, but the Authorized Version sometimes uses ought; when combined with the negative, naught, or nought.
augment, increase, add, again *verb* {3254 yacaph} to add to; to repeat.
Augustus *transliterated name* [828 Augoustos] August; Venerable.
aunt *noun* {1733 dodah} a father's or mother's sister.
authority *noun* [1849 exousia] to have the right.
authorize *verb* [1850 exousiazo] to grant the right.
authorize over *verb* [2715 katexousiazo] to be granted the right; to exercise authority.
automatically *adverb* [844 automatos] self–moved; acting without intervention or instigation of another.
avarice *noun* [147 aiskrokerdees] [150 aiskros] [4124 pleonexia] greedy gain.
avaricious *adjective* [146 aiskrokerdees] [4123 pleonektees] greedy of shameful gain.
avenge *verb* {5358 naqam} [1556 ekdikeo] to wreak vengeance; to exact satisfaction.
avengement, vengeance *noun* {5359 naqam} {5360 neqamah} revenge; **see** avenge.
avenger *noun* [1558 ekdikos] a punisher.
avow *verb* [1843 exomologeo] to vow; **see** vow *verb.*
Avva *transliterated name* {5755 avva} Perverted.
Avviy, Avviym *transliterated name* {5757 avviy} {*plural* 5761 avviym} Of Avva.
await *adjective* {3175 yachiyl} to wait expectantly.
await, expect, receive, wait *verb* {2442 chakah} {3176 yachal} {6960 qavah} [324 anadekomai] [362 anameno] [553 apekdekomai] [4327 prosdekomai] [4328 prosdokao] [4329 prosdokia] to anticipate; to wait expectantly, patiently; **cp** take.
awake, wake, waken *verb* {5782 uwr} {6974 quts} to wake up.
away from home *verb* [1553 ekdeemeo] to go abroad.
awe, awesome *adjective* {3373 yare} [127 aidos] [5398 phobeetron] [5401 phobos] reverential respect, fear.
awe, awesomeness *noun* {4172 morah} [5400 phobetron] [5401 phobos] reverential respect, fear.
awe, awestricken, awesome *verb* {3372 yare} [5399 phobeo] to respectfully reverence; to fear.
awe, dread, terrify *verb* {6206 arats} to reverence; to harass.
awl *noun* {4836 martsea} an instrument that bores; noun of bore.
Ay, Aya, Ayath *transliterated name* {5857 ay, aya, ayath} Heap.
Ayah *transliterated name* {345 ayah} Hawk.
Ayalon *transliterated name* {357 ayalown} Deer–field; **see** hart.
Ayin *transliterated name* {5871 ayin} [137 ainon] Fountain.
Az Buq *transliterated name* {5802 azbuwq} Strong Hollow.
Azan Yah *transliterated name* {245 azanyah} Hearkened of Yah.
Azar El *transliterated name* {5832 azarel} Helped of El.
Azar Yah *transliterated name* {5838, 5839 azaryah} Helped of Yah.

Azeqah *transliterated name* {5825 azeqah} Walled.
Azi El *transliterated name* {5815 aziel} Recouped of El.
Azzah *transliterated name* {5804 azzah} [1048 gaza] Strong.
Azzahiy *transliterated name* {5841 azzathiy} Of Azzah.
Azzur *transliterated name* {5809 azzuwr} [107 azor] Helper.

B

Baal, Baalim *transliterated title* {1168 baal} {*plural* 1168 baalim} [896 baal] a deity.
baal, married, mastered *transliterated noun* {1167 baal} {1169 beel} one who masters; one who is mastered.
baal, marry, master *verb* {*transliteration* 1166 baal} [1060 gameo] [1918 epigambruo] literally, baal means to be mastered; the ritual of one man and one woman becoming one flesh. **see** baalah.
baalah *transliterated title* {1172 baalah} feminine of baal.
Baal Berith *transliterated name* {1170 baalberith} Baal of the Covenant.
Baal Gad *transliterated name* {1171 baalgad} Baal of the Troop.
Baal Hamon *transliterated name* {1174 baalhamon} Baal of a Multitude.
Baal Hanan *transliterated name* {1177 baalhanan} Baal of Granting Charism.
Baal Hasor *transliterated name* {1178 baalchatsor} Baal of the Courts.
Baal Hermon *transliterated name* {1179 baalhermon} Baal of Abruptness.
Baal Meon *transliterated name* {1186 baalmeon} Baal of Habitation.
Baal Peor *transliterated name* {1187 baalpeor} Baal of Peor (Gap); a deity.
Baal Perasim *transliterated name* {1188 baalperatsim} Baal of the Breaches.
Baal Sephon *transliterated name* {1189 baaltsephon} Baal of the North.
Baal Shalishah *transliterated name* {1190 baalshalishah} Baal of Tripling.
Baal Tamar *transliterated name* {1193 baaltamar} Baal of the Palm Tree.
Baal Yada *transliterated name* {1182 beelyada} Baal Knoweth.
Baal Yah *transliterated name* {1183 bealyah} Baal of Yah.
Baal Zebub *transliterated name* {1176 baalzebub} [954 beelzeboul] Baal of the Fly.
Baalah *transliterated name* {1173 baalah} places in Pelesheth; **see** baalah.
baalah *transliterated noun* {1172 baalah} feminine of baal.
Baalath *transliterated feminine name* {1191 baalath} rule of a baalah; **see** baalah *noun.*
Baalath Beer *transliterated feminine name* {1192 baalathbeer} Baalah of a Well.
Baali *transliterated name* {1180 baali} Master; a title of Yah Veh.
Baalim, Baal *transliterated title* {1168 baal} {*plural* 1168 baalim} [896 baal] a deity.
Baalim Bamoth *plural transliterated name* {1181 baalibamoth} Baalim of the Bamahs; **see** Bamah.
Baale Yah Hudah *plural transliterated name* {1184 baaliyehudah} Baalim of Yah.
Baase Yah *transliterated name* {1202 baaseyah} Work of Yah.
babble *verb* {981 bahtah} [5396 phluareo] to utter nonsense; to make empty charges.
babbler *noun* [5397 phluaros] of one indulging in empty and foolish talk.
Babel *transliterated name* {894, 895 babel} [897 babulon] Mingled; a place; an empire.
Babeliy *transliterated name* {896 babliy} Of Babel.
babes, babies *noun* [3515 neepiazo] [3516 neepios] literally, a very young person; figuratively, immature.
Bachurim *plural transliterated name* {980 bachuriym} Youths.
Bachurimiy *transliterated name* {978 bacharuwmiy} Of Bachurim.
back, bow, brow, rim, arch *noun* {1354 gab} that which is bowed, curved; also the top or rim.
backslide, backsliding *noun* [3900 paraptoma] a side–slip; a lapse or deviation from truth.
badger *noun* {8476 tachash} a clean furred animal; Strong suggests a species of antelope.
bag, bagpipe *noun* {5035 nebel} a skin bag to carry liquids; an instrument with an air supply bag.
bail *verb* {1802 dahlah} {7579 shaab} [501 antleo] to draw water; to let down a pail for drawing out water; verb of pail; **see** pail.
bakings, bakery *noun* {4580 maog} that which is baked, including bakery.
balance *verb* {8625 tekel} to balance, as in a balance scale.
balance, trample *verb* {5537 cala} {5541 calah} as suspended; as weighed; as trampled.
balance, weigh *verb* {8254 shakal} to suspend; to weigh by balancing a set weight against that being weighed; **see** shekel.
balances *dual noun* {3976, 3977 mozenim} a pair of scales to compare weights.
Balaq *transliterated name* {1111 balaq} [904 balak] Waster.
bald, baldy *noun* {7142 qereach} lacking hair on the back of the head.
balden *verb* {7139 qarach} to make bald.
balden, polish, rash *verb* {4178 mowrat} {4803 marat} {4804 merat} to rub (off); to pluck; to cause to be bald.
baldness *noun* {7146} a bald spot on the back of the head.
balm *noun* {6875 tseriy} balsam, as a balm.
Bamah, bamah *transliterated noun* {1116, 1117 bamah} [968 beema] [1041 bomos] Elevated; a tribunal; an elevated seat of judgment; **cp** ramah.
Bamoth Baal *plural transliterated name* {1120 bamothbaal} Baal of Heights; an elevated seat of judgment of Baal; **see** Bamah.
band, bond *noun* {4147 mocerah} {4562 masoreth} a restraint.
bandage *noun* {2848 chittul} loose material that is swathed; **see** swathe.
bandage, channel *noun* {8585 tealah} a bandage, as lifted on a wound; a channel into which water is raised.
bandage, sore *noun* {4205 mazor} in the sense of binding up, a bandage for a sore; an affliction.
bands *plural noun* {7196 qishshur} ornamental bands.
banish *verb* {5077 nada} to exclude.
banister *noun* {4552 micad} a railing of a stairway.
banner bearer *noun* {1713 dagal} one who carries a banner; to set up a standard; figuratively, to be noticeable.
banner *noun* {1714 degel} a standard; a banner.
banquet, drink *noun* {4960, 4961 mishteh} a banquet of eating and drinking; the act of drinking.

- **SUMMARY:**
- **BAPTISM, BAPTIZE, BAPTIZER:**
- **baptism** *transliterated noun* [908 baptisma] immersion in water; an outward expression of inward experience; of identification with Yah Shua Messiah's death, burial, and resurrection; of an inward experience in the Holy Spirit.
- **baptismal** *noun* {7366 rachats} an instrument used for baptizing.
- **baptize** *transliterated verb* {7364 rachats} [907 baptizo] [909 baptismos] [911 bapto] [1686 embapto] to immerse in a body of water; to immerse in the Holy Spirit; **note:** in the Old Covenant, baptism was required for physical purification of humans and animals; in the New Covenant, the baptism of Yahn the Baptizer was unto repentance; those baptisms were **in** water; the new baptism is **in** the Holy Spirit; all who have taken Yah Shua as their Messiah have the Holy Spirit; all who have been metamorphosed by the renewing of the mind are baptized **in** the Holy Spirit; **see** metamorphose.
- **Baptizer** *transliterated participle* [910 baptistees] one who baptizes; used only of Yahn the Baptizer.

Baqbaqqar *transliterated name* {1230 baqbaqqar} Searcher.
Baqbuk Yah *transliterated name* {1229 baqbukyah} Bottle (Emptying) of Yah.
Baqbuq *transliterated name* {1227 baqbuwq} Emptying, as a bottle emptying.
bar *verb* {5702 agan} disallow; prevent.
Bar, bar *transliterated noun* **son** *noun* {1247 bar, 1248 bar} heir apparent to the throne; also a prefix to a compound name indicating, son of; **cp** ben; **see** Psalm 2: where both bar and ben are used.
Bar Abbas *transliterated name* {1247 bar} {5 abagtha} [912 barabbas] Son of Abbas.
Bar Nabi *transliterated name* {1247 bar} {5029 nebiy} [921 barnabas] Son of a Prophet.
Bar Sabah *transliterated name* {1247 bar} {6638 tsabah} [923 barsabas] Son of a Host.
Bar Talmay *transliterated name* {1247 bar} {8526 talmay} [918 bartholomaios] Ridged Son.
Bar Tame *transliterated name* {1247 bar} {2931 tame} [924 bartimaios] Foul Son.

Bar Yah Shua *transliterated name* {1247 bar} {3091 yahshua} [919 barieesous] Son of Yah Shua.
Bar Yonah *transliterated name* {1247 bar} {3124 yonah} [920 barionas] Son of a Dove.
Barach El *transliterated name* {1292 barachel} Blessed of El.
Baraq *transliterated name* {1301 baraq} [913 barak] Lightning.
barb *noun* {7899 sek} {7905 sukkah} a barb or briar, as pricking.
bare *adjective* {2835 chasiph} stripped off, as exposed.
bare, bear, beget, birth, born *verb* {3205 yalad} [1080 gennao] [5088 tikto] to produce from seed; of the male, to cause birth; of the female, to birth.
bare, strip *verb* {2834 chasaph} to strip off as to expose.
Bariach *transliterated name* {1282 bariyach} Fugitive.
barley *noun* {8184 seorah} a grain.
Barqos *transliterated name* {1302 barqos} of uncertain derivative.
barren *adjective* {6185 ariri} as stripped of children.
barren(s) *noun* {4629 maarch} {*plural* 4630 maarah} {*plural* 8205 shephee} bare areas; devoid of growth.
barren, expose *adjective* {8192 shaphah} bare.
Baruch *transliterated name* {1263 baruch} Blessed.
Barzillay *transliterated name* {1271 barzillay} Iron.
base, station *noun* {3653 ken} {4350 mekonah} {4369 mekunah} a base, as in furniture; a base, as in a station, or office.
Basha *transliterated name* {1201 basha} Offensiveness.
basket *noun* {5536 cal} *plural* {5552 calcillah} brush, as woven.
Baslith, Basluth *transliterated name* {1213 batsliyth, batsluwth} Peeling (onion).
bason, threshold *noun* {5592b saph} {5602 sephel} a container; as a vessel, or as a vestibule.
bastard *noun* [3541 nothos] an illegitimate person; **cp** mongrel.
bastinado *verb* [4463 rhabdizo] to beat with a rod or staff.
bath *transliterated noun* {1324, 1325 bath} [943 batos] a measure of liquids.
Bath, bath *transliterated noun* {1323 bath} daughter.
Bath Rabbim *transliterated name* {1337 bathrabbim} Daughter of Rabbim (Rabbis).
Bath Sheba *transliterated name* {1339 bathsheba} Daughter of an Oath.
Bath Shua *transliterated name* {1340 bathshua} Daughter of Opulence.
battering *noun* {6904 qabal} as in a battering ram.
battering ram *noun* {4239 mechiy} an instrument for striking.
Bavvay *transliterated name* {942 bavvay} the meaning uncertain; of Persian origin.
bay *adjective* {8320 saruq} fire colored.
Bayith *transliterated name* {1006 bayith} House; a place in Pelesheth.
bayith, beth, house, household, housing *noun* {1004, 1005 bayith, beth} [3613 oikeeteerion] [3614 oikia] [3624 oikos] usually translated house, as in family or dwelling, except when part of a name, as in Beth Abara; **cp** manse; nave; palace; priestal precinct.
bdellium *noun* {916 bedolach} a stone, separated or set apart.
be, became, become, becometh *verb* {1933, 1934 havah} {1961 hayah} [1096 ginomai] [2071 esomai] to come into existence; to exist; the (Logos) Word, who always existed, that became flesh; hayah is the root of the *name* Yah {3050 yahh}.
beads *noun* {3558 kumaz} *plural* {2737 charuzim} jewels.
beam *noun* 4500 manohr} {6982 qorah} a frame; a structural support.
bear fruit *verb* {6500 para} {6509 parah} [2592 karpophoreo] literally, or figuratively, to be fruitbearing.
bear up, bring up, offer up *verb* [399 anaphero] to take up; to offer up an offering.
bear, beget, birth, born, bare *verb* {3205 yalad} [1080 gennao] [5088 tikto] to produce from seed; of the male, to cause birth; of the female, to birth.
bear, bore, borne *verb* {5445 sabal} [941 bastazo] to bear a burden or load; to lift.
bear, lade, lift, load, spare *verb* {5375 nacah} {5376 nesa} to lift, in a variety of applications.
bear, lift *verb* {5190 natal} {5191 netal} to raise; to lift as to impose.
beard *noun* {2206 zaqan} the beard as a sign of age; **see** aged, elder.
beast *noun* {1165 beiyr} literally, grazers; usually domesticated.
beautiful, handsome (very) *adjective* {3303 yapheh} {3304 yephehphiyah} {8209 shappir} [5611 horaios] timely; flourishing; beautiful.
beautify *verb* {3302 yaphah} to cause to be beautiful.
beauty *noun* {3308 yophiy}.
Bebay *transliterated name* {893 bebay} the meaning uncertain.
became, become, becometh, be *verb* {1933, 1934 havah} {1961 hayah} [1096 ginomai] [2071 esomai] to come into existence; to exist; the (Logos) Word, who always existed, became flesh; hayah is the root of the *name* Yah {3050 yahh}.
because *conjunction* [1360 dioti] on the account of; inasmuch as.
bed *noun* {4903, 4904 mishkab} from the verb, to lie (down); **see** lay, lie.
bed down, spread *verb* {3331 yatsa} to strew as a surface.
Bede Yah *transliterated name* {912 bedeyah} Servant of Yah.
bedstead *noun* {6210 eres} literally, an arch; a bedstead with a canopy.
Beer *transliterated name* {876 beer} Well (of water).
Beer Elim *transliterated name* {879 beerelim} Well of Elim.
Beer Lachay Roi *transliterated name* {883 beerlachayroiy} Well of Living Vision.
Beer Sheba *transliterated name* {884 beersheba} Well of an Oath.
Beera *transliterated name* {878 beera} Well (of water).
Beerah *transliterated name* {880 beerah} Well (of water).
Beeri *transliterated name* {882 beeri} Well (of water).
Beeroth *plural transliterated name* {881 beeroth} Wells (of water).
Beerothiy *transliterated name* {886 beerothiy} Of Beeroth.
Beeroth Bene Yaaqan *plural transliterated name* {885 beerothbeneyaaqan} Wells of the Sons of Yaaqan.
befall, fall, fell, happen *verb* {5307 naphal} {5308 nephal} {7136 qarah} to cause to bring about; fall, fall down, fall away; to fell, as in felling timber.
befit, befitting *verb* {4998 naah} [4241 prepi] to be at home; as to be suitable or proper.
befitteth, befitting *adjective* {5000 naveh} at home; as suitable or proper.
befriend, kiss *verb* {5401 nashaq} [5368 phileo] [5370 phileema] the Hellene is the verb of friend; a soulical expression of fondness; to kiss as a form of attachment; **cp** love; **read** Yahn 21:15–17; **see** eros.
befriend brethren *noun* [5360 philadelphia] fraternal affection.
befriend brethren *verb* [5361 philadelphos] fraternal.
befriend children *verb* [5388 philoteknos] maternal.
befriend Elohim *verb* [5377 philotheos] pious.
befriend men *verb* [5362 philandros] affectionate of a woman to her man.
befriend pleasure *verb* [5369 philedonos] to be voluptuous.
befriend self *verb* [5367 philautos] to be selfish; conceited.
befriend silver *verb* [5365 philarguria] [5366 philarguros] to be fond of money; avaricious.
befriend strangers *verb* [5381 philoxeenia] [5382 philoxenos] to be hospitable.
befriend, graze, tend, attend *verb* {7462 raah} [5256 hupeereteo] to befriend, by attending to; to cause a flock to graze; to tend a flock or to pasture; **see** attendant; **see** Yah Veh Raah.
befriendingly esteem *verb* [5389 philotimeomai] to be fond of honour; emulous.
beget, birth, born, bare, bear *verb* {3205 yalad} [1080 gennao] [5088 tikto] to produce from seed; of the male, to cause birth; of the female, to birth.
beginning, first(s), head, top *noun* {7218 rosh} {7221 rishah} {7225 reshith} {8462 rechillah} the head, in a variety of applications; the head of the body, of time, of the month, of archs.
beginning, hierarchy *noun* [746 arche] origin; chief; as being first, foremost.
behave, overturn, remain, return *verb* [390 anastrepho] [396 anatrepo] to turn; in the manner one turns (behaves); to turn over; to overthrow.
behavior *noun* [391 anastrophee] manner of turning about.
behemoth *transliterated noun* {930 behemoth} a large animal; **see** animal.
behold *interjection* {431 aluw} {718 aruw} {1887 he} {1888 ha} {2005 hen} {2009 hinneh} [2396 ide] [2400 idou] an exclamation of observing with surprise.
Becher *transliterated name* {1071 becher} Dromedary.
Becheriy *transliterated name* {1076 bachriy} Of Becher.

Bechorath *transliterated name* {1064 bechowrath} Firstling.
Bel *transliterated name* {1078 bel} the Baal of the Babeliy.
Bel Adoni *transliterated name* {1081 baladan} Bel (is his) Adoni:
Bel Shats Tsar *transliterated name* {1112, 1113 belshatstsar} a Babeliy sovereign.
belabour *adjective* {3023 yagea} weary of labour; **see** labour.
belabouring *noun* {3024 yegiah} weariness of labour; **see** labour.
Beli Yaal *transliterated name* {1100 beliyaal} [955 belial] Without Worth; a name ascribed to Satan.
belittle, slight, swift, trifle, abase, abate *verb* {6819 tsaar} {6985 qat} {7034 qalah} {7043 qalal} to belittle in contempt; to make light of; to lessen.
belly, matrix, womb *noun* {990 beten} {1512 gachon} {3770 keres} {4579 meah} {6896 qabab} {6897 qobah} {6898 qubbah} {7356 racham} (7358 rechem} [2836 koilia] the interior; a cavity as hollow; the abdominal cavity; sometimes refers to the womb.
beloved *noun* {3033 yediduwth} {3039 yedid} [27 agapeetos] a loved one.
beloved, lover, uncle *noun* {1730 dod} from the root, to boil; literally, an extremely warm caring for; a father's or mother's brother.
Belte Shats Tsar *transliterated name* {1095, 1096 belteshatstsar} the Babeliy name of Dani El.
Ben, ben, son *transliterated noun* {1121, 1122, 1123 ben} son, as builder of the family name; also a prefix to a name; **cp** bar; **note:** both ben and bar appear in Psalm 2:.
Ben Ammi *transliterated name* {1151 benammi} Son of the People.
Ben Deqer *transliterated name* {1128 bendeqer} Son of Stabbing.
Ben Geber *transliterated name* {1127 bengebar} Son of Man of Valour.
Ben Hadad *transliterated name* {1130 benhadad} Son of Hadad.
Ben Hail *transliterated name* {1134 benhail} Son of Valour.
Ben Hanan *transliterated name* {1135 benhanan} Son of Granting Charism.
Ben Hesed *transliterated name* {1136 bencheced} Son of Mercy.
Ben Hur *transliterated name* {1133 benhur} Son of Hur.
Ben Inu *transliterated name* {1148 beninu} Son of Ours.
Ben Oni *transliterated name* {1126 benoni} Son of Mischief.
Ben Regaz *transliterated name* {1123 son} {7266 regaz) [993 boanerges] Son of Rage.
Ben Yamin *transliterated name* {1144 binyamin} [958 beniamin] Son of the Right (as opposed to left).
Ben Yaminiy *transliterated name* {1145 binyaminiy} Of Ben Yamin.
Ben Zocheth *transliterated name* {1132 benzocheth} Son of Zocheth.
Bena Yah *transliterated name* {1141 benayah} Yah Buildeth.
bend, descend, penetrate, press, sink *verb* {5181 nachath} from the root, to sink; to go down; to press or lead down.
bend, pervert, twist *verb* {5753 avah} {5754 avvah} to crook; to overthrow.
Bene Beraq *plural transliterated name* {1139 beneberaq} Sons of Lightning.
Bene Yaaqan *plural transliterated name* {1142 beneyaaqan} Sons of Yaaqan.
beneficial *adjective* [5624 ophelimos] useful; advantageous.
beneficial *adjective* **benefit** *noun* [4851 sumphero] conducive; advantage.
benefit *noun* {8408 tagmuwl} [5622 ophelia] a bestowment; usefulness.
benefit *verb* {3276 yaal} [5623 opheleo] to be useful or valuable.
Beor *transliterated name* {1160 beor} [1007 bosor] Lamp.
Bera Yah *transliterated name* {1256 berayah} Created of Yah.
Berachah/blessing {1294 berachah} Blessing.
bereave, bereft, abort *verb* {7921 shakol} to deprive of; to be deprived of; to miscarry or suffer abortion.
bereaved, bereft *adjective* {7909 shakkul} deprived; left desolate.
bereavement(s) *noun* {7908 shekol} *plural* {7923 shikkulim} deprivation; childlessness.
Berech Yah *transliterated name* {1296 berechyah} [914 barakias] Kneel to Yah.
Bernice *transliterated name* [959 bernikee] Victorious.
Besal El *transliterated name* {1212 betsalel} In the Shadow of El.
Besay *transliterated name* {1153 becay} {1209 betsay} Trampled.
beseech *interjection* {577 anna} literally, Oh now!
beseech *participle* {4994 na} in the sense of pleading; **see** Hoshia Na.
beseech, console *verb* [3870 parakaleo] to invoke by consolation.
beseech, search, seek *verb* {1245 baqash} to search for, including a response to a petition; **cp** inquire, require.
Beser *transliterated name* {1221 betser} Digging (as an inaccessible spot).
besiege, bind, confine, form *verb* {6696 tsur} to confine; to form by shaping.
Besod Yah *transliterated name* {1152 becodyah} Counsel of Yah.
bestowing *verb* [632 aponemo] to confer as a gift.
Betach *transliterated name* {984 betach} Securely; Confidently.
Beth, beth, bayith, house, household, housing *noun* {1004, 1005 bayith, beth} [3613 oikeeteerion] [3614 oikia] [3624 oikos] usually translated house, as in family or dwelling, except when part of a name, as in Beth Abara; **cp** manse; nave; palace; priestal precinct.
Beth Abara *transliterated name* {1004 bayith} {5679 abarah} [962 beethabara] House of the Crossing.
Beth Anath *transliterated name* {1043 bethanath} House of Answers.
Beth Ania *transliterated name* [963 beethania] House of Dates.
Beth Anoth *plural transliterated name* {1042 bethanoth} House of Answers.
Beth Arbel *transliterated name* {1009 bethharbel} House of Lurking of El.
Beth Aven *transliterated name* {1007 bethaven} House of Mischief.
Beth Azmaveth *transliterated name* {1041 bethazmaveth} House of Azmaveth (Strong of Death).
Beth Baal Meon *transliterated name* {1010 bethbaalmeon} House of Habitation of Baal.
Beth Barah *transliterated name* {1012 bethbarah} House of the Plain (Raft).
Beth Biri *transliterated name* {1011 beythbiriy} House of the Creator.
Beth Dagon *transliterated name* {1016 bethdagon} House of Dagon (a fish deity).
Beth Diblathayim *dual transliterated name* {1015 beythdiblathayim} House of Two Lumps.
Beth Eden *transliterated name* {1040 betheden} House of Eden (Pleasure).
Beth El *transliterated name* {1008 bethel} House of El.
Beth Eliy *transliterated name* {1017 betheliy} Of Beth El.
Beth Eqed *transliterated name* {1044 beytheqed} House of Binding.
Beth Gader *transliterated name* {1013 bethgader} House of the Wall.
Beth Gamul *transliterated name* {1014 bethgamul} House of Dealing.
Beth Ha Arabah *transliterated name* {1026 beythhaarabah} House of the Plains.
Beth Ha Emeq *transliterated name* {1025 beythhaemeq} House of the Valley.
Beth Ha Esel *transliterated name* {1018 bethhaetsel} House Beside.
Beth Ha Ram *transliterated name* {1027 beythharam} House Lofted.
Beth Ha Ran *transliterated name* {1028 bethharan} House Lofted.
Beth Ha Yeshimoth *transliterated name* {1020 bethhayeshimoth} House of Desolations.
Beth Hag Gilgal *transliterated name* {1019 bethhaggilgal} House of the Wheel.
Beth Hak Kerem *transliterated name* {1021 bethhakkerem} House of the Vineyard.
Beth Ham Merchaq *transliterated name* {1023 bethhammerchaq} House Afar.
Beth Hash Shittah *transliterated name* {1029 beythhashshittah} House of Shittah (a species of tree).
Beth Hesed *transliterated name* {1004 bayith} {2617 hesed} [964 bethesda] House of Mercy.
Beth Hoglah *transliterated name* {1031 bethchoglah} House of a Partridge.
Beth Horon *transliterated name* {1032 bethchoron} House on the Boundary.
Beth Kar *transliterated name* {1033 beythkar} House of Meadow.
Beth Lebaoth *plural transliterated name* {1034 bethlebaoth} House of the Roaring Lionesses.

Beth Lechem *transliterated name* {1035 bethlechem} [965 bethleem] House of Bread.
Beth Lechemiy *transliterated name* {1022 bethhallechemi} Of Beth Lechem.
Beth Markaboth *plural transliterated name* {1024 bethmarkaboth} House of Chariots.
Beth Nimrah *transliterated name* {1039 bethnimrah} House of the Leopard.
Beth Pag *transliterated name* {1004 bayith} {6291 pag} [967 bethphagee] House of Unripened.
Beth Pases *transliterated name* {1048 bethpatsets} House of Scattering.
Beth Pelet *transliterated name* {1046 bethpelet} House of Escape.
Beth Peor *transliterated name* {1047 bethpeor} House of the Gap; a deity.
Beth Rapha *transliterated name* {1051 bethrapha} House of Healing.
Beth Rechob *transliterated name* {1050 bethrechob} House of the Broadway.
Beth Sayad *transliterated name* {1004 bayith} {6719 tsayad} [966 bethsaida] House of the Hunt.
Beth Shean, Beth Shan *transliterated name* {1052 beythshean, beythshan} House of Relaxation.
Beth Shemesh *transliterated name* {1053 bethshemesh} House of the Sun.
Beth Shemeshiy *transliterated name* {1030 bethhashshimshiy} Of Beth Shemesh.
Beth Sur *transliterated name* {1049 bethtsur} House of Rock.
Beth Tappuach *transliterated name* {1054 beythtappuwach} House of the Apple.
Bethu El *transliterated name* {1328 bethuwel} {1329 bethuwl} Desolated of El.
betray, deliver, surrender *verb* [3860 paradidomi] to deliver to an enemy; to release; to give to possession of another.
betroth, betrothe, congregate *verb* {781 aras} {3259 yaad} [718 harmozo] to join together as in marriage; to congregate.
betrothals *plural noun* {3623 kelulah} engagements for marriage.
better *adjective* [2909 kretton] more useful; more excellent.
beyond acme [5230 huperakmos] past the prime of youth.
Bezeq *transliterated name* {966 bezeq} Flash.
Bidqar *transliterated name* {920 bidqar} Stabber.
Bigvay *transliterated name* {902 bigvay} the meaning uncertain.
Bichri *transliterated name* {1075 bichriy} Firstling.
Bilam *transliterated name* {1109 bilam} [903 balaam] Not of the People.
Bilgay *transliterated name* {1084 bilgay} Relaxed.
Bina *transliterated name* {1150 bina} of unceratin derivative.
bind, bound *verb* {6123 aqad} {8244 saqad} to tie; to fasten.
bind, confine, form, besiege *verb* {6696 tsur} to confine; to form by shaping.
bind, conspire *verb* {7194 qashar} {7405 rakac} to tie; to tie together.
bind, harness *verb* {2280 chabash} to tie, or wrap.
bind, tyrranize *verb* {631 acar} {6014 amar} to bind with a bond; to bind a captive; to tyrranize.
Binnuy *transliterated name* {1131 binnuwy} Built Up.
bird *noun* {6833 tsippor} {6853 tsephar} a feathered vertabrate; **cp** flyer.
birth, born, bare, bear, beget *verb* {3205 yalad} [1080 gennao] [5088 tikto] to produce from seed; of the male, to cause birth; of the female, to birth.
Birzoth *plural transliterated name* {1269 birzowth} Holes (as pierced).
bit *noun* {4964 metheg} the bit of a harness.
bit, bit by bit, few, little, petty, shortly *adjective, adverb* {4592 meat} diminutive; a few; a little.
bit of land *noun* {3530 kibrah} a short distance.
bite, blink, nip *verb* {7169 garats} a pinch, of the lids, of the lips, of the hands as forming.
bite, usure *verb* {5391 nashak} literally, as in usury, to take a bite.
Bith Yah *transliterated name* {1332 bithyah} Daughter of Yah.
bitter *adjective* {3992 maar} {4751 mar} {4815 meriri} {*plural* 8563 tamrurim} [4089 pikros] pungent; acrid; embittered; painful.
bitter, bitterness *noun* {4470 memer} {*plural* 4472 mamrorim} {4786 morah} {4787 morrah} {4814 meriruth} [4088 pikria] pungent; acridity; trouble; grief.
bitter, gall, venom *noun* {*plural* 4844 merarim} {4845 mererah} {4846 merorah} bile; venom; a bitter herb.
bitterly *adverb* [4090 pikros] with poignant grief.
bitumin *noun* {2564 chemar} as frothing to the surface.
Bizyoth Yah *transliterated name* {964 bizyotheyah} Despised of Yah.
black tile *noun* {5508 sochereth} tessara; a border tile.
blade, flame *noun* {3851 lahab} a flame of fire; a flashing blade of a sword.
blameless *adjective* **blamelessly** *adverb* [273, 274 amemptos] without blame.
blanket *noun* {8063 semikah} a large covering.
blaspheme *transliterated verb* {1442 gadaph} {4167 muq} {5006 naats} [987 blaspheemeo] to vilify; to slander.
blasphemous *transliterated adjective* [989 blaspheemos] vilifying.
blasphemy *transliterated noun* {5007 neatsah} [988 blaspheemia] a vilification.
blast *verb* {7710 shadaph} to scorch; to blight.
blast, blasting *noun* {7711 shedephah} a scorch; a blight.
blast, clang, clap, shout, stake *verb* {7321 ruwa} {8628 taqa} [4078 peegnumi] [4717 stauroo] to sound loudly; to celebrate by shouting, and/or blasting trumpets unto Yah Veh; to shout and/or blast a battle cry; to stake a tabernacle or tent; to stake for execution.
blast(ing), clang(ing), clap(ping), shout(ing), stake(ing) *noun* {8619 taqowa} {8643 teruah} a loud sound; the celebration of shouting, and/or blasting trumpets unto Yah Veh; also of shouting, and/or blasting a battle cry; a stake of a tent, or tabernacle; a stake for execution.
bleeding, menstruous *adjective* {1742 davvay} sick, as in having a period.
blemish *noun* {3971 mum} [3470 momos] imperfection.
blemish *verb* [3469 momeomai] become imperfect.
bless, kneel *verb* {1288 barak} {1289 berak} [3107 makarios] to beatify; the Hebrew also means to kneel in adoration.
blessed *noun* [3106 makarizo] beatified.
blessedness *noun* [3108 makarismos] beatification.
blessing *noun* {1293, 1294 berakah} an adoration.
blind *verb* {5786 avar} to cause blindness.
blind, blindness *noun* {5787 ivver} {5788 ivvaron} literally, or figuratively, undiscerning; without sight; sightlessness.
blink *adverb* {6621 petha} to open momentarily.
blink *noun* {7281 rega} {8160 shaah} the blink of the eye; a quick look; a moment.
blink, calm, rest, split *verb* {7280 raga} this word is derived from two roots; blink and split, as momentary; calm and rest, as soothing.
blink, nip, bite *verb* {7169 qarats} to pinch the lids, the lips, or the hands as forming.
blister *noun* {3555 keviyah} a branding.
blister *verb* {3554 kavah} to prick; to penetrate, as to blister.
blithe *noun* {835 esher} pleasant; **cp** blessed.
blithe *verb* {833 ashar} to please; **cp** bless.
blithesome *adjective* {837 ohsher} pleasing.
blood *noun* {1818 dam} [129 haima] the soul sustaining fluid in the arteries.
blood pouring *verb* [130 haimatekchusia] an effusion of blood.
bloody *adjective* {1741 devay} sickly; menstrous; loathing.
blossom *noun* {5322 nets} {5328 nitstsah} {5339 nitstsan} {5563 semadar} {6525 perach} {6733 tsitsah} {6734 tsitsith} [438 anthos] a bloom.
blossom, flourish *verb* {6524 parach} {6692 tsuts} to bloom.
blossom, wing *noun* {6731 tsits} a blossom, as blooming brightly; a wing, as gleaming.
blow away *verb* {6284 paah} from the root of puff.
blow *verb* {5380 nashab} to disperse; **cp** puff.
blush *verb* {2659 chapher} to express shame by blushing.
board *noun* {7175 qeresh} a slab or plank.
boast *verb* [2744 kaukaomai] to brag; to vaunt; in either a good or bad sense.
boast, boasting *noun* [2745 kaukeeme] [2746 kaukeesis] bragging; vaunting; in either a good or bad sense.
Boaz *transliterated name* {1162 boaz} [1003 booz] derivative uncertain.
bodily *adjective* [4984 somatikos] relating to the body; corporeal, or physical.
bodily *adverb* [4985 somatikos] relating to the body; corporeally, or physically.
body *noun* {1465 gevah} {1472 geviah} {1610 gaph} {1655 geshem} [4983 soma] the physical housing of the soul and spirit.

boil *verb* {7570 rathach} to boil.
boilings *noun* {7571 rethach} that which is boiled.
Bocheru *transliterated name* {1074 bocheruw} Firstborn.
Bochim *plural transliterated name* {1066 bochiym} Weepers.
boldly *adverb* **(having) boldness** *noun* [3954 parreesia] [3955 parreesiazomai] unreserved in speech; confident.
bond *noun* {632, 633 ecar} a binding declaration.
bond, band *noun* {4147 mocerak} {4562 masoreth} a restraint.
bonds *plural noun* {4575 maadannahoth} clusters.
bone, skeleton *noun* {1634, 1635 gerem} {6106 etsem} [3747 osteon] a framework; a substance; usually of the body.
boot *noun* {5430 seon} a military boot; a protection.
booted *participle* {5431 saan} shod with a military boot.
border, enclosure *noun* {1367 gebulah} {4526 micgereth} that outward bounds which encloses.
border, wing *noun* {3671 kanaph} {4020 migbalah} literally, extreme edge.
bore, pierce, appoint *verb* {5344 naqab} to point out; to thrust or make a hole through.
born *adjective* {3209 yillod} brought forth.
born *noun* {3211 yalid} that which is brought forth.
born, bare, bear, beget, birth *verb* {3205 yalad} [1080 gennao] [5088 tikto] to produce from seed; of the male, to cause birth; of the female, to birth.
borne, bear, bore *verb* {5445 sabal} [941 bastazo] to bear a burden or load; to lift.
borrow, join, lend *verb* {3867 lavah} literally, to entwine; to become wrapped up in; as a borrower, or as a lender.
Boses *transliterated name* {949 bowtsets} Bleached.
Bosmath *transliterated name* {1315 bosmath} Spices.
bosom *noun*{2436 cheq} {2683 chetsen} {2684 chotsen} [2859 kolpos] the breast; symbolic of one's inner self.
bosom, bowl *noun* {6747 tsallacheth} deep; as a bowl, as a bosom.
Bosqath *transliterated name* {1218 botsqath} Swell (of ground).
Bosrah *transliterated name* {1224 botsrah} Fold.
botany *transliterated noun* [1008 botanee] herbs and plants.
bound *noun* {615 acir} {616 accir} persons that are bound, as in imprisoned.
bound, bind *verb* {6123 agad} {8244 sagad} to tie; to fasten.
boundary *noun* [3725 horion] [3734 horothesia] as a boundary line; limit.
boundary, cord, line, pang *noun* {2256 chebel} literally, a rope; as a boundary line, or as binding one in a pang.
bounty *noun* {8228 shepha} {8636 tarbith} a premium; an abundance; an excess.
bow *noun* {7198 qesheth} {7199 qashshath} that which is bent; a bow in the heavens; the bow of an archer.
bow *verb* {6915 qadad} to bend in reverence or respect.
bow, brow, rim, arch, back *noun* {1354 gab} that which is bowed, curved; also the top or rim.
bowl, hollow, palm, paw, sole *noun* {3709 kaph} {6447 pas} {8168 shoal} a hollow of the hand, foot, paw, or body; also utensils with a hollow.
braggadocio *verb* [212 alazoneia] bragging.
braggard *noun* [213 alazon] one that brags.
braid *noun* {6616 pathil} that which is entwined.
braids *plural noun* {4253 machlaphoth} ringlets of hair.
branch *noun* {5342 netser} {6056, 6057 anaph} {*plural* 6073 opheim} {7754 sok} [902 baion] [2798 klados] [2814 kleema] a limb; a bough of a tree; a descendant; also of the Messiah; **cp** twig.
branch, ear, stream *noun* {7641 shibboleth} a branch or an ear of grain, as growing; a stream, as flowing.
branch, spear *noun* {7973 shelach} {7976 shilluchah} a spear, as a missile; a branch, as sprouting.
branching *adjective* {6058 aneph} as covering.
brand, etching, mark, tattoo *noun* {7085 qaaqa} {8420 tab} [5480 karagma] a scratched marking; a mark on animals; an x or a + as a signature of an illiterate; a mark of protection; **read** Yechezq El 9:4–6; **read** Apocalypse 13:16,17, 14:9–11, 15:2, 16:2, 19:20, 20:4; **cp** brand *verb.*
brand, mark, tattoo *verb* {8427, 8428 tavah} to mark an animal; to mark an x or + as a signature of an illiterate, or to mark for protection.
branded *verb* {5348 nagod} marked by piercing.
brander *noun* {5349 noqed} one who brands.
bray *verb* {5101 nahaq} a screaming from hunger; **cp** growl.
breach, break *noun* {7667 sheber} {7670 shibron} a breach; a break; a ruin.
breach, break *verb* {7665 shabar} to breach; to break open.
breach, break (off) (loose), craunch, crunch, separate, split *verb* {6561 paraq} {6562 peraq} {6555 parats} to breach; to separate from; to split.
breach, plunder *noun* {6563 pereq} a breach; that which was broken away from.
breach, separate, split *noun* {6556 perets} a breach; a separation from; a split.
breaches *dual noun* {4370 miknac} in the sense of concealing.
bread *noun* {3899 lechem} literally, food; consider our Adonay Yah Shua Messiah as the food – that which sustains life.
break (down), dismay, terrify *verb* {2865, 2866 chathath} to cause to prostrate; to break down by violence, or fear.
break (forth) *verb* {6476 patsach} usually in singing; also break bones.
break (off) (loose), craunch, crunch, separate, split, breach *verb* {6561 paraq} {6562 peraq} {6555 parats} to breach; to separate from; to split.
break (open) *verb* {6626 pathath} to break open.
break neck *verb* {6202 araph} to break the neck, as to destroy.
break, breach *noun* {7667 sheber} {7670 shibron} a breach; a break; a ruin.
break, breach *verb* {7665 shabar} to breach; to break open.
break, broken *verb* {6565 parar} to break; to violate; especially a covenant.
breakers *noun* {4867 mishbar} a breaker of the sea.
breakwater *noun* {4664 miphrats} break is literal; water is implied; from the root, break.
breast *noun* {2373 chazeh} {7699 shad} [3149 mastos] the bosom; **see** bosom; **cp** chest.
breath *noun* {5396 nishma} {5397 neshamah} air inhaled and exhaled.
breathe cold *verb* [674 apopsucho] [5594 psucho] to inhale and exhale; from the root of soul.
breathe *verb* [1709 empneo] to inhale and exhale; from the root of spirit.
breathe, puff *verb* {6315 puwach} to exhale the breath; to blow air; **cp** spirit {7307 ruwach}.
breather *noun* {6314 pugah} breathing space.
bribe *verb* {7809 shachad} to donate.
bribe, ransom *noun* {7810 shachad} a donation.
bribes *plural noun* {8021 shalmon} extortions.
brick (make), whiten *verb* {3835 laban} to make a brick; to cause to be white; this is a derivative of two words; **see** brick *noun*; **see** white.
brick *noun* {3843 lebenah} a block of white clay.
bride *noun* [3565 numphee] a man's woman.
bridechamber *noun* [3567numphon] bridal suite.
bridegroom *noun* [3566 numphios] a woman's man.
brier *noun* {5636 carpad} {8068 shamir} [942 batos] [5146 tribolos] a thorny or prickly stem.
brigandine *noun* {5630 siryon} a coat of mail.
bright vine *noun* {8321 soreqah} [288 ampelos] the Hebrew indicates a burning bright.
brilliance, brilliancy *noun* {5051 nogahh} {*plural* 5053 nogahoth} brightness; splendor.
brilliant copper *noun* {2830 chashmal} a polished metal.
bring near, oblate, approach *verb* {7126 qarab} {7127 qereb} to draw near; to bring near; to offer for worship.
bring up, offer up, bear up *verb* [399 anaphero] to take up; to offer up an offering.
bring, embark *verb* [321 anago] to bring out; to embark in sailing.
broad, large *noun* {7341 rochab} {7342 rachab} wide, width; roomy.
broaden, enlarge *verb* {7337 rachab} to widen; to make larger.
broadness *noun* {7338 rachab} width.
broadway *noun* {7339 rechob} [4113 plateia] a broad way; a wide street.
brocades *plural noun* {4865 mishbetsahim} fabrics into which gold, silk, or silver are woven.
brood *verb* {1716 dagar} to brood over eggs or chicks.
broom *noun* {4292 matate} an instrument for sweeping.
brother *noun* {251 ach} [80 adelphos] a male child born of one's parents; also used figuratively.
brotherhood *noun* {264 achavah} [81 adelphotees] brotherliness; a fraternity.
brow, rim, arch, back, bow *noun* {1354 gab} that which is bowed, curved; also the top or rim.
brush arbors, sukkoth, Sukkoth/Brush Arbors *transliterated noun*

{5520 cok} {5521 cukkah} {5522 cikkuwth} {5523 cukkowth} {7900 sok} [4634 skeenopeegia] name of places in Pelesheth and Misrayim; a brush arbor to harbor animals; a celebration of harvest, of spreading of branches, of Hoshia Na; Leviticus 23:33–44, Yahn 7:37, Psalm 118:25,26, Matthaios 21:9–15, Markos 11:9,10, Yahn 12:13, Apocalypse 7:9,10; **see** Hoshia Na.
bubble *verb* {7370 rachash} to gush.
buck (goat) *noun* {6841 tsephir}{6842 tsaphir} a male goat.
buck, hairy *adjective* {8163 sair} shaggy; also a he goat.
buckler *noun* {4043 magen} {5507 socherah} a protector, as surrounding.
buckler *verb* {4042 magan} to protect to another's care.
bud, flee *verb* {5132 nuts} to flash, as in color; to flee in a flash.
build, edify *verb* {1124 benah} {1129 banah} [2026 epoikodomeo] [3618 oikodomeo] to build; to build up; to confirm; to construct; to erect.
building *noun* {1146, 1147 binyan} [3619 oikodomee] that which is erected or constructed.
bull *noun* {8450 tor} a male animal.
bullock *noun* {6499 par} a young bull, as breaking forth with strength.
bundle, kernel *noun* {6872 tseror} a package: as a parcel; as a particle.
Buqqi *transliterated name* {1231 buqqiy} Vacated; Evacuated.
Buqqi Yah *transliterated name* {1232 buqqiyah} Evacuating of Yah.
burden *noun* {2960 torach} {4614 maamacah} {4853 massa} {4858 massaah} [922 baros] a weight; **see** load; **see** overload.
burden *noun* {5447 sebel} {5448 sobel} {5450 sebalah} the load; the responsibility.
burden, lade, laden, load *verb* {6006 amas} to load a load; to impose a burden.
burden, uplift, uprise *noun* {4864 maseth} a raising; a reproach, as a burden.
burdenbearer *noun* {5449 sabbal} one that bears burdens; a porter.
burdened *adjective* [916 bareo] [925 baruno] weighed down.
burdenless *noun* [4 abares] not burdensome.
burn (down) *verb* {3344 yaqad} [2618 katakaio] to wholly consume.
burn *verb* {6272 atham} to glow.
burn *verb* {8313 saraph} to fire; **see** seraph.
burn, kindle *verb* {3341 yatsah} {5400 nasaq} {6919 qadach} to set on fire; to desolate.
burner, burnings *noun* {3350 yeqod} {4168 moqed} {4169 moqadah} a fire; a fuel.
burning *noun* {8316 serephah} a firing; a cremation; **see** seraph.
burning *participle* {3345 yeqad} {3346 yeqeda} a conflagration.
burning (coal) (flash) *noun* {7565 resheph} a burning coal; a burning flash as of a flaming arrow.
burnished *adjective* {7044 qalal} brightened.
burst (open), liberated *adjective* {6359 patir} {6362 patar} burst open, as a flower; liberate, as a person.
burster *noun* {6363 pitrah} a firstborn; the first to burst the matrix.
bury, hide *verb* {2934 taman} to hide by covering.
bush *noun* {5572 ceneh} a shrub with branches.
butler, drink (give), drown, moisten, wet *verb* {8248 shaqah} {8257 shaga} to butler, as a bartender; to drink to quench thirst; to drink unto drowning; to cause to be wet.
butlership, drinking, moistened, moisture *noun* {4945 mashqeh} to cause to be moistened, or drunken.
butt, push *adjective* {5056 naggach} butting, as vicious.
butt, push *verb* {5055 nagach} to butt with the horns; to war against.
buttocks *noun* {8357 shethah} the rump.
by, from, of *preposition* In most versions, these three words are used interchangeably as the translators desired; in the Hebrew, they are most often inferred; in the Hellene, two words [575 apo] [1537 ek, ex] (among others) are translated into more than thirty words; most often the context must decide their proper use; for example, it is not feasible to build a doctrine on the phrase, the trust **of** Yah Shua Messiah.
byssus *noun* {3768 karpac} a yellow flax.

C

cage *noun* {5474 sugar} an inclosure.**cake** *noun* {809 ashishah} a bakery, usually of grapes.
cakes *plural noun* {8601 tuphinim} those which have been caked by baking; **see** bake.
calamity *noun* {6365 pid} to ruin by piercing.
calcinations, cremations *plural noun* {4955 misraphahoth} calcinations as of lime; cremations of bones.
calf *noun* {5695 egel} male calf; as frisking round; **cp** heifer.
call back *verb* [479 antikaleo] to return an invitation.
call, proclaim, recall *verb* {7121 qara} {7123 qera} [1941 epikaleomai] [2564 kaleo] [4341 proskaleomai] [4377 prosphoneo] to call forth; to call out; to call upon; to address; **cp** name.
called *noun* {7148 qari} the called ones.
calling *noun* {7150 qeriah} having been called.
callous, heavy *adjective* {3515 kabed} [3975 pakunomai] as in grievous; as in thickskinned.
callous, heavy, honour *verb* {3513 kabad} to weigh down; to callous; to esteem.
callous, prevail, strengthen, uphold *verb* {553 amats} {555 omets} {2388 chazaq} {2393 chezqah} {5810 azaz} to become thickskinned; to enable physically.
calm, rest, split, blink *verb* {7280 raga} this word is derived from two roots; blink and split, as momentary; calm and rest, as soothing.
camel *transliterated noun* {1581 gamel} [2574 kameelos] burdenbearer.
camp *noun* {4264 machaneh} a tenting area; an army.
camp, encamp *verb* {2583 chanah} {8497 takah} [63 agrauleo] [835 aulizomai] to pass the night in the open air; to tent; **see** pull stakes; **see** court, courtyard.
camphire, koper/atonement, pitch *noun* {3724 koper} camphor, a medication; a sealant for the ark of the flood; also an atonement: **see** koper/atonement.
can, enable, prevail, able *verb* {3201 yakol} {3202 yekel} {3546 kehal} [1410 dunamai] [2427 hikanoo] the dynamis to do; **see** dynamis.
cankerworm *noun* {3218 yeleq} a devourer.
canon *transliterated noun* [2583 kanon] a measured rule or regulation.
canopy *noun* {2646 chuppah} a cover.
cap *noun* {3805 kothereth} {6858 tsepheth} the top cap of a column.
capable, possible *adjective* [1415 dunatos] having sufficient dynamis; **see** dynamis.
captivate, capture, adhere *verb* {3920 lachad} {3921 leked} [259 halosis] to catch; to cause to stick.
captive, captivity *noun, adjective* {7622 shebiyth} {7628 shebiy} {7633 shibyah} [161 aichmalosia] [162 aichmaloteuo] [164 aichmalotos] one that is captured; the state of being captured.
captive, captor *noun* **capture** *verb* {7617 shabah} [163 aikmalotizo] captive, as one captured; captor, as one who captures; capture, to transport into captivity; **see** survive.
capture, adhere, captivate *verb* {3920 lakad} {3921 leked} [258 halosis] to catch; to cause to stick.
capture, manipulate *verb* {8610 taphas} to manipulate; to seize with the hands; to use without warrant.
caravan *noun* {736 orechah} {1979 helikah} a group of travelers.
caravan *verb* {732 arach} to travel in groups.
carcase heap *noun* {7419 ramuth} a heap of carcases.
carcase *noun* {1480 guphah} {5038 nebelah} {6297 peger} [2966 kolon] [4430 ptoma] corpse.
carousal, potion *noun* {5435 cobe} a drinking revelry; a potion of carousing.
carouse *verb* **carouser** *participle* {5433 caba} to revel by drinking; one who carouses.
carousing *noun* [2970 komos] a drinking revelry.
carve *verb* {6605 pathach} {7049 qala} to hew in wood or stone; to plow the ground.
carve, chop *verb* {2404 chatab} to hew or cut.
carving *noun* {*plural* 2405 chatubah} {4734 miqlaath} {6603 pittuach} {6816 tsatsua} that which is carved or hewn.
cast (away) (down) (forth) (out) *verb* {2904 tuwl} to pitch away, down, forth, or out.
cast, hurl, throw *verb* {7993 shalak} to throw out, down, or away.
cast, lie, put *verb* [906 ballo] to throw.
castle *noun* {2038 harmon} a tall building.
castrated *adjective* {4790 meroach} literally, bruised testis.
castrated *noun* {1795 dakkah} literally, crushed testis.

cataract *noun* {8400 teballul} as flowing; a cataract in the eye.
catastrophe *transliterated noun* [2692 katastrophe] a calamity; a demolition.
catechize *transliterated verb* [2727 kateekeo] to doctrinate by question and answer.
cathedra *transliterated noun* [2515 kathedra] a seat of one in authority.
cathedra (preeminent) *transliterated noun* [4410 protokathedria] first seat of one in authority.
cauldron *noun* {4802 marchesheth} a stewing instrument.
cause, accusation *noun* [156 aitia] [157 aitiama] [158 aition] as asked; as inquired into.
causer *noun* [159 aitios] one that causes to be; **cp** Creator.
cauterize *transliterated verb* [2743 kauteriazo] to sear or burn with a caustic.
cavalry *noun* {6571 parash} combat troops on horseback.
cave, cavern *noun* {4631 mearah} {*plural* 4492 minharoth} [3692 opee] an opening in the earth.
cease *verb* {988 batel} {989 betel} to desist; to stop.
cease, consummate *verb, participle* {1584 gamar} {1585 gemar} to bring to conclusion.
cease, decease, desist, abandon *verb* {2308 chadal} to be lacking; to stop.
cedar *noun* {8391 teashshur} a species of tree.
ceil, ciel *verb* {5603 saphan} to cover with a ceiling.
ceiling, cieling *noun* {5604 sippun} a ceiling as a cover.
celebrate *verb* {2287 chagag} {8567 tanah} [1858 heortazo] to commemorate by ceremony.
celebration *noun* {2282 chag} [1859 heortee] a ceremonial commemoration; a festive occasion; Elohim's intent was for the earthly life of humanity to be one celebration after another.
cement *noun* {4423 melet} literally, smooth.
censer *noun* {4730 miqtereth} [2369 thumiasterion] an incense holder; **see** incense; **see** frankincenser.
census, mandate *noun* **specified** *adjective* {4662 miphqad} an enumeration; a designated spot; an order, or command.
centurion *transliterated noun* [1543 hekatontarchees] [2760 kenturion] an arch over a hundred.
ceremonial, ceremony *noun* [2356 threeskia] the form of commemorating an event.
ceremonious *adjective* [2357 threeskos] formal; ritual.
certain, secure *adjective* **certainly, securely** *adverb* {3330 yatstsib} [804 asphalees] [806 asphalos] assuredly; safely.
certainty, security *noun* {3321 yetseb} [803 asphalia] safety; an undoubtable truth.
cesspool *noun* {5122 nevaluw} from the root, to foul; a pool that collects filthy waste.
chaff *noun* {4671 mots} {5784 ur} [892 akuron] that which is winnowed from the grain.
chaff, flakes *noun* {4651 mappal} that which falls off; that which is pendulous.
chain *noun* {6060 anaq} {7242 rabid} a collar; a chain of adornment.
chain *noun* {7569 rattoq} {7572 rattiqah} {*plural* 7577 rethuqahoth} {8331 sharshah} {8333 sharsherah} a chain as woven; a chain as linked.
chain *verb* {6059 anaq} to adorn with a chain.
chain *verb* {7576 rathaq} to chain with a woven chain.
chalice *noun* {6907 qubbaath} a goblet.
chamber *noun* {3326 yatsuah} {3957 lishkah} {5393 nishkah} {8372 taah} a bedchamber; a cell; a room.
chameleon, swan *noun* {8580 tanshemeth} hard breather.
change, double, duplicate, fold, reiterate, repeat, alter *verb* {8132 shana} {8133 shena} {8138 shanah} to reinforce by folding, by doubling; may include disguise, camouflage.
change, exchange *verb* {3235 yamar} {4171 mur} [236 allasso] to alter; to change places.
changes *noun* {2487} chaliphah} alterations of ways of life; of clothing.
channel, bandage *noun* {8585 tealah} a channel into which water is raised; a bandage, as lifted on a wound.
charge *verb* [1291 diastellomai] to enjoin.
chariot, upper millstone *noun* {4817 merkab} {4818 merkabah} {7393 rekeb} {7396 rikbah} {7398 rekub} a vehicle; a rider; **cp** millstones.
charioteer *noun* {7395 rakkab} one that drives a chariot.

- **SUMMARY:**
- **CHARISM, CHARISMA, CHARISMATIC, CHEERS:**

- **charism** *transliterated noun* {2580 chen} [5485 charis] grace; an unmerited spiritual enduement bestowed on all who trust in Adonay Yah Shua Messiah as Savior: most versions give chen seven different renderings, and charis fourteen renderings.
- **charism (bestow)** *verb* [5487 charitoo] verb of charism; to endue, or to be endued with charism.
- **charism (grant)** *transliterated verb* {2589 channoth} {2603, 2604 chanan} [5483 charizomai] [5486 charisma] verb of charism; to grant charism.
- **charisma** *transliterated singular noun* **charismata** *plural noun* {2594 chaninah} [5486 charisma] a spiritual enduement.
- **charismatic** *adjective* {2587 channun} having charisma.
- **cheers** *noun* [5463 chairo] a salute of approval, of welcome; often used as a greeting; chairo is the prime root of words indicating charism.

charmer *noun* {2267 cheber} one who casts spells.
chart, inscribe *verb* {3789 kathab} {3790 kethab} {3799 katham} [1449 engrapho] to scribe; **see** scribe.
chase, flap, flee, wander *verb* {5074 nadad} {5323 natsa} to flap up and down; to shoo away.
chasm *noun* {6178 aruts} {7745 shuehah} [5490 chasma] a breach in a rock; an abyss.
chattel *noun* {4735 miqneh} {4736 miqnah} {7075 qinan} any human, animal, or material possession, except real estate.
chattel, chattelize *verb* {7069 qanah} to aquire chattel; to cause to be a chattel.
chatter *verb* {6527 parat} to scatter words.
cheat, deprive *verb* [650 apostereo] to deprive of some right.
checkered *adjective* {8665 tashbets} as reticulated.
cheek, jaw *noun* {3895 lechi} the side, or the bottom of the face.
cheer *noun* [5479 chara] cheerfulness; delight; **see** SUMMARY: charism, cheers.
cheer *verb* {4010 mabliygiyth} {8055 samach} to cheer.
cheerful *adjective* {8056 sameach} blithe.
cheerfulness *noun* {8057 simehah} blithsomeness.
charm, join *verb* {2266 chabar} literally, to join objects; to cast spells.
cherish befriending *verb* [5387 philostorgos] to have affection for being a friend.
cherub, cherubim *transliterated noun* {*singular* 3742 cherub} [*plural* 5502 cheroubim] figures which guarded the Garden of Eden and the Ark; **cp** seraph.
chesnut *noun* {6196 armon} a nut bearing tree.
chest *noun* [4738 steethos] the thorax of the body; **cp** breast.
chew out *verb* {399 akal} to eat at; to gnaw at.
chew out *verb* {7170 qerats} to chastize verbally.
chew, cut *verb* {1262 barah} chew food; to cut as in choosing.
chicks *plural noun* {667 ephroachim} as in bursters of a shell.
child, children (young) *noun* {2056 valad} {3206 yeled} {3207 yeled} [3808 paidarion] [3813 paidion] [5043 teknon] young person or persons.
childbearer *noun* [5041 teknogoneo] a person who bears children.
childhood *noun* {3208 yalduth} [3812 paidiothen] the life period of a young person.
childless *adjective* [815 ateknos] without children.
children (fostered) *verb* [5044 teknotrophee] to bring up another person's children.
children (little) *noun* [5040 teknion] children of small stature.
chiliarch *transliterated noun* {441 alluph} [5506 chiliarchos] a ruler of a thousand.
chip away *verb* {7111 qetsaphah} to fragment.
chirp *verb* {6850 tsaphaph} to chirp or coo as a bird.
choice *adjective* {4004 mibchor} {4005 mibchar} select; best.
choir *plural noun* {1960 huyedah} a group of singers.
chomer, heap, mortar *transliterated noun* {2563 chomer} a dry measure as mixed, or heaped.
choose, chose *verb* {977 bacher} to select.
chop off *verb* {7112 qatsats} {7113 qetsats} literally, or figuratively, to chop off.
chop, carve *verb* {2404 chatab} to hew; to cut.
chop, chopping *noun* {4553 misped} [2870 kopetos] [2871 kopee] a beating of the breast as an expression of lamenting, mourning, or wailing.
chop, chopping *verb* {5594 saphad} [2875 kopto] to beat the breast as in expression of lamenting, mourning, or wailing.
chop, curtail, harvest, shorten *verb* {7114 qatsar} literally, or

figuratively, to cut off.
chops, cuttings *noun* {1279 biryah} a cut or chop of meat.
chorus *transliterated noun* [5525 choros] a band of singers.
chosen *adjective* {972 bachirr} a select people whom Yah Veh chose.
ciel, ceil *verb* {5603 saphan} to cover with a ceiling.
cieling, ceiling *noun* {5604 sippun} a ceiling as a cover.
circle *noun* {2329 chug} a round.
circle *verb* {2328 chug} to go around.
circuit, crutch, spindle *noun* {6418 pelek} to be round; a spindle as whirled; hence a crutch.
circuit, revolution *noun* {8622 tequphah} a revolution of days; a revolving around.
circumcise *verb* {4135 mul} [4059 peritemno] to cut the foreskin; **cp** incise.
circumcision *noun* {4139 mulah} {*plural* 4139 muloth} [4061 peritomee] the cutting of the foreskin; **cp** decircumcision; **cp** incision; **cp** uncircumcision.
cistern *noun* [999 bothunos] a hole for storing water.
citadel *noun* {759 armown}a fortified dwelling.
citizen *noun* [4177 politees] a member of a nation.
citizenize *verb* [4176 polituomai] to cause to be, or become a citizen; citizenlike.
citizenship *noun* [4174 politia] [4175 polituma] membership in a nation.
city *noun* {5892 ayar} {6144 ar} {7149, 7151 qiryah} {7176 qereth} [4172 polis] (as in metropolis) a large town.
clamors *plural noun* {8663 teshuah} crashings; loud clamors.
clang, clap, shout, stake, blast *verb* {7321 ruwa} {8628 taqa} [4078 peegnumi] [4717 stauroo] to sound loudly; to celebrate by shouting, and/or blasting trumpets unto Yah Veh; to shout and/or blast a battle cry; to stake a tabernacle or tent; to stake for execution.
clang(ing), clap(ping), shout(ing), stake(ing), blast(ing) *noun* {8619 taqowa} {8643 teruah} a loud sound; the celebration of shouting, and/or blasting trumpets unto Yah Veh; also of shouting, and/or blasting a battle cry; a stake of a tent, or tabernacle; a stake for execution.
clap *verb* {4222 macha} to strike, especially hands.
clap, slap, slurp *verb* {5606 saphaq} as in clapping hands, slapping the thigh, slurping vomit; **see** gluttony.
clasp *noun* {6781 tsamid} a bracelet, as an arm clasp.
Claudius *transliterated name* [2804 klaudios] the name of a kaisar.
clay *noun* {2635 chacaph} [3749 ostrakinos] [4081 peelos] a substance of the earth; implies frailty.
clean *adjective* {5343 neqe} pure.
cleanse for sin, sin (against) *verb* {2398 chata} [264 hamartano] to misaim.
cleanse, polish, purge *verb* {1305 barar} [1571 ekkathairo] clarify, catharize; **cp** purify.
clear *adjective* [573 haplous] able to see distinctly, pure.
clear *adjective* **clearly** *adverb* {6703 tsach} bright; evident.
clear, gold *noun* {2091 zahab} literally, yellow shimmer.
clearing *adjective* {6708 tsechichi} as on the top of a rock.
clearing *noun* {6706 tsechiyach} as on the top of a rock.
cleave, pierce *verb* {6398 palach} to split in half; to pierce through.
cleaver *noun* {6393 peladah} a divider.
cleavered, cleft, clove, cloven *verb* {8156 shaca} {8158 shacaph} to split.
cleft *noun* {8157 sheca} a split.
cleft, clove, cloven, cleavered *verb* {8156 shaca} {8158 shacaph} to split.
cleft, twig *noun* {5585 caiph} a fissure of rocks; a small branch.
cliff *noun* [2911 kreemnos] the steep side of an elevation.
clip *verb* {5243 namal} to clip; to be clipped; as pruning; as circumcising.
clip *verb* {7094 qatsab} to clip or chop off.
clip, cut off *verb* {1219 batsar} to clip a crop; a city cut off by fortifying.
cloak *noun* {3737 karbela} {*feminine* 4304 mitpachath} a full outer garment.
cloak *verb* {3736 karbel} to put on a cloak; **see** cloak *noun*.
clot *noun* [2361 thronos] a large thick drop, especially of clotted blood.
cloth, clothes, covering *noun* {899 beged} {8008 salmah} {8071 simlah} that which is used to cover.
clothe *verb* {3271 yaat} [294 amphiennumi] to enrobe.
cloud *noun* {6050, 6051 anen} [3507 nephelee] [3509 nephos] a mist in the atmosphere.
cloud over, overcloud *verb* {6049 anan} to cover over with a cloud.
cloudiness *noun* {6053 ananah} the condition of mist in the atmosphere.
clove, cloven, cleavered, cleft *verb* {8156 shaca} {8158 shacaph} to split.
club *noun* {8455 tothach} a smiting instrument.
cluster *noun* [1009 botrus] a bunch or group.
coal *noun* [440 anthrax] anthracite.
coalfire *noun* [439 anthrakia] a fire of anthracite.
coat *noun* {3801 kethoneth} a covering; the first human covering in the Garden of Eden.
cocktail *noun* {4197 mezeg} {4469 mimcak} a mixed intoxicant.
cohabitation *noun* {5772 onah} the state of living together.
coil *verb* [1507 hellisso] [1667 helisso] to roll tightly; **cp** furl.
coincidence, incident *noun* {6294 pega} casual impact.
cold *noun* {7120 qor} {7135 qarah} chilly.
cold, hook, shield *noun* {6793 tsinnah} coldness, as piercing; a hook, as pointed; a shield, as a prickler.
colleague *noun* {3674, 3675 kenath} literally, one with the same title.
colts *plural noun* {5895 ayir} sons of a burro.
columns *plural noun* {8490 timarah} a round, vertical substance; a support; also of smoke.
comingle, mingle, pledge *verb* {6148, 6151 arab} to become colateral; **see** mingle.
comingling *noun* {8397 tebel} a mixing together; bestiality.
commander *noun* {5057 nagid} one who takes charge.
commander *noun* {7101 qatsin} one that determines.
commentary *noun* {4097 midrash} a treatise of notes or remarks.
common, profane *adjective* {2455 chol} [2839 koinos] that which is common; that which is held in common; that which is not hallowed.
commotion *noun* {7267 rogez} a quivering; **see** quiver.
commune *verb* [2843 koinonikos] to participate; to partake in common.
communicant, partaker *noun* [2844 koinonos] one who communes or partakes in common, or in communion.
communion *noun* [2842 koinonia] an act of sharing; the ceremony known as the Lord's Supper.
compacted *adjective* {4568 maabeh} compressed.
companion *noun* {2269 chabar} {2271 chabbar} {2270 chaber} {2273 chabrah} {2278 chabereth} {4828 merea} a personal associate.
companionship *noun* {2274 chebrah} personal association.
company *noun* {7277 rigmah} a throng.
compare, liken *verb* {1819 dahmah} [3666 homoioo] to liken unto; to compare; to resemble; to consider; homoioo is the verb of likeness.
compassion *noun* [3627 oikteiro] [3628 oiktirmos] empathy.
compassion, compassionate *participle* {2551 chemlah} commiseration.
compassion, spare *verb* {2550 chamal} [3629 oiktirmon] to exercise compassion; to spare.
compel *verb* [315 anagkazo] to necessitate; to oblige.

- **SUMMARY:**
- **COMPLETE, COMPLETELY, COMPLETER, COMPLETION: also see SHALOM.**
- **complete** *noun* [3651 holotelees] [5046 telios] perfect; finished; finalized; satisfaction, as in a state of being, or as payment of a debt
- **complete** *verb* [658 apoteleo] [4931 sunteleo] [5048 telioo] [5055 teleo] to perfect; to finish; to finalize; to satisfy.
- **complete (fully)** *verb* [1615 ekteleo] [2005 epiteleo] to fully finish, finalize, perfect, satisfy.
- **completely** *adverb* [3651 holoteles] [3838 panteles] [5049 telios] fully; totally.
- **completer** *noun* [5051 teliotees] one who completes, fully satisfies, pays in full.
- **completion** *noun* [4930 suntelia] [5047 teliotees] [5050 teliosis] [5056 telos] full satisfaction; full payment.
- **completion (bring to)** *verb* [5052 telesphoreo] to bring to full satisfaction.

comprehend *verb* **comprehending, comprehension** *participle* {7919 sakal} {7920 sekal} [3539 noieo] [4920 sunieme] a

mental grasp; to understand.
comprehending *adjective* [4908 sunetos] a mental grasping; understanding.
comprehension *noun* {7922 sekel} {7924 soklethanu} [3540 noeema] [4907 sunesis] a mental grasp; understanding.
compulsion *noun* [317 anagkastos] the act of compelling.
comrade *noun* [2083 hetairos] a close companion.
conceal, cover (over) *verb* {3680 kacah} to fill up hollows.
conceal, cut off *verb* {3582 kachad} to secrete by act or word; to destroy.
conceal, veil *verb* {5956 alam} to conceal; to veil from sight.
concealed, concealment *noun* {8587 taalummah} that which is veiled; covered over.
conceive *verb* {2029 harah} {3179 yacham} to become pregnant.
conceive, hath conceived *adjective* {2030 hareh} pregnant.
concentrate, shut *verb* {5462 sagar} {5463 segar} shut; shut tight; cold as shut tight, or concentrated.
conception *noun* {2031 harhor} {2032 heron} that which is conceived mentally, or physically.
concern *noun* {1674 dagah} to have care; anxiety.
concern *verb* {1672 deagah} to care about; to be anxious.
conclude, finish (off), fully finish *verb* {3615 kalah} {3635 kelal} to cease; to cause to decease; to bring to an end; **cp** complete.
conclusion *noun* {8502 tiklah} {8503 taklith} the finality.
conclusion, consummation, end *noun* {5490 soph} {5491 soph} {7093 qets} {7097 qetseh} {7098 qatsah} the end, of an eon, of a scroll.
concubine *noun* {3904 lechenah} {6370 pilegesh} one who cohabits without a marital relationship.
condemn *verb* [2607 kataginosko] to have knowledge against; to find fault with.
condemn *verb* [2613 katadikazo] [2632 katakrino] to judge against.
condemnation *noun* [2631 katakrima] [2633 katakrisis] a judgment against.
confide *verb* {982 batach} to place confidence in; **see** trust.
confidence *noun* {985 bitchah} [986 bittahchohn} with assurance.
confidence *noun* {4009 mibtach} a refuge; assurance; **cp** hope; **cp** trust.
confident *plural noun* {987 battuchoth} assured.
confidently *adverb* {983 batach} with confidence.
configuration *noun* [4976 scheema] a schematic; an arrangement of a form.
configure *verb* [4964 suscheematizomai] to form according to a schematic.
confine, form, besiege, bind *verb* {6696 tsur} to confine; to form by shaping.
confines, distress, narrows, straits *noun* {4689 matsoq} {4691 metsuqah} {4712 metsar} from the root, belly; a narrow place; a confinement.
confiscate *verb* {6065 anash} to penalize by confiscation; a confinement for a fine.
conform *verb* [4832 summorphos] [4833 summorpho] to bring to the same form of another; **see** metamorphose.
confront, meet *verb* {7122 qara} {7125 qirah} to encounter.
confront, precede, anticipate *verb* {6923 qadam} to front; **cp** east.
confusion *noun* {4103 mehumah} to question reluctantly; uproar.
congregate *verb* {6950 qahal} {7035 qahall} to congregate a congregation.
congregate, betroth, betrothe *verb* {781 aras} {3259 yaad} [718 harmozo] to join together as in marriage; to congregate.
congregating, expectation *noun* {4723 miqveh} a collecting of troops, of water, of expectation.
congregation *noun* {4721 maqhel} {6951 qahal} {6952 qehillah} the assemblage of Yah Veh's selected people; the Hebrew and Aramaic corresponds to the Hellene, ecclesia.
congregation, season *noun* {4150, 4151 moed} [2540 kairos] an assemblage; an occasion of celebration; a season of the year, of existence.
Congregationer *noun* {6953 qoheleth} the one that ministers to the congregation; the Preacher of Ecclesiastes.
consider (well) *verb* [2648 katamanthano] to examine thoroughly.
consider, perceive *verb* [2657 katanoeo] to observe attentively.
considering *verb* [872 aphorao] to consider attentively.
consolation *noun* {*plural* 8575 tanchumuhoth} [3874 parakleesis] [3889 paramuthia] [3890 paramuthion] [3931 pareegoria] compassion; solace.
console, beseech *verb* [3870 parakaleo] to invoke by consolation.
conspiracy *noun* {7195 qesher} a tying together.
conspiracy *noun* {7285 regesh} renunciation; resistance.
conspire *verb* {7283 ragash} {7284 regash} to renounce, resist.
conspire, bind *verb* {7194 qashar} to tie; to tie together.
constellations *plural noun* {4208 mazzalah} {4216 mazzaroth} the stellar heavens.
constricted *adjective* **tribulation, tribulator** *noun* {6862 tsar} {6869 tsarah} a constriction; a time of constriction; a constricted place; one that constricts.
consume, consummate *verb* **integrious** *adjective* {8552 tamam} to finish off; to cause to be in consummate wholeness.
consummate, cease *verb* {1584 gamer} {1585 gemar} to bring to conclusion.
consummate, consume *verb* {5486, 5487 suph} [355 analisko] to end; to finish off; to be used up.
consummation, end, conclusion *noun* {5490 soph} {5491 soph} {7093 qets} {7097 qetseh} {7098 qatsah} the end, of an eon, of a scroll.
consumption *noun* {8399 tablith} the consuming.
contain, maintain, measure, sustain *verb* {3557 kuwl} to keep in.
contemplate *verb* {6448 pacag} to disect; to analyze thoroughly.
contend *verb* {6229 asaq} to press upon.
contend, defend, plead, strive *verb* {7378 rub} to hold a controversy.
Contention *name* {6230 eseq} Strife.
contention *noun* {*plural* 4079 midyanim} {*plural* 4090 medanim} {4695 matstsuth} [119 athleesis] [2054 eris] argument.
contention, defence, plea, strife *noun* {7379 rib} a personal, or legal contest.
contest, agony *noun* [73 agon] [74 agonia] a struggle; a contest.
continual, continually, continuance *noun* {8548 tamid} to stretch out indefinitely.
contort, form, idolize *verb* {6087 atsab} to form; to contort; as in idolizing, to writhe in pain.
contorting *participle* {6088 atsab} writhing as in pain.
contorting, contortion, idol *noun* {6089 etseb} {6090 otseb} {6092 atseb} {6093 itstsabon} an earthen vessel; a writhing as in pain; **see** contort *verb.*
contortion, scar *noun* {6094 atstsebeth} contortion, as in pain; scars as causing contortion; **see** contort *verb.*
contradict *verb* [470 antapokrinomai] [483 antilego] to word against; to answer against.
contrive, join, attach *verb* {6775 tsamad} to link; to gird; mentally, to contrive.
control *noun* {4623 matsar} restraint.
controversy *noun* [485 antilogio] words against.
convocation *noun* {4744 miqra} a called meeting.
cool *adjective* {7119 qar} chilly.
cooling *noun* {4747 meqerah} a cooling off.
copper *noun* {5154 nechushah} {5174 nechash} {5178 nechosheth} a species of metal; that made of the metal.
copper, coppery *adjective* {5153 nachush} {5180 nechushtan} reddish; copper colored.
copulate *verb* {7250 raba} {7903 shekobeth} to squat; to lie out flat in copulation.
copulation, lying *noun* {7902 shekabah} the lying of the dew; the copulation of persons.
cord, hope *noun* {8615 tiqvah} hope, as to hang on to; a cord, to hang on to.
cord, line, pang, boundary *noun* {2256 chebel} literally, a rope; as a boundary line; as binding one in a pang.
cords *noun* {*plural* 4189 moshechoth} {4340 meythar} that which draws tight.
corner *noun* {4740 maqtsowa} {*plural* 4742 mequtsoth} an angle or recess.
corner *noun* {6434 pen} an angle; **cp** edge.
corner, chief *noun* {6438 pinnah} an angle; a pinnacle; a high person; **cp** edge.
corner, scrape *verb* {7106 qatsa} to corner off; to strip off.
corona *noun* {6843 tsephirah} as circling the head.
corrupt, corruptible *adjective* {7844 shechath} [5349

phthartos] decayable.
corrupt, destroy, destruct, lose, ruin, vanish *verb* {6 abad} {7 abad} {8 obed} {7843 shachath} [622 apollumi] [1311 diapthiro] [2704 kataphthiro] [5351 phthiro] to corrupt through decay.
corruption *noun* {7845 shachath} [1312 diaphthora] [5356 phthora] decay.
corruption, disfigured {*participle* 2763 charam} {*noun* 4893 mishchath} **see** devote; **see** destroy.
cosmic power *noun* [2888 cosmokrator] power over the cosmos; **see** cosmos.
cosmic *transliterated adjective* [2886 cosmikos] [2887 cosmios] cosmetic; mundane; orderly.
cosmos *transliterated noun* [2889 cosmos] the globe on which we now exist; **see** world; **cp** earth.
counsel (private), councilmen *noun* {*plural* 4176 moetsoth} {5475 cowd} {5483 eta} {6098 etsah} [1012 boulee] [1013 boouleema] purpose; advice; advisors.
counsel, consult *verb* {3272 yeat} {3289 yaats} {5779 uts} [1011 bouleuo] [4824 sumboulion] [4323 prosanatitheemi] to advise.
counsel, support *noun* {8454 tushiah} {*plural* 8458 tachbuloth} advice; support.
counsellor *noun* {*plural* 1907 haddabar} [1010 boulutees] [4825 sumboulos] adviser.
courage *noun* [2293 tharseo] [2294 tharsos] boldness; bravery.
courageous, encouraged *adjective* [2292 tharreo] to exercise courage.
courier *noun* {6432 pelethi} an official messenger (not angel); **cp** angel.
court, courtyard *noun* {2681 chatsir} {2691 chatser} [833 aulee] a residential court; a court of the tabernacle; a court for owls; a court as a village; often in conjuction with the name of the court.
court, ledge *noun* {*plural* 4052 migraah} {5835 azarah} {*plural* 7948 shalab} that which is surrounded; that which surrounds.
cousin *noun* [431 anepsios] the offspring of one's uncle or aunt.
covenant *noun* {1285 berith} [1242 diatheekee] literally, a cutting; in Scripture, a contract that was cut between Elohim and humanity; the shedding of blood is strongly implied.
covenant, covenantor *verb* [1303 diatithemai] [4934 suntitheemi] the act of covenanting; one who covenants.
covenant, cut *verb* {3772 karath} [4934 suntitheemi] literally, to cut; to covenant; to cut off; to cut down; to cut a cutting; to covenant a covenant.
cover *noun* {7184 qasah} a cover of an instrument.
cover *verb* {2643 chaph} {2645 chaphah} {2653 chophaph} in the sense of protection; of sins being covered.
cover *verb* {2926 talal} to strew over; to cover in.
cover *verb* {3728 kahphash} to cover, in the sense of atoning.
cover *verb* {7159 qaram} to cover.
cover, covering *noun* {3681 kacuy} {3682 kecuth} {4372 mikceh} {4374 mekeacceh} a protective covering; a veiling.
cover, covering *noun* {4539 masak} {4540 mesukkah} {4541 massekah} a cover as a veil, as a curtain.
cover, covert, covertly *noun, adjective* {5643 sether} a covering over; a concealment; also a hiding place of protection.
cover, demolish, hide *verb* {5641 sathar} {5642 sethar} to conceal by covering; to demolish and cover over.
cover, hedge *verb* {5526 sakak} to cover over; to hedge with a brush; **see** brush arbor.
cover, languish, veil *verb* {5848 ataph} {5968 alaph} to shroud; to cover over; to languish.
cover, vail, veil *verb* {3874 luwt} {5844 atah} {6809 tsaiph} [2619 katakaluptomai] to cover; to enrobe; to wrap; to withhold from view.
cover (over), conceal *verb* {3680 kacah} to fill up hollows.
coveralls *plural noun* {6446 pasim} a tunic many widths wide.
covering, cloth, clothes *noun* {899 beged} {8008 salmah} {8071 simlah} that which is used to cover.
covert *noun* {4563 mictowr} {4565 mictar} a protective cover; a refuge.
covertly *adverb* {2644 chapha} under cover.
covertly, enchantingly *adjective* {3909 lat} whispering a spell; under cover.
cowardice *noun* [1167 dilia] timidity.
cowardly *adjective* [1168 diliao] [1169 dilos] timid.
co–bound *verb* [4887 sundeomai] bound together.
co–citizens *noun* [4847 sumpolitees] citizens together.
co–destruct *verb* [4881 sunapollumi] to destroy or be destroyed in company with.
co–die *verb* [4880 sunapothneesko] die together.
co–elders *noun* [4850 sumpresbuteros] elders together.
co–enliven *verb* [4806 suzoopolio] enliven together.
co–heirs *noun* [4789 sunkleeronomos] heirs together.
co–judge *verb* [4793 sunkrino] judge together.
co–partake *verb* [4791 sunkoinonos] [4830 summetokos] to partake together.
co–partaker *noun* [4790 sunkoinoneo] [4829 summerizomai] [4830 summetokos] one who partakes with another.
co–scion *noun* [4853 sumphuletees] scions together.
co–seated *verb* [4775 sunkatheemai] [4776 sunkathizo] seated together.
co–servant *noun* [4889 sundoulos] servant together.
co–settle *verb* [4924 sunoikeo] [4925 sunoikodomeomai] to settle together.
co–souled *verb* [4861 sumpsukos] souled together.
co–staked *verb* [4957 sustauroo] staked together.
co–witness *verb* [4828 summartureo] [4901 sunepimartureo] to witness together.
crack, crush *verb* {2827 chashal} {7533 ratsats} {7779 shuph} to crack or crush to pieces; to weaken.
crafty *adjective* {3596 kiylay} withholding.
crag, ivory, tooth, tusk *noun* {8127, 8128 shen} {*plural* 8143 shenhabbim} [3599 adous] as being sharp.
cranium *transliterated noun* {1538 gulgoleth} [2898 kranion] the skull.
craunch bone, mighted, mightier, mightily, mighty *verb* {6105 atsam} to become mighty; to overpower a bone; to be powerful; to be numerous.
craunch, crunch, separate, split, breach, break (off) (loose) *verb* {6561 paraq} {6562 peraq} {6555 parats} to breach; to separate from; to split.
craw *noun* {4760 murah} an enlargement of the gullet of some birds to store food prior to gestation.
create, creator *verb* {1254 bara} [2936 ktizo] to cause to be; **cp** make; **cp** work.
creation *noun* {1278 beiryah} [2937 ktisis] that which is caused to be; **cp** work.
Creator *noun* [2939 ktistees] He who caused to be.
creature *noun* [2938 ktisma] that which the Creator caused to be.
creature, full breast *noun* {2123 ziyz} full breast in the sense of conspicuous, or "out in the open"; a moving creature.
creep *verb* {7430 ramas} to move on or near the ground.
creeper *noun* {2119 zachal} {7431 remes} [2062 herpeton] that which creeps.
cremate *verb* {5635 saraph} cremation of bones.
cremations, calcinations *plural noun* {4955 misraphahoth} cremations of bones; calcinations as of lime.
crimson *noun* {3758 karmil} carmine; a deep red.
crooked *noun* {4625 maaqash} [4646 skolios] bent; warped; wicked.
crooked, trap, trip *adjective* {6121 aqob} {6128 aqalqal} {6129 aqallathon} a trap; one that trips; crooked, as full of traps.
crop *noun* {1210 batssiyr} a harvest that has been cropped (clipped); **see** clip *verb*.
crop *noun* {1715 dagan} as an increase of growth.
crossway *noun* [296 amphodon] the place where two ways cross.
crotch *noun* {4667 miphsaah} the place of branching.
crouch *verb* {7251 raba} to sprawl on all fours.
crowd *noun* {5519 cak} a thicket of persons.
crown *noun* {5850 atarah} a circular headpiece; **cp** diadem; **cp** wreath.
crown *noun* {6936 qodqod} the circle of the head.
crown *verb* {5849 atar} to encircle with a crown.
crucible *noun* {4715 mitsreph} that in which metals are melted, and refined.
crumble, subjugate *verb* {7287 radah} to bring under; to conquer.
crumbs *plural noun* {5350 niqqud} as fragmented.
crunch, separate, split, breach, break (off) (loose), craunch *verb* {6561 paraq} {6562 peraq} {6555 parats} to breach; to separate from; to split.
crush *verb* {1792 daka} {1794 dakah} {4277 machaq} to crush physically, or in spirit.
crush, crack *verb* {2827 chashal} {7533 ratsats} {7779 shuph} to crack or crush to pieces; to weaken.

crushed *adjective* {1793 dakkah} physically, or in spirit.
crutch, spindle, circuit *noun* {6418 pelek} to be round; a spindle as whirled; hence a crutch.
crutch, support *noun* {4938 mishenah} that on which one leans.
cry *noun* {2201 zaaq} {6818 tsaaqah} [2906 kraugee] an exclamation; a scream.
cry *verb* {2199 zaaq} {2200 zeiq} {4798 marzeach} {6817 tsaaq} {7768 shava} {7769 shua} {7773 sheva} {7775 shavah} [310 anaboao] [994 boao] [1916 epiboao] [2896 krazo] [2905 kraugazo] to exclaim; to scream; **note:** {7768 shava} is the verb of salvation.
crystal, frost, ice *noun* {7140 qerach} as being smooth.
cubit *noun* {520 ammah} a linear measure, thought to be a forearm in length.
cucumber field *noun* {4750 miqshah} a cucumbered field.
cucumbers *plural noun* {6498 paqquahoth} as splitting open to shed its seeds.
cultivation *noun* [1091 georgion] that which is cultivated.
cultivator *noun* {406 ikkar} [1092 georgos] a digger of the soil.
culvert *noun* {6794 tsinnur} a hollow.
cunning *noun* [3834 panourgia] [3835 panourgos] trickery.
cup, little owl *noun* {3563 kowe} a container; an owl, from the cup–like cavity of its eye.
curdle *verb* {7087 qapha} to thicken.
cure *noun* {1456 gahah} that which heals.
cure *verb* {1455 gahah} [2323 therapeuo] the Hellene is the verb of therapy; **see** therapy.
curl, trough *noun* {7298 rahat} {*plural* 4857 mashabim} {8268 shoqeth} a ringlet of hair; a drinking trough for animals.
curled *adjective* {4748 miqsheh} turned; rounded.
curse *noun* {8381 taalah} [2671 katara] an imprecation; a pronouncement of doom.
curse, cursing *verb* {779 arar} {3994 meerah} {6895 qabab} [685 ara] [1944 epikataratos] [2672 kataraomai] to pronounce doom.
curtail *verb* {2179 zanab} literally, to cut the tail; **see** tail.
curtail, harvest, shorten, chop *verb* {7114 qatsar} literally, or figuratively, to cut off.
custom *noun* [1485 ethos] a usage prescribed by habit or law.
custom *noun* {1983 halak} a toll on goods.
cut (off) *verb* {5533 sakan} from the root, knife.
cut off *verb* {1219 batsar} to clip a crop; a city cut off by fortifying.
cut off, conceal *verb* {3582 kachad} to destroy; to secrete by act or word.
cut off, loathe, lothe *verb* {6962 qut} {6990 qatat} literally, or figuratively, to be cut off.
cut *verb* {1504 gazar} to cut down, cut off, cut out.
cut, chew *verb* {1262 barah} chew food; to cut as in choosing.
cut, covenant *verb* {3772 karath} [4934 suntitheemi] literally, to cut; to cut off; to cut down; to cut a cutting (covenant a covenant); Elohim's covenants were cut; this cutting may imply shedding of blood; **see** circumcision; **see** covenant.
cut, decide, determine, point *verb* {2782 charats} {2852 chathak} to be cut; to cut a decision, or a determination; to point.
cut, scrape *verb* {7096 qatsah} to cut off; to scrape off, by cutting; to destroy.
cutting, separation *noun* {1508 gizrah} a cutting as of a stone; a place set apart.
cuttings, chops *noun* {1279 biryah} a cut or chop of meat.
cymbal, harpoon, locust, whirring *noun* {6767 tselatsal} a clattering, as of a cymbal; a whirring, as of wings; a rattling, as of a harpoon.
cymbals *dual noun* {4700 metseleth} large double jinglers; **see** jinglers.
cypress *noun* {8645 tirzah} a kind of tree.

D

Dabbesheth *transliterated name* {1708 dabbesheth} Hump.
Daberath *transliterated name* {1705 daberath} Word.
Dagon *transliterated name* {1712 dagon} a fish deity.
Dahava *transliterated name* {1723 dahava} of uncertain derivative.
daily *adjecive* [2184 epheemeros] for a day.
daily, by day *adjecive* {3119 yomam} [2522 kathemerinos] during the period between sunrise and sunset, or sunrise to sunrise.
damage *noun* {2257 chabal} {5143 nezeq} hurt or injury.
damage (cause) (experience) *verb* {5142 nezaq} to suffer or inflict hurt, or injury.
damask *transliterated noun* {1833 demeshek} a fabric of Dammeseq.
Dammeseq *transliterated name* [*plural* 1153 damaskeenos] of Dammeseq.
Dammeseq *transliterated name* {1834 dammeseq} [1154 damaskos] a city of Syria; **see** damask.
Dan Yaan *transliterated name* {1842 dan yaan} Judge of Purpose.
dance *verb* {7540 raqad} [3738 orkeomai] to stomp; to spring about.
Dani El *transliterated name* {1840 daniel} {1841 daniel} [1158 daniel] Adoni of El.
darics *plural transliterated noun* {150 adarkon} Persian coins.
dark *adjective* {2841 chashrah} {7838 shachor} {7840 shecharchoreth} as in cloudy, dusky, swarthy.
dark *noun* {7835 shachar} dim, or dark in color.
darken *verb* {2821 chashak} {2825 chashekah} {6937 qadar} removing of light.
darkness *noun* {2816 chashok} {2821 chashach} {2822 choshek} {2824 cheshkah} {2825 chashechah} {3990 maaphel} {4285 machshak} {4588 mauph} {5890 eyphah} {6940 qadruth} {7815 shechor} absence of light.
darnel *noun* [2215 zizanion] darnel or false grain; resembling wheat except that the grains are black.
Darqon *transliterated name* {1874 darqown} of uncertain derivative; one of Shelomoh's servants.
dart *noun* {3591 kiydon} an instrument for striking.
Daryavesh *transliterated title* {1867, 1868 daryavesh} a title of several Persian sovereigns.
daughter *noun* {1323 bath} [2364 thugateer] a female offspring.
daughter in law *noun* {3618 kallah} a son's woman.
daughterling *noun* [2365 thugatrion] little daughter.
David *transliterated name* {1732 david} [1138 dabid] Loving.
dawn (at), dawning *noun* {4891 mishchar} {5053 nogahh} {7837 shachar} {7839 shacharuth} {8238 shepharphar} [827 augee] [3719 orthrizo] [3721 orthrios] [3722 orthros] daybreak.
dawn, dawning *verb* [1306 diaugazo] [2020 epiphosko] [3720 orthrinos] the breaking of day.
day, yom *transliterated noun* {3117, 3118 yom} [2250 heemera] including, but not limited to dawn to down, or dawn to dawn; 24 hours, or a nonspecific period such as the Day of Yah Veh, Yom Kippurim.
daylight *noun* {5105 neharah}.
dazzling white *verb* {6705 tsachach} as glaring.
dead (half) *noun* [2253 heemithanees] as in entirely exhausted.
dead *noun* [3498 nekros] necro; **see** necrosis; lifeless.
dead, death *noun* {4192 muth} {4193 moth} {4194 maveth} {*plural* 4463 mamoth} {8546 temuthah} [2288 thanatos] [5054 telutee] the cessation of life.
deaden *verb* [3499 nekroo] to cause to be lifeless.
deadly *adjective* [2286 thanasimos] fatal.
deal, ripen, wean *verb* {1580 gamal} transact.
dealing *noun* {1576 gemuwl} {1578 gemuwlah} transaction.
death (doomed to) *verb* [1935 epithanatios] destined to die.
deathbearing *adjective* [2287 thanateephoros] fatal.
deathify, die, necro– *verb* {4191 muth} [2289 thanatoo] to die; to put to death.
debate, discern, discriminate, doubt *verb* {995 biyn} [1252 diakrino] [1253 diakrisis] to distinguish; to thoroughly judge.
debtor *noun* [3781 ophiletees] used metaphorically of one who is under an obligation.
Decapolis *transliterated name* [1179 dekapolis] Ten City; a city which is tenth in size or influence; or a city over ten.
decease, desist, abandon, cease *verb* {2308 chadai} to be lacking; to stop.
deceased *noun* {2309 chedel} the state of the dead.
deceit *noun* **deceitful** *adjective* {4820 mirmah} {4860 mashshaon} {5231 nekel} {7423 remiah} fraud; treachery.
deceitfully/to Tormah *adverb, transliterated name* {8649 tormah} fraud.
deceive *verb* **deceiver** *participle* {5230 nakal} {8591 taa} to cheat.
deceive, deny, disown, emaciate *verb* {3584 kachash} [550 apeipomen] to be untrue in word, or deed.
deceive, hurl *verb* {7411 ramah} {7412 ramah} to throw; to betray.
deceive, mislead *verb* {5377 nasha} {7952 shalah} to lead

astray; to wrong.
deception *noun* {7944 shal} a fault.
deception, denial, emaciation *noun* {3585 kachash} a failure of flesh.
deceptive *adjective* {3586 kechash} untrue in word, or deed.
decide, determine, point, cut *verb* {2782 charat} {2852 chathak} to be cut; to cut a decision, or a determination; to point.
decircumcision *noun* [1986 epispaomai] a circumcision which has been undone; **cp** circumcision.
decision *noun* {6600 pithgam} a judicial sentence.
decision, decisive, incision, incisor, ore, sickle, trench *adjective, noun* {2742 charuts} physically, soulically, or mentally, an incising.
decision, opinion *noun* [1106 gnomee] a personal judgment.
declaration *noun* [1335 diegesis] a setting forth in detail.
declare *verb* [1334 diegeomai] [1555 ekdiegeomari] [1834 exegeomai] the verb of exegesis; to set forth in detail.
decorous *adjective* [2158 uskeemon] respectable.
decorously *adverb* [2156 uskeemonos] in a seemly manner; decently.
decorum *noun* [2157 uskeemosunee] that which is befitting.
decree *noun* {1510 gezerah} {1881, 1882 dath} {2942 teem} [3724 horizo] a regulatory order.
decree, taste *noun* {2941, 2942 teem} judgment; flavor.
decreer *noun* {1884 dethabar} one who decrees.
dedicated *adjective* {2593 chaniyk} from hanukkah; initiated; practised.
deed *noun* {4659 miphalah} that which is done; noun of the verb do.
deed *noun* {6467 poal} {6468 peullah} an act or work; **see** do, make.
deep fried *verb* {7246 rabak} bake by soaking in oil.
deep *noun* {4688 metsulah} far down; **cp** depths.
deep, deeper, depth *adjective* {6011 omeq} {6012 ameq} further below; far lower.
deepen *verb* {6009 amaq} to be deep; to make deep.
defamation *noun* [1426 duspheemia] a bringing into disrepute; dishonour; disgrace.
defat, fatten *verb* {1878 dashen} depending on the case, to make fat, or to remove fat; to enrich.
defence, plea, strife, contention *noun* {7379 rib} a personal, or legal contest.
defend, plead, strive, contend *verb* {7378 rub} to hold a controversy.
defile *verb* [3392 miaino] contaminate.
defraud *verb* {6906 qaba} to cover over.
degrees, steps *noun* {4609 maalah} steps; stations; a progression; 1/360th of a circle.
Dela Yah *transliterated name* {1806 delayah} Bailed of Yah.
delay, slack *verb* [1019 braduno] to be slow.
delicacies *noun* {*plural* 4303 matammoth} {*plural* 4516 manamim} {6598 pathbag} dainties; delicious foods.
delicate *adjective* {6028 anog} dainty; luxurious.
delicate *participle* **delight, luxuriate** *verb* {6026 anag} to be, or to become soft; to delight in; to deride.
delicately *adverb* {4574 maadan} cheerfully.
delight, desire *adjective* {2655 chaphets} pleased with.
delight, desire *noun* {2531 chemed} {2532 chemdah} {2656 chephets} {2837 chesheq} {*plural* 3970 maavayim} {4261 machmad} {*plural* 4262 machmadim} {8588 taanug} a delight; a pleasure; an object of desire, or pleasure, or of value.
delight, desire *verb* {2654 chaphets} literally, to bend toward; to be inclined toward.
delight, luxuriate *verb* **delicate** *participle* {6026 anag} to be, or to become soft; to delight in; to deride.
delights *plural noun* {8191 shaashua} pleasant strokes.
deliver, surrender, betray *verb* [3860 paradidomi] to release; to give to possession of another; to deliver to an enemy.
delude *verb* [538 apatao] to cheat; to deceive.
delusion *noun* {*plural* 4123 mahathallahoth} [539 apatee] a misleading of the mind.
demand *verb* [523 apaiteo] to demand back.
demand *verb* [1809 exaiteomai] to demand (for trial).
demolish *verb* {2040 harac} utterly destroy; break; break through.
demolish, hide, cover *verb* {5641 sathar} {5642 sethar} to conceal by covering; to demolish and cover over.
demolition *noun* {2034 haricah} {2035 haricuwth} {2041 herec} utter destruction.
demon *noun* {7700 shed} [1140 daimonion] [1142 daimon] an evil spirit; **see** spirit; **cp** Diabolos.
demondreader *noun* [1174 disidaimonesteros] a kind of worshipper.
demondreading *verb* [1175 disidaimonia] the dreading of demons.
demonic *adjective* [1141 daimoniodees] demon in character.
demonized *verb* [1139 daimonizomai] to be infused or overtaken by a demon.
denarion *transliterated noun* [1220 denarion] a Latin coin; a silver tenthpiece (dime).
denial, emaciation, deception *noun* {3585 kachash} a failure of flesh.
deny *verb* [533 aparneomai] [720 arneomai] to disown; to recant; to renounce.
deny, disown, emaciate, deceive *verb* {3584 kachash} [550 apeipomen] to be untrue in word, or deed.
depart, remove *verb* {5253 nacag} to retreat.
dependant, necessary *adjective* [316 anagkaios] needed; depend upon.
depose, deposit, descend *verb* {5182 nechath} to go down; to bring away.
deprive, cheat *verb* [650 apostereo] to deprive of some right.
depth, deep, deeper *adjective* {6011 omeq} {6012 ameq} further below; far lower.
depths *plural noun* {4615 maamaqim} **cp** deep; lower region.
Deqer *transliterated name* {1857 deqer} Stab.
deride *verb* {3931 laab} {3932 laag} to ridicule.
derision *noun* {3933 laag} a ridicule.
descend *verb* [2597 katabaino] to go down.
descend, depose, deposit *verb* {5182 nechath} to go down; to bring away.
descend, lower, topple *verb* {3381 yarad} to go lower; to tip over.
descend, penetrate, press, sink, bend *verb* {5181 nachath} from the root, to sink; to go down; to press or lead down.
descendant *noun* [1549 ekgonon] one in the line of ancestors.
descending *adjective* {5185 nacheth} going down.
descent, festoon *noun* {4174 mowrad} a place of going down; an ornamental hanging; a garland or wreath.
desert dwellers *noun* {6728 tsiyiy} they who dwell in the desert.
desert *noun* {6707 tsechichah} {6723 tsiah} {6724 tsion} a barren place.
designate, indicate *verb* {5567 saman} [322 anadiknumi] to show; to appoint.
desirables *plural noun* {2532 chemdah} valuables.
desire *noun* {8375 taabah} {8378 taavah} {8669 teshuqah} a longing for; **cp** will.
desire *verb* {183 avah} {8373 taab} to long for; **cp** will.
desire *verb* {2530 chamad} to delight in.
desire, delight *adjective* {2655 chaphets} pleased with.
desire, delight *noun* {2531 chemed} {2532 chemdah} {2656 chephets} {2837 chesheq} {*plural* 3970 maavayim} {4261 machmad} {*plural* 4262 machmadim} {8588 taanug} a delight; a pleasure; an object of desire, or pleasure, or of value.
desire, delight *verb* {2654 chaphets} literally, to bend toward; to be inclined toward.
desist, abandon, cease, decease *verb* {2308 chadai} to be lacking; to stop.
desolate, dry, parch *adjective* {2720 chareb} {8076 shamen} parched; ruined.
desolate, dry, parch *verb* {2717, 2718 charab} {3456 yashem} {8045 shamad} {8046 shemad} [2049 ereemoo] to lay waste; to destroy.
desolate, strive *verb* {5327 natsah} to struggle; to lay waste.
desolate, stun, astonish *verb* {8074 shamem} {8075 shemam} to lay waste; to stun, as in to stupefy or devastate.
desolation *noun* **desolate** *adjective* {2723 chorbah} {*plural* 3451 yeshiymah} {3452 yeshimon} {4923 meshammah} {8047 shammah} {8077 shemamah} [2048b ereemos] [2050 ereemosis] an area which has been abandoned and left to ruin; **cp** wilderness.
despise *verb* {7750 suwt} to contemn.
despoil, pledge, spoil *verb* {2254, 2255 chabal} literally, to bind tightly; as in spoiling or as in binding a pledge.
despotes *transliterated title* [1203 despotes] a title ascribed to a lord of servants, to Yah Veh, and to Yah Shua; an absolute ruler; the present day connotation of tyrant did not appear until centuries later.

destroy, destruct, lose, lost *verb* {6 abad} {7 abad} [622 apollumi] to destroy fully.
destroy, destruct, lose, ruin, vanish, corrupt *verb* {6 abad} {7 abad} {8 obed} {7843 shachath} [622 apollumi] [1311 diapthiro] [2704 kataphthiro] [5351 phthiro] to corrupt through decay.
Destroyer *title* [3644 olothrutees] a ruiner; the Hellenic translation of the Hebrew, Abbaddon; **see** Abbaddon.
destroying *participle* {4892 mashcheth} ruining.
destruct, lose, lost, destroy *verb* {6 abad} {7 abad} [622 apollumi] to destroy fully.
destruction *noun* {8 obed} {12 abdan} {13 obdan} {3589 kiyd} {4889 mashchith} [684 apolia] [3639 olethros] ruin.
determine, point, cut, decide *verb* {2782 charat} {2852 chathak} to be cut; to cut a decision, or a determination; to point.
Deu El *transliterated name* {1845 deuel} Known of El.
devastation *noun* {7722 shoah} ruin.
deviate *noun* {7846 set} one who turns aside.
deviate *verb* {7847 satah} to turn aside.
devote, doom *verb* {2763 charam} to set apart for dedication; to set apart for destruction; **see** disfigure.
devoted, doomed *noun* {2764 cherem} that which is set apart in dedication; that which is set apart for destruction.
dewdrops *plural noun* {7447 raciyc} drippings; droppings.
Di Zahab *transliterated name* {1774 diyzahab} Of Gold.
Diabolos *transliterated name* **diabolic** *adjective* [1228 diabolos] the Hellenic name of Satan; also used adjectively; **see** Satan; **cp** demon.
diadem *transliterated noun* {3804 kether} [1238 diadeema] a royal headpiece; **cp** crown; **cp** wreath.
diadem *verb* {3803 kathar} to place a diadem.
dialect *transliterated noun* [1258 dialektos] a provincial form of a language; **read** Acts 2:8–11.
dialogue *noun* [1261 dialogismos] a reasoning of words.
dialogue *transliterated verb* [1256 dialegomai] [1260 dialogizomai] to reason words, in argument or exhortation.
diaphanous *transliterated adjective* [1307 diaphanees] transparent; translucent.
diaspora *transliterated noun* [1290 diaspora] dispersion.
diatribe *transliterated noun* [3859 paradiatribe] a harangue.
Diblayim *dual transliterated name* {1691 diblayim} Two Lumps.
dichotomize *transliterated verb* [1371 dikotomeo] to cut into two parts.
didactic *transliterated adjective* [1317 didaktikos] able to doctrinate.
didrachma *transliterated noun* [1323 didrachmon] double drachma.
die *verb* [599 apothneesko] [2348 thneesko] to become lifeless in the sense of dying off.
die *verb* [5053 telutao] to become lifeless in the sense of having come to completion.
die, necro–, deathify *verb* {4191 muth} [2289 thanatoo] to die; to put to death.
difficult *adjective* [1422 duskolos] impractible.
difficultly *adverb* [1423 duskolos] impractibly.
dig, explore *verb* {2658 chaphar} to pry into.
dig, pierce *verb* {3738, 3739 kahrah} to bore; to dig.
dig, undermine *verb* {6979 qur} to trench; to estop.
digging *noun* {4290 machtereth} a burglary committed by digging into a building.
Dilan *transliterated name* {1810 dilan} of uncertain derivative.
dilute *verb* {4107 mahal} to cut down; to reduce.
dim, fade *adjective* {3544 kehah} obscure; dull.
dim, fade *verb* {3543 kahah} to become obscure, dull.
diminish, lessen *verb* {4591 maat} to reduce; to pare off.
dimness *noun* [887 aklus] dimness of sight.
Dioscuri *transliterated noun* [1359 dioskouroi] Twins of Zeus.
Diotrephes *transliterated noun* [1361 diotrephes] Nourished of Zeus.
Diqlah *transliterated name* {1853 diqlah} of foreign origin; a region of Arabia.
disadvantageous *adjective* [255 alusiteless] without advantage; without gain.
disallow, discourage, annul *verb* {5106 nuw} to refuse; dissuade.
disappear *verb* {6461 pacac} to disperse.
disapproved *verb* [593 apodokimazo] to refuse to accept as true.
discern, discriminate, doubt, debate *verb* {995 biyn} [1252 diakrino] [1253 diakrisis] to distinguish; to thoroughly judge.
discern, distinguish, estrange, notice, recognize *verb* {5234 nakar} to acknowledge; to scrutinize; to distinguish between; to ignore, hence to be estranged.
discernment *noun* {998, 999 binah} distinguishment; understanding.
discernment *noun* {8394 tabun} [144 aistheesis] detection; distinguishment.
disciple *noun* [3101 matheetees] [*feminine* 3102 matheetria] a learner.
disciple *verb* {3925 lamad} [3100 matheetuo] to learn; to teach; **note:** not to be confused with discipline.
discipled *adjective* {3928 limmud} one who has learned, who has been taught; **see** learn, teach.
discipline *noun* {*plural* 4000 mabim} {4148 mucar} {4561 mocar} tutorial; may or may not include punishment; the Hellene is the verb of pedagogue; to tutor; **note:** not to be confused with disciple.
discipline *verb* {3256 yacar} {4148 mucar} [3809 paidia] [3811 paiduo] to tutor; may or may not include punishment; the Hellene is the verb of pedagogue; to tutor; **note:** not to be confused with disciple; **cp** disciple.
discourage, annul, disallow *verb* {5106 nuw} to refuse; dissuade.
discriminate, doubt, debate, discern *verb* {995 biyn} [1252 diakrino] [1253 diakrisis] to distinguish; to thoroughly judge.
disease *noun* {4064 madveh} {4245 machalah} {*plural* 4251 machluyim} sickness.
disesteem *verb* {2107 zuwl} [2706 kataphphroneo] to belittle.
disfigured, corruption {*participle* 2763 charam} {*noun* 4893 mishchath} **see** devote; **see** destroy.
disgrace, folly, wither *verb* {5034 nabel} from the root, to wilt; to fall away; to fail.
disguise, search *verb* {2664 chaphas} to discover; to uncover; to mask.
dish *noun* {7086 qearah} as hollowed.
dishonour *noun* [819 atima] [820 atimos] disesteem.
dishonour *verb* [818 atimazo] to disesteem.
dishonourably *adverb* [821 atimoo] disesteemingly.
disintegrate, harass *verb* {7492 raats} to break in pieces.
disintegrator *noun* {4660 mappats} {4661 mappets} that which disintegrates.
dislocated *adjective* {4154 muwedeth} as slipped out of place.
dismay, terrify, break (down) *verb* {2865, 2866 chathath} to cause to prostrate; to break down by violence, or fear.
dismember *verb* {5408 nathach} to separate members of a body, human or animal; **see** members.
disown, emaciate, deceive, deny *verb* {3584 kachash} [550 apeipomen] to be untrue in word, or deed.
disperse *verb* {5086 nadaph} [1287 diaskorpizo] [1289 diaspiro] to scatter.
disperse, express, wound *verb* {6567 parash} to separate; to specify; to wound.
disregard *verb* [272 ameleo] as being unconcerned.
disrespect *noun* {937 buwz} {939 buwzah} abasement.
disrespect *verb* {936 buwz} to abase.
dissipate *noun* {3988 maac} to flow away.
dissolve *noun* {8557 temec} liquifaction; disappearance.
dissolve, flow, melt *verb* {4529 masah} to dissolve.
dissolve, melt *verb* {4127 muwg} to soften; to dissipate.
dissolve, vanish *verb* {4743 maqaq} [1262 dialuo] to dissolve; to dwindle; to vanish.
distant past, far, afar *adjective* {7350 rachoq} {7352 rachiq} {7369 racheq} remote; in time, or distance.
distant, receive in full *verb* [568 apeko] to have out; to keep away.
distend, extend *verb* {8311 sara} to extend oneself, as in stretching out; to distend, as an appendage.
distinction *noun* [1293 diastoles] [1243 diairesis] the difference between; a variation.
distinctly *participle* {6568 perash} to separate, as in words.
distinguish *verb* {6395 palah} [1243 diairesis] to differentiate.
distinguish, estrange, notice, recognize, discern *verb* {5234 nakar} to acknowledge; to scrutinize; to distinguish between; to ignore, hence to be estranged.
distortion *noun* {4297 mutteh} a stretching out of shape.
distress *noun* **distressful** *adjective* {6695 tsuqah} a strait.
distress, narrows, straits, confines *noun* {4689 matsoq} {4691 metsuqah} {4712 metsar} from the root, belly; a narrow place; a confinement.

distress, oppress *verb* {6693 tsuq} to compress.
distrust *verb* [544 apitheo] [569 apisteo] to lack trust.
distrust, trustlessness *noun* [543 apeitheia] [570 apistia] without trust; obstinate and rebellious.
distrusting *adjective* [545 apithees] lacking trust.
divide *verb* {6385 palag} {6386 pelag} to split.
dividing *noun* {6387 pelag} the division of a half.
divination *noun* {4738 miqcam} {7081 qecem} foreknowledge by magic.
divine *verb* {7080 qacam} to foreknow by magic.
diviner *noun* {1505 gezar} one who foreknows by magic.
division, rivulet *noun* {6390 pelaggah} {6391, 6392 peluggah} division of families; a split in the ground where a rivulet flows.
divorce *noun* {3748 keriythuth} a cutting of the marriage bond.
divulge *verb* [1583 eklaleo] to speak out.
do, keep, make, serve *verb* {5648 abad} in the sense of serving.
do, make *verb* {6466 paal} [4160 poieo] to assemble; to practice; to perform; **cp** create.
doctor *noun* [1320 didaskalos] one who doctrinates; the Hellene translation of rabbi, rabboni.
doctor of the torah *noun* [3547 nomodidaskalos] one who doctrinates the torah.
doctrinate *verb* [1318 didaktos] [1321 didasko] to teach.
doctrinate otherwise, other doctrine *verb* [2085 heterodidaskaleo] to doctrinate differently; to doctrinate different doctrines.
doctrinator of good *noun* [2567 kalodidaskalos] teacher of good.
doctrine *noun* {3948 leqach} [1319 didaskalia] [1322 didakee] teaching.
Doda Yah *transliterated name* {1735 dowdavahuw} Beloved of Yah.
Doday *transliterated name* {1737 dowday} Amatory.
doe *noun* {8166 seirah} a she animal.
doe goat *noun* {5795, 5796 ez} a she goat, as strong.
dogma *transliterated noun* [1378 dogma] a definite and authoritative doctrine.
dogmatic *transliterated adjective* [1379 dogmatizomai] true to the doctrine; **see** dogma.
dominant *noun* {7984 shilton} {7989 shalliyt} one that prevails.
dominate *verb* [2634 katakuriuo] [2961 kuriuo] to lord over.
dominate *adjective* {7990 shalliyt} mighty over; **cp** reign.
dominate *verb* {7786 sur} {7980 shalat} {7981 shelet} [831 authenteo] to be mighty over; **cp** reign.
domineering *adverb* {7986 shalleteth} ability to prevail.
doom, devote *verb* {2763 charam} to set apart for liturgy; to set apart for destruction; **see** disfigured.
doomed, devoted *noun* {2764 cherem} that which is set apart in liturgy; that which is set apart for destruction.
Dophqah *transliterated name* {1850 dophqah} Knock.
Dorcas, gazelle, Tabitha *noun* {6643 tsebiy} {6646 tsebiyah} [5000 tabitha] a gazelle, as beautiful; Tabitha is the Hellene transliteration of tsebiyah; Dorcas is the Hellene translation of tsebiyah.
double *adjective* [1362 diplous] two–fold.
double *verb* [1363 diploo] to repay or render two–fold.
double, duplicate, fold, reiterate, repeat, alter, change *verb* {8132 shana} {8133 shena} {8138 shanah} to reinforce by folding, by doubling; may include disguise, camouflage.
double, duplicate, second *noun* {4932 mishneh} a copy of; a double amount; a repetition.
doublemouthed *adjective* [1366 distomos] two–edged.
doublesouled *adjective* [1374 dipsukos] in the sense of being twofaced; **cp** doubleworded.
doubleworded *adjective* [1351 dilogos] as in wording differently on different occasions; in the sense of being twofaced; **cp** doublesouled.
doubt, debate, discern, discriminate *verb* {995 biyn} [1252 diakrino] [1253 diakrisis] to distinguish; to thoroughly judge.
doughboard *noun* {4863 mishereth} a board on which the dough rises.
downcast *adjective* {7807 shach} sunken.
downing *noun* {4606 meal} the downing, usually of the sun; **cp** dawn, dawning.
downing *verb* [1416 dumi] to go down, usually of the sun; **cp** dawn, dawning.
downpour *noun* {1653 geshem} [5494 kimon] a heavy rain.
downpour *verb* {1652 gasham} {1656 goshem} to rain heavily.
downward *adverb* {4295 mattah} in the direction of down.
dowry *noun* {4119 mohar} {*plural* 7964 shilluach} the price paid to marry a woman.
drachma *transliterated noun* [1406 drachme] a silver coin; literally, a handful of silver; **cp** didrachma.
drachmim *plural noun* {1871 darkmohneem} Persian coins.
drag *verb* {5498 sachab} to trail along.
drag net *noun* {4365 mikmereth} a net that is dragged; **see** net.
dragon *transliterated noun* [1404 drakon] a kind of serpent.
drape *noun* {7757 shul} that which hangs down; **cp** train.
draughts *plural noun* {8514 talubah} desications.
draw *verb* {8025 shalaph} as a drawn sword.
draw, pour *verb* {7324 ruq} to pour in; to pour out.
drawn *adjective* {8305 seriyqah} flax, as drawn.
dread, terrify, awe *verb* {6206 arats} to harass; to reverence.
dream *noun* {2472 chalom} {2493 chelem} [1798 enupnion] [3677 onar] thoughts, images, or emotions occurring during sleep.
dream *verb* {2492 chalam} [1797 enupniazomai] to experience a thought, image, or emotion during sleep.
dregs *plural noun* {8105 shemer} the settlings of the wine.
drift, shake, stagger, totter, wag, wander, waver *verb* {5128 nuwa} to waver.
drink (give), drown, moisten, wet, butler *verb* {8248 shaqah} {8257 shaga} to butler, as a bartender; to drink to quench thirst; to drink unto drowning; to cause to be wet.
drink *noun* {8354 shathah} a liquid.
drink, banquet *noun* {4960, 4961 mishteh} the act of drinking; a banquet of eating and drinking.
drink, moisture *noun* {8249 shiqquv} {8250 shiqquw} a beverage.
drinking *noun* {8358 shethy} intoxicating.
drinking, moistened, moisture, butlership *noun* {4945 mashqeh} to cause to be moistened, or drunken.
drip, drop *noun* {1812 deleph} a dripping.
drip, drop *verb* {1811 dahlaph} {5197, 5198 nataph} {6201 araph} {7491 raaph} to drip; to descend in drops; as in weeping.
dripping darkness *noun* {6205 araphel} gloom; as of a lowering sky.
dripping, fresh *adjective* {2961 tariy} to be moist.
drive (out), expel *verb* {1644 garash} {2957 terad} {5080 nadach} {5090 nahag} to expatriate; to push off; to carry away.
drive, alight *verb* {6795 tsanach} to cause to descend; to come down; to drive down.
drive, ride *verb* {7392 rakab} to place upon; to dispatch.
drop, spoil *verb* {7997 shalal} to let drop; to strip, or plunder.
dross *noun* {5509 sug} scoria.
drought, parch *noun* {2721 choreb} {2725 charabon} very dry.
drove *noun* {5739 eder} [34 agelee] an arrangement of; a herd, as being driven.
drown, moisten, wet, butler, drink (give) *verb* {8248 shaqah} {8257 shaga} to butler, as a bartender; to drink to quench thirst; to drink unto drowning; to cause to be wet.
drowsiness *noun* {5124 numah} {8572 tenuwm} sleepiness; **see** sleep.
drudgery *noun* {6045 inyan} difficult task.
dry, parch, desolate *adjective* {2720 chareb} {8076 shamen} parched; ruined.
dry, parch, desolate *verb* {2717, 2718 charab} {3456 yashem} {8045 shamad} {8046 shemad} [2049 ereemoo] to lay waste; to destroy.
dry, wither *noun* {3002 yabesh} {3004 yabbashah} {3006, 3007 yabbesheth} lands and waters dry; plants, persons wither.
dry, wither *verb* {3001 yabesh} {5405 nashath} {7060 qamal} lands and waters dry; plants, persons wither.
dugout *noun* {1358 gob} {1360 gebe} a digging.
dull *verb* {6949 qahah} to unsharpen.
dumbfounded *verb* {1724 dahham} to cause to be speechless.
dung *noun* {*plural* 2755 charey yonim} {6569 peresh} {6675 tsoah} {6832 tsephua} excrement.
dungball *noun* {1557 gahlal} {1561 gehlel} a ball of excrement.
dunghill *noun* {830 ashpoth} {4087 madmenah} a heap of excrement.
dungy *adjective* {6674 tso} dunglike.
dupe, entice *verb* {6601 pathah} to delude; to tempt; **cp** test.
duplicate, fold, reiterate, repeat, alter, change, double *verb* {8132 shana} {8133 shena} {8138 shanah} to reinforce by folding, by doubling; may include disguise, camouflage.
duplicate, second, double *noun* {4932 mishneh} a copy of; a double amount; a repetition.

dusk, duskward *noun* {4628 maarabah} {5939 alatah} in the sense of shade.
dust *noun* {6083 aphar} [2868 koniortos] [5522 choos] fine particles of matter.
dust *verb* {6080 aphar} to dust with dust.
dusty *adjective* [5517 choikos] dirty; soil–like.
dwell, settle *verb* [1460 egkatoikeo] [2730 katoikeo] [3611 oikeo] to reside.
dye *noun* {6648 tseba} a dye.
dye *verb* {6647 tseba} to dip into a dye.
dyed scarlet *participle, verb* {8529 tala} to dye a scarlet color.
dynamic *adjective* [1414 dunateo] able; capable.
dynamis *transliterated noun* [1411 dunamis] dynamic ability.
dynamize *verb* [1412 dunamoo] [1743 endunamoo] to endue with dynamis.
dynast, dynasty *noun* [1413 dunastees] one endued with dynamis; the seat of dynamis; **see** dynamis.

E

eagle *noun* {5403 neshar} {5405 nesher} from the root, to lacerate; as a bird of prey.
ear *noun* {241 ozen} [5621 otion] the organ for hearing.
ear, stream, branch *noun* {7641 shibboleth} a branch or an ear of grain, as growing; a stream, as flowing.
early (rise) (seek) *verb* {7836 shachar} to be early.
early start, start early *verb* {7925 shakam} to start early.
earrings *noun* {5694 agil} as being round; **cp** nosering.
earth, land *noun* {772 ara} {776 erets} {778 araq} [1093 gee] **cp** soil; **cp** cosmos.
earthly *adjective* [1919 epigios] as of the earth.
east, easterly, eastern, eastward, formerly, preceding, ancient, antiquity *noun* {6921 qadim} {6924 qedem} {6925 qodam} {6926 qidmah} {6927 qadmah} literally, the forefront; from the front.
east, eastern, ancient(s) *adjective* {6930 qadmon} {6931 qadmoniy} anterior.
eat, fight *verb* {3898 lacham} literally, to feed on food, to feed on an enemy.
eating *verb* **food** *noun* [1034 brosimos] literally, feeding; the act of eating.
Ebed Melech *transliterated name* {5663 ebedmelech} Servant of the Sovereign.
Eben Ezer *transliterated name* {72 ebenhaezer} Stone of Help.
Eber *transliterated name* {5677 eber} [1443 eber] Beyond; Crossover.
Ebes *transliterated name* {77 ebets} Conspicuous.
Ebron {5683 ebron} Over Against.
ecclesia *singular* **ecclesiae** *plural transliterated noun* [1577 ekklesia] refers to the congregation of the Messianists, and corresponds to the Hebrew word, congregation (except in Acts 2:38); **see** congregation.
echo *transliterated noun* [2279 echos] a reverberation; figuratively a rumor.
echo *transliterated verb* [2278 echeo] to reverberate.
Echud *transliterated name* {261 echuwd} United.
eclipses *plural noun* {3650 kimriyrim} obscurages, as of lights.
ecstasis *transliterated noun* [1611 ekstasis] enraptured in a state of mental absorption.
Eden *transliterated name* {5729 eden} {5731 eden} Pleasure: **see** pleasure.
Eder *transliterated name* {5738 eder} Arrangement.
edge *noun* {6285 peah} {6366 peyah} from mouth, as the edge of the head.
edge, end *noun* {7093 qets} {7097 qetseh} {7098 qatsah} {7099 qetsev} an extremity.
edge, lip *noun* {8193 saphah} [5491 kilos] an edge; a shoreline; the physical lip; a language; **cp** tongue.
edict *noun* {3982 maamar} {3983 memar} {7010 qeyam} a spoken decree.
edify, build *verb* {1124 benah} {1129 banah} [2026 epoikodomeo] [3618 oikodomeo] to build; to build up; to confirm; to construct; to erect.
Edom, Edomiy *transliterated name* {123 edom} {130 edomi} [2401 idoumaia] Red; Ruddy; a region; people of the region; **cp** Adam.
effulgence *noun* [541 apaugasma] radiance.
effusion *verb* [401 anakusis] a pouring out.
Eglayim *dual transliterated name* {97 eglayim} Double Drops.

- **SUMMARY:**
- **EL, ELAH, ELI, ELOHAH, ELOHIM, ELOI:**
- Most versions translate the many Hebrew, Aramaic, and Hellene words of deity without any distinction.
- The *exeGeses* transliterates all the Hebrew and Arami titles of deity of the Old Covenant, and translates all the Hellene titles of the New Covenant corresponding to the Hebrew and Arami.
- **El, Eli** *transliterated title* {410 el} [2241 eli] El, as being almighty.
- **Elah, Elohah, Eloi** *transliterated singular title* {426 elah} {433 elohah} [1682 eloi] a male god.
- **Elohim, elohim** *transliterated plural title* {430 elohim} plural of {433 eloahh, elowahh}; this plural title has a dual interpretation; at times it refers to pagan gods, and at times to the triune Father, Son, and Holy Spirit.
- **Elohimic** *adjective* [2304 thios] Elohim–like.
- **Elohimic** *noun* [2305 thiotees] Elohim–likeness.
- **Elohimic** *noun* [2320 theotees] the total essence of Elohim.
- **Elyon** *transliterated title* **uppermost** *adjective* {5943 illay} {5945, 5946 elyon} [5310 hupsistos] an uppermost place or position; a title of Elohim.
- **Elohim–doctrinated** *verb* [2312 theodidaktos] doctrinated by Elohim.
- **Elohim–hater** *noun* [2319 theostugees] one who hates Elohim.
- **Elohim–opponent** *noun* [2314 theomakos] one who opposes Elohim.
- **Elohim–resister** *noun* [2313 theomakeo] one who resists Elohim.
- **Elohim–reverence** *noun* [2317 theosebia] reverence to Elohim.
- **Elohim–revering** *adverb* [2318 theosebees] reverent of Elohim.
- **Elohim–spirited** *verb* [2315 theopnustos] spirited by Elohim.
- **goddess** *title* [2299 thea] a female deity.
- **theos** *title* [2316 theos] a male deity; **note:** when theos refers to Elohim, the *exeGeses* so translates.

El Ad *transliterated name* {496 elad} Witnessed of El.
El Adah *transliterated name* {497 eladah} El Adorneth.
El Aleh *transliterated name* {500 elaleh} El Ascendeth.
El Asah *transliterated name* {501 elasah} El Worketh.
El Azar *transliterated name* {499 elazar} [1648 eleazar] [2976 lazaros] El Helpeth.
El Beth El *transliterated name* {416 elbeythel} El of the House of El.
El Daah *transliterated name* {420 eldaah} El Knoweth.
El Dad *transliterated name* {419 eldad} El Beloved.
El Elohe Yisra El *transliterated name* {415 eleloheyyisrael} Mighty El of Yisra El.
El Hanan *transliterated name* {445 elchanan} El Granteth Charism.
El Naam *transliterated name* {493 elnaam} El Pleaseth.
El Nathan *transliterated name* {494 elnathan} El Giveth.
El Paal *transliterated name* {508 elpaal} El Maketh.
El Paran *transliterated name* {364 eylparan} El of Paran.
El Qanah *transliterated name* {511 elqanah} El Chattelizeth.
El Sabaoth *transliterated title* {410 el} {6635 tsebaah} **see** Sabaoth.
El Saphan *transliterated name* {469 elitsaphan} El of Treasure.
El Teqeh *transliterated name* {514 elteqeh} of unceratin derivative.
El Teqon *transliterated name* {515 elteqon} El Straighteneth.
El Tolad *transliterated name* {513 eltolad} El of Generations.
El Uzay *transliterated name* {498 eluwzay} El Recoupeth.
El Yachba *transliterated name* {455 elyachaba} El Hideth.
El Yah Enay *transliterated name* {454 elyehoweynay} Towards El are my Eyes.
El Yaqim *transliterated name* {471 elyaqiym} [1662 eliakeim] El Raiseth.
El Yasaph *transliterated name* {460 elyacaph} El Increaseth.
El Yashib *transliterated name* {475 elyashiyb} El Returneth.
El Zabad *transliterated name* {443 elzabad} El Endoweth.
Elamiy *transliterated name* {5867 elam} [1639 elamiy] Of Elam.
Elamiy *transliterated name* {5962 almiy} Of Elam.
elbow *noun* {679 atstsiyl} literally, joint.

elder *noun* {2205 zaqen} {7868 sib} [4244 presbuterion] [4245 presbuteros] an elder, as grayed; a presbyter.
elephantine *transliterated adjective* [1661 elephantinos] of an elephant; ivory.
elevation *noun* {5131 noph} a raised area.
Eli *transliterated name* {5941 eli} [2242 heeli] Holocauster.
Eli, El *transliterated name, transliterated title* {410 el} [2241 eli] El, as being mighty.
Eli Ab *transliterated name* {446 eliab} El the Father.
Eli Ada *transliterated name* {450 eliada} El Knoweth.
Eli Am *transliterated name* {463 eliam} El of the People.
Eli Athah *transliterated name* {448 eliyathah} El of Consent.
Eli Dad *transliterated name* {449 elidad} El Beloved.
Eli El *transliterated name* {447 eliel} El of El.
Eli Enay *transliterated name* {462 eliyeynay} El the Eye; **see** El Yah Enay.
Eli Ezer *transliterated name* {461 eliezer} [1663 eliezer] El Helpeth.
Eli Horeph *transliterated name* {456 eliychoreph} El of Winter.
Eli Hu *transliterated name* {453 elihu} El of Him.
Eli Melech *transliterated name* {458 elimelech} El Sovereign.
Eli Phal *transliterated name* {465 eliphal} El of Prayer.
Eli Phaz *transliterated name* {464 eliphaz} El of Pure Gold.
Eli Phelehu *transliterated name* {466 eliyphelehuw} El Distinguisheth.
Eli Phelet *transliterated name* {467 eliphelet} El of Escape.
Eli Qa *transliterated name* {470 eliyqa} El Vomiteth.
Eli Shah *transliterated name* {473 elishah} meaning uncertain.
Eli Shama *transliterated name* {476 elishama} El Hearkeneth.
Eli Shaphat *transliterated name* {478 elishaphat} El Judgeth.
Eli Sheba *transliterated name* {472 elisheba} [1665 elisabeth] El of Oath.
Eli Shua *transliterated name* {474 eliyshuwa} {477 eliysha} [1666 elissaios] El is Salvation.
Eli Sur *transliterated name* {468 elitsur} El of the Rock.
Eli Ud *transliterated name* {410 el} {1935 howd} [1664 eliud] El of Majesty.
Eli Yah *transliterated name* {452 eliyah} [2243 eelias] El of Yah.
Ellasar *transliterated name* {495 ellacar} an early country of Asia.
Elon *transliterated name* {356 elown} Oak Grove.
Elon Beth Hanan *transliterated name* {358 eylownbeythchanan} Oak Grove of the House of Charism.
Eloniy *transliterated name* {440 elowniy} Of Elon.
Elqoshiy *transliterated name* {512 elqoshiy} Of Elqosh.
Elyon *transliterated title* **uppermost** *adjective* {5943 illay} {5945, 5946 elyon} [5310 hupsistos] an uppermost place or position; a title of Elohim.
emaciate *verb* {7329 razah} to thin.
emaciate, deceive, deny, disown *verb* {3584 kachash} [550 apeipomen] to be untrue in word, or deed.
emaciated *adjective* {7330 razeh} {7534 raq} as flattened out; thin; skinny.
emaciation *noun* {7332 razon} {7334 raziy} thin; skinny.
emaciation *noun* {7829 shachepheth} as peeled thin.
emaciation, deception, denial *noun* {3585 kachash} a failure of flesh.
embalm, ripen, spice *verb* {2590 chanat} from the root, to spice.
embitter *verb* {4843 marar} [4087 pikraino] to cause to be bitter.
embroider *verb* **emroiderer** *participle* {7551 raqam} {7660 shabats} to variegate color; usually threads of gold.
embroidered mail *noun* {7661 shabats} a woven, or mesh armour.
embroidery *noun* {7553 riqmah} of variegated color.
embryo *noun* {1564 golem} a wrapped unformed mass.
Emim *plural transliterated name* {368 eymiym} Terrors.
eminence, eminent *noun* {5057 nagid} one that stands out.
eminent, oversee, perpetual, perpetuity (in) *adjective, participle* {5329 natsach} {5331 netsach} [1336 dieenekes] continual, on and on; to oversee work; to be eminent.
Emmaus *transliterated name* {3222 yem} [1695 emmaous] Warm Spring.
Emoriy *transliterated name* {567 emoriy} Mountaineer.
empower, overpower, prevail *verb* {8280 sarah} {8630 taqaph} [2616 katadunastuo] [2729 katiskuo] [2901 krataioo] [2902 krateo] to have ability over; to cause to have power.
empowerment *noun* {8632 teqoph} power.
empty, pour out, strip naked *verb* {6168 arah} {6379 pakah} to empty; to empty by pouring; to strip bare; **see** naked.
empty, req, vain, vanity, void *adjective* {1892 hebel} {*transliteration* 7385 riq} {*transliteration* 7386 req} {7723 shav} [*transliteration* 4469 rhaka] emptiness, voidness; figuratively, stupid.
empty, vainly, void *adverb* {7387 reqam} emptily; without effect; **cp** req.
En Eglayim *dual transliterated name* {5882 eyneglayim} Fountain of Two Calves.
En Haq Qore *transliterated name* {5875 eynhaqqowre} Fountain of Calling.
En Harod *transliterated name* {5878 eyncharod} Fountain of Trembling.
En Hasor *transliterated name* {5877 eynchatsowr} Fountain of a Court.
En Tappuach *transliterated name* {5887 eyntappuwach} Fountain of an Apple (Tree).
enable, prevail, able, can *verb* {3201 yakol} {3202 yekel} {3546 kehal} [1410 dunamai] [2427 hikanoo] the dynamis to do; **see** dynamis.
encamp, camp *verb* {2583 chanah} {8497 takah} [63 agrauleo] [835 aulizomai] to pass the night in the open air; to tent; **see** pull stakes; **see** court, courtyard.
encampment *noun* {8466 tachanah} [3925 parembolee] a place to camp, to pitch tents.
enchant *verb* **enchanters** *participle* {3907 lachash} to whisper a spell; whisperers of spells.
enchanter *noun* {825 ashshaph} {826 ashshaph} [1114 goees] a conjurer; a whisperer of spells.
enchantingly, covertly *adjective* {3909 laht} whispering a spell; under cover.
enchantment *noun* {3908 lachash} a whispered spell.
enclose, inclose, lock, shod *verb* {5274 naal} {7000 qatar} to fasten; **see** shoe.
encounter, intercede, reach *verb* {6293 paga} to impinge.
encourage, abuse *verb* {7292 rahab} in the sense of urging; of pressuring.
end, conclusion, consummation *noun* {5490 soph} {5491 soph} {7093 qets} {7097 qetseh} {7098 qatsah} the end, of an eon, of a scroll.
end, edge *noun* {7093 qets} {7097 qetseh} {7098 qatsah} {7099 qetsev} an extremity.
end, part *noun* {7117, 7118 qetsath} a portion; a termination.
endow *verb* {2064 zabad} {4117 mahar} a bestowment of a dowry or a valuable; **cp** endue.
endowment *noun* {2065 zehved} a bestowment, a dowry.
endurance *noun* [5281 hupomonee] constancy.
endure *verb* [4722 stego] to keep by covering, to bear.
endure, abide *verb* [5278 hupomeno] [5297 hupophero] to bear, persevere.
endure, tolerate *verb* [430 anekomai] to hold oneself up against.
endure evil *verb* [420 anexikakos] to forbear.
enemy *noun* {340 ayab} {341 oyeb} {6145, 6146 ar} [2190 ekthros] one who hates.
energize, energizing *transliterated verb* [1753 energeia] [1754 energeo] [1755 energeema] [1756 energees] to impart energy.
enfold, gather *verb* {3664 kanac} to collect; to wrap.
engrave, (set) statute *verb* **statute setter** *participle* {2710 chaqaq} [1795 entupoo] to engrave; to prescribe; **see** statue.
engrave *verb* **engraving** *participle, noun* {2707 chaqah} {2799 charosheth} {2801 charath} to carve; a carved work; **see** statute.
engrave, open, pethach *verb* {6605 pathach} {6606 pethach} [*transliterated* 2188 ephphatha] to open; to loosen; to engrave.
engraver *noun* {2791 cheresh} {2794 choresh} {2796 charash} {*plural* 2798 chaarashim} {2800 charosheth} a skilled engraver of any material.
engraving *noun* {2799 charosheth} {6603 pittuach} a sculpting.
enlarge, broaden *verb* {7337 rachab} to widen; to make larger.
enlighten *verb* {2094 zahar} *participle* {2095 zehar} to cause to gleam; to cause to understand.
enliven *verb* [2227 zoopoieo] to bestow life.
enmity *noun* {342 eybah} {4895 mastemah} [2189 ekthra] hatred.
Enosh *transliterated name* {583 enosh} [1800 enos] Man, Mortal.
enquire, examine, inquire, require, seek *verb* {1875 dahrash} to ask; to seek; **cp** beseech.
enrage *verb* {2194 zaam} {2196 zaaph} {7107 qatsaph} {7108 qetsaph} [3949 parorgizo] [3951 parotruno] to cause one to rage; to rage.

enraged *adjective* {2198 zaeph} angered.
enrich *verb* {6238 ashar} to cause to be rich; **see** rich.
enrobe *verb* {3847 labesh} {3848 lebash} to wrap around; **cp** robe.
ensign (raise an) *verb* {5264 nacac} to lift up; as fluttering in the wind.
ensign, pole, sail *noun* **Nissi** *transliterated title* {5251 nec} an ensign; the pole of an ensign; part of the title, Yah Veh Nissi, which means, Yah Veh Ensign.
ensign, sign *noun* {226 owth} [3902 parasemos] [4592 seemion] as emblematic, or as a signal; the sun, moon, and stars are for signs and seasons; Yonah was a sign to the Ninevehiy and the Yah Hudiy; turning water into wine was Yah Shua's first sign; some signs are miraculous, some are not.
ensign bearer *noun* {5263 nacac} one who bears an ensign.
enslave *verb* [2615 katadouloo] to bring into bondage (to one's self).
ensnare, snare *verb* {3369 yaqosh} {5367 naqash} {6351 pachah} {6983 qosh} to lay, or spring a snare.
entangle *verb* {8308 sarqak} to interlace.
entangle, pawn, pledge *verb* {5670 abat} to entangle a people; to entangle a pledge by pawning.
enter *verb* {5954 alal} to enter, in the sense of thrusting.
entertain, laugh, ridicule *verb* {6711 tsachaq} {6712 tsechoq} {7832 sechag} to laugh; to laugh at; to laugh at in defiance.
entice, dupe *verb* {6601 pathah} to delude, to tempt; **cp** test.
entomb *verb* {6912 qabar} [2290 thapto] to deposit in a tomb; to bury, **see** tomb.
entombment *noun* [5027 taphee] burial.
entorahed *verb* [1772 ennomos] under the torah; **cp** untorahed.
entrap *verb* [64 agreuo] [1185 deleazo] to trap; to trip up.
entrust, trust *verb* {539 aman} {540 aman} [4100 pistuo] [4104 pistoo] **see** amen; to confidently rely upon; **note:** whereas believing is a psyching up of the mental attributes, trust is the abandonment of self into the care of another.
entwine *verb* {5440 sabak} {8276 sarag} [4553 sargane *a transliteration of the Hebrew 5440*] entangle; as woven.
enumeration *noun* {4510 minyan} a counting up of numbers.
environ, round, surround *noun* {3603 kikkar} literally, circle; the environs of an area; a round of material, usually of precious metals.
envy, jealousy, suspicion *noun* {7068 qinah} zeal, as jealousy, or envy.
envy, suspect *verb* **jealous, zealous** *adjective* {7065 qana} {7067 qanna} {7072 qannow} to be zealous, as jealous, or envious.
enwisen, wisen *verb* {2449 chakam} [4679 sophizo] to cause to be wise.
eon, eon of the eons *transliterated noun* [165 aion] unlimited; limitless periods of time.
Epaphroditus *transliterated name* [1891 epaphrodites] Devotee of Aphrodite (a deity).
ephah *transliterated noun* {374 ephah} a measure.
ephod *transliterated noun* {642 ephuddah} { 646 ephod} a shoulderpiece of clothing.
Ephrath *transliterated name* {672 ephrath} another name of Beth Lechem.
Ephrathiy *transliterated name* {673 ephrathiy} Of Ephrath.
Ephrayim *transliterated name* {669 ephrayim} {6085 ephron} [2187 ephraim] Double Fruit, or Fawn–like.
Epicurean *transliterated name* [1946 ephikourios] a follower of the philosopher Epikouroos.
epigraph *transliterated noun* [1923 epigraphee] a superscription; **cp** inscription.
epigraph *transliterated verb* [1924 epigrapho] to scribe an epigraph.
epiphanous *adjective* [2016 epiphanees] bright.
epiphany *noun* [2015 epiphania] a manifestation; usually, a manifestation of Christ as divine.
episcopate, visitation *transliterated noun* [1984 episcope] [1985 episcopos] one who scopes; an inspector; inspection.
epistle *transliterated noun* {104 iggera} {107 iggereth} {5406, 5407 nishtevan} [1992 epistolee] a letter.
epistolize *transliterated verb* [1989 epistello] to communicate by epistle.
Eqer *transliterated name* {6134 eqer} Uprooted.
Eqron *transliterated name* {6138 eqrown} Eradication.
Eqroniy *transliterated name* {6139 eqroniy} Of Eqron.
equal, reign *noun* {4915 moshel} equal, in the sense of being able to liken unto, or compare with; reign, of being more than equal, of being over.
equal to angels *adjective* [2465 isangelos] like angels; angelic.
equate, equalize *verb* {7737 shavah} {7739 shevah} to level; to resemble.
equidistant *participle* {7947 shalab} of equal distance.
equip, rescue, strip *verb* {2502 chalats} literally, to strip for hostility; to strip out of danger.
Er *transliterated name* {6147 er} [2262 er] Awake.
Eraniy *transliterated name* {6198 eraniy} Of Eran.
erase, wipe, wipe out *verb* {4229 machah} [1813 exalipho] to rub; to rub out; to erase sins, tears, names.
Erastos *transliterated name* [2037 erastos] of eros; **see** Eros.
erect *noun* {6968 qomemiuth} high, as straightened out.
erect *verb* {5446 sebal} to raise up.
Erech *transliterated name* {751 erech} Length.
Erechiy *transliterated name* {756 archevay} Of Erech; **see** Archiy.
Eri *transliterated name* {6179 eriy} Waken.
Eriy *transliterated name* {6180 eriy} Of Eri.
Eros *transliterated title* **eros** *transliterated noun* Although eros does not appear in Scripture, it is worthy of definition; a deity; the expression of the physical emotion, often sexual; **cp** love, the spiritual expression; **cp** befriend, the soulical expression; **see** Erastos.
err inadvertently, inadvertently err *verb* {7683 shagag} {7686 shagah} to err unintentionally.
error (inadvertent) *noun* {7684 shegagah} {*plural* 7691 shegiyahoth} unintentional error.
error *noun* {4870 mishgeh} {4879 meshugah} {7691 shegiah} {8442 toah} a moral or spiritual mistake.
erupt *verb* {8368 sathar} to break out.
Esav *transliterated name* {6215 esav} [2269 esau] Worker.
Esbon *transliterated name* {675 etsbon} of uncertain derivative.
escape, rescue *verb* {4422 malat} literally, to smooth; to slip away; to be slipped away.
escape, rescue, strip *verb* {5337, 5338 natsal} to snatch away; favorably, or unfavorably.
escape, slip (away) (out) *verb* {6403 palat} {6405 peletah}.
escapee, escaped, escaping *noun* {6412 palit} {6413 peleytah} that which has escaped.
Esem *transliterated name* {6107 etsem} Bone.
Eseq *transliterated name* {6230 eseq} Contend.
Eser *transliterated name* {687 etser} Treasure.
Esh Baal *transliterated name* {792 eshbaal} Man of Baal.
Eshan *transliterated name* {824 eshan} Lean.
Esheq *transliterated name* {6232 esheq} Oppression.
Eshkol *transliterated name* {812 eshkol} Cluster.
Eshtaol *transliterated name* {847 eshtaol} Ask.
Eshtaoliy *transliterated name* {848 eshtauliy} Of Eshtaol.
Esli *transliterated name* [2069 esli] meaning uncertain; possibly, Of El.
establish *verb* [950 bebaioo] to make sure.
establish, prepare *verb* {3559 kuwn} to set up.
establishment *noun* [951 bebaiosis] stability.
establishment *noun* {4349 makown} a base, as set up; **see** establish.
esteem *noun* {3367 yeqar} the regard; the value.
esteem *verb* {1921, 1922 hadar} to hold in honour; **cp** honour.
esteem *verb* {3365 yaqar} to value highly; to regard highly.
esteem, estimation *noun* {3366 yeqar} the value.
esteemed *adjective* {3357, 3358 yaqqiyr} highly valued; highly regarded.
Ester *transliterated name* {635 ecter} the meaning uncertain; of Persian derivative.
estimate *verb* {3699 kacac} to appraise.
estrange, notice, recognize, discern, distinguish *verb* {5234 nakar} to acknowledge; to scrutinize; to distinguish between; to ignore, hence to be estranged.
estrange, strange *verb* {2114 zuwr} to cause to be strange; although a verb, often carries the force of a noun; **see** strange.
Esyon Geber *transliterated name* {6100 etsyongeber} Spine–like of a Man.
et cetera *participle* {3706 keeneth} and so on.
etching, mark, tattoo, brand *noun* {7085 qaaqa} {8420 tab} [5480 karagma] a scratched marking; a mark on animals; an x or a + as a signature of an illiterate; a mark of protection; **read** Yechezq El 9:4–6; **read** Apocalypse 13:16,17, 14:9–11, 15:2, 16:2, 19:20, 20:4; **cp** brand.
eternal, eternally, eternity, original *noun, adjective, adverbally* {5703 ad} {5769 olam} {5865 elom} {5957 alam} [126 aidios] [166 aionios] a limitless period – either past, present, or future.

Eth Qasin *transliterated name* {6278 ethqatsiyn} Time of a Commander.
ethnarch *transliterated title* [1481 ethnarchees] an arch over the ethnics.

- **SUMMARY:**
- **EUCHARIST, EUCHARISTIC, EUCHARISTIZE:**
- **eucharist** *transliterated noun; also used verbally* [2169 eucharistia] an offering of charism: verb; to offer charism; usually related to the commemoration of memorial of our Lord's final communion service; **see** charism.
- **eucharistic** *transliterated adjective* [2170 eucharistos] of good charism; **see** charism.
- **eucharistize** *transliterated verb* [2168 eucharisteo] [2169 eucharistia] to express or offer charism; **see** charism.

- **SUMMARY:**
- **EULOGIZE, EULOGY:**
- **eulogize** *transliterated verb* [1757 eneulogeomai] [2127 eulogeo] to word well.
- **eulogized** *transliterated adjective* [2128 eulogeetos] well worded.
- **eulogy** *transliterated noun* [2129 eulogia] a well word.

eunuch *transliterated noun* {5631 saric} {*plural* 5632 sarek} [2135 eunouchos] one who has gone beyond circumcision by castration.
eunuchize *transliterated verb* [2134 eunouchizo] to castrate; to become a eunuch.
euphonious *transliterated adjective* [2163 eupheemos] well sounding; praiseworthy.
euphony *transliterated noun* [2162 eupheemia] agreeableness of sound; a praise.
Euphrates *transliterated name* {6578 perath} [2166 euphratees] name of a river; Bursting; Rushing.
evaluation *noun* {4373 mikcah} an evaluation based on an enumeration (census); **see** assessment.

- **SUMMARY:**
- **EVANGELISM, EVANGELIST, EVANGELIZE:**
- **evangelism** *transliterated noun* {1309 besorah} {4400 malakuth} [31 angelia] [2098 euangelion] [3852 parangelia] the Helene is from the root, angel; the evangelism is Elohim's message to humanity.
- **evangelist** *transliterated noun, participle* {1319 basar} [2099 euangelistees] one who evangelizes the evangelism.
- **evangelize** *transliterated verb* {1319 basar} [312 anangello] [518 apangello] [1229 diangello] [1804 exangello] [2097 euangelizo] [2605 katangello] [3853 parangello] to disperse the evangelism.
- **evangelizer** *transliterated noun* [2604 katangelus] one who evangelizes.
- **pre–evangelism** *transliterated noun* [1860 epangelia] [1862 epangelma] an evangelism previously prepared, or previously evangelized; **see** evangelism; **cp** angel.
- **pre–evangelize** *transliterated verb* [1861 epangello] [4279 proepangellomai] [4283 prouangelizomai] [4293 prokatangello] previously evangelized; an evangelism previously prepared for future evangelizing.

eve, even, evening *noun* {6153 ereb} [2073 hespera] [3796 opse] the end of day; dusk.
evening *adjective* [3797 opsimos] duskward.
evening, obscure *verb* {6150 arab} in the sense of dusking; of becoming obscure.
evening breeze *noun* {5399 nesheph} a breeze at dusk.
ever *adverb* [104 ai] at any; at all; **cp** eon.
Evil Merodach *transliterated name* {192 eviylmerodach} possibly, Soldier of Merodach.
evil (do) *verb* [2554 kakopoyeo] to injure; to sin; **see** vilify.
evil *adjective* {7451 ra} [2556 kakos] injurious.
evil *noun* {7455 ra} [4189 poneeria] [4190, 4191 poneeros] an opposition of all that is good, right, and whole.
evildoer *noun* [2555 kakopoyos] one who does evil.
evilworker *noun* [2557 kakourgos] one who works evil.
ewe *noun* {7353 rachel} a young female.
ewe lamb *noun* {3535 kabsah} {3776 kisbah} a young female sheep.
exact *verb* **exactor** *participle* {5065 nagas} {5378 nasha} {5383 nashah} to extract; one that extracts by tax or tyrrany.
exact, forget *verb* {5382 nashah} to neglect; to remove from.
exact, transact *verb* [4238 prasso] to extract dues; to execute; to perform repeatedly.
exactly as, even as *participle*[2509 kathaper] [2531 kathos] [5618 hosper] just as.
exalt, extol, raise (up) *verb* {5549 salal} from the root, to mound up; **see** selah; **cp** halal.
exalt, lift, loft, raise *verb* {7311, 7313 rum} {7318 romam} {7426 ramam} to lift hand, heart, offering, voice; to oath; **see** exalt.
exalt, loft *verb* {7682 sagab} to lift high.
exaltation *noun* {7319 romemah} {7427 romemuth} {7863 siy} elevation; praise.
exalting, lifting, swelling *noun* {7613 seeth} an elevation; from the verb, lift {5375}.
exaltment *noun* {8641 terumah} {8642 terumiah} the celebration of lifting a sacrificial exaltment unto Yah Veh.
examination, judgment *noun* [351 anakrisis] investigation.
examine, expect *verb* {7663 sabar} to scrutinize with expectation.
examine, inquire, require, seek, enquire *verb* {1875 darash} to ask; to seek; **cp** beseech.
examine, judge, plead *verb* {8199 shaphat} {8200 shephat} [350 anakrino] [2919 krino] to scrutinize; to investigate.
exceeding, greatly, increasing, many, mighty, much, very *adjective* {7689, 7690 saggiy} superlatively mighty, or large.
exceeding, remainder, remnant, rest *noun* {3499 yether} the remainder, those left over.
excellent, exceeding *adjective* **exceedingly** *adverb* {3493 yattiyr} preeminent; very.
exchange (in) *noun* {8545 temurah} [465 antallagma] to barter; to trade.
exchange, change *verb* {3235 yamar} {4171 mur} [236 allasso] to alter; to change places.
excise *noun* {1093 beloh} a tax on articles consumed.
excite *verb* [383 anasio] [2042 erethizo] to quake; to stir up.
exclaim *verb* [400 anaphoneo] to cry out.
exclusion *noun* {5079 niddah} one chased away; excluded, as a menstruous woman.
excrement *noun* {2716 chere} {*plural* 2755 charim} {*plural* 4280 macharaah} {6627 tsaah} human or animal dung.
executioners *plural noun* {3746 kariy} {3774 kerethi} guards in charge of executing.
exhale *adjective* {3307 yapheach} puffing.
exhaust, exhale *verb* {6313 pug} to exhale; to let out the breath.
exhausted *adjective* {4198 mazeh} sucked out.
exhausted *noun* {6296 pagar} to be exhaled; out of breath.
exile *noun* {1473 golah} {1546, 1547 gauwth} one who is expelled; an expulsion.
exile, expose *verb* {1540 galah} {1541 gelah} to expel; to expose.
exodus, exit *transliterated noun* {*plural* 8444 totsaahoth} [1841 exodos] an exit; of death as an exodus from life.
exonerate *verb* {5352 naqah} verb of innocent; to declare innocent; **see** innocent.
exonerated, innocent *adjective* {5355 naqi} [172 akakos] not guilty.
exoneration basins *plural noun* {4518 menaqqithoth} sacrifice basins which held blood; from the verb, exonerate.
expand *verb* {7554 raqa} to expand by pounding thin; verb of expanse.
expanded *adjective* {7555 riqqua} thinned.
expanse *noun* {4800 merchab} an enlargement.
expanse *noun* {7549 raqia} noun of expand; of the heavens; **read** Genesis 1:8.
expect, examine *verb* {7663 sabar} to scrutinize with expectation.
expect, receive, wait, await *verb* {2442 chakah} {3176 yachal} {6960 qavah} [324 anadekomai] [362 anameno] [553 apekdekomai] [4327 prosdekomai] [4328 prosdokao] [4329 prosdokia] to anticipate; to wait expectantly, patiently; **cp** take.
expectation *noun* {4007 mabbat} {7664 seber} anticipation.
expectation, congregating *noun* {4723 miqveh} this Hebrew word has two roots; a congregating of troops, of water; of expectation.
expel, drive (out) *verb* {1644 garash} [2957 terad] {5080 nadach} {5090 nahag} to carry away; to expatriate; to push off.
expiration *noun* {4646 mappach} an exhausting of breath.

expire soul, pressure, puff *verb* {5301 naphach} [1634 ekpsucho] to breathe away one's soul; to pressure, as in a pressure cooker; and to puff; **cp** expire spirit.
expire spirit *verb* [1606 ekpneo] to breathe away one's spirit; **cp** expire soul.
expire *verb* {1478 gava} to breathe one's last breath.
explain *verb* {874 bahar} [1956 epiluo] to make plain; **cp** interpret; **cp** translate.
explanation *noun* [1955 epilusis] a making plain; **cp** interpretation; **cp** translation.
exploit, exploitation *noun* {4611 maalal} {5949 alilah} {5950 aliliah} an act or accomplishment.
exploit, glean *verb* {5953 alal} to pick up after; in a good sense, to glean; in a bad sence, to exploit.
exploits, freaks *plural noun* {8586 taalul} deeds as exploitations.
explore, dig *verb* {2658 chaphar} {8446 tur} to pry into.
expose *verb* {5783 uwr} {6544 para} to loosen; to cause to be bare.
expose, exile *verb* {1540 galah} {1541 gelah} to expel; to expose.
expound *verb* [5419 phrazo] to define; to explain in detail.
express, wound, disperse *verb* {6567 parash} to separate; to specify; to wound.
exscind *verb* [1575 ekklao] [1581 ekkopto] to cut off or out.
exsynagogue *transliterated verb* [656 aposunagogos] to excommunicate from a synagogue.
extend hands, wring hands *participle* {3029 yeda} {3034 yadah} {8426 todah} to extend hands in praise; to wring hands in sorrow.
extend *verb* {3447 yahshat} to reach out.
extend, distend *verb* {8311 sara} to extend oneself, as in stretching out; to distend, as an appendage.
extend, happen *verb* {4291 meta} to extend unto the heavens; to happen upon.
extend, send *verb* {7971 shalach} {7972 shelach} to send; to send forth.
extend, spread (thin), stretch *verb* {5186 natah} {5628 sarach} to bend away; to spread out; to stretch.
extending, sending *participle* {4916 mishloach} a sending out; from the verb, send.
extention *noun* {5629 serach} an augmentation.
exterminate *verb* {6789 tsamath} to eradicate; to wipe out.
extermination *noun* {7171 qerets} extirpation.
extol, raise (up), exalt *verb* {5549 salal} from the root, to mound up; **see** selah; **cp** halal.
extort, oppress *verb* {6231 ashaq} to press out of; to oppress.
extortion, oppression *noun* {6233 osheq} a pressing out of; an oppressing.
extortioner of gold *noun* {4062 madhebah}.
eye, fountain *noun* {5869, 5870 ayin} [3788 ophthalmos] as the eye of the landscape; the organ for seeing; **see** fountain.
eye against *verb* [503 antophthalmeo] to stare against.
eyelids *plural noun* {6079 aphaph} as fluttering.
eyeservice *noun* [3787 ophthalmodoulia] a deceitful ascent to agree; **cp** lipservice.
eyewitness *noun* [845 autoptees] one who physically witnessed.
Ezra *transliterated name* {5830, 5831 ezrah} Helper.
Ezrah *transliterated name* {5834 ezrah} Helper.
Ezri *transliterated name* {5836 ezri} Help.
Ezri El *transliterated name* {5837 ezriel} Help of El.
Ezri Qam *transliterated name* {5840 azriyqam} Help of an Enemy.

F

fabricate, machinate *verb, participle* {2803, 2804 chashab} to interpenetrate; to weave; to contrive; physically, to fabricate; mentally, to machinate.
fabricated *adjective* {6247 esheth} fabricated; machinated.
fabricated girdle *noun* {2805 chesheb} a girdle, as interlaced.
fabrication, machination *noun* {2808 cheshbohn} {*plural* 2810 chishshabonth} {4284 machashebeth} a contrivance of machine, or mind.
face bread, prothesis bread *compound noun* {6440 paneh} {3899 lechem} [*transliteration* 4286 prothesis] [740 artos] the bread of the holy of holies as displayed; the face bread of the Old Covenant is identical to the prothesis bread of the New Covenant.
face *noun* {6440 paneh} [4383 prospon] the front of the head; also used verbally.
face *verb* {6437 panah} to turn face toward; facing.
fade, dim *adjective* {3544 kehah} obscure; dull.
fade, dim *verb* {3543 kahah} to become obscure, dull.
fade, shade *verb* {6004 amam} in the sense of concealing; of fading.
fail, fall (away),(off) (out) *verb* [1601 ekpipto] to be without effect; to be driven out of one's course.
fail, hoe, lack, arrange *verb* {5737 adar} to miss having; to arrange a vineyard, as in hoeing.
failing *noun* {3631 killayon} as in finished off.
fall (away) (off) (out), fail *verb* [1601 ekpipto] to be without effect; to be driven out of one's course.
fall, fell, happen, befall *verb* {5307 naphal} {5308 nephal} {7136 qarah} fall, fall down, fall away; to fell, as in felling timber; to cause to bring about.
false *adjective* {3538 cedab} deceitful.
false, falsehood *noun* {8267 sheqer} an untruth.
falsify *verb* {8266 shaqar} to cheat; to be untrue.
falter, stumble, trip *verb* {3782 kashal} to totter; to waver.
fame, hearing, notoriety, report *noun* {8052 shemuah} {8088 shema} {8089 shoma} [189 akoee] that which is heard; an announcement; a rumor.
family *noun* {4940 mishpachah} parents and their offspring, ancestors and their descendants.
famine *noun* {7458 raab} {7459 reabon} a dearth of food.
famish *adjective* {7457 raeb} experiencing famine.
famish *verb* {7456 raeb} to experience famine.
far be it *interjection* {2486 chaliylah} in the sense of that which is profane.
far removed, removed far *verb* {7368 rachaq} from the root, to widen.
far, afar, distant past *adjective* {7350 rachoq} {7352 rachiq} {7369 racheq} remote; in time, or distance.
fascinate *verb* [940 baskaino] to lead away into error by wicked arts.
fast *verb* {6684 tsum} to abstain from eating.
fast, fasting *noun* {6685 tsom} {8589 taanith} [776 asitia] abstinence from eating.
fasting *adjective* [777 asitos] without food.
fat *adjective* {1879 dashen} {8082 shamen} fat symbolizes health and prosperity.
fat *noun* {6309 peder} the fat of the holocaust sacrifices.
fat, fatness *noun* {1880 deshen} {1881 dath} {2459 cheleb} {4924 mashman} the grease of the body; the richness, fertility; fat symbolizes health and prosperity.
Fate *name* {4507 meniy} Destiny; perhaps the name of an idol.
father in law *noun* {2524 cham} [3995 pentheros] the father of a man's woman or a woman's man.
father, ab, abba *transliterated noun* {1 ab} {2 ab} [5 abba] [3962 pater] ab is Hebrew for father; **abba** is a Hellenic transliteration; **pater** is the Hellenic translation.
fatherland *noun* [3968 patris] one's native home.
fatherless *adjective* [540 apator] without father.
fatling *noun* {4806 meriy} that which is stall fed.
fatten, defat *verb* {1878 dashen} {2954 taphash} {8080 shaman} depending on the case, to make fat, or to remove fat; to enrich.
fatten, plump *verb* {2492 chalam} {3780 kasah} to cause to be fat, to plump; to cover with flesh.
fattlings *plural noun* {4220 meachim} that which is fattened; prosperous.
faultless *adjective* [176 akatagnostos] literally, unfaulted.
fawn *noun* {6082 opher} from its dusty color.
fear *noun* {6343 pachad} {6345 pachdah} alarm; **cp** awe.
fear *verb* {3025 yagor} {6342 pachad} {7297 rahah} to be alarmed; to be afraid; **cp** awe.
feast *noun* [1403 doche] a reception.
feast *noun* {3900 lechem} literally, a feeding.
feast of mourning *noun* {4798 marzeach} a cry of grief.
feast of revelling *noun* {4797 mirzasch} a cry of joy.
feel, grope *verb* {4959 mashash} from the root, to feel of.
fell, happen, befall, fall *verb* {5307 naphal} {5308 nephal} {7136 qarah} to fell, as in felling timber; to cause to bring about; fall, fall down, fall away.
fellow settler *noun* [4040 perioikos] associates or mates who settle together.
female *noun* {5347 neqebah} [2338 theelia] the species that births, whether human, animal, or plant.
fennel flower *noun* {7100 qetsach} from its pungency.
ferment, foam *verb* {2556 chamets} {2560 chamar} [2220

zumoo] to cause to ferment; action of enzymes induced by yeast or bacteria.
fermentation *noun* {2557 chamets} {2561 chemer} {2562 chamar} [2219 zumee] the action of enzymes induced by yeast or bacteria; **see** yeast.
fermented *adjective* {2558 chomets} that which is fermented.
festive mantle *noun* {6614 pethigil} a mantle for festive occasions.
festoon, descent *noun* {4174 mowrad} a place of going down; an ornamental hanging; a garland or wreath.
fetter *noun* [254 halusis] a restraint.
fetus *noun* {7698 sheger} {7988 shilyah} that which is finally ejected.
fever *noun* {2746 charchur} {6920 qaddachath} as hot; inflamed.
few, few men, men *plural noun* {4962 mathim} **see** Theological Wordbook of the Old Testament, 1263.
few, little, petty, shortly, bit, bit by bit *adjective, adverb* {4592 meat} diminutive; a few; a little.
fewer, lesser, little, pinky, younger *adjective* {6810 tsaor} {6995 qoten} {6996 qatan} less in age, number, size; little finger.
field *noun* {7704 sadeh} {7709 shedemah} {*plural* 8309 sheremahoth} [68 agros] land set aside for tillage, pasture, or sport.
fiery *adjective* [4447 purinos] inflamed.
fiery *noun* [4449 purrazo] [4450 purros] reddened; flame colored.
fiery, fired *verb* [4448 puroomai] to be inflamed; to burn; of the heat of passions; of anger.
fig *noun* {8384 tenah} [4810 sukon] a species of fruit.
fight, eat *verb* {3898 lacham} literally, to feed on food; to feed on an enemy.
fighting *noun* {3901 lachem} literally, a feeding on the enemy.
figtree *noun* [4808 sukee] a species of fruit tree.
figurine *noun* {5566 semel} a likeness; a carved figure; a statuette; an idol.
fill *verb* [1072 gemizo] [1705 empiplao, empleetho] to occupy wholly, including liquid in a bottle, a position of leadership; **cp** fill full, fulfill.
fill full, fulfill, fully fill *verb* {4390 mala} {4391 mela} {4395 meleah} [378 anapleeroo] [4130 pleetho] [4137 pleeroo] [4845 sumpleero] to bring to a conclusion; **cp** complete; **cp** shalom; **see** worship.
filling, fulfillment *noun* {*plural* 4394 milluim} {4396 milluah} {4402 milleth} that which has filled; that which is fulfilled; of sacrifices; of stones which fill mountings.
filth *noun* {7516 rephesh} as mud; **cp** foul.
final, finality [2078 eskatos] extreme; last in time or in place.
find *verb* {7912 shekach} [429 anurisko] to discover.
finger *verb* [2345 thigo] to point out; to touch with the finger.
finger, toe *noun* {676 etsba} {677 etsba} [1147 daktulos] literally, a digit as a grasper; **cp** great toe, thumb.
finial *noun* {3730 kaphtor} a chaplet; the top of a stem, or column.
finish (full) (final) *noun* {3617 kalah} the end; full and final cessation; **cp** completion.
finish (off), fully finish, conclude *verb* {3615 kalah} {3635 kelal} to cease; to cause to decease; to bring to an end; **cp** complete.
finished off *adjective* {3616 kaleh} to cease.
finishing *noun* [535 apartismos] completion.
fire, fiery *noun* {5135 nur} also used adjectively; from the root, to shine.
firing *noun* [4451 purosis] trials as a test; burning by which metals are refined.
firing *noun* {801 ashshah} a celebration of a firing as a sacrifice unto Elohim.
firm, form, pour *verb* {3332 yatsaq} to pour out; to shape by pouring into a mold; to make firm.
first(s), head, top, beginning *noun* {7218 rosh} {7221 rishah} {7225 reshith} {8462 rechillah} the head, in a variety of applications; the head of the body, of time, of the month, of archs.
first, head *adjective* {7223 rishon} {7224 rishoniy} head, as at the top; first, as at the beginning.
firstborn *noun* {*feminine* 1067 bekirah} {*masculine* 1069 bakar} the first to burst the womb.
firstborn, firstling *noun* {1060 bekor} {*plural* 1061 bikkuwr} [536 *plural* aparkee] [4416 prototokos] the first offspring of a family or of a harvest.
firstrights, firstling *noun* {1062 bekorah} [4415 prototokia] the rights afforded a firstborn.
firstripe *noun* {1073 bakkurah} that which ripens first.
fists *dual noun* {2651 chophen} clenched hands.
fistsful *plural noun* {6653 tsebeth} as much as the clenched hand can hold.
flake *noun* [3016 lepton] a flake, or shaving.
flakes, chaff *noun* {4651 mappal} that which falls off; that which is pendulous.
flambeau *noun* {3940 lappid} a flaming torch.
flame *noun* {3827 labbah} {3852 lehabah} {7631 sebib} {7632 shabib} {7957 shalhebeth} a flame, or a flare of fire as split into tongues; **read** Acts 2:3.
flame, blade *noun* {3851 lahab} a flame of fire; a flashing blade of a sword.
flame, inflame *verb* **flaming** *adjective* {3857 lahat} {3859 laham} to blaze; that which is inflamed by fire.
flamed, inflamed *adjective* {6867 tsarebeth} [4092 pimpramai] as burning.
flamings *plural noun* {3858 lahatim} flames, as enwraping.
flank *noun* **flanks** *dual noun* {3409 yarek} {3410 yarka} {3411 yerechah} figuratively, the rear; the thigh, or thighs, as being soft.
flank, folly *noun* {3689 kecel} {3690 kiclah} silliness; the flank of the body; the flanks as symbolic of hope.
flap, flee, wander, chase *verb* {5074 nadad} {5323 natsa} to flap up and down; to shoo away.
flap, rebel *verb* {4754 mahrah} to flap one's self; to flap one's wings; to rebel.
flash, shine *verb* {3313 yapha} from the root, to shine.
flask *noun* {6378 pak} a container from which a liquid may flow.
flax *noun* {6593 pishteh} {6594 pishtah} flax as woven; flax as a wick
flee *verb* {5075 nedad} {5111 nud} {5127 nuwc} to depart; to flit.
flee, bud *verb* {5132 nuts} to flash, as in color; to flee in a flash.
flee, wander, chase, flap *verb* {5074 nadad} {5323 natsa} to flap up and down; to shoo away.
flesh *noun* {1320 basar} {1321 besar} [4561 sarx] literally, the substance of the living body; symbolically, the entire nature of man, sense and reason.
flesh, kinflesh *noun* {7607 sheer} {7608 shaarah} flesh, as food; flesh, as near of kin.
fleshly *adjective* [4559 sarkikos] under the control of animal appetites.
fleshy *adjective* [4560 sarkinos] consisting of flesh; soft.
flight, retreat *noun* {4498 manohs} {4499 menusah} a place to flee to; a fleeing.
flint *noun* {6862 tsar} {6864 tsor} a hard pebble; a tight place.
flip, flit, paddle *verb* {7751 shuwt} to flit forth and back; to flip oars.
flit, flitter, fly *verb* {5774 uph} {1675 daah} [4072 petomai] to move through the air.
flit, paddle, flip *verb* {7751 shuwt} to flit forth and back; to flip oars.
float, overflow *verb* {6687 tsuph} to float; to flow over.
flock *noun* {6629 tson} {6792 tsone} a group, usually of animals or birds.
flog *verb* [1194 dero] to scourge.
flood *noun* {2230 zerem} {3999 mabbuwl} an overflowing.
flood *verb* {2229 zaram} to overflow.
floor *noun* {7172 qarqa} a slab or board laid down.
flour *noun* {5560 soleth} flour, as stripped.
flour *noun* {7058 qemach} that which is ground.
flourish, blossom *verb* {6524 parach} {6692 tsuts} to bloom.
flourish, germinate *verb* {5107 nub} from the root, to germinate; to flourish.
flow, flux *verb* {2100 zoov} of land as flowing with milk and honey; of woman as fluxing with blood.
flow, melt, dissolve *verb* {4529 masah} to dissolve.
flow, pour *verb* {5047 negad} {5064 nagar} {5140 nazal} to flow out, as to clear the way; to pour out.
flow, sparkle *verb* {5102 nahar} to flow, as to assemble; to be cheerful; to sparkle.
flush {*adjective* 2447 chakliyl} {*noun* 2448 chakliluth} flush in color.
flushness *noun* {6289 parur} a glowing flushness.
flute *noun* {2485 chaliyl} as being perforated.

flute *noun* {4953 mashroqiy} {5155 nechiylah} [836 aulos] as a musical pipe, blown, or whistled.
flute *verb* [832 auleo] to blow or whistle the flute.
flutist *noun* [834 auleetees] one who flutes.
flux, flow *noun* {2101 zohv} {2231 zirmah} the flow as of blood or pus.
flux, flow *verb* {2100 zuwb} of land as flowing with milk and honey; of woman as fluxing with blood.
fly, flit, flitter *verb* {5774 uph} {1675 daah} [4072 petomai] to move through the air.
flyer *noun* {5775, 5776 oph} [4071 petinon] [4421 pteenon] one who can fly.
foam, ferment *verb* {2556 chamets} {2560 chamar} [2220 zumoo] to cause to ferment; action of enzymes induced by yeast or bacteria.
fodder, mingle, mix up *verb* {1101 balal} to mix together; to mix up; **see** Beli Yaal; **see** comingle.
fold, reiterate, repeat, alter, change, double, duplicate *verb* {8132 shana} {8133 shena} {8138 shanah} to reinforce by folding, by doubling; may include disguise, camouflage.
foliage *noun* {6074 ophi} {6288 purah} {6788 tsammereth} whatever sprouts from a tree, vine, or plant.
foliage, rope, wreath, wreathen *noun* {5688 abothah} as entwined; a wreath of victory; **cp** crown; **cp** diadem.
folly *noun* {200 ivveleth} {5039 nebalah} {5529 sekel} {5531 sikluth} silliness; foolishness.
folly *verb* {5528 sakal} to do foolishly; to act silly.
folly, flank *noun* {3689 kecel} {3690 kiclah} silliness; the flank of the body; the flank, as symbolic of hope.
folly, wither, disgrace *verb* {5034 nabel} from the root, to wilt; to fall away; to fail.
food *noun* **eating** *verb* [1034 brosimos] that which is eaten.
food *noun* {3894 lachuwm} [1033 broma] that which is eaten.
food *noun* {3978 maakal} {4202, 4203 mazown} an edible.
fool, foolish *adjective* {5036 nabal} stupid.
fool *noun* **Kesil** *transliterated name* {3684 kecil} {5530 sakal} a constellation; stupid, or silly.
foolish *adjective* {191 eviyl} {196 eviliy} {3687 keciyluth} silly.
foolish *adjective* {3688 kecal} to be silly.
foot (on) *noun* {7273 ragli} persons on foot; infantry.
foot (step) *noun* {4772 margelah} {7271 regal} {7272 regel} [4228 pous] the foot; a footstep.
foot (to the) *noun* [4158 podeerees] full length.
foothold *noun* {4613 moomad} a place to secure the foot.
footstool *noun* {3534 kebesh} [5286 hupopodion] as trodden upon; as under foot.
forage *noun* [5527 chortasma] animal feed.
force, lizard, substance *noun* {3581 koach} {3981 maamats} pressure, physical or intellectual; also a lizard.
forehead *noun* {4696 metsach} [3359 metopon] the upper front of the head.
foreknow *verb* [4267 proginosko] to know prior to occurrence.
foreleg, arm *noun* {2220 zeroah} [1023 brakion] arm (human), foreleg (animal); denoting force, strength.
foresay *verb* [4280 proereo] to say prior to occurrence.
foresee *verb* [4308 prooraо] to see prior to occurrence.
foreshabbath *transliterated noun* [4315 prosabbaton] shabbath eve.
foreskin, uncircumcised *noun* {6190 orlah} [203 akrobustia] the foreskin of the penis; the foreskin not removed; **cp** circumcision; **cp** decircumcision.
forespeak *verb* [4302 prolego] to speak prior to occurrence.
forest *noun* {2793 choresh} {3264 yaor} {3293 yaar} {3295 yaarah} [5208 hulee] a growth of trees.
foretell *verb* [4277 proepo] to tell prior to occurrence.
forget *adjective* {7913 shekach} oblivious.
forget *verb* {7911 shakach} to be oblivious of.
forget, exact *verb* {5382 nashah} to neglect; to remove from.
forging *noun* {4300 metil} a metal as hammered out.
forgive *verb* {5545 salach} to grant charism.
forgive, forsake, leave, release, allow *verb* [863 aphieemi] to send forth.
forgiveness *noun* {5547 celichah} [859 aphesis] charism granted.
forgiving *noun* {5546 callach} a granting of charism.
fork *noun* {4207 mazleg} {*plural* 4207 mezlagoth} an instrument to draw up.
form *noun* {3333 yetsukah} {*plural* 3338 yatsurim} {8389 toar} [3444 morphee] [3446 morphosis] that which is formed; **see** metamorphose.
form *noun* {3336 yetser} to form of the thought.
form *noun* {6699 tsurah} a form, as shaped.
form *verb* {3335 yatsar} [3445 morphoomai] to shape; **see** metamorphose.
form, besiege, bind, confine *verb* {6696 tsur} to confine; to form by shaping.
form, idolize, contort *verb* {6087 atsab} to form; to contort; as in idolizing, as in pain.
form, pour, firm *verb* {3332 yatsaq} to pour out; to shape by pouring into a mold; to make firm.
formation, rank, arrangement *noun* {4633 maarak} {4634 maarakah} {4635 maareketh} an arrangment (physical or mental).
formerly, preceding, ancient, antiquity, east, easterly, eastern, eastward *noun* {6921 qadim} {6924 qedem} {6925 qodam} {6926 qidmah} {6927 qadmah} literally, the forefront; from the front.
formula, quantity *noun* {4971 mathkuneth} a measured proportion of portions.
forsake, leave (behind), release *verb* {5800 azab} [1459 enkatalipo] to leave behind; in a good sense, to let remain over; in a bad sense, to abandon.
forsake, leave, release, allow, forgive *verb* [863 aphieemi] to send forth.
forsaking, leaving, releasing *noun* {5805 azubah} a desertion.
fortifications *plural noun* {8284 sharoth} reinforcements.
fortified, fortress, fortressed *noun, adjective* {4013 mibtsar} [3794 okuroma] a reinforced building, or city.
forum *noun* [60 agoraios] a market; including a forum for open discussion, of the judiciary; **see** market.
foul *verb* {2930 tame} {2933 tamah} {2936 tanaph} {7515 raphas} [4510 rupoo] to become offensive to the senses; **cp** filth.
foul, foulness *noun* {2932 tumah} [4507 ruparia] [4508 ruparos] [4509 rupos] loathsome; offensive to the senses.
fouled *adjective* {2931 tame} loathed.
found, foundation *verb* {3245 yacad} [2311 themelioo] to lay a base or basis for.
foundation *noun* {3246 yecud} {3247 yecod} {3248 yecudah} {4143 muwcad} {4144 mowcad} {4145 muwcadah} {*plural* 4146 mowcadah} {4328 meuccadah} {4527 maccad} {8356 shathah} [2310 themelios] [2602 kataboelee] the base or basis, whether of a fact, or ediface.
fountain *noun* {1543 gulah} {4002 mabbua} {4599 mayan} {5033 nebek} a source, usually of water.
fountain *noun* {4726 maqor} a gusher; including tears, and menstruation of a woman.
fountain, eye *noun* {5869, 5870 ayin} [3788 ophthalmos] as the eye of the landscape; the organ for seeing.
foursquare, square *verb* {7251 raba} to cause to be quadrate.
fowl *noun* {1257 barbur} {6853 tsephar} [3732 orneon] a species of flyer.
fracture *noun* {4386 mekittah} a crushing break.
fragment *noun* {7518 rats} {*plural* 7616 shabahim} [2801 klasma] of remnants of food, a broken piece.
frail *adjective* [770 astheneo] [772 asthenees] feeble.
frailty *noun* [769 asthenia] feebleness of body or mind.
frailty *noun* [771 astheneema] error arising from weakness of mind; a scruple of conscience.
framing *noun* {4746 meqareh} the frame of a building, as the meeting of timbers.
frankincense *noun* {3828 lebonah} [3030 libanos] a species of incense; **see** incense.
frankincenser *noun* [3031 libanoton] a censer for a species of incense; **see** censer.
fraud *noun* {8496 tok} {*plural* 8501 takakim} {*plural* 8595 tatuaim} in the sense of cutting up; also errors.
freaks, exploits *plural noun* {8586 taalul} deeds as exploitations.
fresh *adjective* {3892 lach} new, as unused; as undried.
fresh, dripping *adjective* {2961 tahiy} new, as moist.
freshness *noun* {3893 leach} vigor.
friend *noun* {5997 amith} {7453 rea} {7463 reeh} {7464 reah} {7468 reuth} {7474 raah} [5384 philos] a fond one; a soulical attraction.
friendly minded *noun* [5390 philophronos] [5391 philophron] agreeable.
friendship *noun* [5373 philia] relationship with a fond one.
fright *noun* {1205 beathah} extreme fear.
frighten *verb* {1204 baath} {7738 shavah} to cause extreme fear.

frivolity *noun* {8604 tiphlah} silliness.
frost, ice, crystal *noun* {7140 qerach} as being smooth.
froth *verb* [875 aphrizo] to foam at the mouth.
frothiness *noun* {6350 pachazuth} frothy; foamy; unimportant.
frothy *adjective* {6348, 6349 pachaz} frothy; foamy; as boiling over; as unimportant.
fruit (stray) *noun* {6528 peret} fruit left for strangers to glean.
fruit *noun* {5108 nob} {6529 peri} [2590 karpos] species of produce of the ground, usually self–seeded.
fuel *noun* {3980 maakoleth} a feed for fire.
fuel pile *noun* {4071 medurah} an accumulation of fuel.
fugitive *noun* {1280 beriach} {1281 bariach} {4015 mibrach} {5211 niye} one who flees.
fulfillment, filling *noun* {*plural* 4394 milluim} {4396 milluah} {4402 milleth} that which has filled; that which is fulfilled; of sacrifices; of stones which fill mountings.
full, fulness *adjective* {4392 male} [1073 gemo] [4134 pleerees] filling; filled full.
fully fill, fill full, fulfill *verb* {4390 mala} {4391 mela} {4395 meleah} [378 anapleeroo] [4130 pleetho] [4137 pleeroo] [4845 sumpleeroo] to bring to a conclusion; **cp** complete; **cp** shalom; **see** worship.
fully finish, conclude, finish (off) *verb* {3615 kalah} {3635 kelal} [535 apartismos] to cease; to cause to decease; to bring to an end; **cp** complete.
fulness *noun* [4138 pleeroma] the whole filling; the totality.
fulness, fulfillment *noun* {4395 meleah} that which is brought to a conclusion; an abundance.
fuming *adjective* {2740 charon} {2750 choriy} burning anger; **see** kindle, inflame.
function *noun* {4612 maamad} job; assigned activity.
function, acts *noun* [4234 praxis] something done; a deed.
furl *verb* [4428 ptusso] to roll up; **cp** coil; **cp** unfurl.
furnace, oven *noun* {8574 tannur} a fire pot.
furrow *noun* {6170 arugah} {8525 telem} a furrow, as dug and piled.
fury *noun* {2528 chema} {5678 ebrah} [2372 thumos] an outburst of passion.
fury, poison *noun* {2534 chemah} heat; an outburst of passion as poison.

G

Gabbatha *transliterated name* {1355 gab} [1042 gabbatha] Arch, Bow.
Gabbay *transliterated name* {1373 gabbay} Collective.
Gabri El *transliterated name* {1403 gabriel} [1043 gabrieel] Man of El.
Gacham *transliterated name* {1514 gacham} Flame.
Gacher *transliterated name* {1515 gacher} Lurker.
Gad *transliterated name* {1408, 1410 gad} [1045 gad] Treasure.
Gaddi *transliterated name* {1426 gaddiy} Treasured.
Gadi *transliterated name* {1424 gadiy} Treasured.
Gadi El *transliterated name* {1427 gaddiyel} Treasure of El.
Gadiy *transliterated name* {1425 gadiy} Of Gad; a Yisra Eliy.
gain, greed *noun* {1215 betsa} that which is greedily gained; **see** the verb; **read** Yechezq El 22:27, where the noun and the verb are used together.
gain, greed *verb* {1214 batsa} gaining through greed; **see** the noun.
Gal Ed *transliterated name* {1567 galed} Heap of Witness; a memorial cairn east of the Yarden.
galbanum *transliterated noun* {2464 chelbenah} a gum.
Galiyl *transliterated name* {1551 galiyl} [1056 galilaia] Circle; Corona.
Galiyliy *transliterated name* [1057 galilaios] Of Galiyl.
gall, venom, bitter *noun* {*plural* 4844 merarim} {4845 mererah} {4846 merorah} bile; venom; a bitter herb.
Gamli El *transliterated name* {1583 gamliel} [1059 gamalieel] Reward of El.
Gammadim/warriors *plural transliterated name* {1575 gammadim} Warriors, as grasping instruments.
gangrene *transliterated noun* [1044 gangraina] an ulcer, as gnawing.
gape, gasp *verb* {6473 paar} {6475 patsah} to open the mouth in gasping, or in gaping.
garden *noun* {1588 gan} {1593 gannah} {1594 ginnah} [2779 keepos] a ground for growing edibles and flowers; **cp** paradise.
gardener *noun* [2780 keepouros] one who tends a garden.
garment *noun* {4063 medev} a garment, as measured.
garment (masculine) *noun* {7897 shith} a masculine garment, as being put on.
garrison *verb* {1598 ganan} to hedge round about.
Gath Rimmon *transliterated name* {1667 gathrimmown} Winepress of the Pomegranate.
Gath Shemen *transliterated name* {1660 gath} {8081 shemen} [1068 gethseemanee] Treader of (anointing) Oil.
gather *verb* {622 aseaph} {6908 qabats} {7197 qashash} to bring together; **cp** congregate.
gather, enfold *verb* {3664 kanac} {3673 kenash} to wrap; to collect.
gathering, ingathering *noun* {*plural* 624 acuppim} {625 oceph} {626 acephah} {*plural* 627 acuppah} {628 acpecuph} {6910 qebutsah} a collection of offerings, fruits, people, or learned persons.
gauge *noun* {8506 token} {8508 toknith} a measure of all dimensions; including, but not limited to size, volume, weight.
gauge *verb* {8505 takan} to measure all dimensions; including, but not limited to size, volume, weight.
Gay, valley *transliterated noun* {1516 gay} valley; sometimes transliterated when used in compound names.
Gay Chazi/Valley of the Seer *transliterated name* {1522 gechaziy} Valley of the Seer.
Gay Haregah/Valley of Slaughter *transliterated name* {1516 gay} {2028 haregah} Valley of Slaughter.
Gay Hinnom/Valley of Burning *name* {1516 gay} {2011 hinnom} [1067 geenna] used figuratively, as a name for the place (or state) of everlasting punishment; may be transliterated, Gay Hinnom.
Gay Hizzayon/Valley of Vision *transliterated name* {1516 gay} {2384 chizzayown} Valley of Vision.
Gay Melach/Valley of Salt *transliterated name* {1516 gay} {4417 melach} Valley of Salt.
gazelle, Tabitha, Dorcas *noun* {6643 tsebiy} {6646 tsebiyah} [5000 tabitha] a gazelle, as beautiful; Tabitha is the Hellene transliteration of tsebiyah; Dorcas is the Hellene translation of tsebiyah.
Geba *transliterated name* {1387 geba} Hillock.
Gedal Yah *transliterated name* {1436 gedalyah} Greatness of Yah.
Gederothayim *dual transliterated name* {1453 gederothayim} Double Wall.
Gemar Yah *transliterated name* {1587 gemaryah} Consummated of Yah.
genealogize *transliterated verb* {3187 yachas} [1075 genealogeo] literally, to sprout; to sequence by birth.
genealogy *transliterated noun* {3188 yachas} [1076 genealogia] the sequence by birth.
generation *noun* {1755 dor} {1859 dar} a revolution of time.
generation *noun* {*plural* 8435 toledahoth} [1074 genea] descendants; history.
genesis, genetics *transliterated noun* [1078 genesis] beginning; birth.
genos *transliterated noun* [1085 genos] species; kinds.
gerah *transliterated noun* {1626 gerah} a small measure of weight, a coin.
germinate, flourish *verb* {5107 nub} from the root, to germinate; to flourish.
Geshur *transliterated name* {1650 geshuwr} Bridge.
Geshuriy *transliterated name* {1651 geshuwriy} Of Geshur.
Geu El *transliterated name* {1345 geuel} Triumph of El.
ghosts *plural noun* {7496 raphaim} the spirits of departed beings; **cp** spirit.
Giach *transliterated name* {1520 giyach} Fountain.
Giba *transliterated name* {1388 giba} Hill.
Gibah *transliterated name* {1390 gibah} Hillock.
Gibath *transliterated name* {1394 gibath} Hilliness.
Gibathiy *transliterated name* {1395 gibathiy} Of Gibath.
gibe *noun* {8148 sheninah} a snide; a scoff.
Gibon *transliterated name* {1391 gibown} Hilly.
Giboniy *transliterated name* {1393 giboniy} Of Gibon.
Gichon *transliterated name* {1521 gichown} Stream; a river of Paradise.
Gidon *transliterated name* {1439 gidown} [1066 gedeon] Feller; Toppler.
Gidoni *transliterated name* {1441 gidoniy} Felled; Cut Off.
gift *noun* {4976 mattan} {4978 mattena} {4979 mattanah} {4991 mattath} {5379 nisseth} {7862 shay} {8670 teshurah} [1390 doma] that which is voluntarily presented without compensation in return; **note:** in some versions, the word is

often inserted without reason, and at other times mistranslated.
Gilad *transliterated name* {1568 gilad} a region east of Yarden.
Giladiy *transliterated name* {1569 giladiy} Of Gilad.
Gilalay *transliterated name* {1562 gilalay} Dungy.
gird *verb* {2296 chagar} {8151 shanas} to bind.
girdle *noun* {2289 chagohr} {2290 chagorah} {4206 maziyach} {4228 machagoreth} a binding, or belt for the waist.
Girgashiy *transliterated name* {1622 girgashiy} [1086 gergesenos] of uncertain derivative; Of Kenaan.
girt *verb* [4024 perizonnumi] to fasten by a girdle, to equip.
Gishpa *transliterated name* {1658 gishpa} of uncertain derivative.
Gittayim *dual transliterated name* {1664 gittayim} Double Winepress.
give *verb* {3051 yahab} {3052, 3053 yehab} [1325 didomi] [1394 dosis].
give, allow *verb* {5414 nathan} {5415 nethan} literally, to give; to give permission.
give over *verb* [325 anadidomi].
give (over) *verb* [1929 epididomi] to surrender.
give (up) (back) *verb* [591 apodidomi] to give away.
giver *noun* [1395 dotees] one who gives.
glean (after) *verb* {3950 laqat} {3953 laqash} to pick up after the harvest.
glean, exploit *verb* {5953 alal} to pick up after; in a good sense, to glean; in a bad sence, to exploit.
gleaning *noun* {3951 leqet} that which is left after the harvest.
glitter, resound *verb* {6670 tsahal} to stand out; in color, or in sound.
glittering *participle* {6668 tsahab} from the root, to glitter.
glorify, glorifying *verb* {8231 shaphar} {8232 shephar} {8235 shiphrah} [1392 doxazo] [1740 endoxazomai] to brighten; to splendor.
glorious, glories *adjective* {8233 shepher} [1741 endoxos] splendorous; praiseworthy.
glory *noun* [1391 doxa] splendor; praise.
glory pavilion *noun* {8237 shaphrur} a canopy of splendor.
glutton, quake, shake *participle* {2151 zalal} to quake; to shake; to eat in excess; **cp** drunkard.
gluttony *noun* {5607 sepheq} overeating; **cp** drunkard.
gnash *verb* [1031 bruko] to grate the teeth in pain or rage.
gnashing *noun* [1030 brugmos] a grating of the teeth.
gnaw *verb* {6207 araq} to eat at; to pain.
gnawing *noun* {7469 reuth} {7475 rayah} a feeding upon, in the sense of desiring.
go (about) (around), surround, turn (about) (around) *verb* {5437 cabab} to border; to revolve; to surround.
go, walk, went *verb* {3212 yahlach} literally, to walk.
goad *verb* {5496 cuth} to prick; to stimulate.
goats (he) *plural noun* {6260 attud} as prepared; as full grown.
GOD see • SUMMARY: EL, ELAH, ELI, ELOHAH, ELOHIM, ELOI:
Gog *transliterated name* {1463 gog} [1136 gog] derivative uncertain; an Yisra Eliy; a northern area.
gold, clear *noun* {2091 zahab} literally, yellow shimmer.
Golyath *transliterated name* {1555 golyath} Uncoverer (as in exposing).
Gomer *transliterated name* {1586 gomer} Ceased; Consumated.
good *adjective* [2570 kalos] valuable; praiseworthy.
govern *verb* {8323 sarar} to domineer.
governess *noun* {8282 sarah} the dominant female.
governing *noun* [2231 heegemonia] the time period of governing.
governor *noun* {6346, 6347 pechah} {8269 sar} {8660 tirshatha} [2230 hegemoneuo] [2232 hegemon] [2233 hegeomai] the dominant male; one who governs.
goy, goyim *transliterated noun* {*singular* 1471 goy} {*plural* 1471 goyim} [1484 ethnos] other nations; sometimes includes Yisra Eliy and Yah Hudiy; a transliteration of the Hebrew; a translation of the Hellene.
goyim (as the) *adverb* [1482 ethnikos] [1483 ethnikos] **see** goy, goyim.
grain *noun* {1250 bar} grain of any species.
granary *noun* {4200 mezev} {*plural* 4460 mammegoroth} a building for storing grain.
granary, terror *noun* {4035 megurah} a fright; a place to store grain.
grant *verb* [1433 doreomai] to permit.
grant charism; see charism (grant).
grapevines *plural noun* {8291 saruq} vines of grapes.
grass *noun* {2682 chatsir} the lawn of a courtyard.
gratis, gratuitous *adjective,* **gratuitously** *adverb* {2600 chinnam} [77 adapanos] [1432 dorean] free; freely; bestowed freely.
gratuity *noun* [1431 dorea] [1434 doreema] an honorarium.
gray *verb* {7867 siyb} to grow gray; to age.
grayed, grayness *noun* {7869 seyb} {7872 seybah} aged.
graze, tend, attend, befriend *verb* {7462 raah} [5256 hupeereteo] to cause a flock to graze; to tend a flock or to pasture; to befriend, by attending to; **see** attendant; **see** Yah Veh Raah.
great toe, thumb *noun* {931 bohen} literally, large digit.
great, greater, abundant *adjective* {1419 gadol} {7227, 7229 rab}{7260 rabrab} {7690 saggiy} large; older; plentiful.
greaten *adjective* {1432 gadel} large.
greaten, abound *verb* {7235 rabah} {7236 rebah} to be greatened, in any dimension; to increase.
greaten, grow *verb* {1431 gadal} to enlarge.
greatly, increasing, many, mighty, much, very, exceeding *adjective* {7689, 7690 saggiy} superlatively mighty, or large.
greatness, greatnesses, abundance *noun* {1420 gedullah} {1433 godel} {7230 rob} {7238 rebu} increase; magnitude; mighty acts.
greed, gain *noun* {1215 betsa} that which is greedily gained; **see** the verb; **read** Yechezq El 22:27, where the noun and the verb are used together.
greed, gain *verb* {1214 batsa} gaining through greed; **see** the noun.
green *adjective* {7387, 7488 raanan} as flourishing; as prosperous.
green, greens *noun* {3418 yereq} {3419 yareq} as edibles.
green (pale) *adjective* {3420 yeraqon} [5515 chloros] a paleness; of plants from drought, or of people from fright.
griddle *noun* {4227 machabath} a baking pan.
grief *noun* {3015 yagah} {8424 tugah} affliction; oppression.
grieve *verb* {3013 yagah} {5701 agam} to be sad.
grinderteeth *plural noun* {4459 maltaaoth} the teeth that grind; the molars.
grits *plural noun* {7383 riphah} grits, as pounded.
groan, groaning *noun* {5009 neaqah} an audible, nonverbal expressing of grief; **cp** growl; **cp** sigh.
groan, groaning *verb* {5008 naaq} to express an audible, nonverbal utterance expressing grief; **cp** growl; **cp** sigh.
grope, feel *verb* {4959 mashash} from the root, to feel of.
grow, greaten *verb* {1431 gadal} to enlarge.
grow, scatter, spread *verb* {6335 push} [837 auxano] to grow, to enlarge; as in spreading out.
growl *verb* {5098, 5099 naham} {5286 naar} to snarl; **cp** groan.
growling *noun* {5100 nahamah} snarling; **cp** groan.
growth (spontaneous) *noun* {5599 caphiach} that which grows of itself, sometimes without nurturing.
growth *noun* [838 auxeesis] increase.
guard *noun* {4929 mishmar} {4931 mishmereth} {*plural* 8109 shemurah} [5441 phulax] one that protects; the guard of the night.
guard *verb* [1314 diaphulasso] [5442 phulasso] to protect; to obey.
guard, guardhouse *noun* [5438 phulakee] a person or place that guards.
guard, hearing, audience *noun* {4928 mishmaath} an audience; also obedience; a subject.
guard, on guard, regard *verb* {5201 natar} {5202 nater} {5341 natsar} {8104 shamar} {*plural* 8107 shimmurim} {8108 shomrah} {8176 shaar} [5083 tereo] in the sense of protecting from harm, observing observances, obeying misvahs.
guide, sustain *verb* {5095 nahal} literally, to lead with light.
guilt (for the) *noun* {819 ashmah} an offering to Elohim for having guilted; **see** guilt.
guilt, guiltiness *noun* {817 asham} a breach of code; **cp** subject to.
guiltless *adjective* [121 athoos] without guilt.
guilty *adjective* {818 ashem} {2054 vazar} to bear guilt; to have breached.
guilty *verb* {816 asham} to have breached a code.
Gulgoleth *transliterated name* {1538 gulgoleth} [1115 golgotha] Cranium; **cp** cranium.
gullible *adjective* {6612 pethai} seducible.
gullible *noun* {6615 pethayuth} seducible.
gulp *verb* {3886 luwa} to swallow; to be rash.
gulp *verb* {7602 shaaph} to inhale; to gulp.
Gur Baal *transliterated name* {1485 gurbaal} Sojourn of Baal.
gush *verb* {5042 naba} to gush the Spirit, water, words.

H

Haba Yah *transliterated name* {2256 habayah} Hidden of Yah.
Habaqqaq *transliterated name* {2265 chabaqquwq} Embrace.
habergeon *noun* {8302 shiryonah} {8473 tachara} a mesh garment of metal as armour; of linen as woven.
habitation *noun* {4583 maon} {4585 meonah} a habitat; an area in which to abide.
habitation (rest in) *verb* {5115 navah} to abide in rest.
habitation of rest *noun* {5116 navah} a restful abode.
Hadad *transliterated name* {111 adad} {2301 chadad} Sharp.
hades, sheol *noun* {7585 sheol} [86 hades] literally, the unseen; sheol is a transliteration of the Hebrew; hades is a transliteration of the Hellene, which is a translation of the Hebrew; both refer to a temporary abode of the body and soul; there is a progressive distinction of purpose of sheol/hades from its inception to its final state; **read** Yechezq El 31:15–17, 32:18–29, Loukas 16:19–31, Apocalypse 20:13,14; **cp** Psalm 16:10, Acts 2:27.
Hadrach *transliterated name* {2317 chadrach} of uncertain derivative; a Syriaiy deity.
Hagab *transliterated name* {2285 hagab} [13 agabos] Locust.
Hagaba *transliterated name* {2286 chagaba} Locust.
Hagar *transliterated name* {1904 hagar} [28 agar] mother of Yishma El.
Hagariy *transliterated name* {1905 hagriy} Of Hagar.
Haggay *transliterated name* {2292 chaggay} Celebrative.
Hah! *interjection* {1929 hahh} {1930 how} an expression of grief.
hair, hairy *noun* {8177 sear} {8181 saar} {8185 saarah} [2359 thrix, trikos] [5155 trikinos] a filament protruding from the skin; **cp** tresses.
hairy, buck *adjective* {8163 sair} shaggy; also a he goat.
Hachal Yah *transliterated name* {2446 chachalyah} Flushness of Yah.
Hachilah *transliterated name* {2444 chachiylah} Flushness.
Hachmoni *transliterated name* {2453 chachmowniy} Enwisen.
Halach *transliterated name* {2477 chalach} of foreign origin; a region in Ashshur.
halal *noun* [133 ainesis] [136 ainos] [1868 epainos] laud.
halal *transliterated noun* {*plural* 1974 hillul} {4110 mahalal} {8416 tehillah} a hail; a reverent salutation; **cp** selah.
halal *transliterated verb* {1984 halal} to hail; to salute reverently; as in Halalu Yah.
halal *verb* [134 aineo] [1867 epaineo] to laud.
haloled one *transliterated title* {1966 heylel} hailed one; a title of Satan.
Halalu Yah *transliterated verb* {1984 halal} {3050 yah} [239 allelouya] Hail Yah.
Halchul *transliterated name* {2478 chalchuwl} Writhed.
half, mid–, midst *preposition* {2676 chatsoth} {2677 chetsiy} {4275 mechetsah} {4276 machatsith} among; a half of a whole; the middle of.
hallow see • SUMMARY: HOLY, HOLIES, HALLOW:
halloo *verb* [214 alalazo] to sound out loudly.
haloed, haloing *verb* [4034 perilampo] to encircle as with a halo; to shine around.
halve *verb* {2673 chatsah} to separate one whole into two halves.
Hamath *transliterated name* {2574 chamath} Walled.
Hamath Rabbah *transliterated name* {2579 chamathrabbah} Wall of Rabbah (Great).
Hamath Sobah *transliterated name* {2578 chamathtsowbah} Wall of Sobah (Station).
Hamathiy *transliterated name* {2577 chamathiy} Of Hamath.
hammer *verb* {1986 halam} to pound; to strike down.
hammer, quarry *noun* {4717 maqqabah} {4718 maqqebeth} that which is used to pound; a quarry, from which is pounded.
hammerings *plural noun* {4112 mahalummah} poundings of a hammer.
hammock *noun* {4412 maluwnah} a restingplace; **see** lodge.
Hammu El *transliterated name* {2536 chammuwel} Heat of El.
Hamor *transliterated name* {2544 chamor} [1697 emmor] Burro.
hamstring, uproot *verb* {6131, 6132 aqar} to pluck up the root; to cut the tendons.
Hanan El *transliterated name* {2606 chananel} Granted Charism of El.
Hanan Yah *transliterated name* {2608 chananyah} [367 ananias] [452 annas] Granted Charism of Yah.
hand *noun* {3027, 3028 yad} [5495 cheir] the body part below the wrist; **note:** the *exeGeses* places *hand* in *oblique type* when it has been added by the translators.
hand toss *verb* {3034 yadah} to toss by hand.
handle *noun* {5325 nitstab} a fixed handle.
handle *verb* {3032 yadad} {7061 qasmats} {7062 qomets} [5496 cheiragogeo] to manipulate with the hands.
handlead *verb* [5497 cheiragogos] to lead by the hand.
handmade *adjective* [5499 cheiropoietos] made by hand.
hands (extend) (wring) *participle* {3029 yeda} {3034 yadah} {8426 todah} to extend hands in praise; to wring hands in sorrow.
handscribing *noun* [5498 cheirographon] that which is scribed by hand.
handsome, beautiful (very) *adjective* {3303 yapheh} {3304 yephehphiyah} {8209 shappir} [5611 horaios] beautiful; timely; flourishing.
hang, suspend *verb* **prone** *participle* {8511 tala} {8518 talah} to suspend.
Hannah *transliterated name* {2584 channah} [451 anna] Endued with Charism.
Hanni El *transliterated name* {2592 channiel} Granted Charism of El.
Hanoch *transliterated name* {2585 chanoch} [1802 enok] Hanukkahed.
hanukkah *transliterated noun* {2597 chanukkah} {2598 chanukkah} [1456 enkainia] a celebration of hallowing.
hanukkah *transliterated verb* {2596 chanuk} [1457 enkainizo] to celebrate a hanukkah.
Haparayim *dual transliterated name* {2663 chapharayim} Double Pit.
happen, befall, fall, fell *verb* {5307 naphal} {5308 nephal} {7136 qarah} to cause to bring about; fall, fall down, fall away; to fell, as in felling timber.
happen, extend *verb* {4291 metah} to extend unto the heavens; to happen upon.
happening, occurrence *noun* {4745 miqreh} that which happens to occur.
Haqupha *transliterated name* {2709 chaquwpha} Crooked.
Har Megiddo *transliterated name* {2022 har} {4023 megiddo} [717 armageddon] Rendezvous Mountain.
Haran *transliterated name* {2771 charan} [5488 charrhan] Parched.
Harashim/engravers *plural transliterated name* {2798 charashiym} Engravers.
harass, disintegrate *verb* {7492 raats} to break in pieces.
harbor *noun* [3040 limeen] a shelter or haven, usually for boats.
Harchas *transliterated name* {2745 charchac} possibly, Shining.
Harchur *transliterated name* {2744 charchuwr} Inflammation.
hard, stern *adjective* {7186 qasheh} [4642 skleeros] harsh; severe.
hard, stern *verb* {7188 qashach} severe.
harden *verb* {7185 qashah} [4645 skleeruno] literally, or figuratively, to become obstinate.
hardheartedness *noun* [4641 skleerokardia] hardness of heart.
hardnaped *adjective* [4644 skleerotrakeelos] obstinate.
Harha Yah *transliterated name* {2736 charayah} Fearing Yah.
harness, bind *verb* {2280 chabash} to tie, or wrap.
harp *noun* {3658 kinnor} an instrument on which to twang.
harpoon, locust, whirring, cymbal *noun* {6767 tselatsal} a clattering, as of a cymbal; a whirring, as of wings; a rattling, as of a harpoon.
harrow *verb* {7702 sadad} to harrow a field.
hart *noun* {354 ayal} a stag; a male of the red deer.
Harum Aph *transliterated name* {2739 charuwmaph} Devoted Nostrils.
Harus *transliterated name* {2743 charuwts} Earnest.
harvest *noun* {7105 qatsir} [2326 therismos] the harvest as clipped.
harvest *verb* {103 agar} [2325 therizo] to ingather.
harvest, shorten, chop, curtail *verb* {7114 qatsar} literally, or figuratively, to cut off.
harvester *noun* [2327 theristees] one that harvests.
Hasad Yah *transliterated name* {2619 chacadyah} Mercy of Yah.
Hasar Addar *transliterated name* {2692 chatsaraddar} Court of Addar.
Hasar Enan *transliterated name* {2704 chatsareynan} Court of Springs.
Hasar Enon *transliterated name* {2703 chatsareynown} Court of Fountains.

Hasar Gaddah *transliterated name* {2693 chatsargaddah} Court of Treasure.
Hasar Hat Tichon *transliterated name* {2694 chatsarhattiychowa} Court of the Middle.
Hasar Maveth *transliterated name* {2700 chatsarmaveth} Court of Death.
Hasar Shual *transliterated name* {2705 chatsarshuwal} Court of the Fox.
Hasar Susah *transliterated name* {2701chatsarcuwcah} Court of Cavalry.
Hasar Susim *plural transliterated name* {2702 chatsarcuwciym} Court of Horses.
Haserim *plural transliterated name* {2699 chatseriym} (masculine) Courts.
Haseroth *plural transliterated name* {2698 chatserowth} (feminine) Courts.
Haseson Tamar *transliterated name* {2688 chatsetsowntamar} Row of the Palm Tree.
Hashab Yah *transliterated name* {2811 chachabyah} Fabricated of Yah.
Hashabne Yah *transliterated name* {2813 chashabneyah} Machinated of Yah.
Hashbad Danah *transliterated name* {2806 chashbaddanah} Fabricated Rule.
Hashshub *transliterated name* {2815 chashshuwb} Fabricated.
Hasi Ham Menuchiy *transliterated name* {2680 chatsiyhammenachtiy} Of Hasi Ham Menuchoth.
Hasi Ham Menuchoth *plural transliterated name* {2679 chatsiyhammenuchowth} Midst of the Resting Places.
Hasor *transliterated name* {2674 chatsowr} Court.
Hasor Hadattah *transliterated name* {2675 chatsowrchadattah} New Hasor (Court).
haste *noun* {2649 chippazown} hurriedness.
haste, hasten *verb* {2363 chush} {2439 chiysh} {2648 chaphaz} {4116 mahar} to hurry up; to be eager.
hastily chew *verb* {3216 yala} to utter inconsiderately.
hasting, skillful *adjective* {4106 mahir} to hurry along; to be skillful; quick, as skillful.
hasty *adjective* **hastily** *adverb* {4118 maher} hurry; hurriedly.
hate *verb* {8130 sane} {8131 sene} [3404 misseo] to have an intense aversion.
hated *adjective* {8146 sani} disliked intensely.
hateful *adjective* [4767 stugeetos] full of hate.
Hathach *transliterated name* {2047 hathach} of foreign origin; a Persian eunuch.
hatred *noun* {8135 sinah} an intense aversion.
haughtily, high *adverb* {7315 rom} {7317 romah} aloft; proudly.
haughtiness, haughty, height *noun* {7312, 7314 rum} haughty, as in highminded; height, as altitude.
haven *noun* {2348 choph} a place of covering, protection; **see** spare.
Havran *transliterated name* {2362 chavran} Cavernous.
Havvah *transliterated name* {2332 havvah} [2096 Eva] Lifegiver; name of the first female; Adam's woman.
Haza El *transliterated name* {2371 chazael} Seer of El; Seer, as seeing into the future; **cp** prophet.
Haza Yah *transliterated name* {2382 chazayah} Seer of Yah; Seer, as seeing into the future; **cp** prophet.
Hazi El *transliterated name* {2381 haziel} Seer of El; Seer, as seeing into the future; **cp** prophet.
he burro *noun* {2543 chamor} a male burro.
he goat *noun* {8495 tayish} that which butts.
he goats *plural noun* {6260 attud} as prepared; as full grown.
head *noun* [2776 kephalee] the top of the body.
head, first *adjective* {7223 rishon} {7224 rishoniy} head, as at the top; first, as at the beginning.
head, sum *noun* {7217 resh} the top of the body; the sum total.
head, top, beginning, first(s) *noun* {7218 rosh} {7221 rishah} {7225 reshith} {8462 rechillah} the head, in a variety of applications; the head of the body, of time, of the month, of archs.
headpieces *plural noun* {4763 meraashoth} as a headrest.
headships *plural noun* {4761 marashoth} one that heads others.
headstone *noun* {68 eben} {7222 roshah}.
headstruck *verb* [2775 kephalaioo] a strike or wound on the head.
heal *verb* {7495 raphah} [2390 iaomai] to cause to be whole; **see** Yah Veh Raphah.
heal, healed, healthy [*verb* 5198 hugiaino] [*adjective* 5199 hugiees] to cause to be hygenized; to be hygenic; healthy, or healed in body, or in doctrine.
healer *noun* {*plural* 7499 rephuah} [2395 iatros] one who causes another to be whole, healthy; a medicine.
healing *noun* {724 arukah} {4832 marpe} {8644 teruphah} [2386 iama] [2392 iasis] wholeness.
health *noun* {7500 riphuth} the state of wholeness.
heap *noun* {5067 ned} {8510 tel} a mound; as piling up.
heap *noun* {6194 arem} {6652 tsibbur} a pile.
heap *verb* {6192 aram} {6651 tsabar} to pile up; to aggregate.
heap, mortar, chomer *transliterated noun* {2563 chomer} a dry measure as mixed, or heaped.
heaps *noun* {5856 iy} piles of rubble.
hear *verb* {8085 shama} {8086 shema} [191 akouo] to ear.
hearer *noun* [202 akroatees] one that hears.
hearing *noun* {4926 mishmag} that which the ear hears.
hearing, audience, guard *noun* {4928 mishmaath} an audience; also obedience; a subject.
hearing, notoriety, report, fame *noun* {8052 shemuah} {8088 shema} {8089 shoma} [189 akoee] that which is heard; an announcement; a rumor.
hearken *adjective* {7183 qashshab} attending to the ear.
hearken *verb* {238, 239 azan} emphatic of hear.
hearken *verb* {7181 qashab} {7182 qesheb} to attend to the ear.
heart *noun* {3820, 3821 leb} {3824, 3825 lebab} [2588 kardia] the blood pump of the body; symbolically of the center of the will.
hearth *noun* {4018 mebashshelah} a hearth for boiling, or cooking.
heartknowing *adjective* [2589 kardiognostees] knowing the heart.
heat *verb* {2552 chamam} to be, or cause to be hot.
heat, hot *noun* {2527 chom} literally, or figuratively.
heaven, heavens *noun* {*dual* 8064, 8065 shamayim} [3772 ouranos] the lofties; the name of the expanse surrounding the earth; **read** Genesis 1:6–8; in the Old Covenant, the heavens is always dual; in the New Covenant, sometimes singular, sometimes plural.
heavenlies *noun* [2032 epouranios] in the sphere of the heavens.
heavenly *adjective* [3770 ouranios] belonging to, or of the heavens.
heavens (from the) *adverb* [3771 ouranothen].
heaviness, heavy *noun* {3514 kobed} {3517 kebeduth} as in grievous.
heavy, callous *adjective* {3515 kabed} as in grievous; as in thickskinned.
heavy, heaviness *noun* {3514 kobed} {3517 kebeduth} as in grievous.
heavy, honour, callous *verb* {3513 kabed} to esteem; to weigh down; to callous.
Hebraic *transliterated adjective* [1444 hebraikos] [1446 hebrais] [1447 hebraisti] the Hebrew tongue.
Hebrew *transliterated name* {5680, 5681 ibriy} [1445 Hebraios] Of Eber.
hedge *noun* [5418 phragmos] a row of bushes; figuratively, a partition; a separation.
hedge *verb* {5473 cuwq} {7735 sug} {7753 suk} [5418 phragmos] to hedge in; to hem in; to inclose; to plant a row of bushes; to partition; to separate.
heel (restrain the) (trip the) *verb* {6117 aqab} to seize by holding the heel.
heel, heelprint, heel trippers, trip the heel *noun* {6119 aqeb} [4418 pterna] the back of the foot; a print made by the heel; ones that trip the heel by trapping.
Hege *transliterated name* {1896 hege} of Persian origin; a eunuch of Xerxes.
heifer *noun* {5697 eglah} {6510 parah} [1151 damalis] female calf; as being round; as being tame; **cp** calf.
height, haughtiness, haughty *noun* {7312, 7314 rum} haughty, as in highminded; height, as altitude.
height, high *noun* {6967 qomah} the highness.
heir *noun* [2818 kleeronomos] a possessor; one who received by allotment.
Helday *transliterated name* {2469 chelday} Transcient.
Heleph *transliterated name* {2501 cheleph} [256 alphaios] Change; Exchange.
Heleq *transliterated name* {2507 cheleq} Allotment.
Heleqiy *transliterated name* {2516 chelqiy} Of Heleq.
Heleq Dam *transliterated name* {2506 cheleq} {1818 dam} [184

akeldama] Allotment of Blood.
Heles *transliterated name* {2503 chelets} Equipped.
Helqath *transliterated name* {2520 chelqath} Smoothness.
Helqath Has Surim *plural transliterated name* {2521 chelqathhatstsuriym} Smoothness of the Rocks.
Hellas *transliterated name* [1671 hellas] the nation now known as Greece.
Hellene *transliterated name* [1672 hellen] of Hellas.
Hellenic *transliterated name, adjective* [1673 hellenikos] [1676 hellenisti] the tongue of Hellas.
Hellenist *transliterated name* [1674 hellenis] [1675 hellenistees} Of Hellas.
helmet *noun* {3553 kowbah} as being arched.
help *noun* {5828 ezer} aid.
help *verb* **helper** *participle* {5826 azar} to protect; to aid.
Helqai *transliterated name* {2517 helqay} Allotted.
hemorrhage *noun* [131 haimorroeo] a heavy bleeding.
hemorrhoid, mound *noun* {2914 techor} a rising of earth; a rising by inflamation.
Hephsi Bah *transliterated name* {2657 chephtsiybahh} My Delight is in Her.
herb, herbage, herbs *noun* {6211 asab} {6212 eseb} [3001 lakanon] [5528 chortos] annual seed plants used primarily for healing and seasoning.
herbs *plural noun* {2235 zehrohgim} that which is sown.
heresy *transliterated noun* [139 hairesis] an opposing opinion.
Hereth *transliterated name* {2802 chereth} Forest.
heretical *transliterated adjective* [141 hairetikos] that of heresy.
Hermas *transliterated name* [2057 hermas] Of Hermes.
Hermes *transliterated name* [2060 hermees] An angel of Hellene deities.
Hermogenes *transliterated name* [2061 hermogenees] Of the genes of Hermes; **see** Hermes.
Herod *transliterated name* [2264 heerodees] Hero; Heroic.
Herodias *transliterated name* [2266 heerodias] Of Herod.
Herodion *transliterated name* [2267 heerodion] Of Herod.
Hesro *transliterated name* {2695 chetsrow} Court (inclosure).
Hesron *transliterated name* {2696 chetsrown} [2074 esrom] Courtyard.
Hesroniy *transliterated name* {2697 chetsrowniy} Of Hesron.
heterogenetic inductions *dual noun* {3610 kilayim} crossbreed; mix together.
Heth *transliterated name* {2845 cheth} Terrified.
Hethiy *transliterated name* {2850 chittiy} Of Heth.
hew *verb* {2672 chatsab} to cut or carve; as in lumbering, mining, or quarrying.
hewed, hewn *adjective* {4274 machtseh}.
hexsect *verb* {8338 shawshaw} {8341 shashah} to divide into sixths.
Hezyon *transliterated name* {2383 chezyown} Seer; One who foresees.
Hi El *transliterated name* {2419 chiel} Life of El.
Hidday *transliterated name* {1914 hidday} of uncertain derivative.
hidden treasure *noun* {4301 matmon} {*plural* 4362 mikman} {*plural* 4710 mitspunim} {6840 tsaphin} {8226 saphan} a secreted valuable.
Hiddeqel *transliterated name* {2313 chiddeqel} of foreign origin; the Tigris river.
hide *verb* {2244 chaba} {2247 chabah} to withhold from view.
hide, bury *verb* {2934 taman} to hide by covering.
hide, cover, demolish *verb* {5641 sathar} {5642 sethar} to conceal by covering; to demolish and cover over.
hide, treasure *verb* {6845 tsaphan} to hide by covering over; to reserve, or protect.
hiding *noun* {2253 chebon} a withholding from view.
Hierapolis *transliterated name* [2404 hieropolis] Holy City.
hierarch, vapour *noun* {5387 nasi} [747 archeegos] a chief leader; as being first, foremost; also a vapour, as a rising mist.
hierarchy, beginning *noun* [746 arche] chief; origin; as being first, foremost.
high, haughtily *adverb* {7315 rom} {7317 romah} aloft; proudly.
high, height *noun* {4791 marom} {5299 naphah} elevation; elation.
high, height *noun* {6967 qomah} the highness.
high forehead *adjective* {1371 gibbeagh} as a frontal balding.
high forehead *noun* {1372 gabbachath} frontal baldness.
highway *noun* {4546 mecillah} {4547 masluwl} [1327 diexodes] an exitway.
hilarious *noun* [2431 hilaros] merriness; promptness or willingness.
hilarity *adjective* [2432 hilarotees] merry; prompt or willing.
hill *noun* {5316 nephet} a height.
Hillel *transliterated name* {1985 hillel} Halal; **see** halal.
Hilqi Yah *transliterated name* {2518 hilqiyah} Alloted of Yah.
hin *transliterated noun* {1969 hiyn} a unit of liquid measure.
hind leg, leg *noun* {7785 shoq} the leg of a biped; the hind leg of a quadruped.
hindrance *noun* {4622 matsor} an obstacle.
hire *noun* {4909 maskoreth} {7938 seker} {7939 sakar} reward, or return of that earned as a hireling.
hire *verb* {7936 sakar} {8566 tanah} to employ.
hireling *noun* {7916 sakir} {7917 sekirah} [3407 misthios] [3411 misthotos] one that is hired; an employee.
hiss *verb* {659 epha} {8319 sharaq} the sound of a prolonged s; used to show disapproval.
hisser *noun* {660 epheh} {6848 tsepha} that which hisses.
hisses, hissing *noun* {*plural* 8292 sheruqah} {8322 shereqah}.
Hizqi *transliterated name* {2395 chizqi} Strong.
ho *transliterated participle, interjection* {1945 howy} an interjection of surprise, delight, exultation.
hoarfrost, tankard *noun* {3713 kephor} a covering; hoarfrost, as covering the ground; a tankard, as a covered vessel.
Hodav Yah *transliterated name* {1938, 1939 hodavyah} Majesty of Yah.
Hodev Yah *transliterated name* {1937 howdevah} Majesty of Yah.
Hodi Yah *transliterated name* {1940, 1941 hodiyah} Majesty of Yah.
hoe *noun* {4282 macharesheth} {4576 mader} an instrument for picking; **cp** pick.
hoe, lack, arrange, fail *verb* {5737 adar} to miss having; to arrange a vineyard, as in hoeing.
Hoglah *transliterated name* {2295 choglah} possibly, a Partridge.
holding, holdings *noun* {4943 mesheq} {5232 nekac} {5233 nekec} [*plural* 5224 huparkonta] from the verb, hold: one's possessions including investments.
hole *noun* {3975 meurah} a crevice.
hole *noun* {5357 naqiyq} a boring in the rock.
hollow *noun* {5014 nabab} that which is empty inside.
hollow, palm, paw, sole, bowl *noun* {3709 kaph} {6447 pas} {8168 shoal} a hollow of the hand, foot, paw, or body; also utensils with a hollow.
hollow depressions *plural noun* {8258 sheqarurah}.
holocaust *noun* {*plural* 1890 habhabim} {5928 alah} {5930 olah} [*transliteration* 3646 holokautoma] a sacrificial burning.
holocaust, ascent *noun* {5930 olah} an ascent to a higher area; an offering that has been holocausted; **see** holocaust, *verb.*
holocaust, mount, regurgitate, ascend *verb* {5927, 5928 alah} to ascend, as a mountain; to mount an animal; to regurgitate food; to ascend a holocaust; **see** holocaust, *noun.*

- **SUMMARY:**
- **HOLY, HOLIES, HALLOW:**
- **holies** *noun* {4720 miqdash} {6944 qodesh} [39 hagion] the outer court of the tabernacle; where the congregation congregated, where the doctrinating took place; the Old Covenant equivalant of the New Covenant priestal precinct; **cp** holy of holies; **see** congregation; **see** tabernacle.
- **holily** *adverb* [55 hagnos] in a holy manner.
- **holiness** *noun* [38 hagiasmos] [41 hagiotees] [42 hagiosunee] [47 hagnia] [54 hagnotees] the character of being holy.
- **holy (one)** *adjective* {6918 qadosh} {6922 qaddish} spiritually whole; set apart unto Elohim.
- **holy (the)** *noun* [40 hagios] that which has been hallowed; they who have been hallowed – set apart unto Elohim; whereas many versions interchange the words holy and saints, the *exeGeses* abides with holy.
- **holy of holies** *noun* {6944 qodesh} [39 hagion] the inner court of the tabernacle; corresponds to the nave in the New Covenant; **see** SUMMARY: TABERNACLE, TEMPLE, TENT:.
- **hallow, hallowing** *verb* {6942 qadash} [37 hagiazo] [48 hagnizo] [49 hagnismos] [53 hagnos] verb of holy; whereas many versions interchange the words sanctify and hallow, the *exeGeses* abides with hallow.
- **hallowed whore** *noun* {6948 qedeshah} a female whore for religious service.
- **hallowed whoremonger** *noun* {6945 qadesh} a male whore for religious service.

home (at) *verb* [1736 endeemeo] figuratively, as in the body.
home (away from) *verb* [1553 ekdeemeo] figuratively, as out of the body.
homolies *transliterated noun* [3657 homilia] wording together.
homologize *transliterated verb* [3656 homileo] [3662 homoiazo] to word together.
homosexual *noun* [733 arsenokoitees] sexual desires for one of the same sex.
honour *noun* {3519 kabod} esteem.
honour, heavy, callous *verb* {3513 kabad} to esteem; to weigh down; to callous.
honour, honourable *adjective* {3520 kebuddah} [1784 entimos] one of esteem.
honour, price *noun* [5092 timee] of esteem; of value; money paid.
honour, price *verb* [5091 timao] to esteem; to value.
hoof *noun* {6541 parcah} the horn-like foot of some animals.
hook *noun* {2397 chach} {2443 chakkah} {*dual* 8240 shaphath} as an ornament, or as a grappler.
hook, shield, cold *noun* {6793 tsinnah} coldness, as piercing; a hook, as pointed; a shield, as a prickler.
hook, thorn *noun* {5518 sirah} {*plural* 7165 qeresim} literally, a boiler; a hook; a thorn.
hope *noun* {3689 kecel} {8431 towcheleth} {8615 tiqvah} [1680 elpis] a high expectation.
hope *verb* [1679 elpizo] to fully expect.
hope, cord *noun* {8615 tiqvah} hope, as to hang on to; a cord, to hang on to.
Hor Hag Gidgad *transliterated name* {2735 chorhaggidgad} Hole of the Cleft.
horn *noun* {7161, 7162 qeren} [2768 keras] a bonelike growth on the head of some animals; a music instrument.
Horonayim *dual transliterated name* {2773 choronayim} Double Hole.
horoscopist *noun* {1895 habar} {2748 chartom} {2749 chartom} one who foretells events by the zodiac.
horrible *adjective* **horribly** *adverb* {8186 shaarurith} of horror.
horror, whirling *noun* {8178 saar} a whirling of a storm; a shuddering of horror.
horse, swallow *noun* {5483 cuc} {5484 cucah} a horse as leaping; a swallow as flitting.
Hosay *transliterated name* {2335 chowzay} Seer, as seeing into the future; **cp** prophet.
Hosha Yah *transliterated name* {1955 hoshayah} Salvation of Yah; **cp** Hoshia Na.
Hoshea *transliterated name* {1954 hoshea} [5617 hosee] Deliverer.
Hoshia Na *transliterated saying* {3467 yasha} {4994 na} [5614 hosanna] Save, we beseech; **see** beseech.
host, hosting *verb* {6633 tsaba} to assemble a host.
host, hosts *noun* **Sabaoth** *transliterated title* {6635 tsebaah *plural* tsabaoth} [3841 pantokrator] [*plural* 4519 sabaoth] of hosts; a vast array of warriors; often compounded with El and with Yah Veh; [4519 sabaoth] is the Hellenic transliteration of sabaoth, only in Romans 9:29, and Yaaqovos 5:4; [3841 pantokrator] is the Hellenic translation of sabaoth, only in 2 Corinthians 6:18, and throughout the Apocalypse; **see** host.
host, swell *verb* {6638 tsabah} to assemble a host; to swell up.
hot [2200 zestos] boiling hot; metaphorically of fervor of mind and zeal.
hot springs *plural noun* {3222 yamim}.
hot, heat *noun* {2527 chom} literally, or figuratively.
hour (half) *noun* [2256 heemiorion] one half of one literal hour.
hour *noun* [5610 hora] a specific period of time; an indefinite period of time, as the hour of Yah Shua's parousia.
house (whole) *noun* [3832 panoiki] with the whole family.
house *noun* [3612 oikeema] a house to guard persons.
house, household, housing, bayith, beth *noun* {1004, 1005 bayith, beth} [3613 oikeeteerion] [3614 oikia] [3624 oikos] usually translated house, as in family or dwelling, except when part of a name, as in Beth Abara; **cp** manse; nave; palace; priestal precinct.
houseguard *noun* [3626 oikouros] one who guards a house.
household *noun* [3609 oikios] [3615 oikiakos] members of a house; domestics, and all who are under the authority of the same householder.
housekeeper *noun* [3610 oiketees] one who keeps house.
housedespotes *masculine noun* [3617 oikodespotes] despotes (head) of the house; **see** despotes.
housedespotes *feminine verb* [3616 oikodespoteo] to be despotes (head) of the house.
hover *verb* {7363 rachaph} to hover over; to brood as a bird over her chicks.
howl (caused us to) *verb* {8437 tolal} to cause to emit a wailing cry.
howl *verb* {3213 yalal} a wailing cry.
howling *adjective* {3214 yelel} a wailing cry.
howling *noun* {3215 yelalah} a wailing cry.
hubris *transliterated noun* [5196 hubris] insolence; arrogance; violence.
hubs *plural noun* {2840 chishshur} as attached; **see** spokes.
human, humanity *noun* {119 adam} {120 adam} {121 adam} [444 anthropos] Adam {121 adam} is the name of the first adami (human) {120 adam}; who is the first anthropo (human) [444 anthropos]; Yah Shua Messiah, the son of Yah Veh, was born by the Holy Spirit through a woman; He is the son of humanity, not the son of man; a human being consists of at least three attributes: body, soul, spirit.
human, humanly *adjective* [442 anthropinos] as human.
humanity pleaser *noun* [441 anthropareskos] one who tries to please humanity.
humble *adjective* {6035 anav} {6041 aniy} [5011 tapinos] lowered in esteem or status.
humble, humbling, subdue *verb* {3665 kana} {6031 anab} {6033 anah} {6039 enuth} {6800 tsana} [5013 tapino] to cause to bend the knee; to knuckle under; to lower in esteem or status.
humblemindedness *noun* [5012 tapinophrosunee] of humble mind.
humbleness *noun* {6037 anvah} lowered in esteem or status.
humbling, subdue, humble *verb* {3665 kana} {6031 anab} {6033 anah} {6039 enuth} {6800 tsana} [5013 tapino] to cause to bend the knee; to knuckle under; to lower in esteem or status.
humiliation *noun* {6040 oniy} a disesteeming humbling.
humility *noun* {6038 anavah} humbleness.
hunt *verb* {6679 tsud} [2614 katadioko] to lurk for, and hunt down.
hunt, hunter *noun* {6718 tsaid} {6719 tsaad} {6720 tsedah} that which is hunted; one that hunts.
hunthold, lair, lure *noun* {4679 metsadah} {4685 metsodah} {4686 matsudah} a hunter's hideout; a lair; a lure.
Huqqoq *transliterated name* {2712 chuqqoq} Statute Setter.
Hur *transliterated name* {2354 chur} White.
hurl, deceive *verb* {7411 ramah} {7412 ramah} to throw; to betray.
hurl, throw, cast *verb* {7993 shalak} to throw out, down, or away.
hurricane *noun* {5492 cuphah} {5591 caar} a violent cyclone.
hurricaned *verb* {5590 caar} to toss.
hurry *verb* {5789 uwsh} to hasten.
hush *verb* {*imperative* 2013 hacah} {2814 chashah} to quiet.
hush, plow *verb* {2790 charash} literally, to scratch; to silence.
hush, subside *verb* {8367 shathaq} from the root, to subside.
Hushay *transliterated name* {2365 chuwshay} Hasty.
Hymenaeus *transliterated name* [5211 humenaios] God of Marriage.
hymn *transliterated noun* [5215 humnos] a song of praise.
hymn *transliterated verb* [5214 humneo] to sing in praise.
hyssop *transliterated noun* {231 ezob} [5301 hussopos] an aromatic plant used as a remedy for bruises.

I

I AM *title* {1961 hayah} [1473 ego] [1510 eimi] the eternal existant one; **cp** Yah; **note:** Whenever the scripture presents Yah Veh or Yah Shua as the eternal existant one, the *exeGeses* indicates with all capital letters, thus: **I AM.**
Ibsan *transliterated name* {78 ibtsan} Splendid.
ice, crystal, frost *noun* {7140 qerach} as being smooth.
icon (sun) *noun* {2553 chamman} an image of the sun.
icon *transliterated noun* [1504 ikon] a likeness; an image.
idol *transliterated noun* {434, 457 eliyl} {*plural* 1544 gillul} {6091 azab} [1497 idolon] an image or other object of worship.
idol, contorting, contortion *noun* {6089 etseb} {6090 otseb} {6092 atseb} {6093 itstsabon} an earthen vessel; a writhing as in pain; **see** contort *verb*.
idol, worthless *noun* {434 elul} {457 elil} of no worth.
idol of awe *noun* {4656 miphletseth} an idol of reverence.
idol sacrifice *noun* [1494 idolothuton] a sacrifice to an idol.

idolater *transliterated noun* [1496 idololatrees] an idol worshipper.
idolatrous (downright) *transliterated adjective* [2712 katidolos] utterly idolatrous.
idolatry *transliterated noun* [1495 idolotatria] a worship of an idol.
idoleon *transliterated noun* [1493 idolion] a place of idol worship.
idolize, contort, form *verb* {6087 atsab} to form; to contort; as in idolizing, to writhe in pain.
if not, unless *participle* {3884 looleh}.
if only, if though, O that *interjection* {3863 luw} as a petition.
ignoble *adjective* [36 agenes] without genos.
Ilay *transliterated name* {5866 iylay} Ascended.
image *noun* {6754, 6755 tselem} semblance.
imagery, imagination *noun* {4906 maskiyth} images of stone; images of the imagination.
Immanu El *transliterated name* {6005 immanuel} [1694 emmanoueel] El With Us.
immeasurably *adverb* [280 ametros] without measure; unable to measure.
immoveable *adjective* [277 ametakineetos] not moveable.
immutable *adjective* **immutability** *noun* [276 ametathetos] unchangeable; unchangeability.
impartial *adjective* [87 adiakritos] not critical.
imparting, partaking *verb* [2841 koinoneo] communing and partaking by imparting.
impending, ready, treasured *adjective* {6259, 6264 athud} {6263 athid} prepared; treasured.
impossible *adjective* [418 anendekton] unable to be.
impossible, impotent *adjective* [101 adunateo] [102 adunatos] not able; without ability.
impoverish *verb* [4433 ptokuo] to be poor.
impoverish *verb* {4134 mowk} to become lean.
impoverish *verb* {7567 rashash} to cause to be poor by demolishing.
impoverish, lack *verb* {7326 rush} verb of poverty; to be destitute; **see** poverty.
impudence *noun* [335 anaidia] insolence.
impudent *adjective* {6277 athaq} in the sense of being carried away.
impure *adjective* [169 akathartos] not pure; **cp** pure.
impurity *noun* [167 akatharsia] [168 akathartees] without purity; **cp** purity.
in law *noun* {2860 chathan} a relative through marriage.
in order to, on account of, so (as) (that) *participle* {4616 maan} {5668 abur} for the purpose of.
inactivate *verb* [2673 katargeo] to render inactive; to abolish.
inadvertent error *noun* {7684 shegagah} unintentional error.
inadvertently err, err inadvertently *verb* {7683 shagag} {7686 shagah} to err unintentionally.
incense *adjective* [2367 thuinos] fragrant.
incense *noun* {6988 qetorah} {7002 qitter} {7004 qetoreth} [2368 thumiama] aromatic fumes; **cp** frankincense.
incense *verb* {4729 miqtar} {6999 qatar} {7002 qitter} {7004 qetoreth} [2370 thumiao] to fume aromatics.
incident, coincidence *noun* {6294 pega} casual impact.
incise *verb* {8295 sarat} to cut the flesh; forbidden by Yah Veh; **cp** circumcise; **cp** eunuchize.
incision *noun* {8296 sareteth} a cutting in the flesh; forbidden by Yah Veh; **cp** circumcision; **cp** eunuchize.
incision, incisor, minings, sickle, trench, decision, incisors *noun* [2699 katatome] mutilators; **cp** circumcise; **cp** eunuchize.
incision, incisor, ore, sickle, trench, decision, decisive *adjective, noun* {2742 charuts} literally, mentally, or soulically, an incising.
inclose, lock, shod, enclose *verb* {5274 naal} {7000 qatar} to fasten; **see** shoe.
inconvenient *adjective* [428 anuthetos] not wellsuited.
incorruptibility *noun* [861 aphtharsia] not decayable.
incorruptible *adjective* [862 aphthartos] not subject to decay.
incorruptible *noun* [90 adiaphthoria] not corrupt.
increase *noun* {6451 piccah} an expansion.
increase *noun* {7679 saga} an increase through growth.
increase *noun, adjective* **increasingly** *adverb* {4766 marbeh} {4767 mirbah} {4768 marbith} an oversupply; an oversupplying.
increase *verb* {7680 sega} {7685 sagah} to increase through growth.
increase, add, again, augment *verb* {3254 yacaph} to add to; to repeat.
increasing, many, mighty, much, very, exceeding, greatly *adjective* {7689, 7690 saggiy} superlatively mighty, or large.
indebted *verb* [3784 ophilo] to be under obligation; to owe.
indeed *adverb* [3689 ontos] in reality; in truth.
indeed, therefore, then *adverb* [686 ara] truly; in point of fact; the idea of drawing a conclusion.
indescribable *adjective* [411 ankdieegeetos] unable to describe; **cp** inexpressible.
indicate, designate *verb* {5567 caman} [322 anadiknumi] to show; to appoint.
indignation *noun* [24 aganakteesis] resentment.
indignify *verb* [23 aganakteo] to resent.
indwell *verb* [1774 enoikeo] to dwell within.
inexcusable *adjective* [379 anapologeetos] without pleadability.
inexhaustible *adjective* [413 anekliptos] unable to explore competely.
inexpressible *adjective* [412 aneklaleetos] [731 arreetos] unable to express; **cp** indescribable.
infant *noun* {5768 olal} [1025 brephos] a young baby; **see** suckling.
inflame, flame *verb* **flaming** *adjective* {3857 lahat} {3859 laham} to blaze; that which is inflamed by fire.
inflame, kindle, scorch *verb* {2734 charah} {2787 charar} {6866 zarab} literally, or soulically, to glow; to blaze up.
inflamed, flamed *adjective* {6867 tsarebeth} [4092 pimpramai] as burning.
ingathering, gathering *noun* {*plural* 624 acuppim} {625 oceph} {626 acephah} {*plural* 627 acuppah} {628 a**cp**ecuph} {6910 qebutsah} a collection of offerings, fruits, people, or learned persons.
ingot *noun* {7192 qesitah} an ingot, as weighed and stamped for a coin.
ingraft *verb* [1461 enkentrizo] to cut into for the sake of inserting a scion; to graft in.
inherit *verb* {5157 nachal} [2816 kleeronomeo] [2820 kleero–omai] to come into possession by allotment.
inheritance *noun* {5159 nachalah} [2817 kleeronomia] the acquisition of a possession by allotment.
injure *verb* [91 adikeo] verb of injustice; to be unjust; **see** injustice.
injustice *noun* [92 adikeema] [93 adikia] an injury; **see** unjust.
inkling *noun* {8102 shemets} a slight emission
inkwell *noun* {7083 qeceth} a container for ink.
inner, inward *adjective* {6442 peniymiy} the inside of; **cp** out, outward.
innermost depths *noun* {4278 mechqar} that which is scrutinized.
innocency *noun* {5356 niqqaon} guiltlessness.
innocent, exonerated *adjective* {5355 naqi} [172 akakos] not guilty.
inopportune *adjective* [170 akaieomai] without opportunity.
inopportunely *adverb* [171 akairos] without opportunity.
inquire precisely *verb* [198 akriboo] to interrogate exactly.
inquire, require, seek, enquire, examine *verb* {1875 darash} to ask; to seek; **cp** beseech.
insane *noun* {7696 shaga} one that raves.
insanity *noun* {7697 shiggaon} a raving.
inscribe, chart *verb* {3789 kathab} {3790 kethab} {3799 katham} [1449 engrapho] to scribe; **see** scribe.
inscribing *noun* {3791, 3792 kethab} {4385 miktab} [1121 gramma] a writing; **cp** scribe.
inscription *noun* {3793 kethobeth} a tattoo on the skin; a caption; **see** superscription.
insignificant *adjective* **lessen** *verb* {6994 qaton} [1642 elattoo] a diminishing in rank or influence.
inspection *noun* {4935 mishiy} to examine thoroughly.
instability *adjective* [181 akatastasia] disorder; **see** unstable.
instead, in stead *participle* {8478 tachath} in lieu of.
instrument *noun* {3627 keliy} including, but not limited to music, ornament, weapon.
insubordinate, unsubjected *adjective* [506 anupotaktos] not subject to; refusing subordination.
integrious *adjective* **integriously** *adverb* {8535 tam} {8549 tamim} in consummate wholeness.
integrious *noun* **consummate, consume** *verb* {8552 tamam} to finish off; to cause to be in consummate wholeness.
integrity *noun* {4974 methom} {8537 tom} {8538 tummah} consummate wholeness.

intent, intention *noun* {6656 tseda} {7454 rea} {7470 reuth} {7476 raon} that which one attends to do; **see** tend.
intently *adverb* [1616 ektenia] [1617 ektenesteron] earnestly.
intercede *verb* [1793 entunkano] to intervene in behalf of.
intercede, reach, encounter *verb* {6293 paga} to impinge.
interest *noun* {4855 mashsha} a loan, interest on a loan; **cp** usuary.
intermarry, in law *verb* {2859 chathan} to contract affinity by marriage.
interpret *verb* {6590 peshar} to give the meaning of; **cp** translate; **note:** dreams are interpreted; tongues are translated.
interpretation *noun* {6591 peshar} {6592 pesher} {6623 pithron} an explanation of the meaning of; **cp** translation; **note:** dreams are interpreted; tongues are translated.
interval *noun* [1292 diasteema] a space between.
intimidate *verb* [1286 diasio] to make timid or fearful.
intoxicant *noun* {7941 shekar} [4608 sikera] that which intoxicates; an intoxicating agent.
intoxicate *verb* {7937 shakar} [3182 methuskomai] [3184 methuo] to drink unto intoxication; to cause intoxication.
intoxicated *adj* {7910 shikkor} one who is intoxicated.
intoxicated, intoxication *noun* {7943 shekar} [3178 methee] the state of being intoxicated.
intoxicator *noun* [3183 methusos] one who intoxicates.
intreat *verb* {6279 athar} to petition with urgency.
intrigue *noun* {2154 zimmah} {2162 zamam} {4209 mezimmah} conspiracy; strategy.
intrigue *verb* {2161 zamam} to conspire, to strategize.
invalidate *verb* [208 akuroo] to unconfirm.
invigoration *noun* {4241 michyah} from the root of enliven; the sustenance of life.
inviolable *adjective* [531 aparabatos] not violated.
invisible *adjective* [517 aoratos] incapable of being seen.
inward, inner *adjective* {6442 peniymiy} the inside of; **cp** out, outward.
inward, middle, midst, within, among *noun* {7130 qereb} {8432 tavek} the nearest part; the center.
inwards *plural noun* {4577, 4578 meah} the innards; the intestines; figuratively, of sympathy, or empathy.
iota *transliterated noun* [2503 iota] the tenth letter of the Hebrew alphabet, and the eighth letter of the Hellenic alphabet; the minutest part.
Iqqesh *transliterated name* {6142 iqqesh} Perverted.
Ir Ham Melach/City of Salt *transliterated name* {5898 iyrhammelach} City of Salt.
Ir Nachash/City of the Serpent *transliterated name* {5904 iyrnachash} City of the Serpent.
iron *noun* {1270 barzel} {6523 parzel} as an ore; as an instrument of cutting.
irreverence *plural noun* [763 asebia] without reverence.
irreverent *adjective* [765 asebees] without reverence.
irreverently *adverb* [764 asebeo] to act without reverence for.
irritate, thunder *verb* {7481 raam} to agitate; to be agitated.
Ish Bosheth *transliterated name* {378 ishbosheth} Man of Shame.
Ish Hod *transliterated name* {379 iyshhowd} Man of Majesty.
Ish Tob *transliterated name* {382 ishtob} Man of Goodness.
island *noun* {336, 339 iy} [3520 nesos] a habitable spot of land.
island howlers *plural noun* {338 eieyim} a howler of an island.
isle *noun* [3519 neesion] a small island.
Ithi El *transliterated name* {384 ithiel} Blithed of El.
Ittay *transliterated name* {863 ittay} Near.
ivory, tooth, tusk, crag *noun* {8127, 8128 shen} {*plural* 8143 shenhabbim} [3599 adous] as being sharp.
Iy Ezer *transliterated name* {372 iyezer} No Help.
Iy Ezeriy *transliterated name* {373 iyezriy} Of Iy Ezer.
Iy Chabod *transliterated name* {350 iychabowd} No Honour.
Iy Thamar *transliterated name* {385 iythamar} Coast of the Palm.
Iy Zebel *transliterated name* {348 iyzebel} [2403 iezabeel] No Residing.
Iye Ha Abarim *plural transliterated name* {5863 iyeyhaabariym} Heaps of the Passers.
Iyim *plural transliterated name* {5864 iyiym} Heaps.
Iyob *transliterated name* {347 iyowb} [2492 iob] Persecuted.
Iyon *transliterated name* {5859 iyown} Heap.

J

Jambres *transliterated name* [2387 iambrees] the meaning uncertain.
jasper *noun* [2393 iaspis] a precious stone of divers colors; thought to be dark green or opalescent.
javelin *noun* {7420 romach} from being hurled.
jaw, cheek *noun* {3895 lechi} the side, or the bottom of the face.
jealous, zealous *adjective* **envy, suspect** *verb* {7065 qana} {7067 qanna} {7072 qannow} to be zealous, as jealous, or envious.
jealousy, suspicion, envy *noun* {7068 qinah} zeal, as jealousy, or envy.
jeering *adjective* {3934 laeg} **see** deride.
jinglers *plural noun* {4698 metsillah} little bells that jingle; **see** cymbals.
join *verb* {2338 chut} literally, to thread together; **see** thread.
join, attach, contrive *verb* {6775 tsamad} to link; to gird; mentally, to contrive.
join, charm *verb* {2266 chabar} literally, to join objects; to cast spells.
join, lend, borrow *verb* {3867 lavah} literally, to entwine; to become wrapped up in, as a borrower, or as a lender.
join, stick, adhere *verb* {1692 dabaq} {1693 debaq} [4347 proskollao] to join one's self to closely; stick to; to remain attached.
joint *noun* {2279 chobereth} {4225 machbereth} {*plural* 4226 mechabberoth} a place of joining.
journey *verb* [3593 hodeuo] [3596 hodoiporeo] [4922 sunodeuo] to travel; **see** sojourn.
journey, way *noun* {1870 derek} a road, as trodden; a walkway; figuratively, the journey of life.
journey, way *noun* {4550 macca} [3597 hodiporia] [3598 hodos] a trip; **see** sojourn.
joy *noun* {4885 masows} from the verb, rejoice.
jubile *transliterated noun* {3104 yobel} the celebration of the year of jubile; **read** Leviticus 25:10–54, 27:17–24.

- **SUMMARY:**
- **JUDGE, JUDGMENT, JUST, JUSTNESS,**
- **JUSTIFICATION, JUSTICE:**
- **judge, plead, examine** *verb* {8199 shaphat} {8200 shephat} [350 anakrino] [2919 krino] to scrutinize; to investigate.
- **judge, judger** *noun* {6414 palil} [1348 dikastees] [2923 kritees] [2924 kritikos] one that decides; one that sentences.
- **judgment (under)** *verb* [5267 hupodikos] under sentence.
- **judgment** *adjective, noun* {6416 pelili} {6417 peliliah} [2917 krima] [2920 krisis] [2922 kriterion] decision; crisis; criterion.
- **judgment, examination** *noun* [351 anakrisis] investigation.
- **judgment, justification** *noun* {1779 duwn} {4941 mishpat} {8196 shephut} {*plural* 8201 shephet} [1345 dikaioma] [1347 dikaiosis] [1349 dikee] a judicial verdict; a sentence; also, an unsentencing.
- **judicators** *plural noun* {8614 tiphtay}.
- **jurisdiction** *noun* {4082, 4083 mediynah} a district under a judge.
- **just, justness** *adjective* {6662 tsaddiq} {6664 tsedeq} {6665 tsidqah} {6666 tsedaqah} [1342 dikaios] [1343 dikaiosunee] [1738 endikos] having justness; innocent in the sense of not having unjustness: whereas most versions alternate between just, justness and righteous, righteousness, just and justness are more accurate; this is the root of the Hellene word, Sadducees, transliterated Sadoqiy; **see** Yah Veh Sidqenu.
- **just judgment** *noun* [1341 dikaiokrisia] a just sentence.
- **justice** *noun* {6415 pelilah} a right judgment of that which is just.
- **justification, judgment see judgment, justification.**
- **justify, justified** *verb* {6663 tsadaq} [1344 dikaioo] to cause to be just; **see** just.
- **justly** *adverb* [1346 dikaios] **see** just.

juice *noun* {3955 leshad} {8492 tirosh} as freshly squeezed.
jump *verb* {5539 salad} to leap.
jump for joy *adjective* {5938 alez} {5947 alliyz} a physical expression of praise.
jump for joy *verb* {5937 alaz} {5970 alats} [20 agalliasis] [21 agalliao] to physically express praise.
jumping for joy *noun* {5951 alitsuth} a physical expression of praise.
juniper *noun* {7574 rethem} a species of evergreen shrub.
just, justness, see • SUMMARY: JUDGE, JUDGEMENT:

K

Kaisar *transliterated title* [2541 kaisar] title of the Roman sovereign; the Hellene form for Tsar.
Kaisaria *transliterated name* [2542 kaisaria] Kaisar City.
Kaleb *transliterated name* {3612 kaleb} Dog.
Kaleb Ephrathah *transliterated name* {3613 kalebephrathah} Dog of Fruitbearing.
Kalebiy *transliterated name* {3614 kalebiy} Of Kaleb.
Kalkol *transliterated name* {3633 kalkol} Sustenance.
Kalubay *transliterated name* {3621 keluwbay} Dog.
Kaluhay *transliterated name* {3622 keluwhay} Finished.
kammon *transliterated noun* {3646 kammon} [2951 kuminon] a dill or fennel.
Kaphar Nachum *transliterated name* {3723 kaphar} {5151 nachum} [2584 kapernaoum] Comfort Village.

- **SUMMARY: KAPPORETH, KAPUR/ATONE,**
- **KIPPURIM/ATONEMENTS, KOPUR/ATONEMENT**
- **kapporeth** *noun* {3727 kapporeth} [2435 hilasteerion] the atonement cover of the holy ark.
- **kapur/atone** *verb* {3722 kapar} [2433 hilaskomai] [2436 hileos] to expiate the guilt of by sufferance of penalty or some equivalent; to make complete satisfaction for.
- **kippurim/atonements** *plural transliterated noun* {3725 kippurim} expiations; **see** Yom Kippurim.
- **koper/atonement** *noun* {3724 kopher} [2434 hilasmos] an expiation: **see** camphire, pitch.

Karmel/orchard *transliterated name, noun* {3759 karmel} a planting of fruit trees; an orchard.
Karmeliy *transliterated name* {3761 karmeliy} Of Karmel.
keep, make, serve, do *verb* {5648 abad} in the sense of serving.
Kelach *transliterated name* {3625 kelach} Maturity.
Kenaan *transliterated name* **merchant** *noun* {3667 kenaan} [5477 chanaan] merchant; made to bend the knee; humiliated; name of a person; name of a land.
Kenaanah *transliterated name* {3668 kenaanah} Humiliated.
Kenaaniy *transliterated name* {3669 kenaaniy} [2581 kananitees] [5478 chananaios] Of Kenaan; **see** Kenaan.
Kenan Yah *transliterated name* {3663 kenanyah} Planted of Yah.
Kepha *transliterated name* {3710 keph} [2786 keephas] Rock; Kepha is the Hellene transliteration of the Hebrew Keph; Petros is the Hellenic translation of Keph; **cp** Petros.
Keran *transliterated name* {3763 keran} of uncertain derivative.
kernal, bundle *noun* {6872 tseror} a package, as a parcel, as a particle.
kernel *noun* {*plural* 6507 perudah} {7666 shabar} {7668 sheber} [2848 kokkos] a seed within a hard shell; grain, as broken into kernels.
kernels (market for) *verb* {7666 shabar} to purchase kernels.
Kesediy, Kesediym *transliterated name* {3679 kacday} {*plural* 3778 kasdiym} {3779 kasday} [5466 chaldaios] Of Kesed.
Kesil *transliterated name* **fool** *noun* {3684 kecil} {5530 sakal} a constellation; stupid, or silly.
key *noun* [2807 klis] an instrument for shutting a lock; figuratively, used to denote power and authority.
Kil Ab *transliterated name* {3609 kilab} Restraint of His Father.
Kilyon *transliterated name* {3630 kilyown} Failing.
kin, kindred *noun* {4129 moda} {4130 modaath} {4138 moledeth} [4772 sungenia] [4773 sungenees] blood relatives.
kind, kinder, kindness [5543 kreestos] as useful; benevolent.
kindle, burn *verb* {3341 yatsah} {5400 nasaq} {6919 qadach} to set on fire; to desolate.
kindle, inflame, scorch *verb* {2734 charah} {2787 charar} {6866 zarab} literally, or soulically, to glow; to blaze up.
kinflesh, flesh *noun* {7607 sheer} {7608 shaarah} flesh, as food; flesh, as near of kin.
Kinneroth *transliterated name* {3672 kinnerowth} [1082 genneesaret] Harpist.
kiss (ardently) *verb* [2705 kataphileo] to kiss earnestly.
kiss *noun* {5390 neshiqah} to touch with the lips.
kiss *verb* {5401 nashaq} as attaching; as fastening.
kiss, befriend *verb* {5401 nashaq} [5368 phileo] [5370 phileema] the Hellene is the verb of friend; a soulical expression of fondness; to kiss as a form of attachment; **cp** love; **read** Yahn 21:15–17.
Kithlish *transliterated name* {3798 kithliysh} Wall of a Man.
Kittiy *transliterated name* {3794 kittiy} Of Cyprus; an islander.
Kiymah *transliterated noun* {3598 kiymah} the name of a cluster of stars.
Kiyun *transliterated name* {3594 kiyun} [4481 remphan] an idolic statue; the Hellene is an incorrect transliteration of the Hebrew.
knee *noun* {1290, 1291 bereck} [1119 gonu] the joint between the upper and lower leg.
kneel, bless *verb* {1288 barak} {1289 berak} [3107 makarios] to beatify; the Hebrew also means to kneel in adoration.
kneel, knuckle under *verb* {3766 kara} [1120 gonupeteo] to bend the knee; to fall to the knee.
knife, razor, sheath *noun* {8593 taar} a knife, or a razor, as making bare; a sheath, as being bare.
knobs *plural noun* {6497 peqaim} literally, openers.
knock *verb* {5368 neqash} {6375 piq} as in knees knocking.
know *verb* [1097 ginosko] to be aware of facts.
know, acknowledge *verb* [1921 epiginosko] to recognize; to become acquainted with.
know, perceive *verb* {3045 yada} {3046 yeda} [143 aisthanomai] [1492 eido] [5274 hupolambano] to be aware through the senses.
know exactly *verb* [1231 diaginosko] to diagnose.
knower *noun* {3049 yiddoni} one who has the spirit (not necessarily holy) of knowledge; **cp** seer.
knowledge *noun* **knowingly** *adverb* {4093 madda} intelligence; conssciousness.
knowledge, perception *noun* {1843 dehag} {1844 dehgah} {1847 dahgath} [1108 gnosis] an awareness of facts.
known (become) (cause to be) *verb* [319 anagnorizomai] [1107 gnorizo] to cause to become known.
known, acquaintance *noun* [1110 gnostos] one who is known by another.
Kol Hozeh *transliterated name* {3626 kolchozeh} Every Seer.
Kon Yah *transliterated name* {3659 konyah} Established of Yah.
Konan Yah *transliterated name* {3562 konanyah} Established of Yah.
kor *transliterated noun* {3734 kor} [2884 koros] a large dry measure.
Kor Ashan *transliterated name* {3565 kowrashan} Furnace of Smoke.
Koresh *transliterated name* {3566, 3567 koresh} a Persian sovereign.
Kush *transliterated name* {3568 kush} the son of Ham; that which is now Ethiopia.
Kushan Rishathaim *dual transliterated name* {3573 kuwshanrishathayim} Kushan of Double Wickedness.
Kushiy *transliterated name* {3569, 3570 kuwshiy} Of Kush.
Kushiyth *transliterated name* {3571 kuwshiyth} a female Kushiy.
Kuth *transliterated name* {3575 kuwth} the meaning uncertain; a province in Ashshur.

L

La El *transliterated name* {3815 lael} Of El.
labor, labour *noun* {3018 yegiya} {3022 yaga} the labor, including the result thereof.
labor, labour *verb* {3021 yaga} to labor; to toil; **see** belabour.
Lachmam *transliterated name* {3903 lachmam} Bread–like.
Lachmi *transliterated name* {3902 lachmiy} Bread.
lack *adjective* {2638 chacer} {2639 checer} {2640 chocer} {4270 machor} without; destitute of.
lack, abate *verb* {2637 chacer} to lack, to lessen; spoken of the prophecy of the Messiah having become flesh; **read** Psalm 8:5.
lack, arrange, fail, hoe *verb* {5737 adar} to miss having; to arrange a vineyard, as in hoeing.
lack, impoverish *verb* {7326 rush} verb of poverty; to be destitute; **see** poverty.
lacking *adverb* {2642 checrohn} deficiency.
lad *noun* {5288, 5289 naar} {5290 noar} {5958 elem} [3816 pais] male child; **cp** lass.
Ladah *transliterated name* {3935 ladah} the meaning uncertain.
Ladan *transliterated name* {3936 ladan} the meaning uncertain.
lade, laden, load, burden *verb* {6006 amas} to load a load; to impose a burden.
lade, lift, load, spare, bear *verb* {5375 nacah} {5376 nesa} to lift, in a variety of applications.
ladhood *noun* {5290 noar} the eon of being a lad.
lady *noun* {1377 gebiyrah} {1404 gebereth} [2959 kuria] feminine of lord.
lair, lure, hunthold *noun* {4679 metsudah} {4685 metsodah} {4686 matsudah} a hunter's hideout; a lair; a lure.
lake *noun* [3041 limnee] an inland body of water, as nearness of a shore.

Lamb (the), lamb *noun* [721 arnion] is used of Christ, as a sacrifice to expiate the sins of men; a small sheep.
lamb (ewe) *noun* {3535 kabsah} {3776 kisbah} a young female sheep.
lamb, lambs *noun* {563 immar} {2922 tela} {2924 taleh} {3532 kebes} {3775 keseb} {7716 seh} [286 amnos] [704 areen] small sheep.
lame *noun* [5560 kolos] limping; as deprived of a foot.
lament *verb* {5091 nahah} {6969 qun} [2354 threeneo] [2360 throeomai] to mourn; to express deep sorrow for.
lamentation *noun* {4553 micped} {5089 noahh} {5092 nehiy} {5093 niyah} {5204 niy} {7015 qinah} [2355 threenos] a mourning.
lamp *noun* {5216 nerah} that which glistens; a light.
land, earth *noun* {772 ara} {776 erets} {778 araq} [1093 geel the soil; terra frima; **cp** cosmos.
languid *noun* {5889 ayeph} weak; wasted away.
languish *verb* {5888 ayeph} {5969 ulpeh} to weaken.
languish, veil, cover *verb* {5848 ataph} {5968 alaph} to shroud; to cover over; to languish.
Laodicea *transliterated name* [2993 laodikia] Laity of Judgment.
Laodicean *transliterated name* [2994 laodikus] Of Laodicea.
lap *verb* {3952 laqaq} to lick up with the tongue; **cp** lick.
Lappidoth *plural transliterated name* {3941 lappiydowth} Flambeaus.
Laqqum *transliterated name* {3946 laqquwm} possibly, Fortification.
large, broad *noun* {7341 rochab} {7342 rachab} wide; width; roomy.
largess *noun* {5023 nebizbah} liberality; a bounty as owed.
larynx *transliterated noun* [2995 larunx] the body structure housing the vocal cords.
lash *noun* {2250 chabburah} the wound of a lashing or whipping.
lass *noun* {5291 naarah} [3814 paidiskee] female child; **cp** lad.
latter rain *noun* {4456 malqosh} the spring rain.
lattice, net, netting *noun* {7638 sabak} that which is entwined.
laud, soothe *verb* {7623 shabach} {7624 shecach} to extol with words; to smooth it over.
laugh, ridicule, entertain *verb* {6711 tsachaq} {6712 tsechoq} {7832 sechag} to laugh; to laugh at; to laugh at in defiance.
laughingstock *noun* {4890 mischaq} an object of ridicule.
laughter, ridicule *noun* {7814 sechoq} a laugh; a laughing at; a laughing at in defiance.
launder *verb* {3526 kabac} to wash by treading; used only of ceremonial cleansing of clothing after their contamination, except in 2 Shemu El 19:24.
lay waste *verb* {3765 kircem} to despoil.
lay, lie (down) *verb* {7901 shakab} to lie down; **see** bed.
lay, repose *verb* [2621 katakimai] to lie down; recline at a meal.
layer *noun* {5073 nidbak} that which is laid vertically; a stratum.
laying aside *verb* [595 apothesis] to put away; to abandon for a time or permanently.
lead, led *verb* {5148 nachah} to guide; to transport.
leaders, leaderships *plural noun* {6546 parah} persons at the beginning; persons at the front.
leaf, leaves *noun* {5929 aleh} a foliage of a tree.
lean *verb* {8172 shaan} to rely on for support.
leap for joy *verb* {5965 alaz} to exult physically; **cp** jump for joy.
leap, lighten, loose *verb* {5425 nathar} [242 hallomai] to leap; to loosen; to untie.
leap, solidify *verb* {6339 pazaz} to become solid; to spring.
leaper *noun* {1788 dishon} that which leaps.
learn, teach *verb* {3925 lamad} literally, to goad; to disciple; to be discipled; **see** disciple *verb*.
lease *verb* [1554 ekdidomi] to give out; to let out for hire.
leave (behind), release, forsake *verb* {5800 azab} [1459 enkatalipo] to leave behind; in a good sense, to let remain over; in a bad sense, to abandon.
leave off, loose *verb* [447 anieemi] to loosen; to let go of.
leave, let, set, abandon, allow *verb* {3240 yanach} {5203 natash} to allow to be; to allow to be set; to abandon.
leave, release, allow, forgive, forsake *verb* [863 aphieemi] to send forth.
leaves *noun* [5444 phullon] as sprouts.
leaving, releasing, forsaking *noun* {5805 azubah} deserting.
lechery *noun* [766 aselgia] unrestrained lust; selfish pleasure.
Lechi *transliterated name* {3896 lechiy} Cheek.
ledge, court *noun* {*plural* 4052 migraah} {5835 azarah} {*plural* 7948 shalab} that which is surrounded; that which surrounds.
left *adjective* {8042 semaliy} leftward.
left *noun* {8040 semol} that which is opposite the right; **cp** right; example: when facing north, the west; most versions erroneously insert the words *hand*, or *side*; we sit not on Yah Shua's right hand, or on his left hand; but at his left, and at his right.
left over, leftovers *noun* {5736 adaph} a surplus.
left *verb* {8041 samal} to pass leftward.
leftover *noun* {5669 abur} that which has been passed over, or kept over.
leg *noun* {3767 kara} {8243 shaq} [4628 skelos] a limb of a human or animal.
leg, hind leg *noun* {7785 shoq} the leg of a biped; the hind leg of a quadruped.
Lekah *transliterated name* {3922 lekah} Walk.
Lemech *transliterated name* {3929 lemech} [2984 lamech] the meaning uncertain.
Lemu El *transliterated name* {3927 lemuel} Of El.
lend, borrow, join *verb* {3867 lavah} literally, to entwine; to become wrapped up in, as a borrower, or as a lender.
lend, loan, ask {7592 shael} {7593 sheel} [154 aiteo] to inquire; to request or demand.
lender *noun* {4874 mashsheh} {5386 neshiy} one to whom another is indebted.
lentiles *plural noun* {5742 adashim} an edible pealike vegetable, usually cooked whole, or ground.
leopard *noun* {5245 nemar} {5246 namer} as being spotted.
leper, leprous *verb* {6879 tsara} to be stricken with leprousy.
leprosy *noun* {6883 tsaraath} a disease of the skin.
Lesha *transliterated name* {3962 lesha} Break Through.
lessen *verb* **insignificant** *adjective* {6994 qaton} [1642 elattoo] a diminishing in rank or influence.
lessen, diminish *verb* {4591 maat} to pare off; to reduce.
lesser, little, pinky, younger, fewer *adjective* {6810 tsaor} {6995 qoten} {6996 qatan} less in age, number, size; little finger.
let (down) (fall) (go) (loose), loose, loosen up, slacken *verb* {7503 raphah} to slacken.
let, set, abandon, allow, leave *verb* {3240 yanach} {5203 natash} to allow to be; to allow to be set; to abandon.
lethek *transliterated noun* {3963 lethek} a dry measure.
level, plain, straight, straightness *noun* {4334 miyshor, *plural* miyshorim} {4339 meyshar} {6160 arabah} plain, as unadorned; as a level land area; as of straight character; as just.
Levi, Leviy, Leviym *transliterated name* {3878 levi} {*plural* 3879, 3881 leviym} [3018 lui] [*plural* 3019 luitees] Attached; Joined; name of a person; of a scion of Yisra El.
leviathan *transliterated noun* {3882 livathan} a wreathed monster.
levir *noun* {2993 yabam} the one who is to levirate.
levirate *verb* {2992 yabam} to impregnate a deceased brother's widow to preserve his seed.
Levitical *transliterated adjective* {3878 levi} [3020 luitikos] of Levi.
libate, pour, anoint *verb* {4886 mashach} {5258 nacak} {5260 necak} {5480 cuwk} {8210 shaphach} [218 alipho] [4689 spendomai] [5548 chrio] symbolic of setting apart by libating (pouring on) of oil; of pouring a molten image.
libated, anointed *noun* {5257 necik} symbolic of one set apart by libating (pouring on) oil.
libation, pouring *noun* {5261 necak} {5262 necek} a pouring of worship; a pouring of images.
liberal, liberty *noun* {1865 derowr} from the root, to move rapidly; freedom.
liberality *noun* [572 haplotees] not restricted in giving, granting, or yielding.
liberate *verb* {2666 chaphash} {7804 shezab} [1659 elutheroo] to release; to free.
liberated *adjective* {2670 chopshiy} [1658 elutheros] released.
liberated *noun* [558 apelutheros] one released.
liberated, burst (open) *adjective* {6359 patir} {6362 patar} burst open, as a flower; liberate, as a person.
liberation *noun* {2667 chophesh} {2668 chuphshah} a releasing.
liberty *adjective* {2669 chophshuth} spoken of a house; possibly in contrast to a guarded house.

lick *verb* {3897 lachak} to lap with the tongue; **cp** lap.
lie (down), lay *verb* {7901 shakab} to lie down.
lie *verb* {3576 kazab} to deceive.
lie, put, cast *verb* [906 ballo] to throw.
life (physical) *noun* {2424 chayuth} [2222 zoee] the portion of existence following birth and preceding death wherein a being grows, decides, and decays; life is sustained by the soul; **read** Leviticus 17:11; physical life is superceded by eternal life with Yah Veh, or eternal death in the lake of fire.
life, live, lively, living *adjective* {2416, 2417 chay} {2422 chayeh} the Hebrew and Arami adjective is used as a noun in English; **see** live.
lifestyle *noun* [72 agogee] a mode of living.
lift *verb* {7213 raam} to raise.
lift, bear *verb* {5190 natal} {5191 netal} to lift, as to impose; to raise.
lift, load, spare, bear, lade *verb* {5375 nacah} {5376 nesa} to lift, in a variety of applications.
lift, loft, raise, exalt *verb* {7311, 7313 rum} {7318 romam} {7426 ramam} to lift hand, heart, offering, voice; to oath; **see** exalt.
lift, take *verb* [142 airo] to take up; to take away.
lifting, swelling, exalting *noun* {7613 seeth} an elevation; from the verb, lift {5375}.
light *noun* {3974 maor} a luminary.
light, lit *verb* [381 anapto] to light a fire.
lighten, loose, leap *verb* {5425 nathar} [242 hallomai] to leap; to loosen; to untie.
lightning *noun* {1300 baraq} {2385 chaziz} [796 astrapee] a flashing light produced by an atmospheric discharge.
like *adjective* [3664 homoios] similar to.
like, likewise *adverb* [3668 homoios] same as; samewise.
like manner (in) *adverb* [5615 hosautos] in the same way.
likeminded *noun* [3675 homophron] of similar thoughts.
liken, compare *verb* {1819 dahmah} [3666 homoioo] to liken unto; to compare; to resemble; to consider; homoioo is the verb of likeness.
liken, proverbialize *verb* {4911 mashal} to present as a proverb; liken, as being equal; **see** equal.
likeness *noun* {1823 demuwth} {1825 dimyohn} [3665 homoiotees] [3667 homoioma] [3669 homoiosis] resemblance; noun of liken.
likesouled *noun* [2473 isopsuchos] with similar emotions.
lilies *plural noun* [2918 krinon] plants possessing a bell–like blossom.
lily, trumpet *noun* **Shoshanna** *transliterated name* {7799 shoshanna} [4677 sousanna] lily, as a flower, or as an ornament; trumpet, from its lily shaped bell.
limp *verb* {6760 tsala} to limp; as one–sided.
limp, limping *noun* {6761 tsela}.
line *noun* {6957 qav} {6961 qaveh} a line for measuring.
line up, rank, appraise, apprize, arrange, array *verb* {6186 arak} to line up in a row; to put in order.
line, pang, boundary, cord *noun* {2256 chebel} literally, a rope; as a boundary line; as binding one in a pang.
linen *transliterated noun* [3043 linon] a thread or cloth made of flax.
linen (bleached) *noun* [4616 sindon] a cloth or clothing of linen that has been lightened by bleaching.
linen (white) *noun* {948 buwts} [1039 bussinos] [1040 bussos] made of flax.
linen (white), marble (white) *noun* {8336 shesh} white, as bleached.
linger *verb* {4102 mahahh} to question; to hesitate.
lintel *noun* {4947 mashqoph} an overhang.
lion *noun* {3918 layish} a lion, as a crusher, from his destructive blows.
lion (roaring) *noun* {3833 lebia, *plural* lebaim} {7826 shachal} a lion, as a roarer.
lioness (roaring) *noun* {3833 *singular* lebeoth, *plural* lebaoth} a female lion, as the fiercer.
lip (upper) *noun* {8222 sapham} as the place for hair.
lip, edge *noun* {8193 saphah} [5491 kilos] an edge; a shoreline; the physical lip; a language; **cp** tongue.
Liqchi *transliterated name* {3949 liqchiy} Learned.
litra *transliterated noun* [3046 litra] a measured weight.
little *noun* {4705 mitsar} little in size, or significance.
little owl, cup *noun* {3563 kowe} a cup; a little owl, from the cup–like cavity of its eye.
little, petty, shortly, bit, bit by bit, few *adjective, adverb* {4592 meat} diminutive; a few; a little.
little, pinky, younger, fewer, lesser *adjective* {6810 tsaor} {6995 qoten} {6996 qatan} less in age, number, size; little finger.
liturgist *transliterated noun* [3011 litourgos] one who ministers a religious service.
liturgize *transliterated verb* [3000 latruo] [3008 litourgeo] to minister a religious service.
liturgizing *transliterated adjective* [3010 liturgikos] of religious service.
liturgy *transliterated noun* [2999 latria] [3009 litourgia] religious service.
live beings *noun* {2423 cheva} [2226 zoon] as in animal sacrifices in Hebrews 13:11; of irrational blasphemers in 2 Petros 2:12 and Yah Hudah 10; of live beings who worship throughout the Apocalypse; **see** life; **see** live.
live *verb* {2418, 2421 chayah} {2425 chayay} [2198 zao] to live; to enliven; **see** life.
liver *noun* {3516 kabed} the largest glandular organ of the body.
living areas, Havoth *noun* {2333 chavvah} a residential area; **see** life; **see** live.
lizard *noun* {8079 semamith} as being poisonous.
lizard, substance, force *noun* {3581 koach} {3981 maamats} pressure; physical, or intellectual; also a lizard.
Lo Ammi *transliterated name* {3818 loammi} Not My People.
Lo Debar *transliterated name* {3810 lodebar} Not Pastured.
Lo Ruchamah *transliterated name* {3819 loruchamah} Not Mercied.
load *noun* {5385 nesuah} a load, as bearing, or lifting.
load, burden, lade, laden *verb* {6006 amas} to load a load; to impose a burden.
load, spare, bear, lade, lift *verb* {5375 nacah} {5376 nesa} to lift, in a variety of applications.
loan *noun* {4859 mashshaah} a loan; **cp** interest.
loan, lend, ask {7592 shael} {7593 sheel} [154 aiteo] to inquire; to request or demand.
loathe, lothe *verb* {1602 gaal} {2092 zaham} {5354 naqat} {8374 taab} to dislike intensely.
loathe, lothe, cut off *verb* {6962 qut} {6990 qatat} literally, or figuratively, to be cut off.
Lochesh *transliterated name* {3873 lowchesh} Enchanter.
lock *noun* {4514 manul} {4515 manal} a bolt.
lock, shod, enclose, inclose *verb* {5274 naal} {7000 qatar} to fasten; **see** shoe.
locksmith, lockup *noun* {4525 mager} one that makes or services locks; a place of lockup.
locust *noun* [200 akris] as pointed; or as lightning on the top of vegetation.
locust, whirring, cymbal, harpoon *noun* {6767 tselatsal} a clattering, as of a cymbal; a whirring, as of wings; a rattling, as of a harpoon.
Lod *transliterated name* {3850 lod} [3069 ludda] meaning uncertain.
lodge *noun* {4411 malown} a restingplace; **see** hammock.
loft, exalt *verb* {7682 saqab} to lift high.
loft, raise, exalt, lift *verb* {7311, 7313 rum} {7318 romam} {7426 ramam} to lift hand, heart, offering, voice; to oath; **see** exalt.
lofty *participle* {8524 talal} to elevate.
logic *transliterated noun* [3053 logismos] reasoning.
logical *transliterated adjective* [3050 logikos] rational.
logomachize *transliterated verb* [3054 logomakeo] to dispute words.
logomachy *transliterated noun* [3055 logomakia] disputation of words.
loins *noun* {*plural* 2504 chalats} {*dual* 4975 mothen} [*plural* 3751 osphus] the lower parts of the back; symbolically the seat of reproductive vigor.
long, longing *verb* {16 ebeh} to breathe after.
look (around) (at) (away) *verb* {5027 nabat} {8159 shaah} to look at; to regard favorably.
look, appear *verb* {8259 shaqaph} [398 anaphainoman] to become apparent; to gaze; **see** manifest.
lookout *noun* {8260 sheqeph} {*plural* 8261 shaquph} peep hole to look through.
lookout tower *adjective, noun* {969 bachown} a high structure for guarding by looking.
loose, leap, lighten *verb* {5425 nathar} [242 hallomai] to leap; to loosen; to untie.

loose, leave off *verb* [447 anieemi] to loosen; to release.
loose, loosen up, slacken, let (down) (fall) (go) (loose) *verb* {7503 raphah} to slacken.
loose, release *verb* [3089 luo] to set free, unbind.
lop (off) *verb* {7082 qacac} {8456 tazaz} to whack off.
lop *verb* {5586 caaph} to detwig.
lord *noun* {1376 gebiyr} a dignitary; one who prevails mightily; **cp** lady.
lord, Lord *title,* **LORD** *name*: **note:** in both the old and new covenants, **lord** may refer to one's superior, whether landlord, or a woman's man; **see** adoni, adonim: **lord** may also refer to an absolute ruler, Elohim or human; **see** despotes: in the New Covenant, **Lord** (capitalized) may refer to Yah Veh, the angel of Yah Veh, and to Yah Shua Messiah; **see** Adonay: **LORD** (all caps) is a mistranslation for the name of Yah Veh; **see** Yah Veh.
lordship *noun* [2963 kuriotees] lord over; see lord.
lose *verb* [2210 zeemioo] to sustain damage; to suffer loss.
lose, lost, destroy, destruct *verb* {6 abad} {7 abad} [622 apollumi] to destroy fully.
lose, ruin, vanish, corrupt, destroy, destruct *verb* {6 abad} {7 abad} {8 obed} {7843 shachath} [622 apollumi] [1311 diapthiro] [2704 kataphthiro] [5351 phthiro] to corrupt through decay.
loss, lost *noun* {9 abedah} [2209 zeemia] loss; destruction.
Lot *transliterated name* {3876 lot} [3091 lot] Veiled.
lot *noun* [2819 kleeros] an object used for casting lots; that which is obtained by lot; an allotted portion.
lothing *noun* {1604 goal} intense dislike.
lotuses *plural noun* {6628 tseelim} of the lotus tree, as being slender.
Loukas *transliterated name* [3065 loukas] perhaps Enlightener.
Loukia *transliterated name* [3073 loukia] perhaps Enlightenment.
Loukios *transliterated name* [3066 loukios] perhaps Enlightening.
love *noun* {160 ahabah} [26 agapee] a spiritual caring for, above and beyond that which is soulical, or physical; **cp** friend; **cp** eros.
love *verb* {157 ahab} {*plural* 158 ahab} {*plural* 159 ohab} [25 agapao] to care for spiritually, above and beyond that which is soulical, or physical; **cp** befriend; **cp** eros.
loves, uncle, beloved *noun* {1730 dod} literally, from the root, to boil; an extremely warm caring for; an uncle.
low, lower, lowly *adjective* {8215 shephal} {8217 shaphal} humiliating; depressed.
lower, abase *verb* {8213 shaphel} {8214 shephal} to humiliate.
lower, topple, descend *verb* {3381 yarad} to go lower; to tip over.
lowland *noun* {8218 shiplah} {8219 shephelah} a depression of land.
lowliness *noun* {8216 shephel} as in humility.
Lubiym *plural transliterated name* {3864 luwbiym} Of the interior of Africa.
Luchith *transliterated name* {3872 luwchiyth} Slab.
Lud *transliterated name* {3865 luwd} the meaning uncertain; the name of two nations.
Ludiy *transliterated name* {3866 luwdiy} Of Lud.
lump *noun* {1690 debelah} that which is pressed together; usually of figs.
lure, hunthold, lair *noun* {4679 metsudah} {4685 metsodah} {4686 matsudah} a hunter's hideout; a lair; a lure.
lurk *noun* {695 ereb} {3993 maarab} {6660 tsediah} a place from which to lie in wait; an ambush.
lurk *verb* {693 arab} {696 oreb} {6658 tsadah} [1747 enedra] [1748 enedreno] [1749 enedron] to lie in wait; to ambush.
lurking *noun* {698 orobah} that which is gained by lying in wait.
Lush *transliterated name* {3889 luwsh} Kneading.
luxuriate, delight *verb* **delicate** *participle* {6026 anag} to be, or to become soft; to delight in; to deride.
luxurious *adjective* **luxury** *noun* {6027 oneg} in luxury.
lyric poem *noun* {7692 shiggayon} a rambling poem.

M

Ma Halal El *transliterated name* {4111 mahalalel} [3121 malaeeel] Halal of El.
Maad Yah *transliterated name* {4573 maadyah} Adorned of Yah.
Maaday *transliterated name* {4572 maaday} Adornment.
Maachah *transliterated name* {4601 maachah} Pinched.
Maachahiy *transliterated name* {4602 maachathiy} Of Maachah.
Maas *transliterated name* {4619 maats} Closure.
Maase Yah *transliterated name* {4641 maaseyah} Work of Yah.
Maaz Yah *transliterated name* {4590 maazyah} Recouped of Yah.
Mach Nadbay *transliterated name* {4367 machnadbay} What is Like a Volunteer?
Machalath *transliterated name* {4258 machalath} Sickness.
Machanayim *dual transliterated name* {4266 machanayim} Double Camp.
Machaneh Dan *transliterated name* {4265 machanehdan} Camp of Dan.
Machath *transliterated name* {4287 machath} Erasure.
Machaviym *plural transliterated name* {4233 machaviym} Of Machaveh.
Machazioth *plural transliterated name* {4238 machaziyowth} Visions.
Machbena *transliterated name* {4343 machbena} Hilly.
Machbeniy *transliterated name* {4344 machbannay} Of Machbena.
Machi *transliterated name* {4352 machiy} Impoverished.
machinate, fabricate *verb, participle* {2803, 2804 chashab} to interpenetate; to contrive; physically, to fabricate; mentally, to machinate.
machination, fabrication *noun* {2808 cheshbohn} {*plural* 2810 chishshabonth} {4284 machashebeth} a contrivance of machine, or mind.
Machir *transliterated name* {4353 machiyr} Sell.
Machiriy *transliterated name* {4354 makchiyriy} Of Machir.
Machlah *transliterated name* {4244 machlah} Sickness.
Machli *transliterated name* {4249 machliy} Sick.
Machliy *transliterated name* {4250 machliy} Of Machli.
Machlon *transliterated name* {4248 machlown} Sick.
Machol *transliterated name* {4235 machowl} Round Dancing.
Machpelah *transliterated name* {4375 machpelah} Double.
Machse Yah *transliterated name* {4271 machceyah} Refuge of Yah.
Maday *transliterated name* {4074, 4075, 4076, 4077 maday} [3370 meedos] a country of central Asia.
madness *participle* {1947 holelah} {1948 holelooth} in the sense of folly.
Magdala *transliterated name* {4026 migdalah} [3093 magdala] Tower.
Magdalene *transliterated name* {4026 migdalah} [3094 magdalene] of Magdala.
Magdi El *transliterated name* {4025 magdiel} Precious of El.
maggot eaten *verb* [4662 skoleekobrotos] eaten by maggots.
maggot *noun* {7415 rimmah} [4663 skoleex] a wormlike larva.
maggot, scarlet *noun* {8438 tolaath} a wormlike larva; scarlet, the color of the maggot.
magi *plural,* **magus** *singular noun* {*plural* 2445 chakkim} {7248 rabmag} [3097 magos] a title of wise ones; and in Acts 13: 6, 8 of sorcerers.
magnificent *adjective* **magnificently** *adverb* [3171 megalos] [3176 megistos] very great.
magnify *verb* [3170 megaluno] to extol; to greaten.
Magog *transliterated name* {4031 magowg} [3098 magog] a northern region of prophecy; **read** Yezek El 38:2, 39:6; **cp** Gog.
Magor Mis Sabib *transliterated name* {4036 magowrmiccabiyb} Terror Round About.
Magpi Ash *transliterated name* {4047 magpiyash} Smiter of Herbage.
Maharay *transliterated name* {4121 maharay} Hasty.
maid *noun* {519 amah} {8198 shiphchah} [1399 doulee] female servant.
maiden *noun* {7361 rachamah} [2877 korasion] an unmarried woman.
maimed *participle* {7038 qalat} [376 anapeeros] castrated; crippled.
maintain, measure, sustain, contain *verb* {3557 kuwl} to keep in.
majesty *noun* **majestic** *adjective* {1925 heder} {1926 hadar} {1927 hadarah} [3168 megaliotees] [3169 megaloprepees] [3172 megalosunee] greatness; splendor.
make, do *verb* {6466 paal} [4160 poieo] to assemble; to practice; to perform; **cp** create.
make, serve, do, keep *verb* {5648 abad} in the sense of serving.
Malachi *transliterated name* {4401 malachiy} Angel.
male *noun* {2138 zakur} {2145 zakar} [730 arreen] the species that fertilizes the female, whether human, animal, or plant.

malice *noun* [2549 kakia] ill will.
Malkam, Milkom *transliterated name* {4445 malkam, milkown} the meaning uncertain; the national idol of the Ammoniy.
Malki El *transliterated name* {4439 malkiyel} Sovereign of El.
Malki Eliy *transliterated name* {4440 malkiyeliy} Of Malki El.
Malki Ram *transliterated name* {4443 malkiyram} Sovereign of Exaltation.
Malki Sedeq *transliterated name* {4442 malkiytsedeq} [3198 melkisedek] Sovereign of Justness; sovereign of the Sadoq priesthood.
Malki Shua *transliterated name* {4444 malkiyshuwa} Sovereign of Salvation.
Malki Yah *transliterated name* {4441 malkiyah} Sovereign of Yah.
mallet *noun* {4650 mephiyts} an instrument that breaks.
Malluch *transliterated name* {4409 malluwch} Reigned.
mammon *transliterated noun* [3126 mammonas] avarice.
mammy *transliterated noun* [3125 mammee] granny.
man *noun* {376 iysh} {582 enosh} {606 enosh} [435 aneer] the human male adult; **cp** woman; **cp** human.
Manachath *transliterated name* {4506 manachath} Rest.
manager *noun* [2012 epitropos] one in charge of.
mandate *noun* {7595 sheela} the decision of an asking.
mandate, census *noun* **specified** *adjective* {4662 miphqad} an enumeration; a designated spot; an order, or command.
mandrake *noun* {1736 duwday} an herb, considered to be aphrodesiac.
maneh *transliterated noun* {4488 maneh} a measure.
manger *noun* {18 ebuwc} a foddering place.
manifest *adjective* [5318 phaneros] apparent.
manifestation *noun* [5321 phanerosis] [5324 phantazomai] an exhibition; a spectacle.
manifestation *noun* {8544 temunah} from species {4327 miyn} a specification.
manifested *verb* [5319 phaneroo] to render apparent.
manifestly *adverb* [5320 phaneros] clearly; openly.
manipulate, capture *verb* {8610 taphas} to manipulate; to seize with the hands; to use without warrant.
manly *adjective* {377 iysh} [407 andrizomai] to behave in manner of a man.
manna *transliterated noun* {4478 man} literally, a whatever.
Manoach *transliterated name* {4495 manowach} Rest.
manse *noun* {1964, 1965 heykal} usually mistranslated temple or palace; a large house for rulers, and also for Yah Veh; **see** tabernacle; **cp** nave; **cp** priestal precinct.
manslayer *noun* [409 androphonos] one who slays man.
mantle (mighty) *noun* {145 eder} {155 adaereth} a covering as symbolic of authority, power.
mantle *noun* {*plural* 4254 mechalatsah} {4594 maateh} {*plural* 4595 maataphah} {4598 meiyl} {*plural* 5622 carbal} [4018 peribolaion] a covering, as easily stripped off.
manure *noun* {1828 domen} **cp** dung.
many, mighty, more, much *adjective* {3524 kabbiyr} vast.
many, mighty, much, very, exceeding, greatly, increasing *adjective* {7689, 7690 saggiy} superlatively mighty, or large.
Maoch *transliterated name* {4582 maowch} Pierced.
Maon *transliterated name* {4584 maown} Habitation.
Maoniym *plural transliterated name* {4586 meuwniy} Of Maon.
Maqas *transliterated name* {4739 maqats} End.
Maqheloth *plural transliterated name* {4722 maqheloth} Congregations.
Maqqedah *transliterated name* {4719 maqqedah} Branded.
maranatha [3134 maran atha] our Adonay cometh.
marble (white), linen (white) *noun* {8336 shesh} white, as bleached.
march, anklet *noun* {685 etsadah} {6807 tseadah} a pacing; an ornament of that which paces; an ankle chain.
mare *noun* {7424 rammak} a brood mare.
Mareshah *transliterated name* {4762 mareshah} Summit.
mark, tattoo, brand *verb* {8427, 8428 tavah} to mark an animal; to mark an x or + as a signature of an illiterate, or to mark for protection.
mark, tattoo, brand, etching *noun* {7085 qaaqa} {8420 tab} [5480 karagma] a scratched marking; a mark on animals; an x or a + as a signature of an illiterate; a mark of protection; **read** Yechezq El 9:4–6; **read** Apocalypse 13:16,17, 14:9–11, 15:2, 16:2, 19:20, 20:4; **cp** brand.
market (for) kernels *verb* {7666 shabar} to aquire kernels at the market; **see** kernels.
market *noun* {5801 izzabon} [58 agora] a place to market, to purchase; **see** forum.
market *verb* [59 agorazo] [1805 exagorazo] to market in the sense of purchasing; Yah Shua marketed us to Elohim with His blood; Apocalypse 5:9.
Markos *transliterated name* [3138 markos] the meaning uncertain.
marriage *noun* [1062 gamos] the holy ritual wherein one man and one woman become one flesh.
married, mastered, baal *transliterated noun* {1167 baal} {1169 beel} one who masters; one who is mastered.
marrow *noun* {4221 moach} [3452 muelos] the tissue within the bone; fat.
marrowed *verb* {4229 machah} to fatten.
marry off *verb* [1547 ekgamizo] [1548 ekgamiskomai] to give in marriage.
marry, master, baal *verb* {*transliteration* 1166 baal} [1060 gameo] [1918 epigambruo] literally, baal means to be mastered; the ritual of one man and one woman becoming one flesh.
marsh, rush *noun* {98 agam} {99 agem} {100 agmone} a stagnant water, or that which grows therefrom.
Martha *transliterated name* [3136 martha] possibly Minister, in the sense of serving.
marvel *noun* {4652 miphlaah} {8540 temahh} a consternation; a miracle; a wonder.
marvel *verb* **marvels** *noun* **marvelous** *adjective* {6381 pala} {6382 pele} {6383 pali} [2295 thauma] [2297 thaumasios] [2298 thaumastos] an amazing miraculous sight.
marvel *verb* {8429 tevahh} {8539 tamahh} [2296 thaumazo] to be in consternation at the miraculous sight of.
Masay *transliterated name* {4640 masay} Workable.
masculine garment *noun* {7897 shith} a masculine garment, as being put on.
Masreqah *transliterated name* {4957 masreqah} Vineyard.
massage *verb* {4799 marach} to soften by rubbing.
Massah *transliterated name* **testing** *noun* {4531 maccah} Testing.
mast *noun* {8650 toren} a pole as a mast.
master *noun* {1397 geber} {1399 gebar} {1400 gebar} {1401 gibbar} one who prevails in power; **cp** mistress.
master *noun* {4756 marah} one that dominates.
master, baal, marry *verb* {*transliteration* 1166 baal} [1060 gameo] [1918 epigambruo] literally, baal means to be mastered; the ritual of one man and one woman becoming one flesh.
mastered, baal, married *transliterated noun* {1167 baal} {1169 beel} one who masters; one who is mastered.
mataeologist *transliterated noun* [3151 mataiologos] a babbler of words.
mataeology *transliterated noun* [3150 mataiologia] vain, unprofitable discourse or inquiry.
matricide *noun* [3389 meetraloees] mother murder.
matrix *noun* {4866 mishber} [3388 meetra] the mothering organ.
matrix, womb, belly *noun* {990 beten} {1512 gachon} {3770 keres} {4579 meah} {6896 qabab} {6897 qobah} {6898 qubbah} {7356 racham} (7358 rechem} [2836 koilia] the interior; a cavity as hollow; the abdominal cavity; sometimes refers to the womb.
matsah *transliterated noun* {4682 matstsah} [106 azumos] unfermented bakery.
Mattan *transliterated name* {4977 mattan} [3157 matthan] Gift.
Mattatha *transliterated name* [3160 mattatha] form of Gift of Yah.
Mattattah *transliterated name* {4992 mattattah} form of Gift of Yah.
Mattenay *transliterated name* {4982 mattenay} Gift.
Matthaios *transliterated name* [3156 matthaios] form of Gift of Yah.
Matthat *transliterated name* [3158 matthat] form of Gift of Yah.
Matthias *transliterated name* [3159 matthias] form of Gift of Yah.
Mattith Yah *transliterated name* {4993 mattithyah} [3161 mattathias] Gift of Yah.
maturity *noun* {3624 kelach} to be fully finished.
may, mayest, might, mightest *auxiliary verbs* these auxiliary verbs are not in the manuscripts, but have been supplied by the translators to smooth the verbal flow: **see** shalt, shalt, should, shoudest; **see** will, wilt, would, wouldest; **cp** might, mighty, mightily.
Mayim Meribah/Waters of Strife *plural transliterated name* {4325 mayim, 4809 meriybah} Waters of Strife.

Mayim Nephtoach/Waters of Nephtoach *plural transliterated name* {4325 mayim, 5318 nephtowach} Waters of a Spring; **see** Nephtoach.
Me Hay Yarqon *transliterated name* {4313 meyhayyarqown} Waters of the Pale Green.
Me Zahab *transliterated name* {4314 meyzahab} Waters of Gold.
meadow *noun* {3741 karah} a grassland.
meadow, ram, saddle *noun* {3733 kar} literally, plumpness, as in a full grown lamb; padding, as in a saddle; a meadow for sheep.
measure *noun* {4884 mesurah} a liquid measure.
measure *verb* {4058 madad} to fit; to size up.
measure, measurement, tailoring *noun* {4060 middah} {4067 madown} {*plural* 4461 memadim} size.
measure, sustain, contain, maintain *verb* {3557 kuwl} to keep in.
Mebunnay *transliterated name* {4012 mebunnay} Built Up.
Mechida *transliterated name* {4240 mechiyda} Propound.
Mechir *transliterated name* {4243 mechiyr} Price.
Mecholathiy *transliterated name* {4259 mecholathiy} Of Abel Mecholah.
Mechuya El *transliterated name* {4232 mechuyael} Erased of El.
Medatha *transliterated name* {4099 medatha} the meaning uncertain; the father of Haman.
mediate *verb* [3315 mesituo] to be in the middle of persons, usually to resolve differences.
mediator *noun* [3316 mesitees] one who is in the middle of persons, usually to resolve differences.
meditate *verb* {7742 suwach} {7878 siyach} to muse pensively; to ponder.
meditate, mutter *verb* {1897 hagah} to contemplate upon; to utter in a low voice.
meditation *noun* {1899 hegeh} {1900 haguth} {1901 hagig} {1902 higgayon} {7808 seach} {7879 siyach} {7881 siachah} a pensive musing; a pondering.
meet *verb* {6298 pagash} to contact; **cp** reach.
meet, confront *verb* {7122 qara} {7125 qirah} to encounter.
mega *adjective* [3173 megas] great.
Megiddo *transliterated name* {4023 megiddo, megiddon} Troop; in the New Covenant, it is transliterated with the prefix, Har, as in Armegeddon; the Valley of Troops; **read** Apocalypse 16:16.
Mehetab El *transliterated name* {4105 mehetabel} Well—pleased of El.
Mecherahiy *transliterated name* {4382 mecherathiy} Of Mekerah.
Mechonah *transliterated name* {4368 mechonah} Base.
Melech *transliterated name* {4428, 4429 melech} [3124 malchos] [3197 melchi] Sovereign.
melech *transliterated title* {4428 melech} {4430 melech} sovereign.
melt away *adjective* {4523 mac} as in pining away.
melt *verb* {4549 macac} to liquify.
melt, dissolve *verb* {4127 muwg} to soften; to dissipate.
melt, dissolve, flow *verb* {4529 masah} to dissolve.
melt, pour *verb* {5413 nathak} to flow; to liquify.
member *noun* [3196 melos] a body part.
members *noun* {5409 nethach} parts of a body, human or animal.
memorial *noun* {234 azkarah} {2143 zeker} {2146 zikron} [3422 mneemosunon] a remembrance.
memorialize, remember *verb* {2142 zakar} {7876 shayah} [3403 mimeeskomai] [3415 mnaomai] [3421 mneemonuo] [5279 hupomimneesko] an acting of the memory; to hold in remembrance.
Memuchan *transliterated name* {4462 memuwchan} the meaning uncertain; a Persian satrap.
men subduers *noun* [405 andrapodistees] they that bring men to their feet.
men, few, few men *plural noun* {4962 mathim} **see** Theological Wordbook of the Old Testament, 1263.
Menachem *transliterated name* {4505 menachem} Sigh.
Menash Sheh *transliterated name* {4519 menashsheh} [3128 manassees] Forgetful.
Menash Shiy {4520 menashshiy} Of Menash Sheh.
menorah *transliterated noun* {4501 menorah} {5043 nebresha} [3087 luchnia] the holy candelabrum with seven candles.
menstrual *plural adjective* {5708 ed} as of a woman's period.
menstruate *verb* {1738 dahvah} to be sick, as in menstruation; **cp** bleed.
menstruation *adjective* {1739 dahveh} **cp** bleed.
Meonothay *plural transliterated name* {4587 meownothay} Habitations.
Mephi Bosheth *transliterated name* {4648 mephiybosheth} Dispeller of Shame.
Merayah *transliterated name* {4811 merayah} Rebellion.
Merayoth *transliterated name* {4812 merayowth} Rebellions.
merchandise *noun* {4627 maarab} {*plural* 4728 maqqechoth} {4819 markoleth} articles of exchange.
merchandise *noun* {7404 rekullah} that which a merchant peddles.
merchandise *verb*, **palpitate** *verb* **merchant** *participle* {5503 cachar} to peddle; a peddler (pedlar); to merchandise by travelling; to pound.
merchandise, merchant *noun* {5504, 5505 cachar} {5506 cechorah} that which is peddled; a peddler (pedlar).
merchandising *noun* {4536 micchar} buying and selling.
merchant *noun* **Kenaan** *transliterated name* {3667 kenaan} [5477 chanaan] merchant; made to bend the knee; humiliated; name of a person; name of a land.
merchant *noun* {7402 rachal} an itinerant trader; a peddler (pedlar).
mercies *noun* {7356 racham} {*plural* 7356 rachamim} {7359 rechem} [1654 eleeemosunee] compassions; retributions withheld.
merciful, mercied *adjective* {2623 chacid} {7349 rachum} {7362 rachmani} [1655 eleeemon] [3741 hosios] compassionate.
mercifully *adverb* [3743 hosios] compassionately.
mercy *noun* [1656 eleos] [3742 hosiotees] compassion; a retribution withheld.
mercy *noun* {2617 checed} literally, a bowing of the neck in kindness.
mercy *verb* {7355 racham} [1653 eleeo] to give mercy; to be mercied; to give compassion; to withhold retribution.
mercy, shame *verb* {2616 chaced} literally, to bow the neck in kindness; to reprove.
Meri Baal *transliterated name* {4810 meriybaal} Rebellion of Baal.
Merib Baal *transliterated name* {4807 meribbaal} Strife of Baal.
Meribah *transliterated name* {4809 meribah} Strife.
Merodach Bel Adoni *transliterated name* {4757 merodachbaladan} a sovereign.
Merodach *transliterated name* {4781 merodach} an idol.
Meshach *transliterated name* {4335, 4336 meyshach} the meaning uncertain; the Babel name of Misha El.
Meshech *transliterated name* {4902 meshech} Sowing.
Meshelem Yah *transliterated name* {4920 meshelemyah} Shalom of Yah.
Meshezab El *transliterated name* {4898 meshezabel} Liberated of El.
Mesoba Yah *transliterated name* {4677 metsobayah} Found of Yah.
Messiah *transliterated title* **anointed** *noun* {4899 mashiach} [5547 christos] anointed; Messiah is a transliteration of the Hebrew mashiach, and a translation of the Hellene christos; Yah Shua Messiah is the Anointed of Yah Veh; **see** Messias; **note:** the *exeGeses* indicates whenever Messiah is preceded by the article, as in "the Messiah".
Messianists *title* {4899 mashiach} [5546 kristianos] of the Messiah; all who trust in the Messiah.
Messias *transliterated title* [3323 messias] the Hellene transliteration of the Hebrew, Messiah; **see** Messiah.
metamorphose *transliterated verb* [3339 metamorphoomai] to change from one form to another; only in Matthaios 17:2, Markos 9:2, Romans 12:2, 2 Corinthians 3:18; **see** form; **cp** transfigure.
meteorite *noun* [1356 diopetees] a body which has fallen from the heavens.
Methu Shelach *transliterated name* {4968 methushelach} [3103 mathousala] Man of Security; Man of Spear.
Methusha El *transliterated name* {4967 methushael} Man of El.
Mi Yamin *transliterated name* {4326 miyamin} From the Right.
Mibchar *transliterated name* {4006 mibchar} Choice.
Mibsar *transliterated name* {4014 mibtsar} Fortified.
Michah El *transliterated name* {4317 michahel} [3413 mikaeel] Who is Like unto El; or, O That El.
Michah *transliterated name* {4316, 4318 michah} Who is Like; or, O That.
Michah Yah *transliterated name* {4319 michahuw} {4320

miychayah} {4321 michayehuw} {4322 michayahuw} Who is Like unto Yah; or, O That Yah.
Michal *transliterated name* {4324 michal} Streamlet.
Michmash *transliterated name* {4363 michmash} Stored.
Michmethath *transliterated name* {4366 michmethath} Concealment.
Michri *transliterated name* {4381 michriy} Sell.
mid, middle, pupil *noun* {380 iyshown} literally, the middle man of the eye; the middle of the night.
middle *adjective* {8484 tikon} central.
middle, midst, within, among, inward *noun* {7130 qereb} {8432 tavek} the nearest part; the center.
midheaven *noun* [3321 mesouraneema] in the middle of the heavens.
midnight *noun* [3317 mesonuktion] the moment between two consecutive days.
midst, within, among, inward, middle *noun* {7130 qereb} {8432 tavek} the nearest part; the center.
Midyan *transliterated name* {4080 midyan} [3099 madian] Contentious; a son of Abraham.
Midyaniy, Midyaniym *transliterated name* {4084 midyaniy} {*plural* 4092 medyaniym} Of Midyan.
mid–, midst, half *preposition* {2676 chatsoth} {2677 chetsiy} {4275 mechetsah} {4276 machatsith} among; a half of a whole; the middle of.
Migdal Eder *transliterated name* {4029 migdaleder} Tower of Droves.
Migdal El *transliterated name* {4027 migdalel} Tower of El.
Migdal Gad *transliterated name* {4028 migdalgad} Tower of Troops.
Migdol *transliterated name* **tower** *noun* {4024 migdol} {4026 migdal} tower; a place in Misrayim.
might *noun* {353 eyal} {360 eyaluth} {1369, 1370 geburah} {6108 otsem} {6109 otsmah} {*plural* 6110 atstsumah} [2479 iskus] authority; power.
mighty diviner *noun* {148 adargazer} mighty prognosticator.
mighty enough *adjective* [2480 iskuo] to have, or exercise force.
mighty mantle *noun* {145 eder} {155 adaereth} a covering as symbolic of authority, power.
mighty *noun* {193 uwl} {352 ayil} strong; powerful.
mighty oaks *noun* {436 elown} a forest of strong oaks.
mighty *verb* {142 adar} to be great.
mighty, mighted, mightier, mightily, craunch bone *verb* {6105 atsam} to become mighty; to be powerful; to be numerous; to overpower a bone.
mighty, mightier *adjective* {47 abbiyr} {117 addiyr} {1368 gibbor} {6099 atsum} {8623, 8624 taqqiph} [2478 iskuros] mighty; powerful; **see** Almighty.
mighty, mightily *adverb* {3966 meod} sometimes duple.
mighty, more, much, many *adjective* {3524 kabbiyr} vast.
mighty, much, very, exceeding, greatly, increasing, many *adjective* {7689, 7690 saggiy} superlatively mighty, or large.
migrate *verb* {6813 tsaan} to load up.
Milalay *transliterated name* {4450 milaly} Utter.
Milchah *transliterated name* {4435 milchah} Sovereigness.
millstone (upper), chariot *noun* {4817 merkab} {4818 merkabah} {7393 rekeb} {7396 rikbah} {7398 rekub} a vehicle; a rider; **cp** millstones.
millstones *dual noun* {7347 recheh} an upper and a lower millstone, as used to mill grain.
Min Yamin *transliterated name* {4509 minyamiyn} From the Right.
mina *transliterated noun* [3414 mna] a Latin coin of a hundred weight.
mind *noun* [1271 dianoyia] [1771 ennoia] [1963 epinoia] [3563 nous] that mental facility of the spirit which remembers, and wills.
mingle, mix up, fodder *verb* {1101 balal} to mix together; to mix up; **see** Beli Yaal; **see** comingle.
mingle, pledge, comingle *verb* {6148 arab} to become colateral.
minister *noun* [1249 diakonos] one who serves.
minister *verb* {8120 shemash} {8334 sharath} [1247 kiakoneo] to serve.
ministry *noun* {8335 shareth} [1248 diakonia] the serving; the service.
Miqloth *transliterated name* {4732 miqlowth} Staffs.
Miqne Yah *transliterated name* {4737 miqneyah} Chattel of Yah.
mirage *noun* {8273 sharab} a mirage, as glaring.
Mirmah *transliterated name* {4821 mirmah} Defraud.
mirror *noun* {7209 reiy} that which reflects that which is seen.
Miryam *transliterated name* {4813 miryam} [3137 mariam] Rebellious; the true transliteration of Mary.
miscarriage *noun* {5309 nephel} as having fallen.
mischief *noun* {205 aven} {611 acown} {*plural* 8383 teunim} harm; hurt.
Misha El *transliterated name* {4332, 4333 mishael} Who is Like unto El; or: O That El.
mislead, deceive *verb* {5377 nasha} {7952 shalah} to lead astray; to wrong.
misleading *noun* {7955 shalah} {7960 shaluw} wrongful.
Mispeh *transliterated name* {4708 mitspeh} {4709 mitspah} Watchtower.
Misrayim *transliterated name* {4713 mitsriy} {*dual* 4714 mitsrayim} [124 aiguptios] [125 aiguptos] **note:** Misrayim of the Old Covenant is translated to Egypt in the New Covenant.
Misrephoth Mayim *plural transliterated name* {4956 misrephowthmayim} Calcinations/Cremations of Water.
missile *noun* [956 belos] [1002 bolis] as a spear, or arrow.
mistress *noun* {1404 gebereth} feminine of {1376 gebiyr} {1400 gebar}.
mistress *noun* {7694, 7695 shegal} one that copulates with.
mistress of mistresses *noun* {7705 shiddah} a woman of the house.
mistress *transliterated title* {1172 baalah} feminine of {1167 baal}.
misvah *verb* {6680 tsavah} [1781 entellomai] the Hebrew is from the noun misvah; **see** misvah *noun*.
misvah, *plural* **misvoth** *transliterated noun* {4687 mitsvah} {6673 tsav} [1785 entolee] [1778 entalma] a command; commandments; **see** command *verb*.
Mithqah *transliterated name* {4989 mithqah} Sweetness.
mix up, fodder, mingle *verb* {1101 balal} to mix together; to mix up; **see** Beli Yaal; **see** comingle.
mix *verb* {4537 macak} as a cocktail.
mixture *noun* {4538 mecek} a cocktail.
Moad Yah *transliterated name* {4153 moadyah} Congregation of Yah.
mock *verb* {2048 hathal} to deride.
mockers *plural noun* {2049 hathollim} deriders.
moist *adjective* {7373 ratob} moist with sap.
moist *verb* {7372 ratab} to wetten.
moisten, rain *verb* [1026 breko] to moisten by a shower.
moisten, wet, butler, drink (give), drown *verb* {8248 shaqah} {8257 shaga} to butler, as a bartender; to drink to quench thirst; to drink unto drowning; to cause to be wet.
moistened, moisture, butlership, drinking *noun* {4945 mashqeh} to cause to be moistened, or drunken.
moisture, drink *noun* {8249 shiqquv} {8250 shiqquw} a beverage.
molars *plural noun* {4973 methalleah} literally, biters.
mold *verb* [4111 plasso] to form by molding.
molded *noun* [4110 plasma] the product that was formed by molding.
Molech *transliterated name* {4432 molech} Sovereign; an Ammoniy deity.
Molecheth *transliterated name* {4447 molecheth} Reigned.
molten *noun* {4541 maccekah} that which has been cast by a molten metal.
momentary *noun* [3910 parautika] at that very instant.
mongrel *noun* {4464 mamzer} one born of parents of different races; **cp** bastard.
mongrel, woof *noun* {6154 ereb} a crossed race of persons; the transverse threads.
monolith, stump *noun* {4676 matstsebah} {4678 matstsebeth} a singular block of stone.
monster *noun* {8565 tan} {*plural* 8568 tannoth} {8577 tannim} [2785 keetos] a malformed and/or huge animal.
month *noun* {3393 yerach} [3376 men] the period between two new moons; **see** month, moon (new).
month, moon (new) *noun* {2320 chodesh} [3561 noumeenia] a period of time from which events were scheduled; **see** month.
monument *noun* {6725 tsiun} any substance to memorialize.
moon (full) *noun* {3677 keceh} its festival.
moon, month *noun* {3391 yerach} {3393 yerach} {3394 yareach} {3842 lebanah} [4582 seleenee] the sign in the heavens by which seasons are measured; the body in the heavens which reflects the sun; known as the lesser light; **cp** new moon.

Mordechay *transliterated name* {4782 mordechay} meaning uncertain.
more, much, many, mighty *adjective* {3524 kabbiyr} vast.
Moreshethiy *transliterated name* {4183 morashiy} Of Moresheth Gath.
Mori Yah *transliterated name* {4179 moriyah} Seen of Yah.
morning (early) *noun* {1242 boqer} [4404 proi] [4407 proinos] the first part of daylight.
morology *transliterated noun* [3473 morologia] silly words.
morphosis *transliterated noun* [3446 morphosis] form; figure; **cp** metamorphose.
morrow (the), tomorrow *noun* {4279 machar} {4283 mochorath} [839 aurion] [1887 epaurion] the following day.
morsel *noun* {6595 path} a bit.
mortal *adjective* [2349 thneetos] subject to death.
mortar, chomer, heap *transliterated noun* {2563 chomer} a dry measure as mixed, or heaped.
Mosa *transliterated name* {4162 mowsta} Proceeding.
Mosah *transliterated name* {4681 motsah} Wrung.
Moserah, *plural* **Moseroth** *transliterated name* {4149 mowcerah, mocerowth} Band(s).
Mosheh *transliterated name* {4872, 4873 mosheh} [3475 moseus, moses, mouses] Drawn (as from the water).
moth *noun* {5580 cac} {6211 ash} an insect known for eating cloth.
motheaten *verb* {6244 ashesh} eaten by moths.
mother in law *noun* {2545 chamoth} [3994 penthera] the mother of a man's woman, or a woman's man.
mother *noun* {517 em} [3384 meeteer] a female parent.
motherless *noun* [282 ameetor] without mother; possibly, unmothered.
moulding *noun* {2213 zer} a border.
mound, hemorrhoid *noun* {2914 techor} a rising of earth; a rising by inflamation.
mound, mount *noun* {5550 solelah} as raised.
Mount El *noun, name* {2025 harel} Mount of El.
mount, mountain *noun* {2022 har} {2042 harar} [3714 orinos] [3735 oros] a high landmass.
mount, regurgitate, ascend, holocaust *verb* {5927, 5928 alah} to ascend, as a mountain; to mount an animal; to regurgitate food; to ascend a holocaust; **see** holocaust, *noun.*
mourn *verb* {578 anah} to lament through groaning.
mourning *noun* {8386 taaniyah} a lamenting.
mouth *noun* {6310 peh} {6433 pum} [4750 stoma] in the sense of edge.
much, many, mighty, more *adjective* {3524 kabbiyr} vast.
much, very, exceeding, greatly, increasing, many, mighty *adjective* {7689, 7690 saggiy} superlatively mighty, or large.
muffle *verb* {3813 lahat}.
Multitude of Gog *noun, name* {1996 hamongog} Multitude of Gog.
murder *noun* {7524 retsach} the killing of a person with malice aforethought; **cp** slaughter.
murder *verb* {7523 ratsach} to kill of a person with malice aforethought; **cp** slaughter.
murderer *noun* [443 anthropoktonos] one that kills a person with malice aforethought; **cp** slaughter.
murmurings *plural noun* {8519 telunnoth} grumblings.
mustard *noun* [4615 sinapi] a plant which grows from a very small seed to a remarkable size; refers to a small quantity which becomes great.
muster, oversee, visit *verb* {6485 paqad} to visit with friendly intent, to oversee; or to visit with hostile intent, to take care of; to muster for display.
muster, overseer, oversight, visitation *noun* {6486 pequddah} a visit with friendly intent, to oversee; or a visit with hostile intent, to take care of; a muster for display.
mute *noun* {482 elem} a silenced one.
mute, tie *verb* {481 alam} as in silencing by tying the tongue, or lips; tying bundles.
Muth, Muth Labben *transliterated name* {4192 muwth, muwthlabben} To Die for the Son.
mutilator *verb* [2699 katatomee] cutter; one who would go beyond circumcision.
mutter, meditate *verb* {1897 hagah} to contemplate upon; to utter in a low voice.
muzzle *noun* {4269 machcowm} a muzzle.
myriads (abound by the) *verb* {7231 rabab} to multiply by the myriads.
myriads *noun* {7233 rebabah} {*plural* 7239 ribboth} {7240 ribbo} [3461 murias] [3463 murioi] an innumerable abundance; the number of ten thousand.
myrrh (tincture of) *transliterated noun* [4669 smurnizomai] a myrrh concentrate.
myrrh *transliterated noun* {3910 lot} {4753 mowr} [3464 muron] [4666 smurna] an anointing ointment.
myrrh *transliterated verb* [3462 murizo] to anoint with myrrh.
mystery *noun* {7328 raz} that which is hidden.
myth *transliterated noun* [3454 muthos] a religious legend.

N

Naaman *transliterated name* {5283 naaman} [3497 neeman] Pleasant.
Naamaniy *transliterated name* {5280 naamiy} Of Naaman.
Naarah *transliterated name* {5292 naarah} Lass.
Naaray *transliterated name* {5293 naaray} Youthful.
Nachali El *transliterated name* {5160 nachaliyel} Wadi of El; **see** wadi.
Nacham *transliterated name* {5163 nacham} Consolation.
Nachamani *transliterated name* {5167 nachamaniy} Consolatory.
Nachash *transliterated name* {5176 nachash} Serpent.
Nachath *transliterated name* {5184 nachath} Rest.
Nachbi *transliterated name* {5147 nachbiy} Hide.
Nachor *transliterated name* {5152 nachowr} [3493 nachor] Snorer.
Nachray *transliterated name* {5171 nachray} Snorter.
Nachshon *transliterated name* {5177 nachshon} [3476 naasson] Prognosticator.
Nachum *transliterated name* {5151 nachuwm} [3486 naoum] Comfortable.
nail *noun* {6856 tsipporen} the nail of a finger; a nail, as being pointy, for scratching.
Nain *transliterated name* [3484 nain] Home.
naked (be) *verb* [1130 gumneetuomai] to be stripped; to be scantily clothed.
naked *adjective* [1131 gumnos] unclothed; scantily or poorly clothed.
naked tree *noun* {6176 arar} a tree, as stripped.
naked, nakedness *adjective* {5903 eyrom} {6174 arom} nudity; partial, or total.
naked, nakedness *noun* {4626 maar} {*plural* 4636 maaromim} {6172 ervah} {6173 arvah} that which is stripped bare.
naked, nude *noun* {6181 eryah} stripped.
nakedness *noun* [1132 gumnotees] want of clothing, nakedness of the body.
nakednesses *noun* {*plural* 6169 arahoth} plots of land that are stripped bare.
Nachon *transliterated name* {5225 nachown} Prepared.
name *noun* {8034 shem} [3686 onoma] [5122 tounoma] a title by which a person is distinguished.
name *verb* [3687 onomazo] to bestow a title.
Naphtali *transliterated name* {5321 naphtali} [3508 nephthalim] Wrestler.
Naphtuchim *transliterated name* {5320 naphtuchiym} the meaning uncertain.
Narcissus *transliterated name* [3488 narkissos] Erotic.
nard *transliterated noun* {5373 nerd} [3487 nardos] an aromatic anointing oinment.
narrowness *noun* {4164 muwtsaq} a pressing in.
narrows, straits, confines, distress *noun* {4689 matsoq} {4691 metsuqah} {4712 metsar} from the root, belly; a narrow place; a confinement.
Nathan *transliterated name* {5416 nathan} [3481 nathan] Given.
Nathan Melech *transliterated name* {5419 nathanmelech} Given of the Sovereign.
nation *noun* {523, 524 ummah} [3816 leom] a people united by a government; **cp** goyim; **cp** people.
nature *noun* [5449 phusis] the natural according to physics.
naught, nought, aught, ought *noun* {3972 meumah} [3361 me] [3762 oudeis, oudemia, ouden] nil; several words, and combinations of words are used to indicate nil; these include the double negative, not aught, which the *exeGeses* renders as naught; most versions use the word, thing, which indicates an object; the *exeGeses* avoids thing, as an object is not implied; **note:** ought is correctly aught, but the Authorized Version sometimes uses ought; when combined with the negative, naught, or nought.
nave *transliterated noun* [3485 naos] one of two Hellenic words mistranslated temple; the nave corresponds to the holy of holies of the tabernacle where, prior to the Messiah's staking,

only the archpriest was allowed to enter; when the Messiah completed complete satisfaction for the sins of humanity, the veil of the nave was split from above to below so that all Messianists may now freely enter into his presence; **see** • SUMMARY: HOLY, HOLIES, HALLOW; **see** • SUMMARY: TABERNACLE, TEMPLE, TENT:.

navel *noun* {8270 shor} {8306 sharir} {8326 shorer} the umbilicus of the body.

navesweeper *noun* [3511 neokoros] one who sweeps the nave.

Navith *transliterated name* {5121 naviyth} Habitation.

Nazarene *transliterated name* [3479 nazareenos] [3480 nazoraios] of Nazareth; **cp** Separatist.

Nazareth *transliterated name* [3478 nazareth] derivation uncertain; not to be confused with Old Covenant separatist vow of separation.

Neapolis *transliterated name* [3496 neapolis] New City.

Near Yah *transliterated name* {5294 nearyah} Lad of Yah.

near, nearby, neighbor, nigh *adjective* {7138 qarob} near in place, kindred, or time.

Nebayoth *plural transliterated name* {5032 nebayowth} Fruitfulnesses.

Nebukadnets Tsar *transliterated name* {5019, 5020 nebukadnetstsar} a Tsar of Babel.

Nebushazban *transliterated name* {5021 nebuwshazban} the meaning uncertain; Nebukadnets Tsar's chief eunuch.

necessary, dependant *adjective* [316 anankaios] needed; depend upon.

necessity, need *noun* [318 anankee] distress.

Nechem Yah *transliterated name* {5166 nechemyah} Consolation of Yah.

Nechlamiy *transliterated name* {5161 nechelamiy} Dreamed; Of Nechlam.

Nechum *transliterated name* {5149 nechuwm} Sighed Over.

Nechushta *transliterated name* {5179 nechushta} Copper.

Nechushtan *transliterated name* {5180 nechushtan} Copper.

neck *noun* {1621 gargeroth} {4665 miphreketh} {6203 oreph} {6676, 6677 tsavvar} [5137 trakeelos] the part connecting the head to the body.

necklace *noun* {2002 hamniyk} necklace or neck chain.

necromancer *noun* {178 ob} {*plural* 328 atim} one who communicates with the dead.

necrosis *transliterated noun* [3500 nekrosis] decease.

necro–, deathify, die *verb* {4191 muth} [2289 thanatoo] to die; to put to death.

Nedab Yah *transliterated name* {5072 nedabyah} Volunteer of Yah.

need, necessity *noun* [318 anankee] distress.

needy *noun* {34 ebyon} one who lacks necessities; **cp** poor.

Nei El *transliterated name* {5272 neiel} Wanderer of El.

neighbor, nigh, near, nearby *adjective* {7138 qarob} near in place, kindred, or time.

neighbour *noun* [1069 geton] [4139 plesion] one who dwells nearby; a fellow.

neighing *noun* {*plural* 4684 mitshalah} a whinnying; a whining.

Necho *transliterated name* {5224 nechow} the meaning uncertain; a Misrayim sovereign.

Nemu El *transliterated name* {5241 nemuel} (at the) Right of El.

Nemu Eliy *transliterated name* {5242 nemuweliy} Of Nemu El.

neophyte *transliterated noun* [3504 neophutos] a new convert; a proselyte.

Nephilim *transliterated plural name* {5303 nephilim} literally, Fellers; they who cause others to be felled; that is, to be toppled; **see** fall.

Nephisim *plural transliterated name* {5300 nephuwsheciym} {5304 nephiyciym} Expansions.

Nephtoach *transliterated name* {5318 nephtowach} Opened, as a spring.

Neqeb *transliterated name* {5346 neqeb} Mounting.

Nergal Shareser *transliterated name* {5371 nergalsharetser} the meaning uncertain.

Neri Yah *transliterated name* {5374 neriyah} [3518 neeri] Light of Yah; Overseen of Yah.

Nesiach *transliterated name* {5335 netsiyach} Conspicuous.

Nesib *transliterated name* {5334 netsiyb} Station.

nest *noun* {7064 qen} a nest, as fixed; figuratively, a dwelling.

nest *verb* {7077 qanan} to build, or occupy a nest.

net (drag) *noun* {4365 mikmereth} [293 amphibleestron] a net that is dragged.

net *noun* {4346 makbar} {4364 makmar} {4365 mikmereth} {7568 resheth} {*plural* 7636 shabie} that which is woven; a hair net; **cp** screen.

net, netting, lattice *noun* {7638 sabak} that which is intwined.

Nethan El *transliterated name* {5417 nethanel} [3482 nathanaeel] Given of El.

Nethan Yah *transliterated name* {5418 nethanyah} Given of Yah.

nether, nethermost *adjective* {8481 tachton} {8482 tachti} the lower, or lowest.

Nethinim *transliterated plural noun* {5411 nathinim} {5412 nethinim} those devoted exclusively to holy worship.

new, fresh, anew *adjectice* [2537 kainos] new, especially in freshness, of a new kind.

new, newness *adjective* {2319 chadash} **see** renew, renovate.

new moon, month *noun* {2320 chodesh} [3561 noumeenia] a period of time from which events were scheduled; **see** month.

newness *noun* [2538 kainotees] in a new state.

Nibchaz *transliterated name* {5026 nibchaz} the meaning uncertain; a deity of the Avviy.

Nicodemus *transliterated name* [3530 nikodemos] Public Triumphant.

Nicolaitees *transliterated name* [3531 nikolaitees] Laity Triumphant.

Nicolas *transliterated name* [3532 nikolainos] Triumphant.

Nicopolis *transliterated name* [3533 nikopolis] Triumphant City.

Niger *transliterated name* [3526 niger] Black.

nigh, near, nearby, neighbor *adjective* {7138 qarob} near in place, kindred, or time.

night *noun* {3915 layil} {3916 leyleyla} [3571 nux] literally, a twisting away (of the light); the part of day from sunset to sunrise.

nightday *noun* [3574 nuktheemeron] a full day; **cp** day.

Nineveh *transliterated name* {5210 nineveh} [3535 nineui] meaning uncertain.

Nineviy *transliterated name* [3536 ninuitees] of Nineveh.

nip, bite, blink *verb* {7169 qarats} a pinch; of the lids, of the lips, of the hands as forming.

nipple *noun* {1717 dad} the small protuberance of a breast or udder.

Nisroch *transliterated name* {5268 nisroch} the meaning uncertain; a Babel idol.

Nissi *transliterated title* **pole, sail, ensign** *noun* {5251 nec} an ensign; the pole of an ensign; part of the title, Yah Veh Nissi, which means, Yah Veh Ensign.

nitre *nun* {5427 nether} named from its effervescing acid.

Noach *transliterated name* {5146 noach} [3575 noe] Rest; the patriarch of the flood.

Noad Yah *transliterated name* {5129 noadyah} Congregated (Betrothed) of Yah.

Noah *transliterated name* {5270 noah} Movement; a Yisra Eliyth.

Nobach *transliterated name* {5025 nobach} Bark.

Nobay *transliterated name* {5109 nowbay} Fruitful.

noble *noun* {7261 rabreban} a magnate.

nobles *plural noun* {2715 chor} persons of eminent character.

nobles *plural noun* {6579 partam} grandees.

Nochah *transliterated name* {5119 nowchah} Rest.

nocturnal spectre *noun* {3917 lilith} a night spectre.

nod, nodding, nodded *verb* [1769 enneos] [1770 enneuo] [2656 kataneuo] [3506 neuo] to signal with the head.

Nogah *transliterated name* {5052 nogahh} [3477 naggai] Brilliant.

noncircumcised *verb* [564 aperitmeetos] not circumcised; **cp** circumcised; **cp** decircumcised.

nonpseudo *adjective* [893 apseudees] not phony; **cp** pseudo.

Noomi *transliterated name* {5281 noomiy} Pleasantness.

noon, window *dual noun* {6672 tsohar} double light, as a window; double light, as noon.

noose *noun* [1029 brokos] figuratively, a snare.

noose *noun* {5364 niqpah} a rope, as encircling.

Nophach {5302 nophach} Gust.

north, northerly, northern, northward, north quarter *noun* {6828 tsaphon} literally, of the dark; used only of the north.

northern *adjective* {6830 tsephoniy} of the north.

nosering *noun* {5141 nezem} meaning uncertain; a circular ornament.

nostril, snout, wrath *noun* {639 aph} {*plural* 5156 nechirim} [3709 orgee] the snorter, as in expressing wrath; **see** snorting.

nothing; **see** naught, nought, aught, ought.

notice, recognize, discern, distinguish, estrange *verb* {5234 nakar} to acknowledge; to scrutinize; to distinguish between; to ignore, hence to be estranged.

notoriety, report, fame, hearing *noun* {8052 shemuah} {8088 shema} {8089 shoma} [189 akoee] that which is heard; an announcement; a rumor.
nourish *verb* {2109, 2110 zuwn} to plumpen.
nourishment *noun* {4361 makkoleth} eats.
number, appoint *verb* {4483 menah} {4484 mene} {4487 manah} to enumerate.
Nun *transliterated name* {5126 nun} Perpetual.
nurture *verb* [397 anatrepho] soulically, and mentally, to nourish.
Nymphas *transliterated name* [3564 numphas] Veiled Oblation; a mythical Hellene goddess.

O

O that, if only, if though *interjection* {3863 luw} as a petition.
O that, whoever *participle pronoun* {4310 miy}.
O, Oh *interjection* {994 biy} in the sense of pleading.
oak *noun* {8410 tidhar} a species of tree.
oar, scourge *noun* {7885 shait} a whip; a paddle.
oath *noun* {7621 shebuah} [3727 horkos] literally, a seven; figuratively, the number of completion; a solemn affirmation.
oath *verb* {422 alah} {7650 shaba} [1964 epiokeo] [3660 omnumi, omnuo] [3726 horkizo] [3728 horkomosia] literally, to seven; figuratively, to complete; to solemnly affirm.
Obad Yah *transliterated name* {5662 obadyah} Server of Yah.
Obed *transliterated name* {5744 obed} [5601 obed] Server.
Obed Edom *transliterated name* {5654 obededom} Server of Edom.
oblate, approach, bring near *verb* {7126 qarab} {7127 qereb} to offer for worship; to draw near; to bring near.
oblation *noun* [1435 doron] an oblation; a transliteration of the Hebrew qorban, and of the Hellenic qorban; **see** qorban; **read** Markos 7:11.
oblivion *noun* {5388 neshiyah} forgotten.
obscure, evening *verb* {6150 arab} in the sense of dusking; of becoming obscure.
obscure, uncertain *adjective* [82 adelos] [83 adelotes] unclear.
obscurity *noun* {4155 muwaph} shielded from view.
observant *noun* {7907 sekviy} one that observes.
observation *noun* {7914 sekiyah} that which is observed.
observe, prowl *verb* {7789 shur} to spy out; to survey; **see** stroll.
observer, prowler *noun* {7790 shur} a foe, as lying in wait; **see** stroll.
obstinate *participle* [3267 yaaz] to be bold.
occasion *noun* {8385 taanah} opportunity; opportune time.
occurrence, happening *noun* {4745 miqreh} that which happens to occur.
ode *transliterated noun* [5603 ode] a poem set to music.

- **SUMMARY:**
- **OFFER, OFFERING:**

note: most versions insert the words **offer** and **offering,** even though they are not indicated in the manuscripts; the *exeGeses* indicates these with *oblique type*; **cp** holocaust; sacrifice; libation; **read** Leviticus 23:37.

- **offer up, bear up, bring up** *verb* [399 anaphero] to offer up an offering; to take up.
- **offer** *verb* [4374 prosphero] to offer an offering.
- **offering** *noun* {4503, 4504 minchah} [4376 prosphora] a tribute; **note:** most versions often imply offer and offering even when not in manuscripts; **see** qorban.
- **offering** *noun* {5379 nisseth} an offering, as received.

officer *noun* {2951 tiphcar} {7860 shoter} [4233 praktor] an official invested with an office.
offscouring *verb* {5501 cechiy} a scouring off; **see** scrape off.
offscraping *noun* [4067 peripsoma] what is scraped off; scum.
offspring *adjective* {3329 yetsiy} an issue.
offspring *noun* {5209 nin} {6526 pirchach} {*plural* 6631 tseetsim} that which issued of; progeny; produce; **see** posterity.
ogling *participle* {8265 saqar} to blink coquettishly, playfully.
Oholah *transliterated name* {170 oholah} Her Tent.
Oholi Ab *transliterated name* {171 oholiyab} Tent of Father.
Oholi Bah *transliterated name* {172 oholiybah} My Tent is in Her.
Oholi Bamah *transliterated name* {173 oholiybamah} Tent of the Bamah (Height).
oil *noun* {3323 yitshar} {8081 shemen} oil for anointing.
Ochran *transliterated name* {5918 ochran} Troubler.
old *adjective* [3820 palaios] not recent; worn out.
olive *noun* {2132 zayith} [*plural* 1636 elaia] an oily fruit.
olive (good) *noun* [2565 kallielaios] as cultivated; as improved.
olive (wild) *noun* [65 agrielaios] as uncultivated; as natural.
olive oil *noun* [1637 elaion] the oil of anointing.
olive orchard *noun* [1638 elaion].
Olympas *transliterated name* [3652 olumpas] Heavenly.
omega *transliterated noun* [5598 omega] the last letter of the Greek alphabet; figuratively, finality.
omen *noun* {852 ath} {*plural* 852 atheen} {4159 mopeth} [5059 teras] a phenomenon.
omer *transliterated noun* {5995 amir} {6016 omer} a dry measure of grain.
on account of, so (as) (that), in order to *participle* {4616 maan} {5668 abur} for the purpose of.
on guard, regard, guard *verb* {5201 natar} {5202 nater} {5341 natsar} {8104 shamar} {*plural* 8107 shimmurim} {8108 shomrah} {8176 shaar} [5083 tereo] in the sense of protecting from harm, observing observances, obeying misvahs.
onager *noun* {6167 arad} {6171 arod} a wild burro.
Onesimus *transliterated name* [3682 oneesimos] Profitable.
Onesiphorus *transliterated name* [3683 oneesiphoros] Tribute Bearer.
open, pethach, engrave *verb* {[*transliterated* 6605 pathach} {[*transliterated* 6606 pethach} [*transliterated* 2188 ephphatha] to open; to loosen; to engrave.
open, opening *verb* {6491 paqach} [455 anoigo] [457 anoixis] to open up.
opener *noun* {4668 maphteach} that which opens.
openeyed *adjective* {6493 piqqeach} clear sighted.
opening *noun* {4669 miphtach} as an arperture.
opening *noun* {6495 peqachqoach} as a way of escape.
opening, portal *noun* {6607 pethach} {6608 pethach} {6610 pithchon} {8179 shaar} {8651 tera} [2374 thura] an entrance or an exit.
Ophay *transliterated name* {5778 owphay} Flyer–like.
Ophel *transliterated name* {6077 ophel} Mound.
Opheniy *transliterated name* {6078 ophniy} Of Ophen.
opinion, decision *noun* [1106 gnomee] a personal judgment.
opinions *plural noun* {5587 saiphim} {8312 saraphim} literally, of divided mind; **see** skeptics.
opponent *noun* {7009 giym} one that rises against.
opponent *noun* {8324 sharar} one that opposes.
opportunity *noun* [874 aphorme] a starting point.
oppose *verb* [496 antipipto] [498 antitassomai] to set against.
oppose *verb* {7852 satam} to lurk for; for noun, **see** satan.
opposite, toward, –ward *adjective* {4136 mowl} [481 antikru] [492 antiparerkomai] [495 antiperan] across from.
opposition *noun* {7855 sitnah} **see** oppose.
oppress *verb* {3238 yanah} to maltreat.
oppress, distress *verb* {6693 tsuwq} to compress.
oppress, extort *verb* {6231 ashaq} to press out of; to oppress.
oppress, press *verb* {3905 lachats} literally, to press; to distress.
oppression *noun* {3906 lachats} {4157 muwaqah} {*plural* 4642 maashaqqah} {4835 merutsah} {6125 aqah} {*plural* 6217 ashuq} [2347 thlipsis] constraint; oppression; pressure.
oppression, extortion *noun* {6233 osheq} a pressing out; an oppressing.
oppression, race *noun* {4793 merots} {4794, 4835 merutsah} a test of running; the pressures of life.
oppressor *noun* {4160 muwts} {6216 ashoq} one who oppresses.
opulent, outcry *noun* {7771 showa} one that is opulent; an outcry; **see** cry.
oracle *noun* {5001 naam} {5002 neum} [3051 logion] [5538 chrematismos] a verbal revelation or affirmation.
oracle *verb* [5537 chrematizo] to utter an oracle.
orator *noun* [3052 logios] one who words.
orator *noun* [4489 reetor] one who rhetorizes.
orchard *noun,* **Karmel** *transliterated name* {3759 karmel} a planting of fruit trees; an orchard.
ordain *verb* [1299 diatasso] [5021 tasso] to set apart for ministry; to establish by appointment.
order *noun* [2003 epitage] [5001 tagma] [5010 taxis] an arrangement; a command.
order *verb* [2004 epitasso] [4367 protasso] [4929 suntasso] [5002 taktos] to arrange; to command.
ordinance *noun* [1296 diatage] [1297 diatagma] an order.
ore *noun* {3800 kethem} as carved out; as mined.
ore, sickle, trench, decision, decisive, incision, incisor

adjective, noun {2742 charuts} literally, a mental, soulical, or material incising.
origin *noun* {4351 mekorah} as being dug; as if a mine.
original, eternal, eternally, eternity *noun, adjective, adverbally* {5703 ad} {5769 olam} {5865 elom} {5957 alam} [126 adidios] [166 aionios] a limitless period – either past, present, or future.
ornament *noun* {2481 chaliy} {2484 chelyah} a trinket as polished.
ornament *noun* {5716 adiy} an ornament that adorns.
ornament, adornment, tiara *noun* {6287 peer} an embellishment; a tiara, as an adornment.
orphan *transliterated noun* {3490 yathom} [3737 orphanos] without parents; bereft.
orphanize *transliterated verb* [642 aporphanizomai] to cause to become orphan.
Osem *transliterated name* {684 otsem} Strong.
Osnapper *transliterated name* {620 ocnapper} the meaning uncertain; an Ashshuriy sovereign.
ostriches *plural noun* {7443 renen} named from its cry.
other doctrine, doctrinate otherwise *verb* [2085 heterodidaskaleo] to teach differently; to teach different doctrines.
Othni *transliterated name* {6273 othni} Force.
Othni El *transliterated name* {6274 othniel} Force of El.
ought, naught, nought, aught *noun* {3972 meumah} [3361 me] [3762 oudeis, oudemia, ouden] nil; several words, and combinations of words are used to indicate nil; these include the double negative, not aught, which the *exeGeses* renders as naught; most versions use the word, thing, which indicates an object; the *exeGeses* avoids thing, as an object is not implied; **note:** ought is correctly aught, but the Authorized Version sometimes uses ought; when combined with the negative, naught, or nought.
out, outside, outskirt, outward, outway, without *noun, adverb* {2351 chuts} a separated area.
outburst *noun* {8241 shetseph} an emotional outburst.
outcasts *plural noun* {6849 tsephiah} that which is cast out.
outcry *noun* {6682 tsevachah} a crying out.
outcry, opulent *noun* {7771 showa} one that is opulent; an outcry; **see** cry.
outresurrection *noun* [1815 exanastasis] a resurrection out of.
outrun, run *verb* **runner** *participle* {7323 ruts} {7325 rur} to run; to run faster than.
oven, furnace *noun* {8574 tannur} a fire pot.
overburden *verb* [1912 epibareo] to put a heavy load upon; to be burdensome.
overcast *verb* {5743 ub} to be dense.
overcloud, cloud over *verb* {6049 anan} to cover over with a cloud.
overflow *noun* {3502 yithrah} the surplus.
overflow *verb* {7857 shataph} to inundate.
overflow, float *verb* {6687 tsuph} {7783 shuq} to float; to flow over.
overflowing *noun* {7858 sheteph} an inundation.
overlay *noun* {6826 tsippuy} an encasement.
overlay, watch *verb* **watcher** *participle* {6822, 6823 tsaphah} to observe; to await; to sheet over.
overlay, subdue *verb* {7286 radad} to conquer; to sheet over.
overload *verb* {2959 tarach} to overburden; **cp** burden.
overlook *verb* [3865 paratheoreo] [5237 huperido] to disregard.
overlord *verb* [2634 katakuriuo] [2961 kuriuo] to lord over; **see** lord.
overpass, pass (over) (through), surpass, trespass *verb* {5674 abar} to cross over; this verb is unrelated to the mistranslation of passover.
overpower, prevail, empower *verb* {8280 sarah} {8630 taqaph} [2616 katadunastuo] [2729 katiskuo] [2901 krataioo] [2902 krateo] to have ability over; to cause to have power.
oversee, perpetual, perpetuity (in), eminent *adjective, participle* {5329 natsach} {5331 netsach} [1336 dieenekes] continual, on and on; to oversee work; to be eminent.
oversee, scope over *verb* [1983 episkopeo] to episcopate; to inspect over.
oversee, visit, muster *verb* {6485 paqad} to oversee; to visit with friendly intent, to visit with hostile intent, to take care of; to muster for display.
overseeing *noun* {6487 piqqadon} that which is being overseen, or watched over.
overseeing others *verb* [244 allotriepiskopos] in the sense of not minding one's own matters.
overseer *noun* {6488 peqiduth} {6496 paqid} one that oversees, or watches over.
overseer, oversight, visitation, muster *noun* {6486 pequddah} a visit with friendly intent, to oversee; or a visit with hostile intent, to take care of; a muster for display.
overshadow, overshadowing *verb* {6751 tsalal} to shade, as hovering over.
oversight, visitation, muster, overseer *noun* {6486 pequddah} a visit with friendly intent, to oversee; or a visit with hostile intent, to take care of; a muster for display.
overspread, spread over *verb* {5259 nacak} to interweave.
overspreading *adjective* {4473 mimshach} expanding over.
overtake, reach, attain *verb* {5381 nasag} to attain by reaching for.
overtake, take over *verb* [2638 katalambano] to lay hold of; to seize.
overthrow *noun* {2925 taltelah} {4072 midcheh} {*plural* 4073 medachphah} {4114 mahpechah} an overthrow; a rejection.
overthrow *verb* {1760 dahghah} to overthrow by pushing down.
overturn, remain, return, behave *verb* [390 anastrepho] [396 anatrepo] to turn over; to overthrow; to turn; in the manner one turns (behaves).
overworking [4020 periergazomai] [4021 periergos] to bustle about uselessly.
owl (little), cup *noun* {3563 kowe} a container; an owl, from the cup–like cavity of its eye.
ox, oxen *noun* {7794 shor} an ox, or oxen as strolling; **see** stroll.

P

Paaray *transliterated name* {6474 paaray} Yawning.
pace *noun* {4703 mitsad} {6806 tsaah} a marching pace; the measured movement from one step to another; **cp** step.
pace *verb* {6805 tsaad} to pace; to march; **see** march.
Pachath Moab *transliterated name* {6355 pachathmowab} Pit of Moab.
pacify *verb* [1514 iereneuo] [1517 eirenopoieo] the verb of peace; to make peace; to be peaceful.
Paddan *transliterated name* {6307 paddan} Plateau.
Paddan Aram *transliterated name* {6307 paddanaram} Plateau of Aram.
paddle, flip, flit *verb* {7751 shuwt} to flit forth and back; to flip oars.
Pagi El *transliterated name* {6295 pagiel} Coincidence of El.
pail *noun* {1805 deli} [502 antlema] a container for drawing water; noun of bail.
pail *noun* {5845 atiyn} container.
pain *noun* {3511 keeb} physically, soulically, or mentally, suffering.
pain *verb* {3510 kaab} to hurt; to feel pain.
palace *noun* {1001 bira} {1002 birah} {1055 bithan} {*plural* 1003 birahanith} a large house; **cp** house; manse; nave; priestal precinct.
Palal *transliterated name* {6420 palal} Prayer.
Palal Yah *transliterated name* {6421 palalyah} Prayer of Yah.
palanquin *noun* {668 appiryown} a passenger conveyance borne on shoulders by poles.
palanquin, tortoise *noun* {6632 tsab} a wagon, as covered; a tortoise, as covered.
palate *noun* {2441 chek} the roof of the mouth.
pale *verb* {2357 chavar} to turn pale; to blanch.
Pallu *transliterated name* {6396 palluw} Distinguished.
Palluiy *transliterated name* {6384 palluiy} Of Pallu.
palm, paw, sole, bowl, hollow *noun* {3709 kaph} {6447 pas} {8168 shoal} a hollow of the hand, foot, paw, or body; also utensils with a hollow.
palm (tree) *noun* {8558 tamar} {8560 tomer} {8561 timmor} a species of tree; symbolic of triumph; of being erect.
palm leaf *noun* {3712 kippah} as having a hollow as a palm.
palmspan *verb* {2946 taphach} to span with the palm.
palmspan, support *noun* {2947 tephach} {2948 tophach} the span of a palm; a support; **see** span.
Paloniy *transliterated name* {6397 pelowniy} Separate; Of Palon.
Palti El *transliterated name* {6409 paltiel} Escape of El.
Palti *transliterated name* {6406 paltiy} Escaped.
Paltiy *transliterated name* {6407 paltiy} Of Palti.
pamper *verb* {6445 panaq} to treat daintily.
pang *noun* **ambassador** *title* {6735 tsir} an ambassador, as a

representative; a pang, as writhing.
pang *noun* {2427 chiyl} a throe, especially of childbirth.
pang, boundary, cord, line *noun* {2256 chebel} literally, a rope; as a boundary line, or as binding one in a pang.
pannag *transliterated noun* {6436 pannag} an article of trade or barter.
panoply *transliterated noun* [3833 panoplia] a full suit of armour.
pant (after) *verb* {5689 agab} [1937 epithumeo] to breathe hard after; **cp** sigh.
panter *noun* [1938 epithumeetees] one who pants.
panting *noun* {5691 agabah} {*plural* 5690 egeb} [1939 epithumia] a breathing hard after; **cp** the Hebrew agabah with the Hellenic agape.
parable *transliterated noun* [3850 parabole] similitude; a short narrative of a possible event in life, from which a moral or spiritual truth is drawn.
Paraclete *transliterated noun* [3875 parakleetos] one who consoles, guides, intercedes; Yah Shua is the Paraclete; 1 Yahn 2:1; the Holy Spirit is the "another Paraclete" whom Yah Shua sent after His rapture; **read** Yahn 14:16,26, 15:26, 16:7.
paradise, park *noun* {6508 pardec} [3857 paradisos] a park; refers to the original garden, the new garden in Apocalypse, as well as the third heaven in 2 Corinthians 12; **cp** garden.
paradox *transliterated noun* [3861 paradoxos] a contradiction.
Paran *transliterated name* {6290 paran} Ornamental.
parapet *noun* {4624 maaqeh} a rampart to protect warriors.
parcel *noun* [5564 chorion] a plot of land.
parch *noun* **parched** *adjective* {6704 tsicheh} {*plural* 6710 tsachtsachah} {6723 tsiyah} {6724 tsiywon} {7039 qaliy} parched land, throat, kernels.
parch, desolate, dry *adjective* {2720 chareb} {8076 shamen} parched; ruined.
parch, desolate, dry *verb* {2717, 2718 charab} {3456 yashem} {8045 shamad} {8046 shemad} [2049 ereemoo] to lay waste; to destroy.
parch, drought *noun* {2721 choreb} {2725 charabon} very dry.
parched (area) *noun* {2723 chorbah} {2724 charabah}.
parched *adjective* {6704 tsicheh} from the root, to glow; parched.
parchment *noun* [3200 membrana] membrane.
parents *noun* [1118 gonus] father and mother.
Parnach *transliterated name* {6535 parnach} of uncertain derivative.
Paroh *transliterated title* {6547 paroh} [5328 pharao] title of Misrayim sovereigns.
Paroh Hophra *transliterated title and name* {6548 parohchophra} a Misrayim sovereign.
Paroh Nechoh *transliterated title and name* {6549 parohnechoh} a Misrayim sovereign.
parousia, appearance *transliterated noun* [3952 parousia] the presence to be; of the coming of ministers; especially of the return of our Adonay Yah Shua Messiah.
Parpar *transliterated name* {6554 parpar} Rapid.
part, end *noun* {7117, 7118 qetsath} a portion; a termination.
partake, partaking *verb* [3335 metalambano] [3352 metochee] [3348 metecho] to take part together; to share in.
partake, support *verb* [482 antilambanomai] [484 antileepsis] to take part; to support.
partaker, communicant *noun* [2844 koinonos] one who communes or partakes in common, or in communion.
partaker, partner *noun* [3335 metalambano] [3336 metaleepsis] [3353 metokos] one who takes part.
partaking, imparting *verb* [2841 koinoneo] communing and partaking by imparting.
partiality *noun* [4380 prosopolepteo] [4382 prosopoleepsia] favoritism.
partiality *noun* {4856 massoh} as in lifting one above another.
Paruach *transliterated name* {6515 paruwach} Blossomed.
Parvayim *transliterated name* {6516 parvayim} an Oriental region.
Pas Dammim {6450 pacdammiym} Coverall of Blood.
pasach *transliterated noun* {6453 pecach} [3957 pascha] a celebration of Elohim's protection; a celebration sacrifice of a lamb; Adonay Yah Shua Messiah as our protection; often mistranslated passover; **cp** suffer [3958 pasko]; **read** Vine; **read** Theological Wordbook of the Old Testament.
pasach *transliterated verb* {6452 pacach} to protect.
Pasach *transliterated name* {6457 pasach} Protection.
Pashchur *transliterated name* {6583 pashchuwr} Liberation.
pass (away) (over) (through) *verb* {2498, 2499 chalaph} from the root, to slide by; to pass on.
pass (over) (through), surpass, trespass, overpass *verb* {5674 abar} to cross over; this verb is unrelated to the mistranslation of passover.
pass, passage *noun* {4569 maabarah} a place to cross over; **see** route.
pasture *noun* {4829 mireh} {4830 miriyth} {5097 nahalol} a place of feeding.
pasture *noun* {4999 naah} {7471 reiy} [3542 nome] grazing land.
patch *verb* {2950 taphal} literally, to patch clothes; to patch lies.
patch, spot *verb* {2921 tala} to color in spots; to repair in spots.
path, way *noun* {734, 735 orach} also includes the manner of a person.
pathos *transliterated noun* [3806 pathos] a suffering; a passion.
Pathrosiym *transliterated name* {6625 pathruciym} Of Pathros.
patriarch *transliterated noun* [3966 patriarches] [3967 patrikos] [3971 patroos] the arch fathers; the early fathers.
patriarchal tradition *noun* [3970 patroparadotos] the tradition of the arch fathers.
patriarchy *noun* [3965 patria] the reign of the arch fathers, past or present.
patricide *noun* [3964 patraloees] a parricide; a murderer of, or the murder of one's father.
patroness *noun* [4368 prostatis] a female who sponsors or supports.
pattern *noun* {8403 tabnith} a model to be reproduced or followed.
Paulos *transliterated name* [3972 paulos] Little.
pause *verb* [3973 pauo] to stop.
pavement, red hot stones *noun* {7528 ratsaph} {7529 retseph} as used for baking; as used for laying a pavement.
pavilion *noun* {643 appeden} {8237 shaphrur} a large tent.
paw, sole, bowl, hollow, palm *noun noun* {3709 kaph} {6447 pas} {8168 shoal} a hollow of the hand, foot, paw, or body; also utensils with a hollow.
pawn, pledge, entangle *verb* {5670 abat} to entangle a people; to entangle a pledge by pawning.
payoff *noun* {866 ethnah} {868 ethnan} {5078 nedeh} {5083 nadan} usually the price paid to a whore.
peacocks *plural noun* {8500 tukkim} a species of imported creature.
pearls *plural noun* {6443 paniyn} as being round.
pebble *noun* {1486 goral} casting pebbles was a common manner of determining who received what; **see** Apocalypse 2:17.
peculiar aquisition *noun* [4047 peripoiesis] private, personal property; Messianists are Elohim's private personal property.
peculiar people *adjective* [4041 periousios] private personal people; Messianists are Elohim's private personal people.
peculiar treasure *noun* {5459 cegullah} private treasure, as held close to the breast; private property.
pedagogue *transliterated noun* [3807 paidagogos] [3810 paidutees] one who disciplines children; a tutor.
Pedah El *transliterated name* {6300 pedahel} Redeemed of El.
Pedah Sur *transliterated name* {6301 pedatsur} Redeemed of the Rock.
Pedah Yah *transliterated name* {6305 pedayah} Redeemed of Yah.
peel *noun* {4286 machsoph} a peeling.
peel *verb* {6478 patsal} to strip, as tree bark.
peelings *plural noun* {6479 petsalah} that which is peeled.
peer *verb* {7688 shagach} to peep; to peer.
peeved *adjective* {5620 car} annoyed.
Pela Yah *transliterated name* {6411 pelayah} Marvel of Yah.
Pelat Yah *transliterated name* {6410 pelatyah} Escape of Yah.
Peleg *transliterated name* {6389 peleg} [5317 phalek] Split.
Pelesheth *transliterated name* {6429 pelesheth} Wallow; original name of Palestine.
Peleshethiy *transliterated name* {6430 pelishtiy} Of Pelesheth.
pelican *noun* {6893 qaath} from its vomiting.
penalize *verb* {6064 anash} to inflict a penalty; to fine.
penalty *noun* {6066 onesh} a fine; **see** confiscate.
pendant *noun* {7720 saharon} a round ornament for the neck.
pendants *plural noun* {5188 netiyphahoth} pendants for the ears.
pendulous *plural noun* {8534 taltalim} vibrations.
penetrate, press, sink, bend, descend *verb* {5181 nachath}

from the root, to sink; to go down; to press or lead down.
Peni El *transliterated name* {6439 peniel} [5323 phanouel] Face of El.
pentecost *transliterated noun* [4005 pentekostee] fiftieth; the fiftieth day following the pasach; **read** Leviticus 23:15–17, Acts 2:1–4.
Penu El *transliterated name* {6439 punuel} Face of El.
people, peoples *noun* {5971, 5972 am} [2992 laos] the body of citizens of a place, group, or class; **cp** goyim; **cp** nations.
Peqach *transliterated name* {6492 peqach} Open.
Peqach Yah *transliterated name* {6494 peqachyah} Opened of Yah.
Peqod/visitation *transliterated name, noun* {6489 peqowd} refers to Babel as a place of Yah Veh's visitation.
perceive, consider *verb* [2657 katanoeo] to observe attentively.
perceive, know *verb* {3045 yada} {3046 yeda} [143 aisthanomai] [1492 eido] [5274 hupolambano] to be aware through the senses.
perception *noun* {4486 manda} [144 aitheesis] [145 aistheeteerin] an awareness through the senses.
perception, knowledge *noun* {1843 dehag} {1844 dehgah} {1847 dahgath} [1108 gnosis] an awareness of facts.
perennial, permanent *adjective* {386 ethan} {7011 qayam} continually abiding; lasting.
Peres *transliterated name* {6557 perets} [5329 phares] Separatist; **see** Peresiy.
Peres Uzza *transliterated name* {6560 peretsuzza} Separatist of Strength; **see** Peresiy.
Peresiy *transliterated name* {6558 partsi} [*plural* 5330 pharisaios] Separatist; one who separates from.
perfect *adjective*, **totality** *noun*, **totally** {3642 kaliyl} all inclusive; naught to be added.
perfect *verb* {3634 kalal} to finish to perfection.
perfection *noun* {*plural* 4357 miklah} {4359 miklal} splendid; with splendor.
perforated *adjective* {2751 choriy} full of holes.
perfume *noun* {7544 reqach} {7545 roqach} {*plural* 7547 raqquachim} an aromatic; a scented substance.
perfume *verb* {7543 raqach} to perfume.
perfumer *noun* {*masculine* 7546 raqqach} {*feminine* 7548 raqqachah} one that perfumes.
Perizziy *transliterated name* {6522 perizziy} Of the suburbs.
permanent, perennial *adjective* {386 ethan} {7011 qayam} continually abiding; lasting.
permit *noun* {7558 rishyon} a permission.
perpetual, perpetuity (in), eminent, oversee *adjective, participle* {5329 natsach} {5331 netsach} [1336 dieenekes] continual, on and on; to oversee work; to be eminent.
perpetually *adverb* {8411 tedira} continually on and on.
perpetuate *verb* {5125 nun} to continue on and on.
perplex *verb* {6323 pun} {7672 shebash} to confuse, to entangle.
persecuted, persecution *verb, noun* {4783 murdaph} {4788 marud} a maltreatment; to maltreat.
Persia, Persian *transliterated name* {6539, 6540 parac} {6542, 6543 parsciy} the land of Persia; including settlers.
perverse *adjective* {2019 haphakpak} [1294 diastrepho] devious; distorted.
perverseness *noun* {3891 lezuwth} {5758 ivya} {5558 seleph} a turning from; a mental twistedness.
perversion *noun* **perverted** *adjective* {6143 iqqeshuth} as in perversion of mouth.
perversion, perversity *noun* {5771 avon} deviation.
perversities *plural noun* {5773 aveh} deviations.
pervert *noun* {5760 avil} perverse.
pervert *verb* {3868 luwz} {6140 aqash} to distort; to turn away from.
pervert *verb* {5686 abath} to interlace.
pervert, subvert *verb* {5557 calaph} to turn from; to undermine.
pervert, twist, bend *verb* {5753 avah} {5754 avvah} to crook; to overthrow.
perverted *adjective* {6141 iqqesh} distorted; turned away from.
pestle *verb* {3795 kathiyth} {3806 kathash} {3807 kathath} to pulverize with a pestle.
pestle, socket *noun* {4388 maktesh} {5940 eliy} the pestle of a mortar; a socket.
Pethach Yah *transliterated name* {6611 pethachyah} Opened of Yah.
pethach, engrave, open *verb* {[*transliterated* 6605 pathach} {[*transliterated* 6606 pethach} [*transliterated* 2188 ephphatha] to open; to loosen; to engrave.
Pethu El *transliterated name* {6602 pethuel} Duped of El.
petition *noun* {7596 shelah} [1162 deesis] an asking; a solemn request.
petition *verb* {8469 tachanun} [1189 deomai] to solemnly request.
petrifaction *noun* [4457 porosis] rocklikeness; **see** Petros.
petrified *verb* [4456 poroo] become rocklike; **see** Petros.
Petros *transliterated name* {3710 keph} [4074 petros] Rock; **see** Kepha; **note:** Petros is a Hellene translation of the Hebrew Keph, whereas Kepha is a transliteration of the Hebrew.
petty, shortly, bit, bit by bit, few, little *adjective, adverb* {4592 meat} diminutive; a few; a little.
Peullthay *transliterated name* {6469 peullthay} Laborious.
phantasm *transliterated noun* [5326 phantasm] a figment of the imagination.
pharmacist *transliterated noun* [5332 pharmakus] [5333 pharmakos] drug pushers; originally pharmacists were associated with drugs in the occult.
pharmacy *transliterated noun* [5331 pharmakia] the dispensary of drugs.
Pharsin *verb* {6537 peras} separated; split.
Philadelphia *transliterated noun* [5359 philadelphia] Friendship City.
philanthropically *transliterated adverb* [5364 philanthropos] friendly giving.
philanthropy *transliterated noun* [5363 philanthropia] friend of humanity; also friend of giving.
Philemon *transliterated name* [5371 philemon] Friendly.
Philetos *transliterated name* [5372 philetos] Friendly.
Philippos *transliterated name* [5376 philippos] Friend of Horses.
Philologos *transliterated name* [5378 philologos] Friend of Words; Philological.
phoenix *transliterated noun* [5404 phoinix] a type of palm.
phylactery *noun* {2903 towphaphah} [*transliteration* 5440 phulakterion] a guardcase worn on the forehead containing scripture passages.
physical *adjective* [5446 phusichos] of the physique; instinctive.
physically *adv*[5447 phusichos] instinctively.
Pi Ha Hiroth *plural transliterated name* {6367 pihachiyroth} Mouth of the Holes.
pick *noun* {4281 machareshah} an instrument for picking; **cp** hoe.
pierce *verb* {3735 kara} to be pierced in spirit.
pierce, appoint, bore *verb* {5344 naqab} to point out; to thrust or make a hole through.
pierce, dig *verb* {3738, 3739 kahrah} to bore; to dig through.
pierce, pinch *verb* {4600 maak} from the root, to press; to pierce.
pierce, pluck, profane *verb* {2490 chalal} {2610 chaneph} [2840 koinoo] to pierce a person; to pluck an instrument; to desecrate the hallowed.
pierced, profane *adjective* {2455 chol} {2491 chalal} [952 bebeelos] of pierced (slaughtered) and profaned persons.
Pichol *transliterated name* {6369 piychol} Mouth of All.
Pilcha *transliterated name* {6401 pilcha} Slicing.
pilgrim *noun* [3927 parepidemos] a wanderer in a foreign land.
pillar *noun* {4690 matsuq} {5982 ammud} {*plural* 8564 tamrurim} [4769 stulos] a column; a vertical structural support; of smoke; of fire; **cp** statue.
Piltay *transliterated name* {6408 piltay} Escaped.
pinch, pierce *verb* {4600 maak} from the root, to press; to pierce.
Pinechas *transliterated name* {6372 piynechac} Mouth of a Serpent.
pinion *noun* {83 eber} {84 ebrah} the bone of the wing.
pinky, younger, fewer, lesser, little *adjective* {6810 tsaor} {6995 qoten} {6996 qatan} less in age, number, size; little finger.
Pirathoniy *transliterated name* {6553 pirathoniy} Of Pirathon.
Pisgah *transliterated name* {6449 picgah} Contemplation.
Pishon *transliterated name* {6376 piyshown} Spread.
Pisses *transliterated name* {6483 pitstsets} Dispersive.
pit *noun* {4379 mikreh} {6354 pachath} as dug.
pit, pitfall *noun* {7825 shechith} {7882 shichah} as a depression.
pitch, camphire, koper/atonement *noun* {3724 koper} camphor, a medication; a sealant for the ark of the flood; also

an atonement: **see** koper/atonement.
pitted *noun* {6356 pechetheth} pitted with holes or blemishes as in oxidation.
place (by), set (by), stand (by), station (by) *verb* {3320 yatsab} {3322 yatsag} {5324 natsab} from the root, to place, so as to stay.
place *noun* {8499 tekunah} a fixed, or certain place.
place, put, set *verb* {7760, 7761 suwm} {7896 shith} {8239 shaphath} {8271 shathah} to put in place.
placing *noun* {8667 tesumeth} a placing of the hand.
plague *noun* {4046 maggephah} a pestilence.
plague *transliterated noun* {5061 nega} {5063 negeph} [4127 plege] a heavy touch, or strike; an infliction of disease.
plague, reach, touch *verb* {5060 naga} to touch heavily; to strike.
plain, straight, straightness, level *noun* {4334 miyshor, *plural* miyshorim} {4339 meyshar} {6160 arabah} plain, as unadorned; as a level land area; as of straight character; as just.
plant *noun* {3657 kannah} {3661 kanan} [5451 phutia] organic produce which cannot move of itself.
plant *verb* {5193 nata, *plural* natiaim} [5452 phutuo] to place seed in the ground.
plant, plantation *noun* {5194 neta} a planting; a place of planting.
plant, planting, plantation *noun* {4218 mizra} {4302 matta} a field, as planted.
plea, pleading *noun* {1779, 1780 diyn} a defence; a petition.
plea, strife, contention, defence *noun* {7379 rib} a personal, or legal contest.
plead *verb* [626 apologeomai] to defend.
plead, examine, judge *verb* {8199 shaphat} {8200 shephat} [350 anakrino] [2919 krino] to scrutinize; to investigate.
plead, strive, contend, defend *verb* {7378 rub} to hold a controversy.
plead (for) *verb* {1777, 1778 diyn} to petition; to act in defence of.
pleader *noun* {1781, 1782 dayan} one who pleads.
pleading *noun* [627 apologia] words in defence.
pleading, plea *noun* {1779, 1780 diyn} a defence; a petition.
pleasant, pleasure *adjective* {5273 naiym} {6156 areb} delightful.
pleasantness *adjective* {5278 noam} delightful; agreeableness.
please, be pleased, pleasing, (have the) (take) pleasure *verb* {5276 naem} {5727 adan} {6149 areb} {7521 ratsah} [700 aresko] [701 arestos] to please; to please (satisfy) a debt; **cp** shalom.
pleasing, pleasure *noun* {7522 ratson} a delight.
pleasure *noun* {5730 eden} **see** Eden.
pledge (heavy) *noun* {5667 abot} that which has been pledged, or pawned.
pledge *noun* {2258 chabol} {6161 arubbah} {6162 arabon} [728 arrabon] an agreement as bound; that which is pledged for colateral.
pledge, comingle, mingle *verb* {6148, 6151 arab} to become colateral.
pledge, entangle, pawn *verb* {5670 abat} to entangle a people; to entangle a pledge by pawning.
pledge, spoil, despoil *verb* {2254, 2255 chabal} literally, to bind tightly; as in spoiling or as in binding a pledge.
pledges *plural noun* {8594 taarubahoth} sons, as security.
plough *verb* {2758 charish} literally, to slice.
plow, hush *verb* {2790 charash} literally, to scratch; to silence.
plowed fields *plural* {3010 yageb} literally, plowings, as in fields to plow.
plowers *participle* {3009 yagab} diggers; ploughers.
pluck *verb* {5394 nashal} to pluck off.
pluck, plucking, psalm, psalming *noun* {2158, 2159 zamir} {2170 zemar} {2172 zimrah} {2176 zimrath} {4210 mizmor} a string, fruit, or twig as plucked.
pluck, profane, pierce *verb* {2490 chalal} {2610 chaneph} [2840 koinoo] to pierce a person; to pluck an instrument; to desecrate the hallowed.
pluck, pull, pull stakes *verb* {5265 naca} to pluck; to pull up; to pull the tent stakes when moving; **read** Numbers 33:3–48.
pluck, strip *verb* {6998 qataph} {7059 qamat} to pluck out; to strip off.
plucker, psalmist *noun* {2171 zammar} plucker.
plumage *noun* {5133 notsah} the entire covering of feathers on a bird.
plumbline *noun* {4949 mishqeleth} a weight with a line attached for surveying.
plump *noun* {2109 yahsan} {6371 pimah} fat.
plump, fatten *verb* {2492 chalam} {3780 kasah} to cause to be fat, to plump; to cover with flesh.
plunder *noun* {957 baz} {961 bizzah} {4933 mechiccah} [724 harpage] a pillage.
plunder *verb* {962 bazaz} {8154 shasah} {8155 shacac} [1283 diarpazo] to seize apart; to pillage.
pockets *plural noun* {2754 charitim} literally, cutouts.
poem *noun* {4387 miktam} a metrical composition.
poet *transliterated noun* [4163 poietes] one who composes metrical compositions.
point, cut, decide, determine *verb* {2782 charat} {2852 chathak} to be cut; to cut a decision, or a determination; to point.
point, pointen *verb* {8150 shanan} to point; to cause to be pointy; to pierce.
poison, fury *noun* {2534 chemah} heat; as anger, as poison.
Pochereth Sebayim *transliterated name* {6380 pocherethtsebayiym} Trap of Gazelles.
pole, sail, ensign *noun* **Nissi** *transliterated title* {5251 nec} an ensign; the pole of an ensign; part of the title, Yah Veh Nissi, which means, Yah Veh Ensign.
pole, yoke pole *noun* {4132 mowt} the slip pole of a yoke.
polish, purge, cleanse *verb* {1305 barar} [1571 ekkathairo] clarify, catharize; **cp** purify.
polish, rash, balden *verb* {4178 mowrat} {4803 marat} {4804 merat} to rub (off); to pluck; to cause to be bald.
polish, scour *verb* {4838 maraq} to polish, so as to sharpen.
politarche *transliterated noun* [4173 politarches] arch politicians of the city.
pollution *noun* [234 alisgeema] a contamination.
polylogy *transliterated noun* [4180 polulogia] multiwordedness.
pomp *noun* {1344 geah} {1346 gaavah} {1347 gaoun} {1348 qeuwth} ostentation; majesty.
pompous *adjective* {1341 ge} {1343 geeh} {1349 gaayon} ostentatious.
pond *noun* {4950 mishqa} a settling (of water).
poor *adjective* {1800 dal} weak; thin: **cp** needy; **note:** one can be poor without being needy.
poor *noun* [4434 ptokos] begging; lacking in anything.
Porkios *transliterated name* [4201 porkios] Porky.
portal, opening *noun* {6607, 6608 pethach} {6610 pithchon} {8179 shaar} {8651 tera} [2374 thura] an opening for entering and exiting.
portalguard *noun* {8652 tara} [2377 thuroros] one who guards a portal.
porter *noun* {7778 shoer} a janitor.
portico *noun* {4329 meycak} {4528 micderown} [4745 stoa] a porch, as being covered.
portion *noun* {4490 manah} a portion as measured out; **see** meneh.
portion, smooth, allotment *noun* {2506 cheleq} {2508 chalaq} {2511 challaq} {2513 chelqah} {2515 chaluqqah} {4255 machleqah} {4256 machaloqeth} {4521 menath} smoothness of tongue; usually an inheritance allotted by pebble.
possess *verb* {270 achaz} to have by seizing; verb of possession.
possess *verb* {3423 yaresh} [2932 ktaomai] to take hold; in some Hebrew stems, to dispossess.
possession *noun* {272 achuzzah} something seized.
possession *noun* {3424 yereshah} {3425 yerushshah} {4180 morash} {4181 morashah} {4476 mimshaq} that which is held on to.
possible, capable *adjective* [1415 dunatos] having sufficient dynamis; **see** dynamis.
posterity *noun* {5220 neked} from the root, to propagate; **see** offspring.
potentate *noun* {7333 razon} {7336 razan} one who possesses power.
Poti Phera *transliterated name* {6319 powtiyphera} the meaning uncertain; of Misrayim derivative.
potion, carousal *noun* {5435 cobe} a drinking revelry; a potion of carousing.
potsherd, pottery *noun* {2789 cheres} a piece of pottery.
pottage *noun* {5138 nazid} that which is boiled.
pouch *noun* {3219 yalqut} for gleanings, or for scrip.
pouch *noun* {3599 kiyc} [905 balantion] a money bag.
pounce *verb* {2907 tuws} to pounce upon, as a bird of prey.

pour, anoint, libate *verb* {4886 mashach} {5258 nacak} {5260 necak} {5480 cuwk} {8210 shaphach} [218 alipho] [4689 spendomai] [5548 chrio] symbolic of setting apart by libating (pouring on) of oil; of pouring a molten image.
pour, draw *verb* {7324 ruq} to pour in; to pour out.
pour, firm, form *verb* {3332 yatsaq} to pour out; to shape by pouring into a mold; to make firm.
pour, flow *verb* {5047 negad} {5064 nagar} {5140 nazel} to pour out; to flow out, as to clear the way.
pour, melt *verb* {5413 nathak} to flow; to liquify.
pour blood *verb* [130 haimatekchusia] as an effusion of blood.
pour (out) *verb* {6694 tsuwq}.
pour out, strip naked, empty *verb* {6168 arah} {6379 pakah} to empty; to empty by pouring; to strip bare; **see** naked.
poured (forth), (out) *verb* [1632a echeo] [1632b echuno] to pour forth; to bestow.
pouring *noun* {8211 shephek} a place where ashes are poured.
pouring, libation *noun* {5261 necak} {5262 necek} a pouring of worship; a pouring of images.
poverty *noun* {4544 mickenuth} {7389 rish} destitution.
power *noun* {2632 checen} {8632 teqoph} {8633 toqeph} [2904 kratos] ability.
powerful *adjective* {2626 chacin} {2634 chacon} [2900 krataios] [2903 kratistos] able.
praetorium *transliterated noun* [4232 praitorion] courtroom.
prancer *noun* {3753 karkarah} an animal that prances; probably a dromedary.
pray *verb* {6419 palai} {6739 tsela} [4336 proseuchomai] to entreat.
prayer *noun* {8605 tephillah} [4335 proseuche] an entreaty.
pre–evangelism *transliterated noun* [1860 epangelia] [1862 epangelma] an evangelism previously prepared, or previously evangelized; **see** evangelism; **cp** angel.
pre–evangelize *transliterated verb* [1861 epangello] [4279 proepangellomai] [4283 prouangelizomai] [4293 prokatangello] previously evangelized; an evangelism previously prepared for future evangelizing.
preach, preaching *verb* [2784 kerusso] to proclaim.
preacher *noun* [2783 keerux] proclaimer.
preaching *noun* [2782 keerugma] proclaiming.
prearrange *verb* [4384 protasso] previously arranged.
precede, anticipate, confront *verb* {6923 qadam} to front; **cp** east.
preceding, ancient, antiquity, east, easterly, eastern, eastward, formerly *noun* {6921 qadim} {6924 qedem} {6925 qodam} {6926 qidmah} {6927 qadmah} literally, the forefront; from the front.
precepts *plural noun* {6490 piqqudim} mandates.
precious (vastly) *adjective* [4185 polutelees] [4186 polutimos] extremely valuable.
precious *noun* {4022 meged} highly regarded.
preciousnesses *plural noun* {4030 migdanahoth} that which is highly regarded.
precipitate *verb* {4048 magar} to yield up; to hurl from a precipice; to hurry.
precise (most) *adjective* [196 akribestatos] most exact.
precisely (inquire) *verb* [198 akriboo] to be exact.
precisely (more) *adverb* [197 akribesteron] [199 akribos] more exactly.
preciseness *noun* [195 akribia] exactness.
predetermine *verb* [4309 proorizo] [4388 protitheemi] to determine prior to occurrence.
preeminent cathedras *noun* [4410 protokathedria] the foremost seat; preeminence in council.
preeminent leader *noun* [4414 protostates] the most prominent leader at celebrations.
preeminent *noun* {5330 netsach} most prominent.
preeminent recliner *noun* [4411 protoklisia] the most prominent reclining place.
preevident *adjective* [4271 prodelos] known before all.
prefect, statue, station *noun* {5333 netsib} {*plural* 5460 seganin} {*plural* 5461 saganim} {6346, 6347 pechah} a stationed officer; that which is stationary; a station; also a statue.
preinscribe *verb* [4270 prographo] to write previously.
premeditate *verb* [4304 promeletao] to meditate prior to occurrence.
preparation *noun* [2091 hetoimasia] a making ready.
prepare *verb* [2090 hetoimazo] [2680 kataskuazo] [3903 paraskuazo] to prepare; make ready; equip.
prepare, establish *verb* {3559 kuwn} to set up.
prepared *adjective* [2092 hetoimos] prepared; ready.
preparedly *adverb* [2093 hetoimos] readily.
presbyter *transliterated noun* [4243 presbuo] [4245 presbuteros] an elder representative; the Hellene word for the congregational and ecclesiastical representatives.
presbytry *transliterated noun* [4242 presbia] the office of elder representative; corresponds to Old Covenant elder.
present *noun* {7862 shay} a gift.
press *noun* {6333 purah} a grape crusher.
press oil *verb* {6671 tsahar} to press out oil.
press, oppress *verb* {3905 lachats} literally, to press; to oppress.
press, sink, bend, descend, penetrate *verb* {5181 nachath} from the root, to sink; to go down; to press or lead down.
pressure, puff, expire soul *verb* {5301 naphach} [1634 ekpsucho] to breathe away one's soul; to pressure, as in a pressure cooker; and to puff; **cp** expire spirit.
presume, swell *verb* {6075 aphal} to assume aforehand; an ascending, as swollen.
pretext *noun* {5931 illah} [4392 prophasis] a pretense.
prevail, able, can, enable *verb* {3201 yakol} {3202 yekel} {3546 kehal} [1410 dunamai] [2427 hikanoo] the dynamis to do; **see** dynamis.
prevail, empower, overpower *verb* {8280 sarah} {8630 taqaph} [2616 katadunastuo] [2729 katiskuo] [2901 krataioo] [2902 krateo] to have ability over; to cause to have power.
prevail, strengthen, uphold, callous *verb* {553 amats} {555 omets} {2388 chazaq} {2393 chezqah} {5810 azaz} to enable physically; to become thickskinned.
prevail mightily *verb* {1396 gabar} might in verbal form, for which there is no English equivalent.
previously preached *verb* [4296 prokerusso] that which was proclaimed in advance; **cp** pre–evangelize.
prewitness *verb* [4303 promarturomai] to witness prior to occurrence.
prey, tear *noun* {2964 tereph} {2966 terephah} {5706 ad} a prey, as an object of attack; as being torn.
price *noun* {4242 mechiyr} the payment.
price *noun* {4377 meker} the evaluation; the value to be paid; **cp** sell.
price, honour *noun* [5092 timee] of esteem; of value; money paid.
price, honour *verb* [5091 timao] to esteem; to value.
prickle *noun* {5544 cillon} a type of brier.
pride *noun* {7293 rahab} {7296 rohab} a vociferous boasting.
pride *noun* {7830 shachats} as in strutting.

- **SUMMARY:**
- **PRIEST, PRIESTAL PRECINCT, PRIESTHOOD:**
- **priest** *noun* {3548 kohen} {3549 kahen} [2409 hierus] an officer of sacrifices and ministries of the holies and the holy of holies of the tabernacle; the emminent priests were classified as: **head** {7218 rosh}, **great** {1419 gadol}, and **arch** [749 archiereus] [758 archon].
- **priest, priested, priesting** *verb* {3547 kahan} [2407 hieratuo] [2418 hierourgeo] to officiate as a priest.
- **priestal** *adjective* [2413 hieros] hallowed.
- **priestal precinct** *noun* [2411 hieron] one of two Hellenic words mistranslated temple; the priestal precinct refers to the holies area of the tabernacle where the doctrinating took place; **see** SUMMARY: TABERNACLE, TEMPLE, TENT:.
- **priestal precinct stripper** *noun* [2416 hierosuleo] [2417 hierosulos] one who strips priestal precincts, either by removing or desecrating.
- **priesthood** *noun* {3550 kehunnah} [2405 hieratia] [2406 hieratuma] [2420 hierosune] the office of the priest.
- **priestlike, priestly** *adjective* [2412 hieroprepes] hallowed.

prince *noun* {*plural* 4502 minnezarim} set apart.
prison guard *noun* [1200 desmophulax] one that guards a prison.
prison *noun* {3608 kele} {3628 kelu} [1201 desmoteerion] a place of binding.
prisoner *noun* [1202 desmotees] one that is bound.
private assembly *noun* {6116 atsereth} an assembly; a festival.
private counsel, councilmen *noun* {*plural* 4176 moetsoth} {5475 cowd} {5483 eta} {6098 etsah} [1012 boulee] [1013 booulema] purpose; advice; advisors.
probe *verb* {2713 chaqar} to penetrate.
probe, probing *noun* {2714 chaqar} penetration.

proceeding, procedure, rising, springing *noun* {4161 motsa} {*plural* 4163 motsaoth} literally, the source of going forth, whether of persons, of water, of the sun.
procession *noun* {8418 tahalukah} an orderly walk; from the verb, to walk.
proclaim, recall, call *verb* {7121 qara} {7123 qera} [1941 epikaleomai] [2564 kaleo] [4341 proskaleomai] [4377 prosphoneo] to call out; to call upon; to address; **cp** name.
proconsul *noun* [445 anthupatuo] [446 anthupatos] the highest officer.
produce *noun* {2981 yebuwl} {8393 tebuah} {8570 tenubah} the product of the soil.
produce, progeny *noun* [1081 gennema] offspring.
produce, promote *verb* {6329 puq} to bring forth.
profane, common *adjective* {2455 chol} [2839 koinos] that which is common; that which is held in common; that which is not hallowed.
profane *noun* {1352 goel} desecration.
profane *verb* {1351 gaal} [953 bebeloo] to cross the threshold in the sense of desecrating the holy.
profane, pierce, pluck *verb* {2490 chalal} {2610 chaneph} [2840 koinoo] to pierce a person; to pluck an instrument; to desecrate the hallowed.
profane, pierced *adjective* {2455 chol} {2491 chalal} [952 bebeelos] of pierced (slaughtered) and profaned persons.
profaner *noun* {2611 chaneph} a desecrater.
profanity *noun* {2612 choneph} {2613 chanuphah} desecration.
profess *verb* [437 anthomologeomai] [3670 homologeo] to homologize; to agree with words.
professedly *adverb* [3672 homologoumenos] confessedly.
profession *noun* [3671 homologia] homology.
profound *adjective* {5994 amiq} as unsearcheable.
progenitors *noun* [4269 progonos] ancestors; forefathers.
progeny, produce *noun* [1081 gennema] offspring.
prognosis *transliterated noun* [4268 prognosis] foreknowledge.
prognosticate *verb* {5172 nachash} to predict.
prognostication *noun* {5173 nachash} a prediction.
prone *participle* **suspend, hang** *verb* {8511 tala} {8518 talah} to suspend.
proof *noun* [1382 dokime] a test; that which is tested.
proof *verb* {974 bachan} to test, as in a crucible.
proofing *verb* [1383 dokimion] that by which something is tested or proved.
prop, sustain, uphold *verb* {5564 camak} {8551 tamak} to prop up; with the hands, or with props.
proper *adjective* [433 aneko] to be proper; to attain unto.
prophecy *transliterated noun* {5016 nebuah} {5017 nebuah} [4394 prophetia] a foretelling prior to occurrence; does not mean a telling forth.
prophesy *transliterated verb* {5012 naba} {5013 neba} [4395 propheetuo] to foretell prior to occurrence; does not mean to tell forth.
prophet *transliterated noun* {5029 nebiy} {5030 nabiy} [4396 prophetes] one who foretells prior to occurrence; does not mean one who tells forth.
prophetess *transliterated feminine noun* {5031 nebiah} [4398 prophetis] a female who foretells prior to occurrence; does not mean one who tells forth.
prophetic *transliterated adjective* [4397 prophetikos] a foretelling; does not mean a telling forth.
propound *verb* {2330 chud} [394 anatithemi] to propose for consideration; **see** shew, show.
proselyte *transliterated noun* [4339 proselutos] one who has changed religions.
prosper, succeed *verb* {3787 kasher} {6743 tsaleach} {6744 tselach} to succeed; to press on.
prosperity *noun* {3574 kowsharah} {3788 kishron} success.
prostrate *verb* {5456 cagad} {5457 cegid} {7511 raphas} {7812, 7817 shachah} to lie with face to the soil as in doing obeisance.
protected *noun* {5336 natsiyr} delivered.
prothesis bread, face bread *transliterated noun* {6440 paneh} {3899 lechem} [4286 prothesis] [740 artos] the bread of the holy of holies as displayed; the face bread of the Old Covenant is identical to the prothesis bread of the New Covenant.
prothesis *transliterated noun* [4286 prothesis] a setting forth of a thesis; the bread of the holies as displayed.
prototype *noun* [5296 hupotuposis] a type to be patterned after.
proud *adjective* {7295 rahab} as insolent; **note:** Yah Veh was never proud of His Son; but well–pleased.
prove, reprove, approve *verb* {3198 yakach} [1381 dokimazo] to prove; to accept or reject the proving.
proverb *noun* {4912 mashal} {4914 meshol} [3942 paroimia] an adage; a general truth of conduct expressed in a sententious form.
proverbialize, liken *verb* {4911 mashal} to present as a proverb; liken, as being equal; **see** equal.
prowl, observe *verb* {7789 shur} to survey; to spy out; **see** stroll.
prowl, yearn *verb* {8264 shaqaq} to prowl as an animal; to greedily yearn for.
prowler, observer *noun* {7790 shur} a foe, as lying in wait; **see** stroll.
psalm *noun* [5568 psalmos] a sacred ode.
psalm, pluck *verb* {2167, 2168 zamar} [5567 psallo] as in plucking strings; **cp** strum.
psalm, psalming, pluck, plucking *noun* {2158, 2159 zamir} {2170 zemar} {2172 zimrah} {2176 zimrath} {4210 mizmor} a string, fruit, or twig as plucked.
psalmist, plucker *noun* {2171 zammar} plucker.
psalmpicks *plural noun* {4211 mazmerah} **note:** when the shalom of Yah Veh reigns, spears are turned into psalmpicks.
psalterion *transliterated noun* {6460 pecanterin} a transliteration of the Hellene psalterion; a lyre.
transliterated noun [5571 pseudes] phony.
pseudo apostles *transliterated noun* [5570 pseudapostolos] phony apostles.
pseudo brethren *noun* [5569 pseudadelphos] phony brethren.
pseudo doctors *noun* [5572 pseudodidaskalos] phony doctors.
pseudo messiah *noun* [5580 pseudochristos] phony messiah.
pseudo prophets *transliterated noun* [5578 pseudoprophetes] phony prophets.
pseudo witnesses *noun* [5575 pseudomartur] phony witnesses.
pseudo witnessing *verb* [5576 pseudomarturia] phony witnessing.
pseudologists *transliterated noun* [5572 pseudologos] phony wordists.
pseudonym *transliterated noun* [5581 pseudonumos] phony name.
Puah, Puvvah *transliterated name* {6312 puwah, puvvah} Blow Away.
pudenda *noun* {*plural* 4016 mabushim} {4589 maor} exposed part.
pudenda, socket *noun* {6596 poth} literally, a hole.
puff *verb* [4154 pneo] [4157 pnoee] to blow hard; from pneuma (spirit).
puff *verb* {5301 naphach} [1720 emphusao] to blow hard; from nephesh; the Septuagint translates naphach to emphuzao; this word is used of Yah Veh puffing into Adam; of the Holy Spirit puffing into the dry bones; and of Yah Shua puffing into the disciples.
puff *verb* {5395 nasham} {5398 nashaph} to blow away; from nephesh.
puff, breathe *verb* {6315 puwach} **cp** spirit {7307 ruwach}.
puff, expire soul, pressure *verb* {5301 naphach} [1634 ekpsucho] to breathe away one's soul; to pressure, as in a pressure cooker; and to puff; **cp** expire spirit.
puffed up *adjective* [5448 phusioo] as in proud.
puffings up *noun* [5450 phusiosis] as in proud.
pull (down) (out) *verb* {5421 natha} {5422 nathats} to tear out; to tear down.
pull, pull stakes, pluck *verb* {5265 naca} to pluck; to pull up; to pull the tent stakes when moving; **read** Numbers 33:3–48.
pull, take, put (down) [2507 kathaireo] to take down, demolish.
pulling down *noun* [2506 kathairesis] a taking down, demolition.
pulpit *noun* {1687 debir} the furniture from whence the word is worded.
pulverize *verb* {1854 dahkak} {1855 dekak} {7833 shachaq} to crush to powder; to vapourize.
pulverized, thin *adjective* {1851 dak} thin; beaten small; emaciated.
punch *verb* [2852 kolaphizo] to strike with the fist; treat with violence.
Puniy *transliterated name* {6324 puwniy} Of Pun.
pupil *noun* {892 babah} the hollow of the eye.

pupil, mid, middle *noun* {380 iyshown} literally, the middle man of the eye; the middle of the night.
Pur, Purim *transliterated name, noun* {6332 puwr, *plural* puriym} a celebration of deliverance; **read** Ester 9:24–32.
Purah *transliterated name* {6513 purah} Foliage.
pure *adjective* {1249 bar} {2889 tahor} physically, soulically, or mentally, completely pure.
pure *adjective* {2134 zak} {2135 zakah} [2513 katharos] clean; clear; catharized.
pure *noun* {2890, 2891 tehor} completely pure.
pure *noun, participle* {6337 paz} {6338 pazaz} refined; made pure.
purge, cleanse, polish *verb* {1305 barar} [1571 ekkathairo] clarify; catharize; **cp** purify.
purification *noun* {*plural* 4795 maruqim} {8562 tamruq} clarification; catharization.
purify *verb* {2135 zakah} {2141 zakak} {2891 taher} [2511 katharizo] physically, soulically, or mentally, to cause to be completely pure.
purifying *noun* [2512 katharismos] [2514 katharotees] a washing off; an expiation.
purity *noun* {1252 bor} {2136 zakuw} clarity; catharized.
purity, purification *noun* {2890 tehor} {2891 taher} {2892 tohar} {2893 tohorah} physically, soulically, or mentally, completely pure.
pursue *verb* {7291 radaph} to run after.
pus *verb* {2990 yabbel} the excretion of a running sore.
push, butt *adjective* {5056 naggach} butting, as vicious.
push, butt *verb* {5055 nagach} to butt with the horns; to war against.
pustules *plural noun* {76 ababuah} eruptions of pus.
Put *transliterated name* {6316 put} a son of Ham; his descendants.
put, cast, lie *verb* [906 ballo] to throw.
put, set, place *verb* {7760, 7761 suwm} {7896 shith} {8239 shaphath} {8271 shathah} to put in place.
Puthiy *transliterated name* {6336 puwthiy} Hinge; Of Puth.
Puti El *transliterated name* {6317 putiel} Contempt of El.
putrefied *adjective* [4550 sapros] [4595 seepo] rotten; worthless.
putrid *adjective* {8182 shoar} offensive; **cp** horrible.
putridity *noun* {4716 maq} a moldy mess.
Python *transliterated name* [4436 puthon] a species of snake used in pagan worship.

Q

qab *transliterated noun* {6894 qab} a scoop of dry measure.
Qabse El *transliterated name* {6909 qabtseel} Gathered of El.
Qadesh *transliterated name* {6946 qadesh} Hallowed.
Qadesh Barnea *transliterated name* {6947 qadeshbarnea} Hallowed Field of Wandering.
Qadmi El *transliterated name* {6934 qadmiel} Ancient of El.
Qadmoniy *transliterated name* {6935 qadmoniy} Ancient.
Qallay *transliterated name* {7040 qallay} Trifle.
Qamon *transliterated name* {7056 qamown} Raised.
Qanah *transliterated name* {7071 qanah} [2580 kana] Reedy; **cp** Reed Sea.
Qareach *transliterated name* {7143 qareach} Balden.
Qarqa *transliterated name* {7173 qarqa} Floor.
Qarqor *transliterated name* {7174 qarqor} Undermine.
Qartah *transliterated name* {7177 qartah} City.
Qartan *transliterated name* {7178 qartan} City.
Qatan *transliterated name* {6997 qatan} Small.
Qattath *transliterated name* {7005 qattath} Littleness.
Qayin *transliterated name* {7014 qayin} [2535 kain] Chattelizer.
Qayiniy *transliterated name* {7014 qayin} {7017 qeyniy} Of Qayin.
Qedar *transliterated name* {6938 qedar} Drakened.
Qedemah *transliterated name* {6929 qedemah} Precedence.
Qedemoth *transliterated name* {6932 qedemowth} Precedings.
Qedesh *transliterated name* {6943 qedesh} Hallowed.
Qehath *transliterated name* {6955 qehath} Allied.
Qehathiy *transliterated name* {6956 qohathiy} Of Qehath.
Qehelathah *transliterated name* {6954 qehelathah} Congregated.
Qeilah *transliterated name* {7084 qeiylah} Citadel.
Qelayah *transliterated name* {7041 qelayah} Abased.
Qelita *transliterated name* {7042 qeliyta} Maiming.
Qemu El *transliterated name* {7055 qemuel} Raised of El.
Qenath *transliterated name* {7079 qenath} Chattel.
Qenaz *transliterated name* {7073 qenaz} Hunter.
Qenaziy *transliterated name* {7074 qenizziy} Of Qenaz.
Qeren Hap Puch *transliterated name* {7163 qerenhappuwch} Horn of Stibium.
Qerioth *plural transliterated name* {7152 qeriyowth} Cities.
Qeros *transliterated name* {7026 qeroc} Ankled.
Qesem *transliterated name* {7081 qecem} {2973 kosam} Divination.
Qesiah *transliterated name* {7103 qetsiyah} Cassia.
Qesis *transliterated name* {7104 qetsiyts} Chopped Off.
Qeturah *transliterated name* {6989 qetuwrah} Incensed.
Qeynan *transliterated name* {7018 qeynan} [2536 kainan] Nest.
Qibroth Hat Taavah *plural transliterated name* {6914 qibrowthbattaavah} Tombs of Desire.
Qibsayim *dual transliterated name* {6911 qibtsayim} Double Heap.
Qidron *transliterated name* {6939 qidron} [2748 kedron] Dusky.
Qinah *transliterated name* {7016 qiynah} Lamentation.
Qir *transliterated name* {7024 qiyr} Wall.
Qir Hareseth *transliterated name* {7025 qiyrchareseth} Wall of Pottery.
Qiryath Arba *transliterated name* {7153 qiryatharba} City of the Four Giants.
Qiryath Arim *transliterated name* {7157 qiryathariym} City of Forests.
Qiryath Husoth *plural transliterated name* {7155 qiryathchutsowth} City of Outways.
Qiryath Sannah *transliterated name* {7158 qiryathcannah} City of Twigs.
Qiryath Sepher *transliterated name* {7158 qiryathcepher} City of a Scroll.
Qiryathaim *dual transliterated name* {7156 qiryathayim} Double City.
Qish *transliterated name* {7027 qish} [2797 kis] Bow.
Qishi *transliterated name* {7029 qiyshiy} Bowed.
Qishon *transliterated name* {7028 qiyshown} Ensnared.
Qishyon *transliterated name* {7191 qishyown} Stubborn.
Qitron *transliterated name* {7003 qitrown} Incensed.
Qola Yah *transliterated name* {6964 qolayah} Voice of Yah.
Qorach *transliterated name* {7141 qorach} [2879 kore] Baldened.
Qorachiy *transliterated name* {7145 qorchiy} Of Qorach.
qorban *transliterated noun* {7133 qorban} [2878 korban] a hallowed oblation; **see** oblation.
Qore *transliterated name* {6981 qore} Called.
Qos *transliterated name* {6976 qowts} Thorn.
quadruped *noun* [5074 tetrapous] four footed.
quake *noun* {7494 raash} a vibrating; a quivering.
quake *verb* {1949 huwm} {7322 ruph} {7493 raash} to vibrate; to quiver.
quake *verb* [5120 noot] to quake.
quake, glutton *participle* {2151 zalal} to shake; to eat in excess.
quake, quiver *verb* {7264 ragaz} {7265 regaz} to quiver; in anger, or fear.
quake, shake, glutton *participle* {2151 zalal} to quake; to shake; to eat in excess; **cp** drunkard.
quantity, formula *noun* {4971 mathkuneth} a measured proportion of portions.
quarried rock *noun* [2991 laxutos] a rock, as fashioned, as distinct from a natural rock.
quarry, arrow *noun* {4551 macca} a quarry, in which stones are ejected; a missle, as projecting.
quarry, hammer *noun* {4717 maqqabah} {4718 maqqebeth} that which is used to pound; a quarry, from which is pounded.
quarter *noun* [2835 kodrantes] a quarter coin.
quickly *adverb* {4120 meherah} promptly.
quicksand *noun* [4950 surtis] sand that yields to pressure.
quietly *adverb* {3814 lat} silently; **cp** hush.
quit *verb* {2976 yaash} to desist.
quiver, quake *verb* {7264 ragaz} {7265 regaz} to quiver; in anger, or fear.
quiver, tingle *verb* {6750 tsalal} to vibrate.
quivering *adjective* {7268 raggaz} timid.
quivering *noun* {7269 rogsah} trepidation.
Qusha Yah *transliterated name* {6984 qushayah} Snared of Yah.

R

Raam Yah *transliterated name* {7485 raamyah} Thunder of Yah.
Rab Shaqeh *transliterated name* {7262 rabshaqeh} Great Butler.
Rabbah *transliterated feminine name* {7237 rabbah} Feminine of {7227 rab} rabbi.

rabbi *noun* [1988 epistates] a doctor who doctrinates; the Hellene translation of the Hebrew and Arami word for rabbi; scribed only by Loukas who spoke no Hebrew.
rabbi *transliterated noun* {7227 rab} [4461 rhabbi] a great doctor who doctrinates; the Hebrew transliteration for doctor as scribed by Yahn, Matthaios, and Markos; **see** great.
rabboni *transliterated noun* {7229 rab} [4462 rhabboni] the Arami transliteration for doctor as spoken by others, and scribed by Yahn and Markos; **see** great.
race *noun* [1408 dromos] figuratively, the course of life, or occupation.
race, oppression *noun* {4793 merots} {4794, 4835 merutsah} a test of running; the pressures of life.
Rachab *transliterated name* {7343 rachab} [4460 rhaab] [4477 rhachab] Large; Broad.
Racham *transliterated name* {7357 racham} Mercy.
Rachel *transliterated name* {7354 rachel} [4478 rhachel] Ewe (lamb).
Radday *transliterated name* {7288 radday} Domineering.
rafts *plural noun* {7513 raphcodah} as a flat on the water.
rage *noun* {2195 zaam} {7108 qetsaph} {7109 qetsaph} {7110 qetseph} [3950 parorgismos] raving anger.
rags *plural noun* {5499 cechabahoth} as ripped or torn.
Rahab *transliterated name* {7294 rahab} Proud.
railing *noun* {7507 rephidah} as spread along.
rain (early) *noun* {3138 yoreh} {4175 moreh} autumnal showers.
rain *noun* {4306 matar} [1028 brokee] [5205 huetos] showers; **cp** downpour.
rain *verb* {4305 matar} to rain; **cp** downpour.
rain, moisten *verb* [1026 breko] to moisten, as by a shower.
raise (up), exalt, extol *verb* {5549 salal} from the root, to mound up; **see** selah; **cp** halal.
raise, exalt, lift, loft *verb* {7311, 7313 rum} {7318 romam} {7426 ramam} to lift hand, heart, offering, voice; to oath; **see** exalt.
raise, rise, rose, rouse, arise, arose *verb* {6965, 6966 qum}[450 anisteemi] [1453 egiro] to stand forth; to rise; to be stirred up, awakened.
raisin cakes *plural noun* {6778 tsammuq} bakings of dried grapes.
Rachal *transliterated name* {7403 rachal} Merchant.
Ram *transliterated name* {7410 ram} [689 aram] Lofted.
Ram Yah *transliterated name* {7422 ramyah} Lofted of Yah.
ram, saddle, meadow *noun* {3733 kar} literally, plumpness, as in a full grown lamb; padding, as in a saddle; a meadow for sheep.
Ramah *transliterated name* {7414 ramah} [707 arimathaia] [4471 rhama] Lofty Altar; **cp** bamah.
Ramah *transliterated name* {7484 ramah} Thunder.
ramah *transliterated noun* {7413 ramah} a lofted altar; **cp** bamah.
Ramah Ham Mispeh *transliterated name* {7434 ramathhammitspeh} Ramah of the Watch Tower.
Ramah Lechi *transliterated name* {7437 ramathlechiy} Ramah of a Jaw.
Ramahayim Sophim *transliterated name* {7436 ramathayimtsowphiym} Double Ramah of Watchers.
Ramahiy *transliterated name* {7435 ramathiy} Of Ramah.
ramble on *verb* {7300 rud} mentally, soulically, or physically, to wander about.
rampart, siege *noun* {4692 matsur} {4694 matsor} a mound for protection; a seizing.
rank, appraise, apprize, arrange, array, line up *verb* {6186 arak} to line up in a row; to put in order.
rank, arrangement, formation *noun* {4633 maarak} {4634 maarakah} {4635 maareketh} an arrangment (physical or mental).
rank, row, shingle *noun* {7713 sederah} {7795 sorah} that which is regulated in rows.
ranks of five *noun* {2571 chamush} regulated rows of five.
ransom, bribe *noun* {7810 shachad}.
rape *verb* {7693 shagal} to ravish in copulation; **see** ravage.
Rapha, Raphaim *transliterated name* {*singular* 7497, 7498 rapha} {*plural* 7497 rephaim} Healer.
Rapha El *transliterated name* {7501 raphael} Healer of El.
Rapha Yah *transliterated name* {7509 rephayah} [4488 rhesa] Healer of Yah.
Raphu *transliterated name* {7505 raphu} Healed.
Raqqath *transliterated name* {7557 raqqath} Expanded.
Raqqon *transliterated name* {7542 raqqown} Emaciated.
rash, balden, polish *verb* {4178 mowrat} {4803 marat} {4804 merat} to rub (off); to pluck; to cause to be bald.
rasp *noun* {4883 massor} an instrument for rasping.
ravage *noun* {7701 shod} a devastation.
ravage *verb* {7703 shadad} {7736 shud} to devastate.
razor, sheath, knife *noun* {8593 taar} a knife, or a razor, as making bare; a sheath, as being bare.
Rea Yah *transliterated name* {7211 reayah} Seen of Yah.
reach, attain, overtake *verb* {5381 nasag} to attain by reaching for.
reach, encounter, intercede *verb* {6293 paga} to impinge.
reach, touch, plague *verb* {5060 naga} to touch heavily; to strike.
read *verb* [314 anaginosko] to decipher.
reading *noun* 320 anagnosis] that which is read.
ready *verb* {6257 athad} to prepare.
ready, treasured, impending *adjective* {6259, 6264 athud} {6263 athid} prepared; treasured.
rebel *verb* {4775 marad} {4784 marah} {6586 pasha} {7279 ragan} to renounce; to resist.
rebel, flap *verb* {4754 mahrah} to flap one's self; to flap one's wings; to rebel.
rebellion *noun* {4776 merad} {4777 mered} {4805 meriy} {6588 pesha} renunciation; resistance.
rebellious *adjective* {4779 marad} {4780 maruth}.
rebirth *verb* [313 anagennao] to be reborn.
rebuild *verb* [456 anoikodomeo] to build again.
rebuke *noun* {1606 geahrah} a chiding.
rebuke *verb* {1605 gahgar} to chide.
rebuke, admonish *verb* [2008 epitimao] to charge sharply.
recall, call, proclaim *verb* {7121 qara} {7123 qera} [1941 epikaleomai] [2564 kaleo] [4341 proskaleomai] [4377 prosphoneo] to call out; to call upon; to address; **cp** name.
receive in full, distant *verb* [568 apeko] to have out; to keep away.
receive, wait, await, expect *verb* {2442 chakah} {3176 yachal} {6960 qavah} [324 anadekomai] [362 anameno] [553 apekdekomai] [4327 prosdekomai] [4328 prosdokao] [4329 prosdokia] to anticipate; to wait expectantly, patiently; **cp** take.
Rechab Am *transliterated name* {7346 rechabam} [4497 rhoboam] Enlarged the People.
Rechab Yah *transliterated name* {7345 rechabyah} Enlarged of Yah.
Rechob *transliterated name* {7340 rechob} Broadway.
Rechoboth *plural transliterated name* {7344 rechoboth} Broadways.
Rechum *transliterated name* {7348 rechuwm} Merciful.
recline *verb* [347 anaklino] the posture when eating; **cp** repose.
recognize, discern, distinguish, estrange, notice *verb* {5234 nakar} to acknowledge; to scrutinize; to distinguish between; to ignore, hence to be estranged.
recompense *noun* [468 antapodoma] [469 antapodosis] that which is given back.
recompense *verb* [467 antapodidomi] to give back.
reconcile (fully) *verb* [604 apokatallasso] completely restore.
reconcile *verb* [2644 katallasso] to restore.
reconciliation *noun* [2643 katallagee] restoration.
record *noun* {1799 dikrown} a register.
recoup *verb* {5756 uz} to restore strength.
red hot stones, pavement *noun* {7528 ratsaph} {7529 retseph} as used for baking; as used for laying a pavement.
redeem *verb*, **redeemer** *participle* {1350 gaal} {6299 padah} [3084 lutroo] [3086 lutrotes] to ransom; a ransomer; **cp** market.
redeemed *noun* {*plural* 6302 paduim} the ransomed.
redemption *noun* {1353 geullah} {6304 peduth} {6306 pidon} [487 antilutron] [629 apolutrosis] [3083 lutron] [3085 lutrosis] the ransom; the setting free.
Reed (Sea) *name* {5488 cuph} {5492 cuphah} [2063 eruthra] [2281 thalassa] of reeds; Reed Sea; **note:** Reed is mistranslated Red.
Reela Yah *transliterated name* {7480 reelayah} Shaken of Yah.
reem *noun* {7214 reem} a wild ox.
refine *verb* {2212 zaqaq} {6884 tsaraph} to purify; **cp** test; **cp** proof.
refiner *noun* {6885 tsorephi} one that refines.
refire *verb* [329 anazopureo] to fire up again.
reflourish *verb* [330 anathallo] to flourish again.

refrain, restrain, retain *verb* {3607 kala} {6113 atsar} to restrict; to hold back.
refresh *verb* [404 anapsuko] recovery of breath.
refreshing *noun* [403 anapsuxis] recovery of breath.
refuge *noun* {4152 muwadah} {4224 machabe} {*plural* 4224 machabeim} {4268 machaceh} {4733 miqlat} a place of protection.
refuge (seek) *verb* {2620 chacah} {2622 chacuth} to flee to for protection.
refuse *adjective* {3986 maen} {*plural* 3987 maenim} unwilling.
refuse *verb* {3985 maen} {3988 maac} to reject; to spurn; also to disappear.
refute *verb* [471 antepo] an answer instead of; as opposed to.
regard, guard, on guard *verb* {5201 natar} {5202 nater} {5341 natsar} {8104 shamar} {*plural* 8107 shimmurim} {8108 shomrah} {8176 shaar} [5083 tereo] in the sense of protecting from harm, observing observances, obeying misvahs.
regenesis *noun* [3824 palingenesia] rebirth; renovation; restoration.
region *noun* [5561 chora] an area.
regirt *verb* [328 anazonnumi] to girt again.
regret *verb* [3338 metamellomai] to be sorry; **cp** repent.
regurgitate, ascend, holocaust, mount *verb* {5927, 5928 alah} to ascend, as a mountain; to mount an animal; to regurgitate food; to ascend a holocaust; **see** holocaust, *noun*.
reign *noun* {4474 mimshal} {4475 memshalah} the office of a sovereign.
reign *verb* **sovereign** *participle* {4427 malak} {4910 mashal} [936 basiluo] to rule; the officiating of a sovereign; **see** sovereign.
reign, equal *noun* {4915 moshel} equal, in the sense of being able to liken unto, or compare with; reign; of being more than equal; of being over.
reinforce *verb* {5790 uth} to hasten; to encourage.
reinforcement *noun* {8136 shinan} to reinforce by doubling, or by duplicating.
reinforcing *participle* {4834 marats} pressuring; irritating.
reins *plural noun* {2910 tuwchah} {3629 keliy} [3510 nephros] literally, kidneys; symbolic of the innermost thoughts.
reiterate, repeat, alter, change, double, duplicate, fold *verb* {8132 shana} {8133 shena} {8138 shanah} to reinforce by folding, by doubling; may include disguise, camouflage.
reject *verb* {5010 naar} to not accept.
rejoice *verb* {2302 chadah} {2868 teeb} {7797 sus} to cheer.
rejoicing *noun* {8342 sason} a cheerfulness.
rejoicing *verb* {2304, 2305 chedvah} cheering.
rejuvenate *verb* {7375 rutaphash} made juvenile.
Rekah *transliterated name* {7397 rekah} Tenderized.
relax *verb* {7599 shaan} to loll.
relaxation, relaxed *noun* {7600 shaanan} [425 anesis] relaxation, as being secure; relief.
release *noun* {8059 shemittah} the negation of a debt.
release *verb* {8058 shamat} [525 apallasso] to loose; to let fall, or drop.
release, abandon *verb* {8281 sharah} to free.
release, allow, forgive, forsake, leave *verb* [863 aphieemi] to send forth.
release, forsake, leave (behind) *verb* {5800 azab} [1459 enkatalipo] to leave behind; in a good sense, to let remain over; in a bad sense, to abandon.
release, loose *verb* [3089 luo] to set free; to unbind.
release, unravel *verb* {8271 shere} to let loose.
released *noun* {8293 sheruth} set free; separate; freedom of persons.
releasing, forsaking, leaving *noun* {5805 azubah} the letting loose of, or from.
relive *verb* [326 anazao] to live again.
remain, remaining *verb* {3498 yathar} to be left over.
remain, return, behave, overturn *verb* [390 anastrepho] [396 anatrepo] to turn; in the manner one turns (behaves); to turn over; to overthrow.
remainder, remnant, rest, exceeding *noun* {3499 yether} the remainder, those left over.
Remal Yah *transliterated name* {7425 remalyah} Bedecked of Yah.
remeasure *verb* [488 antimetreo] to remeter.
remember, memorialize *verb* {2142 zakar} {7876 shayah} [3403 mimeeskomai] [3415 mnaomai] [3421 mneemonuo] [5279 hupomimneesko] an acting of the memory; to hold in remembrance.
remember, remind *verb* [363 anamimnesko] to recollect; to remind.
remembrance *noun* [364 anamneesis] [3417 mnia] [3420 mneemee] [5280 hupomneesis] a recollection; a memory.
remind *verb* [3560 noutheteo] to caution; to recall to mind; **see** mind.
remnant, rest, exceeding, remainder *noun* {3499 yether} the remainder, those left over.
remove *verb* [522 apairo] to lift off.
remove *verb* [851 aphaireo] to take away.
remove, depart *verb* {5253 nacag} to retreat.
remove, transcribe, antiquate *verb* {6275 athaq} that which has aged; to take away; to take down, as in transcribing.
removed far, far removed *verb* {7368 rachaq} from the root, to widen.
renew, renewing, renovate *verb* {2318 chadash} [340 anakainizo] [341 anakainoo] [342 anakainosis] [365 ananeoo] to make new again; to rebuild; to retore; **see** new.
repartee *verb* [2160 eutrapelia] to say in ready and witty reply.
repeat, alter, change, double, duplicate, fold, reiterate *verb* {8132 shana} {8133 shena} {8138 shanah} to reinforce by folding, by doubling; may include disguise, camouflage.
repent *verb* [3340 metanoeo] to be sorry afterwards; **cp** regret.
repentance *noun* [3341 metanoya] being sorry afterwards.
Rephach *transliterated name* {7506 rephach} Support.
report *verb* [1310 diapheemizo] to divulge; to tell thoroughly.
report, fame, hearing, notoriety *noun* {8052 shemuah} {8088 shema} {8089 shoma} [189 akoee] that which is heard; an announcement; a rumor.
repose *noun* {7258 rebets} a place of rest.
repose *verb* {7252 reba} [345 anakimai] [376 anapipto] [1879 epanapauomai] to prostrate; to rest; the posture when eating; **cp** recline.
repose, lay *verb* [2621 katakimai] to lie down; recline at a meal.
reproach *noun* {2781 cherpah} [3680 onidismos] [3681 onidos] a discredit; disgrace.
reproach *verb* {2778 charaph} [3679 onidizo] to discredit; to disgrace.
reproof *noun* {8433 tokachath} correction; refutation; noun of reprove; **see** reprove.
reprove, approve, prove *verb* {3198 yakach} [1381 dokimazo] to prove; to accept or reject the proving.
reputation *noun* {5082 nedibah} as of nobility.
req, vain, vanity, void, empty *adjective* {1892 hebel} {*transliteration* 7385 riq} {*transliteration* 7386 req} {7723 shav} [*transliteration* 4469 rhaka] emptiness; voidness; figuratively, stupid.
Reqem *transliterated name* {7552 reqem} Embroidered.
request *noun* {4862 mishalah} an asking.
require, seek, enquire, examine, inquire *verb* {1875 darash} to ask; to seek; **cp** beseech.
rescue *verb* {6308 pada} [4506 rhuomai] to retrieve; to pull from the current.
rescue, escape *verb* {4422 malat} literally, to smooth; to slip away; to be slipped away.
rescue, strip, equip *verb* {2502 chalats} literally, to strip for hostility; to strip out of danger.
rescue, strip, escape *verb* {5337, 5338 natsal} to snatch away; favorably, or unfavorably.
resend *verb* [375 anapempo] to send again.
Reseph *transliterated name* {7530 retseph} Red Hot Stones.
reservior *noun* {650 aphiyq} a gathering of water; **see** gather.
reservoir *noun* {4724 miqvah} a congregating of waters; **see** congregate.
reside, residence *verb* {2082 zabal} {7871 shibah} to dwell.
residence *noun* {2073 zebul} a dwelling.
resident *noun* [1927 epidemeo] a dweller.
Resin *transliterated name* {7526 retsiyn} Pleasing.
resistance *noun* {8617 tequmah} ability to rise up against.
resound, glitter *verb* {6670 tsahal} to stand out; in color, or in sound.
respiration, respite *noun* {7305 revach} {7309 revachah} the inspiration and expiration; a spiritual respite; a spirit of rest; **see** spirit; **see** wind.
respire, scent *verb* {7304 ravach} {7306 ruwach} ruwach is the verb of spirit, wind; literally, to breathe freely; to refresh; to sense through the movement of air; **cp** breathe.
resplend *verb* [1584 eklampo] to be resplendent; to shine brilliantly.

respond, restore, return, turn (away) (back) (from) (to) *verb* {7725 shub} {8421 tub} from the root, to turn back; as to reply, to come back.
response, return, turn *noun* {8666 teshubah} a reccurence; a reply, as returned.
rest *adjective* {7282 ragea} restful.
rest *noun* {1679 dobe} {4494 manoach} {4496 menuchah} {4774 margeah} {5118 nuwach} {5183 nachath} {8253 sheqet} [372 anapausis] repose; tranquility.
rest *verb* {5117 nuwach} {8252 shaqat} [373 anapauo] to repose.
rest, exceeding, remainder, remnant *noun* {3499 yether} the remainder, those left over.
rest, split, blink, calm *verb* {7280 raga} this word is derived from two roots; blink and split, as momentary; calm and rest, as soothing.
rest in habitation *verb* {5115 navah} to rest, as at home; **see** habitation of rest.
restake *verb* [388 anastauroo] to stake again; **see** stake; **read** Hebrews 6:6.
resting place *noun* {4769 marbets} {4771 margoa} a place to rest.
restless *adjective* [180 akatapaustos] without rest; pauseless.
restore *verb* [600 apokathistemi] to reconstitute.
restore *verb* {8627 teqan} to set straight.
restore, return, turn (away) (back) (from) (to) respond *verb* {7725 shub} {8421 tub} from the root, to turn back; as to reply, to come back.
restrain the heel, trip the heel *verb* {6117 aqab} to seize by holding the heel.
restrain, retain, refrain *verb* {3607 kala} {6113 atsar} to restrict; to hold back.
restrainer *noun* {6115 etser} one that holds back; **see** abstinence.
restraint *noun* {6115 otser} a holding back; **see** abstinence.
resurrection *noun* [386 anastasis] a rising again.
retain, refrain, restrain *verb* {3607 kala} {6113 atsar} to restrict; to hold back.
retreat *verb* {7734 sug} to back off.
retreat, flight *noun* {4498 manohs} {4499 menusah} a place to flee to; a fleeing.
retribution *noun* {8005 shillem} {8011 shillumah} [489 antimisthia] retribution; reward in a negative sense.
return, behave, overturn, remain *verb* [390 anastrepho] [396 anatrepo] to turn; in the manner one turns (behaves); to turn over; to overthrow.
return, turn (away) (back) (from) (to) respond, restore *verb* {7725 shub} {8421 tub} from the root, to turn back; as to reply, to come back.
return, turn, response *noun* {8666 teshubah} a reccurence; a reply, as returned.
returning *noun* {7870 shibah} a turning back.
Reu *transliterated name* {7466 reu} [4466 rhagan] Friend.
Reu Ben *transliterated name* {7205 reuben} [4502 rouben] See Ye a Son.
Reu Beniy *transliterated name* {7206 reuwbeniy} Of Reu Ben.
Reu El *transliterated name* {7467 reuel} Friend of El.
revere (well), reverence (well) *verb* [2124 eulabia] [2125 eulabeomai] [2150 eusebia] [2151 eusebeo] to well venerate.
reverently *adverb* [2153 eusebos] veneratively.
revolt *noun* {5627 carah} turned away.
revolt, revolting *verb* {5637 sarar} turning away.
revolution, circuit *noun* {8622 tequphah} a revolution of days; a revolving around.
rhema *transliterated noun* [4487 rhema] a verbalization; the noun of rhetorize; **cp** word.
rhetorically *transliterated adverb* [4490 rhetos] verbally.
rhetorize *transliterated verb* [4483 reo] to express verbally.
rib, side *noun* {5967 ala} {6763 tsela} literally, a curve or an arch; a rib of a body; a rib of a structure.
Ribay *transliterated name* {7380 riybay} Contentious.
Riblah {1689 diblah} {7247 riblah} Fertile.
Ribqah *transliterated name* {7259 ribqah} [4479 rhebekka] Fetterer.
rich, riches *noun* {6223 ashir} {6239 osher} {*plural* 6251 ashteroth} enriched with riches; **see** enrich.
riddle *noun* {2420 chidah} a question, proposition, or rhyme worded so as to rouse conjecture.
riddle, vertebrae *noun* {7001 qetar} a knot; as that which is to be unravelled.
ride, drive *verb* {7392 rakab} to place upon; to despatch.
ridges *plural noun* {7406 rekec} a mountain ridge.
ridicule *noun* {7047 qelec} {7048 qallacah} a disparagement.
ridicule *verb* [2606 katagelao] to laugh at; to deride.
ridicule *verb* {7046 qalac} to disparage.
ridicule, entertain, laugh *verb* {6711 tsachaq} {6712 tsechoq} {7832 sechag} to laugh; to laugh at; to laugh at in defiance.
ridicule, laugh, laughter *noun* {6712 tsechoq} {7814 sechoq} laughter; a laughing at; a laughing at in defiance.
right *adjective* {3227 yeminiy} {3233 yeminay} **see** right *noun*; **cp** left.
right *noun* {3225 yamiyn} that which is opposite the left; **cp** left; example: when facing north, the east; most versions erroneously insert the words *hand*, or *side*; we sit not on Yah Shua's right hand, or on his left hand; but at his left, and at his right.
right *verb* {3231 yaman} to cause to go to the right.
rim *noun* {3749 karkob} a rim as encircling.
rim, arch, back, bow, brow *noun* {1354 gab} that which is bowed, curved; also the top or rim.
Rimmon Peres *transliterated name* {7428 rimmonperets} Pomegranate Split (of Separation).
ringleaders, rims *plural noun* {5633 ceren} instigators; rims of wheels.
ringstraked *adjective* {6124 aqod} round, circular stripes.
rip, shred *verb* {7167 qara} from the root, to rend.
ripen, spice, embalm *verb* {2590 chanat} from the root, to spice.
ripen, wean, deal *verb* {1580 gamal} transact.
ripped *verb* [1284 diarrhesso] to tear apart with force.
rise early, seek early *verb* {7836 shachar} to be early.
rise, rose, rouse, arise, arose, raise *verb* {6965, 6966 qum} [393 anatello] [450 anisteemi] [1453 egiro] to stand forth; to rise; to be stirred up, awakened.
risen being *noun* {3351 yequm} a being who has risen.
rising *noun* {4217 mizrach} [395 anatole] the rising (of the sun); the east; **cp** lowering.
rising *noun* {7012 qimah} an arising.
rising, springing, proceeding, procedure *noun* {4161 motsa} {*plural* 4163 motsaoth} literally, the source of going forth, whether of persons, of water, of the sun.
Rispah *transliterated name* {7532 ritspah} Hot Stone.
Risya *transliterated name* {7525 ritsya} Pleased.
rivalry *noun* [2052 erithia] a desire to put one's self forward; factiousness.
river, rivulet *noun* {2975 yeor} {5103 nehar} {5104 nahar} {6388 peleg} a stream of water.
roaming *verb* {7904 shakah} to roam.
roar *verb* {1993 hamah} to hum, as in commotion.
roar *verb* {7580 shaag} to rumble.
roar, uproar, waste *noun* {7588 shaon} a rumble; a destruction.
roaring *noun* {7581 shagah} a rumbling.
roaring lion *noun* {3833 lebia *plural* labaim} {7826 shachal} a lion, as a roarer.
roaring lioness *noun* {3833 lebeoth *plural* lebaoth} a lioness, as the fiercer.
roaring waste *noun* {7584 shaavah} a wasting away.
robe, robing *noun* {1545 gelowm} {3830, 3831 lebush} {4403 malbwsh} {8509 takrik} {8516 talbosheth} a wraparound; **see** enrobe.
rock *noun* {2906 tur} {5553 cela} {6697 tsur} [4073 petra] [4074 petros] a rock; a piece of rock; **cp** Petros.
rock *noun* {*plural* 3710 kephim} a hollow rock; **cp** Kepha.
rocky *adjective* [4075 petrodees] rock–like; **cp** Petros.
rod *noun* {2415 choter} [4464 rhabdos] rod, or twig; also a rod of royalty.
rod *noun* {4294 mattah} an offshoot, branch, sprout of a tree; of a people; **note:** both rod and scion are translated *tribe* in both covenants of most versions; **cp** scion; **cp** sceptre.
Rohagah *transliterated name* {7303 rowhagah} Outcry.
roll *noun* {1549 gillayon} {4039 megillah} something rolled up; a roll of a scroll; a little scroll.
roll *noun* {megillah} a roll of a scroll.
roll *verb* {1556 gahlal} to roll; to roll up; to roll away.
roll *verb* {6428 palash} to roll, as in dust or ashes; an expression of humbling.
Roman *transliterated name* [4513 rhomaikos] [4514 rhomaios] [4515 rhomaisti] of Rome.
Rome *transliterated name* [4516 rhome] Strength.

roof *noun* {1406 gag} usually the top of a house or altar.
rooster *noun* [220 alektor] a male fowl.
roostervoice *noun* [219 alektorophonia] the sound of a rooster.
root *noun* {8328 sheresh} {8330 shoresh} the underground part of a plant.
root, uproot *verb* {8327 sharash} {8332 sheroshu} to plant a root; to pull out by the root.
rope, wreath, wreathen, foliage *noun* {5688 abothah} as entwined; a wreath in victory; **cp** crown; **cp** diadem.
rose, rouse, arise, arose, raise, rise *verb* {6965, 6966 qum}[450 anisteemi] [1453 egiro] to stand forth; to rise; to be stirred up, awakened.
Rosh *transliterated name* {7220 rosh} Head; Top.
rosh *transliterated noun* {7219 rosh} a poisonous plant.
rot *verb* {5685 abash} to dry up.
rot *verb* {7537 raqab} to decay.
rotten, rotteness *noun* {7538 raqab} {7539 riqqabon} decay.
round about *advery* {5439 cabiyb} all around; surrounding.
round *adjective* {5696 agol} circular.
round dance *noun* {4246 mechol} a dance in which participants form a ring.
round dancing *verb* {4234 machol} to dance with participants forming a ring.
round, strike (round about), surround *verb* {5362 naqaph} to strike; to strike all around; to surround; to round off the beard.
round, surround, environ *noun* {3603 kikkar} literally, circle; the environs of an area; a round of material, usually of precious metals.
rouse up *verb* [387 anastatoo] soulically, to be roused.
rouse, arise, arose, raise, rise, rose *verb* {6965, 6966 qum}[450 anisteemi] [1453 egiro] to be stirred up, awakened; to stand forth; to rise.
route *noun* {4570 magalah} a rampart; a track; **see** pass, passage.
row, shingle, rank *noun* {7713 sederah} {7795 sorah} that which is regulated in rows.
row, turn *noun* {8447 tor} a succession of occasion; a row of.
rub, shake, wave *verb* {5130 nuph} to rub a bed with aromatics; to shake a hand; to wave an offering.
rub, sicken, stroke, worn (out) *verb* {2470 chalah} to wear out; to stroke the face as in appeasement.
rubbing rags *noun* {4418 malachim} literally, rubbers; that which is used to rub.
ruin *noun* {4288 mechittah} {4596 meiy} {4654 mappalah} {4658 mippeleth} {4875 meshoah} {4876 *plural* mashshooth} {6986 qeteb} {6987 qoteb} [3639 olethros] utter destruction; death.
ruin, vanish, corrupt, destroy, destruct, lose *verb* {6 abad} {7 abad} {8 obed} {7843 shachath} [622 apollumi] [1311 diapthiro] [2704 kataphthiro] [5351 phthiro] to corrupt through decay.
ruling *adverb* {4431 melak} adverb of reign.
rump *noun* {451 alyah} the hind of the body.
run, outrun *verb* **runner** *participle* {7323 ruts} {7325 rur} to run; one who runs; to run faster than.
rush *noun* {1999 hamullah} the sound of rushing.
rush, marsh *noun* {98 agam} {99 agem} {100 agmone} a stagnant water, or that which grows therefrom.
rushing *participle* {5584 caah} as a wind.
Ruth *transliterated name* {7327 ruth} [4503 routh] Friend.

S

Saanan *transliterated name* {6630 tsaanan} Flock.
Saanannim, Saanayim *plural transliterated name* {6815 tsaananniym, tsaanayim} Migrates.
Sabaoth *transliterated title* **host, hosts** *noun* {6635 tsebaah *plural* tsabaoth} [3841 pantokrator] [*plural* 4519 sabaoth] of hosts; a vast array of warriors; often compounded with El and with Yah Veh; [4519 sabaoth] is the Hellenic transliteration of sabaoth, only in Romans 9:29, and Yaaqovos 5:4; [3841 pantokrator] is the Hellenic translation of sabaoth, only in 2 Corinthians 6:18, and throughout the Apocalypse; **see** host.
Sabtecha *transliterated name* {5455 cabtecha} the meaning uncertain; a son of Kush, and the region settled by him.
sack *noun* {6861 tsiqion} a sack, as tied at the mouth; **cp** saq.
sackbut *noun* {5443 sabbeka} a lyre, as being stringed.
sacrifice *noun* {1685 debach} {2077 zebach} [2378 thusia] an offering – usually an animal; Yah Shua Messiah became our sacrifice as a lamb unblemished.
sacrifice *verb* {1684 debach} {2076 zabach} [2380 thuo] to offer up – usually an animal.
sacrifice (idol) *noun* [1494 eidolothuton] a sacrifice to an idol.
sacrifice altar *noun* {4056 madbach} {4196 mizbeach} [2379 thusiasterion] a furniture on which sacrifices are sacrificed; the Hebrew is from the root of the verb, sacrifice {2076 zabach}; **see** sacrifice.
saddle, meadow, ram *noun* {3733 kar} literally, plumpness, as in a full grown lamb; padding, as in a saddle; a meadow for sheep.
Sadoq *transliterated name* {6659 tsadowq} [4524 sadok] Just; a scion of the priesthood; **see** justness.
Sadoqiy *transliterated name* {6659 tsadowq} [4523 saddoukaios] of Sadoq; the name of a religious sect who claimed the virtue of justness; **see** Sadoq; **see** justness.
saffron *noun* {3750 karkom} the crocus.
sail, ensign, pole *noun* **Nissi** *transliterated title* {5251 nec} an ensign; the pole of an ensign; part of the title, Yah Veh Nissi, which means, Yah Veh Ensign.
sailer *noun* {2259 chobel} one that handles riggings of rope on a sailor.
Sair *transliterated name* {6811 tsaiyr} Little.
Sachar *transliterated name* {7940 sachar} Hire.
Sal Monah *transliterated name* {6758 tsalmonah} Shade of Death.
Sal Munna *transliterated name* {6759 tsalmunna} Shade is Withheld.
Salaph *transliterated name* {6764 tsalaph} the meaning uncertain.
sale *noun* {4466 mimkereth} **see** sell.
Salchah *transliterated name* {5548 calchah} Walking.
Sallu, Sallay *transliterated name* {5543 calluw, callay} Balanced.
Salmah *transliterated name* {8009 salmah} Clothing.
Salmay *transliterated name* {8014 salmay} Clothed.
Salmon *transliterated name* {6756 tsalmown} Shady.
Salmon *transliterated name* {8012 salmon} [4533 salmon] [4534 salmone] Clothed.
salt *noun* **salty** *adjective* {4420 melechah} [358 analos] salted; an unfertile land caused by a high salt content.
salt *noun* {4415, 4416 melach} {4417 malach} [217 halas] [251 hals] [252 halukos] salt, as pulverized.
salt *verb* {4414 malach} [233 halizo] to rub on salt.
salutation *noun* [783 aspasmos] a greeting of welcome.
salute *verb* [782 aspazomai] to welcome.

- **SUMMARY:**
- **SALVATION, SAVE, SAVIOUR:**
- **salvation** *noun* {3468 yesha} {8668 teshuah} [4991 soteria] [4992 soterion] the rescue; the restoration to wholeness.
- **salvational** *adjective* [4991 soteerios] rescue.
- **save, saviour** *verb, noun* {3467 yasha} [1295 diasozo] [4982 sozo] to rescue; one who rescues; to restore in the sense of preservation or wholeness.
- **Saviour** *title* [4990 soter] a title reserved for our Adonay Yah Shua Messiah; one who saves, rescues, restores to wholeness.

Sancherib *transliterated name* {5576 cancheriyb} the meaning uncertain; an Ashshur sovereign.
sand *noun* {2344 chowl} [285 ammos] pulverized rock.
sanhedrim *transliterated noun* [4892 sunedriom] a Yah Hudiy tribunal.
Saphon *transliterated name* {6829 tsaphown} Northern.
saplings *plural noun* {3242 yeniqah} young trees.
sapphire *transliterated noun* {5601 sapir} a gem.
saq *transliterated noun* {8242 saq} [4526 sakkos] a mesh cloth; **cp** sack.
Sarah *transliterated name* {8283 sarah} [4564 sarrha] Marshaless (female marshal); **cp** Saray.
Saray *transliterated name* {8297 saray} Governess; **cp** Sarah.
Sardis *transliterated name* [4554 sardis] Asked.
Sarephath *transliterated name* {6886 tsarephath} [4558 sarepta] Refinement.
Sarethan *transliterated name* {6891 tsarethan} Pierced.
Sarsechim *transliterated name* {8310 sarcechiym} a Babeliy general.
satan *transliterated verb* {7853 satan} to oppose.
Satan *transliterated name* {7854 satan} [4566 satan] [4567 satanas] the Hebrew name of Diabolos; an opposer; the Hellene is a transliteration of the Hebrew; **see** satan; **see**

- **SUMMARY:**
- **SATIATE, SATISFY, SATURATE, SUFFICIENT:**
- **satiate, satisfy** *verb* {7646 sabea} to fill to satisfaction.
- **satiate, saturate** *verb* {7301 ravah} to satisfy the appetite of hunger, or thirst.
- **satiated, satisfied** *adjective* {7649 sabea} sufficiently satisfied; sufficiently satiated.
- **satiated, saturated** *noun* {7310 revayah} satisfied.
- **satiation, saturated** *noun, adjective* {7302 raveh} satisfaction.
- **satiaty, satisfaction** *noun* {7648 soba} {7654 sobah} sufficiently satisfied; sufficiently satiated.
- **satisfaction** *noun* {7966 shillum} as a recompense for something owed; **see** shalom.
- **satisfied, sufficient** *verb* [714 arkeo] to be satisfactory.

satrap *noun* {323, 324 achashdarpan} a governor.
savage *adjective* [434 aneemeros] uncivilized.
savour of rest *noun* {5207, 5208 nichoach} a species of offering.
saw *verb* {7787 sur} to saw with a saw.
say, said, saith, saying *verb* {559, 560 amar} [2031 epos] [2036 epo] [2046 ereo] [5345 pheemi] to express in words.
saying, sayings *noun* {561 emer} {562 omer} {565 imrah} a statement, usually quoted, often as a proverb.
scab *noun* {5597 cappachath} a mange, as falling off.
scale *noun* {7193 qasqeseth} a scale of a fish; a scale of an armor.
scall *noun* {5424 netheq} a scurf.
scalp *noun* {6936 qodqod} the scalp of the head.
scan, tan *verb* {7805 shazaph} to scan; to be scanned by the sun; hence, to tan.
scandal *transliterated noun* [4625 skandalon] a trap; a stumblingblock; **see** stumblingblock.
scandal, scandalize *transliterated verb* [4624 scandalizo] to entice to sin; to be a stumblingblock.
scapegoat *noun* {5799 azazel} a goat which bears the sins of another; **read** Leviticus 16:8–26.
scar, contortion *noun* {6094 atstsebeth} contortion, as in pain; scars as causing contortion; **see** contort *verb*.
scarlet *noun* {8144 shaniy} the color; **see** crimson.
scarlet, maggot *noun* {8438 tolaath} a wormlike larva; scarlet, as the color of the maggot.
scarring *noun* {3587 kiy} a scar or brand caused by searing.
scatter, shatter, splatter *verb* {5310 naphats} {5311 nephets} {6327 puts} {6340 pazar} {7376 ratash} to disperse; to disperse by shattering.
scatter, spread, grow *verb* {6335 push} [837 auxano] to grow, to enlarge; as in spreading out.
scattering *noun* {8600 tephowtsah} a dispersal.
scatterings *plural noun* {4215 mezarehim} of winds.
scent *noun* {7381, 7382 reyach} an inspiration and expiration of a being; an aroma that is emitted.
sceptre, scion *noun* {7625 shebat} {7626 shebet} {8275 sharbit} [5443 phule] an offshoot, branch, sprout of a tree; a family of people; a symbol of rule; **cp** rod.
scholar *noun* {8527 talmid} a teacher or learner.
scion, sceptre *noun* {7625 shebat} {7626 shebet} {8275 sharbit} [5443 phule] an offshoot, branch, sprout of a tree; a family of people; a symbol of rule; **cp** rod.
scion (another) [246 allophulos] **see** scion.
scions (twelve) *noun* [1429 diodekaphulon] the twelve scions of Yisra El.
scope over, oversee *verb* [1983 episkopeo] to episcopate; to inspect over.
scorch *adjective* [2739 kaumatizo] burn; scorch; sear.
scorch, kindle, inflame *verb* {2734 charah} {2787 charar} {6866 zarab} literally, or soulically, to glow; to blaze up.
scorch, scorching *noun* [2738 kauma] [2740 kausis] [2742 kauson] painful and burning heat.
scorches *plural noun* {2788 charim} parched areas.
scorn *verb* {3887 luwts} {5006 naats} to mouth off; to deride.
scorn, scorner *verb, participle* {3945 latsats} to despise; a despiser.
scorn, scorning *noun* {3944 latsohn} {5007 neatsah *plural* neatsahoth} a derision.
scorpion *transliterated noun* [4651 skorpios] a species of lizard with a sting in its tail.
scour, polish *verb* {4838 maraq} to polish, so as to sharpen.
scourge *noun* {7850 shotet} a whip.
scourge, oar *noun* {7885 shait} a whip; a paddle.
scrape (off) (away) (together) *verb* {5500 cachah} {5595 caphah} {5596 caphach} to scrape; **see** offscouring.
scrape, cut *verb* {7096 qatsah} to cut off; to scrape off, by cutting; to destroy.
scream *verb* {6463 paah} [349 anakrazo] to utter a shrill screech.
screen *noun* {4345 makber} as woven; **cp** net.
scribe *noun* {5613 capher} [1122 grammatus] a writer; one that scribes; **see** scripture; **see** scroll.
scribe *verb* {5608 saphar} [1123 graptos] [1125 grapho] to write; to scribe; **see** inscribe, chart.
scribing *noun* {5610 sephar} {5615 sephorah} [1121 gramma] that which is scribed; **see** scroll.
scripture *noun* [1124 graphee] the writing, especially of Elohim; scripture *singular* usually encompasses the whole scroll of Elohim; scriptures *plural* usually encompasses segments of scripture *singular*.
scroll *noun* {5609 cephar} {5612 ciphrah} [975 biblion] [976 biblos] a roll or series of rolls which contain scribings.
scrollette *noun* [974 biblaridion] diminutive of scroll; **cp** roll.
sculpt *verb* {6458 pacal} to sculpt a sculptile.
sculptiles *noun* {*plural* 6456 pecil} {6459 pecel} that which is sculpted.
sea, seaward *noun* {3220, 3221 yam} [2281 thalassa] a great expanse of salt water; toward the sea.
seah *transliterated noun* {5429 ceah} {5432 caceah} [4568 saton] a measure of grain.
seal *noun* {2368 chotham} [4973 sphragis] a signature ring used to seal scrolls to indicate that they have not been tampered with; **see** signet.
seal *verb* {2856, 2857 chatham} [4972 sphragizo] [5420 phrasso] to affix a seal; to close up.
search *noun* {2665 chephes} an uncovering; a discovery; a masking.
search *verb* [2045 erunao] to seek; to examine into.
search, disguise *verb* {2664 chaphas} to uncover; discover; to mask.
search, seek, beseech *verb* {1245 baqash} to search for, including a response to a petition; **cp** inquire, require.
season *noun* [2540 kairos] an occasion; a measure of time; a fixed or proper time.
season, congregation *noun* {4150, 4151 moed} [2540 kairos] an assemblage; an occasion of celebration, of the year, of existence.
seat *verb* [2525 kathistemi] to place down.
Sebaiym *plural transliterated name* {5436 cebaiym} Of Seba.
Sebam, Sibmah *transliterated name* {7643 sebam, sibmah} Spice.
Seboim *plural transliterated name* {6636 tseboiym} Gazelles.
Seboim *plural transliterated name* {6650 tseboiym} Stripes.
second, double, duplicate *noun* {4932 mishneh} a copy of; a double amount; a repetition.
secondly *adverb* {8579 tinyanuth} a second time.
section *noun* {1335 bether} that which has been cut.
section *verb* {1333 bathaq} {1334 bathar} to cut into sections.
secure *verb* [805 asphalizo] to make firm, secure.
secure, certain *adjective* **securely, certainly** *adverb* {3330 yatstsib} [804 asphalees] [806 asphalos] assuredly; safely.
secure loft *noun* {4869 misgab} a lofty place; figuratively, an elevated refuge.
security, certainty *noun* {3321 yetseb} [803 asphalia] safety; an undoubtable truth.
Sedad *transliterated name* {6657 tsedad} Side.
Sedom *transliterated name* {5467 cedom} [4670 sodoma] Scorch.
seduce, wander *verb* [4105 planao] to go; be led astray.
seducing *adjective* **seducer** *noun* [4108 planos] raving; a misleader.
seduction, wandering *noun* [4106 planee] a straying from.
seductions *plural noun* {4065 madduach} allurements.
see *adjective* {7202 raeh} as experiencing.
see *verb* {2370, 2372 chazah} to gaze; to envision; **see** seer.
see *verb* {7200 raah} [308 anablepo] the prime verb of to see; to see again.
see, spectacle *noun* {7210 roiy} from the root, sight.
seed *noun* {2221 zeruwa} {2233 zera} {2234 zerah} a seed, as planted; posterity.
seed *verb* {2232 zahrah} to plant seed.
seeing *participle* {7212 reith} sight.

seek *verb* [327 anazeeteo] to search for.
seek, beseech, search *verb* {1245 baqash} to search for, including a response to a petition; **cp** inquire, require.
seek, enquire, examine, inquire, require *verb* {1875 darash} to ask; to seek; **cp** beseech.
seek early, rise early *verb* {7836 shachar} to be early.
seek refuge *verb* {2620 chacah} {2622 chacuth} to flee to for protection.
seer *noun* {2374 chozeh} the former name of a prophet; one that sees into the future; **cp** knower.
seethe *verb* {2102, 2103 zuwd} literally, or soulically, to boil.
Seirah *transliterated name* {8167 seiyrah} Roughness.
Sechachah *transliterated name* {5527 sechachah} Covered; Hedged.
Sechu *transliterated name* {7906 sechuw} Observatory.
Sela *transliterated name* {6762 tsela} Limping.
Sela Ham Machleqoth *plural transliterated name* {5555 celahammachleqowth} Rock of the Allotments.
selah *transliterated noun* {5542 celah} a suspension in music; from the same root as halal; **see** exalt, extol; **cp** halal.
select *verb* [1586 eklegomai] to pick out; to choose.
selected [1588 eklektos] [1589 eklogee] picked out; chosen.
Selel Poni *transliterated name* {6753 tselelpowniy} Shadow–Facing.
Seleq *transliterated name* {6768 tseleq} Fissure.
self–control *noun* **control self** *verb* **self–controlled** *adjective* [1466 enkratia] [1467 enkratuomai] [1468 enkrates] restraint of one's own desires and passions, especially his sensual appetites.
sell (out) *verb* {4376 makar} {4465 mimkar} to sell merchandise; to sell persons; **see** price.
Seloph Had *transliterated name* {6765 tselophchad} the meaning uncertain.
Selsach *transliterated name* {6766 tseltsach} Clear Shade.
Semach Yah *transliterated name* {5565 semachyahuw} Upheld of Yah.
Semarayim *dual transliterated name* {6787 tsemarayim} Double Wool.
Semariy *transliterated name* {6786 tsemariy} Of the Kenaaniy.
semblance *noun* [1491 eidos] a likeness; resemblance.
Senan *transliterated name* {6799 tsenan} Flock.
send, extend *verb* {7971 shalach} {7972 shelach} to send; to send forth.
sending, extending *participle* {4916 mishlach} from the verb, to send; a sending out.
sending, shooting *participle* {4917 mishlachath} from the verb, send; a release; an army.
senesce *verb* [1095 gerasko] to grow old.
senescence *noun* [1094 geeras] a growing old; aging.
sentence *noun* {6599 pithgam} [610 apokrima] the verdict of a judgment.
sentiments *plural noun* {5587 saiph} mentally divided; mixed feelings.
Senuah *transliterated name* {5574 cenuwah} Pointed.
separate *verb* [673 apokorizomai] to rend apart.
separate *verb* {914 badal} to divide; to segregate; to distinguish.
separate *verb* {5144 nazar} to set apart; **see** separatist, separatism.
separate, split *verb* {6536 parac} {6537 perac} to separate from; to split.
separate, split, breach *noun* {6556 perets} a breach; a separation from; a split.
separate, split, breach, break (off) (loose), craunch, crunch *verb* {6561 paraq} {6562 peraq} {6555 parats} to breach; to separate from; to split.
separate, spread *verb* {6504 parad} to break through; to separate from; to spread out.
separation, cutting *noun* {1508 gizrah} a cutting as of a stone; a place set apart.
Separatist *title* **separatism** *noun* {5139 nazir} {5145 nezir} a person or object set apart for service; an emblem of the Separatist; sometimes mistranslated, Nazarite; **cp** Nazarene.
Sephan Yah *transliterated name* {6846 tsephanyah} Hidden (Treasured) of Yah.
Sepharvayim *dual transliterated name* {5617 cepharvayim} the meaning uncertain; a place in Ashshur.
Sepharviy *transliterated name* {5616 cepharviy} Of Sepharvayim.
Sephath *transliterated name* {6857 tsephath} Watcher.
Sephathah *transliterated name* {6859 tseph} Watcher.
Sephi *transliterated name* {6825 tsephiy} Watcher.
Sepho *transliterated name* {6825 tsephow} Watcher.
Sephon *transliterated name* {6827 tsephown} Watcher.
Sephoniy *transliterated name* {6830 tsephowniy} Of Sephon.
sequins *plural noun* {5351 nequddoth} those which are little and punctured.
Ser *transliterated name* {6863 tser} Narrow.
Sera Yah *transliterated name* {8304 serayah} Prevailed of Yah.
Seraph *transliterated name* {8315 saraph} Burning; **see** seraph, seraphim.
seraph, seraphim *transliterated noun* {8314 *singular* saraph *plural* saraphim} literally, on fire; a kind of serpent.
Seredah *transliterated name* {6868 tseredah} {6888 tserarah} Pierced.
Serediy *transliterated name* {5625 cardiy} Of Sered.
serenity *noun* {7959 shelev} {7962 shalvah} {7963 shelevah} complete satisfaction; **see** shalom *adjective.*
serene, serenity *adjective* {7961 shelevah}
serenely *adverb* {7987 sheliy}
serene, serenify serenize *verb* {7951 shalah, shalav} {7954 shelah} to make or become serene.
Sereth *transliterated name* {6889 tsereth} Splendor.
Sereth Hash Shachar *transliterated name* {6890 tserethhashshachar} Splendor of the Dawn.
Seri *transliterated name* {6874 tseriy} Balm.
Seror *transliterated name* {6872 tseror} Bundle.
serpent *noun* {5175 nachash} [3789 ophis] a reptile; figuratively of Satan, or one who is cunning.
Seruah *transliterated name* {6871 tseruwah} Leprous.
Serug *transliterated name* {8286 serug} [4562 sarouch] Tendril.
Seruyah *transliterated name* {6870 tseruyah} Balm.
servant *noun* {5649 abad} {5650 ebed} [1401 doulos] male servant; **see** serve; **cp** maid.
servantry *noun* {5657 abuddah} that which serves.
serve *verb* **server** *participle* {6399 pelach} to serve; that which serves.
serve, servient *verb* {5647 abad} [1398 douluo] to serve in servitude; to serve the soil, as in agriculture.
serve, do, keep, make *verb* {5648 abad} in the sense of serving.
service *noun* {5652 abad} {5656 abodah} {5673 abidah} a deed.
service *noun* {6402 polchan} as worship.
servient (be), (in) servitude, subservient *verb, adjective* [1396 doulagogeo] [1402 douloo] to enslave.
servitude *noun* {5659 abduth} [1397 douliei] [1400 doulon] slavery.
set (apart) *verb* [873 aphorizo] to set off by boundary.
set (apart) *verb* {4560 macar} to separate from.
set (by), stand (by), station (by), place (by) *verb* {3320 yatsab} {3322 yatsag} {5324 natsab} from the root, to place, so as to stay.
set the torah *verb* [3548 nomothesia] to establish the torah.
set, abandon, allow, leave, let *verb* {3240 yanach} {5203 natash} to allow to be; to allow to be set; to abandon.
set, place, put *verb* {7760, 7761 suwm} {7896 shith} {8239 shaphath} {8271 shathah} to put in place.
settings *plural noun* {6183 ariph} the droopings of the sky.
settle *verb* {3427 yashab} {3488 yethib} [1460 enkatoikeo] [2730 katoikeo] [3611 oikeo] [3939 paroikeo] to settle down, as in a community, or as on a throne.
settle around *verb* [4039 perioikeo] to be a neighbor.
settlement *noun* {4186 moshab} [2731 katoikeesis] [2732 katoiketerion] [2733 katoikia] a place of settling; the act of settling; the state of being settled; **see** settle.
settler *noun* {8453 toshab} [3941 paroikos] one who has settled.
settling *verbal noun* [3940 paroikia] settlement.
seven *noun* {7651 shibah} a prime number; a week of days; symbolic of completion; the root of the verb, oath.
seven, seventh *adjective* {7637 shebiyiy} {7655 shibah} {7658 shibanah} [2033 hepta] **see** seven *noun.*
sevenfold *dual noun* {7659 shibathayim} literally, sevens; double seven.
sever *verb* {2685 chatsaph} {6991 qatal} {6992 qetal} {6993 qetel} {7088 qaphad} to cut off; to deathify.
severance *noun* {7089 qephadah} a cutting off.
Shaalbim *plural transliterated name* {8169 shaalbiym} Fox Holes.
Shaalbimiy *transliterated name* {8170 shaalboniy} Of Shaalbim.
Shaalim *transliterated name* {8171 shaaliym} Foxes.
Shaarayim *dual transliterated name* {8189 shaarayim} Double

Portals.
shabbath *transliterated noun* {7676 shabbath} [2663 katapausis] [4521 sabbaton] a celebration of rest which Elohim commands humanity to guard.
shabbathism *transliterated noun* {4868 mishbath} {7674 shebeth} {7677 shabbathon} [4520 sabbatismos] a celebration of rest.
shabbathize *transliterated verb* {7673 shabath} [2664 katapauo] to celebrate a shabbathism.
Shabbethay *transliterated name* {7678 shabbethay} Restful.
Shacharayim *transliterated name* {7842 shacharayim} Double Dawn.
Shachasom *transliterated name* {7831 shachatsowm} Proudly.
shackle *verb* {3729 kephath} to bind, or confine the limbs to prevent free motion.
shackles *noun* [3976 pede] a ring or band that confines the feet to prevent their free motion.
Shadday *transliterated title* {7706 shadday} Nourisher; Nurturer; sometimes compounded with El; **cp** Almighty; **see** Theological Wordbook.
shade *noun* {4699 metsullah} a hovering over.
shade *verb* {2927 telal} to cover over.
shade, fade *verb* {6004 amam} in the sense of concealing; of fading.
shade, shadow *noun* {6738 tsel} {6752 tselel} literally, or figuratively, shade; shadow.
shadow of death *noun* {6757 tsalmaveth} the shade, or shadow of death.
Shadrach *transliterated name* {7714, 7715 shadrach} the Babeliy name of one of Dani El's companions.
shaggy *adjective* {5569 camar} bristling.
shake *verb* {1607 gaash} {5287 naar} {5363 noqeph} {5426 nethat} {7477 raal} to thresh; **cp** quake.
shake, glutton, quake *participle* {2151 zalal} to quake; to shake; to eat in excess; **cp** drunkard.
shake, stagger, totter, wag, wander, waver, drift *verb* {5128 nuwa} to waver.
shake, wave, rub *verb* {5130 nuph} to rub a bed with aromatics; to shake a hand; to wave an offering.

- **SUMMARY:**
- **SHALAM, SHALOM, SHELAMIM:**
- **ALSO SEE COMPLETE.**
- **shalam** *verb* {*transliterated* 7999 shalam} {*transliterated* 8000 shelam} (to cause) to be at shalom; to complete; to satisfy a debt. **Note:** The Hellene uses two different root forms: the first root form [1514 eireneuo] [1517 eirenopoieo] [1518 eirenopoios] relates primarily to the area of personal satisfaction and contentment: the second root form [658 apoteleo] [4931 sunteleo] [5048 telioo] [5055 teleo] relates primarily to the area of satisfying a debt.
- **shalom** *noun* {7965 shalom} {7966 shillum} [5046 telios] complete satisfaction, as in a state of being, or as payment of a debt.
- **Mighty Important Consideration:** The translators of the Septuagint, the Old Covenant from Hebraic and Aramaic into Hellene, have translated the words of **shalom** and **shalam** into the following Hellenic words: [467 autapodom] to recompense; [591 apadidom] to give back; [661 apotino] to repay; [1515 eireneuo] to be at peace; [1516 eirenikos] peace; [1517 eirenopoleo] to make peace; [3648 holokieuos] whole; [4982 sozo] heal, save; [4992 soteria] save; [5046 telios] perfect; [5055 teleo] finished, **see** Yahn 19:30. Since we know that Adonay Yah Shua Messiah spoke Aramaic and/or Hebrew on the stake, is it possible that His word for **teleo** was literally, **shalam?**
- **shalom (of)** *transliterated noun, adjective* {8001 shelam} {8003 shalem} [1515 eirene] [1516 eirenikos] of inward satisfaction.
- **shelamim** *transliterated plural noun* {8002 shelamim} from {7999 shalam}; sacrifices of shalom.

Shalem *transliterated name* {8004 shalem} [4530 salim] [4532 shaleem] Complete; **see** complete.
Shalishah *transliterated name* {8031 shalishah} Triple.
shall, shalt, should, shouldest *auxiliary verbs* these auxiliary verbs are not in the manuscripts, but have been supplied by the translators to smooth the verbal flow: they do not indicate a future tense except when coupled to a future verb: **see** may, mayest, might, mightest; **see** will, wilt, would, wouldest.
Shallecheth *transliterated name* {7996 shallecheth} Cast.
Shalmaneser *transliterated name* {8022 shalmanecer} an Ashshuriy sovereign.
Shalmay *transliterated name* {8073 shamlay} Clothed; one of the Dedicates.
Shalome *transliterated name* {7965 shalom} [4539 salomee] Completely Satisfied; **see** shalom.
shame *noun* {955 buwshah} humiliation; disgrace.
shame *verb* {954 bush} {3001 yabesh} {3637 kalam} [1788 entrepo] [2617 kataiskuno] to humiliate; to disgrace.
shame, mercy *verb* {2616 chaced} literally, to bow the neck in kindness, or in reproof.
shame, shamefulness *noun* {1322 bosheth} {3639 kelimmah} {3640 kelimmuth} [149 aiskron] [151 aiskrotes] [152 aiskune] [1791 entropee] the feeling, and condition of shame; of disgrace.
shameful words *noun* [148 aiskrologia] disgraceful words.
Shammay *transliterated name* {8060 shammay} Destructive.
Shamsheray *transliterated name* {8125 shamsheray} Sunlike.
Shamur *transliterated name* {8053 shamuwr} Observed.
Shaphat *transliterated name* {8202 shaphat} Judge.
Shaphat Yah *transliterated name* {8203 shephatyah} Judge of Yah.
Shaphir *transliterated name* {8208 shapiyr} Glorified.
Sharay *transliterated name* {8298 sharay} Hostile.
Shareser *transliterated name* {8272 sharetser} the meaning uncertain.
Sharon *transliterated name* {8289 sharon} [4565 saron] Straight.
Sharoniy *transliterated name* {8290 sharowniy} Of Sharon.
sharp *adjective* {2299 chad} {*plural* 2303 chaddud} [3691 oxus] as pointed keen.
sharpen *verb* {2300 chadad} to cause to be sharp.
sharpen *verb* {3913 latash} to hammer out an edge.
sharpened *adjective* {4593 maot} an edge, as thinned.
Sharuchen *transliterated name* {8287 sharuwchen} Abode of Charism.
Shashaq *transliterated name* {8349 shashaq} Pedestrian.
Shashay *transliterated name* {8343 shashay} Whitish.
shatter, splatter, scatter *verb* {5310 naphats} {5311 nephets} {6327 puts} {6340 pazar} {7376 ratash} to disperse; to disperse by shattering.
shatter, vilify, vilifying *verb* {7489 raa} {7490 rea} [2551 kakologeo] [2558 kakoucheo] [2559 kakoo] verb of evil; to make or declare evil; to vilify by shattering; **see** evil.
Shaul *transliterated name* {7586 shaul} [4549 saoul] [4569 saulos] Asked; Loaned.
Shaveh *transliterated noun* {7740 shaveh} Plain; Plains; also a prefix to names of plains.
Shaveh Qiryathayim *dual transliterated name* {7741 shavehqiryathayim} Plain of a Double City.
she burro *noun* {860 athown} a female burro.
Shealti El *transliterated name* {7597, 7598 shealtiyel} [4528 salathieel] Asked (Loaned) of El.
Shear Yah *transliterated name* {8187 shearyah} Guard of Yah.
Shear Yashub *transliterated name* {7610 shearyashuwb} A Remainder Returneth.
shear *verb* {1494 gazaz} {3697 kacam} to cut, usually hair or fleece.
shearing *noun* {1488 gez} {1492 gazzah} that which is sheared.
sheath *noun* {5084 nadan} {5085 nidneh} a receptacle of a sword; figuratively, the body, as a receptacle of the soul.
sheath, knife, razor *noun* {8593 taar} a knife, or a razor, as making bare; a sheath, as being bare.
Sheba *transliterated noun* {7652 sheba} Seven.
Sheba, Shebaiym *transliterated noun* {7614 sheba} {*plural* 7615 shebaiym} the meaning uncertain; three progeniters of scions; a district in Ethiopia.
Shebaiym *transliterated name* {7615 shebaiym} Of Sheba.
Sheban Yah *transliterated noun* {7645 shebanyah} Grown of Yah.
Shebat *transliterated noun* {7627 shebat} the name of a month.
Shebu El, Shuba El *transliterated noun* {7619 shebuel, shubael} Captured of El.
Shechar Yah *transliterated noun* {7841 shecharyah} Early Seeker of Yah.
Shedey Ur *transliterated name* {7707 shedeyuwr} Spreader of Light.
sheep *noun* [4263 probaton] a wooly domestic animal.
sheep gate *noun* [4262 probatikos] a gate through which sheep are led.
Sheerah *transliterated name* {7609 sheerah} Kinflesh.
sheets, snare *noun* {6341 pach} a sheet, as pounded thin; a

snare of lumina, as made to spring shut.
Shekan Yah *transliterated name* {7935 shekanyah} Tabernacle of Yah.
shekel *transliterated noun* {8255 sheqel} a set weight of a balance scale.
Shechem *transliterated name* {7927, 7928 shechem} [4966 suchem] Shoulder.
Shechemiy *transliterated name* {7930 shichmiy} Of Shechem.
Shelach *transliterated name* {7974 shelach} [4527 sala] Spear; Branch.
Shelah *transliterated name* {7956 shelah} Ask; Loan.
Shelahiy *transliterated name* {8024 shelaniy} Of Shelah.
Shelem Yah *transliterated name* {8018 shelemyah} Completed of Yah; from {7965 shalom}; **see** complete.
Shelomi *transliterated name* {8015 shelomi} Complete; from {7965 Shalom}; **see** complete.
Shelomith *transliterated name* {8019 shelomith} Complete; from {7965 shalom}; **see** complete.
Shelomoh *transliterated name* {8010 shelomoh} [4672 solomon] Complete; from {7965 shalom}; **see** complete.
Shelomoth *transliterated name* {*feminine plural* 8013 shelomoth} Complete; from {7965 shalom}; **see** complete.
Shelumi El *transliterated name* {8017 shelumiel} Completed of El; from {7965 shalom}; **see** complete.
Shem *transliterated name* {8035 shem} [4590 seen] means Name.
Shem Eber *transliterated name* {8038 shemeber} Name of Pinion.
Shema *transliterated name* {8087 shema} {8090 shema} Annunciation.
Shema Yah *transliterated name* {8098 shemayah} Heard of Yah.
Shemar Yah *transliterated name* {8114 shemaryah} Guarded of Yah.
Shemer *transliterated name* {8106 shemer} Dregs.
Shemi Da *transliterated name* {8061 shemiyda} Name of Knowing.
Shemi Daiy *transliterated name* {8062 shemiydaiy} Of Shemi Da.
Shemi Ramoth *plural transliterated name* {8070 shemiyramowth} Name of Ramoth.
Shemu El *transliterated name* {8050 shemuel} [4545 samouel] Heard by El.
Shenassar *transliterated name* {8137 shenatstsar} Of Babel.
sheol, hades *noun* {7585 sheol} [86 hades] literally, the unseen; sheol is a transliteration of the Hebrew; hades is a transliteration of the Hellene, which is a translation of the Hebrew; both refer to a temporary abode of the body and soul; there is a progressive distinction of purpose of sheol/hades from its inception to its final state; **read** Yechezq El 31:15–17, 32:18–29, Loukas 16:19–31, Apocalypse 20:13,14; **cp** Psalm 16:10, Acts 2:27.
Shepham *transliterated name* {8221 shepham} Bare.
Shephamiy *transliterated name* {8225 shiphmiy} Of Shepham.
Shepher *transliterated name* {8234 shepher} Glorious.
shepherd *noun* [4166 poimen] one who tends.
shepherd *verb* [4165 poimaino] to tend.
shepherddom *noun* [4167 poimnee] [4168 poimnion] the sovereigndom of a shepherd.
Shephuphan, Shephupham *transliterated name* {8197 shephuwphan, shephuwpham} Adderlike.
Shereb Yah *transliterated name* {8274 sherebyah} Mirage of Yah.
Sheshach *transliterated name* {8347 sheshach} a symbolic name of Babel.
Sheshay *transliterated name* {8344 sheshay} Whitish.
Sheth *transliterated name* {8352 sheth} [4589 seeth] Set, as in authority; a son of Adam.
Shethar Bozenay *transliterated name* {8370 shetharbowzenay} the meaning uncertain; a Persian officer.
shew, show *verb* {2324 chava} {2331 chavah} to propose for consideration; **see** propound.
shewing, showing *noun* [323 anadixis] display.
Sheya *transliterated name* {7864 sheya} False.
Shibah *transliterated noun* {7656 shibah} Seven.
shibboleth *transliterated noun* {7641 shibboleth} a stream, as flowing; **cp** sibboleth; **see** Judges 12:6.
Shichor *transliterated name* {7883 shichor} Dark.
Shichor Libnath *transliterated name* {7884 shiychowrlibnath} Darkish Whiteness.
shield *noun* {{7982 shelet} a protector.
shield, cold, hook *noun* {6793 tsinnah} coldness, as piercing; a hook, as pointed; a shield, as a prickler.
Shikkeron *transliterated name* {7942 shikkerown} Intoxication.
Shilchi *transliterated name* {7977 shilchiy} Spear; Branch.
Shilchim *plural transliterated name* {7978 shilchiym} Spears; Branches.
Shillem *transliterated name* {8006 shillem} Retribution.
Shillemiy *transliterated name* {8016 shillemiy} Of Shillem.
Shiloach *transliterated name* {7975 shiloach} [4611 siloam] Spear; Branch.
Shiloh *transliterated title, name* {7886, 7887 shiloh} Tranquility; a title of the Messiah; a place in Pelesheth.
Shilohiy *transliterated name* {7888 shiloniy} Of Shiloh.
Shima *transliterated name* {8092 shima} Annunciation.
Shimah *transliterated name* {8039 shimah} {8093 shimah} Annunciation.
Shimahiym *plural transliterated name* {8101 shimathiym} Of Shimah.
Shimam *transliterated name* {8043 shimam} Annunciation.
Shimi *transliterated name* {8096 shimiy} [4584 semei] Famous.
Shimiy *transliterated name* {8097 shimiy} Of Shimi.
Shimon *transliterated name* {7889 shimon} Desolation.
Shimon *transliterated name* {8095 shimon} [4613 simon] [4826 sumeon] Hearer.
Shimoniy *transliterated name* {8099 shimoniy} Of Shimon {8095}.
Shimron *transliterated name* {8110 shimrown} Guardianship.
Shimroniy *transliterated name* {8117 shimroniy} Of Shimron.
Shimshay *transliterated name* {8124 shimshay} Sunny.
Shimshon *transliterated name* {8123 shimshon} [4546 sampson] Sunlight.
shine, flash *verb* {3313 yapha} from the root, to shine.
shine, think *verb* {6245 ashath} {6246 ashith} as polishing.
shingle *noun* {7824 shachiph} a board, as a chip.
shingle, rank, row *noun* {7713 sederah} {7795 sorah} that which is regulated in rows.
shinquards *plural noun* {4697 mitschah} a piece of armor protecting the shin.
ship *noun* {590 oniy} {591 oniyah} {6716 tsiy} a large boat.
ship *noun* {5600 sephinah} a vessel as ceiled; a ship with a deck; **see** ceiled; **cp** sailer.
Shitray *transliterated name* {7861 shitray} Official.
shittah, shittim *transliterated noun* {7848 *singular* shittah, *plural* shittim} a species of tree, or the timber thereof.
Shiyon *transliterated name* {7866 shiyown} Devastation.
Shobach *transliterated name* {7731showbach} Thicket.
Shobay *transliterated name* {7630 shobay} Captor.
Shobeq *transliterated name* {7733 showbeq} Forsaking.
Shobyah *transliterated name* {7634 shobyah} Captive.
shod, enclose, inclose, lock *verb* {5274 naal} {7000 qatar} to fasten; **see** shoe.
shoe *noun* {5275 naalah} **see** shod.
Shomeron *transliterated name* {8111 shomeron} {8115 shomrain} [4540 samaria] Guard Station.
Shomeroness *transliterated name* [4542 samaritis] a female of Shomeron.
Shomeroniy *transliterated name* {8118 shomeroniy} [4541 samarites] Of Shomeron.
shoot *verb* {7232 rabab} to shoot an arrow.
shooting, sending *participle* {4917 mishlachath} from the verb, send; a release; an army.
Shophach *transliterated name* {7780 showphach} Poured.
short *adjective* {7116 qatser} short, in a variety of applications.
shorten, chop, curtail, harvest *verb* {7114 qatsar} literally, or figuratively, to cut off.
shortly, bit, bit by bit, few, little, petty *adjective, adverb* {4592 meat} diminutive; a few; a little.
shortness *noun* {7115 qotser} impatience.
Shoshanna *transliterated name* **trumpet, lily** *noun* {7799 shoshanna} [4677 sousanna] Lily, as a flower, or as an ornament; trumpet, from its lily shaped bell.
shoulder *noun* {3802 katheph} {7926 shechem} [5606 omos] literally, a side piece; figuratively, the place of bearing a burden; the shoulder.
shoulder blade *noun* {7929 shikma} the bone of the shoulder.
shout *noun* {7440 rinnah} {7445 renanah} a shriek; a shout for joy.
shout *verb* {7438 ron} to shriek for deliverance; to shout for joy.
shout(ing), stake(ing), blast(ing), clang(ing), clap(ping) *noun* {8619 taqowa} {8643 teruah} a loud sound; the celebration of shouting, and/or blasting trumpets unto Yah Veh; also of

shouting, and/or blasting a battle cry; a stake of a tent, or tabernacle; a stake for execution.
shout, blast *verb* {6681 tsavach} {7442 ranan} {7244 renen} {7321 ruwa} [2019 epiphoneo] to sound forth loudly, instrumentally or vocally.
shout, shouting *verb* {7442 ranan} {7444 rannen} to shriek; to shout for joy.
shout, stake, blast, clang, clap *verb* {7321 ruwa} {8628 taqa} [4078 peegnumi] [4717 stauroo] to sound loudly; to celebrate by shouting, and/or blasting trumpets unto Yah Veh; to shout and/or blast a battle cry; to stake a tabernacle or tent; to stake for execution.
shout, thunder *noun* {7452 rea} a crashing sound.
shove away *verb* [683 apotheomai] to push off; to reject.
shower *noun* {7377 riy} {*plural* 8164 saiyr} moisture.
shred *noun* {2636 chacpac} from the root, to peel; a shred; a scale.
shred, rip *verb* {7167 qara} from the root, to rend.
shreds *plural noun* {7168 qeraim} rags.
shriek *verb* {603 anaqah} to screech.
shrieker *noun* {604 anaqah} a shrieking animal.
shriveled *adjective* {5384 nasheh} shrunken and wrinkled.
shrub *noun* {7880 siach} bush.
Shu Telach *transliterated name* {7803 shuwthelach} Waste of Breakage.
Shu Telachiy *transliterated name* {8364 shuthalchiy} Of Shu Telach.
Shuach *transliterated name* {7744 shuwach} Dell.
Shuachiy *transliterated name* {7747 shuchiy} Of Shuach.
Shual *transliterated name* {7586 shauwl} [4549 saoni] [4569 saulos] Asked.
Shualiy *transliterated name* {7587 shauwliy} Of Shaul.
Shuchah *transliterated name* {7746 shuwchah} Chasm.
Shucham *transliterated name* {7748 shuwcham} Humbly.
Shuchamiy *transliterated name* {7749 shuwchamiy} Of Shucham.
shudder, whirl away *verb* {8175 saar} to storm; to shudder, as in fright; to be stormed away.
Shulammith *transliterated name* {7759 shuwlammiyth} Completely Satisfied.
Shumahiy *transliterated name* {8126 shumathiy} Garlic; Of Shumah.
Shunem *transliterated name* {7766 shuwnem} Quietly.
Shunemiyth *transliterated name* {7767 shuwnammiyth} a female of Shunem.
Shuni *transliterated name* {7764 shuwniy} Quiet.
Shuniy *transliterated name* {7765 shuwniy} Of Shuni.
Shuphamiy *transliterated name* {7781 shuwphamiy} Of Shephupham.
Shushanchiy *transliterated name* {7801 shuwshanchiy} the meaning uncertain.
shut (up) (in) *verb* {5534 sakar} {5535 sakath} to shut up, as a mouth; to shut in, as a people.
shut (up), stop (up) *verb* {5640 satham} to stop up; figuratively, to keep secret.
shut, concentrate *verb* {5462 cagar} {5463 cegar} to shut; to shut tight; cold as shut tight, or concentrated.
Siba *transliterated name* {6717 tsiyba} Station.
Sibbechay *transliterated name* {5444 cibbechay} Entwined.
sibboleth *transliterated noun* {5451 cibboleth} an ear of grain; **cp** shibboleth; **see** Judges 12:6.
Sibon *transliterated name* {6649 tsibown} Dyes.
Sibrayim *dual transliterated name* {5453 cibrayim} Double Will.
Sibya *transliterated name* {6644 tsibya} Gazelle.
Sibyah *transliterated name* {6645 tsibyah} Gazelle.
Sicha *transliterated name* {6727 tsicha} Parched.
Sichon *transliterated name* {5511 ciychown} Tempestuous.
sicken, stroke, worn (out), rub *verb* {2470 chalah} to wear out; to stroke the face as in appeasement.
sickle *noun* {2770 chermesh} an incisor.
sickle, trench, decision, decisive, incision, incisor, ore *adjective, noun* {2742 charuts} physically, soulically, or mentally, an incising.
sickness *noun* {2483 choliy} {*plural* 8463 tachalim} a malady.
Siddim *plural transliterated name* {6661 tsiddim} Sides.
side, rib *noun* {5967 ala} {6763 tsela} literally, a curve or an arch; a rib of a body; a rib of a structure.
Sidon *transliterated name* {6721 tsiydon} [4605 sidon] Hunt (as provision).
Sidoniy *transliterated name* {6722 tsiydoniy} [4606 sidonios] Of Sidon.
Sidqenuw (Yah Veh) *transliterated title* {3072 yehovah tsidqenuw} a combined form of {3068 yehovah} and {6664 tsedeq} Yah Veh of Justness.
Sidqi Yah *transliterated name* {6667 tsidqiyah} Justness of Yah; of the priesthood of Yah.
siege, rampart *noun* {4692 matsur} {4694 matsor} a mound for protection; a seizing.
sigh deeply *verb* [389 anastenazo] to express deep emotion.
sigh *verb* {584 anach} {3306 yaphach} {5162 nacham} [1690 embrimaomai] an expressing of emotion; to sigh over, as in empathy; does not mean regret.
sigh, sighing *noun* {585 anachah} {592 aniyah} {5164 nocham} an expression of emotion.
sight *noun* {7203 roeh} {7207 roeh} [309 anablepsis] a vision; a seeing again.
sign *verb* {7560 resham} to signature.
sign, ensign *noun* {226 owth} [3902 parasemos] [4592 seemion] as emblematic, or as a signal; the sun, moon, and stars are for signs and seasons; Yonah was a sign to the Ninevehiym and the Yah Hudahiym; turning water into wine was Yah Shua's first sign; some signs are miraculous, some are not.
signal *verb* [2678 katasio] to make a sign; to signal.
signet *noun* {2858 chothemeth} {2885 tabbaath} {5824 izqa} a signet ring used for sealing; **see** seal.
signify *verb* {7559 rasham} [4591 seemaino] [4593 seemioomai] to distinguish; to indicate; to signal.
silence *noun* {1745 duwmah} from the root, to be mute.
silent *adjective, adverb* {1747 duwmiyah} {1748 duwmahm} mute; still.
Sillah *transliterated name* {6741 tsillah} Shade.
Sillethay *transliterated name* {6769 tsillethay} Shady.
silver *noun* [693 argurous] made of silver.
silver *noun* {3701 keceph} [696 arguros] the metal, especially as a medium of exchange.
simplicity *noun* [858 aphelotes] smoothness.
simultaneously *adverb* [260 hama] at the same time.
Sin *transliterated name* {6790 tsin} Crag.
sin (against), cleanse for sin *verb* {2398 chata} [264 hamartano] to misaim.
sin (offering) (for the) *noun* {2399 chet} {2401 chataah} {2402 chattaah} {2403 chattath} {2408 chatiy} {2409 chattaya} [265 hamartema] [266 hamartia] a misaiming; in some instances implies an offering for sin.
Sinay *transliterated name* {5514 ciynay} [4614 sina] a mountain of Arabia.
sinew *noun* {1517 giyd} a tendon.
sing *verb* **songster, songstress** *participle* {7891 shiyr, shuwr} [103 ado] to sing; a male singer; a female singer.
singe *verb* {2760, 2761 charak} to scorch.
Siniy *transliterated name* {5513 ciyniy} Of one of the sons of Kenaan.
sink *verb* {7743 shuwach} literally, or figuratively, to sink.
sink, bend, descend, penetrate, press *verb* {5181 nachath} from the root, to sink; to go down; to press or lead down.
sinless *adjective* [361 anamartetos] one who is not misaiming.
sinner *noun* {2400 chatta} [268 hamartolos] one who misaims.
Sior *transliterated name* {6730 tsiyor} Belittle.
Siphyon *transliterated name* {6837 tsiphyown} Watcher.
Sippay *transliterated name* {5598 cippay} Bason–like.
Sippor *transliterated name* {6834 tsippowr} Bird.
Sipporah *transliterated name* {6855 tsipporah} Bird.
Siqlag *transliterated name* {6860 tsiqlag} uncertain derivative.
Sis *transliterated name* {6732 tsiyts} Blossom.
Sismay *transliterated name* {5581 cicmay} of uncertain derivative.
sister in law *noun* {2994 yebemeth} the sister of a man's woman, or of a woman's man.
sister *noun* {269 achowth} [79 adelphe] a female child of the same parents.
sistrum *noun* {*plural* 4517 menanaim} an instrument consisting of metal frame and metal rods, which jingle; **cp** tambourine.
Sithri *transliterated name* {5644 cithriy} Protective.
Siyon *transliterated name* {6726 tsiyown} [4622 sion] Monument.
skeleton, bone *noun* {1634, 1635 gerem} {6106 etsem} [3747 osteon] a framework; a substance, usually of the body.
skeptics *plural noun* {5588 ceeph} literally, of divided mind; **see** opinions.

skillet *noun* {6517 parur} {6745 tselachah} a utensil; as flattened, as being spread out.
skillful, hasting *adjective* {4106 mahir} to hurry along; to be skillful; quick, as skillful.
skin *noun* {1539 geled} {5785 owr} [5559 chros] the covering of the body.
skin *noun* {2573 chemeth} {4997 nod} as tied to hold contents, usually liquid.
skip about *verb* {6852 tsaphar}.
sky, powder *noun* {7834 shachaq} the upper atmosphere; a substance of pulverized particles.
slab *noun* [4109 plax] a slab for engraving.
slab *noun* {3871 luach} a slab, as polished; usually of stone; figuratively, of the heart.
slack *adjective* {7504 rapheh} lacking energy.
slack, delay *verb* [1019 braduno] to be slow.
slacken, let (down) (fall) (go) (loose), loose, loosen up *verb* {7503 raphah} to slacken.
slackness *noun* {7510 riphion} a lack of energy.
slander *noun* {1681 dibbah} [2636 katalalia] defamation.
slander *verb* [2635 katalaleo] to be a cause of sin to; to defame.
slanderer *noun* [2637 katalalos] one who slanders.
slap, slurp, clap *verb* {5606 saphaq} as in clapping hands, slapping the thigh, slurping vomit; **see** gluttony.
slaughter *noun* {2027 hereg} {2028 haregah} {2874 tebach} {2878 tibehah} {4293 matbeach} {7821 shechitah} [4967 sphagee] [4968 sphagion] to slaughter for sacrifice; a massacre.
slaughter *verb* {2026 harag} {2873 tabach} {7819, 7820 shachat} [615 apoktino] [2695 katasphatto] [4969 sphatto] [4372 prosphatos] to sacrifice; to massacre.
slaughterer *noun* {2876, 2877 tabbach} {2879 tabbachah} a butcher; an executioner.
slave *noun* {4522 mac, mic} one in forced servitude; **cp** servant; **cp** maid.
sledge *noun* {4173 morag} a sledge for threshing.
sledgehammers *plural noun* {3597 keylaph} from the root, to strike with noise.
sleep (sound) *noun* {8639 tardemah} also lethargy.
sleep *noun* {8139, 8142 shenah} {8153 shenath} to slumber.
sleep soundly *verb* {7290 radam} to stun; to stupify with sleep, or with death.
sleep *verb* {5123 nuwm} to slumber from drowsiness; **see** drowsiness.
slice *noun* {6400 pelach} a split; a division off a whole.
slice, slicer *noun* {2757 charits} slice of milk; may be cheese.
slight, swift, trifle, abase, abate, belittle *verb* {6819 tsaar} {6985 qat} {7034 qalah} {7043 qalal} to belittle in contempt; to make light of; to lessen.
slime *noun* {8602 taphel} soft, moist earth reduced to the consistency of slime; that which is slimy in consistency.
slime, saliva *noun* {7388 rir} from its broth texture.
sling *noun* {7050 qela} that which slings stones.
slinger *noun* {7051 qaila} one that slings stones.
slip (away) (out), escape *verb* {6403 palat} {6405 peletah}.
slothful *verb* {6101 atsal} *adjective* {6102 atsel} *noun* {6103 atslah} {6104 atsluth} slow; sluggish.
slurp, clap, slap *verb* {5606 saphaq} as in clapping hands, slapping the thigh, slurping vomit; **see** gluttony.
smite *verb* {5062 nagaph} to touch heavily.
smite, smitten *verb* {5221 nakah} to strike lightly, or heavily; **cp** strike.
smiter *adjective* {5222 nekeh} a traducer; **cp** striker.
smitten *adjective* {5223 nakeh} maimed; dejected; **cp** stricken.
smoke *noun* {6227 ashan} literal, figurative smoke.
smoke *noun* {7008 qitor} as the fume of a fire.
smoke *verb* {6225 ashan} literally, or figuratively, to smoke.
smoking, smoky *adjective* {6226 ashen} literally, or figuratively, smoky.
smooth *adjective* {2509 chalaq} {2512 challuq} smooth of tongue; smooth stones.
smooth it over, allot *verb* {2505 chalaq} literally, to smooth; as tossing smooth pebbles to allot lands, inheritances; as smoothing over through flattery.
smooth *verb* {4452 malats} as in soothing.
smooth, allotment, portion *noun* {2506 cheleq} {2508 chalaq} {2511 challaq} {2513 chelqah} {2515 chaluqqah} {4255 machleqah} {4256 machaloqeth} {4521 menath} smoothness of tongue; usually an inheritance allotted by pebble.
snare *noun* {4170 moqesh} {4204 mazor} {7407 rokes} that which entangles; as in turning aside from truth.
snare, ensnare *verb* {3369 yaqosh} {5367 naqash} {6351 pachah} {6983 qosh} to lay, or to spring a snare.
snare, sheets *noun* {6341 pach} a sheet, as pounded thin; a snare of lumina, as made to spring shut.
snarer *noun* {3352 yaqosh} {3353 yaqosh} one who snares.
snatch away *verb* {3261 yaah} from the root, to brush aside.
snatch *verb* {6642 tsabat} to reach for.
sneezing *noun* {5846 atiyshah} from the root, to sneeze.
snorting *participle* {5170 nacharah} as expressing wrath; **see** nostrils.
snout, wrath, nostril *noun* {639 aph} {*plural* 5156 nechirim} [3709 orgee] the snorter, as in expressing wrath; **see** snorting.
snow *noun* {7950 sheleg} {8517 telag} [5510 chion] frozen atmospheric vapor.
snow–white *verb* {7949 shalag} to be white as snow.
so (as) (that), in order to, on account of *participle* {4616 maan} {5668 abur} for the purpose of.
Soan *transliterated name* {6814 tsoan} meaning uncertain.
Soar *transliterated name* {6820 tsoar} Belittle.
Sobah *transliterated name* {6678 tsowbah} Station.
Sobebah *transliterated name* {6637 tsobebah} Palanquin.
sober up *verb* [366 ananepho] [1594 eknepho] to become sober; metaphorically, to return to soberness of mind.
Sochar *transliterated name* {6714 tsochar} White.
socket, pestle *noun* {4388 maktesh} {5940 eliy} the pestle of a mortar; a socket.
socket, pudenda *noun* {6596 poth} literally, a hole.
soil *noun* {127 adamah} ruddy; the soil of the earth: **cp** Adam; **cp** cosmos.
sojourn *verb* {1481 gur} to travel; **see** journey.
sojourner, sojourning *noun* {1616 ger} {4033 magur} a traveler; a travelling; **see** journey.
Sochoh *transliterated name* {7755 sochoh} Hedge.
solaces *plural noun* {5150 nichum} consolings.
sole, bowl, hollow, palm, paw *noun noun* {3709 kaph} {6447 pas} {8168 shoal} a hollow of the hand, foot, paw, or body; also utensils with a hollow.
solidify, leap *verb* {6339 pazaz} to become solid; to spring.
son *noun* [5207 huios] a male offsrping; figuratively, kinship.
son, bar *noun* {1247, 1248 bar} a son; as heir apparent to the throne; also a prefix to a name; **cp** ben; **note:** both ben and bar appear in Psalm 2:.
son, ben, Ben *transliterated noun* {1121, 1122, 1123 ben} a son, as builder of the family name; also a prefix to a name; **cp** bar; **note:** both ben and bar appear in Psalm 2:.
song *noun* {7892 shir, shirah} words set to music.
songster, songstress *participle* **sing** *verb* {7891 shiyr, shuwr} [103 ado] to sing; a male singer; a female singer.
sonship *noun* [5206 huiothesia] the placing as a son; much closer than adoption.
soothe, laud *verb* {7623 shabach} {7624 shecach} to extol with words; to smooth it over.
soothings *plural noun* {2514 chalaqqah} {2519 chalaqlaqqah} smoothings over; **see** smooth.
soothsaying *verb* [3132 mantuomai] predicting.
Sophach *transliterated name* {6690 tsowphach} Breadth.
Sophar *transliterated name* {6691 tsowphar} Skip About.
Sophim *plural transliterated name* {6839 tsophiym} Watchers.
Sophnath Paneach *transliterated name* {6847 tsophnathpaneach} Yoseph's Misrayim name.
Sor *transliterated name* {6865 tsor} [5184 turos] Flint; often rendered as Tyre, Tyrus.
Sorah *transliterated name* {6881 tsorah} Hornet.
Sorahiy *transliterated name* {6882 tsorathiy} Of Sorah.
sorcerer {*participle* 3784 kashaph} {*noun* 3786 kashshaph} one who does sorceries through evil spirits.
sorceries *plural noun* {3785 keshephim} the use of powers of evil spirits.
sore, bandage *noun* {4205 mazor} an affliction; in the sense of binding up; a bandage for a sore.
Soreq *transliterated name* {7796 sowreq} Choice.
Soriy *transliterated name* {6865 tsor} {6876 tsoriy} [5183 turios] Of Sor.
sorrow *noun* {4341 makob} [3077 lupe] sadness; **note:** not to be confused with sorry.
sorrow *verb* [3076 lupeo] to be sad; **note:** not to be confused with sorry.
sort, straighten *verb* {8626 taqan} to unbend; to become

upright; to sort out.
Sotay *transliterated name* {5479 cowtay} Swerving.
soundmind *verb* [4994 sophronizo] to make soundminded.
soundminded *noun, adjective* [4993 sophroneo] [4995 sophronismos] [4998 sophron] of a sound mind; figuratively, self–controlled.
soundmindedly *adverb* [4996 sophronos] to make mindfully; of sound mind.
soundmindedness *noun* [4997 sophrosunee] soundness of mind.
sounds (empty) *noun* [2757 kenophonia] vain voices; figuratively, a useless discussion.
sounds *noun* [5353 phthoggos] an audible sensation perceived by the ear.

- **SUMMARY:**
- **SOUL, SOULICAL, SOULLESS:**
- **soul** *noun* {5315 nephesh} [5590 psuchee] the psyche; the soul is the center of the emotional attributes; the soul of the flesh is in the blood; **read** Leviticus 17:11; the inhalation of breath brings oxygen to the blood, which brings life to the flesh; the soul sustains life, but is not life itself; Yah Veh puffed (exsouled) into Adam's nostrils and Adam became a living soul; **see** puff; **read** Genesis 2:7; all live beings have souls; **note:** most versions render nephesh into more than forty differents words, and psuchee into seven; only soul is correct; **cp** spirit.
- **soulical** *adjective* [5591 psuchikos] emotional; **cp** spiritual.
- **soulless** *noun* [895 apsuchos] without soul; figuratively, without emotion.

sound sleep *noun* {8639 tardemah} also lethargy.
soup *noun* {6564 paraq} soup, as full of crumbled meat.
sour grape *noun* {1154 becer} {1155 bocer} an unripe grape.
southerly, southward *adjective* {8486 teman} on the right when facing dawnward.
sovereign *adjective* [934 basilios] [937 basilikos] the character of the priesthood of the Messianists, of a person, place, or thing.
sovereign *noun* {4428, 4430 melech} [935 basilus] the office of a male who reigns over a sovereigndom; **see** reign; **cp** title.
sovereign *participle* **reign** *verb* {4427 malak} {4910 mashal} [936 basiluo] to rule; the officiating of a sovereign; **see** sovereign.
sovereign palace *noun* [933 basilion] the area in which a sovereign resides.
sovereigndom *noun* {4410 melukah} {4437 malku} {4438 malkuth, malkuyah} {4467 mamlakah} {4468 mamlakuth} [932 basilia] the area or peoples over which a sovereign reigns.
sovereigness *noun* {4436 malkah} {4433 malka} {4446 melecheth} [938 basilissa] a sovereign's woman; the title of a female who reigns over a sovereigndom.
sowing *participle* {4901 meshek} a sowing.
span *noun* {1574 gomed} {2239 zereth} the breadth of a hand.
Spania *transliterated name* [4681 spania] a region of Europe.
spanned in the palms *plural verb* {2949 tippuch} held in the span of a palm.
spare *verb* {2347 chue} to cover as in protection; **see** haven.
spare *verb* {2820 chasak} to preserve.
spare, bear, lade, lift, load *verb* {5375 nacah} {5376 nesa} to lift, in a variety of applications.
spare, compassion *verb* {2550 chamal} [3629 oiktirmon] to compassion; to spare.
sparkle, flow *verb* {5102 nahar} to flow, as to assemble; to sparkle, as to be cheerful.
speak *verb* [2980 laleo] [4354 proslaleo] to express thoughts or articulate sounds.
spear *noun* {2595 chaniyth} {7013 qayin} a lance for thrusting.
species (in), (to) species *noun* {2177, 2178 zan} {4327 min} by specific kinds.
specified *adjective* **census, mandate** *noun* {4662 miphqad} an enumeration; a designated spot; an order, or command.
spectacle, see *noun* {7210 roiy}from the root, sight; a vision.
speech *noun* [2981 lalia] that which is spoken.
speechless *noun* [216 alalos] without speech.
spelt *noun* {3698 kuccemeth} a variety of grain.
sperma *transliterated noun* [4690 sperma] the seed from which anything develops.
spermalogist *transliterated noun* [4691 spermologos] a seedy worder; an empty talker.
spice, embalm, ripen *verb* {2590 chanat} from the root, to spice.
spice, spicery *noun* {5219 nekoth} {5238 nekoth} an aromatic gum, as pounded out; **see** smitten.
spicy broth *noun* {4841 merqachah} an effusion of spiced seasonings.
spicy *plural adjective* {4840 merqachim} spicy seasonings.
spin, twirl, twist *noun* {1524 giyl} {1525 giylah} a physical expression of joy.
spin, twirl, twist *verb, noun* {1523 giyl, guwl} {3769 karar} [4761 strebloo] to spin around, as in rejoicing; **cp** whirl.
spindle, circuit, crutch *noun* {6418 pelek} to be round; a spindle as whirled; hence a crutch.
spine *noun* {6096 atseh} the backbone.
spinning *noun* {4299 matveh} that made by spinning.
spinnings, spun *noun* {4749 miqshah} turned, as in a lathe.
spiral stairs *plural noun* {3883 lowlim} circular steps.
spiral upward *verb* {55 abak} to coil upward.
spiraling *participle* {4141 muwcab} a coiling.

- **SUMMARY:**
- **SPIRIT, SPIRITS, SPIRITUAL, SPIRITUALS:**
- **Spirit, spirit, spirits** *name, noun* {7307, 7308 ruwach} [4151 pneuma] the Hebrew and Arami word ruwach has the twofold meaning of spirit and wind; the Hellene word pneuma has the single meaning of spirit; **cp** wind.
- **The Holy Spirit** is that essence of triune Elohim who participated in the creation, and Who conceived the flesh body of Elohim, Yah Shua the Messiah; the Holy Spirit guides the spiritually unborn to the Messiah; **read** Yahn 3:1–8; the Holy Spirit guides the spiritually born into all truth; the Holy Spirit is the Messianist's "another Paraclete"; **read** Yahn 15:26, 16:7–11; the Holy Spirit endues Messianists with the spirituals of energies, ministries, and charismata; **read** 1 Corinthians 12:1–11; the King James Version sometimes translates Holy Spirit as Holy Ghost; in Germanic languages, their word for spirit is rooted in our word for ghost; in Latin languages, their word for spirit is rooted in our word for spirit; in modern day English, ghost is a dead spirit; Yah Shua became flesh of the the living Holy Spirit of Elohim, and thus we translate Holy Spirit throughout; we are well aware that many Spirit–filled Messianists prefer Holy Ghost – and this is by no means an effort to alter their personal convictions.
- **the human spirit** is the center of the mental attributes; the will, memory, thought, including, but not limited to wisdom, knowledge, prophecy; all Messianists are born of, and have the Holy Spirit; but not all Messianists are filled with the Holy Spirit; Messianists may also have "in Spirit" experiences; **read** Apocalypse 4:2:
- **demon spirits** are evil spirits which may possess and control the spiritually unborn, and attack the Messianist.
- **spiritual** *adjective* [4152 pneumatikos] that mental attribute which is beyond that of the physical, or soulical.
- **spiritually** *adverb* [4153 pneumatikos] in a spiritual manner.
- **spirituals** *noun* [4152 pneumatikos] the spirituals bestowed upon humanity are often referred to as spiritual gifts; they are, more accurately, spirituals which the Holy Spirit endues as He wills upon whom He wills; here are nine of the spirituals as presented in I Corinthians 12:1–11:
- **(1) word of wisdom** *nouns* [3056 logos] [4678 sophia] the spiritual of the promise of the ability to decide well.
- **(2) word of knowledge** *nouns* [3056 logos] [1108 gnosis] the spiritual of the promise of the awareness of facts not necessarily gained through experiences of self or others.
- **(3) trust** *noun* [4102 pistis] **note:** trust is a more accurate translation than the usual words, belief and faith; whereas belief and faith imply a directing of the mind, trust implies a total reliance of the being; the Hebrew word for trust is rooted in the word, amen; **see** amen.
- **(4) charismata of healings** *plural nouns* [5486 charisma] [2386 iama] the spiritual of having the abilities of healings of various ailments.
- **(5) energizing** *transliterated verb* **dynamis** *transliterated noun* [1755 energema] [1411 dunamis] the spiritual of energizing the ability; of having the energy and the ability.
- **(6) word of prophecy** *nouns* [3056 logos] [4394 prophetia] the spiritual of the promise of the ability to foretell;

foretell is not to be confused with tell forth; **read** I Corinthians 12:10 with 2 Petros 1:19–21.

• **(7) discernments of spirits** *plural nouns* [1253 diakrisis] [4151 pneuma] the spiritual ability to distinguish species or qualities of spirits; to test the spirits, whether they be of Elohim.

• **(8) genos of tongues** *adjective/noun* [1085 genos] [1100 glossa] the spiritual of the ability to express in species of tongues other than those acquired through experience; including foreign and spiritual tongues.

• **(9) translation of tongues** *nouns* [2058 hermeneia] [1100 glossa] the ability to hear a tongue or language other than than learned by human experience, and rendering its meaning; **note:** dreams are interpreted; tongues are translated.

spit *verb* {7556 raqaq} to expectorate.
spit, spittle *noun* {7536 roq} **cp** saliva.
splatter, scatter, shatter *verb* {5310 naphats} {5311 nephets} {6327 puts} {6340 pazar} {7376 ratash} to disperse; to disperse by shattering.
spleen (large) *noun* [4184 polusplanknos] the spleen as figurative of much compassion.
spleen (sympathetic) *noun* [4697 splanknizomai] the spleen as symbolic of sympathetic compassion.
spleen (tender) *noun* [2155 eusplanknos] the spleen as symbolic of tender compassion.
spleen *noun* [4698 splankna] a large lymphatic organ which modifies the blood structure, symbolic of compassion.
splendidly *adverb* {4358 miklowl} with splendor.
splendour *noun* {3314 yiphah} {*plural* 4360 miklulim} beauty.
split *verb* {1234 baqa} [4977 skizo] to separate into more than one.
split, blink, calm, rest *verb* {7280 raga} this word is derived from two roots; blink and split, as momentary; calm and rest, as soothing.
split, breach, break (off) (loose), craunch, crunch, separate *verb* {6561 paraq} {6562 peraq} {6555 parats} to breach; to separate from; to split.
split, breach, separate *noun* {6556 perets} a breach; a separation from; a split.
split, schism *transliterated noun* [4978 schisma] a gap; a split.
split, separate *verb* {6536 parac} {6537 perac} to separate from; to split.
spoil *noun* {7998 shalal} that which is plundered.
spoil, despoil, pledge *verb* {2254, 2255 chabal} literally, to bind tightly; as in spoiling or as in binding a pledge.
spoil, drop *verb* {7997 shalal} to let drop; to strip, or plunder.
spokes *plural noun* {2839 chishshuq} as attached; **see** hubs.
spontaneous growth *noun* {5599 caphiyach} a self–growing growth.
spontaneous sprout *noun* {7823 shachic} a self–sprouting sprout.
spot, patch *verb* {2921 tala} to color in spots; to repair in spots.
spread (thin), stretch, extend *verb* {5186 natah} {5628 sarach} to bend away; to spread out; to stretch.
spread over, overspread *verb* {5259 nacak} to interweave.
spread *verb* {3331 yatsa} {6566 paras} {6576 parshez} {6581 pasah} to disperse; to spread thin.
spread *verb* {4969 mathach} as in stretching nets, or tents.
spread *verb* {7502 raphad} {7849 shatach} to expend.
spread, bed down *verb* {3331 yatsa} to strew as a surface.
spread, grow, scatter *verb* {6335 push} [837 auxano] to grow, to enlarge; as in spreading out.
spread, separate *verb* {6504 parad} to break through; to separate from; to spread out.
spread, strip *verb* {6584 pashat} to spread out; to deploy; to strip clothing; to flay the skin.
spreads *plural noun* {4765 marbadim} oversized spreads.
sprigs *plural noun* {2150 zalzal} small twigs.
springing, proceeding, procedure, rising *noun* {4161 motsa} {*plural* 4163 motsaoth} literally, the source of going forth, whether of persons, of water, of the sun.
sprinkle *verb* {2236 zaraq} [4472 rhantizo] to sprinkle solids or liquids.
sprinkle *verb* {5137 nazah} {7450 racac} a ceremonious libating of blood, oil, or water.
sprinkler *noun* {4219 mizraq} a bowl or bason used to sprinkle.
sprout (forth) *verb* {1876 dasha} [1631 ekphuo] [5453 phuo] to newly grow.
sprout (spontaneous) *noun* {7823 shachic} a self–sprouting sprout.
sprout *noun* {1877 deshe} {1883 dethe} {3126 yoneq} {3127 yoneqeth} {4731 maqqelah} a sprout; a grass.
sprout *noun* {6780 tsemach} a sprout; also a prophetic title of the Messiah; **cp** rod; **cp** scion.
sprout *verb* {6779 tsamach} [985 blastano] to germinate; to sprout.
spurn *verb* {3973 maowc} to refuse with disdain.
spy, step, tread *verb* {7270 ragal} verb of foot; to measure out with the foot; **see** foot.
squad *noun* [4686 spira] a small group in a quad.
square, foursquare *verb* {7251 raba} to cause to be quadrate.
squeezed juice *nount* {6071 acic} juice, as freshly trodden.
squeezings *noun* {5332 netsach} as bright red juice of grapes.
stab *verb* {1856 daqar} {2944 taan} {*plural* 4094 madqarah} to stab through.
staff bearer *noun* [4465 rabdoukos] one that bears a staff.
staff, staves, timber *noun* {905 bad} [3586 xulon] [4464 rhabdos] timber, or staves made therefrom.
stagger *verb* {7478 raal} to reel; to stagger.
stagger, stray, wander *verb* {8582 taah} to reel; to stray.
stagger, totter, wag, wander, waver, drift, shake *verb* {5128 nuwa} to waver.
staggering *noun* {6330 puqah} stumbling; **see** waver, wiggle.
staggering *noun* {8653 tarelah} reeling.
stain *noun* [3436 molusmos] blackish.
stain *noun* [4696 spilos] soil.
stain *verb* [3435 moluno] to blacken.
stain *verb* [4695 spiloo] to soil.
stake *noun* {3489 yathed} [4716 stauros] a tabernacle or tent stake; an upright stake on which our Adonay was staked.
stake(ing), blast(ing), clang(ing), clap(ping), shout(ing) *noun* {8619 taqowa} {8643 teruah} a loud sound; the celebration of shouting, and/or blasting trumpets unto Yah Veh; also of shouting, and/or blasting a battle cry; a stake of a tent, or tabernacle; a stake for execution.
stake, blast, clang, clap, shout *verb* {7321 ruwa} {8628 taqa} [4078 peegnumi] [4717 stauroo] to sound loudly; to celebrate by shouting, and/or blasting trumpets unto Yah Veh; to shout and/or blast a battle cry; to stake a tabernacle or tent; to stake for execution.
stalk *noun* {7054 qamah} {7070 qaneh} the stem of a plant.
stallion *noun* {7409 rekesh} as set aside.
stalls *dual noun* {4942 mishpathim} stalls for animals.
stammerer, stammering *adjective* {5926 illeg} stuttering.
stand (by), station (by), place (by), set (by) *verb* {3320 yatsab} {3322 yatsag} {5324 natsab} from the root, to place, so as to stay.
stand guard *verb* {7520 ratsad} to look with suspicion.
stand, standing, station *noun* {4673 matsab} {4674 mutstsab} {4675 mitstsabah} {5979 emdah} a stand; a military station.
stand, stay, withstand *verb* {5975 amad} {5977 omed} [436 anthistemi] [478 antikathistemi] to stand steady; to stand against.
star *noun* {3556 kowkab} [792 aster] [798 astron] a luminous body in the heavens.
start early, early start *verb* {7925 shakam} to start early.
stater *transliterated noun* [4715 stater] a coin with a standard of value.
station (by), place (by), set (by), stand (by) *verb* {3320 yatsab} {3322 yatsag} {5324 natsab} from the root, to place, so as to stay.
station, base *noun* {3653 ken} a base, as in furniture; a base as in a station, or office.
station, stand, standing *noun* {4673 matsab} {4674 mutstsab} {4675 mitstsabah} {5979 emdah} a stand; a military station.
statue, station, prefect *noun* {5333 netsib} {*plural* 5460 seganin} {*plural* 5461 saganim} {6346, 6347 pechah} a stationed officer; that which is stationary; a station; also a statue.
statute (set) *verb* **statute setter** *participle* **engrave** *verb* {2710 chaqaq} [1795 entupoo] to engrave; to prescribe; **cp** statue.
statute *noun* {2706 choq} {2708 chuqqah} a law engraved in stone; **cp** statue.
statute *noun* {2711 cheqeq} an enactment.
staves, timber, staff *noun* {905 bad} [3586 xulon] [4464 rhabdos] timber, or staves made therefrom.
stay around, surround *verb* {3803 kathar} to enclose.
stay overnight *verb* {3885 lun, lin}.
stay, withstand, stand *verb* {5975 amad} {5977 omed} [436

anthistemi] [478 antikathistemi] to stand steady; to stand against.
steal *verb* {1589 ganab} to thieve; to deceive; **see** thief.
stedfast *adjective* [949 bebaios] stable.
steep steps *noun* {4095 madregah} a steep, or inaccessible place.
steepings *noun* {4952 mishrah} maceration; a steeped juice.
stench *noun* {6292 piggul} {6709 tsachanah} a stink; a putrefaction.
step *noun* {4096 midrak} a treading.
step, support, time, anvil *noun* {6471 paamah} anvil, as a support; support, as a pedestal or column in a structure; a "stepper", as a supporter of the body; time, as an occasion or occurrence – but not as measured time.
step, tread, spy *verb* {7270 ragal} verb of foot; to measure out with the foot; **see** foot.
Stephanas *transliterated name* [4734 stephanas] Wreathed.
Stephanos *transliterated name* [4736 stephanos] Wreathed.
steps, degrees *noun* {4609 maalah} steps; stations; a progression; 1/360th of a circle.
sterile *adjective* {1565 galmuwd} {6135 aqar} barren; desolate.
stern *adjective* **harden** *verb* {7188 qashach} severe; without feeling.
stern, hard *adjective* {7186 qasheh} [4642 skleeros] harsh; severe.
steward *noun* {4453 meltsar} the tsar over the household.
stibium *noun* {6320 puk} a stibium dye for the face.
stick, adhere, join *verb* {1692 dabaq} {1693 debaq} [4347 proskollao] to join one's self to closely; stick to; to remain attached.
stinger *noun* {3654 ken} a stinging insect.
stink *noun* {889 beosh} a bad smell.
stink *verb* {887 baash} {888 beesh} to smell bad; to be offensive.
stinkweed *noun* {890 boshah} {*plural* 891 beushiym} bad smelling weeds.
stitching *noun* {8278 serad} as pierced with a needle.
Stoic *transliterated name* [4770 stoikos] one of pantheistic philosophy.
stokade *noun* {4115 mahpecheth} a stokade, as being wrenched in.
stone *noun* {5619 caqal} [3035 lithinos] [3036 lithoboleo] [3037 lithos] a detached piece of rock.
stone *verb* {7275 ragam} [3034 lithazo] to hurl stones.
stoneheap *noun* {4773 margemah} a heap of stones.
stones (red hot), pavement *noun* {7528 ratsaph} {7529 retseph} as used for baking; as used for laying a pavement.
stood on end *verb* {5568 camar} to be erect; to bristle.
stool *noun* {1916 hadom} as a place to tromp or set the foot; **see** trample.
stop (up), shut (up) *verb* {5640 satham} to stop up; figuratively, to keep secret.
storage *plural adjective* {4543 mickenoth} an area to store valuables.
storm *noun* **stormy** *adjective* {5591 saar} {5592 caph} a weather storm.
storm *verb* {5590 caar} to agitate; to rush.
stoutness *noun* [100 hadrotes] plumpness in the sense of growth.
straight *adjective* {3474 yashar} {3477 yashar} [3717 orthos] as in upright; not crooked.
straight, straightness, level, plain *noun* {4334 miyshor, *plural* miyshorim} {4339 meyshar} {6160 arabah} plain, as unadorned; as a level land area; as of straight character; as just.
straight–footed [3716 orthopodeo] to go directly forward.
straighten *verb* [461 anorthoo] to straighten.
straighten, sort *verb* {8626 taqan} to unbend; to become upright; to sort out.
straightforward, straightforwardness *adjective* {5228 nakoach} {5229 nekochah} as integrious.
straightness *noun* {3476 yosher} {3483 yishrah} as in uprightness; as in integrious.
straightway *adverb* [2112 utheos] [2117 uthus] at once; immediately.
straits, confines, distress, narrows *noun* {4689 matsoq} {4691 metsuqah} {4712 metsar} from the root, belly; a narrow place; a confinement.
strange, estrange *verb* {2114 zuwr} to cause to be strange; although a verb, often carries the force of a noun.
strange, stranger *adjective* {5237 nokriy} [3579 xenizo] alien.
strange, stranger *noun* {2114 zur} {5235 noker} {5236 nekar} [3581 xenos] an alien; a cality.
strangers (lodge) *verb* [3580 zenodokeo] to be hospitable.
strangle *verb* {2614 chanaq} [519 apankomai] [4155 pnigo] [4846 sumpnigo] to choke.
strangled *noun* [4156 pniktos] that which is choked.
strangling *noun* {4267 machanaq} by choking.
strategize *verb* {6191 aram} to plot subtly.
strategoi *transliterated plural noun* [4755 strategos] strategists.
strategy *noun* {6193 orem} {6195 ormah} a subtle plot.
straw *noun* {8401 teben} stalk on which grain grows.
stray fruit *noun* {6528 peret} a stray fruit; a single fruit.
stray, wander, stagger *verb* {8582 taah} to reel; to stray.
stream *noun* {2988 yabal} {3105 yubal} a current of water.
stream, branch, ear *noun* {7641 shibboleth} a branch or an ear of grain, as growing; a stream, as flowing; **see** shibboleth.
streamlet *noun* {4323 miykal} a little stream.
street *noun* {7784 shuq} [4505 rhume] a road midst houses.
strength *noun* {202 own} {556 amtsah} {2391 chezeq} {2392 chozeq} {5797 oz} {5807 ezuz} physical ability.
strength *noun* {5326 nitsbah} {*plural* 8443 toaphah} firmness; speed.
strengthen, uphold, callous, prevail *verb* {553 amats} {555 omets} {2388 chazaq} {2393 chezqah} {5810 azaz} to enable physically; to become thickskinned.
stretch, extend, spread (thin) *verb* {5186 natah} {5628 sarach} to bend away; to spread out; to stretch.
stricken *adjective* {5218 naka} smitten.
stride *noun* {6587 pesa} a spread of the legs.
stride, spread *verb* {6585 pasa} {6589 pasaq} a spreading of the legs, or the lips.
strife *noun* {4066 maddown} {4683 matstsah} {4808 meribah} a struggle of words; a quarrel; a contest.
strife, contention, defence, plea *noun* {7379 rib} a personal, or legal contest.
strike (round about), surround, round *verb* {5362 naqaph} to strike; to strike all around; to surround; to round off the beard.
strike *verb* {4223 mecha} {4272 machats} to strike in pieces; to impale.
strip bare *verb* {6209 arar} to bare; figuratively, to demolish.
strip naked, empty, pour out *verb* {6168 arah} {6379 pakah} to empty; to empty by pouring; to strip bare; **see** naked.
strip *verb* {1497 gazal} to flay, or cut.
strip, bare *verb* {2834 chasaph} to strip off as to expose.
strip, equip, rescue *verb* {2502 chalats} literally, to strip for hostility; to strip out of danger.
strip, escape, rescue *verb* {5337, 5338 natsal} to snatch away; favorably, or unfavorably.
strip, pluck *verb* {6998 qataph} {7059 qamat} to pluck out; to strip off.
strip, spread *verb* {6584 pashat} to spread out; to deploy; to strip clothing; to flay the skin.
stripped *noun* {7758 sholal} bare.
stripped *verb* [554 apekduomai] [555 apekdusis] to despoil.
stripped, stripping *noun* {1498 gazel} {1499 gezel} {1500 gezelah} that which has been flayed, or cut.
strive, contend, defend, plead *verb* {7378 rub} to hold a controversy.
strive, desolate *verb* {5327 natsah} to struggle; to lay waste.
stroke *noun* {4273 machats} {4347 makkah} a strike.
stroke, worn (out), rub, sicken *verb* {2470 chalah} to wear out; to stroke the face as in appeasement.
stroll *verb* {6808 tsaah} to pace at leisure; **see** pace.
stroll *verb* {7788 shur} to wander about; as a whore, as a merchant.
strong, tough *adjective* {533 ammits} {554 amots} {2389 chazaq} {5794 az} {5808 izzuz} forceful; harsh; physically able.
stronger *adjective* {2390 chazeq} more powerful.
stronghold *noun* {4581 mauz} a place of protection.
strongly *adverb* {2394 chozqah} vehemently.
structure *noun* {8498 tekunah} the architecture.
strum *verb* **strummers** *participle* {5059 nagan} to strum, as on a musical instrument; one who strums; **cp** pluck.
strummer, strumming *noun* {5058 neginah} a musical instrument.
strums, strummings *plural noun* {4482 minim} a musical chord as parted into strings.
stubble *noun* {7179 qash} the stubs left in the soil after

harvesting.
stumble *noun* {3783 kishshalon} ruin.
stumble *verb* [4417 ptaio] to trip up; to err; to sin.
stumble, trip, falter *verb* {3782 kashal} to totter; to waver.
stumbling *noun* [4348 proskomma] [4349 proskopee] an obstacle; to provide an occasion for sinning.
stumblingblock *noun* {4383 mikshol} {4384 makshelah} an obstacle; an enticement.
stump *noun* {6136 iqqar} the underground part of a tree.
stump, monolith *noun*{4676 matstsebah} {4678 matstsebeth} a singular block of stone.
stun, astonish, desolate *verb* {8074 shamem} {8075 shemam} to stun, as in to stupefy or devastate; to lay waste.
stupid *adjective* {1198 baar} gullible; one who swallows.
stupidity *noun* {6580 pash} degeneracy.
stylus *noun* {2747 cheret} {5842 et} {8279 sered} an instrument for engraving or inscribing.
Suach *transliterated name* {5477 cuwach} Sweeping.
Suar *transliterated name* {6686 tsuwar} Belittle.
subdue *verb* {3533 kabash} literally, to tread down.
subdue *verb* {4355 makak} literally, to tumble.
subdue, humble, humbling *verb* {3665 kana} {6031 anab} {6033 anah} {6039 enuth} {6800 tsana} [5013 tapino] to cause to bend the knee; to knuckle under; to lower in esteem or status.
subdue, overlay *verb* {7286 radad} to conquer; to sheet over.
subject to *noun* [1777 enochos] as in, liable to a penalty.
subject *verb* [5293 hupotasso] to obey; to subordinate.
subjugate, crumble *verb* {7287 radah} to bring under; to conquer.
submit *verb* [5226 hupiko] to yield; to surrender.
subside, hush *verb* {8367 shathaq} from the root, to subside.
substance, force, lizard *noun* {3581 koach} {3981 maamats} pressure, physical or intellectual; also a lizard.
substrata *noun* [2737 katoteros] underlayer; figurative of sheol/hades.
subterranean *noun* [2709 katakthonios] underground; of the world of departed souls.
subtil, subtle *adjective* {6175 arum} cunning.
suburb *noun* {4054 migrash} {6503 parbar} {6518 paraz} {*plural* 6519 perazah} a surrounding area.
suburban *adjective* {6521 peraziy; *plural* perozim} of a surrounding area.
suburbanite *noun* {6520 perazon} one that settles in a suburb; **cp** urbanite.
subvert, pervert *verb* {5557 calaph} to turn from; to undermine.
succeed, prosper *verb* {3787 kasher} {6743 tsaleach} {6744 tselach} to succeed; to press on.
successor *noun* {4497 manown} one who perpetuates.
such a one *noun* {6422 palmoniy} so and so.
such *noun* {6423 peloniy} a specific one.
suck (up) (out) *verb* {4041 megammah} {4711 matsats} {5966 ala} to suck up; to suck out.
suck, suckle, suckling *verb* {3243 yanaq} {5134 nuq} {5763 ul} to feed at the breast.
suck, sweeten *verb* {4985, 4988 mathaq} to be sweet; to relish.
suck, wring *verb* {4680 matsah} to wring, or squeeze out; to suck out.
suckling *noun* {5764 ul} {5768 olal} one who feeds at the breast; **see** infant.
sudarium *transliterated noun* [4676 soudarion] a cloth used to wipe perspiration from the face or to wrap the head of a corspe.
suddenly *adverb* {6597 pithom} instantly.
sufficiency *noun* {7647 saba} an overflow; plenty.
satire *noun* {4426 melitsah} {4485 manginah} a literary work holding up follies or shortcomings for ridicule.
sufficient *adjective* [566 apeki] adequate.
sufficient *adjective* [713 arketos] satisfactory.
sufficient, satisfied *verb* [714 arkeo] to be satisfactory.
Suchahiy *transliterated name* {7756 suwchathiy} Of Sukah.
Sukkoth Benoth *transliterated noun* {5524 cukkowthbenowth} Brush Arbor of the Daughters.
Sukkoth/Brush Arbors, sukkoth, brush arbor *transliterated noun* {5520 cok} {5521 cukkah} {5522 cikkuwth} {5523 cukkowth} {7900 sok} [4634 skeenopeegia] Brush Arbor; name of places in Pelesheth and Misrayim; a brush arbor to harbor animals; a celebration of harvest, of spreading of branches, of Hoshia Na; Leviticus 23:33–44, Yahn 7:37, Psalm 118:25, 26, Matthaios 21:9–15, Markos 11:9,10, Yahn 12:13, Apocalypse 7:9,10; **see** Hoshia Na.
sulphur *noun* {1614 gophriyth} [2303 thion] as ignited.
sulphurous *adjective* [2306 thiodes] sulphur-like.
sum *noun* {6575 parashah} the full exposition; the total.
sum up *verb* [346 anakephalaiomai] to total.
sum, head *noun* {7217 resh} the top of the body; the sum total.
summer (fruit) (house) *noun* {7019 qaits} the summer season; summer fruit; a summer house.
summit *noun* {2872 tabbuwr} top of the pile.
summon *verb* {6817 tsaaq} [2753 keluo] [3343 metapempo] to call to convene.
summons *noun* [2752 keleuma] a call to convene.
sun *noun* {8121, 8122 shemesh} [2246 helios] the brightest body in the heavens.
sun icons *plural noun* {2553 chamman} sun pillars.
sup, supping *verb* [1172 dipneo] to dine.
superabound *verb* [4052 perissuo] [4121 pleonazo] to exceed adundantly.
superabundance *noun* [4051 perissuma] a surplus.
superabundant *adjective, adverb* [4053 perissos] [5250 huperpleonazo] in the sense of beyond; excessive, supreme.
superabundantly (more) *adverb* [4054 perissoteron] [4055, 4056 perissoteros] [4057 perissos] [5249 huperperissos] more exceedingly.
superior *adjective* [5242 hupereko] to stand out; to excel; to be above.
Suph *transliterated name* {6689 tsuwph} Honeycomb.
supper *noun* [1173 dipnon] a formal meal usually in the evening
supplement *verb* [466 antanapleeroo] to fullfil; to fill up.
supplication *noun* {8467 techinnah} {*plural* 8469 tachanunim} entreaty; petition.
support, counsel *noun* {8454 tushiah} {*plural* 8458 tachbuloth} advice; support.
support, crutch *noun* {4938 mishenah} that on which one leans.
support, palmspan *noun* {2947 tephach} {2948 tophach} the span of a palm; a span; a support.
support, partake *verb* [482 antilambanomai] [484 antileepsis] to take part; to support.
support, supply *noun* {4937 mishen} that on which one leans.
support, time, anvil, step *noun* {6471 paamah} anvil, as a support; support, as a pedestal or column in a structure; a "stepper", as a supporter of the body; time, as an occasion or occurrence – but not as measured time.
support, uphold *verb* {5582 scaad} to support; usually, figuratively; **cp** prop.
Sur *transliterated name* {6698 tsur} Rock.
Suri El *transliterated name* {6700 tsuriel} Rock of El.
Suri Shadday *transliterated name* {6701 tsurishadday} Rock of Shadday; **see** Shadday.
surpass, trespass, overpass, pass (over) (through) *verb* {5674 abar} to cross over; this verb is unrelated to the mistranslation of passover.
surrender, betray, deliver *verb* [3860 paradidomi] to give to possession of another; to deliver to an enemy; to release.
surround, environ, round *noun* {3603 kikkar} literally, circle; the environs of an area; a round of material, usually of precious metals.
surround, round, strike (round about) *verb* {5362 naqaph} to strike; to strike all around; to surround; to round off the beard.
surround, stay around *verb* {3803 kathar} to enclose.
surround, turn (about) (around), go (about) (around) *verb* {5437 cabab} to border; to revolve; to surround.
survey *verb* {8376 taah} {8388 taar} to mark off; to designate.
survive *verb* {7604 shaar} {8277 sarad} as having escaped.
survive, survivors *noun* {7605, 7606 shear} {7611 sheeriyth} {8300 sariyd} as escaped.
survivor *noun* {2475 chaloph} as being orphaned.
suspect, envy *verb* **jealous, zealous** *adjective* {7065 qana} {7067 qanna} {7072 qannow} to be zealous, as jealous, or envious.
suspend, hang *verb* **prone** *participle* {8511 tala} {8518 talah} to suspend.
suspicion, envy, jealous *noun* {7068 qinah} zeal, as jealousy, or envy.
sustain, contain, maintain, measure *verb* {3557 kuwl} to keep in.
sustain, guide *verb* {5095 nahal} literally, to lead with light.
sustain, uphold, prop *verb* {5564 camak} {8551 tamak} to prop

up; with the hands, or with props.
swallow *verb* [2666 katapino] to drink down; to destroy; to be overwhelmed with sorrow.
swallow, horse *noun* {5483 cuc} {5484 cucah} a horse as leaping; a swallow as flitting.
swan, chameleon *noun* {8580 tanshemeth} hard breather.
swarmers *noun* {6157 arob} insects as swarming; **cp** teemers.
swathe *verb* {2853 chathal} {2854 chathullah} to wrap as a baby, as a bandage.
sway, wag over, wander, waver *verb* {5110 nud} to waver.
sweater *noun* {3154 yeza} a garment that causes sweat.
sweep (away) *verb* {5502 cachaph} to scrape off.
sweepings *noun* {5478 suwchah} that which is swept away.
sweeten, suck *verb* {4985, 4988 mathaq} to be sweet; to relish.
sweeter, sweetness *adjective* {4966 mathoq} {4986 metheq} {4987 motheq} sweet; pleasantness.
swell *adjective* {6639 tsabeh} swollen.
swell, host *verb* {6638 tsabah} to assemble a host; to swell up.
swell, presume *verb* {6075 aphal} to assume aforehand; an ascending, as swollen.
swelling within *adjective* [1471 enkuos] pregnant.
swelling, exalting, lifting *noun* {7613 seeth} an elevation; from the verb, lift {5375}.
swerve *participle* **swerver** *noun* {7750 sut} {*plural* 7750 sutim} one that turns to avoid.
swift *adjective* {7031 qal} rapid.
swift, trifle, abase, abate, belittle, slight *verb* {6819 tsaar} {6985 qat} {7034 qalah} {7043 qalal} to belittle in contempt; to make light of; to lessen.
swim *noun* {7813 sachu} from the verb, to swim.
swim *verb* {7811 sachah} to inundate; to swim.
swoop *verb* {5860 it} literally, or figuratively, to swoop down.
swooper *noun* {5861 ait} a being that swoops.
sword *noun* {2719 chereb} {4380 mekerah} a cutting instrument; a stabber.
sycamine fig *noun* [4807 sukaminos] a species of fig.
sycamore *transliterated noun* {8256 shaqam} [4809 sukomoraia] a species of tree.
Sychar *transliterated name* {7941 shekar} [4965 suchar] Intoxicant.
sycophant *transliterated noun* [4811 sukophanteo] a fig informer; a tattletale.
sympathy *noun* {4263 machmal} compassion.
symphonia *transliterated dual noun* {5481 ciyphoneya} Hellenic; literally, a sounding as one; a soundbag with dual pipes.
symphonize *verb* [4856 sumphoneo] [4859 sumphonos] literally, to sound as one; to harmonize; to agree.
symphony *transliterated noun* [4857 sumpheesis] [4858 sumphonia] literally, a sounding as one; harmony; a group of instruments sounding together.
synagogue *transliterated noun* [4864 sunagogee] Hellenic translation of the Hebrew congregation.
synagogue arch *transliterated noun* [752 archchisunagogos] the arch over a synagogue.
synagogue together *transliterated verb* [1997 episunagoge] to co–congregate.
Syria *transliterated name* {6865 tsor} [4947 suria] Rock; **cp** Sor.
Syriaiy *transliterated name* {6865 tsor} [4948 suros] Of Syria.

T

Taanak *transliterated name* {8590 taanak} the meaning uncertain; a place in Pelesheth.
Taarea *transliterated name* {8390 taarea} possibly, Earthly.

- **SUMMARY:**
- **TABERNACLE, TEMPLE, TENT:**
- **tabernacle** *noun* {4907, 4908 mishkan} {7933 sheken} [4633 skene] [4636 skenos] [4638 skenoma] the structure surrounding the holies {6944 qodesh} [39 hagion] which is the priestal precinct [2411 hieron]; and the holy of holies {6944 qodesh} [39 hagion] which is the nave [3485 naos]; the holies/priestal precinct, the outer court of the tabernacle, is the place of doctrinating where Yah Shua doctrinated; although Yah Shua referred to the holy of holies/nave, He did not enter the holy of holies/nave until after he split the veil; tabernacle is also the housing of the human body; and the human body is also the nave of the Holy Spirit; **cp** manse; **see** holies, holy of holies, priestal precinct, nave; **note:** the *exeGeses* accurately distinguishes between tent, and tabernacle.
- **tabernaclemaker** *noun* [4635 skenopoios] a maker of tabernacles; **note:** it is quite possible that Paulos manufactured tabernacles in which to congregate; there is no evidence that Paulos was a tentmaker.
- **tabernacler (fellow) (nearby)** *adjective* {7934 shaken} a fellow who tabernacles nearby; a neighbour.
- **tabernacle (over) (upon)** *verb* {7931 shakan} {7932 shekan} [1981 episkenoo] [4637 skenoo] to abide in a tabernacle; to abide over, upon.
- **tabernaclestaking** *verb* [4634 skenopeegia] the setting up of the tabernacle; **see** Sukkoth/Brush arbor.
- **temple** *noun,* in the Authorized King James and most other versions, are mistranslations; temple, as a place of worship, is unknown in Scripture: for {1964, 1965 heykal} **see** manse: for [2411 hieron] **see** priestal precinct: for [3485 naos] **see** nave.
- **tent** *noun* {168 ohel} a portable lodging; a portable covering of cloth and/or skins; tent is designated as the abode of the Yisra Eliy, and tent is also designated as the covering of the tabernacle; **note:** the *exeGeses* accurately distinguishes between tent and tabernacle.
- **tent** *verb* {167 ahal} to abide in a tent.

Tab Rimmon *transliterated name* {2886 tabrimmown} Goodly to Rimmon.
Tabe El *transliterated name* {2870 tabeel} Goodly of El.
Tabitha, Dorcas, gazelle *noun* {6643 tsebiy} {6646 tsebiyah} [5000 tabitha] a gazelle, as beautiful; Tabitha is the Hellene transliteration of tsebiyah; Dorcas is the Hellene translation of tsebiyah.
table *noun* {7979 shulchan} a table, as spread out.
tablet *noun* [4093 pinakidion] a small slab for scribing; **cp** slab.
Tachan *transliterated name* {8465 tachan} Encamped.
Tachaniy *transliterated name* {8470 tachaniy} Of Tachan.
Tachash *transliterated name* {8477 tachash} Badger.
Tachath *transliterated name* {8480 tachath} Beneath.
Tachkemoni *transliterated name* {8461 tachkemoniy} Enwisen.
Tachpanches *transliterated name* {8471 tachpanchec} the meaning uncertain; a place in Misrayim.
Tachpenes *transliterated name* {8472 tachpeneyc} the meaning uncertain; a Misrayim woman.
Tachrea *transliterated name* {8475 tachrea} possibly, Earthly.
tail *noun* {2180 zahnab} literally, a flapper; **see** curtail.
tailoring *noun* {4055 mad} measured, or fitted clothing.
tailoring, measure, measurement *noun* {4060 middah} {4067 madown} {*plural* 4461 memadim} size.
take heed *verb* [4337 proseko] to hold the mind towards; to be cautious about.
take out *verb* [336 anairesis] [337 anaireo] in the sense of deathifying.
take over, overtake *verb* [2638 katalambano] to lay hold of; to seize.
take *verb* [618 apolambano] [2983 lambano] to take hold of; to take aside.
take, lift *verb* {142 airo} to take up; to take away.
take, undertake *verb* {6901 qabal} {6902 qebal} [353 analambano] to acquire; to take up; **cp** receive.
taken up *verb* [354 analepsis] ascended.
taking *noun* [3028 lepsis] receipt.
talebearer *noun* {7400 rakil} a scandalmonger, as travelling about.
Talmay *transliterated name* {8526 talmay} Ridged.
Tamar *transliterated name* {8559 tamar} [2283 thamar] Erect.
tambourine *noun* {8596 toph} {8611 topheth} as being shaken; a shallow drum, played with the hands.
tambourining *verb* {8608 taphaph} to play the tambourine.
tame *verb* {3711 kaphah} to bend into submission.
Tanchumeth *transliterated name* {8576 tanchumeth} Consolations.
tankard, hoarfrost *noun* {3713 kephor} a covering; hoarfrost, as coversing the ground; a tankard, as a covered vessel.
Taom *transliterated name* {8380 taomim} [2381 thomas] Twin; **see** Twin.
Tappuach *transliterated name* {8599 tappuwach} Apple.
target, target area *noun* {4307 mattarah} {4645 miphga} that which is aimed at; an area for aiming.
tarry *verb* [1304 diatribo] to remain.
Tarshish *transliterated name* {8659 tarshish} a place in the Mediterranean.
Tartaq *transliterated name* {8662 tartaq} the meaning uncertain;

a deity of the Avviym.
Tartaros (incarcerate in) *verb* [5020 tartaros] possibly the lowest abyss in sheol/hades; **see** sheol/hades.
tassel *noun* {6731 tsits} as a tassel of hair; as an ornament.
taste *noun* {2940 taam} taste includes the full gestation.
taste *verb* {2938 taam} [1089 guomai] to taste; taste includes the full gestation.
taste, decree *noun* {2941, 2942 teem} judgment; flavor.
Tattenay *transliterated name* {8674 tattenay} the meaning uncertain; a Persian.
tattoo, brand, etching, mark *noun* {7085 qaaqa} {8420 tab} [5480 karagma] a scratched marking; a mark on animals; an x or a + as a signature of an illiterate; a mark of protection; **read** Yechezq El 9:4–6; **read** Apocalypse 13:16,17, 14:9–11, 15:2, 16:2, 19:20, 20:4; **cp** brand.
tattoo, brand, mark *verb* {8427, 8428 tavah} to mark an animal; to mark an x or + as a signature of an illiterate, or to mark for protection.
teach *plural verb* {4000 mabowm} to cause to discern.
teach, learn *verb* {3925 lamad} literally, to goad; to disciple; to be discipled; **see** *verb* disciple.
tear (away) (up) *verb* {5420 nathac} {5423 nathaq} to tear off; to tear up.
tear *verb* [1145 dakruo] to shed tears.
tear *verb* {6533 param} {6582 pashach} to rip.
tear, prey *noun* {2964 tereph} {2966 terephah} {5706 ad} a prey, as an object of attack; as being torn.
Tebach *transliterated name* {2875 tebach} Slaughter.
Tebal Yah *transliterated name* {2882 tebalyah} Dipped of Yah.
Tebes *transliterated name* {8405 tebets} Whiteness.
Techinnah *transliterated name* {8468 techinnah} Supplication.
teem *verb* {8317 sharats} to become prolific.
teemer *noun* {8318 sherets} one who becomes prolific; **cp** swarmer.
teeth, tusks *plural noun* {6374 piphiah} {8143 shenhabbim} teeth of a person, animal, or instrument.
Tel Aviv *transliterated name* {8512 telaviv} Heap of Unripe.
Tel Harsha *transliterated name* {8521 telcharsha} Heap of an Engraver.
Tel Melach *transliterated name* {8528 telmelach} Heap of Salt.
Telach *transliterated name* {8520 telach} Breach.
tell *verb* {5046 nagad} to relate.
Temach *transliterated name* {8547 temach} the meaning uncertain; one of the Dedicates.
Teman *transliterated name* {8487 teman} Southerly.
Temaniy *transliterated name* {8489 teymaniy} Of Teman.
temple *noun* {7541 raqqah} the side of the head as being thin.
tend, attend, befriend, graze *verb* {7462 raah} [5256 hupeereteo] to tend a flock or to pasture; to befriend, by attending to; to cause a flock to graze; **see** attendant; **see** Yah Veh Raah.
tender *adjective* {7390 rak} [527 apalos] tender; as soft, as weak.
tender *noun* {7473 roiy} one that tends flocks.
tender *verb* {7401 rakak} to tenderize; to soften; to weaken.
tenderness *noun* {7391 rok} tenderness; as softness; as weakness.
tendril *noun* {5189 netishah} {8299 sarig} a spiral shoot of a plant which attaches itself for support.
Teqoa *transliterated name* {8620 teqowa} Blast.
Teqoaiy *transliterated name* {8621 teqoiy} Of Teqoa.
Terach *transliterated name* {8646 terach} [2291 thara] derivative uncertain.
teraphim *transliterated plural noun* {8655 teraphim} family idols.
terrify *verb* {926 bahal} {927 behal} {1763 dechal} to panic; to hasten anxiously.
terrify, awe, dread *verb* {6206 arats} to harass; to reverence.
terrify, break (down), dismay *verb* {2865, 2866 chathath} to cause to prostrate; to break down by violence, or fear.
terror *noun* {928 behalah} {4032 magor} {4034 megorah} {7374 retet} panic.
terror *noun* {2844 chath} {2847 chittah} {2851 chittiyth} {*plural* 2849 chatchathim} in the sense of crushing.
terror, granary *noun* {4035 megurah} a fright; a place to store grain.
tertiary, thrice, tierce, triangle *noun* {7991 shalosh} an officer of the third rank; three times; an interval of a third; a three sided music instrument.
test *noun* [3984 pira] attempt.
test *verb* {5254 nacah} [426 anetazo] [1598 ekpirazo] [3985 pirazo] to test; to attempt; to try as in a court.
testi *noun* {6344 pachad} a testicle.
testing *noun* [3986 pirasmos] a putting to proof.
testing *noun* **Massah** *transliterated name* {4531 maccah} name means Testing.
tetrarch *transliterated title* [5075 tetrarcheo] [5076 tetrarchees] a ruler over a fourth part.
thatch *noun* [4721 stege] thatched roof.
then *adverb* [687 ara] denoting an interrogation to which a negative answer is presumed.
then, therefore, indeed *adverb* [686 ara] the idea of drawing a conclusion; in point of fact.
thence (from) [2547 kakithen] (of place) thence; (of time) thereafter, afterward.
Theo Philos *transliterated name* [2321 theophilos] Friend of God/Elohim.
therapist *transliterated noun* [2324 therapon] one skilled in therapeutics.
therapy *transliterated noun* [2322 therapia] cure.
therefore, then, indeed *adverb* [686 ara] the idea of drawing a conclusion; in point of fact.
thick (cloud), thicket, thickness *adjective* {5645, 5646 ab} {5672 abiy} {5687 aboth} thick; enveloping as a cloud.
thicken *verb* {5666 abah} to cause to be dense.
thicket *noun* {5441 cobek} {5442 cebak} {7730 sobek} trees or shrubs closely set.
thief *noun* {1590 gannab} one who steals.
thigh *noun* [3382 meros] the upper leg.
thin, pulverized *adjective* {1851 dak} thin; beaten small; emaciated.
thing, things *noun* **note:** These two word are never used throughout manuscripts; most often, they have been added by the translaters to satisfy the English idiom. At times, they are a mistranslation of the word, **word**, and a very few other words. These instances are brought out in the *exeGeses* thus: *thing* **word.**
think, shine *verb* {6245 ashath} {6246 ashith} as polishing.
think, think well, well thinking *verb* [1380 dokeo] [2106 eudokeo] [2107 eudokia] [5426 phroneo] the (well) exercise of the mind.
thinketh amiss *verb* [5422 phrenapatao] to be misled in mind.
thirst *noun* {6772 tsama} {6773 tsimah} a dryness.
thirst *noun* {6774 tsimmaon} a place of thirst.
thirst *verb* {6770 tsame} [1372 dipsao] literally, or figuratively, to thirst for; to long for.
thirsty *adjective* {6771 tsame} literally, to thirst; figuratively, to be longing for.
thistle *noun* {*plural* 5621 carabim} {7057 qimosh} {7063 qimmashon} a prickly plant.
thong *noun* [2438 himas] a strap or strip of leather; a whip to lash or to bind criminals; also a fastener, as a of a sandal.
thorn, hook *noun* {5518 sirah} {*plural* 7165 qeresim} literally, a boiler; a hook; a thorn.
thorn, thorns *noun* {5518 cirah} {5544 cillon} {6791 tsen} {*plural* 6796 tsaninim} {6975 qots} {7898 shaith} [173 akantha] [174 akanthinos] [4647 skolops] a sharp projection on the stem of a plant.
thought *noun* {*plural* 6248 ashtoth} {*plural* 6250 eshtonahoth} [1270 dianoema] [5424 phren] [5427 phronema] [5428 phronesis] that which results from thinking.
thought deluder *noun* [5423 phrenapates] a mind misleader; a deceiver.
thoughtful *adjective* [5429 phronimos] [5431 phrontizo] exercising thought.
thoughtfully *adv* [5430 phronimos] in a thoughtful manner.
thoughtless *adjective* [878 aphron] without thought; as ignorant; as rash.
thoughtlessness *noun* [877 aphrosunee] unthoughtful.
thread *noun* {2339 chut} from the root, to sew; a string.
three yesters ago *adverb* {8032 shilshom} {8543 temol} these two words are usually used in combination; day before yesterday.
three yesters ago *noun* {865 ethmowl} may refer to day before yesterday, or recently.
thresh *verb* [248 aloao] to tread out grain.
threshing floor *noun* {1637 goren} [257 halon] a smooth and/or hard place to thresh grain.
threshold waiter *noun* {5605 saphaph} one that waits upon the threshold; a doorperson.
threshold, bason *noun* {5592 caph} {5602 cephel} a container;

as a vessel, or as a vestibule.
thrice, tierce, triangle, tertiary *noun* {7991 shaloah} an officer of the third rank; three times; an interval of a third; a three sided music instrument.
throat *noun* {1621 gargeroth} {1627 garon} {3930 loa} the forepart of the neck.
throne *noun* {3676 kec} {3678 kicceh} {3764 korce} [2362 thronos] a seat of authority.
throng *noun* {6899 qibbuts} a crowd.
throng, abundance *noun* {8229 shiphah} a crowd, plenty.
throttle *verb* {1624 gahrah} to throttle the throat, to stir.
throw, cast, hurl *verb* {7993 shalak} to throw out, down, or away.
thrush *noun* {5693 aguwr} literally, to twitter; a species of bird.
thumb, great toe *noun* {931 bohen} literally, the large digit.
thunder *noun* {7482 raam} {7483 ramah} [1027 bronte] the voice caused by lightning.
thunder *verb* {7481 raam} to sound the voice caused by lightning.
thunder, irritate *verb* {7481 raam} to agitate; to be agitated.
thunder, shout *noun* {7452 rea} a crashing sound.
thunderstorm *noun* [3655 ombros].
tiara *noun* {4701 mitsnepheth} headpiece of a sovereign or archpriest.
tiara, ornament, adornment *noun* {6287 peer} an embellishment; a tiara, as an adornment.
Tibchath *transliterated name* {2880 tibchath} Slaughter.
tie, mute *verb* {481 alam} as in silencing by tying tongue, or lips; tying bundles.
tier, thirds, three, triple *noun* {8027 shalash} layers, or lofts; a whole, severed into three; three; threefold.
tierce, triangle, tertiary, thrice *noun* {7991 shaloah} an officer of the third rank; three times; an interval of a third; a three sided music instrument.
Tilgath Pilneser, Tilgath Pileser *transliterated name* {8407 tilgathpilnecer, tilgathpilecer} an Ashshuriy sovereign.
till *verb* {5214 niyr} to furrow the soil.
Timaeus *transliterated name* [5090 timaios] Fouled.
timber, staff, staves *noun* {905 bad} [3586 xulon] [4464 rhabdos] timber, or staves made therefrom.
timber, tree *noun* {6086 ets} {6097 etsah} a tree; timber; sticks of timber.
time *noun* {5732 iddan} not a specific measured period of time; rather an era of indeterminable length; as in this time, next time; of Arami origin, and appears only in Dani El.
time *noun* {6256 eth} [5550 chronos] chrono; a measured period of existence; including, but not limited to seconds, minutes, hours, days, weeks, months, years; **see** Apocalypse 10:6 for the prophecy when measured time ends and eternity begins; **cp** season.
time, anvil, step, support *noun* {6471 paamah} anvil, as a support; support, as a pedestal or column in a structure; a "stepper", as a supporter of the body; time, as an occasion or occurrence – but not as measured time.
time (at this) (by this) (from this) *adverb* {6258 attah} now; this present moment.
time (take) *verb* [5549 chronizo] to take a measured portion of time; **see** time.
time (waste) *verb* [5551 chronotribeo] to waste a measured portion of time; **see** time.
timely *adjective* {6261 itti} opportunely.
timidity *noun* {4816 morek} literally, soft.
timidsouled *adjective* [3642 oligopsukos] shy; lacking courage.
Timna *transliterated name* {8555 timna} Withhold.
Timnah *transliterated name* {8553 timnah} Portion.
Timnahiy *transliterated name* {8554 timniy} Of Timnah.
Timnath Heres *transliterated name* {8556 timnathcherec} Portion of the Sun.
Timo Theos *transliterated name* [5095 timotheos] Honoured of God/Elohim.
tingle, quiver *verb* {6750 tsalal} to vibrate.
tinkle *verb* {5913 akac} to tinkle with tinklers.
tinkler *noun* {5913 ecec} an ornament that tinkles.
Tiphsach *transliterated name* {8607 tiphcach} Ford.
Tiqvah *transliterated name* {8616 tiqvah} Cord.
Tirahiy *transliterated name* {8654 tirathiy} Gate; Of Tirah.
Tirchanah *transliterated name* {8647 tirchanah} the meaning uncertain; a Yisra Eliy.
Tireya *transliterated name* {8493 tiyreya} Awe.
Tirhaqah *transliterated name* {8640 tirhaqah} the meaning uncertain; a sovereign of Kush.
Tirsah *transliterated name* {8656 tirtsah} Pleasure.
Tisbehiy *transliterated name* {8664 tishbiy} Recourse; Of Tishbeh (in Gilad).
Tisiy *transliterated name* {8491 tiytsiy} Of Tis.
tithe *noun* {4643 maasrah} [1181 dekate] one tenth.
tithe *verb* {6237 asar} [586 apodekatoo] [1183 dekatoo] to offer or receive one tenth.
title *transliterated noun* [5102 titlos] the rank of a person; a caption; **cp** inscription; **cp** superscription; **cp** epigraph.
tittle *noun* [2762 keraia] an infintismal part.
Titus *transliterated name* [5103 titos] meaning uncertain.
Tormah/deceitfully *transliterated name* {8649 tormah} Fraud.
Toach *transliterated name* {8430 towach} Humbled.
Tob Adoni Yah *transliterated name* {2899 tobadoniyah} Goodly of Adoni Yah.
Tobi Yah *transliterated name* {2900 tobiyah} Goodly of Yah.
Tochu *transliterated name* {8459 tochuw} Abasement.
toddler *noun* {2945 taph} little ones that toddle.
toe, finger *noun* {676 etsba} {677 etsba} [1147 daktulos] literally, a digit as a grasper; **cp** great toe, thumb.
together, unitedly, altogether *adverb* {3162 yachad} as one; **see** united.
toil *adjective* {6001 amel} hard working.
toil *noun* {5999 amal} to work hard.
toil *verb* {5998 amal} hard work.
Token *transliterated name* {8507 token} Gauge.
Tola *transliterated name* {8439 towla} Maggot.
Tolaiy *transliterated name* {8440 towlaiy} Of Tola.
tolerance *noun* [463 anokee] ability to restrain.
tolerate, endure *verb* [430 anekomai] to hold oneself up against.
tomb *noun* {6900 qeburah} {6913 qeber} [5028 taphos] burial; **see** entomb; **cp** grave.
tomorrow, morrow (the) *noun* {4279 machar} {4283 mochorath} [839 aurion] [1887 epaurion] the following day.
tongue *name* {3956 leshonah} {3961 lishshan} [1100 glossa] the physical body part in the mouth; a language; **cp** lip.
tonguelash *verb* {3960 lashan} to wag the tongue.
tongues (divided) *noun* [1266 diamerizo] also implies distributed.
tongues (foreign) *noun* {3937 laaz} foreign languages.
tongues (other) *noun* [2084 heteroglossos] another language; only in 1 Corinthians 14:21.
tongues of fire *noun* [1100 glossa] [4442 pur] licking flames; **note:** in Acts 2:1–4, divided (or, distributed) tongues of fire sat on each of the apostles; they spoke in other tongues, and were heard in many dialects; **see** dialect.
tooth, tusk, crag, ivory *noun* {8127, 8128 shen} {*plural* 8143 shenhabbim} [3599 adous] as being sharp.
top, beginning, first(s), head *noun* {7218 rosh} {7221 rishah} {7225 reshith} {8462 rechillah} the head, in a variety of applications; the head of the body, of time, of the month, of archs.
Topheth *transliterated name* {8612 topheth} {8613 tophteh} meaning uncertain; Theological Wordbook suggests a place of spitting; Strong suggests a place of cremation; Scofield suggests a place in Gay Hinnom/Valley of Burning where humans were sacrificed; **read** Yesha Yah 30:33, Yirme Yah 7:31, 32, 19:6–14.
topple, descend, lower *verb* {3381 yarad} to go lower; to tip over.
topple, totter, waver *verb* {4131 mowt} {4571 maad} to waver; to fall over.
Toqahath *transliterated name* {8445 towqahath} Obedience.
torah *transliterated noun* {8451, 8452 torah} [3551 nomos] Elohim's holy statute; the first five scrolls of the Scripture.
torah (doctors of the) [3547 nomodidaskalos] doctrinators of the torah, including rabbis and rabbonis.
torah (set the) *verb* [3549 nomotheteo] to legislate the torah.
torah (setting the) *verb* [3548 nomothesia] legislating the torah.
torah (violating the) *noun* [3891 paranomeo] to be opposed to the torah.
torah setter *noun* [3550 nomothetees] one who legislates the torah.
torah violation, violation of the torah *noun* [458 anomia] [3892 paranomia] a disregarding of the torah.
torahically *adverb* [3545 nomimos] according to the torah.
torahist *noun* [3544 nomikos] an expert of the torah.

torrential *adjective* {5464 cagrid} rushingly.
tortoise, palanquin *noun* {6632 tsab} a wagon, as covered; a tortoise, as covered.
tossings *plural noun* {5076 nadud} flailings.
totality *noun,* **totally, perfect** *adjective* {3642 kaliyl} all inclusive; naught to be added.
totter, wag, wander, waver, drift, shake, stagger *verb* {5128 nuwa} to waver.
totter, waver, topple *verb* {4131 mowt} {4571 maad} to waver; to fall over.
touch *verb* {3237 yamash} {4184 muwsh} to touch.
touch, plague, reach *verb* {5060 naga} to touch heavily; to strike.
tough, strong *adjective* {533 ammits} {554 amots} {2389 chazaq} {5794 az} {5808 izzuz} forceful; harsh; physically able.
toward, –ward, opposite *adjective* {4136 mowl} [481 antikru] [492 antiparerkomai] [495 antiperan] across from.
tower *noun* **Migdol** *transliterated name* {4024 migdol} {4026 migdal} tower; a place in Misrayim.
tower *noun* {5470 cohar} a dungeon surrounded by walls.
tower *noun* {6877 tseriach} a citadel.
tracks *noun* [2487 ichnos] a way or path beaten by the feet; metaphorically used of imitating the example of another.
trail *noun* {5410 nathiybah} as trodden.
train *noun* {7640 shebel} the train of a gown, as flowing after; **cp** drape.
trample *verb* {1915 hadak} to crush with the foot; **see** stool.
trample *verb* {6072 acac} {7429 ramac} {7512 rephac} [3961 pateo] to tread; to squeeze underfoot.
trample, balance *verb* {5537 cala} {5541 calah} as suspended; as weighed; as trampled.
trampled *adjective* {4001 mebuwcah} {4823 mirmac} {4833 mirpas} trodden; treaded upon.
trampling *noun* {8395 tebucah} a treading down.
tranquil *adjective* {7946 shalanan} serene.
transact, exact *verb* [4238 prasso] to extract dues; to execute; to perform repeatedly.
transcience *adjective* **transient** *adverb* {2465 cheled} the fleeting of life.
transcribe, antiquate, remove *verb* {6275 athaq} that which has aged; to take away; to take down, as in transcribing.
transcript *noun* {6572, 6573 parshegen} a copy.
transfigure *verb* [3345 metaschematizo] to alter the figure; **cp** metamorphose.
transgress *verb* [3845 parabaino] to overstep.
transgression *noun* [3847 parabasis] an overstepping of the basis.
transgressor *noun* [3848 parabatees] one who oversteps.
translate thoroughly *verb* [1329 diermenuo] to translate exactly, in detail.
translate *verb* {8638 tirgam} [2058 hermenia] [2059 hermeenuo] [3177 methermenuo] the rendering of words from one language to another; **note:** languages are translated; dreams are interpreted; **cp** interpret.
translator *noun* {3887 luwts} [1328 diermenutees] one who translates from one tongue to another; **cp** interpreter.
transparent *adjective* {3840 libnah}.
transplace *verb* [3346 metatithemi] to put in another place; to transpose.
transplant *noun* {8363 shethil} that which has removed and planted elsewhere.
transplant *verb* {8362 shathal} to remove and plant elsewhere.
trap, trip, crooked *adjective* {6121 aqob} {6128 aqalqal} {6129 aqallathon} a trap; one that trips; crooked, as full of traps.
trauma *transliterated noun* [5134 trauma] a wound.
traumatize *transliterated verb* [5135 traumatizo] to wound or injure.
travail *noun* [5604 odin] pain; a pang of birthing.
travail *noun* {8513 telaah} a distress.
travail *verb* [5605 odino] to experience the pains of birth.
tray *noun* {4289 machtah} a tray to remove live coals, or ashes.
tread, spy, step *verb* {7270 ragal} verb of foot; to measure out with the foot; **see** foot.
treason *noun* {4604 maal} a covert act.
treason *verb* {4603 maal} to act covertly.
treasure (hidden) *noun* {4301 matmon} {*plural* 4362 mikman} {*plural* 4710 mitspunim} {6840 tsaphin} {8226 saphan} a secreted valuable.
treasure (peculiar) *noun* {5459 cegullah} private treasure, as held close to the breast; private property.
treasure *noun* [2344 thesauros] something precious; a treasury, that which is laid up in a treasury.
treasure *noun* {5458 cegor} as withheld at the heart.
treasure *verb* {686 atsar} [2343 thesaurizo] to reserve; to store up.
treasure, hide *verb* {6845 tsaphan} to hide by covering over; to protect; to reserve.
treasure, treasury *noun* {214 owtsar} {*plural* 1595 genezim} {1596 genaz} {1597 ginzak} a gathering place of valuables.
treasured, impending, ready *adjective* {6259, 6264 athud} {6263 athid} prepared; treasured.
treasurer *noun* {*plural* 1411 gedabar} {1489 gizbar} {1490 gizbar} one that oversees a treasury.
tree *noun* {363 iylan} [1186 dendron].
tree, timber *noun* {6086 ets} {6097 etsah} a tree; timber; sticks of timber.
tremble *verb* {2729 charad} {2730 chared} {6426 palats} {7460 raad} to shudder with terror.
trembling *noun* {2731 charadah} {6427 pallatsuwth} {7461 raad} {8606 tiphletseth} a shudder; fear.
trench *noun* {2430 cheylah} {2434 chayits} a trench for protection.
trench, decision, decisive, incision, incisor, ore, sickle *adjective, noun* {2742 charuts} mentally, soulically, or physically, an incising.
trench, valiant *noun* {2426 chel} character of a person who protects; a trench for protection.
trespass, overpass, pass (over) (through), surpass *verb* {5674 abar} to cross over; this verb is unrelated to the mistranslation of passover.
tresses *noun* [2863 komao] [2864 kome] a long lock of hair; hair as hanging; **cp** hair.
triangle, tertiary, thrice, tierce *noun* {7991 shaloah} an officer of the third rank; three times; an interval of a third; a three sided music instrument.
tribulate *verb* [2346 thlibo] to press hard upon.
tribulate *verb* {6887 tsarar} to constrict.
tribulation *noun* [2347 thlipsis] a pressing together.
tribulation *noun* **tribulator** *noun* **constricted** *adjective* {6862 tsar} {6869 tsarah} a constriction; a time of constriction; a constricted place; one that constricts.
tribute *noun* {4061 middah} a tribute of money.
trickery *noun* {6122 oqbah} to trip or trap by trickery.
trifle, abase, abate, belittle, slight, swift *verb* {6819 tsaar} {6985 qat} {7034 qalah} {7043 qalal} to belittle in contempt; to make light of; to lessen.
trip the heel, heel, heelprint, heel trippers *noun* {6119 aqeb} [4418 pterna] the back of the foot; a print made by the heel; ones that trip the heel by trapping.
trip the heel, restrain the heel *verb* {6117 aqab} to seize by holding the heel.
trip, crooked, trap *adjective* {6121 aqob} {6128 aqalqal} {6129 aqallathon} a trap; one that trips; crooked, as full of traps.
trip, falter, stumble *verb* {3782 kashal} to totter; to waver.
troop against *verb* {1464 guwd} to attack with a troop.
troop *noun* {1409 gad} {1416 geduwd} a crowd, usually military.
trouble *verb* {5916 akar} to disturb.
trough *noun* {3342 yeqeb} a trough for treading wine.
trough, curl *noun* {7298 rahat} {*plural* 4857 mashabim} {8268 shoqeth} a drinking trough for animals; a ringlet of hair.
true (being) *noun* [226 aleethuo] to be true.
true *adjective* [227 alethes] accurate; genuine; honest.
true, truly, truth *noun* {571 emeth} [225 alethia] literally, of a truth.
truly *adverb* {551 omnam} {552 umnam} [230 alethos] **note:** the Hebrew are from the root of amen; **see** amen.
truly, truth *noun* {7187 qeshot} {7189 qoshet} from the root, to balance; equity.
trumpet, lily *noun* **Shoshanna** *transliterated name* {7799 shoshanna} [4677 sousanna] lily, as a flower, or as an ornament; trumpet, from its lily shaped bell.
trumpet, trump *noun* {2689 chatsotsrah} {7782 shophar} [4536 salpinx] a trumpet which sounds.
trumpet, trumpeting *verb* {2690 chatsar} [4537 salpizo] to blow on a trumpet.
trumpeter *participle* {2690 chatsar} [4538 salpistees] one who trumpets.

- **SUMMARY:**
- **TRUST, ENTRUST, TRUSTLESS, TRUSTWORTHY:**
- **trust (little)** *noun* [3640 oligopistos] literally, puny truster.
- **trust, amen, amenable** *transliterated verb* {539 aman} to confirm; to confide it.
- **trust, entrust** *verb* {539 aman} {540 aman} [4100 pistuo] [4104 pistoo] **see** amen; to confidently rely upon; **note:** whereas believing is a psyching up of the mental attributes, trust is the abandonment of self into the care of another.
- **trust, trustworthiness** *noun* {529 emuwn} {2622 chacuth} [4102 pistis] **see** amen; the spiritual of the ability of total reliance in another; **note:** whereas faith is a psyching up of the mental attribute, trust is the abandonment of self into the care of another; **note:** the *exeGeses* indicates whenever trust is preceded by the article, as in "the trust".
- **trustless** *adjective, noun* [571 apistos] without trust.
- **trustlessness** *noun* [570 apistia] to not trust.
- **trustlessness, distrust** *noun* [543 apeitheia] obstinate and rebellious.
- **trustworthily, trustworthiness, trustworthy, trusting** *adjective, adverb* {530 emunah} [4101 pistikos] [4103 pistos].

truthful *noun* [228 alethinos] factual.
Tubal Qayin *transliterated name* {8423 tuwbalqayin} Offspring of Qayin.
tubes *plural noun* {6804 tsantarah} hollows.
tuft *noun* {5296 neoreth} that which is shaken out, as the tuft from the flax.
Tulon *transliterated name* {8436 tuwlon} Lofty.
tumult *noun* {8351 sheth} [2351 thorubos] uprising; riot.
tumulting *verb* [2350 thorubeo] to make a noise or uproar; to disturb.
turban *noun* {*plural* 4021 migbaahoth} {6797 tsaniph} a wraparound headdress.
turn (about) (around), go (about) (around), surround *verb* {5437 cabab} to border; to revolve; to surround.
turn (aside) (in), twist (off) *verb* {5493 sur} from the root, to turn off.
turn (away) (back) (from) (to) respond, restore, return *verb* {7725 shub} {8421 tub} from the root, to turn back; as to reply, to come back.
turn *noun* {5438 cibbah} a providential turn of affairs.
turn, response, return *noun* {8666 teshubah} a reccurence; a reply, as returned.
turn, row *noun* {8447 tor} a succession of occasion; a row of.
turtledove *noun* {8449 tor} a ringdove; a term of endearment.
tusk, crag, ivory, tooth *noun* {8127, 8128 shen} {*plural* 8143 shenhabbim} [3599 adous] as being sharp.
tusks, teeth *plural noun* {6374 piphiah} {8143 shenhabbim} teeth of a person, animal, or instrument.
tutor *noun* [2519 kathegetes] teacher; **cp** doctor.
tweezers *noun* {*plural* 4212 mezammeroth} {*dual* 4457 malqachim} literally, pluckers or tweezers used to trim the menorah.
twig *noun* {2156 zemor} [2595 karphos] a small branch; figuratively, a smaller fault.
twig *noun* {5577 cancin} {5589 ceappah} {5634 carappah} **cp** branch.
twig, cleft *noun* {5585 caiph} a fissure of rocks; a small branch.
Twin, twins *name, noun* {*plural* 8380 taomim} [1324 didumos] Twin; **see** Taom.
twin, twinned *verb* {8382 taam} to bear twins; to twin; to twine; to duplicate.
twinkle *verb* {7335 razam} to twinkle the eye, as in mockery; **cp** blink.
twirl, twist, spin *noun* {1524 giyl} {1525 giylah} a physical expression of joy.
twirl, twist, spin *verb, noun* {1523 giyl, guwl} {3769 karar} [4761 strebloo] to spin around, as in rejoicing; **cp** whirl.
twirl, whirl, writhe *verb* {1752, 1753 duwr} {2342 chiyl} {3769 karar} {6801 tsanaph} to gyrate; to move in a circle; to dance.
twist (off), turn (aside) (in) *verb* {5493 sur} from the root, to turn off.
twist *verb* {5791 avath} {6127 aqal} to wrest away from.
twist, bend, pervert *verb* {5753 avah} {5754 avvah} to crook; to overthrow.
twisted *adjective* {5494 cuwr} of a plant as being twisted.
twisted *adjective* {6129 aqallathon} {6618 pethaltol} contorted, tortuous.
type *noun* [5179 tupos] an example for imitation or warning.
tyranny *noun* {6531 perek} violence.
tyranny, tyrant *noun* {6184 aryts} a despotic rule; a despotic ruler.
tyrant *noun* **tyrannical** *adjective* {6530 perits} violent; one that is violent.
tyrranize, bind *verb* {631 acar} {6014 amar} to bind with a bond; to bind a captive; to tyrranize.

U

U El *transliterated name* {177 uel} possibly, Whether of El.
Ukal *transliterated name* {401 ukal} Devoured.
ulcer *noun* {7822 shechin} an inflamation.
umbilical cord *noun* {8270 shor} the navel cord connecting unborn infant to the mother.
unaccusable *adjective* [410 anegkletos] without cause of accusation.
unaccused *adjective* [338 anaitios] not accused; without accusation.
unadulterated *adjective* [185 akeraios] without mixture; without dilution.
unanxious *adjective* [275 amerimnos] without anxiety.
unapprehendable *adjective* [423 anepileptos] unable to take.
unapproved *adjective* [96 adokimos] not approved.
unashamed *adjective* [422 anepaischuntos] not ashamed.
unavaricious *adjective* [866 aphilarguros] undesiring of greedy gain.
unbend *verb* [352 anakupto] to rise; figuratively, to be elated.
unbeneficial *noun, adjective* [512 anopheles] without benefit.
unblemished *adjective* [298 amometos] [299 amomos] without imperfection.
unceasing *adjective* [88 adialiptos] not ceasing.
unceasingly *adverb* [89 adialiptos] not ceasingly.
uncertain, obscure *adjective* [82 adelos] [83 adelotess] unclear.
uncertainly *adverb* [84 adelos] unclear.
uncircumcise *verb* {6188 arel} as having the foreskin of the penis; as not having been circumcised; **cp** circumcision; **cp** decircumcision.
uncircumcised *adjective* {6189 arel} as having the foreskin of the penis; as not having been circumcised; **cp** circumcision; **cp** decircumcision
uncircumcised, foreskin *noun* {6190 orlah} [203 akrobustia] the foreskin of the penis; the foreskin not removed; **cp** circumcision; **cp** decircumcision.
uncle, beloved, loves *noun* {1730 dod} from the root, to boil; literally, an extremely warm caring for; an uncle.
uncomprehending *adjective* [801 asunetos] not having a mental grasp; without understanding.
uncontrollable *adjective* [193 akrates] not controllable.
uncovenantal *adjective* [111 athemitos] against, outside, or without covenant; **see** covenant.
uncovenanted *adjective* [113 athesmos] [802 asunthetos] against, outside, or without covenant; **see** covenant.
undeceitful *adjective* [97 adolos] not deceitful.
undergarment *noun* {6361 pattish} a thin garment.
undermine, dig *verb* {6979 qur} to trench; to estop.
undertake, take *verb* {6901 qabal} {6902 qebal} [353 analambano] to acquire; to take up; **cp** receive.
undiluted *adjective* [194 akratos] lliterally, without pouring together.
undisciplined *adjective* [521 apaidutos] without discipline; stupidly conjectured.
uneucharistic *adjective* [884 acharistos] without charism; **see** charism; **cp** eucharist.
unexplorable *adjective* [419 anexerunetos] unable to explore completely.
unfathered *verb* [540 apator] the negative of fathered; that is, no record of having been fathered; **cp** ungenealogized.
unfortunate *adjective* {2489 cheleka} literally, wretched.
unfortunates *plural noun* {2489 chelekim}.
unfriendly *adjective* [865 aphilagathos] not friendly.
unfruitful *adjective* [175 akarpos] barren.
unfurl *verb* [380 anaptusso] to unroll; **cp** furl.
ungenealogized *adjective* [35 agenealogetos] unrecorded genealogy; without genealogy.
ungrieving *adjective* [253 alupoteros] without grief.
unhypocritical *adjective* [505 anupokritos] without hypocrisy; sincere.
unintelligent *adjective* [801 asunetos] without intelligence.
unite *verb* {3161 yachad} to become one.

unitedly, altogether, together *adverb* {3162 yachad} as one; **see** unite.
unjust *adjective* [94 adikos] not just; **see** injure; **see** injustice.
unjustly *adverb* [95 akidos] without justness.
unknowing *adjective* [50 agnoeo] not knowing.
unknowingness *noun* [51 agnoema] [52 agnoia] [56 agnosia] without knowledge.
unknown *adjective* [57 agnostos] not known.
unlearned *noun* [261 amathes] [2399 idiotes] idiot.
unless, if not *participle* {3884 luwley} if not.
unlettered *adjective* [62 agrammatos] not grammatic; unable to scribe; illiterate.
unmarried *noun* [22 agamos] not married.
unmercied *adjective* [448 anileos] [462 anosios] without being mercied.
unmerciful *adjective* [415 anele emon] without compassion.
unmindful *noun* [453 anoetos] without mind.
unmindfulness *noun* [454 anoia] stupidity.
unmothered *adjective* [540 apator] the negative of mother; that is, no record of having been mothered; **cp** ungenealogized.
unpolluted *adjective* [283 amiantos] not polluted; **see** polluted.
unquestionable *adjective* [368 anantirrhetos] no room for rhetoric.
unquestioning *adverb* [369 anantirrhetos] without room for rhetoric.
unravel, release *verb* {8271 shere} to separate; to free.
unregrettable *adjective* [278 ametameletos] without regret.
unrepentant *adjective* [279 ametanoetos] without repentance.
unrestrained *adjective* [180 akatapaustos] [183 akatasketos] [192 akrasna] without restraint.
unripe *adjective* **Abib** *transliterated name* {3, 4 eb} {24 abib} an unripened or tender produce; a month of the Hebrew calender; also a syllable in the name of the city, Tel Abib.
unripe figs *noun* {6291 pag}.
unsentenced *adjective* [178 akatakritos] not sentenced.
unshod *adjective* {3182 yacheph} without footwear.
unstable *adjective* [182 akatastatos] not constant; **see** instability.
unstumbling *verbal noun* [679 aptaistos] not stumbling; without sin.
unsubjected, insubordinate *adjective* [506 anupotaktos] not subject to; refusing subordination.
unteased *adjective* [46 agnaphos] of cloth that has not been carded or combed.
untestable *adjective* [551 apirastos] unable to test.
untested *adjective* [552 apiros] inexperienced; ignorant.
until when *participle adverb* {4970 mathay} extent of time.
untorahed *adjective* [459 anomos] [460 anomos] without torah; **cp** entorahed; **see** torah.
untraceable *adjective* [421 anexichniastos] unable to track out.
untranslatable *adjective* [1421 dusermenutos] not translatable.
unutterable *adjective* [215 alaletos] unable to utter.
unveil *verb* [343 anakalupto] [601 apokalupto] to uncover.
unveil *verb* {8365 shatham} to lift the lid.
unveiled *adjective* [177 akatakaluptos] uncovered.
unwashen *adjective* [449 aniptos] not washed.
unwavering *adjective* [186 aklines] without wavering.
unwise *adjective* [781 asophos] not wise.
unwitnessed *adjective* [267 amaturos] without witness.
unworthily *adverb* [371 anaxios] undeservingly; **see** worthy.
unworthy *adjective* [370 anaxios] undeserving; **see** worthy.
up, upper, above *adverb* [507 ano] upward; the top.
uphold *verb* [472 antechomai] to hold on to.
uphold, callous, prevail, strengthen *verb* {553 amats} {555 omets} {2388 chazaq} {2393 chezqah} {5810 azaz} to enable physically; to become thickskinned.
uphold, prop, sustain *verb* {5564 camak} {8551 tamak} to prop up; with the hands, or with props.
uphold, support *verb* {5582 scaad} to support; usually, figuratively; **cp** prop.
upholding *participle* {5583 cead} aiding.
uplift, uprise, burden *noun* {4864 maseth} a raising; a reproach, as a burden.
upper millstone, chariot *noun* {4817 merkab} {4818 merkabah} {7393 rekeb} {7396 rikbah} {7398 rekub} a vehicle; a rider; **cp** millstones.
upper room *noun* {5944 aliyah} {5952 alliyth} [508 anogeon] a space above earth; an upper loft.
upper, uppermost, above *adjective* [509 anothen] [510 anoterikos] [511 anoteron] from above; the source of the rebirth; **read** Yahn 3:1–8.
uppermost *adjective* **Elyon** *transliterated title* {5943 illay} {5945, 5946 elyon} [5310 hupsistos] an uppermost place or position; a title of Elohim.
upright *plural adjective* {3651 ken} literally, set upright.
uprise, burden, uplift *noun* {4864 maseth} a raising; a reproach, as a burden.
uproar, waste, roar *noun* {7588 shaon} a rumble; a destruction.
uproot *verb* {5255 nacach} {5256 necach} {5428 nathash} to pluck up; to tear away.
uproot, hamstring *verb* {6131, 6132 aqar} to pluck up the root; to cut the tendons.
uproot, root *verb* {8327 sharash} {8332 sheroshu} to plant a root; to pull out by the root.
uprooted *adjective* {4535 maccach} {6133 eqer} usually of persons who are forced to move.
upset *verb* [384 anaskuazo] to pack up; figuratively, to upset.
Urbane *transliterated name* [3773 ourbanos] Urbane; of the city.
urbanite (the) *noun* {377 ish} {7149 qirah} [2469 iskariotes] City Man.
urge *verb* {6484 patsar} to peck at.
urgent *verb* {5169 nachats} to press for immediate action.
Uri *transliterated name* {221 uri} Flame.
Uri El *transliterated name* {222 uriel} Flame of El.
Uri Yah *transliterated name* {223 uriyah} [3774 ourias] Flame of Yah.
urinate *verb* {8366 shathan} from the root, to make water.
urines *plural noun* {7890 shain} the fluids secreted from the body.
Us *transliterated name* {5780 uwts} Consultation.
use, used, useful, accustomed *verb* {5532 cakan} to be familiar by use; to be serviceable to.
useful *adjective* [2173 euchreestos] easy to make use of.
useless *adjective* [888 achrios] [890 achreestos] unprofitable.
useless *verb* [889 achreioo] to render unserviceable.
usure, bite *verb* {5391 nashak} literally, as in usury, to take a bite.
usurpation *noun* [725 harpagmos] the act of seizing and holding in possession by force, or without right.
usury *noun* {5392 neshek} interest on a debt, usually excessive.
Uthay *transliterated name* {5793 uwthay} Reinforcing.
utter *verb* {4448 malal} {4449 melal} [2044 erugomai] [5350 phtheggomai] to express vocally; **cp** speak; **cp** word.
utterance *noun* {4008 mibta} {4405, 4406 millah} [669 apophtheggomai] a vocal expression; **see** utter.
Uzzen Sheerah *transliterated name* {242 uzzensheerah} Hearkened of Sheerah.
Uzzi El *transliterated name* {5816 uzziel} Strength of El.
Uzzi Eliy *transliterated name* {5817 ozziyeliy} Of Uzzi El.
Uzzi Yah *transliterated name* {5814 uzziya} {5818 uzziyah} [3604 ozias] Strength of Yah.

V

Veheb *transliterated name* {2052 vaheb} of uncertain derivative; a place in Moab.
vail *noun* {6532 poreketh} the separatrix in the tabernacle.
vail, veil *noun* {3875 lowt} {4044 meginnah} {4533 masveh} {*plural* 4555 micpachahoth} {5497 cuth} {6777 tsammah} {6809 tsaiph} {7289 radid} {7479 raalah} [2571 kaluma] a covering; that which is fastened on.
vail, veil, cover *verb* {3874 luwt} {5844 atah} {6809 tsaiph} [2572 kalupto] [2619 katakaluptomai] to cover; to enrobe; to wrap; to withhold from view.
vain (become) *verb* {1891 habal} to empty; to void; the Hebrew verb is not translatable into one English verb.
vain, vanity, void, empty, req *adjective* {1892 hebel} {*transliteration* 7385 riq} {*transliteration* 7386 req} {7723 shav} [*transliteration* 4469 rhaka] emptiness, voidness; figuratively, stupid.
vainly *adverb* [1500 eikee] [2756 kenos] idly; without reason.
vainly, void, empty *adverb* {7387 reqam} emptily; without effect; **cp** req.
valiant, trench *noun* {2426 chel} character of a person who protects; a trench for protection.
valiant, valour, valuable, virtue *noun* {2428, 2429 chayil} usually of persons of character; of valuables.
Valley of Burning/Gay Hinnom *name* {1516 gay} {2011 hinnom} [1067 geenna] used figuratively, as a name for the place (or state) of everlasting punishment; may be

transliterated, Gay Hinnom.
Valley of Engravers *transliterated plural name* {1516 gay} {2798 charashim} Valley of Engravers.
Valley of Salt/Gay Melach *transliterated name* {1516 gay} {4417 melach} Valley of Salt.
Valley of Slaughter/Gay Haregah *transliterated name* {1516 gay} {2028 haregah} Valley of Slaughter.
Valley of Vision/Gay Hizzayon *transliterated name* {1516 gay} {2384 chizzayon} Valley of Vision.
valley *noun* {1237 biqah} {6010 emeq} a lowland or split area between two heights.
valley, Gay *transliterated noun* {1516 gay} sometimes transliterated when used in compound names.
valour, valuable, virtue valiant *noun* {2428, 2429 chayil} usually of persons of character; of valuables.
Van Yah *transliterated name* {2057 vanyah} Answer of Yah.
vanish *verb* {4414 malach} to rub away; **see** salt *verb*.
vanish, corrupt, destroy, destruct, lose, ruin *verb* {6 abad} {7 abad} {8 obed} {7843 shachath} [1311 diaphthiro] [2704 kataphthiro] [5351 phthiro] to corrupt through decay.
vanish, dissolve *verb* {4743 maqaq} [1262 dialuo] to dissolve; to dwindle; to vanish.
vanity, void, empty, req, vain *adjective* {1892 hebel} {*transliteration* 7385 riq} {*transliteration* 7386 req} {7723 shav} [*transliteration* 4469 rhaka] emptiness, voidness; figuratively, stupid.
vanquish *verb* {2522 chalash} to cause to prostrate.
vanquished *noun* {2523 challash} one caused to prostrate.
vapour, hierarch *noun* {5387 nasi} [747 archeegos] a vapour, as a rising mist; a chief leader; as being first, foremost.
vassal *noun* {4522 mac} one that is under homage.
Vayezatha *transliterated name* {2055 vayezatha} of foreign origin; a son of Haman.
Vedan *transliterated name* {2051 vedan} the meaning uncertain; a place in Arabia.
veil, conceal *verb* {5956 alam} to conceal; to veil from sight.
veil, cover, languish, shroud *verb* {5848 ataph} {5968 alaph} to cover over; to languish.
venerable *adjective* [4575 sebastos] adorable in the sense of able to adore.
venerant *noun* [4586 semnos] worthy of adoration.
venerate *verb* [4573 sebazomai] [4576 sebomai] to adore.
veneration *noun* [4574 sebasma] [4587 semnotes] adoration.
vengeance *noun* [1557 ekdikesis] punishment inflicted in return for an injury, or an offense.
vengeance, avengement *noun* {5359 naqam} {5360 neqamah} revenge; **see** avenge.
venom *noun* [2447 ios] as emitted.
venom, bitter, gall *noun* {*plural* 4844 merarim} {4845 mererah} {4846 merorah} bile; venom; a bitter herb.
vermillion *noun* {8350 shashar} as a piercing red.
vertebrae, riddle *noun* {7001 qetar} a knot; as that which is to be unravelled.
very, exceeding, greatly, increasing, many, mighty, much *adjective* {7689, 7690 saggiy} superlatively mighty, or large.
vex *verb* {3707 kaac} [3791 ochleo] to harass; to irritate; to agitate; to trouble.
vexation *noun* {3708 kaac} an agitation; a harassment; an irritation.
vile *adjective* {5240 nemibzeh} evil.
vilification *noun* [2561 kakosis] a declared evil.
vilify, vilifying, shatter *verb* {7489 raa} {7490 rea} [2551 kakologeo] [2558 kakoucheo] [2559 kakoo] verb of evil; to make or declare evil; to vilify by shattering; **see** evil.
village *noun* [2968 kome] [2969 komopolis] a small assemblage of houses.
village, whelp *noun* {3715 kephiyr} a young lion, as covered with a mane; a village, as covered by walls.
vine (bright) *noun* {8321 soreqah} [288 ampelos] literally, a burning bright; a vine, as producing grapes.
vinedresser *noun* {3755 korem} [289 ampelourgos] one who tends the vines.
vineyard *noun* {3754 kerem} [290 ampelon] a plantation of grapevines.
violate *verb* [3845 parabaino] to go contrary.
violate *verb* {2554 chamac} to ravish.
violating the torah *verb* [3891 paranomeo] to disregard the torah.
violation *noun* [3847 parabasis] nonobservance; transgression.
violation of the torah, torah violation *noun* [458 anomia] [3892 paranomia] a disregarding of the torah; **see** torah.
violator *noun* [3848 parabates] one who violates the torah.
violence *noun* {2555 chamac} {4637 maaratsah} ravishment.
virgin *noun* {1330 bethulah} {5959 almah} {5961 alamoth} [3933 parthenos] one who has had no sexual intercourse.
virginity *noun* {1331 bethulim} [3932 parthenia] the quality or state of a virgin.
virtue valiant, valour, valuable *noun* {2428, 2429 chayil} usually of persons of character; of valuables.
visable *adjective* [3707 horatos] able to be seen.
visage *noun* [3799 opsis] appearance.
visage, vision *noun* {4758 mareh} {4759 marah} a vision, or visage, especially one of beauty.
vision *noun* {2376 chezev} {2377 chazon} {2378, 2379 chazoth} {2380 chazuth} {2384 chizzayon} {4236 machazeh} [3701 optasia] [3705 horama] [3706 horasis] that which is seen beyond eyesight.
visit, muster, oversee *verb* {6485 paqad} to visit with friendly intent, to oversee; or to visit with hostile intent, to take care of; to muster for display.
visitation, episcopate *transliterated noun* [1984 episcope] [1985 episcopos] one who scopes; an inspector; inspection.
visitation, muster, overseer, oversight *noun* {6486 pequddah} a visit with friendly intent, to oversee; or a visit with hostile intent, to take care of; a muster for display.
visitation/Peqod *noun, transliterated name* {6489 peqowd} refers to Babel as a place of Yah Veh's visitation.
voice *noun* {6963 qol} {7032 qal} [5456 phonee] sound.
voice *verb* [5455 phoneo] to voice out; to emit a sound.
voiceless *noun* [880 aphonos] without voice.
void *noun* {4003 mebuwqah} empty.
void *verb* {6331 pur} to cause to be empty.
void, empty, req, vain, vanity *adjective* {1892 hebel} {*transliteration* 7385 riq} {*transliteration* 7386 req} {7723 shav} [*transliteration* 4469 rhaka] emptiness, voidness; figuratively, stupid.
void, empty, vainly *adverb* {7387 reqam} emptily; without effect; **cp** req.
voluminous *noun* {6282 athar} increased in volume.
voluntary *noun* {4530 miccah} an offering, as flowing.
voluntary, voluntarily *noun, adverb* {5071 nedabah} a willing offer.
volunteer, voluntarily *verb* {5068 nadab} {5069 nedab} to offer willingly.
volunteers, voluntary *noun, adjective* {5081 nadyb} a willing offer; one who willingly offers.
voluptuous *adjective* {5719 adiyn} sensual gratification.
vomit *noun* {6892 qiy} that which is spewed.
vomit *verb* {6958 qow} {7006 qayah} to spew.
votive *noun* [334 anatheema] an offering of a vow; **cp** anathema.
vow *noun* {5088 neder} [2171 euchee] a binding word.
vow *verb* {5087 nadar} [2172 euchomia] to bind by word.
vulture *noun* {7201 raah} from its sharp sight.
vulva *noun* {5040 nabluth} the female pudenda.

W

wadi *noun* {5158 nachal} a watercourse which is dry, except in the rainy season.
wafers *plural noun* {3561 kavvanim} as prepared; wafers used in sacrifice.
wag over, wander, waver, sway *verb* {5110 nud} to waver.
wag, wander, waver, drift, shake, stagger, totter *verb* {5128 nuwa} to waver.
wagon *noun* {5699 agalah} that which has revolving wheels.
wait, await, expect, receive *verb* {2442 chakah} {3176 yachal} {6960 qavah} [324 anadekomai] [362 anameno] [553 apekdekomai] [4327 prosdekomai] [4328 prosdokao] [4329 prosdokia] to anticipate; to wait expectantly, patiently; **cp** take.
wake, waken, awake *verb* {5782 uwr} {6974 quts} to wake up.
waker *noun* {5894 iyr} one that is awake; one that wakens.
walk gently *verb* {1718 dadah}.
walk *noun* {4109 mahalak} literally, a walk; a passage.
walk, went, go *verb* {3212 yahlach} literally, to walk.
wall *noun* {1444 geder} {1447 gader} {1448 gederah} {7023 qir} an encircling enclosure.
wall *noun* {2346 chomah} a divider, or separator.
wall *noun* {2918 tiyrah} a protective wall.
wall *noun* {3796 kothel} {3797 kethal} a barrier that holds in

confinement.
wall *noun* {7791 shur} as surrounding.
wall *verb* {1443 gadar} {5823 azaq} to install a wall; to wall in.
wallet *noun* [4082 pera] a leather pouch for carrying provisions.
wander (around) *verb* [4022 perierkomai] to go about.
wander, chase, flap, flee *verb* {5074 nadad} {5323 natsa} to flap up and down; to shoo away.
wander, seduce *verb* [4105 planao] to go or be led astray.
wander, stagger, stray *verb* {8582 taah} to reel; to stray.
wander, waver, drift, shake, stagger, totter, wag *verb* {5128 nuwa} to waver.
wander, waver, sway, wag over *verb* {5110 nud} to waver.
wandering *noun* **Nod** *transliterated noun* {5112, 5113 nod} exile.
wandering, seduction *noun* [4106 planee] a straying from.
war *noun* {7128, 7129 qerab} an encounter.
war, warfare, warrior *noun* {4421 milchamah} a fight; a fighter; **see** fight.
wardrobe *noun* {4458 meltachah} room where clothing is spread.
warp *noun* {8307 sheriruth} bent out of shape.
warp *noun* {8359 shethiy} a fixture; the warp in weaving.
warriors/Gammadim *plural noun* {1575 gammadim} as grasping instruments.
waste *noun* {7591 sheiyah} {7612 sheth} a devastation; a ruin.
waste *verb* {1110 balaq} {7582 shaah} to devastate; to ruin.
waste, roar, uproar *noun* {7588 shaon} a rumble; a destruction.
watch *verb* **watcher** *participle* **overlay** *verb* {6822, 6823 tsaphah} to observe; to await; to sheet over.
watch *verb* {8245 shaqad} [69 agrupmeo] to be alert; unsleeping.
watching *noun* {6836 tsephiah} [70 agrupnia] unsleeping.
watchtower *noun* {6844 tsaphith} a sentry post.
water *noun* {*dual* 4325 mayim} [5204 hudor] a common liquid.
waterless *adjective* [504 anudros] without water; dry.
wave *noun* {8573 tenuphah} the celebration of undulating a loaf or a breast unto Yah Veh.
wave, rub, shake *verb* {5130 nuph} to rub a bed with aromatics; to shake a hand; to wave an offering.
waver *verb* [1365 distazo] to stand in two ways, implying uncertainty of which way to take.
waver, drift, shake, stagger, totter, wag, wander *verb* {5128 nuwa} to waver.
waver, sway, wag over, wander *verb* {5110 nud} to waver.
waver, topple, totter *verb* {4131 mowt} {4571 maad} to waver; to fall over.
waver, wiggle *verb* {6328 puq} emotionally, to waver; physically, to wiggle.
way, journey *noun* {1870 derek} a road, as trodden; a walkway; figuratively, the journey of life.
way, journey *noun* {4550 macca} [3597 hodiporia] [3598 hodos] a trip; **see** sojourn.
way, path *noun* {734, 735 orach} also includes the manner of a person.
wean, deal, ripen *verb* {1580 gamal} transact.
weaned, antiquated *adjective* {6267 attiq} removed; that which has endured.
weapon *noun* {2021 hotsen} from the root sharp, and/or strong.
weary *adjective* {3287 yaeph} fatigued.
weary *verb* {3286 yaaph} {3288 yeaph} {3811 laah} to fatigue.
web *noun* {4545 macceketh} as expanded.
week, weeks *noun* {7620 shabua} literally, a seven; symbolic of an oath; **see** oath.
weigh *verb* {6424 palac} a literal weighing; a weighing (considering) of thought.
weigh, balance *verb* {8254 shakal} to weigh by balancing a set weight against that being weighed; **see** shekel.
weight *noun* {4946 mishqol} {4948 mishqal} a measure of heaviness.
weight *noun* {6425 pelec} a balance of a scale.
weighty *adjective* {5192 netel} a burden.
well *noun* {875 ber} {*plural* 877 bor} {953 bor} that which is dug; **cp** pit.
well–approve *verb* [2106 eudokeo] to well–please; to think well of.
well–approved *noun* [2107 eudokia] to be well–thought of.
well–please *verb* {3190 yatab} {3191 yetab} [2100 euaresteo] to cause to well–please.
well–pleasing *adjective* [2101 euarestos] fully agreeable.
well–receiving *adjective* [2126 eulabes] taking hold well.
well–souled *adjective* [2174 eupsucheo] of beneficient soul.
well–working *adverb* [2109 euergeteo] beneficently; doing well.
well–working *noun* [2108 uergesia] beneficence.
went, go, walk *verb* {3212 yahlach} literally, to walk.
wet, butler, drink (give), drown, moisten *verb* {8248 shaqah} {8257 shaga} to butler, as a bartender; to drink to quench thirst; to drink unto drowning; to cause to be wet.
What trouble! *interjection* {4972 mattelaah} An Hebraic idiom.
wheat *noun* [4621 sitos] a cereal grain.
wheel, whirler *noun* {1534, 1535 galgal} {1536 gilgal} something that whirls.
whelp, village *noun* {3715 kephiyr} a young lion, as covered with a mane; a village, as covered by walls.
whip *noun* {7752 shot} literally, or figuratively, a lash.
whir *noun* [4500 rhoizedon] a sound of whirling.
whirl away, shudder *verb* {8175 saar} to storm; to shudder, as in fright; to be stormed away.
whirl *noun* {6802 tsenephah} a rapid revolving.
whirl, writhe, twirl *verb* {1752, 1753 duwr} {2342 chiyl} {3769 karar} {6801 tsanaph} to gyrate; to move in a circle; to dance.
whirler *noun* {1754 dur} one who whirls.
whirler, wheel *noun* {1534, 1535 galgal} {1536 gilgal} that which whirls.
whirling *noun* {4070 medar} a spinning around, as in wandering.
whirling, horror *noun* {8178 saar} a whirling of a storm; a shuddering of horror.
whirlwind *noun* [2978 lailaps] a whirling wind.
whirring, cymbal, harpoon, locust *noun* {6767 tselatsal} a clattering, as of a cymbal; a whirring, as of wings; a rattling, as of a harpoon.
whisperer *noun* {5372 nirgan} [*plural* 5588 psithuristes] one who speaks without their vocal cords; figuratively, a slanderer.
whisperings *noun* {8103 shimtsah} [*plural* 5587 psithurismos] speaking without vocal cords; figuratively, slanderings.
white *adjective* {3836 laban}.
white linen, white marble *noun* {8336 shesh} white, as in bleached.
whiten, brick (make) *verb* {3835 laban} to make a brick; to cause to be white; this is a derivative of two words; **see** brick; **see** white.
whoever, O that *participle pronoun* {4310 miy} An Hebraic idiom.
whoop *verb* {6873 tsarach} to express a shrill sound.
whore *noun* [4204 porne] one who commits sexual acts for hire; in Scripture, also includes deviation from Elohim's misvoth.
whore (hallowed) *noun* {6948 qedeshah} a female whore for religious service.
whore, whoring *verb* {2181 zanah} [1608 ekpornuo] [4203 pornuo] to commit idolatry; to commit forbidden sexual acts for hire.
whoredoms *noun plural* {2183 zanunim} {2184 zenuwth} {8457 taznuth} [4202 pornia] physical or spiritual infidelity.
whoremonger (hallowed) *noun* {6945 qadesh} a male whore for religious service.
whoremonger *noun* [4205 pornos] a male whore.
wicked (deal) (declare) (do) *verb* {5765 avel} {7561 rasha} to do or declare evil.
wicked *adjective* {5766 avel} {7563 rasha} evil.
wicked *noun* {4849 mirshaath} {5767 avval} evil; an evil doer.
wickedly *adverb* {5766 avel} evilly.
wickedness *noun* {2248 chabulah} {5766 aval} {5932 alvah} {7562 resha} {7564 rishah} evil.
widow noun {490 almanah} [5503 chera] an unmarried woman whose man deceased.
widowhood *noun* {489 almon} {491 almanuth} the position of being a widow.
width *noun* {6613 pethay} the wideness.
wiggle, waver *verb* {6328 puq} emotionally, to waver; physically, to wiggle.
wild *noun* [66 agrios] as pertaining to the undeveloped, the natural, as the field.
wild olive *noun* [65 agrielaios] the natural growing olive.
wild runner *noun* {6501 pere} untamed runner.
wilderness *noun* {4057 midbar} [2047 eremia] [2048 eremos] an uninhabited and undeveloped area; **cp** desolation.
will *noun* {17 abowy} {35 abiyonah} {6640 tsebuw} [2307

thelema] [2308 thelesis] the volition; the attribute of the spirit that decides.
will, willeth, willing *verb* {14 abah} {2974 yaal} {5452 cebar} {6634 tseba} [1014 boulomai] [2309 thelo] to volitionate; the exercise to volition in deciding or determining; **cp** will, wilt, would, wouldest *auxiliary verbs.*
will, wilt, would, wouldest *auxiliary verbs* these auxiliary verbs are not in the manuscripts, but have been supplied by the translators to smooth the verbal flow: when used as auxiliary verbs, the *exeGeses* renders them thus: *will* **shall**, *wilt* **shalt**, *would* **should**, *wouldest* **shouldest**: when they refer to the volition, they are so indicated: **cp** will, willeth, willing; **see** may, mayest, might, mightest; **see** shall, shalt, should, shouldest.
willceremony *verb* [1479 ethelothreskeia] a mental, or intellectual type ceremony.
wind *noun* {7307 ruach} [417 anemos] air in motion; ruach is the Hebrew word for both spirit and wind; great discernment must be exercised in some instances; therefore there are instances where the *exeGeses* renders ruach as Spirit/wind; anemos is the Hellene word for wind; this distinction is important doctrinally; for most versions have mistranslated Spirit as wind in Yahn 3:8; **see** spirit.
window *noun* {2474 challown} as perforated.
window *noun* {4237 mechezah} as a look through.
window, noon *dual noun* {6672 tsohar} double light, as a window; double light, as noon.
windtossed *noun* [416 anemizo] tossed by the wind.
wine *noun* {3196 yayin} effervescence, as in fermentation.
wing *noun* [4419 pterugion] extremity; the top of the corner.
wing, blossom *noun* {6731 tsits} a blossom, as blooming brightly; a wing, as gleaming.
wing, border *noun* {3671 kanaph} {4020 migbalah} literally, extreme edge.
winnow *verb* {2219 zarah} to toss, as seed.
winnowing basket *noun* {4214 mizreh} a basket used to scatter chaff.
winnowing fork *noun* {7371 rachath} a fork used to scatter chaff.
winter (in) *verb* [3914 parakimazo] to stay with, or at a place over the winter season.
wipe, wipe out, erase *verb* {4229 machah} [1813 exalipho] to rub; to rub out; to erase sins, tears, names.
wisdom *noun* {2451, 2452 chokmah} {2454 chokmoth} {4678 sophia] the ability to decide well.
wise *adjective* {2450 chakam} [4680 sophos] deciding well.
wisen, enwisen *verb* {2449 chakam} [4679 sophizo] to cause to be wise.
withdraw *noun* {7873 siyg} removal into privacy.
withdraw *verb* {5756 uz} [402 anakoreo] to retire; to save by flight.
wither, disgrace, folly *verb* {5034 nabel} from the root, to wilt; to fall away; to fail.
wither, dry *noun* {3002 yabesh} {3004 yabbashah} {3006, 3007 yabbesheth} {7060 qamal} lands and waters dry; plants, persons wither.
wither, dry *verb* {3001 yabesh} {5405 nashath} {6798 tsanam} {7060 qamal} lands and waters dry; plants, persons wither.
within *adverb* {6441 penimah} literally, faceward; inside; **see** inward; **cp** without.
within, among, inward, middle, midst *noun* {7130 qereb} {8432 tavek} the nearest part; the center.
without, out, outside, outskirt, outward, outway *noun, adverb* {2351 chuts} a separated area.
withstand, stand, stay *verb* {5975 amad} {5977 omed} [436 anthistemi] [478 antikathistemi] to stand steady; to stand against.
witness *noun* {5707 ed} {7717 sahed} {8584 teuwdah} [3141 marturia] [3144 martus] [3142 marturion] evidence.
witness *noun* {5712 edah} {5713 edah} a people as a witness.
witness *noun* {5715 eduth} the witness; especially the ark of the witness.
witness, witnessing *verb* {5749 ud} [1263 diamarturomi] [1957 epimartureo] [3140 martureo] [3143 marturomai] to give evidence; the Hellene is from the root, martyr; one who through martyrdom became a witness of Yah Shua.
witness against *verb* [2649 katamartureo].
woe *interjection* [3759 ouai] exclamation of grief
wolf *noun* [3074 lukos] a wild dog.
woman, women *noun* {802 ishshah} {*plural* 802 nashim} {*plural* 5389 nashin} {7695 shegal} {7705 shiddah} [1134 gunaiikios] [1135 gunee] an adult female; when married, the female becomes a man's woman.
womb (to have in) *verb* [1064 gaster] to be bearing in womb; pregnant.
womb, belly, matrix *noun* {990 beten} {1512 gachon} {3770 keres} {4579 meah} {6896 qabab} {6897 qobah} {6898 qubbah} {7356 racham} {7358 rechem} [2836 koilia] the interior; a cavity as hollow; the abdominal cavity; sometimes refers to the womb.
women (little) *noun* [1133 gunaikarion] used in a belittling sense.
woodwinds *noun* {5748 uggab} a breath controlled music instrument.
woof, mongrel *noun* {6154 ereb} the transverse threads; a crossed race of persons.
word *noun* {1697 dabar} {1699 dibber} {1700 dibrah} {1701 dibrah} {*plural* 1703 dabroth} [3056 logos] an utterance or scribing of a thought; a promise, or guarantee (to give one's word); a manifestation; **note:** the noun, logos, is the outward expression of the verb, lego (Adonay Yah Shua Messiah is the physical manifestation of Elohim's word}; **read** Yahn 1:1-14.
word *verb* {1696 dabar} [3004 lego] in Hebrew and Hellene, word implies much more than uttering, or scribing one's thought; word also includes that of promising, or guaranteeing, or having been given one's word; when Yah Veh states, I have worded, or when Yah Shua states, Amen! Amen! I word unto you, they are saying, I have given my word, and that's final.
words (kind) *plural noun* [5542 chrestologia].
work *noun* {4639 maasch} {4399 melakah} an employment; a product; a transaction; **cp** creation.
work *verb* [2038 ergazomai] to do; to labor.
work *verb* {6213 asah} to be engaged in, or with; to do or make; **cp** create; **note:** {6213 asah} is the verb of work *noun* {4639 maasch}.
work, working, effort *noun* [2039 ergasia] [2041 ergon] occupation; toil.
worker *noun* [2040 ergates] a toiler.
world *noun* {8398 tebel} [3625 oikoumene] the inhabited earth; the universe; **cp** cosmos.
wormwood, absinthe *transliterated noun* {3939 laanah} [894 apsinthos] a bitter plant.
worn (out), rub, sicken, stroke *verb* {2470 chalah} to wear out; to stroke the face as in appeasement.
worship *verb* [4352 proskuneo] to do obesience, as by bowing and/or kissing.
worshipper *noun* [4353 proskunetes] one who worships.
worthily *adverb* [516 axios] deserving.
worthless, idol *noun* {434 elul} {457 elil} of no worth.
worthy (deem) *verb* [515 axioo] deserving.
worthy *adjective* [514 axios] deserving.
wound *noun* {6482 petsa} an open split.
wound *verb* {6481 patsa} to split open.
wound, disperse, express *verb* {6567 parash} to separate; to specify; to wound.
wraps *noun* {*singular* 5466 cadiyn} {*plural* 5156 nechirim} wraparounds.
wrath, nostril, snout *noun* {639 aph} {*plural* 5156 nechirim} [3709 orgee] the snorter, as in expressing wrath; **see** snorting.
wrathful *adjective* [3711 orgilos] intense anger.
wreath *noun* {3880 livyah} {*plural* 3914 loyoth} [4725 stemma] [4735 stephanos] as entwined; a wreath of victory; **cp** crown; **cp** diadem.
wreath, wreathen, foliage, rope *noun* {5688 abothah} as entwined; a wreath of victory; **cp** crown; **cp** diadem.
wreathe *verb* [4737 stephanoo] to wreathe in victory; **cp** crown; **cp** diadem.
wrestle *verb* {6617 pathal} to struggle; to entwine.
wrestlings *plural noun* {5319 naphtuim} strugglings.
wring hands, extend hands *participle* {3029 yeda} {3034 yadah} {8426 todah} to extend hands in praise; to wring hands in sorrow.
wring, suck *verb* {4680 matsah} to wring, or squeeze out; to suck out.
writhe, twirl, whirl *verb* {1752, 1753 duwr} {2342 chiyl} {3769 karar} {6801 tsanaph} to gyrate; to move in a circle; to dance.
writhing *noun* {5792 avvathah} twisting, as in pain.
wroth *adjective* [3710 orgizo] full of wrath.

Y

Yaalah *transliterated name* {3279 yaalah} Roe.
Yaanay *transliterated name* {3285 yaanay} Responsive.
Yaaqan *transliterated name* {3292 yaaqan} Tortuous.
Yaaqov, Yaaqovos *transliterated name* {3290 yaaqob} [2384 iakob] [2385 iakobos] Heel Seizer.
Yaaqovah *transliterated name* {3291 yaaqobah} Heel Seizer.
Yaare Oregim *plural transliterated name* {3296 yaarey oregiym} Forests of Weavers.
Yaaresh Yah *transliterated name* {3298 yaareshyah} of uncertain derivative and Yah.
Yaasi El *transliterated name* {3300 yaasiel} Worked of El.
Yaasu *transliterated name* {3299 yaasuw} They Worketh.
Yaazan Yah *transliterated name* {2970 yaazanyah} Hearkened of Yah.
Yaazi El *transliterated name* {3268 yaziel} Obstinate of El.
Yaazi Yah *transliterated name* {3269 yaaziyah} Obstinate of Yah.
Yabal *transliterated name* {2989 yabal} Stream.
Yabboq *transliterated name* {2999 yabboq} Pouring Forth.
Yabes *transliterated name* {3258 yabets} Sorrowful.
Yabesh *transliterated name* {3003 yabesh} Dry.
Yabin *transliterated name* {2985 yabyn} Discerning.
Yabne El *transliterated name* {2995 yabneel} Built of El.
Yabneh *transliterated name* {2996 yabneh} Built.
Yachath *transliterated name* {3189 yachath} Unity.
Yachazi El *transliterated name* {3166 yachaziel} Seer of El.
Yachazi Yah *transliterated name* {3167 yachaziyah} Seer of Yah.
Yachdi El *transliterated name* {3164 yachdiel} United of El.
Yachdi Yah *transliterated name* {3165 yechdiyah} United of Yah.
Yachdo *transliterated name* {3163 yachdo} United.
Yachle El *transliterated name* {3177 yachleel} Awaiting El.
Yachle Eliy *transliterated name* {3178 yachleeliy} Of Yachle El.
Yachmay *transliterated name* {3181yachmay} Hot.
Yachse El *transliterated name* {3183 yachtseel} Halved of El.
Yachse Eliy *transliterated name* {3184 yachtseeliy} Of Yachse El.
Yachsi El *transliterated name* {3185 yachtsiyel} Halved of El.
Yachzerah *transliterated name* {3170 yachzerah} Protection.
Yada *transliterated name* {3047 yada} Knowing.
Yaddua *transliterated name* {3037 yadduwa} Knowing.
Yadon *transliterated name* {3036 yadown} Thankful.
Yael *transliterated name* {3278 yael} Wild Goats.
• **Yah** *transliterated name* {3050 yah} name of Deity in basic form: Eternal Existent One; **see** following for compound forms.
• **Yah Shua** *transliterated name* {3091 yehowshua} {3442, 3443 yeshuwa} [2424 ieesous] Yah Saveth; the name of Mosheh's successor, the name of our Adonay Messiah, and the name of other persons.
• **Yah Veh** *transliterated name* {3068, 3069 yehovah} Eternal Existent One.
• **Yah Veh Nissi** *transliterated name* {3071 yehovahnissi} Yah Veh Ensign.
• **Yah Veh Raah** *transliterated name* {3068 yehovah} {7462 raah} Yah Veh Tendeth; see Psalm 23:1.
• **Yah Veh Raphah** *transliterated name* {3068 yehovah} {7495 raphah} Yah Veh Healer.
• **Yah Veh Sabaoth** *transliterated name* {3068 yehovah} {6635 tsabaah *plural* sabaoth} [3841 pantokrator] Yah Veh of Hosts; **see** Sabaoth.
• **Yah Veh Sadakah** *transliterated name* {3068 yehovah} {6666 sadakah} Yah Veh of Justness.
• **Yah Veh Shalom** *transliterated name* {3073 yehovahshalom} Yah Veh Shalom; **see** complete.
• **Yah Veh Sham** *transliterated name* {3068 yehovah} {8033 sham} Yah Veh's Presence; see Yechezq El 48:35.
• **Yah Veh Sidqenu** *transliterated name* {3072 yehovahtsidqenuw} a combined form of {3068 yehovah} and {6664 tsedek} Yah Veh of Justness.
• **Yah Veh Yireh** *transliterated name* {3070 yehovahyireh} Yah Veh Seeth.

Yah Ab *transliterated name* {3097 yowab} Yah Fathered.
Yah Ach *transliterated name* {3098 yowach} Yah Brothered.
Yah Achaz *transliterated name* {3059 yehowachaz} {3099 yowachaz} Yah Possessed.
Yah Addah *transliterated name* {3085 yehowaddah} Yah Adorneth.
Yah Addan *transliterated name* {3086 yehaddan} Yah Pleaseth.
Yah Arib *transliterated name* {3080 yehowyariyb} Yah Contendeth.
Yah Ash *transliterated name* {3060 yehowash} Yah Fired.
Yah Ash *transliterated name* {3101 yowash} Yah Fired.
Yah Ash *transliterated name* {3135 yowash} Yah Hurrieth.
Yah Dai *transliterated name* {3056 yehday} Yudaic.
Yah El *transliterated name* {3100 yowel} [2493 ioeel] Yah El.
Yah Ezer *transliterated name* {3134 yowezer} Yah Helpeth.
Yah Ha *transliterated name* {3109 yowcha} Revived of Yah.
Yah Hanan, Yahn *transliterated name* {3076 yehowchanan} {3110 yowchanan} [*contraction* 2491 ioannees] Yah Granteth Charism.
Yah Hanna, Yah Hannas *transliterated name* [2489 ioanna] [2490 ioannas] Yah Granteth Charism.
Yah Hu *transliterated name* {3058 yewhu} Yah is He.

• **SUMMARY:**
• **YAH HUDAH, YAH HUDIY, YAH HUDIYM:**
• In Strong's Concordance, Old Covenant, between {3050 Yah} and {3068 Yah Veh} are most of the words which pertain to Yah Veh's people which are called by His name (2 Chronicles 7:14). There is a difference of vowel points between the words referring to Yah, and the words referring to Yah Hudah. However, these vowel points were not added until the seventh century A.D. in the masoretic text – long after the Hebrews decided that it was not proper to refer to Yah Veh by His name – even though Yah Veh had so commanded; **read** Genesis 29:24, Exodus 3:15, 2 Chronicles 7:14, Psalms 68:4, 83:18, Yesha Yah 12:2, 42:8, 52:6, Yirme Yah 33:2, Ephesians 3:15, Apocalypse 14:1; **see** Yah Veh.
• **Yah Hudah, Yah Hudaim; Yah Hudiy;** *transliterated names* {a place 3055 yehud} {the land, the people 3061 yehud} {the peoples 3062 yehudaim} {the scion 3063 yehudah} {a people, a person 3064, 3065 yehudi} [a land 2448, 2449 ioudaia] [a people, a person 2453 ioudaios] [a people, a person, a scion 2455 ioudas] Celebrated of Yah.
• **Yah Hudaic, Yah Hudaically** *transliterated name* {3066 yehudith} [2451, 2452 ioudaikos] the Yah Hudahiy tongue; as a Yah Hudiy.
• **Yah Hudaism** *noun* [2454 ioudaismos] the Yah Hudahiy religion, and usages.
• **Yah Hudaize** *participle* {3054 yahad} [2450 ioudaizo] to cause to be Yah Hudahiy.

Yahudiah *transliterated name* {3057 yehudiyah} a female Yah Hudiy.
Yahudith *transliterated name* {3067 yehudith} a female Yah Hudiy.
Yah Chebed *transliterated name* {3115 yowchebed} Honoured of Yah.
Yah Nadab *transliterated name* {3082 yehownadab} {3122 yownadab} Yah Volunteereth.
Yah Nathan *transliterated name* {3083 yehownathan} {3129 yownathan} Yah Given.
Yah Qim *transliterated name* {3137 yowqiym} [885 acheim] Yah Riseth.
Yah Ram *transliterated name* {3088 yehowram} {3141 yowram} [2496 ioram] Yah Raiseth.
Yah Sadaq *transliterated name* {3087 yehowtsadaq} {3136 yowtsadaq} Yah Justifieth.
Yah Shabath *transliterated name* {3090 yehowshabath} Yah Oatheth; may be a form of Yah Sheba.
Yah Shah *transliterated name* {3144 yowshah} Equateth of Yah.
Yah Shama *transliterated name* {1953 howshama} Yah Heareth.
Yah Shaphat *transliterated name* {3092 yehowshaphat} {3146 yowshaphat} [2498 iosaphat] Yah Judgeth.
Yah Shavah *transliterated name* {3145 yowshavyah} Equateth of Yah.
Yah Sheba *transliterated name* {3089 yehowsheba} Yah Oatheth.
Yah Shua *transliterated name* {3091 yahshua} {3442, 3443 yahshua} [2424 ieesous] Yah Saveth; the name of Mosheh's successor, the name of our Messiah, and the name of other persons; see SUMMARY: YAH, YAH SHUA.
Yah Tham *transliterated name* {3147 yowtham} [2488 ioatham] Yah Integrious.
Yah Veh Shammah *transliterated name* {3074 yehovahshammah} Yah Veh's presence; symbolic name of Yeru Shalem.
Yah Yada *transliterated name* {3077 yehowyada} {3111 yowyada} Known of Yah.
Yah Yachin *transliterated name* {3078 yehowyachiyn} {3112 yowyachiyn} Yah Establisheth.
Yah Yaqim *transliterated name* {3079 yehowyaqiym} {3113

yowyaqiym} Yah Raiseth.
Yah Yarib *transliterated name* {3114 yowyariyb} Yah Contendeth.
Yah Zabad *transliterated name* {3075 yehowzabad} {3107 yowzabad} Yah Endowed.
Yah Zachar *transliterated name* {3108 yahzachar} Yah Remembereth.
Yahn, Yah Hanan *transliterated name* {3076 yehowchanan} {3110 yowchanan} [*contraction* 2491 ioannees] Yah Granteth Charism.
Yahsah *transliterated name* {3096 yahtsah} possibly, Threshing (floor); a place east of the Yarden.
Yair *transliterated name* {2971 yaiyr} [2383 iairos] Enlightener.
Yairiy *transliterated name* {2972 yairiy} Of Yair.
Yachan *transliterated name* {3275 yachan} Troublesome.
Yachin *transliterated name* {3199 yachiyn} Establisheth.
Yachiniy *transliterated name* {3200 yachiyniy} Of Yachin.
Yalam *transliterated name* {3281yalam} Concealed; Veiled.
Yalon *transliterated name* {3210 yalown} Stay Overnight.
Yamin *transliterated name* {3226 yamiyn} Right.
Yaminiy *transliterated name* {3228 yemiyniy} Of Yamin.
Yamlech *transliterated name* {3230 yamlech} Reign.
Yanah *transliterated name* {3238 yanah} [2388 ianna] Oppressor.
Yanim *transliterated name* {3241 yaniym} Slumber.
Yanochah *transliterated name* {3239 yanowchah} Allowed to Stay.
Yaphia *transliterated name* {3309 yaphiya} Shining.
Yaphlet *transliterated name* {3310 yaphlet} He Escapeth; He Slippeth Away.
Yaphletiy *transliterated name* {3311 yaphletiy} Of Yaphlet.
Yapho *transliterated name* {3305 yapho} [2445 ioppee] Beautiful.
Yaqeh *transliterated name* {3348 yaqeh} Obedient.
Yaqim *transliterated name* {3356 yaqiym} He Raiseth.
Yarah *transliterated name* {3294 yarah} Forest; Honeycomb.
Yarcha *transliterated name* {3398 yarcha} the meaning uncertain.
Yarden *transliterated name* {3383 yarden} [2446 iordanees] Descender.
Yareb *transliterated name* {3377 yareb} He Contendeth.
Yarib *transliterated name* {3402 yariyb} He Contendeth.
Yarmuth *transliterated name* {3412 yarmuwth} Lofty.
Yaroach *transliterated name* {3386 yarowach} Born At the New Moon.
Yarob Am *transliterated name* {3379 yarobam} Contender of People.
Yashen *transliterated name* {3464 yashen} Asleep.
Yashob Am *transliterated name* {3434 yashobam} People Returneth.
Yashub *transliterated name* {3437 yashuwb} He Returneth.
Yashubi Lechem *transliterated name* {3433 yashubiylechem} Returner of Bread.
Yashubiy *transliterated name* {3432 yashubiy} Of Yashub.
Yathni El *transliterated name* {3496 yathniel} Saved of El.
Yattir *transliterated name* {3492 yattiyr} Remaining.
Yaur *transliterated name* {3265 yauwr} Forest; Honeycomb.
Yavan *transliterated name* {3120 yavan} Effervescing.
Yavaniy *transliterated name* {3125 yevaniy} Of Yavan.
Yazer *transliterated name* {3270 yazer} Helpful.
Ye Halal El *transliterated name* {3094 yehallalel} Halal to El.
yea [3483 nai] [3513 ne] a particle of affirmation.
year, yearling *noun* {8140 shenah} {8141 shaneh} [1763 eniautos] [2094 etos] [4070 perusi] the time span of the revolution of the earth around the sun; that which is a year in age.
Yearim *plural transliterated name* {3297 yeariym} Forests.
yearn *verb* {3642 kamahh} {3648 kamar} {3700 kacaph} to pine after.
yearn, prowl *verb* {8264 shaqaq} to seek for greedily; to prowl as an animal.
yearning *verb* [2442 himiromai] desiring; longing for.
yeast *noun* {7603 seor} that which ferments.
Yeatheray *transliterated name* {2979 yeatheray} Stepping.
Yeberech Yah *transliterated name* {3000 yeberechyah} Blest of Yah.
Yebus *transliterated name* {2982 yebuwc} Trampled.
Yebusiy *transliterated name* {2983 yebuwciy} Of Yebus.
Yechezq El *transliterated name* {3168 yechezqel} Strengthened of El.
Yechi El *transliterated name* {3171 yechiel} Enlivened of El.
Yechi Eliy *transliterated name* {3172 yechiyeliy} Of Yechi El.
Yechi Yah *transliterated name* {3174 yechiyah} Enlivened of Yah.
Yechizqi Yah *transliterated name* {2396, 3169 yechiziqiyah} [1478 ezekias] Strenghthened of Yah.
Yechubbah *transliterated name* {3160 yechubbah} Hidden.
Yeda Yah *transliterated name* {3042 yedayah} Extended Hands of Yah.
Yeda Yah *transliterated name* {3048 yedayah} Known of Yah.
Yedi *transliterated name* {3260 yediy} Congregate; Betroth.
Yedia El *transliterated name* {3043 yediyael} Known of El.
Yedid Yah *transliterated name* {3041 yedideyah} Beloved of Yah.
Yedidah *transliterated name* {3040 yedidah} Beloved.
Yeduthun *transliterated name* {3038 yeduthuwn} Extended Hands.
Yegar Sahadutha *transliterated name* {3026 yegarsahaduwtha} Heap of the Witness.
Yehuchal *transliterated name* {3081yehuwchal} Able.
Yei El *transliterated name* {3273 yeiyel} Snatched Away of El.
Yeish *transliterated name* {3274 yeiysh} Hurried.
Yechol Yah *transliterated name* {3203 yecholyah} Yah Enableth.
Yechon Yah *transliterated name* {3204 yechonyah} [2423 iechonias] Established of Yah.
Yemimah *transliterated name* {3224 yemiymah} Warm.
Yemu El *transliterated name* {3223 yemuel} Day of El.
Yepheth *transliterated name* {3315 yepheth} Delude; Entice.
Yephunneh *transliterated name* {3312 yephunneh} He Faceth.
Yeqabse El *transliterated name* {3343 yeqabtseel} Gathered of El.
Yeqam Am *transliterated name* {3360 yeqamam} The People Riseth.
Yeqam Yah *transliterated name* {3359 yeqamyah} Raised of Yah.
Yequthi El *transliterated name* {3354 yequthiel} Obedient of El.
Yerach *transliterated name* {3392 yerach} Moon.
Yerachme El *transliterated name* {3396 yerachmeel} Mercy of El.
Yerachme Eliy *transliterated name* {3397 yerachmeeliy} Of Yerachme El.
Yered *transliterated name* {3382 yered} [2391 iared] Toppler.
Yeremay *transliterated name* {3413 yeremay} Lofted.
Yeremoth, Yerimoth *plural transliterated name* {3406 yeriymowth, yereymowth} Elevations.
Yeri El *transliterated name* {3400 yeriel} Formed of El.
Yeri Yah *transliterated name* {3404 yeriyah} Formed of Yah.
Yeribay *transliterated name* {3403 yeriybay} Contentious.
Yericho *transliterated name* {3405 yericho} [2410 hieriko] Fragrant.
Yerioth *plural transliterated name* {3408 yeriyowth} Curtains.
Yerocham *transliterated name* {3395 yerocham} Merciful.
Yeru El *transliterated name* {3385 yeruel} Formed of El.
Yeru Shalem *transliterated name* {3389 yerushalaim} {3390 yerushalem} [2414 hierosoluma] [2419 hierousaleem] Founded Shalem.
Yeru Shalemiy *transliterated name* [2415 hierosolumites] Of Yeru Shalem.
Yerub Baal *transliterated name* {3378 yerubbaal} Contender of Baal.
Yerub Besheth *transliterated name* {3380 yerubbesheth} Contender of Shame.
Yerushah *transliterated name* {3388 yerushah} Possessed.
Yesar Elah *transliterated name* {3480 yesarelah} Straight Towards El.
Yeser *transliterated name* {3337 yetser} Form; Conception.
Yeseriy *transliterated name* {3340 yitsriy} Of Yeser.
Yesha Yah *transliterated name* {3470 yeshayah} [2268 hesaias] Saved of Yah.
Yeshanah *transliterated name* {3466 yeshanah} Old.
Yesheb Ab *transliterated name* {3428 yeshebab} Seat of His Father.
Yesher *transliterated name* {3475 yesher} Straight, as in right.
Yeshishay *transliterated name* {3454 yeshiyshay} Aged.
Yeshocha Yah *transliterated name* {3439 yeshochayah} Hungered of Yah.
Yeshurun *transliterated name* {3484 yeshuruwn} Straight, as in upright.
Yesima El *transliterated name* {3450 yesimael} Placed of El.
yesterday *adjective* [5504 chthes] the previous day.
Yetheriy *transliterated name* {3505 yithriy} Of Yether.
Yetheth *transliterated name* {3509 yetheth} of uncertain derivative.
Yetur *transliterated name* {3195 yetur} [2484 ituraea] Encircled.
Yeu El *transliterated name* {3262 yeuel} Snatched Away of El.

Yeus *transliterated name* {3263 yeuwts} Consultant.
Yeush *transliterated name* {3266 yeuwsh} Hurried.
Yezan Yah *transliterated name* {3153 yezanyah} Hearkened of Yah.
Yezav El *transliterated name* {3149 yezavel} Sprinkled of El.
Yezav Yah *transliterated name* {3150 yezziyah} Sprinkled of Yah.
Yibchar *transliterated name* {2984 yibchar} Choice.
Yible Am *transliterated name* {2991 yibleam} Swallowing People.
Yibne Yah *transliterated name* {2997 yibneyah} Built of Yah.
Yibni Yah *transliterated name* {2998 yibniyah} Building of Yah.
Yibsam *transliterated name* {3005 yibsam} Spice.
Yidalah *transliterated name* {3030 yidalah} of uncertain derivative.
Yidbash *transliterated name* {3031 yidbash} Honeyed.
Yiddo *transliterated name* {3035 yiddow} Praised.
Yidlaph *transliterated name* {3044 yidlaph} Tearful.
Yigal *transliterated name* {3008 yigal} Redeemer.
Yigdal Yah *transliterated name* {3012 yigdalyah} Greatened of Yah.
Yimlah *transliterated name* {3229 yimlah} Full.
Yimna *transliterated name* {3234 yimna} Withhold; Hinder.
Yimnah *transliterated name* {3232 yimnah} Prosperity.
Yimrah *transliterated name* {3236 yimrah} Exchange.
Yiphde Yah *transliterated name* {3301 yiphdeyah} Redeemed of Yah.
Yiphtach *transliterated name* {3316 yiphtach} [2422 iephthae
Yiphtach El *transliterated name* {3317 yiphtachel} Opened of El. Opener.
Yiri Yah *transliterated name* {3376 yiriyah} Awed of Yah.
Yirme Yah *transliterated name* {3414 yirmeyah} [2408 hieremias] Raised of Yah.
Yiron *transliterated name* {3375 yirown} Awesomeness.
Yirpe El *transliterated name* {3416 yerpeel} Healed of El.
Yischaq *transliterated name* {3327 yitschaq} {3446 yischaq} [2464 isaak] Laughter; Ridicule.
Yischar *transliterated name* {3328 yitschar} He Shineth.
Yishar *transliterated name* {3324 yitshar} Oil (anointing).
Yishariy *transliterated name* {3325 yitshariy} Of Yishar.
Yishay *transliterated name* {3448 yishay} [2421 iessai] Existent.
Yishbach *transliterated name* {3431 yishbach} He Laudeth.
Yishbaq *transliterated name* {3435 yishbaq} He Leaveth.
Yishbo Be Nob *transliterated name* {3430 yishbowbenob} He Settleth in Nob.
Yishi *transliterated name* {3469 yishiy} Saving.
Yishma *transliterated name* {3457 yishma} Desolate.
Yishma El *transliterated name* {3458 yishmael} Hearkened of El.
Yishma Eliy *transliterated name* {3459 yishmaeliy} Of Yishma El.
Yishma Yah *transliterated name* {3460 yishmayah} Hearkened of Yah.
Yishmeray *transliterated name* {3461 yishmeray} Guarded.
Yishpah *transliterated name* {3472 yishpah} He Exposeth.
Yishpan *transliterated name* {3473 yishpan} He Hideth.
Yishshi Yah *transliterated name* {3449 yishshiyah} Exacted of Yah.
Yishvah *transliterated name* {3438 yishvah} He Equalizeth.
Yishvi *transliterated name* {3440 yishviy} Equalized.
Yishviy *transliterated name* {3441 yishviy} Of Yishvi.
Yiskah *transliterated name* {3252 yickah} Observant.
Yismach Yah *transliterated name* {3253 yicmachyah} Upheld of Yah.
Yisra El *transliterated name* {3478, 3479 yisrael} [2474 israel] Ruled of El.
Yisra Eliy *transliterated name* {3481 yisreeliy} [2475 israeelitees] Of Yisra El.
Yisra Eliyth *transliterated name* {3482 yisreeliyth} a female Yisra Eliy.
Yisri *transliterated name* {3339 yitsriy} Formative.
Yissachar *transliterated name* {3485 yissachar} [2466 isakar] Exalted Hireling.
Yithlah *transliterated name* {3494 yithlah} It Hangeth.
Yithmah *transliterated name* {3495 yithmah} Orphaned.
Yithnan *transliterated name* {3497 yithnan} Monster.
Yithra *transliterated name* {3501yithra} Remainder.
Yithran *transliterated name* {3506 yithran} Remaining.
Yithre Am *transliterated name* {3507 yithream} Remainder of People.
Yithro *transliterated name* {3503 yithrow} His Remainder.
Yizliah *transliterated name* {3152 yizliyah} Drawn.
Yizrach *transliterated name* {3155 yizrach} Risen.
Yizrach Yah *transliterated name* {3156 yizrachyah} Risen of Yah.
Yizre El *transliterated name* {3157 yizreel} Seeded of El.
Yizre Eliy *transliterated name* {3158 yizreeliy} Of Yizre El.
Yizre Eliyth *transliterated name* {3159 yizreeliyth} a female of Yizre El.
Yobab *transliterated name* {3103 yowbab} Howler.
Yoed *transliterated name* {3133 yowed} Congregate; Betroth.
Yoelah *transliterated name* {3132 yowelah} Furthermore.
Yogbehah *transliterated name* {3011 yogbehah} Height.
Yogli *transliterated name* {3020 yogliy} Exiled.
yoke *noun* {5923 ol} [2218 zugos] that which joins; that which connects; figuratively, of bondage.
yoke *verb* {7573 ratham} to yoke a yoke pole.
yokepole, pole *noun* {4132 mowt} the slip pole of a yoke.
Yom Kippurim *transliterated plural noun* {3117 yom} {3725 kippurim} day of atonements; **see** kippurim/atonements.
yom, day *transliterated noun* {3117, 3118 yom} [2250 heemera] including, but not limited to dawn to down, or dawn to dawn; 24 hours, or a nonspeific period such as the Day of Yah Veh; **see** Yom Kippurim.
Yonah *transliterated name* {3124 yonah} [2495 ionas] Dove.
Yoqde Am *transliterated name* {3347 yoqdeam} Burning of the People.
Yoqme Am *transliterated name* {3361 yoqmeam} The People Raiseth.
Yoqne Am *transliterated name* {3362 yoqneam} The People Lamenteth.
Yoqshan *transliterated name* {3370 yoqshan} Ensnare.
Yoqtan *transliterated name* {3355 yoqtan} He Maketh Little.
Yoqthe El *transliterated name* {3371 yoqtheel} Obedient of El.
Yorah *transliterated name* {3139 yowrah} Pouring.
Yoray *transliterated name* {3140 yowray} Pouring (rain).
Yorqe Am *transliterated name* {3421 yorqeam} People Poureth Out.
Yoseph *transliterated name* {3084 yehowceph} {3130 yowceph} [2501 ioseph] Addeth; the name of several persons, including the name of the man of Miryam, the mother of Yah Shua.
Yoses *transliterated name* [2499, 2500 iosees] Addeth.
Yoshbe Qashah *transliterated name* {3436 yoshbeqashah} Hard Seat.
Yosheb Bash Shabbath *transliterated name* {3429 yoshebbashshebeth} Sitting in the Seat.
Yoshi Yah *transliterated name* {2977 yoshiyah} [2502 iosias] Founded of Yah.
Yoshib Yah *transliterated name* {3143 yoshibyah} Settled of Yah.
Yosiph Yah *transliterated name* {3131 yowciphyah} Yah Addeth.
Yotbah *transliterated name* {3192 yotbah} Well–**pleas**ing.
Yotbathah *transliterated name* {3193 yotbathah}Well–**pleas**ing.
young *adjective* [3555 nossia] not born long.
younger, fewer, lesser, little, pinky *adjective* {6810 tsaor} {6995 qoten} {6996 qatan} less in age, number, size; little finger.
youngling *noun* {1469 gozal} [3502 neossos] [3556 nossion] the young of any species.
youngness *adjective* {6812 tseirah} smallness of age.
youth *noun* {970 bachur} {979 bechuroth} {979 bechurim} {*plural* 5271 neurah} {*plural* 5934 alum} [3494 neanias] [3495 neaniskos] [3503 neotees] a young person.
youthful *adjective* [3512 neoterikos] acting, being, or feeling young.
Yubal *transliterated name* {3106 yuwbal} Stream.
Yuchal *transliterated name* {3116 yuwchal} Able.
Yushab Hesed *transliterated name* {3142 yuwshabcheced} Mercy Returneth.
Yuttah *transliterated name* {3194 yuttah} Extended.

Z

Zabdi El *transliterated name* {2068 zabdiel} Endowment of El.
Zabdi *transliterated name* {2067 zabdi} [2199 zebedaios] Endowment.
Zakkay *transliterated name* {2079 zabbay} {2140 zakkay} [2195 zakchaios] Pure.
Zakkur *transliterated name* {2139 zakkuwr} Memorialize.
Zamzomiym *plural transliterated name* {2157 zamzomim} Intriguing; Of Pelesheth.
Zanoach *transliterated name* {2182 zanowach} Abandoned.
zeal *noun* [2205 zelos] used favorably, ardor; unfavorably, jealousy.
zealot *transliterated noun, transliterated title* [2207 zelotes] one burning with zeal; a title of Shimon.

zealous *adjective* [2206 zeloo] to have warmth of feeling for or against.
zealous, jealous *adjective* **envy, suspect** *verb* {7065 qana} {7067 qanna} {7072 qannow} to be zealous, as jealous, or envious.
Zebach *transliterated name* {2078 zebach} Sacrifice.
Zebidah *transliterated name* {2080 zebiydah} Endowed.
Zebulun *transliterated name* {2074 zebulun} [2194 zaboulon] Residence.
Zechar Yah *transliterated name* {2148 zecharyah} [2197 zakarias] Memorial of Yah.
Zecher *transliterated name* {2144 zecher} Memorial.
Zemirah *transliterated name* {2160 zemiyrah} Psalm.
Zerach *transliterated name* {2226 zerach} [2196 zara] Rising, Dawn.
Zerach Yah *transliterated name* {2228 zerachyah} Rising of Yah.
Zerachiy *transliterated name* {250 ezrachiy} {2227 zarchiy} Of Zerach.
Zerub Babel *transliterated name* {2216, 2217 zerubbabel} [2216 zorobabel] Of Babel.
Zeus *transliterated name* [2203 zeus] deity of the Hellenes.
Zichri *transliterated name* {2147 zichriy} Memorable.
Ziph *transliterated name* {2128 ziyph} Flowing.
Ziphah *transliterated name* {2129 ziyphah} Flowing.
Ziphiy *transliterated name* {2130 ziyphiy} Of Ziph.
Zocheleth *transliterated name* {2120 zocheleth} Creeper.
Zocheth *transliterated name* {2105 zowcheth} of uncertain derivative.
Zuziym *plural transliterated name* {2104 zuwziym} Prominent; Of Pelesheth.